Bookman's Price Index

CUMULATIVE INDEX TO VOLUMES 47-54

Bookman's Price Index

CUMULATIVE INDEX TO VOLUMES 47-54

A Consolidated Index to 160,000 Citations Describing Antiquarian Books Offered For Sale by Leading Dealers

Anne F. McGrath
Managing Editor

Richard Grazide
Editor

DETROIT · NEW YORK · TORONTO · LONDON

Anne F. McGrath, *Managing Editor*
Richard Grazide, Editor
Kathy Hinkle, *Contributing Editor*

Gale Research Staff

Kelly L. Sprague, *Coordinating Editor*
Paula Cutcher-Jackson, Kathleen Dallas, Shelly Dickey, Nancy Franklin, William H. Harmer,
Debra M. Kirby, Alesia Lawson, Charles B. Montney, and Dana Shonta, *Contributors*
Ann V. Evory, *Managing Editor*

Eleanor Allison, *Manager, Data Entry Services*
Kenneth Benson, *Data Entry Coordinator*
Civie Ann Green, *Senior Data Entry Associate*
Timothy Alexander, Nikkita Bankston, Frances L. Monroe, Cynthia Morgan, Elizabeth Pilette,
Nancy Sheridan, Shanitta L. Watkins, and Constance J. Wells, *Data Entry Associates*

Mary Beth Trimper, *Production Director*
Deborah L. Milliken, *Production Assistant*

Cynthia D. Baldwin, *Product Design Manager*
Christi Fuson, *Macintosh Artist*

Theresa Rocklin, *Manager, Technical Support Services*
Wayne D. Fong, *Programmer/Analyst*

While every effort has been made to ensure the reliability of the information presented in this publication, Gale Research does not guarantee the accuracy of the data contained herein. Gale accepts no payment for listing; and inclusion in the publication of any organization, service, or individual does not imply endorsement of the editors or publisher.

Errors brought to the attention of the publisher and verified to the satisfaction of the publisher will be corrected in future editions.

∞™ This book is printed on acid-free paper that meets the minimum requirements of American National Standard for Information Sciences—Permanence Paper for Printed Library Materials, ANSI Z39.48-1984.

 This book is printed on recycled paper that meets Environmental Protection Agency standards.

This publication is a creative work fully protected by all applicable copyright laws, as well as by misappropriation, trade secret, unfair competition, and other applicable laws. The authors and editors of this work have added value to the underlying factual material herein through one or more of the following: unique and original selection, coordination, expression, arrangement, and classification of the information.

All rights to this publication will be vigorously defended.

Copyright © 1998
Gale Research
835 Penobscot Bldg.
Detroit, MI 48226-4094

All rights reserved including the right of reproduction in whole or in part in any form.

ISBN 0-7876-2214-1
ISSN 0068-0141

Printed in the United States of America

Contents

Introduction vii

Cumulative Index to *Bookman's Price Index*, Volumes 47-54 1

This work provides speedy access to the 160,000 book titles contained in Volumes 47-54 of the *Bookman's Price Index*, which were published between 1993 and 1997. Additional information is available about these titles in the individual volumes.

Introduction

The *Bookman's Price Index* (*BPI*), published since 1964, indicates the availability and price of antiquarian books in the United States, Canada, and the British Isles. Since the *BPI* now numbers over 50 volumes, searching for specific titles has become a time consuming task for the user.

This volume is the seventh "cumulative index to the index." It references the entries in Volumes 47 through 54, which were published between 1993 and 1997. Since each of these *BPI* volumes includes, on average, 20,000 entries, this work provides access to 160,000 entries from the original *BPI* volumes.

What Is Included?

Since the primary purpose of this volume is speedy access to tens of thousands of book titles, the complete entry in the original *BPI* volume is not repeated here. Such a repetition would necessarily negate the ability to include all this information in one volume, thus defeating its purpose of quick and easy access. This index includes sufficient information for rapid identification of a specific title including the author, date of publication, and place of publication, followed by a list of all the *BPI* volumes in which that book is included.

BPI's regular volumes provide extensive information so that the user can identify a rare book and get some indication of how the particular dealer arrived at its price. This information, taken from rare book dealer catalogs, includes not only the author, title, date and place of publication, publisher, edition and price, but a thorough description of the book and notes on its condition. The description and condition information includes physical size, illustrations, binding, authors' signatures, general physical condition, specific flaws, and relative scarcity whenever this information has been given by the dealer listing the book.

Arrangement

Entries appear in a single alphabetic sequence, based on the name of the author: in cases of personal authorship, the author's last name; in cases of books produced by corporate bodies such as governments of countries or states, the name of that entity; in cases of anonymous books, the title; and in cases of anonymous classics such as *Arabian Nights*, the customary or well-known title. The editors have tried their best to duplicate the sorting rules of the original volumes, but as these rules have changed over the years that *BPI* has been published, this has been a difficult task. Users are advised to check the listings for possible variants to ensure they find all appropriate entries.

Extensive efforts were made to standardize the names of authors so that all titles belonging to the same author appeared together. However, in compiling the original volumes of the *BPI* covered herein, some inconsistencies appeared in the way the authors' names were presented between volumes. The editors have brought as much consistency as possible to this index, but in certain cases, changing an author's name for the sake of consistency might have made it impossible for the user to find the entry in the original *BPI* volume. Therefore, some latitude is necessary when searching for a specific author.

Under the author's name, works are arranged in alphabetical sequence according to the first word of the title, excepting initial articles. References to the same title are grouped together unless such grouping would have made it difficult for the user to locate the entry in the original *BPI* volume. Different editions of a single work are arranged according to the date of publication, with the earliest dates first. If the date of publication is the same but the place of publication is different, these entries are then organized alphabetically by the place of publication. Bearing all of this in mind, it would be advisable for users to scan the entire list of an author's works so as not to miss locating information for a specific title.

Sample Entry

The following sample illustrates the components of a typical entry:

① **DE QUINCY, THOMAS**
　　② *Confessions of an English Opium Eater.* ③Oxford: ④1930.
　　　　⑤　V. 47; 52; 54

① Author's name
② Title
③ Place of publication
④ Date of publication
⑤ Volumes of the *BPI* in which the complete descriptive entry for copies of this edition can be found

Acknowledgments

My thanks to Kelly Sprague, coordinating editor at Gale Research, and to her associates Paula Cutcher-Jackson, Kathleen Dallas, Shelly Dickey, Nancy Franklin, William Harmer, Debra Kirby, Alesia Lawson, Charles Montney, and Dana Shonta for their guiding hands throughout this project, to Richard Grazide for his assistance in research and editing, and to Kathy Hinkle for her many hours of reviewing and correcting some 160,000 entries in order to bring consistency to this index.

Suggestions and Comments Welcome

Suggestions are always welcome. This index volume is, in part, a result of the suggestions of *BPI* users. The editor invites all comments, especially those that might improve the usefulness of the *Bookman's Price Index*. Please contact:

>Editor
>*Bookman's Price Index*
>Gale Research
>645 Griswold St.
>Detroit, MI 48226-4094
>Phone: 313-961-2242
>Toll-Free: 800-347-GALE
>Fax: 313-961-6083

>Anne F. McGrath
>Managing Editor

Bookman's Price Index

CUMULATIVE INDEX TO VOLUMES 47-54

A

A B C. 1983. V. 54
A B C. New York, Dusseldorf: 1983. V. 47

A B C for Booklovers. Valparaiso: 1992. V. 49

ABC for Tiny Schools. Los Angeles: 1975. V. 52

A B C in Living Models. V. 54
A B C in Living Models. London: 1930's. V. 48; 51
A B C in Living Models. London: 1940's. V. 49

ABC Picture Book in Little Learner's Toy Book... London. V. 48; 51

THE ABC With the Church of England Catechism. Philadelphia: 1785. V. 52

A., D.
The Whole Art of Converse: Containing Necessary Instructions For All Persons, Of What Quality, and Condition Soever. London: 1683. V. 51

A., M.
Co-Operation in Land Tenure. London: 1879. V. 53

A., T.
A Rich Storehouse or Treasurie for the Diseased Wherein are many Approved Medicines. London: 1630. V. 49

AA, PIETER VAN DER
Vues des Villes. Leiden: 1707?. V. 50

AA Today. New York: 1960. V. 51

ABAILARD, PIERRE
The Letters of Abelard and Heloise. London: 1925. V. 48
Opera. Paris: 1616. V. 48

ABATI, BALDO ANGELO
De Admirabili Viperae Natura & de Mirificis Eiusdem Facultatibus Liber... Nurnberg: 1603. V. 47

ABAUZIT, FIRMIN
Miscellanies of the Late Ingenious and Celebrated M. Abauzit, on Historical, Theological and Critical Subjects. London: 1774. V. 47

ABBADIE, JACQUES
Chemical Change in the Eucharist. London: 1867. V. 54
The History of the Late Conspiracy Against the King and the Nation. London: 1696. V. 51; 52; 53
A Vindication of the Truth of Christian Religion, Against the Objections Of All Modern Opposers. London: 1694. V. 48; 51

ABBE, DOROTHY
Caslon Flowers. Boston: 1913. V. 48
The Dwiggins Marionettes. New York: 1969. V. 47; 48; 49; 50; 53; 54
The Dwiggins Marionettes, a Complete Experimental Theatre in Miniature. New York: 1970. V. 48; 51
Stencilled Ornament and Illustration. 1979. V. 48

ABBEY, EDWARD
Abbey's Road. New York: 1979. V. 53
Appalachian Wilderness. New York: 1970. V. 47; 51; 52; 53
Beyond the Wall. New York: 1984. V. 47; 49; 50; 51
Black Sun. New York: 1971. V. 52; 53; 54
The Brave Cowboy. Salt Lake City: 1993. V. 50; 53; 54
Cactus Country. New York: 1973. V. 53
Desert Images: an American Landscape. New York: 1979. V. 48; 51
Desert Solitaire. New York: 1968. V. 47; 50; 51; 52; 54
Fire On the Mountain. New York: 1962. V. 47; 49; 50; 51; 52; 53; 54
The Fool's Progress. New York: 1968. V. 49
The Fool's Progress. New York: 1988. V. 52
Good News. New York: 1980. V. 51; 52; 53
The Hidden Canyon. New York: 1977. V. 51; 52; 53
In Praise of Mountain Lions. Albuquerque: 1984. V. 51
Jonathan Troy. New York: 1954. V. 48; 50; 51; 52; 53
The Journey Home. New York: 1977. V. 50; 52
The Monkey Wrench Gang. Philadelphia and New York: 1975. V. 48; 50; 51; 52; 53; 54
The Monkey Wrench Gang. Edinburgh: 1978. V. 53; 54
The Monkey Wrench Gang. 1985. V. 48; 49; 50
The Monkey Wrench Gang. Salt Lake City: 1985. V. 51; 53
One Life at a Time, Please. New York: 1988. V. 53
Slickrock - The Canyon of Southeast Utah. New York: 1971. V. 54
Slickrock. The Canyon Country of Southeast Utah. San Francisco: 1971. V. 49; 51; 52; 53; 54
Slumgullion Stew: an Edward Abbey Reader. New York: 1984. V. 50
Sunset Canyon. London: 1972. V. 52; 53
Vox Clamantis in Deserto. Santa Fe: 1989. V. 47; 51; 52

ABBEY, JOHN ROLAND
Catalogue of the Valuable Printed Books and Fine Bindings (and) Manuscripts. London: 1965-89. V. 51
Catalogue of Valuable Printed Books and Fine Bindings from the Celebrated Collection. London: 1956-78. V. 50
Catalogue of Valuable Printed Books and Fine Bindings, from the Celebrated Collection of... London: 1965-70. V. 50; 52
Catalouge of Valuable Printed Books and Fine Bindings. London: 1965-78. V. 49; 54
The Italian Manuscripts in the Library of J. R. Abbey. 1969. V. 53
The Italian Manuscripts in the Library of Major J. R. Abbey. London: 1969. V. 51; 54
Life in England in Aquatint and Lithography 1770-1860. London: 1953. V. 49; 52; 54
Life in England in Aquatint and Lithography 1770-1860. Folkestone & London: 1972. V. 48
Life in England in Aquatint and Lithography, 1770-1860, Architecture, Drawing Books, Art Collections, Magazines, Navy and Army, Panoramas, Etc.... San Francisco: 1991. V. 49
Scenery of Great Britain and Ireland in Aquatint and Lithography 1770-1860. London: 1952. V. 49; 52; 54
Scenery of Great Britain and Ireland in Aquatint and Lithography 1770-1860. London: 1972. V. 48
Scenery of Great Britain and Ireland in Aquatint and Lithography, 1770-1860... San Francisco: 1991. V. 47; 49
Scenery of Great Britain and Ireland in Aquatint and Lithography 1770-1860. (with) Life in England in Aquatint and Lithography 1770-1860. (with) Travel in Aquatint and Lithography 1770-1860. London. V. 50
Scenery of Great Britain and Ireland in Aquatint and Lithography 1770-1860. (with) Life in England in Aquatint and Lithography. (with) Travel in Aquatint and Lithography. London: 1952/53/57. V. 51
Travel in Aquatint and Lithography 1770-1860. Folkestone & London: 1972. V. 52
Travel in Aquatint and Lithography 1770-1860. Mansfield: 1995. V. 54

THE ABBEY of Weyhill. London: 1805. V. 49; 54

ABBOT, DOWNING CO.
Manufacturers of Coaches & Wagons. Concord: 1871. V. 47

ABBOT, FREDERIC V.
History of the Class of 'Seventy-Nine: at the U.S. Military Academy, West Point, New York. New York & London: 1884. V. 47

ABBOT, GEORGE
Sketches About Kurrah, Mannickpore. London: 1831. V. 49

ABBOT, GORMAN
Mexico and the United States Their Mutual Relations and Common Interests. New York: 1869. V. 53

ABBOT, HENRY LARCOM
Testing of Medium and High Tension Fuzes. N.P: 1879. V. 51

ABBOT, JOHN
The Natural History of the Rarer Lepidopterous Insects of Georgia, Including Their Systematic Characters, the Particulars of Their Several Metamorphoses and the Plants on Which They Feed. London: 1797. V. 47

ABBOT, WILLIS J.
The Panama Canal. London: 1914. V. 48; 49

ABBOTT, ARTHUR V.
Testing Machines, their History, Construction and Use. New York: 1884. V. 50

ABBOTT, BELLE K.
Leah Mordecai. New York: 1875. V. 51; 53

ABBOTT, BERENICE
Photographs. New York: 1970. V. 50; 51
A Portrait of Maine. New York: 1968. V. 51
The View Camera Made Simple. Chicago & New York: 1948. V. 54
The World of Atget. New York: 1964. V. 50

ABBOTT, CARLISLE S.
Recollections of a California Pioneer. New York: 1917. V. 48

ABBOTT, CHARLES
Tratado Sobre as Leys Relativas a Navios Mercantes, e Marinheiros... Liverpool: 1819. V. 47
A Treatise of the Law Relative to Merchant Ships and Seamen (etc.). London: 1802. V. 52
A Treatise of the Law Relative to Merchant Ships and Seamen (etc.). London: 1827. V. 50

ABBOTT, CHARLES C.
Primitive History; or Illustrations of the Handiwork, in Stone, Bone and Clay of the Native Races of the Northern Atlantic Seaboard of America. Salem: 1881. V. 52

ABBOTT, CHARLES D.
Howard Pyle, a Chronicle... New York: 1925. V. 48

ABBOTT, CLARE
Rowland Ward's "Game Animals of Africa". N.P: 1979. V. 47

ABBOTT, DAN
Colorado Midland Railway: Daylight through the Divide. Denver: 1989. V. 53

ABBOTT, E. C.
We Pointed Them North, Recollections of a Cowpuncher. New York: 1939. V. 48; 53

ABBOTT, EDWIN ABBOTT
Flatland: a Romance of Many Dimensions. London: 1884. V. 51
Flatland, a Romance of Many Dimensions. San Francisco: 1980. V. 47; 52

ABBOTT, HENRY
Catalogue of a Collection of Egyptian Antiquities, the Property of Henry Abbott, M.D. Now exhibiting at the Stuyvesant Inst. New York: 1854. V. 49; 51

ABBOTT, JACOB
A Description of the Mount Vernon School in 1832. Boston: 1832. V. 54
The Harper Establishment; or, How the Story Books are Made. New York: 1855. V. 47
New England, and Her Institutions. Boston: 1835. V. 49

ABBOTT, JAMES
Narrative of a Journey from Heraut to Khiva, Moscow and St. Petersburgh, During the Late Russian Invasion of Khiva; with Some Account of the Court of Khiva and the Kingdom of Khaurism. London: 1843. V. 48; 53
Narrative of a Journey from Heraut to Khiva, Moscow, and St. Petersburgh, During the Late Russian Invasion to Khiva. London: 1884. V. 47

ABBOTT, JOHN S. C.
Christopher Carson: Familiarly Known as Kit Carson. New York: 1873. V. 47
The Life of Napoleon Bonaparte. London: 1883. V. 50
The Life of Napoleon Bonaparte. New York: 1883. V. 50

ABBOTT, LYMAN
Henry Ward Beecher: a Complete History of His Career... Hartford: 1887. V. 51

ABBOTT, MAUDE
Atlas of Congenital Cardiac Disease. New York: 1936. V. 48
Atlas of Congenital Cardiac Disease.. New York: 1954. V. 53
Classified and Annotated Bibliography of Sir William Osler's Publications. Montreal: 1939. V. 49; 50; 52
Sir William Osler Memorial Number: Appreciations and Reminiscences. Montreal: 1927. V. 51

ABBOTT, R. T.
American Seashells, The Marine Mollusca of the Atlantic and Pacific Coasts of North America. New York: 1974. V. 51
Indo-Pacific Mollusca. Philadelphia & Delaware: 1959-76. V. 50

ABBOTT, STEPHEN
The First Regiment New Hampshire Volunteers in the Great Rebellion. London: 1890. V. 47

ABBOTT, T. K.
Catalogue of the Fifteenth-Century Books in the Library of Trinity College Dublin and in Marsh's Library, Dublin, with a Few From Other Collections... 1905. V. 47
Celtic Ornaments from the Book of Kells. Dublin: 1895. V. 53

ABD-ALLAH, BEN ABD-EL-KADER
Translations from the Hakayit Abdulla (Bin Abdulkadar), Munshi. London: 1874. V. 53

ABD AL-RASHID TATTAVI
Moontukhub-ool-loghaut, or a Dictionary of Arabic Words, With a Persian Translation... Calcutta: 1808. V. 51

ABDILL, GEORGE B.
Rails West. Seattle: 1960. V. 54

ABDY, ROBERT
Choice and Valuable Collection of English, Greek & Roman Coins and Medals, of the Late Sir Robert Abdy, Bart, Deceased 1748. London: 1841. V. 48

ABE, KOBO
The Woman in the Dunes. New York: 1964. V. 47; 52

A' BECKETT, ARTHUR WILLIAM
The A'Becketts of "Punch": Memories of Father and Sons. Westminster: 1903. V. 51

A' BECKETT, GILBERT ABBOTT
The Comic Blackstone. London: 1846. V. 48; 51
The Comic Blackstone. Chicago: 1869. V. 49
The Comic Blackstone. London: 1887. V. 49; 50
The Comic Blackstone of 'Punch'. Philadelphia: 1844-46. V. 50
The Comic History of England. London: 1846-48. V. 51
The Comic History of England. London: 1847-48. V. 51
The Comic History of England. London: 1850. V. 51
The Comic History of England. London: 1860. V. 54
The Comic History of England. London: 1864. V. 47
The Comic History of England. London: 1897?. V. 51
The Comic History of England and Rome. London: 1880. V. 54
The Comic History of England. (with) The Comic History of Rome. London: 1847-48 & n.d. V. 47; 50; 52; 54
The Comic History of Rome. London. V. 49
The Comic History of Rome. London: 1851. V. 51
The Comic History of Rome. London: 1851-52. V. 49; 51
The Comic History of Rome. London: 1852. V. 50
The Comic History of Rome. London: 1860. V. 54
The Comic History of Rome. London: 1880. V. 48
George Cruikshank's Tablebook. London: 1869. V. 51

ABEEL, DAVID
Journal of a Residence in China, and the Neighboring Countries... New York: 1836. V. 51; 52

ABEL, ANNIE HELOISE
Chardon's Journal at Fort Clark, 1843-1839. Pierre: 1932. V. 48

ABEL, CLARKE
Narrative of a Journey in the Interior of China. London: 1818. V. 47; 49; 51; 54

ABEL, HENRY I.
Traveller's and Emigrant's Guide to Wisconsin & Iowa. Philadelphia: 1838. V. 47

ABEL, JOHN
Crystalline Insulin. 1926. V. 48
Crystalline Insulin. London: 1927. V. 53
On the Removal of Diffusible Substances from The Circulating Blood by Means of Dialysis. 1913. V. 48

ABELING, JAMES
The History of Roche Abbey, Yorkshire, From Its Foundation to Its Dissolution. Worksop: 1870. V. 53

ABELL, WILLIAM
The Copie of a Letter (in verse) Sent From the Roaring Boyes in elizium; to the Two Arrant Knights of the Grape, in Limbo, Alderman Abell and M. Kilvert, the Two Great Projectors for, Wine... London: 1641. V. 49
A Dialogue or Accidental Discourse Betwixt Mr. Alderman Abell, and Richard Kilvert, the Two Main Projectors for Wine, and Also Aldermans Abels (sic) Wife, etc. London: 1641. V. 49

ABERCONWAY, CHRISTABEL
The Story of Mr. Korah. London: 1954. V. 49

ABERCROMBIE, JOHN
The British Fruit-Gardener; and Art of Pruning... London: 1799. V. 53
The Garden Vade Mecum...Flower Garden, Pleasure Ground, Shrubbery and Plantations, Fruit-Garden and Kitchen Garden, Greenhouse and Hot-House. Dublin: 1790. V. 49
The Hot-House Garadener on the General Culture of the Pine-Apple and Methods of Forcing Early Grapes, Peaches, Nectarines and Other Choice Fruits, in Hot-Houses, Vineries, Fruit-Houses, Hot-Walls &c. London: 1789. V. 53
Inquiries Concerning the Intellectual Powers and the Investigation of the Truth. Edinburgh: 1830. V. 48; 51
Pathological and Practical Researches on Diseases of the Brain and Spinal Cord. Edinburgh: 1828. V. 47; 51
Pathological and Practical Researches on Diseases of the Brain and Spinal Cord. Philadelphia: 1843. V. 47
The Universal Gardener and Botanist; or, a General Dictionary of Gardening and Botany. London: 1778. V. 50

ABERCROMBIE, LASCELLES
Lyrics and Unfinished Poems. Newtown: 1940. V. 48; 51; 52

ABERCROMBIE, PATRICK
A Civic Survey and Plan for the City and Royal Burgh of Edinburgh. Edinburgh: 1949. V. 51
Cumbrian Regional Planning Scheme, Prepared for the Cumbrian Regional Joint Advisory Scheme. 1932. V. 52
The Martial Achievements of the Scots Nation. Edinburgh: 1711-15. V. 48

ABERCROMBY, HELEN
Susie's and Little Hugh's Alphabet. Aberdeen;. V. 48

ABERCROMBY, JOHN
A Study of the Bronze Age Pottery of Great Britain and Ireland and Its Associated Grave-Goods. Oxford: 1912. V. 49; 51; 53

ABERG, NILS
The Anglo Saxons in England During the Early Centuries After the Invasion. Uppsala: 1926. V. 48

ABERNETHY, ANDREW
The Pocket Chronological Directory; or, Compend of General History, in the Form of Questions and Answers. Hartford: 1817. V. 50

ABERNETHY, JOHN
Lectures on the Theory and Practice of Surgery. London: 1830. V. 48
The Surgical and Physiological Works of... London: 1830. V. 47; 48; 49; 50; 51; 52; 53
Surgical Observations, Containing a Classification of Tumours, with Cases to Illustrate the History of Each Species... London: 1804. V. 50
Surgical Observations on Injuries of the Head; and On Miscellaneous Subjects. Philadelphia: 1811. V. 52
Surgical Observations On the Constitutional Origin and Treatment of Local Diseases; and On Aneurisms. Philadelphia: 1811. V. 48; 51
Surgical Observations On the Constitutional Origin and Treatment of Local Diseases; and On Aneurisms. London: 1817. V. 50; 53
Surgical Observations on Tumours and on Lumbar Abscesses. London: 1811. V. 47; 48; 49

ABERT, JAMES WILLIAM
Report of the Secretary of War Communicating in Answer to a Resolution of the Senate, a Report and Map of the Examination of New Mexico. Washington: 1848. V. 52; 53
Through the Country of the Comanche Indians in the Fall of the Year 1845... San Francisco: 1970. V. 48; 49; 50
Western America in 1846-1847. San Francisco: 1966. V. 48; 50; 52; 54

ABINGDON, ROGERT
The Green Mat - a Romance of Askew People. London: 1925. V. 48

ABINGDON, WILLOUGHBY BERTIE, EARL OF
Thoughts on the Letter of Edmund Burke, Esq; to the Sheriffs of Bristol, on the Affairs of America. Oxford: 1777. V. 47

ABISH, WALTER
Duel Site. New York: 1970. V. 51
How German Is It. Wie Deutsch Ist Es. New York: 1980. V. 53

ABLANCOURT, SIEUR D'
Memoirs of the Sieur d'Ablancourt. London: 1703. V. 48

THE ABORIGINES of Minnesota: a report Based on the Collections of Jacob V. Brower and on the Field Surveys and Notes of Alfred J. Hill and Theodore H. Lewis. St. Paul: 1911. V. 48

ABOUNDING Grace: a Poem. Taunton: 1775. V. 50; 54

ABRAHALL, JOHN HOSKYNS
Western Woods and Waters: Poems and Illustrative Notes. London: 1864. V. 51

ABRAHAM, A. P.
Rock Climbing in Skye. London: 1908. V. 53

ABRAHAM A SANTA CLARA
Grammatica Religiosa, Quae Pie Docet Declinare a Malo, & Facere Bonum... Salzburg: 1691. V. 53
Wohl Angefulter Wein-Keller, In Welchem Mance Durstige Seel Sich Mit Einem Geistlichen Geseng-Gott Erquickon Kan. Wurzberg: 1710. V. 47

ABRAHAM, GEORGE D.
British Mountain Climbs. London: 1909. V. 49
The Complete Mountaineer. London: 1907. V. 54
Motor Ways in Lakeland. London: 1913. V. 52
Mountain Adventures at Home and Abroad. London: 1910. V. 54
Rock-Climbing in North Wales. London: 1906. V. 53

ABRAHAM, JAMES JOHNSTON
Lettsom. His Life, Times, Friends and Descencants. London: 1933. V. 54

ABRAHAMS, PETER
Mine Boy. London: 1946. V. 54

ABRAM.
A *Military Poem, by A. Young Rebelle, Esq. of the Army.* Richmond: 1863. V. 51

ABRAM, WILLIAM ALEXANDER
A History of Blackburn, Town and Parish, Parish of Blackburn, County of Lancaster. Blackburn: 1877. V. 48; 54

ABRAMS, ALBERT
Transactions of the Antiseptic Club. New York: 1895. V. 52

ABRAMS, ALEXANDER SAINT CLAIR
The Trials of the Soldier's Wife: A Tale of the Second American Revolution. Atlanta: 1864. V. 51

ABRAMS, L.
Illustrated Flora of the Pacific States: Washington, Oregon and California. Stanford: 1940-60/61-65. V. 50

ABRANTES, MIGUEL CALMON DU PIN E ALMEIDA, MARQUEZ DE
Americus: Cartas Politiicas Extrahidas do Padre Amaro. London: 1835. V. 48

ABRANTES E CASTRO, BERNARDO JOSE DE
Memoria Sobre a Conducta Do...Desde a Retirada de Sua Alteza Real o Principe Regente Nosso Senhor Para a America. London: 1810. V. 48

ABREGE de l'Histoire Francaise avec les Effigies... Rouen: 1612. V. 47

AN ABRIDGEMENT of Geography. Adorned with Cuts Representing the Dress of Each Country. London: 1800. V. 48; 50

ABRIDGEMENTS of Specifications Relating to the Manufacture of Iron and Steel 1621-1865. London: 1857-58. V. 50

AN ABRIDGMENT of the Prerogatives of St. Ann, Mother of the Mother of God. London: 1688. V. 50

ABROAD.. London: 1890. V. 49

ABSE, DANNIE
After Every Green Thing: a Selection of Poems. London. V. 53

ABSOLON, JOHN
Rural Pickings; or, Attractive Points in Country Life and Scenery. London: 1846. V. 48; 50
Visits to Beechwood Farm: or, Country Pleasures and Hints for Happiness. London: 1848. V. 48

ABSTRACT of Title to Lands of the Market and Fourteenth Streets Homestead Association. San Francisco: 1876. V. 49

ABSTRACTS OF Somersetshire. London: 1887-89. V. 51

ABURBIDGE, F. W.
Cool Orchids and How to Grow Them... London: 1874. V. 47

ABY, JOE C.
The Tales of Rube Hoffenstein. New York: 1882. V. 47; 49

ACADEMY OF PACIFIC COAST HISTORY
Publications. Berkeley;: 1910-11. V. 52
Publications. Berkeley: 1910-19. V. 52

ACADEMY OF SCIENCE OF ST. LOUIS
Transactions. 1857-91. V. 48; 52

ACCADEMIA DE' GELATI, BOLOGNA
Memorie, Imprese, e Ritratti de' Signori Accademici Gelati di Bologna Reccolte ne Principato del Signor Conte Valerio Zani il Ritardato. Bologna: 1672. V. 54

ACCENT Anthology. New York: 1946. V. 49

ACCIDENTS at the Opening of Hungerford Market. and Mr. Grahams Fatal Descent in the Balloon. 1836?. V. 47

THE ACCOMPLISHED Letter-Writer; or, Universal Correspondent. London: 1779. V. 54

AN ACCOUNT Of All the Manors, Messuages, Lands, Tenements and Hereditaments in the Different Counties of England and Wales, Held by lease from the Crown. London: 1787. V. 52

AN ACCOUNT of Some Remarkable Passages in the Life of a Private Gentleman; With Reflections Thereon. London: 1711. V. 47; 49

AN ACCOUNT of the Burman Empire and the Kingdom of Assam... Calcutta: 1839. V. 53

AN ACCOUNT of the Celebrations of the Jubilee, on the 25th October 1809...of George the Third... Birmingham: 1809. V. 54

AN ACCOUNT of the Ceremony in Westminster Hall on Thursday May 9th, 1935... 1935. V. 52

AN ACCOUNT of the Coal Bank Disaster at Blue Rock, Ohio... Malta: 1856. V. 48

AN ACCOUNT of the Constitution and Present State of Great Britain. London. V. 49

ACCOUNT of the County Stock Levied and raised by the County of Cumberland, and Of Other Sums Cararied to the Credit Thereof, for the Year Ending at the Easter Quarter Sessions, 1849... Carlisle: 1849. V. 52

AN ACCOUNT of the Dedication of the West Window of St. John's Church, Beverly Farms, Whitsunday, May thirty first MDCCCCXXV. V. 47

AN ACCOUNT of the Discovery of the South Part of the World, Which is Thought to be One Quarter of the Earth... London: 1759. V. 47; 50

ACCOUNT of the Escape of the French King; His Recapture and the Proceedings of the National Assembly, in Consequence Thereof. London. V. 50

AN ACCOUNT of the Free-School Society of New York. New York: 1814. V. 51

AN ACCOUNT of the Institution of the Society for the Establishment of a Literary Fund: Constitutions...Transactions of the Committee in the Application of Subscriptions... London: 1800. V. 53

AN ACCOUNT of the Manner, of the Behaviour of the Prisoners, Who Recieved Sentence of Death, on Friday the 27th of April, 1688. London: 1688. V. 53

AN ACCOUNT of the New Sheriffs, Holding Their Office. Made Public Upon Reason of Conscience, Respecting Themselves and Others, in Regard to the Act for Corporations. London: 1680. V. 52

AN ACCOUNT of the Origin, Progress and Consequences of the Late Discontents of the Army on the Madras Establishment. London: 1810. V. 52

AN ACCOUNT of the Present English Conspiracy, Taken from the Report of the Secret Committee of the House of Commons, Just Now Published... London: 1799?. V. 48

AN ACCOUNT of the Proceedings at the Guild-Hall of the City of London, on Saturday September 12, 1679. London: 1679. V. 52

AN ACCOUNT of the Receipts and Expenditures of the United States, for the Year 1831. City of Washington: 1832. V. 50

AN ACCOUNT of the Rise and Progress of the Indian or Spasmodic Cholera; with a Particular Description of the Symptoms Attending the Disease. New Haven: 1832. V. 52

ACCOUNT of the Russian Discoveries Between Asia and America to Which are Added the Conquest of Siberia and the History of the Transactions and Commerce Between Russia and China. London: 1780. V. 54

AN ACCOUNT of the Terrible Explosion at Fales and Gray's Car Manufactory, Hartford, Connecticut, Which Occurred on Thursday, March 2nd, 1854.. Hartford: 1854. V. 53

ACCOUNT of the Terrific and Fatal Riot at the New York Astor Place Opera House...With the Quarrels of Forrest and Macready, Including All the Causes Which Led to that Awful Tragedy!. New York: 1849. V. 50; 53; 54

AN ACCOUNT of the True Author of Two Infamous Libels, Entitled, I. A Letter from Count Sinzendorf, &c. to Mr. DePalm...II.A Memorial Presented by Mr. De Palm, &c. London: 1727. V. 53

AN ACCOUNT of the Visit of His Royal Highness the Prince Regent, with Their Imperial and Royal Majesties... (with) An Account of the Entertainment Given to Field Marshall His Grace the Duke of Wellington, by the Corporation.. London: 1815. V. 49; 53

AN ACCOUNT of the Visit of His Royal Highness The Prince Regent and Their Imperial...Majesties The Emperor of Russia and the King of Prussia to the University of Oxford in June MDCCCXIV. Oxford: 1815. V. 48; 53

AN ACCOUNT of (together with) the Writing Itself That Was Found in the Pocket of Lawrence Hill, at the Time He and Green Were Executed...for the Murder of Sr. Edmond-Berry Godfrey Kt. 1679. V. 53

ACCOUNT of..."Great Eastern" Steam Ship. London: 1857. V. 48

ACCUM, FREDERICK
Chemical Amusement, Comprising a Series of Curious and Instructive Experiments in Chemistry. London: 1817. V. 48
Chemical Amusement Comprising a Series of Curious and Instructive Experiments in Chemistry... London: 1821. V. 50
Culinary Chemistry. London: 1821. V. 48; 53
A Practical Essay on Chemical Re-Agents or Tests. London: 1816. V. 50
A Practical Treatise on Gas-Light... London: 1815. V. 47; 48; 50; 52; 53; 54
A Practical Treatise on Gas-Light... London: 1818. V. 51
System of Theoretical and Practical Chemistry. Philadelphia: 1808. V. 48; 50; 54
A Treatise on the Art of Making Fruits; Exhibiting the Chemical principles Upon Which the Art of Wine Making Depends; the Fruits Best Adpated for Home Made Wines and The Method of Preparing Them. London: 1820. V. 51

AN ACCURATE Account of the Trial of William Corder for the Murder of Maria Marten...To Which are Added, An Explantory Preface and Fifty-Three of the Letters Sent by Various Ladies, in Answer to Corder's Matrimonial Advertisements... London: 1828. V. 51

AN ACCURATE Description and History of the Cathedral and Metropolical Church of St. Peter, York, from It's Foundation to the Present Year. London: 1790/70. V. 51

AN ACCURATE Description and History of the Metropolitan and Cathedral Churches of Canterbury and York, from Their First Foundation to the Present Year. London: 1755. V. 53

ACERBI, JOSEPH
Travels through Sweden, Finland, and Lapland to the North Cape, in the Years 1798 and 1799. London: 1802. V. 47; 54

ACHAD, FRATER
The Egyptian Revival: or the Evercoming Sun in the Light of the Tarot. Chicago: 1923. V. 52

ACHARYA, PRASANNA KUMAR
Architecture of Manasara. London: 1933. V. 49

ACHDJIAN, A.
A Fundamental Art of the Rug. Paris: 1949. V. 48

ACHEBE, CHINUA
Christmas in Biafra and Other Poems. Garden City: 1973. V. 53
Morning Yet on Creation Day - Essays. London: 1975. V. 53
No Longer at Ease. New York: 1961. V. 53; 54
Things Fall Apart. New York: 1959. V. 52; 53

ACHERLEY, ROGER
The Britannic Constitution; or, the Fundamental Form of Government in Britain. London: 1727. V. 51
Free Parliaments; or, an Argument on Their Constitution; Proving Some of Their Powers to Be Independent. London: 1731. V. 48

ACHESON, WILLIAM
An Enquiry Into the Origin, Progress and Material of Ancient Personal Ornaments. Dublin: 1856. V. 53

ACHILLES TATIUS
De Dlitophontis et leucippes Amoribus Libri VIII. Heidelberg: 1606. V. 52
The Loves of Clitophon and Leucippe. Oxford: 1638. V. 52
The Loves of Clitophon and Leucippe. London: 1923. V. 51
The Loves of Clitophon and Leucippe. Oxford: 1923. V. 53

ACHINTRE, A.
From the Atlantic to the Pacific. A Journey to Vancouver and British Columbia. Prospectus. Montreal: 1872. V. 53

ACKERLEY, J. R.
Hindoo Holiday. London: 1932. V. 47; 53; 54
Hindoo Holiday. London: 1952. V. 54
My Dog Tulip. London: 1956. V. 51
The Prisoners of War. London: 1925. V. 47; 50; 51; 53; 54

ACKERMAN, JAMES S.
The Architecture of Michelangelo. New York: 1961/64. V. 51; 53

ACKERMANN, JAMES S.
The Architecture of Michelangelo. 1964. V. 48

ACKERMANN, R.
Six Progressive Lessons for Flower Painting.. London: 1810. V. 53

ACKERMANN, RUDOLPH
The History of Rugby School. London: 1816. V. 49
The History of the Abbey Church of St. Peters Westminster. London: 1812. V. 47; 48; 49; 50; 51; 52; 54
The History of the Charter-House. London: 1816. V. 52
The History of the Colleges of Winchester, Eton and Westminster, with the Charterhouse, the Schools of Saint Paul's, Merchant Taylors, Harrow and Rugby and the Free School of Christ's Hospital. London: 1816. V. 47; 48; 52
A History of the University of Cambridge, Its Colleges, Halls and Public Buildings. London: 1814-16. V. 47
A History of the University of Cambridge, its Colleges, Halls and Public Buildings. London: 1815. V. 49; 52
A History of the University of Oxford, Its Colleges, Halls and Public Buildings. London: 1814. V. 47; 48; 49; 50; 52; 54
The Microcosm of London. London: 1808-10. V. 51; 52
The Microcosm of London. London: 1810. V. 47
The Microcosm of London or London in Miniature. London: 1904. V. 48; 49; 50
A Suite of Six Aquatint Views of Landscapes and Ruins. London: 1797. V. 48

ACKERMANN'S Drawing Book for 1824. London: 1824. V. 53

ACKERMANN'S New Drawing Book of Light and Shadow, in Imitation of Indian Ink. London: 1812, plates. V. 53

ACKLAND, VALENTINE
Country Conditions. London: 1936. V. 54
Twenty-Eight Poems. London: 1957. V. 53

ACKLEY, MARY E.
Crossing the Plains and Early Days in California: Memories of Girlhood Days in California's Golden Age. San Francisco: 1928. V. 51

ACKROYD, PETER
Chatterton. London: 1987. V. 54
Country Life. London: 1978. V. 52
Dickens. London: 1990. V. 49; 51; 53
Dressing Up: Transvestism and Drug: The History of an Obsession. New York: 1979. V. 54
English Music. London: 1992. V. 48; 49; 51; 53
The Great Fire of London. London: 1982. V. 50; 54
The Last Testament of Oscar Wilde. London: 1983. V. 53
London Lickpenny. London: 1973. V. 52; 53
Notes for a New Culture - an Essay on Modernism. London: 1976. V. 47; 54
Ouch (Poems). 1971. V. 51

ACLAND, ALICE
Caroline Norton. London: 1948. V. 50

ACLAND, HENRY WENTWORTH
Memoir on the Cholera at Oxford, in the Year 1854... Oxford: 1856. V. 48
The Oxford Museum. London: 1859. V. 52

ACORN, MILTON
Jawbreakers. Toronto: 1963. V. 47; 51

ACOSTA, CHRISTOVAL
Tratado en Contra y Pro de la Vida Solitaria Con Otros dos Tratados; Uno de la Religion y Religioso, Otro Contra los Hombres Que Mal Viven. Venice: 1592. V. 53
Trattato...Della Historia, Natura et Virtu Delle Droghe Medicinali & altri Semplici Rarissimi, che Vengono Portraiti dalle Indie Orientali in Europa... Venice: 1585. V. 48

ACOSTA, JOSE DE
De Natura de Novi Orbis. Cologne: 1596. V. 54
Historia Natural Y Moral De Las Indias. Seville: 1590. V. 52

ACOSTA, OSCAR ZETA
The Revolt of the Cockroach People. San Francisco: 1973. V. 51

ACRELIUS, ISRAEL
Beskrifning Om de Swenska Forsamlingars Forna Och Narwarande Tilstand, Det sa Kallade Nya Swerige... Stockholm: 1759. V. 47

ACRES, W. MARSTON
The Bank of England From Within, 1694-1900. London: 1931. V. 48; 50

AN ACROBATIC Alphabet. London: 1986. V. 53

THE ACT for Permitting the Free Importation of Cattle from Ireland, Considering with a View to the Interests of Both Kingdoms. London: 1760. V. 54

ACTIUS, THOMAS
De Ludo Scacchorum in Legali Methodo Tractatus. Pesaro: 1583. V. 54

ACTIVE Anthology. London: 1933. V. 47; 51

ACTON, HAROLD
Cornelian. London: 1928. V. 48; 49
The Last of the Medici. Florence: 1930. V. 48; 51
The Last of the Medici. London: 1932. V. 49
Memoirs of an Aesthete. London: 1948. V. 52
More Memoirs of an Aesthete. London: 1970. V. 53
This Chaos. Paris: 1930. V. 50
Tuscan Villas. London: 1973. V. 47

ACTON, JOHN
An Essay on Shooting... London: 1791. V. 48; 49; 50; 54

ACTON, WILLIAM
A Complete Practical Treatise on Venereal Diseases and Their Immediate and Remote Consequences. New York: 1846. V. 53
Prostitution, Considered In Its Moral, Social and Sanitary Aspects, in London and Other Large Cities. London: 1857. V. 52

ACUNA, CHRISTOVAL DE
Voyages and Discoveries in South America. London: 1698. V. 47

ADAIR, F. E. S.
A Summer in High Asia, Being a Record of Sport and Travel in Baltistan and Ladakh... 1899. V. 54

ADAIR, JAMES
The History of the American Indians; Particularly Those Nations Adjoining to the Mississippi, East and West Flordia, Georgia, South and North Carolina and Virginia. London: 1775. V. 47; 48
A Philosophical and Medical Sketch of the Natural History of the Human Body and Mind. Bath: 1787. V. 54

ADAIR, JOHN
Hints on the Culture of Ornamental Plants in Ireland. London: 1878. V. 52

ADAIR, ROBERT
Sketch of the Character of the Late Duke of Devonshire. London: 1811. V. 52

ADAIR, W. P.
Memorial of the Indian Delegates from the Indian Country, Protesting Against the Passage by Congress of the Bill "Providing for the Establishment of a United States Court in the Indian Territory and for Other Purposes.". Washington?: 1872. V. 48

ADALBERT, PRINCE OF PRUSSIA
Travels in the South of Europe and in Brazil: With a Voyage Up the Amazon and Its Tributary the Xingu... London: 1849. V. 48

ADAM, ALEXANDER
Roman Antiques: or an Account of the Manners and Customs of the Romans... London: 1825. V. 47
Roman Antiquities; or, An Account of the Manners and Customs of the Romans. London: 1792. V. 49
A Summary of Geography and History, Both Ancient and Modern. Edinburgh;: 1794. V. 53

ADAM, G. MERCER
Toronto, Old and New: a Memorial Volume - Historical, Descriptive and Pictorial... Toronto: 1891. V. 50

ADAM, HELEN DOUGLAS
Shadow of the Moon. London. V. 48

ADAM, JOHN
Catalogue Raisonne of Books in a Private Library. Greenock: 1867. V. 49

ADAM, MELCHIOR
Vitae Germanorum Medicorum: Qui Saeculo Superiori et Qui Excurrit Claruenrunt... Heidelberg: 1620. V. 51; 53; 54

ADAM, P.
Australian Rainforests. London: 1992. V. 48; 50; 51

ADAM, PAUL
Practical Bookbinding. New York: 1903. V. 47

ADAM, R. B.
The R. B. Adam Library Relating to Dr. Samuel Johnson and His Era. London: 1929. V. 50; 52

ADAM, ROBERT
Color Schemes of Adam Ceilings. New York: 1928. V. 47
Ruins of the Palace of the Emperor Diocletian at Spalatro in Dalmatia... London: 1764. V. 50

ADAM, W.
The Gem of the Peak; or Matlock Bath and Its Vicinity. Derby: 1845. V. 48; 52
The Gem of the Peak; or Matlock Bath and Its Vicinity. London: 1851. V. 54

ADAMS, A. LEITH
Field and Forest Rambles, With Notes & Observations on the Natural History of Eastern Canada. London: 1873. V. 48; 49; 50; 51; 52; 53
Travels of a Naturalist in Japan and Manchuria. London: 1870. V. 48
Wanderings of a Naturalist in India. Edinburgh: 1867. V. 52

ADAMS, ABIGAIL SMITH
Letters of Mrs. Adams, the Wife of John Adams. Boston: 1840. V. 53

ADAMS, ANDREW N.
A Genealogical History of Henry Adams of Braintree, Mass. Rutland: 1898. V. 54

ADAMS, ANDY
Log of a Cowboy. Boston: 1903. V. 48; 51; 53
The Log of a Cowboy. New York: 1903. V. 50
The Outlet. Boston: 1905. V. 49
The Ranch on the Beaver. Boston: 1927. V. 47; 48; 49

ADAMS, ANSEL
The American Wilderness. Boston: 1990. V. 53
Ansel Adams. New York: 1972. V. 49
Ansel Adams Images 1923-1974. Boston: 1974. V. 51
Born Free and Equal. New York: 1944. V. 47; 52
The Camera. Boston: 1981. V. 47
Camera and Lens: The Creative Approach, Studio, Laboratory and Operation. Boston: 1976. V. 50
Death Valley. San Francisco: 1959. V. 47
Examples. The Making of 40 Photographs. Boston: 1984. V. 49
Fiat Lux. New York: 1967. V. 47
The Four Seasons in Yosemite National Park. Los Angeles: 1936. V. 47
Images 1923-1974. Boston: 1974. V. 47; 48; 53; 54
Images 1923-1974. Boston: 1981. V. 47; 50; 53
Making a Photograph: an Introduction to Photography. London & New York: 1935. V. 52
My Camera in the National Parks. Boston: 1950. V. 47; 51; 52; 53
My Camera in Yosemite Valley. Boston: 1949. V. 47; 51
The Negative. Boston: 1981. V. 47
The Pageant of History and the Panorama of Today in Northern California. San Francisco: 1954. V. 47; 50; 52
Photographs of the Southwest. Boston;: 1976. V. 47; 53
Polaroid Land Photography. Boston: 1980. V. 47
The Portfolios. 1977. V. 52
The Portfolios of Ansel Adams. Boston: 1981. V. 48
Shamrock Over Ireland!. San Francisco: 1939. V. 47
Sierra Nevada: the John Muir Trail. Berkeley: 1938. V. 52
Singular Images. Dobbs Ferry: 1974. V. 53
Taos Pueblo. Boston: 1977. V. 51; 52
These We Inherit, the Parklands of America. San Francisco: 1962. V. 48; 51
This Is the American Earth. San Francisco: 1960. V. 47; 50
Yosemite and the Range of Light. Boston: 1979. V. 47; 48; 49; 50; 51; 52; 53
Yosemite Trails and Tales. San Francisco: 1934. V. 47

ADAMS, ARTHUR
A Genealogy of the Lake Family of Great Egg Harbor, in old Gloucester County, in New Jersey, Descended from John Lake of Gravesend, Long Island. N.P: 1915. V. 47; 49; 51
Travels of a Naturalist in Japan and Manchuria. London: 1870. V. 48

ADAMS, B. M. G.
England. Paris: 1923. V. 50

ADAMS, BERNARD
London Illustrated, 1604-1851. London: 1983. V. 50; 51; 54
London Illustrated, 1604-1851. Phoenix: 1983. V. 50

ADAMS, CHARLES FRANCIS
A Chapter of Erie. Boston: 1869. V. 53
Chapters of Erie, and Other Essays. Boston: 1871. V. 51
How to Settle The Texas Question. Boston: 1845. V. 49

ADAMS, CLINTON
Fritz Scholder Lithographs. Boston: 1975. V. 51

ADAMS, CYDNEY
Flesh of Best Intention. Tuscaloosa: 1989. V. 51

ADAMS, DANIEL
The Medical and Agricultural Register, for the Years 1806 and 1807. Boston: 1806-07. V. 52

ADAMS, DOUGLAS
The Hitch Hiker's Guide to the Galaxy. London: 1980. V. 54

ADAMS, EDWARD
The Polychromatic Ornament of Italy. London: 1846. V. 52

ADAMS, ELEANOR B.
The Missions of New Mexico, 1776. Albuq: 1975. V. 48

ADAMS, ELIZABETH LAURA
Dark Symphony. New York: 1942. V. 54

ADAMS, ELONIE
Those Not Elect. New York: 1925. V. 51

ADAMS, EMMA HILDRETH
Digging the Top Off and Other Stories. San Francisco: 1892. V. 47

ADAMS, F. C.
Manuel Pereira; or, the Sovereign Rule of South Carolina. Washington: 1853. V. 54

ADAMS, F. W.
Theological Criticisms, or Hints of the Philosophy of Man and Nature. Montpelier: 1843. V. 51; 54

ADAMS, FRANCIS
A Child of the Age. London: 1894. V. 50
Tiberius: a drama. London: 1894. V. 50; 54

ADAMS, FRANCIS COLBURN
Our World; or, the Democrat's Rule. London: 1855. V. 52

ADAMS, FRANK
The History of Sam the Sportsman. London. V. 54
State of Texas Buildings. Austin: 1937. V. 47
Texas Democracy: a Centennial History of Politics and Personalities of the Democratic Party (1836-1936). Austin: 1937. V. 47; 53

ADAMS, FRANK DAWSON
The Birth and Development of the Geological Sciences. Baltimore: 1938. V. 54

ADAMS, FRANKLIN P.
Innocent Merriment: an Anthology of Light Verse. New York: 1942. V. 50

ADAMS, FREDERICK B.
Bookbindings by T. J. Cobden-Sanderson. An Exhibition at the Pierpont Morgan Library. New York: 1969. V. 52
Radical Literature in America, an Address, to Which is Appended a Catalogue of an Exhibition held at the Grolier Club in New York City. Stamford: 1939. V. 49; 54
The Sadleir Collection - Addresses Delivered by Frederick B. Adams, Jr. and David A. Randall at the Dedication Ceremonies... Los Angeles: 1953. V. 50
To Russia with Frost. Boston: 1963. V. 49

ADAMS, FREDERICK UPHAM
John Henry Smith. A Humorous Romance of Outdoor Life. New York: 1905. V. 52

ADAMS, GEORGE
Astronomical and Geographical Essays... London: 1790. V. 52
Astronomical and Geographical Essays... Whitehall: 1800. V. 51
An Essay on Vision, Briefly Explaining the Fabric of the Eye, and the Nature of Vision. London: 1792. V. 53
Essays on the Microscope. London: 1798. V. 52
The Maine Register, and Business Directory for the Year 1856... South Berwick: 1856. V. 54
Micrographia Illustrata, or the Knowledge of the Microscope Explain'd... London: 1747. V. 53
A Treatise Describing and Explaining the Construction and Use of New Celestial and Terrestial Globes. London: 1766. V. 48; 51
A Treatise Describing the Construction and Explaining the Use, of New Celestial and Terrestial Globes. London: 1769. V. 51; 54

ADAMS, H.
The Smaller British Birds. London: 1874. V. 53

ADAMS, H. G.
Beautiful Shells: Their Nature, Structure and Uses. London: 1855. V. 48
Humming Birds. London: 1856. V. 49
Humming Birds Described and Illustrated. London. V. 49
The Language and Poetry of Flowers. New York: 1858. V. 47
The Smaller British Birds, with Descriptions of Their Nests, Eggs, Habits, etc. London: 1874. V. 47
The Smaller British Birds, with Descriptions of their Nests, Eggs, Habits, Etc. London: 1894. V. 52
The Smaller British Feeding Birds. London: 1894. V. 50

ADAMS, H. M.
Catalogue of Books Printed on the Continent of Europe, 1501-1600, in Cambridge Libraries. Cambridge: 1967. V. 47; 53

ADAMS, HANNAH
An Alphabetical Compendium of the Varous Sects Which Have Appeared in the World... Boston: 1784. V. 47; 49

ADAMS, HANNAH continued
A Narrative of the Controversy Between the Rev. Jedidiah Morse, D.D. and the Author. Boston: 1814. V. 53
A Summary History of New-England, from the First Settlement at Plymouth to the Acceptance of the Federal Constitution. Dedham: 1799. V. 50
The Truth and Excellence of the Christian Religion Exhibited. Boston: 1804. V. 50; 51
A View of Religions, in Two Parts. Boston: 1791. V. 50; 51; 53
A View of Religions, in Two Parts. Boston: 1801. V. 51; 54

ADAMS, HENRY
A Catalogue of the Books of John Quincy Adams Deposited in the Boston Athenaeum. Boston: 1938. V. 50
Democracy. New York: 1880. V. 47; 49; 51; 52; 53; 54
Democracy. London: 1882. V. 47; 49; 51; 52; 54
Democratie. Roman Americain. Paris: 1883. V. 47
The Education of Henry Adams. Boston: 1942. V. 47; 52; 54
History of the United States. New York: 1889-90. V. 53
History of the United States of America. New York: 1898. V. 49
A Letter to American Teachers of History. Washington: 1910. V. 54
Letters of Henry Adams (1858-1891). Boston: 1930. V. 49
Memoirs of Arii Taimai E Marama of Eimeo, Teriirere of Tooarai. Paris: 1901. V. 49; 51
Mont Saint Michel and Chartres. New York: 1957. V. 47; 48; 53; 54

ADAMS, J. N.
A Bibliography of Nineteenth Century Legal Literature. London: 1992-95. V. 52

ADAMS, JAMES
The Dartmoor Prison; or, a Faithful Narrative of the Massacre of American Seamen. To which is Added a Sketch of the Treatment of Prisoners, During the Late War, by the British Government. Pittsburgh: 1816. V. 52

ADAMS, JAMES H.
Message of His Excellency James H. Adams to the Legislature of South Carolina, at Session in 1855. Columbia: 1855. V. 52

ADAMS, JEREMY DUQUESNAY
A Leaf From the Letters of St. Jerome First Printed by Sixtus Riessinger, Rome c. 1466-1467. Los Angeles/London: 1981. V. 51; 52

ADAMS, JOHN
An Address to the Convention for Framing a New Constitution of Government, for the State of Massachusetts Bay to Their Constituents. Boston: 1780. V. 52
Anecdotes, Bons-Mots, and Characteristic Traits of the Greatest Princes, Politicians, Orators and Wits of Modern Times. London: 1789. V. 50
A Collection of State Papers Relative to His First Acknowledgement of the Sovereignty of the United States of America, and the Reception of Their Minister Plenipotentiary by the States-General of the United Netherlands. The Hague: 1782. V. 49
Correspondence of the Late President Adams, Originally Published in the Boston Patriot, in a Series of Letters: Number 1. Boston: 1809. V. 47
Curious Thoughts On the History of Man... London: 1789. V. 49
A Defence of the Constitutions of Government of the United States of America. London: 1787/88. V. 47; 53
A Defence of the Constitutions of Government of the United States of America. Boston: 1788. V. 50
A Defence of the Constitutions of Government of the United States of America, Against the Attack of M. Turgot in His Letter to Dr. Price, Dated the Twenty-Second Day of March, 1778. London: 1794. V. 52
Defense des Constitutions Americaines. Paris: 1792. V. 51
Flowers of Ancient History: Comprehending On a New Plan, the Most Remarkable and Interesting Events, as Well As Characters of Antiquity. Leesburg: 1822. V. 51
The Flowers of Modern Travels... Boston: 1797. V. 50
Index Villaris or an Exact Register...of All the Market Towns, Parishes, Villages (&c)... London: 1690. V. 54
Legal Papers of John Adams. Cambridge: 1965. V. 50; 51
Sketches of the History, Genius, Disposition, Accomplishments, Employments, Customs, Virtues and Vices of the Fair Sex. Philadelphia: 1797. V. 50; 51
Sketches of the History, Genius, Disposition, Accomplishments, Employments, Customs, Virtues and Vices of the Fair Sex, In All Parts of the World. Boston: 1807. V. 48; 50; 51; 53
Twenty-Six Letters, Upon Interesting Subjects... New York: 1789. V. 47
Woman. Sketches of the History, Genius, Disposition, Accomplishments, Employments, Customs and Importance of the Fair Sex, In All Parts of the World. London: 1790. V. 47

ADAMS, JOHN GREGORY
Reminiscences of the Nineteenth Massachusetts Regiment. Boston: 1899. V. 47

ADAMS, JOHN, MRS.
Commonplace Book. Washington: 1826. V. 54

ADAMS, JOHN QUINCY
An Answer to Paine's Rights of Man. Dublin: 1793. V. 48
Discurso del Ex-President de los Estados Unidos...en la Camara de Representantes de Washington. mayo 25 de 1836. Mejico: 1836. V. 52
The Duplicate Letters, the Fisheries and the Mississippi. Louisville: 1823. V. 51
The Jubilee of the Constitution. New York: 1839. V. 47; 51
Letters from the Hon. John Quincy Adams, to Edward Livingston, Grand High Priest of the General Grand Royal Arch Chapter of the United States. Hartford: 1834. V. 47
Poems of Religion and Society with Notices of His Life and Character by John Davis and t. H. Benton. New York: 1848. V. 49
Poems of Religion and Society...with Notices of His Life and Character... Auburn: 1850. V. 47
The Social Compact, Exemplified in the Constitution of the Commonwealth of Massachusetts, with Remarks on the Theories of Divine Right of Hobbes and Filmer, and the Counter Theories of Sidney, Locke, Montesquieu and Rousseau. Providence: 1842. V. 54
The Writings of... New York: 1913. V. 53

ADAMS, JOHN, RIDING MASTER
An Analysis of Horsemanship; Teaching the Whole Art of Riding, in the Manege, Military, Hunting, Racing and Travelling System. Together with the method of Breaking Horses. London: 1805. V. 47

ADAMS, JOHN S.
Answers to Seventeen Objections Against Spiritaul Intercourse and Inquiries Relating to the Manifestions of the Present Time. New York: 1853. V. 52

ADAMS, JULIUS J.
Challenge: a Study in Negro Leadership. New York: 1949. V. 52

ADAMS, LEONIE
Midsummer. Pasadena: 1929. V. 54
Those Not Elect. New York: 1925. V. 47; 49

ADAMS, NATHANIEL
Annals of Portsmouth (New Hampshire), Comprising a Period of Two Hundred Years from the First Settlement of the Town... Portsmouth: 1825. V. 52

ADAMS, OSCAR FAY
The Story of Jane Austen's Life. Boston: 1897. V. 47; 49

ADAMS, RAMON F.
The Adams One-Fifty: a Checklist of the 150 Most Important Books on Western Outlaws and Lawmen (with) Six Score: the 120 Best Books on the Range Cattle Industry. Austin: 1976. V. 48; 52
Burrs Under the Saddle. Norman: 1964. V. 48; 49; 50; 52; 53; 54
Charles M. Russell. The Cowboy Artist. Pasadena: 1948. V. 51; 53; 54
Charles M. Russell, the Cowboy Artist: a Biography. Pasadena: 1954. V. 53
Cowboy Lingo. Boston: 1936. V. 47; 53
The Cowman and His Code of Ethics. Austin: 1969. V. 50
The Cowman and His Philosophy. Austin: 1967. V. 53
The Horse Wrangler and His Remuda. Austin: 1971. V. 50
More Burrs Under the Saddle: Books and Histories of the West. Norman: 1979. V. 52; 54
The Old Time Cowhand. New York: 1961. V. 48; 50; 52
Poems of the Canadian West. Vancouver: 1919. V. 50
The Rampaging Herd. Norman: 1959. V. 50; 53
Six-Guns and Saddle Leather. Norman: 1954. V. 48; 49; 51; 52; 54
Six-Guns and Saddle Leather. Norman: 1969. V. 50; 53

ADAMS, RICHARD
The Legend of the Tuna. Los Angeles: 1982. V. 51
The Plague Dogs. London: 1977. V. 49
The Plague Dogs. New York: 1978. V. 49
The Tyger Voyage. London: 1976. V. 48
Watership Down. London: 1972. V. 50
Watership Down. New York: 1972. V. 49
Watership Down. London: 1974. V. 49
Watership Down. New York: 1974. V. 53; 54
Watership Down. 1976. V. 51

ADAMS, ROBERT
The Narrative of Robert Adams, a Sailor, Who Was Wrecked on the Western Coast of Africa, in the Year 1810, was Detained Three Years in Slavery by the Arabs of the Great Desert... London: 1816. V. 50

ADAMS, SAMUEL
An Oration Delivered at the State House in Philadelphia, to a Very numerous Audience on Thursday the 1st of August, 1776... London: 1776. V. 50

ADAMS, THOMAS
The Humble Petition of the Worshipful Thomas Adams, John Langham and James Bunce, Aldermen of London Presented to the Lords...April 25, 1648. London: 1648. V. 53
A Study of Rural Conditions and Problems in Canada. Ottawa: 1917. V. 52; 54

ADAMS, THOMAS R.
The American Controversy. A Bibliographical Study of the British Pamphlets About the American Disputes, 1764-1783. New York: 1980. V. 54

ADAMS, W. A.
Bores and Loads for Sporting Guns for British Game Shooting. London: 1894. V. 49

ADAMS, WILLIAM
The Modern Voyager and Traveller Through Europe, Asia, Africa and Americana. London: 1828. V. 48
Sacred Allegories. London: 1856. V. 51

ADAMS, WILLIAM HENRY DAVENPORT
Dwellers on the Threshold or Magic and Magicians. London: 1865. V. 48
The Eastern Archipelago. London: 1880. V. 48; 50
In the Far East. London: 1879. V. 53
Windsor Castle and the Water-Way Thither. London: 1880. V. 52; 54

ADAMS, WILLIAM LORING
The Iconography of the Battery and Castle Garden. New York: 1901. V. 50

ADAMS, WILLIAM TAYLOR
The Boat Club; or, the Bunkers of Rippleton. Boston: 1855. V. 54
The Great Bonanza. Boston: 1876. V. 47
Hatchie, the Guardian Slave; or, the Heiress of Bellevue. Boston: 1853. V. 48

ADAMSON, ARCHIBALD R.
North Platte and Its Associations. North Plate: 1910. V. 54

ADAMSON, C. E.
A History of the Manor and Church of Haltwhistle. South Shields. V. 47

ADAMSON, JAMES
Sketches of Our Information as To Rail-Roads. Also, an Account of the Stockton and Darlington Rail-Way with Observations on Railways. Newcastle: 1826. V. 54

ADAMSON, JOHN
Memoirs of the Life and Writings of Luis de Camoens. London: 1820. V. 48

ADAMSON, R. S.
Flora of the Cape Peninsula. Cape Town: 1950. V. 51

ADAMSON, WILLIAM AGAR
Salmon-Fishing in Canada by a Resident. London: 1860. V. 51

ADANSON, MICHEL
Familles des Plantes... Paris: 1763. V. 49
Histoire Naturelle du Senegal. Coquillages. Avec la Relation Abregee d'n Voyage fait en ce Pays, Pendant les Annees 1749, 50, 51, 52, 53. Paris: 1757. V. 54
A Voyage to Senegal, in the Isle of Goree, and the River Gambia. London: 1759. V. 47; 49; 51; 54

ADCOCK, MARION ST. JOHN
The Littlest One. London: 1915. V. 49

ADCOCK, ST. JOHN
Wonderful London. London: 1926-27. V. 52

ADDAMS, CHARLES
Drawn and Quartered - an Album of Drawings. London: 1943. V. 47
Favorite Haunts. New York: 1976. V. 48

ADDAMS, JANE
The Long Road of Woman's Memory. New York: 1916. V. 50
The Second Twenty Years at Hull-House, September 1909 to September 1929; With a Record of a Growing World Consciousness. New York: 1930. V. 48
The Spirit of Youth and the City Streets. New York: 1909. V. 47
Twenty Years at Hull House. New York: 1910. V. 48

ADDENBROOKE, JOHN
A Short Essay on Free-Thinking. London: 1714. V. 53

ADDERLEY, C. B.
Review of The Colonial Policy of Lord J. Russell's Administration: and of Subsequent Colonial History. London: 1869. V. 54

ADDICKS, BARBARA O'SULLIVAN
Essay on Education; in Which the Subject is treated as a Natural Science... Philadelphia: 1831. V. 54

ADDINGTON, SARAH
Tommy Tingle-Tangle. Joliet: 1927. V. 49

ADDIS, J. M.
Chinese Ceramics from Datable Tombs. London: 1978. V. 49

ADDISON, CHARLES GREENSTREET
Damascus and Palmyra: a Journey to the East. London: 1838. V. 48; 49; 50; 53
The Knights Templars. London: 1853. V. 52

ADDISON, FRANK
The Wellcome Excavations in the Sudan. London: 1949-51. V. 49; 51

ADDISON, GEORGE AUGUSTUS
Indian Reminiscences or the Bengal Moofussul Miscellany. London: 1837. V. 51; 52

ADDISON, JOSEPH
Beauties: Selected from the Writings of... London: 1822. V. 48
The Campaign, a Poem, To His Grace the Duke of Marlborough. London: 1705. V. 51; 54
Cato. London: 1713. V. 50
Cato, a Tragedy. Firenze: 1725. V. 51; 54
A Criticism and Notes Upon the Twelve Books of Paradise Lost. London: 1765. V. 49; 54
Dialogues Upon the Usefulness of Ancient Medals Especially in Relation to the Latin and Greek Poets. London: 1726. V. 50
Dialogues Upon the Usefulness of Ancient Medals, Especially in Relation to the Latin and Greek Poets. Glasgow: 1751. V. 48; 53
A Discourse on Ancient and Modern Learning. London: 1739. V. 54
The Free-Holder, or Political Essays. London: 1716. V. 49; 50; 51; 53
The Free-Holder; or, Political Essays. London: 1758. V. 49; 51
Interesting Anecdotes, Memories, Allegories, Essays and Poetical Fragments... London: 1795. V. 54
Letter from Italy, to the Right Honourable Charles, Lord Halifax... London: 1709. V. 50
The Miscellaneous Works in Verse and Prose. London: 1765. V. 48; 49; 51; 52; 54
Notes Upon the Twelve Books of Paradise Lost. London: 1719. V. 54
Remarks on Several Parts of Italy, &c. in the Years 1701, 1702, 1703. London: 1705. V. 52
Remarks on Several Parts of Italy, Etc. in the Years 1701, 1702, 1703. London: 1733. V. 54
Remarks on Several Parts of Italy, etc. In the Years 1701-1703. London: 1736. V. 51; 52; 54
The Sir Roger De Coverley Papers. New York: 1945. V. 51; 54
The Works. London: 1721. V. 50
The Works. Birmingham: 1761. V. 47; 48; 50; 51
The Works. London: 1761. V. 51
The Works. London: 1856-93. V. 51
Works. London: 1883. V. 51

ADDISON, LANCELOT
West Barbary, or a Short Narrative of the Revolutions of the Kingdoms of Fez and Morocco. Oxford: 1671. V. 48

ADDISON, ROBERT
Poetry on the Year's Revolution, Solar System and Some Other Subjects. Scarborough: 1824. V. 54

ADDISON, THOMAS
A Collection of the Published Writings. London: 1868. V. 48; 50; 52; 53
On the Constitutional and Local Effects of Disease of the Supra-Renal Capsules. London: 1968. V. 47; 51

AN ADDRESS, Delivered Before the Brewster Lyceum, on Wednesday Evening, Feb. 3, 1836. Barnstable: 1836. V. 51

ADDRESS of a Committee Appointed by the Citizens, July 20, 1831, on the Subject of a Rail Road, from the Western Termination of the Pennsylvania Canal to the Ohio Canal. Pittsburg: 1832. V. 53

AN ADDRESS of Members of the House of Representatives...on the Subject of the War with Great Britain. Hartford: 1812. V. 54

AN ADDRESS of Thanks to the Broad-Bottoms for the Good Things They Have Done and the Evil Things They Have Not Done, Since their Elevation. London: 1745. V. 48; 53

ADDRESS of the Louisiana Native American Association to the Citizens of Louisiana and the Inhabitants of the United States. New Orleans: 1839. V. 48

ADDRESS to Chambers of Commerce, Boards of Trade and to Congress, As to Fort St. Philip Canal. New Orleans: 1872. V. 50

AN ADDRESS to the Christian Proprietors and Freeholders of Great Britain by an Unrepresented Christian Layman. London: 1830. V. 53

AN ADDRESS To the Inhabitants of Pennsylvania, by Those Freemen of the City of Philadelphia, Who Are Now Confined in the Mason's Lodge by Virtue of a General Warrant... Philadelphia: 1777. V. 47; 48; 53

ADDRESS to the People of New-Jersey, Relative to a Bridge Over the Delaware River at Trenton and a Rail-Road from Trenton to New-Brunswick. N.P: 1834. V. 47; 51

ADDRESS to the People of North Carolina. Raleigh: 1861. V. 50

AN ADDRESS to the People of the United States, Adopted at a Conference of Colored Citizens, Held at Columbia, S.C. July 20-21, 1876. Columbia: 1876. V. 53

ADDRESS to the People of the United States, by the Covnention of the People of South Carolina. Charleston?: 1832. V. 50

AN ADDRESS to the People of the United States on the Policy of Maintaining a Permananet Navy. Philadelphia: 1802. V. 50

AN ADDRESS to the Proprietors and Managers of Coal-mines...Respecting the Means of Destroying the Fire-Damp. London: 1806. V. 50; 54

ADDRESS to the Reformers of Fawdon, to Their Brothers and Pitmen, Keelmen and Other Labourers on Tyne and Wear. Newcastle-upon-Tyne: 1819. V. 49

AN ADDRESS to the Soldiery of Great Britain. N.P: 1800. V. 54

AN ADDRESS to the Worshipful Company of Barbers in Oxford; Occasioned by the Late Infamous Libel Intitled, "The Barber and Fireworks".... Oxford: 1749. V. 54

AN ADDRESS To the Yeomanry of England. London: 1795. V. 48

ADDRESSES and Memorials, Together with Articles, Reports &c. &c, from the Public Journals, Upon the Occasion of the Retirement of Sir James Douglas, K.C.B. from the Governorship of the Colonies of Vancouver's Island, and British Columbia. Deal: 1864. V. 47

THE ADDRESSES of the Freeholders of the County of Middlesex, Made and Delivered in Writing the Third Day of This Instant March 1680 at Hampstead Heath Unto Sir William Roberts Kt. and Bt. and William Ranton, Esq. after they were Declared to be... London: 1680. V. 52

ADE, GEORGE
Fables in Slang. (with) More Fables. Chicago: 1900/1900. V. 51; 54
The Girl Proposition: a Bunch of He and She Fables. New York: 1908. V. 52
The Old-Time Saloon Not Wet - Not Dry/ Just History. New York: 1931. V. 51
People You Know. New York: 1903. V. 48
Stories of the Streets and of the Town. Chicago: 1941. V. 51; 53

ADELER, MAX
Elbow Room. London: 1883. V. 49

ADELMANN, HOWARD B.
Marcello Malpighi and the Evolution of Embryology. Ithaca: 1966. V. 47; 50
Marcello Malpighi and the evolution of Embryology. New York: 1966. V. 48

ADES, DAWN
Dada and Surrealism Reviewed. London: 1978. V. 47; 50; 53

ADGER, JOHN B.
The Religious Instruction of the Colored Population. Charleston: 1847. V. 50

ADHEMAR, JEAN
Degas: The Complete Etchings, Lithographs and Monotypes. London: 1973. V. 51

ADHEMR, JEAN
Toulouse-Lautrec, His Complete Lithographs and Drypoints. New York: 1965. V. 47; 50; 51

THE ADJUSTMENT and Testing of Telescope Objectives. York & London: 1921/1891. V. 48

ADLER, ALFRED
The Neurotic Constitution: Outlines of a Comparative Individualistic Psychology and Psychotherapy. New York: 1916. V. 52

ADLER, CYRUS
Catalogue of a Hebrew Library, Being the Collection, with a Few Additions, of the Late Joshua (Cohen, M.D. of Baltimore). Baltimore: 1887. V. 53

ADLER, JANKEL
Jankel Adler. London: 1948. V. 52

ADLER, JEREMY
To Cythera! Four Poems. 1993. V. 52; 54
Triplets: 24 Poems. 1980. V. 52

THE ADMINISTRATION of the Post Office, From the Introduction of Mr. Rowland Hill's Plan of Penny Postage Up to the Present Time, Grounded on Parliamentary Documents, and the Evidence Taken Before the Select Committee on Postage at the Conclusion... London: 1844. V. 54

ADOLF IN Blunderland. London: 1939. V. 51

ADOLPH, KARL
Daughters of Vienna. London: 1922. V. 49

ADOLPHUS, J. H.
A Correct, Full and Empartial Report, of the Trial of Her Majesty, Caroline, Queen Consort of Great Britain. London: 1820. V. 50
The Last Days, Death, Funeral, Obsequies, &c. of Her Late Majesty Caroline Queen Consort of Great Britain... London: 1822. V. 53
The Royal Exile; or Memoirs of the Public and Private Life of Her Majesty, Caroline, Queen Consort of Great Britain. London: 1821. V. 53
Voyages and Travels of Her Majesty, Caroline Queen of Great Britain... London: 1822. V. 53

ADOLPHUS, JOHN
Memoirs of John Bannister, Comedian. London: 1839. V. 51; 52
The Political State of the British Empire; Containing a General View of the Domestic and Foreign Possessions of the Crown; the Laws, Commerce, Revenues, Offices and Other Establishments, Civil and Military. London: 1818. V. 50; 53

ADRIAN, E. D.
The Mechanism of Nervous Action, Electrical Studies of the Neurone. London: 1932. V. 47

ADRIANI, GOTZ
Toulouse-Lautrec, the Complete Graphic Works. New York: 1988. V. 50

ADRICHEM, CHRISTIAAN VAN
Vrbis Hierosolimae Qvemadmodvm ea Christi Tempore Floruit... Cologne: 1585. V. 51

THE ADVANTAGE of Misfortune: a Poem. London: 1773. V. 49

THE ADVENTURER. London: 1752-54. V. 53
THE ADVENTURER. London: 1753-54. V. 47; 48; 49
THE ADVENTURER. London: 1777. V. 49
THE ADVENTURER. Dublin: 1788. V. 48; 50; 54
THE ADVENTURER. London: 1794. V. 50

ADVENTURES and Conversations of a Summer Morning, Intended to Entertain and Instruct the Minds of Youth. London: 1813. V. 48

ADVENTURES at Espiegleries de Lazarille de Tormes, ecrites par Luimeme. Paris: 1801. V. 47

ADVENTURES in Borneo. London: 1849. V. 54

THE ADVENTURES of a Watch!. London: 1788. V. 54

THE ADVENTURES of Andolocia, with the Purse and Cap of His Father Fortunatus: a Tale for the Nursery. London: 1804. V. 50

THE ADVENTURES of Captain Gulliver, in a Voyage to Lilliput. Glasgow: 1815. V. 51

The ADVENTURES of Cinderella; or the History of a Glass Slipper. York: 1820. V. 48

THE ADVENTURES of Doctor Comicus or the Frolics of Fortune. London: 1815. V. 54

THE ADVENTURES Of Don Juan De Ulloa, in a Voyage to Calicut, Soon After the Discovery of India by Vasco de Gama. London: 1825. V. 49

THE ADVENTURES of Jack and Jill and Old Dame Jill. London: 1803. V. 47

THE ADVENTURES Of John M'Alpine, a Native Highlander. Glasgow: 1985. V. 48

ADVICE and Select Hymns, for the Instruction of Little Children. Seventh Series No. 10. Concord: 1837. V. 48

ADVICE to Proprietors, On the Care of Valuable Pictures Painted in Oil, with Instructions for Preserving, Cleaning and Restoring Them When Damaged or Decayed. London: 1835. V. 50

ADVICE to Sabbath School Children. Andover: 1830. V. 48

ADY, JOHN
The Case of Our Fellow-Creatures, the Oppressed Africans, Respectly Recommended to the Serious Consideration of the Legislature of Great Britain, by the People Called Quakers. London: 1783. V. 51

ADYE, WILLETT
Musical Notes. London: 1869. V. 51

AELFRIC
A Saxon Treatise Concerning the Old and New Testament...and...a Second Edition of a Testimonie of Antiquitie, &c... London: 1623. V. 50
A Testimonie of Antiqvitie. London: 1567. V. 50

AELIANUS, CLAUDIUS
De Historia Animalium Libri XVII. Leyden: 1565. V. 50; 54
De Historia Animalium Libri XVII. Leyden: 1575. V. 52
Variae Historiae Libri XIII. Lyon: 1587. V. 49

AELIANUS TACTICUS
The Tactiks of Lian or Art of Embattailing an Army After Ye Grecian Manner Englished and Illustrated with Figures... London: 1616. V. 51

THE AERO Manual, a Manual of Mechanically Propelled Human Flight... London: 1909. V. 50

AERONAUTICAL SOCIETY OF GREAT BRITAIN
Aeronautical Classics. London: 1910-11. V. 49

AESCHYLUS
Agamemnon, a Tragedy. London: 1876. V. 47; 49
Ai Tou Aischylos Tragodiai Epta. Glasgow: 1795. V. 48
Fragments. Alabama: 1992. V. 54
Fragments. 1993. V. 54
Fragments. Alabama: 1993. V. 51
(Greek title, then) *Tragoediae Quae Extant Septem.* Glasguae: 1746. V. 47; 48; 49
Oresteia. 1904. V. 47
The Oresteia. London: 1904. V. 47
The Oresteia: Agamemnon, The Libation-Bearers and the Furies. New York: 1961. V. 53; 54
The Oresteian Trilogy. 1982-83. V. 54
The Oresteian Trilogy. Greenbrae: 1982-83. V. 48; 53
Six Dramas. Paris: 1552. V. 48
Tentmen de Metris ab Aeschylo in Choricis Cantibus Adhibitis... Cambridge: 1809. V. 47

AESOPUS
Aesop Junior in America, Being a Series of Fables... New York: 1834. V. 47
Aesopi Phrygis Fabulae Elegantissimis Iconibus Veras Animalium Species ad Vivum Adumbrantes. Coloniae Allobrogum: 1619. V. 53
Aesop's Fables. London: 1812. V. 49
Aesop's Fables. London: 1848. V. 52
Aesop's Fables. New York: 1850. V. 49
Aesop's Fables. London: 1895. V. 52
Aesop's Fables. London: 1912. V. 47; 48; 49; 51; 53; 54
Aesop's Fables. London: 1915. V. 48
Aesop's Fables. London: 1919. V. 50
Aesop's Fables. London: 1927. V. 49
Aesop's Fables. London: 1930. V. 51
Aesop's Fables. New York: 1933. V. 50
Aesop's Fables. Oxford: 1933. V. 50; 53
Aesop's Fables. London: 1936. V. 47
Aesop's Fables. Hampstead: 1964. V. 52
Aesop's Fables: a New Version, Chiefly from Original Sources by the Rev. Thomas James. London: 1852. V. 50
Aesop's Fables for Little Readers. London: 1888. V. 47
Aesop's Fables, New Versified, From the Best English Editions. Hull: 1803. V. 48
Aesop's Fables, With His Life in English, French and Latin. London: 1703. V. 48
Aesop's Fables with Instructive Morals and Reflections Abstracted from all Party Considerations Adapted to All Capacities and Designed to Promote Religion, Morality and Universal Benevolence. London: 1760. V. 47
Aesop's Frog Fables. Santa Cruz: 1990. V. 49; 52; 54
Baby's Own Aesop. London: 1887. V. 52
Fabellae Graece et latine. Venetiis: 1561. V. 53
The Fables. London: 1651. V. 51
Fables. London: 1766. V. 51
The Fables. London: 1793. V. 47; 50; 51; 54
The Fables... London: 1793. V. 48
The Fables. London: 1818. V. 52
The Fables. London: 1818. V. 50; 51
The Fables. Newcastle: 1823. V. 48
Fables. London: 1848. V. 51
The Fables. London: 1857. V. 51
The Fables. London: 1909. V. 49; 50; 51; 53; 54
The Fables. Waltham St. Lawrence: 1926. V. 52; 53
Fables. New York: 1933. V. 47
Fables. Ithaca: 1950. V. 51
Fables. According to Sir Roger L'Estrange. New York, Paris: 1931. V. 50; 51
Fables... Avec Les Explications et les Principaux Traits de Savie. Paris: 1801. V. 53
Fables of Aesop. 1931. V. 51
Fables of Aesop and Other Eminent Mytholgoists. London: 1694. V. 52
Fables of Aesop and Other Eminent Mythologists... (with) Fables and Storyes Moralized. London: 1704/1699. V. 51
The Fables of Aesop, and Others with Designs On Wood by Thomas Bewick. New Castle: 1818. V. 47
Fabularum Aesopiarium Libri V. Amsterdam: 1701. V. 47; 50; 53
Four Fables. N.P.: 1972. V. 47
The History and Fables. Ilkey: 1976. V. 49
The Little Aesop. London: 1841. V. 54
The Little Esop. London: 1835. V. 52

AESOPUS continued
Select Fables of Aesop and Other Fabulists. Gainsborough: 1809. V. 51
Select Fables of Aesop and Others. London: 1878. V. 48
Select Fables of Esop and Other Fabulists. Birmingham: 1764. V. 51
Some of Aesop's Fables with Modern Instances. London: 1883. V. 49; 51; 52
Three Hundred Aesop's Fables. London & New York. V. 49
Twelve Fables of Aesop Newly Narrated by Glenway Westcott. New York: 1954. V. 47; 48; 50; 52
Twenty Four Fables of Aesop and Other Eminent Mythologists... London: 1928. V. 51

AETHELGIFU
The Will of Aethelgifu. Oxford: 1968. V. 52

AETIUS
Contractae ex Veteribus Medicinae Tetrabiblios. Basel: 1542. V. 47
The Gynecology and Obstetrics of the 6th Century, A.D. Philadelphia: 1950. V. 50

AEVOLUS NEAPOLITANUS, CAESAR
De Divinis Attributis, Quae Sephirot Ab Hebraeis Nuncupta. Venice: 1580. V. 50

AF-BEELDINGHE Van D'Eerste Eeuwe der Societyt jesu. Antwerp: 1640. V. 49; 50

AFBEELDING der Marmor Sorten...(A Representation of Different Sort of Marble). Amsterdam: 1776. V. 47

L'AFFAIRE Crainquebille. Stamford: 1937. V. 51

AN AFFECTING History of the Captivity and Sufferings of Mrs. Mary Velnet, an Italian Lady, Who Was Seven Years a Slave in Tripoli. Boston: 1804?. V. 47

THE AFFECTING Story of the Children in the Wood. London: 1854. V. 49

THE AFFIANCED One. London: 1832. V. 47

LES AFFICHES Etrangeres Illustrees. Paris: 1897. V. 47

AFIFI, AWAD
Tale of the Sands. Del Mar: 1980. V. 47

AFLALO, F. G.
The Encyclopaedia of Sport. London: 1897. V. 50
A Fisherman's Summer in Canada. London: 1911. V. 47
Sport in Europe. London: 1901. V. 49
Sunshine and Sport in Florida and the West Indies. London: 1907. V. 47; 50

AFTER Ffity Years: a Lincoln Day Program. Cincinnati: 1905. V. 52

AFTERNOON Tea. Boston: 1891. V. 54

AGAINST Women, a Satire. Waltham St. Lawrence: 1953. V. 49

AGAR, HERBERT
Who Owns America?. Boston: 1936. V. 50

AGARD, ARTHUR
The Repertorie of Records... London: 1631/27. V. 50

AGAR-ELLIS, GEORGE
Catalogue of the Principal Pictures in Flanders and Holland. London: 1826. V. 47

AGASSIZ, ALEXANDER
The Coral Reeefs of the Tropical Pacific. Cambridge: 1930. V. 48
The Islands and Coral Reefs of Jiji. Cambridge: 1899. V. 51
Natural History Pamphlets. V.P. V. 53
Three Cruises of the United States Coast and Geodetic Survey Steamer "Blake" in the Gulf of Mexico, in the Caribbean Sea, and Along the Atlantic Coast of the United States from 1877 to 1880. Boston: 1888. V. 51; 54
Three Cruises of the United States Coast and Geodetic Survey Steamer "Blake" in the Gulf of Mexico, in the Caribbean Sea, and Along the Atlantic Coast of the United States, from 1877 to 1880. London: 1888. V. 50; 53

AGASSIZ, ELIZABETH C.
Seaside Studies in Natural History: Marine Animals of Massachusetts Bay. Boston: 1865. V. 53

AGASSIZ, LOUIS
Bibliographia Zoologiae et Geologiae. New York: 1968. V. 50
Contributions to the Natural History of the United States. Boston: 1857. V. 50
Contributions to the Natural History of the United States. Boston: 1857-62. V. 48; 54
Geological Sketches. Boston and New York: 1893-94. V. 50; 51
A Journey to Brazil. Boston & London: 1868. V. 48; 54
Lake Superior; its Physical Character, Vegetation and Animals, Compared with Those of Other Similar Regions. Boston: 1850. V. 48
Methods of Study in Natural History. Boston: 1863. V. 50
Nomenclator Zoologicus. Soloduri: 1842-46. V. 48
The Structure of Animal Life. Six Lectures Delivered at the Brooklyn Academy of Music in January and February 1862. New York: 1866. V. 50

AGATE, JAMES
Buzz, Buzz! Essays of the Theatre. London: 1918. V. 51
The Contemporary Theatre 1923-1926. London: 1924-27. V. 51
Here's Richness!. London: 1942. V. 48; 49; 52; 54
Kingdoms for Horses. London: 1936. V. 50
Responsibility - a Novel. London: 1919. V. 48
A Shorter Ego. Autobiography. London: 1946. V. 47; 52; 54
Their Hour Upon the Stage. Cambridge: 1930. V. 54

THE AGE of Johnson. Essays Presented to Chauncey Brewster Tinker. New Haven: 1949. V. 54

AGEE, GEORGE W.
Rube Burrow. King of Outlaws. Chicago: 1890. V. 47; 53

AGEE, JAMES
Agee on Film. Reviews and Comments. New York: 1958/60. V. 51
A Death in the Family. New York: 1957. V. 47; 49; 50; 51; 53
Four Early Stories. West Branch: 1964. V. 49; 51; 54
The Last Letter of James Agee to Father Flye. Boston: 1959. V. 48; 51
Let Us Know Praise Famous Men. Boston: 1941. V. 47; 48; 49; 52
Letters of James Agee to Father Flye. New York: 1962. V. 53
Permit Me Voyage. New Haven: 1934. V. 47; 49; 50; 51; 52; 53
A Way of Seeing: Photographs by Helen Levitt with an Essay by James Agee. New York: 1965. V. 47

THE AGELESS Story, With Its Antiphons Pictured By... New York: 1939. V. 48

AGG, JOHN
The General-Post-Bag; or, News!. London: 1814. V. 51
Lord Byron's Pilgrimage to the Holy Land. London: 1817. V. 53; 54
A Month at Brussels, a Satirical Novel. London: 1815. V. 47
A Month in Town. London: 1814. V. 51

AGLIONBY, WILLIAM
Painting Illustrated in Three Diallogues, Containing some Choice Observations Upon the Art. Together with the Lives of the Most Eminent Painters... London: 1685. V. 49; 53

AGNER, DWIGHT
The Books of WAD - A Bibliography of the Books Designed by W. A. Dwiggins. Baton Rouge: 1974. V. 52

AGNES Arlington; Life, Times, Troubles, Tribulations and Sad End of Anges Arlington, the Cotton Planter's Daughter, a Beautiful and Accomplished Young Lady from Georgia, Whose Body Was Found Floating in the North River, a Few Miles Above New York... Baltimore, Philadelphia: 1854. V. 47

AGNESI, MARIA GAETANA
Istituzioni Analitiche. Milan: 1748. V. 50

AGNEW, ANDREW
The Hereditary Sheriffs of Galloway, Their "Forebears" and Friends, Their Courts and Customs of their Times. Edinburgh: 1893. V. 51

AGNEW, ELEANOR C.
Geraldine: a Tale of Conscience. London: 1837-39. V. 48; 51

AGNEW, FRANKLIN H.
The Lay of a Summer's Day, or "Love is Mightier than All". Los Angeles: 1933. V. 54

AGNEW, GEORGETTE
Elaine's Party. London: 1920. V. 50
Let's Pretend. London: 1927. V. 47; 48
Let's Pretend. New York: 1927. V. 48

AGOSTINHO DE SANTA MARIA, F.
Historia da Fundacao do Real Convento de Santa Monica da Cidade de Goa, Corte do Estado da India & Do Imperio Lusitano do Oriente. Lisbon: 1699. V. 48
Sanctuario Mariano, e Historia das Imagens Milagrosas de Nossa Senhora... Lisbon: 1707-23. V. 48

AGRICOLA, GEORGIUS
De Re Metallica. Basil: 1621. V. 54
De Re Metallica. London: 1912. V. 47; 49; 50; 51; 52
De Re Metallica. New York: 1950. V. 49; 51; 52; 53; 54
De Re Metallica Libri XII. Basel: 1556. V. 53; 54
De Re Metallica Libri XII. Basle: 1561. V. 47

AGRICULTURAL SOCIETY OF IRELAND
Report of the Gentlemen Who Formed a Deputation to Inspect and Inquire into the Success of the Bog Improvements Executed by John Featherston H. (sic) Esq... Dublin: 1836. V. 50

AGRIPPA VON NETTESHEIM, HEINRICH CORNELIUS
De Incertitudine et Vanitate Scientiarum Declamatio Invectiva, ex Postrema Authoris Recognitione. Coloniae: 1575. V. 49
Fourth Book of Occult Philosophy: of Geomancy, Magical Elements of Peter De Abano, Astronomical Geomancy, the Nature of Spirits, Arbatel of Magick. London: 1978. V. 52
Opera in Duos Tomas Concinne Digesta... Leyden: 1600?. V. 48
Three Books of Occult Philosophy. London: 1651. V. 48
The Vanity of Arts and Sciences... London: 1676. V. 49

AGUILAR, GRACE
The Jewish Faith: its Spiritual Consolation, Moral Guidance and Immortal Hope. Philadelphia: 1864. V. 52
Woman's Friendship: A Story of Domestic Life. New York: 1850. V. 49
The Women of Israel. New York: 1872. V. 53

AGUILON, FRANCOIS D'
Opticorum Libri Sex. Antwerp: 1613. V. 48

AHERN, GEORGE P.
Compilation of Notes On the Most Important Timber Tree Species of the Philippine Islands. Manila: 1901. V. 50

AHLBERG, GUDRUN
Fighting on Land and Sea in Greek Geometric Art. Stockholm: 1971. V. 50

AHLBERG, HAKON
Swedish Architecture of the 20th Century. London: 1925. V. 48; 50; 51
Swedish Architecture of the 20th Century. New York: 1925. V. 52

AHMAD, ARDABILI
A Series of Poems, Containing the Plaints, Consolations and Delights... Bristol: 1797. V. 48; 51

AHMAD, J. D.
Afghanistan. A Brief Survey. Kabul: 1934. V. 51

AHMED, R.
The Black Art. 1936. V. 49; 54

AHMED, ROLLO
I Rise: the Life Story of a Negro. London: 1937. V. 52

AHRONS, E. L.
The British Steam Railway Locomotive 1825-1925. London: 1927. V. 49

AI
Cruelty. Poems. Boston: 1973. V. 49; 50

AICKMAN, R.
Sub Rosa. London: 1968. V. 48
We Are for the Dark. London: 1951. V. 49

AICKMAN, ROBERT
Painted Devils - Strange Stories. New York: 1979. V. 50

AIKEN, CONRAD
Among the Lost People. New York: 1934. V. 54
Blue Voyage. New York: 1927. V. 48; 49; 52; 54
Bring! Bring! and Other Stories. New York: 1925. V. 52
Brownstone Eclogues and Other Poems. New York: 1942. V. 51
Cats and Bats and Things with Wings. New York: 1965. V. 51
The Clerk's Journal Being the Diary of a Queer Man. New York: 1971. V. 47
Costumes by Eros. New York: 1927. V. 54
Costumes by Eros. New York: 1928. V. 47; 52
Great Circle. New York: 1933. V. 47; 50
The Jig of Forslin. 1916. V. 49; 53
King Coffin. New York: 1935. V. 47; 48; 49
Selected Poems. New York: 1929. V. 47; 50; 51; 53
Senlin: a Biography. London: 1925. V. 48; 51; 52
The Soldier - a Poem. London: 1946. V. 54
Thee. A Poem. New York: 1967. V. 51
Ushant: an Essay. New York: 1971. V. 48

AIKEN, JOAN
Hate Begins at Home. London: 1967. V. 53
Trouble with Product X. London: 1966. V. 53

AIKEN, JOHN
Biographical Memoirs of Medicine in Great Britain from the Revival of Literature to the Time of Harvey. London: 1780. V. 48; 49; 50
England Delineated; or, a Geographical Description of Very County in England and Wales... London: 1788. V. 51
Essays on Song Writing: With A Collection of Such English Songs as Are Most Eminent for Poetical Merit... London: 1772. V. 48
A View of the Character and Public Services of the Late John Howard, Esq. London: 1792. V. 53

AIKEN, LUCY
Memoirs of the Court of King James the First. London: 1822. V. 54

AIKENS, ASA
Practical Forms; with Notes and References Explanatory of the Laaw Governing the Cases to Which They Are Applicable (etc.). Windsor: 1823. V. 51

AIKIN, ARTHUR
A Dictionary of Chemistry and Mineralogy...(with) An Account of the Most Important Recent Discoveries and Improvements in Chemistry and Mineralogy... London: 1807-14. V. 53
Journal of a Tour Through North Wales and Part of Shropshire, With Observations on Mineralogy... London: 1797. V. 49; 50
A Manual of Mineralogy. London: 1814. V. 47

AIKIN, C. R.
A Concise View Of All the Most Important Facts Which Have Hitherto Appeared Concerning the Cow-Pox. London: 1801. V. 53

AIKIN, J.
Geographical Delineations or a Compendious View of the Natural and Political State of all Parts of the Globe. London: 1806. V. 50
The Natural History of the Year. London: 1821. V. 54

AIKIN, JOHN
Annals of the Reign of King George the Third; From Its Commencement in the Year 1760, to the General Peace in the Year 1815. London: 1816. V. 48; 52
The Arts of Life: I. Of Providing Food, II. Of Providing Clothing. III. Of Providing Shelter... London: 1802. V. 49
A Description of the Country from Thirty to Forty Miles Round Manchester... London: 1795. V. 49
An Essay on the Application of Natural History to Poetry. 1777. V. 54
Essays on Song Writing. London: 1772. V. 47; 48; 49; 50; 51; 52; 53
Essays on Song Writing: With A Collection of Such English Songs as Are Most Eminent for Poetical Merit. Warrington: 1774. V. 47; 49
Essays on Song-Writing. London: 1810. V. 47
The Lives of John Selden, Esq. & Archbishop Usher. 1812. V. 49; 50
A View of the Life, Travels and Philanthropic Labours of the Late John Howard. New York: 1814. V. 50
The Woodland Companion. London: 1802. V. 47; 50; 52; 54

The Woodland Companion. London: 1820. V. 52; 53

AIKIN, LUCY
The Life of Joseph Addison. London: 1843. V. 54
Memoirs of the Court of King Charles I. London: 1833. V. 49; 51
Memoirs of the Court of King James the First, in Two Volumes. London: 1822. V. 49; 50; 51; 53
Memoirs of the Court of Queen Elizabeth. London: 1819. V. 49; 50
Memoirs of the Court of Queen Elizabeth. London: 1826. V. 49

AIMARD, GUSTAVE
The Border Rifles. A Tale of the Texan War. Philadelphia. V. 49
The Prairie Flower. A Tale of the Indian Border. London: 1865. V. 49

AIME, JEAN JACQUES
Narrative of the Deportation to Cayenne, and Shipwreck Off the Coast of Scotland, of J. J. Job Aime, Written by Himself. London: 1800. V. 51

AIMOIN
Historiae Francorum Lib. V. Ex Veterib. Exemplaribus Multo Emedatiores... Parisiis: 1567. V. 48; 50; 53

AINSLIE, DOUGLAS
Chosen Poems. London: 1926. V. 49; 51

AINSLIE, GEORGE ROBERT
Illustrations of the Anglo-French Coinage: Taken From the Cabinet of a Fellow of the Antiquarian Socieites of London, and Scotland... London: 1830. V. 48

AINSLIE, HEW
A Pilgrimage to the Land of Burns... Deptford: 1822. V. 51

AINSLIE, JOHN
A Comprehensive Treatise on Land Surveying... London: 1842. V. 47

AINSLIE, KATHLEEN
Catharine Susan and Me's Coming Out. London: 1905. V. 51
Catharine Susan in Hot Water. London: 1905. V. 49
Catharine Susan's Little Holiday. London: 1905. V. 49
Lady Tabitha and Us. London: 1905. V. 49
Me and Catharine Susan. London: 1903. V. 49
Me and Catharine Susan. London: 1905. V. 48
Votes for Catharine Susan and Me. 1910. V. 54

AINSLIE, ROBERT
A Selection of the Most Interesting of Sir Robert Ainslie's Celebrated Collection of Views in Egypt, Asia Minor, &c. London: 1812. V. 53

AINSLIE, WHITELAW
Materia Indica; or Some Account of Those Articles Which are Employed by the Hindoos and Other Eastern Nations... London: 1826. V. 49
Observations on the Cholera Morbus of India. London: 1825. V. 52

AINSWORTH, ED
The Cowboy in Art. New York: 1968. V. 47
Golden Checkerboard. Palm Desert: 1965. V. 47; 48; 53
Painters of the Desert. Palm Desert: 1960. V. 47; 49; 54

AINSWORTH, G. C.
Fungi: an Advanced Treatise. New York: 1965-73. V. 50
Introduction to the History of Plant Pathology. London: 1981. V. 49

AINSWORTH, HENRY
Annotations Upon the Book of Psalmes. Amsterdam?: 1617. V. 50

AINSWORTH, RICHARD
History of the Parkinson Family of Lancahsire. London: 1936. V. 50

AINSWORTH, WILLIAM FRANCIS
A Personal Narrative of the Euphrates Expedition. London: 1888. V. 50; 53

AINSWORTH, WILLIAM HARRISON
Beatrice Tyldesley. London: 1878. V. 54
Cardinal Pole. London: 1863. V. 49; 52; 53; 54
The Collected Novels. London: 1900. V. 50
Collected Works. London: 1880. V. 50
The Constable de Bourbon. London: 1866. V. 54
Crichton. New York: 1837. V. 52
The Fall of Somerset. London: 1877. V. 51; 54
Le Gentilhomme des Grandes-Routes. Colophon Paris: 1859. V. 51
The Good Old Times: The Story of the Manchester Rebels of '45. London: 1873. V. 47
Guy Fawkes; or, the Gunpowder Treason. London: 1841. V. 49
Guy Fawkes, or, the Gunpowder Treason. London: 1857. V. 51
Historical Romances. Philadelphia: 1898. V. 48; 51
Jack Sheppard. London: 1839. V. 47; 48; 49; 50; 51; 52; 54
James the Second; or the Revolution of 1688. London: 1848. V. 52
John Law: the Projector. London: 1864. V. 54
The Lancashire Witches. London: 1849. V. 50; 53
The Leaguer of Lathom. London: 1876. V. 51
The Lord Mayor of London; or, City Life in the Last Century. London: 1862. V. 54
Merry England; or, Nobles and Serfs. London: 1874. V. 53; 54
The Miser's Daughter. London: 1842. V. 47; 50; 51
The Miser's Daughter: a Tale. London: 1848. V. 54
Novels. London. V. 47; 49
Old Saint Paul's: A Tale of the Plague and the Fire. London: 1841. V. 50; 51; 53

AINSWORTH, WILLIAM HARRISON continued
Rookwood: a Romance. London: 1834. V. 50; 52
Saint James's; or, The Court of Queen Anne. London: 1846. V. 51
The Spanish Match or Charles Stuart at Madrid. London: 1865. V. 49; 50; 54
The Spendthrift: a Tale... London: 1857. V. 50; 54
Stanley Brereton. London: 1881. V. 54
The Star-Chamber: an Historical Romance. London: 1854. V. 48; 53
The Star-Chamber: an Historical Romance. London: 1857. V. 54
The Tower of London. London: 1840. V. 49; 50; 54
Windsor Castle. London: 1843. V. 49; 50; 51
The Works. London: 1850-51. V. 54
Works. London: 1895. V. 50
The Works of.. London: 1901. V. 48

AIR Service Medical. Washington: 1919. V. 50; 52

AIREY, JOHN
Railway Junction Diagrams... London: 1872. V. 47

AIRY, GEORGE BIDDELL
Six Lectures on Astronomy, Delivered at the Meeting of the Friends of Ipswich Museum...March 1848. London: 1849. V. 50

AIRY, OSMUND
Charles II. London: 1901. V. 49; 50; 54
Charles II. Paris: 1901. V. 53; 54

AIRY, WILFRID
Iron Arches. London: 1870. V. 49

AITCHISON, J.
The Zoology of the Afghan Delimitation Commission. London: 1887. V. 48

AITKEN, JAMES
A Genuine Account of the Life, Transactions, Confession and Execution of James Aitken, Alias John Hill, Commonly Called John the Painter, Who Was Tried at the Castle of Winchester, on Thursday the 7th of March 1777, and Convicted of Setting Fire... London: 1777. V. 49
The Trial (at large) of James Hill; Otherwise, James Hind; Otherwise James Actzen; for...Setting fire to the Rope-House, in His Majesty's Dock-Yard at Portsmouth.. London: 1777. V. 47; 52

AITKEN, JOHN
Principles of Midwifery, or Puerperal Medicine. London: 1786. V. 52

AITKEN'S General American Register and Calendar, for the Year 1774. Philadelphia: 1774. V. 49

AITON, JOHN
Clerical Economics; or Hints, Rural and Household, to Ministers and Others of Limited Income. Edinburgh: 1942. V. 54
Eight Weeks in Germany: Comprising Narratives, Descriptions and Directions for Economical Tourists. Edinburgh: 1842. V. 49

AITON, WILLIAM
A History of the Rencounter at Drumclog and Battle at Bothwell Bridge... Hamilton: 1821. V. 51; 54
Hortus Kewensis; or, a Catalogue of the Plants Cultivated in the Royal Botanic Garden at Kew. London: 1789. V. 49
Hortus Kewensis; or, a Catalogue of the Plants Cultivated in the Royal Botanic Garden at Kew... London: 1810-13. V. 49; 52
A Treatise on the Origin, Qualities and Cultivation of Moss-Earth, with Directions for Converting It Into Manure... 1811. V. 50

AJOURDAIN, M.
English Decoration and Furniture of the Later XVIIth Century (1760-1820). New York: 1923. V. 47

AKEHURST, B. C.
Tobacco. London: 1981. V. 52

AKELEY, CARL E.
In Brightest Africa. London: 1924. V. 54

AKEN, DAVID
Pioneers of the Black Hills. N.P. V. 53
Pioneers of the Black Hills of Gordon's Stockade Party of 1874... Milwaukee: 1911. V. 53
Pioneers of the Black Hills; or, Gordon's Stockdale Party of 1875. Milwaukee: 1920. V. 48; 50; 54

AKENSIDE, MARK
An Epistle to Curio. London: 1744. V. 53
An Ode to the Country Gentlemen of England. London: 1758. V. 52
Odes on Several Subjects. London: 1745. V. 48; 51
Les Plaisirs de l'Imagination. Amsterdam: 1759. V. 49
The Pleasures of Imagination. London: 1744. V. 48; 49; 52; 54
The Pleasures of Imagination. Glasgow: 1775. V. 53
The Pleasures of Imagination. London: 1814. V. 49
The Poems. London: 1772. V. 48; 51; 54
The Poetical Works of... London: 1866. V. 51

AKERMAN, JOHN YONGE
A Descriptive Catalogue of Rare and Unedited Roman Coins: From the Earliest Period of the Roman Coinage, to the Extinction of the Empire Under Constantinus Paleologos. London: 1834. V. 48
Illustrations to Tales of Other Days, Designed by George Cruikshank... London: 1830. V. 49
Spring Tide; or, the Angler and His Friends. London: 1850. V. 48

Tradesmen's Tokens Current in London and Its Vicinity Between the Years 1648 and 1672, Described From the Originals in the British Museum and in Several Private Collections. London: 1849. V. 48

AKHMATOVA, ANNA
Forty Seven Love Poems. London: 1927. V. 52
U Samovo Morya. (By the Sea.). Petersburg: 1921. V. 49; 50
Vecher. St. Petersburg: 1912. V. 50

AKIN, EMMA E.
Ideals and Adventures. Oklahoma City: 1938. V. 53

AKIN, JAMES
Journal of James Akin, Jr. Norman: 1919. V. 50

AKINS, THOMAS B.
Selections from the Public Documents of the Province of Nova Scotia. Halifax: 1869. V. 50

AKIYAMA, TERUKAZU
Arts of China. Tokyo: 1970/69/70. V. 48

AKOEV, G. N.
Sensory Hair Cells, Synaptic Transmission. Berlin: 1993. V. 50

AKSAKOV, SERGEI TIMOFEYEVICH
Years of Childhood. New York: 1916. V. 47

AKSYONOV, VASSILY
The Burn. New York: 1984. V. 51; 54
The Island of Crimea. New York: 1983. V. 51
Surplussed Barrelware. Ann Arbor: 1985. V. 51

AKURGAL, EKREM
The Art of the Hittites. New York: 1962. V. 49; 50; 51; 54

AKUTAGAWA, RYUNOSUKE
Hell Screen and Other Stories. 1948. V. 53
Rashomon and Other Stories. Rutland: 1952. V. 48

AL- MUBASHSHIR IBN FATIK, ABU AL-WAFA
The Dictes and Sayings of the Philosophers. Detroit: 1901. V. 49

ALABAMA. LAWS, STATUTES, ETC.
An Act of the General Assembly of Alabama to Aid in Arresting Deserters and Stragglers from the Army, Adopted at the Called Session, 1864, Held in the City of Montgomery, Commencing on the Twenty-sixth Day of September A.D., 1864. Montgomery: 1864. V. 52

ALABAMA. UNIVERSITY
Rare Books and Collections of the Reynolds Historical Library. A Bibliography. Birmingham: 1968. V. 49

ALADDIN and His Wonderful Lamp. London: 1919. V. 50

ALADDIN; or, the Wonderful Lamp. London: 1820. V. 48; 50

ALADDIN or the Wonderful Lamp and Ali Baba and the Forty Thieves. Chicago: 1929. V. 51

ALAMANNI, LUIGI
La Coltivatione. Florence: 1549. V. 50

ALANSON, EDWARD
Practical Observations Upon Amputation, and the After-Treatment. London: 1779. V. 54

ALARCON, FRANCISCO X.
De Amor Oscuro?Of Dark Love. Santa Cruz: 1993. V. 52

ALARCON, PEDRO ANTONIO DE
The Three Corner Hat. New York: 1944. V. 52
The Three Corner Hat. Los Angeles: 1959. V. 53

ALASKA Tours to the National Wonderland. Chicago: 1989. V. 50

ALASKA TRANSPORTATION TRADING AND MINING CO.
The Prospectus of the Alaska Transportation Trading and Mining Company. San Francisco: 1898. V. 50

ALASKAN BOUNDARY TRIBUNAL
Atlas of Award. Washington: 1904. V. 53
British Atlas. Maps and Charts Accompanying the Case of Great Britain. Washington: 1904. V. 53
The Counter Case of the United States Before the Tribunal Convened at London Under the Provisions of the Treaty Between the United States and Great Britain, Concluded January 24, 1903. Washington: 1903. V. 48
Proceedings of the Alaskan Boundary Tribunal, Convened at London,..with Respect to the Boundary Line Between the Territory of Alaska and the British Possessions in North America. Washington: 1904. V. 52
United States Atlas. Maps and Charts Accomapnying the Case and Coutner Case of the United States. Washington: 1904. V. 53

ALASTAIR
Fifty Drawings by Alastair with an Introduction by Carl Van Vechten. New York: 1925. V. 53

ALBAUGH, WILLIAM A.
Confederate Arms. Harrisburg: 1957. V. 49
Confederate Faces. Solano Beach: 1970. V. 48; 49; 50
Confederate Swords, The Handbook Of... 1951. V. 49
More Confederate Faces. Washington: 1972. V. 49; 50; 54

ALBEDA, MOSES BEN JACOB
Sha'Arei Dimah. Venie: 1586. V. 47

ALBEE, EDWARD
The American Dream. New York: 1961. V. 52
Box and Quotations from Chairman Mao Tse-Tung. New York: 1969. V. 54
A Delicate Balance. New York: 1966. V. 51; 52; 54
Everything in the Garden. New York: 1968. V. 54
The Lady from Dubuque. New York: 1980. V. 49
Malcolm. New York: 1966. V. 54
Tiny Alice. New York: 1965. V. 52; 53
Who's Afraid of Virginia Woolf?. New York: 1962. V. 51; 52
The Zoo Story and Other Plays. London: 1962. V. 51
The Zoo Story and Other Plays. London: 1962. V. 47; 50; 51
The Zoo Story, The Death of Bessie Smith and the Sandbox. New York: 1960. V. 51; 52; 53; 54

ALBEE, FRED HOUDLETT
Bone Graft Surgery. Philadelphia: 1915. V. 50; 54
Bone-Graft Surgery. Philadelphia: 1917. V. 52; 53
Orthopedic and Reconstruction Surgery, Industrial and Civilian. Phildelphia: 1919. V. 50

ALBEE, LOUIS RANKIN
A List of Books on Angling, Fishes and Fish Culture in Harvard College Library. Cambridge: 1896. V. 47

ALBEMARLE, GEORGE THOMAS KEPPEL
Fifty Years of My Life... London: 1876. V. 54
Fifty Years of My Life. New York: 1876. V. 50

ALBEMARLE, WILLIAM COUTTS KEPPEL, 7TH EARL OF
Cycling. London: 1887. V. 49; 53
Cycling. London: 1901. V. 54

ALBERS, JOSEF
Despite Straight Lines. New Haven: 1961. V. 47; 50; 51

ALBERT, ALLEN D.
History of the Forty-Fifth Regiment: Pennsylvania Veteran Volunteer Infantry, 1861-1865. Williamsport: 1912. V. 53

ALBERT Camus and the Men of Stone. San Francisco: 1971. V. 54

ALBERT Einstein, Philosopher-Scientist. Evanston: 1949. V. 54

ALBERT, JOHN
The Fatal Book Opened! An Authentic Account of John Albert, a Young Gentleman in Hambrugh, Who by the Constant Study of the Works of Friar Bacon and Doctor Faustus and Other Books of Magic and astrology... Otley: 1830. V. 48

ALBERT, NEAL
February Trouble. 1992. V. 51
The January Corpse. 1991. V. 51; 54

ALBERT, PRINCE CONSORT
The Principal Speeches and Addresses of His Royal Highness the Prince Consort. London: 1862. V. 49

ALBERT The Good: a Nation's Tribute to the memory of a Truly Virtuous Prince. London: 1862. V. 48

ALBERTI, LEANDRO
Descrittione di Tutta Italia. Bologna: 1550. V. 47; 53
Descrittione di Tutta Italia... London: 1550. V. 47

ALBERTI, LEON BATTISTA
The Architecture...of Painting...and of Statuary, . London: 1762. V. 47

ALBERTI, RAFAEL
El Negro Motherwell. New York: 1982. V. 52
Selected Poems. New York: 1944. V. 49

ALBERTS, S. S.
A Bibliography of the Works of Robinson Jeffers. New York: 1933. V. 48

ALBERTUS MAGNUS
Compendium Theologice Veritatis. Venice: 1510. V. 52
Enchiridion Verae Perfectaeque Virtutis, Cum Eiusdem Inductivis, Signis, Ac Argumentis Paradisus Animae Merito Nuncupatum. Bologna: 1555. V. 50
Philosophia Pauperum, sive Philosophia Naturalis. Venice: 1496. V. 51

ALBIN, ELEAZAR
Natural History of English Song Birds, and Such of the Foreign as Are Usually brought Over and Esteem'd for Their Singing. London: 1759. V. 48
A Natural History of English Song Birds and Such of the Foreign as are Usually Brought Over and Esteemed for Their Singing. London: 1741. V. 49; 51; 52
A Natural History of Singing Birds and Particularly, That species of Them Most Commonly Bred in Britain, To Which Are Added... Edinburgh: 1776. V. 48

ALBINUS, BERNHARD SIEGFRIED
The Explanation of Albinus's Anatomical Figures of the Human Skeleton and Muscles. London: 1754. V. 53; 54
Explicatio Tabularum anatomicarum Bartholomaei Eustachii... Leiden: 1744. V. 48
Historia Musculorum Hominis. 1734. V. 53

ALBO, JOSEPH
(Hebrew:) *Sefer Ha-Ikkarim....* Venice: 1618. V. 52

ALBORGHETTI, TOMASSO
Tratto della Mirabili Fecolta' et Effeti Della Polvere, O Elixir Vitae. Rome: 1699. V. 48

ALBRIGHT, GEORGE LESLIE
Official Explorations for Pacific Railroads. Berkeley: 1921. V. 53

ALBRIGHT, WILLIAM FOXWELL
Eretz-Israel: Archaeological, Historical and Geographical Studies. Jerusalem: 1969. V. 49; 51
The Excavation of Tell Beit Mirsim. New Haven: 1932-43. V. 49; 51
The Excavation of Tell Beit Mirsim. Volume III. The Bronze Age. New Haven: 1938. V. 51
The Excavation of Tell Beit Mirsim. Volume III: The Iron Age. New Haven: 1924. V. 49
The Excavation of Tell Ben Mirsim. Volume III. The Iron Age. New Haven: 1943. V. 51

ALBRIZZI, GIROLAMO
Esatta Notitia del Peloponnoso Volgarmente Penisola della Morea. Venice: 1687. V. 49

ALBUCASIS
Albucasis on Surgery and Instruments. Los Angeles: 1973. V. 51; 52
On Surgery and Instruments. London: 1973. V. 47; 50; 53

THE ALBUM. New York: 1824. V. 52

ALBUM Of Celebrated American Indian Chiefs.... Richmond: 1890. V. 54

ALBUM of Indian and Persian Miniatures of the XVI-XVIIIth Centuries. Moscow: 1962. V. 51

ALBUM of Old Japanese Prints of the Ukiyo-ye School Reproduced from the Collection of Ken-Ichi Kawaura. Tokyo: 1919. V. 47

ALBUM of San Diego and Coronado Beach, California. Columbus: 1887. V. 47

ALBUM of the Union Pacific Railway. Omaha: 1881. V. 49

ALBUM Vilmorin, the Vegetable Garden. London: 1986. V. 48; 50; 51; 52; 54

ALCALA Y HERRERA, ALONSO DE
Varios Effetos de Amor en Cinco Novelos Exemplares. Lisbon: 1641. V. 53

ALCAREZ, RAMON
The Other Side; or Notes for the History of the War Between Mexico and the United States Written in Mexico. New York: 1850. V. 49

ALCEDO, DON ANTONIO DE
The Geographical and Historical Dictionary of America and the West Indies. London: 1812. V. 47; 51

ALCHEMIAE Quam Vocant Artisque Metallicae, Doctrina. Basileae: 1572. V. 47; 50; 53

ALCIATI, ANDREA
Emblemata. Lyon: 1600. V. 50
Emblemata cum Commentarius... Padua: 1661. V. 47
Emblematum Libellus. Parisiis: 1542. V. 47; 49; 50
Emblematum Libellus. Venetiis: 1546. V. 47
Omnia Andreae Alciati V. C. Emblemata: Cum Commentariis Quibus. Antwerp: 1577. V. 50

ALCIATUS, ANDREA
Omnia Emblemata: cum Commentariis... Parisiis: 1583. V. 48; 51

ALCIBIADES
The Dream of Alcibiades. London: 1749. V. 54

ALCOCK, A. W.
A Naturalist in Indian Seas or Four Years with Royal Indian Marine Survey Ship 'Investigator'. London: 1902. V. 50
Report on the Natural History Results of the Pamir Boundary Commission... Calcutta: 1898. V. 51

ALCOCK, C. W.
Famous Cricketers and Cricket Grounds. London: 1895. V. 48; 51; 52

ALCOCK, JOHN
Harmonia Festi, or a Collection of Canons... Lichfield: 1791. V. 48
Harmonia Festi, or a Collection of Canons; Cheerful and Serious Glees and Catches. 1791. V. 52

ALCOCK, RUTHERFORD
The Capital of the Tycoon: a Narrative of a Three Years' Residence in Japan. London: 1863. V. 47

ALCOCK, T.
An Essay on the Use of Chloruerts of Oxide of Sodium and of Lime as Powerful Disinfecting Agents...in the Treatment of Hospital Gangrene... 1827. V. 51

ALCOCK, THOMAS
Travels in Russia, Persia, Turkey and Greece in 1828-9. London: 1831. V. 53

ALCOCK, W. A.
Report on the Natural History Results of the Pamir Boundary Commission. Calcutta: 1898. V. 47

ALCOFORADO, MARIANA SOROR
Letters from a Portuguese Nun. Andoversford: 1986. V. 50; 51
Letters from a Portuguese Nun. London: 1986. V. 50
Letters of a Portuguese Nun. North Wales: 1929. V. 50
Portuguese Letters. Switzerland: 1948. V. 51

ALCOHOLICS Anonymous. New York: 1954. V. 51
ALCOHOLICS Anonymous. New York: 1955. V. 51

ALCOHOLICS Anonymous Comes of Age. New York: 1957. V. 51

ALCOTT, AMOS BRONSON
Concord Lectures on Philosophy Comprising Outlines of all the Lectures at the Concord Summer School of Philosophy in 1882... Cambridge: 1883. V. 50
The Concord Summer School of Philosophy. Concord: 1883. V. 51
Conversations with Children on the Gospels. Boston: 1836. V. 47

ALCOTT, AMOS BRONSON continued
Observations on the Principles and Methods of Infant Instruction. Boston: 1830. V. 54
Ralph Waldo Emerson. An Estimate of His Character and Genius in Prose and Verse. Boston: 1882. V. 49
Tablets. Boston: 1868. V. 48
Tablets. Boston: 1888. V. 47

ALCOTT, LOUISA MAY
Aunt Jo's Scrap Bag. Boston: 1872-82. V. 49
Aunt Jo's Scrap-Bag. 1872. V. 50
Aunt Jo's Scrap-Bag. My Girls, etc. Boston: 1878. V. 47
Aunt Jo's Scrap-Bag. Shawl-Straps. Boston: 1872. V. 47
Eight Cousins. Boston: 1875. V. 47
Flower Fables. Boston: 1855. V. 48; 49; 53
Good Wives. London: 1913. V. 48
Her Life, Letters and Journals. Boston: 1889. V. 54
Hospital Sketches. Boston: 1863. V. 47; 48; 51; 52
Jack and Jill. Boston: 1880. V. 52
Jo's Boys, and How they Turned Out. Boston: 1886. V. 47; 52
Jo's Boys and How they Turned Out. Toronto: 1887. V. 51
Little Men: Life at Plumfield with Jo's Boys. Boston: 1871. V. 47; 50; 51; 53; 54
Little Women. Boston: 1868/69. V. 50; 52
Little Women. London: 1922. V. 47; 49; 51
Little Women. Racine: 1934. V. 50
Little Women. (with) Little Women Part Second. (with) Little Men. Boston: 1868-71. V. 49
Louisa May Alcott: Her Life, Letters and Journals. London: 1889. V. 50
An Old Fashioned Girl. London: 1870. V. 47
Rose in Bloom. Boston: 1876. V. 47; 53
Silver Pitchers: and Independence,, a Centennial Love Story. Boston: 1876. V. 48
Spinning-Wheel Stories. Boston: 1884. V. 53
Three Proverb Stories. Boston: 1870. V. 54
Under the Lilacs. Boston: 1878. V. 47

ALDAN, DAISY
The Destruction of Cathedrals and Other Poems. Paris/New York: 1963. V. 52

ALDANA, COSME DE
Discourso Contro il Volgo in Cui Con Buone Regioni si Reprovano Molte Sue False Opinioni... Florence: 1578. V. 48

ALDE, JOHN
Souvenir and Official Programme of the Centennial Celebration of George Washington's Inauguration. New York: 1889. V. 53

ALDEN, JOHN
European Americana. New Canann: 1980-88. V. 47; 50
European Americana. New York: 1980/82. V. 50

ALDEN, JOHN ELIOT
Rhode Island Imprints 1727-1800. New York: 1949. V. 50

ALDEN, TIMOTHY
A Collection of American Epitaphs and Inscriptions with Occasional Notes. New York: 1814. V. 49

ALDER, J.
Birds and Flowers of the Castle of Mey. London: 1993. V. 51; 53

ALDER, ROBERT
A Sermon, Delivered in the Wesleyan Chapel, City Saint John, on Occasion of the Death of Mrs. Elizabeth Bennett... Saint John: 1825. V. 47

ALDERMAN, EDWIN ANDERSON
Library of Southern Literature. Atlanta: 1913. V. 47; 49

ALDERMAN'S Feast, a New Alphabet. London: 1845. V. 50

ALDERSON, E. G.
Studies in Ampullaria. Cambridge: 1925. V. 54

ALDERSON, M. A.
An Essay On the Nature and Application of Steam, with an Historical Ntoice of the Rise and Progressive Improvement of the Steam Engine. London: 1834. V. 50

ALDERTON, D.
The Atlas of Parrots. London: 1991. V. 49; 52

ALDIN, CECIL
Aldin's Painting Books: the Doggy Book. London: 1920. V. 53
An Artist's Models. London: 1930. V. 48; 49; 50
The Bob-Tail Puppy Book. London: 1910. V. 47
Cathedrals and Abbey Churches of England. London: 1929. V. 54
Cathedrals of England. London. V. 54
Dogs of Character. London: 1927. V. 51
A Gay Dog. London: 1905. V. 49
Hunting Scenes... New York: 1936. V. 50
Just Among Friends. London: 1934. V. 49
Just Among Friends. London: 1935. V. 48; 54
Mac. London: 1915. V. 53
The Mongrel Puppy Book. London. V. 54
Old Inns. London: 1923. V. 50
Ratcatcher in Scarlet. London: 1933. V. 54
The Romance of the Road. London: 1928. V. 54
Scarlet to M. F. H. London: 1933. V. 47; 48
Scarlet to M. F. H. New York: 1933. V. 48; 52
A Sporting Garland. London: 1902. V. 47
Time I Was Dead. London: 1934. V. 48
Time I Was Dead. New York: 1934. V. 54
The Twins. London: 1905. V. 50
The Twins. London: 1910. V. 52

ALDINGTON, CYRIL
In Shabby Streets and Other Verses. London: 1942. V. 47

ALDINGTON, HENRY
Some Acount of the Abbey Church of St. Peter and St. Paul, at Dorchester, Oxfordshire. Oxford: 1845. V. 54

ALDINGTON, JOHN HENRY
The Cyclopaedia of Law, or, the Correct British Lawyer... Oxford: 1820. V. 49

ALDINGTON, RICHARD
A. E. Housman and W. B. Yeats. Two Lectures. Hurst, Berkshire: 1955. V. 48; 53
All Men Are Enemies. 1933. V. 49; 54
All Men Are Enemies. London: 1933. V. 48; 53
The Colonel's Daughter. London: 1931. V. 53
The Colonel's Daughter. London: 1931. V. 51; 52; 54
D. H. Lawrence. London: 1930. V. 49
Death of a Hero. London: 1929. V. 50; 54
A Dream in the Luxembourg. London: 1930. V. 50
Ezra Pound & T. S. Eliot: a Lecture. London: 1954. V. 49
Fifty Romance Lyric Poems. New York: 1928. V. 53
A Fool i' the Forest. London: 1925. V. 49
Images. London: 1919. V. 48
Images of Desire. London: 1919. V. 47; 54
Images of War. Poems. Boston: 1921. V. 49
Last Straws. Paris: 1930. V. 48; 49; 52; 54
Lawrence of Arabia. 1954. V. 54
Love and the Luxembourg. New York: 1930. V. 50; 53
Roads to Glory. London: 1930. V. 47; 51; 52; 53; 54
Soft Answers. 1932. V. 49; 54
Stepping Heavenward. Florence: 1931. V. 47; 49; 49; 52; 54
Stepping Heavenward. London: 1931. V. 54
Stepping Heavenward. Florence: 1932. V. 50
War and Love (1915-1918). Boston: 1919. V. 51

ALDINI, GIOVANNI
Essai Theorique et Experimental sur Le Galvanisme.... Paris: 1804. V. 47; 48

ALDINUS, TOBIAS
Exactissima Descriptio Rariorum Quarundam Plantarum, que Continentur Rome in Horto Farnesiano. Roma: 1625. V. 54
Exactissima Descriptio Rariorum Quarundam Plantarum, Que Continentur Rome in Horto Farnesiano. Roma: 1625. V. 53

ALDIS, H. G.
A Dictionary of printers and Booksellers in England, Scotland and Ireland and of Foreign Printers of English Books 1557-1640. London: 1910. V. 48

ALDISS, BRIAN
A Brian Aldiss Omnibus. London: 1969. V. 51; 53
The Brighfount Diaries. London: 1955. V. 52
Frankenstein Unbound. London: 1973. V. 48
The Hand Reared Boy. London: 1970. V. 51
Hothouse. London: 1962. V. 54
The Malacia Tapestry. London: 1976. V. 51
My Country 'Tis Not Only of Thee'. London: 1986. V. 51
Space Time and Nathaniel. London: 1957. V. 48; 52

ALDRICH, ARMISTEAD ALBERT
The History of Houston County, Texas. San Antonio: 1943. V. 48

ALDRICH, HENRY
Elementa Architecturae Civilis ad Vitruvii Veterumque Disciplinam, et Recentiorum Praesertim a Palladii Exempla Probatiora Concinnata. Oxford: 1789. V. 49
Elements of Civil Architecture According to Vitruvius and Other Ancients. Oxford: 1789. V. 48; 50; 51; 53
The Elements of Civil Architecture According to Vitruvius and Other Ancients and the Most Approved Practice of Modern Authors... Oxford: 1824. V. 49

ALDRICH, LORENZO D.
A Journal of the Overland Route to California and the Gold Mines. Los Angeles: 1950. V. 53

ALDRICH, THOMAS A.
The History of Battery A, First Regiment Rhode Island Light Artillery in the War to Preserve the Union 1861-1865. Providence: 1904. V. 48; 50; 52

ALDRICH, THOMAS BAILEY
The Ballad of Babie Bell and Other Poems. New York: 1859. V. 50; 51; 54
The Bells: a Collection of Chimes. New York: 1855. V. 54
The Course of True Love Never Did Run Smooth. New York: 1858. V. 54
Friar Jerome's Beautiful Book. Boston: 1896. V. 48; 49
Judith of Bethulia: a Tragedy. Boston: 1904. V. 54
Marjorie Daw. Boston and New York: 1908. V. 54
Out of His Head. A Romance. New York: 1857. V. 47
Prudence Palfrey. Boston: 1874. V. 47
A Sea Turn and Other Matters. Boston & New York: 1902. V. 54

ALDRICH, THOMAS BAILEY continued
The Story of a Bad Boy. Boston & New York: 1894. V. 51
The Writings of Thomas Bailey Aldrich. Cambridge: 1897. V. 54
The Young Folks Library, Selections from the Choicest Literature of All Lands. Boston: 1901. V. 49

ALDRIDGE, REGINALD
Life on a Ranch. London: 1884. V. 53
Life on a Ranch: Ranch Notes in Kansas, Colorado, the Indian Territory and Northern Texas. New York: 1884. V. 49; 50

ALDRIDGE, T. J.
The Sherebo and its Hinterland. London: 1901. V. 47

ALDRIN, EDWIN E.
Return to Earth. New York: 1973. V. 52

ALDROVANDI, ULISSE
De Piscibvs Libri V, et De Cetis Lib. Vnvs. Bologna: 1612. V. 49
De Piscibvs Libri v, et De Cetis Lib. Vnvs. Bologna: 1613. V. 47
Musaeum Metallicum in Libros IIII Distributum... colophon Bologna: 1648. V. 47
Serpentum, et Craconu Historiae Libri Duo. (with) *De Reliquis Animalibus Exanguibus Libri Quatuor.* Rome/Bologna: 1640/42. V. 53

ALDWINCKLE, STELLA
Christ's Shadow in Plato's Cave. Oxford: 1990. V. 49

ALDYNE, NATHAN
Slate. New York: 1984. V. 54

ALECHINSKY, PIERRE
Pierre Alechinsky. New York: 1977. V. 47; 48; 50; 52

ALEMAN, MATEO
The Life of Guzman d'Alfarache; or, the Spanish Rogue. London: 1708. V. 54
The Rogue; or the Life of Guzman de Alfarache. London: 1622. V. 53
The Rogue, or, The Life of Guzman de Alfarache Written in Spanish by Matheo Aleman and Done Into English Anno 1623. London: 1924. V. 54

ALEMBERT, JEAN LEROND D'
An Account of the Destruction of the Jesuits in France. Glasgow: 1766. V. 47
An Account of the Destruction of the Jesuits in France. London: 1766. V. 51
Encyclopedie Methodique. Mathematiques. Paris: 1784. V. 50
Miscellaneous Pieces in Literature, History and Philosophy. London: 1764. V. 48; 50
Reflexions sur la Cause Generale des Vents. Paris: 1747/46. V. 47
Traite de Dynamique, Dans Lequel les Loix de L'Equilibre & du Mouvement des Corps sont Reduites au Plus Petit Nombre Possible. Paris: 1758. V. 52; 54

ALEMBIC PRESS
Specimens of Wood Type Held at the Alembic Press. Oxford: 1993. V. 52

ALEXANDER, ALEXANDER
The Life of Alexander Alexander Written by Himself... Edinburgh: 1830. V. 51

ALEXANDER, ANN
An Address to the Inhabitants of Charleston, South Carolina. Philadelphia: 1805. V. 48; 49; 53

ALEXANDER, BOYD
From the Niger to the Nile. London: 1907. V. 47
From the Niger to the Nile. London: 1908. V. 47

ALEXANDER, C.
The Life and Mysteries of the Celebrated Dr. "Q". Los Angeles: 1921. V. 47

ALEXANDER, CHARLES W.
The Convent Horror; or the True Narrative of Barbara Ubryk, a Sister of the Carmelite Convent at Cracow, Who Has Been Walled Up in a Dungeon Eight Feet Long by Six Feet Wide!. Philadelphia: 1869. V. 51; 53

ALEXANDER, CONSTANCE G.
Francesca Alexander. A "Hidden Servant" Memories. Cambridge: 1927. V. 50

ALEXANDER, DOROTHY
The German Single-Leaf Woodcut 1600-1700. New York: 1977. V. 48; 50

ALEXANDER, EDWARD PORTER
Military Memoirs of a Confederate. New York: 1907. V. 49

ALEXANDER, EVELINE MARTIN
Among the Pimas. Albany: 1893. V. 49; 54

ALEXANDER, GABRIEL
Robert Bruce, the Hero-King of Scotland. London: 1852. V. 47

ALEXANDER, GRAND DUKE OF RUSSIA
Once a Grand Duke. New York: 1932. V. 54

ALEXANDER, HARTLEY BURR
Bertram Grosvenor Goodhue, Architect and Master of Many Arts. New York: 1925. V. 47
God's Drum and Other Cycles from Indian Lore. New York: 1927. V. 51
Pueblo Indian Painting. Santa Fe: 1979. V. 50
The Religious Spirit of the American Indians, As Shown In the Development of His Religious Rites and Customs. Chicago: 1910. V. 51

ALEXANDER, J.
An Early Breton Gospel Book. Cambridge: 1977. V. 47
The Italian Manuscripts in the Library of Major J. R. Abbey. London: 1969. V. 48

ALEXANDER, J. A.
The Life of George Chaffey: A story of Irrigation Beginnings in California and Australia. Melbourne: 1928. V. 47

ALEXANDER, JAMES
The Jack Rabbit Poem. San Francisco: 1966. V. 51

ALEXANDER, JAMES EDWARD
L'Acadie; or, Seven Years' Explorations in British America. London: 1849. V. 53
Narrative of a Voyage of Observation Among the Colonies of Western Africa, In the Flag Ship Thalia; and a Campaign in Kaffir-Land... London: 1837. V. 49; 53
Travels from India to England: Comprehending a Visit to the Burman Empire, and a Journey through Persia, Asia Minor, European Turkey &c. in the Years 1825-26... London: 1827. V. 50

ALEXANDER, JAMES LYNNE
Wonders of the West. York: 1825. V. 53

ALEXANDER, JOHN H.
Mosby's Men. New York: 1907. V. 49

ALEXANDER, KARL
Time After Time. New York: 1979. V. 51

ALEXANDER, L.
The Book of Three. London: 1966. V. 49; 54

ALEXANDER, L. D.
Catalogue of the Large and Valuable Library of L. D. Alexander; Part the First and Part the Second; to be sold at Auction March 25-30, 1895 (and) April 15-19, 1895. New York: 1895. V. 47

ALEXANDER, L. M.
Candy. New York: 1934. V. 48; 49

ALEXANDER, PHILIP W.
History of San Mateo County. Burlingame: 1916. V. 53

ALEXANDER, RUSSELL GEORGE
The Engraved Work o F. L. Griggs, A.R.A., R.E., Etchings and Dry-Points 1912-1928. Stratford-upon-Avon: 1928. V. 47; 51; 53; 54

ALEXANDER, W. B.
Birds of the Ocean, a Handbook for Voyagers Containing Descriptions of All the Sea-Birds of the World... New York: 1928. V. 52

ALEXANDER, W. D.
History of Later Years of the Hawaiian Monarachy and the Revolution of 1893. Honolulu: 1896. V. 50

ALEXANDER, WILLIAM
The Costume of the Russian Empire. London: 1803. V. 50; 51
Costume of the Russian Empire. London: 1810. V. 51
An Experimental Enquiry Concerning the Causes Which Have Generally Been Said to Produce Putrid Diseases. London: 1771. V. 51
The History of Women, from the Earliest Antiquity, to the Present Time. London: 1779. V. 53
A Journey to Beresford Hall, The Seat of Charles Cotton Esq. The Celebrated Author and Angler. London: 1841. V. 47
Plan and Description of the Original Electro-magnetic Telegraph with Prefatory Note to the Royal Commissioners of the Exhibition of the Works of Industry of All Nations, and Relative Documents. London: 1851. V. 54

ALEXANDER AB ALEXANDRO
Genialivm Dierum. Parisiis: 1579. V. 53

ALEXANDER TRALLIANUS
(De Arte Medica). Libri Duodecim, Graeci et Latini. Basel: 1556. V. 47; 50
De singularum Corporis Partium, ab Hominis Coronide ad Imum Usque Calcaneum, vitiis, Aegritudinibus... Basle: 1533. V. 49

ALEXANDRE, ARSENE
The Decorative Art of Leon Bakst. London: 1913. V. 50

ALEXANDROVNA, B.
Spring on the Kholkoz (Communal Farm). Moscow: 1932. V. 53

ALEYN, CHARLES
The Battailes of Crescey and Poictiers, Under the Fortunes and Valour of King Edward the Third of that Name, and His Sonne Edward Prince of Wales, Named the Black. London: 1633. V. 53

ALFAU, FELIPE
Locos. New York: 1936. V. 47; 50

ALFONSO VI, KING OF PORTUGAL
Regimento da Forma Por Que Se Ham de Cobrar os Reaes Impostos Na Carne, & Vinho Nesta Cidade... Lisbon: 1674. V. 48

ALFORD, D.
A Colour Atlas of Pests of Ornamental Trees, Shrubs and Flowers. London: 1991. V. 48

ALFRED A. *Knopf, Quarter Century.* New York: 1940. V. 54

ALFRED, H. J.
A Complete Guide to Spinning and Trolling Shewing How and Where to Take Pike & Jack with Instructions in the Art of Spinning for Trout & Perch. London: 1860. V. 47
Views of the Thames...Marlow Weir, Near Marlow Bridge, Bisham Abbey, Temple Lock, Hurley Harleyford. London: 1857. V. 52

ALGAE *Abstracts. A Guide to Literature Up to 1974.* New York: 1973-76. V. 52

ALGAROTTI, FRANCESCO
An Essay on Painting. London: 1763. V. 50

ALGAROTTI, FRANCESCO continued
An Essay on Painting. London: 1764. V. 52; 54
An Essay on the Opera Written in Italian. London: 1767. V. 47
The Philosophy of Sir Isaac Newton Explained in Six Dialogues on Light and Colours Between a Lady and the Author. Glasgow: 1765. V. 52; 54
Sir Isaac Newton's Philosophy Explain'd for the Use of the Ladies. London: 1739. V. 53

ALGER, HORATIO
Ben, the Luggage Boy; or, Among the Wharves. Boston: 1870. V. 47
Ben's Nugget; or a Boy's Search for Fortune. Philadelphia: 1882. V. 50
Bertha's Christmas Vision: an Autumn Sheaf. Boston: 1855. V. 54
Fame and Fortune; or, the Progress of Richard Hunter. Boston: 1868. V. 47
Ragged Dick; or. Street Life in New York with Boot-Blacks. Boston: 1868. V. 53
The Western Boy. 1878. V. 48
The Young Miner; or Tom Nelson in California. Boston: 1879. V. 51
The Young Outlaw; or Adrift in the Streets. Boston: 1875. V. 53

ALGER, R. A.
The Spanish American War. New York: 1901. V. 47

AN ALGONQUIN Sampler: Excerpts from Forthcoming Fiction. Chapel Hill: 1990. V. 48; 50

ALGREN, NELSON
Chicago: City on the Make. Garden City: 1951. V. 49; 52; 53
Chicago: City on the Make. Garden City: 1952. V. 48
Galena Guide. Galena: 1937. V. 48
The Last Carousel. New York: 1973. V. 47
The Man With the Golden Arm. Garden City: 1949. V. 47
The Neon Wilderness. Garden City: 1947. V. 47; 49; 51; 53
Never Come Morning. London: 1958. V. 53; 54
Somebody in Boots. New York: 1935. V. 51
Walk on the Wild Side. New York: 1956. V. 47; 48; 49; 53; 54
Who Lost an American?. New York: 1963. V. 48

ALI, S.
Birds of Kerala. London: 1969. V. 49; 54
The Birds of Sikkim. London: 1962. V. 54
The Birds of Sikkim. Oxford: 1962. V. 49
The Birds of Travancore and Cochin. London: 1953. V. 49
Compact Edition of Handbook of the Birds of India and Pakistan... Oxford: 1987. V. 51
Compact Edition of Handbook of the Birds of India and Pakistan, Together With Those of Bangladesh, Nepal, Bhutan and Sri Lanka. Oxford: 1988. V. 50
Handbook of the Birds of India and Pakistan Together with Those of Nepal, Sikkim, Bhutan and Ceylon. London: 1968-74. V. 51; 54

ALI, TARIQ
The Thoughts of Chairman Harold. London: 1967. V. 47

ALIBERT, JEAN LOUIS
Clinica del Parigino Spedale di S. Luigi Ossia Trattato Compiuto Delle Malattie Della Pelle. Venice: 1835. V. 49

ALIBONE, S. AUSTIN
A Critical Dictionary of English Literature, British and American Authors, Living and Deceased to the Latter Half of the 19th Century. Philadelphia & London: 1871-91. V. 50

ALICE Aforethought. Dublin: 1938. V. 53

ALICE Aforethought. Guinness Carols for 1938. London: 1938. V. 50

ALICE, GRAND DUCHESS OF HESSE
Biographical Sketch and Letters. London: 1884. V. 51

ALICE in Police Court Land with Some Legal Fictions and Other Diversions. London: 1936. V. 51

ALICE, the Negro; and the Good Old Indian; to Which are Added a Memoir of Ann Watson, and the Advice of Thomas Gwin &c. New York: 1826?. V. 47

ALICE Versary. London: 1959. V. 54

THE ALICE Versary. The Guiness Birthday Book. 1959. V. 53

ALICE Versary. The Guinness Birthday Book. Ipswich: 1959. V. 50

ALICE Where Art Thou?. 1948. V. 49

ALINDER, J.
Roy De Carava Photographs. 1981. V. 52

ALISHAN, LEO M.
Armenian Popular Songs Translated Into English. Venice: 1852. V. 50; 51

ALISON, ARCHIBALD
England in 1815 and 1845; or a Sufficient and a Contracted Currency. Edinburgh & London: 1846. V. 51
Essays on the Nature and Principles of Taste. London and Edinburgh: 1790. V. 48; 49; 54
Essays On the Nature and Principles of Taste. Edinburgh: 1825. V. 50; 52; 54
History of Europe From the Commencement of the French Revolution in 1789 to the Restoration of the Bourbons in 1815. Edinburgh: 1839-44. V. 49
History of Europe from the Commencement of the French Revolution in MDCCLXXXIX tot he Restoration of the Bourbons in MDCCCXV. London: 1848. V. 51
History of Europe from the Commencement of the French Revolution (to the Accession of Louis Napoleon in 1852). London: 1849-59. V. 47; 53
A History of Europe from the Commencement of the French Revolution to the Restoration of the Bourbons in 1815... London: 1853-59. V. 47
The History of Europe from the Commencement of the French Revolution to the Restoration of the Bourbons in MDCCCXV. Edinburgh: 1858. V. 54
History of Europe from the Commencement of the French Revolution to the Restoration of the Bourbons in MDCCCXV. (with) History of Europe from the Fall of Napoleon in MDCCCXV to the Accession of Louis Napoleon in MDCCCLII. London: 1860/1854-59/75. V. 51
The Principles of Population, and their Connection with Human Happiness. Edinburgh: 1840. V. 49; 52
Travels in France, During the Years 1814-15. London: 1816. V. 47

ALKEN, HENRY
The Art and Practice of Etching with Directions for Other Methods of Light and Entertaining Engraving. London: 1849. V. 48; 49
The Beauties and Defects in the Figure of the Horse, Comparatively Delineated. London: 1816. V. 48
The Beauties and Defects in the Figure of the Horse Comparatively Delineated. London: 1881-66. V. 50
Driving Discoveries. London: 1817. V. 47; 49; 50; 54
Ideas, Accidental and Incidental to Hunting and Other Sports; Caught in Leicestershire. London: 1826-30. V. 53
Military Occurrences. N.P: 1820. V. 52
National Sports of Great Britain. London: 1820. V. 47
A Panorama of the Progress of Human Life... London: 1930. V. 54
Qualified Horses and Unqualified Riders, or the Reverse of Sporting Phrases, from the Work Intitled Indispensable Accomplishments by Ben Tally-Ho. London: 1815. V. 51; 52
Specimens of Riding Near London. Drawn from Life. London: 1821. V. 48; 53
Sporting Discoveries, or the Miseries of Hunting, in a Series of Seven Plates... London: 1816. V. 47
The Sporting Repository. London: 1822. V. 52
Symptoms of Being Amused. London: 1822. V. 47
A Touch at the Fine Arts. London: 1824. V. 53

ALL The Funny Folks: the Wonder Tale of How the Comic-Strip Characters Live and Love 'Behind the Scenes'. New York: 1926. V. 49

ALLAIN, MARIE FRANCOISE
One November day in 1980 the Other Graham Greene Burst through His Shadow. London: 1983. V. 53

ALLAIS, ALPHONSE
Story for Sara: What Happened to a Little Girl. New York: 1971. V. 51

ALLAN, FRANCIS D.
A Collection of Southern Patriotic Songs, Made During Confederate Times. Galveston: 1874. V. 49

ALLAN, JAMES
The Life of James Allan, the Celebrated Northumberland Piper and other Branches of His Extraordinary Family. Blyth: 1818. V. 50

ALLAN, JOHN HAY
The Bridal of Caolchairn and Other Poems. London: 1822. V. 53; 54

ALLAN, M.
The Tradescants, Their Plants, Gardens and Museum 1570-1662. London: 1964. V. 54

ALLAN, R.
The Sportsman in Ireland. 1840. V. 54

ALLAN, W.
My Early Soldiering Days, Including the Crimea Campaign. Edinburgh: 1897. V. 50

ALLAN, WILLIAM
The Army of Northern Virginia in 1862. Boston and New York: 1892. V. 54
A Narrative of the Expedition Sent by Her Majesty's Government to the River Niger in 1841 Under the Command of Capt. H.D. Trotter, R.N. London: 1848. V. 48

ALLARD, WILLIAM ALBERT
Vanishing Breed: Photographs of the Cowboy and the West. Boston: 1982. V. 53; 54

ALLARDICE, ROBERT BARCLAY
Agricultural Tour in the United States and Upper Canada, with Miscellaneous Notices. Edinburgh: 1842. V. 53

ALLARDYCE, ALEXANDER
Balmoral: a Romance of the Queen's Country. London: 1893. V. 54

ALLBEURY, TED
A Choice of Enemies. London: 1973. V. 53
Show Me a Hero. Bristol: 1992. V. 52; 54

ALLDAY, JOSEPH
Truth is Stranger than Fiction. Birmingham: 1853. V. 50

ALLDRIDGE, W. J.
The Universal Merchant, in Theory and Practice. Philadelphia: 1797. V. 50; 54

ALLEINE, RICHARD
Vindiciae Pietatis; or, a Vindication of Godliness, in the Greatest Strictnesse and Spirituality Of It. London: 1664. V. 53

ALLEMAGNE, HENRY RENE D'
Les Cartes a Jouer du XIVe au XXe Siecle. Paris: 1906. V. 49; 50
Recreations et Passe-Temps. Paris: 1906. V. 47
La Toile Imprimee et Les Indiennes de Traite. Paris: 1942. V. 47

ALLEMAN, TILLIE PIERCE
At Gettysburg or What a Girl Saw and Heard of the Battle. New York: 1889. V. 49

ALLEN & TICKNOR
Allen & Ticknor's Medical Catalogue. A Catalogue of Medical Books, for Sale by Allen and Ticknor, Corner of Washington and School Streets, Boston. Boston: 1833. V. 51

ALLEN, A. J.
The American Pioneer: With a New and Useful Plan to Establish Free Labour, in the United States. Boston: 1855. V. 49
Ten years in Oregon, Travels and Adventures of Doctor E. White and Lady, West of the Rocky Mountains. Ithaca: 1848. V. 49; 54

ALLEN, A. S.
The City of Seattle, 1900. Seattle: 1900. V. 48
Dawson, Yukon Territory, the Golden City in the Land of the Midnight Sun. The Mining and Commercial Metropolis of the Far North. Dawson: 1901. V. 50

ALLEN, ALFRED
The Journal of the Postal Miscroscopical Society: A Miscellany of Natural and Microscopical Science. London: 1882-85. V. 50; 54

ALLEN, ARTHUR CHARLES
The Skin, a Clinicopathologic Treatise. St. Louis: 1954. V. 54

ALLEN, ARTHUR S.
Under Sail to Greenland. New York: 1931. V. 51

ALLEN, BRASSEYA JOHNSON
Pastorals, Elegies, Odes, Epistles and Other Poems. Abingdon: 1806. V. 53

ALLEN, BUNNY
First Wheel. Clinton: 1983. V. 53

ALLEN, C. BRUCE
Rudimentary Treatise. Cottage Building: or, Hints for Improving the Dwellings of the Labouring Classes. London: 1849-50. V. 50

ALLEN, CHARLES
A New and Improved Roman History, from the Foundation of the City of Rome, to its Final Dissolution as the Seat of Empire, in the Year of Christ 476... London: 1798. V. 52
The Operator for the Teeth. London: 1969. V. 47
The Polite Lady; or, a Course of Female Education. London: 1760. V. 52
The Polite Lady; or, a Course of Female Education. London: 1785. V. 48

ALLEN, CHARLES DEXTER
American Bookplates. London: 1895. V. 53
Ex Libris. Essays of a Collector. Boston and New York: 1896. V. 47

ALLEN, DOUGLAS
N. C. Wyeth. Collected Paintings, Illustrations and Murals. New York: 1972. V. 50

ALLEN, ELIZABETH ANN CHASE AKERS
Poems. Boston: 1866. V. 53

ALLEN, ETHAN
Allen's Captivity: Being a Narrative of Colonel Ethan Allen, Containing His Voyages, Travels...Inerspersed with Political Observations. Boston: 1845. V. 47

ALLEN, EVERETT S.
Arctic Odyssey - the Life of Admiral Doanld B. Macmillan. New York: 1963. V. 53

ALLEN, FRANCIS
The Complete English Dictionary... London: 1765. V. 52

ALLEN, FRANCIS H.
A Bibliography of Henry David Thoreau. Boston & New York: 1908. V. 54

ALLEN, FRANK J.
The Great Church Towers of England, Chiefly of the Perpendicular Period. Cambridge: 1932. V. 51; 53

ALLEN, G. M.
Bats. Cambridge: 1939. V. 53
Mammals of China and Mongolia. New York: 1938-40. V. 54
The Mammals of China and Mongolia. Volume I. Tupaiidae to Ochotonidae. New York: 1938. V. 49; 52

ALLEN, G. N.
Incidents and Sufferings in the Mexican War; with Accounts of Hardships Endured; Treacheries of the Mexicans... Boston and New York: 1848. V. 49

ALLEN, GEORGE
An Appeal to the People of Massachusetts, on the Texas Question. Boston: 1844. V. 49

ALLEN, GRANT
An Army Doctor's Romance. London: 1893. V. 47
Michael's Crag. Chicago & New York: 1893. V. 50

ALLEN, H. WARNER
A History of Wine. London: 1961. V. 52

ALLEN, HARRISON
Report of an Autopsy on the Bodies of Chang and Eng Bunker, Commonly Known as the Siamese Twins. Phiadelphia: 1875. V. 48

ALLEN, HENRY T.
Report of an Expedition to the Copper, Tanana and Koyukuk Rivers, in the Territory of Alaska, in the Year 1885. Washington: 1887. V. 49; 52; 53

ALLEN, HERVEY
Anthony Adverse. New York: 1933. V. 51
Anthony Adverse. New York: 1934. V. 50
Anthony Adverse. Mount Vernon: 1937. V. 53
Israfel, the Life and Times of Edgar Allan Poe. New York: 1926. V. 49; 50; 51; 53
It Was Like This: Two Stories of the Great War. New York: 1940. V. 54
New Legends. Poems. New York: 1929. V. 50
Poe's Brother. The Poems of William Henry Leonard Poe. New York: 1926. V. 48; 49

Sarah Simon: Character Atlantean. Garden City: 1929. V. 50
Wampum and Old Gold. New Haven: 1921. V. 49

ALLEN, I. N.
Diary of a March through Sinde and Affghanistan, with Troops Under the Command of General Sir William Nott. 1843. V. 54

ALLEN, IRA
A Concise Summary of the Second Volume of the Olive Branch, a Book... Philadelphia: 1806. V. 52
A Narrative of the Transactions Relative to the Capture of the American Ship Olive Branch. Philadelphia?: 1804. V. 52

ALLEN, J.
Synopsis Medicinae; or, a Summary View of the Whole Practice of Physick. London: 1761. V. 47
Ten Years in Oregon. Travels and Adventures of Doctor E. White and Lady West of the Rocky Mountains. Ithaca: 1848. V. 54

ALLEN, J. A.
History of North American Pinnipeds, a Monograph of the Walruses, Sea-Lions, Sea-Bears, and Seals of North America. Washington: 1880. V. 53
Ontogenetic and Other Variations in Muskoxen. U.S.A: 1913. V. 50

ALLEN, J. FISK
A Practical Treatise on the Culture and Treatment of the Grape Vine... Boston: 1848. V. 51; 54

ALLEN, J. ROMILLEY
Celtic Art in Pagan and Christian Times. London: 1904. V. 50

ALLEN, JAMES
A Collection of Hymns for the Use of Those that Seek , and Those that Have Redemption in the Blood of Christ. Kendal: 1757. V. 50; 54
Schoolcraft and Allen Expedition to Northwest Indians. Washington: 1834. V. 47; 52

ALLEN, JAMES LANE
A Kentucky Cardinal and Aftermath. New York and London: 1900. V. 49; 51

ALLEN, JAMES S.
The Negro Question in the United States. London: 1936. V. 50

ALLEN, JAY
Forty Carats. New York: 1968. V. 50

ALLEN, JOHN
Modern Judaism; or, a Brief Account of the Opinions, Traditions, Rites and Ceremonies of the Jews in Modern Times. London: 1816. V. 52
An Oration, Upon the Beauties of Liberty... Wilmington: 1775. V. 54
The Trial of the Reverend John Allen, Taken Exact from the Proceedings on the King's Commission of the Peace, Oyer and Terminer, and Goal-Delivery for the City of London. Boston: 1773. V. 53

ALLEN, JOHN H.
Southwest. Philadelphia: 1952. V. 53

ALLEN, JOHN LOGAN
Passage through the Garden, Lewis and Clark and the Image of the American Northwest. Urbana: 1975. V. 54

ALLEN, JOSEPH
Battles of the British Navy. London: 1905. V. 47

ALLEN, JUNIS M.
Rhymes, Tales and Rhymed Tales. Topeka: 1906. V. 53

ALLEN, L. F.
The American Herd Book-1846, Containing Pedigrees of Short Horn Cattle... Buffalo: 1846. V. 50; 52

ALLEN, L. L.
A Thrilling Sketch of the Life of the Distinguished Chief Okah Tubbe, Alias, Chubbee...of the Choctaw Nation of Indians. New York: 1848. V. 47; 49

ALLEN, LAWRENCE J.
Man's Greatest Adventure. Selah: 1974. V. 50

ALLEN, LEWIS F.
Rural Architecture: Being a Complete Description of Farm Houses, Cottages and Out Buildings. New York: 1852. V. 54

ALLEN, LEWIS M.
Printing With the Hand Press. Herewith a Definitive Manual... Kentfield: 1969. V. 47

ALLEN, NATHAN
The Opium Trade: Including a Sketch of Its History, Extent, Effects, etc. as Carried On In India and China. Lowell: 1853. V. 48; 54

ALLEN, OSRIC
Philip Larkin Talks to Eboracum. London: 1982. V. 47

ALLEN, OSWALD
History of the York Dispensary... London: 1845. V. 51

ALLEN, PAUL
Beresford Egan: An Introduction to His Work. London: 1966. V. 50
A History of the American Revolution... Baltimore: 1819. V. 47; 50

ALLEN PRESS
The Allen Press Bibliography. 1981. V. 54
The Allen Press Bibliography. San Francisco;: 1985. V. 47; 48; 50; 52; 54

THE ALLEN Press Bibliography. Greenbrae: 1981. V. 49

ALLEN, R.
A Souvenir of Newstead Abbey, Formerly the Home of Lord Byron. London: 1874. V. 51

ALLEN, REGINALD
The First Night Gilbert and Sullivan. New York: 1958. V. 52

ALLEN, SAMUEL A.
My Own Home and Fireside: Being Illustrative of the Speculations of Martin Chuzzlewit and Co... Philadelphia: 1846. V. 49

ALLEN, T.
Hell Upon Earth; or, Devils Let Loose. London: 1822. V. 48

ALLEN, THOMAS
The Commerce and Navigation of the Valley of the Mississippi: and Also that Appertaining to the City of St. Louis. St. Louis: 1847. V. 48
History of the Counties of Surrey and Sussex. London: 1829. V. 50; 53
A New and Complete History of the County of York. London: 1828-31. V. 49
The Panorama of London, and Visitor's Pocket Companion, in a Tour through the metropolis. London: 1830. V. 50

ALLEN, THOMAS GASKELL
Across Asia on a Bicycle. New York: 1894. V. 53
Across Asia on a Bicycle. London: 1895. V. 49

ALLEN, THOMAS GEORGE
The Egyptian Book of the Dead Documents in the Oriental Institute Museum of the University of Chicago. Chicago: 1960. V. 49

ALLEN, V. C.
Rhea and Meigs Counties (Tennessee) in the Confederate War. 1908. V. 54
Rhea and Meigs Counties (Tennessee) in the Confederate War. 1909. V. 49

ALLEN, W. W.
California Gold Book; First Nugget, its Discovery and Discoverers and Some of the Results Proceeding Therefrom. San Francisco and Chicago: 1893. V. 47; 50; 51; 53

ALLEN, WALTER
Governor Chamberlain's Administration in South Carolina a Chapter of Reconstruction in the Southern States. New York: 1888. V. 54

ALLEN, WALTER C.
Hendersonia. The Music of Fletcher Henderson...a Bio-Discography. Highland Park: 1973. V. 47

ALLEN, WILLIAM
Five Years in the West...With Reminiscences and Sketches of Real Life, by a Texas Preacher. Nashville: 1884. V. 47
Killing No Murder; Briefly Discoursed in Three Questions. London?: 1689. V. 49
A Narrative of the Expedition Sent By Her Majesty's Government to the River Niger, in 1841. London: 1848. V. 50
Picturesque Views on the River Niger, Sketched During Lander's Last visit in 1832-33. London: 1840. V. 48

ALLEN, WILLIAM A.
Adventures With Indians and Game or Twenty Years in the Rockies. Chicago: 1903. V. 50; 52

ALLEN, WILLIAM FRANCIS
Slave Songs of the United States. New York: 1867. V. 54

ALLEN, WILLIAM G.
Sea Weeds Collected on the British Coast...Presented to the Boston Anti-Slavery Bazaar Collected by... Leeds: 1853. V. 53

ALLEN, WILLIAM M.
Bismarck, the Pig of Genius; His Life and Labors... Philadelphia: 1871. V. 51

ALLEN, WOODY
Don't Drink the Water. New York: 1967. V. 51
The Floating Light Bulb. New York: 1982. V. 53
Getting Even. 1971. V. 50
Play It Again, Sam. New York: 1969. V. 50
Without Feathers. New York: 1975. V. 47; 50

ALLENDE, ISABEL
The House of the Spirits. New York: 1985. V. 49; 53; 54

ALLESTREE, RICHARD
The Art of Contentment. London: 1675. V. 49
The Art of Contentment. Oxford: 1675. V. 47
The Art of Contentment. Oxford: 1694. V. 49
The Gentleman's Calling. London: 1696. V. 51; 54
The Government of the Tongue. Oxford: 1674. V. 47; 48; 52; 53; 54
The Government of the Tongue. Oxford: 1675. V. 54
Holl Ddled-Swydd Dyn... Ynghyd a Dwywolder Neillduol ar Amryw Achosion... (The Whole Duty of Man, in Welsh). Llundain: 1711. V. 50
The Ladies Calling. Oxford: 1677. V. 50
The Ladies Calling in Two Parts. Oxford: 1673. V. 50; 51; 53; 54

ALLETZ, PONS AUGUSTIN
Les Ornemens de la memoire, ou les Traits Brillans des Poetes Francois les plus Ce'lebres (sic)...Pour Perfectionner l'Education de la Jeunesse. Detroit: 1811. V. 47

ALLEY, FREDERICK J.
Myopia Races and Riders 1879-1930, Being an Account of the Various Races Under the Auspices... Hamilton: 1931. V. 47

ALLEY, GEORGE
Observations on the Hydragyria; of that Vascular Disease Arising from the Exhibition of Mercury. London: 1810. V. 47; 50

ALLEY, JEROME
The Judge, an Estimate of the Importance of the Judicial Character, Occassioned by the death of the Late Lord Clare, Lord Chancellor of Ireland. London: 1803. V. 51

ALLFREY, PHYLLIS SHAND
In Circles. Poems. London: 1940. V. 52

ALLHANDS, J. L.
Boll Weevil: Recollections of the Trinity & Brazos Valley Railway. Houston: 1946. V. 49
Gringo Builders. 1931. V. 48; 49; 50
Gringo Builders. Iowa City: 1931. V. 51
Gringo Builders. Joplin: 1931. V. 53
Railroads to the Rio. Salado: 1960. V. 54

ALLIBONE, S. AUSTIN
A Critical Dictionary of English Literature and British and American Authors... Philadelphia and London: 1877. V. 49
A Critical Dictionary of English Literature and British and American Authors. Philadelphia: 1897. V. 53
A Critical Dictionary of English Literature and British and American Authors... Philadelphia: 1990. V. 50

THE ALLIES' Fairy Book. London: 1961. V. 50

ALLIN, THOMAS
Mechanics' Institutions Defended on Christian Principles. Sheffield: 1833. V. 52

ALLINGHAM, HELEN
Happy England. London: 1903. V. 49; 50
Happy England as Painted. London: 1904. V. 52
The Homes of Tennyson. London: 1905. V. 48
Letters to William Allingham. London: 1911. V. 49

ALLINGHAM, MARGARET
The Case of the Late Pig. London: 1937. V. 50

ALLINGHAM, MARGERY
The Fashion in Shrouds. Garden City: 1938. V. 50
Mr. Campion: Criminologist - Seven Important Episodes from the Casebook of Albert Campion. New York: 1937. V. 52

ALLINGHAM, WILLIAM
The Ballad Book. 1879. V. 48
The Ballad Book. London: 1879. V. 52
Blackberries. London: 1890. V. 49
Blackberries Picked of Many Bushes. 1884. V. 47
Blackberries Picked of Many Bushes. London: 1884. V. 53
Evil May Day, &c. London: 1882. V. 51; 54
Life and Phantasy. London: 1889. V. 51; 54
The Music Master, a Love Story. London: 1855. V. 51
Thought and Word and Ashby Manor. London: 1890. V. 51; 53; 54

ALLIS, OSCAR
An Inquiry Into the Difficulties Encountered in the Reduction of Dislocations of the Hip. Philadelphia: 1896. V. 53

ALLISON, CHARLES E.
History of Yonkers. London: 1896. V. 49

ALLISON, DAVID
History of Nova Scotia. Halifax: 1916. V. 53

ALLISON, DOROTHY
Bastard Out of Carolina. New York: 1992. V. 50; 51; 52; 53; 54
Trash. Ithaca: 1988. V. 51
The Women Who Hate Me. Ithaca: 1991. V. 51

ALLISON, DRUMMOND
The Poems of Drummond Allison. 1978. V. 50; 52
The Yellow Night - Poems - 1940-41-42-43. London: 1944. V. 47; 50; 52

ALLISON, EDWIN H.
The Surrender of Sitting Bull. Dayton: 1891. V. 47

ALLISON, THOMAS
An Account of a Voyage from Archangel in Russia, in the Year 1697. London: 1699. V. 47

ALLISON, WILLIAM
Blair Athol. London: 1881. V. 51
The British Thoroughbred Horse, His History and Breeding, Together with an Exposition of the Figure System. London: 1901. V. 54

ALLIX, PIERRE
Reflections Upon the Opinions of Some Modern Divines, Concerning the Nature of Government in General and that of England in Particular. London: 1689. V. 52
Some Remarks Upon the Ecclesiastaical History of the Ancient Churches of Piedmont. (with) Remarks Upon the Ecclesiastaical History of the Ancient Churches of the Albigenses... London: 1690/92. V. 49

ALLMAN, G. J.
Greek Geometry from Thales to Euclid. Dublin: 1889. V. 50; 52; 54
A Monograph of the Gymnoblastic or Tubularian Hydroids. London: 1871-72. V. 51

ALLOM, THOMAS
China, in a Series of Views, Displaying the Scenery, Architecture and Social Habits of that Ancient Empire. London: 1843. V. 54
Constantinople and the Scenery of the Seven Churches of Asia Minor Illustrated... London. V. 47
Lake and Mountain Scenery. London. V. 52
Westmorland, Cumberland and Durham and Northumberland. London: 1832. V. 50; 51; 52

ALLOT, ROBERT
Englands Parnassus; or the Choysest Flowers of Our Moderne Poets, with Their Poeticall Comparisons. London: 1600. V. 48; 51
Wits Theater of the Little World. London: 1599. V. 47; 49

ALLOTT, KENNETH
Poems. London: 1938. V. 49

ALLOUSE, B. E.
Birds of Iraq. Baghdad: 1960-62. V. 49

ALLOWAY, L.
Roy Lichtenstein. New York: 1983. V. 47

ALLSOP, THOMAS
Letters, Conversations and Recollections of S. T. Coleridge. New York: 1836. V. 49

ALLSOPP, BRUCE
Decoration and Furniture. London: 1952. V. 51
Decoration and Furniture. London: 1952-53. V. 53

ALLSOPP, FRED W.
Folklore of Romantic Arkansas. N.P: 1931. V. 50

ALLSTON, WASHINGTON
Outlines and Sketches... Boston: 1850. V. 52
The Sylphs of the Seasons, with Other Poems. Boston: 1813. V. 51; 52

ALLWOOD, PHILIP
Literary Antiquities of Greece; as Developed in an Attempt to Ascertain Principles for a New Analysis of the Greek Tongue...(with) Remarks On some Observations Edited in "The British Critic" Relating to a Work Lately Published... London: 1799/1800. V. 50; 52

ALLYN, JOSEPH PRATT
By Horse, Stage & Packet. The Far West Letters of Joseph Pratt Allyn. San Francisco: 1988. V. 47; 50

ALMACK, EDWARD
Fine Old Bindings with Other Interesting Miscellanea in Edward Almack's Library. London: 1913. V. 52
Fine Old Bindings with Other Interesting Miscellanea in Edward Almack's Library. London: 1913/14. V. 50
The History of the Second Dragoons, 'Royal Scots Greys'. London: 1908. V. 50

ALMANAC for the Year 1386. London: 1812. V. 52

ALMANACH.. Paris: 1778. V. 52

ALMANACH Dedie Aux Demoiselles. Paris: 1826. V. 54

ALMANACH der Wiener Werkstatte. Vienna & Leipzig: 1911. V. 50; 52

ALMANACH Royal, Annee 1777. Paris. V. 47

ALMANACH Royal, Annee Bissextile 1776. Paris. V. 47

ALMANACK 1929. London: 1928. V. 52

ALMANACK for 1793. London: 1793. V. 52

ALMANACK for the Year of Christ 1850. London: 1849. V. 52

AN ALMANACK for the Year of Our Lord 1701. London: 1701. V. 54

ALMEIDA, ANTONIO D'
Tratado Completo de Medicina Opratoria... Lisbon: 1800. V. 48

ALMER, CHRISTIAN
A Facsimile of Christian Almer's Fuhrerbuch 1856-1894. London: 1896. V. 48

ALMETTE, ALBERT
Venoms, Venomous Animals and Antivenomous Serum-Therapeutics. London: 1908. V. 48

ALMIRALL, LEON V.
From College to Cow Country. Caldwell: 1956. V. 50

ALMOGUERA, JUAN DE
Instruccion de Sacerdotes...de las Indias Donde se Escrive. Madrid: 1671. V. 47

ALMON, JOHN
Anecdotes of the Life of the Right Honourable William Pitt, Earl Chatham. London: 1792. V. 54
An Asylum for Fugitive Pieces in Prose and Verse, No In Any Other Collection. London: 1785. V. 49; 51
Biographical, Literary and Political Anecdotes of Several of the Most Eminent Persons of the Present Age... London: 1797. V. 51
An History of the Parliament of Great Britain, From the Death of Queen Anne, to the Death of King George II. London: 1764. V. 50; 51
A Letter to the Earl of Bute. London: 1771. V. 53
A New and Impartial Collection of Interesting Letters from the Public Papers... London: 1767. V. 47
William Pitt, Earl of Chatham: Anecdotes of the Life of... Dublin: 1792. V. 50

ALMON, ROBERT
The Portrait of a Generation. Paris: 1926. V. 47

AL MUBASHSHIR IBN FATIK, ABU AL-WAFA
The Dictes and Sayings of the Philosophers. Detroit: 1901. V. 49

ALPATOV, M. V.
Early Russian Icon Painting. Moscow: 1974. V. 54

AN ALPHABET in Prose, Containing some Important Lessons in Life, for the Use and Edification of All Great and Small Children in New England. Worcester: 1800. V. 53

THE ALPHABET of Creation. New York: 1954. V. 49

THE ALPHABET of Flowers. London: 1848. V. 47

THE ALPHABET of Flowers and Fruit. London: 1910. V. 51

AN ALPHABET of Verses in My Pretty Story Book. London. V. 49

ALPHABETICAL. New York: 1983. V. 50

ALPHERAKY, SERGIUS
The Geese of Europe and Asia. London: 1905. V. 50

ALPHONSO X, KING OF CASTILE AND LEON
Tabulae Alphonsinae Perpetuae Motuum Coclestium Denu Restitutae & Illustratae a Francisco Garacia Ventanas Mathematico. Matriti (Madrid): 1640. V. 50

ALPINE CLUB
Peaks, Passes and Glaciers. A series of Excursions by Members of the Alpine Club. London: 1859/62. V. 48

ALPINE CLUB OF CANADA
The Canadian Alpine Journal. Banff: 1930. V. 51

ALPINUS, PROSPER
De Plantis Aegyptis Liber...De Balsamo, Dialogvs (etc.). Venice: 1592. V. 48; 52
De Praesagienda Vita et Morte Aegrotantium Libri Septem... Venetiis: 1751. V. 47

ALSBERG, HENRY G.
American Stuff: an Anthology of Prose & Verse by Members of the Federal Writers' Projects. New York: 1937. V. 53

ALSBERG, J. L.
Ancient Sculpture from Western Mexico. Berkeley: 1968. V. 54

ALSOP, GEORGE
A Character of the Province of Maryland. New York: 1869. V. 47

ALSOP, RICHARD
The Echo. New York: 1807. V. 51; 52
A Poem: Sacred to the Memory of George Washington, Late President of the United States and Commander in Chief of the Armies of the United States, Adapted to the 22d of Feb. 1800. Hartford: 1800. V. 51

ALSTED, JOHANN H.
Philomela Theologico-Philosophica, Recitans, Fundamenta Pietatis & Humanitatis... Herbornae Nassoviorum: 1627. V. 48

ALSTON, E. R.
Biologia Centrali-Americana: Mammalia. London: 1879-82. V. 51; 52

ALSTON, J. W.
Hints to Young Practioners in the Study of Landscape Painting. London: 1808. V. 52
Hints to Young Practioners in the Study of Landscape Painting, Intended to Show the Different Stages of the Neutral Tint... London: 1820. V. 47; 50

ALSTON, R. C.
A Bibliography of the English Language from the Invention of Printing to the Year 1800. Leeds: 1965. V. 53

THE ALTAR Book: Containing the Order for the Celebration of the Holy Eucharist According to the Use of the American Church. Boston: 1896. V. 47

ALTER, J. CECIL
James Bridger, Trapper, Frontiersman, Scout and Guide. Salt Lake City: 1925. V. 50; 53
James Bridger, Trapper, Frontiersman, Scout and Guide. Salt Lake City: 1945. V. 53
James Bridger: Trapper, Frontiersman, Scout and Guide. Columbus: 1951. V. 53
Utah, the Storied Domain. Chicago/New York: 1932. V. 51; 53

ALTGELD, JOHN PETER
Live Questions Including Our Penal Machinery and its Victims. New York: 1890. V. 50
Reasons for Pardoning Fielden, Neebe and Schwab. Chicago: 1893. V. 50

ALTHAMER, ANDREAS
Diallage, Hoc Est. Conciliatio Locorum Scripturae... Nuremberg: 1527. V. 52

ALTHANS, HENRY
Scripture Natural History, with Reflections Designed for the Young. London: 1828. V. 53

ALTHAUS, J.
A Treatise on Medical Electricity, Theoretical and Practical... London: 1859. V. 51

ALT-LEININGEN, FRIEDRICH
Comite-Bericht des Vereines zum Schutz Deutscher Einwanderer in Texas. Wiesbaden: 1850. V. 49

ALTOMARE, DONATO ANTONIO
Omnia, Qvae Hvcvsqve in Lvcem Prodiervnt, Opera, Nunc Primum in Unum Collecta & ab Eodem Auctore Diligentissime Recognita... Venetiis: 1574. V. 47; 48; 49; 50; 51; 53

ALTSHELER, JOSEPH A.
The Sun of Saratoga. New York: 1897. V. 51

AL TUSI, MUHAMMAD IBN MUHAMMAD IBN AL-HASAN
Astronomica Quaedam ex Traditione Shah Cholgii Prsae; Una Cum Hypothesibus Planetarum: Studio et Opera Johannis Gravii... London: 1652. V. 48

ALVAREZ DEL VAYO
Freedom's Battle. London: 1940. V. 49

ALVAREZ, J. M.
Instituciones De Derecho Real De Castilla Y De Indias...Para El Curso, De Los Discipulos De P. A. Jose Martinez, En Taso De Nuevo Mexico.... Taos: 1842. V. 52

ALVAREZ, JULIA
How the Garcia Girls Lost Their Accents. Chapel Hill: 1991. V. 51; 53

ALVAREZ, WALTER
The Mechanics of the Digestive Tract. New York: 1922. V. 53
Nervous Indigestion. New York: 1931. V. 53

ALVAREZ DE COLMENAR, JUAN
Les Delices de l'Espagne & du Portugal. Leiden: 1707. V. 54

ALVERDES, PAUL
Changed Men. London: 1933. V. 47

ALVES, JAMES
The Banks of Esk...a Poem Descriptive, Historical and Moral... Edinburgh: 1800. V. 47; 51; 54

ALVES, ROBERT
Poems. Edinburgh: 1782. V. 51; 54
Sketches Of a History of Literature... Edinburgh: 1794. V. 47; 49; 51

ALVORD, CLARENCE WALWORTH
First Explorations of the Trans-Allegheny Region by the Virginians 1650-1674. Cleveland: 1912. V. 47
The Mississippi Valley In British Politics. Cleveland: 1917. V. 49; 50

AMADO, JORGE
The Miracle of the Birds. New York: 1983. V. 51; 54

AMANTIUS, BARTHOLOMAEUS
Flores Celebriorum Sententiarum Graecarum ac Latinarum, Definitionum, Item Virtutem et Vitiorum, Omnium Exemplorum, Proverbiorum, Apopthegmatum, Apologorum, Similium et Dissimilium... Dillingen: 1556. V. 52

AMARALL, ANTHONY
Mustang, Life and Legends of Nevada's Wild Horse. Reno: 1977. V. 53

THE AMARANTH; or, Religious Poems: Consiting of Fables, Visions, Emblems, &c. London: 1767. V. 50

AMARI, MICHELE
History of the War of the Sicilian Vespers. London: 1850. V. 54

AMAT, JUAN CARLOS
Fructus Medicine ex Variis Galeni Locis Decerpti...Nunc Primum Prodit in Lucem. Lyon: 1623. V. 47

THE AMATEUR, Or Guide to the Stage. Philadelphia: 1850. V. 50

AMBERG, GEORGE
Art in Modern Ballet. New York: 1946. V. 49

AMBERLEY
The Amberley Papers - the Letters and Diaries of Lord and Lady Amberley. London: 1937. V. 52

AMBLER, CHARLES
Reports of Cases Argued and Determined in the High Court of Chancery, with Some Few In Other Courts. London: 1790. V. 53

AMBLER, CHARLES HENRY
A History of Transportation in the Ohio Valley... Glendale: 1932. V. 53; 54

AMBLER, ERIC
The Ability to Kill and Other Pieces. London: 1962. V. 47
The Army of the Shadows. Helsinki: 1986. V. 48
Background to Danger. New York: 1937. V. 48; 49; 53
The Care of Time. New York: 1981. V. 48; 49; 50; 54
Epitaph for a Spy. New York: 1952. V. 49
Journey Into Fear. London: 1940. V. 48; 50
Judgment on Detchev. London: 1951. V. 48
Passage of Arms. London: 1959. V. 54
Passage of Arms. New York: 1960. V. 47; 48; 49
The Schirmer Inheritance. New York: 1953. V. 53

AMBLER, LOUIS
The Old Halls and Manor Houses of Yorkshire. London: 1913. V. 54

AMBROSE, D. L.
History of the Seventh Regiment, Illinois Volunteer Infantry. Springfield: 1868. V. 54

AMBROSE, SAINT
Christian Offices Crystall Glasse. London: 1637. V. 48
De Officiis. Milan: 1474. V. 53
Divi Ambrosii Mediolanensis Episcopi Opera... Paris: 1584-86. V. 51
Omni Quotuot Extant D. Ambrosii Episcopi Mediolanensis Opera. Basel: 1555. V. 51
Omnia Opera. Parisiis: 1539. V. 50
Operum Tomus Quartus. Basileae: 1527. V. 50

THE AMBULATOR; or a Pocket Companion... London: 1811. V. 50

THE AMBULATOR; or, the Stranger's Companion in a Tour Round London; Within the Circuit of Twenty five Miles. London: 1774. V. 50; 54

AMBULATOR (sic): or, A Pocket Companion in a Tour Round London, Within the circuit of Twenty Five Miles... London: 1792. V. 50

AMEDEO, LUIGI
On the "Polar Star" in the Arctic Sea. London: 1903. V. 49; 54

AMERICA and Alfred Stieglitz. New York: 1934. V. 54

AN AMERICAN ABC by Maud and Miska Petersham. New York: 1941. V. 52

AMERICAN ACADEMY OF ARTS AND SCIENCES
Memoirs... Volume I. To the end of the Year 1783. Boston: 1785. V. 50

AMERICAN ACADEMY OF POLITICAL AND SOCIAL SCIENCE
The Annals of the American Academy of Political and Social Science. Philadelphia: 1975-84. V. 54

AN AMERICAN Album of Incidental Printers. N.P: 1948. V. 50

AMERICAN AND FOREIGN ANTI-SLAVERY SOCIETY
An Address to the Anti-Slavery Christians of the United States. New York: 1852. V. 49

THE AMERICAN Anti-Slavery Almanac for 1838. Boston: 1838. V. 53

AMERICAN ART ASSOCIATION
The Stephen H. Wakeman Collection of Books. New York: 1924. V. 50

AMERICAN BATTLE MONUMENTS COMMISSION
93rd Division Summary of Operations in the World War. Washington: 1944. V. 53; 54

THE AMERICAN Bible. Original Leaves From Rare and Historic Bibles Printed in the Colonies and the United States During the Seventeenth, Eighteenth and Nineteenth Centuries, Collected, Described and with a Preface by Michael Zinman. New York: 1993. V. 48

AMERICAN Big Game Fishing. New York: 1935. V. 49

AMERICAN Biographical and Historical Dictionary. Cambridge: 1809. V. 53

AMERICAN Boy Scouts Plays and Pastimes. Chicago: 1912. V. 53

THE AMERICAN Caravan. New York: 1927. V. 48
THE AMERICAN Caravan. London: 1928. V. 48; 51

AMERICAN Churches. New York: 1915. V. 53

AMERICAN COLONIZATION SOCIETY
Information About Going to Liberia: With Things Which Every Emigrant Ought to Know... Washington: 1852. V. 47

AMERICAN Country Houses of Today. New York: 1912. V. 51

AMERICAN Criticisms of Mrs. Trollope's "Domestic Manners of the Americans". London: 1833. V. 54

AMERICAN Decorative Papermakers. The Work and Specimens of Twelve Craft Artists. Mattapoisett: 1983. V. 52

AMERICAN Dictionary of Printing and Bookmaking. New York: 1894. V. 47

THE AMERICAN Dream Book, or the Origin, Interpretation and History of Dreams. Philadelphia: 1850?. V. 49

AMERICAN Esoterica. 1927. V. 50

AMERICAN ETHNOLOGICAL SOCIETY
Transactions of the American Ethnological Society. New York: 1845-48. V. 47

AMERICAN GEOGRAPHICAL AND STATISTICAL SOCIETY
Bulletin. New York: 1852. V. 47

AMERICAN GREENHOUSE MANUFACTURING CO.
American Greenhouses. Chicago: 1928. V. 51

AMERICAN GUANO COMPANY
Prospectus of the American Guano Company. New York: 1855. V. 48; 54

AMERICAN Horse Show Blue Book. New York & Chicago: 1902. V. 54
AMERICAN Horse Show Blue Book. New York & Chicago: 1903. V. 54

AMERICAN Indian Fairy Tales. London: 1921. V. 49

AMERICAN Indian Legends. Los Angeles: 1968. V. 53

AMERICAN Indian Life. New York: 1922. V. 50

AMERICAN INSTITUTE OF ELECTRICAL ENGINEERS LIBRARY
Catalogue of the Wheeler Gift of Books. New York: 1909. V. 54

AMERICAN INSTITUTE OF GRAPHIC ARTS
Fifty Books of the Year: 1924-1934. New York: 1924-34. V. 48

AMERICAN IRIS SOCIETY
Alphabetical Iris Check List. 1939. Baltimore: 1940. V. 51

AMERICAN IRON & STEEL ASSOCIATION
Annual Reports, 1868, 1871, 1874-78, 1880-89. V. 53

AMERICAN JEWISH PUBLICATION SOCIETY
Constitution and By-Laws...(Founded on the 9th of Heshvan 5606) Adopted at Philadelphia, on Sunday, Nov. 30, 1845, Kislev 1, 5606. Philadelphia: 1845. V. 52

AMERICAN Journal of Mathematics, Pure and Applied. Baltimore: 1878-86. V. 50

AMERICAN Journal of Science. Volume I. New York: 1818-19. V. 50

AMERICAN Journal of the Medical Science. Philadelphia: 1827. V. 48; 52; 53

THE AMERICAN Jurist and Law Magazine. Volume I. Boston: 1829. V. 52

THE AMERICAN Keepsake for 1851. New York: 1850. V. 48

THE AMERICAN Lady's Preceptor... Baltimore: 1815. V. 53

THE AMERICAN Law Journal and Miscellaneous Repertory. Philadelphia: 1810. V. 51

THE AMERICAN Lumberman: The Personal History and Public and Business Achievements of One Hundred Eminent Lumberman of the United States. Third Series. Chicago: 1906. V. 49

THE AMERICAN Medical and Philosophical Register, or Annals of Medicine, Natural History, Agriculture and the Arts. New York: 1812. V. 51

AMERICAN MEDICAL ASSOCIATION
Code of Ethics...Adopted...1847. Philadelphia: 1848. V. 52
Constitution, Ordinances and Code of Ethics of the American Medical Association. Louisville: 1859. V. 51
Laws and Regulations...with a Sketch of Detroit, and a Brief History of the University of Michigan, and of the Development of the State... Detroit: 1856. V. 48

THE AMERICAN Medical Recorder. Philadlephia: 1823. V. 48

THE AMERICAN Mercury. New York: 1924. V. 54

AMERICAN Negro Poetry. New York: 1963. V. 54

THE AMERICAN Negro; the Annals. Volume CXXXX. November. 1928. Philadelphia: 1928. V. 47; 49

AMERICAN NUMISMATIC SOCIETY
Catalogue of the International Exhibition of Contemporary Medals, The American Numismatic Society, March 1910. New York: 1911. V. 48

AMERICAN PHILOSOPHICAL SOCIETY
Transactions of the American Philosophical Society. Philadelphia: 1771. V. 50
Transactions of the American Philosophical Society. Philadelphia: 1786. V. 50
Transactions of the American Philosophical Society. Philadelphia: 1804. V. 50

AMERICAN Poems, Selected and Original. Litchfield: 1793. V. 49; 54

AMERICAN Poetry 1922: a Miscellany. New York: 1922. V. 50

THE AMERICAN Primer; or, an Easy Introduction to Spelling and Reading. Philadelphia: 1813. V. 53

THE AMERICAN Remembrancer....Essays, Resolves, Speeches &c. Relative, or Having Affinity, to the Treaty with Great Britain. Philadelphia: 1795. V. 53

THE AMERICAN Republican Harmonist; or, a Collection of Songs and Odes... Philadelphia: 1803. V. 47

AMERICAN SCHOOL OF ORIENTAL RESEARCH IN JERUSALEM
The Annual of the American School of Oriental Research in Jerusalem. Volume I for 1919-20. New Haven: 1920. V. 51
The Annual of the American School of Oriental Research in Jerusalem. Volume II and III for 1921-22. New Haven;: 1923. V. 51

AMERICAN Shropshire Sheep Record. Lafayette: 1886-89. V. 49

AMERICAN SOCIETY FOR MELIORATING THE CONDITION OF THE JEWS
The First Report...Presented May 9, 1823; with an Appendix. New York: 1823. V. 48

THE AMERICAN Soldier and Sailor in War, A Pictorial History of the Campaigns and Conflicts of the War Between the States, from the First Bllodshed in the Street of Baltimore to Our Country's War with Spain. New York. V. 50

THE AMERICAN Stage of To-Day. New York: 1910. V. 52

THE AMERICAN Star. Richmond: 1817. V. 52

AMERICAN SUNDAY SCHOOL UNION
Catalogue of Sunday School Books. Philadelphia: 1832. V. 54

AMERICAN TEMPERANCE SOCIETY
First Annual Report of the Executive Committee of the American Society for the Promotion of Temperance for the Year Ending Nov. 1827. Andover: 1828. V. 53

AMERICAN TRACT SOCIETY
Proceedings of the First Ten Years of the American Tract Society, Instituted at Boston, 1814. N.P: 1824. V. 51

AMERICAN Turf Register and Sporting Magazine... Baltimore & New York: 1829-44. V. 47

AMERICAN TYPE FOUNDERS CO.
American Specimen Book of Type Styles. Jersey City: 1912. V. 49
Specimens of Type Borders and Ornaments, Brass Rules and Cuts, Etc. Cleveland: 1897. V. 48
Summary of the Industrial Graphic Arts Library and Museum. Jersey City: 1934. V. 48
Wood-Type. Boston: 1900. V. 52

AMERICAN UNION OF ASSOCIATIONISTS
Industrial Association. An Address to the People of the United States. Boston?: 1850. V. 47

AMERICAN WATER COLOR SOCIETY
Illustrated Catalogue Twentieth Annual Exhibition of the American Water Color Society Held at the Galleries of the National Academy of Design... New York: 1887. V. 52
Illustrations of Pictures and Catalogue of the twenty-Second Annual Exhibition. New York: 1889. V. 52

AMERY, L. C.
Aristophanes at Oxford. London: 1894. V. 51

AMERY, LEOPOLD
The Times History of the War in South Africa 1899-1902. London: 1900-09. V. 48; 50

AMES, B.
Drawings of Florida Orchids. 1947. V. 52

AMES, BLANCHE
Adelbert Ames, 1835-1933, General Senator, Governor: The Story of His Life. North Easton: 1964. V. 49

AMES, ERNEST, MRS.
An ABC for Baby Patriots. London: 1900. V. 47; 49

AMES, JOSEPH
A Catalogue of English Heads; or, an Account of About Two Thousand Prints, Describing What Is Peculiar On Each... London: 1748. V. 52
Typographical Antiquities; or an Historical Account of the Origin and Progress of Printing in Great Britain and Ireland... London: 1785-90. V. 52

AMES, NATHANIEL
An Astronomical Diary; or, Almanack for the Year of Our Lord Christ 1771. Boston: 1770. V. 49; 53
An Astronomical Diary, or an Almanack for 1761. Boston: 1760. V. 52
Astronomical Diary; or an Almanack for the Year of Our Lord Christ, 1755. Boston: 1754. V. 47
An Astronomical Diary...1768. Boston;: 1767. V. 53
The Essays, Humor and Poems of Nathaniel Ames, Father and Son of Dedham, Massachusetts, from Their Almanacs 1726-1775... Cleveland: 1891. V. 48
A Mariner's Sketches. Providence: 1830. V. 53

AMES, O.
Orchidaceae. Boston: 1908. V. 52
Orchidaceae, Illustrations and Studies of the Fmaily Orchidaceae. Boston: 1915. V. 52
Orchids of Guatemala. Chicago: 1952-53. V. 52; 53
Orchids of Guatemala. London: 1952-53. V. 53

AMES, RICHARD
The Character of a Bigotted Prince; and What England May Expect from the Return of Such a One. London: 1691. V. 53
The Siege and Surrender of Mons. London: 1691. V. 49

AMHERST, ALICIA
Bibliography of Works on Gardening. N.P: 1897. V. 47
A History of Gardening in England. London: 1896. V. 48
London Parks and Gardens. London: 1907. V. 51

AMHURST, NICHOLAS
The British General; a Poem, Sacred to the Memory of His Grace John, Duke of Marlborough. London: 1722. V. 48
A Collection of Poems on Several Occasions, Publish'd in the Craftsman. London: 1731. V. 52
Oculus Britanniae: an Heroi-Panegyrical Poem on the University of Oxford. London: 1724. V. 54
Terrae-Filius; or, the Secret History of Oxford; in Several Essays. London: 1754. V. 52
Terrae-Filius: or, the Secret History of the University of Oxford... London: 1726. V. 47; 48; 49; 52; 53

AMICHAI, YEHUDA
Amen. New York: 1977. V. 54
Songs of Jerusalem and Myself. New York: 1973. V. 54
Time. New York: 1979. V. 54

AMICIS, EDMONDO DE
Holland. Philadelphia: 1894. V. 48

AMICO, BERNARDINO
Trattato Delle Piante & Immagini de Sacri Edifizi di Terra Santa Disegnate in Jerusalemme... Firenza: 1620. V. 51; 54

AMIDON, R. W.
The Effect of Willed Muscular Movements on the Temperature of the Head: New Study of Cerebral Localization. New York: 1880. V. 49; 50

AMIET, PIERRE
Art of the Ancient Near East. New York: 1977. V. 47
Art of the Ancient Near East. New York: 1980. V. 47; 51

AMIRAN, RUTH
Ancient Pottery of the Holy Land from its Beginnings in the Neolithic Period to the End of the Iron Age. Jerusalem: 1969. V. 49
Ancient Pottery of the Holy Land from Its Beginnings in the Neolithic Period to the End of the Iron Age. 1970. V. 54
Early Arad: the Chaloclithic Settlement and Early Bronze City I: First-Fifth Seasons of Excavations, 1962-66. Jerusalem: 1978. V. 51

AMIS, KINGSLEY
The Anti-Death League. London: 1966. V. 52; 54
Bright November. London: 1947. V. 47; 51; 54
Collected Short Stories. London: 1987. V. 54
The Crime of the Century. New York: 1989. V. 49; 51; 52; 53
The Darkwater Hall Mystery. Edinburgh: 1978. V. 51
Dear Illusion. London: 1972. V. 51
The Fantasy Poets - Number Twenty Two. Swinford, Eynsham: 1954. V. 53
I Like It Here. New York: 1958. V. 52; 54
Jake's Thing. London: 1978. V. 54
A Look Round the Estate - Poems. London: 1967. V. 50
Lucky Jim. London: 1953. V. 47; 50; 51; 52; 53

AMIS, KINGSLEY continued
Lucky Jim. Garden City: 1954. V. 52
Lucky Jim. New York: 1954. V. 47
The Old Devils. 1986. V. 47; 54
One Fat Englishman. London: 1966. V. 52
The Riverside Villas Murder. London: 1973. V. 49
Socialism and the Intellectuals. London: 1957. V. 47
That Uncertain Feeling. London: 1955. V. 54
That Uncertain Feeling. New York: 1956. V. 49
You Can't Do Both. London: 1994. V. 53; 54

AMIS, MARTIN
Dead Babies. London: 1975. V. 47; 48; 49; 50; 53
Dead Babies. New York: 1975. V. 53; 54
Dead Babies. New York: 1976. V. 47; 51; 53; 54
The Information. London: 1995. V. 51; 53; 54
The Information. New York: 1995. V. 54
Invasion of the Space Invaders. London: 1982. V. 47; 52; 53
The Invasion of the Space Invaders. Millbrae: 1982. V. 49
London Fields. London: 1989. V. 47; 49; 51; 53
Money. London: 1984. V. 51
Other People: a Mystery Story. London: 1981. V. 51; 53
Other People: a Mystery Story. New York: 1981. V. 53
The Rachel Papers. London: 1973. V. 48; 50; 51; 53
The Rachel Papers. New York: 1973. V. 52
The Rachel Papers. New York: 1974. V. 49; 50; 51; 52; 53; 54
Success. London: 1978. V. 47; 49; 50; 54
Time's Arrow. 1991. V. 49
Time's Arrow. London: 1991. V. 53
Two Stories. London: 1994. V. 51; 53

AMIS ET AMILES
Of the Friendship of Amis and Amile. 1894. V. 51

AMMAN, JOST
Stand Und Orden der H. Romischen Catholischen Kirchen, Darinn aller Geistlichen Personen, H. Ritter und Dero Verwandten Herkommen, Constitution Regeln, Habit und Kleidung, Beneben Schonen und Kunstlichen Figurn Fleissig Beschrieben... Frankfurt a.m: 1585. V. 52

AMMANN, OTHMAR H.
Verrazano-Narrow Bridge: Conception of design and Construction Procedure... New York: 1964. V. 49

AMMEN, S. Z.
History and Description of the Luray Cave. Baltimoe: 1880. V. 50

AMMIANUS MARCELLINUS
Ammiano Marcellino Delle Guerre de Romani. Vinetia aperesso: 1550. V. 49
Delle Gverre de Romani. Venice: 1550. V. 51
Rerum Gestarum Qui XXXI Supersunt Libri XVIII... Hamburg: 1609. V. 53

AMMONS, A. R.
Shit List: or, Omnium-Gatherum of Diversity into Unity. Winston Salem: 1979. V. 47

AMON CARTER MUSEUM, FORT WORTH
America from Amerigo Vespucci to the Louisiana Purchase. An Exhibition at the Amon Carter Museum, Fort Worth and the Lyndon Baines Johnson Library, Austin.... Fort Worth: 1976. V. 47

AMONG the Mountains: a Guidebook to Colorado Springs and the Scenery in the Neighborhood, Including Soda Springs at Manitou, Canon and Falls of the Fountain, the Ute Pass... Colorado Springs: 1873. V. 50; 54

AMONG the Rockies. Denver: 1910. V. 50

AMORIM, GASPAR DE
Sermao em a Solemne Celebracao Dos Prodigiosos Milagres, que Christo Senhor Nosso Obrou em Hum Crucifixo, Que Esta Sobre o Arco do Coro do Insigne, & Mui Observante... Lisbon: 1647. V. 50; 53

AMORY, JOHN, MRS.
The Journal of Mrs. John Amroy...1775-1777. Boston: 1923. V. 49

AMORY, ROBERT
A Treatise on Elecctrolysis and Its Applications to Therapeutical and Surgical Treatment in Disease. New York: 1886. V. 53

AMORY, THOMAS
The Life of John Buncle, Esq. London: 1756-66. V. 47; 49; 54
The Life of John Buncle Esq. London: 1766. V. 53
Transfer of Erin; or the Acquistion of Ireland by England. Philadelphia: 1877. V. 54

AMOS, ANDREW
Observations on the Statutes of the Reformation Parliament in the Reign of Henry the Eighth. London: 1859.. V. 50
Ruins of Time Exemplified in Sir Matthew Hale's History of the Pleas of the Crown. London: 1856. V. 51

AMOS, SHELDON
Political and Legal Remedies for War. New York: 1880. V. 53

AMOS, W.
Minutes in Agriculture Planting. Boston: 1804. V. 54

AMPERE, ANDRE MARIE
Expose Methodique des Phenomenes Electro-Dynamiques, et des Lois de ces Phenomenes. Paris: 1823. V. 47

AMPHLETT, JOHN
The Botany of Worcestershire. Birmingham: 1909. V. 48

AMPLE Instructions for the Barometer and Thermometer: Containing Particular Directions for the Marine and House Barometers, of Weather Glasses... New York: 1841. V. 51

AMRAM, DAVID WERNER
The Makers of Hebrew Books in Italy. Philadelphia: 1909. V. 53

AMRSTRONG, WALTER
Sir Henry Raeburn. London: 1901. V. 54

AMSBARY, WALLACE BRUCE
The Ballads of Bourbonnais. Indianpolis: 1904. V. 48

AMSDEN, CHARLES AVERY
Navajo Weaving, Its Technic and History. Santa Ana: 1934. V. 47
Navajo Weaving, It's Technique and History. Albuquerque: 1949. V. 51; 52

AMSDORFF, NICOLAUS VON
Auff Die Kuenstliche Spoettische und Bitter-Hoenische Oration so D. Ziegler zu Leipzig Oster Montag Widder die Bestendigen Lutherischen Recitirt Hat. Magdeburgk: 1549. V. 47

AMSINCK, PAUL
Tunbridge Wells and Its Neighbourhood. London: 1810. V. 52

AMTMANN, BERNARD
Contributions to a Short-Title Catalogue of Canadiana. Montreal: 1971-73. V. 49

AMUCHASTEGUI, A.
Some Birds and Mammals of Africa. London: 1979. V. 49; 50; 51; 52
Some Birds and Mammals of North America. London: 1971. V. 47; 50; 51; 53
Some Birds and Mammals of South America. London: 1966. V. 48; 50; 51; 52; 54
Some Birds and Mammals of South America. London: 1971. V. 52
Studies of Birds and Mammals of South America. 1967. V. 54

AMUNDSEN, ROALD
The North West Passage, Being the Record of a Voyage of Exploration of the Ship "Gjoa" 1903-1907... 1908. V. 54
The Northwest Passage. New York: 1908. V. 49
Our Polar Flight. The Amundsen-Ellsworth Polar Flight. New York: 1925. V. 50
The South Pole. London & New York: 1913. V. 53
The South Pole. London: 1976. V. 49; 50
Sydpolen. Kristiania: 1912. V. 48; 49

AMYX, D. A.
Corinthian Vase-Painting of the Archaic Period. Berkeley: 1989. V. 50

ANACREON
Anacreon Done Into English Out of the Original Greek. Oxford: 1683. V. 48
Anacreon Done Into English Out of the Original Greek by Abraham Cowley... London: 1923. V. 47; 48; 50; 52; 54
Anacreon Teius, Poeta Lyricus... Cambridge: 1705. V. 48
Anacreon: With Thomas Stanley's Translation. London: 1893. V. 48
Anacreontis Odaria, ad Textus Barnesiani Fidem Emendata. London: 1813. V. 47
Anacreontis Teij Odae (title in Creek and Latin). Paris: 1554. V. 50
Carmina, Plurimis Quibus Hactenus Scatebant Mendis Purgavit...Willielmus Baxter. London: 1695. V. 47
The Extant Fragments. 1991. V. 54
The Extant Fragments. University of Alabama: 1991. V. 53
Five Odes of Anacreon. 1985. V. 52
Odari. Parmae: 1784. V. 53; 54
Odes of Anacreon. London: 1802. V. 50
The Odes of Anacreon. London: 1804. V. 54
Odes of Anacreon. Philadelphia: 1804. V. 51
The Odes of Anacreon. London: 1869. V. 49
Twenty-nine Odes. London: 1926. V. 52; 54
The Works of Anacreon. London: 1735. V. 54

THE ANALYST: a Monthly Journal of Pure and Applied Mathematics. Des Moines: 1874-83. V. 50

ANAND, MULK RAJ
Curries and Other Indian Dishes. London: 1932. V. 53
The Lost Child and Other Stories. London: 1934. V. 53

ANARCHY at an End. Lives, Trial and Conviction of the Eight Chicago Anarchists. Chicago: 1886. V. 49

ANBUREY, THOMAS
Travels through the Interior Parts of America. London: 1789. V. 47; 48; 49; 53; 54

ANCELL, SAMUEL
A Journal of the Late and Important Blockade and Siege of Gibraltar, from the Twelfth of September 1779 to the Third Day of February 1783. Edinburgh: 1786. V. 53

THE ANCIENT British Drama. (with) The Modern British Drama. London: 1810/11. V. 52

ANCIENT Laws of Ireland - Brehon Law Tracts. Volume IV. London: 1879. V. 49

ANCIENT Lives of Scottish Saints. Paisley: 1895. V. 54

ANCIENT Maya Paintings of Bonampak Mexico. Washington: 1955. V. 52

ANCIENT MONUMENTS SOCIETY
Transactions. London: 1953-60. V. 48

ANCOURT, D'ABBE
The Lady's Preceptor. London: 1745. V. 53

ANDERDON, JOHN LAVICOUNT
The Life of Thomas Ken, Bishop of Bath and Wells. London: 1851. V. 50; 54
The River Dove With some Thoughts on the Happy Practice of Angling. London: 1847. V. 48; 49; 51; 52; 53; 54

ANDERSEN, HANS CHRISTIAN
Andersen's Fairy Tales. New York: 1933. V. 48; 53; 54
Andersen's Later Tales. London: 1869. V. 49; 53; 54
Andersen's Tales for Children. London: 1887. V. 50
Beauty and the Beast. London: 1875. V. 51
The Complete Andersen: All of the 168 Stories by Hans Christian Andersen. New York: 1949. V. 49; 51; 53
Danish Fairy Legends and Tales. London: 1846. V. 47
The Dream of Little Tuk, and Other Tales. London: 1847. V. 47
The Dream of Little Tuk and Other Tales. London: 1848. V. 48
Es Ist Ganz Gewiss. Einbach/Han: 1940. V. 51
Fairy Book. London: 1932. V. 48
Fairy Tales. London. V. 47
Fairy Tales. London: 1872. V. 51
The Fairy Tales. London: 1899. V. 49; 52
Fairy Tales. London: 1911. V. 48
Fairy Tales. London: 1913. V. 48; 54
Fairy Tales. London: 1916. V. 49; 51
Fairy Tales. London: 1924. V. 49; 50; 51; 52; 53
Fairy Tales. New York: 1924. V. 51
Fairy Tales. London: 1930. V. 50
Fairy Tales. London: 1931. V. 48; 49
Fairy Tales. London: 1932. V. 47; 48; 49; 50; 51; 52
Fairy Tales. New York: 1932. V. 53; 54
Fairy Tales... New York: 1942. V. 47; 48; 51; 54
Fairy Tales. New York: 1945. V. 49
Fairy Tales and Legends. London: 1935. V. 47; 48; 54
Four Tales from Hans Andersen. 1935. V. 48
Hans Andersen's Fairy Stories. London: 1938. V. 48
Hans Andersen's Fairy Stories. London: 1944. V. 48
Hans Andersen's Fairy Tales. London. V. 49
Hans Andersen's Fairy Tales. New York: 1899. V. 49
Hans Andersen's Fairy Tales. London: 1911. V. 48
Hans Andersen's Fairy Tales. London: 1913. V. 48
Hans Andersen's Fairy Tales. London: 1920. V. 51
Hans Andersen's Fairy Tales. London: 1930. V. 47; 49
The Ice-Maiden. London: 1863. V. 49
The Ice-Maiden and other Tales. Philadelphia: 1863. V. 51
The Improvisatore: Or, Life in Italy. London: 1845. V. 48; 49
The Improvisatore; or, Life in Italy. London: 1857. V. 52
The Improvisatore: or Life in Italy. London: 1875. V. 54
Maerchen. Munchen. V. 49
The Nightingale and Other Stories. London: 1912. V. 51
The Nightingale and Other Stories from Hans Andersen. London: 1915. V. 49
Only a Fiddler. London: 1845. V. 50; 51
A Picture Book Without Pictures Or What the Moon Saw. 1928. V. 48
Rambles in the Romantic Regions of the Hartz Mountains, Saxon, Switzerland, &c. London: 1848. V. 53
The Sand-Hills of Jutland. 1860. V. 48; 50; 52
The Sand-Hills of Jutland. London: 1860. V. 47; 48; 51
The Shoes of Fortune and Other Tales. London: 1846. V. 47
The Snow Queen. London: 1918. V. 50
The Snow Queen. New York: 1972. V. 54
Stories. New York & London: 1911. V. 47; 48; 49; 50; 52; 53; 54
Stories and Fairy Tales. London: 1893. V. 53
Stories for Children; Tommelise and the Rose Elf. London: 1846. V. 54
Stories for the Household. London: 1866. V. 51; 53
Stories from Hans Andersen. London: 1911. V. 53
Stories from Hans Andersen. London: 1920's. V. 52
The Story of My Life. London: 1872. V. 53
Tales for the Young. London: 1847. V. 51
The True Story of My Life. London: 1847. V. 51
The Ugly Duck and Other Tales. London: 1847-48. V. 47
Wonderful Stories for Children. London: 1846. V. 50

ANDERSEN, K.
Catalogue of the Chiroptera in the Collection of the British Museum. London: 1912. V. 52

ANDERSON, A.
A Bibliography of the Wirtings of Frances Cornford. 1975. V. 54

ANDERSON, A. C.
A Brief Account of the Province of British Columbia, Its Climate and Resources. Victoria: 1883. V. 47

ANDERSON, ABRAHAM C.
Trails of Early Idaho. The Pioneer Life of George W. Goodhart and His Asssociation With the Hudson's Bay and American Fur Traders. Caldwell: 1940. V. 49

ANDERSON, ADAM
Anderson's Historical and Chronological Deduction of the Origin of Commerce, from the EArliest Accounts. Dublin: 1790. V. 50; 54
An Historical and Chronological Deduction of the Origin of Commerce, from the Earliest Accounts. London: 1787-89. V. 48; 49

ANDERSON, AENEAS
A Narrative of the British Embassy to China. London: 1795. V. 53
A Narrative of the British Embassy to China in the Years 1792, 1793, and 1794. 1795. V. 51
A Narrative of the British Embassy to China, in the Years 1792, 1793 and 1794... Dublin: 1796. V. 52
A Narrative of the British Embassy to China, in the Years 1792, 1793 and 1794. London: 1796. V. 50

ANDERSON, ALAN ORR
Early Sources of Scottish History, A.D. 500 to 1286. Stamford: 1990. V. 50

ANDERSON, ALEX D.
The Silver Country of the Great Southwest. New York: 1877. V. 49; 52

ANDERSON, ALEXANDER
Exercitationum Mathematicarum Decas Prima. Paris: 1619. V. 47

ANDERSON, ALEXANDER CAULFIELD
The Dominion at the West. Victoria: 1872. V. 49

ANDERSON, ANNE
All About Old Goodie Goose. London. V. 51
All About Old Goodie Goose. London: 1912. V. 54
The Betty Book. London: 1912. V. 54
The Dandy-Andy Book. London. V. 49
The Dickie-Birdie Book. London: 1913. V. 49
Hop O-My Thumb. London: 1920. V. 49
Little Folks Picture Story book. London. V. 50
The Maisie-Daisie Book. London: 1913. V. 49
Snowdrop and the Seven Dwarfs. London: 1920. V. 49

ANDERSON, ARCHER
The Campaign and Battle of Chickamauga. Richmond: 1881. V. 49

ANDERSON, ARTHUR J. O.
Florentine Codex. Santa Fe: 1950-69. V. 50; 52

ANDERSON, AVRIL
Whist, Listen a Minute. Belfast: 1935. V. 50

ANDERSON, C. L. G.
Old Panama and Castilla del Oro: a Narrative History of the Discovery, Conquest and Settlement by the Spaniards of Panama, dArien, Veragua, Santo Domingo, Santa Marta... New York: 1944. V. 50

ANDERSON, CARL
Henry. London: 1940's. V. 49

ANDERSON, CAROLINE D.
The Three Paths; or, Truth, Vanity and Profession. London: 1852. V. 54

ANDERSON, CHARLES C.
Fighting by Southern Federals. New York: 1912. V. 49

ANDERSON, CHARLES LOFTUS GRANT
Arizona as a Health Resort. V. 53
Arizona as a Health Resort. Hagerstown: 1890. V. 54
Old Panama and Castilla Del Oro: a Narrative History of the Discovery, Conquest and Settlement by the Spaniards of Panama, Darien, Veragua, Santo Domingo, Santa Marta, Cartagena, Nicaragua and Peru. New York: 1944. V. 53

ANDERSON, CHRISTOPHER
Historical Sketches of the Native Irish and Their Descendants... Edinburgh: 1830. V. 50; 51
The Native Irish and Their Descendants. London: 1846. V. 51

ANDERSON, DAVID
Canada: or, A View of the Importance of the British American Colonies... London: 1814. V. 48
The Winner of Souls: a New Year Ordination Sermon, Preached at Saint John's Church, Red River on Tuesday, Jan. 1, 1856. London: 1856. V. 49

ANDERSON, EMILY
The Pursuit of Happy Results: Barry Spann and the making of Twenty Seven Landscapes. Boston: 1991. V. 49

ANDERSON, EUSTACE
Chamouni and Mont Blanc. London: 1856. V. 53

ANDERSON, F.
Hints on Polo and the Care of Polo Ponies in India. Allahabad: 1921. V. 47

ANDERSON, FLORENCE MARY
The Little Wee Cupid. London: 1916. V. 49
The Rainbow Twins. London: 1919. V. 50

ANDERSON, FULTON
Addresses Delivered Before the Virginia State Convention...February 1861. Richmond: 1861. V. 47

ANDERSON, GARLAND
Uncommon Sense: the Law of Life in Action. New York: 1933. V. 53

ANDERSON, GEORGE
A Reinforcement of the Reasons Proving that the Stage is an Unchristian Diversion. Edinburgh: 1733. V. 49

ANDERSON, GEORGE B.
History of New Mexico, Its Resources and People. New York: 1907. V. 50

ANDERSON, GEORGE WILLIAM
A New, Authentic and Complete Collection of Voyages Round the World... London: 1784. V. 52
A New Authentic And Complete Collection of Voyages Round the World, Undertaken and Performed by Royal Authority. London: 1784-86. V. 49; 50

ANDERSON, GREGG
Recollections of the Grabhorn Press. Los Angeles: 1935. V. 47

ANDERSON, HENRY
An Enquiry Into the Natural Right of Mankind to Debate Freely Concerning Religion. London: 1737. V. 52
The Medical and Surgical Aspects of Aviation. London: 1919. V. 50; 52

ANDERSON, ISABEL
The Great Sea Horse. Boston: 1909. V. 49

ANDERSON, J.
The New Practical Gardener and Modern Horticulturist. London: 1870. V. 52

ANDERSON, J. M.
Prodromus of South African Megafloras, Devonian to Lower Cretaceous. Rotterdam: 1985. V. 52

ANDERSON, J. MARTIN
Cartoons, Social and Political. London: 1893. V. 47
Symbols and Metaphors. London: 1892. V. 47

ANDERSON, JAMES
Anatomical and Zoological Researches: Comprising an Account of the Zoological results of the Two Expeditions to Western Yunnan in 1868 and 1875... London: 1878-79. V. 51
Constitutions of the Ancient Fraternity of Free and Accepted Masons... London: 1784. V. 54
Memorable Women of the Puritan Times. London: 1862. V. 49
Miscellaneous Observations of Planting and Training Timber-Trees... Edinburgh: 1777. V. 47
The New Book of Constitutions of the Antient and Honourable Fraternity of Free and Accepted Masons. London: 1738. V. 48
Recreations in Agriculture, Natural History, Arts and Miscellaneous Literature. London: 1799-1803. V. 48

ANDERSON, JOHN
Dura Den a Monograph of the Yellow Sandstone and Its Remarkable Fossil Remains. Edinburgh: 1859. V. 47; 54
Mandalay to Momien: a Narrative of the Two Expeditions to Western China of 1868 and 1875. London: 1876. V. 50; 52
Mission to the East Coast of Sumatra, in MDCCCXXIII, Under the Directions of the Government of Prince of Wales Island... Edinburgh: 1826. V. 53
A Practical Essay on the Good and Bad Effects of Sea-Water and Sea-Bathing. London: 1795. V. 47; 53
A Preliminary Introduction to the Act of Sea-Bathing... Margate: 1795. V. 53
The Unknown Turner: Revelations Concerning the Life and Art of J. M. W. Turner. New York: 1926. V. 49; 51

ANDERSON, JOHN E.
The Contract for the Purchase of Western Territory, Made with the Legislature of Georgia in the Year 1785 (i.e. 1795), Considered with a Reference to the Subsequent Attempts of the State, to Impair Its Obligation. Augusta: 1799. V. 47

ANDERSON, JOHN L.
The River Dove, with Some Quiet Thoughts on the Happy Practice of Angling. London: 1847. V. 49

ANDERSON, JOHN W.
From the Plains to the Pulpit. Goose Creek: 1907. V. 54

ANDERSON, JON
Counting the Days. Lisbon: 1974. V. 54

ANDERSON, JONATHAN
Attention, Union Men! Organized Labor is Threatened and the Time for Action Has Arrived. Spokane: 1899. V. 50

ANDERSON, JOSEPH
Recollections of a Peninsular Veteran. London: 1913. V. 50
Scotland in Early Christian Times. (and) Scotland in Pagan Times. London: 1881/83/86. V. 47; 49; 50; 53

ANDERSON, KENT
Sympathy for the Devil. New York: 1987. V. 51

ANDERSON, MABEL WASHBOURNE
The Life of General Stand Watie and Contemporary Cherokee History. Pryor: 1931. V. 54

ANDERSON, MARGARET
The Autobiography: My Thirty Years' War: the Fiery Fountains; the Strange Necessity. New York: 1969. V. 48

ANDERSON, MARTA
Dho Tsu Hwi/Gifts of the Tsetseka Season. Wisconsin: 1974. V. 51

ANDERSON, MARTIN
The Satires of Cynicus. London: 1890. V. 53
The Satires of Cynicus. London: 1892. V. 48

ANDERSON, MARY AUDENTIA SMITH
Ancestry and Posterity of Joseph Smith and Emma Hale... Independence: 1929. V. 50

ANDERSON, MARY E.
Scenes in the Hawaiian Islands and California. New York: 1865. V. 48

ANDERSON, MAXWELL
Anne of the Thousand Days. New York: 1948. V. 54
Barefoot in Athens. New York: 1951. V. 54
Joan of Arc. New York: 1948. V. 54
Joan of Lorraine. Washington: 1946. V. 50; 51; 54
Key Largo. Washington: 1939. V. 53
Mary of Scotland. New York: 1933. V. 50
Mary of Scotland. Garden City: 1934. V. 51; 54
Winterset. Washington: 1935. V. 54

ANDERSON, MAYBELLE HARMON
The Journals of Appleton Milo Harmon, a Participant in the Mormon Exodus from Illinois and the Early Settlement of Utah 1846-1877. Glendale: 1946. V. 53

ANDERSON, POUL
Brain Wave. London: 1955. V. 48; 52
Brain Wave. 1969. V. 51
The Broken Sword. 1954. V. 49; 54
The Broken Sword. New York: 1954. V. 47; 51
Perish by Sword. New York: 1959. V. 51; 54
Shield. London: 1965. V. 54
Star Ways. New York: 1956. V. 51
Star Ways. 1957. V. 47
Tau Zero. Garden City: 1970. V. 51
Tau Zero. New York: 1970. V. 48; 52
Three Hearts and Three Lions. Garden City: 1961. V. 51
Three Hearts and Three Lions. New York: 1961. V. 49; 54
Three Hearts and Three Lions. 1962. V. 47
The Trouble Twisters. Garden City: 1966. V. 51
Twilight World. 1961. V. 48; 52
The Worlds of Poul Anderson. Boston: 1978. V. 52

ANDERSON, R.
Ballads in the Cumberland Dialect... Wigton: 1808. V. 52
Ballads in the Cumberland Dialect... Wigton: 1815. V. 50; 52
Cumberland Ballads. Wigton: 1830. V. 52
The Cumberland Dialect Entitled the Borrowdale Letter... 1820?. V. 47
The Poetical Works... Carlisle: 1820. V. 47

ANDERSON, R. C.
Nematode Parasites of Vertebrates: Their Development and Transmission. Wallingford: 1992. V. 50
The Rigging of Ships in the Days of the Spritsail Topmast 1600-1720. Salem: 1927. V. 51

ANDERSON, R. D.
Catalogue of Eygptian Antiquities in the British Museum III: Musical Instruments. London: 1976. V. 49

ANDERSON, R. E.
Gastronomy as a Fine Art. London: 1877. V. 49

ANDERSON, RICHARD
Lightning Conductors. London: 1880. V. 48

ANDERSON, ROBERT
Tea and Sympathy. New York: 1953. V. 50; 53
To Hit a Mark, as Well Upon Ascents and Descents, As Upon the Horizon... London: 1690. V. 53

ANDERSON, RUFUS
The Hawaiian Islands. Boston: 1864. V. 53
The Hawaiian Islands. Boston: 1865. V. 53

ANDERSON, SHERWOOD
Alice and the Lost Novel. London: 1929. V. 53
Beyond Desire. New York: 1932. V. 53; 54
Dark Laughter. 1925. V. 50
Dark Laughter. New York: 1925. V. 51; 52
Hello Towns!. New York: 1929. V. 48; 49; 51
Home Town. New York: 1940. V. 51
Horses and Men. New York: 1923. V. 47; 48; 49
Many Marriages. New York: 1923. V. 48; 49; 51
Mid-American Chants. New York: 1918. V. 53
The Modern Writer. San Francisco: 1925. V. 53
Nearer the Grass Roots. San Francisco: 1929. V. 50; 51; 52; 54
A New Testament. New York: 1927. V. 47; 48; 51
Plays Winesburg and Others. New York: 1937. V. 54
Puzzled America. New York: 1935. V. 47; 48; 49
Sherwood Anderson's Notebook. New York: 1926. V. 48; 53; 54
Six Mid-American Chants. Highlands: 1964. V. 47; 51
A Story Teller's Story. New York: 1924. V. 48; 49; 51; 53
Tar. New York: 1926. V. 48; 51; 52; 54
The Triumph of the Egg. New York: 1921. V. 48; 51; 54
Winesburg, Ohio. New York: 1919. V. 47; 50; 51; 52; 53
Winesburg, Ohio. New York: 1921. V. 50
Winesburg, Ohio. New York: 1978. V. 47; 51

ANDERSON, T.
The Battle of Magnolia Hills...(and Five Other Poems). Mississippi?: 1863?. V. 47

ANDERSON, T. continued
Report on the Eruptions of the Soufriere in St. Vincent in 1902 and on a Visit to Montagne Pelee, in Martinique. London: 1903-08. V. 49
Volcanic Studies in Many Lands. London: 1903. V. 53

ANDERSON, WALTER
The History of Coresus in IV Parts. Edinburgh: 1755. V. 52

ANDERSON, WILLIAM
Japanese Wood Engravings. Their History, Technique and Characteristics. London: 1895. V. 51
A New Authentic and Complete Collection of Voyages Round the World... London: 1784-86. V. 51
The Scottish Nation; or the Surnames, Families, Literature, Honours and Biographical History of the People of Scotland. Edinburgh &c: 1867. V. 49; 50

ANDERSON, WILLIAM JAMES
The Life of F.M., H.R.H. Edward, Duke of Kent, Illustrated by His Correspondence With the De Salaberry Family, Never Before Published, Extending from 1791 to 1814. Oshawa/Toronto: 1870. V. 53

ANDERSON, WILLIAM MARSHALL
The Rocky Mountain Journals of William Marshall Anderson, the West in 1834. San Morino: 1960. V. 54

ANDERSON, WILLIAM WEMYSS
Jamaica and the Americans. New York: 1851. V. 51

ANDERSSON, ARON
English Influence in Norweigian and Swedish Figure Sculpture in Wood 1220-1270. Stockholm: 1949. V. 47

ANDERSSON, KARL JOHAN
Lake Ngami: or, Explorations and Discoveries During Four Wanderings in the Wilds of South Western Africa. London: 1856. V. 53
Notes on the Birds of Damara Land and the Adjacent Countries of South-West Africa. London: 1872. V. 50
The Okavango River: a Narrative of Travel, Exploration and Adventure. New York: 1861. V. 51

ANDRADA, JACINTO FREIRE DE
The Life of Don John De Castro. London: 1693. V. 50

ANDRADE, ANTONIO DE
Relatione del Novo Scoprimento del Gran Cataio, Overo Regno di Tibet Fatto dal P. Antonio di Andrade Portoghese Della Compagnia di Giesu l'anno 1624. Rome: 1627. V. 48

ANDRADE, BENJAMIN
Trade Truths and Fireside Fallacies. London: 1873. V. 53

ANDRADE, CARLOS DRUMMOND DE
Souvenir of the Ancient World. 1976. V. 53

ANDRADE, FRANCISCO DE
Cronica do Muyto Alto e Muito Poderoso Rey Destes Reynos de Portugal dom Joao o III deste Nome. Lisbon: 1613. V. 53

ANDRADE, JOSE IGNACIO DE
Cartas Escriptas da India e da China Nos Annos de 1815 a 1835. Lisbon: 1843. V. 53

ANDRAE, WALTER
Coloured Ceramics from Ashur and Earlier Ancient Assyrian Wall Paintings. London: 1925. V. 51

ANDRAL, G.
Medical Clinic: Diseases of the Encephalon with Extracts from Ollivier's Work on Diseases of the Spinal Cord and Its Membranes. Philadelphia: 1843. V. 47

ANDRASY, MANO
Hazai Vadaszatok es Sport Magyarorszagon. Budapest: 1857. V. 47

ANDRE, E.
A Naturalist in the Guianas. London: 1904. V. 49; 50

ANDRE, JOHN
Andre's Journal. Boston: 1903. V. 47; 49; 50; 51

ANDRE, R.
A Dream of the Zoo. London: 1880. V. 52
Shakespearian Tales in Verse. London: 1880. V. 51

ANDREAE, BERNARD
The Art of Rome. New York: 1977. V. 52
The Art of Rome. New York: 1978. V. 47

ANDREAE, JOHANNES
Processus Judiciarus...et Juris Defensorium: Vna Cum Procuratorum Manuali. Nuremberg: 1512. V. 47
Quaestiones Mercuriales Super Regulis Iuris. Strassburg: 1475. V. 51; 53
Summa Sup. Quarto Decretalium... Nuremberg: 1507. V. 47
Super Arboribus Consanguinitatis, Affinitatis, et Cognationis Spiritualis. Nuremberg: 1476. V. 53; 54
Super Arboribus Consanguinitatis, Affinitatis et Cognationis Spiritualis et Legalis. Leipzig: 1498. V. 47; 50; 53

ANDREAS, A. T.
Illustrated Historical Atlas of the State of Iowa. Chicago: 1875. V. 50
Illustrated Historical Atlas of the State of Iowa. 1970. V. 48

ANDREE, A. A.
The Andree Diaries, Being the Diaries and Records of A. A. Andree, Nils Strindberg and Knut Fraenkel, Written During Their Balloon Expedition to the North Pole in 1897 and Discovered on White Island in 1930. London: 1931. V. 54

ANDREE, KARL
Nord-Amerika in Geographischen und Geschichtlichen Umrissen... Braunschweig: 1854. V. 49

ANDREE, S. A.
Andree's Story, the Complete Record of His Polar Flight, 1897. New York: 1930. V. 47; 50

ANDREEV, LEONID
The Dark. London: 1922. V. 48; 50
The Dark. Richmond: 1922. V. 51

ANDRELINUS, PUBLIUS FAUSTUS
Epistole P(ro)uerbiales & Morales Longe Lepidissime Nec Minus Sententiose. Strasbourg: 1508. V. 48

ANDREOSSY, FRANCOIS
Histoire du Canal du Midi, ou Canal de Languedoc, Considere Sous les Rapports d'Invention, d'Art, d'Administration, d'Irrigation, et dans ses relations avec les Etangs de l'interieur des Terres qui l'Avoisinent... Paris: 1804. V. 51; 54

ANDRES, GLENN
The Art of Florence. New York: 1988. V. 47

ANDRESEN, ANDREAS
Das Deutche Peintre-Graveur. German Graphic Artists Catalogued from 1560-1800. New York. V. 54

ANDREW, J. R. H.
The Southern Ark. London: 1987. V. 53

ANDREW, JOHN A.
Speeches of John A. Andrew....Together with His Testimony Before the Harper's (sic) Ferry Committee of the Senate in Relation to John Brown. Boston: 1860. V. 48

ANDREW Marvell 1621-1678: Tercentenary Tributes. London: 1922. V. 48; 51

ANDREW, W. P.
India and Her Neighbours. London: 1878. V. 52

ANDREW, WILLIAM
A Comprehensive Synopsis fo the Elements of Persian Grammar... London: 1830. V. 51

ANDREWES, LANCELOT
Ninety-six Sermons. London: 1629. V. 52
Ninety-six Sermons. Oxford: 1853-61. V. 53
The Pattern of Catechistical Doctrine at Large; or, a Learned and Pious Exposition of the Ten Commandments. London: 1650. V. 50
A Sermon Preached Before His Majestie, at Whitehall, on Easter Day Last, 1614. London: 1614. V. 47

ANDREWS, ALEXANDER
The History of British Journalism, from the Foundation of the Newspaper Press in England. London: 1859. V. 47

ANDREWS, ALICE E.
Christopher C. Andrews, Pioneer in Forestry Conservation in the United States for Sixty Years a Dominant Influence in the Public Affairs of Minnesota... Cleveland: 1928. V. 50; 52

ANDREWS, BENAJAH
A Narrative of Mrs. Elizabeth Andrews... Stockbridge: 1800. V. 50

ANDREWS, BERT
In the Shadow of the Great White Way: Images from the Black Theatre. New York: 1989. V. 52

ANDREWS, BYRON
The Facts About the Candidate. Chicago: 1904. V. 47; 49

ANDREWS, C. C.
Minnesota and Dakota. Washington: 1857. V. 48; 50

ANDREWS, C. W.
Catalogue of the Tertiary Vertebrata of the Fayum, Egypt. London: 1906. V. 48
Memoir of Mrs. Anne R. Page. Philadelphia: 1844. V. 53
A Monograph of Christmas Island (Indian Ocean)... London: 1900. V. 47; 51

ANDREWS, CAROL A. R.
Jewelry Catalogue of Egyptian Antiquities in the British Museum, VI: from the Earliest Times to the Seventeenth Dynasty. London: 1981. V. 49

ANDREWS, E. WYLLYS
The Archaeology of Southwestern Campeche. Washington: 1943. V. 52

ANDREWS, ETHAN A.
Slavery and the Domestic Slave-Trade in the United States. Boston: 1836. V. 49

ANDREWS, F. H.
Ancient Chinese Figures Silks Excavated by Sir Aurel Stein at Ruined Sites of Central Asia. London: 1920. V. 50

ANDREWS, G. H.
Modern Husbandry. A Practical and Scientific Treatise On Agriculture, Illustrating the Most Approved Practices in Draining, Cultivating, and Manuring the Land... London: 1853. V. 54

ANDREWS, H. C.
Coloured Engravings of Heaths. London: 1802. V. 48; 49

ANDREWS, H. C. continued
Coloured Engravings of Heaths... London: 1802-09. V. 52
Coloured Engravings of Heaths... London: 1802-09-(28?). V. 49
Geraniums: Or a Monograph of the Genus Geranium: Containing Coloured Figures Of All Known Species and Numerous Beautiful Varities, Drawn, Engraved, Described and Coloured from the Living Plants. London: 1805. V. 48

ANDREWS, H. K.
The Technique of Byrd's Vocal Polyphony. London: 1966. V. 49

ANDREWS, JAMES
Studies in Flower Painting: a Series of Plates, for Instruction in Drawing and Coloring Flowers. New York: 1852. V. 48

ANDREWS, JAMES PETTIT
Anecdotes, &c. Antient and Modern. London: 1789. V. 50
The History of Great Britain Connected with the Chronology of Europe; with Anecdotes of the Times, Lives of the Learned. London: 1794. V. 47; 53

ANDREWS, JOHN
An Analysis of the Principal Duties of Social Life... London: 1783. V. 50
History of the War With America, France, Spain and Holland... London: 1785-86. V. 49
Letters to a Young Gentleman, on His Setting Out for France... London: 1784. V. 47
Remarks on the French and English Ladies, in a Series of Letters... London: 1783. V. 50; 51

ANDREWS, KEITH
Catalogue of Italian Drawings. 1971. V. 49

ANDREWS, LORRIN
A Dictionary of the Hawaiian Language, to Which is Appended an English-Hawaiian Vocabulary and a Chronological Table of Remarkable Events. Honolulu: 1865. V. 51; 53
Grammar of the Hawaiian Language. Honolulu: 1854. V. 48; 52; 53; 54
A Vocabulary of Words in This Hawaiian Language. Lahainaluna: 1836. V. 47

ANDREWS, MICHAEL
Machu Picchu. Hermosa Beach: 1978. V. 50

ANDREWS, R. C.
Ends of the Earth. 1929. V. 52
Monographs of the Pacific Cetacea. New York: 1914-16. V. 51

ANDREWS, R. MC CANTS
John Merrick: a Biographical Sketch. Durham: 1920. V. 52

ANDREWS, ROY CHAPMAN
The New Conquest of Central Asia, a Narrative of the Explorations of the Central Asiatic Expeditions in Mongolia and China, 1921-1930. New York: 1932. V. 50

ANDREWS, STEPHEN PEARL
Discoveries in Chinese or the Symbolism of the Primitive Characters of the Chinese System of Writing. New York: 1854. V. 52
Love, Marriage and Divorce and the Sovereignty of the Individual. New York: 1853. V. 53
The Primary Synopsis fo Universology and Alwato, the New Scientific Universal Language. New York: 1871. V. 49
The Science of Society. New York: 1851-51. V. 53

ANDREWS, THOMAS
The Scientific Papers of... London: 1889. V. 49

ANDREWS, W. D.
Swimming and Life-Saving. Toronto: 1889. V. 53

ANDREWS, W. L.
Haunting Years - the Commentaries of a War Territorial. London: 1930. V. 49

ANDREWS, WILLIAM
Bygone Derbyshire. Derby: 1892. V. 54
The Doctor in History, Literature, Folk-Lore, Etc. London: 1896. V. 52

ANDREWS, WILLIAM LORING
Bibliopegy in the United States and Kindred Subjects. New York: 1902. V. 47
The Heavenly Jerusalem: a Mediaeval Song of the Joys of the Church Triumphant. New York: 1908. V. 50; 52
The Journey of Iconophiles Around New York in Search of Historical and Picturesque. New York: 1897. V. 47; 48; 50
A Prospect of the Colleges in Cambridge New England. New York: 1897. V. 49
A Trio of Eighteenth Century French Engravers of Portraits in Miniature. New York: 1898. V. 48; 50

ANDREYEV, LEONID
Abysss. Waltham St. Lawrence: 1929. V. 49

ANDREZEL, PIERRE
The Angelic Avengers. New York: 1947. V. 47

ANDRIAN, LEOPOLD
Der Garten der Erkenntnis. The Hague: 1913. V. 50

ANDRIC, IVO
Bosnian Story. London: 1961. V. 52; 53

ANDRIES, JUDOCUS
Het Ghedurigh Kruys Jesu Christi...(with) Gheestelycke Oeffeningen voor de Ghebroeders ende Chesusters des H. Roosen-Kransken van de Alder-Weerdighste Maghet ende Moeder Godts Maria... Brussels: 1645. V. 50

ANDRIEUX, PIERRE D'
Catalogue des Plantes, Arbres, Arbrisseaux, et Arbustes, dont on Trouve des Graines, des Bulbes & du Plant, chez les Sieurs, Andrieux & Vilmorin, Marchands Grainiers-Fleuristes & Botanistes du Roi & Pepinieristes. Paris: 1778. V. 49

ANDROS, EDMUND
The Andros Tracts: Being a Collection of Pamphlets and Official Papers Issued During the Period Between the Overthrow of the Andros Government and the Establishment of the Second Charter of Massachusetts. Boston: 1868-74. V. 51

ANDROUET DU CERCEAU, JACQUES
Lecons de Perspective Positive. Paris: 1676, i.e. V. 53

ANDRY, NICHOLAS
An Account of the Breeding of Worms in Human Bodies. London: 1701. V. 52; 53

AN ANECDOTE Concerning a Cherry-Tree and George Washington, General and Commander of the Armies of America. Stanford: 1932. V. 53

THE ANECDOTE Library. London: 1822. V. 51

ANECDOTES for Our Soldiers. No. 3. Charleston. V. 54

ANECDOTES of Mr. Hogarth and Explantory Descriptions of the Plates of Hogarth Restored. London: 1803. V. 50

ANECDOTES of Napoleon Bonaparte and His Times: With an Interesting Account of His Disinterment at St. Helena, and His Second Interment in France. Liverpool: 1841. V. 50

ANECDOTES on the Origin and Antiquity of Horse-Racing, from the Earliest Times. London: 1825. V. 47

ANECDOTES Secrets du Dix-Huitieme Siecle, Redigees avec Soin d'Apres la Correspondance Secrete, Politique et Litteraire. Paris: 1808. V. 48

ANESAKI, M.
Buddhist Art In Its Relation to Buddhist Ideals. Boston: 1923. V. 50

ANET, CLAUDE
Mayerling. Paris: 1930. V. 48

ANGAS, GEORGE FREDERICK
Australia: a Popular Account of its Physical Features, Inhabitants, Natural History and Productions, with the History of Its Colonization. London: 1865. V. 51
Polynesia: a Popular Description of the Physical Features, Inhabitants, Natural History and Productions of the Islands of the Pacific. London: 1866. V. 47; 51

ANGAS, GEORGE FRENCH
The New Zealanders. London. V. 49
Savage Life and Scenes in Australia and New Zealand. London: 1847. V. 53

ANGEL, JOSEPH K.
A Treatise on the Law of Watercourses with an Appendix Containing forms of Declaration. Boston: 1840. V. 52

ANGEL, MYRON
History of San Luis Obispo County, California, with Illustrations... Berkeley: 1966. V. 53

THE ANGEL of Mercy, a Little Book of Affection. London: 1823. V. 49

ANGEL, ROBERT J.
Designs for An Iron Roof. London: 1891. V. 52

ANGELI, HELEN ROSSETTI
Dante Gabriel Rossetti. His Friends and Enemies. London: 1949. V. 49

ANGELICA PRESS
Wood Type of the Angelica Press. N.P: 1976. V. 48

ANGELINI BONTEMPI, GIOVANNI ANDREA
Historia Della Ribellione D'Ungheria. Dresden: 1672. V. 52

ANGELIO, PIETRO DA BARGA
Oratione Fvnerale...Fatta Nelle Esseqvie del Sereniss. Florence: 1574. V. 48
Poemata Omnia. Diligenter ab Ipso Recognita... Rome: 1585. V. 47; 52

ANGELL, JOHN
Stenography; or, Short-Hand Improved... London: 1758. V. 50

ANGELL, ROGER
The Summer Game. New York: 1972. V. 50; 53

ANGELO, HENRY
Angelo's Pic Nic. London: 1905. V. 51
Regulations and Instructions for the Cavalry Sword Exercise. Adjutant General's Office, Horse-Gaurds, 10th June 1819. London: 1819. V. 49
The Reminiscences of Henry Angelo, with an Introduction by Lord Howard de Walden and Notes and a memoir by H. Lavers Smith, B.A. Philadelphia: 1904. V. 48
Reminiscences of Henry Angelo, with Memoirs of His Late Father and Friends, Including Numerous Original Anecdotes and Curious Traits of the Most Celebrated Characters that Have Flourished During the Last Eighty Years. London: 1830. V. 47
Reminiscences...With Memoirs of His Late Father and Friends... London: 1828/30. V. 48

ANGELO, VALENTI
A Battle in Washington Square. 1942. V. 48
Come Over and Stay Till Domesday. New York: 1937. V. 49
Nino. New York: 1938. V. 47; 49; 50
Valenti Angelo: Author - Illustrator - Printer. San Francisco: 1976. V. 50; 52; 54
A Very Merry Christmas. N.P: 1973. V. 48

ANGELOU, MAYA
All God's Children Need Traveling Shoes. Franklin Center: 1986. V. 51; 53
Gather Together in My Name. New York: 1974. V. 51; 52; 53
The Heart of a Woman. New York: 1981. V. 53
I Know Why the Caged Bird Sings. New York: 1969. V. 51; 52; 53; 54
I Know Why the Caged Bird Sings. New York: 1970. V. 50

ANGELOU, MAYA continued
Just Give Me a Cool Drink of Water 'Fore I Diiie. New York: 1971. V. 53
Oh Pray My Wings Are Gonna Fit Me Well. New York: 1975. V. 52; 53
On the Pulse of Morning. New York: 1993. V. 51; 53
Swingin' and Swingin' and Gettin' and Merry Like Christmas. New York: 1976. V. 47
Wouldn't Take Nothing for My Journey Now. New York: 1993. V. 50; 51; 52; 53

ANGELUS DE CLAVASIO
Summa Angelica de Casibus Conscientaie. Strassburg: 1491. V. 53

ANGENOUST, NICOLAS
Le Paranymphe des Dames. Troyes: 1629. V. 54

ANGERSTEIN, JOHN JULIUS
Catalogue of the Celebrated Collection of Pictures of the Late John Julius Angerstein, Esq. London: 1823. V. 48

ANGHIERA, PIETRO MARTIRE D'
De Orbe Novo. The Eight Decades... New York: 1970. V. 47
De Rebus Oceanicis et Novo Orbe, Decades Tres... Item Eiusdem de Bablonica Legatione... Cologne: 1574. V. 47; 48
The History of Travayle in the West and East Indies, and Other Countreys Lying Eyther Way, Towardes the Fruitfull and Ryche Moluccas. London: 1577. V. 50

ANGIOLIERI, CECCO
If I Were Fire. Iowa City: 1987. V. 49
Sonette. 1944. V. 52

ANGLER'S CLUB OF NEW YORK
The Anglers' Club Story. Our First Fity Years 1906-1956. New York: 1956. V. 47; 51
The Best of the Anglers' Club Bulletin, 1920-1972. New York: 1972. V. 47; 50

ANGLER'S Evenings. Papers by Members of the Manchester Angler's Association. 1st-3rd Series. Manchester: 1880. V. 47

THE ANGLER'S Guide: Containing Easy Instructions for the Youthful Beginner, with Several Observations on Fishing... London: 1828. V. 47; 52; 53

THE ANGLER'S Note-Book and Naturalist's Record. A Repertory of Fact, Inquiry and Discussion on Field-Spots and Subjects of Natural History... (with) The Angler's Note-Book and Naturalist's Record... London: 1880/88. V. 47

THE ANGLER'S Pocket-Book; or, Compleat English Angler...also, Nobb's Celebrated Treatise on the Art of Trolling. London: 1805. V. 47; 53

ANGLESEY, ARTHUR, EARL OF
England's Confusion: a A True and Impartial Relation of the Late Traverses of State in England... London: 1659. V. 53

ANGLIA Grata: or, a Hearty-English Welcome to King William After a Successful Campaign. London: 1695. V. 53

THE ANGLICAN Friar, and the Fish Which He Took by Hook and by Crook. London: 1851. V. 47

THE ANGLO Saxon. London: 1849. V. 50

ANGLO-Norman Dictionary. London: 1977-92. V. 51

AN ANGLO-Saxon Homily on St. Gregory's Day. London: 1839. V. 53

ANGOLIA, JOHN R.
Daggers, Bayonets & Fighting Knives of Hitler's Germany. Mountain View: 1971. V. 54

THE ANGORA Twinnies. Rochester: 1919. V. 53; 54

ANGULO, JAIME DE
Coyote Man and Old Dcotor Loon. San Francisco: 1973-74. V. 52
The Trial of Ferrer: a Clerical Judicial Murder. New York: 1911. V. 53

ANGUS, H. F.
British Columbia and the United States: The North Pacific slope from Fur Trade to Aviation. Toronto/New Haven/London: 1942. V. 49; 52

ANGUS, WILLIAM
The Seats of Nobility. London: 1787-1815. V. 48; 51; 53
The Seats of the Nobility and Gentry in Great Britain and Wales Engraved by W. Angus. Islington: 1787. V. 48

ANIMADVERSIONS Upon Those Notes Which the Late Observator Hath published Upon the Seven Doctrines and Positions Which the King by Way of Recapitulation (he Saith) Layes Open so Offensive. London: 1642. V. 47; 53

AN ANIMAL ABC. London: 1920. V. 53

ANIMAL Locomotion. The Muybridge Work at the University of Pennsylvania. The Method and the Result. Philadelphia: 1888. V. 47

THE ANIMAL Museum; or, Picture Gallery of Quadrupeds. London: 1826. V. 54

ANIMAL Playtime. London. V. 51

ANIMATED Antics in Playland. New York: 1946. V. 49

ANKER, JEAN
Bird Books and Bird Art. The Hague: 1973. V. 50; 51; 53; 54

ANLEY, CHARLOTTE
Influence: a Moral Tale for Young People. London: 1822. V. 50

ANNABEL, RUSSELL
Hunting and Fishing in Alaska. New York: 1948. V. 53
Tales of a Big Game Guide. New York: 1938. V. 47; 53

ANNALS of Botany. London: 1805-06. V. 54

THE ANNALS of Ireland. Dublin: 1846. V. 54

ANNALS of Lloyd's Register: Being a Sketch of the Origin, Constitution and Progress of Lloyd's Register of British and Foreign Shipping. London: 1884. V. 49; 54

ANNALS of Medical History. 1917-28. V. 52

ANNALS of San Francisco. New York: 1855. V. 53

ANNAN, WILLIAM
Poems, on Various Subjects. Edinburgh: 1818. V. 54

ANNANDALE, N.
Zoological Results of a Tour in the Far East. Calcutta: 1916-25. V. 49; 51

ANNANDALE, THOMAS
On the Pathology and the Operative Treatment of 'Hip' Disease. Edinburgh: 1876. V. 51

ANNENBERG, MAURICE
Type Foundries of America and Their Catalogs. Baltimore: 1975. V. 48

ANNESLEY, ARTHUR, EARL OF
Memoirs of the Right Honourable Earl of Anglesey, Late Lord Privy Seal. London: 1693. V. 48
The Privileges of the House of Lords and Commons Argued and Stated, In Two Conferences Between Both Houses. April 19, and 22, 1671. London: 1702. V. 48

ANNESLEY, GEORGE
Voyages and Travels to India, Ceylon, the Red Sea, Abyssinia and Egypt. London: 1811. V. 54

ANNESLEY, JAMES
Sketches of the Most Prevalent Diseases of India; Comprising a Treatise on the Epidemic Cholera of the East... London: 1829. V. 48; 51

ANNESLEY, WILLIAM
A Description of William Annesley's New System of Naval Architecture As Secured to Him, for the Three Kingdoms and Colonies... London: 1818. V. 51

ANNIGONI, PIETRO
Spanish Sketchbook. London: 1957. V. 54

ANNING BELL, ROBERT
English Lyrics from Milton to Spenser. London: 1898. V. 47

ANNIUS, JOHANNES
De Futuris Christianorum Triumphis in Saracenos. Nuremberg: 1485. V. 53

ANNUAL Abstract of the Sinking Fund, for Michaelmas 1718, When it Was First Stated to Parliament, to the 10th of October, 1763. London: 1764. V. 52

THE ANNUAL Gift-Book: a Drawing-Room Portrait Gallery of Eminent Personages. London: 1859. V. 54

THE ANNUAL Miscellany: for the Year 1694. London: 1694. V. 49

THE ANNUAL Miscellany: for...1694. London: 1708. V. 49

ANNUAL New England Official Directory and General Hand-Book for 1878-79. Boston: 1878. V. 50

AN ANNUAL of New Poetry 1917. London: 1917. V. 47; 48; 50

THE ANNUAL Register, as a View of the History, Politicks and Literature, for the Year 1758-78. London: 1767-79. V. 48

THE ANNUAL Register, or a View of the History, Politics and Literature for the Year 1776. 1777. London: 1777-78. V. 53

ANNUAL Register, or a View of the History, Politics and Literature for the Year 1799. London: 1780. V. 50

ANNUAL Review of Law and Ethics. Berlin: 1993. V. 51; 54

ANNUNZIO, GABRIELE D'
The Daughter of Jorio: a Pastoral Tragedy. Boston: 1907. V. 52
Episcopo and Company. Chicago: 1896. V. 52
The Flame of Life. Boston: 1900. V. 52

ANOTHER Bloudy Fight at Colchester: Upon Tuesday Night Last, Between His Majesties Forces Commanded by Gen. Lucas and the Parliaments Forces, Commanded by Gen. Fairfax, and Playing of Their Great Ordinance from the Town and... London: 1648. V. 50; 54

ANOTHER Great Fight on Sunday Morning Last Between the Shavers of Colchester, and the Parliament Forces, Upon the Sallying Out of General Lucas with Two Thousand Horse and Foot, and His Advancing Up to the Lord Generals Works, and Falling... Yondon (sic): 1648. V. 50

ANOUILH, JEAN
Antigone. Paris: 1947. V. 53
The Fighting Cock. New York: 1960. V. 54
Legend of Lovers. New York: 1952. V. 54
Mademoiselle Colombe. New York: 1954. V. 54
Restless Heart. London: 1957. V. 54
Ring Round the Moon. London: 1950. V. 54
Time Remembered. New York: 1958. V. 54

ANQUETIL, LOUIS PIERRE
A Summary of Universal History... London: 1800. V. 48

ANSEGISUS, ABBAS LUXOVIENSIS
Karoli Magni Et Luvdovici....Capitvla Sive Leges Ecclesiasticae et Civiles. Paris: 1603. V. 51; 53

ANSELL, ROBERT
The Bookplate Designs of Austin Osman Spare. London: 1988. V. 47

ANSEN, ALAN
The Old Religion. New York: 1959. V. 47; 48

ANSICHTEN von Missions-Niederlassungen der Evangelischen Bruder Gemeinde - Vues des Etablissemens Missionaries Fondes par la Communaute Evangelique des Freres-Unis. Basel: 1830. V. 48

ANSIDEI, GIUSEPPE, DI PERUGINO
Trattato Cavalleresco Contra l'Abuso del mantenimento Della private Inimicitie... Perugia: 1691. V. 48

ANSORGE, W. J.
Under the African Sun. London: 1899. V. 53
Under the African Sun: a Description of Native Races in Uganda, Sporting Adventures and Other Experiences. New York: 1899. V. 52; 54

ANSPACH, F. R.
Sons of the Sires. A History of the Rise, Progress and Destiny of the American Party... Philadlephia: 1855. V. 53

ANSTED, DAVID THOMAS
The Channel Islands. London: 1893. V. 52
The Ionian Islands in the Year 1863. London: 1863. V. 49
Scenery, Science and Art: Being Extracts from the Note-Book of a Geologist and Mining Engineer. London: 1854. V. 51; 52; 53; 54

ANSTEY, CHRISTOPHER
Ad C. W. Bampfylde, Arm: Epistola Poetica Familiaris, In Qua Continentur Tabulae Quinque ab Eo Excogitatae... Bathoniae: 1776. V. 50
An Election Ball. Bath;: 1776. V. 53; 54
A Familiar Epistle from C. Anstey, Esq. to C. W. Bampfylde, Esq. London: 1777. V. 48; 51; 54
The New Bath Guide: or Memoirs of the B---R---D Family. London: 1766. V. 53
The New Bath Guide; or, Memoirs of the B---r--d Family. (with) On the Much Lamented Death of the Marquis of Tavistock. (with) The Patriot, a Pindaric Address to Lord Buckhorse. Cambridge: 1766/67/67. V. 52
The New Bath Guide; or Memoirs of the B-n-r-d Family, in a Series of Poetical Epistles. London: 1830. V. 49; 50
The New Bath Guide; or Memoirs of the B-n-r-d Family, in a Series of Poetical Epistles. London: 1832. V. 48
Ode on an Evening View of the Crescent At Bath. Bath: 1773. V. 48
Ode On an Evening View Of the Crescent at Bath. London: 1773. V. 50; 54
The Patriot, a Pindaric Address to Lord Buckhorse. Cambridge: 1767. V. 50
Poetical Works of the Late Christopher Anstey, Esq...With Some Account of the Life and Writings of the Author... London: 1808. V. 49
The Priest Dissected: a Poem. Bath: 1774. V. 50

ANSTEY, HENRY
Munimenta Academica, or Documents Illustrative of Academical Life and Studies at Oxford. London: 1868. V. 49

ANSTEY, JOHN
The Pleader's Guide, a Didactic Poem: Containing the Conduct of a Suit at Law... London: 1804. V. 52
The Pleader's Guide, a Didactic Poem, in Two Books, Containing the Conduct of a Suit at Law... London: 1796-1802. V. 54

ANSTIE, FRANCIS
Stimulants and Narcotics: Their Mutual Relations with Special Researches on the Action of Alcohol, Ether and Chloroform on the Vial Organism. Philadelphia: 1865. V. 53

ANSTIS, JOHN
Observations Introductory to an Historical Essay, Upon the Knighthood of the Bath. London: 1725. V. 54
The Register of the Most Noble Order of the Garter, From Its Cover in Balck Velvet, Usually Called the Blac Book... London: 1724. V. 48

ANSTRUTHER, G. ELLIOT
The Bindings of To-morrow. A Record of the World of the Guild of Women-Binders and of the Hamstead Bindery. London: 1902. V. 48; 49

ANSTRUTHER, JOHN
Remarks on the Drill Husbandry, by Which the Superior Advantages of that Mode of Cultivation are Pointed Out... (bound with) Additional Remarks on the Hoeing Husbandry, With a Description... London: 1796/98. V. 49

AN ANSWER to the Declaration of the King of England, Respecting His Motives for Carrying on the Present War, and His Conduct Towards France. Paris: 1794. V. 47

ANSWERS to the Reasons of Dissent, from the Sentence of the Reverend Commission of the General Assembly on March 11th 1752. Edinburgh: 1752. V. 54

ANTAL, FREDERICK
Hogarth and His Place in European Art. London: 1962. V. 49; 52; 54

ANTAR, a Bedoueen Romance. London: 1820. V. 54

ANTARAH IBN SHADDAD, AL-ABSI
Antar, a Bedoueen Romance. London: 1820. V. 51

ANTES, JOHN
Observations on the Manners and Customs of the Egyptians, the Overflowing of the Nile... Dublin: 1801. V. 49

ANTHEIL, GEORGE
Bad Boy of Music. New York: 1945. V. 54
Bad Boy of Music. London: 1947. V. 50

AN ANTHEM for the Use of the Magdalen Chapel. London: 1760?. V. 48

ANTHOLOGY of Contemporary Latin-American Poetry. 1942. V. 50

ANTHOLOGY of Magazine Verse for 1913. Cambridge: 1913. V. 53

ANTHOLOGY of Magazine Verse for 1920. Boston: 1920. V. 54

ANTHOLOGY of Magazine Verse for 1925. 1925. V. 54

ANTHONY Askabouts Pleasant Exercises for Little Minds: or a New and Entertaining Riddle Book for Young Masters and Misses. London: 1810. V. 52

ANTHONY, EDGAR WATERMAN
Early Florentine Architecture and Decoration. Cambridge: 1927. V. 54
A History of Mosaics. Boston: 1935. V. 50
Romanesque Frescoes. Princeton: 1951. V. 49; 51; 53

ANTHONY, EDWARD
The Fairies Up to Date. London: 1925. V. 48; 51
The Fairies Up to Date. London: 1928. V. 52

ANTHONY, GORDON
Ballet Camera Studies. London: 1937. V. 47; 49; 51; 53
Leonide Massine - Camera Studies. London: 1939. V. 47
Russian Ballet: Camera Studies. London: 1939. V. 49; 52

ANTHONY, SUSAN B.
History of Woman Suffrage. Rochester: 1887. V. 53

ANTHONY, WILLIAM
Bill Anthony's Greatest Hits. Drawings 1963-1987. Highlands: 1988. V. 54

THE ANTI-Weesils. A Poem. London: 1691. V. 52

AN ANTIDOTE Against Melancholy. London: 1749. V. 48

THE ANTIENT and Present State of Military Law in Great Britain Consider'd: With a Review of the Debates of the Army and Navy Bills. London: 1749. V. 47

ANTIMATED Antics in Playland. Akron: 1946. V. 48

ANTIN, DAVID
Code of Flag Behavior. Los Angeles: 1968. V. 51
Meditations. Los Angeles: 1971. V. 54

ANTIN, MARY
The Promised Land. Boston: 1912. V. 48; 51

ANTIQUARIAN and Topographical Cabinet. London: 1807. V. 51

ANTIQUARIAN Horology. London: 1953-79. V. 53

THE ANTIQUARIAN Itinerary. London: 1815-18. V. 49

ANTIQUARIAN Repertory: a Miscellany Intended to Preserve and Illustrate Several Valuable Remains of Old Times. London: 1780-84. V. 51

ANTISELL, THOMAS
The Manufacture of Photogenic or Hydro-Carbon Oils, From Coal or Other Bituminous Substances... New York: 1859. V. 50

ANTOINE, JEAN
Traite d'Architecture, ou Proportions des Trois Ordres Grecs sur un Module de Douze Parties. Treves: 1768. V. 47

ANTOMMARCHI, F.
The Last Days of the Emperor Napoleon. London: 1825. V. 47

ANTON, FERDINAND
Ancient Mexican Art. New York: 1969. V. 47; 50
Art of the Maya. London: 1970. V. 53

ANTON, JAMES
Retrospect of a Military Life. 1840. V. 52

ANTONIN Raymond, Architectural Details. New York: 1947. V. 51

ANTONINUS, BROTHER
Birth of a Poet. Santa Barbara: 1982. V. 48; 51
Black Hills. 1973. V. 49
Black Hills. England: 1973. V. 48
The Blowing of the Seed. New Haven: 1956. V. 49; 52
The Blowing of the Seed. New Haven: 1966. V. 53
A Canticle to the Waterbirds. Berkeley: 1968. V. 47; 48; 53
The Flowering of the Seed. New Haven: 1946. V. 49
The Hazards of Holiness. Poems 1957-1960. Garden City: 1962. V. 51; 52
In Medias Res. San Francisco: 1984. V. 47; 48
In the Fictive Wish. Berkeley: 1967. V. 48; 49; 53; 54
The Last Crusade. Berkeley: 1969. V. 48; 53; 54
The Mate-Flight of Eagles: Two Poems on the Love-Death of the Cross. Newcastle: 1977. V. 53
On Printing. San Francisco: 1992. V. 51; 52
The Poet is Dead. San Francisco: 1964. V. 48
The Poet Is Dead: a Memorial for Robinson Jeffers. Santa Cruz: 1987. V. 47; 49
A Privacy of Speech. Ten Poems in Sequence... Berkeley: 1949. V. 48; 54
Rattlesnake August. Northridge: 1978. V. 54
Renegade Christmas. Northridge: 1980. V. 53
Renegade Christmas. Northridge: 1984. V. 48; 51; 54
The Residual Years. New York: 1948. V. 48
River Root. A Syzygy for the Bicentennial of These States. Berkeley: 1976. V. 47; 49; 54

ANTONINUS, BROTHER continued
San Joaquin. Los Angeles: 1939. V. 48; 54
Single Source. The Early Poems...(1934-1940). Berkeley: 1966. V. 53; 54
Sixty-Five. Boston: 1980. V. 48
The Springing of the Blade. Reno: 1968. V. 48; 49; 53
Ten War Elegies. Waldport: 1943. V. 49; 51; 52
Tendril in the Mesh. San Francisco: 1973. V. 47; 49
These Are the Ravens. San Leandro: 1935. V. 53
Triptych for the Living. Oakland: 1951. V. 48; 50; 53
War Elegies. Waldport: 1944. V. 48
Who Is She That Looketh Forth as the Morning. Santa Barbara: 1972. V. 47; 48; 49; 53
The Year's Declension. Berkeley: 1961. V. 48; 49; 52; 54

ANTONINUS, MARCUS AURELIUS, EMPEROR OF ROME
The Meditations of the Emperor Marcus Aurelius Antoninus. Glasgow: 1749. V. 49

ANTONINUS FLORENTINUS
Confessionale in Vulgare Sermone. Della Dotrina Cristiana. Venice: 1473. V. 47; 53
Repertorin Totius Summe Domini Antonini Archipscopi Floretini Ordinis Predi. Argentinae: 1496. V. 47

ANTONIUS DE BALOCHIO DE VERCELLIS
Sermones Quadragesimales De XII. Mirabilibus Christiane Fidei Excellentiis. Lugduni: 1504. V. 53

ANTRAM, C. B.
Butterflies of India. Calcutta & Simla: 1924. V. 49; 50

ANTREASIAN, G.
The Tamarind Book of Lithography: Art and Techniques. New York: 1971. V. 47

ANTROBUS, CLARA L.
Wildersmoor. London: 1895. V. 51

ANTROBUS, JOHN
Clifton; or, Thoughts and Scenes. London: 1834. V. 47; 54

ANTWERP.
A Journal kept There, Including Also Notices of Brussels and of the Monastery of St. Bernard, Near Westmalle. London: 1847. V. 51

ANVILLE, JEAN BAPTISTE BOURGUIGNON D'
Atlas and Geography of the Antients. London: 1815. V. 53

APES, WILLIAM
The Experience of William Apes, a Native of the Forrest. New York: 1829. V. 47; 50
Indian Nullification of the Unconstitutional Laws of Massachusetts, Relative to the Marshpee Tribe; or the Pretended Riot Explained. Boston: 1835. V. 47

APHORISMS
for Youth, with Observations and Reflections, Religious, Moral, Critical, and Characteristic; Some Original, But Chiefly Selected... London: 1801. V. 49; 52

APHORISMS
for Youth, With Observations and Reflections, Religious, Moral, Critical and Characteristic. London: 1807. V. 49

APHRODITE
a Mythical Journey in Eight Episodes. London: 1970. V. 48

APHTHONIUS
Progymnasmata...cum Scholiss R. Lorichii. Amsterdam: 1642. V. 52

APIANUS, PETRUS
Cosmographia... Cologne: 1574. V. 53
La Cosmographie... Paris: 1553. V. 52
Quadrans Apiani Astronomicus... Ingolstadt: 1532. V. 50

APOLLINAIRE, GUILLAUME
Les Mamelles du Tiresias. Paris: 1918. V. 49

APOLLO ASSN. FOR THE PROMOTION OF FINE ARTS IN THE U. S.
Transactions of the Apollo Association, for the Promotion of the Fine Arts in the United States for the Year 1843. New York: 1844. V. 54

APOLLODORUS
Apollodori Atheniensis Bibliotheces, Sive de Deorum Origine, Tam Graece Qua Latine... Rome: 1555. V. 51

APOLLONIO, UMBRO
Hans Hartung. New York: 1972. V. 50

APOLLONIUS OF PERGA
The Two Books of Apollonius Pergaeus, Concerning Determinate Section... London: 1772. V. 49

APOLLONIUS RHODIUS
Argonautica. New York: 1957. V. 48
Argonautica: Jason and the Golden Fleece. Athens: 1957. V. 53; 54
The Argonautics of Apollonius Rhodius, in Four Books. London: 1780. V. 48
(Greek Title - then) Argonauticorum. Basileae: 1572. V. 53

APOLOGY
for the Conduct of a Late Second-Rate Minister, from the Year 1729, at Which Time He Commenc'd Courtier, Till Within a Few Weeks of His Death, in 1746. London: 1747. V. 49

AN APOLOGY
for the Life and Writings of David Hume, Esq. With a Parallel Between Him and the Late Lord Chesterfield... London: 1777. V. 53

AN APOLOGY
for the Pawnbrokers, Most Respectfully Addressed to the Members of Both Houses of Parliament, the Judges of the Land, and the Justices of the Peace Throughout the Kingdom. London: 1824. V. 49

APPARITIONS:
Poems by John Ashbery, Galway Kinnell, W. S. Merwin, L. M. Rosenberg, Dave Smith. Northridge: 1981. V. 47; 50; 52

AN APPEAL,
From Malice, and Insolence, to Liberality and Benevolence. 1786. V. 50

AN APPEAL
to the Moral and Religious of all Denominations; or, an Exposition of Some of the Indiscretions of General Andrew Jackson, as copied from the Records and Certified by the Clerk of Mercer County, Kentucky. New York: 1828. V. 48

AN APPEAL
to the Nation. Being a Full Vindication of Mr. Mordaunt, and Other Gentlement Employed in the Conduct of the Late Secret Expedition. London: 1757. V. 50

AN APPEAL
To the Public; In Relation to the Tobacco ***: and a Revival of the Old Project, to Establish a General Excise. London: 1751. V. 47

APPENDIX
to the Comment on the Petition of the British Inhabitants of Bengal, Bahar and Orissa to Parliament. 1780. V. 52

APPENDIX
to the Reports of the Court and Evidence Taken Upon the Inquiry into the Tay Bridge Disaster. London: 1880. V. 51

AN APPENDIX
to the Rowfant Library. London: 1900. V. 50

APPERLEY, CHARLES JAMES
The Horse and the Hound Their Various Uses and Treatment, Including Practical Instructions in Horsemanship and a Treatise on Horsedealing by Nimrod. Edinburgh: 1842. V. 47
Hunting Reminiscences. London: 1843. V. 52
The Life of a Sportsman. London: 1842. V. 47; 48; 50; 51; 54
The Life of a Sportsman. London: 1914. V. 47; 49
Memoirs of the Life of the Late John Mytton, Esq. London: 1835. V. 48
Memoirs of the Life of the Late John Mytton, Esq. London: 1837. V. 47; 51; 53
Memoirs of the Life of the Late John Mytton, Esq. London: 1851. V. 47; 54
Memoirs of the Life of the Late John Mytton, Esq. London: 1900. V. 47; 52
Nemrod ou L'Amateur des Chevaux au Courses... Paris: 1838. V. 47
Nimrod's Hunting Tours, Interspersed with Characteristic Anecdotes, Sayings and Doings of Sporting Men... London: 1835. V. 47
Nimrod's Northern Tour. London: 1838. V. 50
Remarks on the Condition of Hunters. London: 1831. V. 50; 52

APPERSON, G. L.
A Jane Austen Dictionary. London: 1932. V. 52

APPERT, FRANCOIS
The Art of Preserving All Kinds of Animal and Vegetable Substances for Several Years. London: 1812. V. 52

APPERT, NICOLAS
The Art of Preserving All Kinds of Animal and Vegetable Substances for Several Years. London: 1811. V. 50
The Art of Preserving all Kinds of Animal and Vegetable Substances for Several Years. New York: 1812. V. 53

APPIANUS, OF ALEXANDRIA
De Ciuilibus Romanorum Bellis Historiarum Libri Quinque. Eiusdem Libri Sex: Illyricus, Celticus, Libycus, Syrius, Parthicus, ^ Mithridaticus. Lvgdvni: 1560. V. 47
De Civilibus Romanoru Bellis Historiarum Libri Quinque. Paris: 1538. V. 53; 54
Historia Romana. (and) De Bellis Civilibus. Venice: 1477. V. 54
Historia Romana, cum. De Bellis Civlibus. Venice: 1500. V. 48; 54
The History of Appian of Alexandria. London: 1690. V. 51
The History of Appian of Alexandria. London: 1703. V. 48
The History...In Two Parts. London: 1679. V. 47; 48; 50
...Romanarum Historiarum. Paris: 1551. V. 48

APPLE
Pie ABC. New York: 1897. V. 52; 54

APPLEGATE, ASHER TUNIS
Aspects of Printing. New Haven: 1951. V. 51

APPLEGATE, JESSE
A Day With the Cow Column. Chicago: 1934. V. 53
Recollections of My Boyhood. Chicago: 1934. V. 47

APPLEGATE, JOHN S.
Reminiscences and Letters of George Arrowsmith of New Jersey, Late Lieutenant-Colonel... New York State Volunteers. Red Bank: 1893. V. 51

APPLETON, ELIZABETH HAVEN
Insurrection at Magellan. Boston: 1854. V. 50

APPLETON, HONOR
Babies Three. London: 1921. V. 53
The Bad Mrs. Ginger. London: 1903. V. 49
Peggy and Joan. London. V. 48

APPLETON, JANE SOPHIA
Voices from the Kenduskeag. Bangor: 1848. V. 54

APPLETON, T. G.
Syrian Sunshine. Boston: 1877. V. 47

APPLETON'S
American Guide Book: Being a Hand-Book for Tourists and Travelers... Philadelphia: 1846. V. 53

APPLETON'S
Cyclopaedia of American Biography. New York: 1888-89. V. 47; 54
APPLETON'S
Cyclopaedia of American Biography. New York: 1888-94. V. 49
APPLETON'S
Cyclopaedia of American Biography. New York: 1889-91. V. 49; 50

APPLETON'S Dictionary of Machines, Mechanics, Engine-Work and Engineering. New York: 1866. V. 47

APPLETON'S Dictionary of Machines, Mechanics, Engine-Work and Engineering. New York: 1867. V. 51

APPLETON'S Hand-Book of American Travel. Southern Tour. New York/London: 1876. V. 47

APPLETON'S Hand-Book of American Travel. Western Tour. New York: 1873. V. 47

APPLETON'S Illustrated Hand-Book of American Summer Resorts, Including Tours and Excursions. New York: 1876. V. 47

APPLETON'S Illustrated Hand-Book of American Travel. New York/London: 1857. V. 47

APPLETON'S Illustrated Hand-Book of American Winter Resorts; for Tourists and Invalids. New York: 1877. V. 48

APPLETON'S New and Complete United States Guide Book for Travellers. New York: 1854. V. 47

APPLETON'S Railraod and Steamboat Companion. New York: 1848. V. 47

APPLETON'S Railway and Steam Navigation Guide. 1864. V. 47
APPLETON'S Railway and Steam Navigation Guide. 1869. V. 47

APPONYI, FLORA H.
The Libraries of California. San Francisco: 1878. V. 54

APPONYI, HENRIK, COUNT
My Big Game Hunting Diary From India and the Himalayas. London: 1937. V. 48; 49; 54

THE APRIL Baby's Book of Tunes. London and New York: 1903. V. 49

APROSIO, ANGELO
Il Vaglio Critico...Sopra Il Mondo Nuovo del...Tomaso Stiglianii da Matera. Rostock: 1637. V. 53

APTHEKER, HERBERT
A Documentary History of the Negro People in the United States. New York: 1951. V. 53

APULEIUS
Amor und Psyche. Munchen: 1881. V. 54
Les Amours de Psyche et de Cupidan, avec la Poeme d'Adonis. Paris: 1795. V. 52
The Amours of Cupid and Psyche. London: 1759. V. 54
Cupid and Psyche. London: 1935. V. 47
Cupid and Psyche and other Tales from the Golden Ass of Apuleius. London: 1904. V. 48
Cupid and Psyche, the Most Pleasant and Delectable Tale of Their Marriage. Waltham St. Lawrence: 1934. V. 49
Cupid and Psyches. London: 1923. V. 47; 50
De Cupidinis et Psyches. London: 1901. V. 47; 50; 51; 52
The Eleven Bookes of the Golden Asse... London: 1924. V. 47; 51; 54
The Excellent Narration of the Marriage of Cupide and Psyches. London: 1897. V. 50; 53
The Golden Ass. New York: 1904. V. 49
The Golden Ass. New York: 1932. V. 51; 54
The Golden Ass. Harmondsworth: 1950. V. 51; 53
The Golden Ass. London: 1951. V. 49
The Golden Ass of Apuleius. 1924. V. 47
The Golden Ass, or The Transformation of Lucius. London: 1960. V. 52
The Golden Asse. London: 1923. V. 51
The Marriage of Cupid and Psyche. New York: 1951. V. 47; 48; 49; 53
Operum, Secunda Pars. Basle: 1560. V. 52
The Story of Cupid and Psyche. New York: 1923. V. 48
The Story of Cupid and Psyche. London and Cambridge: 1974. V. 54
The Transformation of Lucius Otherwise Known as the Golden Ass. Harmondsworth: 1950. V. 48
The Transformations of Lucius, Otherwise Known as the Golden Ass. Middlesex: 1950. V. 50

AQUARIUM Comicum. London: 1870's. V. 48

AQUILA, FRANCESCO
Raccolta di Vasi Diversi Formati Da Illustri Artefici Antichi E Di Varie Targhe... Rome: 1713. V. 48; 50

ARABELLA: a Tale. And the History of Prince Witty and Princess Astrea. Wellington: 1811. V. 49

ARABIAN NIGHTS
Aladdin and the Wonderful Lamp. London: 1928. V. 53
Ali-Baba and the Forty Thieves. London: 1850. V. 47
Ali-Baba and the Forty Thieves. Chicago: 1962. V. 52
The Arabian Nights. London: 1802. V. 47; 48
The Arabian Nights. London: 1810. V. 49; 50
Arabian Nights. London: 1870. V. 52
Arabian Night's. London: 1886-88. V. 51
The Arabian Nights. London: 1910. V. 54
The Arabian Nights. London: 1912. V. 49
The Arabian Nights. London: 1924. V. 49; 53
Arabian Nights. Philadelphia: 1928. V. 49
The Arabian Nights Entertainments. Ipswich: 1954. V. 50
The Arabian Nights Entertainments, Carefully Revised and Occasionally Corrected from the Arabic. Philadelphia: 1826. V. 53
Arabian Nights Entertainments: Consisting of One Thousand and One Stories, Told by the Sultaness of the Indies to Divert the Sultan from the Execution of a Bloody Vow... London: 1736. V. 50
The Arabian Night's Entertainments; or, the Thousand and One Nights. 1815. V. 49
The Arabian Nights, retold by Kate Douglas Wiggin and Nora Smith. London. V. 48
The Arabian Nights Tales from the Thousand and One Nights. London: 1924. V. 52
The Arabian Nights. Tales from the Thousand and One Nights. New York: 1925. V. 47
Arabian Tales: or, a Continuation of the Arabian Nights Entertainments. Edinburgh: 1791. V. 48
Arabische Nachte (One Thousand and One Nights). Weimar: 1914. V. 49
The Book of a Thousand Nights and a Night. London: 1894. V. 54
The Book of a Thousand Nights and a Night. London: 1897. V. 48
The Book of a Thousand Nights and a Night. New York: 1934. V. 47; 48
The Book of the Thousand and One Nights... London: 1901. V. 50
The Book of the Thousand and One Nights. New York: 1930. V. 51
The Book of the Thousand Nights and a Night. 1900. V. 54
The Book of the Thousand Nights and a Night. 1900-20. V. 51
The Book of The Thousand Nights and a Night. New York: 1934. V. 49
The Book of the Thousand Nights and a Night, and Supplemental Nights. 1920. V. 50
The Book of the Thousand Nights and One Night. London: 1923. V. 50
The Book of the Thousand Nights and One Night. New York: 1930. V. 50
The Book of the Thousand Nights and One Night. London: 1953. V. 51
The Book of the Thousand Nights and One Night. London: 1958. V. 48; 49
The Book of the Thousand Nights and One Night. New York: 1972. V. 48
The Book of the Thousand Nights and One Night Rendered into English from the Literal and Complete French Translation of Dr. J. C. Mardrus by Powys Mathers. London: 1947. V. 49
The Book of the Thousand Nights and One Night. (with) Tales from the Arabic. (with) Aladdin and the Enchanted Lamp. (with) The Persian Letters. (with) The Thousand and One Quarter of an Hour. London: 1914. V. 50
The Book of the Thousand Nights and One Nights. London: 1920. V. 50
Dalziel's Illustrated Arabian Nights' Entertainments. London: 1864-65. V. 51
Fairy Tales from the Arabian Nights. London: 1893. V. 48; 54
The Magic Horse, from the Arabian Nights. London: 1930. V. 51
Persian Songs from the Arabian Nights. Greenbrae: 1980. V. 51; 53
A Plain and Literal Translation of the Arabian Nights' Entertainments, Now Entituled The Book of the Thousand Nights and a Night. Boston: 1903. V. 49
A Plain and Literal Translation of the Arabian Nights Entertainments....(with) Supplemental Nights. London: 1920. V. 51
Sinbad the Sailor & Other Stories from the Arabian Nights. 1914. V. 47
Sinbad the Sailor and Other Stories from the Arabian Nights. London: 1911. V. 54
Sinbad the Sailor and Other Stories from the Arabian Nights. London: 1914. V. 48; 53
Stories from the Arabian Nights. London: 1907. V. 50; 52
The Story of Aladdin and His Wonderful Lamp. New York: 1928. V. 48
The Tale of Ali Baba & the Forty Thieves. New York: 1949. V. 47
Tales from the Arabian Nights. London: 1920. V. 54
The Thousand and One Nights. London: 1839-41. V. 50; 51; 53; 54
The Thousand and One Nights, Commonly Called, In England, the Arabian Nights' Entertainments. London & New York: 1865. V. 50
The Thousand and One Nights, Commonly Called...the Arabian Nights' Entertainments. London: 1841. V. 51
The Thousand and One Nights. The Arabian Nights' Entertainments... London: 1883. V. 50

ARAGO, DOMINIQUE FRANCOIS JEAN
Historical Eloge of James Watt. London: 1839. V. 50
Life of James Watt... Edinburgh: 1839. V. 52
Notices Scientifiques. Paris: 1854-58. V. 50

ARAGO, JACQUES
Promenade Autour du Monde, Pendant les Annees 1817, 1818, 1819 and 1820, Sur Les Corvettes du Roi l'Uranie et la Physicienne... Paris: 1822. V. 50; 52

ARAGON, LOUIS
La Grande Gaite. Paris: 1929. V. 51
Henri Matisse. London: 1971. V. 50
Henri Matisse. New York: 1972. V. 47; 48; 50; 50; 52; 53

ARAM, EUGENE
The Genuine Account of the Trial of Eugene Aram, for the Murder of Daniel Clark. Knaresborough, York: 1792. V. 48; 50
The Trial and Life of Eugene Aram... Richmond: 1832. V. 54

ARATUS
(Greek Text); Accesserunt Annotationes in Eratosthenem et Hymnos Dionysii. Oxonii: 1672. V. 50
Phenomena. Lexington;: 1975. V. 52

ARAUJO CARNEIRO, HELIODORO JACINTO DE
Algumas Palavras em Resposta ao Que Certas Pessoas tem Ditto e Avancado a Cerca do Governo Portuguez, Com Algumas Observacoes Tanto a Respeito do Estado Actual de Portugal e de Europa... London: 1832. V. 47

ARBANTES, LAURE SAINT MARTIN PERMON JUNOT, DUCHESSE D'
Memoirs of Napoleon, His Court and Family. New York: 1854. V. 54

ARBER, AGNES
Herbals. Cambridge: 1912. V. 47
Herbals, their Origin and Evolution. Cambridge: 1938. V. 48; 49; 52; 53; 54
Herbals. Their Origin and Evolution. London: 1938. V. 53
Herbals, Their Origin and Evolution... Cambridge: 1953. V. 51; 53

ARBER, EDWARD
An English Garner. London: 1895-96. V. 48; 50
The First Three English Books on America. Birmingham: 1885. V. 50

THE ARBITRATION Between the Dominion of Canada and the Provinces of Ontario and Quebec. Statute and Submission. The Awards on the Interest Question of 2nd November 1893 and 31st August 1894. Toronto: 1894. V. 51

ARBLAY, FRANCES BURNEY D'
Brief Reflections Relative to the Emigrant French Clergy... London: 1793. V. 52
Camilla. London: 1796. V. 48; 49; 50; 53; 54
Camilla. London: 1802. V. 48; 49; 50; 51; 52
Cecilia, or Memoirs of an Heiress. London: 1782. V. 48; 54
Cecilia, or Memoirs of an Heiress. London: 1786. V. 49
Cecilia or Memoirs of an Heiress. London: 1820. V. 48; 53
Cecilia, or Memoirs of an Heiress. London: 1825. V. 52
Cecilia, or Memoirs of an Heiress. London: 1893. V. 47; 48; 53
Diary and Letters. London: 1842-46. V. 48; 49; 51; 54
Diary and Letters of. London: 1842. V. 50
Diary and Letters of. London: 1842. V. 54
Diary and Letters of. London: 1843-46. V. 48
Diary and Letters of. London: 1854. V. 49; 52
Diary and Letters of. 1892. V. 52
Diary and Letters of... London: 1893. V. 53
Diary and Letters of... London, New York: 1904-05. V. 47; 49; 50; 54
Evelina, or the History of a Young Lady's Entrance into the World. London: 1779. V. 48; 50; 51
Evelina, or, The History of a Young Lady's Entrance Into the World. London: 1783. V. 54
Evelina, or. the History of a Young Lady's Entrance Into the World. London: 1784. V. 54
Evelina, or the History of a Young Lady's Introduction to the World. London: 1825?. V. 52
Memoirs of Doctor Burney... London: 1832. V. 47; 48; 49; 53
The Wanderer. London: 1814. V. 49; 50

ARBUCKLE'S Illustrated Atlas of the United States of America. New York: 1889. V. 48

ARBUTHNOT, ARCHIBALD
The Life, Adventures and Many and Great Vicissitudes of Fortune of Simon Lord Lovat, Head of the Family of Frasers... London: 1746. V. 47

ARBUTHNOT, JAMES
Natural History of Those Fishes That are Indigenous to, or Occasionally Frequent the Coasts of Buchan. Aberdeeon: 1815. V. 53

ARBUTHNOT, JOHN
An Essay Concerning the Effects of Air on Human Bodies. London: 1733. V. 49
Law Is a Bottomless Pit. Or, the History of John Bull. London: 1727. V. 47
Lewis Baboon Turned Honest, and John Bull Politician. London: 1712. V. 50
The Miscellaneous Works. Glasgow: 1751. V. 47; 53
A Sermon Preach'd to the People at the Mercat Cross of Edinburgh... N.P: 1706. V. 51
Tables of Ancient Coins, Weights and Measures, Explain'd & Exemplify'd in Several Dissertations. London: 1727. V. 48; 53
Tables of Antient Coins, Weights and Measures... London: 1754. V. 53
Tables of the Grecian, Roman and Jewish Measures, Weights and Coins. London: 1705?. V. 52

ARBUZZI, LUIGI AMEDEO, DUKE OF
On the Polar Star in the Arctic Sea. London: 1903. V. 49

ARCANGELI, FRANCESCO
Graham Sutherland. New York: 1975. V. 47; 48; 50; 52

ARCE, HECTOR
Groucho. New York: 1979. V. 52

ARCEO, FRANCISCO
De Recta Curandorum Vulnerum Ratione, et Aliis Ejus Artis Praeceptis Libri II. Amsterdam: 1658. V. 51

ARCHAEOLOGICAL, Historical and Geographical Studies. Jerusalem: 1951-78. V. 49

ARCHBALD, ROBERT W.
Proceedings of the United States Senate and the House of Representatives in the Trial of Impeachment of Robert W. Archbald, Additional Circuit Judge of the United States from the Third Judicial Circuit. Washington: 1913. V. 52

ARCHBOLD, R.
New Guinea Expedition. Fly River Area 1936-1937. New York: 1940. V. 54

ARCHENHOLZ, JOHANN W. VON
A Picture of England. Dublin. V. 49
A Picture of England. London: 1790. V. 47

ARCHER, CHARLES P.
An Analytical Digest of All the Reported Cases in Several Courts of Common Law in Ireland (etc.). Dublin: 1839. V. 54

ARCHER, G.
The Birds of British Somaliland and the Gulf of Aden. London: 1937-61. V. 49; 51; 52; 54

ARCHER, JEAN C.
Fishy-Winkle. London: 1903. V. 49
Rosalina. London: 1904. V. 47

ARCHER, LOU ELLA
Canyon Shadows. Los Angeles: 1931. V. 53

ARCHER, MILDRED
British Drawings in the India Office Library. London: 1969. V. 49; 51
India and British Portraiture 1770-1825. London: 1979. V. 49

ARCHER, ROBERT
The Night After Christmas. Richmond: 1977. V. 49

ARCHER, THOMAS
Charles Dickens. A Gossip about His Life, Works and Characters. London: 1885. V. 51
Charles Dickens: a Gossip About His Life, Works and Characters with Eighteen Full Page Character Sketches. London: 1894?. V. 49
The Frogs' Parish Clerk; and His Adventures in Strange Lands. London: 1866. V. 50; 52

ARCHER, W. G.
Indian Miniatures. London: 1960. V. 51
Indian Paintings from the Punjab Hills. London: 1973. V. 52

ARCHER, W. S.
In Senate of the United States...Mr. Archer...Submitted the Following Report...On the Subject of Annexaton of Texas... Washington: 1845. V. 49

ARCHER, WILLIAM
Play-Making: a Manual of Craftsmanship. London: 1912. V. 53

THE ARCHER'S Guide, Containing Full Instructions for the Use of that Ancient and Noble Instrument, The Bow... London: 1833. V. 47

THE ARCHER'S Manual; or the Art of Shooting with the Long Bow, as Practised By the United Bowmen of Philadelphia. Philadelphia: 1830. V. 48

ARCHIBALD, A. G.
Letter from A. G. Archibald, Esq. M.P.P. 85 Oxford Terrace, London, 24th Nov. 1866. to the People of Nova Scotia. N.P. V. 53

ARCHILOCOS
The Fragments of Archilocos. Berkeley: 1964. V. 54

ARCHIPENKO, ALEXANDER
Archipenko: Fifty Creative Years, 1908-1958. New York: 1960. V. 47

ARCHITECTONICS, The Tales of Tom Thumtack. New York: 1914. V. 51

THE ARCHITECTURAL Orders. Providence: 1990. V. 51

ARCHITECTURAL Recreations. London: 1822. V. 49

ARCTANDER, JOHN W.
The Apostle of Alaska: the Story of William Duncan of Metlakahtla. New York: 1908. V. 49
The Apostle of Alaska: The Story of William Duncan of Metlakahtla. New York: 1909. V. 47; 50

THE ARCTIC World: its Plants Animals and Natural Phenomena. London: 1876. V. 49; 51; 52; 53; 54

ARDEN, JOHN
Left-Handed Liberty: a Play About Magna Carta. London: 1965. V. 54

ARDINGER, RICHARD
What Thou Lovest Well Remains, 100 Years of Ezra Pound. Boise: 1986. V. 52

ARDITTI, J.
Fundamentals of Orchid Biology. London: 1992. V. 52

ARDIZZONE, EDWARD
Edward Ardizzone's Indian Diary 1952-53. London: 1983. V. 53
Johnny the Cockmaker. Oxford: 1960. V. 50
Little Tim and the Brave Sea Captain. 1936. V. 51
Little Tim and the Brave Sea Captain. Oxford: 1955. V. 50
Lucy Brown and Mr. Grimes. 1937. V. 50
Lucy Brown and Mr. Grimes. New York: 1937. V. 47
Nicholas and the Fast Moving Diesel. London: 1947. V. 49; 52; 53; 54
Nicholas and the Fast Moving Diesel. London: 1959. V. 47
Nicholas and the Fast Moving Diesel. Oxford: 1959. V. 50
Peter the Wanderer. Oxford: 1963. V. 50
Tim All Alone. Oxford: 1956. V. 50
Tim and Charlotte. Oxford: 1951. V. 50
Tim and Lucy Go to Sea. London: 1938. V. 48; 49; 50; 52; 53
Tim and Lucy Go To Sea. Oxford: 1958. V. 50
Tim In Danger. Oxford: 1953. V. 50
Tim to the Lighthouse. Oxford: 1968. V. 50
Tim's Friend Towser. Oxford: 1962. V. 50
Visiting Dieppe. London: 1981. V. 47

ARENAS, REINALDO
Hallucinations. New York: 1971. V. 51

ARETAEUS
On the Causes and Signs of Acute and Chronic Disease. Philadelphia: 1841. V. 50

ARETIN, J. C. F. VON
Uber die Fruhesten Universalhistorische Folgen der Erfindung der Buchdruckerkunst. Munich: 1808. V. 50

ARETINO, PIETRO
Capitoli...Diretti a Gran Signori Sopra Varie & Diverse Materie Molto Deletteuole. Venice: 1541. V. 51
Lettere. Paris: 1609. V. 51
A New and Exact Description of the Pitti Gallery in Florence with a Short Chronological and Biographical Index of all the Painters Herein Mentioned. Florence: 1852. V. 53
Qvattro Comedie... London?: 1588. V. 51
La Terza, et Vltima Parte de Ragionamenti (etc.). London: 1589. V. 53
La Vita di Maria Vergine. Venice: 1540?. V. 52

ARETS Saga. Stockholm: 1931. V. 49

ARGAN, GIULIO CARLO
Henry Moore. Torino: 1948. V. 49; 53

ARGENS, JEAN BAPTISTE DE BOYER, MARQUIS D'
Chinese Letters. London: 1741. V. 48; 51
The Jewish Spy. London: 1765-66. V. 54
Memoirs of the Count du Beauval, Including Some Curious Particulars Relating to the Dukes of Wharton and Ormond, During Their Exiles. London: 1754. V. 51

ARGENSOLA, BARTOLOME LEONARDO DE
Conquesta de Las Islas Malucas. Madrid: 1609. V. 50; 51; 54

ARGENSON, RENE LOUIS VOYER, MARQUIS DE
Essays, Civil, Moral, Literary & Political. Worcester: 1797. V. 47

ARGENTERIO, GIOVANNI
De Morbis Lib. XIIII...ex Secunda Hac Aeditione. Lyon: 1558. V. 49; 52

ARGENTI, PHILIP P.
Chius Liberata, or the Occupation of Chios by the Greeks in 1912. London: 1933. V. 47
The Costumes of Chios. London: 1953. V. 47; 51
The Expedition of Colonel Fabvier to Chios. London: 1933. V. 47; 49
The Expedition of the Florentines to Chios (1599). London: 1934. V. 47; 49
The Occupation of Chios by the Genoese and Their Administration of the Island 1346-1566. Cambridge: 1958. V. 49
The Occupation of Chios by the Germans and Their Administration of the Island... Cambridge: 1966. V. 47

THE ARGUMENTS of Sir Richard Hutton Knight...and Sir George Croke, Knight...Together with the Certificate of Sir John Denham Knight... London: 1641. V. 54

THE ARGUMENTS of the Lord Chief Justice Holt and Judge Powell, in the Controverted Point of Peerage; in the Case of the King and Queen Against Charles Knowles, Otherwise Earl of Banbury. London: 1716. V. 50

ARGUS, ARABELLA, PSEUD.
The Adventures of a Donkey. London: 1815. V. 51
The Adventures of a Donkey. London: 1840. V. 51
Further Adventures of Jemmy Donkey; Interspersed with Biographical Sketches of the Horse. London: 1821. V. 52
The Juvenile Spectator... (with) The Juvenile Spectator: part the Second. London: 1810/12. V. 48; 50
Ostentation and Liberality: a Tale. London: 1821. V. 48; 50

ARGYLE, ARCHIBALD CAMPBELL, 5TH EARL OF
The Speech of...at His Trial..12th of December 1681... London: 1682. V. 47

ARGYLE, ARCHIE
Cupid's Album. New York: 1866. V. 50

ARGYLE, HARVEY
As I Saw It. San Francisco: 1902. V. 47

ARGYLL, JOHN GEORGE EDWARD HENRY DOUGLAS SUTHERLAND
The Canadian North West: A speech Delivered by His Excellency the Marquis of Lorne, Governor General of Canada, Winnipeg. Ottawa: 1881. V. 53
Canadian Pictures Drawn With Pen and Pencil... London: 1884. V. 48
Memoirs of Canada and Scotland: Speeches and Verses. Montreal: 1884. V. 54

ARIAS, P. E.
A History of 1000 Years of Greek Vase Paintings. New York: 1962. V. 52
A History of Greek Vase Painting. London: 1962. V. 54

ARIAS MONTANUS, BENEDICTUS
Humanae Salutis Monumenta... Antwerp: 1571. V. 48

ARIENS-KAPPERS, C. U.
The Evolution of the Nervous System in Invertebrates, Vertebrates, and Man. Haarlem: 1929. V. 47

ARIES, ROBERT S.
Mane-Katz 1894-1962. The Complete Works. London: 1970. V. 54

THE ARIKARA Narrative of the Campaign Against the Hostile June 1876. Bismarck: 1920. V. 50

ARIOSTO, LUDOVICO
Bellezze del (Orlando) Furioso... Venice: 1574. V. 47
La Cassaria Comedia non Meno Piacevole che Ridicolosa... Venetia: 1587. V. 47
La Lena Comedia... Venice: 1551. V. 52
The Orlando... London: 1791. V. 51
Orlando Furiosi Di Lodovico Ariosto. Birmingham: 1773. V. 51
Orlando Furioso. Venice: 1548. V. 54
Orlando Furioso... Venetia: 1556. V. 51
Orlando Furioso... Lyons: 1570. V. 49
Orlando Furioso. Lyons: 1579. V. 48; 51
Orlando Furioso. London: 1607. V. 53
Orlando Furioso. Parigi: 1795-96. V. 50
Orlando Furioso. London: 1799. V. 48; 52
Orlando Furioso. London: 1807. V. 51
The Orlando Furioso. London: 1823-31. V. 53
Orlando Furioso and I Cinque Canti. Venice: 1603. V. 53
Orlando Furioso in English Heroical Verse. London: 1634. V. 47; 53
Orlando Furioso, Tutto Ricorretto, et di Nuove Figure Adornato... Venetia: 1556. V. 48

ARIS, ERNEST
Pirates Three. London. V. 51

Ten Little Bunny Boys. London: 1920. V. 47

ARISTAENETUS
The Love Epistles. London: 1771. V. 48; 52; 54

ARISTOCRACY. A Novel. New York: 1888. V. 52

ARISTOPHANES
The Birds. London: 1971. V. 52
The Eleven Comedies. New York: 1928. V. 48
The Frogs. Oxford: 1785. V. 52
The Frogs. 1937. V. 48
The Frogs. New York: 1937. V. 52; 53
(Greek title) *Aristophanis Facetissimi Commoediae undecim.* Basle: 1532. V. 48
Lysistrata. 1926. V. 52
Lysistrata. London: 1926. V. 48; 50
Lysistrata. New York: 1934. V. 50; 52; 53
A Metrical Version of the Acharnians, the Knights and the Birds. London: 1840.. V. 53
Women in Parliament. London: 1929. V. 47

ARISTOTELES
Aristoteles Art of Poetry. London: 1704. V. 54
Aristoteles Art of Poetry. London: 1705. V. 49
Aristoteles Poetics; or, Discourses Concerning Tragic and Epic Imitation. London: 1775. V. 52
The Complete Works of Aristotle. London: 1984. V. 52
De Optimo Statu Reipub. Libri octo. Paris: 1556. V. 51
De Poetica Liber. Oxford: 1760. V. 52
De Poetica Liber. Oxford: 1794. V. 48; 50
De Rhetorica seu Arte Dicendi Libri Tres... London: 1619. V. 47
Decem Libri Ethicorvm Seu Moralium Secundum Traductionem Ioannis Argyropili... Paris: 1514. V. 51
L'Ethica d'Aristotile. Florence: 1550. V. 47; 48
(Greek & Latin) *De Coloribus Libellus.* Florence: 1548. V. 52
(Greek title - Athenaion Politeia) *On the Constitution of Athens.* London: 1891. V. 47
(Greek title)...*de Moribus ad Nicomachum Libri Decem.* Heidelburgae: 1560. V. 47
Historia De Animalibus... Toulouse: 1619. V. 50
Logica. Lvgdvni: 1584. V. 49
Metaphysicorum Libri XIII. Ingolstadii: 1577. V. 48
The Metaphysics of Aristotle. London: 1801. V. 48
On the Parts of Animals. London: 1882. V. 52; 53
Opera Omnia. Paris: 1629. V. 47; 49; 50
Parva Naturalia. Venetus: 1512. V. 47; 50; 53
Physike Akroasis. (with) *Peri Psyches.* Parisiis: 1556. V. 49; 50
The Politics... Oxford: 1950. V. 49
Politics and Poetics. Lunenburg: 1964. V. 52; 54
Politics and Poetics. New York: 1964. V. 50
Problemata cum Commento...cum Petri de Apono...Commentarijs...Adiunctis Alexandri Aphrodisei: ac Plutarchi...Problematibus. Venice: 1518. V. 52
Problematum...Quaestiones mechanicae. De Miraculis Naturae, Physionomica... Venice: 1585. V. 49
The Rhetoric, Poetic and Nicomanchean Ethics of Aristotle. London: 1818. V. 48
Sententiae Omnes Undiquaque Selectissimae. Lugduni: 1570. V. 47; 49
A Treatise on Government. London: 1776. V. 53
The Works of. London: 1819. V. 50
The Works of... New England: 1831. V. 50; 51; 53

ARISTOTLE, PSEUD.
Aristotle's Compleat Master-Piece. London: 1710. V. 51; 52
Aristotle's Master-Piece Completed. New York: 1793. V. 50; 53
The Problems of Aristotle: with Other Philosophers and Physicians. London: 1689. V. 51
The Works of Aristotle. London: 1772. V. 51; 52; 53
The Works of Aristotle, the Famous Philosopher in Four Parts. New England: 1821. V. 50
The Works of Aristotle, the Famous Philosopher in Four Parts. New England: 1828. V. 53

ARIZONA at the World's Industrial and Cotton Centennial Exposition, New Orleans, 1884-85. Chicago: 1885. V. 49

THE ARIZONA Republican Phoenix, Arizona, August 1892. Phoenix: 1892. V. 52

ARIZONA. (TERRITORY)
Acts, Resolutions and Memorials, Adopted by the Second Legislative Assembly of the Territory of Arizona. Prescott: 1866. V. 49

ARKANSAS. LAWS, STATUTES, ETC. - 1860
Militia Laws of the State of Arkansas: Published by Direction of the Commander-in-Chief of the Army of the State. Little Rock: 1860. V. 48

ARKELL, A. J.
Early Khartoum: an Account of the Excavation of an Early Occupation Site Carried Out by the Sudan Government Antiquites Service in 1944-45. London: 1949. V. 51
Shaheinab: an Account of the Excavation of a Neolithic Occupation Site Carried Out for the Sudan Antiquities Service in 1949-50. London: 1953. V. 49; 51
Wanyanga and an Archaeological Reconnaissance of the south-West Libyan Desert: the British Ennedi Expedition. London: 1964. V. 49; 51

ARKELL, W. J.
English Barthonian Ammonites. London: 1951-58. V. 48; 50

ARKHAM House 1939 - 1964. 25th Anniversary. Sauk City: 1964. V. 47; 51

ARKWAKER, EDMUND
The Second Part of the Vision, a Pindarick Ode Occasioned by Their Majesties Happy Coronation. London: 1685. V. 53

ARKWRIGHT, RUTH
Brownikins & Other Fancies. London: 1910. V. 48

ARKWRIGHT, WILLIAM
The Pointer and His Predecessors. London: 1902. V. 47

ARLAND, MARCEL
Maternite. Paris: 1926. V. 53

ARLDT, C. W.
Ansichten aus dem Park zu Muskau. Muskau: 1850. V. 47

ARLEN, MICHAEL
Babes in the Wood. London: 1930. V. 50
The Green Hat. London: 1924. V. 51
Hell! Said the Duchess. London: 1934. V. 49
The Romantic Lady. London: 1921. V. 53

ARLINGTON, HENRY BENNETT, EARL OF
The Right Honourable Earl of Arlington's Letters to Sir W. Temple Bar. From July 1665, Being the First of His Employments Abroad, to September 1670, When He Was Recall'd... London: 1701. V. 47; 51

ARLOT, M.
A Complete Guide for Coach Painters. Philadelphia & London: 1888. V. 48
A Complete Guide for Coach Painters. Philadelphia: 1899. V. 54

ARLOTT, JOHN
Clausentum. London: 1946. V. 48; 50
Of Period and Place. London: 1944. V. 51

ARMAN, MARK
Fleurons: Their Place in History and in Print. Thaxted: 1988. V. 50
A Legacy of Metal Types. Thaxted: 1987. V. 48; 50; 52
Letterpress, Printers' Types and Decorations. Thaxted: 1993. V. 50

ARMAND
Alte und Neue Heimath. Breslau: 1859. V. 48

ARMENINI, GIOVAN BATTISTA
De' Veri Precetti della Pittura. Ravenna: 1587. V. 52; 54

ARMES, GEORGE A.
Ups and Downs of an Army Officer. Washington: 1900. V. 48; 49; 52

ARMFIELD, MAXWELL
An Artist in America. London: 1925. V. 50; 51; 53; 54

THE ARMIES of Asia and Europe: Embracing Official Reports of the Armies of Japan, China, India, Persia, Italy, Russia, Austria, Germany, France and England... New York: 1878. V. 48

ARMIGER, CHARLES
The Sportsman's Vocal Cabinet Comprising an Extensive Collection of Scarce, Curious and Original Songs and Ballads Relative to Field Sports... London: 1831. V. 47

ARMISTEAD, WILSON
A Tribute for the Negro: Being a Vindication of the Moral, Intellectual, and Religious Capabilities of the Coloured Portion of Mankind... Manchester: 1848. V. 50

ARMITAGE, ELLA S.
The Early Norman Castles of the British Isles. London: 1912. V. 53

ARMITAGE, JOHN
The History of Brazil, from the Period of the Arrival of the Barganza Family in 1808 to the Abdication of Don Pedro I in 1831. London: 1836. V. 47; 48; 51

ARMITAGE, MARY
Tales from Fairyland. London: 1930. V. 51

ARMITAGE, MERLE
Dance Memoranda. New York: 1947. V. 49; 52
The Lithographs of Rich and Day. New York: 1932. V. 47; 54
Martha Graham. Los Angeles: 1937. V. 49; 52
Napolitano. New York: 1935. V. 50
Rockwell Kent. New York: 1932. V. 48; 54
Schoenberg. New York: 1937. V. 49
Warren Newcombe. New York: 1932. V. 51

ARMITAGE, ROBERT
Doctor Johnson: His Religious Life and His Death. London: 1850. V. 51

ARMITT, M. L.
Ambleside Town and Chapel... Kendal: 1906. V. 48
Rydal. Kendal: 1916. V. 50; 52

ARMOR, SAMUEL
History of Orange County, California. Los Angeles: 1911. V. 52

ARMORY, THOMAS C.
Transfer of Erin; or the Acquisition of Ireland by England. Philadelphia: 1877. V. 51

ARMOUR, EDWARD DOUGLAS
A Treatise on the Investigation of Titles to Real Estate in Ontario etc. Toronto: 1887. V. 51

ARMOUR, GEORGE DENHOLM
Bridle and Brush, Reminiscences of an Artist Sportsman. London: 1937. V. 47; 48
A Hunting Alphabet. London: 1929. V. 47; 50
Pastime with Good Company. London: 1914. V. 47
Sport - "And There's the Humour of It". London. V. 49

Sport 'and there's the Humour of it'. London: 1935. V. 47

ARMOUR, JAMES
A Premonitor Warning; or Advice, by a True Lover of His Country. Edinburgh?: 1702. V. 54

ARMOUR, MARGARET
The Eerie Book. London: 1898. V. 49

ARMOUR, PHILIP DANFORTH
The Present Condition of the Live Cattle and Beef Markets of the United States and Causes Therefor. Chicago: 1889. V. 50

ARMS, DOROTHY NOYES
Churches of France. New York: 1929. V. 47

ARMS, J. T.
Twenty-One Years of Drawing: a Retrospective Exhibition of the Work of... New York: 1937. V. 53

ARMSTRONG, A. M.
The Place-Names of Cumberland. Cambridge: 1950-52. V. 50; 52

ARMSTRONG, A. N.
Oregon... Chicago: 1857. V. 53

ARMSTRONG, ALEX
Shantung (China): a General Outline of the Geography and History of the Province... Shanghai: 1891. V. 48

ARMSTRONG, AMZI
A Syllabus of Lectures on the Visions of the Revelation. Morris-town: 1815. V. 49; 52

ARMSTRONG, ARCHIE
Archie Armstrong's Banquet of Jests Together with Archie's Dream. London: 1872. V. 49

ARMSTRONG, E. A.
The Folklore of Birds. Collins: 1958. V. 51
The Wren. London: 1955. V. 48

ARMSTRONG, ELIZABETH
Robert Estienne, Royal Printer. Cambridge: 1954. V. 47; 51; 52

ARMSTRONG, G.
Early Life Among the Indians, Reminiscences from the Life of Benj. G. Armstrong, Treaties of 1835, 1837, 1842 and 1854. Habits and Customs of the Red Men of the Forest. Ashland: 1892. V. 53

ARMSTRONG, GEORGE
An Account of the Diseases Most Incident to Children, From the Birth Till the Age of Puberty... London: 1783. V. 49

ARMSTRONG, GEORGE W.
Memoirs of George W. Armstrong. Austin: 1958. V. 47

ARMSTRONG, HARRY
Aero-Space Medicine. Baltimore: 1961. V. 48; 53
Principles and Practice of Aviation Medicine. Baltimore: 1939. V. 49
Principles and Practice of Aviation Medicine. Baltimore: 1941. V. 50; 52

ARMSTRONG, JAMES
Carolina Light Infantry's Record in the Great War: The Story of a Gallant Company, Most of the Members of Which Were Boys. Charleston: 1912. V. 49

ARMSTRONG, JAMES LESLIE
Scenes in Craven: in a Series of Letters, Containing Interesting Sketches of Characters, and Notices of Some of the Principal Natural Curiosities. York: 1835. V. 47

ARMSTRONG, JOHN
The Art of Preserving Health. London: 1744. V. 47; 48; 50; 52; 54
The Art of Preserving Health. Kennebunk: 1804. V. 51
Miscellanies. London: 1770. V. 47; 48; 54
Of Benevolence: an Epistle to Eumenes. London: 1751. V. 51
Practical Illustrations of Typhus and Other Fevers: of Pulmonary Consumption, Measles, &c. Boston: 1829. V. 50; 53

ARMSTRONG LEAGUE OF HAMPTON WORKERS
Memories of Old Hampton. Hampton: 1909. V. 50

ARMSTRONG, LOUIS
Satchmo My Life in New Orleans. New York: 1954. V. 53
Swing that Music. London: 1936. V. 51
Swing That Music. New York: 1936. V. 47; 48

ARMSTRONG, MARGARET
Western Wild Flowers. New York and London: 1915. V. 52

ARMSTRONG, MARTIN
The Puppet Show. Waltham St. Lawrence: 1922. V. 47
Saint Hercules and Other Stories. London: 1927. V. 49; 52

ARMSTRONG, MOSTYN JOHN
An Actual Survey of the Great Post-Roads Between London and Edinburgh, with the country Three Miles, On Each Side, Drawn On a Scale of Half an Inch to a Mile. London: 1776. V. 47; 52

ARMSTRONG, NEVILL
After Big Game in the Upper Yukon. London: 1937. V. 47; 48; 53

ARMSTRONG, ORLAND K.
Old Massa's People: The Old Slaves Tell Their Story. Indianapolis: 1931. V. 48

ARMSTRONG, W. G.
The Industrial Resources of the District of the Three Northern Rivers. London: 1864. V. 50
Modern Naval Artillery. Newcastle: 1890. V. 48

ARMSTRONG, WALTER
Celebrated Pictures Exhibited at the Glasgow International Exhibition. London: 1888. V. 51
Memoir of Peter de Wint. London/New York: 1888. V. 50; 53
Sir Henry Raeburn. London: 1901. V. 52; 53; 54
Sir Joshua Reynolds. London: 1900. V. 51; 53
The Thames from its Rise to the Nore. London: 1887. V. 51

ARMSTRONG, ZELLA
Notable Southern Families. Chattanooga & Bristol: 1974. V. 52

ARMY Register for 1864. Washington: 1864. V. 47

ARNALDI, ENEA, CONTE
Idea di Un Teatro Nelle Principali Sue Parti Simile a'Teatri Antichi. Venice: 1762. V. 52

ARNALD OF VILLANOVA
The Earliest Printed Book on Wine... New York: 1943. V. 50

ARNALL, WILLIAM
The Complaint of the Children of Israel, Representing Their Grievances Under the Penal Law... London: 1736. V. 48

ARNASON, H. H.
Robert Motherwell. New York: 1977. V. 53

ARNAULD, ANTOINE
Logic; or, the Art of Thinking. London: 1693. V. 54
Logic; or, the Art of Thinking. London: 1696. V. 49
Logic; or the Art of Thinking. London: 1717. V. 54

ARNAY, JEAN RODOLPHE D'
Della Vita Priavata de' Romani. Napoli: 1763. V. 51; 52

ARNE, M.
Fairy Prince a Masque. 1771. V. 51
Lyric Harmony Consisting of Eighteen Entire New Ballads with Colin and Phaebe in Score as Performed at Vaux Hall Gardens... London: 1745. V. 51

ARNE, T. J.
Excavations at Shah Tepe, Iran. Stockholm: 1945. V. 49; 51

ARNE, THOMAS AUGUSTINE
The Guardian Out-Witted. London: 1764. V. 51

ARNETT, ETHEL STEPHENS
Confederate Guns Were Stacked Greensboro, North Carolina. Greensboro: 1965. V. 51

ARNETT, JOHN ANDREWS
Bibliopegia; or the Art of Bookbinding. London: 1835. V. 51
Bibliopegia: or, the Art of Bookbinding. London: 1836. V. 48

ARNHEIM, RUDOLF
Picasso's Guernica. London: 1864. V. 49

ARNO, PETER
Whoops Dearie!. New York: 1927. V. 48; 49; 50; 51

ARNOBIUS
Disputationum Adversus Gentes. Rome: 1542. V. 52
Disputationum Adversus Gentes Libri VIII... 1546. V. 47

ARNOBIUS, AFER
Disputationum Adversus Gentes Libri VIII... Basileae: 1546. V. 50

ARNOLD & SONS
Catalogue of Surgical Instruments and Appliances. London: 1895. V. 50

ARNOLD, ARTHUR
Through Persia by Caravan. London: 1877. V. 54

ARNOLD, C. D.
Official Views of the World's Columbian Exposition Issued by the Department of Photography. N.P: 1893. V. 54

ARNOLD, CHANNING
The American Egypt: a Record of Travel in Yucatan. New York: 1909. V. 52

ARNOLD, E. C.
Bird Reserves. London: 1940. V. 49
Birds of Eastbourne. Eastbourne: 1936. V. 50; 52
British Waders. Cambridge: 1924. V. 47

ARNOLD, EDWIN
Japonica. New York: 1891. V. 48
The Light of Asia... Avon: 1976. V. 47; 48; 53
The Light of Asia, or the Great Renunciation ... London: 1885. V. 54
The Light of Asia: or the Great Renunciation. London: 1889. V. 52; 54
The Light of Asia or, The Great Renunciation, Being the Life and Teaching of Gautama...Founder of Buddhism. London: 1906. V. 47
The Light of Asia: or, The Great Renunciation...The Life and Teaching of Gautama, Pricne of India and Founder of Buddhism. Boston: 1880. V. 50
The Light of Asia or the Great Reununciation. Philadelphia: 1922. V. 50
Seas and Lands. New York: 1891. V. 54
The Song Celestial or Bhagavad Gita. Philadelphia: 1934. V. 49
The Wonderful Adventures of Phra the Phoenician. London: 1891. V. 54

ARNOLD, F. T.
The Art of Accompaniment From a Thorough-Bass as Practised in the 17th & 18th Centuries. London: 1961. V. 49

ARNOLD, GOTTFRIED
A Biographical Sketch of the Life of Taulerus, a Popular Preacher of the Fourteenth Century. Richmond: 1836. V. 51

ARNOLD, HARRIET
A Voice from a Picture. London: 1839. V. 50

ARNOLD, J. B.
Nautical Archeology of Padre Island: The Spanish Shipwrecks of 1554. New York: 1978. V. 52

ARNOLD, JAMES NEWELL
Vital Record of Rhode Island 1636-1850. Providence: 1891-1912. V. 47

ARNOLD, JOSIAS LYNDON
Poems. Providence: 1797. V. 52

ARNOLD, LLOYD R.
High On the Wild with Hemingway. Caldwell: 1968. V. 47; 48; 49; 50

ARNOLD, MATTHEW
Civilization in the United States: First and Last Impressions. Boston: 1888. V. 53
Cromwell: a prize Poem, Recited in the Theatre, Oxford; June 28, 1843. Oxford: 1843. V. 49
Culture and Anarchy: an Essay in Political and Social Criticism. London: 1869. V. 49
Empedocles on Etna. London: 1852. V. 47; 49
Empedocles on Etna. London: 1896. V. 49
Empedocles on Etna. Portland: 1900. V. 52
Essays in Criticism. Boston: 1865. V. 54
Essays in Criticism. London and Cambridge: 1865. V. 47; 49
The Forsaken Merman. London: 1900. V. 48
A French Eton; or, Middle Class Education and the State. London and Cambridge: 1864. V. 49
Isaiah of Jerusalem in the Authorised English Version. London: 1883. V. 49; 51
Literature & Dogma. London: 1873. V. 49
Matthew Arnold on Civilisation in America from the Nineteenth Century for April 1888. Philadelphia: 1888. V. 53
Merope. London: 1858. V. 47
On the Study of Celtic Literature. London: 1867. V. 49
On Translating Homer, Last Words. London: 1862. V. 48; 49; 50; 51
On Translating Homer. Three Lectures Given at Oxford. London: 1861. V. 49
Poems... London: 1853. V. 49
Poems. London: 1855. V. 49
Poems. London: 1885-88. V. 48
Poems. London: 1888. V. 52
Poems. London: 1895. V. 49
Poems. Second Series. London: 1855. V. 47; 48; 49; 50; 51
The Popular Education of France, with Notices of That of Holland and Switzerland. London: 1861. V. 52
The Scholar Gipsy & Thrysis. London: 1919. V. 48
Selected Poems. London: 1878. V. 47; 49
The Strayed Reveller and Other Poems. London: 1849. V. 47; 49; 53
The Works... London: 1903. V. 50; 52

ARNOLD, OF VILLANOVA
Brevarium Practicae Medicinae. Venice: 1494/95. V. 48

ARNOLD, THOMAS
History of Rome. London: 1838-43. V. 50
History of Rome. London: 1840. V. 48
History of Rome. London: 1857. V. 48
Memorials of St. Edmund's Abbey. London: 1890-92. V. 49; 52

ARNOLD, THOMAS JAMES
Reynard the Fox. London: 1855. V. 51

ARNOLD, THOMAS W.
Bihzad and His Paintings in the Zafar-Namah Ms. London: 1930. V. 50; 53; 54
The Library of A. Chester Beatty, a Catalogue of the Indian Miniatures. Bloomsbury: 1936. V. 50
Painting in Islam, A Study of the Place of Pictorial Art in Muslim Culture. London: 1928. V. 50

ARNOLD, WILLIAM HARRIS
First Report of a Book-Collector. New York: 1898. V. 49; 52
A Record of Books and Letters Collected by William Harris Arnold. Jamaica, Queensborough,: 1901. V. 53
A Record of First Editions of Bryant, Emerson, Hawthorne, Holmes, Longfellow, Lowell, Thoreau, Whittier. New York: 1901. V. 48

ARNOLDI, E.
Descrizione Delle Architetture. Vicenza: 1779. V. 51

ARNOLDS & SONS
Catalogue of Surgical Instruments. London: 1888. V. 48

ARNOT, FREDERICK S.
Bihe and Garenganze: a Record of Four Years' Work and Journeying in Central Africa. London: 1893. V. 54

ARNOT, HUGO
A Collection and Abridgement of Celebrated Criminal Trials in Scotland, from A.D. 1536 to 1784. Edinburgh: 1785. V. 51

ARNOT, HUGO continued
An Essay on Nothing. London: 1776. V. 51
The History of Edinburgh. London: 1779. V. 51
The History of Edinburgh...to Which is Added...Improvements of the city from the 1763 (sic) to the Present Period. Edinburgh: 1788. V. 52

ARNOTT, HENRY
Cancer: Its Varieties, Their Histology and Diagnosis. London: 1872. V. 48; 53

ARNOTT, JAMES
The House of Arnot and Some Of Its Branches. Edinburgh: 1918. V. 51; 52

ARNOTT, NEIL
On the Smokeless Fire-Place, Chimney-Valves and Other Means, Old and New of Obtaining Healthful Warmth and Ventilation. London: 1855. V. 53
On Warming and Ventilating; with Directions for Making and Using the Thermometer-Stove, or Self-Regulating Fire and Other New Apparatus. London: 1838. V. 51; 53
Reports on an Inquiry Ordered by the Secretary of State, Relative to the Prevalence of Disease at Croydon, and to the Plan of Sewerage, Together with an Abstract of Evidence Accompanying the Reports. London: 1853. V. 53
A Survey of Human Progress, from the Savage State to the Highest Civilization Yet Attained... London: 1861. V. 49

ARNOTT, SAMUEL
The Column Called the Monument, Described, Erected to Perpetuate the Dreadful Fire of London in the Year 1666; of the Rebuilding the City... London: 1805. V. 47; 53
Keeper of the Monument. London: 1805. V. 50

ARNOULD, JOSEPH
Memoir of Thomas, First Lord Denman. London: 1873. V. 48

ARNOUX, GUY
French Soldiers at War. Paris: 1917. V. 54

ARNOW, HARRIETTE SIMPSON
The Dollmaker. (with) The First Chapter of the Dollmaker. New York: 1954. V. 49
Flowering of the Cumberland. New York: 1963. V. 50
Hunter's Horn. New York: 1949. V. 51; 52; 54

ARNSTEIN, FLORA J.
A Legacy of Hours. San Francisco: 1927. V. 47

ARONSON, BORIS
Sovremennaya Evreiskaya Graphika. (Contemporary Jewish Graphics). Berlin: 1924. V. 47; 53

ARONSON, J. K.
An Account of the Foxglove and Medical Uses, 1785-1985.. London: 1985. V. 52

AROUND the Year. New York: 1957. V. 49

ARP/Delaunay/Magnelli/Taeuber-Arp. Paris: 1950. V. 47

ARRABAL, FERNANDO
And They Put Handcuffs on the Flowers. New York: 1973. V. 51
The Architect and the Emperor of Assyria. New York: 1969. V. 51
Garden of Delights. New York: 1974. V. 51
Pic-Nic on the Battlefield. Columbus: 1983. V. 49
The Tower Struck by Lightning. New York: 1988. V. 53

THE ARRAIGNMENT, Trials, Conviction and Condemnation of Sir. Rich. Grahme...and John Ashton...for High Treason. London: 1691. V. 53

ARRHENIUS, SVANTE
Immunochemistry: The Application of the Principles of Physical Chemistry to the Study of the Biological Antibodies. New York: 1907. V. 48; 51
Quantitative Laws in Biological Chemistry. London: 1915. V. 48; 51

ARRIANUS, FLAVIUS
Arrian's History of Alexander's Expedition. London: 1729. V. 48
The Cynegeticus of the Younger Xenophon. London: 1831. V. 48
(Greek)...De Expeditione sive Rebvs Gestis Alexandri Macedonum Regis Libri Octo. Basel: 1539. V. 54

ARRINGTON, A. W.
The Rangers and Regulators of the Tanaha; or Life Among the Lawless - a Tale of the Republic of Texas. New York: 1856. V. 54

ARROL, WILLIAM, & CO. LTD.
Bridges, Structural Steel Work and Mechanical Engineering Productions. London: 1909. V. 51

ARROW, JOHN
J. C. Squire v. D. H. Lawrence: a Reply to Mr. Squire's Article in "The Observer" of March 9th, 1930. 1930. V. 53

ARROW, SIMON
Count Fanny's Nuptials: Being the Story of a Courtship. London: 1907. V. 50

ARROWMAMMETT WORKS, MIDDLETOWN, CONNECTICUT
Catalogue and Invoice Price List of Bench Planes, and Moulding Tools...Manufactured and for Sale at the Arrowmammett Works, Middletown, Conn. Middletown: 1858. V. 47

ARROWSMITH, A.
A Comparative Atlas of Ancient and Modern Geography. Eton: 1828. V. 51
Orbis Terrarum. A Compartive Atlas of Ancient and Modern Georgraphy. London: 1828. V. 50; 53

ARROWSMITH, H. W.
The House Decorator and Painter's Guide... London: 1840. V. 47; 49; 50

ARROWSMITH, JOSEPH
The Reformation. London: 1673. V. 47; 49

ARS Islamica. Volume IV. Ann Arbor: 1937. V. 54

ARS Notariatus; or, the Art and Office of a Notary PUblic, as the Same Is Practiced in Scotland... Edinburgh: 1762. V. 50; 54

ARSANES
Orations of Arsanes Agaynst Philip the Trecherous Kyng of Macedone... London: 1560. V. 50

ARSENIEV, V. K.
Dersu the Trapper. New York: 1941. V. 49

ARSLAN, EDOARDO
Gothic Architecture in Venice. London: 1971. V. 49; 51; 53; 54

THE ART Album Sixteen Facsimiles of Water-Colour Drawings by George Catermole, T. Sidney Cooper... London: 1861. V. 50; 54

THE ART Amateur. 1887-1890. N.P: 1887-90. V. 49

ART and Letters. London: 1919. V. 49

ART and War: Canadian War Memorials. London. V. 49
ART and War: Canadian War Memorials. London: 1919?. V. 54

ART At Auction: the Year at Sotheby's. New York: 1968-91. V. 50

ART Deco. The Books of Francois Louis Schmied Artist/Engraver/Printer... San Francisco: 1987. V. 51

ART in California. A Survey of American Art with Special Reference to Californian Painting, Sculpture, and Architecture. Irvine: 1988. V. 52

ART in Industry through the Ages. New Delhi: 1982. V. 52

THE ART Journal, 1876. New York: 1876. V. 51

THE ART Journal Illustrated Catalogue: the Industry of All Nations 1851. London. V. 48

THE ART of Anastatic Printing. Kidlington: 1986. V. 48

ART of China. Taiwan. V. 48

THE ART of Dress; or, Guide to the Toilette: With Directions for Adapting the Various Parts of the Female Costume to the Complexion and Figure; Hints on Cosmetics &c. London: 1839. V. 50

THE ART of Engaging the Affections of Wives to Heir Husbands. Berwick: 1793. V. 53

THE ART of Living in London. London: 1768. V. 51; 53

THE ART of Making Fireworks; to Which is Added, the History of Guy Fawks (sic) and Gunpowder Plot... London: 1813. V. 48

THE ART of Manual Defence, or System of Boxing... London: 1799. V. 53

THE ART of Painting in Miniature. London: 1752. V. 51

THE ART of Painting in Oil, Rendered Familiar to Every Capacity... London: 1801. V. 47

ART Work of Middlesex County, New Jersey. Chicago: 1896. V. 47

ART Work of Mississippi. Chicago: 1901. V. 54

ART Work of Seattle and Alaska. Racine: 1907. V. 47; 52

ART Work of Tacoma and Vicinity, Washington. Racine: 1907. V. 48; 53

ART Work of the State of Oregon. Portland: 1909. V. 47

ART Work on Toronto. Toronto: 1984. V. 50

ARTAMONOV, M. I.
Treasures from Scythian Tombs in the Hermitage Museum, Leningrad. London: 1969. V. 52

ARTAUD, ANTONIN
Artaud le Momo. Lyon: 1957. V. 49

ARTEMIDORUS, DALDIANUS
Oneirokriton Biblia Pente/de Somniorum Interpretatione Libre Quinque. Venetiis: 1518. V. 52

ARTEMY, ARARATSKY
Memoirs of the Life of Artemi, of Wagarschapat, Near Mount Ararat, in Armenia. London: 1822. V. 47

ARTHAUD, C.
Enchanted Visions: Fantastic Houses and Their Treasures. New York: 1972. V. 54

ARTHUR, ELIZABETH
Beyond the Mountain. New York: 1983. V. 52
Thunder Bay District. 1821-1892. A Collection of Documents. Toronto: 1973. V. 53

ARTHUR, ERIC R.
The Early Buildings of Ontario. Toronto: 1938. V. 54
Small Houses of the Late 18th and Early 19th Centuries in Ontario. Toronto: 1927. V. 54

ARTHUR, GEORGE
Bushwhacker: a True Story of Bill Wilson. Rolla: 1938. V. 53
The Story of the Household Cavalry. London: 1909. V. 54

ARTHUR, JOHN PRESTON
Western North Carolina: a History (from 1730 to 1913). Raleigh: 1914. V. 48

ARTHUR, STANLEY CLISBY
Old New Orleans: a History of the Vieux Carre, Its Ancient and Historical Buildings. New Orleans: 1936. V. 50

ARTHUR, T. W.
Arthur's Directory of Carlisle... Carlisle: 1880. V. 52

ARTHUR, TIMOTHY SHAY
A Book About Boys. London: 185-?. V. 47; 49
Cast Adrift. Cincinnati: 1873. V. 50
Confessions of a Housekeeper. Philadelphia: 1851. V. 52; 53
Our Little Harry and Other Poems and Stories. Philadelphia: 1852. V. 49
Pierre, the Organ Boy and Other Stories. Philadelphia: 1852. V. 49
The Seamstress. Philadelphia: 1843. V. 52
Ten Nights in a Bar-Room and What I Saw There. Philadelphia: 1854. V. 47

ARTHURIAN SOCIETY
Arthuriana. Proceedings of the Arthurian Society. Oxford: 1928-29/29-30. V. 50

ARTICLES
Drawn Up by order of the Edinburgh Society, with the View to Render More Complete the Laws Concerning Highways, Bridges and Ferries. N.P: 1770?. V. 52

ARTIFICIANA;
or, A Guide to the Principal Trades. Edinburgh: 1820. V. 53

ARTILLEUR
de France. France: 1936. V. 50

ART INSTITUTE, CHICAGO
The Native American Heritage. Chicago: 1977. V. 54

ARTIS, E. T.
Antediluvian Phytology, Illustrated by a Collection of the Fossil Remains of Plants, Peculiar to the Coal Formations of Great Britain. London: 1825. V. 48; 49

THE ARTIST
and the Printer. A Portfolio of Four Prints by Josef Albers, Antonio Frasconi, Gabor Peterdi and Reginald Pollack. New York: 1965. V. 49

ARTISTIC BRONZE CO., BRIDGEPORT
A Catalogue (no. 11) of Unique Creations in Brass and Bronze... Bridgeport: 1930. V. 54

ARTISTS
and Writers Protest Against the War in Viet Nam. N.P: 1967. V. 52

ARTS
and Crafts Essays by Members of the Arts and Crafts Exhibition Society. London: 1893. V. 50

ARTS
and Crafts of China. Peking: 1959. V. 50

ART'S
Masterpiece: or, a Companion for the Ingenious of Either Sex. London: 1721. V. 53

THE ARTS
of the Ch'ing Dynasty: an Exhibition Organized by the Arts Council of Great Britain and the Oriental Ceramic Society. May 26th-July 2nd 1964. V. 54

ARTS
Revealed and Universal Guide... New York: 1853. V. 49

ARTUS, WILIBALD
Hand-Atlas Sammtlicher Medicinisch-Pharmaceutischer Gewachse Oder Naturgetreue Abbildungen Nebst Beschreibungen in Botanischer... Jena: 1876. V. 54

ARUNDEL, THOMAS, EARL OF
The Arundel Cabinet of Gems. 1867. V. 53

ARUNDELL, F. V. J.
Discoveries in Asia Minor; Including a Description of the Ruins of Several Ancient Cities and Especially Antioch of Pisidia. London: 1834. V. 52

ASBJORNSEN, PETER CHRISTEN
At the Back of the North Wind. London: 1871. V. 47
East of the Sun and West of the Moon. London: 1913. V. 48
East of the Sun and West of the Moon. New York: 1913-14. V. 48
East of the Sun and West of the Moon. London: 1914. V. 47; 49; 50
East of the Sun and West of the Moon. Garden City: 1925. V. 53
East of the Sun and West of the Moon. New York: 1927. V. 48; 53
East of the Sun and West of the Moon. London: 1930. V. 54
East of the Sun and West of the Moon. New York: 1930. V. 54

ASBOTH, J. DE
An Offical Tour Through Bosnia and Herzegovina, with An Account of the History, Antiquities, Agrarian Conditions, Religion, Ethnology, Folk Lore and Social Life of the People... London: 1890. V. 50

ASBURY, HERBERT
Up From Methodism. New York: 1926. V. 48; 51

ASBURY, R. O. D.
An Alphabetically Arrranged and an Almost Alliterative Accompaniment, to the Acquisition of the Art of Accurate Available Articulation. Jaffna: 1862. V. 49

ASCH, SHOLEM
The Nazarene. New York: 1939. V. 52
The Prophet. New York: 1955. V. 50

ASCHAM, ROGER
Apologia Pro Caena Dominica. London: 1577. V. 47; 49; 53
Disertissimi Viri Rogeri Aschami Angli, Regiae Olim Maiestate A Latinis Epistolis, Familiarum Epistolaru Libri Tres, Magna Orationis Elegantis Conscripti. Londini: 1590. V. 47; 48; 49
Disertissimi Viri Rogeri Aschami...Familiarium Epistolarum Libri Tres. London: 1590/89. V. 48; 52
The English Works of Roger Ascham Preceptor to Queen Elizabeth. London: 1761. V. 50; 53
The English Works of Roger Ascham Preceptor to Queen Elizabeth. London: 1815. V. 48
Familiarium Epistolarum Libri Tres. London: 1590/89. V. 50
Rogeri Aschami...Familiarum Epistolarum Libri III. Magna Orationis Elegantia Conscripti, Nunc Postremo Emendati U Aucti. Coloniae Allobrogum,: 1611. V. 47
The Scholemaster Or Plaine and Perfite Way of Teaching Children, to Vnderstand, Write and Speake.. London: 1573. V. 47; 49
The Scholemaster: Shewing a Plain and Perfect Way of Teaching the Learned Languages. London: 1743. V. 49; 54
The Schoolmaster; or, Plain and Perfect Way of Teaching Children to Understand, Write and Speak the Latin Tongue... London: 1711. V. 47; 51
Toxophilus, the Schole, or Partitions, of Shooting. Wrexham: 1788. V. 52

ASGILL, JOHN
An Essay on a Registry for Title of Lands. London: 1698. V. 52

ASH, CHARLES BOWKER
Adbaston: a Poem. Bath: 1814. V. 54
The Hermit of Hawkstone: a Descriptive Poem. Bath: 1816. V. 54
The Poetical Works. London: 1831. V. 47

ASH, EDWARD C.
Dogs: Their History and Development. London: 1927. V. 48; 49

ASH, F.
The Radium Seekers. 1908. V. 47; 51

ASH, JOHN
The Easiest Introduction to Dr. Lowth's English Grammar... London: 1768. V. 52
Grammatical Institutes; or an Easy Introduction to Dr. Lowth's English Grammar... London: 1779. V. 53
Grammatical Institutes: or, an Easy Introduction to Dr. Lowth's English Grammar. Philadelphia: 1795. V. 53
Grammatical Institutes; or, an Easy Introduction to Dr. Lowth's English Grammar... London: 1801. V. 47
The New and Complete Dictionary of the English Language... London: 1775. V. 50; 53

ASHBEE, CHARLES ROBERT
American Sheaves and English Seed Corn... London: 1901. V. 49; 50; 51
Conradin. 1908. V. 54
Conradin. London: 1908. V. 52
Echoes from the City of the Sun. London: 1905. V. 47; 49
An Endeavour Towards the Teaching of John Ruskin and William Morris. London: 1901. V. 47; 52; 54
Jerusalem 1918-1920: Being the Records of the Pro-Jerusalem Council During the Period of the British Military Administrataion. London: 1921. V. 49; 51
Last Records of a Cotswold Community. London: 1904. V. 47
The Masque of the Edwards of England. London: 1902. V. 49; 50; 51; 53
Modern English Silverwork... London: 1974. V. 47
The Trinity Hospital in Mile End: an Object Lesson in National History. 1896. V. 54
The Trinity Hospital in Mile End: an Object Lesson in National History. London: 1896. V. 47
Where the Great City Stands, a Study in New Civics. London: 1917. V. 52

ASHBEE, HENRY SPENCER
Bibliography of Prohibited Books. New York: 1962. V. 47; 48
A Bibliography of Tunisia from the Earliest Time to the End of 1888 (in two Parts) Including Utica and Carthage, the Punic Wars, the Roman Occupation, the Arab Conquest, the Expeditions of Louis IX and Charles V, and the French Protectorate. London: 1889. V. 47
Bibliotheca Arcana seu Catalogus Librorum Pentralium. London: 1884. V. 54
An Iconography of Don Quixote 1605-1895. Aberdeen: 1895. V. 48

ASHBERY, JOHN
As We Know. New York: 1981. V. 50
Double Dream of Spring. New York: 1970. V. 47; 50
Fragment. Los Angeles: 1969. V. 47; 49; 50
A Nest of Ninnies. New York: 1969. V. 54
The Poems. New York: 1960. V. 47
Rivers and Mountains. New York: 1966. V. 47; 48; 50
Self-Portrait in a Convex Mirror. New York: 1975. V. 47; 48; 50
Self-Portrait in a Convex Mirror. San Francisco: 1984. V. 47; 53
Shadow Train: Poems. New York: 1981. V. 54
Some Trees. New Haven: 1956. V. 48; 51
The Tennis Court Oath. Middletown: 1962. V. 47; 51
Three Madrigals. New York: 1968. V. 47; 50; 52
Three Plays. Calais: 1978. V. 47
The Vermont Notebook. Los Angeles: 1975. V. 50

ASHBRIDGE, ELIZABETH
Some Account of the Early Part of the Life of Elizabeth Ashbridge... Philadelphia: 1807. V. 47

ASHBURNHAM, JOHN
A Narrative of John Ashburnham of His Attendance on King Charles the First From Oxford to the Scotch Army... London: 1830. V. 47; 50

ASHBURTON, RICHARD BARRE DUNNING, BARON
Genealogical Memoirs of the Royal House of France, Forming a Commentary Upon the Genealogical Table of that Illustrious and Ancient House. London: 1825. V. 49

ASHBY, MATTHEW
Ashby and White: or, the Great Question, Whether an Action Lies at Common Law for an Elector, Who is Deny'd His Vote for Members of Parliament? Debated and Resolv'd. London: 1705. V. 48; 51; 53

ASHBY, N. B.
The Riddle of the Sphinx. Des Moines: 1890. V. 50

ASHBY, PROFESSOR
Helen Howard or the Bankrupt and Broker. Boston: 1845. V. 47; 51
Viola: the Redeemed. Boston: 1845. V. 47; 51; 52

ASHBY, THOMAS ALMOND
The Valley Campaigns Being the Reminiscences of a Non-Combatant While Between the Lines in the Shenandoah Valley During the War of the States. New York: 1914. V. 49

ASHBY, W. ROSS
Design for a Brain. New York: 1952. V. 48; 52; 54
Design for a Brain. London: 1960. V. 48; 50; 52; 54

ASHDOWN, CHARLES H.
British Castles. London: 1911. V. 54

ASHDOWNE, J.
The Churchwarden's and Overseer's Guide and Director, Written and Arranged for the Use of Parish Officers and Others Desirous of Acquiring parochial Information. London: 1824. V. 53

ASHE, ARTHUR R.
A Hard Road to Glory: A History of the African-American Athlete. New York: 1993. V. 52

ASHE, R. P.
Chronicles of Uganda. London: 1894. V. 52; 54
Two Kings of Uganda; or, Life by the Shores of Victoria Nyanza. London: 1889. V. 47

ASHE, SAMUEL A.
The Charge at Gettysburg. Raleigh: 1887. V. 49
Cyclopedia of Eminent and Representative Men of the Carolinas of the Nineteenth Century. Madison: 1892. V. 50

ASHE, THOMAS
History of the Azores or Western Islands. London: 1813. V. 51
The Spirit of "The Book"; or, Memoirs of Caroline, Princess of Hasburgh, a Political and Amatory. London: 1811. V. 47; 49
Travels in America, 1806, for the Purpose of Exploring the Rivers Alleghany, Monongahela, Ohio and Mississippi.. London: 1809. V. 49
Travels in America, Performed in 1806. Newburyport: 1808. V. 53

ASHENDENE PRESS
A Chronological List, with Prices, of The Forty Books printed at the Ashendene Press. MDCCCXCV-MCMXXV. Chelsea: 1935. V. 49; 52; 53; 54
A Descriptive Bibliography of the Books Printed at the Ashendene Press, 1895-1935. London: 1935. V. 47; 50
A Hand-List of the Books Printed at the Ashendene Press MDCCCXCV-MCMXXV. Chelsea: 1925. V. 51; 54

ASHER, ADOLF
A Bibliographical Essay on the Sriptores Rerum Germanicarum. London: 1843. V. 48

ASHFORD, DAISY
The Young Visiters. London: 1918. V. 50
The Young Visiters. New York: 1919. V. 54

ASHFORD, FAITH
Poor Man's Pence. Ditching, Sussex: 1917. V. 52
A Soul Cake. Ditchling: 1919. V. 52
A Soul Cake. Ditchling: 1924. V. 48
Things Unseen. A Book of Verse. Ditchling, Sussex: 1924. V. 49; 52

ASHHURST, J.
The International Encyclopedia of Surgery. New York: 1881-86. V. 53

ASHHURST, WILLIAM
Reasons Against Agreement with a Late printed Paper, Intituled, Foundations of Freedome; or, the Agreement of the People. London: 1648. V. 53

ASHLEY, C. W.
The Ashley Book of Knots. London: 1948. V. 49

ASHLEY, CLIFFORD W.
Whaleships of New Bedford. Boston & New York: 1929. V. 50; 52; 53
The Yankee Whaler. Boston and New York: 1926. V. 50; 51; 52

ASHLEY, DORIS
King Arthur and the Knights of the Round Table. London. V. 51

ASHLEY, JOHN
The Present State of the British and French Trade to Africa and America Consider'd and Compar'd... London: 1745. V. 47

ASHLEY, WILLIAM H.
The West of William Ashley... Denver: 1964. V. 51; 52; 53

ASHMOLE, ELIAS
The Antiquities of Berkshire. London: 1719. V. 52
Autobiographical and Historical Notes, Correspondence and Other contemporary Sources Relating to His Life and Work. London: 1966. V. 50; 51
The Institution, Laws and Ceremonies of the Most Noble Order of the Garter. London: 1672. V. 47; 54
Memoirs of the Life of that Learned Antiquary... London: 1717. V. 48
Theatrum Chemicum Britannicum... London: 1652. V. 48
The Way of Bliss. London: 1658. V. 48

ASHMOLEAN MUSEUM
Catalogue of the Collection of Drawings. 1938/56/80/82. V. 50; 54
Catalogue of the Collection of Dutch and Flemish Still-Life Pictures Bequeathed by Daisy Linda Ward. 1950. V. 54

ASHMUN, JEHUDI
History of the American Colony in Liberia from December 1821 to 1823. Washington City: 1826. V. 52

ASHPITEL, ARTHUR
The Factor, the Miller and the Baker Get More Than the Farmer and Ten Times More Than the Landlord Out of the Loaf. London: 1839. V. 49

ASHTON, DORE
Richard Lindner. New York: 1969. V. 48; 49; 50; 52; 53
Robert Motherwell. Buffalo: 1983. V. 50

ASHTON, JAMES
The Book of Nature... New York: 1861. V. 52

ASHTON, JOHN
Chap-Books of the Eighteenth Century. London: 1882. V. 50; 52
Curious Creatures in Zoology. London: 1890. V. 51
A History of English Lotteries Now for the First Time Written. London: 1893. V. 52; 54
Humour, Wit and Satire of the 17th Century. London: 1883. V. 49; 51; 53
Modern Street Ballads. London: 1888. V. 49
Old Times, a Picture of Social Life at the End of the Eighteenth Century... London: 1885. V. 49
A Righte Merrie Christmasse!. London: 1890. V. 47

ASHTON, LEIGH
The Art of India and Pakistan. A Commemorative Catalogue of the Exhibition at the Royal Academy of Arts London, 1947-48. London: 1950. V. 54
The Art of India and Pakistan: a Commemorative Catalogue of the Exhibition Held at the Royal Academy of Arts, London. London: 1947-48. V. 50
An Introduction to the Study of Chinese Sculpture. New York: 1924. V. 50

ASHTON, S.
The Green Cat. 1915. V. 49

ASHTON, T. J.
On the Diseases, Injuries and Malformations of the Rectum and Anus: with Remarks on Habitual Constipation. London: 1860. V. 53
On the Diseases, Injuries and Malformations of the Rectum and Anus; with Remarks on Habitual Constipation. Philadelphia: 1865. V. 48
Prolapsus Fistula in Ano, and Haemorrhodial Affections: Their Pathology and Treatment. London: 1863. V. 48; 53

ASHTOWN, FREDERICK O. TRENCH, BARON
The Unknown Power Behind the IRish Nationalist Party. London: 1908. V. 47

ASHWAL, STEPHEN
The Founders of Child Neurology. San Francisco: 1990. V. 47; 48; 49; 50; 53; 54

ASHWORTH, CALEB
The Hebrew Grammar, With Principal Rules... London: 1804. V. 51

ASHWORTH, JOHN HENRY
The Saxon in Ireland; or, the Rambles of an Englishman in Search of a Settlement in the West of Ireland. London: 1851. V. 47

ASHWORTH, THOMAS
The Salmon Fisheries of England, 1868...to Which is Added Valuable and Exclusive Information (from) France, America, Norway & Russia. London: 1868. V. 47

ASIATIC Art in Japanese Collections. Tokyo. V. 50

ASIATIC Researches; or Transactions of the Society Instituted in Bengal for Inquiring Into the History and Antiquities, the Arts, Sciences, and Literature of Asia. London: 1799. V. 50

ASIMOV, ISAAC
Asimov's Sherlockian Limericks. New York: 1978. V. 54
The Caves of Steel. London: 1954. V. 54
The Caves of Steel. New York: 1954. V. 48; 51
The Currents of Space. New York: 1952. V. 51; 53
The Day of Eternity. New York: 1955. V. 54
The Dream, Benjamin's Dream and Benjamin's Bicentennial Blast. 1976. V. 47; 51
Earth is Room Enough. New York: 1957. V. 48; 52
The End of Eternity. Garden City: 1955. V. 47
The End of Eternity. New York: 1955. V. 49
Fantastic Voyage. 1966. V. 54
Fantastic Voyage. Boston: 1966. V. 50
Fantastic Voyage II. New York: 1987. V. 48; 50; 52; 54
Foundation. 1951. V. 48; 49; 54
Foundation. New York: 1951. V. 47; 48; 51; 52
Foundation and Earth. New York: 1986. V. 49; 54
Foundation and Empire. New York: 1952. V. 47
Foundation, Foundation & Empire & Second Foundation. 1951-53. V. 48; 50; 52
The Foundation Trilogy. New York: 1963. V. 50
Foundation's Edge. Garden City: 1982. V. 49; 50; 51; 53
The Gods Themselves. New York: 1972. V. 49; 54
I, Robot. 1950. V. 48; 54
I, Robot. 1952. V. 49
An Isaac Asimov Omnibus. 1966. V. 51; 53
Little Brothers. 1988. V. 52; 53
Lucky Starr and the Moons of Jupiter. New York: 1957. V. 48; 52
Marginalia. Cambridge: 1966. V. 51
The Martian Way and Other Stories. New York: 1955. V. 49
The Naked Sun. London: 1958. V. 51; 52

AUDEN, J. E.
A Short History of the Albrighton Hunt. London: 1905. V. 47

AUDEN, WYSTAN HUGH
About the House. London: 1966. V. 53
The Age of Anxiety. New York: 1947. V. 49; 51; 53
The Age of Anxiety. London: 1948. V. 48; 51
Another Time. London: 1940. V. 51
Another Time. New York: 1940. V. 47
The Ascent of F6. London: 1936. V. 51; 53; 54
The Ascent of F6. New York: 1937. V. 47; 49
Auden: Five Poems. Cedar Falls: 1984. V. 51
The Collected Poetry. New York: 1945. V. 53
Collected Shorter Poems, 1927-1957. London: 1966. V. 49
Collected Shorter Poems 1927-1957. New York: 1966. V. 48
Collected Shorter Poems 1930-1944. London: 1950. V. 51
The Dance of Death. London: 1933. V. 48; 49; 51; 52; 53
The Dog Beneath the Skin. London: 1935. V. 47; 50; 54
The Double Man. New York: 1941. V. 47; 48; 51
The Dyer's Hand and Other Essays. New York: 1962. V. 52
Education, Today - and Tomorrow. London: 1939. V. 50
The Enchafed Flood. London: 1950. V. 49
The Enchafed Flood. New York: 1950. V. 50
The English Auden. Poems, Essays and Dramatic Writings 1927-1939. London: 1977. V. 53
Five Poems. Athens: 1983. V. 53; 54
Five Poems. Cedar Falls: 1983. V. 48; 53
For the Time Being. New York: 1944. V. 53
For the Time Being. New York: 1947. V. 53
The Frontier. A Melodrama in Three Acts. London: 1938. V. 48
Homage to Clio. London: 1960. V. 50; 53
Journey to a War. London: 1939. V. 53
Journey to a War. New York: 1939. V. 53
Letters from Iceland. London: 1937. V. 47; 50; 54
Look, Stranger!. London: 1936. V. 50; 51; 53
Louis MacNeice, a Memorial Address. London: 1963. V. 48
The Magic Flute. New York: 1956. V. 54
The Magic Flute. London: 1957. V. 51
Nones. New York: 1950. V. 48; 49
Nones. New York: 1951. V. 52; 53
Nones. London: 1952. V. 48; 49
The Old Man's Road. New York: 1956. V. 48; 54
On the Frontier. London: 1938. V. 47; 49; 51; 54
The Orators. London: 1932. V. 47; 48; 50; 51
The Platonic Blow. New York: 1965. V. 47; 48
Poems. London: 1930. V. 47; 48; 49; 50; 53
Poems. London: 1933. V. 54
Poems. London: 1974. V. 47
Poets of the English Language. New York: 1950. V. 54
Secondary Words. London: 1968. V. 54
Selected Songs of Thomas Campion. Boston: 1973. V. 48
Selections from Poems by Auden. London: 1974. V. 52
The Shield of Achilles. New York: 1955. V. 49
Some Poems. London: 1940. V. 48
Spain. London: 1937. V. 47; 48; 49; 53; 54
Table Talk of W. H. Auden. New York: 1989. V. 54
Three Songs for St. Cecilia's Day. New York: 1941. V. 48; 49; 51; 52; 53
Two Poems. Bryn Mawr: 1934. V. 53
Poems. New York: 1968. V. 52; 53; 54

AUDSLEY, CHARLES, M. G.
Tethys and Tethys. London: 1988. V. 50

AUDSLEY, JOHN
A Visit to Constantinople and some of the Greek Islands, in the Spring and Summer of 1833. London: 1835. V. 52

AUDSLEY, GEORGE A.
Organ Building. 1905. V. 52
Keramic Art of Japan. Liverpool: 1875. V. 48
Keramic Art of Japan. London: 1881. V. 47
The Ornamental Arts of Japan. London: 1882-84. V. 51
The Modern Decorator and Ornamentist. Glasgow: 1892. V. 50

AUDSLEY, W.
Cottage and Villa Architecture. London: 1860. V. 54
The Art of Illuminating and Missal Painting. London: 1862. V. 51
Polychromatic Decoration as Applied to Building in the Medieval Styles. London: 1882. V. 48;

AUDUBON, JOHN JAMES
Audubon Society Baby Elephant Folio, Audubon's Birds of America. New York: 1990.
Birds of America. New York: 1990. V. 53
Birds of America. London: 1937. V. 54
Birds of America. London: 1981. V. 49
Birds of America from Drawings Made in the United States and Their Territories. New York: V. 47

Original Water Color Paintings by J. J. Audubon for The Birds of America. New York: 1966. V. 48; 49; 50; 51; 53; 54
The Original Water Color Paintings for the Birds of America. London: 1966. V. 49
The Original Water-Color Paintings by John James Audubon. 1966. V. 51
Ornithological Biography, or an Account of the Habits of the Birds of the United States of America. Edinburgh: 1831-35. V. 49; 51; 54
Quadrapeds of North America. 1989. V. 53
The Quadrupeds of North America. New York: 1849-54. V. 47; 48
The Quadrupeds of North America. New York: 1856. V. 53
The Viviparous Quadrupeds of North America. New York: 1846-51. V. 52

AUDUBON, JOHN WOODHOUSE
Audubon's Western Journal: 1849-1850. Cleveland: 1906. V. 52; 53

AUDUBON, MARIA R.
Audubon and His Journals. New York: 1897. V. 50; 53

AUEL, JEAN
The Clan of the Cave Bear. The Valley of the Horses. The Mammoth Hunters. 1980/82/85. V. 47

AUENBRUGER, LEOPOLD
Nouvelle methode Pour Reconnaitre les Maladies Internes de La Poitrine Par La Percussion de Cette Cavite... Paris: 1808. V. 48

AUER, ALOIS
Der Polygraphische Apparat oder Die Verschiedenen Kunstfacher der k.k. Hof- und Staatsdruckerei zu Wien. K.k. Vienna: 1853. V. 48

AUER, H. A.
Camp Fires in the Yukon. Cincinnati: 1916. V. 48; 52
Camp-Fires in the Yukon. Cincinnati: 1917. V. 53

AUERBACH, ERNA
Nicholas Hilliard. London: 1961. V. 49; 52; 54

AUFRECHT, LOUIS
The American Hebrew Primer, an Easy Method of Teaching Hebrew Reading. Cincinnati: 1868. V. 51; 53

AUGEREAN, YAROUTHIUN
A Brief Account of the Mechitaristican Society Founded on the Island of St. Lazaro. Venice: 1835. V. 50; 52

AUGUSTA, ANNA
A History of Rhode Island Ferries, 1640-1923. Providence: 1925. V. 50

AUGUSTA, ISABELLA GREGORY
Cuchulain of Muirthemne. 1902. V. 50

AUGUSTIN, GEORGE
History of Yellow Fever. New Orleans: 1909. V. 48

AUGUSTIN, JOHN ALCEE
War Flowers, Reminiscences of Four Years' Campaigning. New Orleans: 1865. V. 54

AUGUSTINUS, AURELIUS, SAINT, BP. OF HIPPO
The Confessions. Philadelphia: 1900. V. 50; 52; 54
The Confessions of.... London: 1921. V. 53
The Confessions of St. Augustine. Ipswich: 1962. V. 54
De Civitate Dei. Basel: 1479. V. 51; 52; 53
De Civitate Dei Libri XXII. Munchen: 1925. V. 53
Explantio Psalmorum. Venice: 1493.. V. 52
In Omniad Aurelli Augustini Scripta Indices Duo Plane Novi, Summaside & Iudicio Nunc Denuo Conscripti & Magnalo... Basileae: 1569. V. 54
Of the Citie of God. London: 1610. V. 49; 51
Of the Citie of God. London: 1620. V. 47; 54
A Pretious Booke of heavenlie Meditations. London: 1612. V. 49
S. Augustine's Confessions... London: 1679. V. 51
Saint Augustines Confessions. London: 1650. V. 51
Soliloquia. Vimperk: 1484. V. 51

AUGUSTINUS DE ANCONA
Summa de Potestate Ecclesiaastica. Augsburg: 1473. V. 51; 52

THE AUK. 1922-94. V. 54

AULARD, A.
The French Revolution: a Political History 1789-1804. London: 1910. V. 49; 52

AULD, J. B.
A Poetical Essay on the First good and the First Fair. With Salutatory Addresses. New York: 1835. V. 52

THE AULD Shop and the New. Katoomba: 1992. V. 54

AULD, WILLIAM MUIR
Genius in Homespun (Robert Burns). Cleveland: 1930. V. 47

AULDJO, JOHN
Narrative of an Ascent to the Summit of Mont Blanc, on the 8th and 9th August 1827. London: 1828. V. 50; 54
Sketches of Vesuvius, With Short Accounts of its Principle Eruptions, From the Commencement of the Christian Era to the Present Time. Naples: 1832. V. 48

AULNOY, MARIE CATHERINE JUMELLE DE BERNEVILLE, COMTESSE D'
Fairy Tales. Philadelphia: 1923. V. 49
Fortunia - a Tale of Mme d'Aulnoy. New York. V. 47
Fortunia: a Tale by Mme. D'Aulnoy. New York: 1974. V. 48; 51; 53

ASIMOV, ISAAC continued
Nemesis. New York: 1989. V. 54
Nightfall. New York: 1969. V. 48; 51; 53
Nightfall. London: 1990. V. 48; 49; 54
Nightfall. New York: 1990. V. 47; 51; 52; 54
Nine Tomorrows. New York: 1959. V. 48; 52
Pebble in the Sky. New York: 1950. V. 49; 50; 52
Pebble in the Sky. New York: 1990. V. 48
Prelude to Foundation. New York: 1988. V. 47; 51; 54
The Rest of the Robots. New York: 1964. V. 47
Robot Dreams. 1986. V. 54
Robot Dreams. Berkeley: 1986. V. 49; 50
Robots and Empire. 1985. V. 54
Robots and Empire. New York: 1985. V. 47; 49
The Robots of Dawn. 1983. V. 51; 52
The Robots of Dawn. New York: 1983. V. 54
Second Foundation. New York: 1953. V. 51
The Stars Like Dust. New York: 1951. V. 49; 54
Tales of the Black Widowers. New York: 1974. V. 53
Three by Asimov: Three Science Fiction Tales. New York: 1981. V. 47; 51; 54

ASINOF, ELIOT
Eight Men Out. New York: 1963. V. 48; 53

ASKEW, JOHN
A Guide to Interesting Places in and Around Cockermouth, with an Account of its Remarkable men and Local Traditions. Cockermouth: 1866. V. 51

ASKIN, JOHN
The John Askin Papers. 1747-1820. N.P: 1928/31. V. 51

ASLIN, MARY S.
Rothamsted Experimntal Station Harpenden. Aberdeen;: 1940/49. V. 49

ASPECTS of Art and Iconography: Anatolia and its Neighbors. Studies in Honor of Nimet Ozguc. Ankara: 1993. V. 49; 51

ASPIAZU, AGUSTIN
Dogmas Del Derecho Internacional. New York: 1872. V. 54

ASPIN, JEHOSHAPHAT
Naval and Military Exploits Which Have Distinguished the Reign of the George the Third. London: 1820. V. 50

ASPINALL, HENRY OSWALD
The Aspinwall and Aspinall Families of Lancashire A.D. 1189-1923. London: 1923. V. 48

ASPINALL, JAMES
Liverpool a Few Years Since. London: 1852. V. 54

ASPLUND, JOHN
The Annual Register of the Baptist Denomination, in North America, to the First of November, 1790. Richmond: 1791?. V. 47; 50

ASQUITH, CYNTHIA
The Mortal Coil. Sauk City: 1947. V. 51

ASQUITH, MARGOT
The Autobiography of Margot Asquith. London: 1920. V. 53

ASSHETON, RALPH
Pedigree of the Family of Feilden, of the County of Lancaster. London: 1879. V. 53

ASSHETON, WILLIAM
The Royal Apology; or, an Answer to the Rebels Plea... London: 1684. V. 50

ASSOCIATED FABRICS CORP., NEW YORK
Associated Fabrics: Costume Material Guide. New York: 1937. V. 50

ASSOCIATION FOR IMPROVING THE CONDITION OF THE POOR
First Report of a Committee on the Sanitary condition of the Working Classes in the City of New York, with remedial Suggestions. New York: 1853. V. 50

ASSOCIATION FOR PROMOTING THE DISCOVERY OF THE INTERIOR PARTS OF AFRICA Proceedings of the Association for Promoting the Discovery of the Interior Part of Africa. London: 1791. V. 47; 53

ASSOCIATION FOR PROMOTING THE DISCOVERY OF THE INTERIOR PARTS OF AFRICA Proceedings of the.... London: 1810. V. 51

ASSOCIATION OF THE BAR OF THE CITY OF NEW YORK
Charter and Constitution of the Association of the Bar of the City of New York. New York: 1873. V. 52

ASSYRIA; Her Manner and Customs, Arts and Arms; Restored from Her Monuments. London: 1852. V. 54

THE ASSYRIAN Dictionary of the Oriental Institute of the University of Chicago. Chicago: 1956-73. V. 52

ASTAIRE, FRED
Steps in Time. New York: 1959. V. 51; 53

ASTELL, MARY
Bart'lemy Fair; or, an Enquiry After Wit; in Which Due Respect is Had to a Letter Concerning Enthusiasm to My Lord. London: 1709. V. 52; 54
An Essay in Defence of the Female Sex. London: 1696. V. 47; 48; 49
An Essay in Defence of the Female Sex. London: 1697. V. 47
Letters Concerning the Love of God, Between the Author of Proposal to the Ladies and Mr. John Norris... London: 1695. V. 51

A Serious Proposal to the Ladies, for the Advancement of Their True and Geatest Interest. London: 1695. V. 47; 49
Some Reflections Upon Marriage. London: 1703. V. 50

ASTLE, THOMAS
The Origin and Progress of Writing: as Well Hieroglyphic as Elementary... London: 1784. V. 50; 51; 52
The Origin and Progress of Writing: as Well Hieroglyphic as Elementary. London: 1876. V. 50; 53
The Origin and Progress of Writing, as Well Hieroglyphic as Elementary by Engravings... London: 1803. V. 50; 52; 53

ASTLEY, CONSTANCE
Catalogue of the Library of Constance Astley at Brinshop Court, Herefordshire. London: 1928. V. 54

ASTLEY, HUBERT DELAVAL
My Birds in Freedom and Captivity. London: 1900. V. 53

ASTLEY, JOHN
The Art of Riding, Set Foorth in a Breefe Treatise, With Due Interpretation of Certaine Places Alledged Out of Xenophon, and Gryson, Verie Expert and Excellent Horsemen... London: 1584. V. 51

ASTLEY, PHILIP
Astley's System of Equestrian Education, Exhibiting the Beauties and Defects of the Horse. London: 1801. V. 47

ASTON, FRANCIS W.
Isotopes. London: 1922. V. 48; 50; 52; 54

ASTON, P. E.
The Raid on Transvaal by Dr. Jameson. London: 1896. V. 53

ASTOR, WILLIAM WALDORF
Pharoah's Daughter and other stories. London: 1900. V. 47

THE ASTROLOGER; or, the Prediction of Guy Mannering. Glasgow: 1836. V. 47

ASTRONOMICA Veterum Scripta Isagogica Graeca & Latina. Heidelberg: 1589. V. 50

ASTRUC, JOHN
A Treatise of Venereal Diseases, in Nine Books... London: 1754. V. 50

ASTRUP, EIVIND
With Peary Near the Pole. London: 1898. V. 53

ASTRY, JAMES
A General Charge to All Gran Juries, with Advice to Those of Life and Death, Nisi Prius &c. London: 1703. V. 53

ASTURIAS, MIGUEL ANGEL
Hombres de Maiz. Buenos Aires: 1949. V. 48
The Talking Machine. Garden City: 1971. V. 52

AN ASYLUM for Fugitive Pieces, in Prose and Verse. London: 1785/86/99/93. V. 49

AT a Meeting of the Friends of the Present Administration Held at the House of Paul I. Evans, in the Town of Winchester... Kentucky: 1828. V. 47

AT Home. London: 1890. V. 49

AT the Graveside of Walt Whitman: Harleigh, Camden, New Jersey, March 30th and Sprigs of Lilac. London: 1892. V. 50

ATALANTA'S Garland - Being the Book of Edinburgh University Women's Union. London: 1926. V. 53

ATALANTA'S Garland: Being the Book of the Edinburgh University Women's Union, 1926. Edinburgh: 1926. V. 48; 50; 53

ATALIE, PRINCESS
The Earth Speaks. New York: 1940. V. 50

ATCHISON, TOPEKA & SANTA FE RAILWAY CO.
1879 Guide to the Arkansas Valley and the Lands of the Atchison, Topeka and Santa Fe R.R. Co. Chicago: 1882. V. 49
Atchison, Topeka and Santa Fe and Southern Pacific Railroads Southern Route to the Pacific Open All the Year Round...and All Pacific Points. Chicago: 1882. V. 47
Eighth Annual Report of the Atchison, Topeka & Santa Fe Railway company for the Fiscal year Ending June 30, 1903. New York: 1903. V. 49
Fifteenth Annual Report of the Atchison, Topeka & Santa Fe Railway Co. for the Fiscal year Ending June 30, 1910. New York: 1910. V. 47; 49
Fourteenth Annual report of the Board of Directors of the Atchison, Topeka and Santa Fe Railroad Co. to the Stockholders for the Year Ending Dec. 31, 1885. Boston: 1886. V. 47; 49
Fourth Annual Report of the Atchison, Topeka & Santa Fe Railway Co. for the Fiscal Year Ending June 30, 1899. New York: 1899. V. 49
Panhandle and South Plains, Texas. Chicago: 1911. V. 54
Plan of Re-Organization, Atchison, Topeka & Santa Fe Railroad Company. Circular No. 63 - October 15, 1889. Boston: 1889. V. 47; 52
Santa Fe Route. Topeka: 1887. V. 50
Seventh Annual Report of the Atchison, Topeka and Santa Fe Railway Co. for the Fiscal Year Ending June 30, 1902. 1902. V. 49
Third Annual Report of the Atchison, Topeka & Santa Fe Railway Co. for the Fiscal Year Ending June 30, 1898. New York: 1898. V. 49

ATCHLEY & CO.
Ornamental and Early English Alphabets, Initial Letters, &c. for Engravers, Designers, Marable Masons, Painters, Decorators, etc. London: 1858. V. 53

ATCHLEY, DANA
ABC Design. New York: 1965. V. 50

ATCHLEY, S. C.
Wild Flowers of Attica. London: 1938. V. 47
Wild Flowers of Attica. Oxford: 1938. V. 47; 48; 51; 52; 54

ATEN, IRA
Six and One Half years in the Ranger Service. 1945. V. 47

ATGET, EUGENE
A Vision of Paris. New York: 1963. V. 47; 48; 50
The Work... New York: 1981-85. V. 52

ATHALINTHIA. *The War Against the Weak.* Hingham: 1948. V. 49

ATHANASIUS, SAINT
(Greek text) *Dialogi V. de Sancta Trinitate. Basilii Libri IIII. Adversus Impium Enunomium Anastasii et Cyrii Ii Compendiaria Orthodoxae Fidei Explicatio...* Geneva: 1570. V. 48
Opera Quae Reperiuntur Omnia. Heidelberg: 1601. V. 50

THE ATHEISTICALL Polition or a Breife Discourse Concerning Ni. Machiavelli. London: 1642. V. 53

ATHENAEUM CLUB, LONDON. LIBRARY
Catalogue of the Library. Together with the Supplement. London: 1845. V. 52

ATHENAEUS
Athenaei Dipnosophistarvm Sive Coenae Sapient Libri XV. Lvgdvni: 1556. V. 47
Dipnosophistarum Sive Coenae Libri XV. Venice: 1556. V. 49

ATHENAGORAS
Apologia pro Christianis, ad Imperatores Antoninum & Commodum. Geneva: 1557. V. 53
Athenagora, Atheniese, Philosopho Christiano, Della Risurrettione de' Morti... Venice: 1556. V. 51

ATHENIAN Letters: or, the Epistoalry Correspondence of an Agent of the King of Persia, Residing at Athens During the Peloponnesian War. London: 1810. V. 47; 51

ATHENIAN SOCIETY
The Athenian Oracle: Being an Entire Collection of All the Valuable Questions and Answers in the Old Athenian Mercuries... 1728. V. 47

ATHERTON, FAXON DEAN
The California Diary of Faxon Dean Atherton, 1836-1839. San Francisco: 1964. V. 48; 52

ATHERTON, GERTRUDE
The Conqueror: Being the True and Romantic Story of Alexander Hamilton. New York: 1902. V. 49; 51
The Jealous Gods. New York: 1928. V. 54
The Splendid Idle Forties. New York: 1902. V. 52; 53
The Splendid Idle Forties: Six Stories of Spanish California. Kentfield: 1960. V. 48
What Dreams May Come. Chicago, New York: 1888. V. 53; 54

ATKIN, G. DUCKWORTH
House Scraps. London: 1887. V. 52

ATKINS, CHARLES E.
Register of Apprentices of the Worship Company of Clockmakers of the City of London from Its Incorporation in 1631. London: 1931. V. 53

ATKINS, J. H. W.
Literary Criticism. London: 1951-52. V. 54

ATKINS, ROBERT
The Power, Jurisdiction and Privilidge of Parliament and the Antiquity of the House of Commons Asserted... London: 1689. V. 51

ATKINS, SAMUEL E.
Some Account of the Worshipful Company of Clockmakers of the City of London. London: 1881. V. 53

ATKINS, WILLIAM
The Art and Practice of Printing...Dealing With the Composing Department, Mechanical Composition, Letterpress Printing...Lithographic Printing... London: 1931. V. 51

ATKINSON, ALEX
The Big City or the New Meyhew. New York: 1959. V. 51

ATKINSON, CHARLES
The Life and Adventures of an Ecentric Traveller. York: 1818. V. 54

ATKINSON, CHRISTOPHER
A Poetical Sermon on the Benefit of Affliction, and the Reasonableness of an Entire Resgination to the Will of the Supreme Being. London: 1765?. V. 54

ATKINSON, CHRISTOPHER WILLIAM
A Guide to New Brunswick, British North America, &c. Edinburgh: 1843. V. 47; 53
A Historical and Statistical Account of New Brunswick, B.N.A. with Advice to Emigrants. Edinburgh: 1844. V. 49; 51

ATKINSON, FREDERICK
The Banquet of Thalia, or the Fashionable Songsters Pocket Memorial, an Elegant Collelction, of the Most Admired Songs from Ancient and Modern Authors. York;: 1790. V. 54

ATKINSON, G. C.
Journal of an Expedition to the Feroe and Westman Islands and Iceland, 1833. Newcastle-Upon-Tyne: 1989. V. 48; 50

ATKINSON, GEORGE M. W.
Sketches in Norway, Taken During a Yachting Cruise in the Summer of 1852. Cork: 1853. V. 47

ATKINSON, HAROLD WARING
The Families of Atkinson of Roxy (Lincs) Thorne and Dearmen of Braithwaite and Families Connected With Them... London: 1933. V. 50

ATKINSON, HENRY
Expedition Up the Missouri. Washington: 1826. V. 47; 48; 50; 54

ATKINSON, HENRY GEORGE
Letters on the Laws of Man's Nature and Development. London: 1851. V. 50

ATKINSON, HERBERT
Cock-Fighting and Game Fowl from the Notebooks of Herbert Atkinson of Ewelme... Bath: 1938. V. 50
The Life and Letters of John Harris, the Cornish Cocker. London: 1910. V. 49

ATKINSON, J. A.
A Picturesque Representation of the Manner, Customs and Amusements of the Russians. London: 1803-04. V. 50
Sixteen Scenes Taken from the Human Life. London: 1807. V. 48

ATKINSON, J. C.
A Glossary of the Cleveland Dialect; Explanatory, Derivative and Critical. London: 1868. V. 52
Memorials of Old Whitby or Historical Gleanings from Ancient Whitby Records. London: 1894. V. 47; 53

ATKINSON, JOSEPH
The History of Newark, New Jersey. Newark: 1878. V. 47; 51

ATKINSON, R. H. M.
Brougham and His Early Friends, Letters to James Loch 1798-1809. London: 1908. V. 50

ATKINSON, RICHARD C.
Stevens' Handbook of Experimental Psychology. New York: 1988. V. 54

ATKINSON, S.
Ackworth Games and the Men Who Made Them. London: 1917. V. 49

ATKINSON, SAMUEL C.
Atkinson's Casket or Gems of Literature, Wit and Sentiment. Philadelphia: 1936. V. 47

ATKINSON, THOMAS
On the Cause of Our National Troubles. A Sermon Delivered in St. James' Church, Wilmington, N.C. Wilmington: 1861. V. 49

ATKINSON, THOMAS WITLAM
Oriental and Western Siberia; a Narrative of Seven Years' Exploration and Adventures in Siberia, Mongolia, the Kirghis Steppes, Chinese Tartary and Part of Central Asia. New York: 1865. V. 48
Oriental and Western Siberia: a Narrative of Seven Years Explorations and Adventures in Siberia, Mongolia, the Kirghis Steppes, Chinese Tartary and Part of Central Asia. London: 1858. V. 49; 50; 51; 53
Travels in the Region of the Upper and Lower Amoor and the Russian Acquisitions on the Confines of India and China. London: 1860. V. 48; 50
Travels in the region of the Upper and Lower Amoor and the Russian Acquisitions On the Confines of India and China. New York: 1860. V. 47; 48; 50; 51
Travels in the Regions of the Upper and Lower Amoor and the Russian Acquisitions on the Confines of India and China. London: 1861. V. 49

ATKINSON, W. N.
Explosions in Coal Mines. 1886. V. 51
Explosions in Coal Mines. London: 1886. V. 50

ATKINSON, WILLIAM
Address and Resolutions Presented to the Republican Convention, for Somerset County. Skowhegan: 1857. V. 48
The Physicians and Surgeons of the United States. Philadelphia: 1878. V. 52
Principles of Political Economy; or, the Laws of the Formation of National Wealth... (with) The Spirit of Magna Charta... London: 1840/41. V. 50

ATKYNS, ROBERT
The Ancient and Present State of Gloustershire. London: 1712. V. 53
An Enquiry into the Power of Dispensing with Penal Statutes. London: 1689. V. 49; 51; 52
Parliamentary and Political Tracts. London: 1741. V. 50
The Power, Jurisdiction and Priviledge of Parliament and the Antiquity of the House of Commons Asserted, Occasioned by an Information in the King's Bench, by the Attorney General, Against the Speaker of the House of Commons. London: 1689. V. 49
A Treatise of the True and Ancient Jurisdiction of the House of Peers... London: 1699. V. 47; 50

ATLANTIC & PACIFIC RAILROAD CO.
Annual Report Atlantic and Pacific Railroad Company to the Stockholders, for the Fiscal Ending December 31st, 1874. New York: 1875. V. 52
Atlantic and Pacific Railroad Co. and Atchison Topeka & Santa Fe, Railroad Co. Boston: 1887. V. 54

ATLANTIC Cable *The Cruise of the "Agamemnon.".* Plymouth: 1869. V. 51

THE ATLANTIC Souvenir: A Christmas and New Year's Offering. 1828. Philadelphia: 1827. V. 48

ATLANTIC Tales. 1866. V. 47; 51

ATLAS Moderne, ou Collection de Cartes sur Toutes les Parties du Globe Terrestre, par Plusieurs Auteurs. Paris: 1771-83. V. 49

THE ATLAS of British Seaweeds. London: 1857. V. 47

ATLAS Of Canada. Ottawa: 1957. V. 49; 52

ATLAS of Canada. Prepared Under the Direction of James White. Ottawa/Toronto: 1906. V. 48

ATLAS of Essex County, New Jersey. From Actual Surveys and Official Records... New York: 1881. V. 47

ATLAS of New Jersey. N.P: 1888. V. 47

ATLAS of Philadelphia and Environs. From Official Records, Private Plans and Actual Surveys. Philadelphia: 1877. V. 47

ATLAS of Province of Prince Edward Island Canada and the World. Toronto: 1920. V. 47

ATLAS of the British Empire. London: 1924. V. 49

ATLAS of the City of Bridgeport. New York: 1876. V. 53

ATLAS of the City of Newport. Springfield: 1907. V. 50

ATLAS of the City of Plainfield, Union County and Borough of North Plainfield, Somerset County, New Jersey. Plainfield: 1894. V. 49; 51

ATLAS of the Lewis and Clark Expedition. Lincoln: 1983. V. 52

ATLAS of the Oranges, Embracing the Cities of Orange and East Orange, Town of West Orange, Village and Township of South Orange, New Jersey. Philadelphia: 1911. V. 47; 49; 51

ATLAS of Western Canada...Manitoba, British Columbia, and Districts of Assinboia, Alberta, Saskatchewan... Ottawa: 1901. V. 50

ATLAS to Accompany the Monograph on the Geology of the Eureka District... Washington: 1883. V. 52

ATLAY, J. B.
Sir Henry Wentworth Acland, Bart. London: 1903. V. 48

ATLEE, WASHINGTON
General and Differential Diagnosis of Ovarian Tumors, With Special Reference to the Operation of Ovariotomy... Philadelphia: 1873. V. 48; 52; 53

ATMORE, CHARLES
A Brief Memoir of the Life and Death of Mr. C. Hopper, Who Departed This life on Firday March 5th, 1802 in the 80th Year of His Age. Manchester: 1802. V. 49; 53; 54

ATRUTEL, J., MRS.
An Easy and Economical Book of Jewish Cookery, Upon Strictly Orthodox Principles. London: 1894. V. 47

ATTANASIO, A. A.
Radix. New York: 1981. V. 53

ATTAWAY, WILLIAM
Let Me Breathe Thunder. New York: 1939. V. 53

ATTERBURY, F.
The Rights, Powers and Priviledges of an English Convocation, Stated and Vindicated in Answer to a late Book of Dr. Wake's, Entituled, The Authority of Christian Princes Over Their Ecclesiastical Synods... (with) Additions to the First Edition of the Rights. London: 1700-01. V. 49; 51

ATTERIDGE, A. HILLIARD
Napoleon's Brothers. London & New York: 1909. V. 50
Towards Khartoum. London: 1897. V. 51; 54

ATTHILL, WILLIAM
Documents Relating to the Foundation and Antiquities of the Collegiate Church of Middleham, in the County of York. London: 1847. V. 53

ATTIC Shells. Selections from the Pacific Coast. Richmond: 1978. V. 49

ATTICUS BOOKS
William S. Burroughs - The Hombre Invisible. San Diego: 1981. V. 52

ATTLEE, CLEMENT
As it Happened. London: 1954. V. 52

THE ATTORNEY'S Compleat Pocket-Book. London: 1743. V. 51

THE ATTORNEY'S Complete Pocket-Book. London: 1780. V. 50

ATTWELL, LUCIE
Attwell's Fairylite Book. London: 1948. V. 53
Lucie Attwell's Painting Book. London: 1934. V. 53
The Seaside: Attwell Kiddies Painting Book. Dundee: 1920's. V. 53
Stich Stich: the Lucie Attwell Needlework Book of Silk Patterns and Weldon's Transfers. London: 1922. V. 53

ATTWELL, MABEL L.
A Wizard of the East. London: 1918. V. 54

ATWATER, CALEB
An Essay on Education. Cincinnati: 1841. V. 52
The General Character, Present and Future Prospects of the People of Ohio. Columbus: 1827. V. 54
Remarks Made on a Tour to Prairie du Chien, Thence to Washington City in 1829. Columbia: 1831. V. 47
The Writings of Caleb Atwater... Columbus: 1833. V. 47

ATWILL, THOMAS H.
The New York Collection of Sacred Harmony, Containing the Necessary Rules of Music with a Variety of Psalm & Hymn Tunes Set Pieces & Anthems... Lansingburg: 1802. V. 50

ATWOOD, HOLMES & REED
The Pocket Atlas of the United States, Containing Separate Copper-Plate Maps of Each State and Territory. Philadelphia: 1884. V. 50

ATWOOD, MARGARET
The Animals in that Country. Boston: 1968. V. 52
The Animals in That Country. Toronto: 1968. V. 53; 54
Anna's Pet. Toronto: 1980. V. 50
Bodily Harm. New York: 1982. V. 47
Dancing Girls. Toronto: 1977. V. 48
Dancing Girls and Other Stories. 1977. V. 49
Double Persephone. Toronto: 1961. V. 51; 53
Encounters with the Element Man. Concord: 1982. V. 50; 51; 52; 54
Hurricane Hazel and Other Stories. Helsinki: 1987. V. 52
The Journals of Susanna Moodie. Toronto: 1970. V. 53
The Journals of Susanna Moodie. Toronto: 1980. V. 51
Lady Oracle. Toronto: 1976. V. 48
Notes Toward a Poem that Can Never Be Written. 1981. V. 51
Notes Toward a Poem That Can Never Be Written. Toronto: 1981. V. 47; 54
Power Politics. New York: 1971. V. 51
Procedures for the Underground. Boston: 1970. V. 53
Procedures for the Underground. Toronto: 1970. V. 48
The Robber Bride. London: 1993. V. 51
Surfacing. Toronto: 1972. V. 47; 48
The Trumpets of Summer: Libretto. Toronto: 1964. V. 53
Up in the Tree Colouring Book - Free!. Toronto: 1978. V. 53

ATWOOD, WILLIAM
Jus Anglorum ab Antiquo: Or, a Confutation of an Impotent Libel Against th by King, Lords and Commons. London: 1681. V. 50

AUBERTIN, DENISE
Van Gogh: Dessins. Paris: 1987. V. 54

AUBESPIN, NICOLAS
La Cordeliere ou Tresor des Indulgences du Cordon St. Francois. Paris

AUBIGNAC, FRANCOIS HEDELIN, ABBE D'
The Whole Art of the Stage. London: 1684. V. 49

AUBIGNE, J. H. MERLE
History of the Reformation in the Sixteenth Century. London: 1842.

AUBIN, PENELOPE
English Nights Entertainments. The Life, Adventures and Distresse and Her Lover Berlanger... London: 1800. V. 54

AUBORN, A. D.'
The French Convert:...From the Errors and Supersitions of P Religion, by Means of a Protestant Gardener, Her Servant... B

AUBREY, F.
King of the Dead. 1903. V. 48

AUBREY, JOHN
Brief Lives, Chiefly of Contemporaries, Set Down by John Aubre and 1696. Oxford: 1898. V. 47
Letters Written by Eminent Persons in the Seventeenth and Ei are Added Hearne's Journeys to Reading, the Seat of Brow V. 49; 50
Miscellanies, Upon the Following Subjects. Day Fatality. II. Omens. V. Dreams. VI. Apparitions... XXI. Second Sigh V. 48
Monumenta Britannica. Boston: 1980. V. 47; 48; 49; 51; 5
Monumenta Britannica. Dorset: 1980. V. 53
The Natural History and Antiquities of the County of Surr Continued to the Present Time. London: 1718-23. V. 5
The Topographical Collections. Devizes,: 1862. V. 52

AUBRY, OCTAVE
The Empress Might Have Been: The Love Story of M York: 1927. V. 50
The King of Rome Napoleon II "L'Aglon". Philadelphia

AUBURN & SYRACUSE RAILROAD CO.
A Report of a Committee to the Board of Director Engineer of the... Auburn: 1837. V. 53

AUCASSIN ET NICOLETTE
Aucassin and Nicolete. Portland: 1907. V. 48; 49
Aucassin and Nicolette. London: 1914. V. 54
Aucassin and Nicolette. London: 1887. V. 48; 50
Aucassin and Nicolette. New York: 1915. V. 52
Aucassin and Nicolette. Prague: 1931. V. 52; 5
Aucassin and Nicolette. Essex: 1947. V. 48
Aucassin et Nicolette. London: 1903. V. 48
Aucassin et Nicolette. New York: 1931. V. 53
Of Aucassin and Nicolette. London: 1925. V.
The Song-Story of Aucassin and Nicolete. 1

AUCASSIN ET NICOLETTE
Aucassin and Nicolette. Portland: 1897. V.

AUCHINCLOSS, LOUIS
The Injustice Collectors. Boston: 1950. V.
A World of Profit. Boston: 1968. V. 54

AUDEBERT, GERMAIN AURELE
Venetiae. Venice: 1583. V. 49

AULNOY, MARIE CATHERINE JUMELLE DE BERNEVILLE, COMTESSE D'
continued
The History of Hypolitus Earl of Douglas. London: 1741. V. 48
Memoires de la Cour d'Espagne. Paris: 1690. V. 48
Memoirs of the Court of England in the Reign of King Charles II. London: 1708. V. 50
Memoirs of the Court of France. London: 1692. V. 52
Memoirs of the Court of France, and City of Paris. London: 1706?. V. 53
Memoirs of the Court of Spain. London: 1692. V. 47; 54
The Prince of Carency. London: 1719. V. 48
The White Cat. Edinburgh and London: 1847. V. 50
The White Cat and other Old French Fairy Tales. New York: 1928. V. 50

AUMONIER, W.
Modern Archtiectural Sculpture. London: 1930. V. 47

AUNGERVILLE, RICHARD
Historie de la Vie de Henri IV, Roi de France et de Navarre. Paris: 1766. V. 47
The Philobiblon. New York: 1889. V. 50; 51; 53; 54
The Philobiblon. New Rochelle: 1901. V. 47; 49
The Philobiblon. New York: 1901. V. 48
Philobiblon. San Francisco: 1925. V. 53
The Philobiblon. New York: 1945. V. 47

AUNIGA, Ignacio. *Rapida Ojeada al Estado de Sonora...* Mexico: 1835. V. 52

AUNT Affable's Story of the Merry Cobbler, or, What Good a Little Boy Can Do. London: 1845. V. 49; 50

AUNT Louisa's Birthday Gift. London: 1875. V. 52

AUNT Louisa's Birthday Gift Book. London: 1880. V. 48

AUNT Louisa's Child's Delight: Comprising Rip Van Winkle, Yankee Doodle, Pochanatas. New York: 1874. V. 47

AUNT Louisa's Favourite Toy Book. London: 1870. V. 51

AUNT Louisa's Keepsake. London. V. 47
AUNT Louisa's Keepsake. London: 1868. V. 49; 50

AUNT Louisa's London Gift Book. London. V. 51

AUNT Louisa's National Album. London: 1880. V. 54

AUNT Louisa's Nursery Favourite. London: 1870. V. 50

AUNT Louisa's Welcome Visitor. London: 1883. V. 47

AUNT Mavor's Toybook. Containing Cock Robin and Jenny Wren, Jack and the Beanstalk, the Little Dog Trusty, The Cherry Orchard, Dick Whittington and His Cat, Old Mother Hubbard. London: 1857. V. 51

AUNT Sally; or the Cross the Way of Freedom. Cincinnati: 1862. V. 50

AUNTIE'S Little Rhyme Book. Philadelphia. V. 47

AUNT LAURA
Bird Stories. Buffalo: 1863. V. 49
Christmas Stories. Buffalo: 1862. V. 52
Fairy Tales. Buffalo: 1862. V. 49
New Testament Stories. Buffalo: 1862. V. 49
Orphan Willie. Buffalo: 1862. V. 49
Our Pic-nic in the Woods. Burralo: 1862. V. 49

AURCHER, OTTO
Gerald Landon. New York: 1917. V. 48

AURELIANUS, CAELIUS
Caelii Aureliani Fisscensis Tardarum Passionum Libri V.D. Oribasii...Euporiston Lib: III. Medicinae Compen: Lib. I. Curationum Lib. I. Trochiscorum Confect: Lib... Basileae: 1529. V. 47; 48; 49

AURELIUS, CORNELIUS
Batavia, sive de Antiquo Veroque Eius Insulae Quam Rhenus in Hollandia Facit Situ, Desciptione et Laudibus. Antwerp: 1586. V. 47; 48

AURELIUS ANTONINUS, MARCUS, EMPEROR OF ROME
The Emepror Marcus Antoninus His Conversation with Himself... London: 1701. V. 48; 53
Marcus Aurelius Antoninus to Himself... London: 1898. V. 51
Meditations... London: 1643. V. 50; 52
The Meditations. Glasgow: 1742. V. 50; 53
The Meditations. Glasgow: 1749. V. 47; 51
Meditations. New York: 1956. V. 51; 54
The Thoughts of the Emperor Marcus Aurelius Antoninus. London: 1902. V. 48
The Thoughts of the Emperor Marcus Aurelius Antoninus. London: 1909. V. 48; 51; 53
The Twelve Books. London: 1896. V. 54

AURENBRUGGER, LEOPOLD
Nouvelle Methode Pour Reconnaitre les Maladies Internes de la Poitrine par la Percussion de Cette Cavite.. Paris: 1808. V. 53

AURORA County, South Dakota, and its Fertile Lands. Plankinton: 1898. V. 52

AUSCHER, E. S.
A History and Description of French Porcelain. London: 1905. V. 52

AUSLANDER, JOSEPH
Letters to Women. New York: 1929. V. 48

AUSONIUS, DECIMUS MAGNUS
Patchwork Quilt. London. V. 49
Poems By...Patchwork Quilt... London: 1930. V. 50

AUST, SARAH MAESE MURRAY
A Companion and Useful Guide to the Beauties of Scotland, to the Lakes...and to the District of Craven. London: 1799. V. 50

AUSTEN, JANE
Austen's Novels. London: 1879. V. 50
Charades Etc. London: 1895. V. 52
Collected Novels. London: 1988. V. 48
The Complete Works. Boston and New York: 1906. V. 47
The Complete Works. London: 1975. V. 49
Emma. London: 1816. V. 47; 49; 51; 52; 53; 54
Emma. London: 1866. V. 49; 52; 54
Emma. London: 1872. V. 49
Emma. Leipzig: 1877. V. 47; 49; 51
Emma. London: 1896. V. 53
Emma. London: 1898. V. 51
Emma. New York: 1964. V. 51; 52; 54
Emma...Mansfield Park...(and) Northanger Abbey, and Persuasion. London: 1849-51-50. V. 48; 51
The Fruits of Jane Austen. London: 1994. V. 54
Jane Austen's Novels. London: 1893-1894. V. 49
Jane Austen's Novels. London: 1898. V. 50
Lady Susan. London: 1925. V. 52; 54
Lady Susan. Oxford: 1925. V. 49; 51; 53; 54
Letters. London: 1884. V. 49; 50; 52; 54
Letters to Her Sister Cassandra and Others. London: 1932. V. 47; 52
Letters to Her Sister Cassandra and Others. London: 1952. V. 54
Letters to Her Sister Cassandra and Others. London: 1964. V. 54
Love and Friendship and Other Early Works. London: 1922. V. 54
Mansfield Park. London: 1814. V. 48; 52; 54
Mansfield Park. London: 1816. V. 49
Mansfield Park. London: 1833. V. 54
Mansfield Park. London: 1837. V. 47; 49
Mansfield Park. London: 1853. V. 47
Mansfield Park. London: 1869. V. 54
Northanger Abbey. Baltimore: 1971. V. 51; 53; 54
Northanger Abbey. New York: 1971. V. 52
Northanger Abbey a Novel. (with) Persuasion. London: 1877. V. 49
Northanger Abbey; and Persuasion. London: 1818. V. 47; 48; 49; 50; 53; 54
Northanger Abbey and Persuasion. London: 1837. V. 54
The Northanger Set of Jane Austen Horrid Novels. London: 1968. V. 50
The Novels. Edinburgh. V. 47
Novels. London: 1833. V. 51
The Novels. London: 1833/47. V. 50
The Novels. London: 1892. V. 47; 52
The Novels. London: 1896-1902. V. 54
The Novels. London: 1898. V. 50
Novels. London: 1900. V. 51
The Novels. London: 1901. V. 52
The Novels. London & New York: 1904-1908. V. 47; 49
Novels. Edinburgh: 1906. V. 50
The Novels. New York: 1906. V. 52; 54
The Novels. London: 1908. V. 54
The Novels. Edinburgh: 1911-12. V. 47; 49
The Novels. New York: 1914. V. 54
The Novels. London: 1922. V. 52
The Novels. London: 1923. V. 48
The Novels. Oxford: 1923. V. 51
The Novels. Oxford: 1926. V. 52
The Novels. Oxford: 1933/4. V. 54
The Novels. Edinburgh: 1950's. V. 49
The Novels. 1953. V. 49
Novels. London: 1975. V. 49
The Novels and Letters. New York: 1906. V. 48; 51
The Novels Of... (and) Minor Works of... 1946/54. V. 50
Persuasion. Philadelphia: 1832. V. 52; 54
Persuasion. London: 1896. V. 49
Persuasion. Paris: 1945. V. 53; 54
Plan of a Novel. Oxford: 1926. V. 54
Pride and Prejudice. London: 1813. V. 48
Pride and Prejudice. London: 1813. V. 47; 49; 54
Pride and Prejudice. London: 1817. V. 50
Pride and Prejudice. London: 1833. V. 47
Pride and Prejudice. London: 1839. V. 50
Pride and Prejudice. London: 1856. V. 47; 49; 51; 53
Pride and Prejudice. London: 1894. V. 53
Pride and Prejudice. Boston: 1940. V. 47; 54
Pride and Prejudice. New York: 1940. V. 47; 48; 52; 54
Pride and Prejudice. New York: 1945. V. 52; 54
Sanditon, Fragment of a Novel... London: 1925. V. 49; 52; 54
Sense and Sensibility. London: 1811. V. 48; 50
Sense and Sensibility. London: 1813. V. 50
Sense and Sensibility. London: 1833. V. 48; 50; 53
Sense and Sensibility. Philadelphia: 1833. V. 53; 54

AUSTEN, JANE continued
Sense and Sensibility. London: 1886. V. 47; 49
Sense and Sensibility. London: 1899. V. 53
Sense and Sensibility. New York: 1957. V. 47; 51; 54
Sense and Sensibility and Persuasion. New York: 1857. V. 52
Sense and Sensibility and Persuasion. New York: 1861. V. 52; 54
Sense and Sensibility. and Persuasion. Boston: 1864. V. 52; 54
Sense and Sensibility and Persuasion. Boston: 1866. V. 49
Sense and Sensibility. (and) Pride and Prejudice. London: 1896/96. V. 49
Sir Charles Grandison, or the Happy Man. London: 1981. V. 52
Three Evening Prayers. San Francisco: 1940. V. 53
Two Chapters of "Persuasion" Printed From Jane Austen's Autograph. London: 1926. V. 52
The Watsons. London: 1927. V. 52
The Watsons. London: 1928. V. 52; 54
Works. London: 1882. V. 50; 52; 54
The Works. Boston: 1898. V. 52
Works. London: 1910. V. 48
The Works in Seven Volumes. London: 1957-63. V. 48
The Works...Together with a Memoir of Jane Austen by Her Nephew. London: 1882-83. V. 50

AUSTEN, JOHN
Historical Notes on Old Sheffield Druggists. Sheffield: 1961. V. 51; 53; 54
Rogues in Porcelain. London: 1924. V. 49

AUSTEN, N. LAURENCE
Natural History Papers and Memoir of... London: 1877. V. 49

AUSTEN, R. A.
A Treatise of Fruit-Trees, Shewing the Manner of Planting, Grafting, Pruning and Ordering of Them in All Respects, Etc. Oxford: 1665. V. 54

AUSTEN-LEIGH, J. E.
A Memoir. London: 1870. V. 47; 49; 51; 53; 54
A Memoir. London: 1871. V. 48; 54
A Memoir. London: 1879. V. 52
A Memoir. London: 1886. V. 54

AUSTEN-LEIGH, M. A.
Personal Aspects of Jane Austen. London: 1920. V. 52; 54

AUSTEN-LEIGH, RICHARD ARTHUR
Austen Papers 1704-1856. London: 1942. V. 49

AUSTEN-LEIGH, W.
Chawton Manor and Its Owners. London: 1911. V. 50
Jane Austen. Her Life and Letters, a Family Record. London: 1913. V. 52; 54

AUSTER, PAUL
The Art of Hunger. London: 1982. V. 54
Auggie Wren's Christmas Story. New York: 1992. V. 51; 52; 53
City of Glass. Los Angeles: 1985. V. 48
City of Glass, Ghosts and The Locked Room. Los Angeles: 1985-86. V. 52
Facing the Music. Barrytown: 1980. V. 54
Ghosts. Los Angeles: 1986. V. 48; 54
Ghosts. New York: 1986. V. 50
Ghosts. San Francisco: 1986. V. 47
In the Country of Last Things. New York: 1987. V. 51
The Locked Room. Los Angeles: 1986. V. 51; 54
Moon Palace. New York: 1989. V. 54
Music of Chance. New York: 1990. V. 51; 54
The New York Trilogy. Los Angeles: 1985-86. V. 47; 51; 53
Wall Writing. Berkeley: 1976. V. 51

AUSTIN, BENJAMIN
Constitutional Republicanism, in Opposition to Fallacious Federalism... Boston: 1803. V. 47

AUSTIN, GILBERT
Chironomia; or a Treatise on Rhetorical Delivery... London: 1806. V. 49; 54

AUSTIN, H. H.
Among Swamps and Giants in Equatorial Africa: an Account of Survey and Adventures in the Southern Sudan and British East Africa. London: 1802. V. 54

AUSTIN, HARRIET
How to Take Baths. Dansville: 1860-65?. V. 53
How to Take Baths. New York: 1860-65?. V. 50

AUSTIN, J. P.
The Blue and the Gray...A Truthful Narrative of Adventure, with Thrilling Reminiscences. Atlanta: 1899. V. 49

AUSTIN, JANE G.
Betty Alden, the First-Born Daughter of the Pilgrims. Boston: 1892. V. 54
Cipher: a Romance. New York: 1869. V. 47
Outpost. Boston: 1867. V. 47

AUSTIN, JOHN C.
Architecture in Southern California. Los Angeles: 1905. V. 54

AUSTIN, JOHN OSBORNE
Ancestry of Thirty-Three Rhode Islanders (Born in the Eighteenth Century). Albany: 1889. V. 54

AUSTIN, MARY
The American Rhythm. New York: 1923. V. 49; 50; 51; 53
The Arrow Maker: a Drama in Three Acts. New York: 1911. V. 47; 50
The Basket Woman: a Book of Fanciful Tales for Children. Boston: 1904. V. 54
The Children Sing in the Far West. Boston: 1928. V. 54
Earth Horizon, Autobiography. Boston: 1932. V. 49
The Flock. Boston: 1906. V. 53
The Land of Journeys' Ending. New York: 1924. V. 53
The Land of Little Rain. Boston: 1903. V. 47; 48; 53
The Land of Little Rain. Boston: 1950. V. 47; 48; 50; 51; 52; 53
The Land of Little Rain. Cambridge: 1950. V. 53
The Lands of the Sun. Boston: 1927. V. 54
Mother of Felipe and Other Early Stories. 1950. V. 50
A Small Town Man. New York: 1925. V. 49
Taos Pueblo. Boston: 1977. V. 50; 54

AUSTIN, OLIVER L.
The Birds of Newfoundland Labrador. Cambridge: 1932. V. 47

AUSTIN, ROLAND
Catalogue of the Gloucestershire Collection Books, Pamphlets and Documents in the Gloucester Public Library. Gloucester: 1928. V. 47; 50

AUSTIN, SARAH
The Story Without an End. London: 1872. V. 50

AUSTIN, STEPHEN F.
The Austin Papers. Washington: 1924-28. V. 47; 50

AUSTIN, WILLIAM
Haec Homo: Wherein the Excellency of the Creation of Woman is Described; By Way of an Essay. London: 1639. V. 48

AN AUTHENTIC Account of the Conversion and Expereience of a Negro. London: 1790. V. 52

AN AUTHENTIC Account of the Proceedings of Their High Mightinesses, the States of Holland and West Friezeland, on the Complaint Laid Before Them by His Excellency Sir Joseph Yorke... London: 1762. V. 50

AN AUTHENTIC and full History of All the Circumstances of the Cruel Poisoning of Mr. Francis Blandy, Gent. London. V. 48

AUTHENTIC and Interesting Memoirs of Mrs. (Mary Ann) Clarke, From Her Infancy to the Present Time... New York: 1809. V. 48; 50; 51; 53

AN AUTHENTIC, Candid and Circumstantial Narrative of the Astonishing Transactions at Stockwell, in the County of Surry (sic)... Containing a Series of the Most Surprising and Unaccountable Events that Ever Happened... London: 1772. V. 47

AN AUTHENTIC Copy of the Last Will and Testament of the Reverend Dr. Swift, Dean of St. Patrick's, Dublin... London: 1746. V. 53

AN AUTHENTIC Detail of Particulars Relative to the Late Duchess of Kingston (Elizabeth Chudleigh). London: 1788. V. 48; 53

AN AUTHENTIC Exposition of the "K. G. C." "Knights of the Golden Circle;" or, a History of Secession from 1834 to 1861. Indianapolis: 1861. V. 50

AN AUTHENTIC Journal of the Remarkable and Bloody Siege of Bergen-op-Zoom, by the French, Under M. de Lowendahl, Begun July 14, and ended Sept. 16 N.S. 1747. London: 1747. V. 47

AUTHENTIC Memoirs of That Wonderful Phenomenon, the Infant Roscius; In Which is Interspersed a Variety of Theatrical Anecdotes, and a Criticism on His Performance. London: 1815. V. 50

AUTHENTIC Memoirs of the Green-Room: Involving Sketches, Biographical, Critical and Characteristic of the Performers of the Theatres-Royal Drury Lane, Covent-Garden and the Haymarket. London: 1801-02. V. 50

AUTHENTIC Memoirs of the Life, Numerous Adventures and Remarkable Escapes, of the Celebrated Patrick Madan.... London: 1782. V. 51

AUTHENTIC Narrative of the Loss of the Ville de Paris, and of All Her Crew Except One, About Five Months After She Was Captured from the Enemy, in the Glorious Victory, Obtained by Admiral Sir George Bridges Rodney, April 12, 1782... London: 1809?. V. 47

AUTHOR'S LEAGUE OF AMERICA
My Maiden Effort. Garden City: 1921. V. 50

THE AUTHORS of England. A Series of Medallion Portraits of Modern Literary Characters... London: 1838. V. 53

AUTHORS Take Sides on the Spanish War. V. 48

AUTHORS Take Sides on Vietnam. London: 1967. V. 47; 53

AUTHOR'S CLUB, NEW YORK
Liber Scriptorum. The Second Book of the Author's Club. New York: 1921. V. 53

AUTOGRAPH Leaves Of Our Country's Authors. Baltimore: 1864. V. 50; 52

AUTOGRAPHS for Freedom. Auburn & Rochester: 1854. V. 52; 53

THE AUTOMOBILE Handbook and Guide, an Illustrated Treatise on Petrol, Steam and Electric Cars for All Purposes. London: 1900. V. 50

AUTOMOBILE Lillian. The Daring Girl Bandit of Arizona. 1910. V. 54

AUTRUM, H.
Handbook of Sensory Physiology. Berlin/Heidelberg/New York: 1971-81. V. 50

AVARY, MYRTA LOCKETT
A Virginia Girl in the Civil War 1861-1865. New York: 1903. V. 53

AVEBURY, JOHN LUBBOCK, BARON
The Scenery of England and the Causes of Which It is Due. London: 1902. V. 49; 51

AVEDON, RICHARD
Avedon: Photographs 1947-1977. New York: 1978. V. 47; 50; 51; 52; 54
In the American West. New York: 1985. V. 48
Observations. New York: 1959. V. 51; 54
Portraits. New York: 1977. V. 47; 48; 50

AVELING, EDWARD BIBBINS
Comic Cricket by the Cockney Sportsman (Alec Nelson). London: 1891. V. 51

AVELING, J. H.
The Chamberlens and the Midwifery Forceps: Memorials of the Family and an Essay on the Invention of the Instrument. London: 1882. V. 50
English Midwives. London: 1872. V. 49

AVELLAR, ANDRE
Chronographia ou Repertorio dos Tempos. Lisbon: 1602. V. 48

AVENARIUS, JOHANN
Hoc Est, Liber Radicum Seu Lexicon Ebraicum, in Quo Omnium Vocabulorum Biblicorum... Wittenberg: 1588. V. 52

AVENI, A. F.
The Lines of Nazca. 1990. V. 54

AVENTURES Singuliers d'Un Voyageur Aerien, Mises au Jour par M. J.***. London: 1785. V. 53

AVERBACH, ALBERT
Handling Accident Cases. Rochester: 1960. V. 49

AVERILL, CHARLES E.
The Corsair King; or, the Blue Water Rovers. Boston: 1847. V. 47

AVERILL, ESTHER
Daniel Boone, Historic Adventures of an American Hunter Among the Indians. Paris: 1931. V. 49; 52; 53
Powder. The Story of a Colt, a Duchess and the Circus. New York: 1933. V. 49

AVERMAETE, ROGER
Frans Masereel. Amsterdam. V. 49
Frans Masereel. London: 1977. V. 47; 48; 50; 52
Franz Masereel. New York: 1977. V. 48

AVERY, CHARLES
Finger Prints of the Artist: European Terra Cotta Sculpture from the Arthur M. Sackler Collections. Cambridge: 1981. V. 53

AVERY, DAVID
A Poem on the Origin and Suppression of the Late Rebellion. Wilmantic: 1865. V. 52

AVERY, HAROLD
The Little Robinson Crusoes or, Ronald and Betty's Adventures on an Uninhabitated Island. London: 1908. V. 49

AVERY, MYRTILLA
The Exultet Rolls of South Italy, Volume II: Plates. Princeton: 1936. V. 48

AVEY, ELIJAH
The Capture and Execution of John Brown: a Tale of Martyrdom, by an Eyewitness. Elgin: 1906. V. 48

AVICENNA
Canon Medicinae. Venice: 1490. V. 47; 50
Canon Medicinae. E. Louvain: 1658. V. 52
Liber Canonis. Venetiis: 1507. V. 47

AVILA, JUAN DE
The Audi Filia, or a Rich Cabinet Full of Spiritual Jewells. St. Omer: 1620. V. 53
Triumph Uber die Welt, Das Fleisch und den Teufel. Munich: 1601. V. 52

AVILER, CHARLES D'
Ausfuehrliche Antleitung zu der Gantzen Civil Baukunst Worinnen Nebst Denen Fuenff Ordnungen von J. Bar. de Vignola... Amsterdam: 1699. V. 53

AVIRETT, JAMES B.
The Memoirs of General Turner Ashby and His Compeers. Baltimore: 1867. V. 50
Who Was the Rebel - the Traitor - the Trans-Susquehanna man or the cis-Susquehanna Man?. N.P: 1897. V. 48

AVISON, CHARLES
An Essay on Musical Expression. London: 1752. V. 47; 49
An Essay on Musical Expression. London: 1753. V. 49
An Essay on Musical Expression. London: 1775. V. 48

AVISON, MARGARET
Winter Sun. Toronto: 1960. V. 54

AVITY, PIERRE D', SIEUR DE MONTMARTIN
Bannissement des Folles Amours, ou Sont Adioustes Quatre Beaux & Excellents Traictes, Tres Curieux & Memorables, Enrichis d'Excellentes Annotations & Beaux Commentaires. Lyon: 1618. V. 52
The Estates, Empires & Principalities of the World. London: 1615. V. 47

L'AVOCAT du Diable: the Devil's Advocate; or, Satan Versus Pictor. London: 1792. V. 51

AVON Fantasy Reader. 1947-52. V. 48

AWDLAY, JOHN
Alia Cantalena de Sancta Maria. Long Crendon: 1926. V. 47; 51

AWOKI, T.
Illustrated Guide Book for Travellers Round the World. Osaka: 1886. V. 50; 53

AWOONOR, KOFI
This Earth, My Brother... Garden City: 1971. V. 52

AWSITER, J.
Thoughts on Brithelmston Concerning Sea-Bathing and Drinking Sea-Water. London: 1768. V. 51

AXELROD, GEORGE
The Seven Year Itch. New York: 1953. V. 53; 54

AXELROD, H. R.
The Atlas of Discus of the World. London: 1991. V. 50
The Complete Coloured Lexicon of Cichlids. London: 1993. V. 52
The Fascination of Breeding Aquarium Fish. London: 1992. V. 49

AXELSON, G. W.
Commy, The Life Story of Charles A. Comiskey. Chicago: 1919. V. 47

AXON, WILLIAM E. A.
The Annals of Manchester: A Chronological Record from the Earliest Times to the End of 1885. Manchester: 1886. V. 48; 53

AXSOME, RICHARD H.
The Prints of Frank Stella: a Catalogue Raisonne 1962-1982. New York: 1983. V. 50; 52

AYCKBOURN, ALAN
The Norman Conquests - a Trilogy of Plays. London: 1975. V. 51

AYER, EDWARD E.
Catalogue of the Edward E. Ayer Ornithological Library. N.P: 1990. V. 47

AYER, HANNAH PALFREY
A Legacy of New England. Letters of the Palfrey Family. N.P: 1950. V. 52

AYER'S American Almanac, 1881. Lowell: 1881. V. 50

AYLIFFE, JOHN
The Antient and Present State of the University of Oxford. London: 1714. V. 47
Parergon Juris Canonici Anglicani: or, a Commentary, By Way of Supplement to the Canyons and Constitutions of the Church of England. London: 1726. V. 51

AYLING, STEPHEN
Photographs from Sketches by Augustus Welby N. Pugin. London: 1865. V. 52

AYLOFFE, JOSEPH
Calendars of the Ancient Charters, and of the Welch and Scotish Rolls, Now Remaining in the Tower of London (etc.). London: 1774. V. 49

AYLWARD, ALFRED
The Transvaal of To-Day: War, Witchcraft, Sport and Spoils in South Africa. London: 1878. V. 47

AYME, MARCEL
Five Short Stories by Marcel Ayme: The State of Grace. The Dwarf. Rue de l'Evangile. Legend of Poldevia. The Seven-League Boots. Newtown: 1994. V. 52

AYME, MAURICE
The Wonderful Farm. New York: 1951. V. 54

AYNGE, G. A.
The Death of Tecumesceh; and Poetical Fragments on Various Subjects. Dartmouth: 1821. V. 47

AYRE, JOSEPH
Practical Observations on the Nature and Treatment Marasmus, and of Those Disorders Allied To it... Northampton: 1822. V. 50

AYRE, WILLIAM
The Life of Alexander Pope, Esq... London: 1754. V. 50

AYRES, ATLEE B.
Mexican Architecture. Domestic, Civil and Ecclesiastical. New York: 1926. V. 52

AYRES, GEORGE B.
How to Paint Photographs in Water Colors. Philadelphia: 1869. V. 47

AYRES, H. B.
The Southern Appalachian Forests. Washington: 1905. V. 47

AYRES, HARRY MORGAN
Carroll's Alice. New York: 1936. V. 54

AYRES, PHILIP
Emblemata Amatorial Emblems of Love... London: 1683. V. 50
Emblems in Four Languages. London: 1683. V. 50; 53
The Voyages and Adventures of Capt. Barth. Sharp and Others, in the South Sea. London: 1684. V. 50

AYRTON, MICHAEL
Drawings and Sculpture. London: 1962. V. 50; 53
Fabrications. London: 1972. V. 50
Giovanni Pisano Sculptor. London: 1969. V. 49; 50; 52; 54
Giovanni Pisano: Sculptor. New York: 1969. V. 52; 53; 54
Golden Sections. London: 1957. V. 49
Hogarth's Drawings - London Life in the 18th Century. 1948. V. 52

AYRTON, MICHAEL continued
The Minotaur. London: 1970. V. 50
Paintings, Drawings, Theatre Designs. Wakefield: 1949. V. 51
The Rudiments of Paradise. London: 1971. V. 50
The Testament of Daedalus. London: 1962. V. 50
Tittivulus or the Verbiage Collector. London: 1953. V. 50; 53

AYRTON, WILLIAM
The Adventures of a Salmon in the River Dee, By a Friend of the Family...Together with Notes for the Fly-Fisher in North Wales. London: 1853. V. 47
Mr. Barnacle and His Boat. N.P: 1855. V. 47

AYSCOUGH, GEORGE EDWARD
Letters from an Officer in the Guards to His Friends in England... London: 1778. V. 47

AYSCOUGH, JAMES
A Short Account of the Eye and Nature of Vision. London: 1752. V. 53

AYTON, RICHARD
A Voyage Round Great Britain, Undertaken between the Years 1813 and 1823, and Commencing from Land's End, Cornwall. London: 1978. V. 51

AYTONA, GUILLEN RAMON DE MONCADA, MARQUES DE
Discurso Militar. Proponense Algunos Inconvenientes de La Milicia Destos Tiempos, y Su Reparo... Valencia: 1653. V. 53

AYTOUN, WILLIAM EDMONSTOUNE
The Book of Ballads. Edinburgh & London: 1860. V. 49; 54
Bothwell. Edinburgh: 1856. V. 54
Lays of the Scottish Cavaliers and Other Poems. Edinburgh: 1863. V. 49
Lays of the Scottish Cavaliers, and Other Poems. Edinburgh & London: 1870. V. 48; 54
Lays of the Scottish Cavaliers and Other Poems. London: 1881. V. 52; 54

AZADI, SIAWOSCH
Turkoman Carpets and the Ethnographic Significance of Their Ornaments. Fishguard, Wales: 1975. V. 48

AZEGLIO, MASSIMO D'
The Challenge of Barletta. London: 1880. V. 51

AZHDERIAN, H. W.
Reference Works in Music & Music Literature in Five Libraries of Los Angeles County. Los Angeles: 1953. V. 49

AZMI, IFTIKHAR
The Garden of the Night. London: 1979. V. 49

AZZINI, GIUSEPPE
The Duties of Man. London: 1862. V. 47

B

B., A.
A Letter from a Friend in Abingdon, to a Gentleman in London, Concerning the Election of Burgesses for the Ensuing Parliament. 1679. V. 50
A Narrative of the Atrocities Committed by the Crew of the Piratical Brig "El Defensor de Pedro" with a Brief Account of the Trial and Execution of the Pirates. London: 1830. V. 52
A Poem on Absolute Predestination. Nottingham: 1785. V. 49

B., W.
Strange and Wonderful News, from the Lords of the Tower, Or a Dialogue Between Them and My Lord Stafford's Ghost. London: 1681. V. 47

BAAS, J. H.
Outlines of the History of Medicine and Medical Profession. New York: 1889. V. 52

THE BABACOMORI Land Grant. 1880?. V. 52

BABB, JAMES T.
The White House Library: a Short Title List. Washington: 1967. V. 47; 48

BABBAGE, CHARLES
The Analytical Engine and Mechanical Notation. London: 1989. V. 52
A Chapter on Street Nuisances. London: 1864. V. 54
The Ninth Bridgewater Treatise. London: 1837. V. 53
The Ninth Bridgewater Treatise. London: 1838. V. 54
On the Economy of Machinery and Manufactures. London: 1832. V. 53
Passages from the Life of a Philosopher. London: 1864. V. 47; 48; 51; 52; 54
Reflections on the Decline of Science in England, and On some Of Its Causes. London: 1830. V. 53
Table of the Logarithms...from 1 to 108000... London: 1834. V. 47
Table of the Logarithms...from 1 to 108000. London: 1841. V. 47
The Works. London: 1989. V. 50

BABBITT, CHARLES
Early Days at Council Bluffs. Washington: 1916. V. 53

BABBITT, EDWIN D.
The Principles of Light & Color... New York: 1896. V. 48

BABCOCK, A. E.
Military Posts...a Report of Inspection of Military Posts. Washington: 1867. V. 48

BABCOCK, HAVILAH
I Don't Want to Shoot an Elephant, and Other Stories. New York: 1958. V. 47
My Health is Better in November: Twenty-Five Stories of Hunting and Fishing in the South. Columbia: 1947. V. 47
Tales of Quails 'n Such. New York: 1951. V. 47
Tales of Quails 'n Such. New York: 1957. V. 53

BABCOCK, PHILIP H.
Falling Leaves. Tales From a Gun Room. New York: 1937. V. 47; 52

BABCOCK, ROBERT
Diseases of the Lungs. New York: 1907. V. 48; 53

BABEL, ISAAC
Red Cavalry. London: 1929. V. 54
Red Cavalry. New York: 1929. V. 50

BABER, ASA
The Land of a Million Elephants. New York: 1970. V. 53

BABES In the Wood. London: 1849. V. 50

THE BABES in the Wood. London: 1851. V. 54

THE BABES In the Wood. London: 1861. V. 53

BABINGTON, C.
Catalogue of the Birds of Suffolk. London: 1884-86. V. 48; 52

BABINGTON, CHURCHILL
The Influence of Christianity in Promoting the Abolition of Slavery in Europe. Cambridge: 1846. V. 50; 52
An Introductory Lecture on Archaeology Delivered Before the University of Cambridge. Cambridge: 1865. V. 51

BABINGTON, GERVASE
A Briefe Conference, Betwixt Mans Frailtie and Faith. London: 1596. V. 48; 50

BABINGTON, WILLIAM
A New System of Mineralogy in the Form of Catalogue, After the Manner of Baron Born's Systymatic Catalogue of the Collection of Fossils of Mlle. Eleonore de Raab. London: 1799. V. 53
A Syllabus of a Course of Chemical Lectures Read at Guy's Hospital. London: 1816. V. 53

BABLE, A. O.
The Cow Boy Schottische. Chicago: 1887. V. 54

BABLET, DENIS
Revolutions in Stage Design of the XXth Century. Paris & New York: 1977. V. 49

BABSON, GRACE K.
A Descriptive Catalogue of the Grace K. Babson Collection of the Works of Sir Isaac Newton and the Material Relating to Him in the Babson Institute Library, Babson Park, Mass. 1950. V. 50; 52
A Descriptive Catalogue of the Grace K. Babson Collection of the Works of Sir Isaac Newton and the Material Relating to him in the Babson Institute Library, with A Supplement to the Catalogue... New York: 1950-55. V. 48; 49; 50; 51

BABTICOCHI, D.
Lesson for the Harpsichord or Piano Forte. London: 1770. V. 52

BABY'S Diary. London: 1925. V. 53

BABY'S Linen Alphabet Book. London: 1890. V. 49

BABY'S Red Letter Days. Syracuse: 1901. V. 47; 49

BACA, MANUEL CABEZA DE
Vicente Silva and His 40 Bandits. Washington: 1947. V. 50

BACCI, ANDREA
De Naturali Vinorum Historia De Vinis Italiae Et de Conviviis Antiquorum Libri Septem... Rome: 1596. V. 51
Del Tevre...Libri Tre... Venice: 1576. V. 48

BACCI, PIETRO GIACOMO
Vita di S. Filippo Neri Fiorentino Fondatore della Congregazione dell' Oratorio Scritta dal P. Pietro Giacomo Bacci Prete dell' Istessa Congregazione, E Accrescinta di Molti Fatti, e Detti del Santo, Cavati da' Processi della sua Coanonizzazione... Rome: 1745. V. 48

BACH, RICHARD
Jonathan Livingston Seagull. New York: 1970. V. 52
Stranger to the Ground. New York: 1963. V. 50

BACHAUS, THEODORE
Private Presses of San Serriffe. Port Clarendon: 1980. V. 54

BACHE, A. D.
Report of the Superintendent of the Coast Survey, Showing the Progress of the Survey During the Year 1854. Washington: 1855. V. 47
Safety Apparatus for Steam Boilers. Philadelphia: 1832. V. 52

BACHE, ANNA
Clara's Amusements. Philadelphia & New York: 1846. V. 47

BACHE, FRANKLIN
The Pharmacopoeia of the United States of America. Philadelphia: 1864. V. 53

BACHE, JULES S.
A Catalogue of Paintings in the Collection of... New York: 1929. V. 48; 50

BACHELDER, JOHN
Bachelder's Illustrated Tourist's Guide of the United States. Boston: 1873. V. 53
Popular Resorts and How to Reach Them. Boston: 1875. V. 53

BACHELLER, IRVING
The Story of a Passion. East Aurora: 1899. V. 47

BACHELOR Belles. New York: 1908. V. 49

BACHELOR, J.
They Further Adventures of Halley's Comet. 1980. V. 54

THE BACHELOR'S Guide and Widow's Manual... New York: 1842. V. 51

BACHER, ROBERT FOX
Atomic Energy States, As Derived From the Analyses of Optical Spectra. New York and London: 1932. V. 50

BACHMAIR, JOHN JAMES
A Complete German Grammar. London: 1771. V. 50

BACHOFEN, J. J.
Walls: Res Sancta/ Res Sacrae. Lexington: 1961. V. 47; 49

BACK, GEORGE
Narrative of the Arctic Land Expedition to the Mouth of the Great Fish River, and Along the Shores of the Arctic Ocean, in the Years 1833, 1834 and 1835. London: 1836. V. 47; 51
Narrative of the Arctic Land Expedition to the Mouth of the Great Fish River, and Along the Shores of the Arctic Ocean in the Years 1833, 1834 and 1835. Philadelphia: 1836. V. 48; 52

BACKHOUSE, E.
Annals and Memoirs of the Court of Peking (from the 16th to the 20th Century). London: 1914. V. 50

BACKHOUSE, JAMES
Narrative of a Visit to Mauritius and South Africa. London: 1844. V. 47; 49; 51
A Narrative of a Visit to Mauritius and South Africa. Hamilton: 1944. V. 47
A Narrative of a Visit to the Australian Colonies. London: 1843. V. 49

BACKHOUSE, JANET
John Scottowe's Alphabet Books. London: 1974. V. 51; 54
The Madresfield Hours, a 14th Century Manuscript in the Library of Early Beauchamp. Oxford: 1975. V. 47; 53

BACKUS, R. H.
Georges Bank. Cambridge: 1987. V. 53

THE BACKWOODS of Canada: Being Letters from the Wife On an Emigrant Officer Illustrative of the Domestic Economy of British America. London: 1836. V. 48

BACON, DELIA
The Bride of Fort Edward, Founded on an Incident of the Revolution. New York: 1839. V. 47; 49; 52

BACON, EDWARD
Among the Cotton Thieves. Detroit: 1867. V. 54

BACON, EDWIN N.
Historic Pilgrimages in New England, Among Landmarks of Pilgrim and Puritan Days and of the Provincial and Revolutionary Periods. Boston: 1898. V. 52

BACON, FRANCIS, VISCOUNT ST. ALBANS
Baconiana. London: 1679. V. 47; 48; 50
Baconiana. London: 1684. V. 51
Bacon's Essays and Colours of Good and Evil. Cambridge & London: 1865. V. 52
Bacon's Essays and Colours of Good and Evil. London: 1891. V. 53
Cabala: Sive Scrinia Sacra. Mysteries of State and Government: In Letters of Illustrious persons and Great Agents... (with) Scrinia Scra; Secrets of Empire, in Letters of Illustrious Persons. A Supplement to the Cabala. London: 1654. V. 48
Cases of Treason. Written by Sir Francis Bacon, Knight, His Maiesties Solicitor Generall. London: 1641. V. 47; 54
Certaine Miscellany Works. London: 1629. V. 47; 48; 49
The Collected Works. London: 1824. V. 48
A Collection of the Proceedings In the House of Commons Against the Lord Verulam, Viscount St. Ablans, Lord Chancellor of England... London: 1740. V. 49
The Elements of the Common Lawes of England, Branched Into a Double Tract. London: 1639. V. 50
The Essaies. London: 1612. V. 47; 49
The Essayes or Counsels, Civill and Moral... London: 1625. V. 49; 51; 52; 53; 54
The Fssayes or Counsels Civill and Morall... London: 1632. V. 53
The Essayes or Counsels Civill and Morall... London: 1639. V. 47; 48; 49; 53
The Essayes, or Covnsels, Civill and Morall. London: 1664. V. 47; 48; 49; 54
The Essayes, or Covnsels, Civill and Morall. London: 1673. V. 48
The Essayes or Covnsels, Civill and Morall of Francis Lo. Verulam... London: 1693. V. 51
Essays. London: 1873. V. 52
The Essays. London: 1907. V. 47
Essays. London: 1912. V. 47
Essays. New York: 1944. V. 47; 48; 49; 50; 51; 52; 53; 54
The Essays: Colors of Good and Evil and Advancement of Learning. London: 1900. V. 52
Essays, Moral, Economical and Political... London: 1798. V. 49; 51
The Essays of Francis Bacon. Tolz: 1920. V. 50; 51; 54
Essays of Lord Bacon. London: 1894. V. 51
The Essays, or Counsels, Civil and Moral... London: 1680. V. 48; 49; 52
The Essays or Counsels, Civil and Moral... London: 1696. V. 50; 53
The Essays or Counsels, Civil and Moral. London: 1890. V. 54
Gardens and Friendship (Essays). London: 1910. V. 49
Historia Regni Henrici Septimi. Lugd. Batavor. 1647. V. 53
Historia Vitae & Mortis... London: 1623. V. 51
Historia Vitae & Mortis. Lugduni Batavorum Leiden: 1636. V. 47
The Historie of the Raigne of King Henry the Seventh. London: 1622. V. 48; 51
The Historie of the Reigne of King Henry the Seventh. London: 1629. V. 48
The Historie of the Reigne of King Henry the Seventh... London: 1641. V. 54
History Natural and Experimental of Life and Death. London: 1638. V. 47; 48; 49; 50; 51
History, Natural and Experimentall (sic), of Life and Death or Of the Prolongation of Life. London: 1650. V. 54
The History of the Reigns of Henry the Seventh, Henry the Eighth, Edward the Sixth and Queen Mary. London: 1676. V. 52; 54
The History of the Reigns of Henry the Seventh, Henry the Eighth, Edward the Sixth and Queen mary... London: 1686. V. 50
Instaur Mag. P.I. of the Advancement and Proficience of Learning or the Partitions of Science... Oxford: 1640. V. 47
Letters of Sir Francis Bacon... V. 48
Letters of Sr. Francis Bacon, Baron of Verulam, Viscount St. Albany, and Lord High Chancellor of England. London: 1702. V. 49; 52
The Naturall and Experimentall History of Winds Etc. London: 1653. V. 50
(Novum Organum) Instauratio Magna. Londini: 1620. V. 53
Of Gardens. London: 1902. V. 47; 49
Of Gardens. Northampton: 1959. V. 48; 51; 52
Of Gardens. London: 1993. V. 50; 52
Of Studies. San Francisco: 1928. V. 52
Of the Advancement and Proficience of Learning, of the Partitions of Sciences. Lichfield: 1640. V. 48
Of the Advancement and Proficience of Learning, or the Partitions of Sciences. Oxford: 1640. V. 51; 53
Of the Advancement and Proficience of Learning, or the Partitions of Sciences... London: 1674. V. 47; 50; 52
Opera Omnia. London: 1730. V. 48; 49
Opervm Moralivm et Civilum (with Novum Organum). Londini: 1620. V. 49
Opervm Moralivm Et Civilvm. Londini: 1638. V. 47; 48
Opuscula Varia Posthuma, Philosophica, Civilia, et Theologica. London: 1658. V. 51; 53
Resuscitatio. London: 1657. V. 48; 50; 51; 52
Resuscitatio... London: 1661. V. 54
Resuscitatio... London: 1671. V. 48; 49
Sermones Fideles, Ethici, Politici, Oeconomici... Leyden: 1641. V. 49
Sylva Sylvarum... London: 1627. V. 48; 49
Sylva Sylvarum... London: 1635. V. 48; 52
Sylva Sylvarum... London: 1664. V. 52
The Two Bookes of Francis Bacon. London: 1605. V. 47; 48; 49; 54
The Two Bookes of Francis Bacon... London: 1605/39. V. 49
The Two Bookes of Sr. Francis Bacon of the Proficience and Advancement of Learning. London: 1629. V. 48; 54
The Two Bookes of Sr Francis Bacon. Of the Proficiencie and Advancement of Learning, Divine and Humane. Oxford: 1633. V. 47; 49; 51; 53; 54
The Two Books of Francis Bacon, of the Proficiencie and Advancement of Learning. London: 1808. V. 54
The Works... London: 1740. V. 47; 51
The Works... London: 1765. V. 52; 54
Works... London: 1824. V. 48; 53
Works. London: 1825-34. V. 51
The Works. London: 1826. V. 48; 49
The Works. London: 1857-59. V. 48

BACON, GEORGE W.
Bacon's Descriptive Handbook of America. London. V. 54
BACON'S Descriptive Handbook of America, Comprising History, Geography, Agriculture, Manufactures, Commerce, Railways, Politics, Education, Laws, Etc. London: 1865. V. 48
Bacon's Guide to America and the Colonies, for the Capitalist, Tourist, or Emigrant. London: 1870. V. 50

BACON, JOHN
Liber Regis, del Thesaurus Rerum Ecclesiasticarum. London: 1786. V. 53
The Life of Edward Jenner. London: 1838. V. 51

BACON, JOHN MACKENZIE
By Land and Sky. London: 1908. V. 51

BACON, LEONARD
The Scrannel Pipe: a Book of Verse. New Haven: 1909. V. 54
The Voyage of Autoleon. New York: 1935. V. 54

BACON, MARY ANN
Flowers and Their Kindred Thoughts. London: 1848. V. 50
Fruits from the Garden and Field. London: 1850. V. 53

BACON, NATHANIEL
The Annalls of Ipswiche. London: 1884. V. 51
An Historical and Political Discourse of the Laws and Government of England... London: 1739. V. 50

BACON, NICHOLAS
The Recreation of His Age. Oxford: 1919. V. 50

BACON, PEGGY
Funerealities. Woodstock: 1925. V. 51; 54

BACON, ROGER
The Mirror of Alchemy. Los Angeles: 1975. V. 48
The Most Famous History of the Learned Fryer Bacon... London: 1720. V. 47

BACON, ROGER continued
Opus Majus ad Clementem Quartum, Pontificem Romanum. London: 1733. V. 49
The Opus Majus of Roger Bacon. Philadelphia: 1928. V. 52; 54
Opus Majus...Nunc Vero Diligenter Recusum. Venice: 1750. V. 47

BACON, THOMAS
Laws of Maryland at Large, with Proper Indexes. Annapolis: 1765. V. 47; 53

BACON-FOSTER, CORRA
Early Chapters in the Development of the Patomac Route to the West. Washington: 1912. V. 50

BACOU, ROSELINE
Bresdin to Redon: Six Letters 1870 to 1881. Northampton: 1969. V. 47

BACQUEVILLE DE LA POTHERIE, CLAUDE CHARLES LE ROY
Histoire de l'Amerique Septentrionale. Paris: 1722. V. 47

BADAWY, ALEXANDER
Architecture in Ancient Egypt and the Near East. Cambridge: 1978. V. 51
A History of Egyptian Architecture: the Empire (the New Kingdom) from the Eighteenth Dynasty to the End of the Twentieth Dynasty 1580-1085 B.C. Berkeley and Los Angeles: 1968. V. 51
A History of Egyptian Architecture: the First Intermediate Period, the Middle Kingdom and the Second Intermediate Period. Berkeley and Los Angeles: 1966. V. 51

BADCOCK, JOHN
Conversations on Conditioning. London: 1829. V. 47; 53
The Groom's Oracle and Pocket Stable Directory... Philadelphia: 1831. V. 51
Slang. A Dictionary of the Turf, the Ring, the Chase, the Pit, of Bon-Ton and the Varities of Life, Forming the Completest and Most Authentic Lexicon... London: 1823. V. 47

BADCOCK, WILLIAM
A New Touch-Stone for Gold and Silver Wares... London: 1679. V. 47

BADDELEY, JOHN
The London Angler's Book, or Waltonian Chronicle... London: 1834. V. 47

BADDELEY, JOHN F.
The Rugged Flanks of the Caucasus. Oxford: 1940. V. 47
The Russian Conquest of the Caucasus. London: 1908. V. 49

BADDELEY, JOHN JAMES
Cripplegate. London: 1921. V. 50; 54

BADEAU, ADAM
Military History of Ulysses S. Grant, From April 1861 to April 1865. New York: 1881. V. 49

BADEN-POWELL, B. F. S.
In Savage Isles and Settled Lands: Malaysia, Australasia and Polynesia 1888-1891. London: 1892. V. 47

BADEN-POWELL, GEORGE S.
New Homes for the Old Country. London: 1872. V. 49; 50

BADEN-POWELL, ROBERT STEVENSON SMYTH
Aids to Scouting for N.-C.O.'s & Men. London: 1900. V. 48; 52
Pigsticking or Hoghunting. London: 1889. V. 47; 49; 53
Sketches in Mafeking and East Africa. London: 1907. V. 47

BADEN-POWELL, WARINGTON
Canoe Travelling: Log of a Cruise on the Baltic, and Practical Hints on Building and Fitting Canoes. London: 1871. V. 50

BADER, BARBARA
American Picture Books from Noah's Ark to the Beast Within. New York: 1976. V. 49; 51; 54

BADGER, GEORGE PERCY
Description of Malta and Gozo. Malta: 1838. V. 47

BADGER, JOSEPH
A Memoir of Rev. Joseph Badger. Hudson: 1851. V. 53

BADGER, T. R.
A Record of Horses, 1900-1936. London: 1937. V. 47; 49

BADHAM, CHARLES DAVID
Prose Haleutics or Ancient and Modern Fish Tattle. London: 1854. V. 47; 48; 50; 51; 53
A Treatise on the Esculent Funguses of England... London: 1847. V. 48; 49
A Treatise On the Esculent Funguses of England... London: 1863. V. 49; 52; 54

BADIN, STEPHEN THEODORE
Origine et Progress de La Mission du Kentucky. Paris: 1821. V. 48

BADIUS ASCENCIUS, JODOCUS
Stultiferae Naves Sensus Animosque Trahentes Mortis in Exitium. Paris: 1500. V. 52

THE BADMINTON Library of Sports and Pastimes. London: 1886-1902. V. 51

BAEDEKER, KARL
The Dominion of Canada with Newfoundland and an Excursion to Alaska... Leipsic: 1900. V. 53
The Dominion of Canada with Newfoundland and an Excursion to Alaska. Leipzig: 1907. V. 51
Palestine and Syria. Leipsic: 1894. V. 49
Palestine and Syria. Leipsic: 1898. V. 49
Russia with Teheran, Port Arthur and Peking. Leipzig, London, & New York: 1914. V. 47; 53
Southern Italy. Leipsic: 1874. V. 49
Switzerland and the Adjacent Portions of Italy, Savoy and the Tyrol. Coblenz: 1869. V. 49
The United States With an Excursion into Mexico... Leipsic & New York: 1893. V. 51; 52
The United States with an Excursion into Mexico. Leipzig, London: 1899. V. 49
The United States with an Excursion into Mexico. Leipzig/London/New York: 1904. V. 47

BAEHNE, G. W.
Practical Applications of the Punched Card Method in Colleges and Universities. New York: 1935. V. 48

BAER, KARL ERNST VON
De Ovi Mammalium et Hominis Genesi... Leipzig: 1827. V. 47; 49

BAERLE, CASPAR
Blyde Inkomst der Allerdoorluchtighste Koninginne Maria de Medicis, t'Amsterdam. Amsterdam: 1639. V. 50

BAERLEIN, HENRY
Belmonte the Matador. New York: 1934. V. 50

BAETA, HENRIQUE XAVIER
Comparative View of the Theories and Practice of Drs. Cullen, Brown and Darwin in the Treatment of Fever and of Acute Rheumatism. London: 1800. V. 52

BAGATTI, B.
Excavations in Nazareth. Jerusalem: 1969. V. 49; 51

BAGBY, GEORGE W.
1860-1880. John Brown and Wm. Malone. An Historical Parallel Foreshadowing Civil Trouble. Richmond: 1880. V. 49
Canal Reminiscences: Recollections of Travel in the Old Days on the James River and Kanawha Canal. Richmond: 1879. V. 49
For Virginians Only. What I Did with My Fifty Millions. Philadelphia: 1874. V. 50

BAGE, ROBERT
The Fair Syrian, a Novel. London: 1787. V. 49; 54

BAGEHOT, WALTER
Collected Works of... London: 1965-86. V. 54
Economic Studies. London: 1880. V. 50
The English Constitution... London: 1867. V. 49
The English Constitution... London: 1872. V. 49; 52
Estimates of Some Englishmen and Scotchmen. London: 1858. V. 50; 51
Literary Studies. London: 1879. V. 49
Lombard Street: a Description of the Money Market. London: 1873. V. 54
Physics and Politics or Thoughts on the Application of the Principles of 'Natural Selection' and 'Inheritance' to Political Society. London: 1872. V. 52
Some Articles on the Depreciation of Silver and On Topics Connected With It. London: 1877. V. 52

BAGG, A. C.
Birds of the Connecticut Valley in Massachusetts. Northampton: 1937. V. 54

BAGGULEY, WILLIAM H.
Andrew Marvell 1621-1678 - Tercentenary Tributes. 1922. V. 50; 52
Andrew Marvell 1621-1678 - Tercentenary Tributes... London: 1922. V. 47

BAGLEY, CLARENCE B.
The Acquisition and Pioneering of Old Oregon. Seattle: 1924. V. 47
Early Catholic Missions in Old Oregon. Seattle: 1932. V. 54
History of King County, Washington. Chicago, Seattle: 1929. V. 52

BAGLEY, GEORGE
A Guide to the Tongues, Antient and Modern; being Short and Comprehensive Grammars of the English, French, Italian, Spanish, German, Latin, Greek, Hebrew, with the Arabic, Chaldaic and Syriac Languages... Shrewsbury: 1804. V. 52

BAGLIVI, GIORGIO
Opera Omnia Medica Practica et Anatomica. Lugduni: 1714. V. 54
The Practice of Physick, Reduc'd to the Ancient Way of Observations Containing a Just Parallel Between the Wisdom and Experience of the Ancients... London: 1723. V. 51
The Practice of Physick, Reduc'd to the Ancient Way of Observations Containing a Just Parallel Between the Wisdom and Experience of the Ancients... London: 1733. V. 54

BAGNALL, A. G.
New Zealand National Bibliography to the Year 1960. Wellington: 1969-80. V. 54

BAGNALL, GEORGE
Piscatorial Ramblings; or, the Fisherman's Pocket Companion. London: 1865. V. 47

BAGNALL, J. E.
The Flora of Warwickshire. London: 1891. V. 50; 51; 53

BAGNALL, ROGER S.
Greek Ostraka. A Catalogue of the Collection of Greek Ostraka in the National Museum of Antiquities at Leiden with a Chapter on the Greek Ostraka in the Papyrological Inst. of the University of Leiden. 1980. V. 50

BAGNOLD, ENID
Enid Bagnold's Autobiography. Boston and Toronto: 1969. V. 54
Letters to Frank Harris, and other Friends. Andoversford: 1980. V. 50
National Velvet. London & Toronto: 1935. V. 48; 49; 50; 53; 54
The Sailing Ships. London: 1918. V. 50

BAGOT, A. G.
Sport and Travel in India and Central America. London: 1897. V. 48

BAGOT, JOSCELINE
Colonel James Grahme of Ievens. Kendal: 1886. V. 50; 52; 54

BAGROW, LEO
History of Cartography. Chicago: 1985. V. 49

BAGROW, LEO continued
A History of the Cartography of Russia Up to 1600. (with) *A History of Russian Cartography Up to 1800.* Ontario: 1975. V. 52; 54

BAGSHAW, SAMUEL
History, Gazetteer and Directory of Shropshire... Sheffield: 1851. V. 51
History, Gazetteer and Directory of the County of Kent. Sheffield: 1847. V. 53

BAGSHAW, WILLIAM
On Man: His Motives, Their Rise, Operations, Oppositions and Results. London: 1833. V. 48

BAGSTER, SAMUEL
The Management of Bees. London: 1834. V. 53

BAHR, A. W.
Early Chinese Paintings from A. W. Bahr Collection. London: 1938. V. 47
Old Chinese Porcelain and Works of Art in China. London: 1911. V. 49; 51; 53

BAHR, HERMANN
Expressionism. London: 1925. V. 53

BAHR, JEROME
All Good Americans. New York: 1937. V. 52; 53

BAIER, JOHANN JAKOB
Monumenta Rerum Pertrificatarum Praeciputa Oryctyographiae Noricae Supplementi Loco Iungenda Interprete Filio Ferdinando Iacobo Baiero... Nurnberg: 1757. V. 47
Norica, sive Rerum Fossilium et ad Minerale Regnum Pertinentium, in Territorio Norimbergensi Eiusque Vicinia Observatarum Succincta Descriptio. Nurnberg: 1708. V. 47

BAIF, LAZARE DE
Annotationes in L. II. De Captivis, et Postliminio Reversis. In Quibus Tractatur De Re Navali. Paris: 1536. V. 52

BAIGELL, MATTHEW
Charles Bruchfield. New York: 1976. V. 47; 48; 49; 50
Thomas Hart Benton. New York: 1973. V. 49
Thomas Hart Benton. New York: 1974. V. 50
Thomas Hart Benton. New York: 1981. V. 53

BAIGENT, WILLIAM
A Book on Hackles for Fly Dressing. Newcastle-upon-Tyne: 1941. V. 53
A Book on Hackles for Fly Dressing. Newcastle upon Tyne: 1943. V. 47

BAIKIE, WILLIAM BALFOUR
Narrative of an Exploring Voyage Up the Rivers Kwo'ra and Bi'nue (Commonly Known as the Niger and Tsadda) in 1854. London: 1856. V. 50

BAIKOV, N.
Big Game Hunting in Manchuria. London: 1936. V. 48

BAILE, B.
A Manual of Navaho Grammar. St. Michaels: 1926. V. 51

BAILEY, A. M.
Birds of Arctic Alaska. Denver: 1948. V. 54

BAILEY, D. M.
A Catalogue of the Lamps in the British Museum. Volume II: Roman Lamps Made in Italy. London: 1980. V. 50; 52

BAILEY, DANIEL
The Essex Harmony Containing a New and Concise Introduction to Musick. Newburyport: 1770. V. 51; 54

BAILEY, FLORENCE MERRIAM
Birds of New Mexico. 1928. V. 52
Birds of New Mexico. Santa Fe: 1928. V. 49

BAILEY, FRANK
The Richest Section of Yale District British Columbia with Up-to-Date maps and Illustrations. Vancouver: 1913. V. 49

BAILEY, GEORGE W.
A Private Chapter of the War (1861-65). St. Louis: 1880. V. 47

BAILEY, HAROLD H.
Birds of Florida. Baltimore: 1925. V. 49; 50; 52; 53

BAILEY, HENRY
Travels and Adventures in the Congo Free State, and Its Big Game Shooting. London: 1894. V. 48; 50

BAILEY, J. M.
The Book of Ensilage; or, the New Dispensation for Farmers, Experience with "Ensilage" at "Winning Farm.". Billerica: 1880. V. 52

BAILEY, JESSIE BROMILOW
Diego De Vargas and the Reconquest of New Mexico. Albuquerque: 1940. V. 47; 54

BAILEY, KENNETH P.
The Ohio Company of Virginia, and the Westward Movement 1748-1792. Glendale: 1939. V. 48; 50

BAILEY, LIBERTY HYDE
Cyclopedia of American Horticulture. New York: 1900-02. V. 51
Cyclopedia of American Horticulture. New York: 1910. V. 47
Hortus Third, A Concise Dictionary of Plants Cultivated in the United States & Canada. New York: 1976. V. 47; 51
Hortus Third, Concise Dictionary of Plants Cultivated in the United States & Canada. New York: 1977. V. 50
The Standard Cyclopedia of Horticulture. New York: 1914. V. 51
The Standard Cyclopedia of Horticulture. New York: 1914-17/19. V. 54
Standard Cyclopedia of Horticulture. New York: 1917. V. 53
The Standard Cyclopedia of Horticulture. New York: 1928. V. 51
Standard Cyclopedia of Horticulture. New York: 1929. V. 51
Standard Cyclopedia of Horticulture. New York: 1935. V. 53
The Standard Cyclopedia of Horticulture. London: 1947. V. 54

BAILEY, NATHANIEL
The Antiquities of London and Westminster... London: 1722. V. 50; 52
Dictionarium Britannicum: or a More Compleat Universal Etymological Dictionary Than Any Extant. London: 1730. V. 53
An Universal Etymological English Dictionary... London: 1726. V. 47
An Universal Etymological English Dictionary... London: 1728/27. V. 48
An Universal Etymological English Dictionary... London: 1731. V. 47
An Universal Etymological English Dictionary... London: 1733. V. 52
An Universal Etymological English Dictionary. London: 1735/31. V. 51
An Universal Etymological English Dictionary. London: 1740. V. 52
An Universal Etymological English Dictionary. London: 1747. V. 53
Universal Etymological English Dictionary. London: 1749. V. 52
Universal Etymological English Dictionary. London: 1751. V. 52
An Universal Etymological English Dictionary. London: 1753. V. 52
Universal Etymological English Dictionary. London: 1763. V. 52
An Universal Etymological English Dictionary. London: 1773. V. 48
An Universal Etymological English Dictionary. London: 1775. V. 53
An Universal Etymological English Dictionary... London: 1776. V. 48
An Universal Etymological English Dictionary. London: 1782. V. 52
An Universal Etymological English Dictionary. London: 1790. V. 52

BAILEY, OLGA
Mollie Bailey, the Circus Queen of the Southwest. Dallas: 1943. V. 48

BAILEY, PEARCE
Accident and Injury, Their Relations to Diseases of the Nervous System. New York: 1899. V. 47

BAILEY, PERCIVAL
Intracranial Tumors. Springfield: 1933. V. 47
Intracranial Tumors. Springfield: 1948. V. 47
Intracranial Tumours of Infancy and Childhood. Chicago: 1939. V. 47; 53
Tumors Arising from the Blood-Vessels of the Brain. Springfield: 1928. V. 49; 50

BAILEY, PHILIP JAMES
The Angel World and other Poems. London: 1850. V. 49

BAILEY, ROBERT G.
Hell's Canyon. Lewistown: 1943. V. 51; 53
River of No Return. Lewiston: 1935. V. 49

BAILEY, ROSALIE FELLOWS
Pre-Revolutionary Dutch Houses and Families in Northern New Jersey and Southern New York. New York: 1936. V. 49; 51

BAILEY, SAMUEL
Letters on the Philosophy of the Human Mind. First Series. London: 1855. V. 49
A Review of Berkeley's Theory of Vision, Designed to Show the Unsoundness of That Celebrated Speculation. London: 1842. V. 49
The Theory of Reasoning. London: 1852. V. 49

BAILEY, VERNON
Empire State: a Pictorial Record of its Construction. New York: 1931. V. 49
Mammals of New Mexico. Washington: 1931. V. 54
Skyscrapers of New York. New York: 1928. V. 53

BAILEY, WILLIAM
The Angler's Instructor. London: 1857. V. 47; 51; 52

BAILEY-KEMPLING, WILLIAM
The Poets Royal of England and Scotland. London: 1908. V. 51

BAILLET, ADRIEN
Autaeurs Deguisez Sous des Nomes Estrangers, Empruntez, Supposez, Feints a Plaisir, Chiffrez, Renversez, Retournez, ou Changez d'une Langue en une Autre. Paris: 1690. V. 53
The Life of Monsieur Descartes... London: 1693. V. 51; 54

BAILLIE, G. H.
Britten's Old Clocks and Watches and Their Makers: a Historical and Descriptive Account of the Different Styles of Clocks and Watches of the Past in England and Abroad... New York: 1956. V. 53
Clocks and Watches: an Historical Bibliography. London: 1978. V. 53
Watches, Their History, Decoration and Mechanism. London: 1929. V. 53

BAILLIE, GEORGE
Memoirs of... London: 1822. V. 52

BAILLIE, JOANNA
A Collection of Poems, Chiefly Manuscript and from Living Authors. London: 1823. V. 48; 49; 50; 51; 54
Complete Poetical Works. Philadelphia: 1832. V. 54
Dramas. London: 1836. V. 48
The Dramatic and Poetical Works. London: 1851. V. 47; 49
Metrical Legends of Exalted Characters. London: 1821. V. 48; 52; 54

BAILLIE, JOANNA continued
A Series of Plays: In Which It Is Attempted to Delineate The Stronger Passions of the Mind... London: 1802. V. 48; 52
A Series of Plays: In Which It Is Attempted to Delineate the Stronger Passions of the Mind. London: 1821. V. 53

BAILLIE, JOHN
A Letter to Dr. ——— in Answer to a Tract in bibliotheque Ancienne & Moderne, Relating to Some Passages in Dr. Freind's History of Physick. London: 1728. V. 47

BAILLIE, M.
First Impressions of a Tour on the Continent in the Summer of 1818, Through Parts of France, Italy, Switzerland, the Borders of Germany and a Part of French Flanders. London: 1819. V. 47
The Morbid Anatomy of Some of the Most Important Parts of the Human Body. Albany: 1795. V. 53

BAILLIE, MARIANNE
Guy of Warwick; a Legende. Kingsbury: 1818. V. 50

BAILLIE, ROBERT
Letters and Journals. Edinburgh: 1775. V. 48

BAILLIE, W. W., MRS.
Days and Nights of Shikar. 1921. V. 54

BAILLIE-GROHMAN, WILLIAM A.
Fifteen Years' Sport and Life in the Hunting Grounds of Western America and British Columbia. London: 1900. V. 47; 49; 50; 52; 53
Sport and Life in Western America and British Columbia. 1900. V. 52; 54
A Sport in Art. London: 1919. V. 49
Sport in the Alps in the Past and Present... 1896. V. 54

BAILLIE-SCOTT, M. H.
Houses and Gardens. London: 1906. V. 53

BAILLIE SCOTT, M. H.
Houses and Gardens. London: 1933. V. 48; 50; 51; 53

BAILLY, JEAN SYLVAIN
Essai sur la Theorie des Satellites de Jupiter, Suivi des Tables de Leurs Mouvemens... Paris: 1766. V. 47

BAILY, FRANCIS
Journal of a Tour in Unsettled Parts of North America in 1796 & 1797. London: 1856. V. 50

BAILY, J. T. HERBERT
Emma, Lady Hamilton. New York. V. 50

BAIN, ALEXANDER
Autobiography. London: 1904. V. 49
Logic. Part First: Deduction; Part Second: Induction. London: 1870. V. 54
Mind and Body. The Theories of Their Relation. New York: 1873. V. 53
The Petition of Alexander Bain Against and the Evidence Before the Committee on, the Electric Telegraph Company Bill. London: 1846. V. 51

BAIN, F. W.
Christina, Queen of Sweden. London: 1890. V. 54

BAIN, IAIN
The Watercolours and Drawings of Thomas Bewick... Cambridge: 1981. V. 47; 51
The Watercolours and Drawings of Thomas Bewick. USA: 1981. V. 50; 53
The Watercolours and Drawings of Thomas Bewick... London: 1989. V. 50

BAIN, ROBERT
History of the Ancient Province of Ross...from the Earliest to the Present Time. London: 1899. V. 53

BAINBRIDGE, BERYL
Another Part of the World. London: 1968. V. 48; 53
The Bottle Factory Outing. London: 1974. V. 48
A Weekend with Claud. London: 1967. V. 47; 48; 49

BAINBRIDGE, GEORGE C.
The Fly Fisher's Guide... Liverpool: 1816. V. 50; 53

BAINBRIDGE, HENRY CHARLES
Peter Carl Faberge. London: 1949. V. 47; 48; 49; 51; 52
Peter Carl Faberge... New York: 1949. V. 47

BAINBRIDGE, JOHN
An Astronomical Description of the Late Comet from the 18 of November 1618 to the 16 of December Following... London: 1619. V. 47

BAINES, EDWARD
A Companion to the Lakes of Cumberland, Westmoreland and Lancashire. London: 1834. V. 54
History, Directory and Gazetteer of the County Palatine of Lancaster... Liverpool: 1824-25. V. 48; 53
History, Directory and Gazetteer of the County Palatine of Lancaster. Liverpool: 1825. V. 53
History of Cotton Manufacture in Great Britain. London: 1835. V. 52; 53
The History of the County Palatine and Duchy of Lancaster. London: 1868. V. 48
The History of the County Palatine and Duchy of Lancaster... London: 1868-70. V. 51; 53
The History of the County Palatine and Duchy of Lancaster. London: 1870. V. 48
Mr. Owen's Establishment at New lanarak, a Failure!. Leeds: 1838. V. 53
Yorkshire Past and Present: a History and a Description of the Three Ridings of the Great County of York... London. V. 47
Yorkshire, Past and Present: a History and a Description of the Three Ridings of the Great County of York... London: 1863. V. 52

BAINES, THOMAS
Explorations in S.W. Africa. Being an Account of a Journey in the Years 1861 and 1862 from Walvisch Bay, on the Western Coast to Lake Ngami and the Victorian Falls. London: 1864. V. 47; 50; 51; 54
The Gold Regions of South Eastern Africa. London: 1877. V. 48; 50; 52; 54
History of the Commerce and Town of Liverpool and of the Rise of Manufacturing Industry in the Adjoining Counties. London and Liverpool: 1852. V. 47; 48; 50; 53
Lancashire and Cheshire Past and Present. London. V. 47; 49
Lancashire and Cheshire Past and Present... London: 1868. V. 52
Lancashire and Cheshire Past and Present... London: 1868-69. V. 48; 53
Liverpool in 1859. The Port and Town of Liverpool, and the Harbour, Docks and Commerce of the Mersey, in 1859. London: 1859. V. 50
The Northern Goldfields, Diaries of Thomas Baines. London: 1946. V. 54

BAINES REED, T.
A History of the Old English Letter Foundries. London: 1887. V. 47

BAINTON, GEORGE
The Art of Authorship. New York: 1890. V. 51

BAIRD, GEORGE
The Story of Barney May, Pioneer. Pittsburg: 1917. V. 50

BAIRD, HUGH
Report on the Proposed Edinburgh and Glasgow Union Canal. Edinburgh: 1813. V. 54

BAIRD, JOSEPH ARMSTRONG
California's Pictorial Letter Sheets 1849-1869. Colophon: 1966. V. 54

BAIRD, SPENCER FULLERTON
Directions for Collecting, Preserving and Transporting Specimens of Natural History. Washington: 1854. V. 54
A History of North American Birds: Land Birds. Boston: 1875. V. 50
A History of North American Birds: Land Birds. Boston: 1905. V. 53
Reports of Explorations and Surveys to Ascertain the Most Practicable and Economical Route for a Railroad from Mississippi River to the Pacific Ocean. Volume 8: Zoology: Mammals. Washington: 1857. V. 51
Reptiles of U. S. Pacific R. R. Exp. and Surveys. Washington: 1857-59. V. 52
United States and Mexican Boundary Survey...Birds of the Boundary. Washington: 1859. V. 48
The Water Birds of North America. Boston: 1884. V. 50

BAIRD, THOMAS
General View of the Agriculture of the County of Middlesex. London: 1793. V. 53

BAIRD, W.
The Natural History of the British Entomostraca. London: 1850. V. 50; 51

BAIRD, W. F., MRS.
The Twentieth Century Retractor, Chess Fantasies, and Letter Problems. London: 1907. V. 47

BAIRD, WILLIAM
John Thomson of Duddingston, Pastor and Painter. Edinburgh: 1895. V. 54

BAIRD, WILLIAM T.
Seventy Years of New Brunswick Life: Autobiographical Sketches. St. John: 1890. V. 50

BAIRNSFATHER, BRUCE
Bullets and Billets. London: 1917. V. 51
Fragments From France, and More Fragments From France. London. V. 48

BAIST, G. WILLIAM
Baist's Real Estate Atlas of Surveys of Los Angeles, California. Philadelphia: 1912. V. 50
Baist's Real Estate Atlas of Surveys of Los Angeles, California. Philadelphia: 1923. V. 54

BAKER, A. B.
Clinical Neurology. Hagerstown: 1974. V. 48

BAKER, AUGUSTINE
Sancta Sophia. 1657. V. 48; 51

BAKER, CHARLES H.
The Gentleman's Companion. New York: 1939. V. 49; 51

BAKER, CHARLES HENRY COLLINS
Crome. London: 1921. V. 49; 51; 53

BAKER, D.
The Royal Gunroom at Sandringham. 1989. V. 52
The Royal Gunroom at Sandringham. London: 1989. V. 48

BAKER, D. W. C.
A Brief History of Texas. New York: 1873. V. 47; 51; 53

BAKER, DAVID ERSKINE
Biographia Dramatica. Dublin: 1782. V. 51
Biographica Dramatica. London: 1782. V. 51
The Companion to the Play-House: or, a Historical Account of all the Dramatic Writers (and Their Works) That Have Appeared in Great Britain and Ireland... London: 1764. V. 50

BAKER, DOROTHY
Young Man With a Horn. Boston: 1938. V. 51

BAKER, EDWARD
A Handbook to Various Publications, Documents and Charts Connected with the Rise and Development of the Railway System... Birmingham: 1893. V. 54
Sport in Bengal. How, When & Where to Seek It. London: 1887. V. 52

BAKER, EDWARD CHARLES STUART
The Birds of Cachar. 1900-01. V. 54
Fauna of British India, Birds. London: 1922-29. V. 50
The Fauna of British India...Birds. London: 1922-30. V. 47; 48; 49; 50; 54
The Game-Birds of India, Burma and Ceylon. London: 1921-30. V. 49; 52; 53
Game-Birds of India, Burma and Ceylon. London: 1930. V. 50
The Game-Birds of India, Burma and Ceylon. Volume II. Snipe, Bustards and Sand-Grouse. London: 1921. V. 50
Indian Ducks and Their Allies. Bombay: 1898-1900. V. 51; 54
The Indian Ducks and Their Allies. London: 1908. V. 49; 52
Indian Pigeons and Doves. London: 1913. V. 49

BAKER, ELLIOTT
A Fine Madness. New York: 1963. V. 47

BAKER, ERNEST A.
Moors, Crags and Caves of the High Peak and the Neighbourhood. Manchester. V. 47
The Netherworld of Mendip. London: 1907. V. 47

BAKER, EZEKIEL
Twenty-Six Years Practice and Observations with Rifle Guns. London: 1806. V. 47

BAKER, F. C.
The Fresh Water Mollusca of Wisconsin. London: 1972. V. 51

BAKER, GEORGE
Opuscula Medica, Iterrum edita. London: 1771. V. 47; 48; 49; 51; 53; 54
Tenby, the Navy of England, and Other Occasional Poetry. London: 1807. V. 49

BAKER, GEORGE PIERCE
Charles Dickens and Maria Beadnell: Private Correspondence. Boston: 1908. V. 51

BAKER, H. A.
Ericas in Southern Africa. Cape Town: 1967. V. 48; 49; 50; 51; 54

BAKER, H. H.
Overland Journey to Carson Valley and California. San Francisco: 1973. V. 54

BAKER, HARRIET
The Organ Grinder; or, Struggles After Holiness. Boston: 1862. V. 52

BAKER, HENRY
An Attempt Towards a Natural History of the Polype. London: 1743. V. 49; 53
Medulla Poetarum Romanorum: or, the Most Beautiful and Instructive Passages of the Roman Poets. London: 1737. V. 51
The Microscope Made Easy. London: 1743. V. 48; 52
The Microscope Made Easy. London: 1744. V. 48; 49; 53
The Microscope Made Easy... London: 1769. V. 53
The Miscroscope Made Easy... London: 1754. V. 54
Of Miscroscopes and the Discoveries Made Thereby. 1785. V. 54
Original Poems: Serious and Humorous. London: 1725. V. 50

BAKER, HENRY BARTON
The London Stage: Its History and Traditions. London: 1889. V. 49
Our Old Actors. London: 1878. V. 51

BAKER, HUMFREY
The Well-Spring of Sciences: Which Teacheth the Perfect Worke and Practise of Arithmetick... London: 1617. V. 51
The Well-Spring of Sciences: Which Teacheth the Perfect Worke and Practise of Arithmeticke... London: 1631. V. 47

BAKER, INEZ
Yesterday in Hall County. Dallas: 1940. V. 52

BAKER, J.
A Complete History of the Inquisition in Portugal, Spain, Italy the East and West-Indies. Westminster: 1736. V. 49
Multum in Parvo. Fasionable Tours, From London to the Pleasant Parts of Lancashire, Yorkshire, Westmorland, Cumberland, Etc., Etc. and the North Coast of Wales, as Far as Holyhead. London: 1802. V. 48

BAKER, J. G.
Flora of Mauritius and the Seychelles. London: 1970. V. 52
Handbook of the Amaryllideae. London: 1888. V. 53
A New Flora of Northumberland and Durham... 1868. V. 54

BAKER, J. H.
English Legal Manuscripts, Catalogue of the Manuscript Year Books, Readings and Law Reports in the Library of Harvard Law School..., Lincoln's Inn and the Bodleian Library and Gray's Inn. 1975-78. V. 51
A Flora of the Lake District. London: 1885. V. 50

BAKER, J. W.
Experiments in Agriculture Made Under the Direction of the...Dublin Society. Dublin: 1765. V. 54

BAKER, JAMES
Home Beauties as Communicated to the Author of the Royal Atlas and Imperial Duide, by Some of the Royal Family, and Nobility, Gentry, &c... London: 1806. V. 47
Pictures from Bohemia Drawn with Pen and Pencil. London. V. 54
Select Landscape Views of the Seats, and Interesting Scenes of Art and Nature, to be Found and Contiguous to the Great Post Roads, Described in the Imperial Guide. London: 1801. V. 47
Turkey. New York: 1877. V. 49

BAKER, JOHN M.
A View of the Commerce Between the United States and Rio de Daneiro, Brazil... Washington: 1838. V. 50

BAKER, JOHN WYNN
An Abridgment of the Six Weeks, and Six Months Tours of Arthur Young, Esq... Dublin: 1771. V. 50; 53

BAKER, JOSEPH BROGDEN
The History of Scarborough, from the Earliest Date. London: 1882. V. 47; 53

BAKER, NICHOLSON
The Mezzanine. New York: 1986. V. 54
The Mezzanine. New York: 1988. V. 50; 51; 53; 54
The Mezzanine. London: 1989. V. 52
Room Temperature. New York: 1990. V. 52; 53
U & I. New York: 1991. V. 47; 53
Vox. New York: 1992. V. 47; 51; 52; 53

BAKER, OSCAR
History of the Antiquities of Sandwich and Richborough Castle in Kent. London: 1848. V. 53

BAKER, R. T.
Building and Ornamental Stones of Australia. New South Wales: 1915. V. 50
The Hardwoods of Australia and Their Economics. Sydney: 1919. V. 52; 54
A Research on the Pines of Australia. Sydney: 1910. V. 52; 53

BAKER, RICHARD
A Chronicle of the Kings of England... London: 1643. V. 52
A Chronicle of the Kings of England... London: 1660. V. 54
A Chronicle of the Kings of England... London: 1665. V. 50
A Chronicle of the Kings of England. London: 1684. V. 47; 50
A Chronicle of the Kings of England... London: 1733. V. 47; 51

BAKER, ROBERT
Remarks on the English Language, in the Nature of Vaugelas's Remarks on the French... London: 1770. V. 52

BAKER, S. JOSEPHINE
The Division of Child Hygiene of the Department of Health of the City of New York. New York: 1912. V. 50

BAKER, SAMUEL WHITE
The Albert N'Yanza, Great Basin of the Nile, and Explorations of the Nile Sources. London: 1866. V. 47; 53
The Albert N'Yanza, Great Basin of the Nile, and Explorations of the Nile Sources. London: 1867. V. 48; 50; 53
The Albert N'Yanza, Great Basin of the Nile, and Explorations of the Nile Sources. London: 1874. V. 52
Eight Years in Ceylon. London: 1855. V. 48
Eight Years in Ceylon. London: 1902. V. 53
Exploration of the Nile Tributaries of Abyssinia. Hartford: 1868. V. 49; 52; 54
Ismailia, a Narrative of the Expedition to Central Africa for the Suppression of the Slave Trade. London: 1874. V. 51
The Nile Tributaries of Abyssinia, and the Sword Hunters of the Hamran Arabs. London: 1867. V. 49; 50
The Nile Tributaries of Abyssinia, and the Sword Hunters of the Hamran Arabs. London: 1874. V. 54
The Rifle and the Hound in Ceylon. London: 1854. V. 50; 54
Wild Beasts and Their Ways. Reminiscences of Europe, Asia, Africa and America. London: 1890. V. 47; 48

BAKER, T.
A Rudimentary Treatise on land and Engineering Surveying... London: 1850. V. 49

BAKER, THOMAS
Hampstead Heath. London: 1706. V. 51
Reflections Upon Learning, Wherein is Shown the Insufficiency Thereof... London: 1699. V. 49; 52
Reflections Upon Learning, Wherein is Shown the Insufficiency Thereof. London: 1738. V. 53
Traite de l'Incertitude des Sciences, Traduit de l'Anglois. Paris: 1714. V. 51

BAKER, THOMAS BARWICK LLOYD
War with Crime, Being a Selection of Reprinted Papers on Crime, Reformatories, etc. London: 1889. V. 52

BAKER, VALENTINE
Clouds in the East: Travels and Adventures on the Perso-Turkoman Frontier. London: 1876. V. 53

BAKER, Z.
The Cottage Builder's Manual. Worcester: 1856. V. 50

BAKER-GABB, RICHARD
Hills and Vales of the Black Mountain District, on the Border of Brecon, Monmouth and Hereford. Hereford: 1913. V. 51

BAKEWELL, ROBERT
An Introduction to Geology. London: 1815. V. 47; 53
An Introduction to Geology... London: 1828. V. 48; 49; 53; 54
An Introduction to Geology... London: 1833. V. 49; 53; 54
An Introduction to Geology... London: 1838. V. 53
An Introduction to Geology. New Haven: 1839. V. 47
Observations on the Influence of Soil and Climate Upon Wool; From Which Is Deduced, a Certain and Easy Method of Improving the Quality of English Clothing Wools... London: 1808. V. 48

THE BAKHTYAR Nama: a Persian Romance. Lanarkshire: 1883. V. 54

BAKST, LEON
The Inedited Works of Bakst. New York: 1927. V. 50; 51
L'Oeuvre de Leon Bakst Pour La Belle ou Bois Dramant. Paris: 1922. V. 47

THE BALANCE and Columbian Repository. Hudson: 1804. V. 49

BALANCHINE, GEORGE
Choreography... A Catalogue of Works. New York: 1983. V. 50; 51

BALBANI, NICCOLO
The Italian Convert, Newes from Italy, of a Second Moses... London: 1655. V. 48

BALCARRES, COLIN LINDSAY, 3RD EARL OF
An Account of the Affairs of Scotland, Relating to the Revolution in 1688. London: 1779. V. 53
Memoirs Touching the Revolution in Scotland, MDCLXXXVIII-MDCXC. Edinburgh: 1841. V. 53

BALCH, EDWIN SWIFT
Glaciers or Freezing Caverns. Philadelphia: 1900. V. 54

BALCH, WILLIAM R.
The Mines, Miners and Mining Interestes of the United States in 1882. Philadelphia: 1882. V. 47

BALCOMB, MARY N.
Nicolai Fechin. N.P: 1975. V. 53

BALD, ROBERT
Report of a Mineral Survey Along the Track of the Proposed North or Level Line of Canal Betwixt Edinburgh and Glasgow, as Projeted by John Rennie, Esq...(and) Observations Occasioned by the Mineral Survey of Mr. Robert Bald...in Which a Comparison is... Leight: 1814. V. 54

BALDASS, LUDWIG VON
Giorgione. London: 1965. V. 50
Heronimus Bosch. Wien-Muchen: 1959. V. 50
Jan Van Eyck. London: 1952. V. 49; 51; 53

BALDI, GUIDO
Le Mechaniche. Venice: 1615. V. 51

BALDICK, ROBERT
The Life of J. K. Huysmans. Oxford: 1955. V. 50

BALDRY, A. L.
Modern Mural Decoration. London: 1902. V. 53
The Practice of Water-Colour Painting. London: 1911. V. 51
Sir John Everett Millais. His Art and Influence. London: 1899. V. 54
A Treatise on Landscape Painting in Watercolours by David Cox. London: 1922. V. 54

BALDWIN, ALICE B.
Memoirs of Major General Frank D. Baldwin. Los Angeles: 1929. V. 49

BALDWIN, C. L.
Quinquivara. New York: 1944. V. 52

BALDWIN, CALEB C.
A Manual of the Foochow Dialect... Foochow: 1871. V. 47

BALDWIN, FAITH
Look Out or Liza. Toronto and New York: 1950. V. 53

BALDWIN, GEORGE RUMFORD
Report Showing the Cost and Income of a Rail-Road As Surveyed from Toledo, Ohio to Chicago, Illinois... Toledo: 1847. V. 54

BALDWIN, J.
The Large and Small Game of Bengal and the North-Western Provinces of India. London: 1877. V. 51

BALDWIN, JAMES
Another Country. New York: 1962. V. 51; 54
Blues for Mister Charlie. New York: 1964. V. 51; 53; 54
The Devil Finds Work. New York: 1976. V. 52
The Fire Next Time. New York: 1963. V. 47; 50; 52; 53
Giovanni's Room. New York: 1956. V. 47; 50; 51; 52; 53; 54
Giovanni's Room. London: 1957. V. 51
Go Tell It On the Mountain. New York: 1953. V. 48; 49; 50; 52; 53; 54
Go Tell It On the Mountain. London: 1954. V. 51; 53
Go Tell It on the Mountain. Franklin Center: 1979. V. 50; 51; 52; 54
Gypsy and other Poems. Leeds: 1989. V. 49; 50; 52
Gypsy and Other Poems. Nevada City: 1989. V. 49; 51
If Beale Street Could Talk. New York: 1974. V. 50; 51; 53
Jimmy's Blues. London: 1983. V. 49; 53
Just Above My Head. New York: 1978. V. 53
Just Above My Head. New York: 1979. V. 47; 48; 49; 50; 54
Little Man Little Man. New York: 1976. V. 52
The Negro Protest. Boston: 1963. V. 50; 51
No Name in the Street. London: 1972. V. 51
No Name in the Street. New York: 1972. V. 48; 51
Nobody Knows My Name. New York: 1961. V. 53; 54
Notes of a Native Son. Boston: 1955. V. 54
Nothing Personal. London: 1964. V. 47
Nothing Personal. Lucerne: 1964. V. 47
Nothing Personal. New York: 1964. V. 47; 48; 50; 51; 52; 54
Nothing Personal. New York: 1965. V. 53
One Day When I Was Lost: A Scenario Based on the Autobiography of Malcolm X. London: 1972. V. 54
The Price of the Ticket. New York: 1985. V. 52
Tell Me How Long the Train's Been Gone. New York: 1968. V. 50; 51; 53; 54

BALDWIN, JAMES MARK
Dictionary of Philosophy and Psychology and... Gloucester: 1960. V. 47

BALDWIN, JOSEPH G.
The Flush Times of Alabama and Mississippi. New York: 1853. V. 47

BALDWIN, LOAMMI
Letter and Documents, in Relation to the Disscolution of the Engagement of Loammi Baldwin with the Union Canal Co. Harrisburg: 1823. V. 53
Report On the Subject of Introducing Pure Water into the City of Boston. Boston: 1834. V. 53

BALDWIN LOCOMOTIVE WORKS
Illustrated Catalogue of Locomotives. Philadelphia: 1881. V. 47

BALDWIN, SETH C.
The Beauties of Jacksonism. Warrensburgh?: 1832. V. 48

BALDWIN, WALTER J.
Punishment Without Crime; or Imprisonment for Debt Proved Unjust, Impolitic... London: 1813. V. 50

BALDWIN, WILLIAM CHARLES
African Hunting and Adventure from Natal to the Zambesi Including Lake Ngami, The Kalahari Desert etc., from 1852 to 1860. London: 1894. V. 47

BALE, JOHN
A Brefe Chronycle Concernynge the Examinacyon and Death of the Blessed Martyr of Christ Syr Johan Oldecastell the Lorde Cobham. Antwerp: 1544. V. 51
The First Two Partes of the Actes or Unchast Examples of the Englysh Votaries Taken Out of Their Owne Legenades (sic) and Chronycles of Johan Bale. London: 1551. V. 52
The First Two Partes of the Actes or Vnchaste Examples of the Englyshe Votaryes... 1560. V. 47
The Image of Both Churches. London: 1570. V. 49; 53
Khynge Johan: a Play in Two Parts. 1838. V. 51
The Pageant of Popes... London: 1574. V. 47

BALES, P. G.
The History of the 1/4th Battalion Duke of Wellington's (West Riding) Regiment, 1914-1919. Halifax: 1920. V. 51; 53

BALESTIER, WOLCOTT
The Average woman: A Common Story: Reffey, Captain My Captain!. London: 1892. V. 49

BALFOUR, ALEXANDER
Characters, Omitted in Crabbe's Parish Register, With Other Tales. Edinburgh: 1825. V. 47; 50
Contemplation; with Other Poems. Edinburgh: 1820. V. 54

BALFOUR, ALICE BLANCHE
Twelve Hundred Miles in a Waggon. London: 1895. V. 50; 52; 54

BALFOUR, ARTHUR JAMES
Speech in the House of Commons on Women's Suffrage. London: 1892?. V. 50

BALFOUR, E.
Cyclopaedia of India. Madras: 1871-73. V. 48
Cyclopaedia of India. Dehra Dun: 1985. V. 50

BALFOUR, FRANCIS
A Collection of Treatises on the Effects of Sol-Lunar Influence on Fevers. 1815. V. 51
A Treatise on Putrid Intestinal Remitting Fevers, In Which the Laws of the Febrile State and Sol-Lunar Influence... Edinburgh: 1790. V. 52; 54

BALFOUR, JAMES
Ancient Heraldic and Antiquarian Tracts. Edinburgh: 1837. V. 49
The Historical Works of Sir James Balfour of Denmylne and Kinnaird, Knight and Baronet... Edinburgh: 1835. V. 54

BALFOUR, MARY
Hope, a Poetical Essay; With Various Other Poems. Belfast: 1810. V. 54

BALFOUR-BROWNE, F.
British Water-Beetles. London: 1940-58. V. 51

BALFOUR-KINNEAR, G. P. R.
Flying Salmon. Spinning Salmon. London: 1973-38. V. 51; 52
Flying Salmon. Spinning Salmon. London: 1973/38. V. 51

BALGUY, JOHN
A Collection of Tracts Moral and Theological: Placed in the Order Wherein They Were First Published... London: 1734. V. 49

BALL, BENJAMIN LINCOLN
Three Days on the White Moutains... Boston: 1856. V. 52

BALL, C. A., MRS.
The Jacket of Grey, and Other Fugitive Poems. Charleston: 1866. V. 47

BALL, C. L.
Manzenita a Flower of the Sierra Nevada. Winchester: 1911. V. 52

BALL, CHARLES
Fifty Years in Chains; or the Life of an American Slave. New York: 1859. V. 52
The History of the Indian Mutiny... 1850. V. 54

BALL, CHARLES continued
The History of the Indian Mutiny... London: 1857-58. V. 47
The History of the Indian Mutiny. London: 1858-59. V. 51; 53; 54
The Rectum, Its Diseases and Developmental Defects. London: 1908. V. 53
Slavery in the United States: a Narrative of the Life and Adventures of Charles Ball, a Black Man, Who Lived Forty Years in Maryland, South Carolina and Georgia. Lewistown: 1836. V. 53

BALL, ELIZA CRAUFURD
The Christian Armour. New York: 1866. V. 50; 51; 52

BALL, EUSTACE HALE
The Gaucho. New York: 1928. V. 53

BALL, GEORGE C.
Inquest on the Death of Agnes E. Lottimer, Before Dr. George C. Ball, Coroner, Brooklyn, New York. New York: 1854. V. 50

BALL, ISAAC
An Analytical View of the Animal Economy. New York: 1808. V. 48

BALL, J.
The Geography and Geology of South-Eastern Egypt. Cairo: 1912. V. 47
The Geography and Geology of West-Central Sinai. Cairo: 1916. V. 47

BALL, JAMES DYER
Things Chinese, Being Notes on Various Subjects Connected with China. Hong Kong: 1893. V. 51

BALL, JAMES M.
Andreas Vesalius, the Reformer of Anatomy. St. Louis: 1910. V. 47

BALL, JAMES MOORE
The Sack-'Em-Up Men. Edinburgh: 1928. V. 51; 52

BALL, JOHN
The Alpine Guide: The Western Alps. London: 1898. V. 49; 53
Autobiography of John Ball. Grand Rapids: 1925. V. 50
In the Heat of the Night. New York: 1965. V. 52
John Ball, Member of the Wyeth Expedition to the Pacific Northwest, 1832... Glendale: 1925. V. 50; 53
Notes of a Naturalist in South America. London: 1887. V. 53
Peaks, Passes and Glaciers. London: 1859. V. 50
Peaks, Passes and Glaciers. London: 1860. V. 49

BALL, JOHNSON
Paul and Thomas Sandby Royal Academicians. Bath: 1985. V. 49

BALL, KATHERINE M.
Decorative Motives of Oriental Art. London: 1927. V. 51; 53

BALL, LUCILLE
Lucy's Notebook. 1951-57. V. 52

BALL, NICHOLAS
The Pioneers of '49 - a History of the Excursion of the Society of California Pioneers of New England. Boston: 1891. V. 47; 49; 54

BALL, ROBERT S.
An Atlas of Astronomy... London: 1892. V. 52
Experimental Mechanics. London: 1871. V. 50

BALL, TIMOTHY HORTON
Northwestern Indiana from 1800 to 1900 or a View of Our Region through the Nineteenth Century. Crown Point: 1900. V. 54

BALL, WILLIAM
An Appendix to the Abridgment of the Statutes of IReland... Dublin: 1794/96. V. 47
The Transcript; also, the Memorial, and Other Poems. 1853. V. 51

A BALLAD Book, or Popular and Romantic Ballads and Songs Current in Annandale and Other Parts of Scotland. Edinburgh: 1883. V. 47

THE BALLAD, or; Some Scurrilous Relfections in Verse, On the Proceedings of the Honourable House of Commons: Answered Stanza by Stanza. London: 1701. V. 50

BALLANCE, CHARLES
The History of Peoria, Illinois. Peoria: 1870. V. 50
Some Points in the Surgery of the Brain and Its Membranes. London: 1907. V. 47; 50; 52
Some Points in the Surgery of the Brain and Its Membranes. London: 1908. V. 54

BALLANTINE, JAMES
One Hundred Songs. Glasgow: 1866. V. 51
Poems. Edinburgh: 1856. V. 51

BALLANTYNE, J. W.
Manual of Antenatal Pathology and Hygiene: the Foetus. Edinburgh: 1902. V. 53

BALLANTYNE, JAMES ROBERT
A Grammar of the Hindustani Language... London: 1838. V. 51

BALLANTYNE, JOHN ALEXANDER
Reply to Mr. Lockhart's Pamphlet entitled 'The Ballantyne-Humbug Handles'. London: 1839. V. 49

BALLANTYNE, ROBERT MICHAEL
Black Ivory. London: 1873. V. 54
Blue Lights or Hot Work in the Soudan. London: 1888. V. 48; 51
The Butterfly's Ball and the Grasshopper's Feast. London: 1857. V. 48; 49; 53
Hudson's Bay; or Every-day Life in the Wilds of North America... Edinburgh: 1848. V. 50
Hudson's Bay; or Every-Day Life in the Wilds of North America... London: 1857. V. 53
Hudson's Bay; or Every-Day Life in the Wilds of North America. Boston: 1859. V. 48
Mee-A-Ow or Good Advice to Cats and Kittens. London: 1859. V. 49
Snowflakes and Sunbeams; or, the Young Fur Traders. London: 1856. V. 51
The Three Little Kittens. London: 1857. V. 50

BALLANTYNE, ROBERT MONTGOMERY
Photographs of Edinburgh, With Descriptive Letterpress by R. M. Ballantyne. Glasgow: 1867. V. 47

BALLARD, ADOLPHUS
The Domesday Inquest. London: 1923. V. 50

BALLARD, C. R.
Kitchener. London: 1930. V. 52

BALLARD, GEORGE
Memoirs of British Ladies, Who Have Been Celebrated for their Writings or Skill in the Learned Language Arts and Sciences. London: 1775. V. 49; 51; 53; 54
Memoirs of Several Ladies of Great Britain, Who Have Been Celebrated for Their Writings or Skill in the Learned Languages, Arts and Sciences. Oxford: 1752. V. 51

BALLARD, J. G.
The Atrocity Exhibition. London: 1970. V. 48; 50; 52
The Atrocity Exhibition. 1990. V. 49; 54
The Atrocity Exhibition. San Francisco: 1990. V. 51; 53
Concrete Island. London: 1974. V. 52
Crystal World. London: 1966. V. 54
The Crystal World. New York: 1966. V. 53
The Day of Creation. 1987. V. 47
The Day of Creation. London: 1987. V. 48; 52; 54
The Drowned World. London: 1962. V. 51; 53
Empire of the Sun. London: 1984. V. 47; 49; 50; 51; 54
The Four Dimensional Nightmare. London: 1974. V. 51; 53
Hello America. London: 1981. V. 49
High Rise. London: 1975. V. 51; 52; 53; 54
Love and Napalm: Export U.S.A. New York: 1972. V. 53
Low-Flying Aircraft and Other Stories. London: 1976. V. 52
Myths of the Near Future. London: 1982. V. 50
News from the Sun. London: 1982. V. 51
The Terminal Beach. London: 1964. V. 51; 52
The Unlimited Dream Company. London: 1979. V. 51; 54
Vermillion Sands. London: 1973. V. 47

BALLENTINE, GEORGE
Autobiography of an English Soldier in the United States Army. New York: 1853. V. 53

BALLIETT, WHITNEY
Dinosaurs in the Morning: 41 Pieces of Jazz. Philadelphia: 1962. V. 50
The Sound of Surprise. New York: 1959. V. 47

BALLIN, ROSETTA
The Statue Room; an Historical Tale. London: 1790. V. 49

BALLIOL College War Memorial Book. 1924. V. 54
BALLIOL College War Memorial Book. London: 1924. V. 49; 53

BALLOONING Chapter of Accidents. Nottingham: 1810-20?. V. 47

BALLOU, ADIN
After Reading Thoreau. Seal Harbor: 1979. V. 52
An Exposition of Views Respecting the Principal Facts, Causes and Peculiarities Involved in Spirit Manifestations, Together with Interesting Phenomenal Statements and Communications. London: 1852. V. 51
History of the Town of Milford, Worcester County, Massachusetts, From Its First Settlement in 1881. Boston: 1882. V. 52
The Inestimable Value of Souls. Boston;: 1830. V. 49; 53
Lecture on the Inspiration of the Bible. Delivered in the Town Hall, Milford, Mass. Sunday evening, Jan. 16, 1859. Milford: 1859. V. 49
Liberty Chimes. Providence: 1845. V. 49
Practical Christianity in Relation Education and Amusements. Hopedale: 1860. V. 53
Practical Christianity in Relation to Marriage and Divorce in a Right Order of Society... Hopedale: 1860. V. 53

BALLOU, ELLIS
An Account of the Coal Bank Disaster at Blue Rock, Ohio, In Which Four Men Were Buried Beneath the Hill for Two Weeks... Malta: 1856. V. 53

BALLOU, MATURIN MURRAY
The Cabin Boy; or, Life on the Wing. Boston: 1848. V. 51
Due South, or Cuba Past and Present. Boston & New York: 1885. V. 47; 52
Fanny Campbell, the Female Pirate Captain. Boston: 1845. V. 47
History of Cuba; or, Notes of a Traveller in the Tropics. Philadelphia: 1854. V. 50

BALLOU, ROBERT
Early Klickitat Days. Goldendale: 1938. V. 51

BALNIEL, LORD
A Commemorative Catalogue of the Exhibition of Italian Art held in...The Royal Academy, Burlington House, London, January - March 1930. 1931. V. 51
A Commemorative Catalogue of the Exhibition of Italian Art Held in...The Royal Academy, Burlington House, London, January- March 1930. London: 1931. V. 48; 53

BALSAM, L. G.
Warshawsky, Master Painter and Humanist. Carmel: 1954. V. 54

BALSTON, J. N.
The Elder James Whatman, England's Greatest Paper Maker (1702-1759). West Farleigh: 1992. V. 49

BALSTON, THOMAS
The Cambridge University Press Collection of Private Press Types, Kelmscott, Ashendene, Eragny, Cranach. 1951. V. 51; 53; 54
The Cambridge University Press Collection of Private Press Types. Kelmscott, Ashendene, Eragny, Cranach. Cambridge: 1951. V. 48; 51
James Whatman, Father and Son. London: 1957. V. 53
Staffordshire Portrait Figures of the Victorian Age. 1958. V. 49
William Balston Paper Maker 1759-1849. London: 1954. V. 48; 49; 53

BALTIMORE & OHIO RAILROAD CO.
List of Officers and Employees in the Service of the Baltimore and Ohio Rail Road Co....For the Month of February 1855. Baltimore: 1855. V. 53

BALTIMORE, FREDERICK CALVERT, 6TH BARON
Coelestes et Inferi. Venice: 1771. V. 49; 53; 54

BALTIMORE MUSEUM OF ART
The History of Bookbinding 525-1950 A.D.: an Exhibition Held at the Balitmore Museum of Art, Nov. 12, 1957 to Jan. 12, 1958. Baltimore: 1957. V. 52; 54

BALTZ, LEWIS
Candlestick Point. Tokyo: 1989. V. 54

BALZAC, HONORE DE
Les Contes Drolatiques. Paris: 1865. V. 50
Droll Stories. New York: 1932. V. 47; 48; 51
Eugenie Grandet. 1960. V. 52
The Hidden Treasures, or, the Adventures of Maitre Cornelius. 1953. V. 54
The Hidden Treasures: or, The Adventures of Maitre Cornelius. Kentfield: 1953. V. 48; 50
The Physiology of Marriage, or Meditations of an Eclectic Philosopher on Happiness and Unhappiness in Marriage. London: 1925. V. 48
The Unknown Masterpiece. San Francisco: 1993. V. 51
The Works... V. 50
The Works... New York: 1895-98. V. 47; 51
Works. New York: 1930. V. 49

BALZAC, JEAN LOUIS GUEZ, SIEUR DE
Aristippus, or, Monsr. De Balzac's Masterpiece, Being a Discourse Concerning the Court, With an Exact Table of the Principall Matter. London: 1659. V. 49
The Letters of Monsievr de Balzac. (with) *New Epistles by Movnsievr d'Balzac.* London ptd. by I.N. & are: 1638/38. V. 49
Politics in Select Discourses of Monsieur Balzac... London: 1709. V. 49

BAMBARA, TONI CADE
The Sea Birds are Still Alive: Collected Stories. New York: 1977. V. 54

BAMBERG, THEODORE
Okito on Magic: Reminiscences. Chicago: 1952. V. 50

BAMBERGER, LOUIS
Memoirs of Sixty Years in the Timber and Pianoforte Trades. London. V. 54

BAMBERGER STERN CO., NEW YORK & PARIS
Paris Models Spring and Summer 1914. 1914. V. 51

BAMBERT, A.
Africa: Tribat Art of Forest and Savana. New York: 1980. V. 51

BAMBURGH CASTLE LIBRARY
Catalogue of the Library at Bamburgh Castle, in the County of Northumberland. London: 1859. V. 53

BAMFORD, P. G.
1st King George V's Own Battalion the Sikh Regiment. The 14th King George's Own Ferozepore Sikhs... Aldershot: 1948. V. 51

BAMFORD, SAMUEL
Early Days. London: 1849. V. 47
Poems. Manchester: 1843. V. 51

BAMPBIELD, FRANCIS
All In One. All Useful Sciences and Profitable Acts in One Book of Jehovah Aelohim. 1677. V. 54

BANARESCU, P.
Zoogeography of Fresh Waters. Volume 2. Distribution and Dispersal of Freshwater Animals in North America and Eurasia. Wiesbaden: 1992. V. 50

BANCKS, JOHN
The History of the Life and Regin of the Czar Peter the Great, Emperor of All Russia. London: 1740. V. 48; 53

BANCROFT, A. L., & CO.
Bancroft's Tourist Guide to the Geyesers. San Francisco: 1871. V. 47

BANCROFT, EDWARD
An Essay on the Natural History of Guiana, in South America... London: 1769. V. 52; 53
Experimental Researches Concerning the Philosophy of Permanent Colours and Best Means of Producing Them, by Dyeing, Calico Printing, &c. Philadelphia: 1814. V. 48; 52; 54

BANCROFT, FREDERIC
Surgical Treatment of the Nervous System. Philadelphia: 1946. V. 47

BANCROFT, GEORGE
History of the United States, from the Discovery of the American Continent to the Declaration of Independence. London: 1875. V. 54
Poems. Cambridge: 1823. V. 49; 50
Prospectus of a School to be Established at Round Hill, Northampton, Mass. N.P: 1823. V. 51
Some Account of the School for the Liberal Education of Boys, Established at Round Hill, Northampton, Massachusetts. N.P: 1825. V. 51

BANCROFT, HUBERT HOWE
The Book of the Fair... the Columbian Exposition at Chicago. Chicago: 1893. V. 51
The Book of the Fair...The Columbian Exposition at Chicago in 1893. Chicago and San Francisco: 1895. V. 47
History of Arizona and New Mexico 1539-1888. San Francisco: 1889. V. 54
History of British Columbia 1792-1887. San Francisco: 1887. V. 52
History of California. San Francisco: 1884. V. 49
History of California. Santa Barbara: 1963. V. 50; 52; 54
History of California. Santa Barbara: 1963-70. V. 53
History of Mexico. San Francisco: 1883/85/86/87. V. 52
History of Mexico. San Francisco: 1886-88. V. 51; 53
History of Oregon. San Francisco: 1886/88. V. 54
History of Texas and North Mexican States. San Francisco: 1886-89. V. 49
History of the Life of William Gilpin. San Francisco: 1889. V. 52
History of the North Mexican States and Texas: 1531-1889. San Francisco: 1883. V. 54
History of the North Mexican States and Texas, 1531-1889. San Francisco: 1884/89. V. 50; 53; 54
History of the Northwest Coast. New York. V. 49
History of the Northwest Coast. San Francisco: 1884. V. 51; 54
History of the Northwest Coast... San Francisco: 1886. V. 48
History of Utah, 1540-1887. San Francisco: 1889. V. 54
History of Utah, 1540-1887. San Francisco: 1890. V. 52
Index to Bancroft's History of California. Glendale: 1985. V. 47
The Native Races. San Francisco: 1870's. V. 48
The Native Races of the Pacific States of North America. New York: 1875-76. V. 51
Nevada, Colorado and Wyoming. San Francisco: 1890. V. 49
Popular Tribunals. San Francisco: 1871. V. 49; 54
Popular Tribunals. San Francisco: 1887. V. 50; 54
Washington, Idaho and Montana, 1845-1889. San Francisco: 1890. V. 49
The Works... San Francisco: 1883. V. 48
Works. San Francisco: 1883-90. V. 47
The Works of... Volume XXV. History of Nevada, Colorado and Wyoming 1540-1888. San Francisco: 1890. V. 52; 53
The Works of... Volume XXXI. History of Washington, Idaho, and Montana, 1845-1889. San Francisco: 1890. V. 53
The Works of..History of California. Santa Barbara: 1963. V. 47
The Works of...Volume XXVI. The History of Washington, Idaho and Montana. San Francisco: 1890. V. 52
The Works of...Volume XXXII. British Columbia. San Francisco: 1887. V. 52
The Works of...Volume XXXIII. Alaska. San Francisco: 1886. V. 52
The Works of...Volume XXXIV. California Pastoral. San Francisco: 1888. V. 50; 52
The Works of...Volume XXXV. California Inner Pocula. San Francisco: 1888. V. 52
The Works of...Volumes XV and XVI. North American States and Texas. San Francisco: 1887. V. 52
The Works of...Volumes XXIX & XXX. History of Oregon. San Francisco: 1886-87. V. 52

BANCROFT, JOHN
The Tragedy of Sertorius. London: 1679. V. 47

BANCROFT, LAURA
Sugar-Loaf Mountain. Chicago: 1906. V. 53

BANCROFT, ROBERT M.
Tall Chimney Construction. 1885. V. 51
Tall Chimney Construction. Manchester: 1885. V. 50

BANCROFT, WILLIAM L.
A New Railway Outlet from Chicago to the Seaboard. Port Huron: 1866. V. 54

BANCROFT'S *Tourist Guide. The Geysers, San Francisco and Around the Bay, (North).* San Francisco: 1871. V. 49

BANCROFT'S *Tourist's Guide. San Francisco and Around the Bay (South).* San Francisco: 1871. V. 54

BANDAU, R. S.
History of Homes and Gardens of Tennessee. Nashville: 1964. V. 51

BANDEL, EUGENE
Frontier Life in the Army, 1854-1861. Glendalde: 1932. V. 50

BANDELIER, ADOLPHE FRANCIS ALPHONSE
Address of...Of the Archaeological Institute of America. Santa Fe: 1882. V. 49; 54
The Delight Makers. New York: 1890. V. 48
Final Report of Investigations Among the Indians of the Southwestern United States. Part I (only). Cambridge: 1890. V. 54
The Gilded Man (El Dorado) and Other Pictures of the Spanish Occupancy of America. New York: 1893. V. 51
Hemenway Southwestern Archaeological Expedition, Papers of the Archaeological Institute of America. Cambridge: 1890. V. 54
Historical Documents Relating to New Mexico, Nueva Vizcaya and Approaches Thereto to 1773. Washington: 1923-37. V. 54
The Islands of Titicaca and Koati. New York: 1910. V. 50
A Scientist on the Trail. Travel Letters of A. F. Bandelier. Berkeley: 1949. V. 49
The Southwestern Journals of Adolph F. Bandelier. Albuquerque: 1966-75. V. 52
The Unpublished Letters Concerning the Writing and Publishing of "The Delight Makers". El Paso: 1942. V. 48

BANDELIER, ADOLPHE FRANCIS ALPHONSE continued
The Unpublished Letters of Adolphe Bandeleir. New York: 1942. V. 53

BANDELLO, MATTEO
Certain Tragical Discourses. London: 1898. V. 51
The Goodly History of the True and Constant Love Between Rhomeo & Julietta. New Hampshire: 1903. V. 48
L'Histoire Tragique de Romeo Montecchio & Giulietta Capelletta. Paris: 1947. V. 47
The Novels. 1890. V. 50; 52
The Novels. London: 1890. V. 51

BANDINEL, JAMES
The Star of Lovell; a Tale of the Poor Clergy. London: 1862. V. 51

BANDINELLI, RANUCCIO BIANCHI
Rome, the Center of Power: 500 B.C. to A.D. 200. New York: 1970. V. 52

BANDINI, RALPH
Veiled Horizons: Storie sof Big Game Fish of the Sea. New York: 1939. V. 48

THE BANDIT Chief; or, Lords of Urvino. London: 1818. V. 49; 54

BANDLER, SAMUEL
Uterine and Tubal Gestation: a Study of the Embedding and Development of the Human Ovan, The Early Growth of the Embroyo and the Development of the syncytium and Placental Gland. New York: 1903. V. 53

BANERJI, M. L.
Orchids of Nepal Himalaya. London: 1984. V. 51

BANFF and its Beauties. The Grandeur and Magnificence of the Surroundings of This Delightful Pleasure Resort, the Centre of the Alps of America. Toronto. V. 54

BANFIELD, J.
A Guide to Ilfracombe and the Neighbouring Towns, Comprehending a General Sketch of the History and Objects Most Worthy of Remark in the Part of the North of Devon... Ilfracombe: 1838. V. 54

BANGS, JOHN KENDRICK
The Bicyclers and Three Other Farces. New York: 1896. V. 54
The Enchanted Typewriter. New York: 1899. V. 49
From Pilar to Post. New York: 1916. V. 54
A House Boat on the Styx. New York: 1896. V. 53
Katherine. New York: 1888. V. 51
Mr. Munchausen, Account of His Recent Adventures. Boston;: 1901. V. 54
Peeps at People. New York: 1899. V. 47
Uncle Sam Trustee. New York: 1902. V. 47

BANGS, NATHAN
An Authentic History of the Missions... New York: 1832. V. 54
An Authentic History of the Missions... New York: 1932. V. 49

BANHAM, REYNER
Los Angeles - the Architecture of Four Ecologies. New York: 1971. V. 50

BANIM, JOHN
Tales by the O'Hara Family... London: 1825. V. 51

BANIM, MARY
Here and There Through Ireland. 1891. V. 48

BANISTER, JOHN
A Synopsis of Husbandry. London: 1799. V. 49

BANK and Train Robbers of the West - James Boys, Younger Brothers, etc. St. Louis: 1882. V. 54

THE BANK CASE. A Report of the Proceedings in the Cases of the Bank of South Carolina, and the Bank of Charleston, Upon Scire Facias to Vacate Their Charters, for Suspending Specie Payments, with the Final Argument and Determination Thereof... Charleston: 1844. V. 48

BANKART, GEORGE P.
The Art of the Plasterer: an Account of the Decorative Development of the Craft. London: 1907. V. 48
The Art of the Plasterer. An Account of the Decorative Development of the Craft. London: 1909. V. 51

BANKES, THOMAS
A New Royal Authentic System of Universal Geography, Antient and Modern. London: 1790. V. 50

BANKOFF, GEORGE
The Story of Plastic Surgery. London: 1952. V. 52

BANKS, CHARLES EDWARD
The History of Martha's Vinyard, Dukes County, Massachusetts. Boston, Edgartown: 1925. V. 50

BANKS, IAIN
The Player of Games. London: 1988. V. 51
Walking On Glass. London: 1985. V. 53; 54
The Wasp Factory. Boston: 1984. V. 50
The Wasp Factory. London: 1984. V. 47; 49; 50; 51

BANKS, ISABELLA VARLEY
The Manchester Man. London: 1876. V. 53
The Manchester Man. Manchester: 1896. V. 50; 54
The Manchester Man. Manchester: 1897. V. 50

BANKS, JOHN
A Journal of the Life, Labours, Travels and Sufferings (In and For the Gospel) of that Ancient Servant and Faithful Minister of Jesus Christ, John Banks. London: 1712. V. 49; 54
A Short Critical Review of the Political Life of Oliver Cromwell. London: 1739. V. 47; 50
A Short Critical Review of the Political Life of Oliver Cromwell. London: 1747. V. 47
Vertue Betray'd: or, Anna Bullen. London: 1682. V. 52

BANKS, JONATHAN
The Life of the Right Reverend Father in God, Edw. Rainbow, D.D. Late Lord Bishop of Carlisle. London: 1688. V. 52

BANKS, JOSEPH
The Endeavour Journal of Joseph Banks 1768-1771. Sydney: 1962. V. 52; 54
Joseph Banks in Newfoundland and Labrador. London: 1971. V. 52; 53
The Journal of Joseph Banks in the 'Endeavour'. London: 1980. V. 49
Journal...During Captain Cook's First Voyage. London: 1896. V. 54
A Short Account of the Cause of the Disease in Corn, Called by Farmers the Blight, the Mildew and the Rust. London: 1805. V. 49

BANKS, LYNNE REID
The L-Shaped Room. London: 1960. V. 50; 53; 54
The L-Shaped Room. New York: 1961. V. 53

BANKS, RUSSELL
Family Life. New York: 1975. V. 53
The Relation of My Imprisonment. Washington: 1983. V. 51
Snow Meditations of a Cautious Man in Winter. Hanover: 1974. V. 49

BANKS, W.
Stirling and the Scottish Lakes. Edinburgh: 1860. V. 48; 50; 52

BANKS, W. L.
Flora Exotica; or Companion to the Green-House. London: 1893. V. 47

BANKS, WILLIAM
The English Master; or, Student's Guide to Reasoning and Compositions Exhibiting an Analytical View of the English Language, of the Human Mind and of the Principles of Fine Writing. London: 1829. V. 50

BANNATYNE CLUB
The Bannatyne Miscellany.... Edinburgh: 1827-36-55. V. 52

BANNER, HUBERT S.
Romantic Java Is It Was and Is. London: 1927. V. 51

BANNERMAN, ANNE
Tales of Superstition and Chivalry. London: 1802. V. 50

BANNERMAN, DAVID ARMITAGE
Birds of Cyprus. Edinburgh & London: 1958. V. 49; 50; 51; 53; 54
Birds of the Atlantic Islands. Edinburgh & London: 1963-68. V. 49; 51; 52; 53; 54
Birds of the Atlantic Islands. Volume 2. Birds of Madeira, the Desertas and the Porto Santo Islands. London: 1965. V. 53
Birds of the Atlantic Islands. Volume I. London: 1963. V. 48; 53
The Birds of the Balearics. London: 1983. V. 51
The Birds of the British Isles. London: 1953. V. 48; 50; 52
The Birds of the British Isles. London & Edinburgh: 1953-63. V. 47; 48; 49; 50; 51; 52; 53; 54
The Birds of the British Isles. London: 1956. V. 50; 52
Birds of the Maltese Archipelago. London: 1976. V. 50; 52; 53
The Birds of Tropical West Africa. London: 1930-51. V. 49; 53
The Birds of West and Equatorial Africa. London: 1953. V. 47; 49; 52; 53; 54
The Canary Islands, Their History, Natural History and Scenery. 1922. V. 54
The Canary Islands, Their History, Natural History and Scenery. London: 1922. V. 49; 50; 51
Handbook of the Birds of Cyprus and Migrants of the Middle East. London: 1971. V. 49
The History of the Birds of the Cape Verde Islands. London: 1968. V. 52; 53; 54

BANNERMAN, HELEN
Little Black Sambo. London: 1905. V. 48
Little Black Sambo. New York: 1933. V. 49
Little Black Sambo. Arkansas: 1940's. V. 49
Little Black Sambo. New York: 1943. V. 53; 54
Sambo and the Twins, a New Adventure of Little Black Sambo. New York: 1936. V. 52
The Story of Little Black Mingo. New York: 1902?. V. 53
The Story of Little Black Quibba. London: 1901. V. 51
The Story of Little Black Quibba. London: 1902. V. 50
The Story of Little Black Quibba. New York: 1903. V. 49
The Story of Little Black Sambo. London: 1899. V. 47; 49
The Story of Little Black Sambo. London: 1914. V. 49
The Story of Little Black Sambo. Boston: 1925. V. 49
The Story of Little Black Sambo. Garden City: 1933. V. 48; 52

BANNET, IVOR
The Amazons. Waltham St. Lawrence: 1948. V. 47; 50; 52

BANNING, KENDALL
Bypaths in Arcady: a Book of Love Songs. Chicago: 1915. V. 47
Pirates!. Chicago: 1918. V. 49
Songs of the Love Unending: a Sonnet Sequence. 1912. V. 52
Songs of the Love Unending: a Sonnet Sequnece. London: 1912. V. 54

BANNING, WILLIAM
Six Horses. New York: 1930. V. 47; 52

BANNING-Bradley and Associated Familes. Hartford: 1930. V. 49

BANNISTER, J. T.
A Survey of the Holy Land, Its Geography, History and Destiny, Designed to Elucidate the imagery of scripture... Bath: 1843. V. 49; 51

BANTA, DAVID D.
Making a Neighborhood, Delivered at the Shiloh Reunion, May 26, 1887. Franklin: 1887. V. 47

BANTA, R. E.
Indiana Authors and Their Books 1816-1966. Crawfordsville: 1949/74. V. 53

BANTA, THEODORE M.
Sayre Family. Lineage of Thomas Sayre, a Founder of Southampton. New York: 1901. V. 49; 51

BANTA, WILLIAM
Twenty-Seven Years on the Texas Frontier. Council Hill: 1933. V. 49

BANTOCK, NICK
Griffin & Sabine. San Francisco: 1991. V. 53
The Sabine Trilogy: Griffin & Sabine; Sabine's Notebook; The Golden Mean. San Francisco: 1991-93. V. 54

BANVARD, JOHN
Description of Banvard's Panorama of the Mississippi River, Painted on Three Miles of Canvas. London: 1848. V. 49

BANVILLE, JOHN
Doctor Copernicus. London: 1976. V. 49
Doctor Copernicus. New York: 1976. V. 50
Nightspawn. London: 1971. V. 47; 50

BAQUET, CAMILLE
History of the First Brigade, New Jesey Volunteers, from 1861 to 1865. Trenton: 1910. V. 47; 49

THE BAR, with Sketches of Eminent Judges, Barristers, &c, &c.... London: 1825. V. 47; 50

THE BAR, with Sketches of Eminent Judges, Barristers, &c, &c. London: 1826. V. 51

BARAGA, FREDERIC
A Dictionary of the Otchipwe Language, Explained in English. Cincinnati: 1853. V. 50

BARAKA, IMAMU AMIRI
Blues People. New York: 1963. V. 47; 49
Cuba Libre. New York: 1960. V. 47
The Dead Lecturer. New York: 1964. V. 48; 52; 53
Dutchman and the Slave. New York: 1964. V. 54
Home: Social Essays. New York: 1966. V. 52
Preface to a Twenty Volume Suicide Note... 1961. V. 48; 52
Schwartze Musik. (German Music). Augsburg: 1994. V. 54
The System of Dante's Hell. New York: 1965. V. 48
Tales. New York: 1967. V. 47

BARAKAT GALLERY, BEVERLY HILLS
The Barakat Gallery: a Catalogue of the Collection. Volume 1. Beverley Hills: 1985. V. 49; 51

BARAMKI, D. C.
The Coin Collection of the American University of Beirut Museu: Palestine and Phoenicia. Beirut: 1974. V. 48

BARATARIANA. A Select Collection of Fugitive Pieces. Dublin: 1773. V. 51

BARATTI, GIACOMO
The Late Travels of S. Giacomo Baratti, an Italian Gentleman, Into the Remote Countries of the Abissins, or of Ethiopia Interior. London: 1670. V. 49

BARATTIERI, GIOVANNI BATTISTA
Architettura d'Acque... Piacenza: 1699. V. 47

BARBA, ALBARO ALONSO
Arte de Los Metales... Madrid: 1729. V. 50
A Collection of Scarce and Valuable Treatises, Upon Metals, Mines and Minerals. London: 1738. V. 47; 54
Grundlicher Unterricht von den Metallen, Darinnen Beschrieben Wird, Wie Sie Werde in der Erden Generirt... 1763. V. 52; 54

BARBANSON, ADRIENNE
Fables in Ivory: Japanese Netsuke and Their Legends. Rutland: 1961. V. 50

BARBARUS, HERMOLAUS
Castigationes Plinae et Pomponii Melae. Venice: 1493/94. V. 52

BARBAULD, ANNA LAETITIA AIKIN
Evenings at Home or the Juvenile Budget Opened. London: 1807. V. 50
Poems. London: 1773. V. 47; 48; 50; 52
Works of Anna Laetitia Barbauld. New York: 1826. V. 54

BARBAULT, JEAN
Les Plus Beaux Monuments de rome Ancienne, Ou Recueil des Plus Beaux Morceaux de l'Antiquite Romaine Qui Existent Encore... Rome: 1761. V. 50
Recueil de Divers Monumens Anciens Repandus en Plusieurs Endroits de l'Italie. Rome: 1770. V. 54

BARBEAU, MARIUS
The Downfall of Temlaham. Toronto: 1928. V. 48; 51; 54
Folk Songs of French Canada. New Haven: 1925. V. 49
Haida Carvers in Argillite. Ottawa: 1957. V. 51
Haida Myths, Illustrated in Argillite Carvings. Ottawa: 1953. V. 50; 51
Indian Days in the Canadian Rockies. Toronto: 1923. V. 47; 49; 51; 53
Totem Poles... Ottawa: 1929. V. 50; 54
Totem Poles. Ottawa: 1950. V. 54

BARBELLION, P.
Lancer Leger et Poisson de Sport. Paris: 1946. V. 47

BARBE-MARBOIS, FRANCOIS
The History of Louisiana, Particualry of the Cession of that Colony to the United States of America. Philadelphia: 1830. V. 47; 48

BARBER, ANTONIA
The Enchanter's Daughter. London: 1987. V. 49

BARBER, H.
Furness and Cartmel Notes or Jottings of Topographical, Ecclesiastical and Popular Antiquities and of Historical Circumstances... Ulverston: 1894. V. 50; 52

BARBER, H. S.
Tony Tompkins the Lion Tamer. 1908. V. 51; 53

BARBER, JAMES
Tom King's; or, the Paphian Grove. London: 1741. V. 47

BARBER, JOEL D.
'Long Shore. New York: 1939. V. 47
Wild Fowl Decoys. New York: 1934. V. 47; 49; 51

BARBER, JOHN WARNER
Connecticut Historical Collections. 1849. V. 53
Historical Collections of New Jersey: Past and Present. New Haven: 1868. V. 49; 51
Historical Collections of the State of New Jersey... New York: 1845. V. 47; 51
Historical Collections of the State of New Jersey... Newark: 1852. V. 49
Historical Collections of the State of New Jersey... Newark: 1855. V. 51
Historical, Poetical and Pictorial American Scenes, Principally Moral and Religious. New Haven: 1850. V. 53
Historical Religious Events: Illustrated by Forty-Six Copper Plate Engravings. Hartford: 1828. V. 51
History and Antiquities of New Haven... New Haven: 1831. V. 48
History and Antiquities of New Haven. 1856. V. 53
Lectures on the Pilgrim's Progress; in the Form of a Dialogue Between a Teacher and His Pupils. New Haven: 1825. V. 51

BARBER, MARY
Some Drawings of Ancient Embroidery. London: 1880. V. 50
The True Narrative of the Five Years' Suffering & Perilous Adventures... Philadelphia: 1872. V. 47; 54
The True Narrative of the Five Years' Suffering & Perilous Adventures, by Miss Barber, Wife of "Squatting Bear", a Celebrated Sioux Chief... Philadelphia: 1873. V. 47

BARBER, THOMAS
Barber's Picturesque Illustrations of the Isle of Wight. London: 1835. V. 48
Picturesque Illustrations of the Isle of Wight. London: 1834. V. 48

BARBER, WILLIAM HENRY
The Case of Mr. W. H. Barber... London: 1849. V. 48; 52

BARBEY D'AUREVILLY, JULES AMEDEE
What Never Dies. A Romance. 1928. V. 52; 54

BARBIER, GEORGE
Vingt-Cinq Costumes Pour le Theatre. Paris: 1927. V. 51

BARBIERE, JOSEPH
Scraps from the Prison Table, At Camp Chase and Johnson's Island. Doylestown: 1868. V. 47

BARBON, NICHOLAS
An Apology for the Builder or a Discourse Shewing the Cause and Effects of the Increase of Building. London: 1685. V. 49

BARBOSA, P.
Introduction to Forest and Shade Tree Insects. London: 1989. V. 50

BARBOUR, DAVID MILLER
The Theory of Bimetallism and the Effects of the Partial Demonetisation of Silver on England and India. London: 1885. V. 53

BARBOUR, JOHN
The Life and Acts of the Most Victorious Conqueror Robert Bruce, King of Scotland. Edinburgh: 1758. V. 52

BARBOUR, RALPH HENRY
The Lucky Seventh. New York & London: 1915. V. 53

BARBOZA DU BOCAGE, J. V.
Ornithologie d'Angola. Lisbon: 1877-81. V. 51

BARBUSSE, HENRI
Zola. London: 1932. V. 51

BARBUT, JAMES
The Genera Insectorum of Linnaeus... London: 1781. V. 47; 51; 52
The Genera Vermium Exemplified by Various Specimens of the Animals Contained in the Orders of the Intestina at Mollusca Linnaei. Drawn from Nature. London: 1783. V. 51; 52
Les Genres des Insectes de Linne... London: 1781-88. V. 48

BARCIA, D. A. GONZALEZ DE
Barcia's Chronological History of the Continent of Florida. Gainesville: 1951. V. 47
Ensayo Cronologico, Para La Historia General De La Florida. Madrid: 1723. V. 52

BARCKLEY, RICHARD
A Discourse of the Felicitie of Man. London: 1603. V. 47
The Felicitie of man, or, His Summum bonum... London: 1631. V. 50

BARCLAY, A. E.
The Foetal Circulation and Cardiovascular System and the Changes That They Undergo at Birth. Chicago: 1945. V. 53

BARCLAY, A. W.
A Manual of Medical Diagnosis: Being an Analysis of the Signs and Symptoms of Disease. Philadelphia: 1862. V. 53
A Manual of Medical Diagnosis: Being an Analysis of the Signs and Symptoms of Disease. Philadelphia: 1864. V. 48

BARCLAY, CHARLES W.
A History of the Barclay Family. London: 1924-34. V. 50

BARCLAY, EDGAR
Mountain Life in Algeria. London: 1882. V. 54
Stonehenge and its Earth-Works. London: 1895. V. 48

BARCLAY, JAMES
Barclay's Universal Dictionary. London: 1820?. V. 52
A Complete and Universal Dictionary... London: 1799. V. 53
A Complete and Universal Dictionary of the English Language... London: 1848. V. 47
A Complete and Universal Dictionary of the English Language. London: 1856. V. 48
A Complete and Universal English Dictionary on a New Plan. London: 1774. V. 52
The Greek Rudiments; In Which All the Grammatical Difficulties of that Language... Edinburgh: 1754. V. 48; 49
A Treatise on Education: or an Easy Method of Acquiring Language and Introducing Children to the Knowledge of History, Geography, Mythology, Antiquities, Etc. Edinburgh: 1743. V. 53

BARCLAY, JOHN
Argenis. 1630. V. 53
Argenis. Leiden: 1630. V. 49
Argenis. Lugd. Bat: 1630. V. 52
Argenis. Amstelodami: 1659. V. 49
Barclay, His Argenis. London: 1636. V. 50; 52
Euphormionis Lusinini, Partes Quinq. London: 1628. V. 52
Euphormionis Lusinini Sive Ioannis Barclaii Satyricon Partes Quinque cum Clavi. Amsterdam: 1658. V. 49
Euphormionis Lusinini Sive...Satyricon. 1637. V. 52
Euphormionis Lusinini, Sive...Satyricon, Nunc Primum in Sex Partes Dispertitum, & Notis Illustratum... Leyden: 1674. V. 47
His Argenis... London: 1625. V. 49; 51; 53
John Barclay, His Argenis. London: 1628. V. 52
The Mirror of Minds, or Barclay's Icon Animorum. London: 1631. V. 51
The Mirror of Minds or Barclay's Icon Animorum. London: 1633. V. 47; 52

BARCLAY, ROBERT
The Anarchy of the Ranters and Other Libertines, the Hierarchy of the Romanists, and Other Pretended Churches Equally Refused and Refuted in a Two-fold Apology for the Church and People of God... London: 1691. V. 52
Apologie de la Veritable Theologie Chretienne, Ainsi Qu'elle est Soutenue & Prechee, par le Peuple... 1702. V. 47
An Apology for the True Christian Divinity... London: 1678. V. 50
An Apology for the True Christian Divinity... Birmingham: 1765. V. 47; 49; 50; 52; 53
A Catechism and Confession of Faith... the Ancient Testimony of the People Called Quakers... Philadelphia: 1788. V. 52
A Catechism and Confession of Faith... The Ancient Testimony of the People Called Quakers. Troy: 1803. V. 49
Theologiae Vere Christianae Apologia. 1676. V. 49
Theologiae Vere Christianae Apologia. Amsterdam: 1676. V. 50
Theologie vere Christianae Apologia. Londoni: 1686. V. 52
Truth Triumphant Through the Spiritual Warfare, Christian Labours and Writings. London: 1692. V. 49; 52; 54

BARCROFT, JOSEPH
Features in the Architecture of Physiological Function. Cambridge: 1934. V. 49
Researches on Pre-Natal Life. Oxford: 1946. V. 53
The Respiratory Function of the Blood. Cambridge: 1914. V. 49
The Respiratory Function of the Blood. Part I. Lessons from High Altitudes. (with) The Respiratory Function of the Blood. Part II. Haemoglobin. Cambridge: 1925/28. V. 49

BARD, J. P.
Microtextures of Igneous and Metamorphic Rocks. Amsterdam: 1986. V. 52

BARD, SAMUEL
Two Discourses Dealing with Medical Education in Early New York. New York: 1921. V. 50

BARDE, FREDERICK S.
Life and Adventures of "Billy" Dixon of Adobe Walls, Texas Panhandle. Guthrie: 1914. V. 47

BARDON, DANDRE
Costume des Anciens Peuples a l'Usage des Artistes, Contenant les Usages Religieux... Paris: 1784-86. V. 54

BARDSLEY, CHARLES W.
Chronicles of the Town and Church of Ulverston. Ulverston: 1885. V. 50

BARDSLEY, SAMUEL ARGENT
Medical Reports of Cases and Experiments, with Observations Chiefly Derived from Hospital Practice... London: 1807. V. 48; 52

BARDSWEL, FRANCES A.
The Herb-Garden. London: 1930. V. 47

BARDUZZI, BERNARDINO
A Letter in Praise of Verona. Verona: 1974. V. 47; 50; 51

BAREFOOT, ISAAC
A Collection of Psalms and Hymns in the Mohawk Language, For the Use of the Six Nation Indians. Toronto: 1871. V. 49

BARETTI, GIUSEPPE MARCO ANTONIO
An Account of the Manners and Customs of Italy... London: 1768. V. 47; 48; 52
A Dictionary of the English and Italian Languages. London: 1778. V. 50
A Dictionary of the English and Italian Languages... London: 1790. V. 51
An English and Italian Dictionary. Florence: 1816. V. 50
A Grammar of the Italian Language, with a Copious Praxis of Moral Sentences. London: 1778. V. 54
An Introduction to the Italian Language. London: 1755. V. 47; 49
An Introduction to the Most Useful European Languages, Consisting of Select Passages, from the Most Celebrated English, French, Italian and Spanish Authors. London: 1772. V. 47; 49
The Italian Library. London: 1757. V. 47; 49; 51
A Journey from London to Genoa, through England, Portugal, Spain and France. London: 1770. V. 47; 48; 49; 52

BARFIELD, OWEN
Danger, Ugliness and Waste (to All Artists and Men of Letters). London: 1924. V. 53

BARFOOT, JOAN
The Unreasoning Heart. New York: 1946. V. 50

BARFOOT, PETER
The Universal British Directory of Trade, Commerce and manufacture... London: 1793. V. 54

BARFORD, JOHN LESLIE
Fantasies. London: 1923. V. 50

BARGELLINI, PIERO
The Unquiet Conscience. Lexington: 1958. V. 53

BARGHEER, EDOARDO
Monumenta Toscani. Florence: 1945. V. 49

BARHAM, RICHARD HARRIS
The Ingoldsby Legends... London. V. 47; 48
The Ingoldsby Legends. London: 1840/42/47. V. 48; 53
The Ingoldsby Legends... London: 1852. V. 49
The Ingoldsby Legends. London: 1855. V. 51; 53
The Ingoldsby Legends. London: 1864. V. 51; 54
The Ingoldsby Legends. London: 1870. V. 48; 49
The Ingoldsby Legends. London: 1874. V. 51; 53
The Ingoldsby Legends... London: 1887. V. 53
The Ingoldsby Legends... London: 1898. V. 48; 49; 54
The Ingoldsby Legends... London: 1905. V. 53
The Ingoldsby Legends. London: 1907. V. 47; 48; 49; 50; 51; 52
The Ingoldsby Legends... New York: 1911. V. 51
The Ingoldsby Legends. London: 1919. V. 48
The Ingoldsby Legends. London: 1920. V. 47; 52
The Ingoldsby Legends... London: 1922. V. 50
The Ingoldsby Legends... London: 1929. V. 47
Martin's Vagaries; Being a Sequel to "A Tale of a Tub"... London: 1843. V. 52
The Witches' Frolic. London: 1888. V. 48

BARHAM, WILLIAM
Descriptions of Niagara... Gravesend: 1847. V. 54

BARING, ALEXANDER
An Inquiry Into the Causes and Consequences of the Orders in Council; and an Examination of the Conduct of Great Britain Toward the Neutral Commerce of America. London: 1808. V. 49; 50

BARING, M.
Orpheus in Mayfair and Other Stories and Sketches. 1909. V. 48; 50; 52

BARING, MAURICE
Hildesheim. Quatre Pastiches. London: 1924. V. 53
In Memoriam Auberon Herbert, Captain Lord Lucas, Royal Flying Corps, Killed November 3, 1916. Oxford: 1917. V. 47

BARING, THOMAS
Catalogue of the Library of Thomas Baring, Esq. at Sunninghill Park (later at Baring Court). London: 1914. V. 52

BARING-GOULD, SABINE
A Book of Nursery Songs and Rhymes. London: 1895. V. 53
Cliff Castles and Cave Dwellings of Europe. London: 1911. V. 49; 54
Guavas the Tinner. London: 1887. V. 48
Guavas the Tinner. London: 1897. V. 54
Iceland: its Scenes and Sagas. London: 1863. V. 49
In the Roar of the Sea. London: 1892. V. 51
The Lives of the Saints. London: 1914. V. 47; 51
The Silver Store. London: 1868. V. 51; 54

BARK, M. H.
Greenwich Hospital, a Series of Naval Sketches, Descriptive of the Life of a Man-of-War's Man. London: 1826. V. 51

BARKER, BENJAMIN
Francisco, or the Pirate of the Pacific. Boston: 1845. V. 52; 54
Mornilva; or, the Outlaw of the Forest. Boston: 1846. V. 51

BARKER, BURT BROWN
The McLoughlin Empire and its Rulers: Doctor John McLoughlin, Doctor Davd McLoughlin, Marie Louise (Sister St. Henry): an Account of Their Personal Lives... Glendale: 1959. V. 53

BARKER, CICELY MARY
The Book of the Flower Fairies. London. V. 47
Old Rhymes for All Times. London: 1928. V. 48
Rhymes new and Old. London: 1936. V. 48

BARKER, CLIVE
Books of Blood. 1984. V. 47; 50
Books of Blood. London: 1984. V. 51; 52
Books of Blood. London: 1985. V. 51; 53; 54
The Damnation Game. New York: 1987. V. 48; 51
The Great and Secret Show. London: 1989. V. 51
The Great and Secret Show. New York: 1989. V. 50; 53; 54
Hellraiser. Anaheim: 1990. V. 52
The Inhuman Condition. New York: 1986. V. 48; 51
Weaveworld. London: 1987. V. 52
Weaveworld. New York: 1987. V. 51; 52; 54

BARKER, EDMUND HENRY
Literary Anecdotes and Contemporary Reminiscences, of Professor Porson and Others... London: 1852. V. 49

BARKER, EUGENE C.
The Austin Papers. Washington: 1924-28. V. 47
The Life of Stephen F. Austin. Dallas: 1925. V. 53
The Life of Stephen F. Austin... Nashville: 1925. V. 47; 48
Mexico and Texas: 1821-1835. Dallas: 1928. V. 53

BARKER, FRED F.
Compilation of the Acts of Congress and Treaties Relating to Alaska from March 30, 1867 to March 3, 1905, with Indices and Special References to Decisions of the Supreme Court and Opinions of the Attorney-General. Washington: 1906. V. 49

BARKER, GEORGE
At Thurgarton Church. London: 1969. V. 50
Calamiterror. London: 1937. V. 49
Elegy on Spain. Manchester: 1939. V. 48; 49; 51; 52; 53
Poems. London: 1935. V. 50; 51; 53
Thirty Preliminary Poems. London: 1933. V. 51; 53
The True Confession of George Barker. London: 1950. V. 51

BARKER, J. T.
The Beauties of Flowers in Field and Wood. Bath: 1852. V. 54

BARKER, JANE
Poetical Recreations... London: 1688. V. 47; 48

BARKER, LEWELLYS
Nervous System and Its Constituent Neurons. New York: 1899. V. 47

BARKER, MATTHEW
Flores Intellectuales: or, Select Notions Sentences and Observations... London: 1691. V. 48

BARKER, MATTHEW HENRY
Greenwich Hospital... London: 1826. V. 48
Jem Bunt... London. V. 52
Jem Bunt... London: 1841?. V. 49; 51
Jem Bunt... London: 1846. V. 54
Laden with Tales, Yarns, Scraps, Fragments, Etc., Etc. to Please All Hands... London: 1844. V. 49
Land and Sea Tales. London: 1836. V. 49
Tough Yarns: a Series of Tall Tales and Sketches to Please all Hands. London: 1835. V. 52; 54

BARKER, N.
The York Gospels. 1986 (1987). V. 47

BARKER, NICOLAS
Bibliotheca Lindesiana. 1978. V. 48
Bibliotheca Lindesiana. London: 1978. V. 50
In Fair Verona. English Travellers in Italy and Their Accounts from the Middle Ages to Modern Times. London: 1972. V. 48
The Printer and the Poet. Cambridge: 1970. V. 47; 51; 53; 54
The Publication of the Roxburghe Club 1814-1926. Cambridge: 1964. V. 48
The Publications of the Roxburghe Club 1814-1962. Cambridge: 1965. V. 54
Stanley Morison. London: 1972. V. 51

BARKER, R. D.
The Food of Australian Birds. East Melbourne: 1989-90. V. 49

BARKER, S. OMAR
Buckaroo Ballads. Santa Fe: 1928. V. 47

BARKER, SAMUEL BISHOP
Bishop Parker's History of His Own Time. London: 1727. V. 47

BARKER, T. H.
Photographs of Eminent Medical Men... London: 1867. V. 47

BARKER, THOMAS
Barker's Delight; or, the Art of Angling. London: 1820. V. 47

BARKER, W. G. M. JONES
Historical and Topographical Account of Wensleydale The Valley of the Yore... London: 1856. V. 47; 53
The Three Days of Wensleydale: the Valley of the Yore. London: 1854. V. 47; 53

BARKER, WILLIAM BURCKHARDT
Lares and Penates; or, Cilicia and Its Governors... 1853. V. 54
Lares and Penates: or, Cilicia and Its Governors. London: 1853. V. 53

BARKLEY, HENRY C.
Between the Danube and Black Sea, or Five Years in Bulgaria. London: 1876. V. 49

BARKLY, FANNY A.
Among the Boers and Basutos and with Barkly's Horse, the Story of Our Life on the Frontier. Westmisnter: 1896. V. 47
From the Tropics to the North Sea. 1890. V. 50
From the Tropics to the North Sea. London: 1890. V. 51

BARKSTEAD, JOHN
The Speeches, Discourses and Prayers of Col. John Barkstead, Col. John Okey and Mr. Miles Corbet... London: 1662. V. 47; 49

BARLA, JEAN BAPTISTE
Les Champignons de la Province de Nice et Principalement Les Especes Comestibles, Suspectes ou Veneneuses... Nice: 1859. V. 49; 52
Flore Illustree de Nice et des Alpes-Maritmes. Iconographie des Orchidees. 1868. V. 49

BARLAAM AND JOSAPHAT
Barlaam & Josaphat... 1986. V. 52
Barlaam & Josaphat. Greenbrae: 1986. V. 47; 49

BARLAEUS, CASPAR
Medicea Hospes, Sive Descriptio Publicae Gratulationis, Qua Serenissimam, Auguststissmamque Reginam, Mariam de Medicis... Amsterdam: 1683. V. 47; 48
Rerum..in Brasilia...Gestarum...Historia. Amsterdam: 1647. V. 47

BARLER, MILES
Early Days in Llano. Llano: 1905. V. 49

BARLETT, LANDELL
The Vanguard of Venus. New York: 1928. V. 51; 53

BARLOW, ALAN
Chinese Ceramics, Bronzes and Jades in the Collection of Sir Alan and Lady Barlow. London: 1963. V. 54

BARLOW, CRAWFORD
The New Tay Bridge. A Course of Lectures Delivered at the Royal School of Military Engineering at Chatham. London: 1889. V. 51

BARLOW, EDWARD
Barlow's Journal of His Life at Sea in King's Ships, East and West Indiamen and other Merchantmen from 1659 to 1703. London: 1934. V. 49; 51
Meteorological Essays, Concerning the origin of Springs, Generation of Rain and Production of Wind... 1715. V. 54
Meteorological Essays, Concerning the Origin of Springs, Generation of Rain and Production of Wind... London: 1715. V. 53

BARLOW, FRANCIS
Aesop's Life: Newly Translated. London: 1687. V. 47

BARLOW, FREDERICK
The Complete English Dictionary. London: 1772. V. 54

BARLOW, JANE
The Battle of the Frogs and Mice. London: 1894. V. 50
The End of Elfintown. London: 1894. V. 48; 49; 52
The End of Elfintown. London: 1898. V. 52

BARLOW, JOEL
A Letter to the National Convention of France, on the Defects in the Constitution of 1791... London: 1792. V. 48
A Letter to the National Convention of France, on the Defects in the Constitution of 1791... New York: 1793. V. 52; 53
A Letter to the National Convention of France, On the Defects in the Constitution of 1794... New York: 1793. V. 49
The Vision of Columbus; a Poem in Nine Books. Hartford: 1787. V. 51; 52

BARLOW, P.
An Essay on the Strength and Stress of Timber, Founded Upon Experiments Performed in the Royal Military Academy... London: 1826. V. 53

BARLOW, PETER
The Encyclopaedia of Arts, Manufactures and Machinery... London: 1851. V. 50
Experiments on the Transverse Strength and Other Properties of Malleable Iron... London: 1835. V. 54
A Treatise on the Strength Of materials... London: 1867. V. 49
A Treatise on the Strength of Timber,...and Other Materials... London: 1837/45?. V. 49
A Treatise on the Strength of Timber,...and Other Materials... London: 1851. V. 52

BARLOW, T. D.
The Medieval World Picture of Albert Durers Melancholia. Cambridge: 1950. V. 48; 54

BARLOW, THEODORE
The Justice of Peace: a Treatise Containing the Power and Duty of that Magistrate (etc.). London: 1745. V. 47; 53

BARLOW, THOMAS
The Case Concerning Setting Up Images or Painting of them in Churches. London: 1714. V. 52
A Discourse of the Peerage & Jurisdiction of the Lords Spiritual in Parliament. London: 1679. V. 49
Pegasus, or the Flying Horse from Oxford. 1648. V. 47
Pegasus, or the Flying Horse From Oxford. Oxford: 1648. V. 48

BARMAN, CHRISTIAN
The Bridge. London: 1926. V. 49

BARNABAS, SAINT
The Genuine Epistles of the Apostolical Fathers S. Barnabas, S. Ignatius, S. Clement, S. Polycarp. London: 1693. V. 50

BARNABY, HORACE T.
The Long Eared Bat. Akron: 1929. V. 54

BARNARD, ALFRED, MRS.
The Life of a Negro Slave. Norwich: 1846. V. 54

BARNARD, CHRISTIAN
One Life. New York: 1970. V. 54

BARNARD, E.
Virtue the Source of Pleasure. London: 1757. V. 47; 49

BARNARD, E. E.
Photographs of the Milky Way and Of Comets, Made with the Six-Inch Willard Lens and Crocker Telescope During the Years 1892 to 1895. 1913. V. 49

BARNARD, F. A. P.
Report On the Organization of Military Schools, and the the Trustees of the University of Mississippi, November 1861. Jackson: 1861. V. 49

BARNARD, FREDERICK
Scenes and Characters from the Works of Charles Dickens. London: 1908. V. 54

BARNARD, GEORGE
Drawing From Nature... London: 1865. V. 50
Drawing from Nature... London: 1877. V. 49
The Theory and Practice of Landscape Painting in Water Colours. London: 1855. V. 47; 48; 49; 50; 51; 53
The Theory and Practice of Landscape Painting in Water Colours. London: 1871. V. 51

BARNARD, J. G.
The Phenomena of the Gyroscope, Analytically Examined. New York: 1858. V. 51
Report On the North Sea Canal of Holland... Washington: 1872. V. 51; 54

BARNARD, J. H.
Dr. J. H. Barnard's Journal...of Fannin's Regiment, Covering the Period from Dec. 1835 to June 1836. Goliad: 1949. V. 49

BARNARD, JOHN
A Present for an Apprentice: or, a Sure Guide to Gain Both Esteem and an Estate. London: 1740. V. 50
A Present for an Apprentice; or, a Sure Guide to Gain Both Esteem and an Estate. London: 1774. V. 51

BARNARD, JULIAN
The Song of the Reeds. London: 1980. V. 53

BARNARD, K. H.
A Monograph of the Marine Fishes of South Africa. 1925-27. V. 49; 51

BARNARD, M. R.
Sketches of Life, Scenery and Sport in Norway. London: 1871. V. 47; 52

BARNARD, P. M.
Facsimiles from Early Illustrated Books. London: 1900. V. 51

BARNARDISTON, THOMAS
Reports of Cases Determined in the High Court of Chancery From April 25 1740 to May 9, 1741. Savoy: 1742. V. 49

BARNAUD, NICHOLAS
Le Reveille-Matin des Francois, et de Leurs Voisins. Edinburgh: 1574. V. 49

BARNEBY, W. HENRY
Life and Labour in the Far, Far West; Being Notes of a Tour in the Western States, British Columbia, Manitoba and the North-West Territory. London, Paris, New York: 1884. V. 49; 52

BARNES, A. C.
Mechanical Processes for the Extraction of Palm Oil. Lagos: 1925. V. 52

BARNES, ALBERT
The Church and Slavery. Philadelphia: 1857. V. 53

BARNES, BARNABE
Four Bookes of Offices; Enabling Private Person for the Speciall Service of All Good Princes and Policies. London: 1975. V. 51

BARNES, CASS G.
The Sod House: Reminiscent Historical and Biographical Sketches Featuring Nebraska Pioneers 1867-1897. Madison: 1930. V. 48; 54

BARNES, CHARLES MERRITT
Combats and Conquests of Immortal Heroes. San Antonio: 1910. V. 48

BARNES, CLAUDE
John F. Kennedy - Scrimshaw Collector. Boston: 1969. V. 54

BARNES, DJUNA
The Antiphon: a Play. London: 1958. V. 52
The Book. New York: 1923. V. 51; 52
Ladies Almanack. Paris: 1928. V. 47; 49; 51; 52; 53
Ryder. New York: 1928. V. 52; 53
The Selected Works. New York: 1962. V. 52

BARNES, ELEANOR
As the Water Flows. London: 1927. V. 48; 49

BARNES, GILBERT H.
The Letters of Theodore Dwight Weld, Angelina Grimke Weld and Sarah Grimke, 1822-1844. New York: 1934. V. 49

BARNES, JAMES M.
Picture Analysis of Golf Strokes, a Complete Book of Instruction. Philadelphia: 1919. V. 50; 54

BARNES, JOHN
A Tour through the Island of St. Helena with Notices of Its Geology, Mineralogy, Botany... London: 1817. V. 54
A Tour Throughout the Whole of France... London: 1815. V. 49

BARNES, JOSHUA
Gerania: a New Discovery of a Little Sort of People Anciently Discoursed Of, Called Pygmies. London: 1675. V. 50
The History of the Most Victorious Monarch Edward IIId...Together with That of His Most Renowned Son Edward, Prince of Wales... Cambridge: 1688. V. 53
A New Discovery of a Little Sort of People. London: 1750. V. 47

BARNES, JULIAN
Before She Met Me. London: 1982. V. 48; 51; 53; 54
Duffy. London: 1980. V. 48; 49; 51; 52
Fiddle City. London: 1981. V. 52; 53
Flaubert's Parrot. London: 1984. V. 47; 50; 51
Flaubert's Parrot. New York: 1985. V. 48; 49; 51; 52; 53
Going to the Dogs. London: 1987. V. 51; 52
A History of the World in 10 1/2 Chapters. London: 1989. V. 49; 50; 51
Metroland. London: 1980. V. 47; 48; 50; 51; 53; 54
Metroland. New York: 1980. V. 53
Staring at the Sun. London: 1986. V. 47; 49; 51
Talking It Over. London: 1991. V. 48; 51
Talking It Over. New York: 1991. V. 47; 51; 52; 53

BARNES, LINDA
Bitter Finish. 1983. V. 53
A Trouble for Fools. New York: 1987. V. 51

BARNES, R. G.
Babes in the African Wood. London: 1910. V. 52

BARNES, ROBERT
The Supplication of Doctour Barnes Unto the Moost Gracyous Kynge Henrye the Eyght with the Declaration of His Articles Condemned for Heresy by the Byshops. London: 1550?. V. 49

BARNES, THOMAS
A New Method of Propagating Fruit-Trees and Flowering Shrubs... London: 1759. V. 49

BARNES, W.
Contributions to the Lepidoptera of North America. Decatur: 1911-21. V. 49

BARNES, WILLIAM
An Arithmetical and Commercial Dictionary, Containing a Simple Explanation of Commercial and Mathematical Terms and Arithmetical Operations. London: 1840. V. 48
Early England... London: 1869. V. 48; 51; 54
A Few Words on the Advantage of a More Common Adoption of the Mathematics as a Branch of Education... London: 1834. V. 48; 51
A Grammar and Glossary of the Dorset Dialect With the History, Outspreading and Bearings of South-Western English. Berlin: 1863. V. 48; 51
Hwomeley Rhymes. London: 1859. V. 48; 51; 52; 54
A Mathematical Investigation of the Principle of Hanging Doors, Gates, Swing Bridges and Other Heavy Bodies Swinging on Vertical Axes. Dorchester: 1835. V. 48
Notes on Ancient Britian and the Britons. London: 1858. V. 48
An Outline of English Speech-Craft. London: 1878. V. 48; 54
An Outline of Rede-Craft (Logic), with English Wording. London: 1880. V. 48; 51
Poems of Rural Life in Common English. London: 1868. V. 48; 51; 53; 54
Poems of Rural Life, in the Dorset Dialect... London: 1844. V. 48; 49
Poems of Rural Life, in the Dorset Dialect. London: 1847. V. 51
Poems of Rural Life, in the Dorset Dialect. London: 1862. V. 47; 48
Poems of Rural Life, in the Dorset Dialect. London: 1869. V. 48; 51; 54
Poems of Rural Life, in the Dorset Dialect. London: 1888. V. 54
Poems, Partly of Rural Life. London: 1846. V. 48; 51; 54
Se Gefylsta (the Helper): An Anglo-Saxon Delectus. London: 1849. V. 48; 51
Se Gefylsta (the Helper): an Anglo-Saxon Delectus. London: 1866. V. 48; 51
A Selection from Unpublished Poems. 1870. V. 51
A Selection from Unpublished Poems. 1870. V. 48
The Song of Solomon in the Dorset Dialect from the Authorised English Version. London: 1859. V. 48

BARNES, WILLIAM continued
Tiw; or a View of the Roots and Stems of the English as a Teutonic Tongue. London: 1862. V. 48; 51; 52

BARNES, WILLIAM CROFT
Apaches and Longhorns: Reminiscences of Will Barnes. Los Angeles: 1941. V. 53
Tales from the X Bar Horse Camp, The Blue OUtlaw and Other Stories. Chicago: 1920. V. 51; 53; 54
Western Grazing Grounds... Chicago: 1913. V. 49; 54
Western Grazing Grounds... Chicago: 1933. V. 53

BARNES, WILLIAM H.
Prospectus fo the Cieneguita Copper Co. Organized under the Laws of Arizona, 1901 Mines in Sahauripa District, Sonora, Mexico. Gold, Silver, Copper. Phoenix: 1901. V. 49

BARNETT, C. Z.
A Christmas Carol; or, The Miser's Warning. London: 1886. V. 49

BARNETT, JOEL
A Long Trip in a Prairie Schooner. Whittier: 1928. V. 47; 54

BARNETT, JOHN
Report of the Trial of John Barnett, for Forgery, Before Mr. Justice Park, at the Durham Assizes, Feb. 26th 1830. Durham: 1830. V. 53

BARNETT, R. D.
Catalogue of the Jewish Museum. London. V. 48
Catalogue of the Jewish Museum London. New York: 1974. V. 53
Sculptures from the North Palace of Ashurbanipal at Nineveh. London: 1976. V. 49; 51

BARNEY, DANFORD
Chords from Alireo. New York: 1920. V. 47

BARNEY, JAMES M.
Tales of Apache Warfare, True Stories of Massacres, Fights and Raids in Arizona and New Mexico. N.P: 1933. V. 54

BARNEY, JOSHUA
Report of the Survey Estimates, &c. of a Route from St. Louis to the Big Bend of the Red River. Wasahington: 1852. V. 52

BARNEY, WILLIAM C.
Ocean Mail Service. The New Orleans, Havana, Fayal, Santander & Bordeaux U.S. Mail Steamship Line. New York: 1858. V. 48

BARNS, C. R.
The Commonwealth of Missouri, a Centennial Record. St. Louis: 1877. V. 54

BARNS, T. A.
Across the Great Craterland to the Congo. 1923. V. 54
The Wonderland of the Eastern Congo. London: 1922. V. 54

BARNSTONE, HOWARD
The Architecture of John F. Staub, Houston and the South. Austin: 1979. V. 47
The Galveston that Was. New York: 1966. V. 53
The Galveston That Was. New York & Houston: 1966. V. 48; 49; 53

BARNUM, H. L.
Family Receipts, or Practical Guide for the Husbandman and Housewife... Cincinnati: 1831. V. 53

BARNUM, PHINEAS TAYLOR
Auto-Biography of Barnum or the Opening of the Oyster. Danbury: 1889. V. 53
Barnum's American Museum Illustrated. New York: 1840. V. 52
Barnum's American Museum Illustrated. New York: 1850. V. 54
The Life of P. T. Barnum... London: 1855. V. 51
Prospectus of Barnum's Museum Company. New York: 1880. V. 53
Struggles and Triumphs; or, Forty Years' Recollections... London: 1870. V. 48; 54
Struggles and Triumphs; or Forty Years' Recollections. New York: 1871. V. 53
Struggles and Triumphs; or, Forty Years' Recollections... Buffalo: 1879. V. 54

BARNWELL, EDWARD A.
Barnello's Voodoo Incantations, or How to Eat Fire. New York: 1880. V. 53

BARO, GENE
Claes Oldenburg. New York: 1969. V. 50

BARON and Feme. A Treatise of Law and Equity, Concerning Husbands and Wives. In the Savoy: 1738. V. 48

BARON Encore. London: 1952. V. 51

BARON, JOHN
The Life of Edward Jenner, M.D. London: 1827. V. 50
The Life of Edward Jenner, M.D. London: 1838. V. 48; 49
Scudamore Organs, Practical Hints Respecting Organs. London: 1862. V. 52

BARON, S.
A Description of the Kingdom of Tonqueen. 1734. V. 52
A Description of the Kingdom of Tonqueen. London: 1734. V. 50

BARON, WENDY
The Camden Town Group. London: 1979. V. 49; 51; 53

BARONIO, GIUSEPPE
On Grafting in Animals. Boston: 1985. V. 50; 52

BARR, A. E.
Profit and Loss. New York: 1916. V. 53

BARR, ALFRED H.
Matisse: His Art and His Public. New York: 1951. V. 53

BARR, ALWYN
Black Texans. Austin: 1973. V. 52; 53

BARR, AMELIA E.
The Beads of Tasmer. London: 1893. V. 53; 54
A Daughter of Fife. London: 1886. V. 51

BARR, J. S.
Natural History: Containing the Theory of the Earth, A General History of Man of the Brute Creation and of Minerals and Vegetables. (with) Natural History of Birds, Fishes, Reptiles and Insects... London: 1826. V. 54

BARR, JOHN
Natural Wonders: Poems. 1991. V. 52

BARR, LOUISE FARROW
Presses of Northern California and Their Books 1900-1933. Berkeley: 1934. V. 48; 52

BARR, MATHIAS
Hours of Sunshine. London: 1880. V. 51

BARR, NEVADA
Track of the Cat. New York: 1933. V. 54
Track of the Cat. New York: 1993. V. 52; 53

BARR, R.
From Whose Bourne. 1893. V. 48

BARR, ROBERT
Jennie Baxter Journalist. New York: 1899. V. 49
N. B. Strange Happenings. London: 1883. V. 51

BARR, WILLIAM
Journal of a March from Delhi to Peschawur, and From Thence to Cabul, with the Mission of Lieut.-Colonel Sir C. M. Wade... London: 1844. V. 48; 50

BARRA, E. I.
A Tale of Two Oceans; a New Story by an Old Californian. San Francisco: 1893. V. 52; 54

BARRATT, JOSEPH
The Indian of New England and the North Eastern Provinces. Middletown: 1851. V. 48; 52

BARRATT, THOMAS J.
The Annals of Hampstead. London: 1912. V. 50
The Annals of Hampstead. London: 1972. V. 54

BARRAUD, PHILIP
A New Book of Single Cyphers, Comprising Six Hundred Invented and Engraved. London: 1805. V. 50

BARRERA, A. DE
Memoirs of Rachel. London: 1858. V. 52

BARRERE, ALBERT
Argot and Slang; a New French and English Dictionary Of the Cant Words, Quaint Expressions, Slang Forms and Flash Phrases Used in the High and Low Life of Old and New Paris. London: 1889. V. 52

BARRET, GEORGE
The Theory and Practice of Water Colour Painting. London: 1840. V. 48; 50

BARRET, J. V.
Shakespeare Freshly Chiselled on Stone. London: 1850. V. 49

BARRET, ROBERT
The Theorike and Practike of Moderne Warres. London: 1598. V. 49

BARRETT, C. F.
The Black Castle; or the Spectre of the Forest, an Historical Romance. London: 1800. V. 54

BARRETT, C. G.
The Lepidoptera of the British Islands... London: 1893-1907. V. 54

BARRETT, CHARLES RAYMOND BOOTH
Essex: Highways, Byways and Waterways. London: 1892-93. V. 48; 51; 52; 54
The History of the Society of Apothecaries of London. London: 1905. V. 47; 49

BARRETT, DOUGLAS
Paintings of India. 1963. V. 54

BARRETT, EATON STANNARD
All the Talents; a Satirical Poem. London: 1807. V. 51
The Heroine, or Adventures of Cherubina. London: 1815. V. 51
Six Week's at Long's. London: 1817. V. 47
Woman, A Poem. London: 1818. V. 50; 52; 53; 54

BARRETT, ELLEN CATHERINE
Baja California, 1535-1956. Los Angeles: 1957. V. 48
Baja California, 1535-1956. (with) Baja California II 1535-1964. Los Angeles: 1967. V. 48
Baja California 1535-1964. A Bibliography of Literature Relating to the Peninsula...Adjacent Islands... Los Angeles: 1957/67. V. 47; 50

BARRETT, FRANCIS
The Magus, or Celestial Intelligencer... Leicester: 1970. V. 48

BARRETT, FRANKLIN A.
Caughley and Coalport Porcelain. Leigh-on-Sea: 1951. V. 52

BARRETT, JOHN
An Essay on the Earlier Part of the Life of Swift. London: 1808. V. 48; 50; 51
Panama Canal. What It Is. What It Means. Stratford-on-Avon: 1928. V. 51

BARRETT, JOSEPH H.
Life of Abraham Lincoln...also a Sketch of Hannibal Hamlin. Cincinnati: 1860. V. 53

BARRETT, JOSEPH O.
History of 'Old Abe,' the Live War Eagle of the Eighth Regiment Wisconsin Volunteers. Chicago: 1865. V. 49

BARRETT, S. A.
The Material Culture of the Klamath Lake and Modoc Indians of Northeasatern California and Southern Oregon. 1908. V. 51

BARRETT, THOMAS J.
The Annals of Hampstead. London: 1912. V. 52

BARRETT, TIMOTHY
Early vs. Modern Handmade Papers. 1990. V. 51
Nagashizuki: the Japanese Craft of Hand Papermaking. North Hills: 1979. V. 48; 49; 54

BARRETT, W. A.
Flowers and Festivals or Directions for the Floral Decorations of Churches. London: 1868. V. 53

BARRETT, W. P.
LV Book Plates. London: 1900. V. 50

BARRETT, WILLIAM E.
The Lilies of the Field. Garden City: 1962. V. 54
The Lilies of the Field. London: 1963. V. 52

BARRETTE, B.
Eva Hesse Sculpture: Catalogue Raisonne. New York: 1989. V. 54

BARRETT-HAMILTON, GERALD E. H.
A History of British Mammals. London: 1910-21. V. 47; 49; 53

BARRETT-LENNARD, C. E.
Travels in British Columbia, With the Narrative of a Yacht Voyage Round Vancouver Island. London: 1862. V. 48

BARRETT'S Directory of Blackburn and District. Preston: 1925. V. 48
BARRETT'S Directory of Blackburn and District. Preston: 1935. V. 48

BARRETTT'S General and Commercial Directory of Blackpool and the Fylde. Preston: 1938. V. 53

BARRI, GIRALDUS DE
Itinerarium Cambriae Seu Laboriosae Baldvini Cantuariensis Archiepiscopi.... Londini: 1804. V. 51

BARRIE, JAMES MATTHEW
The Admirable Crichton. London. V. 51
Auld Licht Idylls. London: 1888. V. 47
Better Dead. London: 1888. V. 51; 53
Courage. London: 1922. V. 53
Courage. Rectorial Address at St. Andrews University. New York: 1922. V. 53
An Edinburgh Eleven. London: 1889. V. 47; 48; 49; 50; 51
George Meredith. London. V. 51
The Greenwood Hat. Edinburgh: 1930. V. 48
The Greenwood Hat. London: 1930. V. 48
The Little Minister. London: 1880. V. 54
The Little Minister. London, Paris, Melbourne: 1891. V. 47; 48; 49; 52; 53
The Little Minister. New York: 1898. V. 47
My Lady Nicotine, a Study in Smoke. Boston: 1896. V. 50
Novels. Tales and Sketches. New York & London: 1896. V. 52
Peter and Wendy. 1911. V. 54
Peter and Wendy. London: 1911. V. 50
Peter Pan. London: 1912. V. 48
Peter Pan. New York: 1928. V. 49
Peter Pan and Wendy. London. V. 48; 51
Peter Pan and Wendy. London: 1930. V. 49
Peter Pan and Wendy. London: 1932. V. 54
Peter Pan and Wendy. London: 1935. V. 49
Peter Pan In Kensington Garadens. London: 1906. V. 48; 49; 50; 52; 53
Peter Pan in Kensington Gardens. New York: 1906. V. 47; 48
Peter Pan in Kensington Gardens. London: 1907. V. 51
Peter Pan in Kensington Gardens. New York: 1907. V. 50
Peter Pan in Kensington Gardens. London: 1912. V. 48; 50; 51
Peter Pan in Kensington Gardens. 1925. V. 48; 50; 52
Peter Pan in Kensington Gardens. London: 1925. V. 48
Peter Pan or the Boy Who Would Not Grow Up. London: 1928. V. 52
The Peter Pan Picture Book... Racine: 1931. V. 49
Piter Pan dans les Jardins de Kensington. Paris: 1907. V. 47
The Plays of James Matthew Barrie. London: 1928. V. 53
Quality Street. London. V. 51
Quality Street. London: 1913. V. 50; 54
Scotland's Lament: Robert Louis Stevenson. London: 1918. V. 48
Sentimental Tommy. London, Paris: 1896. V. 51; 52
A Tillyloss Scandal. New York: 1893. V. 52
Tommy and Grizel. London: 1900. V. 51
When a Man's Single. London: 1888. V. 48; 50; 51; 52

Works. London: 1913. V. 47; 49; 51
The Works. New York: 1929-40. V. 50

BARRINGTON, DAINES
Miscellanies. London: 1781. V. 49; 50; 52; 53
Observations on More Ancient Statutes, from Magna Charta... London: 1769. V. 47
Observations on More Ancient Statutes, from Magna Charta... London: 1775. V. 52
Observations on the Statutes, Chiefly the More Ancient, From Magna Charta...James the First...with an Appendix... London: 1766. V. 47; 50
The Possibility of Approaching the North Pole Asserted. London: 1818. V. 47; 51

BARRINGTON, E.
The Ladies! A Shining Constellation of Wit and Beauty. Boston: 1922. V. 52

BARRINGTON, EMILIE ISABEL
G. F. Watts, Reminiscences. London: 1905. V. 49
Lena's Picture. Edinburgh: 1892. V. 54
The Life, Letters and Work of Frederick Leighton. London: 1906. V. 54

BARRINGTON, F. H.
Kansas Day. Topeka: 1892. V. 54

BARRINGTON, JOHN SHUTE
Some Arguments Made Use of In the Bishop of Bangor's Preservative against the Principles and Practices of the Nonjurors, Briefly Consider'd. London: 1716. V. 53

BARRINGTON, JONAH
Historic Memoirs of Ireland; Comprising Secret Records of the National Convention, the Rebellion and the Union. 1835. V. 52
Personal Sketches of His Own Times...Judge of the Supreme Court of Admiralty in Ireland. London: 1830/32. V. 48

BARRINGTON, MICHAEL
Grahame of Calverhouse. Viscount Dundee. London: 1911. V. 49

BARRINGTON, R. M.
The Migration of Birds as Observed at Irish Lighthouses and Lightships. London: 1900. V. 48

BARRISTER, HUGHES WILLIAM
The Practical Angler. London: 1842. V. 53

BARRON, EVAN MAC LEOD
Prince Charlie's Pilot. Inverness: 1913. V. 54

BARRON, WILLIAM
History of the Political Connection Between England and Ireland from the Reign of Henry II to the Present Time. 1780. V. 54
A Just Defence of the Royal Martyr K. Charles I. London: 1699. V. 52

BARRONS, JOHN R.
Ubet. Caldwell: 1934. V. 52

BARROW, ALBERT STEWART
Shires and Provinces. London: 1927. V. 47

BARROW, FRANCES ELIZABETH
Carl's Visit to the Child Island. Buffalo: 1863. V. 47

BARROW, ISAAC
A Brief Exposition on the Creed, the Lord's Prayer, and Ten Commandments. London: 1697. V. 53
Of Industry, in Five Discourses: viz In General, in Our General Calling as Christians. London: 1693. V. 50
A Treatise of the Pope's Supremacy. London: 1683. V. 50
The Works... London: 1700-1683-86. V. 54
The Works, Being All His English Works. London: 1722. V. 50

BARROW, JOHN
An Account of Travels Into the Interior of Southern Africa, in the Years 1797 and 1798. London: 1801-04. V. 47; 51
A Chronological History of Voyages Into the Arctic Regions... London: 1818. V. 49; 53
Dictionarium Polygraphicum; or, the Whole Body of Arts Regularly Digested. London: 1735. V. 49; 53
The Eventful History of the Mutiny and Piratical Seizure of H.M.S. Bounty: Its Causes and Consequences. London: 1831. V. 48; 54
A Family Tour Through South Holland: up the Rhine and Across the Netherlands. London: 1831. V. 50
A Family Tour Through South Holland: up the Rhine and Across the Netherlands... London: 1839. V. 50
The Life of Richard Earl Howe, KG Admiral of the Fleet and General of Marines. London: 1836. V. 50
The Life of Richard Earl Howe, K.G., Admiral of the Fleet and General of Marines. London: 1838. V. 48; 54
Mountain Ascents in Cumberland and Westmorland. London: 1886. V. 52; 54
Some Account of the Public Life, and a Selection from the Unpublished Writings of the Earl of Macartney. London: 1807. V. 47; 54
Travels in China... London: 1804. V. 47
Travels in China... Philadelphia: 1805. V. 52
Travels in China. London: 1806. V. 48; 49
Travels Into the Interior of Southern Africa. London: 1806. V. 48; 50; 51
A Voyage to Cochinchina, in the Years 1792 and 1793... London: 1806. V. 47; 49; 50; 54

BARROW, PHILIP
The Method of Physick... London: 1634. V. 47; 48

BARROWS, JOHN R.
Ubet. Caldwell: 1934. V. 53; 54

BARRY, ALFRED
The Life and Works of Sir Charles Barry. London: 1867. V. 47

BARRY, GEORGE
The History of the Orkney Islands: In Which is Comprehended an Account of their Present as Well as Their Ancient State... Edinburgh: 1805. V. 48
History of the Orkney Islands, Including a View of the Manners and Customs of their Ancient and Modern Inhabitants. London: 1808. V. 47; 49; 51

BARRY, HANNAH
Night-Watchmen. New York: 1973. V. 52

BARRY, IRIS
Let's Go to the Pictures. London: 1926. V. 48

BARRY, J. W.
A History of the Strollers Club. Toronto: 1927. V. 49

BARRY, JAMES
A Description of the Series of Pictures Painted by James Barry and Preserved in the Great Room of the Society...for the Encouragement of Art, Manufactures and Commerce... London: 1808. V. 47

BARRY, JAMES BUCKNER
A Texas Ranger and Frontiersman: the Days of Buck Barry in Texas 1845-1906. Dallas: 1932. V. 54

BARRY, JOHN
Barry's Arabian Method of Horsemanship. New York. V. 47

BARRY, JOSEPH
The Annals of Harper's Ferry and Sketches of Its Founder, and Many Prominent Characters Connected With Its History, Anecdotes, &c. Martinsburg: 1872. V. 50

BARRY, ROBERT
German Scenery From Drawings Made in 1820. London: 1823. V. 49

BARRY, T. A.
Men and Memories of San Francisco in the Spring of '50. San Francisco: 1873. V. 52

BARRYMORE, ETHEL
An Autobiography. New York: 195. V. 50

BARRYMORE, JOHN
Confessions of an Actor. Indianapolis: 1926. V. 49

BARRYMORE, LIONEL
Mr. Cantonwine: a Moral Tale. Boston: 1953. V. 48

BARSKY, ARTHUR JOSEPH
Congenital Anomalies of the Hand and Their Surgical Treatment. Springfield: 1958. V. 54
Plastic Surgery. Philadelphia & London: 1938. V. 54

BARSLEY, MICHAEL
Alice in Wunderground and Other Bits and Pieces. London: 1940. V. 51

BARSTOW, GEORGE
The Times; or, the Pressure and its Causes Examined. Boston: 1837. V. 49

BARSTOW, STAN
A Kind of Loving. London: 1960. V. 54

BARTELL, EDMUND
Cromer, Considered as a Watering Place; with Observations on the Picturesque Scenery in the Neighbourhood. London: 1806. V. 50
Hints for Picturesque Improvements in Ornamented Cottages. London: 1804. V. 47

BARTER, CHARLOTTE
Alone Among the Zulus, by a Plain Woman. London: 1866. V. 47

BARTH, H.
A Documentary Study. London: 1975. V. 49

BARTH, HENRY
Travels and Discoveries in North and Central Africa. New York: 1857. V. 47; 51; 54
Travels and Discoveries in North and Central Africa... London: 1857-58. V. 54
Travels and Discoveries in North and Central Africa. Philadelphia: 1859. V. 52

BARTH, JEAN BAPTISTE
A Manual of Auscultation and Percussion. Philadelphia: 1845. V. 52

BARTH, JOHN
Chimera. New York: 1972. V. 49; 50; 51; 52
Don't Count On It: a Note on the Number of the 1001 Nights. Northridge: 1984. V. 48; 51
The End of the Road. Garden City: 1958. V. 48; 49; 50; 51; 53; 54
The End of the Road. London: 1962. V. 50; 52; 53
The Floating Opera. New York: 1956. V. 47; 48; 50; 51; 52; 53
The Floating Opera. New York: 1965. V. 51
Giles Goat Boy. Garden City: 1966. V. 47; 48; 49; 50; 51; 52; 54
Letters. New York: 1979. V. 47; 48; 50; 51; 52; 53
The Literature of Exhaustion and the Literature of Replenishment. Northridge: 1982. V. 48; 51
Lost in the Funhouse. Garden City: 1968. V. 49; 50; 51; 52; 54
Lost in the Funhouse. London: 1969. V. 50
Sabbatical. New York: 1981. V. 51
Sabbatical. New York: 1982. V. 51; 54
The Sot-Weed Factor. Garden City: 1958. V. 54
The Sot-Weed Factor. Garden City: 1960. V. 47; 48; 50; 51; 52; 53
The Sot-Weed Factor. London: 1961. V. 47; 48; 50; 51; 53
The Sot-Weed Factor. Garden City: 1967. V. 51
The Sot-Weed Factor. 1980. V. 49
Tidewater Tales. New York: 1987. V. 51
Todd Andrews to the Author. Northridge: 1979. V. 48; 51

BARTHELEMY, D.
Discoveries in the Judean Desert (of Jordan). Volume I: Qumran Cave I. Oxford: 1956. V. 51
Discoveries in the Judean Desert (of Jordon). Oxford: 1955-56-65. V. 49

BARTHELEMY, JEAN JACQUES
Carite and Polydorus. London: 1799. V. 51
Maps, Plans, Views and Coins, Illustrative of the Travels of Anacharsis the Younger in Greece. London: 1791. V. 54
Travels in Italy. London: 1802. V. 47; 53
Travels of Ahacharsis the Younger in Greece, During the Middle of the Fourth Century Before the Christian Era. London: 1806. V. 54

BARTHELEMY SAINT HILAIRE, JULES
Egypt and the Great Suez Canal. London: 1857. V. 47; 50; 53

BARTHELME, DONALD
Come Back, Dr. Caligari. Boston: 1964. V. 47; 48; 49; 51
The Emerald. Los Angeles: 1980. V. 51
Guilty Pleasures. New York: 1974. V. 49
Here in the Village. Northridge: 1978. V. 47; 48; 49; 51; 52; 53
Paradise. New York: 1986. V. 51
Sixty Stories. New York: 1981. V. 47
The Slightly Irregular Fire Engine. New York: 1971. V. 48; 51
Snow White. New York: 1967. V. 47; 53

BARTHES, ROLAND
Erte. Parma: 1972. V. 52
Roland Barthes. New York: 1977. V. 54

BARTHOLDY
Memoirs of the Secret Societies of the South Of Italy, Particularly the Carbonari. London: 1821. V. 50

BARTHOLINUS, THOMAS
Anatomia, Ex Caspari Bartholini Parentis Institutionibus. The Hague: 1666. V. 49
De Unicornu Observationes Novae. Amstelaedami: 1678. V. 48
Institutions Anatomiques.... Paris: 1647. V. 49

BARTHOLOMEW, ED
The Biographical Album of Western Gunfighters. Houston: 1958. V. 52; 53; 54
Wyatt Earp. Toyahuale: 1963/64. V. 52

BARTHOLOMEW, GEORGE W.
Record of the Bartholomew Family (in America), Historical, Genealogical and Biographical. Austin: 1885. V. 53

BARTHOLOMEW, HARLAND, & ASSOCIATES
A Plan for the City of Vancouver British Columbia Including Point Grey and South Vancouver and a General Plan of the Region 1929. Vancouver,: 1930. V. 47

BARTHOLOMEW, J. G.
Atlas of Zoogeography. Edinburgh: 1911. V. 48; 49; 50; 51; 53
Constable's Hand Atlas of India. London: 1895. V. 50
The Times Survey Atlas of the World. London: 1922. V. 54

BARTHOLOMEW, VALENTINE
A Selection of Flowers Adapted Principally for Students. London: 1821-23. V. 53
A Selection of Flowers Adapted Principally for Students. London: 1822. V. 48

BARTHOLOW, ROBERTS
Manual of Hypodermic Medication. Philadelphia: 1873. V. 53
The Principles and Practice of Disinfection. Cincinnati: 1867. V. 51; 53

BARTLET, JOHN
The Gentleman's Farriery; or a Practical Treatise on the Diseases of Horses... London: 1764. V. 50
The Gentleman's Farriery; or a Practical Treatise on the Diseases of Horses. London: 1785. V. 47; 48

BARTLETT, CHARLES H.
La Salle in the Valley of the St. Joseph. South Bend: 1899. V. 47

BARTLETT, DAVID W.
What I Saw in London, or Men and Things in the Great Metropolis. Auburn and Buffalo: 1853. V. 52

BARTLETT, EDWARD EVERETT
The Typographic Treasures in Europe. New York: 1925. V. 47; 48

BARTLETT, ELISHA
An Essay on the Philosophy of Medical Science. Philadelphia: 1844. V. 50
The History, Diagnosis, and Treatment of the Fevers... Philadelphia: 1847. V. 53
The History, Diagnosis, and Treatment of the Fevers. Philadelphia: 1852. V. 48
The History, Diagnosis, and Treatment of the Fevers... Philadelphia: 1856. V. 48; 51; 53
The History, Diagnosis and Treatment of Typhoid and Typhus Fever... Philadelphia: 1842. V. 51; 52; 53

BARTLETT, FRED
Shoot Straight and Stay Alive. V. 52

BARTLETT, HENRIETTA C.
Catalogue of Early English Books, Chiefly of the Elizabethan Period Collected by William Augustus White. New York: 1926. V. 47
A Census of Shakespeare's Plays in Quarto 1594-1709. New Haven: 1916. V. 47; 48; 52

BARTLETT, I. S.
History of Wyoming. Chicago: 1918. V. 54

BARTLETT, JOHN
A Collection of Familiar Quotations. Cambridge: 1855. V. 47; 54
A Collection of Familiar Quotations. Cambridge: 1858. V. 47
A Collection of Familiar Quotations. Boston: 1868. V. 51

BARTLETT, JOHN RUSSELL
Dictionary of Americanisms, a Glossary of Words and Phrases Usually Regarded as Peculiar to the United States. New York: 1848. V. 50
The Literature of the Rebellion. A Catalogue of Books and Pamphlets Relating to the Civil War... Boston: 1866. V. 50
Personal Narrative of Explorations and Incidents. New York: 1854. V. 47; 53
Personal Narrative of Explorations and Incidents in Texas, New Mexico, California, Sonora and Chihuahua... New York: 1856. V. 47

BARTLETT, JOHN S.
Maize or Indian Corn, Its Advantages as a Cheap and Nutritious Article of Food, With Directions for Its Use. London: 1846. V. 50

BARTLETT, JOSEPH
Aphorisms on Men, Manners, Princciples and Things. Portsmouth: 1810. V. 51
Physiognomy, a Poem, Delivered at the Request of the Society of O B K, in the Chapel of Harvard University, on the Day of Their Anniversary. Boston: 1799. V. 50

BARTLETT, JOSIAH
Speech of Mr. Bartlett, at a Meeting of Citizens Opposed to the Re-election of Andrew Jackson, Holden at Portsmouth, N.H. oct. 15, 1832. Portsmouth?: 1832. V. 51

BARTLETT, N. GRAY, MRS.
Old Friends With New Faces. Boston: 1892. V. 49

BARTLETT, NAPIER
Military Annals Louisiana: Including Biographical and Historical Papers Relating to the Military Organization of the State... New Orleans: 1875. V. 50
A Soldier's Story of the War... New Orleans: 1974. V. 49

BARTLETT, SAMUEL C.
An Appeal for Ministers: a Discussion on the Necessity for a Great Effort to Supply the Country with Preachers of the Gospel. Chicago: 1865. V. 51

BARTLETT, WASHINGTON A.
The Navy Board of 1855 in Review Before the Naval Court of Inquiry, sitting at Washington, 1857;. New York: 1857. V. 49
Reply of Washington A. Bartlett, to the Testimony Taken Before the Naval Committee. Washington: 1856. V. 49

BARTLETT, WILLIAM HENRY
American Scenery. London: 1840. V. 51
Footsteps Of Our Lord and His Apostles in Syria, Greece and Italy. London: 1851. V. 49
Forty Days in the Desert, on the Track of the Israelites; or, a Journey from Cairo, by Wady Feiran, to Mount Sinai and Petra. London: 1848. V. 51
The History of the United States of America. London: 1861. V. 48
Jerusalem Revisited. London: 1855. V. 47; 52
The Nile Boat; or, Glimpses of the Land of Egypt. London: 1850. V. 47
The Nile Boat; or, Glimpses of the Land of Egypt. New York: 1851. V. 54
The Nile Boat; or, Glimpses of the Land of Egypt. London: 1860. V. 48
Pictures from Sicily. London: 1863. V. 49
The Pilgrim Fathers. London: 1853. V. 47; 50; 51; 54
The Pilgrim Fathers... London: 1854. V. 51
The Pilgrim Fathers... London: 1863. V. 49; 51
A Pilgrimage Through the Holy Land, Explanatory of the Diorama of Jerusalem and the Holy Land, Painted Under the Direction of Mr. Beverly (sic) From Original Sketches Made on the Spot, During Repeated Journeys in the East. London: 1851. V. 48
The Scenery and Antiquities of Ireland. London: 1841. V. 50; 51; 52
The Scenery and Antiquities of Ireland. London: 1855. V. 49; 52
Syria, the Holy Land, Asia Minor &c. London: 1836. V. 48
Walks About the City Environs of Jerusalem. London: 1845. V. 53
Walks About the City Environs of Jerusalem. London: 1850. V. 47

BARTOK, BELLA
Hungarian Folk Music. Oxford: 1931. V. 47; 53

BARTOL, B. H.
A Treatise on the Marine Boilers of the United States. Philadelphia: 1851. V. 52

BARTOLI, COSIMO
Del Modo di Misurare. Venetia: 1589. V. 49; 50
Del Modo di Misurare le Distantie, le Superficie i Corpi, le Pianti, le Provincie le Prospettive & Tutte le Altre Cose Terrene. Venice: 1614. V. 54

BARTOLI, DANIELLO
Del Suono de' Tremori Armonici e dell' Udito. Rome: 1679. V. 52; 54
The Learned Man Defended and Reform'd. London: 1660. V. 47

BARTOLI, PIETRO SANTI
Admiranda Romanorum Antiquitatum ac Veteris Sculpturae Vestigia... Rome. V. 47; 53
Le Pitture Antiche Del Sepolcro de Nasonii Nella Via Flaminia...Including, Fragmenta Vestigii Veteris Romae Ex lapidibus Farneasianis... Rome: 1680. V. 48; 51

BARTOLINI, ANNA MARIA
Effleurage. Leeds: 1989. V. 49; 52

BARTON, B. H.
The British Flora Medica, a History of the Medicinal Plants of Great Britain. London: 1877. V. 53
The British Flora Medica, or History of the Medicinal Plants of Great Britain... London: 1837-38. V. 53

BARTON, B. T.
History of the Borough of Bury and Neighbourhood, in the County of Lancaster. Bury: 1874. V. 48

BARTON, BENJAMIN SMITH
Fragments of the Natural History of Pennsylvania. Philadelphia: 1799. V. 47; 48; 50
New Views of the Origin of the Tribes of America. Philadelphia: 1797. V. 50
Professor Cullen's Treatise of Materia medica. Philadelphia: 1812. V. 48; 53

BARTON, BERNARD
Devotional Verses: Founded on, and Illustrative of Select Texts of Scripture. London: 1826. V. 51
Fisher's Juvenile Scrap-Book...1836. London: 1835. V. 49
Memoir, Letters and Poems. Philadelphia: 1850. V. 50
A Memorial of Joseph John Gurney. London: 1847. V. 47
Napoleon, and Other Poems. London: 1822. V. 50
A New Year Offering; for the Queen. Woodbridge: 1847. V. 47
Poems. London: 1820. V. 49; 51
Poetic Vigils... London: 1824. V. 47
A Widow's Tale and Other Poems. London: 1827. V. 48; 51

BARTON, CHARLES
An Historical Treatise of a Suit in Equity. Dublin: 1796. V. 51

BARTON, CLARA
The Red Cross in Peace and War. Washington: 1899. V. 50

BARTON, CUTTS
Modern Characters from Shakespear. London: 1778. V. 51

BARTON, DONALD C.
Gulf Coast Oil Fields: a Symposium on the Gulf Coast Cenozoic by Fifty-Two Authors. Tulsa: 1936. V. 47

BARTON, DUNBAR P.
The Land Law (Ireland) Act, 1896. With Rules and Forms Issued Thereunder in the Land Commission, Supreme Court and County Courts Respectively. Dublin: 1897. V. 49

BARTON, E. H.
The Cause and Prevention of Yellow Fever at New Orleans and Other Cities in America. New York: 1857. V. 51; 53

BARTON, GEORGE A.
Sumerian Business and Administrative Documents from the Earliest Times to the Dynasty of Agade. Philadelphia: 1915. V. 51

BARTON, O. S.
Three Years With Quantrell. A True Story. New York: 1966. V. 47; 53

BARTON, PAULE
The Woe Shirt. Lincoln: 1980. V. 51; 54

BARTON, ROSE
Familiar London. London: 1904. V. 52

BARTON, WILLIAM
Memoirs of the Life....Interspersed with Various Notices of Many Distinguished Men... Philadelphia: 1813. V. 49

BARTON, WILLIAM P. C.
Compendium Florae Philadelphicae.... Philadelphia: 1818. V. 47; 50; 52
A Dissertation On the Chymical Properties and Exhilarating Effects of Nitrous Oxide Gas. Philadelphia: 1808. V. 54
Flora of North America, Illustrated by Coloured Figures Drawn from Nature. Philadelphia: 1821-23. V. 54
Vegetable Materia Medica of the United States... Philadelphia: 1817-18. V. 47; 48; 51

BARTRAM, JOHN
An Account of East-Florida with a Journal Kept by John Bartram of Philadelphia, Botanist to His Majesty for the Floridas... London: 1766. V. 54

BARTRAM, WILLIAM
Botanical and Zoological Drawings, 1756-1788. Philadelphia: 1968. V. 47; 48
Travels Through North and South Carolina, Georgia, East and West Florida, the Cherokee Country... Philadelphia: 1791. V. 48
Travels through North and South Carolina, Georgia, East and West Florida, the Cherokee Country... London: 1792. V. 48; 54
Travels Through North and South Carolina, Georgia, East and West Florida, the Cherokee Country... Dublin: 1793. V. 47; 48

BARTTELOT, W. G.
The Life of Edmund Musgrave Barttelot, Captain and Brevet-Major Royal Fusiliers Commander of the Rear Column of the Emin Pasha Relief Expedition. London: 1890. V. 48

BARUCH, BERNARD M.
American Industry in the War: a Report of the War Industries Board. New York: 1941. V. 54
Report Submitted to the United Nations Atomic Energy commission. 1946. V. 50

BARUCHELLO, GIANFRANCO
Why Duchamp, an Essay on Aesthetic Impact. New York: 1985. V. 49

BARWELL, MRS.
Good in Every Thing or The Early History of Gilbert Harland. London: 1852. V. 49; 51

BARWELL, MRS. continued
Little Lessons for Little Learners, in Words Of One Syllable. London: 1833. V. 51

BARWICK, GEORGE F.
A Book Bound for Mary Queen of Scots. Being a Description of the Binding of a Copy of the Geographia of Ptolemy Printed at Rome, 1490, with Notes on Other Books Bearing Queen Mary's Insignia. London: 1901. V. 54

BARWICK, JAMES
Evidences of the Christian Religion; Briefly and Plainly Stated. Edinburgh: 1786. V. 49

BARWICK, PETER
Vita Johannis Barwick, S.T.P. London: 1721. V. 49; 54

BASEDOW, HERBERT
The Australian Aboriginal. Adelaide: 1929. V. 48

BASHFORD, HERBERT
A Man Unafraid - the Story of John Charles Fremont. San Francisco: 1927. V. 54

BASHKIRTSEFF, MARIE
The Journal of Marie Bashkirtseff. London, Paris, & Melbourne: 1890. V. 47; 49; 51

BASHLINE, L. J.
America's Great Outdoors, The Story of the Eternal Romance Between Man and Nature. Chicago: 1976. V. 50; 52

BASHO, MATSUO
The Records of a Weather-Exposed Skeleton. London: 1969. V. 50; 53
Traveler, My Name: Haiku of Basho. Norwich: 1984. V. 53

BASILE, GIOVANNI BATTISTA
The Pentamerone, or the Story of Stories, Fun for the Little Ones. London: 1850. V. 48
Il Pentamerone; or, the Tale of Tales... London: 1893. V. 48
Stories from the Pentamerone. London: 1911. V. 50; 53

BASILE, GIUSEPPE
Giotto, the Arena Chapel Fescoes. London: 1993. V. 51

BASILIUS, SAINT, THE GREAT, ABP. OF CAESAREA
Divi Basilii...Opera. Cologne: 1523. V. 52
Orationes de Moribus XXIII. Simone Magistro Auctore. (with) Conciones de Vita et Moribus. Paris: 1556/58. V. 47; 52

BASILIUS VALENTINUS
Azoth, ou Le Moyen de Faire l'Or Cache des Philosophes. Paris: 1659. V. 48
Letztes Testament, Fr. Basilii Valentini Darinnen Die Geheime Bucher Vom Grossen STein der Uralten Weisen, Und Andern Verborgenen Geheimnussen der Natur. (with) Von Dem Grossen Stein der Uhralten Daran So Viel Tausend meister Anfangs der Welt Hero... Strassburg: 1651/51. V. 50
The Triumphal Chariot of Antimony... London: 1893. V. 52

BASKERVILLE, JOHN
A Vocabulary, or Pocket Dictionary. Birmingham: 1765. V. 48

BASKIN, ESTHER
An ABC with Best Wishes for 1958 from Esther and Leonard Baskin. Northampton: 1958. V. 54

BASKIN, LEONARD
Ars Anatomica. New York: 1972. V. 48; 49; 50; 51; 52; 53; 54
Caprices and Grotesques. Northampton: 1965. V. 49
Culs de Lampe. Northampton: 1968. V. 49
Demons, Imps and Fiends. Northampton: 1976. V. 48
Figures of Dead Men. 1968. V. 51; 54
Figures of Dead Men. Amherst: 1968. V. 49
Flosculi Sententiarum, Printers Flowers Moralised. Northampton: 1967. V. 49
Grotesques. Leeds: 1991. V. 52
Grotesques... Northampton: 1991. V. 50; 51; 52
Hermaika. Leeds: 1986. V. 51
Horned Beetles and Other Insects. Northampton: 1958. V. 54
Icones Librorum Artifices. Northampton: 1988. V. 47; 49; 51; 52
Irises. Leeds: 1988. V. 47; 49; 50
Jewish Artists of the Early & Late Renaissance. Leeds: 1993. V. 49; 50
Jewish Artists of the Early & Late Renaissance. Northampton: 1993. V. 49; 50; 52; 54
Leonard Baskin. Brunswick: 1962. V. 53
Mokomaki. Leeds: 1985. V. 50
Recollected Fragments of Ornament and Grotesque. Leeds: 1988. V. 51
Six Portraits. San Francisco: 1960. V. 50
To Colour Thought; a Lecture. New Haven: 1967. V. 52; 54
Twelve Sculptors. A Book of Monotypes with Short Notes on the Monotypes and Sculptors. 1988. V. 51

BASKIN, R. N.
Reminiscences of Early Utah. Salt Lake City: 1914. V. 48; 50; 52

BASON, FRED
The Last Bassoon. London: 1960. V. 49

BASON, FREDERICK T.
A Bibliography of the Writings of William Somerset Maugham. London: 1931. V. 53

BASS, ALTHEA
Cherokee Messenger. Norman: 1936. V. 50

BASS, HEINRICH
Grundlicher Bericht von Banadagen... Leipzig: 1720. V. 52

BASS, MICHAEL T.
Street Music in the Metropolis. Correspondence and Observations on the Existing Law, and Proposed Amendments. London: 1864. V. 49

BASS, RICK
The Deer Pasture. College Station: 1985. V. 51; 53; 54
The Ninemile Wolves. Livingston: 1992. V. 49

BASSAN, F.
Cabinet Poullain ou Collection de Cent-vignt Estampes...Gravees d'Apres les Tableaux & Dessins qui Composoient le Cabinet de M. Poullain... Paris: 1781. V. 47

BASSANI, ANTONIO
Viaggio a Roma della S.R.M. di Maria Casimira Regina di Polonia... Rome: 1700. V. 47; 54

BASSANI, GIORGIO
Five Stories of Ferrara. New York: 1971. V. 50
The Heron. New York: 1970. V. 50
The Smell of Hay. New York: 1975. V. 50

BASSETT, M. G.
The Murchison Symposium. London: 1991. V. 50

BASSI, GIULIO
Arimetica, e Geometria Pratica...Libri Otto... Piacenza: 1666. V. 48

BASSLER, R. S.
Shelled Invertebrates of the Past and Present. New York: 1934. V. 53

BAST, WILLIAM
James Dean. New York: 1956. V. 51

BASTABLE, C. FRANCIS
The Theory of International Trade with Some of Its Applications to Economic Policy. Dublin: 1887. V. 52

BASTIAN, HENRY CHARLTON
On Paralysis from Brain Disease in Its Common Forms. New York: 1875. V. 53
Paralyses Cerebral, Bulbar and Spinal: a Manual of Diagnosis for Students and Practioners. London: 1886. V. 53

BASTIAT, FREDERIC
Economic Sophisms. Edinburgh: 1873. V. 47; 49
Harmonies of Political Economy. London: 1860. V. 47; 49; 53

BASTIN, JOHN
Nineteenth Century Prints and Illustrated Books of Indonesia. Utrecht: 1979. V. 54

BASTON, SAMUEL
A Dialogue Between a Modern Courtier, and an Honest English Gentleman. London: 1696. V. 53

BASTWICK, JOHN
Flagellum Pontificis and Episcoporum Latialium; sive Tractatus, De Jurisdictione Episcopali... Holland: 1635. V. 50

BATAILLE, GEORGES
Death and Sensuality. New York: 1962. V. 50
Madame Edwarda. Paris: 1956. V. 49

BATCHELDER, PAUL M.
An Introduction to Linear Difference Equations. Cambridge: 1927. V. 50

BATCHELDER, SAMUEL
Poetry of the Bells. Cambridge: 1858. V. 47; 54

BATCHELOR, JOHN
The Ainu and Their Folklore. London: 1901. V. 53

BATCHELOR, JOHN CALVIN
The Birth of the People's Republic of Antartica. New York: 1983. V. 52
The Further Adventures of Halley's Comet. 1980. V. 49; 50; 52
The Further Adventures of Halley's Comet. New York: 1980. V. 47

BATE, C. S.
A History of British Sessile-Eyed Crustacea. London: 1863. V. 49; 51; 52
A History of the British Sessile-Eyed Crustacea. London: 1863-68. V. 54
A History of the British Sessile-Eyed Crustacea. London: 1963-68. V. 50

BATE, GEORGE
Elenchi Motuum Nuperorum in Anglia. London: 1661-63. V. 47; 50
Elenchi Motuum Nuperorum In Anglia... Londini: 1663. V. 48; 49; 54
Pharmacopoeia Bateana, In Libros Duos Digesta...Cura & Opera Thomae Fuller. London: 1719. V. 50

BATE, PERCY
The English Pre-Raphaelite Painters. London: 1899. V. 49
Modern Scottish Portrait Painters. Edinburgh: 1910. V. 47; 53

BATE, WALTER JACKSON
John Keats. Cambridge: 1963. V. 54

BATEMAN, CHARLES SOMERVILLE LATROBE
The First Ascent of the Kasai: Being Some Records of Service Under the Lone Star. London: 1889. V. 53

BATEMAN, FREDERIC
The Idiot: His Place in Creation and His Claims on Society. London: 1897. V. 47; 54
On Aphasia, or Loss of Speech and the Localization of the Faculty of Articulate Language. London: 1890. V. 47
On Aphasia, or Loss of Speech in Cerebral Disease. London: 1870. V. 48

BATEMAN, GERALD COOPER
A Countryman's Calendar. Sayings for the Months. Ditchling: 1928. V. 49

BATEMAN, H. M.
Considered Trifles. A Book of Drawings. London: 1934. V. 50
The M. F. H. Who Ran Riot!. London: 1934. V. 53

BATEMAN, J.
A Monograph of Odontoglossum. London: 1864-74. V. 48

BATEMAN, JAMES
A Second Century of Orchidaceous Plants. London: 1867. V. 49; 51; 52; 53

BATEMAN, JOHN FREDERIC
Description of a Proposed Cast-Iron Tube for Carrying a Railway Across the Channel Between the Coasts of England and France. London: 1869. V. 51; 53; 54
History and Description of the Manchester Waterworks. London: 1884. V. 54
History and Description of the Manchester Waterworks. Manchester: 1884. V. 49

BATEMAN, ROBERT
The Art of Robert Bateman. New York: 1981. V. 51
Robert Bateman. An Artist in Nature. Markham: 1990. V. 51
The World of Robert Bateman. New York: 1985. V. 51

BATEMAN, THOMAS
Delineations of Cutaneous Diseases. London: 1840. V. 53
A Practical Synopsis of Cutaneous Diseases, According to the Arranement of Dr. Willan... Philadelphia: 1824. V. 48

BATES, ARTHENIA J.
Seeds Beneath the Snow. New York: 1969. V. 54

BATES, CLARA DOTY
On the Treetop. Boston: 1880. V. 47

BATES, D. B., MRS.
Incidents on Land and Water or Four Years on the Pacific Coast... Boston: 1858. V. 50

BATES, DAISY
The Long Shadow of Little Rock: a Memoir. New York: 1962. V. 53

BATES, E. KATHARINE
Egyptian Bonds. London: 1879. V. 47

BATES, EDMUND FRANKLIN
History and Reminiscences of Denton County. Denton: 1918. V. 49; 52; 53

BATES, ELISHA
The Doctrines of Friends: or, Principles of the Christian Religion, as Held by the Society of Friends, Commonly Called Quakers. Dublin: 1828. V. 49

BATES, ELY
Rural Philosophy; or Reflections on Knowledge, Virtue and Happiness, Chiefly in Reference to a Life of Retirement in the Country. London: 1803. V. 52

BATES, GEORGE
Murder: Catalogue the Seventh of Rare and Interesting Books Illustrating the Development of the Detective and Mystery Story. London: 1934. V. 52

BATES, HENRY WALTER
Illustrated Travels: a Record of Discovery, Geography and Adventure. London: 1869-75. V. 53
Naturalist on the River Amazon. London: 1863. V. 52
The Naturalist on the River Amazon. London: 1864. V. 48; 54
Naturalist on the River Amazon. London: 1892. V. 54

BATES, HERBERT ERNEST
Achilles and Diana. London: 1963. V. 50
Achilles and the Twins. London: 1964. V. 48; 52
The Beauty of the Dead and Other Stories. London: 1940. V. 53
The Black Boxer. London: 1932. V. 51; 52
Catherine Foster. London: 1929. V. 51; 53
Catherine Foster. New York: 1929. V. 51; 52
Charlotte's Row. London: 1931. V. 51; 52; 53
Christmas 1930: a Poem. London: 1930. V. 51; 53
Cut and Come Again. London: 1935. V. 47; 50; 51; 52; 53
The Daffodil Sky. London: 1955. V. 48
The Day of Glory - A Play in Three Acts. London: 1945. V. 54
Day's End and Other Stories. London: 1928. V. 51; 52
Day's End and Other Stories. New York: 1928. V. 50
Down the River. London: 1937. V. 48; 51
The Duet. London: 1935. V. 51; 53
The Fallow Land. London: 1932. V. 51; 52; 54
Flowers and Faces. London: 1935. V. 48
Flowers and Faces. Waltham St. Lawrence: 1935. V. 51; 52
The Flying Goat. London: 1939. V. 51; 52
A German Idyll. Waltham Saint Lawrence: 1931. V. 51
A German Idyll. Waltham St. Lawrence: 1932. V. 47; 51; 53
The Great House. 1984. V. 52
The Hessian Prisoner. London: 1930. V. 47; 48; 50; 53
Holly and Sallow. London: 1931. V. 51; 53
A House of Women. London: 1936. V. 48; 51; 52; 53
The House with the Apricot Tales. Waltham St. Lawrence: 1933. V. 53
The Last Bread. London: 1926. V. 48; 50; 51; 54
Love for Lydia. London: 1952. V. 53
Mrs. Esmonds Life. London: 1931. V. 51
The Modern Short Story. London: 1941. V. 48; 51; 53
My Uncle Silas. London: 1939. V. 48; 49; 50; 51
The Poacher. London: 1935. V. 51
The Purple Plain. London: 1947. V. 51
Sally Go Round the Moon. London: 1932. V. 53; 54
The Seekers. London: 1926. V. 47; 51; 53
Seven by Five - Stories. London: 1963. V. 51
Seven Tales and Alexander. London: 1929. V. 50; 51; 52
Seven Tales and Alexander. New York: 1930. V. 51; 52
Something Short and Sweet: Stories. London: 1937. V. 51; 52
Song for December; a Poem. London: 1928. V. 51; 53
Spella Ho; a Novel. London: 1938. V. 51; 52
The Story Without an End and the Country Doctor. London: 1932. V. 51
Sugar for the Horse. London: 1957. V. 51
Thirty One Selected Tales. London: 1947. V. 50; 51; 52
Thirty Tales. London: 1934. V. 49
Through the Woods. London: 1936. V. 49; 51; 52; 54
The Two Sisters. London: 1926. V. 51; 52; 54
The White Admiral. London: 1968. V. 53
The Woman Who Had Imagination and Other Stories. London: 1934. V. 51
The Woman Who Had Imagination and other Stories. New York: 1934. V. 51; 53

BATES, J. C.
History of the Bench and Bar in California. San Francisco: 1912. V. 51; 53

BATES, J. W.
Bryophytes and Lichens in a Changing Environment. London: 1992. V. 50; 52

BATES, JOHN CADWALLADER
Thomas Bates and the Kirklevington Shorthorns. Newcastle-upon-Tyne: 1897. V. 52

BATES, JOSEPH D.
The Art of the Atlantic Salmon Fly. Boston: 1987. V. 51

BATES, MARGARET HOLMES
Manitou. Indianapolis: 1881. V. 50; 54

BATES, RALPH
Lean Men - an Episode in a Life. London: 1934. V. 48
The Miraculous Horde. London: 1939. V. 49
Sierra. London: 1933. V. 49

BATES, ROBERT H.
Mountain Man; the Story of Belmore Browne, Hunter, Explorer, Artist, Naturalist and Preserver of Our Northern Wilderness. Clinton: 1988. V. 52

BATES, RUSSELL
The Man On the Dump. Seattle: 1909. V. 50

BATES, WALTER
The Mysterious Stranger, or the Adventures of Henry More Smith... Charlottetown: 1855. V. 49

BATES, WILLIAM
A Gallery of Illustrious Literary Characters. London: 1873. V. 54
George Cruikshank: The Artist, The Humorist, and the Man... Birmingham: 1878. V. 49; 52
George Cruikshank: the Artist, the Humorist, and the Man... London: 1879. V. 49
Harlequin Mungo, or, a Peep Into the Tower... London: 1788. V. 51
The MacLise Portrait Gallery of Illustrious Literary Characters: with Memoirs. London: 1883. V. 53

BATES, WILLIAM C.
The Stars and Stripes in Rebeldom, a Series of Papers Written by Federal Prisoners (Privates) in Richmond, Tuscalossa, New Orleans, and Salisbury, N.C. Boston: 1862. V. 52

BATES, WILLIAM G.
An Address Delivered in the New Court House, in Springfield, Hampden County, Massachusetts, at the Dedication of the Same... Springfield: 1874. V. 49

BATESON, F. W.
Cambridge Bibliography of English Literature. Cambridge: 1940-57. V. 51

BATESON, GREGORY
Balinese Character: a Photographic Analysis. New York: 1942. V. 49
Steps to an Ecology of Mind. San Francisco: 1972. V. 52; 53

BATESON, WILLIAM
Materials for the Study of Variation. London: 1894. V. 49; 53
Mendel's Principles of Heredity. Cambridge. V. 54
Mendel's Principles of Heredity. Cambridge: 1902. V. 49
Mendel's Principles of Heredity. 1909. V. 54
Mendel's Principles of Heredity. Cambridge: 1909. V. 53
Mendel's Principles of Heredity. Cambridge: 1909/13. V. 48
Mendel's Principles of Heredity. Cambridge: 1913. V. 52
Problems of Genetics. New Haven: 1913. V. 48; 53

BATH & WEST OF ENGLAND SOCIETY
Letters and Papers of Agriculture, Planting &c. for the Encouragement of Agriculture, Arts, Manufactures and Commerce. Bath: 1792-95. V. 49

BATH AGRICULTURAL SOCIETY
Letters and Papers of Agriculture, Planting &c... Bath: 1792-95. V. 47
Letters and Papers on Agriculture, Planting &c. Bath: 1802. V. 50; 53

BATH and London; or, Scenes in Each. London: 1811. V. 49; 54

BATH, DOWAGER MARCHIONESS OF
A Catalogue of the Contents of the Very Valuable Copy of Granger's Biographical History of England... 1826. V. 47

BATH, ELIZABETH
Poems, on Various Occasions... Bristol: 1806. V. 47; 53

BATH, MARQUIS OF
Report on the Manuscripts of the Marquis of Bath at Longleat, Wiltshire. London: 1904-08. V. 52

BATH, WILLIAM PULTENEY, EARL OF
The Politicks On Both Sides, With Regard to Foreign Affairs...With Some Observations on the Present State of Affairs in Great Britain. London: 1734. V. 48
A Proper Answer to the By-Stander. Wherein Is Shewn I. That There Is No Necessity For, But Infallible Ruin in the Maintenenance of a Large Regular (Or Mercenary) Land Force In this Island. II. That By Keeping a Standing Army for Preventing... London: 1742. V. 48
A Review of All that Hath Pass'd Between the Courts of Great Britain and Spain, Relating To Our Trade and Navigation From the Year 1721. To the Present Convention; With Some Particular Observations Upon It. London: 1739. V. 48
A State of the National Debt, As It Stood December the 24th, 1716. London: 1727. V. 48

BATHE, BASIL W.
Seven Centuries of Sea Travel, from the Crusaders to the Cruises. London: 1972. V. 50

BATHURST, CHARLES
Lectures Read at a Mechanics' Institute in the Country. London: 1854. V. 52

BATHURST, EARL
Supplement to the Foxhound Kennel Stud Book. London: 1928. V. 47

BATTARRA, GIOVANNI ANTONIO
Fungorum Agri Ariminensis Historia. Faenza: 1759. V. 49

BATTEL, JOSEPH
The Yankee Boy from Home. New York: 1864. V. 54

BATTELEY, JOHN
Opera Postuma. Viz. Antiquitates Rutupinae et Antiquitates S. Edmundi Burgi ad Annum 1272 Perductae. Oxoniae: 1745. V. 47

BATTEN, A.
Flowers of Southern Africa. Sandton: 1986. V. 50

BATTEN, JOHN H.
The Best of Tiger Hunting. Clinton: 1986. V. 53
Skyline Pursuits. Clinton: 1981. V. 49

BATTEN, JOHN M.
Random Thoughts. 1896. V. 51
Reminiscences of Two Years in the United States Navy. Lancaster: 1881. V. 49

BATTEN, M. I.
English Windmills. London: 1930-32. V. 50

BATTERSHALL, FLETCHER
Bookbinding for Bibliophiles. Greenwich: 1905. V. 47

BATTERSHALL, JESSE
Food Adulteration and Its Detection. New York: 1887. V. 48; 53

BATTEY, THOMAS C.
The Life and Adventures of a Quaker Among the Indians. Boston: 1876. V. 49; 54

BATTLE, KEMP PLUMMER
Sketches of the Early History of the City of Raleigh. Raleigh: 1877. V. 48

THE BATTLE of the Frogs and Mice. 1988. V. 52

BATTLE of the Monkey and the Crab. London & Sydney: 1888. V. 50
BATTLE of the Monkey and the Crab. London: 1900. V. 53

BATTLE, RICHARD JOHN VULLIAMY
Plastic Surgery. London: 1964. V. 54

BATTY, CAPTAIN
Welsh Scenery. London: 1825. V. 48

BATTY, D. T.
Batty's Catalogue of the Copper Coinage of Great Britain, Ireland, British Isles and Colonies, Local and Private Tokens, Jettons, &c. Manchester & London: 1868-98. V. 48

BATTY, ELIZABETH FRANCES
Italian Scenery. From Drawings Made in 1817. London: 1820. V. 52

BATTY, JOSEPH H.
Practical Taxidermy and Home Decoration... New York: 1880. V. 51

BATTY, ROBERT
French Scenery, from Drawings Made in 1819. London: 1822. V. 52
German Scenery. From Drawings made in 1820. London: 1823. V. 52
Scenery of the Rhine, Belgium and Holland. London: 1826. V. 49; 52
Welsh Scenery. London: 1823. V. 47; 51
Welsh Scenery. London: 1825. V. 51; 53

BATTYE, CHRISTINE
The Brewhouse Private Press 1963-1983. Wymondham: 1984. V. 48; 52

BAUCUS, GEORGIANA
In Journeyings Oft. A Sketch of the Life and Travels of Mary C. Nind. New York: 1897. V. 53

BAUDELAIRE, CHARLES
Les Fleurs du Mal. Paris: 1857. V. 47; 51
Les Fleurs du Mal. Paris: 1940. V. 53
Flowers of Evil. London: 1935. V. 53
Flowers of Evil. London: 1939. V. 49
Flowers of Evil. London: 1940. V. 52
Flowers of Evil. New York: 1971. V. 48; 52; 54
Intimate Journals. London, New York: 1930. V. 48; 51
The Intimate Journals. Hollywood: 1947. V. 49
The Letters of Charles Baudelaire to His Mother: 1833-66. London: 1928. V. 48
Little Poems in Prose. London: 1928. V. 47
Little Poems in Prose. Paris: 1928. V. 47; 51
The Mirror of Baudelaire. USA: 1942. V. 53
Oeuvres. Paris: 1916-1930. V. 48
Les Paradis Artificiels. Paris: 1860. V. 49
Poems in Prose... London: 1905. V. 53
Translations from Charles Baudelaire. London: 1869. V. 49

BAUDEMENT, EMILE
Les Races Bovines. Paris: 1861-62. V. 50; 52

BAUDIN, P.
Fetichism and Fetich Worshippers. New York: 1885. V. 49

BAUDOUIN, ALEXANDRE
The Man of the World's Dictionary. London: 1822. V. 52; 54

BAUDUY, JEROME K.
Diseases of Nervous System. Philadelphia: 1892. V. 49; 50

BAUER, FERDINAND
The Australian Flower Paintings of... 1976. V. 50

BAUER, J. J.
Bibliotheca Librorum Rariorum Universalis. Nurnberg: 1770-91. V. 48

BAUER, JOHN I.
William Zorach. New York: 1959. V. 53

BAUER, K. JACK
United States Naval Operations During the Mexican War. Indiana: 1953, 1989. V. 50

BAUER, LOUIS
Hip Disease. Nashville: 1859. V. 50

BAUER, LOUIS HOPEWELL
Aviation Medicine. Baltimore: 1926. V. 49

BAUER, MAX
Precious Stones: a Popular Account of their Characters, Occurrence and Applications... London: 1904. V. 48

BAUER, P.
Himalayan Quest. 1938. V. 53

BAUER, P. V.
The Excavations at Dura-Europos. Final Report IV. Part III: The Lamps. New Haven: 1947. V. 52

BAUERMAN, H.
Report of the Geology of the Country Near the Forty-Ninth Parallel of North Latitutde West of the Rocky Mountains. From Observations Made 1859-1861. Montreal: 1884. V. 50; 52

BAUGHAN, PETER E.
North of Leeds. London: 1966. V. 47; 50; 52; 53

BAUHIN, CASPAR
Pinax Theatri Botanici... Basel: 1623. V. 52; 53

BAUM, DWIGHT JAMES
Great Georgian Houses of America. New York: 1933/37. V. 51

BAUM, JULIUS
Romanesque Architecture in France. London: 1928. V. 47; 48

BAUM, LYMAN FRANK
Annabel. 1906. V. 47
Aunt Jane's Nieces. 1906. V. 48
Aunt Jane's Nieces on Vacation. 1912. V. 48; 50; 52
Bandit Jim Crow. 1906. V. 48
Bandit Jim Crow. Chicago: 1906. V. 52
The Daring Twins. 1911. V. 48
Daring Twins... Chicago: 1911. V. 53
Dorothy and the Wizard in Oz. Chicago: 1908. V. 47; 52; 53
Dot and Tot of Merryland. Chicago: 1901. V. 49
The Emerald City of Oz. Chicago: 1910. V. 49; 53
The Emerald City of Oz. Toronto: 1910. V. 47
The Enchanted Island of Yew, Whereon Prince Marvel Encountered the High Ki of Twi & other Surprising People. Indianapolis: 1903. V. 49
Father Goose: His Book. Chicago: 1899. V. 47
John Dough and the Cherub. 1906. V. 51; 53
L. Frank Baum's Juvenile Speaker. Chicago: 1910. V. 47; 49
The Land of Oz: a Sequel to 'The Wizard of Oz'. Chicago: 1939. V. 51
The Last Egyptian. 1908. V. 51; 53
The Last Egyptian. Philadelphia: 1908. V. 49
The Lost Princess of Oz. 1917. V. 48; 50

BAUM, LYMAN FRANK continued
The Magic of Oz. Chicago: 1919. V. 51
The Magic of Oz. Chicago: 1935. V. 51
The Magical Monarch of Mo and His People. Chicago: 1903. V. 49
The Marvelous Land of Oz. Chicago: 1904. V. 53
Mary Louise Adopts a Soldier. 1919. V. 49
The Master Key. Indianapolis: 1901. V. 47; 48; 49; 52
Mr. Woodchuck. Chicago: 1906. V. 47; 49
Mother Goose in Prose. Chicago: 1896. V. 49
Mother Goose in Prose. Chicago: 1897. V. 47
Mother Goose in Prose. London: 1898. V. 47
Oz-Man Tales: The Yellow Hen. Chicago: 1916. V. 47
Ozma Of Oz. 1907. V. 48; 54
Ozma of Oz. Chicago: 1907. V. 49
The Patchwork Girl of Oz. Chicago: 1913. V. 53
Phoebe Daring. 1912. V. 48
Phoebe Daring. Chicago: 1912. V. 52; 54
Policeman Blue Jay. Chicago: 1907. V. 51
Queen Zixi of Ix. New York: 1905. V. 53
Rinkitink in Oz. 1916. V. 48; 50; 54
The Road to Oz. 1909. V. 54
The Road to Oz. Chicago: 1909. V. 52
The Sea Fairies. Chicago: 1911. V. 49
Sky Island. Chicago: 1912. V. 49
The Songs of Father Goose. For the Kindergarten, the Nursery and the Home. Chicago: 1900. V. 48
Tamawaca Folks. 1907. V. 49; 50; 54
Tik-Tok of Oz. Chicago: 1914. V. 47
The Wizard of Oz. Chicago: 1900. V. 48
Wizard of Oz. London: 1940. V. 47
The Wizard of Oz. West Hatfield: 1985. V. 47
The Wizard of Oz Waddle Book. New York: 1934. V. 52
The Woggle-Bug Book. Chicago: 1905. V. 51
The Wonderful Wizard of Oz. Chicago: 1900. V. 53; 54
The Wonderful Wizard of Oz. West Hatfield: 1985. V. 48; 49; 51; 53
The Yellow Hen. 1916. V. 48

BAUMAN, J. E.
Out of the Valley of the Forgotten, or, From Trinil to New York. Easton: 1923. V. 53

BAUMANN, GUSTAVE
Nearer to Art. Santa Fe: 1993. V. 50

BAUMANN, KURT
Dozy and Hawkeye. 1974. V. 51

BAUME, ANTOINE
A Manual of Chemistry, or a Brief Account of the Operations of Chemistry and Their Products. Warington: 1786. V. 50; 54

BAUME, ERIC
Five Graves at Nijmegen. London: 1945. V. 49

BAUMEL, J. J.
Nomina Anatomica Avium, an Annotated Antomical Dictionary of Birds. London: 1979. V. 54

BAUMGARTEL, ELISE J.
The Cultures of Prehistoric Egypt. Volume II (only). Oxford: 1960. V. 51

BAUR, J. I. H.
New Art in America: 50 Painters of the 20th Century. Greenwich: 1957. V. 47

BAUR, JOHANN WILHELM
Vedute de Giardini. rome: 1636. V. 49

BAVERSTOCK, JAMES
Hydrometrical Obsesrvations and Experiments in the Brewery. London: 1785. V. 54

BAWDEN, EDWARD
Hold Fast by Your Teeth. London: 1963. V. 50
Kynoch Press 1935 Notebook. Witton, Birmingham: 1935. V. 47
Portfolio of Prints. London: 1984. V. 49

BAX, CLIFFORD
Florence Farr, Bernard Shaw and W. B. Yeats. 1941. V. 49; 50; 51; 53; 54
The Traveller's Tale. Oxford: 1921. V. 52

BAXT, GEORGE
A Queer Kind of Death. London: 1967. V. 54

BAXTER
The Birds of Scotland. London: 1953. V. 52

BAXTER, ANDREW
A Letter from Mr. Baxter, Author of an Enquiry Into the Nature of the Human Soul and of Matho. To John Wilkes Esq. N.P: 1753. V. 51

BAXTER, CHARLES
First Light. New York: 1987. V. 50; 53
Shadow Play. New York: 1993. V. 52; 53
The South Dakota Guidebook. New York: 1974. V. 53
Through the Safety Net. New York: 1985. V. 52

BAXTER, D. R.
Superimposed Load Firearms 1360-1860. Hong Kong: 1966. V. 49

BAXTER, EVELYN V.
The Birds of Scotland: Their History, Distribution and Migration. Edinburgh: 1953. V. 48; 49; 50
The Birds of Scotland, Their History, Distribution and Migration. London: 1953. V. 51

BAXTER, FRANCIS WILLOUGHBY
Percy Lockhart; or, the Hidden Will. London: 1872. V. 51

BAXTER, GEORGE R. WYTHEN
Don Juan Junior; a Poem, by Byron's Ghost. London: 1839. V. 47

BAXTER, GLEN
The Falls Tracer - Six Pieces and Five Drawings. London: 1970. V. 53
Glen Baxter: His Life. The Years of Struggle. London: 1983. V. 47

BAXTER, J. H.
Statistics, Medical and Anthropologica of the Provost-Marshall General's Bureau Delivered from Records of the Examintion of Military Service in the Armies of the United States During the late War of the Rebellion, of Over a Million Recruits... Washington: 1875. V. 53; 54

BAXTER, JAMES PHINNEY
A Memoir of Jacques Cartier, Sieur de Limoilou, His Voyages to the St. Lawrence, a Bibliography and a Facsimile of the Manuscript of 1534 with Annotations, etc. New York: 1906. V. 47
Sir Ferdinando Gorges and His Province of Maine. Boston: 1890. V. 47; 50; 51

BAXTER, JOHN
A New and Impartial History of England... London: 1800. V. 51

BAXTER, LUCY
The Life of William Barnes. London: 1887. V. 53; 54

BAXTER, RICHARD
The Cure of Church-Divisions; or, Directions for Weak Christians, to Keep Them from Being Dividers, or Troublers of the Church... London: 1670. V. 48
The Grand Debate Between the Most Reverend the Bishops, & the Presbyterian Divines, Appointed by His Sacred Majesty...Review and Alteration of the Book of Common Prayer. (with) To the Kings Most Excellent Majesty. The Due Account, & Humble Petition of the... London: 1661/61. V. 52; 54
A Key for Catholicks. London: 1659. V. 53
A Petition For Peace; With the Reformation of the Liturgy... London: 1661. V. 48
Poetical Fragments: Heart-Imployment with God and It Self, The Concordant Discord of a Broken-Healed Heart. Sorrowing-Rejoicing. Fearing-Hoping, Dying-Living. London: 1699. V. 52
Preservatives Against Melancholy and overmuch Sorrow. London: 1713. V. 49
Reliquiae Baxterianae; or, Mr. Richard Baxter's Narrative of the Most Memorable Passages of His Life and Times. London: 1696. V. 53
The Saints Everlasting Rest... London: 1651. V. 48
The Saints Everlasting Rest... London: 1653. V. 48
The Saints Everlasting Rest... London: 1659. V. 48; 50; 53
The Saints Everlasting Rest... 1759. V. 49
A Treatise of conversion. London: 1657. V. 49
The Unreasonableness of Infidelity Manifested in Four Discourses... London: 1655. V. 53

BAXTER, S. S.
Brief in the Case of Almanzon Huston. Washington: 1856. V. 54

BAXTER, WILLIAM
Glossarium Antiquitatum Britannicarum Sive Syllabus Antiquitatum Britannicarum sive Syllabus Etymologicus Antiquitatum Veteris Britanniae Atque Iberniae Temporibus Romanorum. London: 1733. V. 54
Glossarium Antiquitatum Romanarum. London: 1731. V. 47

BAY, JENS CHRISTIAN
Danish Fairy and Folk Tales. New York: 1899. V. 49
The Fortune of Books: Essays, Memories and Prophecie of a Librarian. Chicago: 1941. V. 53
A Handful of Western Books... A Second Handful...& A Third Handful... Cedar Rapids: 1935/36/36. V. 51
Three Handfuls of Western Books. Rapid City: 1941. V. 48

THE BAY of San Francisco. The Metropolis of the Pacific Coast and Its Suburban Cities. A History. Chicago: 1892. V. 50

BAYARD, SAMUEL J.
The Life of George Dashiell Bayard, Late Captain, U.S.A. and Brigadier-General of Volunteers, Killed in Battle of Fredericksburg, Dec. 1862. New York: 1874. V. 49
A Sketch of the Life of Com. Robert F. Stockton... New York: 1856. V. 47; 48; 51; 52; 53

BAYER, F., & CO.
Garment Dyeing. Elberfield: 1906. V. 50

BAYER, HERBERT
Bauhaus 1919-1928. New York: 1938. V. 47; 54
Book of Drawings. Chicago: 1961. V. 47
Herbert Bayer. Painter, Designer, Architect. New York: 1967. V. 50; 54
Visual Communication, Architecture, Painting. New York: 1967. V. 50; 54

BAYFIELD, E. G., MRS.
A Winter in Bath. London: 1807. V. 50

BAYFIELD, HENRY WOLSEY
The St. Lawrence Survey Journals of Captain Henry Wolsey Bayfield: 1829-1853. Toronto: 1984/86. V. 51

BAYFIELD, ROBERT
Tractatus de Tumoribus Praeter Naturant or a Treatise of Preternatural Tumors... London: 1662. V. 47

BAYLDON, J. S.
A Treatise on the Valuation of Property for the Poor's Rate... London: 1834. V. 50

BAYLDON, OLIVER
The Paper Makers Craft... 1965. V. 53
The Paper Makers Craft. Leicester: 1965. V. 48; 52; 54

BAYLE, A. L. J.
A Manual of General Anatomy, Containing a Concise Description of the Elementary Tissues of the Human Body. Philadelphia: 1828. V. 51; 53

BAYLE, PIERRE
Dictionaire Historique et Critique. Amsterdam: 1734. V. 50
The Dictionary: Historical and Critical. London: 1734-38. V. 47; 48; 49; 50
An Historical and Critical Dictionary... London: 1826. V. 47
Oeuvres Diverses. The Hague: 1737. V. 50

BAYLESS, FRANCIS
A Narrative of Major General Wool's Campaign in Mexico in the Years 1846, 1847 and 1848. Albany: 1851. V. 49; 54

BAYLEY, FRANK W.
Five Colonial Artists of New England. Boston: 1929. V. 48

BAYLEY, HAROLD
The Lost Language of Symbolism. New York: 1952. V. 50

BAYLEY, JAMES ROOSEVELT
Memoirs of the Right Reverend Simon Wm. Gabriel Brute, D.D. New York: 1860. V. 53

BAYLEY, JOHN
The History and Antiquities of the Tower of London... London: 1812-25. V. 52
The History and Antiquities of the Tower of London... London: 1821-25. V. 50; 52
The History and Antiquities of the Tower of London... London: 1825. V. 47; 54

BAYLEY, NICOLA
La Corona and the Tin Frog. London: 1979. V. 53
Nursery Rhymes. London: 1975. V. 48

BAYLEY, PETER
Idwal: a Poem. London: 1824. V. 48; 51
Sketches from St. George's Fields. London: 1820. V. 47

BAYLEY, RICHARD
Letters from the Health-Office, Submitted to the Common Council, of the City of New-York. New York: 1799. V. 50

BAYLEY, SOLOMON
A Narrative of Some Remarkable Incidents in the Life of Solomon Bayley, Formerly a Slave, in the State of Delaware, North America, Written by Himself. London: 1825. V. 48

BAYLEY, THOMAS
The Royal Charter Granted Unto Kings, by God Himself... London: 1649. V. 50

BAYLEY, THOMAS B.
Thoughts On the Necessity and Advantages of Care and Oeconomy Collecting and Preserving Different Substances of Manure. Manchester: 1796. V. 53

BAYLIES, WILLIAM
Practical Reflections on the Uses and Abuses of Bath Waters. London: 1757. V. 50; 53

BAYLISS, MARGUERITE F.
Bolinvar. New York: 1937. V. 49; 51; 53
The Matriarchy of the American Turn 1875-1930. 1931. V. 52
The Yearbook of Show Horses. New York: 1936. V. 54

BAYLISS, WILLIAM
Intravenous Injection in Wound Shock. London: 1918. V. 53
Principles of General Physiology. London: 1915. V. 48; 53
The Vaso-Motor System. London: 1923. V. 47; 48; 53

BAYLISS, WYKE
Five Great Painters of the Victorian Era. London: 1902. V. 49

BAYLOR, ARMISTED KEITH
Abdul. An Allegory. New York: 1930. V. 47

BAYLOR, BYRD
Yes Is Better than No. New York: 1977. V. 52

BAYLOR, GEORGE
Bull Run to Bull Run; or, Four Years in the Army of Northern Virginia. Richmond: 1900. V. 49

BAYLY, ANSELM
An Introduction to Languages, Literary and Philosophical... London: 1758. V. 51

BAYLY, LEWES
The Practice of Piety, Directing a Christian How to Walk that He May Please God. London: 1685. V. 52

BAYLY, THOMAS
Herba Parientis. Or, The Wall-Flower. London: 1650. V. 49; 54

BAYMA, JOSEPH
The Elements of Molecular Mechanics. London and Cambridge: 1866. V. 47

BAYNARD, EDWARD
Health, a Poem. London: 1740. V. 49

BAYNE, A. D.
A Comprehensive History of Norwich Including a Survey of the City... London: 1869. V. 50
Royal Illustrated History of Eastern England, Civil, Military, Political and Ecclesiastical from the Earliest Period to the Present Time... Great Yarmouth: 1873. V. 50; 54

BAYNE, PETER
Essays in Biography and Criticism. 1st Series. Boston: 1857. V. 54
The Life and Letters of Hugh Miller. London: 1871. V. 54
Two Great Englishwomen, Mrs. Browning & Charlotte Bronte... 1881. V. 54
Two Great Englishwomen, Mrs. Browning & Charlotte Bronte. London: 1881. V. 47; 49; 51

BAYNE, ROBERT
Historical Sketch of Rickmansworth and the Surrounding Parishes. London: 1870. V. 51
Moor Park (Rickmansworth, Hertfordshire) with a Biographical Sketch of Its Principal Proprietors. London: 1871. V. 49

BAYNES, F. J.
Coals and Cooking Ranges: Being a Brief Description of the Combustion of Coals and Construction of Cooking Fires, with a Few Illustrations of Ancient and Modern Kitchen Cooking Stoves. London: 1873. V. 53

BAYNES, HELTON GODWIN
Mythology of the Soul: A Research Into the Unconscious from Schizophrenic Dreams and Drawings. London: 1955. V. 52

BAYNES, ROBERT H.
The Illustrated Book of Sacred Poems. London: 1867. V. 52

BAYRUS, PETER
De Medendis Hunani (sic) Corporis Malis Enchiridion, Quod Vulgo Veni Mecum Vocant... Basel: 1563. V. 48

BAZ, GUSTAVO
History of the Mexian Railway... Mexico: 1876. V. 50

BAZIN, GILLES AUGUSTINE
Le Livre Jaune Contenant Quelques Conversations sur les Logomachies... Basle: 1748. V. 51
The Natural History of Bees. London: 1744. V. 50; 52

BEACH, BELLE
Riding and Driving for Women. New York: 1912. V. 54

BEACH, CHARLES
Lost Lenore; or, the Adventures of a Rolling Stone. London: 1864. V. 47

BEACH, JOSEPH PERKINS
The Log of Apollo: Joseph Perkins Beach's Journal of the Voyage of the Ship Apollo from New York to San Francisco, 1849. San Francisco: 1986. V. 47

BEACH, JOSEPH WARREN
Body's Breviary. Pasadena: 1930. V. 52

BEACH, REX
Big Brother. New York: 1923. V. 54
The Silver Horde. New York: 1909. V. 54

BEACH, S. A.
The Apples of New York. Albany: 1905. V. 48; 50; 51; 52; 53; 54
Apples of New York. New York: 1905. V. 51

BEACH, SYLVIA
Shakespeare and Company. London: 1960. V. 53
Ulysses in Paris. New York: 1956. V. 53

BEACH, WOOSTER
The American Practice Condensed. New York: 1847. V. 48
The American Practice Condensed. Cincinnati: 1862. V. 53; 54
An Improved System of Midwifery, Adapted to the Reformed Practice of Medicine. New York: 1847. V. 52; 53
An Improved System of Midwifery, Adapted to the Reformed Practice of Medicine... New York: 1850. V. 50

BEADLE, CHARLES
A Trip to the United States in 1887. London: 1887. V. 47
A Trip to the United States in 1887. Oxford: 1887. V. 53

BEADLE, DELOS WHITE
Canadian Fruit, Flower and Kitchen Gardener. Toronto: 1872. V. 50; 53

BEADLE, JOHN HANSON
Life in Utah. Philadelphia: 1870. V. 52
Life in Utah... Philadelphia: 1874. V. 50
Western Wilds, and the Men Who Redeem Them. Cincinnati: 1879. V. 47

BEADLE, N. C. W.
Vegetation of Australia, the Evolution of the Vascular Flora... London: 1981. V. 48

BEAGLE, PETER
A Fine and Private Place. New York: 1960. V. 51; 53
The Last Unicorn... London: 1968. V. 48
The Last Unicorn. New York: 1968. V. 49; 50; 51

BEAGLEHOLE, J. C.
The Exploration of the Pacific. London: 1934. V. 47

BEALE, ANNE
Nothing Venture, Nothing Have. London: 1864. V. 50
Poems. London: 1842. V. 50

BEALE, EDWARD F.
Wagon Road - Fort Smith to Colorado River. Washington: 1860. V. 47
Wagon Road from Fort Defiance to the Colorado River. Washington: 1858. V. 49; 54

BEALE, JAMES
The Battle Flags of the Army of the Potomac at Gettysburg, Pennsylvania. July 1st, 2d and 3d, 1863. Philadelphia: 1885. V. 52; 54

BEALE, STEPHEN T.
Trial and Conviction of Dr. Stephen T. Beale, with the Letters of Chief Justice Lewis and Judges Black and Woodward on His Case. Philadelphia: 1855. V. 51

BEALE, THOMAS
The Natural History of the Sperm Whale: Its Anatomy and Physiology... London: 1839. V. 50

BEALS, CARLETON
The Crime of Cuba. Philadelphia: 1933. V. 47; 52

BEAMAN, ARDERN
The Squadroon. London: 1920. V. 47

BEAMISH, NORTH LUDLOW
The Discovery of America by the Northmen, in the Tenth Century, with Notices of the Early Settlements of the Irish in the Western Hemisphere. London: 1841. V. 54

BEAMISH, RICHARD
Memoir of the Life of Sir Marc Isambard Brunel. London: 1862. V. 47; 51; 54

BEAMONT, WILLIAM
A Diary of a Journey from Warrington to the East, in the Autumn of 1854. Warrington: 1855. V. 49

BEAN, LOWELL JOHN
Diaries and Accounts of the Romero Expeditions in Arizona and California 1823-1826. Los Angeles: 1962. V. 48

BEAN, W. J.
The Royal Botanic Gardens, Kew... London: 1908. V. 47; 51; 54
Trees and Shrubs Hardy in the British Isles. London: 1936. V. 52
Trees and Shrubs Hardy in the British Isles. London: 1950-51. V. 48; 50
Trees and Shrubs Hardy in the British Isles. London: 1970-80. V. 48; 50; 51
Trees and Shrubs Hardy in the British Isles. London: 1981. V. 52
Trees and Shrubs Hardy in the British Isles. London: 1989. V. 52
Trees and Shrubs Hardy in the British Isles, Supplement. London: 1988. V. 50; 51

BEANE, J. F.
From Castle to Cabin. New York: 1905. V. 50

BEANLANDS, ARTHUR J.
British Columbia, Its Present Resources and Future Possibilities. Victoria: 1893. V. 54

BEAR, GREG
Early Harvest. Cambridge: 1988. V. 51; 53
Eon. New York: 1985. V. 51; 53
The Wind from a Burning Woman. Sauk City: 1983. V. 51

BEARCROFT, PHILIP
An Historical Account of Thomas Sutton Esq., and His Foundation in Charter-House. London: 1737. V. 54

BEARD, CHARLES R.
A Catalogue of the Collection of Martinware Formed by Mr. Frederick John Nettlefold... London: 1936. V. 49

BEARD, DANIEL CARTER
Moonlight and Six Feet of Romance. New York: 1892. V. 51; 54

BEARD, FRANCES B.
Wyoming - from Territorial Days to the Present. New York: 1933. V. 54

BEARD, GEORGE MILLER
Hay-Fever; or, Summer Catarrh: Its nature and Treatment. New York: 1876. V. 50
A Practical Treatise On Nervous Exhaustion (Neurasthenia): Its Symptoms, Nature, Sequences and Treatment. New York: 1880. V. 52; 53
A Practical Treatise on the Medical & Surgical Uses of Electricity. New York: 1875. V. 47; 48; 52; 53
The Problems of Insanity. A Paper Read Before the Medico-Legal Society, March 3, 1880. V. 53
Sexual Neurasthenia (Nervous Exhaustion). Its Hygiene, Causes, Symptoms...with a Chapter on Diet for the Nervous. New York: 1884. V. 47; 48
Sexual Neurasthenia (Nervous Exhaustion), Its Hygiene, Causes, Symptoms...with a Chapter on Diet for the Nervous. New York: 1891. V. 53
Stimulants and Narcotics; Medically, Philosophically and Morally Considered. New York: 1871. V. 47; 48; 53
The Study of Trance, Muscle-Reading and Allied Nervous Phenomena in Europe and America, with a Letter on the Moral Character of Trance Subjects and a Defence of Dr. Charcot. New York: 1882. V. 53

BEARD, HENRY
Before the Secretary of the Interior. In the Matter of Application of the Southern Pacific Railroad Co. of California for the Appointment of Commissioners to Examine Two Hundred Miles of Railroad Lately Completed by Said Company. Washington: 1883. V. 47

BEARD, JOHN RELLY
The Life of Toussaint L'Ouverture. The Negro Patriot of Hayti. London: 1853. V. 47; 52

BEARD, MARK
Manhattan Third Year Reader. New York: 1984. V. 47; 50; 52
Neo-Classik Comix. New York: 1986. V. 50
New York Portfolio. New York: 1987. V. 52
Nineteen Famous People, Twenty-Two Friends and Six Nudes. New York: 1992. V. 50; 53
Pleasure and Pain. New York: 1987. V. 48; 50
Utah Reader. New York: 1986. V. 50

BEARD, MARY R.
America through Women's Eyes. New York. V. 51

BEARD, PETER HILL
The End of the Game. London: 1965. V. 52
The End of the Game. New York: 1965. V. 49; 54
End of the Game. New York: 1977. V. 48
Eyelids of Morning: The Mingled Destines of Crocodiles and Men. 1973. V. 48
Longing for Darkness. New York: 1975. V. 53

BEARDSLEY, AUBREY VINCENT
Beardsley. St. Petersburg: 1906. V. 49
A Book of Fifty Drawings. London: 1897. V. 50; 51
Keynote Series of Novels and Short Stories. London: 1896. V. 48
Last Letters. London: 1904. V. 48; 51
The Later Work of Aubrey Beardsley. London: 1930. V. 47
Letters to Leonard Smithers,. London: 1937. V. 50
Reproductions of Eleven Designs Omitted from the First Edition of Le Morte D'Arthur Illustrated by Aubrey Beardsley and Published in MDCCCXCIII, Also Those Made for the Covers of the Issue in Parts and a Facsimile Print of the Merlin Drawing. Edinburgh: 1927. V. 47
A Second Book of Fifty Drawings. London: 1899. V. 49; 50
The Story of Venus and Tannhauser in Which is set Forth an Exact Account of the Manner of State Held by Madam Venus, Goddess and Meretrix... London: 1907. V. 51
The Uncollected Work. London: 1925. V. 47; 49; 51
Under the Hill... London: 1904. V. 51
Under the Hill... London: 1921. V. 51
Under the Hill... Paris: 1959. V. 50
Venus and Tannhauser. New York: 1927. V. 53

BEARDSLEY, GRACE HADLEY
The Negro in Greek and Roman Civilization. Baltimore: 1929. V. 52

BEARSE, AUSTIN
Reminiscences of Fugitive-Slave Law Days in Boston. Boston: 1880. V. 53

BEASLAI, PIARAS
Michael Collins and the Making of a New Ireland. London: 1926. V. 50; 53

BEASLEY, GERTRUDE
My First Thirty Years. Paris: 1925. V. 47
My First Thirty Years. Austin: 1989. V. 50; 51

BEASLEY, HENRY
The Book of Prescriptions... Philadelphia: 1855. V. 53

BEATIE, RUSSEL H.
Saddles. Norman: 1981. V. 52; 54

THE BEATITUDES. Hampshire: 1905. V. 49

BEATON, CECIL
Air of Glory - a Wartime Scrapbook. London: 1941. V. 47
Ashcombe: the Story of a Fifteen-Year Lease. London: 1949. V. 48; 54
Ballet. London, New York: 1951. V. 48; 54
The Best of Beaton. London: 1968. V. 47
Cecil Beaton's "Fair Lady". New York: 1964. V. 54
Cecil Beaton's New York. London: 1938. V. 53
Cecil Beaton's New York. Philadelphia & New York: 1938. V. 48
Cecil Beaton's Scrapbook. London: 1937. V. 47
The Face of the World. New York. V. 50; 54
The Face of the World. New York: 1965. V. 54
The Glass of Fashion. Garden City: 1954. V. 48
The Glass of Fashion. London: 1954. V. 50
I Take Great Pleasure. New York: 1956. V. 54
India. Bombay: 1945. V. 47
It Gives Me Great Pleasure. London: 1955. V. 54
Japanese. New York: 1959. V. 49
My Bolivian Aunt - a Memoir. London: 1971. V. 54
Winged Squadrons. London: 1942. V. 54
Winged Squadrons: Impressions of the Men of the R.A.F. & Fleet Air Arm. London: 1944. V. 52
The Years Between 1939-1944. & The Wandering Years 1922-1939. The Diaries. New York: 1961/65. V. 54

BEATON, GEORGE
Jack Robinson: a Picaresque Novel. London: 1933. V. 53

BEATSON, GEORGE
On Spray Producers As Used in Lister's Antiseptic System... Edinburgh: 1881. V. 51

BEATTIE, ANN
Chilly Scenes of Winter. Garden City: 1976. V. 51; 53
Chilly Scenes of Winter. New York: 1976. V. 51; 52; 54
Distortions. Garden City: 1976. V. 47; 50; 51; 52
Jacklighting. 1981. V. 47

BEATTIE, ANN continued
Jacklighting. Worcester: 1981. V. 51; 52

BEATTIE, DAVID J.
Oor Gate-en'. Galashiels: 1915. V. 54

BEATTIE, GEORGE WILLIAM
Heritage of the Valley: San Bernardino's First Century. Pasadena: 1939. V. 53; 54

BEATTIE, JAMES
Dissertations Moral and Critical. London: 1783. V. 50
Elements of Moral Science. Edinburgh: 1790-93. V. 47
An Essay on the Nature and Immutability of Truth, in Opposition to Sophistry and Scepticism. Edinburgh: 1771. V. 53
An Essay on the Nature and Immutability of Truth, in Opposition to Sophistry and Scepticism. 1773. V. 49
An Essay on the Nature and Immutability of Truth, in Opposition to Sophistry and Scepticism. Edinburgh: 1773. V. 50; 54
An Essay on the Nature and Immutability of Truth, in Opposition to Sophistry and Scepticism. London: 1773. V. 51
An Essay on the Nature and Immutability of Truth, in Opposition to Sophistry and Scepticism. London: 1774. V. 47
Essay on the Nature and Immutability of Truth, in Opposition to Sophistry and Scepticism... Edinburgh: 1776. V. 51
An Essay on the Nature and Immutability of Truth, in Opposition to Sophistry and Scepticism. London: 1786. V. 52
Evidences of the Christian Religion: Briefly and Plainly Stated. London: 1786. V. 51
The Minstrel... London: 1771/74. V. 47
The Minstrel... London: 1799. V. 50
The Minstrel... Alnwick: 1807. V. 49
The Minstrel... London: 1807. V. 51
The Minstrel... Alnwick: 1808. V. 47
The Minstrel... London: 1816. V. 48
The Minstrel... London: 1819. V. 54
The Poetical Works of James Beattie. London: 1831. V. 49
The Poetical Works of James Beattie. London: 1866. V. 51

BEATTIE, WILLIAM
The Castles and Abbeys of England from the National Records, Early Chronicles... London. V. 51
The Danube... London: 1840. V. 48; 50; 52; 54
The Danube... London: 1850's. V. 49
The Danube. London: 1855. V. 54
Journal of a Residence in Germany... London: 1831. V. 48
The Ports, Harbours, Watering-Places, and Coast Scenery of Great Britain. London: 1842. V. 48
The Ports, Harbours, Watering-Places, and Coast Scenery of Great Britain. London: 1848. V. 54
Scotland Illustrated in a Series of Views. London: 1838. V. 47; 49; 52
Scotland Illustrated in a Series of Views Taken Expressly for This Work... London: 1842. V. 52; 54
Switzerland... London: 1830-40. V. 52
Switzerland. London: 1836. V. 48; 50; 51; 52; 53; 54
Switzerland... London: 1839/38. V. 54
Switzerland. London: 1936. V. 49
The Waldenses. London: 1838. V. 47; 49; 50; 51; 54

BEATTY, ALEXANDER
The Cleansing of the Sanctuary: a Discourse in Which it is Show that the Millennium may be Expected to Commence about A.D. 1850. Medina: 1843. V. 49

BEATTY, ALFRED CHESTER
The Chester Beatty Library. A Catalogue of the Armenian Manuscripts. Dublin: 1958. V. 47; 48
The Chester Beatty Library. A Catalogue of the Turkish Manuscripts and Miniatures. Dublin: 1958. V. 48
The Library of A. Chester Beatty. 1931. V. 49
Some Oriental Bindings in the Chester Beatty Library. Dublin: 1961. V. 48; 51

BEATTY, CHARLES C.
Record of the Family of Charles Beatty, Who Emigrated from Ireland to America in 1729. Steubenville: 1873. V. 49; 51

BEATTY, DAVID L.
Don't Tread On My Tire Rubber Sandals: a Tale of Vietnam. Boonville: 1969. V. 52

BEATTY, JOHN
The Citizen-Soldier; or, Memoirs of a Volunteer. Cincinnati: 1879. V. 54

BEATTY, K. J.
Human Leopards. London: 1915. V. 48

BEATTY, RICHARD CROOM
A Vanderbilt Miscellany 1919-1944. Nashville. V. 48
The Vanderbilt Miscellany 1919-44. Nashville: 1944. V. 50; 52

BEATTY, WILLIAM
Authentic Narrative of the Death of Lord Nelson With the Circumstance Preceding, Attending and Subsequent to... London: 1807. V. 50

BEAUCHAMP, MARY A.
The April Baby's Book of Tunes. London: 1900. V. 48

BEAUCHAMPS, PIERRE FRANCOIS GODART DE
Recherches sur les Theatres de France, Depuis l'Annee Onze Cens Soixante-un, Jusques a Present. Paris: 1735. V. 52

BEAUCLAIR, RENE
Neue Ideen fur Modernen Schmuck. Stuttgart: 1900. V. 53

BEAUCLERK, CHARLES
Military Operations in Canada, 1837-8-9. Bellevelle: 1980. V. 52

BEAUCLERK, HELEN
The Green Lacquer Pavillon. New York: 1926. V. 50

BEAUCLERK, TOPHAM
Bibliotheca Beauclerkiana. 1781. V. 48; 51
Bibliotheca Beauclerkiana... London: 1781. V. 48; 52

BEAUCOUR, FERNAND
The Discovery of Egypt. Paris: 1990. V. 51

BEAUFORT, HENRY SOMERSET, 9TH DUKE OF
Driving. London: 1889. V. 47; 52; 54

BEAUFORT, JAMES
Hoyle's Games Improved... London: 1788. V. 48

BEAUFOY, MARK
Nautical and Hydraulic Experiments With Numerous Scientific Miscellanies... London: 1834. V. 48; 49; 51; 54
Scloppetaria: or, Considerations on the Nature and Use of Rifled Barrel Guns. London: 1808. V. 48

BEAUJOINT, JULES
The Secret Memoirs of Madame La Marquise de Pompadour. London: 1885. V. 51

BEAUMARCHAIS, PIERRE AUGUSTIN CARON DE
The Follies of a day; or, The Marriage of Figaro. London: 1785. V. 47

BEAUMELLE, M. DE LAURENT ANGLIVIEL
Memoirs of the History of Madame Maintenon and of the Last Age. Dublin: 1758. V. 50

BEAUMONT, C. W.
The Mysterious Toyshop. London: 1924. V. 52
New Paths - Verse - Prose - Pictures. London: 1918. V. 47; 49; 52

BEAUMONT, CHARLES
Charles Beaumont: Selected Stories. 1988. V. 47; 51
The Hunger and Other Stories. New York: 1957. V. 47; 51
The Intruder. 1960. V. 47

BEAUMONT, CYRIL W.
Carnaval. London: 1918. V. 48
The First Score. An Account of the Foundation and Development of the Beaumont Press and its First Twenty Publications. London: 1927. V. 48
The History of Harlequin. London: 1926. V. 53
Impressions of the Russian Ballet: Children's Tales. London: 1919. V. 54
Impressions of the Russian Ballet: Cleopatra. 1918. V. 54
Impressions of the Russian Ballet: La Boutique Fantasque. 1919. V. 54
Impressions of the Russian Ballet: L'Oiseau de Feu. 1919. V. 54
Impressions of the Russian Ballet: Tamar. 1919. V. 54
Impressions of the Russian Ballet: the Good Humoured Ladies. 1918. V. 54
Impressions of the Russian Ballet: the Sleeping Princess (Part Two). 1921. V. 54
Impressions of the Russian Ballet: the Three Cornered Hat. 1919. V. 54
The Romantic Ballet in the Lithographs of Time. London: 1938. V. 48
The Strange Adventures of a Toy Soldier. London: 1926. V. 51

BEAUMONT, FRANCIS
Comedies and Tragedies. London: 1647. V. 47; 48; 50; 52
Fifty Comedies and Tragedies. London: 1679. V. 47; 51
A King and No King. London: 1661. V. 52
The Knight of the Burning Pestle. London: 1635. V. 48
The Knight of the Burning Pestle. London: 1661. V. 51
The Maids Tragedy. London: 1650. V. 48; 52
The Maids Tragedy. London: 1686. V. 53
Philaster, or Love Lies a Bleeding. London: 1687. V. 53
Philaster, or Love Lies a Bleeding. Dublin: 1765. V. 49
Salmacis and Hermaphroditus... Waltham St. Lawrence: 1951. V. 54
Songs & Lyrics from the Plays. 1928. V. 51
Songs & Lyrics from the Plays... London: 1928. V. 47
The Wild-Goose Chase. London: 1652. V. 47
Wit Without Money. London: 1639. V. 51
The Works... London: 1711. V. 50; 54
The Works... London: 1750. V. 49; 51
The Works... Edinburgh;: 1812. V. 47; 50; 51; 54
The Works... London: 1890. V. 53
The Works. London: 1904-12. V. 49

BEAUMONT, GEORGE FREDERICK
A History of Coggeshall, in Essex with an Account of Its Church, Abbey, Manors, Ancient Houses and Biographical Sketches of Its Most Distinguished Men and Ancient Families... London: 1890. V. 49; 54

BEAUMONT, MILES THOMPSON STAPLETON, 8TH BARON
Francesca di Faenza: a Tragedy. London: 1843. V. 51

BEAUMONT, ROBERTS
Colour in Woven Design. London: 1890. V. 48; 52

BEAUMONT, T.
The Complete New Cow Doctor; Being a Treatise on the Disorders Incident to Horned Cattle, With a Description of Their Symptoms and the Most Effectual Methods of Cure... Manchester: 1835. V. 49

BEAUMONT, WILLIAM
Experiments and Observations on the Gastric Juice and the Physiology of Digestion. Plattsburgh: 1833. V. 48; 50; 52; 53; 54
Experiments and Observations on the Gastric Juice and the Physiology of Digestion. Boston: 1834. V. 49; 50; 53; 54
Experiments and Observations on the Gastric Juice and the Physiology of Digestion. Edinburgh: 1838. V. 47; 48; 49; 50; 51; 52; 53; 54
Experiments and Observations on the Gastric Juice and the Physiology of Digestion. Boston: 1929. V. 47; 52; 53
The Physiology of Digestion with Experiments on the Gastric Juice. Burlington: 1847. V. 48; 49; 52
The Physiology of Digestion with Experiments on the Gastric Juice. Burlington: 1848. V. 51; 53; 54

BEAURAIN, JEAN DE
Histoire Militaire de Flandre, Sepuis l'Annee 1690, Jusquen 1694... Paris & La Haye: 1755-59. V. 47

BEAUREGARD, P. G. T.
Gen. Beauregard's Official Report of "The Battle of Manassas". Richmond: 1861. V. 49

BEAUTIES of Music. Boston: 1799. V. 51

THE BEAUTIES of Sidmouth Displayed... Sidmouth: 1810. V. 49

THE BEAUTIES of the Court of King Charles the Second. London: 1833. V. 52

THE BEAUTIES of the English Stage: Consisting of All the Celebrated Passages, Soliloquies, Similies, Descriptions, And Other Poetical Beauties in the English Plays, Ancient and Modern. Continued Down to the Present Year. London: 1737. V. 47; 48

THE BEAUTIFUL Indian; or, the Interesting History of Zoa (Daughter of Henrietta de Belgrave) and of Rodomond, an East Indian Merchant. London: 1824. V. 53; 54

BEAUTY and the Beast. London: 1843. V. 47
BEAUTY and the Beast. London: 1875. V. 52
BEAUTY and the Beast. New York: 1893. V. 48; 54

BEAUTY'S Awakening. A Masque of Winter and Of Spring. 1899. V. 50

BEAUTY'S Awakening. A Masque of Winter and of Spring... London: 1899. V. 49

BEAUVOIR, SIMONE DE
The Blood of Others. London: 1948. V. 53; 54
Le Deuxieme Sexe. Paris: 1949. V. 47; 49
Les Mandarins. Paris: 1954. V. 51
The Mandarins, a Novel. Cleveland and New York: 1956. V. 49; 50
The Second Sex. Franklin Station: 1979. V. 49

BEAUX, CECILIA
Background with Figures. Boston and New York: 1930. V. 47

BEAVEN, JAMES
Recreations of a Long Vacation; or a Visit to Indian Missions in Upper Canada. London/Toronto: 1846. V. 54

BEAVER, HERBERT
Reports and Letters of Herbert Beaver, 1836-38, Chaplain to the Hudson's Bay Company and Missionary to the Indians at Fort Vancouver. Portland: 1959. V. 53

BEAVER, PHILIP
African Memoranda. London: 1805. V. 51; 54

BEAVER, WILFRED N.
Unexplored New Guinea. London: 1920. V. 50

BEAVERBROOK, WILLIAM MAXWELL AIKEN
Don't Trust to Luck. London: 1950. V. 52

BEAZLEY, J. D.
Attic Black-Figure Vase-Painters. New York: 1978. V. 50; 52
Attic Red-figure Vase Painters. Oxford: 1963. V. 50
Etruscan Vase Painting. Oxford: 1947. V. 50; 52
Greek Vases in Poland. Oxford: 1928. V. 50
The Lewes House Collection of Ancient Gems. Oxford: 1920. V. 50; 52

BEBEL, AUGUST
Woman in the Past, Present, and Future. London: 1885. V. 47; 49

BECCARIA, CESARE BONESANA, MARCHESE DI
An Essay on Crimes and Punishments. London: 1767. V. 49
An Essay on Crimes and Punishments. London: 1767. V. 48; 49
An Essay on Crimes and Punishments... London: 1769. V. 47
Essay on Crimes and Punishments. London: 1770. V. 48
An Essay on Crimes and Punishments. London: 1775. V. 48
Essay on Crimes and Punishments. Philadelphia: 1793. V. 48; 50
An Essay on Crimes and Punishments... Philadelphia: 1819. V. 48; 50
The History of the Misfortunes of John Calas, a Victim of Fantaticism. Edinburgh: 1776. V. 48

BECHER, H. C. R.
A Trip to Mexico, Being Notes of a Journey From Lake Erie to Lake Tezcuco and Back... Toronto: 1800. V. 51

A Trip to Mexico, Being Notes of a Journey from Lake Erie to Lake Tezcuco and Back... Toronto: 1880. V. 50; 54

BECHSTEIN, JOHANN MATTHAUS
Cage and Chamber-Birds... London: 1853. V. 51; 53
Cage and Chamber-Birds. London: 1864. V. 51
Cage and Chamber-Birds. London: 1875. V. 54
The Natural History of Cage Birds. London: 1841. V. 54

BECHSTEIN, LUDWIG
The Rabbit Catcher and Other Fairy Tales. New York: 1962. V. 48; 50; 51; 52

BECHTEREV, VLADIMIR M.
General Principles of Human Reflexology. New York: 1932. V. 53

BECHTINGER, J.
Le Sonda Maggiori o l'Arcipelago Malayo. Cairo: 1874. V. 50

BECK, BARONESS VON
Personal Adventures During the Late War of Independence in Hungary. London: 1851. V. 50; 51

BECK, CARL
Surgical Diseases of the Chest. Philadelphia: 1907. V. 48
Surgical Diseases Of the Chest. Philadelphia: 1911. V. 53

BECK, CONRAD
The Miscroscope: a Simple Handbook. London: 1921/24. V. 50

BECK, E.
The Florist and Garden Miscellany 1849. London: 1850. V. 51

BECK, EDWARD JOSSELYN
Memorials to Serve for a History of the Parish of St. Mary, Rotherhithe. Cambridge: 1907. V. 54

BECK, L. C.
Botany of the Northern and Middle States... Albany: 1833. V. 47; 48; 51

BECK, LEWIS
Adulterations of Various Substances Used in Medicine and the Arts with the Means of Detecting Them. New York: 1846. V. 48; 53

BECK, S. WILLIAM
Gloves, Their Annals and Associations: a Chapter of Trade and Social History. London: 1883. V. 53

BECK, THEODRIC ROMEYN
Elements of Medical Jurisprudence. London: 1836. V. 48

BECK, THOMAS ALCOCK
Annales Furnesienses. London: 1844. V. 52

BECKE, DAVID VON DER
Experimenta et Meditationes, Ciraca Naturalium Rerum Principia. Hamburg: 1674. V. 49; 50

BECKER, FREDERICK
The Great Dane. Manchester: 1905. V. 49

BECKER, L.
Les Arachnides de Belgique. Brussels: 1882-96. V. 53

BECKER, LUDWIG
Ludwig Becker. Artist and Naturalist with Burke and Wills Expedition. Melbourne: 1979. V. 50

BECKER, LYDIA E.
Liberty, Equality, Fraternity. Manchester: 1874. V. 50

BECKER, ROBERT HEWITT
Designs on the Land, Disenos of California Ranchos and Their Makers. San Francisco: 1969. V. 47; 48; 49; 53

BECKER, VIVIENNE
Art Nouveau Jewelry. New York: 1985. V. 48

BECKET, ANDREW
A Concordance to Shakespeare. London: 1787. V. 48

BECKETT, JOSEPH
Elements & Practice of Mensuration and Land Surveying, Adapted both to Public and Private Instruction. London: 1804. V. 47; 49

BECKETT, R. B.
Lely. London: 1951. V. 49; 54

BECKETT, SAMUEL
All Strange Away. New York: 1976. V. 50; 51; 52; 53
All That Fall. New York: 1957. V. 48; 50; 52
As the Story Was Told. Cambridge: 1987. V. 48
Assez. Paris: 1966. V. 51
Beginning to End. New York: 1988. V. 47
Breath and Other Shorts. London: 1971. V. 53
Come and Go. London: 1967. V. 50; 53
Comment C'Est. Paris: 1961. V. 47
Company. London: 1980. V. 53
Le Derniere Bande Suivi de Cendres. Paris: 1960. V. 51
Echo's Bones and Other Precipitates. Paris: 1935. V. 47; 48; 53
En Attendant Godot. Paris: 1952. V. 49
En Attendant Godot. Paris: 1954. V. 47

BECKETT, SAMUEL continued
Endgame. London: 1958. V. 48; 49; 50; 51; 54
Happy Days. USA: 1961. V. 53
Happy Days. London: 1962. V. 50
How It Is. London: 1964. V. 47; 50; 52; 53
Ill Seen Ill Said. 1982. V. 48; 54
Ill Seen Ill Said. Northridge: 1982. V. 49; 50; 51; 53
Imagination Morte Imaginez. Paris: 1965. V. 47
L'Issue. Paris: 1968. V. 47
The Lost Ones. Stamford: 1984. V. 50
Malone Dies. New York: 1956. V. 52
Malone Dies. London: 1958. V. 50; 53
Molloy. 1955. V. 54
Molloy. Paris: 1955. V. 49; 50
Molloy/ Malone Dies/ The Unnamable. Paris: 1959. V. 51
Le Monde et le Pantalon. Paris: 1989. V. 50
More Pricks than Kicks. London: 1934. V. 53
More Pricks than Kicks. London: 1970. V. 50
Murphy. London: 1938. V. 53
Murphy. Paris: 1947. V. 51
Murphy. New York: 1957. V. 50; 51; 53; 54
Murphy. New York: 1958. V. 52
Nohow On. New York: 1989. V. 49; 51; 52; 53
The North. London: 1972. V. 48; 52; 53; 54
Play and Two Short Pieces for Radio. London: 1964. V. 47; 51; 54
Poems in English. London: 1961. V. 47; 49; 50; 53
Premier Amour. Paris: 1970. V. 49; 52
Premier Amour. (First Love). Paris: 1970. V. 49
Proust. London: 1931. V. 47; 48; 50
Proust. New York: 1957. V. 52
Quatre Poemes. New York: 1986. V. 47
Sans. Paris: 1969. V. 51
Sejour. Paris: 1970. V. 50; 51
The Unnamable. New York: 1958. V. 51; 52
Waiting for Godot. London: 1956. V. 49; 50; 51; 52
Waiting for Godot. London: 1965. V. 54
Watt. Paris: 1953. V. 51; 53
Watt. 1958. V. 53
Watt. Paris: 1958. V. 50
Watt. New York: 1959. V. 47; 50; 51
Watt. Paris: 1968. V. 49
Whoroscope. Paris: 1930. V. 48; 52

BECKFORD, PETER
Thoughts on Hunting. London. V. 47; 49
Thoughts on Hunting... 1781. V. 50
Thoughts on Hunting. London: 1781. V. 47
Thoughts on Hunting... Sarum, Salisbury: 1781. V. 47; 53
Thoughts on Hunting. 1782. V. 52
Thoughts on Hunting... London: 1782. V. 47
Thoughts on Hunting... London: 1796. V. 51
Thoughts on Hunting... London: 1798. V. 47
Thoughts on Hunting... London: 1802. V. 47
Thoughts on Hunting. London: 1810. V. 47; 48
Thoughts on Hunting... London: 1911. V. 47

BECKFORD, WILLIAM
An Arabian Tale, from an Unpublished Manuscript. London: 1786. V. 50
Biographical Memoirs of Extraordinary Painters. London: 1780. V. 48; 52
Italy: with Sketches of Spain and Portugal. London: 1834. V. 51
Recollections of an Excursion to the Monasteries of Alcobaca and Batalha. London: 1835. V. 48; 49; 51; 54
Thoughts on Hunting, in a Series of Familiar Letters to a Friend. Salisbury: 1781. V. 51
The Valuable Library of Books, in Fonthill Abbey. A Catalogue of the Magnificent, Rare and Valuable Library (of 20,000 volumes). London: 1823. V. 48; 50
Vathek. Lausanne: 1787/86. V. 50
Vathek. Londres: 1815. V. 50; 51
Vathek. London: 1816. V. 50
Vathek. Paris: 1893. V. 52
Vathek. London: 1929. V. 47; 49; 51; 52
Vathek. New York: 1945. V. 47

BECKHAM, BARRY
My Main Mother. New York: 1969. V. 52
Runner Mack. New York: 1972. V. 52

BECKLARD, EUGENE
Physiological Mysteries and Revelations in Love, Courtship and Marriage... Philadelphia: 1848. V. 50

BECKMANN, JOHN
A History of Inventions and Discoveries. London: 1817. V. 47; 48; 49
A History of Inventions, Discoveries and Origins. London: 1846. V. 50

BECKWITH, PAUL
Creoles of St. Louis. St. Louis: 1893. V. 48

BECLARD, P. A.
Additions to the General Anatomy of Xavier Bichat. Boston: 1823. V. 53
Elements of General Anatomy. Edinburgh: 1830. V. 47; 48; 50; 51; 54

BECON, THOMAS
The Reliques of Rome, contaynyng All Such Matters of Religion, as Haue in Times Past Bene Brought Into the Church by the Pope and His Adherents. London: 1563. V. 47; 49

BECQUEREL, ANTOINE CESAR
Traite Experimental de l'Electricite et du Magnetisme et de leurs Rapports avec les Phenomenes Naturels. Paris: 1834-40. V. 47

BEDALES
Poetry - an Anthology of Verse Written by Boys and Girls at Bedales School. London: 1927. V. 50

BEDDARD, FRANK E.
Animal Coloration: an Account of the Principal Facts and Theories Relating to the Colours and Markings of Animals. London: 1892. V. 50
Contributions to the Anatomy of the Anthropoid Apes. London: 1893. V. 49

BEDDEVOLE, DOMINIQUE
Essays of Anatomy, Wherein the Formation of the Organs and Their Mechanical Operations Are Clearly Explained... London: 1696. V. 48

BEDDIE, M. K.
Bibliography of Captain James Cook, R.N., F.R.S., Circumnavigator. Sydney: 1970. V. 51

BEDDOES, THOMAS LOVELL
The Complete Works. London: 1928. V. 51; 53
Hygeia: Essays Moral and Medical on the Causes Affecting the Personal State of Our Middling and Affluent Classes. Bristol: 1802-03. V. 51; 54
Letters. London: 1894. V. 53
Observations on the Medical and Domestic Management of the Consumptive; on the Powers of Digitalis Purpurea... London: 1801. V. 50
The Works of Beddoes. London: 1935. V. 47

BEDDOME, R. H.
The Ferns of British India. New Delhi: 1973. V. 52
The Ferns of Southern India. Madras: 1863. V. 49; 51; 54
The Ferns of Southern India. Madras: 1873. V. 48; 52

BEDE, THE VENERABLE
Ecclesiasticae Historiae Gentis Anglorum. Cologne: 1601. V. 49
The Ecclesiastical History of the English People. London: 1992. V. 49
Historia Ecclesiastaica Gentis Anglorum. Strassburg: 1473-75. V. 50
Historiae Ecclesiastaicae Gentis Anglorum. Cambridge: 1722. V. 50
The History of the Church of England. Antwerp: 1565. V. 49; 50; 52
The History of the Church of England. 1930. V. 48; 52
The History of the Church of England. Oxford: 1930. V. 47; 51; 53
The History of the Church of England... Stratford-upon-Avon: 1930. V. 48; 51
The History of the Church of England. London: 1970. V. 51

BEDFORD, ARTHUR
The Evil and Danger of Stage-Plays... Bristol: 1706. V. 51; 54
The Evil and Danger of Stage-Plays... London: 1706. V. 49
The Great Abuse of Musick. London: 1711. V. 47
The Scripture Chronology Demonstrated by Astronomical Calculations, and Also by the Year of Jubilee, and the Sabbatical Year Among the Jews... London: 1730. V. 49
Serious Reflections on the Scandalous Abuse and Effects of the State. Bristol: 1705. V. 50; 53
The Temple Musick: or, an Essay Concerning the Method of Singing the Psalms of David, in the Temple, Before the Babylonish Captivity... Bristol: 1706. V. 47; 51
The Temple Musick; or, an Essay Concerning the Method of Singing the Psalms of David, in The Temple, Before the Babylonish Captivity. London: 1706. V. 48

BEDFORD, F.
Sketches in York. York: 1841. V. 48; 49; 51

BEDFORD, F. D.
A Night of Wonders. London: 1906. V. 49
The Visit to London. London: 1900. V. 51

BEDFORD, F. G. D.
The Sailor's Handbook. Portsmouth: 1905. V. 53
The Sailor's Pocket Book. Portsmouth: 1877. V. 50

BEDFORD, GUNNING S.
The Principles and Practice of Obstetrics. New York: 1862. V. 52; 53; 54

BEDFORD, HILORY G.
Texas Indian Troubles. Dallas: 1905. V. 54

BEDFORD, JOHN RUSSELL, 6TH DUKE OF
Hortus Ericaeus Woburnensis or a Catalogue of Heaths in the Collection of the Duke of Bedford at Woburn Abbey. London: 1825. V. 49
Outline Engravings and Descriptions of the woburn Abbey Marbles. London: 1822. V. 47; 53

BEDFORD, PAUL
Recollections and Wanderings of Paul Bedford. London: 1864. V. 51

BEDFORD, SYBILLE
The Sudden View - a Mexican Journey. London: 1953. V. 53

BEDFORD, WILLIAM KIKPATRICK
Records of the Woodmen of Arden from 1785. Edinburgh: 1885. V. 51

BEDFORD-JONES, H.
The Mission and the Man. The Story of San Juan Capistrano. Pasadena: 1939. V. 48

BEDFORDSHIRE GENERAL LIBRARY
Catalogue of the Bedfordshire General Library: Established in July, 1830. Bedford: 1831. V. 52

BEDINI, SILVIO A.
The Trail of Time: Time Measurement with Incense in East Asia. Cambridge and New York: 1994. V. 54

BEDLOE, WILLIAM
The Excommunicated Prince; or the False Relic. London: 1679. V. 52

BEDLOW, WILLIAM
The Mails Arrive at the Post Office in New York, From New England and Albany...The Mails Are Closed at the Post Office, in New York, for New England, and Albany... New York?: 1785?. V. 47

BEDWELL, C. E. A.
A Catalogue of the Printed Books in the Library of the Honorable Society of the Middle Temple. Glasgow: 1914-25. V. 53

THE BEE, a Selection of Poetry from the Best Authors. Dublin: 1796. V. 47

BEE, JACOB
Jacob Bee His Booke, Given Him the 29th of August, 1681. (The Diary of Jacob Bee, from 1682 to 1706). Durham: 1819. V. 50

BEEBE, CHARLES WILLIAM
The Arcturus Adventure. London: 1926. V. 48; 50
The Arcturus Adventure. New York: 1926. V. 47; 49
Galapagos: World's End. New York: 1924. V. 52; 53; 54
The Log of the Sun, a Chronicle of Nature's Year. New York: 1906. V. 53
A Monograph of the Pheasants. London. V. 50
A Monograph of the Pheasants. 1918-22. V. 52; 53
A Monograph of the Pheasants. London: 1918-22. V. 48; 54
A Monograph of the Pheasants. New York: 1990. V. 49
Pheasants, Their Lives and Homes. Garden City: 1926. V. 53
Pheasants, Their Lives and Homes. New York: 1926. V. 54
Pheasants, Their Lives and Homes. New York: 1931. V. 47
Pheasants: Their Lives and Homes. New York: 1936. V. 54
Pheasants, Their Lives and Homes. USA: 1936. V. 50; 52; 53
Pheasants, Their Lives and Homes. New York: 1936 or 1937. V. 49
Pheasants, their Lives and Homes. New York: 1937. V. 52
Two Bird-Lovers in Mexico. Boston: 1905. V. 47; 52

BEEBE, LUCIUS
Cable Car Carnival. Oakland: 1951. V. 53
U. S. West The Saga of Wells Fargo. New York: 1949. V. 51
Virginia & Truckee. Oakland: 1949. V. 53

BEECHAM, K. J.
History of Cirencester and the Roman City Corinium. Cirencester: 1886. V. 53

BEECHER, CATHARINE E.
The American Woman's Home. New York: 1869. V. 47; 50
Domestic Receipt-Book. Designed as a Supplement to Her Treatise on Domestic Economy. New York: 1846. V. 51
Letters on the Difficulties of Religion. Hartford: 1836. V. 51
The New Housekeeper's Manual. (with) The Handy cook-Book... New York: 1873. V. 48
Treatise on Domestic Economy... Boston: 1841. V. 53
Woman Suffrage and Woman's Profession. Hartford: 1871. V. 51; 53

BEECHER, EDWARD
Narrative of Riots at Alton; in Connection with the Death of Rev. Elijah P. Lovejoy. Alton: 1838. V. 49

BEECHER, HARRIS H.
Record of the 114th Regiment, New York State Volunteers... Norwich: 1866. V. 47

BEECHER, HENRY WARD
And Even Now. London: 1920. V. 50
Norwood; or, Village Life in New England. London: 1867. V. 54
A Summer in England with Henry Ward Beecher. New York: 1887. V. 53

BEECHER, LYMAN
Lectures on Scepticism. Cincinnati: 1835. V. 51; 54

BEECHEY, FREDERICK WILLIAM
An Account of a Visit to California, 1826-27. San Francisco: 1941. V. 48
Narrative of a Voyage to the Pacific and Beering's Strait... London: 1831. V. 47; 48; 50; 51; 52; 54
Narrative of a Voyage to the Pacific and Beering's Strait... Philadelphia: 1832. V. 48
Narrative of a Voyage to the Pacific and Beering's Strait... Amsterdam and New York: 1968. V. 53
Proceedings of the Expedition to Explore the Northern Coast of Africa... London: 1828. V. 49; 50; 54

BEEDHAM, RALPH JOHN
Wood Engraving... Ditchling: 1925. V. 50
Wood Engraving. Ditchling Common, Hassocks: 1929. V. 50; 53

BEEDOME, R. H.
The Flora Sylvatica for Southern India... Dehra Dun: 1978. V. 52

BEEDOME, THOMAS
Select Poems, Divine and Humane. London: 1928. V. 47; 50; 52; 53; 54

BEEHLER, WILLIAM HENRY
The Cruise of the "Brooklyn". A Journal of the Principal Events of a Three Years' Cruise... Philadelphia: 1885. V. 47; 51

BEEKMAN, E. M.
Carnal Lent. Easthampton: 1979. V. 48
Homage to Mondrian. Easthampton: 1972. V. 48
Narcissus. Easthampton: 1974. V. 48

BEEKMAN, GEORGE C.
Early Dutch Settlers of Monmouth County, New Jersey. Freehold: 1915. V. 49; 51

BEELER, JOE
Cowboys and Indians. Norman: 1967. V. 50

BEER, ARTHUR
Vistas in Astronomy. London & New York: 1955-56. V. 50; 53

BEER, DR.
New Practice of Physic...to Which are Prefixed Candid Remarks on the Illusions of Brilliant Theories. London: 1803. V. 51

BEER, THOMAS
The Fair Rewards. New York: 1922. V. 48; 51
The Road to Heaven. New York: 1928. V. 53
Stephen Crane. New York: 1923. V. 51; 53

BEERBOHM, MAX
And Even Now. London: 1920. V. 47; 52; 54
Around Theatres. London: 1924. V. 49; 52; 53; 54
Caricatures of Twenty-Five Gentlemen. London: 1896. V. 48; 50
Cartoons... London: 1901. V. 52
Cartoons: "The Second Childhood of John Bull.". London: 1911. V. 53
A Christmas Garland. London: 1912. V. 51; 52; 53
Fifty Caricatures. London: 1913. V. 49; 50; 51; 52
Fifty Caricatures. New York: 1913. V. 51
The Happy Hypocrite. New York: 1896. V. 49
Happy Hypocrite. New York & London: 1897. V. 47; 53
The Happy Hypocrite. London: 1915. V. 49; 53
The Happy Hypocrite. London: 1918. V. 53
The Happy Hypocrite... New Fairfield: 1955. V. 47; 48
Heroes and Heroines of Bittersweet. V. 50
Heroes and Heroines of Bittersweet. London: 1931. V. 48
The Illustrated Zuleika Dobson. New Haven & London: 1985. V. 50; 54
Last Theatres - 1904-1910. London: 1970. V. 54
Max in Verse: Rhymes and Parodies. Brattleboro: 1963. V. 53
More. London: 1899. V. 49; 50; 54
Observations. London: 1925. V. 47; 49; 54
Observations. London: 1926. V. 49; 51; 52
The Poet's Corner. London: 1904. V. 49; 50; 51
The Poets' Corner. New York: 1904. V. 53
Rosetti and His Circle. London: 1922. V. 47; 48; 49; 50; 51; 53
Seven Men. London: 1919. V. 47; 49
Seven Men. New York: 1920. V. 47
A Survey. London: 1921. V. 47; 49; 50; 51; 52; 54
A Survey. New York: 1921. V. 50; 51; 53
Things New and Old. London: 1923. V. 49; 50; 51
A Variety of Things. London: 1928. V. 54
William Rothenstein. An Address Delivered by Max Beerbohm at the Memorial Service Held at Saint Martin-in-the-Fields, Tuesday March 6, 1945. London: 1945. V. 48
The Works. New York & London: 1896. V. 47; 49; 51
The Works... London: 1922-24. V. 48
The Works... 1922-28. V. 49
Works. London: 1922-28. V. 51
Yet Again. London: 1909. V. 49
Zuleika Dobson. London: 1911. V. 47; 51; 52; 53; 54
Zuleika Dobson. 1975. V. 53
Zuleika Dobson... Oxford: 1975. V. 48

BEERS, D.
Atlas of Northampton County. Philadelphia: 1874. V. 53

BEERS, F. W.
Atlas of New York and Vicinity... New York: 1867. V. 49
Atlas of New York and Vicinity. New York: 1868. V. 49
Atlas of the Hudson River Valley, from New York City to Troy. New York: 1891. V. 49
County Atlas of Monroe Michigan Under the Superintendence of S. M. Bartlett. New York: 1876. V. 49

BEERS, FANNIE A.
Memories. A Record of Personal Experience and Adventure During Four Years of War. Philadelphia: 1889. V. 49

BEERS, GEORGE A.
Vasquez; or, the Hunted Bandits of San Joaquin. New York: 1875. V. 50

BEERS, J. B.
County Atlas of Westchester, New York. New York: 1872. V. 49

BEES, T. NEEDHAM
Roundway Hill, a Poem. Devizes: 1787. V. 54

BEESLEY, ALFRED
The History of Banbury: Including Copious Historical and Antiquarian Notices of the Neighbourhood. London: 1841. V. 49

BEESON, HARVEY C.
Beeson's Inland Marine Directory. Chicago: 1894. V. 52

BEESON, JOHN
A Plea for the Indians; with Facts and Features of the Late War in Oregon. New York: 1857. V. 48
A Plea for the Indians; with Facts and Features of the Late War in Oregon. New York: 1858. V. 48

BEETON, ISABELLA MARY
The Book of Household Management. London: 1861. V. 47; 48; 49; 50; 51; 52
The Book of Household Management... London: 1888. V. 51
The Book of Household Management. London: 1909. V. 51
The Book of Household Management. London: 1917. V. 54
The Book of Household Management. London: 1920. V. 51
Household Management, a Complete Cookery Book. London: 1923. V. 52
Mrs. Beeton's Every-Day Cookery. London: 1865. V. 52
Mrs. Beeton's Every-Day cookery. London: 1912. V. 47

BEETON, SAMUEL O.
Beeton's Dictionary of Geography. London: 1868. V. 53
Our Soldiers and the Victoria Cross. London: 1867. V. 54

BEETON'S Book of Needlework. London: 1870. V. 53

BEETON'S Housewife's Treasury of Domestic Information. London. V. 54

BEEVER, J.
Practical Fly-Fishing: Founded on Nature... London: 1849. V. 51; 52

BEGBIE, HAROLD
The Political Struwwelpeter. London: 1899. V. 47
The Struwwelpeter Alphabet. London: 1900. V. 47; 49

BEGG, ALEXANDER
History of British Columbia. Toronto: 1894. V. 49; 53
History of the North-West. Toronto: 1894/95. V. 50
Ten Years in Winnipeg. Winnipeg: 1879. V. 54

BEGGARS Bridge. North Yorkshire: 1977. V. 51

BEGIN, LOUIS JACQUES
Application of the Physiological Doctrine of Surgery. Charleston: 1835. V. 49

BEGLEY, LOUIS
Wartime Lies. New York: 1991. V. 53

BEHADER, BEG
Narrative of the proceedings of the Provincial Council at Patna, in the Suit of Behader Beg Against Nadara Begum; and of the Supreme Court of Judicature at Calcutta, in Suit of Nadara Begum against Behader Beg and Others... N.P: 1780. V. 48

BEHAN, BRENDAN
Borstal Boy. London: 1958. V. 48; 51
Brendan Behan's Island - an Irish Sketch-Book. New York: 1962. V. 49; 51
The Hostage. London: 1958. V. 48; 51
The Quare Fellow. London: 1956. V. 47
The Quare Fellow. New York: 1956. V. 48; 49; 51; 52

BEHESNILIAN, KRIKOR
In Bonds. An Armenian's Experiences. London: 1896. V. 47

BEHM, MARC
The Eye of the Beholder. New York: 1980. V. 49
The Queen of the Night. Boston: 1977. V. 50

BEHN, APHRA
All the Histories and Novels Written by the Late Ingenious Mrs. Behn. London: 1705. V. 49
The Dutch Lover: a Comedy. London: 1673. V. 48
Love Letters Between a Nobleman and His Sister (in law); With the History of Their Adventures. London: 1735. V. 54
Plays. London: 1702. V. 53
Plays. London: 1724. V. 49; 51
Poems Upon Several Occasions... London: 1684. V. 47; 48; 49
The Works. London: 1915. V. 50

BEHRENDT, WALTER CURT
Modern Building. Its Nature, Problems, and Forms. New York: 1937. V. 47; 48

BEHRENS, CHARLES
Atomic Medicine. New York: 1949. V. 48; 50; 52; 53

BEHRMAN, SAMUEL NATHANIEL
But for Whom Charlie. New York: 1964. V. 54
The Second Man. 1927. V. 47; 52
Three Plays: Serena Blandish, Meteor, The Second Man. New York: 1934. V. 48

BEIER, ULI
Contemporary Art in Africa. New York: 1968. V. 54

BEIJER, AGNE
Court Theatres of Drottningholm and Gripsholm. Malmo: 1933. V. 47

BEILKE, M.
Shining Clarity: God and Man in the Works of Robinson Jeffers. 1977. V. 53

BEINING, GUY
Stoma. New York: 1984. V. 52; 53; 54

BEKASSY, FERENC
Adriatica and Other Poems. London: 1925. V. 49; 51; 52

BEKE, CHARLES T.
The Sources of the Nile: Being a General Survey of the Basin of that Rivers, and Of Its Head Streams; with the History of Nilotic Discovery. London: 1860. V. 47

BEKYNTON, THOMAS
Memorials of the Reign of King Henry VI... London: 1872. V. 49

BELANY, J. C.
A Treatise Upon Falconry. 1841. V. 48
A Treatise Upon Falconry. Berwick: 1841. V. 49

BELCHER, EDWARD
The Last of the Arctic Voyages... London: 1855. V. 49; 50
Narrative of a Voyage Round the world, Performed In Her Majesty's Chip Sulphur, During the Years 1836-1842, ... London: 1843. V. 50; 51; 52; 53; 54
A Treatise on Nautical Surveying... London: 1835. V. 48

BELCHER, HENRY
Illustrations of the Scenery on the Line of the Whitby and Pickering Railway... London: 1836. V. 50; 52

BELCHER, THOMAS
The Art of Boxing, or Science of Manual Defence, Clearly Displayed on Rational Principles Whereby Every Person May Easily Make Themselves Masters of that Manly Acquirement... London: 1819. V. 50; 52

BELCHER, W. D.
Kentish Brasses. London: 1888-1905. V. 53

BELCOURT, GEORGE ANTOINE
Principles de la Langue des Sauvages Appeles Sauteux. Quebec: 1839. V. 49

BELDAM, GEORGE W.
Great Golfers: their Methods at a Glance. London: 1904. V. 54

BELDEN, BAUMAN L.
Indian Peace Medals Issued in the United States 1979-1889. New Milford: 1966. V. 53

BELDEN, LEMUEL W.
An Account of Jane C. Rider, the Springfield Somnambulist: the Substance of Which Was Delivered as a Lecture Before the Springfield Lyceum, Jan. 22, 1834. Springfield: 1834. V. 52

BELDER, ROBERT DE
A Magnificent Collection of Botanical Books...from the Celebrated Library formed by Robert De Belder. London: 1987. V. 52

BELDON & CO.
Illustrated Atlas of the Dominion of Canada (Kent County). Toronto: 1881. V. 53
Illustrated Atlas of the Dominion of Canada (Lambton County). Toronto: 1880. V. 50

BELFAST, FREDERICK WILLIAM CHICHESTER, EARL OF
Poets and Poetry of the XIXth Century. London: 1852. V. 47

BELFOUR, F. C.
The Life of Sheikh Mohammed Ali Hazin. London: 1830. V. 51

BEL GEDDES, NORMAN
Horizons. Boston: 1932. V. 48; 50
Magic Motorways. New York: 1940. V. 50; 51

BELHAVEN, JOHN HAMILTON, BARON
The Lord Beilhaven's Speech in the Scotch Parliament, Saturday the Second of November, on the Subject Matter of an Union Betwixt the Two Kingdoms of Scotland and England. Edinburgh?: 1706. V. 53

BELICHICK, MEG
Frosting. New York: 1991. V. 54

BELIDOR, BERNARD FOREST DE
Architecture Hydraulique... Paris: 1737-53. V. 47; 48; 53
Architecture Hydraulique. Paris: 1782/82/50/70. V. 52; 54
La Science des Ingenieurs... Paris: 1729. V. 48; 54

BELINAYE, HENRY
The Sources of Health and Disease in Communities; or Elementary Views of "Hygiene"... Boston: 1833. V. 54

BELINDA, or, The Fair Fugitive. London: 1789. V. 49

BELISLE, JOHN G.
History of Sabine Parish, Louisiana. 1912. V. 48

BELITT, BEN
Graffiti. Princeton Junction: 1989. V. 49; 51; 53

BELKNAP, D. C.
The Prints...a Catalogue Raisonne. New York: 1984. V. 54

BELKNAP, D. P.
The Probate Law and Practice of California...with Judicial Decisions of This and Other States... San Francisco: 1861. V. 50

BELKNAP, JEREMY
The Foresters, an American Tale. Boston: 1792. V. 54
The Foresters, an American Tale... Boston;: 1796. V. 49; 54
The History of New-Hampsyire. Dover: 1812. V. 51

BELKNAP, JEREMY continued
The Life and Extraordinary Adventures of Captain John Smith, a Native of Lincolnshire... London: 1803. V. 51

BELKNAP, WALDRON PHOENIX
American Colonial Painting: Materials for a History. Cambridge: 1959. V. 50

BELKNAP, WILLIAM W.
Letter from the Secretary of War, Transmitting a Report Concerning the History and Character of Certain Claims of the State of Texas. Washington: 1872. V. 49
Proceedings of the Senate Sitting for the Trial of Wm. W. Belknap, Late Secretary of War, on the Articles of Impeachment Exhibited by the House of Reps... Washington: 1876. V. 49

BELL, A. MORTON
Locomotives. Their Construction, Maintenance and Operation, with Notes on Electric and Internal Combustion Locomotives. London: 1946. V. 48; 52; 54

BELL, A. N.
Climatology and Mineral Waters of the United States. New York: 1885. V. 48; 50; 52; 53

BELL, ALEXANDER GRAHAM
Establishment for the Study of Vocal Physiology; for the Correction of Stammering, and Other Defects of Utterance, and for Practical Instruction in 'Visible Speech'. Boston: 1872. V. 48
Upon the Formation of a Deaf Variety of the Human Race. Washington: 1883. V. 48

BELL, ANDREW
Extract of a Sermon on the Education of the Poor, Under the Appropriate System. London: 1807. V. 53
History of Canada, from the Time of Its Discovery Till the Union Year 1840-41... Montreal: 1862. V. 49; 51

BELL, ANDREW P.
Modern Law of Personal Property in England and Ireland. 1989. V. 49

BELL, BENJAMIN
A Treatise on the Theory and Management of Ulcers... Edinburgh: 1789. V. 47
A Treatise on the Theory and Management of Ulcers... Edinburgh: 1791. V. 53
A Treatise on the Theory and Management of Ulcers... Boston: 1797. V. 48; 53

BELL, CHARLES
The Anatomy and Philosophy of Expression as Connected with the Fine Arts. London: 1844. V. 53
The Anatomy and Philosophy of Expression as Connected with the Fine Arts. London: 1865. V. 47
The Anatomy of the Brain, Explained in a Series of Engravings. London: 1802. V. 47; 54
The Anatomy of the Brain, Explained in a Series of Engravings... London: 1802/1803. V. 50
The Anatomy of the Brain, Explained in A Series of Engravings... London: 1802/1830. V. 49
Engravings Of the Arteries; Illustrating the Second Volume of the anatomy of the Human Body... London: 1801. V. 48
Essays On the Anatomy and Philosophy of Expressions. London: 1824. V. 53
Essays on the Anatomy of Expression in Painting. London: 1806. V. 47; 50; 52
An Exposition of the Natural System of the Nerves of the Human Body. Philadelphia: 1825. V. 52
The Hand: its Mechanism and Vital Endowments as Evincing Design. London: 1833. V. 52
The Hand: its Mechanism and Vital Endowments as Evincing Design. Philadelphia: 1833. V. 50; 53
The Hand: Its Mechanism and Vital Endowments as Evincing Design. London: 1837. V. 47
Illustrations of the Great Operations of Surgery, Trepan, Hernia, Amputation, Aneurism and Lithotomy. London: 1821. V. 54
Institutes of Surgery: Arranged in the Order of the Lectures Delivered in the University of Edinburgh. Philadelphia: 1840. V. 47; 48; 49; 50; 51; 52
Letters Concerning the Diseases of the Urethra. Boston: 1811. V. 48; 49; 50; 52
A Series of Engravings, Explaining the Course of the Nerves. Philadelphia: 1834. V. 51
A System of Dissections, Explaining the Anatomy of the Human Body, with the Manner of Displaying Parts... Baltimore: 1814. V. 50
A System of Operative Surgery. London: 1814. V. 54
A Treatise on the Diseases of the Urethra, Vesica Urinaria, Prostate and Rectum... London: 1820. V. 47; 51

BELL, CHARLES DENT
The Four Seasons at the Lakes. London: 1878. V. 52
The Four Seasons at the Lakes. London: 1880. V. 50; 52

BELL, CHARLES HENRY
Life of William M. Richardson...Late Chief Justice of the Superior Court in New Hampshire. Concord: 1839. V. 50

BELL, CLIVE
The Legend of Monte Della Sibilla; or, Le Paradis de la Reine Sibille: a Poem. Richmond: 1923. V. 53
On British Freedom. London: 1923. V. 49
Potboilers. London: 1918. V. 51
Proust. London: 1928. V. 49; 53

BELL, DOUGLAS HERBERT
A Soldier's Diary of the Great War. London: 1929. V. 47

BELL, E. WESTON
The Scottish Deerhound. Edinburgh: 1892. V. 49

BELL, ED
Zuni, The Art and the People. Dallas: 1975/76/77. V. 51

BELL, EDWARD
George Bell, Publisher. London: 1924. V. 51

BELL, EDWARD ALLEN
A History of Giggleswick School from Its Foundation 1499 to 1912. Leeds: 1912. V. 51; 53

BELL, FLORENCE
The Letters of Gertrude Bell. New York: 1927. V. 51

BELL, G. J.
A Practical Treatise on Segmental and Elliptical Oblique or Skew Arches Setting Forth the Principles and Details of Construction... Carlisle: 1906. V. 50

BELL, GEORGE JOSEPH
Principles of the Law of Scotland. Edinburgh: 1833. V. 51

BELL, GERTRUDE
The Letters of Gertrude Bell. London: 1927. V. 54
The Letters of Gertrude Bell. New York: 1927. V. 49

THE BELL Gold Mining Company of Dubuque, Iowa. Authorized Capital, $4,000,000, Capita Stock 160,000 Shares Par Value, $25 Per Share.... Chicago: 1880. V. 48; 49

BELL, H. W.
Baker Street Studies. London. V. 53
Sherlock Holmes and Doctor Watson - The Chronology of their Adventures. London: 1932. V. 49; 54

BELL, HENRY
The Perfect Painter; or a Compleat History of the Original Progress and Improvement of Painting. London: 1730. V. 47; 52; 53

BELL, HORACE
On the West Coast: Being Farther Reminiscences of a Ranger. New York: 1930. V. 53
Reminiscences of a Ranger. Los Angeles: 1881. V. 47; 48; 50; 52; 53; 54
Reminiscences of a Ranger. Los Angeles: 1965-67. V. 53

BELL, I. LOWTHIAN
The Iron Trade of the United Kingdom Comparted With That of the Other Chief Iron-Making Nations. London: 1866. V. 50
Principles of the Manufacture of Iron and Steel, With some Notes on the Economic Conditions of Their Production. London: 1884. V. 50

BELL, ISA
The Discipline of Alice Lee. A Truthful Temperance Story. New York: 1870. V. 51

BELL, J. H. B.
A Progress in Mountaineering. London: 1950. V. 54

BELL, JACOB
Historical Sketch of the Progress of Pharmacy in Great Britain. London: 1880. V. 54

BELL, JAMES
The History of Gibraltar... London: 1845. V. 54

BELL, JAMES J.
A Log of Texas-California Cattle Trail 1854. Austin: 1932. V. 53

BELL, JAMES STANISLAUS
Journal of a Residence in Circassia During the Years 1837, 1838, and 1839. London: 1840. V. 49

BELL, JOHN
An Address Delivered at Nashville, October 5th, 1830, Being the First Anniversary of the Alumni Society of the University of Nashville. Nashville: 1830. V. 48
All the Material Facts in the History of Epidemic Cholera... Philadelphia: 1832. V. 51; 53
The Anatomy and Physiology of the Human Body. London: 1829. V. 47; 52; 53; 54
Answer for the Junior Members of the Royal College of Surgeons, Of Edinburgh, to the Memorial of Dr. James Gregory. Edinburgh: 1800. V. 48
Bell's British Theatre. London: 1791-97. V. 50
Bell's New Pantheon, or Historical Dictionary of the Gods, Demi-Gods, Heroes and Fabulous Personages of Antiquity... London: 1790. V. 47; 53
British Theatre. London: 1791-99. V. 49
Discourses on the Nature and Cure of Wounds. Walpole: 1807. V. 48
Engravings of the Bones, Muscles and Joints. Part the First. (with) Part the Second Containing Engravings of the Muscles and of the Joints. Philadelphia: 1815. V. 47
Engravings of the Bones, Muscles and Joints. (with) Part Second containing Engravings of the Muscles and of the Joints. Philadelphia: 1816/15. V. 48; 49; 50; 53
The Principles of Surgery. New York: 1810. V. 52; 53
Report of the Importance and Economy of Sanitary Measures to Cities. New York: 1859. V. 50; 52; 53
Speech of Mr. Bell of Tennessee, on the Bill Making Appropriations For the Suppression and Prevention of Indian Hostilities. Washington: 1838. V. 48
Travels From St. Petersburg in Russia, to Diverse Parts of Asia. Glasgow: 1763. V. 50
A Treatise on Baths: Including Cold, Sea, Warm, Hot, Vapour, Gas and Mudbaths... Philadelphia: 1850. V. 48

BELL, JULIAN
Essays, Poems and Letters. London: 1938. V. 49
We Did Not Fight - 1914-1918 Experiences of War Registers. London: 1935. V. 47
Winter Movement and Other Poems. London: 1930. V. 48; 54
Work for the Winter and Other Poems. London: 1936. V. 51

BELL, KATHARINE M.
Swining the Censer, Reminiscences of Old Santa Barbara. Santa Barbara: 1931. V. 47; 54

BELL, LANDON C.
The Old Free State...Lunenburg County and Southside Virginia. Richmond: 1927. V. 50
Robert E. Lee. An Address... 1929. V. 50

BELL, MAC KENZIE
Christina Rossetti. London: 1898. V. 51

BELL, MADISON SMARTT
Waiting for the End of the World. New York: 1985. V. 54
The Washington Square Ensemble. New York: 1983. V. 48; 49; 50; 51; 52

BELL, MALCOLM
Edward Burne-Jones. London: 1892. V. 49; 52
Edward Burne-Jones. London: 1893. V. 49
Edward Burne-Jones. London: 1894. V. 49
Sir Edward Burne-Jones. London: 1900. V. 47
Sir Edward Burne-Jones. London: 1907. V. 49
Theme Songs of the Dance Band Era. Memphis: 1981. V. 47

BELL, MARVIN
Poems for Nathan and Saul. Mt. Vernon: 1966. V. 54
Things We Dreamt We Died For. Iowa City: 1966. V. 53; 54

BELL, QUENTIN
The Art Critic and the Art Historian - the Leslie Stephen Lecture 1973. Cambridge: 1974. V. 53
The True Story of Cinderella. London: 1957. V. 51
Virginia Woolf: a Biography. London: 1972. V. 52

BELL, RAYMOND
Hacienda de Atotonillo. Durango: 1936. V. 50; 54

BELL, ROBERT
Early Ballads Illustrative of History, Traditions and Customs. London: 1885. V. 54
The Grain Trade of the North-West. Proposed Ship Canal through Canada. Chicago: 1863. V. 48; 49
Reports by Robert Bell, LL.D., M.D., C.E., on the Geology of the Basin of Moose River and Of Lake of the Woods And Adjacent Country. Montreal: 1883. V. 53

BELL, SAMUEL D.
Justice and Sheriff, Practical Forms for the Use of Justices of the Peace, Sheriffs, Coroners and Constables... Concord: 1843. V. 51; 52

BELL, SAUL
Henderson the Rain King. London: 1959. V. 52

BELL, T.
Kalogynomia or the Laws of Female Beauty: Being the Elementary Principles of that Science. London: 1899. V. 50

BELL, THOMAS
The Anatomy, Physiology and Diseases of the Teeth. London: 1829. V. 47; 51
The Anatomy, Physiology and Diseases of the Teeth. London: 1835. V. 52
The Catalogue of 15,000 Volumes of Scarce and Curious Printed Books and Unique Manuscripts... Newcastle-upon-Tyne: 1860. V. 50
An Essay on Opinion and Progress of Gothic Architecture...in Ireland. Dublin: 1829. V. 53
A History of British Quadrupeds. Newcastle-upon-Tyne: 1790. V. 54
A History of British Quadrupeds, Including the Cetacea. London: 1836-37. V. 53
A History of British Quadrupeds, Including the Cetacea. London: 1837. V. 48; 50
The History of Improved Short-Horn or Durham Cattle and of the Kirklevington Herd from the Notes of the Late Thomas Bates. Newcastle-upon-Tyne: 1871. V. 54
A History of the British Stalk-Eyed Crustacea. London: 1853. V. 51
The Ruins of Liveden; with Historical Notices of the Family of Tresham and its Connexion with the Gunpower Plot. London: 1847. V. 47; 51

BELL, VANESSA
Recent Paintings by Vanessa Bell. London: 1930. V. 49

BELL, W. BLAIR
The Pituitary: A Study of the Morphology, Physiology, Pathology and Surgical Treatment of the Pituitary, Together with an Account of the Therapeutical Extracts Made from This Organ. New York: 1919. V. 48; 53

BELL, WALTER DALRYMPLE MAITLAND
Bell of Africa. London: 1960. V. 48; 52; 53
Bell of Africa. Boston: 1961. V. 53
Karamojo Safari. London: 1949. V. 49
Karamojo Safari. New York: 1949. V. 52; 53; 54
The Wanderings of an Elephant House. London: 1923. V. 49; 50

BELL, WALTER GEORGE
The Great Plague in London in 1665. London: 1924. V. 51; 52

BELL, WILLIAM
Elegies. London. V. 52
Mountains Beneath the Horizon. London: 1950. V. 50
Papers Relative to the Regalia of Scotland. Edinburgh: 1829. V. 48; 49; 51
Poetry from Oxford in Wartime. London: 1945. V. 47; 52
Reflections Upon the Utility of a Floating Wet Dock, Recommended to Be Made Near the Mouth of the River Wear... Sunderland: 1816. V. 51

BELL, WILLIAM A.
New Tracks in North America. London: 1869. V. 47; 48; 49
New Tracks in North America... London: 1870. V. 47; 49; 53

BELL, WILLIAM C.
Analysis of Pope's Essay On Man. Lexington: 1836. V. 54

BELL, WILLIAM E.
Carpentery Made Easy; or, the Science and Art of Framing, on a New and Improved System. Philadelphia: 1883. V. 48; 52; 54

BELLAIRS, A. D'A.
Morphology and Biology of Reptiles. London: 1976. V. 50

BELLAIRS, GEORGE
Death in Desolation. London: 1967. V. 48
Fatal Alibi. London: 1968. V. 48
Intruder in the Dark. London: 1966. V. 48
Single Ticket to Deth. London: 1967. V. 48

BELLAMY, CHARLES J.
The Breton Mills. New York: 1879. V. 47; 54

BELLAMY, DANIEL
Back-Gammon: or, the Battle of the Friars. London: 1734. V. 47
Ethic Amusements... London: 1768. V. 48
Ethic Amusements. London: 1768/70. V. 48

BELLAMY, EDWARD
The Blindman's World and Other Stories. Boston & New York: 1898. V. 49; 54
Looking Backward. Boston: 1888. V. 49; 51
Looking Backward. Hollywood: 1941. V. 51; 54

BELLAMY, GEORGE ANNE
An Apology for the Life of... London: 1785. V. 53
Memoirs of George Anne Bellamy, Including All Her Intrigues... London: 1785. V. 51

BELLAMY, JOHN
The Ophion; or the Theology of the Serpent and the Unity of God. London: 1811. V. 50; 54

BELLAMY, JOSEPH
The Religion Delineated; or, Experimental Religion, as Distinguished from Formality on the One Hand and Enthusiasm on the Other, Set in a Scriptural and Rational Light. Boston: 1750. V. 47

BELLAMY, THOMAS
The Trial of Thos. Bellamy, for Forgery, before the Honourable Baron George, and the Hon. Justice Finucane at Dublin the 5th of November 1802. Dublin: 1802. V. 49

BELLARMINO, ROBERTO FRANCISCO ROMOLO, SAINT
De Aeterna Felicitate Sanctorum. Rome: 1616. V. 52
Institutiones Linguae Hebraicae, Postremo Recognitae ac Locupletae. Geneva: 1619. V. 52
Institutionis Linguae Hebraicae, Ex Optimis Quibusque Auctoribus Collectae, Et Quanta Fieri Potuit Brevitate, Ac Perspicuitate in Commodissimum Ordinem Digestae. Cologne: 1580. V. 47

BELLASIS, EDWARD
Westmorland Church Notes. Kendal: 1889. V. 52; 54

BELLASIS, GEORGE HUTCHINS
Views of Saint Helena. London: 1815. V. 51

LA BELLE au Bois Dormant et Quesles Autres Contes de Jadis. Paris: 1910. V. 51

THE BELLE Epoque of French Jewellery 1850-1910: Jewellery Making in Paris 1850-1910. London: 1991. V. 52

BELLEGARDE, JEAN BAPTISTE MORVAN DE
Reflexions on Ridicule; or, What It Is That Makes a Man Ridiculous... London: 1706. V. 49
Reflexions on Ridicule; or, What it Is that Makes a Man Ridiculous... London: 1707. V. 48; 52

BELLERS, FETTIPLACE
A Delineation of Universal Law: Being an Abstract of an Essay Towards Deducing the Elements of Universal Law... London: 1754. V. 49; 51; 52

BELLEW, CHRISTOPHER D.
A Catalogue of Books in the Library of Christopher D. Bellew, Esq. Mount Bellew. Galway: 1813. V. 52; 54
Catalogue of the Mount Bellew Library, 1814. Dublin: 1814. V. 52

BELLEW, HENRY WALTER
From the Indus to the Tigris, a Narrative of a Journey through the Countries of Balochistan, Afghanistan, Khorassan and Iran in 1872. London: 1874. V. 53
The Races of Afghanistan, Being a Brief Account of the Principal Nations Inhabiting That Country. Calcutta: 1880. V. 51

BELLICARD, JEROME CHARLES
Observations on the Antiquities of the Town of Herculaneum, Discovered at the Foot of Mount Vesuvius. London: 1754. V. 47

BELLIIOCENSIS, M. CLAUD
Symbola Heroica. 1600. V. 47

BELLIN, JACQUES NICOLAS
Essai Geographique sur les Isles Britanniques Contenant une Description de l'Angleterre... Paris: 1757. V. 52

BELLINGER, ALFRED R.
Essays On the Coinage of Alexander the Great. New York: 1963. V. 48

BELLINGHAM, SYDNEY
Some Personal Recollections of the Rebellion of 1837 in Canada. Dublin: 1902. V. 50

BELLINGSHAUSEN, FABIAN G. VON
The Voyage of Captain Bellingshausen to the Antarctic Seas 1819-1821. London: 1945. V. 53

BELLINI, JACOPO
Die Skizzenbucher. Herausgegeben Dr. Victor Golubew. Brussels: 1912. V. 51

BELLINI, LORENZO
Opera Omnia. Venice: 1708. V. 49

BELLOC, BESSIE R.
Historic Nuns. London: 1898. V. 49

BELLOC, HILAIRE
Advice to the Rich. 1926. V. 49
The Bad Child's Book of Beasts. London: 1896. V. 52
The Battle Ground. London: 1936. V. 54
Belinda - a Tale of Affection in Youth and Age. London: 1928. V. 52
Cautionary Tales for Children. London: 1907. V. 47
Cranmer. London: 1931. V. 53; 54
The Crusade. London: 1937. V. 53; 54
Economics for Helen. London: 1924. V. 53; 54
The Emerald of Katherine the Great. New York: 1926. V. 50
Emmanuel Burder... London: 1904. V. 51
Esto Perpetua - Algerian Studies and Impressions. London: 1906. V. 49
The Great Inquiry. London: 1903. V. 47; 53
The Hedge and the Horse. London: 1936. V. 54
An Heroic Poem in Praise of Wine. London: 1932. V. 54
The Highway and its Vehicles. London: 1926. V. 48; 49; 51
The Jews. London: 1937. V. 49
Jim Who Ran Away from His Nurse and Was Eaten by a Lion. Providence: 1995. V. 54
Ladies and Gentlemen... London: 1932. V. 53
The Man Who Made Gold. London: 1930. V. 53; 54
The Mercy of Allah. London: 1922. V. 50; 54
Milton. London: 1935. V. 54
The Missing Masterpiece. London: 1929. V. 47
The Modern Traveller. London: 1898. V. 47; 48; 54
Monarchy: a Study of Louis XIV. London: 1938. V. 53
Moral Alphabet. London: 1899. V. 48; 50; 53
More Peers: Verses. London: 1911. V. 53
New Cautionary Tales. London: 1930. V. 54
New Cautionary Tales. New York: 1931. V. 48
On the Place of Gilbert Chesterton in English Letters. London: 1940. V. 54
The Path to Rome. London: 1902. V. 51
Places. Essays. London: 1942. V. 49
The Postmaster General. London: 1932. V. 50; 53; 54
Richelieu. London: 1930. V. 54
A Shorter History of England. London: 1934. V. 54
The Silence of the Sea and Other Essays. London: 1941. V. 54
Sonnets and Verse. London: 1923. V. 52; 53; 54
Verse and Sonnets. London: 1896. V. 47
The Verse of Hilaire Belloc. London: 1954. V. 47; 53
Verses. London: 1910. V. 54

BELLORI, GIOVANNI PIETRO
Le Antiche Lucerne Sepolcrali Figurate, Raccolte Dalle Cave Sotterranee, e Grotte di Roma. Roma: 1691. V. 48
Veteres Arcus Augustorum Triumphis Insignes ex Reliquis Quae Romae Adhuc Supersunt... Rome: 1690. V. 54

BELLOSTE, AUGUSTIN
The Hospital Surgeon; or, a New, Gentle and Easie Way to Cure Speedily all Sorts of Wounds, and Other Diseases Belonging to Surgery. London: 1713. V. 51
The Hospital-Surgeon; or, a New, Gentle and Easy Way to Cure Speedily All Sorts of Wounds and other Diseases Belonging to Surgery. London: 1732. V. 51

BELLOTTO, BERNARDO
Bernardo Bellotto. London: 1972. V. 50

BELLOW, SAUL
The Adventures of Augie March. New York: 1947. V. 51
The Adventures of Augie March. New York: 1953. V. 48; 49; 51; 52; 53
Dangling Man. New York: 1944. V. 49; 50; 51; 52; 53
Dangling Man. London: 1946. V. 51
The Dean's December. New York: 1982. V. 48; 49; 50; 52; 53; 54
Henderson the Rain King. New York: 1956. V. 52
Henderson The Rain King. London: 1959. V. 49; 52
Herzog. New York: 1964. V. 51; 52
Him with His Foot In His Mouth. New York: 1984. V. 52
Humboldt's Gift. New York: 1975. V. 52; 53
It All Adds Up. New York: 1994. V. 50
The Last Analysis. New York: 1965. V. 51
Mr. Sammler's Planet. New York: 1970. V. 49; 51; 53
More Die of Heartbreak. New York: 1987. V. 51
Mosby's Memoirs and Other Stories. New York: 1968. V. 51
Mosby's Memoirs and Other Stories. London: 1969. V. 49
Nobel Lecture. New York: 1979. V. 47; 48; 50; 52; 53; 54
Seize the Day. New York: 1956. V. 52
Seize the Day. 1957. V. 50
Seize the Day. London: 1957. V. 47; 48; 51
A Silver Dish. New York: 1979. V. 47; 48; 50; 51; 53; 54
Something to Remember Me By. New York: 1991. V. 49; 52; 54
To Jerusalem and Back. New York: 1976. V. 52
The Victim. New York: 1947. V. 47; 48; 49; 50; 51; 52; 53

BELLOWS, EMMA S.
George Bellows: His Lithographs. New York: 1928. V. 47; 48; 49; 50; 52

BELLOWS, GEORGE
George W. Bellows: His Lithographs. New York: 1927. V. 47; 50
George W. Bellows: His Lithographs. New York & London: 1928. V. 51
The Paintings of George Bellows. New York: 1929. V. 47; 48; 49; 50; 52

BELLOWS, HENRY W.
An Address Upon the claims of the Drama, Delivered Before the President and Members of the American Dramatic Fund Society, 1857. London: 1857. V. 52
Historical Sketch of the Union League Club of New York...1863-1879. New York: 1879. V. 48

BELL'S British Theatre. London: 1791-97. V. 54

BELNOS, S. C., MRS.
The Sundhya or the Daily Prayers of the Brahmins. N.P: 1851. V. 48

BELOE, WILLIAM
Anecdotes of Literature and Scarce Books. London: 1807. V. 50
Anecdotes of Literature and Scarce Books. London: 1807-12. V. 50; 54
Anecdotes of Literature and Scarce Books. London: 1814/08/10/11/. V. 48
The Sexagenarian; or, the Recollections of a Literary Life. London: 1817. V. 48

BELON DU MANS, PIERRE
Les Observations de Plusieurs Singularitez & Choses Memorables... Paris: 1554. V. 50
Les Observations de Plusieurs Singularitez & Choses Memorables... Paris: 1555. V. 50; 54

BELSHAM, WILLIAM
Memoirs of the Kings of Great Britain of the House of Brunswick-Lunenburg. London: 1793. V. 54
Memoirs of the Reign of George III. To the Session of Parliament ending A.D. 1793. London: 1795. V. 47

BELT, THOMAS
Naturalist in Nicaragua. London: 1874. V. 48; 50; 52
The Naturalist in Nicaragua. London: 1886. V. 53
The Naturalist in Nicaragua. London: 1888. V. 49; 54

BELTRAMI, GIACOMO CONSTANTINO
A Pilgrimage in Europe and America, Leading to the Discovery of the Sources of the Mississippi and Bloody River... London: 1828. V. 47; 48; 49; 53

BELTZ, GEORGE FREDERICK
Memorials of the Most Noble Order of the Garter, from Its Foundation to the Present Time. London: 1841. V. 54

BELZONI, GIOVANNI BATTISTA
Description of the Tomb Discovered by Belzoni. London: 1821. V. 54
Narrative of the Operations and Recent Discoveries, Within the Pyramids, Temples, Tombs and Excavations in Egypt and Nubia... London: 1820. V. 48; 52
Narrative of the Operations and Recent Discoveries Within the Pyramids, Temples, Tombs and Excavations in Egypt and Nubia... London: 1821/20. V. 51
Narrative of the Operations and Recent Discoveries Within the Pyramids, Temples, Tombs and Excavations in Egypt and Nubia... London: 1822. V. 51

BEMATH, DESIRE DE
Cleopatra. London: 1908. V. 54

BEMBO, PIETRO, CARDINAL
De Aetna Liber & Pietro Bembo on Etna. Venice: 1969. V. 49
Gli Asolani. In Vinegia: 1553. V. 47
Gli Asolani. In Venetia: 1586. V. 49
Historiae Venetae Libri XII. Venice: 1551. V. 47; 48; 50; 52
Le Prose...Nelle Quali si Ragiona della Volgar Lingua. Venice: 1561. V. 51
Rerum Venetarum Historiae Libri XII. Paris: 1551. V. 47; 52

BEMBRIDGE Verse. 1936. V. 50

BEMELMANS, LUDWIG
The Donkey Inside. New York: 1941. V. 48; 50; 54
Father, Dear Father. New York: 1953. V. 47; 50
The Golden Basket. New York: 1936. V. 47; 49
Hansi. New York: 1934. V. 49
The Happy Place. Boston: 1952. V. 53
Hotel Splendide. New York: 1941. V. 50
How to Travel Incognito. Boston: 1952. V. 48
Madeline. V. 51
Madeline. London: 1939. V. 53
Madeline and the Bad Hat. New York: 1956. V. 47; 48; 50
Madeline and the Bad Hat. London: 1958. V. 49
Madeline and the Gypsies. New York: 1959. V. 49; 50; 53
Madeline in London. New York: 1961. V. 49
Madeline's Christmas. 1956. V. 51; 53; 54
Madeline's Christmas. New York: 1985. V. 49; 52; 54
Madeline's Rescue. London. V. 51
Madeline's Rescue. New York: 1953. V. 47; 49
Marina. New York: 1962. V. 49
My War with the United States. New York: 1937. V. 48
Noodle. New York: 1937. V. 49
Now I Lay Me Down to Sleep. New York: 1943. V. 48; 54
Now I Lay Me Down to Sleep. New York: 1945. V. 50; 54
Parlsey. New York: 1955. V. 51
Quito Express. New York: 1938. V. 53; 54

BEMELMANS, LUDWIG continued
Sunshine. New York: 1950. V. 49
A Tale of Two Glimps. New York: 1947. V. 47; 53
To the One I Love the Best. New York: 1955. V. 47
Welcome Home!. New York: 1960. V. 49; 53; 54

BEMIS, A. F.
The Evolving House. 1933/34/36. V. 54

BEMISS, ELIJAH
The Dyer's Companion; in Two Parts. New London: 1806. V. 53
The Dyer's Companion; in Two Parts. New York: 1815. V. 48; 50; 53

BEMROSE, WILLIAM
Fret-Cutting and Perforated Carving, With Practical Illustrations. London: 1868. V. 50
Manual of Buhl-Work and Marquetry. London: 1860. V. 51; 52
Mosaicon; or, Paper Mosaic. London: 1870. V. 52

BEN Johnson's Jests; or, the Wit's Pocket Companion. London: 1751. V. 47

BENARDETE, M. J.
And Spain Sings: 50 Loyalist Ballads. New York: 1937. V. 51

BEN-ARI, R.
The Moscow Theatre "Habima". Chicago: 1941.. V. 47; 48

BENATAR, MOLLY
Fairy Tale Adventures. London: 1920. V. 51

BENAVIDES, ALONSO DE
The Memorial of Fray Alonso de Benavides. Chicago: 1916. V. 47; 49; 50; 54

THE BENCH and Bar. Philadelphia: 1839. V. 52

BENCHLEY, PETER
The Deep. Garden City: 1976. V. 52; 53
Jaws. Garden City: 1974. V. 51; 52
Jaws. New York: 1974. V. 50; 53

BENCHLEY, ROBERT
Of All Things. New York: 1921. V. 47; 49; 51; 53

BENCHLEY, ROBERT C.
Of All Things. New York: 1921. V. 51

BENCI, FRANCESCO
Qvinqve Martyres. Cologne: 1594. V. 52

BENDER, G. L.
Reference Handbook on the Deserts of North America. Westport: 1982. V. 53

BENDIRE, CHARLES
Life Histories of North American Birds with Special Reference to Their Breeding Habits and Eggs. Washington: 1892. V. 51

BENDYSHE, THOMAS
The Anthropological Treatises of Johann Friedrich Blumenbach with Memoirs of Him by Marx and Flourens and the Inaugural Dissertation of John Hunter, M.D. London: 1865. V. 53

BENECKE, T.
History of German Guided Missles Development: Agard 1st Guided Missles Seminar, Munich, April 1956. Brunswick: 1957. V. 53

BENEDETTA, MARY
The Street Markets of London. London: 1936. V. 48

BENEDETTI, L'ABBATE ELPIDIO
Pompa Funebre nell' Esequie Celebrate in Roma al Cardinal Mazarini. Rome: 1661. V. 47; 53; 54

BENEDICITE Omnia Opera. London: 1987. V. 50

BENEDICT, CARL P.
A Tenderfoot Kid on Gyp Water. Austin: 1943. V. 53; 54

BENEDICT, ERASTUS C.
The Law of American Admiralty its Jurisdiction and Practice With Forms and Directions. New York: 1940-59. V. 49

BENEDICT, F. G.
The Physiology of Large Reptiles. Washington: 1932. V. 53

BENEDICT, FRANCIS
A Study of Prolonged Fasting. Washington: 1915. V. 48

BENEDICT, FRANK LEE
Her Friend Laurence. London: 1879. V. 54

BENEDICT, GEORGE GRENVILLE
Vermont in the Civil War. A History of the Part Taken by the Vermont Soldiers and Sailors in the War for the Union 1861-65. Burlington: 1886-88. V. 48

BENEDICT, LEO G.
After the Clock Strikes Six. East Aurora: 1906. V. 51

BENEDICT, NICHOLSON
Joseph Wright of Derby. London: 1968. V. 48

BENEDICT, OF NURSIA
Regula b. Patris Benedict a b. Dunstano Diligeter Recognita, cum Pluculis Aliis a Tergo Huius Explicandis. Paris: 1544. V. 54

BENEDICT, PIERCE E.
History of Beverly Hills. Beverly Hills: 1934. V. 50; 51; 54

BENEDICT, PINCKNEY
Town Smokes. Princeton: 1987. V. 51; 54
The Wrecking Yard. New York: 1992. V. 52

BENEDICT, WILLIAM H.
New Brunswick in History. New Brunswick: 1925. V. 47; 49; 51

THE BENEDICTINES of Stanbrook. Worcester: 1957. V. 52

BENEDICTUS
Nouvelles Variations. Soixante-Quinze Motifs Decoratifs en Vingt Planches. Paris: 1925. V. 47
Relais 1930. Quinze Planches Domnant Quarante-Deux Motifs Decoratifs. Paris: 1930. V. 48

BENEDICTUS, EDOUARD
Relais 1930. Paris: 1930. V. 53

BENEDIKT, MORITZ
Anatomcal Studies Upon Brains of Criminals. New York: 1881. V. 48

THE BENEFITS and Privileges of Cuckolds Shewing the Little Disgrace There Is In Being One, and the Obligations Men Sometimes Have to Their Wives... London: 1885. V. 53

BENESCH, O.
Drawings... 1973. V. 48

BENET, LAURA
Enchanting Jenny Lind. New York: 1939. V. 47; 48; 49
Fairy Bread. New York: 1921. V. 49

BENET, STEPHEN VINCENT
The Barefoot Saint. New York: 1929. V. 47
Burning City. New York: 1936. V. 47; 54
The Devil and Daniel Webster. Weston: 1937. V. 53
The Devil and Daniel Webster. New York: 1939. V. 47
Five Men and Pompey. Boston: 1915. V. 48; 51; 52
The Headless Horseman. Boston: 1937. V. 47; 48
Heavens and Earth. New York: 1920. V. 50
James Shore's Daughter. Garden City: 1934. V. 54
James Shore's Daughter. New York: 1934. V. 48
John Brown's Body. Garden City: 1928. V. 51; 52; 53
The John Brown's Body. London: 1948. V. 50
John Brown's Body. New York: 1948. V. 47; 51; 54
John Brown's Body. New York: 1980. V. 52
John Brown's Body. Northampton: 1980. V. 48
John Brown's Body: a Poem... New York: 1948. V. 47
Johnny Pye and the Fool Killer. Weston: 1938. V. 47; 48; 54
King David: The Nation Prize Poem for 1923. V. 47; 48
A Portrait and a Poem. Paris: 1934. V. 51
Tales Before Midnight. New York: 1939. V. 53
Thirteen O'Clock. New York: 1937. V. 54
Tiger Joy: a Book of Poems. New York: 1925. V. 54

BENET, WILLIAM ROSE
The Falconer of God and other Poems. New Haven: 1914. V. 49
The Great White Wall. New Haven: 1916. V. 53; 54
Merchants from Cathay. New York: 1913. V. 49
Moons of Grandeur. New York: 1920. V. 49
The Stairway of Surprise. New York: 1947. V. 54

BENEZET, ANTHONY
The Case of Our Fellow-Creatures, the Oppressed Africans, Respectfully Recommended to the Serious Consideration of the Legislature of Great Britain, by the People Called Quakers. London: 1784. V. 47
A Collection of Religious Tracts. Philadelphia: 1773. V. 48
The Potent Enemies of America Laid Open... Philadelphia: 1774. V. 49
Some Historical Account of Guinea, Its Situation, Produce and the General Disposition of Its Inhabitants. London: 1788. V. 51; 52

BENFORD, G.
Timescape. 1980. V. 47; 51

BENGER, ELIZABETH OGILVIE
Memoirs of Elizabeth Stuart, Queen of Bohemia, Daughter of King James the First. London: 1825. V. 51
Memoirs of the Late Mrs. Elizabeth Hamilton, with a Selection from Her Correspondence and Other Unpublished Writings. London: 1819. V. 54

BENGOUGH, J. W.
A Caricature History of Canadian Politics. Toronto: 1886. V. 54

BEN-GURION, DAVID
Israel: A Personal History. New York: 1971. V. 52

BENIOWSKI, BARTOMIEJ
The Anti-Absurd or Phrenotypic English Pronouncing & Orthographical Dictionary. London: 1845. V. 52

BENIVIENI, ANTONIO
De Abditis Nonnulis Ac Mirandis Morborum et Sanatonum Causis. Springfield: 1954. V. 50

BENJAMIN, ASHER
The American Builder's Companion; or, a New System of Architecture... Boston: 1806. V. 47; 48; 50; 53; 54
The American Builder's Companion; or, A System of Architecture... Boston: 1816. V. 47; 50
The Architect, or Practical House Carpenter... Boston: 1847 (1857). V. 52
The Builder's Guide... Boston: 1839. V. 52
The Practical House Carpenter. New York: 1835. V. 47

BENJAMIN, JONATHAN
Harmonia Coelestis: a Collection of Church Music, in Two, Three and Four Parts. Northampton: 1799. V. 48; 51
Harmonia Coelestis: a Collection of Church Music, in Two Three and Fourt Parts. Northampton: 1799. V. 51

BENJAMIN, MARCUS
The Battle Fields of the Maumee Valley... Washington City: 1896. V. 47
John Bidwell, Pioneer. Washington: 1907. V. 47

BENJAMIN, PARK
Appleton's Cyclopaedia of Applied Mechanics. New York: 1880. V. 54

BENJAMIN, S. G. W.
Contemporary Art in Europe. New York: 1877. V. 52
Persia and the Persians. London: 1887. V. 50

BENJAMIN, W. S.
The Great Epidemic in New Berne and Vicinity, September & October, 1864. New Berne: 1865. V. 48

BENJAMIN BEN JOHAN, OF TUDELA
Itinerarium Beniamini Tudelensis: In Quo Res memorabiles, Quas Ante Quadringentos Annos Totum Fere Terrarum Orbem Notatis... Antwerp: 1575. V. 52

BENJAMIN BEN JONAH, OF TUDELA
Itinerarium D. Benjaminis cum Versione & Notis Constantini L'Emereur. Leyden: 1633. V. 49; 50; 53

BENKARD, ERNST
Undying Faces - a Collection of Death Masks. London: 1929. V. 47

BENKARD, J. B.
Historical Sketch of the German Emperors and Kings. London: 1855. V. 50

BENKOVITZ, MIRIAM J.
A Bibliography of Ronald Firbank. London: 1963. V. 50

BENN, EDITH FRASER
An Overland Trek from India by Side-Saddle, Camel and Rail... London: 1909. V. 53

BENNET, E.
Shots and Snapshots in British East Africa. London: 1914. V. 48

BENNET, J. W.
The Coco-nut Tree...More Extensive Cultivation of This Invaluable Palm in the British West Indies and African Colonies... London: 1836. V. 47

BENNET, JOHN
Poems on Several Occasions. London: 1774. V. 49; 54
Poems on Several Occasions. Oxford: 1774. V. 49

BENNET, S. S. R.
Thirty Seven Bamboos Growing in India. Dehra Dun: 1990. V. 52

BENNETT, A. W.
A Selection of Rare and Curious Fishes Found Upon the Coast of Ceylon, From Drawings made in that Island, and Coloured from Life. London: 1841. V. 49

BENNETT, AGNES MARIA
Anna; or Memoirs of a Welch Heiress. Dublin: 1786. V. 49
The Beggar Girl and Her Benefactors. London: 1791. V. 54
The Beggar Girl and Her Benefactors. London: 1797. V. 48

BENNETT, ALAN
Getting On. London: 1972. V. 50

BENNETT, ARNOLD
Anna of the Five Towns. London: 1902. V. 47
The Bright Island. London: 1924. V. 47; 48; 52; 53; 54
Clayhanger - Hilda Lessways - These Twain. London: 1910/11/16. V. 52
The Clayhanger Family. I. Clayhanger. II. Hilda Lessways. III. These Twain. London: 1925. V. 48
Don Juan de Marana. London: 1923. V. 48
Elsie and the Child. London: 1929. V. 48; 49; 50; 52; 53
The Feast of St. Friend. Toronto: 1911. V. 48
The Human Machine. New York: 1911. V. 53
Journal 1929. London: 1930. V. 50
Journalism for Women... London: 1895. V. 50
Journalism for Women. London: 1898. V. 51
Liberty! - A Statement of the British Case. New York: 1914. V. 47
Lillian. London: 1922. V. 49; 52
The Lion's Share. London: 1916. V. 48
A Man from the North. London & New York: 1898. V. 47; 48; 49; 54
A Man From the North. London & New York: 1989. V. 52
Mediterranean Scenes. London: 1928. V. 54
Mr. Prohack. New York: 1922. V. 48
The Old Wive's Tale. Toronto. V. 48
The Old Wives' Tale. London: 1908. V. 47; 51; 52; 54
The Old Wive's Tale. Toronto: 1910. V. 48
The Old Wive's Tale. London: 1927. V. 49; 50
The Old Wive's Tale. 1941. V. 47
The Old Wive's Tale. New York: 1941. V. 49
The Old Wive's Tale. Oxford: 1941. V. 51; 52; 54
The Old Wive's Tale. Oxford: 1952. V. 54
Our Women - Chapters on the Sex-Discord. London: 1920. V. 47; 50
Polite Farces for the Drawing Room. London: 1900. V. 48; 53; 54
Polite Farces for the Drawing Room. London: 1900/1899. V. 47
The Roll Call. New York: 1918. V. 48
These Twain. London: 1916. V. 48
These Twain. Toronto: 1916. V. 48
Things...Interested Me: Third Series. Burslem: 1908. V. 49
Things...Interested Me. Third Series. London: 1916. V. 48
Venus Rising from the Sea. London: 1931. V. 53

BENNETT, C. N.
The Handbook of Kinematogrpahy: the History, Theory and Practice of Motion Photography and Projection. London: 1911. V. 53

BENNETT, CHARLES
Lightsome and the Little Golden Lady. London: 1867. V. 50
London People: Sketched from Life. London: 1863. V. 49
The Sorrowful Ending of Noodledoo, with the Fortunes and Fate of Her Neighbours and Friends. London: 1865. V. 49

BENNETT, CHARLES H.
Shadow and Substance. London: 1859. V. 50
Shadows. London: 1857. V. 54
Shadows. London: 1860's. V. 49
The Surprising, Unheard of and Never-to-be-Surpassed Adventures of Young Munchausen... London: 1865. V. 51

BENNETT, D. M.
Trial of D. M. Bennett in the United States Circuit Court....Upon the Charge of Depositing Prohibited Matter in the Mail. New York: 1879. V. 50; 54

BENNETT, EDWARD TURNER
The Gardens and Menagerie of the Zoological Society Delineated. 1830-31. V. 54
The Gardens and Menagerie of the Zoological Society Delineated. London: 1830-31. V. 50; 52
The Gardens and Menagerie of the Zoological Society Delineated. 1831. V. 49
The Gardens and Menagerie of the Zoological Society Delineated, Quadrupeds, Birds. Chiswick: 1831. V. 51
The Gardens and Menagerie of the Zoological Society Delineated. Volume 2. Birds. London: 1831. V. 47; 48; 50; 51

BENNETT, EMERSON
Clara Moreland; or, Adventures in the Far South-West. Philadelphia: 1853. V. 51
Viola; or, Adventures in the Far Southwest. Philadelphia: 1852. V. 52

BENNETT, FRANK M.
The Steam Navy of the United States. Pittsburgh: 1896. V. 51

BENNETT, FREDERICK DEBELL
Narrative of a Whaling Voyage Round the Globe... London: 1840. V. 50; 52; 54
Narrative of a Whaling Voyage Round the Globe... Amsterdam/New York: 1970. V. 47

BENNETT, GEORGE
The History of Bandon, and the Principal towns in the West Riding of County Cork. 1869. V. 48
Wanderings in New South Wales, Batavia, Pedir Coast, Singapore and China.. London: 1834. V. 50; 53

BENNETT, GEORGIANA
Woman and Her Duties. London: 1860. V. 50; 51

BENNETT, H. S.
English Books and Readers 1474 to 1557 (volume 1) 1558-1603 (volume 2) 1603 to 1640 (volume 3). 1952-70. V. 47
English Books and Readers 1475 to 1640. 1952-70. V. 54

BENNETT, HAL
Seventh Heaven. Garden City: 1976. V. 53

BENNETT, JOHN
The Artificer's Complete Lexicon for Terms and Prices. London: 1833. V. 47
Letters to a Young Lady, on a Variety of Useful and Interesting Subjects. Hartford: 1792. V. 48
Letters to a Young Lady on a Variety of Useful and Interesting Subjects... London: 1793. V. 47
Letters to a Young Lady, on a Variety of Useful and Interesting Subjects. New York: 1796. V. 48; 50; 51; 53
Letters to a Young Lady, On a Variety of Useful and Interesting Subjects. Worcester: 1798. V. 50; 51; 53
Letters to a Young Lady, on a Variety of Useful and Interesting Subjects... London: 1812. V. 52
Master Skylark. A Story of Shakespeare's Time. New York: 1897. V. 54
The Pathology and Treatment of Pulmonary Tuberculosis... Philadelphia: 1854. V. 48; 53
Strictures on Female Education; Chiefly As It Relates to the Culture of the Heart. Norwich: 1792. V. 53

BENNETT, JOHN B.
The Evil of Theatrical Amusements, Stated and Illustrated in a Sermon, Preached in the Wesleyan Methodist Chapel, Abbey St., Dublin, on Sunday, Nov. 4, 1838. London: 1839. V. 52

BENNETT, JOHN COOK
The History of the Saints; or, an Expose of Joe Smith and Mormonism. Boston: 1842. V. 48

BENNETT, JOHN WHITCHURCH
A Selection of the Most Remarkable and Interesting of the Fishes Found on the Coasts of Ceylon. London: 1834. V. 53

BENNETT, JOSEPH M.
Bennett's Illustrated Toilet of Fashion. Philadelphia: 1858. V. 47

BENNETT, LEONORA
Historical Sketch and Guide to the Alamo. San Antonio: 1904. V. 48; 54

BENNETT, LERONE
Before the Mayflower: a History of the Negro in America 1619-1964. Chicago: 1964. V. 52
The Shaping of Black America. Chicago: 1975. V. 52
Wade in the Water: Great Moments in Black History. Chicago: 1979. V. 54
What Manner of Man: A Biography of Martin Luther King Jr. Chicago: 1964. V. 52

BENNETT, M. M.
Christison of Lammermoor. London: 1928. V. 48

BENNETT, MELBA BERRY
Robinson Jeffers and the Sea. San Francisco: 1936. V. 48; 49

BENNETT, NATHANIEL
The Pacific Law Magazine. January 1867. San Francisco: 1867. V. 52
Reports of Cases Argued and Determined in the Supreme Court of the State. San Francisco/New York: 1851. V. 49; 50

BENNETT NEWS CO.
The Picturesque Land of Gold. Its Magnificent Mountain and Water Scenes, Its Peaks, Passes and Canyons. The Home of the Midnight Sun. A Land With a Summer Charm. White Horse: 1903-04?. V. 48
A Yukon Souvenir. The Picturesque Land of Gold. White Horse: 1903-05?. V. 48

BENNETT, PAUL A.
Bouquet for B. R. New York: 1950. V. 52
Postscripts on Dwiggins. New York: 1960. V. 48

BENNETT, R. A.
Which One?. 1912. V. 54

BENNETT, RICHARD
History of Corn Milling. London and Liverpool: 1898-1904. V. 49; 50
The Story of Bovril. Bovril: 1953. V. 52
The Story of Bovril. London: 1953. V. 48

BENNETT, ROBERT
The Wrath of John Steinbeck. Los Angeles: 1939. V. 51

BENNETT, T. P.
Architectural Design in Concrete. London: 1927. V. 52

BENNETT, WENDELL
The Tarahumara, an Indian Tribe of Northern Mexico. 1935. V. 48
The Tarahumara, an Indian Tribe of Northern Mexico. Chicago: 1935. V. 51

BENNETT, WHITMAN
A Practical Guide to American Nineteenth Century Color Plate Books. New York: 1949. V. 49; 52

BENNETT, WILLIAM
A Letter to a Friend, In Reply to the Question, What is Vegetarianism?. London: 1849. V. 50

BENNETT, WILLIAM P.
The First Baby in Camp: a Full Account of the Scenes and Adventures During the Pioneer Days of '49. Salt Lake City: 1893. V. 47; 50

BENNEVILLE, GEORGE DE
A True and Most Remarkable Account of Some Passages in the Life of Mr. George De Benneville... London: 1791. V. 54

BENNION, ELISABETH
Antique Medical Instruments. London: 1979. V. 52

BENOIT, PIERRE
Les Puits de Joseph. Paris: 1927. V. 50

BENSEN, D. R.
Irene, Godd-Night. New York: 1982. V. 51
Irene, Good-Night. New York: 1982. V. 50; 51; 52

BENSERADE, ISAAC DE
Ballet Royal de Flore. Paris: 1669. V. 51

BENSON, ARTHUR CHRISTOPHER
The Book of the Queen's Dolls'-House. London: 1924. V. 48
Monnow: an Elegy. Eton: 1896. V. 50
Thomas Gray. Eton: 1895. V. 47

BENSON, C. E.
British Mountaineering. London: 1909. V. 54
Crag and Hound in Lakeland. London: 1902. V. 51; 52; 54

BENSON, EDWARD FREDERIC
Dodo: a Detail of the Day. London: 1893. V. 47; 54
The Freaks of Mayfair. London: 1916. V. 48
The Life of Alcibiades. London: 1928. V. 52
The Luck of the Vails. London: 1901. V. 53
Male Impersonator. London: 1929. V. 47; 51; 54
Mammon and Co. London: 1899. V. 53
Paul. London: 1906. V. 51
Raven's Brood. 1934. V. 51
Trouble for Lucia. London: 1939. V. 51

BENSON, FRANK SHERMAN
Catalogue of the Valuable Collection of Greek Coins Formed by the Late Frank Sherman Benson, Esq. of Brooklyn, New York, Comprising Choice and Interesting Examples of the Ancient Coinages of Italy and Sicily, Greece and the Islands, Asia Minor &c. ... London: 1909. V. 48

BENSON, HENRY C.
Life Among the Choctaw Indians and Sketches of the Southwest. Cincinnati: 1860. V. 51; 52

BENSON, JOHN HOWARD
The Elements of Lettering. Newport: 1940. V. 48

BENSON, L.
The Cacti of the United States and Canada. Stanford: 1982. V. 50

BENSON, MARY ELEANOR
At Sundry Times and in Divers Manners. London: 1891. V. 54

BENSON, NATHANIEL A.
Poems. Toronto: 1927. V. 48

BENSON, ROBERT
State Credit and banking During the War and After. London: 1918. V. 50

BENSON, ROBERT HUGH
Collected Novels. London: 1920-35. V. 51
Richard Raynal, Solitary. Chicago: 1956. V. 51

BENSON, STELLA
Hope Against Hope and Other Stories. London: 1931. V. 47; 48
The Man Who Missed the Bus. London: 1928. V. 50
Twenty. New York: 1918. V. 52

BENSON, THOMAS
Vocabularium Anglo-Saxonicum, Lexico Gul. somneri. Oxford: 1701. V. 47; 48; 49; 50; 51; 52

BENSON, THOMAS W.
Fundamentals of Television. New York: 1930. V. 54

BENSON, WILLIAM
A Letter to Sir J--- B--- (Jacob Bancks), by Birth a Swede, but Naturaliz'd and a M---4 of the Present P---5... London: 1711. V. 52
Manual of the Science of Colour on the True Theory of the Colour-Sensations and the Natural System. London: 1871. V. 54

BENT, A. C.
Life Histories of North American Birds. Washington: 1919-68. V. 49; 50; 53
Life Histories of North American Birds. Washington: 1939-58. V. 53

BENT, J. THEODORE
The Ruined Cities of Mashonaland... London: 1892. V. 48; 50
The Ruined Cities of Mashonaland. London: 1893. V. 47; 51; 54
Southern Arabia. London: 1900. V. 54

BENT, SILAS
Report Made to Commodore M. C. Perry Upon the Kuro-Siwo, or Gulf Stream of the North Pacific Ocean. 1857. V. 50

BENTES, ALBERTUS
Bibliotheca Bentesiana Sive Catalogus Librorum, Quos Collegit vir Amplissimus Albertus Bentes. Amsterdam: 1702. V. 47

BENTHAM, EDWARD
An Introduction to Moral Philosophy. Oxford: 1746. V. 48

BENTHAM, G.
Flora Australiensis: a Description of the Plants of the Australian Territory. London: 1863-78. V. 52

BENTHAM, JAMES
The History and Antiquities of the Conventual and Cathedral Church of Ely. Cambridge: 1771. V. 47; 51; 53
The History and Antiquities of the Conventual and Cathedral Church of Ely... Cambridge: 1771/1817. V. 53

BENTHAM, JEREMY
Benthamiana; or, Select Extracts from the Works of Jeremy Bentham. Edinburgh: 1843. V. 52
Defence of Usury; Shewing the Impolicy of the Present Legal Restraints on the Terms of Pecuniary Bargains... Dublin: 1788. V. 48
Defence of Usury; Shewing the Impolicy of the Present Legal Restraints on the Terms of Pecuniary Bargains. London: 1790. V. 54
The Elements of the Art of Packing, as Applied to Special Juries, Particularly in Cases of Libel Law. London: 1821. V. 52
Emancipate Your Colonies! Addressed to the National Convention of France, Ao 1793, Shewing the Uselessness and Mischievousness of Distant Dependencies to an European State. London: 1830 & 1793. V. 52
Fragment on Government. London: 1823. V. 54
An Introduction to the Principles of Morals and Legislation. London: 1823. V. 52
Jeremy Bentham to His Fellow Citizens of France on Death Punishment. London: 1831. V. 53
Plan of Parliamentary Reform, in the Form of a Catechism... London: 1817. V. 51; 52; 54

BENTHAM, JEREMY continued
Plan of Parliamentary Reform, in the Form of a Catechism... London: 1818. V. 48; 50; 52; 54
Rhyme and Reason; or, A Fresh Stating of the Arguments Against an Opening Through the Wall of Queen's Square, Westminster. London: 1780. V. 50
Scotch Reform; Considered, with Reference to the Plan, Proposed in the Late Parliament, for the Regulation of the Courts and the Administration of Justice, in Scotland... London: 1811. V. 47; 48
Supply Without Burthen; or Escheat Vice Taxation: Being a Proposal for a Saving in Taxes by an Extension of the law of Escheat... to which is prefixed A Protest Against Law Taxes, Shewing the Peculiar Mischievousness of All Such Impositions... London: 1795/93. V. 52
Theorie des Peines et des Recompenses. Londres: 1811. V. 53; 54
The Works of Jeremy Bentham. Edinburgh: 1843. V. 52

BENTHAM, JOSEPH
A Disswasive from Error Much Increased. London: 1669. V. 53

BENTHAM, T.
An Illustrated Catalogue of the Asiatic Horns and Antlers in the Collection of the Indian Museum. Catalogue: 1908. V. 49

BENTINE, MICHAEL
The Long Banana Skin. London: 1975. V. 50

BENTLEY, E. C.
Trent's Last Case. 1913. V. 53
Trent's Last Case. London: 1913. V. 51
Trent's Own Case. London: 1936. V. 48; 49; 51

BENTLEY, EDMUND CLERIHEW
Biography for Beginners. London: 1905. V. 54

BENTLEY, ELIZABETH
Poems: Being the Genuine Compositions of... Norwich: 1821. V. 53

BENTLEY, GEORGE
Mr. Dickens and Mr. Bentley. London: 1871. V. 50

BENTLEY, GERALD EADES
Blake Books. Annotated Catalogues of William Blake's Writings in Illuminated Printing. Oxford: 1977. V. 48
The Jacobean and Caroline Stages, Dramatic Companies and Players. Oxford: 1949-56. V. 50

BENTLEY, H. CUMBERLAND
The Legend of the Black Loch. London: 1880. V. 53

BENTLEY, HENRY
A Correct Account of All the Cricket Matches...from the Year 1786 to 1822. London: 1823. V. 50

BENTLEY, JOHN
Halifax and its Gibbet-Law Placed in a True Light. Halifax: 1761. V. 47; 51

BENTLEY, RICHARD
Designs for Six Poems by Mr. Gray. London: 1789. V. 53
Designs...for Six Poems by Mr. Gray. London: 1753. V. 53
A Dissertation Upon the Epistles of Phalaris. London: 1699. V. 49
Epistolae, Partim Mutuae. London: 1807. V. 48
Remarks Upon a Late Discourse of Free-Thinking: in a Letter to F(rancis) H(are) D.D.... London: 1713. V. 49
Remarks Upon a Late Discourse of Free-Thinking: in a Letter to F(rancis) H(are) D.D. Cambridge: 1743. V. 49
Remarks Upon a Late Discourse of Free-Thinking In a Letter to N.N. (with) Part the Second. Cambridge: 1725/25. V. 49
Richardi Bentleii Opuscula Philologica Disserationem in Phalarides Epistolas et Epistolam ad Ioannem Millium Complectentia. Lipsiae: 1781. V. 49
A Short Account of Dr. Bentley's Humanity and Justice, to Those Authors Who Have Written Before Him... London: 1699. V. 53
The Works. London: 1836-38. V. 52

BENTLEY, SAMUEL
Poems on Various Occasions... London: 1774. V. 48

BENTLEY, W. A.
Snow Crystals. New York and London: 1931. V. 51

BENTLEY, WILLIAM
Bentley's Hand-book of the Pacific Coast... Oakland: 1884. V. 47
Catalogue of the Part of the Late Dr. Bentley's Library, Not Bequeathed to Literary Institutions, to be sold at Auction, on Wednesday and Thursday, June 14, and 15, 1820, at 9 o'clock A.M. and 3 P.M. at Blake & Cunningham's Office... Boston: 1820. V. 52

BENTLY, JOHN
A Book of Discarded Things. London: 1992. V. 52

BENTON, J. A.
The California Pilgrim; A Series of Lectures. Sacramento: 1853. V. 47; 50

BENTON, JOEL
In the Poe circle. New York: 1899. V. 48

BENTON, M. J.
The Phylogeny and Classification of Tetrapods. Oxford: 1988. V. 50; 51

BENTON, THOMAS HART
An Artist in America. New York: 1937. V. 47
An Artist in America. New York: 1951. V. 53
Discourse of Mr. Benton, of Missouri, Before the Boston Mercantile Library Association, on the Physical Geography of the Country Between the States of Missouri and California, with a View to Show its Adaptation to Settlement and to the Construction... Washington: 1854. V. 50
In Senate of the United States...from the Committee on Indian Affairs. Washington: 1824. V. 47; 50
Speech of Hon. T. H. Benton, to the People of Missouri, Delivered in the Capitol in the City of Jefferson, May 26, 1849. Jefferson City: 1849. V. 48
Speech of Thomas H. Benton of Missouri...in Secret Session on the Treaty for the Annexation of Texas to the United States. Little Rock: 1844. V. 49
Thirty Years' View; or, a History of the Working of the American Government for Thirty Years, 1820-1850. New York: 1854. V. 49; 53
Thirty Years' View; or a History of the Working of the American Government for Thirty Years, 1820-1850. New York: 1856. V. 48

BENWELL, J.
An Englishman's Travels in America: His Observataions of Life and Manners in the Free and Slave States. London & Bath colophon: 1853. V. 50; 53

BENYOWKSY, MAURITIUS AUGUSTUS, COUNT DE
Memoirs and Travels...His Exile into Kamchatka, His Escape and Voyage From that Peninsula Through the Northern Pacific Ocean, Touching at Japan and Formosa. London: 1790. V. 47

BENZ, ADOLPH CHRISTOPH
Thesaurus Processum Chimicorum. Nuremberg: 1715. V. 47; 53

BENZONI, GIROLAMO
History of the New World by Girolamo Benzoni, of Milan... London: 1857. V. 54
Novae Novi Orbis Historia... Geneva: 1581. V. 47

BEOWULF
Beowulf. New York: 1932. V. 48; 53
Beowulf. 1952. V. 48
Beowulf. Market Drayton: 1984. V. 48
Ellor-Gast. Eight Anglo-Saxon texts from Beowulf with translations by the Artist. 1986. V. 52
The Tale of Beowulf. Hammersmith: 1895. V. 54

BERAIN, JEAN
Ornemens Inventez Par J. Berain. (Oeuvres de jean Berain). Paris: 1710. V. 50
Ornemens Inventez...Desseins de Cheminees... Paris: 1709. V. 53

BERANGER, PIERRE
Songs. London: 1837. V. 53

BERBEROVA, NINA
The Italics Are Mine. New York: 1969. V. 52

BERDOE, MARMADUKE
An Enquiry into the Influence of the Electric Fluid in the Structure and Formation of Animated Beings. Bath: 1771. V. 53

BERENDSOHN, W. A.
Selma Lagerlof: Her Life and Work. London: 1931. V. 48

BERENDT, JOHN
Midnight in the Garden of Good and Evil. New York: 1994. V. 53; 54

BERENS, EDWARD
Christmas Stories. Oxford: 1823. V. 49
Christmas Stories. Oxford: 1830. V. 49

BERENSON, BERNARD
The Drawings of Florentine Painters. Chicago: 1938. V. 51; 53; 54
The Italian Painters of the Renaissance. Garden City: 1953. V. 51
Lorenzo Lotto... London: 1956. V. 52
Lorenzo Lotto. New York: 1956. V. 48
Three Essays in Method. 1927. V. 52

BERESFORD, CHARLES
The Break-Up of China with an Account of Its Present Commerce, Currency, Waterways, Armies, Railways, Politics and Future Prospects. 1899. V. 51
Nelson and His Times. London: 1910. V. 50

BERESFORD, J. D.
Goslings. London: 1913. V. 48
The Hampdenshire Wonder. 1911. V. 52
The Hampdenshire Wonder. London: 1911. V. 53
The Wonder. 1917. V. 49; 54

BERESFORD, JAMES
The Miseries of Human Life; or the Groans of Samuel Sensitive and Timothy Testy. London: 1806. V. 51; 53
The Miseries of Human Life; or, the Groans of Samuel Sensitive and Timothy Testy. London: 1806-07. V. 48
The Miseries of Human Life; or the Groans of Timothy Testy and Samuel Sensitive. London: 1825. V. 48

BERESFORD HOPE, ALEXANDER JAMES
Oratio Latina Aureo Numismate ab Honoratissimo viro Roberto Peel Baronetto Quotannis Proposito Dignata et in Auditorio Recitata Scholae Harroviensis VII. ID. IVN. MDCCCXXXVII. London: 1837. V. 47

THE BERGEN County Democrat's History of Hackensack, N.J. Its Olden Story, Present Annals, Prospective Growth. Hackensack: 1898. V. 47

BERGER, JOHANNES
Hans Berger on the Electroencephalogram of Man. Amsterdam: 1969. V. 53

BERGER, JOHN
Permanent Red. London: 1960. V. 49
Toward Reality, Essays in Seeing. New York: 1962. V. 53

BERGER, KLAUS
Odilon Redon. Fantasy and Colour. London: 1964. V. 54

BERGER, THOMAS
Arthur Rex. New York: 1978. V. 54
Crazy in Berlin. New York: 1958. V. 48; 49; 50; 52
Granted Wishes. Northridge: 1984. V. 48; 53
Little Big Man. New York: 1964. V. 48; 50; 51; 52; 53
Orrie's Story. Boston: 1990. V. 54
Reinhart in Love. New York: 1962. V. 47; 48; 51; 54
Reinhart's Women. New York: 1981. V. 54
Sneaky People. New York: 1975. V. 54
Vital Parts. New York: 1970. V. 54

BERGER, VICTOR
Berger's Broadsides. Milwaukee: 1912. V. 50

BERGERAT, EMILE
A Wild Sheep Chase. New York: 1894. V. 52

BERGERON, LOUIS ELOY
Manuel Du Tourneur, Ouvrage dans Lequel on Enseigne Aux Amateurs la Maniere d'Executer sur le Tour a Pointes... Paris: 1792-96. V. 48

BERGH, PETER
The Art of Ogden M. Pleissner. Boston: 1984. V. 47

BERGHOLD, ALEXANDER
The Indians Revenge; or, Days of Horror. Some Appalling Events in the History of the Sioux. San Francisco: 1891. V. 48; 49; 54

BERGMAN, RAY
Fresh Water Bass. New York: 1942. V. 47

BERGMAN, S.
In Korean Wilds and Villages. London: 1938. V. 52
Sport and Exploration in the Far East, a Naturalist's Experiences in and Around the Kurile Islands. London: 1933. V. 51

BERGMAN, TORBERN
A Dissertation on Elective Attractions... London: 1785. V. 48
An Essay on the Usefulness of Chemistry and Its Application to the Various Occasions of Life. London: 1783. V. 48
Physical and Chemical Essays. London: 1788. V. 53
Physical and Chemical Essays. London/Edinburgh: 1788/91. V. 53

BERGMANN, W.
Nutritional Disorders of Plants, Development, Visual and Analytical Diagnoses. Jena: 1992. V. 50

BERGSTROM, INGVAR
Dutch Still-Life Painting in the Seventeenth Century. London: 1956. V. 47; 48; 49; 51; 54
Dutch Still-Life Painting in the Seventeenth Century. New York: 1956. V. 51

BERINGTON, JOSEPH
The History of the Lives of Abeillard and Heloisa... Birmingham: 1787. V. 48; 50

BERINGTON, SIMON
The Adventures of Sigr. Gaudentio di Lucca. London: 1748. V. 48; 50; 52
The Adventures of Sigr. Gaudentio di Lucca... London: 1776. V. 49

BERJEAU, CHARLES
The Horses of Antiquity, Middle Ages and Renaissance from the Earliest Monuments Down to the XVITH Century. London: 1864. V. 53

BERKEBILE, DON H.
Carriage Terminology: an Historical Dictionary. Washington: 1978. V. 54

BERKELEY, ANTHONY
The Roger Sheringham Stories. London: 1994. V. 51; 54

BERKELEY, COMYNS
On Safari. A Chat to the medical Society of the Middlesex Hospital. London: 1910. V. 48

BERKELEY, EDMUND CALLIS
Giant Brains; or Machines that Think. New York: 1949. V. 51; 52; 54

BERKELEY, G. F. H.
Italy in the Making 1815-48. 1968. V. 52

BERKELEY, GEORGE BERKELEY, 1ST EARL OF
Historical Applications and Occasional Meditations Upon Several Subjects. London: 1670. V. 47

BERKELEY, GEORGE, BP. OF CLOYNE
Alciphron: or, the Minute Philosopher. London: 1732. V. 47; 48
Life and Letters...and an Account of His Philosophy. Oxford: 1871. V. 49
A Miscellany, Containing Several Tracts on Various Subjects... London: 1744. V. 48
A Miscellany, Containing Several Tracts on Various Subjects... London: 1752. V. 49
The Querist. London: 1760. V. 47
Siris: a Chain of Philosophical Reflexions and Inquiries Concerning the Virtues of Tar Water, and Divers Other Subjects Connected Together and Arising from One Another. Dublin, London: 1744. V. 48; 53
A Treatise Concerning the Principles of Human Knowledge... London: 1734. V. 49; 50
A Treatise Concerning the Principles of Human Knowledge. London: 1776. V. 53

The Works of... London: 1871. V. 49; 50
The Works of... Oxford: 1871. V. 48; 50; 52
The Works of... London: 1897-98-98. V. 47; 50
The Works. To Which is Added an Account of His Life and Several of His Letters. London: 1784. V. 50

BERKELEY, GEORGE MONCK
Literary Relics: Containing Original Letters from King Charles Ii, King James II, The Queen of Bohemia, Swift, Berkeley, Addison, Steele, Congreve, the Duke of Ormond and Bishop of Rundle. London: 1789. V. 52; 53

BERKELEY, GRANTLEY F.
The English Sportsman in the Western Prairies. London: 1861. V. 47
Fact Against Fiction. London: 1874. V. 49
A Month in the Forests of France. London: 1857. V. 47
My Life and Recollections. London: 1865-66. V. 47; 49; 51
Reminiscences of a Huntsman. London: 1854. V. 52
Sandron Hall, or the Days of Queen Anne. London: 1840. V. 49; 52

BERKELEY, HASTINGS
Japanese Letters: Eastern Impressions of Western Men and Manners, as Contained in the Correspondence of Tokiwara and Yashiri. London: 1891. V. 53

BERKELEY, JOHN
Memoirs... London: 1699. V. 50; 53

BERKELEY, M. J.
Handbook of British Mosses. London: 1863. V. 47; 50; 52; 53
Outlines of British Fungology.... London: 1860-91. V. 49; 54

BERKELEY, WILLIAM
The Lost Lady. London: 1639. V. 54

BERKELL, JOHN
A Dissertation Upon the Subject of Circumcision. London: 1763. V. 48

BERKENHOUT, JOHN
Clavis Anglica Linguae Botanicae; or, a Botanical Lexicon. London: 1789. V. 49; 52
Outlines of the Natural History of Great Britain and Ireland. London: 1769-72. V. 52
Synopsis of the Natural History of Great Britain and Ireland... London: 1789. V. 49

BERKMAN, ALEXANDER
Deportation. Its Meaning and Menace. New York: 1919. V. 51
Prison Memoirs of an Anarchist. New York: 1912. V. 47; 48; 49; 50
Trials and Speeches. New York: 1917. V. 51

BERKO, PATRICK
Dictionary of Belgian Painters Born Between 1750 and 1875. Brussels: 1981. V. 54

BERKOVITS, ILONA
Illuminated Manuscripts from the Library of Matthias Corvinus. Budapest: 1964. V. 51

BERKOWITZ, DAVID S.
In Remembereance of Creation: Evolution of Art and Scholarship in the Medieval and Renaissance Bible. Waltham: 1968. V. 50

THE BERKSHIRE *Lady's Garland, In Four Parts.* N.P: 1785-1800. V. 48

BERLEPSCH, HERMANN ALEXANDER VON
The Alps or Sketches of Life and Nature in the Mountains. London: 1861. V. 48

BERLEPSCH-VALENDAS, H. E.
Dekorative Anregungen. (Decorative Inspirations). Leipzig: 1899. V. 48; 49

BERLI, AGOSTINO
Opuscoli. Parma: 1785. V. 47

BERLIC-MAZURANIC, I.
Croatian Tales of Long Ago. London: 1924. V. 47

BERLIN, C.
Hebrew Printing and Bibliography. New York: 1976. V. 50

BERLIN, IRA
Freedom: a Documentary History of Emancipation. Series II: The Black Military Experience. Cambridge: 1982. V. 53

BERLIN IRON BRIDGE CO.
Berlin Bridges and Buildings. East Berlin: 1898/99. V. 52
The Berlin Iron Bridge Co., Engineers, Architects and Builders in Iron and Steel. East Berlin: 1895. V. 52
The Berlin Iron Bridge Company. A Trade Catalogue. East Berlin: 1889. V. 52

BERLIN, ISAIAH
Historical Inevitability. London: 1954. V. 52

BERLIN, KONIGS MUSEEN. MUSEUM FUR VOLKERKUNDE
The North-West Coast of America, Being Results of Recent Enthological Researches, From the Collections of the Royal Museums at Berlin, Published by the Directors of the Ethnological Department. New York: 1883. V. 48

BERLIN, SVEN
The Dark Monarch. London: 1962. V. 53
Sven Berlin. An Artist and His Work. 1981. V. 49; 51; 53

BERLING, K.
Festive Publication to Commemorate the 200th Jubilee of the Oldest European China Factory. Dresden: 1911. V. 47

BERLIOZ, LOUIS HECTOR
Autobiography of Hector Berlioz... London: 1884. V. 54

BERLU, J. J.
The Treasury of Drugs Unlocked. London: 1724. V. 47

BERLYN, ANNIE
Rambles in Eastern England. London: 1894. V. 48
Sunrise-Land Rambles in Eastern England. London: 1894. V. 48

BERMAN, LOUIS
The Religion Called Behaviorism. New York: 1927. V. 49

BERNACCHI, L. C.
Saga of the 'Discovery'. London and Glasgow: 1938. V. 52

BERNAL, RALPH
Catalogue of the Celebrated Collection of Works of Art...of that Distinguished Collector, Ralph Bernal, March 5th, 1855. London: 1855. V. 47; 49
Illustrated Catalogue of the Distinguished Collection of Works of Art and Vertu, from the Byzantine Period to that of Louis Seize Collected by the Late Ralph Bernal, Esq. London: 1855. V. 47; 49; 52

BERNANOS, GEORGES
The Diary of a Country Priest. New York: 1986. V. 47; 48

BERNARD, APRIL
Prayers and Sermons for the Stations of the Cross. New York: 1983. V. 54

BERNARD, AUGUSTE
Geofroy Tory. Painter and Engraver... Cambridge: 1909. V. 47; 49; 51; 52; 53

BERNARD, CLAUDE
Introduction a l'Etude de la Medecine Experimentale. Paris: 1865. V. 47
An Introduction to the Study of Experimental Medicine. New York: 1927. V. 52
Lecons de Physiologie Operatoire. Paris: 1879. V. 54

BERNARD, DAVID
A Revelation of Free Masonry, As Published to the World by a Convention of Seceding Masons, Held at Le Roy, Genesee County, New York. Rochester: 1828. V. 52

BERNARD, EDWARD
Catalogi Librorum Manuscriptorum Angliae et Hiberniae in Unum Collecti cum Indice Alphabetico. Oxoniae: 1697. V. 54
De Mensuris et Ponderibus Antiquis Libri Tres. Oxoniae: 1688. V. 50; 54

BERNARD, GEORGE SMITH
War Talks of Confederate Veterans...the Battle of the Crater. Petersberg: 1892. V. 49; 53

BERNARD, JEAN FREDERIC
The Praise of Hell... London: 1760. V. 48; 49
The Praise of Hell... London: 1765. V. 48; 52; 53

BERNARD, JOHN
Retrospection of the Stage. London: 1830. V. 47

BERNARD, KENNETH
Two Stories. Mt. Horeb: 1973. V. 54

BERNARD, NICHOLAS
The Penitent Death of A Woefull Sinner. London: 1651. V. 49

BERNARD, OF CLUNY
De Contemptu mundi: a Bitter Satirical Poem of 3000 Lines Upon the Morals of the XIIth Century. London: 1929. V. 48

BERNARD, OLIVER P.
Cock Sparrow - a True Chronicle. London: 1936. V. 49

BERNARD, PHILIPPA
Antiquarian Books: a Companion for Booksellers, Librarians and Collectors. England: 1994. V. 52

BERNARD, PIERRE JOSEPH
Oeuvres... Paris: 1797. V. 47; 52

BERNARD RIVER LAND DEVELOPMENT CO.
Homestead Gardens, Almeda, Texas. Five and Ten-Acre Tracts for Homes, Orchards, Gardens and Farms. Close to Houston, Texas. Sold on Small Monthly Payments. Houston: 1910. V. 49

BERNARD, THOMAS
Spurinna or the Comforts of Old Age. London: 1816. V. 51

BERNARD, TRISTAN
Tableau de la Box. Paris: 1922. V. 47

BERNARD, W. D.
Narrative of the Voyages and Services of the Nemesis, From 1840 to 1843... London: 1844. V. 50

BERNARD DE CLAIRVAUX, SAINT
Opera Omnia. Lyons: 1520. V. 50

BERNARDIS, CALOGERO DE
Insurrection in Sicily, 1820. Sicily: 1820. V. 51

BERNARDUS, CARTHUSIENSIS
Dialogus Virginis Mariae Misericordiam Elucidans. Leipzig: 1497. V. 52

BERNATH, DESIRE DE
Celopatra, Her Life and Reign. London: 1908. V. 53

BERNATZ, JOHANN MARTIN
Bilder Aus Athiopien...In Zwei Abtheilungen. I. Aden und das Heisse Vulkanische Tiefland der Danakil. II. Das Hochland von Sud-Abyssinien oder Schoae. Hamburg: 1854. V. 50

BERNAU, J. H.
Missionary Labours in British Guiana: with Remarks on the Manners, Customs and Superstitious Rites of the Aborigines. London: 1847. V. 50

BERNDT, R. M.
Australian Aboriginal Art. Sydney: 1964. V. 50
Djanggawul. London: 1952. V. 48; 50
Kunapipi. Melbourne: 1951. V. 50
A Preliminary Report of Field Work in the Ooldea Region. Sydney: 1945. V. 50
Sexual Behavior in Western Arnhem Land. New York: 1951. V. 50

BERNE HISTORICAL MUSEUM
The North American Indian Collection. Berne: 1977. V. 54

BERNEGGER, MATHIAS
Manuale Mathematicum, Darinn Begriffen, die Tabulae Sinnum, Tangentiu(m), Secantium... Strassburg: 1619. V. 47

BERNERS, GERALD HUGH TYRWHITT-WILSON
Percy Wallingford and Mr. Pidger. Oxford: 1941. V. 52

BERNERS, JULIANA, DAME
The Boke of Saint Albans. London: 1881. V. 48
The Boke of St. Albans. London: 1901. V. 49
The Boke of Saint Albans... London: 1905. V. 47
The Treatyse of Fysshynge Wyth an Angle. London: 1827. V. 47; 48; 49; 54
Treatyse of Fysshynge Wyth an Angle. New York: 1875. V. 47
A Treatyse of Fysshynge Wyth an Angle. London: 1880. V. 47
A Treatyse of Fysshynge wyth an Angle. London: 1883. V. 49
A Treatyse of Fysshynge Wyth an Angle. 1903. V. 49; 52
A Treatyse of Fysshynge wyth an Angle. Chelsea: 1903. V. 47; 50; 51

BERNERS, LORD
The Camel. London: 1936. V. 51
Count Omega. London: 1941. V. 50; 51
A Distant Prospect, a Sequel to First Childhood. London: 1945. V. 50
Far From the Madding War. London: 1941. V. 50
First Childhood. London: 1934. V. 53

BERNHARD, RUTH
The Eternal Body: a Collection of 50 Nudes. Carmel: 1986. V. 52

BERNHARD KARL, DUKE OF SAXE-WEIMAR EISENACH
Travels through North America, During the Years 1825 and 1826. Philadelphia: 1828. V. 47

BERNHARDT, C.
Indian Raids in Lincoln County, Kansas, 1864 and 1869. Lincoln: 1910. V. 47

BERNHARDT, SARAH
Dans les Nuages. Impressions d'une Chaise. Paris: 1878. V. 52
Memoirs of My Life. New York: 1907. V. 50

BERNHEIM, BERTRAM
Blood Transfusion, Hemorrhage and the Anaemias. Philadelphia: 1917. V. 48; 53
Surgery of the Vascular System. Philadelphia: 1913. V. 48

BERNHEIM, H.
Suggestive Therapeutics. A Treatise on Nature and Uses of Hypnotism. New York: 1889. V. 47

BERNI, FRANCESCO
The Enchanted Lake of the Fairy Morgana. New York: 1806. V. 53
The Orlando. Edinburgh: 1823. V. 51

BERNIER, JOSEPH E.
Report on the Dominion of Canada Government Expedition to the Arctic Islands and Hudson Strait on Board the D.G.S. "Arctic". Ottawa: 1910. V. 53

BERNIER, R. L.
Art in California: a Survey of American Art. San Francisco: 1916. V. 47; 50; 51; 53

BERNIERES, LOUIS DE
Corelli's Mandolin. New York: 1994. V. 51
Senor Vino and the Coca Lord. London: 1991. V. 53

BERNOULLI, JAKOB
Ars Conjectandi, Opus Posthumum. Basel: 1713. V. 52

BERNSTEIN, ALINE
The Martha Washington Doll Book. 1945. V. 51
The Martha Washington Doll book. U.S.A: 1945. V. 49
Three Blue Suits. New York: 1933. V. 48; 51; 52

BERNSTEIN, HARRY
Pedro Craesbeeck & Sons, Seventeenth Century Publishers to Portugal and Brazil. Amsterdam: 1987. V. 50

BERNSTEIN, LEONARD
The Infinite Variety of Music. New York: 1966. V. 47

BEROALDUS, PHILIPPUS
De Felicitate Opusculum. Bologna: 1499. V. 47
Declamatio Lepidissima Ebriosi Scortatoris Aleatoris de Vitiositate Discepantium. Bologna: 1499. V. 52
Libellus Quo Septem Sapientum Sententia Discutiuntur. Paris: 1505. V. 48
Oratio Prouerbiorum. Paris: 1505. V. 48

BERQUIN, ARNAUD
The Children's Friend. London: 1793. V. 47
The Children's Friend. Newbury-port: 1794?. V. 49; 53
The Children's Friend... Boston: 1833. V. 49
The Friend of Youth. London: 1788. V. 52
The Looking-Glass for the Mind; or Intellectual Mirror... London: 1803. V. 52
Oeuvres de... Paris: 1848. V. 49; 50; 51

BERQUIN-DUVALLON
Travels in Louisiana and the Floridas, in the Year 1802. New York: 1806. V. 48
Vue de la Colonie Espagnole du Mississipi, ou des Provinces de Louisiane et Floride Occidentale, en l'Annee 1802. Paris: 1803. V. 48; 49; 54

BERRIAN, WILLIAM
Travels in France and Italy in 1817 and 1818. New York: 1821. V. 49

BERRIDGE, JOHN
The Christian World Unmasked. London: 1773. V. 50

BERRIGAN, DANIEL
Lost and Found. Montclair: 1989. V. 49; 50; 51; 52

BERRIGAN, TED
In a Blue River. New York: 1981. V. 49
Sonnets. New York: 1982. V. 49
Train Ride. New York: 1971. V. 48; 51

BERRIMAN, A. E.
Notes on the Materials of Motor-Car Construction. London: 1912. V. 47

BERRY, ALICE EDNA
The Bushes and the Berrys. Los Angeles: 1941. V. 54

BERRY, C. D.
Loss of the Sultana and Reminiscences of Survivors. History of a Disaster Where Over One Thousand Five Hundred Human Beings Were Lost, Most of Them being Exchanged Prisoners of War On Their Way Home After Privation and Sufferings...in Cahaba and... Lansing: 1892. V. 49

BERRY, DON
A Majority of Scoundrels: an Informal History of the Rocky Mountain Fur Company. New York: 1961. V. 52

BERRY, FRANCIS
Ghosts of Greenland. London: 1966. V. 48; 50
The Iron Christ. London: 1938. V. 49

BERRY, HARISON
A Reply to Ariel. Macon: 1869. V. 49

BERRY, JAMES
My Experiences as an Executioner. Bradford & London: 1892. V. 47

BERRY, MARY
Extracts from the Journals and Correspondence of Miss Berry, from the Years 1783 to 1852. London: 1865. V. 47; 50

BERRY, PENNY
Bricks: a Study of Brick Making and Building in East Anglia. Colchester: 1989. V. 54

BERRY, R. J.
The Natural History of Orkney. London: 1985. V. 48; 52
The Natural History of Shetland. London: 1980. V. 48; 52; 54

BERRY, ROBERT POTTER
A History of the Formation and Development of the Volunteer Infantry from the Earliest Times Illustrated by the Local Records of Huddersfield and its Vicinity from 1794 to 1894. London: 1903. V. 50

BERRY, THOMAS FRANKLIN
Four Years with Morgan and Forrest. Oklahoma City: 1914. V. 47; 49

BERRY, W. TURNER
Catalogue of Specimens of Printing Types by English and Scottish Printers and Founders 1665-1830. 1935. V. 51; 52
Catalogue of Specimens of Printing Types by English and Scottish Printers and Founders 1665-1830. London: 1935. V. 47; 48; 50

BERRY, WENDELL
The Broken Ground. New York: 1964. V. 53
Clearing. New York: 1977. V. 49; 53
An Eastward Look. Berkeley: 1974. V. 52; 53
The Farm: a Poem. 1995. V. 54
Findings. Iowa City: 1969. V. 49; 52; 53
The Long-Legged House. New York: 1969. V. 49
The Memory of Old Jack. New York: 1974. V. 48; 52; 54
Nathan Coulter. Boston: 1960. V. 47; 48; 49; 51; 53
November Twenty Six Nineteen Hundred Sixty Three. New York: 1964. V. 48; 49; 52; 53; 54
Openings. New York: 1968. V. 53
A Place on Earth. New York: 1967. V. 49
A Place on Earth. Revision. San Francisco: 1983. V. 47; 48
The Rise. Lexington: 1968. V. 47
Sayings and Doings and an Eastward Look. Frankfort: 1990. V. 52; 53
Standing On Earth. Selected Essays. Ipswich: 1941. V. 53
There Is Singing Around Me. Austin: 1976. V. 52; 53; 54
Three Memorial Poems. Berkeley: 1977. V. 47; 49; 50; 52
Travelling at Home. Lewisburg: 1988. V. 53
The Unforseen Wilderness. Lexington: 1971. V. 48
The Unsettling of America. San Francisco: 1977. V. 47; 53

BERRY, WILLIAM
County Genealogies. Pedigrees of the Families in the County of Kent. London: 1830. V. 47
The History of the Island of Guernsey, Part of the Ancient Duchy of Normandy, from the Remotest Period of Antiquity to the Year 1814. London: 1815. V. 50

BERRY-HILL, HENRY
Chinnery and China Coast Paintings. Leigh-on-Sea: 1970. V. 50; 54

BERRYMAN, JOHN
Delusions, Etc. New York: 1972. V. 50; 54
The Dispossessed. New York: 1948. V. 48; 49; 51; 53
The Dream Songs. New York: 1969. V. 51
His Thought Made Pockets & the Plane Buckt. Pawlett: 1958. V. 48; 53; 54
Homage to Mistress Bradstreet. New York: 1956. V. 47; 48; 49; 51; 52; 53; 54
Homage to Mistress Bradstreet... London: 1959. V. 50
Love and Fame. New York: 1970. V. 48; 49; 50; 51; 52
Poems. Norfolk: 1942. V. 48; 49; 52; 53
Seventy-seven Dream Songs. London: 1964. V. 52
Seventy-seven Dream Songs. New York: 1964. V. 51
Stephen Crane. New York: 1950. V. 47; 48; 53
Two Dream Songs. Season's Greetings. Kate, Martha & John Berryman. 1969. V. 48

BERSENBRUGGE, MEI-MEI
Hiddenness. Poems. New York: 1987. V. 53
Mizu. Tucson: 1990. V. 49

BERSEY, W. C.
The Motor Card Red Book, 1916. London: 1916. V. 50

BERT, PAUL
Barometric Pressure. Researches in Experimental Physiology. Columbus: 1943. V. 49; 53

BERTHA S. *Goudy, First Lady of Printing. Remembering the Distaff Side of the Village Press.* New York: 1958. V. 54

BERTHAUD, L'ABBE
Le Quadrille des Enfans ou Systeme Nouveau de Lecture. Yverdon: 1785. V. 50

BERTHELET, A.
The Use of Tools by Human and Non-Human Primates. London: 1993. V. 49

BERTHET, E.
The Pre-Historic World. 1879. V. 51

BERTHOLD, VICTOR M.
The Pioneer Steamer California, 1848-1849. Boston: 1932. V. 47; 49; 54

BERTHOLLET, CLAUDE LOUIS
Elements of the Art of Dyeing; with a Description of the Art of Bleaching by Oxymuriatic Acid. London: 1824. V. 49
Essai de Statique Chimique... Paris: 1803. V. 50

BERTHOUD, FERDINAND
De La Mesure du Temps, Ou Supplement au Traite des Horloges Marines, et a l'Essai sur l'Horlogerie... Paris: 1787. V. 53
Essai sur l'Horlogerie... Paris: 1763. V. 53
Histoire de la Mesure de Temps. Paris: 1802. V. 53

BERTHOUD, LOUIS
Entretiens sur l'Horlogerie a l'Usage de la Marine... Paris: 1812. V. 53

BERTI, ALESSANDRO P.
Catalogo Della Libreria Capponi o sia de' Libri Italiani del fu Marchese Alessandro Gregorio Capponi... Rome: 1747. V. 47

BERTILLON, ALPHONSE
Signaletic Instructions Including the Theory and Practice of Anthropometrical Identification. Chicago: 1896. V. 48

BERTIN, CHARLES
Christopher Columbus. New York: 1992. V. 51

BERTIN, R. J.
Treatise On the Diseases of the Heart. Philadelphia: 1833. V. 53

BERTOLACCI, ANTHONY
A View of the Agricultural, Commercial and Financial Interests of Ceylon. London: 1817. V. 48

BERTOLDI, GIUSEPPE
Memoirs of the Secret Societies of the South of Italy, Particularly the Carbonari. London: 1821. V. 49; 52

BERTON, PIERRE
The Klondike Quest: a Photographic Essay, 1897-99. Toronto: 1983. V. 49

BERTOTTI SCAMOZZI, OTTAVIO
Il Forestiere Istrutto Delle Cose Piu Rare di Architettura e di Alcune Pitture Della Citta di Vicenza. Vicenza: 1761. V. 53

BERTRAM, ANTHONY
Here We Ride. London: 1927. V. 50

BERTRAM, CHARLES
Britannicarum Gentium Historiae Antiquae Scriptores Tres... Havniae: 1757. V. 48

BERTRAM, JAMES G.
The Harvest of the Sea. London: 1865. V. 52

BERTRAM, JAMES G. continued
The Starlit Mire. London: 1911. V. 50

BERTRAM, R. J. S.
Old Newcastle. Newcastle-Upon-Tyne: 1916. V. 47; 53

BERTRAMUS
The Book of Bertram the Priest, Concerning the Body and Blood of Christ in the Sacrament... London: 1686. V. 52

BERTRAND, ALFRED
The Kingdom of the Barotsi Upper Zambezia. London: 1899. V. 49

BERTRAND, LOUIS JACQUES NAPOLEON
Gaspard de La Nuit. Paris: 1903. V. 54

BERTRAND DE MOLEVILLE, ANTOINE FRANCOIS
Annals of the French Revolution; or, A Chronological Account of its Principal Events; with a Variety of Anecdotes and Characters Hietherto Unpublished. London: 1800. V. 48

BERVE, HELMUT
Greek Temples, Theaters and Shrines. New York: 1962. V. 52

BERVEROVA, NINA
The Italics Are Mine. New York: 1969. V. 50

BERWICK, EDWARD
The Rawdon Papers, Consisting of Letters on Various Subjects... London: 1819. V. 47

BERWICK, JAMES FITZJAMES, DUKE OF
Memoirs of the Marshal Duke of Berwick. Edinburgh: 1707. V. 47

BERZELIUS, J. J.
The Kidneys and Urine.... Philadelphia: 1843. V. 50

BESANCON, FRANCE
Ordonnances, Reglemens et Status es Arts & Metiers de la Cite Royale de Besancon. Besancon: 1689. V. 52

BESANT, ANNIE
The Story of the Great War, Some Lessons from the Mahabharata for Use of Hindu Students in the Schools of India. London: 1899. V. 47

BESANT, WALTER
All in a Garden Fair, a Simple Story of Three Boys and a Girl. London: 1883. V. 48; 51; 54
Armorel of Lyonesse. A Romance of Today. London: 1890. V. 51; 53
The Golden Butterfly. London: 1876. V. 51
Herr Paulus: His Rise, His Greatness and His Fall. London: 1888. V. 54
The Ivory Gate. London: 1892. V. 54
London. New York: 1892. V. 52
South London. London: 1899. V. 50
The Survey of London. London: 1903-1925. V. 49
The World Went Very Well Then. London: 1887. V. 54

BESCHER, RENE FRANCOIS
Les Rois et Reines de France en Estampes, Ou Abrege Historique et Chronologique de Chaque Regne... Paris: 1826. V. 48

BESCHKE, WILLIAM
The Dreadful Sufferings and Thrilling Adventures of an Overland Party of Emigrants to California, Their Terrible conflicts with Savage Tribes of Indians!!. St. Louis: 1850. V. 51; 52
To All American Patriots. America and Europe. Washington: 1858. V. 51

BESHOAR, MICHAEL
All About Trinidad and Las Animas County Colorado. Denver: 1882. V. 49

BESLER, B.
The Besler Florilegium, Plants of the Four Seasons. New York: 1989. V. 47

BESNIER, ERNEST
A Pictorial Atlas of Skin Diseases and Syphilitic Affections in Photo-lithochromes from Models in the Museum of the Saint Louis Hospital, Paris. London: 1895/97. V. 49

BESSE, JOSEPH
An Abstract of the Sufferings of the People Called Quakers for the Testimony of a Good Conscience... London: 1733-38. V. 49
Life and Posthumous Work of Joseph Claridge, Being Memoirs and manuscripts Relating to His Experiences and Progress in Religion... London: 1726. V. 49; 54

BESSEMER, HENRY
An Autobiography. London: 1905. V. 47

BESSIE, ALVAH
The Heart of Spain. New York: 1952. V. 49
Men in Battle. A Story of Americans in Spain. New York: 1939. V. 49
The Symbol. New York: 1966. V. 54

BESSON, MAURICE
The Scourge of the Indies, Buccaneers, Corsairs & Filibusters. London: 1929. V. 52
The Scourge of the Indies, Buccaneers, Corsairs & Filibusters... New York: 1929. V. 54

THE BEST American Short Stories 1983. Boston: 1983. V. 51

BEST, ELSDON
Maori Religion and Mythology Being an Account of the Cosmogony, Anthrogeny, Religious Beliefs and Rites... Wellington: 1924. V. 50

THE BEST of the Best A Show of Concern to Benefit AIDS Research and Care Metropolitan Opera House at Lincoln Center Sunday, Nov. 3, 1985. New York: 1985. V. 50

THE BEST Plays 1894-1895 to 1986-1987. V. 54

THE BEST Plays of 1960-1961...(1988-1989). New York: 1961-89. V. 54

BEST Radio Plays of 1982; The Giles Cooper Award Winners. London: 1983. V. 54

BEST, SAMUEL
Notes On Building and Road-Making, with Rules for Estimating Repairs to Tanks and Channels. Madras: 1856. V. 49

THE BEST Short Stories of 1937. Boston: 1937. V. 49

BEST, THOMAS
The Art of Angling. London: 1814. V. 47
A Concise Treatise on the Art of Angling... London: 1798. V. 47
A Concise Treatise on the Art of Angling. London: 1804. V. 47
A Concise Treatise on the Art of Angling. London: 1807. V. 49; 54
A Concise Treatise on the Art of Angling... Market Drayton: 1992. V. 49; 50; 52
A Concise Treatise on the Art of Angling. Shropshire: 1992. V. 51

BEST, WILLIAM
The Merit and Reward of a Good Intention. London: 1742. V. 52

BESTARICK, D. D.
Hawaii 1778-1920 from the Viewpoint of a Bishop Being the Story of English and American Churchmen in Hawaii with Historical Sidelights. Honolulu: 1924. V. 47

BESTER, ALFRED
The Demolished Man. 1953. V. 47; 48; 49; 51; 52; 53; 54
The Demolished Man. Chicago: 1953. V. 54
Tiger! Tiger!. 1956. V. 47

BESTER, JOHN
Tiger! Tiger!. London: 1956. V. 54

BESTERMAN, THEODORE
Old Art Books Collected and Catalogued By... London: 1975. V. 48
The Pilgrim Fathers, a Journal of Their Coming in the Mayflower to New England and Their Life and Adventures There. 1939. V. 47
The Pilgrim Fathers, a Journal of Their Coming in the Mayflower to New England and Their Life and Adventures There. Waltham St. Lawrence: 1939. V. 50; 53
A World Bibliography of Bibliographies and of Bibliographical Catalogues, Calendars, Abstracts, Digests, Indexes... London: 1947-49. V. 49
A World Bibliography of Bibliographies and of Bibliographical Catalogues, Calendars, Abstracts, Digests, Indexes... Geneva: 1955-56. V. 49; 51
A World Bibliography of Bibliographies and of Bibliographical Catalogues, Calendars, Abstracts, Digests, Indexes... Lausanne: 1956-66. V. 54
A World Bibliography of Bibliographies and of Bibliographical Catalogues, Calendars, Abstracts, Digests, Indexes... Lausanne: 1965. V. 54

BESTON, HENRY
Herbs and the Earth. Garden City: 1935. V. 51

BETENSON, LULA
Butch Cassidy My Brother. Provo: 1975. V. 53

BETHAM, GEOFFREY
The Golden Gallery. The Story of the Second Punjab Regiment 1761-1947. Oxford: 1956. V. 50

BETHAM, MARY MATILDA
A Biographical Dictionary of the Celebrated Women of Every Age and Country. London: 1804. V. 52; 53; 54
The Lay of Marie: a Poem. London: 1816. V. 50

BETHAM, WILLIAM
The Gael & Cymbri; or An Inquiry into the Origin...of the Irish Scoti, Britons and Gauls. London: 1834. V. 47
Irish Antiquarian Researches. Dublin: 1826-27. V. 54

BETHEL BAPTIST ASSOCIATION
Minutes of the Thirteenth Bethel Baptist Association, Held at Mt. Zion, Todd County, Kentucky, on the 23d, 24th & 25th days of September 1837. Russellville: 1837. V. 50

BETHEL, SLINGSBY
The Interest of Princes and States. London: 1680. V. 54
The Interest of the Princes and States of Europe. London: 1681. V. 52
The World's Mistake in Oliver Cromwell; or, a Short Political Discourse, Shewing that Cromwell's Mal-administration, (During His Four Years, and Nine Months Pretended protectorship)... London: 1668. V. 50; 54

BETHUNE, GEORGE A.
The Uncertainties of Travel. Boston: 1880. V. 47

BETHUNE, GEORGE W.
British Female Poets with Biographical and Critical Notices. Philadelphia: 1849. V. 49; 51

BETJEMAN, JOHN
Antiquarian Prejudice. London: 1939. V. 50
Church Poems. London: 1980. V. 49
Collected Poems. London: 1958. V. 51; 52
Continual Dew - a Little Book of Boureois Verse. London: 1937. V. 49
Devon. London: 1936. V. 50
A Few Late Chrysanthemums. London: 1954. V. 48; 50; 51
First and Last Loves. London: 1952. V. 50
Ghastly Good Taste. London: 1933. V. 49; 50; 51; 52
Ghastly Good Taste... 1970. V. 49
Ghastly Good Taste... London: 1970. V. 51; 52

BETJEMAN, JOHN continued
Ground Plan to Skyline. London: 1960. V. 53
High and Low. London: 1966. V. 48; 49; 50; 51
London's Historic Railway Stations. London: 1972. V. 50
Metro-Land. Verses. London: 1977. V. 53
Moments of Truth - Nineteen Short Poems by Living Poets. London: 1965. V. 50
Mount Zion or In Touch with the Infinite. 1931. V. 49
Mount Zion or In Touch with the Infinite. London: 1931. V. 53
Murray's Buckinghamshire Architectural Guide. London: 1948. V. 54
New Bats in Old Belfries. London: 1945. V. 53
A Nip in the Air. London: 1974. V. 48; 50; 53
An Oxford University Chest, Comprising a Description of the Present State of the Town and University of Oxford, With an Itinerary Arranged Alphabetically. London: 1938. V. 48
A Ring of Bells - Poems of John Betjeman. London: 1962. V. 47
Selected Poems. London: 1948. V. 49
Sir John Piers. London: 1938. V. 49
Slick but not Streamlined. Poems and Short (Prose) Pieces. New York: 1947. V. 48
Summoned by Bells. London: 1960. V. 50; 53; 54
Uncollected Poems. 1982. V. 49
Uncollected Poems. London: 1982. V. 53
Victorian and Edwardian Oxford from Old Photographs. London: 1971. V. 50

THE BETRAYAL of the Left. London: 1941. V. 52

BETT, W. R.
A Short History of Some Common Diseases. London: 1934. V. 50

BETTEN, H. L.
Upland Game Shooting. V. 47

BETTENCOURT PITTA, NICOLAU CAETANO
Account of the Island of Madeira. London: 1812. V. 53

BETTERTON, THOMAS
The History of the English Stage... London: 1741. V. 51
The History of the English Stage. Boston: 1814. V. 49
The Life of Mr. Thomas Betterton, the Late Eminent Tragedian. London: 1710. V. 48; 52

BETTI, BENEDETTO
Orazione Fvnerale...Nelle Esequie dei Sereniss. Cosimo Medici Gran Duca di Toscana Celebrate il di 13. di Giugnio 1574... Florence: 1574. V. 48

BETTI, GIOVANNI BATTISTA
A'Dilettanti delle Bell'Arti. Firenze: 1785. V. 49; 53

BETTRIDGE, WILLIAM
A Brief History of the Church in Upper Canada... London: 1838. V. 52

BETTS, ALEXANDER DAVIS
Experiences of a Confederate Chaplain, 1864-1864. Sanford. V. 47

BETTS, DORIS
The Gentle Insurrection and Other Stories. New York: 1954. V. 47; 49; 50; 52
The Insurrection. New York: 1954. V. 50

BETTY Bolaine: the History of Betty Bolaine the Canterbury Miser. Rochester: 1825. V. 50

BETTY, WILLIAM HENRY WEST
The Young Roscius. New York: 1806. V. 50

BETZINEZ, JASON
I Fought With Geronimo. Harrisburg: 1959. V. 50

BEUBE, DOUGLAS
24 Hours a Day. New York: 1991. V. 54

BEUGHEM, CORNELIUS
Syllabus Recens Exploratorum in re Medica Physica & Chemica Prout in Miscellaneis Medico-Physicis Nature Curiosorum Germaniae, Galliae, Daniae, Belgii Sparsim Extant. Amsterdam: 1696. V. 47

BEURDELEY, CECILE
L'Amour Bleu. New York: 1978. V. 53; 54

BEURDELEY, MICHEL
The Chinese Collector Through the Centuries from the Han to the 20th Century. Fribourg: 1966. V. 52
Porcelain of the East India Company. London: 1962. V. 48; 54

BEUTEL, TOBIAS
Churfuerstlicher Saechsischer stets Gruenender hoher Cedern-Wald...Electorale Saonicum...Cedretum. Dresden: 1683. V. 47

BEUYS, JOSEPH
Joseph Beuys Drawings. London: 1983. V. 49

BEVAN, ANEURIN
What We Saw In Russia. London: 1931. V. 51

BEVAN, EDWARD
The Honey Bee. London: 1870. V. 51

BEVAN, EDWYN R.
The House of Seleucus. London: 1902. V. 48

BEVAN, JOSEPH GURNEY
Memoirs of the Life of Isaac Penington: To Which is Added a Review of His Writings. London: 1807. V. 47

BEVAN, WILLIAM
York Illustrated In a Series of Views. London: 1850. V. 48; 51
York Illustrated in a Series of Views. York: 1850. V. 47; 50

BEVER, THOMAS
The History of the Legal Polity of the Roman State an of the Rise, Progress and Extent of the Roman Laws. London: 1781. V. 51

BEVERIDGE, ALBERT JEREMIAH
Abraham Lincoln 1809-1858. Boston and New York: 1928. V. 48; 53; 54
The Life of John Marshall. Boston and New York: 1916. V. 50
The Life of John Marshall. Boston: 1919. V. 52
The Life of John Marshall. New York: 1980. V. 51

BEVERIDGE, WILLIAM
Institutionum Chronologicarum Libri II, Una Cum Totidem Arithmetices Chronologicae Libellis... London: 1705. V. 53

BEVERIDGE, WILLIAM H.
Social Insurance and Allied Services. London: 1942. V. 48; 50
Unemployment - a Problem of Industry. London: 1931. V. 52

BEVERLEY, ROBERT
Historie de la Virginie: Contenant, I. L'Histoire du Premier Etablissement dans la Virginie... Paris: 1707. V. 47
The History and Present State of Virginia, in Four Parts. London: 1705. V. 47; 48; 53
The History of Virginia, in Four Parts... London: 1722. V. 47; 49; 54

BEVERLEY, THOMAS
A Catholick Catechism: shewing the Impossibility the Catholick Religion Should Be Varied to a Degree of a Thought... London: 1683. V. 53
The Whole Duty of Nations. London: 1681. V. 53
The Woe of Scandal. London: 1682. V. 53

BEVERLY, BOB
Hobo of the Rangeland. Lovingston. V. 52

BEVERWYCK, JAN VAN
De Calcvi Renum et Vesicae Singularia. Leyden: 1638. V. 47

BEVIER, ROBERT S.
History of the First and Second Missouri Confederate Brigades 1861-1865. St. Louis: 1879. V. 49

BEWER, D. S.
The Thornton Manuscript. 1978. V. 53

BEWICK, ELIZABETH
Comfort Me with Apples and Other Poems. 1987. V. 47; 52; 54
Comfort Me with Apples and Other Poems. London: 1987. V. 50

BEWICK, JOHN
Tales for Youth: in Thirty Poems... London: 1794. V. 48

BEWICK, JOSEPH
Geological Treatise on the District of Cleveland in North Yorkshire, Its Ferruginous Deposits, Lias, and Oolites; with Some Observations on Ironstone Mining. London: 1861. V. 48

BEWICK Memento. London. V. 54

BEWICK, THOMAS
Bewick's British Birds. Newcastle-upon-Tyne: 1817. V. 48
Bewick's Select Fables. New Hampshire: 1965. V. 53
Bewick's Select Fables of Aesop and Others. London: 1871. V. 50; 54
Bewick's Select Fables of Aesop and Others. London: 1886. V. 54
The British Champion; or, Honour Rewarded. York: 1795?. V. 53
Figures on British Land Birds. Newcastle-upon-Tyne: 1800. V. 50
A General History of Quadrupeds. London: 1790. V. 53; 54
A General History of Quadrupeds. Newcastle-upon-Tyne: 1790. V. 48; 50; 52
A General History of Quadrupeds. London: 1791. V. 51; 52; 53; 54
A General History of Quadrupeds. Newcastle-upon-Tyne: 1791. V. 48; 50
A General History of Quadrupeds. Newcastle-upon-Tyne: 1792. V. 50; 53
A General History of Quadrupeds. Newcastle-upon-Tyne: 1800. V. 48; 49
A General History of Quadrupeds... London: 1807. V. 51; 54
A General History of Quadrupeds. London: 1811. V. 52; 53
A General History of Quadrupeds. Newcastle-upon-Tyne: 1811. V. 48; 51
A General History of Quadrupeds. Newcastle-upon-Tyne: 1820. V. 49; 50; 51
A General History of Quadrupeds. Newcastle-upon-Tyne: 1824. V. 48; 50
History of British Birds. Newcastle-upon-Tyne: 1797. V. 52; 54
History of British Birds. London: 1797-1804. V. 53; 54
History of British Birds. Newcastle: 1797-1804. V. 47; 48; 50; 51; 53; 54
History of British Birds... London: 1797-1807. V. 54
History of British Birds. Newcastle-Upon-Tyne: 1804. V. 48; 49; 50; 53
A History of British Birds. London: 1809. V. 52
A History of British Birds. Newcastle-upon-Tyne: 1809. V. 48; 49; 50; 53
A History of British Birds. London: 1809-21. V. 52; 53
The History of British Birds. Newcastle-upon-Tyne: 1816. V. 48; 54
A History of British Birds. Newcastle: 1826. V. 48; 50; 54
A History of British Birds. London: 1832. V. 51
A History of British Birds. Newcastle-upon-Tyne: 1832. V. 53
A History of British Birds. Newcastle: 1847. V. 50; 51; 53
A History of British Birds. Volume 2 (only). Newcastle: 1826. V. 49
Memoir of Thomas Bewick. London: 1924. V. 50

BEWICK, THOMAS continued
Memoir of Thomas Bewick Written by Himself. London: 1862. V. 48
A Memoir of Thomas Bewick, Written by Himself. Newcastle-upon-Tyne: 1862. V. 48
Memorial Edition of Thomas Bewick's Works. London: 1885-87. V. 50
A Portfolio of Thomas Bewick Wood Engravings. Chicago: 1970. V. 47
Select Fables. Newcastle: 1820. V. 54
Select Fables: With Cuts Designed and Engraved by Thomas and John Bewick. London: 1820. V. 49
Select Fables: with Cuts Designed and Engraved by Thomas and John Bewick. Newcastle: 1820. V. 49; 51; 54
Thomas Bewick's ABC. New York: 1926. V. 52
The Watercolours and Drawings of Thomas Bewick. Cambridge: 1981. V. 49; 53
The Watercolours and Drawings of Thomas Bewick... London: 1981. V. 51
The Watercolours and Drawings of Thomas Bewick. USA: 1981. V. 52
The Watercolours of Thomas Bewick. London: 1981. V. 50
Wood Engravings... London: 1953. V. 53
Wood Engravings. Newcastle-upon-Tyne: 1978. V. 52
The Works of Thomas Bewick. Newcastle-upon-Tyne: 1822. V. 48

BEWICK, WILLIAM
Life and Letters of William Bewick, Artist. London: 1871. V. 48

BEWLEY, GEORGE
The Examiner Examined. London: 1781. V. 53

BEYER, HARTMANN
Quaestiones Novae in Libellum de Sphaera. Parisiis: 1551. V. 47

BEYLE, MARIE HENRI
La Chartreuse de Parme. New York: 1895. V. 53
La Chartreuse De Parme. London: 1896. V. 53
The Chartreuse of Parma. New York: 1925. V. 51
The Life of Haydn, in a Series of Letters Written at Vienna. Followed by the Life of Mozart, with Observations on Metastasio, and on the Present State of Music in France and Italy. London: 1817. V. 48
On Love. New York: 1916. V. 48

BEZA, THEODORE
Poematum. Geneva: 1569. V. 51

BEZOUT, ETIENNE
Theorie Generale des Equations Algebriques. Paris: 1779. V. 47

BEZZERIDES, A. I.
Long Haul. New York: 1938. V. 51

BHAGAVAD GITA
Bhagavad Gita: The Son Celestial. Bombay: 1965. V. 53

BHAT, K. S.
Soma - Number Three. London: 1932. V. 49

BHUSHAN, JAMILA BRIJ
Indian Jewellery, Ornaments and Decorative Designs. Bombay: 1955. V. 53

BIALOSTOCKI, JAN
The Art of the Renaissance in Eastern Europe - Hungary Bohemia, Poland. Oxford: 1976. V. 49

BIANCHI, DANIEL BERKELEY
The Merrymount Press. A Centenary Keepsake. V. 48

BIANCHI, MARC ANTONIO
Tractatus de Indiciis Homicidii ex Proposito Commissi & de Alijs Indicijs Homicidij & Furti... Lugduni: 1546. V. 51

BIANCHI, V.
Aves Expeditionis P.K. Kozlowi per Mongoliam et Tibetiam Orientalem 1899-1901. St. Petersberg: 1907. V. 51

BIANCHI BANDINELLI, RANUCCIO
Rome, the Center of Power, 500 B.C. to A.D. 200. New York: 1970. V. 53; 54

BIANCHINI, FRANCESCO
Camera ed Inscrizioni Sepulcrali De' Liberti, Servi, de Ufficiali della Casa di Augusto Scoperte nella Via Appia... Roma: 1727. V. 47

BIANCHINO, GLORIA
Italian Fashion. New York: 1987. V. 53

BIANCO, MARGERY WILLIAMS
The Adventures of Andy. New York: 1927. V. 48
The Hurdy-Gurdy Man. New York: 1933. V. 47
Poor Cecco: The Wonderful Story of a Wonderful Wooden Dog. New York: 1925. V. 47
The Skin Horse. New York: 1927. V. 53

BIBB, HENRY
Narrative of the Life and Adventures of Henry Bibb, an American Slave. New York: 1849. V. 50

THE BIBELOT. New York. V. 49

BIBER, EDWARD
Life and Trials of Henry Pestalozzi... Philadelphia: 1833. V. 51

BIBIENA, FERDINANDO GALLI
L'Archiecture Civile Preparata Su La Feometria, E. Rideotta Alle Prosettive, Considerazioni Pratiche... Parma: 1711. V. 47

BIBLE. ACCRA - 1872
The New Testament in Accra (West Africa). Basle: 1872. V. 48

BIBLE. ARABIC - 1776
(Bible. New Testament, Arabic, Gospels.). Mt. Kerouan, Lebanon: 1776. V. 49; 52

BIBLE. ARMENO-TURKISH - 1831
The New Testament in Armenian Character. Malta: 1831. V. 49

BIBLE. BLACKFOOT - 1890
The Gospel According to St. Matthew. Translated into the Language of the Blackfoot Indians. London: 1890. V. 49; 52

BIBLE. BRAILLE - 1850
The Book of Nehemiah, in Embossed Type for the Blind. Brighton: 1850. V. 49

BIBLE. CHEROKEE - 1850
The Book of Isaiah in Cherokee Language. Park Hill: 1850. V. 48

BIBLE. CHEROKEE - 1856
Genesis or the First Book of Moses. Park Hill: 1856. V. 47

BIBLE. CREE - 1876
The New Testament Translated Into the Cree Language. London: 1876. V. 52

BIBLE. DAKOTA - 1887
Dakota, Wowapi Wakan. The Holy Bible, in the Language of the Dakotas. New York: 1887. V. 49

BIBLE. DUTCH - 1557
Ghesneden Figveren Vvy ten Ouden (Nieuvven) Testamente. Lyons: 1557. V. 54

BIBLE. DUTCH - 1583
Bible in Dutch. Tot Dordrecht: 1583. V. 50

BIBLE. DUTCH - 1701
Biblia Dat is, De Gantsche H. Schrifture Vervattende Alle de Boecken des Ouden Ende Nieuwen testaments. Amsterdam: 1701-03. V. 49

BIBLE. DUTCH - 1855
Al de Boeken van het Oude Testament.... (with) Al de Boeken van het Nieuwe Testament. Gouda: 1855-56. V. 51

BIBLE. ENGLISH
The Book of Psalms. New York. V. 51
Ecclesiastes, or the Preacher and The Song of Solomon. London. V. 50
The Large-Print Paragraph Bible...The New Testament. London. V. 52
The Song of Songs. London. V. 48

BIBLE. ENGLISH - 1560
Here Beginneth the Epistles & Gospels, of Euery Sunday and Holday Day in the Yeare. London: 1560. V. 50

BIBLE. ENGLISH - 1572
Apocrypha, Extracted from the Second Folio Edition of the Bishop's Bible of 1572. London: 1572. V. 51

BIBLE. ENGLISH - 1578
Bible in English. (Geneva Version). London: 1578. V. 50

BIBLE. ENGLISH - 1579
Bible in English. New Testament. (Geneva-Tomson Version.). London: 1579. V. 50

BIBLE. ENGLISH - 1582
Bible in English. New Testament (Rheims Version). Rheims: 1582. V. 47; 50

BIBLE. ENGLISH - 1589
Bible in English. New Testament. London: 1589. V. 50

BIBLE. ENGLISH - 1594
The Whole Booke of Psalmes, Collected Into English... London: 1594. V. 48; 51

BIBLE. ENGLISH - 1597
The Bible, That is, The Holy Scriptures Conteined in the Olde and New Testament. London: 1597. V. 50

BIBLE. ENGLISH - 1600
Bible in English. New Testament (Rheims Version). Antwerp: 1600. V. 50

BIBLE. ENGLISH - 1601
Bible in English. New Testament. (Fulke Version). London: 1601. V. 50; 53

BIBLE. ENGLISH - 1609
The Holie Bible Faithfully Translated into English Out of the Authentical Latin... (with) The New Testament of Jesus Christ Faithfully Translated. Rouen: 1609/35/1600. V. 49

BIBLE. ENGLISH - 1611
The Bible. London: 1611. V. 50

BIBLE. ENGLISH - 1613
Bible in English. (King James Version). London: 1613. V. 50

BIBLE. ENGLISH - 1616
The Bible, That Is the Holy Scriptures Contained in the Old and New Testament. London: 1616. V. 50

BIBLE. ENGLISH - 1619
The New Testament. (with) The Whole Booke of Pslames. London: 1619-20. V. 47

BIBLE. ENGLISH - 1629
Bible in English. (King James Version). Cambridge: 1629. V. 50

BIBLE. ENGLISH - 1630
The Whole Booke of Psalmes Collected into English Meeter by T. Sternhold, I. Hopkins and others. London: 1630. V. 51

BIBLE. ENGLISH - 1631
Bible in English. (King James Version). London: 1631. V. 50
The New Testament of Our Lord and Saviour Jesus Christ. London: 1631. V. 50

BIBLE. ENGLISH - 1634
Bible in English. (King James Version). London: 1634. V. 50

BIBLE. ENGLISH - 1635
The Second Tome of the Holy Bible. London: 1635. V. 47
The Whole Booke of Psalmes Collected into English Meeter by T. Sternhold, I. Hopkins and Others. London: 1635. V. 49; 51; 52

BIBLE. ENGLISH - 1636
The New Testament... Edinburgh: 1636. V. 54

BIBLE. ENGLISH - 1637
Bible in English. (King James Version). 1637. V. 50

BIBLE. ENGLISH - 1638
Bible in English. (King James Version, Corrected). Cambridge;: 1638. V. 50

BIBLE. ENGLISH - 1640
The Holy Bible. London: 1640. V. 50

BIBLE. ENGLISH - 1647
The Holy Bible... London: 1647. V. 48

BIBLE. ENGLISH - 1667
Le Nouveau Testament. Amsterdam: 1667. V. 51

BIBLE. ENGLISH - 1668
The Holy Bible Containing the Old Testament and the New... Cambridge: 1668. V. 52

BIBLE. ENGLISH - 1671
The Holy Bible, Containing the Old Testament and the New. London: 1671. V. 49

BIBLE. ENGLISH - 1672
The Holy Bible. London: 1672. V. 50

BIBLE. ENGLISH - 1678
The New Testament of Our Lord and Saviour Jesus Christ... London: 1678. V. 50

BIBLE. ENGLISH - 1683
The Holy Bible containing the Old Testament and New. Cambridge: 1683. V. 50

BIBLE. ENGLISH - 1685
The Holy Bible Containing the Old Testament and the New... London: 1685. V. 49; 53

BIBLE. ENGLISH - 1687
The Holy Bible in Shorthand. 1687. V. 47

BIBLE. ENGLISH - 1714
The Holy Bible. Edinburgh: 1714. V. 50; 52

BIBLE. ENGLISH - 1715
The Holy Bible. Edinburgh: 1715. V. 54

BIBLE. ENGLISH - 1727
Biblia, or a Practical Summery of ye Old and New Testaments. London: 1727. V. 53
Holy Bible Containing the Old and New Testaments. Oxford: 1727. V. 54

BIBLE. ENGLISH - 1735
The Holy Bible Containing the Old Testament and the New. London: 1735. V. 48

BIBLE. ENGLISH - 1746
The Holy Bible, Containing the Old and New Testaments... Oxford: 1746. V. 48; 49

BIBLE. ENGLISH - 1759
An Illustration of the New Testament... London: 1759. V. 52; 53

BIBLE. ENGLISH - 1763
The Holy Bible. Containing the Old Testament and the New... Cambridge: 1763. V. 50

BIBLE. ENGLISH - 1764
The Song of Solomon, Newly Translated from the Original Hebrew. London: 1764. V. 47

BIBLE. ENGLISH - 1765
The Holy Bible. Oxford: 1765. V. 47
The Psalms, Translated or Paraphrased in English Verse. Reading: 1765. V. 47; 48

BIBLE. ENGLISH - 1772
The Holy Bible. Containing the Old and New Testaments... (with) The Psalms of David in Metre... Edinburgh: 1772/72. V. 51

BIBLE. ENGLISH - 1774
The Holy Bible, Containing the Old Testament and New. Oxford: 1774. V. 53

BIBLE. ENGLISH - 1778
The Holy Bible... Edinburgh: 1778. V. 50

BIBLE. ENGLISH - 1780
The Bible in Miniature, or a Concise History of the Old and New Testaments. London: 1780. V. 50; 52; 54

BIBLE. ENGLISH - 1785
The Complete Family Bible. London: 1785. V. 48

BIBLE. ENGLISH - 1788
The Holy Bible, Containing the Old and New Testaments and Also the Apocrypha. Birmingham: 1788. V. 47

BIBLE. ENGLISH - 1791
The Holy Bible. Edinburgh: 1791. V. 51
The Holy Bible, Containing the Old and New Testaments. Trenton: 1791. V. 47; 48; 50; 51

BIBLE. ENGLISH - 1792
The Holy Bible Containing the Old and New Testaments (Also Contains the Apocrypha). London: 1792. V. 53

BIBLE. ENGLISH - 1795
The Holy Bible Ornamented With Engravings, by James Fittler From Celebrated Pictures by Old Masters. The Letter Press by Thomas Bensley. London: 1795. V. 48

BIBLE. ENGLISH - 1796
The Holy Bible, Containing the Old and New Testaments. Cambridge: 1796. V. 51

BIBLE. ENGLISH - 1797
The Holy Bible Abridged; or, the History of the Old and New Testament. Wilmington: 1797. V. 48

BIBLE. ENGLISH - 1800
The Old Testament (New Testament), Embellished with Engravings from Pictures and Designs by the Most Eminent English Artists. London: 1800. V. 47; 51

BIBLE. ENGLISH - 1801
The Family Testament and Learner's Assistant. London and Coventry: 1801. V. 51

BIBLE. ENGLISH - 1802
The Holy Bible. Philadelphia: 1802. V. 47

BIBLE. ENGLISH - 1805
Abridgment of the New Testament, or the Life Miracles and Death of Our Lord & Saviour Jesus Christ. Glasgow: 1805-15. V. 51

BIBLE. ENGLISH - 1807
Bible. New York: 1807-06. V. 51
Universal Family Bible: or, Christian's Divine Library Containing the Sacred Texts of the Old and New Testaments. London: 1807. V. 53

BIBLE. ENGLISH - 1808
The Holy Bible, Containing the Old and New Covenant, Commonly Called the Old and New Testament. Philadelphia: 1808. V. 47; 53

BIBLE. ENGLISH - 1809
The Holy Bible. Philaldelphia: 1809. V. 53

BIBLE. ENGLISH - 1811
The Holy Bible Abridged or the History of the Old and New Testament... Boston: 1811. V. 51
The Holy Bible, Containing the Old and New Testaments. Edinburgh: 1811. V. 47

BIBLE. ENGLISH - 1812
The Holy Bible, Containing the Old and New Testaments, According to the Publick Version... London: 1812. V. 50

BIBLE. ENGLISH - 1815
The Book of Psalms. London: 1815. V. 52
The Holy Bible Containing the Old and New Testaments, and the Apocrypha. London: 1815/14. V. 49; 52

BIBLE. ENGLISH - 1816
Miniature Bible, or Abstract of Sacred History. Brattleborough: 1816. V. 50
The Old (and New) Testaments Embellished with Engravings. Together with the Apocrypha. London: 1800/16. V. 49; 50

BIBLE. ENGLISH - 1821
A Miniature History of the Holy Bible, Embellished with Nearly 50 Engravings. Hartford: 1821. V. 47; 51

BIBLE. ENGLISH - 1822
The Columbian Family, and Pulpit Bible... Boston: 1822. V. 51

BIBLE. ENGLISH - 1823
The Holy Bible, Containing the Old and New Testaments; Together with the Apocrypha. New York: 1823. V. 52
The Psalmes of David. London: 1823. V. 48

BIBLE. ENGLISH - 1824
The Devotional Diamond Pocket Bible. (with) The Devotional Diamond Testament. London: 1824/1816. V. 52

BIBLE. ENGLISH - 1827
The Holy Bible... Oxford: 1827. V. 51

BIBLE. ENGLISH - 1830
The Holy Bible. Oxford: 1830. V. 53
The New Testament. Pittsburgh: 1830. V. 50

BIBLE. ENGLISH - 1832
The First Epistle of Paul the Apostle to Timothy. London: 1832. V. 50; 51

BIBLE. ENGLISH - 1835
The Book of the Prophet Jeremiah and Lamentations. London: 1835. V. 50

BIBLE. ENGLISH - 1837
Psalms of David in Metre. London: 1837. V. 47

BIBLE. ENGLISH - 1838
The Holy Scriptures, Faithfully and Truly Translated by Myles Coverdale, Bishop of Exeter, 1535. London: 1838. V. 49

BIBLE. ENGLISH - 1840
Miniature Bible with Engravings. Philadelphia: 1840. V. 51

BIBLE. ENGLISH - 1841
The Holy Bible, Containing the Old and New Testaments... Oxford: 1841. V. 47; 49

BIBLE. ENGLISH - 1844
The Imperial Holy Bible Containing the Old and New Testaments According to the Authorised Version. London: 1844. V. 48
The Sermon on the Mount. London: 1844. V. 53

BIBLE. ENGLISH - 1846
The Illuminated Bible, Containing the Old and New Testaments... New York: 1846. V. 47

BIBLE. ENGLISH - 1847
Parables of Our Lord. London: 1847. V. 51

BIBLE. ENGLISH - 1848
The New Testament in English Translated by John Wycliffe Circa MCCCLXXX. London: 1848. V. 47; 51

BIBLE. ENGLISH - 1849
The Preacher. London: 1849. V. 51
The Thumb Bible. London: 1849. V. 52

BIBLE. ENGLISH - 1850
The Book of Ruth, from the Holy Scriptures. London: 1850. V. 51
The Holy Bible (King James). London: 1850?. V. 47; 48

BIBLE. ENGLISH - 1853
The Holy Bible, Containing the Old and New Testaments. Oxford: 1853. V. 49

BIBLE. ENGLISH - 1854
The Twenty-Four Books of the Holy Scriptures. Philadelphia: 1854. V. 53

BIBLE. ENGLISH - 1857
The Holy Bible. London: 1857. V. 49

BIBLE. ENGLISH - 1861
The Holy Bible, Containing the Old and New Testaments. London: 1861. V. 50
The New Testament of Our Lord and Saviour Jesus Christ. Nashville: 1861. V. 48
The Psalms of David Illuminated by Owen Jones. London: 1861-62. V. 48; 50
The Sermon on the Mount. London: 1861. V. 50; 52; 54
The Victoria Psalter...or Psalms of David. London: 1861. V. 51

BIBLE. ENGLISH - 1861.
The Victoria Psalter...Psalms of David. 1861. V. 51

BIBLE. ENGLISH - 1862
The Psalms of David. London: 1862. V. 47; 49

BIBLE. ENGLISH - 1865
The New Testament of Our Lord and Saviour Jesus Christ. London: 1865. V. 47; 50; 52

BIBLE. ENGLISH - 1866
The Holy Bible Containing the Old and New Testaments. London: 1866-70?. V. 49; 54

BIBLE. ENGLISH - 1867
Golden Verses from the New Testament with Illuminations and Miniatures From Celebrated Missals and Books of Hours of the XIV and XV Centuries. London: 1867. V. 49; 51
The Victoria Psalter. The Pslams of David Illuminated By Owen Jones. London: 1867. V. 48

BIBLE. ENGLISH - 1870
The Child's Bible. London: 1870. V. 50

BIBLE. ENGLISH - 1876
The Holy Bible: Containing the Old and New Testaments. Hartford: 1876. V. 47; 49; 53

BIBLE. ENGLISH - 1880
Brown's Self-Interpreting Family Bible: Containing the Old and New Testaments. Southport: 1880. V. 51
The National Comprehensive Family Bible, Holy Bible with the Commentaries of Scott and Henry... London: 1880. V. 51
The Self-Interpretating Bible. Containing the Old and New Testaments. London: 1880. V. 54

BIBLE. ENGLISH - 1881
The Bible Containing the Old New Testaments. Oxford: 1881. V. 51

BIBLE. ENGLISH - 1882
The New Testament... London: 1882. V. 47
The Old Testament... New York: 1882. V. 47

BIBLE. ENGLISH - 1885
Biblia Pauperum. (i.e. Selections from the New Testament). London: 1885. V. 54

BIBLE. ENGLISH - 1887
The Song of Songs. Philadelphia: 1887. V. 52

BIBLE. ENGLISH - 1894
Psalmi Penitentiales. Hammersmith: 1894. V. 50

BIBLE. ENGLISH - 1896
The Book of Job. London: 1896. V. 51; 53
Book of Ruth and the Book of Esther. London: 1896. V. 47
The Book of Rvth Pictvred and Designed by W. B. MacDougall. New York: 1896. V. 48
The Holy Bible. Glasgow: 1896. V. 53
The Journal of Koheleth Being a Reprint of the Book of Ecclesiastes. East Aurora: 1896. V. 50
The Song of Songs Which is Solomons. East Aurora: 1896. V. 53

BIBLE. ENGLISH - 1897
The Book of Ruth and the Book of Esther. New York: 1897. V. 47; 49
The Song of Solomon. London: 1897. V. 47; 51; 53

BIBLE. ENGLISH - 1901
The Holy Bible, Containing the Old and New Testaments... Glasgow: 1901. V. 49; 52

BIBLE. ENGLISH - 1902
Ecclesiastes; or, the Preacher and the Song of Solomon. London: 1902. V. 47
Ecclesiastes; or, the Preacher and the Song of Solomon. 1902. V. 53
The Psalter or Psalms of David from the Bible of Archbishop Cranmer. London: 1902. V. 48
The Song of Songs Which is Solomon's. 1902. V. 54

BIBLE. ENGLISH - 1903
The English Bible. 1903-05. V. 48; 49; 50
The English Bible. Hammersmith: 1903-05. V. 50; 51
The New Testament. Glasgow: 1903. V. 49
The Parables from the Gospels. 1903. V. 51
The Parables from the Gospels. London: 1903. V. 50; 52

BIBLE. ENGLISH - 1904
The Book of Ruth. Indianapolis: 1904. V. 50
A Book of Songs and Poems from the Old Testament and the Apocrypha. 1904. V. 47
A Book of Songs and Poems from the Old Testament and the Apocrypha. Chelsea: 1904. V. 52; 54
The Holy Bible. London: 1904. V. 47
(The Four Gospels). Matthew; Mark; Luke; John. London: 1904. V. 50

BIBLE. ENGLISH - 1906
Ecclesiastes. Boston: 1906. V. 54

BIBLE. ENGLISH - 1909
The Song of Songs Which Is Solomon's. London: 1909. V. 49

BIBLE. ENGLISH - 1911
In Principio. The First Chapter of Genesis. Hammersmith: 1911. V. 47; 50
The Sermon on the Mount. London: 1911. V. 50

BIBLE. ENGLISH - 1913
The Song of Songs Which is Solomon's. London: 1913. V. 49

BIBLE. ENGLISH - 1914
The Book of Genesis. London: 1914. V. 53

BIBLE. ENGLISH - 1916
The Book of Job. London: 1916. V. 47

BIBLE. ENGLISH - 1919.
The Holy Bible. London: 1919. V. 47

BIBLE. ENGLISH - 1919
The Holy Bible Containing the Old and New Testaments. New York: 1919. V. 50

BIBLE. ENGLISH - 1920
The Book of Kells. London: 1920. V. 47

BIBLE. ENGLISH - 1923
The Book of Ruth. London: 1923. V. 52

BIBLE. ENGLISH - 1924
The Apocrypha Reprinted According to the Authorised Version 1611. London: 1924. V. 51
Genesis. London: 1924. V. 49; 52
Genesis. Soho: 1924. V. 47; 50
The Holy Bible. London: 1924-25. V. 53
The Holy Bible and Apocrypha. London: 1924-27. V. 52; 53; 54
The Holy Bible Reprinted According to the Authorised Version 1611. (with) The Apocrypha. Bloomsbury: 1924-27. V. 51
The Sermon on the Mount. San Francisco: 1924. V. 48

BIBLE. ENGLISH - 1925
The Birth of Christ from the Gospel According to Saint Luke. 1925. V. 47
The Birth of Christ from the Gospel According to Saint Luke. Berkshire: 1925. V. 54
The Birth of Christ from the Gospel According to Saint Luke. Waltham St. Lawrence: 1925. V. 50
The Holy Bible Reprinted According to the Authorised Version 1611. (with) The Apocrypha. London: 1925-27/24. V. 47; 51
Samson and Delilah. From the Book of Judges. Waltham St. Lawrence: 1925. V. 54
The Song of Songs. Berkshire: 1925. V. 48
The Song of Songs. Waltham St. Lawrence: 1925. V. 49; 50; 52; 53
The Song of Songs Called by Many the Canticle of Canticles. Waltham St. Lawrence: 1925. V. 47

BIBLE. ENGLISH - 1926
The Book of Ruth. San Francisco: 1926. V. 54

BIBLE. ENGLISH - 1927
The Book of Ruth. San Francisco: 1927. V. 51; 53
The Gentle Cynic: being a Translation of the Book of Koheleth Known as Ecclesiastes. San Francisco: 1927. V. 49; 51
The Song of Solomon. Philadelphia: 1927. V. 47

BIBLE. ENGLISH - 1928
Judith. 1928. V. 53
Judith. London: 1928. V. 48; 49
The Psalms of David in Metre. Cambridge: 1928. V. 49; 53

BIBLE. ENGLISH - 1929
The Apocrypha. London: 1929. V. 49; 50; 51; 53
The Book of Tobit and History of Susanna. London: 1929. V. 48; 49; 51
The Psalms of the Singer David. San Francisco: 1929. V. 51

BIBLE. ENGLISH - 1930
The Sermon on the Mount from the Gospel of St. Matthew. Flansham: 1930. V. 48; 50
The Story of How Amnon Ravished His Sister Absalom Killed Him, As Is Written in the Second Book of Kings. Buckinghamshire: 1930. V. 49
The Wisdom of Jesus the Son of Sirach, Commonly Called Ecclesiasticus. 1930. V. 52

BIBLE. ENGLISH - 1931
Canticum Canticorum Salomonis. 1931. V. 54
The Four Gospels of the Lord Jesus Christ According to the Authorised Version of King James I. Waltham St. Lawrence: 1931. V. 48; 50; 51; 53
The Revelation of Saint John the Divine. London: 1931. V. 49
The Song of Songs. New York: 1931. V. 47; 54

BIBLE. ENGLISH - 1932
The Four Gospels... Leipzig: 1932. V. 47; 48
The Revelation of Saint John the Divine. Newtown: 1932. V. 48; 53; 54
The Wisdom of Jesus the Son of Sirach, Commonly Called Ecclesiasticus. 1932. V. 48; 49; 51; 52; 54
The Wisdom of Jesus The Son of Sirach, Commonly Called Ecclesiasticus. Chelsea: 1932. V. 47; 50
The Wisdom of Jesus the Son of Sirach, Commonly Called Ecclesiasticus. London: 1932. V. 47; 50; 53; 54

BIBLE. ENGLISH - 1933
The Book of Ruth. London: 1933. V. 52; 53
The Lamentations of Jeremiah. Newtown: 1933. V. 48; 52; 53

BIBLE. ENGLISH - 1934
Ecclesiasates, or the Preacher. London: 1934. V. 51
Ecclesiastes or the Preacher. Waltham St. Lawrence: 1934. V. 53; 54
The Lamentations of Jeremiah. Newtown: 1934. V. 54
The New Testament. London: 1934. V. 51

BIBLE. ENGLISH - 1935
The Book of Esther. New York: 1935. V. 47
The Song of Songs Which is Solomon's. New York: 1935. V. 51; 54

BIBLE. ENGLISH - 1936
The Book of Ruth. San Francisco: 1936. V. 52

BIBLE. ENGLISH - 1937
The Song of Songs. 1937. V. 48; 51

BIBLE. ENGLISH - 1939
The New Testament. 1939. V. 48; 50

BIBLE. ENGLISH - 1941
Ecclesiastaes, Reprinted from the Authorised Version. 1941. V. 52
Ecclesiastes: reprinted from the Authorised Version. Cambridge: 1941. V. 48

BIBLE. ENGLISH - 1944
The Book of Job from the King James Bible. Cummington: 1944. V. 47; 53
The Ninety-First Psalm. London: 1944. V. 49
The Ninety-First Psalm. Waltham St. Lawrence: 1944. V. 47

BIBLE. ENGLISH - 1946
The Book of Job. New York: 1946. V. 49; 54

BIBLE. ENGLISH - 1947
The Book of Ruth, From the Translation Prepared at Cambridge, 1611, for King James I. New York: 1947. V. 48; 50; 52; 54
The Ten Commandments. Philadelphia: 1947. V. 48; 49; 51

BIBLE. ENGLISH - 1949
The Book of Ruth and Boaz According to the King James VErsion of the Holy Bible. New York: 1949. V. 47

BIBLE. ENGLISH - 1953
Ecclesiastes; Words of the Preacher. Iowa City: 1953. V. 53

BIBLE. ENGLISH - 1960
The Book of Psalms... New York: 1960. V. 49
The Book of Ruth. 1960. V. 54
The Sixth Chapter of St. Matthew Containing the Lord's Prayer. 1960. V. 49

BIBLE. ENGLISH - 1961
The Sixth Chapter of St. Matthew Containing the Lord's Prayer. New York: 1961. V. 51

BIBLE. ENGLISH - 1962
The Holy Gospel According to Matthew, Mark, Luke and John. 1962. V. 54
The Holy Gospel According to Matthew, Mark, Luke and John. Verona: 1962. V. 47; 50; 51

BIBLE. ENGLISH - 1963
The Book of Proverbs from the Authorized King James Version... New York: 1963. V. 50; 53
The Holy Bible. The Authorized or King James Version of 1611 Now Reprinted with the Apocrypha. London: 1963. V. 48; 53

BIBLE. ENGLISH - 1965
Ecclesiastes or, The Preacher. New York: 1965. V. 47; 48; 53

BIBLE. ENGLISH - 1967
Ecclesiastes. Paris: 1967. V. 50; 51; 53; 54
Genesis. Boston: 1967. V. 47

BIBLE. ENGLISH - 1968
The Book of Ecclesiasates. New York: 1968. V. 48; 50; 52; 54

BIBLE. ENGLISH - 1969
The Book of Jonah from the Authorized King James Version. Bronxville: 1969. V. 48

BIBLE. ENGLISH - 1970
The Book of Genesis. King James Bible. Kentfield: 1970. V. 49; 53
The Jerusalem Bible. Garden City: 1970. V. 50; 52
The Jerusalem Bible. New York: 1970. V. 51

BIBLE. ENGLISH - 1972
The Book of the Prophet Ezekiel. Los Angeles: 1972. V. 48

BIBLE. ENGLISH - 1974
The Book of Kells: Reproductions from the Manuscript in Trinity College Dublin. New York: 1974. V. 47; 48

BIBLE. ENGLISH - 1976
The Book of Kells. London: 1976. V. 47

BIBLE. ENGLISH - 1977
The Book of Jonah, Taken from the Authorised Version of King James I. Cambridge: 1977. V. 52
The Book of Jonah, Taken from the Authorised Version of King James I. London: 1977. V. 51
The Book of Kells, Reproductions from the Manuscript in Trinity College, Dublin. New York: 1977. V. 48
Oracles: Six Versions from the Bible. Durham: 1977. V. 47
The Pslams of David. Dawson, Folkestone: 1977. V. 49; 50
The Pslams of David and Others. San Francisco: 1977. V. 53
The Sermon on the Mount. Oxford: 1977. V. 48; 50
Song of Solomon. London: 1977. V. 50

BIBLE. ENGLISH - 1979
The Book of Jonah. London: 1979. V. 49; 54
The Book of the Prophet Isaiah in the King James Version. 1979. V. 47; 53
The Book of the Prophet Isaiah. In the King James Version. New York: 1979. V. 47; 48; 52; 54

BIBLE. ENGLISH - 1980
The Gospel According to Saint Mark Translated into English in 1380 by John Purvey. 1980. V. 52

BIBLE. ENGLISH - 1984
The First Epistle of John. 1984. V. 49
Jonah, Judith, Ruth: Three Stories from the Old Testament. Greenbrae: 1984. V. 50; 53

BIBLE. ENGLISH - 1985
The Song of Songs by Solomon. Utrecht: 1985. V. 52

BIBLE. ENGLISH - 1988
The Four Gospels. 1988. V. 47
The Four Gospels. London: 1988. V. 50
The Four Gospels... Wellingborough: 1988. V. 47
The Gospel According to Saint Matthew. Shropshire: 1988. V. 52

BIBLE. ENGLISH - 1990
The Book of Jonah. 1990. V. 48
The Song of Songs. New York: 1990. V. 47

BIBLE. ENGLISH - 1991
Cantica Canticori. Salamons Lovelist Song. Market Drayton: 1991. V. 52

BIBLE. ENGLISH - 1994
The Book of Ruth. 1994. V. 52
The Book of Ruth. Market Drayton: 1994. V. 52
The History of Susanna. 1994. V. 52

BIBLE. ENGLISH - 1995
Sermon on the Mount. From the Gospel According to Matthew. 1995. V. 54
The Song of Songs. London: 1995. V. 54

BIBLE. FRENCH - 1533
Divi Anselmi...In Epistolas Beati Pauli Apostoli Explanationes. Paris: 1533. V. 47

BIBLE. FRENCH - 1570
Le Novveav Testament. Geneve: 1570. V. 53
Les Pseaumes mis en Rime Francoise, par Clement Marot & Theodore de Beze. Geneva: 1570. V. 48; 50; 54

BIBLE. FRENCH - 1616
Bible in French. (Geneva Version). La Rochelle: 1616. V. 50

BIBLE. FRENCH - 1667
Le Nouveau Testament... Amsterdam: 1667. V. 47

BIBLE. FRENCH - 1730
Les Pseaumes de David, mis en Vers Francois, Revus & Approuvez par le Synode Walon des Provinces-Unies. Amsterdam: 1730. V. 47

BIBLE. FRENCH - 1738
Version du Nouveau Testament Selon La Vulgate... Paris: 1738. V. 52

BIBLE. FRENCH - 1779
La Sainte Bible Qui Content le Vieux et Le Nouveau Testament...Par J. F. Ostervald...(with) Apocrypha. Neuchatel: 1779. V. 47

BIBLE. FRENCH - 1811
Le Nouveau Testament de Notre Seigneur Jesus-Christ... Boston: 1811. V. 50

BIBLE. FRENCH - 1930
Ruth et Booz. Paris: 1930. V. 47; 52; 53

BIBLE. FRENCH - 1931
Cantique des Cantiques de Salomon. 1931. V. 52

BIBLE. FRENCH - 1952
Cantique des Cantiques. Paris: 1952. V. 52

BIBLE. GAELIC - 1767
Tiomnadh Nuadh...(New Testament, Scottish Gaelic). Dun-Eudain: 1767. V. 48

BIBLE. GALLA - 1872
The Book of Psalms Translated into the Galla Language. 1872. V. 48

BIBLE. GERMAN - 1528
Das New Testament... Leipzig: 1528. V. 53

BIBLE. GERMAN - 1556
Bible in German. Coln: 1556. V. 50

BIBLE. GERMAN - 1712
Biblia, Das ist: Die Gantze Heilige Schrifft Alten und Neuen Testaments...Durch Doct. Mart. Luthur... Marburg: 1712. V. 47

BIBLE. GERMAN - 1763
Biblia, Das Ist: Die Heilige Schrift Altes und Neues Testaments... Germantown: 1763. V. 48

BIBLE. GERMAN - 1776
Biblia, Das Ist: Die Ganze Goettliche Heilige Schrift Alten Und Neuen Testaments. Germantown: 1776. V. 48

BIBLE. GERMAN - 1810
Das Neue Testament Unsers Herrn und Heilandes Jesu Christi... Germantown: 1810. V. 50

BIBLE. GERMAN - 1815
Das Neue Testament Unsers Herr und Heilandes Jesu Christi... Somerset: 1815. V. 48

BIBLE. GERMAN - 1910
Das Buch Judith. Berlin: 1910. V. 48

BIBLE. GERMAN - 1926
Biblia, das 1st; Die Gantze Heilige Schrifft-Deudsch D. Martin Luther. 1926-28. V. 52; 54

BIBLE. GREEK - 1524
Bible in Greek. New Testament. Argentorati: 1524. V. 50

BIBLE. GREEK - 1546
Bible in Greek. (New Testament). Lvtetiae: 1546. V. 50
Novum Testamentum. Paris: 1546. V. 50

BIBLE. GREEK - 1559
Novum Jesu Christi Domini Nostri Testamentum. Zurich: 1559. V. 47

BIBLE. GREEK - 1568
Noveum Testamentum. Paris: 1568. V. 54
Novum Testamentum. Ex Bibliotheca Regia. Paris. V. 48

BIBLE. GREEK - 1569
Bible in Greek. New Testament. Lvtetiae: 1569-68. V. 50
Nouum Testamentum. Paris: 1568, 1569. V. 52

BIBLE. GREEK - 1619
(Greek title, then) Novum Jesu Christi... Coloniae Allobrogum: 1619. V. 52

BIBLE. GREEK - 1628
Bible in Greek. New Testament. Sedani: 1629. V. 50

BIBLE. GREEK - 1632
(Greek Letter) Novum Testamentum. Cambridge: 1632. V. 50

BIBLE. GREEK - 1633
Bible in Greek. New Testament. Amsterdam: 1633. V. 48; 49
Bible in Greek. New Testament. Londini: 1633. V. 50

BIBLE. GREEK - 1653
Old Testament. Londini: 1653. V. 53

BIBLE. GREEK - 1658
Novum Testamentum. Amsterdam: 1658. V. 48

BIBLE. GREEK - 1665
(Greek script) Veus Testamentum Graecum ex Versione septuaginta Interpretum Juxta Exemplar Vaticanum Romae Editum. Cantabrigiae: 1665. V. 47

BIBLE. GREEK - 1723
Novum Testamentum Graecum. Leipzig: 1723. V. 52; 54

BIBLE. GREEK - 1763
(Greek) Novum Testamentum. Oxonii: 1763. V. 48; 49

BIBLE. GREEK - 1798
Quator Evangelia Graece. (Four Gospels in Greek). Oxford: 1798. V. 51

BIBLE. GREEK - 1808
Novum Testamentum Graece Lectiones Variantes... Oxford: 1808. V. 50

BIBLE. GREEK - 1813
New Testament in Greek. London: 1813. V. 53

BIBLE. GREEK - 1828
Novum Testamentum Graecum. Londini: 1828. V. 54

BIBLE. GREEK - 1863
Noveum Testamentum Sinaiticum... Leipzig: 1863. V. 52

BIBLE. GREEK - 1932
The Four Gospels in the original Greek. Oxford: 1932. V. 48

BIBLE. HAIDA - 1891
Saint Matthew Gie Giatlan Las. London: 1891. V. 47

BIBLE. HARAUTI - 1821
The Holy Bible, containing the Old and New Testaments. Seramproe: 1821. V. 49

BIBLE. HAWAIIAN - 1843
Ka Pala-Pala Hemolele... Honolulu: 1843. V. 50

BIBLE. HEBREW - 1530
Psalmi Davidici ad Hebraicam Veritatem Castigati... Venice: 1530. V. 51

BIBLE. HEBREW - 1566
Psalterium Recens Editum ac Diligentissime Correctum per M. Hieronymum Opitium Iuniorem. Wittenberg: 1566. V. 50

BIBLE. HEBREW - 1584
Biblia Hebraica. Antuerpie: 1584. V. 48

BIBLE. HEBREW - 1656.
The Hebrew Text of the Psalmes and Lamentations, Revised and Corrected According to the Best of Plantin and Stephan's Impressions. London: 1656. V. 47

BIBLE. HEBREW - 1666
The Book of Psalms. Amsterdam: 1966. V. 48

BIBLE. HEBREW - 1740
Biblia Hebraica. Lipsiae: 1740. V. 48

BIBLE. HEBREW - 1776
Vetus Testamentum Hebraicum, Cum Variis Lectionibus. Oxonii: 1776-1780. V. 47

BIBLE. HEBREW - 1825
Biblia Herbraica, Secundum Ultimam Editionem Jos. Athiae, a Johanne Leusden Denuo Recognitam... Londoni: 1825. V. 47

BIBLE. HEBREW - 1930
Megillot Esther. Jerusalem: 1930's. V. 53

BIBLE. HIEROGLYPHIC - 1565
The Hieroglyphick Bible, or, Select Passages in the Old and New Testaments, Represented with Emblematical Figures for the Amusement of Youth... Plymouth: 1820. V. 47

BIBLE. HIEROGLYPHIC - 1789
A Curious Hieroglyphick Bible... Dublin: 1789. V. 51

BIBLE. HIEROGLYPHIC - 1791
A Curious Hieroglyphick Bible... London: 1791. V. 50

BIBLE. HIEROGLYPHIC - 1796
A Curious Hieroglyphic Bible; or, Select Passages in the Old and New Testaments. London: 1796. V. 53

BIBLE. HIEROGLYPHIC - 1813
New and Complete Hieroglyphical Bible... London: 1813. V. 50

BIBLE. INDO-PORTUGESE - 1851
O Evangelho Conforme de Santo Mattheos. London: 1851. V. 47

BIBLE. IRISH - 1827
Leabhuir an Tsean Tiomna. Dublin: 1827. V. 50

BIBLE. IRISH - 1852
An Bioblia Naomhtha. London: 1852. V. 47

BIBLE. ITALIAN - 1567
Discorsi Spirituali, Sopera il Giardino de Peccatori: nella Espos-izione de Sette Salmi Penitentiali...(Psalms). Vinegia: 1567. V. 48

BIBLE. ITALIAN - 1753
Epistole ed Evangeli... Venice: 1753. V. 54

BIBLE. LATIN - 1480
Bible in Latin. Strassburg: 1480. V. 50
Bible in Latin. Venice: 1480. V. 47; 50

BIBLE. LATIN - 1484
Biblia Latina. Venice: 1484. V. 48

BIBLE. LATIN - 1486
Bible in Latin. Speier: 1486. V. 50

BIBLE. LATIN - 1491
Bible in Latin. Basel: 1491. V. 54

BIBLE. LATIN - 1495
Biblia Integra. Basel: 1495. V. 48; 50

BIBLE. LATIN - 1498
Biblia Cum Tabula Nuper Impressa et Cum Summariis Noviter Editis. Venice: 1498. V. 50

BIBLE. LATIN - 1509
Biblia Cum Pleno Apparatu. Basel: 1509. V. 47

BIBLE. LATIN - 1522
Bibliorvm Opvs Integrvm...ex Athanasio Fragmentum... Basle: 1522. V. 51

BIBLE. LATIN - 1525
Novi Testamenti Totius Editio Longe Optima & Accuratissima, Divo Hieronymo Interprete: Una Cum Utriusque Instrumenti Concordantiis... Cologne: 1525. V. 51

BIBLE. LATIN - 1528
Bible in Latin. Parisiis: 1528. V. 50

BIBLE. LATIN - 1533
Epistles of Paul. Paris: 1533. V. 49

BIBLE. LATIN - 1536
Bible in Latin. Lugduni: 1536. V. 50

BIBLE. LATIN - 1540
Bible in Latin. Lvgdvni: 1540. V. 50

BIBLE. LATIN - 1545
Bible in Latin. Lvtetiae: 1545. V. 50
Biblia. Paris: 1545. V. 52
(Noveum Testamentum Latine). Evangelium Secundum Matthaeum... Paris: 1545. V. 54

BIBLE. LATIN - 1549
Biblia Sacra Iuxta Vulgatam Quam Dicunt Editionem. Paris: 1549. V. 52

BIBLE. LATIN - 1551
Biblia Sacra. Lyons: 1551. V. 54

BIBLE. LATIN - 1554
Biblia, Interprete Sebastian Castalione. Basileae: 1554. V. 53

BIBLE. LATIN - 1555
Bible in Latin. Geneva: 1555. V. 50

BIBLE. LATIN - 1558
Biblia Sacra ad Optima Quaeque Veteris... Lyons: 1558. V. 47

BIBLE. LATIN - 1562
Bible in Latin. Basel: 1562?. V. 50

BIBLE. LATIN - 1565
Testamenti Novi. Dillingen: 1565. V. 47; 53

BIBLE. LATIN - 1567
Biblia, ad Vetustissima Exemplaria Castigata. Antwerp: 1567. V. 49
Novum I. C. Testamentum. Antwerp: 1567. V. 50; 52; 54

BIBLE. LATIN - 1569
Bible in Latin. Genevae: 1569. V. 50

BIBLE. LATIN - 1574
Biblia Sacra Veteris et Novi Testamenti... Geneva: 1574. V. 47

BIBLE. LATIN - 1576
Bible in Latin. Venice: 1576. V. 49; 50

BIBLE. LATIN - 1579
Testamenti Veteris Biblia Sacra. Frankfurt: 1579. V. 51

BIBLE. LATIN - 1581
Noveum Jesu Christi Testamentum. Venice: 1581. V. 51

BIBLE. LATIN - 1585
Bible in Latin. Londini: 1585. V. 50
Canticum Canticorum Salomonis. (Song of Solomon). Paris: 1585. V. 49

BIBLE. LATIN - 1587
Biblia Sacra. Antwerp: 1587. V. 53
Novum Testamentum. Londini: 1587. V. 50
Novum Testamentum. Novum. 1587. V. 47

BIBLE. LATIN - 1588
Vetvs Testamentvm Secvndvm LXX Latine Redditvm et ex Avctoritate Sixti V Pont. Max. editvm. Rome: 1588. V. 51

BIBLE. LATIN - 1592
Testamenti Veteris Biblia Sacra. London: 1592-97. V. 51
Testamenti Veteris Biblia Sacra...ab Immanuele Tremellio & Francisco Iunio...Etiam Novi Testamenti Libros... London: 1592-93. V. 47

BIBLE. LATIN - 1602
Testamenti Verteris Biblia Sacra. Hanover: 1602. V. 51

BIBLE. LATIN - 1603
Bible in Latin. Hanoviae: 1603. V. 50
Biblia Sacra Vulgatae Editionis; Sixti Quinti Pont. Max. Iussu Recognita, Atque Edita. Venetiis: 1603. V. 47

BIBLE. LATIN - 1608
Bible in Latin. Antverpiae: 1608. V. 50
Biblia Sacra Vulgate Editionis Sixti Quinti Pont. Max... Venice: 1608. V. 53

BIBLE. LATIN - 1618
Biblia Sacra Vulgatae. Rome: 1618. V. 48

BIBLE. LATIN - 1642
Jesu Christi Domini Nostri Novum Testamentum, Sive Novum Foedus... Cantabrigiae: 1642. V. 53

BIBLE. LATIN - 1664
Biblia Sacra Vulgatae Editionis Sixti V. Pont. Max. Iussu Recognita Atque Edita. Antwerp: 1664. V. 48; 49

BIBLE. LATIN - 1681
Novum Jesu Christi Testamentum. Amsterdam: 1681. V. 50

BIBLE. LATIN - 1729
Selectae e Veteri Testamento Historiae, ad Usum Eorum qui Latinae Linguae Rudiments... Paris: 1729. V. 47

BIBLE. LATIN - 1742
Biblia Sacra Vulgate Editionis Sixti V & Clem VIII Pont Max Auctoritate Recognita... Venetiis: 1742. V. 49

BIBLE. LATIN - 1840
Biblia Latina. Venice: 1480. V. 49

BIBLE. LATIN - 1894
Psalmi Penitentiales. Found in a Manuscript...Written at Gloucester about the Year 1440... Hammersmith: 1894. V. 54

BIBLE. LATIN - 1926
Passio Domini Nostri Jesu Christi; Being the 26th and 27th Chapters of Saint Matthew's Gospel from the Latin Text. Waltham St. Lawrence: 1926. V. 49; 50; 54

BIBLE. LATIN - 1954
The Holkham Bible Picture Book. London: 1954. V. 54

BIBLE. LATIN - 1961
Biblia Sacra. Paterson: 1961. V. 50
A Facsimile of the Gutenberg Bible. Patterson: 1961. V. 49

BIBLE. LATIN - 1963
Sanctum Evangelium Secundum Matthaeum Marcum Lucam Iohannem; the Vulgate Text of... 1963. V. 54

BIBLE. LATIN - 1968
Biblia. New York: 1968. V. 50

BIBLE. MENDE - 1872
La Yia Yekpe Nanisia Wotenga Mende-Bela Ti Kenye-Lei Hu... (Gospels in the Mende Language). 1872. V. 48

BIBLE. NAVAHO - 1910
Mozes Bi Naltsos Alesedihigi Godesziz Holyehigi (Genesis), Inda Yistainilla Ba Hani Mark Naltsos Ye Yiki-Iscinigi (Mark). Tohatacidi Enisoti Dine Bizadkyehgo Ayila. New York: 1910. V. 51

BIBLE. POLYGLOT - 1539
Bible in Greek and Latin. New Testament. Basileae: 1539. V. 50

BIBLE. POLYGLOT - 1543
Novum Testamentum Graece & Latine... Paris: 1543. V. 52

BIBLE. POLYGLOT - 1558
Il Nuovo Testamento di Iesu Christo Nostro Signore. Latino & Volgare. Lyon: 1558. V. 47; 48

BIBLE. POLYGLOT - 1559
Bible in Greek and Latin. New Testament. Tigvri: 1559. V. 50

BIBLE. POLYGLOT - 1570
Bible in Greek & Latin. New Testament. Basileae: 1570. V. 50

BIBLE. POLYGLOT - 1582
Bible in Greek and Latin. New Testament. Geneva: 1582. V. 50

BIBLE. POLYGLOT - 1583
Novum Testamentum. Paris: 1583. V. 49

BIBLE. POLYGLOT - 1584
Biblia Hebraica. Eorumdem Latina Interpretatio Xantis Pagnini Lucensis... Antwerp: 1584. V. 54
New Testament in Greek, Hebrew and Latin. Anteurpiae: 1584. V. 50

BIBLE. POLYGLOT - 1588
Bible in Greek and Latin. New Testament. Geneva: 1588. V. 50

BIBLE. POLYGLOT - 1591
Evangelia et Epistolae Graece et Latine, Domincorum Festorumque Dierum, eo Quo in Tempolis Legi Oridine Consuerunt. Innsbruck: 1591. V. 50

BIBLE. POLYGLOT - 1610
Bible in Greek and Latin. New Testament. Colonia Allobrogvm: 1610-11. V. 50

BIBLE. POLYGLOT - 1619
Sacrosancta Quatuor Iesu Chriti N. Evangelia. Romae: 1619. V. 54

BIBLE. POLYGLOT - 1649
Liber Psalmorum Hebraice Cum Versione Latina Santis Pagnini. Basil: 1649. V. 48

BIBLE. POLYGLOT - 1831
Biblia Sacra Polyglotta Textus Archetypos Versionesque Praecipuas ab Ecclesia Antiquitus Receptas Necnon Versiones Recentiores Anglicanam... Londini: 1831. V. 50
The Gospel According to St. John. (Menwahjemoowin Kahezhebeegaid Owe St. John). London: 1831. V. 48

BIBLE. POLYGLOT - 1884
The Lord's Prayer in the Principal Languages, Dialects and Versions of the World, Printed in Type and Vernaculars of the Different Countries. Chicago: 1884. V. 51

BIBLE. POLYGLOT - 1925
Le Livre D'Esther. Paris: 1925. V. 48

BIBLE. POLYGLOT - 1940
The Song of Solomon. Jerusalem: 1940's. V. 52

BIBLE. POLYGLOT - 1965
The Ten Commandments. Los Angeles: 1965. V. 52

BIBLE. POLYGLOT - 1990
The Song of Songs. Woodmere: 1990. V. 54

BIBLE. POLYGLOT - 1991
The Book of Jonah. Southbury: 1991. V. 50

BIBLE. SCOTTISH - 1767
Tiomnadh Nuadh... Dun Eudain: 1767. V. 50

BIBLE. SIOUX - 1913
Dakota Wowapi Wakan Kin. (New Testament in Sioux Language). New York: 1913. V. 50

BIBLE. SIOUX - 1919
Dakota Wowapi Woken Sioux Holy Bible. New York: 1919. V. 50

BIBLE. SPANISH - 1820
El Nuevo Testamento. 1820. V. 51; 54

BIBLE Stories and Pictures. London: 1885. V. 48

BIBLE. SYRIAC - 1664
Novum Testamentum Syriacum....(with) Notae Criticae in Novum Testamentum Syriacum. Hamburg: 1664. V. 50

BIBLE. WELSH - 1630
Bible in Welsh. Llundain: 1630. V. 50

BIBLE. WELSH - 1861
Y Bibl Cyssegr-lan sef yr hen Destament a'r Newydd. London: 1861. V. 50

BIBLE. WELSH - 1927
Llyfr y Pregeth-wr (The Book of Ecclesiastes). Newtown: 1927. V. 52

BIBLE. WELSH - 1929
Psalmau Dafydd. Newtown: 1929. V. 51; 54

BIBLIA Pauperum. Venice: 1480. V. 47; 49
BIBLIA Pauperum. Strassburg: 1490. V. 47; 49

BIBLIOGRAPHICA. Papers on Books, Their History and Art. London: 1895-97. V. 47; 48; 49; 50; 51; 52; 53

THE BIBLIOGRAPHICAL and Retrospective Miscellany. London: 1830. V. 51

A BIBLIOGRAPHICAL Catalogue of English Writers on Angling and Ichthyology. London: 1856. V. 47

A BIBLIOGRAPHICAL Checklist and Index to the Published Writings of Albert Einstein. Paterson: 1960. V. 54

BIBLIOGRAPHICAL SOCIETY OF AMERICA
Rhode Island Imprints, 1727-1800. New York: 1949. V. 48

BIBLIOGRAPHICAL SOCIETY, LONDON
Hand-Lists of English Printers 1501-1556. Part I (-IV). London: 1895-1913. V. 47

THE BIBLIOGRAPHY of American Literature. New Haven: 1955. V. 54
THE BIBLIOGRAPHY of American Literature. New Haven: 1991. V. 54

BIBLIOGRAPHY of British History: the Eighteenth Century, 1714-1789. Oxford: 1951. V. 50

A BIBLIOGRAPHY of the History of Printing in the Library of Congress. Spingwater: 1987. V. 48; 51; 54

A BIBLIOGRAPHY of the Writings of Harvey Cushing. Springfield: 1939. V. 47; 50; 51; 52; 53; 54

BIBLIOPHILE SOCIETY
The Fourteenth Year Book 1915. Boston: 1905. V. 48

A BIBLIOPHILE'S Los Angeles: Essays for the International Association of Bibliophiles on the Occasion of Its XIV Congress. Los Angeles: 1985. V. 51

BIBLIOTHECA Anglo-Poetica: or, a Descriptive Catalogue of a Rare and Rich Collection of Early English Poetry.... London: 1815. V. 51; 53

BIBLIOTHECA Curiosa. The Political Songs of England, From the Reign of John to that of Edward II. Edinburgh: 1884. V. 48

BIBLIOTHECA Lichenologica. Berlin: 1973-92. V. 51

BIBLIOTHECA Lindesiana. Catalogue of English Broadsides 1505-1897. New York: 1968. V. 54

BIBLIOTHECA Lindesiana. Handlist of Proclamations Issued by Royal and Other Constitutional Authorities 1714-1910 George I to Edward VII... Wigan: 1913. V. 54

BIBLIOTHECA Lindesiana. The Lives and Collections of Alexander William, 25th Early of Crawford and 8th Earl of Balcarres and James Ludovic, 26th Earl of Crawford and 9th Earl of Balcarres. London: 1977. V. 48

BIBLIOTHECA Lindesiana. The Lives and Collections of Alexander William, 25th earl of Crawford and 8th Earl of Balcarres and James Ludovic, 26th Earl of Crawford and 9th Earl of Balcarres. 1978. V. 48; 54

BICHAT, XAVIER
Anatomie Generale Appliquee au la Physiologie et a La Medecine. Paris: 1801. V. 53
Pathological Anatomy. Philadelphia: 1827. V. 48; 53
Physiological Researches Upon Life and Death. Philadelphia: 1809. V. 53
Recherches Physiologiques Sur La Vie et La Mort. Paris: 1800. V. 47; 48; 53
Traite des Membranes en General et de Diverse membranes in Particulier. Paris: 1800. V. 47
A Treatise on the Membranes in General and on Different Membranes in Particular. Boston: 1813. V. 47; 48; 53

BICK, EDGAR
History and Source Book of Orthopaedic Surgery. New York: 1933. V. 50
Source Book of Orthopaedics. Baltimore: 1937. V. 52

BICK, MALCOLM W.
Poems. Northampton: 1965. V. 50

BICKEL, KARL A.
The Mangrove Caost: the Story of the West Coast of Florida. New York: 1942. V. 47

BICKELL, L.
Bookbindings from the Hessian Historical Exhibition. Leipzig: 1893. V. 47; 48; 53

BICKERSTAFF, LAURA M.
Pioneer Artist of Taos. Denver: 1915. V. 49
Pioneer Artist of Taos. Denver: 1955. V. 48; 52; 54

BICKERSTAFFE, ISAAC
Love in a Village. London: 1762?. V. 52

BICKERTON, THOMAS H.
A Medical History of Liverpool from the Earliest Days to the Year 1920... London: 1936. V. 48; 53

BICKHAM, GEORGE
The British Monarchy; or, a New Chorographical Description Of All the Dominions Subject to the King of Great Britain. London: 1743. V. 51
Deliciae Britannicae, or the Curiosities of Kensington, Hampton Court and Windsor Castle... London: 1742. V. 50
The Penman's Companion, Containing Specimens in All Hands, by the Most Eminent English Masters, Viz. Ayres, More, Snell, Shelley, Snow, Clark, Ollyffe, Brooks, Nicholas, Chambers, Bland, Webster &c. London: 1730. V. 50
The Universal Penman. London: 1741. V. 51
The Universal Penman. London: 1743. V. 48; 50; 54
The Universal Penman. New York: 1941. V. 48

BICKHAM, WARREN STONE
Operative Surgery Covering the Operative Technic Involved in the Operations of General and Special Surgery. Philadelphia: 1930. V. 49; 50

BICKHAM, WILLIAM D.
From Ohio to the Rocky Mountains. Dayton: 1879. V. 47; 48; 49; 52

BICKNELL, ALEXANDER
Painting Personified; or, the Caricature and Sentimental Pictures, of the Principal Artists of the Present Times, Fancifully Explained. London: 1790. V. 47

BICKNELL, AMOS JACKSON
Bicknell's Village Builder. Tory, New York: 1870. V. 48
Bicknell's Village Builder. (with) Supplement to Bicknell's Village Builder. New York: 1872/71. V. 50
Detail, Cottage and Constructive Architecture. New York: 1873. V. 50; 52

BICKNELL, ARTHUR C.
Travel & Adventure in Northern Queensland. London: 1895. V. 48; 50

BICKNELL, JOHN
Musical Travels through England. London: 1775. V. 47
Musical Travels through England. London: 1776. V. 48

BICKNELL, JOHN LAURENS
The Modern Church; a Satirical Poem... London: 1820. V. 54

BICKNELL, LESLIE
The Art of Gravitating Upwards. London: 1986. V. 52
Elsewhere. London: 1987. V. 52
Thirteen Potential Poems: the Incomplete Works. London: 1986. V. 51; 52

BICKNELL, W. I.
The Natural History of the Sacred Scriptures, and a Guide to General Zoology... London: 1850. V. 49
The Natural History of the Sacred Scriptures, and a Guide to General Zoology. London: 1850-51. V. 54

BIDDELL, HERMAN
The Suffolk Stud-Book: a History and Register of the County Breed of Cart Horses from the Earliest Records to the Present Date to Which are Added Tables of Winners, Pedigree Charts, Sales, etc... Norfolk: 1880. V. 51

BIDDLE, ELLEN McGOWAN
Reminiscences of a Soldier's Wife. Philadelphia: 1907. V. 47; 49; 51; 53; 54

BIDDLE, GEORGE
Boardman Robinson: Ninety Three Drawings. Colorado Springs: 1937. V. 48; 49; 50; 52

BIDDLE, NICHOLAS
An Ode to Bogie, July 16, 1829. Philadelphia: 1865. V. 50
Oration Delivered Before the Pennsylvania State Society of Cincinnati, on the Fourth of July. Philadelphia: 1811. V. 53

BIDDLE, RICHARD
A Memoir of Sebastian Cabot; with a Review of the History of Martime Discovery. London: 1832. V. 53

BIDDLECOMBE, GEORGE
The Art of Rigging... London: 1848. V. 52
The Art of Rigging, Containing an Explanation of Terms and Phrases and the Progressive Method of Rigging Expressly Adapted for Sailing Ships. Salem: 1925. V. 51

BIDDLECOMBE, GEORGE continued
Changes in the Royal Navy During the Last Half Century. Glasgow: 1872. V. 54

BIDDULPH, JOHN
The Nineteenth (Hussars) and Their Times... London: 1899. V. 50

BIDERMANAS, IZIS
Paris Enchanted: Photographs. 1951. V. 53

BIDIE, GEORGE
Report on Neilgherry Loranthaceous Parasitical Plants Destructive to Exotic Forest and Fruit Trees. Madras: 1874. V. 51

BIDLAKE, JOHN
The Year, a Poem. London: 1813. V. 54

BIDLOO, GOVARD
Anatomia Humani Corporis, Centum et Quinque Tabulis... Amsterdam: 1685. V. 48; 49; 50; 51
Komste van Zyne Majesteit Willem III. 'sGraavenhaage: 1691. V. 50

BIDMAN, DAVID
The Complete Graphic Works of William Blake. New York: 1978. V. 53

BIDPAI
A Fable of Bidpai. West Burke: 1974. V. 51; 52; 53; 54
Kalil and Dimna, or the Fables of Bidpai. Oxford: 1819. V. 52
The Panchatantra. New York: 1972. V. 53

BIDWELL, JOHN
Early American Papermaking: Two Treatises on Manufacturing Techniques Reprinted from James Cutbush's American Artist's Manual (1814). New Castle: 1990. V. 48
Echoes of the Past: an Account of the First Emigrant Train to California, Fremont in the Conquest of California, the Discovery of Gold and Early Reminiscences. Chico: 1914. V. 50
A Journey to California. San Francisco: 1937. V. 53

BIEBER, MARGARET
Ancient Copies: Contributions to the History of Greek and Roman Art. New York: 1977. V. 52
The History of the Greek and Roman Theater. Princeton: 1961. V. 50
The Portraits of Alexander the Great. Philadelphia: 1949. V. 52
The Sculpture of the Hellenistic Age. New York: 1961. V. 52
Sculpture of the Hellenistic Age. New York: 1967. V. 48

BIEBER, RALPH P.
Exploring Southwestern Trails 1846-54. Glendale: 1938. V. 47
Frontier Life in the Army 1854-1861. Glendale: 1932. V. 48
The Southwest Historical Series. Glendale: 1943. V. 50

BIEBUYCK, D.
The Arts of Central Africa, An Annotated Bibliography. Boston: 1987. V. 54
Lega Culture: Art, Initiation and Moral Philosophy Among a Central Africa People. Berkeley: 1973. V. 54
The Power of Headdresses. A Cross-Cultural Study of Forms and Functions. Brussels: 1984. V. 51

BIEN, H. M.
Ben Beor. A Story of the Anti-Messiah. Baltimore: 1891. V. 53

BIEN, JOSEPH R.
Atlas of the Metropolitan District and Adjacent Country, Comprising the Counties of New York, Kings, Richmond, Westchester and Part of Queens in the State of New York... New York: 1891. V. 49
Atlas of Westchester County, New York. New York: 1893. V. 49

BIENS, P. C.
Goddelike Liefde-Vlammen Van een Boetvaardige, Geheiligde, Liefheebende... Amsterdam: 1691. V. 52

BIERBRIER, M. L.
Hieroglyphic Texts from Egyptian Stelae, etc. part 10. London: 1982. V. 51

BIERCE, AMBROSE
Battle Sketches. 1930. V. 48
Battlefields & Ghosts. Palo Alto: 1931. V. 51
Black Beetles in Amber. San Francisco & New York: 1892. V. 47; 48; 49; 51; 52; 53; 54
Cobwebs from an Empty Skull. London: 1874. V. 48
The Collected Works of Ambrose Bierce. New York: 1909-12. V. 52
The Cynic's Word Book. New York: 1906. V. 47; 48; 50; 52; 54
The Dance of Death. San Francisco: 1877. V. 47
The Devil's Dictionary. V. 48
The Devil's Dictionary. New York: 1972. V. 53
Fantastic Fables. New York & London: 1899. V. 47; 48; 51; 53
The Fiend's Delight. London: 1873. V. 49
The Fiend's Delight. New York: 1873. V. 48; 51
In the Midst of Life... London: 1892. V. 49
In the Midst of Life... New York: 1898. V. 50
In the Midst of Life. New York: 1901. V. 47
An Invocation. San Francisco: 1928. V. 50
The Letters of Ambrose Bierce. San Francisco: 1922. V. 49
My Favorite Murder. New York: 1916. V. 49
Nuggets and Dust Panned Out in California by Dod Grile. London: 1873. V. 50
The Shadow on the Dial. San Francisco;: 1909. V. 48; 49; 50; 51; 52; 54
Shapes of Clay. San Francisco: 1903. V. 49; 51

A Son of the Gods and a Horseman in the Sky. San Francisco & New York: 1907. V. 47; 49; 50
Tales of Soldiers and Civilians. New York: 1891. V. 49
Tales of Soldiers and Civilians. San Francisco: 1891. V. 48; 49; 53; 54
Tales of Soldiers and Civilians. Brattleboro: 1943. V. 53
Ten Tales. London: 1925. V. 49; 51
Twenty-One Letters of Ambrose Bierce. Cleveland: 1922. V. 54
Write it Right. New York: 1909. V. 48; 49; 54

BIERMANN, A.
60 Photos. Berlin: 1930. V. 52

BIERSTADT, EDWARD HALE
Satan Was a Man. New York: 1935. V. 54

BIERSTADT, O. A.
The Library of Robert Hoe. A Contribution to the History of Bibliophilism in America. New York: 1895. V. 51

BIESE, NICOLAS
De Methodo Medicine Liber Unus. Antwerp: 1564. V. 47

BIESTA, LABOULAYE & CIE.
Epreuves de Caracteres. Paris: 1843 (1845). V. 47

THE BIG Bend of Texas. Brooklyn: 1928. V. 53

THE BIG Book of Fables. London and Glasgow: 1912. V. 54

THE BIG Game of Asia and North America. London: 1915. V. 50

BIGELOW, FRANK H.
Eclipse Meteorology and Allied Problems. Washington: 1902. V. 52

BIGELOW, H. B.
Fishes of the Western North Atlantic. Part 2. Sawfishes, Quitarfishes, Skates, Rays and Chimaeroids. New Haven: 1953. V. 50

BIGELOW, HENRY JACOB
Ether and Chloroform. A Compendium of Their History Surgical Uses, Dangers, and Discovery, Anaesthetic Agents, Their Mode of Exhibition and Physiological Effects. Boston: 1848. V. 50; 52
A Lecture Introductory to the Course of Surgery Delivered at the Massachusetts Medical College. Boston: 1850. V. 50; 52
The Mechanism of Dislocation and Fracture of the Hip. (and) Litholapaxy; or, Rapid Lithotrity with Evacuation. Boston: 1900. V. 52
Orthopedic Surgery and Other Medical Papers. Boston: 1900. V. 52

BIGELOW, HORATIO
Gunnerman. New York: 1939. V. 47
Gunnerman's Gold: Memories of Fifty Years Afield with a Scatter Gun. Huntington: 1943. V. 47; 48
An International System of Electro-Therapeutics. Philadelphia: 1895. V. 47; 48; 50; 52; 53

BIGELOW, JACOB
American Medical Botany. 1817-1821. 1970. V. 48
American Medical Botany 1817-1821. North Hill & Boston: 1979. V. 47
Brief Expositions of Rational Medicine: to Which is Prefixed the Paradise of Doctors, a fable. Boston: 1858. V. 50; 52
Discourse on Self-Limited Diseases Delivered Before the Massachusetts Medical Society... Boston: 1835. V. 53
Elements of Technology. Boston: 1829. V. 50
Florula Bostoniensis. Boston: 1824. V. 47; 50
Nature in Disease, Illustrated in Various Discourses and Essays. Boston: 1854. V. 48; 50; 52; 53
A Treatise on the Materia Medica.... Boston: 1822. V. 48; 50; 52; 53
The Useful Arts, Considered in Connexion witht he Applications of Science. New York: 1855. V. 53

BIGELOW, JOHN
The Campaign of Chancellorsville a Strategic and Tactical Study. New Haven: 1910. V. 52; 53; 54
Jamaica in 1850; or, the Effects of Sixteen Years of Freedom On a Slave Colony. New York and London: 1851. V. 54
Memoir of the Life and Public Services of John Charles Fremont. New York: 1856. V. 48; 54
William Cullen Bryant. Boston & New York: 1890. V. 54

BIGELOW, JOSEPH
Florula Bostoniensis. Boston: 1824. V. 51

BIGG, JAMES
The Bookselling System. Letter to the Right Hon. Lord Campbell, Respecting the Late Inquiry into the Regulations of the Bookseller's Association, More Particularly in Reference to the Causes Which Led to Its Dissolution... London: 1852. V. 54

BIGG, WILLIAM
The Ten day Tourist; or Sniffs of the Mountain Breeze. London: 1865. V. 52

BIGGAR, E. B.
Anecdotal Life of Sir John Maconald. Montreal: 1891. V. 50

BIGGE, JOHN
Contes des Fous, and Other Trifles in Verse...with Notes Critical and Explanatory. London: 1812. V. 47

BIGGER, RUBY VAUGHAN
My Miss Nancy. Macon: 1924. V. 51

BIGGERS, DON HAMPTON
A Biggers Chronicle: Consisting of a Reprint of the Extremely Rare History that Will Never Be Repeated by Lan Franks. Lubbock: 1961. V. 52

BIGGERS, DON HAMPTON continued
German Pioneers in Texas, A Brief History of their Hardships, Struggles and Achievements. 1925. V. 48
German Pioneers in Texas, a Brief History of Their Hardships, Struggles and Achievements. Fredericksburg: 1925. V. 52

BIGGERS, EARL DERR
Charlie Chan Carries On. Indianapolis: 1930. V. 47; 48; 49; 54
Charlie Chan Carries On. New York: 1931. V. 50
Love Insurance. 1914. V. 53
Seven Keys to Baldpate. Indianapolis: 1913. V. 51

BIGGERS, JOHN
Ananse: The Web of Life in Africa. Austin: 1962. V. 49

BIGGS, E. R. J.
Historical Record of the 76th Overseas Battalion of the Canadian Expeditionary Force, 1915-1916. Toronto: 1916. V. 48

BIGGS, JAMES
The History of Don Francisco de Miranda's Attempt to Effect a Revolution in South America. Boston: 1808. V. 47

BIGHAM, CLIVE
The Roxburghe Club Its History and Its members 1812-1927. 1928. V. 48; 54
The Roxburghe Club Its History and Its members 1812-1927. London: 1928. V. 48

BIGHAM, R. W.
California Gold-Field Scenes. Nashville: 1886. V. 48; 49

BIGLAND, JOHN
The History of Spain, from the Earliest Period the the close of the Year 1809. London: 1810. V. 52
A Natural History of Animals... Philadelphia: 1828. V. 52
A Natural History of Birds, Fishes, Reptiles and Insects. Philadelphia: 1845. V. 51; 53
A Selection of Miscellaneous Pieces of Prose and Verse. Doncasater: 1814. V. 51; 54
Yorkshire. The Beauties of England and Wales. Volume XVI. London: 1812. V. 47

BIGLAND, THOMAS
Sutton-in-Holderness: the Manor, the Berewic and the Village Community. Hull: 1896. V. 49

BIGMORE, E. C.
Bibliography of Printing. London: 1880-86. V. 50; 52
A Bibliography of Printing. London: 1969. V. 53
A Bibliography of Printing. London: 1978. V. 50; 53

BIGSBY, JOHN JEREMIAH
The Flora and Fauna of the Devonian and Carboniferous Periods. London: 1878. V. 49; 52; 54
The Shoe and Canoe: or, Pictures of Travel in the Canadas. London: 1850. V. 47; 52; 54

BIGSBY, ROBERT
Boldon Delaval; A Love Story. Derby: 1850. V. 47

BIGUS, RICHARD
The Mystique of Vellum. Boston: 1984. V. 47

BIHALJI-MERIN, OTO
Art Treasures of Yugoslavia. New York. V. 54
Masters of Naive Art; a History. New York: 1970. V. 53; 54
Primitives. Naive Painting from the Late Seventeenth Century Until the Present Day. London: 1971. V. 50
Spain Between Birth and Death. London: 1938. V. 49

THE BIJOU. London & Philadelphia: 1828. V. 51

BIJOU Almanack 1850. London: 1849. V. 53

BIJOU Illustrations of the Holy Land. Philadelphia: 1845. V. 49

BILGRAMI, SYED HOSSAIN
Verses. Hyderabad (Deccan): 1895. V. 47

BILGUER, JOHANN ULRIC
A Dissertation on the Inutility of the Amputation of Limbs. London: 1764. V. 53

BILIBIN, IVAN YAKOLOVICH
The Frog Princess. St. Petersburg: 1901. V. 53
Ivan the Tsar's Son and the Firebird. St. Petersburg: 1901. V. 53
Little Ivanushka and His Sister Alyonushka and the White Duck. (with) Sister Alyonushka and Brother Ivanushka. St. Petersburg/Moscow: 1903/77. V. 50
Vasilisa the Beautiful. St. Petersburg: 1902. V. 53
Volga. St. Petersburg: 1904. V. 53

BILL, E. G. W.
A Catalogue of Manuscripts in Lambeth Palace Library MSS... Oxford: 1872-76. V. 53

BILL, LEDYARD
Pen-Pictures of the War, Lyrics, Incidents and Sketches of the War of the Rebellion. New York: 1864. V. 50

BILLET, ANNE LOUISE FRANCOISE DEFORME
Historical Memoirs of Stephanie Louise de Bourbon Conti. Newbern: 1801. V. 54

BILLETS in the Low Countries, 1814 to 1817. London: 1818. V. 49

BILLICH, ANTON GUNTER
Observationum ac Paradoxorum Chymiatricorum Libri Duo: Quorum Unus Medicamentorum Chymicorum Praparatione(m)... Leiden: 1631. V. 49

BILLING, ARCHIBALD
The Science of Gems, Jewels, Coins and Medals, Ancient and Modern. London: 1875. V. 48; 51

BILLING, MARTIN
Directory and Gazetter of the County of Devon, Containing a Descriptive Account of Every Town, Village Hamlet, etc. Followed by a General Directory. Birmingham: 1857. V. 47

BILLINGS, C. K. G.
Fort Tyron Hall, a Descriptive and Illustrated Catalogue... Washington Heights: 1910. V. 47

BILLINGS, FRANK
The Relation of Animal Diseases to the Public Health and their Prevention. New York: 1884. V. 51

BILLINGS, JOHN D.
Hard Tack and Coffee or the Unwritten Story of Army Life. Boston: 1887. V. 47; 49

BILLINGS, JOHN SHAW
Description of the Johns Hopkins Hosptial. Baltimore: 1890. V. 50; 52
Hospitals, Dispensaries and Nursing... Baltimore & London: 1894. V. 49
Hospitals, Dispensaries and Nursing. New York: 1984. V. 50; 52
Physiological Aspects of the Liquor Problems... Boston: 1903. V. 53
A Report On the Hygiene of the United States Army with Descriptions of Military Posts. New York: 1974. V. 50; 52

BILLINGS, JOSH
Old Probability, Perhaps Rain-Perhaps Not. New York: 1879. V. 47; 48

BILLINGS, ROBERT WILLIAM
Architectural Illustrations and Description of the Cathedral Church at Durham. London: 1843. V. 53
Architectural Illustrations, History and Description of Carlisle Cathedral. London: 1840. V. 50; 52
The Baronial and Eccleiastical Antiquities of Scotland... Edinburgh: 1845-52. V. 48; 50
The Baronial and Ecclesiastical Antiquities of Scotland. London: 1845-52. V. 52; 54
The Barronial and Ecclesiastical Antiquities of Scotland... Edinburgh: 1901. V. 47
Illustrations of the Architectural Antiquities of the County of Durham. Durham: 1846. V. 49
The Power of Form Applied to Geometric Tracery. Edinburgh: 1851. V. 52

BILLINGTON, ELIZABTH
Memoirs of Mrs. Billington, from Her Birth... London: 1792. V. 51

BILLINGTON, MARY FRANCES
Woman in India. London: 1895. V. 53

BILLINGTON, RAY ALLEN
Westward Expansion. A History of the American Frontier. New York: 1949. V. 53

BILLON, FREDERIC L.
Annal of St. Louis in Its Early Days. St. Louis: 1886-88. V. 49; 54
Annals of St. Louis In Its Territorial Days from 1804 to 1821. St. Louis: 1888. V. 48

BILLON, JEREMIE DE
Instructions Militaires, Divisees en Six Livres. Lyon: 1617. V. 54

BILLROTH, CHRISTIAN ALBERT THEODOR
General Surgical Pathology and Therapeutics in Fifty-One Lectures. New York: 1883. V. 52

BILLROTH, THEODOR
General Surgical Pathology and Therapeutics, in Fifty Lectures... New York: 1987. V. 50
The Medical Sciences in the German Universities. New York: 1924. V. 50; 52

BILLY, JACQUES DE
Sonnets Spirituels. Paris: 1577. V. 52

BILSON, BENJAMIN
The Hunters of Kentucky; or, the Trials and Toils of Trappers and Traders. New York: 1847. V. 47

BILSON, THOMAS
The Effect of Certaine Sermons Touvching the Fvll Redemption of mankind by the Death and Bloud of Christ Jesvs. London: 1599. V. 48; 50
The Effect of Certaine Sermons Tovching the Redemption of Mankind by the Death and Bloud of Christ jesvs. (with) The Perpetual Government of Christs Church. London: 1610. V. 48
The Perpetual Government of Christs Church. London: 1610. V. 53
The Survey of Christs Svfferings for Mans Redemption: and of His Descent to Hades or Hel for Our Deliuerance. London: 1604. V. 50

BILTON, WILLIAM
The Angler in Ireland; or an Englishman's Ramble through Connaught and Munster During the Summer of 1833. London: 1834. V. 48

BINACHI, LEONARDO
A Text-Book of Psychiatry for Physicians and Students. New York: 1906. V. 52

BINDLEY, CHARLES
The Old Book Collector's Miscellany; or, a Collection of Readable Reprints of Literary Rarities, Illustrative of the History, Literature Manners, Biography of the English Nation During the Sixteenth and Seventeenth Centuries. London: 1871-73. V. 51
The Pocket and the Stud; or, Practical Hints on the Management of the Stable. London: 1848. V. 48
Sporting Facts and Sporting Fancies. London: 1853. V. 47
Stable Talk and Table Talk, or Spectacles for Young Sportsmen. London: 1845-46. V. 50; 51

BINDLEY, JAMES
A Catalogue of the Very Extensive, Choice and Valuable Collection of medals, in Gold, Silver and Bronze. London: 1819. V. 48

BINDLEY, JAMES continued
A Catalogue of the Very Valuable Collection of British Portraits... London: 1819. V. 48; 50

BINDMAN, DAVID
The Complete Graphic Works of William Blake. New York: 1978. V. 51

BINDON, DAVID
Some Thoughts on the Woollen Manufactures of England... London: 1731. V. 50; 53; 54

BINET, ALFRED
The Development of Intelligence in Children... Baltimore: 1916. V. 49
Intelligence of the Feeble Minded. Baltimore: 1916. V. 47; 49; 54

BING, ROBERT
Compendium of Regional Diagnosis of Lesions of the Brain and Spinal Cord... New York: 1911. V. 53
Compendium of Regional Diagnosis of Lesions of the Brain and Spinal Cord. St. Louis: 1940. V. 53
A Textbook of Nervous Diseases for Students and Practising Physicians in Thirty Lectures. New York: 1915. V. 53

BING, S.
Artistic Japan. London: 1889. V. 49

BINGHAM, CLIFTON
The Animals' Picnic. London: 1902. V. 54
The Animals' Trip to Sea. London: 1900. V. 53
Comical Kittens and Their Frolics. London: 1896. V. 49
Funny Favorites. London. V. 49
Funny Favourites. London: 1904. V. 50
Laugh and Play, a Collection of Original Stories. London. V. 49
Peepshow Pictures: a Novel Colour Book. London: 1890. V. 49
Six and Twenty Boys and Girls. London: 1902. V. 52
Surprise Pictures from Fairy Land. London: 1910. V. 49

BINGHAM, HELEN
In Tamal Land. San Francisco: 1906. V. 49; 54

BINGHAM, HIRAM
Memoir of Mrs. Sally Fornis, Who Died at Beverly, Massachusetts, July 31, 1817, Aet. 19. Andover: 1819. V. 53
A Residence of Twenty-One Years in the Sandwich Islands. Hartford/New York: 1847. V. 47
A Residence of Twenty-One Years in the Sandwich Islands. Hartford: 1848. V. 48

BINGHAM, J. ELLIOT
Narrative of the Expedition to China; from the Commencement of the War to Its Termination in 1842... London: 1843. V. 54

BINGHAM, JOHN A.
Trial of the Conspirators for the Assassination of President Lincoln, &c. Argument of... Washington: 1865. V. 47

BINGHAM, JOSEPH
Origines Ecclesiasticae. The Antiquities of the Christian Church. London: 1867. V. 48

BINGHAM, MILLICENT TODD
Ancestor's Brocades. New York: 1945. V. 53

BINGHAM, PEREGRINE
The Law of Infancy and Coverture. Burlington: 1824. V. 51
The Law of Infancy and Coverture. Exeter: 1824. V. 48

BINGHAM, WILLIAM T.
Ka Hana Kapa, the Making of Bark Cloth in Hawaii. Honolulu: 1911. V. 48

BINGLEY, WILLIAM
Animal Biography; or, Authentic Anecdotes of the Lives, Manners and Economy of the Animal Creation... London: 1805. V. 54
Animal Biography...Authentic Anecdotes of the Animal Creation. London: 1813. V. 48
Correspondence Between Frances, Countess of Hartford, (afterwards Duchess of Somerset) and Henrietta Louisa, Countess of Pomfret, Between the Years 1738 and 1741. London: 1805. V. 48
Memoirs of British Quadrupeds. London: 1809. V. 54
North Wales, Including Its Scenery, Antiquities, Customs and Some Sketches of its Natural History. London: 1804. V. 51
A Practical Introduction to Botany... London: 1827. V. 50; 51
Travels in Africa, From Modern Writers, With Remarks and Observations... London: 1819. V. 50
Travels in North America, from Modern Writers... London: 1821. V. 54

BINION, SAMUEL AUGUSTUS
Ancient Egypt or Mizraim. New York: 1877. V. 50
Ancient Egypt or Mizraim. New York: 1887. V. 52

BINKLEY, WILLIAM CAMPBELL
The Expansionist Movement in Texas: 1836-1850. Berkeley: 1925. V. 52

BINNEY, GEORGE
The Eskimo Book of Knowledge/Aglait Ilisimatiksat: Inungnut Ilingnajut. London: 1931. V. 50

BINNEY, HORACE
An Eulogium Upon the Hon. William Tilghman, Late Chief Justice of Pennsylvania. Philadelphia: 1827. V. 50
An Eulogy on the Life and Character of John Marshall, Chief Justice of the United States. Philadelphia: 1835. V. 53
The Opinion of Mess. Binney and Chauncey on the Acts of the Legislature of New Jersey, Respecting the Delaware and Raritan Canal, and Camden and Amboy Rail-Road Companies. Trenton: 1834. V. 47; 51

BINNEY, W. G.
Land and Fresh Water Shells of North America. London: 1865-73. V. 49
Land and Fresh Water Shells of North America. Washington: 1865-73. V. 49; 51
Report of the Invertebrata of Massachusetts... Boston: 1870. V. 53

BINNIE, A. R.
Water Supply, Rainfall, Reservoirs, Conduits & Distribution. London: 1887. V. 49; 53

BINNS, JOHN
Dictionarium Musica, Being a Complete Dictionary; or, Treasury of Music. London: 1770. V. 48; 51

BINNS, R. W.
A Century of Potting in the City of Worcester... London: 1865. V. 49

BINNS, T.
Lithographic Views. London: 1837. V. 47

BINYON, LAURENCE
Asiatic Art in the British Museum (Sculpture and Painting). Paris & Brussels: 1925. V. 50; 53; 54
Brief Candles. V. 53
Brief Candles. Waltham St. Lawrence: 1938. V. 49
Catalogue of Drawings by British Artists and Artists of Foreign Origin Working in Great Britain, Preserved in the Department of Prints and Drawings in the British Museum. London: 1898-1907. V. 49
A Catalogue of Japanese & Chinese Woodcuts...in the British Museum. London: 1916. V. 48; 49; 51; 53
Chinese Paintings in English Collections. Paris & Brussels: 1927. V. 52; 53
The Court Painters of the Grand Moguls. V. 51; 53
The Court Painters of the Grand Moguls. 1921. V. 54
The Court Painters of the Grand Moguls. London: 1921. V. 49
The Drawings and Engravings of William Blake. London: 1922. V. 50; 54
Dream-Come-True. 1905. V. 47
Dream-Come-Ture. Hammersmith: 1905. V. 50; 51
The Engraved Designs of William Blake. London: 1926. V. 51
The Followers of William Blake. London: 1925. V. 48; 49; 52; 53
Japanese Colour Prints. London: 1923. V. 52
Landscape in English Art and Poetry. London: 1931. V. 53
Lyric Poems. London: 1894. V. 48
Persephone. Oxford: 1890. V. 50
Persian Miniature Painting Including a Critical and Descriptive Catalogue of the Miniatures Exhibited at Burlington House Jan.-March 1931. 1933. V. 53
Persian Miniature Painting Including a Critical and Descriptive Catalogue of the Miniatures Exhibited at Burlington House Jan.-March 1931. London: 1933. V. 48
Poems. Oxford: 1895. V. 51; 52; 53
The Poems of Nizami. London: 1928. V. 47; 53

BIOGRAPHIA Britannica; or, the Lives of the Most Eminent persons Who Have Flourished in Great Britain and Ireland. London: 1747-66. V. 49; 51; 53

BIOGRAPHIA Dramatica; or, a Companion to the Playhouse. London: 1812. V. 47; 52

BIOGRAPHICA and Descriptive History of the First Congressional District of New Jersey. New York: 1900. V. 49

BIOGRAPHICAL and Genealogical History of Morris County, New Jersey. New York: 1899. V. 47; 49; 51

BIOGRAPHICAL and Genealogical History of the City of Newark and Essex County, New Jersey. New York: 1898. V. 47

BIOGRAPHICAL And Historical Memoirs of Northwest Louisiana... Nashville: 1890. V. 48

THE BIOGRAPHICAL Encyclopedia of New Jersey of the Nineteenth Century. Philadelphia: 1877. V. 51

BIOGRAPHICAL, Genealogical and Descriptive History of the First Congressional District of New Jersey. New York: 1900. V. 47; 51

BIOGRAPHICAL History of Northern Michigan Containing Biographies of Promient Citizens. N.P: 1905. V. 50

BIOGRAPHICAL History of Westchester County. Chicago: 1899. V. 49

BIOGRAPHICAL Review...Containing Life Sketches of Leading Citizens of Burlington and Camden Counties, New Jersey. Boston: 1897. V. 47; 49; 51

BIOGRAPHICAL Review...Sketches of Leading Citizens of Cumberland County, New Jersey. Boston: 1896. V. 47

A BIOGRAPHICAL Sketch of the Celebrated Salem Murderer, Who For Ten Years Has Been the Terror of Essex County, Mass. Boston: 1830. V. 51

BIOGRAPHICAL Souvenir of the State of Texas. Chicago: 1889. V. 52; 53

BIOGRAPHIE Universelle, Ancienne et Moderne. Paris: 1811-62. V. 47

BIOGRAPHIES of Physicians and Surgeons, Illustrated. Chicago: 1904. V. 52

BIOGRAPHY of Joseph Lane, "Not Inappropriately Styled by His Brother Officers and Soldiers, the Marion of the War...". Washington: 1852. V. 47; 50

A BIOLOGICAL Survey of the Waters of Woods Hole and Vicinity. 1913. V. 53

BION
(Opera) Quae Supersunt. Oxford: 1748. V. 48

BION, NICOLAS
The Construction and Principle Uses of Mathematical Instruments. London: 1972. V. 53

BION, OF SMYRNA
The Lament for Adonis Bion the Smyrnaean. London: 1918. V. 47

BIONDI, FRANCIS
An History of the Civil Warres of England, Betweene the Two Houses of Lancaster and Yorke. London: 1641/46. V. 54

BIONDI, GIOVANNI FRANCESCO
An History of the Ciuill Warres of England, Between the Two Houses of Lancaster and Yorke. London: 1641. V. 47; 51

BIONDO, FLAVIO
Roma Ristavrata, et Italia Illustrata. Venice: 1542. V. 47

BIONDO, MICHEL ANGELO
De Diebvs Decretoriis, et Crisi Eorvmqve Verissimis Cavsis in Via Galeni (etc.). Rome: 1544. V. 49

BIORKLUND, GEORGE
Rembrandt's Etchings, True and False. Stockholm/London: 1955. V. 53
Rembrandt's Etchings True and False. Stockholm, London, New York: 1968. V. 50; 54

BIOY-CASARES, ADOLFO
Diary of the War of the Pig. New York: 1969. V. 49

BIRAGO AVOGARO, GIOVANNI BATTISTA
Mercurio Veridico, Overo Annali Universali d'Europa. Bologna: 1650. V. 50

BIRBECK, MORRIS
Notes On a Journey through France, From Dieppe Through Paris and Lyons, to the Pyrennees and Back through Toulouse, in July, August and September 1814... London: 1815. V. 52

BIRCH, BUSBY
City Latin, or Critical and Political Remarks on the Latin Inscription on Laying the First Stone of the Intended New Bridge at Black-Fryars. London: 1761. V. 51

BIRCH, JOHN
Examples of Labourers' Cottages, with Plans for improving the Dwellings of the Poor in large Towns. London: 1871. V. 54
Examples of Stables, Hunting-Boxes, Kennels, Racing Establishments, &c. London: 1892. V. 50

BIRCH, JOHN GRANT
Travels in North and Central China. London: 1902. V. 50

BIRCH, JONATHAN
Fifty-One Original Fables, with Morals and Ethical Index. London: 1833. V. 47; 52

BIRCH, SAMUEL
Fac-Similes of the Egyptians Relics, Discovered at Thebes in the Tomb of Queen Aah-Hotep (ca. B.C. 1800)... London: 1863. V. 53
History of Ancient Pottery. London: 1858. V. 48; 49; 54

BIRCH, THOMAS
A Collection of the Yearly Bills of Mortality, from 1657 to 1758 Inclusive. London: 1759. V. 47
The Heads of Illustrious Persons of Great Britain Engraved by Mr. Houbraken and Mr. Vertue, with their Lives and Characters. London: 1813. V. 49
An Historical View of the Negotiations Between the Courts of England, France and Brussels from the Year 1592 to 1617. London: 1749. V. 50
The History of the Royal Society of London... 1756-57. V. 54
The History of the Royal Society of London... London: 1756-57. V. 48; 49
The History of the Royal Society of London... Brussels: 1968. V. 48; 49
The Life of the Honourable Robert Boyle. London: 1744. V. 47; 48

BIRCH, WALTER DE GRAY
A History of Maram Abbey (Glamorgan) Derived from the Original Documents in the British Museum. London: 1897. V. 49
Seals. New York: 1907. V. 50

BIRCK, BETULEIUS
...In M. T. Ciceronis Libros III. De Natura Deorum & Paradoxa, Commentarii,... Basel: 1550. V. 52

THE BIRD and Bull Commonplace Book. North Hills: 1971. V. 48

BIRD And Bull, Number 13. North Hills: 1972. V. 48

BIRD, ARTHUR
Looking Forward a Dream of the United States of the Americas in 1999. Utica: 1899. V. 50

BIRD, CHARLES
Picturesque Old Bristol. Bristol: 1885. V. 48; 49; 54

BIRD, D. T.
A Catalogue of Sixteenth-Century Medical Books in Edinburgh Libraries. Edinburgh: 1982. V. 47

BIRD, F. J.
The American Practical Dyer's Companion... Philadelphia: 1882. V. 48

THE BIRD Fancier's Recreation: Being Curious Remarks on the Nature of Song-Birds. London: 1770. V. 47

BIRD, GOLDING
Urinary Deposits, Their Diagnosis, Pathology and Therapeutical Indications. Philadelphia: 1845. V. 48; 53

BIRD, JAMES
Dunwich; a Tale of the Splendid City. London: 1828. V. 54
Framlingham: a Narrative of the Castle. London: 1831. V. 47; 54
Poetical Memoirs. The Exile, a Tale. London: 1823. V. 54

BIRD, JAMES BARRY
The Laws Respecting Tithes. London: 1801. V. 49

BIRD, MARK B.
The Victorious. A Small Poem on the Assassination of President Lincoln.. Kingston: 1866. V. 49

BIRD, ROBERT MONTGOMERY
The Hawks of Hawk-Hollow: a Tradition of Pennsylvania. London: 1839. V. 54
The Infidel; or the Fall of Mexico. Philadelphia: 1835. V. 47
Peter Pilgrim, or a Rambler's Recollections. Philadelphia: 1838. V. 51
Peter Pilgrim: or a Rambler's Recollections. London: 1839. V. 51
Sheppard Lee. New York: 1836. V. 48; 51

BIRD, WILLIAM
A Treatise of the Nobilitie of the Realm. London: 1642. V. 49; 50

BIRDS and Flowers; or, the Children's Guide to Gardening and Bird-Keeping. London: 1862. V. 54

A BIRD'S-Eye View of Foreign Parts; and a Look at Home. London: 1831. V. 47

BIRDSONG, JAMES C.
Brief Sketches of the North Carolina State Troops in the War Between the States. Raleigh: 1894. V. 49

BIRGE, JOHN K.
The Bektashi Order of Dervishes. London: 1937. V. 49

BIRGE, JULIUS C.
The Awakening of the Desert. Boston: 1912. V. 47

BIRINGUCCIO, VANNOCCIO
The Pirotechnia... New York: 1942. V. 48; 52
The Pirotechnia of Vannoccio Biringuccio. New York: 1943. V. 53
La Pyrothecnie, ou Art Du Feu, Contenant Dix Livres. Rouen: 1627. V. 53

BIRKBECK, GEOFFREY
Old Norfolk Houses. London. V. 50

BIRKBECK, GEORGE
A Lecture on the Preservation of Timber by Kyan's Patent for Preventing Dry Rot. London: 1834. V. 50

BIRKBECK, MORRIS
Letters from Illinois. London: 1818. V. 47; 49; 53
Letters from Illinois. Philadelphia: 1818. V. 47
Notes On a Journey in America, from the Coast of Virginia to the Territory of Illinois. Philadelphia: 1817. V. 53
Notes On a Journey in America, from the Coast of Virginia to the Territory of Illinois. London: 1818. V. 49; 53; 54
Notes On a Journey through France, From Dieppe through Paris and Lyons to the Pyrennees and Back through Toulouse, in July, August and September 1814... London: 1815. V. 48; 51

BIRKENHEAD, JOHN
Cabala, Mysteries of State. London: 1654. V. 51

BIRKET-SMITH, KAJ
The Eskimos. New York. V. 53

BIRKETT, JOHN
The Diseases of the Breast and Their Treatment. London: 1850. V. 53

BIRKHIMER, WILLIAM EDWARD
Historical Sketch of the Organization, Administration, Material and Tactics of the Artillery, United States Army. Washington: 1884. V. 47

BIRKS, WILLIAM
Evidence of William Birks, Maltster and Cheesemonger, Charnes Old Hall, County of Stafford, on the Trial of the Cause, Sparrow and Others v. Crewe, Which Took Place at the Stafford Lent Assizes, on March 18 & 19, 1822. London: 1822. V. 49

BIRLEY, ERIC
Research on Hadrian's Wall. Kendal: 1961. V. 47; 48; 50; 52; 53

BIRMINGHAM, GEORGE A.
Gossamer. London: 1915. V. 54
The Island Mystery. London: 1918. V. 54

THE BIRMINGHAM Six: an Appealing Vista. Dublin: 1990. V. 52

BIRNBAUM, MARTIN
Introductions: Painters, Sculptors and Graphic Artists. New York: 1919. V. 52
Oscar Wilde: Fragments and Memories. New York: 1914. V. 53

BIRNBAUM, URIEL
Moses: a Biblical Cycle in Fifty Pictures. Vienna and Berlin: 1924. V. 48

BIRNEY, EARLE
The Beginnings of Chaucer's Irony. New York. V. 48
The Beginnings of Chaucer's Irony (an Essay). New York: 1939. V. 52
David and Other Poems. Toronto: 1942. V. 47; 52; 53
Near False Creek Mouth (Poems). Toronto and Montreal: 1964. V. 52
Now is the Time. Toronto: 1945. V. 47; 48; 49; 52
The Strait of Anian. Selected Poems. Toronto: 1948. V. 52
Trial of a City and Other Verses. Toronto: 1952. V. 47; 48; 49

BIRNEY, JAMES GILLESPIE
An Appeal to the Friends of the Slave. New York: 1838. V. 47
Letters of James Gillespie Birney, 1831-1857. New York: 1938. V. 49

BIRNIE, WILLIAM
The Blame of Kirk-Buriall. London: 1833. V. 51

BIRRELL, AUGUSTINE
Frederick Locker-Lampson. London: 1920. V. 48; 49; 50; 53; 54
Seven Lectures on the Law and History of Copyright in Books. London: 1899. V. 51

BIRRELL, FRANCIS
The Art of Dying. An Anthology. London: 1930. V. 53

BIRREN, FABER
Monument to Color. New York: 1938. V. 48

THE BIRTH of Jesus. A Peepshow Book. Holland: 1950. V. 51

THE BIRTH-Place, Home, Churches and Other Places Connected with the Author of "The Christian Year.". Winchester: 1867. V. 52

THE BIRTHDAY. New York: 1954. V. 53

THE BIRTHDAY Party or I and My Young Friends and How We Amused Ourselves. London: 1835. V. 53

BISBEE, WILLIAM H.
Through Four American Wars. The Impressions and Experiences of Brigadier General William Haymond Bisbee. Boston: 1931. V. 49

BISBY, F. A.
Chemosystematics: Principles and Practice. London: 1980. V. 53

BISCHOFF, HERMANN
Deadwood the the Big Horns 1877. Bismarck: 1931. V. 48; 50; 54

BISCHOFF, JAMES
Sketch of the History of Van Diemen's Land. London: 1832. V. 48; 53

BISHOP, ABRAHAM
Oration, in Honor of the Election of President Jefferson, and the Peacable Acquisition of Louisiana... New Haven: 1804. V. 48
The Triumph of Truth. Boston: 1791. V. 47

BISHOP, ELIZABETH
The 1934 Vassarion. Poughkeepsie: 1934. V. 49
An Anthology of Twentieth Century Brazilian Poetry. Middletown: 1972. V. 48
The Ballad of Burglar of Babylon. New York: 1968. V. 49; 52
The Complete Poems. New York: 1969. V. 48; 51; 53
The Complete Poems. New York: 1970. V. 49; 52
Geography III. New York: 1976. V. 52; 53; 54
North and South. Boston: 1946. V. 49; 53; 54
North and South. Cambridge: 1946. V. 49
Poems. London: 1956. V. 50
Poems. North and South - A Cold Spring. Boston: 1955. V. 48; 50; 52
Questions of Travel. New York: 1965. V. 49; 51; 52
Selected Poems. London: 1967. V. 47; 51

BISHOP, FREEMAN C.
The Alaska Highway. 1944. V. 50

BISHOP, G. W.
Barry Jackson and the London Theatre. London: 1933. V. 49

BISHOP, GEORGE
Every Woman Her Own Lawyer. A Private Guide in all Matters of Law, of Essential Interest to Women, and by the aid of Which Every Female May, in Whatever Situation, Understand Her Legal Course and Redress, and be Her Own Legal Adviser (etc.). New York: 1858. V. 47

BISHOP, HARRIET E.
Floral Home; or, First Years of Minnesota. New York: 1857. V. 53

BISHOP, ISABEL
Prints and Drawings 1925-1964. 1964. V. 54

BISHOP, ISABELLA LUCY BIRD
Among the Tibetans. Chicago: 1894. V. 52
The Golden Chersonese and the Way Thither. London: 1883. V. 48; 54
The Hawaiian Archipelago. Six Months Among the Palm Groves, Coral Reefs, and Volcanoes of the Sandwich Islands. London: 1876. V. 47
The Hawaiian Archipelago: Six Months Among the Palm Groves, Coral Reefs, and Volcanoes of the Sandwich Islands. London: 1906. V. 49
Journeys in Persia and Kurdistan. London: 1891. V. 50
Korea and Her Neighbours. Chicago: 1898. V. 52
Unbeaten Tracks in Japan... New York: 1880?. V. 48
Unbeaten Tracks in Japan. New York: 1881. V. 48
Unbeaten Tracks in Japan. London: 1900. V. 50; 51; 52; 53
The Yangtze Valley and Beyond... London: 1899. V. 51; 52
The Yangtze Valley and Beyond. New York: 1900. V. 48; 52

BISHOP, J.
The History of Little Emily. London: 1845. V. 49; 51

BISHOP, J. LEANDER
A History of American Manufactures from 1608 to 1860... Philadelphia: 1861-64. V. 50; 52; 54

BISHOP, JOEL PRENTISS
Commentaries on the Law of Contracts Upon a New and Condensed Method. Chicago: 1887. V. 50; 52
Practical Directions and forms for the Grand-Jury Room, Trial Court and Court of Appeal in Criminal Causes With... Boston: 1885. V. 50; 52

BISHOP, JOHN GEORGE
The Brighton Chain Pier: In Memoriam. Brighton: 1897. V. 48
The Brighton Chain Pier: in Memoriam... London: 1897. V. 49

BISHOP, JOHN PEALE
Green Fruit. Boston: 1917. V. 51
Minute Particulars. New York: 1935. V. 47
Minute Particulars. New York: 1938. V. 48

BISHOP, MICHAEL
No Enemy But Time. New York: 1982. V. 51

BISHOP, MORRIS
The Odyssey of Cabeza de Vaca. New York: 1933. V. 50

BISHOP, NATHANIEL H.
Four Months in a Sneak-Box... Boston: 1879. V. 51
Four Months in a Sneak-Box. Edinburgh: 1880. V. 53
Voyage of the Paper Canoe. Boston: 1878. V. 47

BISHOP, RICHARD EVETT
Bishop's Wildfowl. St. Paul: 1948. V. 47; 48
Bishop's Wildfowl. USA: 1948. V. 50; 52

BISHOP, ROBERT
American Decorative Arts: 360 Years of Creative Design. New York: 1982. V. 53

BISHOP, SAMUEL
Feriae Poeticae; Sive Carmina Anglicana Elegiaci Plerumque Argumenti Latine Reddita... Londini: 1766. V. 48; 51

BISHOP, W. J.
A Bio-Bibliography of Florence Nightingale. London: 1962. V. 52

BISHOP, WILLIAM HENRY
Old Mexico and Her Lost Provinces. New York: 1883. V. 48

BISHOP, ZEALIA
The Curse of Yig. Sauk City: 1953. V. 51

BISHOP ABRAHAM
An Oration on the Extent and Power of Political Delusion. Delivered in New Haven...September, 1800. Newark: 1800. V. 47

BISHOP'S Bonus, Seabury College, Divine Right of Presbyterianism, and Divine Right of Episcopacy... New Haven: 1816. V. 47

BISHTON, DEREK
Home Front. London: 1984. V. 50

BISLAND, ELIZABETH
The Life and Letters of Lafcadio Hearn. Boston and New York: 1906. V. 47; 54

BISSCHOP, JAN DE
Paradigmata Graphices Variorum Artificum. Amsterdam: 1671. V. 52

BISSELL, RICHARD
7 1/2 Cents. Boston: 1953. V. 48; 50; 54
Say, Darling. Boston: 1957. V. 50

BISSET, JAMES
Bisset's Magnificent Guide, or, Grand Copperplate Directory for the Town of Birmingham. Birmingham: 1808. V. 50
A Poetic Survey Round Birmingham; with a Brief Description of the Different Curiosities and Manufactories of this Place. Birmingham: 1800. V. 47

BISSET, ROBERT
The Life of Edmund Burke. London: 1798. V. 52

BISSETT, BILL
The Jinx Ship and Other Trips. Vancouver: 1966. V. 47

BITTER Root Valley. Chicago: 1912. V. 54

BITTING, KATHERINE GOLDEN
Gastronomic Bibliography. San Francisco;: 1939. V. 48; 50
Gastronomic Bibliography. London: 1981. V. 49; 50

BIXBY-SMITH, SARAH
Adobe Days. Cedar Rapids: 1925. V. 52

BJORNSON, BJORNSTJERNE
Arne. A Sketch of Norwegian Country Life. London & New York: 1866. V. 47
Bjornson's Works. Boston: 1885. V. 48

BLAAUW, F. E.
A Monograph of the Cranes. Leiden and London: 1897. V. 51

BLACK, A. P.
The End of the Long Horn Trail. Selfridge. V. 50

BLACK, ALEXANDER
A Capital Courtship. New York: 1897. V. 54
Miss Jerry. New York: 1895. V. 47

BLACK and White War Album. Soudan No. 1: Omdurman. London: 1898. V. 50

BLACK and White War Album. Soudan No. 2: Atbara. London: 1898. V. 50

BLACK, CHARLES CHRISTOPHER
Michael Angelo Buonarroti. Sculptor, Painter, Architect. The Story of His Life and Labors. London: 1875. V. 47

BLACK, DAVIDSON
Asia and the Dispersal of Priamtes. Peking: 1925. V. 54

BLACK, GLENN A.
Angel Site: an Archaeological, Historical and Ethnological Study. Indianapolis: 1967. V. 48; 50

BLACK, HELEN C.
Notable Authors of the Day. Glasgow: 1893. V. 47

BLACK, HENRY
History and Antiquities of the Worshipful Company of Leathersellers. London: 1871. V. 50; 52

THE BLACK Hills: Their Wonderful Mineral Wealth and Products... Chicago: 1883. V. 48

BLACK, JOHN
Poems. Ipswich: 1799. V. 54

BLACK List of Traffickers and Persons Implicated in the Illicit Traffic in Heroin, Cocaine, Morphine and Allied Drugs. Cairo: 1930. V. 51

BLACK, PATTI CARR
Eudora. 1984. V. 49

THE BLACK Pirate: or, the Phantom Ship. London: 1848. V. 49

BLACK, R. D. COLLISON
A Catalogue of Pamphlets on Economic Subjects Published Between 1750 and 1900 and Now Housed in Irish Libraries. Belfast: 1969. V. 48

BLACK, READING W.
The Life and Diary of Reading Black a History of Early Uvalde. Uvalde: 1934. V. 52

BLACK Republican Imposture Exposed! Fraud Upon the People! The Accounts of Fremont Explained... Washington: 1856. V. 48

BLACK, ROBERT
Horse-Racing in England. London: 1893. V. 48
Jacob Epstein. Cleveland: 1942. V. 49

BLACK, SAMUEL
Black's Rocky Mountain Journal 1824. London: 1955. V. 50
A Journal of a Voyage from Rocky Mountain Portage in Peace River to the Sources of Finlays Banch and North West Ward in Summer 1824. London: 1955. V. 48; 51

BLACK, WILLIAM
Beautiful Wretch. The Four Macnichols. The Pupil of Aureluis. Three Stories in Three Volumes. London: 1881. V. 51
Green Pastures and Piccadilly. London: 1877. V. 51
The Handsome Humes. London: 1893. V. 51
An Historical Sketch of Medicine and Surgery, from Their Origin to the Present Time... London: 1782. V. 48
Judith Shakespeare. London: 1884. V. 54
The Privileges of the Royal Burrows as Contained in Their Particular Rights. Edinburgh: 1707. V. 49; 53
Reflections on the Relicks of Ancient Trandeur, and the Pleasing Retirements of South Wales. London: 1823. V. 48
Sabina Zembra. London: 1887. V. 54
The Strange Adventures of a Phaeton. London: 1874. V. 49
Sunrise, a Story of These Times. London: 1881. V. 54
Yolande. London: 1883. V. 51

BLACKADDER, H. HOME
Observations on Phagedaena Gangraenosa. Edinburgh: 1818. V. 51; 52; 54

BLACKALL, JOHN
Observations on the Nature and Cure of Dropsies, and Particularly on the Presence of the Coagulable Part of the Blood in Dropsical Urine... Philadelphia: 1820. V. 47

BLACKBURN, ALEXANDER
A Sunrise Brighter Still. The Visionary Novels of Frank Waters. Athens: 1991. V. 50

BLACKBURN, EDWARD L.
An Architectural and Historical Account of Crosby Place, London... London: 1834. V. 50

BLACKBURN, FRANCIS
Remarks on Johnson's Life of Milton. London: 1780. V. 50

BLACKBURN, HENRY
The Harz Mountains: a Tour in the Toy Country. London: 1873. V. 52
The Pyrenees: a Description of Summer Life at French Watering Places... London: 1867. V. 50
Randolph Caldecott: a Personal Memoir of His Early Art Career. London: 1886. V. 54

BLACKBURN, ISAAC WRIGHT
Illustrations of the Gross Morbid Anatomy of the Brain of the Insane... Washington: 1908. V. 47; 48; 50
Intracranial Tumors Among the Insane. Washington: 1903. V. 47; 52; 53

BLACKBURN, JANE
Birds Drawn from Nature. Edinburgh: 1862. V. 48
Birds from Moidart and Elsewhere. Edinburgh: 1895. V. 54

BLACKBURN, JOHN
Description of a Parabolic Sounding Board, Erected in Attercliffe Church. London: 1829. V. 52

BLACKBURN, PAUL
The Assassination of President McKinley. Mt. Horeb: 1970. V. 54
The Dissolving Fabric. Palma de Mallorca: 1955. V. 51; 53; 54
Gin: Four Journal Pieces. Mt. Horeb: 1970. V. 54
Guillem de Poitou. His Eleven Extant Poems. Mt. Horeb: 1976. V. 47; 51; 53; 54
In. On. Or About the Premises. London: 1968. V. 47; 54
The Journals: Blue Mounds Entries. Mt. Horeb: 1971. V. 54
The Omitted Journals. Mount Horeb: 1983. V. 51; 54
Poem of the Cid. New York: 1966. V. 51
Proensa. Majorca: 1953. V. 52
The Reardon Poems. Madison: 1967. V. 53; 54
The Reardon Poems. Mt. Horeb: 1967. V. 51; 53; 54
The Selection of Heaven. Mount Horeb: 1980. V. 51; 54
Two New Poems. Mt. Horeb: 1969. V. 52; 53

BLACKBURN, WILLIAM
A Duke Miscellany. Durham: 1970. V. 52
Under Twenty-Five: Duke Narrative and Verse, 1945-1962. Durham: 1963. V. 50

BLACKBURNE, E. L.
Suburban and Rural English Architecture, English and Foreign. London: 1869. V. 52

BLACKBURNE, FRANCIS
Remarks on Johnson's Life of Milton. 1780. V. 48
Remarks on Johnson's Life of Milton. London: 1780. V. 49; 54

BLACKBURNE, MR.
Mr. Blackburne's Games at Chess. London: 1899. V. 50

BLACKBURNE-MAZE, C. I.
From Oriental to Occidental Africa. Maidstone: 1914. V. 53

BLACKER, C. P.
The Chances of Morbid Inheritance. London: 1934. V. 53

BLACKER, W.
Art of Angling and Complete System of Fly Making, Actual Flies and Materials Inserted. London: 1843. V. 53

BLACKFORD, CHARLES M.
Annals of the Lynchburg Home Guard. Lynchburg: 1891. V. 50
Campaign and Battle of Lynchburg, Va. Lyncburg: 1901. V. 49; 50; 54

BLACKFORD, J. H.
The Manor and Village of Cherhill, a Wiltshire Village from Early Times to the Present Day. London: 1941. V. 54

BLACKIE, W. G.
The Imperial Gazetteer, a General Dictionary of Geography, Physical, Political, Statistical and Descriptive... London: 1874. V. 51

BLACKLEY, R. JOHN
Beyond Dust. San Francisco: 1964. V. 53

BLACKLOCK, AMBROSE
A Treatise on Sheep; with the Best means for Their Improvement, General Management and the Treatment of Their Diseases. New York: 1841. V. 47

BLACKLOCK, THOMAS
Poems on Several Occasions. Edinburgh: 1754. V. 47

BLACKMAN, AYLWARD M.
The Rock Tombs of Meir, Parts 1-6. London: 1914-53. V. 51

BLACKMAR, FRANK W.
Spanish Institutions of the Southwest. Baltimore: 1891. V. 49; 54

BLACKMER, HENRY MYRON
Greece and the Levant. The Catalogue of the Henry Myron Blackmer Collection of Books and manuscripts. London: 1989. V. 47; 48; 52
The Library of...Sold at Sotheby's London 11-13 October 1989. London: 1989. V. 47; 48; 49; 52

BLACKMORE, JOHN
Views on the Newcastle-Upon-Tyne and Carlisle Railway... Newcastle: 1836-38. V. 54
Views on the Newcastle-Upon-Tyne and Carlisle Railway... Newcastle: 1836/37. V. 52; 53

BLACKMORE, R. D.
The Farm and Fruit of Old. London: 1862. V. 52

BLACKMORE, RICHARD
Eliza, an Epick Poem. London: 1705. V. 47; 52
Essays Upon Several Subjects. London: 1716/17. V. 49
Essays Upon Several Subjects. London: 1717. V. 47
A Hymn to the Light of the World. London: 1703/02. V. 53
King Arthur. London: 1697. V. 47
Prince Arthur. London: 1695. V. 47; 51; 53; 54
Prince Arthur. London: 1696. V. 47; 49
A Treatise of Consumptions and Other Distempers Belonging to the Breast and Lungs. London: 1724. V. 51
A True and Impartial History of the Conspiracy Against the Person and Government of King William III of Glorious Memory, in the Year 1695. London: 1723. V. 54

BLACKMORE, RICHARD DODDRIDGE
Alice Lorraine, a Tale of the South Downs. London: 1875. V. 53
Cradock Nowell. London: 1866. V. 54
Fringilla. Cleveland: 1895. V. 47; 50
Lorna Doone. 1869. V. 53
Lorna Doone... London: 1869. V. 51
Lorna Doone... New York: 1890. V. 49

BLACKMORE, RICHARD DODDRIDGE continued
Lorna Doone. London: 1910. V. 53
Lorna Doone. London: 1968. V. 50
Mary Anerley. A Yorkshire Tale. London: 1880. V. 48; 51; 53
The Picture Story of Lorna Doone. London: 1933. V. 54
Slain by the Doones and Other Stories. New York: 1895. V. 47
Springhaven: a Tale of the Great War. London: 1888. V. 51

BLACKMORE, S.
Pollens and Spores, Patterns of Diversification. London: 1992. V. 49; 50

BLACKMUR, R. P.
Dirty Hands or the True-Born Censor. Cambridge: 1930. V. 52
The Double Agent. New York: 1935. V. 51; 52
The Expense of Greatness. New York: 1940. V. 52
From Jordan's Delight. New York: 1937. V. 52
The Good European. Cummington: 1947. V. 48; 49; 51; 54
The Second World. Cummington: 1942. V. 50; 51; 52
T. S. Eliot. 1928. V. 52; 54

BLACKNER, JOHN
The History of Nottingham, Embracing Its Antiquities, Trade and Manufactures, from the Earliest Authentic Records to the Present Period. Nottingham: 1815. V. 51

BLACK'S Picturesque Guide to the English Lakes. Edinburgh: 1849. V. 52
BLACK'S Picturesque Guide to the English Lakes. Edinburgh: 1858. V. 50; 52
BLACK'S Picturesque Guide to the English Lakes. Edinburgh: 1879. V. 52

BLACK'S Picturesque Tourist and Road and Railway Guide Book through England and Wales. Edinburgh: 1851. V. 54

BLACKSTONE, WILLIAM
An Analysis of the Laws of England. Oxford: 1759. V. 48
An Analysis of the Laws of England. Oxford: 1762. V. 52
The Case of the Late Election for the County of Middlesex, Considered On the Principles of the Constitution and the Authorities of Law. London: 1769. V. 51
Commentaire sur le Code Criminel d'Angleterre. Paris: 1776. V. 52
The Commentaries of Sir William Blacktone. London: 1796. V. 53
Commentaries on the Laws of England. Oxford: 1765-66-68-69. V. 48; 49
Commentaries on the Laws of England. Oxford: 1765-69. V. 50; 54
Commentaries on the Laws of England. London: 1766-69. V. 53
Commentaries on the Laws of England. Oxford: 1766-69. V. 47; 48; 54
Commentaries on the Laws of England. Dublin: 1766-70. V. 52
Commentaries on the Laws of England. Oxford: 1766-70. V. 49
Commentaries on the Laws of England. Oxford: 1768-69. V. 48; 49; 53
Commentaries on the Laws of England. Oxford: 1768/67/68/70. V. 50
Commentaries on the Laws of England. America: 1771. V. 48
Commentaries on the Laws of England. Dublin: 1773. V. 50
Commentaries on the Laws of England. London: 1774. V. 50; 52; 53
Commentaries on the Laws of England. Dublin: 1775. V. 48
Commentaries on the Laws of England. Dublin: 1788. V. 47
Commentaries on the Laws of England. London: 1791. V. 49; 50; 52
Commentaries on the Laws of England. London: 1809. V. 47; 53
Commentaries On the Laws of England. London: 1813. V. 47; 50
Commentaries on the Laws of England... New York: 1832. V. 47
Commentaries on the Laws of England... New York: 1847. V. 54
Commentaries on the Laws of England. London: 1857. V. 49
Commentaries on the Laws of England... Philadelphia: 1860. V. 50
Commentaries On the Laws of England. Philadelphia: 1897. V. 49
Commentaries on the Laws of England. Abingdon: 1982. V. 54
A Discourse on the Study of the Law (etc.). Oxford: 1758. V. 47; 50
Dissertation on the Accounts of All Souls College, Oxford. London: 1898. V. 48; 54
The Great Charter and Charter of the Forest, with Other Authentic Instruments to Which is Prefixed an Introductory Discourse, Containing the History of the Charters. Oxford: 1759. V. 52
An Interesting Appendix to Sir William Blackstone's Commentaries on the Laws of England... Philadelphia: 1772. V. 47
A Letter to the Author of the Question Stated. London: 1769. V. 51
The Pantheon: a Vision. London: 1747. V. 47
A Summary of the Constitutional Law of England, Being an Abridgement of the Commentaries of Sir William Blackstone, Knt. Dublin: 1790. V. 54
Tracts Chiefly Relating to the Antiquities and Laws of England. Oxford: 1771. V. 54

BLACKWALL, ANTHONY
The Sacred Classics Defended and Illustrated. London: 1725. V. 49

BLACKWALL, JOHN
A History of Spiders of Great Britain and Ireland. London: 1861-64. V. 49; 51; 52; 53
Researches in Zoology. London: 1834. V. 49

BLACKWELL, A.
A Curious Herbal... London: 1737-39. V. 54

BLACKWELL, BASIL
Fifty New Poems for Children. Oxford. V. 49

BLACKWELL, MISS
Poverty and Affluence. Brussels: 1851. V. 51; 52; 54

BLACKWELL, THOMAS
An Enquiry into the Life and Writings of Homer. London: 1735. V. 52; 54
An Enquiry into the Life and Writings of Homer. London: 1736. V. 52

BLACKWOOD, ALGERNON
Day and Night Stories. London: 1917. V. 49
Full Circle. London: 1929. V. 47; 49; 53
The Garden of Survival. London: 1918. V. 49
A Prisoner in Fairyland. London: 1913. V. 54
Shocks!. London: 1935. V. 49
The Wave. London: 1916. V. 51

BLACKWOOD, ALICIA
Scutari, The Bosphorus and The Crimea. 1857. V. 53
Scutari, the Bosphorus and the Crimea. Isle of Wight: 1857. V. 54

BLADEN, MARTIN
Solon: Or, Philosophy No Defence Against Love. London: 1705. V. 52

BLADES, WILLIAM
An Account of the German Morality Play Entitled Depositio Cornuti Typoraphici, as Performed in the 17th and 18th Centuries. London: 1885. V. 52
Bibliographical Miscellanies Nos. 1-5. London: 1890. V. 50
The Biography and Typography of William Caxton, England's First Printer. London & Strassburg: 1877. V. 52
The Enemies of Books. London: 1880. V. 49; 52
The Enemies of Books. London: 1896. V. 54
The Pentateuch of Printing. Chicago: 1891. V. 48; 51; 54
The Pentateuch of Printing... London: 1891. V. 47
William Caxton. San Francisco: 1926. V. 48

BLADES, WILLIAM F.
Fishing Flies and Fly Tying. Harrisburg: 1951. V. 47

BLAES, GERARD
Anatome Animalium, Terrestrium Variorum, Volatilium, Aquatilium, Serpentum, Insectorum, Ovorumque, Structuram Naturalem... Amstelodami: 1681. V. 52

BLAEU, WILLEM JANSZOON
Institution Astronomique de l'Usage des Globes et Spheres Celestes & Terrestres... Amsterdam: 1642. V. 47

BLAGDON, FRANCIS WILLIAM
The Modern Geographer: Being a General and Complete Description of Europe, Asia, and America with the Oceans, Seas and Islands in Every Part of the World. London: 1820. V. 51
Orme's Graphic History of the Life, Exploits and Death of Horatio Nelson. London: 1806. V. 49
Paris As It Was and As it Is; or, a Sketch of the French Capital. London: 1803. V. 47; 49

BLAGRAVE, JOSEPH
Blagrave's Astrological Practice of Physick. London: 1689. V. 47
The Epitome of the Art of Husbandry. London: 1685. V. 51

BLAGROVE, WILLIAM
The Elements of Chess: a Treatise Combining Theory with Practice and Comprising the Whole of Philidor's Games and Explanatory Notes... Boston: 1805. V. 54

BLAHILL, THOMAS
Sutton-in-Holderness: the Manor, the Berewic and the Village Community. Hull: 1896. V. 54

BLAIKIE, JOHN
Among the Goths and Vandals. London: 1870. V. 50; 53

BLAIKIE, WALTER BIGGAR
Itinerary of Prince Charles Edward Stuart from His Landing in Scotland July 1745 to His Departure in September 1746. Edinburgh: 1897. V. 50

BLAINE, DELABERE PRITCHETT
Canine Pathology, or a description of the Diseases of Dogs... London: 1817. V. 48
A Concise Description of the Distemper in Dogs... London: 1806. V. 47
An Encyclopaedia of Rural Sports... London: 1840. V. 50
An Encyclopaedia of Rural Sports... London: 1870. V. 50

BLAINE, G.
Falconry. London: 1936. V. 49

BLAIR, ADAM
History of the Waldenses. Edinburgh: 1833. V. 47

BLAIR, C. N. M.
Guerilla Warfare. London: 1957. V. 49

BLAIR, CHARLES
Indian Famines. Edinburgh and London: 1874. V. 51

BLAIR, DAVID
The Universal Preceptor: Being a General Grammar of Arts, Sciences and Useful Knowledge. Philadelphia: 1817. V. 54

BLAIR, DOROTHY
A History of Glass in Japan. New York: 1973. V. 54

BLAIR, HENRY
Biological Effects of External Radiation. New York: 1954. V. 53

BLAIR, HENRY W.
Speech of...in the Senate of the United States. December 8, 1886. Woman Suffrage. Washington: 1886. V. 50

BLAIR, HUGH
Lectures on Rhetoric and Belles Lettres. Philadelphia: 1774. V. 53

BLAIR, JOHN
The History of the Life, Adventures and Heroic Actions of the Celebrated Sir William Wallace, General and Governor of Scotland. New York: 1820. V. 52

BLAIR, MONTGOMERY
In the General Land Office. Survey of El Sobrante, Juan Jose Castro and Victor Castro, Confirmees. Brief of Montgomery Blair for Claimants. Washington: 1880. V. 49

BLAIR, ROBERT
The Grave... London: 1743. V. 48; 49
The Grave. London: 1749. V. 47; 51
The Grave. London: 1808. V. 48; 49; 53
The Grave. London: 1813. V. 49; 50

BLAIR, VILRAY PAPIN
Cancer of the Face and Mouth. Diagnosis, Treatment, Surgical Repair. St. Louis: 1941. V. 53
Surgery and Diseases of the Mouth and Jaws; a Practical Treatise on the Surgery and Diseases of the Mouth and Allied Structures. St. Louis: 1917. V. 54

BLAIR, WALTER A.
A Raft Pilot's Log: A History of the Great Rafting Industry on the Upper Mississippi, 1840-1915. Cleveland: 1930. V. 48; 50; 54

BLAIR, WILLIAM
An Opium-Eater in America and The Fraticide's Death. Aurora: 1941. V. 52

BLAISHER, JAMES
Travels in the Air. London: 1871. V. 47

BLAIZOT, GEORGE
Masterpieces of French Modern Bindings. 1947. V. 51

BLAKE, D. W. C.
Texas Scrap-Book Made Up of the History, Biography and Miscellany of Texas and Its People. New York: 1875. V. 53

BLAKE, E. R.
Manual of Neotropical Birds. Volume 1, Spheniscidae (Penguins) to Laridae (Gulls and Allies). Chicago: 1977. V. 49

BLAKE, E. VALE
Arctic Experiences... New York: 1874. V. 50

BLAKE, ELI W.
Original Solutions of Several Problems in Aerodynamics. London: 1882. V. 50

BLAKE, J. A.
Hand-Book of Colorado with Maps and Illustrations. Denver: 1872. V. 48

BLAKE, J. L.
The Family Encyclopedia of useful Knowledge and General Literature. New York: 1834. V. 49

BLAKE, JOHN B.
A Short Title Catalogue of Eighteenth Century Printed books in the National Library of Medicine. Bethesda: 1979. V. 48; 54

BLAKE, MARION ELIZABETH
Ancient Roman Construction in Italy from the Prehistoric Period to Augustus: a Chronological Study Based in Part Upon the Material Accumulated by the Late Dr. Esther Boise Van Deman. Washington: 1947. V. 52
Roman Construction in Italy from Tiberius through the Flavians. Washington: 1959. V. 52

BLAKE, MARY E.
On the Wing. Rambling Notes of a Trip to the Pacific. Boston: 1883. V. 49

BLAKE, MAURICE C.
Postal Markings of Boston Massachusetts, to 1890. Portland: 1949. V. 53

BLAKE, MRS.
The Realities of Freemasonry. 1879. V. 52

BLAKE, PETER
Architecture For the New World. Sydney: 1973. V. 48; 50; 51; 53; 54

BLAKE, W. H.
Brown Waters. Toronto: 1940. V. 49; 53

BLAKE, W. O.
The History of Slavery and the Slave Trade... Columbus: 1857. V. 50
The History of Slavery and the Slave trade. Columbus: 1860. V. 48; 50

BLAKE, W. W.
Catalogue of the Collections, Historical and Archaeological, of the National Museum of Mexico. Mexico: 1884. V. 47

BLAKE, WILLIAM
All Reglions Are One. London: 1970. V. 48
All Religions are One. 1970. V. 54
All William Blake's Woodcuts (i.e. Woodcuts to Thornton's Virgil). London: 1902/03. V. 48
America... Edmonton: 1887. V. 52
America. 1977. V. 52
Auguries of Innocence. Northampton: 1959. V. 49
Auguries of Innocence. New York: 1968. V. 53
Blake's Pencil Drawings: Second Series. London: 1956. V. 52
The Book of Ahania. 1973. V. 54
The Book of Los. 1976. V. 54
The Book of Los. London: 1976. V. 48
The Book of Los. Paris: 1976. V. 53
The Book of Urizen. London: 1958. V. 49
The Complete Portraiture of William and Catherine Blake. 1977. V. 54
The Complete Portraiture of William and Catherine Blake... London: 1977. V. 48
A Cradle Song. The Divine Image. A Dream Night. New York: 1949. V. 48; 49
The Divine Image. New York: 1949. V. 52
The Drawings and Engravings of William Blake. London: 1922.. V. 48; 53
The Engraved Designs of William Blake. London: 1926. V. 48
Etchings From His Works. London: 1878. V. 47
Europe... Edmonton: 1887. V. 52
Europe. 1969. V. 54
Europe... London: 1969. V. 48; 50
Europe... Paris: 1969. V. 54
Illustrations for the Morning of Christ's Nativity. London: 1981. V. 48
Illustrations of the Book of Job. London: 1826. V. 49; 50
Illustrations of the Book of Job. London: 1902. V. 50
Illustrations of the Book of Job. New York: 1935. V. 48; 50
Illustrations of the Book of Job. New York: 1935. V. 54
The Illustrations of William Blake for Thornton's Virgil. London: 1937. V. 53; 54
Illustrations to the Divine Comedy of Dante. London: 1922. V. 50
Illustrations to Young's Night Thoughts Done in Water-Colour by William Blake. Cambridge: 1927. V. 52
Jerusalem. London. V. 47
Jerusalem. London: 1951. V. 48; 51; 54
Jerusalem. London & New York: 1955. V. 50
Jerusalem. 1974. V. 54
Jerusalem. London: 1974. V. 48; 49; 51; 53
The Ladies Charity School-House Roll of Highgate; or a Subscription of Many Noble, Well Disposed Ladies for the Easie Carrying of It On. London: 1670. V. 52
Laocoon. A Last Testament. With Related Works: on Homers' Poetry and On Virgil, The Ghost of Abel. 1976. V. 54
A Letter from William Blake. 1944. V. 54
A Letter from William Blake. Northampton: 1964. V. 49
Little Engravings Classical and Contemporary Number II. Edinburgh: 1902. V. 51
Le Mariage du Ciel et de l'Enfer. Paris: 1946. V. 47
The Marriage of Heaven and Hell... New York: 1927. V. 47
The Marriage of Heaven and Hell. 1960. V. 54
The Note-Book of William Blake: Called the Rossetti Manuscript. London: 1935. V. 49; 53; 54
The Paintings and Drawings of William Blake. London: 1981. V. 47
The Paintings and Drawings of William Blake. New Haven: 1981. V. 48
Pencil Drawings. London: 1927. V. 47; 48; 50; 51; 52; 53
Pencil Drawings: Second Series. London: 1956. V. 48; 51; 53; 54
The Poems. Basel: 1874. V. 50
The Poems... London: 1874. V. 48; 51
Poems. London: 1893. V. 48
The Poems... Cambridge: 1973. V. 47; 51; 53
Poetical Sketches... London: 1868. V. 53
Poetical Sketches. London: 1899. V. 52
Poetical Sketches... London: 1927. V. 53
The Poetical Works. Oxford: 1905. V. 48
The Poetical Works... London: 1913. V. 47
Poetry and Prose. London: 1927. V. 49; 51
The Prophetic Writings. London: 1926. V. 48
The Prophetic Writings. Oxford: 1926. V. 48; 53
Selections from the Writings of William Blake. London: 1893. V. 52
The Song of Los. 1975. V. 54
The Song of Los. Paris: 1975. V. 52; 53
Songs of Experience. New York: 1927. V. 49
Songs of Innocence. London. V. 51
Songs of Innocence. London: 1911. V. 47
Songs of Innocence. London: 1912. V. 47; 52
Songs of Innocence. Clairvaux: 1954. V. 51
Songs of Innocence. London: 1954. V. 49; 53
Songs of Innocence and of Experience... London: 1839. V. 49
Songs of Innocence and of Experience... London: 1868. V. 50
There Is No Natural Religion. London: 1886. V. 54
There is No Natural Religion. 1971. V. 54
Vala or the Four Zoas. Oxford: 1963. V. 49
Visions of the Daughters of Albion. 1957. V. 52
Visions of the Daughters of Albion. 1959. V. 54
William Blake's Designs for Edward Young's Night Thoughts. 1980. V. 48
William Blake's Designs for Edward Young's Night Thoughts. Oxford: 1980. V. 47; 51
William Blake's Designs for Gray's Poems Reproduced Full Size...From the Unique Copy Belonging to His Grace the Duke of Hamilton. London: 1922. V. 48
William Blake's Illustrations to the Bible. Clairvaux: 1957. V. 54
William Blake's Illustrations to the Bible. London: 1957. V. 48
William Blake's Illustrations to Thornton's Pastorals of Virgil in Ambrose Phillips' Imitation of Virgil's First Eclogue. 1821. 1912. V. 52
William Blake's Water-Colour Designs for the Poems of Thomas Gray. 1971. V. 54
William Blake's Water-Colour Designs for the Poems of Thomas Gray. London: 1972. V. 51; 53; 54
Works by William Blake. London: 1876. V. 54
The Works of William Blake. London: 1893. V. 54
The Writings... London: 1925. V. 50; 53

BLAKE, WILLIAM P.
Geographical Notes Upon Russian America and the Stickeen River, Being a Report Addressed to the Secretary of State Seward. Washington: 1868. V. 50
Preliminary Geological Report. Washington: 1854. V. 47
Tombstone and Its Mines: a Report on the Past and Present Conditions of the Mines of Tombstone, Cochise County, Arizona to the Development Company of America. New York: 1902. V. 53

BLAKEMAN, ELISHA D'ALEMBERT
The Youth's Guide in Zion, and Holy Mother's Promises. Canterbury: 1842. V. 52

BLAKEMORE, TREVOR
The Art of Herbert Schmalz. London: 1911. V. 49; 52

BLAKENEY, ROBERT
A Boy in the Peninsular War, the Services, Adventures and Experiences of Robert Blakeney, Subaltern in the 28th Regiment... London: 1899. V. 50

BLAKESTON, OSWELL
The Cat with the Moustache. London: 1935. V. 49
Murder Among Friends. London: 1933. V. 49

BLAKEY, DOROTHY
The Minerva Press 1790-1820. London: 1939. V. 48; 51; 54
The Minerva Press, 1790-1820. Oxford: 1939. V. 53
The Minerva Press 1790-1820. London: 1939 for 1935. V. 54

BLAKEY, ROBERT
An Essay Towards an Easy and Useful System of Logic. London: 1834. V. 47; 51
Hints on Angling. London: 1846. V. 48; 52
Historical Sketch of the Angling Literature of All Nations, to which is added a Bibliography. London: 1856. V. 47; 53
The History of Political Literature from the Earliest Times. London: 1855. V. 47; 51
Old Faces in New Masks. London: 1859. V. 49

BLAKISTON, T. W.
A Birds of Japan. Tokyo: 1882. V. 48; 51

BLAKSTON, W. A.
The Illustrated Book of Canaries and Cage Birds British and Foreign. London: 1877-80. V. 52; 53
The Illustrated Book of Canaries and Cage Birds, British and Foreign. London: 1880. V. 54

BLALOCK, ALFRED
The Papers of Alfred Blalock. Baltimore: 1953. V. 52
The Papers of Alfred Blalock. Baltimore: 1966. V. 47; 48; 50

BLAMIRES, DAVID
Adults' Alphabets: Examples of English Press Alphabet Books from the Last Hundred Years... 1990. V. 52
Margaret Pilkington: 1891-1974. 1995. V. 54

BLANC, HENRY
A Narrative of Captivity in Abyssinia: With Some Account of the Late Emperor Theodore, His Country and People. London: 1868. V. 53

BLANC, LOUIS
Letters on England. London: 1866. V. 52

BLANCH, H. J.
A Century of Guns: a Sketch of the Leading Types of Sporting and Military Small Arms. London: 1909. V. 49

BLANCH, LESLEY
Round the World in Eighty Dishes. London: 1946. V. 53

BLANCHARD, JEAN PIERRE
Principles, History and Use of Air-Balloons. 1993. V. 52; 54

BLANCHARD, RUFUS
The Discovery and Conquests of the Northwest. Chicago: 1880. V. 47; 54

BLANCHE, JAQUES EMILE
Portraits of a Lifetime. & More Portraits of a Lifetime. London: 1937/39. V. 53

BLANCHONUS, JACOBUS
Naphsi Phileloai, Auctoris Graeci... Lyon: 1553. V. 51

BLANCHOT, MAURICE
Celui Qui ne m'Accompagnait Pas. Paris: 1953. V. 52
Thomas l'Obscur. Paris: 1941. V. 54

BLANCK, JACOB
Bibliography of American Literature. New Haven. V. 48
Bibliography of American Literature. New Haven: 1955-91. V. 48
Bibliography of American Literature. New Haven: 1965-91. V. 51; 53
Bibliography of American Literature. New Haven: 1968-91. V. 53
Merle Johnson's American First Editions. New York: 1936. V. 51
Peter Parley to Penrod: a Bibliographical Description of the Best Loved American Juvenile Books. New York: 1938. V. 53

BLANCO County Heritage Book. Blanco: 1996. V. 54

BLANCO, J. F.
Documentos Para la Historia de la Vida Publica del Libertador de Colombia, Peru, y Bolivia. Caracas: 1875-78. V. 47

BLANCO Y CRESPO, JOSE MARIA
Vargas; a Tale of Spain. London: 1822. V. 49

BLAND, DAVID
A History of Book Illustration. London: 1958. V. 48

BLAND, E.
Annals of Southport and District. Southport: 1903. V. 48

BLAND, HARCOURT
The Exposure Dissected, and the Foul Calumnies of Aitken & Co. Fully Established; or the Theatrical Profession Thoroughly Vindicated. Glasglow: 1857. V. 52

BLAND, HUMPHREY
A Treatise of Military Discipline... London: 1759. V. 51

BLAND, J. O. P.
China, Japan and Korea. London: 1921. V. 54
Recent Events and Present Policies in China. London: 1912. V. 50

BLAND, JANE COOPER
Currier & Ives, a Manual for Collectors. Garden City: 1931. V. 51

BLAND, MILES
The Elements of Hydrostataics: With Their Application to the Solution of Problems. Cambridge: 1824. V. 49

BLAND, WILLIAM
Experimental Essays on the Principles of Construction in Arches, Piers, Buttresses &c. London: 1839. V. 51; 52
Hints on the Principles Which Should Regulate the Form of Ships and Boats; Derived from Original Experiments. London: 1852. V. 50

BLANDFORD, GEORGE FIELDING
Insanity and Its Treatment: Lectures on the Treatment, Medical and Legal, of Insane Patients. Philadelphia: 1871. V. 47; 48; 52
Insanity and Its Treatment: Lectures on the Treatment, Medical and Legal, of Insane Patients. New York: 1886. V. 52

BLAND-SUTTON, JOHN
Tumours Innocent and Malignant; Their Clinical Features and Appropriate Treatment. Philadelphia: 1893. V. 48; 53

BLANDY, MARY
The Genuine Trial at Large of Mary Blandy, Spinster, for Poisoning her Late Father Francis Blandy, Gent. Town-Clerk, of Henley Upon the Thames, Oxfordshire, at the Assizes held at Oxford...on Tuesday the third of March 1752. Edinburgh: 1752. V. 54
Miss Mary Blandy's Own Account of the Affair Between Her and Mr. Cranstoun, From the Commencement of their Acquaintance in the Year 1746... London: 1752. V. 54

BLANE, WILLIAM
Cynegetica; or, Essays on Sporting: Consisting of Observations on Hare-Hunting... London: 1788. V. 47
Essays on Hunting. Southampton: 1781. V. 47; 51

BLANFORD, W. T.
Eastern Persia. London: 1876. V. 51
Observations on the Geology and Zoology of Abyssinia. London: 1870. V. 51; 53
Scientific Results of the Second Yarkand Mission: Based Upon the Collections and Notes of the Late Ferdinand Stolickza. Mammalia. Calcutta: 1879. V. 52

BLANKAART, STEPHEN
The Physical Dictionary. London: 1715. V. 51

BLANKENBERG-VAN DELDEN, C.
The Large Commemorative Scarabs of Amenhotep III. Leiden: 1969. V. 49; 51

BLANQUI, JEROME ADOLPHE
History of Political Economy in Europe. New York and London: 1885. V. 47; 49
Voyage a Madrid, (Aout et Septembre 1826). Paris: 1826. V. 49

BLANSHARD, HENRY
An Appeal to the Inhabitants of Great Britain on Behalf of the Native Population of India. London: 1836. V. 53

BLANTON, JOSEPH EDWIN
The Organ in Church Design. Albany: 1957. V. 47; 48; 49

BLANTON, THOMAS LINDSAY
Pictorial Supplement to "Interwoven".... Albany: 1953. V. 47

BLANTON, WYNDHAM B.
Medicine in Virginia in the Nineteenth Century. Richmond: 1933. V. 50; 52
Medicine in Virginia in the Seventeenth Century. Richmond: 1930. V. 49

BLANVILLE, S. R. K.
Catalogue of Demotic Papyri in the British Museum. Volume 1: A Theban Archive of the Reign of Ptolemy I, Soter. London: 1939. V. 49

BLAQUIERE, EDWARD
Narrative of a Residence in Algiers... London: 1830. V. 52

BLASCHE, BERNARD HEINRICH
The Art of Working in Pasteboard. London: 1827. V. 48
Papyro-Plastics, or the Art of Modeling in Paper: Being an Instructive Amusement for Young Persons of Both Sexes. London: 1825. V. 54

BLASCO-IBANEZ, VICENTE
Mare Nostrum (Our Seas). New York: 1919/18. V. 48

BLASER, W.
Mies Van Der Eohe: the Art of Sculpture. 1965. V. 50; 51; 53

BLASHFIELD, EDWIN HOWLAND
Italian Cities. New York: 1902. V. 51

BLASHFIELD, EDWIN HOWLAND continued
The Works of Edwin Howland Blashfield. New York: 1937. V. 47

BLASHILL, THOMAS
Sutton-in-Holderness, the Manor, the Berewic and the Village Community. Hull and London: 1896. V. 52

BLASIS, CARLO
The Code of Terpsichore. London: 1830. V. 47; 51

BLASIUS, GERARD
Anatome Animalium, Terrestrium Variorum, Volatilium, Aquatilium, Serpentum... Amsterdami: 1681. V. 48

BLATCHFORD, ROBERT
Merrie England: a Series of Letters on the Labour Problem. London: 1893. V. 52
The Sorcery Shop: an Impossible Romance. London: 1907. V. 50

BLATCHFORD, THOMAS W.
Observations on Equivocal Generation: Prepared as Evidence in a Suit for Slander. Albany: 1844. V. 48

BLATCHLEY, W. S.
An Illustrated Descriptive Catalogue of the Coleoptera or Beetles Known to Occur in Indiana. Indianapolis: 1910. V. 53

BLATCHLY, A.
Property of the Consolidated Silver Mining Company, Resse River and Union Districts, Nevada. Boston: 1865. V. 48

BLATHERWICK, CHARLES
Miss Nancy Stocker. London: 1887. V. 51

THE BLATHWAYT Atlas... Providence: 1970. V. 52

BLATTER, ETHELBERT
Beautiful Flowers of Kashmir. London: 1927-28. V. 49
Beautiful Flowers of Kashmir. London: 1928. V. 53
Beautiful Flowers of Kashmir. London: 1928-29. V. 52
Beautiful Flowers of Kashmir. London: 1929. V. 48

BLATTY, WILLIAM PETER
The Exorcist. New York: 1971. V. 50; 51; 52; 54

BLAU, ERNEST E.
The Queen's Falcon. Philadelphia: 1947. V. 54

BLAUKOPF, K.
Mahler, a Documentary Study. New York: 1976. V. 49

BLAVATSKY, HELENA PETROVNA
From the Caves and Jungles of Hindostan. London: 1892. V. 50; 51; 53
A Modern Panarion: a Collection of Fugitive Fragments. London: 1895. V. 48

BLAYLOCK, J.
Paper Dragons. 1986. V. 48; 52

BLAYNEY, BENJAMIN
Jeremiah and Lamentations. Oxford: 1784. V. 51

BLAYRE, CHRISTOPHER
The Purple Sapphire, and Other Posthumous Papers, Selected from the Unofficial Records of the University of Cosmopoli. London: 1921. V. 50

BLAZEBY, WILLIAM
Rotherham: the Old Meeting House and Its Ministers, with Supplementary Chapters. Rotherham: 1906. V. 53

BLAZE DE BURY, MARIE PAULINE ROSE, BARONNE
Germania: its Courts, Camps and People. London: 1850. V. 52

BLEASE, WALTER LYON
The Emancipation of English women. London: 1910. V. 50

BLEDSOE, ALBERT TAYLOR
Is Davis a Traitor: or Was Secession a Constitutional Right Previous to the War of 1861. Baltimore: 1866. V. 54

BLEECK, OLIVER
No Questions Asked. New York: 1976. V. 49

BLEEKER, SYLVESTER
Gen. Tom Thumb's 3 Years Tour Around the World Accompanied by His-Wife Lavinia Warren Strattion, Commodore Nutt, Miss Minnie Warren and Party. New York: 1872. V. 49

BLEGEN, CARL W.
Corinth. Volume XIII: The North Cemetery. Princeton: 1964. V. 52

BLEGNY, ETIENNE DE
Les Elemens ou Premieres Instructions de la Jeunesse. Paris: 1691. V. 53

BLEGNY, NICOLAS DE
Le Bon Usage du The, du Caffe, et du Chocolat pour la Preservation & Pour la Guerison des Maladies. Lyon: 1687. V. 50; 51

BLENNERHASSETT, HARMAN
The Blennerhassett Papers, Embodying the Private Journal of H. B. and Devleoping the Aims of the Attempted Wilkinson and Burr Revolution... Cincinnati: 1861. V. 54

BLENNERHASSETT, LADY
Madame de Stael. London: 1889. V. 54

BLES, JOSEPH
Rare English Glasses of the XVII & XVIII Centuries. Boston: 1925. V. 47

BLESSINGTON, JOSEPH PALMER
The Campaigns of Walker's Texas Division. New York: 1875. V. 49; 53

BLESSINGTON, MARGUERITE POWER FARMER GARDINER, COUNTESS OF
The Confessions of an Elderly Gentleman. (with) *The Confessions of an Elderly Lady.* London: 1836-38. V. 47
The Confessions of an Elderly Lady. London: 1838. V. 50
Heath's Book of Beauty. London: 1835. V. 50
The Idler in France. London: 1842. V. 52
The Idler in Italy. Paris: 1839. V. 48
The Literary Life and Correspondence of the Countess of Blessington. London: 1855. V. 50; 54
Sketches and Fragments. London: 1822. V. 50

BLEULER, PAUL EUGEN
Dementia Praecox Oder Gruppen der Schizophrenien. Handbuch der Psychiatrie, Herausgegeben von G(ustav) Aschaffenburg Spezieller Teil, 4. Abteilung, 1. Halfte. Leizig und Wien: 1911. V. 52
Textbook of Psychiatry. New York: 1924. V. 52

BLEW, WILLIAM C. A.
Brighton and Its Coaches. London: 1894. V. 49
A History of Steeplechasing. London: 1901. V. 47; 49
The Quorn Hunt and its Masters. London: 1899. V. 48

BLEWETT, GEORGE
An Enquiry Whether a General Practice of Virtue Tends to the Wealth or Poverty, Benefit or Disadvantage of a People. London: 1725. V. 52

BLEWITT, JONATHAN
The Matrimonial Ladder. London: 1841. V. 49

BLEWITT, MARY
Surveys of the Seas: a Brief History of British Hydrography. London: 1957. V. 50

BLEWITT, OCTAVIAN, MRS.
The Rose and the Lily: How They Became the Emblems of England and France. London: 1877. V. 49

BLEWITT, REGINALD JAMES
The Court of Chancery: a Satirical Poem. London: 1827. V. 49; 52; 54

BLIGH, WILLIAM
Bligh's Voyage in the Resource from Coupang to Batavia, Together with the Log of His Subsequent Passage to England in the Dutch Packet Vlydt and His Remarks on Morrison's Journal. London: 1937. V. 49; 51
Captain Bligh's Second Voyage to the South Sea. London, New York, Bombay: 1920. V. 54
The Log of H.M.S. Providence 1791-1793. Guildford: 1976. V. 49; 54
The Log of the Bounty, Being Lieutenant William Bligh's Log of the Proceedings of His Majesty's Armed Vessel Bounty in a Voyage to the South Seas. Waltham St. Lawrence: 1937. V. 51
A Narrative of the Mutiny on Board His Majesty's Ship Bounty... London: 1790. V. 49; 50; 51; 52
The Voyage of the Bounty's Launch. Waltham St. Lawrence: 1934. V. 50
The Voyage of the Bounty's Launch as Related in William Bligh's Despatch to the Admiralty and Journal of John Fryer. London: 1934. V. 50
A Voyage to the South Seas... London: 1792. V. 50; 52
A Voyage to the South Seas. 1975. V. 47
A Voyage to the South Seas. Adelaide: 1975. V. 48; 52; 53
A Voyage to the South Seas... Melbourne: 1979. V. 47

BLILLROTH, CHARLES ALBERT THEODORE
The Medical Sciences in the German Universities. New York: 1924. V. 53

BLIN DE SAINMORE, ADRIEN MICHEL HYACINTHE
Lettres en Vers, ou Epitres Heroiques et Amoureuses. Paris: 1766. V. 50

BLINKY Bill. Racine: 1935. V. 54

BLINN, CAROL J.
Arno Werner: One Man's Work. Easthampton: 1982. V. 51
A Fowl Letter Book. Easthampton: 1989. V. 50
From Stripper to Publisher; or, How Printing Changed My Life. Northampton: 1986. V. 50; 54

BLISH, HELEN H.
A Pictographic History of the Oglala Sioux. Lincoln: 1967. V. 54

BLISH, JAMES
Black Easter. New York: 1968. V. 48; 52
A Case of Conscience. London: 1958. V. 52
Doctor Mirabilis. London: 1964. V. 49; 51; 52; 54
Doctor Mirabilis. New York: 1968. V. 51
Earthman, Come Home. New York: 1955. V. 51
The Frozen Year. 1957. V. 47; 51
Jack of Eagles. New York: 1952. V. 51
They Shall Have Stars. London: 1956. V. 51

BLISS, CAREY S.
Julius Firmicus Maternus and the Aldine Edition of the Sciptores Astronomica Veteres. Los Angeles: 1981. V. 48; 50
A Leaf From the 1583 Rembert Dodoens Herbal printed by Christopher Plantin. San Francisco: 1977. V. 50; 51; 52; 53; 54
A Pair on Printing... North Hills: 1982. V. 54

BLISS, CAREY S. continued
The Willow Dale Press, 1879: with Notes on the Amateur Press in California. Los Angeles: 1975. V. 48

BLISS, D. E.
The Biology of the Crustacea. London: 1982-86. V. 50; 52

BLISS, DOUGLAS PERCY
Border Ballads. London: 1925. V. 49
Edward Bawden. Godalming and Toronto. V. 47
Edward Bawden. London: 1797. V. 48
A History of Wood Engraving. New York: 1928. V. 47; 48

BLISS, GEORGE
An Address to the Members of the Bar of the Counties of Hampshire, Franklin and Hampden, at Their Annual Meeting at Northampton, September 1826. Springfield: 1827. V. 50

BLISS, PHILIP
Bibliographical Miscellanies, Being a Selection of Curious Pieces, in Verse and Prose. Oxford: 1813. V. 48

BLISS, ROBERT WOODS
Pre-Columbian Art. Robert Woods Bliss Collection. New York: 1957. V. 48
Pre-Columbian Art. Robert Woods Bliss Collection. New York: 1959. V. 47

BLISS, SYLVESTER
Memoirs of William Miller, Generally Known as a Lecturer on the Prophecies and the Second Coming of Christ. Boston: 1853. V. 47
Phenomena of the Rapping Spirits. Boston: 1853. V. 47

BLISS, WILLIAM D. P.
The Encyclopedia of Social Reforms, Including Political Economy, Political Science, Sociology and Statistics. New York: 1898. V. 52

BLITH, WALTER
The English Improver Improved or the Survey of Husbandry Surveyed... London: 1652. V. 47; 51; 52

BLITZ, ANTONIO
Fifty Years in the Magic Circle; Being an Account of the Author's Professional Life... San Francisco: 1871. V. 51

BLITZSTEIN, MARC
The Cradle Will Rock. New York: 1938. V. 47

BLIXEN-FINECKE, BROR VON
African Hunter. New York: 1938. V. 48

BLOCH, E. MAURICE
George Caleb Bingham. The Evolution of an Artist. Berkeley/Los Angeles: 1967. V. 49; 50

BLOCH, ERNST
Geist der Utopie. Berlin: 1923. V. 51

BLOCH, ROBERT
Blood Runs Cold. 1961. V. 52
The Dead Beat. 1960. V. 54
The Dead Beat. 1961. V. 47
The King of Terrors: Tales of Madness and Death. New York: 1977. V. 51
The Night of the Ripper. New York: 1984. V. 51
The Opener of the Way. Sauk City: 1945. V. 47; 51
Out of the Mouths of Graves. New York: 1979. V. 51; 54
Pleasant Dreams. Sauk City: 1960. V. 51; 52
Pleasant Dreams... 1967. V. 54
Psycho. 1959. V. 54
Psycho. New York: 1959. V. 50; 53
Psycho. 1976. V. 52; 53
The Scarf. 1947. V. 47; 48
The Scarf. New York: 1947. V. 52
Screams: Three Novels of Suspense. San Rafael: 1989. V. 51
The Selected Stories of Robert Bloch. 1987. V. 47; 54
Selected Stories of Robert Bloch. Los Angeles: 1987. V. 51; 53
Strange Eons. Browns Mills: 1978. V. 51

BLOCK, ADELBERT J.
Confederate War Etchings. Philadelphia?: 1880's?. V. 47

BLOCK, ANDREW
The English Novel 1740-1850... London: 1961. V. 53
The English Novel 1740-1850. London: 1968. V. 48; 51; 54

BLOCK, LAURIE
An Odd Bestiary. Easthampton: 1982. V. 51

BLOCK, LAWRENCE
Eight Million Ways to Die. New York: 1982. V. 51
Ronald Rabbit is a Dirty Old Man. 1966. V. 53
Ronald Rabbit is a Dirty Old Man. 1995. V. 54
The Sins of the Father. Arlington Heights: 1992. V. 51; 52
Writing the Novel. Cincinnati: 1979. V. 53

BLOCK, M. E.
Allgemeine Naturgeschichte der Fische. New York: 1993. V. 52

BLODGET, LORIN
Climatology of the United States. Philadelphia: 1857. V. 47; 49; 51; 53; 54

BLODGETT, M. F.
At the Queen's Mercy. 1896. V. 48

BLOGG, MINNIE WRIGHT
Bibliography of the Writings of Sir William Osler. Baltimore: 1921. V. 52

BLOME, RICHARD
A Description of the Island of Jamaica: With the Other Isles and Territories in America. London: 1672. V. 48
A Geographical Description of the World, Taken from the Works of the Famous Monsieur Sanson late Geographer to the Present French King... N.P: 1680. V. 53
Hawking or Faulconry. London: 1929. V. 48

BLOMEFIELD, FRANCIS
An Essay Towards a Topographical History of the County of Norfolk... London: 1805-10. V. 49; 54
A Supplement to Blomefield's Norfolk. London: 1929. V. 52

BLOMFIELD, REGINALD
A History of Renaissance Architecture in England 1500-1800. London: 1897. V. 47; 53

BLONDEL, DAVID
A Treatise of the Sibyls, So Highly Celebrated, as Well by the Ancient Heathens, as the Holy Fathers of the Church. London: 1661. V. 51; 53

BLONDEL, JACQUES
Emily Bronte. 1955. V. 52

BLONDEL, JACQUES FRANCOIS
Cours d'Archtiecture, ou Traite de la Decoration, Distribution and Construction des Batiments. Paris: 1771-77. V. 50
De la Distribution des Maisons de Plaisance, et de la Decoration des Edifices en Generale. Paris: 1737-38. V. 53

BLONDUS, FLAVIUS
Roma Instaurata. De Origine et Gestis Venetorum. Italia Instaurata. Verona: 1482. V. 52

BLOOD, BENJAMIN PAUL
The Bridge of the Iconoclast. A Poem. Boston and Cambridge: 1854. V. 54
Optimism - the Lesson of Ages. Boston: 1860. V. 53

BLOOD, GERTRUDE ELIZABETH
Topo. A Tale About English Children in Italy. London: 1878. V. 47

BLOOD, KATIE E.
Memoirs of a Forty-Niner. New Haven: 1907. V. 53

BLOOD, THOMAS
The Narrative of Col. Tho. Blood, Concerning the Design Reported to Be Lately Laid Against the Life and Honour of His Grace George Duke of Buckingham. London: 1680. V. 47

BLOODGOOD, JAMES, & CO.
Catalogue of Fruit and Forest Trees, Flowering Shrubs and Plants, for Sale by James Bloodgood & Co. at Their Nursery, Flushing, Long Island, Near New York. New York: 1820. V. 47
Catalogue of Fruit and Forest Trees, Flowering Shrubs and Plants, for Sale by James Bloodgood & Co. at Their Nursery, Flushing, Long Island, Near New York. New York: 1822. V. 54

BLOODGOOD, JOSEPH
Operations on 459 Cases of Hernia in the John Hopkins Hosptial from June 1889 to January 1899. The Special Consideration of 268 Cases Operated On by the Halsted Method. Baltimore: 1899. V. 53

BLOODGOOD, SIMEON DEWITT
An Englishman's Sketch-Book; or Letters from New York. New York: 1828. V. 51

THE BLOODY Game at Cards. *As it Was Played Betwixt the King of Hearts and the Rest of His Suite, Against the Residue of the Packe of Cards...* London: 1643. V. 49

THE BLOODY Massacre Perpetrated in King Street Boston on March 5th 1770 by a Party of the 29th Regiment. Barre: 1970. V. 51; 53

BLOOM, HAROLD
The Flight to Lucifer. New York: 1979. V. 54

BLOOM, VERA
Empress Eugenie 1290. New York: 1923. V. 48

BLOOMFIELD, GEORGINA, BARONESS
Reminiscences of Court and Diplomatic Life. London: 1883. V. 50

BLOOMFIELD, MAX
Bloomfield's Illustrated Historical Guide. St. Augustine: 1885. V. 47

BLOOMFIELD, NATHANIEL
An Essay on War, in Blank Verse: Honington Green, a Ballad. Bury. V. 50

BLOOMFIELD, ROBERT
The Banks of the Wye; a Poem. London: 1811. V. 47
The Farmer's Boy; a Rural Poem. London: 1800. V. 48; 49; 52; 53
The Farmer's Boy; a Rural Poem... London: 1800/02. V. 50; 51
Good Tidings; or, News from the Farm. London: 1804. V. 47; 54
The Horkey. London: 1882. V. 51; 52
May Day with the Muses. London: 1822. V. 51
Rural Tales, Ballads and Songs. London: 1802. V. 48; 49; 50; 51; 53; 54
Wild Flowers; or, Pastoral and Local Poetry. London: 1806. V. 47; 49; 50; 51

BLORE, EDWARD
The Monumental Remains of Noble and Eminent Persons... London: 1824-26. V. 49

BLORE, EDWARD continued
The Monumental Remains of Noble and Eminent Persons... London: 1826. V. 50; 52; 54

THE BLOSSOMS Of Morality. London: 1796. V. 52

BLOSSOMS of Morality... New York: 1800. V. 51

BLOUIN DE LA PIQUETIERRE, MICHEL
The Portugal History; or, a Relation of the troubles that Happened in the Court of Portugal in the Years 1667 and 1668. London: 1677. V. 50

BLOUNT, GODFREY
The Story of the Sower. London: 1910. V. 54

BLOUNT, HENRY
A Voyage Into the Levant. London: 1636. V. 48

BLOUNT, THOMAS
The Academy of Eloquence. London: 1670. V. 53
Boscobel; or, the Compleat History of the most Miraculous Preservation of King Charles II. After the Battle of Worcester (and) Claustrum Regale Reseratum; or, the King's Concealment at Trent. London: 1725. V. 52
Fragmenta Antiquitatis. London: 1679. V. 50; 52
Fragmenta Antiquitatis... York: 1784. V. 53
Glossographia; or a Dictionary, Interpreting the Hard Words of Whatsoever Language, Now Used In Our Refined English Tongue... London: 1670. V. 52
Glossographia; or a Dictionary, interpreting the Hard Words of Whatsoever Language, Now used In our refined English Tongue... London: 1674. V. 52

BLOUNT, THOMAS POPE
De Re Poetica. London: 1694. V. 47; 49; 50; 53; 54
Essays On Several Subjects. London: 1692. V. 51
A Natural History: Containing Many Not Common Observations... London: 1693. V. 48; 50

BLOW, JOHN
Amphion Anglicus. A Work of Many Compositions, for One, Two, Three and Four Voices. London: 1700. V. 52

BLOWER, J. G.
Myriapoda. London: 1974. V. 52

BLUE Beard. New York. V. 53

BLUE Blanket Valley Lands Improved and Unimproved Farm and Ranch Lands in Walworth, Campbell and Edmunds Counties South Dakota and Emmons and McIntosh Counties North Dakota... Aberdeen: 1902. V. 50

THE BLUE Book, A Bibliographical Attempt to Describe the Guide Books to the Houses of Ill Fame in New Orleans As They Were Published There. 1936. V. 50

BLUM, ANDRE
The Origin and Early History of Engraving in France in Woodcut, Metalcut and Blockbook. Frankfurt: 1930. V. 53

BLUMBERG, FANNIE BURGHEIM
Rowena Teena Tot and the Blackberries. Chicago: 1934. V. 53

BLUME, DIETER
The Sculpture of Anthony Caro 1942-1989. Cologne: 1981-90. V. 50; 54

BLUME, JUDY
Otherwise Known as Sheila the Great. New York: 1972. V. 47; 51

BLUMENBACH, JOHANN FRIEDRICH
The Anthropological Treatises of Johann Friedrich Blumenbach. London: 1865. V. 54
Elements of Physiology... Philadelphia: 1795. V. 48; 53

BLUMENTHAL, JOSEPH
Robert Frost and His Printers. 1985. V. 54
Typographic Years: a Printer's Journey through a Half Century 1925-1975. 1982. V. 52
Typographic Years: a Printer's Journey Through a Half Century 1925-1975. New York: 1982. V. 47; 48

BLUMENTHAL, WALTER HART
Formats and Foibles. Worcester: 1955. V. 53

BLUM'S Farmers' and Planters' Almanac for the Year 1864... Salem: 1864. V. 50

BLUNDELL, JOSEPH HIGHT
Toddington: Its Annals and People. Isle of Wight: 1925. V. 54

BLUNDEN, EDMUND CHARLES
An Anthology of War Poems. London: 1930. V. 50
Choice or Chance. London: 1934. V. 48
De Bello Germanico - a Fragment of Trench History - Written in 1918 by the Author of Undertones of War. Hawstead: 1930. V. 47; 54
Dead Letters. London: 1923. V. 48; 50; 53
Great Short Stories of the War. London: 1930. V. 50; 54
Halfway House. Poems. London: 1932. V. 49
The Harbingers. 1916. V. 47; 49
The Harbingers. Uckfield: 1916. V. 48
Japanese Garland. London: 1928. V. 51
Masks of Time... London: 1925. V. 47
Near and Far: New Poems. London: 1929. V. 49; 54
Pastorals: A Book of Verses. London: 1916. V. 47; 48; 51; 52
The Poems of Edmund Blunden. London: 1930. V. 49; 53
Retreat. London: 1928. V. 52
Shakespeare's Significances. A Paper Read Before the Shakespeare Association, 25th January 1929 at King's College, London. London: 1929. V. 48
Some Seventeenth-Century Latin Poems by English Writers. Toronto: 1957. V. 47
A Summer's Fancy. 1930. V. 47
To Nature... London: 1923. V. 49; 52
To Themis. Poems on Famous Trials with Other Pieces. London: 1931. V. 52
Undertones of War. London: 1928. V. 47; 48; 49
Votive Tablets: Studies Chiefly Appreciative of English Authors and Books. London: 1931. V. 50
The Waggoner and other Poems. London: 1920. V. 48; 50; 51

BLUNDEVILLE, THOMAS
Mr. Blundevil His Exercises... London: 1636. V. 50

BLUNT, ANNE
A Pilgrimage to Nejd, the Cradle of the Arab Race. London: 1881. V. 50
The Stealing of the White Mare. Newtown: 1930. V. 47

BLUNT, ANTHONY
Baroque & Rococo: Architecture and Decoration. London: 1978. V. 54
Drawings of G. B. Castiglione and Stefano Della Bella. London: 1954. V. 52; 54
Nicolas Poussin... Washington: 1966. V. 50
Nicolas Poussin. New York: 1967. V. 49; 51; 53; 54
Nicolas Poussin. New York: 1976. V. 50
The Paintings of Nicolas Poussin. (with) Nicolas Poussin. London: 1966/67. V. 54
Roman Drawings of the XVII and XVIII Centuries. London: 1960. V. 52; 54
Sicilian Baroque. New York: 1968. V. 53

BLUNT, C. F.
The Beauty of the Heavens. London: 1842. V. 54

BLUNT, DAVID ENDERBY
Elephant... London: 1933. V. 50

BLUNT, JOSEPH
The Merchant's and Shipmaster's Assistant... New York: 1822. V. 47; 50
The Merchant's and Shipmaster's Assistant... New York: 1832. V. 47

BLUNT, REGINALD
The Carlyle's Chelsea Home. London: 1895. V. 52
The Cheyne Book of Chelsea and Pottery. London: 1924. V. 50

BLUNT, WILFRED
The Art of Botanical Illustration. London: 1950. V. 47; 48; 51; 54
The Art of Botanical Illustration. London: 1951. V. 47
The Art of Botanical Illustration. New York: 1951. V. 48
The Art of Botanical Illustration. London: 1955. V. 47; 49
The Art of Botanical Illustration. London: 1971. V. 49
Flora Superba. London: 1971. V. 52; 53
The Illustrated Herbal. London: 1979. V. 54

BLUNT, WILFRID SCAWEN
Fand of the Fair Cheek: A Three Act Tragedy in Rhymed Verse. London: 1904. V. 47
In Vinculis. London: 1889. V. 47; 50; 53; 54
The Land War in Ireland, Being a Personal Narrative of the Events. 1912. V. 48
The Love Lyrics and Songs of Proteus. Hammersmith: 1892. V. 48; 51; 52; 54
The Love Lyrics and Songs of Proteus. London: 1892. V. 47; 50; 51
The Love Sonnets of Proteus. London: 1881. V. 54
The Poetry of Wilfred Blunt. 1898. V. 49; 54
The Poetry of Wilfred Blunt. London: 1898. V. 50; 51

BLUXOME & CO., NEW YORK
Trade Catalogue of Hats. Spring and Summer 1883. V. 54

BLY, ROBERT
Basho. San Francisco: 1972. V. 49; 51
The Light Around the Body. New York: 1967. V. 48; 53
The Lion's Tail and Eyes, Poems Written Out of Laziness and Silence. Madison;: 1962. V. 52
Mirabai Versions. New York: 1980. V. 52; 53; 54
The Teeth-Mother Naked at Last. Minnesota: 1970. V. 53
This Tree Will Be Here for a Thousand Years. New York. V. 51
This Tree Will Be Here for a Thousand Years. New York: 1979. V. 52
The Traveller Who Repeats His Cry. New York: 1982. V. 52; 53
Visiting Emily Dickinson's Grave and Other Poems. Madison: 1979. V. 52
Visiting Emily Dickinson's Grave and Other Poems. New York: 1979. V. 54
The Whole Moisty Night. New York: 1983. V. 52; 54

BLYDEN, EDWARD WILMOT
Philip and the Eunuch; or, the Instruments and methods of Africa's Evangelization. Cambridge: 1883. V. 49

BLYTH, E.
The Natural History of the Cranes. London: 1881. V. 49; 50

BLYTH, R. H.
Haiku. 1: Eastern Culture; 2: Spring; 3: Summer-Autumn; 4: Autumn-Winter. Tokyo: 1949-52. V. 49

BLYTON, ENID
The Play's The Thing!. London: 1927. V. 47
Silver and Gold. London: 1925. V. 48

B'NAI B'RITH Constitution of the Independent Order B'nai B'rith, Adopted in the General Convetion of the Order, Held in the City of New York, July 19-27, 1868. New York: 1868. V. 48

BOADEN, JAMES
An Inquiry into the Authenticity of Various Pictures and Prints, Which, From the Decease of the Poet to Our Own Times, Have Been Offered to the Public as Portraits of Shakespeare, etc. London: 1824. V. 49
The Life of Mrs. Jordan... London: 1831. V. 49; 51; 52; 53; 54
The Maid of Bristol: a Play in Three Acts. New York: 1803. V. 54

BOAK, ARTHUR E. R.
Karanis: The Temples, Coin Boards, Botanical and Zoological Reports, Seasons 1924-31. Ann Arbor: 1933. V. 52

BOAKE, BARCROFT
Where the Dead Men Lie and Other Poems. Sydney: 1896. V. 52
Where the Dead Men Lie and Other Poems. Sydney: 1897. V. 47; 54

BOAM, HENRY J.
Twentieth Century Impressions of Canada. Its History, People, Commerce, Industries and Resources. London: 1914. V. 53

BOARD OF GENERAL PROPRIETORS OF THE EASTERN DIVISION OF NEW JERSEY
The Minutes of the Board...from 1685 to 1705 (1725-1744, 1745-1764). Perth Amboy: 1949-60. V. 47

BOARDMAN, JAMES
America and the Americans. London: 1833. V. 53

BOARDMAN, JOHN
Catalogue of the Engraved Gems and Finger Rings: I. Greek and Etruscan. Oxford: 1978. V. 50; 52
The Cretan Collection in Oxford: the Dictaean Cave and Iron Age Crete. Oxford: 1961. V. 50; 52
Excavations at Tocra 1963-1965. London: 1966-73. V. 50
Greek Art and Architecture. New York: 1967. V. 52
Greek Gems and Finger Rings... New York. V. 54
Greek Gems and Finger Rings. London: 1970. V. 52
Greek Gems and Finger Rings... New York: 1970. V. 48
Greek Gems and Finger Rings. New York: 1972. V. 47; 50

BOARDMAN, MABEL THORP
Under the Red Cross Flag At Home and Abroad. Philadelphia & London: 1915. V. 47; 49; 53

BOARDMAN, PETER
The Shining Mountain. London: 1978. V. 54

BOARDMAN, SAMUEL L.
The Agriculture and Industry of the County of Kennebec, Maine, with Notes Upon Its History and Natural History. Augusta: 1867. V. 48

BOARDMAN, THOMAS
A Dictionary of the Veterinary Art. London: 1805. V. 48

BOAS, FRANZ
Anthropology and Modern Life. New York: 1928. V. 52
Ethnology of the Kwakiutl. Washington: 1921. V. 50
Folk-Tales of Salishan and Sahaptin Tribes. Lancaster/New York: 1917. V. 48
Kathlamet Texts. Washington: 1901. V. 52; 54
Kutenai Tales...Together with Texts Collected by Alexander Francis Chamberlain. Washington: 1918. V. 54
Tsimshian Mythology. Washington: 1916. V. 50

BOASE, FREDERICK
Modern English Biography, Containing Many Thousand Concise Memoirs of Persons Who Have died Between the Years 1851-1900. London: 1965. V. 47

BOATFIELD, ROSAMOND
The King's Fairy Air Force. London. V. 47

BOATRIGHT, MODY C.
Tall Tales from Texas Cow Camps. Dallas: 1934. V. 53; 54

BOAZ, HERMAN
The Angler's Progress: a Poem. London: 1820. V. 49

BOBART, H. H.
Records of the Basketmaker's Company. London: 1911. V. 47

BOBER, PHYLLIS PRAY
Drawings After the Antique Sketchbooks in the British Museum. 1957. V. 54

BOBO by the Sea.
1930's. V. 49

BOBO, WILLIAM M.
Glimpses of New York City. Charleston: 1852. V. 47

BOCALINI, TRAJANO
Advices from Parnassus, in Two Centuries. London: 1706. V. 47
I Ragguagli Di Parnasso; or, Advertisements from Parnassus... London: 1656. V. 48
I Ragguagli Di Parnasso; or, Advertisements from Parnassus... London: 1657. V. 50
I Ragguagli Di Parnasso; or, Advertisements from Parnassus... London: 1669. V. 47

BOCANGEL Y UNZUETA, GABRIEL
La Fiesta Real, y votiva de Toros, Que a Honor de San Juan Bautista, Celebro Madrid, a 6. de Julio de 1648. Madrid: 1648. V. 48
La Lira de las Musas, de Humanas, y Sagradas Vozes: Junto con las Demas Obras Poeticas Antes Divulgadas. Madrid: 1637?. V. 48

BOCCACCIO, GIOVANNI
Amorous Fiammetta. London: 1926. V. 48
Le Decameron. Lyons: 1558. V. 51; 52
Le Decameron. Paris: 1559. V. 52
The Decameron. London: 1741. V. 48; 50; 51; 52; 53
The Decameron... London: 1804. V. 50
The Decameron... London: 1822. V. 49
The Decameron... London: 1895. V. 47; 48
The Decameron. London: 1903. V. 51
The Decameron... London: 1920. V. 47; 51
The Decameron. New York: 1925. V. 48; 49; 52; 54
The Decameron. Philadelphia: 1928. V. 51
The Decameron... London: 1930. V. 47
The Decameron. New York: 1930. V. 50; 53; 54
The Decameron. London: 1932. V. 48
Decameron... Oxford: 1934/35. V. 47
The Decameron. New York: 1940. V. 51
The Decameron. Garden City: 1949. V. 48; 50; 52
The Decameron. London: 1969. V. 49; 51
Il Decamerone. London: 1702. V. 52
Il Decamerone. London: 1712. V. 47; 49
Il Decamerone... 1729. V. 51; 54
Il Decamerone... Pasinello: 1729. V. 47
The Fall of Princys Princessys and Other Nobles. London: 1976. V. 51
La Fiammette Amoureuse... Paris: 1609. V. 53
Il Filocolo. In Firenze: 1594. V. 53
Genealogiae Deorum. Venice: 1494/95. V. 48; 53; 54
I Philocopo. Venegia: 1538. V. 51
Laberinto D'Amore di...Con Una Epistola Confortatoria a Messer Pino di Ross del Medesimo Autore. Venezia: 1529. V. 47
The Life of Dante. Greenbrae: 1992. V. 54
The Modell of Wit, Mirth, Eloquence and Conversation. (With) The Decameron. London: 1625/20. V. 48
The Novels and Tales of... London: 1684. V. 47; 48
The Novels and Tales of... London: 1764. V. 47
The Nymphs of Fiesole. Verona: 1952. V. 47; 52
Opera dell'Huomo Dotto et Famoso Giovanni Boccaccio... Venice: 1530?. V. 54
The Story of Griselda. London: 1909. V. 51; 54
The Tale of the Falcon. San Francisco: 1926. V. 54
Thirteene Most Pleasaunt and Delectable Questions. London: 1927. V. 48; 54
The Tragedies... London: 1554. V. 53
The Tragedies... London: 1555?. V. 47; 49; 50
A Translation of Boccaccio's Life of Dante. New York: 1900. V. 47; 53
Trattatello in Laude de Dante, by Boccaccio. Verona: 1955. V. 50

BOCCHI, FRANCESCO
Le Bellezze Della Citta di Firenze... Firenze: 1677. V. 51

BOCCIUS, GOTTLIEB
A Treatise on the Management of Fresh-Water Fish, with a View to Making Them a Source of Profit to Landed Proprietors. London: 1841. V. 47; 53

BOCK, CARL
The Head-Hunters of Borneo: a Narrative of Travel Up the Mahakkam and Down the Barito; also Journeyings in Sumatra. London: 1881. V. 47; 53
Temples and Elephants: the Narrative of a Journey of Exploration through Upper Siam and Lao. London: 1884. V. 53

BOCKENHEIMER, P. H.
Atlas of Typical Operations in Surgery. New York & London: 1906. V. 48

BOCKES, BERNARD
Sixteen Poems in Verse and Wood. Boston: 1965. V. 51; 54

BOCKETT, ELIAS
Geneva: a Poem. London: 1729. V. 47; 51

BOCKLER, GEORGE ANDREAS
Architectura Curiosa Nova, Das Ist: Neue, Ergotzliche, Sinnund Kunstreiche, Auch Nutzliche Bau und Wasserkunst. Nurnberg: 1675. V. 53

BOCKSTOCE, JOHN R.
American Whalers in the Western Arctic. Fairhaven: 1983. V. 49

BODDAM-WHETHAM, J. W.
Roraima and British Guiana with a Glance at Bermuda, West Indies and Spanish Main. London: 1879. V. 54

BODDINGTON, MARY
Slight Reminiscences of the Rhine, Switzerland and a Corner of Italy. Philadelphia: 1835. V. 52

BODE, CLEMENT AUGUSTUS DE
Travels in Luristan and Arabistan. London: 1845. V. 50

BODE, WILHELM
Florentine Sculptors of the Renaissance. London: 1908. V. 50; 52

BODE, WILLIAM
Lights and Shadows of Chinatown. San Francisco: 1896. V. 48; 53

BODE, WINSTON
A Portrait of Pancho. Austin: 1965. V. 50; 52; 54

BODENHAUSEN, EBERHARD, FREIHERR VON
Gerard David and His School. New York. V. 51

BODENHEIM, MAXWELL
Minna and Myself. New York: 1918. V. 49
Replenishing Jessica. New York: 1925. V. 47; 53; 54
The Sardonic Arm. Chicago: 1923. V. 49

BODENHEIMER, F. S.
Animal and Man in Bible Lands. Leiden: 1960-72. V. 52
The Aphidoidea of the Middle East. Jerusalem: 1957. V. 50
A Biologist in Israel. Jerusalem: 1959. V. 54

BODIAM Castle, a Poem, in Six Cantos. London: 1818. V. 54

BODIAN, MARTIN
Fibrocystic Disease of the Pancreas: a Congenital Disorder of Mucus Production, Mucosis. London: 1952. V. 53

BODIN, JEAN
De La Demonomanie des Sorciers. Antwerp: 1586. V. 52
De La Demonomanie des Sorciers. Anvers: 1592/93. V. 48
De La Demonomanie des Sorciers. Antwerp: 1593. V. 53
De Magorum Demonomania Libri IV. Basel: 1581. V. 50
De Magorum Demonomania... Libri IV. Francofurti: 1590. V. 52
Les Six Livres de la Republique. Lyon: 1580. V. 47; 50; 53

BODINE, L.
Off the Face of the Earth. 1894. V. 48; 52

BODIO, STEPHEN
Atlantic Salmon. Easthampton: 1988. V. 51

BODKIN, THOMAS
Four Irish Landscape Painters... Dublin: 1920. V. 49
Four Irish Landscape Painters. London: 1920. V. 47
Twelve Irish Artists. Dublin: 1940. V. 48; 50; 53
Twelve Irish Artists. London: 1940. V. 47; 53

THE BODLEY Head - 1887-1957. London: 1970. V. 49

BODLEY, THOMAS
Letters...to the University of Oxford 1598-1611. Oxford: 1927. V. 48
Pietas Oxoniensis. Oxford: 1902. V. 50
Reliquiae Bodleianae: or Some Genuine Remains of Sir Thomas Bodley. London: 1703. V. 47

BODONI, GIOVANNI BATTISTA
Bodoni's Preface to the Manuale Tipografico of 1818. London: 1925. V. 48
Manuale Tipografico. London: 1960. V. 47

BODROGI, T.
Art in Africa. Corvina: 1968. V. 54
Art of Indonesia. Budapest: 1972. V. 51

BOECE, HECTOR
The Buik of the Cronicli of Scotland; or, a Metrical Version of the History of Hector Boece... London: 1858. V. 49; 52

BOECK, WILHELM
Picasso. New York: 1955. V. 47; 50
Picasso. London: 1961. V. 53
Picasso Linoleum Cuts: Bacchanals, Women, Bulls & Bullfights. New York: 1962. V. 48

BOECKELMANN, ANDRIES
Nootwendig Bericht van Mr. Andries Boekelman, Chirurgyn, Breuck, en Vroetmeester der Stadt Amsterdam... Amsterdam: 1677. V. 52

BOECKH, AUGUSTUS
The Public Economy of Athens; to Which is Added a Dissertation on the Silver Mines of Laurion. London: 1842. V. 52

BOEHL VON FABER, CECILIA
The Sea Gull. London: 1867. V. 53

BOEHME, JAKOB
The Way to Christ Discovered and Described... Bath: 1775. V. 48

BOEHN, MAX VON
Modes and Manners. London: 1932. V. 51

BOELTER, HOMER H.
Portfolio of Hopi Kachinas. Hollywood: 1969. V. 52

BOEMUS, JOANNES
The Fardle of Facion... 1888. V. 47
The Manners, Lawes and Customs of All Nations...With Many Other Things... London: 1611. V. 47

BOERHAAVE, HERMANN
Academical Lectures on the Theory of Physic. London: 1751-43-44-57. V. 53
Aphorisms: Concerning the Knowledge and Cure of Diseases. London: 1735. V. 49
De Viribus Medicamentorum; or, a Treatise of the Virtue and Energy of Medicines. London: 1720. V. 53
Elements of Chemistry. London: 1735. V. 50; 51; 54
Materia Medica, or the Druggist's Guide and the Physician and Apoethecary's Table-Book... London: 1755. V. 51
A New Method of Chemistry... London: 1741. V. 50
A Treatise on the Powers of Medicines. London: 1740. V. 47

BOERIN, EDWARD
Etchings of the West... Santa Barbara: 1950. V. 47

BOERSMA, J. S.
Athenian Building Policy from 561/0 to 405/4 BC. Groningen: 1970. V. 50; 52

BOESCH, GOTTFRIED
The Glory of the Rose. London: 1965. V. 48

BOESIGER, W.
Richard Neutra: Buildings and Projects. Zurich: 1951. V. 51; 54
Richard Neutra: Buildings and Projects... New York: 1964. V. 53

BOETHIUS, ANICIUS MANLIUS
Boetius de Consolatione Philosophae... Lyon: 1493. V. 47; 50
De Consolatione Philosophie Libri Quinque. Amsterdam: 1620. V. 47
Consolationis Philosophiae Libri Quinque. Glasgow: 1751. V. 48; 52
Consolationis Philosophiae Libri V... Oxoniae: 1698. V. 48
De Consolatione Philosophiae. Basel: 1522. V. 49
Della Consolatione de la Filosofia. Fiorenza: 1551. V. 53
Dialectica, in Qua Emendanda Tantam Adhibuit Martianvs Rota Diligentiam. Venice: 1570. V. 52
His Consolation of Philosophy. London: 1730. V. 47; 49; 54
In Topica Ciceronis Commentarius. Paris: 1540. V. 53

BOETHIUS, AXEL
Etruscan and Roman Architecture. Harmondsworth: 1970. V. 50
The Golden House of Nero: Some Aspects of Roman Architecture. Ann Arbor: 1960. V. 50; 52

BOETHIUS, BERDA
Anders Zorn. An International Swedish Artist-His Life and Work. Stockholm: 1954. V. 54

BOETTICHER, ERNST
La Troie de Schliemann. Une Necropole a Incineration a la Maniere Assyro-Babylonienne. Louvain: 1889. V. 52

BOFFITO, GIUSEPPE
Biblioteca Aeronautica Italiana Illustrata...(with) Primo Supplemento Decennale (1927-36). Florence: 1929-37. V. 49

BOGAERT, LUDO VAN
First International Congress of Neurological Sciences...Brussels 21-28 July 1957. London: 1959. V. 52

BOGAN, LOUISE
The Blue Estuaries. Poems: 1923-68. New York: 1968. V. 52
Body of This Death. New York: 1923. V. 48; 49; 51; 52
Dark Summer. New York: 1929. V. 47; 48; 49; 52
Poems and New Poems. New York: 1941. V. 52
Selected Criticism - Poetry & Prose. London: 1955. V. 52
The Sleeping Fury. New York: 1937. V. 50; 52

BOGAN, P. M.
Yaqui Indian Dances of Tucson, Arizona. Tucson: 1925. V. 51

BOGAN, ZACHARY
Archaeologiae Atticae... Oxford: 1654. V. 53

BOGATZKY, CARL HEINRICH VON
The Golden Treasury for the Children of God, Whose Treasure Is In Heaven... Boston: 1796. V. 50
A Golden Treasury for the Children of God, Whose Treasure Is In Heaven... York: 1796. V. 54
A Golden Treasury for the Children of God, Whose Treasure is in Heaven... York: 1799. V. 48

BOGDANOVICH, PETER
Pieces of Time...On the Movies. 1973. V. 53

BOGG, EDMUND
From Edenvale to The Plains of York: A Thousand Miles in the Valleys of the Nidd and Yore. Leeds & York. V. 47; 53
A Thousand Miles in Wharfedale and the Wharfe. London. V. 54
A Thousand Miles of Wandering Along the Roman Wall, the Old Border Region, Lakeland and Ribblesdale. Lees: 1898. V. 54
Two Thousand Miles in Wharfedale... London: 1904. V. 54
Two Thousand Miles of Wandering in the Border Country, Lakeland and Ribblesdale. Leeds: 1898. V. 52; 53; 54

BOGGIS, R. J. E.
A History of the Diocese of Exeter. Exeter: 1922. V. 49; 54

BOGGS, JEAN SUTHERLAND
Portraits by Degas. Berkeley: 1962. V. 51

BOGGS, MAE HELEN BACON
My Playhouse Was a Concord Coach. Oakland: 1942. V. 47; 49; 51

BOGGS, TOM
American Decade. Cummington: 1943. V. 50

BOGGS, WILLIAM R.
Military Reminiscences of Gen. Wm. R. Boggs, C.S.A. Durham: 1913. V. 49

BOGOLYUBOV, ANDREI ANDREYEVICH
Carpets of Central Asia. 1973. V. 54

BOHEMIA: a Symposium of Literary and Artistic Impressions by Men and Women Distinguished in Journalism, Art, Romance, Literature, Finance, Diplomacy... Philadelphia: 1904. V. 49

BOHLKE, J. E.
Fishes of the Bahamas and Adjacent Tropical Waters. Philadelphia: 1968. V. 49
Fishes of the Bahamas and Adjacent Tropical Waters. Philadelphia: 1970. V. 53

BOHME, JAKOB
Drievoudigh Leven des Menschen. N.P: 1636. V. 53

BOHME, PALL W.
Highlights In the History of American Whaling. Bookhaven: 1968. V. 47

BOHN, HENRY GEORGE
Bohn's Catalogue of Books (spine title). 1948. London: 1841. V. 49
Catalogue of the Second Portion of the Very Extensive and Valuable Stock of Mr. Henry George Bohn. London: 1870. V. 51
Polyglot of Foreign Proverbs. London: 1857. V. 50; 54

BOHNM-BAWERK, EUGEN V.
Capital and Interest. A Critical History of Economical Theory... London: 1890. V. 53

BOHNY, NICHOLAS
The New Picture Book. Edinburgh: 1858. V. 52

BOHR, NIELS HENRIK DAVID
On the Quantum Theory of Line-Spectra. Copenhagen: 1918-22. V. 47
Studier Over Metallernes Elektrontheorie. Copenhagen: 1911. V. 50; 54

BOHTE, J. H.
A Catalogue of Books, Consisting Chiefly of Imported Greek and Latin Classics and Miscellaneous Literature in Various Languages, Including a Most Complete and Select Collection of German Literature... London: 1821. V. 49

BOHUN, EDMUND
An Address to the Free-Men and Free-holders of the Nation. London: 1682. V. 50; 54

BOHUN, RALPH
A Discourse Concerning the Origin and Properties of Wind.. Oxford: 1671. V. 50; 54

BOHUN, WILLIAM
A Collection of Debates, Reports, Orders and Resolutions, of the House of Commons, Touching the Right of Electing Members to Serve in Parliament, for the Several Counties, Cities, Burroughs, and Towns Corporate in England and Wales. London: 1700?. V. 47; 52
Declarations and Pleadings in the Most Usual Actions Brought in the Several Courts of King's Bench and Common-Pleas at Westminster, viz, in Actions of Scandal of Peers Respecting Their Honour. In the Savoy: 1733. V. 50
The Law of Tithes... London: 1731. V. 50; 52
The Law of Tithes... London: 1744. V. 50
Privilegia Londini: or, the Laws, Customs and Privileges of the City of London. London: 1702. V. 52
Privilegia Londini: or, the Rights, Liberties, Privileges, Laws and Customs of the City of London. London: 1723. V. 52

BOIES, HENRY M.
Prisoners and Paupers. New York: 1893. V. 50
The Science of Penology, the Defence of Society Against Crime. New York: 1901. V. 51

BOILEAU, D.
The Art of Working in Pasteboard, Upon Scientific Principles: To Which is Added, an Appendix... London: 1827. V. 52

BOILEAU, DANIEL
An Introduction to the Study of Political Economy; or Elementary View of the Man in Which the Wealth of Nations is Produced... London: 1811. V. 48; 52

BOILEAU, JACQUES
The History of Flagellants... London: 1777. V. 49
Memorials of Human Superstition... London: 1784. V. 49; 54

BOILEAU-DESPREAUX, NICOLAS
Les Oeuvres... Paris: 1740. V. 49
Oeuvres. Glasgow: 1759. V. 52
Oeuvres Diverses. Paris: 1674. V. 53
Posthumous Works...viz. I. A Satire Upon Equivocation... II. Seventeen New Epigrams. III. The Heroes Romances... London: 1736. V. 49
The Works... London: 1711-12. V. 47

BOISDUVAL, J. A.
Histoire General et Iconographie des Leipdopteres et des Chenilles de l'Amerique Septentrionale. Paris: 1829-33. V. 47

BOISGELIN, LOUIS DE
Travels through Denmark and Sweden. London: 1810. V. 47

BOISGILBERT, EDMUND
Caesar's Column: a Story of the Twentieth Century. London: 1891. V. 47

BOISSARD, JEAN JACQUES
Emblematum Liber. Emblemes Latins, Avec l'Interpretation Francoise du I. Pierre Ioly Messin. Metz: 1588. V. 49
Icones Quinquaginta Virorum Illustrium Doctrina & Erudtione Praest Antium ad Virum, Cum Eorum Vitis Descriptis. Frankfurt: 1597-1631/32. V. 50
Tractatus Posthumus de Divinatione et Magicis... Oppenheim: 1605. V. 49; 53; 54
Tractatus Posthumus...de Divinatione et Magicis... Oppenheim: 1615?. V. 47
Tractatus Posthumus...De Divinatione et Magicis Praestigiis. Oppenheimii: 1616?. V. 50
Vitae et Icones Sultanorum Turcicorum, Principum Persarum Aliorumque Illustrium Heroum Heroin-Arumque Ab Osmane Usque ad Mahometem II. Franckofurti: 1596. V. 50

BOISSET, LOUIS
Monaco-Monte Carlo. Nice: 1884. V. 51

BOISSIER, E.
Voyage Botanique dans le Midi de l'Espagne...Pendant l'Annee 1837. Paris: 1839-45. V. 49

BOISSIER, PIERRE EDMOND
Flora Orientalis Sive Enumeratio Plantarum in Oriente a Graecia et Aegypto ad Indiae Fines Hucusque Observatarum. Basel: 1867-88. V. 53

BOISSLIER, JEAN
The Heritage of Thai Sculpture. New York: 1975. V. 50
Thai Painting. Tokyo: 1976. V. 54

BOITO, ARRIGO
Re Orso; Two Verse Legends. Milan: 1948. V. 52

BOIVIN, MARIE ANNE VICTORIE
Traite Pratique des Maladies de l'Uterus et de ses Annexes. Bruxelles: 1834. V. 49; 50; 51; 52; 53; 54

BOK, CURTIS
Commonwealth v. Gordon et al: the Opinion of Judge Bok, March Eighteenth 1949. San Francisco: 1949. V. 47

BOK, EDWARD W.
Beecher Memorial; Contemporaneous Tributes to the Memory of Henry Ward Beecher. Brooklyn: 1887. V. 48

THE BOKE of Noblesse... 1860. V. 52
THE BOKE of Noblesse... London: 1860. V. 54

THE BOKE of Noblesse. London: 1890. V. 51; 52

BOKER, GEORGE H.
The Book of the Dead. Philadelphia: 1882. V. 53
The Podesta's Daughter and Other Miscellaneous Poems. Philadelphia: 1852. V. 49

BOLAM, GEORGE
Birds of Northumberland and the Eastern Borders. 1912. V. 52
Wild Life in Wales. London: 1913. V. 50; 52

BOLAND, D. J.
Forest Trees of Australia. East Melbourne: 1984. V. 51

BOLAND, E.
The Journey and Other Poems. Dublin: 1986. V. 48

BOLAND, MAUREEN
Garden Lore: Extracts from Old Wives' Lore for Gardeners. London: 1976. V. 53

BOLDONI, OTTAVIO
Theatrum Temporaneum Aeternitati Caesaris Monti S.R.E. Cardinalis et Archiep. Mediolanen. Sacrum. Milan: 1636. V. 47

BOLDREWOOD, ROLF
Robbery Under Arms. London: 1888. V. 51

BOLINGBROKE, HENRY ST. JOHN, 1ST VISCOUNT
A Collection of Political Tracts. London: 1748. V. 47
A Congratulatory Letter to a Certain Right Honourable Person, Upon His Late Disappointment. London: 1743. V. 47
Le Crafts-man. Amsterdam: 1737. V. 54
The Craftsman Extraordinary. London: 1729. V. 48
A Disseration Upon Parties; in Several Letters to Caleb D'Anvers. Dublin: 1735. V. 47; 53
A Letter to Sir William Windham. II. Some Reflections on the Present State of the Nation. III. A letter to Mr. Pope. London: 1753. V. 47; 51; 53
Letters and Correspondence, Public and Private of... London: 1798. V. 47; 49
Letters, on the Spirit of Patriotism: on the Idea of a Patriot King; and on the State of Parties, at the Accession of King George the First. London: 1749. V. 47; 48; 53
Letters on the Study and Use of History. 1752. V. 47
Letters on the Study and Use of History. London: 1752. V. 47; 53
Memoires Secrets de Mylord Bolingbroke, sur les Affaires d'Angleterre Depuis 1710, Jesqu'en 1716. Londres i.e. Berlin: 1754. V. 54
Memoirs of the Life and Ministerial Conduct... of the Late Lord Viscount Bolingbroke. London: 1752. V. 49
The Miscellaneous Works.... Edinburgh: 1768. V. 50
The Works. London: 1751-71. V. 47
Works... London: 1753. V. 48
The Works. London: 1754-79. V. 54

BOLIO, ANTONIO MEDIZ
The Land of the Pheasant and the Deer. Mexico City: 1935. V. 47

BOLL, HEINRICH
Acquainted with the Night. London: 1955. V. 54
Adam, Where Are Thou?. London: 1955. V. 47; 48; 49
Group Portrait with Lady. New York: 1973. V. 47

BOLLAERT, WILLIAM
Antiquarian, Ethnological and Other Researches in New Granada, Ecquador, Peru and Chile, with Observations on the Pre-Incarial, Incarial and Other Monuments of Peruvian Nations. London: 1860. V. 47

BOLLAN, WILLIAM
A Succinct View of the Origin of Our Colonies, with Their Civil State, Founded by Queen Elizabeth, Corroborated by Succeeding Princes, and Confirmed by Acts of Parliament... London: 1766. V. 51

BOLLAND, WILLIAM
Saint Paul at Athens. Cambridge: 1800. V. 54

BOLLER, ALFRED P.
Practical Treatise on the Construction of Iron Highway Bridges... New York: 1878. V. 49
Practical Treatise On the Construction of Iron Highway Bridges. New York: 1893. V. 50

BOLLER, HENRY A.
Among the Indians. Chicago: 1959. V. 50

BOLLES, JOHN S.
Las Monjas: a major Pre-Mexican Architectural Complex at Chichen Itza. Norman: 1977. V. 50

BOLLI, H. M.
Plankton Stratigraphy. Cambridge: 1985. V. 52

BOLLOTEN, BURNETT
The Grand Camouflage. The Communist Conspiracy in the Spanish civil War. London: 1961. V. 49

BOLSEC, JEROME HERMES
De Vita et Rebvs Gestis Martini Lvtheri, et Aliorum Speudapostolorum (sic) Haereseos... Paris: 1581. V. 53

BOLTON, ARTHUR T.
The Architecture of Robert and James Adam (1758-1794). London: 1922. V. 48; 50; 51; 52
The Gardens of Italy. London: 1919. V. 53

BOLTON, CHARLES KNOWLES
The Founders: Portraits of Persons Born Abroad Who Came to the Colonies in North America Before the Year 1701. Boston: 1916-26. V. 54
The Founders: Portraits of Persons Born Abroad Who Came to the Colonies in North America Before the Year 1701. Boston: 1919-26. V. 53
On the Wooing of Martha Pitkin. Boston: 1894. V. 47; 49

BOLTON, CLAIRE
The Alembic Press Guide to Sundry Printing Places & Sources that Might Be of Interest to Other Private Press Printers. Oxford: 1991. V. 51
Awa Gami: Japanese Handmade Paper from Fuji Mills, Tokushima. 1992. V. 54
Awa Gami: Japanese Handmade Paper from Fuji Mills, Tokushima. London: 1992. V. 52
Maziarczyk Paste Papers. Oxford: 1991. V. 50; 51
Payhembury Marbled Papers Sampler. Winchester: 1987. V. 49; 53
A Winchester Bookshop and Bindery 1729-1991. London: 1991. V. 52

BOLTON, ETHEL STANWOOD
American Samplers. 1921. V. 50
American Samplers. Boston: 1921. V. 51

BOLTON, HEBERT EUGENE
Anza's California Expeditions. Berkeley: 1930. V. 50; 52; 53; 54

BOLTON, HERBERT EUGENE
Coronado Knight of Pueblos and Plains. New York and Albuquerque: 1949. V. 54
Coronado on the Turquoise Trail: Knight of Pueblo and Plains. Albuquerque: 1949. V. 48; 49; 52; 54
Fray Juan Crespi: Missionary Explorer on the Pacific Coast. Berkeley: 1927. V. 54
Kino's Historical Memoir of Pimeria Alta, A Contemporary Account of the Beginnings of California, Sonora and Arizona. Berkeley: 1948. V. 52
New Spain and the Anglo-American West. Los Angeles: 1932. V. 47; 50; 54
Outpost of Empire. New York: 1931. V. 48; 50
Pageant in the Wilderness, The Story of the Escalante Expedition to the Interior Basin, 1776. Salt Lake City: 1950. V. 49; 53; 54
Pageant in the Wilderness. The Story of the Escalante Expedition to the Interior Basin, 1776. Salt Lake City: 1951. V. 54
Rim of Christendom. New York: 1936. V. 49; 52; 53; 54
Rim of Christendom. New York: 1960. V. 54
Spanish Exploration in the Southwest 1542-1706. New York: 1916. V. 48; 54
Texas in the Middle Eighteenth Century. Berkeley: 1915. V. 50; 52; 53; 54

BOLTON, JAMES
Harmonia Ruralis; or, An Essay Towards a Natural History of British Song-Birds. London: 1794. V. 50
Harmonia Ruralis; or, An Essay Towards a Natural History of British Song-Birds... London: 1794-96. V. 48
Harmonia Ruralis; or An Essay Towards a Natural History of British Song-Birds. London: 1830. V. 48
An History of Funguses, Growing About Halifax. Huddersfield: 1788-91. V. 49
An History of Funguses Growing about Halifax... Halifax;: 1788/91. V. 54

BOLTON, JOHN
Geological Fragments Collected Principally from Rambles Among the Rocks of Furness and Cartmel. London: 1869. V. 54
Geological Fragments Collected Principally from Rambles Among the Rocks of Furness and Cartmel. Ulverston: 1869. V. 48; 50; 52

BOLTON, LOUIS
Medicinal Plants Growing or Cultivated in the Island or Mauritius. Mauritius: 1857. V. 48

BOLTON, REGINALD
Indian Paths in the Great Metropolis. New York: 1922. V. 47

BOLTON, ROBERT
An Answer to the Question, Where Are Your Arguments Against What You Call, Lewdness, If You Make No Use of the Bible? London: 1755. V. 52
History of the County of Westchester. New York: 1848. V. 49; 50
History of the Several Towns, Manors and Patents of the County of Westchester. New York: 1881. V. 48; 49
Letters to a Young Nobleman. London: 1762. V. 47; 50; 52

BOLTON, SARAH K.
Social Studies in England. Boston: 1883. V. 54

BOLTON, THEODORE
The Book Illustrations of Felix Octavius Carr DArley. 1951. V. 49

BOLUS, H.
Icones Orchidearum Austro-Africanarum Extra-Tropicarum; or, Figures with Descriptions of Extra Tropical South African Orchids. London: 1893-1913. V. 47

BOLYAL, JANOS
La Science Absolue de l'Espace Independante de la Verite ou de la Faussete de l'Axiome XI d'Euclide (que l'on ne Pourra Jamais Etablir a Priori); Suivie de la Quadrature Geometrique du Cercle, dans le Cas de la Faussete de l'Axiome XI... Paris: 1868. V. 47

BOLZANIO, URBANO
Institutionum in Linguam Graecam Grammaticarum Libri Duo. Paris: 1543. V. 47; 48

BOMBAL, MARIA LUISA
The Shrouded Woman. New York: 1948. V. 49

BOMBAUGH, C. C.
The Literature of Kissing. Philadelphia: 1876. V. 48

BOMBERG, DAVID
Russian Ballet. 1919. V. 47

BOMER, ANTON
Triumphus Novem Seculorum Imperii Romano-Germanici... Augsburg: 1725. V. 47

BOMPAS, WILLIAM CARPENTER
Diocese of Mackenzie River. London: 1888. V. 49

BOMTEMPO, JOSE MARIA
Trabalhos Medicos Offerecidos a Magestade do Senhor D. Pedro I, Imperador do Brasil... Rio de Janeiro: 1825. V. 48

BONAFOUS, MATTHIEU
Histoire Naturelle, Agricole et Economique du Mais. Paris: 1836. V. 49

BONALDE, MANUEL
La Verdad Protegida. Impugnacion al Manifiesto de los Hechos Que Proporcionaron la Pacificacion a la Provincia de Venezuela, Firmada en 4 de Enero de 1813 por el Presbitero D. Pedro Gamboa y Fr. Pedro Hernandez... Cadiz: 1813. V. 53

BONANNI, FILIPPO
Descrizione degli Istromenti Armonici... Rome: 1776. V. 54

BONAPARATE, MARIE
The Life and Works of Edgar Allan Poe. London: 1949. V. 48

BONAPARTE, LUCIEN JULES LAURENT, CALLED CHARLES LUCIEN
A Geographical and Comparative List of the Birds of Europe and North America. London: 1838. V. 51
Iconographie des Pigeons... Paris: 1857-58. V. 50
Observations on the Nomenclature of Wilson's Ornithology. Philadelphia: 1826. V. 51

BONAR, ANDREW A.
Narrative of a Mission of Inquiry into the Jews from the Church of Scotland in 1839. Philadelphia: 1842. V. 47
Narrative of a Mission of Inquiry to the Jews from the Church of Scotland in 1839. Philadelphia: 1845. V. 47

BONATII, WALTER
On the Heights. London: 1964. V. 54

BONAVENTURA, SAINT, CARDINAL
Breuiloqui Theologie; Quo Omnis Laus. Paris: 1510. V. 52
Diaeta Salutis. Paris: 1500. V. 48; 52
Expositio in Psalmos. Rome: 1588. V. 50
The Life of St. Francis. V. 47
Sermones de Tempore et de Sanctis. Reutlingen: 1485. V. 54
Stimulus Duini Amoris. Paris: 1498-500. V. 52

BONAVERI, DOMENICO MARIA
Freggi dell Architetura Dedicati All' Illmo Sigre Il Sigre Sebastiano M.a. Sighicelli Da Domenico Bonaveri. N.P. V. 51

BONAVIA, DUCCIO
Mural Painting in Ancient Peru. Bloomington: 1985. V. 52

BONAVIA, E.
The Cultivated Oranges and Lemons, Etc. of India and Ceylon. Dehra Dun: 1973. V. 52; 54

BOND, A. L.
Three Gems in One Setting. London: 1860. V. 53

BOND, ALVAN
Memoir of the Rev. Pliny Fisk, A.M., Late Missionary to Palestine. Boston;: 1828. V. 49

BOND, ELIZABETH FORTROSE
Letters of a Village Governess... London: 1814. V. 47; 50

BOND, FRANCIS
An Introduction to English Church Architecture from the Eleventh to the Sixteenth Century. London: 1913. V. 49; 51; 53
Woodcarvings in English Churches. 1910. V. 50

BOND, HORACE MANN
Negro Education in Albama: a Study in Cotton and Steel. Washington: 1939. V. 50

BOND, J. WESLEY
Minnesota and Its Resources to Which are Appended Camp-Fire Sketches of Notes of a Trip from St. Paul to Pembia and Selkirk Settlement on the Red river of the North. Chicago, Philadelphia: 1856. V. 47

BOND, JULIAN
Black Candidates: Southern Campaign Experiences. Atlanta: 1969. V. 52
A Time to Speak, A Time to Act: The Movement in Politics. New York: 1972. V. 53

BOND, N.
The Thirty-First of February. 1949. V. 51

BOND, RICHARD
Poems Divine and Moral. Gloucester: 1769. V. 54

BOND, THOMAS
Topographical and Historical Sketches of the Boroughs of East and West Looe. London: 1823. V. 50; 52

BOND, W. H.
Eighteenth Century Studies in Honor of Donald F. Hyde. New York: 1970. V. 52; 54
The Houghton Library 1942-1967. 1967. V. 52

BONDE, CIMELGUS
Scutum Regale, The Royal Buckler: or, Vox Legis, a Lecture to Traytors... London: 1660. V. 47

BONDT, JACOB DE
An Account of the Diseases, Natural History and Medicines of the East Indies. London: 1769. V. 52

BONE, D. D.
Fifty Years Reminiscences of Scottish Cricket. Glasgow: 1898. V. 51; 52; 54

BONE, DAVID W.
Merchantmen Rearmed. London: 1949. V. 48; 49; 52
Merchantmen-At-Arms. London: 1919. V. 48

BONE, GERTRUDE
The Hidden Orchis. London: 1928. V. 47; 48
On the Western Isles. London: 1925. V. 48

BONE, JAMES
Edinburgh Revisited. London: 1911. V. 54

BONE, MUIRHEAD
War Drawings - from the Collection Presented to the British Museum By His Majesty's Government. London: 1917. V. 47

BONER, CHARLES
Chamois Hunting in the Mountains of Bavaria. London: 1853. V. 48; 52
Chamois Hunting in the Mountains of Bavaria... London: 1860. V. 52

BONET, THEOPHILUS
A Guide to the Practical Physician... London: 1684. V. 47; 49
Sepulchretun: sive, Anatomia Practica ex cadaveribus Morbo Denatis. Geneva: 1679. V. 48

BONFILS, ROBERT
Divertissements de Princesses Qui s'Ennuient, Presentees par Rene Chalupt. Paris: 1918. V. 54

BONFILS, WINIFRED BLACK
The Life and Personality of Phoebe Apperson Hearst. 1928. V. 52; 54
The Life and Personality of Phoebe Apperson Hearst. San Francisco: 1928. V. 50

BONGO, PIETRO
Mysticae Numerorum Significationis... Bergamo: 1585. V. 48

BONHAM-CARTER, VICTOR
A Posy of Wildflowers. 1983. V. 53

BONI, ALBERT
Photographic Literature. An International Bibliographical Guide to General and Specialized Literature on Photographic Processes.... New York: 1962. V. 49; 52
Photographic Literature: an International Bibliographic Guide to General and Specialized Literature on Photographic Processes... New York: 1962/72. V. 47; 52

BONIFACE, JOSEPH XAVIER
Picciola, or, Captivity Captive. London: 1837. V. 49

BONIFACIO, JUAN
De Divae Virginis mariae. Vita et Miraculis. Libri V... Cologne: 1610. V. 50

BONINGTON, R. P.
A Series of Subjects from the Works of the Late R. P. Bonington Drawn on Stone by J. D. Harding. London: 1829-30. V. 53

BONNARD, PIERRE
Correspondances. V. 51
Correspondences. Paris: 1944. V. 49

BONNE *Responce a Tous Propos,...Auquel est Contenu Grand Nombre de Prouerbes & Sentences Ioyeuses...* Lyon: 1567. V. 52

BONNE, RIGOBERT
Atlas de Toutes les Parties Connues du Globe Terrestre, Dresse Pour L'Histoire Philosphique et Politique des Etablissements et du Commerce des Europeens dans les Deux Indes. Geneva?: 1782?. V. 48

BONNEFONS, JEAN
Cupid's Bee-Hive; or the Sting of Love. London: 1721. V. 48
Imitations dv Latin avec Avtres Gayetez Amoureuses de l'Inuention de l'Autheur. Paris: 1610. V. 49

BONNEFONS, N. DE
The French Gardiner...Fruit Trees and Herbs... London: 1691. V. 49

BONNEMAINS, JACQUELINE
Baudin in Australian Waters. The Artwork Of the French Voyage of Discovery to the Southern Lands 1800-1804. London: 1988. V. 52
Baudin in Australian Waters. The Artwork of the French Voyage of Discovery to the Southern Lands 1800-1804. Melbourne: 1988. V. 49; 52

BONNER, CAMPBELL
Studies in Magical Amulets, Chiefly Graeco-Egyptian. Ann Arbor: 1950. V. 52

BONNER, G. W.
Kidd's New Guide to the Lions of London; or, the Stranger's Directory.. London: 1832. V. 50

BONNER, J.
A New Plan for Speedily Increasing the Number of Bee-Hives in Scotland. Edinburgh: 1795. V. 49

BONNER, JOHN STURGIS
My Trip to Central America. Houston: 1913. V. 47
The Three Adventurers. Austin: 1911. V. 49

BONNER, MARY GRAHAM
The Magic Music Shop. New York: 1929. V. 50

BONNER, T. D.
The Life and Adventures of James P. Beckwourth... New York: 1856. V. 47; 48; 52; 54
The Life and Adventures of James P. Beckwourth. New York: 1931. V. 49

BONNEY, EDWARD
The Banditti of the Prairies; or, the Murderer's Doom. Philadelphia: 1855?. V. 47

BONNEY, H. K.
Historic Notices in Reference to Fotheringhay. Oundle: 1821. V. 52; 54

BONNEY, THOMAS GEORGE
Cathedrals, Abbeys and Churches of England and Wales. London. V. 49
Cathedrals, Abbeys and Churches of England and Wales. London: 1891. V. 48
Lake and Mountain Scenery from the Swiss Alps. London: 1874. V. 51
Outline sketches in the High Alps of Dauphine. London: 1865. V. 53

BONNEY, W. P.
History of Pierce County, Washington. Chicago: 1927. V. 54

BONNOT DE MABLY, GABRIEL
Translations from the French. 1770. V. 52
Translations from the French. Lynn: 1770. V. 48

BONNYCASTLE, JOHN
An Introduction to Astronomy. London: 1796. V. 50; 52; 54
An Introduction to Astronomy. London: 1803. V. 48; 49
A Treatise on Plane and Spherical Trigonometry: With Their Most Useful Practical Applications. London: 1818. V. 49

BONNYCASTLE, RICHARD HENRY
The Canadas in 1841. London: 1841. V. 48
Spanish America: or, a Descriptive Historical and Geographical Account of the Dominons of Spain in the Western Hemisphere, Continental and Insular. Philadelphia: 1819. V. 52; 53

BONOMI, JOSEPH
Nineveh and Its Palaces. London: 1852. V. 52
Nineveh and Its Palaces... London: 1853. V. 48; 54
Nineveh and its Palaces. London: 1869. V. 51

BONPLAND, AIME JACQUES GOUJAUD
Description des Plantes Rares Cultivees a la Malmaison et a Navarre. Paris: 1812-13-17. V. 49

BONSAL, STEPHEN
Edward Fitzgerald Beale A Pioneer in the Path of Empire. New York: 1912. V. 47; 50; 52; 54

BONTEMPS, ARNA
Anyplace But Here. New York: 1966. V. 51
Cavalcade of the American Negro: Diamond Jubilee Exposition Authority. Chicago: 1940. V. 52
Chariot in the Sky. Philadelphia: 1951. V. 49; 50
Drums at Dusk. New York: 1939. V. 52
God Sends Sunday. New York: 1931. V. 53
Mr. Kelso's Lion. Philadelphia: 1970. V. 52
Slappy Hooper, the Wonderful Sign Painter. Boston: 1946. V. 50; 52
They Seek a City. Garden City: 1945. V. 47; 54

BONTOUS, J. J.
L'Auguste Piete de la Royale Maison de Bourbon... Avignon: 1750. V. 47

BONVALOT, GABRIEL
Across Tibet. London: 1891. V. 53
Across Tibet. New York: 1892. V. 53
Through the Heart of Asia, Over Pamir to India. 1889. V. 54
Through the Heart of Asia, Over Pamir to India. London: 1889. V. 53

BONWICK, JAMES
Daily Life and Origin of the Tasmanians. London: 1870. V. 48

BONWICK, JAMES continued
The Last of the Tasmanians; or the Black War of Van Diemen's Land. London: 1870. V. 48
The Lost Tasmanian Race. London: 1884. V. 48; 53

BONY, JEAN
French Gothic Architecture of the 12th and 13th Centuries. Berkeley: 1983. V. 53

BOOK ARTS PRESS
Specimens of Wood Type. New York: 1980. V. 50

A **BOOK** for Boston In Which are Gathered Essays, Stories, and Poems by Divers Hand Especially Written in Honor the City Upon the Occasion of the Three Hundred and Fiftieth Anniversary of its Incorporation. Boston: 1980. V. 49

THE **BOOK** of American Negro Poetry. New York: 1922. V. 52

BOOK of Beards. London: 1832. V. 50

A **BOOK** of Belgium's Gratitude. 1915. V. 54
A BOOK of Belgium's Gratitude. London: 1915. V. 52; 53

A **BOOK** of Cape May, New Jersey. Cape May: 1937. V. 47; 49; 51

A **BOOK** of Cats Being a Discourse on Cats... London: 1898. V. 49

THE **BOOK** of Costume; or, Annals of Fashion, from the Earliest Period to the Present Time. London: 1847. V. 53

THE **BOOK** of English Trades, and Library of the Useful Arts. London: 1818. V. 51

THE **BOOK** of English Verse. London: 1926. V. 53

A **BOOK** of Famous and Beautiful Chinese Ladies from all Antiquity. 1920. V. 53

THE **BOOK** of Fate. A New and Complete System of Fortune Telling...In Seven Parts. New York: 1817. V. 52

THE **BOOK** of Fate Formerly in the Possession of Napoleon, Late Emperor of France...of an Ancient Egyptian Manuscript Found in the Year 1801... London. V. 47

THE **BOOK** of Garden Management. London: 1862. V. 53

THE **BOOK** Of Machine. San Francisco;: 1934. V. 54

BOOK OF MORMON
The Book of Mormon: an Account Written by the Hand of Mormon... Liverpool: 1854. V. 48
Book of Mormon Part I. (all Published) & The Deseret Second Book. New York: 1868/69. V. 50

THE **BOOK** of Nature. London: 1771. V. 48

THE **BOOK** of Nursery Tales. London: 1930. V. 53

A **BOOK** of Old Ballads. London: 1934. V. 49

THE **BOOK** of Old Songs and Ballads. London: 1915. V. 50

THE **BOOK** of Poetry. Philadelphia: 1860's. V. 54

THE **BOOK** of Praise from the Best English Hymn Writers. London: 1898. V. 54

A **BOOK** of Prayers. Philadelphia: 1964. V. 52

A **BOOK** of Princeton Verse II. Princeton: 1919. V. 47

THE **BOOK** of Riddles. New York: 1817. V. 48

THE **BOOK** of Sports, British and Foreign; Devoted to the Pictorial Illustration of the Pursuits of the Sportsman in Every Quarter of the Globe. London: 1842-43. V. 47

THE **BOOK** of Sundials and their Mottes. London Edinburgh &: 1914. V. 47

A **BOOK** of Sweethearts. New York: 1908. V. 48

BOOK of the Atmosphere. Boston: 1833. V. 54

THE **BOOK** of the Bench. London: 1900. V. 50

THE **BOOK** of the Camp Fire Girls. New York: 1936. V. 52

THE **BOOK** of the Dead. New York: 1972. V. 47; 50

BOOK of the Governors. 1926. V. 53

THE **BOOK** of the Horace Club. 1901. V. 54

A **BOOK** of the Horace Club. London: 1901. V. 53

THE **BOOK** of, the Proceedings and Correspondence Upon the...Inquiry into the Conduct of...The Princess of Wales, Upon a Commission Appointed by the King...1806. London: 1813. V. 49

THE **BOOK** of the Roycrofters. East Aurora: 1907. V. 49

THE **BOOK** of Trades; or, Circle of the Useful Arts. Glasgow: 1835. V. 47

BOOK of Trades, or Library of the Useful Arts. London: 1806/05. V. 53

BOOK-LORE: a Magazine Devoted to Old-Time Literature. London: 1885-87. V. 50

BOOKANO Stories With Pictures That Sprung Up in Model Form. London: 1949. V. 48

THE **BOOKBINDER**. London: 1887-93. V. 49
THE BOOKBINDER. London: 1888. V. 50

BOOKER, JOHN
The Dutch Fortune-Teller: Discovering XXXVI Several Questions. London: 1705/10?. V. 47
Memorials of the Church in Prestwich. Manchester: 1852. V. 51; 53

BOOKER, LUKE
Tobias: a Poem, in Three Parts. London: 1805. V. 50

BOOKER, RICHARD
Mash. New York: 1968. V. 51

BOOKS and the Public. London: 1927. V. 50

BOOKS Wanted by Frederick Mayhew, 6, Vinegar Yard, Brydges Street, W.C. London: 1870. V. 47

BOOKWALTER, JOHN W.
Siberia and Central Asia. Springfield: 1899. V. 53

BOOKWALTER, THOMAS E.
The Custer Battlefield an Aerial Perspective - from the Crow's Nest to Custer Hill. Louisville: 1976. V. 54

BOOLE, GEORGE
An Investigation of the Laws of Thought, on Which are Founded the Mathematical Theories of Logic and Probabilities. London: 1854. V. 47; 48; 50; 52; 54
A Treatise on Differential Equations. Cambridge: 1859. V. 50; 51
A Treatise on Differential Equations. Cambridge: 1865. V. 50
A Treatise on the Calculus of Finite Differences. Cambridge: 1860. V. 50; 52
A Treatise On the Calculus of Finite Differences. London: 1872. V. 50

BOON, K. G.
Rembrandt: the Complete Etchings. London: 1963. V. 50
Rembrandt, the Complete Etchings. New York: 1963. V. 48; 50; 53; 54

BOONE, JAMES SHERGOLD
The Council of Ten. London: 1822-23. V. 52; 54
The Oxford Spy. Oxford: 1818. V. 47

BOONE, JOEL
A Medical Survey of the Bituminous-Coal Industry. Washington: 1947. V. 53

BOONE, SUSANNA WARING
The Minstrelsy of the Woods; or Sketches and Songs Connected with the Natural History of Some of the Most Interesting British and Foreign Birds. London: 1832. V. 51

BOONE & CROCKETT
American Big Game Hunting. New York: 1893. V. 53
The Black Bear in Modern North America. Pittsburgh: 1979. V. 53
Boone and Crockett Club's 22nd Big Game Awards, 1992-1994. Missoula: 1995. V. 53
Hunting in Many Lands. Edinburgh: 1895. V. 53
North American Big Game... 1934. V. 53
North American Big Game. New York: 1939. V. 53
North American Big Game... Pittsburgh: 1971. V. 53
North American Big Game. Pittsburgh: 1973. V. 53
Record of North American Big Game. New York: 1932. V. 53
Records of North American Big Game... New York: 1952. V. 47; 53
Records of North American Big Game... New York: 1958. V. 53
Records of North American Elk and Mule Deer. Pittsburgh: 1991. V. 53
Records of North American Whitetail Deer. V. 53

BOORDE, ANDREW
The Breviarie of Health. (with) The Second Book of the Breviary of Health, Named the Extravagantes. London: 1575. V. 49
The Pleasant Tales of the Wise Men of Gotam. Newcastle. V. 47

BOOS, FRANK H.
The Cermaic Sculptures of Ancient Oaxaca. South Brunswick: 1966. V. 51; 52

BOOSEY, THOMAS
Piscatorial Reminiscences and Gleanings by an Old Angler and Bibliopolist. London: 1835. V. 47; 49

BOOTH, ANDREW D.
Automatic Digital Calculators. London: 1953. V. 48; 52; 54

BOOTH, BARTH
The Life of that Excellent Tragedian Barton Booth Esq; Late One of the Managers of the Theatre Royal in Drury-Lane, His Birth and Education... London: 1733. V. 51

BOOTH, DAVID
The Art of Brewing on Scientific Principles adapted to the Use of Brewers and Private Families. London: 1852. V. 48
The Principles of English Composition: Illustrated by Examples with Critical Remarks. London: 1831. V. 52

BOOTH, E. J.
Rough Notes on the Birds Observed During Twenty-Five Years Shooting and Collecting in the British Isles. London: 1881-87. V. 50

BOOTH, EDWIN
Australia Illustrated from Drawings. London: 1874-76. V. 53

BOOTH, G. R.
A Popular Treatise on the Strength and Application of Materials Used in Buildings in General Shewing the Advantages to Be Derived from the Principles of the Patent of Messrs. R. Witty & Co. in All Architectural and Engineering... London: 1836. V. 52

BOOTH, GEORGE G.
The Pleasures of Planting and Other Thoughts. Detroit: 1902. V. 49

BOOTH, HENRY
Free Trade, As It Affects the People, Addressed to a Reformed Parliament. Liverpool: 1833. V. 52

BOOTH, STEPHEN
The Book Called Holinshed's Chronicles: an Account of Its Inception, Purpose, Contributors, Contents, Publication, Revision and Influence on William Shakespeare, with a Leaf from the 1587 edition. 1968. V. 49

BOOTH, WILLIAM
In Darkest England and the Way Out. London: 1890. V. 47; 51; 52; 54

BOOTH, WILLIAM BEATTIE
Illustrations and Descriptions of the Plants Which Compose the Natural Order Camellieae, and of the Varieties of Camellia Japonica, Cultivated in the Gardens of Great Britain. London: 1837. V. 48

BOOTH, WILLIAM STONE
Some Acrostic Signatures of Francis Bacon...Together With Some Others All of Which Are Now for the First Time Deciphered and Published. Boston: 1909. V. 47

BOOTHBY, BROOKE
A Letter to the Right Honourable Edmund Burke. London: 1791. V. 51
Sorrows. London: 1796. V. 47

BOOTHBY, GUY NEWELL
Doctor Nikola. London: 1896. V. 51
Dr. Nikola's Experiment. New York: 1899. V. 51
The Lust of Hate. London: 1898. V. 53
My Indian Queen. London: 1901. V. 53
My Strangest Case. London: 1902. V. 53
On the Wallaby or Through the East and Across Australia. New York: 1894. V. 48

BOOTHBY, ROBERT
Recollections of a Rebel. London: 1978. V. 52

BOOTHROYD, B.
The History of the Ancient Borough of Pontefact... Pontefract: 1807. V. 47; 49; 50; 53

BOOTS, JOHN MERCER
Powder River Invasion - War on the Rustlers in 1892. Los Angeles: 1923. V. 54

BOOTT, FRANCIS
A Letter Addressed to William Pratt, Esq... 1819. V. 52

BORAH, W. E.
The Closing Argument of W. E. Borah for the Prosecution, the Great Coeur d'Alene Riot-Murder Trial, Delivered July 27, 1899, Wallace, Idaho. 1899. V. 50
Haywood Trial. Closing Argument of W. E. Borah. Boise: 1907. V. 50

BORASTON, J. H.
Sir Douglas Haig's Despatches (December 1915-April 1919). London: 1920. V. 47

BORBA DE MORAES, RUBENS
Bibliographic Brasiliana. Rare Books About Brazil Published from 1504 to 1900 and Works by Brazilian Authors of the Colonial Period. Los Angeles: 1983. V. 47

BORBON, DON SEBASTIAN GABRIEL
Discurso Inaugural. Madrid: 1868. V. 50

BORCH, OLE
Hermetis, Aegyptiorum, et Chemicorum Sapientia, ab Hermanni Conringii Animadversionibus Vindicata per Olaum Borrichium. Hafniae: 1674. V. 48

BORCHARDT, RUDOLF
Gartenphantasie. 1925. V. 51; 52; 54

BORCKE, HEROS VON
Colonel Heros Von Borke's Journal 26 April - 8 October 1862. 1981. V. 50

BORDA, ANDREAS DE
Practica de Confessores de Monjas, En Que se Explican Los Quatro Votos de Obediencia, Pobreza, Castidad, y Clausura, Por Modo de Dialogo, Dispuesta. Mexico;: 1708. V. 47; 48

BORDALO, FRANCISCO MARIA
Trinta annos de Perigrinacao (1821-1851). Manuscrito Achado na Grunta de Camoes. Macao: 1852. V. 49

BORDE, ANDREW
The Breviarie of Health: Wherein Doth Folow, Remedies, For All Maner of Sicknesses and Diseases. London: 1575. V. 53

BORDE, CHARLES
Parapilla, ou le Vit Deifie Poeme en Cinq Chants, Mis au jour par le Chapitre General... Lyon: 1783. V. 54

BORDEAUX, HENRY
Georges Guynemer, Knight of the Air. New Haven: 1918. V. 47

BORDEAUX, WILLIAM J.
Conquering the Mighty Sioux. Sioux Falls: 1929. V. 53
Custer's Conquerer. V. 49

THE BORDEAUX Wine and Liquor Dealers' Guide: a Treatise on the Manufacture and Adulteration of Liquors, by a Practical Liquor Manufacturer. New York: 1858. V. 48; 53

BORDEN, JOHN
Log of the Auxiliary Schooner Yacht Northern Light...Borden-Field Museum Alaska-Arctic Expedition 1927. Chicago: 1929. V. 48

BORDEN, SPENCER
The Arab Horse. New York: 1906. V. 52

BORDEN, W. C.
The Use of the Rontgen Ray by the Medical Department of the United States Army in the War with Spain. Washington: 1900. V. 50; 52

BORDEON, LAURENT
The Management of the Tongue. London: 1707. V. 52

BORDER Ballads. London: 1895. V. 50

BORDET, JULES
Studies in Immunity... New York: 1909. V. 51

BORDLEY, JAMES
Two Centuries of American Medicine, 1776-1976. Philadelphia: 1976. V. 52

BORDON, COURTNEY LOUISE
The Cruise of the Northern Light: Explorations and Hunting in the Alaskan and Siberian Arctic. New York: 1928. V. 51

BORDONA, J. DOMINGUEZ
Spanish Illumination. 1930. V. 50
Spanish Illumination. London: 1930. V. 48
Spanish Illumination. Paris: 1930. V. 53

BOREIN, EDWARD
Borein's West. Santa Barbara: 1952. V. 53
Etchings of the Far West. Santa Barbara. V. 54

BORELLA, SHIRLEY
Strength Found Gently in Water. Boston: 1969. V. 54

BORELLI, GIOVANNI
On the Movements of Animals. London: 1989. V. 53

BORELLI, GIOVANNI ALFONSO
Euclides Restitutus Denuo Limatus, Sive Prisce Geometriae Brevius & Facilius Contexta. (with) Elementa Conica Apollonii Paergei et Archimedis Opera Nova & Breviori Methodo Demonstrata... Rome: 1679/79. V. 52
Historia et Meteorologia Incendii Aetnaei Anni 1669... Regio Iulio: 1670. V. 50

BOREMAN, THOMAS
A Description of Three Hundred Animals... London: 1759. V. 54
A Description of Three Hundred Animals... London: 1774. V. 47; 49
A Description of...Three Hundred Animals... Glasgow: 1794. V. 50

BORENIUS, TANCRED
Catalogue of the Collection of Drawings by the Old Masters Formed by Sir Robert Mond. London. V. 49
Florentine Frescoes. London: 1930. V. 50; 54

BORG, CARL OSCAR
Cross, Sword and Gold Pan: A Group of Notable Full-Cover Paintings Depicting Outstanding Episodes in the Settlement and Exploration of the West. Los Angeles: 1936. V. 50
The Great Southwest Etchings. 1936. V. 51

BORGES, JORGE LUIS
The Aleph and Other Stories 1933-1969. London: 1971. V. 52
The Book of Imaginary Beings. London: 1970. V. 53; 54
The Congress. 1974. V. 53
Deathwatch on the Southside. Cambridge: 1968. V. 49
Deathwatch on the Southside. New York: 1968. V. 53
Dr. Brodie's Report. New York: 1972. V. 50
Ficciones. Buenos Aires: 1944. V. 53
Ficciones. London: 1962. V. 47; 50; 52
Ficciones. New York: 1962. V. 50; 51; 53
Ficciones. 1984. V. 50
Ficciones. New York: 1984. V. 47; 48; 52
An Introduction to American Literature. Lexington: 1971. V. 51
Irish Strategies. Dublin: 1975. V. 51
Las Kenningar. Buenos Aires: 1933. V. 50
Labyrinths. New York: 1962. V. 53
A Personal Anthology. London: 1968. V. 47
Poems. 1969. V. 53
Siete Poemas Sajones. Seven Saxon Poems. Verona: 1974. V. 52
Texas. Austin: 1975. V. 47; 50; 51

BORGES DE BARROS, JOAO
Relacao Panegyrica das Honras Funeraes, Que as memorias do... Lisbon: 1753. V. 48

BORGHI, PIETRO
...La Nobel Opera de Arithmetica nela Qual se Trata Tite Cosse a Mercantia Pertinente... Venice: 1491. V. 53

BORGIA, STEFANO, CARDINAL
Letters from the Cardinal Borgia, and the Duke of York. London: 1799-1800. V. 53

BORGO, PIETRO
Arithmetca Mercantile. Venice: 1484. V. 53

BORHUN, WILLIAM
A Collection of Debates, Reports, Orders and Resolutions... London: 1700?. V. 54

BORKENAU, FRANZ
The Communist International. London: 1938. V. 47; 49

BORKENAU, FRANZ continued
European Communism. London: 1953. V. 49
The Spanish Cockpit. London: 1937. V. 49

BORLAND, R.
Border Raids and Reivers. Dalbeattie: 1910. V. 52

BORLASE, EDMUND
The Reduction of Ireland to the Crown of England. London: 1675. V. 48

BORLASE, JAMES SKIPP
The King of Conjurors. London: 1888?. V. 50

BORLASE, WILLIAM
Antiquities, Historical and Monumental, of the County of Cornwall. London: 1769. V. 47; 51
The Dolmens of Ireland... London: 1897. V. 47
The Natural History of Cornwall. London: 1758. V. 49
The Natural History of Cornwall. Oxford: 1758. V. 49

BORLASE, WILLIAM COPELAND
Niphon and Its Antiquities. Plymouth: 1876. V. 53

BORN, IGNAZ VON
Monachologia: or, Handbook of the Natural History of Monks... Edinburgh: 1852. V. 51

BORN, INIGO
Testacea Musei Caesarei Vindobonensis, Quae Jussu Mariae Theresiae Augustae Disposuit et Descripsit. Vienna: 1780. V. 53
Travels through the Bannat of Temeswar, Transylvania, and Hugnary, in the Year 1770. London: 1777. V. 53

BORN, MAX
Einstein's Theory of Relativity. London: 1924. V. 48

BORN, WOLFGANG
American Landscape Painting. New Haven: 1948. V. 49

BORNEMAN, HENRY S.
Pennsylvania German Bookplates. A Study. Philadelphia: 1953. V. 49
Pennsylvania German Illuminated Manuscripts. Norristown: 1937. V. 48

BOROUGH of Sheffield. *Visit of Their Royal Highnesses the Prince and Princess of Wales. Monday, August the 16th and Tuesday, August the 17th.* Sheffield: 1875. V. 51

BORRER, DAWSON
Narrative of a Campaign Against the Kabailes of Algeria: with the Mission of M. Suchet to the Emir Abd-el-Kader for an Exchange of Prisoners. London: 1848. V. 53

BORRER, W.
The Birds of Sussex. London: 1891. V. 51; 54

BORRICHIUS, OLAUS
Hermetis, Aegyptiorum et Chemicorum Sapientia ab Hermanni Conringii Animadversionibus Vindicata. Copenhagen: 1674. V. 53
Hermetis, Aegyptiorum, et Chemicorum Sapientia ab Hermanni Conringii Animadversionibus Vindicata... Hafniae: 1674. V. 48; 54

BORROMEO, CHARLES
Pasatorum Instructiones. Antwerp: 1586. V. 52

BORROW, GEORGE HENRY
The Bible in Spain. London: 1843. V. 50; 52; 53
The Bible in Spain. Philadelphia: 1843. V. 50
The Bible in Spain. London: 1896. V. 54
Celebrated Trials and Remarkable Cases of Criminal Jurisprudence, from the Earliest Records to the Year 1825. London: 1825. V. 48; 50
Collected Works. London & New York: 1923-24. V. 51
Lavengro. London: 1851. V. 47; 48; 49; 50; 52; 53
Lavengro.... New York: 1851. V. 53
Lavengro. 1936. V. 48; 51
Lavengro. London: 1936. V. 52
Lavengro. New York: 1936. V. 52; 53; 54
Romantic Ballads. Norwich: 1826. V. 48; 51
The Romany Rye; a Sequel to "Lavengro". London: 1857. V. 47; 52
Works. London: 1914-23. V. 47; 52
The Works. London: 1923. V. 51
Works. London: 1923-26. V. 52
The Zincali; or, an Account of the Gypsies of Spain. New York: 1842. V. 54
The Zincali; or, An Account of the Gypsies of Spain... London: 1845. V. 53

BORSCH-SUPAN, HELMUT
Caspar David Friedrich. London: 1973. V. 49; 51; 53

BORSI, FRANCO
Leon Battista Alberti. New York: 1977. V. 49; 51; 53

BORSOOK, EVE
The Mural Painters of Tuscany, from Cimabue to Andrea Del Sarto. London: 1960. V. 51

BORST, RONALD V.
Graven Images. New York: 1992. V. 49

BORTHWICK, DOUGLAS
History of the Montreal Prison from A.D. 1784 to A.D. 1886... Montreal: 1886. V. 48

BORTHWICK, WILLIAM MURRAY
Proceedings Against William Murray Borthwick, at the Instance of His Majesty's Advocate, and of Robert Alexander, Styling Himself Editor and Proprietor of the Glasgow Sentinel Newspaper. Edinburgh: 1822. V. 53

BORTON, BENJAMIN
On the Parallels or Chapters of Inner History. Woodstown: 1903. V. 49; 51

BORUP, THOMAS LARSEN
Det Menneskelige Livs Fluget, eller Doden-Dands...Besorget til sine Landsmaends Rytte og Fornojelse af... Copenhagen: 1814. V. 50; 53; 54

BORUWLASKI, JOSEPH
Memoirs of the Celebrated Dwarf, Joseph Boruwlaski. Kelso: 1801. V. 50

BORY, ROBERT
Ludwig Van Beethoven, His Life & Work in Pictures. London: 1966. V. 49

BORZESI, GIUSEPPE PERICCIUOLI
The Historical Guide to the Island of Malta and Its Dependencies. Malta: 1830. V. 49; 51

THE BORZOI 1925. New York: 1925. V. 49

BOSANQUET, EUSTACE F.
English Printed Almanacks and Prognostications. London: 1917. V. 48; 50

BOSANQUET, S. R.
A New System of Logic and Development of the Principles of Truth and Reasoning. London: 1839. V. 52

BOSANQUET, THEODORA
Henry James at Work. London: 1924. V. 53

BOSCANA, GERONIMO
Chinigchinich. Santa Ana: 1933. V. 48; 50

BOSCAWEN, WILLIAM
A Treatise on Convictions on Penal Statutes. London: 1792. V. 47; 50

BOSCHE, E.
Allgemeine Beschreibung der Erde... Philadelphia: 1840. V. 53

BOSCO, HENRI
Sites et Mirages. Paris: 1950. V. 52

BOSE, T.
A Bookman's Catalogue: the Norman Colbeck Collection of Nineteenth-Century and Edwardian Poetry and Belle Lettres in the Special Collections of the University of British Columbia. Vancouver: 1987. V. 47

BOSMAN, RICHARD
Hannah Duston. San Francisco: 1987. V. 52

BOSQUES, GILBERTO
The National Revolutionary Party of Mexico: and the Six-Year Plan. Mexico: 1937. V. 47

BOSQUET, ALAIN
Selected Poems. New York: 1962. V. 47

BOSQUI, EDWARD
Memoirs. San Francisco: 1904. V. 54
Memoirs... Oakland: 1952. V. 52

BOSSAGLIA, ROSANNA
1200 Years of Italian Sculpture. New York: 1968. V. 49; 50; 51; 53

BOSSCHERE, JEAN DE
Beasts and Men. London: 1918. V. 51
Christmas Tales of Flanders. London: 1917. V. 50; 51; 54
Christmas Tales of Flanders. New York: 1917. V. 51; 53
The City Curious. London and New York: 1920. V. 53
Marthe and the Madman. New York: 1928. V. 51
Weird Islands. London: 1921. V. 51

BOSSERT, HELMUTH THEODOR
Folk Art of Primitive Peoples. New York: 1955. V. 54
Ornament. London: 1924. V. 49; 54
Ornament in Applied Art. New York: 1924. V. 48; 52
Peasant Art in Europe. London: 1927. V. 47; 49
Peasant Art in Europe. New York: 1927. V. 51

BOSSEWELL, JOHN
Workes of Armorie, Devyded Into Three Bookes, Entituled, the Concordes of Armorie, the Armorie of Honor, and of Coates and Creastes, Collected and Gathered. London: 1572. V. 48

BOSSEY, T.
Piscatorial Reminiscences and Gleanings by an Old Angler and Bibliopolist. London: 1835/36. V. 47

BOSSU, JEAN BERNARD
Travels through That Part of North America Formerly Called Louisiana. London: 1771. V. 49

BOSSUET, JACQUES BENIGNE
An Exposition of the Doctrine of the Catholic Church In... Paris: 1672. V. 53
An Exposition of the Doctrine of the Catholic Church in... London: 1686. V. 48
De Nova Quaestione Tractatus Tres. Paris: 1698. V. 52

BOSSUT, ABBE
French and English Primer; or, an Easy Vocabulary of 1500 cCommon Words, for the Use of Children. London: 1818. V. 49

BOSSUT, C.
Nouvelles Experiences sur la Resistance des Fluides. Paris: 1777. V. 51; 54

BOSSUT, CHARLES
A General History of Mathematics, from the Earliest Times to the Middle of the Eighteenth Century. London: 1803. V. 50

BOSTOCK, JOHN
An Account of the History and Present State of Galvanism. London: 1818. V. 50

BOSTON ARTISTS' ASSOCIATION
The Constitution of the Boston Artists' Association with a Catalogue of the First Public Exhibition of Paintings at Harding's Gallery... Boston: 1842. V. 47

BOSTON ATHENAEUM
Catalogue of Books in the Boston Athenaeum: to Which is Added the By-Laws of the Institution. Boston: 1827. V. 53
Catalogue of the Second Exhibition of Sculpture in the Athenaeum Gallery. Boston: 1840. V. 49

THE BOSTON Directory... Boston: 1820. V. 51

THE BOSTON Directory. Boston: 1827. V. 48

BOSTON Directory for...1806...A General Directory of the Citizens and a Business Directory. Boston: 1859. V. 54

BOSTON MARINE INSURANCE COMPANY
An Act to Incorporate the Boston Marine Insurance Company. Boston: 1799. V. 47

BOSTON MARINE SOCIETY
The Constitution and Laws of the Boston Marine Society, Instituted in the Year 1742. Boston: 1792. V. 50

BOSTON MEDICAL ASSOCIATION
Rules and Regulations of the Boston Medical Association. Boston: 1820. V. 50; 51

BOSTON Miscellany of Literature and Fashion. Boston and New York: 1842. V. 48

BOSTON. MUSEUM OF FINE ARTS
The Artist and the Book 1860-1960 in Western Europe and the United States. Boston: 1961. V. 53
Illustrated Catalogue of a Special Loan Exhibition of Art Treasures from Japan. Boston: 1936. V. 48; 49
Paul Gauguin, Woodcuts in the Museum of Fine Arts, Boston. New York. V. 48

BOSTON-NEW YORK RAILWAY
A Chart and Description of the Rail-Road from Boston to New York, via Worcester, Springfield, Hartford, and New Haven. Boston: 1850. V. 54

BOSTON Prize Poems and Other Specimens of Dramatic Poetry. Boston: 1824. V. 51

BOSWELL, ALEXANDER
The Poetical Works, Now First Collected and Edited. Glasgow: 1871. V. 48
Songs, Chiefly in the Scottish Dialect... Edinburgh: 1803. V. 50

BOSWELL, C. S.
An Irish Precursor of Dante: A Study on the Vision of Heaven and Hell Ascribed to... 1908. V. 49; 52

BOSWELL, EDWARD
The Civil Division of the County of Dorset, Methodically Digested and Arranged... Dorchester: 1833. V. 50; 54

BOSWELL, H.
Complete Historical Descriptions of a New and Elegant Collection of Picturesque Views and Representations of the Antiquities of England and Wales. London: 1790. V. 47

BOSWELL, JAMES
An Account of Corsica. Dublin: 1768. V. 47
An Account of Corsica... Glasgow: 1768. V. 47; 48
An Account of Corsica... London: 1768. V. 48; 50
An Account of Corsica... London: 1769. V. 48
An Account of Corsica... London: 1791. V. 49
Boswell on Grand Tour. London: 1953/55. V. 54
Boswell on the Grand Tour... London: 1953. V. 51; 53
The Boswell Papers: Boswell the Ominous Years, 1774/1776. London: 1963. V. 53
Boswelliana. Folium Reservatum. London: 1856. V. 49
Boswell's Journal of a Tour to the Hebrides... London: 1963. V. 53
Boswell's London Journal... London: 1950. V. 49
Boswell's London Journal 1762-1763. Together with Journal of My Jaunt. London: 1951. V. 53
Boswell's Note Book 1776-1777, Recording Particulars of Johnson's Early Life... London: 1925. V. 48
British Essays in Favour of the Brave Corsicans... London: 1769. V. 52
Carminum Rariorum Macaronicarum Delectus: In Usum Ludorum Apollinarum... Edinburgi: 1813. V. 52
Correspondence of Boswell with David Garrick, Edmund Burke and Edmond Malone. London: 1986. V. 50; 53
The Decision of the Court of Session, Upon the Question of Literary Property; In the Case of John Hinton of London, Bookseller, Pursuer; Against Alexander Donaldson and John Wood, Booksellers in Edinburgh and James Meurose Bookseller in Kilmarnock, Defenders. Edinburgh: 1774. V. 53
The English Experiment, 1785-1789. 1986. V. 53
Everybody's Boswell. London: 1930. V. 51; 52; 54
The Hypochondriack. Stanford: 1928. V. 54
Jacob Boswells, Esq. Historich-Geographische Beschreibung von Corsica Nebst Vielen Wichtigen Nachrichten und Anecdoten vom Pascal Paoli dem General der Corsen. Leipzig: 1769. V. 52
James Boswell's Life of Johnson. Edinburgh and New Haven: 1994. V. 53
The Journal of a Tour to Corsica & Memoirs of Pascal Paoli. Cambridge: 1923. V. 52
The Journal of a Tour to the Hebrides... Dublin: 1785. V. 52; 54
The Journal of a Tour to the Hebrides... London: 1785. V. 47; 48; 49; 51; 52; 53; 54
The Journal of a Tour to the Hebrides... London: 1786. V. 48; 49; 51; 54
The Journal of a Tour to the Hebrides... London: 1786/91. V. 50
The Journal of a Tour to the Hebrides... London: 1807. V. 49
The Journal of a Tour to the Hebrides... London: 1810. V. 48
Journal of a Tour to the Hebrides... New York: 1810. V. 54
The Journal of a Tour to the Hebrides... London: 1813. V. 50; 51; 53
Journal of a Tour to the Hebrides... London: 1852. V. 54
The Journal of a Tour to the Hebrides... London: 1885. V. 53
The Journal of a Tour to the Hebrides. London: 1901. V. 53
The Journal of a Tour to the Hebrides... New York: 1936. V. 50; 51; 53; 54
The Journal of a Tour to the Hebrides... London: 1968. V. 53
The Journal of a Tour to the Hebrides... 1974. V. 48
The Journal of a Tour to the Hebrides... Avon: 1974. V. 47; 48; 53
The Journal of a Tour to the Hebrides, with Samuel Johnson. London: 1785. V. 52
A Letter to Samuel Johnson. Edinburgh, 3 March, 1772. Buffalo: 1900. V. 50
A Letter to the People of Scotland, on the Alarming Attempt to Infringe the Articles of the Union... London: 1785. V. 47; 48
Letters Between the Honourable Andrew Erskine, and James Boswell, Esq. London: 1763. V. 49
Letters of James Boswell. London: 1857. V. 51; 53
Letters of James Boswell. Oxford: 1924. V. 50
The Life of Samuel Johnson. London: 1791. V. 47; 48; 50; 51; 52; 54
The Life of Samuel Johnson... Dublin: 1792. V. 48
The Life of Samuel Johnson... London: 1793. V. 47; 48; 49; 50; 51; 54
The Life of Samuel Johnson... London: 1804. V. 47; 48
The Life of Samuel Johnson. Boston: 1807. V. 47; 48; 49; 50; 53
The Life of Samuel Johnson... London: 1807. V. 51
The Life of Samuel Johnson... London: 1811. V. 48; 50
The Life of Samuel Johnson... London: 1816. V. 51
The Life of Samuel Johnson... London: 1822. V. 48
The Life of Samuel Johnson... London: 1823. V. 48
The Life of Samuel Johnson... Bellows Falls: 1824. V. 50
The Life of Samuel Johnson. Oxford & London: 1826. V. 49; 50; 51
The Life of Samuel Johnson... London: 1831. V. 53
The Life of Samuel Johnson... London: 1835. V. 47; 49; 51; 54
The Life of Samuel Johnson... London: 1839. V. 52; 53
The Life of Samuel Johnson... London: 1844. V. 49
The Life of Samuel Johnson... London: 1859. V. 49
The Life of Samuel Johnson... London: 1860-67. V. 51
The Life of Samuel Johnson... London: 1872. V. 48; 52
The Life of Samuel Johnson... London: 1874. V. 54
The Life of Samuel Johnson... London: 1880. V. 48; 50
The Life of Samuel Johnson... London: 1884. V. 48; 50
The Life of Samuel Johnson... London: 1885. V. 48; 53
The Life of Samuel Johnson... Oxford: 1887. V. 48; 49; 52
The Life of Samuel Johnson... New York: 1891. V. 48; 50
The Life of Samuel Johnson. London: 1901. V. 48; 51; 53
The Life of Samuel Johnson. New York: 1909. V. 48
The Life of Samuel Johnson. New York: 1922. V. 49; 51; 54
The Life of Samuel Johnson. London: 1924. V. 48; 51; 52
The Life of Samuel Johnson... Bath: 1925. V. 48
The Life of Samuel Johnson. London: 1925. V. 48; 52
The Life of Samuel Johnson... Oxford: 1934-50. V. 48
Life of Samuel Johnson. 1938. V. 48; 52
Life of Samuel Johnson. London: 1938. V. 50; 53
The Life of Samuel Johnson. New York: 1963. V. 48; 52
The Life of Samuel Johnson. London: 1968. V. 47; 48
The Principal Corrections and Additions to the First Edition of Mr. Boswell's Life of Dr. Johnson. London: 1793. V. 48; 51; 52

BOSWELL, JAMES H.
American Blue Book: Texas Attorneys. 1926. V. 47

BOSWELL, JOHN
The Case of the Royal Martyr Considered with Candour or an Answer to Some Libels Lately Published... London: 1758. V. 47; 51

BOSWELL, ROBERT
Dancing in the Movies. Iowa City: 1986. V. 49; 52

BOSWELL, THOMAS ALEXANDER
The Journal of an Exile. London: 1825. V. 48
Recollections of a Pedestrian. London: 1826. V. 47; 49

BOSWORTH, JOSEPH
An Anglo-Saxon Dictionary Based on the Manuscript Collections of the Late Joseph Bosworth. Oxford: 1882. V. 52
A Dictionary of the Anglo-Saxon Language, etc. London: 1838. V. 52
The Elements of Anglo-Saxon Grammar with Copious Notes, Illustrating the Structure of the Saxon and the Formation of the English Language. London: 1823. V. 52

BOSWORTH, WELLES
Gardens of Kijkuit. 1919. V. 52
The Gardens of Kijkuit. Baltimore: 1919. V. 50

THE BOTANICAL Keepsake; an Arrangement of British Plants. London: 1843. V. 54

THE BOTANICAL Keepsake: an Arrangement of British Plants. London: 1846. V. 51; 52; 53; 54

BOTANICAL Sketches of the Twenty-Four Classes in the Linnaean System... London: 1825. V. 54

THE BOTANIST'S Calendar, and Pocket Flora... London: 1797. V. 47

BOTCHKAREVA, MARIA
Yashka - My Life as Peasant. London: 1919. V. 53

BOTELER, THOMAS
Narrative of a Voyage of Discovery to Africa and Arabia, Performed in His Majesty's Ships Leven and Barracouta...Under the Command of Capt. F. W. Owen. London: 1835. V. 50

BOTERO, GIOVANNI
Raison et Govvernement d'Estat, en Dix Livres. Paris: 1599. V. 51
Le Relationi Universali...Divise in Sette Parti...(and) Aggiunta Alla Quarta Parte dell'Indie... Venice: 1622/23. V. 47

BOTFIELD, BERIAH
The Catalogue of the Minister's Library in Collegiate Church of Tong, in Shropshire, with Some Notices of that Structure. London: 1858. V. 54
Some Account of the First English Bible. London: 1856. V. 54
Stemmata Botevilliana. Memorials of the Families of De Boteville, Thynne and Botfield in the Counties of Salop and Wilts. London: 1858. V. 47; 53

BOTHEMER, BERNARD V.
Egyptian Sculpture of the Late Period 700 B.C. to A.D. 100. Brooklyn: 1960. V. 51

BOTKIN, B. A.
Folk-Say, a Regional Miscellany. Norman: 1929. V. 54
Lay My Burden Down. Chicago: 1945. V. 53

BOTREL, THEODORE
Songs of Botrel. London: 1916. V. 50

BOTTA, CHARLES
History of the War of Independence of the United States... New Haven: 1834. V. 50
History of the War of Independence of the United States... New Haven: 1836. V. 52

BOTTARI, GIOVANNI
Sculpture Pitture Sagre...Roma Sotterranea... Rome: 1737-54. V. 51

BOTTAZZO, GIOAN IACOPO
Dialogi Maritimi...et Alcvne Rime Maritime de M. Nicolo Franco et d'Altri Diuersi Spiriti... Mantua: 1547. V. 51

BOTTGER, ADOLF
Die Pilgerfahrt der Blumengeister. Leipzig: 1857. V. 53

BOTTOMLEY, GORDON
Chambers of Imagery, Together with Chambers of Imagery (Second Series). London: 1907-12. V. 52
King Lear's Wife and Other Plays. London: 1920. V. 49; 52; 53
Laodice and Danae. London: 1909. V. 52
Midsummer Eve: a Play. 1905. V. 52
The Riding to Lithend. Flansham: 1909. V. 48
Scenes and Plays. London: 1929. V. 52; 54

BOTTOMS, DAVID
Jamming with the Band at the VFW. 1978. V. 48

BOTTRALL, RONALD
The Collected Poems of Ronald Bottrall. London: 1961. V. 54
Poems 1955-1973. London: 1974. V. 54
Reflections on the Nile - Poems Cairo-London-Rome. London: 1980. V. 54

BOTZUM, A.
Nouveaux Modeles de Lettres. Paris: 1890. V. 50; 53

BOUCARD, A.
Genera of Humming Birds... London: 1893-95. V. 53

BOUCAUT, JAMES PENN
The Arab the Horse of the Future. London: 1900. V. 47

BOUCAUX, JEAN
Memoire, Pour Jean Boucaux, Negre, Demandeur. Contre Le Sieur Verdelin, Defendeur. Paris: 1738. V. 49

BOUCH, C. M. L.
The Lake Counties 1500-1830. Manchester: 1961. V. 50; 54

BOUCHER, ANTHONY
The Case of the Baker Street Irregulars. New York: 1940. V. 51

BOUCHER, FRANCOIS
20,000 Years of Fashion. New York: 1967. V. 48

BOUCHET, JEAN
Les Ancienes et Modernes Genealogies des Roys de France. Paris: 1537. V. 49; 53
Les Annales d'Aquitaine. Poitiers: 1557. V. 47

BOUCHET, MAX POL
Johnny Friedlaender: Oeuvre 1961-1965. New York. V. 50

BOUCHETTE, JOSEPH
The British Dominions in North America: or a Topographical and Statistical Description of the Province of Lower and Upper Canada, New Brunswick, Nova Scotia... (with) A Topographical Dictionary of the Province of Lower Canada. London: 1832. V. 52
A Topographical Description of the Province of Lower Canada, with Remarks Upon Upper Canada, and On the Relative Connection of Both Provinces with the United States of America. London: 1815. V. 52; 53

BOUCHOT, HENRI
Catherine de Medicis. Paris: 1899. V. 49; 53

BOUCICAULT, DION
Arrah-Na-Pogue; or, The Wickow Wedding. London: 1864. V. 47

BOUDIER, JEAN LOUIS EMILE
Icones Mycologicae ou Iconographie des Champignons de France Principalement Discomycetes. Piantanida,: 1981. V. 49

BOUDIER DE VILLEMERT, PIERRE JOSEPH
The Ladies Friend; Being a Treatise on the Virtues and Qualifications Which are the Brightest Ornaments of the Fair Sex, and Render Them Most Agreeable to the Sensible Part of Mankind. New Haven: 1784. V. 49
The Ladies Friend; Being a Treatise on the Virtues and Qualifications Which are the Brightest Ornaments of the Fair Sex, and Render Them Most Agreeable to the Sensible Part of Mankind. New Haven: 1789. V. 51; 53

BOUDINOT, ELIAS
Address, of the New-Jersey Bible Society to the Publick; with an Appendix. New Brunswick: 1810. V. 51
Journal of Historical Recollections of American Events During the Revolutionary War. Philadelphia: 1894. V. 47; 49; 51
Memoirs of the Life of the Rev. William Tennent, Formerly Pastor of the Presbyterian Church at Freehold, in New Jersey... Poughkeepsie: 1815. V. 51
The Second Advent, or Coming of the Messiah in Glory... Trenton: 1815. V. 51
A Star in the West; or a Humble Attempt to Discover the Long Lost Ten Tribes of Israel, Preparatory to Their Return to Their Beloved City, Jerusalem. Trenton: 1816. V. 47; 50

BOUDRYE, LOUIS NAPOLEON
Historic Records of the Fifth New York Cavalry, First Ira Harris Guard. Albany: 1865. V. 52; 54

BOUFFONIDOR
Le Proces des Trois Rois, Louis XVI...Charles III...et George III. London: 1780. V. 47

BOUGAINVILLE, LOUIS ANTOINE DE
A Voyage Round the World, Performed by Order of His Most Christian Majesty in the Years 1766, 1767, 1768, and 1769. London: 1772. V. 50; 52

BOUGARD, RENE
The Little Sea Torch; or True Guide for Coasting Pilots... London: 1801. V. 49; 54

BOUGEANT, GUILLAUME HYACINTHE
A Philosophical Amusement Upon the Language of Beasts and Birds. London: 1740. V. 51
Voyage Merveilleux du Prince Fan-Feredin dans La Romance. Paris: 1735. V. 52

BOUGUER, PIERRE
Nouveau Traite de Navigation, contenant la Theorie et la Pratique du Pilotage. Paris: 1753. V. 48
Traite du Navire, de sa Construction, et de ses Mouvemens. Paris: 1746. V. 48; 53; 54

BOUHOURS, DOMINIC
The Life of St. Ignatius, Founder of the Society of Jesus... London: 1686. V. 50

BOUILLAUD, JEAN B.
Traite Clinique des Maladies Du Coeur. Paris: 1835. V. 51; 53

BOUILLON, JEAN PAUL
Art Nouveau 1870-1914. New York: 1985. V. 50

BOULAINVILLIERS, HENRI, COUNT DE
An Historical Account of the Ancient Parliaments of France, or States General of the Kingdom. London: 1739. V. 53

BOULANGER, NICOLAS ANTOINE
The Origins and Progress of Despotism. Amsterdam: 1764. V. 51

BOULDER And Surroundings. Boulder: 1887. V. 49

BOULENGE, JACQUES
Miroir a Deux Faces. Paris: 1933. V. 51

BOULENGER, G. A.
Catalogue of the Freshwater Fishes of Africa. London: 1964. V. 48
Catalogue of the Lizards in the British Museum. London: 1885-87. V. 52; 54
Catalogue of the Reptiles and Batrachians of Barbary. London: 1891. V. 49
The Fauna of British India...Reptilia and Batrachia. London: 1890. V. 49
The Tailless Batrachians of Europe. London: 1897-98. V. 51
A Vertebrate Fauna of the Malay Peninsula...Reptilia and Batrachia. London: 1912. V. 48

BOULET, ROGER H.
The Tranquility and the Turbulence: the Life and Works of Walter J. Phillips. Markham: 1981. V. 53

BOULGER, DEMETRIUS C.
The Life of Gordon. London: 1897. V. 54

BOULGER, G. S.
Familiar Trees. London: 1885-88. V. 49; 50
Familiar Trees... London: 1892. V. 54

BOULLE, PIERRE
The Bridge of the River Kwai. New York: 1954. V. 51
Planet of the Apes. 1963. V. 51

BOULNOIS, HELEN MARY
Into Little Thibet. London: 1923. V. 54

BOULTER, HUGH
Letters Written by Hugh Boulter, Lord Primate of All Ireland...to Several Ministers of State in England and Others. Oxford: 1769. V. 49

BOULTON, CHARLES A.
Reminiscences of the North-West Rebellions, with a Record of the Raising of Her Majesty's 100th Regiment in Canada, and a Chapter on Canadian Social and Political Life by Major Boulton, Commanding Boulton's Scouts. Toronto: 1886. V. 49; 51

A BOUQUET of Pheasants. Brighton: 1981. V. 54

BOURCHIER, THOMAS
Historia Ecclesiastica de Martyrio Fratrum Ordinis Divi Francisci. Paris: 1586. V. 49

BOURDILLON, FRANCIS WILLIAM
The Early Editions of the Roman de la Rose. London: 1906. V. 48; 50
Sursum Corda. London: 1893. V. 49

BOUREAU DELANDES, ANDREW FRANCOIS
An Essay on Maritime Power and Commerce: Particularly Those of France. London: 1743. V. 47

BOURET, JEAN
The Barbizon School and 19th Century French Landscape Painting. Greenwich: 1973. V. 48

BOURGADE, ARMAND
Polichinelle. Le Diable Rosse. Paris: 1880. V. 52

BOURGELAT, CLAUDE
A New System of Horsemanship. From the French of Monsieur Bourgelat. London: 1754. V. 47

BOURGEOIS, CONSTANT
Voyage Pittoresque a la Grande Chartreuse. Paris: 1821. V. 49; 52

BOURGEOIS, LOUISE
The Puritan. New York: 1990. V. 49

BOURGET, D. JOHN
The History of the Royal Abbey of Bec, Near Rouen in Normandy. London: 1779. V. 53

BOURGOING, CHARLES AUGUSTIN
La Perspective Affranchie, Contenant la Vraye et Naturele Pratique Jusques Icy Inconnue... Paris: 1661. V. 49

BOURGOING, JEAN FRANCOIS, BARON DE
Travels in Spain; containing a New, Accurate and Comprehensive View of the Present State of that Country. London: 1789. V. 52

BOURJAILY, VANCE
The End of My Life. New York: 1947. V. 47; 48; 51

BOURKE, ALGERNON
Bourke Collection Catalogue of Prints After Morland, in the Possession of Hon. Algernon Bourke. London: 1894. V. 50

BOURKE, JOHN
On the Border With Crook. New York: 1891. V. 53

BOURKE, JOHN GILBERT
Compilation of Notes and Memoranda on the Use of Human Ordure and Urine in Rites of a Religious or Semi-Religious Character Among Various Nations. Washington: 1888. V. 48; 49
The Moquis of Arizona, The Snake Dance. New York: 1884. V. 47; 48; 52
Notes Upon the Gentile Organization of the Apaches of Arizona. 1890's. V. 49
Our Neutrality Laws. Fort Ethan Allen: 1896?. V. 48
Popular Medicine, Customs and Superstitions of the Rio Grande. Washington: 1891. V. 48
Popular Medicine, Customs and Superstitions of the Rio Grande. 1894. V. 49
Scatalogic Rites of All Nations. Washington: 1891. V. 49
The Urine Dance of the Zuni Indians of New Mexico. Ann Arbor: 1885. V. 48; 49; 50

BOURKE, RICHARD SOUTHWELL
St. Petersburg and Moscow; a Visit to the Court of the Czar. London: 1846. V. 48

BOURKE, ULICK J.
The College Irish Grammar. 1856. V. 48; 52

BOURKE-WHITE, MARGARET
Dear Fatherland, Rest Quietly. New York: 1946. V. 48; 51
Eyes on Russia. London: 1931. V. 47
Eyes on Russia. New York: 1931. V. 47
Halfway to Freedom - a Report on the New India in the Words and Photographs of Margaret Bourke-White. New York: 1949. V. 53
Newsprint. Montreal: 1935. V. 47
Newsprint: a Book of Pictures Illustrating the Operations in the Manufacture of Paper on Which to Print the World's News. Montreal: 1939. V. 47
North of the Danube. New York: 1939. V. 47
Portrait of Myself. New York: 1963. V. 47; 50; 52; 54
A Report on the American Jesuits. New York: 1956. V. 47
Say Is This the U.S.A. New York: 1941. V. 47
They Called It "Purple Heart Valley". New York: 1944. V. 48; 51
You Have Seen Their Faces. New York: 1937. V. 47

BOURNE, BENJAMIN FRANKLIN
The Captive in Patagonia, or Life Among the Giants, a personal Narrative. Boston: 1853. V. 49

BOURNE, G. H.
The Chimpanzee. Baltimore: 1969-73. V. 53

BOURNE, GEORGE
The Book and Slavery Irreconcilable with Animadversions Upon Dr. Smith's Philosophy. Philadelphia: 1816. V. 51

BOURNE, HENRY
Observations on Popular Antiquities, Including the Whole of Mr. Bourne's Antiquitates Vulgates... London: 1810. V. 54

BOURNE, HERMON
Flores Poetici. The Florist's Manual... Boston: 1833. V. 48; 54

BOURNE, JOHN
A Treatise on the Steam Engine In Its Application to Mines, Mills, Steam Navigation and Railways. London: 1846. V. 48; 50; 53

BOURNE, VINCENT
Miscellaneous Poems: Consisting of Originals and Translations. London: 1772. V. 53
Poematia Latinae Partim Reddita. London: 1840. V. 48

BOURRIENNE, LOUIS ANTOINE FLAUVELET DE
Memoirs of Napoleon Bonaparte. London: 1836. V. 48; 49; 53
Memoirs of Napoleon Bonaparte. London: 1885. V. 51

BOURRIT, MARC THEODORE
A Relation of a Journey to the Glaciers, in the Dutchy of Savoy. Norwich: 1775. V. 50; 52

BOUSSARD, GEOFFROY
De Continentia Sacerdotum... Nuremberg: 1510. V. 47

BOUSSINGAULT, J. B.
Rural Economy, In Its Relations with Chemistry, Physics and Meteorology... New York: 1845. V. 50; 52

BOUSSUET, BP. OF MEAUX
The History of France from Pharamond to Charles IX. Edinburgh: 1672. V. 47

BOUSSUET, FRANCOIS
De Natura Aquatilium Carmen, in Universam Guilemi Rondeletii... Lyons: 1558. V. 52

BOUTCHER, WILLIAM
A Treatise on Forest Trees. Edinburgh: 1775. V. 47; 51; 52; 53
A Treatise on Forest Trees... Dublin: 1784. V. 47; 49

BOUTELL, CHARLES
A Manual of British Archaeology. London: 1858. V. 47
The Monumental Brasses of England. London: 1849. V. 48; 49

BOUTELLE, JOHN A.
The Burke and Alvord Memorial; a Genealogical Account of the Descendants of Richard Burke of Sudbury, Mass. and of the Descendants of Alexander Alvord of Windsor, Conn. Boston: 1864. V. 53

BOUTERWEK, FREDERICK
History of Spanish and Portuguese Literature. London: 1823. V. 54

BOUTET, CLAUDE
The Art of Painting in Miniature: Teaching the Speedy and Perfect Acquisition of that Art Without a Master... London: 1729. V. 53

BOUTFLOWER, DOUGLAS SAMUEL
The Boutflower Book. London: 1889. V. 53
The Boutflower Book. Newcastle-upon-Tyne: 1930. V. 50; 52; 54

BOUTON, EDWARD
Events of the Civil War. Los Angeles: 1906. V. 47

BOUTON, LOUIS
Medicinal Plants Growing or Cultivated in the Island of Mauritius. Mauritius: 1857. V. 53

BOUVET, FRANCIS
Bonnard. The Complete Graphic Work. London: 1981. V. 49

BOUYS, THEODORE
Nouvelles Considerations Puisees Dans la Clairvoyance Instinctive de l'Homme, sur Les Oracles, Les Sibylles et les Prophetes... Paris: 1806. V. 48

BOVALLIUS, CARL
Nicaraguan Antiquities. Stockholm: 1886. V. 47; 52

BOVILL, E. W.
Missions to the Niger. Cambridge: 1962-66. V. 50
Missions to the Niger. London: 1964-66. V. 47; 48

THE BOW in the Cloud; Or, the Negro's Memorial. London: 1834. V. 49; 50

BOW, WILLIAM FORRESTER
Notions of the Nature of Fever, and of Nervous Action... London: 1829. V. 47

BOW-Wow's Rag Book. London: 1910. V. 54

BOWAMN, JAMES CLOYD
John Henry. The Rambling Black Ulysses. Chicago: 1942. V. 50

BOWDEN, AMBROSE
A Treatise On Dry Rot, In Which are Described, the Nature and Causes of that Disease in Ships, Houses, Mills &c. London: 1815. V. 51

BOWDEN, B. V.
Faster than Thought: a Symposium on Digital Computing Machines. London: 1957. V. 52; 54

BOWDEN, CHARLES
Street Signs Chicago. Chicago: 1981. V. 52

BOWDEN, EVERETT L.
Both Profiles. Richmond: 1964. V. 54

BOWDEN, J.
The Naturalist in Norway; or, Notes on the Wild Animals, Birds, Fishes, and Plants of That Country. London: 1869. V. 48

BOWDEN, JAMES
The History of the Society of Friends in America. London: 1850/54. V. 49

BOWDEN, SAMUEL
Poems on Various Subjects; with Some Essays in Prose, Letters to Correspondents, etc. Bath: 1754. V. 54

BOWDICH, THOMAS EDWARD
An Account of the Discoveries of the Portuguese in the Interior of Angola and Mozambique. London: 1824. V. 53
Excursions in Madeira and Porto Santo, During the Autumn of 1823, While on His Third Voyage to Africa. London: 1825. V. 49
Mission from Cape Coast Castle to Ashantee... London: 1819. V. 50; 53

BOWDITCH, CHARLES P.
Mexican and Central American Antiquities, Calendar Systems and History. Washington: 1904. V. 49

BOWDITCH, HENRY I.
Public Hygiene in America. Boston: 1877. V. 50
The Young Stethoscopist; or, the Students Aid to Auscultation. New York: 1848. V. 48

BOWDITCH, NATHANIEL
Bowditch's Useful Tables. New York: 1844. V. 48
Mathematical Papers from the Fourth Volume of the Memoirs of the American Academy of Arts and Sciences. Boston: 1820. V. 51
The New American Practical Navigator. Newburyport: 1802. V. 48; 54
The New American Practical Navigator. New York: 1848. V. 53
The New American Practical Navigator. Washington: 1874. V. 53

BOWDITCH, NATHANIEL INGERSOLL
A History of the Massachusetts General Hospital, (to August 5, 1851)...with a Continuation to 1872. Boston: 1872. V. 52
Memoir of Nathaniel Bowditch. Boston: 1840. V. 47; 52
Suffolk Surnames. Boston: 1857. V. 54
Suffolk Surnames. London: 1861. V. 53

BOWDITCH, T. E.
An Introduction to the Ornithology of Cuvier, for the Use of Students and Travellers. Paris: 1821. V. 51

BOWDLER, THOMAS
Letters Written in Holland. (with) Papers Relating to the Journey of the Princess of Orange. London: 1788. V. 54

BOWDOIN, JAMES
A Paraphrase on Part of the Oeconomy of Human Life. Boston: 1759. V. 47
A Philosophical Discourse, Addressed to the American Academy of Arts and Sciences, Assembled at the Meeting House, in Brattle Street, Boston, on the Eighth of November, 1780. Boston Printed: 1785. V. 48

BOWDOIN, W. G.
The Rise of the Bookplate, Being an Exemplification of the Art, Signified by Various Bookplates from Its Earliest to Its Most Recent Practice. New York: 1910. V. 48

BOWE, WILLIAM FORRESTER
Notions of the Nature of Fever and of Nervous Action. Alnwick: 1829. V. 52

BOWEN, ABEL
Bowen's Picture of Boston... Boston: 1833. V. 51
Bowen's Picture of Boston. Boston: 1838. V. 54

BOWEN, AYLWIN
In New Japan: the Narrative - A Travel Record in the Main-of a Post-War Sojourn. 1932. V. 54

BOWEN, CLARENCE WINTHROP
The History of the Centennial Celebration of the Inauguration of George Washington as First President of the United States. New York: 1892. V. 47; 54

BOWEN, ELIZABETH
Anthony Trollope. New York: 1946. V. 51
Collected Impressions. New York: 1950. V. 48; 50
The Death of the Heart. London: 1938. V. 47
Eva Trout. London: 1968. V. 53
The Heat of the Day. New York: 1948. V. 51
The Heat of the Day. London: 1949. V. 54
The House in Paris. London: 1935. V. 48
Joining Charles and Other Stories. London: 1929. V. 48; 49
The Last September. London: 1929. V. 50
Look at All those Roses. New York: 1941. V. 54
Seven Winters. Dublin: 1942. V. 48
The Shelbourne Hotel. New York: 1951. V. 49

BOWEN, FRANCIS
American Political Economy... New York: 1870. V. 50; 54

BOWEN, FRANK C.
The Golden Age of Sail. London: 1925. V. 51; 53
The Sea, Its History and Romance. London: 1924-26. V. 50
The Sea, its History and Romance. London: 1925. V. 49

BOWEN, GEORGE FERGUSON
The Ionian Islands Under British Protection. London: 1851. V. 54

BOWEN, JAMES L.
History of the Thirty Seventh Regiment Mass. Volunteers. Holyoke: 1884. V. 47

BOWEN, MARJORIE
The Bishop of Hell and Other Stories. London: 1949. V. 50

BOWEN, NATHANIEL
A Pastoral Letter, on the Religious Instruction of the Slaves of members of the Protestant Episcopal Church in the State of South-Carolina, Prepared at the Request of the Convention of the Churches of Diocese. Charleston: 1835. V. 51

BOWEN, RICHARD LE BARON
Archaeological Discoveries in South Arabia. Baltimore: 1958. V. 51; 52; 53

BOWEN, T. J.
Grammar and Dictionary of the Yoruba Language. Washington: 1858. V. 52

BOWEN, THOMAS
An Historical Account of the Origin, Progress and Present State of Bethlem Hospital... London: 1783. V. 48; 49

BOWEN'S New Guide to the City of Boston and Vicinity: State of Massachsetts. Boston: 1849. V. 48

BOWER, ARCHIBALD
A Faithful Account of Mr. Archibald Bower's Motives for Leaving His Office of Secretary to the Court of Inquisition; Including Also, a Relation of the Horrid Treatment of an Innocent Gentleman... London: 1750. V. 52
The History of the Popes from the Foundation of the See of Rome, to the Present Time. London: 1750-66. V. 48

BOWER, DONALD E.
Fred Rosenstock. A Legend in Books and Art. 1976. V. 47

BOWER, JOHN
Description of the Abbeys of Melrose and Old Melrose, with Their Traditions. Kelso: 1813. V. 52; 54

BOWER, SAMUEL
The People of Utopia; or, the Sufficiency of Socialism for Human Happiness... Bradford: 1838. V. 53

BOWERBANK, J. S.
A History of the Fossil Fruits and Seeds of the London Clay. Part 1. London: 1840. V. 51
A Monograph of the British Spongladae. London: 1864. V. 52

BOWERING, GEORGE
Points on a Grid. Toronto: 1964. V. 47

BOWERS, C. G.
Rhododendrons and Azaleas... New York: 1936. V. 51; 52

BOWERS, FREDSON
Studies in Bibliography. Charlottesville: 1948-89. V. 50
Studies in Bibliography... Charlottesville: 1959-92. V. 49
Studies in Bibliography... Charlottesville: 1977-88. V. 50

BOWERS, GEORGINA
Canters in Crampshire. I. Gallops from Gorseborough; II. Scrambles with Scratch Packs. III. Studies with Staghounds. London: 1878. V. 47
Idyls of the Rink. London: 1877. V. 47

BOWERS, LESLIE
Plantation Recipes. New York: 1959. V. 53

BOWERS, STEPHEN
A Remarkable Valley and an Interesting Tribe of Indians. San Buena Ventura: 1888. V. 53

BOWERS, W. H.
Researches into the History of the Parish and Parish Church of Stone, Staffordshire. Birmingham: 1929. V. 53

BOWES, JAMES L.
Japanese Enamels. London: 1886. V. 50
Japanese Pottery with Notes Describing the Thoughts and Subjects Employed in Its Decoration. Liverpool: 1890. V. 47

BOWES, ROBERT
A Catalogue of Books Printed at or Relating to the University Town & County of Cambridge from 1521 to 1893. (with) Index. Cambridge: 1894. V. 47; 51; 54
A Dictionary of Printers and Booksellers, in England, Scotland and Ireland and of Foreign Printers of English Books 1557-1640. London: 1910. V. 50
John Siberch. Bibliographical Notes 1886-1905. 1906. V. 51; 54

BOWIE, HENRY P.
On the Laws of Japanese Painting. San Francisco: 1911. V. 48

BOWIE, THEODORE
The Carrey Drawings of the Parthenon Sculptures. Bloomington: 1971. V. 50; 52

BOWING, L.
Paintings in the Louvre. London: 1987. V. 50

BOWKER, PIERPONT F.
The Indian Vegetable Family Instructer. Boston: 1836. V. 51

BOWLER, THOMAS W.
Pictorial Album of Cape Town with Views of Simon's Town, Port Elizabeth and Graham's Town, with Historical and Descriptive Sketches by W. R. Thompson. Cape Town: 1966. V. 47

BOWLES, CARRINGTON
The Art of Drawing Without a Master from the French of Sieur P.B. London: 1785. V. 52
The Artist's Assistant; or School of Science, Being an Introduction to Painting in Oil, Water and Crayons... London: 1807. V. 53
Bowles's Art of Painting in Water-Colours... London: 1783. V. 54
Bowles's New London guide; Being an Alphabetical Index... London: 1790. V. 50; 52
The Draughtmen's Assistant; or, Drawing Made Easy... London: 1776. V. 52
The Draughtsman's Assistant; or, Drawing Made Easy... London: 1786. V. 53

BOWLES, J. M.
Some Examples of the Work of American Designers. Philadelphia, New York: 1918. V. 51

BOWLES, JANE
In the Summer House. New York: 1954. V. 52
Two Serious Ladies. New York: 1943. V. 48; 51; 53

BOWLES, JOHN
Thoughts on the Late General Election, as Demonstrative of the Progress of Jacobinism. London: 1802. V. 50; 53

BOWLES, PAUL
The Delicate Prey. New York: 1950. V. 48
The Hours After Noon. London: 1959. V. 51; 52
In the Red Room. Los Angeles: 1981. V. 51; 53
In Touch: the Letters of Paul Bowles. New York: 1994. V. 51; 52; 53; 54
Let It Come Down. 1952. V. 50
Let It Come Down. London: 1952. V. 49; 54
Let it Come Down. New York: 1952. V. 47; 49; 51; 52; 54
Let It Come Down. Santa Barbara: 1980. V. 50; 52
A Little Stone. London: 1950. V. 48; 49; 50; 51; 53
Midnight Mass. Santa Barbara: 1981. V. 48; 49; 51; 53
Morocco. Sausalito: 1993. V. 50
Next to Nothing. Kathmandu: 1976. V. 48; 50; 51; 54
Next to Nothing... Santa Barbara: 1981. V. 52
Once a Lady Was Here. New York: 1946. V. 52
The Sheltering Sky. 1949. V. 49
The Sheltering Sky. London: 1949. V. 47; 53
The Sheltering Sky. New York: 1949. V. 47; 53
The Spider's House. New York: 1955. V. 49; 52; 53; 54
The Spider's House. London: 1957. V. 49; 52
The Spider's House. Santa Barbara: 1982. V. 51; 52
The Spider's House. Santa Barbara: 1983. V. 50; 51
Un The Au Sahara (The Sheltering Sky). Paris: 1952. V. 49
Their Heads are Green and Their Hands are Blue. New York: 1963. V. 53
The Thicket of Spring. Los Angeles: 1972. V. 53
Things Gone and Things Still Here. Santa Barbara: 1977. V. 52
The Time of Friendship: a Volume of Short Stories. New York: 1967. V. 50
Too Far From Home. 1994. V. 53
Too Far from Home. London: 1994. V. 52
Two Poems. New York: 1933. V. 51; 52
Up Above the World. New York: 1966. V. 52; 54
Up Above the World. London: 1967. V. 49
Without Stopping: an Autobiography. New York: 1972. V. 51
Yallah. New York: 1957. V. 48; 51

BOWLES, SAMUEL
Across the Continent. Springfield New York: 1865. V. 47
The Pacific Railroad - Open. How to Go: What to See, Guide for Travel to and Through Western America. Boston: 1869. V. 47

BOWLES, WILLIAM LISLE
Elegy Written at the Hot-Wells, Bristol. Bath: 1791. V. 54
Ellen Gray; or, the Dead Maiden's Curse. Edinburgh: 1823. V. 54
The Grave of the Last Saxon; or, the Legend of the Curfew. London: 1822. V. 54
Monody, Written at Matlock, October 1791. Salisbury: 1791. V. 54
A Poetical Address to the Right Honourable Edmund Burke. London: 1791. V. 47
Sonnets, and Other Poems. Bath: 1796. V. 47; 53
Sonnets and Other Poems... Bath: 1801-05. V. 51
Sonnets and Other Poems. Bath: 1802. V. 51
The Sorrows of Switzerland: a Poem. Bath: 1801. V. 54
Verses on the Benevolent Institution of the Philanthropic Society for Protecting and Educating the Children of Vagrants and Criminals. Bath: 1790. V. 54
Verses to John Howard, F.R.S.... His State of ... Prisons and Lazarettos. Bath: 1789. V. 54
Verses to John Howard, F.R.S... His State of Prisons and Lazarettos. London: 1789. V. 54

BOWLES'S Florist. London: 1777(98). V. 52

BOWLKER, CHARLES
The Art of Angling... Birmingham: 1786. V. 47
The Art of Angling... London: 1792. V. 49; 51; 53
Art of Angling. London: 1826. V. 53
The Art of Angling... Ludlow: 1833. V. 49; 54
Art of Angling. Ludlow: 1854. V. 49

BOWMAN, AMOS
Maps of the Principal Auriferous Creeks in the Cariboo Mining District, British columbia. Ottawa: 1895. V. 50
Report On the Geology of the Mining District of Cariboo Mining District, British Columbia. Montreal: 1888. V. 50

BOWMAN, ANNE
The Bear-Hunters of the Rocky Mountains. 1861. V. 54
The Bear-Hunters of the Rocky Mountains. London: 1861. V. 50

BOWMAN, DAVID
Let the Dog Drive. New York: 1992. V. 51; 52; 53; 54
Let the Dog Drive. New York: 1993. V. 52

BOWMAN, HENRY
The Churches of the Middle Ages. London: 1845/53. V. 49

BOWMAN, JAMES
John Henry. Chicago: 1942. V. 48; 50

BOWMAN, S. M.
Sherman and His Campaigns: a Military Biography. New York: 1865. V. 52

BOWNAS, SAMUEL
An Account of the Life, Travels and Christian Experiences in the Work of the Ministry of Samuel Bownas. London: 1756. V. 48; 49; 53; 54
A Description of the Qualifications Necessary to a Gosepl Minister... London: 1767. V. 49; 50

BOWNESS, ALAN
Alan Davie. London: 1967. V. 49
Barbara Hepworth, Drawings from a Sculptor's Landscape. London: 1966. V. 54
The Complete Sculpture of Barbara Hepworth 1960-1969. London: 1971. V. 47; 48; 50; 51; 53; 54
Victor Pasmore: a Catalogue Raisonne of the Painting, Constructions and Graphics, 1926-1979. New York: 1980. V. 53

BOWNESS, S.
Model Ships and Power Boats, Incorporating Ships and Ship Models. London: 1950-56. V. 53

BOWNESS, W.
Rustic Studes in the Westmorland Dialect; with Other Scraps from the Sketch Book of an Artist. London: 1868. V. 50

BOWRA, C. M.
Memories. 1898-1939. London: 1966. V. 51
Poetry and Politics. 1900-1960. Cambridge: 1966. V. 51

BOWRING, JOHN
Ancient Poetry and Romances of Spain. London: 1824. V. 51
The Decimal System in Numbers, Coins and Accounts... London: 1854. V. 47
The Kingdom and People of Siam. London: 1857. V. 47; 51; 54
Matins and Vespers: with Hymns and Occasional Devotional Pieces. London: 1823. V. 54
Minor Morals for Young People. London: 1834. V. 49
Minor Morals for Young People. London: 1835-5-9. V. 51
Specimens of the Polish Poets; with Notes...on the Literature of Poland. London: 1827. V. 48

BOWYER, GEORGE
Commentaries on the Constitutional Law of England. London: 1846. V. 52

BOWYER, JOHN WILSON
The Annals of Elder Horn: Early Life in the Southwest. New York: 1930. V. 47

BOWYER, WILLIAM
The Origin of Printing: in Two Essays. London: 1774. V. 48; 51; 52; 54

BOX, MICHAEL JAMES
Capt. James Box's Adventures and Explorations in New and Old Mexico. New York: 1869. V. 49; 54

BOXER, CHARLES RALPH
The Dutch in Brazil 1624-1654. Oxford: 1957. V. 50

BOXER, F. N.
Hunter's Hand Book of the Victoria Bridge, Illustrated with Wood-Cuts... Montreal: 1860. V. 51

THE BOY Who Drew Cats. Tokyo: 1898. V. 48

BOYCE, A. P.
Boyce's Modern Ornamenter and Interior Decorator. Boston: 1874. V. 52

BOYCE, CHARLES WILLIAM
A Brief History of the Twenty-Eighth Regiment New York State Volunteers First Brigade, First Division, Twelfth Corps, Army of the Potomac... Buffalo: 1896?. V. 52

BOYCE, ROBERT
Mosquito or Man? The Conquest of the Tropical World. London: 1909. V. 51
Mosquito or Man? The Conquest of the Tropical World. London: 1910. V. 48

BOYCE, W. B.
Notes on South-African Affairs. London: 1839. V. 47

BOYD, A. W.
A Country Parish. London: 1951. V. 48

BOYD, ALEXANDER KENNEDY HUTCHINSON
Twenty-Five Years of St. Andrews. London: 1892. V. 49; 54

BOYD, ANDREW
Chinese Architecture and Town Planning 1500 BC - AD 1911. London: 1962. V. 48

BOYD, ARTHUR
Arthur Boyd Drawings 1934-1970. Catalogue... London: 1973. V. 49

BOYD, BELLE HARDINGE
Belle Boyd in Camp and Prison. New York: 1865. V. 49

BOYD, DAVID
A History: Greeley and the Union Colony of Colorado. Greeley: 1890. V. 47

BOYD, E.
Popular Arts of Spanish New Mexico. Santa Fe: 1974. V. 49

BOYD, ERNEST
H. L. Mencken. New York: 1925. V. 49

BOYD, J. D.
The Human Placenta. Cambridge: 1970. V. 48

BOYD, JAMES
Drums. New York London: 1925. V. 50
Drums. New York: 1928. V. 47; 49
Long Hunt. New York: 1930. V. 53

BOYD, JAMES D.
The Drawings of Sir Frank Brangwyn. 1967. V. 51; 53
The Drawings of Sir Frank Brangwyn... England: 1967. V. 49

BOYD, JULIA
Bewick Gleanings: Being Impressions from Copperplates and Wood Blocks... Newcastle-upon-Tyne: 1886. V. 51; 53

BOYD, NANCY
Distressing Dialogues. New York: 1924. V. 47

BOYD, ROBERT
The Office, Powers and Jurisdiction of His Majesty's Justices of the Peace and Commissioners of Supply. Edinburgh: 1787. V. 52; 54

BOYD, WALTER
A Letter to the Right Honourable William Pitt, on the Influence of the Stoppage of Issue in Specie at the Bank of England; on the Prices of Provisions, and Other Commodities. London: 1801. V. 53

BOYD, WILLIAM
The Blue Afternoon. London: 1990. V. 53
The Blue Afternoon. London: 1993. V. 51; 54
Brazzaville Beach. London: 1990. V. 47; 48; 49; 51; 54
Cork. 1994. V. 51; 53
Cork. London: 1994. V. 52; 54
A Good Man in Africa. London: 1981. V. 47; 49; 51; 52; 53
A Good Man in Africa. New York: 1982. V. 49; 51
An Ice-Cream War. London: 1982. V. 49; 51; 53
An Ice-Cream War. New York: 1983. V. 53
On the Yankee Station. London: 1981. V. 47; 49; 52
On the Yankee Stations... London: 1982. V. 49
On Yankee Station - Stories. New York: 1984. V. 54

BOYDELL, JOHN
Catalogue Raisonne d'un Recueil d'Estampes d'Apres les plus Beaux Tableaux qui Soient en Angleterre. London: 1779-83. V. 54
Description of the Picture of the Death of Major Peirson, and the Defeat of the French Troops in the Island of Jersey, in 1781. London: 1784. V. 54
An History of the River Thames. London: 1794. V. 50
An History of the River Thames. London: 1794-96. V. 49

BOYDELL'S Illustrations of the Dramatic Works of Shakespeare by the Most Eminent Artists of Great Britain... New York: 1852. V. 49

BOYDEN, CHARLES M.
The Cruise of the Snapshot, Chicago to Memphis 1897. 1898. V. 47

BOYDEN, D. D.
The History of Violin Playing from its Origins to 1761 and Its Relationship to the Violin and Violin Music. London: 1965. V. 49

BOYD HARTE, GLYNN
Temples of Power: the Architecture of Electricity in London... 1979. V. 52

BOYER, ABEL
Characters of the Virtues and Vices of the Age; or, Moral Reflections, Maxims, and Thoughts Upon Men and Manners. London: 1695. V. 50
The Compleat French Master, for Ladies and Gentlemen... London: 1699. V. 47; 50
The Complete French Master for Ladies and Gentlemen... London: 1764. V. 52
Le Dictionnaire Royal (The Royal Dictionary, French and English and English and French)... London: 1753. V. 47
The History of Queen Anne... London: 1722. V. 49
The History of Queen Anne. London: 1735. V. 47; 50; 53
Memoirs of the Life and Negotiations of Sir W. Temple... London: 1714. V. 49; 51; 52
The Royal Dictionary Abridged. London: 1728. V. 49; 54

BOYER, ALEXIS
The Lectures of Boyer Upon Diseases of the Bones. Philadelphia: 1805. V. 52

BOYER, C. S.
The Diatomaceae of Philadelphia and Vicinity. Philadelphia: 1916. V. 50; 52

BOYER, MARTHA
Catalogue of Japanese Lacquers in the Walters Art Gallery. Baltimore: 1970. V. 49

BOYES, JOHN
The Company of Adventurers. London: 1928. V. 49

BOYES, JOSEPH
On the Shoulders of Giants: Notable Names in Hand Surgery. Philadelphia: 1976. V. 52

BOYKIN, EDWARD M.
The Boys and Girls Stories of the War. Richmond: 1863?. V. 47
The Falling Flag. Evacuation of Richmond, Retreat and Surrender at Appomatox. New York: 1874. V. 50

BOYKIN, RICHARD M.
Captain Alexander Hamilton Boykin. New York: 1942. V. 50

BOYLAN, GRACE DUFFIE
Kids of Many Colors. Chicago: 1901. V. 47

BOYLE, ELEANOR VERE
Beauty and the Beast. London: 1875. V. 51
Child's Play. London: 1852. V. 52
Child's Play. London: 1859. V. 51
Child's Play. London: 1865. V. 49
Days and Hours in a Garden. London: 1884. V. 50
A Dream Book. London: 1870. V. 52
A Garden of Pleasure. London: 1895. V. 52
In the Fir Wood. London: 1866. V. 49
A New Child's Play. London: 1877. V. 51
A New Child's Play. London: 1879. V. 47; 51

BOYLE, FREDERICK
The Golden Prime. London: 1882. V. 52
The Woodlands Orchids Described and Illustrated with Stories of Orchid Collecting. London: 1901. V. 50

BOYLE, JACK
Boston Blackie. New York: 1919. V. 52

BOYLE, JAMES
A Letter...to Wm. Lloyd Garrison, Respecting the Clerical Appeal, Sectarianism, True Holiness, &c. Boston: 1838. V. 49

BOYLE, KAY
The First Lover and Other Stories. 1933. V. 51
Plagued by the Nightingale. New York: 1931. V. 48
Short Stories. Paris: 1929. V. 51; 53
Three Hundred and Sixty-five Days. New York: 1936. V. 51
Wedding Day and Other Stories. New York: 1930. V. 47; 49
The White Horses of Vienna and Other Stories. New York: 1936. V. 48
Year Before Last. New York: 1932. V. 54

BOYLE, MARIE
Three Little Maids from School. London: 1890. V. 52

BOYLE, MARY LOUISA
The State Prisoner, a Tale of the French Regency. London: 1837. V. 47; 49; 50; 53

BOYLE, P.
The Fashionable Court Guide, or Town Visiting Dictory, for the Year 1793... London: 1793. V. 50; 52

BOYLE, PATRICK
At Night All Cats Are grey and Other Stories. New York: 1969. V. 47
Like Any Other Man. 1966. V. 47

BOYLE, ROBERT
Chymista Scepticus... Geneva: 1680/94. V. 54
A Continuation of New Experiments Physico-Mechanical, Touching the Spring and Weight of the Air, and Their Effects. Oxford: 1669. V. 49; 53
An Essay Of the Great Effects of Even Languid and Unheeded Motion. London: 1690. V. 52
The Martyrdom of Theodora and of Didymus. London: 1687. V. 52
Medicina Hydrostatica; or Hydrostaticks... London: 1690. V. 48
Medicinal Experiments: or, a Collection of Choice Remedies, for the Most Part Simple... London: 1693. V. 48
Medicinal Experiments; or, a Collection of Choice... Remedies, for the Most Part Simple... London: 1712. V. 52
New Experiments and Observations Touching Cold, or an Experimental History of Col, Begun. London: 1683. V. 52; 54
New Experiments Physico-Mechanical, Touching the Spring of the Air, and Its Effects, (Made for the Most Part, in a New Pneumatical Engine)... Oxford: 1662. V. 47; 49
Occasional Reflections Upon Several Subjects. London: 1665. V. 48; 50; 52
Of the Reconcileableness of Specifick Medicines to the Corpuscular Philosophy. London: 1685. V. 52; 54
The Philosophical Works Abridged, Methodized and Disposed Under the General Heads of Physics, Statics, Pneumatics, Natural History, Chymistry and Medicine. London: 1725. V. 47; 48
The Sceptical Chymist: or Chymico-Physical Doubts and Paradoxes... London: 1680. V. 52
The Sceptical Chymist; or, Chymico-Physical Doubts and Paradoxes. London: 1965. V. 48
Some Considerations About the Reconcileableness of Reason and Religion. London: 1675. V. 52
Some Considerations Touching the Style of the Holy Scriptures. London: 1668. V. 52; 54

BOYLE, ROBERT continued
Some Considerations Touching the Usefulness of Experimental Natural Philosophy. (with) Some Considerations Touching the Usefulnesse of Experimental Naturall Philosophy...the Second Tome. Oxford: 1664/71. V. 52
Some Considerations Touching the Usefulnesse of Experimental Naturall Philosophy, Propos'd in Familiar Discourses to a Friend, by Way of Invitation to the Study Of It. Oxford: 1663. V. 52
Some Motives and Incentives to the Lord of God, Pathetically Discours'd of In a Letter to a Friend. London: 1678. V. 53
Tracts Consisting of Observations About the Saltness of the Sea... London: 1674. V. 48; 52; 54
The Water Hustlers. San Francisco: 1971. V. 48; 53
The Works... London: 1699-1700. V. 54
The Works... London: 1744. V. 48
The Works... London: 1772. V. 47; 53; 54

BOYLE, T. CORAGHESSAN
Budding Prospects. New York: 1984. V. 49; 53
Descent of Man. Boston: 1979. V. 47; 48; 49; 50; 51; 53; 54
Descent of Man. London: 1980. V. 49; 50; 54
Greasy Lake. New York: 1985. V. 53
If the River Was Whiskey. New York: 1989. V. 52
Water Music. Boston: 1981. V. 48; 50; 51; 52; 53; 54
Water Music. London: 1982. V. 53
World's End. New York: 1987. V. 49; 52; 53

BOYLE, WILLIAM
Christmas at the Zoo. London. V. 49

BOYLE'S Fashionable Court and Country Guide and Town Visiting Director. London: 1831. V. 54

BOYNE, WILLIAM
Tokens Issued in the Seventeenth, Eighteenth and Nineteenth Centuries, in Yorkshire, by Tradesmen, Overseers of the Poor, Etc. in gold, Silver, Brass and Copper. Headingly: 1858. V. 48
Trade Tokens Issued in the Seventeenth Century in England, Wales and Ireland... London: 1889-91. V. 48

BOYNINGEN-HUENE, GEORGE
Baalbek Palmyra. New York: 1946. V. 53

BOYNTON, CHARLES B.
The History of the Navy During the Rebellion. New York: 1867-68. V. 51
A Journey through Kansas: With Sketches of Nebraska. Cincinnati: 1855. V. 47; 50

BOYNTON, H. W.
The Golfer's Rubaiyat. Chicago: 1901. V. 52

BOYNTON, S. R.
The Painter Lady: Grace Carpenter Hudson. Eureka: 1978. V. 47; 50; 54

BOYS, EDWARD
Narrative of a Captivity and Adventures in France and Flanders, Between the Years 1803 and 1809. London: 1827. V. 49

BOY'S Illustrated Annual. Volume I. 1892-93. V. 51

BOY'S Illustrated Annual. Volume II. 1893-94. V. 51

BOYS, JOHN
A General View of the Agriculture of the County of Kent... London: 1796. V. 47; 50; 52

THE BOY'S Own Conjuring Book: Being A Complete Hand Book of Parlour Magic and Containing Over One Thousand Optical, Chemical, Mechanical, Magnetical and Magical Experiments... New York: 1860. V. 50

BOYS, THOMAS SHORTER
London As It Is. London: 1842. V. 50
Picturesque Architecture in Paris, Ghent, Antwerp, Rouen, Etc. Drawn from Nature and On Stone. London: 1839. V. 49

THE BOY'S Treasury of Sports, Pastimes and Recreations. New York: 1850. V. 49

BOYS, W.
Testacea Minuta Rariora... London: 1784. V. 53

BOYS, WILLIAM
Practical Treatise on the Office and Duties of Coroners in Upper Canada. Toronto: 1864. V. 53

BOYSE, SAMUEL
Deity: a Poem. London: 1749. V. 47; 54

BOZIUS, THOMAS
den Antiquo et Novo Italiae Stataue Adversus Macchiavellum. Rome: 1596. V. 48

BR Today: a Selection of His Books, with Comments. New York: 1982. V. 52; 54

BRAAM, ANDRE EVERARD VAN
An Authentic Account of the Embassy of the Dutch East-India Company, To the Court of the Emperor of China, in the Years 1794 and 1795. London: 1798. V. 53

BRAASCH, WILLIAM
Clinical Urography: an Atlas and Textbook of Roentgenologic Diagnosis. Philadelphia: 1951. V. 53
Urography. Philadelphia: 1928. V. 53

BRABANT, A. J.
Vancouver Island and Its Missions 1874-1900. New York: 1900. V. 49

BRABOURNE, LORD
The Birds of South America. London: 1912-17. V. 48
The Birds of South America. Volume I. Checklist. London: 1912. V. 52; 53

BRABROOK, EDWARD W.
The Royal Society of Literature of the United Kingdom. London: 1891. V. 51

BRACE, CHARLES LORING
The Dangerous Classes of New York and Twenty Years Work Among Them. New York: 1872. V. 49
The New West or California in 1867-69. New York: 1869. V. 54

BRACEBRIDGE, SELINA
Notes Descriptive of a Panoramic Sketch of Athens, Taken May 1839, Sold in Aid of the London Benevolent Repository. London: 839. V. 47

BRACHT, VIKTOR
Texas in 1848. 1931. V. 48; 51

BRACKEN, HENRY
Farriery Improv'd. London: 1737. V. 47
Farriery Improv'd... London: 1738. V. 50
Farriery Improv'd... London: 1740-42. V. 47
Farriery Improv'd... London: 1742. V. 47
Farriery Improv'd. London: 1752. V. 47
Ten Minutes Advice to Every Gentleman Going to Purchase a Horse Out of a Dealer, Jockey, or Groom's Stables. Philadelphia: 1787. V. 54

BRACKENBURY, HENRY
The Ashanti War... Edinburgh & London: 1874. V. 47; 51; 52; 54

BRACKENRIDGE, HENRY MARIE
Early Discoveries by Spaniards in New Mexico: Containing an Account of the Castles in Cibola... Pittsburgh: 1857. V. 49
History of the Western Insurrection in Western Pennsylvania, Commonly Called the Whiskey Insurrection, 1794. Pittsburgh: 1859. V. 47; 50
Istoria Della Guerra Fra Gli Stati Uniti d'America e L'Inghilterra Negli Anni MDCCCXII-XIII-XIV E XV. Milano: 1821. V. 52
Recollection of Persons and Places in the West. Philadelphia: 1834. V. 48; 50
Views of Louisiana; Together with a Jouranl of the Voyage Up the Mississippi Rier in 1811. Pittsburgh: 1814. V. 47; 50; 52; 54
Voyage to South America, Performed by Order of the American Government in the Years 1817 and 1818, in the Frigate Congress. Baltimore: 1819. V. 47; 51; 54
Voyage to South America, Performed by Order of the American Government in the Years 1817 and 1818, in the Frigate Congress. London: 1820. V. 49

BRACKENRIDGE, HUGH HENRY
Gazette Publications. Carlisle: 1806. V. 48
Incidents of the Insurrection in the Western Parts of Pennsylvania, in the Year 1794. Philadelphia: 1795. V. 47
Modern Chivalry. Philadelphia: 1797. V. 51; 54
Modern Chivalry... Philadelphia: 1804-07. V. 51

BRACKETT, ALBERT G.
History of the United States Cavalry, from the Formation of the Federal Government to the 1st of June, 1863. New York: 1865. V. 47; 49; 52

BRACKETT, CHARLES
Entirely Surrounded. New York: 1934. V. 47; 48; 49

BRACKETT, GEORGE A.
A Winter Evening's Tale. New York: 1880. V. 48

BRACKETT, L.
The Sword of Rhiannon. 1955. V. 48; 52

BRACKETT, OLIVER
Thomas Chippendale, a Study of His Life, Work and Influence. London: 1930. V. 48; 49

BRACTON, HENRY DE
De Legibus et Consuetudinibus Angliae Libri Quinq. London: 1569. V. 47; 52
De Legibus et Consuetudinibus Angliae. London: 1878-83. V. 49; 52

BRADBURY, JOHN
Travels In the Interior of America, in the Years 1809, 1810 and 1811. Liverpool: 1817. V. 52
Travels in the Interior of America, in the Years 1809, 1810 and 1811. London: 1819. V. 47; 50

BRADBURY, MALCOLM
Contemporary Criticism. 1970. V. 53
Eating People Is Wrong. London: 1959. V. 48; 49; 51
The History of Man. London: 1975. V. 51
Stepping Westward. London: 1965. V. 53; 54

BRADBURY, OSGOOD
Louise Kempton; or, Vice and Virtue Contrasted. Boston: 184-. V. 47
The Old Distiller; a Tale of Truth. New York: 1851. V. 52

BRADBURY, RAY
About Norman Corwin. 1979. V. 51
The Anthem Sprinters. 1963. V. 48; 50; 52
The Aqueduct. 1979. V. 49; 50
The Attic Where the Meadow Greens. Northridge: 1979. V. 50
Beyond 1984: Remembrance of Things Future. New York: 1979. V. 47; 51
Beyond 1984: Remembrance of Things Future. New York: 1979/65. V. 48
The Climate of Palettes. Northridge: 1989. V. 48
Dandelion Wine. 1957. V. 52

BRADBURY, RAY continued
Dandelion Wine. Garden City: 1957. V. 54
Dandelion Wine. London: 1957. V. 50
Dandelion Wine. New York: 1957. V. 51
Dandelion Wine. New York: 1975. V. 50
Dark Carnival. Sauk City: 1947. V. 47; 48; 49; 50; 51; 52; 53
Dark Carnival. London: 1948. V. 50; 52
The Day It Rained Forever. 1959. V. 50; 51
Death Has Lost Its Charm for Me. Northridge: 1987. V. 48
Death is a Lonely Business. New York: 1985. V. 47; 48; 50; 51; 52
The Dragon. 1988. V. 49; 50; 54
Fahrenheit 451. New York: 1933. V. 49
Fahrenheit 451. 1953. V. 47; 51
Fahrenheit 451. New York: 1953. V. 49
Fahrenheit 451. London: 1954. V. 47; 50
Fahrenheit 451. New York: 1967. V. 48
Fahrenheit 451. 1982. V. 52; 54
Fahrenheit 451. New York: 1982. V. 47; 49
The Ghosts of Forever. New York: 1980. V. 49
The Golden Apples of the Sun. Garden City: 1953. V. 52; 54
The Golden Apples of the Sun. London: 1953. V. 47; 48; 53
The Golden Apples of the Sun. New York: 1953. V. 48; 49; 50; 51; 52
Graveyard for Lunatics. New York: 1990. V. 51
Green Shadows, White Whale. 1992. V. 51; 53; 54
Green Shadows, White Whale. New York: 1992. V. 49
The Halloween Tree. New York: 1972. V. 49
Hollerbochen Comes Back or the Voyage of the Neuralgia. 1938. V. 47
The Illustrated Man. Garden City: 1951. V. 47
The Illustrated Man. New York: 1951. V. 48; 50; 52
The Last Circus and the Electrocution. Northridge: 1980. V. 50
The Last Good Kiss. 1984. V. 49
Long After Ecclesiastes; New Biblical Texts by Ray Bradbury. Santa Ana: 1985. V. 52
The Machineries of Joy. Garden City: 1964. V. 54
The Machineries of Joy. New York: 1964. V. 48; 54
The Martian Chronicles. Garden City: 1950. V. 52
The Martian Chronicles. New York: 1950. V. 48; 49
The Martian Chronicles. 1974. V. 48; 50; 52
The Martian Chronicles. Avon: 1974. V. 47; 49
A Medicine for Melancholy. Garden City: 1959. V. 54
A Medicine for Melancholy. New York: 1959. V. 50
A Medicine for Melancholy. Garden City: 1962. V. 54
Nineteen Eighty-four Will Not Arrive. A Prediction for the Greening of Scripps. Los Angeles: 1975. V. 49
The October Country. 1955. V. 51
The October Country. 1956. V. 48; 52
The Pedestrian. 1946. V. 49
The Pedestrian. 1951. V. 50
The Pedestrian. Glendale: 1964. V. 47; 48
R is For Rocket. Garden City: 1962. V. 50; 54
Ray Bradbury Review. 1988. V. 47; 49; 51; 54
S is for Space. Garden City: 1966. V. 54
S is for Space. London: 1968. V. 51
The Silver Locusts. 1951. V. 54
The Silver Locusts. London: 1951. V. 52
The Silver Locusts. 1952. V. 50
Something Wicked This Way Comes. V. 49
Something Wicked This Way Comes. New York: 1962. V. 52
Something Wicked This Way Comes. London: 1963. V. 50
The Stories. New York: 1980. V. 52
Switch On the Night. 1955. V. 49; 50; 54
Switch On the Night. New York: 1955. V. 49
That Son of Richard III. 1974. V. 47; 48
The Toynbee Convector. New York: 1988. V. 49; 50
Twice 22. New York: 1966. V. 51
The Vintage Bradbury. 1965. V. 51
The Vintage Bradbury. New York: 1965. V. 49

BRADBURY, ROBERT
The Day It Rained Forever. 1959. V. 47

BRADBY, CHRISTOPHER
Well on the Road. London: 1935. V. 51

BRADDON, EDWARD
Thirty Years of Shikar. London: 1895. V. 48

BRADDON, LAWRENCE
Essex's Innocency and Honour Vindicated: or, Murther, Subornation, Perjury and Oppression, Justly Charg'd on the Murtherers of that Noble Lord and True Patriot, Arthur (Late) Earl of Essex... London: 1690. V. 50

BRADE, DANIEL
Picturesque Sketches In Italy. London: 1886. V. 50; 52

BRADFIELD, WESLEY
Cameron Creek Village, a Site in the Mimbres Area in Grant County, New Mexico. Santa Fe: 1929. V. 50
Cameron Creek Village, A Site in the Mimbres Area in Grant County, New Mexico. Santa Fe: 1931. V. 49; 52

BRADFORD, ALDEN
History of Massachusetts, for Two Hundred Years from the Year 1620 to 1820. Boston: 1835. V. 51; 54
History of Massachusetts from 1764 (...to 1820). Boston: 1822-25-29. V. 51
Memoirs of the Life and Writings of Rev. Johnathan Mayhew, D.D., Pastor of the West Church and Scoeity in Boston from June 1747 to July 1866. Boston: 1838. V. 53

BRADFORD, ALEXANDER W.
American Antiquities and Researches into the Origin and History of the Red Race. New York: 1841. V. 49; 53

BRADFORD, JOHN
Holy Meditations Upon the Lords Prayer, the Beleife, and Ten Commandements. London: 1614. V. 54
John Bradford's Historical &c Notes on Kentucky from the Western Miscellany. San Francisco: 1932. V. 52
Tales of the Moor. London: 1841. V. 50

BRADFORD, PETER
Born With the Blues. New York: 1967. V. 51

BRADFORD, ROARK
Kingdom Coming. New York: 1933. V. 53
Let the band Play Dixie and Other Stories. New York: 1934. V. 47
Ol' King David an' the Philistine Boys. New York: 1930. V. 47
Ol' Man Adam An' his Chillun. New York & London: 1928. V. 51; 52; 54
This Side of Jordan. New York: 1929. V. 48

BRADFORD TEXTILE SOCIETY
The Journal. Bradford: 1962-70. V. 47; 53

BRADFORD: The Post-Office Bradford Directory, 1900. Bradford: 1900. V. 53

BRADFORD, THOMAS
History of the Homoeopathic Medical College of Pennsylvania: The Hahnemann Medical College and Hospital of Philadelphia. Philadelphia: 1898. V. 50

BRADFORD, THOMAS LINDSLEY
The Bibliographer's Manual of American History.... Philadelphia: 1907-10. V. 49; 50; 53
The Bibliographer's Manual of American History Containing an Account of All State, Territory, Town and County Histories Relating to the United States of North America, with Verbatim Copies of their Titles, and Useful Bibliographical Notes... Detroit: 1968. V. 52

BRADFORD, WILLIAM
The Arctic Regions Illustrated with Photographs Taken on an Art Expedition to Greenland. London: 1873. V. 51
Sketches of the Country, Character and Costume, in Portugal and Spain, Made During the Campaign and on the Route of the British Army in 1808 and 1809. London: 1813-22. V. 48

BRADFORD, WILLIAM J. A.
Notes on the Northwest, or Valley of the Upper Missisippi. New York: 1846. V. 48

BRADLAUGH, CHARLES
Fruits of Philosophy. A Treatise on the Population Question. 188-. V. 48
Labor and Law, with Memoir and Two Portraits. London: 1891. V. 50

BRADLEY, CHARLES WILLIAM
Patronomatology; for an Essay on the Philosophy of Surnames, Read Before the Connecticut State Lyceum, Nov. 13, 1839. Baltimore: 1842. V. 47

BRADLEY, CUTHBERT
The Foxhound of the Twentieth Century. London: 1914. V. 48
Good Sport. London. V. 50; 53

BRADLEY, DAVID
The Chaneysville Incident. New York: 1981. V. 48; 51; 53
South Street. New York: 1975. V. 49; 52; 53

BRADLEY, EDWARD
College Life. A Series of Original Etchings. Oxford. V. 54
Fox Hunting from Shire to Shire. London & New York: 1912. V. 49
Glencraggan: or, A Highland Home in Cantire. London: 1861. V. 47; 51; 52; 54
Little Mr. Bouncer and His Friend Verdant Green, also Tales of College Life. Boston: 1893. V. 54
Mattins and Mutton's; or, the Beauty of Brighton. London: 1866. V. 48
Nearer and Nearer; a Tale Out of School. London: 1857. V. 53
Photographic Pleasures; Popularly Portrayed with Pen and Pencil. London: 1853. V. 52

BRADLEY, ELIZA
An Authentic Narrative of the Shipwreck and Sufferings of... Boston: 1820. V. 50; 53
An Authentic Narrative of the Shipwreck and Sufferings Of.... Boston: 1823. V. 51

BRADLEY, F. H.
Collected Papers. Oxford: 1935. V. 47
Ethical Studies. London: 1876. V. 49

BRADLEY, HELEN
And Miss Carter Wore Pink. London: 1971. V. 51; 52
The Queen Who Came to Tea. London: 1978. V. 52

BRADLEY, MARION ZIMMER
The Mists of Avalon. New York: 1982. V. 51; 53

BRADLEY, MARY HASTINGS
On the Gorilla Trail. New York: 1922. V. 54

BRADLEY, O. CHARNOCK
Bailliere's Atlas of the Horse. London: 1918. V. 51

BRADLEY, RICHARD
A General Treatise of Husbandry and Gardening... London: 1721-22. V. 51
A General Treatise of Husbandry and Gardening. London: 1724. V. 49
The Gentleman and Farmer's Guide Abridg'd. London and Bulin: 1729. V. 47
New Improvements of Planting and Gardening, Both Philosophical and Practical... London: 1717/17/18. V. 52
New Improvements of Planting and Gardening, both Philosophical and Practical. London: 1724. V. 53
New Improvements of Planting and Gardening, Both Philosophical and Practical. London: 1731. V. 53
New Improvements of Planting and Gardening, Both Philosophical and Practical. London: 1739. V. 47; 48; 50
A Philosophical Account of the Works of Nature... London: 1721. V. 48; 49

BRADLEY, THOMAS H.
Letter from the Secretary of War, Transmitting a Report Concerning the History and Character of Certain Claims of the State of Texas. Washington: 1872. V. 49

BRADLEY, TOM
The Old Coaching Days in Yorkshire. Leeds: 1889. V. 47; 51; 53

BRADLEY, W. A.
Souvenir History of Bruce Beach. N.P: 1938. V. 50

BRADLEY, WILL
Bradley: His Book. Springfield. V. 51
Bradley: His Book. Springfield: 1896. V. 53
Bradley: His Book. Springfield: 1896-97. V. 51; 53
Bradley His Book. Wayside: 1896-Jan. 1897. V. 51
Peter Poodle, Toy Maker to the King. New York: 1906. V. 51; 54

BRADLEY, WILLIAM
A Voyage to New South Wales. The Journal of Lieutenant William Bradley, RN of HMS Sirius 1786-1792. Sydney: 1969. V. 53

BRADLEY-BIRT, F. B.
Persia through Persia from the Gulf to the Caspian. Boston and Tokyo: 1910. V. 54
Through Persia from the Gulf to the Caspian. London: 1909. V. 47

BRADLOW, EDNA
Thomas Bowler of the Cape of Good Hope, His Life and Works with a Catalogue of Extant Paintings... Cape Town & Amsterdam: 1955. V. 49; 51

BRADSHAW, HENRY
A Catalogue of the Bradshaw Collection of Irish Books in the University Library. Cambridge: 1916. V. 48; 51

BRADSHAW, HERBERT C.
History of Prince Edward County, Virginia. Richmond: 1955. V. 52

BRADSHAW, JOHN
Dedham Park. London: 1885. V. 54

BRADSHAW, PERCY V.
Art in Advertising. A Study of British and American Pictorial Publicity. London: 1925. V. 47; 50
The Art of the Illustrator. London: 1920's. V. 48
Drawn from Memory. London: 1943. V. 51

BRADSHAW, W. R.
The Goddess of Atvatabar. 1892. V. 48; 52

BRADSHAW, WILLIAM
A Protestation of the Kings Supremacie, Made by the Non-Conforming Ministers, Which Were Suspended or Deprived... London: 1647. V. 47
Puritanismus Anglicanvs. Frankfurt: 1610. V. 53

BRADSHAW'S
Canals and Navigable Rivers of England and Wales. London: 1918. V. 50; 52
Railway Companion, Containing the Times of Departure, Fares &c. of the Railways in England and Also Hackney Coach Fares from the Principal Railway Stations. Manchester: 1841. V. 47

BRADSTREET, ANNE
The Poems of Mrs. Anne Bradstreet (1612-1672) Together with Her Prose Remains. New York: 1897. V. 49
Several Poems Compiled with Great Variety of Wit and Learning, Full of Delight... Boston: 1678. V. 47
The Works of Anne Bradstreet in Prose and Verse. Charlestown: 1867. V. 47; 49; 51; 52

BRADSTREET, ROBERT
The Sabine Farm, a Poem. London: 1810. V. 52

BRADSTREET'S
Cincinnati Annual Trade Directory of the Principal Mercantile and Manufacturing Firms of Cincinnati, Ohio.... Cincinnati: 1867. V. 53

BRADY, AIDEN FINBAR
Aiden. New York: 1992. V. 50

BRADY, JOHN
Clavis Calendaria; or, a Compendious Analysis of the Calendar. London: 1814. V. 49

BRADY, JOHN H.
The Visitor's Guide to Knole, with Catalogues of the Pictures...and Biographical Notices. Sevenoaks: 1839. V. 53

BRADY, ROBERT
A Complete History of England, from the First Entrance of the Romans...(with) A Continuation of the Complete History... London: 1685/1700. V. 54
An Historical Treatise of Cities and Burghs or Boroughs. London: 1711. V. 48
An Introduction to the Old English History, Comprehended in Three Several Tracts... London: 1684. V. 47
The Story of One Regiment the Eleventh Maine Infantry Volunteers In the War of the Rebellion. New York: 1896. V. 47
A True and Exact History of the Succession of the Crown of England. London: 1681. V. 47

BRADY, SAMUEL
Sketches of the Life and Indian Adventures of Captain Samuel Brady, a Native of Cumberland County, Born 1758, a Few Miles Above Northcumberland. Lancaster: 1891. V. 48

BRADY, WILLIAM
Glimpses of Texas: its Divisions, Resources, Development and Prospects. Houston: 1871. V. 52; 53

BRAEGGER, MARGRIT
Prince Mido. Bienne: 1951. V. 52

BRAGDON, DUDLEY A.
Billy Bounce. Chicago: 1906. V. 49

BRAGG, G. F.
Progressive Sketches for the Lead Pencil. London: 1835. V. 49

BRAGG, GEORGE F.
The First Negro Priest on Southern Soil. Baltimore: 1909. V. 54

BRAGGE, FRANCIS
A Practical Treatise of the Regulation of the Passions. London: 1708. V. 49

BRAHE, TYCHO
Tycho Brahe's Description of His Instruments and Scientific Work as Given in Astronomiae Instauratae Mechanica. Kobenhavn: 1946. V. 54

BRAIN: a Journal of Neurology. Volume VI. London: 1884. V. 52

BRAINARD, JOHN G. C.
The Literary Remains...with Sketch of His Life. Hartford: 1832. V. 50; 52
The Poems... Hartford: 1842. V. 53

BRAINE, JOHN
Life at the Top. London: 1962. V. 54
Room at the Top. London: 1957. V. 47; 48; 50; 51; 54

BRAINERD, CHAUNCEY NILES
My Diary; or Three Weeks on the Wing. New York: 1868. V. 52

BRAINERD, GEORGE W.
The Archaeological Ceramics of Yucatan. Berkeley and Los Angeles: 1958. V. 52

BRAINERD, IRA H.
Edwin Davis French, a Memorial. New York: 1908. V. 49

BRAINES, W. W.
The Site of the Globe Playhouse Southwark... London: 1924. V. 50

BRAITHWAITE, E. R.
Paid Servant. London: 1962. V. 53
To Sir, With Love. London: 1959. V. 53; 54

BRAITHWAITE, EDWARD
Islands. London: 1969. V. 53
Masks. London: 1968. V. 53
Rights of Passage. London: 1967. V. 49

BRAITHWAITE, G. E.
The Braithwaite Clan. 1975. V. 50
Generoso germine Gemmo. Kendal: 1965. V. 50

BRAITHWAITE, GEORGE FOSTER
The Salmonidae of Westmorland, Angling Reminiscences and Leaves from an Angler's Note Book. Kendal: 1884. V. 50; 51; 52

BRAITHWAITE, J. W.
Guide to Kirkby Stephen, Appleby, Brough, Warcop, Ravenstonedale, Mallerstang, &c... 1884. V. 50
Guide to Kirkby Stephen, Appleby, Brough, Warcop, Ravenstonedale, Mallerstang, &c. Kirkby: 1884. V. 52

BRAITHWAITE, JOSEPH BEVAN
Memoirs of Joseph John Gurney. Norwich: 1854. V. 49; 54
Memoirs of Joseph John Gurney. Norwich: 1855. V. 54

BRAITHWAITE, ROBERT
The British Moss Flora. London: 1880-1905. V. 48; 50; 51; 53
The British Moss Flora. London: 1887-1905. V. 49; 51; 52; 53; 54

BRAITHWAITE, WILLIAM STANLEY
Anthology of Magazine Verse for 1913. Cambridge: 1913. V. 51
Anthology of Magazine Verse for 1915. New York: 1915. V. 49
Anthology of Magazine Verse for the Year 1923. Boston: 1923. V. 47; 51; 54
Braithwaite's Anthology of Magazine Verse for 1926... Boston: 1926. V. 51
The House of Falling Leaves with Other Poems. Boston: 1908. V. 54
Lyrics of Life and Love. Boston: 1904. V. 51
Our Lady's Choir: A Contemporary Anthology of Verse by Catholic Sisters. Boston: 1931. V. 54
The Story of the Great War. New York: 1919. V. 54

BRAIVE, MICHEL F.
The Photograph: a Social History. New York: 1966. V. 47; 52; 54

BRAKE, HEZEKIAH
On Two Continents. Topeka: 1896. V. 47

BRAKHAGE, JANE
From the Book of Legends. New York: 1989. V. 54

BRAMAN, D. E.
E. Braman's Information About Texas. Philadelphia: 1858. V. 50

BRAMHALL, JOHN
A Just Vindication of the Church of England, from the Unjust Apsersion of Criminal Schisme. London: 1654. V. 50
The Works... Dublin: 1677. V. 47; 52

BRAMHALL, MAE ST. JOHN
Japanese Jingles. Tokyo: 1891. V. 48

BRAMLEY MOORE, WILLIAM
The Book of Martyrs. London: 1850's. V. 54

BRAMMER, WILLIAM
The Gay Place. 1961. V. 50; 51
The Gay Place. Boston: 1961. V. 48; 54

BRAMSTON, JAMES
The Art of Politicks, in Imitation of Horace's Art of Poetry. London. V. 52
The Art of Politicks, in Imitation of Horace's Art of Poetry. London: 1729. V. 48; 49; 53
The Man of Taste. London: 1733. V. 48; 49; 54

BRAMWELL, BYROM
Anaemia and Some of the Diseases of the Blood-forming Organs and Ductless Glands. Edinburgh: 1899. V. 48; 53
Atlas of Clinical Medicine. Edinburgh: 1892-96. V. 47
Diseases of the Heart and Thoracic Aorta. New York: 1884. V. 53
Diseases of the Spinal Cord. New York: 1882. V. 47
Diseases Of the Spinal Cord. New York: 1886. V. 53

BRAMWELL, CLARENCE C.
The Construction of a Gasolene Motor Vehicle. New York: 1901. V. 47

BRAMWELL, D.
Plants and Islands. London: 1979. V. 48

BRANAGAN, THOMAS
The Excellency of the Female Character Vindicated... Harrisburg: 1828. V. 48; 50
The Excellency of the Female Character Vindicated... New York: 1839. V. 51
The Flowers of Literature. Trenton: 1810. V. 53
The Penitential Tyrant; or, Slave Trader Reformed... New York: 1807. V. 49

BRANCH, DOUGLAS
The Cowboy and His Interpreters. New York: 1926. V. 52

BRANCH, WILLIAM
Life, a Poem in Three Books. Richmond: 1819. V. 49

BRANCHE, THOMAS
Principia Legis & Aequitatis: Being an Alphabetical Collection of Maxims, Principles or Rules, Definitions and Memorable Sayings in Law and Equity. London: 1753. V. 48

BRAND, CHRISTIANNA
London Particular. London: 1952. V. 50
Nurse Matilda Goes to Hospital. London: 1974. V. 49
The Three Cornered Halo. London: 1957. V. 50
Tour de Force. London: 1955. V. 54

BRAND, DONALD D.
So Live the Works of Men: Seventieth Anniversary Volume, Honoring Edgar Lee Hewett. Albuquerque: 1939. V. 47; 53

BRAND, JOHN
Bibliotheca Brandiana. London: 1807. V. 51; 53
Observations on Popular Antiquities... Newcastle-upon-Tyne: 1777. V. 49; 53
Observations on Popular Antiquities. London: 1813. V. 48; 50; 52; 54
On Illicit Love. Newcastle upon Tyne: 1775. V. 47

BRAND, MAX
Call of the Blood. New York: 1934. V. 53
Gunman's Gold. New York: 1939. V. 48
The Happy Valley. 1931. V. 50
Silvertip's Chase. New York: 1944. V. 48
Silvertip's Trap. New York: 1943. V. 51
Singing Guns. New York: 1938. V. 50
Streak. New York: 1937. V. 53
The Ten-Foot Chain: or, Can Love Survive the Shackles. New York: 1920. V. 50
Wine on the Desert. New York: 1940. V. 48; 53

BRANDAU, ROBERTA SEAWELL
History of Homes and Gardens of Tennessee. Nashville: 1936. V. 51
History of Homes and Gardens of Tennessee. Nashville: 1964. V. 47

BRANDBOIS, ALAIN
Selected Poems. Toronto: 1964. V. 47

BRANDE, WILLIAM THOMAS
A Manual of Chemistry... London: 1819. V. 50
A Manual of Chemistry... London: 1821. V. 50
Manual of Chemistry... New York: 1821. V. 48
A Manual of Chemistry... New York: 1829. V. 47
A Manual of Chemistry. London: 1830/30-27. V. 50
Outlines of Geology. London: 1829. V. 54

BRANDEIS, LOUIS D.
Other People's Money and How the Bankers Use It. New York: 1914. V. 52

BRANDES, RAY
Troopers West: Military and Indian Affairs on the American Frontier. San Diego: 1970. V. 51; 52

BRANDFORD, W. E.
Christmas Eve Tales by Six Poor Travellers. Newcastle-upon-Tyne: 1880. V. 50

BRANDIS, D.
Indian Trees. London: 1906. V. 47

BRANDLING JUNCTION RAILWAY
Brandling's Junction Railway, to Connected the Towns of Gateshead, South Shields, and Monk Wearmouth... London: 1835. V. 54

BRANDON, ISAAC
Fragments in the Manner of Sterne. London: 1798. V. 49; 54

BRANDON, RAPHAEL
An Analysis of Gothic Architecture. London: 1849. V. 53
An Analysis of Gothic Architecture. Edinburgh: 1903. V. 48

BRANDT, BILL
Camera in London. London & New York: 1948. V. 47; 50; 52; 53; 54
The English at Home. London: 1936. V. 47; 54
The English at Home. New York: 1936. V. 47; 52
Literary Britain. London: 1951. V. 47; 50
Perspective of Nudes. New York: 1961. V. 47; 48; 54
Shadow of Light. New York: 1966. V. 47; 49; 52

BRANDT, FRANCIS FREDERICK
Habet! A Short Treatise on the Law of the Land As it Affects Pugilism. London: 1857. V. 47; 50

BRANDT, HERBERT
Alaska Bird Trails: Adventures of an Expedition By Dog Sled to the Delta of the Yukon River at Hooper Bay. Cleveland: 1943. V. 48; 51; 54
Arizona and its Bird Life. Cleveland: 1951. V. 50; 52; 54

BRANDT, J. H.
Asian Hunter. 1989. V. 52; 54
Asian Hunter. Mesilla: 1991. V. 52

BRANGWYN, FRANK
A Book of Bridges. London: 1916. V. 48
Bookplates by... London: 1920. V. 50
The British Empire Panels Designed for the House of Lords. London: 1933. V. 52
British Royal Bookplates. London: 1992. V. 50

BRANN, WILLIAM COWPER
Brann, the Iconoclast. Waco: 1898-99. V. 51

BRANNER, ROBERT
Manuscript Painting in Paris During the Reign of Saint Louis. A Study of Styles. Berkeley: 1977. V. 52; 53

BRANNON, GEORGE
Brannon's Shilling Pocket Guide to the Isle of Wight. London: 1883. V. 53
Graphic Delineations of the Most Prominent Objects in the Isle of Wight, Serving Equally the Purposes of a Useful Accompaniment to Any of the Un-Illustrated Local Guides... Isle of Wight: 1857. V. 52
Vectis Scenery: Being, a Series of Original and Select Views, Exhibiting the Picturesque Beauties...(of) the Isle of Wight, Drawn from Nature and Engraved by George Brannon. Southampton: 1826. V. 54

BRANSOM, PAUL
An Argosy of Fables. New York: 1921. V. 49

BRANSON, LEVI
First Book in Composition, applying the Principles of Grammar to the Art of Composing... Raleigh: 1863. V. 47

BRANT, JOSEPH
Memoir of the Distinguished Mohawk Indian Chief, Sachem and Warrior, Capt. Joseph Brant. Brantford: 1872. V. 53

BRANT, SEBASTIAN
Navis Stultifera. Paris: 1506. V. 50

BRANTOME, PIERRE DE BOURDEILLE, SEIGNEUR DE
Famous Women. London: 1908. V. 51
The Lives of Gallant Ladies. Waltham St. Lawrence: 1924. V. 47; 49

BRAQUE, GEORGES
Cahier de Georges Braque, 1917-1947. New York/Paris: 1948. V. 47; 48; 50
Catalogue de l'Oeuvre de Georges Braques. Paris. V. 49
Georges Braque: His Graphic Work. New York: 1961. V. 50

BRASAVOLA, ANTONIO MUSA
In Octo Libros Aphorismorum Hippocratis & Galeni. Commentaria & Annotationes. Basel: 1541. V. 51; 52; 53

BRASCH, FREDERICK E.
Sir Isaac Newton, 1727-1927. Baltimore: 1928. V. 52; 54

BRASHER, REX
Birds and Trees of North America. New York: 1961. V. 50
Birds and Trees of North America. New York: 1961-62. V. 47; 48; 49

BRASS, ARNOLD
Atlas of Histology. London: 1897. V. 51; 53

BRASS, JOHN
The Art of Ready Reckoning; or Mental and Practical Arithmetic. Toronto: 1851. V. 52

BRASSAI
Camera in Paris. London/New York: 1949. V. 48; 50
Seville en Fete. Paris: 1954. V. 52

BRASSBRIDGE, JOSEPH
Fruits of Experience; or, memoir... London: 1824. V. 48

BRASSEY, ANNIE ALLNUTT, BARONESS
The Last Voyage to India and Australia in the "Sunbeam". London: 1889. V. 47; 48; 54
Sunshine and Storm in the East, or Cruises to Cyprus and Constantinople. London: 1880. V. 50
Sunshine and Storm in the East, or Cruises to Cyprus and Constantinople. London: 1881. V. 50
A Voyage in the "Sunbeam". London: 1879. V. 49; 53
A Voyage in the "Sunbeam"... Toronto: 1879. V. 53
A Voyage in the "Sunbeam". London: 1903. V. 49; 53

BRASSEY, T. A.
Brassey's Naval Annual. Portsmouth: 1890. V. 50

BRASSINGTON, W. SALT
Historical Buildings in the Bodleian Library, Oxford, with Reproductions of Twenty-Four of the Finest Bindings. London: 1891. V. 50; 53
A History of the Art of Bookbinding. London: 1894. V. 47; 48; 50; 53

BRATHWAITE, RICHARD
Barnabae Itinerarium, or Baranbee's Journal. London: 1638. V. 47; 48; 49
Barnabae Itinerarium, or Barnabee's Journal. London: 1818. V. 50
Barnabae Itinerarium, or Barnabee's Journal. London: 1876. V. 51
Drunken Barnaby's Four Journeys to the North Of England. London: 1716. V. 48
Drunken Barnaby's Four Journeys to the North of England. London: 1723. V. 47; 49; 51; 54
Drunken Barnaby's Four Journeys to the North of England. London: 1805.. V. 52; 53
Drunken Barnaby's Four Journeys to the North of England. London: 1822. V. 50; 52; 53
The English Gentleman... London: 1633. V. 47
A Strappado for the Divell. Epigrams and Satyres Eluding to the Time, with Divers Measurs of No Lesse Delight. (with) Loves Labyrinth: or the True-Lovers Knot. London: 1615. V. 50
A Survey of History; or, a Nursery for Gentry. London: 1638. V. 47

BRATT, JOHN
Trails of Yesterday. Lincoln: 1921. V. 53

BRAUN, HEINRICH
Local Anaesthesia, Its Scientific Basis and Practical Use. Philadelphia: 1914. V. 47

BRAUN, LILIAN JACKSON
The Cat Who Turned On and Off. New York: 1968. V. 53

BRAUN, LILLIAN JACKSON
The Cat Who Could Read Backwards. New York: 1966. V. 53

BRAUN, THOMAS
L'An. Poemes. Bruxelles: 1847. V. 49
L'An. Poemes... Bruxelles: 1897. V. 52

BRAUNE, WILHELM
Topographisch-Anatomischer Atlas, Nach Durschnitten an Gefrornen Cadavern. Leipzig: 1872. V. 48

BRAUNSTEIN, TERRY
A Tale from the Fire. Washington: 1994. V. 53

BRAUTIGAN, RICHARD
The Abortion: an Historical Romance,. New York: 1971. V. 53
A Confederate General from Big Sur. New York: 1964. V. 47; 49; 50; 51; 52; 53
A Confederate General from Big Sur. London: 1970. V. 49
Dreaming of Babylon. New York: 1977. V. 52; 53
The Hawkline Monster. New York: 1974. V. 48; 54
In Watermelon Sugar. San Francisco: 1968. V. 52
In Watermelon Sugar. London: 1970. V. 49
Knock On Wood (Part 2) from Trout Fishing in America. Lexington. V. 48
The Octopus Frontier. San Francisco: 1960. V. 51; 54
The Pill Versus the Springhill Mine Disaster. San Francisco: 1968. V. 52
Please Plant this Book. San Francisco: 1968. V. 50; 51
Revenge of the Lawn. New York: 1971. V. 50; 51; 53
Richard Brautigan's Trout Fishing in America, The Pill Versus the Springhill Mine Disaster and In Watermelon Sugar. New York: 1969. V. 49
So The Wind Won't Blow It All Away. New York: 1982. V. 49
The Tokyo-Montana Express. New York: 1979. V. 47; 49; 50; 51; 53; 54
The Tokyo-Montana Express. London: 1980. V. 49; 51; 54
Trout Fishing in America. London: 1970. V. 49
Would You Like to Saddle Up a Couple of Goldfish and Swim to Alaska?. Berkeley: 1995. V. 53

BRAVO, FRANCISCO
The Opera Medicinalia. Folkstone: 1970. V. 49

BRAWLEY, BENJAMIN
Negro Builders and Heroes. Chapel Hill: 1937. V. 54
Your Negro Neighbor. New York: 1918. V. 48

BRAY, ANNA ELIZA
Fitz of Fitz-Ford; a Legend of Devon. London: 1830. V. 50
Life of Thomas Stothard, R.A. London: 1841. V. 52
Life of Thomas Stothard, R.A. London: 1851. V. 47; 49; 52; 54
Traditions, Legends, Supersititions and Sketches of Devonshire on the Borders of the Tamar and the Tavy...in a Series of Letters to Robert Southey. London: 1838. V. 50
Trials of the Heart. London: 1839. V. 49; 50

BRAY, ANNE ELIZA
Fitz of Fitz-Ford; a Legend of Devon. London: 1830. V. 47

BRAY, CHARLES
The Philosophy of Necessity; or, Natural Law as Applicable to Moral, Mental and Social Science. London: 1863. V. 52

BRAY, CLAUDE ARTHUR
To Save Himself. London: 181. V. 54

BRAY, JOHN
Hull's Victory. Philadelphia: 1812-13. V. 52

BRAY, JOHN FRANCIS
Labour's Wrongs and Labour's Remedy; or, the Age of Might and the Age of Right. Leeds: 1839. V. 49

BRAY, N. E.
A Paladin of Arabia. The Biography of Brevet Lieut. Col. G. E. Leachman, C.I.E., D.S.O. London: 1936. V. 47

BRAY, ROBERT
An Introduction to the Old English History. London: 1684. V. 50
The Theory of Dreams: in Which an Inquiry Is Made Into the Poers and Faculties of the Human Mind... London: 1808. V. 51

BRAY, WILLIAM
Memoirs, Illustrative of the Life and Writings of John Evelyn, Esq. London: 1818. V. 49
Memoirs, Illustrative of the Life and Writings of John Evelyn, Esq... London: 1819. V. 47; 51
Sketch of a Tour into Derbyshire and Yorkshire... London: 1778. V. 49; 52
Sketch of a Tour into Derbyshire and Yorkshire. London: 1783. V. 49
True Excellency of God and His Testimonies, and Our Nationall-Lawes, against Titular Excellency. 1649. V. 50

BRAYBROOKE, NEVILLE
Four Poems for Christmas. 1986. V. 53
T. S. Eliot: a Symposium for His Seventieth Birthday. London: 1958. V. 50

BRAYBROOKE, PATRICK
Great Children in Literature. London: 1929. V. 51
Oscar Wilde - a Study. London: 1930. V. 51

BRAYBROOKE, RICHARD
The History of Audley End, to Which are Appended Notices of the Town and Parish of Saffron Walden in the County of Essex. London: 1836. V. 47

BRAYER, HERBERT O.
William Blackmore. Denver: 1949. V. 54

BRAYLEY, ARTHUR W.
Bakers and Baking in Massachusetts, Including the Flour, Baking Supply and Kindred Interests from 1620 to 1909. Boston: 1909. V. 50

BRAYLEY, EDWARD WEDLAKE
A Concise Account, Historical and Descriptive of Lambeth Palace. London: 1806. V. 50; 52
History of Survey. London: 1870. V. 50
The History of the Ancient Palace and Late Houses of Parliament at Westmisnter. London: 1836. V. 49
Lambeth Palace. London: 1806. V. 51
Londiniana; or, Reminiscences of the British Metropolis... London: 1829. V. 50
A Topographical History of Surrey. Dorking: 1841. V. 52
A Topographical History of Surrey... Dorking: 1841-48. V. 50; 52
A Topographical History of Surrey. London: 1841-48. V. 51
A Topographical History of Surrey. London: 1850. V. 48; 49; 53
A Topographical History of Surrey. London: 1860. V. 52
Views in Suffolk, Norfolk and Northamptonshire... London: 1806. V. 54

BRAYSHAW, THOMAS
Giggleswick Church As It Was and As It Is. Settle: 1898. V. 53
Guide to Settle. Cheltenham: 1910. V. 47
A History of the Ancient Parish of Giggleswick. London: 1932. V. 47; 53
Hurtley's Poems on the Natural Curiosities of Malham, in Craven, Yorkshire. Settle: 1917. V. 53
Notes on Giggleswick Church. Settle: 1905. V. 53

BRAYTON, ALICE
George Berkeley in Newport. Newport: 1954. V. 52

BRAYTON, MATTHEW
The Indian Captive. Cleveland: 1860. V. 47
The Indian Captive. Fostoria: 1896. V. 54

BRAZEAL, BRAILSFORD R.
The Brotherhood of Sleeping Car Porters. New York: 1946. V. 52

BRAZIL, ANGELA
A Terrible Tomboy. London: 1904. V. 51

BREACKENBURY, JOSEPH
Natale Solum, and Other Pieces. London: 1810. V. 47

BREAD and Puppet: St. Francis Preaches to the Birds. 1978. V. 52

BREAD and Puppet: the Dream of the Dirty Woman. 1980. V. 52

BREADALBANE, MARCHIONESS OF
The High Tops of Black Mount. London: 1907. V. 52; 54

BREADE, WINWOOD
The African Sketch Book. London: 1873. V. 47

BREAKENRIDGE, WILLIAM M.
Helldorado. Bringing the Law to the Mesquite. Boston and New York: 1928. V. 50; 52; 53

BREAKING Ice. New York: 1990. V. 47

BREASTED, JAMES HENRY
Egyptian Servant Statues. Washington: 1948. V. 49; 51
Oriental Forerunners of Byzantine Painting. Chicago: 1924. V. 49; 51

BREAZEALE, J. W. M.
Life As it Is. Knoxville: 1842. V. 53

BREBEUF, JEAN DE
The Travels and Sufferings of Father Jean Brebeuf among the Hurons of Canada as Described by Himself. Waltham St. Lawrence: 1938. V. 47; 49; 50; 51; 53

BRECHT, BERTOLT
A Penny for the Poor. London: 1937. V. 51
A Penny for the Poor. New York: 1938. V. 47
The Private Life of the Master Race. New York: 1944. V. 49; 50; 53
The Seven Deadly Sins of the Lower Middle Class. New York: 1992. V. 50
The Threepenny Opera. New York: 1982. V. 48; 50; 54

BRECKINRIDGE, MARGARET E.
Memorial of Margaret E. Beckinridge. Philadelphia: 1865. V. 48

BRECKINRIDGE, SOPHONISBA P.
The Child in the City. A Series of Papers Presented at the Conferences Held During the Chicago Child Welfare Exhibit. Chicago: 1912. V. 48

BREDON, JULIET
Peking a Historical and Intimate Description of Its Chief Places of Interest... Shanghai: 1922. V. 50

BREE, C. R.
A History of the Birds of Europe Not Observed in the British Isles. London: 1875-76. V. 52; 54

BREE, JOHN
The Cursory Sketch of the State of the naval, Miltiary and Civil Establishment, Legislative, Judicail and Domestic Oeconomy of this Kingdom... London: 1791. V. 47; 50; 51; 53; 54

BREEDEN, S.
A Natural History of Australia. Sydney: 1970-73. V. 49; 53

BREEN, HUGH
A Treatise on the Summation of Series. Belfast: 1827. V. 52

BREEN, PATRICK
The Diary of Patrick Breen. San Francisco: 1946. V. 53

BREENWOOD, JAMES
The Hatchet Throwers. London: 1866. V. 48

BREES, S. C.
A Glossary of Civil Engineering, Comprising Its Theory and Modern Practice. London: 1841. V. 52
The Illustrated Glossary of Practical Architecture and Civil Engineering... London: 1852. V. 49
Railway Practice. London: 1837. V. 49
Second Series of Railway Practice... London: 1840. V. 49

BREESE, LOUIS V.
Some Unwritten Laws of Organized Foxhunting and Comments on the Usage of the Sport of Riding to Hounds in America. N.P: 1909. V. 47

BREESKIN, ADELYN DOHME
Mary Cassatt: a Catalogue Raisonne of the Graphic Work. Washington: 1979. V. 51
Mary Cassatt, a Catalogue Raisonne of the Oils, Pastels, Watercolors and Drawings. Washington: 1970. V. 47
Scholder Indians. Flagstaff: 1972. V. 48

BREEZE, RYDER E. N.
Lays of Scottish Highlands. London: 1893. V. 47

BREHME, HUGO
Picturesque Mexico: The Country, the People and the Architecture. Berlin: 1925. V. 50

BREMER, FREDERIKA
Father and Daughter. Philadelphia: 1859?. V. 50
The Home... London: 1843. V. 50; 51
The Homes of the New World... London: 1853. V. 51; 54
The Homes of the New World... New York: 1853. V. 50; 51; 53
The Neighbours... London: 1842. V. 50
The Neighbours... London: 1843. V. 50; 51

Strife and Peace, or Scenes in Norway. (with) *The Bondmaid.* London: 1844. V. 54

BREMNER, ARCHIE
City of London Ontario, Canada. The Pioneer Period and the London of To-day. London: 1900. V. 48

BRENAN, GERALD
Doctor Partridge's Almanack for 1935. London: 1934. V. 48
The Face of Spain. London: 1950. V. 50
St. John of the Cross _ His Life and Poetry. Cambridge: 1973. V. 50
South from Granada. London: 1957. V. 51
The Spanish Labyrinth - an Account of the Social and Political Background of the Civil War. 1943. V. 53
The Spanish Labyrinth. An Account of the Social and Political Background of the Civil War. Cambridge: 1943. V. 49
Spanish Scene. 1946. V. 49

BRENCHLEY, JULIUS L.
Jottings During the Cruise of H. M. S. Curacoae Among the South Sea Islands in 1865. London: 1873. V. 49

BRENNAN, JOSEPH PAYNE
The Borders Just Beyond. 1986. V. 48
Scream at Midnight. 1963. V. 48; 52

BRENNER, ANITA
Idols Behind Altars. New York: 1929. V. 53

BRENT, JOHN
The Battle Cross: a Romance of the Fourteenth Century. London: 1845. V. 50

BRENT, JOSEPH LANCASTER
Memoirs Of the War Between the States. New Orleans: 1940. V. 54

BRENTON, EDWARD PELHAM
The Naval History of Great Britain, from the Year 1783 to 1836. London: 1837. V. 47
The Naval History of Great Britain, from the Year MDCCLXXXIII to MDCCCXXII. London: 1823-25. V. 53

BRENTON, HOWARD
Weapons of Happiness. London: 1976. V. 50

BRENTZ, JOHANN
Zwo Und Zwaintzig Predig Den Turckischen Krieg (bound with unidentified work). Nuremberg: 1532. V. 47

BRERA, VALERIAN LEWIS
A Treatise on Verminous Diseases, Preceded by the Natural History of Intestinal Worms and Their Origin in the Human Body. Boston: 1817. V. 51

BRERETON, AUSTIN
The Lyceum and Henry Iriving. London: 1903. V. 50; 52

BRERETON, F. S.
The Great Aeroplane. 1911. V. 48; 52

BRERETON, JOHN
A Briefe And True Relation of the Discoverie of The North Part of Virginia. New York: 1903. V. 53

BRERETON, MRS.
Woman's Influence. London: 1845. V. 49

BRERETON, ROBERT MAITLAND
Reminiscences of an Old English Civil Engineer 1858-1908. Portland: 1908. V. 49

BRERWOOD, EDWARD
Enquiries Touching the Diversity of Languages, and Religion, through the Chiefe Parts of the World. London: 1622. V. 49; 53

BRES, JEAN PIERRE
Simples Histoires, Trouvees Dans un Pot au Lait. Paris: 1825. V. 51

BRESADOLA, J.
Iconographia Mycologica. Milan and Trento: 1927-40. V. 48; 50; 51

BRESDIN
Bresdin to Redon: Six Letters, 1870-1881. Northampton: 1969. V. 49

BRESLAUER, BERNARD H.
Bibliography, Its History and Development. New York: 1984. V. 50; 52; 53; 54

BRESLAUER, MARTIN
Fine Books in Fine Bindings: Catalogue 104, Part II. New York: 1985. V. 50

BRESSEY, L. MARNEZIA, MARQUISE DE
Letters from Julia, the Daughter of Augustus, to Ovid. London: 1753. V. 47

BRESSON, HENRI CARTIER
The Decisive Moment. New York: 1952. V. 48
The Europeans. 1955. V. 51; 52

BRET, ANTOINE
Ninon de Lenclos. London: 1904. V. 51; 53

BRETON, ANDRE
Andre Masson. Paris: 1940. V. 48
Arcane 17, Together with: Ajours. Paris: 1947. V. 47
The Automatic Message. V. 48
Humour Noir. Paris: 1950. V. 50
The Magnetic Fields. London: 1985. V. 47

BRETON, ANDRE continued
Manifeste du Surrealisme. Paris: 1924. V. 54
Nadja. Paris: 1928. V. 50; 54
Pleine Marge. New York: 1940. V. 47
Young Cherry Trees Secured Against Hares. New York: 1946. V. 50
Yves Tanguy. New York: 1946. V. 50

A BRETON Maiden. London: 1888. V. 54

BRETON, NICHOLAS
A Mad World My Masters and Other Prose Works. London: 1929. V. 48; 49
No Whipping, Nor tripping; But a Kinde Friendly Snippping. London. V. 49; 54
The Twelve Months. London: 1927. V. 48
The Twelve Months. Waltham St. Lawrence: 1927. V. 51

BRETON DE LA MARTINIERE, JEAN BAPTISTE JOSEPH
China: its Costume, Arts, Manufactures &c... London: 1813. V. 48
La Chine en Miniature, ou Choix de Costumes, Arts et Metiers de cet Empire Representes par 74 Gravures...a l'Usage de la Jeunesse. Paris: 1811. V. 52

BRETSCHNEIDER, E.
Mediaeval Researches from Eastern Asiatic Records. London: 1887. V. 49

BRETT, EDWIN J.
A Pictorial and Descriptive Record of the Origin and Development of Arms and Armour. London: 1894. V. 54

BRETT, JOHN WATKINS
The Illustrated Sales Catalogue of the Valuable Collection of Pictures and Other Works of Art of the Egyptian, Greek, Roman and Mediaeval Periods... London: 1864. V. 47

BRETT, THOMAS
An Account of Church-Government and Governours. London: 1701. V. 52; 54

BRETT, WILLIAM HENRY
The Indian Tribes of Guiana. New York: 1853. V. 48; 50
Legends and Myths of the Aboriginal Indians of British Guiana. London. V. 48
Legends and Myths of the Aboriginal Indians of British Guiana. London: 1880. V. 50; 51

BRETTELL, RICHARD
Catalogue of Drawings by Camille Pisarro in the Ashmolean Museum. Oxford: 1980. V. 50; 54

BREUER, JOSEPH
Studien Uber Hysterie. Leipzig: 1922. V. 53; 54

BREUER, LEE
The Warrior Ant. New York: 1992. V. 51

BREUIL, HENRI
Rock Paintings of Southern Andulasia. 1929. V. 49
Rock Paintings of Southern Andulasia. Oxford: 1929. V. 54

BREVAL, JOHN DURANT
The History of the Most Illustrious House of Nassau, continued from the Tenth Century...to this Present Time. London: 1734. V. 52
Remarks on Several Parts of Europe, Relating Chiefly to Their Antiquities and History. London: 1738. V. 51; 54

BREVINT, DANIEL
Missale Romanum, or the Depth and Mystery of (the) Roman Mass. 1672. V. 50
Missale Romanum, or the Depth and Mystery of (the) Roman Mass. Oxford: 1672. V. 48

BREVOORT, HENRY
The Letters of Henry Brevoort to Washington Irving. Garden City: 1916. V. 52

BREWER, D. S.
The Thornton Manuscript (Lincoln Cathedral MS. 91). London: 1978. V. 50

BREWER, FRANCES J.
The Fables of Jean de La Fontaine. Los Angeles: 1964. V. 50; 52

BREWER, GEORGE
The Juvenile Lavater; or a Familiary Explanation of the Passions of Le brun... London: 1812. V. 48; 49
The Juvenile Lavater or,...The Passions of Le Brun...Interspersed with Moral and Amusing Tales... London: 1813. V. 50

BREWER, J.
Flora of Surrey...From the MSS. of the Late J.D. Salmon and From Other Sources... London: 1863. V. 49

BREWER, J. MASON
Negro Legislators of Texas and Their Descendants... Dallas: 1935. V. 47
Negro Legislators of Texas and Their Descendants... Austin: 1970. V. 47

BREWER, J. S.
The Reign of Henry VIII from His Accession to the Death of Wolsey. London: 1884. V. 52

BREWER, JAMES NORRIS
A Descriptive and Historical Account of Various Palaces and Public Buildings (English and Foreign)... London: 1821. V. 53
Historionic Topography; or, the Birth-Places, Residences and Funeral Monuments of the Most Distinguished Actors. London: 1818. V. 50; 54

BREWER, JOSIAH
A Residence at Constantinople, in the Year 1827. New Haven: 1830. V. 49; 51

BREWER, LUTHER A.
My Leigh Hunt Library. Cedar Rapids: 1932. V. 48; 50

BREWER, S. S.
The Jubilee Harp. Concord: 1855. V. 52

BREWER, THOMAS M.
North American Oology. Part 1. Raptores and Fissirosters. Cambridge: 1856. V. 51
North American Oology. Part 1, Raptores and Fissirosters. Washington: 1857. V. 51

BREWER, WILLIAM HENRY
Such a Landscape!. Yosemite: 1987. V. 47
Up and Down California in 1860-1864. New Haven: 1930. V. 54

BREWER, WILLIS
Alabama: Her History, Resources, War Record and Public Men. From 1540 to 1872. Montgomery: 1872. V. 50

BREWERTON, G. DOUGLAS
The Automaton Regiment, or Infantry Soldiers Practical Instructor, for All Regimental Movements in the Field. New York: 1862. V. 52; 53

BREWINGTON, MARION VERNON
Kendall Whaling Museum Paintings (&) Kendall Whaling Museum Prints. Sharon: 1965/69. V. 51

BREWSTER, A.
The Hill Tribes of Fiji. London: 1922. V. 54

BREWSTER, DAVID
Letters on Natural Magic Addressed to Sir Walter Scott. London: 1832. V. 47; 48
Letters on Natural Magic Addressed to Sir Walter Scott... New York: 1832. V. 49; 53
Letters on Natural Magic Addressed to Sir Walter Scott. New York: 1839. V. 48
Letters on Natural Magic Addressed to Sir Walter Scott. London: 1842. V. 54
The Life of Sir Isaac Newton. London: 1831. V. 50; 51; 54
Plates Illustrative of Ferguson's Astronomy; and of the Twelve Supplementary Chapters. London: 1811. V. 54
A Treatise on Magnetism. Edinburgh: 1837. V. 53
A Treatise on the Microscope, Forming the Article Under that Head in the Seventh Edition of the Encyclopaedia Britannica. Edinburgh: 1837. V. 54

BREWSTER, JOHN
Meditations of a Recluse, Chiefly on Religious Subjects. London: 1800. V. 50
The Parochial History and Antiquities of Stockton Upon Tees: an Account of the Trade of the Town... Stockton: 1796. V. 47; 52

BREYDENBACH, BERNHARD VON
Peregrinatio in Terram Sanctam. Mainz: 1486. V. 54

BREYMEYER, A. I.
Grasslands, Systems Analysis and Man. Cambridge: 1980. V. 52; 53

BREYTENBACH, BREYTEN
Sinking Ship Blues. Toronto: 1977. V. 51; 54

BRICHARD, P.
Book of Cichlids and All the Other Fishes of lake Tanganyika. London: 1989. V. 48

BRICKDALE, ELEANOR FORTESCUE
Eleanor Fortescue Brickdale's Golden Book of Famous Women. London: 1920. V. 53
Golden Book of Famous Women. London: 1919. V. 48
Golden Book of Songs and Ballads. London: 1915. V. 49; 51

BRICKELL, JOHN
The Natural History of North Carolina. Dublin: 1737. V. 48
The Natural History of North Carolina... Raleigh: 1911. V. 48

BRICKER, CHARLES
Landmarks of Mapmaking. New York: 1976. V. 50; 51

BRICKERHOFF, SIDNEY B.
Lancers for the King, a Study of the Frontier Military System of Northern New Spain... Phoenix: 1965. V. 53

BRICKWORK in Italy: a Brief Review from Ancient to Modern Times. Chicago: 1925. V. 47

BRICUSSE, LESLIE
Christmas 1993. London: 1987. V. 47

THE BRIDAL Souvenir. London: 1857. V. 52

THE BRIDE'S Confession... Paris. V. 47

BRIDGE, HORATIO
Journal of an African Cruiser. New York: 1845. V. 47; 53

BRIDGE, JAMES HOWARD
The History of the Carngie Steel Company. New York: 1903. V. 47

BRIDGEABOUT, TIMOTHY, PSEUD.
Rinology; or, a Description of the Nose and Particularly, of that Part of It, Call'd the Bridge. London: 1736. V. 53

BRIDGEMAN, CHARLES
Stowe Gardens in Buckinghamshire, Belonging to the Right Honourable, the Lord Viscount Cobham... London: 1987. V. 54

BRIDGEMAN, G. T. O.
Some Account of the Parish of Church Eaton, In the County of Stafford. London: 1884. V. 50

BRIDGEMAN, WILLIAM
Translations from the Greek, viz. The Golden Sentences of Demophilus and the Pythagoric Symbols... London: 1804. V. 50

BRIDGENS, RICHARD
Sefton Church. London: 1822. V. 47

BRIDGES, C. A.
Catalogue of Hesperiidae (Lepidoptera: Rhopalocera). Urbana: 1988. V. 50; 51

BRIDGES, GEORGE WILSON
Alpine Sketches, Comprising a Short Tour through Parts of Holland, Flanders, France, Savoy, Switzerland and Germany, During the Summer of 1814. London: 1814. V. 48

BRIDGES, JAMES
View of the Political State of Scotland, at Michaelmas, 1811... Edinburgh: 1812. V. 52; 54

BRIDGES, JOHN
Catalogus Librorum Johannis Bridges, Armigeri; Nuper ex Hospitio Lincolniensi. London: 1725. V. 47

The Supremacie of Christian Princes, Over All Persons Throughout Their Dominions, In All Causes So Wel Ecclesiastaical as Temporall, Both Against the Counterblast of Thomas Stapleton... London: 1573. V. 52

BRIDGES, JOHN HENRY
The Unity of Comte's Life and Doctrine. London: 1866. V. 52

BRIDGES on the Backs. A Series of Drawings by David Gentleman. Cambridge: 1961. V. 53

BRIDGES, ROBERT SEYMOUR
Carmen Elegiacum Roberti Bridges de Nosocomio Sti Bartolomaei Londinensi in Quo Narratur Historia Fundationis Nosocomii... London: 1877. V. 47

Eight Plays. London: 1885-94. V. 51
Eros and Psyche. Newtown: 1935. V. 48; 50; 51; 52; 54
The Growth of Love. Oxford: 1890. V. 53
The Growth of Love. Portland: 1894. V. 51
Hymns. Oxford: 1899. V. 53
The Message of One of England's Greatest Poets to a Printer. London: 1931. V. 48
New Verse... London: 1925. V. 52
New Verse. Oxford: 1925. V. 47; 50; 51
Now In Wintry Delights. Oxford: 1903. V. 48
October and Other Poems. London: 1920. V. 53; 54
Overheard in Arcady. New York: 1894. V. 48; 50
Peace. 1903. V. 52
Poems. London: 1873. V. 49; 50
Poems. London: 1879. V. 53
Poems. Oxford: 1884. V. 53
Poems Written in the Year MCMXIIII. 1914. V. 47; 51
Poems Written in the Year MDMXIII. London: 1914. V. 51
A Practical Discourse on Some Principles of Hymn-Singing. Oxford: 1901. V. 53
Prometheus the Firegiver. Oxford: 1883. V. 47
Purcell Ode and Other Poems. Chicago: 1896. V. 47; 49
Shorter Poems of Robert Bridges. Oxford: 1893-94. V. 47
The Tapestry. Poems. London: 1925. V. 47; 50
The Testament of Beauty. London: 1929. V. 48
The Testament of Beauty. New York: 1929. V. 51
The Testament of Beauty... Oxford: 1929. V. 52; 54

BRIDGES, ROY
From Silver to Steel. Melbourne: 1920. V. 54

BRIDGES, THOMAS
A Burlesque Translation of Homer. London: 1797. V. 48; 54

BRIDGES, WILLIAM
The Hand-Book for Life Assurers. London: 1842. V. 48

BRIDGET, SAINT
Revelationes...Olim a card. Romae: 1628. V. 51

BRIDGMAN, CLARE
The Bairn's Coronation Book. London: 1902. V. 54
A Book of Days for Little Ones. London: 1901. V. 54

BRIDGMAN, L. J.
Mother Wild Goose and Her Wild Beast Show. Boston: 1900. V. 49

BRIDGMAN, ORLANDO
Conveyances: Being Select Precedents (re) Estates in England. London: 1682. V. 47

BRIDGMAN, RICHARD WHALLEY
An Analytical Digested Index of the Reported Cases in the Several Courts of Equity, and the High Court of Parliament (in Both England and Ireland), from the Earliest Authentic Period to the Present Time. London: 1813. V. 52
A Short View of Legal Bibliography... London: 1807. V. 50

BRIDLE, WILLIAM
A Narrative of the Rise and Progress of the Improvements Effected in His Majety's Goal at Ilchester, in the County of Somerset, Between July 1808, and November 1821... Bath: 1822. V. 50

BRIDOUL, TOUSSAINT
The School of the Eucharist Established Upon the Micraculous Respects and Acknoledgments, Which Beasts, Birds and Insects...Have Rendered to the Holy Sacrament of the Altar... London: 1687. V. 50

BRIDSON, D. G.
The Quest of Gilgamesh. London: 1972. V. 53

BRIDSON, G. D. R.
Plant, Animal and Anatomical Illustrataion in Art and Science... Winchester: 1990. V. 51; 52; 53

A BRIEF Account of the Associated Presbyteries; and a General View of Their Sentiments Concerning Religion and Ecclesiastical order. Catskill: 1796. V. 49

A BRIEF Account of the Lodiana Mission, From Its Commencement in November 1834, to the Beginning of November, 1844. Allahabad: 1845. V. 49

A BRIEF Account of the Proceedings of the Committee, Appointed by the Yearly Meeting of Friends, Held in Baltimore, For Promoting the Improvement and Civilization of the Indian Natives. London: 1806. V. 48

A BRIEF Account of the Rise, Progress and Present State of the Theological Seminary of the Presbyterian Church in the United States at Princeton. Philadelphia;: 1822. V. 53

A BRIEF Account of the Tagore Family. Calcutta: 1868. V. 52

BRIEF Astronomy Translated From the English Original (in Armenian). Smyrna: 1841. V. 49

A BRIEF Collection Out of the Records of the City, Touching Elections of the Sheriffs of London and the County of Middlesex. London: 1682. V. 52

BRIEF Deductions Relative to the Aid and Supply of the Executive Power, According to the Law of England. In Cases of Infancy, Delirium, or Other Incapacity of the King. London: 1788. V. 52

A BRIEF Description of England and Wales. London: 1798. V. 47

A BRIEF Description of Places of Interest in the County of York, Within Twenty-Six Miles of the City. York: 1843. V. 51

A BRIEF Description of the Future History of Europe, from 1650 to An. 1710. London: 1650. V. 54

A BRIEF Discourse Betwen (sic) A Sober Tory and a Moderate Whigg. London: 1682. V. 47

A BRIEF Enquiry, Whether It Be Reasonable to Oblige Dissenters to Serve the Office of Sheriff of the City of London; or, On Their Refusal, Pay the Fine, Usually Impos'd on Those Who Refuse to Serve That Office. London: 1738. V. 48

BRIEF Extracts from High Authorities Exposing the Evils of Vaccination: Great Medical Delusion of the 19th Century: Now Inciting Popular Imagination. Providence: 1891. V. 51; 52; 53

BRIEF Historical Account of the Romance of British Columbia. 1934. V. 54

A BRIEF History of the Life of Mary Queen of Scots. London: 1681. V. 53

BRIEF Remarks on the Proposed Regent's Canal. By an Observer. March 1812. London: 1812. V. 51

BRIEF View of the Baptist Missions and Translations; with specimens of Various Languages in which the Scriptures are Printing at the Mission Press, Serampore. London: 1815. V. 49

BRIEGER, PETER
Illuminated Manuscripts of the Divine Comedy. London: 1969. V. 48
Illuminated Manuscripts of the Divine Comedy. Princeton: 1969. V. 53

BRIER CREEK ASSOCIATION
Minutes of the Fortieth Annual Session of the Brier Creek Association Convened at Cook spring Meeting House Wilkes County, N.C. Saturday Before the 4th Lord's Day in September 1861. Salem: 1861. V. 49

Minutes of the Forty-Third Annual Session of the Brier Creek Association, Convened at Grassy Knob Meeting House, Iredell County, N.C...in Sept., 1864. 1864. V. 49

BRIERLEY, BEN
Ab-oth-Yate Sketches and Other Short Stories. Oldham: 1896. V. 53; 54

BRIERLEY, HENRY
The Registers of Brough Under Stainmore. Part 1 1556-1706. Kendal: 1923. V. 51

The Registers of Caton, Claughton, Gressingham, Hornby and Tatham. Preston: 1922. V. 48

The Registers of St. Michael's Pennington in Furness 1612-1702; The Registers of Urswick in Furness 1608-1695. Cambridge: 1907. V. 50

The Registers of the Parish Church of Skelton, Cumberland 1580-1812. Kendal: 1918. V. 52

The Registers of the Parish Church of Torver 1599-1792; the Registers of the Parish Church of Kirkby Ireleth 1681-182. Rochdale: 1911. V. 50

BRIERRE DE BOISMONT, ALEXANDRE
Hallucinations; or, the Rational History of Apparitions, Visions, Dreams, Ecstasy, Magnetism and Somnambulism. Philadelphia: 1853. V. 51

On Hallucinations: a History and Explanation of Apparitions, Visions, Dreams, Ecstacy, Magnetism and Sonambulism. London: 1859. V. 51; 53

BRIEUX, EUGENE
Three Plays by Brieux. London: 1911. V. 54

BRIFFAULT, ROBERT
The Mothers. New York: 1927. V. 50; 51; 53

BRIGANTI, GIULIANO
Italian Mannerism. London: 1962. V. 53
The View Painters of Europe. London: 1970. V. 50; 54

BRIGGS & CO.
Patent Transferring Papers. New York. V. 50
Patent Transferring Papers. Manchester: 1882/83. V. 51

BRIGGS, CHARLES F.
Homes of American Authors. New York: 1853. V. 50

BRIGGS, GRACE M.
The Honnold Library. The William W. Clarey Oxford Collection. A Descriptive Catalogue. Oxford: 1956. V. 52
The William W. Clary Oxford Collection. A Descriptive Catalogue. 1956-65. V. 52
The William W. Clary Oxford Collection. A Descriptive Catalogue. Claremont: 1956-65. V. 49

BRIGGS, HAROLD E.
Frontiers of the Northwest. New York: 1940. V. 52

BRIGGS, HENRY
Trigonometria Britannica: sive De Doctrina Triangvlorvm Libri Dvo (etc.). Gouda: 1633. V. 51; 53

BRIGGS, HENRY GEORGE
The Parsis; or, Modern Zerdusthians. Bombay: 1852. V. 47

BRIGGS, HORACE
Letters from Alaska and the Pacific Coast. Buffalo: 1889. V. 48; 50

BRIGGS, HOWARD R.
Westward America. New York: 1942. V. 47

BRIGGS, J. P.
Heathen and Holy Lands: or, Sunny Days on the Salween, Nile and Jordan. London: 1859. V. 49

BRIGGS, JOHN
The Lonsdale Magazine, or Provincial Repository... Kendal: 1820. V. 52
The Lonsdale Magazine, or Provincial Repository... Kendal: 1820-22. V. 52; 54
The Lonsdale Magazine, or Provincial Repository... Kendal: 1822. V. 52
Poems on Several Subjects. Ulverston: 1818. V. 54
The Remains of John Briggs... Kirkby Lonsdale: 1825. V. 50; 52

BRIGGS, LLOYD VERNON
Arizona and New Mexico 1882, California 1886, Mexico 1891. Boston: 1932. V. 52; 54
Experiences of a Medical Student in Honolulu, and On the Island of Oahu, 1881. Boston: 1926. V. 54
The Manner of Man That Kills: Spencer - Czolgosz - Richeson. Boston: 1921. V. 48; 52

BRIGGS, MARTIN SHAW
Muhammadan Architecture in Egypt and Palestine. Oxford: 1924. V. 52

BRIGGS, RAYMOND
Father Christmas. London: 1973. V. 49
Ring-a-Ring o' Roses - A Picture Book of Nursery Rhymes. London: 1962. V. 50
The Snowman. London: 1978. V. 50
When the Wind Blows. London: 1982. V. 50

BRIGGS, RICHARD
The New Art of Cookery, According to the Present Practice... Philadelphia: 1792. V. 50
The New Art of Cookery, According to the Present Practice... Boston: 1798. V. 49

BRIGGS, SOPHIA
The Gitana: a Tale. London: 1845. V. 50

BRIGGS, WALTER
Without Noise of Arms. Flagstaff: 1976. V. 51; 54

BRIGHAM, AMARIAH
An Inquiry Concerning the Diseases and Functions of the Brain, the Spinal Cord and the Nerves. New York: 1840. V. 49; 50
Mental Exertion in Relation to Health. London: 1864. V. 53; 54
Remarks ont he Influence of Mental Cultivation and Mental Excitment Upon Health. Glasgow: 1836. V. 52; 53
A Treatise on Epidemic Cholera: Including an Historical Account of Its Origin and Progress to the Present Period. Hartford: 1832. V. 49

BRIGHAM, CLARENCE S.
History and Bibliography of American Newspapers, 1690-1820. Worcester: 1947. V. 48
Paul Revere's Engravings. Worcester: 1954. V. 49

BRIGHAM, T. W.
Ka Hana Kapa, the Making of Bark-Cloth in Hawaii. Honolulu: 1911. V. 53

BRIGHAM, WILLIAM
The Compact, with the Charter and Laws of the Colony of New Plymouth. Boston: 1836. V. 48

BRIGHAM, WILLIAM T.
Guatemala. The Land of the Quetzal. New York: 1887. V. 48
Handbook for Visitors to the Bernice Pauahi Bishop Museum of Polynesian Ethnology and Natural History. V. 50
Ka Hana Kapa: The Making of Bark Cloth in Hawaii. Honolulu: 1911. V. 49

BRIGHT, HENRY
The Praxis; or, a Course of English and Latin Exercises. Oxford: 1783. V. 47

BRIGHT, JOHN
Public Addresses... London: 1879. V. 52

BRIGHT, P. M.
A Monograph of the British Aberrations of the Chalk-Hill Blue Butterfly Lysandra Coridon. Bournemouth: 1938. V. 49; 52

BRIGHT, RICHARD
Clinical Memoirs on Abdominal Tumours and Intumescence. London: 1860. V. 48; 53
Travels from Vienna through Lower Hunbary... Edinburgh: 1818. V. 47

BRIGHT, TIMOTHY
A Treatise of Melancholy. London: 1613. V. 53

BRIGHTMAN, L. J.
Farmer Fox and Other Rhymes. Boston: 1900. V. 47

BRIGHTON; or, The Steyne. London: 1818. V. 54

BRIGHTWELL, CECILIA LUCY
Memorials of the Life of Amelia Opie. Norwich: 1854. V. 48

BRIGODE, EMILIE DE PELLAPRA, COMTESSE
Daughter of Napoleon: Memoirs of Emilie de Pellapra, Comtesse de Brigode, Princess de Chimay. New York: 1922. V. 50

BRILL, ABRAHAM
Psychoanalysis. Its Theory and Practical Application. Philadelphia: 1912. V. 53

BRILL, CHARLES J.
Conquest of the Southern Plains: Uncensored Narrative of the Battle of the Washita and Custer's Southern Campaign. Oklahoma City: 1938. V. 47

BRILLANT, RICHARD
The Arch of Septimius Severus in the Roman Forum. Roma: 1967. V. 50; 52
Gesture and Rank in Roman Art. New Haven: 1963. V. 50; 52

BRILLAT-SAVARIN, JEAN ANTHELME
The Handbook of Dining; or, Corpulency and Leanness Scientifically Considered. New York: 1865. V. 54
The Handbook of Dining, or, How to Dine. London: 1859. V. 50; 52
Physiologie Du Gout, a Handbook of Gastronomy. New York: 1884. V. 49; 52
The Physiology of Taste... London: 1925. V. 51; 52
The Physiology of Taste... New York: 1926. V. 47; 48
The Physiology of Taste. New York: 1949. V. 53
The Physiology of Taste. San Francisco: 1994. V. 51

BRILLIANT, ALAN
Unicorn Folio Series Three Number One: a Canadian Folio. 1969. V. 54

BRIM, CHARLES
Medicine in the Bible, the Pentateuch Torah. New York: 1936. V. 52

BRIMLOW, GEORGE FRANCIS
The Bannock Indian War of 1878. Caldwell: 1938. V. 53; 54

BRIMMER, MARTIN
Egypt: Three Essays on the History, Religion and Art of Ancient Egypt. Cambridge: 1892. V. 49; 51

BRIN, DAVID
Earth. 1960. V. 54
Earth. 1990. V. 49
Startide Rising. 1985. V. 48; 49; 52; 54
The Tides of Kithrup. London: 1983. V. 51
The Tides of Kithrup. New York: 1983. V. 51
The Uplift War. 1987. V. 47; 51; 52

BRINCKERHOFF, SIDNEY B.
Lancers for the King. A Study of the Frontier Military System in Northern New Spain... Phoenix: 1965. V. 48; 49; 50; 51; 53

BRINDESI, JEAN
Elbicei Atika Muse des Anciens Costumes Turcs de Constaninople. Paris: 1855. V. 51

BRINDLEY, JAMES
Queries Proposed by the Committee of the Common-Council of the City of London, About the Intended Canal from Monkey Island to Isleworth, Answered. London: 1770. V. 54

BRINDLEY, JOHN
Public Discussion on Socialism, Held at the New Theatre, Leicester, on the Evenings of Tuesday and Wednesday, April 14th and 15th, 1840, Between Mr. Brindley and Mr. Hollick, Socialist Missionary. Leicester: 1840. V. 50

BRINE, MARY DOW
Grandma's Attic. New York: 1893. V. 48; 52
Somebody's Mother. Baltimore. V. 50

BRININSTOOL, E. A.
Crazy Horse. Los Angeles: 1949. V. 47; 53; 54
The Custer Fight. Hollywood: 1933. V. 53
Dull Knife. Hollywood: 1935. V. 49; 50
A Trooper With Custer and Other Historic Incidents of the Battle of Little Big Horn. Columbus: 1925. V. 54

BRINKERHOFF, DERICKSEN M.
A Collection of Sculpture in Classical and Early Christian Antioch. 1970. V. 53

BRINKERHOFF, HENRY R.
Ivah-Nee-Ta, a Tale of the Navajo. Washington: 1886. V. 53

BRINKLEY, FRANK
Japan Described and Illustrated by the Japanese. Boston;: 1897. V. 53
Japan Its History, Arts and Literature. and China Its History, Arts and Literature. Boston and Tokyo: 1901/02. V. 54
Oriental Series: Japan... Boston and Tokyo: 1901-02. V. 52
Oriental Series: Japan... Boston: 1901-12. V. 49

BRINLEY, FRANCIS
Life of William T. Porter. New York: 1860. V. 47

BRINLEY, GEORGE
Catalogue of the American Library of the late Mr. George Brinley, of Hartford, Conn. Hartford: 1878-93. V. 47

BRINNIN, JOHN MALCOLM
No Arch, No Triumph. New York: 1945. V. 47; 48

BRINSLEY, JOHN
Ludus Literarius, or, Grammar Schoole. London: 1627. V. 50

BRINTON, ANNA COOK
A Pre-Raphaelite Aeneid of Virgil in the Collection of Mrs. Edward Laurence Doheney of Los Angeles, Being an Essay in Honor of the William Morris Centenary, 1934. Los Angeles: 1934. V. 54

BRINTON, DANIEL G.
Essays on an Americanist. Philadelphia: 1890. V. 53
Library of Aboriginal American Literature. Philadelphia: 1885. V. 53

BRINTON, JOHN
Tour in Palestine and Syria. London: 1893. V. 53

BRINTON, JOHN H.
Personal Memoir of John H. Brinton, Major and Surgeon U.S.V. 1861-1865. New York: 1914. V. 49

BRINTON, SELWYN
The Renaissance; Its Art and Life. London: 1908. V. 51

BRISBANE, ALBERT
Social Destiny of Man; or, Association and Reorganization of Industry. Philadelphia: 1840. V. 47

BRISBANE, JOHN
The Anatomy of Painting; or a Short and Easy Introduction to Anatomy. London: 1769. V. 47

BRISBANE, REDELIA
Albert Brisbane. Boston: 1893. V. 49

BRISBANE, WILLIAM HENRY
Slaveholding Examined in the Light of the Holy Bible. Philadelhia: 1847. V. 47

BRISBIN, JAMES S.
The Beef Bonanza; Or How to Get Rich on the Plains. Philadelphia: 1881. V. 53; 54

BRISSEAU, MICHEL
Observations Faites Par Mr. Brisseau. A Douay: 1716. V. 49

BRISSON, BARNABE
Essai sur le Systeme-General de Navigation Interieure de la France, Suivi d'un Essai sur l'art de Projeter les Canaux a Point de Partage. Paris: 1829. V. 51

BRISSON, MATHURIN JACQUES
Ornithologia sive Synopsis Methodica.... Paris: 1760. V. 54

BRISSOT DE WARVILLE, JACQUES PIERRE
J. P. Brissot to His Constituents. Dublin: 1793. V. 47
New Travels in the United States of America, Performed in 1788. Dublin: 1792. V. 47
New Travels in the United States of America, Performed in 1788. New York: 1792. V. 53
Nouveau Voyage dans les Etats-Unis de L'Amerique Septentrionale, fait en 1788. Paris: 1791. V. 53
To His Constituents, on the Situation of the National Convention; on the Influence of the Anarchists. London: 1794. V. 47

BRISTED, JOHN
America and Her Resources; Or a View of the Agricultural, Commercial, Manufacturing, Financial, Political, Literary, Moral and Religious Capacity and Character of American People. London: 1818. V. 48; 50; 54
The Resources of the United States of America; or, a View of the Agricultural, Commercial, Manufacturing, Financial, Political, Literary, Moral and Religious Capacity and Character of the American People. New York: 1818. V. 52

BRISTER, BO
The Golden Crescent. Houston: 1969. V. 53

BRISTOL & EXETER RAILWAY
Resolutions of the Committee of the House of Commons, with Extracts from the Evidence of Traffic and Outlay on the Line and Absract of the Traffic to Bridgwater. Bristol: 1838. V. 54

BRISTOL, CHARLES BIRD
Picturesque Old Bristol, a Series of Fifty-Two Etchings. Bristol: 1885. V. 52

BRISTOL NATURALISTS' SOCIETY
Proceedings. Bristol: 1866-1940. V. 52

BRISTOW, AMELIA
Emma de Lissau; a Narrative of Striking Vicissitudes, and Peculiar Trials... London: 1829. V. 50
The Orphans of Lissau and Other Interesting Narratives... London: 1830. V. 52; 53; 54

BRISTOW, GWEN
Deep Summer. New York: 1937. V. 48
The Invisible Host. New York: 1930. V. 50

BRISTOW, H.
The Geology of the Isle of Wight. London: 1889. V. 48

BRISTOWE, WILLIAM S.
The Comity of Spiders. London: 1939. V. 54
The Comity of Spiders. London: 1939-41. V. 47

BRITAINE, WILLIAM DE
Human Prudence; or, the Art by Which a man May Raise Himself and His Fortune to Grandeur. London: 1697. V. 50; 51
Human Prudence; or, the Art by Which a man May Raise Himself and His Fortune to Grandeur. Dublin: 1728. V. 47

BRITAIN'S Mistakes (with: a Supplement to Britain's Mistakes) in the Commencement and Conduct of the Present War. London: 1740. V. 47

BRITANNIA.. London: 1774. V. 53

BRITANNIA In Mourning: or, A Review of the Politicks and Conduct of the Court of Great Britain With Regard to France, The Ballance of Power, and the True Interest of These Nations... London: 1742. V. 48

BRITANNIA SMELTING CO. LTD.
Memorandum and Articles of Association. Victoria: 1905. V. 50

BRITISH & FOREIGN BIBLE SOCIETY
Reports of the British and Foreign Bible Society, with Extracts of Correspondence, &c... London: 1805-16. V. 50; 52

THE BRITISH Almanac of the Society for the Diffusion of Useful Knowledge, for the Year of Our Lord 1863. (with) The Companion to the Almanac...for 1863. London: 1863. V. 47

THE BRITISH Almanac...for the Year of Our Lord 1841, 1842, 1849, 1850, 1857, 1859 and 1860. London: 1840-59. V. 49

BRITISH ARCHAEOLOGICAL ASSOCIATION
Transactions of the British Archaeological Association, at Its Third Annual Congress, Held at Gloucester, August 1846... London: 1848. V. 54

BRITISH Artists at the Front. Eric Kennington. London: 1918. V. 47

BRITISH Artists at the Front. Sir John Lavery. London: 1918. V. 47

BRITISH ASSOCIATION FOR THE ADVANCEMENT OF SCIENCE
Index to Reports and Transactions of the British Association for the Advancement of Science, from 1831 to 1860 Inclusive. London: 1864. V. 50
Report of the 48th Meeting Held at Dublin, in August 1878. 1879. V. 52

THE BRITISH Bell-Man. London: 1648. V. 54

THE BRITISH Bookmaker. 1890-91. V. 50
THE BRITISH Bookmaker. Raithby: 1890-94. V. 49

BRITISH Botany Familarly Explained and Described in a Series of Dialogues. Dublin: 1835. V. 54

BRITISH Bridges: an Illustrated Technical and Historical Record. London: 1933. V. 50

BRITISH COLUMBIA
Report of Conferences Between the Provincial Government and Indian Delegates from Fort Simpson and Naas River. The Superintendent of Indians and Indian Reserve Commissioner Being Present, 3rd and 8th Feb. 1887. Victoria: 1887. V. 53
Second Annual Report of Immigration Agents. British Columbia for the Year Ending 31st December, 1884. Victoria: 1885. V. 51

BRITISH COLUMBIA. DEPARTMENT OF PUBLIC WORKS
Journal of the Department of Public Works. Victoria: 1936. V. 51

BRITISH Columbia: its Resources and Capabilities: Reprinted from "Canada: a Memorial Volume". Montreal: 1889. V. 50; 52

BRITISH Columbia Medical Register, Printed and Published Under the Direction of the Medical Council of Physicians and Surgeons of British Columbia...May 1890. Victoria: 1890. V. 47; 54

BRITISH COLUMBIA MOUNTAINEERING CLUB
The Northern Cordilleran. Vancouver: 1913. V. 48; 49

BRITISH Cowhide Leathers. London: 1960. V. 54

BRITISH Curiosities... London: 1713. V. 54
BRITISH Curiosities... London: 1728. V. 48

BRITISH ECOLOGICAL SOCIETY
The Journal of Animal Ecology. Cambridge & Oxford: 1949-68. V. 49

THE BRITISH Essayists. London: 1817. V. 52

BRITISH Essayists. London: 1827. V. 48

BRITISH-INDIAN SUBMARINE TELEGRAPH CO.
Souvenir of the Inaugural Fete, in Commemoration of the Opening of Direct Submarine Telegraph with India, June 23rd, 1870. London: 1870. V. 50

BRITISH INSTITUTION
An Account of All the Pictures Exhibited in the Rooms of the British Institution from 1813 to 1823... London: 1824. V. 47

BRITISH Journal Photographic Almanac, and Photographer's Daily Companion for 1883-(1889). London: 1883-89. V. 50

BRITISH Liberties, or the Free-Born Subject's Inheritance... London: 1766. V. 48

BRITISH Liberty; or, Sketches Critical and Demonstrative, of the State of English Subjects. London: 1804. V. 50

BRITISH LIBRARY
Catalogue of Books from the Low Countries 1601-1621 in the British Library. London: 1990. V. 50
Catalogue of Seventeenth Century Italian Books in the British Library. London: 1986. V. 50
General Catalogue of Printed Books to 1955. New York: 1967-80. V. 47

THE BRITISH Metropolis in 1851. London: 1851. V. 47

BRITISH MUSEUM
Assyrian Sculptures in the British Museum from Shalmaneser III to Sennacherib. London: 1938. V. 47; 50; 54
Bookbindings from the Library of Jean Grolier. A Loan Exhibition. London: 1965. V. 53
British Graham Land Expedition 1934-37. Scientific Reports. London: 1940-41. V. 47; 51
Catalogue of Birds. Volume 1. Accipitres or Diurnal Birds of Prey. London: 1874. V. 52
Catalogue of Birds. Volume 10. Fringilliformes, Part I. London: 1885. V. 52
Catalogue of Birds. Volume 11. Fringilliformes, part 2. London: 1886. V. 50
Catalogue of Birds. Volume 12. Fringilliformes, Part 3: Fringillidae. London: 1888. V. 52
Catalogue of Birds. Volume 13. Sturniformes: Artamidae, Sturnidae, Ploceidae, Alaudidae. London: 1890. V. 50
Catalogue of Birds. Volume 14, Oligomyodae: Tyrannidae, Oxyrhamphidae, Pipridae, Cotingidae, Phytotomidae, Philepittidae... London: 1890. V. 50; 51; 54
Catalogue of Birds. Volume 15. Tracheophonae; Dendrocolaptidae, Formicariidae, Conopophagidae and Pteropthochidae. London: 1890. V. 49; 50; 51
Catalogue of Birds. Volume 16; Upupae and Trochili. London: 1892. V. 49; 52
Catalogue of Birds. Volume 17. Leptosomatidae, Coraciidae, Meropidae, Alcedinidae, Momotidae, Todidae, Collidae. London: 1892. V. 52
Catalogue of Birds. Volume 19. Scansores and Coccyges: Rhamphastidae, Galbulidae and Bucconidae. London: 1891. V. 52
Catalogue of Birds. Volume 21. Columbae. London: 1893. V. 52
Catalogue of Birds. Volume 22. Game Birds: Pterocletes, Gallinae, Opisthocomi and Hemipodii. London: 1893. V. 5; 53
Catalogue of Birds. Volume 23. Fulicariae (Rallidae and Heliornithidae) and Alectorides (Aramidae, Eurypygidae, Mesitidae, Rhinochetidae, Gruidae, Psophiidae and Otididae). London: 1894. V. 49; 52; 53
Catalogue of Birds. Volume 24. Limicolae. London: 1896. V. 50; 51
Catalogue of Birds. Volume 25. Gaviae and Tubinares. London: 1896. V. 50; 51; 54
Catalogue of Birds. Volume 26. Plataleae and Herodiones. London: 1898. V. 51; 52; 53; 54
Catalogue of Birds. Volume 27. Chenomorphae, Crypturi and Ratitae. London: 1895. V. 52
Catalogue of Birds. Volume 4. Passeriformes, Cichlomorphae Part 1. London: 1879. V. 52
Catalogue of Birds. Volume 6. Cichlomorphae. Part 3. London: 1881. V. 52
Catalogue of Books in the Library of the British Museum Printed in England, Scotland and Ireland, and of Books in English, Printed Abroad to the Year 1640. London: 1884. V. 51
Catalogue of Books, Manuscripts, Maps and Drawings. London: 1903-15/64. V. 50
Catalogue of Books printed in the XVth Century Now in the British Museum. London: 1971. V. 48
Catalogue of Books Printed in the XVth Century Now in the British Museum. Part X. Spain and Portugal. London: 1971. V. 49
Catalogue of British Drawings XVI and XVII Centuries. London: 1960. V. 54
Catalogue of Carnivorous Pachydermatous and Edente Mammalia in the British Museum. 1869. V. 52; 54
Catalogue of Demotic Papyri in the British Museum. Volume I. A Theban Archive of the Reign of Ptolemy I, Soter. London: 1939. V. 51
Catalogue of Early German and Flemish Woodcuts Preserved in the Department of Prints and Drawings in the British Museum 1903-11. London: 1903-11. V. 50
Catalogue of Egyptian Antiquities in the British Museum I (only): Mummies and Human Remains. London: 1968. V. 51
Catalogue of Egyptian Antiquities in the British Museum III: Musical Instruments. London: 1976. V. 51
Catalogue of Egyptian Antiquities in the British Museum. V: Early Dynatic Objects. London: 1980. V. 51
Catalogue of Egyptian Antiquities in the British Museum. VI: Jewellery I. From the Earliest Times to the Seventeenth Dynasty. London: 1981. V. 51
Catalogue of Egyptian Scarabs, etc. in the British Museum. London: 1913. V. 51
A Catalogue of Engraved British Portraits Preserved in the Department of Prints and Drawings in the British Museum. London: 1908-25. V. 51
Catalogue of Fossil Cephalopoda in the British Museum. London: 1888-1934. V. 53
Catalogue of Fossil Mammalia in the British Museum. London: 1885-87. V. 51
Catalogue of Greek and Etruscan Vases in the British Museum. London: 1893-1925. V. 50
A Catalogue of Hebrew and Samaritan Manuscripts in the British Museum. London: 1899/1905. V. 51
Catalogue of Maps, Prints, Drawings, etc., Forming the Geographical and Topographical Collection Attached to the Library of King George the Third and Presented by King George the Fourth to the British Museum. London: 1829. V. 47
Catalogue of Printed Books. London: 1882-1900. V. 52
Catalogue of the Birds in the British Museum. London: 1875-98. V. 50; 51; 54
Catalogue of the Blasatoidea in the Geological Department of the British Museum (Natural History). London: 1886. V. 54
Catalogue of the Books, Manuscripts, Maps and Drawings. London: 1903-40. V. 49
Catalogue of the Books, Manuscripts, Maps and Drawings in the British Museum (Natural History). New York: 1991. V. 50; 52
Catalogue of the Books, Manuscripts, Maps and Drawings in the British Museum (Natural History). London: 1992. V. 48; 50
Catalogue of the Books, Manuscripts, Maps and Drawings in the British Museum (Natural History). New York: 1992. V. 48; 49; 52; 53; 54
Catalogue of the Carved Amber in the Department of Greek and Roman Antiquities. London: 1966. V. 54
Catalogue of the Fifty Manuscripts and Printed Books Bequeathed to the British Museum by Alfred H. Huth. London: 1912. V. 49; 52
Catalogue of the Fossil Sponges in the Geological Department of the British Museum (Natural History). London: 1883. V. 52; 53; 54
Catalogue of the Freshwater Fishes of Africa in the British Museum. London: 1909-16. V. 50; 51
Catalogue of the Greek and Etruscan Vases in the British Museum. London: 1893-1925. V. 52
Catalogue of the Lizards in the British Museum. London: 1885-87. V. 51
Catalogue of the Madreporarian Corals in the British Museum (Natural History). London: 1893-1928. V. 53; 54
Catalogue of the Stowe Manuscripts in the British Museum. London: 1895-96. V. 47
Catalogue of the Terracottas in the Department of Greek and Roman Antiquities, British Museum. London: 1959. V. 50
Catalogue of the Ungulate Mammals in the British Museum. London: 1913-16. V. 51
A Catalogue of the Works of Linnaeus (and Publications More Immediately Relating Thereto) Preserved in the Libraries of the British Museum. London: 1933. V. 51
Chinese Natural History Drawings Selected from the Reeves Collection in the British Museum (Natural History). London: 1974. V. 54
A Description of the Collection of Ancient Terracottas in the British Museum, with Engravings. London: 1810. V. 48
The Drawings of John White 1577-1590... London: 1964. V. 50
Egyptian Sculptures in the British Museum. London: 1914. V. 51
Egyptian Texts of the Earliest Period from the Coffin of Amamu in the British Museum. London: 1886. V. 51
Facsimiles of Biblical Manuscripts in the British Museum. London: 1900. V. 52
Franks Bequest. Catalogue of British and American Book Plates Bequeathed to the Trustees of the British Museum by Sir Augustus Wollaston Franks. London: 1903-04. V. 53
General Catalogue of Printed Books. London: 1975. V. 49
General Catalogue of Printed Books to 1955. New York: 1967. V. 53
Greek Printing Types 1465-1927. 1927. V. 48
Hieratic Papyri in the British Museum. Fifth Series. The Abu Sir Papyri. London: 1968. V. 51
Hieratic Papyri in the British Museum. Fourth Series: Oracular Amuletic Decrees of the Late New Kingdom. Volumes I-II. London: 1960. V. 51
Hieroglyphic Texts from Egyptian Stelae & C., in the British Museum. Parts I-IV. London: 1911-13. V. 51
Hieroglyphic Texts from Egyptian Stelae, Etc. Part 1. London: 1961. V. 49; 51
Hieroglyphic Texts from Egyptian Stelae, etc. Part 9. London: 1970. V. 49; 51
History of the Collections. London: 1904-12. V. 50
Illuminated Manuscripts in the British Museum. London: 1903. V. 54
An Illustrated Catalogue of the Rothschild Colletion of Fleas (Siphonaptera) in the British Museum. London: 1953-81. V. 51
Illustrations of Typical Specimens of Lepidoptera Heterocera...in the British Museum. London: 1879. V. 51
Italian Drawings in the Department of Prints and Drawings in the British Museum. London: 1967. V. 51
Italian Drawings in the Department of Prints and Drawings in the British Museum. Fourteenth and Fifteenth Centuries. London: 1950. V. 50; 54
Japanese and Chinese Paintings in the British Museum, a Descriptive and Historical Catalogue. London: 1886. V. 50
List of Catalogues of English Book Sales 1676-1900. Now in the British Museum. London: 1915. V. 49; 51
A List of the Books of Reference in the Reading Room of the British Museum. London: 1871. V. 54
List of the Specimens of British Animals in the Collection, with Synonyms and References to Figures. London: 1848-56. V. 49; 52
List of the Specimens of Dipterous Insects in the Collection of the British Museum. London: 1848-55. V. 51
Nomenclature (and Catalogue) of Coleopterious Insects. London: 1847-56. V. 50
Prints in the Dotted Manner and Other Metal-Cuts of the XV Century in the Department of Prints and Drawings, British Museum. London: 1937. V. 48; 49
Queen Mary's Psalter Miniatures and Drawings by an English Artist of the 14th Century Reproduced from Royal MS.2B.VII in the British Museum. London: 1912. V. 50
Reproductions from Illuminated Manuscripts. Series IV. London: 1928. V. 47
Short Title Catalogue of French Books 1601-1700 in the Library of the British Museum. Folkestone and London: 1969-73. V. 49
Short-Title Catalogue of Books Printed in Italy and of Italian Books Printed in Other Countries from 1465 to 1600 Now in the British Museum. London: 1962. V. 49
Short-Title Catalogue of Books Printed in Italy and of italian Books Printed in Other Countries from 1465 to 1600 Now in the British Museum. London: 1986. V. 50
Short-Title Catalogue of Books Printed in the German-Speaking Countries and German Books Printed in Other Countries from 1455 to 1600 Now in the British Museum. London: 1962. V. 49
Three Hundred Notable Books Added to the Library of the British Museum Under the Keepership of Richard Garnett, 1890-1899. London: 1899. V. 50; 51
World, an Excerpt from the British Museum Catalogue of Printed Maps, Charts, and Plans, Photographic Edition to 1964. London: 1967. V. 54

BRITISH National Bibliography. London: 1971-87. V. 47

BRITISH National Bibliography. Cumulated Indices 1950-1970. London: 1950-70. V. 47

BRITISH Novelists: with an Essay and Prefaces biographical and Critical, by Mrs. Barthauld. London: 1820. V. 49

THE BRITISH Orpheus; Being a Selection of Two Hundred and Seventy Songs and Airs... Stourport: 1810. V. 48

THE BRITISH Phoenix: or, the Gentleman and Lady's Polite Literary Entertainer. London: 1758. V. 51

THE BRITISH Plutarch, Containing the Lives of the Most Eminent Statesmen, Patriots, Divines, Warriors, Philosophers, Poets and Artists of Great Britain and Ireland, from the Accession of Henry VIII to the Present Time... Perth: 1795. V. 51

BRITISH Poets. Including Translations. Chiswick: 1822. V. 51

BRITISH PORTLAND CEMENT ASSOCIATION
Concrete Bridges. London: 1930. V. 49

BRITISH REINFORCED CONCRETE ENGINEERING CO.
B.R.C. Structure. A Photographic Record of the Use of Reinforced Concrete in Modern Building Construction. London: 1923. V. 50; 54

THE BRITISH Representative; or, a General List of the Knights, Commissioners of Shires, Citizens and Burgesses, Returned to All the Parliaments of Great Britain, Which are Eight in Number... London: 1736. V. 49

BRITISH SCHOOL OF ARCHAEOLOGY IN JERUSALEM
Journal of the British School of Archaeology in Jerusalem. London: 1969. V. 52

BRITISH Sports and Sportsmen. Shooting and Deerstalking. London: 1913. V. 48; 52

THE BRITISH Story Briefly Told, from Early Times to the Present Period. London: 1834. V. 49

BRITISH Yachts and Yachtsmen. London: 1907. V. 52; 53

BRITO, C.
The Mukkuva Law: or, the Rules of Succession Among the Mukkuvars of Ceylon. Colombo: 1876. V. 48

BRITO DE MENEZES, FRANCISCO
Sanctissimae Reginae Elisabethae Poeticum Certamen Dedicat, & Consecrat Academia Conimbricensis... Coimbra: 1626. V. 47

BRITO FREIRE, FRANCISCO DE
Relacao da Viagem Que fez ao Estado do Brazil a Armada da Companhia, Anno 1655. Lisbon: 1657. V. 48

BRITTAIN, HARRY E.
Canada: There and Back. London: 1908. V. 49

BRITTAIN, VERA
England's Hour. London: 1941. V. 47
Honourable Estate: A Novel of Transition. London: 1936. V. 47; 53
Thrice a Stranger - New Chapters of Autobiography. London: 1938. V. 54

BRITTAINE, GEORGE
Irishmen and Irishwomen. Dublin: 1831. V. 51

BRITTEN, BENJAMIN
Children's Crusade. London: 1973. V. 48

BRITTEN, F. J.
Old Clocks and Watches and their Makers. London: 1911. V. 53
Old Clocks and Watches and Their Makers... London: 1932. V. 52; 53
Old English Clocks (The Wetherfield Collection). London: 1907. V. 53
Old English Clocks (The Wetherfield Collection). London: 1980. V. 52

BRITTEN, JAMES
A Dictionary of English Plant Names. London: 1878-86. V. 52; 53
European Ferns. London: 1880. V. 48; 49

BRITTON, BURT
Self Portrait: Book People Picture Themselves. New York: 1976. V. 50

BRITTON, JOHN
The Architectural (and Cathedral) Antiquities of Great Britain. London: 1807-26/14-30. V. 48; 50
The Architectural Antiquities of Great Britain. London: 1807. V. 49
The Architectural Antiquities of Great Britain... London: 1807-26. V. 48
The Architectural Antiquities of Great Britain, Represented and Illustrated in a Series of Views, Elevations, Plans, Sections and Details of Ancient English Edifices... London: 1835. V. 47; 49
The Beauties of England and Wales; or Delineations, Topographical, Historical and Descriptive. London: 1801-15. V. 51
The Beauties of England and Wales; or Delineations, Topographical, Historical and Descriptive of Each County. Volume 2: Cambridgeshire, Cheshire and Cornwall. London: 1801. V. 48
The Beauties of England and Wales; or Delineations, Topographical, Historical and Descriptive... Volume 5: Durham, Essex and Gloucestershire. London: 1803. V. 47
The Beauties of England and Wales or Original Delineations, Topographical, Historical and Descriptive of Each County. London: 1801-18. V. 54
The Beauties of England and Wales: Volume IV. Devonshire and Dorset. London: 1803. V. 47; 53
The Beauties of England and Wales...Volume 12 Part 1: Northumberland, Nottinghamshire and Rutlandshire. London: 1813. V. 47
The Beauties of England and Wales...Volume 16: Yorkshire. London: 1812. V. 47
The Beauties of England and Wales....Volume 2: Cambridgeshire, Cheshire and Cornwall. London: 1801. V. 53
Brief Memoir of Sir John Soane. London: 1834. V. 50
A Brief Memoir of the Life and Writings of John Britton. London: 1825. V. 50; 52
Britton (On the Laws of England). London: 1640. V. 52
Devonshire and Cornwall Illustrated. Cornwall Illustrated. Ireland Illustrated. London: 1832-31. V. 51
Graphic Illustration, with Historical and Descriptive Accounts of Toddington, Gloucestershire, the Seat of Lord Sudeley... London: 1840. V. 52
The History and Antiquities of Bath Abbey Church; including Biographical Anecdotes of the Most Distinguished Persons Interred in that Edifice. London: 1825. V. 47; 53
The History and Antiquities of The Cathedral Church of Oxford. London: 1836. V. 48
The History and Antiquities of the Cathedral Church of Wells... London: 1824. V. 50
The History And Antiquities of the Metropolitan Church of Canterbury... London: 1836. V. 50
The History and Antiquities of the Metropolitical Church of York... London: 1819. V. 48; 51
Illustrations of the Early Domestic Architecture of England... London: 1846. V. 51
Modern Athens! Displayed in a Series of Views: or Edinburgh in the Nineteenth Century. London: 1831. V. 54
The Original Picture of London. London: 1835. V. 50
The Picture of London. London: 1824. V. 50
Picturesque Antiquities of the English Cities. London: 1830. V. 47; 50
The Pleasures of Human Life, Investigated Cheerfully, Elucidated, Satirically, promulgated Explicitly and Discussed Philosophically in a Dozen Dissertations on Male, Female and Neuter Pleasures. London: 1807. V. 49; 50
The Union of Architecture, Sculpture and Painting... London: 1827. V. 47; 48

BRITTON, N. L.
The Bahama Flora. New York: 1920. V. 51
Botany of Porto Rico and the Virgin Islands. New York: 1923-30. V. 51
The Cactacceae, Descriptions and Illustrations of Plants of the Cactus Family. Los Angeles: 1931-35-37-37. V. 48
The Cactaceae. New York: 1963. V. 54
The Cactaceae. 1964. V. 50; 51
The Cactaceae, Descriptions and Illustrations of Plants of the Cactus Family. Washington: 1919-23. V. 53
An Illustrated Flora of the Northern United States, Canada and the British Possessions... New York: 1896-97-98. V. 48

BRITTON, WILEY
The Civil War on the Border. New York: 1891. V. 47
The Civil War on the Border. New York and London: 1899-1904. V. 49
Memoirs of the Rebellion on the Border, 1863. Chicago: 1882. V. 48; 53
Pioneer Life in Southwest Missouri. Columbia: 1923. V. 49
The Union Indian Brigade in the Civil War. Kansas City: 1922. V. 49; 50; 52

BROAD, AMOS
The Trial of Amos Broad and His Wife, on the Several Indictments for assaulting and Beating Betty, a Slave and Her Little Female Child Sarah, Aged Three Years. New York: 1809. V. 51; 52

BROAD, C. D.
Examination of McTaggart's Philosophy. Cambridge: 1933/38. V. 47

BROAD Grins; or, Fun for the New year. Boston: 1832. V. 53

BROADBENT, WILLIAM H.
Heart Disease: with Special Reference to Prognosis and Treatment. New York: 1898. V. 53
The Pulse. London: 1890. V. 48; 50
Selections from the Writings Medical and Neurological of Sir William Broadbent. London: 1908. V. 47; 50

BROADDUS, JOHN ERIC
The Sphinx and The Bird of Paradise. 1991. V. 54

BROADFOOT, W.
Billiards. London: 1896. V. 54
The Career of Major George Broadfoot. London: 1888. V. 47

BROADHOUSE, JOHN
How to Make a Violin. The Violin: its Construction Practically Treated... London: 1910. V. 51

BROADLEY, A. M.
The Last Punic War. Edinburgh: 1882. V. 54
Napoleon in Caricature 1795-1821. London: 1911. V. 50

BROADMOOR CRIMINAL LUNATIC ASYLUM
Report from a Committee Appointed to Inquire Into Certain Matters. London: 1877. V. 53

BROADSIDE Ballads of the Restoration Period from the Jersey Collection Known as the Osterley Park Ballads. London: 1930. V. 52

BROADUS, JOHN ERIC
Sphinx and the Bird of Paradise. New York Dusseldorf: 1981. V. 47

BROCA, PAUL
On the Phenomena of Hybridity in the Genus Homo. London: 1864. V. 53

BROCARD, PIERRE RENE JEAN BAPTISTE HENRI
Notes de Bibliographie des Courbes Geometriques (-Partie Complemetaire). Bar-le-Duc: 1897-99. V. 47

BROCH, HERMANN
The Death of Virgil. 1945. V. 50
The Death of Virgil. New York: 1945. V. 53
The Death of Virgil. London: 1946. V. 51
James Joyce und die Gegenwart. Zurich: 1936. V. 52
Die Schuldosen. Munich: 1950. V. 54
Der Tod des Vergil. New York: 1945. V. 49
The Unknown Quantity. New York: 1935. V. 49

BROCH, THEODOR
The Mountains Wait. St. Paul: 1942. V. 49

BROCK, C. E.
The Children's Hour. Boston: 1929. V. 47

BROCK, CHARLES E.
Twelve Extra Illustrations to the "Pickwick Papers". Leamington Spa: 1921. V. 54

BROCK, R. A.
General Robert Edward Lee, Soldier, Citizen and Christian Patriot. Atlanta: 1897. V. 49
Virginia and Virginians. Richmond & Toledo: 1888. V. 54

BROCK, R. C.
The Life and Work of Astley Cooper. Edinburgh: 1952. V. 50

BROCKBANK, EDWARD
Sketches of the Lives and Work of the Honorary Medical Staff of the Manchester Infirmary. Manchester: 1904. V. 50

BROCKBANK, OLIVER
Diary of a Journey through the Siani Peninsula and Arabia in 1914. 1915. V. 50

BROCKEDON, WILLIAM
Egypt and Nubia. London: 1846-49. V. 54
Finden's Illustrations of the Life and Works of Lord Byron. London: 1833. V. 54

BROCKEDON, WILLIAM continued
Finden's Landscape Illustrations to Mr. Murray's First Complete and Uniform Edition of the Life and Works of Lord Byron. London: 1834. V. 48
Illustrataions of the Passes of the Alps By Which Italy Communicates with France, Switzerland and Germany. London: 1850. V. 48
Illustrations of the Life and Works of Lord Byron. London: 1833-34. V. 47
Road-Book From London to Naples. London: 1835. V. 49

BROCKETT, JOHN TROTTER
A Catalogue of the Very Valuable and Extensive Collection of Ancient Coins and Medals, Collected By... London: 1823. V. 50
A Glossary of North Country Words, In Use. Newcastle-upon-Tyne: 1825. V. 50; 53; 54

BROCKETT, JOSHUA ARTHUR
Zipporah: the Maid of Midian. Chicago: 1926. V. 52

BROCKETT, L. P.
Battle-Field and Hospital; or, Lights and Shadows of the Great Rebellion. Philadelphia: 1888. V. 48
Epidemic and Contagious Diseases: Their History, Symptoms and Treatment Illustrated, with the Best Colored plates of the Various Contagious and Eruptive Diseases Ever Executed in this Country... New York: 1873. V. 50; 51; 52
Woman's Work in the Civil War: a Record of Heroism, Patriotism and Patience. Philadelphia: 1867. V. 48; 53

BROCKETT, L.P.
Our Western Empire: or the New West Beyond the Mississippi. Philadelphia: 1882. V. 47

BROCKETT, PAUL
Bibliography of Aeronautics. Washington: 1910. V. 49

BROCKLEBANK, HUGH
A Turn or Two I'll Walk to Still My Beating Mind. London: 1955. V. 53; 54

BROCKLEHURST, H. C.
Game Animals of the Sudan, a handbook for Hunters and Naturalists. London: 1931. V. 47; 48; 49; 50

BROCKLEHURST, THOMAS
Mexico To-Day: A Country with a Great Future and a Glance at the Prehistoric Remains and Antiquities of the Montezumas. London: 1883. V. 50; 53

BROCKMAN, CARL HEINRICH
Die Metallurgischen Krankheiten des Oberharzes. Osterode;: 1851. V. 49; 52; 54

BROCKWAY, FENNER
Inside the Left. Thirty Years of Platform, Press, Prison and Parliament. London: 1942. V. 49

BROD, MAX
The Biography of Franz Kafka. London: 1947. V. 51

BRODER, PATRICIA JANIS
The American West, The Modern Vision. New York: 1984. V. 50; 52
Bronzes of the American West. New York: 1973. V. 51; 54
Bronzes of the American West. New York: 1974. V. 54
Shadows on Glass, the Indian World of Ben Wittick. Savage: 1990. V. 52

BRODERIP, FRANCES FEELING
Mamma's Morning Gossip or, Little Bits for Little Birds. London: 1866. V. 48

BRODHEAD, JOHN ROMEYN
History of the State of New York, 1609-1691. New York: 1853/71. V. 50

BRODHEAD, L. W.
The Delaware Water Gap: Its Scenery, Its Legends and Early History. Philadelphia: 1867. V. 49
The Delaware Water Gap: Its Scenery, Its Legends and Early History. Philadelphia: 1870. V. 53

BRODIE, BENJAMIN COLLINS
Lectures Illustrative of Certain Local Nervous Affections. London: 1837. V. 52
Lectures on Diseases of the Urinary Organs. London: 1832. V. 47; 49
Psychological Inquiries: in a Series of Essays, Intended to Illustrate the Mutual Relations of the Physical Organization and the Mental Faculties. London: 1854. V. 48; 51
The Works of... London: 1865. V. 51

BRODIE, GEORGE
A History of the British Empire from the Accession of Charles I to the Restoration. Edinburgh: 1822. V. 50

BRODIE, ROBERT
The Reminiscences of a Civil Engineering Contractor. Bristol: 1943. V. 49; 54

BRODIGAN, THOMAS
A Botanical, Historical and Practical Treatise on the Tobacco Plant, in Which the Art of Growing and Curing Tobacco in the British Isles Is made Familiar to Every Capacity, as Deduced from the Observations of the Author in the United States... London: 1830. V. 52

BRODKEY, HAROLD
First Love and Other Sorrows. New York: 1957. V. 49; 50; 51
First Love and Other Sorrows. London: 1958. V. 47
A Poem About Testimony and Argument. New York: 1986. V. 54
Stories in an Almost Classical Mode. New York: 1988. V. 52; 53

BRODRICK, ALAN HOUGHTON
Parts of Barbary. London. V. 47

BRODRICK, GEORGE C.
English Land and English Landlords, an Enquiry into the Origin and Character of the English Land System with Proposals for Its Reform with an Index. London: 1881. V. 54

BRODSKY, JOSEPH
A Part of Speech. New York: 1980. V. 52; 53; 54
Selected Poems. New York: 1973. V. 47; 52; 53; 54
To Urania. New York: 1988. V. 50; 52
Verses on the Winter Campaign 1980. London: 1981. V. 48; 52; 53

BRODY, CATHERINE TYLER
Checklist: Stone House Press Books and Ephemera 1978-1988. New York: 1989. V. 50

BRODY, G. S.
Flora of Weston...and Botanical Memoranda of Steep Holm, Chapwick Moor and Cheddar Cliffs... Weston-super-Mare,: 1856. V. 54

BRODZKY, HORACE
Henri Gaudier-Brzeska - 1891-1915. London: 1933. V. 52

BROGGER, A. W.
The Viking Ships, Their Ancestry and Evolution. Oslo: 1951. V. 51; 52

BROGGER, W. C.
Fridtiof Nansen 1861-1893. London: 1896. V. 50; 54

BROGIOTTI, ANDREA
Indice de Caratteri con l'Inventori e Nomi de Essi, Esistenti Nella Stampa Vaticana, e Camerale. Rome: 1628. V. 50

BROGLIE, LOUIS CESAR VICTOR MAURICE DE
Ondes et Mouvements. Paris: 1926. V. 47

BROINOWSKI, G. J.
The Birds of Australia... Melbourne: 1887-91. V. 48; 52
The Cockatoos and Nestors of Australia and New Zealand. Melbourne: 1981. V. 54

BROKE, ARTHUR DE CAPELL
Sketches in Spain and Morocco... London: 1831. V. 49
Travels through Sweden, Norway and... London: 1835. V. 51
Winter Sketches in Lapland, or Illustrations of a Journey from Alten...through Norwegian, Russian and Swedish Lapland, to Nornen. London: 1827. V. 47

BROKE, GEORGE
With Sack and Stock in Alaska. London: 1891. V. 47

BROKESBY, FRANCIS
The Life of Mr. Henry Dodwell; with an Account of His Works and an Abridgment of Several Of Them... London: 1715. V. 52

BROME, ALEXANDER
Rump; or an Exact Collection of the Choycest Poems and Songs Relating to the Times. London: 1662. V. 47; 50
Songs and Other Poems. London: 1661. V. 53
Songs and Other Poems. London: 1664. V. 50
Songs and Other Poems. London: 1668. V. 48

BROME, RICHARD
The Northern Lasse, a Comoedie. London: 1632. V. 50

BROMFIELD, LOUIS
A Modern Hero. New York: 1932. V. 49; 52
Twenty-Four Hours. New York: 1930. V. 52

BROMHALL, THOMAS
A Treatise of Specters. Or, an History of Apparitions, Oracles, Prophecies...and the Cunning Delusions of the Devil. London: 1658. V. 54

BROMIGE, DAVID
The Ends of the Earth. Los Angeles: 1968. V. 54
Threads. Los Angeles: 1971. V. 54
Tight Corners and What's Around Them. Los Angeles: 1974. V. 54

BROMLEY, F. W.
Atlas of Westchester County, New York. New York: 1881. V. 49

BROMLEY, G. W.
Atlas of Westchester County, New York. Philadelphia: 1910-11. V. 49

BROMLEY, GEORGE T.
The Long Ago and the Later On - or Recollections of Eighty Years. San Francisco: 1904. V. 54

BROMLEY, THOMAS
The Way to the Sabbath of Rest; or the Soul's Progress in the Work of the New-Birth... Leeds: 1744. V. 47

BROMLEY, W.
Treatise on the Acknowledged Superiority of the French Over the English Officer in the Field. London: 1810?. V. 50

BROMLEY, WILLIAM
Remarks in the Grand Tour of France and Italy. London: 1705. V. 53
Several Years Travels through Portugal, Spain, Italy, Germany, Prussia, Sweden, Denmark and the United Provinces. London: 1702. V. 47

BROMLEY-DAVENPORT, W.
Sport; Fox-Hunting; Salmon-fishing; Covert-Shooting; Deer-Stalking. London: 1885. V. 49

BROMME, TAUGOTT
Comite des Vereins zum Schutze Deutscher Eiswanderer in Texas. Weisbaden: 1850. V. 49

BRON, WILLIAM
Careless Love and its Apostrophes. New York: 1985. V. 52

BRONAUGH, WARREN CARTER
The Younger's Fight for Freedom. Columbia: 1906. V. 52; 53

BRONEER, OSCAR
Corinth. Volume I. Part IV: The South Stoa and Its Roman Successors. Princeton: 1954. V. 52
The Lion Monument at Amphipolis. Cambridge: 1941. V. 52

BRONGERSMA, L. D.
European Atlantic Turtles. Leiden: 1972. V. 53

BRONK, WILLIAM
Careless Love and Its Apostrophes. New York: 1985. V. 54
Light and Dark. Ashland: 1956. V. 54
Light In a Dark Sky. Concord: 1982. V. 47; 48; 49
Six Duplicities. New York. V. 54

BRONOWSKI, J.
The Poet's Defence. Cleveland: 1966. V. 54

BRONOWSKI, JACOB
For Wilhelmina, Queen of the Netherlands. Cambridge: 1929. V. 52
Spain 1939: Four Poems. Hull: 1939. V. 47; 49

BRONSON, BERTRAND H.
Johnson and Boswell - Three Essays. Berkeley & Los Angeles: 1944. V. 54

BRONSON, EDGAR BEECHER
Red Blooded. Chicago: 1910. V. 53

BRONSON, HENRY
Medical History and Biography. Articule dans L'Hemisphere Gauche. 1876. V. 48

BRONSON, J.
The Domestic Manufacturer's Assistant, and Family Directory, in the Arats of Weaving and Dyeing. Utica: 1817. V. 51

BRONSON, MILES
A Spelling Book and Vocabulary in English, A'sa'mese, Singpho, and Na'ga. Jaipur: 1839. V. 49

BRONTE, ANNE
The Complete Poems of... London: 1920. V. 54
The Tenant of Wildfell Hall. New York: 1848. V. 54
The Tenant of Wildfell Hall. London: 1854. V. 49; 54
The Tenant of Wildfell Hall. New York: 1858. V. 54
The Tenant of Wildfell Hall. London: 1867. V. 50
The Tenant of Wildfell Hall. London: 1895. V. 50
The Tenant of Wildfell Hall. 1931. V. 52; 54

BRONTE, CHARLOTTE
The Complete Poems. London: 1923. V. 52; 54
Jane Eyre. London: 1847. V. 52; 54
Jane Eyre. New York: 1848. V. 47; 48; 49; 52; 53; 54
Jane Eyre. Leipzig: 1850. V. 54
Jane Eyre. London: 1855. V. 54
Jane Eyre. New York: 1855. V. 54
Jane Eyre. New York: 1856. V. 49
Jane Eyre. London: 1857. V. 50; 54
Jane Eyre. London: 1859. V. 53
Jane Eyre. Paris: 1859. V. 52; 54
Jane Eyre. Paris: 1860. V. 47
Jane Eyre. London: 1875. V. 47
Jane Eyre. London: 1883. V. 47
Jane Eyre. London: 1898. V. 54
Jane Eyre. New York & London: 1920's. V. 48
Jane Eyre. Paris: 1923. V. 52; 54
Jane Eyre, an Autobiography. Ilkley: 1991. V. 49
Latest Gleanings. London: 1918. V. 50; 51
The Poems of... New York: 1887. V. 54
The Professor. London: 1857. V. 47; 48; 49; 51; 52; 53; 54
The Professor. New York: 1857. V. 47; 52; 54
The Professor. London: 1860. V. 50; 52; 54
The Professor. New York: 1865. V. 52; 54
Le Proffesuer. Paris: 1869. V. 53
Saul and Other Poems. London: 1913. V. 50
Shirley. London: 1849. V. 47; 49; 51
Shirley. New York: 1850. V. 54
Shirley. London: 1857. V. 52; 54
Shirley. London: 1860. V. 49; 51; 53
Shirley. London: 1979. V. 52
Shirley et Agnes Grey. Paris: 1877. V. 52; 54
The Spell, an Extravaganza. London: 1931. V. 54
The Twelve Adventurers and Other Stories. London: 1925. V. 52; 54
Two Tales "The Secret Hart" & "Lily Hart". 1978. V. 52; 54
Villette. Leipzig: 1853. V. 50
Villette. London: 1853. V. 47; 49
Villette. New York: 1853. V. 52; 53; 54
Villette. London: 1855. V. 52
Villette. New York: 1855. V. 52; 54
Villette. New York: 1857. V. 50; 52; 54
Villette. New York: 1858. V. 54
Villette. 1931. V. 52; 54
Villette. New York: 1931. V. 52
Villette. Oxford: 1984. V. 54
Works. London: 1899. V. 48

BRONTE, EMILY
The Complete Poems. London: 1910. V. 54
The Complete Poems of... London: 1923. V. 52; 54
The Complete Poems of... New York: 1941. V. 52; 54
Gondal Poems. V. 54
Gondal's Queen. Austin: 1955. V. 52
Les Hauts de Hurle-Vent. (Wuthering Heights). Paris: 1925. V. 49
The Outcast Mother. London: 1860. V. 51
Wuthering Heights. New York: 1848. V. 47; 49; 51
Wuthering Heights. London: 1911. V. 52
Wuthering Heights. London: 1924. V. 48
Wuthering Heights. London: 1931. V. 50; 54
Wuthering Heights. New York: 1931. V. 47; 52; 54
Wuthering Heights. New York: 1944. V. 48
Wuthering Heights. Paris: 1947. V. 52; 54
Wuthering Heights. 1970. V. 54
Wuthering Heights. London: 1970. V. 52
Wuthering Heights. Oxford: 1976. V. 54

BRONTE PARSONAGE MUSEUM
Catalogue of the Bonnell Collection in the Bronte Parsonage Museum. Haworth: 1932. V. 50

BRONTE, PATRICK
Bronteana: His Collected Works and Life. London: 1898. V. 54
The Cottage in the Wood; or the Art of Becoming Rich and happy... Bradford: 1818. V. 47
The Cottage in the Woods, or the Art of Becoming Rich and Happy. London: 1818. V. 54
Cottage Poems... Halifax: 1811. V. 49

BRONTE, THE SISTERS
The Bronte Novels. London: 1890. V. 49
The Complete Works... 1923. V. 54
The Complete Works. London: 1931/33. V. 52
The Complete Works. Oxford/Boston: 1931/33. V. 54
The Complete Works. London: 1931/36. V. 52
The Complete Works. Oxford: 1931/36. V. 54
Life and Works of Charlotte Bronte and Her Sisters. London: 1872-78. V. 49
Life and Works of Charlotte Bronte and Her Sisters. London: 1882-85. V. 50
The Life and Works of Charlotte Bronte and Her Sisters. London: 1883-84. V. 50
Life and Works of Charlotte Bronte and Her Sisters. London: 1889-91. V. 50
The Life and Works of Charlotte Bronte and Her Sisters. London: 1893. V. 48
The Life and Works of Charlotte Bronte and Her Sisters. London: 1910. V. 51
The Life and Works of the Sisters Bronte. New York: 1900. V. 49
The Novels. London: 1888-96. V. 52
The Novels. New York: 1899. V. 54
Novels. Edinburgh: 1905. V. 53
The Novels. London: 1905. V. 48
The Novels. New York: 1905. V. 54
The Novels. Edinburgh: 1907. V. 52; 54
The Novels. Edinburgh: 1911. V. 51
Novels. Edinburgh: 1911 or 1924. V. 49
The Novels. London: 1915. V. 54
The Novels. London: 1922. V. 48; 49
The Novels. Edinburgh: 1924. V. 51; 52; 54
The Novels. London: 1924. V. 47
Novels. Oxford: 1931. V. 49; 50
The Novels. London: 1991. V. 52
Pocket Edition of the Life and Works of Charlotte Bronte...and Her Sisters, Emily and Anne Bronte. London: 1895?. V. 50
Poems. London: 1846/48. V. 49
Poems. New York: 1902. V. 54
Poems by Currer, Ellis and Acton Bell. London: 1846. V. 47; 48
Poems by Currer, Ellis and Acton Bell. London: 1846/48. V. 49; 51; 52
Poems by Currer, Ellis and Acton Bell. Philadelphia: 1848. V. 49
Uniform Edition of the Works of Currer Bell,...Together with the Works of Ellis and Action Bell. London: 1859-61. V. 50
The Works. London: 1878-82. V. 50
The Works. London: 1880/87. V. 52
The Works. London: 1893. V. 48; 53
The Works. London: 1893-96. V. 53
The Works. London: 1893/98. V. 52
The Works. London: 1898-1900. V. 54
Works. Edinburgh: 1924. V. 51
Works. London: 1949. V. 48
Wuthering Heights & Jane Eyre. New York: 1943. V. 52
Wuthering Heights and Agnes Grey. Leipzig: 1851. V. 50
Wuthering Heights and Agnes Grey. London: 1858. V. 50

THE BRONTES - Their Lives, Friendships and Correspondence. 1980. V. 54

BROOK, A. W.
Witch's Hollow or the New Babes in the Wood. London: 1920. V. 50

BROOK, BENJAMIN
Memoir of the Life and Writings of Thomas Cartwright. London: 1845. V. 49

BROOK, G.
Catalogue of the Madreporarian Corals in the British Museum. London: 1893-1928. V. 49

BROOK, H. M. BERNARD
Catalogue of the Madreporarian Corals in the British Museum. London: 1893-1928. V. 52

BROOK, HARRY ELLINGTON
Irrigation in Southern California: issued for the Use of Delegates to the International Irrigation Congress, Los Angeles, California, Oct. 10-15, 1893. Los Angeles: 1893. V. 54

BROOK, RICHARD
New Cyclopaedia of Botany and Complete Book of Herbs... 1853. V. 54
New Cyclopaedia of Botany and Complete Book of Herbs... Huddersfield: 1853. V. 51
New Cyclopaedia of Botany and Complete Book of Herbs... London: 1854. V. 54

BROOK, ROBERT
Elements of Style in Furniture and Woodwork. London: 1889. V. 50; 52
The Reading of M. Robert Brook, Serjeant of the Law, and Recorder of London, Upon the Stat. of Magna Charta. Chap. 16. London: 1641. V. 51

BROOKAW, IRVING
The Art of Skating, Its History and Development, with Practical Directions. London: 1910. V. 48

BROOKE, CHARLOTTE
Reliques of Irish Poetry... Dublin: 1789. V. 51

BROOKE Crutchley: a Printer's Christmas Books. Cambridge: 1974. V. 51; 53

BROOKE, EMMA FRANCES
The Heir without a Heritage: a Novel. London: 1887. V. 54

BROOKE, FRANCES
The History of Lady Julia Mandeville. London: 1763. V. 49; 51; 53; 54

BROOKE, FULKE GREVILLE, 1ST BARON
Caelica. Newtown: 1936. V. 48
Caelica. Newtown: 1936-37. V. 47
Caelica. Newtown: 1937. V. 49; 52; 54
Certaine Learned and Elegant Workes... London: 1633. V. 47; 50; 51
The Remains...Being Poems of Monarchy and Religion. London: 1670. V. 52; 54

BROOKE, GEOFFREY
The Way of a Man with a Horse. London: 1929. V. 47

BROOKE, HENRY
The Fool of Quality; or History of Henry Earl of Moreland. London: 1767-70. V. 51; 52; 54
The Fool of Quality, or the History of Henry Earl of Morland. London. V. 47
Juliet Grenville; or, the History of the Human Heart. London: 1774. V. 47
The Poetical Works. Dublin: 1792. V. 50
The Tryal of the Cause of the Roman Catholics; On a Special Commission Directed to Lord Chief Justice Reason, Lord Chief Baron Interest, and Mr. Justice Clemency... Dublin: 1761. V. 48

BROOKE, HENRY K.
Book of Murders Containing an Authentic Account of the Most Awful Tragedies That Have Been Committed in This Country. Philadelphia. V. 51

BROOKE, JAMES
The Duty and Advantage of Singing to the Lord. A Sermon Preach'd in the Cathedral Church of Worcester, at the Anniversary Meeting of the Choirs of Worcester, Gloucester and Hereford, Sept. 4, 1728. London: 1738?. V. 47

BROOKE, JAMES WILLIAMSON
The Democrats of Marylebone. London: 1839. V. 49

BROOKE, JOCELYN
The Crisis in Bulgaria or Ibsen to the Rescue. London: 1956. V. 52
December Spring - Poems. London: 1946. V. 50; 53
The Flower in Season: a Calendar of Wild Flowers. London: 1952. V. 53
The Military Orchids. London: 1948. V. 53
The Military Orchids. London: 1951. V. 50
A Mine of Serpents. London: 1949. V. 53
The Orchard Trilogy. London: 1948-50. V. 48
The Passing of a Hero. London: 1953. V. 53
The Scapegoat. London: 1948. V. 53
The Wild Orchids of Britain. London: 1950. V. 50; 53; 54

BROOKE, RALPH
A Catalogue and Succession of the Kings, Princes, Dukes, Marquesses, Earles and Viscounts of This Realme of England, Since the Norman Conquest to 1622. London: 1622. V. 47; 51

BROOKE, RICHARD
Liverpool As It Was During the Last Quarter of the Eighteenth Century 1775 to 1800. Liverpool: 1853. V. 48; 52

BROOKE, ROBERT
La Graunde Abridgement. London: 1573. V. 52
La Graunde Abridgement. London: 1576. V. 51

BROOKE, RUPERT
The Collected Poems. London: 1918. V. 47; 50; 51
Collected Poems. London: 1919. V. 48; 49
The Collected Poems of Rupert Brooke: With a Memoir. London: 1929. V. 48
Democracy and the Arts. London: 1946. V. 49
Four Poems: Drafts and Fair Copies in the Author's Hand. Ilkley: 1974. V. 49
Four Poems: The Fish, 1911; Grantcheter 1912; the Dead, 1914. The Soldiers, 1914. London: 1974. V. 48
John Webster and the Elizabethan Drama. London: 1916. V. 50; 51
The Letters. London: 1968. V. 53
Letters from America. London: 1916. V. 47; 49
Letters from Rupert Brooke to His Publisher 1911-1914. New York: 1975. V. 51
The Letters of Rupert Brooke. London: 1968. V. 50
Lithuania. 1915. V. 48; 49; 53
Nineteen Fourteen. London: 1915. V. 47; 49; 51; 52; 53; 54
The Old Vicarage Grantchester. London: 1916. V. 47; 49; 51
Poems. London: 1911. V. 51

BROOKE, STOPFORD
On Ten Plays of Shakespeare. (with) Ten More Plays of Shakespeare. London: 1914/13. V. 53

BROOKE, SUSAN W.
Stately Progress. A Tale of Ducal Profigacy and Providence. New York: 1980. V. 54

BROOKE, THOMAS
A Catalogue of the Manuscripts and Printed Books Collected by... London: 1891. V. 51

BROOKER, WILLIAM
Texas: an Epitome of Texas History. Columbus: 1897. V. 53

BROOKE-ROSE, CHRISTINE
A Grammar of Metaphor. London: 1958. V. 50

BROOKES, IVESON L.
A Discourse, Investigating the Doctrine of Washing the Saints Feet: Delivered at Monticello. Macon: 1830. V. 48

BROOKES, RICHARD
The Art of Angling. London: 1740. V. 47; 48; 53
The Art of Angling. London: 1770. V. 47
The Art of Angling. London: 1774. V. 49
The Art of Angling... London: 1790. V. 49
The Art of Angling. London: 1799. V. 47
The Art of Angling in Two Parts... London: 1801. V. 47
Brooke's General Gazetteer Improved: or, a New and Compendious Geographical Dictionary... Philadelphia: 1806. V. 50
The General Gazetteer; or Compendious Geographical Dictionary. London: 1809. V. 49
The General Gazetteer; or, Compendious Geographical Dictionary. London: 1815. V. 51
The General Practice of Physic... London: 1763. V. 48; 49; 50; 51; 52; 53; 54
The London General Gazetteer... London: 1837. V. 51

BROOKES, THOMAS
The Unsearchable Riches of Christ or Meat for Strong Men and Milk for Babes, Held Forth in 22 Sermons. London: 1657. V. 53

BROOKFIELD, ARTHUR MONTAGUE
The Apparition. Edinbrugh: 1884. V. 51
The Autobiography of Thomas Allen. Edinburgh & London: 1882. V. 49

BROOKLYN MUSEUM
Africa in Antiquity: The Arts of Ancient Nubria and the Sudan I-II. Brooklyn: 1978. V. 49; 51
Cleopatra's Egypt, Age of the Ptolemics. Brooklyn: 1988. V. 51
Coptic Textiles in the Brooklyn Museum. Brooklyn: 1971. V. 51
A Papyrus of the Late Middle Kingdom in the Brooklyn Museum. Brooklyn: 1972. V. 51

BROOKNER, ANITA
Family and Friends. London: 1985. V. 48
Hotel de Lac. London: 1984. V. 48; 51
Jacques-Louis David. London: 1980. V. 52
Providence. London: 1982. V. 51
A Start in Life. London: 1981. V. 54

BROOKS & HEDGER
Monthly Register of Estates for Sale, Likewise of Farms, Residences, and Manors, To Be Let. London: 1834. V. 53

BROOKS, BRYANT B.
Memoirs of Bryant B. Brooks: Cowboy, Trapper, Lumberman, Stockman, Oilman, Banker and Governor of Wyoming. Glendale: 1939. V. 50; 52; 53

BROOKS, CLEANTH
Modern Poetry and the Tradition. Chapel Hill: 1939. V. 52
Modern Poetry and the Tradition. London: 1948. V. 54
A Shaping Joy - Studies in the Writers' Craft. London: 1971. V. 54
Tragic Themes in Western Literature. New Haven: 1955. V. 50
Understanding Drama, Together with Understanding Drama - Eight Plays. New York: 1945. V. 47

BROOKS, E. W.
The Journal of a Forty-Niner. London: 1967. V. 47; 48; 50

BROOKS, ELISHA
A Pioneer Mother of California. San Francisco: 1922. V. 47; 54

BROOKS, ELIZABETH
Prominent Men of Texas. Akron: 1896. V. 49
Prominent Women of Texas. Akron: 1896. V. 48; 52; 53; 54

BROOKS, GEORGE R.
The Southwest Explorations of Jedidiah S. Smith, His Personal Account of the Journey to California 1826-27. Glendale: 1977. V. 49

BROOKS, GWENDOLYN
Annie Allen. New York: 1949. V. 47; 48; 49; 50
The Bean Eaters. New York: 1960. V. 53
Bronzeville Boys and Girls. New York: 1956. V. 53
For Illinois: a Sesquicentennial Poem. New York: 1968. V. 47; 51
In the Mecca. New York: 1968. V. 47; 51; 52; 54
In the Time of Detachment, in the Time of Cold. 1965. V. 47
Maud Martha. New York: 1953. V. 48; 54
Report from Part One. Detroit: 1972. V. 52
Selected Poems. New York: 1963. V. 49; 52
A Street in Bronzeville. New York: 1945. V. 49
Winnie. Chicago: 1988. V. 48

BROOKS, H. ALLEN
Prairie School Architecture, Studies from the Western Architect. Toronto: 1975. V. 50

BROOKS, H. C.
Compendiosa Bibliografia Di Edizioni Bodoniane. Italy: 1980. V. 50

BROOKS, HENRY
The Fool of Quality, or the History of Henry, Earl of Moreland. London. V. 48
Natal: a History and Description of the Colony: Including Its Natural Features, Productions, Industrial Condition and Prospects. London: 1876. V. 54

BROOKS, JEROME E.
Tobacco: Its History Illustrated by the Books, Manuscripts and Engravings in the Library of George Arents, Jr. Together with an Introductory Essay, a Glossary and Bibliographic Notes. New York: 1937-69. V. 49

BROOKS, JOHN
A Discourse Delivered Before the Humane Society of the Commonwealth of Massachusetts, 9th June, 1795. Boston: 1795. V. 52

BROOKS, JUANITA
John Doyle Lee. Glendale: 1961. V. 53
John Doyle Lee... Glendale: 1962. V. 53
The Mountain Meadows Massacre. Stanford: 1950. V. 51; 53; 54

BROOKS, S. H.
Designs for Cottage and Villa Architecture. London: 1839. V. 48; 52

BROOKS, SARA W.
Alamo Ranch, a Story of New Mexico. Cambridge: 1903. V. 50

BROOKS, SHIRLEY
The Gordian Knot. London: 1860. V. 49
Sooner or Later. London: 1868. V. 51

BROOKS, T.
The Sword of Shannara. 1977. V. 49; 52

BROOKS, THOMAS
A Cabinet of Choice Jewels, or, a Box of Precious Ointment. London: 1669. V. 50

BROOKS, ULYSSES R.
Butler and His Cavalry in the War of Secession 1861-65. Columbia: 1909. V. 49
Stories of the Confederacy. Columbia: 1912. V. 49

BROOKS, VAN WYCK
The Flowering of New England. Boston: 1941. V. 49

BROOKS, WALTER R.
Freddy the Magician. New York: 1947. V. 49

BROOKS, WILLIAM ALEXANDER
Treatise on the Improvement of the Navigation of Rivers; with a New Theory on the Cause of the Existence of Bars. London: 1841. V. 54

THE BROOM Drill. New York: 1882. V. 53

BROOM, R.
The Mammal-Like Reptiles of South Africa and the Origin of Mammals. London: 1932. V. 48

BROOME, MARY ANNE BARKER
Station Life in New Zealand. London: 1870. V. 47

BROOME, RALPH
The Letters of Simkin the Second, Poetic Recorder of all the Proceedings Upon the Trial of Warren Hastings, Esq. London: 1791. V. 51
Simkin Redivivus to Simon: a Satirical and Poetical Epistle, Describing Edmund Burke's Letter to a Nobel Lord in Defence of His Pension... London: 1796. V. 48

BROOME, WILLIAM
The Oak and the Dunghill. London: 1728. V. 49
Poems on Several Discoveries. London: 1727. V. 52
Poems On Several Occasions. London: 1750. V. 49; 54

BROPHY, JOHN
The Bitter End. New York: 1928. V. 51
Soldiers Songs and Slang, 1914-1918. London: 1930. V. 51
The Soldier's War. A Prose Anthology. London: 1929. V. 51

BROPHY, TRUMAN WILLIAM
Cleft Lip and Palate. Philadelphia: 1923. V. 54

BROSNAN, C. J.
History of the State of Idaho. New York: 1918. V. 54

BROSSAIS DU PERRAY
A Historical Remarks on the Castle of the Bastille. London: 1789. V. 53

BROSSES, CHARLES DE
Histoire des Navigations aux Terres Australes. Paris: 1756. V. 50

BROTHERHEAD, W.
Forty Years Among the Old Booksellers of Philadelphia With Bibliographical Remarks. Philadelphia: 1891. V. 49
General Fremont, and the Injustice Done Him by Politicians and Envious Military Men. Philadelphia: 1862. V. 48

THE BROTHERS a Novel, for Children. 1795. V. 54
THE BROTHERS a Novel, for Children. London: 1795. V. 49

BROTHERS, MARY HUDSON
A Pecos Pioneer. Albuquerque: 1943. V. 49; 51; 53

THE BROTHERS; or, Consequences. London: 1818. V. 47

BROTHERS, RICHARD
A Dissertation of the Existence, Nature and Extent of the Prophetic Powers in the Human Mind... London: 1794. V. 48; 53

BROUARDEL, PAUL
Death and Sudden Death. New York: 1897. V. 53

BROUE, PIERRE
The Revolution and Civil War in Spain. London: 1972. V. 49

BROUGH, ROBERT
Life of Sir John Falstaff. London: 1857. V. 51
The Life of Sir John Falstaff. London: 1858. V. 47; 49; 53
The Vacant Frame. 1983. V. 53

BROUGHAM, HENRY
General Theorems, Chiefly Porisms, in the Higher Geometry. V. 50
Lives of Men of Letters and Science Who Flourished in the Time of George III. London: 1845. V. 48
Present State of the Law. The Speech...in the House of Commons...On His Motion...to Issue a Commission for Inquiring Into the Defects. Philadelphia: 1828. V. 48

BROUGHAM, JOHN
Dombey and Son. New York: 1875. V. 49; 54
Dombey and Son. London: 1883?. V. 49

BROUGHAM & VAUX, HENRY PETER BROUGHAM, 1ST BARON
Albert Lunel. London: 1844/72. V. 54
Albert Lunel; or, The Chateau of Lanquedoc. London: 1844. V. 49
British Constitution. London: 1844. V. 52
Historical Sketches of Statesmen Who Flourished in the Time of George III. London: 1839. V. 49
Historical Sketches of Statesmen Who Flourished in the Time of George III. London: 1845. V. 47
An Inquiry into the Colonial Policy of the European Powers. Edinburgh: 1803. V. 51; 54
Installation Address (as Chancellor of the University of Edinburgh) Delivered in the 18th May. Edinburgh: 1860. V. 52; 54
A Letter on National Education, to the Duke of Bedford, K.G. from Lord Brougham. Edinburgh: 1839. V. 49
The Life and Times, Written by Himself. London: 1871. V. 51
Lives of Men of Letters and Science, Who Flourished in the Time of George III. London: 1845-47. V. 54
Lives of Men of Letters and Science, Who flourished in the Time of George III. London: 1845/46. V. 49; 50
Lives of Men of Letters and Statesmen Who Flourished in the Time of George III. London: 1839-43. V. 51
Speeches of Henry Lord Brougham, Upon Questions Relating to Public Rights, Duties, and Ineterests; with Historical Introductions. Philadelphia: 1841. V. 47
Speeches of Henry Lord Brougham, Upon Questions Relating to Public Rights, Duties and Interests... Edinburgh: 1838. V. 53
The Speech...In the House of Commons, on Tuesday, the 16th of June, 1812. Upon the Present State of Commerce and Manufacatures... London: 1812. V. 50

BROUGH-SMYTHE, R.
The Goldfields and Mineral Districts of Victoria. London: 1869. V. 47

BROUGHTON, A.
Enchiridion Botanicum... London: 1782. V. 53

BROUGHTON, BRIAN
Six Picturesque Views in North Wales, Engraved in Aquatint by Alken... London: 1801. V. 47; 49

BROUGHTON, EDWARD
State of Louisiana, Parish of Cordia. At a Polic Jury...Town of Vidalia...1st Day of May...1820. Vidalia: 1820. V. 48

BROUGHTON, JAMES
A Long Undressing: Collected Poems 1949-1969. New York: 1971. V. 47

BROUGHTON, JOHN
Remarks Upon the Bank of England, with Regard More Especially to Our Trade and Government. London: 1705. V. 54

BROUGHTON, RHODA
Belinda. London: 1883. V. 49; 51; 53
Cometh Up as a Flower. London: 1878. V. 47
Second Thoughts. London: 1880. V. 51

BROUGHTON, RICHARD
(Greek title, then..) Oratio ad Genevenses de Descensu ad Inferos, quid Locutio Velit. Mainz: 1601. V. 53

BROUGHTON, ROSA
Scylla or Charybdis?. London: 1895. V. 48; 49

BROUGHTON, THOMAS DUER
Selections from the Popular Poetry of the Hindoos. London: 1814. V. 54

BROUGHTON, WILLIAM ROBERT
A Voyage of Discovery to the North Pacific Ocean. London: 1804. V. 47
A Voyage of Discovery to the North Pacific...Performed In His Majesty's Sloop Providence, and Her Tender, in the Years 1795, 1796, 1797, 1798. Amsterdam: 1967. V. 53

BROUMAS, OLGA
Soie Sauvage. Port Townsend: 1979. V. 54

BROUN, HEYWOOD
Seeing Things at Night. New York: 1921. V. 49; 51

BROUSSAIS, F. J. V.
History of Chronic Phlegmasiae, or Inflammations, Founded on Clinical Experience and Pathological Anatomy. Philadelphia: 1831. V. 53

BROWDER, EARL
The People's Front in the United States. London: 1938. V. 49

BROWN, AARON V.
Oregon Territory. Washington: 1844. V. 48
Texas and Oregon. Letter and Speeches, in Reply to J. Q. Adams, on the Annexation of Texas, and on the Bill for the Organization of a Territorial Government Over Oregon. Washington: 1845. V. 50

BROWN, ABBIE FARWELL
The Lonesomest Doll. Boston & New York: 1928. V. 49; 53

BROWN, ABIEL
Genealogical History, with Short Sketches and Family Records of the Early Settlers of West Simsbury, No Canton, Connecticut. Hartford: 1856. V. 51

BROWN, ALEXANDER
The First Republic in America. Boston & New York: 1898. V. 48; 50
The Genesis of the United States. Boston and New York: 1890. V. 52

BROWN, ALFRED
Old Masterpieces in Surgery. Omaha: 1928. V. 48; 52; 53; 54

BROWN, ALICE
Robert Louis Stevenson a Study by A. B. With a Prelude and A Postlude by L.I.G. Boston: 1895. V. 47; 49

BROWN, ALONZO LEIGHTON
History of the Fourth Regiment of Minnesota Infantry Volunteers During the Great Rebellion 1861-1865. St. Paul: 1892. V. 47

BROWN, ANDREW, OF GLASGOW
History of Glasgow; and of Paisley, Greenock, and Port-Glasgow...Population, Commerce, Manufacture, Arts and Agriculture. Glasgow: 1795. V. 53

BROWN, B. GRATZ
Speech of Hon. B. Gratz Brown, of St. Louis, on the Subject of Gradual Emancipation in Missouri. Jefferson City: 1857. V. 48

BROWN, BASIL
Astronomical Atlases, Maps and Charts: an Historical and General Guide. London: 1932. V. 50

BROWN, BEATRICE BRADSHAW
A Paris Pair. Their Day's Doings. New York: 1923. V. 50

BROWN, BENJAMIN
Testimonies for the Truth: a Record of Manifestations of the Power of God... Liverpool: 1853. V. 47; 50; 53

BROWN, BOB
Readies for Bob Brown's Machine. Cagnes-sur-Mer: 1931. V. 50
Words. Paris: 1931. V. 49

BROWN, C. BARRINGTON
Canoe and Camp Life in British Guiana. London: 1876. V. 49
Canoe and Camp Life in British Guiana... London: 1877. V. 49

BROWN, C. C.
Samuel Morris, a Spirit Filled Life. Kingswood: 1900. V. 52

BROWN, CARLETON
A Register of Middle English Religious and Didactic Verse. Oxford: 1916. V. 50
A Register of Middle English Religious and Didactic Verse. Oxford: 1916-20. V. 48

BROWN, CATHERINE HAYES
Letters to Mary. New York: 1940. V. 47; 48

BROWN, CHARLES
Descriptive Pamphlet of Marysville, Kansas, the Commercial and Manufacturing Metropolis of the Great Blue Valley. Marysville: 1887. V. 52

BROWN, CHARLES BROCKDEN
An Address to the Government of the United States, On the Cession of Louisiana to the French; and the Late Breach of Treaty by the Spaniards... Philadlephia: 1803. V. 48
Arthur Mervyn. Philadelphia: 1799. V. 54
Arthur Mervyn. London: 1803. V. 49
Carwin the Biloquist and Other American Tales and Pieces. London: 1822. V. 54
Wieland, or the Transformation, an American Tale. New York printed: 1811. V. 54

BROWN, CHRISTY
My Left Foot. London: 1954. V. 53

BROWN, CLAUDE
Manchild in the Promised Land. New York: 1965. V. 49; 53

BROWN, COLIN RAE
The Beggar's Benison; or, a Hero Without a Name, But with an Aim. London: 1866. V. 54

BROWN, CORNELIUS
A History of Nottinghamshire. London: 1891. V. 54

BROWN, D. S.
America in 48 Hours, India and Back in a Fortnight, Being Suggestions for Certain Improvements in the Construction of Steam Vessels. London: 1852. V. 51; 52

BROWN, DAVID
The Planter: or, Thirteen Years in the South. Philadelphia: 1853. V. 49

BROWN, DEE
Bury My Heart at Wounded Knee. New York: 1970. V. 50; 51; 53

BROWN, DON
Fragments. Champaign: 1971. V. 49

BROWN, E. H.
Trinity River Canalization: the Story of the Navigation of the Trinity River - Past, Present and Future. N.P: 1930. V. 47

BROWN, EDMUND RANDOLPH
The Twenty-Seventh Indiana Volunteer Infantry in the War of the Rebellion, 1861 to 1865, First Division, 12th and 20th Corps, a History of its Recruiting, Organization, Camp Life, Marches and Battles, Together with a Roster of the Men Composing It... Monticello: 1899. V. 54

BROWN, EDWARD
A Brief Account of Some Travels in Divers Parts of Europe, Viz. Hungaria, Austria, Servia, Styria, Bulgaria, Carinthia... London: 1685. V. 50
A Brief Account of Some Travels in Divers Parts of Europe, Viz. Hungaria, Servia, Bulgaria, Macedonia, Thessaly, Austria, Styria, Carinthia, Carniola and Friuli. London: 1687. V. 52

BROWN, ELIZA
Mamma's Lessons for Her Little Boys and Girls. London: 1835. V. 51

BROWN, ELIZABETH CULLEN
Passion and Reason; or, the Modern Quintilian Brothers. London: 1831. V. 50

BROWN, ERASTUS
The Trial of Cain, the First Murderer, in Poetry, by Rule of Court... 1834. V. 52

BROWN, ERNEST W.
An Introductory Treatise on the Lunar Theory. 1896. V. 48

BROWN, EVERETT SOMERVILLE
The Constitutional History of the Louisiana Purchase, 1803-1812. Berkeley: 1920. V. 51

BROWN, FORD MADOX
Catalogue of an Exhibition of Collected Works by Ford Madox Brown. London: 1909. V. 51

BROWN, FRANCIS F.
Volunteer Grain. Chicago: 1895. V. 47; 49

BROWN, FRANK LONDON
The Myth Maker. Chicago: 1969. V. 53

BROWN, FRED R.
History of the Ninth U.s. Infantry 1799-1909. Chicago: 1909. V. 50

BROWN, FREDERICK, MRS.
Little Margaret's Ride or, the Wonderful Rocking Horse. London: 1880. V. 48

BROWN, FREDRIC
And the Gods Laughed. West Bloomfield: 1987. V. 47; 51; 52; 54
Angels and Spaceships. New York: 1954. V. 51; 52
Before She Kills. San Diego: 1984. V. 52
The Bloody Moonlight. New York: 1949. V. 52
Brother Monster. Miami Beach: 1987. V. 52; 54
Carnival of Crime. 1975. V. 47; 51
The Case of the Dancing Sandwiches. New York: 1950. V. 52
The Case of the Dancing Sandwiches. 1985. V. 52
Compliments of a Fiend. New York: 1950. V. 52
The Dead Ringer. New York: 1948. V. 52
Death Has Many Doors. New York: 1951. V. 52
The Deep End. New York: 1952. V. 52
The Fabulous Clipjoint. New York: 1947. V. 52
The Far Cry. New York: 1951. V. 52
The Five Day Nightmare. New York: 1962. V. 52
The Freak Show Murders. Belen: 1985. V. 52
Here Comes a Candle. New York: 1950. V. 48; 52; 54
His Name Was Death. New York: 1954. V. 52
Homicide Sanitarium. San Antonio: 1984. V. 52
Knock Three-One-Two. London: 1959. V. 52
Knock, Three-One-Two. New York: 1959. V. 52
The Late Lamented. New York: 1959. V. 52
The Lenient Beast. New York: 1956. V. 52
The Lights in the Sky are Stars. New York: 1953. V. 52
Madman's Holiday. 1985. V. 52
Martians, Go Home. New York: 1955. V. 52

BROWN, FREDRIC continued
Mrs. Murphy's Underpants. New York: 1963. V. 52
Mitkey Astromouse. 1970. V. 47
Mostly Murder. New York: 1953. V. 48; 52
The Murderers. New York: 1961. V. 48; 52
Night of the Jabberwock. New York: 1950. V. 52
The Office. New York: 1958. V. 47; 52
The Office. New York: 1961. V. 48
Paradox Lost and Twelve Other Great Science Fiction Stories. New York: 1973. V. 52
Pardon My Ghoulish Laughter. 1986. V. 52
Project Jupiter. London: 1954. V. 52
Red is the Hue of Hell. Miami Beach: 1986. V. 48; 52
Rogue in Space. New York: 1957. V. 52
Science Fiction Carnival. Chicago: 1953. V. 52
The Screaming Mimi. New York: 1949. V. 49; 52; 53; 54
Sex Life on the Planet Mars. Miami Beach: 1986. V. 52
The Shaggy Dog and Other Murders. New York: 1963. V. 52
Space on My Hands. Chicago: 1951. V. 47; 49; 51; 52; 54
Thirty Corpses Every Thursday. Belen: 1986. V. 52
We All Killed Grandma. New York: 1952. V. 52
The Wench is Dead. New York: 1955. V. 52
What Mad Universe. New York: 1949. V. 52
What Mad Universe. 1951. V. 51

BROWN, G. P.
Drainage Channel and Waterway: a History of the Effort to Secure...The Disposal of the Sewage of the City of Chicago. Chicago: 1894. V. 54

BROWN, GEORGE
Arithmetica Infinita or the Accurate Accomptant's Best Companion Contriv'd and Calculated by the Reverend George Browne A.M.... Edinburgh: 1718. V. 50
Melanesians and Polynesians. London: 1910. V. 50
The New and Complete English Letter-Writer; Or, Whole Art of General Correspondence... London: 177-?. V. 49
South Durham and Lancashire Union, and Eden Valley Railway Companies. 1863. V. 54

BROWN, GEORGE MAC KAY
In the Margins of Shakespeare. London: 1991. V. 51; 52; 53
Stone. Verona: 1987. V. 47; 48

BROWN, GEORGE R.
Reminiscences of Senator William M. Stewart of Nevada. New York: 1908. V. 49

BROWN, GEORGE WASHINGTON
Old Times in Oildom. Youngsville: 1909. V. 54
Old Times in Oildom. Oil City: 1912. V. 54

BROWN, GEORGIANA
Water Babies Circus and Other Stories. Boston: 1940. V. 53

BROWN, GLENN
History of the United States Capitol. Washington: 1900/03. V. 48

BROWN, HENRY ROWLAND
A Virgin Widow. London: 1886. V. 54

BROWN, HORATIO F.
The Venetian Printing Press. New York: 1891. V. 51

BROWN, HUGH STOWELL
Lectures to Working Men. London: 1870. V. 50

BROWN, IRVING
Ballads of a Book Worm. East Auroa: 1899. V. 48

BROWN, ISAAC V.
Memoirs of the Rev. Robert Finley, D.D. Late Pastor of the Presbyterian Congregation of Basking Ridge New-Jersey and President of Franklin College, Located at Athens... Georgia. New Brunswick: 1819. V. 51

BROWN, J. A.
The Family Guide to Health, Containing a Description of the Botanic Thomsonian System of Medicine. Providence: 1837. V. 50

BROWN, J. CABELL
Calabazas, or Amusing Recollections of an Arizona "City". San Francisco: 1892. V. 53

BROWN, J. GUTHRIE
Hydro-Electric Engineering Practice. London: 1958. V. 53

BROWN, J. H.
Spectropia; or, Surprising Spectral Illusions. London: 1864. V. 48; 51
Spectropia; or, Surprising Spectral Illusions... London: 1865. V. 48

BROWN, J. L.
The Story of Kings County California. Berkeley: 1941. V. 54

BROWN, J. M.
Astyanax. 1907. V. 51

BROWN, J. MACMILLAN
Peoples and problems of the Pacific. New York: 1927. V. 48

BROWN, J. ROSS
Report Upon the Mineral Resources of the State and Territories West of the Rocky Mountains. Washington: 1860. V. 50

BROWN, J. WOOD
An Enquiry into the Life and Legend of Michael Scot. Edidnburgh: 1897. V. 50; 52; 54

BROWN, JAMES
The Forester. A Practical Treatise on the Planting, Rearing and General Management of Forest Trees. Edinburgh: 1851. V. 47
The History of Sanquhar. Dumfries: 1891. V. 54
The Injustice of American Slavery. A Sermon, Preached in Keokuk, Iowa July 13, 1856. Keokuk: 1856. V. 51
The New Deeside Guide. Aberdeen: 1866. V. 48

BROWN, JAMES B.
Journal of a Journey Across the Plains in 1859. San Francisco: 1870. V. 48
Views of Canada and the Colonists Embracing the Experience of an Eight Years' Residence. Edinburgh: 1851. V. 54

BROWN, JAMES BALDWIN
Memoirs of the Public and Private Life of John Howard the Philanthropist. London: 1818. V. 52; 54
Memoirs of the Public and Private Life of John Howard, the Philanthropist. London: 1823. V. 51

BROWN, JAMES H.
Catalogue of the Extensive Dramatic Collection of the Late James H. Brown, Esq. of Malden, Mass. Boston: 1898. V. 51

BROWN, JAMES S.
California Gold an Authentic History of the First Find. Oakland: 1894. V. 48; 50
Life of a Pioneer Being the Autobiography of... Salt Lake City: 1900. V. 47; 50; 54

BROWN, JANE
Fulbrook: The Sketchbook, Letters, Specification of Works and Accounts for a House by Edward Lutyens 1896-1899. London: 1989. V. 50
Fulbrook: The Sketchbook, Letters, Specification of Works and Accounts for a House by Edward Luytens 1896-1899. 1989. V. 47

BROWN, JESSE
The Black Hills Trails. A History of the Struggles of the Pioneers in the Winning of the Black Hills. Rapid City: 1924. V. 49; 53; 54

BROWN, JOHN
Address of John Brown to the Virginia Court, Nov. 2, 1859, on Receiving the Sentence of Death, For His Heroic Attempt At Harper's Ferry, to Give Deliverance to the Captives and to Let the Oppressed Go Free. Boston: 1859. V. 47
The Elements of Medicine: or, a Translation of the Elementa Medicinae Brunonis. Philadelphia: 1790. V. 50
The Elements of Medicine; or a Translation of the Elementa Medicinae Brunonis. Philadelphia: 1795. V. 48
An Essay on Satire: Occasion'd by the Death of Mr. Pope. London: 1745. V. 47
Essays on the Characteristics. London: 1751. V. 49; 51; 52
An Estimate of the Manners and Principles of the Times. London: 1757. V. 47; 49
An Estimate of the Manners and Principles of the Times. (with) An Explanatory Defence of the Estmate. London: 1757/58/58. V. 49
The History of the Rise and Progress of Poetry, Through Its Several Species. Newcastle: 1764. V. 52
Honour. London: 1743. V. 47; 54
Horae Subsecivae. Edinburgh: 1858-61-82. V. 47
Horae Subsecivae. London: 1897. V. 53; 54
The North-west Passage and the Plans for the Search for Sir John Franklin. London: 1860. V. 47; 49
Notes on an Excursion into the Highlands of Scotland, in Autumn 1818. Edinburgh: 1819. V. 47
A Short Catechism for Young Children. Morris-Town: 1818. V. 51
Thoughts on Civil Liberty, on Licentiousness and Faction. Newcastle-Upon-Tyne: 1765. V. 52
The Works... London: 1804. V. 53

BROWN, JOHN, & CO., LTD.
Atlas Works, Sheffield: Shipyard and Engineering Works, Clydebank... London: 1903. V. 53

BROWN, JOHN C.
Argument of John C. Brown, Vice President Texas and Pacific Railway Company, Before House Committee on Pacific Railroads, Jan. 25, 1878, in Behalf of the Texas and Pacific Railway Co. Washington City: 1878. V. 49
A Letter from Jno. C. Brown, Vice-President. To the People of the south. Pulaski: 1878. V. 49

BROWN, JOHN CARTER
Bibliotheca Americana, a Catalogue of Books Relating to North and South America in the Library of John Carter Brown of Providence, R.I. Part I - 1482 to 1601; Part II 1600 to 1700. Providence: 1875, 1882. V. 47

BROWN, JOHN E.
Memoirs of a Forty-Niner. New Haven: 1907. V. 47

BROWN, JOHN HENRY
History of Dallas County Texas from 1837 to 1887. Dallas: 1887. V. 50; 54
History of Texas 1685-1892. St. Louis: 1892. V. 47; 48; 49; 52
History of Texas, 1685-1892. St. Louis: 1892-93. V. 53
Indian Wars and Pioneers of Texas. Austin: 1896. V. 47; 48; 49; 50; 52; 53
Reminiscences and Incidents, of "The Early Days" of San Francisco (1845-50). San Francisco: 1933. V. 47; 53; 54

BROWN, JOHN P.
Old Frontiers to Story of the Cherokee Indians from Earliest Times to the Date of their Removal to the West in 1838. Kingsport: 1938. V. 54

BROWN, JOHN WILLIAM
The Life of Leonardo Da Vinci... London: 1828. V. 48

BROWN, JOSEPH EMERSON
Message of His Excellency Joseph E. Brown to the Extra Session of the Legislature, Convened March 10th, 1864. Milledgeville: 1864. V. 49

BROWN, L.
Eagles, Hawks and Falcons of the World. London: 1968. V. 50; 51; 54
Eagles, Hawks and Falcons of the World. New York: 1968. V. 54

BROWN, L. H.
Birds of Africa. London: 1982-88. V. 49

BROWN, LARRY
Dirty Work. Chapel Hill: 1989. V. 51; 53
Facing the Music. Chapel Hill: 1988. V. 49; 50; 51; 52; 53; 54
Joe. Chapel Hill: 1991. V. 51

BROWN, LEONARD
Poems of the Prairies. Des Moines: 1865. V. 49; 52

BROWN, LLOYD A.
Revolutionary War: Journals of Henry Dearborn, 1775-1783. Chicago: 1939. V. 47

BROWN, LOUISE NORTON
Block Printing and Book Illustration in Japan. London: 1924. V. 47; 49; 50

BROWN, MABEL
Neuropsychiatry and the War. A Bibliography with Abstracts. New York: 1918. V. 53

BROWN, MALCOLM
Seven Stranded Coal Towns: a Study of an American Depressed Area. Washington: 1941. V. 54

BROWN, MARCIA
Felice. New York: 1958. V. 52

BROWN, MARGARET WISE
Baby Animals. New York: 1941. V. 52; 53
The Noisy Bird Book. New York: 1943. V. 53

BROWN, MARION
San Francisco Old and New. San Francisco: 1939. V. 47

BROWN, MONTY
Hunter Away. The Life and Times of Arthur Henry Neumann. 1850-1907. V. 52

BROWN, OLIVER MADOX
The Dwale Bluth, Hebditch's Legacy and Other Literary Remains. London: 1876. V. 47; 49; 52; 54
Gabriel Denver. London: 1873. V. 49

BROWN, P. CLEMENT
Art in Dress. New York: 1922. V. 53

BROWN, P. HUME
History of Scotland, to the Present Time. 1911. V. 49
John Knox a Biography. London: 1895. V. 54
Our Journall into Scotland anno domini 1629, 5th of November... Edinburgh: 1894. V. 52; 54

BROWN, PAUL
Aintree, Grand Nationale -- Past and Present. New York: 1930. V. 47; 49; 53
Crazy Quilt. New York: 1934. V. 50
Hits and Misses (on Polo). New York: 1935. V. 49; 54
Piper's Pony. The Story of Patchwork. New York: 1935. V. 49
Spills and Thrills. New York: 1933. V. 47
Three Rings, a Circus Book. New York: 1938. V. 50; 52
Ups and Downs. New York: 1936. V. 54

BROWN, PHILIP F.
Reminiscences of the War of 1861-1865. Richmond: 1917. V. 50

BROWN, R.
Chloris Melvilliana. London: 1823. V. 49
Prodromus Florae Novae Hollandiae et Insulae Van-Diemen Exhibens Characteres Plantarum Quas Annis 1802-1805... Nuremberg: 1827. V. 48; 50

BROWN, R. ALLEN
The History of the King's Works. London: 1963. V. 49

BROWN, RICHARD
Domestic Architecture: Containing a History of the Science, and the Principles of Designing Public Edifices, Private Dwelling-Houses, Country Mansions, and Suburban Villas. London: 1842. V. 48
The London Bookshop. Parts I and II. London: 1971/77. V. 52
The Principles of Practical Perspective; or Scenographic Projection. London: 1815. V. 47; 53
The Rudiments of Drawing Cabinet and Upholstery Furniture... London: 1820. V. 52

BROWN, RICHARD BLAKE
The Blank Cheque - a Novel. London: 1934. V. 48

BROWN, RITA MAE
The Hand That Cradles the Rock. New York: 1971. V. 47; 51
Songs to a Handsome Woman. Baltimore: 1973. V. 53

BROWN, ROBERT
The Book of the Landed Estate. Edinburgh: 1869. V. 52
Miscellaneous Botanical Works. London: 1866-68. V. 47; 48
Notes on the Earlier History of Barton-on-Humber. London: 1908. V. 51
Poems, Principally on Sacred Subjects. London: 1826. V. 54

BROWN, ROBERT CARLTON
The Remarkable Adventures of Christopher Poe. Chicago: 1913. V. 47; 48; 51

BROWN, ROBERT E.
The Book of the Landed Estate Containing Directions for the Management and Development of the Resources of Landed Property. London: 1869. V. 47

BROWN, ROBERT NEAL RUDMOSE
A Naturalist at the Poles. London: 1923. V. 50; 52; 53

BROWN, ROSE
Amazing Amazons. London: 1943. V. 51

BROWN, SAM
The Cowboy Po 8, May Day Dreams, Passions, Flowers, Poetic Flights and Prosy Thoughts. Denver: 1890. V. 49

BROWN, SAMUEL R.
Views of the Campaigns of the North-Western Army, &c. Burlington: 1814. V. 51; 54
The Western Gazetteer; or Emigrant's Directory, Containing a Geographical Description of the Western States and Territories. Auburn: 1817. V. 47; 54

BROWN, SOLYMAN
A Comparative View of the Systems of Pestalozzi and Lancaster: in an Address Delivered Before the Society of Teachers of the City of New York. New York: 1825. V. 54
Dentologia: a Poem on the Diseases of the Teeth. New York: 1833. V. 51
An Essay on American Poetry, With Several Miscellaneous Pieces on a Variety of Subjects... New Haven: 1818. V. 47

BROWN, STERLING
The Collected Poems of Sterling Brown. New York: 1980. V. 48; 54
The Last Ride of Wild Bill and Eleven Narrative Poems. Detroit: 1975. V. 51

BROWN, STEWARDSON
Alpine Flora of the Canadian Rocky Mountains. New York: 1907. V. 47

BROWN, SUSAN ANNA
Home Topics: a Book of Practical Papers on House and hOme Matters. New York: 1881. V. 52

BROWN, T. ALLSTON
History of the American Stage. New York: 1870. V. 49

BROWN, T. H.
A History of the English Turf, 1904 to 1930. London: 1931. V. 47; 49

BROWN, T. JULIAN
The Stonyhurst Gospel of Saint John. Oxford: 1969. V. 52; 54

BROWN, THOMAS
An Account of the People Called Shakers: their Faith, Doctrines and Practice, Exemplified in the Life, Conversations and Experience of the author During the Time He Belonged to the Society. Troy: 1812. V. 50
Amusements Serious and Comical, Calculated for the Meridian of London. London: 1700. V. 47
Amusements Serious and Comical, Calculated for the Meridian of London. London: 1702. V. 52
The Book of Butterflies, Sphinxes and Moths. London: 1832. V. 49; 50; 53
The Bower of Spring, With Other Poems. Edinburgh: 1817. V. 54
Brighton; or, the Steyne. London: 1818. V. 51; 52
The Conchologist's Text-Book... Glasgow: 1833. V. 48
The Conchologist's Text-Book. Glasgow: 1835. V. 51
The Conchologist's Text-Book. Glasgow: 1836. V. 48
The Elements of Chonchology; or Natural History of Shells... London: 1816. V. 48; 49; 54
The Englishman in Paris: a Satirical Novel. London: 1819. V. 51
Illustrations of the Fossil Conchology of Great Britain and Ireland. London: 1849. V. 51
Illustrations of the Land and Fresh Water Conchology of Great Britain and Ireland with Figures and Descriptions and Localities of All the Species. London: 1845. V. 49
Illustrations of the Recent Conchology of Great Britain and Ireland. London: 1844. V. 51
Inquiry Into the Relation of Cause and Effect. Edinburgh: 1818. V. 49
The Late Converts Exposed; or the Reasons of Mr. Brays's. London: 1690. V. 52
Lectures on the Philosophy of the Human Mind. Edinburgh: 1820. V. 53
Legacy for the Ladies. London: 1705. V. 47
Letters from the Dead to the Living... London: 1702. V. 47; 49; 50
Memoirs Relating to the Late Famous Mr. Tho. Brown. London: 1704. V. 50
Miscellanea Aulica: or, a Collection of State-Treatises. London: 1702. V. 51; 54
Observations on the Zoonomia of Erasmus Darwin, M.D. Edinburgh: 1798. V. 53; 54
On Dreams. London. V. 52
Popular Natural History, or the Characteristics of Animals Portrayed in a Series of Illustrative Anecdotes. London, Dublin, & Edinburgh: 1848. V. 54
The Reasons of Mr. Joseph Hains the Player's Conversion and Re-Conversion. London: 1690. V. 52
The Reminiscences of an old Traveller Throughout Different Parts of Europe. Edinburgh: 1840. V. 52
The Taxidermist's Manual; or the Art of Collecting, Preparing and Preserving Objects of Natural History. London: 1881. V. 48; 50
The Weesils. London: 1691. V. 53
The Works of Mr. Thomas Brown, Serious and Comical, in Prose and Verse. London: 1730. V. 52
The Works of Mr. Thomas Brown, Serious and Comical, In Prose and Verse. London: 1760. V. 53

BROWN, TOM, PSEUD.
News From the Dead, in a Letter from Tom Brown the Poet. London: 1716. V. 48

BROWN UNIVERSITY
Bibliotheca Americana. Catalogue of the John Carter Brown Library in Brown University. New York: 1919-31. V. 53

BROWN, W.
The Natural History of the Salmon, as Ascertained by the Recent Experiments in the Artificial Spawning and Hatching of the Ova and Rearing of the Fry... Glasgow: 1862. V. 50
Privilegia Parlaimentaria Senatus Consensu Sublata. Being Remarks Upon the Acts of Parliament...For Preventing any Inconveniences That May Happen by Privilege of Parliament. London: 1704. V. 52

BROWN, W. LLEWELLYN
The Etruscan Lion. Oxford: 1960. V. 50

BROWN, W. M.
The Queen's Bush: A Tale of the Early Days of Bruce County. London: 1932. V. 50

BROWN, W. NORMAN
A Descriptive and Illustrated Catalogue of Miniature Paintings of the Jaina Kalpasutra as Executed in the Early Western Indian Styles. Washington: 1934. V. 49

BROWN, WILLIAM
Antiquities of the Jews. Philadelphia: 1823. V. 53
Documents and Proceedings Connected with the Donation of a Free Public Library and Museum to the Town of Liverpool. Liverpool: 1858. V. 53
The History of the Propagation of Christianity Among the Heathen Since the Reformation. New York: 1816. V. 47

BROWN, WILLIAM F.
National Field Trial Champions. An Authentic and Detailed History of the National Field Trial Championship Association Since Its Inception in 1896. Harrisburg: 1955. V. 47
Retreiver Gun Dogs. West Hartford: 1945. V. 47

BROWN, WILLIAM H.
The History of the First Locomotives in America. New York: 1871. V. 48
Portrait Gallery of Distinguished American Citizens. New York: 1931. V. 51

BROWN, WILLIAM HARVEY
On the South African Frontier. The Adventures and Observations of an American in Mashonaland and Matabeleland. New York: 1899. V. 47; 51; 54

BROWN, WILLIAM LAWRENCE
An Essay on the Natural Equality of Men. Philadelphia: 1793. V. 52

BROWN, WILLIAM ROBINSON
The Horse of the Desert. New York: 1929. V. 47; 49; 54
The Horse of the Desert. 1936. V. 48

BROWN, WILLIAM WELLS
A Lecture Delivered Before the Female Anti-Slavery Society of Salem, at Lyceum Hall, Nov. 14, 1847. Boston: 1847. V. 47
Narrative of...a Fugitive Slave. Boston: 1847. V. 53
The Negro in the American Rebellion, His Heroism and His Fidelity. Boston: 1867. V. 54

BROWNBILL, J.
A Calendar of that Part of the Collection of Deeds and Paper of the Moore Family of Bankhall, Co. Lanc. Now in the Liverpool Public Library. London: 1913. V. 53

BROWNE, ARTHUR
Miscellaneous Sketches: or, Hints of Essays. London: 1798. V. 50

BROWNE, B.
The Conquest of Mount McKinley. 1956. V. 53
The Conquest of Mount McKinley. London: 1956. V. 52

BROWNE, CHARLES FARRAR
Artemus Ward (his Travels) Among the Mormons. London: 1865. V. 49
The Complete Works. London: 1871. V. 49

BROWNE, D. J.
The Field Book of Manures; or, the American Muck Book... New York: 1855. V. 50; 52

BROWNE, EDMOND CHARLES
The Coming of the great White Queen, a Narrative of the Acquisition of Burma. London: 1888. V. 47

BROWNE, EDWARD
A Brief Account of some Travels in Divers Parts of Europe. London: 1685. V. 52

BROWNE, EDWARD GRANVILLE
A Literary History of Persia. Cambridge: 1929-30. V. 53
A Year Amongst the Persians. 1926. V. 50

BROWNE, F. F.
Volunteer Grain. 1895. V. 50

BROWNE, FELICIA
Drawings by Felicia Browne. Killed in Action with the Spanish Government Militia August 29th 1936. London: 1936. V. 49

BROWNE, FELICIA DOROTHEA
Poems. Liverpool: 1808. V. 47

BROWNE, FRANCIS F.
Bugle-Echoes: a Collection of Poems of the Civil War...Northern and Southern... New York: 1886. V. 48

BROWNE, G. F.
Ice-Caves of France and Switzerland... London: 1865. V. 50

BROWNE, G. ST. J. O.
The Vanishing Tribes of Kenya. Philadelphia: 1925. V. 54

BROWNE, G. WALDO
Japan: the People and the Place. Boston: 1904. V. 49; 53; 54

BROWNE, GEORGE
The History of the British and Foreign Bible Society, From Its Institution in 1804, to the Close of Its Jubilee in 1854. London: 1859. V. 48

BROWNE, HABLOT KNIGHT
Dombey and Son. London: 1848. V. 49
Home Pictures, Sixteen Domestic Scenes of Childhood. London: 1851. V. 50
Phiz and Dickens As They Appeared to Edgar Browne. London: 1913. V. 49

BROWNE, HAROLD
The Taste of Ashes. New York: 1957. V. 49

BROWNE, HOWARD
Warrior Of the Dawn: the Adventures of Tharn. Chicago: 1940. V. 49

BROWNE, ISAAC HAWKINS
Poems on Various Subjects, Latin and English. London: 1768. V. 47; 48; 49

BROWNE, JAMES
The History of Scotland, its Highlands, Regiments and Clans. Edinburgh: 1909. V. 52
The History of Scotland, Its Highlands, Regiments and Clans. London: 1913. V. 50
A History of the Highlands and of the Highland Clans. Glasgow: 1838. V. 50; 51; 53
A History of the Highlands, and of the Highland Clans... London: 1845. V. 50; 52
A History of the Highlands and of the Highland Clans. Edinburgh: 1859. V. 52

BROWNE, JEFFERSON BEALE
Key West the Old and the New. St. Augustine: 1912. V. 50

BROWNE, JOHN
History of Congregationalism and Memorials of the Churches in Norfolk and Suffolk. London: 1878. V. 47
Myographia Nova. London: 1684. V. 53
Myographia Nova. Amsterdam: 1694. V. 48; 49; 53
Myographia Nova. 1970. V. 48
Myographia Nova. London: 1980. V. 49
Poetical Translations from Various Authors. London: 1786. V. 48; 51; 54

BROWNE, JOHN HUTTON BALFOUR
The Medical Jurisprudence of Insanity. San Francisco: 1880. V. 48; 52

BROWNE, JOHN ROSS
Adventures in Apache Country: a Tour through Arizona & Sonora, with Notes on the Silver Regions of Nevada. New York: 1869. V. 47; 51; 54
Crusoe's Island - A Rambler in the Wilderness of Alexander Selkirk with Sketches of Adventures in California and Washoe. New York: 1864. V. 48; 49; 54
Crusoe's Island: a Ramble in the Footsteps of Alexander Selkirk. New York: 1867. V. 47; 51; 54
Etchings of a Whaling Cruise, with Notes of a Sojourn on the Island of Zanzibar. New York: 1846. V. 47; 48; 51
The Indians of California. San Francisco: 1944. V. 54
Letter from the Sec. of the Treasury Transmitting Report Upon the Mineral Resources West of the States and Territories West of the Rocky Mountains. Washington: 1867. V. 52; 53
Report Of the Debates in the Convention of California, on the Formation of the State Constitution. Washington: 1850. V. 49; 53
Report on the Late Indian War in Oregon and Washington. Washington: 1848. V. 51

BROWNE, JOSEPH
The Circus; or, British Olympicks. London: 1709. V. 47

BROWNE, LEWIS
The Graphic Bible: From Genesis to Revelation in animated Maps and Charts. New York: 1928. V. 50

BROWNE, M.
Artistic and Scientific Taxidermy and Modelling. London: 1896. V. 47; 49; 50; 54

BROWNE, MAGGIE
The Book of Betty Barber. London: 1910. V. 47

BROWNE, MATTHEW
Little Ben Bute. Edinburgh: 1882. V. 48

BROWNE, MOSES
Angling Sports: in Nine Piscatory Eclogues. London: 1773. V. 47; 52

BROWNE, O'DONEL T. D.
The Rotunda Hospital, 1745-1945. London: 1947. V. 54

BROWNE, P.
The History of Norwich, from the Earliest Records to the Present Time. Norwich: 1814. V. 53

BROWNE, PATRICK
The Civil and Natural History of Jamaica... London: 1789. V. 54

BROWNE, PATRICK WILLIAM
Where the Fishers Go: The Story of Labrador. Toronto: 1909. V. 53

BROWNE, PETER
Things Divine and Supernatural Conceived by Analogy with Things Natural and Human. London: 1733. V. 53

BROWNE, PETER A.
Reports of Cases Adjudged in the Court of Common Pleas of the First Judicial District of Pennsylvania. St. Louis: 1871. V. 54

BROWNE, RICHARD
The Lord Digbies Design to Betray Abingdon, Carryed On for Divers Weeks by an Intercourse of Letters. London: 1645. V. 54

BROWNE, ROBERT DILLON
Debate on the First Reading of the Protection of Life (Ireland) Bill. London: 1846. V. 54

BROWNE, T. H.
History of the English Turf 1904-1930. New York: 1931. V. 47

BROWNE, THOMAS
Browne's Religio Medici. London: 1909. V. 50
Christian Morals. London: 1756. V. 47; 48; 49
A Dictionary of Ancient Classical and Scriptural Proper Names... Burlington: 1812. V. 51
Essai sur les Erreurs Populaires, ou Examen de Plusieurs Opinions Recues Comme Vrayes, Qui Sont Fausses ou Douteuses. Paris: 1733. V. 54
Essays. Religio Medici: Urn Burial: Chritian Morals: Letter to Friend: On Dreams. London: 1902. V. 48
Hydriotaphia. London: 1658. V. 50
Hydriotaphia. London: 1893. V. 54
Hydriotaphia. Cambridge: 1907. V. 47; 49
A Letter to a Friend Upon the Occasion of the Death of an Intimate Friend, Together with Christian Morals. Waltham St. Lawrence: 1923. V. 52
A Letter to a Friend Upon the Occasion of the Death of His Intimate Friend. Boston: 1971. V. 54
Of Garlands and Coronary of Garland Plants... Northampton: 1962. V. 48; 49
Of Unicornes Hornes. Easthampton: 1984. V. 54
Of Unicornes Hornes. Williamsburg: 1984. V. 47
Posthumous Works of the Learned Sir Thomas Browne... London: 1712. V. 48; 52
Pseudodoxia Epidemica... London: 1650. V. 47; 53; 54
Pseudodoxia Epidemica... Frankfurt and Leipzig: 1680. V. 47
Pseudodoxia Epidemica; of Unicornes Hornes. Easthampton: 1984. V. 48
Pseudodoxia Epidemica: of Unicornes Hornes. Williamsburg: 1984. V. 52
Pseudodoxia Epidemica: or, Enquires into Very Many Received Tenents and Commonly Presumed Truths. London: 1658. V. 48; 53; 54
Pseudodoxia Epidemica; or, Enquiries Into Very Many Received Tenents. London: 1646. V. 47; 48; 49; 50
Pseudodoxia Epidemica; or, Enquiries Into Very Many Received Tenents and Commonly Presumed Truths. London: 1650. V. 48; 49; 51; 52; 53
Pseudodoxia Epidemica; or, Enquiries into Very May Received Tenents, and Commonly Presumed Truths... London: 1646. V. 47
Pseudodoxia Epidemica....Whereunto are Now Added Two Disccourses the One Urn-Burial, or Sepulchrall Urns, later Found in Norfolk. The Other the Garden of Cyrus... London: 1658. V. 52
Pseudodoxia Epidemica...(with) Religio Medici... London: 1658/59. V. 53
Religio Medici. Leiden: 1644. V. 47; 48; 49; 50; 51; 52; 53; 54
Religio Medici. Paris: 1644. V. 47
Religio Medici. Argentorati: 1665. V. 47
Religio Medici. London: 1678. V. 50
Religio Medici. London: 1682. V. 54
Religio Medici. London: 1736. V. 49; 50
Religio Medici. London: 1738. V. 48; 49
Religio Medici. Boston: 1862. V. 47; 48; 49
Religio Medici. London: 1902. V. 47; 51
Religio Medici. New York: 1903. V. 48
Religio Medici. London: 1911. V. 53
Religio Medici. New York: 1915. V. 50
Religio Medici. Eugene: 1939. V. 53; 54
Religio Medici. New York: 1939. V. 52; 54
Religio Medici. San Francisco: 1939. V. 51
Repertorium; or, Some Account of the Tombs and Monuments in the Cathedral Church of Norwich. London: 1712. V. 47
The Union Dictionary... London: 1806. V. 52
The Union Dictionary; Containing All That is Truly Useful in the Dictionaries of Johnson, Sheridan and Walker... London: 1810. V. 52
Urne Buriall and the Garden of Cyrus. London: 1932. V. 51; 52; 53
The Works... London: 1686. V. 47; 48; 50; 52; 53; 54
Works. London: 1836. V. 48; 49; 50
Works. London: 1846. V. 49
The Works. Edinburgh: 1927. V. 52
The Works. London: 1928. V. 53
The Works. London: 1964. V. 47

BROWNE, W. H.
Firework Making for Amateurs: Being Complete and Explicit Instructions in the Art of Pyrotechny. London: 1888. V. 48

BROWNE, WALDO
Altgeld of Illinois. A Record of His Life and Work. New York: 1924. V. 49

BROWNE, WILLIAM
Britannia's Pastorals. London: 1616?. V. 47
Britannia's Pastorals. London: 1625. V. 47

BROWNE, WILLIAM GEORGE
Travels in Africa, Egypt and Syria, from the Year 1792 to 1798. London: 1799. V. 49

BROWNE, WOGAN
Bibliotheca Browniana. A Catalogue of the Valuable and Extensive Library of the Late Wogan Browne, Esq. of Castle Browne in the County of Kildare... Dublin: 1812. V. 51

BROWNELL, CHARLES DE WOLF
The Indian Races of America... Boston: 1855. V. 47
Indian Races of North and South America. Cincinnati: 1853. V. 54

BROWNELL, WILLIAM
Original Poems on Various Subjects. Sheffield: 1815. V. 54

BROWNING, COLIN ARROTT
The Convict Ship. London: 1844. V. 53

BROWNING, ELIZABETH BARRETT
Aurora Leigh. London: 1857. V. 50; 52
Aurora Leigh. New York: 1857. V. 47; 49; 50
Aurora Leigh. London: 1859. V. 52; 53; 54
Aurora Leigh. Leipzig: 1872. V. 49
The Battle of Marathon. London: 1891. V. 52
Casa Guidi Windows. London: 1851. V. 47; 49; 50; 52; 54
The Complete Poetical Works of Elizabeth Barrett Browning. Boston & New York: 1900. V. 48
A Drama of Exile; and Other Poems. New York: 1845. V. 49; 50; 54
An Essay on Mind, With Other Poems. London: 1826. V. 52
The Greek Christian Poets and the English Poets. London: 1863. V. 47; 48; 50
Lady Geraldine's Courtship. New York: 1870. V. 53
Last Poems. London: 1862. V. 47; 48; 53
Last Poems. New York: 1862. V. 47; 49
Leila. London: 1913. V. 52
Letters to B. R. Haydon. New York: 1939. V. 53
Letters...Addressed to Richard Hengist Horne, with Comments on Contemporaries. London: 1877. V. 47; 50; 51; 52
Napoleon III in Italy and Other Poems. New York: 1860. V. 47; 50
Poems. London: 1844. V. 47; 49; 50; 51; 54
Poems. London: 1850. V. 50; 54
Poems. London: 1856. V. 47; 48; 50; 52
Poems. London: 1862. V. 49; 54
Poems Before Congress. London: 1860. V. 47; 49; 50; 52
Poems Before Congress. London: 1918. V. 51
Poems Before Congress. (with) Last Poems. London: 1860-62. V. 49
Poetical Works. London: 1873. V. 50; 51
The Poetical Works. London: 1889-1890. V. 49; 52
The Poetical Works. London: 1890. V. 53; 54
Poetical Works. London: 1906. V. 50
The Poetical Works. London: 1951. V. 48
Prometheus Bound and Other Poems. New York: 1854. V. 47
A Selection from the Poetry. London: 1866. V. 52
A Selection from the Poetry....First Series (-Second Series). London: 1884. V. 52
The Seraphim and Other Poems. London: 1838. V. 47; 48; 49; 50; 52; 54
The Seraphim and Other Poems. London: 1839. V. 47
Sonnets. London. V. 48
Sonnets from the Portuguese. Boston: 1896. V. 47
Sonnets from the Portuguese. London: 1897. V. 48
Sonnets from the Portuguese. London: 1900. V. 48
Sonnets from the Portuguese. New York: 1902. V. 48
Sonnets from the Portuguese. Venice: 1906. V. 52
Sonnets from the Portuguese. London: 1914. V. 48
Sonnets from the Portuguese. Montagnola: 1925. V. 47
Sonnets from the Portuguese. San Francisco: 1927. V. 47
Sonnets from the Portuguese. Chicago: 1933. V. 48
Sonnets from the Portuguese. New York: 1938. V. 54
Sonnets from the Portuguese. Cambridge: 1939. V. 48
Sonnets From the Portuguese. New York: 1948. V. 47; 48; 51
Two Poems. London: 1854. V. 49; 52; 54

BROWNING, GEORGE
The Domestic and Financial Condition of Great Britain; Preceded by a Brief Sketch Of her Foreign Policy... London: 1834. V. 50; 54
Footprints. London: 1871. V. 49

BROWNING, ROBERT
An Account of the Illness and Death of His Father, Robert Browning the Second. London: 1921. V. 52
Asolando: Fancies and Facts. London: 1890. V. 51; 53
Balaustion's Adventure: Including a Transcript from Euripides. Boston: 1871. V. 48
Bells and Pomegranates. No I - Pippa Passes. (No. II-No. VIII). London: 1841-46. V. 52
Browning's Men and Women. London: 1855. V. 48
Browning's Men and Women. London: 1907. V. 48
Christmas Eve and Easter Day. London: 1850. V. 47; 49; 53
Complete Works. New York: 1898. V. 48
Dramatic Romances and Lyrics. London: 1899. V. 47; 49; 50; 54
Dramatis Personae. London: 1864. V. 51
Dramatis Personae. 1910. V. 49; 51; 52
Dramatis Personae. London: 1910. V. 48; 52
Dramatis Personae and Dramatic Romances and Lyrics. London: 1909. V. 50
Fifine at the Fair. London: 1872. V. 54
Flight of the Duchess. London: 1905. V. 51
Gold Hair: a Legend of Pornic. 1864. V. 52
Helen's Tower. 1897. V. 52
A History of Golf, the Royal and Ancient Game. London: 1955. V. 48
History of Golf. The Royal and Ancient Game. New York: 1955. V. 47
The Last Ride. 1900. V. 49
The Last Ride Together. New York: 1906. V. 48

BROWNING, ROBERT continued
Letters from Le Croisic. London: 1917. V. 52
Letters from Robert Browning to Various Correspondents. London: 1895-96. V. 52
Letters of Robert Browning. London: 1933. V. 50
The Letters of Robert Browning and Elizabeth Barrett Browning 1845-1846. London: 1899. V. 48
Letters of...To Miss Isa Blagden. Waco: 1923. V. 49
Men and Women. London: 1855. V. 47; 48; 53
Men and Women. London: 1908. V. 50; 53; 54
Paracelsus. London: 1835. V. 48; 50; 52
Parleyings with Certain People of Importance in Their Day. London: 1887. V. 47; 48
Pauline, a Fragment of a Confession. London: 1886. V. 50
Pictor Ignotus, Fra Lippo Lippi Andrea del Sarto. Waltham St. Lawrence: 1925. V. 50; 52
The Pied Piper of Hamelin. London, Glasgow, & New York: 1888. V. 48; 49; 54
The Pied Piper of Hamelin. London: 1898. V. 47; 48; 50; 52
The Pied Piper of Hamelin. London: 1903. V. 48
The Pied Piper of Hamelin. London: 1905. V. 49
The Pied Piper of Hamelin. London: 1912. V. 54
The Pied Piper of Hamelin. Chicago: 1927. V. 53
The Pied Piper of Hamelin. London: 1934. V. 47; 48; 49; 50; 51; 53
The Pied Piper of Hamelin. New York: 1936. V. 51; 52
The Pied Piper of Hamlin. Portland: 1980. V. 52
Pippa Passes and Men and Women. London: 1908. V. 50; 53
Poems. London: 1849. V. 52
The Poems of Robert Browning. Cambridge: 1969. V. 48
The Poetic and Dramatic Works of Robert Browning. Boston and New York: 1899. V. 47; 51
The Poetical Works. London: 1863. V. 52
The Poetical Works. London: 1868. V. 52
The Poetical Works. London: 1875. V. 54
The Poetical Works. London: 1875-78. V. 50
The Poetical Works. London: 1888-94. V. 52
Poetical Works. London: 1889. V. 48; 51
The Poetical Works. London: 1889-1914. V. 47; 48; 50
The Poetical Works. New York: 1894. V. 54
The Poetical Works. Boston: 1899. V. 49
The Poetical Works... London: 1902. V. 54
The Poetical Works. London: 1924/1896. V. 48
Rabbi Ben Ezra. Concord: 1902. V. 48; 50
Rabbi Ben Ezra. Concord: 1904. V. 49
The Ring and the Book. London: 1868. V. 47; 50; 52
The Ring and the Book. London: 1868-69. V. 48; 51; 52; 53
The Ring and the Book. Boston: 1869. V. 52
The Ring and the Book. London: 1872. V. 52
The Ring and the Book. Los Angeles: 1949. V. 53; 54
The Ring and the Book. New York: 1949. V. 48
La Saisiaz: The Two Poets of Croisic. London: 1878. V. 48
A Selection from the Works of Robert Browning. London: 1865. V. 52
So Here Then Is the Last Ride. Aurora: 1900. V. 47
Some Poems. 1904. V. 47; 52; 54
Some Poems. London: 1904. V. 48
Sordello. London: 1840. V. 47; 48; 51
Strafford: an Historical Tragedy. London: 1837. V. 47; 50; 52
Two Poems. London: 1854. V. 47
The Works. London: 1912. V. 48; 50; 52

BROWNING SOCIETY
The Browning Society's Papers...Parts I-V, VII-XIII (all published). London: 1881-91. V. 52

BROWNJOHN, ALAN
Philip Larkin. London: 1975. V. 49

BROWNLIE, G.
The Pteridophyte Flora of Figi. London: 1977. V. 51

BROWNLOW, WILLIAM GANNAWAY
Helps to the Study of Presbyterianism...to Which is added a Brief Account of the Life and Travels of the Author. Knoxville: 1834. V. 54
Ought American Slavery to Be Perpetuated?. Philadelphia: 1858. V. 53
Sketches of the Rise, Progress and Decline of Secession, with a Narrative of Personal Adventures Among the Rebels. Philadelphia: 1862. V. 47; 49; 53

BROWNRIG, RALPH
Forty Sermons. London: 1685. V. 52

BROWNRIGG, WILLIAM
The Art of Making Common Salt, As Now Practised in Most Parts of the World... London: 1748. V. 51

BROWN-SEQUARD, C. E.
Course of Lectures on the Physiology and Pathology of the Central Nervous System. Philadelphia: 1860. V. 47; 48
Lectures on the Diagnosis and Treatment of Principal Forms of Paralysis of the Lower Extremities. Philadelphia: 1861. V. 47; 54

BROWNSON, ORESTES A.
An Address on the Fifty-Fifth Anniversary of American Independence Delivered at Ovid, Seneca Co., New York:. Ithaca: 1831. V. 49
Essays and Reviews Chiefly on Theology, Politics and Socialism. New York: 1852. V. 54
New Views of Christianity, Society and the Church. Boston: 1836. V. 54
Social Reform. An Address Before the Society of the Mystical Seven in the Wesleyan University, Middletown, Conn., August 7, 1844. Boston: 1844. V. 54
The Ten Squaws: a Serio-Comic Drama. Dubuque: 1870. V. 51

BROWSE, LILLIAN
Barbara Hepworth - Sculptress. London: 1946. V. 52
Degas Dancers. London: 1949. V. 47; 50; 51; 53
William Nicholson. London: 1956. V. 48; 50; 52

BROXBOURNE LIBRARY
Catalogue of Valuable Printed Books Illustrating the Spread of Printing. London: 1977-78. V. 48

THE BRUCE and Wallace; Published From Two Ancient Manuscripts Preserved in the Library of the Faculty of Advocates. Glasgow: 1869. V. 49

BRUCE, ARCHIBALD
Free Thoughts on the Toleration of Popery, Deduced from a Review of Its Principles and History. Edinburgh: 1780. V. 47

BRUCE, CARLTON
Mirth and Morality: a Collection of Original Tales. London: 1834. V. 50

BRUCE, CHARLES GRANVILLE
The Assault of Everest. 1922. London: 1923. V. 48; 53
The Assault on Mount Everest, 1922. New York: 1923. V. 48
Kulu and Lahoul. London: 1914. V. 53
Twenty Years in Borneo. London: 1924. V. 53
Twenty Years in the Himalaya. 1910. V. 54

BRUCE, GEORGE
The Land Birds in and Around St. Andrews... Dundee: 1895. V. 50; 52; 54
Poems and Songs, on Various Occasions. (with) Poems, Ballads and Songs on Various Occasions. Edinburgh: 1811/13. V. 52
Poems, Ballads and Songs, on Various Occasions. Edinburgh: 1813. V. 54

BRUCE, GEORGE ANSON
The Twentieth Regiment of Massachusetts Volunteer Infantry 1861-1865. Boston & New York: 1906. V. 48

BRUCE, HENRY AUSTIN
Life of General Sir William Napier. London: 1864. V. 50

BRUCE, I. M.
The History of Aberdeenshire Shorthorn. Aberdeen: 1923. V. 54

BRUCE, J.
Select Views of Brighton, taken on the Spot and Executed by Mr. Bruce. 1827. V. 47
Travels to Discover the Source of the Nile in the Years 1768-73. London: 1790. V. 54

BRUCE, J. COLLINGWOOD
The Hand-Book to the Roman Wall. London: 1885. V. 50; 52; 53
The Wall of Hadrian: With Especial Reference to Recent Discoveries. Newcastle-upon-Tyne: 1874. V. 53; 54

BRUCE, JAMES
Travels Between the Years 1768 and 1773, through Part of Africa, Syria, Egypt & Arabia into Abyssinia, to Discover the Source of the Nile. Glasgow: 1818. V. 47
Travels to Discover the Source of the Nile in the Years 1768, 1759, 1771 and 1773. Dublin: 1790. V. 49
Travels to Discover the Source of the Nile, in the Years 1768, 1769, 1770, 1771, 1772 and 1773. Edinburgh: 1790. V. 47; 50; 53
Travels to Discover the Source of the Nile in the Years 1768, 1769, 1770, 1771, 1772 and 1773. Dublin: 1790-91. V. 50
Travels to Discover the Source of the Nile in the Years 1768, 1769, 1770, 1771, 1772 and 1773. Edinburgh: 1805. V. 52; 54

BRUCE, JOHN
Report on the Arrangements Which Were Made...When Spain, By Its Armada, Projected the Invasion. London: 1798. V. 52
Review of the Events and Treaties Which Established the Balance of Power in Europe and the Balance of Trade in Favor of Great Britain. 1796. V. 54

BRUCE, LEWIS
The Happiness of Man the Glory of God. A Sermon Preached Before the Honourable Trustees for Establishing the Colony of Georgia in America, and the Associates of the Late Rev. Dr. Bray... London: 1744. V. 48

BRUCE, MICHAEL
Poems on Several Occasions. Edinburgh: 1782. V. 50

BRUCE, PETER
Memoirs...an Account of His Travels in Germany, Russia, Tartary, Turkey, the West Indies. London: 1782. V. 47; 54

BRUCE, PHILIP A.
History of Virginia. Chicago and New York: 1924. V. 54
Institutional History of Virginia in the Seventeenth Century. New York: 1910. V. 54

BRUCE, ROBERT
Custer's Last Battle. New York: 1927. V. 53

BRUCE, THOMAS
Heritage of the Trans-Alleghany Pioneers or Resources of Central West Virginia. Baltimore: 1894. V. 53

BRUCE, WALLACE
The Hudson River by Daylight. New York: 1890. V. 48; 49

BRUCE-LOCKHART, R. H.
Jan Masaryk. A Personal Memoir. London: 1951. V. 54

BRUCE-MITFORD, RUPERT
The Sutton-Hoo Ship-Burial. London: 1975-83. V. 48; 50

BRUCE'S NEW YORK TYPE-FOUNDRY
Specimens of Printing Types. New York: 1882. V. 48; 50

BRUCKER, JOHANN JAKOB
Historia Critica Philosophiae... Leipzig: 1766-67. V. 54

BRUCKMAN, FRED
A Juvenile Gallery. London: 1879. V. 50

BRUCKMANN, P.
Neue Formen Silberner Gefasse. Heilbrunn am Neckar: 1851-60. V. 53

BRUDICK, ARTHUR J.
The Mystic Mid-Region: the Deserts of the Southwest. New York: 1904. V. 53

BRUEHL, ANTON
Photographs of Mexico. New York: 1933. V. 47

BRUEL, WALTER
Praxis Medicinae, or, the Physicians Practice. London: 1632. V. 52

BRUELL, WALTER
Praxis Medicinae, or the Physitians Practise.. London: 1648. V. 54

BRUFF, HARALD JOHN
T'Miners. York. V. 54

BRUFF, J. GOLDSBOROUGH
Gold Rush, the Journals, Drawings and other Papers of... New York: 1944. V. 47; 50; 53
Gold Rush. The Journals, Drawings and Other Papers of... New York: 1949. V. 52; 54

BRUGSCH, HEINRICH
Thesaurus Inscriptionum Aegyptiacapum. Leipzig: 1883-91. V. 49; 51

BRUGSCH-BEY, HEINRICH
Egypt Under the Pharaohs. London: 1902. V. 49

BRUGUIERE, FRANCIS
San Francisco. San Francisco: 1918. V. 47; 52

BRUHL, GRAF VON
Lalla Roukh, Divertissement Mele de Chants et de Danses, Execute au Cahteau Royal de Berlin... Berlin: 1822. V. 49; 53

BRUHNS, KARL
Life of Alexander Von Humboldt. London: 1873. V. 50; 51

BRUMMEL, BEAU
Male and Female Costume. Grecian & Roman Costume, British Costume from the Roman Invasion Until 1822 and the Principles of Costume Applied to the Improved Dress of the Present Day. Garden City: 1932. V. 51

BRUMMER, ERNEST
The Ernest Brummer Collection. 1879. V. 53
Ernest Brummer Collection. Zurich: 1979. V. 49; 50; 51; 52

BRUN, ANDRES
The Writing Book of Andres Brun, Calligrapher of Saragosse. Paris: 1928. V. 50

BRUNDAGE, FRANCIS
Daughters of Colonial Days. Boston: 1890. V. 47

BRUNEL, I. K.
The Great Eastern Steam Ship: A Description of Mr. Scott Russell's Great Ship, Now Building at Millwall, for the Eastern Steam Navigation Company. London: 1857. V. 51
History of the Great Eastern. A Memento of Her Present and Past Condition. Manchester: 1890. V. 54
The Leviathan. History of the "Great Eastern" Steamship. London: 1886. V. 51; 54
Report of the Commissioners Appointed to Inquire into the Present State of the River Tyne, together with the Minutes of Evidence and Appendix. London: 1855. V. 54

BRUNEL, M. I.
A Letter to the Proprietors of the Thames Tunnel. London: 1832. V. 54
The Origin, Progress and Present State of the Thames Tunnel; and the Advantages Likely to Accrue from It, Both to the Proprietors and to the Public. London: 1827. V. 51; 54
Sketches and Memoranda of the Works for the Tunnel Under the Thames from Rotherhithe to Wapping. London: 1828. V. 50; 53
The Thames Tunnel. London: 1833. V. 50

BRUNET, G.
Life of William Bedell, D.D., Bishop of Kilmore in Ireland. 1685. V. 52

BRUNET, JACQUES CHARLES
Manuel du Libraire det de l'Amateur. Paris: 1860-80. V. 47

BRUNET, THOMAS
Doctrina Antiqua de Rerum Originibus; or, an Inquiry into the Doctrine of the Philosophers of All Nations... London: 1736. V. 53

BRUNHOFF, JEAN DE
Babar and Father Christmas. London: 1940. V. 47
Babar and His Children. New York: 1938. V. 54
Babar and that Rascal Arthur. London: 1948. V. 48; 50
Babar the King. New York: 1935. V. 47; 49
Babar the King. London: 1936. V. 53
Picnic at Babar's. London: 1950. V. 48; 53
The Story of Babar. New York: 1933. V. 53; 54

BRUNI, LEONARDO ARETINO
Epistaloarum Familiarum Libri VIII. Venice: 1495. V. 50

BRUNNER, ARNOLD
Interior Decoration. New York: 1887. V. 50

BRUNNER, J.
Stand on Zanzibar. New York: 1968. V. 48

BRUNNMARK, GUSTAVUS
A Short Introduction to Swedish Grammar... London: 1805. V. 50

BRUNNOW, F.
Spherical Astronomy. London: 1865. V. 53

BRUNO, GIORDANO
De Umris Idearum. Implicantibus Artem, Quaerendi, Inveniendi, Judicani, Ordinandi... Paris: 1582. V. 50

BRUNS, HENRY P.
Angling Books fo the Americas...Assisted by Marian K. Bruns. Atlanta: 1975. V. 47

BRUNS, THOMAS
Old Scottish Communion Plate... Edinburgh: 1892. V. 48

BRUNSCHWIG, HIERONYMUS
Das New Gross Distillier Buch. Franckfurt: 1545. V. 47; 50; 53
The Noble Experyence of the Vertuous Handy Warke of Surgeri... Southwark: 1525. V. 47
The Noble Expryence of the Vertuous Handy Warke of Surgeri, Practysyd & Complyed by the Moost Experte Mayster Jherome of Bruynswyke... London: 1525. V. 51

BRUNSDON, JYOTI
The Cure. Katoomba: 1992. V. 54

BRUNSON, ALFRED
Prairie du Chien. Its Present Position and Future Prospects. Milwaukee: 1857. V. 50

BRUNSWICK & FLORIDA RAILROAD CO.
Report of the President of the...With the Proceedings of the Stockholers, at Their Annual Meeting, Held at Brunswick Georgia, May 3d, 1855. New York: 1855. V. 54

BRUNTON, GUY
Lahun I-II. London: 1920-23. V. 51
Mostagedda and the Tasien Culture. London: 1937. V. 51
Qua and Badari I (only). London: 1927. V. 51

BRUNTON, MARY
Discipline. Edinburgh: 1814. V. 49; 51; 54
Discipline: a Novel. Edinburgh: 1815. V. 50
Emmeline. Edinburgh: 1819. V. 47; 49; 50; 51; 54
Self Control, a Novel. Edinburgh: 1811. V. 47; 50

BRUNTON, T. LAUDER
Collected Papers on Circulation and Respiration. First Series. London: 1906. V. 48; 50; 53
An Introduction to Modern Therapeutics Being the Croonian Lectures on the Relationship Between Chemical Structure and Physiological action in Relation to the Prevention, Control and Cure of Disease. London: 1892. V. 53
Lectures on the Actions of Medicines. New York: 1897. V. 48
On Disorders of Assimilation, Digestion, Etc. London: 1901. V. 48; 53
Therapeutics of the Circulation. London: 1908. V. 53
Therapeutics of the Circulation. London: 1914. V. 48; 53

BRUNTON, WINIFRED
Great Ones of Ancient Egypt. London: 1929. V. 49; 51
Kings and Queens of Ancient. London: 1924. V. 49; 51

BRUNUS, ARETINUS
Epistolarum Familiarum Libri VIII. Venice: 1495. V. 48

BRUSENDORFF, OVE
Love's Picture Book. New York: 1969. V. 48

BRUSHER, JOSEPH S.
Popes Through the Ages. Princeton: 1959. V. 51

BRUSHFIELD, T. N.
A Bibliography of Sir Walter Raleigh, Knt. Exeter: 1908. V. 52

BRUSONIUS, LUCIUS DOMITIUS
Facetiarum Exemplorumq Libri VII. 1518. V. 50
Facetiarvm Exemplorvmqve. Lugduni: 1562. V. 53

BRUSSEL, I. R.
Anglo-American First Editions. London: 1935. V. 47
Anglo-American First Editions 1826-1900 East to West. London: 1935-36. V. 51
Anglo-American First Editions. Part Two: West to East 1786-1930. London: 1936. V. 49; 51

BRUTON, JOHN HILL
Life and Correspondence of David Hume. Edinburgh: 1846. V. 52

BRUTUM Fulmen: or the Bull of Pope Pius V. London: 1681. V. 48

BRUTUS, DENNIS
Stubborn Hope: Selected Poems of South Africa & A Wider World Including China Poems. London: 1978. V. 54

BRUYERE, JEAN DE
The Characters of...Newly Rendered into English by Henri Van Laun. London: 1885. V. 47

BRUYERE, L.
Etudes Relatives a l'Art des Constructions. Paris: 1823/28. V. 52

BRUYN, AMBROSIUS DE
A Narration, Briefly Contayning the History of the French Massacre, Especially that Horrible One at Paris... London: 1618. V. 47

BRUYN, CORNELIUS DE
Reizen door Vermaardste Deelen van Kleinasia, die Eylanden Scio, Rhodus, Cyprus, Meteling, Stanchio &c... Delft: 1698. V. 48
Travels Into Muscovy, Persia, and Part of the East-Indies... London: 1737. V. 51

BRY, THEODOR DE
America, Das Ist Erfindung Und Offenbahrung Der Newen Welt... Frankfurt am Main: 1617. V. 47
Emblemata Saecularia, Mira et Iucunda Varaietate Saeculi Huius Mores ita Exprimentia, Ut Sodalitatum Symbolis Insigniisque... Frankfurt: 1596. V. 50

BRYAN, ASHLEY
The Ox of the Wonderful Horns and Other African Folktales. New York: 1971. V. 52

BRYAN, C. D. B.
Beautiful Women; Ugly Scenes. Garden City: 1983. V. 51

BRYAN, DANIEL
The Appeal for Suffering Genius: a Poetical Address for the Benefit of the Boston Bard; and the Triumph of Truth, a Poem. Washington City: 1826. V. 54

BRYAN, DOROTHY
Michael and Patsy on the Golf Links. London: 1934. V. 52

BRYAN, EMMA LYON
1860-1865, A Romance of the Valley of Virginia. Harrisonburg: 1892. V. 52

BRYAN, GEORGE
Chelsea, in the Olden and Present Times. Chelsea: 1869. V. 50; 54

BRYAN, HUGH
Living Christianity Delineated, in the Diaries and Letters to Two Eminently Pious Persons Lately Deceased... Both of South Carolina. London: 1760. V. 48

BRYAN, J. E.
Bulbs. London: 1989. V. 49; 51; 52; 54
Bulbs. Portland: 1989. V. 51

BRYAN, JOHN STEWART
Joseph Bryan: His Times, His Family, His Friends. A Memoir. Richmond: 1935. V. 48

BRYAN, JULIEN H.
Ambulance 464 - Encore des Blesses. New York: 1918. V. 47

BRYAN, M.
Bryan's Dictionary of Painters and Engravers. London: 1915/19. V. 49
Dictionary of Painters and Engravers. London: 1909. V. 49; 51
Dictionary of Painters and Engravers. London: 1909-10. V. 52

BRYAN, MARGARET
A Compendious System of Astronomy, in a Course of Familiar Lectures. London: 1797. V. 54
Lectures on Natural Philosophy. London: 1806. V. 53; 54

BRYAN, PEARL
The Mysterious Murder of Pearl Bryan, the Headless Horror. Cincinnati: 1896. V. 51

BRYAN, WILLIAM ALANSON
Natural History of Hawaii. Honolulu: 1915. V. 51; 52

BRYAN, WILLIAM S.
Our Islands and Their People as Seen with Camera and Pencil. St. Louis/New York: 1899. V. 47

BRYANT, C.
A Dictionary of the Ornamental Trees, Shrubs and Plants... Norwich: 1790. V. 49

BRYANT, EDWIN
Voyage en Californie. Bruxelles: 1850. V. 47
What I Saw in California. London: 1849. V. 47
What I Saw in California. New York: 1849. V. 47
What I Saw in California. Santa Ana: 1936. V. 48; 53

BRYANT, G. E.
The Chelsea Porcelain Toys, Scent-Bottles, Bonbonnieres, Etuis, Seals, and Statuettes, Made at the Chelsea Factory 1745-1769. London: 1925. V. 52

BRYANT, HENRY G.
The Peary Auxiliary Expedition of 1894. Philadelphia: 1895. V. 47; 52

BRYANT, J. R. M.
Address Delivered Before the Philomathean Soceity of Wabash College, July 13, 1836. Crawfordsville: 1836. V. 54

BRYANT, JACOB
A New System, or an Analysis of Ancient Mythology... London: 1807. V. 47; 48; 52
Observations and Inquiries Relating to Various Parts of Ancient History... Cambridge: 1767. V. 51
Observations Upon the Plagues Inflicted Upon the Egyptians. London: 1810. V. 53

BRYANT, JOSHUA
Bryant's Treatise on the Use of Indian Inks and Colours. London: 1808. V. 53

BRYANT, LOUISE
Mirrors of Moscow. New York: 1923. V. 51

BRYANT, SARA CONE
The Gingerbread Man and Other Stories for Little Ones. London: 1926. V. 49

BRYANT, WILLIAM CULLEN
A Forest Hymn. New York: 1860. V. 50
The Fountain and Other Poems. New York & London: 1842. V. 47; 54
Letters from the East. London: 1869. V. 49
A New Library of Poetry. New York: 1883. V. 48
A New Library of Poetry and Song. New York: 1878. V. 51
Picturesque America. London: 1872. V. 47
Picturesque America. New York: 1872. V. 47; 48; 49; 50; 52; 54
Picturesque America. New York: 1872-74. V. 47
Picturesque America... London: 1894-5-6-7. V. 50
Poems. Cambridge: 1821. V. 47; 49; 50; 51; 52; 53; 54
Poems. London: 1832. V. 51
Poems. New York: 1856. V. 50
Poems. London: 1858. V. 51
Poems. New York: 1863. V. 48
Poems. New York & London: 1872. V. 52
Poems. New York: 1947. V. 51
The Snow Shower. London: 1929. V. 53
Thirty Poems. New York: 1864. V. 47; 49; 50; 51; 53
Unpublished Poems by Bryant and Thoreau. Boston: 1907. V. 54
Washington Irving. Mr. Bryant's Address on His Life and Genius. New York: 1860. V. 49
The White-Footed Deer and Other Poems. New York: 1844. V. 50

BRYCE, DAVID
Bryce's Thumb English Dictionary. Glasgow: 1890's. V. 47

BRYCE, GEORGE
Everyman's Geology of the Three Prairie Provinces of the Canadian West. Winnipeg: 1907. V. 53
A History of Manitoba. Its Resources and People. Toronto: 1906. V. 49
The Siege and Conquest of the North Pole. London: 1910. V. 48
Sketch of the Life and Discvoeries of Robert Campbell. Winnipeg: 1898. V. 50

BRYCE, JAMES
The American Commonwealth. London: 1888. V. 48; 51; 52; 53
The American Commonwealth. London: 1889-90. V. 53
Modern Democracies. London: 1921. V. 48
Transcaucasia and Ararat: Being Notes of a Vaction Tour in the Autumn of 1876,. London: 1877. V. 54

BRYCE, VISCOUNT
The Treatment of Armenians in the Ottoman Empire 1915-1916. London: 1916. V. 47

BRYDALL, JOHN
Jura Coronae. His Majesties Royal Rights and Prerogatives Asserted. London: 1680. V. 50; 51

BRYDEN, H. ANDERSON
Great and Small Game of Africa, an Account of the Distribution, Habits and Natural History of the Sporting Mammals... London: 1899. V. 48; 50; 51
Gun and Camera in Southern Africa. London: 1893. V. 47; 48
How to Buy a Gun. London: 1903. V. 49
Kloof and Karroo: Sport Legend and Natural History in Cape Colony, with a Notice of the Game Birds... London: 1889. V. 47; 51; 54

BRYDEN, M. M.
Research on Dolphins. London: 1986. V. 49

BRYDEN, ROBERT
Castles of Carrick. London: 1910. V. 54

BRYDGES, CHARLES JON
The Letters Of...Volume I: 1879-1882. Volume II: 1883-1889. Winnipeg: 1977/81. V. 47; 48; 53; 54

BRYDGES, SAMUEL EGERTON, BART.
The Autobiography, Times, Opinions, and Contemporaries of... London: 1834. V. 50
Censura Literaria. London: 1805-09. V. 50
Human Fate, and an Address to the Poets Wordsworth and Southey: Poems. Totham: 1848. V. 47
Letters From the Continent. Kent: 1821. V. 52
Letters on the Character and Poetical Genius of Lord Byron. London: 1824. V. 50
A Note on the Suppression of Memoirs Announced by the Author in June, 1825... Paris: 1825. V. 47
Occasional Poems, Written in the Year MDCCCXI. Kent: 1814. V. 47
Opartisk Skildring af Lord Byron, Sasom Skald Och Menniska....(Impartial Account of Lord Byron...). Stockholm: 1831. V. 52
Restituta; or, Titles, Extracts and Characters of Old Books in English Literature. London: 1814. V. 52; 53
Restituta; or Titles, Extracts and Characters of Old Books in English Literature, Revived. London: 1814-16. V. 49

BRYDONE, PATRICK
A Tour through Sicily and Malta. London: 1773. V. 53; 54
A Tour through Sicily and Malta. London: 1775. V. 49; 53
A Tour Through Sicily and Malta. Dublin: 1780. V. 49

BRYDSON, A. P.
Some Records of Two Lakeland Townships (Blawith and Nibthwaite) Chiefly from Original Documents. London. V. 50; 52

BRYER, ANTHONY
The Byzantine Monuments and Typography of the Pontos. Washington: 1985. V. 49

BRYK, F.
Voodoo-Eros, Ethnological Studies int he Sex-Life of the African Aborigines. New York: 1933. V. 54

BRYNILDSEN, E. NORTH
The Dancing Annual - 1923. London: 1923. V. 50

BRYSKETT, LODOWICK
A Discourse of Civill Life... London: 1606. V. 48

BUB, H.
Bird Trapping and Bird Banding. Ithaca: 1991. V. 50

BUBER, MARTIN
I and Thou. New York: 1970. V. 49

BUBIER, E. T.
How to Build Automobiles. Lynn: 1904. V. 50

BUCHAN, ANNA
Alistair Buchan. London: 1917. V. 49

BUCHAN, DAVID STEUART ERSKINE, 11TH EARL OF
Essays on the Lives and Writings of Fletcher of Saltoun and the Poet Thomson. London: 1792. V. 50; 51

BUCHAN, JAMES WALTER
A History of Pebbleshire. Glasgow: 1925. V. 49

BUCHAN, JOHN
The African Colony. Edinburgh: 1903. V. 47; 51
The African Colony. London: 1903. V. 52
Andrew Jameson, Lord Ardwall. London: 1913. V. 49; 52; 53
Andrew Lang and the Border. London: 1933. V. 49
Augustus. 1937. V. 54
Augustus. London: 1937. V. 53
Balliol College War Memorial Book. London: 1924. V. 52
The Battle of Jutland. 1916. V. 54
The Battle of Jutland. London: 1916. V. 49; 51; 52; 53
The Battle-Honours of Scotland, 1914-1918. London: 1919. V. 49
The Blanket of the Dark. London: 1931. V. 49; 52; 53
A Book of Escapes and Hurried Journeys. London: 1922. V. 52
A Book of the Horace Club. London: 1901. V. 49; 52
Collection of His Famous Novels. London: 1922-48. V. 50
The Courts of Morning. London: 1929. V. 47; 49; 53
The Dancing Floor. 1926. V. 54
The Dancing Floor. London: 1926. V. 49
Days to Remember. 1923. V. 54
Essays of Lord Bacon. London: 1894. V. 52
The Fifteenth (Scottish) Division. 1914-1919. 1925. V. 54
The Fifteenth (Scottish) Division. 1914-1919. London: 1926. V. 52; 53
Francis and Riversdale Grenfell - a Memoir. London: 1920. V. 47; 53
The Free Fishers. 1934. V. 54
The Free Fishers. London: 1934. V. 49; 52; 53
The Gap in the Curtain. 1932. V. 47
The Gap in the Curtain. London: 1932. V. 49; 52; 53
Greenmantle. 1916. V. 54
Greenmantle. London: 1916. V. 52; 53
Grey Weather. London: 1899. V. 49; 52; 53
The Half-Hearted. London: 1900. V. 52
History of Brasenose College. London: 1898. V. 53
A History of the Great War. London: 1921. V. 47
History of the Great War. London: 1921-22. V. 49; 52; 53
The History of the Royal Scots Fusilers. (1678-1918). 1925. V. 54
The History of the South African Forces in France. London: 1920. V. 49; 52; 53
Homilies and Recreations. London: 1926. V. 49; 50; 53
The House of the Four Winds. London: 1935. V. 50; 52
The Island of Sheep. 1920. V. 53
The Island of Sheep. 1936. V. 53; 54
The Island of Sheep. London: 1936. V. 52; 53
John Buchan. 1847-1911. 1912. V. 53
John Burnet of Barnes. 1898. V. 54
John Burnet of Barnes. London: 1898. V. 49; 51; 52
John MacNab. Boston: 1925. V. 47
The King's Grace. 1935. V. 53; 54
The King's Grace. London: 1935. V. 48; 49; 50; 52
The Kirk in Scotland. 1930. V. 53; 54
The Kirk in Scotland. London: 1930. V. 49; 52
The Last Secrets - the Final Mysteries of Exploration. London: 1923. V. 51; 52; 53
The Lodge in the Wilderness. 1906. V. 53
The Lodge in the Wilderness. London: 1907. V. 52
The Long Traverse. London: 1941. V. 52; 53
Lord Minto. A Memoir. 1924. V. 53; 54
Lord Minto. A Memoir. London: 1924. V. 52
A Lost Lady in Old Years. 1899. V. 53; 54
A Lost Lady of Old Years. London: 1899. V. 52; 53
The Magic Walking-Stick. London: 1932. V. 53
The Marquis of Montrose. London: 1913. V. 52
The Massacre of Glencoe. London: 1933. V. 53
Men and Deeds. London: 1935. V. 50
Menin Gate Pilgrimage. St. Barnabas 1927. London: 1927. V. 52
Mr. Standfast. London: 1919. V. 52
Montrose. London, Edinburgh: 1928. V. 49; 54
Montrose and Leadership. London: 1930. V. 52
The Moon Endureth. London: 1912. V. 52
Mountain Meadow. Boston: 1941. V. 54
Musa Piscatrix. 1896. V. 49
Musa Piscatrix. London: 1896. V. 54
The Nine Brasenose Worthies. 1909. V. 49
The Nine Brasenose Worthies. London: 1909. V. 52
The Northern Muse. London: 1924. V. 49; 52
Oxford and Cambridge. London: 1909. V. 52
The Path of the King. London: 1921. V. 52
The Pilgrim Fathers. London: 1898. V. 47
The Power-House. London: 1916. V. 52
Prester John. New York. V. 47
Prester John. 1910. V. 49; 53; 54
Prester John. London: 1910. V. 52; 53
A Prince of Captivity. 1933. V. 53
Prince of Captivity. London: 1933. V. 49; 52
Principles of Social Service. 1933. V. 53; 54
Principles of Social Service. Glasgow: 1933. V. 48
Principles of Social Service. London: 1933. V. 52
The Runagates Club. 1928. V. 53
Salute to Adventurers. 1915. V. 53
Salute to Adventurers. London: 1915. V. 48
Scholar Gipsies. 1896. V. 49; 53; 54
Scholar Gipsies. London: 1896. V. 47; 48; 49; 50; 52
Scholar Gypsies. London & New York: 1906. V. 54
Sick Heart River. London: 1941. V. 52; 53
Sir Quixote of the Moors. 1895. V. 53; 54
Sir Quixote of the Moors. London: 1895. V. 49; 52
Sir Walter Raleigh. 1897. V. 53
Sir Walter Raleigh. 1911. V. 49; 53; 54
Sir Walter Raleigh. London: 1911. V. 52
Sir Walter Scott. London: 1932. V. 52; 53; 54
Some Eighteenth Century Byways and Essays. 1908. V. 49; 53; 54
Some Eighteenth Century Byways and other Essays. London: 1908. V. 52
The Story of the South African Brigade. 1921. V. 54
The Thirty-Nine Steps. 1915. V. 49; 53
The Thirty-Nine Steps. London: 1915. V. 47; 50; 52; 53
Two Ordeals of Democracy. 1925. V. 53; 54
The Watcher by the Threshold. 1902. V. 53

BUCHAN, PATRICK
Legends of the North. The Guidman o' Inglismill, and the Fairy Bride. Edinburgh: 1873. V. 50

BUCHAN, PETER
Ancient Ballads and Songs of the North of Scotland, Hitherto Unpublished. Edinburgh: 1875. V. 50

BUCHAN, SUSAN
Aunt Lily. 1921. V. 53
The Funeral March of a Marionette. London: 1935. V. 48

BUCHAN, TELFER J.
Crimea & Transcaucasia; Being the Narrative of a Journey in the Kouban in Gouria, Georgia, Armenia, Ossety, Imeritia, Swannety and Mingrelia and in the Tauric Range. London: 1876. V. 54

BUCHAN, WILLIAM
Domestic Medicine. 1776. V. 54
Domestic Medicine. 1779. V. 54
Domestic Medicine. London: 1791. V. 47
Domestic Medicine. London: 1792. V. 49; 51
Domestic Medicine. London: 1797. V. 47
Domestic Medicine. New York: 1797. V. 50
Domestic Medicine. Fairhaven: 1798. V. 54
Domestic Medicine. Leonminster: 1804. V. 48; 50
Every Man His Own Doctor; or, a Treatise on the Prevention and Cure of Disease... New Haven: 1816. V. 47; 48; 50

BUCHANAN, A. W. PATRICK
The Buchanan Book. Montreal: 1911. V. 49

BUCHANAN, BRIGGS
Catalogue of Ancient Near Eastern Seals in the Ashmolean Museum. Oxford: 1988. V. 50

BUCHANAN, CLAUDIUS
Christian Researches in Asia. Boston: 1811. V. 47
Christian Researches in Asia. Edinburgh: 1812. V. 47
Christian Researches in Asia. London: 1812. V. 47; 50
Christian Researches in Asia... Philadelphia: 1813. V. 47
Colonial Ecclesiastical Establishment. London: 1813. V. 47; 50; 53; 54

BUCHANAN, DONALD W.
James Wilson Morrice: a Biography. Toronto: 1936. V. 52; 53

BUCHANAN, G. D.
Observations on the Character and Present State of the Military Force of Great Britain. London: 1806. V. 50

BUCHANAN, GEORGE
De Ivre Regni Apvd Scotos Dialogvs... Edinburgh: 1580. V. 47
De Marai Scotorum Regina...Plena et Tragica Plane Historia. 1571. V. 49; 53
A Detection of the Actions of Mary Queen of Scots Concering the Murder of Her Husband and Her Conspiracy, Adultery and Pretended Marraige with Earth Bothwell... London: 1721. V. 51; 54
Georgii Buchanani Scoti, Poetarum Sui Seculi Facile Principis, Parapharasis Psalmorum Davidis Poetica. Glasguae: 1750. V. 47
The History of Scotland, from the Earliest Accounts of that Nation to the Reign of James VI. Edinburgh: 1762. V. 54
Jephtha. Paisley: 1902. V. 49
Jephtha. Paisley: 1903. V. 48
Paraphrasis Psalmorum Davidis Poetica. Glasgow: 1750. V. 49
Poemata. Leyden: 1628. V. 50
Poemata Quae Extant. Amsterdam: 1676. V. 53
Rerum Scoticarum Historia. Edinburgh: 1700. V. 47; 53
Rervm Scoticarvm Historia. Edimbvrgi (but London?): 1583. V. 52

BUCHANAN, ISAAC
The Relations of the Industry of Canada with the Mother Country and the United States... (with) Various Valuable Documents. Montreal: 1864. V. 47; 53

BUCHANAN, J. CROSS
Edith, a Tale of the Azores and Other Poems. London: 1838. V. 50

BUCHANAN, JAMES
The British Grammar; or, an Essay in Four Parts, Towards Speaking and Writing the English Language Grammatically and Inditing Elegantly. Oxford: 1913. V. 52
The British Grammar; or Essay in Four Parts, Towards Speaking and Writing the English Language Grammatically... Boston: 1784. V. 47
Correspondence Between Great Britain and the U.S. In Relation to Central American Affairs and the Enlistment Question. Washington: 1856. V. 48
Difficulties on Southwestern Frontier. Washington: 1860. V. 49
Execution of Colonel Crabb and Associates. Washington: 1858. V. 48
A New Pocket-Book for Young Gentlemen and Ladies; or, a Spelling Dictionary. London: 1757. V. 52
A Regular English Syntax. London: 1767. V. 48
A Regular English Syntax. Philadelphia: 1792. V. 53
Sketches of the History, Manners and Customs of the North American Indians. London: 1824. V. 50

BUCHANAN, JOHN
Albert: a Poem in Two Cantos. Hilda: and Other Poems. London: 1828. V. 50

BUCHANAN, JOHN LANE
Travels in the Western Hebrides; from 1782 to 1790. London: 1793. V. 52

BUCHANAN, JOSEPH
The Philosophy of Human Nataure. Richmond: 1812. V. 51; 53

BUCHANAN, JOSEPH R.
Outlines of Lectures on the Neuroogical system of Anthropology, as Discovered, Demonstrated and Taught in 1841 and 1842. Cincinnati: 1854. V. 50

BUCHANAN, R.
The Culture of the Grape, and Wine-Making. Cincinnati: 1855. V. 53
The Fleshly School of Poetry and Other Phenomena of the Day. London: 1872. V. 49

BUCHANAN, ROBERT
An Exposure of the Falsehoods, Calumnies, and Misrepresentations of a Pamphlet Entitled "The Abominations of Socialism Exposed". Manchester: 1840?. V. 53
The Fleshly School of Poetry. London: 1872. V. 47; 51
The Land of Lorne Including the Cruise of the "Tern" to the Outer Hebrides. London: 1871. V. 54
The Life and Adventures of John James Audubon. London: 1868. V. 54
The Life and Adventures of John James Audubon, the Naturalist. London: 1869. V. 48
On Descending into Hell: a Letter Addressed to the...Home Secretary Concerning the Proposed Suppression of Literature. London: 1889. V. 51
The Piper of Hamelin: Fantastic Opera in Two Acts. London: 1893. V. 52; 54
Saint Abe and His Seven Wives. London: 1872. V. 50; 52
Undertones. London: 1863. V. 49
The Wandering Jew. London: 1893. V. 52

BUCHANAN, ROBERTSON
A Practical Treatise On Propelling Vessels by Steam. Glasgow: 1816. V. 49

BUCHANAN, THOMAS
Physiological Illustrations of the Organ of Hearing, More Particularly of the Secretion of Cerumen... London: 1828. V. 47

BUCHANAN, W.
Memoirs of Painting, with a Chronological History of the Importation of Pictures by the Great Masters into England Since the French Revolution. London: 1824. V. 47; 52

BUCHANAN-JARDINE, JOHN
Hounds of the World. London: 1937. V. 47; 54

BUCHER, FRANCOIS
The Pamplona Bibles. New Haven: 1970. V. 48

BUCHHEIM, LOTHAR GUNTER
The Graphic Art of German Expressionism. New York: 1960. V. 53; 54

BUC' HOZ, PIERRE JOSEPH
Herbier Ou Collection des Plantes Medicinales de la Chine. (bound with) Les Dons Merveilleux et Diversement Colories de la Nature Dans le Regne Mineral. Paris: 1781/82. V. 47
Herbier Ou Collection des Plantes Medicinales de la Chine. (with) Les Dons Merveilleux et Diversement Colories de la Nature dans le Regne Mineral. Paris: 1781. V. 48
The Toliet of Flora; or, a Collection of the Most Simple and Approved Methods of Preparing Baths, Essences, Pomatums, Powders, Perfumes... London: 1775. V. 50

BUCK, ALBERT
A Reference Handbook of the Medical Sciences Embracing the Entire Range of Scientific and Practical Medicine and Allied Science by Various Writers. New York: 1907. V. 53
A Treatise on Hygiene and Public Health. New York: 1879. V. 48; 50

BUCK, DANIEL
Indian Outbreaks. Mankato: 1904. V. 53

BUCK, EDWARD J.
Simla Past and Present. Calcutta: 1904. V. 54

BUCK, FRANK
On Jungle Trails. New York: 1937. V. 47

BUCK, G. W.
A Practical and Theoretical Essay on Oblique Bridges. London: 1839. V. 49
A Practical and Theoretical Essay on Oblique Bridges... London: 1857. V. 47; 50; 54

BUCK, GEORGE
The History of the Life and Reigne of Richard the Third. London: 1646. V. 49
The History of the Life and Reigne of Richard the Third. London: 1647. V. 50

BUCK, MITCHELL
Book Repair and Restoration. Philadelphia: 1918. V. 53

BUCK, PEARL SYDENSTRICKER
For Spacious Skies: Journey in Dialogue. New York: 1966. V. 54
God's Men. New York: 1951. V. 54
The Patriot. New York: 1939. V. 54
Pavilion of Women. New York: 1946. V. 49; 54
Stories For Little Children. New York: 1940. V. 47
Tell the People. New York: 1959. V. 54
The Young Revolutionist. New York: 1932. V. 48; 53

BUCK, SAMUEL
Antiquities, or Venerable Remains of Castles, Monasteries, Palaces, &c. in England and Wales... London: 1737. V. 50
Antiquities, or Venerable Remains of Castles, Monasteries, Palaces &c. in England and Wales... London: 1744. V. 49

BUCKBEE, EDNA BRYAN
The Saga of Old Tuolumne. New York: 1935. V. 50; 54

BUCKE, CHARLES
Amusements in Retirement; or, the Influence of Science, Literature and the Liberal arts, on the Manners and Happiness of Private Life. London: 1818. V. 52
On the Beauties, Harmonies and Sublimities of Nature... London: 1821. V. 51

BUCKEYE Cookery and Practical Housekeeping. Minneapolis: 1877. V. 47

BUCKINGHAM, CLARENCE
The Clarence Buckingham Collection of Japanese Prints. Chicago: 1955/65. V. 54
The Clarence Buckingham Collection of Japanese Prints. Chicago: 1965. V. 47

BUCKINGHAM, GEORGE VILLIERS, 1ST DUKE OF
The Rehearsal. London: 1709. V. 54

BUCKINGHAM, GEORGE VILLIERS, 2ND DUKE OF
The Genuine Works of His Grace... Glasgow: 1752. V. 50
The Genuine Works of His Grace George Villiers, Duke of Buckingham. London: 1752. V. 47
Miscellaneous Works... London: 1705. V. 52
The Rehearsal, As it Is Now Acted... London: 1675. V. 51

BUCKINGHAM, JAMES SILK
America, Historical, Statistic and Descriptive. London: 1841. V. 48; 49; 50
America, Historical, Statistic and Descriptive. New York: 1841. V. 53
Appeal to the British Nation, on the Greatest Reform Yet Remaining to be Accomplished... London: 1846. V. 50; 54
Appendix to Travels in Mesopotamia. London: 1826. V. 49
Canada, Nova Scotia, New Brunswick, and other British Provinces in North America. London & Paris: 1843. V. 49; 53
The Eastern and Western States of America. London: 1842. V. 53
The Slave States of America. London and Paris: 1842. V. 49
Travels in Assyria, Media and Persia. London: 1830. V. 47
Travels in Palestine, through the Countries of Bashan and Gilead, East of the River Jordan. London: 1821. V. 47

BUCKINGHAM, JOHN SHEFFIELD, 1ST DUKE OF
The Works. London: 1723. V. 47
The Works. London: 1729. V. 50
The Works. London: 1740. V. 49

BUCKINGHAM, JOSEPH T.
Miscellanies from the Public Journals. Boston: 1822. V. 51; 54

BUCKINGHAM, NASH
Blood Lines. Tales of Shooting and Fishing. New York: 1938. V. 47; 49; 51
De Shootin'est Gent'man and Other Hunting Tales. New York: 1961. V. 50

BUCKINGHAM, NASH continued
De Shootinest Gent'man and Other Tales. New York: 1934. V. 51; 53
Game Bag: Tales of Shooting and Fishing. New York: 1945. V. 47; 53
Mark Right! Tales of Shooting and Fishing. New York: 1936. V. 47; 52
Ole Miss'. New York: 1937. V. 47
Tattered Coat. New York: 1944. V. 47

BUCKLAND, F.
Fish Hatching. London: 1863. V. 54

BUCKLAND, W.
Geology and Mineralogy. London: 1836. V. 53
Geology and Mineralogy. London: 1837. V. 53
Geology and Mineralogy... London: 1858. V. 48
Plates of Dr. Buckland's Bridgewater Treatise 1836. London: 1837. V. 48
Reliquiae Diluvianae. London: 1823. V. 51; 54
Reliquiae Diluvianae or Observation on the Organic Remains Contained in Caves, Fissures and Diluvial Gravel and On Other Geological Phenomena. London: 1824. V. 48; 49; 50; 53

BUCKLAND WRIGHT, JOHN
Baigneuses: Engravings. Denby Dale: 1995. V. 54
Bathers and Dancers: the White Line and Silhouette Engravings. London: 1993. V. 50; 52; 53
Engravings. Aldershot: 1990. V. 48
The Engravings of John Buckland Wright. London: 1990. V. 47; 51; 54

BUCKLE, A.
Yorkshire Etchings with Sonnets and Descriptions. Leeds: 1885. V. 47; 53

BUCKLE, HENRY THOMAS
Essays with a Biographical Sketch of the Author. New York: 1863. V. 49; 51; 53
History of Civilization in England. London: 1857-61. V. 49
History of Civilization in England. London: 1861. V. 51

BUCKLE, RICHARD
Jacob Epstein, Sculptor. London: 1963. V. 49

BUCKLE, THOMAS
Essays with a Biographical Sketch of the Author. New York: 1863. V. 50

BUCKLE, THOMAS HENRY
Miscellaneous and Posthumous Works. London: 1872. V. 48

BUCKLER, BENJAMIN
A Complete Vindication of the Mallard of All-Souls College, Against the Injurious Suggestions of the Rev. Mr. (John) Pointer. London: 1751. V. 52
A Philosophical Dialogue Concerning Decency. Oxford: 1751. V. 52
Stemmata Chicheleana: or, a Genealogical Account of Some of the Families Derived from Thomas Chichele, of Higham-Ferrers in the County of Northampton... Oxford: 1765. V. 47
Stemmata Chicheleana; or, A Genealogical Account of some of the Families Derived from Thomas Chichele, of Higham-Ferrers in the County of Northampton. (with) A Supplement to the Stemmata Chicheleana... Oxford: 1765-75. V. 47

BUCKLER, ERNEST
The Mountain and the Valley. New York: 1952. V. 50

BUCKLER, J.
The South West View of the Collegiate Church of Saint Wilfrid, Ripon. Bermondsey: 1809. V. 47

BUCKLER, W.
The Larvae of the British Butterflies and Moths. London: 1886-1901. V. 52

BUCKLEY, J. M.
Two Weeks in the Yosemite and Vicinity. New York: 1883. V. 50

BUCKLEY, MICHAEL J.
Day at the Farm; a Poem. San Francisco: 1937. V. 52; 54

BUCKLEY, W.
Big Game Hunting in Central Africa. London: 1930. V. 47

BUCKLEY, WILLIAM F.
Racing Through Paradise, a Pacific Passage. New York: 1987. V. 49; 50

BUCKLEY'S Ethiopian Melodies. New York: 1853. V. 47

BUCKMAN, GEORGE REX
Colorado Springs, Colorado and Its Famous Scenic Environs. Colorado Springs: 1893. V. 54
The Story of Cripple Creek Up to Date. A Plain Statement of Facts Concerning Colorado's Foremost Gold District. Colorado Springs: 1894. V. 54

BUCKMAN, JAMES
Illustrations of the Remains of Roman Art, in Cirencester, the Site of Antient Corinium. London: 1850. V. 50

BUCKNALL, THOMAS SKIP DYOT
The Orchardist; or a System of Close Pruning and Medication... London: 1797. V. 53

BUCKNER, ROBERT
Sigrid and the Sergeant. New York: 1957. V. 53

BUCKNILL, J. C.
A Manual of Psychological Medicine... London: 1879. V. 47; 53

BUCKNILL, JOHN A.
The Birds of Surrey. London: 1900. V. 49; 53

THE BUCK'S Bottle Companion: Being a Complete Collection of Humorous, Bottle and Hunting Songs. London: 1775. V. 48

BUCKTON, ALICE MARY
Through Human Eyes. Poems. Oxford: 1901. V. 49; 52; 53

BUCKTON, G. B.
Monograph of the British Cicadae or Tettigidae. (with) *The Natural History of Eristalis Tenax or the Drone-Fly.* London: 1890-95. V. 52; 53
The Natural History of Eristalis Tenax or the Drone-Fly. London: 1895. V. 52

THE BUD Of Texas, or Little Jennie. Philadelphia: 1845. V. 49

BUDD, GEORGE
On Diseases of the Liver. Philadelhia: 1846. V. 48; 53
On Diseases of the Liver. Philadelphia: 1857. V. 48; 53
On the Organic Diseases and Functional Disorders of the Stomach. Philadelphia: 1856. V. 53

BUDD, WILLIAM
Typhoid Fever: Its Nature, Mode of Spreading and Preventio. London: 1873. V. 51
Typhoid Fever: its Nature, Mode of Spreading and Prevention. New York: 1931. V. 50; 53

BUDDEN, LIONEL B.
The Book of the Liverpool School of ARchitecture. Liverpool: 1932. V. 53

BUDDEN, MARIA ELISABETH
Always Happy!!! or, Anecdotes of Felix and His Sister Serena. London: 1815. V. 48; 51

BUDDLE, JOHN
The Marquis of Worcester's Century of Inventions. Newcastle: 1813. V. 50

BUDGE, ERNEST ALFRED WALLIS THOMPSON
Amulets and Superstitions. 1930. V. 48
Assyrian Sculptures in the British Museum, Reign of Ashur-Nasir-Pal, 885 to 1860 B.C. London: 1914. V. 49; 50
The Book of the Cave of Treasures... London: 1927. V. 48
The Book of the Dead... London: 1898. V. 51
The Book of the Dead. London: 1901. V. 48
By Nile and Tigris. London: 1920. V. 48; 49
The Chapters of Coming Forth by the Day or the Theban Recension of the Book of the Dead. London: 1910. V. 49
Coptic Biblical Texts in Dialect of Upper Egypt. London: 1912. V. 49; 51
An Egyptian Hieroglyphic Dictionary. New York: 1960. V. 49; 51
Egyptian Sculptures in the British Museum. London: 1914. V. 49; 53
Facsimiles of the Papyri or Hunefor, Anhai, Karasher and Netchemet with Supplementary text from the Papyrus of Nu. London: 1899. V. 49; 51
From Fetish to God in Ancient Egypt. London: 1934. V. 48
From Fetish to God in Ancient Egypt. Oxford: 1934. V. 49; 51
The Greenfield Papyrus in the British Museum. London: 1912. V. 51
A History of Egypt from the End of the Neolithic Period to the Death of Cleopatra VII, B.C. 30. New York: 1902. V. 51
The History of Esarhaddon (Son of Sennacherib) King of Assyria, B.C. 681-668. Boston: 1881. V. 47
The Life of Takla Haymanot... London: 1906. V. 50
The Monks of Kublai Khan Emperor of China. London: 1928. V. 48
The Mummy. Cambridge: 1893. V. 48
The Mummy. London: 1894. V. 51
The Mummy. A Handbook of Egyptian Funerary Archaeology. Cambridge: 1925. V. 48; 51
Osiris: The Egyptian Religion of Resurrection. London: 1911. V. 49; 51
The Sarcophagus of Anehnesraneferab, Queen of Ahmes II, King of Egypt, About B.C. 564-526. London: 1885. V. 51
Some Account of the Collection of Egyptian Antiquities in the Possession of Lady Meux, of Theobold's Park, Waltham Cross. London: 1896. V. 49; 51
Tutankhamen...Egyptian Monotheise... New York: 1923. V. 53

BUDGE, J.
The Practical Miner's Guide... London & Devonport: 1825. V. 48

BUDGELL, EUSTACE
A Short History of Prime Ministers in Great Britain. London: 1733. V. 48

BUDGEN, L. M.
Episodes of Insect Life. London: 1849-50-51. V. 50; 54

BUDGEN, LOUIS H.
The Grasshoppr's Fall. London: 1835. V. 47

BUDGEN, M. L.
Episodes of Insect Life by Acheta Domestica M.E.S. London: 1849-51. V. 49
Episodes of Insect Life. First and Second Series. London: 1849-50. V. 49

BUDRYS, A. J.
Cerberus. 1989. V. 47

BUECHNER, THOMAS S.
Norman Rockwell, Artist and Illustrator. New York: 1970. V. 47; 49; 50; 53
Norman Rockwell, Artist and Illustrator. New York: 1975. V. 47

BUEL, J. W.
The Border Outlaws...the Younger Brothers, Jessie & Frank Maes and Their Comrades in Crime. St. Louis: 1881. V. 47; 53; 54

BUEL, JAMES WILLIAM
Heroes of the Plains. St. Louis: 1881. V. 53

BUELL, SAMUEL
A Copy of a Letter from the Reverend Mr. Buell, of East-Hampton, On Long Island, to the Reverend Mr. Barber of Groton, in Connecticut, North America. London: 1764. V. 49

BUERGER, GOTTFRIED AUGUST
Leonora. London: 1796. V. 52

BUERJA, ABEL
Der Mathematische Maler, Oder Grundliche Anweisung zur Perspective... Berlin: 1795. V. 53

BUFFA, JOHN
Travels through the Empire of Morocco. London: 1810. V. 49

BUFFALO Bill's Store Vovestykee en Fortaelling Fra Det Vestlige Amerika. St. Paul: 1900. V. 54

BUFFEN, F. F.
Musical Celebrities. London: 1889/93. V. 49

BUFFET, BERNARD
Bernard Buffet: Lithographs 1952-1966. New York: 1968. V. 50
Lithographs 1952-1966. New York: 1968. V. 51

BUFFON, GEORGE LOUIS LECLERC, COMTE DE
Buffon's Animated Nature. London: 1828-21. V. 49
Buffon's Natural History... London: 1792. V. 49
Histoire Naturelle... Paris: 1799-1801. V. 51
Histoire Naturelle Generale et Particliere, Oiseaux. 1785-87. V. 54
Histoire Naturelle Generale et Particuliere avec la Description du Cabient du Roy. Paris: 1750-67. V. 54
The History of Singing Birds. Edinburgh: 1791. V. 48
Natural History, General and Particular. London: 1785. V. 54
Natural History, General and Particular. London: 1791. V. 47; 49; 51
Natural History, General and Particular. London: 1791/93. V. 49
Natural History, General and Particular. London: 1812. V. 47; 52; 54
A Natural History, General and Particular... London: 1834. V. 48; 49
The Natural History of Birds. London: 1792. V. 47; 51; 54
Natural History of Birds, Insects and Reptiles Embellished with Upwards of 200 Engravings. London: 1793. V. 50
The Natural History of Quadrupeds. Edinburgh: 1830. V. 48; 51
Natural History of the Globe and of Man; Beasts, Birds, Fishes, Reptiles and Insects. London: 1831. V. 54
The Natural History of the Horse. London: 1762. V. 47; 49

BUFFORD'S Colored Views of the White Mountains and the Vicinity. Boston: 1863. V. 50

BUFFUM, EDWARD GOULD
Six Months in the Gold Mines: from a Journal of Three Years' Residence in Upper and Lower California, 1847-8-9. Philadelphia: 1850. V. 47
Six Months in the Gold Mines: from a Journal of Three Years' Residence in Upper and Lower California, in 1847-8-9. London: 1850. V. 51

BUFFUM, GEORGE T.
On Two Frontiers. Boston: 1918. V. 48

BUFFUM, W. ARNOLD
The Tears of Heliades; or, Amber as a Gem. London: 1897. V. 53

BUGBEE, L. G.
Slavery in Early Texas. Boston: 1898. V. 48

BUGDEN, M. L.
Episodes of Insect Life. London: 1849-51. V. 48

BUGENHAGEN, JOHAN
Der XXIX. Psalm Ausgelegt. Wittenberg: 1542. V. 50

BUGLER, ARTHUR
HMS Victory Building, Restoration and Repair. London: 1966. V. 49; 50

BUGNEY, T. O.
A Month with the Muses. Colorado Tales and Legends of the Earlier Days. Pueblo: 1875. V. 47

BUHL, HERMANN
Nanga Parbat Pilgrimage. London: 1956. V. 51; 52; 53

BUHLER, K. C.
American Silver: Garvan and Other Collections in the Yale University Art Gallery. New Haven: 1970. V. 47

BUICHARD, CLAUDE
Funerailles & Diverses Manieres d'Enseuelir des Rommains, Grecs & Autres Nations. Lyon: 581. V. 49

THE BUILDER'S Practical Directory, or, Building for All Classes. (with) Supplemental Series. Leipzig & Dresden: 1855-58. V. 50

BUIST, ROBERT
The Rose Manual. Philadelphia: 1844. V. 50
The Rose Manual... Philadelphia: 1847. V. 47

BUJOLD, L.
Barrayar. 1991. V. 48; 52
The Vor Game. 1990. V. 48; 52

BUKOWSKI, CHARLES
Aftermath of A Lengthy Rejection Slip. 1983. V. 50
All Assholes in The World and Mine. Bensenville: 1966. V. 47; 49; 50; 51; 53
Art. Los Angeles: 1977. V. 49
Art. Santa Barbara: 1977. V. 53
At Terror Street and Agony Way. 1968. V. 54
At Terror Street and Agony Way. Los Angeles: 1968. V. 49
Barfly. 1984. V. 51
Barfly. Sutton West & Santa Barbara: 1984. V. 48; 49; 50
Barfly. 1987. V. 52
Bring Me Your Love. Santa Barbara: 1983. V. 47; 48; 49; 50
A Bukowski Sampler. Madison: 1969. V. 49; 51
The Bukowski/Purdy Letters 1964-1974. Santa Barbara: 1983. V. 48; 50
Burning in Water, Drowning in Flame. Los Angeles: 1974. V. 49; 50; 53
Cold Dogs in the Courtyard. Chicago: 1965. V. 47; 49; 50; 53
Confessions of a Man Insane Enough to Live with Beasts. Bensenville: 1965. V. 47; 49; 50; 52; 53
Crucifix in a Deathhand. New Orleans: 1965. V. 52
Crucifix in a Deathhand. New York: 1965. V. 47; 49; 50; 51; 53
The Curtains are Waving and People Walk through the Afternoon Here. San Francisco: 1967. V. 48; 49; 51; 52
Dangling in the Tournefortia. 1981. V. 54
Dangling in the Tournefortia. Santa Barbara: 1981. V. 47; 48; 49; 50
The Day It Snowed in L.A. Santa Barbara: 1986. V. 50
The Day it Snowed in L.A. Sutton West: 1986. V. 49
The Days Run Away Like Wild Horses Over the Hills. Los Angeles: 1969. V. 49; 51
The Days Run Away Like Wild Horses Over the Hills. Santa Barbara: 1969. V. 52
Dear Mr. Bukowski... San Luis Obispo: 1979. V. 50; 52
Erections, Ejaculations, Exhibitions and General Tales of Ordinary Madness. 1972. V. 53
Factotum. 1975. V. 54
Factotum. Santa Barbara: 1975. V. 49; 50
A Fine Man, A Fine Book. V. 48
Flower Fist and Bestial Wail. Eureka: 1959. V. 49; 51
Flower Fist and Bestial Wail. Eureka: 1960. V. 54
The Genius of the Crowd. Ohio: 1966. V. 49; 51
Ham on Rye. Santa Barbara: 1982. V. 47; 48; 49; 50; 54
Hollywood. 1989. V. 52; 54
Horsemeat. Santa Barbara: 1982. V. 48; 50
Hot Water Music. 1983. V. 54
Hot Water Music. Santa Barbara: 1983. V. 47; 49; 51
If We Take. Los Angeles: 1970. V. 50
In the Shadow of the Rose. 1991. V. 54
In the Shadow of the Rose. Santa Rosa: 1991. V. 49
It Catches My Heart In its Hands. New Orleans: 1963. V. 49; 50
The Last Generation. Santa Barbara: 1982. V. 51
The Last Night of the Earth Poems. 1992. V. 48
The Last Night of the Earth Poems. Santa Rosa: 1992. V. 47; 49
Life and Death in the Charity Ward. London: 1974. V. 53
Longshot Poems for Broke Players. New York: 1962. V. 49; 50; 51
Love is A Dog from Hell. 1977. V. 54
Love Is a Dog From Hell. Santa Barbara: 1977. V. 49; 50
A Love Poem. Santa Barbara: 1979. V. 50
Me and Your Sometimes Love Poems. Los Angeles: 1971. V. 49
Mockingbird Wish Me Luck. 1972. V. 54
Mockingbird Wish Me Luck. Los Angeles: 1972. V. 49
Mockingbird Wish Me Luck. Santa Barbara: 1974. V. 50
The Movie "Barfly": An Original Screenplay. Santa Rosa: 1987. V. 49
The Movie: Barfly. 1987. V. 54
Notes of a Dirty Old Man. North Hollywood: 1969. V. 52; 53
Now. 1992. V. 54
Play the Piano Drunk Like a Percussion Instrument Until the Fingers Begin to Bleed a Bit. Santa Barbara: 1978. V. 50
Play the Piano Drunk Like a Percussion Instrument Until the Fingers Begin to Bleed a Bit. Santa Barbara: 1979. V. 50; 52
Poems and Drawings. Crescent City: 1962. V. 49
Poems Written Before Jumping Out of an 8 Story Window. Berkeley. V. 54
Poems Written Before Jumping Out of an 8 Story Window. Berkeley: 1968. V. 49; 51
Poems Written Before Jumping Out of an 8 Story Window. Glendale: 1968. V. 50
Post Office. Los Angeles: 1971. V. 49
Pulp. Santa Rosa: 1994. V. 51
Pulp. 1995. V. 54
Red. Hollywood: 1989. V. 49
The Rooming-House Madrigals: Early Selected Poems 1946-1966. Santa Rosa: 1988. V. 47; 48
Run With the Hunted. Chicago: 1962. V. 49
Run with the Hunted. 1993. V. 54
Run with the Hunted. New York: 1993. V. 53
Scarlet. Santa Barbra: 1976. V. 49
Screams from the Balcony. 1993. V. 52; 53
Screams from the Balcony. Selected Letters. 1994. V. 54
Septaugenarian Stew, Stories and Poems. Santa Rosa: 1990. V. 49; 50; 54
Shakespeare Never Did This. San Francisco: 1979. V. 49; 50; 52
Shakespeare Never Did This. Santa Fe: 1979. V. 50
South of North. 1973. V. 54
South of North. Los Angeles: 1973. V. 49
South OF North. Los Angeles: 1975. V. 48
Sparks. Santa Barbara: 1983. V. 50

BUKOWSKI, CHARLES continued
There's No Business. 1984. V. 52; 53
There's No Business. Santa Barbara: 1984. V. 49; 50; 51
This. Andernach: 1990. V. 49
Two Poems. Los Angeles: 1967. V. 47; 49
Under the Influence. Sudbury: 1984. V. 50
War All the Time. 1984. V. 54
War All the Time. Santa Barbara: 1984. V. 49; 50
What They Want. Santa Barbara: 1977. V. 50
Women. Santa Barbara: 1978. V. 49
You Get So Alone At Times That It Just Makes Sense. Santa Rosa: 1986. V. 49; 50; 54
You Kissed Lilly. Santa Barbara: 1978. V. 49

BULFINCH, S. G.
Poems. Charleston: 1834. V. 51; 52; 54

BULFINCH, THOMAS
The Age of Fable; or, Stories of Gods and Heroes. Boston: 1855. V. 47; 48
A Book for Young Men. The Boy Inventor; a memoir of Matthew Edwards, Mathematical Instrument Maker. Boston: 1860. V. 54

BULGER, GEORGE ERNEST
Leaves from the Records of St. Hubert's Club; or, Reminiscences of Sporting Expeditions in Many Lands. London: 1864. V. 49; 51

BULKELEY, JOHN
A Voyage to the South-Seas, in the Years 1740-41. London: 1743. V. 49

BULKLEY, CHARLES
A Vindication of My Lord Shaftesbury, on the Subject of Ridicule. London: 1751. V. 47

BULKLEY, DUNCAN
Eczema and its Management. New York: 1882. V. 48; 53

BULL, CLARENCE SINCLAIR
The Faces of Hollywood. South Brunswick: 1968. V. 51

BULL, FREDERICK W.
A History of Newton Pagnell. Kettering: 1900. V. 53

BULL, GEORGE
Opera Omnia. London: 1703. V. 50
The Works of... London: 1725. V. 49

BULL, H. G.
The Herfordshire Pomona... Hereford: 1876-85. V. 48
Notes on the Birds of Herefordshire. London: 1888. V. 52

BULL, MARCUS
Experiments to Determine the Comparative Value of the Principal Varieties of Fuel Used in the United States, and Also in Europe. Philadelphia: 1827. V. 47

BULL, ROGER, PSEUD.
Grobianus; or the Compleat Booby. London: 1739. V. 52

BULL, WILLIAM PERKINS
From Brock to Currie: The Military Development and Exploits of Canadians in General and of the Men of Peel in Particular, 1791 to 1930. Toronto: 1935. V. 53
From Hummingbird to Eagle: an Account of North American Birds Which Appear to Have Appeared in the County of Peel. Toronto: 1936. V. 51
From Rattlesnake Hunt to Hockey: The History of Sports in Canada and of the Sportsmen of Peel, 1798 to 1934. Toronto: 1934. V. 53
From Strachan to Owen: How the Church of England Was Planted and Tended in British North America. Toronto: 1938. V. 53
Spadunk, or, From Paganism to Davenport United: a Study of Community Development of the Religious Life Around Which it Centered... Toronto: 1935. V. 51

BULLANT, JEAN
Reigle Generalle D'Architecture des Cinq manieres de Colonnes. Paris: 1568. V. 50

BULLAR, JOSEPH
A Winter in the Azores and a Sumemr at the Baths of the Furnas. London: 1841. V. 50; 54

BULLART, ISAAC
Academie des Sciences et des Arts, Contenant les Vies & les Eloges Historiques des Hommes Illustres, Qui Ont Excelle en Ces Professions Depuis Environ Quatres Siecles Parmy Diverses Nations de l'Europe... Bruxelles: 1682. V. 50

BULLEID, ARTHUR
The Meare Lake Village. 1948-66. V. 52

BULLEIN, WILLIAM
Bulleins Bulwarke of Defence Againste All Sicknes, Sores and Woundes that Dooe Daily Assaulte mankinde... London: 1562. V. 52
Bulwark of Defence Against All Sicknesse, Soarnesse and Woundes. London: 1579. V. 49

BULLEN, A. H.
Davison's Poetical Rhapsody. London: 1890-91. V. 50
England's Helicon. London: 1887. V. 50; 53
Lyrics From the Dramatists of the Elizabethan Age. London: 1889. V. 50
Lyrics from the Dramatists of the Elizabethan Age. London: 1891. V. 47; 51
More Lyrics from the song-Books of the Elizabethan Age. London: 1888. V. 50
Musa Proterva: Love-Poems of the Restoration. London: 1889. V. 48
Poems, Chiefly Lyrical, from Romances and Prose-Tracts of the Elizabethan Age: with Chosen Poems of Nicholas Breton. London: 1890. V. 50
Speculum Amantis: Love Poems. London: 1902. V. 49; 52; 54
Speculum Amantis: Love-Poems. London: 1889. V. 50

BULLEN, FRANK T.
The Cruise of the Cachalot Round the World After Sperm Whales. London: 1898. V. 48; 51
The Cruise of the Cachalot Round the World After Sperm Whales. London: 1899. V. 54

BULLEN, GEORGE
Caxton Celebration 1877. Catalogue of the Loan Collection of Antiquities, Curiosities and Appliances Connected with the Art of Printing, South Kensington. London: 1877. V. 47; 52
Specimens of Printing Types for Book, Newspaper and General Work. 1876. V. 47

BULLEN, HENRY LEWIS
Nicolas Jenson, Printer of Venice: His Famous Type Designs and Some Comment Upon the Printing Types of Earlier Printers. San Francisco: 1926. V. 52

BULLEN, K. B.
We Stand Alone...and Other War Sonnets. Cairo: 1942. V. 47

BULLER, FRANCIS
The Charge of Sir Francis Buller, Bart. One of the Commissioners Appointed for Trying Arthur O'Conner, Favey, Binns, Allen and Leary, On a Charge of High Treason, at Maidstone on Wednesday 11th April, 1798 to the Grand Jury... Dublin: 1798. V. 53
An Introduction to the Law Relative to Trials at Nisi Prius. Dublin: 1773. V. 50; 52
An Introduction to the Law Relative to Trials at Nisi Prius, Containing Additions to the Present Time... New York: 1806. V. 53

BULLER, WALTER L.
Birds of New Zealand. London: 1967. V. 49; 52
A History of New Zealand. New Zealand: 1967. V. 50
A History of the Birds of New Zealand. London: 1888. V. 48; 50
A History of the Birds of New Zealand. London: 1888-1906. V. 47
A History of the Birds of New Zealand. London: 1967. V. 52; 53; 54
Manual of the Birds of New Zealand. Wellington: 1882. V. 51; 54

BULLETT, GERALD
Seed of Israel. Tales from the English Bible and Apocrypha. London: 1927. V. 53

BULLEY, ELEANOR
Life of Queen Alexandra. London: 1902. V. 54

BULLIET, C. J.
Venus Castina: Famous Female Impersonators Celestial and Human. New York: 1928. V. 47; 48

BULLINGER, EDWIN W.
The Mercantile Agency Special Edition of Bullinger's Postal and Shippers Guide for the United States and Canada Containing Every Post Office, Railroad Station, and United States For, with the Railroad or Water Route on Which Every Place... New York: 1882. V. 47

BULLINGER, HEINRICH
The Christian State of Matrimony. London: 1575. V. 51

BULLINS, ED
Five Plays. Indianapolis: 1969. V. 52
How Do You do. New York: 1965. V. 53

BULLOCH, JOHN
George Jamesone. The Scottish Vandyck. Edinburgh: 1885. V. 54

BULLOCH, WILLIAM
The History of Bacteriology. London: 1938. V. 50; 51; 52

BULLOCK, BARBARA
Wynn Bullock. San Francisco: 1971. V. 47; 50

BULLOCK, GEORGE
Soul Retrievers. New York: 1974. V. 53

BULLOCK, R. E.
How to Vote!...the Working Man's Candidate: Hon. R. B. Bullock, of Richmond County. Constitution of Man's Candidate. Atlanta: 1868. V. 48

BULLOCK, T. H.
The Chinese Vindicated, or Another View of the Opium Question... London: 1840. V. 54

BULLOCK, TOM
The Ideal Bartender. St. Louis: 1917. V. 54

BULLOCK, WILLIAM
A Companion to Mr. Bullock's Museum...of...Natural and Foreign Curiosities, Antiquities...Fine Arts...in the Great Room, 22 Piccadilly, London. London: 1811. V. 52
A Concise and Easy Method of Preserving Objects of Natural History... London: 1818. V. 48
Six Months' Residence and Travels in Mexico... London: 1824. V. 47; 48; 52

BULLOCK, WYNN
The Widening Stream. San Francisco: 1965. V. 47

BULLOUGH, CHARLES P.
The Tale of a Trout With a Moral. Cambridge: 1903. V. 49; 53

BULMER, GEORGE BERTRAM
Architectural Studies in Yorkshire. London: 1887. V. 53

BULMER, JOHN
The Vicar of Llandovery, or Light from the Welshman's Candle. Haverfordwest: 1821. V. 54

BULMER, T., & CO.
History, Topography and Directory of Cumberland, Comprising Its History and Archaeology... Preston: 1901. V. 50; 52
History, Topography and Directory of East Cumberland... Manchester: 1884. V. 50; 52; 54
History, Topography and Directory of East Yorkshire (with Hull) Comprising Its Ancient and Modern History...Family History and Genealogical Descent. London: 1890. V. 52

BULMER, T., & CO. continued
History, Topography and Directory of West Cumberland... Preston: 1883. V. 50; 52
History, Topography and Directory of Westmoreland... Manchester: 1885. V. 50
History, Topography and Directory of Westmoreland. Preston;: 1906. V. 50; 52
T. Bulmer's History, Topography and Directory of Lancaster & District. Preston: 1912. V. 51

BULOW, ERNIE
Navajo Taboos. Gallup: 1991. V. 51; 52; 53; 54
Words, Weather and Wolfmen. Gallup: 1989. V. 49; 52

BULPETT, C.
A Picnic Party in Wildest Africa...the Upper Nile. London: 1907. V. 48

BULPIN, T. V.
The Hunter is Death. Johannesburg: 1962. V. 53
The Hunter is Death. London: 1962. V. 48

BULSTRODE, EDWARD
The Reports of...His Highness Chief Justice of North-Wales. London: 1657-8-9. V. 47

BULSTRODE, RICHARD
Memoirs and Reflections Upon the Reign and Government of King Charles the 1st and K. Charles the IId. London: 1721. V. 47

BULSTRODE, WHITELOCKE
An Essay on Transmigration, in Defence of Pythagoras. London: 1692. V. 52

BULTMANN, BERNHARD
Oskar Kokoschka. New York: 1961. V. 50

BULWER, JOHN
Anthropometamorphosis: Man Transform'd; or, the Artificial Changeling. London: 1650. V. 52; 53

BULWER-LYTTON, HENRY
France, Social, Literary, Political. (with) The Monarachy of the Middle Classes. New York: 1835/36. V. 52

BUMKE, OSWALD
Handbuch der Neurologie. Berlin: 1935. V. 53

BUMP, G.
The Ruffed Grouse, Life History, Propagation, Management. Albany: 1947. V. 54

BUMPUS, J. & E.
Catalogue of an Exhibition. London: 1934. V. 52

BUNBURY, CHARLES J. F.
Journal of a Residence at the Cape of Good Hope; with Excursions into the Interior, and Notes on the Natural History and the Native Tribes. London: 1848. V. 47

BUNBURY, HENRY WILLIAM
An Academy for Grown Horseman. London: 1809. V. 53
An Academy for Grown Horsemen. London: 1808. V. 49
An Academy for Grown Horsemen. New York: 1929. V. 50
An Academy for Grown Horsemen. (with) Annals of Horsemanship. London: 1825/25. V. 51
Annals of Horsemanship. London W. Dickinson, S: 1791/88. V. 51
Annals of Horsemanship. London: 1812. V. 52

BUNBURY, SELINA
The Abbey of Innismoyle: a Story of Another Century. Dublin: 1829. V. 50
Rides in the Pyrenees. London: 1847. V. 51

BUNBURY, WILLIAM
Reports of Cases in the Court of Exchequer, from the Beginning of the Reign of King George the First, Until the Fourteenth Year of the Reign of King George the Second. London: 1755. V. 47

BUNCE, F. W.
An Encyclopedia of Buddhist Deities, Demigods, Godlings, Saints and Demons... New Delhi: 1994. V. 51

BUNCE, JOHN THACKRAY
Cloudland and Shadowland. London: 1860. V. 54
History of Old St. Martin's, Birmingham... Birmingham: 1875. V. 48; 51
History of Old St. Martin's, Birmingham. London: 1875. V. 49; 52

BUNCHER, RICHARD
Tretchikoff. Cape Town: 1953. V. 48

BUND, J. W. WILLIS
Oke's Game Laws, Containing the Whole Law as to...Poaching Prevention, Trespass, Rabbits, Deer, Ground Game, Dogs, Birds... London: 1897. V. 54

BUNDGAARD, J. A.
The Excavation of the Athenian Acropolis 1882-1890. Copenhagen: 1974. V. 50

BUNGAY, GEORGE W.
Nebraska: a Poem, Personal and Political. Boston: 1854. V. 51

BUNGENER, LAURENCE F.
France Before the Revolution; or, Priests, Infidels and Huguenots in the Reign of Louis XV. Edinburgh: 1854. V. 51

BUNIM, MIRIAM SCHILD
Space in Medieval Painting and the Forerunners of Perspective. New York: 1940. V. 47

BUNIN, I. A.
The Gentleman from San Francisco & Other Stories. London: 1922. V. 47; 51; 54
The Gentleman from San Francisco and Other Stories. Richmond: 1922. V. 53

BUNIN, IVAN
Memoirs and Portraits. London: 1951. V. 52

BUNKER, CHANG
An Account of Chang and Eng, the World Renowned Siamese Twins. New York: 1853. V. 53

BUNKER, EDWARD
No Beast So Fierce. New York: 1973. V. 53

BUNN, ALFRED
Old England and New England, In a Series of Views Taken on the Spot. London: 1853. V. 49; 53
The Stage Both Before and Behind the Curtain in Two Volumes. Philadelphia: 1840. V. 49; 53

BUNNELL, J. H.
Telephone Catalogue and Manual of Telegraphy with Description of Instruments Adapted for Use on Private Telegraph Lines. New York: 1900. V. 51

BUNNELL, LAFAYETTE HOUGHTON
Discovery of the Yosemite and the Indian War of 1851 Which Led to that Event. Chicago: 1880. V. 54

BUNNER, HENRY CUYLER
Airs from Arcady and Elsewhere. New York: 1884. V. 54
The Suburban Sage. New York: 1896. V. 54
A Woman of Honor. Boston: 1883. V. 54

BUNT, CYRIL G. E.
The Art and Life of William James Muller 1812-1845. Leigh on Sea: 1948. V. 49
The Goldsmiths of Italy. London: 1926. V. 51

BUNTING, BABRIDGE
John Gaw Meew, Southwestern Architect. Albuquerque: 1983. V. 50

BUNTING, BASIL
Briggflatts. London: 1966. V. 47; 51
Collected Poems. London: 1968. V. 49; 52
Collected Poems. Oxford: 1978. V. 53
Loquitur. London: 1965. V. 47; 49; 50; 52; 53; 54
The Pious Cat. London: 1986. V. 51
The Spoils. Newcastle-upon-Tyne: 1965. V. 51
What the Chairman Told Tom. Cambridge: 1967. V. 48; 49; 50; 51; 52
What the Chairman Told Tom. USA: 1967. V. 53

BUNTING, EDWARD
The Ancient Music of Ireland Arranged for Piano-Forte... 1840. V. 48; 52

BUNYAN, JOHN
The Acceptable Sacrifice; or the Excellency of a Broken Heart... London: 1698. V. 53
The Barren Fig-Tree; or, the Doom and Downfal of the Fruitless Professor. London: 1692. V. 47
A Book for Boys and Girls: or, Country Rhymes for Children. London: 1890. V. 51
Eines Christen Riese. (Pilgrim's Progress). Germantaun: 1796. V. 53
The Church Book of Bunyan Meeting 1650-1821. London: 1928. V. 49
Divine Emblems or Temporal Things Spiritualized Calculated for the Use of Young People. London: 1817. V. 47
Den Heyligen Oorlogh. Amsterdam: 1685. V. 48
The Jerusalem Sinner Saved; or, Good News for the Vilest of men... London: 1715. V. 52
The Land of Beulah: Being an Extract from the Pilgrim's Progress. London: 1974. V. 53
The Life and Death of Mr. Badman... London: 1680. V. 54
The Life and Death of Mr. Badman Presented to the World in a Familiar Dialogue Between Mr. Wiseman and Mr. Attentive... New York: 1900. V. 51
The Pilgrim's Progress. London. V. 52
The Pilgrim's Progress. London: 1758. V. 51
The Pilgrim's Progress. London: 1760. V. 48
Pilgrim's Progress. London: 1789-93. V. 51
The Pilgrim's Progress. London, Edinburgh: 1847. V. 53
The Pilgrim's Progress. London: 1849. V. 50
The Pilgrim's Progress. London: 1856. V. 54
The Pilgrim's Progress. Glasgow: 1860's. V. 54
The Pilgrim's Progress. London: 1861. V. 54
The Pilgrim's Progress. London: 1881. V. 49
The Pilgrim's Progress. London: 1895. V. 48
The Pilgrims Progress. 1899. V. 50; 51; 54
The Pilgrims Progress. London: 1899. V. 49; 54
The Pilgrims Progress. London: 1901. V. 49
The Pilgrim's Progress. Guildford: 1902. V. 50
The Pilgrim's Progress. London: 1903. V. 50
The Pilgrim's Progress. London: 1905. V. 53
The Pilgrim's Progress. London: 1906. V. 47; 49
The Pilgrim's Progress. London: 1928. V. 47; 50; 51; 52
Pilgrim's Progress... New York: 1939. V. 49
The Pilgrim's Progress. New York: 1941. V. 47; 52; 53
The Pilgrim's Progress, the Holy War Etc. Edinburgh: 1860. V. 49
The Pilgrim's Progress, to Which is Prefixed the Life of the Author... London: 1796. V. 51
A Relation of the Imprisonment of Mr. John Bunyan...in November, 1660. London: 1765. V. 50
The Select Works. Glasgow & London: 1866. V. 48
Solomons Temple spiritualiz'd, or Gospel-Light Fecht Out of the Temple at Jerusalem, to Let Us More Easily into the Glory of New Testament Truths. London: 1691. V. 52
The Works. London: 1692. V. 49

BUNYAN, JOHN continued
Works. London: 1856. V. 49; 51

BUNYARD, E.
Eggs of Rarer Limiccolae and Variations. London: 1994. V. 52

BUNYARD, EDWARD
Old Garden Roses. London: 1936. V. 54

BUNZEL, RUTH L.
Introduction to Zuni Ceremonialism, Zuni Origin Myths, Zuni Ritual Poetry, Zuni Katcinas; the Acoma Indians, Isleta, New Mexico. Washington: 1932. V. 48

BUONAIUTI, M.
Italian Scenery: Representing the Manners, Customs and Amusements of the Different States of Italy... London: 1806. V. 47

BUONANNI, F.
Recreatio Mentis, et Oculi in Observatione Animalium Testaceorum Curiosis Naturae Inspectoribus. Rome: 1684. V. 53

BUONAROTTI, MICHEL ANGELO
The Complete Works of Michelangelo. New York. V. 47; 48
His Sonnets. 1991. V. 52; 54
The Letters. London: 1963. V. 52
Letters. Stanford: 1963. V. 54

BUONARROTI, MICHEL ANGELO
Poesie. Montagnola: 1923. V. 51
Sonnet XLIV of Machelangelo Buonarroti. London: 1912. V. 53

BURBANK, LUTHER
His Methods and Discoveries and Their Practical Application. New York: 1914-15. V. 54
Luther Burbank, His Methods and Discoveries and Their Practical Application. New York and London: 1914. V. 50
Luther Burbank. His Methods and Discoveries and Their Practical Application. New York & London: 1914-15. V. 48

BURBANK, W. H.
The Photographic Negative. New York: 1888. V. 47; 54

BURBIDGE, F. W.
The Gardens of the Sun; or, a Naturalist's Journal on the Mountains and in the Forests and Swamps of Boreno and Sulu Archipelago. London: 1880. V. 53
Narcissus: its History and Culture. London: 1875. V. 51

BURBRIDGE, WILLIAM F.
A Biographical Sketch of Lawrence of Arabia. London: 1940's. V. 53

BURBURY, E. J., MRS.
Florence Sackville, or Self-Dependence: an Autobiography. London: 1851. V. 54

BURCHARD, PETER
One Gallant Rush: Robert Gould Shaw and His Brave Black Regiment. New York: 1965. V. 54

BURCHETT, JOSIAH
A Complete History of the Most Remarkable Transactions at Sea... London: 1720. V. 48; 54

BURCHETT, R.
Linear Perspective. London: 1872. V. 47

BURCKHARDT, JACOB
The Civilisation of the Period of the Renaissance in Italy. London: 1878. V. 50

BURCKHARDT, JOHN LEWIS
Notes on the Beduoins and Wahabys, Collected During His Travels in the East. London: 1831. V. 48; 49
Travels in Arabia. London: 1829. V. 51; 54
Travels in Nubia... London: 1819. V. 48
Travels in Nubia. London: 1822. V. 47; 49; 51; 53; 54
Travels in Syria and the Holy Land. London: 1822. V. 51; 54

BURDEKIN, RICHARD
Memoir of the Life and Character of Mr. Robert Spence, of York. York: 1827. V. 51

BURDEN, MRS.
Short Tales in Short Words About the Lame Boy; The Sea Shore; The Cross Boy; and the Stray Child. London: 1855. V. 49
The Three Baskets or How Henry, Richard and Charles Were Occupied While Papa Was Away. London: 1845. V. 47

BURDETT, C. D.
English Fashionless Abroad. London: 1827. V. 51

BURDETT, CHARLES
The Gambler; or, the Policeman's Story. New York: 1848. V. 54

BURDETT, H. C.
Hospitals and Asylums of the World... London: 1891-93. V. 47; 48

BURDETT, ROBERT J.
The Drums of the 47th. Indianapolis: 1914. V. 47; 53

BURDETT, SARAH
Poems, with Biographical Notes. 1841. V. 48; 51

BURDICK, ARTHUR J.
The Mystic Mid-Region. The Desert of the Southwest. New York: 1904. V. 54

BURDICK, USHER L.
David F. Barry's Indian Notes On "The Custer Battle". Baltimore: 1937. V. 53
The Last Battle of the Sioux Nation. Stevens Point: 1929. V. 47
Some of the Old-Time Cow Men of the Great West. Baltimore: 1957. V. 54

BURDON, HENRY
The Fountain of Health; or, a View of Nature. London: 1734. V. 48

BURDSALL, R.
Men Against the Clouds. London: 1935. V. 52; 53

BURFORD, J.
Description of a View of the City of Mexico and Surrounding Country...Painted by the Proprietors... London: 1826. V. 47

BURFORD, ROBERT
Description of a View of the City of Damascus and the Surrounding Country. London: 1841. V. 48

BURFORD, THOMAS
Six Landscapes from Original Paintings. London: 1779. V. 52

BURGE, C. O.
The Adventures of a Civil Engineer. London: 1909. V. 49

BURGER, GOTTFRIED AUGUST
Leonora. London: 1796. V. 54
Leonora. London: 1809. V. 54

BURGER, JOHN F.
African Adventures. London: 1957. V. 52
African Jungle Memories. London: 1958. V. 52
American Buffalo Trails. London: 1957. V. 49

BURGES, JAMES BLAND
The Dragon Knight. London: 1818. V. 49

BURGES, TRISTAM
Battle of Lake Erie with Notices of Commodore Elliot's Conduct in the Engagement. Philadelphia: 1839. V. 51

BURGES, WILLIAM
Architectural Drawings. London: 1870. V. 50

BURGESS, ANTHONY
Beds in the East. London: 1959. V. 48; 50
A Clockwork Orange. London: 1962. V. 47; 49; 50; 53
Devil of a State. London: 1961. V. 47
The Doctor is Sick. London: 1960. V. 49; 50
The Enemy in the Blanket. London: 1958. V. 47; 53
Here Comes Everybody. London: 1965. V. 49; 53
Honey for the Bears. London: 1963. V. 50
Inside Mr. Enderby. London: 1963. V. 49
Joysprick: An Introduction to the Language of James Joyce. London: 1973. V. 47
Nothing Like the Sun: a Story of Shakespeare's Love-Life. London: 1964. V. 47
The Novel Now. London: 1967. V. 49
One Hand Clapping. London: 1961. V. 48; 49; 51
Time for a Tiger. London: 1956. V. 50
Tremor of Intent. London: 1966. V. 49
A Vision of Battlements. London: 1965. V. 47; 50; 51
The Wanting Seed. London: 1962. V. 47; 50; 51
The Wanting Seed. New York: 1963. V. 47
Will and Testament. Verona: 1977. V. 48; 49; 54
The Worm and the Ring. London: 1961. V. 47; 50

BURGESS, EDWARD
English and American Yachts, Illustrating and Describing the Most Famous Yachts Now Sailing in English and American Waters. London: 1888. V. 52

BURGESS, GELETT FRANK
Bayside Bohemia, Fin de Siecle San Francisco and Its Little Magazines. San Francisco;: 1954. V. 52; 54
Blue Goops and Red. New York: 1909. V. 49
Gelett Burgess Behind the Scenes. San Francisco: 1968. V. 47
Goop Tales Alphabetically Told. New York: 1904. V. 51; 52
The Lark. San Francisco: 1896-97. V. 54
The Master of Mysteries. Indianapolis: 1912. V. 47; 48; 50
The Purple Cow. San Francisco: 1895. V. 51; 54
The Romance of the Commonplace. San Francisco: 1902. V. 48

BURGESS, GELLETT FRANK
The Romance of the Commonplace. 1902. V. 53

BURGESS, H. W.
Studies of Trees. London: 1828. V. 49
Studies of Trees. London: 1837. V. 47; 48; 50

BURGESS, JAMES
The Lives of the Most Eminent Modern Painters, Who Have Lived Since, or Were Omitted by Mons. De Piles. London: 1754. V. 50
The Rock Temples of Elephanta or Gharapuri. Bombay: 1871. V. 49

BURGESS, JOHN CART
An Easy Introduction to Perspective. London: 1840. V. 47; 53

BURGESS, MOLLY
Still. New Jersey: 1975. V. 52

BURGESS, N. G.
The Photograph Manual: a Practical Treatise Containing the Cartes De Visite Process and the Method of Taking Stereoscopic Pictures. New York: 1865. V. 52

BURGESS, RENATE
Portraits of Doctors & Scientists in the Wellcome Institute of the History of Medicine. 1973. V. 52

BURGESS, THORNTON W.
Bedtime Stories. Racine: 1929. V. 53
The Bedtime Story Books. Boston: 1913-18. V. 49
The Burgess Flower Book for Children. Boston: 1923. V. 49
Mother West Wind "How" Stories. Boston: 1916. V. 49
Mother West Wind 'Why' Stories. Boston: 1915. V. 49
The Neatness of Bobby Coon. New York: 1927. V. 53
Tommy's Change of Heart. Boston: 1921. V. 47

BURGH, ALLATSON
Anecdotes of Music, Historical and Biographical; by a Series of Letters from a Gentleman to His Daughter. London: 1814. V. 51; 52

BURGH, JAMES
The Art of Speaking. London: 1775. V. 52
The Dignity of Human Nature. London: 1754. V. 48; 49; 52
Political Disquisitions; or, an Enquiry into Public Errors, Defects and Abuses. London: 1774-75. V. 50
Thoughts on Education, Tending Chiefly to Recommend to the Attention of the Public, Some Particulars Relating To that Subject... London: 1747. V. 48

BURGHER, GOTTFRIED AUGUSTUS
Leonora. London: 1796. V. 53

BURGHLEY, WILLIAM CECIL, BARON
A Collection of State Papers Relating to Affairs in the Reigns of King Henry VIII, King Edward VI, Queen Mary and Queen Elizabeth, from the Year 1542 to 1570 (Volume I), 1571-1596 (Volume 2). London: 1740/59. V. 51

BURGOYNE, J. JOHN
The Dramatic and Poetical Works. London: 1808. V. 47

BURGOYNE, JOHN
The Heiress. London: 1786. V. 48; 51
A Letter from Lieut. Gen. Burgoyne to His Constituents, Upon His Late Resignation; with the Correspodences... London: 1779. V. 47
Rudimentary Treatise on the Blasting and Quarrying of Stone for Building and Other Purposes. London: 1849. V. 49
Rudiments of the Art of Constructing and Repairing Common Roads and a General Survey of the Principal Metropolitan Roads... London: 1861-62. V. 49
A State of the Expedition From Canada, As Laid Before the House of Commons...and Verified by Evidence; with a Collection of Authentic Documents... London: 1780. V. 47; 48
The Substance of General Burgoyne's Speeches, on Mr. Vyner's Motion...and Upon Mr. Hartley's Motion...of May, 1778. London: 1778. V. 47

BURGUM, JESSAMINE S.
Zebula or Pioneer Days in the Smoky Water Country. Valley City: 1937. V. 47; 49

BURHANS, ROBERT D.
The First Special Service Force, a War History of the North Americas 1942-44. Washington: 1947. V. 52

BURK, P. H.
Arts and Crafts of Hawaii. London: 1957. V. 51

BURKE, BERNARD
Burke's Genealogical and Heraldic History of the Landed Gentry. London: 1937. V. 50
A Genealogical and Heraldic Dictionary of the Peerage and Baronetage, Together with Memoirs of the Privy Councillors and Knights. London: 1884. V. 54
A Genealogical and Heraldic History of the Peerage and Baronetage, the Privy Council, Knightage and Companionage. London: 1913. V. 50
Peerage and Baronetage, the Privy Council and Knightage, Privy Council. London: 1928. V. 50
Vicissitudes of Families. London: 1883. V. 54

BURKE, BILLIE
With a Feather On My Nose. New York: 1949. V. 54

BURKE, CLIFFORD
Bone Songs. Newark: 1992. V. 54
Bone Songs. West Burke: 1992. V. 48; 49; 52
A Chiroxylographic Book. Anacortes: 1981. V. 52
A Landscape With Cows In It. 1987. V. 52

BURKE, EDMUND
An Account of the European Settlements in America. London: 1757. V. 47
An Account of the European Settlements in America. London: 1758. V. 47
An Account of the European Settlements in America. London: 1770. V. 47
An Account of the European Settlements in America. London: 1777. V. 52
An Appeal from the New to the Old Whigs, in Consequence of some Late Discussions in Parliament, Relative to the Reflections on the French Revolution. London: 1791. V. 50; 52; 54
An Authentic Copy of Mr. Pitt's Letter to His Royal Highness the Prince of Wales, with His Answer. London: 1789. V. 47
Correspondence of Edmund Burke and William Windham. Cambridge: 1910. V. 48; 54
Correspondence of the Right Honourabe...Between the Year 1744 and the Period of His Decease in 1797. London: 1844. V. 49
The Early Life, Correspondence and Writings Of... Cambridge: 1923. V. 50
An Impartial History of the War in America Between Great Britain and Her Colonies... London: 1780. V. 47
A Letter from Edmund Burke, Esq; One of the Representatives in Parliament for the City of Bristol, to John Farr and John Harris...Sheriffs of that City, on the Affairs in America. London: 1777. V. 47
A Letter from the Rt. Honourable Edmund Burke to His Grace the Duke of Portland on the Conduct of the Minority in Parliament. London: 1797. V. 47; 52
Observations on a Late State of the Nation. London: 1769. V. 48; 51; 52
On Conciliation with the Colonies. New York: 1975. V. 52; 53; 54
On Conciliation With the Colonies & Other Papers On the American Revolution. Lunenburg: 1975. V. 47; 48; 52; 53
A Philosophical Enquiry into the Origin of Our Ideas of the Sublime and Beautiful. London: 1757. V. 48
A Philosophical Enquiry into the Origin of Our Ideas of the Sublime and Beautiful. London: 1782. V. 52; 54
A Philosophical Enquiry Into the Origin of Our ideas of the Sublime and Beautiful. London: 1798. V. 53
A Philosophical Enquiry into the Origin of Our Ideas of the Sublime and Beautiful. (with) A Vindication of Natural Society; or a View of the Miseries and Evils Arising to Mankind from Every species of Artificial Society. London: 1767/57. V. 49
A Philosophical Inquiry Into the Origin of Our Ideas of the Sublime and Beautiful. London: 1810. V. 52; 54
Reflections on the Revolution in France. Dublin: 1790. V. 50; 52
Reflections on the Revolution in France. London: 1790. V. 47; 48; 50; 51; 52; 53
Reflections on the Revolution in France. Dublin: 1791. V. 54
Reflections on the Revolution in France. London: 1791. V. 48; 52
Reflections on the Revolution in France. New York: 1791. V. 54
Reflections On the Revolution in France. Philadelphia: 1792. V. 48
Speech of Edmund Burke, Esq., Member of Parliament for the city of Bristol, on Presenting to the House of Commons (on the 11th of Feb., 1780), a Plan for the Better Security of the Independence of Parliament and the Oeconomical Reformation... London: 1780. V. 52; 53; 54
The Speech of Edmund Burke, Esq; on Moving His Resolutions for Conciliation with the Colonies, March 22, 1775. Dublin: 1775. V. 47
Speech...Debate on Army Estimates.... London: 1790. V. 53
Speeches at His Arrival at Bristol, and at the Conclusion of the Poll. London: 1775. V. 47
The Speeches of the Right Honourable Edmund Burke, in the House of Commons and in Westminster Hall. London: 1816. V. 53
Substance of the Speeches Made in the House of Commons, on Wednesday, the 15th of December, 1779. London: 1779. V. 48
Thoughts and Details on Scarcity, Originally Presented to the Right Hon. William Pitt, In the Month of November, 1795. London: 1800. V. 47
A Vindication of Natural Society... London: 1757. V. 52
The Work... Dublin: 1792-93. V. 49; 52
The Works. London: 1808-13. V. 51
Works. London: 1823. V. 49; 50
The Works. London: 1826. V. 47; 49
The Works. London: 1826-27. V. 49
The Works. London: 1897. V. 54
The Works. London: 1899. V. 48
The Works and Correspondence. London: 1852. V. 51
The Writings and Speeches of... London. V. 54

BURKE, EMILY P.
Reminiscences of Georgia. Oberlin: 1850. V. 47

BURKE, J. BERNARD
Anecdotes of the Aristocracy, and Episodes in Ancestral Story. London: 1850. V. 54
Anecdotes of the Aristocracy, and Episodes in Ancestral Story. First and Second Series. London: 1849/50. V. 47
A Genealogical History of the House of Gwysaney. London: 1847. V. 53
Peerage and Baronetage and Knightage, Privy Council and Order of Precedence. London: 1926. V. 54
Peerage and Baronetage, the Privy Council and Knightage, Privy Council. London: 1928. V. 54
The Royal Families of England, Scotland and Wales. London: 1851. V. 53

BURKE, JAMES HENRY
Days in the East. A Poem. London: 1842. V. 53

BURKE, JAMES LEE
Black Cherry Blues. Boston: 1989. V. 52
Burning Angel. New Orleans: 1995. V. 53; 54
Cadillac Jukebox. New Orleans: 1996. V. 54
The Convict. 1985. V. 54
Dixie City Jam. New York: 1994. V. 50; 52; 54
Half of Paradise. Boston: 1965. V. 51; 52; 53
Half of Paradise. Fribourg: 1965. V. 52
Heaven's Prisoners. New York: 1988. V. 52; 54
In the Electric Mist With Confederate Dead. New York: 1993. V. 49; 50; 51; 52; 53
In the Electric Mist with Confederate Dead. Northridge: 1993. V. 54
Lay Down My Sword and Shield. New York: 1971. V. 50; 52; 54
The Lost Get-Back Boogie. Baton Rouge: 1986. V. 47; 50; 51; 52; 53
The Neon Rain. New York: 1987. V. 49; 50; 51; 52; 54
Texas City 1947. Northridge: 1992. V. 51; 54
To the Bright and Shining Sun. New York: 1970. V. 51; 52; 53; 54
To the Bright and Shining Sun. Huntington Beach: 1992. V. 51; 52; 53; 54
Two for Texas. New York: 1982. V. 52
Two For Texas. Huntington Beach: 1992. V. 51; 53; 54
Winter Light. Huntington Beach: 1992. V. 49; 51; 52

BURKE, JANE
Messages On Healing Understood to Have Been Dictated by William James, Sir William Osler, Andrew Jackson Davis, and Others and Received by Jane Revere Burke Sitting with Edward S. Martin. London: 1936. V. 50
Messages on Healing Understood to Have Been Dictated by William James, William Osler, Andrew Jackson Davis and Others and Received by Jane Revere Burke Sitting with Edward Martin. 1936. V. 52

BURKE, JOHN
A Genealogical and Heraldic History of the Commoners of Great Britain and Ireland. London: 183-38. V. 54

BURKE, JOHN BERNARD
A Visitation of the Seats and Arms of the Noblemen and Gentlemen of Great Britain. (First and Second Series). London: 1852-3-4-5-. V. 50

BURKE, JOSEPH
Hogarth: The Complete Engravings. New York: 1968. V. 53

BURKE, MARY LOUISE
Kamehameha: King of the Hawaiian Islands. San Francisco: 1939. V. 51; 53

BURKE, OLIVER J.
The History of the Lord Chancellors of Ireland, from A.D. 1186 to A.D. 1874. Dublin: 1879. V. 51

BURKE, PETER
Celebrated Trials Connected with the Aristocracy in the Relations of Private Life. London: 1849. V. 48
The Romance of the Forum, or Narratives, Scenes and Anecdotes from Courts of Justice. London: 1852. V. 54

BURKE, THOMAS
Limehouse Nights: Tales of Chinatown. London: 1916. V. 51; 53
Living in Bloomsbury. London: 1939. V. 50
More Limehouse Nights. New York: 1921. V. 50
The Pleasantries of Old Quong. London: 1931. V. 54
The Song Book of Quong Lee of Limehouse. London: 1920. V. 51
The Wind and the Rain: a Book of Confessions. London: 1924. V. 51; 53

BURKE, W. S.
Official Military History of the Kansas Regiments During the War for the Suppression of the Great Rebellion. Leavenworth: 1870. V. 47

BURKE, WILLIAM
An Examination of the Commercial Principles of the Late Negotiation Between Great Britain and France in MDCCLXI. London: 1762. V. 53
The Mineral Springs of Western Virginia; with Remarks on their Use... New York: 1846. V. 47

BURKER, ROBERT TRAVERS
Tremora: an epic Poem of Ossian in Eight Cantos... Perth: 1818. V. 48

BURKE'S Genealogical and Heraldic History of the Peerage, Baronetage and Knightage. Founded 1826 by John Burke and Sir Bernard Burke, C.B... London: 1963. V. 48

BURKE'S Texas Almanac for 1882 Containing Some Information About Texas. Houston: 1881. V. 53

BURKILL, H. M.
The Useful Plants of West Tropical Africa. Volume 1. Families A-D. 1984. V. 48

BURKILL, I. H.
A Dictionary of the Economic Products of the Malay Peninusla. London: 1935. V. 53

BURKITT, F. CRAWFORD
The Hymn of Bardaisan. London: 1899. V. 47; 49

BURKITT, WILLIAM
Expository Notes, with Practical Observations. London: 1734. V. 53
Expository Notes, with Practical Observations. New York: 1796. V. 49

BURKLUND, C.
New Michigan Verse. Ann Arbor: 1940. V. 49

BURLAMAQUI, JEAN JACQUES
The Principles of Natural Law. London: 1780. V. 48
The Principles of Politic Law: Being a Sequel to the Principles of Natural Law. London: 1752. V. 50

BURLAND, BRIAN
A Fall from Aloft. New York: 1969. V. 47
St. Nicholas & the Tub. New York: 1964. V. 47

BURLAND, C.
Gods and Demons in Primitive Art. Prague: 1973. V. 54

BURLAND, H.
The Gold Worshipers. 1906. V. 48; 52

BURLEIGH, CHARLES G.
The Anti-Slavery History of the John Brown Year... New York: 1861. V. 50

BURLEIGH, GEORGE S.
Elegiac Poem on the Death of Nathaniel Peabody Rogers. Hartford: 1846. V. 52

BURLEIGH, WILLIAM CECIL
A Declaration of the Favourable Dealing of Her Majesties Commissioners Appointed for the Examination of Certaine Traitours and of Tortures Unjustly Reported to Be Done On Them for Matters of Religion. London: 1583. V. 53

BURLEIGH, WILLIAM HENRY
Poems. Philadelphia: 1841. V. 53

BURLEND, REBECCA
A True Picture of Emigration: or Fourteen Years in the Interior of North America... London: 1848. V. 47; 50

BURLESON, CLYDE W.
The Panoramic Photography of Eugene O. Goldbeck. Austin: 1986. V. 51

BURLESON, GEORGIA J.
The Life and Writings of Rufus C. Burleson... 1901. V. 47

BURLEY, WALTER
Expositio in Artem Veterem Porphyrii et Aristotelis. Venice: 1492/93. V. 53

BURLINGAME, H. J.
Herrmann the Great. The Famous Magician's Wonderful Tricks. Chicago: 1897. V. 47

BURLINGAME, MERRILL G.
The Montana Frontier. Helena: 1942. V. 52; 53

BURLINGTON & MISSOURI RIVER RAILROAD
1878. B. & M. Railroad. Keep in the Right Latitude. 750,000 Acres of the Best Lands for Sale. Southern Iowa and Southeastern Nebraska Have the Largest and Finet Crops, the Best Class of Settlers, the Most Successful Farmers, the Best and Cheapest... St. Louis: 1878. V. 47
The Old B. & M. Ahead Railroad. St. Louis. V. 54
Report of the Directors of the Burlington and Missouri River Railroad Company in Nebraska to The Stockholders for the Year 1873. Boston: 1874. V. 47

BURLINGTON, CHARLES
The Modern Universal British Traveller; or a Complete and Accurate Tour through England, Wales and Scotland, and the Neighbouring Islands. London: 1779. V. 47; 51; 54

BURLINGTON County Directory for 1872, Containing the Names of the Inhabitants of Bordertown, Burlington and Mount Holly, together with a Business Directory of Burlington County... Burlington: 1872. V. 49; 51

BURLINGTON FINE ARTS CLUB
Catalogue of a Collection of Early Drawings and Pictures of London, with Some contemporary Furniture. London: 1920. V. 47; 49
An Exhibition of Ancient Greek Art. London: 1904. V. 52
Exhibition of Bookbindings. 1891. V. 48
Exhibition of Bookbindings. London: 1891. V. 51; 53
Exhibition of English Embroidery Executed Prior to the Middle of the SVI Century. London: 1905. V. 47
French Art of the Eighteenth Century. London: 1914. V. 51; 53
Illustrated Catalogue of Illuminated Manuscripts. Exhibition Catalogue 269. London: 1908. V. 52
The Venetian School: Pictures by Titian and His Contemporaries. 1915. V. 52

BURMA through the Stereoscope. New York & London: 1907. V. 47

BURMAN, C. CLARK
An Account of the Art of Typography, as Practised in Alnwick from 1781 to 1815... Alnwick: 1896. V. 53

BURMAN, JAN
Thesaurus Zeylanicus, Exhibiens Plantas in Insula Zeylana Nascentes. Amstelaedami: 1737. V. 49; 53

BURMEISTER, H.
The Organization of Trilobites, Deduced from Their Living Affinities... London: 1846. V. 48

BURN, ANDREW
Memoirs Of the Late Major-General Andrew Burn, of the Royal Marines... London: 1816. V. 50

BURN, DAVID WILL M.
Cantilenosae Nugae Being Volume I (all published) of the Poetical Works of... Oamaru: 1891. V. 49

BURN, EDWARD
A Reply to the Reverend Dr. Priestley's Appeal to the Public,on the Subject of the Late Riots at Birmingham, in Vindication of the Clergy, and Oter Respectable Inhabitants...(with) Birmingham, Thurs. April 19, 1792. To the Public. Birmingham: 1792. V. 52

BURN, J. H.
A Descriptive Catalogue of the London Traders, Tavern and Coffee-House Tokens...in the Seventeenth Century, Presented by Beaufoy. London: 1855. V. 52

BURN, JAMES DAWSON
Three Years Among the Working-Classes in the United States During the War. London: 1865. V. 53

BURN, JOHN ILDERTON
A Digested Index to the Modern Reports of the Courts of Common Law. London: 1804. V. 54

BURN, RICHARD
A Digest of the Militia Laws. London: 1760. V. 53
A Digest of the Militia Laws. London: 1778. V. 53
Ecclesiastical Law. London: 1763. V. 47
Ecclesiastical Law. London: 1788. V. 48; 49
The History of the Poor Laws; with Observations. London: 1764. V. 53
The Justice of the Peace and Parish Officer. London: 1755. V. 48; 52
The Justice of the Peace, and Parish Officer. London: 1764. V. 49; 52
The Justice of the Peace, and Parish Officer... London: 1820. V. 54

BURN, ROBERT SCOT
The Practical Directory for the Improvement of Landed Property. Edinburgh: 1882. V. 52

BURN, ROBERT SCOTT
Modern Building and Architecture: a Series of Working Drawings and Practical Designs... Edinburgh: 1869. V. 52
The New Guide to Carpentry, General framing & Joinery. Murdoch: 1870. V. 49

BURNABY, ANDREW
Travels Through the Middle Settlements in North America, in the Years 1759 and 1760. London: 1775. V. 49

BURNABY, FRED
A Ride to Khiva. London: 1876. V. 50; 54
A Ride to Khiva. London: 1877. V. 50

BURNABY, FRED, MRS.
The High Alps in Winter; or Mountaineering in Search of Health. London: 1883. V. 50

BURNABY, FREDERICK
On Horseback through Asia Minor. London: 1877. V. 52

BURNABY, WILLIAM
The Ladies Visiting-Day. London: 1701. V. 47; 51
The Modish Husband: a Comedy. London: 1702. V. 51

BURNAND, F. C.
A New Light Thrown Across the Keep it Quite Darkest Africa. London: 1890. V. 47
One-and-Three. London: 1878. V. 47
Present Pastimes of Merrie England, Interpreted from Ancient Mss. and Annotated by F. C. Burnand. London: 1873. V. 54

BURNAP, WILLARD
One Man's Life: 1840-1920. Fergus Falls: 1923. V. 50

BURNAT-PROVINS, MARGUERITE
Petits Tableaux Valaisans. Vevey: 1903. V. 53

BURNE-JONES, EDWARD
The Beginning of the World. London: 1902. V. 49; 50; 53
Drawings of Sir Edward Burne-Jones. London: 1905. V. 53
Fifty-Seven Plates. London. V. 53
Letters to Katie. London: 1925. V. 49
Memorials of Edward Burne-Jones. London: 1904. V. 47; 48; 49; 50; 51

BURNE-JONES, GEORGIANA
Memorials of Edward Burne-Jones. New York: 1904. V. 49; 51
Memorials of Edward Burne-Jones. London: 1906. V. 49

BURNES, ALEXANDER
Cabool: a Personal Narrative of a Journey to and Residence in that City in the Years 1836, 7 and 8. London: 1843. V. 53
Travels into Bokhara: Being the Account of a Journey from India to Cabool, Tartary, and Persia... 1834. V. 54
Travels Into Bokhara: Containing the Narrative of a Voyage on the Indus, and an Account of a Journey from India to Cabool, Tartary and Persia. London: 1839. V. 47

BURNES, JAMES
A Narrative of a Visit to the Court of Sinde: a Sketch of the History of Cutch, From Its First Connexion with the British Government in India... Edinburgh: 1831. V. 53

BURNET, GILBERT, BP. OF SALISBURY
The Abridgment of the History of the Reformation of the Church of England. London: 1682. V. 50
The Abridgment of the History of the Reformation of the Church of England... London: 1683. V. 52
Bishop Burnet's History of His Own Time. Dublin: 1724/34. V. 51
Bishop Burnet's History of His Own Time. London: 1724/34. V. 47; 49; 50; 51; 53; 54
Bishop Burnet's History of His Own Time. London: 1734. V. 47
Bishop Burnet's History of His Own Time. London: 1766. V. 48
Bishop Burnet's History of His Own Time... Oxford: 1833. V. 53
Bishop Burnet's History of His Own Time: With the Suppressed Passages of the First Volume, and Notes by the Earls of Dartmouth and Hardwicke, and Speaker Onslow, Hitherto Unpublished. Oxford: 1823. V. 51
A Discourse of the Pastoral Care. (with) Four Discourses Delivered to the Clergy of the Diocess of Sarum. London: 1692-94. V. 50
An Enquiry into the Measures of Submission to the Supream Authority. London: 1688. V. 53
An Enquiry Into the Present State of Affairs: and In Particular, Whether We Owe Allegience to the King In Thos Circumstances. London: 1689. V. 53
An Essay on the Memory of the Late Queen. London: 1695. V. 52
An Exhortation to Peace and Union, in a Sermon Preached at St. Lawrence - Jury, on Tuesday the 16th of Novemb. Licens'd the 29th 1689. N.P: 1689. V. 53
History of His Own Time. London: 1833. V. 51
History of His Own Time. Oxford: 1897-1900. V. 53
The History of the Reformation of the Church of England. London: 1681-1715. V. 47
The History of the Reformation of the Church of England... London: 1681-83. V. 48
History of the Reformation of the Church of England. London: 1715. V. 51; 53
The History of the Reformation of the Church of England. Dublin: 1758. V. 51
The History of the Reformation of the Church of England. London: 1837. V. 47
The Life and Death of Sir Matthew Hale... London: 1705?. V. 47
The Life and Death of Sir Matthew Hale, Kt., Sometime Lord Chief Justice of His Majesties Court of Kings Bench. London: 1853. V. 53
Life of William Bedell, D.D., Bishop of Kilmore in Ireland. London: 1685. V. 47
Lives of Sir Matthew Hale and John, Earl of Rochester. London: 1829. V. 50
The Memoires of the Lives and Actions of James and William, Dukes of Hamilton and Castleherald, &c. London: 1677. V. 47; 50; 51; 52

Reflections on Mr. Varillas's History. (with) A Defence of the Reflections. (with) A Continuation of Reflections. Amsterdam: 1686-87. V. 48; 50
A Sermon Preached at the Coronation of William III and Mary II...in the Abby-Church of Westminster April 11, 1689. Edinburgh: 1689. V. 53
A Sermon Preached at the Funeral of the Honourable Robert Boyle at St. Martins in the Fields, Jan. 7, 1691/2. London: 1692. V. 47; 53
Some Account of the Life and Death of John Wilmot, Earl of Rochester... Albany: 1797. V. 50
Some Letters Containing, an Account of What Seemed Most Remarkable in Switzerland, Italy &c. Rotterdam: 1686. V. 52
Some Letters, Containing an Account of What Seemed Most Remarkable in Travelling through Switzerland, Italy, Some Parts of Germany &c. in the Years 1685 and 1686. Rotterdam: 1687. V. 54
Some Passages in the Life and Death of the Right Honourable John Earl of Rochester, Who Died the 26th of July, 1680. London: 1680. V. 47; 48; 49; 50; 53
A Supplement to Burnet's History of My Own Time Derived from His Original Memoirs... Oxford: 1902. V. 50
Three Letters Concerning the Present State of Italy, Written in the Year 1687. London: 1688. V. 48; 50
A Vindication of the Authority, Constitution and Laws of the Church and State of Scotland (with) Observations on the First and Second of the Canons... Glasgow: 1673. V. 50

BURNET, JACOB
Notes On the Early Settlement of the North Western Territory. New York: 1847. V. 49

BURNET, JOHN
The Battle of Trafalgar A Descriptive Key to the Engraving of...Now In Progress. London: 1855. V. 49
Practical Hints on Colour in Painting, Illustrated by Examples fromt he Works of the Venetian, Flemish and Dutch Schools. London: 1827. V. 50; 52
A Practical Treatise on Painting. London: 1827. V. 51
The Progress of a Painter in the Nineteenth Century... London: 1854. V. 47; 50
A Treatise on Painting. London: 1864-65. V. 48; 51

BURNET, MAC FARLANE
The Clonal Selection Theory of Acquired Immunity. Cambridge: 1959. V. 50

BURNET, ROSS
A Bookseller's Diary. Katoomba: 1993. V. 54

BURNET, THOMAS
De Fide & Officiis Christianorum Liber. Londini: 1722. V. 52
Essays Divine, Moral and Political. Viz. I. Of Religion. II. Of Christianity. III. Of Priests. IV. Of Virtue. V. Of Friendship. VI. of Government. VII. of Parties. VIII. Of Plots. London: 1714. V. 50; 52
Homerides; or a Letter to Mr. Pope, Occasion'd by His Intended. London: 1715. V. 47; 49
The Sacred Theory of the Earth. London: 1722. V. 52
The Sacred Theory of the Earth...With a Review of the Theory... London: 1734. V. 52
A Second Iale of a Tub; or, the History of Robert Powel the Puppet-Show man. London: 1715. V. 47; 50; 51
A Synopsis of the Most Important Prophecies Relative to the Future Restoration of the Jews, According to Thomas Burnet. London: 1828. V. 49
The Theory of the Earth. London: 1684-90. V. 48
The Theory of the Earth... London: 1697. V. 54
Thesaurus Medicinae Practicae, ex prastantissimorum tum Vereum Tum Recentiorum Medicorum Observationibus... London: 1673. V. 47; 48

BURNETT, DAVID
Vines. 1984. V. 53

BURNETT, FRANCES HODGSON
Barty Crusoe and His Man Saturday. London: 1909. V. 47
Dolly. London: 1893. V. 54
Editha's Burglar. Boston: 1888. V. 52; 53
Giovanni and the Other: Children Who Have Made Stories. New York: 1892. V. 48
In Connection with the De Willoughby Claim. London: 1899. V. 54
In the Closed Room. New York: 1904. V. 49
The Lass o' Lowrie's. New York: 1877. V. 49
Little Lord Fauntleroy. London: 1886. V. 49
Little Lord Fauntleroy. New York: 1886. V. 49; 50; 51; 52; 53
Little Lord Fauntleroy. New York: 1936. V. 50
A Little Princess. London: 1905. V. 49
The Makers of the XXth Century. 1894. V. 51
The Making of a Marchioness. New York: 1901. V. 53; 54
My Robin. New York: 1912. V. 53; 54
Queen Silver-Bell. New York: 1906. V. 49
Queen Silver-Bell. London: 1907. V. 51; 52
Racketty-Packetty House. London: 1907. V. 48
Racketty-Packetty House, as Told by Queen Crosspatch. New York: 1914. V. 49
The Secret Garden. London: 1911. V. 48; 51
The Secret Garden. New York: 1911. V. 50; 51
The Spring Cleaning, as Told by Queen Crosspatch. New York: 1911. V. 49
That Lass O'Lowrie's. New York: 1877. V. 50; 54
That Lass O'Lowrie's. New York: 1890. V. 50
The White People. New York & London: 1917. V. 54

BURNETT, G. T.
An Encyclopaedia of Useful and Ornamental Plants...Used in the Arts... London: 1852. V. 48; 50; 51

BURNETT, GILBERT
The Life and Death of Sir Matthew Hale, Kt., Sometime Lord Chief Justice of His Majesties Court of Kings Bench. London: 1682. V. 48

BURNETT, PETER H.
Recollections and Opinions of an Old Pioneer. New York: 1880. V. 47; 50; 52; 53

BURNETT, W. R.
Good-Bye, Chicago: 1928: End of an Era. New York: 1981. V. 50
High Sierra. New York: 1940. V. 47; 54
Little Caesar. New York: 1929. V. 48; 51

BURNETT, WILLIAM
A Practical Account of the Mediterranean Fever, As It Appeared in the Ships and Hospitals of His Majesty's Fleet on That Station. London: 1816. V. 48

BURNETT, WILLIAM HALL
Old Cleveland. London: 1886. V. 47

BURNETT, WILLIAM HICKLING
Views of Cintra. London: 1835. V. 49; 52

BURNEY, CAROLINE
Seraphina; or, a Winter in Town. London: 1809. V. 52

BURNEY, CHARLES
Account of an Infant Musician. London: 1779. V. 47
An Account of the Musical Performances in Westminster Abbey and the Pantheon...1784. In Commemoration of Handel. Dublin: 1784. V. 48
An Account of the Musical Performances in Westminster Abbey, and the Pantheon...in Commemoration of Handel. London: 1785. V. 48; 49; 51; 53
An Account of the Musical Performances in Westminster-Abbey, and the Pantheon, May 26th, 27th, 29th and June the 3rd and 5th, 1784. In Commemoration of Handel. Dublin: 1785. V. 47
Dr. Burney's Musical Tours in Europe. London: 1959. V. 52
An Essay Towards a History of the Principal Comets That Have Appeared Since the Year 1742. London: 1769. V. 51
A General History of Music, from the Earliest Ages to the Present Period. London: 1776-82. V. 47; 49
A General History of Music, from the Earliest Ages to the Present Period. London: 1776-89. V. 49; 54
A General History of Music, from the Earliest Ages to the Present Period. London: 1782-89. V. 48
Memoirs of Doctor Burney. London: 1832. V. 53
Memoirs of the Life and Writings of the Abate Metastasio... London: 1796. V. 48; 51
The Present State of Music in Germany, the Netherlands, & United Provinces. (with) The Present State of Music in France and Italy. London: 1773-75. V. 48; 51
The Present State of Music in Germany, the Netherlands and the United Provinces. London: 1773. V. 51

BURNEY, FRANCES
Tragic Dramas... London: 1818. V. 52

BURNEY, JAMES
A Chronological History of the Discoveries in the south Sea or Pacific Ocean. London: 1803-17. V. 50
A Chronological History of the North-Eastern Voyages of Discovery and of the Early Eastern Navigations of the Russians, by Captain James Burney, F.R.S. Amsterdam: 1969. V. 52

BURNEY, SARAH HARRIET
Geraldine Fauconberg. London: 1808. V. 50
Tales of Fancy. London: 1816-20. V. 49
Traits of Nature... London: 1812. V. 47; 52

BURNHAM, DANIEL H.
Report on a Plan for San Francisco...Presented to the Mayor and Board of supervisors by the Association for the Improvement and Adornment of San Francisco. San Francisco: 1905. V. 47; 50

BURNHAM, FREDERICK R.
Taking Chances. Los Angeles: 1904. V. 53
Taking Chances. Los Angeles: 1944. V. 54

BURNHAM, HAROLD B.
Keep Me Warm One Night: Early Handweaving in Eastern Canada. Toronto: 1975. V. 47; 52

BURNHAM, JOHN B.
The Rim of Mystery: a Hunter's Wanderings in Unknown Siberian Asia. New York: 1929. V. 54

BURNHAM, S. W.
Measures of Proper Motion Stars, Made with 40 Inch Refractor of the Yerkes Observatory in the Years 1907 to 1912. Washington: 1913. V. 48

BURNIER, RAYMOND
Hindu Medieval Sculpture. Paris: 1950. V. 49

BURN-MURDOCH, WILLIAM GORDON
From Edinburgh to the Antarctic an Artist's Notes and Sketches During the Dundee Expedition of 1892-93. London: 1894. V. 49

BURNOUF, EMILE
Memoires sur l'Antiquite: l'Age du Bronze, Troie, Santorin, Delos, Ycenes, le Parthenon, les Courbes, les Propylees, un Faubourg d'Athenes. Paris: 1879. V. 52

BURNS, ALLAN
Observations on the Surgical Anatomy of the Head and Neck. Edinburgh: 1811. V. 52
Observations on the Surgical Anatomy of the Head and Neck. Baltimore: 1823. V. 51

BURNS, ARCHIBALD
Picturesque "Bits" from Old Edinburgh. Edinburgh: 1868. V. 54

BURNS, B. J.
The Stetefeldt Furnace: its Results and Advantages. San Francisco: 1871. V. 47

BURNS, GEORGE
All My Best Friends. 1989. V. 53

BURNS, JOHN
Burn's Obstetrical Works. New York: 1809. V. 54
Dissertations on Inflammation. Albany: 1812. V. 47
An Historical and Chronological Remembrancer. Dublin: 1775. V. 47; 49; 53
Popular Directions for the Treatment of the Diseases of Women and Children. London: 1811. V. 52
The Principles of Midwifery; Including the Diseases of Women and Children. Philadelphia: 1810. V. 54

BURNS, JOHN H.
Memoirs of a Cow Pony, As Told by Himself. Boston: 1906. V. 53

BURNS, JOHN HORNE
The Gallery. New York: 1947. V. 51

BURNS, OLIVE ANN
Cold Sassy Tree. New York: 1984. V. 50

BURNS, R. F.
The Life and Times of the Rev. Robert Burns, D.D. Toronto: 1872. V. 52

BURNS, ROBERT
An Address to the Devil...with Explanatory Notes. London: 1830. V. 49; 54
Aloway Kirk; or Tam o'Shanter. 1796?. V. 52
Auld Lang Syne. London: 1859. V. 54
The Complete Poetical Works of... New York: 1900. V. 48
Complete Works. Edinburgh: 1883. V. 52
The Complete Works. Philadelphia: 1896. V. 49
Complete Works. Philadelphia: 1905. V. 49
The Complete Works. New York: 1910. V. 51
The Complete Writings. London: 1927. V. 53
The Correspondence Between Burns and Clarinda. Edinburgh: 1843. V. 50; 52
Fac-Simile of Burns's Celebrated Poem, Entitled The Jolly Beggars. Glasgow: 1823. V. 51
Illustrated Songs with a Portrait After the Original by Nasmyth. London: 1861. V. 54
The Jolly Beggars. Northampton: 1963. V. 49; 52
Letters of Robert Burns. Boston: 1820. V. 51
The Letters of Robert Burns. Oxford: 1931. V. 47
The Letters of Robert Burns, Chronologically Arranged from Dr. Currie's Collection. London: 1819. V. 52
The Life and Works. Edinburgh: 1851-52. V. 54
The Merry Muses, a Choice Collection of Favourite Songs Gathered from Many Sources. 1872?. V. 49; 51
The National Burns, Including the Airs of All the Songs... London: 1870. V. 50
Poems. Glasgow: 1965. V. 51
Poems and Letters in the Handwriting of Robert Burns. Saint Louis: 1908. V. 52; 54
Poems Ascribed to Robert Burns, the Ayrshire Bard, not Contained in Any Edition of His Works Hitherto Published. Glasgow: 1801. V. 49
Poems, Chiefly in the Scottish Dialect. Edinburgh: 1787. V. 47; 48; 49; 50
Poems Chiefly in the Scottish Dialect... London: 1787. V. 52
Poems Chiefly in the Scottish Dialect... New York: 1788. V. 49
Poems, Chiefly in the Scottish Dialect... Edinburgh: 1798. V. 48
Poems, Chiefly in the Scottish Dialect. New York: 1799. V. 52
Poems, Chiefly in the Scottish Dialect. Edinburgh: 1817. V. 48
Poems, Chiefly in the Scottish Dialect. London: 1824. V. 48
Poems Chiefly in the Scottish Dialect. Glasgow: 1900. V. 50; 52
Poems Chiefly in the Scottish Dialect. London: 1927. V. 48
The Poems of Robert Burns. 1965. V. 50
Poems Published in 1786. London: 1911. V. 47
The Poetical Works. London: 1830. V. 48
The Poetry. London: 1859. V. 52
The Poetry. London: 1861. V. 52
The Poetry. Edinburgh: 1896. V. 51; 52; 54
The Poetry. Edinburgh: 1896-97. V. 48
The Prose Works... Newcastle-Upon-Tyne: 1819. V. 48
Reliques...Consisting Chiefly of Original Letters, Poems and Critical Observations on Scottish Songs. London: 1808. V. 52
Reliques...Consisting Chiefly of Original Letters, Poems and Critical Observations on Scottish Songs. Philadelphia: 1809. V. 51; 52
Sir Patric Spens, The Wife of Usher's Well and The Bonnie Rle of Moray. London: 1930. V. 52
The Soldier's Return. London: 1857. V. 54
Songs from Robert Burns. Waltham St. Lawrence: 1925. V. 48; 51
Tam O'Shanter. London: 1855. V. 54
Tam O'Shanter. New York: 1868. V. 47
Tam O'Shanter. London: 1902. V. 50; 52
The Works... Liverpool: 1800. V. 49
The Works. London: 1803. V. 47; 51
The Works. London: 1809. V. 54
The Works. London: 1819. V. 54
The Works. Glasgow & Edinburgh: 1834. V. 54
The Works. London: 1834. V. 51
Works. London: 1859. V. 51; 54
The Works. London: 1861. V. 51; 54
The Works. London: 1866. V. 51

BURNS, ROBERT continued
The Works. 1877. V. 52
The Works. London: 1887. V. 54
Works. London: 1891. V. 49

BURNS, ROBERT HOMER
Wyoming Pioneer Ranches. Laramie: 1955. V. 53

BURNSIDE, HELEN MARION
A Birthday Present. London: 1890. V. 52
Wonderland Pictures. London: 1890. V. 52

BURNSIDE, WESLEY M.
Maynard Dixon, Artist of the West. 1974. V. 51; 53
Maynard Dixon: Artist of the West. Provo: 1974. V. 49; 52

BURNYEAT, JOHN
The Truth Exalted in the Writings of that Eminent and Faithful Servant of Christ, John Burnyeat... London: 1691. V. 49; 50; 52

BURPEE, LAWRENCE J.
Among the Canadian Alps. New York: 1914. V. 48; 50
Among the Canadian Alps. London: 1915. V. 48
The Search for the Western Sea. Toronto: 1908. V. 49; 50; 51
The Search for the Western Sea. Toronto: 1935. V. 48; 51; 53

BURR, AARON
The Private Journal of Aaron Burr, During His Residence of Four Years in Europe. New York: 1838. V. 52; 54
Reports of the Trials of Col. Aaron Burr...for Treason and for a Misdeameanor...in the Circuit Court of the United States. Philadelphia: 1808. V. 52

BURR, FEARING
Field and Garden Vegetables of America: Containing Full Descriptions of Nearly Eleven Hundred Species and Varities... Boston: 1863. V. 47; 50

BURR, FREDERICK M.
The Life and Works of Alexander Anderson, M.D., the First American Wood Engraver. New York: 1893. V. 47; 48; 51

BURR, THOMAS BENGE
The History of Tunbridge-Wells. London: 1766. V. 48

BURR, WILLIAM H.
Revelations of Antichrist, Concerning Christ and Christianity. Boston: 1879. V. 54

BURRA, PETER
Virginia Woolf. London: 1934. V. 51

BURRAGE, HENRY S.
Burnside's East Tennessee Campaign. Boston: 1910. V. 48; 50

BURRARD, G.
Big Game Hunting in the Himalalyas and Tibet. London: 1925. V. 48; 51; 52; 53; 54
Big Game Shooting in the Himalayas and Tibet. London: 1925. V. 49

BURRARD, GERALD
The Modern Shotgun. (with) The Identification of Firearms and Forensic Baliistics. London: 1944/34. V. 54

BURRARD, SIDNEY GERALD
Records of the Survey of India. Volume VI. Dehra Dun: 1914. V. 53

BURRELL, H.
The Platypus: Its Discovery, Zoological Position, Form and Characteristics. Sydney: 1927. V. 49

BURRELL, ROBERT
The First Step in the Ladder to Political Knowledge; or the Young Man's Catechism. Glasgow: 1843. V. 54

BURRETT, EDWARD
My Wartime Caricatures. 1992. V. 54

BURRIDGE, RICHARD
A New Review of London: Being an Exact Survey, Lately Taken of every Street, Lane, Court, Alley, alphabetically Digested. London: 1728. V. 48

BURRILL, ALEXANDER M.
A Treatise on the Nature, Principles and Rules of Circumstantial Evidence... New York: 1859. V. 54

BURRITT, ELIHU
Elihu Burritt's Miscellaneous Writings. Worcester: 1850. V. 49
Sparks from the Anvil. Worcester: 1846. V. 53

BURROUGH, EDWARD
A Declaration of the Sad and Great Persecution and Martyrdom of the People of God Called Quakers, in New England... London: 1661. V. 48
A Declaration of the Sad and Great Persecution and Martyrdom of the People of God Called Quakers, in New England. London: 1661. V. 54

BURROUGHS, ALAN
Art Criticism from a laboratory. Boston: 1938. V. 49

BURROUGHS, EDEN
A Faithful Narrative of the Wonderful Dealings of God Towards Polly Davis, of new Grantham, in the State of New Hampshire. Worcester: 1793. V. 47

BURROUGHS, EDGAR RICE
At the Earth's Core. Chicago: 1922. V. 47; 51; 52
Back to the Stone Age. Tarzana: 1937. V. 48; 49; 50; 51; 53
The Beasts of Tarzan. Chicago: 1916. V. 47; 50; 51; 52; 53
Beyond Thirty and the Man-Eater. New York: 1957. V. 50
Carson of Venus. 1939. V. 48; 49; 50; 52
The Cave Girl. Chicago: 1925. V. 54
The Chessmen of Mars. London: 1923. V. 48; 52
The Deputy Sheriff of Comanche County. Tarzana: 1940. V. 49; 50; 51; 53
The Deputy Sheriff of Comanche County. Tarzana: 1941. V. 51
The Edgar Rice Burroughs Library of Illustration. 1976/77/84. V. 47
The Edgar Rice Burroughs Library of Illustrations. West Plains: 1976. V. 53
Escape on Venus. 1946. V. 51
Escape on Venus. Tarzana: 1946. V. 48; 50; 51; 53
The Eternal Lover. Chicago: 1925. V. 51
The Eternal Lover. New York: 1927. V. 51
A Fighting Man of Mars. 1931. V. 49; 54
A Fighting Man of Mars. New York: 1931. V. 51
The Girl from Hollywood. 1923. V. 51
Gods of Mars. Chicago: 1918. V. 53
Gods of Mars. Tarzana: 1948. V. 51; 53
I Am a Barbarian. Tarzana: 1967. V. 52
John Carter of Mars. New York: 1964. V. 52
Jungle Girl. 1933. V. 47; 49; 51
Jungle Tales of Tarzan. 1919. V. 49; 53; 54
Jungle Tales of Tarzan. Chicago: 1919. V. 47; 49; 51
The Lad and the Lion. Tarzana: 1938. V. 49; 51
The Lad and the Lion. 1939. V. 48
Land of Terror. 1944. V. 49
Land Of Terror. Tarzana: 1944. V. 50; 51; 53; 54
The Land that Time Forgot. Chicago: 1924. V. 51
Llana of Gathol. Tarzana: 1948. V. 48; 51; 52; 53
Lost on Venus. 1935. V. 48
Lost on Venus. Tarzana: 1935. V. 51
The Mad King. Chicago: 1926. V. 51
The Man Without a Soul. London: 1922. V. 47
The Man Without a Soul. London: 1927. V. 51
The Master Mind of Mars. London: 1939. V. 49; 54
The Monster Men. Chicago: 1929. V. 51
The New Adventures of Tarzan "Pop-Up". Chicago: 1935. V. 47
The Outlaw of Torn. Chicago: 1927. V. 49; 51; 53
Pirates of Venus. Tarzana: 1934. V. 49; 51; 53
A Princess of Mars. 1917. V. 48
A Princess of Mars. Chicago: 1917. V. 53
A Princess of Mars. New York: 1965. V. 52
The Return of Tarzan. Leipzig: 1921. V. 48
The Son of Tarzan. Chicago: 1917. V. 49; 53
Swords of Mars. Tarzana: 1936. V. 51; 53
Synthetic Men of Mars. Tarzana: 1940. V. 47; 49; 50; 51; 52; 53
Tanar of Pellucidar. New York: 1930. V. 50
Tanar of Pellucidar. London: 1939. V. 47; 51
Tarzan and the Apes. New York: 1940. V. 51
Tarzan and the City of Gold. Tarzana: 1933. V. 51
Tarzan and the Forbidden City. 1938. V. 48; 50; 52
Tarzan and the Forbidden City. Tarzana: 1948. V. 51
Tarzan and the Foreign Legion. Tarzana: 1947. V. 52; 53
Tarzan and the Golden Lion. Chicago: 1923. V. 48; 49; 51; 52
Tarzan and the Golden Lion. London: 1924. V. 47; 51
Tarzan and the Jewels of Opar. 1918. V. 49
Tarzan and the Leopard Man. Tarzana: 1935. V. 48; 49; 51
Tarzan and the Lion Man. 1934. V. 48
Tarzan and the Lion Man. Tarzana: 1934. V. 51
Tarzan and the Lost Empire. 1929. V. 47
Tarzan and the Lost Empire. New York: 1929. V. 53
Tarzan at the Earth's Core. 1930. V. 47
Tarzan at the Earth's Core. New York: 1930. V. 51
Tarzan: Lord of the Jungle. Chicago: 1928. V. 48; 50; 51
Tarzan of the Apes. 1917. V. 50; 52
Tarzan: the Invincible. Tarzana: 1931. V. 50; 53; 54
Tarzan the Magnificent. Tarzana: 1939. V. 48; 50; 51; 54
Tarzan the Magnificent. Tarzana: 1948. V. 51; 53
Tarzan the Terrible. 1921. V. 49
Tarzan the Untamed. Chicago: 1920. V. 48; 50; 51; 54
Tarzan Triumphant. Tarzana: 1932. V. 48; 50; 51
Tarzan's Quest. Tarzana: 1936. V. 48; 50; 51; 53
The War Chief. Chicago: 1927. V. 51; 53
The War Chief. London: 1928. V. 51
The Warlord of Mars. 1919. V. 47
The Warlord of Mars. Chicago: 1919. V. 51; 52; 53
The Warlord of Mars. New York: 1920. V. 51

BURROUGHS, EDWARD
The Case of Free Liberty of Conscience in the Exercise of Faith and Religion. London: 1661. V. 53

BURROUGHS, JOHN
Bird and Bough. Boston: 1906. V. 49
The Complete Writings of John Burroughs. Boston: 1904. V. 54

BURROUGHS, JOHN continued
Notes on Walt Whitman, as Poet and Person. New York: 1871. V. 47
Songs of Nature. New York: 1901. V. 51
Wake-Robin. New York: 1871. V. 51; 53
Winter Sunshine. New York: 1876. V. 51

BURROUGHS, JOHN ROLFE
Guardian of the Grasslands. Cheyenne: 1971. V. 52; 53

BURROUGHS, RAYMOND DARWIN
The Natural History of the Lewis and Clark Expedition. 1961. V. 52

BURROUGHS, STEPHEN
Memoirs of Stephen Burroughs. Hanover: 1798. V. 51
Sketch of the Life of the Notorious Stephen Burroughs, Containing the Most Interesting Events of His Life. Ostego: 1810. V. 47

BURROUGHS, WILLIAM
Time and Change. Boston: 1912. V. 51

BURROUGHS, WILLIAM S.
The Adding Machine. New York: 1986. V. 50; 51
Ah Pook is Here and Other Texts - The Book of Breething - Electronic Revolution. London: 1979. V. 54
The Book of Breeething. Berkeley: 1975. V. 50
The Book of Breeething. Berkeley: 1980. V. 50
Brion Gysin Let the Mice In. West Glover: 1973. V. 50
The Cat Inside. New York: 1986. V. 54
Catalogue of the William S. Burroughs Archive. London: 1973. V. 50
Cities of the Red Night. New York: 1981. V. 47; 48; 50; 51; 53; 54
Cobble Stone Gardens. Cherry Valley: 1976. V. 50; 51
Dead Fingers Talk. 1963. V. 49; 52; 53; 54
Doctor Benway. Santa Barbara: 1979. V. 48; 50; 51
Early Routines. Santa Barbara: 1981. V. 48; 50; 51
The Exterminator. San Francisco: 1960. V. 50; 51
Exterminator. New York: 1973. V. 50; 51; 52; 53
Exterminator!. London: 1974. V. 54
Junkie. New York. V. 51
Junkie. New York: 1953. V. 52; 53
The Last Words of Dutch Schultz. London: 1970. V. 48; 50; 52; 53; 54
The Last Words of Dutch Schultz. New York: 1975. V. 50
The Last Words of Hassan-I-Sabbah. 1981/82. V. 49
Letters to Allen Ginsberg 1953-1957. New York: 1982. V. 50; 54
Minutes to Go. Paris: 1960. V. 47; 50
Naked Lunch. New York: 1959. V. 50; 51
The Naked Lunch. Paris: 1959. V. 49; 50; 51
Naked Lunch. New York: 1962. V. 51
The Naked Lunch. London: 1964. V. 52
Naked Lunch. New York: 1984. V. 50; 51
Nova Express. New York: 1956. V. 54
Nova Express. New York: 1964. V. 47; 50; 53
The Place of Dead Roads. New York: 1983. V. 48; 50; 51; 54
The Place of Dead Roads. New York: 1984. V. 54
Port of Saints. London: 1973. V. 50
Port of Saints. Berkeley: 1980. V. 50; 51
Queer. New York: 1985. V. 49; 50
The Retreat Diaries. New York: 1976. V. 50; 53
Roosevelt After Inauguration. New York: 1964. V. 50
Ruski. New York: 1984. V. 50
The Seven Deadly Sins. New York: 1991. V. 50
Sinki's Sauna. New York: 1982. V. 50
The Soft Machine. New York: 1966. V. 47; 51; 52; 53
The Streets of Chance. New York: 1981. V. 50; 52
The Third Mind. New York: 1978. V. 47
The Ticket that Exploded. Paris: 1962. V. 53
The Ticket That Exploded. 1967. V. 49
The Ticket That Exploded. New York: 1967. V. 50; 53; 54
The Ticket that Exploded. London: 1968. V. 54
Time. New York: 1965. V. 49; 50; 53
Valentine's Day Reading. New York: 1965. V. 51
The Western Lands. New York: 1987. V. 51; 54
The Wild Boys - a Book of the Dead. New York: 1971. V. 50

BURROW, F. R.
Law Tennis, The World Game Today. London. V. 50

BURROW, J. C.
'Mongst Mines and Miners; or Underground Scenes by Flash-Light. London: 1893. V. 51

BURROWES, JOHN FRECKLETON
The Piano-Forte Primer... London: 1819. V. 50
The Piano-forte Primer, or New Musical Catechism... Philadelphia: 1820. V. 50

BURROWES, THOMAS H.
Pennsylvania School Architecture. Harrisburg: 1855. V. 47; 51

BURROWS, C. ACTON
The Annals of the Town of Guelph 1827-1877. Guelph: 1877. V. 54

BURROWS, GEORGE
On Disorders of the Cerebral Circulation: and on the Connection Between Affections of the Brain and Diseases of the Heart. Philadelphia: 1848. V. 47; 53

BURROWS, GEORGE MAN
An Inquiry into Certain Errors Relative to Insanity; and Their Consequences; Physical, Moral and Civil. London: 1820. V. 52

BURROWS, GUY
The Curse of Central Africa... London: 1903. V. 53

BURROWS, HAROLD
Biological Actions of Sex Hormones. Cambridge: 1945. V. 53
Oestrogens and Neoplasia. Springfield: 1952. V. 48; 53

BURROWS, J. E.
Southern African Ferns and Fern Allies. 1990. V. 52
Southern African Ferns and Fern Allies. Sandton: 1990. V. 51

BURROWS, LARRY
Larry Burrows: Compassionate Photographer. New York: 1972. V. 47; 51

BURROWS, MONTAGU
The Family of Brocas of Beaurepaire and Roche Court...With Some Account of the English Rule in Aquitaine. London: 1886. V. 54

BURROWS, WILLIAM
Adventures of a Mounted Trooper in the Australian Constabulary... London: 1859. V. 51

BURRUS, ERNEST J.
Kino and Manje, Explorers of Sonora and Arizona, Their Vision of the Future. Rome: 1971. V. 48
Kino and the Cartography of Northwestern New Spain. Tucson: 1965. V. 48; 50; 52

BURSCOUGH, ROBERT
A Discourse, I. Of the Unity of the Church. II. Of the Separation of the Dissenters from the Church of England. III. Of Their Setting Up Churches Against the Conforming Churches; and of the Ordination of Their Teachers. Exeter: 1704. V. 53
A Discourse of Schism: Address'd to Those Dissenters, Who Conform'd Before the Toleration... London: 1699. V. 53

BURSILL, HENRY
Hand Shadows to be Thrown Upon the Wall. London: 1859. V. 48; 49; 51
Hand Shadows to be Thrown Upon the Wall. London: 1860. V. 52

BURT, JOHN S. G.
Report of the Indiana Canal Company, on the Improvement of the Falls of the Ohio, to the Senate and House of Representatives of the United States. Cincinnati: 1856. V. 48

BURT, JOHN T.
Convict Discipline in Ireland; Being an Examination of Sir Walter Crofton's Answer to "Irish Facts and Wakefield Figures". London: 1865. V. 48; 53

BURT, KATHARINE NEWLIN
The Branding Iron. Boston: 1919. V. 48
A Man's Own Country. Boston: 1931. V. 48; 53

BURT, S. W.
The Rocky Mountain Gold Regions. Denver: 1962. V. 47

BURT, STRUTHERS
The Deletable Mountains. New York: 1927. V. 53

BURTON, ALFRED
The Adventures of Johny Newcome in the Navy; A Poem in four Cantos. London: 1818. V. 50
Rush-Bearing: an Account of the Old Custom of Strewing Rushes... Manchester: 1891. V. 48; 53

BURTON, E. F.
An Indian Olio. London: 1880. V. 54

BURTON, EDWARD
A Description of the Antiquities and Other Curiosities of Rome. Oxford: 1821. V. 47
A Description of the Antiquities and Other Curiosities of Rome... London: 1828. V. 49

BURTON, F. A.
The Roman Fort at Manchester. Manchester: 1909. V. 49

BURTON, F. R.
American Primitive Music, with Special Attention to the songs of the Ojibways. New York: 1909. V. 51; 54

BURTON, GILBERT
The Life of Sir Philip Musgrave, Bart, of Hartley Castle, Westmorland and of Edenhall, Co. Cumberland, Governor of the City of Carlisle... Carlisle: 1840. V. 50; 52; 54

BURTON, H. W.
The History of Norfolk, Virginia 1736-1877. Norfolk: 1877. V. 54

BURTON, HARLEY TRUE
A History of the JA Ranch. Austin: 1928. V. 50; 53; 54

BURTON, ISABEL
The Inner Life of Syria, Palestine and the Holy Land. From My Private Journal... London: 1875. V. 51

BURTON, JAMES E.
Selections From Official Records of the Criminal Department of the Rajpootana States and North-Western Provinces, of the Murder of Europeans by Mtineers During the Mutiny of 1857... Allahabad: 1874. V. 49

BURTON, JOHN
Lectures on Female Education and Manners. London: 1793. V. 51
Lectures on Female Education and Manners.. Dublin: 1794. V. 53
Lectures on Female Education and Manners. Elizabeth-Town: 1799. V. 50
Monasticon Eboracense; and the Ecclesiastical History of Yorkshire. London: 1758. V. 47; 49
Monasticon Eboracense: and The Ecclesiastical History of Yorkshire. York: 1758. V. 47; 50; 51; 52
The Parish Priest: a Poem. London: 1800. V. 49
Trackless Winds. San Francisco: 1930. V. 47

BURTON, JOHN EDWARD BLOUNDELLE
His Own Enemy; the Story of a Man of the World. London: 1887. V. 49

BURTON, JOHN HILL
The Book-Hunter, Etc. Edinburgh: 1882. V. 54
Communism. Edinburgh: 1854. V. 54
A History of the Reign of Queen Anne. Edinburgh & London: 1880. V. 53
Narratives from Criminal Trials in Scotland. London: 1852. V. 47; 48; 54

BURTON, M.
The Secret of High Eldersham. 1931. V. 54

BURTON, MARIA AMPARO RUIZ
The Squatter and the Don. San Francisco: 1885. V. 51; 52

BURTON-ON-TRENT NATURAL HISTORY AND ARCHAEOLOGICAL SOCIETY
Transactions of the Burton-on-Trent Natural History and Archaeological Society. London: 1889-1927. V. 52

BURTON, PETER J.
Police Court Pictures at Richmond, Virginia. Richmond: 1892. V. 50

BURTON, R. G.
Sport and Wild Life in the Deccan. Philadelphia: 1928. V. 47

BURTON, REGINALD G.
Tropics and Snows, a Record of Travel and Adventure. 1898. V. 54

BURTON, RICHARD
Admirable Curiosities, Rarities and Wonders in England, Scotland and Ireland, Being an Account of Many Remarkable Persons and Places... Westminster: 1811. V. 49
Meeting Mr. Jenkins. New York: 1966. V. 54

BURTON, RICHARD FRANCIS
Ananga-Ranga. Cosmopoli: 1885. V. 51
Arabic Proverbs, or the Manners and Customs of the Modern Egyptians... London: 1875. V. 53
Book of the Sword. London: 1884. V. 50; 53; 54
The Captivity of Hans Stade of Hesse, in A.D. 1547-1555... London: 1874. V. 47
The City of the Saints and Across the Rock Mountains to California. London: 1861. V. 47; 53; 54
The City of the Saints, and Across the Rocky Mountains to California. New York: 1862. V. 49; 54
Etruscan Bologna: a Study. London: 1876. V. 48; 49; 50; 51; 54
Explorations of the Highlands of Brazil... London: 1869. V. 47; 51; 53; 54
Falconry in the Valley of the Indus. London: 1852. V. 50; 52
First Footsteps in East Africa; or, an Exploration of Harar. London: 1856. V. 47; 53
First Footsteps in East Africa, or, an Exploration of Harrar... London: 1894. V. 51
The Gold Mines of Midian and the Ruined Midianite Cities. London: 1878. V. 47; 48; 50; 51
The Guide-Book. A Pictorial Pilgrimage to Mecca and Medina. London: 1865. V. 47
The Jew, the Gypsy and El Islam. Chicago & New York: 1898. V. 52
The Kasidah of Haji Abdu El-Yezdi. London: 1880. V. 48
The Kasidah of Haji Abdu El-Yezdi. Portland: 1915. V. 48; 54
The Kasidah of Haji Abdu El-Yezdi. London: 1925. V. 50
The Kasidah of Haji Abdu El-Yezdi. New York: 1937. V. 48; 52; 53; 54
Lacerda's Journey to Cazembe in 1798. London: 1873. V. 47
The Lake Regions of Central Africa. London: 1860. V. 47; 50
The Land of Midian. London: 1879. V. 47; 48; 51
The Lands of Cazembe. London: 1873. V. 47
Letters from the Battle-Fields of Paraguay. London: 1870. V. 52; 53
A Mission to Gelele, King of Dahome. London: 1864. V. 49
A Mission to Gelele, King of Dahome with Notices of the So Called 'Amazons', The Grand Customs, the Yearly Customs, the Human Sacrifices... London: 1893. V. 51
A Mission to Gelele of Dahome... London: 1864/93. V. 51
Narrative of a Pilgrimage to Meccah and Medinah. London: 1879. V. 53
Il Pentamerone; or the Tale of Tales. London: 1893. V. 54
Personal Narrative of a Pilgriamge to El-Madinah & Meccah. London: 1893. V. 48; 50; 51
Personal Narrative of a Pilgrimage to El-Madinah & Mecca. London: 1898. V. 51
Personal Narrative of a Pilgrimage to El-Medinah and Meccah. London: 1855. V. 54
Personal Narrative of a Pilgrimage to El-Medinah and Meccah. London: 1855-56. V. 54
Personal Narrative of a Pilgrimage to El-Medinah and Meccah. London: 1857. V. 47; 51; 54
A Pilgrimage to El Medinah and Meccah. New York: 1856. V. 47
The Prairie Traveler, a Hand-Book for Overland Expeditions. London: 1863. V. 54
Scinde; or, the Unhappy Valley. London: 1851. V. 47
Selected Papers on Anthropology, Travel and Exploration... London: 1924. V. 47; 50; 54
To the Gold Coast for Gold. London: 1883. V. 47
Ultima Thule; or, a Summer in Iceland. London: 1875. V. 47; 53
Unexplored Syria. visits to the Libanus, the Tulul El Safa, The Anti-Libanus, the Northern Libanus, and the Alah. London: 1872. V. 49
Voyage aux Grands Lacs de l'Afrique Orientale. Paris: 1862. V. 54
Wanderings in Three Continents. London: 1901. V. 47; 51; 54
Wit and Wisdom from West Africa; or, A Book of Proverbial Philosophy, Idioms, Enigmas and Laconisms. London: 1865. V. 47

BURTON, ROBERT
The Anatomy of Melancholy... Oxford: 1621. V. 47; 49; 51; 52; 54
The Anatomy of Melancholy. Oxford: 1624. V. 53
The Anatomy of Melancholy. Oxford: 1628. V. 47
The Anatomy of Melancholy. London: 1652. V. 50
The Anatomy of Melancholy. London: 1660. V. 49; 53
The Anatomy of Melancholy. Oxford: 1660. V. 54
The Anatomy of Melancholy. London: 1676. V. 48
The Anatomy of Melancholy... London: 1800. V. 47; 48; 49; 50; 51; 52; 53
The Anatomy of Melancholy. London: 1806. V. 48; 50; 53
The Anatomy of Melancholy. London: 1821. V. 50; 54
The Anatomy of Melancholy. London: 1849. V. 50; 52
The Anatomy of Melancholy. London: 1883. V. 47; 48
The Anatomy of Melancholy. New York: 1885. V. 54
The Anatomy of Melancholy. London & New York: 1893. V. 49; 53
The Anatomy of Melancholy. London: 1925. V. 48; 50; 51; 53; 54
The Anatomy of Melancholy. New York: 1927. V. 52
The Anatomy of Melancholy. London: 1971. V. 51
The Library of Robert Burton. Oxford: 1988. V. 51

BURTON, THOMAS
Diary of Thomas Burton, Esq., Member in the Parliaments of Oliver and Richard Cormwell, from 1656 to 1659... London: 1828. V. 49; 53
The History and Antiquities of the Parish of Hemingbrough in the County of York. York: 1888. V. 53

BURTON, VIRGINIA LEE
Mike Mulligan and His Steam Shovel. Boston: 1939. V. 47

BURTON, W.
The Pleasures of Belief. London: 1812. V. 48

BURTON, W. K.
The Water Supply of Towns and Construction of Waterworks... 1898. V. 51

BURTON, WARREN
My Religious Experience, at My Native Home. Boston: 1829. V. 49
White Slavery: a New Emancipation Cause, Presented to the People of the United States. Worcester: 1839. V. 48

BURTON, WILLIAM
A Commentary on Antoninus His Itinerary, or Journies of the Roman Empire... London: 1658. V. 47; 48; 53; 54
The Cyclopedia of Wit and Humor. New York: 1858. V. 48
The Description of Leicester Shire. London: 1622. V. 48; 52
The Description of Leicestershire: Containing, Matters of Antiquity, History, Armoury and Genealogy. (King's) Lynn: 1777. V. 47
A General History of Porcelain. London: 1921. V. 48

BURTON, WILLIAM E.
Bibliotheca Dramatica. New York: 1860. V. 48

BURY, ADRIAN
John Varley of the "Old Society". Leigh-on-Sea: 1946. V. 49; 50; 52
Joseph Crawhall, the Man and the Artist. London: 1957. V. 53
Joseph Crawhall, the Man and the Artist. London: 1958. V. 49
Shadow of Eros: a Biographical and Critical Study of the Life and Works of Sir Alfred Gilbert. London: 1952. V. 53

BURY, CHARLOTTE
The Executives. London: 1830. V. 50
Family Records; or, The Two Sisters. Paris: 1841. V. 47

BURY, ELIZABETH
An Account of the Life and Death of Mrs. Elizabeth Bury, Who Died May the 11th, 1720... Bristol: 1720. V. 49

BURY, G. WYMAN
Arabia Infelix, or The Turks in Yamen. London: 1915. V. 47; 49

BURY, JAMES
Pickings Up In Ireland. London: 1859. V. 54

BURY, T. T.
Coloured Views on the Liverpool and Manchester Railway... London: 1831. V. 48; 54
Remains of Ecclesiastical Woodwork. London: 1847. V. 54

BUSBECQ, OGIER GHISLAIN DE
Travels Into Turkey... London: 1744. V. 53

BUSBY, CHARLES AUGUSTINE
A Series of Designs for Villas and Country Houses. London: 1808. V. 53

BUSBY, J.
Journal of a Recent Visit to the Principal Vineyards of Spain and France, Giving a Minute Account of the Different Methods Pursued in the Cultivation of the Vine and the Manufacture of Wine... New York: 1835. V. 47

BUSBY, THOMAS
A Complete Dictionary of Music. Philadelphia: 1827. V. 50

BUSCARLET, K.
Twelve Pencil Drawings of Sedbergh. Sedbergh: 1924. V. 53

BUSCH, FREDERICK
I Wanted a Year Without Fall. London: 1971. V. 53

BUSCH, GEORGE B.
Duty, the Story of the 21st Infantry Regiment. 1953. V. 47

BUSH & SON & MEISSNER
Illustrated Descriptive Catalogue of American Grape Vines. St. Louis: 1883. V. 47; 50; 52

BUSH, BENJAMIN
The Drunkard's Emblem; or, an Enquiry into the Effects of Ardent Spirits Upon the Human Body and Mind. Winchester: 1811. V. 52

BUSH, I. J.
Gringo Doctor. Caldwell: 1939. V. 52

BUSH, J.
Hibernia Curiosa: a Letter from a Gentleman in Dublin. London: 1769. V. 47; 48; 52

BUSH, JAMES
The Choice: or Lines on the Beatitudes. London: 1841. V. 52

BUSH, M.
The Passion of Sacco and Vanzetti. Syracuse: 1968. V. 49; 54

BUSHBY, ANNE S.
The Danes Sketched by Themselves. London: 1864. V. 54

BUSHE, PETER KENDAL
Through the Troposcope. London & Paris: 1966. V. 51

BUSHELL, KEITH
Papuan Epic. London: 1936. V. 50

BUSHNELL, HORACE
Women's Suffrage; the Reform Against Nature. New York: 1869. V. 54

BUSHYHEAD, D. W.
To the Cherokees and Other Indians. Cherokee Nation: 1885. V. 48

BUSINESS Directory and Historical and Descriptive Hand-Book of Tulare County, California...
Tulare City: 1888. V. 54

BUSINESS Man's Assistant and Legal Guide.
Chicago: 1856. V. 47

BUSK, M. M., MRS.
Tales of Fault and Feeling. London: 1825. V. 50

BUSS, HENRY
Wanderings in the West, During the Year 1870. London: 1871. V. 53

BUSSING, CASPAR
Einleitung zu der Herolds-Kunst. Hamburg: 1694. V. 50

BUSSY, ROGER DE RABUTIN, COMTE DE
The Amorous History of the Gauls. London: 1725. V. 47

BUSTI, BERNARDINO DE
Mariale. Lyon: 1511. V. 48

BUSWELL, JOHN
An Historical Account of the Knights of the Most Noble ORder of the Garter. London: 1757. V. 47

BUSWELL, LESLIE
Ambulance No. 10 - Personal Letters From the Front. Boston and New York: 1916. V. 47

THE BUSY Body, or Men and Manners.
London: 1816. V. 47

BUTCHER, DAVID
The Stanbrook Abbey Press. 1956-1990. Herefordshire: 1992. V. 48; 51
The Stanbrook Abbey Press 1956-1990. London: 1992. V. 47; 50
The Whittington Press. A Bibliography 1971-1981. Andoversford: 1982. V. 51

BUTCHER, E.
Sidmouth Scenery, or Views of the Principal Cottages and Residence of the Noblity and Gentry. Sidmouth: 1817. V. 47

BUTCHER, RICHARD
The Survey and Antiquity of the Towns of Stamford in the County of Lincoln and Tottenham-High-Cross in Middlesex. London: 1717. V. 51

BUTLER, A. G.
Foreign Finches in Captivity. London: 1904. V. 48
Illustrations of Typical Specimens of Lepidoptera Heterocera in the Collection of the British Museum. London: 1886-93. V. 48

BUTLER, A. S. G.
The Architecture of Sir Edward Lutyens. London: 1950. V. 49
The Domestic Architecture of Sir Edwin Lutyens. London: 1989. V. 54

BUTLER, A. W.
The Birds of Indiana, a Descriptive Catalogue of the Birds that Have Been Observed Within the State, with an Account of Their Habits. Indianapolis: 1898. V. 52

BUTLER, ALBAN
The Lives of the Fathers, Martyrs and Other Principal Saints. London: 1880. V. 53

BUTLER, ARTHUR GARDINER
Birds of Great Britain and Ireland. London: 1900. V. 51
Birds of Great Britain and Ireland. London: 1908. V. 50
Birds of Great Britain and Ireland: Order Passeres. London: 1907-08. V. 47
British Birds' Eggs: a Handbook of British Oology. London: 1886. V. 47
British Birds With Their Nests and Eggs. London: 1896-98. V. 49
British Birds, with Their Nests and Eggs. London: 1896-99. V. 47; 52; 53
Foreign Finches in Captivity. London: 1894-96. V. 49
Foreign Finches in Captivity. Hull & London: 1899. V. 49
Illustrations of Typical Specimens of Lepidoptera Heterocera in...the British Museum. Part III. London: 1879. V. 49

BUTLER, BENJAMIN
Butler's Book; a Review of His Legal, Political and Military Career. Boston: 1892. V. 47; 48

BUTLER, BENJAMIN CLAPP
Lake George and Lake Champlain, from Their First Discovery to 1759. New York: 1869. V. 49

BUTLER, CHARLES
The Life of Erasmus. The Life of Hugo Grotius. Memoir of the Life of Henry-Francis D'Aguesseau. London: 1825-30. V. 47
The Life of Fenelon... London: 1819. V. 50
Reminiscences of Charles Butler. London: 1822. V. 48
Reminiscences of Charles Butler...with...Considerations on the Present Proceedings for the Reform on (sc) the English Courts of Equity... Boston: 1827. V. 50

BUTLER, CONSTANCE
Illyria, Lady. London: 1934. V. 49

BUTLER, E. A.
A Biology of the British Hemiptera-Heteroptera. London: 1923. V. 48; 53
A Catalogue of the Birds of Sind, Cutch, Ka'thia'wa'r, North Gujarat and Mount Abo (the Southern Portion of the bombay Presidency). Bombay: 1879-80. V. 48

BUTLER, ELIZABETH
A Memoir of the Very Rev. Richard Butler, Vicar of Trim. 1863. V. 52

BUTLER, ELLIS PARKER
Philo Gubb: Correspondence School Detective. Boston: 1918. V. 47
Pigs is Pigs. Chicago-New York: 1905. V. 47

BUTLER, FREDERICK
The Farmer's Manual: Being a Plain Practical Treatise on the Art of Husbandry, Designed to Promote an Acquaintance with the Modern Improvements in Agriculture... Weathersfield: 1821. V. 47

BUTLER, GEORGE
Thomas Butler and His Descendants. New York: 1886. V. 48

BUTLER, GERALD
Kiss the Blood Off My Hands. New York: 1946. V. 52

BUTLER, HARCOURT
A Big Game Shoot in Upper Burma, 1923. Rangoon: 1923. V. 54

BUTLER, HENRY
South African Sketches Illustrataive of the Wild Life of a Hunter on the Frontier of the Cape Colony. London: 1841. V. 47; 49

BUTLER, HILLARY
The Mayor of Wigan, a Tale. London: 1760. V. 54

BUTLER, HOWARD CROSBY
Sardis. Volume I (only): The Excavations, Part I. 1910-1914. Leyden: 1922. V. 52
Sardis. Volume II: Architecture. Part I (only), The Temple of Artemis. Leyden: 1925. V. 52

BUTLER, JAMES
American Bravery Displayed, in the Capture of Fourteen Hundred Vessels of War and Commerce, Since the Declaration of War by the President... Carlisle: 1816. V. 48
Fortune's Foot-Ball: or, the Adventures of Mercutio... Harrisonburgh: 1797-98. V. 50

BUTLER, JAMES D.
Butleriana. Genealogica et Biographica; or Genealogical Notes Concerning Mary Butler and Her Descendants. Albany: 1888. V. 49
A September Scamper. 1877. V. 52

BUTLER, JAMES DAVIS
Nebraska. Its Characteristics and Prospects. Nebraska City: 1873. V. 48

BUTLER, JAMES LEE
A Good Scent from a Strange Mountain. New York: 1992. V. 53

BUTLER, JOHN C.
Historical Record of Macon and Central Georgia. Macon: 1879. V. 49

BUTLER, JOSEPH
The Analogy of Religion, Natural and Revealed, to the Constitution and Course of Nature. London: 1736. V. 47; 48; 54
Fifteen Sermons Preached at the Rolls Chapel... London: 1736. V. 49
The Works. London: 1828. V. 49
The Works. 1896. V. 50

BUTLER, M. B.
In the Ranks with Company A, My Story of the Civil War and Underground Railroad. Huntington: 1914. V. 54

BUTLER, MANN
A History of the Commonwealth of Kentucky. Lexington: 1834. V. 53
A History of the Commonwealth of Kentucky. Louisville: 1834. V. 47; 48
Report on Monotorial Education; to the Hon. Mayor and Council of Louisville. Louisville: 1829. V. 54

BUTLER, OCTAVIA
Clay's Ark. New York: 1984. V. 53
Survivor. Garden City: 1978. V. 53

BUTLER, OCTAVIA E.
Patternmaster. Garden City: 1976. V. 51

BUTLER, RACHEL
Jessie Cameron: a Highland Story. Edinburgh: 1857. V. 50

BUTLER, ROBERT OLEN
The Alleys of Eden. New York: 1981. V. 51; 52; 53; 54
Countrymen of Bones. New York: 1983. V. 51
The Deuce. New York: 1989. V. 50; 53
A Good Scent from a Strange Mountain. New York: 1992. V. 50; 51; 52; 53
On Distant Ground. New York: 1985. V. 52; 53
Sun Dogs. New York: 1982. V. 50; 51; 52; 53; 54
They Whisper. Huntington Beach: 1993. V. 51
They Whisper. Huntington: 1994. V. 52
Wabash. New York: 1987. V. 53

BUTLER, SAMUEL
Alps and Sanctuaries of Piedmont and the Canton Ticino. London: 1882. V. 52
Alps and Sanctuaries of Piedmont and the Canton Ticino. London: 1913. V. 52
The Authoress of the Odyssey. London: 1897. V. 51; 52
Butleriana. Bloomsbury: 1932. V. 47; 50; 52
The Collected Works. London: 1926. V. 52
Erewhon. London: 1872. V. 48; 49; 50; 51; 52; 53
Erewhon. London: 1873. V. 52
Erewhon. London: 1880. V. 52
Erewhon. London: 1890. V. 52
Erewhon. London: 1901. V. 52
Erewhon. London: 1913. V. 47
Erewhon. Newtown: 1923. V. 52
Erewhon. Newtown: 1931. V. 50
Erewhon. Newtown: 1932. V. 50
Erewhon. Newtown: 1933. V. 54
Erewhon. New York: 1934. V. 48; 51; 52; 53
Erewhon Revisited. London: 1872. V. 52
Erewhon Revisited. London: 1901. V. 50; 51; 52; 53; 54
Essays on Life, Art and Science. London: 1904. V. 52
Evolution Old and New... London: 1879. V. 50; 52
Evolution, Old and New. Salem: 1879. V. 49
Evolution, Old and New. London: 1882. V. 52
Ex Voto; an Account of the Sacro Monte or New Jerusalem at Varallo-Sesia. London: 1890. V. 52
Ex Voto: an Acocunt of the Sacro Monte of New Jerusalem at Varallo-Sesia. London: 1888. V. 52
The Fair Haven. London: 1873. V. 52
A First Year in Canterbury Settlement. London: 1863. V. 49; 52
Gavottes, Minuets, Fugues and Other Short Pieces for the Piano by Samuel Butler. London and New York: 1885. V. 52
The Genuine Poetical Remains Of... London: 1827. V. 49
The Genuine Remains in Verse and Prose. London: 1759. V. 49; 51; 54
God the Known and God the Unknown. London: 1909. V. 52
Hudibras. London: 1663. V. 50; 51; 54
Hudibras. London: 1663/64/78. V. 51
Hudibras. London: 1674/78. V. 50
Hudibras. London: 1678/80. V. 53
Hudibras. London: 1684/84/79. V. 48; 49
Hudibras. London: 1689. V. 54
Hudibras. London: 1694. V. 50
Hudibras. London: 1694/93/94. V. 53
Hudibras. London: 1716. V. 51
Hudibras. London: 1720. V. 52; 54
Hudibras. Cambridge: 1744. V. 48; 49; 53; 54
Hudibras. London: 1744. V. 50
Hudibras. Londres: 1757. V. 47
Hudibras. London: 1793. V. 48; 53
Hudibras. London: 1806. V. 50
Hudibras. London: 1810. V. 53
Hudibras. London: 1819. V. 47; 48; 49; 50; 51; 52; 54
Hudibras. London: 1820. V. 51
Hudibras... London: 1835. V. 52
Hudibras. (with) The Genuine Poetical Remains of Samuel Butler. London: 1819/27. V. 50
Hudibras. (with) The Genuine Remains in Verse and Prose. Cambridge: 1744-59. V. 50
The Humour of Homer. Cambridge: 1892. V. 52
The Humour of Homer and Other Essays. London: 1913. V. 52
A Letter from Mercurius Civicus to Mercurius Rusticus: or London's Confession But Not Repentance. Oxford: 1643. V. 49
A Letter to Philograntus, by Eubulus. London: 1822. V. 50
Life and Habit. London: 1878. V. 49
The Life and Letters of Dr. Samuel Butler, Head-Master of Shrewsbury School 1798-1836... London: 1896. V. 52
Luck, or Cunning, as the Main Means of Organic Modification?. London: 1887. V. 52
The Medical Register and Directory of the United States... Philadelphia: 1874. V. 50
Narcissus. London: 1888. V. 52
The Note-books of Samuel Butler, Author of "Erewhon". London: 1912. V. 52; 54
On the Trapanese Origin of the Odyssey. Cambridge: 1893. V. 50; 52
The Poetical Works of Samuel Butler. London: 1803-04. V. 49
The Poetical Works of Samuel Butler. London: 1866. V. 51
Prose Observations. London: 1979. V. 54
Seven Sonnets and a Psalm of Montreal. Cambrdige: 1904. V. 48; 52
Shakespeare's Sonnets Reconsidered. London: 1899. V. 52
A True and Perfect Copy of the Lord Roos, His Answer to the Marquesse of Dorchester's Letter, Written the 25 of February 1659. London: 1660. V. 47
Ulysses: a Dramatic Oratorio in Vocal Score... London: 1904. V. 52
Unconscious Memory. London: 1880. V. 52
The Way of All Flash. London: 1903. V. 47; 50; 51; 52; 53; 54
The Way of All Flesh. New Haven: 1936. V. 53; 54
The Way of All Flesh. New York: 1936. V. 47; 52; 54
Works. London: 1923. V. 50

BUTLER, SAMUEL, BP. OF LICHFIELD & COVENTRY
An Atlas of Ancient Geography. London: 1827. V. 48
An Atlas of Antient Geography. Philadelphia: 1832. V. 51
An Atlas of Antient Geography. Philadelphia: 1834. V. 50
An Atlas of Antient Geography. Philadelphia: 1838. V. 48
An Atlas of Modern Geography. London: 1826. V. 53
A General Atlas of Ancient and Modern Geography. 1826. V. 54

BUTLER, THOMAS
The Case of Thomas Butler, Bookseller and Stationer in Pall-Mall, London. Who Was Most Cruelly Treated at New-Market, Oct. 6, 1753. London: 1754. V. 48; 53

BUTLER, W. F.
The Campaign of the Cataracts. London: 1887. V. 49
The Campaign of the Cataracts. London: 1887. V. 52
Sir William Butler: an Autobiography. London: 1911. V. 48

BUTLER, WILLIAM
Exercises on the Globes... London: 1811. V. 54
The Land of the Veda. New York: 1871. V. 53
The Land Of the Veda. New York: 1906. V. 50; 54

BUTLER, WILLIAM F.
Akim-Foo: The History of a Failure. London: 1875. V. 47; 50
The Great Lone Land: a Narrative of Travel and Adventure in the North West of America. London: 1872. V. 47
The Wild North Land: the Story of a Winter Journey With Dogs Across Northern North America. London: 1915. V. 50

BUTLER, WILLIAM H. A.
Nothing to Wear. New York: 1857. V. 51

BUTLIN, JOHN ROSE
The Sabbath Made for Man, or, Defence of the Crystal Palace. London: 1853. V. 54

BUTLIN, MARTIN
The Paintings of J. M. W. Turner. New Haven: 1977. V. 48; 53
The Paintings of J. M. W. Turner. New Haven & London: 1984. V. 50; 53

BUTOR, MICHEL
Octal. Munich: 1972. V. 52

BUTT, ISAAC
The History of Italy, from the Abdication of Napoleon I. London: 1860. V. 47; 49; 50
The Irish People and the Irish Land: a Letter to Lord Lilford: with Comments on the Publications of Lord Dufferin and Lord Rosse. Dublin: 1867. V. 54

BUTT, JOHN
Memoirs of the Late Anthony Metcalfe-Gibson. Kendal: 1903. V. 50

BUTTERFIELD, C. W.
An Historical Account of the Expedition Against Sandusky Under Col. William Crawford in 1782... Cincinnati: 1873. V. 50

BUTTERFIELD, CARLOS
United States and Mexico. Commerce, Trade and Postal Facilities... New York: 1861. V. 47

BUTTERFIELD, CONSUL WILLSHIRE
History of Brule's Discoveries and Explorations 1610-1626. Celveland: 1898. V. 47

BUTTERFIELD, LINDSAY P.
Flora Forms in Historic Design. London. V. 54

BUTTERICK PUBLISHING CO.
(Trade Catalogue): Masquerade and Carnival: Their Customs and Costumes. 1892. V. 53

BUTTERWORTH, ADELINE M.
William Blake. Mystic: a Study. 1911. V. 53

BUTTERWORTH, BENJAMIN
The Growth of Industrial Art. Washington: 1892. V. 50; 53

BUTTERWORTH, E.
Macaws. London: 1993. V. 52

BUTTERWORTH, EDWIN
A Statistical Sketch of the County Palatine of Lancaster. London: 1841. V. 53

BUTTERWORTH, JAMES
The Antiquities of the Town and a Complete History of the Trade of Manchester... Manchester: 1822. V. 48

BUTTERWORTH, JAMES continued
A Complete History of the Cotton Trade, Including...the Silk, Calico-Printing & Hat Manufactories... Mancheter: 1823. V. 50

BUTTERWORTH, JOSEPH
A General Catalogue of Law-Books. London: 1801. V. 49

BUTTERWORTH, JOSEPH, & SON
A Catalogue of Modern Law Books, Also of the Old Reports, by Joseph Butterworth and Son. London: 1826. V. 54

BUTTON, EDWARD
A New Translation of the Persian Tales; From an Original Version of the Indian Comedies of Mocles... London: 1754. V. 51

BUTTRE, J. C.
Catalogue of Engravings by J. C. Buttre, Publisher, Engraver and Plate Printer. New York: 1870. V. 51; 52

BUTTRICK, GEORGE ARTHUR
The Interpreter's Dictionary of the Bibl. New York: 1962. V. 49

BUTTS, CHARLES
Geology of the Appalachian Valley in Virginia. 1940. V. 51

BUTTS, MARY
Armed with Madness. London: 1928. V. 49; 54
The Crystal Cabinet - My Childhood at Salterns. London: 1937. V. 50; 51; 53
Imaginary Letters. Paris: 1928. V. 50; 53
Scenes from the Life of Cleopatra. London: 1935. V. 51; 53
Scenes from the Life of Cleopatra. London: 1937. V. 54
Speed the Plough. London: 1923. V. 47; 49
Traps for Unbelievers. London: 1932. V. 48; 54

BUTT-THOMPSON, F. W.
West African Secret Societies: Their Organisations, Officials and Teaching. London: 1929. V. 54

BUXTON, BERTHA H.
Sceptre and Ring. London: 1881. V. 51

BUXTON, CHARLES
Memoirs of Sir Thomas Fowell Buxton. London: 1849. V. 54

BUXTON, EDWARD NOEL
On Either Side of the Red Sea. London: 1895. V. 50

BUXTON, EDWARD NORTH
Short Stalks; or Hunting Camps North and South, East and West. London: 1892. V. 47; 50; 51; 52
Short Stalks; or Hunting Camps North, South, East and West. London: 1893. V. 50
Short Stalks; or Hunting Camps North, South, East and West. First and second Series. London: 1893/98. V. 49
Short Stalks: or Hunting Camps North, South, East and West with Second Series. 1893/98. V. 54
Two African Trips with Notes and Suggestions on Big Game Preservation in Africa. London: 1902. V. 47

BUXTON, RICHARD
A Botanical Guide to the Flowering Plants, Ferns, Mosses and Algae, Found Indigenous Within Sixteen Miles of Manchester... London: 1849. V. 54

BUXTON, THOMAS FOWELL
The African Slave Trade. London: 1839. V. 52; 54
Memoirs of Sir Thomas Fowell Buxton. London: 1848. V. 53
Memoirs of Sir Thomas Fowell Buxton, Baronet. Philadelphia: 1849. V. 50

THE BUYERS Manual and Business Guide, Being a Description of the Leading Business Houses, Manufactories, Inventions, etc., of the Pacific Coast. San Francisco: 1872. V. 47

BY the Lords Justices, a Proclamation. Given at the Court at Whitehall the Twenty Seventh Day of May 1697. London: 1697. V. 47

BY-LAWS and Regulations of the 'Petersburg Light Infantry Guards'. Petersburg: 1846. V. 50

BYATT, A. S.
Angels and Insects. London: 1992. V. 48; 49; 50; 53
Degrees of Freedom - the Novels of Iris Murdoch. London: 1965. V. 52
The Game. London: 1967. V. 51; 52
Shadow of a Sun. London: 1964. V. 52
Still Life. London: 1985. V. 53
Still Life. New York: 1985. V. 47
The Virgin in the Garden. London: 1978. V. 52

BYATT, A S.
Wordsworth and Coleridge in Their Time. London: 1970. V. 53

BYER, A. P.
Conquest of Coomassie: an Epic of the Mashanti Nation. Los Angeles: 1923. V. 53

BYERLY, STEPHEN
Byerly's New American Spelling Book, Calculated for the Use of Schools in the United States. Philadelphia: 1827. V. 53

BYERS, DOUGLAS S.
The Prehistory of the Tehuacan Valley. Austin and London: 1967-72. V. 52

BYERS, H. M.
With Fire and Sword. New York: 1911. V. 48

BYERS, WILLIAM N.
Encyclopedia of Biography of Colorado. History of Colorado. Chicago: 1901. V. 51

BYINGTON, LEWIS FRANCIS
The History of San Francisco. Chicago & San Francisco: 1931. V. 49; 52; 54

BYINGTON, MARGARET F.
Homestead: The Households of a Mill Town. New York: 1910. V. 52

BYNE, ARTHUR
Majorcan Houses and Gardens: a Spanish Island in the Mediterranean. New York: 1928. V. 48
Provincial Houses in Spain. New York: 1925. V. 48
Rejeria of the Spanish Renaissance. New York: 1914. V. 48
Spanish Architecture of the Sixteenth Century. New York: 1917. V. 48; 53
Spanish Gardens & Patios. Philadelphia: 1924. V. 48; 53

BYNE, MILDRED STAPLEY
Spanish Gardens and Patios. Philadelphia: 1924. V. 50
Spanish Gardens and Patios. Philadelhpia & New York: 1928. V. 47; 48

BYNG, JOHN
An Exact Copy of a Remarkable Letter from Admiral Byng to the Right Hon. W(illiam) P(itt), Esq; Dated March 12, 1757, Two Days Before His Execution. London: 1757. V. 48
The Torrington Diaries. London: 1934-38. V. 48; 49
The Trial of the Honouruable Admiral John Byng, at a Court Martial, as Taken by Mr. Charles Fearne, Judge Advocate of His Majesty's Fleet. London: 1757. V. 51; 52

THE BYNG Papers Selected from the Letters and Papers of Admiral Sir George Byng, First Viscount Torrington and His Son Admiral the Hon. John Byng. London: 1930-31. V. 52

BYNKERSHOEK, CORNELIUS VAN
A Treatise on the Law of War. Philadelphia: 1810. V. 48

BYNNER, EDWIN LASSETER
Nimport. Boston: 1877. V. 47

BYNNER, WITTER
Journey with Genius; Recollections and Reflections Concerning the D. H. Lawrences. London: 1953. V. 50
An Ode to Harvard and Other Poems. Boston: 1907. V. 48
The Persistence of Poetry. San Francisco: 1929. V. 48
Tiger. London: 1913. V. 48

BYRD, CECIL K.
A Bibliography of Indiana Imprints 1804-1853. Indianapolis: 1955. V. 51; 52; 53

BYRD, RICHARD EVELYN
Alone. New York: 1938. V. 50; 53
Antarctic Discovery. London: 1936. V. 50
Discovery. The Story of the Second Byrd Antarctic Expedition. New York: 1935. V. 48
Little America. New York, London: 1930. V. 47; 50; 53
Skyward. New York & London: 1928. V. 48

BYRD, WILLIAM
The Westover Manuscripts: Containing the History of the Dividing Line Betwixt virginia and North Carolina; a Journey to the Land of Eden, A.D. 1733 and a Progress to the Mines. Petersburg: 1841. V. 49; 51
The Writings of Colonel William Byrd of Westover in Virginia. New York: 1901. V. 50; 54

BYRNE, DONN
Brother Saul. New York: 1927. V. 51
Stories Without Women. New York: 1915. V. 47

BYRNE, JULIA CLARA BUSK
Curiosities of the Search-Room. London: 1880. V. 51

BYRNE, M. ST. CLAIR
The Elizabethan Zoo: a Book of Beasts Both Fabulous and Authentic. London: 1926. V. 51; 54

BYRNE, MATTHEW J.
Ireland Under Elizabeth. 1903. V. 54

BYRNE, MILES
Memoirs on Miles Byrne. Dublin: 1907. V. 51

BYRNE, OLIVER
The First Six Books of the Elements of Euclid in Which Coloured Diagrams and Symbols are Used Instead of Letters for the Greater Ease of Learners. London: 1847. V. 48
The Handbook for the Artisan, Mechanic and Engineer. Philadelphia: 1853. V. 50
The Practical Cotton Spinner, and Manufacturer, the Managers' Overlookers' and Mechanics' Companion. Philadelphia: 1851. V. 48
Spon's Dictionary of Engineering, Civil, Mechanical, Military and Naval. London: 1869-73. V. 53
Spons' Dictionary of Engineering, Civil, Mechanical, Military and Naval... London: 1869-74. V. 49; 52

BYRNE, RAYMOND
Annual Review of Irish Law. Dublin: 1987-89. V. 49
Annual Review of Irish Law. Dublin: 1990. V. 49

BYRNES, THOMAS
Professional Criminals of America. New York: 1886. V. 47

BYROM, JOHN
Careless Content 1814 (a Poem). Chichester: 1932. V. 48

BYROM, JOHN continued
A Catalogue of the Library of the Late John Byrom, Esq., M.A., F.R.S., formerly Fellow of Trinity College. London: 1848. V. 50; 52; 54
Miscellaneous Poems... Manchester: 1773. V. 47; 50; 53; 54
The Private Journal and Literary Remains. London: 1854-57. V. 48
The Universal English Short-Hand; or, the Way of Writing English... Manchester: 1767. V. 47; 48; 52

THE BYRON Gallery: a Series of Historical Embellishments to Illustrate the Poetical Works of Lord Byron. London: 1833. V. 54

BYRON, GEORGE ANSON
Voyage of the H.M.S. Blonde to the Sandwich Islands, in the Years 1824-1825. London: 1826. V. 47; 52; 54

BYRON, GEORGE GORDON NOEL, 6TH BARON
The Age of Bronze; or, Carmen Seculare et Annus Haud Mirabilis. London: 1823. V. 51
Beppo, a Venetian Story. London: 1818. V. 47; 51; 53; 54
The Bride of Abydos. London: 1813. V. 47; 48; 53; 54
The Byron Gallery. London: 1833. V. 48; 49
Byron's Works. London: 1813-16. V. 53
Cain. A Mystery. Paris: 1822. V. 54
Childe Harold. Canto the Third and Canto the Fourth. London: 1816. V. 51
Childe Harold's Pilgrimage. London: 1812. V. 49
Childe Harold's Pilgrimage. Philadelphia: 1812. V. 51
Childe Harold's Pilgrimage. London: 1818. V. 48
Childe Harold's Pilgrimage. New York: 1931. V. 51
Childe Harold's Pilgrimage. Paris: 1931. V. 48; 51; 52
Childe Harold's Pilgrimage. Canto the Fourth. London: 1816. V. 48
Childe Harold's Pilgrimage. Canto the Fourth. London: 1818. V. 47; 48
Childe Harold's Pilgrimage, Complete. Paris: 1818. V. 47
The Complete Poetical Works. Oxford: 1980-93. V. 52
Correspondence of Lord Byron, with a Friend, Including His Letters to His Mother, Written from Portugal, Spain, Greece and the Shore of the Mediterranean, in 1809, 1810, 1811. Paris: 1825. V. 52
The Corsair. London: 1814. V. 47; 48; 49; 51
The Corsair. London: 1824. V. 53; 54
The Corsair, a Tale. (with) The Giaour, a Fragment of a Turkish Tale. (with) The Bryde of Abydos. London: 1814/13/13. V. 49
The Curse of Minerva. Philadelphia: 1815. V. 53
Don Juan. London: 1819. V. 51; 53
Don Juan. London: 1822-23-24. V. 48; 50
Don Juan. London/New York: 1926. V. 49; 53
Don Juan, Cantos III, IV, and V. London: 1821. V. 49
Don Juan. Cantos III, IV and V. London: 1828. V. 47
English Bards and Scotch Reviewers. London: 1809. V. 48; 49; 52
English Bards, and Scotch Reviewers. London: 1810. V. 47; 48; 51; 53
English Bards and Scotch Reviewers. London: 1811. V. 53
English Bards and Scotch Reviewers. London: 1812. V. 53; 54
English Bards and Scotch Reviewers. Paris: 1818. V. 53
English Bards and Scotch Reviewers. London: 1819. V. 53; 54
English Bards and Scotch Reviewers. New York: 1865. V. 54
Fugitive Pieces, a Facsimile Reprint of the Suppressed edition of 1806. London: 1886. V. 47
The Genuine Rejected Addresses, Presented to the Committee of Management for Drury-Lane Theatre... London: 1812. V. 47
The Giaour, a Fragment of a Turkish Tale. London: 1813. V. 47; 48; 50
The Giaour, a Fragment of a Turkish Tale. Philadelphia: 1813. V. 50
Hebrew Melodies. London: 1815. V. 51; 53
Hours of Idleness, a Series of Poems. Newark: 1807. V. 48; 50; 51; 52; 53; 54
Hours of Idleness: a Series of Poems, Original and Translated. (with) English Bards and Scotch Reviewers... London: 1820/10. V. 52
The Island, or Christian and His Comrades. London: 1823. V. 52; 54
A Journal of the Conversations of Lord Byron with the Countess of Blessington. London: 1893. V. 51
The Lament of Tasso. London: 1825. V. 53; 54
Lara, a Tale. London: 1814. V. 47; 48; 49; 51; 53
Letter *** ****** on the Rev. W. L. Bowles' Strictures on the Life and Writings of Pope. London: 1821. V. 47; 48; 50; 51; 52; 54
Letters and Journals. London: 1830. V. 50; 51; 52; 53
Letters and Journals of Lord Byron... London: 1833. V. 49
The Liberal. Verse and Prose from the South. London: 1822-23. V. 48
The Life, Letters and Journals of Lord Byron. London: 1860. V. 48
Manfred. London: 1817. V. 49; 51; 53; 54
Marino Faliero: a Tragedy. The Prophecy of Dante: a Poem. London: 1821. V. 47; 48; 49; 50; 51; 52; 53
Mazeppa, a Poem. London: 1819. V. 47; 48; 49; 50; 51; 53; 54
Monody on the Death of the Right Honourable R. B. Sheridan. London: 1816. V. 48; 49; 51
A Nonce Collection of Byron's Poetical Works... London: 1814-19. V. 47
The Parliamentary Speeches of Lord Byron. London: 1824. V. 53; 54
A Poem. (with) Beppo. London: 1819/18. V. 49
Poems. London: 1816. V. 47
Poems and Letters of Lord Byron. Chicago: 1912. V. 48
Poems of Lord Byron, on His Own Domestic Circumstances. London: 1816. V. 53; 54
Poems on His Domestic Circumstances. London: 1817. V. 47
Poems Original and Translated... Newark: 1808. V. 47
The Poetical Works. London: 1839. V. 48; 51
The Poetical Works. London: 1851. V. 51
The Poetical Works. London: 1854. V. 48; 50
The Poetical Works. London: 1855. V. 48; 49; 51
Poetical Works. London: 1866. V. 49
The Poetical Works. New York: 1867. V. 52
Poetical Works. London: 1870. V. 49
The Poetical Works. London: 1879. V. 54
Poetical Works. London: 1896. V. 52
The Prisoner of Chillon. London: 1816. V. 47; 48; 49; 51
The Prisoner of Chillon. London: 1865. V. 52
Sardanapalis...The Two Foscari...Cain. London: 1821. V. 47; 48; 49; 50; 51; 52
Sardanapalus; a Tragedy. Paris: 1822. V. 54
The Siege of Corinth. London: 1816. V. 48; 49; 53
Sunset from the Parthenon. 1875. V. 52
Three Poems, Not Included in the Works of Lord Byron: Lines to Lady J—, the Aenigma, The Curse of Minerva... London: 1818. V. 47
The Unpublished Letters of Lord Byron. London: 1872. V. 53
A Venetian Story. 1963. V. 54
A Venetian Story. Kentfield: 1963. V. 53
Waltz: an Apostrophic Hymn. London: 1813. V. 47; 51
Waltz: an Apostrophic Hymn. London: 1821. V. 48; 54
Werner. London: 1822-23. V. 47; 49
Werner. London: 1823. V. 48; 49; 51; 52
The Works. London: 1815. V. 50
The Works. London: 1815-20. V. 48
The Works. London: 1818. V. 47; 48; 50
The Works. London: 1819. V. 51
The Works. London: 1821. V. 47
The Works. London: 1823. V. 49; 52; 53
The Works. London: 1823-33. V. 53
The Works. Philadelphia: 1825. V. 49; 52
The Works. London: 1825-26. V. 54
The Works. London: 1827. V. 48
The Works. London: 1828. V. 54
The Works. London: 1832. V. 53
The Works. London: 1832-33. V. 51; 54
The Works. London: 1833. V. 50; 51
The Works. London: 1847. V. 54
The Works. London: 1898. V. 54
The Works. London: 1898-1901. V. 53
The Works. London: 1903. V. 49
Works. London: 1904-22. V. 48; 51

BYRON, JOHN
The Narrative of the Honourable John Byron... London: 1768. V. 47
Voyage of H.M.S. Blonde to the Sandwich Islands, 1824-25. London: 1826. V. 49

BYRON, MAY
Cat's Cradle. New York: 1908. V. 51
Peek-A-Book Pam. London. V. 54
Sambo and Susanna. London: 1920. V. 47
The Teddy Bear Book. London: 1920. V. 48

BYRON, MEDORA GORDON
Celia in Search of a Husband. London: 1809. V. 49

BYRON, ROBERT
The Birth of Western Painting - a History of Colour, Form and Iconography. London: 1930. V. 49
The Birth of Western Painting: a History of Colour, Form and Iconography, Illustrated from the Paintings of Mistra and Mount Athos of Giotto and Duccio and of El Greco. New York: 1931. V. 49
The Byzantine Achievement. London: 1929. V. 54
An Essay on India. London: 1931. V. 49
Europe in the Looking Glass. London: 1926. V. 50
First Russia Then Tibet. London: 1933. V. 54
How We Celebrate the Coronation. London: 1937. V. 48
Imperial Pilgrimage. London: 1937. V. 48
Innocence and Design. London: 1935. V. 48
The Road to Oxiana. London: 1937. V. 49; 54

BYRON-CURTISS, A. L.
The Life and Adventures of Nat Foster, Trapper and Hunter of the Adirondacks. Utica: 1897. V. 53

BYRONIANA Bozzies and Piozzies. London: 1825. V. 53

BYSSHE, EDWARD
The Art of English Poetry. London: 1702. V. 49; 52; 54
The Art of English Poetry. London: 1705. V. 49; 52; 54
The Art of English Poetry. London: 1718. V. 54
The Art of English Poetry. London: 1725. V. 47; 49; 50; 54
The Art of English Poetry. London: 1737. V. 49; 50; 52; 53; 54
A Visitation of the County of Essex. London: 1888. V. 49

BYTHNER, VICTORINUS
Lyra Prophetica Davidis Regis... 1664. V. 47

BZILIKAZI
Tales of Zululand and Other Stories. London: 1953. V. 54

C

C., A.
The Lives of Dr. Edward Pocock, the Celebrated Orientalist... London: 1816. V. 52

C., R.
Arcana Parliamentaria. Or Precedents Concerning Elections, Proceedings, Privileges, and Punishments in Parliament. London: 1685. V. 48; 51

C., T.
The History of the Commons Warre of England throughout These Three Nations; Begun from 1740, and Continued Till This Present Year 1662. London: 1662. V. 50

C., W. E.
The Lays of the Pharisee. 1913. V. 48; 50

CABALA, Mysteries of State, in Letters of the Great Ministers of K. James and K. Charles. London: 1654. V. 50

CABALA, Sive Scrinia Sacra, Mysteries of State and Government: In Letters of Illustrious Persons and Great Ministers of State...In the Reigns of King Henry the Eighth, Q. Elizabeth, K. James and K. Charles... London: 1663. V. 47

CABALLERIA Y COLLELL, JUAN
History of San Bernardino Valley from the Padres to the Pioneers. San Gernardino: 1902. V. 47

CABANEL, DANIEL
Poems and Imitations. London: 1814. V. 54

CABANES, DON FRANCISCO XAVIER DE
Memoria que Tiene por Objeto Manifestar la Posibilidad y Facilidad de Hacer Navegable el Rio Taijo desde Aranjuez Hasta el Atlantico, las Ventajas de Esta Empresa, y las Concesiones Hechas a la Misma Para Realizar la Navegacion. Madrid: 1829. V. 54

CABANIS, PIERRE JEAN GEORGE
On the Relations Between the Physical and Moral Aspects of Man. Baltimore: 1981. V. 49

CABANNE, P.
The Brothers Duchamp: Jacques Villon, Raymond Duchamp-Villon, Marcel Duchamp. Boston: 1976. V. 47; 50; 51; 53; 54

CABATON, ANTOINE
Java, Sumatra and Other Islands of the Dutch East Indies. London: 1912. V. 52

CABBE, GEORGE
The Village: a Poem. London: 1783. V. 48

CABELL, JAMES BRANCH
Branchiana, Being a Partial Account of the Branch Family in Virginia. Richmond: 1907. V. 52
Chivalry. New York: 1909. V. 51; 52; 54
The Cords of Vanity. New York: 1920. V. 52
Domnei: a Comedy of Woman Worship. New York: 1920. V. 52
The Eagle's Shadow. New York: 1940. V. 50
The First Gentleman of America. New York: 1942. V. 48
Gallantry. New York: 1907. V. 48; 52
The High Place - a Comedy of Disenchantment. London: 1923. V. 48
The Jewel Merchants. 1928. V. 47
Jurgen. New York: 1919. V. 48; 50; 53; 54
Jurgen. New York: 1919/28. V. 49
Jurgen. London: 1921. V. 47
Jurgen. 1923. V. 51
Jurgen. London: 1923. V. 47; 50
Jurgen. 1926. V. 47
Jurgen. London: 1949. V. 49; 51
Jurgen. Waltham St. Lawrence: 1949. V. 47; 50; 52
Ladies & Gentlemen. 1932. V. 48
Ladies and Gentlemen. 1934. V. 50; 52
The Line of Love. New York & London: 1905. V. 48; 49
The Majors and their Marriages. Richmond: 1915. V. 51
The Music From Behind the Moon. New York: 1926. V. 48
Notes on Figures of Earth. New York: 1929. V. 49
The Rivet in Grandfather's Neck. London: 1924. V. 48
Smirt. 1934. V. 48
Smirt. New York: 1934. V. 54
Something About Eve. London: 1927. V. 48
Something About Eve. New York: 1927. V. 51; 52; 53
Special Delivery. New York: 1923. V. 50
The Way of Ecben. London: 1929. V. 48
The Way of Ecben. New York: 1929. V. 48

CABET, ETIENNE
Voyage en Icarie, Roman Philosophique et Social... Paris: 1842. V. 54

THE CABINET Cyclopaedia. A Treatise on the Origin, Progressive Improvement and Present State of the Silk Manufacture. Philadelphia: 1832. V. 52

CABINET Maker's Album of Furniture: Comprising a Collection of Designs for the Newest and Most Elegant Styles of Furniture. Philadelphia: 1868. V. 49; 53

THE CABINET of Fiction, Science and Entertainment. London: 1837. V. 54

THE CABINET of Interesting Tales, Moral and Entertaining, Selected From the Best Authors int he English Language. Bungay: 1820. V. 48

THE CABINET of the Scottish Muses; Selected from the Works of the Most Esteemed Bards of Caledonia. Edinburgh: 1808. V. 52; 54

THE CABINET of Useful Arts and Manufactures: designed for the Perusal of Young Persons. London: 1825. V. 49

THE CABINET, or, A Collection of Choice Things; Comprising the Beauties of American Miscellanies for the Last Thirty Years. New York: 1815. V. 54

CABLE, GEORGE WASHINGTON
Bonaventure. New York: 1899. V. 54
The Cavalier. New York: 1901. V. 50
The Grandissimes: a Story of Creole Life. New York: 1880. V. 51; 54
Madame Delphine. New York: 1881. V. 51
Old Creole Days. New York: 1879. V. 47; 49; 51
Old Creole Days. New York: 1897. V. 50
Old Creole Days. New York: 1905. V. 54
Strange True Stories of Louisiana. New York: 1889. V. 49; 51; 52
Strong Hearts. New York: 1899. V. 54

CABLE, MILDRED
Apostle of Turkestan. 1948. V. 51

CABOT, RICHARD
Differential Diagnosis Presented through an Analysis of 383 Cases. Philadelphia: 1911. V. 53
The Serum Diagnosis of Disease. New York: 1899. V. 51; 53

CABOT, WILLIAM BROOKS
In Northern Labrador. Boston: 1912. V. 50; 53
Labrador. London: 1921. V. 47

CABRAL, ANTONIO JACINTO XAVIER
Explicacao Analitica do Quadro Alegorico Da Regeneracao da Monarquia Portugueza, Feito a Bico de Pena Por Seu Auctor... Lisbon: 1822. V. 48

CABRERA INFANTE, G.
Infante's Inferno. London: 1984. V. 54
Three Trapped Tigers. New York: 1971. V. 49

CACHIN, FRANCOISE
Paul Signac. Greenwich: 1971. V. 51

CADDICK, JOHN
Illustrated Catalogue of Bricks, Finials, Roofing Ridge and Floor Tiles, Terra Metallic Garden Edging, Chimney Pots, Sanitary Ware &c. Stoke-on-Trent: 1870's. V. 52

CADDY, F.
Adrian Bright. London: 1883. V. 54
Through the Fields with Linnaeus. London: 1887. V. 51

CADELL, WILLIAM ARCHIBALD
A Journey in Carniola, Italy and France, in the years 1817, 1818. Edinburgh: 1820. V. 53

CADET DE GASSICOURT, CHARLES LOUIS
Voyage en Autriche En Moravie et en Baviere. Paris: 1818. V. 50

CADET-DE-VAUX, ANTOINE ALEXIS
L'Art de faire Le Vin, d'Apres La Doctrine De Chaptal Instruction Destinee Aux Vignerons... Paris: 1803. V. 49

CADMAN, SAMUEL PARKES
The Parables of Jesus. Philadelphia: 1931. V. 49; 54

CADOGAN, WILLIAM
A Dissertation on the Gout, and all Chronic Diseases, Jointly Considered, as Proceeding from the Same Causes... London: 1771. V. 48; 51
An Essay Upon Nursing, and the Management of Children, from Birth to Three Years of Age. London: 1752. V. 53

CADWALADER, JOHN
A Reply to General Joseph Reed's Remarks on a Late Publication in the Independent Gazetteer, with some Observations on His Address to the People of Pennsylvania. Philadelphia: 1783. V. 47

CADY, BERTHA CHAPMAN
The Way Life Begins. New York: 1917. V. 51

CADY, JOHN H.
Arizona's Yesterday: Being the Narrative of John H. Cady, Pioneer. Patagonia: 1916. V. 54

CAEMMERER, H. P.
Washington: The National Capital. Washington: 1932. V. 47

CAEN, HERB
San Francisco, City on Golden Hills. New York: 1967. V. 48

CAESAR, GAIUS JULIUS
C. Iulii Caesaris Quae Extant. Lugduni Batavorum: 1635. V. 49; 51; 54
Commentaria. 1569. V. 53
The Commentaries. London: 1655. V. 47; 48
Commentaries. London: 1712. V. 48
Commentaries. Waltham St. Lawrence: 1951. V. 47; 51; 52
Commentarii ab Aldo Manutio Pavlii F. Aldi N. Emendati et Scholiis Illvstrati. Venice: 1575. V. 50; 54
The Eyght Bookes of Caius Iulius Caesar... London: 1565. V. 51; 52
The Gallic Wars. New York: 1954. V. 47
The Gallic Wars. Verona: 1954. V. 50; 51; 53; 54
Ivlii Caesaris Commentarii Ab Aldo Manvccio Pavlii F. Aldi. N. Emendati et Scholiis Illustrati. Venetiis: 1588. V. 48

CAESAR, GAIUS JULIUS continued
Opera. Glasguae: 1750. V. 48; 54
Opera Omnia. London: 1790. V. 48
(Opera) quae extant, Accuratissime cum Libris Editis et MSS. Optimis Collata... London: 1712. V. 49; 53

CAESARIUS, JOANNES
Dialectica. Lugduni: 1541. V. 53
Dialectica... Cologne: 1577. V. 51

CAFFARO, FATHER
A Defence of the Drama... New York: 1826. V. 49; 53

CAFFEY, THOMAS E.
Battle-Fields of the South, From Bull Run to Fredericksburg... London: 1863. V. 49; 50
Battle-Fields of the South, from Bull Run to Fredericksburg... New York: 1864. V. 53

CAFFIN, CHARLES H.
Photography as Fine Art. New York: 1901. V. 47

CAFFYN, KATHLEEN
Anne Mauleverer. London: 1899. V. 50
A Comedy in Spasms. London: 1895. V. 50

CAFKY, MORRIS
Colorado Midland. Denver: 1945. V. 54
Colorado Midland. Denver: 1965. V. 54

CAFMEYER, PETRUS DE
Hooghweidighe Histoire van het Ailer-Heylighste Sacrament van Mirakel. Brussels: 1720-35. V. 47; 50

CAGE, JOHN
Empty Words. Writings '73-78. Middletown: 1979. V. 52
Mud Book: How to Make Pies and Cakes. New York/London: 1983. V. 51
Silence. 1961. V. 49

CAGLE, WILLIAM R.
A Matter of Taste. Bibliographical Catalogue of the German Collection of Books on Food and Drink. New York: 1990. V. 47

CAGNOLA, LUIGI
Le Solenni Esequie di Mosignor Filippo Visconti, Archivescovo di Milano... Milan: 1802. V. 47

CAHAN, ABRAHAM
Yekl: a Tale of the New York Ghetto. New York: 1896. V. 47; 53

CAHEN, EDWARD
The Mineralogy of the Rarer Metals. London: 1920. V. 54

CAHILL, HOLGER
George O. Hart, "Pop". Twenty-Four Selections from His Work. New York: 1928. V. 47
Max Weber. New York: 1930. V. 47; 49; 51

CAHN, SAMMY
I Should Care: the Sammy Cahn Story. New York: 1974. V. 53

CAHOON, HERBERT
Thanatopsis. New York: 1949. V. 48

CAHUSAC, LOUIS DE
La Danse Ancienne et Moderne, ou Traite Historique de la danse. La Haye: 1754. V. 49

CAIGER, G.
Dolls on Display: Japan in Miniature. Nishikicho. V. 53

CAILLE, AUGUSTUS
Differential Diagnosis and Treatment of Disease. New York: 1906. V. 48; 53

CAILLIAUD, FREDERIC
Voyage a l'Oasis de Thebes et dans les Deserts Situes a l'Orient et a l'Occident de la Thebiade. Paris: 1821-62. V. 47
Voyage a l'Oasis de Thebes et dans les Deserts Situes a l'orient et a 'Occident de la Thebiade... Paris: 1821. V. 48

CAILLIE, RENE
Travels through Central Africa to Timbuctoo and Across the Great Desert to Morocco, Performed in the Years 1824-28. London: 1830. V. 54

CAILLOIS, ROGER
Pierres. Paris: 1966. V. 53

CAIN, J.
The Officer's Guide and Farmer's Manual... Indianapolis: 1837. V. 53

CAIN, JAMES M.
The Butterfly. New York: 1947. V. 50
Galatea. New York: 1953. V. 47; 51; 52
Loves Lovely Counterfeit. New York: 1942. V. 50; 51; 52
Mildred Pierce. New York: 1941. V. 47; 49; 50; 52
The Moth. New York: 1948. V. 52
Our Government. New York: 1930. V. 48; 49; 51; 54
Past All Dishonor. New York: 1946. V. 49; 54
The Postman Always Rings Twice. London: 1934. V. 53; 54
Serenade. New York: 1937. V. 51; 52
Three of a Kind. New York: 1943. V. 48; 53

CAIN, JOHN
Officer's Guide and Farmer's Manual... Indianpolis: 1837. V. 49

CAIN, JULIEN
The Lithographs of Chagall. Monte Carlo/New York: 1960. V. 47
The Lithographs of Chagall 1962-1968. Boston: 1969. V. 50; 51

CAIN, PAUL
Fast One. Garden City: 1933. V. 52; 54

CAINCROSS, DAVID
The Origin of the Silver Eel, with Remarks on Bait and Fly Fishing. London: 1862. V. 49

CAINE, CAESAR
Cleator and Cleator Moor: Past and Present. Kendal: 1916. V. 50; 52

CAINE, HALL
The Bondman. A New Saga. London: 1890. V. 52
The Bondman Play. London: 1906. V. 52
The Manxman. London: 1894. V. 54
Recollections of Dante Gabriel Rossetti. London: 1882. V. 51
Recollections of Rossetti. London: 1928. V. 51
The Scapegoat. London: 1891. V. 49
The Shadow of a Crime. London: 1885. V. 51
Sonnets of Three Centuries: a Selection Including Many Examples Hitherto Unpublished. London: 1882. V. 51
The Woman Who Gavest me. London: 1913. V. 48

CAINE, N.
History of the Royal Rock Beagle Hunt. Liverpool: 1895. V. 47; 49

CAINE, W. RALPH HALL
Lancahsire. Biographies, Rolls of Honour. London: 1917. V. 48

CAIRD, JAMES
Prairie Farming in America. London: 1859. V. 53

CAIRD, MONA
The Morality of Marriage and Other Essays on the Status and Destiny of Woman. London: 1897. V. 48

CAIRE, HELEN
Santa Cruz Island: a History and Recollections of an Old California Rancho. Spokane: 1993. V. 50

CAIRNES, D. D.
Report On a Portion of Conrad and Whitehorse Mining Districts, Yukon. Ottawa: 1908. V. 53

CAIRNES, JOHN E.
The Character and Logical Method of Political Economy. London: 1875. V. 48; 51
Essays on Political Economy, Theoretical and Applied. London: 1873. V. 49; 51; 52; 53
The Slave Power: Its Character, Career & Probable Designs. London: 1862. V. 47; 54
The Slave Power: Its Character, Career and Probable Designs. London: 1863. V. 49
Some Leading Principles of Political Economy Newly Expounded. New York: 1874. V. 49; 53

CAIRNS, HUNTINGTON
The Limits of Art: Poetry and Prose Chosen by Ancient and Modern Critics. Washington: 1949/48. V. 51

CAIROLA, ALDO
The Palazzo Pubblico di Siena. Roma: 1964. V. 53

CAIUS, J.
Works. Cambridge: 1912. V. 47

CAIUS, JOHN
Iohannis Caij Angli, de Pronunciatione Grecae & Latinae Linguae Cum Scriptione Nova Libellus. London: 1574. V. 47; 48

CAJETAN, TOMASO DE VIO
Parabolae Salomonis ad Veritatem Haebraicam Castigatae & Per Reverendissimum Dominum, D. Thomam De Vio Caietanum Cardinalem Sancti Xisti Ordinis Praedicatorum Enerratae, Recens in Lumen Editae. Rome: 1542. V. 47

CALABRELLA, E. C. DE, BARONESS
Evenings at Haddon Hall. London: 1846. V. 51

CALAMY, EDMUND
The Nonconformist's Memorial: Being an Account of the Ministers Who Were Ejected or Silenced After the Restoration by the Act of Uniformity, Which Took Place On Bartholomew-Day, Aug. 24, 1662. London: 1775. V. 51

CALAS, NICOLAS
Confound the Wise. New York: 1942. V. 50

CALAVERAS County Illustrated and Described, Showing Its Advantages for Homes. Oakland;: 1885. V. 54

CALCOTT, JOHN W.
A Musical Grammar in Four Parts. Boston: 1810. V. 48

CALCRAFT, JOHN WILLIAM
A Defence of the Stage, or an Inquiry into the Real Qualities of Theatrical Entertainments, Their scope and Tendency. Dublin: 1839. V. 52

CALDANI, LEOPOLDO
Icones Anatomicae, Quotquot Sunt Celbriores, ex Optimis Neotericorum Operibus Summa Diligentia Depromtae et Collectae. (with) Oconum Anatomicarum Explicatio. Pars Prima, Partis Secundae Sectio Prima et Alterqa. Partis Tertiae Sectio Prima et Altera. Venetiis: 1801/2/4/5/8/14. V. 52; 53

CALDAS BARBOSA, DOMINGOS
Recopilacao dos Successos Principaes da Historia Sagrada em Verso... Lisbon: 1793. V. 48

CALDAS PEREIRA E CASTRO, FRANCISCO DE
Singularis, et Excellens Tractatus et Analyticus Commentarius, et Syntagma De Nominatione Emphyteutica, Eiusque Successione, & Progressu... Lisbon: 1585. V. 48

CALDECOTT, RANDOLPH
Breton Folk, an Artistic Tour in Brittany. London: 1880. V. 49
Caldecott's Picture Books. Volume II. London: 1880. V. 48
The Complete Collection of Pictures and Songs by Randolph Caldecott. London: 1887. V. 49
Gleanings From the Graphic. London: 1889. V. 49
Last Graphic Pictures. London: 1888. V. 49; 51
More Graphic Pictures. London: 1887. V. 51; 53
The Panjandrum Picture Book. London. V. 50
Picture Book No. 1. John Gilpin, The Three Jovial Huntsmen and The Mad Dog. London: 1890. V. 48; 51
Picture Book No. 3. Hey Diddle Diddle and Baby Bunting; Ride a Cock-Horse to Banbury Cross... The Milkmaid; A Frog He Would a Wooing Go. London. V. 48
Randolph Caldecott's "Graphic" Pictures. London: 1883. V. 48
A Sketch-Book. London. V. 49
A Sketch-Book. London: 1883. V. 48

CALDER, ALEXANDER
Alexander Calder's Universe. London: 1977. V. 48
Calder's Circus. New York: 1965. V. 47
Mobiles - Stabiles - Constellations. Paris: 1946. V. 47

CALDER, ROBERT
Miscellany Numbers Relating to the Controvrsie about the Book of Common Prayer, Epsicopal Government, &c. Edinburgh: 1712?. V. 49

CALDERARI, OTTONE
Disegni et Scritti d'Architettura di ottone Calderari. Vicenza: 1808. V. 52

CALDER-MARSHALL, ARTHUR
Occasion of Glory - a Novel. London: 1955. V. 48

CALDERON, V. G.
The Lottery Ticket. Waltham St. Lawrence: 1945. V. 47; 52

CALDERON, W. F.
The Painting and Anatomy of Animals. London: 1936. V. 51; 53; 54

CALDERON DE LA BARCA, MARQUESA
Life in Mexico, During a Residence of two Years in that Country. London: 1843. V. 48; 49; 52

CALDERONE, MARY STEICHEN
The First Picture Book: Everyday Things for Babies. New York: 1991. V. 47

CALDERWOOD, DAVID
The True History of the Church of Scotland, from the Beginning of the Reformation, Unto the End of the Reigne of King James VI. London: 1678. V. 50

CALDERWOOD, MRS.
Letters and Journals of Mrs. Calderwood of Polton... Edinburgh: 1884. V. 52

CALDICOTT, J.
The Values of Old English Silver and Sheffield Plate, from the XVth to the XIXth Centuries. London: 1906. V. 50

CALDWALL, THOMAS
A Select Collection of Ancient and Modern Epitaphs and Inscriptions; to Which are Added Some on the Decease of Eminent Personages. London: 1796. V. 50

CALDWELL, ANNE MARSH
Emilia Wyndham. London: 1846. V. 47

CALDWELL, CHARLES
A Discourse On the Genius and Character of the Rev. Horace Holley, Late President of Transylvania University with an Appendix. Boston: 1828. V. 54
Essays on Malaria, and Temperament. Lexington: 1831. V. 47; 48
Medical Theses, Selected from Among the Inaugural Dissertations... Philadelphia: 1806. V. 50

CALDWELL, ERSKINE PRESTON
Afternoons in Mid-America. New York: 1976. V. 54
All-Out on the Road to Smolensk. New York: 1942. V. 48; 51
American Earth. New York: 1931. V. 47
The Bastard. New York: 1929. V. 48
God's Little Acre. New York: 1933. V. 50; 54
Hamrick's Polar Bear. Helsinki: 1984. V. 48
Journeyman. New York: 1935. V. 52; 54
Kneel to the Rising Sun. New York: 1935. V. 47; 48; 50; 51; 52; 54
A Message for Genevieve. Mount Vernon: 1933. V. 48; 53
Molly Cottontail. Boston & Toronto: 1958. V. 49; 52
Poor Fool. New York: 1930. V. 48; 53; 54
La Route au Tabac. Paris: 1946. V. 52; 54
Russia at War. London: 1942. V. 51
The Sacrilege of Alan Kent. Portland: 1936. V. 51; 53
Say, Is this the U.S.A. New York: 1941. V. 47; 48; 49; 50; 51; 53
Some American People. New York: 1935. V. 51; 53
Tenant Farmer. New York: 1935. V. 48; 49; 52; 53
Tobacco Road. New York: 1932. V. 53
Tobacco Road. New York: 1940. V. 53
Tobacco Road. New York: 1960. V. 54
We Are the Living. New York: 1930. V. 51
We Are The Living. New York: 1933. V. 48; 49; 51

CALDWELL, H. R.
Blue Tiger. London: 1925. V. 48; 52
South China Birds. Shanghai: 1931. V. 49

CALDWELL, JAMES
Debates Relative to the Affairs of Ireland; in the Years 1763 and 1764. Dublin: 1766. V. 47

THE CALEDONIAN
Bee; or, A Select Collection, of Interesting Extracts, from Modern PUblications. Perth: 1795. V. 47

THE CALEDONIAN
Jester; Being a Choice Selection of Repartees, Puns and Bon-Mots, Well Adapted to Excite Mirth and Afford General Amusement. London: 1806. V. 47

CALENDAR
for 1894. New York: 1894. V. 52

A CALENDAR
of all the Prisoners in His Majesty's Gaol, Within the City and County of Bristol, for Felony and Other Criminal Matters, This Ninth Day of July, 1821. Bristol: 1821. V. 48

CALENDAR
of State Papers, Colonial Series - America and West Indies. London: 1889-1963. V. 51

CALENDAR
of State Papers, Foreign Series...Preserved in the State Paper Department of Her Majesty's Public Record Office. London: 1861-1940. V. 51

CALENDAR
of Twelve Travellers Through the Pass of the North. 1947. V. 49; 51

CALENDAR
of Virginia State Papers. Richmond: 1875. V. 54

CALEPINUS, AMBROSIUS
Dictionarium. Geneva: 1594. V. 54

CALEY, EARLE R.
Analyses of Ancient Glasses 1790-1957. Corning: 1962. V. 51

CALGARY..
London: 1912?. V. 53

CALHOUN, CHARLES M.
Liberty Dethroned. Greenwood: 1903. V. 49

CALHOUN, J. C.
Life of John C. Calhoun. Presenting a Condensed History of Political Events. New York: 1843. V. 47
Report on...Fitting Out and Prosecuting the Expedition to the Yellow Stone River, and Concerning the Objects Intended to Be Accomplished by the Expedition. Washington: 1820. V. 48

CALHOUN, WILLIAM B.
Rights of Indians. Boston: 1830. V. 48

CALHOUN, WILLIAM LOWNDES
History of the 42nd Regiment Georgia Volunteers, Confederate States Army. Atlanta: 1900. V. 49; 50

CALIBAN PRESS
Type Specimens of Caliban Press. On the Occasion of Its Sixth Anniversary. Montclair: 1991. V. 47

CALIFORNIA. BOARD OF PRISON DIRECTORS
Second Annual Report of the State Board of Prison Directors of the State of California. Sacramento: 1881. V. 54

CALIFORNIA CAMERA CLUB
Catalogue of the Fifth International Photographic Salon at the Palace Hotel, November Twenty-Fifth to December Second, 1916. San Francisco: 1916. V. 47

CALIFORNIA. DEPARTMENT OF NATURAL RESOURCES
Geology of Southern California: Bulletin 170. San Francisco: 1954. V. 47

A CALIFORNIA
Gold Rush Miscellany. San Francisco: 1934. V. 47

CALIFORNIA HISTORICAL SOCIETY
Papers of the California Historical Society: Volume I, Parts I and II. San Francisco: 1887. V. 47; 52

CALIFORNIA. LAWS, STATUTES, ETC.
An Act in Relation to a Sea-Wall or Bulkhead in the City and County of San Francisco. San Francisco: 1858. V. 49
The General Railroad Laws of California, the Pacific Railroad Act of Congress, and the By-Laws of the Central Pacific Railroad Company of California, Together With ... Sacramento: 1862. V. 54
The Statutes of California Passed at the First Session of the Legislataure. Begun the 15th Day of Dec. 1849 and Ended the 22d Day of April, 1850, at the City of Pueblo de San Jose. San Jose: 1850. V. 54
The Statutes of California, Passed at the Second Session of the Legislature. San Jose: 1851. V. 50; 53

CALIFORNIA. LEGISLATURE
Journal of the Senate of the State of California at the Tenth Session of the Legislature... Sacramento: 1859. V. 47
Journals of the Legislature of the State of California at Its Second Session. San Jose: 1851. V. 50

THE CALIFORNIA
Star. Yerba Buena and San Francisco. Volume I, 1847-1848. Berkeley: 1965. V. 53

CALIFORNIA. STATE BOARD OF HEALTH
Second Biennial Report of the State Board of Health of California, for the Years 1871, 1872 and 1873. Sacramento: 1873. V. 52

CALIFORNIA. STATE LIBRARY
Catalogue of the California State Library, January 1, 1855. Sacramento: 1855. V. 49

CALIFORNIA. SURVEYOR GENERAL
Annual Report of the Surveyor General, for 1856. Sacramento: 1856. V. 49
Annual Report of the Surveyor General for 1857. Sacramento: 1858. V. 49
Annual Report of the Surveyor General for the year 1858. Sacramento: 1859. V. 49
Annual Report of the Surveyor General of the State of California...Northern Boundary Survey... Sacramento: 1855. V. 49
Annual Report of the Surveyor-General for the Year 1859. Sacramento: 1859. V. 49
Annual Report of the Surveyor-General, for the Year 1860. Sacramento: 1860. V. 49
Report of the Surveyor General of the State of California. Sacramento: 1854. V. 49
Special Report of the Surveyor General of the State of California. Sacramento: 1852. V. 49

CALIFORNIA. UNIVERSITY. BERKELEY. BANCROFT LIBRARY
The Bancroft Library, University of California, Berkeley. Catalog of Printed Books. Boston: 1964. V. 53

CALISHER, HORTENSE
The Collected Stories of Hortense Calisher. New York: 1975. V. 53
Eagle Eye. New York: 1973. V. 53
False Entry. London: 1961. V. 53
Tale for the Mirror. Boston: 1962. V. 53

CALKINS, ALONZO
Opium and the Opium-Appetite: With Notices of Alcoholic Beverages, Cannabis Indica, Tobacco and Coca, and Tea and Coffee in Their Hygienic Aspects and Pathologic Relations. Philadelphia: 1871. V. 47; 48

CALKINS, D.
Strange Adventures in the Spider Ship. 1935. V. 47

CALL, GEORGE A.
Letters from the Frontiers. Written During a Period of Thirty Years' Service in the Army of the United States. V. 47

CALL, HUGHIE
Golden Fleece. Boston: 1942. V. 53

CALL, LEWIS W.
United States Military Reservations, National Cemeteries and Military, Title, Jurisdiction, Etc. Washington: 1907. V. 50

CALLAGHAN, MORLEY
A Broken Journey. New York: 1932. V. 51
It's Never Over. New York: 1930. V. 50; 51
More Joy in Heaven. New York: 1937. V. 51
No Man's Meat. Paris: 1931. V. 49; 51; 52; 54
Strange Fugitive. New York: 1928. V. 48; 53
The Varsity Story. Toronto: 1948. V. 51

CALLAHAN, HARRY
Harry Callahan: Color. Providence: 1980. V. 47; 48; 49
Harry Callahan: Photographs. Santa Barbara: 1964. V. 47; 52
The Multiple Image. Chicago: 1961. V. 54
Water's Edge. Lyme: 1980. V. 47

CALLAN, HUGH
From the Clyde to the Jordan; Narrative of a Bicycle Journey. London: 1895. V. 54

CALLAN, N. J.
An Abstract of a Course of Lectures on Electricity and Galvanism, Delivered in the R. C. College of Maynooth. Dublin: 1832. V. 49

CALLAWAY, NICHOLAS
Georgia O'Keefe: One Hundred Flowers. New York: 1987. V. 52

CALLAWAY, S.
20th Century Decoration. New York: 1988. V. 50

CALLCOTT, MARIA DUNDAS GRAHAM, LADY
Three Months Passed in the Mountains East of Rome, During the Year 1819. London: 1820. V. 52
Voyage of HMS Blonde to the Sandwich Islands: in the Years 1824-1825. London: 1826. V. 51

CALLENDER, JAMES
Sketches of the History of America. Philadelphia: 1798. V. 53

CALLENDER, JAMES T.
Deformities of Dr. Samuel Johnson. Edinburgh: 1782. V. 49
Deformities of Dr. Samuel Johnson. London: 1782. V. 50; 52

CALLIMACHUS
Callimaco Greco-Itlaiano Ora Pubblicato. Parma: 1792. V. 51
Hymns and Epigrams. Glasgow: 1755. V. 50
The Hymns of Callimachus. London: 1755. V. 48; 52; 54
The Works. London: 1793. V. 48

CALLISON, JOHN
Bill Jones of Paradise Valley, Oklahoma. Chicago: 1914. V. 53

CALLOT, JACQUES
La Vie de l'Enfant Prodique. Paris: 1635. V. 50

CALLOW, WILLIAM
William Callow, R.W.S.,F.R.G.S. An Autobiography. London: 1908. V. 54

CALLOWAY, CAB
Of Minnie the Moocher and Me. New York: 1976. V. 54

CALLOWAY, S.
20th Century Decoration. 1988. V. 51; 53; 54

CALMER, ALAN
Salud! Poems, Stories and Sketches of Spain by American Writers. New York: 1938. V. 49

CALMET, AUGUSTIN
Antiquities Sacred and Profane... London: 1727. V. 50

CALMETTE, ALBERT
Tubercle Bacillus Infection and Tuberculosis in Man and Animals. Baltimore: 1923. V. 51
Venoms, Venomous Animals and Antivenomus Serum Therapeutics. London: 1908. V. 53

CALMOUR, ALFRED C.
Rumbo Rhymes. London: 1911. V. 47; 48; 49; 51

CALONNE, CHARLES ALEXANDER DE
A Catalogue of All that Noble and Superlatively Capital Assemblage of Valuable Pictures, Drawings, Miniatures and Prints, the Property of the Right Hon. Charles Alexander de Calonne...which will be sold by Auction by Messrs. Skinner & Dyke... London: 1795. V. 47; 54

CALSEY, DAVID
A Catalogue of the Manuscripts of the King's Library. (with) An Appendix to the Catalogue of the Cottonian Library; Together with an Account of Books Burnt or Damaged by a Late Fire. London: 1734. V. 47

CALTHROP, DION CLAYTON
English Costume. London: 1906. V. 50

CALTHROP, HENRY
Reports of Special Cases Touching Several Customes and Liberties of the City of London, Whereunto is Annexed Divers Ancient Customes and Usages of the Said City of London. London: 1670. V. 52

CALVERLEY, WILLIAM SLATER
Notes on the Early Sculptured Crosses, shrines and Monuments in the Present Diocese of Carlisle. Kendal: 1899. V. 50; 52

CALVERT, ALBERT F.
Mineral Resources of Minas Geraes (Brazil). London: 1915. V. 47
My Fourth Tour in Western Australia. London: 1897. V. 50
Nigeria and Its Tin Fields. London: 1912. V. 54
Spain: an Historical Descriptive Account of Its Architecture, Landscape and Arts. London: 1924. V. 52

CALVERT, F. CRACE
Lectures on Coal Tar Colours, and on Recent Improvements and Progress in Dyeing and Calico Printing. Philadelphia: 1863. V. 52

CALVERT, FREDERICK
The Isle of Wight Illustrated in a Series of Coloured Views... London: 1846. V. 48; 50
A Series of Sketches of Cottages, Landscapes, Trees, Bridges, Water-Falls, Ruins, Castles, Boats, &c. 1830. V. 50
The Young Artist's Instructor. London: 1823. V. 47; 49

CALVERT, GEORGE H.
Illustrations of Phrenology. Baltimore: 1832. V. 52

CALVERT, HARRY
Regulations and Instructions for the Infantry Sword Exercise. London: 1819. V. 47

CALVERT, J.
The Gold Rocks of Great Britain and Ireland and a General Outline of the Gold Regions of the World. London: 1853. V. 50; 52

CALVESI, MAURIZIO
Alberto Burri. New York: 1975. V. 50

CALVIN, JEAN
An Abridgement of the Instivtion of Christian Religion... Edinburgh: 1587. V. 47
A Commentarie of John Caluine Vpon the First Book of Moses Called Genesis. London: 1578. V. 50
The Commentaries of M. Iohn Calvin Upon the Actes of the Apostles. Londini: 1585. V. 50
Commentarii in Isaiam Prophetam. Geneva: 1583. V. 50
A Commentary on the Prophecie of Isaiah. London: 1609. V. 50
The Institution of Christian Religion. London: 1587. V. 50
The Institution of Christian Religion. London: 1611. V. 50
Tractatus Theologici Omnes, In Unum Volumen Certis Classibus Congesti. Geneva: 1597. V. 49

CALVINO, ITALO
The Baron in the Trees. London: 1959. V. 51
The Baron in the Trees. New York: 1959. V. 52; 53
Before You Say Hello. Cottondale: 1985. V. 51; 53; 54
Cosmicomics. New York: 1971. V. 51
Invisible Cities. New York: 1972. V. 54
Invisible Cities. New York: 1974. V. 51
The Nonexistent Knight and The Cloven Viscount. New York: 1962. V. 51; 52
The Path to the Nest of Spiders. Boston: 1957. V. 51; 54
The Silent Mr. Palomar. New York: 1981. V. 48; 50; 51; 52; 53; 54
T Zero. New York: 1969. V. 52
Time and the Hunter. London: 1970. V. 52
The Watcher and Other Stories. New York: 1971. V. 50; 53

CALVIUS, CHRISTOPH
Geometria Practica. Mainz: 1606. V. 47

CALZADA, JUAN
Tratado de Las Indulgencias en General y en Particular, Compuesto en dos Tomos. Havana: 1838-40. V. 53

CAMBELL, SYLVIA
The Practical Cook-Book... Cincinnati: 1855. V. 47

CAMBIAIRE, CELESTINE PIERRE
The Influence of Edgar allan Poe in France. New York: 1927. V. 48

CAMBITOGLOU, ALEXANDER
Apulian Red-Figured Vase-Painters of the Plain Style. New York: 1961. V. 52

CAMBON, MARIA GEERTRUIDA DE
Young Grandison. London: 1790. V. 49

CAMBRAY, CHEVALIER DE
Maniere De Fortifier de Mr. De Vauban... Amsterdam: 1689. V. 48

CAMBRELANG, CHURCHILL CALDOM
An Examination of the New Tariff Proposed by the Hon. Henry Baldwin, a Representative in congress. New York: 1821. V. 51

THE CAMBRIAN *Directory. Or, Cursory Sketches of the Welsh Territories.* Salisbury: 1801. V. 48

CAMBRIDGE Ancient History. Cambridge: 1924-36. V. 48
CAMBRIDGE Ancient History. Cambridge: 1927-39. V. 50

THE CAMBRIDGE Economic History of Europe. 1963-67. V. 52

CAMBRIDGE History of English Literature. Cambridge: 1907-16. V. 49
CAMBRIDGE History of English Literature. Cambridge: 1932. V. 49

THE CAMBRIDGE History of Iran. 1968-86. V. 52

CAMBRIDGE History of Latin America. Cambridge: 1984-91. V. 47; 50

CAMBRIDGE Medieval History. 1911-36. V. 49

CAMBRIDGE Modern History. Cambridge: 1902. V. 47; 50
CAMBRIDGE Modern History. New York: 1902. V. 47

THE CAMBRIDGE Modern History. 1902-24. V. 49
THE CAMBRIDGE Modern History. Cambridge: 1934. V. 50

CAMBRIDGE Modern History. London: 1934. V. 52

CAMBRIDGE, RICHARD
The Works. London: 1803. V. 50

CAMBRIDGE, RICHARD OWEN
An Account of the War in India, Between the English and French, on the Coast of Coromandel, from the Year 1750 to the Year 1760. London: 1761. V. 50; 51; 54
The Fakeer. London: 1756. V. 47
The Scribleriad: an Heroic Poem. London: 1751. V. 48; 52
The Works.. London: 1803. V. 48; 52; 53

THE CAMBRIDGE Tart: Epigrammatic and Satiric-Poetical Effusions, etc. by Cantab's on Various Occasions. London: 1823. V. 47

CAMBRILL, RICHARD
Sporting Stables and Kennels. New York: 1935. V. 47

CAMDEN, CHARLES PRATT, 1ST EARL OF
A Letter from Candor, to the Public Advertiser. London: 1764. V. 53

THE CAMDEN Miscellany. 1847-171. V. 53

CAMDEN, Ouachita County, Arkansas. Resources and Advantages of Camden, With a Description of Soil, Climate, Timber...for Those Seeking Homes in the Southwest. Little Rock: 1883. V. 48

CAMDEN, WILLIAM
Annales Rerum Anglicarum, et Hibernicarum, Regnante Elizabetha. Leyden: 1625. V. 47; 50
Annals, or History of the Most Renowned and Victorious Princesse Elizabethe, Late Queene of England. London: 1635. V. 51; 54
Britain, or a Chorographical Description of the Most Flourishing Kingdomes, England, Scotland and Ireland... London: 1610. V. 49
Britain, or, A Chorographicall Description of the Most Flourishing Kingdomes, England, Scotland and Ireland... London: 1637. V. 48
Britannia. Londini: 1587. V. 47; 49
Britannia. Frankfurt: 1590. V. 47; 49; 53; 54
Britannia. London: 1594. V. 47; 49; 53
Britannia. Londini: 1600. V. 47
Britannia. London: 1695. V. 53
Britannia. Oxford: 1695. V. 48
Britannia. London: 1722. V. 49
Britannia. London: 1730. V. 48
Britannia. London: 1753. V. 50
Britannia. London: 1772. V. 49; 51; 54
Britannia. London: 1789. V. 51
Britannia. London: 1806. V. 48; 49
The History of the Most Renowned and Victorious Princess Elizabeth, Late Queen of England... London: 1675. V. 47
Reges, Reginae Nobiles, & Alii in Ecclesia Collegiata B. Petri Westmonastererii Sepulti, Usque ad Annum Reparatae Salutis 1600. London: 1600. V. 48; 50; 52
Regis, Reginae, Nobiles, et Alii in Ecclesia Collegiata Petri Westmonasterii Septulti, Usque ad Annum Reparatae Salutis 1606. London: 1606. V. 47
Remaines, Concerning Britaine: But Especially England, and the Inhabitants Thereof. London: 1614. V. 47; 54
Remains Concerning Britain... London: 1674. V. 47
Remains Concerning Britain: Their Languages, Names Surnames, Allusions, Anagrammes, Armories, Moneys, Empreses, Apparell, Artillarie, Wise Speeches, Proverbs, Poesies, Epitaphes. London: 1636. V. 47
Remains Concerning Britaine: Their Languages, Names...Armories...Artillarie. London: 1637. V. 48; 50; 54

CAMDEN'S Compliment to Walt Whitman May 31, 1889. Philadelphia: 1889. V. 47

CAMEHL, ADA WALKER
The Blue-China Book. New York: 1916. V. 47

CAMERARIUS, JOACHIM
Hortus Medicus et Philosophicus, In Quo Plurimarum Stirpium Breves Descriptiones, Novae Icones non Paucae... Frankfurt (colophon): 1588. V. 47

CAMERARIUS, PHILIP
The Living Librarie, or Meditations and Observations Historical, Natural, Moral, Political and Poetical. London: 1625. V. 54
Operae Horarum Subcisivarum...Centuria Prima. (with) *Centuria Altera (and) Centuria Tertia.* 1615/20/18. V. 50

CAMERON, A. G.
The Wild Red Deer of Scotland. 1923. V. 54

CAMERON. A Novel. London: 1832. V. 47; 52

CAMERON, AGNES DEANS
The New North. London: 1910. V. 48

CAMERON, CHARLES
The Baths of the Romans Explained and Illustrated. London: 1772. V. 49; 52

CAMERON, D. Y.
The District of Meteith. Stirling: 1930. V. 50
The Etchings of D. Y. Cameron. London: 1924. V. 49

CAMERON, JOHN
Researches in Craniometry. Halifax: 1928-31. V. 47; 48; 49; 50; 51; 54

CAMERON, JULIA MARGARET
Victorian Photographs of Famous Men and Fair Women. London: 1926. V. 49
Victorian Photographs of Famous Men and Fair Women. New York: 1926. V. 47

CAMERON, KENNETH NEILL
The Carl H. Pforzheimer Library: Shelley and His Circle 1773-1822. Cambridge: 1961. V. 50
Shelley and His Circle 1773-1822, the Carl H. Pforzheimer Library. 1961. V. 49; 51

CAMERON, MRS.
The Fruits of Education; or, the Two Guardians. Wellington: 1827. V. 49; 51

CAMERON, P.
A Monograph of the British Phytophagous Hymenoptera. London: 1882-93. V. 48; 50; 51

CAMERON, VERNEY LOVETT
Across Africa. London: 1877. V. 47
Across Africa. London: 1885. V. 52

CAMERS, JOANNES
Commentaria in C. Ivlii Solini Polyhistora, et Lvcii Flori de Romanorum Rebus Gestis, Libros, Ac Tabvlam Cebetis...Ionne Camerte Autore... Basileae: 1557. V. 49; 50

CAMFIELD, WILLIAM A.
Francis Picabia, His Art, Life and Times. Princeton: 1979. V. 49; 52; 54

CAMILLI, CAMILLO
Imprese Illustri di Diversi, Coi Discorsi. Venice: 1586. V. 53; 54

CAMINOS, RICARDO
Late-Egyptian Miscellanies. London: 1954. V. 51

CAMMAN, WILLIAM C.
History of Troop "A" New York Cavalry U.S.V., from May 2 to November 28, 1898, in the Spanish American War. New York: 1899. V. 49

CAMOENS, LUIZ DE
The Lusiad; or, The Discovery of India. Oxford: 1778. V. 47
The Lyrics (Sonnets, Canzons, Odes and Sextines). London: 1884. V. 47

CAMOES, LUIZ DE
The Lusiad; or, the Discovery of India. Dublin: 1791. V. 50; 53

CAMP, ANTONIO
Cremona, Fedelissima Citta et Nobilissima Colonia de Romani, Rappresentate in Disegno, Col Suo Contado... Cremona: 1585. V. 53

CAMP, C.
Philo White's Narrative of a Cruize In the Pacific to South America and California...1841-1843. Denver: 1965. V. 53

CAMP, C. L.
Bibliography of Fossil Vertebrates. New York: 1962-68. V. 51

CAMP, CHARLES L.
Essays for Henry R. Wagner. San Francisco: 1947. V. 47
James Clyman, American Frontiersman 1792-1881. San Francisco: 1928. V. 54
James Clyman Frontiersman 1792-1881. Portland: 1960. V. 54
James Clyman, Frontiersman, The Adventures of a Trapper and Overland Emigrant as Told in His Own Reminiscences and Diaries. Portland: 1966. V. 49

THE CAMP Guide: In a Series of Letters, From Ensign Tommy Toothpick, to Lady Sarah Toothpick, and From Miss Nelly Brisk, to Miss Gadabout. London: 1778. V. 49

THE CAMP Kettle. Beaufort: 1863. V. 48

CAMP, WALTER
American Football. New York: 1892. V. 51
Drives and Puts. A Book of Golf Stories. Boston: 1899. V. 54
Football. Boston and New York: 1896. V. 51

CAMPA, MIGUEL DE LA
A Journal of Explorations Northward Along the Coast from Monterey in the Year 1775. San Francisco: 1964. V. 50

CAMPAIGNS of 1793, 1794: An Accurate and Impartial Narrative of the War, by an Officer of the Guards Comprising the Campaigns of 1793, 1794 and the Retreat Through Holland to Westphalia, in 1795. London: 1796. V. 51

CAMPAN, JEANNE LOUISE HENRIETTE
Memoirs of the Court of Marie Antoinette. London: 1895. V. 52
Memoirs of the Private Life of Marie Antoinette... New York: 1917. V. 54

CAMPANA, GIOVANNI PIETRO
Antiche Opere in Plastica Discoperte, Raccolte e Dichiarate. Rome: 1851. V. 53

CAMPANELLA, TOMMASO
De Monarchia Hispanica: Discursus. Hardovici: 1640. V. 47
De Sensu Rerum et Magia, Libri Quatuor, Pars Mirabilis Occultae Philosophiae, Ubi Demonstratur, Mundum. Francofurti: 1620. V. 47
De Sensv Rervm, et Magia. Libros Qvatvor. Paris: 1637. V. 48; 52

CAMPANI, FABRICE
La Vie Civile. Paris: 1608. V. 51

CAMPBELL, A.
Nests and Eggs of Australian Birds. Sheffield: 1901. V. 48; 51; 54

CAMPBELL, A. G.
History of the 11 Canadian Army Field rEgiment R.C.A. from 1 September 1939 to 5 May 1945. Utrecht. V. 54

CAMPBELL, ALBERT
Pacific Wagon Roads...a Report Upon the Several Roads Constructed. Washington: 1859. V. 47; 49

CAMPBELL, ALEXANDER
A Journey from Edinburgh through Parts of North Britain. London: 1802. V. 54
Speech of Sir Alexander Campbell on the Second Reading of a Bill to Incorporate the Pacific Railway Company in the Senate, Ottawa, Thursday Feb. 3, 1881. Ottawa: 1881. V. 52

CAMPBELL, ALFRED WALTER
Histological Studies on the Localization of Cerebral Function. Cambridge: 1905. V. 53

CAMPBELL, ARCHIBALD
The Doctrines of a Middle State Between Death and the Resurrection: Of Prayers for the Dead: and the Necessity of Purification. London: 1721. V. 49
A Journey from Edinburgh through Parts of North Britain Containing Remarks on Scotish Landscape... London: 1802. V. 52
Lexiphanes, a Dialogue. London: 1767. V. 48
Lexiphanes, a Dialogue. Dublin: 1774. V. 48; 49
Lexiphanes, a Dialogue. London: 1783. V. 51; 52; 54
Records of Argyll. Edinburgh & London: 1885. V. 49
Reports Upon the Survey of the Boundary Between the Territory of the United States and the Possessions of Great Britain from the Lake of the woods to the Summit of the Rocky Mountains, Authorized by An Act of Congress... Washington: 1878. V. 49
A Voyage Round the World, from 1806 to 1812. Edinburgh: 1816. V. 47; 50; 51; 54
A Voyage Round the World...In Which Japan, Kamschatka, the Aleutian Islands and the Sandwich Islands Were Visited. New York: 1817. V. 53

CAMPBELL, BEBE MOORE
Sweet Summer: Growing Up with and Without My Dad. New York: 1989. V. 52
Your Blues Ain't Like Mine. New York: 1992. V. 52

CAMPBELL, DONALD
Arabian Medicine and its Influence on the Middle Ages. London: 1826. V. 50
A Narrative of Extraordinary Adventures and Sufferings by Shipwreck and Imprisonment, of...in an Overland Journey to India. London: 1797. V. 47
A Narrative of the Extraordinary Adventures, and Sufferings by Shipwreck and Imprisonment of Donald Campbell, Esq. of Barbeck... London: 1801. V. 50
A Narrative of the Extraordinary Adventures and Sufferings by Shipwreck and Imprisonment, or Donald Campbell, Esq. of Barbreck. London: 1796. V. 52

CAMPBELL, DUNCAN
Nova Scotia In Its Historical, Mercantile and Industrial Relations. Montreal: 1873. V. 50

CAMPBELL, GEORGE
India as it May Be; an Outline of a Proposed Goverment and Policy. London: 1853. V. 51
Lectures on Ecclesiastical History... Aberdeen: 1815. V. 49
The Philosophy of Rhetoric. Edinburgh: 1819. V. 47
White and Black: the Outcome of a Visit to the United States. London: 1879. V. 53

CAMPBELL, HARRY
Flushing and Morbid Blushing. Their Pathology and Treatment. London: 1890. V. 48; 53

CAMPBELL, HELEN
Darkness and Daylight; or, Lights and Shadows of New York Life. Hartford: 1891. V. 51
Prisoners of Poverty Abroad. Boston: 1889. V. 52

CAMPBELL, HEYWORTH
The Body Beautiful. Volume Three. New York: 1937. V. 54

CAMPBELL, J.
The Black Star Passes. 1953. V. 51
Invaders from the Infinite. 1961. V. 51
Islands of Space. 1956. V. 54
The Moon is Hell. 1951. V. 47; 51
Who Goes There?. 1948. V. 47; 48; 49; 51; 52

CAMPBELL, J. A.
Biology of the Pitvipers. Tyler: 1993. V. 50

CAMPBELL, J. EDWIN
Driftings and Gleanings. Charleston: 1887. V. 54

CAMPBELL, J. F.
Popular Tales of the West Highlands. Edinburgh: 1880-62. V. 53

CAMPBELL, J. L.
Geology and Mineral Resources of the James River Valley. New York: 1882. V. 50

CAMPBELL, J. MENZIES
A Dental Bibliography British and American 1682-1800. London: 1949. V. 49

CAMPBELL, J. RAMSEY
The Doll Who Ate His Mother. 1976. V. 48; 52
The Face that Must Die. Santa Cruz: 1983. V. 51; 52
The Inhabitant of the Lake and Less Welcome Tenants. Sauk City: 1964. V. 48; 50; 52
New Tales of the Cthulhu Mythos. Sauk City: 1980. V. 48; 50; 52
Scared Stiff. Los Angeles: 1987. V. 49
Scared Stiff. London: 1989. V. 49

CAMPBELL, JAMES HAVELOCK
McClellan: a Vindication of the Military Career of General George B. McClellan. New York: 1916. V. 47; 49

CAMPBELL, JOHN
An Account of the Spanish Settlements in America. Edinburgh: 1762. V. 49
Candid and Impartial Considerations On the Nature of the Sugar Trade... London: 1763. V. 48; 50
The History of the Bible. Oxford: 1817. V. 51
Journey to the Moon, and Interesting Conversations with Inhabitants, Respecting the Condition of Man. London: 1815. V. 49
Lives of the Admirals and Other Eminent British Seamen. London: 1742-44. V. 50
Lives of the Admirals and Other Eminent British Seamen... London: 1761. V. 53
Lives of the British Admirals, and Naval History of Great Britain Fro the Time of Caesar to the Chinese War of 1841. Glasgow: 1841. V. 48
Lives of the British Admirals: Containing a New and Accurate Naval History, from the Earliest Periods... London: 1785. V. 49
The Lives of the Chancellors and Keepers of the Great Seal of England from the Earliest Times till the Reign of King George IV. First, Second and Third Series. London: 1845-47. V. 47; 48
Lives of the Chief Justices of England. London: 1849-57. V. 50
The Lives of the Chief Justices of England. Philadelphia: 1851. V. 53
The Lives of the Chief Justices of England. New York: 1873-75. V. 52
The Lives of the Chief Justices of England. London: 1874. V. 50
The Lives of the Chief Justices of England. Long Island: 1894-99. V. 52
The Lives of the Lord Chancellors and Keepers of the Great Seal of England, From the Earliest Times Till the Reign of King George IV. London: 1845-47. V. 50; 53
The Lives of the Lord Chancellors and Keepers of the Great Seal of England, from the Earliest Times Till the Reign of King George IV. London: 1846-69. V. 52
Lives of the Lord Chancellors and Keepers of the Great Seal of England from the Earliest Times to the Reign of King George IV. London: 1856. V. 50
The Lives of the Lord Chancellors and Keeprs of the Great Seal of England, from the Earliest Times Till the Reign of King George IV. London: 1846-57. V. 47
The Naval History of Great Britain, Commencing with the Earliest Period of History and Continuing to the Expedition Against Algiers...in 1816. London: 1818. V. 50
A Personal Narrative of Thirteen Years Service Amongst the Wild Tribes of Khondistan for the Suppression of Human Sacrifice. London: 1864. V. 53
A Political Survey of Britain... London: 1774. V. 47; 48; 49; 51; 53
The Spanish Empire in America. London: 1747. V. 50
Thirty Years' Experience of a Medical Officer in the English Convict Service. London: 1884. V. 47
The Travels and Adventures of Edward Brown, Esq.; Formerly a Merchant in London. London: 1739. V. 48
Travels in South Africa, Undertaken at the Request of the London Missionary Society... London: 1822. V. 47; 48
Travels in South Africa, Undertaken at the Request of the Missionary Society. London: 1815. V. 50; 51
Travels in South Africa...(with) A Second Journey into the Interior of That Country. London: 1822. V. 50; 51

CAMPBELL, JOHN FRANCIS
Frost and Fire: Natural Engines, Tool-marks and Chips, with Sketches Taken at Home and Abroad by a Traveller. Edinburgh: 1865. V. 49

CAMPBELL, JOHN L.
Idaho: Six Months in the New Gold Diggings. New York: 1864. V. 52

CAMPBELL, JOHN LORNE
Highland Songs of the Forty-Five. Edinburgh: 1933. V. 54

CAMPBELL, JOHN P.
An Essay. Negotiations for Peace at the Court of Heaven, the Only Way to Close the War Honorably to the South. Jackson: 1863. V. 49

CAMPBELL, JOHN P. continued
Nashville Business Directory. Nashville: 1857. V. 49

CAMPBELL, JOHN W.
Cloak of Aesir. Chicago: 1952. V. 51
Islands of Space. 1956. V. 49

CAMPBELL, JOSEPH
The Mythic Image. Princeton: 1974. V. 49; 50; 53

CAMPBELL, KEN
Father's Hook. Bath: 1978. V. 47
Horse. 1985. V. 47
In the Door Stands a Jar. 1987. V. 47
Night Feet on Earth. 1986. V. 47
Night Feet on Earth. 1987. V. 52

CAMPBELL, M. G. GUNNING
Delhi Hunt. Hints on Riding to Hounds. Simla: 1929. V. 47

CAMPBELL, M. M.
Circular to the Good People of Kansas... Lecompton: 1859. V. 48

CAMPBELL, MARGARET O.
A Memorial History of the Campbells of Melfort, Argyllshire (including) Records of the Different Highland and Other Families with Whom they Have Intermarried. (with) Supplement. London: 1882-94. V. 47; 53

CAMPBELL, MARIA HULL
Revolutionary Services and Civil Life of General William Hull. New York: 1848. V. 49; 51; 53

CAMPBELL, MARIE
Folks Do Get Born. New York: 1946. V. 48; 53

CAMPBELL, MUNGO
The Trial of Mungo Campbell, Before the High Court of Justiciary in Scotland, for the Murder of Alexander Earl of Eglintoun... London: 1770. V. 48

CAMPBELL, PATRICK
Travels in the Interior Inhabited Parts of North America in the Years 1791 and 1792. Toronto: 1937. V. 47; 50

CAMPBELL, R.
The London Tradesman. London: 1747. V. 47

CAMPBELL, RACHEL
The Prodigal Daughter, or, the Price of 'Virtue'. Grass Valley: 1885. V. 48

CAMPBELL, ROBERT
Two Journals of Robert Campbell (Chief Factor Hudson's Bay Company) 1808 to 1853. Seattle: 1958. V. 54

CAMPBELL, ROBERT ALLEN
Campbell's Gazetteer of Missouri. St. Louis: 1874. V. 54

CAMPBELL, ROY
Adamastor: Poems. London: 1930. V. 47; 50; 51; 53
Broken Records. London: 1934. V. 51
Choosing a Mast. London: 1931. V. 50
Collected Poems. London: 1949. V. 51
Collected Poems. London: 1949-57. V. 49
The Flaming Terrapin. London: 1924. V. 48; 51; 53
Flowering Reeds - Poems. London: 1933. V. 53
Flowering Rifle. London: 1939. V. 49; 53
The Georgiad. London: 1931. V. 51; 53
Light on a Dark Horse. An Autobiography 1901-1935. London: 1951. V. 47; 49
Mithraic Emblems. London: 1936. V. 49
Talking Bronco. London: 1946. V. 49
Taurine Provence. London: 1932. V. 50; 51; 53

CAMPBELL, SANDY
B: Twenty-Nine Letters from Coconut Grove. Verona: 1974. V. 47; 51

CAMPBELL, STUART
King Arthur and His Knights. London: 1930. V. 54

CAMPBELL, THOMAS
Gertrude of Wyoming. London: 1809. V. 48; 50; 51; 53
Inaugural Discourse of Thomas Campbell, Esq. On Being Installed Lord Rector of the University of Glasgow, Thursday, April 12th, 1827. Glasgow: 1827. V. 50; 54
The Journal of a Residence in Algiers. London: 1837. V. 51; 54
Life of Mrs. Siddons. London: 1834. V. 49; 51
The Life of Mrs. Siddons. London: 1839. V. 51; 54
A Philosophical Survey of the South of Ireland in a Series of Letters. London: 1777. V. 47
A Philosophical Survey of the South of Ireland, in a Series of Letters to John Watkinson, M.D. Dublin: 1778. V. 47; 49
The Pleasures of Hope. Edinburgh: 1808. V. 51
The Pleasures of Hope. London: 1821. V. 50
The Pleasures of Hope... London: 1822. V. 53
The Poetical Works. London: 1828. V. 49; 53
The Poetical Works. London: 1837. V. 47; 53; 54
The Poetical Works. London: 1843. V. 54
The Poetical Works. London: 1854. V. 49; 51
The Poetical Works. London: 1858. V. 54
The Poetical Works. (with) Theodric. Paris: 1825/25. V. 49
Theodric: a Domestic Tale; and Other Poems. London: 1824. V. 54

CAMPBELL, THOMAS MONROE
The Movable School Goes to the Negro Farmer. 1936. V. 50; 52
The Movable School Goes to the Negro Farmer. Tuskegee: 1936. V. 53

CAMPBELL, W. R.
Insulin: its Use in the Treatment of Diabetes. Baltimore: 1925. V. 53

CAMPBELL, WALTER
My Indian Journal. Edinburgh: 1864. V. 50; 51
The Old Forest Ranger; or, Wild sports of India on the Neilgherry Hills, in the Jungles and on the Plains. London: 1845. V. 49
The Old Forest Ranger; or, Wild Sports of India, The Neilgherry Hills, in the Jungles and on the Plains. New York: 1853. V. 47

CAMPBELL, WILFRED
The Scotsman in Canada. Toronto: 1911. V. 48

CAMPBELL, WILLIAM
Materials for a History of the Reign of Henry VII, from Original Documents Preserved in the Public Record Office. London: 1873-77. V. 49; 52

CAMPBELL, WILLIAM J.
The Collection of Franklin Imprints in the Museum of the Curtis Publishing co. Philadelphia: 1918. V. 50

CAMPBELL, WILLIAM W.
Annals of Tryon County; or, the Border Warfare of New York, During the Revolution. New York: 1831. V. 48

CAMPBELL IRON CO., ST. LOUIS.
Catalog No. 25 of Blacksmith Implements, Machinist and Industrial Supplies and Tools. St. Louis: 1922. V. 51

CAMPBELL-JOHNSTON, R. C.
The Story of the Totem. Vancouver: 1924. V. 53

CAMPE, JOACHIM HEINRICH
The New Robinson Crusoe; an Instructive and Entertaining History. Boston: 1790. V. 49
Polar Scenes, Exhibited in the Voyages of Heemskirk and Barenz to the Northern Regions. London: 1822. V. 49
Polar Scenes, Exhibited in the Voyages of Heemskirk and Barenz to the Northern Regions. London: 1823. V. 52

CAMPELLO DE MACEDO, JOAO
Instancia Que Faz o Cerimonial dos Bispos, as Opinioes, Que o Lecenciado Christovao Martinez, Fundado, Nas Rubricas do Missal Romano.. Lisbon: 1654. V. 53

CAMPEN, JACOB VAN
Afbeelding Van't Stadt Huys Van Amsterdam... Amsterdam: 1661. V. 48; 52

CAMPEN, JEAN DE
Enchiridium Psalmorum. Lyons: 1540. V. 47

CAMPER, CHARLES
Historical Record of the First Regiment Maryland Infantry. Washington: 1871. V. 48; 52

CAMP FIRE GIRLS, INC.
The Book of the Camp Fire Girls. New York: 1936. V. 47

CAMPION, EDMUND
Edmundi Campiani Angli e Soc. Iesu Decem Rationes Propositae in Causa Fidei, et Opuscula Eius Selecta. Antwerp: 1631. V. 52

CAMPION, G.
Introduction to Ornamental Writing for the Use of Artists, Painters and Sculptors. London: 1830. V. 49

CAMPION, J. S.
On the Frontier, Reminiscences of Wild Sports, Personal Adventures and Strange Scenes. London: 1878. V. 48; 50; 52

CAMPION, THOMAS
Campion's Works. Oxford: 1909. V. 52
Fifty Songs. London: 1896. V. 50; 51
The Maske by Thomas Campion, as Produced at Hatfield Palace on May 30th and 31st 1924 for the Benefit of the Hertfordshire County Nursing Association. London: 1924. V. 52
Selected Poems of Thomas Campion. Boston: 1973. V. 47
Selected Songs of... Boston: 1973. V. 47; 49; 51
Songs and Masques: With Observations in the Art of English Posey. London: 1903. V. 48
The Works. London: 1889. V. 53

CAMPOS, JULES
Jose De Creeft. New York: 1945. V. 48; 49; 50
The Sculpture of Jose De Creeft. New York: 1972. V. 51; 53; 54

CAMSELL, CHARLES
The MacKenzie River Basin. Ottawa: 1919. V. 49

CAMUS, ALBERT
Caligula and Cros Purpose. New York: 1947. V. 54
L'Envers et l'Endroit. Alger: 1937. V. 54
The Fall. New York: 1957. V. 50
The Fall. Kentfield: 1960. V. 49; 54
Les Justes. Paris: 1950. V. 47
The Outsider. London: 1946. V. 47; 49; 51; 52
The Plague. London: 1948. V. 52
The Rebel. New York: 1957. V. 51
September 15th, 1937. Bronxville: 1963. V. 47

CAMUS, ALBERT continued
The Stranger. Brattleboro: 1971. V. 49; 51

CAMUS, E. G.
Iconographie des Orchidees d'Europe et du Bassin Mediterraneen. London: 1921. V. 50; 51
Iconographie des Orchidees d'Europe et du Bassin Mediterraneen. Paris: 1921-29. V. 47; 48; 51

CAMUS, JACQUES
Idees. Paris: 1923?. V. 54

CAMUS, JEAN PIERRE
L'Esprit de Saint Francois De Sales. A Lyon: 1816. V. 51
Natures Paradox; or, the Innocent Imposter. London: 1652. V. 47; 53
The Triumphs of Love. Glasgow: 1784. V. 51

CANADA a Year of the Land. Ottawa: 1969. V. 52

CANADA At the Universal Exhibition of 1855. Toronto: 1856. V. 52

CANADA. DEPARTMENT OF AGRICULTURE
Tenant-Farmer Delegates' Visit to Canada in 1890 and Their Reports Upon the Agricultural Resources of the Provinces of Prince Edward Island, Nova Scotia, New Brunswick, Quebec, Ontario, Manitoba, the North-West Territories, and British Columbia. Ottawa: 1892. V. 47

CANADA. DEPARTMENT OF MARINE & FISHERIES - 1911
Report on the Dominion Government Expedition to the Northern Waters and Arctic Archipelago of the D.G.S. "Arctic" in 1910. Ottawa: 1911. V. 53

CANADA FOUNDRY CO.
Architectural Catalogue No. 11. Toronto: 1920's. V. 54

CANADA. GEOLOGICAL SURVEY - 1857
Report of Progress for the Years 1853-54-55-56. Toronto: 1857. V. 48; 53

CANADA. GEOLOGICAL SURVEY - 1865
Petroleum its Geological Relations Considered with Especial Reference to its Occurence in Gaspe. Quebec: 1865. V. 49

CANADA. Indian Treaties and Surrenders from 1680 to 1890. Ottawa: 1891. V. 53

CANADA Indian Treaties and Surrenders from 1680 to 1890 in Two Volumes. (with) Canada. Indian Treaties and Surrenders from No. 281 to 483. Volume III. Ottawa: 1905/12. V. 50

CANADA. LEGISLATIVE ASSEMBLY - 1858
Report on the Exploration of the Country Between Lake Surperior and the Red River Settlement. Toronto: 1858. V. 53

CANADA. LEGISLATIVE COUNCIL - 1853
Standing Orders of the Legislative Council. Of Canada: Adopted in the 1st Session of the 4th Parliament, 16 Victoria, 1852-53. Quebec: 1853. V. 53

CANADA. LEGISLATURE
Parliamentary Debates on the Subject of the Confederation of the British North American Provinces, 3rd Session, 8th Provincial Parliament of Canada. Quebec: 1865. V. 50

CANADA. PARLIAMENT
Parliamentary Debates on the Subject of the Confederation of the British North American Provinces, 3rd Session, 8th Provincial Parliament of Canada. Quebec: 1865. V. 52
Report from the Select Committee On the Civil Government of Canada. Quebec: 1829. V. 52

CANADA West and the Hudson's Bay Company: a Political and Humane Question of Vital Importance to the Honour of Great Britain. London: 1856. V. 54

THE CANADIAN Almanac, and Repository of Useful Knowledge, for the Year 1875. Toronto: 1874. V. 54

CANADIAN Farming: an Encyclopedia of Agriculture,,,. Toronto: 1881. V. 52

THE CANADIAN Handbook and Tourists Guide Giving a Description of Canadian Lake and River Scenery and Places of Historical Interest with the Best Spots for Fishing and Shooting. Montreal: 1867. V. 47

CANADIAN INSTITUTE
The Canadian Journal of Industry, Science and Art. Toronto: 1856-58. V. 53

THE CANADIAN Mining Manual and Mining Investor's Year Book. 1899. V. 50

CANADIAN NORTHERN RAILWAY
The Canadian Northern Rockies through the Yellowhead Pass. Chicago: 1917. V. 49
Homeseekers and Settler's Guide to Western Canada. Chicago: 1917. V. 52
Peace River Guide. Toronto?: 1917. V. 49

CANADIAN PACIFIC RAILWAY
British Columbia. The Most Westerly Province of Canada.... 1900. V. 50
The Canadian Pacific. The New Highway to the East Across the Mountains Prairies and Rivers of Canada. Montreal: 1887. V. 52

CANADIAN Poems 1850-1952. Toronto: 1952. V. 47

CANADIAN PUBLICITY CO.
Prominent People of the Maritime Provinces. St. John: 1922. V. 47

THE CANADIAN Temperance Minstrel.... Montreal: 1842. V. 49

CANALE, FLORIANO
De Secreti Universale Raccolti, et Esperimentati...Trattati Nove Ne'Quali si Hanno Rimedii per Tutte... Venice: 1666. V. 47; 48

CANBY, E. R. S.
Headquarters, Department of Louisiana and Texas. General Orders No. 13. New Orleans: 1865. V. 48

CANBY, HENRY SEIDEL
Thoreau. Boston: 1939. V. 51; 54

CANDELARIA WATERWORKS & MILLING CO.
Memorandum of Association and Articles of Association of the Candelaria Waterworks and Milling Co. Ltd. London: 1885. V. 50

CANDID Camera Shots of Mr. D. W. Hogan. On the Occasion of a Meeting, Saturday, October 6, 1934 at Continental House, 1000 E. Grand Ave., Ponca City, Oklahoma in Honor of Mr. Frank Bartow and Mr. William Ewing. Ponca City: 1934. V. 49

CANDIUS, PSEUD.
The Theatre; or The Letters of Candius &c. On the Performances of the Edinburgh Stage in 1802. Edinburgh: 1802. V. 53

CANDLER, ALLEN D.
The Confederate Records of the State of Georgia. Atlanta: 1909-11. V. 52

CANDLER, E.
The Dinosaur's Egg. 1926. V. 51

CANDLER, EDMUND
On the Edge of the World. London: 1919. V. 50; 53
The Unveiling of Lhasa. London: 1905. V. 50

CANDOLLE, A. J.
Astragalogia, Nempe Astragali, Biserrulae et Oxytropidis... Paris: 1802. V. 54

CANE, CLAUDE
Summer and Fall in Western Alaska: the Record of a Trip to Cook's Inlet After Big Game. London: 1903. V. 49

CANEPARIUS, PETRUS MARIA
De Atramentis Cuiuscunque Generis. Venetiis apud: 1619. V. 53

CANER, HENRY
A Sermon Preached at King's Chapel, in Boston, Before His Excellency Francis Bernard, Esq., Captain General and Governor in Chief...January 1, 1761 Upon Occasion of the Death of Our Late Most Gracious Sovereign King George the Second. Boston: 1761. V. 48

CANES, JOHN VINCENT
Fiat Lux. London: 1662. V. 53

CANESTRELLI, PHILIP
A Kootenai Grammar. Spokane: 1959. V. 54

CANETTI, ELIAS
Auto Da Fe. London: 1946. V. 51
Crowds and Power. London: 1962. V. 49; 52
Komodie der Eitelkeit. Munich: 1950. V. 54

CANEVARI, DEMETRIO
De Ligno Sancto Commentarium, in Quo Praecipuae Qualitates Eius and Facultates Omnes Exacta Diligentia Exprimuntur... Rome: 1602. V. 52

CANFIELD, FREDERICK A.
A History of Thomas Canfield and of Matthew Camfield with a Genealogy of Their Descendants in New Jersey. Dover: 1897. V. 49; 51

CANFIELD, THOMAS HAWLEY
Life of Thomas Hawley Canfield...and His Connection with the Erly History of the Northern Pacific Railroad. Burlington: 1889. V. 54
Northern Pacific Railroad...Report to the Board of Directors of a Reconnaisance Made in the Summer of 1869... New York: 1870. V. 50; 54

CANIFF, WILLIAM
History of the Settlement of Upper Canada, (Ontario)... Toronto: 1869. V. 53

CANIN, ETHAN
Emperor of the Air. Boston: 1988. V. 53

CANINA, LUIGI
The Vicissitudes of the Eternal City; or, Ancient Rome... London: 1849. V. 52

CANISIUS, PETRUS
Authoritatum Sacrae Scripturae, et Santorum Patrum, Quae in Summa Doctrinae Christianae... Venice: 1571. V. 51

CANNAN, EDWIN
A History of the Theories of Production and Distribution in English Political Economy from 1776 to 1848. London: 1903. V. 54

CANNAN, GILBERT
Mendel - a Story of Youth. London: 1916. V. 48

CANNE, JOHN
The Discover. London: 1649. V. 50; 53
A Seasonable Word to the Parliament-Men. London: 1659. V. 50

CANNEY, M.
University of London Library Catalogue of the Goldsmiths' Library of Economic Literature. Cambridge: 1970-82. V. 52
University of London Library Catalogue of the Goldsmiths' Library of Economic Literature. 1982/83. V. 54

CANNEY, MARGARET
Catalogue of the Goldsmiths' Library of Economic Literature. Cambridge: 1970. V. 49

CANNEY, MARGARET continued
Catalogue of the Goldsmiths' Library of Economic Literature. Cambridge: 1970-83. V. 49; 53

CANNIFF, WILLIAM
The Medical Profession in Upper Canada 1783-1850. Toronto: 1894. V. 49; 51

CANNING, ALBERT
Baldearg O'Donnell. London: 1867. V. 51

CANNING, ELIZABETH
The Case of Elizabeth Canning Fairly Stated. London: 1753. V. 51
Curious and Remarkable Life and Trial of Elizabeth Canning... London: 1810?. V. 49
Genuine and Impartial Memoirs of Elizabeth Canning, Containing a Complete History of that Unfortunate Girl, from Her Birth to the Present Time, and Particularly Every Remarkable Occurrence from the Day of Her Absence, Jan. 1, 1753... London: 1754. V. 52
The Hard Case of Mary Squires, the Gipsey, and Susanna Wells. London: 1753. V. 51
A Refutation of Sir Crisp Gascoyne's Account of His Conduct, in the Cases of Elizabeth Canning and Mary Squires. London: 1754. V. 51; 52
The Trial of Elizabeth Caning, Spinster, for Wilful and Corrupt Perjury; at Justice Hall in the Old Bailey... London: 1754. V. 52
The Truth of the Case; or Canning and Squires Fairly Opposed. London: 1753. V. 52
The Unfortunate Maid Exemplified, in the Story of Elizabeth Canning Vindicated from Every Mean Aspersion Thrown Upon it. London: 1754. V. 51

CANNING, GEORGE
The Microcosm; a Periodical Work... London: 1825. V. 47
The Speeches. London: 1830. V. 49
The Speeches and Public Addresses...During the Late Election in Liverpool, and On a Public Occasion in Manchester. Liverpool: 1812. V. 51
The Speeches of the Right Honourable George Canning. London: 1828. V. 53
Substance Of the Speech of the Right Honourable George Canning, in the House of Commons, On Wednesday the 30th of April, 1823, on Mr. MacDonald's Motion Respecting the Negotiations, at Verona, Paris and Madrid. London: 1823. V. 50

CANNING, JOSIAH D.
Poems. Greenfield: 1838. V. 51

CANNING, T.
The Wedding and Bedding; or, John Bull and His Bride Fast Asleep. London: 1800. V. 48

CANNON, POPPY
A Gentle Knight: My Husband, Walter White. New York: 1952. V. 54

CANNON, RICHARD
Historical Record of the 72nd Foot. London: 1848. V. 50
Historical Record of the 73rd Foot, First Raised as the Second Battalion of the Forty Second Royal Highlanders in 1780 and Its Subsequent Services to 1851. London: 1851. V. 50
Historical Record of the First Regiment of Foot (Royal Scots Regiment of Foot). London: 1847. V. 50
Historical Record of the Sixth, or the Inniskilling Regiment of Dragoons. London: 1843. V. 50
Historical Record of the Thirty-First, or, the Huntingdonshire Regiment of Foot... London: 1850. V. 48; 50
Historical Record of the Thirty-Ninth or the Dorsetshire Regiment of Foot. 1853. V. 50

CANNON, WALTER
Bodily Changes in Pain, Hunger, Fear and Rage... New York: 1915. V. 54
The Mechanical Factors of Digestion. London: 1911. V. 48; 49; 53
Traumatic Shock. New York: 1923. V. 53

CANOE and Camp Cookery: a Practical Cook Book for Canoeists, Corinthian Sailors and Outers. New York: 1885. V. 52

CANSLER, CHARLES W.
Three Generations: The Story of a Colored Family in Eastern Tennessee. 1939. V. 53

CANTICA Natalia Viginti Hymni in Honorem Nativitatis Domini Nostri Jesu Christi. Ditchling: 1926. V. 50

THE CANTICLE of the Sun. New York: 1951. V. 49

CANTILLON, RICHARD
Essai sur la Natuare du Commerce en General. London: 1931. V. 54

CANTINELLI, R.
Joseph Bernard. Paris: 1928. V. 54

CANTON, FRANK
Frontier Trails. Boston: 1930. V. 53

CANTON, WILLIAM
The True Annals of Fairyland, The Reign of King Herla. London: 1900. V. 49

CANTOR, EDDIE
My Life Is In Your Hands. New York & London: 1928. V. 48

CANTWELL, J. C.
Report on the Operations of the U.S. Revenue Steamer Nunivak on the Yukon River Station, Alaska, 1899-1901. Washington: 1902. V. 52

CAP and Gown. Third Series. Boston: 1903. V. 47

CAPA, CORNELL
The Concerned Photographer. New York: 1968-72. V. 47

CAPA, ROBERT
Images of War. New York: 1964. V. 47
Slightly Out of Focus. New York: 1947. V. 50; 52

CAPEFIGUE, J. B. H. R.
Madame de Pompadour. London: 1908. V. 54

CAPEK, KAREL
The Absolute at Large. London: 1927. V. 47; 51
Krakatit. London: 1925. V. 51
Krakatit. New York: 1925. V. 48; 50
Meteor. London: 1935. V. 51; 52
War With the Newts. 1937. V. 49

CAPEL, ARTHUR
Excellent Contemplations, Divine and Moral. London: 1683. V. 47

CAPELL, EDWARD
Prolusions; or, Selected Pieces of Antient Poetry... 1759/60. V. 53

CAPELLE, PIERRE ADOLPHE
La Cle Du Caveau a l'usage de Tous les Chansonniers Francais, des Amateurs, Auteurs, Acteurs du Vaudeville et de Tous les Amis de la Chanson. Paris: 1811. V. 49

CAPELLEN, JOAN DERK VAN DER
An Address to the People of the Netherlands, on the Present Alarming and Most Dangerous Situation of the Republick of Holland... London: 1782. V. 48

CAPELLMANN, CARL
Pastoral Medicine. New York: 1879. V. 48; 53

CAPEN, ELWIN A.
Oology of New England: A Description of the Eggs, Nests and Breeding Habits of the Birds Known to Breed in New England... Boston: 1908. V. 51

CAPEN, O. B.
Country Homes of Famous Americans. New York: 1905. V. 50; 51

CAPERS, HENRY DICKSON
The Life and Times of C. G. Memminger. Richmond: 1893. V. 49

CAPERS, WALTER B.
The Soldier-Bishop. New York: 1912. V. 50

CAPES, WILLIAM WOLFE
Scenes of Rural Life in Hampshire. London: 1901. V. 52

CAPETANAKIS, DEMETRIOS
The Poetry of Demetrios Capetanakis. Madison: 1966. V. 52; 53; 54

CAPGRAVE, JOHN
Ye Solace of Pilgrimes. London: 1911. V. 50; 53
Ye Solace of Pilgrimes. A Description of Rome, ca. A.D. 1450. 1911. V. 48

CAPITAL City Cook Book Published by the Ladies of the Christian Church, Guthrie, Oklahoma. Guthrie: 1898. V. 49

CAPITANEIS, THOMAS DE
Oratio...ad Sixtu III Pon. Max. Rome: 1483. V. 47; 49

THE CAPITOL Land Reservation in the Panhandle of Texas Now Offered for Sale...3,000 Acres Fine Agricultural or Grazing Land, Low Prices, Easy Terms Perfect Titles... Chicago: 1901. V. 52

CAPITOLI de' Regolamenti dell' Albergo Generale de' Poveri... Palermo: 1772. V. 54

CAPITULA Sive Constiutiones Ecclesiasticae. London: 1597. V. 47

CAPON, PAUL
The World at Bay. New York: 1954. V. 51; 53

CAPONIGRO, PAUL
Megaliths. Boston: 1986. V. 54
Sunflower. New York: 1974. V. 54

CAPOTE, TRUMAN
Breakfast at Tiffany's. 1956. V. 50
Breakfast at Tiffany's. London: 1958. V. 47
Breakfast at Tiffany's. New York: 1958. V. 47; 51; 52; 53; 54
A Christmas Memory. 1966. V. 50
A Christmas Memory. New York: 1966. V. 47
The Dogs Bark. New York: 1973. V. 53
The Grass Harp. New York: 1951. V. 47; 48; 49; 51; 52; 54
The Grass Harp. New York: 1952. V. 47; 49; 52; 53; 54
House of Flowers. New York: 1968. V. 51
In Cold Blood. New York: 1965. V. 48; 49; 50; 51; 52; 53; 54
Local Color. 1950. V. 50
Local Color. New York: 1950. V. 53
Miriam. Mankato: 1982. V. 51; 52
The Muses are Heard. New York: 1956. V. 51; 53
Observataions. Lucerne: 1959. V. 48
Observations. New York: 1959. V. 47; 51; 52
One Christmas. New York: V. 48; 52
One Christmas. New York: 1983. V. 48
Other Voices, Other Rooms. London: 1948. V. 49; 50
Other Voices, Other Rooms. New York: 1948. V. 47; 48; 49; 50; 51; 53; 54
Other Voices, Other Rooms. New York: 1949. V. 52
Other Voices, Other Rooms. Franklin Center: 1979. V. 51
Selected Writings of Truman Capote. New York: 1963. V. 54
A Tree of Night. London: 1949. V. 50
A Tree of Night. New York: 1949. V. 48; 49; 51; 52

CAPP, AL
The World of Little Abner. New York: 1953. V. 48; 51

CAPPARONI, GIUSEPPE
Raccolta Della Gerarchia Ecclesiastaica. (and) Raccolta Degli Ordini Religiosi. (and) Raccolta degli Ordini Religiosi delle Vergine a Dio Dedicate. Rome: 1826. V. 50; 53

CAPPE, CATHARINE
Thoughts on Various Charitable and Other Important Institutions, and on the Best Mode of Conducting Them. York: 1814. V. 52

CAPPER, B. P.
A Compendious Geographical Dictionary, Containing a Description of Every Remarkable Place in Europe, Asia, Africa and America. London: 1813. V. 51

CAPPER, JAMES
Observations on the Winds and Monsoons: Illustrataed with a Chart and Accompanied with Notes, Geographical and Meterological... London: 1801. V. 48

CAPPER, JOHN
The Three Presidencies of India: a History of the Rise and Progress of the British Indian Possessions. London: 1853. V. 47; 52

CAPPIELLO, L.
Nos Actrices. Preface de Marcel Prevost. Paris: 1899. V. 47

CAPPON, LESTER J.
Atlas of Early American History: the Revolutionary Era, 1760-1790. Princeton: 1976. V. 50; 53
Virginia Newspapers 1821-1935. New York and London: 1936. V. 52

CAPRA, ALESSANDRO
La Nuova Architectura Famigliare. Bologna: 1678. V. 53; 54

CAPRA, FRANK
The Name Above the Title. New York: 1971. V. 50

CAPRANICA, DOMENICUS
Speculu Artis Bene Moriendi. Cologne: 1493. V. 47; 49

CAPRIATA, PIETRO GIOVANNI
Dall'Historia...Ne'Quali si Contengono Tutti I Movementi d'Arme Successi in Italia dal MDCXIII fina al (MDCL). Genova: 1638-1663. V. 48

CAPRON, ELIAB WILKINSON
Singular Revelations, Explanation and History of the Mysterious Communion with Spirits, Comprehending the Rise and Progress of the Mysterious Noises in Western New York, Generally Received as Spiritual Communications. Aubrun: 1850. V. 48

CAPRON, ELISHA S.
History of California, from Its Discovery to the Present Time. Boston: 1854. V. 47; 49

CAPSTICK, P. H.
Peter Capstick's Works... 1977-91. V. 54

CAPTIVITY of Hanna Duston. San Francisco: 1987. V. 48

CAPUTO, PHILIP
Horn of Africa. New York: 1980. V. 54
A Rumor of War. New York: 1977. V. 54

CAR and Locomotive Cyclopedia of American Practice, 1966. New York: 1966. V. 53

CARACCIOLA, GALEACIUS
The Italian Convert: newes from Italy of a Second Moses; or The Life of Galeacius Caracciolus. London: 1662. V. 47

CARACCIOLI, CHARLES
The Antiquities of Arundel; the Peculiar Privilege of Its Castle and Lordship, With an Abstract of the Lives of the Earls of Arundel. London: 1766. V. 52

CARACCIOLI, LOUIS ANTOINE DE, MARQUIS
Advice from a Lady of Quality to Her Children, in the Last Stage of a Lingering Illness. Boston: 1796. V. 52
The Language of Reason. Dublin: 1802. V. 49
The Travels of Reason in Europe. London: 1780. V. 53

CARACCIOLO, ROBERTO
Sermones Fratis Roberti de Peccatis. Venice: 1490. V. 51; 52
Sermones Quadragesimales de Peccatis. Venice: 1490. V. 51

CARACTERES de la Fonderie de J. Gille, Graveur et Fondeur du Roi Pour les Caracteres de l'Imprimerie de la Loterie Royales de France... Paris: 1778. V. 47

CARANDENTE, GIOVANNI
Voltron: David Smith. Philadelphia: 1964. V. 53

CARBONE, LODOVICO
L'Hvomo Givsto, o la Centvria delle Lodi dell'hvomo Christiano... Venice: 1594. V. 47; 52

CARBUTT, MARY RHODES
Five Months' Fine Weather in Canada, Western U.S. and Mexico. London: 1889. V. 47

CARCO, FRANCIS
L'Amour Venal. Paris: 1926. V. 54
Perversity. Chicago: 1928. V. 48

CARD, HENRY
Beauford; or, a Picture of High Life. London: 1811. V. 54

CARD, O. S.
Cardography. 1987. V. 51; 54
Ender's Game. Toronto: 1985. V. 48
The Folk of the Fringe. 1989. V. 47; 51
The Memory of Earth. Toronto: 1992. V. 51
Songmaster. 1980. V. 51
Speaker For the Dead. 1986. V. 49; 51; 54
The Tales of Alvin Maker Trilogy: SeventhSon, Red Prophet, Prentice Alvin. New York: 1987-89. V. 54
Unaccompanied Sonata. 1981. V. 51
Xenocide. 1990. V. 49; 54

CARDANO, GIROLAMO
De Rerum Varietate Libri XVII. Basle: 1557. V. 49
De Rerum Varietate, Libri XVII. Iam Denuo Ab in Numeris mendis Summa Cura Ac Studio Repurgati, & Pristino Nitori Restituti. Basel: 1581. V. 49; 50

CARDEN, ALLEN D.
The Missouri Harmony. Cincinnati: 1834. V. 49
The Missouri Harmony... Cincinnati: 1842. V. 50

CARDEW, MARGARET
A French Alphabet. London: 1940. V. 51
A French Alphabet. London: 1950. V. 51

CARDIGAN, JAMES THOMAS, EARL OF
The Trial of James Thomas Earl of Cardigan Before the Right Honorable The House of Peers, in Full Parliament, For Felony (etc.). London: 1841. V. 54

CARDILUCIUS, JOHANNES HISKIAS
Artzneyísche Wasser-Und Signatur-Kunst. Nurnberg: 1680. V. 47

CARDINAL, CATHERINE
Watchmaking in History, Art and Science: Masterpieces in the Musee International d'Horlogerie. Lausanne: 1984. V. 53

CARDINALL, A. W.
In Ashanti and Beyond. 1927. V. 52

CARDINELL, CHARLES
Adventures on the Plains. San Francisco: 1922. V. 47; 49

CARDONNEL, ADAM DE
Numismata Scotiae; or, a Series of the Scottish Coinage, from the Reign of William the Lion to the Union. Edinburgh: 1786. V. 52
Picturesque Antiquities of Scotland. London: 1778. V. 47
Picturesque Antiquities of Scotland. London: 1788. V. 49

CARDOZO, BENJAMIN N.
Law Is Justice, Notable Opinions of Mr. Justice Cardozo. New York: 1938. V. 52
The Paradoxes of Legal Science. New York: 1928. V. 51
What Medicine Can Do for Law. New York: 1930. V. 51

CARDWELL, K. H.
Bernard Maybeck, Artisan, Architect, Artist. Santa Barbara: 1977. V. 51

CARE, HENRY
Draconica; or, an Abstract of All the Penal-Laws Touching Matters of Religion and the Several Oaths and Tests Thereby Enjoyned, Now so Much Controverted, with Brief Observations Thereupon. London: 1687. V. 49
English Liberties; or, the Free-Born Subject's Inheritance. London: 1680?. V. 50; 52
English Liberties; or, the Free-Born Subject's Inheritance. London: 1691. V. 47; 53
English Liberties, or the Free-born Subject's Inheritance... London: 1719. V. 47
A Vindication of the Proceedings of His Majesties Ecclesiastaical Commissioners, Against the Bishop of London and the Fellows of Magdalen-College. London: 1688. V. 54

CARELESS, JOHN
The Old English Square. London: 1821. V. 49; 51

CAREW, BAMPFYLDE MOORE
An Apology for the Life of Mr. Bampfylde-Moore Carew. London: 1760?. V. 54
The Life and Adventures of.... London: 1793. V. 54
The Surprising Adventures of...King of the Beggars. London: 1813. V. 52

CAREW, HAROLD
History of Pasadena and the San Gabriel Valley, California with Personal Sketches of...Men and Women, Past and Present... Chicago: 1930. V. 53

CAREW, PATRICK J.
An Ecclesiastical History of Irleand...to the Commencement of the Thirteenth Century. Dublin: 1835. V. 53

CAREW, RICHARD
The Survey of Cornwall. London: 1602. V. 47
The Survey of Cornwall. 1723. V. 54

CAREW, THOMAS
Poems and Masque. London: 1893. V. 53
Poems with a Maske... London: 1651. V. 53
A Rapture. 1927. V. 47
A Rapture. Berkshire: 1927. V. 48
A Rapture. Waltham St. Lawrence: 1927. V. 49; 50; 52; 54
The Works of Thomas Carew. Edinburgh: 1824. V. 51

CAREWE, NICHOLAS
The Voyage of Sir Nicholas Carewe to the Emperor Charles V in the Year 1529. Cambridge: 1959. V. 50

CAREY, DAVID
Life in Paris... London: 1822. V. 47; 48; 51; 53
The Reign of Fancy, a Poem. London: 1804. V. 54

CAREY, HENRY
A Learned Dissertation on Dumpling: Its Dignity, Antiquity and Excellence. London: 1726. V. 53
The Musical Century, in One Hundred English Ballads, on Various Subjects and Occasions. London: 1737-40. V. 49
Songs and Poems. Waltham St. Lawrence: 1924. V. 47; 49

CAREY, HENRY C.
A Complete Historical, Chronological and Geographical American Atlas... Philadelphia: 1823. V. 50
Principles of Social Science. Philadelphia: 1858. V. 48
Review of the Report of the Late Commissioners for Investigating the Affairs of the Joint Companies... Philadelphia: 1850. V. 51
The Slave Trade, Domestic and Foreign: Why It Exists, and How it May be Extinguished. Philadelphia: 1862. V. 50

CAREY, JOHN
Vegetable Gardening: an Essay. 1989. V. 52; 54

CAREY, MATHEW
Letters on the Colonization Society; and On Its Probable Results... Philadelphia: 1833. V. 52
The Olive Branch: or, faults on Both Sides, Federal and Democratic. Winchester: 1817. V. 49
A Short Account of the Malignant Fever, Lately Pervalent in Philadelphia. Philadelphia: 1793. V. 47; 49
Twenty-One Golden Rules to Depress Agriculture, Impede the Progress of Manufactures, Paralize Commerce... Salem: 1824. V. 49

CAREY, P.
Marine Interstitial Ciliates, an Illustrated Key. London: 1991. V. 48

CAREY, PETER
Bliss. London: 1981. V. 50
Oscar and Lucinda. St. Lucia: 1988. V. 51

CAREY, ROSA NOUCHETTE
Barbara Heathcote's Trial. London: 1871. V. 50
Heriot's Choice. London: 1879. V. 50; 51
Life's Trivial Round. London: 1900. V. 50
Little Miss Muffet. London: 1894. V. 50
Lover or Friend?. London: 1890. V. 50
Nelli's Memories. London: 1868. V. 50
The Old, Old Story. London: 1894. V. 50
The Search for Basil Lyndhurst. London: 1889. V. 50
Uncle Max. London: 1887. V. 50
Wee Wifie. London: 1869. V. 50

CAREY, W. H.
The Good Old Days of Honorable John Company, Being Curious Reminiscences Illustrating Manners and Customs of the British in India During the Rule of the East India Company from 1600 to 1858. Calcutta: 1906-07. V. 54

CAREY, WILLIAM
A Grammar of the Mahratta Language to Which are Added Dialogues on Familiar Subjects. Serampore: 1825. V. 52
Travel and Adventure in Tibet... London: 1902. V. 50; 53

CAREY, WILLIAM PAULET
Ridolfi's Critical Letters on the Style of Wm. Etty, Esq. R.A. and On His Destroying Angel... Nottingham: 1833. V. 50
Variae. Historical Observations on Anti-British and Anti-Contemporarian Prejudices. London: 1822. V. 53

THE CARIBBEAN Poetry of Derek Walcott and the Art of Romare Bearden. New York: 1983. V. 48

CARION, JOHANN
The Thre Bokes of Cronicles, Whyche John Carion Gathered Wyth Great Diligence of the Beste Authors that Have Written in Hebrue, Greke or Latine. London: 1550. V. 54

CARISBRICK, EDWARD
The Life of the Lady Warner of Parham in Suffolk. London: 1691. V. 49; 50; 54

CARLETON, J. HENRY
The Prairie Logbooks. Dragoon Campaigns to the Pawnee Villages in 1844. Chicago: 1943. V. 47

CARLETON, GEORGE, BP. OF CHICHESTER
The Life of Bernard Gilpin, a Man Most Holy and Renowned Among the Northerne English... London: 1552. V. 50
The Life of Bernard Gilpin, a Man Most Holy and Renowned Among the Northerne English. London: 1629. V. 50
A Thankfvll Remembrance of Gods Mercy. London: 1625. V. 48; 50; 52

CARLETON, GEORGE, BP. PF CHICHESTER
A Thankfull Remembrance of Gods Mercie. London: 1630. V. 49

CARLETON, HENRY GUY
Lectures Before the Thompson Street Poker Club. New York: 1889. V. 54
The Thompson Street Poker Club. Paris: 1888. V. 52

CARLETON, JOHN WILLIAM
Recreations in Shooting. London: 1846. V. 47; 52

CARLETON, L. A.
History of Hunting Trip in Sierra Madres, Northern Mexico. Houston?: 1922. V. 54

CARLETON, WILLIAM
Denis O'Shaughnessy Going to Maynooth. London: 1845. V. 47
Farm Ballads. New York: 1873. V. 53
The Life...Being His Autobiography and Letters and an Account of His Life and Writings... London: 1896. V. 51
Parra Sastha; or, the History of Paddy Go-Easy and His Wife Nancy. Dublin: 1845. V. 51
Rody the Rover; or, the Ribbonman. Dublin: 1845. V. 51
The Squanders of Castle Squander. London: 1852. V. 47; 51
Stories from Carleton. London & New York: 1889. V. 47; 53
Traits and Stories of the Irish Peasantry. Dublin: 1835. V. 47
Traits and Stories of the Irish Peasantry. London: 1836. V. 51; 53
Traits and Stories of the Irish Peasantry... Dublin: 1843. V. 47; 51
Traits and Stories of the Irish Peasantry. London: 1852. V. 50
Valentine McClutchy, the Irish Agent; or, the Chronicles of Castle Cumber... Dublin: 1854. V. 50
Valentine M'Clutchy, the Irish Agent; or, Chronicles of the Castle Cumber. Dublin: 1845. V. 50
Willy Reilly and His Dear Cooleen Bawn. Dublin: 1857. V. 51
The Works of... New York: 1881. V. 52

CARLILE, JAMES
The Fortune-Hunters; or, Two Fools Well Met. London: 1689. V. 47
Thoughts on the Mixed Character of Government Institutions in Ireland, with Particular Reference to the New System of Education. London: 1833. V. 52

CARLILE, RICHARD
The Report of the Proceedings of the Court of King's Bench...Being the Mock Trials of Ricahrd CArlile, for Alledged Blasphemous Libels, in Publishing Thomas Paine's Theological Works and Elihu Principles of Nature. London: 1826. V. 47

CARLISLE, ANTHONY
An Essay on the Disorders of Old Age, and On the Means for Prolonging Human Life. London: 1817. V. 50; 52
An Essay on the Disorders of Old Age, and On the Means for Prolonging Human Life. Philadelphia: 1819. V. 53
The Hunterian Oration, Delivered Before the Royal College of Surgeons...1820. London: 1820. V. 50

CARLISLE, EARL OF
Diary in Turkish and Greek Waters. London: 1854. V. 47

CARLISLE, FREDERICK HOWARD, 5TH EARL OF
Poems. London: 1807. V. 48; 51; 53
Thoughts Upon the Present Condition of the Stage and Upon the Construction of a New Theatre. London: 1808. V. 54

CARLISLE, GEORGE WILLIAM FREDERICK HOWARD, 7TH EARL OF
Two Lectures on the Poetry of Pope, and On His Own Travels in America. Leeds: 1850. V. 53

CARLISLE NATURAL HISTORY SOCIETY
Transactions. Carlisle: 1909-28. V. 52

CARLISLE, NICHOLAS
A Concise Account of the Several Foreign Orders of Knighthood and Other Marks of Honourable Distinction. London: 1839. V. 47; 53
A Memoir of the Life and Works of William Wyon, Esq., A.R.A., Chief Engraver of the Royal Mint. 1837. V. 48

CARLISLE, ROBERT
An Account of Bellevue Hospital with a Catalogue of the Medical and Surgical Staff from 1736-1894. New York: 1893. V. 50

CARLISLE, WILLIAM
An Essay on Evil Spirits; or, Reasons to Prove Their Existence. Bradford: 1825. V. 51
An Essay on Evil Spirits; or, Reasons to Prove Their Existence... 1827. V. 51

CARLL, LEWIS BUFFETT
A Treatise on the Calculus of Variations. New York: 1881. V. 48; 52; 54

CARLL, M. M.
Infant Instructer, and Mothers' Manual, Designed for Infant or Primary Schools and Families. Philadelphia: 1832. V. 51

CARLOCK, WILLIAM BRYAN
A Compilation of the Historical and Biographical Writings of William B. Carlock. 1923. V. 49; 50

CARLOS IV, KING OF SPAIN
Real Cedula Por la Qual su Magestad Funda un Colegio de Nobles Americanos en la Ciudad de Granada. Madrid: 1792. V. 48

CARLQUIST, S.
Island Biology. New York: 1974. V. 51
Island Life, a Natural History of the Islands of the World. New York: 1965. V. 54

CARLSON, P. S.
The Biology of Crop Productivity. London: 1980. V. 52

CARLTON, AMBROSE B.
The Wonderlands of the Wild West With Sketches of the Mormons. 1891. V. 52

CARLYLE, J. D.
Poems, Suggested Chiefly by Scenes in Asia-Minor, Syria and Greece with Prefaces... London: 1805. V. 50
Specimens of Arabian Poetry, from the Earliest Time to the Extinction of the Khaliphat With some Account of the Authors. Cambridge: 1796. V. 53

CARLYLE, JANE WELSH
Letters and Memorials. London: 1883. V. 47; 48; 49; 50; 51; 53

CARLYLE, THOMAS
Chartism. Boston: 1840. V. 49; 54
Chartism. London: 1840. V. 47; 48
Collected Works. London: 1870. V. 48; 50
The Complete Works. Boston. V. 51
The Complete Works. London: 1880. V. 50; 51
Complete Works. Boston: 1884. V. 51; 52
The Correspondence of Thomas Carlyle and Ralph Waldo Emerson, 1834-1872. Boston: 1883. V. 51
Critical and Miscellaneous Essays. Boston: 1838-39. V. 49
Critical and Miscellaneous Essays. London: 1840. V. 48; 49
Critical and Miscellaneous Essays. London: 1869. V. 54
Critical and Miscellaneous Essays... London: 1895. V. 50
The French Revolution. London. V. 51
The French Revolution. London: 1837. V. 48; 49; 50
The French Revolution. Boston: 1838. V. 47
The French Revolution. London: 1848. V. 48
The French Revolution. London: 1857. V. 51
The French Revolution. London: 1903. V. 47
The French Revolution. London: 1910. V. 51
The French Revolution. London: 1911. V. 50; 54
The French Revolution. New York: 1956. V. 53; 54
German Romance: Specimens Of its Chief Authors... Edinburgh: 1827. V. 47; 51; 52
History of Frederick II of Prussia: Called Frederick the Great. Leipzig: 1858-65. V. 52
History of Friedrich II of Prussia, Called Frederick the Great. London: 1890. V. 49; 52
Inaugural Address at Edinburgh, April 2nd, 1866. London: 1866. V. 50
Latter-Day. Boston: 1850. V. 54
Latter-Day Pamphlets. London: 1850. V. 47; 51; 53
The Life of Friedrich Schiller. London: 1825. V. 47; 50; 51
On Heroes, Hero-Worship and the Heroic in History. London: 1841. V. 47
On Heroes, Hero-Worship and the Heroic in History. New York: 1841. V. 54
On the Choice of Books. London: 1866. V. 49; 51
Past and Present. London: 1843. V. 47; 51
Samuel Jackson. London: 1853. V. 54
Sartor Resartus. London: 1834. V. 47
Sartor Resartus. Boston: 1836. V. 49
Sartor Resartus. London: 1838. V. 49; 51; 52; 54
Sartor Resartus. London: 1889. V. 49
Sartor Resartus. London: 1898. V. 52
Sartor Resartus. Hammersmith: 1907. V. 51; 54
Sartor Resartus. London: 1931. V. 54
Shooting Niagara: and After?. London: 1867. V. 49
Thomas Carlyle's Counsels to a Literary Aspirant. Edinburgh: 1886. V. 47
The Works. London: 1898-1905. V. 49

CARMACK, GEORGE W.
My Experiences in the Yukon. Seattle: 1933. V. 50

CARMAN, BLISS
Ballads of Lost Haven. Boston: 1987. V. 47
By the Aurelian Wall and Other Elegies. Boston, New York & London: 1898. V. 52
The Gate of Peace. A Poem. New York: 1907. V. 47
The Girl in the Poster: for a design by Miss Ethel Reed. 1897. V. 49
A Painter's Holiday. New York: 1911. V. 49
The Princess of the Tower, The Wise Men from the East and to the Winged Victory. 1906. V. 52
The Rough Rider and Other Poems. New York: 1909. V. 54
Talks on Poetry and Life. Toronto: 1926. V. 49

CARMAN, W. Y.
Military Uniforms - Regiments of Scotland. 1970. V. 50

CARMICHAEL, A. C., MRS
Domestic Manners and Social Condition of the White, Coloured and Negro Population of the West Indies. London: 1833. V. 49; 50

CARMICHAEL, A. C., MRS.
Domestic Manners and Social Condition of the White, Coloured and Negro Population of the West Indies. 1834. V. 53

CARMICHAEL, ANDREW
A Memoir of the Life and Philosophy of Spurzheim. Boston: 1833. V. 49

CARMICHAEL, JOHN
A Self-Defensive War Lawful, Proved in a Sermon, Preached at Lancaster Before Captain Ross's Companyof Militia...June 4, 1775. Philadelphia: 1775. V. 48

CARMICHAEL, MARY
A New Dress for an Old Friend...Being a Fable of Aesop in Rhyme. London: 1857. V. 50

CARMICHAEL, PHILIP
The Man from the Moon. New York: 1909. V. 52

CARMICHAEL, R.
An Essay on Veneral Diseases... London: 1825. V. 47; 51
An Essay on Venereal Diseases and the Uses and Abuses of Mercury in Their Treatment. Philadelphia: 1825. V. 48

CARMICHAEL, SARAH E.
Poems...A Brief Selection, Published by Persmission of the Authoress, for Private Circulation. San Francisco: 1866. V. 51; 54

CARMINA
Quinque Illustrium Poetarum; Parapharasis in Triginta Psalmos. Florence: 1552. V. 53

CARMON, EZRA
Special Report On the History and Present Condition of the Sheep Industry of the United States. Washington: 1892. V. 52

CARNAC, CAROL
The Greenwell Mystery. New York: 1934. V. 50

CARNAHAN, MELISSA STEWART MC KEE
Personal Experiences of the San Francisco Earthquake of April, 1906. Pittsburgh: 1908. V. 51

CARNAN, T.
The Gentleman and Lady's Key to Polite-Literature, or a Compendious Dictionary of Fabulous History. London: 1788. V. 52

CARNARVON, H. J. G. HERBERT, EARL OF
Catalogue of Books Selected from the Library of an English Amateur. London: 1893-97. V. 51
Portugal and Gallicia, with a Review of the Social and Political State of the Basque Provinces; and a Few Events in Spain. London: 1836. V. 54
Reminiscences of Athens and the Morea; Extracts from a Journal of Travels in Greece in 1839. London: 1869. V. 54

CARNE, JOHN
Syria, The Holy Land, Asia Minor, &c. London Paris & America: 1836. V. 52
Syria, The Holy Land, Asia Minor, &c. London: 1836-38. V. 48; 51; 53

CARNEGIE, ANDREW
An American Four-in-Hand in Britain. New York: 1914. V. 47
Autobiography of Andrew Carnegie. Boston: 1920. V. 51
Our Coaching Trip: Brighton to Inverness. New York: 1882. V. 47; 49

CARNEGIE, DAVID
The History of Munitions Supply in Canada 1914-1918. London: 1925. V. 54

CARNEGIE, DAVID WYNFORD
Spinifex and Sand a Narrative of Five Years' Pioneering and Exploration in Western Australia. London: 1898. V. 53

CARNEGY, PATRICK
Kachahri Technicalities or a Glossary of Terms Rural, Official and General in Daily Use in the Courts of Lawa. Allahabad: 1877. V. 48

CARNES, J. A.
Journal of a Voyage from Boston to the West Coast of Africa... Boston: 1952. V. 54

CARNES, JAMES E.
Use: a Poem: Delivered June 16, 1858, Before the Washington Society of Bethel College, Russellville, Ky. Galveston: 1858. V. 49

CARNEVALI, EMANUEL
A Hurried Man. Paris: 1925. V. 51; 53

CARNOCHAN, JANET
History of Niagara. Toronto: 1914. V. 54

CARO, ANNIBALE
Apologia de Gli Academici di Banchi di Roma, Contra M. Lodovico Castelvetro da Modena. Parma. V. 48
Commento Di ser AGresto Da Ficarvolo Sopra la Prima Ficata Del Padre Siceo. Con la Diceria de Nasi. Bengodi: 1584. V. 47
Rime. 1569. V. 47
Rime. Venice: 1584. V. 50

CAROCHI, HORACIO
Compendio del Arte de la Langua Mexicana. Mexico City: 1759. V. 47; 54

A CAROL, Good King Wencesias. London: 1920. V. 54

CAROL, MARK
Ancient Needs. Easthampton: 1989. V. 50
The Banging Rock.... Easthampton: 1990. V. 49; 50

CAROLINE Hargrave, the Merchant's Daughter. Salem: 1845. V. 49

CAROLINE Lindsay, the Laird's Daughter. Edinburgh: 1827. V. 47

CAROLINE AMELIA ELIZABETH, QUEEN OF GREAT BRITAIN
The Trial at Large of Her Majesty Caroline Amelia Elizabeth, Queen of Great Britain, in the House of Lords, on Charges of Adulterious Intercourse... London: 1821. V. 49; 50; 51
The Trial at Large of Her Majesty Caroline, Queen Consort of Great Britain; Before the House of Peers; on the bill of Pains and Penalties. London: 1820. V. 53
The Whole Proceedings on the Trial of Her Majesty, Caroline Amelia Elizabeth, Queen of England... London: 1820. V. 50; 51

CAROLINO, PEDRO
English As She Is Spoke. The New Guide of the Conversation in Portuguese and English. London: 1960. V. 53
The New Guide of the Conversation in English. London: 1884. V. 47
The New Guide of the Conversation in Portugese and English. Boston: 1883. V. 47; 51; 53
The New Guide of the Conversation in Portuguese and English. 1960. V. 54

CARON, BOB
I Saw It First - From the Eyewitness Account of Bob Caron, Tail Gunner Aboard the Enola Gay. Reynoldsburg: 1993. V. 54

CAROSO, FABRIZIO
Il Ballarino... Venice: 1581. V. 51

CAROVE, FRIEDRICH WILHELM
Story Without an End. Boston: 1836. V. 51
The Story Without an End. London: 1868. V. 51; 52; 53
The Story Without an End. New York: 1868. V. 49

CARP, AUGUSTUS
Augustus Carp, by Himself. London: 1924. V. 52

CARPENTER, AURELIUS O.
Picturesque Mendocino. 1900. V. 53

CARPENTER, CHARLES H.
Gorham Silver, 1831-1981. New York: 1982. V. 53
Tiffany Silver. London: 1979. V. 47; 53

CARPENTER, EDWARD
Angel's Wings. A Series of Essays on Art and Its Relation to Life. London: 1899. V. 54
Love's Coming of Age... London & Manchester: 1909. V. 51
Never Again! - a Protest and a Warning addressed to the Peoples of Europe. London: 1916. V. 47
Sex-Love, and its Place in a Free Society. Manchester: 1894. V. 49
Who Shall Command the Heart. Towards Democracy Part IV. London: 1902. V. 54
Woman, and Her Place in a Free Society. Manchester: 1894. V. 49

CARPENTER, EDWIN H.
A Sixteenth Century Mexican Broadside from the Collection of Emilio Valton: Described, with a Checklist. Los Angeles: 1965. V. 47

CARPENTER, G. W.
Essays on Some of the Most Important Articles of the Materia Medica...To Which Is Added, a Catalogue of Medicines, Surgical Instruments &c, &c. Philadelphia: 1834. V. 48

CARPENTER, GEOFFREY DOUGLAS HALE
A Naturalist on Lake Victoria... London: 1920. V. 50; 54
A Naturalist on Lake Victoria.... New York: 1920. V. 53

CARPENTER, J. ESTLIN
The Life and Work of Mary Carpenter. London: 1881. V. 50

CARPENTER, MARY
Six Months in India. London: 1868. V. 49

CARPENTER, R. P.
Catalogue of the Reigen Collection of Mazatlan Mollusca in the British Museum. Warrington: 1855-57. V. 48; 50

CARPENTER, R. R. M.
Game Trails from Alaska to Africa. 1938. V. 47; 54

CARPENTER, STEPHEN CULLEN
The Mirror of Taste, and Dramatic Censor. Philadelphia: 1810. V. 48; 51

CARPENTER, W. H.
The Baltimore Book. Baltimore: 1838. V. 48

CARPENTER, WILLIAM
The Angler's Assistant: Comprising Practical Directions for Bottom-Fishing, Trolling, &c. London: 1848. V. 47
The Angler's Assistant: Comprising Practical Directions for Bottom-Fishing, Trolling, &c. London: 1852. V. 47

CARPENTER, WILLIAM B.
The Microscope and Its Revelations. Philadelphia: 1856. V. 50
The Microscope and Its Revelations. Philadelphia: 1881. V. 53
The Microscope and Its Revelations. New York: 1883. V. 53
The Microscope and Its Revelations. London: 1901. V. 52; 53

THE CARPENTER'S New Guide: Being a Complete Book of Lines for Carpentry and Joinery... London: 1814. V. 47

CARPENTIER, ALEJO
The Kingdom of This World. N.P: 1987. V. 48; 51

CARPENTIER, WILLIAM E.
Introduction to the Study of Foraminifera. London: 1862. V. 52

CARPUE, J. C.
An Account of Two Successful Operations for Restoring a Lost Nose from the Integuments of the Forehead with Foreword and Biography By Frank McDowell. Birmingham: 1981. V. 52

CARR, CALEB
The Alienist. Franklin Center: 1994. V. 53
The Alienist. New York: 1994. V. 52
Casing the Promised Land. New York: 1980. V. 52; 54

CARR, EMILY
Hundreds and Thousands. The Journals of Emily Carr. Toronto: 1966. V. 50

CARR, EZRA S.
The Patrons of Husbandry on the Pacific Coast. San Francisco: 1875. V. 50

CARR, FRANCIS
Mary Fitton, Dark Lady of the Sonnets. London: 1980. V. 51

CARR, FRANK
Characteristics of Leight Hunt, as Exhibited in that Typical Literary Periodical, "Leigh Hunt's London Journal". London: 1878. V. 51

CARR, J. COMYNS
King Arthur. London: 1893. V. 51

CARR, J. L.
The Battle of Pollocks Crossing. New York: 1985. V. 53
The Harpole Report. London: 1972. V. 53
How Steeple Sinderby Wanderers Won the F.A. Cup. London: 1975. V. 53
A Month in the Country. London: 1990. V. 51
A Season in Sinji. London: 1967. V. 53
What Hetty Did or Life and Letters. Kettering: 1988. V. 53

CARR, JOHN
A Northern Summer or Travels Round the Baltic... London: 1805. V. 48; 50
Pioneer Days in California. Eureka: 1891. V. 47; 51; 54
A Tour through Holland, Along the Right and Left Banks of the Rhine, to the South of Germany, in the Summer and Autumn of 1806. Philadelphia: 1807. V. 52; 54
A Tour through Holland, Along the Right and Left Banks of the Rhine, to the South of Germany...in 1806. London: 1807. V. 54
A Vulcan Among the Argonaut, Being Vivid Excerpts From Those Most Original and Amusing Memories of John Carr, Blacksmith. San Francisco: 1936. V. 49; 53

CARR, JOHN DICKSON
The Cavalier's Cup. New York: 1953. V. 52
Death Turns the Tables. New York: 1941. V. 52
Eight Poems. In a Book of Hill School Verse 1920-1926. New York: 1927. V. 51
The Emperor's Snuff Box. New York: 1942. V. 52; 53
A Graveyard to let. New York: 1949. V. 47
He Who Whispers. New York: 1946. V. 52
Most Secret. 1964. V. 53
My Late Wives. New York: 1946. V. 52
Night at the Mocking Widow. New York: 1950. V. 52
Till Death Do Us Part. New York: 1944. V. 47

CARR, MARY FRANCES
Life Among the Shakers. New York: 188-. V. 53
Shakers: a Correspondence Between Mary F. C. of Mt. Holley City and a Shaker Sister, Sarah L. of Union Village. Cincinnati: 1869. V. 48

CARR, RALPH
The Mahumetane or Turkish Historie, Containing Three Bookes... London: 1600. V. 49

CARR, WILLIAM
An Accurate Description of the United Netherlands, and of the Most Considerable Parts of Germany, Sweden & Denmark... London: 1691. V. 47
The Dialect of Craven, in the West-Riding of the County of York, with a Copious Glossary... London: 1828. V. 52
Horae Momenta Cravenae, or the Craven Dialect Exemplified in Two Dialogues. London: 1824. V. 50

CARR, WILLIAM G.
John Swett, the Biography of an Education Pioneer. Santa Ana: 1933. V. 48

CARR, WILLIAM WINDLE
Poems on Various Subjects. London: 1791. V. 48

CARRANZA, BARTHOLOME DE, ABP. OF TOLEDO
Summa Conciliorum et Pontificum. Paris: 1550. V. 50

CARREL, ALEXIS
The Treatment of Infected Wounds. New York: 1917. V. 48
Uniterminal and Biterminal Venous Transplantations. 1906. V. 48

CARRERAS, LUIS
The Glory of Martyred Spain. London: 1939. V. 49

CARRICK, GEORGE L.
Koumiss, or Fermented Mare's Milk and Its Uses in the Treatment and Cure of Pulmonary Consumption and Other Wasting Diseases. Edinburgh: 1881. V. 53

CARRICK, T. W.
The Story of Wigton. Carlisle: 1949. V. 51

CARRIER'S Address to the Patrons of the Haverhill Gazette, on the Commencement of the Year 1837. Haverhill: 1837. V. 47

CARRINGTON, CHARLES
A Subaltern's War. London: 1929. V. 47
Untrodden Fields of Anthropology. Paris: 1898. V. 48

CARRINGTON, DORA
Carrington - Letters and Extracts from Her Diaries. London: 1970. V. 47
Paintings, Drawings and Decorations. London: 1978. V. 53

CARRINGTON, FRANCIS
Army Life on the Plains. Philadelphia: 1910. V. 50

CARRINGTON, HENRY B.
Ab-Sa-Ra-Ka, Land of Massacre, Being the Experiences of An Officer's Life Out on the Plains with an Outine of Indian Operations and Conferences from 1865 to 1878. Philadelphia: 1878. V. 52
The Indian Question. Boston: 1884. V. 50
The Indian Question... Boston: 1909. V. 48

CARRINGTON, HENRY E.
The Plymouth and Devonport Guides with Sketches of the Surrounding Scenery. Devonport: 1833. V. 49

CARRINGTON, LEONORA
The Oval Lady. Six Surreal Stories. Santa Barbara: 1975. V. 50

CARRINGTON, MARGARET I.
Ab-Sa-Ra-Ka. Home of the Crow. New York: 1869. V. 49

CARRINGTON, NICHOLAS TOMS
The Collected Poems of Lake N. T. Carrington. London: 1834. V. 54
Dartmoor: a Descriptive Poem. London: 1826. V. 48; 51

CARRINGTON, NOEL
Carrington: Paintings, Drawings and Decorations. 1978. V. 54

CARRION Y MORCILLO, ALFONSON
Magnifica Parrentacion y Funere Pompa en la Ocasion de Trasladarse de los Sres. Funebre Pompa en la Ocasion de Trasladarse de la Sepultura de los Sres. Lima: 1744. V. 53

CARROLL, ANNA ELLA
The Great American Battle; or, the Contest Between Christianity and Political Romanism. New York and Auburn: 1856. V. 47
The Union of the States. Boston: 1856. V. 53

CARROLL, B. H.
Standard History Of Houston Texas from a Study of the Original Sources. Knoxville: 1912. V. 53

CARROLL, CAMPBELL
Three Bar: the Story of Douglas Lake. Vancouver: 1958. V. 49; 51; 54

CARROLL, CHARLES
Journal of Charles Carroll of Carrollton, During the Visit to Canada in 1776, as One of the Commissioners from Congress... Baltimore: 1845. V. 53

CARROLL, GEORGE D.
Diamonds from Brilliant Minds. New York: 1881. V. 52

CARROLL, H. BAILEY
The Texan Santa Fe Trail. Canyon: 1951. V. 50

CARROLL, JIM
4 Ups and 1 Down. New York: 1970. V. 53
The Basketball Diaries. Bolinas: 1978. V. 51
The Book of Nods. New York: 1986. V. 48
Living at the Movies. New York: 1973. V. 52
Organic Trains. 1968. V. 53

CARROLL, JOHN
Eggenhofer: the Pulp Years. Fort Collins: 1975. V. 53

CARROLL, JOHN M.
The Unpublished Papers of the Order of the Indian Wars, Book 1 Through Book E10. New Brunswick: 1977. V. 47
4 on Custer by Carroll. New York: 1976. V. 47
The Black Military Experience in the American West. New York: 1971. V. 51
The Elanor Hinman Interviews On the Life and Death of Crazy Horse. 1976. V. 52
I, Varnum, The Autobiographical Reminiscences of Custer's Chief of Scouts. Glendale: 1982. V. 47
Just Such a Time. Recollections of a Childhood on the Texas Frontier 1858-1867. Austin: 1987. V. 49; 51

CARROLL, JONATHAN
Black Cocktail. London: 1990. V. 49
The Land of Laughs. New York: 1980. V. 49; 50; 51

CARROLL, L.
A Handbook of the Literature of the Rev. C. L. Dodgson. London: 1931. V. 47

CARROLL, W.
The Angler's Vade Mecum. Edinburgh: 1818. V. 47

CARROTHERS, JULIA D.
Japan's Year. Tokyo: 1905. V. 52

CARROW, JOHN MONSON
Cases Relating to Railways and Canadls, Argued and Adjuded in the Courts of Law and Equity. 1842-1846. London: 1846. V. 49

CARRUTH, HAYDEN
The Adventures of Jones. New York: 1895. V. 53
Almanach du Printemps Vivarois. New York: 1979. V. 53
Loneliness. Newark, West Burke: 1976. V. 52; 53
Mr. Milo Bush and Other Worthies. New York: 1899. V. 53
Track's End. New York: 1911. V. 53

CARRUTHERS, DOUGLAS
Beyond the Caspian, a Naturalist in Central Asia. Edinburgh: 1949. V. 51
Beyond the Caspian, a Naturalist in Central Asia. London: 1949. V. 50; 54
Unknown Mongolia, a Record of Travel and Exploration in North-West Mongolia and Dzungaria... 1913. V. 54
Unknown Mongolia, a Record of Travel and Exploration in North-West Mongolia and Dzungaria. London: 1913. V. 49

CARRUTHERS, JOHN
Retrospect of Thirty-Six Years' Residence West: Being a Christian Journal and Narrative. Hamilton: 1861. V. 47; 49; 51

CARRYL, CHARLES E.
Davy and the Goblin of What Followed Reading "Alice's Adventures in Wonderland". Boston: 1886. V. 54
The River Syndicate and Other Stories. New York: 1899. V. 54

CARRYL, GUY WETMORE
The Garden of Years and Other Poems. New York: 1904. V. 54
Grimm Tales Made Gay. Boston: 1902. V. 52; 54
Mother Goose for Grown-Ups. New York & London: 1900. V. 47

CARSON, HAMPTON L.
History of the Celebration of the One Hundredth Anniversary of the Promulgation of the Constitution of the United States. Philadelphia: 1889. V. 50; 52

CARSON, JAMES H.
Recollections of the California Mines - an Account of the Early Discoveries of Gold, with Anecdotes and Sketches of California and Miner's Life... Oakland: 1950. V. 54

CARSON, JOSEPH
A History of the Medical Department of the University of Pennsylvania, From Its Foundation in 1765. Philadelphia: 1869. V. 49
Illustrations of Medical Botany... Philadelphia: 1847. V. 47

CARSON, KIT
Kit Carson's Own Story of His Life. Taos: 1926. V. 54

CARSON, R. A. G.
Essays in Roman Coinage Presented to Harold Mattingly. London: 1956. V. 48

CARSON, RACHEL
The Edge of the Sea. Boston: 1955. V. 53
Of Man and the Stream of Time. Claremont: 1962. V. 51
The Sea Around Us. New York: 1951. V. 50; 54
The Sea Around Us. 1980. V. 48; 51
The Sea Around Us. New York: 1980. V. 47; 48; 52; 54
Silent Spring. Boston: 1962. V. 51; 52; 53; 54
Under the Sea-Wind. 1941. V. 50
Under the Sea-Wind... New York: 1942. V. 52

CARSON, THOMAS
Ranching, Sport and Travel. London: 1911. V. 52; 54

CARSTAIRS, CARROLL
A Generation Missing. London: 1930. V. 47; 50

CARSTARIS, JOHN PADDY
Honest Injun!...Autobiography. London: 1942. V. 53

CARSTARPHEN, JAMES
My Trip to California in '49. 1914. V. 47; 50

CARSTENSEN, A. RIIS
Two Summers in Greenland. London: 1890. V. 48; 53

CARTA Escrita de Un Solado Oran a un Consejero de Su Magestad, en Respuesta de Una Suya de 20. de Iulio de 1622. Madrid: 1622. V. 48

CARTAS de Tejas y Venida de Santa-Anna. Mexico: 1836. V. 49

CARTE, THOMAS
A General History of England. London: 1747-55. V. 47
An History of the Life of James Duke of Ormonde... London: 1736/5. V. 51; 54
A History of...Life of James, Duke of Ormonde... 1736/35. V. 48

CARTE Topographique de l'Egypte, et de Plusieurs Parties des Pays Limitrophes... Paris: 1818. V. 49

CARTER & CO.
Manufacturers of Encaustic Mosaic Tesselated Majolica Enamelled & Other Tiles. Leicester: 1890. V. 50

CARTER, ANGELA
Black Venus. London: 1985. V. 51
Black Venus's Tale. London: 1980. V. 51
The Donkey Prince. New York: 1970. V. 52; 53
The Passion of New Eve. London: 1977. V. 53
Several Perceptions. London: 1968. V. 51; 53
Sleeping Beauty and Other Favourite Fairy Tales. London: 1982. V. 47; 50
Unicorn. Leeds: 1966. V. 52
The War of Dreams. New York: 1974. V. 51

CARTER, C. F.
The Wedding Day in Literature and Art. New York: 1900. V. 48

CARTER, CHARLOTTE
Sheltered Life. New York: 1975. V. 54

CARTER, CLARENCE EDWIN
The Territorial Papers of the United States: The Territory of Indiana 1800-1816. Washington: 1939. V. 52

CARTER, DENNY
Henry Farney. New York: 1978. V. 49

CARTER, E. S.
The Life and Adventures of E. S. Carter Including a trip Across the Plains and Mountains in 1852, Indian Wars in the Early Days of Oregon... St. Joseph: 1896. V. 54

CARTER, ELIZABETH
Memoirs of the Life... London: 1816. V. 48
Poems on Several Occasions. London: 1762. V. 50; 52
Poems on Several Occasions. London: 1766. V. 50
A Series of Letters Between...and Miss Catherine Talbot, from the Year 1741 to 1770. London: 1809. V. 49; 50

CARTER, ERNEST
The Blonde Donna: or, The Fiesta of Santa Barbara. New York: 1936. V. 47

CARTER, F.
Gold Like Glass. London: 1932. V. 48; 50; 52

CARTER, FOREST
George & Lurleen Wallace. Centre: 1967. V. 47

CARTER, FORREST
The Education of Little Tree. 1976. V. 50; 53
The Education of Little Tree. New York: 1976. V. 49; 53
Gone to Texas. 1973. V. 50
Gone to Texas. New York: 1975. V. 53
The Vengeance Trail of Josey Wales. 1976. V. 50
The Vengeance Trail of Josey Wales. New York: 1976. V. 51
Watch For me on the Mountain. New York: 1978. V. 50

CARTER, FREDERICK
D. H. Lawrence and the Body Mystical. London: 1932. V. 48

CARTER, GEORGE
A Narrative of the Loss of the Grosvenor East Indiamen, Which was Unfortunately Wrecked Upon the Coast of California, Somewhere Between the 27th and 32nd Degree of Southern Latitude, on the 4th of August, 1782. London: 1791. V. 54

CARTER, H. B.
Sir Joseph Banks Bibliography. Winchester: 1987. V. 49

CARTER, HARRY
Fournier on Typefounding. London: 1930. V. 51; 52

CARTER, HARVEY LEWIS
Dear Old Kit: The Historical Christopher Carson. Norman: 1968. V. 52; 54

CARTER, JAMES EARL
Always A Reckoning. New York: 1995. V. 52; 53; 54
Everything to Gain. New York: 1987. V. 48; 49; 53
A Government As Good As its People. New York: 1977. V. 50
Keeping Faith. Memoirs of a President. New York: 1982. V. 47; 53
Keeping Faith. Memoirs of a President. Norwalk: 1982. V. 50
Negotiation, the Alternative to Hostility. Macon: 1984. V. 49
Turning Point. New York: 1992. V. 50; 54

CARTER, JOHN
The Ancient Architecture of England, Including the Orders During the British, Roman, Saxon and Norman Eras.. London: 1837. V. 53
Binding Variants in English Publishing 1820-1900. 1932. V. 47; 48
Binding Variants in English Publishing 1820-1900. London: 1932. V. 50; 52
Binding Variants in English Publishing 1820-1900. (with) More Binding Variants. London: 1932/1938. V. 49
Binding Variants with More Vinding Variants in English Publishing 1820-1900. 1989. V. 53
An Enquiry Into the Nature of Certain 19th Century Pamphlets. London, New York: 1934. V. 48; 51; 52; 54
An Enquiry into the Nature of Certain 19th Century Pamphlets... London: 1934/48. V. 47
A Handlist of the Writings of Stanley Morison. Cambridge: 1950. V. 51
More Binding Variants. London: 1938. V. 52
Printing and the Mind of Man. London: 1963. V. 51
Printing and the Mind of Man. London, New York: 1967. V. 47; 48; 50; 51; 52; 53; 54
Printing and the Mind of Man. Munchen: 1983. V. 47; 49; 50; 51; 53
Printing and the Mind of Man. London: 1987. V. 48
The Progress of Architecture. London: 1830. V. 50; 54
Specimens of Gothic Architecture and Ancient Buildings in England... London: 1824. V. 47
Specimens of the Ancient Sculpture and Painting Now Remaining... London: 1780-87-94. V. 48
Specimens of the Ancient Sculpture and Painting Now Remaining in England. London: 1887. V. 48; 51

CARTER, JOHN BROWN
Bibliotheca Americana: Catalogue of the John Carter Brown Library in Brown University, Providence, Rhode Island. Providence: 1919-31. V. 54

CARTER, JOSEPH COLEMAN
The Sculpture of the Sanctuary of Athena at Priene. London: 1983. V. 52

CARTER, LILLIAN
Away from Home: Letters to My Family. New York: 1977. V. 54

CARTER, MARY ELIZABETH
Juliet. London: 1883. V. 51

CARTER, MATTHEW
Honor Redivivus; or an Analysis of Honor and Armory. London: 1655. V. 49
Honor Redivivus; or, the Analysis of Honor and Armory. London: 1673. V. 47; 53
A Most True and Exact Relation of that as Honourable as Unfortunate Expedition of Kent,, Essex, and Colchester. London: 1650. V. 50; 52

CARTER, RAY
An Exhibition of Works by Sir John Betjeman from the Collection of Ray Carter, in the Art Gallery of St. Paul's School, February-March, MCMLXXXIII. London: 1983. V. 49

CARTER, RICHARD
Short Sketch of the Author's Life, and Adventures From His Youth Until 1818, in the First Part. Versailles: 1825. V. 49

CARTER, ROBERT
The Case of the Planters of Tobacco in Virginia, as Represented by Themselves; Signed by the President of the Council and the Speaker of the House of Burgesses. London: 1733. V. 48

CARTER, ROBERT BRUDENELL
On the Influence of Education and Training in Preventing Diseases of the Nervous System. London: 1855. V. 53

CARTER, ROBERT GOLDTHWAITE
Four Brothers in Blue or Sunshine and Shadows of the War of the Rebellion a Story of the Great Civil War from Bull Run to Appomatox. Washington: 1913. V. 52; 54
The Old Sergeant's Story. New York: 1926. V. 47; 48
On the Border With Mackenzie. Washington: 1935. V. 50; 54
On the Border with Mackenzie... New York: 1961. V. 50; 53

CARTER, SAMUEL
The Law of Executions, or, a Treatise Shewing and Explaining the Nature of Executions... London: 1706. V. 52
Lex Custumaria; or, a Treatise of Copy-Hold Estates, in Respect of the Lord... London: 1696. V. 52; 54
Lex Custumaria; or, a Treatise of Copy-hold Estates, in Respect of the Lord, Copy-Holder. London: 1701. V. 47

CARTER, SEBASTIAN
A Printer's Dozen. Cambridge: 1993. V. 51; 52

CARTER, SUSANNAH
The Frugal Housewife: or, Complete Woman Cook. Philadelphia: 1796. V. 48; 49

CARTER, THOMAS
Medals of the British Army and How They Were Won... London: 1861. V. 48; 50; 51

CARTER, THOMAS FRANCIS
The Invention of Printing in China. New York: 1925. V. 52

CARTER, W. A.
Great Inducements to Those Who Desire to Ship Cattle by the U.P. Railroad. Fort Bridger: 1877. V. 52
McCurtain County and Southeast Oklahoma. Idabel: 1923. V. 49; 51

CARTER, WILL
The First 10. Some Ground Covered at the Rampant Lions Press by Will Carter 1949-58. Cambridge: 1958. V. 52
The Paper Makers Craft. Leicester: 1965. V. 51
The Rampant Lions Press Miscellany. Cambridge: 1988. V. 51

CARTER, WILLIAM H.
From Yorktown to Santiago With the Sixth U.S. Cavalry... Baltimore: 1900. V. 48; 49
Horses, Saddles and Bridles. Baltimore: 1902. V. 54
Horses Saddles and Bridles. Baltimore: 1906. V. 47

CARTER, WILLIAM RANDOLPH
History of the First Regiment of Tennessee Volunteer Cavalry in the Great War of the Rebellion, with the Armies of the Ohio and Cumberland, Under Generals Morgan, Rosencrans, Thomas, Stanley and Wilson. 1862-1865. Knoxville: 1902. V. 49

CARTERET, PHILIP
Carteret's Voyage Round the World 1766-1769. Cambridge: 1965. V. 54

CARTHEW, THOMAS
Reports of Cases Adjudged in the Court of King's Bench, from the Third Year of King James the Second to the Twelfth Year of King William the Third. London: 1738. V. 51
Reports of Cases Adjudged in the Court of King's Bench, from the Third Year of King James the Second, to the Twelfth Year of King William the Third... London: 1741. V. 52

CARTIER, E.
Edd Cartier: The Known and the Unknown. 1977. V. 51

CARTIER-BRESSON, HENRI
About Russia. New York: 1974. V. 49
Beautiful Jaipur. Bombay: 1948. V. 47
Cartier-Bresson Photographer. Boston: 1979. V. 50
The Decisive Moment. New York: 1952. V. 47; 48; 50; 52
The Europeans. New York: 1955. V. 51; 54
From One China to the Other. New York: 1956. V. 47; 52
Henri Cartier Bresson Photographer. 1979. V. 52
The People of Moscow. London: 1955. V. 50; 53
The People of Moscow. New York: 1955. V. 47; 48; 49; 50; 52; 53; 54
World of Henri Cartier Bresson. New York: 1968. V. 50; 52

CARTLAND, BARBARA
I Search for Rainbows. London: 1967. V. 50; 53

CARTWRIGHT, DAVID W.
Natural History of Western Wild Animals and Guide for Hunters, Trappers and Sportsmen... Toledo: 1875. V. 48

CARTWRIGHT, EDMUND
Poems. 1786. V. 48
The Prince of Peace; and other Poems. London: 1779. V. 53

CARTWRIGHT, FAIRFAX LEIGHTON
The Mystic Rose from the Garden of the King. London?: 1898. V. 52
Olga Zanelli: a Tale of an Imperial City. London: 1890. V. 54

CARTWRIGHT, GEORGE
Captain Cartwright and His Labrador Journal. Boston: 1911. V. 53

CARTWRIGHT, GEORGE continued
A Journal of Transactions and Events, During a Residence of Nearly Sixteen Years on the Coast of Labrador... Newark: 1792. V. 48; 53; 54

CARTWRIGHT, JAMES J.
The Memoirs of Sir John Reresby of Thrybergh, Bart, M.P. for York, &c. 1634-1689. London: 1875. V. 53; 54

CARTWRIGHT, JOHN
Address to the Electors of Westminster... London: 1819. V. 49
An Appeal, on the subject of the English Constitution. Boston: 1797. V. 54
A Bill of Rights and Liberties; or, an Act for a Constitutional Reform of Parliament... London: 1817. V. 49
Give Us Our Rights!. London: 1782. V. 52
A Letter to Mr. Lambton...A Petition to the Commons, Maintaining that Ninety-Seven Lords Appear to Usurp Two Hundred Seats in the Commons House... London: 1820. V. 49
A Letter to the Freeholders of Lincolnshire, Written During the Late Contested Election for that County. Boston: 1807. V. 49
The People's Barrier Against Undue Influence and Corruption; or the Commons' House of Parliament According to the Constitution. London: 1780. V. 48; 49
Reasons for Reformation... London: 1809. V. 54
The State of the Nation; in a Series of Letters to His Grace the Duke of Bedford. Harlow: 1805. V. 47

CARTWRIGHT, ROBERT, MRS.
Ambrose the Sculptor: An Autobiography of Artist Life. London: 1854. V. 49

CARTWRIGHT, THOMAS
A Confutation of the Rhemists Translation, Glosses and Annotations on the New Testament. Leyden: 1618. V. 53; 54
In Librum Salomonis...Cum Metaphrasi, Homiliae (etc.). London: 1604. V. 49

CARTWRIGHT, W. C.
Gustave Bergenroth a memorial Sketch. Edinburgh: 1870. V. 49

CARTWRIGHT, WILLIAM
Comedies, Tragi-Comedies, with other Poems... London: 1651. V. 48; 50; 51
Rambles and Recollections of a Fly-Fisher. London: 1854. V. 53

CARTY, T. J.
A Dictionary of Literary Pseudonyms in the English Language. London: 1994. V. 52

CARUSO, ENRICO
Rare Art Treasures Collected by the Late Enrico Caruso, to be Sold at Unrestricted Public Sale, March 5, 6, 7, 8 at the American Art Galleries. New York: 1923. V. 49

CARUS WILSON, WILLIAM
The Children's Friend. Kirby Lonsdale: 1831-38. V. 52
The Friendly Visitor. 1847. V. 51
The Friendly Visitor. 1853. V. 51

CARUTHERS, ELI WASHINGTON
Interesting Revolutionary Incidents: and Sketches of Character, Chiefly in the "Old North State". Second Series. Philadelphia: 1856. V. 48

CARUTHERS, WILLIAM ALEXANDER
The Cavaliers Of Virginia, Or the Recluse of Jamestown. New York: 1834-35. V. 53; 54

CARVALHO, JORGE DE
Relacado Verdadeira dos Sucessos do Conde de Castel Melhor, Preso na Cidade de Cartagena de Indias, & Hoje Liure, por Particular Merce do Geo. & Favor del Rey Dom Ioao Iv Nosso Senhor, na Cidade de Lisboa. Lisbon: 1642. V. 53

CARVALHO, SOLOMON NUNES
Incidents of Travel and Adventure in the Far West... New York: 1857. V. 48; 53

CARVEL, J. L.
The Alloa Glass Work. London: 1953. V. 49

CARVER, GEORGE WASHINGTON
How to Make Sweet Potato Flour, Starch, Sugar Bread and Mock Coconut. Tuskegee: 1918. V. 53

CARVER, JONATHAN
Fires. Santa Barbara: 1983. V. 53
Three Years' Travels Throughout the Interior Parts of North America... Portsmouth: 1794. V. 47
Three Years' Travels Throughout the Interior Parts of North America... Walpole: 1813. V. 48
Travels through the Interior Parts of North America, in the Years 1766, 1767 and 1768. London: 1778. V. 50; 53

CARVER, NORMAN F.
Form and Space of Japanese Arachitecture. Tokyo: 1955. V. 51; 52

CARVER, RAYMOND
At Night the Salmon Move. Santa Barbara: 1976. V. 47; 51; 53; 54
Carnations. Vineburg: 1992. V. 52
Cathedral. New York: 1983. V. 47; 49; 51; 52; 53
Cathedral. New York: 1984. V. 51
Dostoevsky and King Dog. Santa Barbara: 1985. V. 51
Elephant... Fairfax: 1988. V. 53
Elephant. London: 1988. V. 53
Fires. Santa Barbara: 1983. V. 47; 49; 50; 54
Furious Seasons. Santa Barbara: 1977. V. 51; 52; 53
If It Pleases You. Northridge: 1984. V. 48; 52
In a Marine Light: Selected Poems. London: 1987. V. 50
Intimacy. Concord: 1987. V. 52
Music. Concord: 1985. V. 51; 52
My Father's Life. 1986. V. 47
My Father's Life. Derry & Ridgewood: 1986. V. 53; 54
Near Klamath. Sacramento: 1968. V. 52
A New Path to the Waterfall. New York: 1989. V. 48; 53
No Heroics, Please. New York: 1992. V. 47; 52
The Painter and the Fish. 1988. V. 50
The Pheasant. Worcester: 1982. V. 47; 54
Put Yourself In My Shoes. Santa Barbara: 1974. V. 48; 52; 54
The Stories of Raymond Carver. London: 1983. V. 53
The Stories of Raymond Carver. London: 1985. V. 50
This Water. Concord: 1985. V. 52; 53
This Water. Ewert: 1985. V. 50
The Toes. Ewert: 1988. V. 50
Two Poems. Salisbury: 1982. V. 52; 53; 54
Ultramarine. New York: 1986. V. 48; 52; 53
Vitamins. V. 51
What We Talk About When We Talk About Love. New York: 1981. V. 52; 53; 54
Where I'm Calling From. 1988. V. 47
Where I'm Calling From. Boston: 1988. V. 48
Where I'm Calling From. Franklin Center: 1988. V. 53
Where I'm Calling From. New York: 1988. V. 48; 50; 51; 52; 53
Where Water Comes Together with other Water. New York: 1985. V. 53
Will You Please Be Quiet, Please?. Santa Cruz: 1970. V. 51
Will You Please Be Quiet, Please?. New York: 1976. V. 48; 50; 51; 53; 54
Winter Insomnia. Santa Cruz: 1970. V. 48; 51; 53

CARWITHEN, I. B. S.
A View of the Brahminical Religion, In its Confirmation of the Truth of the Sacred History, and In Its Influence on the Moral Character... London: 1810. V. 52

CARY, ALICE
Hagar. A Story of To-Day. New York: 1852. V. 47
The Josephine Gallery. New York: 1859. V. 51
Poems. Boston: 1855. V. 49

CARY, HENRY FRANCIS
The Early French Poets, a Series of Notices and Translations. London: 1846. V. 51

CARY, JOHN
Cary's New and Correct English Atlas... London: 1787. V. 48; 49
Cary's New and Correct English Atlas... London: 1793. V. 48
A Discourse Concerning the Trade of Ireland and Scotland, as They Stand in Competition with the Trade of England, Being Taken Out of an Essay on Trade. Bristol: 1696. V. 54

CARY, JOYCE
The African Witch. London: 1936. V. 48; 50; 53
The African Witch. New York: 1936. V. 47; 48; 49; 53
Aissa Saved. New York: 1962. V. 48; 53
Art and Reality. Cambridge: 1957. V. 48
The Drunken Sailor. London: 1947. V. 48; 53
Except the Lord. New York: 1953. V. 48
Herself Surprised. New York: 1941. V. 48
The Horse's Mouth. New York: 1944. V. 48; 50; 53
The Horse's Mouth. London: 1957. V. 48
Illustrations by Joyce Cary for the Old Strife at Plant's. Oxford: 1956. V. 49
Not Honour More. London: 1955. V. 53
Power in Men. London: 1939. V. 48; 51
Spring Sowing and Other Stories. London: 1960. V. 48
To Be a Pilgrim. New York: 1942. V. 48

CARY, LORENE
Black Ice. New York: 1991. V. 49

CARY, MELBERT B.
A Bibliography of the Village Press, 1903-1938. New York: 1938. V. 53

CARY, R. MILTON
Skirmisher's Drill and Bayonet Exercise (As Now Used in the French Army). Richmond: 1861. V. 49

CARY, ROBERT
Palaeologia Chronica. London: 1677. V. 47; 52; 54

CARY, S. F.
The National Temperance Offering, and Sons and Daughters of Temperance Gift. New York: 1850. V. 50

CARY, VIRGINIA
Letters On Female Character, Addressed to a Young Lady on the Death of Her Mother. Richmond: 1828. V. 48; 50; 51; 53
Letters On Female Character, Addressed to a Young Lady On the Death of Her Mother. Richmond: 1830. V. 53

CARYLL, JOHN
Naboth's Vinyard; or, the Innocent Traytor: Copied from the Original of Holy Scripture in Heroic Verse. London: 1679. V. 47
Sir Salomon; or the Cautious Coxcomb; a Comedy. London: 1671. V. 52

CARY'S New Itinerary: or an Accurate Delineation of the Great Roads Both Direct and Cross throughout England and Wales... London: 1817. V. 54

CARYSFORT, WILLIAM, EARL OF
The Pageants of Richard Beauchamp Earl of Warwick. Oxford: 1908. V. 47

CASA, GIOVANNI DELLA
The Refin'd Courtier, or, a Correction of Several Indencencies Crept Into Civil Conversation. London: 1679. V. 52
Rime, et Prose. Fiorenza: 1564. V. 52; 53

CASADO, S.
The Last Days of Madrid. The End of the Second Spanish Republic. London: 1939. V. 49

CASALIS, EUGENE
The Basutos; or, Twenty-Three Years in South Africa. London: 1861. V. 50; 52

CASANOVA DE SEINGALT, GIOVANNI GIACOMO
History of My Life. London: 1967. V. 51
Memoires. Paris: 1924-35. V. 50
The Memoirs. London. V. 47; 48
The Memoirs. 1894. V. 54
The Memoirs. London: 1929. V. 51
Memoirs. Edinburgh: 1940. V. 53; 54
The Memoirs. New York & London: 1940's?. V. 48
The Memoirs of... Haarlem: 1972. V. 53

CASANOVA DE SEINGALT, GIOVNNI GIACOMO
The Memoirs. 1940. V. 52

CASAS, BARTOLOME DE LAS, BP. OF CHIAPA
The Log of Christopher Columbus' First Voyage to America in the Year 1492. New York: 1938. V. 51

CASATI, GAETANO
Ten Years in Equatoria and the Return with Emin Pasha. London: 1891. V. 47; 51; 53; 54

CASAUBON, MERIC
A Treatise Concerning Enthusiasm, as...an Effect of Nature; But...Mistaken...for Either Divine Inspiration or Diabolicall Possession. London: 1656. V. 49

CASCOYNE, CRISP
An Address to the Liverymen of the City of Lodon, from Sir Crisp Cascoyne, Knt. Late Lord Mayor, Relative to His Conduct in the Cases of Elizabeth Canning and Mary Squires. London: 1754. V. 52

CASE, ARTHUR E.
A Bibliography of English Poetical Miscellanies 1521-1750. London: 1935. V. 48; 51
A Bibliography of English Poetical Miscellanies 1521-1750. Oxford: 1935. V. 50

THE CASE Between the Lord Maryor and Commons of London Concerning the Election of Sheriffs for the Year Ensuing, Clearly Stated. London: 1682. V. 52

CASE, DAVID
The Cell. Three Tales of Horror. 1969. V. 51

CASE, NELSON
History of Labette County, Kansas. Topeka: 1893. V. 47

THE CASE of Leon Trotsky. London: 1937. V. 51

THE CASE of Mr. Benjamin Leech Bricklayer, a the Old Baily, the Fourteenth Day of Oct. 1682. London: 1682. V. 52; 53

THE CASE of Mrs. Mary Catharine Cadiere, Against the Jesuit Father John Baptist Girard... London: 1732. V. 48

THE CASE of Sir Thomas Pilkington, Ktd. (Now Lord Mayor of London), Sir Thomas Player, Kt. Deceased; Slingsby Bathell, Esq; Henry Cornish, Esq; Deceas'd; Samuel Shute, Esq; Deceas'd; Samuel Swynock, John Deagle, Francis Jenks, deceas'd; Richard Freeman, ... London: 1689. V. 47

THE CASE of the British and Irish Manufacture of Linen, Threads and Tapes, Fairly Stated; In Answer to the Impartial Considerer. N.P: 1738. V. 52

THE CASE of the Earl of Stamford, Relating to the Wood Lately Cut in Enfeild-Chace (sic). London: 1701. V. 50

THE CASE of the Hertfordshire Witchcraft Consider'd. Being an Examination of a Book Entitl'd, A Full and Impartial Account of the Discovery of Sorcery & Witchcraft Practis'd by Jane Wenham of Walkern, Upon the Bodies of Anne Thorne, Anne Street, &c. London: 1712. V. 48

THE CASE of the Journeymen Taylors by the Bill Now Depending in the Right Honourable the House of Peers. N.P: 1721?. V. 50

THE CASE Of the Lord Mayor and Aldermen of London, Upon the Petition of some of the Common Council Men, Presented to the Honourable House of Commons, with His Lordships and the Aldermens Answer to the Charge Exhibited... London: 1690. V. 52

THE CASE of the Noblemen, Gentlemen and Others, Having Right of Common in the New Forest.... London?: 1720-40. V. 47

THE CASE of the Planters of Tobacco in Virginia... London: 1733. V. 48; 51; 52

THE CASE of the United States, to be Laid Before the Tribunal of Arbitration, to be Convened at Geneva (etc.). Washington: 1871. V. 48

CASELIUS, JOHANNES
Ludo Litterario Recte Aperiendo, Liber. 1619. V. 47

CASEMENT, DAN
Random Recollections. Kansas City: 1955. V. 50; 53

CASEY, E.
Judgments of the Court of Criminal Appeal. Dublin: 1984-89. V. 49

CASEY, JOHN
An American Romance. New York: 1977. V. 49

CASEY, R.
The Ammonidea of the Lower Greensand. London: 1960-80. V. 47; 49; 51; 53; 54

CASEY, SILAS
Infantry Tactics. New York: 1862. V. 47; 49

CASH, J.
The British Freshwater Rhizopoda and Heliozoa. London: 1905-19. V. 52
British Freshwater Rhizopoda and Heliozoa. London: 1905-21. V. 49

CASH, THOMAS M.
A Plain Statement of Facts for the Perusal of Those Interested. New York: 1872. V. 48

CASH, W. J.
The Mind of the South. New York: 1941. V. 48; 52; 53

CASHIN, HERSCHEL V.
Under Fire with the Tenth U.S. Cavalry. Chicago: 1902. V. 48; 49

CASIGLIONI, ARTURO
A History of Medicine. New York: 1947. V. 52

CASKEY, L. D.
Attic Vase Paintings in the Museum of Fine Arts, Boston. Boston: 1931-63. V. 50; 52
Catalogue of Greek and Roman Sculpture. Cambridge: 1925. V. 50

CASLER, JOHN O.
Four Years in the Stonewall Brigade. Guthrie: 1893. V. 49

CASLON, H. W., & CO., LTD.
Specimens of Printing Types and Illustrated Catalogue of Printing Materials. 1905? or 1906?. V. 47
Specimens of Types and Borders and Illustrated Catalogue of Printer's Joinery and Materials. 1911. V. 47

CASLON. Poetry of Nature, Comprising a Selection of the Most Sublime and Beautiful Apostrophes, Histories, Songs, Elegies &c from the Works of the Caledonian Bards, the Typographical Execution in a Style Entirley New and Decorated with.... London: 1789. V. 48

CASLON, WILLIAM
Letter Founder to His Majesty. London: 1786. V. 51
A Specimen of Printing Types, by William Caslon, Letter Founder to His Majesty. London: 1785. V. 47; 48; 53
A Specimen of Printing Types by Wm. Caslon, Letter Founder to the King. (with) A Specimen of Cast Ornaments by Wm. Caslon. London: 1796/95. V. 47

CASO, ALFONSO
Interpretation of the Codex Bodley 2858. Mexico City: 1960. V. 51

CASPAR, WHITNEY
Musk-ox, Bison, Sheep and Goat. New York: 1904. V. 48

CASPER, JOHANN LUDWIG
A Handbook of Forensic Medicine, Based Upon Personal Experience... London: 1861. V. 48; 52
A Handbook of the Practice of Forensic Medicine, Based Upon Personal Experience. London: 1861-65. V. 48; 49

CASS, LEWIS
France, Its King, Court and Government. New York: 1840. V. 54
Treatment of the Indians by the United States and Great Britain. Boston: 1827. V. 54

CASSELBERRY, EVANS
A Discovery in the Science of Electricity. St. Louis: 1873. V. 51

CASSELL'S Gazetteer of Great Britain and Ireland; a Complete Topographical Dictionary of the United Kingdom. London: 1894-98. V. 53

CASSELL'S Gazetteer of Great Britain and Ireland, Being a Complete Topographical Dictionary of the United Kingdom. London: 1893. V. 48

CASSELL'S History of the War Between France and Germany 1870-1871. London: 1871-72. V. 50

CASSELL'S Household Guide to Every Department of Practical Life... London Paris & New York: 1877-78. V. 49

CASSELL'S Household Guide to Every Department of Practical Life... London: 1880. V. 49

CASSELL'S Illustrated History of England. London: 1875-85. V. 47

CASSERIO, GUILO
De Vocis Auditusque Organis Historia Anatomica singulari Fide methodo ac Industria Concinnata Tractatibus Duobus Explicat ac Varis Iconibus Aere Excusis Illustrata. Ferrariae: 1600-01. V. 53

CASSERIUS
Tabulae Anatomicae & De Formato Poetu Tabulae. New York: 1970. V. 54

CASSIN, JOHN
Illustrations of the Birds of California, Texas, Oregon, British and Russian America. Philadelphia: 1856. V. 50
Illustrations of the Birds of California, Texas, Oregon, British and Russian America. Philadelphia: 1865. V. 48

CASSINI, JACQUES
Tables Astronomiques de Soleil, de la Lune, des Planetes, des etoiles Fixes, et des Dstellites de Jupiter et de Saturne... Paris: 1740. V. 47

CASSINO, SAMUEL
The Naturalist's Directory 1884. Boston: 1884. V. 50; 52

CASSIODORUS, FLAVIUS MAGNUS AURELIUS
Psalterii Davidici Expositio. Paris: 1519. V. 48

CASSLER, LA FAYETTE
Thrilling Experiences of Frontier Life in the Early Days of Western Oklahoma. Cincinnati: 1910. V. 49

CASSON, A. J.
My Favourite Watercolours 1919 to 1957. 1982. V. 53

CASSON, HUGH
The Sketch Book. 1975. V. 54
The Sketch Book. London: 1975. V. 53

CASSON, S.
Sculpture Of To-day. London: 1939. V. 50; 51

CASSON, STANLEY
Macedonia, Thrace and Illyria: Their Relations to Greece from the Earliest Times Down to the Time of Philip, Son of Amyntas. Oxford: 1926. V. 52

CASSOU, JEAN
Antoni Clave. Greenwich: 1960. V. 50
The Sources of Modern Art. London: 1962. V. 49

CASTANAEUS, HENRICUS LODOVICUS
Celebriorum Distinctionum Philosophicarum Synopsis. Oxoniae: 1657. V. 53

CASTANEDA, CARLOS E.
The Mexican Side of the Texas Revolution. Dallas: 1928. V. 47
Our Catholic Heritage in Texas. New York. V. 50
Our Catholic Heritage in Texas... Austin: 1936. V. 50
Our Catholic Heritage in Texas... Austin: 1936/38/39/42. V. 48
The Teachings of Don Juan. Berkeley & Los Angeles: 1968. V. 51

CASTANEDA, PEDRO DE
The Journey of Francisco Vazquez de Coronado 1540-1542... San Francisco: 1933. V. 54

CASTEL, LOUIS BERTRAND
Le Vrai Systeme de Physique Generale de M. Isaac Newton, Expose et Analyse en Parallele avec Celui de Descartes... Paris: 1743. V. 47

CASTELFRANCO, GIORGIO
Donatello. London: 1963. V. 51

CASTELL, EDMUND
Lexicon Heptaglotton, Hebraicum, Chaldaicum, Syriacum, Samaritanum, Aethiopicum, Arabicum, Conjunctim... London: 1686. V. 47

CASTELL, ROBERT
The Villas of the Ancients Illustrated. London: 1728. V. 50

CASTELLI, BARTOLOMMEO
Lexicon Medicum, Primum a Bartholomaeo Castello Messanensi Inchoatum... Norimbergae: 1688. V. 47

CASTELLI, BENEDETTO
Della Misura dell' Acque Correnti. Rome: 1628. V. 49
Delle Misure dell'Acque Correnti. Rome: 1639. V. 54

CASTENEDA, C. E.
A Report of the Spanish Archives in San Antonio. (Texas). San Antonio: 1937. V. 52

CASTENS, EDWARD H.
The Story of the 446th Bomb Group (8th A.F.). San Angelo: 1945?. V. 47

CASTERA, JEAN HENRI
History of Catherine II, Emperress of Russia. London: 1800. V. 52

CASTIANI, ESTELLA
Piedmont. London: 1913. V. 47

CASTIGATOR, JOHN, PSEUD.
It Is! It Can! It Shall be No Mistake!!. London: 1828. V. 47

CASTIGLIONE, BALDASSARE
Baltasaris Castilionis Comitis de Curiali Sive Aulico... Londini: 1593. V. 49
Il Cortegiano. Lyons: 1553. V. 52
Il Cortegiano... London: 1727. V. 47; 48; 51
Il Cortegiano... London: 1737. V. 54
The Courtier... London: 1724. V. 49
The Courtyer... London: 1900. V. 47; 48
Libri IV De Curali sive Aulico ex Italico Sermone in Latinum Conversi. Cambridge: 1713. V. 47
Il Libro del Cortegiano. Venice: 1528. V. 54
Il Libro del Cortegiano. 1530. V. 47
Il Libro del Cortegiano. 1532. V. 50; 53
Il Libro Del Cortegiano... Venice: 1538. V. 51
Le Parfait Covrtisan. Lyons: 1579. V. 48; 52
Les Quatre Livres du Courtisan du Conte Baltazar de Castillon. 1537. V. 52

CASTIGLIONE, SABBA DA
Ricordi Overo Ammaestramenti... Milan: 1561. V. 51

CASTIGLIONI, ARTURO
A History of Medicine. New York: 1941. V. 49; 50; 51; 53; 54
A History of Medicine. New York: 1947. V. 52; 54

CASTILLO SOLORZANO, ALONSO DEL
The Spanish Pole-Cat; or the Adventures of Seniora Rufina in Four Books. London: 1717. V. 47

CASTLE, EGERTON
English Book Plates. London: 1892. V. 47
English Book Plates. London: 1894. V. 48

CASTLE, FREDERICK A.
Wood's Household Practice of Medicine, Hugiene and Surgery. New York: 1880-81. V. 51

THE CASTLE Howell School Record, Comprising a List of Pupils from the Beginning, Papers on the Origin, Name and Changes by Principals and Miscellaneous Articles Contributed by Old Boys. Lancaster: 1888. V. 53

CASTLE, THOMAS
An Essay on Animal, Mineral and Vegetable Poisons. London: 1822. V. 54
An Introduction to Medical Botany. London: 1829. V. 54
An Introduction to Systematical and Physiological Botany. London: 1829. V. 54

CASTLEDEN, GEORGE
Conscience: an Essay in Blank Verse... London: 1842. V. 51

CASTLEREAGH, FREDERICK, VISCOUNT
A Journey to Damascus through Egypt Nubia, Arabia Petraea, Palestine and Syria. London: 1847. V. 47; 49

CASTLEREAGH, ROBERT STEWART, VISCOUNT
Memoirs and Correspondence. London: 1848-49. V. 53

CASTRO, C.
Mexico y sus Alrededores. Mexico: 1855-56. V. 47

CASTRO, JUAN JOSE
Treatise on the South American Railways and the Great International Lines. Montevideo: 1893. V. 51

CASTRO, LORENZO
The Republic of Mexico in 1882. New York: 1882. V. 53

CASTRO, NUNO DE
Chinese Porcelain and the Heraldry of the Empire. Porto: 1988. V. 47; 50

CASTRO, RODRIGO DE
De Universa Mulierum Medicina... Hamburg: 1603-04. V. 47

CASTRO ALVES, ANTONIO DE
A Cachoeira de Paulo-Affonso. Poema Original Brazileiro. Fragmento dos Escravos, sob o Titulo de Manuscriptos de Stenio. Bahia: 1876. V. 50

CASTRO ZAMORENSE, ALFONSO DE
...Adversus Omnes Haereses, Libri. XIIII. Opus Hoc Nunc Postremo ab Autore Recognitum Est... Antwerp. V. 48

CASWALL, EDWARD
Sketches of Young Ladies. London: 1837. V. 49

A CATAECHISM of American Law. Philadelphia: 1852. V. 52

CATALAN Art from the Ninth to the Fifteenth Centuries. London: 1937. V. 47

CATALINA: California's Magic Isle. 1926. V. 54

CATALOGUE des Livres Imprimes sur Velin de la Bibliotheque du Roi. New York: 1965. V. 50

CATALOGUE of Five Hundred Celebrated Authors of Great Britain, Now Living... London: 1788. V. 51

A CATALOGUE Of Friends Books; Written by Many of the People Called Quakers. London: 1708. V. 49

A CATALOGUE of Shakespeareiana With a Prefatory Essay by Sidney Lee. London: 1899. V. 49

CATALOGUE of Some Five Hundred Examples of the Printing of Edwin and Robert Grabhorn 1917-1960 Two Gentlemen from Indiana Now Resident in California, Offered for Sale at the Book Shop of David Magee. San Francisco. V. 53

CATALOGUE of the Anglo-Jewish Historical Exhibition, Royal Hall. London: 1887. V. 50

A CATALOGUE of the Baronets of This Kingdom of England. London: 1667. V. 48; 49

CATALOGUE of the Chapel Library, Little Portland Street. London: 1880. V. 47

A CATALOGUE of the Contents of the Library of the Incorporated Law Society of Liverpool. 1892. V. 51

A CATALOGUE of the Exhibition of Rare and Valuable Books Relating to the Early Catholic Missionary Work in Japan. Tokyo & Osaka: 1932. V. 48

A CATALOGUE of the Five Conquerors of This Island and Theire Armes...Viz. the Britaynes the Romanes, the Saxons ye Danes & Lastly the Normans and of Theire Succession. (with) A Catalogue of the Armes Belonging to England, With the Causes of Alteracon... England: 1606. V. 49

CATALOGUE of the Goldsmiths' Library of Economic Literature. Printed Books to 1850. Cambridge: 1970. V. 47

A CATALOGUE of the Large and Valuable Freehold Estate of the Most Nob William, Duke of Powis, Deceased, Situated in the County of Northampton... 1758. V. 53

A CATALOGUE of the Library at Knowsley Hall, Lancashire. London: 1893. V. 52

A CATALOGUE of the Lords, Knights and Gentlemen That Have Compounded for Their Estates. London: 1655. V. 53

A CATALOGUE of the Most Eminently Venerable Relics of the Roman Catholic Church; Collected by the Pious Care of Their Holiness the Popes, the Most August Emperors, Kings, Princes and Prelates of the Christian World, Which are to be Disposed... London: 1818. V. 49

A CATALOGUE of the Mount Bellew Library. Dublin: 1814. V. 54

CATALOGUE of the names of the Lords That Subscribed to Levie Horse to Assist His Majestie in Defence of His Royall Person, the Two Houses of Parliament, and the Protestant Religion. Yorke: 1642. V. 47

Catalogue of the Printed Books and Manuscripts in the John Rylands Library, Manchester. Manchester: 1899. V. 53

A CATALOGUE of the Valuable Library of Books, in Excellent Condition and Handsomely Bound: Which Will be sold by Auction, by Mr. J. P. Bradford, at the Large Room, at the King's Arms Inn, Leonminster on Wednesday the 2nd of April 1845. Leonminster: 1845. V. 49

CATALONIA, a Poem; With Notes Illustrative of the Present State of Affairs in the Peninsula. Edinburgh: 1811. V. 49

CATE, WIRT ARMISTEAD
Lucius Q. C. Lamar Secession and Reunion. Chapel Hill: 1935. V. 51; 52; 54

CATES, CLIFF
Pioneer History of Wise County. Decatur: 1907. V. 53

CATESBY, MARK
The Natural History of Carolina, Florida and the Bahama Islands. Savannah: 1974. V. 47; 50; 51; 52; 53

CATHARINAE Mediceae Reginae Matris, Vitae, Actorum & Consiliorum...Enarratio. Geneva: 1575. V. 49

CATHCART, GEORGE
Correspondence of Lieut.-General the Hon. Sir George Cathcart, K.C.B. Relative to His Military Operations in Kaffraria... London: 1857. V. 49

CATHCART, JOHN
A Letter to the Honorable Edward Vernon Esq.; Vice Admiral of the Red, &c. from John Cathcart, Director of the Hospital in the Late Expedition to the West-Indies... London: 1744. V. 48

CATHCART, WILLIAM
The Ancient British and Irish Churches... Philadelphia: 1894. V. 51; 54

CATHER, WILLA SIBERT
Alexander's Bridge. Boston & New York: 1912. V. 47; 50; 53; 54
April Twilights. Boston: 1903. V. 47; 49; 51; 53; 54
April Twilights. New York: 1923. V. 47; 49; 51
Death Comes for the Archbishop. New York: 1927. V. 47; 49; 51; 52; 53; 54
Death Comes for the Archbishop. New York: 1929. V. 54
December Night. New York: 1933. V. 50; 53
Father Junipero's Holy Family. Lexington: 1956. V. 48
A Lost Lady. New York: 1923. V. 47; 49; 50; 51; 53; 54
A Lost Lady. New York: 1983. V. 47; 48; 51
Lucy Gayheart. New York: 1935. V. 47; 49; 50; 51; 53; 54
My Antonia. Boston: 1918. V. 47; 49; 51
My Mortal Enemy. New York: 1926. V. 47; 48; 49; 50; 51; 52; 53
Not Under Forty. New York: 1936. V. 49; 51
The Novels and Stories of Willa Cather. Boston: 1937-41. V. 47
O Pioneers. Boston, New York: 1913. V. 48; 49; 52
O Pioneers!. Boston: 1937. V. 47
Obscure Destinies. New York: 1932. V. 48; 49; 50; 51; 53
The Old Beauty and Others. New York: 1948. V. 47; 52
One of Ours. New York: 1922. V. 49
The Professor's House. New York: 1925. V. 47; 49; 50; 51; 52; 53
Sapphira and the Slave Girl. New York: 1940. V. 47; 48; 49; 50; 51; 52
Shadows on the Rock. New York: 1926. V. 48
Shadows on the Rock. New York: 1931. V. 47; 49; 50; 51; 53; 54
The Song of the Lark. Boston: 1915. V. 50
The Troll Garden. 1905. V. 50
The Troll Garden. New York: 1905. V. 49
Youth and the Bright Medusa. New York: 1920. V. 47; 51

CATHERINE OF SIENA, SAINT
Dialogo de la Seraphica Vergine... Venice: 1517. V. 52

CATHERINE THE GREAT, EMPRESS OF RUSSIA
Memoirs of the Empress Catherine II, Written by Herself. London: 1859. V. 51

CATHERWOOD, FREDERICK
Incidents of Travel in Central America, Chiapas and Yucatan. London: 1854. V. 51
Views of Ancient Monuments in Cental America, Chiapas and Yucatan. Barre: 1965. V. 50
Views of Ancient Monuments in Central America, Chiapas and Yucatan. London: 1844. V. 48

CATHERWOOD, JOHN
A New Method of Curing the Apoplexy. London: 1715. V. 49; 50; 51; 52; 53

CATHERWOOD, MARY HARTWELL
Lazarre. Indianapolis: 1901. V. 50

CATHOLIC CHURCH
Regvlae Constitutiones et Reseruationes Sanctissimi Dni, Nostri Dni, Leonis Pape Decimi... Rome: 1513. V. 48

CATHOLIC CHURCH.
Rituum Ecclesiasticorum sive Sacrarum Ceremoniarum. S. S. Romanae Ecclesiae. Libri Tres non Ante Impressi. Venice: 1516. V. 47

CATHOLIC CHURCH. COUNCILS
Conciliorum Quatuor Generalium Niceni, Constantinopolitani, Ephesini & Calcedonensis. Paris: 1535. V. 52

CATHOLIC CHURCH. LITURGY & RITUAL
Missae Episcopales Pro Sacris Ordinibus Conferendis Secundum Ritu(m) Sacrosancte Romane Ecclesie...Breve Compendium Diversorum Casuum... Venetiis: 1563. V. 49

CATHOLIC CHURCH. LITURGY & RITUAL. BREVIARY
Breviarium Romanum Ex Decreto Sacrosancti Concilij Tridentini Restitutm, Pii V. Pont. Max. Iussu Editum, et Clementis VIII... Antverpiae: 1628. V. 48
Diurnal du Breviarie Romain. Lyon: 1740. V. 52

CATHOLIC CHURCH. LITURGY & RITUAL. HOURS
Ces P(re)sentes Heures a Lusaige de (Poitiers). 1502. V. 47; 51
Ces Presentes Heures a Lusaige de Rome. Paris: 1520. V. 47
A Child's Book of Hours. London: 1921. V. 51
Les Heures a L'Usaige de Romme. Paris: 1508. V. 47; 51
Heures de Nostre Dame a l'Usage de Rome, en Latin et en Francois. Paris: 1582. V. 50
Heures du Moyen Age. Paris: 1862. V. 50
Horae Beatae Virginis Mariae Juxta Ritum Sacri Originis Praedicatorum Jussu Editae. 1923. V. 52
Horae Beate Virginis Marie Secundum Usum Romanum. Paris: 1516. V. 49; 51
Horae Beatissime Virginis Marie ad Legitimu Sarisburiensis Ecclesie Ritum. Paris: 1535. V. 51
Horae B.M.V. Horae in Laudem Beatissime Virginis Marie, ad Usum Romanum. Paris: 1546. V. 50
Horae B.M.V. Hore Diue V(ir)ginis Marie Scd'm Vsum Romanu. Paris: 1505. V. 47; 50
Horae B.V.M. as Usum Romanum cum Calendario. Paris: 1520. V. 50
Horae Diue Virginis Marie Secundum Vxum Romanum... Paris: 1511. V. 50
Horae Dive Virginis Marie, Secundum Usum Romanum. Paris: 1514. V. 52
Le Livre De Heures de La Riene Anne De Bratagne. Paris: 1860. V. 50
Livre d'Heures. Satirique et Libertin du XIXme Siecle. Brussels: 1890. V. 47
The Madresfield Hours. A Fourteenth Century Manuscript In the Library of the Early Beauchamp. Oxford: 1975. V. 47; 48; 54
Officium Beatae Mariae Virginis. Paris: 1616. V. 51; 54
The Sobieski Hours. 1977. V. 47
Use of Rome (Hore Intemerate Dive Virginis Marie, Secundum Usum Ecclesie Romane). Paris: 1503. V. 50
The Visconti Hours. London: 1973. V. 50

CATHOLIC CHURCH. LITURGY & RITUAL. MISSAL
Canon Missae ad Usum Episcoporum, ac Praelatorum Solemniter, Vel Private Celebrantium. Venetiis: 1784. V. 50
Missae in Agenda Defunctorum... Venice: 1736. V. 50
Missale ad Usum Insignis ac Famose Ecclesie Saru. Paris: 1503. V. 52
Missale Magdeburgense. Magdeburg: 1480. V. 50
Missale Romanum. Venice: 1763. V. 52
Missale Romanum ex Decreto... Antverpiae: 1655. V. 48; 51
Missale Romanum ex Decreto Sacrosancti Concilii Tridentini Restitutum... Venice: 1766. V. 52; 54
Missale Secundum Morem Sancte Romane Ecclesie. Venice: 1490 (1493-98). V. 52

CATHOLIC CHURCH. LITURGY & RITUAL. OFFICE
Office de la Semaine. Paris: 1683. V. 47
L'Officio di Maria Vergine. Vienna: 1672. V. 52; 54
Officium B. Mariae Virginis. Brescia: 1583. V. 52
Officium B. Mariae Virginis, Nuper Reformatum... Antwerp: 1731. V. 52; 54

CATHOLIC CHURCH. LITURGY & RITUAL. PONTIFICAL
Pontificale Romanum Clementis VIII. Primum; Nunc Denuo Urbani VIII. Parisiis: 1664. V. 50

CATHOLIC Encyclopedia. New York: 1907-14. V. 51

THE CATHOLIC Religion Vindicated. Being an Answer to a Sermon Preached by the Rev. Mr. Cuyler, in Poughkeepsie, on the 30th day of July 1812, the Day Set Apart for Fasting and Prayer in the State of New York... 1813. V. 52

CATHRALL, WILLIAM
The History of Oswestry, Comprising British, Saxon, Norman and English Eras... Oswestry: 1855. V. 54

CATICH, EDWARD M.
Letters Redrawn from the Trajan Inscription in Rome. Davenport: 1961. V. 48; 53
The Origin of the Serif. Brush Writing and Roman Letters. Iowa: 1968. V. 47

CATLIN, GEORGE
The Breath of Life or Mal-Respiration and Its Effects Upon the Enjoyments and Life of Man. London: 1864. V. 53
Catlin's Notes of Eight Years' Travels and Residence in Europe, With His North American Indian Collection. New York: 1848. V. 47
Drawings of the North American Indians. Garden City: 1984. V. 51; 53
Drawings of the North American Indians. New York: 1984. V. 50
Episodes from Life Among the Indians and Last Rambles. Norman: 1959. V. 54
Illustrations of the Manners, Customs and Condition of the North American Indians... London: 1845. V. 47; 51
Illustrations of the Manners, Customs and Condition of the North American Indians. London: 1851. V. 51
Illustrations of the Manners, Customs and Condition of the North American Indians... London: 1866. V. 49; 50; 51
Letters and Notes on the Manners, Customs and Condition of the North American Indians. London: 1841. V. 47; 48; 53

CATLIN, GEORGE continued
Letters and Notes on the Manners, Customs and Conditions of the North American Indian. New York: 1841. V. 54
Letters and Notes on the Manners, Customs and Conventions of the North American Indians... Philadelphia: 1857. V. 51
North American Indian Portfolio. Chicago: 1970. V. 48; 51; 53
North American Indians. Edinburgh: 1903. V. 49; 52; 53
The North American Indians. Philadelphia: 1913. V. 48; 51
North American Indians. Edinburgh: 1926. V. 47; 49; 50; 54
North American Indians... Edinburgh: 1927. V. 54
Rambles Among the Indians of the Rocky Mountains and the Andes. London: 1895. V. 50
Shut Your Mouth. New York: 1865. V. 49

CATLING, D.
Rice in Deep Water. London: 1992. V. 49

CATLOW, AGNES
Popular Conchology; or the Shell Cabinet Arranged... London: 1843. V. 54
Popular Field Botany. London: 1848. V. 54
Sketching Rambles; or, Nature in the Alps and Apennines. London: 1861. V. 49; 52
Sketching Rambles; or, Nature in the Alps and Apennines. London: 1862. V. 53

CATLOW, E. M.
Popular Geography of Plants, a Botanical Excursion Round the World. London: 1855. V. 53

CATLOW, JOSEPH PEEL
On the Principles of Aesthetic Medicine, or the Natural Use of Sensation and Desire in the Maintenance of Health and Treatment of Disease, as Demonstrated by Induction from the Common Facts of Life. London: 1867. V. 54

CATO: Or, *Interesting Adventures of A Dog: Interspersed with Real Anecdotes.* London. V. 49

CATON, JOHN D.
The Last of the Illinois and a Sketch of the Pottawatomies. Chicago: 1870. V. 53

CATON, JOHN DEAN
Early Bench and Bar of Illinois. Chicago: 1893. V. 48

CATON-THOMPSON, G.
Kharga Oasis in Prehistory. London: 1952. V. 49; 51

CATS & *Landladies' Husbands: T. E. Lawrence in Bridlington.* Denby Dale: 1995. V. 54

CATS, JACOB
Alle de Wercken. Amsterdam: 1659-59. V. 53
Silenus Alcibiadis, Sive Proteus: Humanae Vitae Ideam, Emblemate Trifarium Variato. Amsterdam. V. 50
Spiegel van den Ouden ende Nieuvven Tijdt. 1632. V. 49

CATTAN, CHRISTOPHER DE
The Geomancie of Maister Christopher Cattan Gentleman. London: 1591. V. 52; 54

CATTERMOLE, RICHARD
The Great Civil War of Charles I and His Parliament. London: 1845. V. 52
The Great Civil War of the Times of Charles I and Cromwell. London: 1852. V. 51

THE CATTLE Industry and the Cattlemen of Texas. New York: 1959. V. 50

CATTON, CHARLES
Thirty-Six Animals, Drawn from Nature and Engraved in Aqua-Tint. New Haven: 1825. V. 48

CATULLUS, C. VALERIUS
The Carmina... London: 1894. V. 51; 52; 53
Catulii, Tibulii, et Propertii. Birmingham: 1772. V. 47; 48; 49; 50; 51; 52; 54
Catulli, Tibulli, Propertii, Nova Editio... Paris: 1577. V. 51
Catulli, Tibulli, Propertii, Nova Editio. Antwerp: 1582. V. 47
Catullus, Tibullus et Propertius. (Works). Londini: 1824. V. 51
Catullus, Tibullus, Propertius. Venice: 1502. V. 51
Catullus, Tibullus, Propertius. Venice: 1515. V. 51
Catvllvs Cvm Commentario Achillis Statii Lvsitani. Venice: 1566. V. 47
The Complete Poetry... London: 1929. V. 48; 51; 54
Et in Eum Commentarius M. Antonii Mureti. Venice: 1554. V. 51
Opera. Birminghamiae: 1772. V. 47; 48; 49
(Opera). Caius Valerius Catullus et in Eum Isaaci Vossi Observationes. 1684. V. 52
The Poems. Omaha: 1978. V. 51

CATUREGLI, PIETRO
Ephemerides Motuum Caelestium ex Anno 1833 ad Annum 1836 Quas ad Meridianum Bononiae Supputavit... Bologna: 1832. V. 53

CAUCHON, JOSEPH
The Union of the Provinces of British North America. Quebec: 1865. V. 47

CAUCHY, AUGUSTIN-LOUIS
Memoire sur les Integrales Definies, Prises Entre des Limites Imaginaires. Paris: 1825. V. 47

CAUDLE, PHOEBE, PSEUD.
The Precious Secret of Taming Husbands, Discovered and Practised with the Most Perfect Success... London: 1858. V. 50

CAUDWELL, CHRISTOPHER
Illusion and Reality - a Study of the Sources of Poetry. London: 1937. V. 48
The Six Queer Things. London: 1937. V. 50
Studies in a Dying Culture. London: 1938. V. 50

CAULFIELD, A. ST. G.
The Temple of the Kings at Abydos (Sety I). London: 1902. V. 49; 51

CAULFIELD, JAMES
Calcographiana: The Printsellers Chronicle and Collectors Guide to the Knowledge and Value of Engraved British Portraits. London: 1814. V. 48; 49
Cromwelliana. A Chronological Detail of Events in Which Oliver Cromwell was Engaged; from the Year 1642 to His Death in 1658: with a Continuation of Other Transactions to the Restoration. Westminster: 1810. V. 51
The High Court of Justice... London: 1820,. V. 54
Memoirs of the Celebrated Persons Composing the Kit-Cat Club... London: 1821. V. 49
Portraits, Memoirs and Characters of Remarbkle Persons, from the Revolution in 1688 to the End of the Reign of George II. London: 1819-20. V. 47
The Reply of the Rev. Doctor Caulfield...and of the Roman Catholic Clergy of Wexford, to the Misrepresentations of Sir Richard Musgrave Bart. Dublin: 1801. V. 49

CAUNTER, HOBART
The Oriental Album, Lives of the Moghul Emperors. London: 1837. V. 52

CAUS, SALOMON DE
Les Raisons de Forces Mouvantes avec Diverses Machines Tant Utiles que Plaisantes. Frankfurt am Main: 1615. V. 49; 53

THE CAUSE Of the Riots in the Yangtse Valley. Hankow: 1891. V. 49

CAUSEY, ANDREW
Edward Burra. Complete Catalog. London: 1985. V. 49; 51; 53
Paul Nash. Oxford: 1980. V. 49; 53
Peter Lanyon, His Painting. England: 1971. V. 49

CAUSLEY, CHARLES
Timothy Winters. London: 1970. V. 53
Twenty-One Poems. London: 1986. V. 47
Underneath the War. Bow, near Crediton, Devon: 1969. V. 53

CAUSSIN, NICOLAS
The Christian Diurnal. London: 1686. V. 51
Entertainments for Lent, Written in French. Liverpool: 1755. V. 51
The Holy Court in Five Tomes... London: 1663. V. 47; 54
The Unfortunate Politique. Oxford: 1638. V. 51

A CAUTION Against Deceivers, with Respect to the Subordination of the Son of God; and a Defence of Several Eminent Divines. Exeter: 1719. V. 52

CAUTY, WILLIAM
Natura, Philosophia, & Ars in Concordia. London: 1772. V. 47; 48

CAUVET, GILLES PAUL
Receuil d'Ornemens a l'Usage des Jeunes Artistes qui se Destinent a la Decoration des BAtimens. Parls: 1777. V. 47; 53

CAUX, J. W. DE
The Herring and the Herring Fishery, with Chapters on Fishes and Fishing and Our Sea Fisheries in the Future. London: 1881. V. 52

CAVAFY, C. P.
Fourteen Poems By... London: 1966. V. 52
Three Poems of Cavafy. 1980. V. 49; 52
Three Poems of Cavafy. London: 1980. V. 53

CAVALCANTI, BARTOLOMEO
La Rhetorica di...in Questa Seconda Editione... Vinegia: 1559. V. 49

CAVALCANTI, GUIDO
Le Rime: Ballate, Sonetti, Canzoni. 1966. V. 52; 54
Sonnets and Ballate of Guido Cavalcante. London: 1912. V. 50
Thirty-Three Sonnets of Guido Cavalcanti. San Francisco: 1991. V. 51; 53

CAVALERIO, BONAVENTURA
Geometria Indivisiblibus Continuorum Nova Quadam Ratione Promota. Bologna: 1653. V. 50
Trigonometria Plana, et Sphaerica, Linearis, & Logarithmica... Bologna: 1643. V. 47; 49; 50

CAVALIER, JEAN
Memoirs of the Wars of the Cevennes, Under Col. Cavallier, in Defence of the Protestants Persecuted in that Country. Dublin: 1726. V. 48; 52

CAVALLO, TIBERIUS
A Complete Treatise on Electricity, in Theory and Practice, with Original Experiments. London: 1782. V. 48
A Complete Treatise on Electricity, in Theory and Practice, with Original Experiments. London: 1786-95. V. 50
The Elements of Natural Experimental Philosophy. London: 1803. V. 48; 53
The History and Practice of Aerostation. London: 1785. V. 48

CAVALRY Sword Exercises. (with) The Manual and Platoon Exercises, for Percussion Carbine. London: 1840. V. 50

CAVAN, RICHARD LAMBART, EARL OF
A New System of Military Discipline, Founded Upon Principle. Philadelphia: 1776. V. 50; 53; 54

CAVANAGH, MICHAEL
Memoirs of Gen. Thomas Francis Meagher - Comprising the Leading Events of His Career. 1892. V. 54

CAVE, FRANCIS O.
Birds of the Sudan. Edinburgh: 1955. V. 49
Birds of the Sudan. London: 1955. V. 48; 49; 52; 54

CAVE, H. B.
Murgunstrumm and Others. 1977. V. 51

CAVE, HENRY
Picturesque Buildings in York. London: 1870. V. 51

CAVE, HENRY W.
Golden Tips. London: 1900. V. 48

CAVE, RODERICK
The Private Press. New York & London: 1983. V. 48
Private Press Books 1959 to 1960. Pinner: 1960-92. V. 48
Typographia Naturalis. 1967. V. 54
Typographia Naturalis. Wymondham: 1967. V. 47; 49; 50

CAVE, WILLIAM
Apostolici: or, the History of the Lives, Acts, Death and Martyrdoms of Those Who Were Contemporary With, or Immediately Succeeded the Apostles. London: 1677. V. 50
Apostolici: or the History of the Lives, Acts, Death and Martyrdoms Of Those Who Were Contemporary With, or Immediately Succeeded the Apostles. London: 1716. V. 49
Apostolici or The Lives of the Primitive Fathers for the Three First Ages of the Christian Church. London: 1677. V. 47; 50
Ecclesiastici or the History of the Lives, Acts, Death & Writings of the Most Eminent Fathers of the Church That Flourished in the Fourth Century... London: 1683/82. V. 47; 48; 50
Primitive Christianity: or, The Religion of the Ancient Christians in the First Ages of the Gospel. London: 1676. V. 49; 52

A CAVEAT Against the Methodists. Dublin: 1808. V. 53

CAVENDISH, GEORGE
The Life of Cardinal Wolsey. 1852. V. 53
The Life of Thomas Wolsey... Hammersmith: 1893. V. 50
The Life of Thomas Wolsey... London: 1893. V. 50
The Memoirs of that Great Favorite, Cardinal Woolsey, with Remarks on His Rise and Fall and Other Secret Transactions of His Ministry in Church and State... London: 1706. V. 54
The Negotiations of Thomas Woolsey, the Great Cardinall of England. London: 1641. V. 52

CAVENDISH, RICHARD
Man, Myth & Magic: An Illustrated Encyclopedia of the Supernatural. New York: 1970. V. 47

CAVENDISH, WILLIAM
The Humorous Lovers. London: 1677. V. 53

CAVENDISH-BRADSHAW, MARY ANNE
Memoirs of Maria, Countess d'Alva; Being Neither Novel Nor Romance, but Appertaining to Both. London: 1808. V. 52

CAVENESS, WILLIAM F.
Atlas of Electroencephalography in the Developing Monkey: Macaca Multatta. Palo Alto: 1962. V. 52

CAVERHILL, JOHN
A Treatise of the Cause and Cure of the Gout. London: 1769. V. 49

CAVERLEY, WILLIAM SLATER
Notes on the Early Sculptured Crosses, Shrines and Monuments in the Present Diocese of Carlisle... Kendal: 1899. V. 52

THE CAVERN of Death, a Moral Tale. Batlimore: 1801. V. 51

CAVINESS, MADELINE HARRISON
The Early Stained Glass of Canterbury Cathedral. Princeton: 1977. V. 52

CAW, JAMES L.
Scottish Painting Past and Present 1620-1908. Edinburgh: 1908. V. 51; 53
William McTaggart. A Biography and an Appreciation. Glasgow: 1917. V. 54

CAWDELL, JAMES
The Miscellaneous Poems. Sunderland: 1785. V. 47; 49; 53

CAWEIN, MADISON J.
Accolon of Gaul with Other Poems. Louisville: 1889. V. 51; 52
Moods and Memories. Poems. New York: 1892. V. 47
Myth and Romances. New York & London: 1899. V. 54
An Ode Read August 15, 1907 at the Dedication of the Monument Erected at Gloucester, Massachusetts, in Commemorataion of the Founding of the Massachusetts Bay Colony in the Year Sixteen Hundred and Twenty Three. Louisville: 1908. V. 54

CAWSTON, GEORGE
The Early Chartered Companies (A.D. 1296-1858). London: 1896. V. 52

CAWTHORN, JAMES
Poems. London: 1771. V. 52

CAWTHORNE, GEORGE JAMES
Royal Ascot, Its History and its Associations. London: 1902. V. 48

CAXTON CLUB
Catalogue of an Exhibition of Nineteenth Century Bookbinding. Chicago: 1898. V. 48

CAXTON, WILLIAM
Caxton's Prologues and Epilogues. London: 1927. V. 48

CAYET, PIERRE VICTOR-PALME
Chronolgie Septenaire de l'Histoire de la Paix entre les Roys de France et d'Espagne. Paris: 1605. V. 47
Chronologie Septenaire de Histoire de la Paix Entre les Roys de Frane et d'Espagne. Paris: 1606. V. 53

CAYLEY, ARTHUR
The Life of Sir Walter Raleigh. London: 1805. V. 50

CAYLEY, CORNELIUS
The Seraphical Young Shepherd. London: 1762. V. 47
The Seraphical Young Shepherd... London: 1779. V. 52

CAYLEY, GEORGE
Aeronautical and Miscellaneous Note-Book. Cambridge: 1933. V. 50

CAYLEY, N. W.
Australian Parrots, Their Habits in the Field and Aviary. Sydney: 1938. V. 50; 52; 53

CAYLEY-WEBSTER, H.
Through New Guinea and the Cannibal Countries. London: 1898. V. 48

CAYLUS, ANNE CLAUDE PHILIPPE, COMTE DE
Histoire de Joseph, Accompagnee de Dix Figures, Relatives Aux Principaux Evenemens de la Vie de ce Fils du Patriarche Jacob, et Gravees sur les Modeles du Fameux Reimbrandt... Amsterdam: 1757. V. 47
Receuil d'Antiquites Exgytiennes, Etrusques, Grecques et Romaines. Paris: 1752-67. V. 53

CAZALET, VICTOR
With Sikorski to russia. London: 1942. V. 47

CAZOTTE, JACQUES
The Devil in Love. New York: 1810. V. 51
The Devil in Love. London: 1925. V. 48

CECCHI, GIANMARIA
Gli Incantesimi. Comedia. Venetia: 1585. V. 50

CECIL, DAVID
Modern Verse in English, 1900-1950. New York: 1958. V. 53

CECIL, EVELYN
London Parks and Gardens. London: 1907. V. 54

CECIL, HENRY
Independent Witness. London: 1963. V. 52
Portrait of a Judge and Other Stories. London: 1964. V. 52

CEDAR RAPIDS & MISSOURI RIVER RAILROAD
Articles of Incorporation, and By-Laws of the Cedar Rapids and Missouri River Railroad Company. Cedar Rapids: 1867. V. 47
Statement of the Affairs of the Cedar Rapids and Missouri River Railroad Company, to December 25th, 1865. Blairstown: 1865. V. 47

CEELY, R.
Observations (Further Observations) on the Variolae Vaccinae as They Occasionally Appear in the Vale of Aylesbury, with an Account of Some Recent Experiments in the Vaccination, Retro-Vaccination and Varioaltion of Cows. Worcester: 1840-42. V. 51

CELA, CAMILO J.
Pascual Duarte's Family. London: 1946. V. 53

CELAN, PAUL
Todesfuge. 1984. V. 54
Todesfuge. New York: 1984. V. 47

CELANT, GERMANO
The Power of Theatrical Madness. London: 1986. V. 49

A CELEBRATION for Edith Sitwell. Norfolk: 1948. V. 54

CELIBACY; or, Good Advice to Young fellows to keep Single. London: 1739. V. 47

CELINE, LOUIS FERDINAND
Death on the Installment Plan. Boston: 1938. V. 53
Journey to the End of Night. London: 1934. V. 47; 51
Mea Culpa. Boston: 1937. V. 51; 54
Mea Culpa. Paris: 1937. V. 54
Voyage au Bout de la Nuit. Paris: 1932. V. 53

CELIZ, FRANCISCO
Diary of the Alarcon Expedition Into Texas 1718-1719. Los Angeles: 1935. V. 50; 52

CELLARIUS, CHRISTOPHER
Geographia Antiqua. London: 1731. V. 47
Nucleus Geographiae Antiqvae et Novae... Jena: 1676. V. 47

CELLARIUS, HENRI
The Drawing-Room Dances. London: 1847. V. 51

CELLI, ROSE
Baba Yaga. A Popular Russian Tale. New York: 1935. V. 53

CELLIER, ELIZABETH
The Tryal and Sentence of Elizabeth Cellier, for Writing, Printing and Publishing a Sandalous Libel, Called Malice Defeated...Saturday the 11th and Monday the 13th of Sept. 1680. London: 1680. V. 52

CELLINI, BENVENUTO
The Autobiography. Garden City: 1946. V. 49
The Life... Dublin: 1772. V. 49
The Life... London: 1900. V. 48; 50; 52
The Life... New York: 1906. V. 48; 54
The Life... Verona: 1937. V. 47; 51; 52; 54
Memoirs... London: 1822. V. 51; 54
Memoirs... London: 1823. V. 47; 51
Vita Di Benvenuto Cellini, Orefice e Scultore Fiorentino, Da Lui Medisimo Scritta. In Colonia: 1728. V. 48; 54

CELOTTI, ABATE L.
A Catalogue of a Highly Valuable and Extremely Curious Collection of Illuminated Miniature Paintings. 1825. V. 47

CELSUS, AURELIUS CORNELIUS
De Re Medica, Octo Libri Eruditissimi. Salingiaci: 1538. V. 48
Medicinae, Libri Octo Ex Recensione Leonardi Targae. Edinburgh: 1831. V. 50
Medicinae Libri VIII. Venetiis: 1528. V. 47

CENDRARS, BLAISE
The African Saga. New York: 1927. V. 48

CENNICK, JOHN
A Treatise of the Holy Ghost. 1751. V. 53

CENNINI, CENNINO
A Treatise on Painting, Written in the Year 1437 and First Published in Italian in 1821. London: 1844. V. 49; 52

THE CENTENNIAL History of the Harvard Law School 1817-1917. 1918. V. 47

THE CENTENNIAL of the Settlement of Upper Canada by the United Empire Loyalists, 1784-1884. Toronto: 1885. V. 53

CENTLIVRE, SUSANNAH
The Works of Celebrated Mrs. Centlivre. London: 1761-60. V. 49; 54

CENTRAL ARGENTINE RAILWAY CO.
The General Credit and Finance Co. of London and the London Financial Association Invite Subscriptions for the Capital of the Central Argentine Railway Co. from Rosario to Cordova (with) Map...(with) The Central Argentine Railway Co... London: 1864. V. 49

THE CENTRAL London Railway. London: 1894. V. 54

CENTRAL PACIFIC RAILRAOD
Information Concerning the Terminus of the Railroad System of the Pacific Coast. Oakland: 1871. V. 47

CENTRAL PACIFIC RAILROAD
Railroad Communication with the Pacific, With an Account of the Central Pacific Railroad of California: The Character of the Work, Its Progress, Resources, Earnings and Future Prospects and the Advantages of Its First Mortgage Bonds. New York: 1867. V. 47
Report of Chief Engineer Upon Recent Surveys, Progress of Construction and an Approximate Estimate of Cost of First Division of Fifty Miles of the Central Pacific Railroad of California, July 1st, 1863. Sacramento: 1863. V. 47
Report of the Chief Engineer on the Preliminary Survey and Cost of Construction of the Central Pacific Railroad, of California, Across the Sierra Nevada Mountains, from Sacramento to the Eastern Boundary of California. Sacramento: 1861. V. 47
Report of the Chief Engineer Upon Recent Surveys, Progress of Construction and Estimated Revenue of the Central Pacific Railroad of California. Sacramento: 1864. V. 47

CENTRAL SOUTHERN RAILROAD COMPANY
Sixth Annual Report of the Board of Directors of the Central Southern Railroad Company, to the Stockholders 1861. Nashville: 1861. V. 49

CENTRE FOR NORTH-WEST REGIONAL STUDIES
Occasional Papers 1-15. Lancaster: 1976-86. V. 50

CENTURIE of Prayse: Being Materials for a History of Opinion on Shakespeare and His Works, Culled from Writers of the First Century After His Rise. Birmingham: 1874. V. 50

THE CENTURY Guild Hobby Hrose, June 1889. London. V. 51

A CENTURY of Progress in the Natural Sciences, 1853-1953. San Francisco: 1955. V. 50

CEPHALAS, CONSTANTINE
Anthologiae graecae. Oxford: 1766. V. 47

CERBERUS. Poems by Louis Dudek, Irving Layton, Raymond Souter. Toronto: 1952. V. 51

CERCEAU, JEAN ANTOINE DU
The Compleat History of Thomas Kouli Kan (At Present Called Schah Nadir) Sovereign of Perisa. London: 1742. V. 51

CERDA, MELCHIOR DE LA
Consolatio ad Hispanos Propter Classem in Angliam Profectam Subita Tempestate Submersam. 1621. V. 49; 53

CERDA Y RICO, FRANCISCO
Varonia de Los Ponces de Leon Senores de Villagarcia, Marqueses de Zahara, y Despues Duques de Arcos...Demostrada Con Documentos... Madrid: 1783. V. 48

CEREBERUS.. Toronto: 1952. V. 47

THE CEREMONIES, Form of Prayer, and Services Used in Westminster-Abby at the Coronation of King James the First...With the Coronation of King Charles the First in Scotland. London: 1685. V. 47

CEREMONIES of the Dedication of the Soldiers' Monument in Concord, Mass. Concord: 1867. V. 47

THE CEREMONY to be Observed in the Public Funeral Procession of the Late Vice-Admiral Horatio Viscount Nelson, from Greenwich Hospital to Whitehall Stairs, and Thence to the Admiralty on Wednesday, the 8th Day of Janu... London: 1806. V. 51

CERESOLO, CARLO F.
Petrisyndon Evolvens Nova Volucria, Quadrupedia et Serpentia... Bergamo: 1680. V. 52

CERNY, J.
Coptic Etymological Dictionary. Cambridge: 1976. V. 49

CERTAIN Necessary Directions, As-Well for the Cure of the Plague, as for Preventing the Infection. London: 1636. V. 53

CERTAIN Sermons or Homilies Appointed to be Read in Churches, in the Time of Queen Elizabeth... London: 1673. V. 49; 51

CERTAINE Sermons or Homilies Appointed to Be Read in Churches, in the Time of Queen Elizabeth... London: 1633. V. 52; 54

CERUTI, BENEDETTO
Musaeum Franc Calceolari... 1622. V. 49

CERVANTES SAAVEDRA, MIGUEL DE
Adventures of Don Quixote de La Mancha. London. V. 54
Adventures of Don Quixote de la Mancha. London: 1866. V. 50
The Dialogue of the Dogs. Kentfield: 1969. V. 48; 53
The Diverting Works of the Famous Miguel de Cervantes... London: 1709. V. 47
Don Quixote... London: 1818. V. 48; 49; 53
Don Quixote... London: 1819. V. 47; 49; 52
Don Quixote. Exeter: 1828. V. 47
Don Quixote... London: 1837-39. V. 48
Don Quixote. Edinburgh: 1879. V. 48
Don Quixote... London: 1900. V. 50
Don Quixote. Strasburg: 1905. V. 54
Don Quixote... London: 1922. V. 54
Don Quixote... Cambridge: 1930. V. 53
Don Quixote... London: 1930. V. 48; 51; 52
The History...Don Quixote... London: 1620. V. 48
The History...Don Quixote... London: 1675. V. 47
The History...Don Quixote... London: 1725. V. 51
The History...Don Quixote... London: 1731. V. 49
The History...Don Quixote... London: 1743. V. 47
History...Don Quixote. London: 1755. V. 53; 54
The History...Don Quixote... Dublin: 1783. V. 48
The History...Don Quixote. History: 1796. V. 47
The History...Don Quixote. London: 1833. V. 48
The History...Don Quixote. London: 1860. V. 49
The History...Don Quixote... Edinburgh: 1908. V. 54
The History...Don Quixote... London: 1908. V. 53
The History...Don Quixote... Edinburgh: 1910. V. 50
The History...Don Quixote... New York: 1923. V. 51
The History...Don Quixote... Chelsea: 1927/28. V. 49; 50; 51
The History...Don Quixote... London: 1933. V. 54
L'Ingenieux Don Quichotte de la Manche. Paris: 1926/27. V. 51
El Ingenioso Hidalgo Don Quijote De La Mancha. Madrid: 1876... V. 53
El Ingenioso Hidalgo Don Quixote de la Mancha. Madrid: 1780. V. 49
El Ingenioso Hidalgo Don Quixote de la Mancha... Madrid: 1797-98. V. 47
El Ingenioso Hidalgo Don Quixote De La Mancha. Paris: 1814. V. 51
The Ingenious Gentleman Don Quixote of La Mancha. New York: 1926. V. 47
The Ingenious Gentleman Don Quixote of La Mancha. Barcelona: 1933. V. 49
Journey to Parnassus. London: 1883. V. 52
The Life and Adventures of Don Quixote de la mancha. London: 1820. V. 48; 50; 54
The Life and Exploits of Don Quixote... London: 1742. V. 48; 50
The Life and Exploits of Don Quixote... London: 1766. V. 51
The Life and Exploits of Don Quixote... London: 1801. V. 49; 54
The Life and Exploits of Don Quixote. 1824. V. 49
The Life and Exploits of Don Quixote. London: 1828. V. 50
The Life and Exploits of Don Quixote... London: 1833. V. 50
Novelas Exemplares. Brussels: 1614. V. 49
Novellas Exemplares: or, Exemplary Novels, in Six Books. London: 1743. V. 48
Persiles and Sigismunda: a Celebrated Novel. London: 1741. V. 51
The Spirit of Cervantes, or Don Quixote Abridged. London: 1820. V. 47
Vida y Hechos del Ingenioso Hidalgo Don Quixote de la Mancha. London: 1738. V. 48

CESCINSKY, HERBERT
The Antique Dealer. V. 47
The Antique Dealer... London: 1940. V. 51
Early English Furniture & Woodwork. London: 1922. V. 47; 48; 49; 50; 52; 53
English Domestic Clocks. London: 1914. V. 47
English Furniture of the Eighteenth Century. London: 1909-11. V. 50; 54
The Gentle Art of Faking Furniture. London: 1931. V. 51
Old English Master Cockmakers. London: 1938. V. 49; 53
The Old World House, Its Furniture and Decoration. London: 1924. V. 50; 51

CESNOLA, LOUIS PALMA DI
Cyprus: Its Ancient Cities, Tombs and Temples. London: 1877. V. 48
Cyprus: Its Ancient Cities, Tombs and Temples. New York: 1878. V. 47; 49
Salaminia. (Cyprus). The History, Treasures & Antiquities of Salamis in the Island of Sypurs. London: 1882. V. 49

CESSOLIS, JACOBUS DE
The Game of Chesse... London: 1855. V. 48
The Game of Chesse. London: 1860. V. 47
Game of Chesse. London: 1883. V. 53
The Game of Chesse. Ilkley: 1976. V. 49

CEVALLOS, PEDRO
Exposition of the Practices and Machinations Which Led to the Usurpation of the Crown of Spain... Boston: 1808. V. 47

CEYLON Almanac and Annual Register for the Year of Our Lord, 1858. Colombo: 1858. V. 54

CEZANNE, PAUL
Les Baigneuses. London: 1947. V. 51
Paul Cezanne Sketchbook Owned by the Art Institute of Chicago. New York: 1951. V. 51

CHABERT, JEAN LOUIS
Reflexions Medicales sur la Maladies Spasmodico-Liprienne des pays Chauds, Vulgairement Appelee Fievre Jaune. New Orleans,: 1821. V. 49

CHABERT, JOSEPH BERNARD DE
Voyage Fait par Ordre du Roi en 1750 et 1751, Dans 'Amerique Septentrionale Pour Rectifier les Cartes des Cotes de l'Acadie, de L'Isle Royale & del L'Isle de Terre-Neuve. Paris: 1753. V. 47; 52

CHABOT, CHARLES
The Handwriting of Junius: Professionally Investigated... London: 1871. V. 50; 52

CHABOT, FREDERICK C.
Corpus Christi and Lipantitlan, A Story of the Army of Texas Volunteers, 1842. San Antonio: 1942. V. 47
Perote Prisoners. San Antonio: 1934. V. 50
Texas Expeditions of 1842... 1942. V. 49
Texas Expeditions of 1842. San Antonio: 1942. V. 52
Texas Letters. San Antonio. V. 52

CHACE, ARNOLD BUFFUM
The Rhind Mathematical Papyrus. Oberlin: 1927. V. 48

CHADOUR, ANNA BEATRIZ
Rings: Forty Centuries Viewed by Four Generations. The Alice and Louis Koch Collection. 1994. V. 53

CHADWICK, ELLIS H., MRS.
In the Footsteps of the Brontes. New York: 1914. V. 54
Mrs. Gaskell. Haunts, Homes and Stories. 1910. V. 54

CHADWICK, G. F.
The Park and the Town, Public Lanscape in the 19th and 20th Centuries. New York: 1966. V. 51

CHADWICK, HENRY
Sports and Pastimes of American Boys: a Guide and Text-Book of Games of the Play-Ground the Parlor and the Field, Adapted Especially for American Youth. New York: 1884. V. 52

CHADWICK, MRS.
Rectitude; or, Virginia of the Wye. London: 1875. V. 54

CHADWICK, NORA K.
Celt and Saxon: Studies in the Early British Border. 1963. V. 52

CHADWICK, OWEN
The Victorian Church. London: 1970. V. 49

CHADWICK, WILLIAM
The Life and Times of Daniel DeFoe. London: 1859. V. 51

CHAFETZ, SIDNEY
The Story of Wu-Kut and Pren-Ting. Columbus: 1979. V. 49

CHAFF, GUMBO
The Ethiopian Glee Book: A Collection of Popular Negro Melodies. Boston: 1848. V. 48

CHAFF, SANDRA
Women in Medicine: A Bibliography of the Literature on Women Physicians. Metuchen: 1977. V. 52

CHAFFERS, WILLIAM
A Catalogue of Ancient and Modern Coins and Medals, Which may Be Obtained at the prices Attached to Each. London: 1851-55. V. 48
Gilda Aurifabrorum: a History of English Goldsmiths and Plateworkers, and Their Marks Stamped on Plate, Etc. London: 1883. V. 48

CHAFIN, WILLIAM
The Anecdotes and History of Cranbourn Chase. London: 1818. V. 50
A Second of the Anecdotes and History of Cranborn Chase... London: 1818. V. 47

CHAGALL, MARC
The Biblical Message of Marc Chagall. New York: 1973. V. 48
The Ceiling of the Paris Opera. New York: 1966. V. 50; 52; 53
Chagall. New York: 1943. V. 48
Chagall in Jerusalem. New York: 1983. V. 51
His Graphic Work. New York: 1957. V. 47; 51
The Jerusalem Windows. New York: 1962. V. 47
The Lithographs... Monte Carlo & New York: 1960-86. V. 50; 51
The Lithographs... Boston and New York: 1960/1963/1969/. V. 48
The Lithographs. Boston: 1969. V. 49
Lithographs... New York: 1986. V. 49
My Life. 1960. V. 54
My Life. New York: 1960. V. 53

CHAGEINU (Our Holidays), The Season of Rejoicing. New York: 1928. V. 50

CHAILLU, PAUL
The Land of the Midnight Sun. New York: 1882. V. 52

CHAKOTIN, SERGE
The Rape of the Masses. The Psychology of Totalitarian Political Propaganda. London: 1940. V. 49

CHALFANT, W. A.
Outposts of Civilization. Boston: 1928. V. 47; 53

CHALIAPIN, FEODOR
Man and Mask - Forty Years in the Life of a Singer. London: 1932. V. 48

CHALK, THOMAS
Journals of the Lives, Travels and Gospel Labours of Thomas Wilson, and James Dickinson. London: 1847. V. 50; 54

CHALKHILL, JOHN
Thelma and Clearchus: a Pastoral. London: 1820. V. 49

CHALKLEY, LYMAN
Records of Augusta County, Virginia 1745-1800. Baltimore: 1966. V. 52

CHALKLEY, THOMAS
A Collection of the Works of that Ancient, Faithful Servant of Jesus Christ, Who Departed This Life in the Island of Tortola, The Fourth Day of the Ninth Month, 1741. With a Journal of His Life, Travels and Christian Experiences, Written by Himself. London: 1791. V. 49

A CHALLENGE to Colored Men in Philadelphia, N. York and Boston; or Any of the Free States Which Shall Produce the First Ship Manned with Captain, Mates and All Hands Colored People!. Philadelphia: 1854. V. 50

CHALLIS, C. E.
A New History of the Royal Mint. 1992. V. 48

CHALLONER, RICHARD
The Catholick Christian Instructed. London: 1737. V. 51
Instructions for the Time of Jubilee, Anno 1751... 1751. V. 48
Martyrs to the Catholic Faith. Memoirs of Missionary Priests and Other Catholics of Both Sexes That Have Suffered Death in England on Religious Accounts from the Year 1577 to 1684... Edinburgh: 1878. V. 52; 54
Memoirs of Missionary Priests, as Well As Regular and Of Other Catholics, of Both Sexes, That Have Suffered Death in England, on Religious Accounts, from the Year of Our Lord 1577 to 1684. London: 1741-2. V. 49
The True Principles of a Catholic. Philadelphia: 1789. V. 52

CHALMERS, ALEX
A History of the Colleges, Halls and Public Buildings, Attached to the University of Oxford... Oxford: 1810. V. 48

CHALMERS, GEORGE
The Arrangements with Ireland Considered. London: 1785. V. 51
Caledonia: or, a Historical and Topographical Account of North Britian from the Most Ancient to the Present Times. Paisley: 1888-1902. V. 51
An Estimate of the Comparative Strength of Britain... London: 1782. V. 48
An Estimate of the Comparative Strength of Great Britain... London: 1786. V. 54
An Estimate of the Comparative Strength of Great Britain... London: 1794. V. 50
An Estimate of the Comparative Strength of Great Britain. London: 1802. V. 53
The Life of Mary, Queen of Scots... London: 1818. V. 52
The Life of Thomas Ruddiman...of the Library Belonging to the Faculty of Advocates at Edinburgh... Edinburgh: 1794. V. 50; 54
The Life of Thomas Ruddiman...of the Library Belonging to the Faculty of Advocates at Edinburgh. London: 1794. V. 48; 53
Opinions on Interesting Subjects of Public Law and Commercial Policy. London: 1785. V. 54

CHALMERS, GEORGE F.
Descriptive Astronomy. Oxford: 1867. V. 50

CHALMERS, JAMES
The Channel Railway, Connecting England and France. London: 1861. V. 51
Pioneering in New Guinea. London: 1887. V. 50
Plain Truth: Addressed to the Inhabitants of America, containing Remarks on a Late Pamphlet Intitled Common Sense. London: 1776. V. 53
Work and Adventure in New Guinea 1877 to 1885. London: 1886. V. 50

CHALMERS, JOHN P.
A Bookbinders' Florilegium. Austin: 1988. V. 51

CHALMERS, PATRICK R.
Birds Ashore and A-Foreshore. London: 1935. V. 48; 50; 52; 53; 54
A Dozen Dogs Or So. London: 1928. V. 48; 49
A Dozen Dogs Or So. New York: 1928. V. 47
Forty Fine Ladies. London: 1929. V. 48
Forty Fine Ladies. New York: 1929. V. 47
Gun-Dogs. London: 1931. V. 48
Kenneth Grahame. Life, Letters and Unpublished Work. London: 1933. V. 51

CHALMERS, THOMAS
The Application of Christianity to the Commercial and ordinary Affairs of Life, in a Series of Discourses. Glasgow: 1820. V. 52
On Political Economy, in Connexion with the Moral State and Moral Prospects of society. Glasgow: 1832. V. 52
On Political Economy, in Connexion with the Moral State and Moral Prospects of Society. Columbus: 1833. V. 52
On the Power, Wisdom and Goodness of God as Manifested in the Adaptation of External Nature to the Moral and Intellectual Constitution of Man. London: 1833. V. 52
On the Use and Abuse of Literary and Ecclesiastical Endowments. Glasgow: 1827. V. 50; 54
On the Wisdom and Goodness of God as Manifested in the Adaptation of External Nature to the Moral and Intellectual Constitution of Man. London: 1839. V. 47; 49

CHALMERS, THOMAS continued
A Sermon Delivered in the Tron Church, Glasgow, on Wednesday, Nov. 19th, 1817, the day of the Funeral of Her Royal Highness the Princess Charlotte of Wales. Glasgow: 1817. V. 52
Sermons, Preached in the Tron Church Glasgow. Glasgow: 1819. V. 54

CHALON, H. BERNARD
Chalon's Drawing Book of Animals and Birds of Every Description. London: 1804. V. 53

CHALONER, THOMAS
An Answer to the Scotch Papers Delivered in the House of Commons in Reply to the Votes of both Houses of Parliament of England, concerning the Disposall of the Kings Person, As It Was Spoken When the Said Papers Were Read in the House. London: 1646. V. 54

CHALONS, VINCENT CLAUDE
The History of France: from the Establishment of that Monarchy Under Pharamond, to the Death of Lewis XIII... London: 1752. V. 49

CHAMBERLAIN, ARTHUR B.
Hans Holbein the Younger. London: 1913. V. 49

CHAMBERLAIN, B. H.
The Serpent With Eight Heads. London: 1888. V. 48

CHAMBERLAIN, BRENDA
Poems with Drawings. 1969. V. 51

CHAMBERLAIN, CHARLES
The Servant-Girl of the Period. New York: 1873. V. 52

CHAMBERLAIN, F. W.
Atlas of Avian Anatomy: Osteology, Arthrology, Myology. East Lansing: 1943. V. 51

CHAMBERLAIN, GEORGE AGNEW
African Hunting Among the Thongas. New York: 1923. V. 47

CHAMBERLAIN, HENRY
A New and Compleat History and Survey of the Cities of London and Westminster, the Borough of Southark and parts Adjacent... London: 1770. V. 52

CHAMBERLAIN, JACOB CHESTER
First Editions of American Authors Collected by Jacob Chester Chamberlain. New York: 1909. V. 47; 51

CHAMBERLAIN, PAUL M.
It's About Time. New York: 1941. V. 53
Watches. The Paul M. Chamberlain Collection at the Art Institute of Chicago. 1921. V. 53

CHAMBERLAIN, SAMUEL
Tudor Homes of England... New York: 1929. V. 48

CHAMBERLAIN, SARAH
A Bestiary. Wallertown: 1979. V. 49
A Frog He Would A-Wooing Go. Portland: 1981. V. 49

CHAMBERLAINE, WILLIAM W.
Memoirs of the Civil War Between the Northern and Southern Sections of the United States of America, 1861 to 1865. Washington: 1912. V. 49

CHAMBERLAYNE, EDWARD
Angliae Notitia; or, the Present State of England. London: 1682. V. 47; 52
Angliae Notitia Sive Praesens Status Angliae Succincte Enucleatus... Oxford: 1686. V. 50
The New State of England, Under Our Present Monarch K. William III. London: 1702. V. 47

CHAMBERLAYNE, JOHN
Magnae Britanniae Notitia... London: 1708. V. 49
Magnae Britanniae Notitia... London: 1723. V. 52
Magnae Britanniae Notitia... London: 1726. V. 53
Magnae Britanniae Notitia... London: 1729. V. 50
Memoirs of the Royal Academy of Sciences in Parish Epitomized. With Lives of the Late Members... London: 1721. V. 52
Oratio Dominica in Diversas Omnium Fere Gentium Linguas Versa et Propriis Cujusque Linguae Characteribus Expressa, Una Cum Ddissertationibus Nonnullis de Linguarum Origine... Amstelaedami: 1715. V. 48

CHAMBERLAYNE, JOHN HAMPDEN
Ham Chamberlayne - Virginian Letters and Papers of an Artillery Officer in the War for Southern Indepdence 1861 to 1865. Richmond: 1932. V. 49; 50

CHAMBERLEN, PAUL
An Impartial History of the Life and Reign of Our Late Most Gracious Sovereign Queen Anne...Incidents of the Life of the Late Duke of Ormond... London: 1738. V. 47

CHAMBERLIN, EDWIN M.
The Sovereigns of Industry. Boston: 1875. V. 50

CHAMBERLIN, HARRY D.
Riding and Schooling Horses. New York: 1934. V. 47

CHAMBERS, A.
British Essayists. London: 1817. V. 51

CHAMBERS, ANDREW JACKSON
Recollections. N.P: 1947. V. 47; 49; 54

CHAMBERS, ANNE
The Principal Antique Patterns of Marbled Papers. Burford: 1984. V. 47; 50

CHAMBERS, DAVID
Cock-a-Hoop a Sequel to Chanticleer, Pertelote and Cockalorum Being a Bibliography of the Golden Cockerel Press Sept. 1949-Dec. 1961...with a List of Prospectuses 1920-62. 1976. V. 54
Divine Worship in England in the Thirteenth and Fourteenth Centuries. London: 1877. V. 49
Gogmagog: Morris Cox & The Gogmagog Press. Pinner: 1991. V. 52; 54
Joan Hassall Engravings and Drawings. 1985. V. 47; 54
Joan Hassall Engravings and Drawings. London: 1985. V. 50; 53

CHAMBERS, E. K.
The Elizabethan Stage. 1951. V. 47
The Elizabethan Stage. Oxford: 1951. V. 50
The Mediaeval Stage. Oxford: 1954. V. 50
William Shakespeare: a Study of Facts and Problems. London: 1930. V. 51
William Shakespeare, a Study of Facts and Problems. Oxford: 1930. V. 54

CHAMBERS, EPHRAIM
Cyclopaedia; or, an Universal Dictionary of Arts and Sciences... London: 1741. V. 48
Cyclopaedia; or, an Universal Dictionary of Arts and Sciences. London: 1741-43. V. 54
Cyclopaedia; or an Universal Dictionary of Arts and Sciences. London: 1750. V. 50
Cyclopaedia; or an Universal Dictionary of Arts and Sciences. London: 1779-86. V. 47; 48; 50
Cyclopaedia; or and Universal Dictionary of Arts and Sciences. London: 1786/83. V. 53

CHAMBERS, ERNEST J.
Canada's Fertile Northland: a Glimpse of the Enormous Resources of Part of the Unexplored Regions of the Dominion - Evidence Heard Before a Select Commitee of the Senate of Canada During the Parliamentary Session of 1906-07. and the Report Based Thereon. Ottawa: 1907. V. 49; 52
The Canadian Militia: a History of the Origin and Development of the Force. Montreal: 1907. V. 54
The Queen's Own Rifles Of Canada. Toronto: 1901. V. 49

CHAMBERS, GEORGE F.
East Bourne Memories of the Victorian Period. 1845 to 1901. East-Bourne: 1910. V. 54
A Handbook for Eastbourne, Seaford, Pevensey & Herstmonceux Castles... London: 1883. V. 49

CHAMBER'S Information for the People. No. 83 -Angling. London: 1842. V. 53

CHAMBERS, JACK
Jack Chambers. Toronto: 1978. V. 50

CHAMBERS, JAMES
The Poetical Works of James Chambers, Itinerant Poet, With the Life of the Author. Ipswich: 1820. V. 51

CHAMBERS, ROBERT
Ancient Sea-Margins as Memorials of Changes in the Relative Level of Sea and Land. Edinburgh: 1848. V. 48; 52
A Biographical Dictionary of Eminent Scotsmen. Glasgow: 1835. V. 52
A Biographical Dictionary of Eminent Scotsmen. London: 1852-55. V. 53
The Book of Days... London: 1866. V. 52
The Book of Days. London: 1880. V. 51
Cyclopaedia of English Literature. Edinburgh: 1844. V. 50; 51
Domestic Annals of Scotland from the Reformation to the Revolution. Edinburgh & London: 1861. V. 47; 49
Minor Antiquities of Edinburgh. Edinburgh: 1833. V. 52; 54
The Picture of Scotland. Edinburgh: 1830. V. 54
Traditions of Edinburgh. Edinburgh: 1825. V. 47; 52; 54
Traditions of Edinburgh... Edinburgh: 1825/33. V. 49

CHAMBERS, ROBERT WILLIAM
The Maker of Moons. 1896. V. 51
The Mystery of Choice. 1897. V. 51
Police!!!. New York: 1915. V. 48; 50; 52
The Red Republic: a Romance of the Communes. New York: 1895. V. 51
River-Land a Story for Children. New York: 1904. V. 49
The Rogue's Moon. New York: 1928. V. 53
The Sun Hawk. London: 1928. V. 47

CHAMBERS, THEODORE FRELINGHUYSEN
The Early Germans of New Jersey. Their History, Churches and Genealogies. 1895. V. 47

CHAMBERS, THOMAS
Catalogue of...Library of Books. Sheffield: 1870. V. 54

CHAMBERS, W.
Traite des Edifices, Meubles, Habits, Machines et Ustensiles des Chinois... Paris: 1776. V. 50

CHAMBERS, WHITTAKER
Witness. New York: 1952. V. 54

CHAMBERS, WILLIAM
American Slavery and Colour. London: 1857. V. 54
The Book of Scotland. Edinburgh: 1830. V. 53
California. Edinburgh: 1850. V. 54
California. London: 1850. V. 49
Chambers's Encyclopaedia; or a Dictionary of Universal Knowledge. London: 1895. V. 52
Chambers's Encyclopaeida; a Dictionary of Universal Knowledge. London: 1906. V. 52
Desseins des Edifices, Meubles, Habits Machines et Ustencles (sic) des Chinois, Graves sur les Originaux Dessines a la Chine. London: 1757. V. 53
A Dissertation on Oriental Gardening. London: 1772. V. 47; 53
A Dissertation on Oriental Gardening. London: 1773. V. 51
Things As They Are in America. Philadelphia: 1854. V. 51
A Translation of the Persian Abridgment of the Regulations of the 5th of July, 1781 for the Sudder and Mufussul Dewanny Adaulets. Calcutta: 1783. V. 47

CHAMBERS, WILLIAM continued
A Treatise On Civil Architecture, In Which the Principles of Art Are Laid down... London: 1759. V. 52; 54
A Treatise on the Decorative Part of Civil Architecture. London: 1825. V. 52
A Treatise on the Decorative Part of Civil Architecture. London: 1862. V. 48; 51

CHAMBLIN, THOMAS S.
The Historical Encyclopedia of Wyoming. V. 53

CHAMBLISS, J. E.
The Life and Labors of David Livingstone Covering His Entire Career in Southern and Central Africa. Philadelphia: 1875. V. 52

CHAMBLISS, WILLIAM H.
Chambliss' Diary; or, Society As It Really Is. New York: 1895. V. 50

CHAMBRAY, ROLAND FREART, SIEUR DE
An Idea of the Perfection of Painting: Demonstrated From the Principles of Art, and by Examples Conformable to the Observations... London: 1668. V. 50

CHAMBRUN, C. LONGWORTH DE
An Explanatory Introduction to Thorpe's Edition of Shakespeare's Sonnets 1609. Aldington, Kent: 1950. V. 50

CHAMEROVZOW, LOUIS ALEXIS
The Chronicle of the Bastile (La Bataudiere). London: 1847. V. 51
The Yule Log, for Everybody's Christmas Hearth: Showing Where It Grew. London: 1847. V. 49; 51

CHAMFORT, SEBASTIEN ROCH NICOLAS
The Maxims and Considerations of Chamfort. Waltham St. Lawrence: 1926. V. 47; 53

CHAMIER, FREDERICK
The Arethusa. London: 1837. V. 51
The Unfortunate Man. London: 1835. V. 54

CHAMISSO, ADELBERT VON
Peter Schlemihl: from the German. London: 1824. V. 49
The Shadowless Man; or the Wonderful History of Peter Schlemihl. London: 1857-70. V. 47

CHAMPION, IVAN F.
Across New Guinea from the Fly to the Sepik. London: 1932. V. 50

CHAMPION, RICHARD
Comparative Reflections on the Past and Present Political, Commercial and Civil State of Great Britain... London: 1787. V. 53

CHAMPION, THOMAS EDWARD
History of the 10th Royals and of the Royal Grenadiers from the Formation of the Regiment Until 1896. Toronto: 1896. V. 53

CHAMPLAIN, SAMUEL DE
The Works of Samuel De Champlain. Toronto: 1971. V. 50

CHAMPMIER, P. A.
Statement of the Sugar Crop, Made in Louisiana in 1861-62. New Orleans: 1862. V. 49

CHAMPNEYS, AMIAN L.
Public Libraries. A Treatise on Their Design, Construction and Fittings. London: 1907. V. 51

CHAMPNEYS, ARTHUR C.
Irish Ecclesiastical Architecture with Some Notice of Similar or Related Work in England, Scotland and Elsewhere. London: 1910. V. 49; 51; 53

CHAMPOLLION, JEAN FRANCOIS
L'Egypte sous les Pharaons, ou Recherches sur la Geographie, la Religion, la Language, les Ecritures et l'Histoire de l'egypte avant 'Invasion de Chambyse. Paris: 1814. V. 49; 51
Monuments d'l'Egypte, et de la Nubie d'Apre les Dessins Executes sur les Lieux, sous la direction de Champollion le jeune... Paris: 1834-45. V. 49

CHAMPOMIER, P. A.
Statement of the Sugar Crop, Made in Louisiana, in 1851-52. New Orleans: 1852. V. 53
Statement of the Sugar Crop, made in Louisiana in 1861-62. New Orleans: 1862. V. 52

CHANCE BROS.
Designs for Coloured Ornamental Windows. Birmingham: 1853. V. 52

CHANCE, JAMES FREDERICK
The Pattinsons of Kirklinton. 1899. V. 50; 52
The Pattinsons of Kirklinton. Witherby: 1899. V. 54

CHANCELLOR, E. BERESFORD
The Lives of the Rakes. London: 1924. V. 47; 50

CHANCELLOR, J. W.
Through the Visograph. 1928. V. 48; 52

CHANDLER, BRUCE
Lovejoy, Excerpts from a Memoir. Boston: 1988. V. 48; 51
Lovejoy, Excerpts from a Memoir. Boston: 1989. V. 47
Samen met de Andere Dieren. Ten Etchings from the Nieuwe Zon. Kasterlee: 1977. V. 53

CHANDLER, ELIZABETH MARGARET
Essays, Philanthropic and Moral...Principally Relating to the Aboliton of Slavery in America. Philadelphia: 1836. V. 49
The Poetical Works... (with) Essays Philanthropic and Moral... Philadelphia: 1836. V. 47; 49; 51; 53

CHANDLER, LLOYD H.
A Summary of the Work of Rudyard Kipling. New York: 1930. V. 49

CHANDLER, M. E. J.
Lower Tertiary Floras of Southern England. London: 1961-64. V. 54

CHANDLER, MARY
The Description of Bath. London: 1738. V. 53

CHANDLER, MELBOURNE C.
Garryowen in Glory the History of the Seventh United States Regiment of Cavalry. Annandale: 1960. V. 47; 54

CHANDLER, RAYMOND
Backfire: Story for the Screen. Santa Barbara: 1984. V. 51; 54
The Big Sleep. New York: 1939. V. 48; 50; 51; 53
The Big Sleep. London: 1975. V. 50
The Big Sleep. San Francisco: 1986. V. 47
The Blue Dahlia. Carbondale & Edwardsville: 1976. V. 52
Chandler Before Marlow. Columbia: 1973. V. 50
Farewell My Lovely. New York: 1940. V. 47; 48; 50; 51; 53
The Finger Man. New York: 1946. V. 47
The High Window. New York: 1942. V. 47; 49; 50
Killer in the Rain. Boston: 1964. V. 48; 49; 50; 54
Killer in the Rain. London: 1964. V. 49; 50; 53
The Lady in the Lake. New York: 1943. V. 52; 53; 54
The Lady in the Lake. London: 1944. V. 51
Letters. Santa Barbara: 1978. V. 50
The Little Sister. 1949. V. 53
The Little Sister. Boston: 1949. V. 49; 50
The Little Sister. London: 1949. V. 48; 51
The Long Goodbye. 1953. V. 54
The Long Goodbye. London: 1953. V. 47; 48; 50
The Long Goodbye. 1954. V. 53
The Long Goodbye. Boston: 1954. V. 49; 50
The Midnight Raymond Chandler. Boston: 1971. V. 51
Playback. 1958. V. 53
Playback. Boston: 1958. V. 49; 51
Playback. London: 1958. V. 47; 48; 49; 50; 51; 52
Playback. London: 1960. V. 50
Poodle Springs. London: 1989. V. 50
Red Wind. Cleveland and New York: 1946. V. 52; 53
The Simple Art of Murder. Boston: 1950. V. 52
Smart Aleck Kill. London: 1958. V. 47
The Smell of Fear. London: 1965. V. 49; 51
Spanish Blood - a Collection of Short Stories. Cleveland and New York: 1946. V. 52

CHANDLER, RICHARD
The Life of William Waynflete, Bishop of Winchester, Lord High Chancellor of England in the Reign of Henry VI and Founder of Magdalen College, Oxford. London: 1811. V. 54
Travels in Asia Minor...an Account of a Tour Made at the Expense of the Society of Dilettanti. London: 1776. V. 48
Travels in Asia Minor...an Account of a Tour Made at the Expense of the Society of Dilettanti. London: 1817. V. 47

CHANDLER, THOMAS BRADBURY
The Life of Samuel Johnson, D.D., the First President of King's College, in New York... New York: 1805. V. 49

CHANDLESS, WILLIAM
Ved Saltsoen. Et Besog hos Mormonerne I Utah af William Chandless. Kjobenhavn: 1858. V. 47
A Visit to Salt Lake: Being a Journey Across the Plains and a Residence in the Mormon Settlements at Utah. London: 1857. V. 47; 51; 52

CHANGING Pictures. A Book of Transformation Pictures. London: 1894. V. 47

CHANIN, ADA
This Land, These Voices. Flagstaff: 1975. V. 51

CHANLER, ISAAC
The Doctrines of Glorious Grace Unfolded, Defended, and Practically Improved... Boston: 1744. V. 50

CHANLER, JOHN ARMSTRONG
Four Years Behind the Bards of "Bloomingdale", or the Bankruptcy of Law in New York. Roanoke Rapids: 1906. V. 52

CHANLER, WILLIAM ASTOR
Through Jungle and Desert. London: 1896. V. 53

CHANNEL BRIDGE & RAILWAY CO.
Avant-Projets de M. M. Schneider et Cie (Usines du Creusot) et H. Hersent... Paris: 1889. V. 51

THE CHANNEL Tunnel. 1. London and the Tunnel. International Parliamentary Commercial Conference - The Tunnel In its Commercial Aspects. 3. History, benefits and Prospects of the Tunnel. From London to the Cape by Rail. London: 1918. V. 51

CHANNEL Tunnel. Full Details of the Present Scheme - Military, Engineering, Financial. London: 1913. V. 47; 51

CHANNING, WILIAM ELLERY
Carta al Honorable Henrique Clay Sobre la Agregacion de Tejas a los Estados-Unidos, por Guillermo E. Channing. Megico: 1837. V. 50

CHANNING, WILLIAM ELLERY
The Duty of the Free States, or Remarks Suggested by the Case of the Creole. (and) The Duty of the Free States. Second Part. Boston: 1842. V. 51; 53

CHANNING, WILLIAM ELLERY continued
Letter to the Hon. Henry Clay of the Annexation of Texas to the United States. Boston: 1837. V. 49; 51
Memoir of, with Extracts from His Correspondence and Manuscripts (1780-1893). London: 1848. V. 47
Poems. Boston: 1843. V. 49; 52; 53; 54
Thoreau: the Poet-Naturalist. Boston: 1873. V. 54
The Works. Glasgow: 1840. V. 48

CHANSON DE ROLAND
The Song of Roland. New York: 1906. V. 50
The Song of Roland. New York: 1938. V. 48; 52; 53; 54

CHANT, J.
Red Moon and Black Mountain. 1970. V. 48

CHANT, LAURA ORMISTON
Why We Attacked the Empire. London: 1895. V. 50

CHANTER, CHARLOTTE
Ferny Combes. London: 1856. V. 51
Ferny Combes. London: 1857. V. 54

CHANTICLEER: A Bibliography of the Golden Cockerel Press, April 1921-1936. 1936. V. 53

CHANTICLEER: a Bibliography of the Golden Cockerel Press, April 1921-1936 August. London: 1936. V. 51

CHANTICLEER. A Bibliography of the Golden Cockerel Press, April 1921-1936 August. Waltham St. Lawrence: 1936. V. 49; 50

CHANTICLEER. Pertelote. Cockalorum. Cock-A-Hoop. Waltham St. Lawrence: 1936-76. V. 54

CHANTREY, FRANCIS LEGATT
Illustrations of Derbyshire. London: 1818-22. V. 52

CHANTS et Chansons Populaires de la France. Paris: 1848. V. 47

CHAPAIS, J. C.
The Canadian Forester's Illustrated Guide. Montreal: 1885. V. 47

CHAPELLE, HOWARD IRVING
The Baltimore Clipper, its Origin and Development. Salem: 1930. V. 48

CHAPIN, ANNA ALICE
The Everyday Fairy Book. London: 1924. V. 47
The Everyday Fairy Book. London: 1930. V. 52
The Now-A-Days Fairy Book. New York: 1911. V. 47; 49

CHAPIN, FREDERICK H.
Mountaineering in Colorado: The Peaks About Estes Park. Boston: 1889. V. 50

CHAPIN, HOWARD M.
Rhode Island Privateers in King George's War, 1739-1748. Providence: 1926. V. 49

CHAPIN, J. P.
The Birds of the Belgian Congo. New York: 1932-54. V. 48; 49; 52
The Birds of the Belgian Congo Part 3. New York: 1953. V. 48; 52
The Birds of the Belgian Congo Part 4. New York: 1954. V. 48
The Birds of the Belgian Congo, Part I (General Survey and Struthioniformes to Turniciformes). New York: 1932. V. 52

CHAPIN, LON F.
Thirty Years in Pasadena: with an Historical Sketch of Previous Eras. 1929. V. 52

CHAPIN, S.
Statement and Reports Concerning the Uncle Sam Senior and Gold Canon Silver Lodes in Nevada. Boston: 1865. V. 48

CHAPIN, SAMUEL
The Detective's Manual and Officer's Guide. Springfield: 1868. V. 50

CHAPIN, WILL E.
The Switzerland of America (Rock Creek Resort). Hollywood: 1927. V. 53

CHAPIN, WILLIAM
Villages Sketches; or, Tales of Somerville. Norristown: 1825. V. 49

CHAPIUS, ALFRED
Automata: a Historical and Technological Study. London: 1958. V. 52
Automata: a Historical and Technological Study. New York & Neuchatel: 1958. V. 49; 53
The History of the Self-Winding Watch 1770-1931. Neuchatel: 1956. V. 49; 51; 53
Le Monde des Automates Etude Historique et Technique. Paris: 1928. V. 53

CHAPLIN, JOSEPH
The Trader's Best Companion... Newburyport: 1795. V. 50; 54

CHAPLIN, RALPH
Bars and Shadows. The Prison Poems. New York: 1922. V. 49

CHAPMAN, A. B. WALLIS
The Black Book of Southampton 1388-1503. Southampton: 1912. V. 53

CHAPMAN, ABEL
Bird Life of the Borders. London: 1889. V. 47; 49; 53
Bird-Life of the Borders... London: 1907. V. 49; 52
The Borders and Beyond. London: 1924. V. 49; 51
First Lessons in the Art of Wildfowling. London: 1896. V. 49
The Gun at Home and Abroad: British Game Birds and Wildfowl. London: 1912. V. 52
Memories of Fourscore Years Less Two. London: 1930. V. 49; 54
On Safari, Big-Game Hunting in British East Africa. London: 1908. V. 49; 50; 53; 54
Retrospect. London: 1928. V. 49; 54
Savage Sudan. London: 1921. V. 48; 49; 50
Unexplored Spain. London: 1910. V. 49; 52; 54
Unexplored Spain. Madrid: 1978. V. 54
Wild Norway. 1897. V. 48; 54
Wild Norway. London: 1897. V. 49
Wild Spain (Espana Agreste). Records of Sport with Rifle, Rod & Gun. London: 1892. V. 48
Wild Spain (Espana Agreste). Records of Sport with Rifle, Rod & Gun... London: 1893. V. 51

CHAPMAN, ALVAN WENTWORTH
Flora of the Southern United States... New York: 1860. V. 50
Flora of the Southern United States... New York: 1872. V. 48

CHAPMAN, ARTHUR
The Pony Express; The Record of a Romantic Adventure in Business. New York: 1932. V. 48

CHAPMAN, C. I. A.
Franklin's Oath: A Tale of Wyoming One Hundred Years Ago. Pittson: 1880. V. 49; 54

CHAPMAN, CHARLES
The Ocean Waves: Travels by Land and Sea. London: 1875. V. 53

CHAPMAN, CHARLES EDWARD
The Founding of Spanish California. The Northwestward Expansion of New Spain, 1687-1783. New York: 1916. V. 50

CHAPMAN, EDWARD JOHN
A Song of Charity. Toronto: 1857. V. 51

CHAPMAN, F. M.
The Distribution of Bird Life in Columbia. New York: 1917. V. 53
The Distribution of Bird Life in Ecuador. New York: 1926. V. 49
The Warblers of North America. New York: 1907. V. 48; 52; 53
The Warblers of North America. New York: 1923. V. 50

CHAPMAN, GEORGE
An Anthology of His Work. London: 1934. V. 52
The Tragedie of Chabot Admiral of France; as it Was Presented by Her Majesties Servants, at the Private House in Drury Lane. London: 1639. V. 52
A Treatise on Education. Edinburgh: 1773. V. 49
A Treatise on Education. London: 1790. V. 52

CHAPMAN, GUY
A Bibliography of William Beckford. London: 1930. V. 54
A Passionate Prodigality - Fragments of Autobiography. London: 1933. V. 47
A Passionate Prodigality - Fragments of Autobiography. New York, Chicago: 1966. V. 52
Vain Glory - a Miscellany of the Great War 1914-1918 Written by Those who Fought In It On Each Side and All Fronts. London: 1937. V. 47

CHAPMAN, HENRY
A Manual of Medical Jurisprudence and Toxicology. Philadelphia: 1893. V. 53
On Treatment of Ulcers of the Leg, Without Confinement, With an Inquiry Into the Best Mode of Effecting the Permanent Cure of Varicose Veins. Cincinnati: 1853. V. 48

CHAPMAN, HILARY
The Wood Engravings of Ethelbert White. London: 1992. V. 50

CHAPMAN, J.
An Essay on the Evils of Scandal, Slander and Misrepresentation. London: 1821. V. 50

CHAPMAN, JOHN
Eusebius, or the True Christian's Defense Against a Late Book Entitul'd The Moral Philosopher. Cambridge & London: 1739-41. V. 53
Theater '53. New York: 1953. V. 54

CHAPMAN, JOHN JAY
Deutschland uber Alles or Germany Speaks. New York: 1914. V. 54
Emerson and Other Essays. New York: 1898. V. 53
Homeric Scenes. New York: 1914. V. 54
Practical Agitation. New York: 1909. V. 51
The Treason and Death of Benedict Arnold. New York: 1910. V. 47; 54

CHAPMAN, JOHN KEMBLE
A Complete History of Theatrical Entertainments...at the English Court... London: 1849?. V. 54
The Court Theatre, and Royal Dramatic Record... London: 1849. V. 49

CHAPMAN, JOHN RATCLIFFE
Instructions to Young Marksmen...The Improved American Rifle. New York: 1848. V. 51

CHAPMAN, KENNETH M.
The Pottery of Santo Domingo Pueblo... Santa Fe: 1936. V. 50; 52
The Pottery of Santo Domingo Pueblo... Santa Fe: 1953. V. 50; 52
Pottery of Santo Domingo Pueblo, a detailed Study of its Decoration. Santa Fe: 1936/38. V. 51

CHAPMAN, MARIA WESTON
Right and Wrong in Massachusetts. Boston: 1839. V. 51; 53

CHAPMAN, NATHANIEL
Elements of Therapeutics and Materia medica. Philadelphia: 1823-24. V. 52
The Philadelphia Journal of the Medical and Physical Sciences. Philadelphia: 1825. V. 49

CHAPMAN, PRISCILLA
Hindoo Female Education. London: 1839. V. 50; 51; 53

CHAPMAN, R. W.
Cancels. London: 1930. V. 48; 50; 52
Specimens of Books Printed at Oxford with the Types Given to the University by John Fell. Oxford: 1925. V. 47

CHAPMAN, ROGER G.
Charles Darwin... London: 1982. V. 47
Charles Darwin... Wellington: 1982. V. 51; 54

CHAPMAN, WALTER
Dutchie Doings. London. V. 51

CHAPMAN, WILLIAM
Observations on the Various Systems of Canal Navigation and Inferences, Practical and Mathematical... London: 1797. V. 53; 54
Report on the Harbour of New Shoreham (Sussex). (and) Supplementary Report on the Efficacy of the Measure Proposed fro the Improvement of the Harbour of New Shoreham. Brighton: 1815/1815. V. 52

CHAPONE, HESTER
Miscellanies in Prose and Verse. London: 1775. V. 47; 48; 52
Miscellanies in Prose and Verse. London: 1783. V. 54

CHAPPE D'AUTEROCHE, JEAN
A Voyage to California, to Observe the Transit of Venus... London: 1778. V. 47; 50; 53; 54

CHAPPELL, EDWARD
Narrative of a Voyage to Hudson's Bay In His Majesty's Ship Rosamond... London: 1817. V. 53
Reports Relative to Smith's Patent Screw Propeller, as Used on Board the Archimedes Steam Vessel, in Various Trials with Her Majesty's Steam Packet Widgeon, at Dover... London: 1840. V. 54
Voyage of His Majesty's Ship Rosamond to Newfoundland and the Southern Coast of Labrador. London: 1818. V. 48; 53

CHAPPELL, FRED
The Gaudy Place. New York: 1973. V. 54
The Inkling. New York: 1965. V. 50; 51
It is Time, Lord. New York: 1963. V. 52
Moments of Light. Los Angeles: 1980. V. 50; 51

CHAPPELL, GEORGE S.
A Basket of Poses. New York: 1924. V. 50; 51

CHAPPELLE, HOWARD I.
The National Watercraft Collection. Maine: 1976. V. 49

CHAPPUIS, ADRIEN
The Drawings of Paul Cezane: a Catalogue Raisonne. London: 1973. V. 50

CHAPTAL, JEAN ANTOINE CLAUDE
Chimie Appliquee Aux Arts. Paris: 1807. V. 48
Traite Theorique et Pratique Sur La Culture de la Vigne, Avec L'Art De Faire Le Vin. Paris: 1801. V. 49

CHAR, RENE
Elizabeth Petite Fille. Ales: 1958. V. 52

CHARACTERISTIC Sketches of Young Gentlemen. London: 1838. V. 49; 54

CHARACTERS and Anecdotes Collected in the Reigns of William Rufus, Charles the Second and King George the Third, by the Celebrated Wandering Jew of Jerusalem. London: 1791. V. 47; 52

CHARACTERS And Anecdotes of the Court of Sweden. London: 1790. V. 52

CHARAKA CLUB
Proceedings of... New York: 1902-85. V. 54
Proceedings of... Volume 2. New York: 1906. V. 50; 51; 52; 53; 54
Proceedings of... Volume 3. New York: 1910. V. 47; 48; 49; 50; 51; 53; 54
The Proceedings of... Volume 4. New York: 1916. V. 47; 48; 49; 50; 51; 52; 53; 54
The Proceedings of... Volume 5. New York: 1919. V. 50; 52
Proceedings of... Volume 8. New York: 1938. V. 50; 53
The Proceedings of... Volume 9. New York: 1938. V. 50; 51; 52; 54
Proceedings of...Volume 1. New York: 1902. V. 48; 54

CHARARA, ADNAN
Fables - Visual Metaphors. Boston: 1993. V. 51

CHARCOT, JEAN MARTIN
Clinical Lectures on Senile and Chronic Diseases. London: 1881. V. 50; 53
Clinical Lectures on the Diseases of Old Age. New York: 1881. V. 47; 48; 50; 52; 53
Lectures on Bright's Diseases of the Kidneys, Delivered at the School of Medicine of Paris... New York: 1878. V. 52
Lectures on Localisation of Cerebral and Spinal Diseases. London: 1883. V. 47
Lectures on Localization in Diseases of the Brain Delivered at the Faculte de Medecine, Paris, 1875. New York: 1878. V. 53
Lectures on the Diseases of the Nervous System. London: 1877. V. 53
Lectures oN the Diseases of the Nervous System. London: 1877-89. V. 50
Lectures on the Pathological Anatomy of the Nervous System. Diseases of the Spinal Cord. Cincinnati: 1881. V. 52
Neue Vorlesungen Uber die Krankheiten des Nervensystems Insbesondere Uber Hysterie. Leipzig und Wien: 1886. V. 50; 51; 52

CHARD, THOMAS
A Short and True Narrative of a Swindling Scheme Which was the Ruin of an Industrious Family... London: 1794. V. 50

CHARD, THOMAS S.
California Sketches. Chicago: 1888. V. 48

CHARDIN, JOHN
Travels in Persia. London: 1927. V. 49; 54
The Travels of Sir John Chardin into Persia and the East Indies, through the Black Sea, and the Country of Colchis. London: 1691. V. 47; 51; 54

CHARDON, FRANCIS A.
Chardon's Journal at Fort Clark, 1834-1839: Descriptive of Life on the Upper Missouri; a Fur Trader's Experiences Among the Mandans, Gros Ventres and Their Neighbors' of the Ravages of the Small-Pox Epidemic of 1837. Pierre: 1932. V. 52

CHARFY, GUINIAD, PSEUD.
The Fisherman: or, The Art of Angling Made Easy. London: 1800. V. 47

THE CHARGE of Sir Francis Bacon, Kt. His Majesties Attourney General, Touching the Duells. Upon Information in the Star-Chamber...with the Decreee of the Star-Chamber in the Same Cause. London: 1670. V. 50

CHARING Cross to Bagdad. A Great Inter-allied Reconstruction Scheme. London: 1917. V. 51

CHARLES, C. J.
Elizabethan Interiors. London. V. 52

CHARLES Darwin 1809-1882. A Centennial Commemorative. Wellington: 1982. V. 48; 49

CHARLES Dickens in the Cloth. Los Angeles: 1982. V. 49

CHARLES Dickens. The Story of His Life. By the author of the "Life of Thackeray". London: 1871?. V. 49

CHARLES, EDWARD STUART
A Full Collection of All Poems Upon Charles, Prince of Wales, Regent of the Kingdoms of Scotland, England, France and Ireland and Dominions Thereunto Belonging, Published Since His Arrival in Edinburgh the 17th Day of Sept. Till 1st Nov. 1745. Edinburgh: 1745. V. 50

CHARLES, WILLIAM RICHARD
Life in Corea. London: 1888. V. 50

CHARLES D'ORLEANS
Poemes. Paris: 1950. V. 47

CHARLES I, KING OF GREAT BRITAIN
His Majesties Answer, to a Booke, Intituled, the Declaration, Remonstrance of the Lords and Commons of the 19 of May 1642. Imprinted at Yorke and: 1642. V. 47
His Majesties Declaration, To all His Loving Subjects. London: 1641. V. 47
His Majesties Declaration: to All His Loving Subjects, of the Causes Which Moved Him to Dissolve the Last Parliament. London: 1640. V. 52
His Majesties Speech Spoken to the Mayor, Alderman, and Commonaltie of the Citie of Oxford, and to the High Sheriffes of the Countries of Oxford and Berks... Oxford: 1643. V. 50
The Kings Majesties Most Gracious Message in Foure Letters: One of Which His Majesty Received from London, and Three Written by His Majesties Own Hands... London: 1647. V. 47
A Perfect Copie of Prayers Used by His Majesty In the Time of His Sufferings... London: 1649. V. 50
Reliquiae Sacrae Carlinae. or the Works fo that Great Monarch and Glorious Martyr. Hague: 1651. V. 50
Reliquiae Sacrae Carolinae: The Works of that Great Monarch and Glorious Martyr King Charles the 1st, Both civil and Sacred. Hague: 1658. V. 50
The Royall Legacies of Charles the First of that name, of Great Britaine, France and Ireland, King & Martyr, to His Persecutors and Murderers. London: 1649. V. 47
The Workes of King Charles the Martyr, with a Collection of Declrations, Treaties and Other Papers... London: 1662. V. 47
The Works of that Great Monarch, and Glorious Martyr... Aberdeen: 1766. V. 49

CHARLES II, KING OF GREAT BRITAIN
His Majesties Gracious Answer to the Earle of Manchesters Speech, Made in the Name of the House of Peers, At the Arrival of His Majesty at White-Hall, on the 29th of May, 1660. London: 1660. V. 50

CHARLES ROUX, EDMONDE
Chanel and Her World. London: 1981. V. 50; 54

CHARLESWORTH, E. G.
Poems. London: 1856. V. 53

CHARLESWORTH, EDWARD PARKER
Remarks on the Treatment of the Insane, and the Management of Lunatic Asylums. London: 1828. V. 51

CHARLET, GASTON
La Decoration Moderne dans le Textile. Paris: 1927. V. 48

CHARLETON, RICE
A Treatise on the Bath Waters: Wherein are Discover'd the Several principles of Which They Are Compos'd: the Cause of Their Heat; and the Manner of Their Production. Bath: 1754. V. 48

CHARLETON, T. W.
The Art of Fishing. A Poem. North Shields: 1819. V. 51

CHARLETON, WALTER
Two Discourses. I. Concerning the Different Wits of Men. II. of the Mysterie of Vintners. London: 1669. V. 50

CHARLEVOIX, PIERRE FRANCOIS XAVIER DE
Histoire et Description Generale de la Nouvelle France, Avec le Journal Historique d'un Voyage Fait par Ordre du Roi dans l'Amerique Septentrionnale. Paris: 1744. V. 52; 53; 54
History and General Description of New France. Chicago: 1962. V. 53
Journal of a Voyage to North America. London: 1761. V. 47; 48; 49
Journal of a Voyage to North America. Chicago: 1923. V. 47

CHARLEY Chalk; or, the Career of an Artist: Being Sketches from Real Life... London: 1839. V. 51

CHARLIE Wyndham; or, the Adventures of a Modern Midshipman. Hanley: 1887. V. 47

CHARLIP, REMY
Arm in Arm. New York: 1969. V. 54
Fortunately. New York: 1964. V. 54

CHARLOT, JEAN
Charlot Murals in Georgia. 1945. V. 53
Picture Book. New York: 1933. V. 50; 53
Picture Book II. Los Angeles: 1973. V. 54

CHARLTON, EDWIN A.
New Hampshire As It Is. Claremont: 1856. V. 47

CHARLTON, JOHN
Royal Naval and Military Bazaar, Organized by Charles Peter Little in Aid of H.R.H. Princess Christian's Homes for Disabled Soldiers and Sailors on June 19, 20, 21, 1900. London. V. 49

CHARLTON, ROBERT MILLEDGE
Poems. Boston: 1839. V. 54

CHARLTON, WILLIAM HENRY
Four Months in North America. Hexham: 1873. V. 53
Poems. London: 1834. V. 51

THE CHARMS of Liberty: a Poem. 1709. V. 53

CHARNAY, DESIRE
The Ancient Cities of the New World: Being Voyages and Explorations in Mexico and Central America from 1857-1882. New York: 1887. V. 47

CHARNES, JEAN ANTOINE, ABBE DE
Conversations sur la Critique de la Princesse de Cleves. Paris: 1679. V. 54

CHARNOCK, JOHN
Biographia Navalis: or, Impartial Memoirs of the Lives and Characters of Officers of the Navy of Great Britain, from the Year 1660 to the Present Time. London: 1794-98. V. 49
Biographical Memoirs of Lord Viscount Nelson, &c. &c. With Observations Critical and Explanatory. London: 1806. V. 49; 50; 52
An History of Marine Architecture. London: 1800-02. V. 52; 54

CHARNOCK, RICHARD STEPHEN
A Glossary of the Essex Dialect. London: 1880. V. 50

CHARPENTIER, FRANCOIS
Relation de l'Establissement de la Compagnie Francoise Pour le Commerce des Indes Orientales. Dediee au Roi. Amsterdam: 1666. V. 49

CHARPENTIER, HENRI
Food and Finesse. Chicago: 1945. V. 47; 48

CHARPENTIER, JEAN DE
Essai Sur les Glaciers et sur le Terrain Erratique du Bassin du Rhone. Lausanne: 1841. V. 48

CHARPY, EDMOND
Imperatorum XII...Effigies Resque Gestae Iconibus. Paris: 1610. V. 53; 54

CHARRIERE, GEORGES
Scythian Art: Crafts of the Early Eurasian Nomads. New York: 1979. V. 50

CHARRON, PIERRE, SIEUR DE
Of Wisdom: The Second and Third Books. London: 1697. V. 49

THE CHARTER and Laws of the States of Ohio, Indiana, Michigan and Illinois, Relating to the Michigan Southern and Northern Indiana Rail-Road Co. New York: 1855. V. 50

THE CHARTER of the British Colonies in America. London: 1774. V. 47

CHARTERIS, LESLIE
The Happy Highwayman. Garden City: 1939. V. 49
Prelude For War. Garden City: 1938. V. 49
Saint Errant. London: 1949. V. 49
The Saint in New York. London: 1935. V. 49
The Saint on Guard. London: 1945. V. 53
The Saint on the Spanish Main. London: 1956. V. 53
The Saint Sees It Through. London: 1947. V. 52; 53
The Saint Steps In. Garden City: 1943. V. 53
The Saint to the Rescue. London: 1961. V. 53
Senor Saint. London: 1959. V. 53
Thanks to the Saint. London: 1958. V. 53
Trust the Saint. London: 1962. V. 53
Vendetta for the Saint. London: 1965. V. 53
X Esquire. London: 1929. V. 52

CHARTERS, ANN
Scenes Along the Road. Photographs of the Desolation Angels 1944-1960. New York: 1970. V. 52

THE CHARTERS of the British Colonies in America. Dublin: 1776. V. 52

THE CHARTERS of the City of London. London: 1745. V. 53

CHASE, CHARLES M.
The Editor's Run in New Mexico and Colorado: Embracing Travels and Observations. Lyndon: 1882. V. 49

CHASE, CHARLES S.
The Trial of Christ, Represented by 23 Figures in Statuary the Size of Life... Portland: 1850. V. 54

CHASE, FREDERICK
A History of Dartmouth College and the Town of Hanover, N.H. Cambridge: 1891-1913. V. 52

CHASE, GEORGE H.
Catalogue of Arretine Pottery. Boston: 1916. V. 50; 52

CHASE, HEBER
The Final Report of the Committee of the Philadelphia Medical Society on the Construction of Instruments and Their Mode of Action in the Radical Cure of Hernia. Philadelphia: 1837. V. 53

CHASE, LEVI B.
A Genealogy and Historical Notices of the Family of Plimpton of Plympton in America and of Plumpton in England. Hartford: 1884. V. 53

CHASE, LEWIS
Poe and His Poetry. London: 1913. V. 48

CHASE, OWEN
Narratives of the Wreck of the Whale-Ship Essex... Waltham St. Lawrence: 1935. V. 50; 54

CHASE, PHILANDER
Bishop Chase's Address Delivered Before the Convention of the Protestant Espicopal Church, Springfield, Illinois, June 16, 1845. St. Louis: 1845. V. 52
Constitution and Canons of the Diocese of Illinois. 1847. V. 52
Defense of Kenyon College. Columbus: 1831. V. 51

CHASE, SALMON P.
Speech of Salmon P. Chase in the Case of the Colored Woman, Matilda, Who was Brought Before the Court of Common Pleas of Hamilton County, Ohio by Writ of Habeas Corpus. Cincinnati: 1837. V. 53

CHASE, SAMUEL
The Answer and Pleas of Samuel Chase. Washington City: 1805. V. 49

CHASHIN, A.
In Remembrance of the Fallen Jewish Watchmen and Workers in the Land of Israel. New York: 1917. V. 53

CHASSEAUD, GEORGE WASHINGTON
The Druses of the Lebanon; Their Manners, Customs and History. London: 1855. V. 49

CHASSEPOL, FRANCOIS DE
A Treatise of the Revenue and False Money of the Romans. London: 1741. V. 50; 54

CHASTEL, ANDRE
The Age of Humanism: Europe 1480-1530. London: 1963. V. 52
The Flowering of the Italian Renaissance. New York: 1965. V. 53; 54
Studios and Styles of the Italian Renaissance. New York: 1966. V. 53; 54

CHASTELLUX, FRANCOIS JEAN, MARQUIS DE
Travels in North America, in the Years 1780, 1781 and 1782. London: 1787. V. 47; 50; 51; 54

CHATEAUBRIAND, FRANCOIS AUGUSTE RENE, VICOMTE DE
Atala. Bath: 1802. V. 47
The Interesting History of Atala, the Beautiful Indian of the Mississippi... New York: 1818. V. 50
A Letter from Rome, Addressed to M. De Fontanes, by the Vicomte de Chateaubriand. London: 1815. V. 50
The Natchez; an Indian Tale. London: 1827. V. 49
Recollections of Italy, England and America... London: 1815. V. 53
Recollections of Italy, England and America. Philadelphia: 1816. V. 53
Sketches of English Literature, with Considerations on the spirit of the Times, Men and Revolution. London: 1836. V. 51
Travels in Greece, Palestine, Egypt and Barbary During the Years 1806 and 1807. Philadelphia: 1813. V. 48

CHATELAIN, CLARA DE PONTIGNY
The Silver Swan. London: 1847. V. 54

CHATELAIN, HENRI ALBERT
Atlas Historique, Ou Nouvelle Introduction a l'Histoire, a la Chronologie & a la Geographie Ancienne & Moderne... Amsterdam: 1713-20. V. 48

CHATELAIN, JEAN
The Biblical Message of Marc Chagall. New York: 1973. V. 49; 51; 53
Marc Chagall. London: 1964. V. 49

CHATER, CATCHICK PAUL
The Chater Collection, Pictures Relating to China, Hong Kong, Macao, 1655-1860... London: 1924. V. 51

CHATER, JAMES
A Grammar of the Cingalese Language. Colombo: 1815. V. 49

CHATFIELD, ROBERT
An Historical Review of the Commercial, Political and Moral State of Hindoostan. London: 1808. V. 50

CHATHAM, RUSSELL D.
The Angler's Coast. Garden City: 1976. V. 53; 54
The Angler's Coast. 1990. V. 53
The Angler's Coast. Livingston: 1991. V. 47; 48
One Hundred Paintings by Russell Chatham. 1990. V. 53
Silent Seasons: 21 Fishing Adventures by 7 American Experts. New York: 1978. V. 48; 50; 54
Striped Bass on the Fly: a Guide to California Waters. San Francisco: 1977. V. 54

CHATHAM, WILLIAM PITT, 1ST EARL OF
Anecdotes of the Life and of the Principal Events of His Time, With His Speeches in Parliament from 1736 to 1778. London: 1792. V. 47
Anecdotes of the Life of the Right Honourable William Pitt. London: 1793. V. 52
Letters Written by the Late Earl of Chatham to His Nephew Thomas Pitt, Esq... London: 1804. V. 53

CHATTAWAY, E. D.
Railways: Their Capital and Dividends, with Statistics of Their Working in Great Britain and Ireland... London: 1855-56. V. 49

CHATTERBOX. London: 1917. V. 49

CHATTERING Jack's Picture Book. London. V. 48

CHATTERJEE, RAMANANDA
The Golden Book of Tagore: a Homage to Rabindrath Tagore from India and the World in Celebration of His Seventieth Brithday. Calcutta: 1931. V. 50

CHATTERTON, ALFRED
Experiments on the Strength of Building Materials Used in Southern India. Madras: 1900. V. 52

CHATTERTON, EDWARD KEBLE
Old Sea Paintings the Story of Maritime Art as Depicted by the Great Masters. London: 1928. V. 51
Old Ship Prints. London: 1927. V. 47; 48
Sailing Models, Ancient and Modern. London: 1934. V. 54
Ship Models. London: 1923. V. 48; 51; 53
Steamship Models. London: 1924. V. 50; 51; 53
Steamship Models. London: 1925. V. 48

CHATTERTON, HENRIETTA GEORGIANA, LADY
The Lost Bride. London: 1872. V. 47
The Pyrenees with Excursions Into Spain. London: 1843. V. 49

CHATTERTON, THOMAS
Miscellanies in Prose and Verse. London: 1778. V. 47; 49
Poems by Thomas Chatterton. London: 1865. V. 54
Poems Supposed to Have Been Written at Bristol, by Thomas Rowley. London: 1777. V. 47; 48; 50; 51; 53
Poems Supposed to Have Been Written at Bristol, by Thomas Rowley. London: 1778. V. 48; 49; 50; 51; 52
Poems, Supposed to Have Been Written at Bristol, by Thomas Rowley... London: 1782. V. 48
Poems Supposed to Have Been Written at Bristol by Thomas Rowley. Cambridge: 1794. V. 48; 50; 51; 54
The Rowley Poems. London: 1898. V. 48; 51; 52
The Works. London: 1803. V. 49; 50

A CHATTO & Windus Almanack. 1927. London: 1927. V. 47

CHATTO, WILLIAM ANDREW
The Angler's Souvenir. London: 1835. V. 50
The History and Art of Wood Engraving. London: 1848. V. 53
A Paper of Tobacco...Smoking...Pipes and Tobacco Boxes. London: 1839. V. 53
Playing Cards. Facts and Speculations ont he Origin and History. London: 1848. V. 53
Scenes and Recollections of Fly-Fishing, in Northumberland, Cumberland and Westmorland. London: 1834. V. 54
A Treatise on Wood Engraving Historical and Practical. London: 1861. V. 48

CHATTOCK, R. S.
Wensleydale. London: 1872. V. 47
Wensleydale. Seeley: 1872. V. 53

CHATWIN, BRUCE
The Attractions of France. London: 1993. V. 49; 50; 51; 52; 53
In Patagonia. London: 1977. V. 50; 51; 53; 54
In Patagonia. New York: 1977. V. 49; 51; 52; 53; 54
In Patagonia. New York: 1978. V. 51; 52
The Morality of Things. Francestown: 1993. V. 52; 53; 54
On the Black Hill. London: 1982. V. 49; 51; 52; 53; 54
On the Black Hill. New York: 1983. V. 47
Patagonia Revisited. 1985. V. 50
Patagonia Revisited. London: 1985. V. 52; 53
Patagonia Revisited. Salisbury: 1985. V. 48; 49; 50; 54
Patagonia Revisited. Wilton: 1985. V. 50; 54
Photographs and Notebooks. London: 1993. V. 53
The Songlines. Franklin Center: 1987. V. 49; 51; 52; 53; 54
The Songlines. London: 1987. V. 49; 50; 51; 52; 53
The Songlines. New York: 1987. V. 51; 52
The Viceroy of Ouidah. London: 1980. V. 47; 49; 51; 53; 54

The Viceroy of Ouidah. New York: 1980. V. 51

CHAUCER, GEOFFREY
The Booke of the Duchesse... Lexington: 1954. V. 51; 52
The Canterbury Tales... London: 1775-78. V. 54
The Canterbury Tales... Oxford: 1798. V. 53
The Canterbury Tales. London: 1822. V. 50; 51
The Canterbury Tales. London: 1913. V. 47; 48; 49; 50; 51; 52; 54
The Canterbury Tales. London: 1929. V. 49
The Canterbury Tales. Waltham St. Lawrence: 1929-31. V. 47; 50; 51; 52; 54
The Canterbury Tales. London: 1934. V. 50; 51; 53; 54
Canterbury Tales. New York: 1934. V. 49; 51
Canterbury Tales. London: 1935. V. 51
The Canterbury Tales. New York: 1946. V. 48; 49; 50; 51
The Canterbury Tales. Cambridge: 1973. V. 48
Chaucer's Romaunt of the Rose, Troilus and Creseide, and the Minor Poems. London: 1846. V. 49
The Complete Poetical Works. New York: 1912. V. 47; 49
The Complete Works... Oxford: 1894-97. V. 51
Complete Works. Oxford: 1899. V. 49
The Complete Works. Oxford: 1952. V. 50
The Floure and the Leafe, & the Boke of Cupide, God of Love, or the Cuckow and the Nightingale. Hammersmith: 1896. V. 51
The Flower and the Leaf. 1902. V. 51
Flower and the Leaf. London: 1902. V. 47; 52
Geoffrey Chaucer's ABC called La Priere de Notre Dame. San Francisco: 1967. V. 47; 49
Major Poetry. London: 1963 i.e. 1964. V. 54
The Nun's Priest's Tale of Chaucer. London: 1950. V. 49
The Pardoner's Tale. Chicago: 1966. V. 47; 48; 50; 52
The Parlement of Foules. Boston: 1904. V. 50; 52
The Poetical Works. London: 1845. V. 50
Poetical Works. London: 1854-56. V. 51
The Poetical Works. London: 1882. V. 49
Poetical Works. London: 1888. V. 54
The Prioresses Tale, from the Canterbury Tales. Guildford: 1902. V. 50
The Prologue to the Canterbury Tales... Los Angeles: 1975. V. 49
The Prologue to the Canterbury Tales. Guildford: 1978. V. 47
The Prologue to the Canterbury Tales. London: 1978. V. 51; 54
The Prologue to the Canterbury Tales. Surrey: 1978. V. 50
The Romaunt of the Rose. 1974. V. 52
Troilus and Cressida. Waltham St. Lawrence: 1927. V. 50; 52; 54
Troilus and Cressida... New York: 1932. V. 49; 51; 53
Troilus and Cressida. London: 1939. V. 52; 54
The Works... London: 1550?. V. 52
The Works... London: 1561. V. 49; 52
The Works... London: 1598. V. 47; 49; 54
The Works... London: 1602. V. 51; 54
The Works... London: 1687. V. 48; 49; 50; 54
Works. London: 1721. V. 50; 51
The Works... Hammersmith: 1896. V. 54
The Works. London: 1905. V. 50; 51; 54
The Works. Cleveland & New York: 1958. V. 48; 50; 51; 52
The Works... London & Ipswich: 1974. V. 50

CHAUDHURI, K. N.
From the Atlantic to the Arabian Sea... Florence: 1995. V. 54

CHAUDON, LOUIS MAYEUL DE
Historical and Critical Memoirs of the Life and Writings of M. de Voltaire. London: 1786. V. 47; 49

CHAUDRON, A. DE V.
Chaudron's Spelling Book. Mobile: 1865. V. 49; 50

CHAULIAC, GUY DE
Guydos Questions, Newly Corrected. London: 1579. V. 48; 49

CHAUMETON, F. P.
Flore Medicale. Paris: 1814-20. V. 51; 54

CHAUNCEY, HENRY
The Historical Antiquities of Hertfordshire. London: 1826. V. 47

CHAUNCY, CHARLES
A Discourse Occasioned by the Death of the Reverend (!). Boston: 1766. V. 51
A Letter to the Reverend Mr. George Whitefield, Vindicating Certain Passages He Has Executed Against, In a Late Book Entitled, Seasonable Thoughts on the State of Religion in New England... Boston: 1745. V. 54
Seasonable Thoughts on the State of Religion in New England. Boston: 1743. V. 54
The Validity of Presbyterian Ordination Asserted and Maintained. Boston: 1762. V. 50; 53

CHAUNCY, HENRY
The Historical Antiquities of Hertfordshire... London: 1700. V. 48; 52; 53
The Historical Antiquities of Hertfordshire. 1826. V. 49
The Historical Antiquities of Hertfordshire. 1826. V. 53

CHAUNDLER, CHRISTINE
Arthur and His Knights. London. V. 51
Arthur and His Knights. London: 1920. V. 52; 54
The Magic Kiss. London: 1916. V. 49

CHAUVEAU, FRANCOIS
Divers Masques. Augsburg. V. 50
Divers Masques. Ausburg: 1680. V. 47

CHAVE, ROSE M.
Youthful Canada: a Book for Boys and Girls. Montreal: 1913. V. 53

CHAVEAU, LEOPOLD
Les Histoires du Petit Renaud. Paris: 1927. V. 54

CHAVES NOGALES, MANUEL
And in the Distance, a Light...? Aspects of the Civil War. London: 1938. V. 49

CHAVEZ, FRAY ANGELICO
Origins of New Mexico Families. Santa Fe: 1954. V. 50

CHAVIGNY, JEAN AIME DE
Commentaires Dv Sr De Chavigny Beavnois Svr Les Centvries et Prognostications de Feu M. Michel de Nostradamus. Paris: 1596. V. 47; 49; 50

CHAYEFSKY, PADDY
Middle of the Night. V. 50

CHAYT, STEVEN
Collotype, Being a History-Practicum-Bibliography. Winter Haven: 1983. V. 47
A Ludlow Anthology. Winter Haven: 1986. V. 47; 51

CHEADLE, WALTER
On Some Cirrhoses of the Liver. London: 1900. V. 53

THE CHEAPSIDE Apprentice; or, The History of Mr. Francis H****. London. V. 50

THE CHEARFUL Companion, Being a Select Collection of Favourite Scots and English Songs, Catches, etc. Glasgow: 1786. V. 54

CHEATLE, GEORGE
Tumors of the Breast. Their Pathology, Symptoms, Diagnosis and Treatment. Philadelphia: 1931. V. 53

THE CHECKERBOARD. New York: 1930. V. 52

CHEDDAR Gorge...English Cheeses. London: 1937. V. 53

THE CHEERFUL Warbler or, Juvenile Song Book. Kendrew, York,: 1830. V. 51

CHEESEMAN, CLARA
A Rolling Stone. London: 1886. V. 54

CHEESMAN, R. E.
In Unknown Arabia. 1926. V. 54

CHEESMAN, T.
Rudiments of Drawing the Human Figure, from Cipriani, Guido, Poussin, Rubens &c. London: 1816. V. 48

CHEETHAM, JAMES
An Answer to Alexander Hamilton's Letter Concerning the Public Conduct and Character of John Adams... New York: 1800. V. 47
An Antidote to John Wood's Poison. New York: 1802. V. 47
The Life of Thomas Paine. New York: 1809. V. 52
A Narrative of the Suppression by Co. Burr, of the History of the Administration of John Adams... New York: 1802. V. 49
Nine Letters on the Subject of Aaron Burr's Political Defection. New York: 1803. V. 47
A Reply to Aristides. New York: 1804. V. 47

CHEETHAM, ROBERT FARREN
Odes and Miscellanies. Stockport: 1796. V. 54

CHEEVER, GEORGE B.
God Against Slavery: and the Freedom and the Duty of the Pulpit to Rebuke It As a Sin Against the God. Cincinnati: 1855?. V. 51
Protest Against the Robbery of the Coloured Race by the Proposed Amendment of the Constitution. New York: 1866. V. 50
The Removal of the Indians. Boston: 1830. V. 50
Wanderings of a Pilgrim in the Shadow of Mont Blanc and the Jungfrau Alp. Glasgow: 1865. V. 50

CHEEVER, HENRY T.
The Island World of the Pacific... Glasgow & London: 1852. V. 53
The Island World of the Pacific. Glasgow: 1860. V. 52
Life in the Sandwich Islands; or, the Heart of the Pacific, As It Was and Is. New York: 1851. V. 47; 51
The Whale and His Captors. London: 1852. V. 54
The Whale and His Captors... New York: 1864. V. 50
The Whaleman's Adventures in the Southern Ocean...on the Homeward Cruise of the "Commodore Preble". London: 1850. V. 50; 53

CHEEVER, JOHN
Atlantic Crossing... 1986. V. 54
Atlantic Crossing. Alabama: 1986. V. 51; 53
Atlantic Crossing. Cottondale: 1986. V. 53
The Brigadier and the Golf Widow. New York: 1964. V. 47; 48; 49; 51; 53
Bullet Park. New York: 1969. V. 47; 49; 51; 53; 54
The Day the Pig Fell Into the Well. Northridge: 1978. V. 48; 49; 51; 52; 53; 54
Elizabeth Ames. Saratoga Springs: 1968. V. 48
The Enormous Radio. London: 1953. V. 52; 53
The Enormous Radio. New York: 1953. V. 48
Excerpts from the Journals of John Cheever. 1986. V. 52
Expelled. Los Angeles: 1987. V. 53; 54
Expelled. 1988. V. 48
Expelled. Los Angeles: 1988. V. 49; 51
Falconer. New York: 1976. V. 49; 50
Falconer. New York: 1977. V. 49; 52; 53
Homage to Shakespeare. 1968. V. 47; 49; 52; 53
The Housebreaker of Shady Hill. New York: 1958. V. 50
The Leaves, The Lion-Fish and the Bear. Los Angeles: 1980. V. 51
The National Pastime. Los Angeles: 1982. V. 51
Oh, What a Paradise It Seems. New York: 1982. V. 49
Some People, Places and Things That Will Not Appear in My Next Novel. New York: 1961. V. 53
The Stories of John Cheever. New York: 1978. V. 47; 48; 50; 51; 52; 53; 54
The Wapshot Chronicle. New York: 1957. V. 48; 49; 51; 53
The Wapshot Chronicle... New York: 1964. V. 54
The Wapshot Chronicle. Franklin Center: 1978. V. 52; 53; 54
The Wapshot Scandal. New York: 1964. V. 53
The Way Some People Live. New York: 1943. V. 47; 48; 51; 53; 54
The World of Apples. New York: 1973. V. 50; 51; 54

CHEEVER, LAWRENCE O.
The House of Morrell. Cedar Rapids: 1948. V. 54

CHEIRO
True Ghost Stories. London. V. 49

CHEKE, JOHN
De Pronvntiatione Graecae...Disputationes cum Stephano Vvintoniensi Episcopo. Basle: 1555. V. 48; 50; 53

CHEKHOV, ANTON
The Black Monk and Other Stories. London: 1903. V. 53
D'trova. St. Petersburg: 1889. V. 53
The Letters of Anton Chekhov. London: 1973. V. 54
Plays. Second Series. (with) Plays. First Series. New York: 1916/16. V. 50
That Worthless Fellow Platonov. London: 1930. V. 49
Two Plays...The Cherry Orchard and Three Sisters. New York: 1966. V. 51; 53; 54

CHELIUS, J. M.
A System of Surgery. Philadelphia: 1847. V. 54

CHELSEA Embankment. Opened by Their Royal Highnesses the Duke and Duchess of Edinburgh on the 9th May, 1874. London: 1874. V. 50

CHELSUM, JAMES
Remarks on the Two Last Chatpers of Mr. Gibbon's History of the Decline and Fall of the Roman Empire, in a Letter to a Friend. London: 1776. V. 47

CHELSUM, JOSEPH
A History of the Art of Engraving in Mezzotint From Its Origin to the Present Times... Winchester: 1786. V. 53

CHELTENHAM, OXFORD & LONDON JUNCTION RAILWAY
Prospectus of the Cheltenham, Oxford and London Junction Railway, Forming also a Direct Route Between Cheltenham and Brighton and Cheltenham and Dover. London: 1845. V. 54

CHEMICAL SOCIETY
Memorial Lectures 1893-1942. London: 1901-51. V. 51

CHEMISTRY As Applied to the Arts and Manufactures. London: 1882. V. 49

CHEMNITZ, MARTIN
Enchiridion de Praecipvis Capitibvs Doctrinae Coelestis... Leipzig: 1588. V. 49; 53

CHEN, JULIE
Listening. Berkeley: 1992. V. 53
River of Stars. 1994. V. 52
River of Stars. Berkeley: 1994. V. 53
You Are Here. Berkeley: 1992. V. 51; 53

CH-EN CHIH-MAI
Chinese Calligraphers and Their Art. Melbourne: 1966. V. 51; 53

CHENEAU, FRANCOIS
The Italian Master; or, Rules for the Italian Tongue... Eton: 1754. V. 48

CHENERY, WILLIAM H.
The Fourteenth Regiment Rhode Island Heavy Artillery (Colored) in the War to Preserve the Union, 1861-1865. Providence: 1898. V. 47; 48; 54

CHENEY, EDNA DOW
Life and Letters of Louisa M. Alcott. Boston: 1889. V. 54

CHENEY, EDNAH DOW
Memoirs of Lucretia Crocker and Abby W. May, Prepared for Private Circulation... Boston: 1893. V. 50

CHENEY, HARRIET
A Peep at the Pilgrims in Sixteen Hundred Thirty-Six. London: 1825. V. 51

CHENEY, JOHN
John Cheney and His Descendants. Banbury: 1936. V. 52

CHENEY, PETER
Dark Hero. London: 1946. V. 52

CHENEY, SHELDON
The New World Architecture. London: 1930. V. 51
Stage Decoration. London: 1928. V. 51

CHENEY, WILLIAM M.
The Sea As Seen by El Sea Powll. Malibu: 1962. V. 47
Type Specimen Book. A Small Book of the letters and Ornaments in the Type Case of My Shop... Los Angeles: 1950-54. V. 51
A Typesticker's Tract on Typefaces: What They Are and What He Thinks They Ought Not to Be... Los Angeles: 1949. V. 54
A Voyage to Trolland: Set Forth in Picture and Prose. Los Angeles: 1922. V. 51

CHENG, T. H.
A Synopsis of the Avifauna of China. Beijing: 1987. V. 49

CHERNAC, LADISLAUS
Cibrum Arithmeticum. Sive, Tabula Continens Numeros Primos, a Compositis Segregatos, Occurentes in Serie Numerorum ab Unitate Progrediendium, Usque ad decies Centens Millia... Deventer: 1811. V. 50

CHERNYSHEVSKY, NIKOLAI G.
A Vital Question; or, What is to Be Done?. New York: 1886. V. 49

CHEROKEE NATION
The Act of Union Between the Eastern and Western Cherokees, the Constitution and Amendments, and the Laws of the Cherokee nation... Tah-Le-Quah: 1870. V. 48
Address of the "Committee and Council of the Cherokee Nation, in General Council Convened", to the People of the United States. 1830. V. 48
Constitution and Laws of the Cherokee Nation. St. Louis: 1875. V. 48
Constitution and Laws of the Cherokee Nation. Parsons: 1893. V. 48
Laws of the Cherokee National: Adopted by the Council at Various periods. Tahlequah: 1852. V. 48; 51; 52
Memorial of the Cherokee Representatives, Submitting the Protest of the Cherokee Nation Against the Ratification, Execution and Enforcement of the Treaty Negotiated at New Echota, in December 1835. Washington: 1836. V. 47

CHERRY, J. L.
Life and Remains of John Clare... Northampton: 1873. V. 51

CHERRY, R. J.
New Techniques of Optical Microscopy and Microspectroscopy. London: 1990. V. 50; 51

CHERRY-GARRARD, APSLEY GEORGE BENET
The Worst Journey in the World. London: 1922. V. 53
The Worst Journey in the World. New York: 1930. V. 54
The Worst Journey in the World. London: 1937. V. 54

CHERRYH, C. J.
Cyteen. 1988. V. 48; 52

CHERTABLON, MONSIEUR DE
Sterben und Erben, das Ist Die Schonste Vorbrereitung zum Tode. Amsterdam: 1702. V. 53

CHERUBINI, LUIGI
A Course of Counterpoint and Fugue. London: 1837. V. 51

CHESAPEAKE & OHIO RAILROAD
The Chesapeake and Ohio Railroad as a Short, Economical and Profitable Line from the Atlantic to the Great West... New York: 1871. V. 47

CHESELDEN, WILLIAM
The Anatomy of the Human Body. London: 1740. V. 47; 49
The Anatomy of the Human Body. London: 1741. V. 52
The Anatomy of the Human Body. London: 1756. V. 54
The Anatomy of the Human Body. London: 1778. V. 47; 52; 53; 54
The Anatomy of the Human Body. Boston: 1806. V. 53

CHESHIRE, JOSEPH B.
Nonnula. Memories, Stories, Traditions, More or Less Authentic. Chapel Hill: 1930. V. 50

CHESNEY, ALAN
Immunity in Syphilis. Baltimore: 1927. V. 51; 53
The Johns Hopkins Hospital and Johns Hopkins University School of Medicine, a Chronicle. Baltimore: 1943/58/63. V. 50; 52; 53
The Johns Hopkins Hospital and the Johns Hopkins University School of Medicine, a Chronicle. Volume I: Early Years, 1867-1893. Baltimore: 1943. V. 50

CHESNEY, CHARLES CORNWALLIS
Campaigns in Virginia and Maryland, etc., etc. London: 1864-5. V. 49
A Military View of Recent Campaigns in Virginia and Maryland...with Maps. London: 1863. V. 49
The Russo-Turkish Campaigns of 1828 and 1829. London: 1854. V. 52

CHESNEY, FRANCIS RAWDON
Narrative of the Euphrates Expedition Carried on by Order of the British Government... London: 1868. V. 49; 50
Observations on the Past and Present State of Fire-Arms and on the Probable Effects in War of the New Musket... London: 1852. V. 49

CHESNEY, GEORGE TOMKYNS
The Battle of Dorking: Reminiscences of a Volunteer. London: 1871. V. 52
The Private Secretary. Edinburgh: 1881. V. 51
A True Reformer. Edinburgh & London: 1873. V. 52

CHESNEY, W.
The Founderd Galleon. London: 1902. V. 47; 51

CHESNUTT, CHARLES WADDELL
The Colonel's Dream. New York: 1905. V. 49; 51; 53; 54
The Conjure Woman. Boston & New York: 1899. V. 49; 51; 52; 53
The Conjure Woman. Cambridge: 1899. V. 54
The House Behind the Cedars. Boston: 1900. V. 51; 53; 54
The Marrow of Tradition. Boston & New York: 1901. V. 48; 49; 51; 53
The Wife of His Youth and Other Stories of the Color Line. Boston: 1899. V. 53

CHESNUTT, HELEN M.
Charles Waddell Chesnutt: Pioneer of the Color LIne. Chapel Hill: 1952. V. 53

CHESSON, NORA HOPPER
Ballads in Prose. London: 1894. V. 54

CHESTER, ALDEN
Courts and Lawyers of New York: a History 1609-1925. New York: 1925. V. 52

CHESTER, ALFRED
The Exquisite Corpse. New York: 1967. V. 54
Jamie Is My Heart's Desire. New York: 1957. V. 48

CHESTER PLAYS
The Chester Play of the Deluge. Waltham St. Lawrence: 1927. V. 51; 52; 54
The Chester Play of the Deluge. London: 1977. V. 48

CHESTER, SAMUEL HALL
Pioneer Days in Arkansas. Richmond: 1927. V. 51; 52

CHESTERFIELD, PHILIP DORMER STANHOPE, 4TH EARL OF
The Case of the Hanover Forces in the Pay of Great Britian, Impartially and Freely Examined. London: 1743. V. 48
Characters of Eminent Personages of His Own Time... London: 1777. V. 47; 48
Choix des Lettres du Lord Chesterfield a son Fils. Londres i.e. Paris: 1776. V. 54
The Fine Gentleman's Etiquette; or, Lord Chesterfield's Advice to His Son. London: 1776. V. 53
The Letters of Philip Dormer Stanhope, 4th Earl of Chesterfield... London: 1847/53. V. 53
The Letters of Philip Dormer Stanhope, 4th Earl of Chesterfield. London: 1932. V. 49
Letters to His Son. London: 1774. V. 47; 48; 51; 52; 53; 54
Letters... to His Son... London: 1775. V. 48; 53
Letters to His Son... London: 1776. V. 48
Letters to His Son. Washington: 1901. V. 51
Letters to His Son. London: 1926. V. 53
Letters...to His Godson and Successor. Oxford: 1890. V. 53
Letters...to His Son. Dublin: 1774. V. 48
Lettres du Comte de Chesterfield a son fils Philippe Stanhope. Venice: 1811. V. 50; 52
The Life of the Late Earl of Chesterfield; or, the Man of the World... Philadelphia: 1774. V. 52
The Life of the Late Earl of Chesterfield; or, the Man of the World... London: 1775. V. 51
Lord Chesterfield's Advice to His Son, on Men and Manners... London: 1792. V. 47
Lord Chesterfield's Advice to His Son, on Men and Manners. London: 1793. V. 53
Miscellaneous Works. London: 1771. V. 53
Miscellaneous Works... London: 1777. V. 48
Miscellaneous Works. London: 1777-78. V. 48
Miscellaneous Works... London: 1778. V. 53
Miscellaneous Works... London: 1779. V. 49; 54
The Oeconomy of Human Life in Two Parts... London: 1769. V. 47
The Poetical Works of... London: 1927. V. 50; 51; 54

CHESTERFIELD, PHILIP STANHOPE, 2ND EARL OF
Correspondence with Various Ladies... London: 1930. V. 51; 52

CHESTERFIELD, RUTH
A New Version of Old Mother Hubbard. Boston: 1866. V. 54

CHESTERTON, GEORGE LAVAL
Peace, War and Adventure. London: 1853. V. 47; 48; 52
Revelations of Prison Life; With an Enquiry Into Prison Discipline and Secondary Punishments. London: 1856. V. 50

CHESTERTON, GILBERT KEITH
All I Survey - a Book of Essays. London: 1933. V. 54
Avowals and Denials - a Book of Essays. London: 1954. V. 54
The Ball and the Cross. London: 1910. V. 51; 52
Blake. London: 1910. V. 49
Christendom in Dublin. London: 1932. V. 54
A Christmas Song for Three Guilds. New York: 1947. V. 50
The Club of Queer Trades. London: 1905. V. 50; 52
The Club of Queer Trades. New York: 1905. V. 52; 53
Collected Poems. London: 1927. V. 48; 50; 52
The Coloured Lands. 1938. V. 47; 51
The Coloured Lands. London: 1938. V. 54
Come To Think Of It... London: 1930. V. 50; 54
The Defendant. London: 1901. V. 47
The End of the Roman Road - a Pageant of Wayfarers. 1924. V. 52
Fancies Versus Fads. London: 1923. V. 50
The Flying Inn. London: 1914. V. 48
The Flying Inn. New York: 1914. V. 54
G. K. C. as M. C. Being a Collection of Thirty-Seven Introductions. London: 1929. V. 50
Generally Speaking - A Book of Essays. London: 1928. V. 50
George Bernard Shaw. London: 1910. V. 54
Gloria in Profundis. New York: 1927. V. 49
Grey-Beards at Play, Literature and Art for Old Gentlemen... London: 1900. V. 49; 53
The Incredulity of Father Brown. London: 1926. V. 48; 50; 53
The Innocence of Father Brown. London: 1911. V. 50
The Innocence of Father Brown. London: 1913. V. 48; 51
London. London: 1914. V. 48
Magic. London: 1920. V. 53
The Man Who Knew Too Much... London: 1922. V. 47

CHESTERTON, GILBERT KEITH continued
The Man Who Knew Too Much. New York: 1922. V. 49; 53
The Man Who Was Thursday. 1908. V. 52
The Man Who Was Thursday. Bristol: 1908. V. 50
The Napoleon of Notting Hil. London: 1904. V. 48; 50
The Nativity. Albany: 1911. V. 54
The New Jerusalem. London: 1920. V. 48; 50
The Poet and the Lunatics. New York: 1929. V. 47; 48; 49
The Queen of Seven Swords. London: 1926. V. 54
The Resurrection of Rome. London: 1930. V. 54
The Return of Don Quixote. 1927. V. 48; 50; 52
The Return of Don Quixote. London: 1927. V. 50; 51; 52; 54
Robert Louis Stevenson. London: 1927. V. 53; 54
Robert Louis Stevenson. New York: 1928/27. V. 49
The Scandal of Father Brown. London: 1935. V. 48; 50; 53
The Secret of Father Brown. New York: 1927. V. 51
The Sword of Wood. London: 1928. V. 50; 54
Tremendous Trifles. London: 1909. V. 50; 54
The Turkey and the Turk. 1930. V. 49
Twelve Types. Essays. London: 1902. V. 50
Ubi Ecclesia. London: 1929. V. 50
The Ultimate Lie. Riverside: 1910. V. 53
The Well and the Shallows. London: 1935. V. 54
The Wild Knight and Other Poems. London: 1900. V. 51
William Cobbett. London: 1925. V. 52
The Wisdom of Father Brown. London: 1914. V. 48

CHESTNUTT, CHARLES WADDELL
The Conjure Woman. 1899. V. 50
The Conjure Woman. Boston: 1927. V. 48

CHESWICKE, LOUIS
South Africa and the Transvaal War. V. 50

CHETHAM, JAMES
The Angler's Vade Mecum; or, a Compendious, Yet Full Discourse of Angling. London: 1681. V. 50
The Angler's Vade Mecum; or, a Compendious, Yet Full Discourse of Angling... London: 1700. V. 47; 50; 52

CHETTLE, E. M.
Tiny Toddlers. London: 1890. V. 54

CHETWOOD, WILLIAM RUFUS
A General History of the Stage, From Its Origin in Greece Down to the Present Time... London: 1749. V. 48
The Voyages and Adventures of Captain Robert Boyle, In Several Parts of the World. London: 1726. V. 51
The Voyages and Adventures of Captain Robert Boyle, in Several Parts of the World. London: 1781. V. 48
The Voyages, Dangerous Adventures and Imminent Escapes of Captain Richard Falconer... London: 1720. V. 47; 52

CHEVALIER, MICHAEL
Society, Manners and Politics in the United States... V. 52

CHEVALIER, MICHEL
On the Probable Fall in the Value of Gold... Manchester: 1859. V. 53
Remarks on the Production of the Precious Metals and on the Depreciation of Gold... London: 1853. V. 53

CHEVES, ELIZABETH WASHINGTON FOOTE
Sketches in Prose and Verse. Baltimore: 1849. V. 54

CHEVES, LANGDON
Speech of Hon. Langdon Cheves, of South Carolina, in the Southern Convention at Nashville, Tenn. November 14, 1850. Nashville: 1850. V. 47

CHEVREUL, MICHEL EUGENE
De la Loi du Contraste Simultane des Couleurs, et de l'Assortiment des Objets Colores. Paris: 1889. V. 47; 49
Expose d'un Moyen de Definer et de Nommer les Couleurs, d'Arpes une Methode Precise et Experimentale... Paris: 1861. V. 54
Laws of Contrast of Colour... London: 1857. V. 50; 51
The Laws of Contrast of Colour... London: 1859. V. 50
The Laws of Contrast of Colour... London: 1868. V. 49
The Laws of Contrast of Colour... London: 1880. V. 51
The Principles of Harmony and Contrast of Colours. London: 1855. V. 50; 52; 54
The Principles of Harmony and Contrast of Colours. New York: 1967. V. 54
The Principles of Harmony and...Contrast of Colours... London: 1870. V. 52

CHEW, BEVERLY
The Library of the Late Beverly Chew. New York: 1924-25. V. 54
The Longfellow Collector's Handbook. New York: 1885. V. 53

CHEWETT, JAMES G.
The Upper Canada Almanac, and Provincial Calendar, for the Year of Our Lord 1831. York: 1831. V. 53

CHEYNE, GEORGE
The English Malady; or, a Treatise of Nervous Diseases of All Kinds. London: 1733. V. 48; 49; 52; 53
An Essay on Health and Long Life. London: 1724. V. 47; 48; 50; 51; 54
An Essay on Health and Long Life. London: 1725. V. 47; 48; 51; 53
An Essay on Regimen. London: 1740. V. 47; 48; 49; 53
An Essay on the True Nature and Due Method of Treating the Gout... (with) An Essay of Health and Long Life. London: 1722/25. V. 48
Philosophical Principles of Natural Religion Containing the Elements of Natural Philosophy... London: 1705. V. 50
Philosophical Principles of Natural Religion: Natural and Revealed: In two Parts. London: 1715. V. 50
Philosophical Principles of Religion, Natural and Revealed in Two Parts... London: 1725/16. V. 50

CHEYNE, JOHN
An Essay on Bowel Complaints of Children, Most Immediately Connected withthe Biliary Secretion... Philadelphia: 1813. V. 48
An Essay on Hydrocephalus Acutus, or Dropsy in the Brain. Philadelphia: 1814. V. 54

CHIANG YEE
Birds and Beasts. London: 1939. V. 54

CHIARI, JOSEPH
Collected Poems. London: 1978. V. 48

CHIARUGI, VINCENZO
Regolamento dei Regi Spedali di Santa Maria Nuovo e di Bonifazio. Florence: 1789. V. 49; 53
Regolamento del Regio Arcispedale di Santa Marai Nuova di Firenze. Florence: 1783. V. 49; 53; 54

CHICAGO & NORTH WESTERN RAILWAY CO.
Sixth Annual Report. June 1865. New York: 1865. V. 47

CHICAGO, BURLINGTON & QUINCY RAILROAD
Estes Park, Colorado and Its Environs. Denver. V. 52
The Heart of the Continent. Chicago: 1882. V. 47

CHICAGO. CHARTER
Charter of the City of Chicago, and Amendments. Chicago: 1849. V. 53

CHICAGO COMMISSION ON RACE RELATIONS
The Negro in Chicago. A Study of Race Relations and a Race Riot. Chicago: 1923. V. 53

CHICAGO HISTORICAL SOCIETY
Charter, Constitution and By-Laws, with a List of Officers, Etc. of the Chicago Historical Society, Organized 1856. Incorporated 1857. Chicago: 1858. V. 47

CHICAGO, KANSAS CITY & TEXAS RAILRAOD
Propsectus of Chicago, Kansas City & Texas Railway Company. Kansas City: 1887. V. 47; 49

CHICAGO, MILWAUKEE & ST. PAUL RAILWAY CO.
A Handy Pocket Volume Containing Facts and Figures About Dakota Together with Information of Lands in Wisconsin, Iowa and Minnesota. Milwaukee: 1886. V. 54

CHICAGO, ROCK ISLAND & PACIFIC RAILROAD
The Chicago Rock Island and Pacific Railroad Is Known as the Best Route to Des Moines, Council Bluffs, Omaha, Denver, Leavenworth, Kansas, Colorado & California. Chicago: 1876. V. 47
THE Great Overland Route!...For California, Oregon, Australia, China and Japan... Chicago: 1875. V. 50
Merry Christmas With the Compliments of the General Ticket & Passenger Department of the Great Rock Island Route. Chicago: 1880's. V. 50
Now Is the Accepted Time. Choose the Right Road! Which is the Great Rock Island. Do You Realize the Fact that More Public Land was Sold and Pre-empted in Dakota During 1881 Than in All the Other States and Territories Combined... Chicago: 1882. V. 47
Oklahoma, Particulary Those Portions Of it Which Are Traversed by the Lines of the Rock Island System. Chicago: 1905. V. 50

CHICKERING, FRANCIS E., MRS.
Cloud Crystals a Snow Flake Album. New York: 1865. V. 47

CHICKERING, JESSE
A Statistical View of the Population of Massachusetts from 1765 to 1840. Boston: 1846. V. 53

CHIDLEY, SAMUEL
An Additional Remonstrance to the Valiant and Wel-Deserving Souldier, and the Rest of the Creditors of the Common-Wealth... London: 1653. V. 51

CHIERA, EDWARD
Sumerian Epics and Myths. Chicago: 1934. V. 49; 51
Sumerian Lexical Texts from the Temple School of Nippur. Chicago;: 1929. V. 49; 51

CHIEREGATUS, LEONELLUS
Propositio Coram Carolo VIII. Facta. Rome: 1488. V. 47; 49

CHIGNELL, ROBERT
The Life and paintings of Vicat Cole, RA. London: 1898. V. 49; 51

CHIHULY, DALE
Baskets. Portland: 1994. V. 51

CHILD, ANDREW
Overland Route to California...Council Bluffs...Platte River...South Pass...Sublette...Bear River... Los Angeles: 1941. V. 50

CHILD, DAVID LEE
An Appeal from David L. Childs (sic), Editor of the Anti-Slavery Standard to the Abolitionists. Albany: 1844. V. 49
A Report of the Trial of Pedro Gilbert, Bernardo de Soto (et al)...Before the U.S. Circuit Court, on an Indictment Charging Them with the Commission of an Act of Piracy, on Board the Brig Mexican of Salem. Boston: 1834. V. 52
The Texan Revolution...Which is Added a Letter on the Annexation of Texas. Washington: 1843. V. 50

CHILD, FRANCIS JAMES
English and Scottish Ballads. London: 1861. V. 53
The English and Scottish Popular Ballads. New York: 1965. V. 53

CHILD, HAMILTON
Gazetteer and Business Directory of Allegany County, New York for 1875. Syracuse: 1875. V. 51

CHILD, JOSIAH
A New Discourse of Trade, Wherein is Recommended Several Weightly Points Relating to Companies of Merchants... London: 1694. V. 50; 54

CHILD, LYDIA MARIA FRANCIS
The American Frugal Housewife... Boston: 1836. V. 47
The American Frugal Housewife. New York: 1844. V. 47
An Appeal in Favor of that Class of Americans Called Africans. Boston: 1833. V. 47
An Appeal in Favor of That Class of Americans Called Africans. New York: 1836. V. 53
The Family Nurse; or Companion of the Frugal Housewife. Boston: 1837. V. 54
Hobomok, a Tale of Early Times. Boston: 1824. V. 49
Letters of... Boston: 1883. V. 49
The Rebels; or, Boston Before the Revolution. Boston: 1850. V. 49

CHILD Pictures from Dickens. London: 1885. V. 54

CHILD, THEODORE
Art and Criticism, Monographs and Studies. New York: 1892. V. 48

CHILDERS, ERSKINE
In the Ranks of the C.I.V. - A Narrative and Diary of Personal Experiences with the C.I.V. Battery (Honourable Artillery Company) in South Africa. London: 1900. V. 49
The Riddle of the Sands - a Record of Secret Service Recently Achieved. London: 1903. V. 51; 52
The Riddle of the Sands, a Record of Secret Service Recently Achieved. Barre: 1971. V. 51

CHILDERS, HUGH
Romantic Trials of Three Centuries. London: 1913. V. 48

CHILDERS, JAMES SAXON
War Eagles - The Story of the Eagle Squadron. London: 1943. V. 51

CHILDHOOD.. London. V. 49

CHILDREN of the Empire. London: 1905. V. 54

CHILDREN Of the Revolution. New York: 1900. V. 50

CHILDREN'S Amusements. New York and Baltimore: 1822. V. 50

THE CHILDREN'S Cargo. London: 1930. V. 50

THE CHILDREN'S Circus Book. 1935. V. 47
THE CHILDREN'S Circus Book. London: 1935. V. 48

THE CHILDREN'S Picture Fable Book. London: 1860. V. 49

A CHILDREN'S Sampler. 1950. V. 48
A CHILDREN'S Sampler. Stamford: 1950. V. 52

THE CHILDREN'S Tableaux. London: 1895. V. 48

CHILDRESS, ALICE
Like One of the Family. Brooklyn: 1956. V. 49; 52; 53

CHILDREY, JOSHUA
Britannia Baconica; or, the Natural Rarities of England, Scotland and Wales. London: 1661. V. 51

A CHILD'S Book of Old Verses. New York: 1910. V. 49; 53

THE CHILD'S Coloured Juvenile Picture and Reading Book. London: 1830. V. 49

CHILDS, FRANCIS J.
Some British Ballads. London: 1918. V. 49

CHILDS, GEORGE
English Landscape Scenery; an Advanced Drawing Book. London: 1850. V. 50
English Landscape Scenery: an Advanced Drawing Book. London: 1860. V. 48

CHILDS, J. RIVES
An Annotated World Bibliography of Jacques Casanova de Seingalt and of Works Concerning Him. Vienna: 1956. V. 50

CHILDS, MARILYN
The Men Behind the Morgan Horse. Leominster: 1979. V. 54

CHILDS, MARY FAIRFAX
De Namin' ob de Twins and Other Sketches from Cotton Land. New York: 1908. V. 50; 51

THE CHILD'S Play-Book. 1840. V. 49

CHILLICOTHE Business Directory, for 1855-6. Chilliccothe: 1855. V. 53

CHILLINGWORTH, WILLIAM
The Religion of Protestants, a Safe Way to Salvation, or an Answer to a Booke (by E. Knott i.e. M. Wilson) entitled Mercy and Truth, or Charity Maintain'd by Catholiques. Oxford: 1638. V. 51

CHILTON, F. B.
Unveiling and Dedication of Monument to Hood's Texas Brigade... Houston: 1911. V. 53

CHILTON, LANCE
New Mexico, A New Guide to the Colorful State. Albuquerque: 1974. V. 54

CHILVERS, HEDLEY
Johannesburg. New York. V. 49

THE CHIMNEY-Sweepers, a Town Eclogue. London: 1773. V. 50; 54

CHIN, FRANK
The Chickencoop Chinaman and the Year of the Dragon. Seattle: 1981. V. 51

THE CHINA Cow and Other Stories. London. V. 48

CHINESE and English Phrase Book and Dictionary. Vancouver: 1897?. V. 54

A CHINESE Chrestomathy, in the Canton Dialect... China: 1839. V. 47

CHINESE, Corean, and Japanese Potteries. A Descriptive Catalogue of Loan Exhibition of Selected Examples... New York: 1914. V. 47

CHINESE Decorated Papers, Chinoiserie for Three, by Hans Schmoller, Tanya Schmoller and Henry Morris. Newtown: 1987. V. 47

CHINESE Love Poems. Mount Vernon: 1942. V. 48

CHING, R.
New Zealand Birds, an Artist's Field Studies. Auckland: 1986. V. 51

CH' ING, SHENG-TSU, EMPEROR OF CHINA
The Sacred Edict... London: 1817. V. 47

CHIN KU CH'I KUAN
The Affectionate Pair, of the History of Sung-Kin. London: 1820. V. 52; 54

CHINQUILLA
Natives of North America. Lame Deer: 1932. V. 50

CHINTAMON, HURRYCHUND
A Commentary on the Bhagavad-Gita, or, the Discourse Between Krishna and Arjuna on Divine Matters. London: 1874. V. 53

CHIPMAN, GEORGE
The American Moralist. Wrentham: 1801. V. 49; 50

CHIPPINDALL, L. K. A.
The Grasses and Pastures of South Africa. Cape Town: 1955. V. 48; 50; 51

CHISHOLM, C. R., & CO.
Chicago and Montreal, Chisholm's All-Round Route and Panoramic Guide of the St. Lawrence... Chicago/Montreal: 1881. V. 47

CHISHOLM, LOUEY
Cinderella and Other Stories for the Seven Year Old. Edinburgh: 1910. V. 53
The Enchanted Land, Tales Told Again. London: 1906. V. 51
The Enchanted Land; Tales told Again. New York: 1906. V. 47
The Golden Staircase. London: 1906. V. 52

CHISHULL, EDMUND
Antiquities Asiaticae Christianam Aeram Antecedentes... London: 1728. V. 52

CHISLETT, R.
Yorkshire Birds. London: 1953. V. 50; 51

CHISOLM, J. JULIAN
A Manual of Military Surgery, for the Use of Surgeons in the Confederate States Army... Columbia: 1864. V. 49

CHITTENDEN, FRED J.
The Royal Horticultural Society Dictionary of Gardening. Oxford: 1951. V. 50

CHITTENDEN, HIRAM MARTIN
The American Fur Trade of the Far West. New York: 1935. V. 48; 49; 52; 53
History of Early Steamboat Navigation on the Missouri River. New York: 1903. V. 52
History of Early Steamboat Navigation on the Missouri River... New York: 1909. V. 49
A History of the American Fur Trade of the Far West. Stanford: 1954. V. 50

CHITTENDEN, L. E.
The Emma Mine. A Statement of the Facts Connected With the Emma Mine: Its Sale to the Emma Silver Mining Company (Limited) of London, and Its Subsequent History and Present Condition. New York: 1876. V. 48

CHITTENDEN, NEWTON H.
Travels in British Columbia. Victoria: 1882. V. 47

CHITTENDEN, RUSSELL
History of the Sheffield Scientific School of Yale Universtiy 1846-1922. New Haven: 1928. V. 50; 52
The Nutrition of Man. New York: 1907. V. 48; 53
On Digestive Proteolysis. New Haven,: 1895. V. 48
Physiological Economy in Nutrition with Special Reference to the Minimal Proteid Requirement of the Healthy Man. New York: 1905. V. 48; 53

CHITTENDEN, WILLIAM
Ranch Verses. New York: 1893. V. 53

CHITTY, EDWARD
The Illustrated Fly-Fisher's Text Book... London: 1845. V. 47

CHITTY, JOSEPH
A Practical Treatise On Bills of Exchange, Checks on Bankers, Promissory Notes, Bankers' Cash Notes and Bank Notes. London: 1807. V. 50
A Practical Treatise on the Law of Nations, Relative to the Legal Effect of War on the Commerce of Belligerents and Neutrals... Boston: 1812. V. 52
A Treatise on the Game Laws and On Fisheries...(with) A Continuation of a Treatise on the Law Respecting Game and Fish... London: 1812/16. V. 47

CHIVERS, HERBERT
Artistic Homes. St. Louis: 1903. V. 49

CHIVERS, THOMAS HOLLEY
The Lost Pleiad; and Other Poems. New York: 1845. V. 47; 54
A Nacoochee; or, the Beautiful Star, With Other Poems. New York: 1837. V. 52; 53; 54
Virginalia; or, Songs of My Summer Nights. Philadelphia: 1853. V. 47; 54

CHLADNI, ERNST FLORENS FRIEDRICH
Die Akustik. Leipzig: 1802. V. 47; 54
Traite d'Acoustique. Paris: 1809. V. 47

CHMURY, B.
Anatol Petritzky. Theater-Trachten. Staatsverlag der Ukraine: 1929. V. 52

CHOATE, RUFUS
Addresses and Orations of Rufus Choate. Boston: 1878. V. 49

CHOCTAW NATION
Constitution and Laws of the Choctaw Nation. Together with the Treaties of 1855, 1865 and 1866. New York: 1869. V. 48

CHOISEUL STAINVILLE, ETIENNE FRANCOIS, DUC DE
Memoire Historque sur la Negociation de la France & de l'Angleterre, Depuis le 26 Mars 1761 jusque'au 20 Septembre de la meme annee, Avec les Pieces Justificatives. Paris: 1761. V. 52

CHOKIER, JOHANNES
Thesavrvs Politicorvm Aphorismorvm... Rome: 1611. V. 54

CHOLMONDELEY, MARY
Moth and Rust... London: 1902. V. 50
Moth and Rust... New York: 1902. V. 50
Prisoners (Fast Bound in Misery and Iron). London: 1906. V. 47; 50
Prisoners (Fast Bound in Misery and Iron). New York: 1906. V. 50
Red Pottage. London: 1899. V. 50
The Romance of His Life and Other Romances. London: 1921. V. 50
Under One Roof: a Family Record. London: 1918. V. 50

CHOLMONDELEY-PENNELL, H.
Fishing. London: 1885. V. 52
Fishing. London: 1901. V. 51
Fishing Gossip. London: 1886. V. 53

CHOPIN, KATE
The Awakening. Chicago: 1899. V. 51
Bayou Folk. Boston: 1894. V. 47; 51; 54
A Night in Acadie. Chicago: 1897. V. 53

CHORLEY, JOHN RUTTER
The Wife's Litany, a Winter-Night's Dream, Ballads and Other Pieces in Verse. London: 1865. V. 54

CHORLTON, WILLIAM
The Cold Grapery, from Direct American Practice... New York: 1853. V. 51

CHOUKRI, MOHAMED
Tennessee Williams in Tangier. Santa Barbara: 1979. V. 48; 49; 53

CHOULANT, LUDWIG
History and Bibliography of Anatomic Illustration. Chicago: 1920. V. 50; 52; 54
History and Bibliography of Anatomic Illustration. New York: 1962. V. 50

CHOULES, JOHN O.
The Origin and History of Missions; a Record of the Voyages, Travels, Labors and Successes of the Various Missionaries... New York: 1851. V. 47; 51

CHRETIEN, CHARLES P.
An Essay on Logical Method. Oxford: 1848. V. 52

CHRETIEN, DOUGLAS
The Battle Book of the O'Donnells. Berkeley: 1935. V. 49

CHRIST, JAY FINLEY
An Irregular Chronology of Sherlock Holmes of Baker Street. Ann Arbor: 1947. V. 49
An Irregular Guide to Sherlock Holmes of Baker Street. New York: 1947. V. 49; 51

CHRISTENSEN, ERWIN O.
Primitive Art. New York: 1955. V. 53

CHRISTIAN, CATHERINE M.
Great Stories of All Time. London: 1930. V. 54

CHRISTIAN, EDWARD
Vindication of the Right of the Universities of Great Britain to a Copy of Every New Publication. Cambridge: 1807. V. 48

CHRISTIAN, EWAN
Architectural Illustrations of Skelton Church, Yorkshire. London: 1846. V. 48; 51; 52

CHRISTIAN, GEORGE L.
North Carolina and Virginia in the Civil War. Nashville: 1904. V. 50

CHRISTIAN, JOACHIM
A Political Discourse Upon the Different Kinds of Militia, Whether National, Mercenary or Auxiliary... London: 1757. V. 48

THE CHRISTIAN *Poet. A Miscellany of Divine Poems.* London: 1728. V. 50

CHRISTIAN DE PISAN
The Epistle of Othea to Hector of the Boke of Knyghthode.... London: 1904. V. 54

IL CHRISTIANO *Occupato.* Rome: 1762. V. 54

CHRISTIE, AGATHA
4:50 from Paddington. London: 1957. V. 47; 48
Absent in the Spring. London: 1944. V. 50; 52
The Adventure of Christmas Pudding and a Selection of Entries. London: 1960. V. 47; 50
After the Funeral. London: 1953. V. 49
And Then There Were None. 1940. V. 53
The Body in the Library. New York: 1942. V. 47; 48
By the Pricking of My Thumbs. London: 1968. V. 48
Cards on the Table. New York: 1937. V. 47
A Caribbean Mystery. 1965. V. 53
Crooked House. London: 1949. V. 47; 48
A Daughter's a Daughter. London: 1952. V. 52
Death Comes as the End. New York: 1944. V. 52
Death Comes as the End. London: 1945. V. 47; 49; 50; 51; 53
Death in the Clouds. London: 1935. V. 48
Death on the Nile. London: 1937. V. 49; 51
Death on the Nile. New York: 1938. V. 48; 52
Destination Unknown. London: 1954. V. 52
Elephants Can Remember. London: 1972. V. 50; 53
Evil Under the Sun. London: 1941. V. 49; 50
Evil Under the Sun. New York: 1941. V. 48; 52
Five Little Pigs. London: 1942. V. 50
Hercule Poirot's Christmas. London: 1939. V. 50
The Hollow. London: 1946. V. 47; 49; 50; 51
The Hollow. New York: 1946. V. 53
The Hollow. London: 1952. V. 52
The Hound of Death. 1933. V. 53; 54
The Hound of Death. London: 1933. V. 48; 51; 52
The Labors of Hercules. 1947. V. 53
The Labors of Hercules. New York: 1947. V. 48
The Labours of Hercules. London: 1947. V. 47; 49; 50; 52
Mrs. McGinty's Dead. London: 1951. V. 51
The Mousetrap. London: 1954. V. 49; 52
The Moving Finger. London: 1943. V. 52
Murder at the Vicarage. London: 1950. V. 52
Murder for Christmas. New York: 1939. V. 49
A Murder is Announced. 1950. V. 47; 49
A Murder is Announced. London: 1950. V. 47
Murder is Easy. London: 1939. V. 52
The Murder of Roger Ackroyd. London: 1926. V. 50; 52
The Mysterious Mr. Quin. London: 1930. V. 48
The Mystery of the Blue Train. London: 1928. V. 48
N or M?. New York: 1941. V. 47; 52
Nesmesis. London: 1971. V. 48
The Pale Horse. London: 1961. V. 52
Partners in Crime. London: 1929. V. 47
Partners in Crime. New York: 1929. V. 54
Poems. London: 1973. V. 54
Poirot and the Regatta Mystery. London: 1940's?. V. 50
Poirot and the Regatta Mystery. London: 1941. V. 52
Poirot's Last Case. London: 1975. V. 53
Sad Cypress. London: 1940. V. 47; 53
Tge Secret of Chimneys. London: 1925. V. 47
Sparkling Cyanide. London: 1945. V. 47; 48; 49; 50; 51; 53; 54
Sparkling Cyanide. London: 1946. V. 50
Star Over Bethlehem and Other Stories. London: 1965. V. 47; 48; 49
Ten Little Niggers. London: 1939. V. 48
Ten Little Niggers. London: 1944. V. 52
They Came to Baghdad. London: 1951. V. 50
Thirteen at Dinner. New York: 1933. V. 47
Three Act Tragedy. London: 1935. V. 54
Towards Zero. London: 1941. V. 49
Towards Zero. 1944. V. 53
Towards Zero. London: 1944. V. 48; 50
The Under Dog. 1929. V. 53
Why Didn't They Ask Evans?. London: 1934. V. 48
The Witness for the Prosecution and Other Stories. New York: 1948. V. 53

CHRISTIE, DUGALD
Thirty Years in Moukden. 1883-1913. London: 1914. V. 48

CHRISTIE, ELLA R.
Through Khiva to Golden Samarkand. London: 1925. V. 50

CHRISTIE, JAMES
A Disquisition Upon Etruscan Vases... London: 1806. V. 52
An Inquiry Into the Antient Greek Game...with Reasons for Believing the Same to Have Been Known from Remote Antiquity in china, and Progressively Improved Into the Chinese, Indian, Persian and European Ches... London: 1801. V. 48
Instructions for Hunting, Breaking Pointers and Finding Out Game... Banff: 1817. V. 54

CHRISTIE, JOHN
The Ancestry of Catherine Thomson Hogarth. The Wife of Charles Dickens, Novelist. Edinburgh: 1912. V. 51

CHRISTIE, W. D.
John Stuart Mill and Mr. Abraham Hayward, Q.C. London: 1873. V. 48

CHRISTIE-MILLER, SYDNEY RICHARDSON
Britwell Handlist or Short-Title Catalogue of the Principal Volumes from the Time of Caxton to the Year 1800 Formerly in the Library of Britwell Court, Buckinghamhire. London: 1933. V. 50
Catalogue of the Library... London: 1873-76. V. 47; 49; 50; 52
Catalogue of Valuable Early English Works on Theology, Divinity, &c. From the Renowned Library Formerly at Britwell Court, Burnham Bucks... London: 1921-27. V. 50

CHRISTINE DE PISAN
The Epistle of Others to Hector of the Boke of Knyghthode... London: 1904. V. 48

CHRISTISON, NEIL
Wedded to a Genius. London: 1894. V. 54

CHRISTISON, ROBERT
A Dispensatory, or Commentary on the Pharmacopoeias of Great Britain. Edinburgh: 1848. V. 51
On Granular Degeneration of the Kidneys and Its Connexxion With Dropsy, Inflmmations and Other Diseases. Edinburgh: 1839. V. 48; 53
A Treatise on Poisons, In Relation to Medical Jurisprudence, Physiology and the Practice of Physic. Edinburgh: 1832. V. 51; 53

CHRIST-JANER, ALBERT
Boardman Robinson. Chicago: 1946. V. 54

CHRISTMAS ABC. Boston: 1899. V. 47
CHRISTMAS ABC. Akron: 1910. V. 53
THE CHRISTMAS Book. New York: 1915. V. 49
CHRISTMAS Carols Old and New. London: 1880. V. 53
THE CHRISTMAS Echo. London: 1919. V. 50
THE CHRISTMAS Eve. Boston: 1842. V. 53
CHRISTMAS Eve with the Spirits; or, the Canon's Wanderings Through Ways Unknown. London: 1870. V. 49

CHRISTMAS, H.
The Shores and Islands of the Mediterranean Including a Visit to the Seven Churches of Asia. London: 1851. V. 48

CHRISTMAS Improvement; or, Hunting Mrs. P. A. Tale, Founded on Facts. London: 1834. V. 49
CHRISTMAS Story Book. New York: 1903. V. 52
A CHRISTMAS Tale. London: 1960. V. 48
THE CHRISTMAS Tale, a Poetical Address and Remonstrance to the Young Ministry. London: 1784. V. 52
CHRISTMAS Tales of Flanders. New York: 1917. V. 52
THE CHRISTMAS Treat; or Gay Companion. Dublin: 1767. V. 47
CHRISTMAS With the Poets. London: 1851. V. 52
CHRISTMAS with the Poets... London: 1862. V. 51

CHRISTO
The Accordion-Fold Book for the Umbrellas, Joint Project for Japan and U.S.A. San Francisco: 1991. V. 53
Christo: Wrapped Walk Ways. Loose Park, Kansas City, Missouri, 1977-78. New York: 1978. V. 49; 53
The Gates Project for Central Park, New York City. New York: 1981. V. 53

CHRISTOPHER, A. B.
The Word Accomplished: Extracts. 1974. V. 52; 54

CHRISTOPHER, JOHN
The Twenty-Second Century. London: 1954. V. 50
The Year of the Comet. London: 1955. V. 50

CHRISTY and Fox's Complete Methodist and Joke-Book. New York: 1858. V. 54

CHRISTY, CUTHBERT
Big Game and Pygmies. London: 1924. V. 47

CHRISTY, HOWARD CHANDLER
Drawings. New York: 1905. V. 53

CHRISTY, MILLER
The Bryant and May Museum of Fire-Making Appliances. Catalogue of the Exhibits...(with) Supplement. London: 1926-28. V. 54
On "Busse Island", One of the Lost Islands of the Atlantic. London: 1897. V. 48

CHRISTYN, J. B.
les Delices des Pais-Bas ou Description Generale. Brussele: 1697. V. 50

THE CHROMOLITHOGRAPH. 1867-69. V. 53

CHRONICA Monasterii S. Albani. London: 1863-76. V. 52

CHRONICLES by the Way: A Series of Letters Addressed to the Montreal 'Gazette' Descriptive of a Trip Through Manitoba and the North-West. Montreal: 1879. V. 50

CHRONICLES of Canada. Toronto: 1914/15/16. V. 52

THE CHRONICLES of Crime: a Series of Memoirs and Anecdotes of Notorious Characters Who Have Outraged the Laws of Great Britain from the Earliest Periods to 1841. London: 1886. V. 47

CHRONICON Saxonicum. Oxonii: 1692. V. 50; 54

CHRYSANTHUS OF BRUSA
(Greek title) Guide to the Holy Places or Outline of the Holy City of Jerusalem and All Palestine. Moscow: 1837. V. 50
(Greek title) Proskunetarion Kai Perigraph... (Guide to the Holy Places or Outline of the Holy City of Jerusalem and all Palestine). Moscow: 1837. V. 49

CHRYSOSTOM, JOHN, SAINT
(Greek title, then) In Omnes Pauli Apostoli Epistolas Accuratissima, Vereque Aurea et Divina Interpretatio. Verona: 1529. V. 49

CHUA CHIA-CHIEN
The Chinese Theatre. London: 1922. V. 51

CHUAN, SHUI HU
All Men Are Brothers. V. 48
All Men Are Brothers. New York: 1948. V. 48

CHUBB, C.
The Birds of British Guiana. London: 1916-21. V. 49; 53

CHUBB, RALPH
A Fable of Love and War. 1925. V. 48; 52
Songs Pastoral and Paradisal. London: 1935. V. 49

CHUBB, THOMAS
The Printed Maps in the Atlases of Great Britain and Ireland... London: 1927. V. 54
The Printed Maps in the Atlases of Great Britain and Ireland. London: 1977. V. 49; 51

CHUDLEIGH, ELIZABETH
An Authentic Detail of Particulars Relative to the Late Duchess of Kingston. London: 1788. V. 50

CHUDLEIGH, MARY
Essays Upon Several Subjects in Prose and Verse. London: 1710. V. 48
Poems on Several Occasions. Together with the Song of the Three Children Paraphras'd. London: 1703. V. 48; 51

CHUINARD. E. G.
Only One Man Died: the Medical Aspects of the Lewis and Clark Expedition. Glendale: 1979. V. 48; 50; 52

CHURCH, A. H.
Introduction to the Plant-Life of the Oxford District. I. General Review. II. The Annual Succcession (Jan.-June 1925). III. The Annual Succession (July-December 1925). (Botanical Memoirs 13-15). London: 1922-25. V. 49
Josiah Wedgewood: Master Potter. London: 1903. V. 51
Some Minor Arts as Practiced in England. London: 1894. V. 48

CHURCH, ALFRED J.
The Story of the Persian War (From Herodotus). London: 1888. V. 54

THE CHURCH and the Indians: the Trouble at Metlakahtla. Victoria: 1882. V. 52

CHURCH, BENJAMIN
The Choice: a Poem, After the Manner of Pomfret. Worcester: 1802. V. 51

CHURCH, EDWARD
Notice on the Beet Sugar... Northampton: 1837. V. 52

CHURCH, ELIHU DWIGHT
A Catalogue of Books Relating to the Discovery and Early History of North and South America. Mansfield: 1995. V. 53; 54
A Catalogue of Books Relating to the Discovery and Early History of North and South America... New York: 1995. V. 52
The E. D. Church Library. A Catalogue of Books Relating to the Discovery and Early History of North and South America. New York: 1951. V. 52

CHURCH, HERBERT E.
An Emigrant in the Canadian Northwest. London: 1929. V. 48
Making a Start in Canada; Letters from two Young Emigrants. London: 1889. V. 48; 53

CHURCH, J.
A Cabinet of Quadrupeds. London: 1805. V. 54

CHURCH OF ENGLAND
Holy Communion with Collects, Epistles, and Gospels According to the Use of the Church of England. 1900. V. 47
Iniunctions Giuen by the Queenes Maiestie. Anno Dom. 1559. London: 1600. V. 51
The Liturgy of the Church of England Adorn'd with 52 Historical Cuts. London: 1773. V. 51
The Order for the Administration of the Holy Communion and Occasional Offices, According to the Use of the Church of England.. London: 1844. V. 53
Visitation Articles. Articles to be Enquired Of in the Visitation in the First Yeere of the Raign of Our Most Dread Soueraign Ladie Elizabeth...1559. London: 1600. V. 51

CHURCH OF ENGLAND. ARCHBISHOPS & BISHOPS
A Declaration of the Arch-Bishop of Canterbury, and the Bishops in and Near London, Testifying Their Abhorrence of the Present Rebellion... London: 1715. V. 53

CHURCH OF ENGLAND. BOOK OF COMMON PRAYER
The Book of Common Prayer... Cambridge: 1638. V. 49
The Book of Common Prayer... London: 1662. V. 47
The Book of Common Prayer... London: 1669. V. 47
Book of Common Prayer. Oxford: 1680. V. 47; 52
Book of Common Prayer... London: 1692. V. 47; 48
Book of Common Prayer. Oxford: 1701. V. 52
The Book of Common Prayer. London: 1702. V. 47
Book of Common Prayer. London: 1707. V. 53
The Book of Common Prayer. London: 1717. V. 47; 48; 50; 51; 52; 54
The Book of Common Prayer... Oxford: 1718. V. 49

CHURCH OF ENGLAND. BOOK OF COMMON PRAYER continued
Book of Common Prayer. London: 1729. V. 52
The Book of Common Prayer... Oxford: 1737. V. 48
Book of Common Prayer... London: 1739. V. 53
Book of Common Prayer. Cambridge: 1743. V. 53
The Book of Common Prayer... London: 1751. V. 52
The Book of Common Prayer... Cambridge: 1754. V. 51
The Book of Common Prayer. Cambridge: 1760. V. 47; 48; 50; 51; 52
The Book of Common Prayer... Cambridge: 1761. V. 48
Book of Common Prayer... Edinburgh: 1761. V. 48
The Book of Common Prayer. Cambridge: 1762. V. 47; 49; 50; 52; 53; 54
The Book of Common Prayer. Cambridge: 1764-66. V. 47
The Book of Common Prayer... Oxford: 1773. V. 52 .
The Book of Common Prayer... Oxford: 1775. V. 50
Book of Common Prayer... Oxford: 1787. V. 48
The Book of Common Prayer... London: 1791. V. 52
The Book of Common Prayer... Oxford: 1791. V. 52
The Book of Common Prayer... Oxford: 1822. V. 47
The Book of Common Prayer. London: 1824. V. 49
The Book of Common Prayer... Oxford: 1840. V. 52
Book of Common Prayer. New York: 1843. V. 53
Book of Common Prayer... Oxford: 1843. V. 47
The Book of Common Prayer. London: 1844. V. 49; 53
The Book of Common Prayer. London: 1845. V. 52
Book of Common Prayer. London: 1850. V. 47
The Book of Common Prayer. London: 1853. V. 49; 51; 52
Book of Common Prayer. Oxford: 1861. V. 54
Book of Common Prayer... London: 1863. V. 54
Book of Common Prayer. Cambridge: 1873. V. 54
The Book of Common Prayer... London: 1885. V. 52
Book of Common Prayer... London: 1890. V. 47
The Book of Common Prayer... 1896. V. 49
The Book of Common Prayer... London: 1898. V. 47; 52
Book of Common Prayer. London: 1903. V. 53
Book of Common Prayer. London: 1904. V. 49
The Book of Common Prayer... London: 1917. V. 52
The Book of Common Prayer. Boston: 1928. V. 49; 54
The Book of Common Prayer... Boston: 1930. V. 47
Book of Common Prayer: in Greek. Cambridge: 1665. V. 47
The Common Prayer Book of the Church of England. Hong Kong: 1879. V. 48
The English Liturgy From the Book of Common Prayer, with Additional Collects... London: 1909. V. 51
Facsimile of the Original Manuscript of the Book of Common Prayer Signed by Convocation December 20th, 1661 and Attached to the Act of Uniformity 1662. London: 1891. V. 49; 51
Holy Communion From the Book of Common Prayer. Bedford Park, Chiswick: 1904. V. 48; 49
Leitoyrgia Brettanike Egoyn Biblos (Greek Letters). London: 1638. V. 47
Liturgia, seu Liber Precum Communium, et Administrationis Sacramentorum, Aliorumque rituum Atque Ceremoniarum Ecclesiae, Juxta Usum... London: 1670. V. 49
Liturgiae ecclesiae Anglicanae Partes Praecipuae...In Linguam Arabicam Traducate... Oxford: 1674. V. 48
A New Family Prayer-Book, Containing the Book of Common Prayer and Administration of the Sacraments... Winchester: 1783. V. 51
The Psalter of David, Taken from the Book of Common Prayer. Waltham St. Lawrence: 1927. V. 47

CHURCH OF JESUS CHRIST OF LATTER-DAY SAINTS
Doctrine and Covenants of the Church of Jesus Christ of Latter-Day Saints. Nauvoo: 1845. V. 52

CHURCH OF SCOTLAND
The Records of the Commissioners of the General Assemblies of the Church of Scotland Holden in Edinburgh...(1646-52). Edinburgh: 1892-1909. V. 51

CHURCH OF SCOTLAND. BOOK OF COMMON PRAYER
Scottish Book of Common Prayer. Edinburgh: 1635. V. 50

CHURCH, PEGGY
Familiar Journey. Santa Fe: 1936. V. 50; 54

CHURCH, PERCY W.
Chinese Turkestan; with Caravan and Rifle. London: 1901. V. 54

CHURCH, RICHARD
The Flood of Life and Other Poems. London: 1917. V. 47; 49; 53
Mereside Chronicle. London: 1948. V. 48
North of Rome. London: 1960. V. 50

CHURCH, THOMAS
The History of Philip's War, Commonly Called the Great Indian War of 1675 and 1676. Boston: 1827. V. 52

CHURCH, WILLIAM CONANT
The Life of John Ericsson. New York: 1891. V. 50

CHURCHER, MADELEINE AMY
Indian Impressions, or the Diary of Our Indian Trip, 1904. London: 1982. V. 48

CHURCHEY, WALTER
An Essay on Man, Upon Principles Opposite to Those of Lord Bolingbroke, in Four Epistles, with a Preface and Notes. London: 1804. V. 47
Poems and Imitations of the British Poets. London: 1789. V. 47; 50

CHURCHILL, CHARLES
The Apology. London: 1761. V. 52
The Author, a Poem. London: 1763. V. 50
(Complete) Poems. London: 1933. V. 51
Poems. London: 1758. V. 47
Poems. London: 1766. V. 50; 51
Poems. (with) The so Called Volume II, a Nonce Collection of Ten Independently Printed Pieces. London: 1763. V. 47
The Poetical Works. London: 1844. V. 50; 51
The Poetical Works... London: 1866. V. 51
The Works. London: 1774. V. 48; 49

CHURCHILL, FLEETWOOD
Essays On the Puerperal Fever and Other Diseases Peculiar to Women. Philadelphia: 1850. V. 50; 51

CHURCHILL, RANDOLPH HENRY SPENCER
Men, Mines and Animals in South Africa. New York: 1892. V. 47

CHURCHILL, RANDOLPH S.
Winston S. Churchill. Boston: 1966-77. V. 50
Winston S. Churchill. London: 1966-88. V. 51; 52
Winston S. Churchill. London: 1967-88. V. 47

CHURCHILL, T. O.
The Life of Lord Viscount Nelson, Duke of Bronte, &c. London: 1808. V. 54

CHURCHILL, WINSTON
Coniston. New York: 1906. V. 47
Divi Britannici: Being a Remark Upon the Lives of All the Kings of This Isle, From the Year of the World 2855 Unto the Year of Grace 1660. London: 1675. V. 48
Richard Carvell. New York: 1899. V. 47; 54

CHURCHILL, WINSTON LEONARD SPENCER
An Address Delivered Before Members of Congress, December 26th, 1941. Stamford: 1942. V. 49
The American Civil War. London: 1961. V. 50; 54
Amid These Storms. New York: 1932. V. 53; 54
Arms and Convenant. Speeches. London: 1938. V. 49; 52
Blood, Sweat and Tears. New York: 1941. V. 49
A Catalogue of His Paintings. London: 1967. V. 52
Churchill & Roosevelt: The Complete Correspondence. Princeton: 1984. V. 49
Churchill His Paintings. London: 1967. V. 51
The Collected Essays of Sir Winston Churchill. London: 1976. V. 49
The Collected Works. London: 1973. V. 53; 54
The Collected Works. London: 1973-76. V. 49; 51; 53
The Collected Works. London: 1974-76. V. 54
The Dawn of Liberation. London: 1945. V. 47
Defending the West. London: 1981. V. 52
Discours de Guerre - 1940-1942. V. 49
The End of the Beginning. Boston: 1943. V. 53
The End of the Beginning... London: 1943. V. 47
Great Contemporaries. London: 1937. V. 48; 53; 54
Great Contemporaries. London: 1938. V. 54
Great Contemporaries. London: 1942. V. 52
The Great War. London. V. 48
The Great War. London: 1930. V. 50
The Great War. London: 1933. V. 50; 51
Here is the Course We Steer!. London: 1945. V. 50
A History of the English Speaking Peoples. London: 1956-58. V. 47; 49; 50; 51; 53; 54
A History of the English Speaking Peoples. New York: 1956-58. V. 48; 51
A History of the English Speaking Peoples. New York: 1956/56/57. V. 47
History of the Second World War. London: 1948-54. V. 54
Ian Hamilton's March. London: 1900. V. 48; 50; 51; 52; 54
Ian Hamilton's March. New York: 1900. V. 47; 49; 53
In the Balance. Speeches, 1949 and 1950. London: 1951. V. 53
India. London: 1931. V. 53
Into Battle. London: 1941. V. 47; 50
The Island Race. London: 1964. V. 47
Liberalism and the Social Problem. London: 1909. V. 47; 53
London to Ladysmith via Pretoria. London: 1900. V. 47; 48; 50; 51; 52; 53; 54
London to Ladysmith via Pretoria. New York: 1900. V. 50; 53
Lord Randolph Churchill. London: 1906. V. 49; 50; 51; 54
Lord Randolph Churchill. New York: 1906. V. 48
Lord Randolph Churchill. London: 1907. V. 53
Marlborough - His Life and Times. London: 1933-38. V. 48; 49; 50; 51; 53; 54
Marlborough His Life and Times. London: 1947-49. V. 48; 49
Mr. Crewe's Career. New York: 1908. V. 54
My African Journey. London: 1908. V. 47; 49; 50; 51; 53; 54
My African Journey. New York: 1909. V. 48
My Early Life. London: 1930. V. 51
My Early Life. London: 1949. V. 47
On the War Problems Facing Britain. New York: 1940. V. 50
Onwards to Victory. Boston: 1944. V. 53
Onwards to Victory. London: 1944. V. 47
The River War. London: 1899. V. 49; 51; 52
A Roving Commission, My Early Life. 1930. V. 50
A Roving Commission, My Early Life. New York: 1930. V. 54

CHURCHILL, WINSTON LEONARD SPENCER *continued*
Savrola. London: 1900. V. 50; 53
Savrola. New York: 1900. V. 49; 51; 53
Savrola... New York: 1956. V. 53
Second World War. London. V. 53
The Second World War. London: 1948. V. 48; 51
The Second World War. Boston: 1948-53. V. 47; 49
The Second World War. London: 1948-54. V. 47; 48; 49; 50; 51; 52; 53; 54
The Second World War... London: 1954. V. 51
The Second World War. London: 1956-58. V. 47
Secret Session Speeches. London: 1946. V. 47; 52
The Sinews of Peace. London: 1948. V. 53; 54
A Speech by the Prime Minister in the House of Commons, August 20th, 1940. London: 1940. V. 48; 49; 50; 51; 54
Step by Step 1936-1939. London: 1939. V. 48; 50; 54
The Story of My Early Life: a Roving Commission. New York: 1945. V. 53
The Story of the Malakand Field Force. London: 1898. V. 47; 48; 52; 53; 54
Their Finest Hour: Speeches, Broadcasts and Messages of Rt. Hon. Winston Churchill Since He Became Prime Minister. Winnipeg. V. 48
Thoughts and Adventures. 1932. V. 50
Thoughts and Adventures. London: 1932. V. 48; 52
Through Terror to Triumph. Edinburgh: 1914. V. 48
To the People of France. New York: 1940. V. 50
The Unrelenting Struggle. Boston: 1942. V. 53
The Unrelenting Struggle. London: 1942. V. 47
Victory. London: 1946. V. 47
War Speeches. London: 1941-46. V. 48; 50; 51
The War Speeches. London: 1943-45. V. 48
What Kind of a People Do They Think We Are?. London: 1942. V. 47
While England Slept. New York: 1938. V. 54
The World Crisis. London: 1923-31. V. 47; 48; 52; 53; 54
The World Crisis. New York: 1931. V. 47; 48; 50
The World Crisis. London: 1933. V. 51

CHURCHMAN, JOHN
An Account of the Gospel Labours. Philadelphia: 1779. V. 47; 53
An Account of the Gospel Labours... Dublin: 1781. V. 49; 54
An Account of the Gospel Labours... London: 1781. V. 54

CHURCHWARD, WILLIAM B.
My Consulate in Samoa. London: 1887. V. 48

CHURCHYARD, THOMAS
Churchyard's Chips Concerning Scotland... London: 1817. V. 48

CHURTON, E.
The Book Collector's Hand-Book: a Modern Library Companion. London: 1845. V. 52

CHURTON, EDWARD
Christian Doctrines. London: 1850. V. 49
The Railroad Book of England: Historical, Topographical and Picturesque... London: 1851. V. 47; 49

CHURTON, WILLIAM RALPH
Remains. London: 1830. V. 51

CHUSIUS, C.
Rariorum Plantarum Historia. Antwerp: 1601. V. 50

CHUTE, CAROLYN
The Beans of Egypt, Maine. London: 1985. V. 51
The Beans of Egypt, Maine. New York: 1985. V. 51; 52; 53; 54
Merry Men. New York: 1994. V. 54

CHUTE, FRANCIS
Beauty and Virtue. London: 1716. V. 54
The Petticoat: an Heroi-comical Poem. London: 1716. V. 53

CHYTRAEUS, DAVID
De Lectione Historiarvm Recte Institvenda. Wittenberg: 1563. V. 48

CIAMPINI, GIOVANNI
De Sacris Aedificiis a Constantino Magno Constructis Synoppsis Historicae. Rome: 1693. V. 53

CIANO, GALEAZZO
Ciano's Diary 1937-1938. London: 1952. V. 49
Ciano's Diplomatic Papers. London: 1948. V. 49

CIARDI, JOHN
Homeward to America. New York: 1940. V. 52
The Man Who Sang the Sillies. Philadelphia: 1961. V. 49
Mid-Century American Poets. New York: 1950. V. 53
The Monster Den or Look What Happened at My House and To It. Philadelphia/New York: 1966. V. 51

CIBBER, COLLEY
Another Occasional Letter from Mr. Cibber to Mr. Pope. London: 1744. V. 48; 53
An Apology for the Life of... London: 1740. V. 52; 54
An Apology for the Life of... London: 1756. V. 50
An Apology for the Life of... London: 1925. V. 48; 52
An Apology for the Life of... Tyford: 1925. V. 52
An Apology for the Life of... Waltham St. Lawrence: 1925. V. 51
The Careless Husband. London: 1705. V. 48
The Double Gallant; or, the Sick Lady's Cure. London: 1707. V. 51
The Dramatic Works. London: 1760. V. 50
The Lady's Last Stake, or, the Wife's Resentment. London: 1707/8. V. 51
A Letter from Mr. Cibber to Mr. Pope, Inquiring Into the Motives that Might Induce Him In his Satyrical Works... London: 1742. V. 48; 51; 53
A Letter from Mr. Cibber, to Mr. Pope, Inquiring Into the Motives that Might Induce Him in His Satyrical Works... London: 1742/44. V. 52
Love's Last Shift; or, the Fool in Fashion. London: 1696. V. 51; 54
Papal Tyrany in the Reign of King John. Dublin: 1745. V. 49
Plays. London: 1721. V. 52

CIBBER, THEOPHILUS
An Epistle from Mr. Theophilus Cibber, to David Garrick, Esq. London: 1755. V. 51
The Lives and Characters of the Most Eminent Actors and Actresses of Great Britain and Ireland... London: 1753. V. 52
The Lives of the Poets of Great Britain and Ireland... London: 1753. V. 50
The Lover. London: 1730. V. 53
Romeo and Juliet, a Tragedy... London: 1748. V. 48
Theophilus Cibber to David Garrick, Esq. London: 1759. V. 49
The Tryal of a Cause (f)or Criminal Conversation Between Theophilus Cibber, Gent, Plaintiff and William Sloper, Esq. Defendant. London: 1739. V. 54

CICERO, MARCUS TULLIUS
Academica Recensuit, Variorum Notis Suas Immiscuit, et Hadr. Cambridge: 1736. V. 47
The Booke of Freendeship. Campden: 1904. V. 49
The Booke of Freendeship... London: 1904. V. 48
Cato Major... Glasgow: 1748. V. 51
Cato Major... Glasgow: 1751. V. 51
Cato; or an Essay on Old Age. 1773. V. 51
Ciceronis De Officiis Libri Tres. Cato Major, Vel de Senectute; Laelius, Vel de Amicitia; Paradoxa Stoicorum Sex; Somnium Scripionis, Ex Libro Sexto de Republica... Venice: 1555. V. 51
Cicero's Books of Friendship, Old Age and Scipio's Dream. London: 1907. V. 52
Cicero's Orations. London: 1799. V. 48
Collected Works. London: 1919-72. V. 48
Cum Optimis Exemplaribus Accurate Collata. Leyden: 1642. V. 50
De Officiis, De Senectute et Amicitia. London: 1821. V. 51; 53
De Officiis, Libri III. Strasbourg: 1564. V. 53
De Officiis, Libri III.... Venice: 1581. V. 51
De Officiis, Libri III. Amsterdam: 1625. V. 51
De Philosophia. Cum Scholiis et Coniecturis Pauli Manutii. Venice: 1552. V. 48
Epistolae ad Atticum Ad M. Brutum, Ad Quintum Fratrem... Venice: 1544. V. 51
Epistolarum ad Atticum, ad Britum, Ad Quintum Fratrem, Libri XX Nuper Exacta Recogniti Cura... Venice: 1521. V. 51
Epistole Famigliari Di Cicerone. Venice: 1548. V. 51
Le Epistole Famigliari di Cicerone. Venice: 1554/55. V. 51
Le Epistole Famigliari, Gia Tradotte, & Hora in Molti Luoghi Corrette da Aldo Mavito. Venice: 1573. V. 52
Les Epistres Familiaries. Lyons: 1543. V. 48
The Familiar Epistles. London: 1620. V. 49; 53
Le Filippiche di Marco T. Cicerone Contra Marco Antonio, Fatte Volgari Per Girolamo Ragazzoni. Venice: 1556. V. 51
Fragmenta Ciceronis, Passim, Dispersa, Caroli Sigonii Diligentia Collecta & Scholiis Illusrata... Venice: 1560. V. 51; 53
The Letters of...to Several of his Friends. London: 1778. V. 49
M. T. Cicero de Oratore. Or His Three Dialogues Upon the Character and Qualifications of an Orator. London: 1755. V. 52
M. Tullii Ciceronis Orationum Volumen Secundum... Venice: 1519. V. 51
M. Tully Cicero's Five Books of Tusculan Disputations. London: 1715. V. 51
Marcus Tullius Cicero His Three Bookes of Duties to Marcus His Sonne, Turned Out of Latine into English, by Nicholas Grimald. London: 1600?. V. 47
Opera. Paris: 1538-39. V. 51
Opera. 1543-44-50. V. 47
Opera. Leyden: 1642. V. 48
Opera... Geneva: 1758. V. 51
Opera. Oxford: 1783. V. 48
Opera Omnia. Paris: 1543-50. V. 49; 53
Orationem, Pars II... Venice: 1550. V. 51
Orationes Diligentius Recognite... Paris: 1522. V. 54
Orationes Selectae. Bruxellis: 1779. V. 53
Orations & Essays. Verona: 1972. V. 47; 48; 51; 54
Orationum. Venice: 1559. V. 51
Philippicae. Francisci Mantvrantii Enarrationes in Philippicas. Venice: 1494. V. 47; 52
Philosophicorvm Librorvm Pars Prima. Argentorati: 1581. V. 53
Rhetoricorum Libri. Rcenter Castigati. Cum Expositoribus Francisco Maturantio. Antonio Mancinello. M. Fabio Victorino. Venice: 1504. V. 47
Tully's Offices in English. London: 1714. V. 48
Tully's Offices in English. London: 1722. V. 49
Tully's Offices, The Three Books. London: 1681. V. 49
Tully's Two Essays of Old-Age, and of Friendship, with His Stoical Paradoxes and Scipio's Dream. London: 1736. V. 49
...Tusculanarum Disputationu Libri Quinque. Accedunt Lectiones Variantes et Doctorum... Glasguae: 1744. V. 47
The Two Last Pleadings of Marcus Tullius Cicero Against Caius Verres. London: 1812. V. 51

CICOGNARA, LEOPOLDO
Le Fabbriche Piu Cospicui di Venzia Illustrati... Venice: 1815-20. V. 50

CICOGNARA, LEOPOLDO continued
Le Fabriche e I Monumenti Cospicui di Venezia. Venice: 1838/40. V. 49

CINCINNATI, Columbus, Cleveland and Erie Railroad Guide. Columbus: 1854. V. 47

CINDERELLA.. New York: 1888. V. 52
CINDERELLA. New York: 1891. V. 49
CINDERELLA. Philadelphia: 1910. V. 47
CINDERELLA. London: 1919. V. 48; 49
CINDERELLA. London: 1940. V. 51
CINDERELLA. New York: 1945. V. 49

CINDERELLA
Cinderella and the Glass Slipper. London: 1854. V. 47; 48; 49

CINDERELLA. A Peepshow Book. London: 1950. V. 49

CINDERELLA: Aunt Louisa's London Toy Books. London: 1830. V. 48

CINDERELLA, or The Little Glass Slipper. London: 1827. V. 48

CINDERELLA Picture Book. New York: 1905. V. 50

CIPRIANI, G. B.
Cipriani's Rudiments of Drawing. London: 1815. V. 52

CIRCIGNANI, NICOLO
Ecclesiae Anglicanae Trophaea Sive Sanctor Martyrum, Qui Prop Christo Catholicae Q' Fidei Vertate Asserenda... Rome: 1584. V. 50

CIRCLE International Survey of Constructive Art. London: 1937. V. 54

CIRCLE of the Sciences. Logic. Made Familiar and Easy to Young Gentlemen and Ladies. London: 1769. V. 48

CIRCLE of the Sciences. Volume 5. Logic Made Familiar and Easy to Which is Added a Compendious System of Metaphysics or Ontology. London: 1777. V. 47

CIRCUS Fun. New York: 1890. V. 48; 51

CIRCUS Sights. Cincinnati: 1870's. V. 48

CIRLOT, J. E.
The Genesis of Gaudian Architecture. Wittenborn: 1967. V. 51

CISNEROS, FRANCISCO JAVIER
Report on the Construction of a Railway from Puerto Berrio to Barbosa. New York: 1878. V. 47; 49; 52

CISNEROS, SANDRA
My Wicked Wicked Ways. Bloomington: 1987. V. 49

CIST, CHARLES
The Cincinnati Directory for the Year 1842. Cincinnati: 1842. V. 53

CISTERNAY DU FAY
Bibliotheca Fayana, seu Catalogus Librorum Bibliothecae. Paris: 1725. V. 54

CITINO, DAVID
A Letter of Columbus. Columbus: 1990. V. 49; 51; 52; 53

THE CITIZEN Of This Village...Are Invited to Meet...Public Sentiment on the Subject of the Lowell, Concord & Keene Rail-Roads!. Nashua-Village: 1835. V. 48

THE CITIZENS' and Strangers' City Guide: With Locations of Hotels, Depots, Omnibuses, Towns on Railroads, and Their Distances, Central Wholesale and Retail Stores, Furnishing All ARticles of Want. Boston: 1852. V. 47

CITRI DE LA GUETTE, SAMUEL
The History of the Triumvirates. London: 1686. V. 48
The History of the Triumvirates. London: 1690. V. 48

CITRON, JULIUS
Immunity Methods of Diagnosis and Therapy and Their Practical Application. Philadelphia: 1912. V. 51; 53

CITY Corruption and Mal-Adminstration Display'd: Occasion'd by the Ill Management of the Public Money in General... London: 1738. V. 50

CITY Cries; or, a Peep at Scenes in Town. Philadelphia: 1851. V. 49

CITY Lights Journal Number One. San Francisco: 1963. V. 54

CITY Men and City Manners. The City; or, The Physiology of London Business; With Sketches on Change and at the Coffee Houses. London: 1842. V. 47

THE CITY of Grand Rapids and Kent County, Michigan Up to Date... 1900. V. 49

CITY Of Kingston Illustrated. V. 48

THE CITY Of London's Plea to the Quo Warranto, (an information) Brought Against Their Charter in Michaelmas Term, 1681. London: 1682. V. 52

CITY of Somerville. Official Fire Alarm Map and Street Directory and Book of General Information. Boston: 1895?. V. 50

THE CITY of Toronto and the Home District Commercial Directory and Register With Almanack and Calendar for 1837. Toronto: 1837. V. 54

CITY Patriotism Displayed: a Poem. Addressed to the Rt. Hon. Frederick Lord North. London: 1773. V. 47

THE CITY Secret; or, Corruption At All Ends of the Town. London: 1744. V. 53

THE CIVIL Record of Major General Winfield S. Hancock, During His Administration in Louisiana and Texas. N.P: 1871. V. 52; 54

CIZEK, FRANZ
Children's Coloured Paper Work. Vienna: 1927. V. 47

CLADEL, JUDITH
Rodin: the Man and His Art with Leaves From his Note-Book. New York: 1917. V. 50; 51

CLAIBORNE, JOHN FRANCIS HAMTRAMCK
Historical Account of Hancock County and the Sea Board of Mississippi. New Orleans: 1876. V. 50

CLAIBORNE, NATHANIEL HERBERT
Notes on the War in the South... Richmond: 1819. V. 48; 49; 52

CLAIM of the Mission of St. James, Vancouver, Washington Territory to 640 Acres of Land. V. 53

THE CLAIMS of the People of England, Essayed. In a Letter from the Country. London: 1701. V. 48

CLAIN-STEFANELLI, E. E.
Numismatic Bibliography. Munchen: 1984. V. 48

CLAIR, COLIN
The Spread of printing. Amsterdam: 1969-72. V. 48

CLAIRMONT, CHRISTOPH W.
The Glass Vessels. New Haven: 1963. V. 50; 52
Gravestone and Epigram: Greek Memorials from the Archaic and Classical Period. Mainz on Rhein: 1970. V. 50; 52

CLAIRON, HYPPOLITE
Memoirs of Hyppolite Clairon the Celebrated French Actress... London: 1800. V. 47

CLAMORGAN, JEAN DE
La Chasse du Loup, Necessaire a la Maison Rustique...En Laquelle est Contenue la Nature des Loups... Lyon?: 1597. V. 48

CLAMPITT, AMY
A Homage to John Keats. 1984. V. 48; 50; 54
The Kingfisher. New York: 1983. V. 51; 54
Manhattan. Iowa City: 1990. V. 50; 51; 52; 54
Manhattan... Iowa City: 1992. V. 47; 49; 51
Multitudes, Multitudes. New York: 1973. V. 52; 53

CLAMPITT, JOHN W.
Echoes from the Rocky Mountains. Chicago: 1888. V. 48; 49; 53

CLANCEY, J. C.
Simplified Stellar Maps and Aspects of the Night Sky Chiefly for Use in Latitude 20 deg. N. Bombay: 1922. V. 54

CLANCEY, P. A.
The Birds of Natal and Zululand. London: 1964. V. 49; 52; 53; 54
A Handlist of the Birds of Southern Mocambique. Lourenco Marques: 1971. V. 49

CLANCY, FOGHORN
My Fifty Years in Rodeo. San Antonio: 1952. V. 53

CLANCY, TOM
Armored Cav. New York: 1994. V. 52
Debt of Honor. New York: 1994. V. 52; 53
Executive Orders. 1996. V. 54
The Hunt for Red October. Annapolis: 1984. V. 48; 49; 51; 53; 54
The Hunt for Red October. London: 1985. V. 49
Patriot Games. New York: 1987;. V. 52
Red Storm Rising. New York: 1986. V. 49; 51; 53
Submarine. New York: 1993. V. 52; 54
The Sum of All Fears. New York: 1991. V. 49
Without Remorse. New York: 1993. V. 49; 52; 53

CLANNY, W. REID
New Researches on flame. 1834. V. 50
A Treatise on the Mineral Waters of Gilsland. Sunderland: 1816. V. 52; 53

CLANRICARDE, ULICK DE BURGH, EARL OF
Memoirs of the Right Honourable the Marquis of Clanricarde, Lord Deputy General of Ireland. London: 1722. V. 52

CLAPHAM, A. R.
Flora of the British Isles. London: 1957-65. V. 49

CLAPHAM, JOHN
The Bank of England: a History. Cambridge: 1944. V. 50

CLAPHAM, RICHARD
Foxes, Foxhounds and Fox-Hunting. London. V. 54
Foxhunting on the Lakeland Fells. London: 1920. V. 51
Rough Shooting for the Man of Moderate Means... London: 1922. V. 48; 50; 52
Sport on Fell, Beck & Tarn. London: 1924. V. 51; 52

CLAPP, FREDERICK MORTIMER
Jacopo Carucci da Ponotmo: His Life and Work. New Haven: 1916. V. 51; 53

CLAPP, WILLIAM W.
A Record of the Boston Stage. Boston and Cambridge: 1853. V. 54

CLAPPE, LOUISE AMELIA KNAPP SMITH
California in 1851 - the Letters of Dame Shirley. San Francisco: 1933. V. 47; 48; 50; 51; 53; 54
The Shirley Letters from California Mines 1851-52. San Francisco: 1922. V. 51; 53

CLAPPERTON, HUGH
Journal of a Second Expedition Into the Interior of Africa, From the Bight of Benin to Soccatoo... London: 1829. V. 50

CLAPPERTON, ROBERT HENDERSON
An Historical Account of Its making by Hand from the Earliest Times Down to the Present Day. Oxford: 1924. V. 48
Modern Paper-Making. Oxford: 1952. V. 53

CLARE, JOHN
Birds Nesting. The Lost Manuscript. 1987. V. 48
The Hue and Cry. London: 1990. V. 50
The Hue and Cry... Market Drayton: 1990. V. 52
John Clare: Verses for His Children. Market Drayton: 1993. V. 50; 52
Madrigals & Chronicles. London: 1924. V. 52
Peterborough Natural History, Scientific and Archaeological Society. 1893. V. 48
Poems. London: 1901. V. 50
Poems. Rugby: 1901. V. 48
Poems. London: 1935. V. 50
Poems... London: 1949. V. 51
Poems Descriptive of Rural Life and Scenery. London: 1820. V. 47; 51; 52
Poems Descriptive of Rural Life and Scenery. London: 1821. V. 54
The Shepheard's Calendar. London: 1978. V. 50
Sketches in the Life of John Clare. London: 1931. V. 47
Trees. London: 1989. V. 54
The Village Minstrel. V. 50
The Village Minstrel... London: 1821. V. 47; 50; 52; 53
The Village Minstrel. London: 1823. V. 53
Woman, Sweet Witchingly Woman. 1993. V. 50

CLARE, MARTIN
The Motion of Fluids, Natural and Artificial... London: 1737. V. 51
The Motion of Fluids, Natural and Artificial... London: 1747. V. 47; 52

CLAREMONT: Or, the Undivided Household. Philadelphia: 1857. V. 49; 52

CLARENCE, C. W.
A Biographical Sketch of the Life of Ralph Farnham, Of Action, Maine... Boston: 1860. V. 47

CLARENDON, EDWARD HYDE, 1ST EARL OF
A Brief View and Survey of the Dangerous and Pernicious Errors to Church and State, in Mr. Hobbes's Book, Entitled Leviathan. Oxford: 1676. V. 53; 54
The History of the Rebellion and Civil Wars... Oxford: 1702-04. V. 48
The History of the Rebellion and Civil Wars in England. Oxford: 1704. V. 53
The History of the Rebellion and Civil Wars in England. Oxford: 1705-06. V. 53
The History of the Rebellion and Civil Wars in England... Oxford;: 1707. V. 47; 54
The History of the Rebellion and Civil Wars in England... Oxford: 1707-12. V. 54
The History of the Rebellion and Civil Wars in England... Oxford: 1732. V. 51
The History of the Rebellion and Civil Wars in England... Oxford: 1760/1807. V. 50
The History of the Rebellion and Civil Wars in England... Basil: 1798. V. 47
The History of the Rebellion and Civil Wars in England... Oxford: 1807. V. 53
The History of the Rebellion and Civil Wars in England... Oxford: 1816. V. 53
The History of the Rebellion and Civil Wars in England. Oxford: 1826. V. 47; 49; 50
The History of the Rebellion and Civil Wars in England... London: 1826/27. V. 49
The History of the Rebellion and Civil Wars in England. London: 1839. V. 52; 54
The History of the Rebellion and Civil Wars in England... London: 1849. V. 47
The History of the Rebellion and Civil Wars in England. Oxford: 1849. V. 54
The History of the Rebellion and Civil Wars in England. Oxford: 1888. V. 49; 50
The History of the Rebellion and Civil Wars in England... 1930. V. 52
The Life of... Oxford: 1759. V. 47; 48; 49; 53; 54
The Life of... Dublin: 1760. V. 54
The Life of... Dublin: 1760/59. V. 50; 51
The Life of... Oxford: 1761. V. 51
The Proceedings in the House of Commons, Touching the Impeachment of Edward Late Earl of Clarendon, Lord High Chancellour of England... 1700. V. 54
Religion and Policy and the Countenance and Assistance Each Should Give the Other. Oxford: 1811. V. 49; 51; 52; 54

CLARENDON, HENRY HYDE, 2ND EARL OF
The State Letters of Henry, Earl of Clarendon Lord Lieutenant of Ireland During the Reign of K. James the Second and His Lordship's Diary for the Years 1687, 1688, 1689 and 1690. Oxford: 1763. V. 53

CLARIDGE, JOHN
The Shepherd of Banbury's Rules to Judge of the Changes of the Weather, Grounded on Forty Years Experience... Edinburgh: 1755. V. 49

CLARIDGE, W. WALTON
A History of the Gold Coast and Ashanti from the Earliest Times to the Commencement of the Twentieth Century. London: 1915. V. 49

CLARK, A. H.
Monograph of the Existing Crinoids. Washington: 1915-67. V. 54

CLARK, A. M.
Starfishes of the Atlantic. London: 1992. V. 48; 50; 51

CLARK, AARON
Communication From His Honor the Mayor, in Relation to the Precautionary Measures Adopted by Him to Secure the Public Peace at the Recent Election in This City, with Documents and a Report from the Comptroller Relative to the Expense... New York: 1839. V. 53

CLARK, ANDREW
Fibroid Diseases of the Lung, Including Fibroid Phthisis. London: 1894. V. 48; 53

CLARK, ANN
About the Grass Mountain Mouse. Lawrence: 1940. V. 50
Singing Sioux Cowboy Reader. Lawrence. V. 50

CLARK, ANTHONY M.
Pompeo Batoni. Oxford: 1985. V. 50

CLARK, AUSTIN S.
Reminiscences of Travel 1852-1865. Middletown. V. 50

CLARK, BADGER
Sun and Saddle Leather. Boston: 1915. V. 53

CLARK, BRACY
On Casting Horses; with a Description of the New Casting Hobbles, Invented by Bracy Clark... London: 1814. V. 49

CLARK, C. M.
A Trip to Pike's Peak and Notes by the Way... Chicago: 1861. V. 47; 50; 54

CLARK, CHARLES
The Doctor's "Do"ings; or the Entrapped Heiress of W-m!. Norwich: 1839. V. 47
Epsom Races: a Poem, Comic, Punning, and Racy. Great Totham, Essex: 1836. V. 51
John Noakes and Mary Styles; or, "An Essex Calf's" Visit to Tiptree Races: a Poem Exhibiting Some of the Most Striking Lingual Localisms peculiar to Essex. London: 1839. V. 50

CLARK, D. L.
The Roving Artist. High Point: 1895. V. 48

CLARK, DANIEL KINNEAR
The Rudiments of Civil Engineering Including a Treatise on Hydraulic Engineering by George R. Burnell. London: 1884. V. 49
The Steam Engine. London: 1890. V. 53
The Steam Engine... London: 1892. V. 50
The Steam Engine. London: 1893. V. 51
Tramways, Their Construction and Working...With Accounts of the Various Modes of Traction... New York: 1894. V. 48

CLARK, E. WARREN
From Hong Kong to the Himalayas; or, Three Thousand Miles through India. 1880. V. 54

CLARK, EDNA MARIA
Ohio Art and Artists. Richmond: 1932. V. 47

CLARK, EDWARD
Catalogue of the Edward Clark Library. London: 1976. V. 51; 53

CLARK, ERLAND FENN
Truncheons. Their Romance and Reality. London: 1935. V. 54

CLARK, F. AMBROSE
The F. Ambrose Collection of Sporting Paintings. New York: 1958. V. 47; 49

CLARK, FRANCIS E.
Our Journey Around the World. Hartford: 1895. V. 49

CLARK, GALEN
Early Days in Yosemite Valley. Los Angeles: 1964. V. 54
Indians of the Yosemite Valley... Yosemite Valley: 1904. V. 50

CLARK, GEORGE
A Glance Backward or Some Events in the Past History of My Life. Houston: 1914?. V. 49
History of England. 1979-87. V. 48
The Oxford History of England. London: 1963-67. V. 49
The Penal Statutes Abridged, and Alphabetically Arranged. London: 1777. V. 48
A Sermon Preached at the Royal Military Asylum, April 1st, 1810, Before His Excellency the Commander in Chief and the Hon. Commissioners on the First Distribution of Rewards to the Children Who Had Completed Apprenticeships. London: 1810. V. 47; 51

CLARK, GEORGE H.
Farm Weeds of Canada. Ottawa: 1906. V. 50
Weeds of Canada. Ottowa: 1909. V. 48

CLARK, GEORGE ROGERS
Col. George Rogers Clark's Sketch of His Campaign in the Illinois in 1778-79. Cincinnati: 1869. V. 48; 52

CLARK, GODFREY, MRS.
Gleanings from an Old Portfolio... 1895-98. V. 52

CLARK, J.
Illustrations to Don Quixote. London: 1819. V. 54

CLARK, J. H.
The Songs of the Seasons...The British Wild Flowers Familiarly Described Under the Months in Which They Bloom... Halifax: 1851. V. 54

CLARK, JAMES
Historical Record and Regimental Memoir of the Royal Scots Fusiliers, Formerly Known as the 21st Royal North British Fusiliers. Edinburgh: 1885. V. 50
Shoeing and Balancing the Light Harness Horse. Buffalo: 1916. V. 48; 54

CLARK, JAMES continued
A Treatise on the Prevention of Diseases Incidental to Horses. Philadelphia: 1791. V. 47; 51
A Treatise on the Prevention of Diseases Incidental to Horses... Edinburgh: 1802. V. 47

CLARK, JAMES A.
The Last Boom. New York: 1972. V. 47
Spindletop. New York: 1952. V. 47

CLARK, JANE INGLIS
Pictures and Memories. London: 1938. V. 52; 54

CLARK, JOHN
The Amateur's Assistant; or a Series of Instructions in Sketching from Nature. London: 1826. V. 47; 48
Elements of Drawing and Painting in Water Colours... London: 1841. V. 47; 50
The Fortunate Discovery, or, Wisdom Found at Last. Trowbridge;: 1807. V. 54
Hymns on Various Subjects and Occasions. Trowbridge: 1799. V. 54
Poems on Several Subjects, and Occasions, Both Moral and Entertaining;. Trowbridge: 1799. V. 54

CLARK, JOHN A.
Gleanings by the Way. Philadelphia: 1842. V. 47

CLARK, JOHN HEAVISIDE
Practical Essay on the Art of Colouring. London: 1812. V. 49

CLARK, JOHN WILLIS
The Care of Books... Cambridge: 1901. V. 50
The Care of Books. London: 1901. V. 54
The Care of Books. Cambridge: 1909. V. 50
The Life and Letters of the Rev. Adam Sedgwick... Cambridge: 1890. V. 48; 50; 54
The Life and Letters of the Rev. Adam Sedgwick. Cambridge: 1980. V. 52
The Observances in Use at the Augustinian Priory of S. Giles and S. Andrew at Barnwell, Cambridgeshire. Cambridge: 1897. V. 49

CLARK, JOSEPH
Texas Gulf Coast: its History and Development - Family and Personal History. New York: 1955. V. 53

CLARK, JOSEPH G.
Lights and Shadows of Sailor Life, as Exemplified in Fifteen Year's Experience... Boston: 1848. V. 47; 52

CLARK, KENNETH
The Drawings of Leonardo Da Vinci in the Collection of Her majesty the Queen at Windsor Castle. London: 1968-69. V. 51
The Florence Baptistery Doors. London: 1980. V. 51; 53
The Gothic Revival. New York: 1929. V. 47
Henry Moore Drawings. New York: 1974. V. 47; 48; 50; 52
Leonardo Da Vinci Drawings at Windsor Castle. London: 1968-69. V. 50
Piero Della Francesca. London: 1951. V. 51; 54
Sidney Nolan. London: 1961. V. 49

CLARK, KIT
Where the Trout Hide. New York: 1889. V. 47

CLARK, L. J.
Wild Flowers of the Pacific Northwest from Alaska to Northern California. Sidney: 1976. V. 52

CLARK, LARRY
The Perfect Childhood. Zurich: 1995. V. 54
Teenage Lust. New York: 1987. V. 47
Tulsa. New York: 1971. V. 47; 52

CLARK, LATIMER
General Description of the Britannia and Conway Tubular Bridges on the Chester and Holyhead Railway. London: 1849. V. 51

CLARK, MARGERY
The Poppy Seed Cakes. Garden City: 1936. V. 51

CLARK, MARK WAYNE
From the Danube to the Yalu. New York: 1954. V. 52

CLARK, ORTON S.
Clay Allison of the Washita First a Cow Man and then an Extinguisher of Bad men. Attica: 1922. V. 49; 53

CLARK, PETER
Statement &c., in Relation to the Richmond and Ohio Rail-road. New York: 1847. V. 54

CLARK, ROBERT A.
The Arthur H. Clark Company: a Bibliography and History 1902-1992. Seattle: 1993. V. 52
The Arthur H. Clark Company. A Bibliography and History 1902-1992. Spokane: 1993. V. 50; 52; 53

CLARK, ROBERT STERLING
Drawings from the Clark Art Institute. A Catalogue Raisonne of the Robert Sterling Clark Collection of European and American Drawings, Sixteenth through Nineteenth Centuries. New Haven/London: 1964. V. 53; 54
Through Shen-Kan: The Account of the Clark Expedition in North China 1908-09. London: 1912. V. 48; 49; 50; 52; 54

CLARK, ROLAND
Gunner's Dawn. New York: 1937. V. 47; 52; 53
Pot Luck... West Hartford: 1945. V. 47
Roland Clark's Etchings. New York: 1938. V. 47; 48; 51; 54

CLARK, RONALD H.
The Development of the English Traction Engine. Norwich: 1960. V. 48

CLARK, SAMUEL
The Little Book of Nature, Comprising the Elements of Geology, Mineralogy, Conchology, Marine Botany and Entomology. London: 1837. V. 54

CLARK, THOMAS
Ways through Bracken. Highlands: 1980. V. 54

CLARK, THOMAS DIONYSIUS
Travels in the Old South: a Bibliography. Norman: 1956-59. V. 48
Travels in the Old South, a Bibliography. Norman: 1969. V. 47

CLARK, TOM
35. Berkeley: 1976. V. 50
When Things Get Tough on Easy Street. Santa Barbara: 1978. V. 48; 51

CLARK, WALTER
Gen. James Johnston Pettigrew. 1920. V. 49
The Papers of Walter Clark. Chapel Hill: 1948-50. V. 52

CLARK, WALTER VAN TILBURG
The Ox-Bow Incident. New York: 1940. V. 51
Strange Hunting. 1985. V. 48; 49
The Track of the Cat. New York: 1949. V. 48; 49

CLARK, WILLIAM
Boy's Own Book, Extended. New York: 1855. V. 51
Marciano; or, the Discovery. Edinburgh: 1871. V. 51

CLARK, WILLIAM G.
Greece and the Greeks. London: 1858. V. 49

CLARK, WILLIAM P.
The Indian Sign Language. Philadelphia: 1885. V. 49

CLARK ART INSTITUTE, WILLIAMSTOWN
Drawings from the Clark Art Institute. A Catalogue Raisonne of the Robert Sterling Clark Collection of European and American Drawings, Sixteenth through Nineteenth Centuries at the Sterling and Francine Clark Art Inst., Williamstown. New Haven: 1964. V. 54

CLARKE, ABRAHAM LYNSEN
The Secrets of Masonry Illustrated and Explained... Providence: 1799. V. 54

CLARKE, ADAM
A Bibliographical Dictionary. Liverpool: 1802-06. V. 50
The Bibliographical Miscellany; or, Supplement to the Bibliographical Dictionary. London: 1806. V. 52
A Dissertation on the Use and Abuse of Tobacco. London: 1798. V. 52
Memoirs of the Wesley Family... London: 1823. V. 49
A Narrative of the Last Illness and Death of Richard Porson, Professor of Greek in the University of Cambridge. London: 1808. V. 48

CLARKE, ARTHUR
An Essay on Warm, Cold and Vapour Bathing with Practical Observations on Sea Bathing, Diseases of the Skin, Bilious, Liver Complaints and Dropsy. London: 1820. V. 52

CLARKE, ARTHUR C.
2001: a Space Odyssey. 1968. V. 49; 50
2001: a Space Odyssey. London: 1968. V. 51; 54
2010: Odyssey Two. 1982. V. 47; 50; 51
2010: Odyssey Two. New York: 1982. V. 47
2061: Odyssey Three. 1988. V. 47; 48; 51; 52; 53
Across the Sea of Stars. 1959. V. 47; 51
Against the Fall of Night. 1953. V. 48; 49; 52; 54
Against the Fall of Night. New York: 1953. V. 52
Childhood's End. 1953. V. 51; 53
Childhood's End. 1954. V. 48; 52; 54
Childhood's End. London: 1954. V. 48
The City and the Stars. New York: 1957. V. 50
The Coast of Coral. New York: 1956. V. 48; 52
Dolphin Island. 1962. V. 47
Dolphin Island. 1963. V. 51
Earthlight. 1955. V. 49; 51; 54
Earthlight. London: 1955. V. 51
Expedition to Earth. 1953. V. 52
Expedition to Earth... New York: 1953. V. 48
Expedition to Earth. London: 1954. V. 47
A Fall of Moondust. 1961. V. 51
A Fall of Moondust. New York: 1961. V. 47; 52
The Fountains of Paradise. London: 1979. V. 51
From the Ocean, From the Stars. 1962. V. 49; 54
Imperial Earth. London: 1975. V. 48; 52
Interplanetary Flight. 1950. V. 48
Interplanetary Flight. New York: 1950. V. 52; 53
Interplanetary Flight. New York: 1951. V. 48; 51; 52
The Nine Billion Names of God. 1967. V. 47
The Other Side of the Sky. 1958. V. 51
The Other Side of the Sky. London: 1961. V. 51; 52
Prelude to Mars. 1965. V. 48; 52
Prelude to Space. London: 1953. V. 49
Rama II. London: 1989. V. 47
Rama II. (with) The Garden of Rama. New York: 189/91. V. 52

CLARKE, ARTHUR C. continued
Reach for Tomorrow. 1956. V. 47; 51
Reach for Tomorrow. London: 1962. V. 47; 48; 49; 51; 52; 54
Rendezvous with Rama. 1973. V. 47; 51
Rendezvous with Rama. London: 1973. V. 49; 51; 52; 54
The Sands of Mars. 1951. V. 47; 49; 54
The Sands of Mars. 1952. V. 49; 54
Tales of Ten Worlds. New York: 1962. V. 51
Tales of Ten Worlds... 1963. V. 51
Tales of Ten Worlds... London: 1963. V. 52

CLARKE, ARTHUR D.
A Tour through the South of England, Wales and Part of Ireland, Made During the Summer of 1791. London: 1793. V. 47

CLARKE, ASA B.
Travels in Mexico and California: Comprising a Journal of a Tour from Brazos Santiago, Through Central Mexico... Boston: 1852. V. 47; 49; 50

CLARKE, AUSTIN
The Cattledrive in Connaught and Other Poems. London: 1925. V. 48; 50
Collected Plays. Dublin: 1963. V. 47
The Collected Poems. London: 1936. V. 48; 51
First Visit to England and Other Memories. Dublin & London: 1945. V. 49
Two Great a Vine - Poems and Satires - Second Series. Dublin;: 1958. V. 52
The Vengeance of Fionn. Dublin: 1917. V. 47

CLARKE, BERNARD
A Trial On an Action for Damages, Wherein Moses Pentland Was Plaintiff, and Bernard Clarke, Defendant; for Criminal Conversation Between the Defendant and the Plaintiff's Wife. Dublin: 1803. V. 49

CLARKE, C. B.
Cyrtandreae. London: 1883. V. 47
A List of Flowering Plants, Ferns and Mosses of Andover. Calcutta: 1866. V. 54

CLARKE, C. STANLEY
Indian Drawings, Thirty Mogul Paintings of the School of Jahangir (17th Century) and four Panels of Calligraphy in the Wantage Bequest. London: 1922. V. 50

CLARKE, CHARLES
Recollections of Writers. London: 1878. V. 54
Sixty Years in Upper Canada. With Autobiographical Recollections. Toronto: 1908. V. 53

CLARKE, CHARLES G.
The Men of the Lewis and Clark Expedition. Glendale: 1970. V. 50; 52; 53; 54

CLARKE COUNTY HISTORICAL SOCIETY
Proceedings. 1941. V. 52
Proceedings. 1941-50. V. 54
Proceedings. 1941-57. V. 52

CLARKE, COWDEN, MRS.
The Complete Concordance to Shakespeare: Being a Verbal Index to All the Passages in the Dramatic Works of the Poet. London: 1875. V. 49

CLARKE, DORUS
Lectures to Young People in Manufacturing Villages. Boston: 1836. V. 54

CLARKE, EDWARD
A Century of American Medicine 1776-1876. Philadelphia: 1876. V. 50

CLARKE, EDWARD DANIEL
The Tomb of Alexander. Cambridge: 1805. V. 47
A Tour through the South of England, Wales and Part of Ireland, Made During the Summer of 1791. London: 1793. V. 48; 50
Travels in Various Countries of Europe, Asia and Africa. 1810-23. V. 52
Travels in Various Countries of Europe, Asia and Africa. London/Cambridge/Broxbourn: 1810-23. V. 51; 54
Travels in Various Countries of Europe, Asia and Africa. London: 1816-24. V. 48
Travels in Various Countries of Europe, Asia and Africa... London: 1819/23. V. 52

CLARKE, EDWARD H.
Sex in Education; or, a Fair Chance for Girls. Boston: 1873. V. 51; 53

CLARKE, EDWIN
The Human Body and Spinal Cord. San Francisco: 1996. V. 54
An Illustrated History of Brain Function. Imaging the Brain from Antiquity to the Present. San Francisco: 1996. V. 54

CLARKE, EWAN
The Rustic: a Poem. London: 1805. V. 52

CLARKE, FLORA
Sisters: Canada and India. Moncton: 1939. V. 51

CLARKE, G. H.
A Treasury of War Verse. Boston & New York: 1917. V. 50

CLARKE, GRAHAM
Balyn and Balan. Boughton, Monchelsea: 1970. V. 48

CLARKE, H. G., & CO.
Her Majesty's State Procession. London: 1875. V. 47

CLARKE, HAROLD GEORGE
Baxter Colour Prints, Pictorially presented. London: 1920-21. V. 51
Colour Pictures on Pot Lids and Other Forms of 19th Century Staffordshire Pottery. London: 1924. V. 51

CLARKE, HARRY
The Year's at the Spring. London: 1920. V. 49; 53

CLARKE, HEWSON
The Cabinet of Arts, or General Instructor in Arts, Science, Trade and Practical Machinery. London: 1839. V. 54
The History of the War, from the Establishment of Louis XVIII on the Throne of France, to the bombardment of Algiers... London: 1817. V. 48

CLARKE, J. B. B.
An Account of the Infancy, Religious and Literary Life of the Rev. Adam Clarke, LL.D. 1833. V. 54

CLARKE, J. G.
The Christian's Looking-Glass, or a Reply to the Animadversions of the Rev. Dr. Redford LL.D. of Worcester... Manchester: 1838. V. 53

CLARKE, J. JACKSON
Congenital Dislocation of the Hip. London: 1910. V. 49; 50; 51; 53

CLARKE, JAMES
The Sanative Influence of Climate. London: 1846. V. 51
A Survey of the Lakes of Cumberland, Westmorland and Lancashire... London: 1787. V. 50; 51; 52
A Survey of the Lakes of Cumberland, Westmorland, and Lancashire... London: 1789. V. 48; 50; 51; 52

CLARKE, JAMES STANIER
The Life and Services of Horatio Viscount Nelson. London: 1840. V. 47; 50
The Life of Admiral Lord Nelson From His Lordship's Manuscripts. London: 1809. V. 51
The Life of Admiral Lord Nelson From His Lordship's Manuscripts. London: 1810. V. 47
The Progress of Maritime Discovery from the Earliest Period to the Close of the Eighteenth Century... London: 1803. V. 50; 52

CLARKE, JOHN
An Essay Upon Study. London: 1737. V. 47
Eutropii Historiae Romanae Breviarium...or Eutropius's Compendious History of Rome. London: 1735. V. 48
Holy Oyle for the Lampes of the Sanctuarie; or, Scripture-Phrases Alphabetically Disposed. London: 1630. V. 54
An Introduction to the Making of Latin... Trenton: 1806. V. 50; 53

CLARKE, JOHN HENRY
A Dictionary of Practical Materia Medica. London: 1900-02. V. 53

CLARKE, JOSEPH
Henry Hudson. 1910. V. 49

CLARKE, LEWIS
Narrative of the Sufferings of Lewis Clarke During a Captivity of More than Twenty-five Years Among the Algerines of Kentucky... Boston: 1845. V. 54
Narratives of the Sufferings of Lewis and Milton Clarke, Sons of a Soldier of the Revolution, During a Captivity of More than Twenty Years Among the Slaveholders of Kentucky... Boston: 1846. V. 47; 54

CLARKE, LEWIS J.
Wild Flowers of British Columbia. Sidney: 1973. V. 48

CLARKE, MARCUS
For the Term of His Natural Life. Sydney: 1929. V. 48

CLARKE, MARTIN
The Motion of Fluids, Natural and Artificial. London: 1747. V. 49

CLARKE, MARY ANNE
Memoirs. London: 1809. V. 47
The Rival Princes; or a Faithful Narrative of Facts Relating to Mrs. Clarke's Political Acquaintance with Col. Wardle, Major Dodd, &c. London: 1810. V. 48; 51; 53
The Rival Princes; or a Faithful Narrative of Facts Relating to Mrs. Clarke's Political Acquaintance with Col. Wardle, Major Dodd &c. &c. New York: 1810. V. 50; 53

CLARKE, MARY CARR
The Memoirs of the Celebrated and Beautiful Mrs. Ann Carson, Daughter of an Officer of the U.S. Navy, and Wife of Another, Whose Life Terminated in the Philadelphia Prison. Philadelphia & New York: 1838. V. 51

CLARKE, MARY COWDEN
The Girlhood of Shakespeare's Heroines: a Series of Fifteen Tales. London: 1884. V. 53; 54
The Girlhood of Shakespeare's Heroines: a Series of Fifteen Tales. London: 1890. V. 53

CLARKE, MARY W.
David G. Burnet, First President of Texas. Austin: 1969. V. 48

CLARKE, MARY WHATLEY
David G. Burnet, First President of Texas. Austin: 1969. V. 47; 48; 50; 52
David Gouverneur Burnet, First President of Texas. Austin: 1969. V. 52

CLARKE, RICHARD
Cardinal Lavigerie and the African Slave Trade. London: 1889. V. 50; 53

CLARKE, S.
The British Botanist... London: 1820. V. 54

CLARKE, S. A.
Pioneer Days in Oregon History. Portland: 1905. V. 54

CLARKE, S. R.
The New Lancashire Gazette, or Topographical Dictionary, Containing an Accurate Description of the Several Hundred, Boroughs, Market Towns, Parishes, Townships and Hamlets in the County of Palatine of Lancaster. London: 1830. V. 53

CLARKE, SAMUEL
A Collection of Papers, Which Passed Between the Late Learned Mr. Leibnitz and Dr. Clarke, in the Years 1715 and 1716. London: 1717. V. 51
A Discourse Concerning the Being and Attributes of God, the Obligations of Natural Religion and the Truth and Certainty of the Christian Revelation. London: 1711. V. 53
The Lives of Sundry Eminent Persons in This Later Age. London: 1683. V. 48
Remarks Upon a Book, Entituled, A Philosophical Enquiry Concerning Human Liberty. London: 1717. V. 52

CLARKE, SIMON H.
Some Considerations on the Present Distressed State of the British West India Colonies, Their Claims on the Government for Relief... London: 1823. V. 50; 54

CLARKE, SOMERS
Ancient Egyptian Masonry: The Building Craft. London: 1930. V. 51

CLARKE, THOMAS
Sir Copp. A Poem for the Times in Six Cantos. Chicago: 1865. V. 54

CLARKE, THOMAS COTTRELL
A Collection of Fugitive Poems. Philadelphia: 1824. V. 51

CLARKE, W. B.
Lays of Leisure. London: 1829. V. 50

CLARKE, W. E. LE GROS
Fossil Mammals of Africa. London: 1951-59. V. 48; 50

CLARKE, W. FAIRLIE
A Treatise on the Diseases of the Tongue. London: 1873. V. 50

CLARKE, W. J.
Baseball. New York: 1915. V. 52

CLARKE, WILLIAM
Clarke's Complete Cellarman: The Publican and Innkeeper's Practical Guide; and Wine and Spirit Dealer's Director and Assistant. London: 1830. V. 51
The Connexion of the Roman, Saxon and English Coins Deduced From Observataions On the Saxon Weights and Money. London: 1767. V. 48
Every Night Book; or, Life After Dark. London: 1827. V. 47; 50
Repertorium Bibliographicum; or, Some Account of the Most Celebrated British Libraries. London: 1819. V. 47; 49
Studies in Bird Migration. London: 1912. V. 48; 50; 52; 53
Three Courses & a Dessert. 1830. V. 51
Three Courses & a Dessert. Branston. 1830. V. 52
Three Courses & a Dessert. London: 1830. V. 49

CLARKE, WILLIAM NELSON
Parochial Topography of the Hundred of Wanting, with Other Miscellaneous Records Relating to the County of Berks. Oxford: 1824. V. 47

CLARK'S Guide and History to Rye, to Which is Added Its Political History, Interspersed with many Pleasing and Interesting Incidents. 1861. V. 52

CLARKSON, CHRISTOPHER
The History and Antiquities of Richmond, in the County of York. Richmond: 1821. V. 47; 53
The History of Richmond, in the County of York... Richmond: 1814. V. 47; 53

CLARKSON, HENRY MAZYCK
Evelyn: a Romance of "The War Between the States". Charleston: 1871. V. 49
Songs of Love and War. Manassas: 1898. V. 49; 54

CLARKSON, L.
The Gathering of the Lilies. Philadelphia: 1877. V. 49
Indian Summer, Autumn, Poems and Sketches. New York: 1881. V. 52
Violet Among the Lilies. New York: 1885. V. 54

CLARKSON, T.
A Portaiture of Quakerism Taken from a View of the Moral Education, Discipline, Peculiar Customs, Religious Principles, Political and Civil Economy and Character, of the Society of Friends. London: 1807. V. 54

CLARKSON, T. CLARKSON
An Essay on the Impolicy of the African Slave Trade in Two Parts. London: 1788. V. 50

CLARKSON, THOMAS
Abolition of the African Slave Trade, by the British Parliament. Augusta: 1830. V. 50
The Cries of Africa, to the Inhabitants of Europe... London: 1822?. V. 50
An Essay on the Impolicy of the African Slave Trade. London: 1788. V. 50; 52
An Essay on the Slavery and Commerce of the Human Species, Particularly the African... Philadelphia: 1786. V. 48
An Essay on the Slavery and Commerce of the Human Species, Particularly the African. London: 1787. V. 48
An Essay on the Slavery and Commerce of the Human Species, Particularly the African. Philadelphia: 1787. V. 49; 50
An Essay on the Slavery and Commerce of the Human Species, Particularly the African. London: 1788. V. 48; 49
An Essay on the Slavery and Commerce of the Human Species, Particularly the African. Georgetown: 1816. V. 49
The History of the Rise, Progress and Accomplishments of the Abolition of the African Slave Trade by the British Parliament. Philadelphia: 1808. V. 49
Memoirs of the Private and Public Life of William Penn. London: 1813. V. 49; 51; 52
Researches Antediluvian, Patriarchal and Historical... London: 1836. V. 50

CLARY, WILLIAM W.
History of the Law Firm of O'Melveny & Myers: 1885-1965. Los Angeles: 1966. V. 47; 48

THE CLASSICAL Journal. London: 1810-29. V. 48

CLASSICAL Selections in Verse. Liverpool: 1808. V. 48

CLATER, FRANCIS
Every Man His Own Cattle Doctor; or, a Practical Treatise on the Diseases of Horned Cattle... Philadelphia: 1815. V. 51

CLAUDE, JEAN
The Catholick Doctrine of the Eucharist In All Ages... London: 1684. V. 48

CLAUDEL, PAUL
The Book of Christopher Columbus: a Lyrical Drama in Two Parts. New Haven: 1930. V. 48
Chine. Geneva: 1946. V. 47

CLAUDET, F. G.
Gold: Its Properties, Modes of Extraction, Values, &c. Vancouver: 1958. V. 50; 52

CLAUDIANUS, CLAUDIUS
Ex Optimorum Codicum Fide. Bassani: 1722. V. 48
Opera. Venice: 1500. V. 48; 54

CLAUDIN, A.
The First Paris Press. London: 1897. V. 48
The First Paris Press. London: 1898. V. 47; 50; 51; 52

CLAUSEN, J.
Experimental Studies on the Nature of Species. Washington: 1940-58. V. 52

CLAVELL, JAMES
King Rat. Boston: 1962. V. 49
King Rat. London: 1963. V. 47; 48; 53
Noble House. New York: 1981. V. 48; 50
Shogun. New York: 1975. V. 51; 52
Tai-Pan. New York: 1966. V. 53; 54

CLAVERING, ROBERT
An Essay on the Construction and Building of Chimneys. London: 1779. V. 52
An Essay on the Construction and Building of Chimneys. London: 1793. V. 47

CLAVERING, VERE
Barcaldine. London: 1889. V. 54
Hugh Deyne of Plas-Idrys. London: 1893. V. 54

CLAVIGERO, D. FRANCESCO SAVERIO
Historical Outline of Lower California... San Francisco: 1862. V. 47
The History of Mexico. London: 1787. V. 47
The History of Mexico... Richmond: 1806. V. 53
Storia Antica del Messico Cavata da' Migliori Storici Spagnuoli, e da' Manoscritti, e Dalle Pitture Antiche... Cesena: 1780-81. V. 50

CLAWSON, JOHN LEWIS
A Catalogue of Early English Books in the Library of John L. Clawson. Philadelphia & New York: 1924. V. 47

CLAXTON, CHRISTOPHER
The Naval Monitor: Containing Many Useful Hints for Both the Public and Private Conduct of the Young Gentleman... London: 1815. V. 48

CLAXTON, FLORENCE
The Adventures of a Woman in Search of Her Rights. London: 1865. V. 52
The Adventures of a Woman in Search of Her Rights. London: 1880. V. 47

CLAY, ALBERT T.
Documents from the Temple Archives of Nippur Dated in the Reigns of Cassite Rulers. Philadelphia: 1906. V. 49; 51

CLAY, ENID
The Constant Mistress. 1934. V. 47
The Constant Mistress. London: 1934. V. 54
The Constant Mistress. Waltham St. Lawrence: 1934. V. 48; 50; 51; 52
Sonnets and Verses. London: 1925. V. 47
Sonnets and Verses. Waltham St. Lawrence: 1925. V. 48; 50; 54

CLAY, FELIX
Modern School Buildings', Elementary and Secondary... London: 1902. V. 52

CLAY, HENRY
An Address... Containing Certain Testimony in Refutation of the Chargers Against Him, Made by Gen. Andrew Jackson. Washington: 1827. V. 53
Life and Speeches of Henry Clay. New York: 1843. V. 48
Remarks of Mr. Clay, of Kentucky, on Introducing His Propositions to Compromise, on the Slavery Question. In the Senate....January 29, 1850. (with) Speech...in Support of His Propositions to Compromise on the Slavery Question. Washington: 1850. V. 48
Valedictory of Henry Clay, in the Seante of the United States Thursday, March 31, 1842. Washington: 1842. V. 47

CLAY, JOHN
My Life On the Range. Chicago: 1924. V. 48; 50; 52
My Recollections of Ontario. Chicago: 1918. V. 49
Tragedy of Squaw Mountain. Chicago. V. 53

CLAY, JOHN CECIL
Cupid's Cyclopedia. New York: 1910. V. 48
Cupid's Fair-Weather Booke. New York: 1911. V. 48
In Love's Garden. Indianapolis: 1904. V. 48
The Lover's Mother Goose. Indianapolis: 1905. V. 48

CLAY, ROTHA MARY
The Hermits and Anchorites of England. London: 1914. V. 49
Julius Caesar Ibbetson 1759-1817. London: 1948. V. 50; 54
The Mediaeval Hospitals of England. London: 1909. V. 50

CLAY, ROTHA MARY continued
Samuel Hieronymous Grimm of Burgdorf in Switzerland. London: 1941. V. 49; 51

CLAY, STEPHEN
An Epistle from the Elector of Bavaria to the French King: after the Battle of Ramilles. London: 1706. V. 53

CLAY, THOMAS
Briefe, Easie and Necessary Tables, of Interest and Rents Forborne: as Also, for the Valuation of Leases, Annuities and Purchases, Either in Present or in Reuersion, According tot he Rates Now Most in Vse. London: 1624. V. 49

CLAYDEN, P. W.
The Early Life of Samuel Rogers. London: 18887. V. 49

CLAYSON, PATRICK
Essays. Viz. I. On the Origin of Colleges, or Universities. II. On the Origin of the Custom of Lecturing in Latin. III. On the Impropriety of this Custom, at Present. Glasgow: 1769. V. 53

CLAYTON, ALEXANDER M.
Centennial Address on the History of Marshall County Delivered...1876. Washington: 1880. V. 50

CLAYTON, AUGUSTIN S.
The Office and Duty of a Justice of the Peace, and a Guide to Clerks, Constables, Coroners...According to the Laws of the State of Georgia... Milledgeville: 1819. V. 48

CLAYTON, BENJAMIN
Notes On Some Phases of Cotton Operations: 1905-1929. V. 53

CLAYTON, DAVID
A Short But Thorough Search Into What May be the Real Cause of the Present Scarcity of Our Silver Coin. London: 1717. V. 54

CLAYTON, ELLEN CREATHORNE
English Female Artists... London: 1876. V. 49; 51
Female Warriors. London: 1879. V. 49; 50
Queens of Song: Being Memoirs of Some of the Most Celebrated Female Vocalists... London: 1863. V. 53
Queens of Song: Being Memoirs of Some of the Most Celebrated Female Vocalists... New York: 1865. V. 49; 52; 53; 54

CLAYTON, H. J.
Clayton's Quaker Cook-Book, Being a Practical Treatise on the Culinary Art Adapted to the Tastes and Wants of All Classes. San Francisco: 1883. V. 53

CLAYTON, JOHN WILLIAM
Scenes and Studies; or Errant Steps and Stray Fancies. London: 1870. V. 54

CLAYTON, RICHARD
A Critical Enquiry into the Life of Alexander the Great. Bath: 1793. V. 53

CLAYTON, ROBERT
The Speech of..., Lord Mayor Elect for the City of London, at the Guild-Hall of the Said City, to the Citizens There Assembled on 29th September 1679... London: 1679. V. 52

CLAYTON, VICTORIA V.
White and Black Under the Old Regime. Milwaukee: 1899. V. 47

CLAYTON, W.
The Invisible Hand. London: 1815. V. 47; 52
The Latter Day Saints' Emigrants' Guide: Being a Table of Distances, Showing All the Springs, Creeks, Rivers, Hills, Mountains... 1930. V. 48

CLAYTON, W. F.
A Narrative of the Confederate States Navy. Weldon: 1910. V. 49

CLAYTON, W. WOODFORD
History Of Union and Middlesex Counties, New Jersey, with Biographical Sketches of Many of Their Pioneers and Prominent Men. Philadelphia: 1882. V. 51

CLAYTON, WILLIAM
William Clayton' Journal a Daily Record of the Journey of the Original Company of "Mormon" Pioneers... Salt Lake City: 1921. V. 47; 49; 54

CLEAR, W.
Address Read from the Chair of the Cork Philosophical and Literary Society on Wednesday evening, 22nd December, 1819. Cork: 1820. V. 49

CLEARY, JON
The High Commissioner. New York: 1966. V. 51

CLEATOR, P. E.
Rockets Through Space. The Dawn of Interplanetary Travel. New York: 1936. V. 48

CLEAVELAND, JOHN
The Idol of the Clownes, or, Insurrection of Wat the Tyler, with His Fellows Kings of the Commons, Gainst the English Church, the King, the Lawes, Mobility and Gentry in the Fourth Yeare of King Richard the 2n Anno 1381. London: 1654. V. 51

CLEAVELAND, NEHEMIAH
Green-Wood: a Directory for Visitors. New York: 1850. V. 51

CLEAVER, ELDRIDGE
Soul on Ice. New York: 1968. V. 49; 53

CLEAVER, ROBERT
Three Sermons Upon Marke, the Ninth Chapter, 22. 23. Verses. London: 1611. V. 53

CLECKLEY, HERVEY M.
The Mask of Sanity: an Attempt to Clarify Some Issues about the So-Called Psychopathic Personality. St. Louis: 1941. V. 52

CLEEVE, BOURCHIER
A Scheme for Preventing a Further Increase of the National Debt and for Reducing the Same. London: 1756. V. 52

CLEGG, SAMUEL
Architecture of Machinery: an Essay on Propriety of Form and Proportion, with a View to Assist and Improve Design. London: 1842. V. 52

CLEGHORN, GEORGE
Observations on the Epidemical Diseases in Minorca, from the Year 1744to 1749... London: 1768. V. 47; 53
Observations on the Epidemical Diseases of Minorca. From the Year 1744 to 1749. Philadelphia: 1809. V. 50

CLELAND, CHARLES
Abstracts of the Several Laws and Rules That Are Now in Force, Relating to the Importation and Exportation of Wines into and Out of Great Britain with Complete Tables. (together with) A Manuscript Table of the Duties in London on Portugal Wine in 1780. London: 1738. V. 47

CLELAND, HENRY WILSON
On the History and Properties Chemical and Medical of Tobacco, a Probationary Essay Presented to the Faculty of Physicians and Surgeons, Glasgow... Glasgow: 1840. V. 48; 52

CLELAND, JAMES
Description of the Banquet Given in Honour of the Right Hon. Sir Robert Peel, Bart, M.P. On His Election as Lord Rector of the University of Glasgow. Glasgow: 1837. V. 50

CLELAND, JOHN
The Dictionary of Love. London: 1753. V. 47
Memoirs of a Coxcomb. London: 1751. V. 47
Memoirs of Fanny Hill. Paris: 1890?. V. 51
Memoirs of Fanny Hill... London: 1908. V. 48

CLELAND, THOMAS MAITLAND
The Decorative Work. New York: 1929. V. 47; 48; 49; 50
Harsh Words. Newark: 1940. V. 47; 48; 49

CLEMENS, JEREMIAH
Bernard Lile: an Historical Romance, Embracing the Periods of the Texas Revolution and the Mexican War. Philadelphia: 1857. V. 47

CLEMENS, SAMUEL LANGHORNE
The $30,000 Bequest. New York: 1906. V. 51; 53
The 1,000,000 Pound Bank Note and Other New Stories. London: 1893. V. 51; 53
The 1,000,000 Pound Bank Note and Other New Stories. New York: 1893. V. 47; 49; 51; 53
1601. Conversation, As It Was by the Social Fireside in the Time of the Tudors. Easthampton: 1978. V. 51; 54
The Adventures of Huckleberry Finn. London: 1884. V. 47; 49; 50; 51; 52; 53; 54
The Adventures of Huckleberry Finn. London: 1884. V. 47
Adventures of Huckleberry Finn. Montreal: 1885. V. 47
Adventures of Huckleberry Finn. New York: 1885. V. 47; 48; 49; 50; 51; 53; 54
The Adventures of Huckleberry Finn. New York: 1885. V. 49; 54
Adventures of Huckleberry Finn. New York: 1886. V. 51
The Adventures of Huckleberry Finn. Leipzig: 1922/23. V. 50
The Adventures of Huckleberry Finn. New York: 1933. V. 50
The Adventures of Huckleberry Finn. New York: 1942. V. 47; 51; 52; 54
Adventures of Huckleberry Finn. Detroit: 1983. V. 48
Adventures of Huckleberry Finn. Northampton: 1985. V. 49
The Adventures of Huckleberry Finn. West Hatfield: 1985. V. 47; 48; 49; 50; 52
The Adventures of Thomas Jefferson Snodgrass. Chicago: 1928. V. 51; 53
The Adventures of Tom Sawyer. Hartford: 1876. V. 47; 48; 49; 51; 52; 53; 54
The Adventures of Tom Sawyer. London: 1876. V. 49; 50
The Adventures of Tom Sawyer. Toronto: 1876. V. 52
The Adventures of Tom Sawyer. Hartford: 1880. V. 52
The Adventures of Tom Sawyer. Hartford: 1902. V. 53
The Adventures of Tom Sawyer. Cambridge: 1939. V. 47; 51; 52; 54
The Adventures of Tom Sawyer. Cambridge: 1939. V. 47; 52
The Adventures of Tom Sawyer. London: 1947. V. 49; 54
The Adventures of Tom Sawyer. Washington: 1982. V. 51
Ah Sin. San Francisco: 1961. V. 47
The American Claimant. London: 1892. V. 47; 48; 51
The American Claimant. New York: 1892. V. 48; 49; 51; 52; 53; 54
Autobiography and First Romance. New York: 1871. V. 47; 48
Les Aventures de Tom Sawyer. Paris. V. 54
A Boy's Adventure... 1928. V. 47; 49
A Boy's Adventure. New York: 1928. V. 54
The Celebrated Jumping Frog of Calaveras County. New York: 1867. V. 47
The Celebrated Jumping Frog of Calaveras County and Other Sketches. New York: 1867. V. 47; 48; 50; 51; 52; 53; 54
A Champagne Cocktail and a Catastrophe. New York: 1930. V. 53
Christian Science. New York: 1907. V. 47; 50; 51; 53; 54
The Complete Works. New York: 1906. V. 51
Concerning Cats: Two Tales. San Francisco: 1959. V. 54
A Connecticut Yankee in King Arthur's Court. New York: 1889. V. 47; 48; 49; 51; 52; 53; 54
A Connecticut Yankee in King Arthur's Court. Toronto: 1890. V. 53
A Connecticut Yankee in King Arthur's Court. New York: 1949. V. 47; 51; 53; 54
Conversation As It Was by the Social Fireside in the Time of the Tudors. 1904. V. 51
Conversation As It Was by the Social Fireside in the Time of the Tudors. 1913. V. 47; 49

CLEMENS, SAMUEL LANGHORNE continued
Conversation As It Was by the Social Fireside in the Time of the Tudors. Chicago: 1936. V. 47
Conversation As It Was by the Social Fireside in the Time of the Tudors. Chicago: 1939. V. 47
The Curious Republic of Gondour. New York: 1919. V. 48; 49; 51; 54
Death-Disk. New York: 1913. V. 47; 51
A Dog's Life. London: 1904. V. 53
A Dog's Tale. London: 1903. V. 49; 50; 51; 54
A Dog's Tale. London: 1904. V. 47; 50
A Dog's Tale. New York: 1904. V. 49; 51
A Double Barrelled Detective Story. New York & London: 1902. V. 47; 49; 50; 51; 53
Editorial Wild Oats. New York: 1905. V. 49; 51
English As She Is Taught... London: 1887. V. 49
English As She Is Taught. Boston: 1900. V. 47; 48; 49; 51
English as She Is Taught. New York: 1900. V. 51
English as She Is Taught. New York: 1901. V. 51
English As She is Taught. Boston: 1930. V. 54
Europe and Elsewhere. New York London: 1923. V. 48
Europe and Elsewhere. New York & London: 1923. V. 48; 49; 51; 54
Eve's Diary. New York: 1906. V. 54
Eve's Diary. Staten Island: 1992. V. 51; 54
Extract from Captain Stormfield's Visit to Heaven. New York & London: 1909. V. 48; 53; 54
Extracts from Adam's Diary. New York & London: 1904. V. 48; 53
Fireside Conversation In the Time of Queen Elizabeth, or 1601, a Fragment. New York: 1920. V. 51
Following the Equator. Hartford: 1897. V. 47; 48; 49; 50; 51; 53; 54
Following the Equator. Hartford: 1898. V. 54
Fra Mississippifloden... (Life on the Mississippi). Kjobenhavn: 1883. V. 49
The Gilded Age. Hartford: 1873. V. 47; 51; 54
The Gilded Age. Hartford & San Francisco: 1874. V. 49; 50; 51; 52; 53; 54
The Gilded Age. London: 1874. V. 51
The Gilded Age. Hartford: 1884. V. 48; 49
Grindringer Fra en Fodtur I Europa. (A Tramp Abroad). Kjobenhavn: 1880. V. 49
A Horse's Tale. New York: 1907. V. 51; 53
How to Tell a Story and Other Essays. New York: 1897. V. 47; 51; 54
Huckleberry Finn and Tom Sawyer. New York: 1940. V. 51
The Innocents Abroad... Hartford: 1868. V. 54
The Innocents Abroad. Hartford: 1869. V. 47; 51; 54
The Innocents Abroad. London: 1869?. V. 49
The Innocents Abroad. Boston: 1895. V. 51; 54
The Innocents Abroad. New York: 1962. V. 48; 49; 51; 54
Is Shakespeare Dead?. New York & London: 1909. V. 48; 49; 51; 52; 53
The Jumping Frog. New York: 1903. V. 51
The Jumping Frog. Easthampton: 1985. V. 50; 52
King Leopold's Soliloquy. Boston: 1905. V. 53
A Letter from Mark Twain to His Publishers, Chatto & Windus of London, Calling Their Attention to the Certain Indiscretions of the Proofreaders of Messrs. Spottiswoode & Co. San Francisco;: 1929. V. 54
Letters from the Sandwich Islands. San Francisco: 1937. V. 47; 50; 53
Letters from the Sandwich Islands. Stanford: 1938. V. 51
Library of Humor. New York: 1888. V. 49
Life on the Mississippi. Boston: 1883. V. 51
Life on the Mississippi. Boston: 1883. V. 47; 48; 49; 51; 52; 53; 54
Life on the Mississippi. London: 1883. V. 51; 52; 54
Life on the Mississippi. Montreal: 1883. V. 51; 53
Life on the Mississippi. New York: 1888. V. 53
Life On the Mississippi. New York: 1944. V. 48; 51; 53
Lotos Leaves. Boston: 1875. V. 51
The Love Letters. New York: 1949. V. 48; 50; 51; 54
The Man that Corrupted Hadleyburg... London: 1900. V. 49
The Man That Corrupted Hadleyburg. New York: 1900. V. 51; 53
Mark Twain Compliments the President's Wife. Boston: 1984. V. 47; 49
Mark Twain in Nevada. 1927. V. 47
Mark Twain: San Francisco Correspondent. Selections from His Letters to the Territorial Enterprise: 1865-66. San Francisco: 1957. V. 53
Mark Twain-Howells Letters. Cambridge: 1960. V. 49; 51; 54
Mark Twain's Autobiography. New York: 1924. V. 47; 48; 51; 53
Mark Twain's (Burlesque) Autobiography and First Romance. New York: 1871. V. 47; 49; 51
Mark Twain's Letter to the California Pioneers. Oakland: 1911. V. 49; 54
Mark Twain's Letter to William Bowen. San Francisco: 1938. V. 49; 51
Mark Twain's Letters. New York: 1917. V. 47; 49; 51; 53; 54
Mark Twain's Letters in the Muscatine Journal. Chicago: 1942. V. 47
Mark Twain's Library of Humor. New York: 1888. V. 49; 51; 54
Mark Twain's Memory Builder. New York: 1891. V. 47; 49
Mark Twain's Notebook. New York: 1935. V. 48; 51
Mark Twain's Rubaiyat. Austin & Santa Barbara: 1983. V. 54
Mark Twain's Scrap Book. New York: 1877. V. 50
Mark Twain's Sketches. London: 1872. V. 49
Mark Twain's Sketches. New York: 1874. V. 51; 53
Mark Twain's Sketches, New and Old. Hartford and Chicago: 1875. V. 47; 49; 50; 51
Mark Twain's Speeches. New York: 1910. V. 49; 51; 54
Merry Tales. New York: 1892. V. 48; 49; 51
The Mississippi Pilot. Glasgow. V. 48; 51
Mississippi Pilot. London: 1877. V. 51
More Tramps Abroad. London: 1897. V. 51; 53; 54
The Mysterious Stranger. New York: 1916. V. 47; 54
The Mysterious Stranger... New York: 1922. V. 47; 51; 53
The New Pilgrims' (sic) Progress. Toronto. V. 51
The New War-Scare. Santa Barbara: 1981. V. 49; 51
The Niagara Book. Buffalo: 1893. V. 53
The Notorious Jumping Frog and Other Stories. New York: 1970. V. 53
Old Times On the Mississippi. Toronto: 1876. V. 48; 51; 52; 54
Old Times on the Mississippi... Toronto: 1878. V. 53
An Open Letter to Commodore Vanderbilt. Boston: 1956. V. 50
Personal Recollections of Joan of Arc. London: 1896. V. 49; 51
Personal Recollections of Joan of Arc. New York: 1896. V. 48; 51; 54
Personal Recollections of Joan of Arc. Salt Lake City: 1924. V. 48
The Prince and the Pauper... Leipzig: 1881. V. 49
The Prince and the Pauper. Montreal: 1881. V. 50; 54
The Prince and the Pauper. Boston: 1882. V. 47; 49; 51; 54
The Prince and the Pauper. Toronto: 1882. V. 53
The Prince and the Pauper. Westerham, Kent: 1964. V. 48; 49; 51; 53; 54
The Private Printing of the "Jumping Frog" Story. Williamsburg: 1985. V. 50; 51
Pudd'nhead Wilson... Hartford: 1894. V. 48; 49; 50; 51; 52; 53; 54
Pudd'nhead Wilson. London: 1894. V. 47; 48; 51; 53; 54
Pudd'nhead Wilson. Avon: 1974. V. 48; 49; 51; 53; 54
Punch, Brothers, Punch! And Other Sketches. Edinburgh: 1878. V. 51
Punch, Brothers, Punch! And Other Sketches. New York: 1878. V. 47; 49; 51; 53; 54
The Quaker City Holy Land Excursion, an Unfinished Play. New York: 1927. V. 54
Queen Victoria's Jubilee. 1910. V. 47
Rambling Notes Of an Idle Excursion. Toronto: 1878. V. 49; 51; 53
Report from Paradise. New York: 1952. V. 51
Roughing It. Hartford: 1872. V. 47; 48; 51; 53; 54
Roughing It. Toronto: 1880. V. 47
Roughing It... Kentfield: 1953. V. 53
Roughing It. New York: 1972. V. 47; 49; 51; 54
Saint Joan of Arc. New York: 1919. V. 47; 49; 50; 51; 54
Samuel Langhorne Clemens. Worcester: 1910. V. 54
The Sandwich Islands. New York: 1920. V. 54
Sketches, New and Old. Hartford & Chicago: 1875. V. 48; 51
Sketches of the Sixties. San Francisco: 1926. V. 51
S.L.C. to C.T. New York: 1925. V. 54
Slovenly Peter. New York: 1935. V. 49
The Stolen White Elephant. Boston: 1882. V. 49
The Stolen White Elephant. London: 1882. V. 49; 51; 54
The Suppressed Chapter of Life on the Mississippi. New York: 1913. V. 49
Three Aces. Westport: 1929. V. 51
To the Person Sitting in Darkness. New York. V. 53
To the Person Sitting in Darkness. New York: 1901. V. 49; 54
Tom Sawyer, a Drama. Washington: 1940. V. 47
Tom Sawyer Abroad. London: 1894. V. 47; 51
Tom Sawyer Abroad. New York: 1894. V. 50; 51; 53; 54
Tom Sawyer Abroad, Tom Sawyer, Detective and Other Stories. New York: 1896. V. 54
Tom Sawyer, Detective. London: 1897. V. 51; 53
Tom Sawyer, Detective. London: 1897/96. V. 48
Tom Sawyer, Detective. Barcelona: 1909. V. 51
A Tramp Abroad. 1880. V. 48; 54
A Tramp Abroad... Hartford & London: 1880. V. 47; 48; 49; 50; 51; 52; 53; 54
A Tramp Abroad. Toronto: 1880. V. 48; 49; 51; 53
A Tramp Abroad. 1966. V. 48
Travels at Home. New York: 1910. V. 51; 53
Travels in History.... New York: 1910. V. 53
Travels with Mr. Brown. New York: 1940. V. 48; 51
A True Story , and the Recent Carnival of Crime. Boston: 1877. V. 47
An Unexpected Acquaintance. New York & London: 1904. V. 49; 54
Wapping Alice... Berkeley: 1981. V. 52
The War Prayer. New York: 1968. V. 51; 54
The Washoe Giant in San Francisco... San Francisco: 1938. V. 51
What Is Man?. London: 1910. V. 49; 51
What Is Man?. New York: 1917. V. 47; 51
Works. New York: 1924. V. 51
The Writings. Hartford: 1899-1907. V. 47
The Writings. New York: 1903. V. 51
The Writings. New York: 1922. V. 48; 52
The Writings... New York: 1929. V. 54
The Writings Of... New York. V. 53
A Yankee at the Court of King Arthur. 1889. V. 52
A Yankee at the Court of King Arthur. London: 1889. V. 49; 50; 51
A Yankee in King Author's Court. New York: 1889. V. 47

CLEMENS, WILL M.
Mark Twain: His Life and Work. San Francisco: 1892. V. 53; 54

CLEMENS ROMANUS
Apostolicarum constitutionum & Catholicae Doctrinae...Livri VIII. Antwerp: 1578. V. 53

CLEMENS V, POPE
Constitutiones (cum Apparatu Joannis Andreae). Venice: 1489. V. 51; 53

CLEMENT, CLARA ERSKINE
Naples, the City of Parthenope. U.S.A: 1894. V. 51

CLEMENT, DAVID
Bibliotheque Curieuse Historique et Critique, ou Catalogue Raisonne de Livres Difficiles a Trouver. Gottingen, Hanover and: 1750-60. V. 51

CLEMENT, ERNEST W.
A Handbook of Modern Japan. Chicago: 1904. V. 54

CLEMENT, HAL
Cycle of Fire. London: 1964. V. 47; 51
Iceworld. New York: 1953. V. 51
Mission of Gravity. New York: 1954. V. 49; 51; 54
Needle. New York: 1950. V. 48; 52

CLEMENT, JOHN
Sketches of the First Emigrant Settlers in Newton Township, Old Gloucester County, West New Jersey. Camden: 1877. V. 47; 49; 51

CLEMENT, LEWIS
Modern Wildfowling. London: 1880. V. 49; 51; 52
Shooting and Fishing Trips, in England, France, Alsace, Belgium, Holland and Bavaria. London: 1876. V. 51; 52

CLEMENT, MARGUERITE
All the World is Colour. New York: 1940. V. 51

CLEMENT, SHAW
Letizia Bonaparte, 1748-1836. New York: 1928. V. 50

CLEMENTS, LEWIS
Modern Wildfowling. London: 1880. V. 49

CLEMENT VIII, POPE
Regulae Ordinationes et Constitutiones Concellariae Apost. Smi. D.N.D. Clementis...VIII. Rome: 1592. V. 47

CLEMONS, WALTER
The Poison Tree. Boston: 1959. V. 50

CLENNETT, ROBERT
Photograms of the Stockton Polytechnic Exhibition. Stockton: 1860. V. 47

CLEOFILO, FRANCESCO OTTAVIO
De Coetu Poetarum Cum Maginarijs Adnotamentis. Basel: 1518. V. 50

CLERCK, CARL
Carl Clerck's Fjarsilsbok Icones Insectorum Rariorum 1759-1764. Stockholm: 1989. V. 49

CLERGUE, LUCIEN
De Cape Qui Caresse et D'Epee Qui Foudroie L'Oeuvre de Picasso. 1992. V. 52

CLERIDES, GLAFKOS
Cyprus: My Deposition. Nicosia: 1989-90. V. 47; 49

CLERIHEWS.. Cambridge: 1938. V. 52

CLERK, JAMES MAXWELL
Colonial Days. Denver: 1902. V. 53

CLERK, JOHN
A Letter to a Friend, Giving an Account How the Treaty of Union Has Been Received Here. Edinburgh: 1706. V. 51

CLERKE, CHARLES
A Voyage Round the World, in His Majesty's Ship the Dolphin, Commanded by the Honourable Commodore Byron. London: 1767. V. 50

THE CLERK'S Instructor in the Ecclesiastical Courts... London: 1740. V. 47

CLERY, JEAN B.
A Journal of Occurrences at the Temple, During the Confinement of Louis XVI, King of France. Cork: 1798. V. 52

CLEVELAND, AGNES MORLEY
No Life for a Lady. Boston: 1941. V. 53

CLEVELAND BRIDGE & ENGINEERING CO.
Bridges, Roofs and Constructional Work in Iron and Steel. Darlington: 1910. V. 49

CLEVELAND, CATHERINE LUCY WILHELMINA STANHOPE POWLETT
The Life and Letters of Lady Hester Stanhope. London: 1897. V. 49

CLEVELAND, JOHN
The Idol of the Clovvnes, or, Insurrections of Wat the Tyler. London: 1654. V. 47; 48; 51
J. Cleaveland Revived: Poems, Orations, Epistles and Other of His Genuine Incomparable Pieces. London: 1660. V. 54
J. Cleaveland Revived: Poems, Orations, Epistles and Other of His Genuine incomparable Pieces. (with) Poems. London: 1662/61. V. 50
Poems... (with) Cleveland Revived: Poems, Orations, Epistles and Other of His Genuine Incomparable Pieces. London: 1668. V. 52
Poems. (with) J. Cleaveland Revived: Poems, Orations, Epistles... London: 1669/68. V. 54
The Works... London: 1687. V. 48; 50; 54

CLEVELAND, P.
An Elementary Treatise on Mineralogy and Geology. Boston and London: 1822. V. 53

CLEVELAND, RAY L.
An Ancient South Arabian Necropolis. Baltimore: 1965. V. 52

CLEVELAND, W.
Extracts From a Journal Kept On Board the Ship 'Madagascar' on Her Passage From Calcutta to England. Deal: 1847. V. 50

CLEVENGER, S. V.
Spinal Concussion: Surgically Considered as a Cause of Spinal Injury, and Neurologically Restricted to a Certain Symptom Group... Philadelphia: 1889. V. 47; 48; 49; 50; 51; 53

CLEVERDON, DOUGLAS
Stanley Morison and Eric Gill 1925-1933. London: 1983. V. 49

CLEYRE, VOLTAIRINE DE
Selected Works. New York: 1914. V. 53

CLIFFE, JOHN HENRY
Notes and Recollections of an Angler: Rambles Among the Mountains, Valleys and Solitudes of Wales. London: 1860. V. 47

CLIFFORD, HENRY H.
California Pictorial Letter Sheets. Catalogue of the Collection of Henry H. Clifford. Austin: 1994. V. 52; 54

CLIFFORD, HERBERT
Crown, Bar and Bridge-work. London: 1885. V. 51

CLIFFORD, HUGH
Further India Being the Story of Exploration from the Earliest Times in Burma, Malaya, Siam and Indo-China... London: 1904. V. 53
Report Expedition: Trengganu and Kelantan. Kuala Lampur: 1938. V. 54

CLIFFORD, ISIDORE E.
Crown, Bar and Bridge-Work; New Methods of Permanently Adjusting Artifical Teeth Without Plates. 1887. V. 54
Crown, Bar and Bridge-Work: new Methods of Permanently Adjusting Artificial Teeth Without Plates. London: 1885. V. 50

CLIFFORD, JAMES L.
Johnsonian Studies, Including a Bibliography of Johnsonian Studies, 1950-1960. Cairo: 1962. V. 48

CLIFFORD, LUCY
Aunt Anne. London: 1892. V. 47
Mrs. Keith's Crime. London: 1885. V. 50

CLIFFORD, M. M.
Egypt: a Poem of that Country and Its Inhabitants. London: 1802. V. 54

CLIFFORD, MARTIN
A Treatise of Humane Reason. London: 1675. V. 47; 52

CLIFFORD, W. K.
Lectures and Essays. London: 1879. V. 49

CLIFFORD, WAYNE
Man in a Window. Toronto: 1965. V. 47

CLIFFORD'S Descriptive Guide of Tunbridge Wells... Tunbridge Wells: 1823. V. 50

CLIFORD, J. HENRY
The Conduct of the Dutch, Relating to Their Breach of Treaties with England... London: 1760. V. 51

CLIFTON, LUCILLE
Good Times (Poems). New York: 1969. V. 51

CLIFTON, M.
They'd Rather Be Right. 1957. V. 51
They'd Rather Be Right. London: 1957. V. 48

CLIFTON, WILLIAM
Poems, Chiefly Occasional by the Late...to Which are Prefixed... New York: 1800. V. 54

CLIMACUS, JOHN
The Illustration of the Heavenly Ladder of John Climacus. Princeton: 1954. V. 48

CLIMENT, ENRIQUE
Ten Linoleum Engravings in Color. Mexico City: 1951. V. 51

CLINCH, GEORGE
Bloomsbury and St. Giles's: Past and Present; With Historical and Antiquarian Notices of the Vicinity. London: 1890. V. 50
English Costume from Prehistoric Times to the End of the Eighteenth Century. London: 1909. V. 50
English Hops. A History of Cultivation and Preparation for the Market From the Earliest Times. London: 1919. V. 48
Marylebone and St. Pancrea: Their History, Celebrities, Buildings and Institutions. London: 1890. V. 49
Mayfair and Belgravia... London: 1892. V. 49

CLINE, L.
God Head. New York: 1925. V. 48; 52

CLING, KONRAD
Svmma Doctrinae Christianae Catholicae. Coloniae: 1570. V. 50

CLINKER, HUMPHREY, PSEUD.
Comical Dialogue Between Maggy and Janet, or "The Folly of Witless Women Displayed". Edinburgh: 1820. V. 50; 51

CLINTON, DE WITT
An Account of Abimelech Coody and Other Celebrated Writers of New York: In a Letter from a Traveller, to His Friend in South Carolina. 1815. V. 51

CLINTON, DE WITT continued
An Address, to the Benefactors and Friends of the Free School Society of New York, Delivered on the Opening of that Institution in Their New and Spacious Building. New York: 1810. V. 52

A Discourse Delivered at Schenectady, July 22nd, 1823, Before the New York Alpha of the Phi Beta Kappa. New York: 1823. V. 52

An Introductory Discourse Delivered Before the Literary and Philosophical Society of New-York on the Fourth of May 1814. New York: 1815. V. 47

Letters on the Natural History and Internal Resources of the State of New York. New York: 1822. V. 49

The Mishaps of an Automobilist. New York: 1902. V. 47

CLINTON, GEORGE
Memoirs and the Life and Writings of Lord Byron. London: 1826. V. 51

CLINTON, HENRY
Authentic Copies of Letters Between Sir Henry Clinton...and the Commissioners for Auditing the Public Accounts. London: 1793. V. 47

The Campaign in Virginia 1781. London: 1888. V. 48

A Letter from Lieut. Gen. Sir Henry Clinton...to the Commissioners of Public Accounts, Relative to Some Observations in Their Seventh Report, Which May Be Judged to Imply Censure on the Late Commander in Chief of His Majesty's Army in North America. London: 1784. V. 47

Memorandums, &c., &c., Respecting the Unprecedented Treatment Which the Army Have Met with Respecting Plunder Taken Under a Siege, and of Which Plunder the Navy Serving with the Army Divided Their More than Ample Share, Now Fourteen years Since. London: 1794. V. 47

The Narrative of Lieutenant-General Sir Henry Clinton, K.B., Relative to His Conduct During Part of His Command of the King's Troops in North America... London: 1783. V. 51; 52

CLINTON-BAKER, H.
Illustrations of Conifers. London: 1909-13. V. 49
Illustrations of Conifers. Hertford: 1909-35. V. 47; 48; 49; 52

CLIO and Euterpe, or British Harmony. London: 1762. V. 48

CLIVE, CAROLINE
IX Poems by V. London: 1840. V. 50

CLIVE, CATHERINE
The Case of Mrs. Clive Submitted to the Publick. London: 1744. V. 49

CLIVE, ROBERT
Lord Clive's Speech in the Commons, 30th March 1772 on the Motion...for...a Bill for the Better Regulation of...the East India Company and...Justice in Bengal. London: 1772. V. 48; 49; 52; 54

CLIVE, ROBERT HENRY
Documents Connected with the History of Ludlow, and the Lords Marchers. London: 1841. V. 53

THE CLOCKMAKERS Outcry Against the Author of the Life and Opinions of Tristram Shandy. London: 1760. V. 47

CLODE, CHARLES M.
The Early History of the Guild of Merchant Taylors... London: 1888. V. 47; 50
Memorials of the Guild of Merchant Taylors of the Fraternity of St. John the Baptist, in the City of London... London: 1875. V. 52

CLONEY, THOMAS
A Personal Narrative of Those Transactions in the County of Wexford, in Which the Author was Engaged... Dublin: 1832. V. 50

CLOPET, LILIANE M. C.
Once Upon a Time. London: 1944. V. 47

CLOUDSLEY-THOMPSON, J. L.
Ecophysiology of Desert Arthropods and Reptiles. Berlin: 1991. V. 50

CLOUET, JEAN BAPTISTE LOUIS, L'ABBE
Geographie Moderne. Paris: 1767. V. 48

CLOUGH, ARTHUR HUGH
Ambarvalia. London: 1849. V. 47; 51
The Bothie of Toper-Na-Fuosich A Long-Vacation Pastoral... Oxford: 1848. V. 50; 53
Letters and Remains of Arthur Hugh Clough. London: 1865. V. 53; 54
Poems. London: 1849. V. 47
The Poems... Boston: 1862. V. 49
The Poems and Prose Remains. London: 1869. V. 53
The Poems and Prose Remains. London: 1969. V. 50; 54

CLOUGH, ROBERT T.
The Lead Smelting Mills of the Yorkshire Dales. 1962. V. 47; 50; 53
The Lead Smelting Mills of the Yorkshire Dales. Keighley: 1962. V. 49
The Lead Smelting Mills of the Yorkshire Dales. Leeds: 1962. V. 49; 51; 53
The Lead Smelting Mills of the Yorkshire Dales. 1980. V. 47; 53

CLOUSTON, J. STORER
Carrington's Cases. London: 1920. V. 48
Mr. Essington in Love. London: 1927. V. 51

CLOUSTON, THOMAS SMITH
Neuroses of Development Being the Morison Lectures for 1890. Edinburgh: 1891. V. 52

CLOUSTON, W. A.
Arabian Poetry for English Readers. Glasgow: 1881. V. 54
Flowers from a Persian Garden and Other Papers. London: 1890. V. 53

CLOUZOT, HENRI
Painted and Printed Fabrics. The History of the Manufactory at Jouy and Other Ateliers in France 1760-1815. New York: 1927. V. 48

CLOWES, FREDERIC
A Description of the East Window of S. Martin's Winderemre... Kendal: 1874. V. 50; 52

CLOWES, G. S. LAIRD
A History. From the Earliest Times to the Present. London: 1897-1903. V. 54

CLOWES, WILLIAM LAIRD
Bibliotheca Arcana Seu Catalogus Librorum Penetralium Being Brief Notices of Books That Have Been Secretly Printed, Prohibited by Law, Seized, Anathematised, Burnt or Bowdlerised. London: 1885. V. 47
The Royal Navy. London: 1897-1903. V. 48; 50; 51; 53

THE CLUB, in a Dialogue Between Father and Son. London: 1817. V. 52

CLUB Women of California: Official Directory and Register, 1907-1908. San Francisco: 1907. V. 54

CLUBB, STEPHEN
A Journal: Containing An Account of the Wrongs, Sufferings and Neglect, Experienced by Americans in France. Boston: 1809. V. 51

CLUBBE, JOHN
Miscellaneous Tracts of the Rev. John Clubbe, Rector of Whatfield, and Vicar of Debenham, Suffolk. Ipswich;: 1770. V. 50; 54

CLUM, WOODWORTH
Apache Agent, the Story of John Clum. Boston & New York: 1936. V. 52; 53

CLUTTERBUCK, ROBERT
The History and Antiquities of the County of Hertford. London: 1815. V. 49; 51
The History and Antiquities of the County of Hertford... London: 1815-27. V. 47; 53; 54
Notes on the Parishes of Fyfield, Kimton, Penton Mewsey, Weyhill and Wherwell, in the County of Hampshire. Salisbury: 1898. V. 51; 52

CLUTTON, CECIL
Watches: a Complete History of the Technical and Decorative Development of the Watch. New York: 1979. V. 53

CLUTTON, HENRY
Remarks With Illustrations of the Domestic Architecture of France. London: 1853. V. 51

CLUTTON-BROCK, ARTHUR
The Miracle of Love and other Poems. London: 1926. V. 48

CLUYSENAAR, J. P.
Chemin de Fer Dendre-et-Waes, et de Bruxelles vers Gand Par Alost. Batiments des Stations et Maisons de Garde. Brussels: 1855. V. 52

CLYDE, NORMAN
Norman Clyde of the Sierra Nevada. Rambles through the Range of Light. San Franicsco: 1971. V. 47

CLYMAN, JAMES
The Adventures of a Trapper and Covered Wagon Emigrant As gold in His Reminiscences and Diaries. Portland: 1960. V. 51
James Clyman, American Frontiersman, 1792-1881. San Francisco;: 1928. V. 52
James Clyman, Frontiersman, 1792-1881. Portland: 1960. V. 47; 52; 53

CLYMER, W. B. SHUBRICK
Robert Frost: a Bibliography. Amherst: 1937. V. 49; 51; 53; 54

CLYNE, GERALDINE
The Jolly Jump-Ups and Their New House. Springfield: 1939. V. 49
The Jolly Jump-Ups On the Farm. Springfield: 1940. V. 52
The Jolly Jump-Ups See the Circus. Springfield: 1944. V. 52

THE COACH-Makers' Illustrated Hand-Book, Containing Complete Instructions in All Different Branches of Carriage Building... Philadelphia: 1875. V. 49

COALE, CHARLES B.
The Life and Adventures of Wilburn Waters... Richmond: 1878. V. 52

COALE, WILLIAM EDWARD
A Practical Essay on Aneurism. Boston: 1861. V. 51; 52; 53

COAN, CHARLES F.
A Shorter History of New Mexico. Ann Arbor: 1928. V. 50

COAN, TITUS
Life in Hawaii: an Autobiographical Sketch of Mission Life and Labors. New York: 1882. V. 54

COAR, THOMAS
A Grammar of the English Tongue. London: 1796. V. 47

COARELLI, FILIPPO
Etruscan Cities. New York: 1975. V. 52

COATES, B. J.
The Birds of Papua New Guinea. 1985-90. V. 49; 50
The Birds of Papua New Guinea. London: 1985-90. V. 51

COATES, CASTELL, MRS.
The Young Princess Fairy Book. London: 1899. V. 54

COATES, CHARLES
The History and Antiquities of Reading. London: 1802. V. 48; 52
The History and Antiquities of Reading. London: 1802-10. V. 51

COATES, HENRY
A Perthshire Naturalist: Charles Macintosh of Inver. London: 1923. V. 52; 54

COATES, JAMES
Human Magnetism or How to Hypnotise. London: 1897. V. 47; 48; 53

COATES, ROBERT
Yesterday's Burdens. New York: 1933. V. 51

COATES, W. BURNETT
Edwy amd Elgiva, a Tale of the Tenth Century. London: 1852. V. 54

COATS, ALICE
The Book of Flowers. London: 1973. V. 48; 50

COATTS, MARGOT
Edible Architecture. London: 1987. V. 53
Portable Pleasures: Picnics for All Seasons. 1992. V. 52

COBB, CHARLIE
Furrows. Tougaloo: 1967. V. 54

COBB, F. C.
Sport on the Setit (Sudan). Canterbury: 1911. V. 48

COBB, HOWELL
Governor Cobb to Governor Means on the Boundary Between Georgia and South Carolina. Athens: 1852. V. 48

COBB, HUMPHREY
Paths of Glory. New York: 1935. V. 50; 54

COBB, J. H.
Manual Containing Information Respecting the Growth of the Mulberry Tree... Boston: 1831. V. 52
A Manual Containing Information Respecting the Growth of the Mulberry Tree... Boston: 1833. V. 51

COBB, JOSEPH BECKHAM
Mississippi Scenes; or, Sketches of southern and Western Life and Adventure, Humorous, Satirical and Descriptive, Including the Legend of Black Creek. Philadelphia: 1851. V. 47

COBB, LYMAN
The Evil Tendencies of Corporal Punishment as a Means of Moral Discipline in Families and Schools, Examined and Discussed. New York: 1847. V. 50

COBBE, FRANCES POWER
Darwinism in Morals and Other Essays. London: 1872. V. 50; 52
The Hopes of the Human Race, Hereafter and Here. London: 1874. V. 50
The Life of Frances Power Cobbe. 1894. V. 52
Religious Duty. Boston: 1883. V. 50; 51

COBBE, SARAH
Julia St. Helen; or, the Heiress of Ellisborough. London: 1800. V. 47

COBBETT, JAMES PAUL
A Ride of Eight Hundred Miles in France...Rural Economy...Manufacturers and Trade...Prices of Land, Food, House, Fuel...a True Picture of the Present State of the People of France. London: 1824. V. 53

COBBETT, THOMAS
An Account of the Expedition of the British Fleet to Sicily, in the Years 1718, 1719 and 1720. London: 1739. V. 47

COBBETT, WALTER WILSON
Cobbett's Cyclopaedic Survey of Chamber Music... Oxford: 1988. V. 49

COBBETT, WILLIAM
Advice to Young Men and (Incidentally) to Young Women, in the Middle and Higher Ranks of Life. Andover: 1829. V. 52
The American Gardener: or, a Treatise on the Situation, Soil, Fencing and Laying-Out of Gardens... London: 1821. V. 49
The American Gardener; or a Treatise on the Situation, Soil, Fencing and Laying-Out of Gardens... New York: 1844. V. 52
The Bloody Buoy, Thrown Out as a Warning to the Political Pilots of America... Paradise: 1823. V. 48; 49
Cobbett's Easy Grammar. London. V. 50
Cobbett's Legacy to Labourers... London: 1834. V. 50
Cobbett's Legacy to Labourers. London: 1835. V. 47; 49
Cobbett's Legacy to Lords: Being Six Lectures on the History of Taxation and Debt in England. London: 1863. V. 47
Cobbett's Tour in Scotland: and in the Four Northern Counties of England; in the Autumn of the Year 1832. London: 1833. V. 47
A Collection of Facts and Observations Relative to the Peace with Bonaparte, Chiefly Extracted from the Porcupine. London: 1801. V. 49; 50
Cottage Economy... London: 1822. V. 47; 51; 52
Cottage Economy. London: 1823. V. 50
Cottage Economy. London: 1828. V. 51
The English Gardener... London: 1829. V. 47
The English Gardener... London: 1833. V. 47; 48; 50; 51
The English Gardener. London: 1838. V. 47; 52
The English Gardener... London: 1845. V. 52
A Grammar of the English Language... London: 1819. V. 51; 52
A History of the Protestant "Reformation" in England and Ireland... London: 1824-26. V. 52
A History of the Protestant "Reformation" in England and Ireland. London: 1824-27. V. 47; 53
A History of the Protestant "Reformation" in England and Ireland... London: 1829. V. 47; 48; 51; 54
Important Considerations for the People of this Kingdom. London: 1803. V. 51
Life of Andrew Jackson, President of the United States of America. London: 1834. V. 54
Le Maitre de'Anglais, ou Grammaire Raisonnee, Pour Faciliter aux Francais l'Etude de la Langue Anglaise. Paris: 1803. V. 47
Mr. Cobbett's Taking Leave of His Countrymen. London: 1817. V. 53
Normandy Farm, Near Ash, Surrey. Catalogue of the Valuable Live and Dead Farming Stock, Garden and Other Seeds. Guildford: 1836. V. 48; 51
Observations on the Debates of the American Congress. (with) Observations of the Emigration of Dr. Joseph Priestley. (and) The Republican Judge... (and) A Letter to the Infamous Tom Paine... London: 1797/98/98/97. V. 49
Observations on the Emigration of Dr. Joseph Priestley, and On the Several Addresses Delivered to Him On His Arrival at New York. London: 1794. V. 51
Paper Against Gold... London: 1817. V. 50
Paper Against Gold... London: 1822. V. 52
The Political Censor, or Monthly Review of the Most Interesting Political Occurrences, Relative to the United States of America. Philadelphia: 1797. V. 47
Rural Rides in the Counties... London: 1830. V. 48; 49; 51; 52; 53
Rural Rides in the Counties. London: 1853. V. 51
Rural Rides...Together with Tours in Scotland...and Letters from Ireland... London: 1930. V. 47; 51
The Soldier's Friend; or, Considerations on the Late Pretended Augmentation of the Subsistence of the Private Soldiers. London?: 1793. V. 47
A Treatise on Cobbett's Corn. London: 1828. V. 48; 50; 54
The Woodland... London: 1825, i.e. 1828. V. 49; 51
A Year's Residence in the United States of America. Andover: 1828. V. 49
A Year's Residence in the United States of America. Part I only. London: 1818. V. 50

COBBING, BOB
Poems for the Aircraft. Cambridge?: 1965. V. 52

COBBOLD, ELIZABETH
Ode on the Victory of Waterloo. Ipswich: 1815. V. 50

COBBOLD, RALPH
Innermost Asia: Travel and Sport in the Pamirs. London: 1900. V. 54

COBBOLD, RICHARD
Freston Tower; or, the Early Days of Cardinal Wolsey. London: 1850. V. 54
Mary Anne Wellington, the Soldier's Daughter, Wife and Widow. London: 1846. V. 50
Valentine Verses; or Lines of Truth, Love and Virtue... Ipswich: 1827. V. 48; 49; 54

COBDEN, EDWARD
Poems on Several Occasions. London: 1748. V. 47; 49; 52

COBDEN, RICHARD
The Political Writings of Richard Cobden. London: 1867. V. 47; 51
Speeches on Questions of Public Policy by Richard Cobden, M.P. London: 1870. V. 54

COBDEN-SANDERSON and the Doves Press. San Francisco: 1929. V. 49

COBDEN-SANDERSON, THOMAS JAMES
Amantium Irae. Hammersmith: 1914. V. 48; 51
The Arts and Crafts Movement. Hammersmith: 1905. V. 50; 52; 53
The Book Beautiful. San Francisco: 1930. V. 48
Credo... 1908. V. 51; 54
Credo. Hammersmith: 1908. V. 47; 54
Credo. Hammersmith: 1917. V. 48
Four Lectures. San Francisco: 1974. V. 47; 48; 54
The Ideal Book or Book Beautiful. Hammersmith: 1900. V. 51
The Journals 1879-1922. London: 1926. V. 49; 52
London, a Paper Read at a Meeting of the Art Workers Guild. London: 1906. V. 48; 49; 50; 51; 52; 53; 54
On a Passage in Julius Caesar. Hammersmith: 1913. V. 51

COBHAM, ALAN J.
The Complete Distiller, Combining Theory and Practice; and Explaining the Mysteries and Most Recent Improvements of Distilling and Brewing... Edinburgh: 1793. V. 48
My Flight to the Cape and Back. London: 1926. V. 48
Twenty Thousand Miles in a Flying-Boat. London: 1930. V. 48

COBHAM, CLAUDE D.
Excerpta Cypria. Materials for a History of Cyprus. New York: 1969. V. 47; 49

COBIN, A.
Short and Plain Principles of Linear Perspective, Particularly Adapted to Shipping &c. London: 1775. V. 53

COBLEY, FRED
On Foot Through Wharfedale... Otley: 1882. V. 47

COBORN, J.
Atlas of Snakes of the World. 1991. V. 53
The Atlas of Snakes of the World. London: 1991. V. 48; 52

COBURN, ALVIN
The Factor of Infection in the Rheumatic State. Baltimore: 1931. V. 51; 53

COBURN, ALVIN LANGDON
Alvin Langdon Coburn Photographer. London: 1966. V. 52
Men of Mark. London: 1913. V. 49; 52
Moor Park, Rickmansworth. A Series of Photographs. London: 1914. V. 47
More Men of Mark. London: 1922. V. 50
More Men of Mark. New York: 1922. V. 52

COBURN, WALLACE
Rhymes from a Roundup Camp. 1899. V. 53

COCCHI, ANTONIO
The Pythagorean Diet of Vegetables Only, Conductive to the Preservation of Health and the Cure of Diseases. London: 1745. V. 48

COCHELET, CHARLES
Narrative of the Shipwreck of the Sophia on the 30th Day of May, 1819... London: 1822. V. 47; 50

COCHIN, CHARLES NICOLAS
Observations Upon the Antiquities of the Town of Herculaneum, Discovered at the Foot of Mount Vesuvius. London: 1756. V. 50
Observations Upon the Antiquities of the Town of Herculaneum, Discovered at the Foot of Mount Vesuvius... London: 1756/53/54. V. 49

COCHISE, CIYE NINO
The First Hundred Years of Nino Cochise. London/New York: 1971. V. 50

COCHRAN, D. M.
The Herpetology of Hispaniola. 1941. V. 51

COCHRAN, JOHN H.
Dallas County, a Record of Its Pioneers & Progress. Dallas: 1928. V. 47

COCHRAN, JOHN S.
Bonnie Belmont, a Historical Romance of the Days of Slavery and Civil War. Wheeling: 1907. V. 48

COCHRANE, ALEXANDER BAILLIE
Poems. Not Published. London: 1838. V. 48

COCHRANE, ALFRED
The Early History of Elswick. Newcastle-upon-Tyne: 1909. V. 50

COCHRANE, CHARLES STUART
Journal of a Residence and Travels in Colombia During the Years 1823 and 1824. London: 1825. V. 47; 49; 51; 52; 53; 54

COCHRANE, JOHN
Hindoo Law. Defence of the Daya Bhaga. Notice of the Case on Prosoono Coomar Tagore's Will. London: 1872. V. 50

COCHRANE, JOHN DUNDAS
Narrative of a Pedestrian Journey through Russia and Siberian Tartary, from the Frontiers of China to the Frozen Sea and Kamchatka... London: 1824. V. 47; 51; 54

COCHRANE, JOHN GEORGE
The Case Stated Between the Public Libraries and the Booksellers. London: 1813. V. 51

COCHRANE-BAILLIE, ALEXANDER
Young Italy. London: 1850. V. 51

COCK Robin. London: 1865. V. 48

COCK Robin and Jenny Wren. London: 1900. V. 48

COCK-A-HOOP. A Sequel to Chanticleer, Pertelote and Cockalorum. 1962. V. 47

COCK-A-HOOP Being a Bibliography of the Golden Cockerel Press Sept. 1949-Dec. 1961. London. V. 51; 52

COCK-A-HOOP...Being a Bibliography of the Golden Cockerel Press Sept. 1949-Dec. 1961. Middlesex: 1976. V. 50

COCK-A-HOOP...Being a Bibliography of the Golden Cockerel Press Sept. 1949-Dec. 1961... Waltham St. Lawrence: 1976. V. 53

COCKALORUM: a Sequel to Chanticleer and Pertelote. Waltham St. Lawrence: 1948. V. 52

COCKALORUM, a Sequel to Chanticleer and Pertelote. Waltham St. Lawrence: 1951. V. 51

COCKAYNE, G. E. C.
Complete Peerage of England, Scotland, IReland, Great Britain and the United Kingdom, Extant, Extinct or Dormant... London: 1887. V. 47

COCKAYNE, T. OSWALD
Leechdoms Wortcunning and Starcraft of Early England... London: 1864-66. V. 49

COCKBURN, ALISON
Letters and Memoir of Her Own Life... Edinburgh: 1900. V. 50

COCKBURN, CLAUD
Reporter in Spain. London: 1936. V. 49

COCKBURN, HENRY
Memorials of His Time (and) Journal of Henry Cockburn, Being a Continuation of the Memorials of His Time, 1831-1854. Edinburgh: 1856/74. V. 49

COCKBURN, HENRY THOMAS
Life of Lord Jeffrey with a Selection from His Correspondence. Edinburgh: 1852. V. 47; 54

COCKBURN, J. A.
Souvenir Views of Alberta: the Land of Sunshine. Grand Rapids: 1906?. V. 50

COCKBURN, JAMES PATTISON
Swiss Scenery. London: 1820. V. 49; 52; 53

COCKBURN, JOHN
A Faithful Account of the Distresses and Adventures of John Cockburn, Mariner and Five Other Englishmen. London: 1740. V. 51
The History of Duels. Edinburgh: 1888. V. 48

COCKBURN, N. C.
Notes on Scent. London: 1905. V. 47; 49

COCKE, SARAH JOHNSON
Bypaths in Dixie: Folk Tales of the South. New York: 1911. V. 53

COCKER, EDWARD
The Young Clerks Tutor: Being a Most Useful Collection of the Best Presidents of Recognizances... London: 1664. V. 50

COCKERAM, HENRY
The English Dictionary of 1623. New York: 1930. V. 54

COCKERELL, CHARLES ROBERT
Iconography of the West Front of Wells Cathedral. London: 1851. V. 51; 54

COCKERELL, S.
The Gorleton Psalter. A Manuscript of the Beginning of the Fourteenth Century in the library of C. W. Dyson Perrins. 1907. V. 47

COCKERELL, SYDNEY M.
The Repairing of Books. London: 1958. V. 50; 52

COCKERMOUTH, KEDWICK & PENRITH RAILWAY
Widening of Line and Additional Lands. Plans and Sections. Session 1893-94. Edinburgh: 1894. V. 51; 52

COCKIN, W.
A Rational and Practical Treatise of Arithmetic. London: 1766. V. 50

COCKIN, WILLIAM
Ode to the Genius of the Lakes in the North of England. London: 1780. V. 47; 50
The Rural Sabbath, a Poem in Four Books; and Other POems. London: 1805. V. 54

COCKLE, MAURICE J. D.
A Bibliography of Military Books Up to 1642. London: 1957. V. 51

COCKRUM, WILLIAM
History of the Underground Railroad: as It Was Conducted by the Anti-Slavery League. Oakland City: 1915. V. 52

COCKS, ANNA SOMERS
The Thyssen-Bornemisza Collection: Renaissance Jewels, Gold Boxes and Objets de Vertu. New York: 1984. V. 49

COCKS, JAMES
Memorials of Hatherlow and of the Old Chadkirk Chapel. Stockport: 1895. V. 54

COCKTAILS and How to Make Them. Providence: 1914. V. 50

COCKTON, HENRY
Life and Adventures of Valentine Fox the Ventrioloquist. London. V. 48; 51
The Life and Adventures of Valentine Vox, the Ventriloquist. London: 1840. V. 48; 50
The Sisters; or England and France. Romance of Real Life. London: 1844. V. 53
Stanley Thorn. London: 1841. V. 48
Stanley Thorn. Philadelphia: 1841. V. 51; 53; 54
The Steward: a Romance of Real Life. London: 1850. V. 47

COCTEAU, JEAN
The Blood of a Poet. New York: 1949. V. 52; 54
The Blood of a Poet... New York: 1968. V. 54
A Call to Order. London: 1926. V. 51
Carte Blanche. Paris: 1920. V. 53
Cocteau on the Film. New York: 1954. V. 54
The Difficulty of Being. New York: 1967. V. 54
The Eagle Has Two Heads. London: 1948. V. 50
The Eagle Has Two Heads. New York: 1948. V. 54
Les Enfants Terribles. North Pomfret: 1992. V. 50
Five Plays. New York: 1961. V. 54
The Head of a Stranger. New York: 1959. V. 54
The Human Voice. London: 1951. V. 54
The Imposter. New York: 1957. V. 54
The Infernal Machine and Other Plays. New York: 1963. V. 54
Le Livre Blanc. Paris: 1928. V. 52
Maalesh: a Theatrical Tour of the Middle East. London: 1949. V. 54
My Contemporaraies. Philadelphia: 1968. V. 54
Opium - The Diary of a Cure. London: 1957. V. 51
Opium. The Diary of an Addict. New York: 1932. V. 50
Paris Album, 1900-1914. London: 1956. V. 54
Picasso. Paris: 1923. V. 50; 52
Poemes: 1916-1955. Paris: 1956. V. 51; 54
Poesie Graphique. Paris: 1973. V. 50
Theatre. Paris: 1957. V. 49; 53
Three Screenplays. New York: 1972. V. 54
The Typewriter: a Play in Three Acts. London: 1947. V. 54

CODE de Procedure Civile. Paris: 1806. V. 49

THE CODE of Criminal Procedure of the Republic of China... Shanghai: 1936. V. 50

A CODE of Gentoo Laws, or, Ordinations of the Pundits. London: 1776. V. 53

A CODE of Gentoo Laws, or, Ordinations of the Pundits... London: 1777. V. 52

A CODE of Gentoo Laws, or, Ordinations of the Pundits. London: 1781. V. 47; 49; 52; 54

A CODE of Laws for the Island of Jersey. St. Helier: 1771. V. 51; 52

CODMAN, E. A.
The Shoulder. Rupture of the Supraspinatus Tendon and Other Lesions in or About the Subacromial Bursa. Boston: 1934. V. 51

CODMAN, JOHN
Sailors' Life and Sailors' Yarns. New York: 1847. V. 51

CODY, H. A.
An Apostle of the North. London: 1908. V. 47
An Apostle of the North... Toronto: 1908. V. 48
Songs of a Bluenose. Toronto: 1925. V. 47

CODY, WILLIAM F.
Buffalo Bill's Wild West and Congress of Rough Riders of the World. Chicago: 1893. V. 47
Life and Adventures of 'Buffalo Bill'. Chicago: 1917. V. 50
The Life of the Hon. William F. Cody. Hartford: 1879. V. 48
True Tales of the Plains. New York: 1908. V. 54

COE, GEORGE WASHINGTON
Frontier Fighter, the Autobiography of George W. Coe. Boston: 1934. V. 53

COE, MICHAEL D.
In the Land of the Olmec. Austin, London: 1980. V. 48; 49; 50; 52
Lords of the Underworld: Masterpieces of Classic Maya Ceramics. Princeton: 1978. V. 50; 51; 52
The Maya Scribe and His World. New York: 1977. V. 50

COEL, MARGARET
The Eagle Catcher. Colorado: 1995. V. 53; 54

COELESTINUS, GEORGIUS
Historia Comitiorum Anno MDXXX Augustae Celebratorum. Frankfurt: 1576. V. 47

COELHO, SIMAO
Compendio das Chronicas da Ordem de Nossa Senhora do Carmo. 1572. Primeira Parte...(and Livro Segundo). Lisbon: 1572. V. 48

COETLOGAN, DENNIS DE
Natural Sagacity the Principal Secret, If Not the Whole in Physick... London: 1742. V. 48; 52
An Universal History of Arts and Sciences; or, a Comprehensive Illustration, Definition and Description of All Sciences, Divine and Human... London: 1745. V. 50

COETZEE, J. M.
Dusklands. Johannesburg: 1974. V. 52
In the Heart of the Country. London: 1977. V. 47
Life and Times of Michael K. New York: 1984. V. 47
Waiting for Barbarians. Johannesburg: 1981. V. 51

COFFEE, a Bibliography. London: 1995. V. 54

COFFEY, BRIAN
Third Person: Poems. 1938. V. 54

COFFEY, CHARLES
The Devil to Pay; or, The Wives Matamorphos'd. London: 1731. V. 52

COFFEY, JAMES V.
A Opinion of Court Denying Application for Probate of Will. San Francisco: 1911. V. 52

COFFIN, ANNE
Jacopo Della Quercia's Fonte Gala. Oxford: 1965. V. 49

COFFIN, CHARLES CARLETON
Our New Way Round the World. Boston: 1869. V. 50
The Seat of Empire. Boston: 1870. V. 52
The Seat of Empire. Boston: 1871. V. 50

COFFIN, J. H. C.
Reports of Observations of the Total Eclipse of the Sun, August 7, 1869. 1885. V. 48

COFFIN, JOSHUA
Sketch of the History of Newbury, Newburyport and West Newburyport from 1635 to 1845. Boston: 1845. V. 47

COFFIN, LEWIS A.
Brick Architecture of the Colonial Period. New York: 1919. V. 51

COFFIN, R. S.
Epistle to Joseph T. Buckingham, Esq. Boston: 1826. V. 52

COFFIN, ROBERT BARRY
Ale: in Prose and Verse. New York: 1866. V. 51

COFFIN, WILLIAM F.
1812: The War, and Its Moral: a Canadian Chronicle. Montreal: 1864. V. 54

COGAN, LEE
Negroes for Medicine: Report of a Macy Conference. Baltimore: 1968. V. 50; 52

COGAN, T.
The Haven of Health. London: 1596 or 1605. V. 51

COGAN, THOMAS
Ethical Questions; or Speculations on the Principal Subjects of Controversy in Moral Philosophy. London: 1817. V. 52

COGGER, H. G.
Reptiles and Amphibians of Australia. Ithaca: 1992. V. 48; 52

COGGESHALL, GEORGE
History of the American Privateers and Letters-of-Marque During Our Own War with England in the Years 1812, '13 and '14... New York: 1856. V. 49
Voyages to Various Parts of the World, Made Between the Years 1799 and 1844... New York: 1851. V. 50

COGGESHALL, WILLIAM TURNER
Five Black Arts. Columbus: 1861. V. 50

COGGINS, J. C.
Abraham Lincoln a North Carolinian. Gastonia: 1927. V. 50

COGGINS, JACK
Rockets, Jets, Guided Missiles and Space Ships. New York: 1951. V. 51

COGGINS & OWENS, BALTIMORE
Catalogue Number 68. Bicycle, Motor Cycle and Automobile Materials, Tires, Tools, Machinery, Etc...The Bicycle and Automobile Supply House of America. Baltimore: 1915. V. 53

COGHLAN, DANIEL
The Ancient Land Tenures of Ireland. Dublin: 1933. V. 51

COGHLAN, MARGARET
Memoirs of ... Dublin: 1794. V. 51
Memoirs of... London: 1794. V. 47; 50; 53
Memoirs of... New York: 1795. V. 47

COGHLAN, T. A.
A Statistical Account of the Seven Colonies of Australasia, 1897-8. Sydney: 1898. V. 49; 54

COGNIAT, RAYMOND
Simon Lissim. Paris: 1933. V. 50

COGSWELL, LEANDER
A History of the Eleventh New Hampshire Regiment Volunteer Infantry in the Rebellion War 1861-1865. Concord: 1891. V. 47

COGSWELL, MARGARET
Margaret Cogswell. 1913-1963 Armory Show 50th Anniversary Exhibition...Sponsored by the Henry Street Settlement, New York. New York: 1963. V. 53

COHAN, GEORGE M.
Broadway Jones. 1913. V. 53

COHAUSEN, JOHANN HEINRICH
Hermippus Redividus; or, The Sage's Triumph Over Old Age and the Grave, Wherein a Method is Laid Down for Prolonging the Life and Vigour of Man. Edinburgh: 1885. V. 50

COHEN, ARTHUR
The Lords and Jews. London: 1853. V. 54
On the Marionette Theater of Heinrich von Kleist. New York: 1988. V. 47
Sonia Delaunay. New York: 1975. V. 51

COHEN, BEN
The River and Firth of Clyde 1549-1993. London: 1994. V. 53
The Thames 1580-1900. A General Bibliography. London: 1985. V. 53

COHEN, I. BERNARD
Introduction to Newton's "Principia". Cambridge: 1971. V. 54

COHEN, LEONARD
Beautiful Losers. New York: 1966. V. 50
Beautiful Losers. London: 1970. V. 51
Let Us Compare Mythologies. Montreal: 1956. V. 47; 51
Selected Poems. New York: 1968. V. 52
The Spice-Box of Earth. 1961. V. 48
The Spice-Box of Earth. Toronto: 1961. V. 47; 50

COHEN, OCTAVUS ROY
Carbon Copies. New York: 1932. V. 54
East of Broadway. New York: 1938. V. 50
The May Day Mystery. New York: 1929. V. 50
The Outer Gate. Boston: 1927. V. 50

COHESON, ANNIE
Captivity Among the Sioux Indians, An Interesting and Remarkable Account...Terrible Sufferings and providential Escape.... Philadelphia. V. 49

COHN, ALBERT
Shakespeare in Germany in the Sixteenth and Seventeenth Centuries... London: 1865. V. 49

COHN, ALBERT M.
A Bibligoraphical Catalogue of...George Cruikshank. London: 1914. V. 48
Catalogue of an Extensive and Important Collection of the Works of George Cruikshank...Which Will Be Sold by Auction by Messrs. Sotheby...July 5th 1920... London: 1920. V. 49
A Few Notes Upon Some Rare Cruikshankiana. London: 1915. V. 49
George Cruikshank: a Catalogue Raisonne of the Work Executed During the Years 1806-1877... London: 1924. V. 49

COHN, LOUIS
A Bibliography of the Works of Ernest Hemingway. New York: 1931. V. 47; 49; 51; 54

COHNHEIM, JULIUS
Lectures On General Pathology. London: 1889-90. V. 48; 53

COIGNEY, RODOLPHE L.
Izaak Walton: a New Bibliography 1653-1987. New York: 1989. V. 47; 49; 50

COILLARD, FRANCOIS
On the Threshold of Central Africa, a Record of Twenty Years' Prioneering Among the Barotsi of the Upper Zambesi... London: 1902. V. 51

COIMBRA, UNIVERSIDADE DE
Estatutos da Universidade de Coimbra Confirmados por el Rey Nosso Snor. Dom Joao o 4o em o anno de 1653. Impressos por Mandaldo e Ordem de manoel de Saldanha... Coimbra: 1654. V. 48

COIT *Correspondence of 1871, of the Second Trip to New Brunswick by the Coit Family.* Worcester: 1872. V. 47

COIT, DANIEL WADSWORTH
An Artist in El Dorado. The Drawings and Letters of. San Francisco: 1937. V. 52
Digging for Gold Without a Shovel: the Letters of Daniel Wadsworth Coit from Mexico City to San Francisco. Denver: 1967. V. 53

COKAIN, ASTON
The Dramatic Works. London: 1874. V. 49

COKAYNE, GEORGE EDWARD
The Complete Peerage of England, Scotland, Ireland, Great Britain and the United Kingdom. London: 1910. V. 47
The Complete Peerage of England, Scotland, Ireland, Great Britain and the United Kingdom... London: 1910-59. V. 51
The Complete Peerage of England, Scotland, Ireland, Great Britain and the United Kingdom. 1987. V. 54

COKE, EDWARD
The Compleate Copy-Holder. London: 1641. V. 51
The First Part of the Institutes of the Lawes of England. London: 1629. V. 52
The First Part of the Institutes of the Lawes of England... London: 1719. V. 47; 50; 54
The First Part of the Institutes of the Lawes of England... London: 1788. V. 48
The First Part of the Institutes of the Lawes of England... London: 1817. V. 51
The Fourth Part of the Institutes of the Laws of England: Concerning the Jvrisdiction of Courts... London: 1644. V. 51
Les Reports. London: 1600/02. V. 47
Les Reports... Londini: 1602-04. V. 50
Les Reports. London: 1604/12. V. 47
The Reports of Sir Edward Coke, Kt. in Verse. Wherein the Name of Each Case, and the Principal Points, Are Contained in Two Lines (etc). London: 1742. V. 48
The Second Part of the Institutes of the Laws of England. London: 1681. V. 47
La Size Part des Reports Sr. Edw. Coke Chiualer,, Chief Iustice del Common Banke (etc.). London: 1607. V. 51; 52
The Third (and Fourth) Part of the Institutes of the Laws of England... London: 1671-71. V. 52
The Third Part of the Institutes of the Laws of England... (with) The Fourth Part of the Institutes... London: 1671. V. 52; 54
La Tierce Part des Reports del Edward Coke, Lattorney General le Roigne, de Divers Resolutions & Judgments Donnes Avec Graund Deliberation (etc.). London: 1697. V. 50
The Twelfth Part of the Reports...of Divers Resolutions and Judgments Given Upon Solemn Arguments...in Cases of Law... London: 1658. V. 47; 50

COKE, HENRY JOHN
A Ride Over the Rocky Mountains to Oregon and California: with a Glance at Some of the Tropical Islands... London: 1852. V. 47; 50

COKE, KATHRYN
A New Edition of the Pulitzer Prize Plays. New York: 1935. V. 53

COKE, ROGER
A Detection of the Court and State of England During the Four Last Reigns, and the Inter-Regnum. London: 1696. V. 52; 53

COKE, THOMAS
A History of the West Indies. Liverpool: 1808/10-11. V. 51; 52; 54
The Life of the Rev. John Wesley, A.M... London: 1792. V. 48

COKE, VAN DEREN
The Painter and the Photograph from Delacroix to Warhol. Albuquerque: 1964. V. 47; 49
Taos and Santa Fe, The Artist's Environment: 1882-1942. Albuquerque: 1963. V. 48; 53

COKE, WILLIAM
A Poetical Essay on the Early Part of Education... Oxford: 1785. V. 54

COKER, MR.
A Survey of Dorsetshire Containing the Antiquities and Natural History of that County. London: 1732. V. 50

COLANGE, L.
Zell's Popular Encylopedia. Philadelphia: 1870-73. V. 50

COLANGE, LEO DE
The Picturesque World, or Scenes from Many Lands. Boston: 1875. V. 48

COLBATCH, JOHN
An Account of the Court of Portugal, Under the Reign of the Present King Don Pedro II. London: 1700. V. 54
A Dissertation Concerning Mistletoe... London: 1730?. V. 51

COLBECK, NORMAN
A Bookman's Catalogue. The Norman Colbeck Collection of 19th Century Literature and Edwardian Poetry and Belles Letters in the Special Collection of the University of British Columbia. British Columbia: 1987. V. 47; 51

COLBERG, NANCY
Wallace Stegner: A Descriptive Bibliography. 1990. V. 51

COLBORNE, JOHN
The Last of the Brave; or Resting Places of Our Fallen Heroes in the Crimea and at Scutari. London: 1857. V. 54

COLBRAN'S Hand-Book and Visitor's Guide for Tunbridge Wells and Its Neighbourhood. Tunbridge Wells: 1855. V. 53

COLBURN, FRONA EUNICE WAIT
In Old Vintage Days. San Francisco: 1937. V. 50

COLBURN, ZERAH
Locomotive Engineering, and the Mechanism of Railways; a Treatise on the Principles and Construction of the Locomotive Engine, Railway Carriages and Railway Plant. London: 1871. V. 47
The Waterworks of London, Together with a Series of Articles on VArious Other Waterworks. London: 1867. V. 51

COLBY, COL
Ordnance Survey of the County of Londonderry. 1837. V. 48

COLCHESTER, ELIZABETH SUSAN LAW, BARONESS
Fitz-Edward. London: 1875. V. 47

COLCORD, CHARLES FRANCIS
The Autobiography of Charles Francis Colcord 1859-1934. Tulsa: 1970. V. 52

COLCQUORN, JOHN
The Moor and the Loch, Containing Minute Instructions In all Highland Sports. London: 1884. V. 53

COLDBATCH, JOHN
A Dissertation Concerning Mistletoe... London: 1730. V. 53

COLDEN, CADWALLADER
The History of the Five Indian Nations of Canada. London: 1747. V. 53
The History of the Five Indian Nations of Canada... London: 1750. V. 48
The History of the Five Indian Nations of Canada. New York: 1902. V. 53

COLDEN, CADWALLADER DAVID
The Life of Robert Fulton... New York: 1817. V. 50

COLDSTREAM, J. N.
Greek Geometric Pottery: a Survey of Ten Local Styles and Their Chronology. London: 1968. V. 52
Kythera: Excavations and Studies Conducted by the University of Pennsylvania Museum and British School at Athens. London: 1972. V. 50; 52

COLDSTREAM, W.
Illustrations of Some of the Grasses of the Southern Punjab... London: 1889. V. 51; 52

COLE, ALFRED W.
The Cape and the Kafirs; or Notes of Five Years' Residence in South Africa. London: 1852. V. 54

COLE, ALPHAEUS P.
Timothy Cole, Wood-Engraver. New York: 1935. V. 52

COLE, BEATRICE PHILLIPS
The Mother You Gave Me. Los Angeles: 1940. V. 50

COLE, BENJAMIN
The Soldier's Pocket-Companion, or the Manual Exercise of Our British Foot, as Now Practised by His Majesty's Special Command... London: 1746. V. 49

COLE, BRUCE
Agnolo Gaddi. Oxford: 1977. V. 54

COLE, CHARLES NALSON
A Collection of Laws Which form the Constitution of the Bedford Level Corporation... London: 1761. V. 51

COLE, CHRISTIAN
Memoirs of Affairs of State: Containing Letters Written by Ministers Employed in Foreign Negotiations from the Year 1697 to the Latter End of 1708. With Treaties, Memorials and Other Transactions. London: 1733. V. 51

COLE, CORNELIUS
California Three Hundred and Fifty Years Ago: Manuelo's Narrative. San Francisco: 1888/87. V. 47
Memoirs of Cornelius Cole, Ex-Senator of the United States from California. New York: 1908. V. 47

COLE, F. J.
The Cole Library of Early Medicine and Zoology. Reading: 1969/75. V. 47; 48; 51; 52; 53

COLE, G. D. H.
The Murder at the Munition Works. New York: 1940. V. 52

COLE, GEORGE WATSON
Bermuda in Periodical Literature: a Bibliography. Brookline: 1907. V. 48

COLE, GILBERT
In the Early Days Along the Overland Trail in Nebraska Territory, in 1852. Kansas City: 1905. V. 47; 54

COLE, GILBERT L.
In the Early days Along the Overland Trail in Nebraska Territory in 1852. Kansas City: 1905. V. 51; 53

COLE, HARRY ELLSWORTH
Stagecoach and Tavern Tales of the Old Northwest. Cleveland: 1930. V. 51

COLE, HENRY
Railway Eccentrics. Inconsistencies of Men of Genius Exemplified in the Practice and Precept of Isambard Kingdom Brunel, Esq... London: 1846. V. 54
The Veritable History of Whittington and His Cat. London: 1847. V. 48; 50

COLE, JOHN
Historical Sketches of Scalby, Burniston and Cloughton. Scarborough: 1829. V. 50; 52
The History and Antiquities of Filey, in the County of York. Scarborough: 1823. V. 47
Reminiscences Tributary to the Memory of Thomas Allen, Author of "History of Lambeth"... Northampton: 1833. V. 49

COLE, JOHN WILLIAM
An Address to the Public, Containing Observations on Some Late Criticisms Connected with the Edinburgh Theatre. Edinburgh: 1822. V. 51
The Life and Theatrical Times of Charles Kean, F.S.A. London: 1859. V. 47; 51

COLE, M.
The Savannas. London: 1986. V. 49

COLE, PETER
Rift. New York: 1986. V. 51; 54

COLE, R. E. G.
History of the Manor and Township of Doddington, Otherwise Doddington-Pigot, in the County of Lincoln... Lincoln: 1897. V. 54

COLE, S.
Kleinholz Graphics: Catalogue Raisonne 1940-75. Miami: 1975. V. 51; 54

COLE, TIMOTHY
Old Spanish Masters. New York: 1907. V. 50

COLE, VAN DEREN
The Painter and the Photograph. Albuquerque: 1972. V. 54

COLE, WILLIAM
Aphorisms. Cambridge: 1992. V. 50
Folk Songs of England, Ireland, Scotland and Wales. New York: 1961. V. 51

COLE, WILLIAM A.
Chemical Literature 1700-1860. A Bibliography with Annotations, Detailed Descriptions, Comparisons and Locations. London. V. 52

COLEBROOK, FRANK
William Morris: Master Printer. 1989. V. 52; 54
William Morris: Master-Printer. Council Bluffs: 1989. V. 53

COLEGATE, ISABEL
The Blackmailer. London: 1958. V. 51; 53

COLEMAN, A. D.
The Grotesque in Photography. New York: 1977. V. 52

COLEMAN, ARTHUR PHILEMON
Canadian Rockies. New and Old Trails. London: 1911. V. 47
The Canadian Rockies: New and Old Trails. Toronto: 1911. V. 47; 51

COLEMAN, EDMUND T.
Scenes From the Snow-Fields; Being Illustrations of the Upper Ice-World of Mount Blanc, from Sketches Made on the spot in the Years 1855, 1856, 1857, 1858; with Historical and Descriptive Remarks and a Comparison of the Chamonix and St. Gervais Routes. London: 1859. V. 52

COLEMAN, EDWARD
Observations on the Structure, Oeconomy and Diseases of the Foot of the Horse, and on the Principles and Practice of Shoeing. Dublin: 1798. V. 50

COLEMAN, J. WINSTON
Stage-Coach Days in Bluegrass. Lexington: 1956. V. 53

COLEMAN, SATIS N.
Bells: Their History, Legends, Making and Uses. Chicago: 1928. V. 50

COLEMAN, VICTOR
In the Streets. 1959. V. 47
Miraculous Montages. 1966. V. 47

COLEMAN, WILLIAM
A Collection of the Facts and Documents Relative to the Death of Major-General Alexander Hamilton; with Comments... New York: 1804. V. 48; 49
Studies in the History of Abraham Colles. London: 1891. V. 50
Studies in the History of Biology. Baltimore: 1977-84. V. 47; 52

COLENSO, JOHN WILLIAM
The Pentateuch and Book of Joshua Critically Examined. London: 1863-65. V. 54

COLERIDGE, ANTHONY
Chippendale Furniture. The Work of Thomas Chippendale. New York: 1968. V. 48

COLERIDGE, CHRISTABEL ROSE
Jack O'Lanthorn. London: 1889. V. 52

COLERIDGE, ERNEST HARTLEY
The Life of Thomas Coutts Banker. London: 1920. V. 48; 54

COLERIDGE, HARTLEY
Biographia Borealis; or Lives of Distinguished Northerns. London: 1833. V. 53; 54
Lives of Northern Worthies. London: 1852. V. 52
Poems. Leeds: 1833. V. 47; 48; 49; 50; 51; 53
Poems. London: 1851. V. 51

COLERIDGE, HENRY NELSON
Six Months in the West Indies in 1825. London: 1825. V. 49; 54
Six Months in the West Indies in 1825. London: 1826. V. 53
Study of the Classic Poets. London: 1834. V. 53

COLERIDGE, S. T., MRS.
Minnow Among Tritons. Mrs. S. T. Coleridge's Letters to Thomas Poole 1799-1834. London: 1934. V. 52

COLERIDGE, SAMUEL TAYLOR
Aids to Reflection. London: 1825. V. 49; 50; 51; 52
Aids to Reflection. London: 1839. V. 54
The Ancient Mariner. London: 1930. V. 47
The Ancient Mariner. London: 1943. V. 51
Biographia Literaria... London: 1817. V. 48; 49; 51; 52; 53
Biographia Literaria... Opinions. London: 1847. V. 49
Blessed Are Ye that Sow Beside All Waters! A Lay Sermon, Addressed to the Higher and Middle Classes, on the Existing Distresses and Discontents. London: 1817. V. 50
Christabel... London: 1816. V. 47; 48; 50; 51; 52
Christabel... London: 1904. V. 49
Christabel. London: 1947. V. 51
Confessions of an Inquiring Spirit. London: 1840. V. 51; 52
Confessions of an Inquiring Spirit. Boston: 1841. V. 47; 54
A Dissertation on the Science of method... London: 1872. V. 49
Essays On His Own Times Forming a Second Series of the Friend... London: 1850. V. 49
The Friend. London: 1818. V. 50
The Friend. Burlington: 1831. V. 54
The Friend... London: 1837. V. 50; 52
The Friend. London: 1844. V. 51; 52; 54
Hints Towards the Formation of a More Comprehensive Theory of Life. London: 1848. V. 47
Kubla Khan, Fancy in Nubius and Song from Zapolya. London: 1904. V. 51
Letters, Conversations and Recollections... London: 1836. V. 50; 51; 53
Letters, Conversations and Recollections. New York: 1836. V. 48; 51
Marriage. London: 1919. V. 48
Notes and Lectures Upon Shakespeare and some of the Old Poets and Dramatists. London: 1849. V. 52
Notes on English Divines. London: 1853. V. 50; 51
Notes, Theological, Political and Miscellaneous. London: 1853. V. 53
Omniana, or Horae Otiosiores. London: 1812. V. 47
Osorio: A Tragedy As Originally Written in 1797. London: 1873. V. 49
The Plot Discovered; or an Address to the People, Against Ministerial Treason. Bristol: 1795. V. 50; 52; 54
Poems. London: 1797. V. 47; 50; 51; 52
Poems Chosen Out of the Works. Hammersmith: 1896. V. 47; 54
Poems on Various Subjects. London: 1796. V. 49; 50; 52; 54
The Poetical Works... London: 1829. V. 49
The Poetical Works... London: 1839. V. 49
Remorse. London: 1813. V. 50
The Rime of the Ancient Mariner. Edinburgh: 1837. V. 49
The Rime of the Ancient Mariner. New York: 1876. V. 53
The Rime of the Ancient Mariner. New York: 1883. V. 48
The Rime of the Ancient Mariner. Philadelphia: 1889. V. 52
The Rime of the Ancient Mariner... London: 1899. V. 47
The Rime of the Ancient Mariner... London: 1899. V. 50
The Rime of the Ancient Mariner. Campden: 1903. V. 50
The Rime of the Ancient Mariner. London: 1903. V. 48
The Rime of the Ancient Mariner. London: 1910. V. 50; 51; 53
Rime of the Ancient Mariner. New York: 1920. V. 53
The Rime of the Ancient Mariner. Bristol: 1929. V. 51
Rime of the Ancient Mariner. London: 1930. V. 48
The Rime of the Ancient Mariner. New York: 1931. V. 50
The Rime of the Ancient Mariner. London: 1943. V. 50; 54
The Rime of the Ancient Mariner. 1945. V. 53
The Rime of the Ancient Mariner. Edinburgh: 1945. V. 54
The Rime of the Ancient Mariner. London: 1945. V. 48
The Rime of the Ancient Mariner. New Haven: 1945. V. 53
The Rime of the Ancient Mariner. New York: 1945. V. 47; 48
The Rime of the Ancient Mariner. New York: 1946. V. 51
The Rime of the Ancient Mariner. London: 1949. V. 52
The Rime of the Ancient Mariner. New York: 1964. V. 49; 51; 52; 53
The Rime of the Ancient Mariner. 1995. V. 54
Selected Poems. London: 1935. V. 47; 48; 50
Selected Poems. Brighton: 1988. V. 47
Seven Lectures on Shakespeare and Milton. London: 1856. V. 47; 50
Sibylline Leaves. London: 1817. V. 47; 48; 49; 50; 52; 54
Specimens of the Table Talk... London: 1835. V. 48; 49; 50; 52; 54
Specimens of the Table Talk. New York: 1835. V. 48; 51
Specimens of the Table Talk. London: 1836. V. 48
The Statesman's Manual; or the Bible the Best Guide to Political Skill and Foresight: a Lay Sermon, Addressed to the Higher Classes of Society... London: 1816. V. 50; 53
Zapolya; a Christmas Tale. London: 1817. V. 47; 48; 50; 51

COLERIDGE, SARA
Memoir and Letters. London: 1873. V. 48; 50
Memoir and Letters... New York: 1874. V. 54
Phantasmion. Boston: 1874. V. 47
Phantasmion. London: 1874. V. 50; 51

COLERIDGE-TAYLOR, S.
Twenty-four Negro Melodies. Boston: 1905. V. 48; 49; 50; 54

COLES, C.
Game Birds. London: 1981. V. 48; 49; 51; 52; 53; 54
Game Birds. New York: 1983. V. 50; 51

COLES, ELISHA
A Dictionary of English-Latin and Latin-English... London: 1730. V. 52
An English Dictionary... London: 1684. V. 52
An English Dictionary... London: 1692. V. 52
An English Dictionary... London: 1713. V. 52; 53
An English Dictionary... London: 1732. V. 48

COLES, JAMES OAKLEY
On Deformities of the Mouth, Congenital and Acquired, with Their Mechanical Treatment. Philadelphia: 1870. V. 50

COLES, MANNING
Not Negotiable. London: 1949. V. 48

COLES, ROBERT
William Carlos Williams. New Brunswick: 1975. V. 47

COLES, WILLIAM
Adam in Eden: or, Natures Paradise. London: 1657. V. 49; 51
A Practical and Familiar Treatise On Ruptures, Containing an Entirely New and Approved Method of Treating These Distressing Afflictions... London: 1825. V. 49

COLETTE, SIDONIE GABRIELLE
Aventures Quotidiennes. Paris: 1924. V. 54
Break of Day. 1983. V. 52
Break of Day. New York: 1983. V. 47
Cheri. New York: 1929. V. 51; 54
For a Flower Album. London: 1959. V. 54
Gigi. Paris: 1945. V. 54
Mitsou or How Girls Grow Wise. New York: 1930. V. 54
La Naissance du Jour. Paris: 1928. V. 47
The Pure and the Impure. New York: 1933. V. 47
La Vagabonde. Paris: 1926. V. 51; 53

COLEY, HENRY
Merlinus Anglious Junior; or the Starry Messenger For the Year of Our Redemption 1694. London: 1694. V. 47

COLGATE, WILLIAM
Canadian Art: Its Origin and Development. Toronto: 1943. V. 47; 50; 51; 53
Horace Walpole on Milton. Toronto: 1953. V. 53

COLIBER, SAMUEL
Columna Rostrata, A Critical History of English Sea Affairs... London: 1727. V. 54

COLIGNY, GASPARD
The Lyfe of the Most Godly, Valeant and Noble Capteine and maintainer of the Trew Christian Religion in Fraunce, Jasper, Colignie, Shatilion, Sometyme Greate Admirall of Fraunce. London: 1576. V. 50

COLLADO, LUIS
Platica Manual de Artilleria. Milan: 1592. V. 49; 54

COLLARD, JOHN
The Life, and Extraordinary Adventures of James Molesworth Hobart, Alias Henry Griffin, Alias Lord Massey, the Newmarket Duke of Ormond, &c. London: 1794. V. 51

COLLARD, WILLIAM
Proposed London and Paris Railway. Westminster: 1928. V. 51; 52

COLLECTANEA Chymica: a Collection of Ten Several Treatises, in Chymistry, Concerning the Liquor Alkahest, the Mercury of Philosophers and Other Curiosities Worthy the Perusal. London: 1684. V. 48

A **COLLECTION** Of Addresses Transmitted by Certain English Clubs and Societies to the National Convention of France. London: 1793. V. 47; 51

A **COLLECTION** of All the Statutes Now in Force Relating to the Excise Upon Beer, Ale and Other Liquors...With an Abridgment of the Said Statutes (etc.). Edinburgh: 1744. V. 49

A **COLLECTION** of Anthems, As The Same Are Now Performed in His Majesty's Chapels Royal. London: 1736. V. 48

A **COLLECTION** of Articles, Canons, Injunctions, &c. Together with Several Acts of Parliament Concerning Ecclesiastical Matters; Some Whereof are to be Read in Churches. London: 1699. V. 47

A **COLLECTION** of Cases, and Other Discourses Lately Written to Recover Dissenters to the Communion of the Church of England. London: 1698. V. 48

A **COLLECTION** Of Chippeway and English Hymns. New York: 1847. V. 54

A **COLLECTION** of English Songs, with an Appendix of Original Pieces. London: 1796. V. 47

A **COLLECTION** of Epigrams. London: 1727. V. 50
A COLLECTION of Epigrams. London: 1735/37. V. 48

A **COLLECTION** of Famous Paintings of the Sung Dynasty Formerly Preserved by the Tien Lai Studio. Shanghai: 1960. V. 48

A **COLLECTION** of Hymns for a Voice, Harpsichord or Guitar. Dublin: 1798. V. 49

A **COLLECTION** of Hymns for Public, Social and Domestic Worship. Charleston: 1847. V. 48

A **COLLECTION** Of Hymns for the Use of Native Christians Who Speak the Mohawk Language. Ottawa: 1892. V. 50

A **COLLECTION** of Hymns, in Muncey and English for the Use of the Native Indians. Toronto: 1874. V. 52

A **COLLECTION** of Hymns in the Oneida Language for the Use of Native Christians. Toronto: 1855. V. 52

A **COLLECTION** of Interesting Biography. Containing, I. The Life of S. Johnson, LL.D. - Abridged, Principally, from Boswell's Celebrated Memoirs. II. The Life of Mr. Elwes... III. The Life of Captain Cook... Dublin: 1792. V. 47

A **COLLECTION** of Letters Relative to Foreign Missions; Containing Several of Melvill Horne's "Letters on Missions" and Interesting Communications from Foreign Missionaries. Andover: 1810. V. 47

A **COLLECTION** Of Loyal Songs Written Against the Rump Parliament, Between the Years 1639 and 1661. London: 1731. V. 47

A **COLLECTION** of Memorials Concerning...Quakers, In Pennsylvania, New Jersey... Philadelphia: 1787. V. 53

COLLECTION of Nebraska Pioneer Reminiscences. Cedar Rapids: 1916. V. 51

COLLECTION of Notes taken at the Kings Tryall, at Westminster Hall, on Tuesday, Last, Jan. 23, 1648, Also a Paper of Instructions Intercepted, Coming from Scotland, to the Scots Commissioners, Concerning the King. London: 1648. V. 51

A **COLLECTION** of Poems. London: 1702. V. 52

A **COLLECTION** of Poems by Several Hands. London: 1693. V. 50

COLLECTION of Poems Relating to State Affairs from Oliver Cromwell to This Present Time. London: 1705. V. 47

A **COLLECTION** of Poems, The Productions of the Kingdom of Ireland... London: 1773. V. 48

COLLECTION of Poems: viz. The Temple of Death (etc.). London: 1702. V. 48

A **COLLECTION** of Poems Written Upon Several Occasions by Several Persons. London: 1673. V. 47

COLLECTION of Portraits of Methodist Ministers. London: 1865-80. V. 49

A **COLLECTION** of Psalms, Hymns and Spiritual songs...Designed for, and Adapted to, The Fraternity of the Brethren... Covington: 1869. V. 49

A **COLLECTION** of Scarce and Valuable Tracts, on the Most Intersting and Entertaining Subjects. London: 1748. V. 53

A **COLLECTION** of Scarce and Valuable Treatises Upon Metals, Mines and Minerals... London: 1740. V. 48; 53; 54

A **COLLECTION** of Scarce, Curious and Valuable Pieces, Both in Verse and Prose; Chiefly Selected From the Fugitive Productions of the Most Eminent Wits of the Present Age. Edinburgh: 1773. V. 48

A **COLLECTION** of Several Treatises, Concerning the Reasons and Occasions of the Penal Laws. London: 1675. V. 47

A **COLLECTION** Of Some Writings of the Most Noted of the People Called Quakers, in their Times. Philadelphia: 1767. V. 52

A **COLLECTION** of State Papers, Relating to Affairs in the Reigns of King Henry VIII, King Edward VI, Queen May and Queen Elizabeth, from the Year 1542 to 1570...Left by William Cecil Lord Burghley... London: 1740. V. 47

A **COLLECTION** of State Tracts, Publish'd on Occasion of the Late Revolution in 1688. And During the Reign of King William III.... London: 1705/6/7. V. 51

COLLECTION of Sundry Publications, and Other Documents, in Relation to the Attack Made During the Late War Upon the Private Armed Brig General Armstrong of New York, Commanded by S. C. Reid, on the Night of the 26th of Sept. 1814, at the Island of... New York: 1833. V. 52

A **COLLECTION** of Tales, Written by Kotzebue, Charlotte Smith, Mitford, Von Messing, Florian (the French Goldsmith), St. Evremond...and Others... Albany: 1808. V. 47

A **COLLECTION** of the Addresses, Songs and Other Papers Which Were Published During the Late Contested Election for the Borough of Grantham; Which Took Place on the 8th, 9th and 10th of March, 1820... Grantham: 1820. V. 52

A **COLLECTION** Of the Several Statutes, and Parts of Statutes, now in Force, Relating to High Treason, and Misprision of High Treason. London: 1709. V. 47

A **COLLECTION** of Upwards of 230 Recipes...Also the Process of Preparing All the Cements for Shopping Carious Teeth. New York: 1836. V. 50

A **COLLECTION** Of Voyages and Travels, Consisting of Authentic Writers in Our Own Tongue, Which Have Not Before Been Collected in English... London: 1745. V. 50

A **COLLECTION** of Voyages and Travels, Some Now Printed from Original Manuscripts. London: 1704. V. 47

A **COLLECTION** of Welsh Tours; or, a Display of the Beauties of Wales, Selected Principally from Celebrated Histories and Popular Tours. London: 1797. V. 51

COLLECTIONS of Passages Refer'd to by Dr. Henry Sacheverell in His Answer to the Articles of His Impeachment. London: 1710. V. 51

COLLEDGE, J. J.
Ships of the Royal Navy: an Historical Index. London: 1987/89. V. 54

COLLEDGE, STEPHEN
The Arraignment, Tryal and Condemnation of Stephen Colledge for High-Treason. (with) The Last Speech and Confession of Mr. Stephen Colledge. (with) An Impartial Account of the Arraignment, Tryal and Condemnation of Stephen Colledge etc. London: 1681/82. V. 50

COLLEN, GEORGE WILLIAM
Britannia Saxonica. London: 1833. V. 54

COLLENDER, H. W.
Modern Billiards. New York: 1881. V. 47

COLLES, ABRAHAM
Practical Observations on the Veneral Disease and on the Use of Mercury. Philadelphia: 1837. V. 48; 51

COLLET, COLLET DOBSON
History of the Taxes on Knowledge, Their Origin and Repeal. London: 1899. V. 52

COLLET, STEPHEN
Relics of Literature. London: 1823. V. 51; 53

COLLIE, J. NORMAN
Climbing on the Himalaya and Other Mountain Ranges. Edinburgh: 1902. V. 48; 50

COLLIE, JEREMY
An Essay Upon Gaming, in a Dialogue Between Callimachus and Dolomedes. Edinburgh: 1885. V. 47

COLLIER, J.
The Literature Relating to New Zealand: a Bibliography. Wellington: 1889. V. 47

COLLIER, JANE
An Essay on the Art of Ingeniously Tormenting. London: 1753. V. 51; 52; 54
An Essay on the Art of Ingeniously Tormenting... London: 1757. V. 49; 54
An Essay on the Art of Ingeniously Tormenting. London: 1808. V. 49
An Essay on the Art of Ingeniously Tormenting... London: 1811. V. 52

COLLIER, JEREMY
A Defence of the Short View of the Immorality and Profaneness of the English Stage. London: 1699. V. 50
A Defence of the Short View of the the Immorality and Profaneness of the English Stage... 1699. V. 47
The Desertion Discuss'd. In a Letter to a Country Gentleman. London: 1689. V. 53
An Ecclesiastical History of Great Britain... London: 1708-14. V. 51
An Ecclesiastical History of Great Britain... London: 1845-46. V. 47
The Great Historical, Geographical, Genealogical and Poetical Dictionary... London: 1701-27. V. 53
A Second Defense of the Short View of the Profaneness and Immorality of the English Stage. London: 1700. V. 49; 53
A Short View of the Immorality and Profaneness of the English Stage... London: 1698. V. 47; 48; 50; 51; 53; 54
A Short view of the Immorality and Profaneness of the English Stage... London: 1698/99. V. 51
A Short View of the Immorality and Profaneness of the English Stage... London: 1698/99/1700. V. 50
A Short View of the Immorality and Profaneness of the English Stage. 1699. V. 47
A Short View of the Immorality and Profaneness of the English Stage. London: 1730. V. 52
Short View of the Immorality and Profaneness of the English Stage... London: 1738. V. 49; 53

COLLIER, JOHN
Defy the Foul Fiend. London: 1934. V. 49; 51
Defy the Foul Fiend. New York: 1934. V. 47; 48; 49
The Devil and All. London: 1934. V. 50
Fancies and Goodnights. Garden City: 1951. V. 54
Fancies and Goodnights. New York: 1951. V. 52
Fancies and Goodnights. New York: 1952. V. 47
Gemini: Poems. London: 1931. V. 49; 51; 53
Green Thoughts. London: 1932. V. 52
His Monkey Wife. New York: 1931. V. 47
His Monkey Wife. London: 1933. V. 51; 53
The Lancashire Dialect; Containing the Adventures and Misfortunes of a Lancashire Town. London: 1785. V. 54
The Miscellaneous Works of Tim Bobbin, Esq... Manchester: 1775. V. 52
No Traveller Returns. London: 1931. V. 51; 52
Tim Bobbin's Lancashire Dialect; and Poems. London: 1828. V. 47; 50; 54
A View of the Lancashire Dialect... London: 1746. V. 52
A View of the Lancashire Dialect... London: 1775. V. 47
Witch's Money. New York: 1940. V. 48; 52; 54
The Works of Tim Bobbin, Esq. in Prose and Verse. Manchester: 1862. V. 47; 53; 54

COLLIER, JOHN PAYNE
History of English Dramatic Poetry and Annals of the Stage to the Restoration. London: 1831. V. 47; 49; 50; 51; 53
The Poetical Decameron, or Ten Conversations on English Poets and Poetry. Edinburgh: 1820. V. 50; 51
Punch and Judy. London: 1828. V. 48; 49; 53
Punch and Judy. London: 1828/27. V. 47
Punch and Judy. New York: 1937. V. 52; 54
Seven Lectures on Shakespeare and Milton. London: 1856. V. 50

COLLIER, MARY
The Woman's Labour: an Epistle to Mr. Stephen Duck... London: 1739. V. 48
The Woman's Labour: an Epistle to Mr. Stephen Duck... London: 1740. V. 48

COLLIGNON, CHARLES
The Miscellaneous Works of Charles Collignon, M.D. Cambridge: 1786. V. 47; 48; 50; 51; 54

COLLIN, VICTOR
A Short Treatise on the Different Methods of Investigating the Diseases of the Chest. Boston: 1829. V. 53

COLLINGRIDGE, W. H.
Comprehensive Guide to Printing and Publishing: a Manual of Information on Matters Connected with Printing, Publishing, etc., etc. London: 1869. V. 48

COLLINGS, ELLSWORTH
The 101 Ranch. Norman: 1937. V. 53

COLLINGWOOD, CUTHBERT
Rambles of a Naturalist on the Shores and Waters of the China Sea. London: 1868. V. 50

COLLINGWOOD, FRANCIS
The Universal Cook, and City and Country Housekeeper. London: 1806. V. 49

COLLINGWOOD, G. L. NEWNHAM
A Selection from the Public and Private Correspondence of Vice Admiral Lord Collingwood... London: 1828. V. 54
A Selection from the Public and Private Correspondence of Vice Admiral Lord Collingwood... London: 1837. V. 50

COLLINGWOOD, STUART DODGSON
The Life and Letters of Lewis Carroll. London: 1898. V. 51; 53
The Life and Letters of Lewis Carroll. New York: 1899. V. 47

COLLINGWOOD, WILLIAM G.
The Book of Coniston. Kendal: 1897. V. 50; 54
Coniston Tales. Ulverstn: 1899. V. 50; 51; 52; 54
The Lake Counties. London: 1932. V. 50; 52
The Life and Work of John Ruskin. London: 1893. V. 52; 54
The Memoirs of Sir Daniel Fleming. Kendal: 1928. V. 52
Northumberian Crosses of the Pre-Norman Age. London: 1927. V. 47; 49; 53
A Pilgrimage to the Saga Steads of Iceland. Ulverston: 1899. V. 51; 52

COLLINS, A. FREDERICK
Experimental Television. Boston: 1932. V. 50; 52; 54

COLLINS, ANTHONY
A Discourse Concerning Ridicule and Irony in Writing, in a Letter to the Rev.d Dr. Nathanael Marshall. London: 1729. V. 47
A Discourse of Free-Thinking, Occasion'd by the Rise and growth of a Sect Call'd Free-Thinkers... London: 1713. V. 48; 49
A Discourse of the Grounds and Reasons of the Christian Religion. 1726. V. 49
A Dissertation on Liberty and Necessity... London: 1729. V. 52
A Philosophical Enquiry Concerning Human Liberty. London: 1717. V. 49; 52; 54

COLLINS, ARTHUR
Letters and Memorials of State in the Reigns of Mary, Elizabeth, James, Charles I, Part of Charles II and Oliver's Usurpation. 1746. V. 48; 52
The Life and Glorious Actions of Edward Prince of Wales... London: 1740. V. 49
The Life of that Great Statesman William Cecil...Secretary of State in the Reign of...Edward the Sixth... London: 1732. V. 51; 53
Proceedings, Precedents, and Arguments, on Claims and Controversies, Concerning Baronies by Writ, and Other Honours. London: 1734. V. 52; 54

COLLINS, ASA W.
Doctor Asa. Los Angeles: 1941. V. 54

COLLINS, CECIL
The Vision of the Fool. London: 1947. V. 51; 53

COLLINS, CHARLES
Juvenile Blossoms. London: 1823. V. 51

COLLINS, CHARLES ALSTON
A Cruise Upon Wheels. London: 1862. V. 47
The Eye-Witness, and His Evidence About Many Wonderful Things. London: 1860. V. 49

COLLINS, D. C.
Practical Political Economy and Social Science, In Their Application To Our Present Condition as a Nation. Covington: 1876. V. 48

COLLINS, D. J.
Plants for Medicines: a Chemical and Pharmacological Survey of Plants in the Australian Region. East Melbourne: 1990. V. 54

COLLINS, DAVID
An Account of the English Colony in New South Wales, from Its First Settlement in January 1788 to August 1801... London: 1804. V. 48; 50

COLLINS, DENNIS
The Indians Last Fight or the Dull Knife Raid. Girard: 1915. V. 47; 49; 54

COLLINS, DOUGLAS TATHAM
A Tear for Somalia, Another Tear for Africa. Clinton: 1980. V. 48; 53

COLLINS, E. T.
The History and Traditions of the Moorfields Eye Hospital. London: 1929. V. 49
In the Kingdom of the Shah. London: 1896. V. 53

COLLINS, FRANCIS
Voyages to Portugal, Spain, Sicily, Malta, Asia-Minor, Egypt. Philadelphia: 1809. V. 54

COLLINS, GEORGE E.
History of the Brocklesbury Hounds 1700-1901. London: 1902. V. 48

COLLINS, GREENVILLE
Great Britain's Coasting Pilot in Two Parts. London: 1767. V. 54

COLLINS, HENRY B.
Archaeology of St. Lawrence Island, Alaska. Washington: 1937. V. 47; 53

COLLINS, HUBERT EDWIN
Warpath and Cattle Trail. New York: 1928. V. 53; 54

COLLINS, J.
A New Look of Shields, Composed of Variety Of Ornaments and Trophies, Calculated for the Use of Artificers in General. London: 1760. V. 53

COLLINS, J. H.
A Handbook to the Mineralogy of Cornwall and Devon. London: 1871. V. 54

COLLINS, JAMES E.
The Private Book of Useful Alloys and Memoranda for Goldsmiths, Jewellers &c. London: 1871. V. 49

COLLINS, JESS
Translations. Los Angeles: 1971. V. 49; 53

COLLINS, JOHN
The City and Scenery of Newport, Rhode Island. Burlington: 1857. V. 48

COLLINS, JOHN S.
Across the Plains in '64. Omaha: 1904. V. 47; 49; 54

COLLINS, MARCIE
The Book of Beasts. Novato: 1971. V. 49

COLLINS, MARVA
Marva Collin's Way. Los Angeles: 1982. V. 50

COLLINS, MORTIMER
Idyls and Rhymes. Dublin: 1855. V. 47

COLLINS, N. G.
The Prospect. The Speech of Rev. N. G. Collins, Chaplain of the 5th Illinois, at Corinth, Miss. on the Day of National Thanksgiving, Aug. 3, '63 to the Officers and men of Col. Bane's Brigade. Chicago: 1863. V. 51

COLLINS, PHILIP
Charles Dickens. the Public Readings. Oxford: 1975. V. 54

COLLINS, R. M.
Chapters from the Unwritten History of the War Between the States; or, the Incidents in the Life of a Confederate Soldier in Camp, on the March, in the Great Battles and in Prison. St. Louis: 1893. V. 52

COLLINS, SAMUEL
The Present State of Russia, in a Letter to a Friend: Written Between...1784 and 1807. Edinburgh: 1811. V. 50
A Systeme of Anatomy, Treating of the Body of Man, Beasts, Birds, Fish, Insects and Plants...After Every Part of Man's Body Hath Been Anatomically described... London: 1685. V. 49

COLLINS, VARNUM LANSING
President Witherspoon. A Biography. Princeton: 1925. V. 51

COLLINS, W.
The Young French Emigrants; or, the Orphans of Montmorency, a Tale for the Moral Instruction and Amusement of Youth of Both Sexes. London: 1823. V. 52

COLLINS, WILKIE
After Dark. London: 1878. V. 51
After Dark. London: 1891. V. 51
Antonia; or, the Fall of Rome. London: 1875. V. 51
Armadale. London: 1866. V. 47
Armadale. New York: 1866. V. 47
Armadale. London: 1872. V. 51
Black and White: a Love Story. London: 1869. V. 48
The Dead Secret. London: 1865. V. 51
The Frozen Deep. V. 54
The Frozen Deep... London: 1875. V. 51
Heart and Science: a Story of the Present Time. London: 1883. V. 54
Hide and Seek. London: 1872. V. 51
The Law and the Lady. New York: 1875. V. 54
The Law and the Lady. London: 1876. V. 51
The Legacy of Cain. London: 1889. V. 49; 52
Man and Wife. London: 1870. V. 51
Man and Wife. New York: 1870. V. 47
Memoirs of the Life of William Collins. London: 1848. V. 51; 54
Miss or Mrs?. London: 1873. V. 48; 51; 52; 54
The Moonstone. London: 1868. V. 48; 49
The Moonstone. New York: 1868. V. 47; 49; 53
The Moonstone. New York: 1869. V. 47
My Miscellanies. London: 1863. V. 51; 54
The New Magdalen: a Novel. London: 1894. V. 51
No Name. London: 1862. V. 47; 49; 51
No Name. Boston: 1863. V. 49

No Name. New York: 1863. V. 53
The Poetical Works. London: 1797. V. 54
Poor Miss Finch. London: 1872. V. 51; 54
The Queen of Hearts. New York: 1859. V. 47; 50
Rambles Beyond Railways; or, Notes in Cornwall Taken a-foot. London: 1851. V. 50
Rambles Beyond Railways; or, Notes in Cornwall Taken a-foot. London: 1852. V. 50
The Woman in White. London: 1860. V. 50; 51
The Woman in White. New York: 1860. V. 47; 54
The Woman in White. London: 1861. V. 47; 52
The Works of Wilkie Collins. New York: 1890. V. 51
The Yellow Mask; or, the Ghost of the Ball Room. Philadelphia: 1862?. V. 50

COLLINS, WILLIAM
Missa Triumphans, Or, The Triumph of the Mass; Wherein All the Sophistical and Wily Arguments of Mr. de Rodon...are Fully, Formally and Clearly Answered... London: 1675. V. 48
Oriental Eclogues. London: 1757. V. 47
Poems. London: 1929. V. 48
The Poetical Works. London: 1798. V. 47; 48; 50; 52
Poetical Works. London: 1800. V. 50
The Poetical Works. London: 1827. V. 47; 48; 50
The Poetical Works... London: 1858. V. 51

COLLINS BAKER, C. H.
Crome. London: 1921. V. 52

COLLIS, MAURICE
The Discovery of L. S. Lowry - a Critical and Biographical Essay. London: 1951. V. 49
On the Diagnosis and Treatment of Cancer and the Tumours Analogous To It. London: 1864. V. 48; 53

COLLIS, SEPTIMA M.
A Women's Trip to Alaska, Being an Account of a Voyage through the Inland Seas of the Sitkan Archipelago in 1890. New York: 1890. V. 50

COLLISON, JOHN
The Beauties of British Antiquity: Selected from the Writings of Esteemed Antiquaries. London: 1779. V. 47

COLLMANN, HERBERT L.
Ballads and Broadsides Chiefly of the Elizabethan Period and Printed in Black letter Most of Which were Formerly in the Heber Collection and are Now in the Library at Britwell Court, Buckinghamshire. Oxford: 1912. V. 50
The Britwell Handlist or Short-Title Catalogue of the Principal Volumes from the Time of Caxton to the Year 1800, Formerly in the Library of Britwell Court, Buckinghamshire. London: 1933. V. 52

COLLODI, CARLO
The Adventures of Pinocchio. New York: 1929. V. 53

COLLS, JOHN HENRY
Ardelia. a Poem. London: 1787. V. 54

COLLUM, RICHARD S.
History of the United States Marine Corps. Philadelphia: 1890. V. 47

COLLYER, ROBERT
Ilkley: Ancient and Modern. Otley: 1885. V. 47; 51; 53

COLLYNS, CHARLES
Notes on the Chase of the Wild Red Deer... London: 1862. V. 47
Notes on the Chase of the Wild Red Deer. London: 1902. V. 49

COLMAN, ANDREW M.
Companion Encyclopedia of Psychology. London: 1994. V. 54

COLMAN, BENJAMIN
The Case of Satan's Fiery Darts in Blasphemous Suggestion and Hellish Annoyances...Preached to the Congregation in Brattle Street, Boston, May 1711, and Lately Repated to Them May 1743. Boston: 1744. V. 50

COLMAN, GEORGE
Barney Buntline and Billy Bowling, or The Advantages of Being at Sea... London: 1835?. V. 49
Broad Grins. London: 1811. V. 51
The Circle of Anecdote and Wit, to Which is Added a Choice Selection of Toasts and Sentiments. London: 1821. V. 47
Inkle and Yarico: an Opera, in Three Acts. London: 1787. V. 48
The Jealous Wife: a Comedy. London: 1761. V. 51
My Night-Gown and Slippers; or Tales in Verse. London: 1797. V. 54
Poetical Vagaries. London: 1812. V. 47; 54
Random Records. London: 1830. V. 51
Some Particulars of the Life of the Late George Colman, Esq. London: 1795. V. 47
Vagaries Vindicated. London: 1813. V. 47; 54

COLMAN, HELEN CAROLINE
Jeremiah James Colman: a Memoir. London: 1905. V. 53

COLMAN, HENRY
The Agriculture and Rural Economy of France, Belgium, Holland and Switzerland... London: 1848. V. 49
European Life and Manners; in Familiar Letters to Friends. Boston: 1849. V. 49

COLMAN, W. A.
A Catalogue of New, Curious and Rare Books... New York: 1837. V. 51

COLMONT, MARIE
Down the River. New York: 1940. V. 53

COLNETT, JAMES
The Journal of Captain James Colnett Aboard the Argonaut, from April 26 1789 to Nov. 3 1791. Toronto: 1940. V. 54
A Voyage to the South Atlantic and Round Cape Horn Into the Pacific Ocean, for the Purpose of Extending the Spermaceti Whale Fisheries, and other Objects of Commerce,... Amsterdam: 1968. V. 49

COLOMBAT DE L'ISERE, MARC C.
A Treatise on the Diseases and Special Hygiene of Females. Philadelphia: 1848. V. 48

COLOMBINA, GIOVANNI BATTISTA
Origine Eccellenza a Necessita dell'Arte Militare. Trevigi: 1608. V. 53; 54

COLOMBO, CHRISTOFORO
Select Letters of Christopher Columbus, with Other Original Documents, Relating to His Four Voyages to the New World. London: 1847. V. 49
The Voyages of Christopher Columbus Being the Journals of His First and Third and the Letters Concerning His First and Last Voyages, To Which is Added the Account of His Second Voyage... London: 1930. V. 49

COLONEL Crockett's Exploits and Adventures in Texas... Philadlephia: 1836. V. 50
COLONEL Crockett's Exploits and Adventures in Texas... Philadelhpia: 1837. V. 47

COLONEY, MYRON
Manomin: A Rhythmical Romance of Minnesota, the Great Rebellion and the Minnesota Massacres. St. Louis: 1866. V. 49; 54

COLONIAL CHURCH & SCHOOL SOCIETY
Annual Report of the..., for Sending Out of Clergymen, Catechist's and Schoolmasters to the Colonies of Great Britain and to British Residents in Other Parts of the World. London: 1851. V. 52

COLONIZATION of Vancouver's Island. London: 1849. V. 49

COLONNA, FRANCESCO
Hypnerotomachia Poliphili, ubi Humana Omnia non Nisisomnium Esse Docet. Venice: 1499. V. 51

THE COLOPHON. New York: 1930. V. 51
THE COLOPHON. New York: 1930-50. V. 47; 49; 50

COLORADO & SOUTHERN RAILWAY
Some Fishing Pools and Pictures Along the Platte. Denver. V. 53

COLORADO. CONSTITUTION
Draft of a Constitution Published Under the Direction of a Committee of Citizens of Colorado for Consideration and Discussion. Denver: 1875. V. 49; 54

COLORADO. LAWS, STATUTES, ETC.
Laws of Gregory District Enacted February 18 & 20, 1860. Denver City: 1860. V. 52

COLOUR Designs for Modern Interiors. London/Stuttgart: 1935. V. 51

COLPOYS, MRS.
The Irish Excursion, or I Fea to Tell You. Dublin: 1801. V. 52

COLQUHOUN, ARCHIBALD ROSS
Across Chryse, Being the Narrative of a Journey of Exploration through the South China Border Lands from Canton to Mandalay. London: 1883. V. 49; 53
Amongst the Shans...and an Historical Sketch of the Shans... London: 1885. V. 49; 50
China in Transformation. London: 1898. V. 48; 50
The Overland to China. New York: 1900. V. 50

COLQUHOUN, JOHN
The Moor and the Loch... Edinburgh: 1840. V. 47
The Moor and the Loch... London: 1878. V. 54
The Moor and the Loch. 1880. V. 52
The Moor and the Loch... 1884. V. 48
Salmon-Casts and Stray Shots, Being Fly-Leaves from the Note-Book of John Colquhoun. London: 1858. V. 53
With the Kurram Field Force, 1878-79. London: 1881. V. 53

COLQUHOUN, PATRICK
A Treatise On the Commerce and Police of the River Thames... London: 1800. V. 49; 53
A Treatise on the Functions and Duties of a Constable... London: 1803. V. 47; 53
A Treatise on the Police of London; Containing a detail of the Various Crimes and Misdemeanors...and Suggesting Remedies for Their Prevention. Philadelphia: 1798. V. 49
A Treatise on the Police of the Metropolis... London: 1796. V. 50
A Treatise on the Police of the Metropolis... London: 1797. V. 50
A Treatise on the Police of the Metropolis... London: 1800. V. 48
A Treatise on the Wealth, Power and Resources, of the British Empire, In Every Quarter of the World... London: 1814. V. 49
A Treatise on the Wealth, Power and Resources of the British Empire, In Every Quarter of the World... London: 1815. V. 48

COLQUHOUN, ROBERT
Poems of Sleep and Dream. London: 1947. V. 49

COLQUITT, ANTHONY
The Second Part of Modern Reports, Being a Collection of Several Special Cases Most of Them Adjudged in the Court of Common Pleas, in the 26th...30th Years of Charles II... London: 1698. V. 49

COLQUITT, HARRIET ROSS
The Savannah Cook Book. New York: 1933. V. 49

COLSON, NATHANIEL
The Mariner's New Calendar. London: 1754. V. 53; 54
The Mariner's New Calendar. London: 1761. V. 48; 53

COLT, ARMIDA MARIA THERESA
Weeds and Wildflowers. London: 1965. V. 47; 54

COLT, H. DUNSCOMBE
Excavations at Nessana (Auja Hafirs, Palestine). London & Princeton: 1950-62. V. 49; 51

COLT, MIRIAM DAVIS
Went to Kansas: Being a Thrilling Account of an Ill-Fated Expedition to that Fairy land and its Sad Results. Watertown: 1862. V. 47; 49

COLT, SAMUEL
Report: the Committee on Military Affairs...Relative Efficiency of the Repeating Pistols, Invented by Samuel Colt. Washington: 1851. V. 47

COLTHORP, HENRY
The Liberties Usages, and Customes of the City of London. London: 1642. V. 50

COLTMAN, ROBERT
The Chinese, Their Present and Future: medical, Political and Social. Philadelphia: 1891. V. 50

COLTON, CALVIN
The Americans. London: 1833. V. 49; 53
A Lecture on the Railroad to the Pacific. Delivered August 12, 1850, at the Smithsonian Institute, Washington, at the Request of Numerous Members of Both Houses. New York: 1850. V. 47

COLTON, CHARLES CALEB
Hypocrisy. Tiverton: 1812. V. 47; 48; 51
Hypocrisy. London: 1823. V. 51

COLTON, HENRY E.
Mountain Scenery. The Scenery of the Mountains of Western North Carolina and Northwestern South Carolina. Raleigh: 1859. V. 54

COLTON, JAMES
Strange Marriage. Los Angeles: 1965. V. 51

COLTON, JOSEPH HUTCHINS
Colton's Traveler and Tourist's Guide-Book through the United States of America and the Canadas. New York: 1850. V. 54
Particulars of Routes, Distances, Fare, Etc. to Accompany Colton's Map of California and the Gold Region. New York: 1849. V. 47; 50

COLTON, ROBERT
Rambles in Sweden and Gottland; with Etchings by the Wayside. London: 1847. V. 52

COLTON, WALTER
Deck and Port; or, Incidents of a Cruise in the United States Frigate Congress to California. New York: 1850. V. 52; 53; 54
Deck and Port; or, Incidents of a Cruise in the United States Frigate Congress to California. New York: 1854. V. 47; 51
Land and Lee in the Bosphorous and Aegean, or Views of Athens and Constantinople. New York: 1851. V. 52
The Sea and the Sailor: Notes on France and Italy and Other Literary Remains of Rev. Walter Colton. New York: 1851. V. 52
Ship and Shore, in Madeira. New York: 1851. V. 49
Three Years in California. New York: 1850. V. 48; 52; 53
Visit to Constantinople and Athens. New York: 1836. V. 47

COLUM, PADRAIC
The Adventures of Odysseus and the Tale of Troy. London: 1920. V. 48
Creatures. New York: 1927. V. 48; 50; 51; 54
Cross Roads in Ireland. New York: 1930. V. 50
The Forge in the Forest. London: 1925. V. 48
The Frenzied Prince: Heroic Stories of Ancient Ireland. Philadelphia: 1943. V. 50
Poems. New York: 1932. V. 50
Ten Poems. Dublin: 1957. V. 49
Wild Earth. Dublin: 1950. V. 50

COLUMBIA Poetry 1935. New York: 1935. V. 51

COLUMBIA Poetry 1939. New York: 1939. V. 49

THE COLUMBIAN World's Fair Atlas... Hopedale: 1893. V. 51

THE COLUMBUS Petition Document of Don Pedro Colon de Portugal y Castro...to Her Royal Highness Mariana of Austria, Queen Regent of Charles II of Spain, for the Island of Jamaica, 1672. San Francisco: 1992. V. 50

COLUMBUS CARRIAGE & HARNESS CO., COLUMBUS
Catalogue No. 26. Columbus: 1901. V. 54

COLUTHUS
The Rape of Helen, from the Greek of Coluthus, with Miscellaneous Notes. London: 1786. V. 52

COLVER, NATHANIEL
The Prophecy of Daniel Literally Fulfilled. Boston: 1843. V. 49

COLVILE, EDEN
London Correspondence Inward from Eden Colvile. London: 1956. V. 47; 50; 52; 54

COLVILL, HELEN HESTER
Mr. Bryant's Mistake. London: 1890. V. 54

COLVILL, ROBERT
The Feast of Holyrood. Edinburgh: 1768. V. 54
The Field of Flowdon, a Descriptive Poem. London: 1768. V. 53

COLVILLE, ARTHUR, MRS.
1,000 Miles in a Machilla: Travel and Sport in Nyasaland, Angoniland and Rhodesia... London: 1911. V. 53

COLVILLE, HENRY
The Land of the Nile Springs. London: 1895. V. 51

COLVIN, F. F.
Diary of the 9th (Q.R.) Lancers During the south African Campaign, 1899 to 1902. South Kensington: 1904. V. 49; 53; 54

COLVIN, H.
A Biographical Dictionary of British Architects 1600-1840. New Haven;: 1995. V. 53

COLVIN, HOWARD
The History of the King's Works. London: 1963-73. V. 48
The History of the King's Works. London: 1976. V. 50
History of the King's Works. London: 1976-81. V. 50

COLVIN, JOHN B.
A Magistrate's Guide; and Citizen's Counsellor... Frederick-Town: 1805. V. 47; 50

COLVIN, SIDNEY
John Keats: His Life and Poetry, His Friends, Critics and After-Fame. London: 1917. V. 48
Keats. London: 1887. V. 51

COLWELL, STEPHEN
Politics for American Christians... Philadelphia: 1852. V. 52

COLWIN, LAURIE
Passion and Affect. New York: 1974. V. 49

COLYER, WILLIAM H.
Sketches of the North River. New York: 1838. V. 47

COMAN, KATHARINE
Economic Beginnings of the Far West - How We Won the Land Beyond the Mississippi. New York: 1912. V. 54

COMANCHE Oil & Gas Company of Oklahoma. Salt lake City: 1918. V. 50

COMAZZI, JOHN BAPTISTA, COUNT
The Morals of Princes: or, an Abstract of the Most Remarkable Passages Contain'd in the History of All the Emperors Who Reign'd in Rome... London: 1729. V. 47

COMBE, ANDREW
The Life and Correspondence of... Edinburgh: 1850. V. 50
Observations on Mental Derangement: Being an Application of the Principles of Phrenology to the Elucidation of the Causes, Symptoms, Nature and Treatment of Insanity. Boston: 1834. V. 52
The Physiology of Digestion Considered with Relation to the Principles of Dietetics. Boston: 1836. V. 48; 53
The Physiology of Digestion Considered with Relation to the Principles of Dietetics. Edinburgh: 1836. V. 48

COMBE, CAROLUS
Nummorum Veterum Populorum et Urbium, Qui In Museo Gulielmi Hunter Asservantur, Descriptio Figuris Illustrata. Londini: 1782. V. 48

COMBE, FLORENCE
Islands of Enchantment. London: 1911. V. 51

COMBE, FRANCES POWER
The Friend of Man: and His Friends - The Poets. London: 1899. V. 54

COMBE, GEORGE
Essays on Phrenology, or an Inquiry into the Principles and Utility of the System of Drs. Gall and Spurzheim, and into the Objections Made Against It. Edinburgh: 1819. V. 50
Essays on Phrenology, or an Inquiry Into the Principles and Utility of the System of Drs. Gall and Spurzheim, and Into the Objections Made Against It. Philadelphia: 1822. V. 53
The Life and Correspondence of Andrew Combe. Edinburgh: 1850. V. 48
Moral Philosophy; or the Duties of Man Considered in His Individual, Social and Domestic Capacities. Edinburgh: 1840. V. 47
Notes on the United States of North America, During a Phenological Visit in 1838-9-40. Edinburgh: 1841. V. 53
A System of Phrenology... New York: 1849. V. 54
Thoughts on Capital Punishment. Edinburgh: 1847. V. 48

COMBE, TAYLOR
Veterum Populorum et Regum Numi Qui In Museo Britannico Adservantur. Londini: 1814. V. 48

COMBE, WILLIAM
The Dance of Life. London: 1817. V. 48; 50; 51; 54
The Devil Upon Two Sticks in England... 1790-1802-02. V. 47
The Devil Upon Two Sticks in England. Dublin: 1790-1802-02. V. 54
Dr. Syntax In Paris. London: 1820. V. 49
Doctor Syntax's Three Tours: In Search of the Picturesque, Consolation and a Wife... London: 1868. V. 49; 51
Doctor Syntax's Three Tours: In Search of the Picturesque, Consolation and a Wife. London: 1869. V. 53
The English Dance of Death. London: 1815-16. V. 51; 52; 54
The English Dance of Death. London: 1815/16/17. V. 50; 54
The English Dance of Death... London: 1905. V. 54
The First of April... Dublin: 1777. V. 47
The First of April... London: 1777. V. 49
The First Tour of Doctor Syntax. London: 1855. V. 48; 49
The Grand Master or Adventures of Qui Hi in Hindostan. London: 1816. V. 50; 54
The History of Johnny Quae Genus, the Little Foundling of the Late Doctor Syntax. London: 1822. V. 49; 51; 52; 54
An History of the River Thames. London: 1794-96. V. 51; 52; 54
Journal of Sentimental Travels in the Provinces of France, Shortly Before the Revolution. London: 1821. V. 49; 51; 52; 54
A Letter to Her Grace the Duchess of Devonshire. London: 1777. V. 49
The Life, Adventures and Opinions of Col. George Hanger, Written by Himself. London: 1801. V. 54
The Life of Napoleon. London: 1815. V. 51
The Philosopher in Bristol. Dublin: 1784. V. 54
The Second Tour of Doctor Syntax... London: 1820. V. 51
The Second Tour of Doctor Syntax... London: 1820/21. V. 47
The Third Tour of Doctor Syntax, in Search of a Wife, a Poem. London. V. 51
The Three Tours of Dr. Syntax. London: 1812-20-21. V. 51
The Three Tours of Dr. Syntax.... London: 1813/20/21. V. 51
The Three Tours of Dr. Syntax.... London: 1823. V. 47; 51; 54
The Tour of Doctor Prosody in Search of the Antique and the Picturesque Through Scotland, the Hebrides, the Orkney and Shetland Isles. London: 1821. V. 50; 54
The Tour of Doctor Syntax... London: 1812. V. 48
The Tour of Doctor Syntax... London: 1813. V. 47; 48
The Tour of Doctor Syntax... London: 1815-21. V. 52
The Tour of Dr. Syntax... London: 1817. V. 47; 52
The Tour of Doctor Syntax... London: 1819-21. V. 51
The Tour of Doctor Syntax. London: 1820. V. 47; 50; 51
The Tour of Dr. Syntax... London: 1823. V. 47; 50; 51
The Tour of Doctor Syntax... London: 1828/23/28. V. 49
The Tour of Doctor Syntax... London: 1838. V. 51
The Tour of Doctor Syntax... London: 1844. V. 51; 53
The Tour of Doctor Syntax... London: 1855. V. 50; 54
A Word in Season, to the Traders and Manufacturers of Great Britain. London: 1792. V. 52

COMBER, JOHN
Sussex Genealogies: Lewes Centre. Cambridge: 1933. V. 49

COMBER, THOMAS
A Companion to the Altar; or a Help to the Worthy Receiving of the Lords Supper... London: 1681. V. 53
A Companion to the Temple. London: 1676. V. 53
Memoirs of the Life and Writings of Thomas Comber, D.D., Sometime Dean of Durham... London: 1799. V. 53
The Occasional Offices of Matrimony, Visitation of the Sick, Burial of the Dead, Churching Of Women... London: 1679. V. 50; 51; 53
A Vindication of the Great Revolution in England in A.D. MDCLXXXVIII... London: 1758. V. 50

COMBERMERLE, MARY WOOLEY GIBBINGS, VISCOUNTESS
A Friar's Scourge. London: 1876. V. 47; 49; 50; 51; 53

COMBIER, CHAUVIN CO.
Paintings to Wear. New York: 1945. V. 49

COMBINATION Atlas Map of Middlesex County, New Jersey. Philadelphia: 1876. V. 51

COMBINED Atlas of the State of New Jersey and the County of Hudson, from Actual Survey (sic) Official Records & Private Plans... Philadelphia: 1873. V. 47

COMBRUNE, M.
An Essay on Brewing. London: 1758. V. 53

COMBS, LESLIE
Gen. Combs' Claim on Texas. 1860. V. 49

COMBS, LOULA LONG
My Reveleation. Longview: 1947. V. 50

COMDEN, BETTY
Applause. New York: 1971. V. 50

COME and Go!. London: 1905. V. 50

COMELIUS, FRED
Tambalear the Tumbleweed and Other Southwestern Stories. El Paso: 1959. V. 51

COMENIUS, JOHANNES AMOS
Janua Linguarum Reserata...the gate of Languages Unlocked; or, a Seed-Plot of All Arts & Tongues... London: 1652. V. 47
The Labyrinth of the World and the Paradise of the Heart. Waltham St. Lawrence: 1950. V. 47
Orbis Sensualium Pictus...The Visible World, or a Nomenclature and Pictures of All the Chief Things That Are in the World. New York: 1810. V. 47; 50

COMERFORD, M.
Collections Relating to the Dioceses of Kildare and Leighlin. London. V. 47; 51; 54

COMERFORD, T.
The History of Ireland. Dublin: 1780. V. 52

COMFORT, J. W.
The Practice of Medicine on Thomsonian Principles...with Practical Directions for Administering a Thomsonian Course of Medicine... Philadelphia: 1843. V. 51; 52

THE COMIC Adventures of Old Mother Hubbard, and her Dog... London: 1850. V. 50

THE COMIC Adventures of Old Mother Hubbard, and her Dog. London: 1860. V. 52

THE COMIC Album: a Book for Every Table. London: 1844. V. 51

THE COMICAL Creatures from Wurtemburg. London: 1851. V. 47; 51

COMICAL Creatures; Picture Book for the Nursery: Comprising I. Comical Folks, Their Doings and Jokes. 2. Comical Creatures with Laughable Features. 3. Pussy's Tea-Party and other Stories. 4. The Weasel Family. London: 1868. V. 49

THE COMICAL Jester: of Laughable Companion. Lambeth: 1808. V. 48

COMINES, PHILIPPE DE, SIEUR D'ARGENTON
The Historie... London: 1596. V. 50; 54
The Historie... London: 1601. V. 52
The Historie. London: 1614. V. 50
The History... London: 1665. V. 50
Les Memoires sur Les Faicts & Gestes Abbregees de Loys XI & Charles VIII. Anvers: 1597. V. 48
The Memoirs. London: 1712. V. 51
The Memoirs. London: 1723. V. 53
The Memoirs. London: 1823. V. 50
The Memoirs. London: 1855. V. 52

COMINI, ALESSANDRA
Egon Schiele's Portraits. 1974. V. 49; 52; 54

COMISKEY, CHARLES A.
Commy. Chicago: 1919. V. 47

COMITIA Westmonasteriensium in Collegio Sti. Petri Habita Die Anniversario Fundatricis Suae Reginae Elizabethae Inauguarate Jan. XV. Londini: 1728. V. 50

COMMELIN, CASPARUS
Beschryvinge Van Amsterdam. Amsterdam: 1693. V. 48
Beschryvinge Van Amsterdam. Amsterdam: 1726. V. 53

COMMEMORATIVE Biographical Record of Dutchess County, New York... Chicago: 1897. V. 50

COMMENTS on the Proceedings and Evidence on the Charges Preferred by Mr. Huntington, M.P. Against the Government of Canada. Montreal: 1873. V. 47

COMMENTS on the Proposed War with France, On the State of Parties, and of the New Act Respecting Aliens. London: 1793. V. 47; 50

COMMERCE and Industry. London. V. 54

COMMERCIAL Advertiser Directory of the City of St. Paul, to Which is Added a Business Directory, 1858-59. Saint Paul: 1858. V. 48

COMMERCIAL CLUB OF NORTH YAKIMA
The Yakima Valley Washington. Yakima: 1904. V. 52

THE COMMERCIAL Handbook of the Telephone Service: Notes on the Business Side of the Telephone Service, for the Private Use of the National Telephone Co. Ltd. London: 1906. V. 50

COMMERELL, ABBE DE
An Account of the Culture and Use of the Mangel Wurzel, or Root of Scarcity. London: 1787. V. 53

COMMON, I. F. B.
Moths of Australia. East Melbourne: 1990. V. 49

COMMON Place Book Three. San Francisco: 1960. V. 48

A COMMON Place-Book of the Holy Bible: or, the Scripture's Sufficiency Practically Demonstrated... London: 1725. V. 49

A COMMON-Place Book With Something For Everybody. Aptos and Woodside: 1969. V. 48

COMMUCK, THOMAS
Indian Melodies. New York: 1845. V. 50

COMO, WILLIAM
Nureyev. New York: 1973. V. 50

COMPAGNO, L. J. V.
Sharks of the Order Carcharhiniformes. Lawrenceville: 1988. V. 50
Sharks of the World. Rome: 1984. V. 52

COMPAIGNON Vanden Verre-sienden Waerschovwer, Thoonende met Veele Redenen Waerom tot Bevestinghe vanden Staet van dese Landen, den Oorlogh veel Dienstiger is Dan den Treves (etc.). 'sGravenhage: 1621. V. 49

A COMPANION for Debtors and Prisoners and Advice to Creditors in Ten Letters. London: 1699. V. 48

A COMPANION to Every Place... London: 1772. V. 50
A COMPANION to Every Place... London: 1774. V. 50

A COMPARISON Between the Two Stages, with an Examen of the Generous Conquerer; and Some Critical Remarks on the Funeral, or Grief Alamode, the False Friend, Tamerlane and others. London: 1702. V. 48

A COMPENDIOUS Geographical and Historical Grammar... London: 1795. V. 51
A COMPENDIOUS Geographical and Historical Grammar... London: 1802. V. 51
A COMPENDIOUS Geographical and Historical Grammar... London: 1802/04. V. 52

COMPENDIOUS Geographical Dictionary, Containing a Concise Description of the Most Remarkable Places, Ancient and Modern, in Europe, Asia, Africa and America... London: 1695. V. 51

A COMPENDIOUS Library of the Law Necessary for Persons of All Degrees and Professions. London: 1743. V. 48
A COMPENDIOUS Library of the Law Necessary for Persons of All Degrees and Professions. London: 1757. V. 47

COMPILATION of Narratives of Explorations in Alaksa. Washington: 1900. V. 53

A COMPLAINT to the House of Commons, and Resolution Taken Up by the Free Protestant Subjects of the Cities of London and Westminster and the Counties Adjacent. Oxford (London): 1642. V. 53

THE COMPLEAT Brewer; or, the Art and Mystery of Brewing Explained. London: 1760. V. 48; 52

THE COMPLEAT Clerk, Containing the Best Forms of All Sorts of Presidents, for Conveyances & Assurances... London: 1677. V. 47

THE COMPLEAT Clerk, Containing the Best Forms of All Sorts of Presidents, For Conveyances & Assurances... London: 1683. V. 48; 52

THE COMPLEAT Dealer's Assistant; or, The Maltster's and Mealman's Useful Pocket Companion. London: 1760. V. 51

THE COMPLEAT Planter & Cyderist; or, Choice Collections and Observations for the Propagating All Manner of Fruit Trees and Most Approved Ways and Methods Yet Known for the Making and Ordering of Cyder and Other English Wines. London: 1685. V. 49

A COMPLETE Account of the Ceremonies Observed in the Coronations of the Kings and Queens of England... London: 1727. V. 48

THE COMPLETE Art of Boxing According to the Modern Method... London: 1788. V. 52

THE COMPLETE Cattle Doctor: a Treatise on the Diseases of Horned Cattle and Calves. Chicago: 1848. V. 54

A COMPLETE Collection of Protests from the Year MDCXLI to the Present Year MDCCXXXVII. London: 1737. V. 47; 50

A COMPLETE Collection of State Trials, and Proceedings for High-Treason, and Other Crimes and Misdeameanours.. London: 1776-81. V. 51

A COMPLETE Collection of State Trials, and Proceedings for High-Treason and Other Crimes and Misdemeanors... London: 1816-28. V. 49

A COMPLETE Collection of the Genuine Papers, &c. in the Case of John Wilkes, Esq... Paris: 1767. V. 48

THE COMPLETE Constable Directing All Constables, Headboroughs, Tithingmen, Churchwardens, Overseers of the Poor, Surveyors of the Highways and Scavengers in the Duty of Their Several Offices... London: 1692. V. 47

THE COMPLETE Distiller; Combining Theory and Practice and Explaining the Mysteries and Most Recent Improvements of Distilling and Brewing, in a Most Simple, Easy and Familiar Manner. Edinburgh: 1793. V. 54

THE COMPLETE Family-Piece; and, Country Gentlemen and Farmer's Best Guide. London: 1736. V. 50

THE COMPLETE Farmer; or a General Dictionary of Husbandry, In all Its Branches... London: 1766. V. 49; 54
THE COMPLETE Farmer; or a General Dictionary of Husbandry, In all Its Branches... London: 1769. V. 54

THE COMPLETE Farmer; or A General Dictionary of Husbandry in All Its Brancches... London: 1793. V. 49

THE COMPLETE Farmer; or, General Dictionary of Agriculture and Husbandry... London: 1807. V. 51

THE COMPLETE Farrier, or, Gentlemen's Travelling Companion. Philadelphia: 1809. V. 47; 54

THE COMPLETE Fisherman; or, Universal Angler; Containing Full Directions for Taking All Kinds of River Fish... London. V. 47

THE COMPLETE Free Mason, or Multa Paucis for Lovers of Secrets. London?: 1764?. V. 47

A COMPLETE Guide to All Persons Who Have Any Trade or Concern and the City of London, and Parts Adjacent... London: 1752. V. 53

A COMPLETE Guide to All Persons Who have Any Trade or Concern with the City of London and Parts Adjacent... London: 1763. V. 50

A COMPLETE Guide to the Leading Hotels... London: 1873. V. 52

A COMPLETE Guide to the Places of Amusement, Objects of Interests, Parks, Clubs, Markets, Docks, Leading Hotels... London: 1897. V. 52

A COMPLETE History of England; with the Lives of All the Kings and Queens Thereof; from the Earliest Account of Time, to the Death of His Late Majesty King William III. London: 1706. V. 53

A COMPLETE History of the "Great Eastern" From Her First Projection in 1850 to Her Visit to the Mersey in 1886. Liverpool: 1886. V. 48

A COMPLETE History of the Present War, From Its Commencement in 1756 to the End of the Campaign 1760. London: 1761. V. 47

THE COMPLETE Letter-Writer... London: 1772. V. 52
THE COMPLETE Letter-Writer... London: 1777. V. 54

THE COMPLETE Letter-Writer. Edinburgh: 1778. V. 52

THE COMPLETE Letter-Writer... Edinburgh: 1786. V. 54

THE COMPLETE Set of Pollock's Characters and Scenes in The Silver Palace or the Golden Poppy. London: 1880?. V. 49

THE COMPLETE Vermin-Killer. London: 1777. V. 49

A COMPLETE View of the Chinese Empire. London: 1798. V. 50

COMPTON, ARTHUR H.
X-Rays and Electrons: an Outline of Recent X-Ray Theory. New York: 1926. V. 54

COMPTON, H.
The Undertaker's Field. 1906. V. 51

COMPTON, HERBERT EASTWICK
A Particular Account of the European Military Adventurers of Hindustan from 1784 to 1803. London: 1892. V. 51; 54

THE COMPTON Marbling Portfolio of Patterns. London: 1992. V. 52

COMPTON, THOMAS
The Northern Cambrian Mountains: or, a Tour through North Wales. London: 1817. V. 47

COMPTON, WALTER A.
One Hundred Masterpieces from the Collection of Dr. Walter A. Compton... New York: 1992. V. 51

COMPTON-BURNETT, IVY
Dolores. Edinburgh and London: 1911. V. 53
A Family and a Fortune. London: 1939. V. 53
A Father and His Fate. London: 1957. V. 53
A Heritage and Its History. London: 1959. V. 53
Pastors and Masters. London: 1925. V. 48; 49; 51; 53
The Present and the Past. London: 1953. V. 53

COMRIE, JOHN DIXON
History of Scottish Medicine. London: 1932. V. 47; 49; 51; 52; 53

COMROE, BERNARD
Arthritis and Allied Conditions. Philadelphia: 1940. V. 48; 53

COMSTOCK, F. G.
A Practical Treatise on Culture of Silk, Adapted to the Soil and Climate of the United States. Hartford: 1839. V. 52; 54

COMSTOCK, J. A.
Butterflies of California. Los Angeles: 1927. V. 49

COMSTOCK, J. L.
The Young Botanist. New York: 1836. V. 49; 54

COMSTOCK, JOHN L.
History of the Greek Revolution... New York: 1828. V. 47
History of the Greek Revolution... New York: 1829. V. 49
History of the Greek Revolution. Hartford: 1853. V. 49

COMSTOCK, JOSEPH
The Tongue of Time, and Star of the States: a System of Human Nature, with the Phenomena of the Heavens and Earth. New York: 1838. V. 49

COMSTOCK, MARY B.
Greek, Etruscan and Roman Bronzes in the Museum of Fine Arts, Boston. Greenwich: 1971. V. 50; 52
Sculpture in Stone: The Greek, Roman and Etruscan Collection of the Museum of Fine Arts, Boston. Boston: 1976. V. 50

COMSTOCK, WILLIAM
Modern Architectural Designs and Details...in the Queen Anne, Eastlake, Elizabethan and Other Modernized Styles. New York: 1881. V. 52

COMSTOCK, WILLIAM T.
Bungalows, Camps and Mountain Houses. New York: 1908. V. 51

COMTE, ACHILLE
The Book of Birds. London: 1841. V. 54

COMTE, AUGUSTE
The Philosophy of Mathematics. New York: 1851. V. 51
The Positive Philosophy. London: 1853. V. 49; 50
System of Positive Polity. London: 1875-77. V. 49

COMTE, T.
Illustrations of Baptismal Fonts. London: 1844. V. 49

COMYN, F. F.
Service and Sport in the Sudan. London: 1911. V. 47

COMYNS, BARBARA
Sisters by a River. London: 1947. V. 47

CONANT, KENNETH JOHN
The Early Architectural History of the Cathedral of Santiago De Compostela. Cambridge: 1926. V. 54

CONANT, THOMAS
Upper Canada Sketches. Toronto: 1898. V. 53

CONARD, H. S.
The Waterlilies, a Monograph of the Genus Nymphaea. Washington: 1905. V. 51
The Waterlilies, a Monograph of the Genus Nymphaea. Bury St. Edmunds: 1991. V. 48

CONARD, HOWARD LOUIS
Uncle Dick Wooton, the Pioneer Frontiersman Of the Rocky Mountain Region. Chicago: 1890. V. 53

THE CONCERNED Photographer. New York: 1968/72. V. 52

CONCIDINE, J. FRANCIS
Singing Rails. Chicago: 1934. V. 49

A CONCISE Account, Historical and Descriptive of Lambeth Palace. London: 1806. V. 50

A CONCISE and Accurate Description of the University, Town and County of Cambridge... Cambridge: 1790. V. 52

A CONCISE Description of Bury St. Edmunds and Its Environs, Within the Distance of Ten Miles. London: 1827. V. 53

CONCISE Dictionary of American Biography. New York: 1990. V. 53

A CONCISE History of Birmingham; Containing an Account of Its Ancient State and the Latest Improvements... Birmingham: 1808. V. 47

A CONCISE Introduction to the Knowledge of the Most Eminent Painters...Intended to Instruct (As Well as to Assist the Memory Of) Those Gentlemen and Connoisseurs... London: 1778. V. 49

CONCLIN, GEORGE
Conclin's New River Guide, or a Gazetteer of All the Towns on the Western Waters... Cincinnati: 1855. V. 47

CONCORD Lectures on Philosophy Comprising Outlines of All the Lectures at the Concord Summer School of Philosophy in 1882 with an Historical Sketch... Cambridge: 1883. V. 54

CONCORDANTIE Maiores Biblie tam Dictionum Declinabilium... Basel: 1496. V. 48; 54

CONCORDATA Principum Nationis Germanicae cum Argumentis...Iam Additis. Strasbourg: 1513. V. 47; 51

CONDAMIND, M. DE LA
Journal of a Tour to Italy containing... London: 1763. V. 49

CONDE, JOSE ANTONIO
History of the Dominion of the Arabs in Spain. London: 1854-55. V. 49

CONDE, LOUIS I. DE
Sommaire Recveil des Choses Memorables. 1564. V. 53

CONDER, CLAUDE REIGNIER
Heth and Moab. Explorations in syria in 1881 and 1882. London: 1883. V. 49
Tent Work in Palestine. London: 1878. V. 48
Tent Work in Palestine. New York: 1878. V. 49; 51
Tent Work in Palestine. London: 1879. V. 49

CONDER, JAMES
An Arrangement of Provincial Coins, Tokens and Medalets, Issued in Great Britain, Ireland and the Colonies, Within the Last Twenty Years... Ipswich: 1798. V. 48
An Arrangement of Provincial Coins, Tokens and Medalets, Issued in Great Britain, Ireland and the Colonies, Within the Last Twenty Years.... Ipswich: 1799. V. 54

CONDER, JOSIAH
Africa. London: 1829. V. 51
The Associate Minstrels. London: 1810. V. 52
Birmah, Siam and Anam (sic). London: 1826. V. 51
Brazil and Buenos Aires. London: 1825. V. 51
Colombia. London: 1825. V. 51
Egypt, Nubia and Abyssinia. London: 1827. V. 51
The Floral Art of Japan. Tokio: 1899. V. 49
Greece. London: 1826. V. 51
India. London: 1828. V. 51
Landscape Gardening in Japan. Tokyo: 1912. V. 54
Mexico and Guatimala (sic). London: 1825. V. 51
North America. London: 1830. V. 51
Russia. London: 1825. V. 51
The Star in the East: with Other Poems. London: 1824. V. 48
The Theory of Japanese Flower Arrangements. Kobe and London: 1935. V. 49
Turkey. London: 1827. V. 51

CONDILLAC, ETIENNE BONNOT, ABBE DE
Traite des Animaux, ou Apres Avoir Fait des Observations Critiques sur le Sentiment de Descartes & sur Celui de M. de Buffon... Paris: 1755. V. 47

CONDIT, JOTHAM H.
Genealogical Record of the Condit Family. Descendants of John Cunditt, a Native of Great Britain, Who Settled in Newark, N.J. 1678-1885. 1916. V. 49; 51

CONDON, RICHARD
The Manchurian Candidate. New York, Toronto: 1959. V. 48; 49; 50; 51

CONDORCET, MARIE JEAN ANTOINE NICOLAS DE CARITAT, MARQUIS DE
Esquisse d'un Tableau Historique des Progres de l'Esprit Humain. Paris: 1795. V. 50
The Life of M. Turgot, comptroller General of the Finance of France in the Years 1774, 1775 and 1776... London: 1787. V. 49; 51
Outlines of an Historical View of the Progress of the Human Mind... London: 1795. V. 47; 49

CONDUCT. A Novel. London: 1814. V. 50

THE CONDUCT of a Certain Member of Parliament. During the Last Session and the Motives On Which He Acted; Explained in a letter to a Friend. Dublin: 1755. V. 49

THE CONDUCT of Queen Elizabeth, Towards the Neighbouring Nations; and Particularly Spain... London: 1629. V. 47

THE CONDUCT of Queen Elizabeth, Towards the Neighbouring Nations, and Particularly Spain... London: 1729. V. 48

THE CONDUCT of the Tories Consider'd. London: 1715. V. 53

CONDUCTOR Generalis, or The Office, Duty and Authority of Justices of the Peace, High-Sherriffs, Under-Sherrifs, Goalers, Coroners, Constables, Jury Men, Over-Seers of the Poor... Philadelphia: 1722. V. 48; 50

CONDY, NICHOLAS
Cothele, on the Banks of the Tamar, the Ancient Seat of the Right Honourable Earl of Mount Edgcumbe. London: 1840. V. 49

CONE, HELEN GRAY
Tiny Toddlers. London: 1890. V. 49

CONE, MARY
Two Years in California. Chicago: 1876. V. 49; 50; 51; 53

CONEL, J. LE ROY
The Postnatal Development of the Human Cerebral Cortex. Cambridge: 1939-47. V. 52

CONESTAGGIO, GIROLAMO
The Historie of the Uniting of the Kingdom of Portugal to the Crowne of Castill. London: 1600. V. 51

THE CONFEDERATE States Almanac...1862. Nashville: 1862. V. 49

THE CONFEDERATE States Almanac...1865. Macon: 1865. V. 49

CONFEDERATE STATES OF AMERICA
An Act to Perpetuate Testimony in Cases of Slaves Abducted or Harbored by the Enemy, and of Other Property Seized, Wasted or Destroyed by Them. Richmond: 1861. V. 48
An Act to Recognize the Existence of War Between the United States and the Confederate States; and Concerning letters of Marque, Prizes and Prize Goods. Montgomery?: 1861. V. 50
Address of Congress to the People of the Confederate States. Richmond: 1864. V. 50
A Bill to be Entitled an Act to Grant a Special Copyright to W. J. Hardee and S. H. Goetzel, for Hardee's Rifle and Infantry Tactics. Richmond: 1863. V. 50
A Bill To Be Entitled an Act to Provide for Organizing, Arming and Disciplining the Militia of the Confederate States... Richmond: 1864. V. 48
A Bill to Increase the Efficiency of the Cavalry of the Confederate States. Richmond: 1865. V. 48
Journal of the Congress of the Confederate States of America, 1861-1865. Washington: 1904-05. V. 52
Letter from Gen. Wise. Headquarters 6th Military District, Department South Carolina, Georgia and Florida, January 3, 1864. To Hon. Jas. Lyons, John R. Chambliss and Others, of the Virginia Delegation in Congress (Endorsing and Enclosing the ...). Richmond: 1864. V. 49
Message of the President. Richmond, Va., Dec. 16, 1863. Richmond: 1863. V. 49
Military Laws of the Confederate States, Embracing All the Legislation of Congress Appertaining to Military Affairs from the First to the Last Session Inclusive... Richmond: 1863. V. 52
Ordnance Instructions for the Confederate States Navy Relating to the Preparation of Vessels of War for Battle, to the Duties of Officers and Others When at Quarters, to Ordnance and Ordnance Stores, and to Gunnery. London: 1864. V. 53
Report of the Attorney General...1st November, 1864. Richmond: 1864. V. 49
Report Of the Special Committee on the Pay and Clothing of the Army. Richmond: 1865. V. 49
Reports of the Operations of the Army of Northern Virginia, from June 1862 to and Including the Battle of Fredericksburg, Dec. 13, 1862. Richmond: 1864. V. 49
Resolutions Adopted by the Officers and Men of the 57th Virginia Regiment... Richmond: 1865. V. 47
Resolutions of Wise's Brigade. Richmond: 1865. V. 47
Rules for Conducting Business in the Senate of the Confederate States of America. Richmond: 1864. V. 47
The Statutes at Large of the Provisional Government of the Confederate States of America...Together with the Constitution for the Provisional Government... Richmond: 1864. V. 50
Substitute for the Bill (H.R. 229) to Provide More Effectually for the Reduction and Redemption of the Currency. Richmond: 1864. V. 53

CONFEDERATE STATES OF AMERICA. ARMY
General Order, No. 11. Petersburg: 1864. V. 54
General Order, No. 12. Petersburg: 1864. V. 54
General Order, No. 6. Petersburg: 1864. V. 54
Regulations for the Army of the Confederate States... Richmond: 1863. V. 49
Regulations for the Army of the Confederate States... Richmond: 1864. V. 49
Regulations for the Army of the Confederate States 1862. Richmond: 1862. V. 49; 52; 54

CONFEDERATE STATES OF AMERICA. BUREAU OF PUBLIC PRINTING
Report of the Superintendent of Public Printing...Apri. 26, 1864. Richmond: 1864. V. 54

CONFEDERATE STATES OF AMERICA. CONGRESS
A Bill to Increase the Efficency of the Cavalry of the Confederate States. Richmond: 186-. V. 51; 54
Report from the Joint Select Committee to Investigate the Management of the Navy Department. Richmond: 1864. V. 54

CONFEDERATE STATES OF AMERICA. CONSTITUTION
Constitution of the Confederate States of America. Richmond: 1861. V. 48
The Constitution of the Confederate States of America, Adopted March 11, 1861. 1861. V. 52

CONFEDERATE STATES OF AMERICA. DEPARTMENT OF JUSTICE
Report of Vessels Sunk and Burnt in the Pamunkey River, by Capt. Chas. S. Carrington, A.Q.M., Under the Orders of General Joseph Johnston and Others. Richmond: 1863. V. 54

CONFEDERATE STATES OF AMERICA. DEPARTMENT OF STATE
Correspondence of the Department of State, in Relation to the British Consuls Resident in the Confederate States. Richmond: 1863. V. 54

CONFEDERATE STATES OF AMERICA. HOUSE OF REPRESENTATIVES
...A Bill Regulating the Granting of Furloughs and Discharges in Hospitals. Richmond: 1863. V. 54
...A Bill to be Entitled an Act to Authorize the 2d Auditor of the Treasury, or a Commissoner, to be Appointed by the Secretary of the Treasury with the consent of the President to Take Proof as to the Expenditures of the State of Tennessee... Richmond: 1864. V. 54
...A Bill to be Entitled An Act to Compensate Charles E. Stuart, Israel C. Ownings and J. H. Taylor for the Use of an Improvement in Instruments for Sighting Cannon. Richmond: 1864. V. 54
...A Bill to Be Entitled an Act to Increase the Efficency of the Army by the Employment of Free Negroes and Slaves in Certain Capacities. Richmond: 1864. V. 54
...A Bill to Be Entitled an Act to Organize the Supreme Court. Richmond: 1864. V. 54
...A Bill to be Entitled an act to Provide for Keeping in Repair the Railraods of the Confederate States Necessary for the Transportation of Troops and Government Supplies. Richmond: 1863. V. 54
...A Bill to Increase the Number of acting Midshipmen in the Navy, and to Prescribe the Manner of Appointment. Richmond: 1864. V. 54
...A Bill to Provide for the Establishment of a Bureau of Special and Secret Service. Richmond: 1864. V. 54
...A Bill to Regulate Furloughs and Discharges to Soldiers in Hospitals. Richmond: 1863. V. 54
Joint Resolution of Confidence in and Thanks to President Jefferson Davis... Richmond: 1865. V. 51
Joint Resolutions Expressing the Sense of Congress on the Subject of the Late Peace Commission. Richmond: 1865. V. 54
...Resolutions Adopted by McGowan's Brigade, South Carolina Volunteers. Richmond: 1865. V. 54

CONFEDERATE STATES OF AMERICA. LAWS, STATUTES, ETC.
An Act to Perpetuate Testimony in Case of Slaves Abducted or Harbored by the Enemy, and Of Other Property Seized, wasted, or Destroyed by Them. Richmond: 1861. V. 54
The Statutes at Large of the Confederate States of America, Passed at the First Session of the Second Congress: 1864... Richmond: 1864. V. 47
The Statutes at Large of the Confederate States of America, Passed at the Fourth Session of the First Congress: 1863-64. Richmond: 1864. V. 47
The Statutes at Large of the Confederate States of America, Passed at the Second Session of the First Congress; 1862... Richmond: 1862. V. 47
The Statutes at Large of the Confederate States of America, Passed at the Third Session of the First Congress: 1863. Richmond: 1863. V. 47

CONFEDERATE STATES OF AMERICA. NAVY DEPARTMENT
Communication from the Secretary of the Navy...Feb. 15, 1865 (Conveying Copies of the Remainder of His Correspondence With the Governor of North Carolina, Relative to "Coals of the Steamer 'Advance'"). Richmond: 1865. V. 54
Ordnance Instructions for the Confederate States Navy Relating to the Preparation of Vessels of War for Battle, to the Duties of Officers and Others When at Quarters, to Ornance and Ordnance Stores, and to Gunnery. London: 1864. V. 54

CONFEDERATE STATES OF AMERICA. POST OFFICE DEPARTMENT
Report of the Postmaster General...May 2, 1864. Richmond: 1864. V. 54
Report of the Postmaster General...November 7, 1864. Richmond: 1864. V. 54

CONFEDERATE STATES OF AMERICA. PRESIDENT
Inaugural Address of President Davis, Delivered at the Capitol, Monday, Feb. 18, 1861, at 1 O'Clock P.M. Montgomery: 1861. V. 49

CONFEDERATE STATES OF AMERICA. SENATE
An Act to Amend an Act Entitled "an Act to Increase the Efficiency of the Army by Employing Free Negroes and Slaves in Certain Capacities, Approved February 17th, 1864". Richmond: 1864. V. 54
Amendment to Senate Bill (S. 129) to Provide for the Employment of Free Negroes and Slaves to Work Upon fortifications, and to Perform Other Labor Connected with the Defences of the Country. Richmond: 1864. V. 54

CONFEDERATE STATES OF AMERICA. TREASURY DEPARTMENT
Communications from the Secretaries of the Treasury and of War Relative to the Amount of Money Forwarded to the Trans-Mississippi Department Since the Adjournment of Congress, and to the Adjustment of Claims for Articles Illegally Impressed. Richmond: 1864. V. 54

CONFEDERATE STATES OF AMERICA. WAR DEPARTMENT
Communication of the Secretary of War...Feb. 3, 1863, (Covering the Reports from the Surgeon General and the Chief of Engineers). Richmond: 1863. V. 54

CONFERENCE OF MINISTERS OF ALL DENOMINATIONS ON THE CORN LAW
Report of the Conference...Held in Manchester, August 17th, 18th, 19th, and 20th, 1841. Manchester: 1841. V. 54

CONFESSIO Fidei, Anno MDXXX in Comitiis Avgvstanis Invictissimo Imperatori Carolo V. Exhibta. Francoforti ad Moenvm: 1591. V. 53

CONFESSIO Fidei Exhibita Inuictiss. Imp. Carolo V. Caesari Aug. In Comicijs Augustae Anno MDXXX. Addita Est Apologia Confessionis. Witebergae: 1531. V. 53

THE CONFESSION and Execution of the Seven Prisoners Suffering at Tyburn on Fryday the 4th of May, 1677. London: 1677. V. 53

CONFESSION of Faith and Covenant of the Independent Presbyterian Church, in Savannah, Georgia, With a Catalogue of its Members, July 1858. Savannah: 1858. V. 50

CONFESSION of Faith Owned and Consented to By the Elders and Messengers of the Churches in the Colony of Connecticut in New-England, Assembled by Delegation at Say-Brook September 9th, 1708. New London: 1710. V. 50

THE CONFESSION of Jesse Strang, Who Was Executed at Albany August 24, 1827, for the Murder of John Whipple. Albany: 1827. V. 47

THE CONFESSIONS of a Gamester. London: 1824. V. 51

THE CONFESSIONS of a Lady's Maid; or, Boudoir Intrigue, Disclosing Many Startling Scenes and Voluptuous Incidents as Witnessed by Her in the Various Families of Distinction With Whom She Lived... London: 1860. V. 51

CONFESSIONS of an English Hashish Eater. London: 1884. V. 50

CONFUCIUS
The Analects... Shanghai: 1933. V. 51; 52; 54
The Analects. Los Angeles: 1970. V. 53; 54
Analects. New York: 1970. V. 47; 48; 51; 52; 53; 54
Confucius Sinarum Philosophus, sive Scientia Siensis Latine Exposita...Eximio Missionum Orientalium, Litterariae Reipublicae Bono e Bibliotheca Regia in Lucem Prodit. Paris: 1686-87. V. 47
Moral Sayings of Confucius, a Chinese Philosopher, Who Lived Five Hundred and Fifty-One Years Before the Christian Era. Cleveland: 1855. V. 49
The Morals of Confucius a Chinese Philosopher... London: 1706. V. 49

CONGAR, STEPHEN
Herbert Wendall: a Tale of the Revolution. New York: 1835. V. 51

CONGDON, LENORE O. KEENE
Caryatid Mirrors of Ancient Greece: Technical, Stylistic and Historical Considerations of an Archaic and Early Classical Bronze Series. Mainz am Rhein: 1981. V. 50; 52

CONGER, ROGER N.
Highlights of Waco History. Waco: 1945. V. 48

CONGREGATIO DE PROPAGANDA FIDE
Librorum Catalogus... Rome: 1765. V. 54

CONGREGATIONAL CHURCH IN THE UNITED STATES
A Book of Plans for Churches and Parsonages...Comprising Designs by Upjohn, Renwick, Wheeler. New York: 1853. V. 52

CONGREGATIONAL CHURCHES OF MASSACHUSETTS
Proceedings of the Convention of Congregational Ministers. Boston: 1795. V. 48

THE CONGRESS of the Beasts, Under the Mediation of the Goat, for Negotiating a Peace Between the Fox, the Ass Wearing a Lion's Skin, the Horse, the Tigress and Other Quadrupeds at War. London: 1748. V. 52

CONGREVE, CELIA
The Transvaal War Alphabet. Manchester: 1900. V. 52

CONGREVE, WILLIAM
Complete Works. London: 1923. V. 48; 50; 53; 54
The Double-Dealer, a Comedy. London: 1694. V. 47; 54
Love for Love: a Comedy... London: 1695. V. 47
The Mourning Bride, a Tragedy. London: 1697. V. 47
The Mourning Muse of Alexis. London: 1695. V. 54
The Way of the World & Love for Love. London: 1929. V. 54
The Way of the World, a Comedy. London: 1700. V. 52; 53
The Works... London: 1710. V. 50
The Works... London: 1730. V. 48; 51
The Works... Birmingham: 1761. V. 47; 48; 49; 50; 52
The Works... London: 1788. V. 54

CONINGESBY, GEORGE
A Sermon Preach'd at the Cathedral Church of Hereford, at the Anniversary Meeting of Three Choirs, Hereford, Worcester and Gloucester, on Wednesday, September 6th, 1732. Oxford: 1733. V. 47

CONJURING; or, Magic Made Easy. New York: 1870. V. 51

CONKLIN, ENOCH
Picturesque Arizona. New York: 1878. V. 47; 51

CONKLING, ROSCOE P.
The Butterfield Overland Mail. Glendale: 1947. V. 47; 49; 50; 53; 54

CONLEY, JOHN
Regional Flaps of the Head and Neck. Philadelphia London: 1976. V. 54

CONLIFFE, MARGARET
The Martyrdom of an Empress. New York: 1902. V. 51

CONN, GEORGE
De Dvplici Statv Religionis Apvd Scotos Libri Duo. Rome: 1628. V. 47; 52

CONN, WILLIAM
Cowboys and Colonels. London: 1888. V. 53

CONNECTICUT. (COLONY). LAWS, STATUTES, ETC. - 1901
Acts and Laws of His Majesties Colony of Connecticut in New England. 1901. V. 47

CONNELL, EVAN S.
The Anatomy Lesson and Other Stories. New York: 1957. V. 47; 49; 50; 53
The Diary of a Rapist. New York: 1966. V. 52
Mesa Verde. New York: 1993. V. 51; 53
Mr. Bridge. New York: 1969. V. 50
Mrs. Bridge. New York: 1959. V. 47; 49; 52
Son of the Morning Star. San Francisco: 1984. V. 47; 48; 50; 51; 52; 53

CONNELL, NICHOLAS
At Fields End Interviews with Twenty Northwest Writers. Seattle: 1987. V. 51

CONNELLAN, OWEN
The Annals of Ireland... Dublin: 1846. V. 51

CONNELLEY, WILLIAM ELSEY
Doniphan's Expedition and the Conquest of New Mexico and California. Kansas City: 1907. V. 52
History of Kansas State and People. Chicago and New York: 1928. V. 53
Quantrill and the Border Wars. Cedar Rapids: 1909. V. 53
Quantrill and the Border Wars. Cedar Rapids: 1910. V. 48; 49; 50
War With Mexico 1846-1847. Doniphan's Expedition and the Conquest of New Mexico and California. Topeka: 1907. V. 53
Wild Bill and His Era. New York: 1933. V. 53

CONNELLY, HENRY
The First Annual Message of Governor Connelly, Delivered Before the Legislative Assembly of the Territory of New Mexico, December 4, 1861. Santa Fe: 1861. V. 48

CONNELLY, MARC
Beggar on Horseback. New York: 1924. V. 50
The Green Pastures. V. 50
The Green Pastures. New York: 1929. V. 47; 51; 54
The Green Pastures. New York: 1930. V. 47; 48; 49; 51; 52

CONNELLY, MICHAEL
The Black Echo. Boston: 1992. V. 52

CONNER, NELLIE VICTORIA
Essence of Good Perfume. A Book of Poems. Burbank: 1940. V. 53; 54

CONNETT, EUGENE V.
American Sporting Dogs. New York: 1948. V. 52
A Decade of Sporting Books and Prints. New York: 1937. V. 47; 51
Duck Shooting Along the Atlantic Tidewater. New York: 1947. V. 47
Feathered Game from a Sporting Journal. New York: 1929. V. 47
Fishing a Trout Stream. New York: 1934. V. 53
Upland Game Bird Shooting in America. New York: 1930. V. 47; 52; 54

CONNICK, CHARLES J.
Adventures in Light and Color. New York: 1937. V. 47; 50; 51; 53

CONNOLD, E. T.
British Vegetable Galls. London: 1910. V. 54

CONNOLLY, CYRIL
The Condemned Playground. Essays 1927-1944. London: 1945. V. 49
Enemies of Promise. London: 1938. V. 52; 53
Enemies of Promise. New York: 1948. V. 50
Enemies of the Realm. London: 1949. V. 47
The Evening Colonnade. London: 1973. V. 50
The Modern Movement. London: 1965. V. 47; 49; 51; 52; 53
The Modern Movement. New York: 1966. V. 52
The Rock Pool. Paris: 1936. V. 49; 51; 52; 54
The Unquiet Grave. 1944. V. 52
The Unquiet Grave. London: 1944. V. 49; 50; 51
The Unquiet Grave. London: 1945. V. 49

CONNOLLY, JAMES B.
An Olympic Victor: a Story of the Modern Games. New York: 1908. V. 53

CONNOLLY, NORA
The Unbroken Tradition. New York: 1918. V. 48

CONNOR, LOUISE S.
Crying' for Daylight. Austin: 1989. V. 53

CONNOR, ROBERT
Buffalo Soldiers. New York: 1993. V. 50

CONNOR, SEYMOUR V.
Dear America: Some Letters of Orange Cicero Connor and Mary America (Aikin) Connor. Austin: 1971. V. 47
The Saga of Texas... 1965. V. 53
Saga of Texas. Austin: 1965. V. 50
Texas Treasury Papers. Austin: 1955/56. V. 53

CONOLLY, JOHN
An Inquiry Concerning the Indications of Insanity with Suggestions for the Better Protection and Care of the Insane. London: 1830. V. 52
The Physician: I. The Cholera. London: 1832. V. 51
The Treatment of the Insane Without Mechanical Restraints. London: 1856. V. 52

CONOR, WILLIAM
The Irish Scene. London: 1944. V. 53

CONOVER, GEORGE W.
Sixty Years in Southwest Oklahoma...Thrilling Incidents of Indian Life in Oklahoma and Texas. Anadarko: 1927. V. 48; 49

CONRAD, BORYS
My Father: Joseph Conrad. London: 1970. V. 53

CONRAD, H. S.
The Waterlilies, a Monograph of the Genus Nymphaea. Washington: 1905. V. 52
The Waterlilies, a Monograph of the Genus Nymphaea. Bury St. Edmunds: 1991. V. 50; 52

CONRAD, JESSIE
A Handbook of Cookery. London: 1923. V. 49; 50; 51; 52
A Handbook of Cookery... New York: 1923. V. 49

CONRAD, JOSEPH
Admiralty Paper. New York: 1925. V. 47
Almayer's Folly. London: 1895. V. 49
Almayer's Folly. New York: 1895. V. 47; 49; 50; 51; 54
Almayer's Folly... London: 1896. V. 54
Almayer's Folly. London: 1898. V. 47
The Arrow of Gold. London: 1919. V. 47; 48; 49; 51
The Arrow of Gold. New York: 1919. V. 49
Chance. New York: 1913. V. 49
Chance... Toronto: 1913. V. 47
Chance. London: 1914. V. 48; 49; 50; 54
The Children of the Sea: A Tale of the Forecastle. New York: 1897. V. 47; 53
Collected Works. Garden City: 1925. V. 52
Collected Works... New York: 1925. V. 51
The Complete Short Stories of Joseph Conrad. London: 1930's. V. 53
Conrad to a Friend: 150 Selected Letters from Conrad to Richard Curle 1928. London: 1928. V. 53
Conrad's Manifesto: Preface to a Career. Philadelphia: 1966. V. 51; 52; 54
The Dover Patrol. Canterbury: 1922. V. 48; 49; 53; 54
Falk. New York: 1903. V. 48; 51; 53
Geography and Some Explorers. London: 1924. V. 51
Heart of Darkness. New York: 1969. V. 53
The Inheritors. 1901. V. 50; 51
The Inheritors. London: 1901. V. 49
The Inheritors. New York: 1901. V. 51
John Galsworthy. An Appreciation. Canterbury: 1922. V. 49; 53; 54
Joseph Conrad on the Art of Writing. New York: 1914. V. 49
Joseph Conrad's Letters to His Wife. London: 1927. V. 47
Last Essays. London: 1926. V. 52
Laughing Anne. London: 1923. V. 47; 49; 53
Letters from Conrad 1892 to 1924. London: 1928. V. 47; 50; 51; 52
Letters of Joseph Conrad to Richard Curle. New York: 1928. V. 48
Letters to Marguerite Poradowska. New Haven: 1940. V. 49
Lord Jim. Edinburgh & London: 1900. V. 50; 51; 52; 53; 54
Lord Jim. New York: 1900. V. 49
Lord Jim. New York: 1916. V. 51; 52
Manifesto: Preface to a Career, The History of the Preface to the Nigger of the 'Narcissus' with Facsimiles of the Manuscripts... Philadelphia: 1966. V. 49; 51
The Medallion Edition of the Works. London: 1925. V. 49
The Medallion Edition of the Works... London: 1925-28. V. 49
The Mirror of the Sea. New York and London: 1906. V. 48; 49; 50; 51; 53; 54
The Nature of a Crime. Garden City: 1924. V. 49
The Nature of a Crime. London: 1924. V. 48; 50; 52; 53
The Nigger of "Narcissus.". London: 1898. V. 47; 48; 53
The Nigger of the "Narcissus.". Nythe: 1902. V. 48
Nostromo. New York & London: 1904. V. 47; 49; 51; 52; 53; 54
Nostromo. London: 1918. V. 51
Nostromo... 1961. V. 52
Notes on Life and Letters. London: 1921. V. 47
Notes on My Books. Garden City: 1921. V. 54
Notes on My Books. London: 1921. V. 48; 49; 53; 54
Novels and Stories. New York: 1925. V. 51
One Day More. London: 1917. V. 49
One Day More. London: 1919. V. 49
One Day More. Garden City: 1920. V. 52; 54
One Day More. New York: 1920. V. 49; 53
An Outcast of the Islands. London: 1896. V. 47; 48; 49; 50; 51; 53; 54
An Outcast of the Islands. New York: 1896. V. 49; 53; 54
An Outcast of the Islands. Connecticut: 1975. V. 47
A Personal Record. New York: 1912. V. 49; 51; 52; 54
A Personal Record. London: 1919. V. 50
The Point of Honor. New York: 1908. V. 49; 50; 51; 52; 54
Preface to The Nigger of the Narcissus. Lebanon: 1927. V. 53
The Rescue. London: 1920. V. 47; 48; 52
Romance. London: 1903. V. 49
Romance. New York: 1904. V. 49; 52
The Rover. Garden City: 1923. V. 47; 48; 49; 51
The Rover. London: 1923. V. 47; 48; 51; 52; 53; 54
The Rover. New York: 1923. V. 51; 54
The Secret Agent. London: 1907. V. 51
The Secret Agent. New York: 1907. V. 47; 51; 54
The Secret Agent. Canterbury: 1921. V. 53
The Secret Agent. London: 1923. V. 48; 49; 50; 52
The Secret Sharer. 1985. V. 52; 54
The Secret Sharer. New York: 1985. V. 48; 50; 51
A Set of Six. London: 1908. V. 49; 51
The Shadow Line, a Confession. London & Toronto: 1917. V. 53; 54
The Shadow Line: a Confession. Garden City: 1923. V. 54
The Sisters. New York: 1928. V. 47; 49; 50; 51; 53
Some Reminiscences. London: 1912. V. 49; 50; 51
Suspense. London & Toronto: 1925. V. 48; 49; 50; 53
Suspense. New York: 1925. V. 51; 53
Tales of Hearsay. London: 1925. V. 48; 49; 50; 51; 52; 53; 54
Tales of the Sea. London: 1919. V. 50
Tales of Unrest. London: 1898. V. 47; 50; 51; 54
Tales of Unrest. New York: 1898. V. 48; 49
To My Brethren of the Pen. London: 1927. V. 53; 54
The Tremolino. New York: 1942. V. 48; 51
Twixt Land and Sea... London: 1912. V. 48; 49; 50; 51
Twixt Land and Sea. New York: 1912. V. 47
Twixt Land and Sea. London: 1925. V. 53
Typhoon. London: 1902. V. 47
Typhoon. London: 1903. V. 47; 48; 50; 51; 53; 54
Under Western Eyes. London: 1911. V. 48; 53; 54
Under Western Eyes. New York: 1911. V. 49; 50; 53
The Uniform Edition of the Works, plus Notes on Life and Letters. London: 1923-24. V. 50
Victory... Garden City: 1915. V. 54
Victory. London: 1915. V. 47; 50; 51
Within the Tides. London: 1915. V. 47; 48; 50
The Works... London: 1921. V. 51; 53
The Works. London: 1921-27. V. 49
The Works.. London: 1923-28. V. 51
The Works... New York: 1924. V. 53
Works. New York: 1925. V. 47
Works. Garden City: 1929. V. 49; 51
The Works... New York: 1938. V. 53
Youth. Edinburgh & London: 1902. V. 47; 49; 50; 51; 53; 54
Youth. 1903. V. 50
Youth. Kentfield: 1959. V. 47; 48; 49; 51; 53; 54

CONRAD, JOSEPH, MRS.
Did Joseph Conrad Return as a Spirit?. Webster Groves: 1932. V. 53

CONRADS, ULRICH
The Architecture of Fantasy - Utopian Building and Planning in Modern Times. New York: 1962. V. 53; 54

CONRADUS DE HALBERSTADT
Concordantie Maiores Biblie tam Dictionum Declinabilium... Basel: 1496. V. 53

CONREAL, FRANCOIS
Voyages de...Aux Indes Occidentales... Amsterdam: 1722. V. 54

CONROY, CAROL
The Jewish Furrier. Atlanta: 1981. V. 48

CONROY, FRANK
Body & Soul. Boston: 1993. V. 53
Stop Time. New York: 1967. V. 49; 51

CONROY, PAT
Beach Music. New York: 1995. V. 54
The Boo. Verona: 1970. V. 47; 49; 51; 52
The Boo. Verona: 1971. V. 49; 51
The Boo. Atlanta: 1988. V. 49; 51; 53; 54
The Boo. New York: 1988. V. 51
The Great Santini. Boston: 1976. V. 48; 49; 50; 51; 52; 53
The Lords of Discipline. Boston: 1980. V. 47; 51; 53
The Lords of Discipline. London: 1981. V. 54
The Prince of Tides. V. 52
The Prince of Tides. Boston: 1986. V. 47; 48; 50; 53; 54
The Prince of Tides. New York: 1986. V. 50
The Water is Wide. Boston: 1972. V. 48; 49; 50; 51; 52; 53; 54
The Water is Wide. Boston: 1976. V. 53

CONSEQUENCES; a Complete Story in the Manner of the Old Parlour Game in Nine Chapters, Each by a Different Author. Waltham St. Lawrence: 1932. V. 47; 52

CONSIDERATIONS Against Laying Any New Duty Upon Sugar; Wherein Is Particularly Shewn, that a New Imposition Will be Ruinous to the Sugar Colonies, Insufficient for the Purposes Intended and Greatly Conducive to the Aggrandizement of France. London: 1744. V. 48; 52

CONSIDERATIONS on the Acts of Parliament Relative to Highways in Scotland, and on the New Scheme of a Tax in Lieu of Statue-Labour. Edinburgh: 1764. V. 48; 52

CONSIDERATIONS on the Bill for the Better Government of the Navy. London: 1749. V. 48

CONSIDERATIONS On the Bill to Permit Persons Professing the Jewish Religion To Be Naturalized by Parliament. London: 1753. V. 48

CONSIDERATIONS on the Expedience of Spanish War: Containing Reflections On the Late Demands of Spain; and on the Negociations of Mons. Bussy. London: 1761. V. 52

CONSIDERATIONS on the Nature and Objects of the Intended Light and Heat Company, Published by Authority of the Committee. London: 1808. V. 50

CONSIDERATIONS on the Political and Commercial Circumstances of G.B. & Ireland. London: 1787. V. 48; 52

CONSIDERATIONS on Two Papers, Published at Antwerp, Respecting a Loan for 3,600,00 Guilders, to be Subscribed at the Houses of Messieurs J. E. Werbrouck and C. J. M. De Wolf, of that City. London: 1791. V. 52

CONSIDERATIONS Relating to a New Duty Upon Sugar. London: 1746. V. 48

CONSIDERATIONS Upon a Proposal for Lowering the Interest of All the Redeemable National Debts to Three Per Cent...To give Immediate Ease to His Majesty's Subjects... London: 1737. V. 47; 52

CONSIDERATIONS Upon the Intended Navigable Communication Between the firth of Forth and Clyde. 1767. V. 52; 54

CONSOLIDATED SILVER MINING CO.
Property of the Consolidated Silver Mining Company, Reese River and Union Districts, Nevada. Boston: 1865. V. 49

CONSTABLE, HENRY
The Poems and Sonnets. 1897. V. 47; 52
The Poems and Sonnets... London: 1897. V. 50

CONSTABLE, HENRY STRICKLAND
Doctors, Vaccination and Utilitarianism. London: 1873. V. 50; 52

CONSTABLE, J.
Wyndham Lewis and I. A. Richards. A Friendship Documented 1928-1957. London: 1989. V. 50

CONSTABLE, JOHN
The Conversation of Gentlemen Considered in Most of the Ways, that Make Their Mutual Company, Agreeable, or Disagreeable. London: 1738. V. 47
English Landscape Scenery. London: 1855. V. 52

CONSTABLE, W. G.
Canaletto, Giovanni Antonio Canal 1697-1768. Oxford: 1976. V. 49; 51; 54
Exhibition of British primitive Paintings from the 12th to the Early 16th Century with Some Related Illuminated manuscripts, Figure Embroidery and Alabaster Carvings... London: 1924. V. 49; 51; 53
Richard Wilson. Cambridge: 1953. V. 51
Richard Wilson. London: 1953. V. 49; 52; 54

CONSTABLE-MAXWELL, ANDREW
Catalogue of the Constable-Maxwell Collection of Ancient Glass. London: 1979. V. 50; 52

CONSTANT, BENJAMIN
Adolphe. Monaco: 1945. V. 54

CONSTANT, SAMUEL VICTOR
Calls Sounds and Merchandise of the Peking Street Peddlers. Peking: 1936. V. 48
Calls, Sounds and Merchandise of the Peking Street Peddlers. Newtown: 1993. V. 50; 51

CONSTANTIA; Or, A True Picture of Human Life, Represented in Fifteen Evening Conversations, After the Manner of Boccace... Dublin: 1751. V. 47

CONSTANTIA; or, a True Picture of Human Life, Represented in Fifteen Evening Conversations After the Manner of Boccace. London: 1751. V. 47

CONSTANTINE, K. C.
Always a Body to Trade. Boston: 1983. V. 50
The Rocksburg Railroad Murders. 1972. V. 53
The Rocksburg Railroad Murders. New York: 1972. V. 47

CONSTANTINE, MILDRED
Tina Modotti. A Fragile Life. New York: 1975. V. 47

CONSTANTINI, ROBERT
Lexicon Graecolatinum... Geneva: 1592. V. 51

A CONSTITUENT'S Answer to the Reflexions of a Member of Parliament Upon the Present State of Affairs at Home and Abroad, Particularly With Regard to Subsidies and the Differences Between Great Britain and France. London: 1755. V. 53

CONSTITUTION of the "United Germans" at Teutonia. Harrisburg?: 1827?. V. 53

THE CONSTITUTIONS of the Several Independent States of America... Phlladelphia (sic): 1781. V. 54

THE CONSTITUTIONS of the United States, According to the Latest Amendments. To Which Are Prefixed, the Declaration of Independence and the Federal Constitution. Philadelphia: 1804. V. 53

CONTACT Collection of Contemporary Writers. Paris: 1925. V. 53

CONTAGIOUS Diseases of Domesticated Animals. Washington: 1881. V. 51; 53

CONTANT, GEORGE C.
A Pardoned Lifer: Life of George Sontag, Former Member Notorious Evans-Sontag Gang Train Robbers. San Bernardino: 1909. V. 50

CONTARINI, GASPARO
La Republica, ei Magistrati di Vinegia.... Venice: 1544. V. 50

CONTARINI, LUIGI
Il Vago, & Diletteuole Giardino ove si Leggono...et in Questa Impressione Accresciuto di Bellissime Figure, et di Noua Aggiunta. Venice: 1619. V. 51

CONTENTMENT; Or Hints to Servants On the Present Scarcity. A Poetical Epistle. London: 1800. V. 53

THE CONTEST. A Poem. London: 1764. V. 54

CONTI, ARMAND DE BOURBON, PRINCE DE
The Works. (with) some Other Pieces, and a Discourse of Christian Perfection, by the Archbishop of Cambray... London: 1711. V. 49; 53

CONTINUATION of the First Principles of Christianity. Halifax: 1810. V. 49

CONTOLI, GIOVANNI BATTISTA
De Lapididvs Podagra, et Chiragra in Humano Corpore Productis... Rome: 1699. V. 54

THE CONTRAST; Or the Evils of War, and the Blessings of Christianity Exemplified, in the Life and Adventures of Paul Placid. London: 1830-35. V. 50

CONTRIBUTIONS to Medical and Biological Research Dedicated to Sir William Osler...In Honor of His Seventieth Birthday July 12, 1919 by His Pupils and Co-Workers. New York: 1919. V. 49; 51; 52

CONTRIBUTIONS to the History Society of Montana. Montana: 1896. V. 50

CONTRIBUTIONS to the Medical Sciences in Honor of Dr. Emanuel Libman by His Pupils, Friends and Colleagues. New York: 1932. V. 49; 50; 52; 54

CONVERSATIONS ON POETRY: Intended for the Amusement and Instruction of Children. London: 1824. V. 48

CONVERSATIONS: Reynolds Price and William Ray. Memphis: 1976. V. 53

CONVERSE, JOHN MARQUIS
Reconstructive Plastic Surgery: Principles and Procedures in Correction, Reconstruction and Transplantation. Philadelphia and London: 1964. V. 54

CONWAY, HERBERT
Tumors of the Skin. Springfield: 1956. V. 48; 53; 54

CONWAY, JAMES
Forays Among Salmon and Deer. London: 1861. V. 47

CONWAY, MONCURE DANIEL
Demonology and Devil-Lore. London: 1879. V. 47
The Life of Thomas Paine. London: 1909. V. 50
My Pilgrimage to the Wise Men of the East. Boston: 1906. V. 54
Testimonies Concerning Slavery. London: 1864. V. 52
Travels in South Kensington. New York: 1882. V. 52

CONWAY, WILLIAM MARTIN
Aconcagua and the Tierra Del Fuego. A Book of Climbing, Travel and Exploration. 1902. V. 53
The Alps... London: 1895. V. 48; 51; 52; 53
The Alps. London: 1904. V. 48; 50; 52
The Bolivian Andes. 1901. V. 53
Climbing and Exploration in the Bolivian Andes. New York & London: 1901. V. 49; 54
Climbing and Exploration in the Karakoram-Himalayas. London: 1894. V. 48; 53; 54
The First Crossing of Spitsbergen. London: 1897. V. 49; 51
The Van Eycks and Their Followers. London: 1921. V. 51; 53

CONWELL, RUSSELL H.
The Life, Travels and Literary Career of Bayard Taylor. Boston: 1881. V. 53

CONYBEARE, EDWARD
Highways and Byways of Cambridge and Ely. London: 1910. V. 54

CONYBEARE, JOHN JOSIAS
Illustrations of Anglo-Saxon Poetry. London: 1826. V. 52

CONYBEARE, W. D.
Outlines of the Geology of England and Wales. Part I. London: 1822. V. 53

CONYERS, ANSLEY
Chesterleigh. London: 1873. V. 54

CONYNGHAM, DAVID P.
Sherman's March through the South. New York: 1865. V. 50

CONZE, EDWARD
Spain Today. London: 1936. V. 49

COOK, ANDREW GEORGE
The New Builder's Magazine and Complete Architectural Library. London: 1819. V. 49

COOK, C. H.
Among the Pimas; or, the Mission to the Pima and Maricopa Indians. Albany: 1893. V. 52

COOK, CLARENCE
The House Beautiful. New York: 1878. V. 47
What Shall We Do With Our Walls?. New York: 1880. V. 53

COOK, DAVID J.
Hands Up; or, Thirty-Five Years of Detetive Life in the Muntains and on the Plains. Denver: 1897. V. 49; 52; 54

COOK, DUTTON
A Book of the Play: Studies and Illustrations of Histrionic Story, Life and Character. London: 1876. V. 47

COOK, E. B.
American Chess-Nuts: a Collection of Problems, by Composers of the Western World. New York: 1868. V. 52

COOK, EDWARD
The History and Romance of the Paisley Shawl. 1922. V. 53

COOK, ELIZA
Melaia and Other Poems. London: 1838. V. 51
Poems. London: 1848. V. 50
Poems. London: 1860. V. 54
Poems... London: 1861. V. 53

COOK, FREDERICK A.
My Attainment of the Pole... New York: 1911. V. 50
My Attainment of the Pole. New York: 1912. V. 52
Through the First Antarctic Night, 1898-1899. London: 1900. V. 50

COOK, FREDERICK A. continued
Through the First Antarctic Night, 1898-1899. New York: 1900. V. 54
Through the First Antarctic Night, 1898-1899... New York: 1909. V. 50
To the Top of the Continent: Discovery, Exploration and Adventure in Sub-Arctic Alaska. New York: 1908. V. 51

COOK, G.
Illustrated Catalogue of Carriages and Special Business Advertiser. New Haven: 1860. V. 53

COOK, GEORGE CRAM
Greek Coins. Poems and Memorabilia. New York: 1925. V. 51

COOK, GEORGE H.
Geology of New Jersey. Newark: 1868. V. 47; 49

COOK, HENRY
Pride, or The Heir of Craven. London: 1841. V. 50; 52; 54

COOK, J.
Beautiful Seaweeds. Paisley: 1877. V. 52
Beautiful Seaweeds... Paisley: 1877/81. V. 48

COOK, J. M.
The Troad: an Archaeological and Topographical Study. Oxford: 1973. V. 50

COOK, JAMES
An Account of the Third Voyage of Captain Cook Around the World, 1776-1780... Toronto: 1930. V. 54
Atlas to Accompany "A Voyage to the Pacific Ocean...for Making Discoveries in the Northern Hemisphere...1776-1780"... London: 1784. V. 47
Captain Cook's Voyages to the Pacific Ocean. Boston: 1797. V. 49
The Charts and Coastal Views of Captain Cook's Voyages - the Voyage of the Endeavour 1768-1771. London: 1988. V. 47; 52
The Charts and Coastal Views of Captain Cook's Voyages: Volume 1. 1988. V. 52
The Charts and Coastal Views of Captain Cook's Voyages. Volume 2... London: 1992. V. 49; 52; 53
A Collection of Voyages Round the World. London: 1790. V. 51
The Explorations of Captain Cook in the Pacific. Adelaide: 1957. V. 54
The Explorations of Captain Cook in the Pacific... New York: 1957. V. 50; 51
Journal, During the First Voyage Round the World Made in H.M. Bark "Endeavour" 1768-67. London: 1893. V. 47; 50; 53
The Journal of H.M.S. Resolution. Guildford: 1981. V. 49
Journals of Captain James Cook. Cambridge: 1955-74. V. 48; 49
The Journals of Captain James Cook... Glasgow: 1961-69. V. 52
The Journals of Captain James Cook... Glasgow: 1961-74. V. 54
Surveyor of Newfoundland. San Francisco: 1965. V. 50; 53
The Three Voyages of Captain James Cook Round the World. London: 1821. V. 51
Troisieme Voyage Abrege du Capitaine Cook, dans L'ocean Pacifique...ou Histoire des Dernieres decouvertes dans la Mer du Sude, Pendant les Annees 1776, 1777, 1778, 1779 and 1780. Paris: 1785. V. 48
Troisieme Voyage du Capitaine Cook Autour du Monde... Lyon: 1834. V. 52
Voyage dans l'Hemisphere Ausral, et Autour du Monde, Fait sur les Vaisseaux de Roi, L'Aventure & la Resolution en 1772-1775. Paris: 1778. V. 50
A Voyage to the Pacific Ocean. London: 1784. V. 50; 51; 53; 54
A Voyage to the Pacific Ocean. London: 1785. V. 47; 49; 51; 53; 54
A Voyage to the Pacific Ocean... London: 1793. V. 50
A Voyage Towards the South Pole, and Round the World, Performed in His Majesty's Ships the Resolution and Adventure, in the Years 1772, 1773, 1774 and 1775 in Which is Included Captain Furneaux's Narrative of the Proceedings in the Adventure During the... London: 1777. V. 48; 53
The Voyages of... London: 1825. V. 47
The Voyages of... London: 1842. V. 48; 50; 53

COOK, JAMES HENRY
Fifty Years on the Old Frontier, as Cowboy, Hunter, Guide, Scout and Ranchman. New Haven: 1923. V. 47; 48; 53

COOK, JANE ELIZABETH
The Sculptor Caught Napping. London: 1874. V. 50; 51
The Sculptor Caught Napping... London: 1911. V. 48

COOK, JOHN
Cursory Remarks on the Subject of Wheel Carriages. London: 1817-18. V. 50
Observations on Fox Hunting, and the Management of Hounds in the Kennel and the Field. London: 1826. V. 47; 48; 53

COOK, JOHN R.
The Border and the Buffalo. Topeka: 1907. V. 52

COOK, MOSES
The Manner of Raising, Ordering and Improving Forest and Fruit Trees... London: 1679. V. 54
The Manner of Raising, Ordering and Improving Forest-Trees... London: 1717. V. 48
The Manner of Raising, Ordering and Improving Forest-Trees... London: 1724. V. 50

COOK, R. L.
The Concord Saunterer. Middlebury: 1940. V. 52; 53

COOK, ROBERT M.
Greek and Roman Pottery. New York: 1979. V. 50

COOK, ROBIN
The Crust On its Uppers. London: 1962. V. 49

COOK, ROY BIRD
Lewis County in the Civil War 1861-1865. Charlestwon: 1924. V. 47

COOK, SAMUEL
The Jenolan Caves: an Excursion in Australian Wonderland. London: 1889. V. 50

COOK, TENNESSEE CELESTE, LADY
Constitutional Equality a Right of Woman, in Consideration of the Various Relations Which She Sustains as a Necessary Part of the Body of Society and Humanity... New York: 1871. V. 47; 48
Essays on Social Topics. Westminster: 188-?. V. 48
Wrongs of Married Men. And Other Essays. Chicago: 1900. V. 49

COOK, THEODORE ANDREA
Eclipse and O'Kelly. London: 1907. V. 47
Sporting Pictures at Lavington Park, with Supplement. London: 1927. V. 47
The Watercolor Drawings of the National Gallery. London: 1904. V. 52; 54

COOK, W. B.
The Curse of Amaris. 1924. V. 47; 51

COOK, WARREN L.
Flood Tide of Empire: Spain and the Pacific Northwest 1543-1819. New Haven: 1973. V. 53

COOK, WILLIAM
Billiards. London: 1890?. V. 48
The Life of Samuel Johnson, LL.D. with Occasional Remarks on His Writings, an Authentic Copy of His Will... Dubin (sic): 1785. V. 48

COOKE, ALAN
The Exploration of Northern Canada: 500 to 1920, a Chronology. Toronto: 1978. V. 53

COOKE, ALEXANDER
Pope Joane. A Dialogue Betweene a Protestant and a Papist. London: 1625. V. 47

COOKE, CHRISTOPHER
Curiosities of Occult Literature. London: 1863. V. 54

COOKE, COLIN
The Life of Stafford Cripps. London: 1957. V. 49

COOKE, CONRAD WILLIAM
Automata Old and New. London: 1893. V. 47

COOKE, E. W.
Grotesque Animals, Invented, Drawn and Described. London: 1872. V. 52

COOKE, EDWARD
Certain Passages Which Happened at Newport, in the Isle of Wight, Novemb. 29, 1648. Relating to Charles I. London: 1690. V. 49
Chronica Juridicialia; or, A General Calendar of the Years of Our Lord God, and Those of the Several Kings of England, from the First Year of William the Conqueror... London: 1685. V. 52
A Voyage to the South Sea, and Round the World, Perform'd in the Years 1708, 1709, 1710 and 1711. London: 1712. V. 48; 50

COOKE, EDWARD WILLIAM
View of the Old and New London Bridges, With Scientific and Historical Notices... London: 1833. V. 50; 51; 53

COOKE, GEORGE ALEXANDER
Topographical and Statistical Description of the County of Cambridge. London: 1804. V. 54
Topographical and Statistical Description of the County of York... Sherwood: 1824. V. 54
The Vicinity fo the River Rhode Displayed in a Series of Views from Original Drawings by P. Dewint... London: 1825. V. 50
Views in London and its Vicinity. London: 1834. V. 50; 52

COOKE, GEORGE PAUL
Moolelo O Molokai. Honolulu: 1949. V. 53

COOKE, GRACE MC GOWAN
Their First Formal Call. New York: 1906. V. 52

COOKE, H. LESTER
Fletcher Martin. New York: 1977. V. 47

COOKE, HENRY
Turpin the Second: or, Cooke Caught at Last. London: 1741. V. 48

COOKE, HEREWARD LESTERN
Eyewitness to Space, Paintings and Drawings Related to the Apollo Mission to the Moon, Selected, with a Few Exceptions... New York: 1976. V. 49

COOKE, J.
A Description of the Royal Hosptial for Seaman, at Greenwich... Greenwich: 1803. V. 54

COOKE, JAMES
Mellificivm Chirurgiae; or, the Marrow Chirurgery. London: 1688. V. 53
Mellificivm Chirurgiae; or, the Marrow Chirurgery. London: 1693. V. 50

COOKE, JAY, & CO.
The Northern Pacific Railroad's Land Grant and the Future Business of the Road. Philadlephia: 1870. V. 48

COOKE, JOHN
A Treatise of Pathology and Therapeutics. Lexington: 1828. V. 48

COOKE, JOHN ESTEN
Hammer and Rapier. New York: 1870. V. 51
A Life of Gen. Robert E. Lee. New York: 1871. V. 49
The Life of Stonewall Jackson. New York: 1863. V. 47; 49
The Life of Stonewall Jackson. Richmond: 1863. V. 49
The Virginia Comedians; or, Old Days in the Old Dominion. New York: 1854. V. 52

COOKE, JOHN H.
Bibliotheca Cestriensis or a Biographical Account of Books, Maps, Plates and Other Printed Matter Relating to, Printed or Published In, or Written by Authors Resident in the County of Chester... Warrington: 1904. V. 51

COOKE, JOSIAH P.
Elements of Chemical Physics. Boston: 1860. V. 48; 53; 54

COOKE, MARY
The Picards of Pychards of Stradewy (now Tretower) Castle and Scethrog, Brecknockshire... London: 1878. V. 49

COOKE, MORDECAI CUBITT
British Desmids... London: 1887. V. 54
British Edibile Fungi How to Distinguish and How to Cook Them. London: 1891. V. 49
British Fresh-Water Algae, Exclusive of Desmidiae and Diatomaceae. London: 1882-84. V. 52
Illustrations of British Fungi. London: 1881-91. V. 47; 49; 50; 52
Mycographia seu Icones Fungorum, Figures of Fungi From All Parts of the World. London: 1875-79. V. 49
A Plain and Easy Account of British fungi. London: 1898. V. 50

COOKE, MR.
The Trial of Mr. Cooke, Malt Distiller, of Stratford, for the Crime of Adultery with Mrs. Walford, Wife of Mr. Walford, of the Same Place, Before Lord Kenyon, and a Special Jury, Who Gave a Verdict for the Plaintiff Three Thousand Five Hundred Pounds Damages. London: 1789. V. 48

COOKE, PHILIP PENDLETON
Froissart Ballads, and other Poems. Philadelphia: 1847. V. 51

COOKE, PHILIP ST. GEORGE
Exploring Southwestern Trails 1846-1854. Glendale: 1938. V. 50
Scenes and Adventures in the Army; or Romance of Military Life. Philadelphia: 1857. V. 47

COOKE, ROBERT
Sketches of the Life of Mgr. de Mazenod, Bishop of Marseilles and Founder of the Oblates of Mary Immaculate, and Of the Missionary Labours and Travels of Members of that Society... London: 1879-82. V. 47; 54
West Country Houses. Bristol: 1957. V. 53

COOKE, ROSE TERRY
Poems. Boston: 1861. V. 47; 49

COOKE, THOMAS
An Epistle to the Right Honouarble the Countess of Shaftesbury, with a Prologue and Epilogue on Shakespeare and His Writings. London: 1743. V. 49
The Mournful Nuptials, or Love the Cure of All Woes, a Tragedy. London: 1739. V. 52
A Practical and Familiar View of the Science of Physiognomy, Compiled Chiefly from the Papers of the Late Mr. T. Cooke of Manchester... London: 1819. V. 47
The Universal Letter-Writer... London: 1794. V. 52
The Universal Letter-Writer. London: 1814. V. 53

COOKE, W. W.
Report on Bird Migration in the Mississippi Valley in the Years 1884-85. Washington: 1888. V. 50; 51

COOKE, WILLIAM
The Beauties of Samuel Johnson. 1804. V. 47
The Elements of Dramatic Criticism. London: 1775. V. 51; 52
The Life of Samuel Johnson, LL.D. with Occasional Remarks On His Writings.... Dublin: 1785. V. 50
The Life of Samuel Johnson, LL.D. with Occasional Remarks on His Writings... London: 1785. V. 48; 54
Poetical Essays on Several Occasions. London: 1774. V. 52

COOKE, WILLIAM BERNARD
Views on the Thames, from the Source to the Sea. London: 1811. V. 48; 50; 53

COOKE, WILLIAM FOTHERGILL
The Electric Telegraph: Was It Invented by Professor Wheatstone?. London: 1854. V. 54
The Electric Telegraph: Was it Invented by Professor Wheatstone?. London: 1856. V. 51
Telegraphic Railways; or, the Single Way Recommended by Safety, Economy and Efficiency Under the Safeguard and Control of the Electric Telegraph. London: 1842. V. 54

COOKE-TRENCH, THOMAS
A Memoir of the Trench Family. London: 1897. V. 50; 54

COOK'S Handbook for London. London: 1888. V. 54

COOLBRITH, INA
California. San Fransico: 1918. V. 48

COOLEY, A.
Cooley's Cyclopaedia. London: 1864. V. 53
A Cyclopaedia of Six Thousand Practical Receipts and Collateral Information in the Arts, Manufactures and Trades... New York: 1846. V. 53

COOLEY, BENJAMIN FRANKLIN
An Exposition and Explanation of the Modern Phenomena Called Spirit Manifestations. Springfield: 1852. V. 48

COOLEY, JEROME EUGENE
Recollections of Early Days in Duluth. Duluth: 1925. V. 49; 50

COOLEY, ROSSA B.
School Acres: an Adventure in Rural Education. New Haven: 1930. V. 53

COOLEY, THOMAS M.
A Treatise on the Constitutional Limitations Which Rest Upon the Legislative Power of the States of the American Union. Boston: 1874. V. 54
A Treatise on the Law of Taxation, Including the Law of Local Assessments. Chicago: 1886. V. 51; 53

COOLEY, TIMOTHY MATHER
Sketches of the Life and Character of the Rev. Lemuel Haynes, for Many Years Pastor of a Church in Rutland, Vt. and Late in Granville, New York. New York: 1839. V. 54

COOLIDGE, CALVIN
The Autobiography of... New York: 1929. V. 47; 54

COOLIDGE, DANE
The Navajo Indians. Boston: 1930. V. 47; 53

COOLIDGE, H. J.
A Revision of the Genus Gorilla. Cambridge: 1929. V. 49; 52

COOLIDGE, RICHARD
Statistical Report on the Sickness and Mortality in the Army of the United States. Washington: 1856. V. 50; 52
Statistical Report on the Sickness and Mortality in the Army of the United States... Washington: 1856/60. V. 50
Statistical Report on the Sickness and Mortality in the Army of the United States... Washington: 1860. V. 49; 50; 52

COOLIDGE, W. A. B.
Swiss Travel and Swiss Guide Books. London: 1889. V. 48

COOMARASWAMY, ANANDA K.
History of Indian and Indoensian Art. New York: 1927. V. 49
Myths of the Hindus and Buddhists. London: 1913. V. 52
Portfolio of Indian Art. Boston: 1923. V. 50; 53
Portfolio of Indian Art... New York: 1923. V. 49

COOMBE, FLORENCE
Islands of Enchantment. London: 1911. V. 50

COOMBES, B. L.
These Poor Hands - the Autobiography of a Miner Working in South Wales. London: 1939. V. 52

COOMBS, ORDE
Drums of a Life: a Photographic Essay on the Black Man in America. Garden City: 1974. V. 52

COONEY, JOHN D.
Amarna Reliefs from Hermopolis in American Collections. Brooklyn: 1965. V. 51

COONEY, LORAINE
Garden History of Georgia 1733-1933. Atlanta: 1933. V. 52

COONEY, ROBERT
A Compendious History of the Northern Part of the Province of New Brunswick and of the District of Gaspe in Lower Canada. Chatham, Miramichi: 1896. V. 53

COONTS, STEPHEN
Flight of the Intruder. Annapolis: 1986. V. 50

COOP, J. O.
The Story of the 55th (West Lancashire) Division. Liverpool: 1919. V. 53

COOPE, ROSALYS
Salomon de Brosse and the Development of the Classical Style in French Architecture from 1565 to 1630. London: 1972. V. 51; 53

COOPER, A.
In and Out of Rebel Prisons. Oswego: 1888. V. 50

COOPER, ASTLEY
The Anatomy and Surgical Treatment of Inguinal and Congenital Hernia. London: 1804. V. 47; 48; 49; 50; 51; 53
A Series of Lectures, on the Most Approved Principles and Practice of Modern Surgery... Boston: 1823. V. 54

COOPER, BRANSBY B.
Lectures on Osteology, Including the Ligaments Which Connect the Bones of the Human Skeleton. London: 1844. V. 53
The Life of Sir Astley Cooper, Bart. London: 1843. V. 52
Surgical Essays: the Result of Clinical Observations Made at Guy's Hospital. London: 1843. V. 47; 48; 49; 50; 51; 53; 54

COOPER, CHARLES HENRY
Athenae Cantabrigienses 1500-1609. Cambridge: 1858-61. V. 51
Memorials of Cambridge. Cambridge: 1858-66. V. 49

COOPER, DEREK
The Work of Graham Sutherland. London: 1962. V. 49

COOPER, DIANA
Autobiography. London: 1958/60. V. 48; 51; 53

COOPER, DOUGLAS
Pablo Picasso, les Dejeuners. London: 1963. V. 50
Picasso: Carnet Catalan. Paris: 1958. V. 48; 52
Picasso Theatre. New York: 1968. V. 47; 48; 50; 52; 53; 54
The Work of Graham Sutherland. London: 1961. V. 49
The Work of Graham Sutherland. London: 1962. V. 52; 54

COOPER, DUFF
Haig. London: 1935. V. 47

COOPER, E. S.
Report on Operation for Removing a Foreign Body from Beneath the Heart. San Francisco: 1857. V. 48

COOPER, F. T.
A Handbook of the Law of Defamation and Verbal Inquiry. Edinburgh: 1894. V. 50

COOPER, FREDERIC TABER
An Argosy of Fables. New York: 1921. V. 53

COOPER, FREDERICK FOX
Hard Times. London: 1886. V. 49
The Tale of Two Cities, or, The Incarcerated Viction of the Bastille. London: 1885. V. 54

COOPER, G. A.
Permian Brachiopods of West Texas. 1972-76. V. 53

COOPER, G. H. C.
Colchester Town Hall. A Brief History. London: 1988. V. 52

COOPER, GEORGE
Cooper's Yankee, Italian and Hebrew Dialect Readings and Recitations. New York: 1891. V. 51
A Treatise of Distresses, Replevins and Avowries... London: 1761. V. 52

COOPER, GEORGE A.
Some Works of Art in the Possession of... London: 1903. V. 53

COOPER, HENRY ST. JOHN
Bulldogs and All About Them. London: 1925. V. 49

COOPER, J.
A Piece of Mine. Navarro: 1984. V. 54

COOPER, J. G.
The Natural History of Washington Territory... New York: 1859. V. 53
Ornithology (of California). Volume 1 Land Birds. Cambridge: 1870. V. 51

COOPER, J. W.
The Experienced Botanist or Indian Physician. Ebensburg: 1833. V. 49; 52
The Experienced Botanist or Indian Physician... Lancaster: 1840. V. 50

COOPER, JAMES FENIMORE
The Borderers. London: 1933. V. 47
The Bravo... London: 1831. V. 50
The Bravo... Philadelphia: 1831. V. 49
The Chainbearer... London: 1845. V. 49
The Chainbearer. New York: 1845. V. 48
Cooper's Novels. New York: 1859-61. V. 53
Cooper's Novels. Boston: 1920. V. 54
The Correspondence of James Fenimore Cooper. New Haven: 1923. V. 50
The Deerslayer. London: 1841. V. 49; 52; 54
The Deerslayer. Philadelphia: 1841. V. 49; 54
The Deerslayer. New York: 1929. V. 49
Eve Effingham; or, Home. London: 1838. V. 47
Excursions in Italy. Paris: 1838. V. 49
The Headsman; or, The Abbaye des Vignerons. London: 1833. V. 49
The Heidenmauer; or the Benedictines. London: 1832. V. 48
The Heidenmauer; or, the Benedictines. Philadelphia: 1832. V. 51; 53; 54
The History of the Navy of the United States of America. Philadelphia: 1839. V. 48
History of the Navy of the United States of America. Philadelphia: 1840. V. 54
The History of the Navy of the United States of America. Philadelphia: 1841. V. 47
Home as Found. Philadelphia: 1838. V. 47; 49; 51
Homeward Bound. Philadelphia: 1838. V. 49; 54
The Jack O'Lantern; or, the Privateer. London: 1842. V. 49
The Last of the Mohicans. London: 1826. V. 47; 49; 50; 54
The Last of the Mohicans. Paris: 1826. V. 49
The Last of the Mohicans. Philadelphia: 1826. V. 53
The Last of the Mohicans. London: 1919. V. 54
The Last of the Mohicans. New York: 1919. V. 54
The Last of the Mohicans. New York: 1925. V. 48
The Last of the Mohicans. New York: 1932. V. 49
A Letter to His Countrymen. New York: 1834. V. 47
Lionel Lincoln... London: 1825. V. 51; 53; 54
Lionel Lincoln... New York: 1825. V. 50
Lionel Lincoln... New York: 1825/24. V. 50; 51; 53; 54
Lionel Lincoln... Boston: 1832. V. 47
Lives of Distinguished American Naval Officers. Philadelhia: 1846. V. 50; 53
Mark's Reef; or, the Crater. London: 1847. V. 49
Mercedes of Castile. Philadelphia: 1840. V. 54
The Monikins. Paris: 1835. V. 48
The Monikins... Philadelphia: 1835. V. 49
Ned Myers; or, a Life Before the Mast. Philadelphia: 1843. V. 47
Notions of the Americans: Picked Up by a Travelling Bachelor. London: 1828. V. 47
Notions of the Americans: Picked Up by a Travelling Bachelor. Philadelphia: 1828. V. 53
The Pathfinder. London: 1840. V. 49; 53
The Pathfinder... Philadelphia: 1840. V. 53; 54
The Pilot; A Tale of the Sea. London: 1826. V. 47
The Pioneers. London: 1823. V. 49
The Pioneers... New York: 1823. V. 51; 53
Les Pionniers ou Les Sources du Susquehannah. (The Pioneers). Paris: 1823. V. 51
The Prairie... Philadelphia: 1827. V. 48
The Prairie. Menasha: 1940. V. 53
Ravensnest; or, the Redskins. London: 1846. V. 47; 50; 51
The Red Rover, a Tale. London: 1827. V. 47
The Red Rover, a Tale. Paris: 1827. V. 52
The Redskins; or, Indian and Injin... New York: 1846. V. 47
The Sea Lions: or the Lost Sealers. New York: 1849. V. 49
Skarprattaren eller Vinskords-Festen. (The Headsman). Stockholm: 1835. V. 54
Sketches of Switzerland. Philadelphia: 1836. V. 53; 54
The Spy... London: 1822. V. 47
The Spy... Paris: 1825. V. 47

COOPER, JAMES FENIMORE
The Spy. London: 1828. V. 49

COOPER, JAMES FENIMORE
The Spy. London: 1831. V. 48; 51
The Two Admirals. London: 1842. V. 47; 49; 50; 51
The Two Admirals. Philadelphia: 1842. V. 52; 53
The Water Witch. London: 1830. V. 50; 51; 54
The Water Witch. Philadelphia: 1831. V. 51
The Wept of Wish-ton-Wish, a Tale. Florence: 1829. V. 52
The Wept of Wish-Ton-Wish: a Tale. Philadelphia: 1829. V. 53; 54
The Works of James Fenimore Cooper. New York: 1861. V. 51
Wyandotte; or, the Hutted Knoll. London: 1843. V. 48
Wyandotte; or, the Hutted Knoll. Paris: 1843. V. 48
Wyandotte, or the Hutted Knoll. Philadelphia: 1843. V. 53

COOPER, JOHN
The Warwickshire Hunt, from 1795 to 1836, Describing Many of the Most Splendid Runs... London: 1837. V. 47

COOPER, JOHN GIBLERT
Epistles to the Great, from Aristippus in Retirement. (with) The Call of Aristippus. London: 1757/58. V. 48; 52

COOPER, JOHN GILBERT
Letters Concerning Taste. London: 1757. V. 52
Poems on Several Subjects. London: 1764. V. 50; 52

COOPER, JOHN IRWIN
The History of the Montreal Hunt. Montreal: 1953. V. 47

COOPER, JOSEPH
Domus Mosaica: sive Legis Sepimentum. London: 1673. V. 50

COOPER, JOSEPH A.
A Survivor of Two Wars. Biographical Sketch of Gen. Joseph A. Cooper with Documents and Letters...War with Mexico and the Rebellion. Knoxville: 1895. V. 48

COOPER, OZ
The Book of Oz Cooper. Chicago: 1949. V. 49

COOPER, PETER
Ideas for a Sentence of Good Government in Addresses, Letters and Articles on a Strictly National Currency, Tariff and Civil Service. New York: 1883. V. 54

COOPER, REV.
A New Roman History. London: 1812. V. 48; 51

COOPER, ROBERT
A Contrast Between the New Moral World and the Old Imoral World. Hulme: 1838. V. 53
A Lecture on Original Sin, Delivered in the Social Institution, Great George Street, Salford. Manchester: 1838. V. 53

COOPER, SAMUEL
A Concise System of Instructions and Regulations for the Militia... Philadelphia: 1836. V. 48
The First Lines of the Practice of Surgery... London: 1807. V. 54
The First Lines of the Practice of Surgery... Boston: 1828. V. 50
A Treatise on the Diseases of the Joints. Hanover: 1811. V. 51

COOPER, SUSAN
Mandrake. 1964. V. 48; 51; 52
Mandrake. London: 1964. V. 53
Over Sea, Under Stone, The Dark is Rising, Greenwitch, The Grey King & Silver on the Tree. 1965-77. V. 47

COOPER, SUSAN FENIMORE
Rural Hours. Philadelphia: 1854. V. 49

COOPER, SUSAN ROGERS
Houston in the Rearview Mirror. New York: 1990. V. 54
The Man in the Green Chevy. New York: 1988. V. 51; 53

COOPER, THOMAS
Address to the Graduates of the South Carolina College, at the Public Commencement 1830. Columbia: 1831. V. 48
Consoldiation. Columbia: 1824. V. 50
Consolidation... Columbia: 1830. V. 48
A Discourse on the Connexion Between Chemistry and Medicine, Delivered in the University of Pennsylvania, Nov. 5, 1818. Philadelphia: 1818. V. 48
The Introductory Lecture, of Thomas Cooper, Esq. Professor of Chemistry at Carlisle College Pennylvania. Carlisle: 1812. V. 47; 48
Lectures On the Elements of Political Economy. Columbia: 1826. V. 48

COOPER, THOMAS continued
Lectures on the Elements of Political Economy. Columbia: 1829. V. 47
Letters On the Slave Trade. Manchester: 1787. V. 48; 49
Men of Mark. Second Series. London: 1877. V. 54
On the Connection Between Geology and the Pentateuch: in a Letter to Professor Silliman...to Which is Added the Defence of Dr. Cooper Before the Trustees of the South Carolina College. Columbia: 1833. V. 48
The Purgatory of Suicides. London: 1845. V. 47; 51
The Right of Free Discussion. New York: 1829. V. 47
The Scripture Doctrine of Materialism. Philadelphia: 1823. V. 47
Some Information Concerning Gas Lights. Philadelphia: 1816. V. 48
Some Information Respecting America. London: 1794. V. 50; 53
Some Information Respecting America. London: 1795. V. 47; 48
Supplement to Mr. Cooper's Letters on the Slave Trade. Warrington: 1788. V. 48; 49
Thesaurus Linguae Romanae & Britannicae. London: 1573. V. 48
Thesaurus Linguae Romanae & Britannicae... London: 1578. V. 47; 51
Thesaurus Linguae Romanae & Britannicae... London: 1584. V. 47; 51
A Treatise of Domestic Medicine... Reading: 1824. V. 54
A View of the Metaphysical and Physiological Arguments in Favor of Materialism. Philadelphia: 1824. V. 47

COOPER, THOMAS THORNVILLE
Travels of a Pioneer of Commerce in Pigtail and Petticoats. London: 1871. V. 50

COOPER, THOMPSON
Men of Mark. London: 1876. V. 54
Men of Mark. London: 1876-83. V. 51; 52

COOPER, W. T.
The Birds of Paradise and Bower Birds. Boston: 1979. V. 54

COOPER, WILLIAM
The Beauties of Church Music and the Sure Guide to the Art of Singing. Boston: 1804. V. 51
The Gardeners' and Poultry Keepers' Guide and Illustrated Catalogue of Goods Manufactured and Supplied by William Cooper. London. V. 50
One Shall Be Taken, and Another Left. A Sermon Preach'd to the Old South Church in Boston, March 22, 1740-41. Boston: 1741. V. 51
Three Marriages. London: 1946. V. 49
Yachts and Yachting. London: 1873. V. 50; 51; 54

COOPER, WILLIAM ARTHUR
A Portrayal of Negro Life. 1936. V. 49

COOPER, WILLIAM DURRANT
The History of Winchelsea, One of the Ancient Towns Added to the Cinque Ports. London & Hastings: 1850. V. 47; 50; 53

COOPER, WILLIAM HEATON
The Hills of Lakeland. London: 1938. V. 50; 52
The Hills of Lakeland. London: 1946. V. 50; 52
Lakeland Portraits. London: 1954. V. 52
The Lakes. London: 1966. V. 50; 52
The Lakes. London: 1970. V. 50; 52
The Tarns of Lakeland. London: 1960. V. 50; 52
The Tarns of Lakeland. Grasmere: 1970. V. 52

COORE, RICHARD
The Practical Expositor of the Most Difficult Texts Throughout the Holy Bible. London: 1683. V. 50

COOTE, EYRE
A Letter From Certain Gentlemen of the Council at Bengal, to the Honourable Secret Committee for Affairs of the Honourable United Company of Merchants of England Trading to the East Indies. London: 1764. V. 48; 52

COOVER, JOHN EDGAR
Experiments in Psychical Research at Leland Stanford Junior University. Stanford: 1917. V. 49; 54

COOVER, ROBERT
The Fallguy's Faith. Chicago: 1975. V. 48
The Origin of the Brunists. New York: 1966. V. 47; 48; 49; 50; 52
The Origin of the Brunists. London: 1967. V. 49; 53
Pricksongs and Descants. New York: 1969. V. 52
Spanking the Maid. Bloomfield Hills: 1980. V. 48
Spanking the Maid. Bloomfield Hills & Columbia: 1981. V. 49; 53
Spanking the Maid. Bloomfield Hills: 1982. V. 52
The Stone Wall Press Book of Short Fiction. Iowa City: 1973. V. 47; 50
A Theological Position. New York: 1972. V. 47; 48; 53
The Universal Baseball Association, Inc. New York: 1968. V. 47; 48; 50; 53
The Water Pourer... Bloomfield Hills, Columbia: 1972. V. 49
The Water Pourer... South Carolina: 1972. V. 48

COPE, E. D.
The Batrachia of North America. Washington: 1889. V. 48
Crocodilians, Lizards and Snakes of North America. Washington: 1900. V. 48; 50; 53
The Vertebrata of the Cretaceous Formations of the West. Washington: 1875. V. 49

COPE, GEORGE W.
The Iron and Steel Interests of Chicago. Chicago: 1890. V. 50

COPE, THOMAS
The Smokers's Text Book. Liverpool: 1889-90. V. 52

COPE, WILLIAM H.
The History of the Rifle Brigade (the Prince Consort's Own). 1877. V. 54
History of the Rifle Brigade (The Prince Consort's Own)... London: 1877. V. 50

COPELAND, JOHN M.
The Trail of the Swinging Lanterns. Toronto: 1918. V. 48

COPELAND, R. MORRIS
Country Life. Boston: 1859. V. 47; 48; 51; 54
Country Life. Boston: 1863. V. 52

COPELAND, THOMAS
Observations On the Principal Diseases of the Rectum and Anus. Philadelphia: 1811. V. 48; 53
Observations on the Principal Diseases of the Rectum and Anus... London: 1824. V. 53

COPELAND, WALTER
Babes and Blossoms. New York. V. 47; 49
The Book of Dollyland. London: 1906. V. 49
The Book of Little J.Ds. (Japanese Dolls). London: 1905. V. 49
The Book of Mandarinfants. London: 1905. V. 49
The Cake Shop. London: 1907. V. 49
The Mad Motor. London: 1906. V. 49
The Silly Submarine. London: 1906. V. 47; 48; 49
The Toy Shop. London: 1905. V. 49

COPEMAN, EDWARD
A Report on the Cerebral Affections of Infancy with a Few Comments and Practical Works. Norwich: 1873. V. 53

COPEMAN, FRED
Reason in Revolt. London: 1948. V. 49

COPERARIO, GIOVANNI
Rules How to Compose. Los Angeles: 1952. V. 49

COPERNICUS, NICHOLAS
On the Revolutions. London: 1978. V. 53

COPIES of Original Letters from the Army of General Bonaparte in Egypt, Intercepted by the Fleet Under the Command of Admiral Lord Nelson... Dublin: 1799. V. 47

COPIES of Original Letters from the French Army in Egypt. Part the Third... London: 1800. V. 54

COPIES of the Letters Patent, the Bishop of London's Grant, and the Original Ordinances, Evidencing the Foundation of Sir Roger Cholmeley's Free Grammar School at Highgate, and referred to in a Bill Now Pending in Parliament... London: 1822. V. 52

COPIES or Extracts of Correspondence Relative to the Discovery of Gold in the Fraser's River District, in British North America. London: 1858. V. 47

COPINGER, H. B.
The Elzevier Press. London: 1927. V. 50

COPINGER, W. A.
Facsimiles of the Incunabula Biblica. London: 1898. V. 50
History and Records of the Smith-Carington Family from the Conquest to the Present Time. London: 1907. V. 52
The Manors of Suffolk. London: 1905. V. 51

COPLAND, DUDLEY
Livingstone of the Arctic. Ottawa: 1967. V. 51

COPLAND, JAMES
Of the Causes, Nature and Treatment of Palsy and Apoplexy: of the Forms, Seats, Complications, and Morbid Relations of Paralytic and Apoplectic Diseases. Philadelphia: 1850. V. 53

COPLAND, SAMUEL
A History of the Island of Madagascar, Comprising a Political Account of the Island, the Religion, Manners and Customs Of Its Inhabitants and its Natural Productions. London: 1822. V. 47; 51; 54

COPLANS, JOHN
A Body of Work: Self Portraits. New York: 1987. V. 54

COPLESTON, EDWARD
The Examiner Examined, or Logic Vindicated. Oxford: 1809. V. 50
A Reply to the Calumnies of the Edinburgh Review Against Oxford. (with) *A Second Reply to the Edinburgh Review.* Oxford: 1810/10. V. 47

COPLESTON, FREDERICK
A History of Philosophy. Westminster: 1946-61. V. 47

COPLESTONE, EDWARD
Advice to a Young Reviewer, With a Specimen of Art. Oxford: 1807. V. 49

COPLEY, ESTHER HEWLETT
The Housekeeper's Guide... London: 1834. V. 52
Housekeeper's Guide. London: 1838. V. 51; 53

COPLEY, JOHN M.
A Sketch of the Battle of Franklin, Tennessee; with Reminiscences of Camp Douglas. Austin: 1893. V. 49

COPLEY, JOSIAH
Kansas and the Country Beyond, on the Line of the Union Pacific Railway, Eastern Division, from the Missouri to the Pacific Ocean... Philadelphia: 1867. V. 50

COPLEY, THOMAS
Letters of Sir Thomas Copley of Gatton, Surrey and Roughley, Sussex...to Queen Elizabeth and Her Ministers from the Originals in the Record Office and British Museum. London: 1897. V. 51

COPPARD, ALFRED EDGAR
Adam and Eve & Pinch Me. Waltham St. Lawrence: 1921. V. 47; 49; 51
The Black Dog, and Other Stories. London: 1923. V. 51
Clorinda Walks in Heaven. Waltham St. Lawrence: 1922. V. 51; 53
Collected Poems. London: 1928. V. 51
Count Stefan. Waltham St. Lawrence: 1928. V. 50; 51; 52; 53
Crotty Shinkwin... 1932. V. 48; 49
Crotty Shinkwin... London: 1932. V. 50
Crotty Shinkwin. Waltham St. Lawrence: 1932. V. 51; 52; 53
Emergency Exit. New York: 1934. V. 54
Fearful Pleasures. Sauk City: 1946. V. 50
The Field of Mustard. London: 1926. V. 51; 54
Fishmonger's Fiddle. London: 1925. V. 47; 48; 52; 54
Good Samaritans. London: 1934. V. 54
Hips and Haws: Poems. Waltham St. Lawrence: 1922. V. 51
The Hundredth Story. London: 1931. V. 54
The Hundredth Story. Waltham St. Lawrence: 1931. V. 47; 48; 50; 53
Judith. Stockholm: 1929. V. 51
The Man from Kilsheelan. London: 1930. V. 47; 49
Ninepenny Flute - Twenty-One Tales. London: 1937. V. 49; 53
Nixey's Harlequin. London: 1931. V. 49; 52
Pelegea and Other Poems. Waltham St. Lawrence: 1926. V. 53; 54
Pink Furniture: a Tale for Lovely Children with Noble Natures. London: 1930. V. 49; 51; 54
Rummy That Noble Game Expounded in Prose, Poetry, Diagram and Engraving... Waltham St. Lawrence: 1932. V. 48; 50; 51
Selected Tales. London: 1946. V. 51
Silver Circus. London: 1928. V. 50; 51; 54
Tapster's Tapestry. London: 1938. V. 51
Tapster's Tapestry. Waltham St. Lawrence: 1938. V. 52
Yokohama Garland and Other Poems. Philadelphia: 1926. V. 50

COPPENS, CHARLES
Moral Principles and Medical Practice, the Basis of Medical Jurisprudence. Cincinnati: 1897. V. 52

COPPER, BASIL
The Black Death. Minneapolis: 1991. V. 52
The Exploits of Solar Pons. Minneapolis: 1993. V. 52

COPPER, SUSAN ROGERS
The Man in the Green Chevy. 1989. V. 51

COPPERTHWAITE, WILLIAM CHARLES
Tunnel Shields and the Use of Compressed Air in Subaqueous Works. New York: 1906. V. 53

COPPETTA DE' BECCUTI, FRANCESCO
Rime. Venice: 1580. V. 47; 52

COPPIN, L. J.
Unwritten History. Philadelphia: 1919. V. 53

COPPING, H.
Character Sketches from Dickens. London: 1924. V. 48

COPPINGER, JOHN B.
The Renegade. New York: 1855. V. 51

COPPINGER, JOSEPH
The American Practical Brewer and Tanner... New York: 1815. V. 48; 50; 52; 53; 54

COPPINGER, RICHARD WILLIAM
Cruise of the 'Alert'. Four years in Patagonian, Polynesian and Masarene Waters. London: 1883. V. 50
Cruise of the 'Alert'. Four Years in Patagonian, Polynesian and Masarene Waters. New York: 1884. V. 50

COPPOCK, PARSON
The Genuine Dying Speech of the Rev. Parson Coppock... Carlisle: 1746. V. 50; 52; 54

COPTIC Studies in Honor of Walter Ewing Crum. Boston: 1950. V. 51

COPWAY, GEORGE
The Life, Letters and Speeches of Kah-Ge-Ga-Gah-bowh or, G. Copway, Chief Ojibway Nation. New York: 1850. V. 51
Recollections of a Forest Life; or, the Life and Travels of George Copway, or, Kah-ge-ga-kah-bowh, Chief of the Ojibway Nation. London: 1860. V. 53
The Traditional History and Characteristic Sketches of the Ojibway Nation. London: 1850. V. 51

A **COPY** of a Letter Sent from the Lords Justices, and the Rest of the Privy Councell in Ireland, Concerning His Majesties Resolution to Go Again Into that His Kingdom. 1642. V. 49

A **COPY** of a Letter Written by Our Blessed Lord and Saviour, Jesus Christ. And Found Under a Great Stone, Sixty-Five Years After His Crucifiction. County of Plymouth: 1787. V. 53

THE **COPY** of a Letter Written to the Lower House of Parliament Touching Divers Grievances and Inconveniences of the State &c. London: 1641. V. 48; 50

A **COPY** of the Poll for the Knights of the Shire for the County of Norfolk Taken at Norwich, March 23, 1768. Norwich: 1768. V. 52

THE COQUETTE; or Florence de Lacey. London: 1846. V. 54

COQUILLETTE, DANIEL R.
The Civilian Writers of Doctors' Commons, London, Three Centuries of Juristic Innovation in Comparative Commercial and International Law. Berlin: 1988. V. 52

CORBET, G. B.
Mammals of the Indo-Malayan Region, a Systematic Review. London: 1992. V. 49; 52

CORBET, JOHN
Self-Employment in Secret. London: 1830. V. 50

CORBET, PHILIP S.
Dragonflies. 1960. V. 54

CORBET, RICHARD
Poems... London: 1672. V. 52; 54

CORBETT, BERTHA L.
The Sun Bonnet Babies. Minneapolis: 1900. V. 47; 50

CORBETT, EDWARD
An Old Coachman's Chatter. London: 1890. V. 47

CORBETT, ELIZABETH
Walt. The Good Gray Poet Speaks for Himself. New York: 1928. V. 51

CORBETT, JAMES J.
The Roar of the Crowd. New York: 1925. V. 50; 51

CORBETT, JULIAN STAFFORD
Drake and the Tudor Navy. London: 1898. V. 47
England in the Seven Years' War. London: 1907. V. 49
Kophetua the Thirteenth. London: 1889. V. 54

CORBETT, P. E.
The Sculpture of the Parthenon. London: 1959. V. 54

CORBETT, THE MISSES
The Busy-bodies, a Novel. London: 1827. V. 49
Tales and Legends. Edinburgh: 1828. V. 49

CORBETT, THOMAS
An Account of the Expedition of the British Fleet to Sicily in the Years 1718, 1719 and 1720. London: 1739. V. 48; 49

CORBETT, THOMAS B.
Colorado Mining Directory. Denver: 1879. V. 49

CORBIN, ALICE
The Sun Turns West. Santa Fe: 1933. V. 50

CORBIN, MARIE OVERTON
Urchins of the Sea. New York: 1900. V. 49

CORBUSIER, WILLIAM T.
Verde to San Carlos. Recollections of a Famous Army Surgeon and His Observant Family on the Western frontier, 1869-1886. Tucson: 1968. V. 53

CORBY, HERBERT
Hampdens Going Over. London: 1942. V. 48
Hampdens Going Over. London: 1945. V. 47; 49; 50; 52

CORCORAN, DENNIS
Pickings from the Portfolio of the Reporter of the New Orleans "Picayune"... Philadelphia: 1846. V. 47; 54

CORCORAN, WILLIAM WATSON
A Grandfather's Legacy: Containing a Sketch of His Life and Obituary Notices of some Members of His Family... Washington: 1879. V. 50

CORDA, A. C. I.
Icones Fungorum Hucusque Cognitorum. Prague: 1837-42. V. 54

CORDASCO, FRANCESCO
American Medical Imprints, 1820-1910. Totawa: 1985. V. 47; 49; 50; 51; 52; 53; 54

CORDEAUX, E. H.
A Bibliography of Printed Works Relating to the University of Oxford. 1968. V. 47

CORDELL, EUGENE FAUNTLEROY
The Medical Annals of Maryland 1799-1899, Prepared for the Centennial of the medical and Chirurgical fAculty. Baltimore: 1903. V. 49; 52

CORDER, E. M.
The Deer Hunter. New York: 1978. V. 51
The Deer Hunter. New York: 1979. V. 52

CORDER, PERCY
The Life of Robert Spence Watson. London: 1914. V. 49

CORDER, WILLIAM
The Trial of William Corder...for the Murder of Maria Marten. London: 1828. V. 52

CORDIER, A. H.
Some Big Hunts. Kansas City: 1911. V. 47

CORDIER, J.
Histoire de la Navigation Interieure, et Particulierement de celle d'Angleterre, Jusqu'en 1803....(with) Histoire de la Navigation Interieure et Particulierement de Celle des États-Unis d'Amerique... Paris: 1819/20. V. 54

CORDINER, CHARLES
Antiquities and Scenery of the North of Scotland. London: 1780. V. 47; 48; 54

CORDINER, JAMES
A Description of Ceylon, Containing an Account of the Country, Inhabitants and Natural Productions... London: 1807. V. 51

CORDLEY, RICHARD
A History of Lawrence Kansas, From the First Settlement to the Close of the Rebellion. Lawrence: 1895. V. 53

CORDRY, D.
Mexican Masks. 1980. V. 54

COREAL, FRANCOIS
Voyages de...Aux Indes Occidentales, Contenant ce qu'il y vu de plus Remarquable Pendant son Sejour Depuis 1666, Jusqu'en 1697. Amsterdam: 1722. V. 50

CORELLI, MARIE
The Life Everlasting. 1911. V. 52; 53
A Life for a Life. London: 1859. V. 53
The Master Christian. New York: 1900. V. 48
The Murder of Delicia. London: 1896. V. 47
The Murder of Delicia. Philadelphia: 1896. V. 49; 51; 53
A Nobel Life. New York: 1866. V. 53
Thelma. London: 1887. V. 50
The Woman's Kingdom. New York: 1868. V. 53
Wormwood, a Drama of Paris. London: 1890. V. 49

COREMANS, P.
The Adoration of the Mystical Lamb. Antwerp: 1948. V. 53

CORENLIUS NEPOS
Imperatorum Vitae Ex Editione Oxoniense. Glasguae: 1749. V. 54

COREY, D. STEVEN
Allen Press Bibliography: A Facsimile with Original Leaves and Additions to Date Including a Checklist of Ephemera. San Francisco: 1985. V. 53

CORFIELD, W. H.
Catalogue of the Collection of Books in Valuable Bindings of the Late Professor W. H. Corfield, M.D. London: 1904. V. 47

CORIOLIS, GASPARD GUSTAVE
Du Calcul de l'Effet des Machines, ou Considerations sur l'Emploi des Moteurs et sur Leur Evaluation, Pour Servir d'Introduction a l'Etude Speciale des Machines. Paris: 1829. V. 47

CORK, RICHARD
Vorticism and Abstract Art in the First Machine Age. London: 1975. V. 49; 51; 53

CORK & ORRERY, JOHN BOYLE, 5TH EARL OF
Letters from Italy in the Years 1754 and 1755... London: 1773. V. 49; 52; 54
Remarks On the Life and Writings of Dr. Jonathan Swift. London: 1752. V. 47; 50; 54

CORKEY, ALEXANDER
The Truth About Ireland, or Through the Emerald Isle with an Aeroplane... 1910. V. 48

CORLE, EDWIN
Death Valley and the Creek Called Furnace. 1962. V. 48
Farewell, My Slightly Tarnished Hero. New York: 1971. V. 54
Fig Tree John. New York: 1935. V. 54
Fig Tree John. Los Angeles: 1955. V. 53
Igor Stravinsky. 1949. V. 52

CORLETT, WILLIAM THOMAS
The Medicine-Man of the American Indian and His Cultural Background. Springfield & Baltimore: 1935. V. 47; 48; 49; 51; 52

CORMACK, W. E.
Narrative of a Journey Across the Island of Newfoundland in 1822. London: 1928. V. 52

CORMAN, CID
All in All. Kyoto: 1964. V. 47
Essays on the Arts of Language. Santa Barbara: 1978. V. 50
In Good Time. Kyoto: 1964. V. 54
In No Time. Kyoto: 1963. V. 54
The Responses. Ashland: 1956. V. 54
Sun Rock Man. Kyoto: 1962. V. 54

CORN, ALFRED
All Roads Are One. New York: 1976. V. 54

CORNABY, W. ARTHUR
A String of Chinese Peach-Stones. London: 1895. V. 50

CORNARIUS, JANUS
Universae rei Medicae. Basel: 1534. V. 54

CORNARO, LUIGI
Sure and Certain Methods of Attaining a Long and Healthful Life, etc. London: 1737. V. 52
The Temperate Man, or the Way of Preserving Life and Health. London: 1678. V. 51

CORNEILLE, PIERRE
Pompey the Great. London: 1664. V. 51
Pulcherie, Comedie Heroique. Paris: 1673. V. 48; 51
Theatre...Avec des Commentaires, et Autres Morceaux Interessans. Geneve: 1774. V. 49

CORNELIUS, BROTHER
Keith, Old Master of California. New York, Berkeley & Fresno: 1942/57. V. 50; 52; 54
Keith, Old Master of California. Fresno: 1956. V. 50

CORNELIUS, C. O.
Furniture Masterpieces of Duncan Phyfe. Garden City: 1922. V. 47

CORNELIUS, ELIAS
The Little Osage Captive, an Authentic Narrative. Boston: 1822. V. 47

CORNELIUS NEPOS
The Lives of Illustrious men. Oxon: 1684. V. 48; 54

CORNELL, F. C.
The Glamour of Prospecting. London: 1920. V. 52

CORNELL, JOSEPH
An Exhibition of Works... Pasadena: 1966-67. V. 47

CORNELL UNIVERSITY
The Cornell Wordsworth Collection. Ithaca: 1957. V. 53

CORNELL, WALTER
Health and Medical Inspection of School Children. Philadelphia: 1913. V. 53

CORNER, CAROLINE
Ceylon, the Paradise of Adam. London: 1908. V. 53

CORNER, E. J. H.
Wayside Trees of Malaya. Singapore: 1952. V. 52

CORNER, GEORGE RICHARD
The Panorama: with Memoirs of Its Inventor, Robert Barker, and His Son, the Late Henry Aston Barker. London: 1857. V. 54

CORNER, J.
The History of China and India... London: 1847. V. 51; 53

CORNER, JOHN
Portraits of Celebrated Painters, With Medallions From Their Best Performances. London: 1825. V. 50

CORNER, JULIA
A Gift to Young Friends: or The Guide to Good in Words of One Syllable. London: 1845. V. 47
The Play Grammar or the Elements of Grammar Explained in Easy Games. London: 1848. V. 49
Spring Flowers; or the Poetical Bouquet... London. V. 47; 49

CORNER, SIDNEY
Rural Churches, Their Histories, Architecture and Antiquities. London: 1869. V. 50

CORNER, WILLIAM
San Antonio de Bexar. San Antonio: 1890. V. 50; 52; 53; 54

CORNET, J.
Art of Africa, Treasures from the Congo. New York: 1971. V. 51

CORNEY, BOLTON
Comments on the Evidence of Antonio Panizzi Esquire Before the Select Committee of the House of Commons on the British Museum, A.D. 1860. London: 1860. V. 54
Curiosities of Literature. Greenwich: 1837. V. 48; 51

CORNEY, BOLTON GLANVILL
The Quest and Occupation of Tahiti by Emissaries of Spain During the Years 1772-1776. London: 1913/15/16. V. 47
The Quest and Occupation of Tahiti by Emissaries of Spain During the Years 1772-1776. 1967. V. 47

CORNEY, PETER
Voyages in the Northern Pacific. Honolulu: 1896. V. 47; 51; 53

CORNFORD, FRANCES
Autumn Midnight. Ditchling: 1923. V. 50
Collected Poems. London: 1954. V. 50
Poems. Hampstead & Cambridge: 1910. V. 50; 53
Spring Morning. Poems. London: 1915. V. 54

CORNFORD, L. COPE
A Century of Sea Trading 1824-1924. London: 1924. V. 49; 52

CORNING, J. LEONARD
Local Anaesthesia in General Medicine and Surgery, Being the Practical Application of the Author's Recent Discoveries. New York: 1886. V. 47

CORNISH, C. J.
The New Forest. London: 1894. V. 52; 53
Sir William Henry Flower, K.C.B. London: 1904. V. 53; 54

CORNISH, GEORGE AUGUSTUS
A Canadian School Geography. Toronto: 1922. V. 54

CORNISH, HENRY
Under the Southern Cross. Madras: 1879. V. 52

CORNPLANTER, JESSE
Legends of the Longhouse. Philadelphia: 1938. V. 50

CORNWALL, BARRY
Mirandola, a Tragedy. London: 1821. V. 53

CORNWALL, BRUCE
Life Sketch of Pierre Barlow Cornwall. San Francisco: 1906. V. 47; 50; 54

CORNWALLIS, EARL
An Answer to that Part of the Narrative of Lieutenant-General Sir Henry Clinton, K.B. which Relates to the Conduct of Lieutenant-General Earl Cornwallis, During the Campaign in North America, in the Year 1781. London: 1783. V. 47; 50

CORNWALLIS, KINAHAN
The New Eldorado; or British Columbia. London: 1858. V. 49

CORNWALLIS, WILLIAM
Essayes. London: 1632. V. 48; 51

CORNWELL, PATRICIA
All That Remains. London: 1992. V. 52
Body of Evidence. New York: 1991. V. 52; 53
Cause of Death. New York: 1996. V. 53; 54
Cruel & Unusual. New York: 1993. V. 53
From Potter's Field. New York: 1995. V. 51
Postmortem. London: 1990. V. 52
Postmortem. New York: 1990. V. 52; 53
A Time for Remembering: the Ruth Bell Graham Story. 1983. V. 53

CORONA, California, The Queen Colony Illustrated. 1902. V. 53

CORONADO, FRANCISCO VASQUEZ DE
The Journey of Francisco Vasquez De Coronado. San Francisco: 1933. V. 51

THE CORONATION: a Poem Humbly Addressed to Nobody Who Was There. London: 1761. V. 48

THE CORONATION of Her Majesty Queen Elizabeth II, 1953. Worcester: 1953. V. 52

THE CORONATION of His Most Sacred Majesty King George the Fourth: Solemnized in the Collegiate Church of Saint Peter Westminster Upon the Nineteenth Day of July MDCCCXXI. London: 1824. V. 54

CORONELLI
Ordinarium Equstrium ac Militarium Brevis Narratio, Cum Imaginibus Exposita, Ap. Coronelli Quamplurimis Additionibus Locupletatis Nempe Curiae Romanae, Hebroerum, Graecorumve... Venice: 1715. V. 48

CORPORATION OF NORWICH
Notices and Illustrations of the Costume, Processions, Pageantry &c., Formerly Displayed by the Corporation of Norwich. Norwich: 1850. V. 52

CORRADO, SEBASTIANO
Commentarius, In Quo M.T. Ciceronis de Claris Oratoribus Liber, Qui Dicitur Brutus & Loci Pene Innumerabiles Quum Aliorum Scriptorum, Tum Ciceronis Ipsius Explicantur. Florence: 1552. V. 48

CORREA, PEDRO
Conspiracao Universal. Combatem os Sete Vicios Matadores com as Sete Virtudes Contrarias Sobre a Posse dal Alma, Servindo o Demonio de General na Liga Viciosa, & Fazendo Christo Officio de Capitao no Santo Exercito. Lisbon: 1615. V. 48

CORREA DE LACERDA, FERNANDO
Catasrophe de Portugal na Deposicao d'El Rei D. Affonso o Sexto, & Subrogacao do Princepe D. Pedro o Unico, Justificada nas Calamidades Publicas, Escrita Para Justificacao dos Portugueses... Lisbon;: 1669. V. 51

A CORRECT Narrative of the Distressing Shipwrecks, the Unhappily Took Place in Seaford Bay, on Thursday Morning Dec. 7th, 1809... 1809 or 1810. V. 53

CORREDOR-MATHEOS, JOSE
Miro's Posters. Barcelona: 1987. V. 47; 48; 50; 52; 53; 54

CORRELL, CHARLES
Sam 'N' Henry. Chicago: 1926. V. 48

CORRELL, D. S.
Aquatic and Wetland Plants of the Southwestern United States. Washington: 1972. V. 54
Manual of the Vascular Plants of Texas. 1979. V. 48; 51; 52
Manual of the Vascular Plants of Texas. Richardson: 1979. V. 47
Native Orchids of North America. Stanford: 1950. V. 54

CORRELL, J. LEE
Through White Men's Eyes: a Contribution to Navajo History. Window Rock: 1979. V. 50

CORRESPODNENCE with Reference to the Proposed Construction of a Channel Tunnel. London: 1882. V. 51

CORRESPONDENCE Relative to Hostilities of the Arickanee Indians. Washington: 1823. V. 54

CORRESPONDENCE Respecting Direct Commerce with the West of China from Rangoon. London: 1865. V. 47

THE CORRESPONDENTS. An Original Novel; in a Series of Letters. London: 1775. V. 47

CORRIE, EDGAR
Letters on the Subject of the Scotch Distillery Laws. Liverpool: 1796. V. 52

CORRINGTON, J. D.
Adventures with the Miscroscope. Rochester: 1934. V. 53

CORRINGTON, JOHN
The Anatomy of Love and Other Poems. Fort Lauderdale: 1964. V. 53

CORROTHERS, JAMES D.
The Black Cat Club. New York: 1902. V. 53

CORROZET, GILLES
Les Antiqvitez Croniqves et Singvlaritez de Paris...Augmentees... Paris: 1586. V. 47

CORRY, J.
The History of Lancashire. London: 1825. V. 53

CORRY, JOHN
Biographical Memoirs of the Illustrious Gen. George Washington. New Haven: 1810. V. 48
Biographical Memoirs of the Illustrious Gen. George Washington... Barnard: 1813. V. 53
The Detector of Quackery; or, Analyser of Medical, Philosophical, Political, Dramatic and Literary Imposture. London: 1802. V. 50
The History of Henry Thomson, or the Reward of Filial Affection. London: 1803. V. 47
The Life of Joseph Priestley... Birmingham: 1804. V. 51
Memoirs of Edward Thornton; or, a Sketch of Modern Dissipation in London. London: 1805. V. 47
A Satirical View of London at the Commencement of the 19th Century. London: 1801. V. 51; 52

CORRY, JOSEPH
Observations Upon the Windward Coast of Africa, the Religion, Character, Customs &c. of the Natives... London: 1807. V. 50

CORRY, TREVOR
Descriptive and Scenic Souvenir. The White Pass and Yukon Route. The Scenic Railway of the World... Seattle: 1900. V. 52

CORRY, WILLIAM
Reflections Upon Liberty and Necessity, &c. London: 1761. V. 48

CORSAN, W. C.
Two Months in the Confederate States, Including a Visit to New Orleans Under the Domination of General Butler. London: 1863. V. 53

THE CORSICAN'S Downfall. The Rise, Name, Regin and Final Downfall of Napoleon, Alias Nicolais Buonaparte... Mansfield: 1814. V. 52

CORSO, GREGORY
The American Express. 1961. V. 49; 53
Ankh. New York: 1971. V. 48; 54
Long Live Man. 1962. V. 48
Mindfield. New York: 1989. V. 48; 49; 50; 51
The Mutation of the spirit. New York: 1964. V. 48
The Vestal Lady on Brattle. Cambridge: 1955. V. 48; 54

CORT, C. F.
A Tribute to Learning, Fame, Science and Genius. London: 1834. V. 50; 54

CORTAZAR, JULIO
All the Fire and Other Stories. New York: 1973. V. 53
Les Armes Secretes. Paris: 1963. V. 49
Bestario. Buenos Aires: 1951. V. 49
End of the Game. New York: 1963. V. 49
End of the Game. New York: 1967. V. 51; 52; 53
A Manual for Manuel. New York: 1978. V. 53
The Winners. New York: 1965. V. 53

CORTE, CLAUDIO
Il Cavallerizzo...ne Qual si Tratta della Natura de Cavalli, Delle Razze, del Mode di Governali, Domarli & Frenarli. Venice: 1573. V. 47

CORTES, HERNANDO
Historia de Neuva-Espana, Escrita por su Esclarecido Conquistador Hernan Cortes,... Mexico: 1770. V. 50

CORTESAO, ARMANDO
History of Portuguese Cartography. Coimbra: 1969. V. 50
The Natutical Chart of 1424. Coimbra: 1954. V. 48; 51

CORTESE, JAMES
What the Owl Said. 1979. V. 52
What the Owl Said... Vermont: 1979. V. 47

CORTI, EGON CAESAR, COUNT
The Reign of the House of Rothschild. New York: 1928. V. 54

CORTISSOZ, ROYAL
Monograph of the Work of Charles A. Platt. New York: 1925. V. 51

CORVISART, J. N.
An Essay on the Organic Diseases and Lesions of the Heart and Great Vessels. Boston: 1812. V. 53

CORWIN, EDWARD TANJORE
The Corwin Genealogy (Curwin, Curwen, Corwine) in the United States. New York: 1872. V. 49; 51

CORY, ALEXANDER TURNER
The Hieroglyphics of Horapollo Nilous. London: 1840. V. 49

CORY, C. B.
Catalogue of Birds of the Americas and Adjacent islands. Chicago: 1918-49. V. 48; 50

CORY, DAVID
The Adventures of Rag and Tag. New York: 1915. V. 50

CORY, H.
African Figurines, Their Ceremonial Use in Puberty Rites in Tanganyika. London: 1956. V. 54

CORY, ISAAC PRESTON
Ancient Fragments of the Phoenician, Chaldean, Egyptian, Tyrian, Carthaginian, Indian, Persian and Other Writers. London: 1832. V. 51

CORY, WILLIAM JOHNSON
Ionica. London and Orpington: 1891. V. 50
Ionica. (with) Ionica II. London: 1858/77. V. 50
Lucretilis. 1951. V. 52
Lucretilis. Cambridge: 1951. V. 48; 51

CORYATE, THOMAS
Coryate's Crudities. London: 1611. V. 52; 53; 54
Coryate's Crudities... Glasgow: 1905. V. 47; 51
Traveller for the English Wits: Greeting from the Court of the Great Mogul, Resident at the Towne of Asmere, in Eastern India. 1616. V. 54

CORYE, JOHN
The Generous Enemies or the Ridiculous Lovers: a Comedy. London: 1672. V. 48

COSENTINO, D. J.
Sacred Hearts of Haitian Vodou. 1995. V. 54

COSENTINO, FRANK F.
Edward Marshall Boehm 1913-1969. Chicago: 1969. V. 47

COSGRAVE, GEORGE
Early California Justice. San Francisco: 1948. V. 47; 48; 49; 52

COSGROVE, RACHEL R.
Hidden Valley of Oz. Chicago: 1951. V. 49; 54

COSIN, JAMES
The Names of the Roman Catholic Nonjurors, and Others, Who Refus'd to Take the Oaths of His Late Majesty King George. London: 1745. V. 54

COSIN, JOHN
A Scholastic History of the Canon of the Holy Scripture or the Certain and Indubitate Books Thereof... London: 1657. V. 49; 51
A Scholastic History of the Canon of the Holy Scripture or the Certain and Indubitate Books thereof... London: 1672. V. 51

COSIN, RICHARD
An Apologie for Sundrie Proceedings by Jurisidiction Ecclesiastaicall, of Late Times by Some Challenged, and Also Diversly by them Impugned... London: 1593. V. 54

COSMO III, GRAND DUKE OF TUSCANY
Travels of Cosmo the Third...through England, During the Reign of King Charles the Second (1669). London: 1821. V. 50

COSTA, E. M. DA
Elements of Conchology... London: 1776. V. 54

COSTA, JOHN C.
Clinical Hematology: a Practical Guide to the Examination of the Blood. Philadelphia: 1902. V. 48

COSTAKIS, GEORGE
Russian Avant-Garde Art. New York: 1981. V. 50; 51; 53

COSTARD, GEORGE
The History of Astronomy, with Its Application to Geography, History and Chronology... London: 1767. V. 48; 52

COSTELLO, DUDLEY
The Cream of Jest; a Fund of Chaste Wit and Humour. Derby: 1826. V. 49
Holidays and Hobgoblins and Talk of Strange Things. London: 1861. V. 49; 51; 54

COSTELLO, J. A.
Th Siwash Their Life, Legends and Tales. Seattle: 1895. V. 50

COSTELLO, LOUISA STUART
The Queen's Poisoner or France in the Sixteenth Century. London: 1841. V. 53
The Rose Garden of Persia. London: 1888. V. 47; 49
Specimens of Early Poetry of France from the Time of the Troubadours...to the Reign of Henri Quatre. London: 1835. V. 51; 52
Venice and the Venetians: With a Glance at the Vaudois and the Tyrol. London: 1850. V. 49

COSTER, FRANCISCUS
Enchiridion Controversiarvm Praecipvarvm Nostri Temporis de Religione. Coloniae Agrippinae: 1590. V. 50

COSTIGAN, JAMES
Little Moon of Alban/A Wind from the South. New York: 1959. V. 54

THE COSTUME, Manners and Peculiarities of Different Inhabitants of the Globe. London: 1830. V. 52; 54

COSTUME of the Russian Empire. London: 1803. V. 47

COSTUMES et Botiques Egyptiens faits par M. Bloch. Partie II. 1840's. V. 49

COSTUMES Suisses. Zurich: 1880. V. 48

COT, PIERRE
Triumph of Treason. Chicago: 1944. V. 49

COTES, ROGER
Hydrostatical and Pneumatical Lectures. Cambridge: 1747. V. 52
Hydrostatical and Pneumatical Lectures... London: 1775. V. 50

COTGRAVE, RANDLE
A Dictionnarie of the French and English Tongues. London: 1611. V. 48

COTTA, JOHN
The Triall of Witch-Craft, Shewing the Trve and Right Methode of the Discovery. London: 1916. V. 53

THE COTTAGE Fireside. Dublin: 1821. V. 52

COTTAGE Tales for Little People; or, the Amusing Repository for All Good Boys and Girls. Glasgow: 1810. V. 53

COTTER, JOSEPH S.
The Band of Gideon: and Other Lyrcis. Boston: 1918. V. 47

COTTERELL, CONSTANCE
Summer Holidays in North East England. London: 1895. V. 52

COTTERILL, ROBERT S.
History of Pioneer Kentucky. Cincinnati: 1917. V. 47

COTTIN, MARIE SOPHIE RISTAUD
Mathilde ou Memoires Tires de l'Histoire des Croisades. Londres: 1809. V. 47

COTTIN, SOPHIE
Malvina, by Madame C****... London: 1804. V. 50

COTTING, URIAH
Boston and Roxbury Mill Corporation. Boston: 1818. V. 51

COTTLE, JOSEPH
Alfred, an Epic Poem, in Twenty-Four Books. London: 1800. V. 54
Alfred: an Epic Poem in Twenty-Four Books. London: 1804. V. 54
Early Recollections; Chiefly Relating to the Late Samuel Taylor Coleridge, During His Long Residence in Bristol. London: 1837. V. 53; 54
The Fall of Cambria, a Poem. London: 1808. V. 54
Malvern Hills, and Other Poems. London: 1802. V. 52
A New Version of the Psalms of David. London: 1801. V. 50; 52

COTTON, ALFRED J.
Cotton's Sketch-Boook. Portland: 1874. V. 51

COTTON, B. C.
South Australian Mollusca: Pelecypoda. 1961. The Molluscs of South Australia: Part II. Scaphopoda, Cephalopoda, Aplacophora and Crepipoda. 1940. Adelaide: 1940-61. V. 51

COTTON, CHARLES
Burlesque Upon Burlesque; or, the Scoffer Scoft. London: 1675. V. 50
The Planter's Manual... London: 1675. V. 53
Poems on Several Occasions. London: 1689. V. 47; 48; 49
Scarronides. London: 1655. V. 48
Scarronides... London: 1664. V. 50; 51; 54
Scarronides... London: 1665. V. 47
Scarronides... London: 1667. V. 47; 49
Scarronides... London: 1678. V. 47
Scarronides... Whiteheaven: 1776. V. 51
The Wonders of the Peake. London: 1681. V. 47

COTTON, CLEMENT
A Complete Concordance to the Bible of the Last Translation. London: 1631. V. 49

COTTON, HENRY
Editions of the Bible and Parts Thereof in English from the Year MDV to MDCCCL. Oxford: 1852. V. 47
Hints on Play with Steel Shafts. Liverpool. V. 49
The Typographical Gazetteer... Oxford: 1825. V. 50; 53

COTTON, JOHN
Beautiful Birds Described. Madgwick: 1860. V. 54
An Exposition Upon the Thirteenth Chapter of the Revelation... London: 1655. V. 49
A Modest and Cleare Answer to Mr. Balls Discourse of Set formes of Prayer. London: 1642. V. 49
A Practical Commentaray, Or an Exposition With Observations, Reasons and Uses Upon the First Epistle Generall of John. London: 1656. V. 48

COTTON, JOSIAH
Vocabulary of the Massachusetts (or Natick) Indian Language. Cambridge: 1829. V. 47

COTTON, NATHANEL
Observations on a Particular Kind of Scarlet Fever, That Lately Prevailed in and about St. Alban's. London: 1749. V. 48

COTTON, NATHANIEL
Visions in Verse, for the Entertainment and Instruction of Younger Minds. London: 1752. V. 50
Visions in Verse, for the Entertainment and Instruction of Younger Minds. London: 1782. V. 49

COTTON, ROBERT BRUCE
Cottoni Posthuma: Divers Choice Pieces of That Renowned Antiquary... London: 1651. V. 49; 51
Cottoni Posthuma: Divers Choice Pieces of that Renowned Antiquary... London: 1672. V. 47; 50; 52; 54
The Danger Wherein the Kingdome Now Standeth and the Remedie. London: 1628. V. 47; 52
An Exact Abridgement of the Records in the Tower of London, From the Reign of King Edward the Second, Unto King Richard the Third... London: 1657. V. 47; 48; 49; 50; 53
The Forme of Governement of the Kingdome of England:... London: 1642. V. 47
A Short View of the Long Life and Raigne of Henry the Third, King of England. London: 1627. V. 47; 50

COTTON, WILLIAM
Sir Joshua Reynolds, and His Works. London: 1856. V. 49

COTTON, WILLIAM A.
The Coins, Tokens and Medals of Worcestershire, with Illustrations and Notes. Bromsgrove: 1885. V. 48

COUCH, JONATHAN
A History of the Fishes of the British Islands. London: 1862-65. V. 54
A History of the Fishes of the British Islands. Groombridge: 1868-69. V. 49
A History of the Fishes of the British Islands. London: 1877. V. 49; 50; 52
A History of the Fishes of the British Isles. London: 1879. V. 48; 49; 53

COUCH, NEVADA
Pages from Cherokee Indian History, as Identified with Samuel Austin Worcester, D.D. for 34 Years a Missionary of the A.B.C.F.M. Among the Cherokees. St. Louis: 1885?. V. 47

COUES, ELLIOTT
The Expeditions of Zebulon Montgomery Pike, to the Headwaters of the Mississippi River. New York: 1895. V. 53
Forty Years a Fur Trader on the Upper Missouri, the Personal Narrative of Charles Larpenteur 1833-1872. New York: 1898. V. 53
Fur-Bearing Animals: A Monograph of North American Mustelidae, in Whichn an Account of the wolverene, the Martens or Sables, the Ermine, the Mink and Various Other Kinds of Weasels, Several Species of Skunks, the Badger, the Land and Sea Otters... Washington: 1877. V. 49
The History of the Lewis and Clark Expedtion. New York: 1893. V. 52
Key to North American Birds... Boston: 1903. V. 49
The Manuscript Journals of Alexander Henry and of David Thompson 1799-1814. V. 53
Monographs of North American Rodentia. Washington: 1887. V. 49; 52; 53
New Light on the Early History of the Greater Northwest. New York: 1897. V. 48
New Light on the Early History of the Greater Northwest. Minneapolis: 1965. V. 52
On the Trail of a Spanish Pioneer: The Diary and Itinerary of Francisco Garces. New York: 1900. V. 52

COUGHLIN, JACK
Grotesques: Etchings. Baltimore: 1970. V. 47

COULSON, ELIZABETH KERR
Dante and Beatrice from 1282 to 1290. London: 1876. V. 48; 49; 51; 52

COULSON, F. RAYMOND
Darwin On Trial at the Old Bailey. Watford: 1899. V. 49

COULTER, EDITH M.
A Camera in the Gold Rush. San Francisco: 1946. V. 48

COULTER, ELLIS MERTON
Travels in the Confederate States. A Bibliography. Norman: 1948. V. 49; 53

COULTER, G. W.
Lake Tanganyika and Its Life. London: 1991. V. 49; 50; 52

COULTER, HARRIS
Divided Legacy: a History of the Schism in Medical Thought. Washington: 1975-82. V. 50; 52

COULTER, JOHN
Adventures on the Western Coast of South America, and the Interior of California... London: 1847. V. 47; 51; 54

COUNCIL Bluffs City Directory for the Year Commencement August 1st, 1889. Omaha: 1889. V. 50

THE COUNCIL of Dogs. Philadelphia: 1809. V. 48

COUNSELL, CHARLES O.
The Stenographer or Self Instructor in the Art of Short-Hand. New York: 1839. V. 53

COUNSELL, GEORGE
The Art of Midwifery; or, the Midwife's Sure Guide... London: 1752. V. 48

COUNT Piper's Packet; Being a Choice and Curious Collection of Manuscript Papers, in Prose and Verse... London: 1732. V. 47

COUNT Roderic's Castle: or, Gothic Times, a Tale. Baltimore: 1795. V. 54

COUNTRY and Seaside. London. V. 51

COUNTRY Architecture in France and England XV. and XVI Centuries. Buffalo: 1896. V. 49

THE COUNTRY Gentleman's Companion... London: 1753. V. 49

THE COUNTRY Life Annual for 1938. London: 1938. V. 49

THE COUNTRY Parson's Companion: or Young Clergyman's Lawyer. London: 1725. V. 50

COUNTRYMAN, A. J.
A Pioneer's Trip Across the Plains. Moville: 1951. V. 47

COUNTY Atlas of Warren, New Jersey, from Actual Surveys by and Under the Direction of F. W. Beers. New York: 1874. V. 47; 49; 51

COUPER, CATHARINE M. A.
Visits to Beechwood Farm: or, Country Pleasures, and Hints for Happiness. London: 1848. V. 49

COUPER, ROBERT
Poetry Chiefly in the Scottish Language. Inverness: 1804. V. 53
Speculations on the Mode and Appearances of Impregnation in the Human Female... Edinburgh: 1797. V. 48

The Tourifications of Malachi Meldrum Esq. of Meldrum-Hall... Aberdeen: 1803. V. 47; 48; 52

COUPER, WILLIAM
Investigations of a Naturalist Between Mingan and Watchicouti, Labrador. Quebec: 1868. V. 54

COUPLAND, R.
The Exploitation of East Africa 1856-1890: the Slave Trade and the Scramble. London: 1939. V. 54

COURNAND, ANDRE
Cardiac Catherization in Congenital Heart Disease: a Clinical and Physiological Study. New York: 1949. V. 48; 53

COURNOS, JOHN
The Lost Leader. New York: 1964. V. 54

COURNOT, ANTOINE AUGUSTIN
Recherches sur les Principes Mathematiques de la Theorie des Richesses... Paris: 1838. V. 50; 54

COURSEY, CLARK
Courthouses of Texas. Brownwood: 1962. V. 49; 53

COURSEY, O. W.
Wild Bill. Mitchell: 1924. V. 53

COURT, D.
Succulent Flora of Southern Africa. Rotterdam: 1981. V. 50; 51

THE COURT Of Adultery: a Vision (in Verse). London: 1778. V. 54

COURT, PIETER DE LA
The True Interest and Political Maxims of the Republic of Holland... London: 1746. V. 53

COURT DE GEBELIN, ANTOINE
Histoire Naturelle De la Parole, ou Precis de l'Origine du Langage & de la Grammaire Universelle. Paris: 1776. V. 49; 50

COURTENAY, JOHN
Juvenile Poems. London: 1795. V. 52
Philosophical Reflections on the Late Revolution in France, and the Conduct of Dissenters in England. London: 1790. V. 51; 52
A Poetical Review of the Literary and Moral Character of the Late Samuel Johnson, LL.D. London: 1786. V. 48
The Rape of Pomona. London: 1773. V. 54

COURTHION, PIERRE
Georges Rouault. New York. V. 47; 48; 50; 52
Georges Rouault. New York: 1961. V. 47; 50; 52
Georges Rouault. New York: 1962. V. 50
Georges Rouault. New York: 1963. V. 51

COURTHOPE, W. J.
A History of English Poetry. London: 1911. V. 49
A History of English Poetry. London: 1926. V. 53

COURTIER, PETER
Poems. London: 1796. V. 54

COURTILZ, GATIEN, SIEUR DE SANDRAS
French Intrigues; or, The History of Their Delusory Promises Since the Pyrenaean Treaty. London: 1685. V. 50
The French Spy. London: 1700. V. 47; 50; 51
The History of the Life and Actions of that Great Captain of His Age the Viscount de Turenne. London: 1686. V. 50; 54
The Life of the Famous John Baptist Colbert, Late Minister and Secretary to Lewis XIV, the Present French King. London: 1695. V. 47

COURTNEY, ABRAM V.
Anecdotes of the Blind... Boston: 1835. V. 51

COURTNEY, W. L.
Life of John Stuart Mill. London: 1889. V. 49

COURTNEY, W. P.
A Bibliography of Samuel Johnson. 1984. V. 48
Dodsleys Collection of Poetry, Its Contents and Contributors. London: 1910. V. 52

COURTONNE, JEAN
Traite de la Perspective Pratique, Avec des Remarques sur l'Architecture, Suivies de Quelques Edifices Considerables Mis en Perspective... Paris: 1725. V. 47

COURTRIGHT, GEORGE S.
An Expedition Against the Indians in 1864. Lithopolis: 1911. V. 54

THE COURTSHIP, Merry Marriage and Pic-Nic of Cock Robin and Jenny Wren. London: 1850. V. 52

COURVILLE, CYRIL
Commotio Cerebri: Cerebral Concussion and the Post concussion Syndrome in Their Medical and Legal Aspects. Los Angeles: 1953. V. 47

COUSE, ERWINA L.
Button Classics. Chicago: 1942. V. 52

COUSENS, HENRY
The Architectural Antiquities of Western India. London: 1926. V. 49

COUSIN Chatterbox's Railway Alphabet. London: 1855. V. 51

COUSIN, JEAN
L'Art de Dessinier. Paris: 1790. V. 47; 54

COUSIN, VICTOR
Course of the History of Modern Philosophy. New York: 1852. V. 54
Lectures on the True, the Beautiful and the Good. New York: 1857. V. 54
Report on the State of Public Instruction in Prussia... London: 1834. V. 52

COUSINS, F.
Colonial Architecture of Philadelphia. Boston: 1920. V. 53; 54
The Wood-Carver of Salem. Boston: 1916. V. 51

COUSTEAU, PIERRE
Pegma, cum Narrationibus Philosophicis. Lyon: 1555. V. 47

COUSTOS, JOHN
The Frauds of Romish Monks and Priests. London: 1704. V. 47

COUTANT, C. C.
The History of Wyoming from Earliest Known Discoveries... Laramie: 1899. V. 49

COUTS, CAVE J.
Arthur M. Ellis Memorial Edition of the Journals and Maps of Cave J. Couts. Los Angeles: 1933. V. 54
From San Diego to the Colorado in 1849: The Journals and Maps of Cave J. Couts. Los Angeles: 1932. V. 53; 54

COUTTS, HENRY T.
Manual of Library Bookbinding. 1911. V. 47
Manual of Library Bookbinding... London: 1911. V. 54

COUZYN, JENI
Twelve to Twelve - Poetry D-Day - Camden Festival 1970. London: 1970. V. 49

COVARRUBIAS, MIGUEL
The Eagle, the Jaguar and the Serpent. New York: 1954. V. 48; 50; 51; 53; 54
Indian Art of Mexico and Central America. New York: 1957. V. 47; 49; 50; 53
Negro Drawings. New York: 1927. V. 48; 51; 54
The Prince of Wales. New York: 1925. V. 50

COVEL, JOHN
Some Account of the Present Greek Church, With Reflections to Their Present Doctrine and Discipline... Cambridge: 1722. V. 51

COVELL, WILLIAM
A Modest and Reasonable Examination, of Some Things in Use in the Church of England, sundrie Times Heretofore Misliked... London: 1604. V. 47

THE COVENT Garden Journal Embellished with Four Views. London: 1810. V. 49

THE COVENTRIAN - Number 143. Coventry: 1933. V. 50

THE COVENTRIAN - Number 152. Coventry: 1936. V. 50

THE COVENTRIAN - Number 154. Coventry: 1937. V. 50

COVENTRY, FRANCIS
The History of Pompey the Little... London: 1751. V. 47; 48; 49; 51
The History of Pompey the Little... London: 1752. V. 51
The History of Pompey the Little... Waltham St. Lawrence: 1926. V. 51; 52; 54

COVENTRY, GEORGE
A Critical Inquiry Regarding the Real Authorship of the Letters of Junius... London: 1825. V. 48

COVENTRY, HENRY
Philemon to Hydaspes; Relating Several Conversations with Hortensius, Upon the Subject of False Religion. London: 1742. V. 47; 49

COVENTRY, PATMORE
Memoirs and Correspondence of Coventry Patmore. London: 1900. V. 50

COVENY, CHRISTOPHER
Twenty Scenes from the Works of Dickens. Sydney: 1883. V. 52; 54

THE COVERDALE Bible: a Leaf from the First Edition of the First Complete Bible in English. San Francisco: 1974. V. 48

COVERDALE, MILES
Certain Most Godly Fruitful, and Comfortable Letters of Such True Saintes and Holy Martyrs of God. London: 1564. V. 47; 50

COVERT, CHRISTINE
Duodecimary: Twelve Marbled Papers Formed Into a Rhythmic Series. Hancock: 1994. V. 53

COVERT, NICHOLAS
The Scrivener's Guide. London: 1695. V. 49
The Scrivener's Guide... London: 1740. V. 50

COVERTE, ROBERT
A True and Almost Incredible Report of an Englishman that...Travelled by Land Thorow Many Unknowne Kingdomes and Great Cities. London: 1631. V. 47; 52

COVILLE, FREDERICK VERNON
Botany of the Death Valley Expedition. Washington: 1893. V. 47; 48; 53
Desert Botanical Laboratory of the Carnegie Institution. Washington: 1903. V. 53

COVNERSE, LORING
Notes of What I Saw, and How I Saw it: a Tour Around the World Including California. Bucyrus: 1882. V. 50

COW, JOHN
Remarks on the Manner of Fitting Boards for Ships of War and Transport: Addressed to the Officers of the Royal Navy. London: 1841. V. 50; 53

COWAN, ALEXANDER
Remains...Consisting of His Verses and Extracts From His Correspondence and Journals. Edinburgh: 1839. V. 49; 54

COWAN, HUGH
Report of the Trial of John Thomson Alias Peter Walker...for the Murder of Agnes Montgomery by Prussic Acid. Edinburgh: 1858. V. 53

COWAN, JAMES
The Maoris of New Zealand. Chirstchurch: 1910. V. 54

COWAN, JOHN
Diseases of the Heart with Chapters on Electro-Cardiograph... Philadelphia: 1914. V. 48; 53

COWAN, ROBERT ERNEST
A Bibliography of the History of California 1510-1930. San Francisco: 1933. V. 53; 54
A Bibliography of the History of California, 1510-1930. San Francisco: 1933/64. V. 47; 53
A Bibliography of the History of California 1510-1930. Los Angeles: 1964. V. 47
A Bibliography of the History of California...1510-1906. San Francisco: 1914. V. 50; 53
A Bibliography of the Spanish Press of California, 1833-1845. San Francisco: 1919. V. 52
The Booklover's Litany. Pasadena: 1930. V. 54

COWAN, SAMUEL K.
Play: a Picture Book of Boys, Girls and Babies. London: 1884. V. 47

COWAN, WILLIAM
A Bibliography of the Book of Common Order and Pslam Book of the Church of Scotland 1556-1644. Edinburgh;: 1913. V. 50

COWARD, NOEL
Bitter Sweet and Other Plays. Garden City: 1929. V. 52
Bon Voyage. Garden City: 1968. V. 54
Chelsea Buns. 1924. V. 54
Chelsea Buns. London: 1925. V. 47; 49
Middle East Diary. Garden City: 1944. V. 54
Middle East Diary. London: 1944. V. 48; 50
The Noel Coward Song Book. London: 1953. V. 53
Not Yet the Dodo and Other Verses. London: 1967. V. 54
Nude with Violin. Garden City: 1958. V. 54
Nude with Violin. New York: 1958. V. 51
Peace In Our Time. Garden City: 1948. V. 52; 54
Play Parade. London: 1934. V. 54
Play Parade. Garden City: 1948. V. 49
Play Parade. London: 1949/50/54. V. 48
The Plays of...First Series. Garden City: 1928. V. 51
Pomp and Circumstance. Garden City: 1960. V. 54
Post-Mortem. Garden City: 1931. V. 49
Post-Mortem... London: 1931. V. 54
Present Indicative. Garden City: 1937. V. 53
Present Indicative. London: 1937. V. 50
Present Indicative. New York: 1937. V. 48
Pretty Polly... London: 1964. V. 53
Pretty Polly. Garden City: 1965. V. 50; 54
Private Lives. London: 1930. V. 50; 53
Quadrille. London: 1952. V. 53
The Railway Book. London: 1952. V. 51
Spangled Unicorn. London. V. 54
Spangled Unicorn... London: 1932. V. 53
Star Quality-Six Stories. Garden City: 1951. V. 54
Suite in Three Keys... London: 1966. V. 49
Suite in Three Keys. Garden City: 1967. V. 54
Tonight at 8:30. New York: 1936. V. 49
The Vortex, a Play in Three Acts. London: 1925. V. 52
Waiting in the Wings. Garden City: 1961. V. 54
A Withered Nosegay. London: 1922. V. 51

COWARD, T. A.
The Birds of the British isles and Their Eggs. London and New York: 1930. V. 49
The Vertebrate Fauna of Cheshire and Liverpool Bay. 1910. V. 53
The Vertebrate Fauna of Cheshire and Liverpool Bay. London: 1910. V. 48
The Vertebrate Fauna of Cheshire and Liverpool Bay. Witherby: 1910. V. 48

COWBOY ARTISTS OF AMERICA
Cowboy Artists of America 1978. Thirteenth Annual Exhibition. Phoenix: 1978. V. 50
Cowboy Artists of America 1980: Fifteenth Annual Exhibition at the Phoenix Art Museum, October 24-November 23, 1980. Flagstaff: 1980. V. 47
Cowboy Artists of America: Eighth Annual Exhibition. Flagstaff: 1973. V. 47
Cowboy Artists of America: Eleventh Annual Exhibition. Flagstaff: 1976. V. 47
Cowboy Artists of America: Fourteenth Annual Exhibition. Kansas City: 1979. V. 47
Cowboy Artists of America: Ninth Annual Exhibition. Flagstaff: 1974. V. 47
Cowboy Artists of America: Seventh Annual Exhibition/1972. Flagstaff: 1972. V. 47
Cowboy Artists of America: Sixth Annual Exhibition/1971. Flagstaff: 1971. V. 47
Cowboy Artists of America: Tenth Annual Exhibition. Flagstaff: 1975. V. 47
Cowboy Artists of America: Thirteenth Annual Exhibition. Kansas City: 1978. V. 47
Cowboy Artists of America: Twelfth Annual Exhibition. Flagstaff: 1977. V. 47

COWDEN, ROBERT
A Brief Sketch of the Organization and Services of the Fifty-Ninth Regiment of United States Colored Infantry and Biographical Sketches. Dayton: 1883. V. 54

COWDEN CLARKE, MARY
Many Happy Returns of the Day. London: 1860. V. 50
My Long Life: an Autobiographic Sketch. London: 1896. V. 50
Recollections of Writers. London: 1878. V. 49; 50

COWDRY, E. V.
Arteriosclerosis: a Survey of the Problem. New York: 1933. V. 52; 53
Cancer Cells. Philadlephia: 1955. V. 53
Special Cytology: The Form and Functions of the Cell in Health and Disease. New York: 1928. V. 53

COWDRY, RICHARD
A Description of the Pictures, Statues, Busto's, Basso-Relievo's and Other Curiosities at the Earl of Pembroke's House at Wilton. London: 1751. V. 53

COWELL, JOHN
Institvtiones Ivris Anglicani, ad Methodvm et Seriem Institvtionvm Imperialium Compositae & Digestae. Frankfurt: 1630. V. 52
The Interpreter... London: 1637. V. 47; 50; 51; 52
The Interpreter... London: 1658. V. 48
The Interpreter... London: 1672. V. 48

COWELL, JOSEPH
Thirty Years Passed Among the Players in England and America, Interspersed with Anecdotes... New York: 1844. V. 47

COWELL, M. H.
A Floral Guide for East Kent. Faversham: 1839. V. 54

COWEN, ESEK
A Treatise on the Civil Jurisidiction of Justices of the Peace in the State of New York. Albany: 1844. V. 51

COWEN, WILLIAM
Characters of Trees. London: 1837. V. 47

COWHAM, HILDA
For Somebody's Baby. London: 1920. V. 47

COWIE, ISAAC
The Company of Adventurers: a Narrative of Seven Years in the Service of the Hudson's Bay Company During 1867-1874.... Toronto: 1913. V. 48; 51; 53

COWIE, J.
Alliterative Anomalies for Infants and Invalids. London: 1913. V. 50

COWING, FANNY
Harvestings: Sketches in Prose and Verse. Boston: 1855. V. 54

COWLES, B. K.
Alaska. Interesting and Reliable Information... Madison: 1885. V. 50

COWLEY, ABRAHAM
The Mistress and other Select Poems... London: 1926. V. 48; 49
Poemata Latina. London: 1668. V. 47
Prose Works Including His Essays in Prose and Verse. London: 1826. V. 50
Select Works in Verse and Prose. London: 1772. V. 50
Wit and Loyalty Reviv'd, In a Collection of Some Smart Satyrs. London: 1682. V. 49
The Works... London: 1668. V. 47; 49; 52
The Works. London: 1672. V. 47; 50
The Works... London: 1678. V. 48
The Works... 1680. V. 47
Works... London: 1681. V. 47; 48; 49
The Works... London: 1684. V. 53
The Works... London: 1688. V. 47; 51; 53
The Works. (with) The Second Part of the Works. London: 1693. V. 50
The Works. (with) The Second Part of the Works. London: 1693/89. V. 53

COWLEY, CHARLOTTE
The Ladies History of England... London: 1780. V. 48

COWLEY, HANNAH
Who's the Dupe?. London: 1780. V. 49

COWLEY, JOHN D.
A Bibliography of Abridgments, Digests, Dictionaries and Indexes of English Lawa to the Year 1800. London: 1932. V. 49

COWLEY, MALCOLM
The Beginning Writer in the University. 1957. V. 54
Blue Juniata. New York: 1929. V. 49; 54
The Dream of the Golden Mountains: Remembering the 1930's. New York: 1980. V. 50
The Dry Season. Norfolk: 1941. V. 53
Exile's Return... New York: 1934. V. 54
Exile's Return. New York: 1981. V. 47; 48; 49; 50; 51; 53; 54
The Literary Situation. New York: 1954. V. 54
A Second Flowering: Works and Days of the Lost Generation. New York: 1973. V. 50

COWLING, ERIC T.
Rombalds Way. Otley: 1946. V. 47; 51; 53

COWPER, ASHLEY
The Norfolk Poetical Miscellany. London: 1744. V. 47

COWPER, EARL
Biographical Catalogue of the Portraits at Panshanger, the Seat of Earl Cowper, K.G. London: 1885. V. 53

COWPER, FRANCIS
Topolski's Legal London. London: 1961. V. 51

COWPER, HENRY
Reports of Cases Adjudged in the Court of King's Bench. London: 1783. V. 54

COWPER, HENRY SWAINSON
Hawkshead. London: 1899. V. 50; 52
The Hill of Graces. A Record of Investigation Among the Trilithons and Megalithic Sites of Tripoli. London: 1897. V. 51
The Oldest Register Book of the Parsih of Hawkshead in Lancashire 1568-1704. London: 1897. V. 50; 52
Registers of the Parish of Aldingham in Furness 1542-1695; Registers of the Parish Church of Coniston, Lancashire 1599-1700. Wigan: 1907. V. 50; 52

COWPER, WILLIAM
Anatomia Corporum Humanorum. Leyden: 1739. V. 47; 49
The Anatomy of Human Bodies. Leyden: 1737. V. 48
The Correspondence. London: 1904. V. 51
Cowper, Illustrated by a Series of Views, in or near the Park of Weston-Underwood, Bucks... London: 1803. V. 50
Hymns in Three Books. London: 1779. V. 49; 54
Life and Letters of William Cowper, Esq., With Remarks... London: 1812. V. 49
The Life and Posthumous Writings of... Chicester: 1803/03/04/06. V. 48; 50
Memoir of the Early Life of... London: 1816. V. 49; 51
Olney Hymns in Three Books. London: 1779. V. 47; 52
Poems. London: 1782. V. 50
Poems... London: 1782/85. V. 47; 48; 52
Poems... London: 1786. V. 52
Poems. London: 1787. V. 49; 51
Poems... Salem: 1792/91. V. 49
Poems. London: 1793. V. 51
Poems. London: 1794. V. 51
Poems. London: 1794-95. V. 49; 52
Poems. London: 1798. V. 48; 52
Poems. London: 1800. V. 48
Poems. London: 1803. V. 50
Poems... London: 1808. V. 47; 51
Poems. London: 1811. V. 49; 53
Poems. London: 1812. V. 52
Poems... London: 1815. V. 50
Poems... London: 1820. V. 47; 51
Poems. London: 1841. V. 47; 48; 49
The Poetical Works. London: 1843. V. 51
The Poetical Works... London: 1851. V. 52; 54
The Poetical Works. London: 1853. V. 47; 51; 54
The Poetical Works. Edinburgh: 1854. V. 47
The Poetical Works... New York: 1860. V. 47
The Poetical Works. London: 1862. V. 54
The Poetical Works. London: 1875. V. 54
Private Correspondence. London: 1824. V. 51
The Task, a Poem in Six Books. Philadelphia: 1787. V. 47; 50
The Works of William Cowper... London: 1835. V. 51

COWTAN, ROBERT
Passages from the Auto-Biography of a "Man of Kent". London: 1866. V. 49

COX, A. B.
Jugged Journalism. London: 1925. V. 49

COX, CHARLES E.
John Tobias, Sportsman. New York: 1937. V. 52

COX, CLIFFORD R.
Strathroy (Red Valley) 1834-1934. V. 48

COX, DAVID
A Series of Progressive Lessons Intended to Elucidate the Art of Landscape Painting in Water Colours. London: 1811. V. 48
A Series of Progressive Lessons Intended to Elucidate the Art of Landscape Painting in Water Colours. London: 1812. V. 48; 49
A Series of Progressive Lessons Intended to Elucidate the Art of Landscape Painting in Water Colours. London: 1820. V. 48
A Series of Progressive Lessons Intended to Elucidate the Art of Landscape Painting in Water Colours... London: 1828. V. 54
A Treatise on Landscape Painting and Effect in Water Colours... London: 1812. V. 47
A Treatise on Landscape Painting and Effect in Water Colours... London: 1814. V. 48; 49
A Treatise on Landscape Painting and Effect in Water Colours... London: 1840-41. V. 48; 50

COX, E.
Out of Silence. 1928. V. 49; 54

COX, E. H. M.
Farrer's Last Journey. Upper Burma, 1919-1920. London: 1926. V. 54
The New Flora and Sylva. London: 1928-38. V. 49
New Flora and Sylva. London: 1928-40. V. 49

COX, EARNEST SEVIER
White America. Richmond: 1923. V. 50

COX, EDWARD GODFREY
A Reference Guide to the Literature of Travel. New York: 1969. V. 47
A Reference Guide to the Literature of Travel... Cambridge: 1992. V. 48; 50

COX, EDWARD YOUNG
The Art of Garnishing Churches at Christmas and Other Festivals. London: 1868. V. 52

COX, FRANCIS AUGUSTUS
The Life of Philip Melanchthon... London and Edinburgh: 1815. V. 51

COX, GEOFFREY
Defence of Madrid. London: 1937. V. 49

COX, GEORGE
Black Gowns and Red Coats, or Oxford in 1834. London: 1834. V. 52

COX, GEORGE W.
The Life of John William Colenso, Bishop of Natal. London: 1888. V. 50
The Mythology of the Aryan Nations. 1878. V. 48

COX, ISAAC
The Annals of Trinity County. Eugene: 1940. V. 47; 52

COX, J. CHARLES
Catalogue of the Muniments and Manuscript Books Pertaining to the Dean and Chapter of Lichfield. London: 1887. V. 54
Notes on the Churches of Derbyshire. London: 1875-79. V. 49
The Parish Church of Giggleswick-in-Craven. Leeds: 1920. V. 47; 53

COX, J. M.
A Cultural Table of Orchidaceous Plants. Sydney: 1946. V. 48; 51; 52

COX, JAMES
Historical and Biographical Record of the Cattle Industry and the Cattlemen of Texas and Adjacent Territory. St. Louis: 1895. V. 53
Historical and Biographical Record of the Cattle Industry and the Cattlemen of Texas and Adjacent Territory. New York: 1959. V. 52; 53; 54
Old and New St. Louis... St. Louis: 1894. V. 54

COX, JAMES ESTEP
Exposition of Thomas W. Bartley, the Present Chief Justice of the State of Ohio, Showing Him to Be the Second Haman That Has Made His Appearance on This Earth. Mansfield: 1857. V. 48

COX, M. J.
The Snakes of Thailand and Their Husbandry. Melbourne: 1991. V. 52

COX, MAMIE WYNNE
The Romantic Flags of Texas. Dallas: 1936. V. 47; 49

COX, MARY L.
History of Hale County. Plainview: 1937. V. 48; 52
Narrative of Dimmock Charlton, a British Subject, Taken from the Brig "Peacock" by the U.S. Sloop "Hornet", Enslaved While a Prisoner of War... Philadelphia?: 1859?. V. 47

COX, MORRIS
An Abstract of Nature. London: 1968. V. 50
Blind Drawings... 1978. V. 49; 52; 54
Crash! An Experiment in Blockmaking and Printing. 1963. V. 52; 54
Crash! An Experiment in Blockmaking and Printing. London: 1963. V. 50; 51
Fourteen Triads. London: 1967. V. 50; 51
An Impression of Autumn: a Landscape Panorama. 1966. V. 52
An Impression of Spring, (Summer, Autumn, Winter): a Landscape Panorama. London: 1965/66. V. 48
An Impression of Winter: a Landscape Panorama. 1965. V. 52
An Impression of (Winter, Spring, Summer, Autumn). London: 1965-66. V. 49
Intimidations of Mortality. London: 1977. V. 51
Ma Gog Ma Gog: Being Random Examples of the Innumerable, Incredible Ideas and Guises of Gog, Ma, Gogma and Magog. London: 1973. V. 53
Mummers' Fool. London: 1965. V. 50; 51
The Warrior and the Maiden. London: 1967. V. 50
The Warrior and the Maiden. London: 1968. V. 51
Young Legs Eleven. London: 1976. V. 50

COX, NICHOLAS
The Gentleman's Recreation. London: 1697. V. 52
The Gentleman's Recreation. London: 1706. V. 48; 49; 52
The Gentleman's Recreation... London: 1721. V. 49; 53
The Gentleman's Recreation. London: 1928. V. 47

COX, PALMER
Brownie year Book. New York: 1895. V. 53
Brownies Abroad. London: 1899. V. 48
The Brownies Abroad. New York: 1899. V. 52
The Brownies Around the World. London: 1894. V. 47
The Brownies Around the World. New York: 1894. V. 49
The Brownies at Home. New York: 1893. V. 49
The Brownies: Their Book. New York: 1887. V. 49
The Brownies through the Union. London: 1895. V. 54
Queer People With Wings and Stings and their Kweer Kapers. Philadelphia: 1888. V. 49

COX, RICHARD
Hibernia Anglicana; or, the History of Ireland from the Conquest Thereof by the English, to this Present Time. 1689/90. V. 54
Hibernia Anglicana; or, the History of Ireland from the Conquest Thereof by the English to This Present Time. London: 1689/90. V. 47; 51
The Present State of His Majesty's Revenue, Compared with that of Some Late Years. Dublin: 1762. V. 51

COX, ROSS
Adventures on the Columbia River... London: 1831. V. 48
Adventures on the Columbia River. New York: 1832. V. 53
The Columbia River; or, Scenes and Adventures During a Residence of Six Years on the Western Side of the Rocky Mountains... London: 1832. V. 51

COX, SIDNEY
Robert Frost Original "Ordinary Man". New York: 1929. V. 51

COX, THOMAS
Westmorland. London: 1720-21. V. 52
Westmorland. London: 1731. V. 52

COX, WALLY
Ralph Makes Good. New York: 1965. V. 52

COX, WARREN E.
Chinese Ivory Sculpture. New York: 1946. V. 51

COX, WILLIAM
Crayon Sketches. New York: 1833. V. 51

COXE, DANIEL
A Description of the English Province, of Carolina, by the Spaniards Called Florida and by the French La Louisiane. St. Louis: 1840. V. 52

COXE, JOHN REDMAN
The American Dispensatory... Philadelphia: 1806. V. 48
The Philadelphia Medical Dictionary. Philadelphia: 1817. V. 52
The Writings of Hippocrates and Galen. Philadelphia: 1846. V. 50; 51; 52

COXE, MARGARET
The Young Lady's Companion: In a Series of Letters. Columbus: 1839. V. 50; 53

COXE, PETER
The Social Day: A Poem, in Four Cantos. London: 1823. V. 48

COXE, RICHARD
Aphorisms Relating to the Kingdom of Ireland, Humbly Submitted to the Most Noble Assembly of Lords and Commons at the Great Convention at Westminster. London: 1689. V. 53

COXE, RICHARD S.
A New Critical Pronouncing Dictionary of the English Language... Burlington: 1813. V. 47; 51

COXE, TENCH
Report of the Case of the Commonwealth vs. Tench Coxe, Esq. Philadelphia: 1803. V. 47
A View of the United States of America, in a Series of Papers, Written at Various Times, Between the Years 1787 and 1794... Philadelphia: 1794. V. 47

COXE, WILLIAM
Account of the Russian Discoveries Between Asia and America. London: 1780. V. 47
Account of the Russian Discoveries Between Asia and America. London: 1787. V. 47; 51; 54
Account of the Russian Discoveries Between Asia and America... London: 1803. V. 54
Account of the Russian Discoveries Between Asia and America. London: 1804. V. 47
Anecdotes of George Frederick Handel, and John Christopher Smith. London: 1799. V. 51
An Historical Tour in Monmouthshire. London: 1801. V. 49
History of the House of Austria...from 1218 to 1792. London: 1807. V. 47; 53
Memoirs of Horatio, Lord Walpole... London: 1820. V. 50
Memoirs of John Duke of Marlborough... London: 1818. V. 47
Memoirs of John Duke of Marlborough... London: 1818/19. V. 50
Memoirs of the Kings of Spain of the House of Bourbon, from the Accession of Philip V to the Death of Charles III. 1700-1788. London: 1815. V. 51
Sketches of the Natural, Civil and Political State of Swisserland... Dublin: 1779. V. 47
Sketches of the Natural, Civil and Political State of Swisserland... London: 1779. V. 47; 49
Travels in Switzerland and the Country of the Grisons: in a Series of Letters to William Melmoth, Esq. London: 1801. V. 54
Travels Into Poland, Russia, Sweden and Denmark. London: 1784. V. 51
Travels into Poland, Russia, Sweden and Denmark. London: 1784-90. V. 47
Travels into Poland, Russia, Sweden and Denmark. London: 1785-90. V. 48
A View of the Cultivation of Fruit Trees, and the Management of Orchards and Cider... Philadelphia: 1817. V. 50; 51; 52; 54

COX-REARICK, JANET
Dynasty and Destiny in Medici Art... Princeton. V. 50

COX REARICK, JANET
Dynasty and Destiny in Medici Art. Princeton: 1984. V. 54

COY, OWEN C.
A Pictorial History of California. Berkeley: 1925. V. 47

COYER, GABRIEL FRANCOIS
The History of John Sobieski, King of Poland. London: 1762. V. 53

COYNE, J. H.
Exploration of the Great Lakes 1669-1670... Toronto: 1903. V. 54

COYNE, JOSEPH STIRLING
The Scenery and Antiquities of Ireland... London: 1841. V. 48
The Scenery and Antiquities of Ireland. London: 1842. V. 54

COZENS, ZACHARIAH
A Tour through the Isle of Thanet, and Some Other Parts of East Kent. London: 1793. V. 47

COZZENS, FREDERIC S.
American Yachts and Yachting. London: 1887. V. 54
Prismatics. New York: 1853. V. 47

COZZENS, ISSACHAR
A Geological History of Manhattan or New York Island, Together with a Map of the Island and a Suite of Sections, Tables and Columns for the Study of Geology, Particularly Adapted for the American Student. New York: 1843. V. 51; 53

COZZENS, JAMES GOULD
Castaway. New York: 1934. V. 51
Confusion, a Novel. Boston: 1924. V. 49
Men and Brethren. New York: 1936. V. 50
Michael Scarlett. New York: 1925. V. 52
A Rope for Doctor Webster. 1976. V. 50
S. S. San Pedro. New York: 1931. V. 49

COZZENS, SAMUEL WOODWORTH
The Marvelous Country: or, Three Years in Arizona and New Mexico... Boston: 1873. V. 51; 52
The Marvelous Country: or, Three Years in Arizona and New Mexico... London: 1874. V. 53
The Marvelous Country: or, Three Years in Arizona and New Mexico... Boston: 1875. V. 47
The Marvelous Country: or, Three Years in Arizona and New Mexico. London: 1875. V. 49

CRABB, GEORGE
English Synonymes, with Copious Illustrations and Explanations, Drawn from the Best Writers. London: 1826. V. 50

CRABB, JAMES
The Gipsies' Advocate; or, Observations on the Origin, Character, Manners and Habits of the English Gipsies. London: 1831. V. 54
The Gipsies's Advocate; or Observations on the Origin, Character, Manners and Habits, of the English Gipsies... London: 1832. V. 54

CRABB, RICHARD
Empire On the Platte. Cleveland and New York: 1967. V. 50

CRABBE, GEORGE
The Borough: a Poem. London: 1810. V. 47; 48; 49; 50; 53; 54
The Complete Poetical Works. Oxford: 1988. V. 52
The Library. A Poem. London: 1781. V. 47; 54
The Library. A Poem. London: 1783. V. 48; 52
The Library. A Poem. London: 1930. V. 53
The Life and Poetical Works. London: 1861. V. 48
The News-Paper: a Poem. London: 1785. V. 48; 49; 51
Peter Grimmes. London: 1985. V. 52
Poems. London: 1808. V. 51
The Poetical Works... With His Letters and Journals... London: 1834. V. 49; 50; 54
The Poetical Works...with His Letters and Journals... London: 1835. V. 52
Tales. London: 1812. V. 47; 48; 49
Tales of the Hall. London: 1819. V. 47; 49; 50; 51; 53
The Village: a Poem. London: 1783. V. 47; 50; 51; 54
Works. London: 1820. V. 50
The Works. London: 1823. V. 48; 49; 52; 53; 54

CRABBE, HARRIETTE
Edith Vernon; or, Contrasts of Character. London: 1855. V. 50; 52

THE CRABBET *Arabian Stud.* London: 1957. V. 54

CRABB ROBINSON, H.
Books and Their Writers. London: 1938. V. 47

CRABTRE, A. D.
The Funny Side of Physic; or, the Mysteries of Medicine... Hartford: 1872. V. 50

CRABTREE, ADAM
Animal Magnetism, Early Hypnotism and Psychical Research, 1766-1925. An Annotated Bibliography. New York: 1988. V. 52

CRACE, JIM
Continent. London: 1986. V. 52

CRACE, JOHN D.
The Art of Colour Decoration. London: 1912. V. 47

CRACKANTHORPE, DAVID
Hubert Crackanthorpe and English Realism in the 1890's. Columbia & London: 1977. V. 53

CRACKANTHORPE, HUBERT
Vignettes - a Miniature Journal of Whim and Sentiment. London: 1896. V. 47
Wreckage, Seven Studies. London: 1893. V. 50; 54

A CRACKER *Bon-Bon for Christmas Parties; Consisting of Christmas Tree Pieces for Private Representation.* London: 1852. V. 52

CRADOCK, C.
Sporting Notes in the Far East. London & Richmond: 1889. V. 49

CRADOCK, H. C., MRS.
Josephine Keeps House. London: 1936. V. 49; 51

CRADOCK, JOSEPH
An Account of some of the Most Romantic Parts of North Wales. London: 1777. V. 52
The Life of John Wilkes, Esq. London: 1773. V. 51
Literary and Miscellaneous Memoirs. London: 1828. V. 48
Village Memoirs; in a Series of Letters Between A Clergyman and His Family in the Country, and His Son in Town. London: 1775. V. 47; 48

CRAFTS, E. F. ROBBINS, MRS.
Pioneer Days in San Bernardino Valley. Redlands: 1906. V. 53

CRAFTS, W. A.
The Southern Rebellion: Being a History of the United States from the Commencement of President Buchanan's Administration Through the War for the Suppression of the Rebellion. Boston: 1867. V. 51

CRAFTS, WILLIAM
A Selection, in Prose and Poetry, from the Miscellaneous Writings of the Late William Crafts. Charleston: 1828. V. 52

CRAHAN, MARCUS ESKETH
Early American Inebriatatis. Los Angeles: 1964. V. 48

CRAIG, CORYDON F.
A Summary of Advantages Offered to Emigrants and Capitalists, by Northwest Missouri, Including the Celebrated Platte Purchase. St. Joseph: 1880. V. 48

CRAIG, EDWARD GORDON
The Black Figures of Edward Gordon Craig. Wellingborough: 1989. V. 47; 50
Books and Theatres. London: 1925. V. 47; 52; 53
Edward Gordon Craig; the Last Eight Years 1958-1966. Andoversford: 1983. V. 47
Gordon Craig's Book of Penny Toys. Hackbridge: 1899. V. 47
Gordon Craig's Paris Diary, 1932-1933. 1982. V. 52
Gordon Craig's Paris Diary, 1932-1933. Newtown: 1982. V. 54
Gordon Craig's Paris Diary, 1932-1933. North Hills: 1982. V. 47; 48; 51; 53; 54
Henry Irving... Chicago: 1899. V. 47
Henry Irving. London: 1930. V. 47
The Last Eight Years 1958-1966. Andoversford: 1983. V. 52
Nothing or the Bookplate. London: 1924. V. 47; 48; 54
On the Art of the Theatre. London: 1911. V. 51
The Page. Christmas 1900. Carshalton: 1900. V. 50
A Production Being Thirty-Two Collotype Plates of Designs Projected or Realised for the Pretenders of Henrik Ibsen and Produced at the Royal Theatre Copenhagen 1926. London: 1930. V. 53
Puppets and Poets. London: 1921. V. 50
Scene. London: 1923. V. 53
Woodcuts and Some Words. New York: 1924. V. 52; 53

CRAIG, GEORGE LILLIE
The Romance of the Peerage, or Curiosities of Family History. London: 1848-50. V. 51

CRAIG, GEORGIANA MARION
Patience Holt. London: 1891. V. 51

CRAIG, HUGH
Grand Army Picture Book from April 12, 1861 to April 26, 1865. New York London: 1890. V. 51

CRAIG, JOHANNE
Theologiae Christianae Principia Mathematica. London: 1699. V. 50; 51

CRAIG, JOHN
The Locks of the Oxford Canal. Andoversford: 1984. V. 48
The Mint: a History of the London Mint from A.D. 287 to 1948. Cambridge: 1953. V. 48

CRAIG, MAURICE
Irish Bookbindings 1600-1800. London: 1954. V. 47; 49; 50; 52; 53

CRAIG, NEVILLE B.
The History of Pittsburgh... Pittsburgh: 1851. V. 47; 50
Recollections of an Ill-Fated Expedition to the Head-Waters of the Madeira River in Brazil. Philadelphia: 1907. V. 47

CRAIG, R. T.
The Mammillaria Handbook... Pasadena: 1945. V. 54

CRAIG, THOMAS
Jus Feudale Tribus Libris Comprehensum (etc.). Edinburghi: 1655. V. 47

CRAIG, W. H.
Spot an Autobiography. London: 1894. V. 49

CRAIG, W. M.
Memoir of Her Majesty Sopha Charlotte, of Mecklenburg Strelitz, Queen of Great Britain... Liverpool: 1818. V. 50

CRAIG, WILLIAM MARSHALL
Description of the Plates Representing the Intinerant Traders of London in Their Ordinary Costume... London: 1804. V. 52

CRAIGE, THOMAS
A Conversation Between a Lady and her Horse. Philadelphia: 1851. V. 47

CRAIGIE, DOROTHY
A Catalogue of the Collection Made by Dorothy Glover and Graham Greene Bibliographically Arranged by Eric Oxborne and Introduced by J. Carter. London: 1966. V. 51
Victorian Detective Fiction. London: 1966. V. 47; 49; 51; 53

CRAIGIE, PEARL MARY TERESA RICAHRDS
The Dream and the Business. London: 1906. V. 47

CRAIGIE, WILLIAM A.
Dictionary of the Older Scottish Tongue: From the Twelfth Century to the End of the Seventeenth. Chicago: 1931-61. V. 49

CRAIGN, JOHN
Ranching With Lords and Commons or Twenty Years on the Range. Toronto: 1903. V. 48

CRAIK, DINAH MARIA MULOCK
A Brave Lady. London: 1870. V. 53
Christian's Mistake. London: 1865. V. 50
The Fairy Book. London: 1913. V. 53
Hannah. London: 1872. V. 54
John Halifax, Gentleman. London: 1856. V. 48; 50; 52; 53; 54
A Legacy. London: 1878. V. 54
A Life for a Life. London: 1859. V. 47; 50; 51; 53
Poems. London: 1859. V. 50
Poems. London: 1860. V. 53
Der Weibliche Beruf. Gedanken Einer Frau. Frei Nach dem Englischen von Anna von Wachter. Stuttgart: 1861. V. 54
A Woman's Thoughts about Women. London: 1858. V. 47; 49; 51; 53; 54
A Woman's Thoughts About Women. New York: 1858. V. 50
A Woman's Thoughts About Women. London: 1859. V. 50

CRAIK, GEORGE LILLIE
English Causes Celebres; or Reports of Remarkable Trials. London: 1844. V. 52
The History of British Commerce, from the Earliest Times. London: 1844. V. 52
The New Zealanders. London: 1830. V. 51

CRAIK, GEORGIANA MARION
Anne Warwick. London: 1877. V. 50
Dorcas. London: 1879. V. 54
Esther Hill's Secret. London: 1870. V. 50
Patience Holt. London: 1891. V. 49; 53

CRAIK, JOHN L.
The New Zealanders... London: 1847. V. 52

CRAIS, ROBERT
The Monkey's Raincoat. New York: 1987. V. 47

CRAKANTHORP, RICHARD
A Sermon of Sanctification, Preached on the Act Sunday at Oxford, Julie 12, 1607. London: 1608. V. 48

CRAKES, SYLVESTER
Five Years a Captive Among the Black-Feet Indians. Columbus: 1858. V. 47; 52

CRAM & FERGUSON
The Work of Cram and Ferguson, Architects... New York: 1929. V. 51

CRAM, GEORGE F.
The Imperial Atlas of the Dominion of Canada and the World. Toronto: 1904. V. 47

CRAM, RALPH ADAMS
Christian Art. Boston: 1908. V. 48

CRAMER, GABRIEL
Introduction a l'analyse des Lignes Courbes Algebriques. Geneva: 1750. V. 50; 52

CRAMER, GERALD
Henry Moore... Geneva: 1973-80. V. 53
Henry Moore... Geneva: 1973-86. V. 53

CRAMER, JOHANN ANDREAS
Anleitung zum Forst-Wesen, Nebst Einer Ausfuhrlichen Beschreibung von Verkohlung des Holzes... 1766. V. 47
Anleitung zum Forst-Wesen, Nebst Einer Ausfuhrlichen Beschreibung von Verkohlung des Holzes. Braunschweig: 1766. V. 49
Elements of the Art of Assaying Metals. London: 1741. V. 48
Elements of the Art of Assaying Metals. London: 1764. V. 50

CRAMER, KARL GOTTLOB
Albert de Nordenshild; or, the Modern Alcibiades. London: 1796. V. 54

CRAMER, RIE
Old Songs in French and English. Philadelphia: 1923. V. 49

CRAMER, ZADOK
The Navigator... Pittsburgh: 1811. V. 47

CRAMP, STANLEY
Handbook of Birds of Europe, the Middle East and North Africa, the Birds of the Western Palearctic. Oxford: 1977-93. V. 54
The Handbook of the Birds of Europe, the Middle East & North Africa. Volume 1. Ostrich to Ducks. London: 1977. V. 50; 52; 53
Handbook of the Birds of Europe, the Middle East & North Africa. Volume 2. London: 1980. V. 50; 52; 53
Handbook of the Birds of Europe, the Middle East & North Africa. Volume 2. Hawks to Bustards. London: 1982. V. 50
Handbook of the Birds of Europe, the Middle East & North Africa. Volume 3. London: 1983. V. 50; 52; 53
Handbook of the Birds of Europe, the Middle East & North Africa. Volume 4. Terns to Woodpeckers. London: 1985. V. 50; 52; 53
Handbook of the Birds of Europe, the Middle East & North Africa. Volume 5. Tyrant Flycatchers to Thrushes. London: 1988. V. 50; 52; 53
Handbook of the Birds of Europe, the Middle East & North Africa. Volume VII. London: 1993. V. 49; 50
Handbook of the Birds of Europe, the Middle East and North Africa. London: 1980-85. V. 48
Handbook of the Birds of Europe, the Middle East and North Africa. (Birds of Western Palearctic) Volume 4 Terns to Woodpeckers. Oxford: 1985. V. 52
Handbook of the Birds of Europe, the Middle East and North Africa. The Birds of the Western Palaearctic. Volumes 1 to 5. Ostrich to Thrushes. London: 1977-88. V. 49
Handbook of the Birds of Europe, the Middle East and North Africa. Volume 6. Warblers. London: 1992. V. 49

CRAMPTON, PHILIP
An Attempt to Explain, on Natural Principles, the Cures, Alledged to be Miraculous, of Miss Lalor and Mrs. Stuart. Dublin: 1823. V. 54

CRANBORNE, JAMES CECIL, VISCOUNT
Ten Weeks from Home in the Spring of 1857...Being Leaves from the Diary of a Blind Traveller. London: 1858. V. 52

CRANCH, CHRISTOPHER PEARSE
The Last of the Huggermuggers, a Giant Story. Boston: 1856. V. 54

CRANDALL, ALLEN
Fisher fo the Antelope Hills. 1949. V. 48

CRANDALL, NORMA
Emily Bronte. 1957. V. 54
Emily Bronte. London: 1957. V. 52

CRANDALL, REUBEN
The Trial of Reuben Crandall, M.D. Charged With Publishing and Circulating Seditious and Incendary Papers... Washington City: 1836. V. 51

CRANE, C. P.
Memories of a Resident Magistrate, 1880-1920. London: 1938. V. 53

CRANE, E.
Bees and Beekeeping, Science, Practice and World Resources. Ithaca: 1990. V. 52

CRANE, EDWARD
Poetical Miscellanies: viz. The Female Parricide, a Tragedy, Founded on the History of Miss Blandy, Who Poison'd Her Father. Saul and Jonathan, a Tragedy... Poems on Several Occasions. Manchester: 1761. V. 49

CRANE, EDWARD A.
Examples of Colonial Architecture in South Carolina and Georgia. Berlin. V. 51
Examples of Colonial Architecture in South Carolina and Georgia. New York: 1895. V. 50

CRANE, GEORGE
Poems from the Novel. New York: 1976. V. 51

CRANE, HART
The Bridge. New York: 1930. V. 47; 49; 52; 53; 54
The Bridge. Paris: 1930. V. 47; 48; 53
The Bridge. New York: 1981. V. 47; 48; 49; 51; 53
The Collected Poems. New York: 1933. V. 47; 48; 51
Porphyro In Akron. Columbus: 1980. V. 51; 53
Voyages: Six Poems from White Buildings. New York: 1957. V. 47; 49; 52
White Buildings. New York: 1926. V. 47; 49; 51

CRANE, J.
Fiddler Crabs of the World, Ocypodidae: Genus Uca. Princeton: 1975. V. 48

CRANE, LEO
Desert Drums: The Pueblo Indians of New Mexico, 1540-1928. Boston: 1928. V. 47
Indians of the Enchanted Desert. Boston: 1925. V. 51

CRANE, LUCY
Art and the Formation of Taste: Six Lectures. London: 1882. V. 50; 52

CRANE, NATHANALIA
The Janitor's Boy. New York: 1924. V. 47

CRANE, RONALD S.
English Literature 1660-1800: a Bibliography of Modern Studies. Princeton: 1950-83. V. 48

CRANE, STEPHEN
Active Service. London: 1899. V. 53
Active Service. New York: 1899. V. 53; 54
A Battle in Greece. Mt. Vernon: 1936. V. 47; 48
The Black Riders and Other Lines. Boston: 1895. V. 52; 53; 54
The Black Riders and Other Lines. 1905. V. 51
The Black Riders and Other Lines. Boston: 1905. V. 54
George's Mother. New York & London: 1896. V. 51; 54
Great Battles of the World. Philadelphia: 1901. V. 48; 49; 50; 51; 52; 53
The Little Regiment... New York: 1896. V. 49; 53; 54
The Little Regiment. London: 1897. V. 47; 52; 53; 54
Maggie... 1893. V. 53
Maggie... London: 1896. V. 49; 50
Maggie... New York: 1896. V. 48; 54
Maggie... 1974. V. 54
Maggie... Avon: 1974. V. 51; 53
Maggie... London: 1974. V. 52
The Monster and Other Stories. New York & London: 1889. V. 48
The Monster and Other Stories. New York and London: 1899. V. 51; 53; 54
The Open Boat. London: 1898. V. 49; 51; 52
The Open Boat... New York: 1898. V. 47; 49; 50
The O'Ruddy. New York: 1903. V. 48; 49; 54
The Red Badge of Courage. New York: 1895. V. 47; 53; 54
The Red Badge of Courage. London: 1896. V. 51
The Red Badge of Courage. New York: 1896. V. 51; 54
The Red Badge of Courage. New York: 1931. V. 49; 52
The Red Badge of Courage. San Francisco: 1931. V. 48; 51
The Red Badge of Courage. New York: 1944. V. 47; 48; 51; 54
The Red Badge of Courage. Washington: 1973. V. 54
The Third Violet. New York: 1897. V. 53

CRANE, STEPHEN continued
War is Kind. New York: 1899. V. 47; 49; 50; 51; 53; 54
Wilholmville Stories. New York: 1900. V. 51; 53
Wounds in the Rain. New York: 1900. V. 47; 54

CRANE, THOMAS
Abroad. London: 1884. V. 47
London Town. London: 1883. V. 52

CRANE, W. J. E.
Bookbinding for Amateurs: Being Descriptions of the Various Tools and Appliances Required and Minute Instructions for Their Effective Use. London: 1885. V. 50

CRANE, WALTER
The Baby's Bouquet. London, New York: 1878. V. 50; 51; 54
The Baby's Bouquet... London: 1879. V. 47
The Baby's Opera. London, New York: 1877. V. 47; 48; 51; 54
The Baby's Opera. London: 1884. V. 53
Baby's Own Aesop. London: 1887. V. 51; 53
The Baby's Own Aesop. London: 1910. V. 50; 51
The Basis of Design. London: 1898. V. 48
The Basis of Design. London: 1902. V. 50
Beauty and the Beast Picture Book. New York: 1905. V. 50
The Bluebeard Picture Book. London: 1875. V. 51
Chattering Jack's Picture Book... London and New York: 1870's. V. 48
Cinderella's Picture Book... London: 1910. V. 51
The Claims of Decorative Art. Boston: 1892. V. 50
The Claims of Decorative Art. London: 1892. V. 51
Columbia's Courtship A Picture History of the United States in Twelve Emblematic Designs in Color with Accompanying Verses by Walter Crane. Boston: 1893. V. 50
Columbus Courtship: a Picture History of the United States in Twelve Emblematic Designs. Boston: 1892. V. 51
Eight Illustrations to Shakespeare's Two Gentlemen of Verona. Dallas: 1894. V. 52
The First of May, a Fairy Masque; Presented in a Series of 52 Designs. Boston: 1881. V. 49; 52
The First of May, a Fairy Masque, Presented in a Series of 52 Designs. London: 1881. V. 49
A Floral Fantasy in an Old English Garden. London: 1899. V. 51
Flora's Feast. A Masque of Flowers. London: 1889. V. 47; 52
A Flower Wedding. London: 1905. V. 49; 51; 52
Flowers from Shakespeare's Garden. London: 1906. V. 48; 50
Goody Two Shoes Picture Book. London. V. 51
Goody Two Shoes Picture Book. New York: 1905. V. 50
Legends for Lionel. London: 1887. V. 53
Little Queen Anne and Her Majesty's Letters. London: 1886. V. 49
A Masque of Days. London: 1901. V. 47; 48; 49
The Necklace of the Princess Fiorimonde. London: 1880. V. 49
Of The Decorative Illustration of Books Old and New. London & New York: 1896. V. 48; 49; 50; 53
The Old Courtier. London: 1870-74. V. 47
Old Mother Hubbard Picture Book. New York: 1905. V. 50
Pan-Pipes. London: 1883. V. 50; 51; 53
Pan-Pipes... London: 1884. V. 52
Pothooks and Perseverance or the ABC-Serpent. London: 1886. V. 53
Queen Summer of the Tourney of the Lily and the Rose. London: 1891. V. 47; 48; 53
Renascence. London: 1891. V. 49
A Romance of the Three R's. London: 1886. V. 51; 54
Rumbo Rhymes or the Great Combine: a Satire. London: 1911. V. 52
Sing a Song of Sixpence and A Gaping-Wide-Mouthed-Waddling Frog in Routledge's Coloured Picture Book... London: 1880. V. 48
Slate and Pencilvania Being the Adventures of Dick on a Desert Island. London: 1885. V. 53
The Sleeping Beauty Picture Book. New York: 1905. V. 50
Valentine and Orson. London: 1895. V. 48
Walter Crane's Baby's Own Alphabet. London. V. 54
Walter Crane's Picture Book. New York: 1903. V. 50
William Morris to Whistler. London: 1911. V. 48; 50

CRANE, WILLIAM CAREY
Life and Select Literary Remains of Sam Houston of Texas. Philadelphia: 1884. V. 47
Life and Select Literary Remains of Sam Houston of Texas. Philadelphia: 1885. V. 50

CRANMER, THOMAS
A Defence of the Trve and Catholike Doctrine of the Sacrament of the Body and Bloud of Our Saviour Christ... London: 1550. V. 48
Sermons or Homilies, Appointed to be Read in Churches in the Time of the Late Queene Elizabeth of Famous Memory. London: 1633. V. 47

CRANNELL, W. WINSLOW, MRS.
Address of Mrs. W. Winslow Crannell...Before the Committee on Resolutions of the Democratic National Convention, at Chicago, July 8th, 1896. Albany: 1896. V. 48

CRANTZ, DAVID
The History of Greenland. London: 1767. V. 53
The History of Greenland... London: 1820. V. 54

CRANWELL, JOHN PHILIPS
Notes On Figures of Earth. New York: 1929. V. 51

CRANWORTH, LORD
Kenya Chronicles. London: 1939. V. 54

CRANZ, DAVID
Select Narratives Extracted From the History of the Church Known by the Name of Unitas Fratrum; or United Brethren. London: 1806. V. 50

CRAPSEY, ADELAIDE
Verse. Rochester: 1915. V. 54

CRARY, CHRISTOPHER G.
Pioneer and Personal Reminiscences. Marshalltown: 1893. V. 48

CRARY, MARY
The Daughters of the Stars. London: 1939. V. 48

CRASHAW, RICHARD
Musicks Duell. London: 1935. V. 48
Steps to the Temple. London: 1646. V. 52
Steps to the Temple... London: 1670. V. 50

CRASTER, EDMUND
History of the Bodleian Library 1845-1945. Oxford: 1952. V. 48; 53

CRATO VON KRAFTHEIM, JOHANNES
Consiliorum & Epistolarum Medicinalium, Liber Primus - Liber Septimus... Hanover: 1609-14-19-11. V. 48

CRAUFURD, DAVID
Love at First Sight. London: 1704. V. 51
Ovidius Britannicus; or, Love's Epistles. London: 1703. V. 51

CRAUFURD, GEORGE
The Doctrine of Equivalents; or an Explanation of the Nature, Value and Power of Money... Rotterdam: 1803. V. 54

CRAUFURD, QUINTIN
Sketches Chiefly Relating to the History, Religion, Learning and Manners of the Hindoos. With a Concise Account of the Present State of the Native Powers of Hindostan. London: 1790. V. 52

CRAVAN, ARTHUR
Maintenant. Paris: 1957. V. 54

CRAVEN, ELIZABETH BERKELEY, BARONESS
A Journey through the Crimea to Constantinople. London: 1789. V. 47; 51; 54

CRAVEN, ELIZABETH BERKELEY, BARONESS CRAVEN
Voyage de Milady Craven a Constantinople... N.P: 1789. V. 48; 50

CRAVEN, JOSEPH
A Bronte Moorland Village and Its People: a History of Stanbury. Keighley: 1907. V. 54

CRAVEN, RICHARD KEPPEL
A Tour through the Southern Provinces of the Kingdom of Naples... London: 1821. V. 54

CRAVENS, R. H.
Brett Weston: Photographs from Five Decades. Millerton: 1980. V. 47

CRAW, WILLIAM
Naval, Poetical Journal: in Twelve Letters. Kilmarnock: 1807. V. 52

CRAWALEY, ERNEST
The Mystic Rose.. London: 1927. V. 50

CRAWFORD, ALAN
C. R. Ashbee, Architect, Designer and Romantic Socialist. New Haven: 1985. V. 52

CRAWFORD, C. H.
Scenes of Earlier Days in Crossing the Plains to Oregon and Experiences of Wester Life. Petaluma: 1898. V. 47

CRAWFORD, EARL STETSON
Lovely Woman. Indianpolis: 1910. V. 48

CRAWFORD, EVERETT LAKE
Let's Ride to Hounds. New York: 1929. V. 47

CRAWFORD, FRANCIS MARION
Corleone. London: 1897. V. 53; 54
Corleone. New York: 1897. V. 53
In the Palace of the King. New York: 1900. V. 53
Khaled: a Tale of Arabia. London: 1891. V. 54
The Novels. New York and London: 1894-1911. V. 51; 52
The Ralstons. New York: 1895. V. 54
Taquisara. New York: 1896. V. 54
The Three Fates. London: 1892. V. 51
To Leeward. London: 1884. V. 54
Via Circus. New York: 1899. V. 53
The Witch of Prague. London: 1891. V. 54
With the Immortals. London: 1888. V. 54
Zoroaster. London: 1885. V. 53

CRAWFORD, ISABELLA VALANCY
Old Spookses' Pas, Malcolm's Katie and Other Poems. 1884/86. V. 51

CRAWFORD, J. MARSHALL
Mosby and His Men: a Record of that Renowned Partisan Ranger, John S. Mosby... New York: 1867. V. 49; 52

CRAWFORD, JAMES LUDOVIC, EARL OF
Bibliotheca Lindesiana: Catalogue of a Collection of English Ballads of the XVIIth and SVIIIth Centuries. Aberdeen: 1890. V. 47
Bibliotheca Lindesiana: Catalogue of Printed Books. A-(HER). Aberdeen?: 190-?. V. 47

CRAWFORD, JAMES LUDOVIC, EARL OF continued
Bibliotheca Lindesiana. Volume III. A Bibliography of the Writings, General, Special and Periodical Forming the Literature of Philately. Aberdeen: 1911. V. 53

CRAWFORD, JOHN F.
The Pearl. San Francisco: 1967. V. 48

CRAWFORD, L. M.
The Art of the Wandjina. Melbourne: 1968. V. 50

CRAWFORD, LEWIS FERANDUS
Rekindling Camp Fires The Exploits of Ben Arnold (Connor). Bismarck: 1926. V. 47; 49; 50; 53; 54

CRAWFORD, M. P.
An Address, Delivered Before the Lancaster Agricultural Society. Lancaster: 1854. V. 50

CRAWFORD, MEDOREM
An Account of His Trip Across the Plains with the Oregon Pioneers of 1842. Eugene: 1897. V. 52
Letter of the Secretary of War Communicating...A Copy of the Report and Journal of Captain Medorem Crawford, Commanding the Emigrant Escort to Oregon and Washington Territory in the Year 1862. Washington: 1863. V. 47

CRAWFORD, MICHAEL H.
Coinage and Money Under the Roman Republic, Italy and the Mediterranean Economy. Berkeley: 1985. V. 48

CRAWFORD, OSWALD
By Path and Trail. 1908. V. 47; 52
The Revelations of Inspector Morgan. New York: 1907. V. 48

CRAWFORD, S. J.
Before the Committee On Public Lands, House of Representatives -- 48th Congress. Adjustment Of Land Grants... Topeka: 1884. V. 47
Message. S. J. Crawford, Governor of Kansas. Lawrence: 1866. V. 50

CRAWFORD, WILLIAM
Remarks on the Late Earl of Chesterfield's Letters to His Son. London: 1776. V. 49

CRAWFORD & BALCARRES, ALEXANDER, EARL OF
The Earldom of Mar. Edinburgh: 1862. V. 54

CRAWFURD, GEORGE
A Genealogical History of the Royal and Illustrious Family of the Stewarts, from the Year 1034 to the year 1710. Edinburgh: 1710. V. 54
A General Description of the Shire of Renfrew. (with) A Genealogical History of the Royal House of Stewart. London: 1818. V. 47
The History of the Shire of Renfrew. Pailsey: 1782. V. 47; 51

CRAWFURD, JOHN
History of the Indian Archipelago. Edinburgh: 1820. V. 47; 51; 54
A View of the Present State and Future Prospects of the Free Trade and Colonisation of India. London: 1828. V. 49

CRAWHALL, JOSEPH
A Beuk o' Newcassel Sangs. Newcastle: 1888. V. 54
Chaplets from Croquet-Side. London: 1873. V. 53
Chorographia, or a Survey of Newcastle-upon-Tyne. Newcastle: 1884. V. 50
A Collection fo Right Merrie Garlands for North Country Anglers. Newcastle-on-Tyne: 1864. V. 47; 48; 52; 53
The Compleatest Angling Book that Euer was Writ, Being Done Out of Ye Hebrewe and Other Tongues, by a Person of Honor. Newe Castle upon Tine: 1881. V. 47
Impresses Quaint. Newcastle-upon-Tyne: 1889. V. 51; 53
Old Ffrendes Wyth Newe Faces. London: 1883. V. 50; 52
Olde Tayles Newly Relayted. London: 1883. V. 47; 48; 50

CRAWSHAY, RICHARD
The Birds of Tierra del Fuego. London: 1907. V. 47; 51; 52; 54

CRAYBILL, FLORENCE CURTIS
Edward Sheriff Curtis. Visions of a Vanishing Race. New York: 1976. V. 54

CRAYON, J. PERCY
Rockaway Records of Morris County, N.J., Families. Cemetery records, Church Records, Military Records, Local History, Genealogies of Old Families, Nearly 20,000 Data. Rockaway: 1902. V. 49

CREAGH, O'MOORE
The V. C. and D.S.O. A Complete Record of All Those Officers, Non-Commissioned Officers and men of His Majesty's Naval, Military and Air Forces Who Have Been Awarded with Descriptions Of the Deeds and Services Which Won the Distinctions... 1930. V. 47

CREALOCK, HENRY HOPE
Among the Red Deer... London: 1870. V. 51
Among the Red Deer. 1983. V. 54
Among the Red Deer... London: 1983. V. 49
Deer-Stalking in the Highlands of Scotland. London: 1981. V. 48

CREASEY, JAMES
Sketches, Illustrative of the Topography and History of New and Old Sleaford... Sleaford: 1825. V. 51

CREASEY, JOHN
Inferno. London: 1965. V. 50; 53
Meet the Baron. London: 1937. V. 50; 53
Murder London - New York. London: 1958. V. 52

CREASY, EDWARD S.
The Fifteen Decisive Battles of the World... London: 1902. V. 50
The Fifteen Decisive Battles of the World. 1969. V. 48
The Fifteen Decisive Battles of the World. New York: 1969. V. 53
History of the Ottoman Turks... London: 1854. V. 50
Memoirs of Eminent Etonians: with Notices of the Early History of Eton College. London: 1850. V. 50

CREECH, WILLIAM
An Account of the Trial of William Brodie and George Smith, Before the High Court of Justiciary... Edinburgh: 1788. V. 48; 50
Edinburgh Fugitive Piece. Edinburgh: 1815. V. 51

CREED, R. S.
Reflex Activity of the Spinal Cord. Oxford: 1923. V. 52
Reflex Activity of the Spinal Cord. Oxford: 1938. V. 47

CREELEY, ROBERT
1. 2. 3. 4. 5. 6. 7. 8. 9. 10. Berkeley: 1971. V. 47
5 Numbers. New York: 1968. V. 47
7 & 6. Albuquerque: 1988. V. 47
Characteristically. Cambridge: 1972. V. 48
The Charm; Early and Uncollected Poems. Madison: 1967. V. 51
The Charm: Early and Uncollected Poems. Mt. Horeb: 1967. V. 47; 51; 54
The Charm: Early and Uncollected Poems. San Francisco: 1969. V. 54
Divisions and Other Early Poems. Madison: 1968. V. 47; 51; 54
Divisions and Other Early Poems. Mt. Horeb: 1968. V. 51; 54
The Finger. Los Angeles: 1968. V. 51
A Form of Women. New York: 1959. V. 54
Le Fou. Columbus: 1952. V. 47; 48; 51
The Gold Diggers. Palma de Mallorca: 1954. V. 47; 54
Hello. New York: 1978. V. 47
If You: Poems by Robert Creeley. San Francisco: 1956. V. 47; 48; 50
The Kind of Act. Palma de Mallorca: 1953. V. 47; 53; 54
Loops: Ten Poems. Kripplebush: 1995. V. 54
Monoprints by Bobbie Creeley. Los Angeles: 1972. V. 51
Numbers. Dusseldorf: 1968. V. 53
Parts. San Francisco: 1994. V. 53
Pieces. Los Angeles: 1968. V. 51
Robert Creeley. Life & Death. Francesco Clemente. New York: 1993. V. 51; 53; 54
Robert Creeley Reads. London: 1967. V. 54
The Whip. Worcester: 1957. V. 54
Words. Rochester: 1965. V. 53; 54
Words. New York: 1967. V. 53

CREENY, WILLIAM F.
A Book of Fac-similes of Monumental Brasses on the Continent of Europe, with Brief Descriptive Notes. Norwich: 1884. V. 48; 50; 53
Illustrations of Incised Slabs on the Continent of Europe... 1891. V. 50

CREER, LELAND HARGRAVE
The Founding of an Empire, The Exploration and Colonization of Utah 1776-1856. Salt Lake City: 1947. V. 53

CREGEEN, ARCHIBALD
A Dictionary of the Manks Language, with the Corresponding Words or Explanations in English... Douglas: 1835. V. 51
A Dictionary of the Manks Language, With the Corresponding Words or Explanations in English. London: 1835. V. 48

CREIGHTON, CHARLES
Contributions to the Physiology and Pathology of the Breast and Its Lymphatic Glands. London: 1878. V. 47; 48; 50
A History of Epidemics in Britain... Cambridge: 1891. V. 50; 51; 52
A History of Epidemics in Britain.. Cambridge: 1891-94. V. 47; 52; 53

CREIGHTON, HELEN
Songs and Ballads from Nova Scotia. Toronto: 1933. V. 50

CREIGHTON, M.
A History of the Papacy During the Period of the Reformation. London: 1892. V. 51

CREIGHTON, MANDELL
Queen Elizabeth. London: 1896. V. 54
The Story of Some English Shires. London: 1897. V. 54

CREIXANS, PEDRO
Infants. Barcelona?. V. 49

CREMER, JOHN DORLAND
Records of the Dorland Family in America, Embracing the Principal Branches Dorland, Dorlon, Dorlan, Durland, Durling in the United States... Washington: 1898. V. 47; 49

CREMER, WILLIAM HENRY
The Magician's Own Book. London: 1871. V. 49; 51

CREMONY, JOHN C.
Life Among the Apaches. San Francisco: 1868. V. 47; 49; 52

THE CREOLE Cookery Book. New Orleans: 1885. V. 47

CREPAZ, ADELE
The Emancipation of Women and Its Probable Consequences. London: 1893. V. 50; 51; 53

CRESHALD, RICHARD
A Legacy Left to the World by that Able Lawyer Richard Creshald... London: 1658. V. 53

CRESPELLE, JEAN PAUL
The Fauves. Greenwich: 1926. V. 48
The Fauves. Greenwich: 1962. V. 47; 50; 51; 53; 54

CRESSENER, A.
The Vindication of A. Cressener, School-Master in Long Acre, from the Apserions of A. Pulton, Jesuit and School-Master in the Savoy; Together with Some Account of His Discourse with Mr. Meredith. London: 1687. V. 53

CRESSETT, EDWARD
A Sermon Preach'd Before the Incorporated Society for the Propagation of the Gospel in Foreign Parts; at Their Anniversary Meeting...Feb. 16, 1753. London: 1753. V. 53

CRESSON, JOSHUA
Meditations Written During the Prevalence of the Yellow Fever in the City of Philadelphia in the Year 1793. London: 1803. V. 52

CRESSWELL, BEATRICE F.
The Royal Progress of King Pepito. London: 1889. V. 48

CRESSY, HUGH PAULIN
The Church History of Brittany From the Beginning of Christianity to the Norman Conquest... Rouen: 1668. V. 48; 49
The Church History of Brittany...from the Beginning of Christianity to the Norman Conquest. London: 1668. V. 47
Exomologesis, or a Faithfull Narration of the Occasion and Motives of the Conversion Unto Catholique Unity. Paris: 1647. V. 53

CREST and Monogram Album. London: 1900. V. 51

CRESWELL, CLARENDON HYDE
The Royal College of Surgeons of Edinburgh. Historical Notes from 1505 to 1905. Edinburgh: 1926. V. 48

CRESWELL, HENRY
Fair and Free. London: 1882. V. 51

CRESWELL, KEPPEL ARCHIBALD CAMERON
Early Muslim Architecture. London: 1969. V. 49

CRESWELL, THOMAS ESTCOURT
A Narrative of the Affair Between Mr. Creswell and Miss S--e, Address'd to G--v--e Sc---e, esq. London: 1747. V. 51; 54

CRESWICK, PAUL
Robin Hood. 1917. V. 47; 51; 53
Robin Hood. Philadelphia: 1917. V. 48

CRESWICK, THOMAS
Picturesque Scenery in Ireland. London: 1880. V. 50

CRESWICK, WILFRED
Essays on the Prevention of Explosions and Accidents in Coal Mines. London: 1874. V. 50

CRESWICKE, LOUIS
South Africa and the Transvaal War. Edinburgh: 1900. V. 49
South Africa and the Transvaal War. London: 1900-02. V. 50

CRESY, EDWARD
An Encyclopedia of Civil Engineering, Historical, Theoretical and Practical. London: 1865. V. 53

CREUZEVAULT, COLETTE
Henri Creuzevault 1905-1971. Paris: 1987. V. 47

CREVECOEUR, MICHEL GUILLAUME ST. JEAN DE
Letters from an American Farmer: Describing Certain Provincial Situations, Manners and Customs, not Generally Known... London: 1782. V. 47; 51
Lettres d'un Cultivateur Americain. Paris: 1784. V. 47; 54
Voyage dans la Haute Pensylvanie et Dans L'Etat de New York, Par un Membre Adoptif de la Nation Oneida. Paris: 1801. V. 47

CREW, BENJAMIN J.
Our Jewels; and the Work of Resetting Them. Philadelphia: 1883. V. 54

CREWDSON, ISAAC
A Beacon to the Society of Friends. London: 1835. V. 49; 50; 52

CREWS, HARRY
Blood and Grits. New York: 1979. V. 54
Car. New York: 1972. V. 47; 51; 52; 53; 54
Car. London: 1973. V. 47; 51; 53
A Childhood. New York: 1978. V. 47; 49; 50; 51; 53; 54
The Enthusiast. 1981. V. 49; 51; 53
The Enthusiast. Winston-Salem: 1981. V. 51; 52
A Feast of Snakes. New York: 1976. V. 47; 49; 50; 51; 52; 53; 54
The Gospel Singer. New York: 1968. V. 47; 50; 51; 52; 53
The Gypsy's Curse. New York: 1974. V. 47; 48; 51; 52
The Gypsy's Curse. London: 1975. V. 47; 52
The Hawk is Dying. New York: 1973. V. 47; 50; 53
The Hawk is Dying. London: 1974. V. 53
Karate Is a Thing of the Spirit. New York: 1971. V. 47; 48; 49; 50; 51; 52; 53; 54
Karate is a Thing of the Spirit. London: 1972. V. 53
The Knockout Artist. New York: 1988. V. 52
Madonna at Ringside. Northridge: 1991. V. 47; 53
Naked in Garden Hills. New York: 1969. V. 47; 48; 49; 51; 52; 53
Scar Lover. New York: 1992. V. 47; 53
This Thing Don't Lead to Heaven. 1970. V. 50
This Thing Don't Lead to Heaven. New York: 1970. V. 47; 51; 52; 53

Two by Crews. Northridge;: 1984. V. 48

CREYKE, W. R.
Book of Modern Receipts...Full Instructions for Producing Enamel, Underglaze and Majolica Colours. London: 1884. V. 47
Book of Modern Receipts...Full Instructions for Producing...Enamel, Underglaze and Majolica Colours. Hanley: 1884. V. 53

CRICHTON, ANDREW
The History of Arabia. Ancient and Modern. New York: 1834. V. 49
Scandinavia, Ancient and Modern; a History of Denmark, Sweden and Norway. 1838. V. 53

CRICHTON, JOHN
A Case of Need. New York: 1968. V. 53

CRICHTON, KYLE S.
Law and Order Ltd., the Rousing Life of El Fego Baca of New Mexico. Santa Fe: 1928. V. 49; 51; 53; 54

CRICHTON, MICHAEL
The Andromeda Strain. London: 1969. V. 52
The Andromeda Strain. New York: 1969. V. 50; 51; 52
Binary. New York: 1972. V. 54
Dealing, or the Berkeley-to-Boston Forty-Brick Lost Bag Blues. New York: 1971. V. 52
Eaters of the Dead. New York: 1976. V. 53
Electronic Life: How to Think About Computers. New York: 1983. V. 50; 51
Five Patients: the Hospital Explained. New York: 1970. V. 50
Jasper Johns. New York: 1977. V. 53
Jurassic Park. New York: 1990. V. 49; 50; 52; 53
Rising Sun. Franklin Center: 1992. V. 53
The Terminal Man. New York: 1972. V. 50

CRICHTON, PATRICK
Observations on a Machine for the Speedy Conveyance of Troops and Report of an Experiment for that Purpose. Edinburgh: 1804. V. 51

CRICK, THRONE
Sketches from the Diary of a Commercial Traveller. London: 1847. V. 48; 49

CRIES of the Metropolis: or, Humble Life in New York. Rutland: 1858. V. 49

CRILE, GEORGE
Anemia and Resuscitation: an Experimental and Clinical Research. New York: 1914. V. 47; 48; 53
Anoci-Association. Philadelphia: 1914. V. 53
Diseases Peculiar to Civilized Man, Clinical Management and Surgical Treatment. New York: 1934. V. 53
Experimental Research Into the Surgery of the Respiratory System.. Philadelphia: 1900. V. 53
Hemorrhage and Transfusion: an Experimental and Clinical Research. New York: 1909. V. 48; 53

THE CRIMES of Reformers. Addressed to The Labouring Classes on the Tyne and Wear. Newcastle-Upon-Tyne: 1819. V. 50

THE CRIMES of the Kings of France from Clovis to Lewis XVI. London: 1791. V. 53

THE CRIMINAL Recorder, or, an Awful Beacon to the Rising Generation of Both Sexes, Erected by the Arm of Justice to Persuade Them from the Dreadful Miseries of Guilt. Philadelphia: 1812. V. 53

CRIMINAL Trials, Illustrative of the Tale Entitled "The Heart of Midlothian". Edinburgh: 1818. V. 48; 52; 54

CRIMP, W. SANTO
Sewage Disposal Works: a Guide to the Construction of Works for the Prevention of the Pollution by Sewage of Rivers and Estuaries. London: 1890. V. 52; 53

CRISP, FRANK
Mediaeval Gardens. London: 1924. V. 51; 52; 54

CRISP, FREDERICK ARTHUR
Memorial Rings. Charles the Second to William the Fourth. London: 1908. V. 50

CRISP, JOHN
On the Methods of Determining Terrestrial Longitudes by the Moon's Right Ascension... Calcutta: 1827. V. 51

CRISP, JOHN ANTHONY
Cuthbert Knope. London: 1869. V. 54

CRISP, MAY FLOWER
A Treatise on Marine Architecture, Elucidating the Theory of the Resistance of Water... Maulmain: 1849. V. 49

CRISP, QUENTIN
All This and Bevin Too. London: 1943. V. 50; 51
Chog - a Gothic Fantasy. London: 1979. V. 51
Colour in Display. London: 1938. V. 50
The Naked Civil Servant. New York: 1977. V. 52; 53

CRISP, STEPHEN
Several Sermons or Declartions. London: 1707. V. 49

CRISPIN, EDMUND
Frequent Hearses - a Detective Story. London: 1950. V. 51
The Moving Toyshop. New York: 1946. V. 53

CRITE, ALLAN ROHAN
Three Spirituals from Earth To Heaven. Cambridge: 1948. V. 51

CRITES, ARTHUR S.
Pioneer Days in Kern County. Los Angeles: 1951. V. 53

A CRITICAL Analysis of Several Striking and Incongruous Passages in Madame de Stael's Work on Germany... London: 1814. V. 48; 50

A CRITICAL, Expatiatory and Interesting Address to a Certain Right Honourable Apostate, On His Present Unaccountable Conduct At Thus Critical Juncture... London: 1747?. V. 48

A CRITICISM on the Verses Addressed to the Rev. Mr. Wh---y, in the Daily Gazetteer of Thursday April 13, 1738. With an Observation or Two on the Introductory Letter to Them... London: 1738. V. 47

CRITTENDEN, HENRY HUSTON
The Crittenden Memoirs. New York: 1936. V. 49; 52; 53

CRITTENDEN, J. J.
Memorial of the Claimants of the New Almaden Mine to the Secretary of State. Washington: 1859. V. 49

CROAL, THOMAS A.
Scottish Loch Scenery... London: 1882. V. 50; 52; 53

CROCCHIOLA, STANLEY
The Grant that Maxwell Bought by F. Stanley. Denver: 1952. V. 50

CROCE, GIULIO CESARE
Bertoldo con Bertoldino e Cacasenno in Ottava Rima Con Argomenti, e Figure in Rame. Bologna: 1736. V. 53

CROCKATT, GILBERT
The Scotch Presbyterian Eloquence... London: 1719. V. 48
Scotch Presbyterian Eloquence... London: 1738. V. 48

CROCKER, A.
The Art of Reading Improved... Bath: 1782. V. 51
The Elements of Land-Surveying, Designed Principally for the Use of Schools and Students. London: 1806. V. 54

CROCKER, CHARLES
Kingley Vale, and Other Poems. Chichester: 1837. V. 51
The Vale of Obscurity, the Lavant and Other Poems. Chichester: 1830. V. 49; 51

CROCKER, CHARLES TEMPLETON
Catalogue of the Library of... Hillsborough: 1918. V. 49

CROCKER, HANNAH MATHER
Observations on the Real Rights of Women, With Their Appropriate Duties, Agreeable to Scripture, Reason and Common Sense. Boston: 1818. V. 51; 53

CROCKER, JAMES F.
Prison Reminiscences. Portsmouth: 1906. V. 49

THE CROCKETT Almanacks: Nashville Series, 1835-1838. 1955. V. 48

CROCKETT, DAVID
An Account of Crockett's Tour to the North and Down East... Philadelphia: 1835. V. 49
The Life and Adventures of Colonel David Crockett, of West Tennessee. Cincinnati: 1833. V. 50

CROCKETT, J. B.
City of San Francisco vs. United States. No. 280. Before U.S. Land Commissioners. San Francisco: 1854. V. 49

CROCKETT, S. R.
The Raiders. London and Glasgow: 1894. V. 49
Sir Toady Crusoe. Wells Gardner: 1905. V. 54
Sweetheart Travellers. London: 1895. V. 48

CROCKETT, WALTER HILL
A History of Lake Champlain. Burlington;: 1909. V. 54

CROESE, GERALD
The General History of the Quakers; Containing the Lives, Tenets, Sufferings, Tryals, Speeches and Letters, of All the Most Eminent Quakers. London: 1696. V. 47

CROFF, G. B.
Model Suburban Architecture. New York: 1870. V. 47
Model Suburban Architecture... Saratoga Springs: 1870. V. 52

CROFFUTT, W. A.
Fifty Years in Camp and Field, Diary of Major General Ethan Allen Hitchcock. New York: 1909. V. 54

CROFT, HERBERT
The Abbey of Kilkhampton; or, Monumental Records for the Year 1960. Dublin: 1780. V. 48; 50; 52
Love and Madness, a Story Too True... Ipswich: 1809. V. 48
Some Animadversions Upon a Book Intituled, The Theory of the Earth. London: 1685. V. 51
The Wreck of Westminster Abbey, Being a Selection from the Monumental Records of the Most Conspicuous Personages, Who Flourished Towards the Latter End of the Eighteenth Century. London: 1788?. V. 53

CROFT, JOHN
Excerpta Antiqua; or, a Collection of Original Manuscripts. York: 1797. V. 49
Memoirs of Harry Rowe: Constructed from Materials Found in an Old Box, After His Decease... York: 1805. V. 50; 52
Scrapeana. Fugitive Miscellany. Sans Souci: 1792. V. 54

CROFT, P. J.
Autograph Poetry in the English Language... London: 1973. V. 50; 53

Autograph Poetry in the English Language... New York: 1973. V. 47; 48; 50

CROFT, WILLIAM
Musica Sacra; or, Select Anthems in Score...to Which is Added, the Burial Service, As It Is Now Occasionally perform'd in Westminster Abbey. London: 1724. V. 48

CROFT-MURRAY, EDWARD
Catalogue of British Drawing: XVI and XVII Centuries. London: 1960. V. 50; 54
Decorative Painting in England 1537-1837. London: 1962/70. V. 53

CROFTS, THOMAS
Bibliotheca Croftsiana. 1783. V. 53

CROFUTT, GEORGE A.
Crofutt's New Overland Tourist, and Pacific Coast Guide. Chicago: 1878. V. 47; 51
Crofutt's New Overland Tourist, and Pacific Coast Guide. Omaha: 1880. V. 47
Crofutt's New Overland Tourist, and Pacific Coast Guide... Omaha and Denver: 1882. V. 47
Crofutt's Overland Tours. Consisting of Nearly Five Thousand Miles of Side Tours. Also Two Thousand Miles by Stage and Water. Chicago: 1888. V. 47
Crofutt's Overland Tours No. 1. Consisting of Over Six Thousand Miles of Main Tours... Chicago and Philadlephia: 1889. V. 50
Crofutt's Trans-Continental Tourist's Guide... New York: 1872. V. 49
Crofutt's Trans-Continental Tourist's Guide... New York and Chicago: 1873. V. 50
No. 2. Crofutt's Overland Tours. Chicago/New York: 1890. V. 47

CROHN, BURRILL
Regional Ileitis. New York: 1949. V. 53

CROIL, JAMES
Dundas; or, a Sketch of Canadian History, and More Particularly of the County of Dundas, One of the Earliest Settled Counties in Upper Canada. Montreal: 1861. V. 51

CROIZAT, L.
Panbiogeography, or an Introductory Synthesis of Zoogeography, Phytogeography and Geology. London: 1958. V. 54

CROKE, GEORGE
The Third Part (though first publish't) of the Reports of...During the First Sixteen Years Reign of King Charles the First. London: 1683. V. 52

CROKER, BITHIA MARY
Two Masters. London: 1890. V. 54

CROKER, J. W.
The Battles of Talavera. London: 1810. V. 49

CROKER, JOHANN MELCHIOR
Der Wohl Anfuhrende Mahler... Jena: 1736. V. 52

CROKER, JOHN WILSON
Familiar Epistles (in verse) to Frederick J(one)s Esq. on the Present State of the Irish Stage. Dublin: 1804. V. 47; 49; 51
Familiar Epistles to Frederick E. Jones, Esq. on the Present State of the Irish Stage. Dublin: 1805. V. 53
Letters to and From Henrietta, Countess of Suffolk and Her Second Husband, the Hon. George Berkeley from 1712 to 1767. London: 1824. V. 53

CROKER, THOMAS CROFTON
Fairy Legends and Traditions of the South of Ireland. London: 1838. V. 54
Letter...to J.S. Refield, of New York, Respectin the Sale by Auction, in London, of the Letters of Thomas Moore. New York: 1854. V. 47
Narratives Illustrative of the Contests in Ireland in 1641 and 1690. 1841. V. 48
Narratives Illustrative of the Contests in Ireland in 1641 and 1690. London: 1841. V. 52; 53
The Popular Songs of Ireland. London: 1839. V. 53
Researches in the South of Ireland, Illustrative of the Scenery, Architectural Remains and the Manners and Superstitions of the Peasantry. London: 1824. V. 48
A Walk from London to Fulham. London: 1860. V. 50; 52

CROLL, OSWALD
Basilica Chymica, Continens Philosophicam Propria Laborum Experientia Confirmatam Descriptionem & Usum Remediorum Chymicorum Selectissimorum e Lumine Gratiae & Naturae Desumptorum. Frankfurt: 1611. V. 47
Chymisch Kleynod. (bound with) D. O. M. A. Crollius Redivivus, das Ist Hermetischer Wunderbaum. Frankfurt: 1647. V. 47

CROLY, GEORGE
The Life and Times of His Late Majesty, George the Fourth: with Anecdotes of Distinguished Persons of the Last Fifty Years. London: 1830. V. 54
May Fair. London: 1827. V. 47; 48; 49; 52
Salathiel... 1828. V. 48; 50; 52
Salathiel. London: 1828. V. 48; 50; 51; 53
Salathiel. New York & Philadelphia: 1828. V. 54
Tales of the Great St. Bernard. London: 1828. V. 47; 50; 53

CROM, THEODORE R.
Horological Shop Tools 1700 to 1900. Melrose: 1980. V. 53

CROMARTY, GEORGE MAC KENZIE, 1ST EARL OF
A Historical Account of the Conspiracies by the Earls of Gowry and Robert Logan...Against King James VI... Edinburgh: 1713. V. 50
A Vindication of Robert III, King of Scotland... Edinburgh: 1695. V. 52; 54

CROMBIE, BENJAMIN W.
Modern Athenians. Edinburgh: 1882. V. 47; 50

CROMBIE, JOHN
Cette Galere. Paris: 1991. V. 52
The Colour Schemers. Paris: 1982. V. 52
Words Words Words. Paris: 1993. V. 51

CROME, ROBERT
The Fiddle New Model'd Or a Useful Introduction for the Violin, Exemplify'd With Familiar Dialogues. London: 1735?. V. 47; 51

CROMEK, R. H.
Remains of Nithsdale and Galloway Song. London: 1810. V. 53; 54

CROMER, EARL
Modern Egypt. London: 1908. V. 48

CROMIE, ROBERT
The Crack of Doom. London: 1895. V. 50
A Plunge into Space. London: 1891. V. 54

CROMMELIN-BROWN, J. L.
Wykehamical Poems and Parodies. Winchester: 1908. V. 54

CROMMELYNCK, ALDO
Picasso 347. New York: 1970. V. 47; 48; 50; 52

CROMPTON, RICHARD
L'Authoritie et Iurisdiction des Courts de la Maiestie de la Roygne. London: 1637. V. 53
The Copie of a Letter to...the Earle of Leicester...With a Report of Certeine Petitions and Declarations Made to the Queenes Majestie...and Her Majesties Answeres. London: 1586. V. 47; 53

CROMPTON, RICHMAL
Just William. London: 1922. V. 48
William's Television Show. London: 1958. V. 47

CROMPTON, SARAH
The Life of Robinson Crusoe in Short Words. London: 1859. V. 50; 52

CROMWELL, OLIVER
Finger-Print Photography. London: 1907. V. 47
His Highness Speech to the Parliament in the Painted Chamber, at Their Dissolution, Upon Monday the 22d of January, 1654-5. London: 1654. V. 50
His Highnesse the Lord Protectors Speeches to the Parliament in the Painted Chamber, The One on Munday the 4th of September, the Other on Tuesday the 12 of September, 1654. London: 1654. V. 47
Memoirs of the Protector, Oliver Cromwell and His Sons Richard and Henry... London: 1820. V. 50
A Most Learned, Conscientious and Devout Exercise or Sermon, Held Forth the Last Lords-Day of April in the Year 1649. London: 1712. V. 53
Oliver Cromwell's Letters and Speeches... London: 1845. V. 47; 48
Oliver Cromwell's Letters and Speeches. London: 1850. V. 54
Oliver Cromwell's Letters and Speeches... London: 1894. V. 51
Writings and Speeches. Oxford: 1988. V. 53

CROMWELL, RICHARD
The Speech of His Highness the Lord Protector, Made to Both Houses of Parliament at their First Meeting, on Thursday the 27th of January 1658. London: 1659. V. 50

CROMWELL, THOMAS KITSON
Excursions in the County of Essex. London: 1818. V. 51
Excursions in the County of Essex... London: 1818-19. V. 52
Excursions in the County of Kent. London: 1822. V. 52
Excursions in the County of Sussex: Comprising Brief Historical Descriptions and Topographical Delineations... London: 1822. V. 48
Excursions through Ireland. 1820. V. 48
History and Description of the Ancient Town and Borough of Colchester in Essex. London & Colchester: 1825. V. 47; 50; 52; 54

CRON, B.
A Handlist of Western Manuscripts from the Library of B. S. Cron. 1965. V. 50

CRONE, RAINER
Andy Warhol. Hamburg: 1970. V. 48; 50; 51; 53; 54
Andy Warhol. New York: 1970. V. 52

CRONIN, A. J.
Hatter's Castle. London: 1931. V. 49
The Keys of the Kingdom. Boton: 1941. V. 52
Three Loves. London: 1932. V. 49

CRONISE, TITUS FEY
The Natural Wealth of California. San Francisco: 1868. V. 47; 52; 53

CRONQUIST, A.
Integrated System of Classification of Flowering Plans. New York: 1981. V. 52
An Integrated System of Classification of Flowering Plants. New York: 1992. V. 49

CROOK, GEORGE
Letter from General Crook on Giving the Ballot to Indians. Whipple Barracks: 1885. V. 50

CROOKE, HELKIAH
Mikrokosmographia, a Description of the Body of Man. Together with the Controversies and Figures Thereto Belonging... London. V. 47

CROOKE, W.
The North-Western Provinces of India. London: 1897. V. 54

CROOKS, JOHN J.
A History of the Colony of Sierra Leone, Western Africa. Dublin: 1903. V. 48; 50; 52

CROOKSHANK, EDGAR
History and Pathology of Vaccination. London: 1889. V. 50; 51; 52

CROPPER, JAMES
Notes and Memories. Kendal: 1900. V. 52
Present State of Ireland... Liverpool: 1825. V. 53
A Vindication of a Loan of 15,000,000 to the West India Planters, Shewing That It May Not Only be Lent with Perfect Safety... London: 1833. V. 53

CROSBIE, ANDREW
Thoughts of a Layman Concerning Patronage and Presentatiaons. Edinburgh: 1769. V. 48

CROSBY, CARESSE
Painted Shores. Paris: 1927. V. 49
The Passionate Years. London: 1955. V. 51

CROSBY, ELIZABETH C.
Correlative Anatomy of the Nervous System. New York: 1962. V. 50; 53

CROSBY, FRANCES JANE
The Blind Girl. New York: 1844. V. 54

CROSBY, HARRY
Anthology. 1924. V. 49
Chariot of the Sun. Paris: 1931. V. 49; 50
Mad Queen. Paris: 1929. V. 48; 51; 53
Red Skeletons. Paris: 1927. V. 51
Shadows of the Sun. Paris: 1928. V. 50
Six Poems. New York: 1928. V. 47
Sleeping Together - a Book of Dreams. Paris: 1931. V. 50; 53
Torchbearer. Paris: 1931. V. 50
Transit of Venus. Paris: 1929. V. 47; 54
Transit of Venus. Paris: 1931. V. 50

CROSBY, HOWARD
Lands of the Moslem. New York: 1851. V. 50

CROSBY, NICHOLS, LEE & CO.
Catalogue of...Publications. Boston: 1860. V. 52

CROSBY, THOMAS
Up and Down the North Pacific Coast by Canoe and Mission Ship. Toronto: 1914. V. 47

CROSBY'S Parliamentary Record of Elections in Great Britain and Ireland. York: 1845. V. 52

CROSFEILD, ROBERT
Justice the Best Support to Government; or, a Brief Account of Some Publick Transactions During the Late War. London: 1697. V. 51

CROSFIELD, A.
The History of North-Allerton, in the County of York. Northallerton: 1791. V. 51

CROSFIELD, GEORGE
Memoirs of the Life and Gospel Labours of Samuel Fothergill... London: 1843. V. 53; 54
Memoirs of the Life and Gospel Labours of Samuel Fothergill... London: 1857. V. 49; 53; 54

CROSIER, JOHN
A Catalogue of the Genuine Household Furniture...Valuable Library of Medical and Other Books...of John Crosier, Esq. Surgeon. London: 1806. V. 48

CROSLAND, T. W.
The Coronation Dumpty Book. London. V. 47

CROSLEGH, CHARLES
Descent and Alliances of Croslegh, or Crossle, or Crossley, of Scaitcliffe and Coddington of Oldbridge; and Evans of Eyteon Hall. London: 1904. V. 50

CROSLEY, WILLIAM F.
The Trenton City Directory, for 1869... Trenton: 1869. V. 49

CROSS, DOROTHY
Archaeology of New Jersey. Trenton: 1941. V. 47; 49; 51
Archaeology of New Jersey... Trenton: 1941-56. V. 49

CROSS, EDWARD
Companion to the Royal Menagerie, Exeter "Change" Containing Concise Descriptions, Scientific and Interesting, of the Curious Foreign Animals Now in that Eminent Collection, Derived from Actual Observation. London: 1820. V. 54

CROSS, HENRY P.
Little Black Sambo, an Operetta for Children. New York: 1936. V. 52; 53

CROSS, IRA B.
Financing an Empire: History of Banking in California. Chicago: 1927. V. 48; 50; 54
Frank Roney, Irish Rebel & California Labor Leader, an Autobiography. Berkeley: 1931. V. 50; 54

CROSS, JAMES WALTER
George Eliot's Life as Related in Her Letters and Journals. Edinburgh & London: 1885. V. 50; 51; 53
George Eliot's Life as Related in Her Letters and Journals. New York: 1885. V. 51

CROSS, JOE
Cattle Clatter: a History of Cattle... Kansas City: 1938. V. 49; 53

CROSS, JOHN KEIR
The Other Passenger - 18 Strange Stories. London: 1944. V. 52

CROSS, JOHN WALTER
Impressions of Dante and of the New World, with a Few Words on Bimetallism. Edinburgh: 1893. V. 49

CROSS, OSBORNE
The March of the Mounted Riflemen...as Recorded in the Journals of...and the Official Report of Colonel Loring. Glendale: 1940. V. 47
Report...of the March of the Regiment of Mounted Riflemen to Oregon. Washington: 1850. V. 50

CROSS, RALPH HERBERT
The Early Inns of California: 1844-1869. San Francisco: 1954. V. 47

CROSS, SAMUEL CREED
The Negro and the Sunny South... Martinsburg: 1899. V. 49

CROSS, THOMAS
The Autobiography of a Stage-Coachman. London: 1861. V. 52
The Autobiography of a Stage-Coachman. London: 1904. V. 47

CROSS, WILBUR L.
The History of Henry Fielding. New Haven: 1918. V. 53; 54
The Life and Times of Laurence Sterne. New Haven: 1925. V. 54
The Life and Times of Laurence Sterne. New Haven: 1929. V. 53

CROSSE, CORNELIA A. H.
Memorials, Scientific and Literary. London: 1857. V. 47
Red-Letter Days of My Life. London: 1892. V. 50

CROSSE, JOHN GREEN
A Treatise on the Formation, Constituents and Extraction of the Urinary Calculus. London: 1841. V. 48

CROSSEN, FOREST
The Switzerland Trail of America. Boulder: 1962. V. 54

CROSSLEY, F. H.
English Church Monuments, A.D. 1150-1550. London: 1921. V. 53

CROSSMAN, CARL L.
The China Trade: Export Paintings, Furniture, Silver and Other Objects. Princeton: 1973. V. 48

CROSSMAN, MARTIN L.
The Philosophy of Mesmerism or Animal Magnetism. Montreal: 1844. V. 51

CROSTHWAITE, PETER
Seven Maps of the Lakes. Keswick: 1809. V. 54

CROSTON, JAMES
Historic Sites of Lancashire and Cheshire. London: 1883. V. 47
Nooks and Corners of Lancashire and Cheshire. London: 1882. V. 47

CROTHERS, SAMUEL MC CHORD
The Pardoner's Wallet. Cambridge: 1905. V. 48

CROTTY, D. G.
Four Years Campaigning in the Army of the Potomac. Grand Rapids: 1874. V. 54

CROUCH, DONALD E.
Carl Rungius: the Complete Prints. Missoula: 1989. V. 53

CROUCH, E. A.
An Illustrated Introduction to Lamarck's Conchology. London: 1827. V. 54

CROUCH, JOSEPH
The Apartments of the House. London: 1900. V. 49

CROUCH, NATHANIEL
Admirable Curiosities, Rarities and Wonders in Great Britain and Ireland. London: 1718. V. 53
Historical Remarks...of London and Westminster... London: 1681. V. 47
Historical Remarks...of London and Westminster. Westminster: 1810. V. 54
The History of the Kingdom of Ireland... Westminster: 1811. V. 54
The History of the Kingdom of Scotland... Westminster: 1813. V. 54
A Journey to Jerusalem, Containing the Travels of Fourteen Englishmen in 1667, to the Holy Land... Hartford: 1796. V. 52
A New View and Observations on the Ancient and Present State of London and Westminster... London: 1730. V. 48; 50; 52
The Wars in England, Scotland and Ireland. London: 1681. V. 50
The Wars in England, Scotland and Ireland... London: 1810. V. 47
Wonderful Prodigies of Judgment and Mercy Discovered in Above Three Hundred Memorable Histories... London: 1685. V. 49

CROUCHER, JOHN H.
Plain Directions for Obtaining Photographic Pictures by the Calotype and Energiatype, also, Upon Albumenied Paper and Glass, by Collodion and Albumen, etc., etc. Philadelphia: 1853. V. 54

CROUSE, RUSSEL
Mr. Currier and Mr. Ives... Garden City: 1930. V. 48
Mr. Currier and Mr. Ives. New York: 1937. V. 48

CROW, BARBARA
An Acrobatic Alphabet. Andoversford: 1986. V. 47
An Acrobatic Alphabet. Gloucestershire: 1986. V. 51

CROW, FANNIE
Little mama Sarah. V. 47

CROW, GERALD H.
William Morris, Designer. London: 1934. V. 49; 54

CROW, MARTHA FOOTE
The World Above. A Duologue. Chicago: 1905. V. 49

CROWE, CATHERINE STEVENS
Light and Darkness; or Mysteries of Life. London: 1856. V. 50
The Night Side of Nature; or, Ghosts & Ghost Seers. London: 1852. V. 48

CROWE, EYRE EVANS
The History of France. London: 1858-68. V. 47; 49; 53; 54
To-day in Ireland. London: 1825. V. 47

CROWE, J. A.
Titian: His Life and Times. London: 1877. V. 47

CROWE, WILLIAM
Lewesdon Hill... Oxford: 1788. V. 50
Lewesdon Hill... London: 1827. V. 48
A Treatise on English Versification. London: 1827. V. 54

CROWELL, CHESTER T.
Liquor, Loot and Ladies. New York: 1930. V. 50

CROWELL, DAVE
Montana's Own. Missoula: 1970. V. 47

CROWELL, MOSES
The Counsellor, or Every Man His Own Lawyer... Ithaca: 1844. V. 52

CROWELL, THOMAS
History and Description of the Ancient Town and Borough of Colchester, in Essex. Colchester: 1825. V. 49

CROWFIELD, CHRISTOPHER
The Chimney Corner. Boston: 1888. V. 52
House and Home Papers. Boston: 1865. V. 52

CROWFOOT, J. W.
The Island of Meroe and Meroitic Inscriptions, Part I. Part II. London: 1911-12. V. 51
Samaria - Sebaste I-III: Reports on the Work of the Joint Expedition in 1931-33 and of the British Expedition in 1935. London: 1938-57. V. 49

CROWLEY, ALEISTER
Ahab and Other Poems. London: 1903. V. 50
Ambergris. Selected Poems. London: 1910. V. 49; 53
Clouds Without Water. London: 1909. V. 51
The Confessions of Aleister Crowley - an Autobiography. London: 1969. V. 52
The Diary of a Drug Fiend. London: 1922. V. 49; 53
The Equinox. 1992. V. 47
Household Gods. Pallanza: 1912. V. 48
In Residence: the Don's Guide to Cambridge. Cambridge: 1904. V. 49
Konx Om Pax. Essays in Light. London, Felling-on-Tyne: 1907. V. 52
Magick... 1929. V. 47; 51
Magick. London: 1929. V. 52
Magick... Paris: 1929. V. 54
Magick... Paris?: 1930. V. 48
Moonchild. London: 1929. V. 48; 51; 53
Olla: an Anthology of Sixty Years of Song. 1946. V. 47
Oracles, the Biography of an Art. 1905. V. 51
Rodin in Rime. London: 1907. V. 52
Rosa Inferni, a Poem. London: 1907. V. 50
Seven Lithographs by Clot from the Water-Colours of Auguste Rodin: With a Chaplet of Verse by Aleister Crowley. London: 1907. V. 49
Songs of the Spirit. London: 1898. V. 49
The Spirit of Solitude. London: 1929. V. 50
The Stratagem and Other Stories. 1929. V. 51; 53
The Stratagem and Other Stories.. London: 1930. V. 48
The Tale of Archais - a Romance in Verse. London: 1898. V. 52
Temperance. London: 1939. V. 50
Thumbs Up!. Rainbow Valley: 1941. V. 47
The Works of Aleister Crowley. London: 1905. V. 50
The Works of Aleister Crowley. 1905-06-07. V. 48

CROWLEY, JOHN
Aegypt. New York: 1987. V. 52; 53
Beasts. Garden City: 1975. V. 52
Beasts. Garden City: 1976. V. 52
The Deep. 1975. V. 48
The Deep. Garden City: 1975. V. 51; 52
Engine Summer. Garden City: 1979. V. 47
Engine Summer. London: 1980. V. 52
Little, Big. New York: 1981. V. 47; 51; 52; 53
Little, Big. London: 1982. V. 47

CROWLEY, MART
The Boys in the Band. New York: 1968. V. 48

CROWLEY, ROBERT
The Confutation of. XIII. Articles, Whereunto Nicolas Shaxton, Late Byshop of Salisburye Subscribed and caussed be Set Forthe in Print the Yere of Our Lorde, MDXLVI Whe(n) He Recanted in Smithfielde at London at the Burning of mestres Anne Askue, Which is .. London: 1546. V. 48

CROWNE, JOHN
The Dramatic Works. Edinburgh: 1873. V. 49

CROWNE, JOHN continued
Henry the Sixth, the First Part. (with) Henry the Sixth, the Second Part. London: 1681/81. V. 50
The History of Charles the Eighth of France or the Invasion of Naples by the French. London: 1672. V. 49
Thyestes. London: 1681. V. 53

CROWNE, WILLIAM
A True Relation of all the Remarkable Places and Passages Observed in the Travels of the Right Honourable Thomas Lord Hovvard, Earle of Arundel and Surrey... London: 1637. V. 47; 51

CROWNINSHIELD, B. B.
Fore-and-Afters. Boston/Cambridge: 1940. V. 51

CROWNINSHIELD, EDWARD A.
Catalogue of the Valuable Private Library of the Late Edward A. Crowninshield, Embracing in the Collection of a Large Number of Valuable and Rare Books...to Be Sold at Auction on Tuesday, Nov. 1, 1859 and 3 Following Days... Boston: 1859. V. 51

CROWNINSHIELD, FRANCES B.
The Story of George Cronwinshield's Yacht Cleopatra's Barge on a Voyage of Pleasure to the Western Islands and the Mediterranean 1816-1817. Boston: 1913. V. 47

CROWNINSHIELD, FRANK
Vogue's First Reader. New York: 1942. V. 50

CROWTHER, J. S.
An Architectural History of the Cathedral Church of Manchester, Dedicated to St. Mary, St. George, and St. Denys. Manchester: 1893. V. 53

CROWTHER, JOHN
Silva Gars (Grass Wood) and Guide to Grassington and Upper Wharfedale. Keighley: 1930. V. 53

CROXALL, SAMUEL
An Original Canto of Spencer: Design'd as Part of His Fairy Queen, but Never Printed. London: 1714. V. 50; 51

CROYDON, MICHAEL
Ivan Albright. New York. V. 48; 49; 50; 52
Ivan Albright. New York: 1978. V. 53

CROZAT, ANTHONY
A Letter to a Member of the P——t of G——t B——n, Occasioned by the Priviledge Granted by the French King to M. Crozat. London: 1713. V. 47

CROZIER, JOHN BEATTIE
Sociology Applied to Practical Politics. London: 1911. V. 49

CRUCHLEY, G. F.
Cruchley's General Atlas, for the Use of Schools and Private Tuition... London: 1849. V. 51

CRUCIGERUS, GEORGIUS
Harmonia Linguarum Quatuor Cardinalium; Hebraicae, Graecae, Latinae & Germanicae... Frankfurt: 1616. V. 51

CRUDEN, ALEXANDER
A Complete Concordance to the Holy Scriptures. London: 1738. V. 48; 49

CRUDEN, R. P.
The History of the Town of Gravesend in the County of Kent and of the Port of London. London: 1843. V. 54

CRUICKSHANK, WILLIAM
An Account of Two Cases of Diabetes Mellitus: with Remarks As They Arose During the Progress of the Cure. London: 1797. V. 51

CRUIKSHANK, BRODIE
Eighteen Years on the Gold Coast of Africa. London: 1853. V. 48; 50

CRUIKSHANK, ERNEST
The Story of Butler's Rangers and the Settlement of Niagara. Welland: 1893. V. 53

CRUIKSHANK, GEORGE
The Bachelor's Own Book. London: 1844. V. 47; 48; 49; 50
The Bachelor's Own Book. London: 1865. V. 49
The Bachelor's Own Book. London: 1868. V. 49
The Betting Book. London: 1852. V. 49
The Bottle. London: 1847. V. 50
The Bottle... London: 1847/48. V. 48
Catalogue of George Cruikshank's Own Original Collection of His Works, Removed from the Royal Westminster Aquarium...Which Will Be sold by Auction by Messrs. Sotheby...May 22, 1903... London: 1903. V. 49
The Comic Almanack... London: 1835-47. V. 48
The Comic Almanack. London: 1835-53. V. 48; 49; 51
The Comic Almanack... London: 1837. V. 53
The Comic Almanack... London: 1841-44. V. 49
The Comic Almanack... London: 1843?. V. 49
The Comic Almanack... London: 1844-47. V. 48
The Comic Almanack. London: 1844-53. V. 51
The Comic Almanack. London: 1850-52. V. 49
The Comic Almanack. London: 1871. V. 50
The Comic Almanack. London: 1874. V. 50
The Comic Almanack. London: 1890. V. 54
The Cruikshankian Momus... London: 1892. V. 49
Cruikshankiana, an Assemblage of the Most Celebrated Works of George Cruikshank. London: 1835. V. 48
Cruikshank's Water Colours. London: 1903. V. 52; 54
Eighty-Two Illustrations on Steel, Stone and Wood by... London: 1860. V. 50
A Few Remarks on the System of General Education as Proposed by the National Education League. London: 1870. V. 49
George Cruikshank's Fairy Library. London: 1853-64. V. 51
George Cruikshank's Fairy Library. London: 1885. V. 49
George Cruikshank's Magazine. London: 1854. V. 50
George Cruikshank's Omnibus. London: 1842. V. 47; 49; 50; 53; 54
George Cruikshank's Omnibus. London: 1842-41-42. V. 49
George Cruikshank's Table Book. London: 1845. V. 47; 49; 51; 53
Hop-O'-My-Thumb and the Seven League Boots. London: 1853. V. 49; 51; 53
The House that Jack Built. London: 1853. V. 49
The Humourist - a Collection of Entertaining Tales, Anecdotes... London: 1892. V. 47
The Humourist: a Collection of Entertaining Tales, Anecdotes... London: 1822-19-20. V. 51; 53
Illustrations of Don Quixote, In a Series of Fifteen Plates... London: 1834. V. 49
Illustrations of Popular Works. London: 1830. V. 49; 50; 51; 53
Illustrations of Time. London: 1827. V. 47
Illustrations to Punch and Judy; Drawn and Engraved by George Cruikshank. London: 1828. V. 52
J. W. Howell's Bubble, of the General Industry Life and Fire Assurance and Sick-Fund Friendly Society, Burst, by George Cruikshank. London: 1856. V. 49
The Life of Napoleon. London: 1815. V. 50
London Characters. London: 1906. V. 52
The Loving Ballad of Lord Bateman. London: 1851. V. 49
Phrenological Illustrations. London: 1826. V. 49
Phrenological Illustrations... London: 1827. V. 48; 50
Points of Humour. London: 1823. V. 54
The Points of Humour. London: 1823-24. V. 49; 53
Points of Humour. London: 1824. V. 51
A Pop-Gun Fired Off. London. V. 51
A Pop-Gun Fired Off... London: 1860. V. 48; 49
A Slice of Bread and Butter Cut by G. Cruikshank. London: 1857. V. 49
Stop Thief; or, Hints to Housekeepers to Prevent Housebreaking. London: 1851. V. 49

CRUIKSHANK, I.
Curious and Remarkable Life and Trial of Elizabeth Canning. London: 1810. V. 54

CRUIKSHANK, ISAAC ROBERT
Lessons of Thrift, Published for General Benefit by a member of the Save-All Club. London: 1820. V. 48; 51

CRUIKSHANK, ROBERT
The Condition of the West India Slave Contrasted With that of the Infant Slave in Our English Factories. London: 1835. V. 49
Cruikshank's Comic Album. London: 1832. V. 49

THE CRUISE: a Poetical Sketch, in Eight Cantos. London: 1808. V. 54

CRUISE, FRANCIS RICHARD
Thomas a Kempis. Notes of a Visit to the Scenes in Which His Life Was Spent, with Some Account of the Examination of His Relics. London: 1887. V. 54

CRULL, JODOCUS
The Antiquities of St. Peter's, or the Abbey Church of Westminster... London: 1711. V. 49
The Antiquities of St. Peter's, or, the Abbey Church of Westminster. London: 1722. V. 49
A Compleat History of the Affairs of Spain, From the First Treaty of Partition, to this Present Time. London: 1708. V. 52

CRUM, F. M.
With Rifleman, Scouts and Snipers - from 1914 - 1919. Oxford: 1921. V. 47

CRUM, H.
Mosses of Eastern North America. New York: 1981. V. 53

CRUM, JOSIE MOORE
The Rio Grande Southern Story. Durango: 1957. V. 54

CRUM, MASON
Gullah. Negro Life in the Carolina Sea Islands. Durham: 1940. V. 48

CRUM, W. E.
A Coptic Ditionary. Parts I-VI. Oxford: 1929-39. V. 49

CRUM, WALTER
An Experimental Inquiry Into the Number and Properties of the Primary Colours and the Source of Colour in the Prism. Glasgow: 1830. V. 53

CRUMLEY, JAMES
Bordersnakes. New York: 1996. V. 54
The Collection. London: 1991. V. 54
Dancing Bear. New York: 1983. V. 52; 53
Mexican Tree Duck. Huntington Beach: 1993. V. 49
The Mexican Tree Duck. New York: 1993. V. 50
The Mexican Tree Duck. Portishead: 1993. V. 54
The Muddy Fork. Northridge: 1984. V. 48; 49; 52; 54
The Muddy Fork... Livingston: 1991. V. 52
One to Count Cadence. New York: 1969. V. 48; 50; 51; 52; 53; 54
The Pigeon Shoot. Santa Barbara: 1987. V. 48; 49; 52; 53; 54
Whores. Missoula: 1988. V. 49; 50; 52; 53; 54
The Wrong Case. New York: 1975. V. 48; 49; 50; 53; 54
The Wrong Case. 1976. V. 53

CRUMMELL, ALEXANDER
The Relations and Duties of Free Colored Men in America to Africa. Hartford: 1861. V. 49; 51; 53

CRUMPTON, HEZEKIAH J.
The Adventures of Two Alabama Boys... Montgomery: 1912. V. 47; 53

CRUNDEN, JOHN
Convenient and Ornamental Architecture, Consisting of Original Designs... London: 1785. V. 52
Convenient and Ornamental Architecture, Consisting Of Original Designs... London: 1791. V. 48; 50

CRUSE, THOMAS
Apache Days and After. Caldwell: 1941. V. 47

CRUSIUS, MARTINUS
Annales Suevici Sieve Chronica Rarum Gestarum Antiquissimae... Frankfurt: 1595. V. 47

CRUSO, S.
Messiah on the Horizon. 1940. V. 51

CRUTCHLEY, BROOKE
A Printer's Christmas Books... Cambridge;: 1959. V. 50
A Printer's Christmas Books. 1974. V. 54
A Printer's Christmas Books. Cambridge: 1974. V. 51; 54
Two Men. Walter Lewis and Stanley Morison at Cambridge. Cambridge: 1968. V. 51; 52; 53; 54

CRUTTWELL, CLEMENT
A Gazetteer of France, Containing Every City, Town and Village, in that Extensive Country. London: 1793. V. 51

CRUZ, MARTIN DE LA
The Badianus Manuscript. Baltimore: 1940. V. 50
The De La Cruz - Badiano Aztec Herbal of 1552. Baltimore: 1939. V. 47

CRUZ E SILVA, ANTONIO DINYS DA
Odes Pindaricas de...Chamado Entre Os Poetas da Arcadia Portugueza, Elpino Nonacriense. London: 1820. V. 50

THE CRYSTAL Palace Described and Illustrated by Beautiful Engravings Chiefly From Daguerreotypes by Beard. London: 1851. V. 48

THE CRYSTAL Palace that Fox Built. A Pyramid of Rhyme. London: 1851. V. 52

CUBITT, JAMES
Church Design for Congregations: Its Developments and Possibilities. London: 1870. V. 48

CUBI Y SOLER, MARIANO
The English Translation: O Neuvo I Practico Sistema de Traduccion, Adaptado al Ingles Para los Que Hablan Espanol. Cambridge: 1828. V. 52

THE CUB'S Triumph. London: 1900. V. 53

CUDMORE, P.
The Irish Republic. St. Paul: 1871. V. 49; 50; 51

CUDWORTH, RALPH
A Treatise Concerning Eternal and Immutable Morality. London: 1731. V. 48
The True Intellectual System of the Universe. London: 1678. V. 48
The True Intellectual System of the Universe... London: 1743. V. 50
The True Intellectual System of the Universe... London: 1845. V. 49

CUDWORTH, WARREN HANDEL
History of the First Regiment (Massachusetts Infantry). Boston: 1866. V. 47

CUDWORTH, WILLIAM
Historical Notes on the Bradford Corporation, with Records of the Lighting and Watching Commissioners and Board of Highway Surveyors. Bradford: 1881. V. 51
Histories of Bolton and Bowling. Bradford: 1891. V. 47; 52; 53
Life and Correspondence of Abraham Sharp.... London: 1889. V. 47; 52; 53
Manningham, Heaton and Allerton (Townships of Bradford) Treated Historically and Topographically. Bradford: 1896. V. 47; 53

CUEVA, PEDRO DE LA
Iconismos, Encomiasticon, o Verdadera Descripcion, y Elogio de la Expedicion de Africa, en que las Reales Armas de su Mag. Reconbraron a Marzaquivir, Oran, y sus Castillos, Con Una Breve Noticia, de Estas Plazas, su Situacion, Pais... Granada: 1732. V. 48

CUFF, JAMES DODSLEY
Catalogue of the Very Extensive, Highly Important and Valuable Cabinet of Coins and Medals Formed with Great Taste and Judgment by the Late James Dodsley Cuff, Esq. London: 1854. V. 48

CUFFEE, PAUL
Narrative of the Life of Paul Cuffee, a Pequot Indian... Vernon: 1839. V. 54

LA CUISINE Creole a Collection of Culinary Recipes from Leading Chefs and Noted Creole Housewives. New Orleans: 1922?. V. 51

CUITT, GEORGE
Six Etchings of Select Parts of Riveaux Abbey, Yorkshire. London: 1824. V. 50; 54
Six Etchings of Selected Parts of the Saxon and Gothic Buildings, Now Remaining in the City of Chester. (with) Eight Etchings, of Old Buildings, in the City of Chester. Chester: 1811/14. V. 51
Wanderings and Pencillings Amongst the Ruins of the Olden Times. London: 1848. V. 47; 49

CUJACIUS, JACOBUS
Recitationes Solemnes... Frankfurt am Main: 1597. V. 52

CULBERT, DICK
A Climber's Guide to the Coastal Rangers of British Columbia (International Boundary to Nass River). 1965. V. 53

CULBERTSON, THADDEUS A.
Appendix - No. IV Journal of an Expedition to the Mauvaises Terres and the Upper Missouri in 1850. Washington: 1851. V. 47

CULE, W. E.
Child Voices. London: 1900. V. 51

CULL, A. TULLOCH
Poems to Pavlova. London: 1913. V. 51

CULLEN, COUNTEE
The Ballad of the Brown Girl. New York: 1927. V. 48; 49; 51; 52; 53; 54
The Black Christ and Other Poems. New York: 1929. V. 48; 54
Caroling Dusk: An Anthology of Verse by Negro Poets. New York: 1927. V. 47; 48; 52
Color. New York: 1925. V. 49; 52
Copper Sun. New York: 1927. V. 53; 54
The Lost Zoo. New York: 1940. V. 54
The Medea and Some Poems. New York: 1935. V. 50; 53
My Lives and How I Lost Them. New York: 1942. V. 54
One Way to Heaven. New York: 1932. V. 52

CULLEN, EDWARD
The Isthmus of Darien Ship Canal. London: 1852. V. 54

CULLEN, STEPHEN
The Castle of Inchvally: a Tale, Alas, Too True. London: 1820?. V. 49

CULLEN, THOMAS
Cancer of the Uterus: its Pathology, Symptomatology, Diagnosis and Treatment, Also the Pathology of the Diseases of the Endometrium. New York: 1900. V. 48; 53

CULLEN, THOMAS S.
The Collected Reprints of... Baltimore: 1925-46. V. 47; 49; 51; 53

CULLEN, WILLIAM
First Lines of the Practice of Physic. Edinburgh: 1796. V. 47
First Lines of the Practice of Physic. New York: 1805. V. 53; 54
First Lines of the Practice of Physic. Philadelphia: 1816. V. 47; 48
Lectures on the Materia Medica... Philadelphia: 1775. V. 48; 52
Lectures on the Materia Medica. Dublin: 1781. V. 47
A Treatise of the Materia Medica. Dublin: 1789. V. 49
Treatise on the Materia Medica... Philadelphia: 1808. V. 50; 53

CULLER, GEORGE W.
Texas County and Road District Atlas. Dallas: 1936. V. 47

CULLEY, GEORGE
Observations on Live Stock... London: 1807. V. 52

CULLEY, JOHN HENRY
Cattle, Horses and Men of the Western Range. Los Angeles: 1940. V. 49; 53; 54

CULLING, LOUIS
The Complete Magick Curriculum of the Secret Order G. B. G. 1969. V. 52

CULLUM, GEORGE W.
Register of the Officers and Graduates of the U.S. Military Academy...from March 16, 1802, to January 1, 1850. New York: 1850. V. 52

CULLYER, JOHN
The Gentleman's and Farmer's Assistant... Norwich: 1798. V. 52
The Gentleman's and Farmer's Assistant... London: 1816. V. 50

CULOT, J.
Noctuelles et Geometres d'Europe. Geneva: 1909-20. V. 50

CULPEPER, NICHOLAS
The British Herbal and Family Physician... Halifax: 1837. V. 54
The Complete Herbal... London: 1835. V. 52
The Complete Herbal. London: 1847. V. 54
Complete Herbal. Manchester: 1860. V. 48
The Complete Herbal. Birmingham: 1953. V. 52
Culpeper's Complete Herbal... London: 1818. V. 48
Culpeper's Complete Herbal. London: 1819. V. 48; 50
Culpeper's Complete Herbal... London: 1823. V. 48
Culpeper's English Physician... London: 1790. V. 52
Culpeper's English Physician... London: 1794-98. V. 52
Culpeper's English Physician... London: 1799. V. 51; 53
Culpeper's English Physician... London: 1807. V. 54
Culpeper's English Physician... London: 1810. V. 51
Culpeper's Family Physician... Exeter: 1824. V. 54
Culpeper's Family Physician. Exeter: 1825. V. 50
The English Physician Enlarged... London: 1669. V. 51
The English Physician Enlarged... London: 1676. V. 49
The English Physician Enlarged... Manchester: 1806. V. 50
Pharmacopeia Londinensis... London: 1659. V. 47; 48
A Physical Directory: Or a Translation of the Sipsensatory Made by the Colledg(e) of Physitians of Lon(d)on, and By Them Imposed Upon All the Apothecaries of England to Made Up Their Medicines By. London: 1651. V. 48; 49

CULS de Lampe. Northampton: 1968. V. 47

CULVER, HENRY B.
The Book of Old Ships and Something of Their Evolution and Romance... Garden City: 1924. V. 47
Forty Famous Ships... Garden City: 1936. V. 51

CULVER, HENRY B. continued
Forty Famous Ships. New York: 1938. V. 54

CUMBERLAND & WESTMORLAND ANTIQUARIAN & ARCHAEOLOGICAL SOC.
Transactions. Kendal: 1883-99. V. 51
Transactions - Old Series. Kendal: 1883-97. V. 51

CUMBERLAND, C. S.
Sport on the Pamirs and Turkistan Steppes. London: 1895. V. 50; 54

THE CUMBERLAND Foxhounds. Carlisle: 1877. V. 52

CUMBERLAND, GEORGE
Thoughts On Outline, Sculpture, and the System That Guided the Ancient Artists in Composing their Figures and Groupes... London: 1796. V. 48; 49; 52; 53

CUMBERLAND, HENRY CLIFFORD, EARL OF
The Declaration of the Right Honourable Henry Earle of Cumberland, Lord Lieutenant Generall of His Majesties Forcs (sic) in York-shire. London: 1642. V. 53

CUMBERLAND, RICHARD
Anecdotes of Eminent Painters in Spain, During the Sixteenth and Seventeenth Centuries... London: 1782. V. 52; 54
Calvary; or the Death of Christ. London: 1792. V. 47
De Legibus Naturae Disquisitio Philosophica... Ottonem & Frankfurt: 1694. V. 48
De Legibus Naturae Disquisitio Philosophica... Dublin: 1720. V. 48
An Essay Toward to Recovery of Jewish Weights and Measures... London: 1686. V. 47; 49; 50; 53
Henry; a novel. London: 1795. V. 47
John De Lancaster. New York: 1809. V. 47
The Observer: Being a Collection of Moral, Literary and Familiar Essays. London: 1791/88. V. 47
Retrospection, a Poem in Familiar Verse. London: 1811. V. 50; 54
A Treatise of the Laws of Nature. London: 1727. V. 51

CUMING, E. D.
British Sport, Past and Present. London: 1909. V. 47; 48; 49
The Three Jovial Puppies. London: 1908. V. 48

CUMINGS, H. F.
Report to the General Assembly fo the Condition of the Railroads in Tennessee. Nashville: 1859. V. 47

CUMMING, ALEXANDER
The Elements of Clock and Watch-Work, Adapted to Practice. London: 1766. V. 47; 48; 50

CUMMING, DAVID
Handbook of Lithography... London: 1904. V. 47; 49

CUMMING, GORDON
At Home in Fijii. London: 1881. V. 53

CUMMING, HILDELITH
The Stanbrook Abbey Press. Worcester: 1970. V. 54

CUMMING, JAMES
A Manual of Electro Dynamics... Cambridge: 1827. V. 50

CUMMING, JEAN
Ten Little Nigger Boys. London: 1930. V. 50

CUMMING, JOSEPH GEORGE
The Isle of Man. London: 1848. V. 49
The Runic and Other Monumental Remains of the Isle of Man. London: 1857. V. 51

CUMMING, KATE
Gleanings From Southland. Birmingham: 1895. V. 49

CUMMING, T. G.
Description of the Iron Bridges of Suspension Now Erecting Over the Straight of Menai, at Bangor, and over the River Conway, in North Wales... London: 1834. V. 51

CUMMING, WILLIAM FULLERTON
Notes On a Wanderer, In Search of Health, Through Italy, Egypt, Greece, Turkey, Up the Danube and down the Rhine. London: 1839. V. 49

CUMMING, WILLIAM P.
The Exploration of North America, 1630-1776. Toronto: 1974. V. 53
The Southeast in Early Maps. Chapel Hill: 1962. V. 50

CUMMINGHAM, J. V.
Dickinson: Lyric and Legend. Los Angeles: 1980. V. 51

CUMMINGS, BYRON
First Inhabitants of Arizona and the Southwest. Tucson: 1953. V. 52
Kinishba. A Prehistoric Pueblo of the Great Pueblo Period. Hohokam: 1940. V. 52
Kinishba. A Prehistoric Pueblo of the Great Pueblo Period. Tucson: 1940. V. 51; 53; 54

CUMMINGS, EDWARD ESTLIN
&. New York: 1925. V. 51
1 x 1. New York: 1944. V. 50; 53
1/20: Poems. London: 1936. V. 51; 53
50 Poems. New York: 1940. V. 53; 54
73 Poems. New York: 1963. V. 48
Christmas Tree. 1960. V. 47; 48
Ciopw. New York: 1931. V. 52
Collected Poems. New York: 1945. V. 53
Complete Poems. London: 1968. V. 49
E. E. Cummings. A Miscellany. New York: 1958. V. 53
Eimi. New York: 1933. V. 47; 48; 49; 50; 51; 54
The Enormous Room. New York: 1922. V. 50; 51; 53; 54
The Enormous Room. London: 1928. V. 47; 49
The Enormous Room. New York: 1934. V. 54
Fairy Tales. New York: 1965. V. 51; 52
Him. New York: 1927. V. 49
Is 5. New York: 1926. V. 48; 52
A Miscellany. New York: 1958. V. 49; 50
Ninety-five Poems. New York: 1958. V. 52
No Thanks. New York: 1935. V. 50; 51; 53
(no title). New York: 1930. V. 52
Nous Gens d'Espagne. Perpignan: 1949. V. 48
Puella Mea. Mount Vernon: 1949. V. 50
Santa Claus. New York: 1946. V. 54
Santa Claus. Paris: 1974. V. 53
Selected Letters of... New York: 1969. V. 48
Selected Poems 1923-1958. London: 1960. V. 53
Seventy-One Poems. New York: 1950. V. 51
Six Non-Lectures. Cambridge: 1953. V. 49
Sketches and Watercolors of the Twenties and Thirties. 1968. V. 53
Tulips and Chimneys. Mt. Vernon: 1937. V. 51
Viva: Seventy New Poems. New York: 1931. V. 51; 53
...Viva Sweet Love. Eleven Poems. Portland: 1989. V. 53
Xaipe, Seventy-One Poems. New York: 1950. V. 51

CUMMINGS, H. F.
Report to the General Assembly of the Condition of the Railroads in Tennessee. Nashville: 1859. V. 47

CUMMINGS, HAYMAN
The College Stamps of Oxford and Cambridge. London: 1905. V. 48

CUMMINGS, JONATHAN
Explanation of the Prophetic Chart and Application of the Truth. Concord: 1854. V. 51

CUMMINGS, MARCUS FAYETTE
Architecture. Designs for Street Fronts, Suburban Houses and Cottages. Troy: 1865. V. 50
Architecture. Designs for Street Fronts, Suburban Houses and Cottages. Troy: 1867. V. 52

CUMMINGS, R.
The Princess of the Atom. 1951. V. 47

CUMMINGS, SARAH
Autobiography and Reminiscences. New York: 1914. V. 54

CUMMINS, ELLA STERLING
The Story of the Files: a Review of Californian Writers and Literature. San Francisco and Chicago: 1893. V. 47; 52; 53

CUMMINS, HENRY
Report on the Horn Silver Mine. New York: 1879. V. 48; 49

CUMMINS, JIM
Jim Cummins' Book, Written by Himself. Denver: 1903. V. 48; 51; 53

CUMMINS, MAUREEN
Aureole to Zingaresca. 1994. V. 52
Aureole to Zingaresca. New York: 1994. V. 54
The Hopeless Romantic's History of the World. New York: 1994. V. 54

CUNARD, NANCY
Authors Take Sides on the Spanish War. V. 49
Authors Take Sides on the Spanish War. 1937. V. 47
Authors Take Sides on the Spanish War. London: 1937. V. 52
Black Man and White Ladyship, an Anniversary. London: 1931. V. 47; 48
Black Man and White Ladyship an Anniversary... Toulon: 1931. V. 49; 51
Negro Anthology. 1934. V. 50
Negro Anthology... London: 1934. V. 53
Outlaws. London: 1921. V. 48
Parallax. London: 1925. V. 47; 51; 53
Poems (Two) 1925. London: 1930. V. 47; 48
Sublunary. London: 1923. V. 48; 49; 51; 53
The White Man's Duty. Manchester: 1945. V. 49

CUNDALL, H. M.
Birket Foster. London: 1906. V. 47; 49; 52; 54
A History of British Water Colour Painting. London: 1929. V. 47
Home Pictures. London: 1851. V. 51

CUNDALL, JOSEPH
On Bookbindings, Ancient and Modern. London: 1881. V. 47; 49; 52
The Poets of the Wood. London: 1853. V. 53; 54
Rhymes and Roundelayes in Praise of a Country Life. London: 1837. V. 51
Songs, Madrigals and Sonnets... London: 1849. V. 53

CUNDY, N. W.
Inland Transit: the Practicability, Utility and Benefit of Railroads... London: 1834. V. 52; 54

CUNELIUS, GEORGIUS
Facilis et Expeditus Modus Constituendarum Figurarum Coelestium, Seu, ut Volgo Vocant, Thematum Natalitiorum... Leipzig: 1582. V. 52

CUNLAP, WILLIAM
Memoirs of the Life of George Frederick Cooke, Late of the Theatre Royal, Covent Garden. New York: 1813. V. 47

CUNNABELL'S Nova-Scotia Almanac for the Year of Our Lord 1845. New Series No. III, Whole No. XII. Halifax: 1845. V. 53

A CUNNING Plot to Divide and Destroy, the Parliament and the City of London Made Knowne...by the Earle of Northumberland. London: 1644. V. 53

CUNNINGHAM, A. B.
Murder at Deer Lick. New York: 1939. V. 48; 52

CUNNINGHAM, A. E.
Patrick O'Brian. Critical Appreciations and a Bibliography. London: 1994. V. 53

CUNNINGHAM, ALEXANDER
The History of Great Britain... London: 1786. V. 53
The History of Great Britain... London: 1787. V. 50; 53

CUNNINGHAM, ALLAN
The Life of Sir David Wilkie; with His Journals, Tours, and Critical Remarks on Works of Art... London: 1843. V. 49; 50
The Lives of the Most Eminent British Painters, Sculptors and Architects. London: 1829-33. V. 54
The Lives of the Most Eminent British Painters, Sculptors and Architects. London: 1830-37. V. 54
The Lives of the Most Eminent British Painters, Sculptors and Architects. London: 1830-39. V. 49
Roorkee Hudraulic Experiments. Roorkee: 1880-81. V. 47
Songs: Chiefly in the Rural Language of Scotland. London: 1813. V. 52
The Songs of Scotland, Ancient and Modern. London: 1825. V. 47; 53

CUNNINGHAM, CHARLES HENRY
The Audiencia in the Spanish Colonies. Berkeley: 1919. V. 50

CUNNINGHAM, D. J.
Zoology. Volume V. Part XVI: Report on Marsupilia. Anatomy of Thylacine, Cuscus & Phascogale. London: 1882. V. 51

CUNNINGHAM, EUGENE
Texas Sheriff, a Novel of "The Territory.". Boston and New York: 1934. V. 54
Triggernometry... New York: 1934. V. 47; 53
Triggernometry. Caldwell: 1941. V. 53

CUNNINGHAM, FRANK
General Stand Watie's Confederate Indians. San Antonio: 1959. V. 52; 54

CUNNINGHAM, GEORGE GODFREY
Lives of Eminent and Illustrious Englishmen, from Alfred the Great to the Latest Times... Glasglow: 1834-38. V. 50
Lives of Eminent and Illustrious Englishmen, From Alfred the Great to the Latest Times. Glasglow: 1835-37. V. 47

CUNNINGHAM, HENRY DUNCAN
The Capabilities and Advantages of Cunningham's Patient Mode of Reefing Topsails &c... 1853. V. 52

CUNNINGHAM, HENRY STEWART
The Heriots. London: 1890. V. 54
Late Laurels. London: 1864. V. 54
Lord Bowen. A Biographical Sketch With Selection From His Verses. London: 1897. V. 48

CUNNINGHAM, HORACE H.
Doctors in Gray: The Confederate Medical Service. Baton Rouge: 1958. V. 47

CUNNINGHAM, J. F.
Uganda and its Peoples, Notes on the Protectorate of Uganda, Especially and Anthropology and Ethnology of Its Indigenous Races. London: 1905. V. 51

CUNNINGHAM, J. V.
Doctor Drink, Poems. Cummington: 1950. V. 53; 54
The Helmsman. San Francisco: 1942. V. 50; 53
The Judge is Fury. New York: 1947. V. 49
The Literary form of the Prologue to the Canterbury Tales. 1952. V. 54
Logic and Lyric. 1953. V. 54
Selected Poems. Mt. Horeb: 1971. V. 53; 54
Some Salt. Mt. Horeb: 1967. V. 53; 54
Trivial, Vulgar & Exhalted: Epigrams. San Francisco: 1957. V. 47; 49

CUNNINGHAM, JAMES
Designs for Farm Cottages and Steadings... London: 1845. V. 50

CUNNINGHAM, JAMES CHARLES
The Truth About Murietta (sic): Anecdotes and Facts Related by Those Who Knew Him and Disbelieve His Capture. Los Angeles: 1938. V. 53

CUNNINGHAM, JOHN
Poems, Chiefly Pastoral. London: 1766. V. 49; 54
Poems, Chiefly Pastoral. Newcastle: 1771. V. 50; 54

CUNNINGHAM, JOHN WILLIAM
The Velvet Cushion. London: 1814. V. 50

CUNNINGHAM, MERCE
Dancers on a Plane: Cage, Cunningham, Johns. 1989. V. 49

CUNNINGHAM, PETER
Saint Anne's Hill. A Poem. London: 1800. V. 54
The Songs of England and Scotland. London: 1835.. V. 50

The Story of Nell Gwyn: and the Sayings of Charles the Second. London: 1852. V. 48; 49
The Story of Nell Gwyn; and the Sayings of Charles the Second. London: 1862. V. 54

CUNNINGHAM, R. O.
Notes on the Natural History of the Strait of Magellan. Edinburgh: 1871. V. 53

CUNNINGHAM, TIMOTHY
A New Treatise on the Laws Concerning Tithes... London: 1765. V. 49

CUNNINGHAM, W.
The Growth of English Industry and Commerce During the Early and Middle Ages. Cambridge: 1922. V. 54

CUNNINGHAME GRAHAME, G.
Father Archangel of Scotland and Other Essays. London: 1896. V. 53

CUNNINGTON, C. WILLETT
English Women's Clothing in the Present Century. London: 1952. V. 51; 54

CUNYNGHAME, ARTHUR THURLOW
My Command in South Africa, 1874-1878... London: 1879. V. 49; 54
Travels in the Caucasus, on the Caspian and Black Seas, Especially in Daghestan and on the Frontiers of Persia and Turkey, During the Summer of 1871. London: 1872. V. 53

THE CUPID: a Collection of Love Songs. Derby: 1891. V. 50

CUPID'S Annual Charter; or St. Valentine's Festival... London: 1810. V. 47

CUPID'S Annual Charter; or St. Valentine's Festival. London: 1825. V. 48

CUPID'S Budget: Being a Collection of New Valentines. York: 1825. V. 50

CUPID'S Horn-Book. Mount Vernon: 1936. V. 48

CUPPE, PIERRE
Letters on the French Nation; by a Sicilian Gentleman Residing in Paris. London: 1749. V. 51

CUPPLES, GEORGE, MRS.
The Story of Our Doll. London: 1873. V. 51

THE CURATE, an Elegiac Poem, by **** *******. London: 1802. V. 49

CURIE, PIERRE
Notice sur les Travaux Scientifiques de Pierre Curie. Paris: 1900. V. 47

CURIONI, ANTONIO
Istoria dei Poeti Italiani, ad Use de' Principianti Nella Lingua Italiana. Londra: 1788. V. 47

CURIOSITIES for the Ingenious: Selected from the Most Authentic Treasures of Nature, Science and Art, Biography, History and General Literature. London: 1821. V. 51
CURIOSITIES for the Ingenious: Selected from the Most Authentic Treasures of Nature, Science and Art, Biography, History and General Literature. London: 1822. V. 52

THE CURIOSITIES Natural and Artificial, of the Island of Great Britain... London: 1780. V. 52

THE CURIOSITIES of London. London: 1815. V. 47

CURIOSITIES of Ornithology. London: 1880. V. 49

CURIOSITIES of Street Literature... London: 1871. V. 54

A CURIOUS Traveller. London: 1742. V. 47; 49; 51; 52

CURLE, ALEXANDER O.
The Treasure of Trapain. Glasgow: 1923. V. 52; 54

CURLE, RICHARD
Collecting American First Editions: Its Pitfalls and Its Pleasures. Indianapolis: 1930. V. 52
A Handlist of the Various Books, Pamphlets, Prefaces, Notes, Articles, Reviews and Letters Written About Joseph Conrad. Brookville: 1932. V. 53
Joseph Conrad 1911-1931. USA: 1932. V. 53
Joseph Conrad, a Study. New York: 1914. V. 47; 53
Joseph Conrad's Last Day. London: 1924. V. 49; 52
The Last Twelve years of Joseph Conrad. London: 1928. V. 51
The Personality of Joseph Conrad. London: 1925. V. 52
The Richard Curle Conrad Collection... New York: 1927. V. 54

CURLEY, EDWIN A.
Nebraska, Its Advantages, Resources and Drawbacks. New York: 1875. V. 48
Nebraska, Its Advantages, Resources and Drawbacks. New York: 1876. V. 54

CURLING, H. ONSLOW
Hints on the Use and Handling of Firearms Generally, and the Revolver in Particular. London: 1885. V. 49

CURLING, HENRY
Geraldine Maynard; or, The Abduction. London: 1864. V. 54

CURLING, T. B.
Observations on the Diseases of the Rectum. London: 1851. V. 48; 53
A Practical Treatise on the Diseases of the Testis, and of the Spermatic Cord and Scrotum... Philadelphia: 1843. V. 51

CURLL, EDMUND
Faithful Memoirs Of the Life, Amours and Performances of...Mrs. Anne Oldfield. London: 1731. V. 50
An Historical Account of the Life and Writings of the Late Eminently Famous Mr. John Toland... London: 1722. V. 48; 51

CURLL, HENRY
A Catalogue of Books, Printed for H. Curll, Over-Against Catherine Street in the Strand. 1726. V. 50

CURMER, LEON
Dresde, Montpelier. (and) Dresde, Paris, Montpellier. Paris: 1858-60. V. 50; 53

CURR, EDWARD M.
Pure Saddle-Horses, and How to Breed Them in Australia. Melbourne: 1863. V. 47; 50; 54

CURRAN, CONSTANTINE P.
Dublin Decorative Plasterwork of the Seventeenth and Eighteenth Centuries. London: 1967. V. 51
The Rotunda Hospital, Its Architects and Craftsmen. Dublin: 1945. V. 54

CURRAN, J. J.
Mr. Foley of Salmon - a Story of Life in a California Village. San Jose: 1907. V. 49; 54

CURRAN, JOHN PHILPOT
Speeches of John Philpot Curran, Esq. London: 1811. V. 52

CURRAN, WILLIAM H.
The Life of Rt. Hon. John Philpot Curran. Edinburgh: 1822. V. 53

CURRENT, W. R.
Greene & Greene, Architects in the Residential Style. Ft. Worth: 1974. V. 48

CURRER, FRANCES MARY RICHARDSON
A Catalogue of the Library Collected by... London: 1833. V. 51; 53; 54

CURREY, LLOYD W.
Bibliography of Yosemite, the Central and the Southern High Sierra, and the Big Trees, 1839-1900. Los Angeles & Palo Alto: 1992. V. 48

CURRIE, BARTON
Fishers of Books. Boston: 1931. V. 48; 50; 53; 54
Officer 666. New York: 1912. V. 50

CURRIE, J. A.
The Red Watch with the First Canadian Division in Flanders. Toronto: 1916. V. 50

CURRIE, JAMES
Medical Reports on the Effects of Water, Cold and Warm, as a Remedy in Fever and Febrile Diseases... Liverpool: 1797. V. 47; 48; 49
Medical Reports on the Effects of Water, Cold and Warm, as a Remedy in Fever and Febrile Diseases... London: 1805. V. 48; 51; 53

CURRIE, MARY MONTGOMERIE LAMB SINGLETON, BARONESS
From Dawn to Noon. Poems. London: 1872. V. 48; 50
Poems. London: 1892. V. 49
Under Cross and Crescent. London: 1896. V. 50

CURRIEHILL, JOHN SKENE, LORD
Regiam Maiestatem. The Auld Lawes and Constitutions of Scotland... Edinburgh: 1609. V. 50; 51

CURRIER, ERNEST M.
Marks of Early American Silversmiths. Portland: 1938. V. 53

CURRIER, NATHANIEL
Caricatures Pertaining to the Civil War. New York: 1892. V. 47

CURRIER, THOMAS FRANKLIN
A Bibliography of Oliver Wendell Holmes. New York: 1953. V. 52

CURRY, EUGENE
Cath Mhuighe Leana, or The Battle of Magh Leana. London: 1855. V. 52

CURRY-LINDAHL, K.
Bird Migration in Africa. London: 1981. V. 52

CURSON, HENRY
The Office and Duty of Executors; or, A Treatise Directing Testators to Form, and Executors to Perform Their Wills and Testaments According to Law. London: 1720. V. 49

CURT VALENTIN GALLERY
Exhibitions 1953-1954. New York: 1954. V. 49

CURTEYS, RICHARD
A Sermon Preached at Greenevviche, Before the Queenes Maiestie, by the Reuerende father in God the Bishop of Chichester, the 14 Day of Marche 1573. London: 1579. V. 47; 49

CURTIES, T. J. HORSLEY
Ancient Records, or, the Abbey of Saint Osythe. London: 1801. V. 51
The Monk of Udolpho: a Romance. London: 1807. V. 54

CURTIN, JEREMIAH
Myths of the Modocs. London: 1912. V. 48

CURTIN, L. S. M.
By the Prophet of the Earth. Santa Fe: 1949. V. 49; 54
Healing Herbs of the Upper Rio Grande. Santa Fe: 1947. V. 52

CURTIS, ALVA
A Fair Examination and Criticism of All the Medical Systems in Vogue. Cincinnati: 1855. V. 50
Synopsis of a Course of Lectures on Medical Science, Delivered to the Students of the Botanico-Medical College of Ohio. Cincinnati: 1846. V. 47

CURTIS, ARIANA WORMLEY
The Spirit of Seventy-Six; or the Coming Woman, A Prophetic Drama. followed by A Change of Base, and Doctor Monschein. Boston: 1868. V. 54

CURTIS, C. DENSMORE
Sardis. Volume XIII: Jewelry and Gold Work. Part I, 1910-1914. Roma: 1925. V. 52

CURTIS, CHARLES P.
Hunting in Africa East and West. Boston: 1925. V. 47

CURTIS, DAVID A.
Stand Pat or Poker Stories from the Mississippi. Boston: 1906. V. 47; 54

CURTIS, EDWARD SHERIFF
In the Land of the Head-Hunters. New York: 1915. V. 50
In the Land of the Head-Hunters. Yonkers-on-Hudson: 1919. V. 50
Indian Days of the Long Ago. Yonkers: 1914. V. 54
Indian Days of the Long Ago. Yonkers-on-Hudson: 1918. V. 48
The North American Indian: the Southwest. Santa Fe: 1980. V. 52; 54
The North American Indian. Volume 15. Norwood: 1926. V. 47
The North American Indian; Written, Illustrated and Published by Edward S. Curtis... 1920. V. 47
Portraits from North American Indian Life. New York: 1972. V. 52; 54

CURTIS, GEORGE TICKNOR
John Charaxes: a Tale of the Civil War in America. Philadelphia: 1889. V. 47; 54
Life of Daniel Webster. New York: 1870. V. 52

CURTIS, GEORGE WILLIAM
Lotos-Eating: a Summer Book. London: 1852. V. 48
Nile Notes. London: 1851. V. 53
Nile Notes of a Howadji. New York: 1851. V. 51; 54
Prue and I. New York: 1856. V. 51
Prue and I. New York: 1858. V. 51
Washington Irving: a Sketch... New York: 1891. V. 52; 53

CURTIS, H. D.
Studies of the Nebulae, Made at the Lick Observatory, University of California. Berkeley: 1918. V. 53

CURTIS, HENRY
Beauties of the Rose. London: 1850-53. V. 48

CURTIS, JOHN
British Entomology... London: 1823-40. V. 48; 49; 54
British Entomology. London: 1824-28. V. 48; 50
Farm Insects... Glasgow, Edinburgh: 1860. V. 47; 52
Farm Insects. London: 1860. V. 50; 51
Farm Insects. London: 1881. V. 52
Farm Insects... London: 1883. V. 48

CURTIS, JOHN HARRISON
A Treatise on the Physiology and Diseases of the Eye: Containing a New Mode of Curing Cataract Without an Operation. London: 1833. V. 53
A Treatise on the Physiology and Pathology of the Ear. Together with Remarks on the Deaf and Dumb. London: 1836. V. 51

CURTIS, NATALIE
The Indians' Book. New York: 1907. V. 54
The Indians' Book... New York: 1907/23. V. 48
The Indians' Book... New York: 1923, c. 1907. V. 51

CURTIS, PAUL A.
Sportsmen All. New York: 1938. V. 47; 49; 52

CURTIS, RICHARD
History of the Famous Battle Between the Iron-Clad Merrimac C.S.N. and the Iron-Clad Monitor and the Cumberland and Congress of the U.S. Navy March the 8th and 9th, 1862... Norfolk: 1907. V. 50
The Life of Malcolm X. Philadelphia: 1971. V. 54

CURTIS, WILLIAM
Flora Londinensis... London: 1817-28. V. 48
Practical Observations on the British Grasses, Especially Such as Are Adapted to the Laying Down or Improving of Meadows and Pastures. London: 1798. V. 50

CURTIS, WILLIAM E.
Oklahoma Indian Territory and Texas. St. Louis: 1905. V. 52

CURTIS, WILLIAM W.
An Interim and Ad Onterim; or Confidential Disclosures of State Secrets by the Correspondent of the 'Alaska Refrigerator'. 1868. V. 50

CURTISS Aeroplanes. 1912. V. 48

CURTIS'S Botanical Magazine. London: 1845-1902. V. 51
CURTIS'S Botanical Magazine. London: 1905-48. V. 51

CURTISS, DANIEL S.
Western Portraiture, and Emigrants' Guide... New York: 1852. V. 47

CURTIUS RUFUS, QUINTUS
De' Fatti d'Alessandro Magni, Re de'Macedoni... Venegia: 1558. V. 48
De la Vida, y Acciones de Alexandro el grande, Traducido de la Lengua Latina... Madrid: 1699. V. 53
De Rebus Gestis Alexandri Magni...Curavit and Digressit Henricus Snakenburg. Delphis & Lugd. Bat: 1724. V. 50
Historiarum Libri, Accuratissime Editi. Amsterdam: 1670. V. 48; 49
The History of the Life and Death of Alexander the Great... London: 1687. V. 50; 51

CURWEN, ANNIE ISABEL
Poems. Barrow-in-Furness: 1899. V. 50; 52

CURWEN, HENRY
Echoes From the French Poets. London: 1870. V. 49
Lady Bluebeard. Edinburgh: 1888. V. 51

CURWEN, J. C.
Hints on Agricultural Subjects, and on the Best Means of Improving the Condition of the Labouring Classes. London: 1809. V. 49
Hints on the Economy of Feeding Stock and the Bettering of the Condition of the Poor. London: 1808. V. 47
Hints on the Economy of Feeding Stock, and the Bettering of the Condition of the Poor. London: 1818. V. 48

CURWEN, J. SPENCER
Memorials of John Curwen. London: 1882. V. 50; 52; 54

CURWEN, JOHN F.
The Ancient Parish of Heversham with Milnthorpe... Kendal: 1930. V. 50; 52
The Castles and Fortified Towers of Cumberland, Westmorland, and Lancashire North-of-the-Sands... London. V. 50
The Castles and Fortified Towers of Cumberland, Westmorland, and Lancashire North-of-the-Sands... Kendal: 1913. V. 50; 52
Historical Description of Levens Hall. Kendal: 1898. V. 52
A History of the Ancient House of Curwen of Workington in Cumberland, and Its Various Branches... Kendal: 1928. V. 50
Kirkbie Kendall. Kendal: 1900. V. 50; 52; 54
The Later Records Relating to North Westmorland or the Barony of Appleby. Kendal: 1932. V. 52

CURWEN PRESS
Catalogue Raisonne of Books Printed at the Curwen Press 1920-1923. London: 1924. V. 51; 53
A Specimen Book of Pattern Papers... Paris: 1819. V. 48
A Specimen Book of Pattern Papers. London: 1928. V. 47; 52
A Specimen Book of Types and Ornaments in Use at the Curwen Press. London: 1928. V. 47; 51

CURWEN, SAMUEL
The Journal of Samuel Curwen, Loyalist. Cambridge: 1972. V. 50; 53

CURWOOD, JAMES OLIVER
The Alaskan: a Novel of the North. New York: 1923. V. 49
Baree: Son of Kazan. Garden City: 1917. V. 48
The Black Hunter: A Novel of Old Quebec. New York: 1928. V. 48
The Country Beyond: a Romance of the Wilderness. New York: 1922. V. 49
Falkner of the Inland Seas. Indianapolis: 1931. V. 48
The Flaming Forest: a Novel of the Canadian Northwest. New York: 1921. V. 49
God's Country: the Trail to Happiness. New York: 1921. V. 50

CURZON, DANIEL
Something You do In the Dark. New York: 1971. V. 54

CURZON, G.
The Violinist of the Quartier Latin. 1884. V. 47

CURZON, GEORGE NATHANIEL, 1ST MARQUIS OF
British Government in India. London: 1925. V. 50; 51
The Pamirs and the Source of the Oxus. 1898. V. 54
Persia and Persian Question. London and New York: 1892. V. 51
Russia in Central Asia in 1889 and the Anglo-Russian Question. London: 1889. V. 49; 54

CURZON, ROBERT
Armenia. A Year At Erzeroom, and On the Frontiers of Russia, Turkey and Persia. New York: 1854. V. 49
Visits to the Monasteries in the Levant. London: 1849. V. 53
Visits to the Monasteries in the Levant. London: 1865. V. 54

CUSACK, MARY FRANCES
A History of the Kingdom of Kerry. London: 1871. V. 52
Woman's Work in Modern Society. 1875. V. 53

CUSHING, CALEB
Reminiscences of Spain, the Country, Its People, History and Monuments. Boston: 1833. V. 53
The Treaty of Washington, Its Negotiation, Execution and Discussions Relating Thereto. New York: 1873. V. 48

CUSHING, FRANK HAMILTON
My Adventures With the Zuni. Santa Fe: 1941. V. 50; 51
Zuni Breadstuff. New York: 1920. V. 47; 48; 53; 54
Zuni Folk Tales. New York: 1901. V. 53

CUSHING, H.
Consecratio Medici and Other Papers. Boston: 1928. V. 52

CUSHING, HARVEY WILLIAMS
A Bibliography of the Writings of Harvey Cushing Prepared on the Occasion of His Seventieth Birthday... Springfield: 1939. V. 48; 49
A Bio-Bibliography of Andreas Vesalius. New York: 1943. V. 47; 48; 50; 52; 53; 54
A Classification of the Tumors of the Glioma Group on a Histogenetic Basis with a Correlated Study of Prognosis. Philadelphia: 1926. V. 47; 48; 49; 51; 54
Consecratio Medici and Other Poems. Boston: 1928. V. 47
The Establishment of Cerebral Hernia as a Decompressive Measure for Inaccessible Brain Tumors... 1905. V. 47; 49; 50
The Establishment of Cerebral Hernia as a Decompressive Measure for Inaccessible brain Tumors... London: 1905. V. 48
From a Surgeon's Journal... Boston: 1936. V. 49
From a Surgeon's Journal. London: 1936. V. 47
From a Surgeon's Journal. Philadelphia: 1936. V. 51; 53; 54
The Harvey Cushing Collection of Books and Manuscripts. New York: 1943. V. 47; 52
Intracranial Tumours: Notes Upon a Series of Two Thousand Verified Cases with Surgical Mortality Percentages Pertaining Thereto. Springfield/Baltimore: 1932. V. 53
The Life of Sir William Osler. London: 1925. V. 54
The Life of Sir William Osler. Oxford: 1925. V. 47; 48; 49; 50; 51; 52; 53; 54
The Life of Sir William Osler. Oxford: 1926. V. 47; 48; 49; 52
The Life of Sir William Osler. Oxford: 1980. V. 49
The Medical Career. Hanover: 1930. V. 47
The Meningiomas Arising from the Olfactory Groove and Their Removal by the Aid of Electro-Surgery. 1927. V. 47
The Meningiomas Arising from the Olfactory Groove and Their Removal by the Aid of Electrosurgery. Glasgow: 1927. V. 54
The Meningiomas (Dural Endotheliomas): Their Sources and Favoured Seats of Origin. Boston: 1922. V. 47
Meningiomas. Their Classification, Regional Behaviour, Life History and Surgical End Results. Springfield: 1938. V. 47; 48; 50; 54
Neurological Surgeons: Wtih the Report on One Case. 1923. V. 47
Papers Relating to the Pituitary Body, Hypothalamus and Parasympathetic Nervous System. Springfield: 1932. V. 47; 48; 53; 54
The Pituitary Body and Its Disorders. Philadelphia & London: 1912. V. 47; 48; 49; 50; 51; 52; 53; 54
Studies in Intracranial Physiology and Surgery. The Third Circulation... 1926. V. 49; 50; 52; 54
Studies in Intracranial Physiology and Surgery. The Third Circulation. London: 1926. V. 48
Studies in Intracranial Physiology and Surgery. The Third Circulation... Oxford: 1926. V. 53
Tumors Arising from the Blood Vessels of the Brain. Springfield: 1928. V. 52; 53; 54
Tumors of the Nervus Acusticus. Philadelphia/London: 1917. V. 53; 54
Xanthochromia and Increased Protein in the Spinal Fluid Above Tumors of the Cauda Equina. 1923. V. 47

CUSHING, JOHN
The Exotic Gardener, in Which the Management of the Hot-House, green-House and Conservatory is Fully Delineated. London: 1812. V. 49

CUSHING, L. S.
An Act for the Relief of Insolvent Debtors and for the More Equal Distribution of their Effects... Boston: 1838. V. 50

CUSHING, S. W.
Wild Oats Sowings; or the Autobiography of an Adventurer. New York: 1857. V. 47

CUSHING, THOMAS
History of the Counties of Gloucester, Salem and Cumberland New Jersey, with Biographical Sketches of Their Prominent Citizens. Philadelphia: 1883. V. 49; 51

CUSHMAN, HORATIO B.
A History of the Choctaw, Chickasaw and Natchez Indians. Greenville: 1899. V. 48; 50; 52

CUSHMAN, J. A.
Foraminifera of the Philippine and Adjacent Seas. 1921. V. 49
The Foraminifera of the Tropical Pacific Collections of the 'Albatross' 1899-1900. Washington: 1932-65. V. 53

CUSHMAN, SAMUEL
The Gold Mines of Gilpin County, Colorado. Historical, Descriptive and Statistical. Central City: 1876. V. 48

CUSHNY, ARTHUR R.
The Actions and uses in Medicine of Digitalis and its Allies. London: 1925. V. 48; 53
The Secretion of the Urine. London: 1917. V. 49
The Secretion of the Urine. London: 1926. V. 49

CUSSANS, JOHN EDWIN
History of Hertfordshire... Hertford: 1870-71. V. 47
History of Hertfordshire. London: 1870-81. V. 47

CUSSLER, CLIVE
Iceberg. New York: 1975. V. 50

CUST, C. LEOPOLD
Naval Battles from the Collection of Prints Formed and Owned By... London: 1911. V. 49

CUST, HENRY
Occasional Poems Chosen by N.C. and R.S. Jerusalem: 1918. V. 49

CUST, LIONEL
History of the Society of Dilettanti. London & New York: 1914. V. 49

CUST, ROBERT H. HOBART
The Life of Benvenuto Cellini. London: 1910. V. 52

CUST, ROBERT NEEDHAM
Pictures of Indian Life Sketched With the Pen from 1852 to 1881. London: 1881. V. 51

CUSTANCE, GEORGE
A Concise View of the Constitution of England. London: 1808. V. 50

THE CUSTER Battlefield National Cemetery. San Francisco: 1937. V. 52

CUSTER, ELIZABETH
Boots and Saddles; or Life in Dakota with General Custer. New York: 1885. V. 54

CUSTER, ELIZABETH B.
Following the Guidon. New York: 1890. V. 51; 54
Following the Guidon. New York: 1899. V. 52
Tenting on the Plains or General Custer in Kansas and Texas. New York: 1887. V. 47; 49; 52

CUSTER, GEORGE A.
My Life on the Plains. New York: 1874. V. 51; 53

CUSTOMS and Privileges of the Manors of Stepney and Hackney in the County of Middlesex. London: 1736. V. 47; 50

THE CUSTOMS of London, Otherwise Called Arnold's Chronicle... London: 1811. V. 47

CUSTON, ROBERT NEEDHAM
Pictures of Indian Life Sketched with Pen from 1852 to 1881. London: 1881. V. 47

CUTBUSH, JAMES
The American Artist's Manual, or Dictionary of Practical Knowledge in the Application of Philosophy to the Arts and Manufactures. Philadelphia: 1814. V. 48; 54
A System of Pyrotechny, Comprehending the Theory and Practice, with the Application of Chemistry... Philadelphia: 1825. V. 52; 53

CUTCHINS, JOHN A.
A Famous Command, the Richmond Light Infantry Blues. Richmond: 1934. V. 52; 53

CUTCLIFFE, H. C.
The Art of Trout Fishing on Rapid Streams... South Molton: 1863. V. 47
The Art of Trout Fishing on the Rapid Streams. Tiverton, Devon: 1982. V. 47; 50; 53

CUTLER, A., & SON
Cutler's Patent Desks. Manufactured by A. Cutler & son. Buffalo: 1884. V. 50

CUTLER, B. D.
Modern British Authors: Their First Editions. New York: 1930. V. 48

CUTLER, BENJAMIN
Twelve Hours on the Wreck; or, The Stranding of the Sheffield. New York: 1844. V. 50

CUTLER, CARL C.
A Descriptive Catalogue of the Marine Collection at India House. Middleton: 1973. V. 47; 49; 52

CUTLER, D. F.
Root Identification Manual of Trees and Shrubs. London: 1987. V. 52

CUTLER, ELLIOTT
Surgery of the Heart and Pericaradium. New York: 1927. V. 53

CUTLER, JERVIS
A Topographical Description of the State of Ohio, Indiana Territory, and Louisiana. Boston: 1812. V. 52

CUTLER, MAX
Tumors of the Breast. Philadelphia: 1962. V. 48; 53

CUTLER, NAHUM S.
A Cutler Memorial and Genealogical History... Greenfield: 1889. V. 54

CUTLER, THOMAS W.
A Grammar of Japanese Ornament and Design... London: 1880. V. 52

CUTRIGHT, PAUL RUSSELL
A History of the Lewis and Clark Journals. Norman: 1976. V. 53; 54
Lewis and Clark: Pioneering Naturalists. Urbana: 1969. V. 54

CUTTEN, GEORGE
Three Thousand Years of Mental Healing. New York: 1911. V. 47; 50

CUTTER, CALVIN
Murder of Caroline H. Cutter by the Baptist Ministers and Baptists Churches. Nashua: 1843. V. 48

CUTTER, CHARLES
Cutter's Guide to the Hot Springs of Arkansas, Illustrated. St. Louis: 1882. V. 51

CUTTER, DONALD C.
Malaspina in California. San Francisco: 1960. V. 48

CUTTER, G. W.
Buena Vista: and other Poems. Cincinnati: 1848. V. 52; 53

CUTTS, EDWARD L.
An Essay on the Christmas Decoration of Churches. London: 1859. V. 52
A Manual for the Study of the Sepulchral Slabs and Crosses of the Middle Ages. London: 1849. V. 52

CUTTS, SIMON
Pianostool Footnotes. Highlands: 1982. V. 47; 48

CUVIER, GEORGES, BARON
The Animal Kingdom... London: 1827-35. V. 54
The Animal Kingdom... London: 1833-34-37. V. 54
The Animal Kingdom. London: 1834. V. 51; 52
A Discourse on the Revolutions of the Surface of the Globe, and the Changes Thereby Produced in the Animal Kingdom... London: 1829. V. 48
Essay On the Theory of the Earth. New York: 1818. V. 48; 51; 54
Essay on the Theory of the Earth. Edinburgh: 1822. V. 51
Essay on the Theory of the Earth. Edinburgh: 1827. V. 50; 53
Essay on the Theory of the Earth... London: 1827. V. 48; 54
Recherches sur les Ossemens Fossiles. Paris: 1834-36. V. 49

CYCLOPAEDIA of Machine and Hand-Tools: a Series of Plans, Sections and Elevations... London: 1869. V. 50

A CYCLOPEDIA of Missions: Containing a Comprehensive View of Missionary Operations Throughout the World... New York: 1855. V. 50

CYNWAL, WILLIAM
In Defence of Woman. Waltham St. Lawrence: 1960. V. 52

CYPRIANUS, SAINT, BP. OF CARTHAGE
The Genuine Works of St. Cyprian... London: 1717. V. 51
Opera. Stuttgart: 1486. V. 51; 52
Opera. Basileae: 1525. V. 50

CYRANO DE BERGERAC, SAVINIEN
The Agreement. A Satyrical and Facetious Dream. 1756. V. 48
A Voyage to the Moon: With Some Account of the Solar World. Dublin: 1754. V. 47

CYRUPAEDIA.. Newtown: 1936. V. 49; 50

CZARNECKA, EWA
Conversations with Czeslaw Milosz. San Diego: 1967. V. 50

CZECH, FRANZ HERMANN
Versinnlichte Denk-und Sprachlehre, mit Anwendung auf Die Religions- und Sittenlehre und auf das Leben. Vienna: 1844. V. 54

CZWIKLITZER, CHRISTOPHER
Picasso's Posters. New York: 1970/71. V. 47; 48; 50; 52
Picasso's Posters. New York: 1971. V. 50

D

DABBS, EDITH M.
Face of an Island: Leigh Richmond Miner's Photographs of Saint Helenea Island. Columbia: 1970. V. 47

DABNEY, ROBERT LEWIS
Life and Campaigns of Lieut. Gen. Thomas J. Jackson. New York: 1866. V. 47; 53

DABNEY, W. P.
Cincinnati's Colored Citizens. Cincinnati: 1926. V. 53

D'ABRANTES, LAURE JUNOT, DUCHESS
Memoirs of Napoleon, His Court and Family. London: 1836. V. 52

D'ABRERA, B.
Butterflies of the Australian Region. Melbourne: 1977. V. 48; 50; 51
Butterflies of the Holarctic Region. Black Rock: 1990-93. V. 50
Butterflies of the Holarctic Region. Parts 1-3. London: 1990-93. V. 51
Butterflies of the Neotropical Region. Part I. Papilionidae and Pieridae. Melbourne: 1981. V. 52; 53
Butterflies of the World. Melbourne: 1980-92. V. 49

DACEY, PHILIP
Gerard Manley Hopkins Meets Walt Whitman in Heaven and Other Poems. Great Barrington: 1982. V. 48

DACIER, ANDRE
The Life of Pythagoras with His Symbols and Golden Verses. Together with the Life of Hierocles... London: 1707. V. 52; 54

DA COSTA, EMANUEL MENDES
Elements of Conchology; or, an Introduction to the Knowledge of Shells. London: 1776. V. 48

DA COSTA, J. M.
Medical Diagnosis With Special Reference to Practical Medicine. Philadelphia: 1864. V. 48

DA COSTA, JOHN C.
Clinical Hematology: a Practical Guide to the Examination of the Blood. Philadelphia: 1902. V. 53

DACRE, ARABELLA SULLIVAN
Recollections of a Chaperon. London: 1833. V. 48; 49; 50; 51

DACRE, CHARLOTTE
Zofloya or the Moor. London: 1928. V. 53

DACRE, CHARLOTTE ROSA MATILDA
The Libertine. London: 1807. V. 50

DACRE, DIANA
Tales of the Peerage and the Peasantry. London: 1835. V. 48

D'ACUGNA, CHRISTOPHER
Voyages and Discoveries in South America. London: 1698. V. 49

DACUS, JOPSEPH A.
Life and Adventures of Frank and Jesse James The Noted Western Outlaws. St. Louis: 1880. V. 49; 54

DACUS, JOSEPH A.
Illustrated Lives and Adventures of Frank and Jesse James and the Younger Brothers, the Noted Western Outlaws. New York and St. Louis: 1880. V. 52; 53
Illustrated Lives and Adventures of Frank and Jesse James and the Younger Brothers, the Noted Western Outlaws. St. Louis: 1881. V. 52
Life and Adventures of Frank and Jesse James, the Noted Western Outlaws. New York: 1882. V. 54

DACY, GEORGE
Four Centuries of Florida Ranching. St. Louis: 1940. V. 53

DAELLI, G.
A Relic of the Italian Revolution in 1849. New Orleans: 1850. V. 54

DAFFAN, KATIE
My Father As I Remember Him Including Autobiographical Sketch... Houston: 1907. V. 49

DAFT, RICHARD
Kings of Cricket. Bristol: 1893. V. 51

DAGGETT, DAVID
Count the Cost. An Address to the People of Connecticut, on Sundry Political Subjects, and Particulary on the Proposition for a New Constitution. Hartford: 1804. V. 51; 52; 54
Sun-Beams May Be Extracted from Cucumbers, But the Process is Tedious. New Haven: 1799. V. 51

DAGLEY, RICHARD
Death's Doings... London: 1826. V. 48; 53
Death's Doings... London: 1827. V. 49
Death's Doings... Boston: 1828. V. 47; 50; 54
Takings: or, The Life of a Collegian. A Poem. London: 1821. V. 48; 52; 54

DAGLISH, ERIC FITCH
Animals in Black and White. London: 1928-29. V. 54
The Birds of the British Islands. London: 1948. V. 49; 50; 51; 52; 53; 54
Woodcuts of British Birds. London: 1925. V. 53

D'AGOULT, MARIE CATHERINE SOPHIE, COMTESSE
Nelida. Paris: 1846. V. 54

DAHL, FOLKE
Dutch Corantos 1618-1650. The Hague: 1946. V. 47

DAHL, GEORGE LEIGHTON
Portals Doorways and Windows of France. New York: 1925. V. 51

DAHL, JOHAN ANDREAS
Norwegian and Swedish Poems. 1872. V. 47

DAHL, ROALD
The BFG. New York: 1982. V. 51
Boy. Tales of Childhood. New York: 1984. V. 47; 51; 52; 53
The Commemorataive Edition. London: 1990. V. 48
The Gremlins. 1943. V. 49
The Gremlins. London: 1944. V. 48; 49
The Magic Finger. London: 1968. V. 50
Over to You. 1946. V. 50
Over to You. New York: 1946. V. 48
Selected Stories of Roald Dahl. New York: 1968. V. 48
Some Time Never: a Fable for Supermen. New York: 1948. V. 48; 51
Someone Like You. New York: 1953. V. 47; 49; 51
Two Fables: (The Princess and the Poacher, Princess Mammalia). 1986. V. 49
The Witches. New York: 1983. V. 52; 53
Works. London: 1991. V. 52

DAHLBERG, EDWARD
Because I Was Flesh. London: 1965. V. 51
Bottom Dogs. London: 1929. V. 52; 53
Bottom Dogs. New York: 1930. V. 48
The Confessions of... New York: 1971. V. 47; 50; 52
Do These Bones Live. New York: 1941. V. 49
The Flea of Sodom. London: 1950. V. 53
From Flushing to Calvary. New York: 1932. V. 51
From Flushing to Calvary. London: 1933. V. 49
The Leafless American. Sausalito: 1967. V. 48; 51
The Owl of Minerva or The Comedy of a Cuckold. New York: 1976. V. 51
The Sorrows of Priapus. Norfolk: 1957. V. 48; 52; 54
Those Who Perish. New York: 1934. V. 51; 52

DAHLGREN, R. M. T.
The Families of the Monocotyledons: Structure, Evolution and Taxonomy. London: 1875. V. 50

DAHN, JULIUS SOPHUS FELIX
A Struggle for Rome. London: 1878. V. 53

DAI, A.
Crabs of the China Seas. Beijing: 1991. V. 48; 50

DAILEY, ABRAM H.
Mollie Fancher, the Brooklyn Enigma. New York: 1894. V. 49; 54

DAILEY, G. A.
Memorial Gardens of the Manila Cemetery. San Francisco: 1954. V. 51

THE DAILY News History of Buchanan County and St. Joseph from the Year of the Platte Purchase to the End of the Year 1898. St. Joseph. V. 51; 53

DAINELLI, GIOTTO
Buddhists and Glaciers of Western Tibet. London: 1933. V. 54

DAIR, CARL
Design with Type. New York: 1952. V. 53
First Proof of Cartier, Roman and Italic. Toronto: 1966. V. 53

THE DAISY; or, Cautionary Stories in Verse. Philadelphia: 1808. V. 48

DAIX, PIERRE
Picasso 1900-1906 (Blue Period). Paris: 1966. V. 50
Picasso: The Blue and Rose Periods. Greenwich: 1967. V. 47; 48; 50; 51; 52; 53; 54

DAKIN, SUSANNA BRYANT
The Christ Child. Pasadena: 1938. V. 54

DAKOTA TERRITORY. LAWS, STATUTES, ETC.
General and Special Laws Passed at the Sixteenth Session of the Legislative Assembly of the Territory of Dakota. Yankton: 1885. V. 54
General Laws and Memorials and Resolutions of the Territory of Dakota Passed at the First Session of the Legislative Assembly... (with) Private Laws of the Territory of Dakota. Yankton: 1862. V. 54
Laws Passed at the Seventeenth Session of the Legislative Assembly of the Territory of Dakota. Bismarck: 1887. V. 54
Laws Passed at the Thirteenth Session of the Legislative Assembly of the Territory of Dakota. Yankton: 1879. V. 54

D'ALBERTIS, L. M.
New Guinea: What I did and What I Saw. London: 1881. V. 48

DALDY, THOMAS
On Disease of the Right Side of the Heart. London: 1866. V. 48

DALE, ANTONIUS VAN
Dissertationes de Origine Ac Progressu Idololatriae et Superstitionum. Amstelodami: 1696. V. 50

DALE, EDWARD EVERETT
The Range Cattle Industry. Norman: 1930. V. 51; 52; 53

DALE, HARRISON CLIFFORD
The Ashley-Smith Explorations and the Discovery of a Central Route to the Pacific... Cleveland: 1918. V. 53
The Ashley-Smith Explorations and the Discovery of a Central Route to the Pacific... Glendale: 1941. V. 49; 50; 53

DALE, NELLIE
The Dale Readers - First Primer. London: 1920. V. 50
Steps to Reading. London: 1917. V. 50

DALE, ROBERT
An Exact Catalogue of the Nobility of England. London: 1697. V. 49; 51

DALE, SAMUEL
The History and Antiquities of Harwich and Dovercourt. London: 1730. V. 47; 48

DALE, THOMAS
The Widow of the City of Nain; and Other Poems; by an Under-Graduate of the University of Cambridge. London: 1819. V. 54

DALE, THOMAS F.
The History of the Belvoir Hunt. Westminster: 1899. V. 47
Polo Past and Present. London: 1905. V. 47
Riding and Polo Ponies. London: 1902. V. 54

DALE, WILLIAM
Tschudi the Harpsichord maker. New York: 1913. V. 49

DALECHAMP, CALEB
Christian Hospitalitie Handled Common-Place-Wise in the Chappel of Trinity Colledge in Cambridge... Cambridge: 1632. V. 52

DALECHAMP, JACQUES
Histoire Generale des Plantes. Lyon: 1653. V. 52; 53

DAL FABBRO, M.
Modern Furniture, Its Design and Construction. New York: 1950. V. 53

DALGAIRNS, MRS.
The Practice of Cookery Adapted to the Business of Every-Day Life. Edinburgh: 1850. V. 49

DALI, SALVADOR
50 Secrets of Magic Craftsmanship. New York: 1948. V. 48; 52
Conquest of the Irrational. New York: 1935. V. 51; 53
Dali. New York: 1968. V. 54
Dali On Modern Art: The Cuckolds of Antiquated Modern Art. New York: 1957. V. 53; 54
Dali's Mustache: a Photographic Interview. New York: 1954. V. 54
Diary of a Genius. Garden City: 1965. V. 49; 54
Diary of Genius. London: 1966. V. 51
Les Diners de Gala. New York: 1973. V. 51; 52
Hidden Faces. London: 1973. V. 50
The Secret Life of Salvador Dali. New York: 1942. V. 48; 50
The Secret Life of Salvador Dali. London: 1949. V. 51; 54
A Study of His Art-in-Jewels: The Collection of the Owen Cheatham Foundation. Greenwich: 1959. V. 49; 50
The Wines of Gala. New York: 1978. V. 47; 48; 50

DALL, CAROLINE H.
Alongside. Boston: 1900. V. 54
The College, the Market and the Court; or, Woman's Relation to Education, Labor and Law. Boston: 1867. V. 50
The Romance of the Association; or, One Last Glimpse of Charlotte Temple and Eliza Wharton. Cambridge: 1875. V. 51
Woman's Right to Labor; or, Low Wages and Hard Work in Three Lectures Delivered in Boston, November, 1859. Boston: 1860. V. 54
Woman's Rights Under the Law. Boston: 1862. V. 47; 51

DALL, W. H.
The Mollusca of Porto Rico. Washington: 1902. V. 48
Notes on the Avifauna of the Aleutian Islands, from Unalashka, Eastward (West of Unalashka). Boston: 1868/73-74. V. 52

DALLAS, 1912: Southwestern Telegraph & Telephone Co. Directory. V. 47

DALLAS, A. J.
Laws of the Commonwealth of Pennsylvania. Volume II. 1781-1790. Philadelphia: 1797. V. 53

DALLAS, GEORGE
System of Stiles, as Now Practicable Within the Kingdom of Scotland; and Reduced to a Clear Method... Edinburgh: 1697. V. 52

DALLAS, GEORGE M.
Mr. Dallas's Letter on the Mexican Treaty: Re-Printed from the Public Ledger of June 15, 1849. Philadelphia: 1849. V. 50

DALLAS in 1873. An Invitation to Immigrants. Dallas: 1980. V. 52

DALLAS, ROBERT CHARLES
Elements of Self Knowledge: Intended to Lead Youth into an Early Acquaintance with the Nature of Man... London: 1802. V. 47
The Morlands. Tales Illustrative of The Simple and Surprising. London: 1805. V. 49; 54
Not at Home: a Dramatic Entertainment as Performed with General Approbation, by the Drury Lane Company, at the Lyceum Theatre. London: 1809. V. 48
Ode to the Duke of Wellington, and Other Poems. London: 1819. V. 49
Recollections of the Life of Lord Byron, from the Year 1808 to the End of 1814... London: 1824. V. 49
Recollections of the Life of Lord Byron, from the Year 1808 to the End of 1814... Philadelphia: 1825. V. 47

DALLAWAY, JAMES
Anecdotes of the Arts in England. London: 1800. V. 49; 50; 51; 54
Antiquities of Bristow in the Middle Centuries... Bristol: 1834. V. 47
A History of the Western Division of the County of Sussex... 1815. V. 53
History of the Western Division of the County of Sussex. London: 1815-32. V. 49; 52
A History of the Western Division of the County of Sussex. London: 1815/19. V. 53
A History of the Western Division of the County of Sussex. London: 1819. V. 51
Inquiries Into the Origin and Progress of the Science of Heraldry in England. 1793. V. 50
Inquiries Into the Origin and Progress of the Science of Heraldry in England. Gloucester: 1793. V. 48; 51
Inquiries Into the Origin and Progress of the Science of Heraldry in England. London: 1793. V. 49
Observations on English Architecture. London: 1806. V. 53

DALLIMORE, W.
A Handbook of Coniferae, Including Ginkgoaceae. London: 1923. V. 51

DALLING AND BULWER, WILLIAM HENRY LYTTON EARL BULWER
France, Social, Literary, Political. Paris: 1834. V. 51

DALLINGTON, RICHARD
Aphorismes Civill and Militaire Amplified With Authorities and Exemplified with Historie Out of the First Quarterne of Fr. Guicciardine. London: 1613. V. 49

DALLISON, CHARLES
The Royalist's Defence: Vindicating the King's Proceedings in the Late Warre Made Against Him. London: 1648. V. 53

DALLY, JOSEPH W.
Woodbridge and Vicinity. New Brunswick: 1873. V. 47

D'ALMEIDA, GEORGE
Memoirs of an Ismaric Spear. Iowa City: 1984. V. 49; 51

D'ALMEIDA, WILLIAM BARRINGTON
Life in Java: With Sketches of the Javanese. London: 1864. V. 53

DALMETTE, ALBERT
Venoms, Venomous Animals and Antivenomous Serum-Therapeutics. London: 1908. V. 51

DALMON, CHARLES
A Poor Man's Riches - a Bundle of Lyrics. London: 1922. V. 49

DALRYMPLE, ALEXANDER
A Collection of English Songs, with An Appendix of Original Pieces. London: 1796. V. 50
A Collection of Voyages Chiefly in the Southern Atlantic Ocean. London: 1775. V. 50
An Historical Collection of the Several Voyages and Discoveries in the South Pacific Ocean. London: 1770-71. V. 50

DALRYMPLE, CHARLES JOHN
Report of the Trial of the Students on the Charge of Mobbing, Rioting and Assault, at the College, on January 11 and 12, 1838. Edinburgh: 1838. V. 50

DALRYMPLE, HUGH
Rodondo; or the State Jugglers. London: 176. V. 54

DALRYMPLE, JOHN
An Essay Towards a General History of Feudal Property in Great Britain. London: 1758. V. 48; 52; 54
Memoirs of Great Britain and Ireland. London & Edinburgh: 1771-1773. V. 47; 53; 54
Memoirs of Great Britain and Ireland from the Dissolution of the Last Parliament of Charles II. London: 1790. V. 54

DALTON, E. A.
History of Ireland...Earliest Times to the Present Day. London: 1910. V. 52
History of Ireland...Earliest Times to the Present Day. London: 1910-25. V. 47

DALTON, EMMETT
When the Daltons Rode. Garden City: 1931. V. 49; 53

DALTON, JOHN
An Epistle to a Young Nobleman, from His Praeceptor. London: 1736. V. 47

D'ALTON, JOHN
The History of Ireland...to...1245, When the Annals of Boyle, Which are Adopted and Embodied at the Running Text Authority, Terminate... Dublin: 1845. V. 53

DALTON, JOHN
History of the College of Physicians and Surgeons in the City of New York: Medical Department of Columbia College. New York: 1888. V. 50; 52; 53

D'ALTON, JOHN
The History of the County of Dublin. Dublin: 1838. V. 51; 53

DALTON, JOHN
Meteorological Observations and Essays. Kendal: 1793. V. 50
A System of Chemistry. Edinburgh: 1807. V. 51
Topographical Anatomy of the Brain. Philadelphia: 1885. V. 47
A Treatise On Human Physiology. Philadelphia: 1859. V. 48

DALTON, JOHN NEALE
The Cruise of Her Majesty's Ship 'Bacchante', 1879-1882. London: 1886. V. 48

DALTON, MICHAEL
The Countrey Justice... London: 1682. V. 50; 52
The Country Justice... London: 1705. V. 47
The Office and Authority of Sheriffs... London: 1670. V. 49

DALTON, O. M.
Byzantine Art and Archaeology. Oxford: 1911. V. 54
East Christian Art. A Survey of the Monuments. Oxford: 1925. V. 47; 48
The Treasure of the Oxus with Other Examples of Early Oriental Metal-Work. London: 1964. V. 52

DALTON, RICHARD
Antiquities and Views in Greece and Egypt; with the Manners and Customs of the Inhabitants: from Drawings made On the Spot A.D. 1749. London: 1791. V. 50

DALTON, WILLIAM
Phaulcon the Adventurer, or, the Europeans in the East. London: 1862. V. 47; 51

DALVIMART, OCTAVIEN
The Costume of Turkey. London: 1804. V. 54
The Costume of Turkey. (with) *The Military Costume of Turkey.* London: 1802/1818. V. 50

DALY, CESAR
Les Theatres de La Place Du Chatelet, Theatre du Chatelet-Theatre Lyrique. Paris: 1865. V. 52

DALY, ELIZABETH
Nothing Can Rescue Me. New York: 1943. V. 49

DALY, LOUISE HASKELL
Alexander Cheves Haskell: the Portrait of a Man. Norwood: 19343. V. 49

DALY, M.
Big Game Hunting and Adventure 1897-1936. London: 1937. V. 49

DALYELL, JOHN GRAHAM
Fragments of Scotish (sic) History. Edinburgh: 1798. V. 52
Scottish Poems of the Sixteenth Century. Edinburgh: 1801. V. 52
Shipwrecks and Disasters at Sea; or Historical Narratives of the Most Noted Calamities and Providential Deliverances... Edinburgh: 1812. V. 47

DALZIEL, HUGH
British Dogs. London: 1880. V. 49
British Dogs: Describing the History, Characteristics, Breeding, Management and Exhibition of the Various Breeds of Dogs Established in Great Britain. London: 1888-89. V. 49

DALZIEL, THE BROTHERS
A Record of 50 Years Work in Conjunction with Many of the Most Distinguished Artists of the Period 1840-1890. London: 1901. V. 48

DAMASE, JACQUES
Rhythms and Colours. London: 1972. V. 50

DAMBERGER, CHRISTIAN FREDERICK
Travels through the Interior of Africa, from the Cape of Good Hope to Morocco... London: 1801. V. 49

D'AMBROSIO, JOE
David. Sherman Oaks: 1993. V. 51

DAME, R. F.
Bivalve Filter Feeders in Estuarine and Coastal Ecosystem Processes. Berlin: 1993. V. 50

DAME Wiggins of Lee and Her Seven Wonderful Cats. London: 1887. V. 48; 50

DAME, WILLIAM MEADE
From the Rapidan to Richmond and the Spottsylvania Campaign: a Sketch in Personal Narrative of the Scenes a Soldier Saw. Baltimore: 1920. V. 49

DAMHOUDER, JOSSE
Promptuarium Theologicum, Morale et Politicum, ex Veteri et Novo Testamento, S.S. Patrum Monumentis, et Prophanis Authoribus. Antwerp: 1596. V. 50

DAMJAN, MISCHA
The False Flamingoes. London: 1968. V. 48

DAMON, S. FOSTER
The Odyssey in Dublin. Cambridge: 1929. V. 47
William Blake: His Philosophy and Symbols. Boston: 1924. V. 49

DAMON, SAMUEL C.
A Journey to Lower Oregon and Upper California 1848-49. San Francisco: 1927. V. 47

DA MORRONA, ALESSANDRO
Ipisa Illustrata nelle Arti del Disegno. Livorno: 1812. V. 53

DAMPIER, WILLIAM
A Collection of Voyages. London: 1729. V. 50
Dampier's Voyages. London: 1906. V. 47
A New Voyage Round the World. London: 1697. V. 47
A New Voyage Round the World... London: 1699/1705/03/09. V. 48
A New Voyage Round the World. London: 1927. V. 49; 50; 51; 52
A New Voyage Round the World. (with) Voyages and Descriptions. London: 1699 & 1705. V. 47; 51; 54
Voyages and Discoveries. London: 1931. V. 50; 52

DAMPIER, WILLIAM JAMES
A Memoir of John Carter. London: 1850. V. 49; 51

DAN Dare: Pilot of the Future. London. V. 48

DAN, HORACE
English Gothic Architecture and Ornament of the 14th, 15th and 16th Centuries. (with) French Gothic Ornament... Boston: 1897. V. 53

DANA, C. W.
The Garden of the World. Boston: 1856. V. 47; 49; 52
The Great West or the Garden of the World, Its History, Its Wealth, Its Natural Advantages and Its Future. 1861. V. 51; 53

DANA, CHARLES
Contributions to Medical and Biological Research Dedicated to Sir William Osler, Bart, M.D., F.R.S. In Honour of His Seventieth Birthday July 12th, 1919. New York: 1919. V. 52
The Peaks of Medical History. New York: 1928. V. 50
Poetry and Doctors: a Catalogue of Poetical Works Written by Physicians with Biographical Notes. Woodstock: 1916. V. 50; 52
Text-Book of Nervous Diseases. New York: 1892. V. 47

DANA, CHARLES A.
Proudhon and His 'Bank of the People' Being a Defence of the Great French Anarachist, Showing the Evils of a specie Currency and That Interest on Capital Can and Ought to be Abolished by a System of Free and Mutual Banking. New York: 1896. V. 52

DANA, DANIEL
Memoirs of Eminently Pious Women, Who Were Ornaments to Their Sex. Newburyport: 1803. V. 50; 51; 53

DANA, E. S.
The System of Mineralogy of James Dwight Dana 1837-1868. London: 1894-1909. V. 53

DANA, EDMUND
Geographical Sketches on the Western Country: Designed for Emigrants and Settlers... Cincinnati: 1819. V. 50

DANA, J. D.
Corals and Coral Islands. New York: 1872. V. 48; 50
Corals and Coral Islands. New York: 1890. V. 47
Manual of Geology: Treating of the Principles of the Science With Special Reference to American Geological History, for the Use of Colleges, Academies and Schools of Science. Philadelphia: 1863. V. 50
Manual of Mineralogy. London: 1872. V. 47
Manual of Mineralogy and Lithology... London: 1879. V. 50; 52

DANA, JAMES
The African Slave Trade. A Discourse Delivered in the City of New Haven, September 9, 1790. New Haven: 1791. V. 51

DANA, JAMES F.
Report on a Disease Afflicting Neat Cattle, in Burton, N. H. Read Before the New Hampshire Medical Society...June, 1822. Concord: 1822. V. 48

DANA, JOHN COTTON
The Far North-West. Newark: 1906. V. 52

DANA, RICHARD HENRY
The Journal of Richard Henry Dana, jr. Cambridge: 1968. V. 50; 54
Poems. Boston: 1827. V. 50
Poems and Prose Writings. New York: 1850. V. 47; 48; 54
Richard Henry Dana, Architect (1879-1933). New York: 1965. V. 48; 50; 51; 53; 54
To Cuba and Back. Boston: 1859. V. 49; 51; 54
Two Years Before the Mast. New York: 1840. V. 47; 49; 53; 54
Two Years Before the Mast. London: 1841. V. 49
Two Years Before the Mast. New York: 1855. V. 47
Two Years Before the Mast. Chicago: 1930. V. 52; 53
Two Years Before the Mast. New York: 1936. V. 53; 54
Two Years Before the Mast. New York: 1947. V. 48; 51; 54
Two Years Before the Mast. Los Angeles: 1964. V. 53

DANA, ROBERT
In a Fugitive Season. Iowa City: 1979. V. 51; 54

DANA, SAMUEL L.
Manures: a Prize Essay. Lowell: 1844. V. 50
A Muck Manual for Farmers. Lowell: 1842. V. 53; 54

DANA, WILLIAM, MRS.
According to Season. New York: 1894. V. 51

DANBY, EARL OF
Copies of Some Letters Written to and From the Early of Danby (Now Duke of Leeds) in the Years 1676, 1677 and 1678. London: 1710. V. 47

DANBY, FRANCIS
Francis Danby: Varieties of Poetic Landscape. New Haven: 1973. V. 48
Three Views, Illustrative of the Scenery of Bristol and Its Vicinity. London: 1823. V. 52

DANCE, CHARLES
Izaak Walton: a Drama in Four Parts. London: 1839. V. 47

DANCE, JAMES
Poems on Several Occasions. Edinburgh: 1754. V. 50

DANCE OF DEATH
The Celebrated Hans Holbein's Alphabet of Death... Paris: 1856. V. 48
The Dance of Death... 1800. V. 48
The Dance of Death. London: 1816. V. 49; 50
The Dance of Death Exhibited in Elegant Engravings on Wood. London: 1833. V. 50
Emblems of Mortality; Representing...Death Seizing All Ranks and Conditions of People. Charleston & New Haven: 1846. V. 49
Emblems of Mortality; Representing...Death Seizing All Ranks and Degrees of People. London: 1789. V. 49
Missae in Agenda Defunctorum... Venice: 1740. V. 50
Missae in Agenda defunctorum... Lucca: 1770. V. 50
S. Avgvstines Manuell, or Litle Booke of the Contemplation of Christ. London: 1586. V. 50; 51

DANCE, S. P.
Seashells of Eastern Arabia. London: 1995. V. 54

DANCER, JOHN
Nicodeme. London: 1671. V. 53

DANCERS On a Plane: Cage, Cunningham, Johns. 1989. V. 51

DANCING With Helen Moller Her Own Statement of her Philosophy and Practice and Teaching Formed Upon the Classic Greek Model... New York: 1918. V. 49

DANCKERTS, CORNELIS
D'volgende Deuren Syn Geteekent Op De Amsterdamse Voetmaet Van II Duyn. Amsterdam: 1625. V. 48

D'ANCONA, PAOLO
The Schifanoia Months at Ferrara. Milan: 1954. V. 53

DANDOLO, VINCENZO, CONTE DE
The Art of Rearing Silk-Worms. London: 1825. V. 47; 53

DANDRIDGE, DOROTHY
Everything and Nothing: The Dorothy Dandridge Tragedy. New York: 1970. V. 54

DANDRIDGE, RAYMOND GARFIELD
The Poet and Other Poems. Cincinnati: 1920. V. 53
Zalka Peetruza and Other Poems. Cincinnati: 1928. V. 53

DANDY, WALTER
Benign Encapsulated Tumors of the Lateral Ventricles of the Brain. Baltimore: 1934. V. 54
Benign Tumors in the Third Ventricle of the Brain: Diagnosis and Treatment. Springfield: 1933. V. 47; 49; 52; 53
Fluoroscopy of the Cerebral Ventricles. 1919. V. 47; 48; 50; 51; 53
Intracranial Arterial Aneurysms. Ithaca: 1944. V. 47
Intracranial Arterial Aneurysms. Ithaca: 1945. V. 47
Intracranial Arterial Aneurysms. Ithaca: 1947. V. 54
Orbital Tumors Results Following the Transcranial Operative Attack. New York: 1941. V. 52; 53; 54
Selected Writings of Walter E. Dandy. 1919. V. 54
Selected Writings of Walter E. Dandy. Springfield: 1957. V. 50; 52

DANE, RICHARD
Sport in Asia and Africa. London: 1921. V. 47

DANERT, THOMAS
The History of Philip de Commines, Knight, Lord of Argenton. London: 1674. V. 54

DANES, PIERRE
Apologie pour Le Roy, Contre les Calomnies des Imperiaulx... Paris: 1551/52. V. 51

DANGERFIELD, THOMAS
Dangerfield's Memoires, Digested Into Adventures, Receipts, and Expences. London: 1685. V. 51; 52

THE DANGERS of Europe From the Growning Power of France. London: 1702. V. 48

DANIEL, FERDINAND EUGENE
Recollections of a Rebel Surgeon. Austin: 1899. V. 47; 49

DANIEL, GABRIEL
The History of France from the Time the French Monarchy Was Established in Gaul, to the Death of Lewis the Fourteenth. London: 1726. V. 50

DANIEL, GEORGE
Catalogue of Most Valuable, Interesting and Highly Important Library of George Daniel, Esq. of Canonbury... V. 47
Catalogue of the Most Valuable, Interesting and Highly Important Library...with His Collection of Original Drawings and Engraved Portraits of Distinguished Actors and Actresses etc. Sotheby July 20-30. London: 1864. V. 54

DANIEL, GEORGE continued
Doctor Bolus; a Serio-comic-Bombastick-Operatick Interlude... London: 1818. V. 52
Garrick in the Green Room. London: 1829. V. 49
Merrie England in the Old Time. London: 1842. V. 49; 51; 52; 54

THE DANIEL Press. Memorials of C. H. O. Daniel with a Bibliography of the Press, 1845-1919. Oxford: 1921. V. 48; 51

DANIEL, ROBERT MAC KENZIE
The Poor Cousin: a Novel. London: 1846. V. 54

DANIEL, ROBERT MAC KENZIE, MRS.
One Golden Summer. London: 1877. V. 47

DANIEL, SADIE IOLA
Women Builders. Washington: 1931. V. 47; 53

DANIEL, SAMUEL
The Collection of the History of England. 1621. V. 53
The Collection of the History of England... London: 1626. V. 49; 51; 54
The Collection of the History of England. London: 1685. V. 52; 53

DANIEL, W. B.
Rural sports. London: 1801-02. V. 48
Rural Sports. London: 1802-13. V. 49
Rural Sports. London: 1805. V. 53; 54
Rural Sports. London: 1807. V. 47
Rural Sports. London: 1812. V. 47

DANIELL, E. T.
Twelve Etchings, with a ....Life... Great Yarmouth: 1882. V. 47

DANIELL, EDMUND ROBERT
Pleading and Practice of the High Court of Chancery. Boston: 1846. V. 54

DANIELL, FREDERICK B.
A Catalogue Raisonne of the Engraved Works of Richard Cosway, R. A. London: 1890. V. 51

DANIELL, J. FREDERIC
Meteorological Essays and Observataions. London: 1827. V. 52

DANIELL, L. E.
Personnel of the Texas State Government - Sketches of Distinguished Texans. Austin: 1889. V. 53
Personnel of the Texas State Government - Sketches of Distinguished Texans. Austin: 1892. V. 53
Texas: the Country and Its Men. London. V. 52
Types of Successful Men of Texas. Austin: 1890. V. 53

DANIELL, THOMAS
A Picturesque Voyage to India by the Way of China. London: 1810. V. 52

DANIELL, WILLIAM
Illustrations of the Island of Staffa, in a Series of Views... London: 1818. V. 48; 51; 52
A Voyage Round Great Britain. London: 1814-25. V. 49

DANIELLS, J. M.
The Life of Stonewall Jackson... New York: 1863. V. 52

DANIELLS, T. G.
California, Its Products, Resources, Industries and Attractions. Sacramento: 1909. V. 54

DANIEL-ROPS, HENRY
The Misted Mirror. London: 1930. V. 52

DANIELS, C. H.
The Cockpit. Flying Adventures. London: 1930's. V. 50

DANIELS, L. E.
Personnel of the Texas State Government, with Sketches of Distinguished Texans, Embracing the Executive and Staff, Heads of the Departments, U.S. Senators and Representatives, Members of the Twenty First Legislature. Austin: 1889. V. 49

DANIELSON, RICHARD E.
Martha Doyle and Other Sporting Memories. New York: 1938. V. 47; 48; 49; 51

DANKERS, JASPAR
Journal of a Voyage to New York and Tour in the Several of the American Colonies. Brooklyn: 1867. V. 50

DANTE ALIGHIERI
The Comedy of... London: 1865. V. 48
The Comedy of Dante Alighieri Rendered into English by Sir Edward Sullivan, Bart. London: 1893. V. 47
Dante con l'Espositioni, di Christophoro Landino, et d'Alessandro Vellutello Sopra Is Sua Comedia dell'Inferno, del Purgatorio, & del Paradiso, con Tauole, Argomenti & Alegorie & Riformato... Venetia: 1578. V. 47
Dante's Hell. Boston: 1857. V. 47
Dante's Inferno. New York: 1875. V. 54
Dante's Inferno. New York & London: 1880. V. 47
Dante's Inferno. Hopewell: 1993. V. 51; 52; 53
La Divina Comedia. 1555/54. V. 48
Divina Comedia. Venice: 1564. V. 50
La Divina Comedia. London: 1822. V. 53
La Divina Comedia. London: 1928. V. 48; 54
La Divina Comedia. Milan: 1878. V. 50
La Divina Commedia. Firenze: 1889. V. 54
La Divina Commedia. Florence: 1919. V. 52
La Divina Commedia... London: 1928. V. 47; 49; 50; 51; 53; 54
The Divine Comedy. London: 1854. V. 49
The Divine Comedy. Boston: 1867. V. 47
The Divine Comedy... Boston & New York: 1906. V. 50; 51
The Divine Comedy. New York: 1909. V. 48
The Divine Comedy. Yonkers-on-Hudson: 1921. V. 54
The Divine Comedy. New York: 1932. V. 48; 52; 53; 54
The Divine Comedy. Verona: 1932. V. 53; 54
The Divine Comedy. 1933. V. 52
The Divine Comedy. New York: 1955. V. 48
The Divine Comedy. London: 1969. V. 53
The Divine Comedy. New York: 1969. V. 47
The Divine Comedy. London: 1983. V. 49
The Divine Comedy, Inferno. A Verse Translation by Tom Phillips. 1983. V. 54
Die Gottliche Komodie. Zurich: 1921. V. 47
In Defence of Woman. London: 1928. V. 52
The Inferno. London: 1805-06. V. 50; 51
Inferno. London: 1903. V. 49
The Inferno. New York: 1931. V. 51
Inferno, Purgatory and Paradise. London: 1903-Sept. 1904. V. 51
Purgatory and Paradise. New York and London: 1875. V. 54
The Stone Beloved. Austin: 1986. V. 48; 52; 54
Le Terze Rime di Dante. (Inferno). Venice: 1502. V. 51; 53
A Translation of the Inferno of Dante. London: 1785. V. 52
The Vision of Hell. London: 1866. V. 49
The Vision; or Hell, Purgatory, and Paradise. London: 1819. V. 47; 48; 50
La Vita Nuova. 1895. V. 54
Vita Nuova. Proemio di Benedetto Croce. Montagnola: 1925. V. 52; 54
La Vita Nuovo. Coventry. V. 49

DANTI, EGNATIO
Dell'uso et Fabricia dell'Astrolabio et del Plaisferio. Florence: 1578. V. 51

DANTO, ARTHUR C.
Mapplethorpe. New York: 1992. V. 51

D'ANVILLE, JEAN B. B.
Atlas and Geography of the Antients. London: 1815. V. 48

D'ANVILLE, M.
A Complete Body of Ancient Geography Neatly Engraved on Thirteen Plates... London: 1818. V. 51

DANZIGER, ADOLPHE
In the Garden of Abdullah: and Other Poems. Los Angeles: 1916. V. 48

DA PORTO, LUIGI
The Original Story of Romeo and Juliet... Cambridge: 1868. V. 48

DAPPER, OLFERT
Description de L'Afrique. Amsterdam: 1686. V. 51
Description Exacte des Isles d l'Archipel, et de...Chypre, Rhodes, Candie, Samos, Chio, Negrepont, Lemnos, Paros... Amsterdam: 1703. V. 48; 49
Naukeurige Beschryving Van Gantsch Syrie, en Palestyn of Heilige Lant. Amsterdam: 1677. V. 47; 50

D'ARANDA, EMANUEL
The History of Algiers and Its Slavery. With Many Remarkable Particularities of Africka. London: 1666. V. 48

D'ARBELOFF, NATALIE
Philosophy: Seventeen Coloured Etchings/Aquatints. 1990. V. 52; 54

DARBY, CHARLES
Bacchanalia: or, a Description of a Druken Club. London: 1680. V. 47; 51

DARBY, JOHN CURTIS
Science and the Healing Art, or A New Book On Old Facts. Louisville: 1880. V. 48

DARBY, WILLIAM
The Emigrant's Guide to the Western and Southwestern States and Territories. New York: 1818. V. 50; 54
A Geographical Description of the State of Louisana. New York: 1817. V. 47; 51; 52
A New Gazetteer of the United States of America. New York: 1833. V. 48
A Tour from the City of New York, to Detroit, in Michigan Territory. New York: 1819. V. 47
View of the United States, Historical, Geographical and Statistical. Philadelphia: 1828. V. 47

DARBY, WILLIAM J.
Food: the Gift of Osiris. London: 1977. V. 51

DARDIS, PATRICK G.
The Occupation of the Land In Ireland in the First Half of the 19th Century. London: 1920. V. 53

D'ARFEY, WILLIAM
Curious Relations. London: 1945. V. 53

DARIOT, CLAUDE
Dariotus Redivivus; or a Briefe Introduction to the Judgement of the Stars. London: 1653. V. 48; 52

DARIUS'S Feast; or, The Force of Truth...Addressed to...the Earls of Salisbury and Exeter. London: 1734. V. 49

DARK as the Grave Wherein My Friend is Laid. New York: 1968. V. 48

DARK, S.
Sir William Orpen, Artist and Man. London: 1932. V. 53

DARKE, S. W.
Salt Lake City Illustrated. St. Louis & New York: 1887. V. 53

DARKNESS At Noon; or, the Great Solar Eclipse, of the 16th of June, 1806, Described and Represented in Every Particular. New York: 1806. V. 50

DARLEY, FELIX OCTAVIUS CARR
A Selection of War Lyrics. New York: 1866. V. 47
Yankee Doodle. New York. V. 53

DARLEY, GEORGE
Nepenthe - a Poem in Two Cantos. London: 1897. V. 49

DARLEY, GEORGE M.
Pioneering in the San Juan. Personal Reminiscences of Work Done in Southwestern Colorado During the "Great San Juan Excitement". Chicago: 1899. V. 52

DARLEY, L.
Bookbinding Then and Now, a Survey of the First Hundred and Seventy Eight Years of James Burn & Co. 1959. V. 47

D'ARLINCOURT, VISCOUNT
The Solitary; or, The Mysterious Man of the Mountain. New York: 1822. V. 48; 49; 50; 51; 53

DARLING, E. B.
The Great Dog Races of Nome, Held Under the Auspices of the Nome Kennel Club, Nome, Alaska. Nome: 1916. V. 50

DARLING, F. FRASER
West Highland Survey. London: 1955. V. 54

DARLING FOUNDATION OF NEW YORK STATE
Early American Silvermsith sand Silver. New York State Silversmiths. Eggertsville: 1964. V. 52
New York State Silversmiths. New York: 1964. V. 50

DARLING, HENRY
Slavery and War: a Historical Essay. Philadelphia: 1863. V. 50

DARLING, JAMES
Cyclopaedia Bibliographica... London: 1854-59. V. 53

DARLING, SISSON
A Practical Course of Mercantile Arithmetic, Adapted to the Capacities of Youth, and Equally Interesting To All... Dublin: 1807. V. 48

DARLINGTON, MARY C.
Fort Pitt and Letters from the Frontier. Pittsburgh: 1892. V. 47; 50

DARLINGTON, W.
Flora Cestrica: an Attempt to Enumerate and Describe the Flowering and Filicoid Plants of Chester County, in the State of Pennsylvania. West Chester: 1837. V. 47; 53
Flora Cestrica: an Herborizing Companion for the Young Botanists of Chester County, State of Pennsylvania. Philadelphia: 1853. V. 51
Memorials of John Bartram and Humphry Marshall, with Notices of Their Botanical Contemporaries. Philadelphia: 1849. V. 52

DARLINGTON, WILLIAM M.
Christopher Gist's Journals with Historical, Geographical and Ethnological Notes and Biographies of His Contemporaries. Pittsburgh: 1893. V. 47

DARLOW, T. H.
Historical Catalogue of the Printed Editions of Holy Scripture in the Library of the British and Foreign Bible Society. Cambridge. V. 53
Historical Catalogue of the Printed Editions of Holy Scripture in the Library of the British and Foreign Bible Society. New York: 1963. V. 53
Historical Catalogue of the Printed Editions of Holy Scripture in the Library of the British and Foreign Bible Society. Cambridge: 1992. V. 50
Historical Catalogue of the Printed Editions of Holy Scripture in the Library of the British and Foreign Bible Society. Cambridge: 1993. V. 48; 49

DARNELL, A. W.
Orchids for the Outdoor Garden. Ashford: 1930. V. 51; 54

D'ARNOUX, CHARLES ALBERT
The Communists of Paris 1871. London: 1874. V. 50

DARR, FRANCIS
Our Pacific Possessions: Railway to the Pacific, Our Future Relations with the Pacific Islands and Mexico. Washington: 1861. V. 47

DARRAH, HENRY ZOUCH
Sport in the Highlands of Kashmir... 1898. V. 54

DARRAH, WILLIAM C.
The World of Stereographs. Gettysburg: 1977. V. 54

DARRELL, S. J.
The Gentleman Instructed in the Conduct of a Virtuous and Happy Life. London: 1720. V. 54

DARRELL, WILLIAM
The History of Dover Castle. London: 1797. V. 47; 53

DARROUGH, MADELINE
Farm on the Hill. New York: 1936. V. 51

DARROW, CLARENCE SEWARD
Debate: Is Man a Machine?. New York: 1927. V. 48
Farmington. Chicago: 1904. V. 49; 50

Resist Not Evil. Chicago: 1903. V. 53
The Story of My Life. New York: 1932. V. 48; 52; 53

DART, JOHN
The History and Antiquities of the Cathedral Church of Canterbury, and the Once Adjoining Monastery. London: 1726. V. 47; 50; 53
Westminster-Abbey: a Poem. London: 1721. V. 47
Westmonasterium or the History and Antiquities of the Abbey Church of St. Peters Westminster. London: 1723. V. 47

D'ARTIGUE, JEAN
Six Years in the Canadian North-West. Toronto: 1882. V. 49

DARTMOUTH, EARL OF
The Manuscripts of the Earl of Dartmouth. London: 1887-96. V. 49

DARTMOUTH Verse. Portland: 1925. V. 52

DARTON, F. J. H.
Essays of the Year (1929-30). London: 1930. V. 54
The Good Fairy; or the Adventures of Sir Richard Whittington, R. Crusoe, Esq.... London: 1920. V. 49; 51
Modern Book Illustration in Great Britain and America. London: 1931. V. 47; 50; 51

DARTON, WILLIAM
Little Truths For the Instruction of Children. Volume II. Philadelphia: 1812. V. 48
The Second Chapter of Accidents and Remarkable Events: Containing Caution and Instruction for Children. Philadelphia: 1807. V. 48
Third Chapter of Accidents and Remarkable Events... Philadelphia: 1807. V. 48

DARTON'S Alphabet of Animals. London: 1855. V. 49

D'ARUSMONT, FRANCES WRIGHT
A Few Days in Athens. London: 1822. V. 54
Views of Society and Manners in America... London: 1821. V. 49; 50; 51; 53
Views of Society and Manners in America... New York: 1821. V. 48; 50; 51

DARVILL, R.
A Treatise on the Care, Treatment and Training of the English Race Horse. London: 1828. V. 48

DARWIN, BERNARD
The Dickens Advertiser: Collection of the Advertisements in the Original Parts of the Novels by Charles Dickens. London: 1930. V. 49
The Golf Courses of the British Isles. London: 1910. V. 49
Golf, Pleasures of Life Series. London: 1954. V. 48
Ishybushy and Topknot. London: 1946. V. 51
Second Shots. London: 1930. V. 48
The Tale of Mr. Tootleoo and the Cockiolly Bird. London: 1925. V. 49; 51; 52
Tootleoo Two. London: 1927. V. 48

DARWIN, CHARLES
Experiments Establishing a Criterion Between Mucaginous and Purulent Matter. Lichfield: 1780. V. 53

DARWIN, CHARLES ROBERT
Charles Darwin's Notebooks 1836-1844. Ithaca: 1987. V. 49; 52
The Correspondence of Charles Darwin. Cambridge: 1985-92. V. 49
The Correspondence of Charles Darwin. Cambridge: 1985-93. V. 52
La Descendance de L'Homme et la selection Sexuelle. Paris: 1872. V. 47; 48; 50
The Descent of Man. London: 1871. V. 47; 48; 49; 54
Descent of Man. New York: 1871. V. 48; 50; 51; 53; 54
The Descent of Man. London: 1877. V. 53
The Descent of Man. London: 1882. V. 49
The Descent of Man. London: 1891. V. 48
The Descent of Man, and Selection in Relation to Sex. Adelaide: 1971. V. 48; 49; 52; 53; 54
The Different Forms of Flower on Plants of the Same Species. London: 1877. V. 48; 52
Different forms of Flowers on Plants of the Same Species. New York: 1877. V. 48
The Different Forms of Flowers on Plants of the Same Species. London: 1892. V. 50; 52
The Effects of Cross and Self-Fertilization in the Vegetable. London: 1876. V. 53
The Effects of Cross and Self-Fertilization in the Vegetable. London: 1878. V. 48; 49
The Expression of Emotion in Man and Animals. London: 1872. V. 47; 48; 49; 50; 51; 52; 53; 54
The Expression of the Emotions in Man and Animals. London: 1873. V. 48; 49; 50; 51; 53
The Expression of the Emotions in Man and Animals. New York: 1873. V. 52; 54
The Expression of the Emotions in Man and Animals. London: 1890. V. 54
The Expression of the Emotions in Man and Animals. New York: 1897. V. 47; 53
The Formation of Vegetable Mould through the Action of Worms. London: 1881. V. 49; 52; 54
The Formation of Vegetable Mould Through the Action of Worms. London: 1882. V. 51
The Formation of Vegetable Mould Through the Action of Worms. London: 1888. V. 49
Geological Observations on the Volcanic Islands and parts of South America Visited During the Voyage of H.M.s. "Beagle". London: 1891. V. 48
Insectivorous Plants. London: 1875. V. 47; 48; 49; 50; 51; 52; 53
Insectivorous Plants. London: 1888. V. 47; 49
The Journal of a Voyage in H.M.S. Beagle. Guildford, Surrey: 1979. V. 48
Journal of Researches... London: 1860. V. 48; 49
Journal of Researches into the Geology and Natural History of the Various Countries Visited by HMS Beagle. London: 1839. V. 48; 49
Journal of Researches into the Geology and Natural History of the Various Countries Visited by H.M.S. Beagle....1832-1836. London: 1840. V. 49; 54
Journal of Researches into the Natural History and Geology of the Countries Visited During the Voyage of H.M.S. Beagle Round the World. London: 1845. V. 54

DARWIN, CHARLES ROBERT continued
Journal of Researches into the Natural History and Geology of the Countries Visited During the Voyage of H.M.S. Beagle Round the World... New York: 1846. V. 48; 51; 54
Journal of Researches...into the Natural History and Geology of the countries Visited During the Voyage of H. M. S. Beagle Under the Command of Capt. Fitz Roy, R.N. Cambridge: 1956. V. 51; 53
Life and Letters... London: 1887. V. 47; 48; 52
The Life and Letters. New York: 1888. V. 52
The Life and Letters. New York: 1888/87. V. 53
Life and Letters, Including an Autobiographical Chapter. London: 1887. V. 48; 49; 50; 52
Life and Letters, Including an Autobiographical Chapter... London: 1888. V. 47; 48; 50; 51; 53; 54
A Monograph on the Fossil Balanidae and Verrucidae of Great Britain. London: 1854. V. 50
A Monograph on the Fossil Lepadidae, or Pedunculated Cirripedes of Great Britain. London: 1851. V. 48
A Monograph on the Fossil Lepadidae or Pedunculated Cirripedes of Great Britain. London: 1851-58. V. 50
A Monograph on the Sub-Class Cirripedia. Volume I. The Lepadidae. London: 1851. V. 51
A Monograph On the Sub-Class Cirripedia, with Figures of All the Species... London: 1851-54. V. 48; 53
More Letters of Charles Darwin. London: 1903. V. 53; 54
The Movements and Habits of Climbing Plants. London: 1875. V. 51; 53
The Movements and Habits of Climbing Plants. London: 1876. V. 49
The Movements and Habits of Climbing Plants. London: 1882. V. 51
The Movements and Habits of Climbing Plants. London: 1888. V. 48; 53; 54
The Movements and Habits of Climbing Plants. London: 1891. V. 49; 52
Narrative of the Surveying Voyages of His Majesty's Ships Adventure and Beagle, Between the years 1826 and 1836... London: 1839. V. 50; 54
A Naturalist's Voyage. Journal of Researches... London: 1879. V. 49
On the Origin of Species. London: 1859. V. 47; 48; 50; 51; 52
On the Origin of Species. London: 1860. V. 47; 50; 51; 52
On the Origin of Species. London: 1861. V. 49
On the Origin of Species... London: 1866. V. 49
On the Origin of Species by Means of Natural Selection. Adelaide: 1963. V. 49; 51; 54
On the Structure and Distribution of Coral Reefs, also Geological Observations on the Volcanic Islands and Parts of South America... London: 1890. V. 54
The Origin of Species. London: 1860. V. 53
The Origin of Species. London: 1861. V. 48; 49
Origin of Species. London: 1866. V. 48
Origin of Species. New York: 1868. V. 48
The Origin of Species. London: 1869. V. 54
The Origin of Species. London: 1872. V. 48; 51; 52; 54
The Origin of Species. London: 1873. V. 48
The Origin of Species. London: 1882. V. 47; 49
Origin of Species. New York: 1898. V. 48
The Origin of...Species. London: 1876. V. 54
The Origin of...Species. London: 1878. V. 54
Power of Movement in Plants. London: 1880. V. 48; 49
Reise Eines Natur-Forschers um Die Welt. Stuttgart: 1875. V. 47; 53
Selected Works. New York: 1900. V. 48
The Variation of Animals and Plants Under Domestication. London: 1868. V. 47; 48; 49; 50; 51; 52; 53; 54
Variation of Animals and Plants Under Domestication. London: 1875. V. 47; 48; 49; 54
The Variation of Animals and Plants Under Domestication. London: 1888. V. 49
The Variation of Animals and Plants Under Domestication. London: 1899. V. 52
The Variation of Animals and Plants Under Domestication. New York: 1968. V. 48
The Various Contrivances by Which British and Foreign Orchids are Fertilized by Insects. London: 1862. V. 47; 48
The Various Contrivances by Which Orchids are Fertilised by Insects. London: 1877. V. 49
The Various Contrivances by Which Orchids are Fertilised by Insects. London: 1882. V. 50
The Various Contrivances by Which Orchids are Fertilised by Insects. London: 1885. V. 54
The Voyage of H. M. S. Beagle. Cambridge: 1956. V. 54
Works. New York: 1896-98. V. 48
The Works. London: 1986. V. 50; 51
Works. New York: 1987. V. 48
Works (Including Life and Letters). New York: 1896-97. V. 49
The Zoology of the Voyage of H.M.S. Beagle During the Years 1832-1836. 1980. V. 47
The Zoology of the Voyage of H.M.S. Beagle, Under the Command of Capt. Fitzroy, 1832-36. Wellington: 1980. V. 50; 53
The Zoology of the Voyage of H.M.S. Beagle, Under the Command of Captain Fitzroy, R.N. During the Years 1832-1836. London: 1994. V. 54

DARWIN, ERASMUS
The Botanic Garden. London: 1791. V. 47; 51; 52
The Botanic Garden. London: 1791/1790. V. 47; 48
The Botanic Garden. London: 1795/91. V. 47
The Botanic Garden. New York: 1798. V. 47; 50
The Botanic Garden. London: 1799. V. 52
The Botanic Garden. London: 1973. V. 48; 52
The Letters of Erasmus Darwin. London: 1981. V. 50
Memoirs of the Life of Dr. Darwin. London: 1804. V. 47; 48; 49
Phytologia; or the Philosophy of Agriculture and Gardening. London: 1800. V. 49; 50
A Plan for the Conduct of Female Education in Boarding Schools. Derby: 1797. V. 47; 49
The Temple of Nature; or, the Origin of Society... London: 1803. V. 47; 49
Zoonomia; or, the Laws of Organic Life. London: 1794-96. V. 50
Zoonomia; or, the Laws of Organic Life. London: 1801. V. 49; 53

THE DARWIN-Wallace Celebration Held on Thursday, 1st July, 1908, by the Linnean Society of London. London: 1908. V. 50

DAS, SARAT CHANDRA
Journey to Lhasa and Central Tibet. London: 1902. V. 53

DASENT, GEORGE WEBBE
Norse Fairy Tales. London: 1910. V. 53
The Story of Burnt Njal or Life in Iceland at the End of the Tenth Century. Edinburgh: 1861. V. 48; 50

DASHWOOD, RICHARD LEWES
Chiploquorgan: or, Life by the Camp Fire in Dominion of Canada and Newfoundland. Dublin: 1871. V. 49; 53
Chiploquorgan; or, Life by the Camp Fire in Dominion of Canada and Newfoundland. London: 1872. V. 53

DASSANAYAKE, M. D.
A Revised Handbook to the Flora of Ceylon. New Delhi: 1980-85. V. 48

D'ASSIGNY, MARIUS
The Art of Memory. London: 1699. V. 48; 49; 53
A Treatise Useful for All, Especially Such as are to Speak in Publick. London: 1706. V. 52

DATHAN, PSEUD.
Dathan's Account of the Political Conduct of the Son of James and His Men, from the Raising of the Siege of Stirling, to the Battle Near Inverness...Being Also the Fourth Book of the Chronicle of William the Son of George. London: 1746?. V. 53
Dathan's Account of the Rebellion: Being the Second Book of the Chronicle of William the Son of George. London: 1745?. V. 53

DATI, CARLO ROBERTO
Vite de Pittori Antichi Scritte e Illustrate da Carlo Dati nell' Academia Della Crusca lo Smarrito... Firenze: 1667. V. 49

DAUBENY, CHARLES
An Introduction to the Atomic Theory, Comprising a Sketch of the Opinions Entertained by the Most Distinguished Ancient and Modern Philosophers with Respect to the Constitution of Matter. Oxford: 1831. V. 52
Lectures on Roman Husbandry Delivered Before the University of Oxford. Oxford: 1857. V. 53

D'AUBIGNE, J. H. MERLE
Germany, England and Scotland; or, Recollections of a Swiss Minister. London: 1848. V. 53
History of the Reformation. Edinburgh: 1853. V. 49
History of the Reformation in the Sixteenth Century. London: 1862. V. 54

DAUBOURG, E.
Interior Architecture. London: 1877. V. 53

D'AUBREE, PAUL
Colonists and Manufacturers in the West Indies. London: 1844. V. 50; 54

DAUDET, ALPHONSE
The Nabob. London: 1878. V. 50
Port Tarascon. New York: 1891. V. 50; 53

DAUGHERTY, HARRY M.
The Inside Story of the Harding Tragedy. New York: 1932. V. 53

DAUGHTERS of Aesculapius. Philadelphia: 1897. V. 53

DAUGHTERS OF THE AMERICAN REVOLUTION
Historical Colletions of the Georgia Chapters... Vidalia: 1960. V. 49

D'AULAIRE, INGRID
Buffalo Bill. New York: 1952. V. 52
Columbus. Garden City: 1955. V. 49
Don't Count Your Chicks. New York: 1943. V. 51

D AULAIRE, INGRID
Leif the Lucky. New York: 1941. V. 51

DAULBY, DANIEL
A Descriptive Catalogue of the Works of Rembrandt, and Of His Scholars, Bol, Livens and Van Vleit... Liverpool: 1796. V. 48; 50; 51; 52

DAUMAS, E.
The Horses of Sahara, and the manners of the Desert. London: 1863. V. 47; 48; 49; 50; 54

DAUNCEY, CAMPBELL, MRS.
The Philippines an Account of their People, Progress, and Condition with Special Contributions. Boston and Tokyo: 1910. V. 54

DAUNCEY, H. M.
Papuan Pictures. London: 1913. V. 50

DAUNCEY, JOHN
The History of His Sacred Majesty Charles the II, King of England, Scotland, France and Ireland, Defender of the Faith, &c... London: 1660. V. 48; 49; 51

DAUNT, ACHILLES
In the Land of the Moose, the Bear and the Beaver. 1885. V. 52; 54

DAUNT, WILLIAM J. O'NEILL
Hugh Talbot: a Tale of the Irish Confiscations of the Seventeenth Century. Dublin: 1846. V. 51

D'AUREVILLY, BARBEY D.
The Anatomy of Dandyism, With Some Observations on Beau Brummell. London: 1928. V. 47; 48

DAUTHORNE, GORDON
Flower and Fruit Prints of the 18th and Early 19th Centuries, Their History, Makers and Uses... Washington: 1938. V. 53

DAVENANT, CHARLES
Circe, a Tragedy. London: 1703. V. 47
An Essay on the East India Trade. London: 1696. V. 51
An Essay On the Probable Methods of Making a People Gainers in the Balance of Trade. London: 1699. V. 49
Essays Upon I. The Ballance of Power. II. The Right of Making War, Peace and Alliances. III. Universal Monarchy. London: 1701. V. 47; 48

DAVENANT, JOHN
Exposito Epistolae D. Pauli ad Colossenses... Cambridge: 1639. V. 51

D'AVENANT, WILLIAM
The Dramatic Works. Edinburgh: 1878. V. 49; 54
Gondibert: an Heroick Poem. London: 1651. V. 48; 50; 52
The Platonick Lovers. London: 1636. V. 48
The Wits, a Comedie; The Platonick Lovers. London: 1665. V. 49
The Works... London: 1673. V. 47; 49; 50; 52; 53; 54

DA VENEZIA, ANGELO
Giornale Sacro o Sia Metodo de Invocare Ogni Giorno Della Settimana. Il Gloriosissimo Taumaturgo Antonio Santo. Padua: 1762. V. 52

DAVENPORT, A. H.
A Narrative of the Cruise of the Yacht Maria Among the Feroe Islands in the Summer of 1854. London: 1855. V. 47
A Narrative of the Cruise of the Yacht Maria Among the Feroe Islands in the Summer of 1854. London: 1856. V. 50

DAVENPORT, BISHOP
A New Gazetteer or Geographical Dictionary of North America and the West Indies. Baltimore: 1833. V. 51
A New Gazetteer, or Geographical Dictionary of North America and the West Indies. Philadelphia: 1836. V. 47

DAVENPORT, CYRIL
Cameos. London: 1900. V. 48; 49; 53
English Embroidered Bookbinding. London: 1899. V. 48; 49; 50; 54
English Heraldic Book-Stamps. London: 1909. V. 49
Mezzotints. London: 1904. V. 53
Roger Payne, English Book-Binder of the Eighteenth Century. Chicago: 1929. V. 48; 49; 50; 51
Royal English Bookbindings. London: 1896. V. 47; 48; 51; 52; 54
Samuel Mearne, Binder to King Charles II. Chicago: 1906. V. 48; 50; 52
Thomas Berthelet, Royal Printer and Bookbinder to Henry VIII. Chicago: 1901. V. 47; 48; 50

DAVENPORT, E. MONTAGU
The Life and Recollections of E. M. Davenport, Major, H.M. 66th Regiment. London: 1869. V. 53

DAVENPORT, GUY
Artists' Sketchbooks. New York: 1991. V. 53
The Bicycle Rider. New York: 1985. V. 47; 53; 54
The Bowman of Shu. New York: 1983. V. 47; 48; 53; 54
The Bowman of Shu. Newtown: 1983. V. 52
Da Vinci's Bicyle. Ten Stories. Baltimore & London: 1979. V. 53
Do You Have a Poem Book on E.E. Cummings?. Penland: 1969. V. 53
Eudora Welty. Millerton: 1981. V. 51
Father Louie: Photographs of Thomas Merton. New York: 1991. V. 48; 52; 53
Flowers and Leaves. A Long Poem. Highlands: 1966. V. 53; 54
The Fragments of Herakleitos. Berkeley: 1991. V. 53
The Geography of the Imagination. San Francisco: 1981. V. 50; 53
Goldfinch Thistle Star. New York: 1983. V. 47; 49; 53; 54
Jonah: a Short Story. 1986. V. 52
Jonah: a Story. New York: 1986. V. 47; 49; 54
The Lark. Story and Drawings. New York: 1993. V. 49
The Medusa. 1984. V. 47; 53
Ralph Eugene Meatyard. Millerton: 1974. V. 53
The Resurrection in Cookham Churchyard. New York: 1982. V. 53; 54
Tatlin!. New York: 1974. V. 51; 53
Trois Caprices. Louisville: 1981. V. 47; 54

DAVENPORT, HOMER
My Quest of the Arabian Horse. New York: 1909. V. 54

DAVENPORT, JEWETTE H.
The History of the Supreme Court of the State of Texas. Austin: 1917. V. 49

DAVENPORT, JOHN
Aphrodisiacs and Anti-Aphrodisiacs: Three Essays on the Powers of Reproduction... London: 1869. V. 47; 50; 52; 53
Curiositates Eroticae Physiologiae; or, Tabooed Subjects Freely Treated. London: 1875. V. 53

DAVENPORT, MILLIA
The Book of Costume. New York: 1948. V. 54

DAVENPORT, MONTAGUE
Under the Gridiron. A Summer in the United States and the Far West. London: 1876. V. 53

DAVENPORT *Past and Present...* Davenport: 1858. V. 50

DAVENPORT, RICHARD A.
The Amateur's Perspective... (with) A Supplement to "The Amateur's Perspective". London: 1828-29. V. 49
The Life of Ali Pasha, of Tepeleni Vizier of Epirus: Surnamed Aslan, or the Lion. London: 1837. V. 47; 54
Sketches of Imposture, Deception, and Credulity. London: 1837. V. 54
Sketches of Imposture, Deception and Credulity. London: 1840. V. 51

DAVENPORT, W.
Historical Portraiture of leading Events in the Life of Alia Pacha, Vizier of Epirus, Surnamed the Lion. London: 1823. V. 49

DAVENPORT ADAMS, W. H.
The Bird World. London: 1885. V. 53

DAVEY, DORIS
My Dolly's Home. Biddy's Adventure. The Story of My Dolly's Home. London: 1921. V. 50

DAVEY, F. H.
Flora of Cornwall. London: 1909-22. V. 50; 51

DAVEY, FRANK
Bridge Force. Toronto: 1965. V. 47
D-Day and After. Oliver: 1962. V. 47

DAVEY, NEIL K.
Netsuke. A Comprehensive Study Based on the M. T. Hindson Collection. London: 1982. V. 54

DAVEY, NORMAN
Poems. London: 1914. V. 51

DAVEY, RICHARD
The Pageant of London. London: 1906. V. 52; 54
The Sultan and His Subjects. London: 1907. V. 47

DAVID, A.
The Charts and Coast Views of Captain Cook's Voyages. Volume I. The Voyage of the Endeavour, 1768-1771. London: 1988. V. 53
Les Oiseaux de la Chine. Paris: 1877. V. 49

DAVID, ELIZABETH
French Country Cooking. London: 1951. V. 52
French Country Cooking. New York: 1952. V. 52

DAVID, ERNEST
Plafonds et Peintures Murales. 1890-1900. V. 47

DAVID, F. A.
Le Museum de Florence, Ou Collection des Pierres Gravees, Statues, Medailles et Peintures...Dessine et Grave... Paris: 1787. V. 48

DAVID, HENRY
An Historical Account of the Curiosities of London and Westminster, In Three Parts. London: 1755. V. 50

DAVID, JOANNES
Occasio Arrepta. Neglecta. Hvivs Commoda: Illivs Incommoda. Antwerp: 1605. V. 50
Paradisvs Sponsi et Sponsae. Antverpiae: 1618. V. 53

DAVID, ROBERT BEEBE
Finn Brunett, Frontiersman: the Life and Adventures of an Indian Fighter, Mail Coach Driver, Miner, Pioneer Cattleman, Participant in the Powder River Expedition, Survivor of the Hay Field Fight... Glendale: 1937. V. 50; 52; 54
Malcolm Campbell, Sheriff. Caspar: 1932. V. 53; 54

DAVID, T. EDGEWORTH, MRS.
Funafuti or Three Months on a Remote Coral Island: an Unscientific Account of a Scientific Expedition. London: 1899. V. 48

DAVID, VILLIERS
The Guardsman and Cupid's Daughter and Other Poems. London: 1930. V. 51; 54
A Winter Firework. Waltham St. Lawrence: 1937. V. 47

DAVID, WILLIAM K.
Secrets of Wise Men, Chemists and Great Physicians. Chicago: 1889. V. 47

DAVIDMAN, JAY
War Poems of the United Nations. New York: 1943. V. 48

DAVIDOFF, LEO
Brain Tumors: Their Pathology, Symptomatology, Diagnosis and Prognosis. Utica: 1931. V. 47

DAVIDS, FRANK MARSHALL
I Am the American Negro. Chicago: 1937. V. 53

DAVIDSON, BASIL
Tir A'Mhurain: Outer Hebrides. London: 1962. V. 47; 54

DAVIDSON, BRUCE
East 100th Street. Cambridge: 1971. V. 47

DAVIDSON, C. J. C.
Diary of Travels and Adventures in Upper India, from Bareilly in Rohilcund, to Hurdward and Nahum, in the Himalayan Mountains, with a Tour in Bundelcund, a Sporting Excursion in the Kingdom of Oude, and a Voyage Down the Ganges. London: 1843. V. 49

DAVIDSON, DIANE MOTT
Catering to Nobody. 1990. V. 53

DAVIDSON, DONAL
The Attack on Leviathan: Regionalism and Nationalism in the United States. Chapel Hill: 1938. V. 48

DAVIDSON, DONALD
An Outland Piper. Boston: 1924. V. 47

DAVIDSON, ELLIS A.
Practical Manual of House-Painting, Graining, Marbling and Sign Writing. London: 1896. V. 47

DAVIDSON, GEORGE
The Alaska Boundary. San Francisco: 1903. V. 47; 48; 54
Coast Pilot of California, Oregon and Washington. Washington: 1889. V. 54

DAVIDSON, GIDEON MINOR
Routes and Tables of Distances Embraced in the Traveller's Guide through the Northern and Middle States and the Canadas. Saratoga Springs: 1833. V. 47

DAVIDSON, GLADYS
All About the Man in the Moon. London. V. 54
Gyp's Hour of Bliss. London: 1919. V. 53

DAVIDSON, GORDON CHARLES
The North West Company. Berkeley: 1918. V. 50

DAVIDSON, HAROLD
The Lost Works of Edward Borein. Santa Barbara: 1978. V. 53

DAVIDSON, HUGH COLEMAN
The Book of the Home: a Practical Guide to Household Management. London: 1906. V. 50

DAVIDSON, JOE
The Art of the Cigar Label. New Jersey: 1989. V. 51

DAVIDSON, JOHN
In a Music Hall and Other Poems. London: 1891. V. 52
Plays: Being an Unhistorical Pastoral: A Romantic Farce; Bruce, A Chronicle Play; Smith A Tragic Farce and Scaramouche In Naxos A Pantomine. London: 1894. V. 50
Smith: a Tragedy. Glasgow: 1888. V. 48

DAVIDSON, LUCRETIA MARIA
Amir Khan and Other Poems: the Remains of...Who Died At Plattsburgh, New York August 27, 1825 aged 16 Years and 11 Months. New York: 1829. V. 47; 49
Poems. New York: 1871. V. 51

DAVIDSON, MARSHALL B.
The American Heritage History of American Antiques. New York: 1967-69. V. 49; 50; 52

DAVIDSON, MICHEL
In Veldi. Chicago: 1926. V. 47

DAVIDSON, PATRICIA F.
Ancient Greek and Roman Gold Jewelry in the Brooklyn Museum. Brooklyn: 1984. V. 50; 52

DAVIDSON, T.
British Fossil Brachiopoda. London: 1851-86. V. 52

DAVIDSON, T. WHITFIELD
Our Scotch Kith and Kin. Austin: 1959. V. 47

DAVIE, DONALD
Purity of Diction in English Verse. London: 1952. V. 49
A Sequence for Francis Parkman. 1961. V. 47

DAVIE, IAN
Oxford Poetry - 1942-1943. Oxford: 1943. V. 52

DAVIE, JOHN CONSTANSE
Letters From Paraguay: Describing the Settlements of Monte Video and Buenos Ayres... London: 1805. V. 48

DAVIE, OLIVER
Methods in the Art of Taxidermy. Columbus: 1894. V. 49; 51
Methods in the Art of Taxidermy. Philadelphia: 1900. V. 49
Nests and Eggs of North American Birds. Columbus: 1889. V. 54

DAVIE, W. GALSWORTHY
Old Cottages and Farmhouses in Kent and Sussex. London: 1900. V. 50; 54
Old Cottages and Farmhouses in Surrey. London: 1908. V. 54
Old English Doorways. London: 1903. V. 48; 54
Old Stone Cottages, Farmhouses and Other Stone Buildings in the Cotswold District. London: 1905. V. 54

D'AVIEDOR, ELIM H.
Loose Reign by 'Wanderer'. London: 1887. V. 47; 52

DAVIES, ADRIANA
Dictionary of British Portraiture. London: 1979-81. V. 47

DAVIES, ARTHUR B.
The Etchings and Lithographs of Arthur B. Davies. New York: 1929. V. 47

DAVIES, BENJAMIN
A New System of Modern Geography, or a General Description of the Most Remarkable Countries throughout the Known World... Philadelphia: 1813. V. 53

DAVIES, BLODWEN
A Study of Tom Thomson: The Story of a man Who Looked for Beauty and For Truth in the Wilderness. Toronto: 1935. V. 52

DAVIES, C. M.
History of Holland, From the Beginning of the Tenth to the End of the Eighteenth Century. London: 1841-44. V. 49

DAVIES, CHARLES
A Treatise on Shades and Shadows and Linear Perspective. New York: 1838. V. 48

DAVIES, E. W. L.
A Memoir of the Rev. John Russell, and His Out-of-Door Life. London: 1878. V. 47

DAVIES, EDWARD
Aptharte, the Genius of Britain. Bath: 1784. V. 47; 54
Celtic Researches, on the Origin, Traditions and Language of the Ancient Britons... London: 1804. V. 48; 51
Celtic Researches on the Origin, Traditions and Language of the Ancient Britons. London: 1904. V. 49

DAVIES, GARETH ALBAN
The Pleasant History of Lazarillo de Tormes. Newtown: 1991. V. 47

DAVIES, GEORGE R.
Collection of Old Chinese Porcelains Formed by George R. Davies, Esq. Purchased by Gorer and Exhibited at the Galleries of Dreicer & Co. London: 1913. V. 47; 49

DAVIES, GERALD S.
Hans Holbein the Younger. London: 1903. V. 47
Renascence: the Sculptured Tombs of the 15th Century in Rome... London: 1910. V. 53

DAVIES, H.
Welsh Botanology...Native Plants of Anglesey... London: 1813. V. 52

DAVIES, HUGH WILLIAM
Devices of the Early Printers 1457-1500, Their History and Development. London: 1935. V. 47; 48; 51; 52; 53

DAVIES, JAMES
Relation of a Voyage to Sagadahoc. Cambridge: 1880. V. 47; 49; 52

DAVIES, JOHN
The Ancient Rites and Monuments of the Monastical and Cathedral Church of Durham. London: 1672. V. 52
A Discoverie of the True Causes Why Ireland Was Neuer Entirely Subdued, Nor Brought Vnder Obedience of the Crowne of England... London: 1747. V. 51; 53
A Discoverie of the True Causes Why Ireland Was Never Entirely Subdued, Nor Brought Under Obedience of the Crowne of England, Until the Beginning of His Majesties Happie Raigne James 1st... Dublin: 1761. V. 50
Historical Tracts. To Which is Prefixed a New Life fo the Author, from Authentic Documents. London: 1786. V. 47; 53
The Innkeeper and Butler's Guide, or a Directory in the Making and Managing of British Wines... Leeds: 1807. V. 49
The Innkeeper's and Butler's Guide, or, a Directory for Making and Managing British Wines with Directions for the Managing, Coloring and Flavoring of Foreign Wines and Spirits.... Leeds: 1811. V. 52
A Memorial for the Learned; or, Miscellany of Choice Collections from the Most Eminent Authors. London: 1686. V. 53
The Original Nature, and Immorality of the Soul. London: 1697. V. 48; 54

DAVIES, K. G.
Letters from Hudson Bay 1703-1740. London: 1965. V. 47; 48
Northern Quebec and Labrador Journals and Correspondence 1819-1835. London: 1963. V. 48; 54

DAVIES, MARGARET
The Miss Margaret Davies Complete Collection of Special Gregynog Bindings. Amsterdam: 1994. V. 52

DAVIES, MARTIN
Rogier Van Der Weyden. An Essay, with a Critical Catalogue of Paintings Assigned to Him and to Robert Campin. New York: 1972. V. 50

DAVIES, MAURICE
Fun, Ancient and Modern. London: 1878. V. 47; 54

DAVIES, MYLES
Athenae Britannicae; or, a Critical History of the Oxford and Cambrige (sic) Writers and Writings... London: 1716. V. 53

DAVIES, N. DE GARIS
The Mastaba of Ptahhetep and Akhethetep at Saqqareh. London: 1900-01. V. 51
Robb de Peyster Tytus Memorial Series Volum I-V. New York: 1917-27. V. 51
The Rock Tombs of Deir el Gebrawi. London: 1902. V. 51
The Rock Tombs of El Amarna. Volumes 1-8. London: 1903-89. V. 51
The Rock Tombs of Sheikh Said. London: 1901. V. 49; 51
The Theban Tomb Series. London: 1915-33. V. 49
The Tomb of Antefoker, Vizier of Sesostris I, and of His Wife, Senet. London: 1920. V. 51
The Tomb of Ken-Amun at Thebes. New York: 1930. V. 51
The Tomb of Nakht at Thebes. New York: 1917. V. 49
The Tomb of Puyemre at Thebes. New York: 1922-23. V. 49
The Tomb of the Two Sculptors at Thebes. New York: 1925. V. 49; 51
The Tomb of the Vizier Ramose. London: 1941. V. 51
The Tombs of Menkheperrasonb, Amenmose and Another. London: 1933. V. 49

DAVIES, NINA
Ancient Egyptian Paintings. Chicago: 1936. V. 49
The Tomb of Huy, Viceroy of Nubia in the Reign of Tut'ankhamun. London: 1926. V. 49

DAVIES, R.
The Historie of the King's Manour House at York. York: 1883. V. 51; 52
Renown at Stratford and Twice Have the Trumpets Sounded. 1953-54. V. 50

DAVIES, RANDALL
Thomas Girtin's Water-Colours. London: 1924. V. 50; 51; 53; 54

DAVIES, RHYS
Aaron. London: 1927. V. 48
Arfon. London: 1931. V. 51; 53
Daisy Matthews and Three Other Tales. Waltham St. Lawrence: 1932. V. 52; 53
A Pig in a Poke: Stories. London: 1931. V. 49; 51
The Red Hills. London: 1932. V. 51
Rings on Her Fingers. London: 1930. V. 51; 53
Selected Stories. London: 1945. V. 51
The Song of Songs and Other Stories. London: 1927. V. 48; 49; 51
The Withered Root. London: 1927. V. 51; 53
A Woman. London: 1931. V. 51; 53

DAVIES, RICHARD
An Account of the Convincement, Exercises, Services and Travels of the Ancient Servant of the Lord. Newtown: 1928. V. 47; 52

DAVIES, ROBERT
Historical Notices of the King's Manor, York, Formerly a Palace of the Abbot of St. Mary's and of the Stuart Kings. London: 1883. V. 47
A Memoir of the York Press, with Notices of Authors, Printers and Stationers in the Sixteenth, Seventeenth and Eighteenth Centuries. London: 1868. V. 47; 50

DAVIES, ROBERTSON
At My Heart's Core. Toronto: 1950. V. 47; 54
The Dignity of Literature. Toronto: 1994. V. 52; 53; 54
Eros at Breakfast. Toronto: 1949. V. 54
Fortune, My Foe. Toronto: 1949. V. 54
The Heart of a Merry Christmas. Grimsby: 1979. V. 49
An Introduction to the Twenty-First Toronto Antiquarian Book Fair. Toronto: 1993. V. 49
Leaven of Malice. New York: 1955. V. 48; 51; 52; 53
The Lyre of Orpheus. London: 1988. V. 49; 50
The Lyre of Orpheus. New York: 1988. V. 48; 51
The Lyre of Orpheus. Toronto: 1988. V. 50
The Manticore. New York: 1972. V. 53
The Manticore. Toronto: 1972. V. 47
A Masque of Mr. Punch. Toronto: 1963. V. 53
A Mixture of Frailties. New York: 1958. V. 47; 48; 51
Murther & Walking Spirits. London: 1991. V. 48; 50; 51; 54
Overlaid: a Comedy. Toronto: 1952. V. 51
The Rebel Angels. Toronto: 1981. V. 53
Samuel Marchbanks' Almanack. Toronto: 1967. V. 53
The Table Talk of Samuel Marchbanks. Toronto: 1949. V. 48; 49; 50; 51; 52
The Table Talk of Samuel Marchbanks. London: 1951. V. 49; 53
Tempest-Tost. New York: 1952. V. 54
Twice Have the Trumpets Sounded. Toronto: 1954. V. 51
A Voice from the Attic. New York: 1960. V. 48; 50; 52; 53; 54
A Voice from the Attic. Toronto: 1960. V. 51; 53; 54
What's Bred in the Bone. Toronto: 1985. V. 47
World of Wonders. Toronto: 1975. V. 47; 51
World of Wonders. London: 1977. V. 52

DAVIES, SAMUEL
The Vessels of Mercy and the Vessels of Wrath, Delineated, in a New, Uncontroverted and Practical Light. London: 1758. V. 47

DAVIES, T. WITTON
Magic, Divination, and Demonology Among the Hebrews and Their Neighbours, Including an Examination of Biblical References and of the Biblical Terms. London: 1898. V. 47; 50

DAVIES, THOMAS
Dramatic Miscellanies. London: 1784/83/84. V. 47; 49
Dramatic Miscellanies... London: 1785. V. 54
A Genuine Narrative of the Life and Theatrical Transactions of Mr. John Henderson, Commonly Called the Bath Roscius. London: 1777. V. 51; 52
Memoirs of the Life of David Garrick, Esq. London: 1780. V. 47; 49; 52; 53
Memoirs of the Life of David Garrick, Esq. London: 1784. V. 47
Memoirs of the Life of David Garrick, Esq. London: 1808. V. 48; 51

DAVIES, VALENTINE
Miracle on 34th street. New York: 1947. V. 49; 50; 52

DAVIES, W. ROBERTSON
Shakespeare's Boy Actors. London: 1939. V. 48; 51

DAVIES, WALTER
General View of the Agriculture and Domestic Economy of North Wales... London: 1810. V. 50; 52

DAVIES, WILLIAM HENRY
The Adventures of Johnny Walker, Tramp. London: 1926. V. 48
Farewell to Poesy and Other Poems. London: 1910. V. 50; 53
Foliage Various Poems.. London: 1913. V. 50; 52; 54
Forty New Poems. London: 1918. V. 47; 51; 53
The Hour of Magic and Other Poems. London: 1922. V. 49; 50
The Lovers' Song-book. London: 1933. V. 47
The Lovers' Song-Book. Newtown: 1933. V. 51; 52; 54
Nature Poems and Others. London: 1908. V. 51
A Poet's Pilgrimage. London: 1918. V. 49; 54
Selected Poems. Newtown: 1928. V. 47; 51; 52; 54
True Travellers: a tramps Opera in Three Acts. London: 1923. V. 48; 49; 50

DAVIES-COLLEY, T. H.
The Family of Colley of Churton Heath in the County Chester... London: 1931. V. 49; 52

D'AVIGDOR, ELIM H.
Fair Diana. London: 1884. V. 51
A Loose Rein. London: 1887. V. 51

DAVILA, ENRICO CATERINO
The Historie of the Civill Warres of France. London: 1647. V. 47; 49; 50; 51; 53
The History of the Civil Wars of France. London: 1678. V. 54

DAVILLE, JOHN
A Sermon Preached at York, on Sunday the 29th of September, 1745. York: 1745. V. 47

DAVIOT, GORDON
Claverhouse. London: 1937. V. 54
The Laughing Woman. London: 1934. V. 50

DAVIS, A.
The Velocipede: Its History and (Practical Hints) How to Use It. London: 1869. V. 50

DAVIS, A. C.
A Hundred Years of Portland Cement. 1824-1924. London: 1924. V. 50; 52

DAVIS, ANDREW JACKSON
The Philosophy of Spiritual Intercourse, Being an Explanation of Modern Mysteries. New York: 1851. V. 50

DAVIS, ANDREW MC FARLAND
Colonial Currency Reprints, 1682-1751. New York: 1964. V. 47
The Journey of Moncacht-Ape, an Indian of the Yazoo Tribe, Across the Continent, About the Year 1700. Worcester: 1883. V. 52

DAVIS, ANGELA
Angela Davis: an Autobiography. New York: 1974. V. 51

DAVIS, ANGELA Y.
If They Come in the Morning: Voices of Resistance. New York: 1971. V. 50

DAVIS, BRITTON
The Truth About Geronimo. New Haven: 1929. V. 52

DAVIS, C. H.
Narrative of the North Polar Expedition. U. S. Ship Polaris... Washington: 1876. V. 48; 52

DAVIS, C. N.
Narrative of the North Polar Expedtiion. Washington: 1876. V. 47

DAVIS, CHARLES AUGUSTUS
Letters of J. Downing, Major, Downingville Militia, Second Brigade, to His Old Friend, Mr. Dwight of the New York Daily Advertiser. Cambridge: 1968. V. 53

DAVIS, CHARLES B.
Report on Interoceanic Canals and Railroads Between the Atlantic and Pacific Oceans. Washington: 1867. V. 51

DAVIS, CHARLES G.
The Ship Model Builder's Assistant. Salem: 1926. V. 51
Ship Models, How to Build Them. Salem: 1925. V. 51
Ships of the Past. Salem: 1929. V. 51
United States vs. Charles G. Davis. Report of the Proceedings at the Examination of Charles G. Davis, Esq. on a Cahrge of Aiding and Abetting in the Rescue of a Fugitive Slave. Held in Boston, February, 1851. Boston: 1851. V. 47

DAVIS, E. O.
The First Five Years of the Railroad Era in Colorado. 1948. V. 53

DAVIS, ELLIS A.
Davis' Commercial Encyclopedia of the Pacific Southwest: California, Nevada, Utah, Arizona. Berkeley: 1914. V. 54
The Historical Encyclopedia of New Mexico. Albuquerque: 1945. V. 48; 50
New Encyclopedia of Texas, Historical Encyclopedia of Texas. 1936. V. 48

DAVIS, FREDERICK
Myths and Legends of Japan. London: 1912. V. 53

DAVIS, FREDERICK C.
He Wouldn't Say Dead. New York: 1939. V. 53

DAVIS, GHERARDI
Alice and I at Larchmont. New York: 1915. V. 47
Alice and I, or Learning to Sail a Boat...(and) Alicq Q and Her Rivals. New York: 1913. V. 47

DAVIS, GWENN
Drama by Women to 1900: a Bibliography of American and British Writers. London: 1992. V. 52
Personal Writings by Women to 1900: a Bibliography of American and British Writers. London: 1989. V. 52
Poetry by Women to 1900: a Bibliography of American and British Writers. London: 1991. V. 52

DAVIS, H. P.
Gold Rush Days in Nevada City. Nevada City: 1948. V. 52

DAVIS, HENRY EDWARDS
An Examination of the Fifteenth and Sixteenth Chapters of Mr. Gibbon's...Decline and Fall... London: 1778. V. 54

DAVIS, HENRY GEORGE
The Memorials of the Hamlet of Knightsbridge. London: 1859. V. 50; 52

DAVIS, HENRY H.
The Fancies of a Dreamer. London: 1842. V. 52

DAVIS, HENRY HARRISON
An Excursion from Lancaster Upon the Vale of Lune and from Kirkby Lonsdale to the Caves of Yorkshire. Kirkby Lonsdale: 1849. V. 50

DAVIS, HENRY T.
Solitary Places Made Glad, Being Observations and Experience for Thirty-Two Years in Nebraska with Sketches and Incidents. Cincinnati: 1890. V. 47; 52

DAVIS, HUBERT
The Symbolic Drawings of Huber Davais for An American Tragedy. New York: 1930. V. 51; 53

DAVIS, J. SCARLETT
Fourteen Plates of Bolton Abbey. London: 1829. V. 52

DAVIS, JAMES
West Yorkshire: an Account of Its Geology, Physical Geography, Climatology and Botany. London: 1878. V. 53
West Yorkshire: an Account of Its Geology, Physical Geography, Climatology and Botany. London: 1880. V. 53

DAVIS, JAMES LUCIUS
The Trooper's Manual: or, Tactics for Light Dragoons and Mounted Riflemen. Richmond: 1862. V. 49

DAVIS, JEFFERSON
Jefferson Davis Constitutionalist His Letters, Papers and Speeches. Jackson: 1923. V. 51
The Rise and Fall of the Confederate Government. London: 1881. V. 51
The Rise and Fall of the Confederate Government. New York: 1881. V. 47; 48; 49; 50; 53
The Rise and Fall of the Confederate Government. New York & London: 1912. V. 49

DAVIS, JOHN
The First Settlers of Virginia... New York: 1806. V. 47; 53; 54
The Life of Thomas Chatterton. London: 1808. V. 48
The Post-Captain; or the Wooden Walls Well Manned: Comprehending a View of Naval Society and Manners. Brooklyn: 1813. V. 50
Travels of Four Years and a Half in the United States of America: During 1798, 1799, 1800, 1801 and 1802. Warrington: 1770-71. V. 48
Travels of Four Years and a Half in the United States of America; During 1798, 1799, 1800, 1801 and 1802. London: 1803. V. 49; 52
Travels of Four Years and a Half in the United States of America During 1798, 1799, 1800, 1801 and 1802. New York: 1909. V. 53

DAVIS, JOHN FRANCIS
The Chinese: a General Description of China and Its Inhabitants. London: 1844/45. V. 48; 53
The Chinese: A General Description...of China and its Inhabitants. London: 1836. V. 48
Chinese Novels. London: 1822. V. 50; 54
Hien Wun Shoo. London: 1823. V. 47; 49
Sketches of China; Partly During an Inland Journey of Four Months, Between Peking, Nanking and Canton... London: 1841. V. 48; 50; 53

DAVIS, JOHN KING
Willis Island: a Storm Warning Station in the Coral Sea. Melbourne: 1923. V. 52

DAVIS, JOHN P.
The Union Pacific Railway: a Study in Railway Politics, History and Economics. Chicago: 1894. V. 47

DAVIS, JOHN S.
Plastic Surgery: its Principles and Practice. Philadelphia: 1919. V. 48; 51; 53

DAVIS, JOSEPH BARNARD
Crania Britannica. London: 1865. V. 52; 53

DAVIS, JOSEPH BERNARD
Thesaurus Craniorum Catalogue of the Skulls of the Various Races of Man in the Collection of... London: 1867. V. 47; 48

DAVIS, L. S.
Penguin Biology. New York: 1990. V. 50

DAVIS, LEOPOLD
Strange Occurrences. Boston: 1877. V. 54

DAVIS, LINDSEY
Shadows in Bronze. London: 1990. V. 53; 54
Time to Depart. London: 1995. V. 53; 54

DAVIS, LOYAL
Neurological Surgery. Chicago: 1936. V. 47

DAVIS, LUCIUS D.
Ornamental Shrubs for Garden, Lawn and Park Planting. New York and London: 1899. V. 53

DAVIS, LUTE L.
Blankets on the Sand. Wichita Falls: 1948. V. 49; 54

DAVIS, MARY ELIZABETH MORAIGNE
The British Partizan: a Tale of the Olden Time. Macon: 1864. V. 49; 53
The British Partizan, a tale of the Times of Old originally Published as a Prize Tale, in the Augusta Mirror. Augusta: 1839. V. 50
Ode to Texas, Written for the Occasion of the Ladies' Bazaar for the Benefit of the San Jacinto Battleground. 1908. V. 51
Poems. Houston: 1872. V. 53

DAVIS, MATTHEW L.
Memoirs of Aaron Burr with Miscellaneous Selections from His Correspondence. New York: 1838. V. 52

DAVIS, NATHAN
Carthage and Her Remains: Being an Account of the Excavations and Researches on the Site of the Phoenician Metropolis in Africa and Other Adjacent Places. London: 1861. V. 49; 52
Carthage and Her Remains: Being an Account of the Excavations and Researches on the Site of the Phoenician Metropolis in Africa and Other Adjacent Places. New York: 1861. V. 49; 51
Ruined Cities with Numidian and Carthaginian Territories. London: 1862. V. 49; 51; 52

DAVIS, NATHAN S.
History of Medical Education and Institutions in the United States from the First Settlement of the British Colonies to the Year 1850... Chicago: 1851. V. 50

DAVIS, NICHOLAS A.
The Campaign from Texas to Maryland. Richmond: 1863. V. 54

DAVIS, NOAH
A Narrative of the Life of Rev. Noah Davis, a Coloured Man, Written by Himself at the Age of Fifty-Four. Baltimore: 1859. V. 52

DAVIS, NORBERT
The Mouse in the Mountain. New York: 1943. V. 50

DAVIS, P. H.
The Flora of Turkey and the East Aegean Islands. Edinburgh: 1965-77. V. 48

DAVIS, PARIS M.
Original and Select Hymns and Sacred Pindoric Odes, Few of Which Have Been Published. Boston: 1803?. V. 50

DAVIS, PERRY
The People's Pamphlet. Providence: 1846. V. 51

DAVIS, REBECCA HARDING
Doctor Warrick's Daughters, a Novel. New York: 1896. V. 54

DAVIS, RICHARD H.
The Lost Road. New York: 1913. V. 51

DAVIS, RICHARD HARDING
Cuba in War Time. New York: 1897. V. 52
The Deserter. New York: 1917. V. 49
The Novels and Stories of... New York: 1916. V. 48; 54
Our English Cousins. New York: 1894. V. 50
Three Gringos in Venezuela and Central America. New York: 1896. V. 52; 54
The West from a Car Window. New York: 1892. V. 53

DAVIS, ROBERT H.
Breathing in Irrespirable Atmospheres, and In Some Cases, also Under Water. 1946. V. 51
Breathing in Irrespirable Atmospheres, and in some Cases, Also Under Water. London: 1947. V. 49
Man Makes His Own Mask. New York: 1932. V. 49; 50

DAVIS, ROGER
Kendrew of Hork and His Chapbooks for Children. Wetherby, West Yorkshire: 1988. V. 47

DAVIS, S. T.
Caribou Shooting in Newfoundland with a History of England's Oldest Colony from 1001 to 1895. Lancaster: 1895. V. 47
Caribou Shooting in Newfoundland with a History of England's Oldest Colony from 1001 to 1895. Lancaster: 1896. V. 47

DAVIS, SAMUEL POST
The History of Nevada. Reno and Los Angeles: 1913. V. 48

DAVIS, SOLOMON
A Prayer Book, in the Language of the Six Nations of Indians Containing the Morning and Evening Service, the Litany, Catechism, Some of the Collects and the Prayers... New York: 1837. V. 49

DAVIS, STANFORD E.
Priceless Jewels. New York: 1911. V. 53

DAVIS, THEODORE M.
Theodore M. Davis' Excavations: Biban el Moluk. London: 1908. V. 49
Theodore M. Davis' Excavations: Biban el Moluk. London: 1910. V. 47; 49

DAVIS, THOMAS
The Love Story of Thomas Davis Told in the Letters of Annie Hutton. 1945. V. 54

DAVIS, W. J.
The Token Coinage of Warwickshire, with Descriptive and Historical Notes. Birmingham: 1895. V. 48

DAVIS, W. M.
The Coral Reef Problem. New York: 1928. V. 53

DAVIS, WALLACE
Corduroy Road: The Story of Glenn Hl. McCarthy. Houston: 1951. V. 47

DAVIS, WALTER BICKFORD
An Illustrated History of Missouri... St. Louis: 1876. V. 50

DAVIS, WASHINGTON
Camp-Fire Chats of the Civil War...as Related by Veteran Soldiers Themselves. Chicago: 1887. V. 49

DAVIS, WILLIAM
A Journey Round the Library of A Bibliomaniac... London: 1821. V. 48; 50

DAVIS, WILLIAM C.
The Image of War 1861-1865. Garden City: 1981-84. V. 48; 53

DAVIS, WILLIAM HEATH
Seventy-Five Years in California, A History of Events and Life in California... San Francisco: 1929. V. 48; 53
Sixty Years in California. San Francisco: 1889. V. 47; 48; 50

DAVIS, WILLIAM M.
Nimrod of the Sea, or, the American Whaleman. London: 1874. V. 50

DAVIS, WILLIAM WATTS HART
El Gringo; or, New Mexico and Her People... New York: 1857. V. 47
The Spanish Conquest of New Mexico. Doylestown: 1869. V. 49; 54

DAVIS, WINFIELD J.
History of Political Conventions in California, 1849-1892. Sacramento: 1893. V. 50; 52; 53; 54

DAVISON, CHARLES
The Hereford Earthquake of December 17, 1896. Birmingham: 1899. V. 53
A History of British Earthquakes. Cambridge: 1924. V. 53

DAVISON, EDWARD
Collected Poems 1917-1939. New York: 1940. V. 54

DAVISON, FRANCIS
Davison's Poetical Rhapsody. London: 1890. V. 49; 51; 52; 54
The Poetical Rhapsody. London: 1826. V. 50; 54
Poetical Rhapsody. London: 1890-91. V. 54

DAVISON, JEAN M.
Attic Geometric Workshops. New Haven: 1961. V. 52

DAVISON, RICHARD ALLAN
Charles & Kathleen Norris, the Courtship Year. San Francisco: 1993. V. 50

DAVISON, THOMAS
Bibliotheca Anglo-Poetica. London: 1815. V. 51

DAVISON, W.
A Descriptive and Historical View of Alnwick...and of Alnwick Castle, Alnwick & Hulne Abbeys, Brislee Tower, The Borough of Alnwick &c. Alnwick: 1822. V. 47

DAVITT, MICHAEL
The Fall of Feudalism in Ireland, or, the Story of the Land League Revolution. New York: 1904. V. 51
Leaves from a Prison Diary; or, Lectures to a Solitary Audience. London: 1885. V. 52

DAVY, HENRY
The Architectural Antiquites of Suffolk. Norwich: 1818. V. 49
A Series of Etchings Illustrative of the Architectural Antiquities of Suffolk... Southwold: 1827. V. 52

DAVY, HUMPHRY
The Collected Works... London: 1839-40. V. 50
Elements of Agricultural Chemistry. London: 1813. V. 48; 50; 52; 53; 54
Elements of Agricultural Chemistry. London: 1814. V. 48; 51; 52; 53
Elements of Agricultural Chemistry. Philadelphia: 1815. V. 48
Elements of Agricultural Chemistry. Glasgow: 1845. V. 50
Elements of Chemical Philosophy. Philadelphia: 1812. V. 51
On the Safety Lamp for Coal Miners; with Some Reflections on Flame. London: 1818. V. 54
Salmonia: or Days of Fly Fishing. London: 1828. V. 52
Salmonia; or Days of Fly Fishing... London: 1829. V. 47
Salmonia: or Days of Fly Fishing. London: 1832. V. 50

DAVY, JOHN
The Angler and His Friend; or Piscatory Colloquies and Fishing Excursions. London: 1855. V. 47; 51
The Angler in the Lake District... London: 1857. V. 47
A Letter from John Davy, M.D., F.R.S., Addressed to the Editors of the Philosophical Magazine... London: 1865. V. 54
Memoirs of the Life of Sir Humphry Davy, Bart. London: 1836. V. 48; 50; 52; 54
Notes and Observations on the Ionian Islands and Malta. London: 1842. V. 47; 49
On Some of the More Important Diseases of the Army, With Contributions to Pathology. London: 1862. V. 50

DAVY, M. J. B.
Lighter-than-Air Craft. London: 1949. V. 49

DAVY DU PERRON, JACQUES, CARDINAL
The Miscellaneous Remains of Cardinal Perron, President Thuanus, Monsr St. Evermont &c. London: 1707. V. 54

DAW, G. H.
Daw's Gun Patents. London: 1864. V. 48

DAWE, GEORGE
Illustrations of the Life of a Nobleman, in Nine Spirited Aquatint Engravings... London: 1825. V. 47; 49
The Life of George Morland. London: 1904. V. 50; 51; 54

DAWKINS, JOHN
Rogues and Marauders. London: 1967. V. 52; 54

DAWKINS, R. M.
Forty-Five Stories from the Dodekanese. Cambridge: 1950. V. 49

DAWKINS, W. BOYD
Cave Hunting, Reasearches on the Evidence of Caves Respecting the Early Inhabitants of Europe. London: 1874. V. 51; 53

DAWSON, CHARLES
Finola: an Opera, Chiefly Composed of Moore's Irish Melodies. Dublin: 1879. V. 52
History of Hastings Castle; the Castle, Rape and Battle of Hastings. London: 1909. V. 47; 49; 52
Pioneer Tales of the Oregon Trail and Jefferson County. Topeka: 1912. V. 52; 53; 54

DAWSON, EMMA FRANCES
A Gracious Visitation. San Francisco: 1921. V. 49

DAWSON, ERNEST
A Visit with Dr. R. Los Angeles: 1948. V. 54

DAWSON, FIELDING
Krazy Kat and One More. San Francisco: 1955. V. 51

DAWSON, G. A. B.
Nilgiri Sporting Reminiscences. Madras: 1880. V. 49

DAWSON, GEORGE
Pleasures of Angling with Rod and Reel for Trout and Salmon. New York: 1876. V. 50

DAWSON, GEORGE M.
British North American Boundary Commission, Report on the Geology and Resources of the Region in the Vicinity of the Forty-Ninth Parallel, From the Lake of the Woods to the Rocky Mountains. Montreal: 1875. V. 49
The Mineral Wealth of British Columbia... Montreal: 1889. V. 50
Preliminary Report on the Physical and Geological Features of that Portion of the Rocky Mountains... Montreal: 1886. V. 53
Report On an Exploration from Port Simpson on the Pacific Coast, to Edmonton on the Saskatchewan, Embracing a Portion of the Northern Part of British Columbia and the Peace River Country, 1879. Montreal: 1881. V. 49
Report On an Exploration in the Yukon District N.W.T. and Adjacent Northern Portion of British Columbia 1887. Montreal: 1888. V. 53
Report on an Exploration in the Yukon District, N.W.T. and Adjacent Northern Portion of British Columbia 1887. Ottawa: 1898. V. 50
Report On Explorations in British Columbia, Chiefly On the Basins of the Blackwater, Salmon and Nechacco Rivers, and on Francois Lake. London: 1877. V. 50
Report On the Queen Charlotte Islands 1878. Montreal: 1880. V. 53

DAWSON, HENRY
Reminiscences of the Park and its Vicinity. New York: 1855. V. 52

DAWSON, HENRY B.
Battles of the United States, by Sea and Land... New York: 1858. V. 48; 49; 50
Battles of the United States by Sea and Land, Embracing Those of the Revolutionary and Indian Wars, and the War of 1812, and the Mexican War. New York: 1860. V. 51

DAWSON, J. W.
Acadian Geology: an Account of the Geological Structure and Mineral Resources of Nova Scotia and Portions of the Neighbouring Provinces of British America. Edinburgh: 1855. V. 47
Contributions Toward the Improvement of Agriculture in Nova-Scotia... Halifax: 1856. V. 52

DAWSON, JAMES
Facts and Fancies from the Farm: Lyrical Poems. London: 1868. V. 49

DAWSON, JOHN FREDERIC
Geodaphaga Britannica. A Monograph of the Carnivorous Ground-Beetles Indigenous to the British Isles. London: 1854. V. 48

DAWSON, KENNETH
From Major to Minor: Some Keys for Anglers. London: 1928. V. 47

DAWSON, LEONARD
The New British Farmer; or a Complete System of Practical Agriculture and Modern Husbandry. Manchester: 1827. V. 49

DAWSON, LIONEL
Sport in War. London: 1936. V. 47; 48; 49

DAWSON, LUCY
Dog As I See Them. London: 1936. V. 54
Dogs Rough and Smooth. New York. V. 49
Lucy Dawson's Dog Book. London: 1939. V. 54

DAWSON, MOSES
A Historical Narrative of the Civil and Military Services of Major-General William H. Harrison... Cincinnati: 1824. V. 51

DAWSON, MUIR
The Aitken Bible: an Original Leaf with an Introduction by Edgar J. Goodspeed. Los Angeles: 1949. V. 54
History and Bibliography of Southern California Newspapers, 1851-1876. Los Angeles: 1950. V. 49; 54

DAWSON, NICHOLAS
Narrative of Nicholas "Cheyenne" Dawson (Overland to California in '41 & '49 and Texas in '51). San Francisco: 1933. V. 47; 49; 52; 53; 54

DAWSON, OSWALD
The Bar Sinister and Licit Love. London: 1895. V. 52

DAWSON, SAMUEL EDWARD
The Saint Lawrence Basin and Its Border Lands Being the Story of Their Discovery, Exploration and Occupation. London: 1905. V. 53

DAWSON, SARAH MORGAN
A Confederate Girl's Diary. Boston: 1913. V. 50

DAWSON, SIMON J.
Report of the Exploration of the Country Between Lake Superior and the Red River Settlement, and Between the Latter Place and the Assiniboine and Saskatchewan. Toronto: 1859. V. 48; 51; 52; 54

DAWSON, THOMAS
Memoirs of St. George, the English Patron; and of the Most Noble Order of the Garter. London: 1714. V. 52; 53

DAWSON, THOMAS F.
The Ute War: a History of the White River Massacre and the Privations and Hardships of the Captive White Women Among the Hostilities on Grand River... Denver: 1879. V. 54

DAWSON, WARREN R.
Catalogue of Egyptian Antiquities in the British Museum I (only): mummies and Human Remains. London: 1968. V. 49
A Leechbook or Collection of Medicinal Recipes of the Fifteenth Century. London: 1934. V. 52
Magician and Leech: a Study in the Beginnings of Medicine with Special Reference to Ancient Egypt. London: 1929. V. 52
The Nelson Collection at Lloyds. London: 1932. V. 49

DAWSON, WILLIAM
The Borderland Illustrated, and the Anglers' Hand-Book to the Rivers and Streams of the Borders, Merse and Lammermuirs. Newcastle-on-Tyne: 1892. V. 47

DAWSON, WILLIAM, & SONS, LTD.
Medicine and Science: a Bibliographical Catalogue of Historical and Rare Books from the 15th to the 20th Century;. London: 1958. V. 49; 50

DAWSON, WILLIAM & SONS, LTD.
Medicine and Science: a Bibliographical Catalogue of Historical and Rare Books from the 15th to the 20th Century. Catalogue No. 91. London: 1956. V. 52
Medicine and Science. A Bibliographical Catalogue of Historical and Rare Books from the 15th to the 20th Century. Catalogue No. 91. London: 1962. V. 51

DAWSON, WILLIAM F.
Christmas: Its Origin and Associations, Together With Its Historical Events and Festive Celebrations During Eighteen Centuries. London: 1902. V. 51

DAWSON, WILLIAM HARBUTT
History of Skipton. Skipton: 1882. V. 47; 53

DAWSON, WILLIAM LEON
The Birds of California. San Diego: 1923. V. 48; 51; 52; 53; 54
The Birds of Ohio. Columbus: 1903. V. 50; 51

DAY, C. L.
English song-Books 1651-1702. London: 1940. V. 48

DAY, F.
British and Irish Salmonidae. London: 1887. V. 48; 50; 51; 54
The Fishes of Great Britain and Ireland. London: 1880-84. V. 52
The Fishes of India. London: 1958. V. 54

DAY, HAROLD
East Anglian Painters. 1969. V. 50
Suffolk School of Painters - the Norwich School of Painters. 1971/79. V. 50

DAY, HORACE B.
The Opium Habit, with Suggestions as to the Remedy. New York: 1868. V. 52

DAY, J. WENTWORTH
Here Are Ghosts and Witches. London: 1954. V. 50

DAY, JAMES M.
The Map Collection of the Texas State Archives. Austin: 1964. V. 53
Texas Almanac: 1857-1873, A Compendium of Texas History. Waco: 1967. V. 52; 53

DAY, JEREMIAH
An Inquiry Respecting the Self-Determining Power of the Will; or Convergent Volition. New Haven: 1838. V. 47; 48; 49
An Introduction to Algebra, Being the First Part of a Course of Mathematics Adapted to the Method of Instruction in the Higher Schools and Academies in the United States. New Haven: 1819. V. 53
A Practical Application of the Principles of Geometry to the Mensuration of Superficies and Solids. New Haven: 1811. V. 54

DAY, L. MEEKER
The Improved American Family Physician; or, Sick Man's Guide to Health... (with) The. New York: 1833/33. V. 50

DAY, LEWIS F.
Art in Needlework, A Book About Embroidery. London: 1900. V. 50
Nature in Ornament. London: 1902. V. 52
Penmanship of the XVI, XVII and XVIIIth Centuries. London. V. 50

DAY, LUELLA
The Tragedy of the Klondike: This Book of Travels Gives the True Facts Of What Took Place in the Gold-Fields Under British Rule. New York: 1906. V. 47; 53

DAY, MATTHEW
(Greek, then) sive Excerpta in Sex Priores Homeri Iliados Libros. London: 1652. V. 50

DAY, RICHARD
A Booke of Christian Prayers, Collected Out of the Ancient Writers, and Best Learned in Our Time, Worthy to be Read with an Earnest Mind of all Christians, in These Dangerous and Troublesome Daies, that God for Christes sake will yet be mercifull Unto Us. London: 1590. V. 47

DAY, SAMUEL PHILLIPS
Down South; or, an Englishman's Experience at the Seat of the American War. London: 1862. V. 53

DAY, T. A.
Illustrations of Mediaeval Costume in England... London: 1851. V. 51; 54

DAY, THOMAS
The Dying Negro, a Poem. London: 1775. V. 50
The History of Sandford and Merton. London: 1783-86-89. V. 47
The History of Sandford and Merton. London: 1786-89. V. 48
The History of Sandford and Merton. London: 1787-88-89. V. 50
The History of Sandford and Merton. London: 1812. V. 53
The History of Sandford and Merton. Baltimore: 1816. V. 49
The History of Sandford and Merton. London: 1816. V. 53
Reflexions Upon the Present State of England, and the Independence of America. London: 1782. V. 48

DAY, WILLIAM
The Racehorse in Training. London: 1925. V. 48
The Shepherd's Boy: Being Pastoral Tales... London: 1804. V. 50

DAYES, EDWARD
A Picturesque Tour in Yorkshire and Derbyshire. V. 47
A Picturesque Tour in Yorkshire and Derbyshire. London: 1825. V. 50; 53
The Works of... London: 1805. V. 53

DAY-LEWIS, CECIL
Beechen Vigil and Other Poems. London: 1925. V. 48; 50; 53
Collected Poems - 1929-1933 - Transitional Poem. London: 1935. V. 52
Country Comets. London: 1928. V. 51
From Feathers to Iron. London: 1931. V. 51
The Magnetic Mountain. London: 1933. V. 51
The Mind in Chains - Socialism and the Cultural Revolution. London: 1937. V. 50
Noah and the Waters. London: 1936. V. 54
A Penknife in My Heart. New York: 1958. V. 52
Poems in Wartime. London: 1940. V. 54
Posthumous Poems. London: 1979. V. 52
The Room and Other Poems. London: 1965. V. 50
Ten Singers: an Anthology. London: 1924. V. 53
Transitional Poem. London: 1929. V. 51
The Whispering Roots - Poems. London: 1970. V. 50
Word Over All. London: 1943. V. 54

THE DAYS of Old and Days of Gold British Columbia. Victoria: 1912. V. 52

DAYS of the Dandies. London. V. 47; 54

DAYS On the Hill by an Old Stalker. London: 1926. V. 52; 54

DAYSH, G. H. J.
A Survey of Whitby and the Surrounding Area. Eton: 1958. V. 47

DAYTON, EDSON C.
Dakota Days, May 1886-Aug. 1898. 1937. V. 53
Dakota Days, May 1886-Aug. 1898. Hartford: 1937. V. 49

D'AZEVEDO, WARREN L.
Straight with the Medicine: Narratives of the Washoe Followers of the Tipi Way. Reno: 1978. V. 50

DAZZI, ROMANO
Self-Development in Drawing as Interpreted by the Genius of Romano Dazzi and Other Children. New York, London: 1928. V. 49

DE BALNEIS Omnia Quae Extant Apud Graecos, Latinos et Arabas... Venice: 1553. V. 48

DE LA BECHE, HENRY T.
Geological Notes. London: 1830. V. 54
The Geological Observer. London: 1851. V. 51; 52; 53
The Geological Observer. London: 1853. V. 47; 48; 50; 53
A Selection of Geological Memoirs Contained in the Annales des Mines... London: 1836. V. 51

DE LA COMBE DE VRIGNY
Travels through Denmark and Some Parts of Germany... London: 1707. V. 47

DE LA CRUZ, MARTIN
The Badianus Manuscript...An Aztec Herbal of 1552. Baltimore: 1940. V. 48
Libellus de Medincalibus Indorum Herbs. Mexico: 1964. V. 48

DE LA FAILLE, J. B.
The Works of Vincent Van Gogh. New York: 1970. V. 47; 51; 54

DE LA MARE, WALTER
Alone. London: 1927. V. 49
Broomsticks and Other Tales. London: 1925. V. 47
The Burning Glass, and Other Poems. London: 1945. V. 50
The Burning Glass and Other Poems. 1955. V. 54
The Captive and other Poems. New York: 1928. V. 47
Come Hither. London: 1928. V. 51
Desert Islands and Robinson Crusoe. London & New York: 1930. V. 47; 48; 49; 51; 54
Ding Dong Bell. London: 1924. V. 47; 50; 51; 52
Flora: a Book of Drawings. London: 1919. V. 48
Flora Book of Drawings...with Illustrative Poems. London. V. 47; 49

DE LA MARE, WALTER continued
Henry Brocken His Travels and Adventures in the Rich, Strange, Scarce-Imaginable Regions of Romance. London: 1904. V. 51
The Hostage. 1925. V. 49
Lispet, Lispett and Vaine. London: 1923. V. 49
The Lord Fish. London: 1933. V. 50
Memoirs of a Midget. London: 1921. V. 47; 49; 52; 53
The Morrow (and the Sun). Bath: 1955. V. 50
Peacock Pie. London: 1913. V. 54
Peacock Pie. New York: 1924. V. 50
Peacock Pie. London: 1946. V. 47
Poems. London: 1906. V. 48
Poems. London: 1937. V. 47
Poems for Children. London: 1930. V. 49
Poems for Children. New York: 1930. V. 50
The Printing of Poetry. Cambridge: 1931. V. 51
The Riddle and Other Stories. London: 1923. V. 48
Seven Short Stories. London: 1931. V. 49; 50
Songs of Childhood. London: 1902. V. 47; 50; 53
Songs of Childhood. London: 1923. V. 47; 50
Songs of Our Grandfathers: Re-set in Guinness Time. Dublin: 1936. V. 53
Stories From the Bible. London: 1929. V. 48
Stuff and Nonsense and So On. London: 1927. V. 47; 51
The Sunken Garden and other Poems. London: 1917. V. 47; 52
This Year: Next Year. London: 1937. V. 51
The Three Mulla-Mulgars. London: 1910. V. 47; 54
Two Poems. (Come! The Strange Spirit). London: 1931. V. 50
The Veil and Other Poems. London: 1921. V. 49; 53
The Veil and Other Poems. London: 1922. V. 51

DE LA MAYNE, THOMAS HALLIE
Love and Honour. London: 1742. V. 48
The Senators: or, a Candid Examinataion into the Merits of the Principal Performers of St. Stephen's Chapel. London: 1772. V. 48

DE LA MERE, HENRY
The Charger to the Grand Jury Held for the Country of Chester on the 25th Day of April 1693. London: 1694. V. 50
The Late Lord Russel's Case with Observations Upon It. London: 1689. V. 50

DE LA MOTTE, FREEMAN GAGE
Primer of the Art of Illumination for the Use of Beginners... London: 1860. V. 50

DE LA MOTTE, GUILLAUME
Traite Complete des Accouchemens Naturels, non Nataurels, et Contre Nature... Paris: 1721. V. 49

DE LA RAMEE, LOUISE
Critical Studies. London: 1900. V. 53
Idalia. London: 1867. V. 53
In Maremma. London: 1882. V. 54
Othmar. London: 1885. V. 50
Pascarel. London: 1873. V. 49
Ruffino &c. London: 1890. V. 51

DE LA ROCHE, JACQUELEIN
Memoirs of the Marchioness. Edinburgh: 1827. V. 54

DE LA ROCHE, MAZZO
Whiteoaks of Jalna. Boston: 1929. V. 53

DE LA RUE, WARREN
Researches on Solar Physics. London: 1865-73. V. 51

DE L' ISLE, GUILLAUME
Nouvelle Introduction a La Geographie. Amsterdam: 1730. V. 48

DE L' ISLE-ADAM, JEAN DE VILLIERS, COUNT
Axel. London: 1925. V. 48

DE LISLE DE SALES, JEAN CLAUDE
C. G. Lamoignon Malesherbes, Formerly First President of the Court of Aids, and Minister of State; Member of the Academy, &c. Edinburgh: 1804. V. 48

DE L' ORME, PHILIBERT
L'Oeuvre de Philibert de L'Orme. Paris: 1894. V. 51

DEACON, S.
An Attempt to Answer the Important Question, What Must I Do to Be Saved?. Pittsburgh: 1826. V. 54

DEACON, WILLIAM F.
Adventures of a Bashful Irishman. London: 1856?. V. 51

THE DEAD Sea Scrolls. New York: 1966. V. 54

DEAD Sea Scrolls. Westerham: 1966. V. 50; 52; 53

DEADRICK, WILLIAM
The Endemic Diseases of the Southern States. Philadelphia: 1916. V. 48; 51; 53

DEAGON, ANN
Indian Summer. Greensboro: 1975. V. 51

DEAKIN, EDWIN
The Twenty-One Missions of California. Berkeley: 1899. V. 54

DEAKIN, RICHARD
Florigraphia Britannica; or, Engravings and Descriptions of the Flowering Plants & Ferns of Britain. London: 1841-48. V. 51
The Flowering Plants of Tunbridge Wells and Neighbourhood. Tunbridge Wells: 1871. V. 54

DEAM, C. C.
Flora of Indiana. Indianapolis: 1940. V. 54

DEAN, B.
A Bibliography of Fishes. New York: 1916-23. V. 47

DEAN, BASHFORD
Catalogue of European Court Swords and Hunting Swords (and) Catalogue of European Daggers. New York: 1929. V. 47
Catalogue of European Daggers 1300-1800. Catalogue of European Court Swords and Hunting Swords. New York: 1929. V. 48

DEAN, G. A.
A Series of Selected Designs for Country Residences. Worthing: 1867. V. 49

DEAN, HENRY
Dean's Analytical Guide to th Art of Penmanship, Containing a Variety of Plates in Which are Exhibited a Complete System of Practical Penmanship... New York: 1808. V. 48
The Whole Art of Legerdemain; or, Hocus Pocus in Perfection. London: 1781. V. 53

DEAN, JAMES
An Alphabetical Atlas, or, Gazetteer of Vermont... Montpelier: 1808. V. 47; 50; 52

DEAN, JOHN WARD
A Memoir of the Rev. Nathaniel Ward, A. M., Author of the Simple Cobbler of Agawam in America. Albany: 1868. V. 48

DEAN, MALLETTE
The Duchow Journal: a Voyage from Boston to California, 1852. Fairfax: 1959. V. 52

DEAN, RICHARD
An Essay on the Future Life of Brute Creatures. London: 1768. V. 47

DEAN, W. G.
Economic Atlas of Ontario. Toronto: 1969. V. 50

DEANE, A. L.
A Guide to Atlantic and Pacific Rail-Road Lands. 1,200,000 Acres for Sale. St. Louis: 1875. V. 47

DEANE, ANN
A Tour through the Upper Provinces of Hindostan; Comprising a Period Between the Years 1804 and 1814. London: 1823. V. 50; 51; 52

DEANE, SAMUEL
The New England Farmer... Worcester: 1790. V. 52; 54
The New-England Farmer; or, Georgical Dictionary. Worcester: 1797. V. 48; 49
The New-England Farmer; or Georgical Dictionary. Boston: 1822. V. 52

DE ANGULO, JAIME
Indian Tales. New York: 1953. V. 50

DEANS, JAMES
Tales from the Totems of the Hidery. Chicago: 1899. V. 48

DEAN'S Moveable Book of Children's Sports and Pastimes. London: 1859. V. 52

DEAN'S New Book of Dissolving Views. London: 1862. V. 49

DEANS, WILLIAM
History of the Ottoman Empire, from the Earliest Period to the Present Time. London: 1854. V. 53

DEAR Alec...A Tribute for His (Alec Robertson's) Eightieth Birthday from His Friends Known and Unknown. Worcester: 1972. V. 48; 54

DEARBORN, F. M.
American Homeopathy in the World War. London: 1923. V. 47

DEARBORN, HENRY
Revolutionary War Journals of Henry Dearborn 1775-1783. Chicago: 1939. V. 49; 52

DEARDEN, ROBERT R.
An Original Leaf from the Bible of the Revolution. San Francisco: 1930. V. 48; 53; 54

DEARDON, ROBERT J.
An Original Leaf from the Bible of the Revolution and an Essay concerning It... San Francisco: 1930. V. 49

DEARING, J. S.
A Drummer's Experiences. Colorado Springs: 1913. V. 51

DEARMER, MABEL
The Cockiolly Bird. New York: 1914. V. 49
Round-About-Rhymes. London: 1900. V. 50

DE ARMOND, DALE
Raven: a Collection of Woodcuts. Anchorage: 1975. V. 50

DEARN, THOMAS DOWNES WILMOT
Hints on an Improved Method of Building; Applicable to General Purposes. London: 1821. V. 52
An Historical Topographical and Descriptive Account of the Weald of Kent. Cranbrook: 1814. V. 47; 49; 53

DEAS, F. T. R.
The Young Tea-Planter's Companion... London: 1886. V. 49

DEASE, EDMUND F.
A Complete History of the Westmeath Hunt from the Foundation... Dublin: 1898. V. 47; 51

DEASE, WILLIAM
Remarks on Medical Jurisprudence, Intended for the General Information of Juries and Young Students. Dublin: 1793. V. 50

DEATH and Burial of Poor Cock Robin. New York: 1864. V. 48

DEATH Blow to Corrupt Doctrines. A Plain Statement of Facts, Published by the Gentry and People. Shanghai: 1870. V. 53

DEATH in the Air - the War Diary and Photographs of a Flying Corps Pilot. London: 1933. V. 47

DEATHERAGE, CHARLES P.
Early History of Greater Kansas City, Missouri and Kansas. Kansas City: 1927. V. 49; 53

DEATH'S Doings. London: 1827. V. 54

DEAVER, JOHN B.
The Breast: Its Anomalies, Its Diseases and Their Treatment. Philadelphia: 1917. V. 48
Enlargement of the Prostate: Its History, Anatomy, Etiology, Pathology, Clinical Causes, Symptons, Diagnosis, Prognosis, Treatment... Philadelphia: 1922. V. 53

DEAVILLE, ALFRED STANLEY
The Colonial Postal Systems and Postage Stamps of Vancouver Island and British Columbia, 1849-1871. Victoria: 1928. V. 50

DE BACA, MANUEL C.
Vicente Silva and His 40 Bandits. Washington: 1947. V. 49

DE BARTHE, JOE
The Life and Adventure sof Frank Grouard, Chief of Scouts. St. Joseph: 1894. V. 54

DEBATE On Censorship Books. New York: 1924. V. 50

DEBATE on the Evidence of Christianity;...Between Robert Owen, of New Lanark, Scotland and Alexander Campbell, of Bethany, Virginia. Bethany: 1829. V. 52

DE BAUSSET, ARTHUR
Aerial Navigation on the Vacuum Principle. Lowell: 1889. V. 53

DE BAZANCOURT, BARON
Secrets of the Sword. London & New York: 1900. V. 52

DE BECK, WILLIAM L.
Murder Will Out. Cincinnati: 1867. V. 50

DE BEER, G. R.
Alps and Men: Pages from Forgotten Diaries of Travellers and Tourists in Switzerland. 1932. V. 53

DE BELLIS, JACK
John Updike: a Bibliography, 1967-1993. Westport: 1994. V. 52

DEBENHAM, FRANK
Navigation with Alice. London: 1961. V. 50

DE BERNIERES, LOUIS
Captain Corelli's Mandolin. London: 1994. V. 52; 53
Senor Vino and the Coca Lord. London: 1991. V. 52; 53
The War of Don Emmanuel's Nether Parts. London: 1990. V. 52; 53

DEBES, LUCAS JACOBSON
Faeroae, & Faeroa Reserata: That Is a Description of the Islands and Inhabitants of Foeroe... London: 1676. V. 47

DE BISSCHOP, JAN
Paradigmata Graphices Variorum Artificum. 1680. V. 50

DE BLANCOURT, FRANCOIS HAUDICQUER
The Art of Glass. London: 1699. V. 48; 50

DE BLEGNY, ETIENNE
Les Elemens ov Premieres Instructions de la Jeunesse. Paris: 1702. V. 49

DEBO, ANGIE
The Road to Disappearance. Norman: 1941. V. 50; 54

DE BODE, C. A., BARON
Travels in Luristan and Arabistan. London: 1845. V. 49

DEBOE, ANGIE
The Cowman's Southwest, Being the Reminiscences of Oliver Nelson, Freighter Camp Cook, Cowboy, Frontersman in Kansas, Indian Territory, Texas and Oklahaoma 1878-93. Glendale: 1953. V. 53

DE BOMARE, M. VALMONT
Dictionnaire Raisonee Universel D'Historie Naturelle... Paris: 1764. V. 49; 53

DE BOSGUERARD, MARIE
Les Amusements de Nos Tout Petits. Paris: 1910. V. 49

DE BOSSCHERE, JEAN
Marthe and the Madman. New York: 1928. V. 48

DE BOSSET, CHARLES PHILIP
Parga, and the Ionian Islands... London: 1821. V. 47

DE BOW, JAMES D. B.
The Interest in Slavery of the Southern Non-Slaveholder. Charleston: 1860. V. 47; 49
Produce Loan-Instructions. Jackson: 1862. V. 49

DE BREBEUF, JEAN
The Travels and Sufferings of Father Jean de Brebeuf Among the Hurons of Canada as Described by Himself. London: 1938. V. 47

DEBRETT, JOHN
The Baronetage of England...A New Genealogical History... London: 1806. V. 54
The Court Companion, Containing the Arms of the Peers, Perreses and Bishops of the United Kingdom. London: 1803. V. 54

DEBRETT'S Correct Peerage of England, Scotland and Ireland With the Extinct and Forfeited Peerages of the Three Kingdoms. London: 1806. V. 48; 54

DEBRETT'S Peerage, Baronetage, Knightage, and Companionage. London: 1900. V. 50

DEBS, EUGENE V.
Debs: His Life, Writings and Speeches. Girard: 1908. V. 50

DE BUCK, ADRIAAN
The Egyptian Coffin Texts I: Texts of Spells 1-75. Chicago: 1935. V. 49
The Egyptian Coffin Texts II (only): Text of Spells 76-163. Chicago: 1938. V. 49
The Egyptian Coffin Texts III: Texts of Spells. Chicago: 1947. V. 49; 51
The Egyptian Coffin Texts V: Texts of Spells 355-471. Chicago: 1954. V. 49

DE BURGH, ULICK
Memoirs of the Right Honourable the Marquis of Clanrickarde, Lord Deputy General of Ireland... London: 1722. V. 48

DE BURGH, ULICK H. H.
The Landowners of Ireland. Dublin: 1878. V. 52

DEBUS, ALLEN G.
Science, Medicine and Society in the Renaissance. Essays to Honor Walter Pagel. New York: 1972. V. 54
World Who's Who in Science, a Biographical Dictionary of Notable Scientists from Antiquity to the Present. Chicago: 1968. V. 49; 51

DE CAMP, L. SPRAGUE
Demons and Dinosaurs. Sauk City: 1970. V. 51; 52
Divide and Rule. 1948. V. 47; 48; 51
Fantasy Twin. Los Angeles: 1953. V. 51
Footprints on Sand. 1981. V. 51
A Gun for Dinosaur and Other Imaginative Tales. Garden City: 1963. V. 49; 51; 54
Land of Unreason. 1942. V. 49; 54
Lest Darkness Fall. 1941. V. 48; 51
Sir Harold and the Gnome King. 1991. V. 52
Solomon's Stone. 1957. V. 51
The Tritonian Ring. New York: 193. V. 51
Wall of Serpents. 1960. V. 47; 48; 51; 52
Wall of Serpents. New York: 1960. V. 51

DECARAVA, ROY
The Sweet Flapper. New York: 1955. V. 47

DECAROLI, P. D. F.
Ammaestramenti Teoricopratici Inderizzati ad Agevolare il Modo d'Imparare da per se la Scrittura Moderna. Torino: 1772. V. 53

DECASTRO, JACOB
The Memoirs of J. Decastro, Comedian... London: 1824. V. 51

DE CASTRO, JOHN P.
The Law and Practice of Hall-Marking Gold and Silver Wares. London: 1926. V. 51

DECAY of Trade. A Treatise Against the Abating of Interest. London: 1641. V. 53

DE CHAIR, SOMERSET STRUBEN
The First Crusade. 1945. V. 47
The First Crusade. Waltham St. Lawrence: 1945. V. 50; 52
The Golden Carpet. London: 1943. V. 47; 50
The Silver Crescent. London: 1943. V. 47; 50; 52
The Silver Crescent. Waltham St. Lawrence: 1943. V. 47; 51
The Story of a Lifetime. Waltham St. Lawrence: 1954. V. 49

DECHARME, PAUL
Euripides and the Spirit of His Dramas. New York: 1906. V. 52; 54

DE CHIRICO, GIORGIO
Hebdomeros. New York: 1966. V. 54

DECHY, MORIZ VON KAUKASUS
Reisen und Forschungen im Kaukasischen Hochgebirge... Berlin: 1905. V. 50

THE DECISIVE Trial; or, the Proceedings in the Court of Common Sense, Between the Supporters of the Bill of the Rights and the Petitioners of Middlesex, London and Surry, Plaintiffs; and the Present Administration, Defendants. London: 1769. V. 48

DECIUS, PHILIPPUS
De Regulis Iuris. Cologne: 1598. V. 49

DECKER, MATTHEW
An Essay on the Causes of the Decline of the Foreign Trade, Consequently of the Value of the Lands of Britain, and on the means to Restore Both. London: 1750. V. 53

DECKER, PETER
A Descriptive Check List Together With Short Title Index Describing Almost 7500 Items of Western Americana...Formed by George W. Soliday. New York: 1960. V. 48
Peter Decker's Catalogues of Rare Americana, 1944-1963. Austin: 1980. V. 47

DECKER, THOMAS
The Gull's Hornbook. Bristol: 1812. V. 50

DECLARATION of Sentiments of the American Anti-Slavery Society. Adopted at the Formation of Said Society, in Philadelphia, on the 4th Day of December, 1833. New York: 1833. V. 48

THE DECLARATION of the County of Oxon to His Excellencie The Lord General Monck. London: 1660. V. 47

A DECLARATION of the General Council of the Officers of the Army; Agreed Upon at Wallingford-House, 27th Oct. 1659... London: 1659. V. 47

THE DECLARATION of the Levellers Concerning Prince Charles, and Their Treaty with His Excellency the Lord General Fairfax... London: 1649. V. 50

A DECLARATION of the Parliament of England, Concerning a Paper Subscriber by the Commissioners of Scotland, Dated 24 Febr. 1648/9. And Sent in a Letter to Mr. speaker to be Communicated to the House. London: 1648. V. 47

A DECLARATION Of the Variance Betweene the Pope, and the Seignory of Venice. 1606. V. 50

DECLE, LIONEL
Three Years in Savage Africa. London: 1898. V. 50

DE CLIFFORD, NORMAN FREDERICK
Egypt the Cradle of Ancient Masonry... Philadelphia: 1902. V. 48; 51

DE COCK, L.
Ansel Adams. 1972. V. 52

DE COETLOGON, CHARLES EDWARD
The Temple of Truth; or, the Best System of Reason, Philosophy, Virtue and Morals... London: 1806. V. 48; 52

DECORATOR'S SUPPLY CO., CHICAGO
Illustrated Catalogue of Plastic Ornaments Cast in Plaster for Interiors & in Composition for Exteriors, Mfg. by the Decorator's Supply Co. Chicago: 1890. V. 48

DE CORDOVA, JACOB
Lecture on Texas: Also a Paper Read by Him Before the New York Geographical Society. Philadelphia: 1858. V. 49
The Texas Immigrant and Traveller's Guide Book... Austin: 1856. V. 49

DE CORDOVA, RAFAEL J.
The Prince's Visit; a Humorous Description of the Tour of His Royal Highness, The Prince of Wales, Through the United States of America, in 1860. New York: 1861. V. 49

DE COSTER, CHARLES
Marvelous Adventures and Rare Conceits of Master Tyll Owlglass. London: 1860. V. 51

DE COU, S. ELLA
The Genealogy of the DeCou Family. 1910?. V. 47; 49; 51

DECRETALES
Gregorii Papae IX. Venice: 1600. V. 52; 54

DE CUGIS, CARLO
England and Italy a Century Ago. 1967. V. 53

DEDHAM Pottery Formerly Known as Chelsea Pottery U.S. A Short History. Boston: 1898. V. 51

DE DIEU, LODOVIC
Historia Christi Persica. Leyden: 1639. V. 50

DEE, ARTHUR
Fasciculus Chemicus; or Chymical Collections. London: 1650. V. 52

DEE, JOHN
A True and Faithful Relation of What Passed for Many Years Between Dr. John Dee and Some Spirits. London: 1659. V. 50
A True and Faithful Relation of What Passed for Many Years Between Dr. John Dee...and Some Spirits... Glasgow: 1974. V. 48

DEEMS, TAYLOR
The Nutcracker Suite from Walt Disney's Fantasia. London: 1940's. V. 51

DEERING, JOHN RICHARD
Lee and His Cause, or the Why and How of the War Between the States. New York and Washington: 1907. V. 51

THE DEESIDE Guide: Descriptive with Traditionary with Photographs and Tourist's Map... Aberdeen: 1885. V. 52; 54

DEFEBAUGH, JAMES ELLIOTT
History of the Lumber Industry of America. Chicago: 1906-07. V. 52

DEFENCE of the Principles of the Equitable Loan Bank and Mont de Piete, Against the Attacks of the Meeting of Pawnbrokers. London: 1824. V. 50

A DEFENCE of True Protestants, Abused for the Service of Popery, Under the Name of Presbyterians. London: 1680. V. 53

DEFENDERS and Offenders. New York: 1885. V. 52

THE DEFENSE of Gracchus Babeuf Before the High Court of Vendome. Northampton: 1964. V. 47; 52

DEFIANCE MACHINE WORKS
Illustrated Descriptive Catalogue Patent Labor-Saving Wood-Working Machinery. 1899. V. 51

DE FILIPPI, FILIPPO
The Ascent of Mount St. Elias (Alaska) by H. R. H. Prince Luigi Amedeo Di Savoia Duke of the Abruzzi. Westminster: 1900. V. 48

Ruwenzori An Account of the Expedition of H.R.H. Prince Lugigi Amedeo of Savoy... New York: 1908. V. 50

DEFOE, DANIEL
Adventures of Robinson Crusoe. London. V. 48
An Answer to the Late K. James's Last Declaration dated at St. Germains, April 17. London: 1693. V. 53
A Brief Reply to the History of Standing Armies in England. London: 1698. V. 52
Caledonia, a Poem in Honour of Scotland, and the Scots Nation. Edinburgh: 1706. V. 50
A Collection of the Writings of the Author of the True-Born Englishman... London: 1703. V. 49
The Compleat English Gentleman. London: 1890. V. 49
A Compleat System of Magick; or, a History of the Black Art. London: 1727. V. 54
A Compleat System of Magick; or the History of the Black Art. London: 1729. V. 54
Conjugal Lewdness; or Matrimonial Whoredom. London: 1728. V. 48
The Consolidator: or, Memoirs of Sundry Transactions from the World in the Moon. London: 1705. V. 48; 53
A Defence of the Allies and the Late Ministry: or, Remarks on the Tories New Idol. London: 1712. V. 49
The Dreadful Visitation, in a Short Account of the Progress and Effects of the Plague, the Last Time it Spread in the City of London, in the Year 1665... Philadelphia: 1774. V. 50
Eleven Opinions About Mr. H-----y; With Observations. London: 1711. V. 48; 49
The Fortunes and Misfortunes of Moll Flanders. New York: 1954. V. 51; 54
The Fortunes and Misfortunes...Moll Flanders. London: 1929. V. 47
The Four Years Voyages of Capt. George Roberts... London: 1726. V. 47; 51
A Further Search into the Conduct of the Allies and the Late Ministry, As to Peace and War. London: 1712. V. 53
A General History of the Pyrates, from Their First Rise and Settlement in the Island of Providence, to the Present Time. London: 1724. V. 50
A General History of the Robberies and Murders of the Most Notorious Pyrates, and also Their Policies, Discipline and Government... London: 1724. V. 51
The History of Mademoiselle de Beleau; or, the New Roxana, the Fortunate Mistress... London: 1775. V. 54
The History of the Devil. London: 1727. V. 54
The History of the Devil. Berwick: 1794. V. 47
The History of the Kentish Petition. 1701. V. 52
The History of the Life and Adventures of Mr. Duncan Campbell... London: 1720. V. 49; 50; 54
The History of the Union Between England and Scotland, with a Collection of Original Papers Relating Thereto and an Introduction. London: 1786. V. 47
An Impartial History of the Life and Actions of Peter Alexowitz, the Present Czar. London: 1722. V. 53
Impeachment or No Impeachment: or, an Enquiry How Far the Impeachment of Certain Persons at the Present Juncture, Would be Consistent with Honour and Justice. London: 1714. V. 53
A Journal of the Plague Year. Oxford: 1928. V. 52
A Journal of the Plague Year, &c. Bloomfield: 1968. V. 53
Jure Divino: a Satyr. London: 1706. V. 47; 48; 50
Jure Divino: a Satyr. London: 1756. V. 49
A Letter from a Gentleman at the Court of St. Germains, to One of His Friends in England... London: 1710. V. 49
A Letter from a Gentleman at the Court of St. Germains, to One of His Friends in England. London: 1715. V. 52
A Letter from a Gentleman in Scotland to His Friend at London. London: 1712. V. 47
The Life, Adventures and Pyracies, of the Famous Captain Singleton... London: 1720. V. 50
The Life and Adventures of Robinson Crusoe. London: 1781. V. 49
The Life and Adventures of Robinson Crusoe. London: 1804. V. 47
The Life and Adventures of Robinson Crusoe. London: 1831. V. 47; 53
The Life and Adventures of Robinson Crusoe. London: 1840. V. 53
The Life and Adventures of Robinson Crusoe. London: 1864. V. 47
The Life and Adventures of Robinson Crusoe. London: 1882. V. 54
The Life and Adventures of Robinson Crusoe. London: 1883. V. 49
The Life and Most Surprising Adventures of Robinson Crusoe. London: 1722. V. 51
The Life and Strange Surprising Adventures (and Farther Adventures) of Robinson Crusoe, of York, Mariner. London: 1772. V. 48
The Life, and Strange Surprising Adventures of Robinson Crusoe. London: 1719. V. 47
The Life and Strange Surprising Adventures of Robinson Crusoe. London: 1719-20. V. 48; 49; 50; 51; 52
The Life and Strange Surprising Adventures of Robinson Crusoe. London: 1784. V. 52
The Life and Strange Surprising Adventures of Robinson Crusoe... London: 1869. V. 51
The Life and Strange Surprising Adventures of Robinson Crusoe. London: 1929. V. 48
The Life and Strange Surprising Adventures of Robinson Crusoe. New York: 1930. V. 48
Life and Strange Surprising Adventures of Robinson Crusoe. Mount Vernon: 1945. V. 51
The Life and Strange Surprising Adventures of Robinson Crusoe. London: 1979. V. 47
The Life and Surprising Adventures of Robinson Crusoe. London: 1790. V. 49
The Life and Surprising Adventures of Robinson Crusoe. London: 1820. V. 51; 54
The Life and Surprising Adventures of Robinson Crusoe. New York: 1884. V. 51
The Life and Surprising Adventures of Robinson Crusoe. London: 1929. V. 48; 49; 50; 51; 52
The Life and Surprising Adventures of Robinson Crusoe Embellished with Eight Elegant Engravings. Glasgow: 1825. V. 49
The Life, Remarkable Adventures and Pyracies, of Captain Singleton... London: 1768. V. 54
Madagascar: or Robert Drury's Journal, During Fifteen Years Captivity on that Island... London: 1729. V. 48; 51
The Meditations of Daniel Defoe. Cummington: 1946. V. 54
Memoirs of a Cavalier... London: 1720. V. 48; 49
The Memoirs of Cap. George Carleton, an English Officer, Who severed in the Last Two Wars Against France and Spain and Was Present in Several Engagements, Both in the Fleet and Army. London: 1743. V. 47

DEFOE, DANIEL continued
Memoirs of Capt. George Carleton, an English Officer... Edinburgh: 1808. V. 50; 51
Minutes of Negotiations of Monsr. Mesnager at the Court of England, Towards the Close of the Last Reign. London: 1717. V. 47; 48; 49
Minutes of the Negotiation of Mons. Mesnager at the Court of England, During the Four Last Years of...Q. Anne. London: 1736. V. 49
A New Test of the Church of England's Loyalty. London: 1702. V. 48; 53
A New Test of the Church of England's Loyalty... Edinburgh: 1703. V. 53
A New Voyage Round the World, by a Course Never Sailed Before. London: 1725. V. 47; 48; 50
A New Voyage Round the World, by a Course Never Sailed Before. London: 1725/24. V. 50
No Queen: or, No General. An Argument, Proving the Necessity Her Majesty Was In, as Well for the Safety of Her Person as of Her Authority, to Displace the D— of M—borough. London: 1712. V. 48; 51; 52
The Novels. Edinburgh: 1810. V. 51; 52
The Novels and Selected Writings of Daniel Defoe. Stratford-upon-Avon: 1928. V. 48; 49; 52; 54
Peace Without Union. London: 1704. V. 53
A Plan of the English Commerce. London: 1728. V. 53
The Political History of the Devil, as Well Ancient as Modern. London: 1726. V. 48; 52
The Political History of the Devil, as Well Ancient as Modern. New York: 1841. V. 49
The Present State of Jacobitism Considered in Two Querys. London: 1701. V. 54
The Pretences of the French Invasion Examined. London: 1692. V. 48
Reflections Up on the Late Great Revolution. London: 1689. V. 48; 51; 53
Robinson Crusoe. London: 1890. V. 49
Robinson Crusoe. Paris: 1890. V. 53
Robinson Crusoe. London: 1979. V. 54
Robinson Crusoeus. Parisiis: 1810. V. 50
Robinson Crusoeus. Paris: 1813. V. 53
Roxana. Avon: 1976. V. 53
Roxana. Connecticut: 1976. V. 47; 48
The Scotch Medal Decipher'd and the New Hereditary Right Men Display'd or Remarks on the Late Proceedings of the Faculty of Advocates at Edinburgh... London: 1711. V. 48
A Seasonable Warning or the Pope and King of France Unmasked. Edinburgh: 1706. V. 47
A Seasonable Warning or the Pope and King of France Unmasked. London: 1706. V. 53
The Secret History of State Intrigues in the Management of the Scepter, in the Late Reign. London: 1715. V. 51; 52
The Secret History of the October Club. London: 1711/11. V. 48
The Secret History of the White-Staff, Being An Account of Affairs Under the Conduct of Some Late Ministers... London: 1712. V. 48
Secret Memoires of the Late Mr. Duncan Campbel, the Famus Deaf and Dumb Gentleman. London: 1732. V. 54
The Secrets of the Invisible World Disclos'd. London: 1729. V. 47
The Secrets of the Invisible World Disclos'd... London: 1735. V. 47; 48; 49
The Secrets of the Invisible World Disclos'd... London: 1738. V. 47; 49; 51
The Shakespeare Head Press Edition of the Novels and Selected Writings of Daniel Defoe. Oxford: 1927. V. 54
A Spectators Address to the Whigs, on the Occasion of the Stabing of Mr. Harley. London: 1711. V. 53
The Storm: or, A Collection of the Most Remarkable Casualties and Disasters Which Happen'd in the Late Dreadful Tempest... London: 1704. V. 47; 48; 49; 50; 52
Strike While the Iron's Hot, or, Now Is the Time to be Happy. London: 1715. V. 53
A System of Magick; or, a History of the Black Art. London: 1727. V. 48; 50
Tories and Tory Principles Ruinous to Both Prince and People. London: 1714. V. 53
A Tour Thro' the Island of Great Britain, Divided into Circuits of Journies... London: 1778. V. 52
A Tour Thro' the Whole Island of Great Britain, Divided Into Circuits of Journies. London: 1724-25-27. V. 48
A Tour thro' the Whole Island of Great Britain, Divided into Circuits of Journies. London: 1927. V. 48; 49; 52; 54
A True Collection of the Writings of the Author of the True Born Englishman. London: 1703. V. 47
The True-Born Englishman. London: 1701. V. 51
The True-Born Englishman. London: 1750. V. 54
The True-Born Englishman. London: 1796. V. 53
The True-born Englishman. London: 1810. V. 51
La Vie et Les Avantures Surprenantes de Robinson Crusoe. Amsterdam: 1720. V. 53
La Vie et Les Aventures Suprenantes de Robinson Crusoe. Paris: 1808. V. 47; 54
The Villainy of Stock-Jobbers Detected and the Causes of the Late Run Upon the Bank and Bankers Discovered and Considered. London: 1701. V. 47
The Whole Life and Strange Surprising Adventures of Robinson Crusoe, of York, Mariner. London: 1785. V. 50
The Works of Daniel Defoe. Boston: 1903. V. 47

DE FONTAINE, FELIX GREGORY
Marginalia: or, Gleanings from an Army Note-Book. Columbia: 1864. V. 49; 50; 51

DE FOREST, EFFINGHAM
The Ancestry of William Henry Moore. New York: 1938. V. 51
Moore and Allied Families. The Ancestry of William Henry Moore. New York: 1938. V. 49

DE FOREST, JOHN W.
History of the Indians of Connecticut from the Earliest Known Period to 1850. Hartford: 1851. V. 47; 54

DE FOREST, LOCKWOOD
Indian Domestic Architecture. 1885. V. 48

DE FOREST, LOUIS E.
Louisbourg Journals 1745. New York: 1932. V. 49

DE FORREST, CYRUS H.
Circular. Schedules of Distances Compiled On the Office of the General Commanding the District of New Mexico. Fort Union: 1867. V. 49

DEFOURI, JAMES H.
Historical Sketch of the Catholic Church in New Mexico. San Francisco: 1887. V. 49

DEGAS, EDGAR
Huit Sonnets. New York/Paris: 1946. V. 53

DE GELLIEU, JONAS
The Bee Preserver; or, Practical Directions for the Management and Preservation of Hives. Edinburgh & London: 1829. V. 48

DEGERING, HERMANN
Lettering: a Series of 240 plates Illustrating Modes of Writing in Western Europe From Antiquity to the End of the 18th Century. London: 1929. V. 48

DE GESVRES, MARQUIS
Case of Impotency Debated, in the Late Famous Tryal at Paris: Between the Marquis de Gesvres and His Lady, Mademoiselle de Mascranny, who After Three Years of Marriage, Commenced a Suit Against Him for Impotency (etc.). London: 1715. V. 47

DEGGE, SIMON
The Parsons Councellor, with the Law of Tithes or Tithing. London: 1681. V. 47

DE GIVRY, GILLOT
Witchcraft Magic and Alchemy. London: 1931. V. 53

DE GOLYER, E.
Across Aboriginal America. The Journey of Three Englishmen Across Texas in 1568. El Paso: 1947. V. 49; 50; 51; 54

DE GOUY, L. P.
The Derrydale Cook Book of Fish and Game. New York: 1937. V. 48; 49

DE GRAAF, REGNER
De Mulierum Organis Generationi... Leiden: 1672. V. 48

DE GRAFF, SIMON
The Modern Geometrical Stair Builder's Guide, Being a Plain practical System of hand-Railing, Embracing All Its Necessary Details... New York: 1845. V. 48

DEGRAND, PETER PAUL FRANCIS
Proceedings of the Friends of a Rail-Road to San Francisco, at their Public Meeting, Held at the U.S. Hotel in Boston, Apri 19, 1849. Boston: 1849. V. 47

DE GRAZIA, TED
De Grazia Paints Cabeza de Vaca: The First Non-Indian in Texas, New Mexico and Arizona, 1527-1536. Tucson: 1973. V. 47
De Grazia Paints the Papago Indian Legends. Tucson: 1975. V. 50
Father Junipero Serra. Los Angeles: 1970. V. 52

DEGREVANT. (ROMANCE)
Sire Degrevaunt. 1896. V. 52

DE GREY, THOMAS
The Compleat Horseman and Expert Farrier. London: 1656. V. 47

DE GROOT, HENRY
British Columbia: Its Condition and Prospects, Soil, Climate and Mineral Resources, Considered. San Francisco: 1859. V. 47; 50
Recollections of California Mining Life. San Francisco: 1884. V. 54

DEGUILEVILLE, GUILLAUME DE
The Pilgrimage of the Life of man. London: 1905. V. 48

DE HAMEL, CHRISTOPHER
Syon Abbey. The Library of the Bridgettine Nuns and the Peregrinations After the Reformation. 1991. V. 54

DE HASS, WILLS
History of the Early Settlement and Indian Wars of Western Virginia. Wheeling: 1851. V. 52; 54

DE HAVEN, TOM
Freaks' Amour. New York. V. 52

DE HEBERAY, NICOLAS
Amadis de Gaul; a Poem in Three Books... London: 1803. V. 48

DEHLI DEVELOPMENT AUTHORITY
Master Plan for Dehli. Dehli: 1962. V. 52

DEIBERT, RALPH C.
A History of the Third United States Cavalry. Harrisburg: 1933. V. 53; 54

DEIGHAN, PAUL
A Complete Treatise on Arithemtic, Rational and Practical... Dublin: 1804. V. 49

DEIGHTON, LEN
Berlin Game. New York: 1983. V. 49
Billion Dollar Brain. London: 1966. V. 49; 50; 53
Catch a Falling Spy. New York: 1976. V. 48
Close-Up. London: 1972. V. 49
Declarations of War. London: 1971. V. 49; 51; 53
An Expensive Place to Die. New York: 1967. V. 48; 52
Funeral in Berlin. London: 1964. V. 53
Hope. 1995. V. 54
Horse Under Water. London: 1963. V. 49; 50; 53
Introduction to the Adventure of the Priory School. Santa Barbara: 1985. V. 48

DEIGHTON, LEN continued
The Ipcress File. 1962. V. 53
The Ipcress File. London: 1962. V. 47; 50; 54
The Ipcress File. New York: 1963. V. 48; 51
London Dossier. London: 1967. V. 52
Mexico Set. London: 1984. V. 50
Only When I Larf. London: 1967. V. 47; 52
The Orient Flight LZ 127 - Graf Zeppelin. A Philatelic Handbook. 1980. V. 48
Ou Est Le Garlic: French Cooking in 50 Lessons. New York: 1977. V. 50
Twinkle, Twinkle, Little Spy. London: 1976. V. 49; 50
Violent Ward. 1993. V. 54
Violent Ward. Bristol: 1993. V. 51; 52
Yesterday's Spy. London: 1975. V. 49; 50

DEISCH, JOHANN ANDREAS
Vermehrte und in der Erfahrung Gegrundete Abhandlung, dass Weder die Wendung Noch Englische Zange in Allen Geburtsfallen vor Mutter und Kind Sicher Gebrauchet... Frankfurt: 1766. V. 47

DEJERINE, JOSEPH
The Psychoneuroses and Their Treatment by Psychotherapy. Philadelphia: 1913. V. 47

DE JONG, MEINDERT
Shadrach. New York: 1953. V. 49; 54

DE JONGE, N.
Forgotten Islands of Indonesia. The Art and Culture of the Southeast Mouluccas. Leiden: 1995. V. 54

DE JOUVANCOURT, HUGHES
Maurice Cullen. Montreal: 1978. V. 50

DE KAY, CHARLES
Barye: Life & Works of Antoine Louis Barye, Sculptor... New York: 1889. V. 48

DE KAY, JAMES ELLSWORTH
Annals of the Lyceum of Natural History of New York. New York: 1824. V. 50
Anniversary Address on the Progress of the Natural Sciences in the United States, Delivered Before the Lyceum of Natural History. New York: 1826. V. 49
Natural History of New York. Part One. Zoology, Mollusca & Crustacea. New York: 1843. V. 47; 48; 49; 50; 51; 53
Sketches of Turkey in 1831 and 1832. New York: 1833. V. 47; 49; 52
The Zoology of New York: Fauna: Part V: Mollusca. Albany: 1843. V. 50
The Zoology of New York or the New York Fauna: Part 1: Mammalia. Albany: 1842. V. 50; 51
The Zoology of New York or the New York Fauna; Part II: Birds. Albany: 1844. V. 49; 50; 51; 54
Zoology of New York, Or the New York Fauna. Part III. Reptiles and Amphibia. Part IV. Fishes. Albany: 1842. V. 50; 53
The Zoology of New York or the New York Fauna: Part IV: Fishes. Albany: 1842. V. 48; 50
Zoology of New York, or the New York Fauna. Part V. and VI. Albany: 1843. V. 54
Zoology of New York. Pt. 5 Mollusca and Pt. 6 Crustacea. Albany: 1843-44. V. 54
Zoology of New York. Volume I: Parts 3, 4, Reptiles, Amphibians and Fishes. Albany: 1842. V. 53

DE KIEWIET, C. W.
Dufferin-Carnarvon Correspondence 1874-1878. Toronto: 1955. V. 51

DEKKER, P. M.
Dredging and Dredging Appliances. London: 1927. V. 49

DEKKER, THOMAS
The Gull's Hornbook. Bristol: 1812. V. 50; 52
The Gull's Hornbook... London: 1812. V. 47
The Gull's Hornbook. London: 1904. V. 47

DE KNIGHT, FREDA
A Date with a Dish: a Cook Book of American Negro Recipes. New York: 1948. V. 54

DE KOONING, WILLEM
De Kooning Drawings. New York: 1967. V. 50; 53

DE KOVEN, ANNA FARWELL
A Sawdust Doll. Chicago: 1895. V. 47

DE KOVEN, JAMES
Dorchester Polytechnic Academy: Dr. Neverasole, Principal. Milwaukee: 1879. V. 54

DE KROYFT, S. H.
A Place in They Memory. New York: 1850. V. 54

DEL Sacristan de Pinos de La Puenta D. Tyburio Cascales...Sombre los Descubrimientos de la Alcazaba de Granada.... Granada: 1761. V. 50

DELACOUR, JAMES
A Prospect of Poetry... Cork: 1807. V. 47; 50
A Prospect of Poetry. London: 1807. V. 54

DELACOUR, JEAN
Curassows and Related Birds. New York: 1973. V. 54
Les Oiseaux de l'Indochine Francaise. London: 1931. V. 47
Les Oiseaux de l'Indochine Francaise. Paris: 1931. V. 49; 52
The Pheasants of the World. London: 1951. V. 49; 52; 53; 54
The Pheasants of the World. London: 1977. V. 50
The Waterfowl of the World. London: 1954-64. V. 48; 49; 50; 51; 52; 53
Waterfowl of the World. London: 1959. V. 52
The Waterfowl of the World. Volume 1. London: 1954. V. 50
The Waterfowl of the World. Volume 1. London: 1954/59. V. 48
The Waterfowl of the World. Volume 2. London: 1956. V. 50
The Waterfowl of the World. Volume 2. London: 1956/66. V. 48
The Waterfowl of the World. Volume 2. London: 1966. V. 53
Waterfowl of the World. Volume 3. London: 1959. V. 53

DELAFIELD, E. M.
Diary of Provincial Lady. London: 1930. V. 47

DELAFIELD, EMILY
Alice in Wonderland. New York: 1898. V. 53

DELAFIELD, FRANCIS
A Manual of Physical Diagnosis. New York: 1878. V. 48; 53

DELAFIELD, JOSEPH
The Unfortified Boundary. A Diary of the First Survey of the Canadian Boundary Line from St. Regis to the Lake of the Woods. New York: 1943. V. 49

DELAFIELD, JULIA
Biographies of Francis Lewis and Morgan Lewis. New York: 1877. V. 50

DELAFIELD, RICHARD
Report on the Art of the War in Europe in 1854, 1855 and 1856. Washington: 1860. V. 49; 53
Report on the Art of the War in Europe in 1854, 1855 and 1856. Washington: 1861. V. 48

DELAFOSSE, PETER H.
Trailing the Pioneers... 1994. V. 54

DE LAGUNA, F.
Under Mt. Saint Elias: the History and Culture of the Yakutat Tlingit. Washington: 1972. V. 50

DELAMAYNE, THOMAS HALLIE
The Patricians; or a Candid Examination into the Merits of the Principal Speakers of the House of Lords. London: 1773. V. 52
The Senators: or, a Candid Examination into the Merits of the Principal Performers of St. Stephen's Chapel. London: 1772. V. 51; 54

DELAMERE, HENRY BOOTH, EARL OF
The Works. London: 1694. V. 50; 51

DELAMOTTE, FREEMAN GAGE
A Primer of the Art of Illumination. London: 1860. V. 47

DELAND, CHARLES
The Sioux Wars: in South Dakota. Pierre: 1930/34. V. 52

DELAND, MARGARET
The Awakening of Helena Richie. New York: 1906. V. 47; 49; 51; 53
Florida Days. Boston: 1889. V. 53
Florida Days. Boston: 1899. V. 47; 48; 50
Old Chester Tales. New York: 1899. V. 48

DELANEY, MATILDA J. SAGER
The Whitman Massacre. Spokane: 1920. V. 54

DELANO, ALONZO
Life on the Plains and Among the Diggings: Being Scenes and Adventures of an Overland Journey to California... Auburn & Buffalo: 1854. V. 49; 54
The Miner's Progress; or, Scenes in the Life of a California Miner. Sacramento: 1853. V. 53
Pen-Knife Sketches or Chips of the Old Block. San Francisco: 1934. V. 53

DELANO, AMASA
A Narrataive of Voyages and Travels, in the Northern and Southern Hemispheres... Boston: 1817. V. 48; 54

DELANY, MARY
Letters from Mrs. Delany to Mrs. Frances Hamilton from the Year 1779 to the Year 1788... London: 1820. V. 50; 51

DELANY, PATRICK
Observations Upon Lord Orrey's Remarks on the Life and Writings of...Swift. London: 1754. V. 48; 54
Reflections Upon Polygamy, and the Encouragement Given to the Practice in the Scriptures of the Old Testament by Phileleutherus Dubliniensis. London: 1739. V. 50

DELANY, S.
The Einstein Intersection. London: 1968. V. 52

DELANY, SAMUEL R.
Nova. Garden City: 1968. V. 49; 51

DELAPLAINES Repository of the Lives and Portraits of Distinguished American Characters. Philadelphia: 1815. V. 48

DE LATOCNAYE, C.
A Frenchman's Walk through Ireland 1796-97. London: 1917. V. 50; 51

DELAUNAY, CHARLES
Hot Discography. New York: 1940. V. 48

DELAUNAY, SONIA
Sonia Delaunay: 27 Tableaux Vivants. Milan: 1969. V. 48

DELAUNE, THOMAS
Angliae Metropolis; or, the Present State of London: With Memorials Comprehending A Full and Succinct Account of the Ancient and Modern State Thereof. London: 1690. V. 48
The Present State of London; or, Memorials Comprehending a Full and Succinct Account of the Ancient and Modern State Thereof. London: 1681. V. 52; 53

DELAURENCE, LAURON
The Great Book of Magical Art, Hindu Magic and Indian Occultism. Chicago: 1939. V. 52

DE LAURENCE, LAURON
The Old Book of Magic. Chicago: 1918. V. 48

DELAVAL, FRANCIS BLAKE
The Trial of Sir Francis Blake Delaval, Knight of the Bath, at the Consistory Court of Doctors Commons, for Committing Adultery with Miss Roach, Alias Miss LaRoche, Alias Miss Le Roche..To which is added, the Trial of George Fitzgerald... London: 1782?. V. 47

DELAWARE & HUDSON CANAL CO.
The Summer Tourist, Descriptive of the Delaware and Hudson Canal Company's Railroads, and their Summer Resorts. 1879. V. 50

DELAWARE & RARITAN CANAL CO.
Address of the Directors of the Camden and Amboy Rail Road and Delaware and Raritan Canal Companies, to the People of New Jersey. Trenton: 1846. V. 47; 51
Address of the Joint Board of Directors of the Delaware and Raritan Canal and Camden and Amboy Railroad Companies, to the People of New Jersey, June 1848. Trenton: 1848. V. 51
First Annual Report of the Delaware and Raritan Canal Company, May 10, 1831. Princeton: 1831. V. 49; 51
An Investigation into the Affairs of the Delaware & Raritan Canal and Camden & Amboy Rail Road Companies, in Reference to Certain Charges... Newark: 1849. V. 51
Reply of the Executive Committee of the Delaware and Raritan Canal...to a Letter...to...G. W. Hopkins...by the Hon. Cave Johnson, Post Master, General. Trenton: 1847. V. 49; 51
Report of Commissioners Appointed to Invesitage Charges Made Against the Directors of the Delaware and Raritan Canal, and Camden and Amboy Railroad and Transportation Companies. Trenton: 1850. V. 51
Report of the Committee Appointed to Offer to the State of New Jersey the Delaware and Raritan Canal and Feeder, and the Camden and Amboy Rail Road, with Their Appendages... Princeton: 1836. V. 51

DELAWARE NATION
Laws of the Delaware Nation of Indians. Lawrence: 1862. V. 48

DE LEIRIS, ALAIN
The Drawings of Edoaurd Manet. Berkeley: 1969. V. 50

DE LEON, DANIEL
Woman's Suffrage. New York: 1909. V. 53

DE LEON, THOMAS C.
Belles, Beaux and Brains of the 60's. New York: 1909. V. 50

DELEUZE, J. P. F.
Practical Instruction in Animal Magnetism. London: 1850. V. 48

DELGADO, PEDRO
Mexican Account of the Battle of San Jacinto. Deepwater: 1919. V. 49

DELILLE, JACQUES
The Gardens, a Poem. London: 1798. V. 53
The Gardens, a Poem. London: 1805. V. 54
Le Malheur et la Pitie, Poeme en Quatre Chants. Londres: 1803. V. 48
The Rural Philosopher; or French Georgics. Newbern: 1804. V. 50

DELILLO, DON
Americana. Boston: 1971. V. 47; 50; 52; 53; 54
End Zone. Boston: 1972. V. 51; 54
Great Jones Street. Boston: 1973. V. 50; 52
Great Jones Street. Boston: 1983. V. 49
The Names. New York: 1982. V. 51; 53
The Names. London: 1983. V. 53
Players. New York: 1977. V. 50
Ratner's Star. New York: 1976. V. 53
White Noise. New York: 1985. V. 51
White Noise. New York: 1986. V. 50

DE LINT, C.
Ascian in Rose. 1986. V. 49; 54

DE LINT, CHARLES
Paperjack. New Castle: 1991. V. 52

DELIUS, R. VON
Mary Wigman. Dresden: 1925. V. 49

DELL, DRAYCOTT M.
Golliwog Island. London: 1930. V. 49

DELL, FLOYD
Intellectual Vagabondage. New York: 1926. V. 52; 53
Janet March. New York: 1923. V. 53
Looking at Life. New York: 1924. V. 52
Runaway. New York: 1925. V. 49; 53; 54
Sweet and Twenty. Cincinnati: 1921. V. 48

DELL, HENRY
The Booksellers. London: 1766. V. 54

DELL, J.
The West Australian Bird Folio. West Perth: 1982. V. 48; 50; 51; 53

DELL, LEIGH
East Coasting. London: 1931. V. 49

DELL, WILLIAM
The Doctrine of Baptisms, Reduced from Its Ancient and Modern Corruptions... London: 1759. V. 51
The Doctrine of Baptisms, Reduced from Its Ancient and Modern Corruptions. Philadelphia: 1759. V. 53
The Trial fo Spirits, Both in Teachers and Hearers... Philadelphia: 1760. V. 47

DELLA BELLA, STEFANO
Recueil de Douze Cartouches... Paris: 1643. V. 50; 52; 54

DELLA CASA, GIOVANNI
Rime et Prose...Riscontrate con i Migliori Originali... Fiorenza: 1564. V. 49

DELLA PORTA, GIOVANNI BATTISTA
Della Fisonomia dell' Humomo...Libri Quattro. In Napli: 1598. V. 51

DELLENBAUGH, FREDERICK S.
Breaking the Wilderness. New York and London: 1905. V. 48; 52
A Canyon Voyage. New Haven: 1926. V. 52
The North America of Yesterday - a Comparative Study of North American Indian Life, Customs and Products on the Theory of the Ethnic Unity of the Race. New York: 1901. V. 54
The Romance of the Colorado River. New York: 1902. V. 51; 53

DELLOYE, H. L.
Chants et Chansons Populaires de la France... Paris: 1843. V. 52

DE LOLME, JEAN LOUIS
The Constitution of England, or an Account of the English Government... London: 1775. V. 47
The Constitution of England, or an Account of the English Government... 1776. V. 47
The Constitution of England, or an Account of the English Government. London: 1784. V. 53
The Constitution of England; or, An Account of the English Government... London: 1790. V. 47
The Constitution of England; or, an Account of the English Government; In Which It is Compared Both with the Republican Form of Government and the Other Monarchies of Europe. London: 1796. V. 51; 54
The History of the Flagellants, or the Advantages of Discipline... London: 1777. V. 52
Memorials of Human Superstition; Being a Paraphrase and Commentary on the Historia Flagellantium of the Abbe Boileau, Doctor of the Sorbonne, Canon of the Holy Chapel. London: 1784. V. 50; 54

DELONEY, THOMAS
The History of Thomas of Reading; or the Six Worthy Yeomen of the West. London: 1827. V. 51; 54
Thomas of Reading; or, the Sixe Worthie Yeoman of the West. Edinburgh: 1812. V. 47; 51

DE LONG, GEORGE
The Voyage of the Jeannette. Boston: 1883. V. 52; 53; 54
The Voyage of the Jeannette. The Ship and Ice Journals of... Boston: 1884. V. 49; 52

DE LOREY, EUSTACHE
Queer Things about Persia. London: 1907. V. 54

DELORIA, ELLA
Dakota Texts. New York: 1932. V. 50

DELOUGAZ, PINHAS
Private Houses and Graves in the Diyala Region. Chicago: 1967. V. 51

DEL POMAR, FELIPE COSSIO
The Art of Ancient Peru. New York: 1971. V. 52
Peruvian Colonial Art: the Cuzco School of Painting. New York: 1964. V. 53

DEL RAY, LESTER
Early Del Ray. Garden City: 1975. V. 47

DEL RENZIO, TONI
Arson - an Ardent Review, Part One. London: 1942. V. 53

DEL REY, LESTER
...And Some Were Human. Philadelphia: 1949. V. 50
Attack from Atlantis. New York: 1953. V. 51; 53
Battle on Mercury. New York: 1953. V. 51; 53
The Mysterious Planet. New York: 1953. V. 51

DELTEIL, JOSEPH
On the River Amour. New York: 1929. V. 50

DE LYRA, NICOLAUS
Praeceptorium (divinae legis), Cum Additionibus et Tractatulis Pulcerrimus Multis. Cologne: 1502. V. 52

DE MADARIAGA, S.
The Sacred Giraffe. New York: 1931. V. 51

DE MANDIARGUES, ANDRE PIEYRE
Chagall. New York. V. 51

DE MARBOT, BARON
The Memoirs of Baron de Marbot, Late Lieutenant-General in the French Army. London: 1892. V. 48

DE MARE, ERIC
The Bridges of Britain. London: 1954. V. 48

DEMAREST, MARY A.
The Demarest Family; David des Marest of the French Patent on the Hackensack and His Descendants. New Brunswick: 1938. V. 47; 49; 51

DE MARGERIE, PIERRE
Eloge de La Typographie. 1931. V. 52

DEMARGNE, PIERRE
The Birth of Greek Art. New York: 1964. V. 54

DEMASE, JACQUES
Rhythms and Colours. London: 1972. V. 54

DEMENTIEV, G. P.
Birds of the Soviet Union. Jerusalem: 1966-70. V. 49

DE MERS, JOE
Alice in Letterland. Hollywood: 1946. V. 53

DE MEZERAY, FRANCOIS ENDES DE
A General Chronological History of France. London: 1683. V. 48; 50

DEMIDOFF, A. DE
Voyage dans la Russie Meridionale et la Crimee... Paris;: 1842. V. 48

DEMIDOFF, E.
After the Wild Sheep in the Altai and Mongolia. 1900. V. 54
A Shooting Trip to Kamchatka. London: 1904. V. 47; 48; 50

DE MIERRE, H. C.
To Stand and Stare. Geneva: 1975. V. 51

DEMIJOHN, T.
Black Alice. Garden City: 1968. V. 50

DE MILLE, AGNES
Lizzie Borden: a Dance of Death. Boston: 1968. V. 54

DE MILLE, JAMES
The Babes in the Wood: A Tragic Comedy. Boston: 1875. V. 47
The Seven Hills. Boston: 1873. V. 47

DE MILT, A. P.
Story of An Old Town with Reminiscences of Early Nebraska and Bibliographies of Pioneers. Omaha: 1967. V. 48

DEMING, ELIZUR
An Address, Delivered at the First Annual Exhibition of the Philomathean Society of Wabash College, September 28, 1835. Crawfordsville: 1835. V. 52

THE DEMOCRATIC Book 1936. V. 53

DEMOCRATIC NATIONAL CONVENTION
Official Proceedings of the Democratic National Convention, Held in 1864 at Chicago. Chicago: 1864. V. 49; 53

DE MOLEYNS, THOMAS
The Landowner's Agent's Practical Guide. Dublin: 1872. V. 49

DE MONTFORT PRESS
Specimens from the De Montfort Press. Volume VII. Leicester: 1894. V. 50

DE MONTI, H.
Strictures On Mr. Logier's System of Musical Education. Glasgow: 1817. V. 49

DE MORAES, R. B.
Bibliographia Brasiliana. Rare Books About Brazil Published from 1504 to 1900 and Works by Brazilian Authors of the Colonial Period. Los Angeles: 1983. V. 50

DE MORGAN, AUGUSTUS
Arithmetical Books from the Invention of Printing to the Present Time. London: 1847. V. 52
A Budget of Paradoxes. Chicago: 1915. V. 47
Differential and Integral Calculus... London: 1842. V. 50
An Essay on Probabilities and on Their Application to Life Contingencies and Insurance Officers. London: 1838. V. 48; 52
Trigonometry and Double Algebra. London: 1849. V. 49

DE MORGAN, J.
Fouilles a Dahehour, 1894-95. Vienne: 1895-1903. V. 51

DE MORGAN, SOPHIA ELIZABETH
Threescore Years and Ten: Reminiscenes; to Which are Added Letters To and From Her Husband the Late Augustus De Morgan, and Others. London: 1895. V. 50

DEMOSTHENES
The Orations. London: 1770. V. 47; 50
The Orations. London: 1771. V. 53
The Orations. London: 1802. V. 48
Orationun Pars Prima (-Secunda & Tertia)... Venice: 1554. V. 51
The Three Orations of Demosthenes Chiefe Orator Among the Grecians, in Favour of the Olynthians, A People in Thracia... London: 1570. V. 47

DEMPSEY, G. DRYSDALE
The Practical Railway Engineer. London: 1847. V. 54
Rudimentary Treatise on the Drainage of Districts and Lands. London: 1849. V. 49; 50
A Rudimentary Treatise on the Locomotive Engine In All Its Phases and Illustrations for Students and Non-Professional men. London: 1866. V. 49

DEMPSTER, HENRY
The Decked-Welled Fishing Boat, and Fisheries and Fish Market Reform... Glasgow: 1868. V. 54

DEMUS, OTTO
The Mosaics of Norman Sicily. London: 1950. V. 53
Romanesque Mural Painting. New York: 1970. V. 49
Romanesque Mural Painting. New York: 1976. V. 47

DENBY, EDWIN
Mediterranean Cities. Sonnets. New York: 1956. V. 53

DENDY, WALTER COOPER
The Philosophy of Mystery. London: 1841. V. 48; 52

DENFFER, JOHANN HEINRICH
Vernunft und Erfahrungsmassiger Discours, Darin Uberhaupt die Wahren Ursachen der Fruchtbarkeit... Halle: 1755. V. 53

DENHAM, DIXON
Narrative of Travels and Discoveries in Northern and Central Africa, in the Years 1822, 1823, and 1824... London: 1826. V. 47; 50; 51; 54
Narrative of Travels and Discoveries in Northern and Central Africa, in the Years 1822, 1823, and 1824... London: 1828. V. 48; 49

DENHAM, JOHN
Cato Major, of Old Age. London: 1669. V. 47
Poems and Translations with the Sophy. London: 1668. V. 47; 50
Poems and Translations; with The Sophy. London: 1671. V. 47; 51
Poems and Translations with the Sophy. London: 1684. V. 50; 51
The Sophy. As It Was Acted at the Private House in Black Friars by His Majesties Servants. London: 1642. V. 54

DENHAM, MICHAEL AISLABIE
The Denham Tracts. London: 1892-95. V. 52

DENHARDT, BOB
The Quarter Horse. Volume Two. 1945. V. 50

DENHOLM, JAMES
The History of the City of Glasgow and Suburbs, To Which is added, a Sketch of a Tour to the Principal Scotch & English Lakes. Glasgow: 1804. V. 50
A Tour to the Principal Scotch and English Lakes. Glasgow: 1804. V. 47

DENIG, EDWIN THOMPSON
Indian Tribes of the Upper Missouri. Washington: 1930. V. 48

DE NIORD, CHARD
River. 1991. V. 54
Train. 1995. V. 54

DENIS, CHARLES
Select Fables. London: 1754. V. 48; 51

DENIS, VALENTINE
The Adoration of the Mystic Lamb. Milano: 1964. V. 47

DENISON, EDMUND BECKETT
A Rudimentary Treatise on Clock and Watch Making... London: 1850. V. 50

DENISON, GEORGE T.
Modern Cavalry: Its Organization, Armament and Employment in War. London: 1868. V. 49

DENISON, MERRILL
Canada's First Bank: a History of the Bank of Montreal. New York: 1966. V. 53

DENISOT, NICOLAS
Le Tombeav de Margverite de Valois Royne de Navarre. Paris: 1551. V. 51

DENMAN, THOMAS
An Introduction to the Practice of Midwifery. New York: 1802. V. 54
An Introduction to the Practice of Midwifery. Brattleborough: 1807. V. 52
An Introduction to the Practice of Midwifery. New York: 1821. V. 53

DENNERY, HENRY E.
Aletha: at the Parting of the Ways. London: 1896. V. 54

DENNIE, JOSEPH
The Lay Preacher. Walpole: 1796. V. 48; 51; 54
The Lay Preacher. Philadelphia: 1817. V. 48; 51; 54
The Port Folio. 1804. Philadelphia: 1804. V. 50

DENNING, C. F. W.
The Eighteenth Century Architecture of Bristol. Bristol: 1923. V. 48

DENNING, W. F.
Telescopic Work for Starlight Evenings. London: 1891. V. 53

DENNIS, FREDERIC S.
System of Surgery. Philadelphia: 1894-96. V. 50
System of Surgery. Philadlephia: 1895. V. 47; 49

DENNIS, GEORGE
The Cities and Cemeteries of Etruria. London: 1848. V. 49; 51; 52
The Cities and Cemeteries of Etruria. London: 1883. V. 50; 52

DENNIS, JOHN
Appius and Virginia. London: 1709. V. 47
The Grounds of Criticism in Poetry... London: 1704. V. 54
Iphigenia. London: 1700. V. 47
A Plot, and No Plot. London: 1697. V. 47
A Proposal for Putting a Speedy End to the War, by Ruining the Commerce of the French and Spaniards, and Securing Our Own, Without Any Additional Expense to the Nation. London: 1703. V. 52
Reflections Critical and Satyrical, Upon a Late Rhapsody, Call'd, an Essay Upon Criticism. London: 1711. V. 50
The Usefulness of the Stage to the Happiness of Mankind. London: 1698. V. 47; 54

DENNIS, R. L. H.
The Ecology of Butterflies in Britian. London: 1992. V. 51

DENNIS, R. W. G.
British Ascomycetes. Vaduz: 1981. V. 52; 53

DENNIS, T. S.
Life of F. M. Buckelew the Indian Captive as Related by Himself. Bandera: 1925. V. 47

DENNISON, W.
Studies in East Christian and Roman Art. New York: 1918. V. 50

DENNISTOUN, JAMES
Memoirs of the Dukes of Urbino, Illustrating the Arms, Arts and Literature of Italy 1440-1630. London: 1909. V. 49; 52

DENNY, ARTHUR
Pioneer Days on Puget Sound. Seattle: 1888. V. 47; 54

DENNY, M. W.
Biology and the Mechanics of the Wave-Swept Environment. Lawrenceville: 1988. V. 50

DENNYS, JOHN
The Secrets of Angling... Edinburgh: 1883. V. 53
Secrets of Angling. London: 1883. V. 47; 53

DENNYS, N. B.
An Account of the Cruise of the St. George on the North American and West Indian Station During the Years... London: 1862. V. 47
The Folk-Lore of China, and Its Affinities with that of the Aryan and Semitic Races. London: 1876. V. 49

DENON, VIVANT
Travels in Upper and Lower Egypt, During...Operations of the French Army Under...Bonaparte... Dublin: 1803. V. 47
Travels in Upper and Lower Egypt, in Company with Several Divisions of the French Army, During the Campaigns of General Bonaparte in That Country... London: 1803. V. 52
Travels in Upper and Lower Egypt, in Company...of the french Army, During the Campaigns of...Bonaparte... New York: 1803. V. 51
Voyage dans la Basse et la Haute Egypte, pendant les Campagnes du General Bonaparte. Paris: 1802. V. 49; 51

DENORES, JASON
Introdvttione...Ridotta Poi in Alcvne Tavole Sopra I Tre Libri Della Rhetorica di Aristotile. Venice: 1578. V. 53

DENSLOW'S *House That Jack Built.* New York: 1903. V. 47

DENSMORE, F.
Nootka and Quileute Music. Washington: 1939. V. 52
Teton Sioux Music. Washington: 1918. V. 54

DENSON, ALAN
Printed Writings by George W. Russell: a Bibliography. Evanston: 1961. V. 49; 50

DENT, CHARLES
The Gerrard Street Mystery and Other Weird Tales. Toronto: 1888. V. 54

DENT, CLINTON THOMAS
Mountaineering. London: 1892. V. 50; 54

DENT, EMMA
Annals of Winchcombe and Sudeley. London: 1877. V. 50

DENT HARDWARE CO.
Catalogue of Refrigerator Hardware and Hardware Specialties. Volume B. Fullerton: 1911. V. 50
Iron Toys. Fullerton: 1910. V. 53

DENT, J.
Catalogue of the Splendid, Curious & Extensive Library of the Late John Dent, Esq. London: 1827. V. 52

DENT, J. M.
The Memoirs of J. M. Dent: 1849-1926. London & Toronto: 1828. V. 48
The Memoirs of J. M. Dent: 1849-1926. London & Toronto: 1928. V. 47; 50

DENT, JOHN
The Candidate; a Farce. London: 1782. V. 49

DENT, JOHN CHARLES
The Last Forty Years: Canada Since the Union of 1841. Toronto: 1881. V. 47
The Story of the Upper Canadian Rebellion; Largely Derived from Original Sources and Documents. Toronto: 1885. V. 48; 54

DENT, OLIV
A V.A.D. in France. London: 1917. V. 50

DENTON, B. E.
A Two-Gun Cyclone: a True Story. Dallas: 1927. V. 48

DENTON, DANIEL
A Brief Description of New York, Formerly Called New Netherlands, with the Places Thereunto Adjoining... New York: 1845. V. 47

DENTON, N.
Catalogue of Short Horn Cattle at Oak Grove Stock Farm, Manchester, Delaware Co., Iowa. Manchester: 1876. V. 52

DENTON, SHERMAN FOOTE
Incidents of a Collector's Rambles in Australia, New Zealand and New Guinea. Boston: 1889. V. 48; 50
Moths and Butterflies of the United States East of the Rocky Mountains. Boston: 1898. V. 53
As Nature Shows Them: Moths and Butterflies of the United States East of the Rocky Mountains. Boston: 1897-1900. V. 50

DENVER & RIO GRANDE RAILROAD
First Annual Report of the Board of Directors...April 1st, 1873. Philadelphia: 1873. V. 47; 49
Rocky Mountain Scenery...Along the Line of the Denver and Rio Grande Railroad. New York: 1888. V. 48

DENVER PUBLIC LIBRARY
Catalog of the Western History Department, Denver Public Library. Boston: 1970. V. 53

DENVER VILLA PARK ASSOCIATION
Articles of Incorporation and By Laws of the Denver Villa Park Association. Denver: 1872. V. 49; 50; 54

DE PALMA, ANTHONY
Diseases of the Knee. Philadelphia: 1954. V. 53

DE PALO, PEDRO
Early Medieval Art in Spain. New York. V. 54

DE PARADES, ROBERT, COUNT
Secret Memoirs of Robert, Count de Parades, Written by Himself... London: 1914. V. 50

DE PAZ, CHRISTOPHER
De Maioratibus, et Eorum Tenuta, Seu Interdicto & Remedio Possessorio Summarissimo, tam mero Quam Mixto. Tractatus II. Pintiae: 1621. V. 48

DEPEW, CHAUNCEY M.
One Hundred Years of American Commerce (1795-1895). New York: 1895. V. 54
Orations and After Dinner Speeches... New York: 1890. V. 49

DE PEYSTER, JOHN WATTS
The Affair at King's Mountain, 7th October, 1780. New York & Chicago: 1880. V. 48
Personal and Military History of Philip Kearny, Major-General United States Volunteers. New York and Newark: 1869. V. 50; 51

DE PILES, ROGER
The Principles of Painting, Under the Heads of Anatomy, Attitude, Accident...Unity. London: 1743. V. 47

DE PISAN
The Epistle of Othea to Hector or the Boke of Knyghthode. London: 1904. V. 47; 50

DE POL, JOHN
Wood Engravings by John de Pol for the Hammer Creek Press. New York: 1957. V. 47

DE PONTIS, LOUIS
Memoirs of the Sieur De Pontis: Who Served in the Army Six and Fifty Years, Under King Henry IV. lewis the XIII. and Lewis the XIV. London: 1694. V. 54

DE PUMA, RICHARD DANIEL
Etruscan Tomb-Groups: Ancient Pottery and Broznes in Chicago's Field Museum of Natural History. Mainz am Rhein: 1986. V. 50

DE PUY, W. H.
The University of Literature. 1896/97/. V. 50

DE QUILLE, DAN
A History of the Comstock Silver Lode and Mines, Nevada and the Great Basin Region: Lake Tahoe and the High Sierras. Virginia: 1889. V. 49

DE QUINCEY, THOMAS
California and the Gold Mania. V. 54
Collected Writings. Edinburgh: 1889-90. V. 50
The Collected Writings. London: 1896-97. V. 47; 52; 53
Confessions of an English Opium-Eater. London: 1822. V. 47; 48; 49; 50; 54
Confessions of an English Opium-Eater. London: 1823. V. 49
Confessions of an English Opium-Eater... London: 1867. V. 49
The Confessions of an English Opium-Eater. London: 1930. V. 53
Confessions of an English Opium-Eater. New York: 1930. V. 51
Confessions of an English Opium-Eater. Oxford: 1930. V. 48; 50; 51; 54
A Diary of Thomas de Quincey 1803. London: 1928. V. 53
A Diary Written in the Year 1803. New York: 1927. V. 53
Dr. Johnson and Lord Chesterfield. New York: 1945. V. 52
Klosterheim: or, the Masque. London: 1832. V. 54
Letters of De Quincey, the English Opium-Eater to a Young Man Whose Education Has Been Neglected. Philadelphia: 1843. V. 53; 54
The Logic of Political Economy. Edinburgh: 1844. V. 50
Revolt of the Tartars. London: 1948. V. 48; 49; 50
Select Essays...Narrative and Imaginative. Edinburgh: 1888. V. 52
Walladmor. London: 1825. V. 47
Works. Boston: 1851-53. V. 50
The Works... Edinburgh: 1862-63. V. 51; 54
Works. Edinburgh: 1862-71. V. 54
The Works. Edinburgh: 1862-74. V. 51; 54

DERANIYAGALA, P. E. P.
A Coloured Atlas of some Vertebrates from Ceylon. Volume I. Fishes. Colombo: 1952. V. 53
Some Extinct Elephants, Their Relatives and the Two Living Species. Colombo: 1955. V. 50; 53
The Tetrapod Reptiles of Ceylon...Volume I: Testudinates and Crocodilians. Colombo: 1939. V. 49

DERBEC, ETIENNE
A French Journalist in the California Gold Rush. The Letters of... Georgetown: 1964. V. 48

DERBY, E. H.
Reality Versus Fiction. Boston: 1850. V. 53

DERBY, EDWARD STANLEY, 14TH EARL OF
The Speech of the Right Honble. Lord Stanley in the House of Lords, on Monday May 25th, 1846. London: 1846. V. 53

DERBY, ELIAS H.
The Overland Route to the Pacific: a Report on the Condition, Capacity and Resources of the Union Pacific and Central Pacific Railways. Boston: 1869. V. 52

Two Months Abroad; or, a Trip to England, France, Baden, Prussia and Belgium. In August and September, 1843. Boston: 1844. V. 47

DERBY, GEORGE HORATIO
Phoenixiana. New York: 1856. V. 48

Phoenixiana. Chicago: 1897. V. 52

Phoenixiana. A Collection of the Burlesques & Sketches of John Phoenix, Alias John P. Squibob, Who Was, in Fact Lieutenant George H. Derby, U.S.A. San Francisco: 1937. V. 47; 54

Report of the Secretary of War...a Reconnoisance of the Gulf of California and the Colorado River by Lieutenant Derby. Washington: 1852. V. 49; 52

The Squibob Papers. New York: 1865. V. 52

DERBY, J. C.
Fifty Years Among Authors - Books and Publishers. New York: 1883. V. 48

Fifty Years Among Authors, Books and Publishers. New York: 1884. V. 52

DERBY, JOHN BARTON
Life Among Lunatics. Boston: 1839. V. 48

Political Reminiscences, Including a Sketch of the Origin and History of the "Statesman Party" of Boston. (and) Second Part. Boston: 1835. V. 54

DERCUM, FRANCIS
A Text-Book of Nervous Diseaes by American Authors. Philadelphia: 1895. V. 47; 48; 53

DE RETZ, JEAN FRANCOIS PAUL DE GONDI, CARDINAL
Memoirs of the Cardinal de Retz... Philadelphia: 1817. V. 49

DERHAM, WILLIAM
The Artificial Clock-Maker. London: 1700. V. 49

Astro-Theology: or, a Demonstration of the Being and Attributes of God, from a Survey of the Heavens. London. V. 51

Astro-Theology: Or a Demonstration of the Being and Attributes of God, from a Survey of the Heavens. London: 1715. V. 47; 54

Astro-Theology; or a Demonstration of the Being and Attributes of God, from a Survey of the Heavens. London: 1719. V. 53

Astro-Theology; or, a Demonstration of the Being and Attributes of God, from a Survey of the heavens. London: 1767. V. 48

Dimostrazione Della Essenza, ed Attributi d' Iddio Dall' Opere Della Sua Creazione. Firenze: 1719. V. 47

Physico-Theology; or, a Demonstration of the Being and Attributes of God. V. 48

Physico-Theology; or, a Demonstration of the Being and Attributes of God, form His Works of Creation. London: 1713. V. 47; 49; 50

Physico-Theology; or, a Demonstration of the Being and Attributes of God, From His Works of Creation. London: 1714. V. 48

Physico-Theology: or, A Demonstration of the Being and Attributes of God, from His Works of Creation. London: 1723. V. 47

Physico-Theology: or, a Demonstration of the Being and Attributes of God, from His Works of Creation. Glasglow: 1758. V. 50

DE RINALDIS, ALDO
Neapolitan Painting of the Seicento. Florence: 1929. V. 52

DERING, EDWARD HENEAGE
The Ban of Maplethorpe. London & Leamington: 1894. V. 54

Sherborne; or, the House at the Four Ways. London: 1875. V. 47

DE RIVER, J. PAUL
The Sexual Criminal: a Psychoanalytical Study. Springfield: 1949. V. 47

DERLETH, AUGUST WILLIAM
100 Books by August Derleth. Sauk City: 1962. V. 48

The Adventure of the Orient Express. 1965. V. 49; 54

The Arkham Collector. Sauk City: 1967-71. V. 47; 49; 51; 54

Dark of the Moon. Sauk City: 1947. V. 47; 49; 51; 52; 54

Dark Things. Sauk City: 1971. V. 52

Death by Design. New York: 1953. V. 51

Fire and Sleet and Candlelight. Sauk City: 1961. V. 52

In Re: Sherlock Holmes. Sauk City: 1945. V. 47; 49; 50

It's A Boy's World. Sauk City: 1948. V. 47; 48

Last Light. Mt. Horeb: 1978. V. 47; 51; 52; 54

Lonesome Places. Sauk City: 1962. V. 52; 54

The Mask of Cthulhu. Sauk City: 1958. V. 51; 54

The Memoirs of Solar Pons. Sauk City: 1951. V. 47; 50; 51

Mischief in the Lane. New York: 1944. V. 51

The Narracong Riddle. New York: 1940. V. 48

Night's Yawning Peal: a New Selection of Supernatural Tales. Sauk City: 1952. V. 51

Not Long for This World. Sauk City: 1948. V. 51; 54

Over the Edge. Sauk City: 1964. V. 52

Praed Street Papers. 1965. V. 48

The Return of Solar Pons. Sauk City: 1958. V. 53

Sentence Deferred. New York: 1939. V. 51

The Shield fo the Valiant. New York: 1945. V. 49

The Sleeping and the Dead - Thirty Uncanny Tales. Chicago: 1947. V. 49

Someone in the Dark. Sauk City: 1941. V. 47; 48; 51; 52

Something Near. Sauk City: 1945. V. 51; 52; 54

Three Problems of Solar Pons. 1952. V. 48

Wind in the Elms. Philadelphia: 1941. V. 49

Wisconsin Murders. Sauk City: 1968. V. 48

DERMODY, THOMAS
The Harp of Erin, Containing the Poetical Works of the Late Thomas Dermody. 1807. V. 47

Poems, Moral and Descriptive. London: 1800. V. 54

DERMOTT, LAURENCE
The Constitution of Freemasonry; or, Ahiman Rezon: to Which is Added a Selection of Masonic Songs. Dublin: 1804. V. 52

DE ROS, JOHN FREDERICK FITZGERALD
Personal Narrative of Travels in the United States and Canada in 1826... London: 1827. V. 47; 48; 51; 53; 54

DERRA DE MORODA, FRIDERICA
The Dance Library a Catalogue. Munich: 1982. V. 50

DERRICK, SAMUEL
The Dramatic Censor. London: 1752. V. 53

A General View of the Stage. London: 1759. V. 50

A Poetical Dictionary; or, the Beauties of the English Poets... London: 1761. V. 47; 50

DERRICK, THOMAS
The Prodigal Son and Other Parables Shown in Pictures... Oxford: 1931. V. 51

DERRIEY, CHARLES
Gravure et Fonderie De C. Derriey. Paris: 1862. V. 50

DERRYDALE PRESS
A Decade of American Sporting Books and Prints by the Derrydale Press 1927-1937. New York: 1937. V. 48; 53

DESAGULIERS, JEAN THEOPHILE
A Course of Experimental Philosophy. London: 1763. V. 47; 48

DE SALIS, HENRY RODOLOPH
Bradshaw's Canals and Navigable Rivers of England and Wales. 1918. V. 54

DE SANA, JIMMY
Submission. New York: 1979. V. 49

DESANI, G. V.
Hali, a Play. London: 1950. V. 52

DE SAULCY, F.
Narrative of a Journey Round the Dead Sea and In the Bible Lands; in 1850 and 1851. Philadelphia: 1854. V. 49; 52

DESAULT, PIERRE JOSEPH
A Treatise on Fractures, Luxations and Other Affections of the Bones Wherein His Opinions and Practice, In Such Cases are Stated and Exemplified. Philadelphia: 1817. V. 48; 52

DE SAUSSURE, L. A. NECKER
Travels in Scotland: Descriptive of the State of Manners, Literature and Science. London: 1821. V. 52; 54

A Voyage to the Hebrides, or, Western Isles of Scotland... London: 1822. V. 52; 54

DE SAUSSURE, W. F.
Report on the Address of a Portion of the Members of the General Assembly of Georgia. Charleston: 1860. V. 50

DESBOROUGH, V. R.
The Last Mycenaens and their Successors, an Archaeological Survey. Oxford: 1964. V. 50

Protogeometric Pottery. Oxford: 1952. V. 52

DESCARTES, RENE
De Homine Figuris et Latinitate Donatus a Florentio Schuyl. Leiden: 1662. V. 52

Discours de La Methode Pour Bien Conduire sa Raison... Paris: 1668. V. 50

Epistolae, Partim ab Auctore Latino Sermone Conscriptae... Amsterdam: 1668/68-83. V. 53

Epistolae...In Quibus Omnis Generis Quaestiones Philosophicae Tractantur... London: 1668. V. 52; 53

Geometria. Amsterdam: 1659. V. 51

Geometria a Renato des Cartes Anno 1637 Gallice Edita... Amsterdam: 1683. V. 48; 50; 52

Opera Philosophica. Amsterdam: 1672. V. 47

Opera Philosophica. Amsterdam: 1677. V. 51

Principia Philosophiae. Amsterdam: 1664. V. 54

Tractatus de Homine, et de Formatione Foetus. Quorum Prior Notis Perpetuis Ludovici De La Forge, M.D. Amsterdami: 1677. V. 51

DE SCENE DES MAISONS, JACQUES
Contrat Conjugal ou Loix eu Mariage, de la Repudiation at du Divorce. Paris?: 1781. V. 50

DESCHARNES, ROBERT
Auguste Rodin. London: 1967. V. 50

Gaudi the Visionary. New York: 1971. V. 51; 53; 54

The World of Salvador Dali. New York: 1962. V. 50; 54

DE SCHAUENSEE, R. M.
The Birds of Columbia, and Adjacent Areas of South and Central America. USA: 1964. V. 50; 52; 53

A Guide to the Birds of South America. London: 1971. V. 52; 53

DE SCHWEINITZ, G. E.
Diseases of the Eye. Philadelphia: 1896. V. 48; 49; 50

DESCLOZEAUX, ADRIEN
Gabrielle D'estrees. London: 1907. V. 51; 52

DESCOLE, H. R.
Genera et Species Pantarum Argentinarum. Buenos Aires: 1943-56. V. 49; 51

DESCRIPTION Exacte de Tout ce Qui s'Est Passe Dans les Guerres Entre le Roy d'Angleterre, le Roy de France, lest Estats des Provinces Unies du Pays-Bas, & l'Eveque de Munster, Commencant de l'an 1664 & Finissant avec lat Conclusion de Paix Faite... Amsterdam: 1668. V. 50; 52

DESCRIPTION la Plus Nouvelle de Toutes les Particularites de la Ville de Vienne. Vienna: 1779. V. 53

DESCRIPTION of a View of the City of Cabul the Capital of Affghanistan, with the Surrounding Country, Now Exhibiting at the Panroama, Leicester Square. London: 1842. V. 51

A DESCRIPTION of East-Bourne and Its Environs. Eastborne: 1819. V. 47; 52

A DESCRIPTION of England and Wales. London: 1802. V. 49

A DESCRIPTION of Fonthill Abbey, Wiltshire. London: 1812. V. 48

A DESCRIPTION of Holland; or, the Present State of the United Provinces...Account of the Hague...Principal Cities and Towns...Manners and Customs...Navigation, Commerce...Universities, Arts, Sciences, Men of Letters.. London: 1743. V. 49

A DESCRIPTION of London; Containing a Sketch of Its History and Present State, And Of All the Most Celebrated Buildings, Etc. London: 1824. V. 51

A DESCRIPTION of the Boston Water Works, Embracing All the Reservoirs, Bridges, Gates, Pipe Chambers, and Other Objects of Interest, from Lake Cochituate to the City of Boston. Boston: 1848. V. 48

A DESCRIPTION of the British Memtropolis; with Historical and Descriptive Accounts of the Different Buildings... London: 1825. V. 50

A DESCRIPTION Of the Colleges, Halls, Public Buildings and Other Objects of Worthy Notice in Oxford... Oxford: 1829. V. 54

A DESCRIPTION of the Colosseum as Re-Opened in MDCCCXLV.... London: 1845. V. 53

A DESCRIPTION of the House and Gardens...at Stowe, in the County of Buckingham. London: 1838. V. 49

A DESCRIPTION of the University, Town and County of Cambridge... Cambridge: 1796. V. 50

DESCRIPTION of the View of the Battle of Vittoria, and the Great Victory Gained by the Marquis of Wellington Over the French Army Under Joseph Bonaparte. London: 1814. V. 48

DESCRIPTIONS des Beautes de Genes. Genoa: 1781. V. 53

DESCRIPTIONS of the Townships of the North West Territories, Dominion of Canada. Ottawa: 1886. V. 47

DESCRIPTIVE Atlas of Western Canada. Ottawa: 1900. V. 53

DESCRIPTIVE Catalogue of the Cosmorama Panoramic Exhibition 29, St. James' Street. London: 1822. V. 54

A DESCRIPTIVE Catalogue of the Marine Collection to be Found at India House. 1935. V. 49

DESCRIZIONE del Solenne Ingresso in Milano delle Loro Maesta...Francesco I e Maria Luigia d'Austria. Milan: 1816. V. 49

DE SCUDERY, M.
Clelia. London: 1655. V. 54

DE SEGUR, COMTESSE
Old French Fairy Tales. Philadelphia: 1920. V. 50

DE SEINGALT, JACQUES CASANOVA
The Memoirs of Jacques Casanova de Seingalt. Haarlem: 1972. V. 47

DESERET. CONSTITUTION
Constitution of the State of Deseret. Memorials of the Legislature and Constitutional Convention of Utah Territory. Washington: 1862. V. 47
Constitution of the State of Deseret, with the Journal of the Convention Which Formed It, and the Proceedings of the Legislature Consquent Thereon. January 28, 1850. Washington: 1850. V. 47

DE SERRES, JEAN
An Historical Collection of the Most Memorable Accidents and Tragicall Massacres of France, Under the Raignes of Henry 2. Francis 2. Charles 9. Henry 3. Henry 4...Until This Present Yeare 1598. London: 1598. V. 51

DE SERVIEZ, JACQUES ROERGAS
The Lives and Amours of the Empresses, Consorts to the First 12 Caesars of Rome. London: 1723. V. 50

DE SEVERSKY, ALEXANDER P.
Air Power: Key to Survivial. New York: 1950. V. 51

DESFONTAINES, PIERRE FRANCOIS GUYOT
The History of the Revolutions of Poland. London: 1736. V. 50

DESFONTAINES, R.
Flora Atlantica. Blanchon: 1799. V. 49
Flora Atlantica, sive Historia Plantarum, Quae in Atlante... Paris: 1798-99. V. 53
Flora Atlantica, Sive Historia Plantarum, Quae in Atlante, Agro Tunetano et Algeriensi Crescunt. Paris: 1798-1800. V. 52

DE SHIELDS, JAMES T.
Border Wars of Texas... Tioga: 1912. V. 47; 50; 52; 53
Cynthia Ann Parker: The Story of Her Capture at the Massacre of Parker's Fort. St. Louis: 1886. V. 54
Cynthia Ann Parker: The Story of Her Capture at the Massacre of the Inmates of Parker's Fort, of Her Quarter of a Century Spent Among the Comanches... Dallas: 1991. V. 48
The Fergusons: "Jim and Ma"; the Stormy Petrels in Texas Politics. Dallas: 1932. V. 47

DESIGNS from the Pennsylvania Dutch. New York: 1954. V. 49

DESIKACHARY, T. V.
Atlas of the Diatoms. Madras: 1986-90. V. 48

DESJARDINS, MARIE CATHERINE HORTENSE, MME. DE VILLEDIEU
The Unfotunate (sic) Heroes; or, the Adventures of Ten Famous men, viz. Ovid, Lentulus, Hortensius, Herennius, Cepion, Horace, Virgil, Corenlius Gallus, Crassus, Agrippa. London: 1679. V. 47

DESLANDES, ANDREW BOUREAU
The Art of Being Easy at all Times and in All Places. London: 1724. V. 54

DES MAIZEAUX, PIERRE
Recueil de Diverses Pieces, sur la Philosophie, la Religion Naturelle l'Histoire, les Mathematiques, &c. Amsterdam: 1740. V. 47

DESMARETS DE SAINT-SORLIN, JEAN
L'Ariane...De Nouveau Reveue, et Augmentee de Plusieurs Histores par l'Autheur, et Enrichie de Plusieurs Figures. Paris: 1639. V. 48
Clovis, ou La France Chrestienne: Poeme Heroique. Paris: 1657. V. 47

DESMOND, R.
Dictionary of British and Irish Botanists and Horticulturists... London: 1977. V. 48

DE SOULIGNE, M.
The Desolation of France Demonstrated. London: 1697. V. 49

DESPIAU, L.
Select Amusements in Philosophy and Mathematics... London: 1801. V. 54

DESPORTES, PHILIPPE
Les Oeuvres. Antwerp: 1596. V. 47

DESSINS. 20 Planches En Couleurs. Paris: 1920's. V. 53

DE STAEL HOLSTEIN, ANNE LOUISE GERMAINE NECKER, BARONNE DE
Considerations of the Principal Events of the French Revolution. New York: 1818. V. 47
Germany. London: 1814. V. 47
Letters and Reflections of the Austrian Field-Marshall Prince de Ligne... Philadelphia: 1809. V. 47

D'ESTERRE-KEELING, ELEONORE
The Music of the Poets. London: 1898. V. 49

DESTUTT DE TRACY, ANTOINE LOUIS CLAUDE, COMTE
A Commentary and Review of Montesquieu's Spirit of Laws... Philadelphia: 1811. V. 53
Treatise on Political Economy, To Which is Prefixed a Supplement to a Preceding Work on the Understanding, or Elements of Ideology... Georgetown: 1818. V. 48

DESTY, ROBERT
The Removal of Causes from State to Federal Courts, with a Preliminary Chapter on Jurisdiction of the Circuit Courts of the United States. San Francisco: 1888. V. 50

DE TABLEY, JOHN BYRNE LEICESTER WARREN, 3RD BARON
Poems Dramatic and Lyrical. London: 1893. V. 50; 52; 54
Poems, Dramatic and Lyrical. (with) ...Second Series. London: 1895. V. 52

DE TABLEY, JOHN FLEMING LEICESTER, 1ST BARON
Poems Dramatic and Lyrical. London: 1893/95. V. 47

DETAILLE, EDOUARD
Types et Uniformes L'Armee Francaise. Paris: 1885-89. V. 47; 51

THE DETECTION of the Views of Those Who Would, in the Present Crisis, Engage an Incumber'd, Trading Nation, as a Principals, in a Ruinous Expensive Land-War... London: 1746. V. 48

DE TOLNAY, CHARLES
The Drawings of Pieter Bruegel the Elder. London: 1952. V. 50
Hieronymus Bosch. London: 1966. V. 47; 50; 51
Hieronymus Bosch. New York: 1966. V. 50; 54
History and Technique of Old Master Drawings. A Handbook. New York: 1943. V. 51; 53

DE TOTT, BARON
Appendix to the Memoirs of...Containing an Answer to the Remarks of M. de Peysonnel, by M. Ruffin... London: 1786. V. 47

DE TRAFFORD, HUMPHREY
The Horses of the British Empire. London: 1907. V. 47

DE TRESSAN, L'ABBE
Mythology Compared with History; or, the Fables of the Ancients Elucidated from Historical Records. London: 1797. V. 51

DETROSIER, ROWLAND
Lecture On the Utility of Political Unions, for the Diffusion of Sound Moral and Political Information Amongst the People. London: 1832. V. 52

DETTLAFF, T. A.
Sturgeon Fishes, Devlopmental Biology and Aquaculture. Berlin: 1993. V. 52

DEUCER, JOHANNES
Metallicorum Corpus Juris Oder Bergkrecht. Leipzig: 1624. V. 52; 54

DEULIN, CHARLES
Johnny Nut and the Golden Goose. London: 1887. V. 51

DEUS, JACINTO DE
Caminho dos Frades menores Para a Vida Eterna. Lisbon: 1689. V. 48
Escudo dos Cavalleiros das Ordens Militares. Lisbon: 1670. V. 48

DEUTSCH, BABETTE
Banners. New York: 1919. V. 49
Take Them, Stranger. New York: 1944. V. 53; 54

DEUTSCH, FELIX
Heart and Athletics, Clinical Researches Upon the Influence of Athletics Upon the Heart. St. Louis: 1927. V. 53

DEUX-PONTS, WILLIAM DE
My Campaigns in America: a Journal Kept by Count William De Deux-Ponts, 1780-81. Boston: 1868. V. 47; 50; 51

DE VAUCOULEURS, GERARD
Reference Catalogue of Bright Galaxies, Being the Harvard Survey of Galaxies Brighter than the 13th Magnitude of H. Shapley and A. Ames, Revised. 1964. V. 51

DE VAUX, MARIE DE MAUPEOU FOUQUET, VICOMTESSE
Recueil de Receptes, Ou est Expliquee la Maniere de Guerir a Peu de Frais Toute Forte de Maux Tant Internes... Lyon: 1676. V. 52

DEVEAUX, SAMUEL
Legend of the Whirlpool and Map of Niagara Falls with Guide Table to All Places of Interest in the Vicinity. Buffalo: 1840. V. 54

DE VEAUX, SAMUEL
The Travellers' Own Book, to Saratoga Springs, Niagara Falls and Canada. Buffalo: 1841. V. 50

DE VEER, GERRIT
The Three Voyages of William Barents to the Arctic Regions (1594, 1595 and 1596). London: 1876. V. 50

DEVENS, R. M.
Our First Century. Springfield: 1876. V. 48

DEVENS, SAMUEL ADAMS
Sketches of Martha's Vineyard and Other Reminiscences of Travel at Home, Etc. Boston: 1838. V. 52

DEVENTER, HENRY
The Art of Midwifery Improv'd. London: 1746. V. 47

DE VERE, AUBREY
Legends of the Saxon Saints. 1879. V. 54
May Crols. London: 1857. V. 54
The Waldenses, or the Fall of Rora. A Lyrical Sketch. Oxford: 1842. V. 51

DE VERE, SCHELE CHARLES
Modern Magic. New York: 1873. V. 53

DE VERE, WILLIAM
Tramp Poems of the West... Tacoma: 1891. V. 47

DEVEVOISE, NEILSON C.
Parthian Pottery from Seleucia on the Tigris. Ann Arbor: 1934. V. 52

DEVEY, LOUISA
Life of Rosina, Lady Lytton... London: 1887. V. 53

DEVICES of Forty-Eight Famous Persons and Vices of Two Not So Famous. 1958. V. 48

THE DEVIL Among the Fancy; or, the Pugilistic. London: 1822. V. 51

DE VILLEMERT, BOURDIER
The Friend of Women. Philadelphia: 1803. V. 50; 51; 53

DE VILLIERS, C. G.
Genealgoies of Old South African Families. Cape Town & Amsterdam: 1966. V. 50

DEVILS at Home. London: 1829. V. 49; 53; 54

THE DEVILS in London. London: 1825. V. 52

DE VINNE, THEODORE LOW
The First Editor: Aldus Pius Manutius. New York: 1983. V. 47; 48; 51; 52
Notable Printers of Italy During the Fifteenth Century. New York: 1910. V. 53
The Plantin Moretus Museum: a Printer's Paradise. San Francisco: 1929. V. 47; 54
The Practice of Typography. New York: 1900-04. V. 48

DEVINNE, THEODORE LOW
The Printer's List. A Manual for the Use of Clerks and Book-Keepers in Job Printing Offices. New York: 1871. V. 48

DE VINNE, THEODORE LOW
Upon Small Types: the Preface to Brilliants. Brooklyn: 1969. V. 51

DEVINNY, V.
The Story of a Pioneer... Denver: 1904. V. 47

DEVLIN, DENIS
Intercessions - Poems. London: 1937. V. 50; 53

DEVOL, GEORGE H.
Forty Years a Gambler on the Mississippi. Cincinnati: 1887. V. 47; 48; 50

DEVOLPI, CHARLES P.
Montreal: a Pictorial Record. Historical Prints and Illustrations of the City of Montreal, Province of Quebec, Canada 1535-1885. Montreal: 1963. V. 52

DE VOLPI, CHARLES P.
Toronto: a Pictorial Record. Montreal: 1965. V. 48

DEVONSHIRE, WILLIAM CAVENDISH, 1ST DUKE OF
The True Copy of a Paper Delivered by the Lord De-shire (sic) to the Mayor of Darby, Where He Quarter'd the One and Twentieth on November, 1688. 1688. V. 47

DEVONSHIRE, WILLIAM CAVENDISH, 7TH DUKE OF
Catalogue of the Library at Chatsworth. London: 1879. V. 53

DE VOTO, BERNARD
Across the Wide Missouri. Boston: 1947. V. 54
Mark Twain at Work. Cambridge: 1942. V. 47; 49
Mark Twain's America. Boston: 1932. V. 47; 54

DE VRIES, PETER
Angels Can't Do Better. New York: 1944. V. 48
The Blood of the Lamb. Boston: 1961. V. 52
But Who Wakes the Bugler?. Boston: 1940. V. 51; 52; 53
No But I Saw the Movie. Boston: 1952. V. 49
The Tunnel of Love. Boston: 1957. V. 50; 54

DE WALD, ERNEST
The Illustrations in the Manuscripts of the Septuagint. Princeton: 1941-42. V. 48

DEWAR, DANIEL
Observations on the Character, Customs and Supersititons of the Irish. London: 1812. V. 49; 51
Observations on the Character, Customs and Superstitions of the Irish. Edinburgh: 1812. V. 48

DEWAR, DOUGLAS
Game Birds. London: 1928. V. 52

DEWAR, GEORGE A. B.
The South Country Trout Streams. London: 1899. V. 54

DEWAR, HUGO
Assassins at Large. London: 1951. V. 49

DEWAR, J. CUMING
Voyage of the Nyanza R.N.Y.C. Edinburgh: 1892. V. 53

DEWDNEY, SELWYN
Indian Rock Paintings of the Great Lakes. Toronto: 1962. V. 53
Indian Rock Paintings of the Great Lakes. Toronto: 1973. V. 50

DEWEES, MARY COBURN
Journal of a Trip from Philadelphia to Lexington in Kentucky, Kept by Mary Coburn Dewees in 1878. Crawfordsville: 1936. V. 53

DE WEES, W. B.
Letters from an Early Settler in Texas. Louisville: 1852. V. 53

DEWEES, W. B.
Letters from an Early Settler of Texas. Louisville: 1858. V. 49

DEWEES, WILLIAM POTTS
An Abridgement of Mr. Heath's Translation of Baudelocque's Midwifery... Philadelphia: 1807. V. 51; 53
An Abridgement of Mr. Heath's Translation of Baudelocque's Midwifery. Philadelphia: 1823. V. 54
A Compendious System of Midwifery. Philadelphia: 1832. V. 53
A Treatise On the Diseases of Females. Philadelphia: 1831. V. 50; 52; 53
A Treatise On the Physical and Medical Treatment of Children. Philadelphia: 1825. V. 54

D'EWES, SIMONDS
A Compleat Journal of the Votes, Speeches and Debates, Both of the House of Lords and House of Commons, Throughout the Whole Reign of Queen Elizabeth. London: 1793. V. 47
The Journal...from the Beginning of the Long Parliament to the Opening of the Trial of the Earl of Strafford. (with) The Journal...from the First Recess of the Long Parliament to the Withdrawal of King Charles from London. New Haven: 1923/42. V. 52
The Journals of All the Parliaments of the House of Lords and House of Commons During the Reign of Queen Elizabeth. 1973. V. 49

DE WET, H. OLOFF
The Valley of the Shadow. London: 1949. V. 52

DE WET, OLOFF
Cardboard Crucifix. The Story of a Pilot in Spain. Edinburgh & London: 1938. V. 49

DEWEY, B.
A True and Concise Narrative of the Origin and Progress of the Church Difficulties in the Vicinity of Dartmouth College, in Hanover, the Same Being the Origin of President Wheelock's Disaffection to the Trustees and Professors... Hanover: 1815. V. 54

DEWEY, JOHN
The Case of Leon Trotsky. New York: 1937. V. 51
The Child and the Curriculum. Chicago: 1902. V. 47
Psychology. New York: 1887. V. 49; 50; 54
Studies in Logical Theory. Chicago: 1903. V. 49

DEWEY, MELVIL
Decimal Classification and Relative Index. Boston: 1885. V. 50

DEWEY, ORVILLE
Moral Views of Commerce, Society and Politics in Twelve Discourses. London: 1838. V. 49
The Old World and the New; or, a Journal of Reflections and Observations Made On a Tour in Europe. New York: 1836. V. 49

DEWEY, SQUIRE P.
The Bonanza Mines and Bonanza Kings of California. San Francisco: 1880. V. 50; 52

DEWHURST, HENRY WILLIAM
The Natural History of the Order Cetacea and the Oceanic Inhabitants of the Arctic Regions. London: 1834. V. 51

DE WILDE, BARBARA
Fiction/Nonfiction. Book Jacket Designs 1987-1993. East Hampton: 1993. V. 53

DE WINDT, HARRY
From Peking to Calais by Land. London: 1889. V. 53
A Ride to India: Across Persia and Baluchistan. London: 1891. V. 54
Through the Gold Fields of Alaska to Bering Straits. London: 1898. V. 48; 50

DE WITT, SIMEON
The Elements of Perspective. Albany: 1813. V. 50

DEWITZ, PAUL W. H.
Notable Men of Indian Territory at the Beginning of the Twentieth Century 1904-05. Muskogee: 1905. V. 50

DE WOLFF, J. H.
Pawnee Bill, His Experience and Adventures on the Western Plains... 1901. V. 53
Pawnee Bill (Major Gordon W. Lillie) His Experiences and Adventures on the Western Plains, or, From the Saddle of a 'Cowboy and Ranger' tot he Chair of a 'Bank President'. 1902. V. 48

DEWS, NATHAN
The History of Deptford, in the Counties of Kent and Surrey... Deptford: 1883. V. 54
The History of Deptford in the Counties of Kent and Surrey. London: 1884. V. 54

DEXTER, CHARLES
In Memoriam. Cambridge: 1866. V. 47

DEXTER, COLIN
The Dead of Jericho. London: 1981. V. 52
The Jewel That Was Ours. Bristol: 1991. V. 51; 54
The Jewel That Was Ours. London: 1991. V. 50
Last Bus to Woodstock. London: 1975. V. 47; 51; 52
Last Bus to Woodstock. New York: 1975. V. 52
Last Seen Wearing. London: 1976. V. 52
Morse's Greatest Mystery. 1993. V. 54
Morse's Greatest Mystery. Bristol: 1993. V. 52
Neighbourhood Watch. 1993. V. 49
Neighbourhood Watch. London: 1993. V. 52
Neighbourhood Watch. Richmond: 1993. V. 48
The Riddle of the Third Mile. London: 1983. V. 52
Service of All the Dead. New York: 1979. V. 52
The Silent World of Nicholas Quinn. London: 1977. V. 52
The Silent World of Nicholas Quinn. New York: 1977. V. 52
The Way through the Woods. 1992. V. 54
The Way through the Woods. Bristol: 1992. V. 51; 52
The Way Through the Woods. London: 1992. 50; 51; 53; 54

DEXTER, PETE
Deadwood. New York: 1986. V. 51
God's Pocket. New York: 1983. V. 50; 51; 53

DEZALLIER D'ARGENVILLE, A. J.
L'Histoire Nataurelle Eclaircie dans une de Ses Parties principales. La Conchyliodlogie... Paris: 1757. V. 53
L'Histoire Naturelle Eclaircie Dans Deux de Ses Parties Principales, La Lithologie et La Conchyliologie. Paris: 1742. V. 54
La Theorie et la Pratique de Jardinage. Paris: 1709. V. 47; 49
The Theory and Practice of Gardening. London: 1712. V. 52

DE ZGLINITZKI, HELEN NICHOLSON, BARONESS
Death in the Morning. A Woman's Experiences of the civil War in Spain. London: 1937. V. 49

D'HARCOURT, RAOUL
Textiles of Ancient Peru and Their Techniques. Seattle: 1962. V. 47

D'HARMONCOURT, ANNE
Marcel Duchamp. New York: 1973. V. 47; 48

D'HERBELOT D'MOLAINVILLE, BARTHELEMY
Bibliotheque Orientale, ou Dictionnaire Universel Contenant Generalment Tout ce Qui Regarade la Connoissance des Peuples de l'Orient. Paris: 1697. V. 48

D'HERELLE, FELIX
The Bacteriophage and Its Clinical Applications. Springfield: 1930. V. 51
Immunity in Natural Infectious Disease. Baltimore: 1924. V. 51

DHU, SKENE
The Angler in Northern India. Allahabad: 1910. V. 52

A DIALOGUE at Oxford Between a Tutor and a Gentleman, Formerly His Pupil, Concerning Government. London: 1681. V. 54

A DIALOGUE Between a Member of Parliament a Divine, A Lawyer, a Freeholder, A Shopkeeper and a Country Farmer; or Remarks on the Badness of the Market (etc.). London: 1703. V. 52

A DIALOGUE Between Death and a Lady. 1790-1810. V. 47

A DIALOGUE Between the Lord R's Ghost and the D. of C. 1683. V. 47

A DIALOGUE Between Two Oxford Schollars. 1680. V. 47

A DIALOGUE Betwixt Sam. The Ferriman of Dochet, Will. A Waterman of London, and Tom, A Bargeman of Oxford. Upon the Kings Calling a Parliament to Meet at Oxford. London: 1681. V. 54

A DIALOGUE Concerning the Times Between Philobelgus and Sophronius. 1688. V. 53

A DIALOGUE Which Lately Pass'd Between the Knight and His Man John. London: 1739. V. 54

DIALOGUES, Poems, Songs and Ballads, by Various Writers, in the Westmoreland and Cumberland Dialects, Now First Collected. London: 1839. V. 52

DIALOGUS CREATURARUM
The Dialogues of Creatures Moralised. London: 1816. V. 48
Dialogues of Creatures Moralised... Kentfield: 1967. V. 48; 53
Herball: from the Dialogues of Creatures Moralised. West Burke: 1979. V. 52; 54

A DIALOUGE on Priestcraft: Founded on Facts. Newburyport: 1835. V. 53

DIAMANT Classics. New York: 1944-53. V. 52

DIAMOND, A. W.
Studies of Mascarene Island Birds. London: 1987. V. 50; 51

DIAPER, WILLIAM
An Imitation of the Seventeenth Epistle of the Eight Books of Horace. London: 1714. V. 49
Nereides, or Sea-Eclogues. London: 1712. V. 49

DIARY of a Nun. London: 1840. V. 51

DIARY of an Excursion, in the Months of August and September, 1814, in a Series of Letters, Wherein an Accurate Idea May be Formed of The Expence Attending a Tour to Paris. Edinburgh: 1814. V. 47

A DIARY of the Wreck on the Western Coast of South America, in May 1835. London: 1836. V. 48

DIAZ, ABBY MORTON
Only a Flock of Women. Boston: 1893. V. 51

DIAZ DEL CASTILLO, BERNAL
The Discovery and Conquest of Mexico. Mexico City: 1942. V. 51; 52; 54
The Memoirs of Conquistador... London: 1844. V. 47
The True History of the Conquest of Mexico. London: 1800. V. 47; 48; 54

DIAZ VARA CALDERON, GABRIEL
Grandezas y Maravillas de la Inclyta y Sancta Cividad de Roma. Madrid: 1677. V. 53

DIBB, ROBERT
The Minstrel's Offering; or Wreath of Poetry. London: 1839. V. 54

DIBBLE, SHELDON
History and General Views of the Sandwich Islands' Mission. New York: 1839. V. 51; 52

DIBDIN, CHARLES
The Gipsies. A Comick Opera, in Two Acts. London: 1778. V. 53
Music Epitomized: a School Book. Goulding: 1820. V. 48
The Musical Tour of Mr. Dibdin. Sheffield: 1788. V. 51; 52; 53; 54
The Overture, Songs, &c. in the Quaker. London: 1777. V. 52
The Padlock a Comic Opera. London: 1768. V. 51
The Professional Life of Mr. Dibdin. London: 1803. V. 54
Songs, Duettos, Glees, Catches, Etc. with an Explanation of the Procession in the Pantomime of Harlequin. London: 1781. V. 54
Songs, Naval and National: With Memoir and Addenda. London: 1841. V. 49
Songs of the Late Charles Dibdin. London: 1841. V. 49

DIBDIN, JAMES C.
The Annals of the Edinburgh Stage. Edinburgh: 1888. V. 48

DIBDIN, MICHAEL
The Last Sherlock Holmes Story. London: 1978. V. 47

DIBDIN, THOMAS
The School for Prejudice. London: 1801. V. 47

DIBDIN, THOMAS FROGNALL
Aedes Althorpianae; or, an Account of the Mansion, Books and Pictures At Althorp; the Residence of George John Earl spencer, K.G. London: 1822. V. 48
A Bibliographical Antiquarian and Picturesque Tour in France and Germany. London: 1821. V. 47; 48; 49; 50; 51; 54
A Bibliographical, Antiquarian and Picturesque Tour in France and Germany. London: 1829. V. 47; 48; 49; 50; 51
A Bibliographical, Antiquarian and Picturesque Tour in the Northern Counties of England and in Scotland. London: 1838. V. 48; 51
The Bibliographical Decameron. London: 1817. V. 48; 49; 50; 52; 53
Bibliography: a Poem. London: 1812. V. 50
The Bibliomania; or Book Madness... London: 1809. V. 48
Bibliomania; or Book Madness... London: 1811. V. 48; 52
Bibliomania; or Book Madness. London: 1842. V. 54
Bibliomania; or Book Madness. London: 1876. V. 47; 48; 50; 52
The Bibliomania, or Book Madness. Boston: 1903. V. 49; 52; 53; 54
Bibliophobia. London: 1832. V. 48; 50
A Descriptive Catalogue of the Books Printed in the 15th Century Lately Forming Part of the Library of the Duke Di Cassano Serra and Now the Property of George John, Earl Spencer. London: 1823. V. 48
The History of Cheltenham and Its Environs... Cheltenham: 1803. V. 47

DIBDIN, THOMAS FROGNALL continued
An Introduction to the Knowldge of Rare and Valuable Editions of the Greek and Latin Classics... London: 1804. V. 48
An Introduction to the Knowledge of Rare and Valuable Editions of the Greek and Latin Classics, Including an Account of the Polyglot Bibles. London: 1808. V. 52
An Introduction to the Knowledge of Rare and Valuable Editions of the Greek and Latin Classics Together with an Account of Polyglot Bibles. London: 1827. V. 47; 48; 51; 53
An Introduction to the Knowledge of Rare and Valuable Editions of the Greek and Roman Classics. Glocester: 1802. V. 53
The Library Companion. London: 1824. V. 47; 48; 49; 50; 51; 52; 54
Library Companion; or, the Young Man's Guide, and Old Man's Comfort, in the Choice of a Library. London: 1825. V. 48; 50; 53; 54
Music Epitomized... Goulding: 1820. V. 49
Poems. London: 1797. V. 50
Reminiscences of a Literary Life. London: 1836. V. 47; 48; 50; 53; 54
Typographical Antiquities or the History of Printing In England, Scotland, and Ireland... London: 1810/19. V. 48; 49; 50
Voyage Bibliographique Archaeologique et Pittoresque en France. Paris: 1825. V. 47

DIBNER, BERN
Agricola On Metals. Norwalk: 1959. V. 50

DICEY, EDWARD
Six Months in the Federal States. London and Cambridge: 1863. V. 50; 53

DICEY, THOMAS
An Historical Account of Guernsey, From Its First Settlement Before the Norman Conquest to the Present Time. London: 1751. V. 51

DICK, MAXWELL
Description of the Suspension Railway Invented by Maxwell Dick. Irvine: 1830. V. 51

DICK, PHILIP K.
The Broken Bubble. New York: 1988. V. 52
Confessions of a Crap Artist. New York: 1975. V. 47
Deus Irae. Garden City: 1976. V. 51; 54
Deus Irae. London: 1978. V. 53
Deus Irae. Newton Abbot: 1978. V. 52
The Divine Invasion. New York: 1981. V. 50
Do Androids Dream of Electric Sheep. New York: 1968. V. 52; 53
Dr. Bloodmoney, or How We Got Along After the Bomb. New York: 1965. V. 50
Eye in the Sky. 1957. V. 51; 53
Eye in the Sky. Boston: 1979. V. 53
Flow My Tears the Policeman Said. Garden City: 1974. V. 51
Flow My Tears, the Policeman Said. New York: 1974. V. 49; 54
The Game Players of Titan. New York: 1963. V. 51
The Game Players of Titan. London: 1974. V. 47; 51
The Golden Man. New York: 1980. V. 49
A Handful of Darkness. 1955. V. 47; 49; 51; 54
A Handful of Darkness. Boston: 1978. V. 51
The Man in the High Castle. 1959. V. 47; 49; 51
The Man in the High Castle. 1962. V. 53
The Man in the High Castle. New York: 1962. V. 49
The Man Who Japed. London: 1978. V. 48; 52
Martian Time-Slip. New York: 1964. V. 50
Martian Time-Slip. 1976. V. 49; 54
Mary and the Giant. New York: 1987. V. 50
A Maze of Death. New York: 1977. V. 50
Now Wait for Last Year. Garden City: 1966. V. 51
Now Wait for Last Year. New York: 1966. V. 47; 51
A Scanner Darkly. Garden City: 1977. V. 51
A Scanner Darkly. New York: 1977. V. 49
The Simulacra. London: 1977. V. 47
The Three Stigmata of Palmer Eldritch. Garden City: 1965. V. 51
The Three Stigmata of Palmer Eldritch. New York: 1965. V. 48; 52
Time Out of Joint. New York: 1959. V. 51
Time Out of Joint. Philadelphia: 1959. V. 47; 48; 51; 52
Time Out of Joint. 1961. V. 49
The Transmigration of Timothy Archer. New York: 1982. V. 52
Ubik. New York: 1969. V. 48; 49; 52
Ubik. New York: 1970. V. 49; 53
Ubik. Boston: 1979. V. 49
Valis. New York: 1981. V. 50
Valis. (with) Costmogony & Cosmology. Surrey: 1987. V. 51
Vulcan's Hammer. Boston: 1979. V. 49
World of Chance. 1957. V. 49; 54
The Zap Gun. New York: 1967. V. 50

DICK, R. A.
The Ghost and Mrs. Muir. Chicago: 1945. V. 50

DICK, STEWART
Arts and Crafts of Old Japan. London: 1914. V. 47
The Cottage Homes of England. London: 1909. V. 48

DICK, WILLIAM BRISBANE
The American Card-Player... New York: 1866. V. 52
Dick's Games of Patience: or Solitaire with Cards. New York: 1884/1983. V. 52

DICKENS, CHARLES
Address Delivered at the Birmingham and Midland Institute on the 27th September, 1869. Birmingham: 1869. V. 49; 54
The Adventures of Oliver Twist. London: 1836. V. 49
The Adventures of Oliver Twist. London: 1846. V. 48; 50; 51; 52; 53
The Adventures of Oliver Twist. London: 1850. V. 54
The Adventures of Oliver Twist. London: 1895. V. 48; 53
The Adventures of Oliver Twist. New York: 1939. V. 54
All the Year Round. London: 1859-67. V. 49
All the Year Round. London: 1859-68. V. 49
All the Year Round. London: 1861-69. V. 51
All the Year Round. London: 1991. V. 49
El Almacen de Antiguedades. (The Old Curiosity Shop). Madrid: 1886. V. 49
American Notes. London: 1842. V. 47; 48; 49; 50; 51; 52; 53; 54
American Notes. New York: 1842. V. 47; 48; 49; 53; 54
American Notes. Paris: 1842. V. 47; 49
American Notes. London: 1850. V. 50; 53; 54
American Notes. London: 1855. V. 53
American Notes. Avon: 1975. V. 53
American Notes, Pictures from Italy and a Child's History of England. London: 1910. V. 47
Barnaby Rudge. London: 1841. V. 49; 51; 53; 54
Barnaby Rudge. Philadelphia: 1842. V. 54
Barnaby Rudge. London: 1860. V. 49
The Battle of Life. London: 1846. V. 47; 48; 49; 50; 51; 52; 53; 54
The Battle of Life and The Haunted Man. Leipzig: 1856. V. 54
Bleak House. London: 1852-53. V. 48; 50; 53; 54
Bleak House. London: 1853. V. 47; 48; 49; 50; 51; 52; 53; 54
Bleak House. New York: 1853. V. 47; 48
Bleak House. London: 1858. V. 54
Bleak House. London: 1860. V. 54
Bleak House. Garden City: 1953. V. 53
Catalogue of the Beautiful Collection of Modern Pictures, Water-Color Drawings and Objects of Art of Charles Dickens Deceased... London: 1870. V. 54
Catalogue of the Library of Charles Dickens from Gadshill Reprinted from Sotheran's Price Current of Literature... London: 1935. V. 54
Character Sketches from Charles Dickens. London. V. 51
The Charles Dickens Birthday Book. London: 1882. V. 47
Charles Dickens Library. London: 1912. V. 49; 54
The Charles Dickens Parlor Album of Illustrations. New York: 1879. V. 54
A Child's Dream of a Star. Boston: 1871. V. 49; 51
A Child's Dream of a Star. Boston: 1871/70. V. 54
A Child's Dream of a Star. London: 1899. V. 49; 54
A Child's History of England. London: 1852. V. 47
A Child's History of England. London: 1852-54. V. 47; 48; 49; 50; 53; 54
A Child's History of England. Boston: 1854. V. 54
A Child's History of England. New York: 1854. V. 47
A Child's History of England. London: 1879. V. 54
A Child's History of England. London: 1890. V. 54
The Chimes. London: 1845. V. 47; 48; 49; 51; 52; 53; 54
The Chimes. New York: 1845. V. 51; 54
The Chimes. London: 1845/44. V. 49; 50; 54
The Chimes. London: 1858. V. 49
The Chimes. London & New York: 1905. V. 52
The Chimes. London: 1913. V. 52; 53; 54
The Chimes. London: 1931. V. 47; 48; 50; 51; 52; 54
The Chimes. New York: 1931. V. 52
The Chimes. 1985. V. 52
The Christmas Books. London: 1843-48. V. 47
The Christmas Books. Leipzig: 1846. V. 54
Christmas Books. London: 1852. V. 49; 52; 54
Christmas Carol. Leipzig: 1843. V. 54
A Christmas Carol. London: 1843. V. 47; 48; 50; 51
A Christmas Carol. London: 1844. V. 49; 54
A Christmas Carol. Philadelphia: 1844. V. 47; 49
A Christmas Carol. London: 1845. V. 49
A Christmas Carol. London: 1846. V. 49; 54
A Christmas Carol. London: 1855. V. 49; 53
A Christmas Carol. London: 1858. V. 49; 54
The Christmas Carol. London: 1890. V. 51
A Christmas Carol. London and New York: 1905. V. 52
A Christmas Carol. London: 1915. V. 47; 48; 51; 52; 53; 54
A Christmas Carol. Cleveland & New York: 1916. V. 52
A Christmas Carol. Boston: 1920. V. 47; 52; 53
A Christmas Carol. London New York & Toronto: 1920. V. 54
A Christmas Carol. London: 1922. V. 53
A Christmas Carol. London: 1934. V. 49
A Christmas Carol. London: 1946. V. 52
A Christmas Carol. London: 1948. V. 54
A Christmas Carol. Cleveland: 1961. V. 54
A Christmas Carol. New York: 1971. V. 54
A Christmas Carol. London: 1978. V. 53
A Christmas Carol. Mission: 1984. V. 47
A Christmas Carol in Prose. London: 1843. V. 49; 51; 52; 53; 54
A Christmas Carol in Prose. Boston: 1934. V. 53

DICKENS, CHARLES *continued*

A Christmas Carol in Prose, Being a Ghost Story of Christmas. Philadelphia Chicago: 1938. V. 51
A Christmas Carol. (with) The Cricket on the Hearth. Leipzig: 1843-46. V. 54
Christmas Stories. Bexhill-on-Sea, E. Sussex: 1984. V. 51
Christmas Stories From "All the Year Round". London: 1863-67. V. 49
Christmas Stories: From "Household Words" and "All the Year Round". London: 1890. V. 48
Christmas Tales: A Christmas Carol in Prose; The Chimes; The Cricket on the Hearth. Leipzig: 1843-46. V. 47
The Collected Works. London: 1873-76. V. 50
The Complete Works. New York: 1890's. V. 51
The Complete Works of Charles Dickens. New York and Chicago: 1910?. V. 49
The Complete Works of Charles Dickens. London: 1937-38. V. 47; 51
Complete Works of Charles Dickens. Bloomsbury: 1938. V. 49
The Cricket on the Hearth. London: 1845. V. 53; 54
The Cricket on the Hearth. London: 1846. V. 47; 48; 49; 50; 51; 52; 53; 54
The Cricket on the Hearth. London: 1864. V. 51
The Cricket on the Hearth. London and New York: 1905. V. 53
The Cricket on the Hearth. London: 1906. V. 54
The Cricket on the Hearth. London: 1933. V. 52
The Cricket On the Hearth. New York: 1933. V. 47; 48
The Cricket on the Hearth. The Chimes. The Battle of Life. The Haunted Man. London: 1844-48. V. 50; 51
A Curious Dance Round a Curious Tree. 1860. V. 49
A Curious Dance Round a Curious Tree. London: 1860. V. 54
Dame Durden, Little Woman. New York: 1855. V. 54
David Copperfield. London: 1920's. V. 53
David Copperfield. London: 1936. V. 50
David Copperfield in Copperplates. Berkeley: 1939. V. 52
De Lotgevallen van Nikolaes Nickleby, Naer het Engelsch. Ghent: 1858. V. 49
Dealings With the Firm of Dombey and Son. London: 1846-April 1848. V. 51
Dealings with the Firm of Dombey and Son. New York: 1847. V. 48
Dealings with the Firm of Dombey and Son. London: 1848. V. 47; 49; 51; 53
A Dickens Friendship, Told in His Own Letters. London: 1931. V. 50
Dickens' Working Notes for His Novels. Chicago: 1987. V. 54
The Dickens-Kolle Letters. Boston: 1910. V. 51
Dickens's Children. New York: 1912. V. 47
Dr. Marigold's Prescriptions, the Extra Christmas Number of all the Year Round, Conducted by Charles Dickens for Christmas 1856. London: 1865. V. 49
Dolly Varden. New York: 1855. V. 53
Dombey and Son. London: 1846-47. V. 49
Dombey and Son. Leipzig: 1847-48. V. 54
Dombey and Son. Boston: 1848. V. 51
Dombey and Son. London: 1848. V. 48; 49; 50; 51; 53; 54
Dombey and Son. New York: 1848. V. 51
Dombey and Son. London: 1858. V. 47; 54
Dombey and Son. London: 1860. V. 54
Dombey and Son. London: 1865. V. 54
Dombey and Son. New York: 1957. V. 53; 54
Dombey and Son. And Barnaby Rudge. Philadelphia: 1848-50. V. 54
The Earliest Letters of Charles Dickens (Written to His Friend Henry Kolle). Cambridge: 1910. V. 49
Edwin Drood. Leipzig: 1870. V. 54
Edwin Drood. London: 1870. V. 54
Edwin Drood. London: 1870-72. V. 54
Edwin Drood. London: 1870/73?. V. 54
Edwin Drood. Brattleboro: 1873. V. 54
The Fireside Dickens. London; 1903-07. V. 49; 54
Florence Dombey, from Dombey & Son. New York: 1855. V. 54
The Gadshill Edition of the Works of Charles Dickens. 1907-08. V. 53
George Silverman's Explanation. Brighton: 1878. V. 49
George Silverman's Explanation. California: 1984. V. 51
Great Expectations. Leipzig: 1861. V. 54
Great Expectations. London: 1861. V. 47; 48; 49; 50; 51; 53; 54
Great Expectations. New York: 1861. V. 47; 51
Great Expectations. Philadelphia: 1861. V. 53
Great Expectations. London: 1862. V. 54
Great Expectations. Mobile: 1863. V. 47
Great Expectations. London: 1864. V. 54
Great Expectations. London: 1876. V. 54
Great Expectations. London: 1925. V. 54
Great Expectations. Edinburgh: 1937. V. 47; 48; 49; 54
Great Expectations. Oxford: 1993. V. 49
Hard Times. Leipzig: 1854. V. 54
Hard Times. London: 1854. V. 47; 49; 50; 51; 53; 54
Hard Times. New York: 1854. V. 47
Hard Times. London: 1857. V. 52
Hard Times. New York: 1966. V. 54
Hard Times. and Great Expectations. London: 1877. V. 54
The Haunted Man and Ghost's Bargain. London: 1848. V. 47; 48; 49; 51; 52; 53; 54
Hern Humphrey's Wanduhr. (Master Humphrey's Clock). Braunschweig: 1840-41. V. 54
The Holly Tree. East Aurora: 1903. V. 51; 52
The Holly Tree Inn and a Christmas Tree. New York. V. 47
Hospital for Sick Children Great Ormond Street. Extract from Chapter IX of "Our Mutual Friend". London: 1865?. V. 49

The Household Narrative of Current Events... London: 1850-53. V. 49
The Household Narrative of Current Events (for the Year 1850-1885). London: 1850-55. V. 49
Household Words. London: 1850-59. V. 49
Household Words. London: 1991. V. 49
Hunted Down. London: 1870. V. 47; 51
Hunted Down. London: 1871. V. 47
Is She His Wife?. Boston: 1877. V. 54
Is She His Wife?. London: 1883. V. 51
Is She His Wife?. London: 1884. V. 49
The Lamplighter. London: 1879. V. 49; 54
The Lazy Tour of Two Idle Apprentices. No Thoroughfare. The Perils of Certain English Prisoners. London: 1890. V. 49; 54
The Letters. London: 1880. V. 53; 54
The Letters. London: 1880-82. V. 49; 54
The Letters. London: 1938. V. 54
The Letters of Charles Dickens. Oxford: 1965. V. 49
The Letters of Charles Dickens. Oxford: 1969. V. 49
The Letters of Charles Dickens. London: 1974. V. 49
The Letters of Charles Dickens. London: 1977. V. 49
The Letters of Charles Dickens. London: 1989. V. 49
The Letters of Charles Dickens. London: 1990. V. 49
The Letters of Charles Dickens. London: 1993. V. 49
The Letters of Charles Dickens 1820-1841. Oxford: 1965/69. V. 51
The Letters. Volume I. 1820-1839. Oxford: 1965. V. 54
The Letters. Volume II: 1840-1841. Oxford: 1969. V. 54
The Letters. Volume III. 1842-1843. Oxford: 1974. V. 54
The Letters. Volume IV. 1844-1846. Oxford: 1977. V. 54
The Letters. Volume V. 1847-1849. London: 1977. V. 54
The Library of Fiction, or Family Story-Teller... London: 1836-37. V. 47; 49
The Life and Adventures of Martin Chuzzlewit. London: 1843-44. V. 47; 51; 53; 54
The Life and Adventures of Martin Chuzzlewit. Leipzig: 1844. V. 54
The Life and Adventures of Martin Chuzzlewit. London: 1844. V. 47; 48; 49; 50; 51; 52; 53; 54
The Life and Adventures of Martin Chuzzlewit. New York: 1844. V. 51
The Life and Adventures of Martin Chuzzlewit. Paris: 1844. V. 49
The Life and Adventures of Martin Chuzzlewit. Philadelphia: 1844. V. 49
The Life and Adventures of Nicholas Nickleby. London: 1838-39. V. 49; 52
The Life and Adventures of Nicholas Nickleby. London: 1838-40. V. 50
The Life and Adventures of Nicholas Nickleby. Paris: 1839. V. 47
The Life and Adventures of Nicholas Nickleby. London: 1848. V. 53
The Life and Adventures of Nicholas Nickleby. London: 1870. V. 48
The Life of Charles James Mathews. London: 1980. V. 48
The Life of Our Lord. London: 1934. V. 47; 48; 49; 53; 54
The Life of Our Lord. New York: 1934. V. 47
The Life of Our Lord. Philadelphia: 1934. V. 51
Little Dorrit. London: 1855. V. 53
Little Dorrit. London: 1855-57. V. 47; 50; 51; 52; 53; 54
Little Dorrit. Leipzig: 1856-57. V. 49; 54
Little Dorrit. London: 1857. V. 47; 48; 49; 50; 51; 52; 53; 54
Little Dorrit. London: 1865. V. 47; 54
Lloyd's Sixpenny Dickens. London: 1909-11. V. 49; 54
The Loving Ballad of Lord Bateman. London: 1839. V. 49; 53
The Loving Ballad of Lord Bateman... London: 1851. V. 49
The Loving Ballad of Lord Bateman. London: 1871. V. 49
Master Humphrey's Clock. London: 1840. V. 48; 50; 51
Master Humphrey's Clock. London: 1840-41. V. 47; 48; 49; 50; 51; 52; 53; 54
Master Humphrey's Clock. Calcutta: 1841-42. V. 54
Master Humphrey's Clock. Leipzig: 1846. V. 54
Memorie di Davide Copperfield... Milano: 1859. V. 49
Mr. Dickens and Mr. Bentley. London: 1871. V. 50
Mr. Nightingale's Diary. Boston: 1877. V. 49; 50; 54
Mister Pickwick. London: 1910. V. 47
Mr. Pickwick's Christmas Being an Account of the Pickwickians' Christmas at Manor Farm... New York: 1906. V. 54
Mrs. Lirriper's Legacy. London: 1864. V. 48; 49
Mrs. Lirriper's Lodgings, The Extra Christmas Number of All the Year Round. London: 1863. V. 48; 49
The Mudfog Papers. London: 1880. V. 49; 54
The Mudfog Papers, etc. New York: 1880. V. 51
Mugby Junction. London: 1866. V. 48; 49; 51; 53
The Mystery of Edwin Drood. London: 1865. V. 51
The Mystery of Edwin Drood. Boston: 1870. V. 47
The Mystery of Edwin Drood. London: 1870. V. 47; 48; 49; 50; 51; 52; 53; 54
Le Neveu de Ma Tante: Histoire Personnelle de David Copperfield. Paris: 1851. V. 49; 54
Nicholas Nickleby. London: 1839. V. 47; 48; 49; 50; 51; 52; 53; 54
Nicholas Nickleby. Leipzig: 1843. V. 54
Nicholas Nickleby. London: 1848. V. 54
Nicholas Nickleby. London: 1865. V. 49
Nicholas Nickleby. London: 1891. V. 49
No Thoroughfare. London: 1867. V. 48; 49; 54
No Thoroughfare. New York: 1868?. V. 54
The Nonesuch Dickens. Bloomsbury: 1937-38. V. 49; 50; 52
The Nonesuch Dickens. London: 1937-38. V. 51
The Novels and Tales. Philadelphia: 1846. V. 54

DICKENS, CHARLES continued
Novels and Tales. London: 1881. V. 51
The Old Curiosity Shop. London: 1841. V. 51
The Old Curiosity Shop. Philadelphia: 1841. V. 53; 54
The Old Curiosity Shop. London: 1848. V. 54
The Old Curiosity Shop. Philadelphia: 1853. V. 49; 54
The Old Curiosity Shop. London: 1860. V. 49
The Old Curiosity Shop. London: 1913. V. 52
Old Lamps for New Ones and Other Sketches and Essays. New York: 1897. V. 51
Oliver Twist. London: 1838. V. 47; 48; 49; 50; 51; 52; 53; 54
Oliver Twist. New York: 1839. V. 51; 54
Oliver Twist... London: 1841. V. 49
Oliver Twist. New York: 1842. V. 49; 54
Oliver Twist. Philadelphia: 1843. V. 54
Oliver Twist. London: 1846. V. 49; 54
Our Mutual Friend. London: 1864-65. V. 47; 48; 49; 50; 51; 53; 54
Our Mutual Friend. London: 1865. V. 47; 48; 49; 50; 51; 52; 53; 54
Our Mutual Friend. New York: 1865. V. 49; 50; 54
Our Mutual Friend. London: 1891. V. 53; 54
The Oxford Illustrated Dickens. London: 1947-58. V. 49
The Oxford India Paper Dickens. London. V. 53
The Personal History of David Copperfield. Leipzig: 1849-50. V. 54
The Personal History of David Copperfield. London: 1849-50. V. 48; 49; 50; 54
The Personal History of David Copperfield. London: 1850. V. 47; 48; 49; 50; 51; 53; 54
The Personal History of David Copperfield. New York: 1852?. V. 49
The Personal History of David Copperfield. London: 1865. V. 54
The Personal History of David Copperfield. London: 1870?. V. 50
The Personal History of David Copperfield. New York & London: 1911. V. 47; 49
La Petite Dorrit. Paris: 1864. V. 54
The Pic Nic Papers. London: 1841. V. 49; 53; 54
The Pic Nic Papers. Paris: 1841. V. 49; 54
The Pic Nic Papers. London: 1858. V. 54
Pickwick Clubbens Efterladte Papirer... Kjobenhavn: 1861. V. 49
The Pickwick Papers. London. V. 48
Pickwick Papers. London: 1836-37. V. 49
Pickwick Papers. London: 1837. V. 49; 54
Pickwick Papers. New York: 1838. V. 49
Pickwick Papers. Philadelphia: 1838. V. 54
Pickwick Papers. Paris: 1839. V. 54
Pickwick Papers. New York: 1842. V. 49
Pickwick Papers. London: 1845. V. 54
Pickwick Papers. Philadelphia: 1846. V. 49; 54
Pickwick Papers. London: 1862. V. 54
Pickwick Papers. London: 1865. V. 54
Pickwick Papers. London: 1875. V. 54
Pickwick Papers. London: 1887. V. 49; 54
Pickwick Papers. London & Bath: 1891. V. 54
Pickwick Papers. London: 1904. V. 54
Pickwick Papers. London: 1910. V. 54
Pickwick Papers. London: 1933. V. 50
Pictures From Italy. London: 1846. V. 47; 48; 49; 50; 51; 52; 53; 54
Pictures from Italy. Paris: 1846. V. 49; 54
Pictures from Italy. New York: 1877. V. 53
Pictures From Italy. Genoa Venice Rome: 1982. V. 48
Pictures From Italy. Greenbrae: 1982. V. 48; 51; 53
The Plays and Poems of Charles Dickens... London: 1885. V. 54
The Poems and Verses of Charles Dickens. London: 1903. V. 49
Poor Traveller: Boots at the Holly-Tree Inn: and Mrs. Gamp. London: 1858. V. 47; 48; 54
The Posthumous Papers of the Pickwick Club. London: 1836. V. 51; 53; 54
The Posthumous Papers of the Pickwick Club. London: 1836-37. V. 47; 48; 53
The Posthumous Papers of the Pickwick Club. Philadelphia: 1836-37. V. 54
The Posthumous Papers of the Pickwick Club. London: 1837. V. 47; 48; 49; 50; 51; 52; 53; 54
The Posthumous Papers of the Pickwick Club. Philadelphia: 1837. V. 47
The Posthumous Papers of the Pickwick Club. London: 1838. V. 49; 51; 52
The Posthumous Papers of the Pickwick Club. Paris: 1838. V. 50
The Posthumous Papers of the Pickwick Club... Paris: 1839. V. 50; 52
The Posthumous Papers of the Pickwick Club. London: 1847. V. 54
The Posthumous Papers of the Pickwick Club. London: 1880. V. 49
The Posthumous Papers of the Pickwick Club. London: 1887. V. 48; 52
The Posthumous Papers of the Pickwick Club. London: 1910. V. 48; 50; 54
The Posthumous Papers of the Pickwick Club. London: 1912. V. 47
The Posthumous Papers of the Pickwick Club. London: 1931. V. 48
The Posthumous Papers of the Pickwick Club. London: 1931-32. V. 48; 54
The Posthumous Papers of the Pickwick Club. London: 1933. V. 49
The Posthumous Papers of the Pickwick Club. New York: 1933. V. 53
The Posthumous Papers of the Pickwick Club. Oxford: 1933. V. 48; 50; 51
Reprinted Pieces and the Lazy Tour of Two Idle Apprentices. New York: 1896. V. 49
The Short Stories of Charles Dickens. New York: 1971. V. 49; 52; 54
Sikes and Nancy: a Reading. London: 1921. V. 49
Sketches by Boz... London: 1836. V. 49
Sketches by Boz. London: 1836/37. V. 47; 48; 49; 50; 54
Sketches by Boz. London: 1839. V. 47; 48; 49; 50; 51; 52; 53; 54
Sketches by Boz. Paris: 1839. V. 49

Sketches by Boz. Philadelphia: 1839. V. 49; 54
Sketches by Boz. London: 1858. V. 47
Sketches by Boz. London: 1877. V. 49
Sketches by Boz. First and Second Series. London: 1836. V. 54
Sketches by Boz. First Series. London: 1837. V. 49
Sketches by Boz, Second Series. London: 1837. V. 47; 50; 54
Sketches by Boz. (together with) Sketches by Boz...Second Series. London: 1836. V. 48; 53; 54
Sketches of Young Couples. London: 1840. V. 49; 54
Sketches of Young Gentlemen. London: 1838. V. 47; 49; 50; 54
Speech of Charles Dickens, Esq. Delivered at the Meeting of the Administrative Reform Association, at the Theatre Royal, Drury lane, Wednesday June 25, 1855. London: 1855. V. 49; 50; 54
Speeches Literary and Social... London: 1870. V. 54
The Speeches of Charles Dickens. Oxford: 1960. V. 54
The Speeches of Charles Dickens. Hemel Hempstead: 1988. V. 54
The Story of Little Dombey. London: 1858. V. 47; 49; 50; 54
The Strange Gentleman. London: 1837. V. 47; 54
The Strange Gentleman. London: 1871. V. 49; 51; 54
The Strange Gentleman. London: 1928. V. 50; 54
Sunday Under Three Heads. London: 1836. V. 49
Sunday Under Three Heads. London: 1884. V. 54
A Tale of Two Cities. Leipzig: 1859. V. 49
A Tale of Two Cities. London: 1859. V. 47; 48; 49; 50; 51; 52; 53; 54
A Tale of Two Cities. Philadelphia: 1859. V. 53
A Tale of Two Cities. London: 1860. V. 48; 49; 54
A Tale of Two Cities. London: 1864. V. 54
A Tale of Two Cities. London: 1896?. V. 49
To Be Read At Dusk and Other Stories, Sketches and Essays. London: 1898. V. 49
The Uncollected Writings of Charles Dickens: Household Words 1850-1859. London: 1969. V. 49
The Uncommercial Traveller. London: 1861. V. 47; 49; 50; 53; 54
The Uncommercial Traveller. London: 1866. V. 54
Unpublished Letters...to Mark Lemon. London: 1927. V. 53; 54
Vie et Aventures de Nicolas Nickleby. Paris: 1865. V. 53; 54
The Village Coquettes. London: 1836. V. 54
The Village Coquettes. London: 1836 (1878). V. 47
The Village Coquettes. London: 1878-1900. V. 49
The Village Coquettes. London: 1883?. V. 49; 54
The Work of Charles Dickens. London: 1900. V. 51
The Works. London: 1858-59. V. 49
Works. New York: 1861-62. V. 47; 49
The Works. London: 1863-66. V. 54
The Works. London: 1871-79. V. 53
The Works. London: 1873. V. 53
Works. New York: 1873. V. 54
Works. London: 1874-76. V. 49; 52
The Works. London: 1875-94. V. 51
The Works. London: 1880. V. 48; 49
Works. New York: 1880. V. 52
Works. New York & London: 1881-86. V. 48
The Works. London: 1885?. V. 49
Works. London: 1887-88. V. 51
Works. Boston: 1890. V. 51
The Works. London: 1890-96. V. 51; 52; 54
The Works. London: 1894-95. V. 53
The Works. London: 1897-98. V. 53
The Works. London: 1897-99. V. 53
The Works. London: 1899. V. 53; 54
The Works. New York: 1899. V. 50
The Works. London: 1899-1901. V. 54
The Works. London: 1900. V. 50; 53
The Works. London: 1900-01. V. 49
The Works. London: 1901. V. 53
The Works. London: 1901-02. V. 54
The Works. London: 1902-03. V. 49; 53
The Works. London: 1906-08. V. 54
The Works. London & Glasgow: 1910. V. 54
The Works. London: 1922-25. V. 54
The Works. London: 1938. V. 49
The Works of the Diamond Edition. Boston: 1867. V. 47
The Wreck of the Golden Mary. Kentfield: 1956. V. 48

DICKENS, MAMIE
Dickens: My Father, As I Recall Him. Westminster: 1887. V. 53; 54
My Father As I Recall Him. London: 1897. V. 49

DICKENS, MARY ANGELA
Children's Stories from Dickens. London: 1893. V. 49
Children's Stories from Dickens. London: 1911. V. 51

DICKENS Pictures. London: 1896. V. 54

DICKENSON, EDMUND
Delphi Phoenicizantes. Oxford: 1655. V. 50

DICKERSON, PHILIP J.
History of the Osage Nation. Pawhuska: 1906. V. 47; 52

DICKERT, D. AUGUSTUS
History of Kershaw's Brigade... Newberry: 1899. V. 49

DICKESON, MONTROVILLE WILSON
The American Numismatic Manual of the Currency or Money of the Aborigines, and Colonial, State and United States Coins... Philadelphia: 1860. V. 53
The American Numismatic Manual of the Currency or Money of the Aborigines, and Colonial, State and United States Coins. Philadelphia: 1865. V. 47

DICKEY, JAMES
Alnilam. Garden City: 1987. V. 53
Buckdancer's Choice. Middletown: 1965. V. 51; 52
The Eye-Beaters, Blood, Victory, Madness, Buckhead and Mercy. Garden City: 1970. V. 51; 52; 53
Four Poems. 1979. V. 49; 51
Head-Deep in Strange Sounds. Winston-Salem: 1979. V. 54
Helmets. Poems. Middletown: 1964. V. 52
The Owl-King. New York: 1977. V. 53
The Suspect in Poetry. Madison: 1964. V. 50; 51
Two Poems of the Air. Portland: 1964. V. 48
Varmland. Poems Based on Poems. 1982. V. 54
The Zodiac. 1976. V. 53
The Zodiac. Bloomfield Hills: 1976. V. 49

DICKEY, ROLAND F.
New Mexico Village Arts. Albuquerque: 1949. V. 51

DICKEY, THOMAS S.
Field Artillery Projectiles of the American Civil War. Atlanta: 1980. V. 53

DICKIE, G.
The Flora of Ulster and Botanist's Guide to the North of Ireland. London: 1864. V. 54

DICKIE, J. F.
Germany. London: 1912. V. 48

DICKINSON, ANNA ELIZABETH
A Ragged Register (Of People Places and Opinions). New York: 1879. V. 49; 50; 54
What Answer?. Boston: 1869. V. 53; 54

DICKINSON, C. J.
Electrophysiological Technique. London: 1950. V. 53

DICKINSON, EDWIN
The Drawings of... New Haven: 1963. V. 53

DICKINSON, EMILY ELIZABETH
Acts of Light. Boston: 1980. V. 49; 51
Bolts of Melody. New York: 1945. V. 52; 53
The Complete Poems of Emily Dickinson. Boston: 1924. V. 48
The Complete Poems of Emily Dickinson. Boston: 1930. V. 48
Emily Dickinson: 7 Poems. Providence: 1995. V. 54
Five Poems. London: 1989. V. 54
From a Letter Sent in October 1870. Paris: 1993. V. 51
Further Poems of Emily Dickinson. Boston: 1929. V. 47; 49; 51; 53; 54
Janvier 1866; Lettre et Poeme Envoyes a Thomas W. Higginson. Paris: 1991. V. 51
Letters of Emily Dickinson. Boston: 1894. V. 47; 49; 50; 51
Letters of Emily Dickinson. Boston: 1899. V. 47
Letters of Emily Dickinson. Cleveland and New York: 1951. V. 54
The Letters of Emily Dickinson. Cambridge: 1958. V. 53
Letters to Emily Dickinson. Boston: 1894. V. 53
The Manuscript Books of Emily Dickinson. Cambridge & London: 1981. V. 51
A Masque of Poets. Boston: 1878. V. 54
Poems. Boston: 1891. V. 47; 51; 53; 54
Poems. London: 1891. V. 47; 48; 49; 51
Poems. Boston: 1892. V. 51
Poems. Boston: 1894. V. 48
Poems. New York: 1952. V. 51; 52
The Poems of Emily Dickinson... Cambridge: 1955. V. 52
The Poems of Emily Dickinson... Cambridge: 1958. V. 53
Poems: Second Series. Boston: 1891. V. 47; 51; 54
Poems: Third Series. Boston: 1896. V. 47; 54
Poems. (with) Poems: Second Series. Boston: 1893. V. 51
Poems... (with) Poems... Second Series (with) Poems... Third Series. Boston: 1890. V. 50
Riddle Poems. 1957. V. 49
Riddle Poems. Northampton: 1957. V. 54
Selected Poems of Emily Dickinson. London: 1924. V. 51
A Selection of Poems by... 1990. V. 50
The Single Hound. Boston: 1914. V. 47; 51
The Single Hound. Boston: 1915. V. 51; 52; 53
Unpublished Poems of Emily Dickinson. Boston: 1935. V. 47; 51; 54
The World in a Frame. New York: 1989. V. 53

DICKINSON, F. A.
Lake Victoria to Khartoum with Rifle and Camera... London: 1910. V. 50

DICKINSON, H. W.
James Watt and the Steam Engine. Oxford: 1927. V. 49
Matthew Boulton. Cambridge: 1936. V. 50
Richard Trevithick. The Engineer and the Man. Cambridge: 1934. V. 50

DICKINSON, J. C.
The Origin of the Austin Canons and Their Introduction to England. London: 1947. V. 52

DICKINSON, JOHN
Letters from a Farmer, in Pennsylvania, to the Inhabitants of the British Colonies. London: 1774. V. 47
A New Essay on the Constitutional Power of Great Britain Over the Colonies in America... Philadelphia: 1774. V. 47

DICKINSON, JOSEPH
The Flora of Liverpool. London: 1851. V. 48

DICKINSON, PATRIC
Soldiers' Verse. London: 1945. V. 54

DICKINSON, R. B.
Los Angeles of Today, Architecturally. Los Angeles: 1896. V. 54

DICKINSON, R. E.
The Geophysiology of Amazonia: Vegetation and Climate Interactions. New York: 1986. V. 49; 52

DICKINSON, ROBERT
A Parlour Companion (Gratis). Hoyle's Rules and Forfeits for the Game of Whist. Table of Taxes and Proper Stamps,...and the Description of a Remedy for all Scorbutic Eruptions and Impurities in the Face, Redress of the Skin and Coarseness of the... London: 1796?. V. 53
The Registers of the Parish Church of Dalton-in-Furness 1565-1691. Preston: 1962-65. V. 48

DICKINSON, RODOLPHUS
A Digest of the Common Law, the Statute Laws of Massachusetts and of the United States, and the Decisions of the Supreme Judicial Court of Massachusetts, Relative to the Powers and duties of Justices of the Peace. Deerfield: 1818. V. 51; 52

DICKINSON, W. H.
On Renal and Urinary Affections. New York: 1885. V. 48; 53
The Tongue As an Indication in Disease. London: 1888. V. 48

DICKINSON, W. HOWSHIP
King Arthur in Cornwall. London: 1900. V. 51

DICKINSON, WILLIAM
A Glossary of the Words and Phrases of Cumberland. London: 1859. V. 50; 52

DICKS, JOHN
The History and Legends of Old Castles and Abbeys. London: 1870. V. 48; 51

DICKSON, A.
A Treatise of Agriculture. London: 1770. V. 47; 48

DICKSON, ARTHUR JEROME
Covered Wagons Days. A Journey Across the Plains in the Sixties and Pioneer Days in the Northwest. Cleveland: 1929. V. 50; 53

DICKSON, C.
He Wouldn't Kill Patience. 1944. V. 50

DICKSON, CARTER
My Late Wives. New York: 1946. V. 48

DICKSON, G.
Necromancer. New York: 1962. V. 48

DICKSON, H. R. P.
The Arab of the Desert. London: 1949. V. 54
The Arab of the Desert. London: 1951. V. 47
Kuwait and Her Neighbors. London: 1956. V. 47; 49

DICKSON, HUGH
The Reasons of Hugh Dickson, for Abjuring the Protestant and Embracing the Catholic Faith. Newry: 1829. V. 53

DICKSON, R. W.
A Complete Dictionary of Practical Gardening... London: 1807. V. 51
An Improved System of Management of Live Stock and Cattle... London. V. 49
An Improved System of Management of Live Stock and Cattle; or a Practical Guide to the Perfecting and Improvement of the Several Breeds and Varieties of Agricultural Stock, and Domestic Animals. London: 1822-24. V. 47
Practical Agriculture; or, a Complete System of Modern Husbandry... London: 1807. V. 47

DICKSON, ROBERT
Annals of Scottish Printing. Cambridge: 1890. V. 47; 48; 50; 52
Examples of Early Scottish Typography. Aberdeen: 1884. V. 53
Introduction of the Art of Printing into Scotland. Aberdeen: 1885. V. 51; 53

DICKSON, SAMUEL
Elements of Medicine: A Compendius View of Pathology and Therapeutics... Philadelphia: 1859. V. 48

DICKSON, W. E.
Railways and Locomotion. London: 1854. V. 49

DICKSON, W. E. CARNEGIE
The Bone-Marrow, A Cytological Study Forming an Introduction to the Normal and Pathological Histology of the Tissue, More Especially with Regard to Blood Formation. London: 1908. V. 48; 53

DICKSON, W. G.
Gleanings from Japan. Edinburgh: 1889. V. 48

DICTAMEN de las Comisiones Unidas de Puntos Constitucionales, Gobernacion y Guerra, del Denado, Sobre el Acuerdo de la Camara de Diputados... Mexico: 1845. V. 48; 49

DICTES and Sayings of the Philosophers. Detroit: 1901. V. 47

DICTIONARIUM Sacrum seu Religiosum. A Dictionary of All Religions, Antient and Modern. London: 1704. V. 52

DICTIONARY Catalog of the Jesse E. Moorland Collection of Negro Life and History. Washington/Boston: 1970/76. V. 48

DICTIONARY Catalogue of the History of printing from John M. Wing Foundation in the Newberry Library. Boston: 1961. V. 48

DICTIONARY Of American Biography. New York: 1943. V. 48
DICTIONARY Of American Biography. New York: 1966. V. 49

DICTIONARY of American History. New York: 1940/61. V. 47

A DICTIONARY of Musicians...to the Present... London: 1824. V. 49

DICTIONARY Of National Biography. London: 1885-1903. V. 50

THE DICTIONARY of National Biography. London: 1885-1939. V. 50
THE DICTIONARY of National Biography. 1937-86. V. 49

DICTIONARY of National Biography. Oxford: 1960. V. 51
DICTIONARY of National Biography. Cambridge: 1975. V. 53
DICTIONARY of National Biography. London: 1975. V. 51; 54

THE DICTIONARY of National Biography. London: 1979-74. V. 51

DICTIONARY of National Biography. Missing Persons. London: 1993. V. 52

DICTIONARY Of National Biography. (with) The Twentieth Century Dictionary. London: 1921-59. V. 53

DICTIONARY of Quotations, in Most Frequent Use. London: 1799. V. 52

DICTIONARY of Scientific Biography. New York: 198-190. V. 47

A DICTIONARY of the Chinook Jargon, Or Indian Trade Language of the North Pacific Coast. Victoria: 1878. V. 52

A DICTIONARY of the English Language. London: 1794. V. 52

DICTIONARY of the Older Scottish Tongue: From the Twelfth Century to the End of the Seventeenth. Chicago: 1931-61. V. 51

DIDAY, P.
A Treatise on Syphilis in New-Born Children and Infants at the Breast. London: 1859. V. 51
A Treatise On Syphilis in New-Born Children and Infants at the Breast. New York: 1883. V. 51

DIDEROT, DENIS
Les Bijoux Indiscretes; or, the Indiscreet Toys. Tobago: 1749. V. 49; 54
Lettres sur les Aveugles, a l'Usage de Ceux Qui voyent. Paris: 1749. V. 49
Memoires sur Differens Sujets de Mathematiques. Paris: 1748. V. 47
Pensees Sur l'Interpretation de La Nature. Paris: 1754. V. 50; 51; 52

THE DIDEROT Encyclopedia: The Illustrations. 1978. V. 50

DIDIER, FRANKLIN J.
Letters from Paris, and Other Cities of France, Holland &c. New York: 1821. V. 49

DIDION, JOAN
A Book of Common Prayer. New York: 1977. V. 53
Play It As It Lays. New York: 1970. V. 51
Run River. New York: 1963. V. 47; 50; 51
Run River. London: 1964. V. 51

DIDUSCH, WILLIAM
A Collection of Urogenital Drawings. New York: 1952. V. 48; 53

DIDYMUS CHALCENTERUS
Interpretiones et Antique, et Perquam Utiles in Homeri Iliada, Nec Non in Odyssea. Venice: 1521. V. 51

DIEHL, CHARLES SANFORD
The Staff Correspondent, How the News of the World is Collected and Dispatched by a Body of Trained Press Writers. San Antonio: 1931. V. 53

DIEHL, EDITH
Bookbinding, Its Background and Technique. New York: 1946. V. 47; 48; 49; 50; 51; 54

DIEHL, G.
The Fauves: the Movement, the Masters, the Percursors and Their Followers. New York: 1975. V. 47

DIENES, PAUL
The Taylor Series. An Introduction to the Theory of Functions of a Complex Variable. Oxford: 1931. V. 50

DIEREVILLE, N. DE
Relation of the Voyage to Port Royal in Acadia or New France. Toronto: 1933. V. 49; 51

DIETRICH, FRIEDRICH GOTTLIEB
Vollstandiges Lexicon der Gartnerei und Botanik Uber Alphabetische Beschreibung vom Bau, Wartung und Nutzen aller in- und Auslandischen Okonomischen Officinellen und zur Zierde Dienenden Gewachese... Weimar and Berlin: 1802-11. V. 49

DIETRICH, MARLENE
Marlene Dietrich's ABC. New York: 1984. V. 54

DIETRICH, WILFRED
Blazing Story of Washington County. 1950. V. 48

DIETZ, AUGUST
The Postal Service of the Confederate States of America. Richmond: 1929. V. 47; 48

DIEULAFAIT, LOUIS
Diamonds and Precious Stones... London: 1874. V. 50
Diamonds and Precious Stones, a Popular Account of Gems. New York: 1874. V. 49

DIEULAFOY, JANE
At Susa, the Ancient Capital of the Kings of Persia. Narrative of Travel through Western Persia and Excavations Made at the Site of the Lost City of the Lilies 1884-1886. Philadelphia: 1890. V. 47

DIGBY, BASSETT
The Mammoth and Mammoth-Hunting in North-East Siberia. New York: 1926. V. 47

DIGBY, EDWARD
Private Memoirs... London: 1827. V. 48; 49; 50; 51; 52; 53

DIGBY, JOAN
A Sound of Feathers. New York: 1982. V. 54

DIGBY, KENELM
The Broad Stone of Honour: or, Rules for the Gentlemen of England... 1823. V. 47
The Broad Stone of Honour: or, Rules for the Gentlemen of England... London: 1823. V. 50
Choice and Experimental Receipts in Physick and Chirurgery... London: 1668. V. 47
The Closet of Sir Kenelm Digby Knight Opened... London: 1910. V. 47
Discours fait en une Celebre Assemblee... Paris: 1658. V. 48; 53
Discours Fait en Une Celebre Assemblee... Rouen: 1673. V. 50
Institutionum Peripateticarum ad mentem Summi Viri, Clarissimique Philosophi Kenelmi Equitis Digbaei... London: 1647. V. 51
A Late Discours Made in a Solemne Assembly of Nobles and Learned Men at Montepellier in France...Touching the Cure of Wounds by the Powder of Sympathy. London: 1658. V. 48; 49; 51
Letters Between the Ld. George Digby and Kenelm Digby Concerning Religion. London: 1651. V. 47; 50; 51
Medicina Experimentalis Digbaeana. Frankfurt: 1670. V. 47; 53
Observations Upon Religio Medici. London: 1644. V. 48; 49; 50; 51; 53
Private Memoirs of Sir Kenelm Digby. London: 1827. V. 48
Theatrum Sympatheticum in Quo Sympathiae Actiones Variae, singulares... Amsterdam: 1661. V. 53
Theatrum Sympatheticum, Ofte Wonderteoneel des Natuers Verborgentheden, Zijnde een Noodigh Vervolgh op de Oratie van den Heere Cancellier Digby... Haerlem: 1662. V. 53
Two Treatises: In the One of Which, The Nature of Bodies; in the Other, The Nature of Mans Soule, Is Looked Into... London: 1645. V. 53
Two Treatises: in the One of Which, the Nature of Bodies; in the Other, the Nature of Mans Soule, Is Looked Into. London: 1658. V. 50; 52

DIGBY, LETTICE
My Ancestors. London: 1928. V. 53

DIGERNESS, DAVID S.
The Mineral Belt. Silverton: 1977/78. V. 54

A DIGEST of Adjudged Cases in the Court of King's Bench from the Revolution to the Present Period...Comprehending...Holt, Parker, Pratt, Raymond, Hardwicke, Lee and Ryder. London: 1775. V. 52

A DIGESTED Index to the Chancery Reports: Containing the Points of Equity Determined in the High Court of Chancery from the Year 1689, to the Year 1801. London: 1802. V. 54

DIGESTORUM Seu Pandectarum Libri Quinquaginta Ex Florentinis Pandectis Repraesentati. Florence: 1553. V. 52

DIGGES, DUDLEY
The Compleat Ambassador; or Two Treaties of the Intended Marriage of Qu: Elizabeth of Glorious Memory... London: 1655. V. 51; 53
A Discourse of Sea-Ports: Principally of the Port and Haven of Dover. London: 1700. V. 51
The Unlawfulness of Subjects Taking Up Armes Against Their Soveraigne, In What Case so Ever. Oxford: 1643/44. V. 47
The Unlawfulness of Subjects Taking Up Armes Against Their Soveraigne, in What Case Soever... London: 1647. V. 49; 54

DIGGES, LEONARD
A Geometrical Practicse, Named Pantometria, Divided Into Three Bookes, Longimetra, Planimetra and Stereometria... London: 1571. V. 51

DIGGINGS From Many Ampersandhogs. New York: 1936. V. 48

DIGGLES, S.
The Ornithology of Australia. Australia: 1990. V. 48

DIGHTON, ROBERT
Book 31. Twelve Prints, Representing the Most Interesting, Sentimental and Humorous Scenes in Tristram Shandy. London: 1785. V. 47

DI GUGLIELMO, L.
A Roentgenologic Study of the Coronary Arteries in the Living. Stockholm: 1952. V. 48

DIKAIOS, PORPHYRIOS
Sotira. Philadelphia: 1961. V. 52
The Stone Age and the Early Bronze Age in Cyprus. Lund: 1962. V. 52

DILKE, CHARLES WENTWORTH
Greater Britain a Record of Travel in English Speaking Countries During 1866-7. Philadelphia/London: 1869. V. 47; 50; 52

DILKE, EMILIA
French Engravers and Draughtsmen of the XVIIIth Century. London: 1902. V. 53
French Furniture and Decoration in the XVIIIth Century. London: 1901. V. 47; 49
The Renaissance of Art in France. London: 1879. V. 47

DILKE, O. A. W.
Roman Books and Their Impact. Leeds: 1977. V. 48; 50

DILL, DAVID BRUCE
Life, Heat and Altitude: Physiological Effects of Hot Climates and Great Heights. Cambridge: 1938. V. 48; 51; 53

DILL, R. G.
The Political Campaigns of Colorado. Denver: 1895. V. 51

DILLARD, ANNIE
Holy the Firm. New York: 1977. V. 53
The Living. 1992. V. 49; 54
The Living. New York: 1992. V. 50; 51
Living by Fiction. New York: 1982. V. 54
Pilgrim at Tinker Creek. New York: 1974. V. 53
Pilgrim at Tinker Creek. New York: 1978. V. 51; 53
Teaching a Stone to Talk. New York: 1982. V. 53
Tickets for a Prayer Wheel. Columbia: 1974. V. 50; 51; 52

DILLENBACK, JACKSON D.
History and Directory of Ionia County, Michigan... Grand Rapids: 1872. V. 53

DILLEY, ARTHUR URBANE
Oriental Rugs and Carpets. New York: 1931. V. 48

DILLIN, JOHN G. W.
The Kentucky Rifle. Washington: 1924. V. 53

DILLIN, JOHN W.
The Kentucky Rifle. York: 1959. V. 53

DILLON, ARTHUR, VISCOUNT
A Winter in Iceland and Lapland. London: 1840. V. 47

DILLON, CHEVALIER P.
Narrative and Successrul Result of A Voyage in the South Seas, Performed by Order of the Government of British India, to Ascertain the Actual Fate of La Perouse's Expedition... Amsterdam/New York: 1972. V. 47

DILLON, GEORGE
Boy in the Wind. New York: 1927. V. 52

DILLON, HENRY AUGUSTUS DILLON-LEE, VISCOUNT
The Life and Opinions of Sir Richard Maltravers, an English Gentleman of the Seventeenth Century. London: 1822. V. 48; 53

DILLON, JOHN
The Case of the Children of His Royal Highness the Duke of Sussex, Elucidated: a Juridical Exercitation. London: 1832. V. 48

DILLON, JOHN F.
Correspondence Concerning a Decision in the Suit Between the Kansas Pacific and Union Pacific Railroads in the United States Circuit Court, District of Nebraska. Washington: 1878. V. 47

DILLON, JOHN JOSEPH
Memoir Concerning the Political State of Malta. London: 1807. V. 50

DILLON, JOHN TALBOT
A Political Survey of the Sacred Roman Empire... London: 1782. V. 49; 52

DILLON, LEO
The Art of Leo and Diane Dillon. 1981. V. 47; 51

DILLON, PETER
Narrative and Successful Result of a Voyage in the South Sea, Performed by Order of the Government of British India to Ascertain the Actual Fate of La Perouse's Expedition... London: 1829. V. 48
Narrative and Successful Result of a Voyage in the South Seas, Performed by Order of the Government of British India... Amsterdam, New York: 1972. V. 52

DILLON, R. C.
The Lord Mayor's Visit to Oxford in the Month of July, 1826. London: 1826. V. 50

DILLON, RICHARD
Bully Waterman and the Voyage of the Clipper Challenge: New York to San Francisco. San Francisco: 1956. V. 54

DILLON, RICHARD H.
Images of Chinatown. San Francisco: 1976. V. 47; 52
Texas Argonauts: Isaac H. Duval and the California Gold Rush. 1987. V. 54
Texas Argonauts: Isaac H. Duval and the California Gold Rush. San Francisco: 1987. V. 52

DILLON, VISCOUNT
An Almain Armourer's Album, Selections from an Original MS in the Victoria and Albert Museum. London: 1905. V. 47
Pageant of the Birth Life and Death of Richard Beauchamp Earl of Warwick K.G. 1389-1439. London: 1914. V. 50

DILLWYN, E. A.
A Burglary: or, Unconscious Influence. London: 1883. V. 54
Chloe Arguelle. London: 1881. V. 54

DILLWYN, GEORGE
Gathered Fragments... London: 1858. V. 49

DILLWYN, J. W.
A Descriptive Catalogue of Recent Shells Arranged According to the Linnean Method. London: 1817. V. 53

DILNOT, GEORGE
The Romance of the Amalgamated Press. London: 1925. V. 51

DILWORTH, THOMAS
A New and Complete Description of the Terrestrial and Celestial Globes, with their Several Uses. London: 1794. V. 51
A New Guide to the English Tongue: In Five Parts. Philadelphia: 1784. V. 53
The Schoolmaster's Assistant: Being a Complete System of Practical Arithmetic... Philadelphia: 1805. V. 53

DILWORTH, W. H.
The Conquest of Peru, by Francis Pizarro. London: 1759. V. 50

DIMAGGIO, JOE
The Joe Dimaggio Albums. New York: 1989. V. 47

DIMITRY, CHARLES PATTON
The House in Balfour Stareet. New York: 1868. V. 54

DIMOCK, A. W.
Wall Street and the Wilds. 1915. V. 52

DIMOND, WILLIAM
Petrarchal Sonnets and Miscellaneous Poems. Bath: 1800. V. 54
The Story of the Broken Sword,. London: 1816. V. 51
The Young Hussar, or Love and Mercy, an Operatic Piece, in Two Acts... Baltimore: 1808. V. 50

DIMPLED Hands. Pictures and Rhymes for Chubby Pets. Boston: 1890. V. 52

DIMSDALE, THOMAS
The Present Method of Inoculating for the Small Pox... London: 1767. V. 48; 51

DIMSDALE, THOMAS JOSIAH
The Vigilantes of Montana. Virginia City: 1921. V. 47

DINAN, W.
Monumenta Historica Celtica; Notices of...Celts in the Writings of the Greek and Latin Authors... London: 1911. V. 52

DINE, JIM
Welcome Home Love Birds. Poems and Drawings. London: 1969. V. 47; 50

DINES, H. G.
The Metalliferous Mining Region of South-West England. London: 1956. V. 49; 51
The Metalliferous Mining Region of South-West England. London: 1969. V. 54

DINESEN, ISAK
Anecdotes of Destiny. London: 1958. V. 50
The Angelic Avengers. London: 1946. V. 52
The Angelic Avengers. New York: 1947. V. 49
Carnival. Chicago: 1977. V. 50
Out of Africa. London: 1937. V. 50
Out of Africa. New York: 1938. V. 47; 48; 50; 51; 52; 53
Seven Gothic Tales. 1934. V. 48; 49; 50; 51; 52
Seven Gothic Tales. London: 1934. V. 49
Seven Gothic Tales. New York: 1934. V. 47; 51; 52; 53
Winter's Tales. New York: 1942. V. 47; 50

DINGLE, EDWIN J.
Across China on Foot. Bristol: 1911. V. 53

DINGLE, REGINALD J.
Woman Under Fire - Six Months in the Red Army. London: 1930. V. 49

DINGMAN, REED
Surgery of Facial Fractures. Philadelphia: 1964. V. 50; 52

DINGS Club Song Book. 1894. V. 54

DINGWALL, ERIC
The Girdle of Chastity: a Medico-Historical Study. London: 1931. V. 50; 52

DINKINS, JAMES
1861 to 1865, by an Old Johnnie. Personal Recollections and Experiences in the Confederate Army. Cincinnati: 1897. V. 49; 52

DINNEEN, PATRICK S.
Me Guidhir Fhearmanach. The Maguires of Fermanagh... Dublin: 1917. V. 54

DINNER to the Hon. Daniel Webster, of Massachusetts...December 2, 1846... Philadelphia: 1847. V. 48

DINNIES, ANNA PEYRE
The Floral Year, Embellished with Bouquets of Flowers, Drawn and Colored from Nature. Boston: 1847. V. 47

DINSDALE, A.
First Principles of Television. New York: 1932. V. 54
Television. London: 1926. V. 53

DINSDALE, FREDERICK P.
A Glossary of Provincial Words Used in Teesdale in the County of Durham. London: 1849. V. 47

DINSDALE, JOHN
Sketches of Scarborough Drawn from Nature by... Darlington: 1881. V. 49

DINSMOOR, ROBERT
Incidental Poems, Accompanied with Letters, and a Few Select Pieces, Mostly Original for Their Illustration, Together with a Preface, and a Sketch of the Author's Life. Haverhill: 1828. V. 50

DINSMOOR, WILLIAM BELL
The Archons of Athens. Cambridge: 1931. V. 50; 52
The Athenian Archon List in the Life of Recent Discoveries. Morningside Heights: 1939. V. 50; 52

DINSTEL, M.
List of French Doctoral Dissertations on Africa, 1884-1961. Boston: 1966. V. 51

DIO COCCEIANUS, CHRYSOSTOMUS, OF PRUSA
De Regno. Bologna: 1493. V. 52

DIODATE, JOHN
Pious Annotations Upon the Holy Bible: Expounding the Difficult Places Thereof Learnedly and Plainly... 1643. V. 47
Pious Annotations Upon the Holy Bible: Expounding the Difficult Places Thereof Learnedly, and Plainly... London: 1643. V. 50

DIODORUS SICULUS
Bibliothecae Historicae Libri VI. Venice: 1481. V. 48; 54
Bibliothecae Historicae Libri VI. Venice: 1496. V. 52
Bibliothecae Historicae Libri XV. Basle: 1578. V. 48
(Greek title, then) Bibliothecae Historicae... Hanoviae: 1604. V. 47; 54
The Historical Library. London: 1721. V. 52
The Historical Library. London: 1814. V. 48

DIOGENES LAERTIUS
De Uita & Moribus Philosophorum. Venice: 1490. V. 48
De Vita, & Moribus, Philosophorum Libri Decem. Basel: 1524. V. 52
De Vite et Moribus Philosphorum Libri X. Antwerp: 1566. V. 48
De Vitis, Decretis, et Responsis Celebrium Philosophorum. Basle: 1533. V. 49
De Vitis, Dogm. & Apophth. Clarorum Philosophorum. Geneva: 1593. V. 51
De Vitis, Dogmatibus et Apophthegmatibus Clarorum Philosophoturm Libri X, Graece et Latine. Amsterdam: 1692. V. 48
De Vitis, Dogmatis & Apopthegmatis Eorum Qui in Philosophia Claruerunt, Libri X. Geneva: 1570. V. 51
De Vita et Moribus Philosophorum. Libri X. Lugduni: 1541. V. 50; 52
Vitae et Sententiae Philosophorum. Bologna: 1495. V. 51

DIONIS, PIERRE
The Anatomy of Humane Bodies Improv'd. London: 1703. V. 48; 53; 54
The Anatomy of Humane Bodies Improv'd. London: 1716. V. 48; 49
A Course of Chirurgical Operations, Demonstrated in the Royal Gardens at Paris. London: 1710. V. 48
A Course of Chirurgical Operations, Demonstrated in the Royal Gardens at Paris. London: 1733. V. 53; 54

DIONYSIUS AEROPAGITA
Coelistis Hierarchia, Ecclesiastica Hierarchia, Divina Nomina Mystica Theologia... Paris: 1515. V. 48

DIONYSIUS HALICARNASSUS
Antiquitates Romanae. Originvm Sive Antiqvitatvm Romanarvm. Treviso: 1480. V. 49; 54
Dionysii Halicarnassei. Responsio ad Gn. Pompeii Epistolam in Qua Ille de Reprehenso ab eo Platonis Stylo Conquerebatur. Paris: 1554. V. 51
Dionysii Halicarnassei Scripta Quae Exstant Omnia et Historica et Rhetorica...Emendata,...Cum Latina Versione ad Graeci Exemplaris Fiden Denuo Collata... Frankfurt: 1586. V. 48
Originvm Sive Antiqvitatvm Romanarvm. Treviso: 1480. V. 48

DIONYSIUS PERIEGETES
De Situ Orbis: Sive Geogrpaphia, Prisciano, aut Fannio Rhenio Interprete Lib. Unicus. Vienna: 1512. V. 50
(Greek) De Situ Orbis Liber. Interprete Andrea Papio Gandensi. (Greek) Museai Hero et Leander, Eordem Interprete. Antwerp: 1575. V. 48
(Greeke title) sive Geographia Emendata and Locupletata, Additione Scil. Geographie Hodiernae Graeco Carmine Pariter Donatae. Oxonii: 1704. V. 53
Sive Dionysii Geographia. London: 1717. V. 51

DIOPHANTUS, OF ALEXANDRIA
Arithmeticorum Libri Sex, et de Numeris Multangulis Liber Unus. Paris: 1621. V. 49

DIOSCORIDES
De Materia Medica Libri Sex, Ioanne Ruellio... Lyon: 1546. V. 48; 49
(Greek title, then) Pedacii Dioscoridis Anazarabaei Opera Qvae Extant Omnia. 1598. V. 47; 48; 49; 53
Opera Quae Exatant Omnia. Francfurti: 1598. V. 49

DIPESO, CHARLES C.
Casas Grandes - a Fallen Trading Center of the Gran Chichimeca. 1974. V. 47

DI PESO, CHARLES C
Casas Grandes - a Fallen Trading Center of the Gran Chichimeca. Flagstaff: 1974. V. 52; 54

DI PESO, CHARLES C.
Casas Grandes: a Fallen Trading Center of the Gran Chichimeca. Dragoon: 1974. V. 50; 52

DIPLOK, JOSEPH BRAMAH
A New System of Heavy Goods Transport on Common Roads. London: 1902. V. 50

DIPLOMATIC Guide. Drawn Up by the Legation of Japan in Paris. Edinburgh and London: 1874. V. 50

DIPPIE, BRIAN W.
Charles M. Russell, Word Painter. Letters: 1887-1926. Fort Worth: 1993. V. 54

DI PRIMA, DIANE
Combination Theatre Poem and Birthday Poem for Ten People. New York: 1965. V. 47

LA DIPUTACION Para la Junta de Gobierno de la Casa de Beneficencia da Cuenta a la Real Sociedad Patriotica de sus Tareas en el Presente Ano de 1796 por Medio del Siguiente Papel. Havanna: 1796. V. 48

DIRAC, PAUL ADRIAN MAURICE
The Principles of Quantum Mechanics. Oxford: 1930. V. 50

DIRCKS, HENRY
The Life, Times and Scientific Labours of the Second Marquis of Worcester. London: 1865. V. 54
Perpetuum Mobile; or, Search for Self-Motive Power, During the 17th, 18th and 19th Centuries... London: 1861. V. 49
The Policy of a Patent Law, a Paper Read at the Social Science Congress, Bristol. (wtih) Statistics of Invention, Illustrating the Policy of Patent Law. London: 1869. V. 54

DIRECCION de Hidrografia. Portulano de la Merica Septentrional... Madrid: 1809. V. 47

DIRECTIONS for the Use of a Scientific Table, in the Collection and Application of Knowledge. Norwich: 1796. V. 47

DIRECTORATE. Alaska Nome Nugget, Ltd. New York: 1898. V. 50

DIRECTORY for Newark, for 1835-36. Newark: 1835. V. 49

DIRECTORY of Boston and Albany Railroad, Between Albany & Pittsfield. East Albany: 1900. V. 53

DIRECTORY of Churches and Religious Organizations in New Mexico 1940. Albuquerque: 1940. V. 52

DIRECTORY of New Brunswick, also Milltown, South River, Sayreville, Piscataway, Bonhamtown, Metuchen, Raritan River Road, Bound Brook, South Bound Brook. 1899-'00. New Brunswick: 1899. V. 49; 51

DIRECTORY of Newark, for 1835-36. Newark: 1835. V. 47; 51

DIRECTORY of the City of Newark, for 1841-42, with a Historical Sketch. Newark: 1841. V. 47

DIRECTORY of the City of Newark, for 1844-45. Newark: 1844. V. 47; 49

DIRECTORY of the City of Newark, for 1849-50. Newark: 1849. V. 49

DIRECTORY of the City of Newark, for 1853-54. Newark: 1853. V. 47; 49

DIRECTORY of the City of Newark, for 1857-58. Newark: 1857. V. 49

DIRINGER, DAVID
The Alphabet. A Key to the History of Mankind. New York: 1968. V. 54
The Hand-Produced Book. London: 1953. V. 49
The Hand-Produced Book. New York: 1953. V. 52
The Illuminated Book, Its History and Production. New York: 1958. V. 48; 50; 52
The Illustrated Book: Its History and Production. London: 1958. V. 47
The Illustrated Book: Its History and Production. New York: 1967. V. 47

DIROM, MAJOR
A Narrative of the Campaign in India... London: 1793. V. 49
A Narrative of the Campaign in India, Which Terminated the War with Tippoo Sultan in 1792. London: 1794. V. 53

DISCH, THOMAS M.
334. 1972. V. 49; 54
Black Alice. Garden City: 1968. V. 49
Black Alice. London: 1969. V. 53
Camp Concentration. London: 1968. V. 53
Echo Round His Bones. 1969. V. 47; 51
The Prisoner. London: 1979. V. 47; 50

THE DISCIPLINE of the Wesleyan Methodist Connection of America. Boston: 1843. V. 54

DISCORD, a Satire. London: 1773. V. 54

A DISCOURSE of Sacrilege, Wherein Is Briefly Shewn, 1. The Just Collation. 2. The Unjust Ablation of the Riches & Honours of the Clergie. London: 1641. V. 53

THE DISCOVERY of Rainbow Bridge, the Natural Bridges of Utah and the Discovery of Betatakin. Tucson: 1959. V. 48

DISCUSSIONS on the Constitution Proposed to The People of Massachusetts by the Convention of 1853. Boston: 1854. V. 49

DISNEY, JOHN
The Laws of Gaming, Wagers, Horse-Racing and Gaming-Houses. London: 1806. V. 51
Thoughts on the Great Circumspection Necessary in Licensing Public Ale-Houses. London: 1776. V. 48

DISNEY, WALT
The Adventures of Mickey Mouse. 1931. V. 51; 53
The Adventures of Mickey Mouse. London: 1931. V. 49
The Adventures of Mickey Mouse Book I. Philadelphia: 1931. V. 53
The Art of Walt Disney. 1945. V. 47
Circus. New York: 1944. V. 49
Dance of the Hours from Walt Disney's Fantasia. New York: 1940. V. 53
Donald and Pluto. London: 1939. V. 53

DISNEY, WALT *continued*
Donald Duck. Racine: 1935. V. 51
Donald Duck Has His Ups and Downs. Racine: 1937. V. 53
Dumbo. Antwerp: 1948. V. 53
Ferdinand the Bull. Racine: 1938. V. 53
The Golden Touch. Racine: 1937. V. 47
Here They Are. Boston: 1940. V. 53
Honest John and Giddy. New York: 1940. V. 53
Mickey Detective. Paris: 1933. V. 49
Mickey Mouse and His Friends. Racine: 1936. V. 53
Mickey Mouse and the Boy Thursday. Racine: 1948. V. 51
Mickey Mouse Goes Fishing. Racine: 1936. V. 51
Mickey Mouse Has a Busy Day. Racine: 1937. V. 47
Mickey Mouse in King Arthur's Court. 1933. V. 49; 50; 54
Mickey Mouse in King Arthur's Court. New York: 1933. V. 51
Mickey Mouse in Pigmy Land. London and Glasgow: 1935. V. 49
Mickey Mouse Stories. Philadelphia: 1934. V. 53
Mickey Mouse Story Book. Philadelphia: 1931. V. 53
Mickey Mouse Story Book. Toronto: 1933. V. 54
Mickey Mouse Waddle Book. New York: 1934. V. 49; 53
Nursery Stories from Walt Disneys Silly Symphony. 1937. V. 49
The Nutcracker Suite. Boston: 1941. V. 47
Pinocchio. Antwerp: 1948. V. 54
The Pop-up Mickey Mouse. New York: 1933. V. 47
The Pop-Up Minnie Mouse. 1933. V. 49
Snow White. Antwerp. V. 53
(Snow White) Sketch Book. London: 1938. V. 54
Stories from Fantasia. New York: 1940. V. 49; 52
Three Little Pigs. 1933. V. 52; 53
Three Little Pigs. New York: 1933. V. 49; 53
Three Little Pigs. 1934. V. 49; 54
Three Little Pigs. London: 1934. V. 54
Toby Tortoise and the Hare. Hollywood: 1938. V. 53
The Victory March or The Mystery of the Treasure Chest. New York: 1942. V. 49
Walt Disney Annual. Racine: 1937. V. 49
Walt Disney's Bambi Cut-Out Book. 1942. V. 49
Walt Disney's Clock Cleaners. Racine: 1938. V. 53
Walt Disney's Pop-Up Book. London: 1950. V. 53
Walt Disney's Snow White and the Seven Dwarfs. London: 1938. V. 52
Walt Disney's Surprise Package. New York: 1944. V. 49
Water Babies' Circus and Other Stories. Boston: 1940. V. 49
The Wise Little Hen. Hollywood: 1937. V. 53

THE DISOBEDIENT Chicken. New York: 1870-80. V. 52

DISRAELI, BENJAMIN
Collected Edition of the Novels and Tales... London: 1870. V. 51
Collected Edition of the Novels and Tales by the Right Honourable B. Disraeli. London: 1878-81. V. 54
Coningsby; or, the New Generation. London: 1844. V. 49
Contarini Fleming. London: 1832. V. 49
The Dunciad of Today - a Satire - and The Modern Aesop. London: 1928. V. 50; 53
Endymion. London: 1880. V. 47; 49; 52; 54
Endymion. Montreal: 1880. V. 49
England and France; or, a Cure for the Ministrerial Gallomania. London: 1832. V. 53
Henrietta Temple, a Love Story. London: 1837. V. 49
The Infernal Marriage. London: 1929. V. 51; 54
The Letters of Runnymede. London: 1836. V. 49; 51; 54
Lord Beaconsfield on the Constitution. London: 1884. V. 49
Lord George Bentinck; a Political Biography. London: 1852. V. 48; 49; 53
Lothair. London: 1870. V. 48; 49; 54
Novels and Tales. London: 1881. V. 50
Novels and Tales... London: 1882. V. 49
Novels and Tales. London, New York: 1900. V. 54
The Novels and Tales. London: 1926. V. 49
Novels and Tales. London: 1926-27. V. 49; 53
Parliamentary Reform. London: 1867. V. 54
Paul Jones, der Kuhne Seeman und Grunder der Amerikanischen Marine. Leipzig: 1826. V. 54
Politics and Politicians, Addressed to the Most Eminent Statesmen Of the Present Time. London: 1840. V. 49
Rumpal Stilts Kin. Glasgow: 1952. V. 54
Sybil; or the Two Nations. London: 1845. V. 49
Tancred: or the New Crusade. London: 1847. V. 49; 52
Vivian Grey. London: 1826-27. V. 49
Vivian Grey. London: 1827. V. 49
The Voyage of Captain Popanilla. London: 1828. V. 47; 50
The Voyage of Captain Popanilla. Philadelphia: 1828. V. 49
The Young Duke. London: 1831. V. 49

D'ISRAELI, ISAAC
Amenities of Literature, Consisting of Sketches and Characters of English Literature. London: 1841. V. 52
Calamities of Authors... London: 1812. V. 50
Curiosities of Literature. London: 1791. V. 52
Curiosities of Literature. London: 1834. V. 51
Curiosities of Literature... London: 1838. V. 48; 54
Curiosities of Literature. London: 1839. V. 49
Curiosities of Literature. London: 1858. V. 54
Curiosities of Literature. Cambridge: 1864. V. 48; 50; 52
A Dissertation on Anecdotes. London: 1793. V. 54
Domestic Anecdotes of the French Nation, During the Last Thirty Years. London: 1794. V. 50
An Essay on the Manners and Genius of the Literary Character. London: 1795. V. 48
The Illustrator Illustrated. London: 1838. V. 48
Miscellanies; or, Literary Recreations. London: 1796. V. 47
Narrative Poems. London: 1803. V. 49; 54
Quarrels Of Authors... London: 1814. V. 47; 48
Romances. London: 1799. V. 49
A Second Series of Curiosities of Literature... London: 1823. V. 52
Vaurien: or, Sketches of the Times... London: 1797. V. 48
Works. London: 1880. V. 51

DISSERTATIO Politica, De Ivre Monarchiae Liberae, Sev De Mutuis Regis Absoluti, & Subditorum Eius Officijs. 1615. V. 51

A DISSERTATION on the Voluntary Eating of Blood. London: 1745. V. 52

A DISSERTATION Upon Earthquakes... London: 1750. V. 53

DISTON, JOHN
The New Seamans Guide and Coasters Companion. Leith Edinburgh: 1800. V. 48
The Seaman's Guide, Chiefly the Experience of the Author... Liverpool and London: 1780. V. 49

A DISTRACTION of Wits. Cambridge: 1958. V. 54

DISTRESSING Calamity. A Brief Account of the Late Fire at Richmond, Virginia in Which the Theatre Was Burnt, and Upwards of One Hundred and Sixty Persons Perished in the Flames. Boston: 1811. V. 53

DISTURNELL, JOHN
Across the Continent and Around the World. Distrunell's Railroad and Steamship Guide... Philadelphia: 1873. V. 52
The Great Lakes, or Inland Seas of America... New York: 1863. V. 51
The Great Lakes, or Inland Seas of America... New York: 1865. V. 50
The Great Lakes, or Inland Seas of America... New York: 1868. V. 54

DITCHFIELD, P. H.
The City Companies of London and Their Good Works: A Record of Their History, Charity and Treasure. London: 1904. V. 49; 51
The Cottages and the Village Life of Rural England. London: 1912. V. 50; 51; 52; 53
Old English Sports, Pastimes and Customs. London: 1891. V. 54
Vanishing England. London: 1911. V. 54

DITSON, GEORGE LEIGHTON
Circassia; or, a Tour to the Caucasus. New York: 1850. V. 53

DITTMER, HEINRICH
Authentische und Vollstandige Beschreibung aller Feyerlichkeiten... Hanover: 1822. V. 49

DITTON, HUMPHRY
An Institution of Fluxions: Containing the First Principles, the Operations, with some of the Uses and Applications of that Admirable Method... London: 1706. V. 51; 52

DIURNALE Pataviense. Augsburg: 1494. V. 52

DIVAEUS, PETRUS
De Galliae Belgicae Antiquitatibus Liber I.... Antwerp: 1584. V. 47

THE DIVINE Miscellany, Consisting of Soliloquies, Meditations, Visions, Contemplations and Orations on Various Subjects; with the Grand Oeconomy of Human Life, in Nine Sections. London: 1751. V. 47

DIX, D. L.
Memorial...Praying an Appropriation of Land for the Relief of the Insane...To the Senate and House of Representatives of the United States in Congress Assembled. Washington: 1850. V. 49
Remarks on Prisons and Prison Discipline in the United States. Boston: 1845. V. 52

DIX, JOHN A.
Speech of General John A. Dix, President of the Mississippi and Missouri Railroad Co., at the Celebration at Iowa City, The Capitol of the State of Iowa, On the Completion of the Road to the Latter Point. January 24, 1856. New York: 1856. V. 52

DIX, THOMAS
A Treatise on Land Surveying in Seven Parts. London: 1819. V. 47; 49

DIXEY, ANNIE
The Lion Dog of Peking: Being the Astonishing History of the Pekingese Dog. New York. V. 47

DIXIE, FLORENCE
Across Patagonia. London: 1880. V. 50
In the Land of Misfortune... London: 1882. V. 50

DIXON, C. M.
The Leaguer of Ladysmith. London: 1900. V. 54

DIXON, CHARLES
The Game Birds and Wild Fowl of the British Islands. Sheffield: 1900. V. 50; 52

DIXON, E.
Fairy Tales from the Arabian Nights and More Arabian Nights. London: 1893/95. V. 54

DIXON, EDWARD H.
Scenes in the Practice of a New York Surgeon. New York: 1855. V. 50

DIXON, F.
The Geology of Sussex. Brighton: 1878. V. 51
The Geology...of Sussex. London: 1850. V. 48; 49; 50
The Geology...of Sussex. London: 1878. V. 51; 52; 53; 54

DIXON, GEORGE
Voyage Autour Du Monde, et Principalement a La Cote Nord-Quest De l'Amerique, Fait en 1785, 1786, 1787, et 1788, A Bord Du King-George Et De La Queene-Charalotte... Paris: 1789. V. 51
A Voyage Round the World; But More Particularly to the North West Coast of America. London: 1789. V. 47; 48; 49; 50; 52; 53; 54
A Voyage Round the World; But More Particularly to the North-West Coast of America...Performed in 1785, 1786, 1787 and 1788, in the King George and Queen Charlotte, Captains Portlock and Dixon. Amsterdam: 1968. V. 48; 50

DIXON, H. H.
Saddle and Sirloin or English Farm and Sporting Worthies (Part North). London: 1870. V. 48

DIXON, J. H.
Chronicles and Stories of the Craven Dales. London: 1881. V. 54
The Wuthering Heights Collection at Oatlands, Harrogate. 1906. V. 54
The Wuthering Heights Collection at Oatlands, Harrogate. London: 1906. V. 52

DIXON, JAMES
Personal Narrative of a Tour through a Part of the United States and Canada. New York: 1849. V. 47; 53

DIXON, JOSEPH K.
The Vanishing Race, the Last Great Indian Council. Garden City: 1914. V. 53
The Vanishing Race. The Last Great Indian Council. Philadelphia: 1925. V. 49

DIXON, JOSHUA
The Literary Life of William Brownrigg, M.D., F.R.S., To Which are Added An Account of the Coal Mines Near Whitehaven... London: 1801. V. 48; 50; 52

DIXON, MAYNARD
Poems and Seven Drawings. San Francisco: 1923. V. 47
Rim-Rock and Sage. San Francisco: 1977. V. 47; 48; 50

DIXON, MICHAEL M.
Life at the Flats. Detroit: 1987. V. 54

DIXON, RICHARD WATSON
Christ's Company and Other Poems. London: 1861. V. 54
Mano. A Poetical History...In Four Books. London: 1883. V. 50
Odes and Eclogues. Oxford: 1884. V. 50
S. John in Patmos. The Prize Poem on a Sacred Subject for 1863. London: 1863. V. 50

DIXON, ROBERT M. W.
Blues and Gospel Records 1902-1942. Harrow: 1963. V. 49

DIXON, SAM HOUSTON
The Heroes of San Jacinto. Houston: 1932. V. 54
The Poets and Poetry of Texas. Austin: 1885. V. 47; 52
Romance and Tragedy of Texas History. Houston: 1924. V. 47; 50

DIXON, THOMAS
The Clansman: an Historical Romance of the Ku Klux Klan. New York: 1907. V. 53
The Fall of a Nation. New York: 1916. V. 48; 52
Living Problems in Religion and Social Science. New York: 1889. V. 53
The Love Complex. New York: 1925. V. 50
The One Woman: a Story of Modern Utopia. New York: 1903. V. 53
The Traitor: a Story of the Fall of the Invisible Empire. New York: 1907. V. 53
The Victim: a Romance of the Real Jefferson Davis. New York: 1914. V. 53

DIXON, W. H.
History of William Penn, Founder of Pennsylvania. London: 1872. V. 48

DIXON, WILLIAM
A Catalogue of the Entire Valuable Collection of Early English Pottery and Porcelain... Norwich: 1874. V. 47
A History of the York and Ainsty Hunt. Leeds: 1899. V. 53

DIXON, WILLIAM HEPWORTH
Diana, Lady Lyle. London: 1877. V. 54
Free Russia. London: 1870. V. 52
Her Majesty's Tower. London: 1865. V. 51
New America. London: 1867. V. 47; 53
Personal History of Lord Bacon. Leipzig: 1861. V. 53
Royal Windsor. London: 1879-80. V. 54
White Conquest. London: 1876. V. 52; 53
White Conquest. London: 1896. V. 49

DIXON, WILLIAM SCARTH
Hunting in the Olden Days. London: 1912. V. 47

DIXON, WILLIE
I Am the Blues The Willie Dixon Story. London and New York: 1989. V. 50

DJURKLOU, G. BARON
Fairy Tales from the Swedish. London: 1901. V. 49

DMITRIEV-MAMONOV, A. I.
Guide to the Great Siberian Railway. St. Petersburg: 1900. V. 50

DOANE, A. SIDNEY
Surgery Illustrated. New York: 1836. V. 48; 51; 52

DOANE, GILBERT H.
About Collected Bookplates: a Letter from Gilbert H. Doane. Madison: 1941. V. 49; 50

DOANE, J.
A Musical Directory for the year 1794. London: 1794. V. 47

DOBBINS, M. D.
Memorial and Affidavits Showing Outrages Perpetrated by the Apache Indians in the Territory of Arizona, During the Years 1869 and 1870. San Francisco: 1871. V. 49

DOBBS, ARTHUR
An Account of the Countries Adjoining to Hudson's Bay, in the North-West Part of America... London: 1744. V. 50

DOBBS, CAROLINE
Men of Champoeg. A Record of the Lives of the Pioneers Who Founded the Oregon Government. Portland: 1932. V. 49

DOBELL, BETRAM
Sidelights On Charles Lamb. London: 1908. V. 49

DOBELL, CLIFFORD
Antony Van Leeuwenhoek and His 'Little Animals':... New York: 1932. V. 51

DOBELL, HORACE
Lectures on the Germs and Vestiges of Disease and on the Prevention of the Invasion and Fatality of Disease by Periodical Examination. London: 1861. V. 48; 51; 53

DOBELL, PERCY JOHN
The Literature of the Restoration Being a Collection of the Poetical and Dramatic Literature Produced Between the Years 1660 and 1700 with Particular Reference to the Writings of John Dryden. (and) Books of the Time of the Restoration Being a Collection... London: 1918-20. V. 51

DOBELL, SYDNEY THOMPSON
Balder. Part the First. London: 1854. V. 51

DOBIE, BERTHA MC KEE
Growing Up in Texas. Austin: 1972. V. 52

DOBIE, CHARLES CALDWELL
The Golden Talisman: A Grove Play... 1941. V. 47
The Golden Talisman: A Grove Play. San Francisco: 1941. V. 49

DOBIE, DUDLEY
Pancho Villa Last Hangout...the Big Bend. Alpine. V. 49

DOBIE, JAMES FRANK
Apache Gold and Yaqui Silver. Boston: 1939. V. 48; 50; 52; 53; 54
As the Moving Finger Writ. Austin: 1955. V. 53
The Ben Lilly Legend. Boston: 1950. V. 49
Bob More, Man and Bird Man. Austin: 1965. V. 47
Bob More: Man and Bird Man. Dallas: 1965. V. 48; 51; 52; 53
Carl Sandburg and Saint Peter at the Gate. Austin: 1966. V. 50; 53
Coronado's Children, Lost Mines and Buried Treasure of the Southwest. Dallas: 1930. V. 47
Coronado's Children: Tales of Lost Mines and Buried Treasures of the Southwest. Dallas: 1980. V. 53
Coyote Wisdom. Austin: 1938. V. 48
The Flavor of Texas. Dallas: 1936. V. 49; 54
Guide to Life and Literature of the Southwest, With a Few Observations. 1943. V. 48; 49; 50
Guide to Life and Literature of the Southwest with a Few Observations. Austin: 1943. V. 49; 50; 51; 54
I'll Tell You A Tale. Boston: 1960. V. 49
John C. Duval: First Texas Man of Letters. Austin: 1939. V. 50
John C. Duval. First Texas Man of Letters. Dallas: 1939. V. 47; 51
Legends of Texas. 1924. V. 49
The Longhorns. Boston: 1941. V. 47; 49; 50
The Longhorns. Boston: 1950. V. 50
Man Bird and Beast. Austin: 1930. V. 47; 50
The Mustangs. Boston: 1952. V. 47; 50; 53; 54
Mustangs and Cow Horses. Austin: 1940. V. 49; 50; 53
On the Open Range. Dallas: 1931. V. 51; 53
On the Open Range. Dallas: 1951. V. 52
Pitching Horses and Panthers. Austin: 1940. V. 49
Storytellers I Have Known. Austin: 1961. V. 53
Tales of Old-Time Texas. Boston: 1955. V. 49; 50
Tales of the Mustang. Dallas: 1936. V. 47; 53
A Texan in England. Boston: 1945. V. 47; 53
Texas and Southwestern Lore. 1927. V. 48; 51
Tongues of the Monte. New York: 1935. V. 47
A Vaquero of the Brush Country. Dallas: 1929. V. 47; 48; 50; 51; 52; 53; 54
The Voice of the Coyote. Boston: 1949. V. 47
Wild and Wiley. Flagstaff: 1980. V. 53

DOBIE, ROWLAND
The History of the United Parishes of St. Giles in the Fields and St. George, Bloomsbury. London: 1829. V. 52

DOBLIN, ALFRED
Alexanderplatz Berlin. New York: 1931. V. 49

DOBREE, BONAMY
Restoration Tragedy 1660-1720. Oxford: 1929. V. 53

DOBRIZHOFFER, MARTIN
An Account of the Abipones. London: 1822. V. 49

DOBSON, AUSTIN
Ballad of Beau Brocade. London: 1892. V. 54
Collected Poems. London: 1907. V. 54
Fielding. London: 1883. V. 52
Life of Oliver Goldsmith. London: 1888. V. 50; 51; 53
Old Kensington Palace and Other Papers. London: 1910. V. 54
Old World Idylls and Other Verses. London: 1893. V. 53
Poems on Several Occasions. New York: 1895. V. 49; 53
Proverbs in Porcelain... London: 1895. V. 52
Proverbs in Porcelain... London: 1905. V. 54
The Story of Rosina and Other Verses. London: 1895. V. 48; 49; 51

DOBSON, EDWARD
A Rudimentary Treatise on the Manufacture of Bricks and Tiles. London: 1850. V. 50
Rudiments of the Art of Building. London: 1849. V. 50

DOBSON, GEORGE
Russia's Railway Advance into Central Asia. London: 1890. V. 53
St. Petersburg. London: 1910. V. 54

DOBSON, JAMES
The Mathematical Repository. London: 1775. V. 49

DOBSON, JESSIE
Anatomical Eponyms Being a Biographical Dictionary of Those Anatomists Who's Names Have Become Incopoarted into Anatomical Nomencalture... London: 1946. V. 49; 50

DOBSON, JOHN
A Sermon Preacht at the funeral of the Honourable the Lady Mary Armor, Relict of Sir William Farmor, Baronet.. London: 1670. V. 51
A Sunday Evening's Conversation, Between Old John Dobson and His Son James... London: 1815. V. 53

DOBSON, MARGARET JANE
Memoir of John Dobson of Newcastle-on-Tyne... London and Newcastle: 1885. V. 47

DOBSON, SUSANNAH DAWSON
The Life of Petrarch. London: 1797. V. 47; 49; 50; 51
Literary History of the Troubadours. London: 1807. V. 53

DOBSON, THOMAS
Index to the Bible, in Which the Various Subjects Which Occur in the Scriptures are Alphabetically Arranged, with Accurate References to All the Books of the Old and New Testaments. Philadelphia: 1804. V. 51

DOBSON, WILLIAM
Kunopaedia. A Practical Essay on Breaking or Training the English Spaniel or Pointer. London: 1814. V. 47
Kunopaedia. A Practical Essay on Breaking or Training the English Spaniel or Pointer. London: 1817. V. 49; 51; 52; 54
Rambles by the Ribble. First and Second Series. Preston: 1877. V. 48
Solomon De Mundi Vanitate. Poema Matthaei Prior Arm. Oxford: 1734. V. 49

DOBYNS, STEPHEN
Concurring Beasts. New York: 1972. V. 50
Man of Little Evils. New York: 1973. V. 53
Saratoga Longshot. New York: 1976. V. 51

DOBYNS, WINIFRED STARR
California Gardens. New York: 1931. V. 47

DOBZHANSKY, THEODOSIUS
Evolutionary Biology. New York: 1967-82. V. 48
Genetics and the Origin of Species. New York: 1937. V. 48; 53

DOCK, GEORGE
Hookworm Disease: Etiology, Pathology, Diagnosis, Prognosis, Prophylaxis and Treatment. St. Louis: 1910. V. 48; 51; 53

DOCKER, ALFRED
The Colour Prints of William Dickes. London: 1924. V. 47

DOCKRILL, A. W.
Australian Indigenous Orchids. Volume I. 1969. V. 53
Australian Indigenous Orchids. Volume I. Picnic Point: 1969. V. 52

DOCKSTADER, FREDERICK J.
Indian Art in America. V. 47; 48
Indian Art in Middle America. Greenwich: 1964. V. 50; 52

THE DOCTOR No Changeling; or, Sacheverell Still Sacheverell. Observations on a Sermon Preach'd at St. Saviour's in Southwark, on Palm-Sunday, 1713. London: 1713. V. 53

DOCTOROW, E. L.
American Anthem. New York: 1982. V. 49; 52
Bad Man From Bodie. London: 1961. V. 47
Big as Life. New York: 1966. V. 51
Billy Bathgate. New York: 1989. V. 49; 50; 51; 52
The Book of Daniel. New York: 1971. V. 47
Drinks Before Dinner. New York: 1979. V. 49; 50; 54
Lives of the Poets. New York: 1984. V. 48; 49; 53
Loon Lake. New York: 1979. V. 49
Loon Lake. New York: 1980. V. 50; 51; 52; 53; 54
The People's Text. Jackson: 1992. V. 52
Ragtime. New York: 1975. V. 47; 48; 49; 50; 51; 52
The Waterworks. Franklin Library: 1994. V. 53
The Waterworks. New York: 1994. V. 50
Welcome to Hard Times. New York: 1960. V. 47; 48; 50; 52
World's Fair. New York: 1985. V. 48; 49; 50; 53

DOCUMENTARY History of the Constitution of the United States of America 1786-1870. Washington: 1894. V. 52

DOCUMENTS and Official Reports, Illustrating the Causes Which Led to the Revolution in the Government of the Seneca Indians, in the Year 1848 and to the Recognition of Their Representative Republican Constiution by the Authorities of the United States... Baltimore: 1857. V. 50

DOCUMENTS Relating to Libels. Published by Order of the Constitutional Association for Opposing the Progress of Disloyal and Seditious Principles. London: 1821. V. 48; 53

DOCUMENTS Relating to the Project of a Rail-Road from Santiago to Valparaiso Chili, South America. Valparaiso: 1852. V. 54

DOCUMENTS Relative to the Colonial History of the State of New York, Procured in Holland, England and France. Albany: 1853-61. V. 49

DODADONI ROVERI, ANNA MARIA
Egyptian Civilization. Milano: 1988. V. 53

DODARIDGE, JOHN
Judge Dodaridge, His Law of Nobility and Peerage. London: 1658. V. 50

DODD, ALLISON
Genealogy and History of the Daniel Dod Family in America, 1646-1940. Bloomfield: 1940. V. 49

DODD, BETHUEL L.
Genealogies of the Male Descendants of Daniel Dod, of Branford, Conn., a Native of England 1646 to 1863. Newark: 1864. V. 49; 51

DODD, DAVID O.
Letters of David O. Dodd. 1917. V. 50

DODD, GEORGE
The Food of London: A Sketch of the Chief Varieties, Sources of Supply, Probable Quantities, Modes of Arrival, Processes of manufacture, Suspected Adulteration and Machinery of Distribution of the Food for a Community of Two Million and a Half. London: 1856. V. 48
Pictorial History of the Russian War, 1854-5-6. London: 1856. V. 47

DODD, RALPH
The Engineering Plagiarist; or Dodd from Phillips Exposed. Newcastle: 1795. V. 54
Report on the First Part of the Line of Inland Navigation from the East to the West Sea by Way of Newcastle and Carlisle, as Originally Projected and Lately Surveyed by R. Dodd, Civil Engineer. Newcastle: 1795. V. 54
Reports, with Plans, Sections, &c. of the Proposed Dry Tunnel, or Passage, from Gravesend, in Kent to Tilbury, in Essex... London: 1798. V. 51
A Short Historical Account of the Greater Part of the Principal Canals in the Known World... Newcastle: 1795. V. 54

DODD, STEPHEN
An Historical and Topographical Account of the Town of Woburn, Its Abbey and Vicinity... Woburn: 1818. V. 50

DODD, WILLIAM
The Beauties of History; or, Pictures of Virtue and Vice... London: 1796. V. 48; 52; 53
The Convict's Address to His Unhappy Brethren. London: 1777. V. 50
A Day in Vacation at College. London: 1751. V. 48; 54
A Familiar Explanation of the Poetical Works of Milton. London: 1762. V. 49; 54
The Magdalen; or, History of the First Penitent Prostitute Recieved into that Charitable Asylum. London: 1805. V. 47
A New Book of the Dunciad Occasion'd by Mr. Warburton's New Edition of the Dunciad Complete. London: 1750. V. 51
An Oration Delivered at the Dedication of Free-Mason's Hall, Great Queen Street, Lincoln's-Inn Fields, on Thursday, May 23, 1776. London: 1776. V. 50
Poems. London: 1767. V. 48; 50; 54
The Sisters; or, the History of Lucy and Caroline Sanson... London: 1791. V. 48; 50
Thoughts in Prison; in Five Parts. London: 1777. V. 51
Thoughts in Prison, in Five Parts. London: 1793. V. 47; 54
Thoughts in Prison; in five Parts... London: 1815. V. 54
Thoughts in Prison...with the Life of the Author, His Last Prayer, and Other Miscellaneous Pieces (etc.). London: 1816?. V. 47
The Visitor. London: 1764. V. 51; 52

DODDRIDGE, JOHN
A Compleat Parson; or, a Description of Advowsons, or Church-Living. London: 1630. V. 54
The History of the Ancient and Modern Estate of the Principality of Wales, Dutchy of Cornwall and Earldome of Chester. London: 1630. V. 47; 54

DODDRIDGE, JOSEPH
Notes On the Settlement and Indian Wars of the Western Parts of Virginia & Pennsylvania... Wellsburgh: 1824. V. 47; 50
Notes on the Settlement and Indian Wars of the Western Parts of Virginia & Pennsylvania. Pittsburgh: 1912. V. 54

DODDRIDGE, PHILIP
The Principles of the Christian religion, Divided Into Lessons, for Children. Hartford: 1796. V. 47
The Rise and Progress of Religion in the Soul... Northampton: 1804. V. 48
Sermons on the Religious Education of Children. Bridgeport: 1810. V. 49
Some Remarkable Passages in the Life of the Honourable Col. James Gardiner, Who Was Slain at the Battle of Preston-Pans, Sept. 21, 1745. London: 1747. V. 52; 54
Some Remarkable Passages in the Life of the Honourable Col. James Gardiner, Who was slain at the Battle of Preston-Pans, Sept. 21, 1745. Wigan: 1782. V. 47

DODDRIDGE, PHILIP continued
Some Remarkable Passages in the Life of the Honourable James Gardiner, Who Was Slain at te Battle of Preston-Pans, Sept. 21, 1745. London: 1747/46. V. 53
Speech of Mr. Doddridge, in the Case of Samuel Houston, Charged with a Contempt and Breach of the Privileges of the House by Assaulting Hon. William Stanberry...May 9, 1832. Washington: 1832. V. 49

DODDS, MADELEINE
The Pilgrimage of Grace 1536-1537 and The Exeter Conspiracy 1538. London: 1915. V. 52

DODDS, MADELEINE HOPE
A History of Northumberland. Volume XII. Newcastle-upon-Tyne: 1930. V. 47

DODGE, DAVID
The British Museum is Falling Down. London: 1965. V. 48

DODGE, G. M.
Report of...Chief Engineer, to the Board of Directors on a Branch Railroad Line from the Union Pacific Railroad to Idaho, Montana, Oregon and Puget's Sound. Washington: 1868. V. 47

DODGE, GRENVILLE M.
Biographical Sketch of James Bridger, Mountaineer Trapper and Guide. Kansas City: 1904. V. 54

DODGE, JIM
Fup. Berkeley: 1983. V. 50

DODGE, JOHN
Narrative of Mr. John Dodge, During His Captivity at Detroit. Cedar Rapids: 1909. V. 48

DODGE, JONATHAN
A Complete System of Stenography, or Short-Hand Writing... 1823. V. 50

DODGE, MARY ABIGAIL
Woman's Worth and Worthlessness. New York: 1872. V. 54
Woman's Wrongs: a Counter-Irritant. Boston: 1868. V. 54

DODGE, MARY MAPES
Along the Way. New York: 1879. V. 54
Hans Brinker; or the Silver Skates. New York: 1866. V. 47; 51
The Two Mysteries. 1892. V. 53

DODGE, ORVIL
The Heroes of Battle Rock: Narrative of the Desperate Encounter of Nine White Men with Three Hundred Indians... 1904. V. 48

DODGE, RICHARD I.
The Black Hills. New York: 1876. V. 48; 50; 52
The Hunting Grounds of the Great West. London: 1877. V. 47; 52
The Hunting Grounds of the Great West. London: 1878. V. 48
Our Wild Indians: Thirty-Three Years' Personal Experience Among the Rid Men of the Great West. Hartford: 1883. V. 54
The Plains of the Great West and Their Inhabitants. New York: 1877. V. 53

DODGE, THEODORE AYRAULT
Riders of Many Lands. New York: 1894. V. 47; 54

DODGE, WALTER PHELPS
The Real Sir Richard Burton. London: 1907. V. 47; 53

DODGE, WILLIAM SUMNER
Robert Henry Hendershot; or, the Brave Drummer Boy of the Rappahannock. Chicago: 1867. V. 54

DODGSON, CAMPBELL
Catalogue of Early German and Flemish Woodcuts Preserved in the Department of prints and Drawings in the British Museum. London: 1923-25. V. 48
The Etchings of Charles Meryon. London: 1921. V. 51
Forain - Draughtsman, Lithographer, Etcher. New York: 1936. V. 49
Old French Colour-Prints. London: 1924. V. 52; 54

DODGSON, CHARLES LUTWIDGE
Adventures d'Alice Au Pays des Merveilles. London: 1869. V. 52
Alice Au Pays Des Merveilles. Paris: 1937. V. 53
Alice Au Pays Des Merveilles. Paris: 1951. V. 52
Alice au Pays des Merveilles. Paris: 1952. V. 49
Alice Au Pays Des Merveilles. Paris: 1955. V. 52
Alice in Wonderland. London. V. 53
Alice in Wonderland. London: 1867/72. V. 51
Alice in Wonderland. London: 1869/72. V. 48
Alice in Wonderland. London: 1883/82. V. 51
Alice in Wonderland. London: 1910. V. 48
Alice in Wonderland. New York: 1914. V. 49
Alice in Wonderland. 1916. V. 49
Alice in Wonderland. Chicago: 1916. V. 52
Alice in Wonderland. London Melborne Toronto: 1916. V. 53
Alice in Wonderland. Mount Vernon: 1920. V. 51
Alice in Wonderland. London: 1921. V. 47
Alice in Wonderland. New York: 1926. V. 49; 53
Alice in Wonderland. London: 1930. V. 53
Alice in Wonderland. Paris: 1930. V. 49; 50
Alice in Wonderland. London: 1932. V. 47
Alice in Wonderland. Stockholm: 1945. V. 48; 49
Alice in Wonderland. London: 1950. V. 53
Alice in Wonderland. London: 1951. V. 53
Alice in Wonderland. London: 1967. V. 50
Alice's Abenteuer im Wunderland. London: 1869. V. 53; 54
Alice's Adventures in Wonderland. London: 1866. V. 47; 54
Alice's Adventures in Wonderland. New York: 1866. V. 47; 48; 53; 54
Alice's Adventures in Wonderland. London: 1866/72. V. 50
Alice's Adventures in Wonderland. London: 1868. V. 48
Alice's Adventures in Wonderland. 1869. V. 50; 52
Alice's Adventures in Wonderland. Boston: 1869. V. 47; 48; 49; 53; 54
Alice's Adventures in Wonderland. Boston/New York: 1872. V. 49
Alice's Adventures in Wonderland. London: 1872. V. 49; 50; 51
Alice's Adventures in Wonderland. London: 1876. V. 54
Alice's Adventures in Wonderland. London: 1886-72. i.e. V. 51
Alice's Adventures in Wonderland. London: 1897. V. 54
Alice's Adventures in Wonderland. Philadelphia: 1897. V. 49
Alice's Adventures in Wonderland. London: 1899. V. 49
Alice's Adventures in Wonderland. New York: 1901. V. 48
Alice's Adventures in Wonderland. New York: 1902. V. 47; 48
Alice's Adventures in Wonderland. London: 1907. V. 47; 48; 49; 50; 52; 53
Alice's Adventures in Wonderland. London: 1911. V. 47
Alice's Adventures in Wonderland. Philadelphia: 1912. V. 53
Alice's Adventures in Wonderland. London: 1914. V. 49; 53
Alice's Adventures in Wonderland. London: 1915. V. 50
Alice's Adventures in Wonderland. Boston: 1917. V. 49
Alice's Adventures in Wonderland. 1918. V. 47; 51
Alice's Adventures in Wonderland. London: 1920. V. 48
Alice's Adventures in Wonderland. London: 1922. V. 48
Alice's Adventures in Wonderland. London: 1923. V. 53
Alice's Adventures in Wonderland. London: 1928/29. V. 49
Alice's Adventures in Wonderland. New York: 1932. V. 48; 49; 50; 51; 52; 53; 54
Alice's Adventures in Wonderland. London: 1932/28. V. 47
Alice's Adventures in Wonderland. New York: 1932/35. V. 54
Alice's Adventures in Wonderland. London: 1934 (1921). V. 50
Alice's Adventures in Wonderland. London: 1940. V. 51; 54
Alice's Adventures in Wonderland. Stockholm: 1946. V. 48
Alice's Adventures in Wonderland. London: 1948. V. 54
Alice's Adventures in Wonderland. London: 1949. V. 50
Alice's Adventures in Wonderland. New York: 1949. V. 53
Alice's Adventures in Wonderland. Paris: 1950. V. 52
Alice's Adventures in Wonderland. London: 1954. V. 49; 54
Alice's Adventures in Wonderland. London: 1965. V. 53
Alice's Adventures in Wonderland. New York: 1965. V. 49
Alice's Adventures in Wonderland. New York: 1969. V. 47; 48; 49; 54
Alice's Adventures in Wonderland. New York: 1971. V. 53
Alice's Adventures in Wonderland. New York: 1977. V. 53
Alice's Adventures in Wonderland. Berkeley & Los Angeles: 1982. V. 50
Alice's Adventures in Wonderland. West Hatfield: 1982. V. 47; 48; 49; 52; 54
Alice's Adventures in Wonderland. New York: 1985. V. 51
Alice's Adventures in Wonderland. (with) Through the Looking Glass. London: 1868/72. V. 49
Alice's Adventures in Wonderland. (with) Through the Looking Glass. New York: 1932/35. V. 49
Alice's Adventures in Wonderland. (with) Through the Looking Glass. New York: 1946. V. 49
Alice's Adventures Under Ground. London: 1886. V. 47; 48; 49; 53
The Animated Picture Book of Alice in Wonderland. New York: 1943. V. 50
Aventures d'Alice au Pays des Merveilles. London: 1849. V. 54
The Children's Alice. London: 1936. V. 48
The Complete Works of Lewis Carroll. New York: 1950. V. 51
Curiosa Mathematica. London: 1893. V. 47
Doublets. London: 1879. V. 51; 52; 54
The Dynamics of a Particle, with an Excursin on the New Methods of Evaluation as Applied... Oxford: 1865. V. 48; 49
Eight or Nine Wise Words About Letter-Writing. Oxford: 1890. V. 50
Eight or Nine Wise Words About Letter-Writing. Oxford: 1907. V. 47
Euclid and His Modern Rivals. London: 1879. V. 48
Feeding the Mind. London: 1906. V. 52
Feeding the Mind. London: 1907. V. 48; 51; 53; 54
The Game of Logic. London: 1886. V. 47; 49
Game of Logic. London: 1887. V. 47; 49; 54
The Hunting of the Snark. London: 1876. V. 47; 48; 49; 51; 52; 54
The Hunting of the Snark. New York: 1891. V. 47
The Hunting of the Snark. Wausau: 1897. V. 49
The Hunting of the Snark. 1903. V. 49
The Hunting of the Snark. New York: 1903. V. 47; 48; 49; 50; 53; 54
The Hunting of the Snark. London: 1910. V. 51
The Hunting of the Snark. London: 1941. V. 49
The Hunting of the Snark. 1975. V. 52
The Hunting of the Snark. London: 1975. V. 49
The Hunting of the Snark. Los Altos: 1981. V. 47
The Hunting of the Snark. 1983. V. 52; 53
The Hunting of the Snark. London & Northampton: 1983. V. 48
The Hunting of the Snark. London: 1993. V. 50; 51; 54
Lewis Carroll and the Kitchins. New York: 1980. V. 54
The Lewis Carroll Picture Book. London: 1899. V. 47; 51

DODGSON, CHARLES LUTWIDGE continued
The New Belfry of Christ Church, Oxford. (with) *Lawn Tennis Tournaments. The True Method of Assigning Prizes with a Proof of the Fallacy of the Present Method.* (with) *Syzygies and Lanrick. A Word-Puzzle and a Game for Two Players.* London: 1893. V. 47
Novelty and Romancement. Boston: 1925. V. 51
The Nursery "Alice". London: 1890. V. 47; 49; 53
The Nursery Alice. London: 1897. V. 50
A Peep-show Alice. Alice's Adventures in Wonderland and Through the Looking Glass. Berkeley: 1989. V. 47
Phantasmagoria. London: 1869. V. 48; 49; 51; 52
The Rectory Umbrella and Mischmasch. London: 1932. V. 48
Rhyme? and Reason?. London: 1883. V. 47; 48; 49; 50; 51; 52; 53
The Russian Journal. New York: 1935. V. 48
A Selection of Letters from Lewis Carroll. Together with Eight or Nine Wise Words About Letter Writing. London: 1933. V. 47
Some Popular Fallacies about Vivisection by Lewis Carroll. Oxford: 1875. V. 47; 51
Songs from Alice in Wonderland & through the Looking Glass. London: 1921. V. 50
Sylvie and Bruno. London: 1889. V. 49; 51; 53
Sylvie and Bruno. London: 1893. V. 47; 48; 49; 52; 53; 54
Sylvie and Bruno Concluded. New York: 1894. V. 47; 53
Sylvie and Bruno. (with) *Sylvie and Bruno Concluded.* London: 1889-93. V. 47; 48; 49; 50; 51; 52
Symbolic Logic. London: 1896. V. 47; 48; 49
A Tangled Tale. London: 1885. V. 48; 51; 54
Three Sunsets and Other Poems. London: 1898. V. 49
Through the Looking Glass. London: 1871/72. V. 49
Through the Looking Glass. London & New York: 1872. V. 47; 49; 50; 51; 52; 53; 54
Through the Looking Glass. London: 1878. V. 53
Through the Looking Glass. London: 1898. V. 49
Through the Looking Glass. New York: 1902. V. 51; 52
Through the Looking Glass. New York: 1909. V. 51
Through the Looking Glass. Mount Vernon: 1920. V. 51
Through the Looking Glass. New York: 1923. V. 52
Through the Looking Glass. New York: 1931. V. 53
Through the Looking Glass. New York: 1935. V. 49; 53
Through the Looking Glass. London: 1962. V. 54
Through the Looking Glass. London: 1972. V. 48
The Two Brothers. 1994. V. 52
The Wasp in a Wig. 1977. V. 48; 50; 52
What the Tortoise Said to Achilles. 1894. V. 47
The Wonderland Postage Stamp Case (with) *Eight or Nine Wise Words About Letter-Writing by Lewis Carroll.* Oxford: 1890. V. 49; 52

DODINGTON, GEORGE BUBB
The Diary. Salisbury: 1784. V. 49; 51; 52; 54
The Diary. London: 1785. V. 49

DODOENS, REMBERT
Medicinalium Observationum Exempla Rara, Recognita & Aucta. Cologne: 1581. V. 52
A New Herbal, or Historie of Plantes: Wherein is Contayned the Whole Discourse and Perfect Description of All Sortes of Herbes and Plantes... London: 1578. V. 48; 53
A New Herbal, or Historie of Plants: Wherein is Contained the Whole Discocurse and Perfect Descriptions of all Sorts of Herbes and Plants... London: 1619. V. 51

DODOREDGE, JOHN
Honors Pedigree, or the Several Fountaines of Gentry. London: 1652. V. 47; 49

DODRIDGE, JOHN
An Historical Account of the Ancient and Modern State of the Principality of Wales, Dutchy of Cornwall (sic)... London: 1714. V. 48; 53
The History of the Ancient and Modern Estate of the Principality of Wales, Dutchy of Cornwall and Earldome of Chester (etc.). London: 1630. V. 49; 52

DODS, MARY DIANA
Tales of the Wild and the Wonderful. London: 1825. V. 50

DODSLEY, J.
A Select Collection of Old Plays. London: 1780. V. 50

DODSLEY, JAMES
A Collection of Poems in Six Volumes. London: 1766/68. V. 48

DODSLEY, JOHN
A Collection of Poems...By Several Hands. London: 1766-68. V. 48

DODSLEY, ROBERT
the Art of Preaching: In Imitation of Horace's Art of Poetry. London: 1738. V. 54
Beauty; or the Art of Charming. London: 1735. V. 52
The Chronicle of the Kings of England. London: 1735. V. 52
A Collection of Poems. London: 1748-58. V. 53
A Collection of Poems...Several Hands... London: 1758. V. 52
A Collection of Poems...Several Hands. London: 1765. V. 53
A Collection of Poems...Several Hands. London: 1782. V. 51
A Collection of Poems...Several Hands. London: 1832. V. 51
The Economy of Human Life. Allentaun: 1813. V. 51
Fugitive Pieces on Various Subjects. London: 1761. V. 48; 51
Fugitive Pieces on Various Subjects. London: 1762. V. 54
Fugitive Pieces, on Various Subjects. London: 1765. V. 52
The General Contents of the British Museum: with Remarks. London: 1762. V. 50
The King and the Miller of Mansfield, a Dramatick Tale. London: 1737. V. 48
The Oeconomy of Human Life. London: 1795. V. 50
The Preceptor. London: 1775. V. 52
The Preceptor... London: 1783. V. 48
Public Virtue: a Poem. London: 1753. V. 48; 54
A Select Collection of Old Plays. London: 1744. V. 47; 48
Trifles. Viz. The Toy Shop; The King and the Miller of Mansfield; The Blind Beggar of Bethnal-Green; Rex & Pontifex; The Chronicle of the Kings of England; The Art of Preaching... London: 1745. V. 50; 52; 53

DODSON, OWEN
Boy at the Window. New York: 1951. V. 50; 54

DODSWORTH, WILLIAM
An Historical Account of the Episcopal See and Cathedral Church of Sarum or Salisbury. London: 1814. V. 50

DODWELL, C. R.
The Canterbury School of Illumination 1066-1200. 1954. V. 49

DODWELL, HENRY
De Parma Equestri Woodwardiana Dissertatio. Oxonii, e Theatro: 1713. V. 48
A Treatise Concerning the Lawfulness of Instrumental Musick in Holy Offices. London: 1700. V. 47; 48; 52

DODWELL, WILLIAM
The Sick Man's Companion: or, the Clergyman's Assistant in Visiting the Sick. London: 1768. V. 47

DOE, JANET
A Bibliography of the Works of Ambroise Pare: Premier Chirurgien & Conseilelr du Roy. Chicago: 1937. V. 50; 51

DOERR, HARRIET
Stones for Ibarra. New York: 1984. V. 51; 52

THE DOG of Knowledge; or, Memoirs of Bob, The Spotted Terrier... London: 1801. V. 51

DOGGEREL Ditties. London: 1900. V. 50

DOHAN, EDITH HALL
Italic Tomb-Groups in the University Museum. Philadelphia: 1942. V. 52

DOHENY, ESTELLE BETZHOLD
The Estelle Doheny Collection. London: 1987-89. V. 50

DOHENY, ESTELLE BETZOLD
Catalouge of Books and Manuscripts in the Estelle Doheny Collection. Los Angeles: 1940-55. V. 54
The Estelle Doheny Collection. New York: 1987-89. V. 49; 52
The Estelle Doheny Collection. 1988-89. V. 52
The Estelle Doheny Collection. New York: 1988-89. V. 49; 51

DOHERTY, TERENCE
The Anatomical Works of George Stubbs. London: 1974. V. 50; 54

DOHERTY, WILLIAM JAMES
Inis-Owen and Tirconnell: Notes, Antiquarian and Topographical. First Series. Dublin: 1891. V. 48; 50

DOHNE, J. L.
Zulu-Kafir Dictionary, Etymologically Explained, with Copious Illustrations and Examples. Cape Town: 1857. V. 54

DOIG, IVAN
The Sea-Runners. 1982. V. 54
This House of Sky: Landscapes of a Western Mind. New York: 1978. V. 50; 52; 54
This House of Sky: Landscapes of a Western Mind. New York: 1988. V. 47
Winter Brothers: a Season at the Edge of America. New York: 1980. V. 54

DOINGS of Kriss Kringle. New York: 1897. V. 53

DOISNEAU, ROBERT
Paris Parade. London: 1956. V. 53
Three Seconds From Eternity. Boston: 1980. V. 48

DOKE, CLEMENT M.
The Lambas of Northern Rhodesia. London: 1931. V. 48

DOLAUS, JOHANNES
Encyclopaedia Chirurgica Rationalis: in Qua Omnes Affectus Externi Corpus Humanum... Venetiis: 1695. V. 47

DOLBEN, DIGBY MACKWORTH
Poems. 1911. V. 48

DOLBY, ANASTASIA
Church Embroidery Ancient and Modern. London: 1867. V. 50

DOLBY, GEORGE
Charles Dickens As I Knew Him: The Story of the Reading Tours in Great Britain and America (1866-1870). London: 1885. V. 49

DOLBY, J.
Six Views of Eton College... Eton: 1838. V. 52

DOLBY, THOMAS
Floreston: or, the New Lord of the Manor. London: 1839. V. 48

DOLCE, LODOVICO
Dialogo Di M. Lodovico Dolce Nel Qvale si Ragiona Del Modo di Accreseere & Conseruar la Memoria. Venice: 1586. V. 53
Dialogo Piacevole Nelqvale Messer Pietro Aretino Parla in Difesa d'i Male Aventvrati Mariti. Venice: 1542. V. 52

DOLE, N. H.
America in Spitsbergen, the Romance of an Arctic Coal-Mine... Boston: 1922. V. 52; 53

DOLGE, ALFRED
Pianos and Their Makers. 1911. V. 48

DOLGIN, I. M.
Climate of Antarctica. Rotterdam: 1986. V. 52

DOLIN, A.
Alicia Markova, Her Life and Art. New York: 1953. V. 49

DOLLAR, JOHN
A Handbook of Horse-Shoeing. New York: 1909. V. 51

DOLLAR, ROBERT
Private Diary of Robert Dollar on His Recent Visits to China. San Francisco: 1912. V. 52

DOLLMAN, F. T.
An Analysis of Ancient Domestic Architecture, Exhibiting Some of the Best Existing Examples in Great Britain... London: 1863. V. 49

DOLLMAN, J. G.
Catalogue of the Selous Collection of Big Game in the British Museum (Natural History). London: 1921. V. 47

D'OLLONE, VICOMTE
In Forbidden China. London: 1911. V. 48
In Forbidden China. London: 1912. V. 53

DOLLS Of Many Lands. Chicago: 1910. V. 53

DOLLY in Town. London: 1900. V. 50

DOLLY'S Mansion. London: 1890's. V. 47

DOLMETSCH, H.
The Historic Styles of Ornament. London: 1912. V. 47

THE DOLPHIN. New York: 1933. V. 49
THE DOLPHIN. New York: 1933-41. V. 54

DOMAT, JEAN
The Civil Law in Its Natural Order. London: 1722. V. 53
The Civil Law In Its Natural Order. London: 1737. V. 50
The Civil Law In Its Natural Order. Boston: 1861. V. 52

THE DOME. London: 1897. V. 50

THE DOME: a Quarterly Containing Examples of All the Arts. London: 1897-98. V. 50

THE DOME: An Illustrated Magazine and Review of Literature, Music, Architecture and the Graphic Arts. London: 1898-1900. V. 48

DOMENECH, EMMANUEL H. D.
Missionary Adventures in Texas and Mexico, a Personal Narrative of Six Years' Sojourn... London: 1858. V. 49
Seven Years Residence in the Great Desert of North America. London: 1860. V. 47; 48; 49; 51; 53; 54
Seven Years' Residence in the Great Deserts of North America. London: 1877. V. 47

DOMESDAY Book: a Survey of England. Chicester: 1983-86. V. 48

THE DOMESTIC Gardener's Manual. London: 1830. V. 53

DOMESTIC Management; or, the Beautiful Cookery-Book. London: 1810. V. 52; 53

THE DOMESTIC Manners of the Americans; or, Sketches of the People of the United States. 1835. V. 47

DOMESTIC Prospects of the Country Under the New Parliament,. London: 1837. V. 49; 52

DOMESTIC Scenes in Greenland and Iceland. London: 1844. V. 52

DOMINGUEZ BORDONA, J.
Spanish Illumination. Florence: 1930. V. 53

DOMINGUIN, LUIS MIGUEL
Pablo Picasso: Toros & Toreros. New York: 1961. V. 52

DOMINICETI, BARTHOLOMEW
An Address from Dr. Dominiceti, of Chelsea. London: 1782. V. 52

DOMINICUS DE FLANDRIA
Questinoum Super XII Libros Metaphisice. Venice: 1499. V. 52

DOMINICY, MARC ANTOINE
Assertor Gallicvs, Contra Vindicias Hispanicas Ioannes Iacobi Chiffletii. Paris: 1616. V. 52
Assertor Gallicvs, Contra Vindicias Hispanicas Ioannes Iacobi Chiffletii. Paris: 1646. V. 48

DOMINION ILLUSTRATING COMPANY
Greater Vancouver Illustrated. Canada's Most Progressive Twentieth Century Metropolis. Vancouver: 1908. V. 50

DOMINIS, MARCO ANTONIO DE
Marcus Antonius Dominus, Archiepiscopus Spalatensis, svae Profectionis Consilium Exponit. Londini: 1616. V. 47

DOMINQUIN, LUIS MIGUEL
Pablo Picasso. Toros y Toreros & Une etude de Georges Boudaile. New York: 1961. V. 50

DOMVILLE-FIFE, C.
Among Wild Tribes of the Amazon...Descriptions of the Savage Head-Hunting. Philadelphia/London: 1924. V. 53

DON, GEORGE
A General History of the Dichlamydeous Plants... London: 1831-38. V. 49; 52

DON Juan: with a Biographical Account of Lord Byron and His Family; Anecdotes of His Lordship's Travels and Residence in Greece, at Geneva &c... London: 1819. V. 53; 54

DON Leon: a Poem by the Late Lord Byron... London: 1900. V. 53

DONAGHY, MICHAEL
O'Ryan's Belt. Eleven Poems: 1990-1991. Madison: 1991. V. 47

DONAHEY, MARY D.
Peter and Prue. Chicago: 1924. V. 51

DONAHUE, CHARLES
The Records of the Medieval Ecclesiastical Courts. Berlin: 1989. V. 48; 50

DONALD, G.
Paul Faber-Surgeon. Philadelphia: 1879. V. 53

DONALD, JAY
Outlaws of the Border. A Complete and Authentic History of the Lives of Frank and Jesse James, the Younger Brothers, and Their Robber Companions... Cincinnati: 1882. V. 53; 54

DONALDSON, ALFRED L.
A History of the Adirondacks. New York: 1921. V. 52

DONALDSON, FLORENCE
Lepcha Land or Six Weeks in the Sikhim Himalayas. London: 1900. V. 50; 51

DONALDSON, JAMES
Modern Agriculture, or the Present State of Husbandry in Great Britain. Edinburgh: 1795-96. V. 54

DONALDSON, M. E. E.
Wanderings in the Western Highlands and Islands. Paisley: 1923. V. 54

DONALDSON, PETER
A Review of the Present Systems of Medicine and Chirurgery of Europe and America... New York: 1821. V. 50

DONALDSON, PROFESSOR
Rudimentary Treatise on Clay Lands and Loamy Soils... London: 1852. V. 50

DONALDSON, S.
The Chronicles of Thomas Covenant the Unbeliever. 1977. V. 54
Epic Fantasy in the Modern World. 1986. V. 48

DONALDSON, STEPHEN R.
The Chronicles of Thomas Covenant. 1977. V. 51

DONALDSON, THOMAS
The George Catlin Indian Gallery in the National Museum with Memoir and Statistics. Washington: 1888. V. 49
Moqui Pueblo Indians of Arizona and Pueblo Indians of New Mexico. Washington: 1893. V. 51
The Public Domain, Its History with Statistics to June 30 and December 1, 1883. Washington: 1884. V. 49

DONALDSON, WILLIAM
A Treatise on the Art of Constructing Oblique Arches with Spiral Courses. London: 1867. V. 49

DONAN, PATRICK
A Scream from the American Eagle in Dakota. Chicago: 1883. V. 50; 54

DONATO D'EREMITA
Dell 'Elixir Vitae Libri Quattro. Naples: 1624. V. 48

DONATUS, AELIUS
Partes Pro Pueris. Paris: 1522. V. 51

DONCASTER AGRICULTURAL ASSOCIATION
Bone Manure. Report of the Committee...on the Advantages of Bones as a Manure. Founded on Returns Received... London: 1834. V. 49

DONDERS, F. C.
New Researches on the Systems of Colour-Sense. Utrecht: 1882. V. 51
Of the Anomalies of Accomodation and Refaction of the Eye. London: 1864. V. 49; 50; 54

DONELAN, A. M.
What 'This to Love. London: 1872. V. 54

DONELLAN, JOHN
The Proceedings at Large on the Trial of John Donellan, Esq. for the Willful Murder (by Poison) of Sir the Edward Allesley Boughton...Tried Before Mr. Justice Buller. London: 1781. V. 47
The Trial of John Donellan, Esq. for the Wilful Murder of Sir Theodosius Edward Allesley Boughton... London: 1781. V. 52

DONELLUS, HUGO
Commentarii ad Titvlvm Digestorum, de Verborum Obligationibus. Francofvrti: 1577. V. 53

DONI, ANTONIO FRANCESCO
La Libraria del Doni Florentino. Vinegia: 1550. V. 48
La Zucca. En Spanol. Venice: 1551. V. 52

DONLEAVY, J. P.
Are You Listening Rabbi Low. New York: 1988. V. 47
Fairy Tales of New York. Harmondsworth: 1961. V. 54
The Ginger Man. London. V. 51
The Ginger Man. Paris: 1955. V. 47; 48; 51; 53; 54
The Ginger Man. London: 1956. V. 52; 53
The Ginger Man. New York: 1958. V. 48; 51
The Ginger Man. Paris: 1958. V. 47; 48; 50; 51; 52; 53

DONN, BENJAMIN
A Map of the County of Devon. London: 1765. V. 48

DONN, BERTRAM
Atlas of Comet Halley 1910 II. Washington: 1986. V. 50

DONN, JAMES
Hortus Cantabrigiensis; or, a Catalogue of Plants Indigenous and Exotic. London: 1815. V. 49
Hortus Cantabrigiensis; or an Accented Catalogue of Indigeonous and Exotic Plants Cultivated in the Cambridge Botanic Garden. London: 1826. V. 52

DONN, ROB
Songs and Poems in the Gaelic Language. Edinburgh: 1899. V. 53

DONNADIEU, ALCIDE
Catalogue of Highly Interesting and Valuable Autograph letters and Historical Manuscripts, Being the Well Known Collection of... London: 1851. V. 54

DONNE, JOHN
Biacanatoe. A Declaration of that Paradoxe, or Thesis, that Self-Homicide is Not so Naturally Sinne... London: 1646-47. V. 49
Bianthanatos (in Greek). A Declaration of That Paradox or Thesis, that Self-Homicide Is Not so Naturally Sin, That It may Never Be Otherwise... London: 1644. V. 52; 54
Biathanatos. A Declaration of that Paradox, or Thesis, that Self-Homicide is not so Naturally Sinne, That It May Never Be Otherwise. London: 1647. V. 47
The Complete Poems of John Donne, D.D. London: 1872-73. V. 50
Complete Poetry and Selected Prose. London: 1929. V. 51
The Courtier's Library, or Catalogus Librorum Aulicorum. London: 1930. V. 47; 50; 52; 53
Death's Duell. Boston: 1973. V. 54
Devotions Upon Emergent Occasions and Several Steps in My Sicknes. London: 1624. V. 52
The Holy Sonnets. London: 1938. V. 48; 49; 51; 53
Ignatius His Conclave; or, His Inthronation in a Late Election in Hell... London: 1634. V. 48
Love Poems. London: 1923. V. 48; 49; 52; 53
LXXX Sermons Preached by That Learned and Reverend Divine, John Donne. (with) Fifty Sermons. London: 1640/49. V. 49; 54
Paradoxes and Problems. London: 1923. V. 48; 50; 51; 53
Poems. London: 1650. V. 49
Poems. London: 1669. V. 51
Poems. London: 1931. V. 52
The Poems... Cambridge: 1968. V. 48; 52
Poems on Several Occasions. London: 1719. V. 48; 52
A Prayer. 1947. V. 52
Sermon of Valediction at His Going Into Germany. London: 1932. V. 50; 53
The Sonnets of John Donne. London: 1938. V. 49
Ten Sermons Preached by the Late Learned and Rev. Devine John Donne... London: 1923. V. 47; 49; 50; 51; 53

DONNE, T. E.
The Game Animals of New Zealand, an Account of Their Introduction, Acclimatization and Development. London: 1924. V. 53

DONNELL, DAVID A.
Poems. Thornhill: 1961. V. 47

DONNELL, EZEKIEL J.
Slavery and 'Protection': an Historical Review and Appeal to the Workshop and the Farm. New York: 1882. V. 50

DONNELL, ROBERT
Thoughts on Various Subjects. Louisville: 1856. V. 50; 53

DONNELLAN, JOHN
The Trial of John Donnellan, Esq. (Late Master of Ceremonies at the Pantheon in Oxford Street) at the Assizes Holden at Warwick on Tuesday the 27th of March, 1781, Before Francis Buller, Esq.. One of the Judges of the Court of King's Bench for the Wilful... London: 1781. V. 49; 51

DONNELLE, A. J.
Custer's Last Battle or the Battle of the Cyclorama of Custer's Last Battle. Boston: 1889. V. 47

DONNELLY, EDWARD
The Manly Art of Self Defence. New York: 1886. V. 47

DONNELLY, ELEANOR C.
A Klondike Picnic: The Story of a Day...with Genuine Letters from Two Gold Seekers. New York Cincinnati: 1898. V. 48; 49

DONNELLY, I.
The American People's Money. Chicago: 1895. V. 50
Atlantis: the Antediluvian World. New York: 1882. V. 53
Caesar's Column - A Story of the Twentieth Century. 1890. V. 48
The Golden Bottle or the Story of Ephraim Benezet of Kansas. 1892. V. 49; 54
The Sonnets of Shakespeare: an Essay. Saint Paul: 1859. V. 51

DONNELLY, NICHOLAS
A Short History of Some Dublin Parishes. 190?-1917. V. 54

DONOSO, JOSE
The Boom in Spanish American Literature. New York: 1977. V. 47
Charleston. Boston: 1977. V. 47; 48; 49; 53
The Obscene Bird of Night. London: 1974. V. 49
Sacred Families. New York: 1977. V. 49
This Sunday. London: 1965. V. 49
This Sunday. New York: 1967. V. 49

DONOVAN, E.
An Epitome of the Natural History of the Insects of China. London: 1798-99. V. 54
The Natural History of British Birds... 1799. V. 53
The Natural History of British Insects. London: 1792-1813. V. 48
The Natural History of British Shells... London: 1799-1800. V. 50
The Natural History of British Shells. London: 1799-1803. V. 53; 54
The Natural History of British Shells. London: 1804/1800/1803. V. 48
Natural History of the Insects of China... London: 1842. V. 53
Natural History of the Insects of India. London: 1842. V. 54

DONOVAN, MIKE
The Science of Boxing. New York: 1893. V. 47

DONOVAN, ROBERT J.
PT 109-John F. Kennedy in World War II. New York: 1961. V. 51

D'ONSTON, ROSLYN
Brief Sketches of the Life of Victoria Woodhull. London: 1893?. V. 50; 53

DOOLEY, JOHN
John Dooley Confederate Soldier His War Journal. Washington: 1945. V. 54

DOOLITTLE, HILDA
By Avon River. New York: 1949. V. 50
Collected Poems of H. D. New York: 1925. V. 52; 54
The Hedgehog. London: 1936. V. 49
Hedylus. Boston: 1928. V. 48; 50; 53
Hedylus. Oxford: 1928. V. 53
Hedylus. Oxford: 1982. V. 49
Heliodora and Other Poems. London: 1924. V. 51
Hippolytus Temporizes. Boston: 1927. V. 47; 48; 51
Hymen. 1921. V. 47; 55
Kora and Ka. 1930. V. 47; 48; 52
Palimpsest. Boston: 1926. V. 50; 51; 53
Priest and Dead Priestess Speaks. Port Townsend: 1983. V. 54
Red Roses for Bronze. New York: 1929. V. 52
The Sea Garden. London: 1916. V. 48; 53; 54
Selected Poems. New York: 1957. V. 48
The Usual Star. London: 1928/34. V. 47; 48
The Walls do Not Fall, Tribute to the Angels and the Flowering of the Rod. London: 1944-46. V. 47
Within the Walls. Iowa City: 1993. V. 49; 54

DOOLITTLE, JAMES ROOD
The Romance of the Automobile Industry... New York: 1916. V. 50

DOOLITTLE, JUSTUS
Social Life of the Chinese. London: 1868. V. 50

DOONER, P. W.
Last Days of the Republic. San Francisco: 1880. V. 50

DOOR and Window Grilles in Bronze and Iron. Boston: 1902. V. 49

DOORLY, ELEANOR
The Microbe Man. London: 1938. V. 53

DOPPELMAYR, JOHANN GABRIEL
Historische Nachricht von den Nurnbergischen Mathematicis und Kunstlern, Welche von Dryen Seculis her Durch ihre Schrifften und Kunst-Bemuhungen die Mathematic und Mehreste Kunste in Nurnberg Trefflich Befordert... Nuremberg: 1730. V. 48; 49; 50

DORAN, ALBAN
Clinical and Pathological Observations on Tumours of the Ovary, Fallopian Tube and Broad Ligament. London: 1884. V. 53

DORAN, DR.
Monarchs Retired From Business. London: 1857. V. 48

DORAN, JOHN
Annals of the English Stage, from Thomas Betterton to Edmund Kean. London: 1864. V. 54
The History of Court Fools... London: 1858. V. 47; 49
Table Traits With Something on Them. New York: 1855. V. 50
Their Majesties' Servants, Annals of the English Stage... London: 1838. V. 49
Their Majesties' Servants: Annals of the English Stage, from Thomas Betterton to Edmund Kean. London: 1864. V. 52; 53
Their Majesties' Servants, Annals of the English Stage from Thomas Betterton to Edmund Kean. London: 1888. V. 52; 54

DORAN, JOHN A.
A Lady of the Last Century. London: 1873. V. 48

DORBIN, SANFORD
A Bibliography of Charles Bukowski. 1969. V. 54

DORE, GUSTAVE
Cassell's Dore Gallery... London: 1870. V. 48; 51
The Dore Bible Gallery. Philadelphia: 1880. V. 52
London. A Pilgrimage. London: 1872. V. 48; 49
Two Hundred Sketches, Humorous and Grotesque. London: 1867. V. 54

DOREY, JACQUES
Legendary Stories of Old Brittany, Normandy and Provence. New York: 1929. V. 50
Three and the Moon Legendary Stories of Old Brittany. New York: 1929. V. 50

DORING, ERNEST N.
How Many Strads? Our Heritage from the Master: a Tribute to the memory... Chicago: 1945. V. 49

DORIS, CHARLES
Amours et Aventures du Vicomte de Barras. Paris and Brussels: 1816-17. V. 51

D'ORLEANS, FR. PIERRE JOSEPH
History of the Two Tartar Conqueors of China, Including the Two Journeys Into Tartary of F. Ferdinand Verbiest... London: 1854. V. 47

DORMAN, LONG & CO.
Bridges: a Few Examples of the Work of a Pioneer Firm in Manufature of Steel and Steelwork. London: 1930. V. 49
Sydney Harbour Bridge. London: 1932. V. 49

DORN, EDWARD
Geography. London: 1965. V. 48; 54
Gunslinger. Book I. Los Angeles: 1968. V. 48
Gunslinger Book I & II. Los Angeles: 1968-69. V. 47

DORNBLASER, T. F.
My Life Story for Young and Old. 1930. V. 54

DORNEY, JOHN
A Briefe and Exact Relation of the Most Material and Remarkable Passages That Hapned in the Late Well-Formed (and as Vailiently Defended) Seige Laid Before the City of Gloucester... London: 1643. V. 48

DOROTHEUS, SAINT
La Doctrine Spiritvelle... Douai: 1597. V. 51

DORR, JULIA C. R.
Vermont. Boston: 1877. V. 53

DORR, NELL
Mother and Child. New York: 1954. V. 47

DORRINGTON, THEOPHILUS
Family Devotions for Sunday Evenings, Throughout the Year. London: 1696. V. 50

DORRIS, MICHAEL
The Benchmark. New York: 1993. V. 51
The Crown of Columbus. New York: 1991. V. 50
Morning Girl. New York: 1992. V. 51
A Yellow Raft in Blue Water. London: 1988. V. 50

D'ORS, EUGENIO
Paul Cezane. Paris: 1930. V. 51; 53

DORSET, CATHERINE ANN
The Lion's Masquerade, a Sequel to the Peacock at Home. London: 1808. V. 53
The Peacock at Home. London: 1807. V. 49
The Peacock At Home. London: 1808. V. 48
The Peacock at Home. London: 1849. V. 50

DORSET NATURAL HISTORY & ANTIQUARIAN FIELD CLUB
Proceedings. Dorchester: 1894-1917. V. 50

DORSET NATURAL HISTORY & ARCHAEOLOGICAL SOCIETY
Proceedings. Dorchester: 1877-1986. V. 54

DORSEY, GEORGE A.
The Araphao Sun Dance. Chicago: 1903. V. 49
The Oraibi Soyal Ceremony. 1901. V. 54
Traditions of the Skidi Pawnee. Boston: 1904. V. 54

DORSEY, JAMES OWEN
The Cegiha Language. Washington: 1890. V. 51; 52

DORSEY, LEO M.
Stair Building-Poems. Canada: 1943. V. 53

DORSEY, SARAH ANNE ELLIS
Recollections of Henry Watkins Allen, Brigadier-General Confederate States Army, Ex-governor of Louisiana. New York: 1866. V. 54

DORTU, M. G.
Toulouse-Lautrec et Son Oeuvre. V. 49; 52; 54

DOSABHAI SOHRABJI, MUNSHI
Idiomatical Sentences in the English Hindostanee, Goozratee and Persian Languages, in Six Parts. Bombay: 1843. V. 50

DOSIO, GIOVANNI ANTONIO
Urbis Romae Aedificorum Illustrium Quae Supersunt Reliquiae Summa Cum Diligentiae Descriptae... Rome: 1569. V. 47

DOS PASSOS, JOHN
Orient Express. New York: 1927. V. 50

DOS PASSOS, JOHN RODERIGO
1919. New York: 1932. V. 47; 51; 52; 53
The 42nd Parallel. New York: 1930. V. 47; 48; 49; 51; 52
Adventures of a Young Man. New York: 1939. V. 51
Airways. New York: 1928. V. 47; 48
The Big Money. London: 1936. V. 49; 51
Facing the Chair. Boston: 1927. V. 48; 53
The Garbage Man. New York: 1926. V. 47
The Garbage Man - a Parade with Shouting. London: 1929. V. 49
The Head and Heart of Thomas Jefferson. Garden City: 1954. V. 53
The Head and the Heart of Thomas Jefferson. New York: 1954. V. 49
In All Countries. New York: 1934. V. 49; 51
Most Likely to Succeed. New York: 1954. V. 49
One Man's Initiation - 1917. London: 1920. V. 51
A Pushcart at the Curb. New York: 1922. V. 47; 50; 51
Rosinante to the Road Again. New York: 1922. V. 47
State of the Nation. Boston: 1944. V. 49; 53
State of the Nation. Cambridge: 1944. V. 49; 51
Three Plays. New York: 1934. V. 49
Three Soldiers. New York: 1921. V. 47; 48; 49; 50; 54
Tour of Duty. Boston: 1946. V. 49
U.S.A. New York: 1930/32/36. V. 54
U.S.A. 1946. V. 50
U.S.A. Boston: 1946. V. 49; 53

DOS SANTOS, REYNALDO
Nuno Goncalves, the Great Portuguese painter of the 15th Century and His Altarpiece for the Convent of St. Vincent. London: 1955. V. 50

DOSSENBACH, MONIQUE
Great Stud-Farms of the World. New York: 1978. V. 48

DOSSIE, ROBERT
The Elaboratory Laid Open, or, the Secrets of Modern Chemistry and Pharmacy Revealed... London: 1758. V. 48; 50; 52; 54
The Elaboratory Laid Open; or, the Secrets of Modern Chemistry and Pharmacy Revealed... London: 1768. V. 48; 52
The Handmaid to the Arts. London: 1764/58. V. 49
The Handmaid to the Arts... York: 1796. V. 47

DOSTER, WILLIAM EMIL
The Conflict Between Literature and Law. Cambridge: 1859. V. 50

DOSTOEVSKII, FEDOR MIKHAILOVICH
Die Beichte Strawrogins. (Stavrogin's Confession). Munich: 1922. V. 50
The Brothers Karamazov. New York: 1933. V. 53
The Brothers Karamazov. New York: 1949. V. 47; 48; 51; 52; 54
The Brothers Karamazov. New York: 1967. V. 53
Buried Alive or Ten Years of Penal Servitude in Siberia. New York: 1881. V. 52
Crime and Punishment. London: 1886. V. 50
Crime and Punishment. New York: 1948. V. 47; 48; 51; 54
The Gambler & Notes from the Underground. New York: 1967. V. 54
A Gentle Spirit. 1931. V. 49; 51
A Gentle Spirit: a Fantistic Story. Paris: 1931. V. 52
The Grand Inquisitor. London: 1930. V. 51; 52
The House of the Dead. New York: 1982. V. 48; 49
The Idiot. New York: 1956. V. 47; 48
Poor Folk. London: 1894. V. 49; 52
The Possessed. Hartford: 1959. V. 50
A Raw Youth. Verona: 1967. V. 53
A Raw Youth. Verona: 1974. V. 47; 48; 49; 52; 54
Stavrogin's Confession. New York: 1947. V. 47
Stavrogin's Confession. (and) The Plan of the Life of a Great Sinner. Richmond: 1922. V. 49

DOTEN, ALFRED
The Journals of Alfred Doten 1849-1903. Reno: 1973. V. 49

DOTEN, LIZZIE
Poems from the Inner Life. Boston: 1864. V. 48

DOTHAN, MOSHE
Ashdod I-IV. Jerusalem: 1967-82. V. 51
Hammath Tiberias: Early Synagogues and the Hellenistic and Roman Remains. Jerusalem: 1983. V. 51

DOTHAN, TRUDE
The Philistines and their Material Culture. New Haven: 1982. V. 49; 51

DOTTER, CHARLES
Angiocardiography. New York: 1952. V. 48

DOTY, WILLIAM KAVANAUGH
The Confectionery of Monsieur Giron. Lexington: 1978. V. 52; 54

DOUBLE CROWN CLUB
The Double Crown Club. Register of Past and Present Members. Cambridge: 1949. V. 51

DOUBLEDAY, FRANCIS
The Coquet-Dale Fishing Songs. London: 1852. V. 50; 53

DOUBLEDAY, THOMAS
A Financial, Monetary and Statistical History of England, from the Revolution of 1688 to the Present Time... London: 1847. V. 49

DOUBLEDAY, THOMAS continued
Matter for Materialists: A Series of Letters in Vindication and Extension of the Principles Regarding the Nature of Existence of the Right Rev. Dr. Berkeley. London: 1870. V. 48

DOUCE, FRANCIS
The Customs of London, Otherwise Called Anrold's Chronicle. London: 1811. V. 47; 51
The Dance of Death. London: 1804. V. 54
The Dance of Death: Exhibited in Elegant Engravings on Wood, with a Dissertation on the Several Representations of that Subject... London: 1833. V. 51; 54
Illustrataions Of Shakespeare and of Ancient Manners: With Dissertations On the Clowns and Fools of Shakespeare... London: 1807. V. 47; 49; 51; 53; 54

DOUGHITT, KATHRINE C.
Romance and Dim Trails, a History of Clay County. Dallas: 1938. V. 49

DOUGHTY, ARTHUR G.
The Elgin Grey Papers. Ottawa: 1937. V. 48
Under the Lily and the Rose: a Short History of Canada for Children. Toronto: 1931. V. 53

DOUGHTY, CHARLES MONTAGU
The Clouds. London: 1912. V. 54
The Dawn in Britain. London: 1906. V. 48; 53
Mansoul or the Riddle of the World. London: 1920. V. 54
Mansoul or the Riddle of the World. London: 1923. V. 48; 50; 54
Travels in Arabia Deserta. London: 1921. V. 50
Travels in Arabia Deserta. London: 1923. V. 51
Travels in Arabia Deserta. New York: 1923. V. 48
Travels in Arabia Deserta... London: 1936. V. 50; 52
Travels in Arabia Deserta. New York: 1937. V. 47; 51; 53; 54
Travels in Arabia Deserta. London: 1943. V. 49
Travels in Arabia Deserta. New York: 1953. V. 48; 51
Wanderings in Arabia. London: 1908. V. 52; 54

DOUGHTY, JOHN
The Cabinet of Natural History and American Rural Sports. Philadelphia: 1830-32. V. 48; 50; 53; 54

DOUGHTY, MARION
Afoot Through the Kashmir Valleys. London: 1902. V. 48; 53

DOUGLAS, ALFRED
The City of the Soul. London: 1899. V. 48
The Collected Satires. London: 1926. V. 48
Hymn to Physical Beauty. 1976. V. 52
In Excelsis. London: 1924. V. 50
Lyrics. (with) Sonnets. London: 1935/35. V. 48
My Friendship with Oscar Wilde: Being the Autobiography of Lord Alfred Douglas. New York: 1932. V. 48
Perkin Warbeck and Some Other Poems. London: 1897. V. 54
Poemes. Paris: 1896. V. 50
The Pongo Papers and the Duke of Berwick. London: 1907. V. 48
The Principles of Poetry, an Address Royal Society of Literature, 1943. London: 1943. V. 48; 50
Sonnets. London: 1909. V. 47
Tails With a Twist. London: 1898. V. 48; 51

DOUGLAS, AMANDA M.
In Trust; or, Dr. Bertrand's Household. Boston: 1866. V. 51

DOUGLAS, ARCHIBALD
Life of Admiral Sir Archibald Lucius Douglas. Totnes: 1938. V. 54

DOUGLAS, C. L.
Cattle Kings of Texas. Dallas: 1939. V. 52; 53

DOUGLAS, CLARENCE B.
The History of Tulsa, Oklahoma, a City with Personality. Chicago: 1921. V. 54

DOUGLAS, D.
The Biographical History of Sir William Blackstone...and a Catalogue of All...Blackstone's Works, Manuscript, as Well as Printed. London: 1782. V. 52; 53

DOUGLAS, DAVID
Journal Kept by David Douglas During His Travels in North America, 1823-1827... London: 1914. V. 50; 53
The Oregon Journals of David Douglas, of His Travels and Adventures Among the Traders and Indians in the Columbia, Willamette and Snake River Regions During the Years 1825, 1826 and 1827. Ashland: 1972. V. 50

DOUGLAS, ELLEN
A Family's Affair. Boston: 1962. V. 48

DOUGLAS, F. C. R.
Land Value Rating. London: 1936. V. 48

DOUGLAS, FREDERICK SYLVESTER NORTH
An Essay on Certain Points of Resemblance Between the Ancient and Modern Greeks. London: 1813. V. 52

DOUGLAS, HENRY H.
Caves of Virginia. Falls Church: 1964. V. 51

DOUGLAS, HERBERT BELL
A Soldier's Diary of the Great War. London: 1929. V. 50

DOUGLAS, HOWARD
Considerations on the Value and Importance of the British North American Provinces, and the Circumstances on Which Depend Their Further Prosperity and Colonial Connection with Great Britain. London: 1831. V. 52

DOUGLAS, J. W.
The British Hemiptera. Volume I. Hemiptera-Heteroptera. London: 1865. V. 50

DOUGLAS, JAMES
A Dissertation on the Antiquity of the Earth, Read At the Royal Society, 12th May, 1785. London: 1785. V. 48
James Douglas in California in 1841. Vancouver: 1965. V. 48
Myographiae Comparata Specimen: or, a Comparative Description of All the Muscles in a Man and in a Quadruped. London: 1707. V. 51
Myographiae Comparata Specimen: or a Comparative Description of all the Muscles in a Man, and In a Quadruped. London: 1763. V. 50
Myographiae Comparatae Specimen; or, a Comparative Description of the Muscles in a Man... Edinburgh: 1775. V. 48
Nenia Britannica; or, a Sepulchra History of Great Britain from the Earliest Period to Its General Conversion to Christianity. London: 1793. V. 51; 52; 54
On the Philosophy of the Mind. Edinburgh: 1839. V. 49
Rules and Regulations for the Working of Gold Mines. Victoria: 1859. V. 47; 50
Travelling Anecdotes through Various Parts of Europe. London: 1785. V. 50; 54

DOUGLAS, JOHN
The Criterion: or, Miracles Examined.... London: 1757. V. 49
A Letter Addressed to Two Great Men, on the Prospect of Peace; and on the Terms Necessary to be Insisted Upon in the Negotiation... London: 1760. V. 47
Milton Vindicated from the Charger of Plagiarism Brought Against Him by William Lauder, and Lauder Himself Convicted of Several Forgeries and Gross Impositions on the Public. London: 1751. V. 54
Pandaemonium; or, a New Infernal Expedition. London: 1750. V. 52

DOUGLAS, KEITH
Alamein to Zem Zem. London: 1946. V. 47; 48; 49; 50; 51; 52; 53
Augury - an Oxford Miscellany of Verse and Prose. Oxford: 1940. V. 47
Collected Poems. London: 1951. V. 52; 53

DOUGLAS, LLOYD CASSEL
More Than a Prophet. Chicago: 1905. V. 51

DOUGLAS, M.
Notes of a Journey from Berne to England through France, Made in the Year 1796. London: 1797. V. 52

DOUGLAS, MARJORY STONEMAN
Road to the Sun. New York: 1952. V. 52

DOUGLAS, NIEL
The African Slave Trade; or a Short View of the Evidence, Relative to that Subject... Edinburgh: 1792. V. 53

DOUGLAS, NORMAN
Alone. London: 1921. V. 53
The Angel of Manfredonia. San Francisco: 1929. V. 48; 52
Birds and Beasts of the Greek Anthology. 1927. V. 49
Birds and Beasts of the Greek Anthology. Florence: 1927. V. 51
Birds and Beasts of the Greek Anthology. London: 1927. V. 50; 54
Birds and Beasts of the Greek Anthology. London: 1928. V. 51
Capri: Materials for a Description of the Island. Florence: 1930. V. 48
D. H. Lawrence and Maurice Magnus. Florence: 1924. V. 53
D. H. Lawrence and Maurice Magnus. A Plea for Better Manner. London: 1924. V. 49; 52
Experiments. 1925. V. 48; 50
Experiments. Florence: 1925. V. 47
Experiments. London: 1925. V. 50
Fountains in the Sand. London: 1912. V. 47; 50
The Fountains in the Sand. London: 1925. V. 50
How About Europe? Some Footnotes on East and West. Florence: 1929. V. 47; 48; 49
In the Beginning. Florence: 1927. V. 48; 49; 50
In the Beginning. New York: 1928. V. 49
London Street Games. London: 1916. V. 48; 52; 53
London Street Games. London: 1931. V. 47; 51
Looking Back. London: 1922. V. 49
Looking Back, an Autobiographical Excursion. London: 1933. V. 48; 51
Nerinda. Florence: 1901. V. 47
Nerinda. Florence: 1929. V. 47; 48; 49; 50; 52; 53
One Day. Eure: 1929. V. 48
Paneros. Florence: 1930. V. 53
Paneros. London: 1931. V. 49; 51
Siren Land. London: 1911. V. 53
Some Limericks Collected for the Use of Students. Florence: 1928. V. 47
South Wind. London: 1917. V. 47; 51
South Wind. London: 1922. V. 48
South Wind. 1929. V. 49
South Wind. New York: 1932. V. 53; 54
Summer Islands: Ischia and Ponza. New York: 1931. V. 47; 48; 49; 51
They Went. London: 1920. V. 51; 54
Together. London: 1923. V. 48; 54
Unprofessional Tales. London: 1901. V. 51; 53

DOUGLAS, R. B.
One Hundred Merrie and Delightsome Stories... Paris: 1898. V. 47
Sophie Arnould. Paris: 1898. V. 51

DOUGLAS, R. J. H.
Catalogue of the Splendid and Unique Collection of the Works of George Cruikshank... London: 1911. V. 49

DOUGLAS, ROBERT
The Form and Order of the Coronation of Charles II. London: 1660. V. 50; 51
General View of the Agriculture of the Counties of Roxburgh and Selkirk; With Observations of the Means of Their Improvement. London: 1798. V. 53

DOUGLAS, ROBERT K.
Society in China. London: 1894. V. 48; 50; 52
Society in China. London: 1901. V. 54

DOUGLAS, STEPHEN A.
Remarks of the Hon. Stephen A. Douglas, on Kansas, Utah and the Dred Scott Decision. Chicago: 1857. V. 52

DOUGLAS, SYLVESTER
Reports of Cases Argued and Determined in the Court of King's bench, in the Nineteenth, Twentieth and Twenty-First Years of the Reign of George III. London: 1786. V. 47

DOUGLAS, WALTER B.
Manuel Lisa, I & II. St. Louis: 1911. V. 50

DOUGLAS, WILLIAM O.
An Almanac of Liberty. Garden City: 1954. V. 50
Beyond the High Himalayas. Garden City: 1952. V. 49
Go East, Young Man, The Early Years, The Autobiography of William O. Douglas. New York: 1974. V. 52
North from Malaya, Adventure on Five Fronts. Garden City: 1953. V. 52
Of Men and Mountains. New York: 1950. V. 52
The Right of the People. Garden City: 1958. V. 52

DOUGLASS, ADAM
Irish Emigrant. An Historical Tale Founded on Fact, by an Hibernian. Winchester: 1817. V. 50

DOUGLASS, FREDERICK
Address of Frederick Douglass, Delivered in the Congregational Church, Washington, D.C., April 16, 1883 on the Twenty-First Anniversary of Emancipation in the District of Columbia. Washington: 1883. V. 53
Eulogy of the Late Hon. Wm. Jay by Frederick Douglass, Delivered on the Invitation of the Colored Citizens of New York City, in Shiloh Presbyterian Church. Rochester: 1859. V. 53
Life and Times of Frederic Douglass Written by Himself. Hartford: 1883. V. 49
The Life and Writings of Frederick Douglass. New York: 1950. V. 48
My Bondage and My Freedom. New York & Auburn: 1855. V. 47; 48
Narrative of the Life Of...an American Slave. Boston: 1845. V. 49; 51
Narrative of the Life of...an American Slave. Boston: 1846. V. 53

DOUGLASS, JAMES WALTER
A Work to Do: the Substance of a Discourse...at the Funeral of Mrs. Winifred Miller. Richmond: 1837. V. 54

DOUGLASS, WILLIAM
A Summary, Historical and Political of the First Planting, Progressive Improvements and Present State of the British Settlements in North America. London: 1760. V. 48

DOUTHIT, MARY
Souvenir of Western Women. Portland: 1905. V. 53

DOUXMENIL
The Memoirs of with Her letters to Monsr. de St. Evremond and Marquis de Sevigne. Dublin: 1778. V. 49
Memoirs of With Her Letters to Monsr. de St. Evremond and...Marquis de Sevigne. London: 1761. V. 48
The Memoirs of...with Her Letters to Monsr. de St. Evremond and...Marquis de Sevigne. London: 1776. V. 54
Memoirs of...With Her Letters to the Marquis of Sevigne and Mons. de S. Evremond. Philadelphia: 1806. V. 54

DOVASTON, JOHN F. M.
The Dove. Scraps of Poetry, Selected...for the Oswestry Herald 1822. London: 1822. V. 53

DOVE at the Windows: Last Letters of Four Quaker Martyrs. Lincoln: 1973. V. 51; 54

DOVE, RITA
Fifth Sunday. Lexington: 1985. V. 51; 53
Lady Freedom Among Us. West Burke: 1994. V. 52
The Only Dark Spot in the Sky. Tempe: 1980. V. 51
Ten Poems. Lisbon: 1977. V. 47; 54
Thomas and Beulah. Pittsburgh: 1986. V. 51

DOVER, CEDRIC
American Negro Art. Greenwich: 1960. V. 53
American Negro Art. 1967. V. 53

DOVES PRESS
Catalogue Raisonne of Books Printed and Published at the Doves Press 1900-1911. London: 1911. V. 50; 51
Catalogue Raisonne of Books Printed and Published at the Doves Press 1900-1916. Hammersmith: 1916. V. 51
Catalogue Raisonne of Books Printed and Published at the Doves Press, No. 1 Hammersmith Terrace. 1908. V. 49

DOVETON, F. B.
Maggie in Mythica; or, What She Saw in Fairyland. 1890. V. 48; 50
Maggie in Mythica; or, What She Saw in Fairyland. London: 1890. V. 52

DOW, ALDEN B.
Reflections. Midland: 1970. V. 48; 50

DOW, ANN ELIZA
The Life and Adventures of Ann Eliza Dow. Burlington: 1845. V. 53

DOW, ARTHUR WESLEY
Composition: a Series of Exercises... Garden City: 1918. V. 50

DOW, CHARLES MASON
Anthology and Bibliography of Niagara Falls. Albany: 1921. V. 50

DOW, GEORGE FRANCIS
The Arts and Crafts in New England 1704-1775. Topsfield: 1927. V. 52; 53
The Sailing Ships of New England. Salem: 1928. V. 50
Slave Ships and Slaving. Salem: 1927. V. 50
Whale Ships and Whaling. Salem: 1925. V. 47; 48

DOW, LORENZO
History of Cosmopolite. Wheeling: 1848. V. 53
The Life and Travels of Lorenzo Dow, Written by Himself... Hartford: 1804. V. 54
Works. (with) Appendix to All the Works. (with) A Collection of Spiritual Songs... Dublin: 1806/06/06. V. 50

DOWD, D. B.
Mustardville: Reports of the Recent Calamity and Commentary Thereupon. St. Louis: 1995. V. 54

DOWDEN, EDWARD
The Life of Percy Bysshe Shelley. London: 1886. V. 52
Robert Southey. New York: 1880. V. 52

DOWDEN, GEORGE
A Bibliography of Works by Allen Ginsberg - Oct. 1943 to July 1967. San Francisco: 1971. V. 54

DOWELL, COLEMAN
The Silver Swanne. 1983. V. 52; 54
The Silver Swanne. New York: 1983. V. 52; 54

DOWELL, JAMES
Norwegian Anglings and Other sportings. London: 1909. V. 47
Norwegian Anglings. Elk, Reindeer and Ryper Shootings and Other Sportings. London: 1912. V. 47

DOWELL, WILLIAM CHIPCHASE
The Webley Story. A History of Webley Pistols and Revolvers and the Development of the Pistol Cartridge. Leeds: 1962. V. 49

DOWLING, D. B.
General Index to the Reports of Progress, 1863-1884. Ottawa: 1900. V. 50

DOWLING, THOMAS H.
Abstract of the Possessory Title to the Island of Yerba Buena in the Harbor of San Francisco. San Francisco: 1866. V. 49
Claim to the Island of Yerba Buena. To the Hon. The Congress of the United States. Washington: 1869. V. 49
District of Columbia, City and County of Washington. Washington: 1871. V. 49
Memorial of Thos. H. Dowling and Accompanying Papers, in Regard to His Claim to the Island of Yerba Buena, in the Harbor of San Francisco, California. Washington: 1868. V. 49
Supplemental Memorial and Brief for Thomas H. Dowling in Regard to His Claim to the Island of Yerba Buena. Washington: 1868. V. 49
Yerba Buena. Brief. San Francisco: 1867. V. 49

DOWN at the Santa Fe Depot. Fresno: 1970. V. 54

DOWN Down the Mountain. New York: 1934. V. 52

DOWNER, SILAS
A Discourse, Delivered in Providence, in the Colony of Rhode Island, Upon the 25th Day of July 1768, at the Dedication of the Tree of Liberty... Providence: 1768. V. 54

DOWNES, HENRY
The Necessity and Usefullness of Laws and the Excellency of Our Own. Oxford: 1708. V. 47

DOWNES, JOHN
Roscius Anglicanus. London: 1789. V. 52
Roscius Anglicanus. London: 1928. V. 49

DOWNES, KERRY
Vanbrugh. London: 1977. V. 48

DOWNES, OLIN
10 Operatic Masterpieces. New York: 1952. V. 54

DOWNES, WILLIAM HOWE
John S. Sargent, His Life and Work. London: 1926. V. 54
John S. Sargent His Life and Work. Oxford: 1945. V. 50

DOWNEY, EDMUND
Charles Lever: His Life in His Letters. London: 1906. V. 51
Dunleary: Humours of a Munster Town. 1913. V. 54
Morrissey. 1924. V. 54

DOWNEY, FAIRFAX
Fyfe, Drum and Bugle. Ft. Collins: 1971. V. 49

DOWNEY, GLANVILLE
A History of Antioch in Syria from Seleucus to the Arab Conquest. Princeton: 1961. V. 52

DOWNHAM, JOHN
Spiritual Physicke to Cure the Diseases of the Soule, Arising from Superfluitie of Choller, Prescribed Out of Gods Word... Edinburgh: 1608. V. 51

DOWNIE, WILLIAM
Hunting for Gold. San Francisco: 1893. V. 47; 50; 51; 53

DOWNING, ALEXANDER G.
Downing's Civil War Diary. Des Moines: 1916. V. 47

DOWNING, ANDREW JACKSON
Cottage Residences; or a Series of Designs for Rural Cottages and Cottage Villas and Their Gardens and Grounds... New York and London: 1842. V. 51
The Fruits and Fruit Trees of America... New York: 1845. V. 50; 51; 52; 54
The Fruits and Fruit Trees of America... New York: 1858. V. 50; 51
The Fruits and Fruit Trees of America... New York: 1888. V. 54
The Fruits and Fruit Trees of America. New York: 1957. V. 47
The Horticulturist and Journal of Rural Art and Rural Taste. Albany: 1846-48. V. 51; 52
The Horticulturist and Journal of Rural Art and Rural Taste. Albany: 1848-49. V. 48; 50; 51
Rural Essays. New York: 1853. V. 51; 54
A Treatise on the Theory and Practice of Landscape Gardening. New York: 1841. V. 51
A Treatise On the Theory and Practice of Landscape Gardening. New York and London: 1844. V. 49; 53
A Treatise On the Theory and Practice of Landscape Gardening. London: 1849. V. 49
A Treatise on the Theory and Practice of Landscape Gardening. London: 1849. V. 54
A Treatise on the Theory and Practice of Landscape Gardening... New York: 1852. V. 48
A Treatise on the Theory and Practice of Landscape Gardening... New York: 1859. V. 48; 54

DOWNING, ANTOINETTE F.
The Architectural Heritage of Newport Rhode Island. Cambridge: 1952. V. 48

DOWNING, FANNY MURDAUGH
Nameless. Raleigh: 1865. V. 49; 54
Nameless. A Novel. Raleigh: 1866. V. 49
Pluto: Being the Sad Story and Lamentable FAte of the Fair Minthe. Raleigh: 1867. V. 49

DOWNING, J.
Letters of J. Downing, Major, Downingville Militia, Second Brigade to His Old Friend, Mr. Dwight, of the New York Daily Advertiser. New York: 1834. V. 47

DOWNING, JACK
The Praepinguida, an Ancient Poem Revived. Wilmington: 1835. V. 53

DOWNING, JACK, PSEUD.
Letters of Major Jack Downing, of Downingville Militia. New York: 1864. V. 54

DOWNMAN, HUGH
The Land of the Muses: a Poem. Edinburgh: 1768. V. 54
Poems to Thespia, to Which are Added, Sonnets, Etc. Exeter: 1791. V. 48

DOWNS, J.
American Furniture: Queen Anne & Chippendale Periods in the Henry Francis du Pont Wintherthur Museum. New York: 1952. V. 47; 48; 51; 53

DOWNS, KARL E.
Meet the Negro. Pasadena: 1943. V. 49

DOWNS, SOLOMON W.
Speech of S. W. Downs, Before a Public Meeting of the People of the Parish of Union, on the Annexation of Texas Delivered at Farmersville, on the 19th June, 1844. New Orleans: 1844. V. 47

DOWSE, THOMAS STRETCH
The Brain and Its Diseases. London: 1879. V. 52

DOWSETT, H. M.
Wireless Telephony and Broadcasting. London: 1924. V. 48

DOWSON, ERNEST
Adrian Rome. London: 1899. V. 54
A Bouquet. Chosen by Desmond Flower. Andoversford: 1991. V. 47; 49
Dilemmas. Stories and Studies in Sentiment. London: 1895. V. 53
Dilemmas. Stories and Studies in Sentiment. London: 1905. V. 53
The Letters of Ernest Dowson. London: 1967. V. 54
Memoirs of Cardinal Dubois. London: 1899. V. 49
New Letters from Ernest Dowson. Andoversford: 1984. V. 49; 53
The Pierrot of the Minute. London: 1897. V. 47; 50
Poems Of... London: 1905. V. 48; 49; 51
The Poems of Ernest Dowson. London and New York: 1906. V. 50
The Poetical Works of Ernest Chrisopher Dowson. London: 1934. V. 49
Studies in Sentiment. Portland: 1915. V. 53
Verses. London: 1896. V. 53

DOY, JOHN
The Narrative of John Doy, of Lawrence Kansas. Boston: 1860. V. 54

DOYLE, ARTHUR CONAN
The Adventure of the Priory School. Santa Barbara: 1985. V. 48
Adventures of Gerard. London: 1903. V. 47; 51; 52
The Adventures of Sherlock Holmes. London: 1892. V. 47; 48; 49
Adventures of Sherlock Holmes. New York: 1892. V. 49; 50; 51
The Adventures of Sherlock Holmes. London: 1898. V. 54
Adventures of Sherlock Holmes. Garden City: 1930. V. 51
The Adventures of Sherlock Holmes. New York: 1948. V. 47
The Adventures of Sherlock Holmes. New York: 1950. V. 50
The Adventures of Sherlock Holmes, The Later Adventures of Sherlock Holmes, the Final Adventures of Sherlock Holmes. Norwalk. V. 53
The Adventures of Sherlock Holmes. (with) The Later Adventures...and The Final Adventures. New York: 1950/52. V. 47; 51; 54
The Adventures of Sherlock Holmes. (with) The Memoirs of Sherlock Holmes. London: 1892/94. V. 47; 49; 50; 51; 52; 53; 54
The Annotated Sherlock Holmes. New York: 1973. V. 49
Beyond the City. Chicago & New York: 1892. V. 51
The British Campaign in France and Flanders. 1914-1918. London: 1916-19. V. 48; 51
The Case-Book of Sherlock Holmes. London: 1927. V. 49; 51; 53; 54
The Casebook of Sherlock Holmes. New York: 1927. V. 49
The Coming of Fairies. London: 1922. V. 47
The Complete Sherlock Holmes. New York: 1953. V. 48
The Crime of the Congo. New York: 1909. V. 48; 51
The Croxley Master. New York: 1907. V. 49
The Croxley Master and Other Tales of the Ring and Camp. New York: 1919. V. 54
The Croxley Master. The Dealings of Captain Sharkey. The Black Doctor. The Great Keinplatz Experiment. Man from Archangel. The Last of the Legions. New York: 1922. V. 54
A Desert Drama: Being the Tragedy of Koroshko. Philadelphia: 1898. V. 51
The Doings of Raffles Haw. London: 1892. V. 48; 50; 51
A Duet. London: 1899. V. 51
A Duet with an Occasional Chorus. London: 1899. V. 53
A Duet; with an Occasional Chorus. New York: 1899. V. 49; 50; 51; 52
The Edge of the Unknown. London: 1930. V. 49
Exploits of Brigadier Gerard. London: 1896. V. 51; 52; 53
The Exploits of Sherlock Holmes. London: 1954. V. 48; 53
The Great Boer War. London: 1900. V. 53
The Great Boer War, a Two Year's Record 1899-1901. London: 1902. V. 54
The Great Shadow. Bristol & London: 1892. V. 50
The Great Shadow and Beyond the City. Bristol: 1893. V. 50
His Last Bow. London: 1917. V. 49; 52
The History of Spiritualism. London: 1926. V. 49; 53
The Hound of the Baskervilles. 1902. V. 47; 52
The Hound of the Baskervilles. London: 1902. V. 48; 49; 52; 53; 54
The Hound of the Baskervilles. New York: 1902. V. 48; 49; 50
The Hound of the Baskervilles. London: 1974. V. 48; 53
The Hound of the Baskervilles. San Francisco: 1985. V. 47; 50; 52; 53
The Land of Mist. London: 1925. V. 49
The Land of Mist. London: 1926. V. 50; 53
The Land of Mist. New York: 1926. V. 49; 53
The Last Galley. Garden City: 1911. V. 48; 52
The Last Galley. London: 1911. V. 47
The Later Adventures of Sherlock Holmes. 1952. V. 53
The Later Adventures of Sherlock Holmes. (with) The Final Adventures of Sherlock Holmes. New York: 1952. V. 49
The Lost World. 1912. V. 52
The Lost World. New York: 1912. V. 47; 48; 49; 53
The Lost World... London: 1914. V. 49
The Memoirs of Sherlock Holmes. 1894. V. 53
The Memoirs of Sherlock Holmes. London: 1894. V. 48; 49; 50; 51; 52; 54
Memoirs of Sherlock Holmes. New York: 1894. V. 49; 50
My Friend the Murderer and other Mysteries and Adventures. New York: 1893. V. 51; 52
The New Revelation. New York: 1918. V. 51
Our American Adventure. New York: 1923. V. 50
Our American Adventure. Toronto and London: 1923. V. 49
Our Second American Adventure. Boston: 1924. V. 49; 52
The Parasite. London: 1894. V. 47
The Parasite. Westminster: 1894. V. 51
The Parasite. New York: 1895. V. 49; 54
Pheneas Speaks. 1926. V. 51; 53
The Poison Belt. New York: 1913. V. 50
The Poison Belt. Toronto: 1913. V. 47; 49; 50; 53
The Refugees. London: 1893. V. 49
The Refugees. New York: 1893. V. 48; 51
The Return of Sherlock Holmes. London: 1905. V. 53
The Return of Sherlock Holmes. New York: 1905. V. 49; 51; 53
Rodney Stone. London: 1896. V. 49; 51
Rodney Stone. New York: 1896. V. 47; 50; 51; 52; 54
Round the Red Lamp. London: 1894. V. 54
Round the Red Lamp. London: 1911. V. 53
Sherlock Holmes. New York: 1950-52. V. 54
The Sherlock Holmes Collected Edition. London: 1974. V. 47
Sherlock Holmes, the Complete Long Stories. London: 1929. V. 52
Sherlock Holmes...Complete Short Stories. London: 1902. V. 53
The Sign of the Four. London: 1893. V. 50
Sir Arthur Conan Doyle Centenary 1859-1959. Garden City: 1959. V. 49
Sir Nigel. Toronto: 1906. V. 53
Songs of Action. London: 1898. V. 51; 54
Stark Munro Letters. London: 1895. V. 53; 54
Strange Secrets. 1895. V. 48; 50
A Study in Scarlet. London: 1888/89. V. 53
A Study in Scarlet. New York: 1890's. V. 54
A Study in Scarlet. London: 1891. V. 53; 54
A Study in Scarlet. London: 1911. V. 53

DOYLE, ARTHUR CONAN continued
Sunlight Year Book for 1898. Port Sunlight: 1898. V. 49
Tales of Sherlock Holmes. 1912. V. 53
Three of Them. London: 1923. V. 51
Through the Magic Door. London: 1907. V. 47
The Tragedy of Korosko. London: 1898. V. 51; 54
Uncle Bernac. London: 1897. V. 51
The Valley of Fear. 1914. V. 50
The Valley of Fear. Toronto: 1914. V. 48
The Valley of Fear. London: 1915. V. 50; 53
The Valley of Fear. New York: 1915. V. 49; 50
A Visit to Three Fronts: Glimpses of the British, Italian and French Lines. London: 1916. V. 52
The Wanderings of a Spiritualist. London: 1921. V. 51; 53
The Wanderings of a Spiritualist. New York: 1921. V. 52
The White Company. Philadelphia. V. 48
The White Company. London: 1903. V. 50
The White Company. 1922. V. 53
The White Company. New York: 1922. V. 50
Works. London: 1903. V. 49; 51; 52
The Works. Garden City: 1930. V. 51; 52

DOYLE, CHARLES WILLIAM
The Military Exploits, Etc., Etc. of Don Juan Martin Diez, the Empeciando; Who First Commenced and Then Organized the system of Guerrilla Warfare in Spain. London: 1823. V. 52

DOYLE, J. B.
Tours in Ulster. 1854. V. 50
Tours in Ulster. London: 1854. V. 51

DOYLE, JAMES E.
The Chronicle of England B.C. 55 - A.D. 1485. London: 1864. V. 49; 50; 53; 54

DOYLE, JAMES W.
An Essay on the Catholic Claims, Addressed to...the Earl of Liverpool. Dublin: 1826. V. 53

DOYLE, JOHN T.
The International Arbitral Court of the Hague. San Francisco: 1906. V. 47
Some Account of the Pious Fund of California and the Litigation to Recover It. San Francisco: 1880. V. 54

DOYLE, MARTIN
Hints Originally Intended for the Small Farmers of the County of Wexford, but Suited to the Circumstances of Most Parts of Ireland. Dublin: 1832. V. 47; 51
Irish Cottagers. Dublin: 1830. V. 51
The Works Containing I. Hints to Small Farmers on Land, Fences, Cottages, Potatoes, Mangel, Wurzel, etc. II. Hints on road Work, Ventilation, Health Dress, etc. III. Hints On Planting Cattle, Fowls, Fisheries, Etc. IV. Irish Cottagers. Dublin: 1831. V. 50

DOYLE, RICHARD
Bird's Eye Views of Society. London: 1864. V. 53
The Foreign Tour of Messrs. Brown, Jones and Robinson. London: 1850. V. 51
The Foreign Tour of Messrs. Brown, Jones and Robinson... London: 1854. V. 47; 50
The Foreign Tour of Messrs. Brown, Jones and Robinson...in Belgium, Germany, Switzerland and Italy. New York: 1877. V. 51
In Fairyland. London: 1869. V. 49
Jack the Giant Killer. London: 1888. V. 47; 48; 49
Manners and Customs of ye Englyshe. London: 1849. V. 49
Manners and Cvstoms of Ye Englyshe. London: 1849-50. V. 50
Rebecca and Rowena. London: 1850. V. 47
Scenes from English History. London: 1886. V. 52; 53; 54
The Sleeping Beauty. London: 1868. V. 49

DOYLE, RODDY
Paddy Clarke Ha Ha Ha. New York: 1993. V. 51; 52
The Snapper. London: 1990. V. 52; 54
War. London: 1989. V. 54

DOYLE, WILLIAM
Two Letters Wherein the Sovereignty of the British Seas, and that the Sole Right of Fishing in Them... London: 1738. V. 47

D'OYLY, CHARLES
The European in India. London: 1813. V. 47; 50; 53
Tom Raw, the Griffin: a Burlesque Poem in Twelve Cantos. London: 1828. V. 48; 50

A DOZEN All Told. London: 1894. V. 52

A DOZEN Pair of Wedding Gloves. London: 1855. V. 51

DR. Comicus or the Frolics of Fortune. London: 1828. V. 51
DR. Comicus or the Frolics of Fortune. London: 1840. V. 51

DR. Last, or the Devil Upon Two Sticks. London: 1771. V. 47; 52

DR. S----'s Real Diary; Being a True and Faithful Account of Himself, for the Week, Wherein He Is Traduc'd by the Author of a Scandalous and Malicious Hue and Cry After Him... London: 1757. V. 53

DRABBLE, MARGARET
Jerusalem the Golden. London: 1967. V. 53
The Millstone. New York: 1966. V. 53
The Needle's Eye. New York: 1972. V. 53
Stratford Revisited: A Legacy of the Sixties. Shipston-on-Stour: 1989. V. 50
The Waterfall. New York: 1969. V. 53

DRACHLER, ROSE
Amulet Against Drought. Tannersville: 1978. V. 51; 54

DRACHMANN, HOLGER
Paul and Virginia of a Northern Zone. Chicago: 1895. V. 47; 49

DRAEGER
Les Beaux Interieurs: Ensembles Decoratifs. Paris: 1920-25. V. 53

DRAGO, HARRY SINCLAIR
Outlaws on Horseback, The History of the Organized Bands of Bank and Train Robbers Who Terrorized the Prairie Towns of Missouri, Kansas, Indian Territory and Oklahoma for a Half a Century. New York: 1964. V. 53
Wild, Woolly and Wicked: the History of the Kansas Cow Towns and the Texas Cattle Trade. New York: 1960. V. 52

DRAKE, BENJAMIN
Cincinnati in 1826. Cincinnati: 1827. V. 50

DRAKE, BURGESS
The Book of Lyonne. London: 1952. V. 48

DRAKE, DANIEL
An Inaugural Discourse On Medical Education Delivered at the Opening of the Medical College Of Ohio in Cincinnati, 11 November 1820... New York: 1951. V. 48
Memoir of Dr. John D. Godman. & Rambles of a Naturalist. Philadelphia: 1833. V. 53
A Systematic Treatise, Historical, Etiological and Practical, on the Principal Diseases of the Interior Valley of North America. Cincinnati: 1850/54. V. 53; 54

DRAKE, FRANCIS
Eboracum; or, the History and Antiquities of the City of York From its Original to the Present Times. London: 1736. V. 48
The English Hero; or Sir Francis Drake Revived. London: 1762. V. 48
The World Encompassed; and Analogous Contemporary Documents Concerning Sir Francis Drake's Circumnavigation of the World. London: 1926. V. 47
The World Encompassed by Sir Francis Drake...Carefully Collected Out of the Notes of Master Francis Fletcher... London: 1635. V. 47
The World Encompassed by Sir Francis Drake...The Relation of a Wonderfull Voiage. Cleveland: 1966. V. 54

DRAKE, FRANCIS S.
The Indian Tribes of the United States: Their History, Antiquities, Customs, Religion, Arts, Language, Tradition, Oral Legends, and Myths. Philadelphia: 1884. V. 49

DRAKE, G. S.
The Old Indian Chronicle. London: 1836. V. 48

DRAKE, JAMES
The Memorial of the Church of England, Humbly Offer'd to the Consideration of All True Lovers Of Our Church and Constitution. London: 1705. V. 49
Some Necessary Considerations Relating to All Future Elections of Members to Serve in Parliament. London: 1702. V. 53

DRAKE, JAMES MADISON
The History of the Ninth New Jersey Veteran Vols.: A Record Of its Service from Sept. 13th, 1861, to July 12th, 1865. Elizabeth: 1889. V. 47; 49; 51
Narrative of the Capture, Imprisonment and Escape of J. Madison Drake. 1868. V. 49

DRAKE, JOSEPH RODMAN
The Croakers. New York: 1860. V. 51
The Culprit Fay. New York: 1835. V. 51; 52
The Culprit Fay. New York: 1867. V. 54

DRAKE, LEAH BODINE
A Hornbook for Witches. Sauk City: 1950. V. 47; 48; 52

DRAKE, M.
A History of English Glass-Painting, With Some Extra Remarks Upon the Swiss Glass Miniatures of the 16th and 17th Centuries. London: 1912. V. 47; 50; 51; 53; 54

DRAKE, MAURICE
Saints and Their Emblems. London: 1906. V. 48
Saints and Their Emblems. London: 1916. V. 48

DRAKE, MILTON
Almanacs of the United States. New York: 1962. V. 52

DRAKE, NATHAN
Winter Nights; or, Fire-side Lucubrations... London: 1820. V. 47

DRAKE, SAMUEL
A Systematic Treatise, Historical, Etiological and Practical, on the Principal Diseases of the Interior Valley of North America. Cincinnati: 1850/54. V. 52

DRAKE, SAMUEL GARDNER
Biography and History of the Indians of North America, From Its First Discovery. Boston: 1848. V. 48
Early History of Georgia, Embracing the Embassy of Sir Alexander Cuming to the Country of the Cherokees, in the Year 1730. Boston: 1872. V. 47; 48; 50

DRAKE, ST. CLAIR
Black Metropolis: a Study of Negro Life in a Northern City. New York: 1945. V. 50; 51; 52

DRAKE-BROCKMAN, R. E.
British Somaliland. London: 1912. V. 52
The Mammals of Somaliland. 1910. V. 52; 54
The Mammals of Somaliland. London: 1910. V. 50

DRAKENBORCH, A.
Maps and Plans, Illustrative of Livy, Containing: Hannibals Expedition... Oxford. V. 48

DRANNAN, WILLIAM F.
Thirty-One Years on the Plains and in the Mountains; or, the Last Voice from the Plains... Chicago: 1899. V. 52

DRANSFIELD, JOHN N.
A History of the Parish of Penistone (West Riding of Yorkshire)...and of the Oldest Pack of Hounds in the World... Penistone: 1906. V. 47

DRAPER, GEORGE
Beleigh (sic) Abbey, Essex. London: 1818. V. 52

DRAPER, JOHN
Human Physiology, Statical and Dynamical; or, the Conditions and Course of the Life of Man. New York: 1856. V. 53
Somerset, with the Severn Sea: a Poem with Historical and Miscellaneous Notes... 1867. V. 47

DRAPER, JOHN W.
A Century of Broadside Elegies Being 9 - English and 10 Scottish Broadsides Illustrating the Biography and Manners of the 17th Century. London: 1928. V. 50

DRAPER, JOHN WILLIAM
Human Physiology, Stataical and Dynamical; or the Conditions and Course of the Life of Man. New York: 1856. V. 48

DRAPER, JOSHUA
An Essay Upon Friendship... London: 1725. V. 52

DRAPIEZ, PIERRE AUGUSTE JOSEPH
Tableau Analytique des Mineraux. Lille, Marlier and Paris: 1804. V. 47

DRAUD, GEORG
Bibliotheca Classica, Sive, Catalogus Officinalis, In Quo Singuli Singularum Facultatum Ac Professionum Libri. Frankfurt: 1611/10. V. 48
Bibliotheca Librorum Germanicorum Classica... Frankfurt: 1611. V. 53; 54

DRAWING Book, Being Studies of Landscape, Containing Twenty Specimens, by J. Hoppner, W. Owen, A. Callcott, J. Gainsborough, J. Owen, J. Varley, T. Girtin, &c. London: 1823. V. 48

DRAWINGS of the Flags in Use at the Present Time by Various Nations. London: 1889. V. 53

DRAYTON, DANIEL
Personal Memoir of Daniel Drayton, for Four Years and Four Months a Prisoner... Boston: 1853. V. 49

DRAYTON, GRACE
Baby Bears Christmas and Other Adventures. New York: 1920. V. 53

DRAYTON, JOHN
A View of South Carolina as Respects Her Natural and Civil Concerns. Charleston: 1802. V. 48

DRAYTON, MARIAN
Ephemeris or Leaves from the Journal of Marian Drayton. London: 1854. V. 54

DRAYTON, MICHAEL
The Ballad of Agincourt and the Ode to the Virginian Voyage. Stratford-upon-Avon: 1926. V. 50
Endimion & Phoebe. Oxford: 1925. V. 48
Endimion and Phoebe. Stratford-upon-Avon: 1925. V. 48
Nimphidia and the Muses Elizium. London: 1896. V. 48; 51
Poems... London: 1613. V. 52
Poems. London: 1619. V. 52; 53; 54
Poems. London: 1953. V. 50
Poly-Olbion, or a Chorographical Description of All the Tracts, Rivers, Mountains, Forests and Other Parts of This Renowned Isle of Great Britain.... London: 1613-22. V. 53

THE DREAM of the Rood. 1992. V. 50

DREAMER, MABEL
The Story of the Seven Young Goslings. London: 1899. V. 47

DREDGE, JAMES
Thames Bridges from the Tower to the Source. London: 1897. V. 51; 52

DREER, HERMAN
The History of Omega Psi Phi Fraternity: a Brotherhood of Negro College Men, 1911-1939. Baltimore: 1940. V. 53
The Immediate Jewel of His Soul: a Romance. St. Louis: 1919. V. 52

DREIER, KATHERINE S.
Shawn the Dancer. New York: 1933. V. 47

DREISER, THEODORE
America Is Worth Saving. New York: 1941. V. 51; 53
An American Tragedy. 1925. V. 53
An American Tragedy. New York: 1925. V. 51
An American Tragedy. 1954. V. 52
An American Tragedy. New York: 1954. V. 48; 51; 53
Chains. 1927. V. 50
Chains. New York: 1927. V. 47; 48; 49; 51; 52; 53
The Color of a Great City. New York: 1923. V. 50; 53
Dawn. 1931. V. 50; 53
Dawn. New York: 1931. V. 48; 49; 52; 53; 54
Epitaph (A Poem). New York: 1929. V. 47; 48; 51; 52; 53; 54
A Gallery of Women. New York: 1929. V. 49; 50; 51; 53; 54
The Genius. New York: 1915. V. 47; 53
The Hand of the Potter. New York: 1918. V. 49; 51; 53
A History of Myself. Dawn. New York: 1931. V. 47
A Hoosier Holiday. New York: 1916. V. 50
Jennie Gerhardt. New York: 1911. V. 50; 51; 53
Moods Cadenced and Declaimed. New York: 1926. V. 49; 50; 53
My City. New York: 1929. V. 47
Sister Carrie. New York: 1939. V. 53; 54
The Titan. New York: 1914. V. 49
A Traveler at Forty. New York: 1913. V. 53; 54

DRESS And Address. London: 1819. V. 51

DRESSER, CHRISTOPHER
Modern Ornamentation. London: 1886. V. 53
Principles of Decorative Design. London: 1874. V. 50; 52

DRESSER, H. E.
A History of the Birds of Europe... London: 1871-96. V. 48; 49; 50; 51; 52
A History of the Birds of Europe. Volume 9. Supplement. London: 1895-96. V. 53; 54
A History of the Birds of Europe. (with) Eggs of the Birds of Europe. London: 1871-1910. V. 50
A Monograph of the Coraciidae, or Family of the Rollers. London: 1893. V. 48; 51
A Monograph of the Meropidae, or Family of the Bee-Eaters. London: 1884-86. V. 48; 51; 53

DRESSER, MATTHAEUS
De Partibus Corporis Humani et de Anima, Eiusdem Potentijs. Wittenberg: 1581. V. 47; 48; 49

DRESSER, PAUL
The Songs of Paul Dresser. New York: 1927. V. 54

DREVON, I. F. HENRY
A Journey through Sweden... London: 1790. V. 51

DREW, SAMUEL
An Original Essay on the Immateriality and Immortality of the Human Soul, Founded Soley on Physical and Rational Principles. Bristol: 1803. V. 52

DREW, THOMAS
The John Brown Invasion: an Authentic History of the Harper's Ferry Tragedy with Full Details of the Capture, Trial and Execution of the Invaders... Boston: 1860. V. 48

DREXEL, JEREMY
The Considerations of Dexelius Upon Eternity. London: 1684. V. 51

DREXELIUS, HIEREMIAS
Heliotropium Seu conformatio Humanae Voluntatis Cum Divina... Coloniae: 1634. V. 50

DREXLER, A.
The Architecture of the Ecole des Beaux-Arts. New York: 1977. V. 51; 54

DREXLER, ARTHUR
The Drawings of Frank Lloyd Wright. New York: 1965. V. 51

DREYFUS, ALFRED
Five Years of My Life. London: 1921. V. 54

DREYFUS, JOHN
Aspects of French Eighteenth Century Typography. 1982. V. 47
Aspects of French Eighteenth Century Typography. Cambridge: 1982. V. 48; 50; 51; 54
Aspects of French Eighteenth Century Typography. London: 1982. V. 50
Eric Gill for Father Desmond. London: 1993. V. 49; 50; 52
Eric Gill for Father Desmond. 1995. V. 54
Four Lectures by T. J. Cobden-Sanderson. San Francisco: 1974. V. 52
Giovanni Mardersteig. An Account of His Work. London: 1966. V. 48
A History of the Nonesuch Press. London: 1981. V. 49; 53
Italic Quartet. 1966. V. 51
Italic Quartet. A Record of the Collaboration Between Harry Kessler, Edward Johnston, Emery Walker and Edward Prince in Making the Cranach Press Italic. Cambridge: 1966. V. 47
Saul Marks and His Plantin Press. Laguna Beach: 1975. V. 54
A Typographical Masterpiece. 1951. V. 54
A Typographical Masterpiece. 1990. V. 48
A Typographical Masterpiece. San Francisco: 1990. V. 49; 54
A Typographical Masterpiece. 1991. V. 52; 54
A Typographical Masterpiece. London: 1993. V. 50; 52
William Caxton and His Quincentenary. San Francisco: 1976. V. 52
The Work of Jan Van Krimpen. Haarlem: 1952. V. 52; 53

DREYFUSS, HENRY
Industrial Design. Volume V. New York: 1957. V. 53; 54

DRIAULT, EDOUARD
Pictorial History of Napoleon. Paris: 1932. V. 49

DRIGGS, B. W.
History of the Teton Valley Idaho. Caldwell: 1926. V. 48; 50

DRIGGS, FRANK
Black Beauty, White Heat. A Pictorial History of Classic Jazz. New York: 1982. V. 47; 51; 52; 53

DRIGGS, HOWARD R.
The Pony Express Goes Through: an American Saga Told by Its Heroes. New York: 1935. V. 48
Westward America. New York: 1942. V. 48

THE DRINKER'S Farm Tragedy. Trial and Convention of James Jeter Phillips for the Murder of His Wife. Richmond: 1868. V. 48

DRINKWATER, JOHN
Abraham Lincoln - A Play. London: 1918. V. 50
Abraham Lincoln - A Play. London: 1923. V. 52
All About Me: Poems for a Child. London: 1928. V. 48
The Collected Plays. London: 1925. V. 49
Collected Poems: 1908-1922. London: 1923. V. 48
Cotswold Characters. New Haven: 1921. V. 47; 52
From the German. Verses written from German Poets. London: 1924. V. 51
A History of the Late Seige of Gibraltar. London: 1786. V. 50
Loyalties. London: 1918. V. 52
Peresphone: a Poem. New York: 1926. V. 47; 52; 54
Swinburne: an Estimate. London: 1913. V. 52; 54

DRIPS, J. H.
Three Years Among the Indians in Dakota. Kimball: 1894. V. 51

THE DROPMORE Poems. 1946-48. V. 49

DROST, WILLIAM E.
Clocks and Watches of New Jersey. Elizabeth: 1966. V. 47

DROWN, WILLIAM
Compendium of Agriculture or Farmer's Guide, in the Most Essential Parts of Husbandry and Gardening... Providence: 1824. V. 52

DRUCE, G. C.
The Flora of Berkshire... Oxford: 1897. V. 50; 51; 54
The Flora of Buckinghamshire... Arbroath: 1926. V. 50; 51
The Flora of Oxfordshire. London: 1886. V. 51
The Flora of Oxfordshire. London: 1927. V. 52

DRUCE, GEORGE
A Genealogical Account of the Family of Druce of Goreing in the County of Oxon. London: 1853. V. 53

DRUCKER, JOHANNA
The Century of Artists Books' by Johanna Drucker. New York: 1995. V. 54
The Word Made Flesh. Cambridge: 1989. V. 47

DRUMHELLER, DAN
Uncle Dan Tells Thrills of Western Tales in 1854. Spokane: 1925. V. 49; 54

DRUMMON, GEORGE W. A. HAY
A Town Eclogue. Edinburgh: 1804. V. 53

DRUMMOND, ALEXANDER
Travels through Different Cities of Germany, Italy, Greece and Several Parts of Asia, as Far as the Banks of the Euphrates. London: 1754. V. 53; 54

DRUMMOND, DAVID THOMAS KERR
Scenes and Impressions in Switzerland and the North of Italy Together with Some Remarks on the Religious State of These Countries, Taken from the Notes of a Four Months' Tour During the Summer of 1852. Edinburgh: 1853. V. 49

DRUMMOND, HENRY
Baxter's Second Innings. London: 1892. V. 51
Histories of Noble British Familes with Biographical Notices of the Most Distinguished Individuals in Each. London: 1846. V. 49
The Monkey That Would Not Kill. London: 1898. V. 47; 51
A Plea for the Rights and Liberties of Women Imprisoned for Life Under the Power of Priests. London: 1851. V. 54
Speeches in Parliament and Some Miscellaneous Pamphlets of the Late Henry Drummond, Esq. London: 1860. V. 54

DRUMMOND, JAMES
Ancient Scottish Weapons. Edinburgh & London: 1881. V. 47; 52; 54

DRUMMOND, ROBERT B.
Erasmus, His Life and Character. London: 1873. V. 49

DRUMMOND, THOMAS
Musci Scotici; or Dried Specimens of the Mosses that Have Been Discovered in Scotland. Volume 1 Only. London: 1800. V. 52
Poems Sacred to Religion and Virtue. London: 1756. V. 54

DRUMMOND, V. H.
Mrs. Easter and the Starks. London: 1957. V. 50

DRUMMOND, W., & SONS
A General Priced Catalogue of Implements, Seeds, Plants &c. Sold by W. Drummond and Sons, Seedsmen and Nurserymen, Agricultural Museum, Stirling and Dubling. Stirling: 1844. V. 49

DRUMMOND, W. H.
The Large Game and Natural History of South and South-East Africa. Edinburgh: 1875. V. 49

DRUMMOND, WILLIAM
The History of Scotland, from the Year 1423, Until the Year 1542. London: 1655. V. 53
Memoir on the Antiquity of the Zodiacs of Esneh and Dendera. London: 1821. V. 47
Odin. London: 1817. V. 50; 54
The Poetical Works... Manchester: 1913. V. 51
The Works of William Drummond of Hawthornden... Edinburgh: 1711. V. 54

DRUMMOND, WILLIAM HAMILTON
The Giants' Causeway. Belfast: 1811. V. 48; 50

The Giants' Causeway, a Poem. London: 1811. V. 48

DRUMMOND, WILLIAM HENRY
The Habitant and Other French Canadian Poems. New York: 1897. V. 50
Johnnie Corteau and Other Poems. New York: 1901. V. 53
Phil-o-rum's Canoe and Madeleine Vercheres. New York: 1898. V. 47

DRUMMOND DE ANDRADE, CARLOS
Souvenir of the Ancient World. New York: 1976. V. 47

DRURY, DRU
Illustrations of Exotic Entomology. London: 1837. V. 54
Illustrations of Natural History; Wherein are Exhibited Upwards of 240 Figures of Exotic Insects... London: 1770. V. 53

DRURY, ROBERT
Madgascar; or Robert Drury's Journal, During Fifteen Years Captivity on that Island... London: 1729. V. 54

DRURY, W. P.
The Peradventures of Private Pagett. London: 1910. V. 47

DRUTEN, JOHN VAN
The Druid Circle. New York: 1948. V. 54
I've Got Sixpence. New York: 1953. V. 54
The Mermaids Singing. New York: 1946. V. 54

DRY, JOHN
Merton Walks, or the Oxford Beauties, a Poem. Oxford: 1717. V. 49

DRYANDER, JONAS
Catalogus Bibliothecae Historico-Naturalis Josephi Banks. London: 1798-1800. V. 48

DRYBROUGH, T. B.
Polo. London: 1898. V. 50
Polo. London: 1906. V. 47

DRYDEN, JOHN
Absalom and Achitophel. London: 1708. V. 49
Alexander's Feast. London: 1904. V. 48; 52
All for Love, Or, the World Well Lost. London: 1678. V. 48
All for Love; or, the World Well Lost. London: 1692. V. 47
All for Love, or, The World Well Lost. San Francisco: 1929. V. 48; 50; 53
All for Love, or the World Well Lost... 1932. V. 51; 52; 54
Amboyna: a Tragedy. London: 1673. V. 54
Amboyna: a Tragedy. London: 1691. V. 49
The Assignation; or, Love in a Nunnery... London: 1678. V. 47; 50
Aureng-Zebe: a Tragedy. London: 1676. V. 48; 53; 54
Britannia Rediviva: a Poem on the Birth of the Prince. London: 1688. V. 48; 53
Cleomenes, the Spartan Heroe. London: 1692. V. 48; 49; 53
The Comedies, Tragedies and Operas. London: 1701. V. 52; 54
Don Sebastian, King of Portugal... London: 1692. V. 49
Dramatic Works. London: 1725. V. 53; 54
The Dramatic Works. London: 1735/17 (vol 4). V. 52
The Dramatic Works. London: 1762-63. V. 50
The Dramatic Works. London: 1931. V. 47; 48; 49; 52
The Dramatic Works. London: 1931-32. V. 49; 50; 51; 54
Eleonora: a Panegyrical Poem. London: 1692. V. 48; 50; 54
An Evening's Love. London: 1671. V. 48; 49; 50
Examen Poeticum: being the Third Part of Miscellany Poems. London: 1693. V. 51
The Fables. London: 1797. V. 49; 51; 53; 54
The Fables. London: 1798. V. 49
Fables Ancient and Modern. London: 1700. V. 47; 52; 54
Fables Ancient and Modern. (with) Poems on Various Occasions; and Translations from Several Author. London: 1700/01. V. 49; 52
Hind and the Panther Transvers'd to the Story of the Country-Mouse and the City-Mouse. London: 1687. V. 50
The History of the League. London: 1684. V. 47
The Kind Keeper; or, Mr. Limberham: a Comedy. London: 1680. V. 49; 50; 54
Love Triumphant; or, Nature Will Prevail. London: 1694. V. 47; 50
Mac Flecknoe: a Poem. London: 1709. V. 51
Marriage-A-la-Mode. London: 1673. V. 54
The Miscellaneous Works. London: 1760. V. 49; 50; 51
Miscellany Poems in Two Parts. (with) Sylvae: or, the Second Part of Poetical Miscellanies. London: 1692/93. V. 54
Oedpius, a Tragedy. London: 1679. V. 48; 54
Of Dramatick Poesie: an Essay. London: 1684. V. 50
Of Dramatick Poesie, an Essay. London: 1693. V. 48; 52
Of Dramatick Poesie. An Essay. London: 1928. V. 48; 51; 53
Original Poems. London: 1743. V. 53
Original Poems. Glasgow: 1756. V. 47
Original Poems. Glasgow: 1775. V. 48
A Poem Upon the Death of His Late Highness Oliver, Lord Protector of England, Scotland and Ireland. London. V. 48
The Poems... Oxford: 1958. V. 52
The Poems. Oxford: 1970. V. 54
Poems on Various Occasions; and Translations from Several Authors. (with) Fables Ancient and Modern. London: 1701/1700. V. 47
The Poetical Works. London: 1811. V. 54
The Poetical Works. London: 1843(?)/32/33. V. 47
The Poetical Works. Edinburgh: 1855. V. 54

DRYDEN, JOHN continued
The Poetical Works. London: 1866. V. 51
The Poetical Works. New York: 1875. V. 47
The Poetical Works. London: 1883. V. 54
Religio Laici, or a Laymans faith. London: 1682. V. 48; 49; 54
Religio Laici Or a Laymans Faith. London: 1683. V. 48
The Rival Ladies. London: 1675. V. 48; 49; 54
Secret Love. London: 1691. V. 49
Secret-Love. London: 1679. V. 50
Songs and Poems. London: 1957. V. 51
Songs and Poems. Waltham St. Lawrence: 1957. V. 49; 51; 52; 54
The Spanish Fryar or, the Double Discovery. London: 1681. V. 47; 53; 54
The State of Innocence. London: 1677. V. 49
The State of Innocence. London: 1678. V. 54
The State of Innocence... London: 1684. V. 49; 54
The State of Innocence. London: 1690. V. 49; 54
Sylvae; or, the Second Part of Poetical Miscellanies. London: 1685. V. 48; 51
Threnodia Augustalis: a Funeral-Pindarique Poem Sacred to the Memory of King Charles II. London: 1685. V. 47
Tyrannick Love: or, the Royal Martyr. London: 1677. V. 50
Unto This Last. Four Essays on the First Principles of Political Economy. Hammersmith: 1907. V. 49
The Vindication: or, the Parallel of the French Holy-League and the English League and Covenant. London: 1683. V. 48; 54
The Wild Gallant: a Comedy. London: 1684. V. 48; 49
The Works. London: 1808. V. 49; 50; 51; 52; 54

DRYGALSKI, ERICH VON
The Southern Ice-Continent: The German South Polar Expedition Aboard the 'Gausss' 1901-1903. Cambridgeshire: 1989. V. 49
Zum Kontinent des Eisigen Suedens. Deutsche Suedpolarexpedition: Fahrten und Forschungen des "Gauss" 1901-1903. Berlin: 1904. V. 49

DRYSDALE, ISABEL
Scenes in Georgia. Philadelphia: 1830. V. 47

DUAINE, CARL
Caverns of Oblivion. Packrat: 1971. V. 52

DUANE, WILLIAM
An Epitome of the Arts and Sciences...Adapted to the Use of Schools in the United States... Philadelphia: 1811. V. 50
An Examination of the Question, Who Is the Writer of Two Forged Letters Addressed to the President of the United States?. 1803. V. 48
Explanation of the Plates of the System of Infantry Discipline fro the United States Army; According to the Rgulation of 19th March, 1813. Philadelphia: 1814. V. 48
A Hand Book for Infantry. Philadelphia: 1812. V. 54
A Military Dictionary... Philadelphia: 1810. V. 50
Politics for American Farmers; Being a Series of Tracts Exhibiting the Blessings of Free Government, As It Is Administered in the United States... Washington City: 1807. V. 51
Sampson Against the Philistines, or the Reformation of Lawsuits; and Justice Made Cheap, Speedy and Brought Home to Every Man's Door. Philadelphia: 1805. V. 50

DUANE, WILLIAM J.
Narrative and Correspondence Concerning the Removal of the Eposites, and Occurrences Connected Therewith. Philadelphia: 1838. V. 47

DU BARTAS, GUILLAUME DE SALLUSTE, SEIGNEUR
Du Bartas His Diuine Weekes and Workes with a Complete Collection of All the Other Most Delight-full Workes. London: 1633. V. 51
His Diuine Weekes, and the Workes with a Compleate Collection... London: 1621. V. 47
His Divine Weekes and Workes: with Complete Collection of All the Other Most Delightful Works. London: 1641. V. 50
The Works. 1935-40. V. 50; 51

DUBE, JEAN SEAL
Let's Save Our Salmon. 1972. V. 47

DUBE-HEYNIG, A.
Kirchner, His Graphic Art. 1961. V. 50; 51; 54
Kirchner, His Graphic Art. Greenwich: 1961. V. 47; 48; 53

DU BELLAY, MARTIN
Memoirs. Paris: 1569. V. 49; 53

DU BELLET, LOUISE PECQUET
Some Prominent Virginia Families. Lynchburg: 1907. V. 47; 52

DUBIE, NORMAN
Popham of the New Song and Other Poems. Port Townsend: 1975. V. 54
The Prayers of the North American Martyrs. Lisbon: 1975. V. 53; 54

DUBIN, ARTHUR D.
Some Classic Trains. Milwaukee: 1964. V. 52

DUBIN, LOIS SHERR
The History of Beads from 30,000 B.C. to the Present. London: 1987. V. 49; 51

DUBLIN Delineated in 28 Views of the Principal Public Buildings. 1843. V. 49

DUBNOW, S. M.
History of the Jews in Russia and Poland from the Earliest Times Until the Presnet Day. Philadelphia: 1916/18/20. V. 53

DU BOCCAGE, MARIE ANNE FIQUET
Letters Concerning England, Holland and Italy. London: 1770. V. 52

DUBOIS, CONSTANCE G.
The Condition of the Mission Indians of Southern California. Philadelphia: 1901. V. 47

DUBOIS, DAVID GRAHAM
...And Bid Him Sing. Palo Alto: 1975. V. 53

DU BOIS, DOROTHEA
The Lady's Polite Secretary, or New Female Letter Writter. London: 177-?. V. 52

DUBOIS, EDWARD
The Fairy of Misfortune; or, the Loves of Octar and Zulima. London: 1799. V. 49
My Pocket Book... London: 1808. V. 49; 51
Old Nick: a Satirical Story. London: 1801. V. 51

DUBOIS, FELIX
Timbuctoo the Mysterious. London: 1897. V. 48; 49; 51; 54

DU BOIS, HENRI PENE
Four Private Libraries of new York. New York: 1892. V. 50
Historical Essay on the Art of Bookbinding. New York: 1883. V. 47; 53

DUBOIS, JACQUES
De Mensibus Mulierum, et Hominis Generatione. Paris: 1561. V. 47
Morborum Internorum Prope Omnium Curatio Brevi Methodo Comprehensa, Ex Galeno Praecipue & Marco Gattinaria. Lyon: 1548. V. 49

DUBOIS, JEAN ANTOINE
Description of the Character, Manners and Customs of the People of Indian, and of Their Institutions, Religious and Civil. Philadelphia: 1818. V. 50

DU BOIS, JOHN VAN DEUSEN
Campaigns in the West, 1856-1861. Tucson: 1949. V. 50

DUBOIS, JUNE
W. R. Leigh, the Definitive Illustrated Biography. Kansas City: 1977. V. 49

DU BOIS, W. E. B.
The African Roots of War. V. 48

DUBOIS, W. E. B.
Black Reconstruction in America 1860-1880. New York: 1956. V. 51
Color and Democracy: Colonies and Peace. New York: 1945. V. 50; 51

DU BOIS, W. E. B.
The Correspondence of W. E. B. Dubois. Amherst: 1973/76. V. 52
Darkwater. New York: 1920. V. 52
Dusk of Dawn. New York: 1940. V. 50; 53
Encyclopedia of the Negro: Prepatory Volume with Reference Lists and Reports. New York: 1946. V. 52

DUBOIS, W. E. B.
The Gift of Black Folk. Boston: 1924. V. 47; 48; 49; 53
In Battle for Peace, the Story of My 83rd Birthday. New York: 1952. V. 49

DU BOIS, W. E. B.
Mansart Builds a School. New York: 1959. V. 52
The Negro. New York: 1915. V. 48; 52; 53
The Negro American Family. Atlanta: 1908. V. 52
The Souls of Black Folks. Chicago: 1903. V. 51; 52; 53
The Souls of Black Folks. London: 1905. V. 52

DUBOIS, W. E. B.
The Souls of Black Folks. New York: 1953. V. 49; 50

DU BOIS, W. E. B.
The World and Africa. New York: 1947. V. 51

DU BOIS, WILLIAM E.
Trial of Lucretia Chapman, Otherwise Called Lucretia Espos Y Mina, Who Was Jointly Indicted with Lino Amalia Espos Y Mina, for the Murder of William Chapman, Esq. Lat of Andalusia, County of Bucks, Pennsylvania.... Philadelphia: 1832. V. 51; 53

DUBOIS-FONTANELLE, JEAN GASPARD
The Shipwreck and Adventures of Monsieur Pierre Viaud, a native of Bordeaux, and Captain of a Ship. London: 1771. V. 47

DUBON, DAVID
Tapestries from the Samuel H. Kress Collection at the Philadelphia Museum of Art. London: 1964. V. 54

DUBOS, JEAN BAPTISTE, ABBE
Critical Reflections on Poetry, Painting and Music. London: 1748. V. 47

DU BOSC, JACQUES
The Excellent Woman Described by Her True Characters and Their Opposites. London: 1692. V. 47

DU BOSE, HENRY KERSHAW
History of Company B, Twenty-First Regiment (Infantry). Columbia: 1909. V. 49

DU BOSE, JOHN WITHERSPOON
General Joseph Wheeler and the Army of Tennessee. New York: 1912. V. 52; 54

DUBOST, ANTOINE
Hunt and Hope. London: 1810. V. 52

DUBOUCHET, JEAN
Histoire Genealogique de la Maison Royale de Courtenay. Paris: 1661. V. 52

DUBOURG, GEORGE
The Violin: Being an Account of That Leading Instrument and its Most Eminent Professors, From Its Earliest Date to the Present Time. Dublin: 1836. V. 48

DUBREUIL, JEAN
Perspective Practical. London: 1698. V. 47
The Practice of Perspective... London: 1726. V. 49
The Practice of Perspective; or, an Easy Method of Representing Natural Objects... London: 1743. V. 50
The Practice of Perspective; or, an Easy Method of Representing Natural Objects According to the Rules of Art. London: 1749. V. 48

DU BROCA, M.
Interesting Anecdotes of the heroic Conduct of Women, During the French Revolution. London: 1802. V. 47

DUBUISSON, A.
Richard Parkes Bonington, His Life and Work. London: 1924. V. 49; 50; 51; 53; 54

DUBUISSON, CHARLES L.
An Inaugural Address...Jefferson College & Washington Lyceum. Natchez: 1836. V. 50

DUBUS, ANDRE
Adultery and Other Choices. Boston: 1977. V. 53
Blessings. Elmwood: 1987. V. 50; 51
Finding a Girl in America. Boston: 1980. V. 50
Land Where My Fathers Died. 1984. V. 54
The Last Worthless Evening. Boston: 1986. V. 52; 53
The Lieutenant. New York: 1967. V. 49; 52; 53; 54
Selected Stories. Boston: 1990. V. 52
Separate Flights. Boston: 1975. V. 50; 51; 52
Voices from the Moon. Boston: 1984. V. 53
We Don't Live Here Anymore. New York: 1984. V. 53

DU CAMBOUT DE PONT CHATEAU, SEBASTIAN JOSEPH
The Moral Practice of the Jesuites; Demonstrated by Many Remarkable Histories of Their Actions In All Parts of the World... London: 1671. V. 52

DU CANE, E. F.
An Account of the Manner In Which Sentences of Penal Servitude are Carried Out in England. London: 1872. V. 53

DU CANE, FLORENCE
The Flowers and Gardens of Japan. London: 1907. V. 47

DU CANGE, CHARLES
Glossarium ad Scriptories Mediae et Infimae Graecitatis. Lyon: 1688. V. 50

DUCAREL, ANDREW COLTEE
Anglo-Norman Antiquities Considered, in a Tour through Part of Normandy. London: 1767. V. 47
The History and Antiquities of the Archiepiscopal Palace of Lambeth from Its Foundation to the Present. London: 1785. V. 53
The History and Antiquities of the Archiepiscopal Palace of Lambeth, from Its Foundation to the Present Time. (with) The History and Antiquities of the Parish of Lambeth, in the County of Surrey... London: 1785/86. V. 52
Some Account of the Town, Church and Archiepiscopal Palace of Croydon. London: 1783. V. 52

DUCAREL, P. J.
Poems, Original and Translated. London: 1807. V. 48

DUCAS, THEODORE
The Travels of...in Various Countries of Europe, at the Revival of Letters and Art. London: 1822. V. 49

DU CHAILLU, PAUL B.
Explorations and Adventures in Equatorial Africa... London: 1861. V. 50; 51
Explorations and Adventures in Equatorial Africa... New York: 1861. V. 52
In African Forest and Jungle. New York: 1903. V. 52
A Journey to Ashango-Land: and Further Penetration Into Equatorial Africa. New York: 1867. V. 49; 52
The Land of the Midnight Sun. London: 1881. V. 50
The Land of the Midnight Sun. New York: 1881. V. 48; 53
The Land of the Midnight Sun. New York: 1882. V. 48; 54
The Land of the Midnight Sun... London: 1888. V. 49
The Viking Age... London: 1889. V. 49; 54
The Viking Age. New York: 1889. V. 47; 53; 54

DUCHAMP, MARCEL
Manual of Instructions for Etant Donnes. Philadelphia: 1987. V. 50
Marcel Duchamp. New York: 1973. V. 50
Marcel Duchamp: a Retrospective Exhibition. Pasadena: 1963. V. 53
Marcel Duchamp Notes. Paris: 1980. V. 51
Not Seen and/ or Less Seen of 1904-64. Houston: 1965. V. 54
Notes and Projects for the Large Glass. New York: 1969. V. 50
Salt Seller. New York: 1973. V. 53

DUCHENNE, G. B.
Physiology of Motion Demonstrated by Means of Electrical Stimulation and Clinical Observation and Applied to the Study of Paralysis and Deformities. Philadelphia: 1949. V. 47; 50; 52
Selections from the Clinical Works of Dr. Duchenne. London: 1883. V. 52

DU CHESNE, ANDRE
Bibliotheque des Autheurs...de la France. Paris: 1618. V. 52

DUCHOCHOIS, P. C.
Industrial Photography... New York: 1901. (1891). V. 54
Photographic Reproduction Processes: a Practical Treatisse of the Photo Impressions Without silver Salts for the Use of Photographers, Architects.... New York: 1891. V. 47

DU CHOUL, GUILLAUME
Discorso Della Religione Antica de Romani...Composti in Franzese.... Lione: 1569. V. 49

DUCHOW, JOHN CHARLES
The Duchow Journal: a Voyage from Boston to California, 1852. 1959. V. 51

DUCK, ARTHUR
The Thresher's Miscellany; or, Poems on Several Subjects. London: 1731. V. 52

DUCK, STEPHEN
Poems on Several Occasions. London: 1736. V. 47; 48; 52
Poems on Several Occasions. London: 1764. V. 54
Poems on Several Subjects. London: 1730. V. 47

DUCKETT, GEORGE
Penal Laws and Test Act; Questions Touching Their Repeal Propounded in 1687-8 by James II. 1883. V. 53

DUCORNET, ERIKA
The Illustrated Universe. Toronto: 1979. V. 47; 48
Weird Sisters. Vancouver: 1976. V. 48
Wild Geraniums. Deal, Kent: 1975. V. 48

DUCORNET, RIKKI
The Butcher's Tales. Toronto: 1980. V. 50

DUCRAY-DUMENIL, FRANCOIS GUILLAUME
Ambrose and Eleanor; or, the Adventures of Two Children Deserted on an Uninhabitaed Island. London: 1796. V. 47
Ambrose and Eleanor, or the Adventures of Two Children Deserted On an Uninhbaited Island...To Which is Added Auguste and Madeline, a Real History... Baltimore: 1799. V. 51

DUCRET, S.
German Porcelain and Faience. New York: 1962. V. 54

DU CROS, ARTHUR
Wheels of Fortune. London: 1938. V. 51

DUCROT, NICOLAS
Andre Kertesz: Sixty Years of Photography, 1912-1972. London: 1972. V. 47

DUDEK, LOUIS
Atlantis. Montreal: 1967. V. 47
East of the City. Toronto: 1946. V. 47; 52
En Mexico. Toronto: 1958. V. 47
Europe. Toronto: 1954. V. 47
Laughing Stalks. Toronto: 1958. V. 47
Patterns of Recent Canadian Poetry (an Essay). Quebec: 1958. V. 52
The Transparent Sea. Toronto: 1956. V. 47

DUDEN, GOTTFRIED
Bericht Uber Eine Reise Nach den Westlichen Staaten Nordamerika's Und Einem Mehrjahrigen Aufenthalt Am Missouri... Elberfeld: 1829. V. 48

DUDEVANT, JEAN F.
The History of Harliquinade. Philadelphia: 1915. V. 53

DUDIN, M.
The Art of the Bookbinder and Gilder. Leeds: 1977. V. 50
The Art of the Bookbinder and Gilder 1772. London: 1977. V. 50

DUDLEY, C. S.
An Analysis of the System of the Bible Society, Throughout its Various Parts. London: 1821. V. 53

DUDLEY, CARRIE
My Peek-A-Book Show Book, Play and Scenery by Carrie Dudley, Performers - Us Kids, Stage Manager - Polly Suzanne Buzza. Minneapolis: 1928. V. 49

THE DUDLEY Castle Miscellany. Wolverhampton: 1860. V. 49

DUDLEY, DONALD R.
Urbs Roma: a Source Book of Classical Texts on the City and Its Monuments. London: 1967. V. 52

DUDLEY, DUD
Dud Dudley's Mettallum Martis; or, Iron Made with Pit-Coale, Sea-Coale &c. West Bromwich: 1851. V. 50

DUDLEY, HENRY BATE
The Travellers in Switzerland, a Comic Opera. 1795. V. 47

DUDLEY, HOWARD
The History and Antiquities of Horsham... London: 1836. V. 47

DUDLEY, JEBB SAMUEL
The Life of Robert Earl of Leicester the Favourite of Queen Elizabeth. London: 1727. V. 52

DUDLEY, ROBERT
Monthly Maxims. Rhymes and Reasons to Suit the Seasons and Pictures New to Suit Them Too. London: 1882. V. 52

DUER, WILLIAM ALEXANDER
A Course of Lectures on the Constitutional Jurisprudence of the United States. Boston: 1856. V. 49

DUER, WILLIAM ALEXANDER continued
A Letter, Addressed to Cadwallader D. Colden...In Answer to the Strictures.... Albany: 1817. V. 47; 50; 51

DUERER, ALBRECHT
The Construction of Roman Letters. Cambridge: 1924. V. 50
Designs of the Prayer Book. London: 1817. V. 52; 53
The Little Passion. London: 1894. V. 47; 50
The Little Passion. Verona: 1971. V. 47; 48; 50
Of the Just Shaping of Letters, from the Applied Geometry of Albrecht Durer Book III. New York: 1917. V. 47
Opera Alberti Dueri. Arnheim: 1604. V. 47; 49
Passion Week. London: 1857. V. 53

DUERRENMATT, FRIEDRICH
A Dangerous Game. London: 1960. V. 54
Once a Greek.... New York: 1965. V. 54
The Pledge. New York: 1959. V. 51; 54
The Visit. New York: 1958. V. 54

DU FAUR, FREDA
The Conquest of Mount Cook and Other Climbs. 1915. V. 53

DUFF, ALEXANDER
A Description of the Durga and Kali Festivals, Celebrated in Calcutta, at an Expense of Three Millions of Dollars. Troy: 1846. V. 52

DUFF, E. GORDON
Catalogue of Printed Books and Manuscripts in the John Rylands Library. Manchester: 1899. V. 54
Early Printed Books. London: 1893. V. 50
Hand Lists of English Printers 1501-1556. London: 1896-1913. V. 48
Hand-Lists of English Printers 1501-1556. Part I (-IV). London: 1895-1913. V. 51; 54
William Caxton. Chicago: 1905. V. 48

DUFF, GRANT
History of the Marat,has (sic). Bombay: 1830. V. 49

DUFF, PATRICK
Sketch of the Geology of Moray. Elgin: 1842. V. 48

DUFFERIN, FREDERICK
Letters from High Latitudes... London: 1857. V. 48; 49; 53
Letters From High Latitudes. London: 1867. V. 49

DUFFERIN, LADY
Songs, Poems and Verses. Together with a Selection of the Songs Set to Music by Herself and Others. London: 1894/95. V. 53

DUFFERIN & AVA, FREDERICK T. H. T. BLACK, MARQUESS OF
Irish Emigration and the Tenure of Land in Ireland. London: 1867. V. 54

DUFFERIN AND AVA, MARCHIONESS OF
My Canadian Journal 1872-8. London: 1891. V. 51

DUFFEY, E. B., MRS.
No Sex in Education; or, An Equal Chance for Both Girls and Boys. Philadelphia: 1874. V. 51; 53

DUFFIELD, A. J.
Recollections of Travels Abroad. London: 1889. V. 49

DUFFIELD, T.
Protected Native Birds of South Australia. Adelaide: 1910. V. 53

DUFFIN, FELIX
Perspective, a Treatise Intended With or Without Models as a Complete Guide for Self Instruction. London: 1852. V. 54

DUFFY, CHARLES G.
Young Ireland: a Fragment of Irish History 1840 to 1845 & Young Ireland, Part II: Or Four Years of Irish History, 1845-49. London: 1884/87. V. 52

DUFIEF, N. G.
The Logic of Facts; or, the Conduct of Wm. Rawle, Esq. Attorney at law, Towards N.G. Dufief, Arraigned Before the Tribunal of Public Opinion... Philadelphia: 1806. V. 49
Nature Displayed in Her Mode of Teaching Language to man. Philadelphia: 1806/06. V. 53

DUFLOT DE MOFRAS, EUGENE
Duflot de Mofras Travels on the Pacific Coast. Santa Ana: 1937. V. 48; 52; 53

DUFORT, GIAMBATTISTA
Trattato dell Ballo Nobile... Naples: 1728. V. 54

DUFOUR, PHILIPPE SYLVESTRE
The Manner of Making of Coffee, Tea and Chocolate. London: 1685. V. 52

DUFOUR, SYLVESTRE
Moral Instructions from a Father to His Son, Ready to Undertake a Long Voyage... Edinburgh: 1780. V. 50

DUFRAN, DORA
Low Down on Calamity Jane. Rapid City: 1932. V. 48; 50

DUFRENE, MAURICE
French Art Nouveau Interior Designs/Un Interieur Moderne. Paris: 190?. V. 48

DUFRESNE, FRANK
Alaska's Animals and Fishes. West Hartford: 1946. V. 47; 50

DU FRESNOY, CHARLES ALPHONSE
L'Art de Peinture. Paris: 1673. V. 48; 50
The Art of Painting. London: 1716. V. 47; 48; 50; 52
The Art of Painting... Dublin: 1783. V. 51; 52
The Art of Painting. York: 1783. V. 47; 51
De Arte Graphica (or) The Art of Painting... London: 1695. V. 47; 49

DUFRESNY, CHARLES
Amusements Serious and Comical; or a New Collection of Bon-mots, Keen-jests, Ingenious Thoughts, Pleasant Tales and Comical Adventures. London: 1719. V. 47; 48

DUGANNE, AUGUSTINE
Bianca. New York: 1854?. V. 47
Camps and Prisons: Twenty Months in the Department of the Gulf. New York: 1865. V. 47; 48
The Fighting Quakers, a True Story of the War for Our Union. New York: 1866. V. 54
The Tenant-House; or, Embers from Poverty's Hearthstone. New York: 1857. V. 50; 54

DUGDALE, FLORENCE E.
The Book of Baby Beasts. London: 1911. V. 52
The Book of Baby Birds. New York: 1912. V. 49; 53

DUGDALE, GILES
William Barnes of Dorset. London: 1953. V. 54

DUGDALE, MICHAEL
An Omelette of Vultures Eggs - Poems 1939-1945. London: 1982. V. 47

DUGDALE, WILLIAM
The Antient Usage in Bearing of Such Ensigns of Honour as are Commonly Called Arms. Oxford: 1682. V. 53; 54
The Antiquities of Warwickshire Illustrated... London: 1656. V. 51
The Antiquities of Warwickshire Illustrated... London: 1730. V. 51
The Baronage of England, or an Historical Account of the Lives and Most Memorable of Our English Nobility... London: 1675/76. V. 50; 51
The History of Imbanking and Draining of Divers Fens and Marshes, Both in Foreign Parts and in This Kingdom... London: 1662. V. 51
The History of Imbanking and Draining of Divers Fens and Marshes, Both in Foreign Parts and In this Kingdom. London: 1772. V. 47
The History of St. Pauls Cathedral in London. London: 1658. V. 49; 50; 52
The History of St. Paul's Cathedral in London, from Its Foundation... London: 1818. V. 54
The Life, Diary and Correspondence... London: 1827. V. 49; 53
Monasatic Anglicanum, or, The History of the Ancient Abbies, and Other Monasteries, Hospitals, Cathedral and Collegiate Churches... London: 1693. V. 48; 50
Monasticon Anglicanum: a History of the Abbies and Monasteries, Hospitals, Frieries and Cathedral and Collegiate Churches, with Their Dependencies, in England and Wales... London: 1846. V. 48; 50
Monasticon Anglicanum: a History of the Abbies and...Monasteries, Hospitals, Frieries and Cathedral and Collegiate Churches, with their Dependencies, in England and Wales. London: 1817-30. V. 49
Monasticon Anglicanum, sive andectae Coenobiorum Benedictionorum, Cluniacensium, Cisterciensium, Carthusianorum... London: 1655-61-73. V. 53
Origines Juridicales, or Historical Memorials of the English Laws, Courts of Justice, Forms of Tryall, Punishment in Cases Criminal, Law Writers, Law Books, Grants and Settlements of Estates, Degree of Serjeant, Innes of Court and Chancery. London: 1666. V. 53
The Restoration of the Beauchamp Chapel at St. Mary's Collegiate Church, Warwick 1674-1742. Oxford: 1956. V. 47; 50
A Short View of the Late Troubles in England. Oxford: 1681. V. 47; 49; 50
Warwickshire; Being a Concise Topographical Description of the Different Towns and Villages in the County of Warwick... Coventry: 1817. V. 50

DUGGAN, G. H.
The Quebec Bridge. Notes on the Work of the St. Lawrence Bridge Company, in Preparing the Accepted Design for the Construction of the Superstructure. Montreal: 1918. V. 49

DUGGER, SHEPHERD MONROE
The Balsam Groves of the Grandfather Mountain: A Tale of the Western North Carolina Mountains. Banner Elk: 1892. V. 47; 54

DUGMORE, A. RADCLYFFE
Camera Adventures in the African Wilds... London: 1910. V. 49
Camera Adventures in the African Wilds... New York: 1910. V. 51
The Romance of the Newfoundland Caribou: an Intimate Account of the Life of the Reindeer of North America. Philadelphia & London: 1913. V. 47; 50; 53

DUGUET, JACQUES JOSEPH
The Institution of a Prince. London: 1740. V. 47

DU HALDE, P.
The General History of China, Containing a Geographical, Historical, Chronological, Political and Physical Description of the Empire of China, Chinese Tartary, Corea and Thibet, Including an Exact and Particular Account of Their Customs.... 1736. V. 54

DUHAMEL DU MONCEAU, HENRI LOUIS
De L'Exploitation des Bois ou Moyens de Tirer un Parti Avantageux des Taillis, Demi-Futaies et Hautes-Futaies, et d'en Faire Une Juste Estimation... Paris: 1764. V. 47
The Elements of Agriculture. London: 1764. V. 51; 52
A Practical Treatise of Husbandry. London: 1759. V. 54
A Practical Treatise of Husbandry... London: 1762. V. 47; 48; 50; 51; 52
Traite des Arbres Fruitiers: Contenant Leur Figure, Leur Description, Leur Culture &c. Paris: 1768. V. 50

DU HAYS, CHARLES
The Percheron Horse. Baltimore: 1886. V. 54

DUHEME, JACQUELINE
Birthdays. San Francisco: 1966. V. 51; 52

DUHIGG, BARTHOLOMEW THOMAS
History of the King's Inns; or, An Account of the Legal Body in Ireland, From Its Connexion with England. Dublin: 1806. V. 48

DUHRING, LOUIS A.
Atlas of Skin Diseases. Philadelphia: 1876. V. 47; 48; 49

DUIGENAN, PATRICK
Pranceriana. Dublin: 1775. V. 54

DU JARRIC, PIERRE
Thesavrvs Rervm Indicarvm. Cologne: 1615. V. 51

DUKE, BASIL W.
History of Morgan's Cavalry. 1867. V. 47
Morgan's Cavalry. New York & Washington: 1906. V. 47; 48; 50; 52; 54

DUKE, F.
The Compleat Florist. London: 1747. V. 51

DUKE, THOMAS S.
Celebrated Criminal Cases of America. San Francisco: 1910. V. 47; 52

DUKE, VERNON
Passport to Paris. Boston: 1955. V. 49

DUKE, WILLIAM
Allergy: Asthma, Hayfever, Urticaria and Allied Manifest-ations of Reaction. St. Louis: 1925. V. 48; 49; 51; 53

DULAC, EDMUND
Edmund Dulac's Fairy Book. London: 1915. V. 48; 49
Edmund Dulac's Fairy-Book. London: 1916. V. 47; 51; 52
Edmund Dulac's Picture-Book for the French Red Cross. 1915. V. 53
Edmund Dulac's Picture-Book for the French Red Cross. London & New York: 1915. V. 48; 50; 51; 52; 53
A Fairy Garland, Being Fairy Tales from the Old French. London & New York: 1928. V. 52; 54
Lyrcis Pathetic and Humorous from A to Z. London: 1908. V. 51; 52
Once Upon A Time Land. London: 1910. V. 48
The Sleeping Beauty and Other Fairy Tales. London: 1910. V. 52

DULANY, PATRICK
Considerations on the Propriety of Imposing Taxes in the British Colonies, for the Purpose of Raising a Revenue by Act of Parliament. London: 1766. V. 47; 48

DULARE, JACQUES ANTOINE
Pogonologia, or a Philosophical and Historical Essay on Beards. Exeter: 1786. V. 53

DU LAURENS, ANDRE
Discursus de Visus Nobilitate et Conserandi Modo. Munich: 1618. V. 47

DULCKEN, H. W.
Rhyme and Reason; a Picture Book of Verses, for Little Folks. London: 1869. V. 49

DUMAS, ALEXANDRE
The Black Tulip. Haarlem: 1951. V. 53; 54
The Black Tulip. London: 1951. V. 54
The Black Tulip. New York: 1951. V. 47
Camille. 1937. V. 52; 53
Camille. London: 1937. V. 48; 51; 52; 53; 54
Camille. New York: 1937. V. 50
Memories of a Physician. London: 1847. V. 49
Peches de Jeunesse. Paris: 1847. V. 47
The Romances. Boston: 1894. V. 48
The Romances of... Boston: 1898. V. 50
The Three Musketeers. Maastricht: 1932. V. 51
The Three Musketeers. New York: 1953. V. 53

DUMAS, CHARLES LOUIS
Principes de Physiologie, ou Introduction a la science Experimentale, Philosophique et Medicale de l'Homme Vivant... Paris: 1806. V. 49

DUMAS, FRANCOISE G.
Modern Artists. London: 1888. V. 49

DUMAS, MATHIEU
Memoirs Of His Own Time; Including the Revolution, The Empire and the Restoration. London: 1839. V. 48

DUMAS, MAURICE
Scientific Instruments of the Seventeenth and Eighteenth Centuries and Their Makers. London: 1989. V. 50

DU MAURIER, DAPHNE
Frenchman's Creek. London: 1941. V. 47
Jamaica Inn. London: 1936. V. 49
Mary Anne. London: 1954. V. 53
My Cousin Rachel. London: 1951. V. 51
My Cousin Rachel. New York: 1952. V. 50
Rebecca. London: 1938. V. 47; 50; 53; 54
Rebecca. New York: 1938. V. 52

DU MAURIER, GEORGE
The Martian. London: 1897. V. 49
The Martian. New York: 1897. V. 53
The Martian. New York: 1898. V. 50
Peter Ibbetson. London: 1892. V. 47; 49; 54
Peter Ibbetson. London: 1892/91. V. 54
Peter Ibbetson. Trilby. The Martian. New York: 1891/94/96. V. 51
Trilby. 1894. V. 54
Trilby. London: 1895. V. 52; 53; 54
Works. London: 1892-98. V. 52

DU MAY, LEWIS
The Estate of the Empire; or, an Abridgement of the Laws and Government of Germany. London: 1676. V. 50

DUMERIL, A. M. C.
Erpetologie Generale ou Histoire Naturelle des Reptiles. Paris: 1834-54. V. 51

DUMMER, JEREMIAH
A Defence of the New-England Charters. Boston: 1745. V. 51; 52
A Defence of the New-England Charters. London: 1765. V. 47; 51

DU MONCEAU, M. DUHAMEL
A Practical Treatise of Husbandry. London: 1759. V. 53

DUMOND, DWIGHT L.
Southern Editorials on Secession (Together with Northern Editorials on Secession). New York: 1931. V. 47

DU MONSTIER, ARTHUR
Neustria Pia seu de Omnibus et Singulis Abbatiis, et Prioratibus Totius Normaniae... Rouen: 1663. V. 50

DUMONT, ETIENNE
Recollections of Mirabeau... London: 1832. V. 51

DUMONT, HENRIETTA
Floral Offering...Comprising the Language and Poetry of Flowers. Philadelphia: 1851. V. 54

DUNAWAY, WAYLAND FULLER
Reminiscences of a Rebel. New York: 1913. V. 49

DUNBAR, A. R.
Dunbar's Western Mining Directory 1901-1902. Denver and San Francisco: 1902. V. 49

DUNBAR, EDWARD E.
The Romance of the Age; or, the Discovery of Gold in California. New York: 1867. V. 48

DUNBAR, FLANDERS
Emotions and Bodily Changes: a Survey of the Literature on Psychosomatic Interrelationships. New York: 1935. V. 52

DUNBAR, J. RIMELL
Park Riding, with Some Remarks on the Art of Horsemanship. London: 1859. V. 47

DUNBAR, PAUL LAURENCE
The Best Short Stories of Paul Laurence Dunbar. New York: 1938. V. 54
Candle-Lightin' Time. New York: 1901. V. 54
Candle-Lightin' Time. New York: 1902. V. 49
The Fanatics. New York: 1901. V. 51; 54
Folks from Dixie. London: 1898. V. 47
Folks from Dixie. New York: 1898. V. 48; 53
The Heart of Happy Hollow. New York: 1904. V. 51; 54
Howdy Honey Howdy. New York: 1905. V. 54
I Greet the Dawn. New York: 1978. V. 52
In Old Plantation Days. New York: 1903. V. 54
The Jest of Fate. London: 1902. V. 54
Joggin' Erlong. New York: 1906. V. 53
Lyrics of Hearthside. New York: 1899. V. 54
Lyrics of Love and Laughter. New York: 1903. V. 51; 53; 54
Lyrics of Lowly Life. New York: 1896. V. 52; 54
Lyrics of Lowly Life. New York: 1898. V. 50
Lyrics of Lowly Life. New York: 1908. V. 49; 51
Lyrics of Sunshine and Shadow. New York: 1905. V. 50
Majors and Minors: Poems by Paul Lawrence (sic) Dunbar. Toledo: 1895. V. 53
Poems of Cabin and Field. New York: 1899. V. 48; 49; 50; 51; 52
Speaking' O' Christmas. New York: 1914. V. 52; 54
The Sport of the Gods. New York: 1902. V. 54
The Stranger of Gideon. New York: 1900. V. 54
The Strength of Gideon and Other Stories. New York: 1900. V. 51
The Uncalled. New York: 1898. V. 47; 50; 54
When Malindy Sings. New York: 1903. V. 49

DUNBAR, REUBEN A.
The Most Foul and Unparalleled Murder in the Annals of Crime. Albany: 1851. V. 50

DUNBAR, ROBERT NUGENT
Indian Hours; or, Passion and Poetry of the Tropics. London: 1839. V. 47

DUNBAR, SEYMOUR
A History of Travel in America. Indianapolis: 1915. V. 48; 49; 50
A History of Travel in America... New York: 1937. V. 53

DUNBAR, WILLIAM
The Poems of William Dunbar. London: 1979. V. 54

DUNCAN, ALASTAIR
Art Nouveau and Art Deco Bookbinding. french Masterpies 1880-1940. New York: 1989. V. 50; 51
Tiffany at Auction. New York: 1981. V. 48

DUNCAN, ANDREW
The Edinburgh New Dispensatory. Worcester: 1805. V. 48; 52; 53
The Edinburgh New Dispensatory... Edinburgh: 1816. V. 48
Observations on the Distinguishing Symptoms of the Different Species of Pulmonary Consumption, the Catarrhal, the Apostematous, and the Tuberculous... Edinburgh: 1816. V. 48; 51; 53

DUNCAN, ARCHIBALD
A Correct Narrative of the Funeral of Horatio Lord Viscount Nelson... London: 1806. V. 51

DUNCAN, CHARLES
A Campaign with the Turks in Asia. London: 1855. V. 48; 50

DUNCAN, DAVID
Picasso's Picassos. New York: 1961. V. 49; 50

DUNCAN, DAVID DOUGLAS
War Without Heroes. New York: 1970. V. 47; 54

DUNCAN, DAVID JAMES
The River Why. San Francisco: 1983. V. 50; 52; 53

DUNCAN, G. S.
A Bibliography of Glass. London: 1960. V. 47; 49

DUNCAN, GEORGE
Present Day Golf. London: 1921. V. 49

DUNCAN, GEORGE, MRS.
Pre-Adamite Man; or, the Story of Our Old Planet and Its Inhabitants. London: 1860. V. 54

DUNCAN Grant. Richmond: 1923. V. 48

DUNCAN, H. O.
The World on Wheels 1926. Paris: 1926. V. 54

DUNCAN, HARRY
Doors of Perception: Essays in Book Typography. Austin: 1983. V. 47; 49; 52; 53; 54

DUNCAN, HENRY
The Young South Country Weaver; or, a Journey to Glasgow; a Tale for the Radicals. Dumfries: 1821. V. 53
The Young South Country Weaver; or, a Journey to Glasgow, a Tale for the Radicals. Edinburgh: 1821. V. 53

DUNCAN, ISABELLA
Geological Monsters of Pre-Adamite Times, As Restored at the Palace Gardens of Sydenham and Their Remains Preserved in Museums of London. London: 1867. V. 47

DUNCAN, ISADORA
The Art of the Dance. New York: 1928. V. 51

DUNCAN, J. GARROW
Corpus of Dated Palestinian Pottery Including Pottery of Gerar and Beth-Pelet dated and Arranged by Sir Flinders Petrie and Beads of Beth-Pelet... London: 1930. V. 49

DUNCAN, JAMES
The Natural History of British Butterflies. Edinburgh: 1835. V. 48; 50

DUNCAN, JAMES F.
The Personal Responsibility of the Insane. Dublin: 1865. V. 50

DUNCAN, JAMES M.
Fecundity, Fertility,, Sterility and Allied Topics. Edinburgh: 1866. V. 49

DUNCAN, JANE E.
A Summer Ride through Western Tibet. London: 1906. V. 53

DUNCAN, JOHN M.
Digest of Entail Cases in Which Deeds Entail Have Been Challenged on the Ground of Alleged Defects in the Prohibitory or Fencing Clauses; with the Clauses Founded On and the Judgments of the Court. Edinburgh: 1856. V. 51
Manual of Summary Procedure, Under the Act for the Amendment of the Law of Entail in Scotland. Edinburgh: 1858. V. 54
Travels through Part of the United States and Canada in 1818 and 1819. Glasgow: 1823. V. 49; 52

DUNCAN, JOHN SHUTE
Hints to the Bearers of Walking Sticks and Umbrellas. London: 1808. V. 48

DUNCAN, JONATHAN
The History of Russia from the Foundation of the Empire to the Close of the Hungarian War. London: 1854. V. 51

DUNCAN, LOUIS
Medical Men in the American Revolution. New York: 1970. V. 50; 52

DUNCAN, P. B.
Essays and Miscellanea. Oxford: 1840. V. 54

DUNCAN, P. M.
The British Fossil Corals. Second Series. London: 1866-72. V. 51; 52; 53; 54
A Monograph of the British Fossil Corals. Second Series. 1866-72. V. 49

DUNCAN, ROBERT
Achilles' Song. New York: 1969. V. 50
As Testimony: The Poem and the Scene. San Francisco: 1964. V. 47
A Book of Resemblances. New Haven: 1966. V. 47; 48; 54
The Cat and the Blackbird. San Francisco: 1967. V. 47; 51
Christmas Present, Christmas Presence!. Los Angeles: 1967. V. 47
The First Decade. Selected Poems 1940-1950. London: 1968. V. 53; 54
The Five Seasons. La Jolla: 1981. V. 51
From the Maginogion. 1963. V. 53
Heavenly City, Earthly City. Berkeley: 1947. V. 53
Letters. Highlands: 1958. V. 51; 54
Names of People. Los Angeles: 1968. V. 47; 48; 50
Notebook Poems: 1953. San Francisco. V. 47
Notebook Poems: 1953. San Francisco: 1991. V. 51; 52; 53
Of the War Passages 22-27. Berkeley: 1966. V. 54
A Paris Visit. 1985. V. 52; 54
A Paris Visit. New York: 1985. V. 53; 54
Roots and Branches. New York: 1964. V. 47
A Selection of 65 Drawings. 1970. V. 47; 48; 49
The Sweetness and Greatness of Dante's Divine Comedy, 1265-1965. San Francisco: 1965. V. 47
Tribunals. Passages 31-35. Los Angeles: 1970. V. 47; 48
The Truth and Life of Myth. New York: 1968. V. 47; 49
The Years As Catches. First Poems (1939-1946). Berkeley: 1966. V. 54

DUNCAN, RONALD
The Dull Ass's Hoof. London: 1940. V. 53

DUNCAN, SARA JEANNETTE
The Simple Adventures of a Memsahib. London: 1893. V. 50

DUNCAN, STANLEY
The Complete Wildfowler. London: 1911. V. 54

DUNCAN, THOMAS D.
Recollections of Thomas D. Duncan, a Confederate Soldier. Nashville: 1922. V. 49; 52; 54

DUNCAN, WILLIAM
The Elements of Logick. London: 1752. V. 47

DUNCAN-JONES, C. M.
The Book of Fairies. London: 1915. V. 50

DUNCANSON, ALEXANDER
Ketchiana; or the Punishment of Death by the Civil Law Proven to Be In Opposition to Enlightened Reason, and Growing Social and Political Policy. London: 1847. V. 54

DUNCKER, MAXIMILIAN WOLFGANG
The History of Antiquity. (with) The History of Greece. London: 1877-83. V. 48

DUNCKLEE, WALES & CO.
The Daily Advertiser Directory for the City of Detroit for the Year 1850. Detroit: 1850. V. 52

DUNCKLEY, HENRY
The Glory and the Shame of Britain. London: 1851. V. 50

DUNCOMBE, CHARLES
Doctor Charles Duncombe's Report Upon the Subject of Education, Made to the parlimanet of Upper Canada, 25th February, 1836. Toronto: 1836. V. 51

DUNCOMBE, JOHN
Collections Towards the History and Antiquities of the County of Hereford. Hereford: 1804-12. V. 48; 49
An Evening contemplation in a College. London: 1753. V. 48
The History and Antiquities of the Two Parishes of Reculver and Herne, in the County of Kent. London: 1784. V. 47

DUNCON, JOHN
The Returnes of Spiritual Comfort and Grief in a Devout Soul. London: 1648. V. 47
The Vertuous, Holy, Christian Life and Death of the Late Lady, Letice, Vi-Countess Falkland. London: 1653. V. 53

DUNCUM, BARBARA M.
The Development of Inhalation Anaesthesia with Special Refence to the Years 1846-1900. London: 1947. V. 49

DUNDAS, C.
Kilimanjaro and its People, a History of the Wachagga, Their Laws, Customs and legends with Some Account of the Mountain. London: 1924. V. 48

DUNDAS, HENRY
Scots Guards. London: 1921. V. 47

DUNDONALD, ARCHIBALD COCHRANE, 9TH EARL OF
The Present State of the Manufacture of Salt Explained... London: 1785. V. 48; 54

DUNDONALD, ARCHIBALD COCHRANE, 9TH EARL OF
A Treatise, Shewing the Intimate Connection that Subsists Between Agriculture and Chemistry. London: 1795. V. 50; 51

DUNDONALD, THOMAS COCHRANE, 10TH EARL OF
The Autobiography of a Seaman. London: 1860. V. 48; 49; 54
Narrative of Services in the Liberation of Chili, Peru and Brazil from Spanish and Portuguese Domination. London: 1859. V. 48

DUNGLISON, ROBLEY
A Dictionary of Medical Science: Containing a Concise Explanation of the Various Subjects and Terms of Physiology, Pathology, Hygiene, Therapeutics, Pharmacology, Obstetrics. London: 1854. V. 47
History of Medicine from the Earliest Ages to the Commencement of the Nineteenth Century. Philadelphia: 1872. V. 49; 50; 52
Human Physiology. Philadelphia: 1846. V. 52
Medical Lexicon. Philadelphia: 1845. V. 50
Medical Lexicon. Philadelphia: 1866. V. 48
Medical Lexicon. Philadelphia: 1874. V. 50; 52; 53
New Remedies. Philadelphia: 1846. V. 48
New Remedies. Philadelphia: 1856. V. 53

DUNGLISON, ROBLEY continued
New Remedies. Philadelphia: 1861. V. 48

DUNHAM, DOWS
El Kurru. Cambridge: 1950. V. 51
Naga-ed Der Stelae of the First Intermediate Period. Boston: 1937. V. 51

DUNHAM, KATHERINE
Katherine Dunham's Journey to Accompong. New York: 1946. V. 53

DUNIWAY, ABIGAIL SCOTT
Captain Gray's Company; or, Crossing the Plains and Living in Oregon. Portland: 1859. V. 48
David and Anna Matson. New York: 1876. V. 47; 50
Path Breaking, an Autobiographical History of the Equal Suffrage Movement in Pacific Coast States. Portland: 1914. V. 53

DUNKIN, JOHN
The History and Antiquities of Bicester, a Market Town in Oxfordshire... London: 1816. V. 49; 50

DUNKIN, ROBERT
The Impossible Island. 1923. V. 52
The Roedeer. A Monograph. 1987. V. 52

DUNKLE, JOHN J.
Prison Life During the Rebellion, Being a Brief Narrative of the Miseries and Suffering of Six Hundred Confederate Prisoners Sent From Fort Delaware to Morris Island to be Punished. Singer's Glen: 1869. V. 49

DUNLAP, DAVID A.
Shahwandahgooze Days. Toronto: 1925. V. 50

DUNLAP, GEORGE T.
The Players at the Chess. New York: 1927. V. 49

DUNLAP, HENRY
History of the Rise and Progress of the Arts of Design in the United States. New York: 1834. V. 53

DUNLAP, WILLIAM
The Father of an Only Child, a Comedy. New York: 1807. V. 52
A History of New York, for Schools in Two Volumes. New York: 1837. V. 47
A History of the American Theatre. New York: 1832. V. 47
History of the New Netherlands,, Province of New York. New York: 1839-40. V. 48
History of the Rise and Progres of the Arts of Design in the United States. New York: 1834. V. 47; 48; 49; 53
The Life of the Most Noble Arthur... New York: 1814. V. 51
Memoirs of George Fred. Cooke, Esq. late of the Theatre Royal, Covent Garden. London: 1813. V. 49; 51; 53
A Narrative of the Events Which Followed Bonaparte's Campaign in Russia to the Period of His Dethronement. Hartford: 1814. V. 49
Peter the Great; or, the Russian Mother: a Play. New York: 1814. V. 54
Thirty Years Ago; or the Memoirs of a Water Drinker. New York: 1836. V. 47

DUNLAVY, JOHN
Plain Evidences by Which the Nature and Character of the True Church of Christ May Be Known... Albany: 1834. V. 53

DUNLOP, ARCHIBALD
Dunlop of that Ilk: Memorabilia of the Families of Dunlop. Glasgow: 1898. V. 54

DUNLOP, DURHAM
The Philosophy of the Bath, or, Air and Water in Health and Disease.... 1868. V. 50
The Philosophy of the Bath; or, Air and Water in Health and Disease. Belfast: 1868. V. 52

DUNLOP, JAMES
Digest of the General Laws of the United States, with References to the Acts Repealed, Supplied, or Modified, and Notes of the Decisions and Dicta of the Supreme Court of the Union Upon Their Constructions. Philadelphia: 1856. V. 48

DUNLOP, JOHN
The History of Fiction... London: 1814. V. 51
The History of Fiction: Being a Critical Account of the Most Celebrated Prose Works of Fiction... London: 1816. V. 50

DUNLOP, JOHN C.
Memoirs of Spain during the Reigns of Philip IV and Charles II from 1621 to 1700. Edinburgh: 1834. V. 49; 53

DUNLOP, ROBERT
Ireland Under the Commonwealth. Manchester: 1913. V. 50

DUNLOP, ROBERT HENRY WALLACE
Service and Adventure with Khakee Ressalah, or, Meerut volunteer Horse, During the Mutinies of 1857-58. London: 1858. V. 50

DUNLOP, WILLIAM
Statistical Sketches of Upper Canada, for the Use of Emigrants: by a Backwoodsman. London: 1832. V. 53

DUNN, DOROTHY
American Indian Painting of the Southwest and Plains Areas. Albuquerque: 1968. V. 54

DUNN, HENRY
Guatimala, or, the Republic of Central America 1827-28. London: 1829. V. 50

DUNN, J. B.
Perilous Trails of Texas. Dallas: 1932. V. 54

DUNN, J. D.
Massacre Of the Mountains, a History of the Indian Wars in the Far West. New York: 1886. V. 49; 50; 53

DUNN, J. E.
Indian Territory, A Pre Commonwealth. Indianapolis: 1904. V. 47

DUNN, KATHERINE
3 Day Fox: a Tattoo. 1979. V. 54
Attic. New York: 1970. V. 49; 53
Geek Love. New York: 1989. V. 54
Mystery Girl's Circus and College of Conumdrum. Ames Lake/Portland: 1991. V. 53
Truck. 1971. V. 53
Truck. New York: 1971. V. 52; 54

DUNN, MATTHIAS
An Historical, Geological and Descriptive View of the Coal Trade of the North of England. Newcastle-upon-Tyne: 1844. V. 49
A Treatise On the Winning and Working of Collieries... Newcastle-upon-Tyne: 1848. V. 47; 49; 50; 54

DUNN, NATHAN
Ten Thousand Chinese Things. Philadelphia: 1839. V. 51

DUNN, P.
Report of a Discussion on Socialism Between Messrs. P. Dunn and C. Leckie, which took place in the Trades' Hall, Glasgow, on the Evening of the 20th and 21st of November, 1839. Paisley: 1839. V. 50

DUNN, ROBERT
The Shameless Diary of an Explorer. New York: 1907. V. 49

DUNN, THOMAS
Tables of Simple Interest, Computed Decimally... Glasgow: 1821. V. 50; 54

DUNNE, CHARLES
Rouge et Noir. London: 1823. V. 51

DUNNE, FINLEY PETER
Mr. Dooley In Peace and in War. Boston: 1914. V. 53

DUNNE, J. W.
An Experiment with Time. London: 1927. V. 49

DUNNETT, DOROTHY
Checkmate. London: 1975. V. 51
The Game of Kings. London: 1961. V. 51
Pawn in Frankincense. New York: 1969. V. 51
Queens' Play. London: 1964. V. 51

DUNNING, J. B.
Handbook of Avian Body Masses. London: 1993. V. 50

DUNNING, JOHN
Booked to Die. New York: 1992. V. 48; 50; 51; 52; 53; 54
The Bookman's Wake. New York: 1995. V. 54
The Dreamer. Huntington Beach: 1995. V. 54
Tune in Yesterday: the Ultimate Encyclopedia of Old-Time Radio, 1925-1976. Englewood Cliffs: 1976. V. 51; 53

DUNNING, RICHARD
A Letter Sent to Mr. James Shepheard, Whilst Prisoner in Newgate, Persuading Him to Repent to His Design to Murder the King. London: 1718. V. 52

DUNNINGTON, GEORGE
A History and Progress of the County of Marion, West Virginia. Fairmont: 1880. V. 53

DUNPHY, THOMAS
Remarkable Trials of All Countries... New York: 1867. V. 50

DUNRAVEN, EDWIN R. WINDHAM WYNDHAM-QUIN, 3RD EARL OF
Notes on Irish Architecture. London: 1875. V. 48

DUNSANY, EDWARD JOHN MORETON DRAX PLUNKETT
The Book of Wonder. 1912. V. 48
The Chronicles of Don Rodriguez. 1922. V. 48; 51
The Chronicles of Rodriguez. London & New York: 1922. V. 47; 48; 49; 50; 51
The Compromise of the King of Golden Isles. New York: 1924. V. 47; 48; 53
The Curse of the Wise Woman. London: 1933. V. 51
The Curse of the Wise Woman. New York: 1933. V. 48; 51
A Dreamer's Tales. 1910. V. 48
A Dreamer's Tales. London: 1910. V. 49
Fifty-One Tales. London: 1915. V. 48; 49
Five Plays. London: 1914. V. 51
The Fortress Unvanquishable, Save for Sacnoth. 1910. V. 48
The Fourth Book of Jorkens. Sauk City: 1948. V. 51
The Gods of Pegana. 1905. V. 48
His Fellow Men. London: 1952. V. 49; 50
Jorkens Has a Large Whiskey. 1940. V. 48
The King of Elfland's Daughter. New York: 1924. V. 48
Lord Adrian. Waltham St. Lawrence: 1933. V. 47; 48; 49
The Old Folk of the Centuries. 1930. V. 48
Patches of Sunlight. London: 1938. V. 48
Plays of Gods and Men. London: 1917. V. 49
Selections from the Writings. Churchtown, Dundrum: 1912. V. 48; 49; 54
The Sword of Welleran and Other Stories. London: 1907. V. 52; 54

DUNSANY, EDWARD JOHN MORETON DRAX PLUNKETT continued
The Sword of Welleran and Other Stories. 1908. V. 48
The Sword of Welleran and Other Stories. London: 1908. V. 54
Tales of Three Hemispheres. London: 1920. V. 49; 51
Tales of War. London: 1918. V. 47
Tales of Wonder. London: 1916. V. 50
Tales of Wonder. 1917. V. 48
Time and the Gods. 1906. V. 48
Time and the Gods. 1922. V. 48
Time and the Gods. London: 1922. V. 49
Unhappy Far-Off Things. London: 1919. V. 48; 51
Up In the Hills. London: 1935. V. 51
The Year. London: 1946. V. 54

DUNSFORD, MARTIN
Historical Memoirs of the Town and Parish of Tiverton in the County of Devon. Exeter: 1790. V. 47

DUNS JOANNES SCOTUS
Perutiles Quaestiones in IIII. Libros Sententiarum, & Quodlibetales, cum Collationibus; Atque Resolutionibus Fidelissime Recognitae, Expurgatae Adnotionibus Exornatae, ac Pristino Candori Restitutae a R. P. F. Paulino Berti Lucense... Venetiis: 1617. V. 48; 49
Scriptum Primum (-Quartum) Oxoniense Super Primo (-Quarto) Sententiarum. (with) Tabula Generalis ac Mare Magnum Scotice Subtilitatis Octo Sectionibus Universas... Venice: 1521-22. V. 50

DUNSTER, CHARLES
Considerations on Milton's Early Reading, and the Prima Stamina of His Paradise Lost. London: 1800. V. 54

DUNSTERVILLE, G. C. K.
Venezuelan Orchids. London: 1959-65. V. 51
Venezuelan Orchids. London: 1959-76. V. 48; 51; 54
Venezuelan Orchids. London: 1960-72. V. 51
Venezuelan Orchids Illustrated. London: 1959. V. 48; 51; 52

DUNSTERVILLE, L. C.
The Adventures of Dunsterforce. London: 1920. V. 50

DUNSTONE, N.
Mammals as Predators. London: 1993. V. 50

DUNTHORNE, GORDON
Catalogue Raisonne of the 18th and Early 19th Century Flower and Fruit Books and Prints. New York: 1970. V. 54
Flower and Fruit Prints of the 18th and Early 19th Centuries. Washington: 1938. V. 47; 48; 49; 50; 51; 52; 53; 54

DUNTON, JOHN
The Athenian Oracle. Being an Entire Collection of All the Valuable Questions and Answers in the Old Athenian Mercuries. London: 1728. V. 52
Athenian Sport: or, Two Thousand Paradoxes Merrily Argued, to Amuse and Divert the Age. London: 1707. V. 49
The Life and Errors of John Dunton, Citizen of London; with the Lives and Characters of More than a Thousand Contemporary Divines... London: 1818. V. 48
The Phenix; or, a Revival of Scarce and Valuable Pieces from the Remotest Antiquity Down to the Present Times. London: 1707-08. V. 53
The Visions of the Soul, Before It Comes Into the Body. London: 1692. V. 49
The Young-Students Library. London: 1692. V. 54

DUOCOUDRAY-HOLSTEIN, H. L. V.
Memoirs of Simon Bolivar, President Liberator of the Republic of Colombia... Boston: 1829. V. 48

DU PERRON, JACQUES
The Reply of the Most Illustrious Cardinall of Perron... Dovay: 1630. V. 49

DUPIN, CHARLES
The Commercial Power Of Great Britain... London: 1825. V. 49
Two Excursions to the Ports of England, Scotland and Ireland, in 1816, 1817 and 1818. London: 1819. V. 54
View of the History and Actual State of the Military Force of Great Britain. London: 1822. V. 48

DUPIN, JACQUES
Joan Miro: Life and Work. New York. V. 47; 48; 50; 54
Joan Miro: Life and Work. New York: 1962. V. 47; 50; 53
Miro. New York. V. 48; 50; 52
Miro Engraver. Volume I, 1928-1960. New York: 1989. V. 52; 53
Miro Engravings. New York: 1989. V. 50; 52

DUPIN, LOUIS ELLIES
A New Ecclesiastical History of the Sixteenth Century... Together with the Lives and Writings of the Eccliastical Authors... London: 1703-06. V. 47

DUPLAIX, GEORGES
Doudou Flies Away. New York: 1937. V. 51

DUPLESSY, F. S.
Des Vegetaux Resineux, Tant Indigenes Qu'Exotiques.. Paris: 1802. V. 49

DU PONCEAU, PETER S.
A Brief View of the Constitution of the United States, Addressed to the Law Academy of Philadelphia. Philadelphia: 1834. V. 53
A Dissertation on the Nature and Character of the Chinese System of Writing in a Letter to John Vaughan, Esq... Philadelphia: 1838. V. 51
A Dissertation On the Nature and Extent of the Jurisdiction of the Courts of the United States. Philadelphia: 1824. V. 48

DU PONT, SAMUEL F.
Official Dispatches and Letters of Rear Admiral Du Pont U.S. Navy 1846-48. Wilmington: 1883. V. 48; 49; 54
Samuel Francis Du Pont a Selection from His Civil War Letters. Ithaca: 1969. V. 52

DUPPA, A.
Elements of the Science of Botany, as Established by Linnaeus. London: 1809. V. 53; 54

DUPPA, RICHARD
A Brief Account of the Subversion of the Papal Governement, 1798. London: 1806. V. 48
A Journal of the Most Remarkable Occurrences that Took Place in Rome, Upon the Subversion of the Ecclesiastical Government in 1798. London: 1799. V. 49; 52
The Life and Literary Works of Michel Angelo Buonarroti. London: 1806. V. 50
Miscellaneous Observations and Opinions on the Continent. London: 1825. V. 47
Travels on the Continent, Sicily and the Lipari Islands. London: 1829. V. 49

DUPRE, WILLIAM
Lexicographia - Neologica Gallica. London: 1801. V. 50

DUPUIS, JOSEPH
Journal of a Residence in Ashantee, Comprising Notes and Researches Relative to the Gold Coast and the Interior of Western Africa... London: 1824. V. 50; 54

DUPUYTREN, GUILLAUME
On Lesions of the Vascular System, Diseases Of the Rectum, and Other Surgical Complaints. London: 1854. V. 48; 53

DUQUESNE, ABRAHAM
A New Voyage to the East Indies in the Years 1690 and 1691. London: 1696. V. 50

DURAN, ANTONIO
Cercos de Mocambique Defendidos por Don Estevan de Atayde... Madrid: 1633. V. 48

DURAND, EDWARD
Rifle, Rod and Spear in the East. 1911. V. 52

DURAND, JEAN B. L.
A Voyage to Senegal, or, Historical, Philosophical and Political Memoirs, Relative to the Discoveries, Establishments and Commerce of Europeans in the Atlantic Ocean, from Cape Blanco to... London: 1806. V. 47; 50; 51; 54

DURAND, JEAN NICOLAS LOUIS
Recueil et Parallele des Edifices de Tout Genre, Anciens et Modernes, Remarquables Par Leur Beaute... Paris: 1801. V. 51

DURANT, SAMUEL W.
History of St. Lawrence County, New York, 1749-1878. Philadelphia: 1878. V. 49

DURANT-DORT CARRIAGE CO.
Famous Blue Ribbon Line. Fling: 1890's. V. 47

DURANTE, CASTORE
Herbario Nuovo...Con Figure, Che Rappresentano le Vive Piante, Che Nascono in Tutta Europa... Venetia: 1636. V. 48
Herbario Nuovo...con Figure che Rappresentatno le vive Piante che Nascono in Tutta Europa & Nell Indie Orientali & Occidentali... Venice: 1718. V. 52

DURANTIUS, JACOBUS CASELLIUS
Variarvm Libri Dvo. Lvtetiae: 1582. V. 47

DURAS, CLAIRE DE DURFORT, DUCHESSE DE
Ourika. Paris: 1824. V. 47; 54
Ourika. Austin: 1977. V. 47; 48; 54

DURAS, MARGUERITE
Hiroshima Mon Amour. 1986. V. 54
Hiroshima mon Amour. Synopsis. New York: 1985. V. 47

DURBIN, JOHN P.
Observations in the East, Chiefly in Egypt, Palestine, Syria and Asia Minor. New York: 1847. V. 47

DURDJIEFF, G.
All and Everything - Ten Books, in Three Series... London: 1950. V. 50

DU REFUGE, EUSTACHE
Arcana Aulica: or Walsingham's Manual of Prudential Maxims for the States-Man and Courtier. London: 1694. V. 50
A Treatise of the Court or Instructions for Courtiers. London: 1622. V. 47

DURENCEAU, ANDRE
An Immoral Anthology Decorated By... 1933. V. 48

DURER, ALBERT
The Stations of the Cross. 1844. V. 49

DURET, THEODORE
Whistler et son Oeuvre. Paris: 1888. V. 52

DURFEE, JOB
Whatcheer, or Roger Williams in Banishment. Providence: 1832. V. 54

D'URFEY, THOMAS
Butler's Ghost; or, Hudibras. London: 1682. V. 47; 48; 49; 50
The Comical History of Don Quixote. London: 1729. V. 50
The Malecontent: a Satyr (in verse). London: 1684. V. 47
New Opera's With Comical Stories and Poems On Several Occasions... London: 1721. V. 48; 51; 52
A Pill to Purge State-Melancholy or a Collection of Excellent New Ballads. London: 1715. V. 49
The Progress of Honesty; or, a View of a Court and City. London: 1681. V. 47; 48; 50

D'URFEY, THOMAS continued
Songs Compleat, Pleasant and Divertive... London: 1719-20. V. 54
Squire Oldsapp. Or, the Night Adventurers. London: 1679. V. 48; 50
Stories, Moral and Comical. Viz. The Banquet of the Gods. Titus and Gissipus; or the Power of Friendship. London: 1707. V. 52
Wit and Mirth: or Pills to Purge Melancholy. V. 48
Wit and Mirth; or Pills to Purge Melancholy. New York: 1959. V. 53

DURHAM, EARL OF
Report on the Affairs of British North America... London: 1839. V. 53
(Sale) Catalogue of the Collection of Valuable Pictures... Newcastle: 1932. V. 47

DURHAM, MARY EDITH
The Burden of the Balkans. London: 1905. V. 49
The Struggle for Scutari (Turk, Slav and Albanian). London: 1914. V. 48

DURHAM, W. E.
Summer Holidays in the Alps, 1898-1914. 1916. V. 53
Summer Holidays in the Alps. 1898-1914. London: 1916. V. 52

DURHAM, W. H.
Coevolution: Genes, Culture and Human Diversity. Stanford: 1991. V. 50

DURIE, JOHN
Confutatio Responsionis Gulielmi Whitakeri... Paris: 1582. V. 49; 52

DU RIETZ, ROLF
Bibliotheca Polynesiana. A Catalogue of Some of the Books in the Polynesiana Collection Formed by the Late Bjarne Kroepelien and Now in the Oslo University Library. Oslo: 1969. V. 48

DURIEU, PAUL
Chinook Bible History. Kamloops: 1899. V. 53

DURLING, RICHARD
A Catalogue of Sixteenth Century Books in the National Library of Medicine. Bethesda: 1967. V. 47; 50; 51; 52; 54

DURNFORD, CHARLES
Reports of Cases Argued and Determined in the Court of King's Bench (1785-1800). Dublin: 1797-1800. V. 49

DURNING-LAWRENCE, EDWIN
Bacon is Shakespeare. New York: 1910. V. 52

DURRANT, VALENTINE
The Cheveley Novels. A Modern Minister. London: 1878. V. 54
The Cheveley Novels. Saul Weir. London: 1879. V. 54

DURRELL, LAWRENCE GEORGE
The Alexandria Quartet. London: 1957/58/58/60. V. 49; 50; 53
The Alexandria Quartet. 1962. V. 54
The Alexandria Quartet. London: 1962. V. 47; 48; 52; 53
The Alexandria Quartet. New York: 1962. V. 54
Ballade of Slow Decay. Bournemouth: 1932. V. 53
Balthazar. 1958. V. 54
Balthazar. London: 1958. V. 47; 50
Beccafico. 1963. V. 51
Beccafico. La Licorne. 1963. V. 52
Beccafico. Montpelier: 1963. V. 47; 48
Bitter Lemons. London: 1947. V. 47
Bitter Lemons. London: 1957. V. 47
The Black Book. Paris: 1938. V. 49; 53; 54
The Black Book. New York: 1960. V. 48; 51
The Black Book. 1973. V. 54
The Black Book. London: 1973. V. 52
Blue Thirst. Santa Barbara: 1975. V. 50
Cefalu. London: 1947. V. 47
Cities, Plains and People. 1946. V. 54
Cities, Plains and People. London: 1946. V. 47; 48; 49; 53
Clea. London: 1960. V. 47; 48; 51; 53
Clea. New York: 1960. V. 51
Collected Poems. London: 1980. V. 50; 51; 52
La Descente du Styx. Lamurene: 1964. V. 48; 50; 51
La Descente du Styx. Montpelier,: 1964. V. 47; 50; 53
Deus Loci. Ischia: 1950. V. 48; 50; 51; 52; 53
Down the Styx. Santa Barbara: 1971. V. 51
Henri Michaux, the Poet of Supreme Solipsism. Birmingham: 1990. V. 49; 50; 51; 53
In Arcadia: a Poem. London: 1968. V. 47; 49
An Irish Faustus: a Modern Morality in Nine Scenes. 1987. V. 48
Justine. New York: 1957. V. 52
Justine. Mountolive. Balthazar. Clea. London: 1957-60. V. 47; 51
Lifelines. Edinburgh: 1974. V. 51
Livia. London: 1978. V. 53
Mountolive. London: 1958. V. 48; 51; 54
Nemea; Song with Pinaforte Accompaniment. London: 1950. V. 53
Nothing Is Lost, Sweet Self. London: 1967. V. 47; 48; 53
Nurse and Mistress of the Crossroads: Arles and the Alyscamps. 1993. V. 53
Nurse and Mistress of the Crossroads: Arles and the Alyscamps. London: 1993. V. 51; 52
On Seeming to Presume. London: 1948. V. 47
On the Suchness of the Old Boy. 1972. V. 54
On the Suchness of the Old Boy. London: 1972. V. 47; 48; 50; 51; 53; 54

Panic Spring. New York: 1937. V. 51
The Parthenon. Rhodes: 1945 or 1946. V. 53
The Plant Magic Man. Santa Barbara: 1973. V. 49; 53
Pope Joan. London: 1954. V. 47; 48
A Private Country. London: 1943. V. 47; 49; 51; 54
Private Drafts. Nicosia: 1955. V. 47; 52; 53
Proems. London: 1938. V. 47
Prospero's Cell, a Guide to the Landscape and Manners of the Island of Corcya. 1945. V. 54
Prospero's Cell A Guide to the Landscape and Manners of the Island of Corcyra. London: 1945. V. 47
The Red Limbo Lingo. New York: 1971. V. 47; 48; 49; 51
Reflections on a Marine Venus. London: 1953. V. 50; 51; 54
Selected Poems. London: 1956. V. 50; 53
Spirit of Place: Letters and Essays on Travel. London: 1969. V. 52
Ten Poems. London: 1932. V. 53
The Tree of Idleness. London: 1955. V. 47; 48; 50; 54
Two Excursions into Reality. Berkley: 1947. V. 49; 53
Ulysses Comes Back. 1970. V. 51
Vega and Other Poems. London: 1973. V. 52
White Eagles Over Serbia. 1957. V. 54
White Eagles Over Serbia. London: 1957. V. 51
Zero and Asylum in the Snow: Two Excursions into Reality. Berkeley: 1946. V. 50

DURRENMATT, FRIEDRICH
Oedipus. 1989. V. 48; 49

DURST, HARRIET
Early Days in Texas. Oklahoma City. V. 50

DURUY, VICTOR
History of Greece, and of the Greek People, from the Earliest Times to the Roman Conquest. Boston: 1890. V. 51
History of Greece, and of the Greek People, from the Earliest Times to the Roman Conquest. London: 1898. V. 48
History of Rome and the Roman People From Its Origin to the Establishment of the Christian Empire. London: 1883-86. V. 48

DUSEJOUR, DIONIS
The Origin of the Graces. London: 1887. V. 53

DU SOLIER, W.
Ancient Mexican Costume. Mexico City: 1950. V. 54

DUSSAUCE, H.
Laboratory of Industrial Chemistry. Hudson: 1869. V. 53
A New and Complete Treatise on the Arts of Tanning, Currying, and Leather Dressing... Philadelphia: 1867. V. 52

DUSSELTHAL Abbey. Count von der Recke's Institution for Destitute Orphans and Jewish Proseltytes. London: 1836. V. 47

DUSTIN, FRED
The Custer Tragedy. Ann Arbor: 1965. V. 53; 54
Echoes from the Little Big Horn Fight, Reno's Positions in the Valley. Saginaw: 1953. V. 53

DUTCH and Quaker Colonies in America. Cambridge: 1903. V. 47

DUTENS, LOUIS
Bibliotheque Completee et Choisie, dans Toutes les Classes et dans la Plupart de Langues. London: 1800. V. 47
An Inquiry into the Origin of the Discoveries Attributed to the Moderns... London: 1769. V. 52

DUTHIE, WILLIAM
A Tramp's Wallet. London: 1858. V. 49; 54

DUTIES Payable By Law On All Goods, Wares and Merchandise, Imported Into the United States of America, After the Last Day of June, 1812. Washington?: 1812. V. 51

DUTOURD, JEAN
Papa Hemingway. Leige: 1961. V. 47

DUTT, R. PALME
The Labour International Handbook 1921... London: 1921. V. 50

DUTT, UDAY CHAND
The Materia Medica of the Hindus. Calcutta: 1922. V. 52

DUTTON, ANNE
A Treatise Concerning the New-Birth. Dalry: 1803. V. 50

DUTTON, BERTHA P.
Excavations at Tajumulco, Guatemala. Santa Fe: 1943. V. 50

DUTTON, CLARENCE E.
Atlas to Accompany the Monograph on the Tertiary History of the Grand Canon District. Washington: 1882. V. 50
Report On the Geology of the High Plateaus of Utah. With Atlas. Washington: 1880/1879. V. 51
Tertiary History of the Grand Canon District. Washington: 1882. V. 50; 51
Tertiary History of the Grand Canyon District. Salt Lake City: 1970's. V. 52
Tertiary History of the Grand Canyon Region. Santa Barbara/Salt Lake: 1977. V. 49
Topographical and Geographical Atlas of the District of the High Plateaus of Utah... New York: 1879. V. 51

DUTTON, E. A. T.
Kenya Mountain. London: 1929. V. 53

DUTTON, E. A. T. continued
Kenya Mountain. 1930. V. 53
Kenya Mountain. London: 1930. V. 50

DUTTON, FRANCIS
South Australia and its Mines, with Historical Sketch of the Colony, Under Its Several Administrations, to the Period of Captain Grey's Departure. London: 1846. V. 50

DUTTON, HELY
Statistical Survey of the County Clare. London: 1808. V. 48; 52

DUTTON, MATTHEW
The Office and Authority of a Justice of the Peace for Ireland... Dublin: 1727. V. 49

DUTTON, WARREN
The Present State of Literature; a Poem, Delivered in New Haven, at the Public Commencement of Yale-College, September 10, 1800. Hartford: 1800. V. 47; 50; 54

THE DUTY of Paying Custom and the Sinfulness of Importing Goods Clandestinely; and of Buying the Goods Thate Are so Imported. London: 1792. V. 53

DUVAL, CHARLES
With a Show through Southern Africa, and Personal Reminiscences of the Transvaal War. London: 1882. V. 48

DU VAL, CHARLES
With a Show Through Southern Africa and Personal Reminiscences of the Transvaal War. London: 1884. V. 50

DUVAL, EDWARD
The Secret of Alchemy, or the Grand Doctrine of Transmutation... Albany?: 1854. V. 53

DUVAL, ELIZABETH W.
T. E. Lawrence: a Bibliography. New York: 1938. V. 49; 51; 53

DUVAL in Newgate; or, the Traitor Jew. New York: 1860. V. 49

DUVAL, ISAAC H.
Texas Argonauts: Isaac H. Duval and the California Gold Rush. San Francisco: 1987. V. 47; 54
Texas Argonauts: Isaac H. Duval and the California Gold Rush. San Francisco: 1988. V. 47; 49

DUVAL, J. C.
Early Times in Texas. Austin: 1892. V. 50

DUVAL, JACQUES
Des Hermaphrodits, Accovchemens des Femmes, et Traitement Qui est Requis Pour Les Releuer en Sante, & Bien Eleuer Leurs Enfans. Rouen: 1612. V. 49; 50

DUVAL, PAUL
A. J. Casson. Toronto: 1975. V. 50
A. J. Casson, a Tribute. Toronto: 1980. V. 47; 54
Canadian Drawings and Prints. Toronto: 1952. V. 51
Canadian Drawings and Prints. Toronto: 1964. V. 53
Eric Freifeld. Toronto: 1977. V. 50
Four Decades: the Canadian Group of Paitners and Their Contemporaries - 1930-1970. Toronto: 1972. V. 47
Group of Seven Drawings. Toronto: 1965. V. 47; 51
The Tangled Garden. Scarborough: 1978. V. 54
The Tangled Garden: the Art of J. E. H. MacDonald. Toronto: 1978. V. 50
York Wilson. Ottawa: 1978. V. 50

DUVAR, J. H.
Annals of the Court of Oberon. 1895. V. 47; 51

DUVEEN, DENIS I.
A Bibliography of the Works of Antoine Laurent Lavoisier 1743-1794. London: 1954. V. 54
A Bibliography of the Works of Antoine Laurent Lavoisier, 1743-1794. London: 1954./1965. V. 54
A Bibliography of the Works of Antoine Laurent Lavoisier, 1743-1794. London: 1965. V. 50
Bibliotheca Alchemica et Chemica... London: 1965. V. 49

DUVOISIN, ROGER
Donkey, Donkey, the Troubles of a Silly Little Donkey. Racine: 1933. V. 49; 53
The Happy Hunter. New York: 1961. V. 52
The House of Four Seasons. New York: 1956. V. 49
Lonely Veronica. New York: 1963. V. 51; 54

DUYCKINCK, EVERT A.
Cyclopedia of American Literature. New York: 1856. V. 48
History of the War for the Union. New York: 1861. V. 49; 54
History of the War for the Union: Civil, Military and Naval. New York: 1862-65. V. 54
Memorial of John Allan. New York: 1864. V. 52; 54
National Portrait Gallery of Eminent Americans. New York: 1862. V. 47; 52
National Portrait Gallery of Eminent Americans. New York: 1863. V. 53

DUYCKINCK, WHITEHEAD CORNELL
The Duyckinck and Allied Families. New York: 1908. V. 47; 49; 51

DWIGGINS, W. A.
22 Printers' Marks and Seals. New York: 1929. V. 48; 50
The Glistening Hill. Athalinthia III: 1950. V. 52
Prelude to Eden: a Drama for Marionettes. Hingham: 1956. V. 54
Towards a Reform of the Paper Currency Particularly in Point of Its Design. New York: 1932. V. 47

DWIGHT, E. W.
Memoir of Henry Obookiah, a Native of the Sandwich islands, Who Died at Cornwall, Connecticut, Feb. 17, 1818 aged 26. New York: 1830's. V. 52

DWIGHT, JAMES
Lawn-Tennis. Boston: 1886. V. 50; 53

DWIGHT, SERENO EDWARDS
The Hebrew Wife; or the Law of Marriage, Examined in Relation to the Lawfulness of Polygamy... Glasgow: 1837. V. 50; 51; 53

DWIGHT, THEODORE
The Northern Traveller, and Northern Tour; With the Routes to the Springs, Niagara, and Quebec and the Coal Mines of Pennsylvania... New York: 1830. V. 47
An Oration Spoken Before "The Connecticut Society, for the Promotion of Freedom and the Relief of persons Unlawfully Holden in Bondage"... Hartford: 1794. V. 49
Travels in England and New York... New Haven: 1821-22. V. 47

DWIGHT, THOMAS
The Intracranial Circulation. Cambridge: 1867. V. 47; 48; 53

DWIGHT, TIMOTHY
The Conquest of Canaan. Hartford: 1785. V. 49; 50
Greenfield Hill: a Poem in Seven Parts. New York: 1794. V. 49
Greenfield Hill: a Poem, in Seven Parts. (with) *The Triumph of Infidelity: a Poem.* New York: 1794/88. V. 52
Travels: In New England and New York. New Haven: 1821-22. V. 47; 48
Travels in New England and New York... London: 1823. V. 47; 48; 51

DWINELLE, JOHN W.
The Colonial History...San Francisco... San Francisco: 1866. V. 52
The Colonial History...San Francisco. San Diego: 1924. V. 52

D'WOLF, JOHN
A Voyage to the South Pacific and a Journey through Siberia More Than Half a Century Ago. Bristol: 1983. V. 53

DWYER, CHARLES
The Anglo-Gallic Grammar. Cork: 1761. V. 47

DWYER, CHARLES P.
The Economic Cottage Builder... Buffalo: 1855. V. 51
The Economy of Church, Parsonage and School Architecture, Adapted to Small Societies and Rural Districts. Buffalo: 1856. V. 52

DWYER, P. W.
The Shield of the United Kingdom of Great Britain and Ireland. London: 1803. V. 52

DYCE, ALEXANDER
Dyce Collection. A Catalogue of the Printed Books and Manuscripts Bequeathed by the Reverend Alexander Dyce. 1875. V. 51
Strictures on Mr. Collier's New Edition of Shakespeare. London: 1859. V. 51

DYCHE, THOMAS
A New General English Dictionary... London: 1737. V. 54
A New General English Dictionary... London: 1744. V. 52
A New General English Dictionary... London: 1754. V. 53

DYCK, PAUL
Brule...The Sioux People of the Rosebud. Flagstaff: 1971. V. 50; 51

DYCKMAN, JACOB
An Inaugural Dissertation on the Pathology of the Human Fluids. New York: 1814. V. 47; 48

DYE, DANIEL SHEETS
A Grammar of Chinese Lattice. Cambridge: 1937. V. 53

DYER, D. B., MRS.
Fort Reno or Picturesque, Cheyenne and Arapahoe Army Life, Before the Opening of Oklahoma. New York: 1896. V. 53

DYER, FRANK LEWIS
Edison His Life and Inventions. New York: 1928. V. 54

DYER, FREDERICK HENRY
A Compendium of the War of the Rebellion. New York: 1959. V. 49; 51

DYER, G.
A Restoration of the Ancient Modes of Bestowing Names on the Rivers, Hills, Vallies, Plains and Settlements of Britain... Exeter: 1805. V. 49

DYER, JOHN
The Fleece: a Poem. London: 1757. V. 48; 49
Grongar Hill. Hackney: 1982. V. 48
Poems: Grongar Hill, The Ruins of rome, The Fleece. London: 1761. V. 51; 52
Poems...I. Grongar Hill. II. The Ruins of Rome. III. The Fleece. London: 1770. V. 52
The Ruins of Rome. London: 1740. V. 48; 54

DYER, JOHN L.
The Snow-Shoe Itinerant. An Autobiography. Cincinnati: 1890. V. 47

DYER, JOHN PERCY
Fightin' Joe Wheeler. 1941. V. 49

DYER SADDLERY CO.
1909 Illustrated Catalogue and Price List of Harness and Strap Work... Milwaukee. V. 53

DYER, T. F. THISELTON
Folk-Lore of Women Illustrated by Legendary and Traditional Tales, Folk-Rhymes, Proverbial Sayings, Supersittions, Etc. London: 1905. V. 50

DYER, T. F. THISTLETON
The Ghost World. London: 1893. V. 49

DYER, THOMAS
Pompeii Photographed. The Ruins of Pompeii. London: 1867. V. 51

DYER, WILLIAM
Chri(st's) Famous Ti(tles) and a Believer'(s) Golden Ch(ain) Handled in Divers Sermons... Glasgow: 1675. V. 53

DYER, WILLIAM H.
The Questions of the Irish Church Calmly Considered. London: 1868. V. 54

DYHRENFURTH, G. O.
To the Third Pole. The History of the High Himalaya. London: 1955. V. 53; 54

DYK, WALTER
Son of Old Man Hat. New York: 1938. V. 50

DYKE, THOMAS
All Round Sport with Fish, Fur, Feather, Also Adventures on the Road, in the Hunting and Cricket Fields, and Over Yachting Courses, Links and Curling Ponds. London: 1887. V. 47

DYKES, FRENCHEVILLE LAWSON BALLANTINE
Isel Church in the Years 1499 and 1864. Cockermouth: 1864. V. 50

DYKES, J. C.
Billy the Kid, the Bibliography of a Legend. Albuquerque: 1952. V. 49; 50; 53; 54

DYKES, JEFF
Fifty Great Western Illustrators: a Bibliographic Check-List. Flagstaff: 1975. V. 49
Fifty Great Western Illustrators: a Bibliographic Check-List. Northland: 1975. V. 48; 49; 50; 51; 54

DYKES, OSWALD
The Royal Marriage. King Lemuel's Lesson of 1. Chasity. 2. Temperance. 3. Clarity. 4. Justice. 5. Education. 6. Industry. 7. Frugality. 8. Religion. 9. Marriage &c.... London: 1722. V. 51; 52

DYKES, W. R.
The Genus Iris. Cambridge: 1913. V. 48; 50; 51; 52; 54
Notes on Tulip Species. London: 1930. V. 47

DYMOCK, CRESSEY
An Invention of Engines of Motion Lately Brought to Perfection. London: 1651. V. 52

DYMOND, EDITH
Eight Evenings at School. London: 1825. V. 49

DYMOND, JONATHAN
An Enquiry into the Accordancy of War with the Principles of Christianity and an Examination of the Philosophical Reasoning by Which It is Defended. Exeter: 1824. V. 53

DYSON, ANTHONY
Pictures to Print. The Nineteenth Century Engraving Trade. London: 1984. V. 47; 48; 50; 52; 53

E

E., B.
A New Dictionary of the Terms Ancient and Modern of the Canting Crew, in Its Several Tribes of Gypsies, Beggards, Thieves, Cheats, &c. London: 1699?. V. 52

THE E. Of Shaftsbury's Expedient for Settling the Nation. Discoursed with His Majesty in the House of Peers, at Oxford,, Mar. 24th, 1680/1. London: 1681. V. 53

EACHARD, JOHN
Mr. Hobb's State of Nature Considered; in a Dialouge Between Philautus and Timothy. London: 1672. V. 51; 53

EACKER, GEORGE I.
Observations on the National Character of the Americans: an Oration. Delivered Before the Tammany Society on the 12th of May, 1798. New York: 1798. V. 52

EADMER
Historiae Novorum, Sive Sui Saeculi Libri VI. London: 1623. V. 47; 50; 53

EADON, JOHN
The Arithmetician's Guide; Being a New Improved and Compendious System of Practical Arithmetic. Sheffield: 1766. V. 49; 52

EADS, JAMES BUCHANAN
Illinois and St. Louis Bridge Company. Report of the Chief Engineer. October 1870. St. Louis: 1870. V. 51
Illinois and St. Louis Bridge Company. Report of the Engineer-in-Chief of the Illinois and St. Louis Bridge Company. (with) Mathematical Investigations and Computations for the Construction of the Illinois and St. Louis Bridge. St. Louis: 1868. V. 51

EAGER, SAMUEL W.
An Outline History of Orange County...Together with Local Traditions and Short Biographical Sketches of Early Settlers, etc. Newburgh: 1846-47. V. 47

EAGLE, DALLAS CHIEF
Winter Count. Colorado Springs: 1967. V. 50
Winter Count. 1969. V. 54

EAGLES, JOHN
The Journal of Llewellin Penrose, a Seaman. London: 1815. V. 51

EAGLETON, WELLS P.
Brain Abscess. Its Surgical Pathology and Operative Technic. New York: 1922. V. 54

EALES, N. B.
The Cole Library of Early Medicine and Zoology. 1969/75. V. 50

EAMES, WILBERFORCE
Americana Collection of Herschel v. Jones. A Check-list (1473-1926). New York: 1964. V. 50
John Eliot and the Indians 1652-1657; Being Letters Addressed to Rev. Jonathan Hanmer of Barnstaple, England. New York: 1915. V. 50

EARBERY, MATHIAS
An Historical Account of the Advantages that Have Accru'd to England... London: 1722. V. 51; 52

EARDLEY, F. S.
Horsted Keynes, Sussex. The Church and Parish of St. Giles. London: 1939. V. 49

EARDLEY, WILMOT S.
Our Journal in the Pacific. London: 1873. V. 47

EARDLEY-WILMOT, JOHN E.
Reminiscences of the Late Thomas Assheton Smith, or the Pursuits of an English Country Gentleman. London: 1860. V. 47; 50

EARHART, AMELIA
20 Hours. 40 Minutes: our Flight in the Friendship. New York: 1928. V. 52
The Fun Of It. New York: 1932. V. 47; 48; 54
Last Flight. New York: 1937. V. 53

EARHART, JOHN F.
The Color Printer. Cincinnati: 1892. V. 50

EARL, GEORGE WINDSOR
The Eastern Seas, or Voyage and Adventures in the Indian Archipelago in 1832-33-34... London: 1837. V. 47; 49

EARLE, ALICE MORSE
China Collecting in America. New York: 1892. V. 47
In Old Narragansett, Romances and Realities. New York: 1898. V. 49
Two Centuries of Costume in America. New York: 1903. V. 53

EARLE, AUGUSTUS
A Narrative of a Nine Month's Residence in New Zealand, in 1827... London: 1832. V. 47; 48; 51; 54

EARLE, C. W.
Pot-pourri from a Surrey Garden. More Pot-pourri. A Third Pot-pourri. Pot-pourri Mixed by Two. London: 1897-1914. V. 51

EARLE, CYRIL
The Earle Collection of Early Staffordshire Pottery Illustrating over 700 Different Pieces. London: 1915. V. 47; 51

EARLE, JOHN
Micro-Cosmographie or, a Piece of the World Discovered in Essayes and Characters. Waltham St. Lawrence: 1928. V. 47

EARLE, THOMAS
The Life, Travels and Opinions of Benjamin Lundy... Philadelphia: 1847. V. 48; 49

EARLE, WILLIAM
Obi; or, the History of Threefingered Jack. Worcester: 1804. V. 50

EARLY History of Atlantic County, New Jersey. Kutztown: 1914. V. 47
EARLY History of Atlantic County, New Jersey. Kutztown: 1915. V. 49; 51

EARLY, JUBAL ANDERSON
Lieutenant General Jubal Anderson Early, C.S.A. Autobiographical Sketch and Narrative of the War Between the States. Philadelphia & London: 1912. V. 48; 49; 50
A Memoir of the Last Year of the War for Independence in the Confederate States of America, Containing an Account of the Operations of His Commands in the Years 1864 and 1865. Toronto: 1866. V. 50

EARLY Korean Typography. 1982. V. 49

EARLY Treatises on the Stage viz Northbrooke's Treatise Against Dicing, Dancing, Plays and Interludes, Etc. London: 1853. V. 52

EARNSHAW, THOMAS
Longitude: an Appeal to the Public: Stating Mr. Thomas Earnshaw's Claim to the Original Invention. 1986. V. 53

EARP, GEORGE BUTLER
The Gold Colonies of Australia... London: 1852. V. 48
New Zealand: Its Emigration and Gold Fields. London: 1853. V. 53

EARP, WYATT
Wyatt Earp. Sierra Vista: 1981. V. 48

EARWAKER, J. P.
East Cheshire, Past and Present, or a History of the Hundred of Macclesfield... London: 1877. V. 52
East Cheshire: Past and Present: or a History of the Hundred of Macclesfield, in the County Palatine of Chester. London: 1877/80. V. 49
East Cheshire: Past and Present; or, a History of the Hundred of Macclesfield, in the County Palatine of Chester, from Original Records. London: 1880. V. 48

EARWAKER, J. P. continued
Lancashire Pedigree Case; or a History of the Various Trials for the Recovery of the Harrison Estates from 1873 to 1886... Warrington: 1887. V. 53
Local Gleanings. Manchester: 1880. V. 48

EASBY, ELIZABETH KENNEDY
Before Cortes: Sculpture of Middle America. New York: 1970. V. 49; 50

EASDALE, JOAN ADENEY
Amber Innocent. London: 1939. V. 51
A Collection of Poems. London: 1931. V. 51

EASON, E. H.
Centipedes of the British Isles. London: 1964. V. 47

EAST Cape May Beach, Cape May City, New Jersey. Philadelphia. V. 47

EAST, HENRY
Humanity Towards the Inerior Animals. London: 1857. V. 54

EAST INDIA CO.
At a Committee of Accounts, 15th February, 1793...Estimate of the Company's Affairs in India, and in Europe, with a View to Ascertain What Will Be the Probable Surplus Resulting from the Whole in Times of Profound Peace. 1793. V. 49
Report of the Committee of Warehouses, on a Memorial from the Manufacturers of Gunpowder and of Other Commodities Made from Saltpetre, Presented to the Right Honourable the Lords of the Committee of Privy Council for Trade. 1793. V. 48; 52
Rules and Regulations for the Establishment and Management of a Fund to Be Provided for the Benefit of the Commodores, Writers, and Laborers, in the Service of the United Company of Merchants of England Trading to the East Indies. London: 1816. V. 54
Seasonable Considerations Relating to the Smugglers. London: 1746. V. 53

THE EAST India Sketch-Book: Comprising An Account of the Present State of Society in Calcutta, Bombay, &c. London: 1832. V. 49

EAST RIDING ANTIQUARIAN SOCIETY
Transactions. London: 1893-1920. V. 50; 52

THE EAST-INDIA Register and Directory for 1807. London: 1807. V. 49

EASTLAKE, CHARLES L.
Contributions to the Literature of the Fine Arts. London: 1848. V. 48; 51
Hints On Household Taste. London: 1868. V. 50; 52
Hints on Household Taste. London: 1869. V. 51
Hints on Household Taste. Boston: 1872. V. 50; 52
Hints on Household Taste... London: 1872. V. 51; 52
Hints on Household Taste. Boston: 1874. V. 52
Hints on Household Taste in Furniture, Upholstery. Boston: 1877. V. 53
A History of the Gothic Revival. London: 1872. V. 47; 52; 53
Materials for a History of Oil Painting. London: 1847. V. 52; 54

EASTLAKE, ELIZABETH RIGBY, LADY
A Residence on the Shores of the Baltic. London: 1841. V. 48; 50; 53

EASTLAKE, WILLIAM
The Bronc People. New York: 1958. V. 50; 51; 53; 54
Castle Keep. New York: 1965. V. 54
Dancers in the Scalp House. New York: 1975. V. 51
Go In Beauty. New York: 1956. V. 50
Go in Beauty. London: 1957. V. 52
Go In Beauty. The Bronc People. Portrait of an Artist with 26 Horses. New York: 1956-63. V. 49; 53
Portrait of an Artist with 26 Horses. New York: 1963. V. 50; 51; 53

EASTMAN, CHARLES A.
Indian Boyhood. New York: 1902. V. 50
Indian Scout Talks. Boston: 1914. V. 50
Old Indian Days. New York: 1907. V. 47
Old Indian Days. New York: 1910. V. 50

EASTMAN, GEORGE
Chronicles of an African Trip. 1927. V. 48; 52
Chronicles of an African Trip. Rochester: 1927. V. 50

EASTMAN, LUKE
Masonick Melodies a Choice Selection of the Most Approved Masonick Songs, Duets, Glees, etc... Boston: 1818. V. 52

EASTMAN, MARY
The American Aboriginal Portfolio. Philadelphia: 1853. V. 51; 53; 54
The American Aboriginal Portfolio. Philadelphia: 1953. V. 47
Chicora and Other Regions of the Conquerors and Conquered. Philadelphia: 1854. V. 47
Dahcotah; or Life and Legends of the Sioux Around Fort Snelling. New York: 1849. V. 47; 52
Jenny Lee of Gettysburg. Philadelphia: 1864. V. 49

EASTON, CHARLES
Life in a Whaler; or, Perils and Adventures in the Tropical Seas. London: 1860. V. 47

EASTON, J.
The Salisbury Guide; Giving an Account of the Antiquities of Old Sarum and of the Ancient and Present State of the City of New Sarum. Salisbury: 1777. V. 52

EASTON, JAMES
Human Longevity. Salisbury: 1799. V. 53

EASTON, JOHN
A Narrative of the Causes Which Led to Philip's Indian War of 1675 and 1676. Albany: 1858. V. 51

An Unfrequented Highway through Sikkim and Tibet to Chumolaori. London: 1928. V. 54

EASTON, PHOEBE
Marbling: a History and a Bibliography. Los Angeles: 1983. V. 49

AN EASY Introduction to the Game of Chess: Containing One Hundred Examples of Games... London: 1806. V. 52

EAT Book. London: 1990. V. 49

EATES, MARGOT
Paul Nash - Paintings, Drawings and Illustrations. London: 1948. V. 51; 52; 54
Paul Nash. The Master of the Image, 1889-1946. New York: 1973. V. 50

EATON, ALLEN H.
Handicrafts of the Southern Highlands, with an Account of the Rural Handicraft Movement in the United States and Suggestions for the Wider Use of Handicrafts in Adult Education and in Recreation. New York: 1937. V. 52; 53

EATON, CHARLOTTE ANNE
Continental Adventures. London: 1826. V. 47; 49; 50

EATON, DANIEL CADY
The Ferns of North America. Salem and Boston: 1879-80. V. 53
The Ferns of North America. Boston: 1893. V. 51

EATON, EDWARD BAILEY
Original Photographs Taken on the Battlefields During the Civil War of the United States by Matthew Brady and Alexander Gardner. Hartford: 1907. V. 53

EATON, ELON HOWARD
Birds of New York. Albany: 1910. V. 52; 54
Birds of New York. Albany: 1910-14. V. 52; 54

EATON, J. C.
70 Years Observations of a Trout Fisherman. Richmond: 1937. V. 51; 52; 54

EATON, J. M.
A Treatise on the Art of Breeding and Managing Tame, Domesticated, Foreign and Fancy Pigeons. London: 1858. V. 49

EATON, L. K.
Landscape Artist in America: the Life and Work... Chicago: 1964. V. 50; 54

EATON, SAMUEL J. M.
Petroleum: a History of the Oil Region of Venango County, Pennsylvania. Its Resources, Mode of Development and Value. Philadelphia: 1866. V. 48

EATON, SEYMOUR
More About Teddy B. and Teddy G., the Roosevelt Bears. Philadelphia: 1907. V. 53
Teddy-B and Teddy-G: The Bear Detectives. New York: 1909. V. 49

EATON, WALTER PRICHARD
Newark: a Series of Engravings on Wood. Newark: 1917. V. 48; 51
The Theatre Guild, The First Ten Years. New York: 1929. V. 48

EAVENSON, HOWARD N.
The First Century and a Quarter of American Coal Industry. Pittsburgh: 1942. V. 53

EBAN, ABBA
My People: The Story of the Jews. New York: 1968. V. 47

EBEL, JOHANN GOTTFRIED
An Atlas to Ebel's Traveller's Guide through Switzerland.... London: 1819. V. 52
Manuel du Voyageur en Suisse. Zurich: 1810-11. V. 54

EBENDORFER, THOMAS
Sermones Dominicales Super Epistolas Pauli. Strassburg: 1478. V. 53

EBERHARDT, WALTER
The Jig-Saw Puzzle Murder. New York: 1933. V. 50

EBERHART, MIGNON G.
Wolf in Man's Clothing. New York: 1942. V. 53

EBERHART, RICHARD
A Bravery of Earth. 1930. V. 49; 53
A Bravery of Earth. London: 1930. V. 48
A Bravery of Earth. New York: 1930. V. 48
Brotherhood of Men. 1949. V. 51; 53; 54
Burr Oaks. London: 1947. V. 52; 54
Collected Verse Plays. Chapel Hill: 1961. V. 48
Collected Verse Plays. Chapel Hill: 1962. V. 47; 54
Fields of Grace. New York: 1972. V. 47; 48
Great Praises. New York: 1957. V. 54
An Herb Basket. Cummington: 1950. V. 47; 48; 50; 51
New Hampshire Nine Poems. Roslindale: 1980. V. 51
Selected Poems. New York: 1951. V. 47; 48
Survivors. Brockport: 1979. V. 47; 51
Ten Poems. 1984. V. 49; 51
Thirty One Sonnets. New York: 1967. V. 47; 48; 49; 51; 54
A World View. 1941. V. 48

EBERLE, JOHN
Notes of Lectures on the Theory and Practice of Medicine: Delivered in the Jefferson Medical College. Philadelphia: 1827. V. 54

EBERLEIN, HAROLD
Historic Houses of George-Town and Washington City. Richmond: 1958. V. 51
The Practical Book of Garden Structure and Design. Philadelphia: 1937. V. 51

EBERS, G.
Egypt: Descriptive, Historical and Picturesque. New York: 1880/83. V. 48

EBERS, GEORGE
Arachne. London: 1898. V. 47

EBERS, JOHN
Seven Years of the King's Theatre. London: 1828. V. 47
Seven Years of the King's Theatre. Philadelphia: 1828. V. 48; 51

EBERSTADT, EDWARD, & SONS
Americana Catalogue. A Collection of Thirty-Odd Catalogues of Americana Issued by This Firm from 1935-1956. New York: 1965. V. 47; 50; 54
The Annotated Eberstadt Catalogs of Americana in Four Volumes Including Index Numbers 103 to 138,. New York: 1965. V. 47
Eberstadt Catalogs of Americana. New York: 1965. V. 53
Texas. Being a Collection of Rare and Important Works and Manuscripts Relating to the Lone Star State. Catalog No. 162. New York: 1963. V. 54

EBORACUM: or, the History and Antiquities of the City of York, From Its Origin to This Time. York: 1788. V. 51

EBY, EZRA E.
A Biographical History of the Eby Family. Berlin: 1889. V. 48

EBY, FREDERICK
The Development of Education in Texas. New York: 1925. V. 47
Education Materials. Austin: 1918. V. 49

EBY, HENRY H.
Observations Of an Illinois Boy in Battle, Camp and Prisons, 1861-1865. Mendota: 1910. V. 49

ECCENTRIC Biography; or, Memoirs of Remarkable Female Characters, Ancient and Modern. Worcester: 1804. V. 51

ECCENTRICITIES of Literature and Life, or the Recreative Magazine. Boston: 1822. V. 50

ECCLES, JOHN CAREW
The Neurophysiological Basis of Mind. The Principles of Neurophysiology. Oxford: 1960. V. 49

THE ECCLESIASTICAL and Architectural Topography of England. Berkshire, Buckinghamshire: 1849. V. 49

THE ECCLESIOLOGIST. Cambridge: 1842-44. V. 49

ECCLESTON, ROBERT
Overland to California and the Southwestern Trail, 1849. Diary of Robert Eccleston. Berkeley & Los Angeles: 1950. V. 49; 50

ECHARD, LAURENCE
An Exact Description of Ireland... London: 1691. V. 53
A General Ecclesiastical History from the Nativity of Our Blessed Saviour to the First Establishment of Christianity...Under Constantine...to Which is Added, a larage Chronological Table. London: 1702. V. 49
The History of England. London: 1720. V. 51
A Most Compleat Compendium of Geography... London: 1691. V. 47
The Roman History. London: 1713. V. 51

ECHEVERRIA, MANUEL GONZALEZ
On Epilepsy: Anatomico-Pathological and Clinical Notes. New York: 1870. V. 53

THE ECHO and Other Poems. New York: 1807. V. 48; 49; 53; 54

L'ECHO des Bardes ou Le Menestrel. Dedie Aux Dames. Paris: 1821. V. 49; 52

ECHOES from the Oxford Magazine - Being Reprints of Seven Years. Oxford and London: 1890. V. 47

THE ECHOES of the Lands and Mountains: or Wonderful Things in the Lake District... London: 1870. V. 50; 52

ECHOLS, SAMUEL ANTHONY
Proceedings of the State Agricultural Society, with the Actions of the Farmers' Convention and the Agricultural and Manufacturing Association of Georgia, In Session in Macon, Georgia, Dec. 9th, 10th, and 11th, 1868. Atlanta: 1869. V. 53

ECK, C.
Traite de Construction en Poteries et fer, a l'Usages des Batimens Civils, Industriels et Militaires. Paris: 1836. V. 52
Traite de l'Application du fer, de la Fonte et de la Tole Dans les Constructions Civiles, Industrielles et Militaires... Paris: 1841. V. 52

ECKE, GUSTAV
Chinese Painting in Hawaii. Honolulu: 1965. V. 48

ECKEL, ALEXANDER
History of the Fourth Tennessee Cavalry U.S.A. War of the Rebellion 1861-1865. Knoxville: 1929. C. 54

ECKEL, JOHN C.
The First Editions of the Writings of Charles Dickens and Their Values. London: 1913. V. 48; 49; 50
The First Editions of the Writings of Charles Dickens. Their Points and Values. New York & London: 1932. V. 48; 49
Prime Pickwick in Parts. New York & London: 1928. V. 52; 53; 54

ECKENRODE, HAMILTON JAMES
James Longstreet, Lee's War Horse. Chapel Hill: 1936. V. 48

ECKER, ALEXANDER
The Cerebral Convolutions of Man, Represented According to Original Observations... New York: 1873. V. 48; 54

ECKFELDT, JACOB R.
A Manual of Gold and Silver Coins of All Nations, Struck within the Past Quarter Century... Philadelphia: 1842. V. 49; 51

ECKHARDT, GEORGE H.
Electronic Television. Chicago: 1936. V. 50

ECKSTEIN, G. F.
A Practical Treatise on Chimneys; with a Few Remarks on Stoves, the Consumption of Smoke and Coal, Ventilation, &c. London: 1852. V. 53

ECO, UMBERTO
The Aesthetics of Chaosmos: the Middle Ages of James Joyce. Tulsa: 1982. V. 52
The Bomb and the General. San Diego: 1989. V. 49
Foucault's Pendulum. New York: 1989. V. 50; 53
Foucault's Pendulum. San Diego: 1989. V. 50
The Island of the Day Before. New York: 1995. V. 54
The Name of the Rose. New York: 1983. V. 49; 50; 51
The Name of The Rose. San Diego: 1983. V. 48
The Picture History of Inventions. New York: 1962. V. 49
Postscript to the Name of the Rose. New York: 1984. V. 49
Postscript to the Name of the Rose. San Diego: 1984. V. 50
A Theory of Semiotics. Bloomington: 1976. V. 54

ECONOMOU, GEORGE
Poems for Self Therapy. Mt. Horeb: 1972. V. 54

ECTON, JOHN
A State of the Proceedings of the Corporation of the Governors of the Bounty of Queen Anne, for the Augmentation of the Maintenance of the Poor Clergy, Giving a Particular Account of Their Constitution, Benefactions and Augmentations, with directions to .. 1725. V. 47
Thesaurus Rerum Ecclesiasticarum. London: 1754. V. 47

EDDA SAEMUNDAR
Icelandic Poetry, or the Edda of Saemund Translated into English Verse. Bristol: 1797. V. 47

EDDINGTON, ARTHUR S.
Fundamental Theory. Cambridge: 1946. V. 53
The Internal Constitution of the Stars. London: 1926. V. 48
The Mathematical Theory of Relativity. 1937. V. 48
Relativity Theory of Protons and Electrons. Cambridge: 1936. V. 48
Report on the Relativity Theory of Gravitation. London: 1918. V. 48
Stellar Movements and the Structure of the Universe. London: 1914. V. 48; 52

EDDISON, E. R.
Egil's Saga. 1930. V. 47
A Fish Dinner in Memison. New York: 1941. V. 48; 52
Mezentian Gate. Plaistow: 1957. V. 51
The Mezentian Gate. 1958. V. 47
Mistress of Mistresses. London: 1935. V. 47; 50; 51
Poems, Letters and Memories of Philip Sidney Nairn. 1916. V. 47; 51
Styrbiorn the Strong. 1926. V. 47
The Worm Ouroboros. 1922. V. 47
The Worm Ouroboros. London: 1922. V. 49; 51; 52; 53; 54
The Worm Ouroboros. 1926. V. 49; 54
The Worm Ouroboros. New York: 1926. V. 53

EDDY, ARTHUR G.
Two Thousand Miles on an Automobile. Philadelphia & London: 1902. V. 52

EDDY, ARTHUR JACKSON
Cubists & Post-Impressionism. Chicago: 1914. V. 48

EDDY, DANIEL
The Percy Family. Boston: 1865. V. 51

EDDY, J. W.
Hunting on Kenai Peninsula and Observations on the Increase of Big Game in North America. Seattle: 1924. V. 47

EDDY, MARY BAKER
Miscellaneous Writings 1883-1896. Boston: 1897. V. 49; 50
Science and Health. Boston: 1875. V. 48; 49
Science and Health; with a Key to the Scriptures. Boston: 1884. V. 49

EDE a Story. London: 1889. V. 53

EDE, BASIL
Wild Birds of America, the Art of Basil Ede. Tuscaloosa: 1991. V. 50

EDE, C.
The Art of the Book. London: 1951. V. 47

EDE, H. S.
Savage Messiah. London: 1931. V. 49

EDE, JAMES
A View of the Gold and Silver Coins Of All Nations... London: 1808. V. 51

EDEES, E. S.
Brambles of the British Isles. London: 1988. V. 49; 51

EDEL, LEON
Henry James. Philadelphia: 1953-72. V. 51
Henry James - the Master - 1901-1916. London: 1972. V. 52
Literary Biography - The Alexander Lectures - 1955-1956. London: 1957. V. 54
Some Memories of Edith Wharton. New York: 1993. V. 53

EDELSTEIN, J. M.
A Garland for Jake Zeitlin of the Occasion of His 65th Birthday and the Anniversary of His 40th Year in the Book Trade. Los Angeles: 1967. V. 48; 51

EDEN, CHARLES HENRY
The Fortunes of the Fletchers: a Story of Life in Canada and Australia. London: 1873. V. 49; 51
The Home of the Wolverene and Beaver: Or, Fur-Hunting in the Wilds of Canada. London: 1870. V. 48
The Home of the Wolverene and Beaver; or, Fur-Hunting in the Wilds of Canada. London: 1898?. V. 54
Japan Historical and Descriptive. London: 1877. V. 53

EDEN, EMILY
The Semi-Attached Couple... London: 1860. V. 48; 50; 52
The Semi-Detached House. London: 1859. V. 48; 50; 52

EDEN, FREDERICK MORTON
On the Maritime Rights of Great Britain. London: 1807. V. 54
The State of the Poor; or, an History of the Labouring Classes in England, from the Conquest to the Present Period... London: 1797. V. 51; 53
The Vision a Poem...Addressed to the Late Rev. Jonathan Boucher. London: 1828. V. 48

EDEN, ROBERT
Jurisprudentia Philologica, Sive Elementa Juris Civilis, Secundum Methodum et Seriem Institutionum Justiniani... Oxford: 1744. V. 47

EDES, PETER
Peter Edes, Pioneer Printer in Maine, a Biography. Bangor: 1901. V. 50

EDGAR, J. DOUGLAS
The Gate to Golf. St. Albans: 1920. V. 49

EDGAR, JOHN G.
The Heroes of England. London: 1893. V. 54

THE EDGAR Rice Burroughs Library of Illustration. London: 1976/77/84. V. 51

EDGAR, ROBERT
The Happy Changes; or, Pride and its Consequences... London: 1830. V. 50
An Introduction to the History of Dumfries. Dumfries: 1915. V. 50

EDGAR, THOMAS
Two Charges As They Were Delivered...One at Easter Publick Quarter-Sessions of the Peace... London: 1650. V. 53

EDGE, A. B. BROUGHTON
The Principles and Practice of Geophysical Prospecting. Cambridge: 1931. V. 49

EDGE, JOHN DALLAS
A Report of the Trial of John Jones Versus Thomas Sheehan for Libel, Tried in the court of Common Pleas...2nd December 1839. Dublin: 1839. V. 50

EDGE-PARTINGTON, JAMES
An Album of the Weapons, Tools, Ornaments, Articles of Dress and Of the Natives of the Pacific Islands. Manchester: 1898. V. 54

EDGER, HENRY
The Positivist Calendar; or, Transitional System of Public Commemoration Instituted by Augustus Comte, Founder of the Positive Religion of Humanity. Long Island: 1856. V. 49

EDGERTON, CLYDE
Raney. Chapel Hill: 1985. V. 47; 48; 50; 51; 52; 53; 54
Walking Across Egypt. Chapel Hill: 1987. V. 52; 53

EDGERTON, WILLIAM F.
Historical Records of Ramses III. Chicago: 1936. V. 49
Medinet Habu Gafiti Facsimiles. Chicago: 1937. V. 49

EDGEVILLE, EDWARD
Castine. Southern Field and Fireside Novelette, No. 2. New Series. Raleigh: 1865. V. 47; 52; 53

EDGEWORTH, HENRY ESSEX
Letters from the Abbe Edgeworth to His Friends, Written Between the Years 1777 and 1807... London: 1818. V. 49

EDGEWORTH, M. L.
The Southern Gardener and Receipt Book... Philadelphia: 1860. V. 48

EDGEWORTH, MARIA
Angelina: ou l'Amie Inconnue. Chelsea: 1933. V. 48
Belinda. London: 1801. V. 48
Castle Rackrent, an Hiberian Tale. London: 1800. V. 48; 54
Castle Rackrent: an Hiberian Tale. London: 1801/1802. V. 50
Castle Rackrent: an Hiberian Tale. London: 1804. V. 50
Comic Dramas, in Three Acts. London: 1817. V. 47; 48; 49; 50; 51; 52; 54
Early Lessons. London: 1801-03. V. 49
Early Lessons, in Six Volumes. Philadelphia: 1827-26. V. 54
Essay on Irish Bulls. London: 1802. V. 53
Extracts from Early Lessons. Philadelphia: 1840. V. 51
Harrington, a Tale; and Ormond, a Tale. London: 1817. V. 47; 48; 49; 50; 51; 53; 54
Harrington, a Tale. Ormond, a Tale. London: 1887. V. 49; 53
Harry and Lucy Concluded. London: 1825. V. 47; 48; 50; 51; 52; 53
Harry and Lucy Concluded. London: 1827. V. 53
Helen, a Tale. London: 1834. V. 48; 50; 52; 54
Leonora. London: 1806. V. 48
Letters for Literary Ladies. London: 1795. V. 52
Letters of Maria Edgeworth and Anna Letitia Barbauld. Waltham St. Lawrence: 1953. V. 52
Letters Selected from the Lushington Papers. Waltham St. Lawrence: 1953. V. 47; 50
The Life and Letters... London: 1894. V. 50
The Life and Letters of Maria Edgeworth. Boston and New York: 1895. V. 51
Memoirs. London: 1820. V. 50
Memoirs of Richard Lovell Edgeworth, Esq., Begun by Himself and Concluded by His Daughter. London: 1856. V. 50
The Modern Griselda. London: 1805. V. 47; 48; 49; 51
Moral Tales. London: 1809. V. 50
Moral Tales. London: 1816. V. 50
The Novels. New York: 1893. V. 50
The Parent's Assistant. London: 1804. V. 51
Patronage. London: 1814. V. 47; 48; 50; 51; 53; 54
Patronage. London: 1815. V. 47
Popular Tales. Philadelphia & New York: 1850. V. 50
Practical Education. London: 1801. V. 48; 52
Practical Education. Providence & Boston: 1815. V. 47; 50
Rosamond. London: 1821. V. 50
Rosamond, a Sequel to Rosamond, in Early Lessons. London: 1850. V. 49
Tales and Miscellaneous Pieces. London: 1825. V. 47; 49; 51; 53
Tales and Novels. London: 1832. V. 49
Tales and Novels. London: 1832-33. V. 47; 50
Tales and Novels. New York: 1832-33-34. V. 54
Tales and Novels. New York: 1839. V. 52
Tales and Novels. London: 1857. V. 47
Tales and Novels. London: 1870. V. 48; 50
Tales from Maria Edgeworth. New York: 1903. V. 50
Tales of Fashionable Life. London: 1809. V. 50
Tales of Fashionable Life. London: 1809-12. V. 50

EDGEWORTH, RICHARD LOVELL
Essay on Irish Bulls. London: 1802. V. 47; 48; 49; 50; 51; 54
Essay on Irish Bulls. 1808. V. 47
An Essay on the Construction of Roads and Carriages. London: 1817. V. 50
Essays on Professional Education. London: 1809. V. 54
Poetry Explained for the Use of Young People. London: 1802. V. 50
Readings on Poetry. London: 1816. V. 53

EDGEWORTH DE FIRMONT, HENRY ESSEX
Letters to His Friends, Written Between the Years 1777 and 1807. London: 1818. V. 48; 51

EDIE, GEORGE
The Art of English Shooting. London: 1780?. V. 48

EDIE, JAMES M.
Russian Philosophy. Chicago: 1965. V. 47

THE EDINBURGH Encyclopaedia. Philadelphia: 1832. V. 49

EDINBURGH New Dispensatory.... Edinburgh: 1786. V. 48

EDIS, ROBERT W.
Decoration and Furniture of Town Houses. London: 1881. V. 50

EDISON, MARGARET E.
Thoreau MacDonald: A Catalogue of Design and Illustration. Toronto: 1973. V. 50

EDISON, THOMAS A.
The Edison System of Incandescent Lighting from Central Stations. New York: 1887. V. 53

THE EDITH Cavell Nurse from Massachusetts. Boston: 1917. V. 50

EDKINS, JOSHUA
A Collection of Poems, Mostly Original by Several Hands. Dublin: 1801. V. 50

EDLIN, ABRAHAM
A Treatise on the Art of Bread Making. London: 1805. V. 52; 54

EDMESTON, JAMES
The Search; and Other Poems. London: 1817. V. 50

EDMONDES, THOMAS
The Edmondes Papers. London: 1913. V. 48; 54

EDMONDS, CLEMENT
Observations Upon Caesar's Commentaries Setting Forth the Practise of ye Art Militarie in the Time of the Romaine Empire for the Better Direction of Our Moderne Warrs... (with) Observations Upon Caesar's Comentaries... London: 1604/09. V. 50

EDMONDS, EMMA
Nurse and Spy in the Union Army... Hartford: 1865. V. 50; 52

EDMONDS, RANDOLPH
Six Plays for a Negro Theatre. Boston: 1934. V. 54

EDMONDS, WALTER
Wilderness Crossing. New York: 1944. V. 49

EDMONDS, WALTER D.
The Big Barn. Boston: 1930. V. 51
Drums Along the Mohawk. Boston: 1936. V. 48; 51

EDMONDSON, JOSEPH
An Historical and Genealogical Account of the Noble Family of Greville... London: 1766. V. 47; 52; 53

EDMONDSTON, ARTHUR
A View of the Antient and Present State of the Zetland Islands... Edinburgh: 1809. V. 48; 50

EDMONTON: Alberta's Capital City. Edmonton: 1914. V. 48

EDMUNDS, A. C.
Pen Sketches of Nebraskans with Photographs. Lincoln and Omaha: 1871. V. 47; 54

EDMUNDS, WILL H.
Pointers and Clues to the Subjects of Chinese and Japanese Art. London. V. 49; 51
Pointers and Clues to the Subjects of Chinese and Japanese Art. London: 1934. V. 47; 50

EDMUNDSON, WILLIAM
A Journal of the Life, Sufferings and Labour of Love in the Work of the Ministry. Dublin: 1715. V. 47
A Journal of the Life, Travels, Sufferings and labour of Love in the Work of the Ministry.. London: 1774. V. 49; 54

EDREHI, M.
An Historical Account of the Ten Tribes Settled Beyond the River Sambatyon, in the East. London & Philadelphia: 1835?. V. 47

EDSON, CARROLL A.
Edson Family History and Genealogy: Descendants of Samuel Edson of Salem and Bridgewater, Mass. Ann Arbor: 1965. V. 52

EDSON, RUSSELL
The Wounded Breakfast. Ten Poems. Madison: 1978. V. 52; 54

EDUCATION in Greece: An Appeal to the Public from the British and Foreign School Society, on the Subject of Education in Greece. London. V. 47

EDUCATION Observations on the Bedford Charity: In A Series of Letters That Were Signed Justus. London: 1761. V. 50

THE EDUCATIONAL Uses of Toys. London: 1854. V. 54

EDWARD and Frances, an Historical Tale, Illustrative of Some Remarkable Events Relative to English History, in the Sixteenth Century. Lancaster: 1829. V. 53

EDWARD, CHARLES
The History and Poetry of Finger-Rings. New York: 1855. V. 53

EDWARD, DAVID
History of Texas; or, The Emigrants, Farmer's and Politician's Guide... Cincinnati: 1836. V. 53; 54

EDWARD, EMILY
Painted Walls of Mexico. Austin: 1966. V. 48

EDWARD, PRINCE OF WALES
Letters of Edward, Prince of Wales 1304-1305. 1931. V. 54

EDWARD Thomas: A Centenary Celebration with Etchings by Arthur Neal. Cambridge: 1978. V. 47

EDWARDES, CHARLES
Rides and Studies in the Canary Islands. London: 1888. V. 48

EDWARDES, H. B.
Memorandum on the Report of the Candallar Mission in 1858. Calcutta: 1868. V. 49
A Year on the Punjab Frontier, in 1848-49. London: 1851. V. 53

EDWARDS, A. CECIL
The Persian Carpet, a Survey of Carpet Weaving Industry of Persia. London: 1960. V. 49

EDWARDS, AMELIA B.
Barbara's History. London: 1864. V. 53
Debenham's Vow. London: 1870. V. 49; 50
In the Days of My Youth. London: 1873. V. 54
A Midsummer Ramble in the Dolomites. London: 1889. V. 49; 53; 54
Pharaohs, Fellahs and Explorers. New York: 1892. V. 50; 51
A Summary of English History; from the Roman Conquest to the Present Time... Toronto: 1869. V. 53
A Thousand Miles Up the Nile...With Upward of Seventy Illustrations Engraved on Wood by G. Pearson... London: 1888. V. 50; 54
Untrodden Peaks and Unfrequented Valleys. London: 1873. V. 51; 52; 54
Untrodden Peaks and Unfrequented Valleys. London: 1890. V. 48
Untrodden Peaks and Unfrequented Valleys. London: 1893. V. 54

EDWARDS, BRYAN
An Historical Survey of the French Colony in the Island of St. Domingo... London: 1797. V. 48; 49; 52; 53
The History, Civil and Commercial of the British Colonies in the West Indies. London: 1793. V. 48
The History Civil and Commercial of the British Colonies in the West Indies. London: 1799. V. 48
The History, Civil and Commercial, of the British Colonies in the West Indies. London: 1801. V. 54
The History, Civil and Commercial of the British West Indies. London: 1819. V. 49

EDWARDS, C. H., & CO.
Catalogue of Ladies' Goods. New York: 1880's. V. 48

EDWARDS. D. B.
Early Days in Abilene. Abilene: 1938. V. 53

EDWARDS, E. I.
Desert Voices. A Descriptive Bibliography. Los Angeles: 1958. V. 47; 52
The Enduring Desert: a Descriptive Bibliography. Los Angeles: 1969. V. 47; 53
Lost Oases Along the Carrizo. Los Angeles: 1961. V. 51; 52
The Valley Whose Name is Death. Pasadena: 1940. V. 47

EDWARDS, EDWARD
Anecdotes of Painters Who Have Resided or Been Born in England... London: 1808. V. 49; 51
A Collection of Views and Studies After Nature. London: 1790. V. 53
Free Town Libraries, Their Formation, Management and History. London: 1869. V. 53
Libraries and Founders of Libraries. London: 1864. V. 47
Memoirs of Libraries, Including a Handbook of Library Economy. London: 1859. V. 54
A Practical Treatise on Perspective. London: 1803. V. 47

EDWARDS, EDWIN
Old Inns. First Division - Eastern England. London: 1873. V. 48; 50; 52

EDWARDS, EMORY
Modern American Locomotive Engines. Their Design, Construction and Management. Philadelphia: 1883?. V. 47
Modern American Locomotive Engines; Their Design, Construction and Management. Philadelphia: 1890. V. 52

EDWARDS, FRANK S.
A Campaign in New Mexico with Colonel Doniphan. Philadelphia: 1847. V. 47; 49; 50

EDWARDS, FREDERICK
A Treatise on Smoky Chimneys, Their Cure and Prevention. London: 1866. V. 51; 53

EDWARDS, GEORGE
An Attempt to Rectify the Public Affairs of the United Kingdom and Empire, and Promote Their Private Prosperity, Illustrated by Many National Projects Hitherto Not Rendered Effectual.. London: 1804. V. 54
Essays Upon Natural History, and Other Miscellaneous Subjects... London: 1770. V. 49; 50; 51; 52
A Natural History of Uncommon Birds, and Of Some Other Rare and Undescribed Animals, Quadrupedes, Reptiles, Fishes, Insects, & Exhibited in Two Hundred and Ten Copper Plates... London: 1743-51. V. 53
A Natural History of Uncommon Birds and of Some Other Rare and Undescribed animals. (with) Gleanings of Natural History... London: 1758-64. V. 48
Three Most Important Objects Proposed; the Original System of Human Economy, or of Providence, at Length Ascertained in All Its Practical Views and Measures... York: 1815. V. 50

EDWARDS, GEORGE WHARTON
A Book of English Love Songs. New York: 1897. V. 48
Vanished Towers and Chimes of Flanders. Philadelphia: 1916. V. 52

EDWARDS, GLADYS BROWN
The Arabian War Horse to Show Horse. Covina: 1973. V. 51
The Arabian War Horse to Show Horse. Denver: 1980. V. 48
A Photographic History of the Polish Arabian. Rockville: 1978. V. 50

EDWARDS, H. S.
The Lyrical Drama, Essays on Subjects, Composers and Executants of Modern Opera. 1881. V. 52

EDWARDS, HARRY S.
Eneas Africanus. New York: 1930. V. 47

EDWARDS, HARRY STILLWELL
Two Runaways and Other Stories. New York: 1900. V. 51

EDWARDS, HENRY SUTHERLAND
The Polish Captivity. London: 1863. V. 47; 49

EDWARDS, I. E. S.
Hieratic Papyri in the British Museum. Fourth Series: Oracular Amuletic Decrees of the Late New Kingdom. London: 1960. V. 49

EDWARDS, J.
The Hemiptera-Homoptera (Cicadina and Psyllina) of the British Islands. London: 1896. V. 47

EDWARDS, J. B.
Early Days in Abilene... V. 47

EDWARDS, J. PERCY
History of London Street Improvements, 1855-1897. London: 1898. V. 51

EDWARDS, JAMES
Bibliotheca Parisina. A Catalogue of a Collection of Books, Formed by a Gentleman in France. London: 1791. V. 48

EDWARDS, JENNIE
John H. Edwards: Biography, Memoirs, Reminiscences and Recollections...Private Letters. Kansas City: 1889. V. 49; 53

EDWARDS, JOHN
Baptism - the Mode (and in) Sequoyah. Vinita, Indian Territory: 1890?. V. 50
The British Herbal, Containing One Hundred Plates of the Most Beautiful and Scarce Flowers and Useful Medicinal Plants. London: 1769-70. V. 47
Polypoikilos Sophia (Graece). A Compleat History or Survey Of all the Dispensations and Methods of Religion, From the Beginning of the World to the Consummation Of All Things... London: 1699. V. 47; 50
Recollections of Filey. Derby: 1835. V. 47
The Tour of the Dove, a Poem: with Occasional Pieces. London: 1821. V. 54

EDWARDS, JOHN ELLIS
The Confederate Soldier: Being a Memorial Sketch of George N. and Bushrod W. Harris Privates in the Confederate Army. New York: 1868. V. 49

EDWARDS, JOHN N.
John N. Edwards. Biography, Memoirs, Reminiscences and Recollections. Kansas City: 1889. V. 50
Noted Guerillas, or the Warfare of the Border. St. Louis: 1877. V. 52
Shelby and His Men; or, the War in the West. Kansas City: 1897. V. 49

EDWARDS, JONATHAN
An Account of the Life of the Late Reverend Mr. David Brainerd, Minister of the Gospel, Missionary to the Indians...and Pastor of a Church of Christian Indians in New Jersey. Boston: 1749. V. 47
An Account of the Life of the Rev. David Brainerd...Missionary to the Indians in New Jersey... Newark: 1811. V. 51
A Careful and Strict Enquiry Into the Modern Prevailing Notions of that Freedom of Will... Boston: 1754. V. 52; 53
The Doctrine of Original Sin, As It Always Held in the Catholick Church of England, Asserted and Vindicated from the Exceptions and Cavils of the Reverend Dr. Daniel Whitby. Oxford: 1711. V. 54
A Faithful Narrative of Surprising Work of God in the Conversion of Many Hundred Souls in Northampton and the Neighbouring Towns and Villages of New Hampshire and New England... Elizabeth-Town: 1790. V. 51
The Great Christian Doctrine of Original Sin Defended... Boston: 1758. V. 49
The Great Christian Doctrine of Original Sin Defended, Evidences of Its Truth Produced, and Arguments to the Contrary Answered. Wilmington: 1771. V. 47; 48
The History of the Work of Redemption. New York: 1786. V. 50; 51
Memoirs of the Rev. David Brainerd; Missionary to the Indians on the Borders of New-York, New-Jersey and Pennsylvania:. New Haven: 1822. V. 51
Observations on the Language of the Muhhekaneew Indians; In Which the Extent of that Langauge in North America as Shewn... London: 1789. V. 47
A Preservative Against Socinianism. Oxford: 1693-1703. V. 47
A Treatise Concerning Religious Affections. Elizabeth-Town: 1787. V. 51
A Treatise Concerning Religious Affections, in Three Parts... Boston: 1746. V. 50
True Grace, Distinguished From the Experience of Devils: in a Sermon Preached Before the Synod of New York. Elizabethtown: 1791. V. 47; 48; 50

EDWARDS, LIONEL
Famous Foxhunters. London: 1932. V. 53
Huntsmen Past and Present. London: 1929. V. 47; 53
A Leicestershire Sketch Book. London: 1933. V. 47
A Leicestershire Sketch Book. London: 1935. V. 47
My Hunting Sketch Book. London: 1928. V. 47
My Hunting Sketch Book. London: 1928-30. V. 47; 51
My Hunting Sketch Book. London: 1930. V. 47
My Hunting Sketch Book Volume I and My Hunting Sketch Book Volume 2. London: 1928-30. V. 47
My Irish Sketchbook. London: 1938. V. 49
My Scottish Sketchbook. London: 1929. V. 47
The Passing Seasons. London: 1927. V. 49; 51
Pink and Scarlet; or, Hunting as a School for Soldiering. London: 1913. V. 47
Seen from the Saddle. New York: 1937. V. 47
Sketches in Stable and Kennel. London and New York: 1933. V. 51
Sketches in Stable and Kennel. London: 1936. V. 48
A Sportsman's Bag. New York: 1937. V. 47
The Wiles of the Fox. Some Notes and Sketches. London: 1932. V. 47

EDWARDS, MATILDA BARBARA BETHAM
Reminiscences. London: 1898. V. 50
Through Spain to the Sahara. London: 1868. V. 50; 52

EDWARDS, MATILDA BARBARA BETHAN
Snow Flakes and the Stories They Told Their Children. London: 1862. V. 49

EDWARDS, NINIAN
Illinois Intelligencer - Extra. An Address, Delivered by Ninian Edwards, Governor of the State of Illinois, to Both Houses of the Legislature. December 7, 1830. Vandalia: 1830. V. 49

EDWARDS, O. M.
Hwiangerddi. 1995. V. 54

EDWARDS, OWEN
Clych Atgof: Penodau yn Hanes fy Addysg. Newtown: 1933. V. 50

EDWARDS, PAUL
The Encyclopedia of Philosophy. New York: 1972. V. 49

EDWARDS, PHILIP LEGET
California in 1837. Sacramento: 1890. V. 49; 53; 54
The Diary of Philip Leget Edwards the Great Cattle Drive from California to Oregon in 1837. San Francisco: 1932. V. 47; 53
Sketch of the Oregon Territory, or Emigrant's Guide. Kansas City: 1951. V. 54

EDWARDS, RALPH
The Dictionary of English Furniture. London: 1954. V. 50

EDWARDS, RICHARD
The Book! Or, the Proceedings and Correspondence Upon the Subject of the Inquiry Into the Conduct of Her Royal Highness the Princess of Wales, Under a Commission Appointed by the King In the Year 1806. London: 1813. V. 52
The Field of Stones. A Study of the Art of Shen Chou (1427-1509). Washington: 1962. V. 49; 53

EDWARDS, SYDENHAM
Cynorophia Brittanica. Horsforth, Leeds: 1991. V. 48
Edward's Botanical Register: or, Ornamental Flower-Garden and Shrubbery... London: 1837. V. 48
The New Botanic Garden. London: 1812. V. 52

EDWARDS, THOMAS
The Canons of Criticism and Glossary. London: 1758. V. 48
The Canons of Criticism and Glossary; The Trial of the letter Y(upsilon), Alias Y and Sonnets. London: 1765. V. 48; 52; 54

EDWARDS, W. H.
Voyage Up the River Amazon Including a Residence at Para. New York & Philadelphia: 1847. V. 52
The Young Artist's Guide to Flower Drawing and Painting in Water Colours, with Instructions and Examples. London: 1820. V. 47

EDWARDS, WELDON NATHANIEL
Memoir of Nathaniel Macon, of North Carolina. Raleigh: 1862. V. 47

EDWARDS, WILLIAM
Art of Boxing and Science of Self Defence, Together with a Manual of Training. New York: 1888. V. 47
Reminiscences of a Bengal Civilian. London: 1866. V. 50
Two Health-Seekers in Southern California. Philadelphia: 1897. V. 50; 52; 53

EDWARDS, WILLIAM H.
Football Days. Memories of the Game and of the Men Behind the Ball. New York: 1916. V. 50; 52

EDWARDS, WILLIAM J.
Twenty-Five Years in the Black Belt. Boston: 1918. V. 52

EDWIN White Newhall. San Francisco?: 1915. V. 48

EDWORDS, C. E.
Campfires of a Naturalist. 1893. V. 48; 52; 54

EELKING, MAX VON
Memoirs, and Letters and Journals, Major General Riedesel, During His Residence in America. Albany: 1868. V. 47

THE EFFECTS O' Drunkenness and Temperance; or Jock and Geordie. Edinburgh: 1806. V. 54

EGAN, BERESFORD
But the Sinners Triumph. London: 1934. V. 49
De Sade: Being a Series of Wounds, Inflicted with Brush and Pen Upon Sadistic Wolves Garbed in Masochists' Wool. Paris: 1929. V. 54
Pollen. London: 1933. V. 51

EGAN, P. M.
History, Guide and Directory of the County and City of Waterford. V. 49; 54
History, Guide and Directory of the County and City of Waterford. London. V. 50; 51

EGAN, PIERCE
Book of Sports and Mirror of Life... London: 1832. V. 49
Boxiana: or Sketches of Antient & Modern Pugilism... 1818-29. V. 50
Boxiana; or Sketches of Antient & Modern Pugilism. 1840. V. 47; 52
Diorama Anglais ou Promenades Pictoresques a Londres. Paris: 1823. V. 51
Every Gentleman's Manual. A Lecture on the Art of Self-Defence. London: 1851. V. 52
Finish to the Adventures of Tom, Jerry and Logic, in Their Pursuits through Life in and Out of London. London: 1830. V. 49
The Finish to the Adventures of Tom, Jerry and Logic, in Their Pursuits through Life In and Out of London. London: 1889. V. 52
Fistiana; or the Oracle of the Ring from 1780 To 1840...Scientific Hints on Sparring, Etc. London: 1841. V. 52
Grose's Classical Dictionary of the Vulgar Tongue. London: 1823. V. 48
The Life and Adventures of Samuel Denmore Hayward, the Modern Macheath, Giving an Account of the Extraordinary Manner in Which He Raised Himself from the Mean Situtation of a Tailor's Apprentice (to) The Most Fashionable Circles of Society... London: 1822. V. 48
Life in London. London: 1821. V. 47; 48; 49; 51; 54
Life in London. London: 1821/30. V. 49
Life in London. London: 1822. V. 48; 49
Life in London. London: 1823. V. 48
Life in London. London: 1830. V. 51
The Life of an Actor. London: 1825. V. 49
Pierce Egan's Anecdotes (Original and Selected) of the Turf, The Chase, The Ring, and The Stage... London: 1827. V. 47
Real Life in London. 1821-22. V. 51; 52
Real Life in London. London: 1824. V. 53
Real Life in London. London: 1824-27. V. 51
Real Life of Ireland: or, The Day and Night Scenes, Rovings, Rambles and sprees, Bulls and Blunders, Bodderation and Blarney of Brian Boru, Esq. and His Elegant Friend Shir Shawn O'Dogherty... London: 1821. V. 48; 52
Robin Hood and Little John or the Merry Men of Sherwood Forest. London: 1850. V. 48
Sporting Anecdotes, Original and Selected. London. V. 47; 49
Sporting Anecdotes, Original and Selected. London: 1820. V. 49
Sporting Anecdotes, Original and Selected.... Philadelphia: 1822. V. 47
Sporting Anecdotes, Original and Selected... London: 1825. V. 47
Tom and Jerry: Life in London, or Day and Night Scenes of Jerry Hawthorn. London: 1869. V. 47; 49
Tom and Jerry. Life in London, or The Day and Night Scenes of Jerry Hawthorn, Esq. and His Elegant Friend Corinthian Tom in Their Rambles and sprees through the Metropolis. London: 1878. V. 49

EGAN, THOMAS J.
History of the Halifax Volunteer Battalion and Volunteer Companies 1859-1887. Halifax: 1888. V. 47

EGE, RALPH
Pioneers of Old Hopewell, with Sketches of Her Revolutionary Heroes. Hopewell: 1908. V. 47; 49; 51

EGE, ROBERT J.
Tell Baker to Strike them Hard, Incidents On the Marias River 23 Jan. 1870. Bellevue: 1970. V. 49

EGEDE, HANS
Description of Greenland. London: 1745. V. 54

EGERTON, DANIEL THOMAS
The Necessary Qualifications of a Man of Fashion. London: 1823. V. 54

EGERTON, FRANCIS
Journal of a Tour in the Holy Land in May and June 184. London: 1841. V. 48; 49; 50; 51; 52; 53

EGERTON, GEORGE
Discords. London: 1894. V. 54
Flies in Amber. London: 1905. V. 52
Keynotes. London: 1893. V. 47

EGERTON, H. C.
Outlines of Irish History. London: 1829. V. 51

EGERTON, JUDY
British Sporting and Animal Paintings, 1655-1867. (and) British Sporting and Animal Drawings 1500-1850. London: 1978. V. 47
British Sporting and Animal Prints, 1658-1874. London: 1981. V. 47

EGERTON, M.
Here and There Over the Water: Being Cullings in a Trip to the Netherlands. London: 1825. V. 53

EGERTON, T.
Egerton's Theatrical Remembrancer, Containing a Complete List of All the Dramatic Performances in the English Language... London: 1788. V. 48

EGERTON, THOMAS
The Speech of the Lord Chancellor of England in the Eschequer Chamber, Touching the Post-nati. London: 1609. V. 52

EGERTON-WARBURTON, ROLAND EYLES
Hunting Songs, Ballads, &c. Chester: 1834. V. 51

EGGENHOFER, NICK
Horses, Horses, Always Horses. 1981. V. 47
Horses, Horses, Always Horses. Cody: 1981. V. 53
Wagons, Mules and Men. New York: 1961. V. 49; 53

EGGERS, REINHOLD
Colditz The German Story. London: 1961?. V. 50

EGGGLESTON, GEORGE CARY
The History of the Confederate War: its Causes and Its Conduct: a Narrative and Critical History. New York: 1910. V. 54

EGGLESTON, EDWARD
The Hoosier School-Boy. New York: 1883. V. 50
The Hoosier School-Master. New York: 1871. V. 51
Roxy. New York: 1878. V. 50

EGGLESTON, GEORGE CARY
A Rebel's Recollections. New York: 1875. V. 54

EGIL'S Saga. Done Into English Out of Icelandic. Cambridge: 1930. V. 51

EGLE, WILLIAM HENRY
Illustrated History of the Commonwealth of Pennsylvania, Civil, Political and Military, From Its Earliest Settlement to the Present Time... Harrisburg: 1876. V. 47; 50

EGLESFIELD, FRANCIS
Monarachy Revived: Being the Personal History of Charles the Second. London: 1822. V. 52

EGLINTON, JOHN
Some Essays and Passages. 1905. V. 54

EGMONT, JOHN PERCEVAL, 1ST EARL OF
An Examination of the Principles and an Enquiry into the Conduct of the Two B*****rs (The Duke of Newcastle and Henry Pelham). London: 1749. V. 48; 49
An Occasional Letter From a Gentleman in the Country, to His Friend in Town. London: 1749. V. 48
A Patriot's Letter to the Duke of Dorset, Written in the Year 1731. Dublin: 1749. V. 53
The Question of the Precedency of the Peers of Ireland in England, Fairly Stated. 1739. V. 47
A Second Series of Facts and Arguments; Tending to Prove, That the Abilities of the Two B——rs, are Not More Extraordinary Than Their Virtues. London: 1749. V. 48

EGNATIUS, JOHANNES BAPTISTA
De Exemplis Illustrium virorum Venetae Civitatis...Cvm Indice. Venice: 1554. V. 47; 48

EGREMONT, MICHAEL
The Bride of Frankenstein. London. V. 50

EGYPT, Paintings from Tombs and Temples. 1954. V. 48

EHLE, JOHN
Move Over, Mountain.. New York: 1957. V. 48; 50; 54
The Road. New York: 1967. V. 50
The Survivor: the Story of Eddy Hukov. New York: 1958. V. 50

EHNINGER, JOHN W.
Illustrations of Longfellow's Courtship of Miles Standish. New York: 1859. V. 47; 54

EHRENBERG, HERMANN
Der Freiheitskampf in Texas im Jahre 1836. Leipzig: 1844. V. 48; 49
Texas und Seine Revolution. Leipzig: 1843. V. 49; 54
With Milam and Fannin. Dallas: 1935. V. 49; 50; 54

EHRENDORFER, F.
Woody Plants - Evolution and Distribution Since the Tertiary. Berlin: 1989. V. 50

EHRENSTEIN, A.
Robbers and Soldiers. New York: 1929. V. 48; 50

EHRET, GEORGE DIONYSIUS
Twelve Coloured Reproductions from the Original Paintings on Vellum... London: 1953. V. 49

EHRLICH, GRETEL
The Solace of Open Spaces. New York: 1985. V. 50

EHRLICH, J. W.
Howl of the Censor, The Four Letter Word on Trial. San Carlos: 1961. V. 52

EHRLICH, PAUL
The Experimental Chemotherapy Of Spirilloses. New York: 1911. V. 51

EHRMAN, JOHN
Catalogue of Valuable Printed Books from the Broxbourne Library Illustrating the Spread of Printing, the Property of John Ehrman, Esq. London: 1977. V. 47

EICHENBERG, FRITZ
The Wood and the Graver. Barre: 1977. V. 47
The Wood and the Graver. New York: 1977. V. 53

EICKEMEYER, CARL
Among the Pueblo Indians. New York: 1895. V. 47
Over the Great Navajo Trail. New York: 1900. V. 49

EICKEMEYER, RUDOLF
Winter. New York: 1903. V. 47

EIDENOFF & RUCHLIS
Atomics for the Millions. New York: 1947. V. 49

EIDLITZ, ROBERT JAMES
Medals and Medallions Relating to Architects...from the Collection of Robert James Eidlitz. New York: 1927. V. 51

EIFFEL, GUSTAVE
The Resistance of the Air and Aviation... London: 1913. V. 50

EIGENMANN, C. H.
Freshwater Fishes of British Guiana. Pittsburgh: 1912. V. 53

EIGHT Harvard Poets. New York: 1917. V. 51

EIGHT Oxford Poets. London: 1941. V. 49

EIGHTEEN New Court-Queries Humbly Offered to the Serious Consideration...of All the Good Honest Hearted People of the Three Nations: of Great Concernment Towards the Stopping Our Breaches... London: 1659. V. 53

EIGHTEENTH Century British Books. An Author Union Catalogue Extracted From the British Museum General Catalogue... London: 1981. V. 50

EIGNER, LARRY
Air the Trees. Los Angeles: 1968. V. 49; 54
From the Sustaining Air. Palma de Mallorca: 1953. V. 49
Things Stirring Together or Far Away. Los Angeles: 1974. V. 54
Waters/Places/A Time. Santa Barbara: 1983. V. 48
The World and Its Streets, Places. Santa Barbara: 1977. V. 48

EIKON Basilike or the King's Book. London: 1903. V. 49

EIKON Basilike: the Portraicture of His Sacred Majestie in His Solitudes and Sufferings. London: 1648. V. 50

EIKON BASILIKE
Eikon Basilicus. The Pourtraicture of His Sacred Majestie in His Solitudes and Sufferings... London: 1649. V. 47
The Pourtraicture of His Sacred Maiestie in His Solitudes and Sufferings. London: 1648/49. V. 47; 51

EILENBURG, CHRISTIAN HEINRICH
Kurzer Entwurf der Koniglichen Naturalienkammer zu Dresden. Dresden and Leipzig: 1755. V. 49

EILENBURGER, C. H.
Description du Cabinet Roiale de Dresde Touchant L'Histoire Naturelle. Dresden and Leipzig: 1755. V. 54

EIMER & AMEND, NEW YORK
Microscopes and Other Apparatus for Biological Laboratories. Catagloue B. New York: 1923. V. 50

EINHORN, MAX
Diseases of the Intestines. New York: 1900. V. 53

EINSTEIN, ALBERT
Die Grundlage der Allgemeinen Relativitatstheorie. Leipzig: 1916. V. 54
Relativity; the Special and General Theory. London: 1920. V. 48; 49
Relativity: the Special and General Theory. New York: 1920. V. 53

EINUNDZWANZIG Kapitel Aus Hisstoria Von D. Johann Fausten. 1992. V. 51; 52; 54

EISELEY, LOREN
The Brown Wasps: Three Essays in Autobiography. Mt. Horeb: 1969. V. 51; 53; 54
Darwin's Century. Garden City: 1958. V. 50; 53
Francis Bacon and Modern Dilemma. Lincoln: 1962. V. 52

EISEN, ALBERT
Paul Jenkins. New York: 1975. V. 51

EISEN, GUSTAV
The Raisin Industry. San Francisco: 1890. V. 50

EISEN, GUSTAVUS A.
Ancient Oriental Cylinder and Other Seals with a Description of the Collection of Mrs. William H. Moore. Chicago: 1940. V. 49
Glass. Its Origin, History, Chronology, Technic and Classification to the Sixteenth Century. New York: 1927. V. 49; 50; 52
The Great Chalice of Antioch. New York: 1923. V. 54
The Great Chalice of Antioch. New York: 1933. V. 54

EISENBERG, BARON D'
Anti-Maquignonnage Pour Eviter la Surprise dans l'Emplette des Chevaux: ou l'on Traite de leur Perfection et de Leurs Defauts. Amsterdam & Leipzig: 1764. V. 47

EISENHART, WILLY
The World of Donald Evans. New York: 1980. V. 47; 50; 53

EISENHOWER, DWIGHT DAVID
Crusade in Europe. New York: 1948. V. 48
Mandate for Change, 1953-1956 with Waging Peace, 1956-61. Garden City: 1963-65. V. 48
Mandate for Change: The White House Years 1953-1956. Garden City: 1963. V. 47
The White House Years: Mandate for Change, 1953-1956. (with) The White House Years: Waging Peace, 1956-1961. Garden City: 1963/65. V. 49

EISENMANN, GEORG HEINRICH
Tabulae Anatomicae Quatuor Uteri Duplicis Observationem Rariorem Sistentes... Strasburg: 1752. V. 49

EISENSTAEDT, ALFRED
People. New York: 1973. V. 48; 51

EISENSTEIN, SERGEI
The Soviet Screen. Moscow: 1939. V. 54

EISGRUBER, ELSA
Spin Top Spin and Rosemarie and Thyme. New York: 1929. V. 49

EISKEN, ED VAN DER
Bagara. Amsterdam: 1958. V. 54

EISLER, MAX
Gustav Klimt. Wien: 1920. V. 50

EISSLER, K. R.
Goethe. A Psychoanalytic Study. 1775-1786. Detroit: 1963. V. 53

EISSLER, M.
The Metallurgy of Gold. London: 1897. V. 52

EITNER, LORENZ
Gericault. His Life and Work. London: 1983. V. 50

EKINS, CHARLES
Naval Battles, from 1744 to the Peace in 1814, Critically Reviewed and Illustrated. London: 1824. V. 48; 52; 54
Naval Battles of Great Britain, from the Accession of the Illustrious House of Hanover to the Throne to the Battle of Navarin. London: 1828. V. 53

EKWALL, EILERT
Scandinavians and Celts in the North-West of England. Sweden & Leipzig: 1918. V. 50

ELAM, CHARLES
Winds of Doctrine: Being an Examination of Modern Theories of Automatism and Evolution. London: 1876. V. 47; 49

ELBERTUS, FRA
The City of Tagaste. East Aurora: 1900. V. 51
Old John Burroughs. East Aurora: 1901. V. 51

ELDER, PAUL
The Old Spanish Missions of California. San Francisco: 1913. V. 50

ELDER, W.
Biography of Elisha Kent Kane. Philadelphia: 1858. V. 53

ELDER, WILLIAM
Aphasia and the Cerebral Speech Mechanism. London: 1897. V. 53

ELDERKIN, JAMES D.
Biographical Sketches and Anecdotes of a Soldier of Three Wars as Written by Himself. Detroit: 1899. V. 49; 54

ELDERSHAW, FLORA S.
The Peaceful Army. A Memorial to the Pioneer Women of Australia 1788-1938. Sydney: 1938. V. 53; 54

ELDERTON, W. PALIN
Frequency-Curves and Correlation. London: 1906. V. 50

ELDREDGE, ROBERT F.
Past and Present of Macomb County, Michigan... Chicago: 1905. V. 51

ELDREDGE, ZOETH SKINNER
The Beginnings of San Francisco from the Expedition of Anza, 1774 to the City Charter of April 15, 1850. San Francisco: 1912. V. 47; 52; 53

ELDRIDGE Cleaver is Running for President: Register Peace and Freedom Attend P&F Convention. San Francisco: 1969. V. 54

ELDRIDGE, ELLEANOR
Memoirs of Elleanor Eldridge. Providence: 1843. V. 48
Memoirs of...(and) Elleanor's Second Book. Providence: 1841. V. 54

ELDRIDGE, GEORGE HOMANS
The Santa Clara Valley, Puente Hills and Los Angeles Oil Districts, Southern California. Washington: 1907. V. 47

ELEGANT Extracts. Being a Copious Selection of Instructive, Moral and Entertaining Passages, From the Most Eminent British Poets. London: 1810-21?. V. 48

ELEGANT Extracts: or Useful and Entertaining Passages in Prose. Also Pieces of Poetry and Elegant Epistles. London: 1808. V. 47

AN ELEGY in a Riding House. London: 1778. V. 54

AN ELEGY On a Most Excellent Man and Much Lamented Friend. London: 1771. V. 48

AN ELEGY Written at a Carthusian Monastery in the Austrian Netherlands. London: 1775. V. 54

ELEMEN, P.
Medieval American Art: a Survey in Two Volumes. New York: 1943. V. 50

ELEMENTS of Chess. Boston: 1805. V. 54

THE ELEMENTS of Geography. London: 1830. V. 49

ELESKA
Our Neighbours. New York: 1944. V. 51

ELFRIDA; or, Paternal Ambition. London: 1786. V. 54

ELGIN, THOMAS BRUCE, 7TH EARL OF
Memorandum on the subject of the Earl of Elgin's Pursuits in Greece. Edinburgh: 1811. V. 53

ELGOOD, GEORGE S.
Some English Gardens. London: 1904. V. 52
Some English Gardens. London: 1920. V. 47

ELI LILY & CO.
The Modern Apothecary: a Compendium. Indianapolis: 1941. V. 51

ELIADE, MIRCEA
No Souvenirs. New York: 1977. V. 52

ELIAS, EDITH
The Story of Hiawatha. London: 1914. V. 49

ELIAS, LEVITA
Grammatica Hebraica Absolutissima... Basel: 1525. V. 52

ELICK, D.
Japonica Magnifica. Portland: 1992. V. 48

ELIOT, ANDREW
A Discourse on Natural Religion Delivered in the Chapel of Harvard College in Cambridge, New England May 8, 1771 at the Lecture Founded by the Hon. Paul Dudley. Boston: 1771. V. 52

ELIOT, CHARLES
Turkey in Europe. London: 1908. V. 52

ELIOT, CHARLES W.
Charles Eliot, Landscape Architect. Boston: 1903. V. 47; 48; 52

ELIOT, FRANCIS PERCIVAL
Six Letters on the Subject of the Armed Yeomanry. London: 1797. V. 54

ELIOT, GEORGE
Felix Holt the Radical. Edinburgh & London: 1866. V. 49

ELIOT, GEORGE, PSEUD.
Adam Bede. Edinburgh & London: 1859. V. 48; 50; 51; 52; 53; 54
Adam Bede. New York: 1859. V. 53
Adam Bede. Paris: 1881. V. 51; 53; 54
Agatha. London: 1869. V. 54
Collected Works. London: 1901. V. 51
The Complete Works. New York, Chicago. V. 49
The Complete Works of George Eliot. New York: 1900. V. 49; 54
Daniel Deronda. Edinburgh & London: 1876. V. 47; 48; 49; 50; 51; 52; 53; 54
Daniel Deronda. New York: 1876. V. 47
Daniel Deronda. New York: 1877. V. 47
Daniel Deronda. Paris: 1882. V. 50
Early Essays. London: 1919. V. 53
Essays and Leaves from a Note-Book. Edinburgh & London: 1884. V. 47; 48; 49; 50; 51; 53; 54

ELIOT, GEORGE, PSEUD. continued
Felix Holt the Radical. Edinburgh & London: 1866. V. 48; 49; 50; 51; 52; 54
George Eliot's Complete Works. Boston. V. 52
George Eliot's Life as Related in Her Letters and Journals. London: 1884. V. 51
George Eliot's Life as Related in Her Letters and Journals. Edinburgh and London: 1885. V. 52; 54
George Eliot's Life as Related in Her Letters and Journals. New York: 1885. V. 47; 50; 54
George Eliot's Life as Related in Her Letters and Journals. Edinburgh & London: 1885-86. V. 54
How Lisa Loved the King. Boston: 1869. V. 49; 53; 54
Impressions of Theophrastus Such. Edinburgh: 1879. V. 49; 50; 54
The Legend of Jubal: and Other Poems. Boston: 1874. V. 50; 54
The Legend of Jubal and Other Poems. Edinburgh & London: 1874. V. 49; 50; 53
The Legends of Jubal and Other Poems. Edinburgh & London: 1875. V. 47
Middlemarch. London: 1871. V. 54
Middlemarch. Edinburgh & London: 1871-72. V. 47; 49; 50; 53
Middlemarch. Berlin: 1872. V. 50
Middlemarch. Edinburgh: 1873. V. 47
Middlemarch. New York: 1873. V. 47
Middlemarch. Edinburgh: 1878. V. 50
The Mill on the Floss. Edinburgh and London: 1860. V. 47; 49; 50; 51; 52; 53; 54; 54
The Mill on the Floss. New York: 1860. V. 47; 51; 53
Novels. Edinburgh: 188-?. V. 53
Novels. Edinburgh & London: 1880. V. 48
The Novels. Edinburgh & London: 1898. V. 47
The Novels. London: 1904. V. 49; 51
Poems. New York: 1883. V. 53
Romola. London: 1863. V. 47; 48; 49; 50; 51
Romola. Edinburgh & London: 1874. V. 54
Romola. London: 1880. V. 53
Romola. London: 1886. V. 51
Romola. Boston: 1890. V. 49; 52; 54
Romola. Philadelphia: 1890. V. 51
Scenes of Clerical Life. Edinburgh & London: 1858. V. 47; 50
Scenes of Clerical Life. New York: 1858. V. 53
Scenes of Clerical Life. London: 1859. V. 54
Scenes of Clerical Life. London and New York: 1906. V. 50; 52; 54
Silas Marner. Edinburgh: 1859. V. 53
Silas Marner. Edinburgh and London: 1861. V. 48; 49; 50; 52; 53; 54
Silas Marner. New York: 1861. V. 53; 54
Silas Marner. London: 1907. V. 52
Silas Marner. 1953. V. 53
Silas Marner. London: 1953. V. 49
The Spanish Gypsy: a Poem. Edinburgh and London: 1868. V. 50; 54
The Works. Edinburgh & London. V. 48
The Works... London: 1876/80. V. 48
The Works. Edinburgh: 1878. V. 54
The Works. 1878-80. V. 54
The Works. Edinburgh & London: 1880. V. 47
The Works. Boston: 1880's. V. 47
The Works. Boston: 1886. V. 51
The Works. Boston and New York: 1890. V. 51
The Works. Edinburgh and London: 1895. V. 48
The Works. Boston: 1910. V. 50
The Works. New York: 1910. V. 50; 51
The Works. Philadelphia & New York: 1920. V. 47
The Writings. Together with George Eliot's Life, as Related in Her Letters and Journals... Boston: 1908. V. 48

ELIOT, HOWARD
Eliot Papers No. 1. 1895. V. 49
Eliot Papers No. 1. John Eliot of London, Merchant 1735-1813. London: 1895. V. 50

ELIOT, THOMAS STEARNS
An Address to Members of the London Library. 1952. V. 47; 48
An Address to Members of the London Library. London: 1952. V. 50; 52
After Strange Gods - a Primer of Modern Heresy - the Page-Barbour Lectures at the University of Virginia. London: 1934. V. 47
After Strange Gods: a Primer of Modern Heresy. New York: 1934. V. 53
The Aims of Poetic Drama, the Presidential Address to the Poets' Theatre Guild. London: 1949. V. 54
Anabasis. London: 1930. V. 49
Animula. London: 1929. V. 47; 49; 52; 53; 54
Ara Vus Prec. London: 1920. V. 51
Ash Wednesday. New York & London: 1930. V. 47; 50; 51; 52; 53
Charles Whibley/ A Memoir. Oxford: 1931. V. 48; 51
The Classics and the Man of Letters. London: 1942. V. 52; 53
The Cocktail Party. London: 1950. V. 49; 50; 51; 52; 53; 54
The Cocktail Party. London: 1953. V. 47; 48
Collected Poems 1901-1935. London: 1936. V. 52
Collected Poems 1909-1935. London: 1936. V. 53
Collected Poems 1909-1935. New York: 1936. V. 49; 50
Collected Poems 1909-1962. London: 1963. V. 50
The Confidential Clerk. London: 1954. V. 48; 51
The Criterion: 1922-1939. London: 1967. V. 49
Dante. London: 1929. V. 48; 50; 51; 52; 54
The Dry Salvages. London: 1941. V. 51
The Elder Statesman - a Play. London: 1959. V. 53
Elizabethan Essays. London: 1934. V. 48
Ezra Pound. His Metric and Poetry. New York: 1917. V. 47; 48; 51; 52
Ezra Pound, His Metric and Poetry. New York: 1918. V. 47; 48; 49; 52
The Family Reunion. London: 1939. V. 54
The Family Reunion. New York: 1939. V. 51
For Lancelot Andrewes. London: 1928. V. 48; 51; 53
Four Quartets. London: 1940-42. V. 48; 49; 53; 54
Four Quartets. New York: 1943. V. 47; 49; 52
Four Quartets. London: 1944. V. 50; 51; 52; 53
Four Quartets. 1950. V. 48
Four Quartets. London: 1960. V. 47; 48; 50; 51; 53; 54
Four Quartets. Verona: 1960. V. 51
Four Quartets. 1996. V. 54
From Poe to Valery. New York: 1948. V. 48
From Poe to Valery - A Lecture Delivered at the Library of Congress on Friday, November 19, 1948. Washington: 1949. V. 52
The Frontiers of Criticism - a Lecture Delivered at the University of Minnesota Williams Arena on April 30, 1956. 1956. V. 51
The Hollow Men. Oxford: 1964. V. 47
Homage to John Dryden. London: 1924. V. 51; 53
The Idea of Christian Society. London: 1939. V. 52
Introducing James Joyce: a Selection of Joyce's Prose. London: 1942. V. 53
John Dryden - The Poet - The Dramatist - The Critic - Three Essays. New York: 1932. V. 48; 49; 50; 53
Journey of the Magi. London: 1927. V. 53
Journey of the Magi. New York: 1927. V. 49
Knowledge and Experience,, in the Philosophy of F. H. Bradley. London: 1963. V. 48
The Letters of T. S. Eliot: Volume 1: 1898-1922. London/New York: 1988. V. 48; 51; 53; 54
The Letters of T. S. Eliot, Volume I 1898-1922. New York: 1989. V. 52
Little Gidding. London: 1942. V. 47
Marina. London: 1930. V. 49; 53
Milton. New York: 1947. V. 47; 48
Murder in the Cathedral. 1935. V. 49
Murder in the Cathedral. Canterbury: 1935. V. 47; 51; 53
Murder in the Cathedral. New York: 1935. V. 48
Murder in the Cathedral. London: 1939. V. 53
The Music of Poetry, the Third W. P. Ker Memorial Lecture Delivered in the University of Glasgow, 24th Feb. 1942. Glasgow: 1942. V. 54
Notes Toward the Definition of Culture. London: 1948. V. 54
Odermarken og Andre Digte. (The Waste Land and Other Poems). Kobenhavn: 1948. V. 52
Old Possum's Book of Practical Cats. London: 1939. V. 47; 48; 49; 50; 52; 53; 54
Old Possum's Book of Practical Cats. New York: 1939. V. 51; 52; 53
Old Possum's Book of Practical Cats. New York: 1982. V. 49
A Play. London: 1939. V. 47
Poems. Richmond: 1919. V. 49
Poems. New York: 1920. V. 48
Poems 1909-1925. London: 1925. V. 47; 54
Poems Written in Early Youth. London: 1967. V. 47; 48
Poetry and Drama. London: 1951. V. 48; 53
Points of View. London: 1941. V. 49; 51
A Presidential Address to the Members of the London Library. London: 1952. V. 50
Prufrock and Other Observations. London: 1917. V. 48; 49; 53
Religious Drama: Mediaeval and Modern. New York: 1954. V. 48
The Rock. London: 1934. V. 47; 48; 50; 51; 53; 54
The Rock. New York: 1934. V. 51; 53
The Sacred Wood. London: 1920. V. 48; 50; 51; 54
Selected Essays. London: 1932. V. 54
A Sermon - Preached in Magdalene College Chapel. Cambridge: 1948. V. 50
A Song for Simeon. London: 1928. V. 49; 51; 52; 53
Sweeney Agonistes. London: 1932. V. 47; 49; 50; 52; 53; 54
Tam Domov Mas (East Coker). 1941. V. 50
Thoughts After Lambeth. London: 1931. V. 51
The Three Voices of Poetry. London: 1953. V. 51; 54
Triumphal March. London: 1931. V. 53
The Undergraduate Poems. Cambridge: 1948. V. 48
The Undergraduate Poems of T. S. Eliot. 1949. V. 49
The Undergraduate Poems of T. S. Eliot. Cambridge: 1949. V. 54
The Use of Poetry and the Use of Criticism - Studies in the Relation of Criticism to Poetry in England - The Charles Eliot Norton Lectures for 1932-1933. Cambridge: 1933. V. 54
The Use of Poetry and the Use of Criticism, Studies in the Relation of Criticism to Poetry in England. London: 1933. V. 53; 54
The Waste Land. New York: 1922. V. 51
The Waste Land. Richmond: 1923. V. 53
The Waste Land. London: 1940. V. 48
The Waste Land. London: 1961. V. 47; 50; 53
The Waste Land. London: 1962. V. 48; 49
The Waste Land. London: 1971. V. 47; 49; 50; 53
Zajojstwo w Katedrze. (Murder in the Cathedral). Kent: 1954. V. 50

ELIOT, WILLIAM GRANVILLE
A Treatise on the Defence of Portugal, with a Military Map of the Country, To Which is Added, A Sketch of the Manners and Customs of the Inhabitants and Principal Events of the Campaigns Under Lord Wellington, in 1808 and 1809. London: 1810. V. 47

ELIOTT, STEPHEN
Vain Is the Help of Man. A Sermon Preached in Christ Church, Savannah ...September 15, 1864... Macon: 1864. V. 49

ELIZA
Grimwood. *A Domestic Legend of the Waterloo Road.* London: 1840. V. 48

ELIZABETH
Masters, the Doubly Affianced: Being the Life of a Southern Belle... Philadelphia: 1859. V. 49

ELIZABETH, QUEEN CONSORT OF CHARLES I, KING OF RUMANIA
How I Spent My Sixtieth Birthday. Guildford: 1904. V. 48; 49

ELIZABETH II, QUEEN OF GREAT BRITAIN
The Address of Her Majesty Queen Elizabeth II. Delivered at Westminster Hall and Guildhall on the Occasion of Her Silver Jubilee 1952-1977. Worcester: 1977. V. 49; 50; 52

ELKHART CARRIAGE & HARNESS MANUFACTURING CO.
Catalogue No. 35. 1896. V. 53

ELKIN, R. H.
The Children's Corner. London. V. 47
Old Dutch Nursery Rhymes. London: 1917. V. 49; 50; 51

ELKIN, STANLEY
A Bad Man. New York: 1967. V. 51
Boswell. New York: 1964. V. 49; 51
Criers and Kibitzers, Kibitzers and Criers. New York: 1965. V. 51
The Dick Gibson Show. New York: 1971. V. 47
Early Elkin. Flint: 1985. V. 51
The Franchiser. New York: 1976. V. 51; 54
The Making of Ashenden. 1972. V. 51
The Six-Year Old Man. Flint: 1987. V. 51
Why I Live Where I Live. University City: 1983. V. 54

ELKINS, A.
The Dark Place. 1983. V. 53
Murder in the Queen's Armes. 1985. V. 53

ELKINS, AARON J.
Murder in the Queen's Armes. New York: 1985. V. 49

ELKINS, JOHN M.
Indian Fighting on the Texas Frontier. Amarillo: 1929. V. 52

ELKO. CHAMBER OF COMMERCE
Elko County the Agricultural Center of Nevada. Elko: 1920's. V. 52

ELKUS, RICHARD J.
Alamos, a Philosophy in Living. 1965. V. 47
Alamos: a Philosophy in Living. San Francisco: 1965. V. 52; 54

ELLA, WHEELER
Drops of Water: Poems. New York: 1872. V. 53

ELLACOMBE, H. T.
Practical Remarks on Belfries and Ringers with an Appendix on Chiming. London: 1859. V. 53

ELLACOMBE, HENRY N.
The Plant-Love and Garden-Craft of Shakespare. Exeter: 1878. V. 51; 53
Shakespeare as an Angler. London: 1883. V. 49

ELLARD, HARRY
Ranch Tales of the Rockies. Canon City: 1899. V. 49

ELLEN
Irving, the Female Victimizer, Who Cruelly Murdered Sixteen Persons in Cool Blood, for Revenge on Her First Love, William Shannon, Who Betrayed Her. Baltimore: 1856. V. 52

ELLENBECKER, JOHN G.
The Jayhawkers of Death Valley. Marysville: 1938. V. 52; 53; 54

ELLENBOGEN, GEORGE
Winds of Unreason. Montreal: 1957. V. 47

ELLENPORT, SAMUEL B.
An Essay on the Development and Usage of Brass Plate Dies,... Boston: 1980. V. 50; 52
The Future of Hand-Bookbinding. Boston: 1993. V. 48; 49; 51; 54

ELLERMAN, J. R.
The Families and Genera of Living Rodents... London: 1940-41. V. 47; 48

ELLERMAN, WINIFRED
Civilians. Territet: 1927. V. 48

ELLERY, ABRAHAM REDWOOD
An Oration, Delivered July 4th, 1796, in the Baptist Meeting-House, in Newport. Warren: 1796. V. 54

ELLES, G. L.
British Graptolites. London: 1901-18. V. 51; 52; 53; 54

THE ELLESMERE
Family: a Tale of Unfashionable Life. Wellington, Salop: 1829. V. 51

ELLESMERE, FRANCIS EGERTON, 1ST EARL OF
Town and Country. London: 1836. V. 47

ELLET, C.
The Mississippi and Ohio Rivers... Philadelphia: 1853. V. 47; 48
Report on a Rail-way Suspension Bridge Across the Connecticut, at Middletown, with a Proposal for Its Construction, to a Committee of the Citizens of Hartford. Philadelphia: 1848. V. 49

ELLICE, EDWARD C.
Place-Names in Glengarry and Glenquoich and Their Origin. London: 1898. V. 52
Place-Names in Glengarry and Glenquoich and Their Origin. London: 1931. V. 54

ELLICOTT, ANDREW
The Journal of Andrew Ellicott...During Part of the Year 1796, the Years 1797, 1798, 1799 and Part of the Year 1800. Philadelphia: 1803. V. 52
The Journal of Andrew Ellicott...During Part of the Year 1796, the Years 1797, 1798, 1799 and Part of the Year 1800... Philadelphia: 1814. V. 47

ELLICOTT, THOMAS
Bank of Maryland Conspiracy as Developed in the Report to the Creditors. Philadelphia: 1839. V. 47

ELLIGEN, J.
The Terrible Deeds of George L. Shaftesbury, Who Killed His Own Mother and Sister, Fled from Justice by Leaping from the Palisades, Swimming the Hudson River, and Taking Refuge in New York City... St. Louis: 1851. V. 54

ELLING, CHRISTIAN
Monumenta Architecturae Danicae. Copenhagen: 1961. V. 48

ELLIOT, ANNE
An Old Man's Favour. London: 1887. V. 54

ELLIOT, CHARLES
Public Notice to Her Majesty's Subjects. Macao: 1839. V. 49

ELLIOT, CHARLES W.
The Working of the American Democracy. 1888. V. 54

ELLIOT, DANIEL GIRAUD
The Birds of Daniel Giraud Elliot... New York: 1872. V. 47
The Birds of Daniel Giraud Elliot... London: 1970. V. 54
The Birds of Daniel Giraud Elliot: a Selection of Pheasants and Peacocks... London: 1979. V. 49; 51; 52; 53; 54
The Gallinaceous Game Birds of North America. New York: 1897. V. 49
The Land and Sea Mammals of Middle America and the West Indies. Chicago: 1904. V. 51
The Life and Habits of Wild Animals. London: 1874. V. 48; 50; 52
A Monogaph of the Paradiseidae or Birds of Paradise. New York and Amsterdam: 1977. V. 50; 51; 53
A Monograph of the Bucerotidae or Family of the Hornbills. London: 1877-82. V. 51
A Monograph of the Felidae or family of the Cats. London: 1883. V. 49
A Monograph of the Pittidae or Family of Antthurshes. London: 1893-95. V. 51
A Monograph of the Pittidae, Parts 1 to 6. New York: 1861-63. V. 49
North American Shore Birds... New York: 1895. V. 53
A Review of Primates. New York: 1912/13. V. 49; 52
Review of the Primates. New York: 1913. V. 52

ELLIOT, EMMA
Up in Arms. London: 1896. V. 47

ELLIOT, JAMES
The Poetical and Miscellaneous Works of James Eliot, Citizen of Guilford, Vermont, and Late a Noncommissioned Officer in the Legion of the United States. Greenfield: 1798. V. 47; 52; 54

ELLIOT, JOHN
An Account of the Nature and Medicinal Virtues of the Principal Mineral Waters of Great Britain and Ireland... London: 1781. V. 48; 53
An Account of the Nature and Medicinal Virtues of the Principal Mineral Waters of great Britain and Ireland... London: 1789. V. 51
Elements of the Branches of Natural Philosophy Connected with Medicine... London: 1786. V. 52

ELLIOT, MARY
Gems in the Mine. Traits and Habits of Childhood in Verse. London: 1824. V. 47
Self-Will, or, Young Heads Not the Wisest. London: 1824. V. 47

ELLIOT, ROBERT H.
Gold, Sport and Coffee Planting in Mysore, With Chapters On Coffee Planting in Coorg, the Mysore Representative Assembly, the Indian Congress, Caste and the Indian Silver Question Being the 38 Years' Experiences of a Mysore Planter. London: 1894. V. 49

ELLIOT, ROBERT HENRY
Sclero-Corneal Trephining in the Operative Treatment of Glaucoma. New York: 1913. V. 54

ELLIOT, W. J.
The Spurs. 1939. V. 48; 53

ELLIOTT, BENJAMIN
The Militia System of South-Carolina. Charleston: 1835. V. 52

ELLIOTT, CLAUDE
Leathercoat. The Life History of a Texas Patriot. San Antonio: 1938. V. 47; 53

ELLIOTT, EBENEZER
The Splendid Village; Corn Law Rhymes; and Other Poems. London: 1833. V. 51
The Village Patriarch; a Poem. London: 1829. V. 48

ELLIOTT, HENRY W.
An Arctic Province. London: 1886. V. 49
A Monograph of the Seal Islands of Alaska. Washington: 1882. V. 49; 52; 53
Report on the Seal Islands of Alaska. Washington: 1880. V. 52
Report on the Seal Islands of Alaska. Washington: 1884. V. 52

ELLIOTT, JAMES WILLIAM
National Nursery Rhymes and Nursery Songs Set to Original Music. London: 1870. V. 49

ELLIOTT, JOHN MALSBURY KIRBY
Fifty Years' Fox-Hunting with the Grafton and other Packs of Hounds. London: 1900. V. 47

ELLIOTT, MARY
The Gift of Friendship or, the Riddle Explained. London: 1822. V. 49
Grateful Tributes or Recollections of Infancy. New York and Baltimore: 1819. V. 50
Plain Things for Little Folks. London: 1824. V. 51
Rural Employments; or, a Peep into Village concerns. London: 1820. V. 49

ELLIOTT, MAUD HOWE
Art and Handicraft in the Woman's Building of the World's Columbian Exposition. Chicago: 1894. V. 51

ELLIOTT, RICHARD SMITH
Notes Taken in Sixty Years. St. Louis: 1883. V. 47; 49; 50; 51
Notes Taken in Sixty Years. St. Louis: 1893. V. 49; 54

ELLIOTT, ROBERT
Views in India, China and on the Shores of the Red Sea. London: 1835. V. 52

ELLIOTT, SIMON G.
Report on the Preliminary Survey of the California and Oregon Railroad. Boston: 1865. V. 47

ELLIOTT, STEPHEN
Address of the Rt. Rev. Stephen Elliott, D.D., to the Thirty-Ninth Annual Convention of the Protestant Episcopal Church, in the Diocese of Georgia. Savannah: 1861. V. 49
New Wine Not to Be Put Into Old Bottles. A Sermon Preached in Christ Church, Savannah, on February 28th, 1862, Being the Day of Humiliation, Fasting and Prayer, Appointed by the President of the Confederate States. Savannah: 1862. V. 49
Pastoral Letter from the Bishops of the Protestant Episcopal Church to the Clergy and Laity of the Church in the Confederate States of America...In St. Paul's Church, Augusta, Saturday, Nov. 22d, 1862. Augusta: 1862. V. 49
A Sketch of the Botany of South Carolina and Georgia. Charleston: 1821-24. V. 48
A Sketch of the Botany of South Carolina and Georgia. Charleston: 1824. V. 48; 51; 52
Vain Is the Help of Man. A Sermon Preached in Christ Church, Savannah, on Thursday, September 15, 1864, Being the Day of Fasting, Humiliation and Prayer, Appointed by the Governor of the State of Georgia. Macon: 1864. V. 49

ELLIOTT, SUMNER LOCKE
Careful, He Might Hear You. New York: 1963. V. 54

ELLIOTT, W. G.
Amateur Clubs and Actors. London: 1898. V. 50

ELLIOTT, W. R.
Encyclopaedia of Australian Plants Suitable for Cultivation. Volume 6 K-M. Melbourne: 1993. V. 52

ELLIOTT, WILLIAM
Carolina Sports, by Land and Water. Charleston: 1846. V. 47; 48
Carolina Sports by Land and Water... New York: 1859. V. 51
Carolina Sports by Land and Water. London: 1867. V. 52
Humbug!! A Poem. London: 1826. V. 49

ELLIS, ANABELLA
Chaperoning Adrienne, A Tale of the Yellowstone National Park. Hot Springs. V. 49

ELLIS, ASA
The Country Dyer's Assistant. Brookfield: 1798. V. 47

ELLIS, BRET EASTON
Less than Zero. New York: 1985. V. 51; 52; 53

ELLIS, CHARLES GRANT
Oriental Carpets in the Philadelphia Museum of Art. Philadelphia: 1988. V. 48

ELLIS, CHARLES MAYO
An Essay on Transcendentalism. Boston: 1842. V. 51

ELLIS, CLEMENT
The Gentile Sinner, or England's Brave Gentleman Character'd in a Letter to a Friend. London: 1679. V. 48

ELLIS, DANIEL
Thrilling Adventures of Daniel Ellis. New York: 1867. V. 47

ELLIS, E.
Colorado Mapology. Frederick: 1983. V. 53

ELLIS, E. H.
International Boundary Lines Across Colorado and Wyoming. Boulder: 1966. V. 53

ELLIS, EDITH M. O.
Seaweed: a Cornish Idyll. London: 1898. V. 50

ELLIS, FRANK H.
Canada's Flying Heritage. Toronto: 1962. V. 50

ELLIS, G. A.
New Britain. A Narrative of a Journey...in the Vast Plain of the Missouri... London: 1820. V. 49

ELLIS, GEORGE
Modern Practical Carpentry. London: 1920. V. 50
Modern Practical Joinery. London: 1924. V. 49
Modern Practical Joinery. London: 1925. V. 53
Specimens of Early English Metrical Romances, Chiefly Written During the Early Part of the Fourteenth Century. Edinburgh: 1805. V. 52
Specimens of Early English Metrical Romances, Chiefly Written During the Early Part of the Fourteenth Century... London: 1805. V. 47; 50; 51
Specimens of Early English Metrical Romances, Chiefly Written During the Early Part of the Fourteenth Century. London: 1811. V. 53
Specimens of the Early English Poets. London: 1790. V. 49; 52; 54
Specimens of the Early English Poets. To Which is Prefixed An Historical Sketch of the Rise and Progress of the English Poetry and Language. London: 1801. V. 47; 48; 49; 50

ELLIS, GEORGE E.
Memoir of Sir Benjamin Thompson, Count Rumford... Boston: 1871. V. 51

ELLIS, GEORGE F.
Bell Ranch As I Know It. Kansas City: 1973. V. 53

ELLIS, GEORGE VINER
Illustrations of Dissections in a Series of Original Coloured Plates the Size of Life Representing the Dissection of the Human Body... London: 1867. V. 47; 48; 49; 50
Illustrations of Dissections in a Series of Original Coloured Plates the Size of Life Representing the Dissection of the Human Body. New York: 1882. V. 49

ELLIS, HENRY
Journal of the Proceedings of the Late Embassy to China Comprising a Correct Narrative of the Embassy... London: 1817. V. 48; 51
Original Letters Illustrative of English History. London: 1824. V. 54
Original Letters, Illustrative of English History. London: 1827/46. V. 47; 48
A Voyage to Hudson's Bay, by the Dobb's Galley and California, in the Year 1746 and 1747, for Discovering a North West Passage. London: 1748. V. 47; 54

ELLIS, HENRY HAVELOCK
Chapman. London: 1934. V. 47; 48; 50; 52; 54
Concerning Jude the Obscure. London: 1931. V. 48; 53
The Criminal. London: 1890. V. 52
Kanga Creek. Waltham St. Lawrence: 1922. V. 47
Kanga Creek. New Jersey: 1938. V. 50
Marriage Today and Tomorrow. San Francisco: 1929. V. 49
Poems. London: 1937. V. 49
Studies in the Psychology of Sex. London: 1897/1900. V. 49
Studies in the Psychology of Sex. Philadelphia: 1918. V. 50
Studies in the Psychology of Sex. Philadelphia: 1928. V. 52
Studies in the Psychology of Sex. New York: 1936. V. 50
A Study of British Genius. London: 1904. V. 54

ELLIS, HENRY T.
Hong Kong to Manilla and the Lakes of Luzon in the Phillipine Isles, in the year 1856. V. 53

ELLIS, J. B.
The North American Pyrenomycetes, A Contribution to Mycologic Botany. Newfield: 1892. V. 49

ELLIS, JOHN
Marriage and Its Violations. Licentiousness and Vice. New York: 1860. V. 48

ELLIS, JOHN B.
Free Love and Its Votaries; or, American Socialism Unmasked. New York et al: 1870. V. 53

ELLIS, ROBERT LESLIE
The Mathematical and Other Writings. Cambridge: 1863. V. 53

ELLIS, ROWLAND C.
Colonial Dutch Houses in New Jersey. Newark: 1933. V. 49; 51

ELLIS, SARAH STICKNEY
The Daughters of England: Their Position in Society, Character and Responsibilities. London & Paris: 1842. V. 49; 50; 51
The Daughters of England, Their Position in Society, Character and Responsibilities. New York: 1842. V. 53
Family Secrets, or Hints to Those Who Would Make Home Happy. London: 1843. V. 47
Summer and Winter in the Pyrenees. London: 1841. V. 54
Summer and Winter in the Pyrenees. London and Paris: 1847. V. 49
The Wives of England, Their Relative Duties, Domestic Influence and Social Obligations. New York: 1843. V. 53
The Women of England, Their Social Duties and Domestic Habits. London: 1839. V. 54
The Women of England, Their Social Duties and Domestic Habits. London: 1842?. V. 50
The Women of England. Their Social Duties and Domestic Habits. New York: 1843. V. 53; 54

ELLIS, STEWART M.
William Harrison Ainsworth and His Friends. London: 1911. V. 53

ELLIS, THOMAS T.
Leaves from the Diary of an Army Surgeon; or Incidents of Field Camp and Hospital Life. New York: 1863. V. 47

ELLIS, W. T.
Memories: My Seventy-Two Years in the Romantic County of Yuba, California. Eugene: 1939. V. 52; 54

ELLIS, WILLIAM
An Authentic Narrative of a Voyage Performed by Captain Cook and Captain Clerke in His Majesty's Ships Resolution and Discovery During the years 1776...1780. London: 1783.
An Authentic Narrative of a Voyage Performed by Captain Cook and Captain Clerke in His Majesty's Ships Resolution and Discovery During the Years 1776...1780. Amsterdam & New York: 1969. V. 51; 54
Chiltern and Vale Farming Explained, According to the Latest Improvements. London: 1733. V. 49

ELLIS, WILLIAM continued
Chiltern and Vale Farming Explained, According to the Latest Improvements. London: 1745. V. 48
A Compleat System of Experienced Improvements, Made on Sheep, Grass-Lambs and House Lambs... London: 1749. V. 48; 54
History of Madagascar. London: 1838. V. 47; 48; 50; 51; 54
The London and Country Brewer. London: 1744. V. 50
Madagascar Revisited Describing the Events of a New Reign and the Revolution Which Followed the Persecutions Endured by the Christians... London: 1867. V. 49
The Modern Husbandman. London: 1750. V. 51
Narrative of a Tour through Hawaii or Owhyhee... London: 1826. V. 48
Narrative of a Tour through Hawaii, or Owhyhee... London: 1827. V. 54
Polynesian Researches During a Residence of Nearly Eight Years in the Society and Sandwich Islands. London: 1832. V. 51; 54
Polynesian Researches During a Residence of Nearly Eight Years in the Society and Sandwich Islands. New York: 1833. V. 47
Polynesian Researches During a Residence of Nearly Six Years in the South Sea Islands. London: 1829. V. 49
Polynesian Researches, During a Residence of Nearly Six Years in the South Sea Islands... London: 1830. V. 51
The Practical Farmer. London: 1732. V. 49
Reminiscences and Reflections of an Old Operative. London: 1852. V. 48
Three Visits to Madagascar, During the Years 1853, 1854, 1856. London: 1858. V. 49
Three Visits to Madagascar, During the Years 1853, 1854, 1856. New York: 1859. V. 47; 50; 53

ELLIS, WILLIAM CHARLES
A Treatise on the Nature, Symptoms, Causes and Treatment of Insanity, with Practical Observations on Lunatic Asylums... London: 1838. V. 52

ELLISON, FRANK
A Journal of a Trip Down East, Aug. 1858. Waltham: 1858. V. 50

ELLISON, HARLAN
Dangerous Visions. Garden City: 1967. V. 48
Dangerous Visions. New York: 1967. V. 49; 51; 54
Love ain't Nothing But Sex Misspelled. 1968. V. 49; 52; 54
Love Ain't Nothing But Sex Misspelled. New York: 1968. V. 48
Medea - Harlan's World. 1985. V. 49; 54
Spider Kiss. 1991. V. 47; 49; 51; 53; 54

ELLISON, JAMES
The American Captive, or the Siege of Tripoli. Boston: 1812. V. 52

ELLISON, RALPH
Invisible Man. New York: 1952. V. 50; 51; 52; 53; 54
Invisible Man. London: 1953. V. 51
Invisible Man. 1980. V. 50
Shadow & Act. New York: 1964. V. 51; 53; 54
Shadow and Act. New York: 1966. V. 51

ELLISON, THOMAS
Decorations Pour Parcs et Jardins... Leipzig: 1800. V. 49

ELLMANN, RICHARD
The Limits of Joyce's Naturalism. London: 1956. V. 47

ELLROY, JAMES
Because the Night. New York: 1984. V. 51
Brown's Requiem. London: 1984. V. 47; 53
L. A. Confidential. 1990. V. 51
Silent Terror. Los Angeles: 1987. V. 53
Silent Terror. New York: 1987. V. 50

ELLWOOD, T.
The Book of the Settlement of Iceland. Kendal: 1898. V. 54
The Landnama Book of Iceland As It Illustrates the Dialect, Place Names, Folk Lore & Antiquities of Cumberland, Westmorland and North Lancashire. Kendal: 1894. V. 52

ELLWOOD, THOMAS
The History fo the Life of Thomas Ellwood... London: 1791. V. 49; 54
A Reply to an Answer Lately Published to a Book Long Since Written By W. P. Entituled, A Brief Examination and State of Liberty, Spiritual &c. London: 1691. V. 51
Sacred History: or the Historical Part of the Holy Scriptures... Burlington: 1804. V. 47

ELLYS, ANTHONY
The Spiritual and Temporal Liberty of Subjects in England. London: 1765. V. 48
Tracts on the Liberty, spiritual and Temporal, of Protestants in England. Addressed to J. N. Esq.; at Aix-la-Chapells. Part I (-II). London: 1763-65. V. 52

ELMER, L.
The Pennsylvania Germans of the Shenandoah Valley. Allentown: 1964. V. 50

ELMER, LUCIUS Q. C.
The Constitution and Government of the Province and State of New Jersey, with Biographical Sketches of the Governors from 1776-1845... Newark: 1872. V. 47; 49; 51
History of the Early Settlement and Progress of Cumberland County, New Jersey... Bridgeton: 1869. V. 49; 51

ELMES, JAMES
The Arts and Artists. London: 1825. V. 49
A General and Bibliographical Dictionary of the Fine Arts...Principal Terms Used...Historical Sketches of....Different Schools...Accounts of the Best Books and Treatises. London: 1826. V. 49; 54
Memoirs of the Life and Works of Sir Christopher Wren. London: 1823. V. 51; 52; 53; 54
Metropolitan Improvements; or London, in the Nineteenth Century... London: 1827. V. 51

A Practical Treatise on Ecclesiastical and Civil Dilapidations, Re-Instatements, Waste, &c. London: 1829. V. 50; 54
Sir Christopher Wren and His Times with Illustrative Sketches and Anecdotes of the Most Distinguished Personages in the Seventeenth Century. London: 1852. V. 50; 51

ELMHIRST, E. PENNELL
Fox-Hound, Forest and Prairie. London: 1892. V. 48; 50

ELMORE, STANTON
A Gentleman of the South. New York: 1903. V. 52

AN ELOGY Against Occasion Requires Upon the Earl of Shaftesbury. Calculated for the Meridian of Eighty One. London: 1681. V. 47

ELPHINSTON, JAMES
Education, in Four Books. London: 1763. V. 48
Propriety Ascertained in Her Picture; or, Inglish Speech and Spelling Rendered Mutual Guides. London: 1787. V. 50

ELPHINSTONE, H.
Patterns for Turning: Comprising Elliptical and Other Figures. London: 1872. V. 52

ELPHINSTONE, MOUNTSTUART
An Account of the Kingdom of Cabul and Its Dependencies in Persia, Tartary, and India... 1815. V. 54
An Account of the Kingdom of Caubul and Its Dependencies in Persia, Tartary and India. London: 1819. V. 52
An Account of the Kingdom of Caubul and Its Dependencies in Persia, Tartary and India. London: 1842. V. 47
The History of India. London: 1841. V. 51

ELRINGTON, DR.
Catalogue of the Rare, Valuable and Extensive Library, in Fine Order, and Beautifully Bound of the Late Rev. Dr. Elrington... Dublin: 1850. V. 50

ELRINGTON, THOMAS
A Review of the Correspondence Between the Earl of Mountcashel and The Bishop of Ferns. London: 1830. V. 47

ELSAM, RICHARD
Hints for Improving the Condition of the Peasantry In all Parts of the United Kingdom... London: 1816. V. 49

ELSBERG, CHARLES
Diagnosis and Treatment of Surgical Diseases of the Spinal Cord and Its Membranes. Philadelphia: 1916. V. 47; 52
Tumors of the Spinal Cord and the Symptons of Irritation and Compression of the Spinal Cord and Nerve Roots. New York: 1925. V. 52

ELSEN, ALBERT
Paul Jenkins. New York. V. 47; 48; 49; 50; 52
Paul Jenkins. New York: 1975. V. 51
The Sculpture of Henri Matisse. New York. V. 47; 48; 50; 52
Seymour Lipman. New York. V. 47; 48; 49; 50; 52

ELSENSOHN, M. ALFREDA, SISTER
Pioneer Days in Idaho Country. Caldwell: 1947. V. 53
Pioneer Days in Idaho County. Caldwell: 1947-51. V. 53
Pioneer Days in Idaho County. Caldwell: 1951-65. V. 53

ELSHOLTZ, JOHANN SIGISMUND
The Curious Distillatory... London: 1677. V. 50

ELSKAMP, MAX
Salutations, Dont D'Angeliques. Brussels: 1893. V. 47; 49

ELSON, HENRY WILLIAM
The Civil War through the Camera... Springfield: 1912. V. 50

ELSTOB, ELIZABETH
The Rudiments of Grammar for the English-Saxon Tongue, First Given in English... London: 1715. V. 52

ELSTOB, PETER
The Armed Rehearsal. London: 1964. V. 49
Spanish Prisoner. London: 1939. V. 49

ELSTOBB, WILLIAM
A Book of References to the Map of Sutton and Mepall levels, Done from a Survey Taken in 1750, by Order of the Gentlemen Commissioners, Appointed by Act of Parliament for the Better Draining and Improving Said Levels. Cambridge: 1750. V. 51

ELSUM, JOHN
The Art of Painting After the Italian Manner. London: 1703. V. 47

ELSYINGE, HENRY
The Ancient Manner of Holding Parliaments in England. London: 1675. V. 49

ELSYNGE, HENRY
The Ancient Method and Manner of Holding Parliaments in England. London: 1679. V. 50

ELTING, VICTOR
A Canadian Expedition. 1933. V. 47

ELTON, C.
Voles, Mice and Lemmings: Problems in Population Dynamics. Oxford: 1942. V. 52; 53

ELTON, G. R.
Studies in Tudor and Stuart Politics and Government: Papers and Reviews 1946-1972. 1974. V. 49

ELTON, JAMES FREDERIC
Travels and Researches Among the Lakes and Mountains of Eastern and Central Africa. London: 1879. V. 53

ELTON, RICHARD
The Compleat Body of the Art Military. London: 1668. V. 48

ELUARD, PAUL
Le Dur Desir de Durer. Philadelphia. V. 50
Misfortunes of the Immortals. New York: 1943. V. 51; 53; 54
Pablo Picasso. Geneva/Paris: 1944. V. 52
Poetry and Truth 1942. London: 1944. V. 53
Thorns of Thunder. London: 1936. V. 51

ELVIN, CHARLES N.
A Hand-Book of Orders of Chivalry, War, Medals and Crosses with Their Clasps and Ribbons and Other Decorations. London: 1893. V. 48; 51

ELWALL, EDWARD
The Triumph of Truth: Being an Account of the Trial of Mr. E. Elwall, for Heresy and Blasphemy, at Stafford Assizes (1726) Before Judge Denton. Leeds: 1771. V. 50

ELWELL, NEWTON W.
The Architecture, Furniture and Interiors of Maryland and Virginia During the Eighteenth Century. Boston: 1897. V. 53
Colonial Furniture and Interiors. Boston: 1896. V. 53

ELWES, D. G. C.
A History of Castles, Mansions, and Manors of Western Sussex. London: 1876. V. 52

ELWES, H. J.
A Monograph of the Genus Lilium. London. V. 48
A Revision of the Oriental Hesperiidae. London: 1897. V. 49
The Trees of Great Britain & Ireland. Edinburgh: 1906-13. V. 47; 48; 49; 50; 51; 52

ELWIN, VERRIER
The Tribal World of Verrier Elwin. An Autobiography. Bombay: 1964. V. 51

ELWOOD, ANNE KATHARINE
Memoirs of the Literary Ladies of England, from the Commencement of the Last Century. London: 1843. V. 47

ELWOOD, P.
American Landscape Architecture. New York: 1924. V. 48; 54

ELWORTHY, FREDERICK THOMAS
The Evil Eye: an Account of the Ancient and Widespread Superstition. London: 1895. V. 50; 52; 53
Horns of Honour and Other Studies in the By-Ways of Archaeology. London: 1900. V. 48; 50

ELY, ALFRED
North American Big Game. New York: 1939. V. 47

ELY, EZRA STILES
The Journal of the Stated Preacher to the Hospital and Almshouse in the City of New York, for the year of Our Lord 1811. New York: 1812. V. 52

ELY, REUBEN POWNALL
An Historical Narrative of the Ely, Revell and Stacye Families, Who Were Among the Founders of Trenton and Burlington in the Province of West Jersey, 1678-1683. New York: 1910. V. 49; 51

ELYOT, THOMAS
The Castel of Helth. New York: 1940. V. 48

ELYTIS, ODYSSEUS
Six and One Remorses for the Sky. Helsinki: 1985. V. 48

EMANUEL, HARRY
Diamonds and Precious Stones: Their History, Value and Distinguishing Characteristics. London: 1867. V. 49
Diamonds and Precious Stones: Their History, Value and Distinguishing Characteristics. London: 1867/84. V. 49

EMANUEL, SOLOMON
An Historical Sketch of the Georgetown Rifle Guards and As Co. A of the Tenth Regiment. 1909. V. 49

EMANUEL, WALTER
A Conceited Puppy: Some Incidents in the Life of a Gay Dog. New York: 1905. V. 49
A Dog Day. New York: 1919. V. 54
The Snob, Some Episodes in a Mis-Spent Youth. London: 1904. V. 49

EMBLEMS for the Entertainment and Improvement of Youth. London: 1750. V. 53

EMBODEN, WILLIAM
Jean Cocteau and the Illustrated Book. Northridge: 1990. V. 50

EMBURY, MISS
Tales for the Young. London: 1848. V. 48

EMDEN, WALTER
Picturesque Westminster. London: 1902. V. 50; 52

EMERSON, CAROLINE
Mickey Sees the U.S.A. London: 1944. V. 53
School Days in Disneyville. Boston: 1939. V. 53; 54

EMERSON, D.
A Book of Old Maps. Cambridge: 1926. V. 48

EMERSON, EDWARD R.
Beverages, Past and Present. New York: 1908. V. 47
The Story of the Vine. New York & London: 1902. V. 47; 48

EMERSON, EDWARD WALDO
Emerson in Concord. A Memoir... Boston & New York: 1889. V. 54

EMERSON, G.
A Report on the Trees and Shrubs Growing Naturally in the Forests of Massachusetts. Boston: 1846. V. 52
Report on the Trees and Shrubs Growning Naturally in the Forests of Mass. Boston: 1878. V. 54

EMERSON, GOUVERNEUR
Medical Statistics: Consisting of Estimates Relating to the Population of Philadelphia, with Its Changes as Influenced by the Deaths and Births, During Ten Years, viz. from 1821 to 1830, Inclusive. Philadelphia: 1831. V. 48

EMERSON, H. H.
The May Blossom or the Princess and Her People. London: 1881. V. 47; 48

EMERSON, JAMES
Letters from the Aegean. New York: 1829. V. 47

EMERSON, JOSEPH
Prospectus of the Female Seminary, at Weathersfield, Ct. Comprising a General Prospectus, Course of Instruction, Maxims of Education and Regulations of the Seminary. Wethersfield: 1826. V. 49

EMERSON, LUCY
The New-England Cookery, or the Art of Dressing All Kinds of Flesh, Fish and Vegetables and All Kinds of Cakes... Montpelier: 1808. V. 51

EMERSON, NATHANIEL B.
Unwritten Literature of Hawaii; the Sacred Songs of the Hula, Collected and Translated with Notes and an Account of the Hula. Washington: 1909. V. 47; 49

EMERSON, P. H.
Birds, Beasts and Fishes of the Norfolk Broadland. London: 1895. V. 49
Marsh Leaves. London: 1895. V. 47
Marsh Leaves from the Norfolk Broad-Land. Stratford Essex: 1898. V. 48
Tales From Welsh Wales: Founded on Fact and Current Tradition. London: 1894. V. 48

EMERSON, RALPH WALDO
An Address Delivered Before the Senior Class in Divinity College. Boston: 1838. V. 52; 54
An Address Delivered in the Court-House in Concord. Boston: 1844. V. 47; 52; 53
Ceremonies at the Dedication of the Soldier's Monument, in Concord. Concord: 1867. V. 47
Complete Works. London: 1894-1903. V. 49
The Complete Works. Boston: 1903. V. 53
The Complete Works. Boston: 1903-04. V. 54
The Complete Works. Boston: 1923. V. 48
The Conduct of Life. Boston: 1860. V. 51; 52
The Conduct of Life. London: 1860. V. 53
The Correspondence of Thomas Carlyle and Ralph Waldo Emerson: 1834-1872. Boston: 1883. V. 50
Emerson. (The Essays of Emerson). London: 1899. V. 48
English Traits. Boston: 1856. V. 48; 49; 51; 52; 53; 54
Essais de Philosophie Americaine... Paris: 1851. V. 47
Essays. Boston: 1841. V. 47; 48; 49; 50; 52; 53; 54
Essays. London: 1841. V. 47
Essays. Boston: 1841-44. V. 53
Essays. 1906. V. 48; 49; 52
Essays. Hammersmith: 1906. V. 49; 51
Essays. London: 1910. V. 52; 54
The Essays. San Francisco: 1934. V. 51; 53; 54
The Essays. Santa Fe: 1934. V. 51
Essays. First Series. Boston: 1847. V. 53; 54
Essays. Second Series. Boston: 1844. V. 47; 49; 51; 52; 53
Essays. Second Series. (with) The Emancipation of the Negroes in the British West Indies. London: 1844. V. 49
Fortune of the Republic. Boston: 1878. V. 47; 48; 52; 53
Friendship. New York: 1993. V. 51
Friendship and Love. New York: 1920. V. 48
Journals. 1820-1872. Cambridge: 1909. V. 47
Journals 1820-1876. Cambridge: 1909-194. V. 53
Letters and Social Aims. Boston: 1876. V. 47; 51
Love, Friendship, Domestic Life. Boston: 1877. V. 48
Man the Reformer: a Lecture on Some of the Prominent Features of the Present Age... London: 1842?. V. 49
May Day and Other Pieces. Boston: 1867. V. 47; 51; 52; 53
May-Day and Other Pieces. London: 1867. V. 51; 52; 53
The Method of Nature. Boston: 1841. V. 52; 53
Miscellanies. Boston: 1856. V. 51; 52; 53
Moments with Emerson. London. V. 52
Nature. Munchen. V. 53
Nature. Boston: 1836. V. 50; 52
Nature. Boston & Cambridge: 1849. V. 47; 52; 53
Nature. Muenchen: 1929. V. 47; 49; 54
Nature. Croton Falls: 1932. V. 49
Nature. New York: 1949. V. 48
An Oration Delivered Before the Literary Societies of Dartmouth College. Boston: 1838. V. 47; 52; 53
Poems. Boston: 1847. V. 53; 54

EMERSON, RALPH WALDO continued
Poems. London: 1847. V. 52; 53
Poems. London: 1850. V. 49
Poems. Boston: 1876. V. 47
The Preacher. Boston: 1880. V. 54
Representative Men. Boston: 1850. V. 51; 52; 53
Society and Solitude. Boston: 1870. V. 48; 51
The Works. Boston. V. 54
Works. Cambridge: 1903. V. 47
The Works. New York: 1920. V. 47
Works. New York: 1930. V. 49

EMERSON, WILLIAM
The Elements of Geometry, In Which the Principal Propositions of Euclid, Archimedes, and Others... London: 1794. V. 50
The Elements of Optics. (with) Perspective: or, the Art of Drawing the Representations of All Objects Upon a Plane. London: 1768. V. 54
Mechanics: or, the Doctrine of Motion. (with) The Projection of the Sphere, Orthographic, Stereographic and Gnomical. (with) The Laws of Centripetal and Centrifugal Force. London: 1769/69/69. V. 50
The Method of Increments Wherein the Principles are Demonstrated... London: 1763. V. 48
Old Bridges of France. New York: 1925. V. 51
The Principles of Mechanics. London: 1800. V. 52; 54
A System of Astronomy. London: 1769. V. 50; 53

EMERSON, WILLIAM C.
Stories and Spirituals of the Negro Slave. Boston: 1930. V. 48

EMERY, JACK
The Putney Debates. 1983. V. 47
The Putney Debates. London: 1983. V. 50

EMERY, M.
Furniture by Architects. New York: 1983. V. 54

EMERY, STEPHEN A.
Elements of Harmony. Boston: 1924. V. 50

EMERY, WALTER B.
Excavations at Buhens and Diagrams with Descriptive Text... London: 1976-79. V. 49; 51
Great Tombs of the First Dynasty I. Cairo: 1949. V. 51
The Royal Tombs of Ballena and Questul. Cairo: 1938. V. 51
The Tomb of Hemaka. Cairo: 1938. V. 51

EMES, THOMAS
A Dialogue Between Alkali and Acid... London: 1699. V. 53

EMICH, KARL, COUNT ZU LEININGEN-WESTERBURG
German Book-plates. An Illustrated Handbook of German & Austrian Ex-libris. London and New York: 1901. V. 47

EMIGRATION Papers Relative to Emigration to the British Provinces in North America, and to the Australian Colonies. London: 1847. V. 54

EMIGRATION Papers Relative to Emigration to the British Provinces in North America. London: 1848. V. 54

EMIGRATION to the United States. (and) Description of the United States. Edinburgh: 1841. V. 54

EMIGRATION to Van Diemens Land and New Zealand. Edinburgh: 1841. V. 54

EMILIO, LUIS F.
A Brave Black Regiment: History of the Fifty-Fourth Regiment of Massachusetts Volunteer Infantry, 1863-65. Boston: 1894. V. 54
Roanoke Island, Its Occupation, Defense and Fall. New York?: 1891. V. 49

EMINENT Authors and Poets with Facsimiles of Their Autographs. 1880. V. 54

EMINESCU, MIHAL
Star and Other Poems. Concord: 1990. V. 53; 54

EMMERICH, A.
Sweat of the Sun and Tears of the Moon. Gold and Silver in Pre-Columbian Art. Seattle: 1965. V. 54

EMMERTON, ISAAC
A Plain and Practical Treatise on the Culture and Management of the Auricula, Polyanthus, Carnation, Pink and the Ranunculus... London: 1819. V. 50; 52

EMMERY, H. C.
Pont d'Ivry en Bois sur Piles en Pierre, Traversant la Seine pres du Confluent de la marne. Paris: 1832. V. 51

EMMET, ROSINA
Pretty Peggy and Other Ballads. New York: 1880. V. 51

EMMETT, A. M.
The Scientific Names of the British Lepidoptera - Their History and Meaning. Colchester: 1991. V. 50

EMMETT, CHRIS
Texas Camel Tales. 1932. V. 47
Texas Camel Tales. San Antonio: 1932. V. 50; 53

EMMETT, DAN
I Wish I Was in Dixie's Land. New York: 1860. V. 48; 49

EMMONS, E.
Agriculture of New York. Albany: 1843-49. V. 52
Agriculture of New York... Albany: 1843-49-51. V. 50
Agriculture of New York. London: 1846. V. 52; 53; 54
Agriculture of New York... New York: 1846-49-51-54. V. 47
Agriculture of New York. Volume 1. Albany: 1846. V. 54
Agriculture of North Carolina. Part II... Raleigh: 1860. V. 52
Geological Report of the Midland Counties of North Carolina. New York: 1856. V. 49
Natural History of New York. Division 5 - Agriculture. Albany: 1845-54. V. 51

EMMONS, RICHARD
The Ferdoniad: or, Independence Preserved. Boston: 1827. V. 50

EMORY, WILLIAM
Report on the United States and Mexican Boundary Survey, Made Under the Direction of the Secretary of Interior. Austin: 1987. V. 53

EMORY, WILLIAM HEMSLEY
Notes of a Military Reconnaissance, from Fort Leavenworth in Missouri, to San Diego, in California... London: 1848. V. 47
Notes of a Military Reconnaissance from Fort Leavenworth, in Missouri, to San Diego, in California, Including Parts of the Arkansas, Del Norte and Gila Rivers. Washington: 1848. V. 47; 49; 51; 52; 53; 54
Report of the U.S. and Mexican Boundary Survey. Washington: 1857. V. 47; 51; 53
Report of the U.S. and Mexican Boundary Survey. College Station: 1987. V. 48
United States & Mexican Boundary Survey. Report of... Washington: 1857-59. V. 52

EMPARAN, MADIE BROWN
The Vallejos of California. San Francisco: 1968. V. 54

THE EMPIRE Gold Mining Company Plymouth, Amador County, California. Capital $2,000,000. Philadelphia: 1879. V. 52

EMPSON, PATIENCE
The Wood Engravings of Robert Gibbings, with Some Recollections of the Artist. 1969. V. 48
The Wood Engravings of Robert Gibbings, with Some Recollections of the Artist. London: 1969. V. 52

EMPSON, WILLIAM
The Gathering Storm. London: 1940. V. 48
Letter IV. Cambridge: 1929. V. 52

ENAULT, LOUIS
Londres. Paris: 1876. V. 50; 52

THE ENCHANTED Mice. London: 1855. V. 50

ENCYCLOPAEDIA Americana. New York: 1973. V. 47

ENCYCLOPAEDIA Britannica. Edinburgh: 1768-71. V. 52
ENCYCLOPAEDIA Britannica. Edinburgh: 1771. V. 54
ENCYCLOPAEDIA Britannica. Edinburgh: 1797. V. 48
ENCYCLOPAEDIA Britannica. Edinburgh: 1797/1824. V. 53
ENCYCLOPAEDIA Britannica. London: 1910-22. V. 51
ENCYCLOPAEDIA Britannica. London: 1910-26. V. 52

THE ENCYCLOPAEDIA Britannica. London: 1926. V. 52

ENCYCLOPAEDIA Britannica. London: 1957. V. 54
ENCYCLOPAEDIA Britannica. London: 1966. V. 51
ENCYCLOPAEDIA Britannica. 1972. V. 54
ENCYCLOPAEDIA Britannica. London: 1975. V. 51

THE ENCYCLOPAEDIA Of Marine Invertebrataes. London: 1983. V. 50

ENCYCLOPAEDIA of Plant Physiology. New Series. Volume 20. Berlin: 1993. V. 50

ENCYCLOPAEDIA of Science and Technology. New York: 1971. V. 47
ENCYCLOPAEDIA of Science and Technology. New York: 1987. V. 47

THE ENCYCLOPAEDIA of Wit. London: 1803. V. 49

ENCYCLOPEDIA Britannica. Edinburgh: 1817. V. 48

ENCYCLOPEDIA Canadiana. Toronto: 1972. V. 51

ENCYCLOPEDIA of Camellias in Color. 1972. V. 51
ENCYCLOPEDIA of Camellias in Color. London: 1972. V. 48

ENCYCLOPEDIA Of World Art. New York: 1959. V. 48

ENCYCOPAEDIA of Sport. London: 1901. V. 50

ENDERS, JOHN O.
Random Notes on Hunting. Hartford: 1955. V. 47

ENDGRAIN: Contemporary Wood Engraving in North America. 1994 i.e. 1995. V. 54
ENDGRAIN: Contemporary Wood Engraving in North America. 1995. V. 52

ENDICOTT, WENDELL
Adventures in Alaska and Along the Trail. New York: 1928. V. 48; 51; 53

ENDLESS Amusement: a Collection of Nearly 400 Entertaining Experiments in Various Branches of Science... London: 1822. V. 47

ENDO, SHUSAKU
Silence. Tokyo: 1969. V. 53

ENDORE, GUY
The Crime at Scottsboro. Hollywood: 1935. V. 53

THE ENDOWED Charities of the City of London; Reprinted at Large from Seventeen Reports of the Commissioners for Inquiring Concerning Charities. London: 1829. V. 50

ENFIELD, WILLIAM
An Essay Towards the History of Liverpool, Drawn Up From Papers Left by the Late Mr. George Perry, and from Other Materials Since Collected... Warrington: 1773. V. 49
Institutes of Natural Philosophy, Theoretical and Experimental. London: 1785. V. 47; 49; 50
Institutes of Natural Philosophy, Theoretical and Experimental. 1799. V. 54
Institutes of Natural Philosophy, Theoretical and Experimental. London: 1799. V. 49
Scientific Amusements in Philosophy and Mathematics. London: 1821. V. 53

ENGEL, JOHANN JACOB
Lorenz Stark, a Characteristic Picture of a German Family. London: 1826. V. 54

ENGEL, LEO
American and Other Drinks. London: 1878. V. 50

ENGEL, MARIAN
Bear. New York: 1976. V. 52
Bear. Toronto: 1976. V. 52

ENGEL, SAMUEL
Essai sur Cette Question: Quand et Comment L'Amerique a-t-elle Peuplee d'Hommes et d'Animaux?. Amsterdam: 1767. V. 53
Memoires et Observations Geographiques et Critiques sur la Situation des Pays Septentrionaux de l'Asie et de l'Amerique... Lausanne: 1765. V. 47

ENGELBACH, LEWIS
Naples and the Campagna Felice. London: 1815. V. 49

ENGELBACH, R.
Harageh. London: 1923. V. 49; 51
Riqqeh and Memphis VI. London: 1915. V. 49; 51

ENGELBACH, WILLIAM
Endocrine Medicine. Springfield: 1932. V. 52

ENGELBRECHT, MARTIN
Elogia Mariana... Augsburg?: 1732. V. 52

ENGELHARDT, H. A.
The Beauties of Nature Combined with Art. Montreal: 1872. V. 53

ENGELHARDT, ZEPHYRIN, FATHER
Franciscans in Arizona. Harbor Springs: 1899. V. 48; 49; 51
The Franciscans in California. Harbor Springs: 1897. V. 47
The Missions and Missionaries of California. San Francisco: 1908-16. V. 50
The Missions and Missionaries of California. Santa Barbara: 1929. V. 48; 53

ENGELMANN, G.
Cactaceae of the Boundary. Washington: 1858. V. 51

ENGELMANN, GEORGE J.
Labor Among Primitive Peoples. St. Louis: 1883. V. 47

ENGELS, FREDERICK
The Origin of the Family, Private Property and the State. Chicago: 1902. V. 53

ENGELS, JOHANN ADOLPH
Ueber Papier und Einige Andere Gegenstande der Technologie und Industrie. Duisburg und Essen: 1808. V. 52; 53

THE ENGINEER and Machinist's Drawing-Book, a Complete Course of Instruction for the Practical Engineer...on the Basis of the Works of M. Le Blanc and MM. Armengaud. Glasgow: 1855. V. 53

ENGINEERING RESEARCH ASSOCIATES
High-speed Computing Devices. New York: 1950. V. 48; 52; 54

ENGLAND, GEORGE ALLAN
The Air Trust. St. Louis: 1915. V. 51
The Golden Blight. New York: 1916. V. 48
Keep Off the Grass. Boston: 1919. V. 48
Out of the Real. 1914. V. 49; 54

ENGLAND Illustrated, or, a Compendium of the Natural History, Geography, Topography and Antiquities Ecclesiastical and Civil of England and Wales. London: 1764. V. 52

ENGLAND, JOHN
The Works of the Rt. Rev. John England. Cleveland: 1908. V. 52

ENGLAND, ROBERT
The Colonization of Western Canada: a Study of Contemporary Land Settlement (1896-1934). London: 1936. V. 49

ENGLAND'S Black Tribunal: Containing the Compleat Tryal of King Charles the First. London: 1720. V. 52

ENGLAND'S Black Tribunal, Containing the Complete Tryal of King Charles the First... London: 1737. V. 53

ENGLAND'S Black Tribunal. Set Forth in the Tryal of Charles I...Together With His Majesties Speech, on the Scaffold...Also a Perfect Relation of the Sufferings, and Death of Divers of the Nobility and Gentry... London: 1680. V. 51

ENGLAND'S Genius; or, Wit Triumphant. London: 1734. V. 48

ENGLE, PAUL
American Song: a Book of Poems. Garden City: 1934. V. 49
Break the Heart's Anger. Garden City: 1936. V. 49; 53
Corn: a Book of Poems. New York: 1939. V. 50; 53
Poet's Choice. New York: 1962. V. 50
West of Midnight. New York: 1941. V. 50

ENGLEFIELD, HENRY C.
A Description of the Principle Picturesque Beauties, Antiquities, and Geological Phenomena, of the Isle of Wight. London: 1816. V. 54
Observations on the Probable Consequences of the Demolition of London Bridge. London: 1821. V. 51
A Walk through Southampton. London: 1801. V. 50
A Walk through Southampton... Southampton: 1805. V. 47; 48; 51; 53

ENGLEFIELD, W. A. D.
The History of the Painter-Stainers Company of London. London: 1923. V. 47

ENGLEHEART, JOHN GARDINER DILLMAN
Journal of the Progress of H.R.H. the Prince of Wales through British North America, and His Visit to the United States, 19th July to 15th Nov. 1860. London: 1860?. V. 53

ENGLEHEART, N. B.
A Concise Treatise on Eccentric Turning... London: 1867. V. 47; 49
A Concise Treatise on Eccentric Turning. London: 1952. V. 52

ENGLEKIRK, JOHN EUGENE
Edgar Allan Poe in Hispanic Literature. New York: 1934. V. 48

ENGLISH, A. L.
History of Atlantic City, New Jersey. Philadelphia: 1884. V. 49; 51

ENGLISH and Gujarati Dictionary with Gujarati Pronunciations. London: 1863. V. 47

ENGLISH As She Is Taught. Genuine Answers to Some Examination Questions Asked in Our Public Schools. New York: 1901. V. 49

ENGLISH Bijou Almanac for 1836. London: 1835. V. 52

ENGLISH Bijou Almanac for 1840. London: 1839. V. 49

THE ENGLISH Cyclopaedia. London: 1854-56. V. 54

ENGLISH Diaries.../More English Diaries. London: 1923-27. V. 54

ENGLISH Fairy Tales. London: 1918. V. 50

AN ENGLISH Florilegium, Flowers, Trees, Shrubs, Fruits, Herbs, the Tradescant Legacy. New York: 1987. V. 51

THE ENGLISH Gardener's New and Complete Kalendar... London: 1778. V. 52

AN ENGLISH Garner In Gatherings from Our History and Literature. London: 1897. V. 52

ENGLISH, HARRIET
Conversations and Amusing Tales. London: 1799. V. 47; 49; 54

THE ENGLISH Lakes in the Neighbourhood of Ambleside. London: 1870. V. 50; 52

ENGLISH Lyrcis from Spenser to Milton. London: 1898. V. 52

THE ENGLISH Poems Collected from the Oxford and Cambridge Verses on the Death of His Royal Highness Frederick Prince of Wales. Edinburgh: 1751. V. 47

ENGLISH Rustic Pictures Drawn by Frederick Walker and G. J. Pinwell and Engraved by the Brothers dalziel. India Proofs. London: 1882. V. 52

ENGLISH, THOMAS H.
A Memoir of the Yorkshire Esk Fishery Association. London: 1925. V. 52
A Memoir of the Yorkshire Esk Fishery Association. Whitby: 1925. V. 51; 54

ENGLISH, WILLIAM B.
Celebrated Trial of Rev. J. H. Fairchild, for the Alledged Seduction of Miss Rhoda Davidson... Boston: 1844. V. 51

ENGLISH, WILLIAM HAYDEN
Conquest of the Country Northwest of the River Ohio 1778-1783; and Life of Gen. George Rogers Clark... Indianapolis: 1896. V. 48; 51

ENIAUTOS Terastios. Mirabilis Annus, or the Year of Prodigies and Wonders, Being a Faithful and Impartial Collection of Several Signs That Have been Seen in the Heavens in the Earth and in the Waters. (with) Mirabilis Annus Secundus, or... 1662. V. 50

ENNEMOSER, JOSEPH
The History of Magic. London: 1854. V. 48

ENNIUS, QUINTUS
Poetae Cum Primus Censendi, Annalium Libb. XIIX... Leiden: 1595. V. 51

AN ENQUIRY Into Some Things That Concern Scotland, Containing Some Remarks Upon a Certain Book... Edinburgh: 1734. V. 50; 51

AN ENQUIRY Into the Nature and Obligation of Legal Rights; With Respect to the Popular Pleas of the Late K. James's Remaining Right to the Crown. London: 1693. V. 52

ENRIGHT, D. J.
Poems of the 1950s an Anthology of New English Verse. Tokyo: 1956. V. 52

ENRIGHT, ELIZABETH
Borrowed Summer. New York: 1946. V. 49

ENRIQUEZ GOMEZ, ANTONIO
La Torre de Babilonia,, Primera Parte (all published). Rouen: 1649. V. 53

ENSCHEDE, CHARLES
Typefoundries in the Netherlands from the 15th to the 19th Century. Haarlem: 1978. V. 48; 49; 51; 52

ENSCHEDE EN ZONEN
Specimen of Dutch Black-Letters and Gothic Initials of the XVth Century. Haarlem: 1925. V. 50

ENSCHEDE, J.
Proef van Letteren, Welke Gegooten Worden in de Nieuwe Haerlemsche Lettergietery van J. Enschede. (with) Oude Hollandse Letteren Zynde Erstelingen der Boek-Drukkonst... (with) Vermeerdering van Meest Nieuw Gesnedene Letteren, in die Haarlemsche... Haarlem: 1768/68/73. V. 47

ENSIGN & THAYER
Travellers' Guide through the States of Ohio, Michigan, Indiana, Illinois, Missouri, Iowa and Wisconsin... New York: 1849. V. 54
Travellers' Guide through the States of Ohio, Michigan, Indiana, Illinois, Missouri, Iowa and Wisconsin with Railroad, Canal, Stage and Steamboat Routes... New York: 1853. V. 47

ENSIGN, Bridgman & Fannings' *Travellers' Guide through the States of Ohio, Michigan, Indiana, Illinois, Missouri, Iowa and Wisconsin, with Railroad, Canal, Stage and Steamboat Routes.* New York: 1857. V. 48; 51

ENSKO, STEPHEN G. C.
American Silversmiths and Their Marks III. New York: 1948. V. 47

ENSLIN, THEODORE
Forms. New Rochelle: 1970-74. V. 51
The Work Proposed. Ashland: 1958. V. 48; 51

ENSOR, GEORGE
The Independent Man; or, an Essay on the Formation and Development of Those Principles and Faculties of the Human Mind Which Constitute Moral and Intellectual Excellence. London: 1806. V. 52

ENSOR, JAMES
Scenes de la Vie du Christ. Brussels: 1921. V. 47

DAS ENTDECKTE Geheimniss des Achten Porcelains, Sowohl des Chinesischen als Sachsischen; von Einem Besitzer Dieses Geheimnisses. Berlin: 1750. V. 50

ENTERTAINING and Instructive Rambles for Young Persons. London: 1827. V. 50

ENTERTAINING Fables for the Instruction of Children. Irongate: 1769-94. V. 50

THE ENTERTAINING Story of Little Red Riding Hood to Which is added Tom Thumb's Toy. York: 1820. V. 49

AN ENTERTAINING Tour, Containing a Variety of Incidents and Adventures, in a Journey through Part of Flanders, Germany & Holland, Historical, Political and Entertaining. London: 1791. V. 48

ENTICK, JOHN
Entick's New Spelling Dictionary... London: 1788. V. 52
Entick's new Spelling Dictionary... London: 1801. V. 52
Entick's New Spelling Dictionary... London: 1803. V. 52
The General History of the Late War...In Europe, Asia, Africa dn America. London: 1763-64. V. 48
A New and Accurate History and Survey of London, Westminster, Southwark... London: 1766. V. 52

ENTRECASTEAUX, ANTOINE RAYMOND JOSEPH DE BRUNI, CHEVAILER D'
Voyage Dentrecasteaux, Envoye a la Recherche de La Perouse... (with) Atlas du voyage de Bruny-Dentrecasteaux...fait par Ordre du Gouvernement en 1791, 1792 and 1793. Paris: 1807. V. 50

ENTREE de Tres Haut et Tres Puissant Prince Henry de Bourbon, Prince de Conde...en la Ville de Dijon. Dijon: 1632. V. 53

ENTWISLE, E. A.
French Scenic Wallpapers 1800-1860. Leigh-on-Sea: 1972. V. 50; 52; 53

EPHRON, PHOEBE
Take Her, She's Mine. New York: 1962. V. 50

EPICTETUS
All the Works of... London: 1758. V. 48; 49; 50; 51
All the Works of Epictetus Which are Now Extant... London: 1768. V. 52
Arte di Correrger la Vita Humana. Venice: 1583. V. 52
Discourses. Berne: 1966. V. 47; 51; 52; 53; 54
Epictetus His Morals, with Simplicius His Comment. London: 1694. V. 50
Epictetus His Morals, with Simplicius His Comment. London: 1721. V. 48

EPICURUS
Epicurus: The Extant Remains of the Greek Text... New York: 1947. V. 47; 48; 52; 53; 54
Epicurus's Morals. London: 1656. V. 48

EPIGRAMMATA et Poematia Vetera. Paris: 1590. V. 50

EPINAY, LOUISE FLORENCE
The Conversations of Emily. London: 1815. V. 53; 54
The Memoirs and Correspondence. London: 1897. V. 51

EPIPHANY 1978 and Happy Birthday. From Laura Evans and Friends. Mt. Horeb: 1978. V. 51

EPISCOPAL CHURCH. BOOK OF COMMON PRAYER
The Book of Common Prayer. New York: 1893. V. 53

THE EPISCOPAL Registers of Carlisle. The Register of Bishop John de Halton, Part I 1293-1300. Kendal: 1906. V. 52

THE EPISCOPAL Registers of Carlisle. The Register of Bishop John de Halton, Part II: 1003-1309. Kendal: 1909. V. 52

THE EPISCOPAL Registers of Carlisle. The Register of Bishop John de Halton. Part III 1292-1324. Kendal: 1913. V. 52

EPISCOPIUS, JAN DE
Paradigmata Graphices Variorum Artificum. The Hague: 1671. V. 49

THE EPISTLE from the Yearly Meeting, Held in London...(1804-13). New Bedford: 1806-13. V. 54

AN EPISTLE of Caution to Friends in General, Relating to the Solemn Affirmation. London: 1721-22. V. 50

AN EPISTLE to Sir Richard Blackmore, Kt. on Occasion of the Late Great Victory in Brabant. Colophon: 1706. V. 53

EPISTOLA de Contemptu Mundi Di Frate Hieronymo De Ferrara Dellordine de Frati Predicatori La Quale Manda ad Elena Buonaccorsi Sua Madre, Per Consolarla Della Morte Del Fratello, Suo Zio. London: 1894. V. 47

EPISTOLIA, Dialogi, Breves, Orativncvlae, Poematia. Paris: 1577. V. 47

EPITHALAMIA Oxoniensia sive Gratulationes in Augustissimi Regis Georgii III et Illustrissimae Principissae Sophiae Charlottae Nupitas Auspicatissimas. Oxonii: 1761. V. 49; 50

AN EPITOME of the History of Algiers, from the First Settlements of the Moors in Those Parts, After the Expulsion from Granada by the Spaniards, to the Time They Rendered themselves Independent of the Ottoman Porte. London: 1750. V. 51

AN EPOSTULARY Letter to a Certain Right Honourable Person (i.e. Earl of Chesterfield) Upon His Promotion. London: 1757. V. 48

EPPES, SUSAN BRADFORD
Through Some Ventful Years by Susan Bradford Eppes. Macon: 1926. V. 47

EPPS, JAMES
The Cacao Plant: a Trip to the West Indies. Croydon: 1897-1903. V. 52

EPSTEAN, EDWARD
A Catalogue of the Epstean Collection on the History and Science of Photography and its Application Especially to the Graphic Arts. New York: 1937. V. 47

EPSTEIN, CLAIRE
Palestinian Bichrome Ware. Leiden: 1966. V. 49; 51

EPSTEIN, JACOB
Drawings. London: 1962. V. 49
Epstein 1956 - a Camera Study of the Sculptor at Work. London: 1956. V. 54
Let There Be Sculpture - an Autobiography. London: 1940. V. 49
The Sculptor Speaks. London: 1931. V. 51

EQUIANO, OLAUDAH
The Interesting Narrative of the Life of Olaudah Equiano, or Gustavus Vassa, the African. New York: 1791. V. 54
The Interesting Narrative of the Life of Olaudah Equiano, or Gustavus Vassa, the African. London: 1793. V. 48; 49

EQUICOLA, MARIO
Libro de natura de Amore... Vinegia: 1526. V. 50

ERASMUS, DESIDERIUS
Adagiorum Epitome. Oxoniae: 1666. V. 48; 50
All the Familiar Colloquies of Desiderius Erasmus, of Roterdam Concerning Men, Manners and Things. London: 1725. V. 47
All the Familiar Colloquies...Concerning Men, Manners and Things. 1733. V. 47
Apopthegmatum. Paris: 1534. V. 47
Apopthegmatum. Paris: 1547. V. 49
Apopthegmatum. 1552. V. 54
Collectanea Adagiorum Veterum... 1513. V. 50
Colloquia Selecta: or, the Select Colloquies... Waterford: 1773. V. 54
The Correspondence of Erasmus. Toronto: 1974-77. V. 50
De Dvplici Copia Verborum & Rerum Commentarij duo... London: 1556. V. 51
Enchiridion Militis Christiani. (with) De Conte(m)ptu Mundi Epistola. (with) Liber De Sarcienda Ecclesiae Concordia. Paris: 1525-28-33. V. 52
Enchiridion Miltis Christiani. (and) Praeparatione ad Mortem. Cantabrigiae: 1685. V. 53
In Novvm Testamentvm Annotationes. Basileae: 1540. V. 50
Moriae Encomium. Basel: 1521. V. 53
Moriae Encomium. Basileae: 1522. V. 49
Moriae Encomium. London: 1709. V. 49; 53
Moriae Encomium. London: 1724. V. 53
Moriae Encomium, an Oration spoken by Folly in Praise of Herself. New York: 1943. V. 52; 54
Opus Epistolarum. Basel: 1529. V. 51
Opus Epistolarum. London: 1992. V. 49
Paraphrasis. Sive Enarratio in Epistolas et Evangelia, Qvae Dominicis & Festis Diebus per Anni Circulum in Ecclesia Legi Consueuerunt. Coloniae: 1555. V. 50
The Pope shut Out o Heaven Gates; or, a Dialogue Between Pope Julius the 2d. His Genius and Saint Peter...Exactly from the Original of the Famous... London: 1673. V. 54
The Praise of Folie. Moriae Encomium... London: 1569/1557?. V. 50
The Praise of Folie. Moriae Encomium. London: 1909/01. V. 48
The Praise of Folly. London: 1709. V. 53
Twenty Select Colloquies,...Pleasantly Representing Several Supporting Levities that Were Crept into the Church of Rome in His Days. London: 1680. V. 54
Twenty Two Select Colloquies. London: 1689. V. 51
Twenty Two Select Colloquies... London: 1711. V. 54

ERASMUS, DESIDERIUS continued
Vita...Additi sunt Epistolarum...Libri Duo... Leyden: 1607. V. 52
Witt Against Wisdom. Oxford: 1683. V. 47; 49

ERB, WILHELM
Diseases of the Peripheral Cerebro-Spinal Nerves. New York: 1876. V. 47
Handbook of Electrotherapeutics. New York: 1883. V. 47; 48

ERBER, CHRISTIAN
A Wealth of Silk and Velvet: Ottoman Fabrics and Embroideries. Bremen: 1990's. V. 52

ERCILLA Y ZUNIGA, A. DE
Primera y Segunda Parte de la Araucana. Madrid: 1578. V. 47

ERCK, JOHN C.
An Account of the Ecclesiastical Establishment in Ireland. Dublin: 1830. V. 49; 50; 51; 54

ERDMANN, KURT
Seven Hundred Years of Oriental Carpets. Berkeley: 1970. V. 48

ERDRICH, LOUISE
The Beet Queen. New York: 1986. V. 50
The Bingo Palace. New York & Northridge: 1994. V. 49; 50; 51; 53
The Crown of Columbus. New York: 1991. V. 51
Jacklight. New York: 1984. V. 47; 48; 49; 50; 51; 52; 53; 54
Love Medicine. New York. V. 52; 54
Love Medicine. New York: 1984. V. 47; 48; 49; 50; 51; 52; 53; 54
Route 2. Northridge: 1991. V. 49; 50
Snares. Middlebury: 1987. V. 49; 50; 51
Tracks. New York: 1988. V. 50

ERFFA, HELMUT VON
The Paintings of Benjamin Wet. New Haven: 1986. V. 50

ERGOTZLICHE und Lehrreiche Bilder Aus dem Leben. Neue Erzahlungen fur die Kinderwelt mit Betweglichen Bildern. 1890. V. 47; 50

ERICHSEN, JOHN E.
Observations on Aneurism Selected From the Works of the Principal Writers On that Disease from the Earliest periods to the Close of the Last Century. London: 1844. V. 48; 50
On Railway and Other Injuries of the Nervous System. London: 1866. V. 53
On Railway and Other Injuries of the Nervous System. Philadelphia: 1867. V. 53
The Science and Art of Surgery. Philadelphia: 1854. V. 54
The Science and Art of Surgery. London: 1864. V. 51
The Science and Art of Surgery. Philadelphia: 1878. V. 51

ERICKSON, ARTHUR
The Architecture... Montreal: 1975. V. 48; 50

ERICKSON, T. C.
Epilepsy and Cerebral Localization. Springfield: 1941. V. 49

ERICSON, JOE
Judges of the Republic of Texas, 1836-1846: a Biographical Directory. Dallas: 1980. V. 53

ERIE RAILROAD CO.
Annual Report. 1896-1913. V. 54

ERIKSON, ERIK H.
Gandhi's Truth. New York: 1969. V. 48

ERIZZO, SEBASTIANO
Le Sei Giornate. Londra: 1794. V. 48

ERLE, THOMAS W.
Letters from a Theatrical Scene-Painter... London: 1880. V. 50

ERLY, C. Y.
Walker-Smith Company, Wholesale Grocers, 1894-1944. 1944. V. 47

ERMAN, ADOLPH
Life in Ancient Egypt. London: 1894. V. 48
Travels in Siberia. London: 1848. V. 47; 50; 51

ERMATINGER, C. O.
1803-1903 Record of the Celebration of the Centenary of the Talbot Settlement Held in the Year of Our Lord 1903. 1910. V. 54
The Talbot Regime or the First Half Century of the Talbot Settlement. St. Thomas: 1904. V. 50

ERNEST, J. H. G.
Die Wol-Ein-Gerichtete Buchdruckery... Nurenberg: 1721. V. 50

ERNEST, JEROME HOPKINS
What Happened in the Mooney Case. New York: 1932. V. 51

ERNST, B. M. L.
Houdini and Conan Doyle. London: 1932. V. 53

ERNST, MAX
At Eye Level and Paramyths. Beverly Hills: 1949. V. 52
Beyond Painting and Other Writings by the Artist and His Friends. 1948. V. 50
Misfortunes of the Immortals. New York: 1943. V. 47; 50
Une Semaine de Bonte, ou Les Sept Elements Capitaux. Paris: 1934. V. 49; 50

ERPENIUS, THOMAS
(Arabic title) Id Est Historia Saracencia. Leyden: 1625. V. 50

ERREGED, JOHN
History of Brightelmston or, Brighton As I View It and Others Knew It. Brighton: 1862. V. 52

ERSKINE, BEATRICE
Beautiful Women. London: 1905. V. 54
Lady Diana Beauclerk, Her Life and Work. London: 1903. V. 48; 51; 53

ERSKINE, CHARLES
Twenty Years Before the Mast. Boston: 1890. V. 52

ERSKINE, FRITH
Naked Murder. London: 1935. V. 53

ERSKINE, JOHN E.
Journal of a Cruise Among the Islands of the Western Pacific, Including the Feejees and Others Inhabited by Polynesian Negro Races. London: 1853. V. 47; 50; 51; 52; 54

ERSKINE, RALPH
Gospel Sonnets, or Spiritual Songs. Boston: 1743. V. 52

ERSKINE, THOMAS
Armata: a Fragment (-The Second Part of Armata). London: 1817. V. 49; 50; 54
The Speech of the Hon. T. Erskine, at the Court of King's Bench...in the Cause of the King v. Williams, for Publishing Paine's Age of Reason. London: 1797. V. 52
Speeches of Thomas Lord Erskine. London: 1870. V. 48
Speeches of...Erskine...on Miscellaneous Subjects. London: 1812. V. 53
Speeches of...Erskine...on Miscellaneous Subjects. Georgetown: 1813. V. 51
The Speeches of...Erskine...on Miscellaneous Subjects. London: 1813-16/12. V. 49
The Speeches of...Erskine...on Subjects Connected with the Liberty of the Press. London: 1810. V. 51
The Speeches of...Erskine...on Subjects Connected with the Liberty of the Press. New York: 1813. V. 54
The Trial of Thomas Paine, from the Speeches of the Hon. Thomas Erskine (Now Lord Erskine), When at the Bar on Subjects Connected With the Liberty of the Press and Against Constructive Treasons. London: 1813. V. 48
Two Actions for Criminal Conversation with the Whole of the Evidence; Both Tried Before the Right Hon. Lord Kenyon, In the Court of King's Bench, Westminster Hall, on Wednesday, June 26, 1790... London: 1790. V. 54
The Whole Proceedings Upon an Information...Against the Right Hon. Sackville Earl of Thanet, Robert Fergusson, Esquire and Others, for a Riot and Other Misdeameanors...to Which are added some Observations by Robert Fergusson on His Own Case. London: 1799. V. 47

ERTE
Costumes and Sets for Der Rosenkavalier in Full Color. 1980. V. 47
Erte Maquettes. Hyattsville: 1984. V. 52
My Life/My Art. New York: 1989. V. 51

ERWIN, ALLEN A.
The Southwest of John H. Slaughter, 1841-1922; Pioneer Cattleman and Trail-Driver of Texas, the Pecos and Arizona and Sheriff of Tombstone. Glendale: 1965. V. 50; 51; 53; 54

ERWIN, MARIE H.
Wyoming Historical Blue Book - a Legal and Political History of Wyoming 1868-1943. Denver: 1946. V. 52

ERWIN, T. L.
Carabid Beetles, Their Evolution, Natural History and Classification. Boston: 1979. V. 54

ESADAILE, KATHARINE A.
English Church Monuments 1510-1840. London: 1946. V. 51

ESAREY, LOGAN
The Indiana Home. Bloomington: 1953. V. 54

ESCARRA, J.
Himalayan Assault. The French Himalayan Expedition 1936. 1938. V. 53

ESCHENBACH, WOLFRAM VON
The Romance of Parzival and the Holy Grail. 1990. V. 47; 52
The Romance of Parzival and the Holy Grail. Newtown: 1990. V. 48; 50

ESCOBAR, MANUEL DE
Verdad Reflexa, Platica Doctrinal Sobre los Varios Sucessos que Intervinieron en la Ciudad de San Luis Potosi Desde el Dia 10 de Mayo de 1767 hasta el Dia 6 de Octubre del Mismo Ano... Mexico: 1768. V. 53

ESCOTT, GEORGE S.
History and Directory of Springfield and North Springfield. Springfield: 1878. V. 53

ESCUDERO, JOSE A. DE
Noticias Estadisticas Del Estado De Chihuahua... Mexico: 1834. V. 52

ESDAILE, ARUNDELL
A List of English Tales and Prose Romances. London: 1912. V. 48; 49; 50; 52

ESDAILE, JAMES
The Introduction of Mesmerism... Perth: 1852. V. 48
Mesmerism in India and its Practical Application. London: 1846. V. 51
Mesmerism in India and Its Practical Application in Surgery and Medicine. Hartford: 1847. V. 47; 50
Mesmerism in India, and Its Practical Application in Surgery and Medicine. Hartford: 1851. V. 52
Natural and Mesmeric Clairvoyance, with the Practical Application of Mesmerism in Surgery and Medicine. London: 1852. V. 48

ESHLEMAN, CLAYTON
Altars. Los Angeles: 1971. V. 54
Brother Stones. Kyoto: 1968. V. 48; 52

ESHLEMAN, CLAYTON continued
Coils. Los Angeles: 1973. V. 54
The House of Ibuki. Fremont: 1969. V. 53
Indiana. Los Angeles: 1969. V. 54
Our Lady of the Three-Pronged Devil. New York: 1981. V. 54

ESKEW, GARNETT LAIDLAW
The Pageant of the Packets: a Book of American Steamboating. New York: 1929. V. 51

ESMONDE, THOMAS
Hunting Memories of Many Lands. 1925. V. 52
More Hunting Memories. London: 1930. V. 51; 52

THE ESOTERIC Book of E. Los Angeles: 1936. V. 54

ESPER, E. J. C.
Die Schmetterlinge in Abbildungen...Europaische Gattungen, Theil I-III... Erlangen: 1777-82. V. 54

ESPIARD DE LA BORDE, FRANCOIS IGNACE
The Spirit of Nations. London: 1753. V. 52

ESPIE, COMTE D'
The Manner of Securing All Sorts of Buildings from Fire. London: 1756. V. 52

ESPINOSA, J. MANUEL
First Expedition of Vargas into New Mexico, 1692. Albuquerque: 1940. V. 54

ESPINOSA, JOSE
Saints in the Valleys. Christian Sacred Images in the History, Life and Folk Art of Spanish New Mexico. Albuquerque: 1960. V. 51
Spanish Folk Tales from New Mexico. New York: 1937. V. 49
A Spanish Voyage to Vancouver and the North-West Coast of America... London: 1930. V. 50

ESPINOSO, TOMAS DE
Heroicos Hechos, y Vidas de Varones Yllustres asy Griegos Como Romanos... Paris: 1576. V. 49; 53

ESPOSITO, VINCENT J.
The West Point Atlas of American Wars. New York: 1959. V. 53

ESPY, J. P.
The Philosophy of Storms. Boston: 1841. V. 52; 53

ESQUIROL, JEAN
Des Maladies Mentales Considerees Sour les Rapports Medical, Hygenique et Modico-Legal...Edition Publiee a Bruxelles en 1838 Entierement Conforme a l'Edition Francaise. Paris: 1838. V. 49; 52
Mental Maladies: a Treatise on Insanity. Philadelphia: 1845. V. 47; 52

ESQUIVEL, LAURA
Like Water for Chocolate. New York: 1992. V. 50; 51; 52; 53; 54

AN ESSAY in Defense of the Female Sex...In a Letter to a Lady. London: 1696. V. 54

AN ESSAY on Civil Government. London: 1743. V. 48

AN ESSAY on Hunting. London: 1733. V. 47

ESSAY on Hunting. London: 1820. V. 47

AN ESSAY on Immorality. London: 1760. V. 48; 54

AN ESSAY on Laughter, Wherein are Displayed, Its Natural and Moral Causes, with The Art of Exciting It. London: 1769. V. 47

AN ESSAY on the Antiquity, Dignity and Advantages of Living in a Garret. London: 1751. V. 47

ESSAY on the Corn Laws; to Evince, on the Most Indubitable Ground, in Opposition to the Inflammatory memorial for the Merchants, Traders and Manufacturers of Glasgow... Edinburgh: 1777. V. 53

AN ESSAY, on the Expediency of Establishing a Literary Society in the Town of Bedford. 1817. V. 51

AN ESSAY on the Present State of Our Public Records; Shewing the Absolute Necessity of a Total Prohibition of the Use of Narrow Wheels, On All Carriages Drawn by Moret than One Horse Lengthways. London: 1756. V. 52

AN ESSAY Upon Study, More Particularly the Study of Philosophy. In a Letter to a Friend. London: 1713. V. 53

ESSAYS by the Pupils at the College of the Deaf and Dumb, Rugby, Warwickshire. London: 1845. V. 48

ESSAYS by the Students of the College of Fort William in Bengal. Calcutta: 1802. V. 49

ESSAYS For Henry R. Wagner by Charles L. Camp: Francis P. Farquhar: George L. Harding: Dorothy H. Huggins and Carl I. Wheat. San Francisco: 1947. V. 47; 48; 51

ESSAYS, Historical, Political and Moral; Being a Proper Supplement to Baratariana. Dublin: 1774?. V. 47; 48

ESSAYS Honoring Lawrence C. Wroth. Portland: 1951. V. 52

ESSAYS On Gothic Architecture. London: 1808. V. 51

ESSAYS on Malory. London: 1963. V. 51

ESSAYS on Various Subjects; Intended to Elucidate the Causes of the Changes Coming Upon all the Earth at This Present Time and the Nature of the Calamities That Are so rapidly Approaching.... New York: 1861. V. 52

ESSAYS Philosophical and Psychological In Honor of William James, Professor in Harvard University. By His Colleagues at University. New York: 1908. V. 49

ESSAYS Presented to Charles Williams. London: 1947. V. 49

ESSAYS Presented to Myron P. Gilmore. Florence: 1978. V. 53

ESSAYS Serious and Comical. Viz. On the Readers of This Book. The Art of Pleasing Women...Play-houses...Town... Universities...Coffee-Houses...Tea-Tables...To which are Added, Characters Satyrical and Panegyrical, Letters Amorous and Gallant... London: 1707. V. 50

ESSEX, ARTHUR CAPEL, EARL OF
Letters Written by H. E., Arthur Capel Earl of Essex, Lord Lieutenant of Ireland in the Year 1675. London: 1770. V. 47

ESSEX FIELD CLUB
The Essex Naturalist: Being the Journal of Essex Field Club. Essex: 1887-93. V. 48

ESSEX, ROBERT DEVEREUX, 2ND EARL OF
Profitable Instructions: Describing What Speciall Observations are to be Taken by Travellers in All Nations. London: 1633. V. 53

ESSICK, ROBERT N.
The Separate Plates of William Blake: a Catalogue. Princeton: 1983. V. 47; 50
William Blake, Printmaker. Princeton: 1980. V. 47

ESSLEMONT, DAVID
Gwasg Gregynog: a Descriptive Catalogue of Printing at Gregynog 1970-1990. 1990. V. 54
Gwasg Gregynog. A Descriptive Catalogue of Printing at Gregynog 1970-1990. Newtown: 1990. V. 48

ESSLIN, MARTIN
Brecht: a Choice of Evils, a Critical Study of the Man, His Work and His Opinions. London: 1959. V. 54

ESSLING, PRINCE DE'
Etudes sur l'Art de la Gravure sur Bois a Venise. Les Livres a Figures Venitiens de la Fin Du XVe Siecle du Commencement du XVIe. Florence & Paris: 1967. V. 53

THE ESTABLISHMENT Of a General Packet Station on the South West Coast of Ireland, Connected by Railways with Dublin and London, Considered with Reference to the Advantages Which It Would Afford...and in Promoting the Improvement of Ireland. London: 1836. V. 47

ESTACO, AQUILES
Illustrium Virorum ut Exstant in Urbe Expressi Vultus. Padua: 1648. V. 53

ESTATE & House Agents' Complete Assistant. London: 1824. V. 49

ESTCOURT, RICHARD
The Fair Example; or, the Modish Citizens. London: 1706. V. 47

ESTE, CHARLES
Carmina Quadragesimilia ab Aedis Christi oxon. Oxonii: 1723. V. 50
A Journey in the Year 1793, through Flanders, Brabant and Germany to Switzerland. London: 1795. V. 47

ESTEE, MORRIS M.
Pleadings, Practice and Forms Adpated to Actions and Special Proceedings Under Codes of Civil Procedure. San Francisco: 1885. V. 50

ESTENS, JOHN LOCKE
The Paraclete and Mahdi or The Exact Testimony to Revelation and Exposition of the Most Ancient Mysteries and Cults. Sydney: 1912. V. 48

ESTES, ELEANOR
The Middle Moffat. New York: 1942. V. 49

ESTES, GEORGE
The Stage Coach. Cedarwood: 1925. V. 48; 53

ESTES, LOUISE REID
Nature and Art, Poems and Pictures from the Best Authors and Artists. London: 1887. V. 49; 51

ESTES, MATTHEW
A Defence of Negro Slavery, As it Exists, in the United States. Montgomery: 1846. V. 50; 52

ESTES, R. D.
The Behaviour Guide to African Mammals. Berkeley: 1991. V. 50

ESTES, WILLIAM K.
Handbook of Learning and Cognitive Processes. Hillsdale: 1975-78. V. 54

ESTIENNE, CHARLES
De re Vestiaria Libellus, ex Baysio Excerptus: Addita Vulgaris Linguae Interpretaatione, in Adulescentulorum Gratiam Atque Utilitatem. Paris: 1535. V. 48
Maison Rustique, or the Countrey Farme... London: 1606. V. 51
Paradoxes...Pour Exerciter les Jeunes Esprits en Causes Difficiles. Paris: 1554. V. 51
Praedivm Rvsticvm, In Quo Cuiusuis Foli vel Culti Vel Inculti Plantarum Vacabula ac Descriptiones...Describuntur. Paris: 1554. V. 49

ESTIENNE, HENRI
The Art of Making Devices... London: 1650. V. 50
Epigrammata Graeca, Selecta ex Anthologia. Geneva: 1570. V. 49; 53
Epistolia, Dialogi Breves, Oratiunculae, Poematia. Geneva: 1577. V. 52
Fragmenta Poetarum. Geneva: 1564. V. 49
The History of the Life of Katharine de Medicis Queen Mother and Regent of France. London: 1693. V. 47
In M. T. Cicero Quamplurimos Locos Castigationes. Geneva: 1557. V. 52
De Latinitate Falso Suspecta...Eivsdem De Plavti Latinitate Dissertatio... Geneva: 1576. V. 47

ESTIENNE, HENRI continued
Nizoliodidascalvs, Siue, Monitor Ciceroniarum Nizolianorum... Geneva: 1578. V. 47
Thesaurus Graecae Linguae. Genevae: 1572-73. V. 47; 48; 49; 50; 51; 53
Thesaurus Graecae Linguae, ab H. Stephano Constructus. London: 1816-28. V. 48
A World of Wonders; or an Introduction to a Treatise Touching the Conformitie of Ancient and Moderne Wonders... London: 1607. V. 53

ESTIENNE, ROBERT
Hebraea, Chaldaea, Graeca et Latina Nomina Virorum, Mulierum, Populorum. Paris: 1537. V. 47
Thesaurus Linguae Latinae. London: 1734. V. 48
Thesaurus Linguae Latinae. London: 1734-35. V. 49

ESTLEMAN, LOREN D.
Motor City Blue. Boston: 1980. V. 50

ESTRACTO de Noticias Del Puerto De Monterey, De La Mission, Y Presido Que Se Han Establecido En El Con La Denominacion De San Carlos, Y Del Sucesso De Las Dos Expediciones De Mar, Y Tierra Que A este Fin Se Despacharon En Al Ano Proxima... Mexico: 1770. V. 52

THE ESTRAY: A Collection of Poems. Boston: 1847. V. 52

ESTVAN, BELA
War Pictures from the South. 1863. V. 53

ETCHECOPAR, R. D.
The Birds of North Africa. London: 1967. V. 49; 50; 52; 53

ETCHES, JOHN
An Authentic Statement of All the Facts Relative to Nootka Sound... London: 1790. V. 51

ETCHINGS of Antiquities in Newcastle Upon Tyne. Newcastle-Upon-Tyne: 1827. V. 48

ETCHINSON, DENNIS
The Complete Masters of Darkness. Novato and Lancaster: 1990. V. 49

ETCHISON, DENNIS
The Complete Masters of Darkness. Lancaster: 1991. V. 49
Lord John Ten. Northridge: 1988. V. 50

ETHEREGE, GEORGE
The Comical Revenge; or, Love in a Tub. London: 1689. V. 48
The Man of Mode; or Sr. Fopling Flutter. London: 1693. V. 53
She Wou'd If She Cou'd. London: 1693. V. 48
Three Plays: the Comical Revenge, or Love in Tub; She Would If She Could, a Comedy; the Man of Mode, or Sir Fopling Flutter. London: 1723. V. 50
The Works of... London: 1704. V. 47; 49; 52

ETHERIDGE, R.
Fossils of the British Islands... Oxford: 1888. V. 49

ETHERTON, P. T.
Across the Roof of the World... 1911. V. 54

ETHIC Travels; With Christian Experience. New England: 1790. V. 51

ETHNOGRAPHIC MUSEUM, ANTWERP
Face of the Spirits. Mask from Zaire Basin (Exhibition Catalogue). Antwerp: 1993. V. 54

ETIQUETTE for the Ladies; Eighty Maxims on Dress, Manners and Accomplishments. London: 1837. V. 52

ETIQUETTE of the Dinner Table, with the Art of Carving. London: 1860. V. 52

ETRENNES aux Amateurs de Venus. Paris: 1788. V. 49

ETS, MARIE HALL
Automobiles for Mice. New York: 1964. V. 51
Oley the Sea Monster. New York: 1947. V. 54
Play With Me. New York: 1955. V. 51
The Story of a Baby. New York: 1939. V. 54

ETTLINGER, LEOPOLD L.
Antonio and Pedro Pollaiuolo. London: 1978. V. 49; 52

ETTMUELLER, MICHAEL
Opera Medica Theoretico-Practica... Frankfurt am Main: 1708. V. 47

ETZLER, J. A.
The New World or Mechanical System, to Perform the Labours of Man and Best by Inanimate Powers. Philadelphia: 1841. V. 49

EUCLIDES
De Gli Elementi Libri Qvindici. Con Gli Scholii Antichi. Urbino: 1575. V. 49
Diligentenmente Rassettato, &...Ridotto, per...Nicolo Tartalea...Di Nuouo...Corretto, e Ristampato. Venice: 1585. V. 52
Elementorum Euclidis Libri Tredecim. Secundum Vetera Exemplaria Restituti. Ex Versione Latina Federici Commandini. London: 1620. V. 52; 54
Elementorum Libri XV. Parisiis: 1598. V. 48; 50; 52
Elementorvm Evclidis Libri Tredecim. London: 1620. V. 52
The Elements of Euclid. Edinburgh: 1775. V. 48
The Elements of Euclid Explain'd, in a New, But Most Easie method... Oxford: 1700. V. 48; 52
The Elements of Euclid with Dissertations, Intended to Assist and Encourage a Critical Examination of these Elements... Oxford: 1781-88. V. 50
The Elements of Geometrie of the Most Auncient Philosopher Eulcide of Megara. London: 1570. V. 53
The English Euclid, Being the First Six Elements of Geometry. Oxford: 1705. V. 49; 53
Euclides' Elementes. London: 1660. V. 50; 54
Euclide's Elements. London: 1751. V. 52
Euclidis Elementorum Libri XV Breviter Demonstrati... Cantabrigiensis: 1659. V. 48
Euclid's Elementes: the Whole Fifteen Books. London: 1660. V. 51
Euclid's Elements. London: 1686. V. 52
Euclid's Elements of Geometry: Book 1. New York: 1944. V. 48
The First Six Books of the Elements of Euclid in Which Coloured Diagrams and Symbols Are Used Instead of Letters... London: 1847. V. 50; 52
Orontii Finaei in Sex Priores Libros Geometricorum Elementorum Euclidis...Demonstrationes. Paris: 1544. V. 47
La Perspectiva, y Especularia de Euclides. Madrid: 1585. V. 53
Die Sechs Erste Bucher Euclidis Vom Anfang der Geometrj. Basle: 562. V. 53
Sex Libri Priores de Geometricis Principiis Graece & Latini...Algebrae Porro Regulae...His Libris Praemissae Sunt. Basel: 1550. V. 51
Solo Introduttore Delle Scientie Mathematice. Venice: 1565. V. 49

EUDORA Welty: a Tribute. 1984. V. 53

EULENSPIEGEL, TILL
The Marvellous Adventures and Rare Conceits of Master Tyll Owlglass. London: 1860. V. 50

EULER, LEONHARD
Elements of Algebra. London: 1797. V. 53
Elements of Algebra. London: 1810. V. 50
Lettres a une Princesse d'Allemagne sur Divers Sujets de Physique & de Philosophie. St. Petersburg: 1768-72. V. 47
Tentamen Novae Theoriae Musicae ex Certissimis Harmoniae Principiis Dilucide Expositae. St. Petersburg: 1739. V. 54

EULOGIUM Historiarum Sive Temporis: Chronicon ab Orbe Conditio Usque ad Annum Domini 1366... London: 1848-63. V. 52

EUNAPIUS
Evnapivs Sardianvs, De Vitis Philosopharvm et Sophistarvm: Nunc Primum Graece & Latine editus. Antwerp: 1568. V. 48

EURIPIDES
Alcestis. London: 1930. V. 51; 53
The Bacchae. Dionysus, the God. Kentfield: 1972. V. 48; 49
Euripides Quae Extant Omnia...Oper & Studio Josuae Barnes. Cambridge: 1694. V. 48
Euripidis Quae Extant Omnia. Oxford: 1778. V. 48; 50
Euripidis Tragoediae XIX. Antwerp: 1571. V. 47; 51
Hecuba. Ad Fidem Manuscriptorum Emandata et Brevibus Notis... London: 1811. V. 48
Hippolytos. Northampton: 1969. V. 48; 54
Ippolytos Stephanephoros cum Scholiss Versione Latina, Variis Lectionibus, Valckenari Notis Integris... Oxford: 1796. V. 48
The Plays. Newtown: 1931. V. 47; 48; 50; 52; 54
Three Plays: Medea, Hippylytus and the Bacchae. New York: 1967. V. 52; 53
The Tragedies. London: 1781. V. 48; 53
The Tragedies of Euripides. London: 1850. V. 47
Tragoediae Octodecim. Basileae: 1537. V. 47
Tragoediae Superstites et Deperditarum Fragmenta. Oxford: 1832-40. V. 48
Tragoediae XIX. Heidelberg: 1597. V. 52
Tres Tragoediae, Phoenissae, Hippolytvs Coronatvs, atqve Andromacha... Antwerp: 1581. V. 52

EUROPE After 8:15. New York: 1914. V. 54

EUROPE Informed. An Exhibition of Early Books Which Acquainted Europe With the East. Cambridge: 1966. V. 47; 50

EUROPEAN Civilization. Its Origin and Development, by Various Contributors... Oxford: 1935. V. 49

EUSEBIUS PAMPHILI, BP. OF CAESAREA
The Auncient Ecclesiastical Histories of the First Six Hundred Yeares after Christ... London: 1619. V. 53
Episcopi Chronicon: Quod Hieronymus... Paris: 1512. V. 51
Sanchoniatho's Phoenician History. London: 1720. V. 48

EUSTACE, JOHN CHETWODE
A Classical Tour through Italy. London: 1815. V. 52
A Classical Tour through Italy. Philadelphia: 1816. V. 53
A Classical Tour through Italy. London: 1817. V. 47
A Classical Tour through Italy. London: 1819. V. 48
An Elegy to the Memory of the Right Honourable Edmund Burke. London: 1798. V. 48; 52
A Tour through Italy...with An Account of the Present State of Its Cities and Towns. London: 1813. V. 54

EUSTACHIUS, BARTOLOMEO
Anatomii Summi Romanae Archetypae Tabulae Anatomicae Novis Explicationibus Illustratae ab Andrea Maximino Romano in Nosocomio... Rome: 1783. V. 51; 52; 53; 54
Tabulae Anatomicae. Rome: 1714. V. 53

EUSTAPHIEVE, ALEXIS
The Resources of Russia, in the Event of a War with France... London: 1813. V. 54

EUSTATHIUS, MACREMBOLITA
Gli Amori d'Ismenio, Composti per Eustathio Filosofo & di Greco... In Venetia: 1560. V. 53

EUTHYMIUS ZIGABENUS
Commentarii in Omnes Psalmos. Paris: 1543. V. 52

EUTROPIUS
De Gestis Romanorum Libri Decem. Paris: 1531. V. 48
De Inclytis Totius Italice Provincie, ac Romanorum Gestis Libri XVIII. Paris: 1512. V. 47

EUTROPIUS continued
Eutropii Historiae Romanae Breviarium... London: 1744. V. 50

EUXINE or Black Sea and Sea of Marmora and Azov Containing Full Instructions for Frequenting the Ports of Constantinople, Galatz, Odessa, Sevastopol, Trebizond, &c. London: 1853. V. 49; 52

EVALENKO, A. M.
The Message of the Doukhobors. A Statement of True Facts by 'Christians of the Universal Brotherhood' and by Prominent Champions of Their Cause. New York: 1913. V. 49; 53

DAS EVANGELIUM des Markus. Offenbach am Main: 1923. V. 47

EVANS, A. E.
Catalogue of Nearly Six Thousand Etchings and Engravings with an Appendix Consisting of a Catalogue Raisonne of Nearly 400 Prints Unknown to Bartsch. London: 1860. V. 47; 49

EVANS, ABEL
The Apparition. London: 1710. V. 47; 54
Vertumnus. London: 1713. V. 54
Vertumnus. Oxford: 1713. V. 49; 51; 52

EVANS, ALBERT EUBULE
A Draught of Lethe. London: 1891. V. 47

EVANS, ALBERT S.
A La California. Sketches of Life in the Golden State. San Francisco: 1873. V. 50
Our Sister Republic. A Gala Trip Through Tropical Mexico in 1869-70. Hartford: 1870. V. 54

EVANS, ARTHUR BENONI
The Cutter, in Five Lectures Upon the Art and Practice of Cutting Friends, Acquaintances and Relations. London: 1808. V. 51
Fungusiana; or the Opinions, and Table Talk of the Late Barnaby Fungus, Esq. to Which are Prefixed Some Biographical Notices, Respecting the True Origin of that Gentleman... London: 1809. V. 51

EVANS, ARTHUR CORNWALLIS
The Cruise of H.M.S. "Calliope" in China, Australian and East African Waters, 1887-1890. Portsmouth: 1890. V. 54

EVANS, ARTHUR J.
The Mycenaean Tree and Pillar Cult and Its Mediterranean Relations. London: 1901. V. 50
The Palace of Minos at Knossos. New York: 1964. V. 52
The Ring of Nestor. A Glimpse Into the Minoan After-World and a Sepulchral Treasure of Gold Signet-Rings and Bead-Seals from the Thisbe, Boeotia. London: 1925. V. 50; 52
Scripta Minoa. Oxford: 1909. V. 50; 51

EVANS, B.
American Indian Dance Steps. New York: 1931. V. 54

EVANS, C. S.
Cinderella. London: 1919. V. 47; 50; 54
The Sleeping Beauty. London: 1920. V. 48; 50; 51; 53

EVANS, CERINDA W.
Collis Potter Huntington. Newport News: 1954. V. 52; 54

EVANS, CHARLES
American Bibliography. Chicago: 1903-34. V. 47; 51

EVANS, DAVID MORIER
Birds of Prey of the British Islands. London: 1980. V. 49; 54
The Commercial Crisis 1847-1848... London: 1848. V. 49
The History of the Commercial Crisis 1857-1858 and the Stock Exchange Panic of 1859. London: 1859. V. 47

EVANS, E. E.
Man of Many Minds. 1953. V. 49

EVANS, E. P.
The Criminal Prosecution and Capital Punishment of Animals. London: 1906. V. 48

EVANS, E. R. G. R.
South With Scott. Glasgow. V. 53

EVANS, EDWARD
Historical and Bibliographical Account of Almanacks, Directories, &c. 1897. V. 54

EVANS, ELIZABETH
Anne Tyler. New York: 1993. V. 50; 51
The Cults of the Sabine Territory. New York: 1939. V. 52

EVANS, ELWOOD
Annual Address Before the Western Washington Industrial Association, At Its Fourth Annual Exhibition, Held in Olympia, Washington Territory By...Friday, October 9th, 1874. Olympia: 1875. V. 50; 52
Oration. Portland, Oregeon, July 4, 1865. Portland: 1965. V. 54
The State of Washington. Washington: 1893. V. 54

EVANS, ESTWICK
Pedestrious Tour of Four Thousand Miles, Through the Western States and Territories, During the Winter and Spring of 1818. Concord: 1819. V. 47; 49

EVANS, EVAN
Some Specimens of the Poetry of the Antient Welsh Bards. London: 1764. V. 47

EVANS, F. W.
Autobiography of a Shaker, and Revelation of the Apocalypse. New York: 1869. V. 54
Shakers. Compendium of the Origin, History, Principles, Rules and Regulations, Government and Doctrines of the United Society of Believers in Christ's Second Appearing. New Lebanon: 1867. V. 48; 51; 53
A Short Treatise on the Second Appearing of Christ, in and Through the order of the Female. Boston: 1853. V. 50; 51

EVANS, G. O.
Principles of Acarology. Wallingford: 1992. V. 49

EVANS, G. P.
Big-Game Shooting in Upper Burma. London: 1911. V. 47

EVANS, GEORGE S.
Wylackie Jake Of Covelo. San Francico: 1904. V. 53

EVANS, HENRY HERMAN
A Contribution Towards a Check List of Bibliographies and Reference material Relating to the History of the States and territories of the American West Including Alaska and Hawaii. San Francisco: 1949-50. V. 48
Western Bibliographies. San Francisco: 1951. V. 47

EVANS, HENRY SMITH
Geology Made Easy; or, the Old and New World. London: 1858. V. 54

EVANS, HERBERT MC LEAN
The Antisterility Vitamin E Fat Soluble E. Berkeley: 1927. V. 50
On the Differential Reaction to Vital Dyes Exhibited by the Two Great Groups of Connective Tissue Cells. Washington. V. 49

EVANS, J.
Letters Written During a Tour through North Wales, in the Year 1798. London: 1804. V. 54

EVANS, J. GWYNOGURON
The Text of the Book of Llan Dav. Oxford: 1893. V. 47; 51; 54

EVANS, J. H.
Ornamental Turning. London: 1886. V. 52

EVANS, JAMES W.
Autobiography of Samuel S. Hildebrand, the Renowned Missouri "Bushwacker" and Inconquerable Rob Roy of America... Jefferson City: 1870. V. 53

EVANS, JOAN
Art in Medieval France, 987-1498. London: 1948. V. 47
Catalogue of Nearly Six Thousand Etchings and Engravings. London: 1860. V. 51
English Jewellery from the Fifth Century A.D. to 1800. London: 1921. V. 53
English Posies and Posy Rings. London: 1931. V. 53
A History of Jewellery 1100-1870. London: 1970. V. 50
A History of Jewellery 1800-1870. New York: 1953. V. 51
Monastic Iconography in France from the Renaissance to the Revolution. 1970. V. 50; 53
Pattern. A Tudy of Ornament in Western Europe from 1180 to 1900. Oxford: 1931. V. 48

EVANS, JOHN
The Ancient Bronze Implements, Weapons and Ornaments of Great Britain and Ireland. New York: 1881. V. 49
The Ancient Stone Implements, Weapons and Ornaments of Great Britain. London: 1872. V. 52
The Ancient Stone Implements, Weapons and Ornaments of Great Britain. London: 1897. V. 52; 54
The Coins of the Ancient Britons. London: 1864-90. V. 48
Gov. Evans' Message. Delivered to the Legislative Assembly of Colroado, in Joint Session, at Denver, Thursday July 17th, 1862. Denver: 1862. V. 48
The Juvenile Tourist; or, Excursions through Various parts of the Island of Great Britain... London: 1804. V. 54
Lectures on Pulmonary Phthisis Comprehending the Pathology, Diagnosis and Treatment of the Disease. Dublin: 1844. V. 48
The Picture of Bristol; or a Guide to Objects of Curiosity and Interest in Bristol, Clifton, the Hotwells and Their Vicinity. Bristol: 1818. V. 54
Picture of Worthing: to Which is Added an Account of the Adjacent Villages. Worthington & London: 1814. V. 47

EVANS, MARI
Singing Black. Indianapolis: 1976. V. 48

EVANS, MARIAN
Essays and Leaves from a Note-Book. London: 1884. V. 52

EVANS, MAX
The One-Eyed sky. Boston: 1963. V. 51
Shadow of Thunder. Chicago: 1969. V. 51

EVANS, MYFANWY
The Painter's Object. London: 1937. V. 50
The Pavilion - a Contemporary Collection of British Art and Architecture. London: 1946. V. 49; 50

EVANS, NATHANIEL
Poems on Several Occasions, with some Other Compositions. Philadelphia: 1772. V. 47; 50; 51

EVANS, OLIVER
The Abortion of the Young Steam Engineer's Guide... Philadelphia: 1805. V. 51; 53
Patent Right Oppression Expressed; or, Knavery Detected. Philadelphia: 1813. V. 53
The Young Mill-Wright and Miller's Guide. Philadelphia: 1836. V. 47; 49; 51; 53; 54

EVANS, SARAH ANN
Resignation. Boston: 1825. V. 54

EVANS, SEBASTIAN
The High History of the Holy Graal. London: 1903. V. 49; 51

EVANS, THOMAS
An English and Welsh Vocabulary; or, an Essay Guide to the Ancient British Language... London: 1816. V. 52
Old Ballads, Historical and Narrative. London: 1777. V. 50
Old Ballads, Historical and Narrative, with Some Modern Date... London: 1784. V. 48; 50; 52

EVANS, WALKER
American Photographs. New York: 1938. V. 47
American Photographs. New York: 1962. V. 49
American Photographs. New York: 1965. V. 47
American Photographs. New York: 1975. V. 49
First and Last. New York: 1978. V. 47; 51
Many Are Called. Boston: 1966. V. 47; 54
Message from the Interior. New York: 1966. V. 47; 54
Walker Evans. 1971. V. 50
Walker Evans. New York: 1971. V. 51

EVANS, WILL F.
Border Skylines, Fifty Years of "Tallying Out" On the Bloys Roundup Ground. A History of the Bloys Cowboy Camp Meeting. Dallas: 1940. V. 52; 54

EVANS, WILLIAM
Art and History of the Potting Business, Compiled from the Most Practical sources, for the Especial use of Working Potters by Their Devoted Friend, William Evans. London: 1846. V. 49
The Mammalian Fauna of the Edinburgh District. 1892. V. 54
The Mammalian Fauna of the Edinburgh District. Edinburgh: 1892. V. 47
The Mammalian Fauna of the Edinburgh District. London: 1892. V. 50; 52; 53

EVANS, WILLIAM JULIAN
The Sugar-Planter's Manual, Being a Treatise on the Art of Obtaining Sugar from the Sugar Cane. Philadelphia: 1848. V. 51

EVANS, WILLIAM SLOANE
A Grammar of British Heraldry. London: 1847. V. 49

EVANS, WILMOT ROBY
Southwest. Boston: 1931. V. 53

EVANS-PRITCHARD, E. E.
Witchcraft, Oracles and Magic Among the Azande. Oxford: 1937. V. 52

EVANSVILLE. BOARD OF TRADE
Annual Report of the Board of Trade of Evansville, Indiana for 1867, with a Historical Sketch of the City. Evansville: 1868. V. 54

EVARTS, R. C.
Alice's Adventures in Cambridge. Cambridge: 1913. V. 52

EVARTS, WILLIAM MAXWELL
Arguments and Speeches of William Maxwell Evarts. New York: 1919. V. 50

EVELEIGH, JOSIAH
An Account of the Reasons Why Many Citizens of Exon Have Withdrawn from the Ministry of Mr. Jos. Hallet and Mr. James Pierce. Exon: 1719. V. 52
A Defence of the Account, &c. London: 1719. V. 52

EVELETH, F. H.
Old Testament Biographical Sketches. Rangoon: 1886. V. 51

EVELYN, CHARLES
The Lady's Recreation; or, The Third and last Part of the Art of Gardening Improv'd... London: 1717. V. 49

EVELYN, JOHN
Diary. London: 1879. V. 53
The Diary. Washington and London: 1901. V. 51
The Diary. London: 1906. V. 48; 53
Diary and Correspondence... London: 1854. V. 49
Diary and Correspondence of John Evelyn... London: 1881. V. 48
Directions for the Gardiner at Says-Court, But Which May Be of Use of Other Gardens. London: 1932. V. 52; 54
The Evleyn Library, Sold by Order of the Trustees of the Wills of J. H. C. Evelyn, Deceased and Major Peter Evelyn, Deceased. London: 1977-78. V. 48
The French Gardiner. London: 1672. V. 51
Fumifugium: or, the Inconvenience of the Aer, and Smoak of London Dissipated. London: 1661. V. 49
Fumifugium; or, the Inconvenience of the Aer, and Smoake of London Disspiated. London: 1772. V. 53
A Letter to John Evelyn, Esq. to the Right Honourable the Lord Viscount Brouncker... 1779?. V. 47
Memoires for My Grand-son. London: 1926. V. 50; 51
Memoires for My Grand-Son. Oxford: 1926. V. 52
Memoirs. London. V. 54
Memoirs... London: 1818. V. 47; 49; 50; 51; 52
Memoirs. London: 1818/19. V. 52
Memoirs. London: 1827. V. 49; 51
Memoirs and Miscellaneous Works. London: 1819/25. V. 51
Memoirs Illustrative of the Life and Writings of... London: 1819. V. 48; 50; 52; 53
The Miscellaneous Writings. London: 1825. V. 48; 49; 54
Navigation and Commerce, Their Original and Progress. London: 1674. V. 47; 50
Numismata. A Discourse of Medals, Antient and Modern. London: 1697. V. 48; 51
A Philosophical Discourse of Earth, Relating to the Culture and Improvement of It for Vegetation, and the Propagation of Plants, Etc. London: 1675. V. 48
A Philosophical Discourse on Earth, Relating to the Culture and Improvement of It for Vegetation, and the Propagation of Plants, Etc., As It Was Presented to the Royal Society, April 29, 1675. London: 1676. V. 52
Sculptura Historico-Technica; or, the History and Art of Engraving. London: 1770. V. 49
Sculptura; or the History and Art of Chalcography and Engraving in Copper... London: 1662. V. 53
Sculptura, or the History and Art of Chalcography and Engraving in Copper. London: 1755. V. 49; 51; 52; 53
Silva. London: 1776. V. 54
Silva, or a Discourse of Forest Trees. London: 1706. V. 50
Silva, or, a Discourse of Forest Trees... London: 1729. V. 47; 52; 53; 54
Silva; or, a Discourse of Forest Trees. York: 1776. V. 48; 50; 52
Silva; or, a Discourse of Forest Trees. London: 1786. V. 51; 52; 53
Silva; or, a Discourse of Forest Trees. York: 1786. V. 47
Silva: or, a Discourse of Forest Trees... York: 1801. V. 54
Sylva, or, a Discourse of Forest Trees. London: 1664. V. 52
Sylva, or, a Discourse of Forest Trees. London: 1670. V. 47; 49

EVELYN WHITE, HUGH G.
The Monasteries of the Wadi N' Natrun. Parts I-II. New York: 1926-32. V. 49; 51

AN EVENING of Poetry at The Skinners' Hall - for the Benefit of the Royal Hospital and Home for Incurables. London: 1973. V. 50

THE EVENING Standard Detective Book. London: 1950. V. 54

EVENINGS At Haddon Hall. London: 1850. V. 52

EVENTFUL History of Three Little Mice and How They Became Blind. Boston: 1858. V. 51

EVERARD, ANNE
Flowers from Nature. London: 1835. V. 49

EVERARD, EDWARD
A Bristol Printing House. London: 1900. V. 50

EVERARD, H.
History of Thos. Farrington's Regiment Subsequently Designated the 29th (Worcester) Foot 1694 to 1891. Worcester: 1891. V. 50

EVERARD, H. S. C.
Golf in Theory and Practice. London: 1898. V. 47

EVEREST, CHARLES WILLIAM
Babylon: a Poem. Hartford: 1838. V. 54

EVEREST, THOMAS
A Popular View of Homoeopathy, with Annotations and a brief Survey of the Progress and Homoeopathia in Europe... New York: 1842. V. 50

EVERETT, EDWARD
An Address Delivered at the Erection of a Monument to John Harvard, Sept. 26, 1828. Boston: 1828. V. 47; 48
Address of Hon. Edward Everett, at the Consecration of the National Cemetery at Gettysburg, 19th November, 1863, with the Dedicatory Speech of President Lincoln, and the Other Exercises of the Occasion... Boston: 1864. V. 47; 48
A Eulogy on the Life and Character of John Quincy Adams, Delivered at the Request of the Legislature of Massachusetts in Faneuil Hall, April 15, 1848. Boston: 1848. V. 47; 48
The Mount Vernon Papers. New York: 1860. V. 47; 50

EVERETT, FRED
Fun with Game Birds: Bird Hunting in Words, Paint and Lines. Harrisburg: 1954. V. 47

EVERETT, HORACE
Regulating the Indian Department. Washington: 1834. V. 47; 49

EVERETT, HOUSTON S.
Gynecological and Obstetrical Urology. Baltimore: 1944. V. 49

EVERETT, JAMES
The Wall's End Miner; or a Brief Memoir of the Life of William Crister... London: 1838. V. 49
Wesleyan Methodism in Manchester and Its Vicinity. Manchester: 1827. V. 48; 49; 53

EVERETT LAND CO.
The City of Smokestacks. Everett. The New Manufacturing and Commercial City at the End of the Great Northern Railway on Puget Sound. Seattle?: 1893. V. 50

EVERETT, M.
The Birds of Paradise and Bowerbirds. London: 1978. V. 50

EVERGREEN Tales. New York: 1949. V. 52

EVERITT, NICHOLAS
Broadland Sport. London: 1902. V. 49

THE EVERLASTING Circle of Fate, or Expounder of Things Thate are to Be... London: 1835. V. 53

EVERMANN, B. W.
General Report on the Investigations in Porto Rico of the U.S. Fish Commission Steamer Fish Hawk in 1899. Washington: 1900. V. 51
Lake Maxinkuckee, a Physical and Biological Survey. 1920. V. 52; 53

EVERSON, R. G.
A Lattice for Momos. Toronto: 1958. V. 47
Three Dozen Poems. Montreal: 1957. V. 47

EVERWINE, PETER
Keeping the Night. Lisbon: 1977. V. 52; 54

EVERY Boy's Annual 1886. V. 53

EVERY Day Occurences. London: 1825. V. 53

EVERY Man Entertained or, Select Histories; Giving an Account of Persons Who Have Been Most Eminently Distinguished by Their Virtues or Vices, Their Perfections or Defects, Either of Body or Mind. London: 1756. V. 52

EVERYMAN.. London: 1911. V. 51
EVERYMAN. London: 1930. V. 47

THE EVERYMAN Encyclopaedia. London: 1913. V. 48

EVERYMAN'S History of the English Church. London: 1914. V. 47

EVIDENCE Concerning Railroads Across the Sierra Nevada Mountains, from Pacific Tide Waters in California, and the Resources, Promises and Action of Companies Organized to Construct the Same. Carson City: 1865. V. 47

EVISON, J.
Compleat Book of Psalmody Containing Variety of Psalm-Tunes, Hymns and Anthems to be Sung in 2, 3 and 4 Parts. 1760. V. 52

EVJEN, JOHN OLUF
The Life of J. H. W. Stuckenberg Theologian - Philosopher - Sociologist Friend of Humanity. Minneapolis: 1938. V. 50

EVSTRATII Et Aliorvm Insignivm Peripateticorvm Commentaria in Libros Decem Aristotelis De Moribvx ad Nicomachvm. Venice: 1536. V. 48

EWALD, ALEXANDER CHARLES
The Right Hon. Benjamin Disraeli, Early of Beaconsfield, K.G. and His Times. London: 1881. V. 48; 54

EWALD, C. A.
The Diseases of the Stomach. New York: 1892. V. 48; 53

EWALD, GEORGE HENRY AUGUSTUS
A Grammar of the Hebrew Language of the Old Testament. London: 1836. V. 48; 51

EWART, GAVIN
A Cluster of Clerihews. Leamington Spa: 1985. V. 49
Poems and Songs. London: 1939. V. 47; 49

EWART, WILFIRD
Scots Guard. London: 1934. V. 47

EWART, WILFRID
When Armageddon Came, Studies in Peace and War. London: 1933. V. 50

EWBANK, JANE M.
Antiquary on Horseback. Kendal: 1963. V. 52

EWBANK, THOMAS
Life in Brazil; or, a Journal of a Visit to the Land of the Cocoa and the Palm. New York: 1856. V. 48; 50; 53; 54

EWELL, JAMES
The Medical Companion, or Family Physician. Baltimore: 1822. V. 50

EWEN, C. L'ESTRANGE
The Familes of Ewen of East Anglia and the Fenland. London: 1928. V. 49; 52

EWEN, DAVID
Complete Book of the American Musical Theater. New York: 1958. V. 54

EWERS, H. H.
Alraune. 1911. V. 48; 52
Blood. 1930. V. 48
Edgar Allan Poe. New York: 1917. V. 48; 53

EWERS, J. C.
Plains Indian Painting: a Description of an Aborginal American Art. Stanford: 1939. V. 51; 53

EWING, CHARLES
In the Matter of the Requisition of the Osage National Council on the Money Arising from the Sale of the Osage Lands, for the Payment of an Osage National Debt. 1873. V. 49

EWING, JAMES
Clinical Pathology of the Blood, a Treatise on the General Principles and Special Applications of Hematology. Philadelphia: 1901. V. 48; 53

EWING, JOHN
The Royal Scots 1914-1919. Edinburgh: 1925. V. 54

EWING, WILLIAM
Arabs and Druze at Home: a Record of Travel and Intercourse with the Peoples East of the Jordan. London: 1907. V. 54

THE EX Libran. Kansas City: 1912. V. 47

AN EXACT Abridgment of all the Irish Statutes. Together With an Abridgment of All the English Statutes in Force in Ireland. Dublin: 1736. V. 49

AN EXACT Abridgment of all the Statutes in Force and Use, from Magna Charta (etc.). London: 1725. V. 51

AN EXACT and Circumstantial History of the Battle of Floddon in Verse, Written About the Time of Queen Elizabeth. Berwick upon Tweed: 1774. V. 47; 50; 53

AN EXACT and Particular Narrative of a Cruel and Inhumane Murder Attempted on the Body of Edward Crispe...by Arundel Coke, Esq.; Barrister at Law and John Woodburn, a Laborer. London: 1722. V. 51

AN EXACT Collection of All Remonstrances, Declarations, Votes, Orders, Ordinances, Proclamations, Petitions, Messages, Answers and Other Remarkable Passages Betweene the Kings Most Excellent Majesty and His Hight Court of Parliament... London: 1643. V. 50; 53

AN EXACT Collection of the Debates of the House of Commons, Held at Westminster Oct. 21, 1680, Prorogued the Tenth and Dissolved the 18th of Jan. Following... London: 1689. V. 50; 53

AN EXACT Collection of the Most Considerable Debates in the Honourable House of Commons, at the Parliament Held at Westminster the One and Twentieth of October, 1680. London: 1681. V. 50

THE EXACT Conformity of the Principles and Practices of the Scots Non-Conformists to the Apostolick Government of the Christian Church. London?: 1703?. V. 53

AN EXACT Journal of the Victorious Expediton of the Confederate Fleet, the Last Year, Under the Command of the Right Honourable Admiral Russel... London: 1695. V. 52

EXAMEN Poeticum: Being the Third Part of Miscellany Poems, Containing Variety of New Translations of the Ancient Poets. London: 1693. V. 49

THE EXAMINATION Of Edward Fitharris, Relating to the Popish Plot, Taken the Tenth Day of March, 1681. London: 1681. V. 53

EXAMINATION of the Controversy Between Georgia and the Creeks. 1825. V. 48

AN EXAMINE of the Expediency of Bringing Over Immediately the Body of Hanoverian Troops Taken Into Our Pay, in Exchange for the Like Number of English to be Sent to Flanders, In Order to a Total Suppression of the Rebellion, the Security of the Royal... London: 1746. V. 48

EXAMPLES of San Bernardino of Siena. 1926. V. 52; 54

EXCEEDING Joyful Newes from York, Being a True Relation of Many Passages of Great Consequence, Happened Very Latelie Between His Majesty and the Inhabitants of Yorkshire... London: 1642. V. 50

EXCEEDING Welcome Newes from Beverley. London: 1642. V. 50

EXECUTORS' Sale. Estate of Joseph Rhoads, Dec'd. Thomas & Sons, Auctioneers. Very Valuable Farm...Situate on the Haverford Plank Road, About Four Miles from Market St. Bridge... Philadelphia, Feb. 1853. Philadelphia: 1853. V. 47

EXERCISE at the Ordination of Five Missionaries... Chicago: 1867. V. 53

THE EXERCISE of the Foot: With the Evolutions, According to the Words of Command, As They Are Explained. London: 1690. V. 47

EXERCISES for Ingenuity: Consisting of Queries, Transpositions, Charades, Rebuses and Riddles. London: 1825. V. 52

EXHIBITION Illustrative of Early English Portraiture - Illustrated Catalogue. 1909. V. 48

THE EXHIBITION of Art-Industry in Dublin. London: 1853. V. 50

EXLEY, FREDERICK
A Fan's Notes. London: 1968. V. 51
A Fan's Notes. New York: 1968. V. 47; 48; 50; 51; 52; 53; 54
Last Notes from Home. New York: 1988. V. 53

EXNER, A. H.
Japan As I Saw It. London. V. 54
Japan As I Saw It. London: 1930. V. 48

EXPANDED METAL & CORRUGATED BAR CO.
Corrugated Bars for Reinforced Concrete. St. Louis: 1906. V. 52

AN EXPLANATION of the Works of the Thames Tunnel Now Completed from Rotherhithe to Wapping. London: 1851. V. 52

AN EXPLANATION of the Works of the Tunnel Under the Thames from Rotherhithe to Wapping. London: 1840. V. 49

THE EXPLORATION of the Colorado River and the High Plateaus of Utah in 1871-72. Salt Lake City: 1949. V. 47

EXPOSITIO Officii Missae Sacrique Canonis. Reutlingen: 1483. V. 52

EXQUEMELIN, ALEXANDRE OLIVIER
Bucaniers of America. London: 1684-85. V. 47; 48; 49; 50
The Buccaneers of America. London: 1893. V. 54
The Buccaneers of America. London: 1911. V. 52
Histoire des Avanturiers Qui se Sont Signalez Dans les Indes, Contenant ce Qu'ils ont fait de Plus Remarquable Depuis Vingt anne'es. Paris: 1688. V. 51
The History of the Bucaniers of America. London: 1771. V. 49

EXTRACTS from an Investigation Into the Physical Properties of Books as They are at Present Published. Boston: 1919. V. 47

THE EXTRAORDINARY Confession, Life and Singular Adventures of Wolfe, Who Was Thirty Years a Notorious Robber, Murder, and Captain of a Gang of Fifty-Three Thieves. London: 1800. V. 51

THE EXTRAORDINARY Red Book... London: 1817. V. 50

EXTRAORDINARY Trial! Crim. Con. and Incest...A Full Report of the Case. Cooke V. Wetherell!...August 16, 1845. London: 1845. V. 51

THE EXTRAVAGANT Wish; a Dream. Dublin: 1749. V. 54

EYCLESHYMER, ALBERT
Anatomical Names Especially the Basle Nomina Anatomica with Biographical Sketches by Roy Lee Moodie. New York: 1917. V. 47

EYER, ALICE
The Famous Fremonts and Their America. Santa Ana: 1948. V. 54

EYKYN, THOMAS
A Peripatetic Parson. Parts of the Pacific. London: 1896. V. 48

EYLAND, E. S.
Working Drawings and Designs in Architecture and Building... London: 1863. V. 50; 52

EYLES, DESMOND
George Tinworth, Chronology of Principal Works. Los Angeles: 1982. V. 52
Royal Doulton ....The Rise and Expansion of the Royal Doulton Potteries. London: 1965. V. 52

EYLOT, THOMAS
The Book Named the Governour. Newcastle-upon-Tyne: 1834. V. 52

EYMERIC, NICOLAS
Directorium Inquisitorum... Rome: 1587. V. 54

EYRE, ALAN MONTGOMERY
Saint John's Wood. Its History, Its Houses, Its Haunts and Its Celebrities. London: 1913. V. 50; 52; 54

EYRE, ALICE
The Famous Fremonts and Their America. 1948. V. 52

EYRE, EDMUND JOHN
Journals of Expeditions of Discovery into Central Australia and Overland from Adelaide to King Georges Sound in the Years 1840-41. London: 1845. V. 52
Observations Made at Paris During the Peace, and Remarks in a Tour from London to Paris, Through Picardy and to England by the Route of Normandy... Bath: 1803. V. 47; 48

EYRE, JOHN
The Exact Surveyor; or, The Whole Art of Surveying of Land. London: 1654. V. 50

EYRE, SELWYN
Sketches of Russian Life and Customs, Made During a Visit in 1876-7. London: 1878. V. 53

EYRE, VINCENT
The Military Operations at Cabal, Which Ended in the Retreat and Destruction of the British Army, Jan. 1842 with a Journal of Imprisonment in Afghanistan... London: 1843. V. 51; 52; 53; 54

EYRIES, J. B. B.
La France, ou Costumes, Moeurs et Usages des Francais. (and) L'Angleterre. Paris: 1821. V. 53

EYTON, T. C.
Osteologia Avium; or, a Sketch of the Osteology of Birds. London: 1867-75. V. 50

EZRA Pound: a Collection of Essays Edited by Peter Russell to Be Presented to Ezra Pound on His 65th Birthday. London: 1950. V. 47

EZZELL, MURRAY, MRS.
Founders and Patriots of the Republic of Texas: The Lineages of the Members of the Daughters of the Republic of Texas, Book II. Austin: 1974. V. 47

F

F., A.
The Ladies' Pocket Book of Etiquett. Waltham St. Lawrence: 1928. V. 47

F., C.
A Ramble on Rumbald's Moor, Among the Dwellings, Cairns and Circles of the Ancient Britons, in the Summer of 1867. Wakefield: 1868-69. V. 53

F., I.
The Two Boys and the Three Dogs or Want of Thought. London: 1836. V. 47

F. Killenberger's New Brunswick City Directory, 1890. New Brunswick: 1890. V. 51

FAAS, EKBERT
Towards a New American Poetics: Essays and Interviews. Santa Barbara: 1978. V. 49
The Unaccomodated Universe. Santa Barbara: 1980. V. 54

FABER, EGIDIUS
Von dem Falschen Blut und Abgott im Thum zu Schwerin. Mit Einer Schonen Vorrede D. Mart. Luth.... Wittenberg: 1533. V. 51; 53

FABER, GEORGE STANLEY
A General and Connected View of the Prophecies, Relative to the Conversion, Restoration, Union and Future Glory of the Houses of Judah and Israel; the Progress and Final Overthrow of the Antichristian Confederacy in the Land of Palestine... Boston: 1809. V. 47
The Origin of Pagan Idolatry Ascertained from Historical Testimony and Circumstancial Evidence. London: 1816. V. 51

FABER, GOTTHILF THEODOR VON
Sketches of the Internal State of France. London: 1811. V. 50; 53

FABES, GILBERT H.
Modern First Editions Points and Values. London: 1929-32. V. 49; 51; 52

FABIAN, RANIER
Masters of Early Travel Photography. New York, Paris: 1983. V. 53

FABLE, LEONARD
The Gingerbread Man. London: 1915. V. 48
The Gingerbread Man. London: 1916. V. 52

FABLES for the Female Sex. London: 1771. V. 50

FABLES of Aesop and Other Eminent Mythologists. London: 1694. V. 54

FABLES, Original and Selected: by the Most Esteemed European and Oriental Authors. London: 1842. V. 51

FABRE, JAN
The Power of Theatrical Madness. London: 1986. V. 50

FABRE, JEAN ANTOINE
Essai Sur La Theorie des Torrens et des Rivieres. Paris: 1797. V. 52

FABRE, JEAN HENRI
Der Abend des Nachtpfauenauges. 1988. V. 52; 54
Book of Insects. New York: 1939. V. 51
Fabre's book of Insects. London. V. 47; 48
Fabre's Book of Insects. London: 1921. V. 48; 49; 51; 52
Fabre's Book of Insects. New York: 1935. V. 52
Fabre's Book of Insects. New York: 1936. V. 50

FABRI, OTTAVIO
Con La Quale Per Teorica et per Pratica Si Misura Geometricamente Ogni Distanza, Altezza, e Profondita... Venetia: 1598. V. 49
L'Uso del la Suqadra Mobile... Padova: 1673. V. 54

FABRICIUS, HIERONYMOUS
The Embryological Treatise of Hieronymous Fabricius of Aquapendente. Ithaca: 1942. V. 48; 50; 52; 53

FABRICIUS, HIERONYMUS
The Embryological Treatises of Hieronymus Fabricius of Aquapendente. Ithaca: 1967. V. 52
Opera Chirugica. Padua: 1647-48. V. 47
Opera Chirugica. Lugdvni Batavorum: 1723. V. 47; 48; 49; 50; 51; 52; 53
L'Opere Cirugiche... Padua: 1671. V. 52

FABYAN, ROBERT
The Chronicle. London: 1559. V. 49
Fabyans Cronycle Newly Prynted with the Cronycle, Actes and Dedes Done in the Tyme of the Reygne of the Moste Excellent Prynce Kynge Henry the VII. London: 1533. V. 47
The New Chronicles of England and France. London: 1811. V. 47; 50; 51; 54

THE FACES of Science Fiction. 1984. V. 51

FACETS: an Anthology of Verse. Nashville: 1928. V. 53

THE FACSIMILE - and - Notes to Accompany a Facsimile Reproduction of the Diploma of Doctor of Medicine Granted by the University of Padua to William Havey 1602. London: 1908. V. 54

FACSIMILES of Choice Examples of the Art of Book-Illumination During the Middle Ages/Facsimiles of Choice Examples Selected from Illuminated Manuscripts, Unpublished Drawings and Illustrated Books of Early Date. London: 1889-92. V. 52

FACT, TOM, PSEUD.
The History of Peter Pindar, From the Memorable Area When He Received a Sound Thrashing Down to the Present Time. London: 1790?. V. 48

FACTS and Arguments in Favour of Adopting Railways in Preference to Canals, in the State of Pennsylvania. Philadelphia: 1825. V. 50

FACTS for the Consideration of the Public at Large, on the High Price of Meat, Shewing the Real Cause of the Same. London: 1795?. V. 47

FACTS; or, A Plain and Explicit Narrative of the Case of Mr. Rudd. London: 1775. V. 48; 50; 51

THE FACTS Respecting Indian Administration in the North-West. Ottawa: 1886. V. 47

FACULTY OF ADVOCATES
Catalogue of the Library of the Faculty of Advocates. Edinburgh: 1742. V. 52

FAERNO, GABRIELLO
Centum Fabulae ex Antiqvis Scriptoribvs Dlectae. Brussels: 1682. V. 50
Emendationes, in Sex Fabulas Terentii. Florence: 1565. V. 51
Fabulae Centum (Cent Fables Choisies des Anciens Auteurs). London: 1743. V. 48; 49
Fabulae Centum ex Antiquis Auctoribus Delectae Carminibusque Explicatae, et Eiusdem Carmina Varia. Parma: 1793. V. 51

FAGAN, LOUIS
The Life of Sir Anthony Panizzi, K.C.B., late Principal Librarian of the British Museum, Senator of Italy &c. London: 1880. V. 53

FAGERSTROM, J. A.
The Evolution of Reef Communities. London: 1987. V. 50

FAGET, JEAN CHARLES
Etude Medicale et Quelques Questiones Importantees Pour la Louisiane, et Expose Succinct d'une Endemie Paludeene, de Forme Catarrhale, Qui a Sevi a la Nouvelle-Orleans... New Orleans: 1859. V. 49

FAGG, MICHAEL
The Life and Adventures of a Limb of the Law... London: 1836. V. 48

FAGG, WILLIAM B.
Afro-Portuguese Ivories. London: 1959. V. 54

FAGGE, CHARLES HILTON
The Principles and Practice of Medicine. London: 1886. V. 53

FAHEY, HERBERT
Early Printing in California. San Francisco: 1956. V. 48; 49; 50; 52; 54

FAHIE, J. J.
Galileo, His Life and Work. London: 1903. V. 51
A History of Electric Telegraphy to the Year 1837. London: 1884. V. 53
A History of Wireless Telegraphy 1838-1899, Including Some Bare-Wire Proposals for Subaqueous Telegraphs. Edinburgh: 1899. V. 52
Memorials of Galileo Galilei, 1564-1642. Leamington & London: 1929. V. 52; 54

FAIFAX, HENRY
An Impartial Relation of the Whole Proceedings Against St. Mary Magdalen Colledge in Oxon, in the Year of Our Lord 1687. London: 1688. V. 47

FAILLE, J. B. DE LA
The Works of Vincent Van Gogh: His Paintings and Drawings. New York: 1970. V. 51

FAINLIGHT, HARRY
Sussicran. London: 1967. V. 47

FAINLIGHT, RUTH
Pigeons at Villa Belmonte. 1974. V. 51

FAIRBAIRN, JAMES
Fairbairn's Crests of the Familes of Great Britain and Ireland... London: 1860. V. 48

FAIRBAIRN, THOMAS
Britannia and Conway Tubular Bridges. Truths and Tubes on Self Supporting Principles... London: 1849. V. 51
Relics of Ancient Architecture and other Picturesque Scenes in Glasgow. Glasgow: 1849. V. 49; 52

FAIRBAIRN, WILLIAM
Iron, Its History, Properties and Processes of Manufacture. Edinburgh: 1861. V. 50
Iron, its History, Properties and Processes of Manufacture. Edinburgh: 1865. V. 50
On the Application of Cast and Wrought Iron to Building Purposes. London: 1854. V. 52
On the Application of Cast and Wrought Iron to Building Purposes. New York: 1854. V. 47
Treatise on Iron Ship Building: Its History and Progress as Comprised in a Series of Experimental Researches on the Laws of Strain... London: 1865. V. 54
Useful Information for Engineers. London: 1856. V. 51
Useful Information for Engineers. London: 1860. V. 50
Useful Information for Engineers. London: 1864. V. 50

FAIRBAIRN'S Book of Crests of the Families of Great Britain and Ireland. London: 1905. V. 52

FAIRBANK, ALFRED
Renaissance Handwriting. London: 1960. V. 48

FAIRBANK, JOHN KING
Modern China: a Bibliographical Guide to Chinese Works 1898-1937. Cambridge: 1950. V. 53

FAIRBANK, TSCHICHOLD
A Book of Scripts. London: 1949. V. 48

FAIRBANKS, ARTHUR
Catalogue of Greek and Etruscan Vases I: Early Vases, Preceding Athenian Black-Figured Ware. Cambridge: 1928. V. 52

THE FAIRBANKS Times "Made in Tanana" Industrial Edition. 1910. V. 50

FAIRBRIDGE, CHARLES A.
The Fairbridge Library. Edinburgh: 1904. V. 53

FAIRBURN, JOHN
Fairburn's Authentic Account of the Bombardment of Copenhagen, and Surrender of the Danish Fleet. London: 1807?. V. 51
Fairburn's Authentic and Copious Account of the Extraordinary Siamese Twins, Eng and Chang (sic).... London: 1830. V. 47

FAIRBURN'S Description of the Popular and Comic New Pantomine, Called Harlequin and Mother Goose, or the Golden Egg. London: 1806. V. 51

FAIRBURN'S Eccentric Songster, Being a Prime Collection of New Songs... London. V. 51

FAIRBURN'S Eccentric Songster, Being a prime Collection of New Songs... London: 1830. V. 49

FAIRCHILD, C. B.
History of the 27th Regiment, New York Volunteers. New York: 1888. V. 49

FAIRCHILD, JOHN F.
Atlas of Mount Vernon and the Town of Pelham. New York: 1899. V. 49

FAIRCHILD, LEE
The Tippler's Vow. New York: 1901. V. 48

FAIRCHILD, T.
The City Gardener...Ever-Greens, Fruit-Trees, Flowering Shrubs, Flowers, Exotick Plants &c. as Will be Ornamental and Thrive Best in the London Gardens. London: 1722. V. 51

FAIRFAX, BRIAN
A Catalogue of the Curious Collection of Pictures of George Villiers, Duke of Buckingham. London: 1758. V. 50

FAIRFAX, FERDINANDO
The Good and Prosperous Successe of the Parliaments Forces in Yorkshire. London: 1642. V. 53
A Miraculous Victory Obtained by the Right Honourable Ferdinando Lrod Fairfax, Against the Army Under the Command of the Earl of Newcastle at Wakefield in Yorkshire. London: 1643. V. 50

FAIRFAX, HENRY
An Impartial Relation of the Whole Proceedings Against St. Mary Magdalen Colledge in Oxon, in the Year of Our Lord 1687 Containing Only Matters of Fact as They Occurred. London: 1688. V. 47

FAIRFAX, THOMAS
The Complete Sportsman: or, Country Gentleman's Recreation... London. V. 49
The Complete Sportsman; or, Country Gentleman's Recreation. London: 1758. V. 47
The Complete Sportsman: or, Country Gentleman's Recreation... London: 1795. V. 47

FAIRFAX MURRAY, CHARLES
Catalogue of Early French Books in the Library of... London: 1961. V. 47
Catalogue of Early German Books in the Library of... London: 1962. V. 47

FAIRFIELD, ASA MERRILL
Fairfield's Pioneer History of Lassen County, California... San Francisco: 1916. V. 47; 54

FAIRFIELD, SUMNER LINCOLN
Abaddon, the Spirit of Destruction; and Other Poems. New York: 1830. V. 51
The Last Night of Pompeii; a Poem. New York: 1832. V. 48; 49; 51; 52; 54
Lays of Melpomene. Portland: 1824. V. 52
The Passage of the Sea; a Poem. With Other Pieces. New York: 1826. V. 49; 52
The Siege of Constantinople. Charleston: 1822. V. 48; 53

FAIRHOLT, FREDERICK WILLIAM
Gog and Magog. The Giants in Guildhall; Their Real and Legendary History. London: 1859. V. 49; 54
Up the Nile and Home Again. London: 1862. V. 53

FAIRLAND, THOMAS
Ackermann's Drawing-Book of Trees, Elementary and Progressive, for 1841. London: 1841. V. 48

FAIRLESS, MICHAEL
Stories Told to Children. London: 1914. V. 49

FAIRLEY, BARKER
Poems of 1922 or Not Long After. Kingston: 1972. V. 47

FAIRLEY, JOHN A.
Relict of Andrew Anderson the King's Printer. A Contribution to the History of Printing in Scotland. Aberdeen: 1925. V. 53

A FAIRY Book. New York: 1923. V. 49

A FAIRY Garland - Being Fairy Tales from the Old French. London: 1928. V. 50; 52

A FAIRY Garland: Being Fairy Tales from the Old French. New York: 1929. V. 52

THE FAIRY Mythology. 1828. V. 48
THE FAIRY Mythology. London: 1828. V. 52

THE FAIRY Shoemaker and Other Fairy Poems. New York: 1928. V. 50; 52; 53

THE FAIRY'S Revel; or, Puck's Trip thro' London by Moon Light. London: 1770. V. 47

A FAITHFUL and Authentic Account of the Siege and Surrender of St. Philip's Fort, in the island of Minorca. London: 1757. V. 50

FAITHFUL Friends. London: 1910. V. 48

A FAITHFUL Picture of the Political Situation of New Orleans, at the Close of the Last and the Beginning of the Present Year 1807. Boston: 1808. V. 48

FAITHFULL, EMILY
Three Visits to America. New York: 1884. V. 50; 52; 53

FAITHHORN, JOHN
Facts and Observations on Liver Complaints and Bilious Disorders in General. Philadelphia: 1822. V. 48; 53

FAKHRY, AHMED
The Egyptian Deserts: Siwa Oasis, Its History and Antiquities. Cairo: 1944. V. 52
The Monuments of Sneferu at Dahshur. Cairo: 1959-61. V. 51

FALADA, GIOVANNI BATTISTA
Le Fontane di Rome nelle Piazze, E Luoghi Publici della Citta... (with) Le Fontane delle Ville di Frascati nel Tusculano con li Loro Prospetti Parte Seconda. (with) Le Fontaine ne Palazzi e ne Giardini di Roma.. (with) Le Fontane del Giardino Estense in ... Rome: 1691/91/91/91. V. 50

FALCKENBERG, ALBERT
Ideen-Magazin fur Buchbinder. Zusammenst(ellung) von Stempeln, Linien &c. Aus Der Graviranstalt. Magdeburg: 1843-50?. V. 48

FALCONER, H.
Fauna Antiqua Sivalensis. London: 1845-49. V. 47

FALCONER, JOHN
Cryptomenisis Patefacta; or the Art of Secret Information Disclosed Without a Key... London: 1685. V. 48
Rules for Explaining and Deciphering All Manner of Secret Writing, Plain and Demonstrative... London: 1692. V. 48

FALCONER, JOHN D.
On Horseback through Nigeria, or, Life and Travel in the Central Sudan. 1911. V. 47
On Horseback through Nigeria, or, Life and Travel in the Central Sudan. London: 1911. V. 54

FALCONER, RICHARD
The Voyages, Dangerous Adventures and Imminent Escapes of Captain Richard Falconer. London: 1720. V. 53; 54

FALCONER, THOMAS
Letters and Notes on the Texan Santa Fe Expedition 1841-1842. New York: 1930. V. 50; 52; 53
On Surnames and the Rules of Law Affecting Their Change. London: 1862. V. 50; 52; 53
The Oregon Question; or, a Statement of the British Claims to the Oregon territory. London: 1845. V. 47; 48
Texan Santa Fe Expedition. New York: 1930. V. 49; 54

FALCONER, WILLIAM
An Account of the Epidemical Catarrahl Fever Commonly called the Influenza, As It Appeared at Bath in the Winter and Spring of the Year 1803. Bath: 1803. V. 52
A New Universal Dictionary of the Marine... London: 1815. V. 48; 49
Observations Respecting the Pulse: Intended to Point Out with Greater Certainty, the Indications Which it Signifies; Especially in Feverish Complaints. London: 1796. V. 51; 53
The Poetical Works of William Falconer. London: 1866. V. 51
Remarks on the Influence of Climate, Situation, Nature of Country, Population, Nature of Food and Way of Life... 1781. V. 54
The Shipwreck. London: 1804. V. 49; 50; 51; 52; 54
The Shipwreck. London: 1811. V. 48
An Universal Dictionary of the Marine. London: 1776. V. 49

FALES, MARTHA GANDY
Joseph Richardson and Family, Philadelphia Silversmiths. Middletown: 1974. V. 50

FALK, BERNARD
Thomas Rowlandson: His Life and Art. London: 1952. V. 54
Thomas Rowlandson, His Life and Art. New York: 1952. V. 50

FALK, TOBY
India Miniatures in the India Office Library. London: 1981. V. 49; 51; 53

FALKE, JACOB VON
Art in the House. Boston: 1879. V. 51

FALKENER, EDWARD
Ephesus and the Temple of Diana. London: 1862. V. 47

FALKINER, FREDERICK B.
A Pedigree, with Personal Sketches of the Falkiners of Mount Falcon. Dublin: 1894. V. 47; 53

FALKIRK IRON CO.
Book of Patterns. London: 1860. V. 50; 52

FALKLAND, AMELIA
Chow-Chow. A Journal Kept in India, Egypt and Syria. London: 1930. V. 49
Chow-Chow; Being Selections from a Journal Kept in India, Egypt and Syria. London: 1857. V. 50

FALKNER, FRANK
The Wood Family of Burslem. London: 1912. V. 51

FALKNER, J. MEADE
A Bath - Its History and Social Tradition. London: 1918. V. 52
A History of Oxfordshire. London: 1899. V. 52
The Lost Stradivarius. London: 1895. V. 53
The Lost Stradivarius. New York: 1896. V. 53

FALKNER, WILLIAM
A Vindication of Liturgies, Shewing the Lawfulness, Usefulness and Antiquity of Performing the Publick Worship of God, by Set Forms of Prayer... London: 1680. V. 52

FALKNER, WILLIAM CLARK
Rapid Ramblings in Europe. Philadelphia: 1844. V. 53
Rapid Ramblings in Europe. Philadelphia: 1884. V. 54

FALL, BERNARD B.
Hell in a Very Small Place. Philadelphia: 1967. V. 51

FALLE, PHILIP
An Account of the Island of Jersey, With an Appendix of Records, &c. Jersey: 1837. V. 48

FALLODON, GREY, EARL OF
The Charm of Birds. London. V. 48

FALLON, W. J.
Practical Wildfowling: A Complete Guide to the Art of the Fowler. London: 1907. V. 49

FALLOPPIO, GABRIELLO
Secreti Diversi, e Miracolosi... Venice: 1650-63?. V. 48

A FAMILIAR Description of Beasts, for the Entertainment of Little Readers. Wendell: 1826. V. 53

A FAMILIAR View, of the Operation and Tendency of Usury Laws... New York: 1837. V. 54

THE FAMILY Guide to Health; or, a General Practice of Physic In a Familiar Way... London: 1767. V. 49; 51

THE FAMILY Magazine: in Two Parts. London: 1741. V. 54

FAMILY Prayers, and Moral Essays in Prose and Verse. London: 1769. V. 51

THE FAMILY Tutor. London: 1851-52. V. 54

THE FAMOUS History of Kasperl and the Adventures He Meet With on His Travels. London: 1857. V. 52

THE FAMOUS History of Valentine and Orson. London: 1801. V. 49

FAMOUS Men of Britain. London: 1835. V. 52

FANCOURT, CHARLES ST. JOHN
The History of Yucatan From Its Discovery to the Close of the Seventeenth Century. London: 1854. V. 49

FANE, HENRY EDWARD
Five Years in India... London: 1842. V. 53

FANE, JULIAN H. C.
Tannhauser; or, the Battle of the Bards. Mobile: 1863. V. 49; 53

FANNING, DAVID
The Narrative of Colonel David Fanning... Richmond: 1861. V. 48; 49

FANNING, EDMUND
Voyages & Discoveries in the South Seas 1792-1832. Salem: 1924. V. 47; 49; 51; 52
Voyages Round the World; with Selected Sketches of Voyages to the South Seas, North and South Pacific Oceans, China, etc., Peformed Under the Command and Agency of the Author. New York: 1833. V. 50; 52

FANNING, J. T.
A Practical Treatise on Water-Supply Engineering: Relating to the Hydrology, Hydrodynamics and Practical Construction of Water-Works in North America with Numerous Tables and Illustrations. 1877. V. 52; 53

FANNING the Embers. Miles City: 1971. V. 50

FANSHAW, RICHARD
Il Pastor Fido; the Faithful Shepherd. London: 1676. V. 52

FANSHAWE, ALTHEA
Easter Holidays, or Domestic Conversations, Designed for the Instruction, and It Is Hoped for the Amusement of Young People. Bath: 1797. V. 47

FANSHAWE, ANNE, LADY
Memoirs of Lady Fanshawe. London: 1829. V. 47; 49; 53

FANSHAWE, CATHERINE MARIA
The Literary Remains. London: 1876. V. 50

FANSHAWE, HERBERT C.
Delhi, Past and Present. London: 1902. V. 54

FANTE, JOHN
1933 Was a Bad Year. Santa Barbara: 1985. V. 53
Ask the Dust. Santa Barbara: 1980. V. 51; 53
Dago Red. New York: 1940. V. 53
Dreams from Bunker Hill. 1982. V. 52
Full of Life. Boston: 1952. V. 52
The Road to Los Angeles. Santa Barbara: 1985. V. 53
Wait Until Spring, Bandini. New York: 1938. V. 53
Wait Until Spring, Bandini. Santa Barbara: 1983. V. 51; 53
The Wine of Youth. Santa Barbara: 1985. V. 53

FARABEE, W. C.
Central Caribs. Philadelphia: 1924. V. 54

FARADAY, MICHAEL
Chemical Manipulations, Being Instructions to Students in Chemistry. London: 1830. V. 49
Copy of Mr. Faraday's Reports on the Electric Light to the Royal Commissioners and Of Those Made by Order of the Trinity Board. London: 1862. V. 53
A Course of Six Lectures on the Chemical History of a Candle... London: 1861. V. 48
A Course of Six Lectures on the Chemical History of a Candle... New York: 1861. V. 51
Experimental Researches in Chemistry and Physics. London: 1859. V. 48; 50; 52; 53; 54
Experimental Researches in Electricity. London: 1839. V. 48
Experimental Researches in Electricity. London: 1839/55/1844. V. 54
Experimental Researches in Electricity. London: 1878. V. 48
Experimental Researches in Electricity... London: 1880. V. 50
The Life and Letters of Faraday. London: 1870. V. 47
On the Alloys of Steel. London: 1822. V. 49
The Subject Matter of a Course of Six Lectures on the Non-Metallic Elements... London: 1853. V. 53

FARADAY, PHILIP MICHAEL
Amasis, an Egyptian Princess. A Comic Opera in 2 Acts. London: 1906. V. 52

FARCY, LOUIS
La Brodierie du IXe Siecle Jusqu-a Nos Jours D'Apres des Specimens Authentiques et les Anciens Inventaires. 1890. V. 49

FAREWELL, GEORGE
Farrago. London: 1733. V. 48

FAREY, JOHN
The Circle of Mechanical Arts... London: 1813. V. 47
A Treatise on the Steam Engine, Historical, Practical and Descriptive. Newton Abbot: 1971. V. 50

FARGO, FRANK F.
A Full and Authentic Account of the Murder of James King..... San Francisco: 1856. V. 51
A True and Minute History of the Assassination of James King of Wm. at San Francisco, Cal. San Francisco: 1856. V. 52

FARGUS, FREDERICK JOHN
Called Back. Bristol: 1885. V. 47

FARHAM, LUTHER
A Glance at Private Libraries. Boston: 1855. V. 54

FARIA Y SOUSA, MANUEL DE
Africa Portuguesa. Lisbon: 1691. V. 50

FARID, SHAFIK
Excavations at Ballana, 1958-1959. Cairo: 1963. V. 49; 51

FARINA, RICHARD
Been Down So Long It Looks Like Up to Me. New York: 1966. V. 52

FARINGTON, J.
Britannia Depicta... London: 1816. V. 50

FARINGTON, JOSEPH
The Diary of Joseph Farington (July 1793 - December 1821). London: 1928. V. 47
The Diary of Joseph Farington (July 1793 - December 1821). New Haven: 1978-1984. V. 47
The Farington Diary. New York: 1923. V. 50
Memoirs of the Life of Sir Joshua Reynolds. London: 1819. V. 48; 50; 53

FARIS, EL-SHIDIAC
A Practical Grammar of the Arabic Language. London: 1866. V. 52

FARIS, JOHN T.
Old Gardens In and About Philadelphia and Those Who Made Them. Indianapolis: 1932. V. 52

FARISH, THOMAS E.
The Gold Hunters of California... Chicago: 1904. V. 47
History of Arizona. Phoenix: 1915-18. V. 53

FARJEON, BENJAMIN LEOPOLD
Devlin the Barber. London: 1888. V. 47; 51
Grif, a Story of Australian Life. London: 1870. V. 54
An Island Pearl. London: 1875. V. 51
The Mesmerists. London: 1900. V. 48

FARJEON, ELEANOR
A Collection of Poems. London: 1929. V. 47
The Eleventh Princess; and Goldfish. V. 53
Elizabeth Myers. Aylesford: 1957. V. 53
The Glass Slipper. London: 1946. V. 51
Heroes and Heroines. London: 1933. V. 53; 54
Kaleidoscope. London: 1963. V. 49
Katy Kruse at the Seaside or the Deserted Islanders. London: 1932. V. 47
Mrs. Malone. London: 1950. V. 51
More Nursery Rhymes of London Town. London: 1917. V. 48
A Sussex Alphabet. 1939. V. 51; 54
Tomfooleries: Verses. London: 1920. V. 49
Town Child's Alphabet. London: 1924. V. 53

FARLEIGH, JOHN
Graven Image: an Autobiographical Textbook. London: 1940. V. 49

FARLEY, HARRIET
Happy Nights at Hazel Nook; or, Cottage Stories. Boston: 1854. V. 53; 54

FARLEY, JOHN
The London Art of Cookery and Housekeeper's Complete Assistant. London: 1804. V. 47; 49

FARLOW, WILLIAM GILSON
Icones Farlowianae. Cambridge: 1929. V. 49; 52; 53

THE FARMER and Gardener's Directory, containing the Most Approved Rules and Directions for Foretelling the Changes... Norwich: 1799?. V. 49

THE FARMER, Corn-Dealer and Miller's New Ready Reckoner of Corn and Cash... London: 1820. V. 51

FARMER, D. S.
Avian Biology. New York: 1971-85. V. 50; 54
Avian Biology. London: 1971-93. V. 50

FARMER, E. J.
The Resources of the Rocky Mountains... Cleveland: 1883. V. 53

FARMER, EDWARD I.
Trade Catalogue of Chinese Lamps. New York: 1920's. V. 50

FARMER, H. G.
The Organ of the Ancients from Eastern Sources. London: 1931. V. 49

FARMER, HUGH
The General Prevalance of the Worship of Human Spirits, in the Ancient Heathen Nations... London: 1783. V. 51

FARMER, JOHN
Memorials of the Graduates of Harvard University, in Cambridge, Massachusetts, Commencing with the First Class, 1642. No. 1, August, 1833. Concord: 1833. V. 47; 48

FARMER, JOHN S.
Merry Songs and Ballads. London: 1897. V. 52
Musa Pedestris. Three Centuries of Canting Songs and Slang Rhymes. London: 1896. V. 49; 51
National Ballad and Song. Merry Songs and Ballads Prior to the Year 1800. London: 1897. V. 48; 53
Slang and its Analogues Past and Present. London: 1890-1904. V. 53
Vocabula Amatoria: a French-English Glossary of Words, Phrases and Allusions Occurring in the Works of Rabelais, Voltaire, Moliere, Rousseau, Beranger, Zola and Others... London: 1896. V. 49

FARMER, PHILIP JOSE
The Fabulous River Boat. 1971. V. 49
The Fabulous River Boat. New York: 1971. V. 54
Flesh. New York: 1968. V. 47; 54
The Green Odyssey. 1957. V. 48; 51; 52
Love Song. San Antonio: 1983. V. 51; 53
The Unreasonable Mask. New York: 1981. V. 54

FARMER, PHILIP JOSE, MRS.
The Captives and Other Poems. Laporte: 1856. V. 52

FARMER, RICHARD
An Essay on the Learning of Shakespeare: Addressed to Joseph Cradock. Cambridge: 1767. V. 48

FARMER, SILAS
The History of Detroit and Michigan and the Annals of Wayne County. Detroit: 1889. V. 53

FARMER, SILAS
History of Detroit and Wayne County and Early Michigan... Detroit: 1890. V. 49

FARMERS' Cyclopedia, Abridged Agricultural Records... Garden City: 1916/12. V. 50; 52

THE FARMER'S Friend; a Record of Recent Discoveries, Improvements and Practical Suggestions in Agriculture. London: 1847. V. 53

THE FARMER'S Instructor; or Every Man His Own Lawyer. Buffalo: 1824. V. 50; 54

THE FARMER'S Lawyer; or Every Country Gentleman His Own Counsellor. London: 1774. V. 47

FARMERS' TRADE UNION OF CLEMENTS, SAN JOAQUIN COUNTY, CA.
By-Laws of the Farmers' Trade Union of Clements, San Joaquin County, California. Lodi: 1885. V. 54

FARNABY, THOMAS
Index Rhetoricus et Oratorius, Scholis and Institutioni Tenerioris... London: 1664. V. 53

FARNBOROUGH, CHARLES LONG, BARON
A Temperate Discussion of the Causes Which Have Led to the Present High Price of Bread. London: 1800. V. 51

FARNESE, ALESSANDRO
Historia de Rebvs in Gallia Gestis. 1663. V. 47
Nvovo Aviso et Particolar Discorso Della Mirabile Espvgnatione D'Anversa, Con le Capitulationi, & Trattati di Essa, Ottenuta dal... Verona: 1585. V. 48

FARNHAM, ELIZA W.
California, In-Doors and Out; or, How We Farm, Mine and Live Generally in the Golden State. New York: 1856. V. 48; 51; 53
Life in Prairie Land. New York: 1846. V. 48; 49
Life in Prairie Land. New York: 1847. V. 47

FARNHAM, THOMAS J.
Early Days of California: Embracing What I Saw and Heard There, with Scenes in the Pacific. Philadelphia: 1860. V. 47
History of Oregon Territory, It Being a Demonstration of the Title of the United States of North America to the Same. New York: 1844. V. 47
Travels in the Great Western Prairies. Poughkeepsie: 1841. V. 47
Travels in the Great Western Prairies. London: 1843. V. 50; 54
Travels in the Great Western Prairies. New York: 1843. V. 47; 49

FARNIE, HENRY BROUGHAM
The Golfer's Manual. London: 1947. V. 49

FARNOL, JEFFREY
The Amateur Gentleman. London. V. 49
The Money Moon, a Romance. London: 1914. V. 48

FARNSWORTH, R. W. C.
A Southern California Paradise, in the Suburbs of Los Angeles: Being a Historic and Descriptive Account of Pasadena, San Gabriel, Sierra Madre and La Canada. Pasadena: 1883. V. 52

FARQUHAR, FERDINAND
The Relicks of a Saint. London: 1816. V. 48; 49

FARQUHAR, FRANCIS P.
The Books of the Colorado River and the Grand Canyon: a Selective Bibliography. Los Angeles: 1953. V. 52
History of the Sierra Nevada. Berkeley: 1965. V. 52; 54
Mount Olympus. San Francisco: 1929. V. 51
Place Names of the High Sierra. San Francisco: 1926. V. 54
Yosemite, the Big Trees and the High Sierra. Berkeley & Los Angeles: 1948. V. 51

FARQUHAR, GEORGE
The Complete Works. London: 1930. V. 48; 53
The Dramatic Works. London: 1892. V. 51
Love and Business: in a Collection of Occasionary Verse and Epistolary Prose. London: 1702. V. 49
The Recruiting Officer: a Comedy. London: 1926. V. 48
Sir Harry Wildair; Being the Sequel of the Trip to the Jubilee. London: 1701. V. 48

FARQUHAR, WILLIAM
Poems on Several Occasions: Consisting of Elegies and Epistles, Miscellanies and Scottish Pieces. Edinburgh: 1794. V. 54

FARR, THOMAS
A Traveller's Rambling Reminiscences of the Spanish War. London: 1838. V. 51

FARR, W.
Vital Statistics, a memorial Volume... London: 1885. V. 47

FARR, WILLIAM
A Medical Guide to Nice: Containing Every Information Necessary to the Invalid as Resident Stranger. London: 1841. V. 51; 53
A Treatise Explanatory of a Method Whereby Occult Cancer May be Cured... London: 1825. V. 51

FARRAR, ELIZA WARE ROTCH
The Young Lady's Friend... London: 1838. V. 53

FARRAR, FERDINANDO RICHARD
Johnny Red, The Confederate and Rip Van Winkle, or the Virginia that Slept Ten Years. Richmond: 1869. V. 49

FARRAR, FRANCIS
The Book of the Roycrofters. East Aurora: 1907. V. 54

FARRAR, FREDERIC WILLIAM
Lives of the Fathers. Edinburgh: 1889. V. 53
Verses. London: 1908. V. 53

FARRAR, MAURICE
Five Years in Minnesota. London: 1880. V. 54

FARRAR, TIMOTHY
Report of the Case of the Trustees of Dartmouth College Against William H. Woodward. Portsmouth: 1819. V. 51

FARRAR, VICTOR
The Annexation of Russian America to the United States. Washington: 1937. V. 52

FARRELL, DAVID
The Stinehours Press - A Bibliographical Checklist of the First Thirty Years. Lunenburg: 1988. V. 47; 52

FARRELL, HENRY
What Ever Happend to Baby Jane?. New York: 1960. V. 49; 51

FARRELL, J. G.
A Girl In the Head. London: 1967. V. 48
The Siege of Krishnapur. London: 1973. V. 50
Troubles. London: 1970. V. 51; 53

FARRELL, JACK W.
North American Steam Locomotive: the Mountains. Edmonds: 1977. V. 53

FARRELL, JAMES T.
$1000 a Week. New York: 1941. V. 52
An American Dream Girl. New York: 1950. V. 48; 51
Calico Shoes and Other Stories. New York: 1934. V. 47; 49; 51
Ellen Rogers. New York: 1941. V. 48; 51
Gas-House McGinty. 1933. V. 51
It Has come to Pass. New York: 1958. V. 54
A Misunderstanding. New York: 1949. V. 47; 48
The Name is Fogarty. New York: 1950. V. 48
A Note on Literary Criticism. New York: 1936. V. 54
The Silence of History. Garden City: 1963. V. 54
A World I never Made. New York: 1936. V. 50
Yet Other Waters. New York: 1952. V. 48; 51
Young Lonigan. New York: 1932. V. 51; 52
Young Lonigan. New York: 1935. V. 48; 49; 51
Young Lonigan. Franklin Center: 1979. V. 54

FARRELL, JOHN
Harrison High. New York: 1959. V. 52

FARRELL, M. J.
Red Letter Days. 1933. V. 49; 50
Red Letter Days. London: 1933. V. 47

FARRELL, NED E.
Colorado, the Rocky Mountain Gem As It Is in 1868. Chicago: 1868. V. 48

FARRELL, WALTER
A Companion to the Summa. New York: 1856-ca. 1960. V. 51

FARREN, ELIZABETH
The Testimony of Truth to Exalted Merit; or, a Biographical Sketch of the Right Honourable the Countess of Derby, in Refutation of a False and Scandalous Libel. London: 1799. V. 47

FARRER, J. A.
Literary Forgeries. London: 1907. V. 54

FARRER, REGINALD
Alpines and Bog Plants. London: 1908. V. 54
Among the Hills, a Book of Joy in High Places. London: 1910. V. 51
Among the Hills: a Book of Joy in High Places. London: 1911. V. 50; 52; 53; 54
The Dolomites. London: 1913. V. 54
The English Rock Garden. London: 1919. V. 52; 53; 54
The English Rock Garden. London: 1922. V. 54
The English Rock Garden. London: 1928. V. 48; 51; 53
The English Rock Garden. London: 1948. V. 48; 49; 50; 52; 53
The English Rock Garden. London: 1948-54. V. 49
The English Rock Garden. London: 1954. V. 49; 53
The English Rock Garden. London: 1955. V. 52
Farrer's Last Journey, Upper Burma 1919-20. London: 1926. V. 54
The Garden of Asia: Impressions from Japan. London: 1904. V. 49; 54
In an Yorkshire Garden. London: 1909. V. 54
My Rock-Garden. London: 1907. V. 54
On the Eaves of the World. London: 1917. V. 52; 54
On the Eaves of the World. London: 1926. V. 51; 52
The Rainbow Bridge. London: 1921. V. 54
The Rainbow Bridge. London: 1926. V. 49; 51; 52

FARRER, RICHARD RIDLEY
A Tour in Greece 1880. Edinburgh: 1882. V. 47

FARRER, WILLIAM
The Chartulary of Cockersand Abbey of the Premonstratensian Order. London: 1989-1909. V. 54
Records Relating to the Barony of Kendale. Kendal: 1924. V. 50; 52
Victoria History of the County of Lancaster. London: 1906-14. V. 47

FARRIES, K. G.
The Windmills of Surrey and Inner London. 1966. V. 51; 54

FARRINGTON, S. KIP
Atlantic Game Fishing. New York: 1937. V. 49; 51; 54
Fishing With Hemingway and Glassell. New York: 1971. V. 51

FARRIS, J.
The Captors. New York: 1969. V. 51
Harrison High. 1959. V. 48; 52
Harrison High. New York: 1959. V. 51
The Long Light of Dawn. London: 1962. V. 49
The Long Night of Dawn. New York: 1962. V. 54
Son of the Endless Night. 1985. V. 54

FARROW, EDWARD S.
Mountain Scouting: a Handbook for Officers and Soldiers on the Frontiers. New York: 1881. V. 49

FARROW, G. E.
The Escape of the Mullingong: a Zoological Nightingale. London: 1907. V. 47; 53
The Missing Prince. London: 1896. V. 49
The Wallypug in the Moon or His Badjesty. London: 1905. V. 47
Wallypug Tales. London: 1907. V. 51
Zoo Babies. London: 1913. V. 49

FARROW, HENRY P.
The Injustice of Poll Taxes. To the Members of the Constitutional Convention. 1868. V. 48

FARTHER Excursions of the Observant Pedestrian, Exemplified in a Tour to Margate... London: 1801. V. 51

FARWELL, W. B.
Misrepresentation of Early California History Corrected. San Francisco: 1894. V. 49

FASCH, JOHANN RUDOLF
Anderer Versuch Seiner Architect...Part Four. Nurnburg: 1725. V. 52

FASCH, JOHANN RUDOLPH
Erster (-Funffter) Versuch Seiner Architect: Werke Bestehend in Allerhand Grund-Haupt Rissen und Profile Unterschiedlicher Gebauden. Nuremberg: 1722-29. V. 49
Versuch Seiner Arachitect: Werke Bestehend in Allerhand Grund-Haupt Rissen und Profile Unterschiedlicher Gebauden. Nuremberg: 1722-29. V. 53

FASCICULUS Ioanni Wiilis Clark Dicatus. Cantabrigiae: 1909. V. 51

FASHION. Dedicated to All the Town. London: 1817. V. 49

THE FASHIONABLE Swindler, or, Villainy Displayed... London: 1822. V. 47

THE FASHIONABLE Tell-Tale; Containing a Great Variety of Curious and Interesting Anecdotes of Emperors, Kings, Queens, Statesmen, Prelates, Divines, Generals, Admirals, Captains, Physicians, Poets and Players. London: 1778. V. 47

FASS, JOHN S.
Some Oriental Versions of the Turtle. Hammer Creek: 1952. V. 52
Some Oriental Versions of the Turtle. New York: 1952. V. 52
The Work of the Hammer Creek Press 1950-1956. New York: 1956. V. 52

FASSAM, THOMAS
An Herbarium for the Fair... London: 1949. V. 48

FASSBENDER, ADOLF
Pictorial Artistry. New York: 1937. V. 47

FAST, HOWARD
Sparatucs. New York: 1951. V. 50

THE FATAL Consequences of Political Adultery Display'd. London?: 1743?. V. 53

THE FATAL Effects of Gambling Exemplified in the Murder of William Weare, and the Trial and Fate of John Thurtell... London: 1824. V. 54

FATE Of the Steam-Ship President, Which Sailed from New York, March 11th, 1841 Bound for Liverpool. Boston: 1845. V. 47

FATHER Abraham's Almanack for the Year of Our Lord 1777. Philadelphia: 1776. V. 47

FATHER Tuck's Little Builders Paper Modelling. Series III. London: 1920. V. 48

FATHER Tuck's Pictorial Panoramas. London. V. 48

FATHERLESS Fanny: or a Young Ladies First Entrance Into Life. London: 1832. V. 50

FATIO, LOUISE
The Christmas Forest. New York: 1950. V. 52
The Happy Lion. London: 1955. V. 49
The Happy Lion and the Bear. New York: 1964. V. 49

FAUCHET, CLAUDE
Origines des Dignitez et Magistrats de France. (with) Origines des Chevaliers, Armoiries et Heraux. Paris: 1600. V. 47

FAUGHT, FRANCIS
Blood-Pressure from the Clinical Standpoint. Philadelphia: 1914. V. 53

FAUJAS DE SAINT-FOND, BARTHELEMY
Description des Experiences de la Machine Aerostatique de M.M. de Montgolfier, et de Celles Auxquelles Cette Decouvert a Donne Lieu. Paris: 1784. V. 52
A Journey through England and Scotland to the Hebrides in 1784. Glasgow: 1907. V. 50

FAULCONER, ALBERT
Foundations of Anesthesiology. Springfield: 1965. V. 52

FAULDING, G. M.
Old Man's Beard and Other Tales. New York: 1909. V. 49; 53; 54

FAULHABER, CHARLES B.
Medieval Manuscripts in the Library of the Hispanic Society of America. Parts I-II. New York: 1983-93. V. 50

FAULK, J. J.
History of Henderson County, Texas. Athens: 1929. V. 53

FAULK, ODIE
General Tom Green - Fightin' Texan. Waco: 1963. V. 53

FAULKENER, EDWARD
Games Ancient and Oriental and How to Play Them. London and New York: 1892. V. 51

FAULKLAND, HENRY
The History of the Most Unfortunate Prince King Edward II, with Choice Political Observations on Him and His Unhappy Favourites... London: 1680. V. 54

FAULKNER, CHARLES JAMES
Speech of Charles Jas. Faulkner (of Berkeley) in the House of Delegates of Virginia, on the Policy of the State with Respect to Her Slave Population. Delivered Jan. 29, 1832. Richmond: 1832. V. 49; 50

FAULKNER, FRITZ
Windless Sky. London: 1936. V. 54

FAULKNER, RAYMOND O.
The Ancient Egyptian Coffin Texts. Warminster: 1977-78. V. 51
The Ancient Egyptian Coffin Texts. Volume II (only): Spells 355-787. Warminster: 1977. V. 49
The Ancient Egyptian Pyramid Texts. Oxford: 1969. V. 51
The Book of the Dead. New York: 1972. V. 51

FAULKNER, THOMAS
An Historical and Descriptive Account of the Royal Hospital and the Royal Military Asylum at Chelsea... London: 1805. V. 50; 52
An Historical and Topographical Description of Chelsea and Its Environs. Chelsea: 1829. V. 50
History and Antiquities of Kensington, Interspersed with biographical Anecdotes of Royal and Distinguished Personages and a Descriptive Catalogue of the Collection of Pictures in the Palace. London: 1820. V. 47; 50
The History and Antiquities of the Parish of Hammersmith. London: 1839. V. 54

FAULKNER, WILLIAM HARRISON
L' Abre aux Souhaits. Paris: 1969. V. 49
Absalom, Absalom!. 1936. V. 50
Absalom, Absalom!. New York: 1936. V. 47; 50; 53
Absalom, Absalom!. London: 1937. V. 49
An Address Delivered by William Faulkner, Oxford, Mississippi, at the Seventeenth Annual Meeting of Delta Council, May 15, 1952. Cleveland: 1952. V. 53
Afternoon of a Cow. Iowa City: 1991. V. 54
As I Lay Dying. New York: 1930. V. 47; 48; 49; 50; 52
As I Lay Dying. London: 1935. V. 49; 50; 53
Big Woods. New York: 1955. V. 47; 48; 49; 51; 52; 54
The Collected Stories. 1950. V. 50
Collected Stories. New York: 1950. V. 54
Collected Stories. London: 1951. V. 48; 50
Doctor Martino and Other Stories. London: 1934. V. 49; 50; 53
Doctor Martino and Other Stories. New York: 1934. V. 48; 49; 50; 51; 52; 53; 54
A Fable. New York: 1954. V. 47; 49; 50; 51; 52; 53; 54
Father Abraham. New York: 1983. V. 53; 54
Faulkner at Nagano. Tokyo: 1954. V. 51
Faulkner at Nagano. Tokyo: 1956. V. 49
Faulkner on Love: a Letter to Marjorie Lyons. Fargo: 1974. V. 48
Go Down, Moses and Other Stories. 1942. V. 50
Go Down Moses and Other Stories. London: 1942. V. 48; 49; 50; 53
Go Down Moses and Other Stories. New York: 1942. V. 47; 48; 49; 51; 52; 53; 54
A Green Bough. New York: 1933. V. 47; 52; 53
A Green Bough. New York: 1953. V. 50
The Hamlet. 1940. V. 50
The Hamlet. London: 1940. V. 49
The Hamlet. New York: 1940. V. 47; 48; 49; 50; 51; 52; 53; 54
Helen: a Courtship. Oxford: 1981. V. 47
Hokum. Wellesley Hills: 1978. V. 48
Hunting Stories. New York: 1988. V. 49; 50; 54
Idyll in the Desert. New York: 1931. V. 47; 53
Intruder in the Dust. New York: 1948. V. 48; 49; 50; 51; 52; 54
Intruder in the Dust. London: 1949. V. 48; 49; 53
L' Invaincu. (Unvanquished). Paris: 1949. V. 49
Jealousy and Episode. Minneapolis: 1955. V. 51; 53
Knight's Gambit. 1949. V. 53
Knight's Gambit. New York: 1949. V. 47; 48; 49; 50; 52; 53
Knight's Gambit: Stories. London: 1951. V. 49
Letter to W. G. Rogers. New York: 1973. V. 48
Letters to His Mother and Father 1918-1921. New York: 1992. V. 48; 49
Light in August. 1932. V. 50
Light in August. London: 1932. V. 49
Light in August. New York: 1932. V. 47; 48; 49; 51; 52; 53; 54
The Mansion. New York: 1959. V. 47; 48; 51; 52; 53; 54
The Marble Faun. Boston: 1924. V. 53
The Marionettes. Charlottesville: 1975. V. 48; 53
Marionettes. Oxford: 1975. V. 47
Mayday. South Bend: 1976. V. 54
Mirrors of Chartres Street. Minneapolis: 1953. V. 49; 52; 53
Miss Zilphia Gant. Dallas: 1922. V. 51
Miss Zilphia Gant. 1932. V. 49
Mississippi Poems. Oxford: 1979. V. 47; 49
Mosquitoes. 1927. V. 51; 54
Mosquitoes. New York: 1927. V. 47; 49; 50; 51; 52; 54
Mosquitoes. Garden City: 1937. V. 53
New Orleans Sketches. Tokyo. V. 50
New Orleans Sketches. 1953. V. 53
New Orleans Sketches. Tokyo: 1955. V. 48
The Nobel Prize Speech. New York: 1951. V. 50
Notes on a Horsethief. Greenville: 1950. V. 47; 51; 53; 54
The Portable Faulkner. New York: 1946. V. 52
Pylon. London: 1935. V. 48; 49; 51; 52; 53; 54
The Reivers. New York: 1962. V. 47; 48; 51; 52; 53; 54
Requiem for a Nun. New York: 1951. V. 47; 48; 49; 50; 51; 52; 53; 54
Requiem For a Nun. London: 1953. V. 49
Requiem for a Nun. New York: 1959. V. 53
Salmagundi. Milwaukee: 1932. V. 48; 51; 54
Sanctuary. London: 1931. V. 49; 53
Sanctuary. New York: 1931. V. 50; 53; 54
Sartoris. New York: 1929. V. 48; 49; 51; 52; 53
Sartoris. London: 1932. V. 49; 53
Sherwood Anderson & Other Famous Creoles. New Orleans: 1926. V. 49; 53; 54
Soldier's Pay. New York: 1926. V. 51
Soldier's Pay. 1930. V. 53
Soldier's Pay. London: 1930. V. 47; 50; 53
A Sorority Pledge. Northport: 1983. V. 48; 51
The Sound and the Fury. New York: 1929. V. 49; 51; 52; 53
The Sound and the Fury. London: 1931. V. 48; 53
The Sound and the Fury. New York: 1931. V. 53
Tandis Que J'Agonise. Paris: 1946. V. 47; 48
These 13. New York: 1931. V. 48; 49; 50; 51; 52; 53; 54
These Thirteen. London: 1933. V. 50
Thinking of Home. New York: 1992. V. 47; 51; 52; 53; 54
This Earth. 1932. V. 53
This Earth. New York: 1932. V. 48; 49; 51
The Town. New York: 1957. V. 47; 49; 52; 53; 54
Uncollected Stories. Franklin Center: 1979. V. 52
The Unvanquished. Leipzig: 1938. V. 50; 51; 53
The Unvanquished. New York: 1938. V. 47; 48; 49; 50; 51; 52; 53; 54
Vesnice, Mesto, Panske Sidlo. (The Mansion, The Town, The Hamlet). Prague: 1985/87. V. 51
Vision in Spring. Austin: 1984. V. 50
The Wild Palms. New York: 1939. V. 47; 48; 49; 51; 52; 53; 54
William Faulkner's Letters to Malcolm Franklin. Irving: 1976. V. 49; 53
Winner Take Nothing. New York & London: 1933. V. 48
The Wishing Tree. New York: 1964. V. 52; 53
The Wishing Tree. New York: 1967. V. 52; 53

FAUNA of Saudi Arabia. Basel: 1980. V. 53

FAUNA of Saudi Arabia. Basel: 1991. V. 50
FAUNA of Saudi Arabia. Basel: 1993. V. 50

FAUNTLEROY, A. M.
Report on the Medico-Military Aspects of the European War from Observations Taken behind the Allied Armies in France. Washington: 1915. V. 51

FAUNTLEROY, HENRY
A Catalogue of the Entire and Very Valuable Library of the Late Henry Fauntleroy, Esq. of Berners Street... London: 1825. V. 50

FAUST, BERHARD CHRISTOPH
Catechism of Health, for the Use of Schools, and for Domestic Instruction. Dublin: 1794. V. 52

FAUST, FREDERICK
Secret Agent Number 1. Philadelphia: 1936. V. 52

FAUSTO DA LONGIANO, SEBASTIANO
Duello...Regolato a le Leggi de l'Honore. Venice: 1552. V. 48
Dvello Regolato a le Leggi de l'Honore... Venice: 1559. V. 51

FAUTEUX, AEGIDIUS
The Introduction of Printing into Canada. Montreal: 1930. V. 50

FAUTHMEL, RICHARD
The Roman Antiquities of Overborough. London: 1746. V. 47

FAUX, WILLIAM
Memorable Days in America: Being a Journal of a Tour to the United States... London: 1823. V. 51; 53

FAVENC, ERNEST
The History of Australian Exploration from 1788 to 1888. London: 1888. V. 54
The History of Australian Exploration from 1788 to 1888. Sydney: 1888. V. 48; 54

FAVORITE Nursery Tales: Red Riding Hood Series. New York: 1896. V. 54

FAVOUR, ALPHEUS H.
Old Bill Williams, Mountain Man. Chapel Hill: 1936. V. 52

THE FAVOURITE Dog. London: 1860. V. 48

FAVRE, ABBE M. DE
Les Quatres Heures de la Toilette des Dames, Poeme Erotique en Quatare Chants, Dedie a Son Altesse Serenissime Madame la Princesse de Lamballe... Paris: 1779. V. 54

FAWCETT, BENJAMIN
The Dying Thoughts of the Rev. Richard Baxter. New York: 1830. V. 48

FAWCETT, F. BURLINGTON
Broadside Ballads of the Restoration Period from Jersey Collection Known as the Osterley Park Ballads. London: 1930. V. 49; 52; 53; 54

FAWCETT, GRAHAM
Poems for Shakespeare 2. London: 1973. V. 52

FAWCETT, HENRY
Pauperism: its Causes and Remedies. London: 1871. V. 53

FAWCETT, MILLICENT GARRETT
Six Weeks in Palestine, Spring, 1921. London. V. 53
Tales in Political Economy. London: 1874. V. 53

FAWCETT, WILLIAM
Rules and Regulations for the Sword Exercise of the Cavalry. London: 1796. V. 51

FAWKES, F. A.
Horticultural Buildings. London: 1881. V. 52

FAWKES, FRANCIS
Original Poems and Translations. London: 1761. V. 47; 49

FAWTIER, ROBERT
Hand List of Characters, Deeds and Similar Documents in the Possession of the John Rylands Library. Manchester: 1935. V. 48

FAXON, ALICIA C.
Dante Gabriel Rossetti. London: 1989. V. 49

FAY, BERNARD
Notes on the American Press at the End of the 18th Century. New York: 1927. V. 47

FAY, ELIZA
Original Letters from India - (1779-1815). London: 1925. V. 52

FAY, FRANK
How to Be Poor. New York: 1945. V. 54

FAY, THEODORE SEDGWICK
The Countess Ida. New York: 1840. V. 53; 54
Sydney Clifton: or, Vicissitudes in Both Hemispheres. New York: 1839. V. 53; 54
Views in New-York and Its Environs, from Accurate, Characteristic and Picturesque Drawings... New York: 1831-34. V. 49; 54

FAYRER, J.
Report and Record of the Operations of the Stafford House Committe, for the Relief of Sick and Wounded Turkish Soldiers...Russo Turkish War 1877-78. London: 1879. V. 47; 51
The Thanatophidia of India...The Venomous Snakes of the Indian Peninsula. London: 1872. V. 47; 48

FAYRER, JOSEPH
Recollections of My Life. London: 1900. V. 47; 50

FAZAKERLEY, JOHN
John Fazakerley, Bookbinder, 40, Paradise St., Liverpool, and 44 Brazennose St. Manchester. 1895. V. 53

FEALES, W.
A True and Exact Catalogue of All the Plays and Other Dramatick Pieces That Were Ever Yet Printed in the English Tongue, Continued Down to april 1732. London: 1732. V. 51

FEAR Itself: The Horror Fiction of Stephen King. San Francisco: 1982. V. 47

FEARFUL Disclosures and Examination of Edwin and Martha Bacon, for the Murder of 2 Children at Walworth. Walworth?: 1820's. V. 48

THE FEARFUL Issue to Be Decided in November Next! Shall the Constitution and the Union Stand or Fall? Fremont, the Sectional Candidate of the Advocates of Dissolution!. 1856. V. 48

FEARING, DANIEL B.
Duplicates from the Library of Hon. Daniel B. Fearing...Comprising Books on Angling, Field Sports, Ornithology, Etc... Albany: 1910. V. 47

FEARING, F.
Reflex Action: a Study in the History of Physiological Psychology. Baltimore: 1930. V. 47; 50; 52

FEARING, KENNETH
Afternoon of a Pawnbroker and Other Poems. New York: 1943. V. 54
The Big Clock. New York: 1946. V. 50
Clark Gifford's Body. New York: 1942. V. 54
New and Selected Poems. Bloomington: 1956. V. 54
Poems. New York: 1935. V. 49

FEARN, J. R.
Creature From the Black Lagoon. 1954. V. 48

FEARN, JOHN
A Review of the First Principles of Bishop Berkeley, - Dr. Reid and Professor Stewart. London: 1813. V. 52

FEARNE, CHARLES
An Essay on the Learning of Contingent Remainders and Executory Devises... London: 1773. V. 54
The Posthumous Works... London: 1797. V. 48

FEARNSIDE, W. G.
Eighty Picturesque Views on the Thames and Medway, Engraved on Steel by the Firsts Artists. London: 1834. V. 48
The History of London: Illustrated by Views in London and Westminster. London: 1838. V. 52

FEARON, HENRY B.
A Narrative of a Journey of Five Thousand Miles through the Eastern and Western States of America. London: 1818. V. 51; 54
A Narrative of a Journey of Five Thousand Miles through the Eastern and Western States of America... London: 1819. V. 50; 53
Sketches of America... London: 1818. V. 52
Sketches of America. London: 1819. V. 50

FEASBY, W. R.
Official History of the Canadian Medical Services 1939-1945. Ottawa: 1953-56. V. 54

FEASEY, J. EATON
Robin Hood and Other Stories of Yorkshire. London: 1913. V. 54

THE FEAST in Galilee. In Humble Imitation of Elijah's Mantle. London: 1807. V. 47

FEATHER, JOHN
English Book Prospectuses. 1984. V. 52; 54
English Book Prospectuses. Newtown & Minneapolis: 1984. V. 47; 50; 52; 53

FEATHER River Hydraulic Mining Company. 1904. V. 50

FEATHERSTON, JOHN
The Visitation of the County of Cumberland in the Year 1615, Taken by Richard St. George, Norroy King of Arms. London: 1872. V. 52

FEATHERSTONHAUGH, G. W.
A Canoe Voyage Up the Minnay Sotor. London: 1847. V. 48
Report of a Geological Reconnoissance Made in 1835, From the Seat of government by the Way of Green Bay and the Wisconsin Territory to the Coteau de Prairie... Washington: 1836. V. 51

FEATHERSTONHAUGH, G.W.
Excursion through the Slave States, from Washington on the Potomac to the Frontier of Mexico... London: 1844. V. 53

FEATLEY, DANIEL
(Part Greek title, then:) The Dippers Dipt, or the Anabaptists Duk'd and Plung'd over Head and Ears... London: 1660. V. 49

FEATON, JOHN
The Waikato War. Together with Some Account of Te Kooti Rikirangi. Auckland: 1923. V. 54

FEATON, MR.
The Art Album of New Zealand Flora. Wellington: 1889. V. 50; 51

FEBURE, MICHELE
Teatro della Turchia Dove si Rappresentano i Disordini di Essa, il Genio, la Natura & I Costumi di Quattordici Nazioni... Milan: 1681. V. 47

FEDDEN, ROBIN
Personal Landscape. London: 1966. V. 47

FEDER, NORMAN
American Indian Art. New York: 1969. V. 48; 50; 52
American Indian Art. New York: 1971. V. 48

THE FEDERAL or New Ready Reckoner and Traders Useful Assistant... Chesnuthill: 1793. V. 50; 54

FEDERAL PARTY. NEW JERSEY
Proceedings and Address of the Second Convention of Delegates, Held at the City of Trenton, on the Fourth of July 1814, to the People of New Jersey. Trenton?: 1814. V. 51

FEDERAL UNION MINING CO.
By-Laws of the Federal Union Mining Company, Clear Creek County Colorado... Greenfield: 1866. V. 49

THE FEDERALIST. New York: 1788. V. 54
THE FEDERALIST. New York: 1802. V. 47; 50
THE FEDERALIST. Washington: 1818. V. 54
THE FEDERALIST. New York: 1945. V. 47; 49; 53

FEDERATION of Canadian Artists. Ontario Region. A Folio of Original Reproductions. Issue Number One. 1950. V. 53

FEDERER, CHARLES
The Ballad of Flodden Field. Manchester: 1884. V. 54
Yorkshire Chapbooks. London: 1889. V. 50

FEDOROV, EVGENY
On the Drifting Ice. A Short Description of the Life of the North Pole Scientific Expedition. Moscow: 1939. V. 47

FEE, NORMAN
Catalogue of Pamphlets, Journals and Reports in the Public Archives of Canada, 1611-1897. Ottawa: 1916. V. 50; 53

FEELINGS, TOM
Black Pilgrimage. New York: 1972. V. 53

FEHER, JOSEPH
Hawaii: a Pictorial History. Honolulu: 1969. V. 52

FEIBLEMAN, JAMES K.
The Dark Bifocals. Lexington: 1953. V. 54

FEIBLEMAN, JAMES KERN
Death of the God in New Mexico. New York: 1931. V. 48

FEIFFER, JULES
Little Murders. New York: 1968. V. 49
Sick Sick Sick. New York: 1958. V. 53

FEILD, JOHN
Truth Commended and Recommended to All; but More Particularly Unto the People that Attend Upon John Atkinson's Ministry at Cockermouth in Cumberland. London: 1709. V. 48

FEILD, ROBERT D.
The Art of Walt Disney. New York: 1942. V. 54

FEINAIGLE, GREGOR VON
The New Art of Memory, Founded Upon the Principles Taught by M. Gregor von Feinaigle... London: 1813. V. 47; 49

FEINGOLD, MCIHAEL
After. New York: 1993. V. 51

FEINSTEIN, ELAINE
The Ecstasy of Miriam Garner. London: 1976. V. 52

FEIST, BERTHA E.
Grunty Grunts and Smiley Smile Indoors. Philadelphia: 1920. V. 54

FEIST, R.
Faerie Tale. 1988. V. 49; 54
Magician. Garden City: 1982. V. 51

FEKULA, PAUL M.
The Paul M. Fekula Collection: a Catalogue. New York: 1988. V. 50

FELBIEN DES AVAUX, M.
Les Plans et Les Descriptions De Deux Des Plus Belles Maisons de Campagne de Pline Le Consul Avec des Ramarques Sur Tous Les Batimens, Et Une Dissertation Touchant l'Architecture Antique et l'Architecture Gothique. Paris: 1699. V. 47

FELD, CHARLES
Picasso. His Recent Drawings 1966-1968. New York: 1969. V. 53

FELDBORG, ANDREAS ANDERSEN
Denmark Delineated; or, Sketches of the Present State of That Country. Edinburgh: 1824. V. 48; 50; 53

FELDMAN, J.
The Eloquent Dead. Los Angeles: 1985. V. 54

FELIBIAN, ANDRE, SIEUR DES AVAUX ET DE JAVERCY
Des Principes de l'Architecture, De La Sculpture, De La Peinture. Paris: 1676. V. 51

FELICIANO, FELICE
Alphabetum Romanum. 1960. V. 49
Alphabetum Romanum. Verona: 1960. V. 47; 50; 51

FELICIANO DA LAZESIO, FRANCESCO
L'Arithmetica et Geometrica Speculativa et Praticale. Venice: 1570. V. 52; 54
Libro di Arithmetica & Geometria Speculativa & Pratticale: Intitulato Scala Grimaldelli: Nuovamente Stampato. Venice: 1563. V. 50

FELISSA; or, the Life and Opinions of a Kitten Sentiment. London: 1811. V. 47

THE FELIX Annual. London. V. 47

FELIX, M. L.
100 Peoples of Zaire and Their Sculpture: the Hand-Book. Brussels: 1987. V. 54

FELKIN, WILLIAM
A History of the Machine-Wrought Hoisery and Lace Manufactures. London: 1867. V. 49

FELL & ROCK CLIMBING CLUB OF THE ENGLISH LAKE DISTRICT
Journal. London: 1907-88. V. 54

FELL, ALFRED
The Early Iron Industry of Furness and District... Ulverston: 1908. V. 50; 54
A Furness Manor: Pennington and its Church. Ulverston: 1929. V. 50
A Furness Military Chronicle. Ulverston: 1937. V. 50; 52

FELL, CHARLES
The Lives of Saints; Collected from Authentick Records, of Church History. London: 1729. V. 49

FELL, H. GRANVILLE
The Art of H. Davis Richter. Benfleet, Essex, England: 1935. V. 47

FELL, JOHN
The Life of that Reverend Divine and Learned Historian, Dr. Thomas Fuller... London: 1661. V. 50
The Life of the Most Learned, Reverend and Pious Dr. H. Hammond. London: 1661. V. 47
Specimens of Books Printed at Oxford with the Types Given to the University by John Fell. Oxford: 1925. V. 48; 50

FELL, RALPH
Memoirs of the Public Life of the Late Charles James Fox. London: 1808. V. 47; 53

FELLIG, ARTHUR
Naked City. New York: 1945. V. 47; 50
Naked Hollywood. New York: 1953. V. 52; 54
Weegee's People. New York: 1946. V. 47; 50; 52; 54

FELLOWES, GEORGINA DE VALCOURT KENDALL
A Short Biographical Sketch of the Kendall Family. San Antonio: 1939. V. 47

FELLOWES, ROBERT
The History of Ceylon, from the Earliest Period to the Year MDCCCXV... London: 1817. V. 51; 52

FELLOWES, W. D.
Historical Sketches of Charles the First, Cromwell, Charles the Second, and the Principal Personages of that Period... London: 1828. V. 47
A Visit to the Monastery of La Trappe in 1817... London: 1818. V. 47
A Visit to the Monastery of La Trappe, in 1817. London: 1823. V. 49; 51; 52

FELLOWS, CHARLES
A Journal Written During an Excursion in Asia Minor. London: 1839. V. 51
The Menu Maker. Chicago: 1910. V. 53
Travels and Researches in Asia Minor...Province of Lycia. London: 1852. V. 52

FELLOWS, JOHN
The Triumphs of the Cross, or Penitent of Egypt. Birmingham: 1766. V. 50

FELLTHAM, OWEN
Resolves: Divine, Moral, Political. London: 1670. V. 50

FELS, CATHARINE
Graphic Work of Louis Monza. 1973. V. 52; 54

FELSENTHAL, B.
History of Kehilath Anshe Ma'arlv (Congregation of the Men of the West)...on the Occasion of Its Semi-Centennial Celebration November 4, 1897. Chicago: 1897. V. 53

FELT, E. P.
Insects Affecting Park and Woodland Trees. Albany: 1905-06. V. 48

FELT, JOEL B.
An Address, Delivered Before Unity Lodge, in Ipswich...in Commemoration of the Nativity of St. John the Baptist, Salem. Salem: 1825. V. 54

FELT, JOSEPH B.
An Historical Account of Massachusetts Currency. Boston: 1839. V. 50

FELTHAM, JOHN
A Guide to All the Watering and Sea-Bathing Places... London: 1803. V. 50
A Guide To All the Watering and Sea-Bathing Places, with a Description of the Lakes, a Sketch of a Tour in Wales. London: 1810. V. 53

FELTHAM, OWEN
Resolves. Divine, Morall, Politicall. London: 1628. V. 51

FELTON, HENRY
A Dissertation on Reading the Classics and Forming a Just Style. London: 1713. V. 49

FELTON, MRS., PSEUD.
American Life. A Narrative of Two Years' City and Country Residence in the United States. Bolton Percy,: 1843. V. 53
Life in America. Hull: 1838. V. 51; 53

FELTON, S.
On the Portraits of English Authors on Gardening. London: 1830. V. 51; 54

THE FEMALE Instructor; or, Young Woman's Companion... Liverpool. V. 48

THE FEMALE Instructor; or Young Woman's Companion, and Guide to Domestic Happiness; being an Epitome of All the Acquirements Necessary to Form the Female Character in Every Class of Life... London: 1824. V. 47; 50

THE FEMALE Instructor; or, Young Woman's Companion; Being a Guide to All the Accomplishments Which Adorn the Female Character, Either as a Useful Member of Society... Liverpool: 1815. V. 52

THE FEMALE Instructor; or Young Woman's Companion Being a Guide to All the Accomplishments Which Adorn the Female Character, Either as a Useful Member of Society, a Pleasing Companion, or a Respectable Mother of a Family. London: 1833. V. 54

FEMALE Robinson Crusoe, a Tale of the American Wilderness. New York: 1837. V. 52

FEMALE SOCIETY FOR INSTRUCTING POOR CHILDREN
Constitution. Hagerstown: 1815. V. 52

FEMININE Fashions Past and Present All About women's Wear, From the Earliest Times to the Present Day. Paris: 1925. V. 48

FENELLOSA, MARY
Blossoms from a Japanese Garden. London: 1913. V. 52

FENELON, FRANCOIS SALIGNAC DE LA MOTHE, ABP.
The Adventures of Telemachus. London: 1792. V. 47
The Adventures of Telemachus. London: 1792-94. V. 49
Les Aventures de Telemaque, fils d'Ulysse. Paris: 1783. V. 50; 51
Les Aventures de Telemaque, Fils d'Ulysse. Paris: 1796. V. 49; 53
Dialogues on Eloquence... Leeds: 1806. V. 48
Fables, Composed for the Use of the Duke of Burgundy, by Mr. Fenelon... London: 1760?. V. 48
Fenelon's Treatise on the Education of Daughters. Cheltenham: 1805. V. 50; 51; 52
Fenelon's Treatise on the Education of Daughters. Albany: 1806. V. 49
The Lives and Most Remarkable Maxims of the Ancient Philosophers. London: 1726. V. 47
A Patern of Christian Education, Agreable to the Precepts and Practice of Our Blessed Lord and Saviour Jesus Christ. Germantown: 1756. V. 51
Undine. London: 1909. V. 49

FENKINS, C. FRANCIS
Vision by Radio, Radio Photographs, Radio Photograms. Washington: 1925. V. 54

FENLEY, FLORENCE
Granddad and I. Leakey: 1951. V. 54
Oldtimers - Their Own Stories. 1939. V. 54
Oldtimers, Their Own Stories. Uvalde: 1939. V. 48

FENN, ELEANOR
The Child's Grammar. London: 1794. V. 47
Cobwebs to Catch Flies; or, Dialogues in Short Sentences Adapted for Children from the Age of Three to Eight Years. London: 1800. V. 51
Juvenile Correspondence: or, Letters, Suited to Children, From Four to Above Ten Years of Age. London: 1783. V. 53
The Mother's Grammar. London: 1795?. V. 47
Sketches of Little Boys. London: 1845. V. 49

FENN, GEORGE MANVILE
A Crimson Crime. London: 1899. V. 53

FENN, GEORGE MANVILLE
George Alfred Henty, the Story of an Active Life. London: 1907. V. 52
Pretty Polly: a Farce in Fyttes. London: 1878. V. 50

FENN, JOHN
Original Letters, Written During the Regins of Henry VI, Edward IV and Richard III. London: 1787. V. 50; 51

FENN, LADY
A Short History of Insects... Norwich: 1797. V. 54

FENN, WILLIAM PURVIANCE
Ah Sin and His Brethren in American Literature. Peiping: 1933. V. 54

FENNEL, JAMES H.
A Natural History of British and Foreign Quadrupeds. London: 1843. V. 50; 53

FENNER, DUDLEY
The Whole Doctrine of the Sacraments, Plainlie and Fullie Set Downe and Declared Out of the Word of God. Middleburgh: 1588. V. 47

FENNING, DANIEL
The British Youth's Instructor; or, a New and Easy Guide to Practical Arithmetic... London: 1754. V. 52
The Ready Reckoner or Trader's Sure Guide, Adapted to the Use of All Who Deal by Wholesale or Retail Exhibiting, At One View, the Amount of Value of Any Number or Quantity of Goods or Merchandize, From One Up to Ten Thousand, At Various Prices... Philadelphia: 1794. V. 49
The Royal English Dictionary. London: 1775. V. 52
The Universal Spelling Book; or a New and Easy Guide to the English Language. London: 1790?. V. 51
Wogan's Improved Universal Spelling-Book... Dublin: 1813. V. 49

FENOLLOSA, ERNEST F.
The Chinese Written Character As a Medium for Poetry. New York: 1936. V. 51
Epochs of Chinese and Japanese Art. New York. V. 53
Epochs of Chinese and Japanese Art. London: 1912. V. 50; 53
Epochs of Chinese and Japanese Art. New York: 1912. V. 47
Epochs of Chinese and Japanese Art. New York: 1913. V. 51
Epochs of Chinese and Japanese Art... London: 1921. V. 52

FENTON, A. W.
Midnight in London and Other poems. Penrith: 1833. V. 54

FENTON, ELIJAH
Poems on Several Occasions. London: 1717. V. 47; 48; 54

FENTON, GEOFFREY
Golden Epistles, Contayning Varitie of Discourse, Both Morall, Philosophicall and Divine... London: 1582. V. 48

FENTON, JAMES
Our Western Furniture. Oxford: 1968. V. 52
Terminal Moraine. London: 1972. V. 51

FENTON, RICHARD
Memoirs of an Old Whig. London: 1815. V. 51
A Tour in Quest of Genealogy through Several Parts of Wales, Somersetshire and Wiltshire... London: 1811. V. 54

FENWICK, GEORGE LEE
A History of the Ancient City of Chester From Its Earliest Times. Chester: 1896. V. 48; 53

FENWICK, JOHN
Observations on the Trial of James Coigly, for High Treason, Together with an Account of His Death. London: 1798. V. 51
The Proceedings Against Sir John Fenwick, Bar, Upon A Bill of Attainder for High Treason. London: 1698. V. 47; 49

FENWICK, STEPHEN
The Mechanics of Construction, Including the Theories of the Strength of materials, Roofs, Arches and Suspension Bridges. London: 1861. V. 49

FEODORA, PRINCESS OF HOHENLOHE-LANGENBURG
Letters of...From 1828 to 1872. London: 1874. V. 48

FEOLI, E.
Computer Assisted Vegetation Analysis. Dordrecht: 1991. V. 50

FERBER, EDNA
American Beauty. Garden City: 1931. V. 54
Dawn O'Hara. New York: 1911. V. 48
A Peculiar Treasure. New York: 1939. V. 53
Saratoga Trunk. Garden City: 1941. V. 48; 51
Show Boat. New York: 1926. V. 47

FERBER, J. J.
Travels through Italy... 1771 and 1772 Described in...Letters to baron Born, on the Natural History... London: 1776. V. 50

FERDOOSEE
Episodes from the Shah Nameh; or Annals of the Persian Kings; by Ferdoosee. London: 1815. V. 52

FEREE, B.
American Estates and Gardens. New York: 1904. V. 47

FERENCZI, SANDOR
Contributions to Psychoanalysis. Boston: 1916. V. 53

FERGUS County Argus Pictorial Edition Lewistown, Montana. Lewistown. V. 52

FERGUSON, ADAM
An Essay on the History of Civil Society. Edinburgh: 1767. V. 48; 49; 52
An Essay on the History of Civil Society. London: 1773. V. 47
An Essay on the History of Civil Society. Boston: 1809. V. 53
The History of the Progress and Termination of the Roman Republic. London: 1783. V. 50; 53
The History of the Progress and Termination of the Roman Republic. Edinburgh: 1825. V. 54
The History of the Progress and Termination of the Roman Republic. London: 1826. V. 53
Remarks on Dr. Price's Observations on the Nature of Civil Liberty, Etc. London: 1776. V. 52

FERGUSON, ALASTAIR MACKENZIE
Souvenirs of Ceylon: a Series of One Hundred and Twenty Illustrations of the Varied Coast, River and Mountain Scenery of the Beautiful 'Eden of the Eastern Wave'. London: 1869. V. 50

FERGUSON, CHARLES D.
The Experiences of a Forty-Niner During Thirty-Four Years residence in California and Australia. Cleveland: 1888. V. 47; 52

FERGUSON, CHARLES J.
A Short Historical and Architectural Account of Lanercost, A Priory of Black Canons, Eight Miles from Carlisle, Upon the North Side of the River Irthing, Close to the Picts Wall. Carlisle: 1870. V. 52

FERGUSON, FREDERICK
The Continental Landscape Annual of European Scenery. London: 1837. V. 49

FERGUSON, HARVEY
Wolf Song. New York: 1927. V. 49

FERGUSON, J. A.
Bibliography of Australia. Canberra: 1975-86. V. 48

FERGUSON, JAMES
The Art of Drawing in Perspective. London: 1775. V. 49
The Art of Drawing in Perspective. 1807. V. 47
Astronomical Tables and Percepts, for Calculating the True Times of New and Full Moons. London: 1763. V. 53
Astronomy Explained Upon Sir Isaac Newton's Principles. London: 1778. V. 49
Astronomy Explained Upon Sir Isaac Newton's Principles. London: 1790. V. 54
The British Essayists. London: 1823. V. 48

FERGUSON, JAMES continued
An Easy Introduction to Astronomy, for Young Gentleman and Ladies. London: 1769. V. 54
An Easy Introduction to Astronomy, for Young Gentlemen and Ladies. London: 1779. V. 53; 54
An Easy Introduction to Astronomy, for Young Gentlemen and Ladies. Philadelphia: 1819. V. 53; 54
Lectures On Select Subjects in Mechanics, Hydrostatics... London: 1764. V. 50; 54
Lectures on Select Subjects in Mechanics, Hydrostatics. London: 1770. V. 52
Lectures on Select Subjects in Mechanics, Hydrostatics. London: 1772. V. 50
Lectures on Select Subjects in Mechanics, Hydrostatics... London: 1803. V. 50
Lectures on Select Subjects in Mechanics, Hydrostatics... Edinburgh: 1823. V. 54
Lectures on Select Subjects in Mechanics, Hydrostatics... London: 1825. V. 48
Papers Illustrating the History of the Scots Brigade in the Service of the United Netherlands, 1572-1782. Edinburgh: 1901. V. 50
Papers Illustrating the History of the Scots Brigade in the Service of the United Netherlands, 1592-1782... Edinburgh: 1899-1901. V. 51
Select Mechanical Exercises; Shewing How to Construct Different Clocks, Orreries and Sun-Dials, on Plain and Easy Principles... London: 1773. V. 52; 53
Tables and Tracts, Relative to Several Arts and Sciences. London: 1767. V. 48
Two Scottish Soldiers, A Solider of 1688 and Bleinheim... Aberdeen: 1888. V. 48

FERGUSON, JOHN
Bibliographical Notes on Histories of Inventions and Books of Secrets. London. V. 47
Bibliographical Notes on Histories of Inventions and Books of Secrets. London: 1981. V. 53; 54
Bibliotheca Chemica: a Catalogue of the Alchemical, Chemical and Pharmaceutical Books in the Collection of the Late James Young of Kelly Durris. London: 1954. V. 54

FERGUSON, JOHN ALEXANDER
Bibliography of Australia.1784-1830. 1831-1838. 1839-1845. 1846-1850. 1851-1900. Canberrra: 1980. V. 50
The Howes and Their Press. Sydney: 1931. V. 54

FERGUSON, LADY
Life of the Right Rev. William Reeves, D.D. 1893. V. 52

FERGUSON, M.
The Printed Books in the Library of the Hunterian Museum in the University of Glasgow. Glasgow: 1930. V. 47

FERGUSON, M. C.
The Story of the Irish Before the Conquest. London: 1868. V. 54

FERGUSON, MUNGO
Printed Books in the Library of the Hunterian Museum in the University of Glasgow: a Catalogue. Glasgow: 1930. V. 50; 52

FERGUSON, R.
The Trial of R. Ferguson, Esq., for Crim. Con. with the Rt. Hon. Lady Elgin...With a Biographical Sketch of the Life of Lady Elgin. London: 1807. V. 49

FERGUSON, RACHEL
Charlotte Bronte. A Play in Three Acts. London: 1933. V. 54

FERGUSON, RICHARD S.
An Accompt of the Most Considerable Estates and Families in the County of Cumberland... Kendal: 1887. V. 50
The Boke off Recorde of Kirkbie Kendall. Kendal: 1892. V. 52
Cumberland and Westmorland M.P.'s (sic) From the Restoration to the Reform Bill of 1867. London: 1871. V. 50; 52; 54
Early Cumberland and Westmorland Friends. London: 1871. V. 49; 50
Miscellany Accounts of the Diocese of Carlisle, with the Terriers Delivered In to Me at My Primary Visitation... London: 1877. V. 52
Old Church Plate in the Diocese of Carlisle; with Makers and Marks. Carlisle: 1882. V. 50
A Short Historical and Architectural Account of Lanercost. London: 1868. V. 50; 52
A Short Historical and Architectural Account of Lanercost... London: 1870. V. 50
Some Municipal Records of the City of Carlisle... Carlisle: 1887. V. 50

FERGUSON, ROBERT
The Design of Enslaving England Discvoered in the Incroachments Upon the Powers and privileges of Parliament, by K. Charles II. London: 1689. V. 50
The History of the Revolution. London: 1706. V. 53
A Just and Modest Vindication of the Proceedings of the Two Last Parliaments. 1681. V. 53
The Northmen in Cumberland and Westmorland. London: 1856. V. 52
The Poetical Works with His Life. Alnwick: 1814. V. 50; 53
The Shadow of the Pyramid. A Series of Sonnets. London: 1847. V. 50
Truth Commended and Recommended to All; but More Particularly Unto the People that Attend Upon John Atkinson's Ministry at Cockermouth in Cumberland. London: 1709. V. 53

FERGUSON, SAMUEL
Father Tom and the Pope; or a Night at the Vatican. Philadelphia: 1861. V. 50
Poems. Dublin: 1880. V. 47; 50

FERGUSON, WILLIAM
America by River and Rail; or, Notes by the Way on the New World. London: 1856. V. 53

FERGUSSON, ADAM
Practical Notes Made During a Tour in Canada and a Portion of the U.S. in 1831. Edinburgh & London: 1883. V. 54

FERGUSSON, DAVID
Report of Major D. Fergusson on the Country, Its Resources and the Route Between Tucson and Lobos Bay. Washington: 1863. V. 49; 54

FERGUSSON, G.
Hounds Are Home. The History of the Royal Calpe Hunt. London: 1979. V. 47; 49

FERGUSSON, HARVEY
Wolf Song. New York: 1927. V. 51; 53; 54

FERGUSSON, J.
The Illustrated Handbook of Architecture... London: 1859. V. 47

FERGUSSON, JAMES
The Cave Temples of India. London: 1880. V. 47
An Essay on the Ancient Topography of Jerusalem with Restored Plans of the Temple &c. and Plans, Sections and Details of the Church Built by Constantine the Great... London: 1847. V. 49
History of Indian and Eastern Architecture. London: 1910. V. 54
History of the Modern Styles of Architecture. London: 1891. V. 53

FERGUSSON, W. N.
Adventure, Sport and Travel on the Tibetan Steppes. 1911. V. 54
Adventure, Sport and Travel on the Tibetan Steppes. London: 1911. V. 49; 50; 53

FERGUSSON, WILLIAM
Notes and Recollections of a Professional Life. London: 1846. V. 52

FERLINGHETTI, LAWRENCE
Back Roads to Far Towns After Basho. San Francisco: 1970. V. 53; 54
Director of Alienation. Northampton: 1976. V. 49; 51
Endless Life. 1980. V. 53
I Am Waiting. Verona: 1977. V. 47
Landscapes of Living and Dying. 1979. V. 50
Landscapes of Living and Dying. New York: 1979. V. 54
The Open Eye. Melbourne: 1972. V. 48
Pictures of the Gone World. San Francisco: 1955. V. 51; 52
The Sea and Ourselves at Cape Ann. Madison: 1979. V. 52; 54
The Secret Meaning of Things. New York: 1969. V. 53; 54
Starting from San Francisco. New York: 1961. V. 52; 54
To Fuck is to Love Again. New York: 1965. V. 53

FERMI, ENRICO
Thermodynamics. New York: 1937. V. 50

FERMOR, PATRICK LEIGH
Between the Woods and the Water - On Foot to Constantinople from the Hook of Holland: the Middle Danube to the Iron Gates. London: 1986. V. 47; 51; 53
Roumeli - Travels in Northern Greece. London: 1966. V. 47; 51; 53
A Time of Gifts. London: 1977. V. 51; 53
A Time to Keep Silence. London: 1953. V. 47
The Traveller's Tree. A Journey through the Caribbean Islands. London: 1950. V. 49

FERNANDES, BENJAMIN DIAS
A Series of Letters on the Evidences of Christianity. Philadelphia: 1859?. V. 53

FERNANDEZ, JOHN
An Address to His Majesty's Ministers, Recommending Efficacious Means for the Most Speedy Termination of African Slavery. London: 1827. V. 52

FERNANDEZ, NICHOLAS
Dying Declaration of Nicholas Fernandez, Who with Nine Others Were Executed in front of Cadiz Harbour, Dec. 29, 1829. For Piracy and Murder in the High Seas. 1830. V. 52

FERNANDEZ DE MEDRANO, SEBASTIAN
El Perfecto Artificial Bombaradero Y Aartillero Que Contiene Los Artificios de Fuego Marciales, Nuevo Uzo de Bompas, Granadas, Etc. Brussels: 1699. V. 48

FERNANDO II, KING OF SPAIN
Ferdinandus Ij. Rex. Hoc est translatum Fideliter Sumptum. Barchione &c. In Nomine Domini Nostri Jesuchristi. Pateat Vniuersis Qui nos Ferinandus Dei Gratia Rex Castelle... Barcelona: 1525. V. 48

FERNEL, JEAN
De Abditis Rerum Causis Libri Duo, Postremo ab Ipso Authore Recogniti, Compluribusque in Locis Aucti. Paris: 1560. V. 47; 48; 49; 50
Vniuersa Medicina. (and) Therapevtices Vniversalis. (and) De Abditis. Francofurti: 1592. V. 49

FERNETT, GENE
Swing Out. Great Negro Dance Bands. Midland: 1970. V. 47
A Thousand Golden Horns. Midland: 1966. V. 47

FERNIE, W. T.
Meals Medicinal: with "Herbal Simples" (of Edible Parts), Curative Foods from the Cook.... Bristol: 1905. V. 48; 53

FERNYHOUGH, THOMAS
Military Memoirs of Four Brothers (John, Robert, Thomas and Henry Fernyhough) Natives of Staffordshire, Engaged in the Service of Their Country, As Well in the New World and Africa, and on the Continent of Europe. London: 1829. V. 48

FERRALL, SIMON ANSLEY
A Ramble of Six Thousand Miles through the United States of America. London: 1832. V. 53

FERRAR, JOHN
A View of the Ancient and Modern Dublin...(and) A Tour to Bellvue, the Sea of Peter La Touche. Dublin: 1796. V. 52

FERRAR, NICHOLAS
Sir Thomas Smith's Misgovernment of the Virginia Company. Cambridge: 1990. V. 51

FERRAR, P.
A Guide to the Breeding Habits and Immature Stages of Diptera Cyclorrapha. Leiden: 1987. V. 50

FERRARI, E. L.
The Frescos in San Antonio De La Florida. Geneva: 1955. V. 48

FERRARI, GIOVANNI BATTISTA
De Florum Cultura Libri IV. Rome: 1633. V. 49
Senenseis Orationes. London: 1657. V. 51

FERRARI, OCTAVIO
Octavii Ferrarii: de Re Vestiaria. Padua: 1642. V. 48

FERRARIO, GIULIO
Storia ed Analisi Degli Antichi Romanzi di Cavaleria e Dei Poemi Romanzeschi d'Italia.. Milan: 1828-29. V. 53

FERRARIO, PHILIPPO
Lexicon Geographicum. London: 1657. V. 51

FERRARS, ELIZABETH
Sequence of Events. Helsinki: 1990. V. 48

FERRARS, MAX
Burma. London: 1900. V. 54
Burma. London: 1901. V. 53

FERREE, B.
American Estates and Gardens. New York: 1904. V. 51; 54

FERREIRA, F. H.
The Trees and Shrubs of South Africa. Pretoria: 1952. V. 50

FERREIRA CARDOSO DA COSTA, VICENTE JOSE
Theses ex Jurisprudentia Naturali, Sacra & Civili, tum Romana, Tum Patria, Necnon ex Utriusque Historia, Quas rro (sic) Repetitionis Actu in Conimbricensi Gymnasio Subeundo... Coimbra: 1785. V. 49

FERREIRA DE FIGUEIROA, DIOGO
Theatro da Mayor Facanha, e Gloria Portugueza... Lisbon: 1642. V. 48

FERREIRA LEOANRDO, MANUEL
Relacao da Viagem, e Entrada, Que fez o Excellentissimo, e Reverendissimo Senhor D. Fr. Miguel de Bulhoens e Sousa, Sagrado Bispo de Malaca, e Terceiro Bispo do Grao Para Para Esta Sua Diocese. Lisbon: 1749. V. 53

FERREL, W.
The Motions of Fluids and Solids, Relative to the Earth's Surface... New York & London: 1860. V. 47

FERRER, IRENE
Pre-Excitation Incuding the Wolff-Parkinson-White and Other Related Syndromes. Mt. Kisco: 1976. V. 53

FERRERS, EDMUND
Illustrations of Hogarth: i.e. Hogarth Illustrated from Passages in Authors He Never Read and Could Not Understand. London: 1816. V. 52

FERRETTI, MARC ANTONIO
Mirinda Favola Pastorale... Venice: 1612. V. 52

FERREY, BENJAMIN
The Antiquities of the Priory of Christchurch, Hants, Consisting of Plans, Sections, Elevations, Details, and Perspective Views. London: 1834. V. 50
Recollections of N. Welby Pugin and His Father Augustus Pugin; with Notices of their Works. London: 1861. V. 52

FERRIAR, JOHN
An Essay Towards a Theory of Apparitions. London: 1813. V. 49; 51
Illustrations of Sterne with Other Essays and Verses. Manchester: 1798. V. 52
Medical Histories and Reflections. Warrington: 1792. V. 53
Medical Histories and Reflections. Volume 3. London: 1798. V. 52

FERRIER, DAVID
The Functions of the Brain. New York: 1876. V. 47; 53
The Functions of the Brain. New York: 1886. V. 53; 54

FERRIER, J. P.
Caravan Journeys and Wanderings in Persia, Afghanistan, Turkistan and Beloochistan... London: 1856. V. 53; 54
History of the Afghans... London: 1858. V. 51

FERRIER, JAMES F.
Institutes of Metaphysics: The Ways of Knowing and Being. Edinburgh & London: 1854. V. 49

FERRIER, SUSAN EDMONSTONE
Destiny. Edinburgh: 1831. V. 48; 50; 53
Destiny; or, the Chief's Daughter. Philadelphia: 1831. V. 54
The Inheritance. Edinburgh: 1824. V. 48; 50; 51; 52; 53; 54
The Inheritance. Philadelphia: 1824. V. 48
Marriage. Edinburgh: 1818. V. 47; 49; 50; 51
Marriage. Edinburgh: 1826. V. 48
Memoir and Correspondence of Susan Ferrier 1782-1854... London: 1898. V. 50
Novels. London: 1878?. V. 50
Novels. 1881-82. V. 50
Novels. London: 1881/82. V. 51
The Novels: Marriage, the Inheritance, Destiny. London: 1894. V. 48

FERRIS, BENJAMIN
The Case of the Seneca Indians in the State of New York. Philadelphia: 1840. V. 48
A Further Illustration of the Case of the Seneca Indians in the State of New York in a Pamphlet Entitled "An Appeal to the Christian Community, &c" by Nathaniel T. Strong, A Chief of the Seneca Tribe... Philadelphia: 1841. V. 48
A History of the Original Settlements on the Delaware, From Its Discovery by Hudson to the Colonization Under William Penn. Wilmington: 1846. V. 47; 51; 53
Utah and the Mormons. New York: 1854. V. 49

FERRIS, CORNELIA (MRS. BENJAMIN)
The Mormons at Home; with Some Incidents of Travel from Mississippi to California, 1852-53. New York: 1856. V. 49; 50; 52

FERRIS, JACOB
The States and Territories of the Great West: Including Wisconsin, Iowa, Minnesota, Kansas, and Nebraska... New York and Auburn: 1856. V. 47

FERRIS, RICHARD
How to Fly, or the Conquest of the Air. London: 1911. V. 53

FERRIS, ROBERT G.
Lewis and Clark Historic Places Associated with Their Transcontinental Exploration (1804-06). Washington: 1975. V. 52; 54

FERRIS, SAMUEL
A Dissertation on Milk. London: 1785. V. 48

FERRIS, SARAH
Mental Perceptions: Illustrated by the Theory of Sensations. London: 1807. V. 49

FERRIS, WARREN ANGUS
Life in the Rocky Mountains... Denver: 1940. V. 52; 54
Life in the Rocky Mountains 1830-1835. Salt Lake City: 1940. V. 49; 51

FERRISS, HUGH
The Metropolis of Tomorrow. New York: 1929. V. 48; 50; 51; 52
Power in Buildings; an Artist's View of Contemporary Architecture. New York: 1953. V. 48; 50

FERRO, GIOVANNI
Teatro D'Impresse. Venetia: 1623. V. 50

FERUSSAC, J. B. L. DE
Histoire Naturelle Generale et Particuliere des Mollusques Terrestres et Fluviatiles. Paris: 1820-51. V. 50; 51

FESSENDEN, THOMAS GREEN
The American Clerk's Companion and Attorney's Prompter...with Observations Relative to the Varities of Practice... Brattleborough: 1815. V. 51
Democracy Unveiled; or, Tyranny Stripped of the Garb of Patriotism. Boston: 1805. V. 47; 51
An Essay on the Law of Patents for New Inventions. Boston: 1810. V. 48; 52
The Ladies Minitor, a Poem. Bellows Falls: 1818. V. 51; 53
The Register of Arts, or a Compendious View of Some of the Most Useful Modern Discoveries and Inventions. Philadelphia: 1808. V. 50
Terrible Tractoration!!!. London: 1803. V. 47

FESTING, GABRIELLE
Strangers Within the Gates. London: 1914. V. 54

FESTING JONES, HENRY
Samuel Butler...a Memoir. London: 1917. V. 53

FESTIVAL of Evenings with the Poets. With Seventy-Three Pictures by members of the National Academy of design. New York: 1866. V. 51

FESTIVAL of the Sons of New Hampshire. With the Speeches of....Celebrated in Boston, Novmber 7, 1849. Boston: 1850. V. 48

THE FESTIVAL of Wit: or, The Small Talker. London: 1783. V. 50

THE FESTOON: a Collection of Epigrams, Ancient and Modern. London: 1766. V. 47

FESTSCRIFT for Marianne Moore's Seventy Seventh Birthday - by Various. London: 1966. V. 53

FETHALAND, JOHN
The Murder at Charters. London: 1939. V. 48

FETHERSTON, JOHN
The Visitation of the County of Cumberland in the Year 1615, Taken by Richard St. George, Norroy King of Arms. London: 1872. V. 54

FETTES, D. J.
Synthesis of the Caledonian Rocks of Britain. London: 1986. V. 52

FEUCHTWANGER, LEWIS
Fermented Liquors: a Treatise on Brewing, Distilling, Rectifying and Manufacture of Sugars, Wines, Spirits and All Known Liquors... New York: 1858. V. 48; 50
A Treatise on Gems, in Reference to Their Practical and Scientific Value... New York: 1838. V. 48; 54

FEUCHTWANGER, LION
Jew Suss: a Historical Romance. London: 1926/25. V. 48
Paris Gazette. New York: 1940. V. 52
Simone. Stockholm. V. 53

FEUERBACH, LUDWIG
The Essence of Christianity. London: 1854. V. 50

FEUILLEE, LUDWIG, FATHER
Beschreibung zur Arznei Dienlicher Pflanzen. Nuremberg: 1756. V. 47; 53

FEWKES, JESSE WALTER
The Aborigines of Porto Rico and Neighboring Islands. Washington: 1907. V. 52
Hopi Katacinas Drawn by Native Artists. Chicago: 1962. V. 54

FEYENS, JOANNES
A New and Needful Treatise of Wind Offending Mans Body. London: 1676. V. 48

FFINCH, MICHAEL
The Dame School at Raisbeck. Kendal: 1984. V. 49; 50; 52
Donald Maxwell 1877-1936. Kendal: 1995. V. 52; 54

FFOLLIOTT, WILLIAM
Cartmel Parish and Parish Church and Sermons Preached therein. London: 1854. V. 52

FFOULKES, CHARLES J.
The Gun-Founders of England. 1937. V. 50
Inventory and Survey of the Armouries of the Tower of London. London: 1916. V. 49

FFRENCH, YVONNE
Ouida - a Study in Ostentation. London: 1938. V. 53

FIALA, ANTHONY
Fighting the Polar Ice. New York: 1906. V. 51
Fighting the Polar Ice. New York: 1907. V. 49

FIALA, F. J. L.
Lilacs, the Genus Syringa. London: 1988. V. 49

FIBONACCI, LEONARDO
Scritti di Leonardo Pisano Matematico del Secodo Decimoterzo Pubblicati di Baldassarre Boncompagni... Rome: 1857-62. V. 47

FICHTE, JOHANN GOTTLIEB
Der Geschlossene Handelsstaat. Tubingen: 1800. V. 52

FICKE, ARTHUR DAVIDSON
Selected Poems. New York: 1926. V. 47
Spectra: a Book of Poetic Experiments. New York: 1916. V. 47; 48; 51

FICORONI, FRANCESCO DE
Dissertatio de Larvis Scenicis et Figuris Comicis Antiquroum Romanorum. Rome: 1754. V. 53

FICORONI, FRANCESO DE
Le Maschere Sceniche e Le Figure Comiche d'Antichi Romani. In Roma: 1736. V. 53

FIDDES, RICHARD
The Life of Cardinal Wolsey... London: 1724. V. 51

FIDLER, ISAAC
Observations on Professions, Literature, Manners and Emigration in the United States and Canada. New York: 1833. V. 48; 52

FIELD, ANDREW
Nabokov, His Life in Art: a Critical Narrative. Boston: 1967. V. 50

FIELD, DAVID DUDLEY
A History of the Country of Berkshire, Massachusetts... Pittsfield: 1829. V. 49; 50
Speeches, Arguments and Miscellaneous Papers. New York: 1884. V. 49

THE FIELD Day Anthology of Irish Writing. 550-1990. New York: 1991. V. 48

FIELD, EUGENE
Christmas Tales and Christmas Verse. New York: 1926. V. 47
Echoes from the Sabine Farm. Chicago: 1893/91. V. 48
The Holy Cross: and Other Tales. Cambridge: 1893. V. 48
How One Friar Met the Devil and two Pursued Him. Chicago: 1900. V. 47
The Land of Make-Believe. Racine: 1931. V. 52; 54
Love-Songs of Childhood. New York: 1894. V. 48
Lullaby-Land, Songs of Childhood. London: 1898. V. 47
The Model Primer. Brooklyn: 1882. V. 48
The Mouse and the Moonbeam. New York: 1919. V. 52
My Book. V. 47
Our Deb to Monkish Men. Council Buffs: 1987. V. 49
Poems of Childhood. New York: 1904. V. 49; 54
Verse and Prose. St. Louis: 1917. V. 48
With Trumpet and Drum. New York: 1892. V. 47; 49
The Writings in Prose and Verse. New York: 1896. V. 47
The Writings in Prose and Verse. New York: 1896-1901. V. 54

FIELD, F. J.
An Armorial for Cumberland. Kendal: 1937. V. 50; 52; 54

FIELD, GEORGE
Chromatography; or a Treatise on Colours and Pigments and Powers in Painting. (with) Chromatics or an Essay on the analogy and Harmony of Colours. London: 1835/17. V. 48; 49
Outlines of Analogical Philosophy: Being a Primary View of the Principles, Relations and Purposes of Nature, Science and Art. London: 1839. V. 49

FIELD, H.
Memoirs of the Botanic Garden at Chelsea Belonging to the Society of Apothecaraies of London. London: 1878. V. 48

FIELD, HENRY
Arabs of Central Iraq: Their History, Ethnology and Physical Characters. Chicago: 1935. V. 50

FIELD, HENRY M.
Blood is Thicker than Water: a Few Days Among Our Southern Brethren. New York: 1886. V. 47
Our Western Archipelago. New York: 1895. V. 49; 51

FIELD, JOHN
Prison Discipline; and the Advantages of the Separate System of Imprisonment... London: 1848. V. 47; 50

FIELD, JOSEPH EMERSON
Three Years in Texas. Boston: 1836. V. 50; 54

FIELD, MICHAEL, PSEUD.
Brutus Ultor. London: 1886. V. 50
Canute the Great: The Cup of Water. London: 1887. V. 47
Fair Rosamund. London: 1897. V. 47; 49; 50; 52
The Father's Tragedy, William Rufus, Loyalty of Love. London. V. 47
Julia Domna. London: 1903. V. 47; 49
A Question of Memory. London: 1893. V. 50
The Race of Leaves. London: 1901. V. 48; 52
Sight and Song. London: 1892. V. 47
Stephania a Trialogue. London: 1892. V. 49
The World at Auction. London: 1898. V. 51; 52

THE FIELD of Mars: Being an Alphabetical Digestion of the Principal Naval and Military Engagements...from the Ninth Century to the Present Period. London: 1781. V. 51; 54

FIELD, RACHEL
Hitty Her First Hundred Years. New York: 1929. V. 49; 54

FIELD, RICHARD
A Stark Fantasy by Daddy Dumps. South Duxbury: 1949. V. 52

FIELD, RICHARD S.
Jasper Johns. Prints 1960-1970. Philadelphia: 1970. V. 50

FIELD, ROBERT D.
The Art of Walt Disney. London: 1944. V. 50

FIELD, SAUL
Bloomsday. 1972. V. 54
Bloomsday. Greenwich: 1972. V. 49

FIELD SPORTS: for the Countryman and Townsman Who Take an Active Part, or are Interested in Country Pursuits, Field Sports, Nature and the Wild Life of the British Countryside. Bradford, Yorkshire: 1947. V. 47

FIELD, STEPHEN J.
Decisions of the Supreme Court of the State of California Upon the Questions...Fremont v. Fowler. San Francisco: 1861. V. 48
Personal Reminiscences of Early Days in California with Other Sketches. San Francisco: 1880. V. 49
Personal Reminiscences of Early Days in California, with Other Sketches. 1893. V. 52; 54
Personal Reminiscences of Early Days in California, with Other Sketches... Washington: 1893. V. 47; 49

FIELD, THOMAS W.
An Essay Towards an Indian Bibliography. Columbus: 1951. V. 54

FIELD, W. B. OSGOOD
Edward Lear on My Shelves. London: 1933. V. 51
John Leech On My Shelves. 1930. V. 54

FIELD, WILLIAM
Memoirs of the Life, Writings and Opinions of Samuel Parr... London: 1828. V. 50

FIELDING, H.
The Soul of a People. London: 1898. V. 52

FIELDING, HENRY
The Adventures of Joseph Andrews. London: 1742. V. 48; 49; 51; 52; 54
The Adventures of Joseph Andrews. London: 1832. V. 51
Amelia. London: 1751. V. 51
Amelia. London: 1752. V. 48; 49; 51; 54
Amelia. London: 1752/51. V. 51
An Apology for the Conduct of the Late Celebrated Second Rate Minister, from the Year 1729, at Which Time he Commenc'd Courtier Till Within a Few Weeks of His Death in 1746. London: 1747. V. 47
An Apology for the Life of Mrs. Shamela Andrews. London: 1925. V. 49
The Beauties of Fielding... London: 1782. V. 52
A Clear State of the Case of Elizabeth Canning, Who Hath Sworn that She Was Robbed and Almost Starved to Death by a Gang of Gipsies and Other Villains in Jan. Last, for Which One Mary Squires Now Lies Under Sentence of Death. London: 1753. V. 53
The Collected Novels. Stratford-upon-Avon: 1926. V. 51
The Complete Works of Henry Fielding. Westminster: 1898. V. 54
The Complete Works of Henry Fielding. London: 1903. V. 48
A Dialogue Between a Gentleman of London, Agent for Two Court Candidates, and an Honest Alderman of the Country Party. London: 1747. V. 49
An Enquiry into the Causes of the Late Increase of Robbers... London: 1751. V. 47; 48; 50; 51; 52
The Fathers; or, the Good-Natur'd Man. London: 1778. V. 47; 51
The Fathers: or, the Good-Natur'd Man. Dublin: 1779. V. 53
Histoire of Tom Jones. France: 1762. V. 53
The Historical Register, for the Year 1736...to Which is Added a Very Merry Tragedy, Called Eurydice Hiss'd, Or, a Word to the Wise. London: 1737. V. 47; 48
The History of Amelia. London: 1832. V. 49

FIELDING, HENRY continued
The History of the Adventures of Joseph Andrews, and Of His Friend Mr. Abraham Adams. London: 1743. V. 52
The History of the Adventures of Joseph Andrews, and of His Friend Mr. Abraham Adams. London: 1749. V. 49; 50; 52
The History of the Adventures of Joseph Andrews, and of His Friend Mr. Abraham Adams. London: 1768. V. 48
The History of the Adventures of Joseph Andrews, and of His Friend Mr. Abraham Adams. Paris: 1794. V. 48; 49; 53
The History of the Adventures of Joseph Andrews, and Of His Friend Mr. Abraham Adams. (and) An Apology for the Life of Mrs. Shamela Andrews. London: 1970. V. 50
The History of the Life of the Late Mr. Jonathan Wild the Great. New York: 1943. V. 51; 54
The History of Tom Jones. London: 1743. V. 49
The History of Tom Jones. London: 1749. V. 47; 48; 49; 50; 51; 52; 53; 54
The History of Tom Jones... London: 1750/49. V. 48; 49; 51
The History of Tom Jones... London: 1759. V. 54
The History of Tom Jones... Edinburgh: 1767. V. 51
The History of Tom Jones... Paris: 1780. V. 48; 49; 50
The History of Tom Jones... London: 1787. V. 48; 49
The History of Tom Jones... London: 1792. V. 47
The History of Tom Jones... Philadelphia: 1810. V. 47
The History of Tom Jones... London: 1819. V. 54
The History of Tom Jones... New York: 1836. V. 54
The History of Tom Jones. London: 1974. V. 51
The Journal of a Voyage to Lisbon. London: 1755. V. 47; 48; 49; 50; 51; 52; 53; 54
A Journey From This World to the Next. Waltham St. Lawrence: 1930. V. 49
A Letter from Mr. Foote, to the Author of the Remarks, Critical and Christian, on the Minor. London: 1760. V. 47
The Letter-Writers; or, a New Way to Keep a Wife at Home. London: 1750. V. 47; 49; 51
The Life of Mr. Jonathan Wild the Great. London: 1754. V. 48; 49
Love in Several Masques. London: 1728. V. 48; 52
Miscellanies. London: 1743. V. 47; 48; 49; 54
The Miser. London: 1733. V. 47
The Modern Husband. London: 1732. V. 48
Novels. Oxford: 1926. V. 48; 49
Pasquin. London: 1736. V. 47; 48; 49; 50; 52; 53
A Plan of the Universal Register-Office, Opposite Cecil-Street in the Strand, and Of that in Bishopsgate-Street, the Corner of Cornhill. London: 1752. V. 49
A Serious Address to the People of Great Britain. London: 1745. V. 52
The Temple Beau. London: 1730. V. 48; 53
Tom Jones. Paris: 1952. V. 50
Tom Jones, ou l'Enfant Trouve. Paris: 1767. V. 47
A True State of the Case of Basavern Penlez, Who Suffered on Account of the Late Riot in the Strand. London: 1749. V. 47; 49; 51
The Wedding Day. London: 1743. V. 48; 52
Works... London. V. 47
The Works... London: 1762. V. 52; 54
The Works. London: 1783. V. 51
The Works. London: 1784. V. 48; 53
The Works... London: 1808. V. 48
The Works. London and Edinburgh: 1821. V. 51; 52; 54
The Works. London: 1845. V. 53
The Works. London: 1871. V. 48; 49; 51
The Works. London: 1871-72. V. 51
The Works... London: 1898-99. V. 52
The Works. London: 1899. V. 50
The Works. London: 1903. V. 51
Works. New York: 1903. V. 49
The Works. 1926. V. 53

FIELDING, JOHN
The Universal Mentor; Containing, Essays on the Most Important Subjects in Life... London: 1763. V. 47

FIELDING, SARAH
The Adventures of David Simple. London: 1744. V. 47; 49; 50; 51; 52
Familiar Letters Between the Principal Characters in David Simple and some Others. London: 1747. V. 49; 50; 52
The History of the Countess of Dellwyn... London: 1759. V. 49

FIELDING, T. H.
The Art of Engraving. London: 1844. V. 48
British Castles; or, A Compendious History of the Ancient Military Structures of Great Britain. London: 1825. V. 49; 51
Cumberland, Westmorland, and Lancashire. London: 1822. V. 47; 52
Index of Colours and Mixed Tints, for the Use of Beginners in Landscape and Figure Painting. London: 1830. V. 48
On Painting in Oil and Water Colours, for Landscape and Portraits... London: 1839. V. 48; 49
On the Theory and Practice of Painting in Oil and Water Colours, for Landscape and Portraits. London: 1846. V. 53
On the Theory of Painting; to Which is added an Introduction to Painting in Water-Colours... London: 1842. V. 48; 49
A Picturesque Tour fo the English Lakes... London: 1821. V. 47; 50

FIELDING, T.H.
A Picturesque Description of the River Wye from the Source. London: 1841. V. 47
The Theory of Painting in Oil and Water Colours for Landscape and Portraits... London: 1852. V. 51

FIELDING, WILLIAM RUSSELL
Drawings. London: 1950. V. 52

FIELDING, XAN
Hide and Seek - The Story of a Wartime Agent. London: 1954. V. 50
The Stronghold. London: 1937. V. 47
The Stronghold - an Account of the Four Seasons in the White Mountains of Crete. London: 1953. V. 49; 54

FIELDING-HALL, H.
Margaret's Book. 1913. V. 48

FIELDS, ANNIE
The Singing Shepherd and Other Poems. Boston: 1895. V. 54

FIELDS, JAMES T.
Anniversary Poem Delivered Before the Mercantile Library Association of Boston, September 13, 1838. Boston: 1838. V. 51; 52
The Boston Book. Boston: 1850. V. 53
Poems. Boston: 1849. V. 53; 54
Yesterdays with Authors. London: 1872. V. 49
Yesterdays with Authors. London: 1873. V. 54

FIELDS, JOSEPH
The Doughgirls. New York: 1943. V. 54
Junior Miss. New York: 1942. V. 54
My Sister Eileen. New York: 1941. V. 53
The Ponder Heart. New York: 1956. V. 51

FIELDS, URIAH J.
The Montgomery Story: the Unhappy Effects of the Montgomery Bus Boycott. New York: 1959. V. 54

FIELDS, WILLIAM
The Literary and Miscellaneous Scrap Book: Consisting of Tales and Anecdotes. Knoxville: 1833. V. 51

FIENNES, CELIA
Through England on a Side Saddle in the Time of William and mary. London: 1888. V. 49

FIERMAN, FLOYD S.
Some Early Jewish Settlers on the Southwestern Frontier. El Paso: 1960. V. 48

FIERSTEIN, HARVEY
Torch Song Trilogy. New York: 1983. V. 54

FIFE-COOKSON, J. C.
Tiger Shooting in the Doon and Ulwar. London: 1887. V. 49

FIFIELD, DASSIGNY
A Serious and Impartial Enquiry into...Free-Masonry in the Kingdom of Ireland...1744, An Answer to the Pope's Bull, 1738. An Impartial Answer to the Enemies of Freemasonry, 1741...and The General Regulations of the F. & A. Masons in...Ireland. 1974. V. 54

FIFIELD, LIONEL
Infections of the Hand. New York: 1927. V. 51; 53

FIFTEEN Poems. Chapel Hill: 1967. V. 53

FIFTEEN Poets. Oxford: 1941. V. 50

FIFTY Years of Robert Frost. Hanover: 1944. V. 52

FIGANIERE, FREDERICO FRANCISCO DE LA
Memorias das Rainhas de Portugal. D. Theresa - Santa Isabel. Lisbon: 1859. V. 47

FIGG, ROYAL W.
Where Men Only Dare to Go!. Richmond: 1885. V. 49

FIGGINS, VINCENT
Specimen Book of Types. London: 1887. V. 51
Specimen of Printing Types. London: 1821. V. 48
Specimen of Printing Types. London: 1835. V. 48

FIGGIS, DARRELL
The Paintings of William Blake. London: 1925. V. 49; 51

FIGHT Talk. New York: 1945. V. 53

FIGLIUCCI, FELICE
De la Filosofia Morale Libri Dieci sopra li Dieci Libri de l'Ethica d'Aristotile. Rome: 1551. V. 54

FIGUERAS, PALL
Decorated Jewish Ossuaries. Leiden: 1983. V. 49

FIGUEROA, JOSE
The Manifesto, Which the General of Brigade...Made to the Mexican Republic, in Regard to His Conduct and That of the Snrs. D. Jose Maris de Hijars and D. Jose Maria Padres, as Directors of Colonization in 1833 and 1834. San Francisco: 1855. V. 48

FIGULUS, BENEDICTUS
A Golden and Blessed Casket of Natures Marvels. London: 1963. V. 52

FIGURE Training; or, Art the Handmaid of Nature. London: 1871. V. 53

THE FIGURES to the First Set of Quadrilles. Newport. V. 50

FILBY, P. WILLIAM
Philadelphia Naturalization Records. Detroit: 1982. V. 48

FILIPE V, KING OF SPAIN
Ragguaglio Delle Nozze delle Maesta di Filippo Quinto, e di Elisabetta Farnese... Parma: 1717. V. 48

FILIPPI, F. DE
The Ascent of Mount St. Elias (Alaska) by H.R.H. Prince Luigi Amedeo Di Savoia Duke of Abruzzi. London: 1900. V. 52; 53

Karakoram and Western Himalay. 1909. An Account of the Expedition of H.R.H. Prince Lugigi Amedeo of Savoy, Duke of Abruzzi. London: 1912. V. 52; 53

Ruwenzori. An Account of the Expedition of H. R. H. Prince Luigi Amedeo of Savoy, Duke of Abruzzi. London: 1908. V. 52; 54

FILIPPI, MARCO
Rome (Vita) di Santa Caterina Vergine, e Martire... Venice: 1586. V. 49; 53

FILIPPI, ROSINA
Duologues and Scenes from the Novels of Jane Austen. London: 1895. V. 52; 54

FILIPPINI, ALESSANDRO
The Table: How to Buy Food, How to Cook It, and How to Serve It. New York: 1889. V. 52
The Table: How to Buy Food, How to Cook It and How to Serve It. New York & Baltimore: 1891. V. 48

FILISOLA, VICENTE
Memorias Para la Historia de la Guerra de Tejas. Mexico: 1848-49. V. 47
Representacion Dirigida al Supremo Gobierno en Defensa de su Honor y Aclaracion de sus Operaciones Como General en Gefe del Ejercito Sobre Tejas. Mexico: 1836. V. 50

FILLEY, WILLIAM
Life and Adventures of William Filley, Who Was Stolen from His Home in Jackson, Mich., by the Indians, August 3d, 1837 and His Safe Return from Captivity, Oct. 19, 1866. Chicago: 1867. V. 51

FILMER, ROBERT
The Free-Holders Grand Inquest, Touching Our sovereign Lord the King and His Parliament. London: 1680. V. 51
Patriarcha; or the Natural Power of Kings. London: 1680. V. 48

FILOW, BOGDAN D.
Early Bulgarian Art. Berne: 1919. V. 54

FILSON, JOHN
The Discovery, Settlement, and Present State of Kentucky. London: 1793. V. 48

FINBERG, ALEXANDER J.
The History of Turner's Liber Sutdiorum. London: 1924. V. 47

FINCH, C.
The Gamut and Time-Table in Verse for the Instruction of Children. London: 1825?. V. 48

FINCH, CATHERINE IRENE
Noureddin, or the Talisman of Futurity. London: 1836. V. 49

FINCH, CHRISTOPHER
The Art of Walt Disney. New York: 1973. V. 47; 48; 50; 51; 52; 53; 54

FINCH, EDWIN
The Frontier, Army and Professional Life of Edwin W. Finch, M.D. New Rochelle: 1909. V. 49

FINCH, G.
The Making of a Mountaineer. 1924. V. 53

FINCH, HENRY
Law, or, a Discourse Thereof, in Four Bookes. London: 1627. V. 51; 52
Law, or a Discourse Thereof, in Four Books. London: 1678. V. 53

FINCH, JOHN
The Accusation and Impeachment of John Lord Finch, Baron of Fordwich, Lord Keeper of the Great Seale of England, by the House of Commons. London: 1640. V. 47

FINCH, PEARL
The History of Burley-on-the-Hill, Rutland with a Short Account of the Owners and Extracts from Their Correspondence and Catalogue of the Contents of the House. London: 1901. V. 52

FINCH, WILLIAM
An Elucidation of the Masonic Plates, Consisting of Sixty Four Different Compartments, viz Forty Six in the First Plate, Nine in the Second and Nine in the Third... London: 1800. V. 47

FINCH, WILLIAM COLES
Watermills & Windmills: a Historical Survey of their Rise, Decline and Fall as Portrayed by Those of Kent. London: 1933. V. 52

FINCHAM, HENRY W.
Artists and Engravers of British and American Book Plates. London: 1897. V. 47; 49; 50; 54
The Order of the Hosptial of St. John of Jerusalem and its Grand Priory of England. London: 1915. V. 48

FINCHAM, JOHN
A Treatise on Masting Ships and Mast Making... London: 1982. V. 54

FINCH-DAVIES, C. G.
The Birds of Southern Africa. Johannesburg: 1982. V. 49

FINCK, HENRY T.
Lotos-Time in Japan. London: 1895. V. 50
The Pacific Coast Scenic Tour from Southern California to Alaska, the Canadian Pacific Railway, Yellowstone Park and the Grand Canyon. New York: 1890. V. 50

FIND the Constellations. Boston: 1956. V. 53

FINDEN, EDWARD
Great Brtain Illustrated: a Series of Original Views from Drawings by William Westall, A.R.A. London: 1830. V. 52

FINDEN, WILLIAM
Byron Beauties; or, the Principal Female Characters in Lord Byron's Poems. London: 1836. V. 50

Landscape Illustrations of the Bible, Consisting of Views of the Most Remarkable Places Mentioned in the Old and New Testaments. London: 1836. V. 53

Landscape Illustrations of the Waverley Novels... London: 1830-31. V. 54

Landscape Illustrations of the Waverly Novels; with Descriptions of the Views. London: 1831-32. V. 50

The Ports, Harbours, Watering Places, Fishing Villages and Picturesque Scenery of Great Britain. London: 1845. V. 52

The Ports, Harbours, Watering-Places and Picturesque Scenery of Great Britain. London: 1874. V. 47

FINDLAY, A. G.
Memoir, Descriptive and Explanatory, of the Northern Atlantic Ocean and Comprising Instructions... London: 1865. V. 49

FINDLEY, PALMER
Priests of Lucina, the Story of Obstetrics. Boston: 1939. V. 50; 52
The Story of Childbirth. Garden City: 1934. V. 50

FINDLEY, WILLIAM
History of the Insurrection, in the Four Western Counties of Pennsylvania; in the Year MDCCXCIV, with a Recital of the Circumstances Specially Connected Therewith... Philadelphia: 1796. V. 47

Observations on "The Two Sons of Oil:" Containing a Vindication of the American Constitutions, and Defending the Blessings of Religious Liberty and Toleration... Pittsburgh: 1812. V. 47

FINE, ORONCE
Arithmetica Practica. Paris: 1542. V. 47
De Mundi Shaera (sic), Libri IIII. Valencia: 1547. V. 47
De Solaribus Holologiis & Quadrantibus Libri Quatuor. Paris: 1560. V. 47; 52
Opere...Divise in Cinque Parti: Arimetica, Geometria, Cosmografia & Orivoli. Venice: 1587. V. 54
Practique de la Geometrie... Paris: 1570. V. 54
Quadratura Circuli. Paris: 1544. V. 47; 48; 50; 52; 54

FINE, RUTH
The Janus Press 1975-80. Catalogue Raisonne. An Exhibition at the Robert Hull Fleming Museum at the University of Vermont in Burlington, 1982. 1982. V. 54
Summer Day/Winter Night. Newark: 1994. V. 52

FINERTY, JOHN F.
War-Path and Bivouac. Chicago: 1890. V. 50

FINETTI, OTTAVIO
Prostasi Fisicomatematica Discorso Apologetico...Intorno le Gare Letterarie Nate fra il. Sig. Dottore Donato Rossetti Professore Filosofo in Pisa, Autore dell' Antignome Fisicomatrematiche... Bologna: 1669. V. 49

FINGER, C.
The Spreading Stain. New York: 1927. V. 48; 52

FINGER, F. L.
Catalogue of the Incunabula in the Elmer Belt Library of Vincina. Los Angeles: 1971. V. 47; 50

FINGLETON, J. H.
The Ashes Crown the Year. London: 1954. V. 48

FINLAY, CARLOS
Selected Papers. Havana: 1894. V. 51
Selected Papers. Havana: 1912. V. 48; 50; 53

FINLAY, GEORGE
A History of Greece From Its Conquest by the Romans to the Present Time. Oxford: 1877. V. 49
A History of Greece From Its Conquest by the Romans to the Present Time, B.C. 146 to A.D. 1864. London: 1877. V. 48
History of the Byzantine Empire from DCCXVI to MLVII. London: 1853. V. 53
History of the Greek Evolution. Edinburgh: 1861. V. 47
Remarks on the Topography of Oropia and Diacria, with a Map. Athens: 1838. V. 49

FINLAY, IAN HAMILTON
Air Letters. 1968. V. 47
Airs/Waters/Graces. 1975. V. 54
The Blue and Brown Poems. Aspen: 1968. V. 54
The Boy's Alphabet Book. Toronto: 1976. V. 47
Canal Stripe Series 3. Edinburgh. V. 54
Cythera. Edinburgh: 1965. V. 49
The Dancers Inherit the Party. London: 1969. V. 54
Evening/Sail 2. 1971. V. 54
A Family. 1973. V. 47
Jibs. 1972. V. 54
Lanes. 1969. V. 54
Ocean Stripe Series 4. Edinburgh: 1966. V. 54
Plakat 5 Fauve Poems. 1966. V. 47
Poems to Hear and See. New York: 1971. V. 54
Rhymes for Lemons. 1970. V. 54
Sail/Sundial. 1972. V. 54
Stonechats. Edinburgh: 1967. V. 54

FINLAY, IAN HAMILTON continued
Thirty Signatures to Silver Catches. East Markham: 1971. V. 48
Wave. 1969. V. 54
The Weed Boat Masters Ticket Preliminary Test Part II. Lanark: 1972. V. 47
The Weed Boat Masters Ticket. Preliminary Test (Part Two). Stonypath: 1972. V. 54

FINLAY, J. R.
Report of Appraisal of Mining Properties of New Mexico, 1921-1922. Santa Fe: 1922. V. 47

FINLAY, JOHN
A Treatise On the Law of Landlord and Tenant in Ireland. Dublin: 1825. V. 51

FINLAY, VIRGIL
The Book of Virgil Finlay. 1971. V. 52
The Book of Virgil Finlay. 1975. V. 48
Virgil Finlay - a Portfolio of Illustrations. 1953. V. 47; 51

FINLAYSON, RODERICK
Biography. Victoria: 1891. V. 47

FINLAYSON, W. F.
A Review of the Authorities as to the Repression of Riot or Rebellion, With Special Reference to Criminal or Civil Liability. London: 1868. V. 52

FINLAYSON, W. J.
Yacht Racing on the Clyde from 1883 to 1890. Glasgow & London: 1891. V. 52

FINLEY, ERNEST LATIMER
The History of Sonoma County, California, its People and Its Resources. Santa Rosa: 1937. V. 54

FINLEY, FLORENCE
Old Timers, Their Own Stories. 1939. V. 53

FINLEY'S Pocket Atlas. Philadelphia: 1826. V. 47

FINN, ELIZABETH ANNE
Reminiscences of Mrs. Finn. London: 1929. V. 52; 53

FINN, F.
Indian Sporting Birds. London: 1915. V. 49; 53

FINN, P.
The Complete Book of Southern African Birds. Cape Town: 1989. V. 48

FINNETT, JOHN
Finetti Philoxenis: som Choice Observations of Sr. John Finett Knight, and Master of Ceremonies to the Two Last Kings, Touching the Reception and Precedence, the Treatment and Audience, the Puntillios and Contests of Forren Ambassadors... London: 1656. V. 50

FINNEY, CHARLES G.
The Circus of Dr. Lao. New York: 1935. V. 52
The Circus of Dr. Lao. 1982. V. 47; 48; 49; 52; 54
The Circus of Dr. Lao. Newark: 1984. V. 51; 52; 54
The Circus of Dr. Lao. Vermont: 1984. V. 49
Guide to the Savior, or Conditions of Attaining to and Abiding in Entire Holiness of Heart and Life. Oberlin: 1848. V. 47
Past the End of the Pavement. New York: 1939. V. 53

FINNEY, JACK
Five Against the House. London: 1954. V. 49
Good Neighbor Sam. New York: 1963. V. 47; 52
House of Numbers. London: 1957. V. 47; 51
Time and Again. New York: 1970. V. 48; 51

FINNIE, RICHARD
Canol: the Sub-Arctic Pipeline and Refinery Project Constructed by Bechtel-Price-Callahan for the Corps of Engineers, United States Army, 1942-44. San Francisco: 1945. V. 50

FINNY, VIOLET GERALDINE
A Daughter of Erin. London: 1898. V. 49; 50

FIONN, MAC CUMHAILL
Fingal, a Fine-Erin: a Poem. London: 1813. V. 54

FIORAVANTI, LEONARDO
Dello Specchio Di Scientia Universale... Venice: 1624. V. 48
Il Reggimento della Peste..., Nel Quale si Tratta che Cosa sia la Peste, & da Che Procede & Quello che Doveriano Fare. Venice: 1594. V. 48

FIORENZA, PIERRE
Encyclopedia of Big Game Animals in Africa. 1983. V. 48

FIRBANK, RONALD
The Artificial Princess. London: 1934. V. 50; 54
Caprice. London: 1917. V. 54
Concerning the Eccentricities of Cardinal Pirelli. London: 1926. V. 47; 48; 49; 53; 54
Extravaganzas. New York: 1935. V. 51; 53
The Flower Beneath the Foot. 1923. V. 54
The Flower Beneath the Foot. London: 1923. V. 49
The Flower Beneath the Foot. New York: 1924. V. 48; 52
A Letter from Arthur Ronald Firbank to Madam Albani. London: 1934. V. 47; 48
Odette - a Fairy Tale for Weary People. London: 1916. V. 47; 49; 52; 53
Odette D'Antrevernes. London: 1905. V. 47; 51; 53
Prancing Nigger. New York: 1924. V. 53; 54
The Princess Zoubaroff. London: 1920. V. 47; 48; 53
La Princesse aux Soleils and Harmonie. London: 1974. V. 51

Santal. London: 1921. V. 48; 49
Sorrow in Sunlight. London: 1924. V. 54
Sorrow in Sunlight. 1925. V. 50
Sorrow in Sunlight. London: 1925. V. 47; 48
Vainglory. London: 1915. V. 50
Valmouth. London: 1919. V. 47; 49

FIRDAWSI
Roostum Zaboolee and Soohrab, from the History of Persia: Entitled Shah Namuh; or, Book of Kings, by Firdousee. Calcutta: 1829. V. 50

FIREBAUGH, ELLEN
The Physician's Wife and the Things that Pertain to Her Life. Philadelphia: 1894. V. 50; 52

FIRENZUOLA, AGNOLO
I Lucidi Comedia di Messer Agnolo firenzuola Fiorentino. Firenze: 1552. V. 47; 50
Prose. Florence: 1548. V. 51
Tales of Firenzuola, Benedictine Monk of Vallombrosa. V. 51

FIRMINGER, THOMAS
A Manual of Gardening for Bengal and Upper India. Calcutta: 1874. V. 49

THE FIRST Chapter of Tear-em the son of Gore'am, in the Apocripha. London: 1750. V. 52

FIRST Church of Christ in Hartford, Commemorative Exercises at Its 250th Anniversary. Hartford: 1883. V. 51

THE FIRST Crusade. The Deeds of the Franks and Other Jerusalemites. London: 1945. V. 47; 50

THE FIRST Crusade. The Deeds of the Franks and Other Jerusalemites. Waltham St. Lawrence: 1945. V. 47

FIRST Day, Wednesday, the 6th of September (1769), Shakespeare's Jubilee. Stratford: 1769. V. 47

FIRST EDITION CLUB
Bibliographical Catalogue of First Editions, Proof Copies and Manuscripts Of Books by Lord Byron Exhibited at the Fourth Exhibition Held by the First Edition Club. Jan. 1925. London: 1925. V. 51

THE FIRST Fleet. The Record of the Foundation of Australia from Its Conception to the Settlement at Sydney Cove. Waltham St. Lawrence: 1937. V. 51; 52

FIRST Help in Accidents and in Sickness. A Guide in the Absence, or Before the Arrival, of Medical Assistance. Boston: 1871. V. 48

FIRST INDEPENDENT CHRISTIAN CHURCH
Constitution and Manual of the First Independent Christian Church, Adopted July 31, 1839. Revised, Jan. 1843. Richmond: 1843. V. 50

FIRST Steamship Pioneers... San Francisco: 1874. V. 47

THE FIRSTBORN; or, a Mother's Trials. London: 1860. V. 54

FIRTH, CHARLES H.
The Last Years of the Protectorate 1656-1658. London: 1909. V. 52

FIRTH, F.
Art and Life in New Guinea. London: 1936. V. 54

FIRTH, HALL & POND
Catalogue of Music, Published by Firth, Hall & Pond, Publishers and Importers of Music...Manufacturers and Importers of All Kinds of Musical Instruments. New York: 1846. V. 48

FIRTH, RAYMOND
Art and Life in New Guinea. London: 1936. V. 48
The Work of the Gods in Tikopia. London: 1940. V. 50

FIRTH, WILLIAM
The Lord Thanet's Case Considered, As to the Question Whether the Judgment be Specific or Arbitrary?. London: 1799. V. 53

FISCHBACK, FRIEDRICH
The Principal Weaving Ornaments Up to the 19th Century. Printed in Germany: 1902-11?. V. 51

FISCHEL, OSKAR
Modes and Manners of the Nineteenth Century as Represented in the Pictures and Engravings of the Time. London and New York: 1909. V. 50
Modes and Manners Ornaments: Lace, Fans, Gloves, Walking Sticks, Parasols, Jewelry and Trinkets. London and Toronto: 1929. V. 50

FISCHER, ALBERT
Tissue Culture: Studies in Experimental Morphology and General Physiology of Tissue Cells in Vitro. London: 1925. V. 48

FISCHER, HANS
Pitschi. New York: 1953. V. 54
Puss in Boots. New York: 1959. V. 53

FISCHER, HENRY GEORGE
Ancient Egyptian Representations of Turtles. New York: 1968. V. 51
Dendera in the Third Millennium B.C. Down to the Theban Domination of Upper Egypt. Locust Valley: 1968. V. 51
The Orientation of Hieroglyps. Part I: The Reversals. New York: 1977. V. 49

FISCHER, JOSEPH
The Discoveries of the Norsemen in America with a Special Relation to the Early Cartographic Representation. St. Louis: 1903. V. 54
The Discoveries of the Norsemen in America with Special Relation to Their Early Cartographic Representation. London: 1903. V. 48

FISCHER, M.
William B. Wherry, Bacteriologist. Springfield: 1938. V. 53

FISCHER, MARJORIE
The Dog Cantbark. New York: 1940. V. 52

FISCHER, MARTIN
Christian R. Holmes: Man and Physician. Springfield: 1937. V. 52
The Lyophilic Colloids (Their Theory and Practice). Springfield: 1933. V. 49

FISCHER VON ERLACH, JOHANN BERNHARD
Entwurff Einer Hisotrischen Arcchitectur, in Abbildung Unterschiedener Beruhmten Gebaude, des Alterthums und Fremder Volcker. Wien: 1721. V. 48

FISH, Flesh and Fowl. A Book of Recipes for Cooking. Portland: 1877. V. 51

FISHBOUGH, WILLIAM
The Macrocosm and Microcosm; or the Universe Without and the Universe Within. New York: 1852. V. 52

FISHER, A. K.
Hawks and Owls of the United States. Washington: 1893. V. 48; 49; 50; 52; 54

FISHER, A. T.
Rod and River or Fly-Fishing for Salmon, Trout and Grayling. London: 1892. V. 54

FISHER, ABBY
What Mrs. Fisher Knows About Old Southern Cooking, Soups, Pickles, Preserves, etc. San Francisco: 1881. V. 47

FISHER, ALBERT KENRICK
The Hawks and Owls of the United States in Their Relation to Agriculture. Washington: 1893. V. 51

FISHER, ALEXANDER
Journal of a Voyage of Discouver, to the Arctic Regions, Performed Between the 4th of April and the 18th of November, 1818.,,. London: 1819. V. 50

FISHER, ANNE
The Pleasing Instructor; or, Entertaining Moralist. Newcastle-upon-Tyne: 1756. V. 53

FISHER, CLARENCE S.
The Minor Cemetery at Giza. Philadelphia: 1924. V. 51

FISHER, CLAY
The Brass Command. Boston: 1955. V. 48; 51

FISHER, DOROTHY CANFIELD
Basque People. New York: 1931. V. 48
The Day of Glory. New York: 1919. V. 52
Understood Betsy. New York: 1917. V. 48

FISHER, ELWOOD
Lecture on the North and the South. Cincinnati: 1849. V. 48
Lecture on the North and the South... Washington: 1849. V. 47

FISHER, F. J.
A Short History of the Worshipful Company of Horners. London: 1936. V. 47; 54

FISHER, G. P.
Life of Benjmain Silliman, M.D., LL.D. New York: 1866. V. 50

FISHER, HARRISON
American Beauties. Indianapolis: 1909. V. 54
Bachellor Belles. New York: 1908. V. 49; 52; 54
A Dream of Fair Women. New York: 1907. V. 50
A Garden of Girls. New York: 1910. V. 50
Harrison Fisher's American Girls in Miniature. New York: 1912. V. 48
The Little Gift Book. New York: 1912. V. 47

FISHER, IRVING
100 Per Cent Money. New York: 1935. V. 50
Stable Money. A History of the Movement. New York: 1934. V. 50

FISHER, J.
The Fulmar. London: 1952. V. 49; 54

FISHER, JAMES
Sea Birds, an Introduction to the Natural History of the Sea Birds of the North Atlantic. London: 1954. V. 53; 54
a Spring Day; or, Contemplations on Several Occurrences Which Naturally Strike the Eye in the Delightful Season. Edinburgh: 1806. V. 47
Wildlife Crisis. London: 1971. V. 48

FISHER, JOHN
defe(n)sio Regie Assertionis Co(n)tra Babylonica(m) Captiuitate(m). (with) Sacri Sacerdotii Defensio Contra Lutherum. Cologne: 1525. V. 50
The Funeral Sermon of Margaret, Countess of Richmond and Derby, Mother to King Henry VII. and Foundress of Christ's and St. John's College in Cambridge... London: 1708. V. 52
The History and Antiquities of Masham and Mashamshire... London: 1865. V. 47
Residence. Two Letters in Verse. London: 1821. V. 54

FISHER, JOHN D.
Description of the Distinct, Conluent, and Inoculated Small Pox, Varioloid Disease, Cow Pox and Chicken Pox. Boston: 1834. V. 48

FISHER, LILLIAN ESTELLE
The Intendant System in Spanish America. Berkeley: 1929. V. 50; 52
Viceregal Adminsitration in the Spanish American Colonies. Berkeley: 1926. V. 50

FISHER, M. F. K.
Boss Dog: a Fable in Six Parts. Covela: 1990. V. 49
Consider the Oyster. New York: 1941. V. 47; 49; 54
A Considerable Town. New York: 1978. V. 51
A Cordiall Water. Boston: 1961. V. 50; 52
The Gastronomical Me. New York: 1943. V. 50
Here Let Us Feast: a Book of Banquets. New York: 1946. V. 49; 54
Peas. From an Alphabet for Gourmets. Athens: 1988. V. 51
Sister Age. New York: 1983. V. 47
Spirits of the Valley. Manhattan: 1985. V. 48; 49; 50; 51; 52; 54

FISHER, M.F.K.
Not Now, But Now. New York: 1947. V. 52; 54
Serve It Forth. New York: 1937. V. 52
With Bold Knife and Fork. New York: 1969. V. 52

FISHER, MURRAY
The Golliwog's Dream and Other Stories for Little Folk. London. V. 47

FISHER, O. C.
It Occurred in Kimble. Houston: 1937. V. 51; 52
Texas Heritage of the Fishers and the Clarks. Salado: 1963. V. 51; 52; 53

FISHER, PAUL
The Angler's Souvenir. London: 1835. V. 49
The Angler's Souvenir. London: 1886. V. 49

FISHER, PAYNE
Marston-Moor: Sive De Obsidione Praelioque Eboracensi Carmen... Londini: 1650. V. 48; 49

FISHER, PHIL J.
Figures and Phases of the War 1916-1919. 1919. V. 47

FISHER, R. A.
A Digest of the Reported Cases (from 1756 to 1870 Inclusive) Relating to Criminal Law, Criminal Information and Extradition... San Francisco: 1871. V. 50; 52; 54

FISHER, RAYMOND H.
The Russian Fur Trade, 1550-1700. Berkeley & Los Angeles: 1943. V. 48

FISHER, RICHARD SWAINSON
A Chronological History of the Civil War in America. New York: 1863. V. 48

FISHER, RONALD AYLMER
Contributions to Mathematical Statistics. New York: 1950. V. 54

FISHER, ROY
Bluebeard's Castle. Surrey: 1972. V. 52
The Left-Handed Punch. Guildford: 1986. V. 54

FISHER, RUTH B.
On the Borders of Pigmy-Land. London: 1910. V. 54

FISHER, SAMUEL
The Testimony of Truth Exalted, by the Collected Labours of that Worthy Many. London: 1679. V. 47; 52

FISHER, SIDNEY GEORGE
The Law of the Territories. Philadelphia: 1859. V. 53

FISHER, THEODORE WILLIS
Plain Talk About Insanity: Its Causes, Forms, Symptoms and the Treatment of Mental Diseases. Boston: 1872. V. 48; 52

FISHER, THOMAS
The Kentish Traveller's Companion... Canterbury: 1799. V. 47; 50; 53
Monumental Remains and Antiquities in the County of Bedford. Hoxton: 1828. V. 52

FISHER, VARDIS
April: a Fable of Love. 1937. V. 48
Children of God. Caldwell: 1939. V. 49; 53
Children of God. New York: 1939. V. 52
Children of God. London: 1940. V. 53
City of Illusion. Caldwell: 1941. V. 47; 50
Gold Rushes and Mining Camps of the Early American West. 1968. V. 54
Idaho: a Guide in Word and Picture. 1937. V. 51; 54
The Idaho Encyclopedia. Caldwell: 1938. V. 50
No Villian Need Be. New York: 1936. V. 50
Orphans in Gethsemane: a Novel of the Past in the Present. 1960. V. 54
Passions spin the Plot. Caldwell & Garden City: 1934. V. 50; 51; 52
Toilers of the Hills. Boston: 1928. V. 47; 48; 51
We Are Betrayed. New York: 1935. V. 50

FISHER, W. K.
Asteroidea of the North Pacific and Adjacent Waters. Washington: 1911-30. V. 49; 51; 52; 53; 54

FISHER, WALTER M.
The Californians. London: 1876. V. 48; 52

FISHER, WILLIAM
The Waiters. Cleveland: 1953. V. 49

FISHER, WILLIAM R.
The Forest of Essex: It's History, Laws, Administration and Ancient Customs and the Wild Deer Which Lived In It. 1887. V. 52
The Law of Mortgage and Other Securities Upon Property. London: 1897. V. 51

THE FISHERMAN'S Hut; or Alzendorf. London: 1805. V. 49; 54

FISHWICK, HENRY
The History of the Parish of Poulton-Le-Fylde, in the County of Lancaster. London: 1885. V. 48
The History of the Parish of Preston in Amoounderness in the County of Lancaster. Rochdale: 1900. V. 49
The History of the Parish of Rochdale in the County of Lancaster. London: 1889. V. 54
Lancashire & Cheshire Church Surveys. 1549-1655. London: 1879. V. 48
The Lancashire Library. A Bibliographical Account of Books on Topography, Biography, History, Science and Miscellaneous Literature Relating to the County Palatine. London: 1875. V. 52
A List of the Lancashire Wills, Proved Within the Archdeaconry of Richmond... London: 1884. V. 48
Rochdale Jubilee. Manchester: 1906. V. 53; 54

FISK, CHARLES B.
Report, on the Examination of Canal Routes from the Potomac River to the City of Baltimore, Especially in Relation to the Supply of Water for Their Summit Levels...to the Governor of Maryland. Annapolis: 1837. V. 50

FISK, GORDON M.
Story of the Female Captive, and the Indian Leap or Great Cove, a Poem. 1844. V. 49

FISK, JAMES L.
Expedition of Captain Fisk to the Rocky Mountains. Washington: 1864. V. 47

FISKE, ABEL
A Sermon Delivered August 15, 1798 at the Ordination of the Rev. Jacob Abbot, to the Pastoral Office Over the Church and Society in Hampton Falls. Newburyport: 1798. V. 50

FISKE, JOHN
American Revolution. Cambridge: 1896. V. 47
Darwinism and Other Essays. London: 1879. V. 47; 53
The Miscellaneous Writings. Boston: 1902. V. 47
Tobacco and Alcohol. New York: 1869. V. 49; 53; 54

FISKE, M.
A Visit to Texas: Being the Journal of a Traveller through Those Parts Most Interesting to America Settlers. New York: 1834. V. 49; 54
A Visit to Texas...with an Appendix, Containing a Sketch of the Late War. New York: 1836. V. 49

FISON, LORIMER
Kamilaoi and Kurnai. Melbourne: 1880. V. 50

FITCH, CHARLES
The Glory of God in the Earth. Boston: 1842. V. 49

FITCH, ELIJAH
The Beauties of Religion. Providence: 1789. V. 52

FITCH, JOSEPH
A Poetical Grammar of the English Language. London: 1820. V. 48

FITCH, MICHAEL HENDRICK
Ranch Life and Other Sketches. Pueblo: 1914. V. 54

FITCH, SAMUEL SHELDON
Six Lectures on the Uses of the Lungs; and Causes, Prevention and Cure of Pulmonary Consumption, Asthma and Diseases of the Heart... New York: 1847. V. 49

FITCHEN, JOHN
The Construction of Gothic Cathedrals. Oxford: 1961. V. 49

FITHIAN, PHILIP VICKERS
Philip Vickers Fithian Journal and Letters, 1767-1774. Princeton: 1900. V. 47; 49; 51

FITSCHEN, M. J.
The School of Design Drawing Book... London: 1865. V. 54

FITT, MARY
Murder Mars the Tour. London: 1936. V. 47

FITTON, SARAH MARY
Conversations on Botany. London: 1817. V. 47

FITZ, REGINALD H.
Perforating Inflammation of the Vermiform Appendix... Philadelphia: 1886. V. 53

FITZCLARENCE, GEORGE A. F.
Journal of a Route Across India through Egypt to England in the Latter End of the Year 1817 and the Beginning of 1818. London: 1819. V. 48

FITZENMEYER, FRIEDA
Once Upon a Time Book Six. Easthampton: 1992. V. 52; 53

FITZGEFFREY, CHARLES
Compassion Towards Captives, Chiefly Towards Our Bretheren and Country-Men Who are in Miserable Bondage in Barbarie, Urged and Pressed in Three Sermons on Heb. 13.3. Preached in Plymouth, in October 1636... Oxford: 1637. V. 48

FITZGERALD, D. J. L.
History of the Irish Guards in the Second World War. London: 1949. V. 51

FITZGERALD, DAVID
A Narrative of the Irish Popish Plot, for the Betraying that Kingdom Into the Hands of the French, Massacring all English Protestants There... London: 1680. V. 52

FITZGERALD, E. A.
Climbs in the New Zealand Alps, being An Account of Travel and Discovery By... London: 1896. V. 52; 53

The Highest Andes. London: 1899. V. 50; 52; 53

FITZGERALD, EDWARD
Agamemnon: a Tragedy Taken from Aeschylus. London: 1876. V. 48
Letters and Literary Remains. London: 1902. V. 49; 50
Letters and Literary Remains. London: 1902-03. V. 48; 50; 51
Letters from Edward FitzGerald to Bernard Quaritch 1853-1883. London: 1926. V. 53
Polonius: a Collection of Wise Saws and Modern Instances. Portland: 1901. V. 52
Readings in Crabbe "Tales of the Hall". London: 1882. V. 47
The Variorum and Definitive Edition of the Practical and Prose Writings... New York: 1967. V. 54

FITZGERALD, FRANCIS SCOTT KEY
Afternoon of an Author. Princeton: 1957. V. 47; 48; 49; 50; 51; 53
All the Sad Young Men. New York: 1926. V. 47; 48; 49; 50; 52; 53; 54
The Beautiful and Damned. New York: 1922. V. 47; 48; 49; 50; 52; 53
The Crack-Up. New York: 1945. V. 53
Dearly Beloved. University of Iowa: 1969. V. 51
The Evil Eye. Cincinnati & New York: 1915. V. 47; 54
The Evil Eye. New York & London: 1915. V. 53
F. Scott Fitzgerald's Preface to This Side of Paradise. Iowa City: 1975. V. 51; 53; 54
Fie! Fie! Fi-Fi!. Cincinnati: 1914. V. 47
Flappers and Philosophers. New York: 1920. V. 47; 48; 49; 50; 51; 53
The Great Gatsby. New York: 1925. V. 47; 48; 49; 50; 51; 53; 54
The Great Gatsby. Washington: 1973. V. 53
The Great Gatsby. 1980. V. 48; 50; 51
The Great Gatsby. Meriden: 1980. V. 53
The Great Gatsby. New York: 1980. V. 48; 51; 52
The Great Gatsby. San Francisco: 1984. V. 47; 48; 51; 52; 53
The Last Tycoon. (with) The Great Gatsby and Selected Stories. New York: 1941. V. 48; 50
Ledger: a Facsimile. Washington: 1972. V. 50
The Mystery of the Raymond Mortgage. 1960. V. 53
The Pat Hobby Stories. New York: 1962. V. 49; 51
The Preface to This Side of Paradise. 1976. V. 50
The Stories of F. Scott Fitzgerald. New York: 1951. V. 47; 48; 51
Tales of the Jazz Age. New York: 1922. V. 48; 50; 51; 52; 54
Tales of the Jazz Age. Toronto: 1922. V. 54
Taps at Reveille. New York: 1935. V. 47; 48; 49; 50; 51; 52; 53; 54
Tender is the Night. New York: 1934. V. 49; 51; 52; 53
Tender is the Night. London: 1953. V. 48; 50; 51; 52
Tender is the Night. New York: 1982. V. 47; 48; 49; 51; 52
Tender is the Night. London: 1995. V. 53
This Side of Paradise. New York: 1920. V. 48; 49; 50; 51; 52; 53
The Vegetable. New York: 1923. V. 47; 48; 49; 50; 51; 52; 53

FITZGERALD, JAMES EDWARD
An Examination of the Charter and Proceedings of the Hudson's Bay Company, with Reference to the Grant of Vancouver's Island. London: 1849. V. 48; 50

FITZGERALD, OSCAR PENN
California Sketches. (with) California Sketches. New Series. Nashville: 1894/92. V. 51

FITZGERALD, PERCY
The Garrick Club. London: 1904. V. 54
Life of James Boswell. London: 1891. V. 53
The Life of Laurence Sterne. London: 1864. V. 51
Memoirs of an Author. London: 1895. V. 51
Memories of Charles Dickens. Bristol: 1913. V. 54
Mildrington the Barrister. London: 1863. V. 54
The Story of the Incumbered Estates Court. London: 1862. V. 52

FITZGERALD, R. A.
Jerks in From Short-Leg. London: 1866. V. 50

FITZGERALD, R. D.
Australian Orchids. Melbourne: 1977-79. V. 47

FITZGERALD, ROBERT
Salt-Water Sweetened; or, a True Account of the Great Advantages of This New Invention Both by Sea and By Land... London: 1683. V. 48

FITZGERALD, S. J. ADAIR
The Zankiwank and the Bletherwitch. London: 1896. V. 49

FITZGERALD, T. P.
The Political and Private Life of the Marquis of Londonderry. 1822. V. 50
The Political and Private Life of the Marquis of Londonderry. London: 1822. V. 51; 54

FITZGERALD, THOMAS
Poems on Several Occasions. London: 1733. V. 48
Poems on Several Occasions. London: 1736. V. 47

FITZGERALD, WILLIAM THOMAS
Nelson's Tomb. London: 1805. V. 50; 54

FITZGERALD, WILLIAM WALTER AUGUSTINE
Travels in the Coastlands of British East Africa. London: 1898. V. 53

FITZGERALD, ZELDA
Save Me the Waltz. New York: 1932. V. 48
Save Me the Waltz. London: 1953. V. 47; 54

FITZGERLAD, THOMAS
Poems on Several Occasions. London: 1733. V. 50

FITZGIBBON, CONSTANTINE
Watcher in Florence. Huntington: 1959. V. 50

FITZGIBBON, EDWARD
A Handbook of Angling: Teaching, Fly-Fishing, Trolling, Bottom and Salmon Fishing. London: 1847. V. 47; 53

FITZGIBBON, GERALD
Ireland in 1868, the Battle-Field for English Party Strife... London: 1868. V. 50; 52

FITZ-HARRIS, EDWARD
The Confession of Edward Fitz-harys, Esquire, Written With His Own Hand...the Frst (sic) of July, 1681. London: 1681. V. 53

FITZHERBERT, ANTHONY
The New Natura Brevium of the Most Reverend Judge Mr. Anthony Fitz-Herbert... London: 1755. V. 47
La Novel Natura Breuium du Iudge Tresreuerend Monsieur Anthony Fitzherbert Dernierement Reuieu & Corrigee per Laueteur... London: 1616. V. 52

FITZMAURICE, EDMOND, LORD
The Life of Sir William Petty, 1623-1687. London: 1895. V. 51

FITZPATRICK, HUGH
A Report of the Trial of H. Fitzpatrick for the Libel Upon the Duke of Richmond. Dublin: 1813. V. 48

FITZPATRICK, J. P.
Jock of Bushveld. London: 1907. V. 48; 49; 50; 51; 54

FITZPATRICK, ROBERT
The Bard's Museum; or, Rational Recreation.... Dublin: 1809. V. 54

FITZPATRICK, T. J.
Rafinesque a Sketch of His Life with Bibliography. Des Moines: 1911. V. 50; 51; 54

FITZPATRICK, WILLIAM JOHN
Lady Morgan: Her Career Literary and Personal. London: 1860. V. 54
The Life of Charles Lever. London: 1879. V. 51
The Life of Charles Lever. London: 1884. V. 51

FITZROY, AUGUSTUS
The Tryal Between Sir William Morris, Baronet, Plaintiff, and Lord Augustus Fitzroy, Defendant for Criminal Conversation with the Plaintiff's Wife at the Kings-Bench for the Wilful Murder of Sir Theodosius Boughton, Bart. Taken in Short-Hand... London: 1781. V. 49

FITZROY, ROBERT
The Weather Book: a Manual of Practical Meteorology. London: 1863. V. 48; 51

FITZSIMMONS, CORTLAND
Death Rings a Bell. Philadelphia: 1942. V. 49

FITZSIMONS, F. W.
The Natural History of South Africa - Mammals. London: 1919-20. V. 52
The Snakes of South Africa. Cape Town: 1912. V. 51; 52

FITZURSE, R.
It Was Not Jones. London: 1928. V. 51

FITZWILLIAM, G. W.
The Pleasures of Love; Being Amatory Poems, Original and Translated... Boston: 1808. V. 47; 52

FITZWILLIAM MUSEUM
Catalouge. An Exhibition of Printing at the Fitzwilliam Museum, 6 May to 23 June 1940. Cambridge: 1940. V. 52

FITZWILLIAMS, DUNCAN
On the Breast. London: 1924. V. 53
The Tongue and Its Diseases. London: 1927. V. 53

FIVE BLIND Men, Poems By: Dan Gerber, Jim Harrison, George Quasha, J.D. Reedd, Charles Simic. Fremont: 1969. V. 52; 54

FIVE Cummington Poems. Cummington: 1939. V. 54

FIVE Cummington Poems, 1939. Northampton. V. 47

FIVE Extraordinary Letters Suppos'd to Be Writ to Dr. B----y, Upon His Edition of Horace and Some Matters of Importance. London: 1712. V. 49

FIVE Eyes. Santa Barbara: 1977. V. 53

THE FIVE Orders of Architecture. Boston. V. 48

FIVE Speciall Passages: viz. Two Petitions of the Countie of Yorke. London: 1642. V. 50

FIVE Young American Poets: George Marion O'Donnell, Randall Jarrell, John Berryman, Mary Barnard, W.R. Moses. Norfolk: 1940. V. 48; 50

FIVE Young American Poets. Third Series, 1944. Eve Merriam, John Frederick Nims, Jean Garrigue, Tennessee Williams, Aleiandro Carrion. Norfolk: 1944. V. 48; 53

FJELDSA, J.
Birds of the High Andes. Copenhagen: 1990. V. 54
Birds of the High Andes. London: 1990. V. 49

FLACHAT, STEPHANE
Histoire des Travaux et de l'Amenagement des Eaux du Canal Caledonian. Paris: 1828. V. 51; 54

FLACIUS ILLYRICUS, MATTHIAS
Nona...Decima...Undecima Centuria Ecclesiasticae Historiae... Basilae: 1565/67/67. V. 52

FLACK, MARJORIE
The Restless Robin. Boston: 1937. V. 53; 54
Tim Tadpole and the Great Bullfrog. Garden City: 1934. V. 49
Up in the Air. New York: 1935. V. 53
Wait for William. Boston & New York: 1935. V. 52

THE FLAG Painting Book. London: 1890's. V. 51

THE FLAG. The Book of the Union Jack Club. London: 1908. V. 48

FLAGG, FANNIE
Coming Attractions. New York: 1981. V. 50

FLAGG, JAMES MONTGOMERY
Roses and Buckshot. New York: 1946. V. 47

FLAGG, THOMAS WILSON
The Woods and By-Ways of New England. Boston: 1872. V. 49; 54

FLAGG, WILLIAM JOSEPH
Woman the Stronger. A Novel. New York: 1879. V. 51

FLAGG, WILSON
Mount Auburn: Its Scenes, Its Beauties and Its Lessons. Boston and Cambridge: 1861. V. 51

FLAHERTY, ROBERT J.
My Eskimo Friends "Nanook of the North". Garden City: 1924. V. 47; 50; 52

FLAMEN, ALBERT
Devises et Emblesmes d'Amour. Paris: 1672. V. 47
Devises et Emblesmes d'Amour Moralisez. Paris: 1648. V. 54
Livre d'Oyseaus, Dedie a Messire Gilles Foucquet. Paris: 1650. V. 49; 53; 54

FLAMENT, ARTHUR
The Private Life of Lady Hamilton. New York London Montreal: 1929. V. 51

FLAMINIO, MARCO ANTONIO
Fifty Select Poems of Marc-Antonio Flaminio... Chester: 1829. V. 48; 54

FLAMMARION, C.
Omega: the Last Days of the World. New York: 1894. V. 48
Urania. 1890. V. 49; 54

FLAMSTEED, JOHN
Atlas Celeste de Flamsteed, Publie en 1776. Paris: 1795. V. 53
Atlas Coelestis. London: 1729. V. 53
A Letter Concerning Earthquakes, Written in the Year 1693, by the Late Celebrated Astronomer, Mr. John Flamsteed... London: 1750. V. 47

FLANAGAN, HALLIE
Shifting Scenes of Modern European Theatre. New York: 1928. V. 47; 52; 54

FLANAGAN, MARY
Bad Girls. London: 1984. V. 51

FLANDERS, RALPH BETTS
Plantation Slavery in Georgia. Chapel Hill: 1933. V. 48

FLANNER, JANET
The Cubical City. New York & London: 1926. V. 51; 52; 53
The Stronger Sex as Seen by Vertes. New York: 1941. V. 51

FLANNERY, L. G.
John Hunton's Diary. Lingle and Glendale: 1956-70. V. 48

FLASH, HENRY LYNDON
Poems. New York: 1860. V. 47

THE FLATELY Book and Recently Discovered Vatican Manuscripts Concerning America as Early as the Tenth Century. London: 1906. V. 54

FLATMAN, THOMAS
On the Death of Our Late Sovereign Lord King Charles II. London: 1685. V. 54
Poems and Songs. London: 1674. V. 52
Poems and Songs. London: 1676. V. 47
Poems and Songs. London: 1686. V. 47; 49; 53

FLAUBERT, GUSTAVE
Bouvard and Peuchet. London: 1896. V. 50; 54
The Complete Works. New York and London: 1904. V. 53
The Complete Works of... London: 1926. V. 53
La Legende de Saint Julien L'Hospitalier. 1900. V. 49
Madame Bovary. Paris: 1857. V. 50; 54
Madame Bovary. London: 1886. V. 52; 53
Madame Bovary. Paris: 1905. V. 54
Madame Bovary. London: 1928. V. 47
Madame Bovary. New York: 1950. V. 48; 52; 54
Salammbo. Paris: 1863. V. 49
Salammbo. London & New York: 1886. V. 47; 49; 52
Salammbo. London: 1930. V. 50
Salammbo. New York: 1930. V. 48; 52; 54

FLAUBERT, GUSTAVE continued
Salammbo. 1960. V. 52; 54
Salammbo. Cambridge: 1960. V. 48; 51; 54
Salammbo. London: 1960. V. 49
Salammbo. New York: 1960. V. 47; 48
Sentimental Education. London: 1898. V. 49; 53; 54
The Temptation of Saint Anthony. London: 1895. V. 49; 54
The Temptation of Saint Anthony. 1910. V. 48; 50; 52
The Temptation of Saint Anthony. New York: 1943. V. 47; 48
The Temptation of Saint Anthony. Kentfield: 1974. V. 48; 51
The Temptation of St. Anthony. London: 1974. V. 52
La Tentation de Saint Antoine. Paris: 1907. V. 54
Le Tentation de Saint Antoine. Paris: 1926. V. 47; 53
Three Tales. New York: 1978. V. 48

FLAVEL, JOHN
Navigation Spiritualized; or a New Compass for Seamen, Consisting of XXXII Points... Newburyport: 1797?. V. 51

FLAXMAN, JOHN
Anatomical Studies of the Bones and Muscles, for the Use of Artists... London: 1833. V. 48; 49
The Classical Compositions of John Flaxman, R.A., Sculptor. London: 1870. V. 47
Compositions from the Works, Days and Theogony of Hesiod. London: 1817. V. 48
Compositions from the Works, Days and Theogony of Hesiod. (with) *Compositions from the Tragedies of Aeschylus.* London: 1795. V. 52
Compositions...from the Divine Poem of Dante Alighieri... London: 1807. V. 47
Composizioni Di Giovanni Flaxman Sculptore Ingleses Tratte Dall'Odissea Di Omero. Milan: 1857. V. 51
Lectures on Sculpture, with a Brief Memoir of the Author. London: 1829. V. 49; 51

FLAYDERMAN, E. NORMAN
Scrimshaw and Scrimshanders. New Milford: 1973,. V. 53

FLEAY, FREDERICK GARD
A Biographical Chronicle of the English Drama. 1559-1642. London: 1891. V. 53

FLECKER, JAMES ELROY
The Bridge of Fire. London: 1907. V. 49; 54
Don Juan. London: 1926. V. 47
The Golden Journey to Samarkand. London: 1913. V. 49
Hassan. London: 1922. V. 52
Hassan. London: 1923. V. 49
Hassan. London: 1924. V. 50; 51
The King of Alsander. London: 1914. V. 54
The Letters of J. E. Flecker to Frank Savery. 1926. V. 47
The Letters of J. E. Flecker to Frank Savery. London: 1926. V. 50; 52

FLEET, WILLIAM HENRY
How I Came to Be Governor of the Island of Cacona. 1989. V. 52; 54
How I Came to be Governor of the Island of Cacona. San Francisco: 1989. V. 50

FLEETWOD, WILLIAM
Chronicon Pretiosum: or an Account of English Gold and Silver Money... London: 1745. V. 48

FLEETWOOD, WILLIAM
Chronicon Preciosum: or, an Account of English Money, The Price of Corn, and Other Commodities for the Last 600 Years. London: 1707. V. 50; 52
The Effect of the Declaration Made in the Guildhall by M. Recorder of London, Concerning the Late Attemptes of the Quenes Maiesties Evill, Seditious and Disobedient Subiectes. London: 1571. V. 53

FLEISCHER, MAX
Noah's Shoes. Detroit: 1944. V. 48

FLEISCHER, NAT
The Ring Record Book. New York: 1952. V. 48

FLEISHER, BENJAMIN W.
Enthronement of the One Hundred Twenty-Fourth Emperor of Japan. Tokyo: 1928. V. 48

FLEMING, A. B.
Address...Upon the Resources of West Virginia. Pittsburgh: 1882. V. 53

FLEMING, A. M.
The Fun Sight Mine. Boston: 1929. V. 53

FLEMING, ALEXANDER
On the Anitbacterial Action of Cultures of a Penicillium. London: 1944. V. 53; 54
Penicillin Its Practical Application. London: 1946. V. 50; 53; 54
Penicillin Its Practical Application. Philadelphia: 1946. V. 51
Recent Advances in Vaccine and Serum Therapy. Philadelphia: 1934. V. 48; 51; 53

FLEMING, FRANCIS PHILLIP
Memoir of Capt. C. Seton Fleming, Of the Second Florida Infantry, C.S.A. Jacksonville: 1884. V. 49

FLEMING, GEORGE
Travels on Horseback in Mantchu Tartary. London: 1863. V. 47; 48; 51

FLEMING, HOWARD A.
Canada's Arctic Outlet. Berkeley & Los Angeles: 1957. V. 47; 54

FLEMING, IAN LANCASTER
Birds of the West Indies. Philadelphia: 1936. V. 49
Casino Royale. 1953. V. 54
Casino Royale. London: 1953. V. 52
Casino Royale. New York: 1954. V. 52
Chitty Chitty Bang Bang. London: 1964. V. 47; 52
Chitty Chitty Bang Bang. London: 1971. V. 51
The Diamond Smugglers. London: 1957. V. 47; 50; 52; 53
Diamonds are Forever. London: 1956. V. 47; 48; 53
Diamonds are Forever. New York: 1956. V. 48
Dr. No. London: 1958. V. 47; 49; 50; 51; 52; 53
For Your Eyes Only. London: 1960. V. 47; 48; 49; 50; 51; 53
From Russia with Love. London: 1957. V. 47; 49; 52
Goldfinger. London: 1959. V. 47; 48; 49; 50; 51; 53; 54
Goldfinger. New York: 1959. V. 53
Live and Let Die. London: 1954. V. 47; 49; 50; 54
Live and let Die. New York: 1954. V. 50
Live and Let Die. 1955. V. 50; 53
Live and Let Die. New York: 1955. V. 49; 50
The Man With the Golden Gun. London: 1965. V. 47; 48; 52; 53; 54
Moonraker. London: 1955. V. 47; 49; 50
Octopussy and the Living Daylights. 1966. V. 54
On Her Majesty's Secret Service. 1963. V. 54
On Her Majesty's Secret Service. London: 1963. V. 50; 53; 54
The Spy Who Loved Me. London: 1962. V. 48; 49; 50; 51; 53; 54
Thunderball. London: 1961. V. 47; 48; 50; 51; 52; 53
You Only Live Twice. London: 1964. V. 47; 51; 52; 53

FLEMING, J. ARNOLD
Flemish Influences in Britain. Glasgow: 1930. V. 49; 52

FLEMING, K.
Can Such Things Be? Or the Weird of the Beresfords - a Study in Occult Will Power. London: 1890. V. 48; 52

FLEMING, LINDSAY
History of Pagham in Sussex... London: 1949-50. V. 47; 54

FLEMING, ROBERT
The Blessedness of Those Who Die in the Lord: a Practical Discourse Occasioned by the Death of King William... London: 1702. V. 48

FLEMING, SANDFORD
Confidential Observataions...On the General Land Policy of the Hudson's Bay Company. London: 1882. V. 49
England and Canada. Montreal: 1884. V. 53
The Intercolonial. A Historical Sketch of the Inception, Location, Construction and Completion of the Line of Railway Uniting the Inland and Atlantic Provinces of the Dominion. Montreal: 1876. V. 53

FLEMING, VIVIAN MINOR
Battles of Fredericksburg and Chancellorsville. Richmond: 1921. V. 48
Campaigns of the Army of Norther Virginia Including the Jackson Valley Campaign 1861-1865. Richmond: 1928. V. 47; 50

FLEMING, W.
Four Days in the Niagara Falls in North America. Manchester: 1840. V. 53

FLEMING, WALTER L.
A Collection of Letters and Documents and Other Material, Chiefly from Private Sources, Relating to the Life and Activities of General William Tecumseh Sherman... Cleveland: 1912. V. 54
General W. T. Sherman as College President: A Collection of Letters, Documents, and Other Material. Cleveland: 1912. V. 48

FLEMMING, ERNST
Encyclopaedia of Textiles. London: 1958. V. 54

FLEMMING, HARFORD
Cupid and the Sphinx. London: 1879. V. 51

FLETA, Seu Commentarius Juris Anglicani sic Nuncupatus, sub Edwardo Rege Primo, Seu Circa Annos ab Hinc CCCXL. ab Anonymo Conscriptus, Atque e Codice Veteri... London: 1685. V. 52

FLETCHER, A.
The Universal Measurer. Whitehaven: 1752/53. V. 47
Within Fort Sumter; or, a View of Major Anderson's Garrison Family For One Hundred and Ten Days. New York: 1861. V. 49; 50

FLETCHER, ANDRES
A Speech Upon the State of the Nation. 1701. V. 52

FLETCHER, ANDREW
A Defence of the Scots Settlement at Darien. Edinburgh: 1699. V. 49
Discorso Delle Cose di Spagna. Naples: 1698. V. 50
A Discourse of Government. Edinburgh: 1698. V. 50
The Political Works. London: 1732. V. 49
The Political Works. Glasgow: 1749. V. 47
A Speech Upon the State of the Nation, in April 1701. Edinburgh: 1701. V. 50
Two Discourses Concerning Affairs of Scotland; Written in the Year 1698. Edinburgh: 1698. V. 50

FLETCHER, BANISTER
Andrea Palladio: His Life and Work. London: 1902. V. 53
A History of Architecture. London: 1987. V. 50

FLETCHER, CORA C.
The Emperor's Lion. Verona: 1976. V. 48

FLETCHER, DANIEL C.
Reminiscences of California and the Civil War. Ayer: 1894. V. 47

FLETCHER, GILES
The Complete Poems of Giles Fletcher. London: 1876. V. 53

FLETCHER, HENRY
The Perfect Politician; or, a Full View of the Life and Actions of O. Cromwell. London: 1680. V. 54

FLETCHER, HENRY CHARLES
History of the American War. London: 1865-66. V. 51

FLETCHER, IFAN KYRLE
Ronald Firbank - a Memoir. London: 1930. V. 50; 54

FLETCHER, J. J.
The Macleay Memorial Volume. Sydney: 1893. V. 53

FLETCHER, J. S.
Behind the Monocle. New York: 1930. V. 49
The Ebony Box: Being the First of the Further Adventures of Ronald Camberwell. New York: 1934. V. 49
The History of the St. Leger Stakes 1776-1901. London: 1902. V. 48

FLETCHER, JAMES C.
International Relations with Brazil. New York: 1865. V. 47

FLETCHER, JOHN
Monsieur Thomas. A Comedy. London: 1639. V. 48; 50
Studies on Slavery, in Easy Lessons. Natchez: 1852. V. 49; 52; 53

FLETCHER, JOHN GOULD
The Black Rock. London: 1928. V. 49
Japanese Prints. Boston: 1918. V. 47
Paul Gauguin. His Life and Art. New York: 1921. V. 49

FLETCHER, JOHN W.
A Vindication of the Rev. Mr. Wesley's "Calm Address to Our American Colonies" in Some Letters to Mr. Caleb Evans. London: 1776. V. 47

FLETCHER, PHINEAS
Piscatory Eclogues, with Other Poetical Misceallanies... Edinburgh: 1771. V. 47; 49; 54
The Purple Island, or the Isle of Man... London: 1633. V. 50
The Purple Island, or the Isle of Man; Together with Piscatory Eclogs and Other Poetical Miscellanies. Cambridge: 1633. V. 47; 48; 49; 50; 54

FLETCHER, R. J.
A Short History of Hazel Grove from Olden Times. Stockport: 1901. V. 53

FLETCHER, ROBERT H.
Free Grass to Fences. The Montana Cattle Range Story. New York: 1960. V. 48; 53

FLETCHER, ROBERT SAMUEL
A History of Oberlin College from Its Foundation through the Civil War. Oberlin: 1943. V. 52

FLETCHER, THOMAS
General George Frederick Alford. Dallas: 1892. V. 54

FLETCHER, THOMAS, & CO.
Economy and Other Advantages of Gas as a Fuel for General Domestic Use. London: 1889. V. 53

FLETCHER, W. A.
Rebel Private Front and Rear: Experiences and Observations from the Early fifties and Through the Civil War. Beaumont: 1908. V. 47

FLETCHER, WILLIAM
English and American Steam Carriages and Traction Engines. London: 1904. V. 47

FLETCHER, WILLIAM J.
Philip Hagreen. The Artist and His work. 1975. V. 52

FLETCHER, WILLIAM YOUNGER
Bookbinding in England and France. London: 1897. V. 50; 53
Bookbinding in France. London: 1894. V. 49; 54
English Bookbindings in the British Museum. London: 1895. V. 47; 48; 49; 50; 51
Foreign Book-Bindings in the British Museum. London: 1896. V. 47; 48; 51

FLEURETTE, MARIE
Words of Ugo Betti. Los Angeles: 1965. V. 48; 49

FLEURIEU, CHARLES PIERRE CLARET, COMTE DE
Discoveries of the French in 1768 and 1769, to the South-East of New Guinea, with the Subsequent Visits to the Same Lands by English Navigators... London: 1791. V. 48; 53; 54
Voyage Autour du Monde, Pendant les Annees 1790, 1791, et 1792... Paris: 1798-1800. V. 50
A Voyage Round the World, Performed...the years 1790, 1791 and 1792... Amsterdam: 1969. V. 47; 49
A Voyage Round the World, Performed...Years 1790, 1791 and 1792... London: 1801. V. 47

THE FLEURON. London: 1923. V. 50; 51

THE FLEURON. London: 1923-30. V. 47; 48; 50; 51
THE FLEURON. London, Cambridge: 1923-30/70. V. 47
THE FLEURON. London: 1923/24/24/25/. V. 48

THE FLEURON. London: 1925. V. 50; 52
THE FLEURON. Cambridge: 1928. V. 52; 54

THE FLEURON. 1929-30. V. 52
THE FLEURON. 1930. V. 52

THE FLEURON. London: 1930. V. 48

THE FLEURON: A Journal of Typography. Number VII. 1930. V. 50

THE FLEURON. No. V. Cambridge: 1926. V. 50; 52

FLEURY, CLAUDE
The History, Choice and Method of Studies. London: 1695. V. 53; 54

FLEXNER, ABRAHAM
Medical Education: a Comparative Study. New York: 1925. V. 52
Medical Education in Europe. A Report to the Carnegie Foundation for the Advancement of Teaching. New York: 1912. V. 49
Prostitution in Europe. New York: 1914. V. 50

FLEXNER, JAMES THOMAS
Doctors On Horseback: Pioneeers of American Medicine. New York: 1937. V. 52
Washington: the Indispensable Man. London: 1975. V. 47

FLICKINGER, ROBERT E.
The Choctaw Freedman and the Story of Oak Hill Industrial Academy. Pittsburgh: 1914. V. 47; 51; 53

FLIGHT, EDWARD D.
The True Legend of St. Dunstan and the Devil. London: 1852. V. 49

FLIGHT, EDWARD G.
The True Legend of St. Dunstan and the Devil... London: 1852. V. 54

FLINDERS, MATTHEW
Matthew Flinder's Narrative of His Voyage in the Schooner Francis: 1798... Waltham St. Lawrence: 1798. V. 47
Matthew Flinders' Narrative of His Voyage in the Schooner Francis: 1798. Waltham St. Lawrence: 1946. V. 47; 48; 53
A Voyage to Terra Australis. Netley: 1989. V. 52

FLINN, ANDREW
A Funeral Discourse Commemorative of the Rev. Isaac S. Keith, D.D. Late One of the Pastors of the Independent or Congreagtional Church in Charleston. Charleston: 1814. V. 50

FLINT, ABEL
A System of Geometry and Trigonometry; Together with a Treatise on Surveying. Hartford: 1804. V. 50

FLINT, AUSTIN
Clinical Medicine: a Systematic Treatise of the Diagnosis and Treatment of Diseses. Philadelphia: 1879. V. 48
Collected Essays and Articles on Physiology and Medicine, 1855-1902. New York: 1903. V. 49
Handbook of Physiology for Students and Practioners of Medicine. New York: 1905. V. 47; 49; 50; 51; 53
Phthisis: its Morbid Anatomy, Etiology, Symptomatic Events in Complications, Fatality and Prognosis, Treatment and Physical Diagnosis. Philadelphia: 1875. V. 48; 51
Physical Exploration and Diagnosis of Diseases Affecting the Respiratoary Organs. Philadelphia: 1856. V. 48; 53
A Practical Treatise On the Diagnosis, Pathology and Treatment of Diseases of the Heart. Philadelphia: 1870. V. 53
A Practical Treatise on the Physical Exploration of the Chest, and the Diagnosis of Diseases Affecting the Respiratory Organs. Philadelphia: 1866. V. 48; 53
A Treatise on the Principles and Practice of Medicine. Philadelphia: 1873. V. 53

FLINT, F. S.
Economic Equilibirium. London: 1940. V. 47
In the Net of the Stars. London: 1909. V. 49
Otherworld - Cadences. London: 1920. V. 48

FLINT, ROBERT
Socialism. London: 1894. V. 54

FLINT, TIMOTHY
Francis Berrian, or the Mexican Patriot. Boston: 1926. V. 54
The History and Geography of the Mississippi Valley. Cincinnati/Boston: 1833. V. 47
The Life and Adventures of Arthur Clenning. Philadelphia: 1828. V. 54
Recollections of the Last Ten Years, Passed in Occasional Residences and Journeyings in the Valley of the Mississippi, from Pittsburg and the Missouri to the Gulf of Mexico and from Florida to the Spanish Frontier. Boston: 1826. V. 51; 54

FLINT, V. E.
A Field Guide to the Birds of the U.S.S.R. Princeton: 1984. V. 48; 50

FLINT, WILLIAM RUSSELL
Breakfast in Perigord. London: 1968. V. 49; 50; 51
Drawings. London: 1950. V. 49; 50; 51
Etchings and Dry Points. London: 1957. V. 49
In Pursuit: an Autobiography. London: 1970. V. 51
The Lisping Goddess. London: 1968. V. 49; 50; 54
The Lisping Goddess: a Figurehead Fantasy. Worcester: 1968. V. 51
Minxes Admonished or Beauty Reproved. London: 1955. V. 48
Minxes Admonished or Beauty Reproved. Waltham St. Lawrence: 1955. V. 47; 52
Models of Propriety; Occasional Caprices for the Edification of Ladies and the Delight of Gentlemen. London: 1951. V. 47; 48; 50

FLINT & WALLING MANUFACTURING CO., KENDALVILLE, INDIANA.
Star Wind Engine 1892. Kalamazoo. V. 54

FLINTOFF, EDDIE
Punting to Islip: a Long Narrative Poem. 1994. V. 52; 54

FLINTOFF, OWEN
The Rise and Progress of the Laws of England and Wales; with an Account of the Origin, History and Customs of Warlike, Domestic and Legal of the Several Nations... London: 1840. V. 51

FLINTOFT, J. JAMES
Collections of Mosses and Specimens of British Mosses from the Lake District. Keswick: 1860. V. 47; 54
Complete Collection of the British Ferns and Their Allies in the English Lake District. 1859. V. 47; 50

FLIPPER, HENRY OSSIAN
The Colored Cadet at West Point. New York: 1878. V. 47
The Western Memoirs of Henry O. Flipper 1878-1916. El Paso: 1963. V. 48

FLITTNER, C. G.
Anmuth und Schonheit Aus de Misterien der Natur und Kunst... Berlin: 1797. V. 52
Die Feyer der Liebe. Aus Einer Handschrift des Oberpriesters zu Paphos... Berlin: 1795. V. 52

FLLOYD, THOMAS
Bibliotheca Biographica: a Synopsis of Universal Biography, Ancient and Modern. London: 1760. V. 48

THE FLOATING Bear. La Jolla: 1973. V. 53

FLODNG, PER GUSTAF
Solemniteter...- Solemnites qui se Sont Passees a Stockholm...Tant a l'Enterrement de Feu Sa majeste... Stockholm: 1772. V. 49; 53

FLOIRE ET JEANNE
The Tale of King Florus and the Fair Jehane. London: 1893. V. 49

FLOOD, WARDEN
Memoirs of the Life and Correspondence of the Right Hon. Henry Flood, M.P., Colonel of the Volunteers... Dublin: 1838. V. 53

FLORA Europaea. Cambridge: 1964-80. V. 50

FLORA, the Roman Martyr. London: 1887. V. 54
FLORA, the Roman Martyr. New York: 1887. V. 54

THE FLORAL Keepsake. New York: 1854. V. 51

FLORAL World Garden Guide and Country Companion 1877. London: 1877. V. 51

FLORAL World Garden Guide and Country Companion 1879. London: 1879. V. 51

FLORE des Dames et Demoiselles. Paris: 1830. V. 50

FLORENCE & KEYPORT COMPANIES
Plan and Charter of the Florence & Keyport Joint Companies. New York: 1856. V. 53
Plan and Charters of the Florence & Keyport Companies. New York: 1853. V. 53

FLORENCE, BERTHA
The Golliwogg's Air-Ship. London: 1902. V. 47

FLORENCE CITY COMPANY
Brief of Title to the Property of the Florence City Company. Chartered by the State of New Jersey, 1849... Philadelphia: 1850. V. 47

FLORENCE: or the Aspirant. London: 1829. V. 50

FLORENCE, WILLIAM J.
The Handbook of Poker. London: 1892. V. 51

FLORENZ, K.
Poetical Greetings from the Far East. 1896. V. 50

FLORES, ANGEL
Franz Kafka. A Chronology and Bibliography. Houlton: 1944. V. 51

FLORES Historiarum. From the Creation to 1326. London: 1890. V. 49; 52

FLOREY, H. W.
Antibiotics: A Survey of Penicillin, Streptomycin and other Antimicrobial Substances From Fungi, Actinomycetes, Bacteria and Plants. Cambridge: 1949. V. 48

FLOREY, M. E.
The Clinical Application of Antibiotics. Penicillin. London: 1952. V. 48

FLOREY, M.E.
Antibiotics. A Survey of Penicillin, Streptomycin and Other Antimicrobial Substances from Fungi, Actinomycetes, Bacteria and Plans. (with) Clinical Application of Antibiotics. 1949/52. V. 50

FLORIAN, JEAN PIERRE CLARIS DE
The Adventures of Numa Pompilius, Second King of Rome. London: 1787. V. 48; 51
Galatee, Roman Pastoral: Imite de Cervantes. Paris: 1793. V. 53
The Orphan Boy; or, the Veiled Statue... London: 1810. V. 47
William Tell or the Patriot Switzerland. London: 1823. V. 47

FLORIANT & Florete. A Metrical Romance Of the Fourteenth Century. Edinburgh: 1873. V. 48

FLORIDA. UNIVERSITY. YONGE LIBRARY
Catalog of the P. K. Yonge Library of Florida History. Boston: 1977. V. 53

FLORILEGIUM Diversorum Epigrammatum In Septem Libros. Venice: 1521. V. 51

FLORINE, MARGARET
Songs of a Nurse. San Francisco: 1917. V. 50

FLORINO DE SOALROLO, LUCA
Tractatus de Prohibitione Duelli. Venice: 1610. V. 48

FLORIO, JOHN
Florio His First Fruites. (and) Florios Second Frutes. London: 1969. V. 51
Queen Anna's New World of Words, or Dictionarie of the Italian and English Tongues. Menston: 1968. V. 52

FLORIO, MICHAELANGELO
Historie de la Vita e de la Morte de...Giovanna Graia. 1607. V. 53

THE FLORIST and Garden Miscellany 1849. V. 48

FLORUS, LUCIUS ANNAEUS
L'Histoire Romaine Sommairement Comprise en Quartre Livres. Paris?: 1580. V. 49
The Roman Histories...from the Foundation of Rome Till Caesar Augustus...from thence to Trajan. London: 1621. V. 47; 50

FLORY, H. C.
An Essay on the Causes of the Indifference to the Study of Modern Languages and Literature in this Town and Vicinity... Sheffield: 1834. V. 52

FLORY, M. A.
A Book About Fans. The History of fans and Fan-Painting. New York and London: 1895. V. 50

FLORY, S. P.
Fragments of Family History. London: 1896. V. 54

FLOURENS, PIERRE
Recherches Experimentales sur Les Properietes et Les Fonctions Du Stysteme Nerveus dan Les Animaux Vertebre. Paris: 1824. V. 48; 49; 50; 51; 53

FLOWER, ALFRED
The Bookplate Annual for 1922, 1923, 1924, 1925. Kansas City: 1922-25. V. 47

FLOWER, B. O.
Fashion's Slaves. Boston: 1892. V. 53
How England Averted a Revolution of Force. Trenton: 1903. V. 50

FLOWER Emblems or the Seasons of Life. London: 1871. V. 48

FLOWER, FRANK A.
History of the Republican Party, Embracing its Origin, Growth and Mission... Springfield: 1884. V. 47

THE FLOWER Garden. London: 1838. V. 48

FLOWER, MARGARET
Victorian Jewellery. London: 1951. V. 50

FLOWER, ROBIN
Loves Bitter Sweet. 1925. V. 50; 51; 54
Love's Bitter-Sweet. Dublin: 1925. V. 51

FLOWER, W. H.
An Introduction to the Study of Mammals, Living and Extinct. London: 1891. V. 54
Recent Memoirs on the Cetacea. London: 1866. V. 47; 49

THE FLOWER-Piece: a Collection of Miscellany Poems. London: 1731. V. 47; 49; 52

THE FLOWERING of Art Nouveau by Maurice Rheims. New York: 1966. V. 53

FLOYD, JOHN B.
Protection of the Frontier of Texas. Washington: 1859. V. 49

FLOYER, CHARLES
Mr. Floyer's Case in the Late Disputes at Madras. 1778. V. 49; 51

FLOYER, JOHN
A Comment on Forty Two Histories Described by Hippocrates in the First and Third Books of His Epidemics. London: 1726. V. 54
Psychrolousia (Graece); or, the History of Cold Bathing: Both Ancient and Modern. London: 1706. V. 54
Psychroloysia (Greek); or, the History of Cold-Bathing Both Ancient and Modern...The wonderful effects of the bath-Waters, Drank Hot from the Pump. London: 1879. V. 51
Psykhrolousia (Greek): Or, The History of Cold-Bathing, Both Ancient and Modern. London: 1722. V. 50
The Sibylline Oracles. London: 1713. V. 48

FLUCKIGER, FRIEDRICH
Pharmacographia. A History of the Principal Drugs of Vegetable Origin, Met With in Great Britain and British India. London: 1874. V. 48; 52
Pharmacographia. A History of the Principal Drugs of Vegetable Origin Met With in Great Britain and British India. London: 1879. V. 48; 50; 53

FLUDD, ROBERT
Utriusque cosmi Maioris Scilicet et Minoris Metaphyscia, Physica Atque Technica Historia... (with) Tractatus Secundus de Naturae Simia seu Technica Microcosmi Historia... Oppenheim: 1617-18. V. 48

FLUGGE, C.
Micro-Organisms With Special Reference to the Etiology of the Infective Diseases. London: 1890. V. 48; 50; 51; 53

FLY-Fishing in Salt and Fresh Water. London: 1851. V. 54

FLYING' Frolic: Love Field - Dallas, Texas - Nov. 8-9. Dallas: 1918. V. 47

FLYNN, P. J.
Irrigation Canals and Other Irrigation Works... San Francisco: 1892. V. 49

FLYNT, JOSIAH
The Little Brother: A Story of Tramp Life. New York: 1902. V. 49

FOA, EDOUARD
After Big Game in Central Africa. London: 1899. V. 53

FOAN, GILBERT A.
The Art and Craft of Hairdressing. London: 1958. V. 54

FOCK, H. C. A. L.
Popular Aesthetic Considerations on the Symmetry of Pleasing Proportions. Cambridge: 1877. V. 53

THE FOCUS of Philosophy, Science and Art; or, a Critical Concentration of all the Practical Knowledge Dispersed through the Scientific Journals of the Day. London: 1821-22. V. 48

FOEMER, F.
Fauna Artica. Jena: 1900-32. V. 47

FOERSTER, HEINZ VON
Music by Computers. New York: 1969. V. 48; 50; 54

FOGELMARK, S.
Flemish and Related Panel-Stamped Bindings: Evidences and Principles. New York: 1990. V. 48

FOGERTY, J.
Robert Leeman's Daughters. London: 1889. V. 47

FOGG, L. D.
The Asbestos Society of Sinners. London: 1906. V. 48

FOGGETT, JOHN S.
The Manufacture of Steel Carriage Springs. London: 1886. V. 48

FOIRADES/FIZZLES: Echo and Allusion in the Art of Jasper Johns. Grunwald Center for the Graphic Arts, Wight Art Gallery, University of California, Los Angeles, Sept. - Nov. 1987 (& other Galleries). V. 54

FOLAN, WILLIAM J.
Coba: a Classic Maya Metropolis. New York: 1983. V. 50

FOLEY, EDWIN
The Book of Decorative Furniture. London: 1910. V. 48
The Book of Decorative Furniture: its Form, Colour & History. London. V. 49

FOLEY, FANNY, PSEUD.
Romance of the Ocean: A Narrative of the Voyage of the Wildfire to California. Philadelphia: 1850. V. 47; 54

FOLEY, HENRY
Records of the English Province of the Society of Jesus. London: 1877-83. V. 49; 54

FOLEY, PATRICK KELVIN
American Authors 1795-1895. A Bibliography of First and Notable Editions Chronologically Arranged. Boston: 1897. V. 51

FOLEY, ROBERT
Laws Relating to the Poor, From the Forty Third of Queen Elizabeth to the Third of King George II. London: 1743. V. 48

FOLEY, THOMAS P.
The Answer of the Rev. Thomas P. Foley, to the World, Who Hath Blaed His Faith in Believing It Was a Command from the Lord to Put in Print Such Parables, As He Printed Last Year... Stourbridge: 1805. V. 47; 48; 50; 51; 53

FOLIO, FRED., PSEUD.
A Book for the Times. Lucy Boston; or woman's Rights and Spiritualism... Auburn and Rochester: 1855. V. 51

FOLKARD, ARTHUR CROUCH
A Monograph of the Family of Folkard of Suffolk. London: 1892-97. V. 54

FOLKARD, H. C.
The Sailing Boat, a Treatise on Sailing Boats and Small Yachts. Stanford: 1901. V. 51
The Wildfowler. 1859. V. 54
The Wildfowler. London: 1859. V. 51; 52
The Wildfowler. London: 1875. V. 49

FOLKES, MARTIN
A Table of English Silver Coins from the Norman Conquest to the Present Time. (with) A Tables of English Gold Coins from the 18th Year of King Edward the Third, When Gold was First Coined in England, to the Present Time. London: 1745. V. 47; 50

FOLLEY, R. W.
Romantic Wycoller. A Haunt of the Brontes. Nelson: 1949. V. 53

FOLSOM, GEORGE
Mexico in 1842...To Which is Added an Account of Texas and Yucatan and of the Santa Fe Expedition. New York: 1842. V. 47; 48; 52

FOLSOM, JOSEPH FULFORD
The Municipalities of Essex County, New Jersey, 1666-1924. New York: 1925. V. 47; 49; 51

FOLSOM, W. H. C.
Fifty Years in the Northwest. St. Paul: 1888. V. 48

FOLWER, JACOB
The Journal of Jacob Fowler. New York: 1898. V. 47

FOMICHOVA, TAMARA
Venetian Painting. Florence/Moscow: 1992. V. 53

FOMON, SAMUEL
Rhinoplasty – New Concepts, Evaluation and Application. Springfield: 1970. V. 54
The Surgery of Injury and Plastic Repair. Baltimore: 1939. V. 54

FONBLANQUE, EDWARD B. DE
Political and Military Episodes in the Latter half of the Eighteenth Century Derived from the Life and Correspondence of the Right Hon. John Burgoyne, General, Statesman, Dramatist. London: 1876. V. 53

FONBLANQUE, JOHN DE GRENIER
Thoughts on the Canada Bill, Now Depending in Parliament. London: 1791. V. 47

FONDA, HENRY
Fonda: My Life. New York: 1981. V. 52

FONERDEN, C.
A Brief History of the Military Career Of Carpenter's Battery. New Market: 1911. V. 49

FONSECA, C. RISTOVAL DE
Devovt Contemplations Expressed in Two and Fortie Sermons Vpon all ye Quadragesimall Gospells... London: 1629. V. 47

FONSECA, JOAO
Satisfacam de Aggravos, e Confusam de Vingativos, por Modo de Dialogo Entre Hum Hermitam, & Hum Soldado. Evora: 1700. V. 48

FONT, FRAY PEDRO
Font's Complete Diary; a Chronicle of the Founding of San Francisco. Berkeley: 1933. V. 48
San Francisco Bay and California in 1776. Providence: 1911. V. 49

FONTAINE, JAMES
Memoirs of a Huguenot Family. London: 1890. V. 52

FONTANON, DENIS
De Morborum Internorum Curatione Libri III. Venice: 1553. V. 48; 49

FONTELLE, BERNARD LE BOVIER DE
A Plurality of Worlds. London: 1688. V. 52

FONTENELLE, BERNARD LE BOVIER DE
Conversations on the Plurality of Worlds. London: 1808. V. 52
Fontenelle's Dialogues of the Dead in Three Parts. London: 1708. V. 52
The History of the Oracles, and the Cheats of the Pagan Priests. London: 1688. V. 47; 49
A Plurality of Worlds. 1929. V. 54
A Plurality of Worlds. London: 1929. V. 47; 48; 50; 52; 53; 54

FONTERIZ, LUIS DE
Red Terror in Madrid. London: 1937. V. 49

FOORD, A.
Catalogue of Fossil Cephalopoda in the British Museum. London: 1888-1934. V. 49; 52

FOORD, J.
Decorative Plant and Flower Studies for the Use of Artists, Designers, Students and Others. London: 1906. V. 54

FOOT, JESSE
The Life of John Hunter. London: 1794. V. 52

FOOT, MIRJAM M.
The Henry Davis Gift. London: 1978-83. V. 50
The Henry Davis Gift: a Collection of Bookbindings. Volume 1, Studies in the History of Bookbinding. London: 1978. V. 52
The Henry Davis Gift: a Collection of Bookbindings. Volume 1, Studies in the History of Bookbinding. London: 1982. V. 49
The Henry Davis Gift, a Collection of Bookbindings. Volume II. A Catalogue of North-European Bindings. London: 1983. V. 49
The Henry Davis Gift. I: Studies in the History of Bookbinding. II. A Catalogue of North European Bookbindings. London: 1978-82. V. 50

FOOTE, ANDREW H.
Africa and the American Flag. New York: 1854. V. 48; 51

FOOTE, HENRY GRANT, MRS.
Recollections of Central America and the West coast of Africa. London: 1869. V. 52

FOOTE, HENRY S.
Texas and the Texans. Philadelphia: 1841. V. 51

FOOTE, HENRY STUART
The Bench and Bar of the South and Southwest. St. Louis: 1876. V. 50
Casket of Reminiscences. Washington: 1874. V. 54

FOOTE, HORACE S.
Pen Pictures from the Garden of the World, or Santa Clara County, California. Chicago: 1888. V. 53

FOOTE, HORTON
Harrison, Texas. New York: 1956. V. 50; 52; 53; 54

FOOTE, JULIA A.
A Brand Plucked from the Fire. Cleveland: 1879. V. 53

FOOTE, MARY HALLOCK
The Desert and the Sown. Boston and New York: 1902. V. 49; 53; 54
John Bodewin's Testimony. Boston: 1886. V. 51

FOOTE, SAMUEL
Bon-Mots of Samuel Foote and Theodore Hook. London: 1894. V. 52

FOOTE, SAMUEL continued
The Dramatic Works. London. V. 49; 54
The Dramatic Works. London: 1765. V. 49; 53
The Dramatic Works. London: 1797?. V. 47; 50; 54
The Dramatic Works... London: 1805. V. 49
A Letter from Mr. Foote, to The Reverend Author of the Remarks, Critical and Christian, on the Minor. London: 1760. V. 53
A Treatise on the Passion, so Far as They Regard the Stage... London: 1747. V. 52

FOOTE, SHELBY
The Civil War. A Narrative. New York: 1958-63-74. V. 48; 49; 50; 52
Jordan County. New York: 1954. V. 54
Love in a Dry Season. New York: 1951. V. 48; 50; 54
Tournament. New York: 1949. V. 47; 48
A View of History. 1981. V. 47

FOOTE, WILLIAM HENRY
Sketches of North Carolina, Historical and Biographical Illustrative of the Principles of a Portion of Her Early Settlers. New York: 1846. V. 48; 50
Sketches of Virginia, Historical and Biographical. Philadelphia: 1850/55. V. 52; 54

FOR Aaron Copland. 1978. V. 47; 48

FOR Britain's Soldiers - a Contribution to the Needs of Our Fighting men and Their Families. London: 1900. V. 50

FOR David Gascoyne on His Sixty-Fifth Birthday - 10 October 1981. London: 1981. V. 49

FOR Ladies & Gentlemen. "Your Manners May Be Your Fortune". True Politeness: or, Good Behaviour and Social Etiquette Guide. London: 1875. V. 47

FOR Love of the King. A Burmese Masque in Three Acts and Nine Scenes. 1921. V. 52

FOR Reynolds Price. Winston-Salem: 1983. V. 53

FOR Reynolds Price: 1 February 1983. 1983. V. 48; 51

FOR Robert Penn Warren. 24-IV-80. 1980. V. 47; 49

FOR Shop Use Only: Curwen & Dent Stock Blocks and Devices. Devizes: 1993. V. 52

FOR the Occasion of Dean. Poems. Iowa City: 1981. V. 54

FOR the Occasion of Death. Iowa City: 1981. V. 50

FOR W. H. Auden. New York: 1972. V. 50

FORAN, R.
A Breath of the Wilds. 1958. V. 54

FORBERG, F. C.
The Manual of Classical Erotology. London: 1887. V. 48

FORBES, ALEXANDER
California: A History of Upper and Lower California. London: 1839. V. 47; 48; 49; 50; 52; 54
California: a History of Upper and Lower California. San Francisco: 1929. V. 48
California: a History of Upper and Lower California. San Francisco: 1937. V. 48; 49; 50; 52; 53; 54
Northernmost Labrador Mapped From the air. New York: 1938. V. 51

FORBES, ALEXANDER P.
Kalendars of Scottish Saints. Edinburgh: 1872. V. 49; 50; 51

FORBES, ALLAN
Sport in Norfolk County. Boston: 1938. V. 50
Yankee Ship Sailing Cards, Presenting Reproductions of Some of the Colorful Cards Announcing Ship Sailings. Boston: 1948/49/52. V. 48; 54

FORBES, ANNA
Insulinde. Edinburgh: 1887. V. 53

FORBES, ARCHIBALD
Battles of the Nineteenth Century. London: 1896-97. V. 50
Chinese Gordon. London: 1884. V. 54
My Experiences of the War Between France and Germany. London: 1871. V. 52

FORBES, BRYAN
Truth Lies Sleeping. London: 1950. V. 48

FORBES, CHARLES
Prize Essay: Vancouver Island: its Resources and Capabilities, as a Colony. Victoria: 1862. V. 47; 50

FORBES, CHARLES S.
Iceland: its Volcanoes, Geysers and Glaciers. London: 1860. V. 54

FORBES, DUNCAN
A Grammar of the Hindustani Language. London: 1862. V. 52
Reflexions on the Sources of Incredulity with regard to Religion. Edinburgh: 1750. V. 47

FORBES, E.
A History of British Mollusca and Their Shells. London: 1848-53. V. 48; 49; 50; 52; 53
A History of British Mollusca and Their Shells. London: 1853. V. 51; 54
A Monograph of the British Naked-Eyed Medusae. London: 1848. V. 49
The Tertiary Fluvio-Marine Formation of the Isle of Wight. London: 1856. V. 51

FORBES, EDWIN
Army Sketchbook. New York: 1890. V. 50
Life Studies of the Great Army. New York: 1876. V. 47; 53

FORBES, ELIZABETH STANHOPE
King Arthur's Wood. London: 1905. V. 50

FORBES, ESTHER
Johnny Tremain: a Story of Boston in Revolt. Boston: 1943. V. 51
A Mirror for Witches. Boston: 1928. V. 54

FORBES, HENRY O.
A Hand-Book to the Primates. London: 1894. V. 49
A Naturalist's Wanderings in the Eastern Archipelago. London: 1885. V. 52; 53
A Naturalist's Wanderings in the Eastern Archipelago. New York: 1885. V. 47; 48; 50
New Guinea; Attempted Ascent of Mount Owen Stanley. Edinburgh: 1888. V. 50

FORBES, HUGH
Extracts from the Manual for the Patriotic Volunteer on Active Service in Regular and Irregular War,... New York: 1857. V. 53

FORBES, J.
Hortus Ericaeus Woburnensis, or a Catalogue of the Heaths in the Collection of the Duke of Bedford at Woburn Abbey. London: 1825. V. 49; 53

FORBES, J. D.
An Account of Some Experiments on the Electricity of Tourmaline and Other Minerals, When Exposed to Heat. Edinburgh: 1834. V. 53
The Glacier Theory; Papers on Glaciers; On the Remarkable Structure Observed...In the Ice of Glaciers; Fourth Letter on the Glacier Theory. Edinburgh: 1842-43. V. 53
Occasional Papers on the Theory of Glaciers. Edinburgh: 1859. V. 47
Travels Through the Alps. 1900. V. 48; 53

FORBES, JAMES
Letters From France, Written in the Years 1803 & 1804. London: 1806. V. 47
Oriental Memoirs: a Narrative of Seventeen Years Residence in India. London: 1834. V. 49
Pinetum Woburnense; or, a Catalogue of Coniferous Plants, in the Collection of the Duke of Bedford, at Woburn Abbey... 1839. V. 50
Pinetum Woburnense; or, a Catalogue of Coniferous Plants, in the Collection of the Duke of Bedford, at Woburn Abbey... London: 1839. V. 48
The Tour of Mont Blanc and Monte Rosa. Edinburgh: 1855. V. 48

FORBES, JOHN
Of Nature and Art in the Cure of Disease. London: 1857. V. 48; 53
Original Cases with Dissections and Observations Illustrating the Use of the Stethoscope and Percussion in the Diagnosis of Diseases of the Chest... London: 1824. V. 53

FORBES, KATHRYN
Transfer Point. New York: 1947. V. 48

FORBES, MALCOLM
Around the World on Hot Air and Two Wheels. New York: 1985. V. 53; 54

FORBES, R. G.
Greenwich Observatory: the Royal Observatory at Greenwich and Herstmonceux, 1675-1975. London: 1975. V. 51

FORBES, R. J.
Studies in Ancient Technology. Leiden: 1955-58. V. 48
Studies in Ancient Technology. Volume VIII and IX. Londoneiden: 1971. V. 50

FORBES, ROBERT BENNET
Personal Reminiscences. Boston: 1876. V. 47; 50
Personal Reminiscences. Boston: 1892. V. 51

FORBES, ROBERT BENNETT
The Voyage of the Jamestown on Her Errand of Mercy. Boston: 1847. V. 54

FORBES, ROBERT H.
The Penningtons Pioneers of Early Arizona. 1919. V. 49; 54

FORBES, ROSITA
Conflict. Angora to Afghanistan. London: 1931. V. 50; 51

FORBES, S. A.
The Fishes of Illinois. Urbana: 1908. V. 50; 51

FORBES, WILLIAM
A Treatise of Church-Lands and Tithes: in Two Parts. Edinburgh: 1705. V. 51

FORBES, WILLIAM ALEXANDER
In Memoriam. The Collected Scientific Papers of... London: 1885. V. 52; 53

FORBES-LEITH, WILLIAM
The Life of Saint Cuthbert... Edinburgh: 1888. V. 47
Narratives of Scottish Catholics Under Mary Stuart and James VI Now First Printed from the Original Manuscripts in the Secret Archives of the Vatican and Other Collections. London: 1889. V. 54

FORBES-MITCHELL, WILLIAM
Reminiscences of the Great Mutiny 1857-59... London: 1897. V. 54

FORBES-ROBERTSON, DIANA
The Battle of Waterloo Road. New York: 1941. V. 49

FORBUSH, E. H.
Birds of Massachusetts and Other New England States. Boston: 1925-27-29. V. 49; 50; 53; 54

FORBUSH, EDWARD HOWE
Birds of Massachusetts and Other New England States. London: 1925-29. V. 49

FORCE, PETER
The Declaration of Independence, or Notes on Lord Mahon's History of the American Declaration of Independence. London: 1855. V. 50
Tracts and Other Papers, Relating Principally to the Origin, Settlement and Progress of the Colonies in North America from the Discovery of the Country to the Year 1776. Washington: 1838/44/46. V. 47; 50; 52

FORCHE, CAROLYN
The Country Between Us. Port Townsend: 1981. V. 54

FORD, ALICE
Audubon's Animals. The Quadrupeds of North America. 1951. V. 51

FORD, ANNA FOSTER
Foster, Ford, Sampson and Allied Families. New York: 1930. V. 49

FORD, ARTHUR PERONNEAU
Life in the Confederate Army Being Personal Experiences of a Private Soldier in the Confederate Army By Arthur P. Ford and Some Experiences and Sketches of Southern Life by Marion Johnstone Ford. New York: 1905. V. 47

FORD, CHARLES HENRI
The Garden of Disorder and Other Poems. Norfolk: 1937. V. 54
A Night with Jupiter. New York: 1945. V. 51
Om Krishna III: Secret Haiku. New York: 1982. V. 52; 54

FORD, DAVID EVERARD
Observations on Psalmody. London: 1827. V. 49

FORD, EDWARD
Bibliography of Australian Medicine, 1790-1900. Sydney: 1976. V. 52

FORD, FORD MADOX
Ancient Lights and Certain New Reflections. London: 1911. V. 49
Antwerp. London: 1914. V. 50; 51
Between St. Dennis and St. George. A Sketch of Three Civilisations. London: 1915. V. 47; 54
The Brown Owl: a Fairy Story. London: 1892. V. 49
Buckshee. Cambridge: 1966. V. 47
A Call: the Tale of Two Passions. London: 1910. V. 53
The Critical Attitude. London: 1911. V. 54
The English Novel. Philadelphia: 1929. V. 48
The Feather. London: 1892. V. 48; 53
The Fifth Queen!. London: 1906. V. 51
Ford Madox Brown - a Record of His Life and Work. London: 1896. V. 49; 51; 53
Great Trade Route. New York: 1937. V. 47; 48
The Heart of the Country. London: 1906. V. 53
Henry for Hugh. Philadelphia: 1934. V. 52
Henry James: a Critical Study. New York: 1916. V. 50
High Germany. London: 1911. V. 51
It Was the Nightingale. Philadelphia: 1933. V. 49; 53
Ladies Whose Bright Eyes - a Romance. London: 1911. V. 51
The Last Post. 1928. V. 49
Last Post. London: 1928. V. 47
The Last Post. New York: 1928. V. 50
A Little Less than Gods. London: 1928. V. 53
A Man Could Stand Up. London: 1926. V. 48; 49; 50; 51; 52
The March of Literature. From Confucius' Day to Our Own. New York: 1938. V. 50; 52; 54
Mister Bosphorus and the Muse. London: 1923. V. 48; 51; 53
Mr. Fleight. London: 1913. V. 48
The Nature of a Crime. New York: 1924. V. 48
New Poems. New York: 1927. V. 49
New York Essays. New York: 1927. V. 51; 52
New York Is Not America. New York: 1927. V. 48
No More Parades: a Novel. London: 1925. V. 53
The Panel: a Sheer Comedy. London: 1912. V. 54
Portraits From Life: Memories and Criticisms. Boston: 1937. V. 48
Provence. From Minstrels to the Machine. Philadelphia: 1935. V. 52
The Rash Act. New York: 1933. V. 48; 51
Ring for Nancy. Indianapolis: 1913. V. 50
Rossetti: a Critical Essay on His Art. London. V. 51
Selected Poems. Cambridge: 1971. V. 51; 52
The Shifting of the Fire. London: 1892. V. 49; 54
Some Do Not... London: 1924. V. 52
Some Do Not. New York: 1924. V. 48
Songs From London. London: 1910. V. 47; 53
The Soul of London. London: 1905. V. 48; 51
Thus to Revisit. London: 1921. V. 49
Women and Men. Paris: 1923. V. 50; 53
The Young Lovell: a Romance. London: 1913. V. 54
Zeppelin Nights - a London Entertainment. London: 1916. V. 47

FORD, GERALD R.
Churchill Lecture. Northridge: 1980. V. 51
Churchill Lecture. Northridge: 1984. V. 48; 49
Global Stability. Northridge: 1981. V. 49
Humor and the Presidency. New York: 1987. V. 49; 54
The Tenth Convention. Northridge: 1988. V. 48; 49; 51
A Time to Heal. New York: 1979. V. 51; 54
Untitled. Northridge. V. 48
A Vision for America. Northridge: 1980. V. 47; 49; 50; 54
The War Powers Resolution: A Constitutional Crisis?. 1992. V. 49

FORD, GUS L.
Texas Cattle Brands. Dallas: 1936. V. 48; 53
Texas Cattle Brands. Dallas: 1958. V. 50

FORD, H. J.
The Olive Fairy Book. London: 1907. V. 54

FORD, H. L.
Shakespeare 1700-1740, a Collation of the Editions and Separate Plays with some Account of T. Johnson and R. Walker. New York: 1968. V. 52

FORD, HELEN C.
Notes Of a Tour in India and Ceylon During the Winter of 1888-89. London: 1889. V. 48; 54

FORD, HENRY CHAPMAN
An Artist Records the California Missions. San Francisco: 1989. V. 52; 54

FORD, HORACE A.
Archery, It's Theory and Practice. London: 1856. V. 52; 54
The Theory and Practice of Archery. London: 1887. V. 51

FORD, JAMES A.
A Comparison of Formative Cultures in the Americas. Diffusion or the Psychic Unity of Man. Washington: 1969. V. 48; 50

FORD, JAMES W.
The Negro and the Democratic Front. New York: 1938. V. 51

FORD, JOHN
The Dramatic Works. London: 1827. V. 47
The Works... London: 1895. V. 52; 53

FORD, JOHN S. FORD
Origin and Fall of the Alamo...March 6, 1836. 1895/94. V. 47

FORD, JOHN SALMON
Rip Ford's Texas. Austin: 1963. V. 49

FORD, JULIA ELLSWORTH
Imagina. New York: 1914. V. 49; 54
Snickerty Nick and the Giant. New York: 1919. V. 49; 51

FORD, LAETITIA
The Butterfly Collector's Vade Mecum. Ipswich: 1824. V. 54
The Butterfly Collector's Vade Mecum. Ipswich: 1827. V. 54

FORD, LEWIS
The Variety Book, Containing Life Sketches and Reminiscences. Boston: 1892. V. 54

FORD, MARGARET L.
Christ, Plato, Hermes Trismegistus. The Dawn of Printing. Catalogue of the Incunabula in the Bibliotheca Philosophica Hermetica. Amsterdam: 1990. V. 50

FORD, PAUL LEICESTER
Franklin Bibliography. Brooklyn: 1889. V. 47; 49; 51; 52
Franklin Bibliography. New York: 1889. V. 50
The Great K. & A. (Train) Robbery. New York: 1897. V. 54
The Journals of Hugh Gaine, Printer. New York: 1902. V. 48
Love Finds the Way. New York: 1904. V. 48
Monographs of the American Revolution: Thomas Jefferson. Cambridge: 1904. V. 52
The New England Primer. A History of Its Origin and Development... New York: 1897. V. 50; 52
Wanted - a Match Maker. New York: 1900. V. 48; 50
Webster Geneology. Brooklyn: 1876. V. 47

FORD, RICHARD
Communist. Derry: 1987. V. 51
English Magnolias. 1992. V. 53
A Hand-Book for Travellers in Spain... London: 1845. V. 49
Independence Day. New Orleans: 1995. V. 53; 54
Independence Day. New York: 1995. V. 53; 54
Juke Joint. Jackson: 1990. V. 48; 51; 53
My Mother, in Memory. Elmwood: 1988. V. 48; 50; 53; 54
A Piece of My Heart. New York: 1976. V. 47; 48; 49; 50; 51; 52; 53; 54
The Sportswriter. New York. V. 49
The Sportswriter. New York: 1986. V. 51; 52; 53
The Ultimate Good Luck. Boston: 1981. V. 47; 48; 50; 52; 53; 54
Wildlife. New York: 1990. V. 47; 48; 49; 52; 53; 54
Wildlife. New York: 1991. V. 51

FORD, ROCHESTER
Tucson, Arizona. Tucson: 1902. V. 52

FORD, SIMON
A Discourse Concerning Gods Judgements: Resolving Many Weighty Questions and Cases Relating to Them... London: 1678. V. 48; 52
Londini Quod Reliquum. Or, London's Remains... London: 1667. V. 49

FORD, THOMAS
A Chalice of Castalian Dew. London: 1873. V. 51
A History of Illinois, from Its commencement as a State in 1818 to 1847. Chicago: 1854. V. 53
Trout Fishing. London: 1881. V. 48; 53

FORD, TREVOR D.
Limestones and Caves of the Peak District. Norwich: 1977. V. 54

FORD, WILLIAM
A Description of Scenery in the Lake District Intended as a Guide to Strangers. Carlisle: 1839. V. 52

FORD, WORTHINGTON CHAUNCEY
George Washington. Paris: 1900. V. 54

FORDE, D.
Select Annotated Bibliography of Tropical Africa. New York: 1956. V. 51

FORDE, EMANUEL
The Famous and Pleasant History of Parismus, the Valiant and Renowned Prince of Bohemia. London: 1790. V. 47

FORDE, GERTRUDE
Driven Before the Storm. London: 1887. V. 54
Geoff. London: 1889. V. 54

FORDE, H. A.
The Fruit of the Spirit. London: 1919. V. 50; 52

FORDHAM, ELIAS PYM
Personal Narrative of Travels in Virginia, Maryland, Pennsylvania, Ohio, Indiana, Kentucky and of a Residence in the Illinois Territory: 1817-1818. Cleveland: 1906. V. 53

FORDHAM, MARY WESTON
Magnolia Leaves. Charleston: 1897. V. 53

FORDRIN, LOUIS
Nouveau Livre de Serrurerie...(with) Livre de Serrurerie de Composition Angloise. Paris: 1723 & n.d. V. 53

FORDTRAN, WILLIAM M.
History of the Order of the Alamo: 1926-1939. V. 49

FORDYCE, ALEXANDER DINGWALL
Family Record of the Name of Dingwall Fordyce, in Aberdeenshire... Toronto: 1885. V. 54

FORDYCE, GEORGE
Elements of Agriculture. Edinburgh?: 1765?. V. 53
Elements of the Practice of Physic, in Two Parts. London: 1777. V. 51
Elements of the Practice of Physic, In Two Parts. London: 1791. V. 53
Five Dissertations on Fever... Boston: 1815. V. 54
Five Dissertations on Fever. Boston: 1823. V. 51
A Treatise On the Digestion of Food. London: 1791. V. 53

FORDYCE, JAMES
Addresses to the Deity. London: 1785. V. 50
Sermons to Young Women. London: 1769. V. 48

FORDYCE, T.
Local Records or, Historical Register of Remarkable Events, Which Have Occurred in Northumberland and Durham, Newcastle-Upon-Tyne, and Berwick-Upon-Tweed... Newcastle-upon-Tyne: 1867. V. 50

FORDYCE, W.
A History of Coal, Coke and Coal Fields and the Manufacture of Iron in the North of England. Newcastle: 1973. V. 53

FOREEST, PIETER VAN
Observationum & Curationum Medicinalium de Febribus Ephemeris et Continuis Libri Duo. (with) Observationum et Curationum Medicinalium Libri Tres... (with) Observataionum & Curationum Medicinalium de Febribus Publice Grassantibus... Leiden: 1593/91/91. V. 52
Observationum et Curationum Medicinalium Liber Decimus-Octavus, de Ventriculi Affectibus....(with) Observationum & Curationum Medicinalium Liber XIX de Hepatis Malis ac Affectibus... Leiden: 1594/95. V. 52
Observationum et Curationum Medicinalium Libri Quinque; Nempe XI. De Morbis Oculorum & Palpebrarum. XII. De Aurium Morbis. XIII. De Nasi Affectibus. XIV. De Aegritudinibus Labiorum, Gingivarum... Leiden: 1591. V. 52
Petri Foresti Alcmariani Observationum et Curationum Chirurgicarum Libri Quinque, de Tumoribus Praeter Naturam. (with) Observationum et Curationum Chirurgicarum Libri Quatuor Posteriores... Leiden: 1610/10. V. 52

FOREMAN, CHARLES
A Letter to the Right Honourable Sir Robert Walpole, for Re-Establishing the Woollen Manufactures of Great Britain Upon Their Ancient Footing... London: 1732. V. 52

FOREMAN, GRANT
The Adventures of James Collier: First Collector of the Port of San Francisco. Chicago: 1937. V. 52; 54
Indian Removal. Norman: 1956. V. 50
The Last Trek of the Indians. Chicago: 1946. V. 51
A Traveler in Indian Territory ... Cedar Rapids: 1930. V. 53; 54

FOREMAN, HARRY E.
Conodoguinet Secrets./North Mountain Shadows and Loudon Road History./ Forbes Road. Parnell's Knob to Burnt Cabins./ History of the Little Cove./Conococheague Headwaters of the Amberson Valley. Fort Loudon Sidelights./Tuscarora, Kittochtinny & North... Chambersburg: 1971. V. 51

FOREMAN, JOHN
The Philippine Islands. London: 1899. V. 48

FOREPAUGH, ADAM
The Progress of Civilization Thrilling Incidents in Actual Border Life in the Wild West. 1887. V. 52

FORES'S Sporting Notes and Sketches. London: 1885-1912. V. 47; 51

FOREST, LOUIS EFFINGHAM DE
Louisbourg Journals, 1745. New York: 1932. V. 48

FOREST, PIETER
Observations et Histories Chyrvrgiqves Tirees des Oeuvres de Qvatre Excellens Medecins... Geneve: 1669. V. 49

FOREST, THOMAS
A Voyage to New Guinea, and the Moluccas, from Balambangan... London: 1779. V. 50

FORESTA, M. A.
George Tooker. 1983. V. 53; 54

FORESTER, CECIL SCOTT
The African Queen. Boston: 1935. V. 47; 49
The Annie Marble in Germany. London: 1930. V. 48; 49; 51
The Barbary Pirates. New York: 1953. V. 52
The Bedchamber Mystery. Toronto: 1944. V. 48; 50; 51
Brown on Resolution. London: 1929. V. 48; 51
The Earthly Paradise. London: 1940. V. 48; 51; 52
Flying Colours. London: 1938. V. 47; 48; 52
The General. Boston: 1936. V. 50
The Gun. London: 1933. V. 48
The Happy Return. London: 1937. V. 47; 51
Horatio Hornblower. London: 1925. V. 51
The Hornblower Companion. London: 1964. V. 48; 49; 50; 51; 52; 53
Josephine, Napoleon's Empress. London: 1925. V. 47; 48; 50
Josephine Napoleon's Empress. New York: 1925. V. 48
Lord Hornblower. Boston: 1946. V. 52
Lord Hornblower. London: 1946. V. 50
Lord Nelson. 1929. V. 50
Lord Nelson. Indianapolis: 1929. V. 48; 51
Louis XIV. 1928. V. 49
Marionettes at Home. London: 1936. V. 48; 51; 53
Napoleon and His Court. London: 1924. V. 48; 49
One Wonderful Week. Indianapolis: 1927. V. 48; 51
Payment Deferred. London: 1926. V. 51
Payment Deferred. 1942. V. 53
Payment Deferred. Boston: 1942. V. 48; 51
Poo-Poo and the Dragon. Boston: 1942. V. 51; 52
Ship of the Line. Boston: 1938. V. 49
Single-Handed. New York: 1929. V. 48; 51
To the Indies. Boston: 1940. V. 48
U 97. A Play. London: 1931. V. 48
Victor Emmanuel II and the Union of Italy. London: 1927. V. 48; 49

FORESTER, THOMAS
Norway in 1848 and 1849; Containing Rambles Among the Fjelds and Fjords of the Central and Western Districts... London: 1850. V. 51
Rambles in the Islands of Corsica and Sardinia. London: 1861. V. 52

FORESTI, JACOPO FILIPPO DA BERGAMO
De Memorabilibvs et Claris Mvlieribvs...Opera.. Paris: 1521. V. 48; 52

FORESTIERE Illuminato Intorno le Cose Piu Rare e Curiose antiche e Moderne della Citta di Venezia... Venice: 1740. V. 53

FORGET Me Not: A Christmas and New Year's Present for MDCCCXXVII. London: 1826. V. 49

FORGUE, NORMAN W.
Bibliography of Miniature Books and Ephemera 1961-1977. Skokie: 1977. V. 51

FORINTI, PIETRO
La Terza Giornata Delle Novelle De' Novizi. Siena: 1811/21?. V. 50

FORLORN Anna, a Poem. Dublin: 1821. V. 54

A FORM of Prayer, to be Used on Friday the Eleventh of April, Being the Fast-Day Appointed by the Kings Proclamation to Seek Reconciliation with Almighty God. London: 1679. V. 53

FORMAGGIO, DINO
A Book of Miniatures. New York: 1962. V. 47

FORMAN, HENRY BUXTON
Between the Lines. Letters and Memoranda Interchanged by H. Buxton Forman and Thomas J. Wise. Austin: 1945. V. 47; 53
The Books of William Morris Described With Some Account of His Doings in Literature and in the Allied Crafts. Chicago: 1897. V. 51
Elizabeth Barrett Browning and Her Scarcer Books. London: 1896. V. 48
The Shelley Library. An Essay in Bibliography. London: 1886. V. 51

FORMAN, HENRY CHANDLEE
Early Manor and Plantation Houses of Maryland: an Architectural and Historical Compendium, 1634-1800. Easton & Haverford: 1934. V. 48; 51

FORMAN, MAURICE BUXTON
A Bibliography of the Writings in Prose and Verse of Geroge Meredith. (with) Meredithiana, Being a Supplement to the Bibliography of Meredith. Edinburgh: 1922-24. V. 48; 50

FORMENI, LORENZO
Indice de' Teatrali Spettacoli... Milan: 1789. V. 52

FORNANDER, ABRAHAM
An Account of the Polynesian Race; Its origin & Migrations and the Ancient History of the Hawaiian People to the Times of Kamehameha I. London: 1880-90. V. 51
Fornander Collection of Hawaiian Antiquities and Folk-Lore. Honolulu: 1916-20. V. 53

FORNARO, CARLO DE
John Wenger. New York: 1925. V. 52
Millionaires of America. Caricatures. New York: 1902. V. 50

FORNEY, JOHN W.
What I Saw in Texas. Philadelphia: 1872. V. 53

FORNEY, MATTHIAS N.
The Car-Builder's Dictionary. New York: 1884. V. 51

FORRER, LEONARD
Biographical Dictionary of Medallists, Coin, Gem and Seal-Engravers, Mint Masters &c. Ancient and Modern, With References to Their Works, B.C. 500 - A.D. 1900. Maastricht: 1980. V. 48
Descriptive Catalogue of the Collection of Greek Coins Formed by Sir Hermann Weber. New York: 1975. V. 48

FORREST, CHARLES RAMUS
A Picturesque Tour Along the Rivers Ganges and Jumna in India... London: 1824. V. 47; 48

FORREST, EARLE R.
Arizona's Dark and Bloody Ground. Caldwell: 1936. V. 53; 54
Lone War Trail of Apache Kid. Pasadena: 1947. V. 52; 53
Missions and Pueblos of the Old Southwest. Cleveland: 1929. V. 48; 50; 53; 54

FORREST, EBENEZER
An Account of What Seemed Most Remarkable in the Five Days Peregrination of the Five Following Persons... London: 1782. V. 48
Hogarth's Frolic. London: 1872. V. 49

FORREST, FENN
The Beat of the Drum and The Whoop of the Dance. New Mexico: 1983. V. 47

FORREST, G.
Details of Specimens of Rhododendrons found by Mr. G. Forrest in 1917, (1921; 1922; 1925). London: 1920-30. V. 47
The Journeys and Plant Introductions of George Forrest. London: 1952. V. 52

FORREST, H. E.
The Fauna of Shropshire Being an Account of All the Mammals, Birds, Reptiles and Fishes Found in the County of Salop. Shrewsbury: 1899. V. 48
The Vertebrate Fauna of North Wales. London: 1840. V. 50
The Vertebrate Fauna of North Wales. London: 1907. V. 47; 48; 54

FORREST, JOHN
Explorations in Australia. London: 1875. V. 52

FORREST, LEON
The Bloodworth Orphans. New York: 1977. V. 52
Divine Days. Chicago: 1992. V. 51

FORRESTER, ALFRED HENRY
The Pickwickians. London: 1837. V. 49; 54
Pictures Picked from the Pickwick Papers. London: 1838. V. 52
Saint George and the Dragon: a Fact. V. 51
Seymour's Humorous Sketches. London: 1843. V. 48
Seymour's Sketches. London: 1838. V. 50
Strange Surprising Adventures of the Venerable Gooroo Simple, and His Five Disciplines... London: 1861. V. 49
The Tutor's Assistant, or Comic Figures of Arithmetic... London: 1843. V. 49; 52

FORRESTER, CHARLES ROBERT
Eccentric Tales, From the German. London: 1827. V. 49

FORRESTER, JAMES
The Polite Philosopher; or, an Essay On that Art Which Makes a Man Happy in Himself, and Agreeable to Others. Dublin: 1734. V. 50; 52
The Polite Philosopher; or, an Essay on that Art Which Makes a Man Happy in Himself, and Agreeable to Others. Edinburgh: 1734. V. 52

FORRESTER, MRS.
My Lord and My Lady. London: 1882. V. 50; 54
Viva. London: 1878. V. 54

FORSHAW, CHARLES F.
The Poets of Keighley, Bingley, Hawaorth and District. 1891. V. 54

FORSHAW, JOSEPH M.
Australian Parrots. Melbourne: 1969. V. 49
Australian Parrots. Wynnewood: 1969. V. 54
Australian Parrots. 1972. V. 54
Birds of Paradise and Bower Birds. Sydney: 1977. V. 52
Kingfishers and Related Birds. Melbourne: 1983-92. V. 51
Kingfishers and Related Birds. Part 1. Alcedinidae. Melbourne: 1983-85. V. 48
Parrots of the World. Garden City: 1973. V. 50; 51; 54
Parrots of the World. London: 1973. V. 50
Parrots of the World. Melborune: 1973. V. 48; 52; 53
Parrots of the World. New York: 1973. V. 49
Parrots of the World. London: 1989. V. 49; 52
Parrots of the World. London: 1990. V. 50; 51

FORSKAL, P.
Flora Aegyptiaco-Arabica sive Descriptiones Plantarum Quas Aegyptum Inferiorem et Arabiam Felicem... Copenhagen: 1775. V. 54

FORSTER, CHARLES
Sinai Photographed: or, Contemporary Records of Israel in the Wilderness... London: 1862. V. 50

FORSTER, EDWARD
Occasional Amusements (in verse). London: 1809. V. 54

FORSTER, EDWARD MORGAN
Abinger, Harvest. London: 1936. V. 48; 51
Abinger Harvest. New York: 1936. V. 51
Alexandria. Alexandria: 1922. V. 51
Alexandria. London: 1922. V. 54
Alexandria. Alexandria: 1938. V. 49; 52
Alexandria. London: 1938. V. 48
Anonymity. London: 1925. V. 51; 53
Aspects of the Novel. London: 1927. V. 48; 49; 51
Battersea Rise. New York: 1955. V. 48; 52; 54
The Celestial Omnibus. London: 1911. V. 51; 54
Commonplace Book. London: 1978. V. 48
The Eternal Moment. 1928. V. 48; 50; 52
The Eternal Moment. London: 1928. V. 47; 48; 49; 50
Forster's Letters to Donald Windham. New York/Verona: 1975. V. 50; 53
The Government of Egypt. London: 1920. V. 47; 48; 51
Howard's End. London: 1910. V. 52
A Letter to Madan Blanchard. London: 1931. V. 51; 53
The Longest Journey. Edinburgh: 1907. V. 51; 52
The Longest Journey. London: 1907. V. 49
Marianne Thornton 1797-1887. London: 1956. V. 48
A Passage to India. London: 1924. V. 47; 48; 49; 50; 51; 52; 54
Passage to India. New York: 1924. V. 53
A Passage to India. Toronto: 1924. V. 52; 54
A Passage to India. London: 1925. V. 51
Pharos and Pharillon. Richmond: 1923. V. 48; 49; 50; 51
Pharos and Pharillon. Surrey: 1923. V. 48
A Room With a View. London: 1908. V. 47; 51
Sinclair Lewis Interprets America. Cambridge: 1932. V. 51
The Story of the Siren. London: 1920. V. 49
The Story of the Siren. Richmond: 1920. V. 51; 53
A View Without a Room. 1973. V. 52
Virginia Woolf. New York: 1942. V. 51; 53
What I Believe. London: 1939. V. 50
Where Angels Fear to Tread. Edinburgh: 1905. V. 51
Where Angels Fear to Tread. New York: 1920. V. 52
Where Angels Fear to Tread. Boston & Toronto: 1965. V. 51

FORSTER, FRANK J.
Country Houses: The Work of Frank J. Forster. New York: 1931. V. 47

FORSTER, J. BURTON
The Sportsman's Vade-Mecum for the Himalayas. London: 1891. V. 49

FORSTER, J. R.
Characteres Generum Plantarum Quas in Itinere ad Insulas Maris Australis Collegerunt. London: 1776. V. 51
History of the Voyages and Discoveries Made in the North. London: 1786. V. 48
Observations Made During a Voyage Round the World on Physical Geography, Natural History and Ethic Philosophy. London: 1778. V. 47; 48; 50
The Resolution Journal of Johann Reinhold Forster 1772-1775. London: 1982. V. 49; 54

FORSTER, JOHANN GEORG ADAM
A Voyage Round the World, in His Britannic Majesty's Sloop Resolution, Commanded by Capt. James Cook, During the Years 1772, 3, 4 and 5. London: 1777. V. 48; 49; 50; 52; 53; 54

FORSTER, JOHN
The Life and Adventures of Oliver Goldsmith. London: 1848. V. 52
The Life and Times of Oliver Goldsmith. London: 1871. V. 54
The Life of Charles Dickens. London: 1872-74. V. 47; 54
The Life of Charles Dickens. London: 1872-77. V. 49
The Life of Charles Dickens. London: 1874. V. 50; 51; 54
The Life of Charles Dickens. London: 1876. V. 54
The Life of Charles Dickens. Boston: 1890. V. 51
The Life of Charles Dickens. London: 1911. V. 50; 54
Sir John Eliot: a Biography. London: 1864. V. 53

FORSTER, MARGARET
Dames' Delight - a Novel. London: 1964. V. 50

FORSTER, NATHANIEL
Reflections on the Natural Foundation of the Hight Antiquity of Government, Arts and Sciences in Egypt. Oxford: 1743. V. 52

FORSTER, R. H.
Corstopitum. Report of the Excavations in 1907-(1914)... 1907-14. V. 49

FORSTER, R. R.
Spiders of New Zealand. Dunedin: 1967-88. V. 54

FORSTER, THOMAS
Norway in 1848 and 1849. London: 1850. V. 50
Numismatology, The Gatherer Up of Fragments. Volumes I-III. Colchester: 1892-94. V. 48
Researches About Atmospheric Phaenomema. London: 1813. V. 49; 51
Researches About Atmospheric Phaenomena. London: 1815. V. 48; 52

FORSTER, WESTGARTH
A Treatise on a Section of the Strata, from Newcastle-upon-Tyne, to the Mountain of Cross Fell, in Cumberland... London: 1821. V. 53; 54

FORSYTH, FREDERICK
The Day of the Jackal. London: 1971. V. 49; 50; 52
The Negotiator. London: 1989. V. 48
No Comebacks. Helsinki: 1986. V. 48

FORSYTH, GEORGE A.
The Story of the Soldier. New York: 1905. V. 49; 53
Thrilling Days in Army Life. New York: 1902. V. 53

FORSYTH, J.
The Highlands of Central India. London: 1872. V. 49

FORSYTH, J. S.
The Citizen's Pocket Chronicle... London: 1827. V. 49
Demonologia; or, Natural Knowledge Revealed... 1827. V. 51

FORSYTH, JAMES BELL
A Few Months in the East; or a Glimpse of the Red, the Dead and the Black Seas. Quebec: 1861. V. 53

FORSYTH, JOSEPH
Remarks on Antiquities, Arts and letters During an Excursion in Italy in the Years 1802, and 1803. London: 1816. V. 49

FORSYTH, ROBERT
The Principles and Practice of Agriculture. Edinburgh: 1804. V. 53
The Principles and Practice of Agriculture. London: 1804. V. 54

FORSYTH, WILLIAM
The History of Lawyers Ancient and Modern. New York: 1875. V. 51
History of the Captivity of Napoleon on St. Helena. London: 1853. V. 50
A Lay of Lochleven. Glasgow: 1887. V. 50; 52
Observations on the Diseases, Defects and Injuries in All Kinds of Fruit and Forest Trees. Dublin: 1791. V. 49; 52
Observations on the Diseases, Defects and Injuries in all Kinds of Fruit and Forest Trees. London: 1791. V. 48; 51
A Treatise on the Culture and Management of Fruit Trees... London: 1802. V. 47; 50; 52
A Treatise on the Culture and Management of Fruit Trees. Philadelphia: 1802. V. 50; 51
A Treatise on the Culture and Management of Fruit Trees... Albany: 1803. V. 47
A Treatise on the Culture and Management of fruit Trees. London: 1803. V. 47; 48; 50
A Treatise on the Culture and Management of Fruit-Trees... Whiting: 1803. V. 52

FORT Brisbane; or, Three Days' Quarantine. London: 1832. V. 47

FORT, C.
Lo!. 1931. V. 47
New Lands. 1923. V. 48; 50; 52

FORT, CHARLES
The Outcast Manufacturers. New York: 1909. V. 50; 51

FORT, GEORGE F.
Medical Economy During the Middle Ages; a Contribution to the History of European Morals, from the Time of the Roman Empire to the Close of the Fourteenth Century. New York: 1883. V. 49

FORT SMITH. CHAMBER OF COMMERCE
Fort Smith, Arkansas, Its History, Its Commerce, Its Location, Itself. Fort Smith: 1892. V. 52

THE FORTAS Catalogue. North Hills: 1970. V. 48; 49; 50; 51; 53

FORTEGUERRI, NICOLO
Ricciardetto di Niccolo Carteromaco. Paris (in fact Venice): 1738. V. 51; 52

FORTESCUE, E. F. K.
The Armenian Church Founded by St. Gregory the Illumiantor... London: 1872. V. 47

FORTESCUE, HUGH
Public Schools for the Middle Classes. London: 1864. V. 52

FORTESCUE, J. W.
A History of the British Army. London: 1899-1912. V. 48
A History of the British Army. London: 1899-1930. V. 49
A History of the British Army. 1910-17. V. 54
A History of the British Army. London: 1910-17. V. 53
A History of the British Army. London: 1935-30. V. 50
The Story of a Red Deer. Newtown: 1935. V. 52
The Story of a Red Deer. Newtown: 1936. V. 47

FORTESCUE, JOHN
De Laudibus Legum Angliae. London: 1616. V. 54
De Laudibus Legum Angliae... London: 1672. V. 49
De Laudibus Legum Angliae. London: 1825. V. 49
The Difference Between an Absolute and Limited Monarchy. London: 1714. V. 48
The Difference Between an Absolute and Limited Monarchy... London: 1719. V. 53
A Learned Commendation of the Politique Lawes of England... London: 1573. V. 51
The Works of Sir John Fortescue, Knight... (with) A History of the Family of Fortescue in All Its Branches... London: 1869. V. 54

FORTH & BRENTFORD, PATRICK RUTHVEN, EARL OF
Letters and Papers of Patrick Ruthven, Earl of Forth and Brentford and of His Family... 1868. V. 54

FORTHERGILL, GEORGE A.
Hunting Racing Coaching & Boxing Ballads. London: 1926. V. 48

FORTHERGILL, JOHN
The Fothergill Omnibus. London: 1931. V. 51

FORTIS, ALBERTO, ABBE
Travels Into Dalmatia... London: 1778. V. 48; 50

FORTITUDO Leonina in Utraque Fortuna Maximiliani Emmanuelis, V.B. ac Sup. Palat. Ducis...et Electoris... Munich: 1715. V. 53

A FORTNIGHT'S Ramble Through London; or, a Complete Display of All the Cheats and Frauds Practiced in the Great Metropolis, With the Best Methods for Eluding Them. London: 1810. V. 52

FORTOUL, HIPPOLYTE
La Danse des Morts Dessinee par Hans Holbein, Gravee sur Pierre par Joseph Schlotthauer. Paris: 1842. V. 52

THE FORTUNATE Orphan; or, Memoirs of the Countess of Marlou. London: 1745. V. 52

THE FORTUNE Anthology - Stories, Critcism and Poems. London: 1942. V. 53

FORTUNE, D.
The Winged Bull. 1935. V. 51; 53

FORTUNE, FRANCIS
General Junction Rail-Road. London: 1831. V. 54

FORTUNE, JAN
Fugitives. The Story of Clyde Barrow and Bonnie Parker. Dallas: 1934. V. 53

FORTUNE, R. F.
Manus Religion. Philadelphia: 1935. V. 50
Sorcerers of Dobu, the Social Anthropology of the Dobu Islanders of the Western Pacific. London: 1932. V. 49; 54

FORTUNE, ROBERT
A Journey to the Tea Countries of China... London: 1852. V. 49
A Residence Among the Chinese: Inland, on the Coast, and at Sea. London: 1857. V. 48; 50; 52

FORTY Illustrations of Lord Byron. London: 1824-25. V. 49

THE FORTY Thieves. London: 1894. V. 48

FORTY-FIVE Wood-Engravers. Wakefield: 1982. V. 52

FORTY-FOUR Turkish Tales. London: 1913. V. 54

FORWARD Into the Past: May Sarton on Her Eightieth Birthday, a Festschrift. Concord: 1992. V. 51; 52

FORWARD MINING DEVELOPMENT CO.
Facts About Goldfield Nevada. The Greatest Gold Camp in the World. Denver: 1904. V. 50
Prospectus of the Foward Mining Development Co. Denver: 1905. V. 50

FORWOOD, GWENDOLEN
Fillida and Corydon with Other Stories. London: 1902. V. 51

FOSBROOKE, THOMAS DUDLEY
British Monachism; or, Manners and Customs of the Monks and Nuns of England. London: 1802. V. 49
British Monachism; or Manners and Customs of the Monks and Nuns of England. London: 1843. V. 51
The Economy of Monastic Life, (As It Existed in England). A Poem... Glocester: 1795. V. 54
Encyclopaedia of Antiquities and Elements of Archaeology, Classical and medieval. (with) Foreign Topography: an Encyclopedick Account of the Ancient Remains in Africa, Asia and Europe. London: 1825-28. V. 47
An Original History of the City of Gloucester. London: 1819. V. 53
The Wye Tour, or Gilpin on "The Wye"... London: 1834. V. 48
The Wye Tour, with Additions; and the Companion to the Tour. London: 1822. V. 53

FOSCOLO, NICCOLO UGO
Essays on Petrarch. London: 1823. V. 52

FOSKETT, DAPHNE
A Dictionary of British Miniature Painters. London: 1972. V. 50

FOSS, EDWARD
Biographia Juridica: a Biographical Dictionary of the Judges of England 1066-1870. London: 1870. V. 47; 49; 53
A Biographical Dictionary of the Judges of England from the Conquest to the Present Time 1066-1870. Boston: 1870. V. 51

FOSSETT, FRANK
Colorado Its Gold and Silver Mines, Farms and Stock Ranges, and Health and Pleasure Resorts. New York: 1879. V. 47; 53
Colorado Its Gold and Silver Mines, Farms and Stock Ranges, and Health and Pleasure Resorts. New York: 1880. V. 47; 51

FOSTER, ARTHUR
A Digest of the Laws of the State of Georgia... Philadelphia: 1820-29. V. 50

FOSTER, BENJAMIN FRANKLIN
Practical Penmanship, being a Developement (sic) of the Carstairian System. Albany: 1830. V. 47

FOSTER, BESS ELEANOR
The New Creative Art Book. Kansas City: 1931. V. 47; 50

FOSTER, BIRKET
Birket Foster's Pictures of English Landscape. London: 1864. V. 52
The Children's Picture Book of Far Famed Country Scenes. London: 1880. V. 47
Pictures of English Landscape. London: 1881. V. 52
Some Places of Note in England: a Series of 25 Drawings. London: 1889. V. 53

FOSTER, CHARLES WILMER
History of the Wilmer Family, Together with Some Account of Its Descendants. Leeds: 1888. V. 52; 53

FOSTER, CLEMENT LE NEVE
A Treatise on Ore and Stone Mining. London: 1905. V. 54

FOSTER, ETHEL TWYCROSS
Little Tales of the Desert. Los Angeles: 1913. V. 53

FOSTER, F. G.
Ferns to Know and Grow. London: 1986. V. 49

FOSTER, GEORGE C.
One Sunday Morning. London: 1929. V. 49

FOSTER, HANNAH
The Boarding School; or, Lessons of a Preceptress to her Pupils... Boston: 1829. V. 47
The Coquette; or, the History of Eliza Wharton. Charlestown: 1802. V. 54

FOSTER, J. W.
The Mississippi Valley. Chicago/London: 1869. V. 47
Pre-Historic Races of the United States of America. Chicago: 1873. V. 52; 54

FOSTER, JAMES
An Account of the Behaviour of the Late Earl of Kilmarnock, after His Sentence, and on the Day of His Execution. Dublin: 1745.. V. 50
An Account of the Behaviour of the Late Earl of Kilmarnock, after His Sentence, and on the Day of His Execution. London: 1746. V. 50; 51
Discourses On All the Principal Branches of Natural Religiion and Social Virtue. London: 1749-52. V. 48; 49; 52

FOSTER, JOHN
An Essay on the Evils of Popular Ignorance. London: 1820. V. 49; 54
An Essay on the Evils of Popular Ignorance: and a Discourse on the Communication of Christianity to the People of Hindoostan. London: 1821. V. 50

FOSTER, JOHN WELLS
Report On the Geology and Topography of a Portion of the Lake Superior Land District, in the State of Michigan. Washington: 1850-51. V. 48

FOSTER, JOHN Y.
New Jersey and the Rebellion: a History of the Services of the Troops and People of New Jersey in Aid of the Union Cause. Newark: 1868. V. 47; 49; 51

FOSTER, JOSEPH
Pedigree of Sir Josslyn Pennington, Fifth Baron Muncasater of Muncaster and Ninth Baronet. London: 1878. V. 50; 52; 53; 54
Pedigree of Wilson of High Wray and Kendal, and the Families Connected With Them. London: 1871. V. 52; 54
Pedigrees of the County Families of England. London: 1873. V. 50
Pedigrees of the County Families of Yorkshire. London: 1874. V. 53; 54
Pedigrees Recorded at the Heralds' Visitations of the Counties of Cumberland and Westmorland... Carlisle: 1891. V. 51
Some Feudal Coats of Arms and Others. London: 1902. V. 54

FOSTER, JOSHUA JAMES
A Dictionary of Painters of Miniatures (1525-1850) with Some Account of Exhibitions, Collections, Sales, Etc., Pertaining to Them. New York: 1968. V. 54
Miniature Painters, British and Foreign. London: 1903. V. 47; 49; 53
Miniature Painters, British and Foreign, With Some Account of Those Who Practised in America in the Eighteenth Century. New York: 1903. V. 54
The Stuarts: Being Illustrations of the Personal History of the Family (Especially Mary Queen of Scots) in 16th 17th and 18th Century Art. New York & London: 1902. V. 49

FOSTER, LE NEVE
A Text-Book of Ore and Stone Mining. London: 1901. V. 49

FOSTER, MARIANA CURTIS
P'Sich. London. V. 50; 53

FOSTER, MICHAEL
The Case of the King Against Alexander Broadfoot, at the Sessions of Oyr and Terminer and Gaol Delivery Held for the City of Bristol and County of the Same City on the 30th of August, 1743. Oxford: 1758. V. 50
A Report of Some Proceedings on the Commission for the Trial of the Rebels in the Year 1746 in the County of Surry... London: 1792. V. 52
A Text Book of Physiology. New York: 1893. V. 48; 50; 51; 53
A Textbook of Physiology. London: 1878. V. 47; 48

FOSTER, ROBERT D.
The North American Indian Doctor, or Nature's method of Curing and Preventing Disease According to the Indians...Also a Treatise on Midwifery... Canton: 1838. V. 48

FOSTER, ROGER
A Treatise on Federal Practice in Civil Causes with Special Reference to Patent Cases and the Foreclosure of Railway Mortgages. Boston: 1892. V. 50

FOSTER, ROXANA C.
The Foster Family, California Pioneers. First Overland Trip...1849, Second Overland Trip...1852, Third Overland Trip...1853. Santa Barbara: 1925. V. 47; 50; 54

FOSTER, SANDYS B.
The Pedigrees of Crewdson of Crook, Whitwell of Kendal, Please of Hutton and Low Cross. London: 1890. V. 50; 52; 54
The Pedigrees of Wilson of Rigmaden Park and Low Nook, Gibson of Whelprigg, Fox of Girsby Co. Linc and Statham, Cheshire, Braithwaite-Wilson of Plumtree Hall, Argles of Eversley, Westmorland and Moser of Kendal. London: 1890. V. 50; 52; 54
Wilson of High Wray and Kendal, Together with the Families Connected With Them. London: 1890. V. 50; 52; 54

FOSTER, STEPHEN S.
The Brotherhood of Thieves, or a true Picture of the American Church and Clergy. London: 1843. V. 51; 54

FOSTER, THOMAS F.
Speech of...of Georgia, on the Bill Providing for the Removal of the Indians West of the Mississippi. Washington: 1830. V. 54

FOSTER, WILLIAM
The Gentleman's Experienced Farrier. Shrewsbury: 1786. V. 47

FOSTER, WILLIAM D.
Cottages, Manoirs and Minor Buildings of Normandy and Brittany. New York: 1926. V. 47

FOSTER, WILLIAM EDWARD
The Royal Descents of the Fosters of Moulton and the Mathesons of Shinness and Lochaalsh. London: 1912. V. 54

FOSTER, WILLIAM HARNDEN
New England Grouse Shooting. New York: 1942. V. 47

FOSTER, WILLIAM Z.
Toward Soviet America. New York: 1932. V. 52

FOSTER-MELLIAR, A.
The Book of the Rose. London & New York: 1894. V. 54

FOTHERGILL, ANTHONY
A New Experimental Inquiry Into the Nature and Qualities of the Cheltenham Water. Bath: 1788. V. 52

FOTHERGILL, CAROLINE
Put to the Proof. A Novel. London: 1883. V. 47

FOTHERGILL, EDWARD
Five Years in the Sudan. London: 1910. V. 50

FOTHERGILL, GEORGE A.
A Gift to the State: the National Stud. London: 1916. V. 53
A North Country Album... Darlington: 1901. V. 54
Notes from the Diary of a Doctor, Sketch Artist and Sportsman. York: 1901. V. 47; 54
An Old Raby Hunt Club Album, 1786-1899. Edinburgh: 1899. V. 47

FOTHERGILL, J. MILNER
The Antagonism of Therapeutic Agents: and What It Teaches. Philadelphia: 1878. V. 53
Digitalis: Its Mode of Action and Its Use, an Enquiry Illustrating the Effect of Remedial Agents Over Diseased Conditions Of the Heart. Philadelphia: 1871. V. 48
Vaso-Renal Change Versus Bright's Disease. London: 1887. V. 53

FOTHERGILL, JESSIE
The First Violin. New York: 1878. V. 51; 53; 54

FOTHERGILL, JOHN
An Account of the Life and Travels in the Work of the Ministry, of John Fothergill. London: 1753. V. 54
A Complete Collection of the Medical and Philsophical Works of John Fothergill.. London: 1781. V. 49; 50
The Fothergill Omnibus. London: 1931. V. 47; 49; 51; 53
Some Account of the Late Peter Collinson...in a Letter to a friend. London: 1770, but 1785. V. 53

FOUCAULT, JEAN BERNARD LEON
Receuil des Travaux Scientifiques... Paris: 1878. V. 47
Sur Divers Signes Sensibles du Mouvement Diurne de la Terre. Paris: 1852. V. 47

FOUCAULT, MICHEL
Histoire de la Folie a L'Age Classique. Paris: 1961. V. 52

FOUCHET, MAX-POL
Johnny Friedlaender: Oeuvre 1961-1965. New York. V. 47; 48; 52
Wifredo Lam. New York: 1976. V. 50; 52; 53

FOUGASSES, THOMAS DE
The Generall Historie of the Magnificent State of Venice. London: 1612. V. 49

FOUGHT, H. W.
The Trail of the Loup-A History of the Loup River Region with Some Chapters on the State. 1906. V. 52

FOUGUERA, KATHERINE GIBSON
With Custer's Cavalry. Caldwell: 1940. V. 53

FOULIS, HENRY
An Exact and True Relation of a Bloody Fight, Performed Against the Earl of Newcastle and His Forces Before Tadcaster and Selby in Yorkshire, in His March Towards London... London: 1642. V. 50
The History of the Wicked Plots and Conspiracies of Our Presented Saints... London: 1662. V. 50

FOULIS, ROBERT
Books Printed by Robert and Andrew Foulis, Printers to the University of Glasgow; Prints Engraved in the Academy at Glasgow and sold by Robert and Andrew Foulis. 1775. V. 47

FOULKE, WILLIAM D.
A Random Record of Travel During Fifty Years. New York: 1925. V. 48; 50; 52

FOULSTON, JOHN
The Public Buildings Erected in the West of England as Designed by John Foulston F.R.I.B.A. London: 1838. V. 52

FOUNTAIN, PAUL
The Great North-West and the Great Lake Region of North America. London: 1904. V. 48

FOUQUERAY, D. CHARLES
Le Front de Mer. Pientre Officiel Du Ministere de la Marine et du Musee le l'Armee. V. 48

THE FOUR Elements: a Poem for Each. 1989. V. 52

FOUR Fictions. Kentfield: 1973. V. 51

FOUR MASTERS
The Annals of Ireland. Dublin: 1846. V. 51

FOUR Negro Poets. New York: 1927. V. 48; 51

FOUR Poets. Melbourne: 1962. V. 50

FOUR Poets for St. Magnus: George Mackay Brown, Ted Hughes, Seamus Heaney, Christopher Fry. Orkney: 1987. V. 48

FOUR Questions Deabated. Q.1. Whether the Exercise of the Government of England Be Totally Subverted. Affirm... Edinburgh: 1689. V. 53

FOUR Visions of America. Santa Barbara: 1977. V. 48; 50

FOURCROY, ANTOINE FRANCOIS DE
Elements of Natural History, and of Chemistry... London: 1788. V. 48; 52
A General System of Chemical Knowledge; and Its Application to the Pheneomena of Nature and Art... Paris: 1804-01. V. 53
Systeme des Connaisances Chimiques, et Leurs Applications aux Phenomenes de la Nature et de l'Art. (with) Table Alphabetique et Analytique des Matieres... Paris: 1802. V. 47

FOURDROY, ANTOINE FRANCOIS DE
Synoptic Tables of Chemistry... London: 1801. V. 50

FOURGEAUD, VICTOR H.
The First California. San Francisco: 1942. V. 48

FOURIER, CHARLES
The Passions of the Human Soul.. London: 1851. V. 54

FOURIER, JEAN BAPTISTE JOSEPH
The Analytical Theory of Heat... Cambridge: 1878. V. 50

FOURNIER, ALAIN
The Wanderer. Boston: 1928. V. 52
The Wanderer. New York: 1958. V. 53

FOURNIER, ALFRED
The Treatment of Prophylaxis of Syphilis. New York: 1907. V. 51; 53

FOURNIER, HENRI ALBAN
The Wanderer. New York: 1958. V. 54

FOURNIER, PIERRE SIMON
Fournier on Typefounding. London: 1930. V. 52
Manuel Typographique. Paris: 1764-66. V. 48; 52; 54

FOURNIVAL, RICHARD DE
Master Richard's Bestiary of Love and Response. 1985. V. 48

THE FOURTH Estate: or the Moral Influence of the Press. London: 1839. V. 48

FOVARGUE, STEPHEN
A New Catalogue of Vulgar Errors. Cambridge: 1767. V. 48

FOWBLE, E. MC SHERRY
Two Centuries of Prints in America, 1680-1880: a Selective Catalogue of the Winterthur Museum Collection. Charlottesville: 1987. V. 53

FOWKE, MARTHA
The Epistles of Clio and Strephon, Being a Collection of Letters that Passed Between an English Lady and an English Gentleman in France, Who Took an Affection to Each Other... London: 1720. V. 47

A FOWL Alphabet. Easthampton: 1986. V. 50

FOWLER, ALFRED
The Woodcut Annual for 1925. Kansas City: 1925. V. 52

FOWLER, CHARLES H.
Historical Romance of the American Negro. Baltimore: 1902. V. 53

FOWLER COLONY IRRIGATION & INDUSTRIAL CO.
Prospectus of the Fowler Colony, Irrigation and Industrial Co. Denver: 1887. V. 51

FOWLER, EDMUND PRINCE
Medicine of the Ear. New York & Edinburgh: 1947. V. 49

FOWLER, GENE
Salute to Yesterday. New York: 1937. V. 50
A Solo in Tom-Toms. New York: 1931. V. 53
A Solo in Tom-Toms. New York: 1946. V. 48

FOWLER, GEORGE
Turkey: or a History of the Origin, Progress and Decline of the Ottoman Empire... London: 1854. V. 53

FOWLER, HENRY W.
The Concise Oxford Dictionary of Current English. Oxford: 1929. V. 51
A Dictionary of Modern English Usage. Oxford and London: 1926. V. 51

FOWLER, JACOB
The Journal of Jacob Fowler Narrating An Adventure from Arkansas through the Indian Territory, Oklahoma, Kansas, Colorado and New Mexico... New York: 1898. V. 48; 49; 50; 54

FOWLER, JAMES
the Diseases of the Lungs. London: 1898. V. 48; 51; 53

FOWLER, JOHN
English Decoration in the 18th Century. London: 1974. V. 53
English Decoration in the 18th Century. Princeton: 1974. V. 54
Journal of a Tour in the State of New York, in the Year 1830... London: 1831. V. 53

FOWLER, L. N.
Marriage: Its History and Ceremonies; with a Phrenological and Physiological Exposition. New York: 1848. V. 54

FOWLER, LAURENCE HALL
The Fowler Agricultural Collection of the John Fowler Hopkins University Catalogue. San Francisco: 1991. V. 47; 54

FOWLER, ORSON S.
A Home for All: or a New, Cheap, Convenient and Superior Mode of Building. New York: 1854. V. 49; 51; 52
Human Science, or Phrenology...as Applied to Health, Mental Philosophy, God, Immortality, Intellect. Philadelphia: 1873. V. 48
Prospectus Of the Fowler Colony, Irrigation and Industrial Company. Denver: 1887. V. 52

FOWLER, PHILEMON HALSTED
Memorials of William Fowler. New York: 1875. V. 49

FOWLER, R. N.
A Visit to Japan, China and India. London: 1877. V. 54

FOWLER, ROBERT LUDLOW
Facsimile of the Laws and Acts of the General Assembly for Their Majesties Province of New York...Printed 1694 at New York. New York: 1894. V. 50

FOWLER, RUSSELL
The Operating Room and the Patient. Philadelphia: 1907. V. 50

FOWLER, W.
The Coleoptera of the British Islands. London: 1887-1913. V. 47

FOWLER, WILLIAM CHAUNCEY
Memorials of the Chaunceys, Including President Chauncy, His Ancestors and Descendants. Boston: 1858. V. 53

FOWLES, JOHN
The Aristos. 1964. V. 50
The Aristos. Boston: 1964. V. 47; 48; 49; 50; 51; 52; 54
The Aristos. 1965. V. 49
The Aristos. London: 1965. V. 49
The Aristos. London: 1980. V. 49
Cinderella. London: 1974. V. 49; 53
The Collector. Boston: 1963. V. 47; 48; 49; 50; 51; 52; 53; 54
The Collector. London: 1963. V. 47; 48; 49; 51; 52; 53
Conditional. Northridge: 1979. V. 48
Daniel Martin. London: 1977. V. 48; 51; 52
Daniel Martin. New York: 1977. V. 49
The Ebony Tower. Boston: 1974. V. 51
The Ebony Tower. London: 1974. V. 47; 52; 53
The Enigma. Helsinki: 1987. V. 48; 49
The Enigma of Stonehenge. London: 1980. V. 48; 50; 54
The French Lieutenant's woman. London: 1969. V. 47; 48; 49; 50; 52; 54
The French Lieutenant's Woman. 1979. V. 49
Introduction: Remembering Cruikshank. Princeton. V. 51
Land. Boston: 1985. V. 47
A Maggot. 1985. V. 49
A Maggot. Boston: 1985. V. 47; 48; 50; 51; 54
A Maggot. London: 1985. V. 47; 49; 51; 52; 53; 54
The Magus. Boston: 1963. V. 49
The Magus. Boston: 1965. V. 50; 52; 54
The Magus. London: 1966. V. 47; 48; 49; 50; 52; 53
The Magus. London: 1977. V. 50
Mantissa. Boston: 1982. V. 47; 49; 50; 52; 54
Mantissa. London: 1982. V. 50; 53
My Recollections of Kafka. Manitoba: 1970. V. 50
The Nature of Nature, and the Tree: Essays. Covelo: 1995. V. 54
Of Memoirs and Magpies. Austin: 1983. V. 52; 53
Poems. New York: 1973. V. 48
Poor Koko. Helsinki: 1987. V. 48
Shipwreck. London: 1974. V. 50; 54
The Tree. London: 1979. V. 54

THE FOX and the Stork and Other Fables. London: 1870. V. 54

FOX, CHARLES DONALD
Mirrors of Hollywood. New York: 1925. V. 51

FOX, CHARLES J.
A Guide to Officers of Towns... Concord: 1866. V. 50

FOX, CHARLES JAMES
A History of the Early Part of the Reign of James the Second... London: 1808. V. 50; 52; 53; 54

Memorials and Correspondence of Charles James Fox. London: 1853. V. 48; 52

Observations on the Historical Works of the Late Right Honorable Charles James Fox... London: 1809. V. 50

The Speech of the Right Honourable Charles James Fox, at a General Meeting of the Electors of Westminster, Assembled in Westminster Hall, July 17, 1782... London: 1782. V. 52

The Speeches of the Right Hon. Charles James Fox, in the House of Commons. London: 1815. V. 53

FOX, CYRIL
The Early Cultures of North-West Europe: H. M. Chadwick Memorial Studies. London: 1950. V. 50; 51

FOX, DOUGLAS
Channel Tunnel. Report of Sir Douglas Fox and Partners. London: 1907. V. 51

The Signs, Disorders and Management of Pregnancy; the Treatment to be Adopted During and After Confinement... Derby: 1834. V. 50

FOX, ERNEST F.
Travels in Afghanistan 1937-1938. New York: 1943. V. 51

FOX, FRANCES MARGARET
Adventures of Sonny Bear. Chicago: 1916. V. 49

FOX, FRANCIS
Geographical Aspects of the Channel Tunnel. London: 1917. V. 51

FOX, FRANK
England. London: 1918. V. 53
Switzerland. London: 1917. V. 54

FOX, GEORGE
A Battle-Door for Teachers & Professors to Learn Singular & Plural... London: 1660. V. 47

Canons and Institutions Drawn Up and Agreed Upon by the General Assembly or Meeting of the Heads of the Quakers... London: 1669. V. 48

A Collection of many Select and Christian Epistles, Letters and Testimonies. London: 1698. V. 48; 50

A General Epistle and a Tender Greeting, Sent Unto the Flock of Christ; Who Meet Together to Worship the Father and Son in the Spirit of Truth. London: 1690. V. 50

Gospel-Truth Demonstrated, in a Collection of Doctrinal Books... London: 1706. V. 48; 49; 51

A Warning to All Teachers of Children Which are Called School-Masters and School-Mistresses, and to Parents, Which Doth Send Their Children to Be taught by Them... London: 1657. V. 47

FOX, GEORGE HENRY
Photographic Atlas of the Diseases of the Skin. Philadelphia: 1905. V. 48
Photographic Illustrations of Cutaneous Syphilis. New York: 1881. V. 53
Photographic Illustrations Of Skin Diseases. New York: 1880. V. 48; 51
Photographic Illustrations of Skin Diseases. New York: 1881. V. 53
Photographic Illustrations of Skin Diseases. New York: 1885. V. 53
Photographic Illustrations of Skin Diseases. 2nd Series. New York: 1887. V. 51

FOX, GEORGE TOWNSHEND
Synopsis of the Newcastle Museum. Newcastle: 1827. V. 47

FOX, GUSTAVUS VASA
Confidential Correspondence of Gustavus Vasa Fox. New York: 1918-19. V. 48; 49; 50; 53
Reports of the Naval Engagements on the Mississippi River. Washington: 1862. V. 50

FOX, H. M.
Patio Gardens. New York: 1929. V. 48; 50

FOX, HENRY
A New Dictionary, in French and English... London: 1769. V. 47

FOX, HERBERT
Disease in Captive Wild Mammals and Birds: Incidence, Description, Comparison. Philadelphia: 1923. V. 48

FOX, JOHN
The Book of Martyrs. London: 1741. V. 49
The Book of Martyrs, or, Christian Martyology... Liverpool: 1807. V. 54
The Book of Martyrs or the Acts and Monuments of the Christian Church. London: 1811. V. 49
The ...Ecclesiasticall History, Contayning the Actes and Monumentes Of Thinges Passed. London: 1576. V. 50
The (First-) Second Volume of the Ecclesiastical History, Conteyining the Actes and monumentes of Martyrs... London: 1576. V. 48
Foxe's Book of Martyrs. London: 1850. V. 49
Foxe's Book of Martyrs. London: 1860. V. 51
Little Shepherd of Kingdom Come. New York: 1931. V. 49; 54
A Mountain Europa. New York & London: 1899. V. 54
An Universal History of Christian Martyrdom... London: 1838. V. 49

FOX, JOSEPH
The Natural History of the Human Teeth, Including a Particular Elucidation of the Changes Which Take Place During the Second Dentition... London: 1803. V. 49

FOX, L. WEBSTER
Diseases of the Eye. New Haven: 1935. V. 49

FOX, MARY ANNA
George Allen, the Only Son. Boston: 1835. V. 47; 49; 54

FOX, NETTIE PEASE
The Phantom Form: Experiences in Earth and Spirit Life. Newton: 1881. V. 50

FOX, R. M.
The Triumphant Machine - a Study of Machine Civilisation. London: 1928. V. 47

FOX, RALPH
Lenin - a Biography. London: 1933. V. 48
This Was Their Youth. London: 1937. V. 50

FOX, RICHARD K.
Life and Battles of James J. Corbett The Champion Pugilist of the World. New York: 1892. V. 47

FOX, ROBERT WERE
Observations on Mineral Veins. Falmouth: 1837. V. 48

FOX, S. P.
Kingsbridge and its Surroundings. Plymouth: 1874. V. 51
Kingsbridge Estuary; With Rambles in the Neighbourhood. Kingsbridge: 1864. V. 51

FOX, SAMUEL MIDDLETON
George. A Story in Drab and Scarlet. London: 1890. V. 53

FOX, STEPHEN
Memoirs of the Life...From His First Entrance Upon the Stage of Action Under the Lord Piercy, Till His Decease. London: 1807. V. 47

FOX, W. J.
Finsbury Lectures. Reports of Lectures Delivered at the Chapel in South Place, Finsbury. No. I. The Morality of Poverty... London: 1835-36. V. 52

FOX, WELLS B.
What I Remember of the Great Rebellion. Lansing: 1892. V. 49; 50

FOX, WILLIAM F.
Regimental Losses in the American Civil War 1861-1865. Albany: 1889. V. 47

FOX, WILSON
The Diseases of the Stomach. London: 1872. V. 48; 53

FOX-DAVIES, ARTHUR CHARLES
Armorial Families. Edinburgh: 1895. V. 50
Armorial Families. London: 1895. V. 54
Armorial Families. Edinburgh: 1899. V. 50
Armorial Families. London: 1902. V. 48; 50; 52; 54
Armorial Families. London: 1910. V. 50
The Maulever Murders. London: 1907. V. 47

FOXON, D. F.
English Verse 1701-1750. Cambridge: 1975. V. 48; 51; 52
English Verse 1701-1750. London: 1975. V. 54

FOXTON, THOMAS
Sereino: or the Character of a Fine Gentleman; With Reference to Religion, Learning and the conduct of Life... London: 1725?. V. 52
The Tower. A Poem. London: 1727. V. 53; 54

FOXY Grandpa's Triumphs. New York: 1907. V. 47

FOY, GEORGE
Anaesthetics, Ancient and Modern: Their Physiological Action, Therapeutic Use and Mode of Administration... London: 1889. V. 48

FOYER, ARCHIBALD
A Defence of the Scots Settlement at Darien. 1699. V. 54

FOY-VAILANT, JEAN
Numismata Imperatorum Romanorum Praestantiora a Julio Caesare ad Postumum et Tyrannos. Lutetiae Parisiorum: 1696. V. 48; 51

FRACASTORO, GIROLAMO
Contagion, Contagious Diseases and Their Treatment. New York: 1930. V. 48; 50; 51; 52; 53
De Sympathia et Antipathia Rerum Liber Unus. De contagione et contagiosis Morbis et Curatione. Venice: 1546. V. 48; 51; 53
Opera Omnia, in Unum Proxime Post Illius Mortem Collecta. Venetiis: 1555. V. 52
Opera Omnia, in Unum Proxime Post Illius Mortem Collecta. Venetiis: 1574. V. 49
The Sinister Shepherd. Los Angeles: 1934. V. 50; 51; 52
Syphilis or the French Disease with a Translation... London: 1935. V. 50

FRAENKEL, MICHAEL
Anonymous. The Need for Anonymity. Paris: 1930. V. 47; 48
Bastard Death. Paris: 1946. V. 49

A FRAGMENT from the Fine Art Folies of Frogmore; or, The Belgian Mystery Unveiled. London: 1869. V. 48

A FRAGMENT of the Voyages of Mr. Verigull Gulliver, (Grandson to the Celebrated Traveleir). To the Island of Ae-ri-si-ter, in the Lake of Spe-cul, Situated in the Province of Fo-li, a Part of China Hitherto Unexplored, &c &c. Middle Hill: 1832/40?. V. 50

FRAME, JANET
Owls Do Cry. New York: 1960. V. 53

FRAMJEE, HORMAJEE
Commercial Calculator, or Tables of Exchange Between England and China, China and Calcutta, & China and Bombay. London: 1851. V. 49

FRANCATELLI, CHARLES ELME
The Royal English and Foreign Confectioner. London: 1862. V. 49

FRANCE
Plan of the French Constitution and Declaration of Rights; as Presented to the National Convention of France. London: 1793. V. 52

FRANCE, ANATOLE
L'Affaire Crainquebile... Stamford: 1937. V. 47
Balthasar et La Reine Balkis. Paris: 1900. V. 47
Bee. London: 1912. V. 48
The Bride of Corinth and Other Poems and Plays. London: 1920. V. 51
Clio. Paris: 1900. V. 49
Crainquebille. Paris: 1903. V. 51
Crainquebille. Providence: 1949. V. 53
The Crime of Sylvestre Bonnard. London: 1891. V. 47
The Crime of Sylvestre Bonnard. New York: 1937. V. 53; 54
Mother of Pearl. London: 1929. V. 47
The Novels and Short Stories of Anatole France. New York: 1915. V. 49
Penguin Island. London: 1924. V. 52
Revolt of the Angels. New York: 1953. V. 53
Les Sept Femmes de La Barbe-Bleue et Autres Contes Merveilleux. Paris: 1909. V. 47
The Seven Wives of Bluebeard. London: 1925. V. 52
Stendhal. London: 1926. V. 52
Vie de Jeanne D'Arc. Paris: 1908. V. 49
Works. New York: 1924. V. 51

FRANCE, GEORGE W.
The Struggles for Life and Home in the North-West. New York: 1890. V. 47

FRANCE, R. S.
Lord Redesdale and the New Railways: a Review of His Lordship as a Railway Legislator... London: 1867. V. 52

FRANCESCHI, DOMENICO DE
Solyman the Magnificent Going to Mosque. Edinburgh: 1877. V. 47

FRANCESCO D'ASSISI, SAINT
Canticle of the Sun. Easthampton: 1983. V. 53
I Fioretti Del Glorioso Poverello di Cristo S. Francesco Di Assisi. 1922. V. 49; 51; 52; 54
Laudes Creaturarum... Hammersmith: 1910. V. 47; 48; 49; 50; 53
Laudes Creaturarum. Hammersmith: 1911. V. 51
Laudes Creaturarum. New York: 1992. V. 53
The Little Flowers. London. V. 47
The Little Flowers... 1909. V. 54
The Little Flowers of S. Francis of Assisi. London: 1909. V. 49; 51
The Little Flowers of Saint Francis of Assisi... New York: 1930. V. 47; 53
The Little Flowers of Saint Francis of Assisi. 1931. V. 50; 52
Selections From the Life and Writings of Saint Francis... Cleveland: 1953. V. 48; 50

FRANCH, JOSE ALCINA
Pre-Columbian Art. New York: 1983. V. 50; 52

FRANCHERE, GABRIEL
Journal of a Voyage on the North West Coast of North America During the Years 1811, 1812, 1813, and 1814. Toronto: 1969. V. 51; 53
Narrative of a Voyage to the Northwest Coast of America in the Years 1811, 1812, 1813 and 1814. New York: 1854. V. 47
Relation d'un Voyage a la Cote du Nord-Ouest de l'Amerique Septentrionale, dans les Annees 1810, 11, 12, 13 et 14. Montreal: 1820. V. 48

FRANCHI, ANNA
The Little Lead Soldier. Philadelphia: 1919. V. 53

FRANCIA, L.
Drawing Book, Being Studies of Landscape, Containing Twenty Specimens... London: 1823. V. 50
Progressive Lessons Tending to Elucidate the Character of Trees, with the Process of Sketch and Painting them in Water Colours. London: 1813. V. 50
Progressive Lessons Tending to Elucidate the Character of Trees, With the Process of Sketching and Painting Them in Water Colours. London: 1835. V. 50
A Series of Progressive Lessons, Intended to Elucidate the Art of Flower Painting in Water Colours. London: 1815. V. 52

FRANCILLON, R. E.
Jack Doyle's Daughter. London: 1894. V. 51

FRANCINE, ALEXANDRE
Livre d'Architecture Contenant Plusieurs Portiques de Differents Inventions sur les Cinq Ordres de Colomnes. Paris: 1631. V. 47

FRANCIS, BENJAMIN
The Conflagration: a Poem on the Last Day, in Fourt Parts. Bristol: 1786. V. 53

FRANCIS, BRUCE
Scenic Route. Northridge: 1990. V. 48; 51

FRANCIS, DICK
Best Racing and Chasing Stories 2. London: 1969. V. 50
Blood Sport. London: 1967. V. 47; 48; 49; 50; 52; 53
Blood Sport. New York: 1967. V. 49; 52; 53
Blood Sport. New York: 1968. V. 51
Bonecrack. London: 1971. V. 47; 48; 49; 51; 52
Dead Cert. London: 1962. V. 49
Dead Cert. New York: 1962. V. 49
Enquiry. London: 1963. V. 48
Enquiry. London: 1969. V. 47; 49; 50; 51
Flying Finish. London: 1966. V. 47; 50; 52; 53
Flying Finish. New York: 1967. V. 53
For Kicks. London: 1965. V. 47; 53
Forfeit. London: 1968. V. 47; 48; 50; 51; 53
In the Frame. London: 1976. V. 52
Knock Down. London: 1974. V. 52
Lester. V. 49
Nerve. 1964. V. 50
Nerve. London: 1964. V. 47; 49; 53
Nerve. New York: 1964. V. 48
Odds Against. London: 1965. V. 47; 48; 49; 50; 52; 53
Odds Against. New York: 1966. V. 49
Rat Race. London: 1970. V. 48; 52
Slay Ride. London: 1969. V. 48
Slay-Ride. London: 1973. V. 47; 50; 52
Smokescreen. London: 1972. V. 47; 48; 50; 52
Smokescreen. London: 1973. V. 51
The Sport of Queens. 1969. V. 53
The Sport of Queens. New York: 1969. V. 49; 51
Twice Shy. London: 1981. V. 52
Wild Horses. 1994. V. 54
Wild Horses. Bristol: 1994. V. 52
Wild Horses. London: 1994. V. 51; 53

FRANCIS, E. F.
History of the 2/3rd East Lancashire Field Ambulance. Salford: 1930. V. 53

FRANCIS, E. T. B.
The Anatomy of the Salamander. Oxford: 1934. V. 48; 51

FRANCIS, ELIZA S.
The Rival Roses; or Wars of York and Lancaster. London: 1813. V. 53

FRANCIS, FRANCIS
A Book of Angling. London: 1867. V. 49; 53
A Book of Angling. London: 1876. V. 53
A Book on Angling. London: 1885. V. 47
Sidney Bellew. London: 1870. V. 53

FRANCIS, GEORGE WILLIAM
The Dictionary of the Arts, Sciences and Manufactures. London: 1842. V. 50

FRANCIS, GRANT R.
Old English Drinking Glasses: Their Chronology and Sequence. London: 1926. V. 49

FRANCIS, HARRIET E.
Across the Meridians and Fragmentary Letters. 1887. V. 53

FRANCIS, JOHN
Annals, Anecdotes and Legends: a Chronicle of Life Assurance. London: 1853. V. 53
A History of the English Railway. London: 1851. V. 49; 53; 54

FRANCIS, JOHN GEORGE
Notes from a Journal Kept in Italy and Sicily, During the years 1844, 1845 and 1846. London: 1847. V. 49

FRANCIS, JOHN W.
Old New York or Reminiscences of the Past Sixty Years. New York. V. 54

FRANCIS, P.
Volcanoes: a Planetary Perspective. London: 1993. V. 50

FRANCIS, ROBERT
Stand With Me Here. New York: 1936. V. 47; 54
The Trouble with God. 1984. V. 52; 54

FRANCIS, VALENTINE MOTT
A Thesis on Hospital Hygiene. New York: 1859. V. 47; 49

FRANCIS, WILLIAM
The Gentleman's, Farmer's and Husbandman's Most Useful Assistant in Measuring.... London: 1818. V. 50

FRANCISCUS DE TOLEDO
Oratio in Funere Leonardi de Robere. Rome: 1481-87. V. 47

FRANCIS DE SALES, SAINT
An Introduction to a Devout Life. London: 1686. V. 50

FRANCIS I, KING OF FRANCE
Exemplaria Literarum...Inter Ipsum & Carolum Quintu(m) Emerserunt. Paris: 1537. V. 48

FRANCK, RICHARD
Northern Memoirs, Calculated for the Meredian of Scotland... Edinburgh: 1821. V. 47; 49

FRANCK, SEBASTIAN
Chronica: Zeytbuch Und Geschycht Bibel Von Anbegyn Biss Inn Diss Gegenwertig 1531 Jar. Strassburg: 1531. V. 47

FRANCKE, A. H.
Antiquities of Indian Tibet. New Delhi: 1972. V. 48

FRANCKE, A. H. continued
A History of Western Tibet. London: 1907. V. 53

FRANCKLIN, THOMAS
Sermons on the Relative Dugies. London: 1765. V. 48
Sermons on the Relative Duties. London: 1770. V. 48
Sermons on Various Subjects, and Preached on Several Occasions. London: 1785-87. V. 47

FRANCKLIN, WILLIAM
The History of the Reign of Shah-Aulum, the Present Emperor of Hindostaun. London: 1798. V. 52

FRANCO, NICCOLO
La Philena. Historia Amorosa Vltimamente Composta. Mantua: 1547. V. 52

FRANCQUART, JACQUES
Pompa Funebris...Alberti Pii Archiducis Austriae... Brussels: 1623. V. 47

FRANK, ANNE
Anne Frank The Diary of a Young Girl. New York: 1952. V. 49
Diary of a Young Girl: Het Achterhius. West Hatfield: 1985. V. 47

FRANK Feignwell's Attempts to Amuse His Friends on Twelfth Night. London: 1811. V. 53

FRANK, HERMAN
Jewish Typography and Bookmaking Art. New York: 1938. V. 50; 53

FRANK, LARRY
Indian Silver Jewelry of the Southwest, 1868-1930. Boston: 1978. V. 52

FRANK, MARK
LI Sermons.. London: 1672. V. 54

FRANK, PAT
Alas, Babylon. New York: 1959. V. 54
Alas, Babylon. Philadelphia: 1959. V. 49; 54

FRANK, PHILIPP
Einstein His Life and Times. New York: 1947. V. 50
Einstein His Life and Times. New York: 1953. V. 54

FRANK, ROBERT
The Americans. New York: 1959. V. 50; 53
The Americans. Millerton: 1978. V. 48; 54
Zero Mostel Reads a Book. New York: 1963. V. 47; 51

FRANK, WALDO
America & Alfred Steiglitz. Garden City: 1934. V. 48; 52
America & Alfred Stieglitz, a Collective Portrait. New York: 1934. V. 47; 50
City Block. Darien: 1922. V. 49
Conferencia de Waldo Frank 2 Por La Causa Del Pueblo Espanol. Mexico: 1937. V. 50
New Year's Eve, a Play. New York: 1929. V. 47
Virgin Spain. New York: 1926. V. 47

FRANKAU, GILBERT
One Of Us. London: 1917. V. 52; 54
The Poetical Works of Gilbert Frankau. London: 1923. V. 47

FRANKEN, H. J.
Excavations at Tell deir Alla I: a Stratigraphical and Analytical Study of the Early Iron Age Pottery. Leiden: 1969. V. 49; 51

FRANKENSTEIN, ALFRED
After the Hunt. William Hartnett and Other Still Life Painters 1870-1900. Berkeley: 1953. V. 53
Karel Appel. New York: 1980. V. 47; 48; 50; 52

FRANKFORT, HENRI
Cylinder Seals: a Documentary Essay on the Art and Religion of the Ancient Near East. London: 1939. V. 51
Cylinder Seals: a Documentary Essay on the Art and religion of the Ancient Near East. London: 1965. V. 51
The Gimilsin Temple and the Palace of the Rulers at Tell Asmar. Chicago: 1940. V. 49
The Mural Painting of El-'Amarneh. 1929. V. 52
The Mural Painting of El-'Amarneh. London: 1929. V. 49; 51

FRANKFURTER, FELIX
The Labor Injunction. New York: 1930. V. 52; 54
Mr. Justice Holmes and the Supreme Court. Cambridge: 1938. V. 50

FRANKIE In Wonderland. New York: 1934. V. 53

FRANKL, PAUL T.
New Dimensions. The Decorative Arts of Today in Words and Pictures. New York: 1928. V. 51; 54
Space for Living: Creative Interior Decoration and Design. New York: 1938. V. 53

FRANKLAND, C. COLVILLE
Narrative of a Visit to the Courts of Russia and Sweden, in the Years 1830 and 1831. London: 1832. V. 52

FRANKLAND, THOMAS
The Annals of King James and King Charles the First. London: 1681. V. 51

FRANKLIN, BENJAMIN
The Almanacs for the Years 1733-1758. New York: 1964. V. 48
The Autobiography. San Francisco. V. 50
Autobiography. Philadelphia: 1868. V. 47
The Autobiography. Cleveland: 1898. V. 49; 51
The Autobiography. San Francisco: 1931. V. 51; 53
Benjmain Franklin's Jugendjahre, von ihm Selbst fur Seinen Sohn Beschrieben. Berlin: 1792. V. 47
Colleccao dos Escriptos Mais Interessantes...em Moral, Encomia e Politica Com Uma Noticia Sobre a Sua Vida por Francisco Ladislao Alvares d'Andrada. London: 1832. V. 53
The Complete Works in Philosophy, Politics and Morals...Now First Collected and Arraned... London: 1806. V. 47
Correspondence Inedite et Secrete du Docteur B. Franklin, Ministre Plenipotentiare des Etats-Unis d'Amerique pres la Cor de France,, depuis l'Annee 1753 Jusqu'en 1790... Paris: 1817. V. 53
Curious and Facetious Letters of Benjamin Franklin Hietherto Unpublished. 1898. V. 50
Enskildta Lefwerne. (The Life of...). Stockholm: 1792. V. 53
Experiences et Observations sur l'Electricite Faites a Philadelphia en Amerique. Paris: 1752. V. 47; 51; 53
Experiences et Observations Sur L'Electricite Faites a Philadelphie en Amerique par M. Benjamin Franklin... Paris: 1756. V. 52
Experiments and Observations on Electricity, Made at Philadelphia in America. London: 1769. V. 48; 52; 53
An Historical Review of the Constitution and Government of Pensylvania, From Its Origin: so Far as Regards the Several Points of Controversy, Which Have, From Time to Time, Arisen Between the Several Governors of that Province... London: 1759. V. 48
The Life and Works of Dr. Benjamin Franklin. Bungay: 1815. V. 48
The Life of Dr. Benjamin Franklin. Montpelier: 1809. V. 51
Memoires de La Vie Privee de Benjamin Franklin... Paris: 1791. V. 47; 50; 51; 52; 54
Memoires de la Vie Privee de Benjamin Franklin. (with) *Vie Publique et Privee de Honore-Gabriel Riquetti, Comte de Mirabeau.* Paris: 1791/92. V. 52
Memoirs of the Life and Writings of Benjamin Franklin, LL.D. London: 1818. V. 53
Observations on Smoky Chimneys, Their Causes and Cure, with considerations On Fuel and Stoves. London: 1793. V. 50; 53
Oeuvres. Paris: 1773. V. 49; 53
Opere Politiche de Beniamino Franklin... Padova: 1783. V. 47
Papers. New Haven: 1960. V. 49
Pictorial Life of...Embracing Anecdotes Illustrative of His Character. Philadelphia: 1847. V. 47
Political, Miscellaneous and Philosophical Pieces. London: 1779. V. 49; 50; 52; 53; 54
Poor Richard's Almanacks for the Years 1733-58. Philadelphia: 1964. V. 51; 53
The Private Life of the Late Benjamin Franklin... London: 1793. V. 47; 49; 51; 54
La Science du Bonhomme Richard, ou Moyen Facile de Payer les Impots. Philadelphia: 1777. V. 52
The Way to Wealth. Paris: 1795. V. 49
The Way to Wealth. New York: 1930. V. 50; 52; 54
Works. London: 1793. V. 49
The Works. Huntingdon: 1800. V. 51
The Works. New York: 1807. V. 51
The Works. Boston: 1840. V. 52
The Writings of Benjamin Franklin. New York: 1905. V. 50

FRANKLIN, COLIN
The Ashendene Press. 1986. V. 53
The Ashendene Press. Dallas: 1986. V. 48; 50; 54
A Catalogue of Early Colour Printing from Chiaroscuro to Aquatint. Culham: 1977. V. 52
A Catalogue of Early Colour Printing from Chiaroscuro to Aquatint. Oxford: 1977. V. 53
Doves Press: the Start of a Worry. Dallas: 1983. V. 54
Emery Walker. Some Light on His Theories of Printing and On His Relations with William Morris and Cobden-Sanderson. Cambridge: 1973. V. 47; 48; 51; 52
The Mystique of Vellum. Boston: 1984. V. 51
Poets of the Daniel Press. Cambridge: 1988. V. 53
The Private Presses. London: 1969. V. 47
Themes in Aquatint. San Francisco: 1978. V. 47; 48; 49; 50; 53

FRANKLIN, JAMES
The Present State of Hayti. London: 1828. V. 53

FRANKLIN, JOHN
Journey to the Shores of the Polar Sea, in Years 1819-20-21 and 22. London: 1824. V. 51
Narrative of a Journey to the Shores of the Polar Sea, in the Years 1819, 20, 21 and 22. London: 1823. V. 54
Narrative of a Journey to the Shores of the Polar Sea, in the years 1819, 20, 21 and 22. London: 1823. V. 47; 50
Narrative of a Journey to the Shores of the Polar Sea, in the Years 1819, 20, 21 and 22. London: 1824. V. 48; 50; 53; 54
Narrative of a Journey to the Shores of the Polar Sea, in the Years 1819, 20, 21 and 22. Philadelphia: 1824. V. 53
Narrative of a Journey to the Shores of the Polar Sea, in the Years 1819, 20, 21 and 22... Edmonton: 1969. V. 54
Narrative of a Journey to the Shores of the Polar Sea, in the Years 1819, 20, 21 and 22. Rutland and Tokyo: 1970. V. 53
Narrative of a Journey to the Shores of the Polar Sea, in the Years 1819, 20, 21 and 22. (with) *Narrative of a Second Expedition to the Shores of the Polar Sea in the Years 1825 and 1827.* London: 1823/28. V. 47
Narrative of a Second Expedition to the Shores of the Polar Sea, in the Years 1825, 1826 and 1827... London: 1828. V. 50
Narrative of a Second Expedition to the Shores of the Polar Sea, in the Years 1825, 1826 and 1827. Edmonton: 1971. V. 47; 49; 54

FRANKLIN, JOHN HOPE
George Washington Williams, Historian. 1946. V. 53

FRANKLIN, JOSEPH
African. A Photographic Essay on Black Women of Ghana & Nigeria. Sebastopol: 1977. V. 48

FRANKLIN, MORRIS JULIUS
Conversion of Morris Julius Franklin: or Proofs of the Messiahship of Jesus of Nazareth. New York: 1855. V. 54

FRANKS, AUGUSTUS WOLLASTON
Catalogue of British and American Bookplates Bequeathed to the Trustees of the British Museum. London: 1903-04. V. 47

FRANZKE, ANDREAS
Dubuffet. New York: 1981. V. 48; 49; 50; 51; 52; 53

FRASCONI, ANTONIO
Birds from My Homeland. New York: 1958. V. 49
The Enduring Struggle: Tom Joad's America. Purchase: 1991. V. 50
Woodcuts. New York: 1957. V. 49

FRASER, A. C.
The Works of George Berkeley. London: 1871. V. 49

FRASER, ALEXANDER, MRS.
A Leader of Society: a Novel. London: 1887. V. 54
A Thing of Beauty. London: 1877. V. 54

FRASER, CLAUD LOVAT
Designs (1890-1921). London: 1922. V. 52
Five New Poems. London: 1913. V. 52
The Lute of Love - an Anthology. London. V. 49
Nursery Rhymes. London: 1919. V. 51
Pirates. London: 1913. V. 49
Pirates. New York: 1922. V. 49
Sixty-three Unpublished Designs. London: 1924. V. 48; 50; 51; 52

FRASER, D.
Torres Straits Sculpture: a Study in Oceanic Primitive Art. New York: 1978. V. 51

FRASER, DAVID
Persia and Turkey in Revolt. Edinburgh: 1910. V. 47
The Short Cut to India. The Record of a Journey Along the Route of the Baghdad Railway. Edinburgh: 1909. V. 47

FRASER, DON
The Young Gentleman and Lady's Assistant... New York: 1791. V. 53

FRASER, DONALD
Proclamations by Governors and Lieutnant Governors of Quebec and Upper Canada. Toronto: 1907. V. 51

FRASER, DUNCAN
Newton's Interpolation Forumlas. London: 1927. V. 52

FRASER, GEORGE
A Catalogue of the Scarabs Belonging to George Fraser. London: 1900. V. 49

FRASER, GEORGE MAC DOANLD
Flashman. New York: 1969. V. 51

FRASER, GEORGE MAC DONALD
Flashman and The Angel of the Lord. 1994. V. 54
Flashman and the Angel of the Lord. London: 1994. V. 51; 53
Flashman in the Great Game. 1975. V. 47
Flashman's Lady. London: 1977. V. 48
Mcauslan in the Rough. London: 1974. V. 49
The Steel Bonnets. London: 1971. V. 54

FRASER, H., MRS.
A Diplomatist's Wife in Japan: Letters from Home to Home. London: 1899. V. 54

FRASER, HUGH
Amid the High Hills. London: 1923. V. 48

FRASER, J.
Irish Texts, Fasciculus I-V. London: 1931-34. V. 47

FRASER, JAMES
The History of Nadir Shah, Formerly Called Thamas Kuli Kahn, the Present Emperor of Perisa. London: 1742. V. 47; 50; 51; 52
John Anderson and The Pickering Press. An Autobiography and a Bibliography. 1995. V. 53

FRASER, JAMES BAILLIE
An Historical and Descriptive Account of Persia, from the Earliest Ages to the Present Time... Edinburgh: 1834. V. 53
Journal of a Tour through Part of the Snowy Range of the Himala Mountains and to the Sources of the Rivers Jumma and Ganges. London: 1820. V. 47; 50
Narrative of a Journey Into Khorasan, in the Years 1821 and 1822. (with) Travels and Adventures in the Persian Provinces... London: 1825/26. V. 50
Travels in Koordistan, Mesopotamia, Etc. London: 1840. V. 49

FRASER, JAMES H.
John Anderson and the Pickering Press. Madison: 1980. V. 52
The Paste Papers of the Golden Hind Press. Florham-Madison: 1983. V. 52

FRASER, JOHN
A Tale of the Sea and Other Poems. Montreal: 1870. V. 47

FRASER, JULIA AGNES
Shilrick the Drummer, or Loyal and True, a Romance of the Irish Rebellion of 1798. London: 1894. V. 54
The Star-Spangled Banner. Plymouth: 1890. V. 53

FRASER, KATHLEEN
Little Notes to You, from Lucas Street. Poems 1970-1971. Urbana: 1972. V. 54

FRASER, LOUIS
Zoologia Typica, or Figures of New and Rare Mammals and Birds. London: 1849. V. 54

FRASER, MARY CRAWFORD
A Diplomatist's Wife in Japan. London: 1899. V. 48
Letters from Japan. London: 1899. V. 53

FRASER, ROBERT W.
Illustrative Views in Tinted Lithography of Interesting and Romantic Parish Kirks and Manses in Scotland. Edinburgh: 1850. V. 49

FRASER, SIMON
The Airs and Melodies Peculiar to the Highlands of Scotland and the Isles... Edinburgh: 1816. V. 49

FRASER, THOMAS
Strophanthus Hispidus: Its Natural History, Chemistry and Pharmacology. Edinburgh: 1891. V. 53

FRASER, THOMAS RODERICK
The Origin of Creation; or the Science of Matter and Force, a New Stystem of Natural Philosophy. Halifax: 1876. V. 47

FRASER, ULIA AGNES
Shilrick the Drummer... London: 1894. V. 51

FRASER, WILLIAM
Coila's Whispers. London: 1872. V. 51; 53; 54

THE FRAUDS and Abuses of Coal-Dealers Detected and Exposed; in a Letter to an Alderman of London. London: 1747. V. 52

FRAULK, ODIE B.
The Leather Jacket Soldier. Pasadena: 1971. V. 54

FRAXI, PISANUS
Bibliography fo Prohibited books. New York: 1962. V. 51

FRAYN, MICHAEL
The Day of the Dog. London: 1962. V. 51

FRAZER, J. G.
The Belief in Immortality and the Worship of the Dead. London: 1913. V. 51

FRAZER, JACK
Inronface, the Adventures of Jack Frazer, Frontier Warrior, Scout and Hunter. Chicago: 1950. V. 47

FRAZER, JAMES
A Hand Book for Travellers in Ireland... Dublin: 1844. V. 53

FRAZER, JAMES GEORGE
Folk-lore in the Old Testament: Studies in Comparative Religion, Legend and Law. London: 1918. V. 48; 50
The Golden Bough. London: 1890. V. 47
The Golden Bough. London: 1926-27. V. 47
The Golden Bough. London: 1955. V. 51
The Golden Bough. London: 1959. V. 54
The Golden Bough. New York: 1969. V. 51
The Golden Bough: a Study in Magic and Religion. New York: 1970. V. 50
The Native Races of Africa and Madagascar. London: 1938. V. 54
Totemica. London: 1937. V. 48
Totemism. Edinburgh: 1887. V. 53
The Worship of Nature. London: 1926. V. 53

FRAZIER, CHARLES H.
Surgery of the Spine and Spinal Cord. New York: 1918. V. 47

FRAZIER, E. FRANKLIN
Black Bourgeoisie. Glencoe: 1957. V. 49
The Negro in the United States. New York: 1949. V. 53; 54

FRAZIER, GEORGE
The One with the Mustache is Costello. New York: 1947. V. 53

FREAR, W. F.
Mark Twain and Hawaii. Chicago: 1947. V. 54

FREART, ROLAND
An Idea of the Perfection of Painting: Demonstrated from the Principles of Art... London: 1668. V. 47

FREDERIC, H.
The Damantion of Theorn Ware. Chicago: 1896. V. 47
The New Exodus. New York: 1892. V. 47

FREDERIC, LOUIS
The Art of India. New York. V. 50
The Art of India: Temples and Sculpture. New York: 1960. V. 49
The Art of Southeast Asia: Temples and Sculpture. New York. V. 54
Japan Art and Civilization. New York: 1969. V. 51

FREDERICA SOPHIA WILHELMINA, PRINCESS OF PRUSSIA
Frederica: or, the Memoirs of a Young lady. Dublin: 1792. V. 51
Memoirs of... London: 1812. V. 47; 51; 53

FREDERICK and Caroline...Forming Part of a New Work. London: 1810. V. 47

FREDERICK, CHARLES
Foxhunting. London: 1930. V. 47

FREDERICK, H.
The Art of Falconry. U.S.A: 1969. V. 47

FREDERICK, J. L.
Ben Holiday - the Stagecoach King. Glendale: 1940. V. 52

FREDERICK, J. V.
Ben Holladay, The Stagecoach King, A Chapter in the Development of Transcontinental Transportation. Glendale: 1940. V. 49; 50; 53

FREDERICKSEN, B.
The Index of Paintings sold in the British Isles During the Nineteenth Century 1801-1810. Oxford: 1988-90. V. 47

FREDERICKSON, A. D.
Ad Orientem. London: 1889. V. 50; 54

FREE, J. B.
Insect Pollination of Crops. London: 1993. V. 50

FREE, JOHN
Tyrocinium Geographicum Londoninense, or the London Geography, Consisting of Dr. Free's Short Lectures... London: 1789. V. 48; 52

FREE Trade; or, an Inquiry into the Pretensions of the Directors of the East India Company, to the Exclusive Trade of the Indian and China Seas... London: 1812. V. 53

THE FREE-MASON'S Vocal Assistant, and Register of the Lodges of Masons in South Carolina and Georgia. Charleston: 1807. V. 53

FREEBURG, VICTOR O.
William Henry Welch at Eighty. New York: 1930. V. 48

FREEDBERG, S. J.
Andrea Del Sarto: Catalogue Raisonne. Cambridge: 1963. V. 53
Painting of the High Renaissance in Rome and Florence. Cambridge: 1961. V. 53
Painting of the High Renaissance in Rome and Florence. New York: 1985. V. 53
Parmigianino, His Works in Painting. Cambridge: 1950. V. 52

FREEDLEY, EDWIN T.
Philadelphia and Its Manufactures: a Hand-Book Exhibiting the Development, Variety and Statistics of the Manufacturing, Industry of Philadelphia in 1857. Philadelphia: 1859. V. 50

FREEDMAN, CLAUDIA
My Toy Cupboard. London: 1930's. V. 51

FREELAND, ROBERT
The Soap Maker's Private Manual. Philadelphia: 1876. V. 52

FREELING, ARTHUR
Dress and Address; or, the Citizen of the World. London: 1848. V. 47
Flowers: Their Use and Beauty, Language and Sentiment. London: 1857. V. 54
Freeling's Grand Junction Railway Companion to Liverpool, Manchester and Birmingham and Liverpool, Manchester and Birmingham Guide... London: 1838. V. 49
The London and Birmingham Railway Companion. London: 1836. V. 48
The Railway Companion, From London to Birmingham, Liverpool and Manchester. (with) Freeling's Grand Junction Railway Companion to Liverpool, Manchester and Birmingham. London: 1838. V. 48; 49

FREELING, G. H.
Catalogue of the Greater Portion of the Valuable Publications of the Revd. T. F. Dibdin, Purchased for Joseph Walter King Eyton...by Messrs Pickering and Thorpe at the Sale of the Library of Sir G. H. Freeling... London: 1842. V. 49

FREELING, M.
The Maize Handbook. Berlin: 1993. V. 50

FREELING, NICHOLAS
Crime and Metaphysics. Helsinki: 1991. V. 48

FREEMAN & CO.
Catalogue of Type, Borders and Cuts. Providence: 1890. V. 50

FREEMAN, ALBERT C.
Hints on the Planning of Poor Law Buildings and Mortuaries. London: 1905. V. 48

THE FREEMAN Book. New York: 1924. V. 50

FREEMAN, DON
Space Witch. New York: 1959. V. 50

FREEMAN, DOUGLAS SOUTHALL
George Washington, a Biography. New York: 1948. V. 50
George Washington, a Biography. New York: 1948-57. V. 47; 50
The Last Parade. Richmond: 1932. V. 49; 54
Lee's Lieutenants. New York: 1942-44-44. V. 47; 49; 50
Lee's Lieutenants. New York: 1943-44. V. 53
Lee's Lieutenants. New York: 1944. V. 51
Lee's Lieutenants. New York: 1945. V. 49
Lee's Lieutenants a Study in Command. New York: 1946. V. 48; 49; 51
Lee's Lieutenants a Study in Command. New York: 1970. V. 50
R. E. Lee A Biography. New York: 1934-35. V. 48; 53
R. E. Lee. A Biography. New York: 1936. V. 49; 52; 53
R. E. Lee. A Biography. New York: 1940. V. 48
R. E. Lee a Biography. New York: 1943-47. V. 48
The South to Posterity an Introduction to the Writing of Confederate History. New York: 1939. V. 49

FREEMAN, EDWARD A.
Historical Essays. London: 1886-92. V. 52
Historical Essays. London: 1896. V. 47; 50
The History of Sicily from the Earliest Times. London: 1891-94. V. 52
The History of Sicily From the Earliest Times. Oxford: 1891-94. V. 48; 49
The History of the Norman Conquest of England, Its Causes and Its Results. London: 1867-79. V. 47; 49
The History of the Norman Conquest of England, Its Causes and Its Results. London: 1877-75-79. V. 52

FREEMAN, GEORGE D.
Midnight and Noonday; or Dark Deeds Unraveled, Giving Twenty Years Experience on the Frontier. Caldwell: 1890. V. 50; 54
Midnight and Noonday; or the Incidental History of Southern Kansas and the Indian Territory. Caldwell: 1892. V. 49; 53

FREEMAN, HARRY C.
A Brief History of Butte, Montana, The World's Greatest Mining Camp. Chicago: 1900. V. 47

FREEMAN, IRA S.
A History of Montezuma County, Colorado. Boulder: 1958. V. 53

FREEMAN, J.
Life of the Rev. William Kirby, Rector of Barham. London: 1852. V. 49
A Narrative of the Persecutions of the Christians in Madagascar... London: 1840. V. 47

FREEMAN, JAMES W.
Prose and Poetry of the Live Stock Industry of the United States. New York: 1959. V. 47; 52; 53; 54

FREEMAN, JOHN R.
On the Proposed Use of a Portion of the Hetch Hetchy, Eleanor and Cherry Valleys...as Reservoirs for...San Francisco. San Francisco: 1912. V. 54

FREEMAN, JONATHAN
A Discourse on Psalmody. Delivered at Newburgh, Before the Presbytery of Hudson... Newburgh: 1801. V. 50

FREEMAN, R.
Kentish Poets. Canterbury: 1821. V. 54

FREEMAN, R. AUSTIN
The Dr. Thorndyke Omnibus. New York: 1932. V. 48
Dr. Thorndyke's Case-Book. London. V. 51
Dr. Thorndyke's Crime File... New York: 1941. V. 48

FREEMAN, RICHARD AUSTIN
Travels and Life in Ashanti and Jaman. London: 1898. V. 49; 51

FREEMAN, ROSEMARY
English Emblem Books. London: 1948. V. 49
English Emblem Books. London: 1967. V. 49; 50

FREEMAN, SAMUEL
The Probate Auxiliary; or, a Director and Assistant to Probate Courts, Executors, Administrators and Guardians. Portland: 1793. V. 52

FREEMAN, SARAH
Medals Relating to Medicine and Allied Sciences in the Numismatic Collection of the Johns Hopkins University. Baltimore: 1964. V. 52

FREEMAN, WALTER JACKSON
Psychosurgery in the Treatment of Mental Disorders and Intractable Pain. Springfield: 1942. V. 53
Psychosurgery: Intelligence, Emotion and Social Behavior Following Prefrontal Lobotomy for Mental Disorder. Springfield: 1950. V. 52; 53

FREEMAN MITFORD, A. B.
The Bamboo Garden. London: 1896. V. 50

FREEMANTLE, BRIAN
Goodbye to an Old Friend. London: 1973. V. 48

FREEMANTLE, W. T.
A Bibliography of Sheffield and Vicinity. Section I, to the End of 1700. Sheffield: 1911. V. 53

FREEMASONS
Proceedings of the M. W. Grand Lodge of Oregon, A. F. & A. M. Special Communication Held in the City of Salem, oct. 8, A. D. 1873 for the Purpose of Laying the Corner-Stone of the State Capital. Portland: 1873. V. 51

FREEMASONS. LOUISIANA
Proceedings of the M.E. Grand Chapter of Royal Arch Masons, of the State of Louisiana, at Its Fifteenth Annual Convocation, Begun and Held in the Masonic Hall, City of New Orleans on Tuesday, Feb. 11, 1862. New Orleans: 1862. V. 49

FREEMASONS. NORTH CAROLINA. GRAND LODGE
Proceedings of the Grand Lodge of Free and Accepted Masons of North Carolina. Raleigh: 1865. V. 48; 49

FREEMASONS. VIRGINIA. GRAND LODGE
Free Masonry and the War. Report of the Committee Under the Resolutions of 1862, Grand Lodge of Virginia... Richmond: 1865. V. 47; 49

FREER GALLERY OF ART, WASHINGTON.
A Descriptive and Illustrative Catalogue of Chinese Bronzes Acquired During the Administration of John Ellerton Lodge (Freer Gallery of Art, Oriental Studies No. 3). Washington: 1946. V. 49; 51; 53
The Freer Chinese Bronzes. Washington: 1967-69. V. 51; 53

FREES, HARRY WHITTIER
The Little Folks of Animal Land. Boston: 1915. V. 53; 54

FREETH, JOHN
New Ballads, to Old Familiar Tunes. Birmingham: 1805. V. 54
The Political Songster, Addressed to the Sons of Freedom and Lovers of Humour. Birmingham: 1771. V. 54
The Political Songster; or, a Touch of the Times on Various Subjects, Adapted to Common Tunes. Birmingham: 1786. V. 54
The Political Songster, or, a Touch On the Times, On Various Subjects and Adapted to Common Tunes. Birmingham: 1790. V. 49

FREHER, PAUL
Theatrum Virorum Eruditione Clarorum in Quo Vitae et Scripta Theologorum, Jureconsultorum, Medicorum et Philosophorum. Noribergae: 1688. V. 47; 53

FREIBURG. LAWS, STATUTES, ETC.
(Freiburg im Breisgau). Nuwe Stattrechten und Statuten der Loblichen Statt Fryburg im Pryssgow Gelegen. 1520. V. 52

FREIBURG IM BREISAGU
Nuwe Stattrechten und Statuten der Statt Fryburg im Pryszgow Gelegen. Basle: 1520. V. 53; 54

FREILIGRATH-KROEKER, KATE
Alice and Other Fairy Plays for Children. London: 1880. V. 53

FREIND, JOHN
An Account of the Earl of Peterborough's Conduct in Spain, Chiefly Since the Raising the Siege of Barcelona, 1706. London: 1707. V. 47; 48; 49; 53
Emmenologia; in Qua Fluxus Muliebris Menstrui Phaenomena, Periodi, Vitia, cum Medendi Methodo... London: 1717. V. 48
Emmenologia: Written, in Latin... London: 1729. V. 52; 54
The History of Physic from the Time of Galen, to the Beginning of the Sixteenth Century. London: 1725-27. V. 47
Nine Commentaries Upon Fevers: and Two Epistles Concerning the Small Pox... London: 1730. V. 47

FREIRE, FRANCISCO JOSE
Memorias das Principaes Providencias, que se Derao no Terremoto, Que Padeceo a Corte de Lisboa no anno de 1755, Ordenadas, e Offerecidas a Magestade Fidelissima de ElRey D. Joseph I Nosso Senhor por Amador Pataricio de Lisboa. 1758. V. 53

FREIRE DE ANDRADA, JACINTO
The Life of Dom John De Castro, The Fourth Vice-roy of India. London: 1664. V. 51

FREITAS, SERAFINO DE
de Justo Imperio Iusitanorum Asiatico... Valladolid: 1625. V. 48

FREJES, FRANCISCO
Historia Breve De la Conquestas de Los Estado Independientes Del Empierio mejicano. Zacatecas: 1838. V. 54

FREKE, WILLIAM
Select Essays Tending to the Universal Reformation of Learning... London: 1693. V. 47; 50

FRELINGHUYSEN, ALICE COONEY
Splendid Legacy, the Havemeyer Collection at the Metropolitan Museum of Art, New York. New York: 1993. V. 52

FREMANTLE, ARTHUR JAMES L.
Three Months in the Southern States April-June 1863. Edinburgh and London: 1863. V. 53; 54
Three Months in the Southern States, April-June 1863. Mobile: 1864. V. 49

FREMANTLE, RICHARD
Florentine Gothic Painters, From Giotto to Masaccio. London: 1975. V. 49; 51; 53

FREMONT - His Supporters and Their Record. The Opinions of Our Great Statesman Upon the Missouri Restriction. 1856. V. 48

FREMONT, JESSIE BENTON
A Year of American Travel...and a Letter from Colonel John Charles Fremont... San Francisco: 1960. V. 47

FREMONT, JOHN CHARLES
Defense of Lieut. Colonel Fremont, Before the Court Martial. 1848. V. 47; 52
The Expeditions of John Charles Fremont. Urbana: 1970/73/84. V. 53
Geographical Memoir Upon Upper California, in Illustration Oregon and California. Washington: 1849. V. 47
Geographical Memoir Upon Upper California, In Illustrations...Oregon and California. Washington: 1848. V. 47
Memoirs of My Life. Chicago: 1886-87. V. 47
Memoirs of My Life... Chicago & New York: 1887. V. 51; 52; 54
Miscellaneous Documents. Washington: 1849. V. 47
Narrative of the Exploring Expedition to the Rocky Mountains in the Year 1842 and to Oregon and North California in the Years 1843-44. V. 53
Narrative of the Exploring Expedition to the Rocky Mountains in the Year 1842 and to Oregon and North California in the Years 1843-44. Washington: 1845. V. 47; 50; 52
Narrative of the Exploring Expedition to the Rocky Mountains in the Year 1842 and to Oregon and North California in the Years 1843-44. New York: 1846. V. 53
Narrative of the Exploring Expedition to the Rocky Mountains in the Year 1842; and to Oregon and North California, in the Years 1843-44. Syracuse: 1847. V. 47; 54
Narrative of the Exploring Expedition to the Rocky Mountains in the Year 1842 and to Oregon and North Carolina in the Years 1843-44. London: 1846. V. 48
Notes on Travel in California. New York: 1849. V. 47; 49
Report of the Exploring Expedition to the Rocky Mountains in the year 1842, and to Oregon and North California in the Years 1843-44. Washington: 1845. V. 47; 48; 49; 51; 54

FREMONT'S Romanism Established. Acknowledged by Archbishop Hughes. How Fremont's Nomination Was Brought About. Huges, Seward, Fremont and the Foreigners - a Most Foul Coalition. 1856. V. 48

FREMOR, PATRICK L.
Roumeli: Travels in Northern Greece. London: 1966. V. 49

FRENCH, A. D. WELD
County Records of the Surnames of Francus, Francis, French, in England 1100-1350. Boston: 1896. V. 52

FRENCH, ALBERT
Billy. New York: 1993. V. 53

FRENCH, ALICE
An Adventure in Photography. New York: 1893. V. 51
A Book of True Lovers. Chicago: 1897. V. 48

FRENCH, ALLEN
The Junior Cup. New York: 1901. V. 47; 48
The Red Keep. Boston: 1938. V. 48

FRENCH Clocks the World Over. Paris: 1981. V. 53

FRENCH, FREDERICK W.
Catalogue of the Valuable Private Library of...to be Sold at Auction April 23rd, 24th, 25th, 1901. Boston: 1901. V. 50

FRENCH, GILBERT J.
The Life and Times of Samuel Crompton, Inventor of the Spinning Machine Called the Mule. London: 1859. V. 48

FRENCH, HANNAH DUSTIN
Bookbinding in American, Three Essays. Portland: 1941. V. 50

FRENCH, HOWARD BARCLAY
Genealogy of the Descendants of Thomas French, Who Came to America from Nether Heyford, Northamptonshire, England, and Settled in Berlinton (Burlington) in the Province and Country of West New Jersey of Which He Was One of the Original Proprietors... Philadelphia: 1909-13. V. 51

THE FRENCH Intrigues Discovered. With Methods and Arts to Retrench the Potency of France by Land and Sea... London: 1681. V. 49

FRENCH, J. H.
Gazetteer of the State of New York... Syracuse: 1860. V. 54

FRENCH, JAMES
Wild Jim - the Texas Cowboy and Saddle King. 1890. V. 54
Wild Jim...the Texas Cowboy and Saddle King. Chicago. V. 54

FRENCH, JAMES WEIR
Machine Tools Commonly Employed in Modern Engineering Workshops. 1911. V. 51
Machine Tools Commonly Employed in Modern Engineering Workshops. London: 1911. V. 52
Modern Power Generators. London: 1908. V. 48

FRENCH, JOHN
The Art of Distillation: or, a Treatise of the Choicest Spagyrical Preparations... London: 1667. V. 48

FRENCH, L. H.
Nome Nuggets. 1901. V. 53
Seward's Land of Gold. Five Seasons Experience with the Gold Seekers in Northwestern Alaska. New York: 1905. V. 47

FRENCH, LEIGH
Colonial Interiors. First and Second Series. New York: 1923/30. V. 54

FRENCH, NICHOLAS
The Historical Works of... Dublin: 1846. V. 53

FRENCH, SAMUEL GIBBS
Two Wars: An Autobiography of Gen. Samuel G. French...Mexican War... Nashville: 1901. V. 48; 49; 50

FRENCH, THOMAS M.
Psychogenic Factors in Bronchial Asthma. Washington: 1941. V. 48

FRENCH, WILLIAM
Some Recollections of a Western Ranchman, New Mexico 1883-1899. London: 1927. V. 54
Some Recollections of a Western Ranchman (New Mexico, 1883-1899) with Further Recollections Western Ranchman. New York: 1965. V. 47

FRENCH-SHELDON, MARY
Sultan to Sultan. 1892. V. 50; 51; 52; 54
Sultan to Sultan. Boston: 1892. V. 47; 51; 54

FREND, WILLIAM
Peace and Union Recommended to the Associated Bodies of Republicans and Anti-Republicans... Cambridge: 1793. V. 50
The Principles of Algebra. London: 1796. V. 53

FRENEAU, PHILIP
Letters on Various Interesting and Important Subjects... Philadelphia: 1799. V. 54
The Miscellaneous Works of... Philadelphia: 1788. V. 51; 53
Poems Written and Pubished During the American Revolutionary War, and Now Republished from the Original Manuscripts... Philadelphia: 1809. V. 47; 50; 51
Poems Written Between the Years 1768 & 1794. Monmouth: 1795. V. 47; 48; 49; 50; 51

FRENZ, LOUIS JACQUES
The Life of Monsr. Louis Jacques, the French Giant. London: 1822. V. 47

FRENZEL, H. K.
Ludwig Hohlwein. Berlin: 1926. V. 48; 50

FRERE, ALICE M.
The Antipodes and Round the World; or, Travels in Australia, New Zealand, Ceylon, China, Japan, and California. London: 1870. V. 50; 51

FRERE, BENJAMIN
The Adventures of a Dramatist, on a Journey to the London Managers. London: 1813. V. 47

FRERE, HENRY BARTLE EDWARD
Memoranda and Letters on Bechuanaland, Written At Various Times (1879-83). London: 1884. V. 50

FRERE, W. H.
Antiphonale Sarisburiense. 1901-15. V. 51

FRERICHS, F. T.
A Clinical Treatise on Diseases of the Liver. London: 1861. V. 53
A Clinical Treatise on Diseases of the Liver. New York: 1879. V. 48

FRESH Hints; or, a New Cambridge Guide; Dedicated Without Permission; to Freshmen. London: 1815. V. 50; 54

FRESH Intelligence of Another New and Great Victory Obtained by the Lord Fairfax His Forces Against the Popish Army in Yorkshire Neere Hull. London: 1643. V. 50

FRESHFIELD, DOUGLAS W.
The Exploration of the Caucasus... London: 1896. V. 48; 49; 50; 54
The Exploration of the Caucasus. London: 1902. V. 54
Italian Alps. Sketches in the Mountains of Ticino, Lombardy, the Trentino and Venetia. London: 1875. V. 51; 54
Round Kangghenjunga. London: 1903. V. 53
Travels in the Central Caucasus and Bashan Including Visits to Ararat and Tabreez and Ascents of Kazbek and Elbruz. London: 1869. V. 47; 51

FRESHFIELD, HENRY, MRS.
A Summer Tour of the Grisons and Italian Valleys of the Bernina. London: 1862. V. 48

FRESHFIELD, JANE
Alpine Byways, or, Light Leaves Gathered in 1859 and 1860 by a Lady. London: 1861. V. 54

FRETTER, V.
British Prosobranch Molluscs, Their Functional anatomy and Ecology. London: 1962. V. 50; 51

FREUD, SIGMUND
The Basic Writings of Sigmund Freud. New York: 1938. V. 51
Beyond the Pleasure Principle. London: 1922. V. 47
Beyond the Pleasure Principle. New York: 1922. V. 53
The Case of the Wolf-Man: from the History of an Infantile Neurosis. 1993. V. 52; 54
Civilization and Its Discontents. London: 1930. V. 51
The Cocaine Papers. Vienna & Zurich: 1963. V. 53
Collected Papers. New York & London: 1924-34. V. 52
Collected Papers. London: 1950. V. 48; 50
Collected Papers. London: 1953-6. V. 52
Collected Papers. New York: 1959. V. 47; 48; 49; 50; 53
Les Diplegies Cerebrales Infantiles. Paris: 1893. V. 51
The Ego and the Id. London: 1927. V. 49
The Future of an Illusion. London: 1928. V. 48
Gesammelte Schriften. Leipzig: 1924-25. V. 51
Gesammelte Schriften. Leipzig: 1924-34. V. 51
Group Psychology and the Analysis of the Ego. London: 1922. V. 49
Inhibitions, Symptoms and Anxiety. London: 1936. V. 49
The Interpretation of Dreams. New York: 1913. V. 48; 50; 52; 54
The Interpretation of Dreams. London: 1954. V. 50; 51
Introductory Lectures on Psycho-Analysis: a Course of Twenty-Eight Lectures Delivered at the University of London. London: 1929. V. 52
Klinische Studie Uber die Halbseitige Cerebrallahmung der Kinder. Wien: 1891. V. 51
Lectures Delivered Before the Department of Psychology...20th Anniversary of the Opening of the Clark University September 1909. 1910. V. 54
The Problem of Anxiety. New York: 1936. V. 51
The Problem of Lay-Analyses. New York: 1927. V. 51
Psychopathology of Everyday Life. New York: 1914. V. 51
Selected Papers on Hysteria and Other Psychoneuroses. New York Washington: 1912. V. 51
Standard Edition of the Complete Psychological Works. London: 1955-73. V. 48
Die Traumdeutung. Leipzig und Wien: 1899. V. 52
Die Traumdeutung. Leipzig und Wien: 1900. V. 51; 54
Die Traumdeutung. Leipzig und Wien: 1909. V. 51
Uber den Bau der Nervenfasern und Nervenzellen Beim Flusskrebs. Wien: 1882. V. 51
Wit and Its Relation to the Unconscious. London. V. 53
Wit and Its Relation to the Unconscious. London: 1916. V. 47; 49
Wit and Its Relation to the Unconscious. New York: 1916. V. 51; 53
Zur Kenntnis der Cerebralen Diplegien des Kindesalters(Im Anschluss an die Little'sche Krankheit). Beitrage zur Kinderheilkunde aus dem I. Offentlichen Kinder-Krankeninstitute in Wien Ueue Folge III. Leipzig und Wien: 1893. V. 50; 51

FREUND, GISELE
Gisele Freund: Photographer. New York: 1985. V. 53

FREUND, PHILIP
The Dark Shore. London: 1946. V. 49

FREUNDLICH, AUGUST L.
William Gropper: Retrospective. Los Angeles: 1968. V. 47; 48; 51; 53

FREVILLE, ANNE FRANCOIS JOACHIM DE
Histoire des Nouvelles Decouvertes Faites dans la Mer du Sud en 1767. Paris: 1774. V. 52

FREWEN, MORETON
Melton Mowbray, and Other Memories. London: 1924. V. 47; 53

FREY, HEINRICH
The Histology and Histochemistry of Man. A Treatise ont he Elements of Composition and Structure of the Human Body. New York: 1875. V. 48; 53

FREY, JOSEPH SAMUEL CHRISTIAN FREDERICK
A Hebrew, Latin and English Dicitionary... London: 1815. V. 47

FREYTAG, GUSTAV
Our Forefathers. London: 1873. V. 54
Pictures of German Life in the XVth, XVIth and XVIIth Centuries. London: 1862. V. 52

FREZIER, AMEDEE FRANCOIS
Relation Du Voyage de La Mer Du Sud Aux Cotes Du Chily et Perou, Fait Pendant Les Annees 1712, 1713, and 1714. Paris: 1716. V. 53
Voyage to the South Sea, and Along the Coasts of Chili and Peru, in the Years 1712, 1713 and 1714. London: 1717. V. 49; 50; 52; 53; 54

FRICERO, KATE J.
Our Visit to France. London: 1905. V. 47

FRICK, GEORGE
A Treatise on the Diseases of the Eye; Including the Doctrines and Practice of the Most Eminent Modern Surgeons... London: 1826. V. 51

FRICK, HENRY CLAY
The Frick Collection. An Illustrated Catalogue of the Works of Art in the Collection of Henry Clay Frick. Pittsburgh: 1949-55. V. 50

FRICKER, KARL
The Antarctic Regions. London: 1900. V. 48
The Antarctic Regions. New York: 1900. V. 52

FRIDGE, IKE
History of the Chisum War; or, Life of Ike Fridge. Electra: 1927. V. 53

FRIED, MICHAEL
Morris Louis. New York. V. 47; 48
Morris Louis. New York: 1979?. V. 50

FRIEDAN, BETTY
The Feminine Mystique. New York: 1963. V. 53; 54

FRIEDENWALD, HARRY
The Jews and Medicine. 1944. V. 47
The Jews and Medicine. Baltimore: 1944. V. 47; 50
The Jews and Medicine, Essays. Baltimore: 1944-46. V. 52

FRIEDLAENDER, JOHNNY
Johnny Friedlaender. Oeuvre 1961-1965. New York: 1965. V. 50

FRIEDLAENDER, WALTER
Claude Lorrain. Berlin: 1921. V. 48
Nicolas Poussin: a New Approach. New York: 1965. V. 51

FRIEDLANDER, LEE
Flowers and Trees. New York: 1981. V. 50; 54

FRIEDLANDER, M. J.
The Painting of Lucas Cranach. 1978. V. 51; 53
The Paintings of Lucas Cranach. Ithaca: 1978. V. 50

FRIEDLANDER, WALTER
Caravaggio Studies. Princeton: 1955. V. 54

FRIEDMAN, BRUCE JAY
Steambath. New York: 1971. V. 54
Stern. New York: 1962. V. 48

FRIEDMAN, CHARLES
Charles Sheeler. New York: 1975. V. 47; 48; 49

FRIEDMAN, I. K.
The Radical. New York: 1907. V. 52

FRIEDMAN, JOSEPH S.
History of Color Photography. Boston: 1944. V. 49

FRIEDMAN, M.
Charles Sheeler: Paintings, Drawings, Photographs. New York: 1975. V. 48; 50; 51; 53

FRIEDMANN, H.
Birds Collected by the Childs Frick Expedition to Ethiopia and Kenya Colony. U.S.A: 1930/37. V. 50; 52; 53

FRIEDRICH DER GROSSE, KING OF PRUSSIA
Familiar and Friendly Correspondence of Frederick the Second, King of Prussia, with U. F. de Suhm, Privy Councillor. London: 1787. V. 47
The History of My Own Times. Dublin: 1791. V. 47

FRIEDRICH II, EMPEROR OF GERMANY
The Art of Falconry. U.S.A: 1969. V. 49; 50; 52; 53

FRIEL, BRIAN
The Gold in the Sea. Stories. London: 1966. V. 52; 53

FRIEND, H.
Flowers and Flower-Lore. London: 1883. V. 50

FRIEND, HERVE
Picturesque Los Angeles County, California. Chicago: 1887. V. 47

A FRIENDLY Address to the Industrious, on the Advantages of a Provident or Savings Bank. Dewsbury: 1822. V. 50

FRIENDLY Advice to Irish Mothers, on Training Their Children. Armagh: 1842. V. 52

FRIENDLY Animals. London: 1930. V. 53

THE FRIENDLY Instructor: or, a Companion for Young Ladies and Gentlemen: In Which Their Duty to God and Their Parents, Their Carriage to Superiors and Inferiors, with several useful and Instructive Lessons are Recommended in Plain & Familiar Dialogues. London: 1810. V. 49

FRIENDS, SOCEITY OF
Epistles from the Yearly Meeting of Friends, Held in London to the Quarterly and Montly Meetings in Great Britain, Ireland and Elsewhere from 1681 to 1875... London: 1858. V. 49

FRIENDS, SOCIETY OF
The Epistle from the Yearly Meeting, Held in London...1744, 1776, 1781-83, 1785-86, 1790-91, 1794, 1796, 1798. 1744-98. V. 48
Further Information Respecting the Aborigines, Containing Extracts from the Proceedings of the Meeting for Sufferings in London and of the Committees on Indian Affairs, of the Yearly Meetings of Philadelphia and Baltimore... London: 1839. V. 49
Report of Friends' London Committee, for the Relief of the Distress in the Manufacturing Districts. London: 1843. V. 53
Transactions of the Central Relief Committee During the Famine in Ireland. 1846 and 1847. 1852. V. 52
Transactions of the Central Relief Committee...During the Famine in Ireland in 1846 and 1847. Dublin: 1852. V. 53
Two Epistles, Taken out of G. Fox's Collection of Epistles, Recommended by This Yearly-Meeting, 1716. London?: 1716?. V. 47

FRIERSON, M.
HPL. 1979. V. 51

FRIES, AMOS
Chemical Warfare. New York: 1921. V. 53

FRIES, B.
A History of Scandinavian Fishes. Stockholm: 1892-95. V. 52; 53

FRIES, E.
Sveriges Atliga Och Giftiga Svampar. Stockholm: 1860. V. 48

FRIES, LORENZ
Spiegel der Artzney. Strassburg: 1529. V. 47

FRIES, W. H.
Story of Audubon's Birds of America. Chicago: 1973. V. 50

FRIKELL, W.
The Secret Out: Or, One Thousand Tricks with Cards and Other Recreations. New York: 1869. V. 51

FRINK, ELISABETH
Sculpture - Catalogue Raisonne. Harpvale: 1984. V. 53
Sculpture. A Catalogue Raisonne.Sculpture. Salisbury: 1984. V. 53

FRINK, MAURICE
Cow Country Cavalcade. Denver: 1954. V. 50
When Grass Was King. Boulder: 1956. V. 52

FRIPP, EDGAR I.
Shakespeare; Man and Artist. London: 1938. V. 51

FRISBEE, JOHN
Family Physician: Designed to Assist Heads of Families, Travellers and Sea-Faring People in discerning, Distinguishing and Curing Diseases. Boston: 1847. V. 48

FRISCH, MAX
Montauk. New York: 1976. V. 50
Three Plays. London: 1962. V. 52
A Wilderness of Mirrors. New York: 1966. V. 52

FRISCH, TERESA G.
The Excavations at Dura-Europos. Final Report IV. Part IV: The Bronze Objects, Fascicule 1: Pierced Bronzes, Enameled Bronzes and Fibulae. New Haven: 1949. V. 52

FRISWELL, JAMES HAIN
Houses with the Fronts Off. London: 1854. V. 47
Life Portraits of William Shakespeare... London: 1864. V. 54

FRISWOLD, CARROLL
The Killing of Chief Crazy Horse. Glendale: 1976. V. 52

FRITH, FRANCIS
Egypt and Palestine. London: 1858. V. 52
Photographs of the Holyland... London, Glasgow: 1863. V. 52
Sinai and Palestine (and) Upper Egypt and Ethiopia (and) Lower Egypt, Thebes and the Pyramids. London: 1862. V. 49

FRITH, WILLIAM POWELL
John Leech, His Life and Work. London. V. 54

John Leech: His Life and Work. London: 1891. V. 53

FRITSCHE, MARCUS
Meteorum, hoc est Impressionum Aerearum et Mirabilium Naturum Operum, Loci Frere Omnes. Nuremberg: 1563. V. 52

A FRIVOLOUS Paper, in Form of a Petition: Framed and Composed by a Disaffected Party in This City of London, Intended by them to Be Presented to the Honourable House of Commons. London: 1642. V. 48; 50

FRIZZELL, LODISA
Across the Plains. New York: 1915. V. 47

FROBENIUS, LEO
The Voice of Africa. London: 1913. V. 50

FROBISHER, MARTIN
The Three Voyages of Martin Frobisher in Search of a Passage to Cathay and India by the North-West, A.D. 1576-78. Amsterdam: 1971. V. 47

FROEBEL, JULIUS
Seven Years' Travel in Central America, Northern Mexico and the Far West of the United States. London: 1859. V. 54

FROGER, FRANCOIS
A Relation Of A Voyage Made in the Years 1695, 1696, 1697, on the Coasts of Africa, Streights of Magellan, Brasil, Cayenna, and the Antilles, by a Squadron of French Men of War, Under the Command of M. de Gennes. London: 1698. V. 50

FROHAWK, F. W.
Natural History of British Butterflies. London: 1924. V. 48; 54
Varieties of British Butterflies. London: 1938. V. 49
Varieties of British Butterflies. London: 1938/46. V. 49

FROHLICH-BUME, L.
Ingres: His Life and Art. 1926. V. 49
Ingres: His Life and Art. London: 1926. V. 51; 52; 54

FROISSART, JEAN
Chronicles of England, France and Spain and the Adjoining Countries. London: 1857. V. 53
Chronicles of England, France, Spain. London: 1842. V. 53
The Chronicles of England, France, Spain and Other Places. New York: 1959. V. 53; 54
Chronicles of England, France, Spain and the Adjoining Countries, from the Latter Part of the Reign of Edward II, to the Coronation of Henry IV. London: 1806. V. 50
Chronicles of England, France, Spain and the Adjoining Countries, From the Latter Part of the Reign of Edward II, to the Coronation of Henry IV. London: 1808. V. 50
Chronicles of England, France, Spain and the Adjoining Countries From the Latter Part of the Reign of Edward II to the Coronation of Henry IV. London: 1844. V. 49
Chronicles of England, France, Spain, Portugal, Scotland, Britanny, Flanders and the Adjoining Countries. London: 1812. V. 47; 49; 50; 51
Cronycles. Oxford: 1927. V. 50
Froissart's Chronycles. Stratford-upon-Avon: 1927-28. V. 47
Here Begynnith the Firste Volum...of the Cronycles of Englande, Fraunce, Spayne, Portyngale, Scotlande, Bretaine, Flaunders and Other Places Adioynynge. (with) Here Beginneth the third and fourth boke... London: 1563/63. V. 54
Histoire det Chroniqve memorable. Paris: 1574. V. 48
Historiarum Opus Omne. Paris: 1537. V. 52
Historiarum Opus Omne. Paris: 1537. V. 47
Le Premier (second, teirs, quart) Volume des Croniques de France. Paris: 1518. V. 47

FROM Incas to Indios. Paris: 1956. V. 47

FROM Under the Rubble. Boston: 1975. V. 47

FROMM, ERICH
Sigmund Freud's Mission. New York: 1959. V. 48

FROMMER, HARVEY
New York City Baseball. The Last Golden Age: 1947-1957. New York: 1980. V. 51; 52

FRONTIER Forts of Pennsylvania. 1896. V. 49

FROST, A. B.
A Portfolio of Twelve Original Illustrations Reproduced from Drawings by A. B. Frost to Illustrate the "Pickwick Papers". London: 1908. V. 54
Stuff and Nonsense. New York: 1884. V. 52

FROST, CHARLES
Notices Relative to the Early History of the Town and Port of Hull. London: 1827. V. 48; 51; 52

FROST, DONALD MC KAY
Notes on General Ashley, The Overland Trail and South Pass. Worcester: 1945. V. 47; 48

FROST, HENRY R.
Elements of the Materia Medica and Therapuetics. Charleston: 1843. V. 50

FROST, J.
The Art of Swimming; a Series of Practical Instructions, on an Original and Progressive Plan... New York: 1818. V. 50

FROST, JOHN
The Mexican War and its Warriors. 1848. V. 53
Mexican War and its Warriors... New Haven: 1848. V. 50
Pictorial History of Mexico and the Mexican War. Philadelphia: 1849. V. 52

FROST, LAWRENCE A.
General Custer's Libbie. Seattle: 1976. V. 51

FROST, ROBERT LEE
Accidentally on Purpose. New York: 1960. V. 49

FROST, ROBERT LEE continued
Acquainted with the Night. Madison: 1993. V. 54
Aforesaid. New York: 1951. V. 51
Aforesaid. New York: 1954. V. 47; 48; 54
Benn's Augustan Books of Poetry: Robert Frost. London: 1932. V. 49
A Boy's Will. London: 1913. V. 48; 49; 51; 53; 54
A Boy's Will. New York: 1915. V. 48; 49; 51; 52; 53; 54
Carpe Diem. New York: 1938. V. 49
Collected Poems. New York: 1930. V. 48; 49; 50; 51; 52; 53
Collected Poems... New York: 1936. V. 53
Collected Poems... New York: 1939. V. 53; 54
Collected Poems 1939. New York: 1939. V. 49
Collected Poems of... New York: 1940. V. 48; 49
Come In and other Poems. New York: 1943. V. 48
Complete Poems. New York: 1949. V. 49; 51; 53
Complete Poems. New York: 1950. V. 47; 48; 50; 51; 54
Complete Poems. 1951. V. 50
Complete Poems. London: 1951. V. 48; 51
A Considerable Speck. Boston: 1939. V. 53
Does No One But Me At All Ever Feel This Way in the Least. New York: 1952. V. 49
Fifty Years of Robert Frost. Hanover: 1944. V. 47
The Four Beliefs. Hanover: 1931. V. 49
From Snow to Snow. New York: 1936. V. 48; 49
A Further Range. New York: 1936. V. 48; 49; 51; 53; 54
The Gold Hesperidee. Cortland: 1935. V. 53
The Guardeen. Los Angeles: 1943. V. 49; 51; 52; 54
Hard Not to Be King. New York: 1951. V. 49; 50
A Hillside Thaw. New York: 1922. V. 47
In the Clearing. New York: 1962. V. 47; 48; 49
The Lovely Shall Be Choosers. New York: 1929. V. 48; 52
Masque of Mercy. New York: 1947. V. 49; 50; 51; 53; 54
A Masque of Reason. New York: 1945. V. 47; 48; 49; 50; 51; 52; 53; 54
Mountain Interval. New York: 1916. V. 47; 48; 49; 50; 53
Mountain Interval. New York: 1921. V. 49; 54
Mountain Interval. New York: 1924. V. 52
Mountain Interval. New York: 1931. V. 47; 53
My November Guest. New York: 1922. V. 47
Neither Out Far Nor in Deep. 1935. V. 48; 51
New Hampshire. New York: 1923. V. 48; 49; 51; 53; 54
New Hampshire. Hanover: 1955. V. 49; 51; 52
North of Boston. 1914. V. 49
North of Boston. London: 1914. V. 47; 53
North of Boston. New York: 1915. V. 49; 50; 52; 53
North of Boston. New York: 1919. V. 48
North of Boston. New York: 1926. V. 52
North of Boston. New York: 1932. V. 54
North of Boston. New York: 1935. V. 53
One Favored Acorn. Ripton: 1969. V. 48
One More Brevity. New York: 1953. V. 49
The Poems of Robert Frost. New York: 1946. V. 53
Selected Poems. London: 1923. V. 53
Selected Poems. New York: 1923. V. 47; 54
Selected Poems. New York: 1928. V. 48; 49; 53
Selected Poems 1934. New York: 1934. V. 49
Several Short Poems. New York: 1924. V. 48; 49
Steeple Bush. New York: 1947. V. 49; 50; 53; 54
The Testing-Time for Loyalties. Hanover: 1942. V. 49
To A Young Wretch. New York: 1937. V. 49
Triple Plate. New York: 1939. V. 47; 48; 49; 51
An Unstamped Letter In Our Rural letter box. New York: 1944. V. 49; 51
A Way Out: a One Act Play. New York: 1929. V. 48; 49; 50; 51; 54
West Running Brook. New York: 1928. V. 47; 48; 49; 50; 51; 53
What Became of New England?. Oberlin: 1938. V. 47; 51
A Witness Tree. New York: 1942. V. 47; 48; 49; 52; 53; 54

FROST, THOMAS
Circus Life and Circus Celebrities. London: 1875. V. 49
Circus Life and Circus Celebrities. London: 1881. V. 52
The Old Showman and the Old London Fairs. London: 1875. V. 52
The Secret Societies of the European Revolution, 1776-1876. London: 1876. V. 52

FROST, W. ADAMS
The Fundus Oculi With an Ophthalmoscopic Atlas Illustrating Its Physiological and Pathological Conditions. Edinburgh: 1896. V. 48

FROST ARTS & CRAFTS WORKSHOP, DAYTON, OHIO.
The Frost Arts and Crafts Workshop...Catalogue Number Fifty-Two. 1910. V. 49

FROSTIANA; or a History of the River Thames in a Frozen State; with An Account of the Late Severe Frost; and the Wonderful Effects of Frost, Snow, Ice and Cold in England... London: 1814. V. 49

FROUDE, JAMES ANTHONY
The English in the West Indies. London: 1888. V. 53
History of England. London: 1858. V. 51
History of England from the Fall of Wolsey to the Death of Elizabeth. London: 1862-70. V. 51
History of England from the Fall of Wolsey to the Death of Elizabeth. New York: 1870-71. V. 53
History of England From the Fall of Wolsey to the Defeat of the Spanish Armada. London: 1872. V. 48
The Nemesis of Faith. London: 1849. V. 48; 49; 51
Oceana, or England and Her Colonies. London: 1886. V. 50
Shadows of the Clouds. London: 1847. V. 50; 54
Thomas Carlyle. A History of the First Forty Years of His Life 1795-1835. (with) A History of His Life in London 1834-1881. London: 1882-84. V. 54
The Two Chiefs of Dunboy, or an Irish Romance of the Last Century. London: 1889. V. 51

FROUDE, RICHARD HURRELL
Remains... London: 1838. V. 53

FROWDE, HENRY
The Christian Year. London: 1895. V. 47

FRY & STEELE & CO.
Fry, Steele's Specimen of Printing Types. London: 1815. V. 51

FRY, C. B.
The Book of Cricket. London: 1899. V. 49; 50

FRY, CAROLINE
Death, and Other Poems. London: 1823. V. 47; 49

FRY, CHRISTOPHER
The Boy with a Cart. London: 1939. V. 48
The Boy with a Cart. New York: 1950. V. 54
Curtmantle. London: 1961. V. 51
Curtmantle. New York: 1961. V. 54
The Dark is Light Enough. 1954. V. 50
The Dark is Light Enough. London: 1954. V. 51; 54
An Experience of Critics and The Approach to Dramatic Criticism. New York: 1953. V. 54
The Lady's Not for Burning. London: 1949. V. 49
The Lady's Not for Burning. New York: 1950. V. 49
The Lady's Not for Burning. Helsinki: 1988. V. 48
A Phoenix Too Frequently. London: 1959. V. 54
A Phoenix Too Frequently. Helsinki: 1985. V. 48
Root and Sky. Cambridge: 1975. V. 50; 53
A Sleep of Prisoners. London: 1951. V. 54
A Sleep of Prisoners. New York: 1951. V. 54
Venus Observed. London: 1950. V. 52; 54
A Yard of Sun - a Summer Comedy. London: 1970. V. 51; 54

FRY, EDMUND
Pantographia... London: 1799. V. 47; 50; 51; 52; 53; 54
Specimen of Modern Printing Types; a New Specimen of Flowers. London: 1824. V. 48

FRY, ELIZABETH
Memoir of the Life of Elizabeth Fry, with Extracts from Her Journal and Letters. London: 1847. V. 49; 50; 54

FRY, FREDERICK
Fry's Traveler's Guide and Descriptive Journal of the Great North-Western Territories. Cincinnati: 1865. V. 47; 50; 54

FRY, JAMES B.
Army Sacrifices or Briefs from Official Pigeon Holes. New York: 1879. V. 49

FRY, JOHN
Bibliographical Memoranda: in Illustration of Early English Literature. Bristol: 1816. V. 54

FRY, LEWIS G.
Oxted, Limpsfield and Neighbourhood. Oxted, Surrey: 1932. V. 50; 51

FRY, LOUISE S.
A Glimpse of Fairyland. London: 1930. V. 54

FRY, ROGER ELIOT
Architectural Heresies of a Painter. London: 1921. V. 50
The Artist and Psycho-Analysis. London: 1924. V. 51
Flemish Art - a Critical Survey. London: 1927. V. 54
Henri-Matisse. Paris. V. 50
Last Lectures. Cambridge: 1939. V. 50
Letters. London: 1972. V. 53
A Sampler of Castile. London: 1923. V. 49; 52
A Sampler of Castile. Richmond: 1923. V. 49; 53; 54
Transformations, Critical and Speculative Essays on Art. London: 1926. V. 48
Twelve Original Woodcuts. Richmond: 1921. V. 50
Twelve Original Woodcuts. London: 1922. V. 49
Vision and Design. London: 1920. V. 47

FRY, STEELE & CO.
A Specimen of Printing Types. London: 1799. V. 47; 49; 50

FRY, WALTER S.
San Francisco-Oakland Directory, Ending June 30, 1907. Oakland: 1907. V. 50

FRY, WILLIAM STORRS
Facts and Evidence Relating to the Opium Trade with China. London: 1840. V. 54

FRYE, F. L.
Biomedical and Surgical Aspects of Captive Reptile Husbandry. Melbourne: 1991. V. 52
Reptile Care: An Atlas of Diseases and Treatments. London: 1991. V. 48; 50

FRYE, JAMES A.
The First Regiment Massachusetts Heavy Artillery, United States Volunteers, in the Spanish-American War of 1898. Boston: 1899. V. 49

FRYE, NORTHROP
Fearful Symmetry: a Study of William Blake. Princeton: 1947. V. 51
The Well Tempered Critic. Bloomington: 1963. V. 54

FRYE, ROLAND MUSHAT
Milton's Imagery and the Visual Arts. Princeton: 1978. V. 54

FRYE, T. C.
Hepaticae of North America. Seattle: 1937-47. V. 53

FRYER, A.
The Potamogetons (Pond Weeds) of the British Isles. London: 1898-1915. V. 51; 54

FRYER, ALFRED C.
Wooden Monumental Effigies in England and Wales. London: 1924. V. 49

FRYER, GEORGE
The Poetry of Various Glees, Songs &c. as Performed at the Harmonists. London: 1798. V. 47; 49; 52

FRYER, JANE EAYRE
The Mary Frances Cook Book, or Adventures Among the Kitchen People. Philadelphia: 1912. V. 47
The Mary Frances Housekeeper. London: 1914. V. 49
The Mary Frances Sewing Book, or Adventures Among the Thimble People. London: 1914. V. 54
The Mary Frances Story Book, or Adventures Among the Story People. London: 1923. V. 48

FRYER, JOHN
A New Account of East India and Persia... London: 1698. V. 48; 51
A New Account of East India and Persia Being Nine Years' Travels. 1672-1681. London: 1909/12/15. V. 52

FRYER, MARY ANN
John Fryer of the Bounty. Waltham St. Lawrence: 1939. V. 51; 52

FRYER, MICHAEL
The Trial and Life of Eugene Aram... Richmond: 1832. V. 49

FRYXELL, FRITIOF
William H. Jackson, Photographer, Artist, Explorer. 1939. V. 47

FU, MARILYN
Studies in Connoisseurship: Chinese Paintings from the Arthur M. Sackler Collection in New York and Princeton. Princeton: 1973. V. 53; 54

FUCHS, DANIEL
Summer in Williamsburg. London: 1935. V. 51

FUCHS, H. ERNST
Text-Book of Ophthalmology. New York: 1924. V. 48

FUCHS, JOHN R.
A Husband's Tribute to His Wife. San Antonio: 1938. V. 54

FUCHS, LEONHARD
Alle Kranckheyt der Augen... Strassburg: 1539. V. 47
De Historia Stirpium Commentarii Insignes. Basel: 1542. V. 47; 50; 53
Hippocratis Coi Medicorvm Omnivm Sine Controuersia Principis Aphorismoru Sectiones Septem... Parisiis: 1545. V. 48; 49
New Kreuterbuch, in Welchem nit Allein die Gantz Histori, das ist, Namen, Gestalt, Statt und Zeit der Wachsung, Natur, Krafft und Wurdkung es Meysten Theyls der Kreuter so in Teutschen unnd andern Landen Wachsen... Basel: 1543. V. 47; 51; 53
Paradoxorum Medicinae Libri Tres. Venetiis: 1547. V. 49

THE FUDGE Family in Edinburgh, in a Series of Poetical Epistles: collected and Arranged by Nehemiah Nettlebottom, Esq. of Brambleside, Near.... Edinburgh: 1820. V. 54

FUENTES, CARLOS
Aura. New York: 1965. V. 49; 52; 53
Aura. New York: 1975. V. 49; 53
A Change of Skin. New York: 1968. V. 50
Christopher Unborn. New York: 1989. V. 48; 49; 50; 51; 53
The Death of Artemio Cruz. New York: 1964. V. 53
The Good Conscience. New York: 1961. V. 49
The Hydra Head. London: 1978. V. 50
The Hydra Head. New York: 1978. V. 50
The Old Morality. Helsinki: 1986. V. 48
Terra Nostra. New York: 1976. V. 52
Where the Air is Clear. New York: 1960. V. 50

FUERST, JULIUS
A Hebrew and Chaldee Lexicon to the Old Testament. Leipzig: 1885. V. 48

FUERST, WALTER RENE
Twentieth Century Stage Decoration. London: 1928. V. 47

FUERTES, L. A.
Album of Abyssinian Birds and Mammals. Chicago: 1930. V. 49
Artist and Naturalist in Ethiopia. New York: 1936. V. 48

FUGARD, ATHOL
Tsotsi. Johannesburg: 1980. V. 50; 51; 53

FUGATE, FRANCIS
Spanish Heritage of the Southwest: Twelve Drawings by Jose Cisneros. El Paso: 1952. V. 51

THE FUGITIVE. Nashville: 1924. V. 51

FUGITIVE Pieces on Various Subjects. Dublin: 1762. V. 48
FUGITIVE Pieces on Various Subjects. London: 1765. V. 53; 54

FUGITIVES. An Anthology of Verse. New York: 1928. V. 52; 53; 54

FUJIOKA, T.
Butterflies of Japan. Tokyo: 1975. V. 48

FUJITA, JUN
Tanka: Poems in Exile. Chicago: 1923. V. 50

FUJIWARA, KANESUKE
The Lady Who Loved Insects. London: 1929. V. 52

FUKAI, SHINI
Telul eth-Thalathat: the Excavation of tell II, the Third Season (1964). (Volume II). Tokyo: 1970. V. 51

FULD, JAMES J.
American Popular Music 1875-1950. (with) Supplement. Philadelphia: 1955/56. V. 49
A Pictorial Bibliography of the First Editions of Stephen C. Foster. Philadelphia: 1957. V. 51; 53

FULGOSUS, BAPTISTA
Factorvm Dictorumqve memorabilivm. Parisiis: 1578. V. 53

FULHAM Gallery Exhibition Catalogue. London: 1967. V. 49

FULKERSON, HENRY S.
Random Recollections of Early Days in Mississippi. Vicksburg: 1885. V. 47; 48

A FULL Account of the Curious and Interesting Proceedings, Instituted in Doctor's Commons, by Rachel Dick Against Her Husband, the Rev. William Dick...for a Nullity of Marriage on the Ground of Impotency; Together with the Sentence Pronounced... London: 1811. V. 51

FULL and By. Garden City: 1925. V. 48

A FULL and Correct Account of the State Trials, held at the Old Bailey...Containing the Whole of the Evidence...With a Copious and Correct Detail of the Various Arrangements Made to...Effect a Revolution in this Country. London: 1820. V. 52

A FULL and Particular Account of All the Circumstances Attending the Loss of the Steamboat Lexington, in Long Island Sound, on the Night of January 13, 1840... Providence: 1840. V. 48

A FULL Answer to a Fallacious Apology Artfully Circulated through the Kingdom, in Favour of the Naturalization of the Jews. London: 1753. V. 53

A FULL Collection of All Poems Upon Charles, Prince of Wales...Published Since His Arrival in Edinburgh 17th Day of September, till the 1st of November 1745. 1745. V. 47

A FULL Relation Concerning the Wonderful and Wholesome Fountain. At First Discovered in Germany, Two Miles from the City of Halberstadt, by a Certain Youth Upon the Fifth of March 1646, as He Was Coming from Schoole. London: 1646. V. 48

FULLARTON, WILLIAM
A View of the English Interests in India, and an Account of the Military Operations in the Southern Parts of the Peninsula, During the Campaigns fo 1782, 1783, and 1784. London: 1787. V. 48; 52

FULLER, ANDREW
The Gospel Its Own Witness; or the Holy Nature and Divine Harmony of the Christian Religion. Clipstone: 1799. V. 54

FULLER, ANDREW S.
The Grape Culturist: a Treatise on the Cultivation of the Native Grape. New York: 1864. V. 48; 50; 52

FULLER, ANNE
Histoire de Miss Nelson. (The Convent; or, the History of Sophia Nelson). Paris: 1792. V. 50
The Son of Ethelolf: an Historical tale. Dublin: 1789. V. 51

FULLER, B.
Nine Chains to the Moon-An Adventure Story of Thought. Philadelphia: 1938. V. 47; 51

FULLER, CLAUD E.
Firearms of the Confderacy. Huntington: 1944. V. 47

FULLER, FRANCIS
Medicina Gymnastica; or, a Treatise Concerning the Power of Exercise, with Respect to the Animal Oeconomy... London: 1705. V. 48

FULLER, FREDERICK T.
Beyond the Selvas. Boston: 1929. V. 51

FULLER, H.
A Grammar of the English Language, Designed for the use of Schools and Private Families. Chelmsford: 1820. V. 48

FULLER, HENRY
On Rheumataism, Rheumatic Gout and Sciatica. New York: 1854. V. 48; 51; 53

FULLER, HENRY CLAY
Adventures of Bill Longley: Captured by Sheriff Milton Mast and Deputy Bill Burrows, near Keatchie, Louisiana in 1877 and Was Executed at Giddings, Texas, 1878. Nacogdoches. V. 50; 52

FULLER, HENRY CLAY continued
A Texas Sheriff. A Vivid and Accurate Account of Some of the Most Notorious Murder Cases and Feuds in the History of East Texas... Nacogdoches: 1931. V. 52; 54

FULLER, HIRAM
North and South. London: 1863. V. 50

FULLER, R. BUCKMINSTER
Isamu Noguchi, a Sculptor's World. London: 1967. V. 49
Nine Chains to the Moon. Philadelphia & New York: 1938. V. 51
Untitled Epic Poem on the History of Industrialization. Highlands: 1962. V. 54
World Science Decade 1965-1975. Carbondale: 1963-67. V. 51

FULLER, RONALD
The Work of Rex Whistler. London: 1960. V. 52

FULLER, ROY
Poems. London: 1940. V. 48; 50
With My Little Eye - A Mystery Story for Teenagers. London: 1948. V. 54

FULLER, S. MARGARET
Woman in the Nineteenth Century. New York: 1845. V. 47

FULLER, SAMUEL
Practical Astronomy, in the Description and Use of Both Globes, Orrery and Telescopes... Dublin: 1732. V. 52

FULLER, THOMAS
Anglorum Speculum, or The Worthies of England, in Church and State. London: 1684. V. 48
The Church History of Britain Until the Year 1648. London: 1842. V. 49
The Church History of Britain...Until the Year 1648. London: 1655. V. 47; 50; 51; 53
The Church History of Britain...Until the Year 1648. London: 1656. V. 48; 50; 52
Exanthematologia; or, An Attempt to Give a Rational Account of Fevers, Especially Measles and Small Pox. London: 1730-29. V. 47; 49
Fuller's Computing Telegraph. New York: 1852. V. 48; 50
The Historie of the Holy Warre. Cambridge: 1647. V. 48
The Historie of the Holy Warre... Cambridge: 1651. V. 47
The Historie of the Holy Warre. (with) The Holy State (and) The Profane State. Cambridge: 1642. V. 51
The History of the Worthies of England. London: 1662. V. 53
The History of the Worthies of England... London: 1811. V. 47; 48; 50; 51; 53
The History of the Worthies of England. London: 1840. V. 51; 53
The Holy State and The Profane State. Cambridge: 1642. V. 47; 53; 54
The Holy State (and) The Profane State. Cambridge: 1648. V. 47
The Holy State and the Profane State. London: 1840. V. 49
Introductio ad Prudentiam; or Directions, Counsels and Cautions Tending to Prudent Management of Affairs in Common Life. London: 1726. V. 54
A Pisgah-Sight of Palestine and the Confines Thereof. London: 1650. V. 47; 54

FULLER, WILLIAM
The Sign of Babinski: a Study of the Evolution of Cortical Dominance in Primates. Springfield: 1932. V. 53
The Whole Life of Mr. William Fuller, Being an Impartial Account of His Birth, Education, Relations and Introduction into the Service of the Late King James and His Queen.... London: 1703. V. 47

FULLERTON, GEORGE
The Zamorano Club: The First Half Century 1928-1978. Los Angeles: 1978. V. 49; 51

FULLERTON, GEORGIANA
Ellen Middleton: a Tale. London: 1844. V. 47; 49
Lady-Bird. London: 1852. V. 50; 54
Laurentia: a Tale of Japan. London: 1861. V. 50
A Stormy Life. Leipzig: 1867. V. 51

FULLMER, JOHN S.
Assassination of Joseph and Hyrum Smith and the Patriarch of the Church of Jesus Christ of Latter-Day Saints. Liverpool: 1855. V. 49

FULLOM, STEPHEN WATSON
The Great Highway: a Story of the World's Struggles. London: 1854. V. 54

FULLONE, ABEL
Descrittione et Uso del Holometro. Venice: 1564. V. 50; 53; 54

FULOP-MILLER, RENE
The Mind and Face of Bolshevism - an Examination of Cultural Life in Soviet Russia. 1927. V. 53
The Russian Theatre. London: 1930. V. 47; 51; 52

FULTON, AMBROSE COWPERTHWAITE
A Life's Voyage a Diary of a Sailor on Sea and Land, Jotted Down During a Seventy-Years' Voyage. New York: 1898. V. 47

FULTON, FRANCES I. SIMS
To and Through Nebraska. Lincoln: 1884. V. 47; 48; 50; 51

FULTON, JOHN F.
Aviation Medicine In its Preventive Aspects. London: 1948. V. 50; 52
Aviation Medicine in Its Preventive Aspects. Oxford: 1948. V. 47
A Bibliographical Study of the Galvani and the Aldini Writings on Animal Electricity. 1936. V. 47; 52
A Bibliographical Study of the Galvani and the Aldini Writings On Animal Electricity. London: 1936. V. 50
A Bibliography of the Honourable Robert Boyle. V. 52
A Bibliography of the Honourable Robert Boyle. Oxford: 1932. V. 54
A Bibliography of the Honourable Robert Boyle Fellow of the Royal Society. London: 1961. V. 51; 54
Harvey Cushing: a Biography. Springfield: 1946. V. 47; 48
Michael Servetus: Humanist and Martyr. New York: 1953. V. 51; 54
Muscular Contraction and the Reflex Control of Movement. Baltimore: 1926. V. 47
Physiology of the Nervous System. London: 1938. V. 47; 48; 49; 50
Selected Readings in the History of Physiology. Springfield: 1930. V. 47; 49; 50; 52
Selected Readings in the History of Physiology... Springfield: 1966. V. 50
The Sign of Babinski. Springfield: 1932. V. 47; 48; 49; 50; 51; 53; 54
Sir Kenelm Digby. Writer, Bibliophile and Protagonist of William Harvey. New York: 1937. V. 51; 52; 53; 54

FULTON, JUSTIN DEWEY
Woman as God Made Her; the True Woman. Boston: 1869. V. 53

FULTON, MAURICE GARLAND
History of the Lincoln County War. Tucson: 1968. V. 49; 53
New Mexico's Own Chronicle. Dallas: 1937. V. 51; 53

FULTON, R.
The Illustrated Book of Pigeons. London: 1874-76. V. 48
The Illustrated Book of Pigeons. London: 1885-89. V. 48

FULTON, ROBERT
De La machine Infernale Maritime, Ou De Le Tactique Offensive et Defensive De La Torpille. Paris: 1812. V. 49

FULTON, ROBERT LARDIN
Epic of Overland. San Francisco: 1924. V. 47; 54

FUN and Fireworks. London: 1850. V. 47

FUN at the Circus. London: 1893. V. 52

FUN Upon Fun, or the Humours of a Fair. Giving a Description of the Curious Amusements in Early Life; Also an Account of a Mountebank Doctor and His Merry Andrew. Glasgow: 1810-15. V. 52

FUNCK, HEINRICH
Eine Restitution, Oder Eine Erklarung Einiger Haupt-Puncten des Tesetzes: Wie es durch Christum Erfullet 1st, und Vollkommen Vollendet Wird Werden an Seinem Grossen Tage... Philadelphia: 1763. V. 49; 51

FUNDABURK, E. L.
Sun Circles and Human Hands. The Southeastern Indians-Art and Industry. Luverne: 1957/65. V. 54

A FUNERAL Discourse, Occasioned by the Much Lamented Death of Mr. Yorick, Prebendary of Y---k and Author of the Much Admired Life and Opinions of Tristram Shandy, Preached Before a very Mixed Society of Jemmies, Jessamies, Methodists and Christians... London: 1761. V. 49

FUNERALI per Carlo III. Palermo: 1789. V. 47

FUNK, CASIMIR
The Vitamins. Baltimore: 1922. V. 48; 53

FUNK, ISAAC K.
A Standard Dictionary of the English Language Upon Original Plans Designed to give, In Complete and Accurate Statement, In the Light of the Most Recent Advances... New York & London: 1900. V. 49

FUNK, JOSEPH
Compilation of Genuine Church Music... Winchester: 1835. V. 49

FUNKAI, SHINJI
Halimehjan I, The Excavation at Shahpir 1976. (and) Halimejhan II. The Excavation at Lameh Zamin. 1978. Tokyo: 1980-82. V. 51

FUNKE, OTTO
Atlas of Physiological Chemistry. London: 1853. V. 49

FUNNELL, WILLIAM
A Voyage Round the World. London: 1707. V. 47; 50

FURBER, GEORGE C.
The Twelve Months Volunteer. Cincinnati: 1850. V. 54

FURBER, ROBERT
The Flower Garden Display'd in Above 400 Curious Representations of the Most Beautiful Flowers... London: 1734. V. 51

FURHANGE, MAGUY
Carzou: Engraver and Lithographer. Nice: 1971. V. 52

FURIETTI, GIUSEPPI ALLESANDRO
Utriusque...De Musivis... Rome: 1752. V. 48

FURLEY, ROBERT
A History of the Weald of Kent. With an Outline of the Early History of the County... Ashford: 1871-74. V. 49

FURLONG, CHARLES WELLINGTON
Let'er Buck. New York: 1923/21. V. 47

FURLONG, JOHN SMITH
Catalogue of the Valuable, Select and Distinguished Library of the Late John Smith Furlong... Dublin: 1846. V. 50

FURLONG, LAWRENCE
The American Coast Pilot. Newburyport: 1798. V. 53

FURLONG, RONALD
Injuries of the Hand. Boston: 1957. V. 54

FURMAN, GABRIEL
Antiquities of Long Island. (with) Notes Geographical and Historical, Relating to the Town of Brooklyn... New York: 1875. V. 50

FURMAN, RICHARD
Exposition of the Views of the Baptists Realtive to the Colored Population In the United States in a Communicataion to the Governor of South Carolina. Charleston: 1833. V. 50

FURNALD, AMOS
Trial of Amos Furnald, for the Murder of Alfred Furnald, Before the Superior Court... Concord: 1825. V. 51

FURNAS, ROBERT W.
An Invitation to South-East Nebraska. Lincoln: 1887. V. 47
Nebraska. Her Resources, Advantages, Advancement and Promises. (with) The School Land Laws. Lincoln: 1885. V. 48

FURNEAUX, H. J.
Glimpses of India: a Grand Photographic History of the land of Antiquity, the Vast Empire of the East. Philadelphia, Bombay: 1896. V. 53

FURNEAUX, J. H.
Glimpses of India. London: 1896. V. 51

FURNESS, C. E.
Land for Emigrants. Lake Superior & Mississippi Railroad. St. Paul to Duluth, Minn. Saint Paul: 1873. V. 52

FURNESS, WILLIAM
History of Penrith, from the Earliest Record to the Present Time. Penrith: 1894. V. 52

FURNESS, WILLIAM HENRY
Records of a Lifelong Friendship 1807-1882. Ralph Waldo Emerson and William Henry Furness. New York: 1910. V. 54

FURNISS, HARRY
P & O Sketches in Pen and Ink. London: 1888. V. 51
Paradise in Piccadilly, the Story of Albany. London: 1925. V. 54
Royal Academy Antics. London: 1890. V. 52

FURNIVALL, FREDERICK J.
The Babees Book... London: 1868. V. 47; 50
Captain Cox, His Ballads and Books... London: 1871. V. 53
Child Marriages, Divorces and Ratifications, &c. in the Diocese of Chester, A.D. 1561-6. London: 1897. V. 48
Mr. Swinburne's "Flat Burglary: on Shakespere". London: 1879. V. 48
Phillip Stubbe's Anatomy of the Abuses in England in Shakespere's Youth. A.D. 1583. London: 1877-82. V. 52

FURSE, CHARLES WELLINGTON
Illustrated Memoir of Charles Wellington Furse, A.R.A. with Critical Papers and Fragments. A Catalogue of Pictures Exhibited at the Club in 1906 and a Chronological List of Works. London: 1908. V. 47

FURST, HERBERT
The Decorative Art of Frank Brangwyn. London: 1924. V. 53
The Modern Woodcut, a Study of the Evolution of the Craft... London: 1924. V. 50; 54
The Woodcut. An Annual Number 11. London: 1927. V. 48

FURST, JILL LESLIE
Pre-Columbian Art of Mexico. New York: 1910. V. 54

FURST, V.
The Architecture of Sir Christopher Wren. London: 1956. V. 48; 49; 50; 51; 53; 54

FURTADO DE MENDONCA, HIPOLYTO JOSE COSTA PEREIRA
Cartas Sobre a Framacomeria. Segunda Edicao Feita Sobre a original de Amsterdam, e Augmentada com Duas Cartas Escriptas em 1778 Sobre o mesmo Assumpto. Madrid: 1805. V. 48

FURTENBACH, JOSEPH
Buechsenmeistereyschul; Darinnen Die New Angehende Buchsenmeister Ind Feuerwerk. Augsburg: 1643. V. 49; 53

FURTHER and Still More Important Suppressed Documents. Boston: 1808. V. 48

FURTHER Communications from the World of Spirits, on Subjects Hightly Important to the Human Family. New York: 1861. V. 52

FURTHER Considerations on the Act to Permit Persons Professing the Jewish Religion, to Be Naturalized by Parliament. London: 1753. V. 48

FURTHER Papers Relative to the Union of British Columbia and Vancouver Island. 1867. V. 53

FURTWANGLER, ADOLF
Sammulung Somzee: Antike Kunstdenkmaler. Munchen: 1897. V. 52

FUSELI, HENRY
Lectures on Painting, Delivered at the Royal Academy. London/Edinburgh: 1820. V. 53

FUSSELL, G. E.
The Old English Farming Books 1523 to 1730. (with) More Old English Farming Books 1731 to 1793. London: 1947-50. V. 53

FUSSELL, L.
A Journey Round the Coast of Kent. London: 1818. V. 47; 53

THE FUTURE of Non-Ferrous Mining in Great Britain and Ireland. London: 1959. V. 54

FYFE, ANDREW
Compedium of the Anatomy of the Human Body. Edinburgh: 1807. V. 48

FYFE, GEORGE
The Cruise of the "St George", R.Y.S. to see the World 1891-92. 1893. V. 53

FYFE, HERBERT C.
Submarine Warfare, Past and Present. London: 1907. V. 54

FYLEMAN, ROSE
Old Fashioned Girls and Other Poems. London: 1928. V. 51
The Rose Fyleman Fairy Book. London: 1923. V. 49
The Sunny Book. London: 1920. V. 49

FYNES-CLYNTON, HENRY
Memoirs of the Clinton Family. London: 1870. V. 53

FYSHER, JOHAN
A Mornynge Remembraunce... London: 1906. V. 47

FYSON, P.
The Flora of the Nilgiri and Pulney Hill Tops. (with) Supplement. Madras: 1915-20. V. 48
The Flora of the South Indian Hill Stations: Ootacamund, Coonoor, Kotagirl, Kodaikanal, Yercaud and the Country Round. Madras: 1932. V. 51

G

G., H.
A Guide to Croft, Dinsdale, Middleton, Darlington, Etc. Comprising Analysis of the Mineral Waters... Darlington: 1834. V. 50

G. K. CHESTERTON - A Criticism. London: 1908. V. 54

GABALLA, G. A.
Narrative in Egyptian Art. Mainz am Rheim: 1976. V. 51

GABLE, KATHLEEN
Clark Gable: a Personal Portrait. Englewood Cliffs: 1961. V. 52

GABLE, WILLIAM F.
Collecting Books and Autographs. V. 51

GABO, NAUM
Circle. International Survey of Constructivist Art. New York: 1971. V. 50

GABRERI, MERCEDES PRECERUTTI
Frescoes from Venetian Villas. London: 1971. V. 49

GABRIEL, RALPH HENRY
The Pageant of America. New Haven: 1925-29. V. 54

GABRIEL, RICHARD
A History of Military Medicine. Westport: 1992. V. 52

GABRIELI, VITTORIO
Sir Kenelm Digby. Un Inglese Italianato Nell-eta Della Controriforma. Roma: 1957. V. 49

GABRIELLI, NAZARENO
The Art of Leather. Tolentino: 1977. V. 54

GABRIELSON, IRA N.
Birds of Alaska. Harrisburg/Washington: 1959. V. 49; 52; 54

GABUTT, BERNARD
The Day of the Horse. Flagstaff: 1976. V. 49

GACON, FRANCOIS
Discours Satiriques en Vers. Lyon or Paris: 1696. V. 52

GADBURY, JOHN
A Ballad. The Third Part, to the Same Tune. London: 1679?. V. 47
Collectio Geniturarum or a Collection of Nativities: Including Genitures, Viz Princely, Prelatical, Causidical, Physical and Mercatorial Twins, etc., with Many Useful Observations. London: 1662. V. 47
Ephemerides of the Celestial Motions and Aspects, Eclipses of the Luminaries &c. for XX Years. London: 1680. V. 52
Ephemerides of the Celestial Motions for X Years: Beginning Anno 1672 (Where the industrious Mr. Wings Expired) and Ending An. 1681. London: 1672. V. 52

GADD, J.
The Stones of Assyria: The Surviving Remains of Assyrian Sculpture, Their Recovery and Their Original Positions. London: 1936. V. 51

GADDIS, WILLIAM
Carpenter's Gothic. New York: 1985. V. 47; 51; 53
Carpenter's Gothic. London: 1986. V. 51
A Frolic of His Own. London: 1994. V. 52; 53
A Frolic Of His Own. New York: 1994. V. 51; 52; 53
A Frolic of His Own. London: 1995. V. 53
J. R. New York: 1975. V. 47; 49; 51; 52; 53
J. R. London: 1976. V. 47
The Recognitions. London: 1955. V. 50; 51
The Recognitions. New York: 1955. V. 47; 49; 51; 52; 53
The Recognitions. London: 1962. V. 48

GADO, FRANK
First Person: Conversations on Writers and Writing with Glenway Wescott, John Dos Passos, Robert Penn Warren, John Updike, John Barth and Robert Coover. Schenectady: 1973. V. 49

GADOW, HANS
Through Southern Mexico, Being an Account of the Travels of a Naturalist. London: 1908. V. 48

GAETKE, H.
Heligoland as an Ornithological Observatory. Edinburgh: 1895. V. 49

GAFFAREL, JACQUES
Unheared-of Curiosities: Concerning the Talismanical Sculpture of the Persians... London: 1650. V. 47

GAFFIKIN, BRIGID
The Bishops' Brothels. Katoomba: 1994. V. 54

GAG, WANDA
The Funny Thing. New York: 1929. V. 50
Gone is Gone or the Story of a Man Who Wanted to Do Housework. New York: 1935. V. 47
Millions of Cats. London: 1928. V. 50
Nothing At All. London: 1942. V. 51
Snippy and Snappy. New York: 1931. V. 53; 54

GAGE, J. D.
Deep-Sea Biology, a Natural History of Organisms at the Deep Sea-Floor. London: 1991. V. 49; 52

GAGE, JOHN
The Christian Sodality, or Catholick Hive of Bees Sucking the Hony of the Churches Prayers from the Blossomes of the Word of God, Blowne Out of the Epistles and Gospels of the Divine Service throughout the Yeare... London: 1652. V. 52
The History and Antiquites of Hengrave, in Suffolk. London: 1822. V. 47; 48; 50; 53
The History and Antiquities of Thingoe Hundred, Suffolk. Bury St. Edmunds: 1838. V. 53

GAGE, MATILDA JOSLYN
Woman, Church and State. A Historical Account of the Status of woman Through the Christian Ages... Chicago: 1893. V. 48; 49; 51

GAGE, THOMAS
The English American Travail By Sea and Land... London: 1648. V. 48; 49

GAGE, WILLIAM
Illustrated Guide to the Black Hills and Picturesque Souvenir of Hot Springs, South Dakota. Battle Creek: 1901. V. 52

GAGUIN, ROBERT
Compendium...Super Francorum Gestis. Paris: 1514. V. 49; 50

GAHAGAN, USHER
Mr. Pope's Temple of Fame. And His Messiah, a Sacred Eclogue, in Imitation of Virgil's Pollio. London: 1748. V. 48

GAIDY, CHARLES
Ephemeras, "Mayflies". New York: 1986. V. 48

GAIMAR, GEOFFREY
Lestorie des Engles Solum la Translacion Maistre Geffrei Gaimar. London: 1888-89. V. 52

GAINE, HUGH
The Journals of Hugh Gaine, Printer. New York: 1902. V. 52

GAINES, EDMUND PENDLETON
Memorial of...to the Senate and House of Representatives of the United States, in Congress Assembled. Memphis: 1840. V. 49

GAINES, ERNEST J.
The Autobiography of Miss Jane Pittman. New York: 1971. V. 52; 53
Catherine Carmier. New York: 1964. V. 48; 51; 52; 53
A Gathering of Old Men. New York: 1983. V. 54
In My Father's House. New York: 1978. V. 53
A Lesson Before Dying. New York: 1993. V. 49; 51; 53
Of Love and Dust. New York: 1967. V. 49

GAINES, W.
Panic. 1954. V. 47

GAINESVILLE: The Great Health Resort of the South. Atlanta: 1888. V. 54

GAINSBOROUGH, THOMAS
A Collection of Prints, Illustrative of English Scenery, from the Drawings and Sketches... London: 1819. V. 47; 48
The Letters... London: 1961. V. 51; 54
Studies of Figures, Selected from the Sketch Books of the Late Thomas Gainsborough... London: 1825. V. 50

GAIRDNER, JAMES
Letters and Papers Ilustrative of the Reigns of Richard III and Henry VII. London: 1861-63. V. 49
Lollardy and the Reformation in England: an Historical Survey. London: 1908-13. V. 50; 52

GALBRAITH, JOHN KENNETH
The Affluent Society. London: 1958. V. 49

GALBRAITH, JOHN S.
The Hudson's Bay Company As an Imperial Factor 1821-1869. Los Angeles: 1957. V. 47

GALE, F.
The Public School Matches, and Those We Meet There... London: 1867. V. 51

GALE, JOHN
Gale's Cabinet of Knowledge... London: 1796. V. 51

GALE, NORMAN
A Book of Quatrains. Old Bilton: 1909. V. 53
The Candid Cuckoo. 1891. V. 49
Cricket Songs. London: 1894. V. 54
Orchard Songs. London: 1893. V. 47; 49
Songs for Little People. London: 1896. V. 48

GALE, RICHARD
Catalogue of the Japanese Paintings and Prints in the Collection of Mr. and Mrs. Richard P. Gale. London: 1970. V. 47; 50
Catalogue of the Japanese Paintings and Prints in the Collection of Mr. and Mrs. Richard P. Gale. Rutland: 1970. V. 54

GALE, ROGER
Registrum Honoris de Richmond Exhibens Terrarum & Villarum Quae Quondam Suerunt Edwini. London: 1722. V. 47; 48; 51

GALE, SAMUEL
The History and Antiquities of the Cathedral Church of Winchester. London: 1715. V. 51
Notices on the Claims of the Hudson's Bay Company and the Conduct of Its Adversaries. Montreal: 1817. V. 53

GALE, THOMAS
Opuscula Mythologica, Ethica et Physica, Grace & Latine. Cambridge: 1671. V. 48

GALE, THOMAS A.
The Wonder of the Nineteenth Century. Rock Oil in Pennsylvania and Elsewhere. 1935. V. 47; 48; 50

GALE, ZONA
The Loves of Pelleas and Etarre. New York: 1907. V. 54
The Secret Way. New York: 1921. V. 54

GALEANO, EDUARDO
Days and Nights of Love and War. New York: 1983. V. 50
Faces and Masks. New York: 1987. V. 50
Genesis. New York: 1985. V. 50

GALENA Guide. Galena: 1937. V. 51

GALENUS
Clauudii Galeni De Locorum Affectorum Notitia Libri Sex... Lyon: 1549. V. 51
De Compositione Medicamentorvm Per Genera Libri Septem. Lugduni: 1552. V. 47; 50; 53
Epitomae Omnium Rerum et Sententiarum, Quae Annotatu Dignae in Commentariis Galeni In Hippocaratem Extant. Lugduni: 1554. V. 47; 50; 53
Galen on the Usefulness of the Parts of the Body. Ithaca: 1968. V. 49; 50; 52; 53; 54
Galen's Method of Physick; or, His Great Master-Peece Being the Marrow and Very Quintessence of All His Writings. Edinburgh: 1656. V. 47; 48
In Hippocratis Librum de Humoribus, Commentarii Tres... Venetiis: 1562. V. 53
Liber De Facvltavm Natvralivm Svbstantia, Gvinteriod Ioanne Andernaco Interpretae... Paris?: 1540. V. 48
On Anatomical Procedures. London: 1956. V. 50
On the Natural Faculties. London: 1916. V. 50; 52
Opera Ex Septima Juntarum Editione. Venetiis: 1596-97. V. 50

GALES, WINIFRED MARSHALL
Matilda Berkely, or, Family Anecdotes. Raleigh: 1804. V. 47

GALIGNANI'S New Paris Guide; or Stranger's Companion through the French Metropolis... Paris & London: 1825. V. 50

GALILEI, GALILEO
Dialogo... Sopra i due Massimi Sistemi del Mondo Tolemaico e Copernicano. In Fiorenza: 1710. V. 51
Nov-Antiqua Sanctissimorum Patrum & Probatorum Theologorum Doctrina, de Sacrae Scripturae Testimoniis, in Conclusionibus Mere Naturalibus... Strasbourg: 1636. V. 48; 49
Le Operationi del Compasso Gemetrico, e Militare...Dedicato al Serenissimo D. Cosimo Medici, Principe di Toscana. Bologna: 1656. V. 50; 54
Opere... Bologna: 1655-56. V. 48; 52
Opere di Galilei Galileo Nobile Fiorentino Accademico Linceo... Florence: 1718. V. 49

GALILEO a Madama Cristina di Lorena (1615). Padova: 1896. V. 47

GALINDO, CATHERINE
Mrs. Galindo's Letter to Mrs. Siddons. London: 1809. V. 48

GALL, JAMES
A Historical Sketch of the Origin and Progress of Literature for the Blind... Edinburgh: 1834. V. 48

GALLAGHER, TESS
On Your Own. 1978. V. 53
Stepping Outside. Poems. Lisbon: 1974. V. 51; 54
Under Stars. 1978. V. 53; 54
Willingly. Port Townsend: 1984. V. 50

GALLAGHER, WILLIAM D.
Facts and Conditions of Progress in the North-West. Cincinnati: 1850. V. 47

GALLAGHER, WILLIAM DAVIS
Facts and Conditions of Progress in the North-West. Cincinnati: 1850. V. 53

GALLANT, MAVIS
The Other Paris. Boston: 1956. V. 50
The Other Paris. London: 1957. V. 50

GALLATIN, ALBERT
The Writings of Albert Gallatin. Philadelphia: 1879. V. 48

GALLATIN, ALBERT E.
American Water Colourists. New York: 1922. V. 54
Art and the Great War. New York: 1919. V. 47; 50; 51; 53
Aubrey Beardsley. Catalogue of Drawings and Bibliography. New York: 1945. V. 50
The Portraits of Albert Gallatin. New York: 1911. V. 53

GALLAUDET, THOMAS H.
An Address Delivered at a Meeting for Prayer, with Reference to the Sandwich Mission, in the Brick Church in Hartford, October 11, 1819. Hartford: 1819. V. 48
A Discourse, Delivered at the Dedication of the American Asylum, for the Education of Deaf and Dumb Persons, May 22nd, 1821. Hartford: 1821. V. 52
A Sermon Delivered at the Opening of the Connecticut Asylum for the Education and Instruction of Deaf and Dumb Persons. Hartford: 1817. V. 52

GALLE, F.
Azaleas. London: 1986. V. 48

GALLE, THEODORE
Ioannis Fabri...In Imagines Illustrium ex Fulvii Ursini Bibliotheca, Antuerpiae a Theodoro Gallaeo Expressas. Commentarius (with) Illustrium Imagines ex Antiquis... Antwerp: 1606. V. 48

GALLEGO, JULIAN
Zurbaran 1598-1664. London: 1977. V. 49; 50; 54

GALLENGA, ANTONIO
Iberian Reminiscences. Fifteen Years' Travelling Impressions of Spain and Portugal. London: 1883. V. 51

GALLERY of Poets, Pall-Mall and Fleet-Street, April 2, 1790. London: 1790. V. 50

THE GALLERY of Portraits: with Memoirs. London: 1833-34. V. 51; 54
THE GALLERY of Portraits: with Memoirs. London: 1833-37. V. 54

GALLICHAN, WALTER M.
Fishing and Travel in Spain: an Angler's Guide. London: 1904. V. 54

GALLICK Reports: or, an Historical Collection of Criminal Cases, Adjudged in the Supreme Courts of Judicature in France. London: 1737. V. 48

GALLICO, PAUL
Adventures of Hiram Holliday. New York: 1939. V. 48; 51
The Snow Goose. London: 1946. V. 48; 50

GALLI DA BIBIENA, FERDINANDO
L'Architettura Civile Preparata su La Geometria, e Ridotta Alle Prospettive Considerazioni Pratiche... Parma: 1711. V. 51

GALLIER, JAMES
The American Builder's General Price Book and Estimator, to Elucidate the Principles of Ascertaining the Correct Value of Every Description of Artificers' Work... Boston: 1836. V. 49; 53

GALLINI, GIOVANNI ANDREA
Critical Observations on the Art of Dancing... London: 1765. V. 47; 52

GALLITZIN, DEMETRIUS
A Defence of Catholic Principles, in a Letter to a Protestant Minister. Pittsburg: 1816. V. 49

GALLO, MIGUEL MUJICA
The Gold of Peru: Masterpieces of Goldsmith's Work of Pre-Incan and Incan Time and the Colonial Period. Recklinghausen: 1967. V. 52

GALLO, PHILIP
Seven Poets, Seven Poems. Minneapolis: 1995. V. 53

GALLOWAY, ARCHIBALD
Observations on the Law and Constitution, and Present Government of India, On the Nature of Landed Tenures and Financial Resources, as Recognized by Moohummudan Law and Moghul Government... London: 1832. V. 52

GALLOWAY, C. F. J.
The Call of the West: Letters from British Columbia. New York: 1916. V. 51; 54
The Call of the West: Letters from British Columbia. London: 1917. V. 47

GALLOWAY, CHARLES J.
Catalogue of Paintings and Drawings at Thorneyholme. Manchester: 1892. V. 47

GALLOWAY, ELIJAH
History and Progress of the Steam Engine: With a Practical Investigation of Its Structure and Application. London: 1830. V. 48

GALLOWAY, JOSEPH
A Reply to the Observations of Lieut. Gen. Sir William Howe, on a Pamphlet Entitled Letters to a Nobleman... London: 1780. V. 48; 52

GALLOWAY, R. I.
Annals of Coal Mining and the Coal Trade. London: 1898-1904. V. 49; 50

GALLOWAY, WILLIAM
The Battle of Tofrek Fought Near Suakin, March 22nd, 1885 under Major General, Sir John Carstairs M'Neill, In Its Relation to the Mahdist Insurrection in the Eastern Sudan and to the Campaigns of 1884 and 1885. London: 1887. V. 51

GALLUP, GEORGE
A Guide to Public Opinion Polls. Princeton: 1944. V. 52

GALLUP, JOSEPH
Observations Made During a Visit to the Clarendon Springs, Vt., in Relation to Their Character and Properties, in a Part of July and August, 1839. Windsor: 1840. V. 53
Sketches of Epidemic Diseases in the State of Vermont... Boston: 1815. V. 50; 51; 52

GALLWEY, NONA
Fairy Moonbeams. 1945. V. 52

GALLWITZ, KLAUS
Picasso at 90, the Late Work. London: 1971. V. 51
Picasso at 90: The Late Work. New York: 1971. V. 47

GALPIN, FRANCIS W.
The Music of the Sumerians and Their Immediate Successors the Babylonians and Assyrians. Cambridge: 1937. V. 49
Old English Instruments of Music. London: 1911. V. 50

GALPINE, J.
A Synoptical Compend of British Botany. Salisbury: 1806. V. 53
A Synoptical Compend of British Botany. London: 1820. V. 53

GALSWORTHY, JOHN
Address to the P.E.N. Club. Kansas City: 1939. V. 48
Author and Critic. New York: 1933. V. 47
Caravan. The Assembled Tales. New York: 1926. V. 49
The Country House. London: 1907. V. 48
The Dark Flower. London: 1913. V. 47
Flowering Wilderness. London: 1932. V. 49; 51
The Forsyte Saga. London: 1921. V. 49
The Forsyte Saga. London: 1922. V. 47; 50
Four Forsyte Stories. New York: 1929. V. 49
From the Four Winds. London: 1897. V. 47; 48; 53; 54
The Inn of Tranquility. London: 1912. V. 52; 54
The Island Pharisees. London: 1904. V. 50
Jocelyn. London: 1898. V. 53
Loyalties, a Drama in Three Acts. London: 1930. V. 49
Maid in Waiting. London: 1931. V. 49
A Man of Devon. Edinburgh & London: 1901. V. 53; 54
The Man of Property. New York: 1906. V. 51
A Modern Comedy. London: 1929. V. 47; 49; 51; 53
A Modern Comedy. London: 1930. V. 49; 54
Novels, Tales and Plays. New York: 1926. V. 51
On Forsyte Change. London: 1930. V. 51; 53
The Plays of John Galsworthy. London: 1929. V. 51; 52; 53; 54
A Rambling Discourse. London: 1929. V. 49
The Rocks. Kansas City: 1943. V. 48
The Silver Spoon. London: 1926. V. 49; 52; 54
Soames and the Flag. London: 1930. V. 51
Swan Song. London: 1928. V. 49; 54
Two Essays on Conrad with the Story of a Remarkable Friendship... Freelands: 1930. V. 51
Two Forsyte Interludes. London: 1927. V. 49; 51; 54
Villa Ruebin. London: 1900. V. 49
The Works. New York: 1922. V. 49
The Works. New York: 1922-36. V. 49
Works. London: 1923-27. V. 49

GALT, JOHN
Annals of the Parish; or The Chonicle of Dalmailing, During the Ministry of the Rev. Micah Balwhidder. Edinburgh: 1821. V. 50; 51; 52
The Entail; or the Lairds of Grippy. Edinburgh: 1823. V. 47; 51
George the Third, His Court and Family. London: 1820. V. 48
The Last of the Lairds; or, the Life and Opinions of Malachi Mailings, Esq. of Auldbiggins. Edinburgh: 1826. V. 47
Lawrie Todd; or, the Settlers in the Woods. London: 1830. V. 50; 51
The Life of Lord Byron. London: 1830. V. 53
The Life of Lord Byron. Niagara: 1831. V. 53
Sir Andrew Wylie of that Ilk... Edinburgh: 1822. V. 50
The Spaewife: a Tale of the Scottish Chronicles. Edinburgh: 1823. V. 54
Works. London: 1895-96. V. 50
The Works of John Galt. Edinburgh: 1936. V. 47; 48; 51

GALTHERUS, ALEXANDER
Alexandreidos Galteri Poetaee Clarissimi. Ingolstadt: 1541. V. 50

GALTHERUS, PHILIPPE
Alexandreidos Libri Decem Nun Primum, in Gallia Gallicique Characteribus editi. Lyons: 1558. V. 48

GALTIER BOISSIERE, JEAN
La Bonne Vie. Paris: 1929. V. 54

GALTON, FRANCIS
English Men of Science: Their Nature and Nurture. London: 1874. V. 53
English Men of Science: Their Nature and Nurture. New York: 1874. V. 49; 50
Finger Prints. London and New York: 1892. V. 50; 52; 54
Hereditary Genius: an Inquiry Into Its Laws, and Consequences. London: 1869. V. 47; 49
Hereditary Genius: an Inquiry Into Its Laws and Consequences. New York: 1870. V. 48; 49; 52
Hereditary Genius: an Inquiry Into Its Laws and Consequences. London: 1892. V. 50; 52; 53
Inquiries into Human Faculty and Its Development. New York: 1883. V. 54
Memories of My Life. London: 1908. V. 54
The Narrative of an Explorer in Tropical Africa. London: 1853. V. 54
Natural Inheritance. London: 1889. V. 47; 53

GALTON, FRANCIS continued
Vacation Tourists and Notes of Travel. London: 1861-64. V. 54
Vacation Tourists and Notes of Travel in 1862-63. London and Cambridge: 1864. V. 48; 53

GALTON, GWENDOLEN DOUGLAS
A Step Aside. London: 1893. V. 54

GALVAO, ANTONIO
The Discoveries of the World From Their First Originall to the Yeere of Our Lord 1555. London: 1601. V. 50

GALVAYNE, SYDNEY
The XXth Century Book on the Horse. London: 1905. V. 47

GALVESTON ARTILLERY CO.
Charter and By-Laws of the Galveston Artillery Company. Galveston: 1871. V. 49

GALVESTON BAY & TEXAS LAND CO.
An Address to Emigrants. Texas. Boston: 1835. V. 47

GALVEZ, BERNARDO DE
Instructions for Governing the Interior Provinces of New Spain, 1786. Berkeley: 1951. V. 48; 52

GALVIN, JOHN
The Etchings of Edward Borein. San Francisco: 1971. V. 48; 52; 53; 54
Through the Country of the Comanche Indians in the Fall of 1845. London: 1970. V. 47

GAMA, JOSE BASILIO DA
O Uraguay, Poema... Lisbon: 1769. V. 53

GAMBARA, LORENZO
Lavrentii Gambarae Brixiani. De Navigatione Christophori Columbi Libri Quattor... Rome: 1585. V. 50

GAMBIER, JAMES EDWARD
An Introduction to the Study of Moral Evidence or that Species of Reasoning Which Relates to Matters of Fact and Practice. London: 1806. V. 47

GAMBLE, C. F. SNOWDEN
The Story of a North Sea Air Station... London: 1928. V. 54

GAMBLE, DAVID
The Descendants of Roger Gower. 1897. V. 54

GAMBLE, GEORGE
The Halls. London: 1899. V. 54

GAMBLE, J. S.
The Bambuseae of British India. Calcutta: 1896. V. 53

GAMBLE, JOHN
Views of Society and Manners in the North of Ireland. London: 1819. V. 53

GAMBLE, SIDNEY G.
A Practical Treatise on Outbreaks of Fire, Being a Systematic Study of Their Causes and Means of Prevention. London: 1931. V. 54

THE GAMBLING World. Anecdotic Memories and Stories of Personal Experience in the Temples of Hazard and Speculation, with some Mysteries and Iniquities of Stock Exchange Affairs, by Rouge et Noir. London: 1898. V. 47

GAMBOA, FRANCISCO JAVIER DE
Comentarios a las Ordenanzas de Minas, Dedicados al Catholico rey, Nuestro Senor, Don Carlos III... Madrid: 1761. V. 54

GAMBOLD, JOHN
The Works of the Late Rev. John Gambold, A.M. Bath: 1779. V. 48

GAMBOLD, W.
A Welsh Grammar; or, A Short and Easy Introduction to the Welsh Tongue. Carmarthen: 1817. V. 54

GAMBRELL, HERBERT
Mirabeau Buonaparte Lamar, Troubadour and Crusader. Dallas: 1934. V. 47; 50; 54

GAMBRILL, RICHARD V. N.
Sporting Stables and Kennels. New York: 1935. V. 47; 48; 50
Sporting Stables and Kennels. London: 1936. V. 48; 50

GAME Pie. A Guiness Indoor Sportfolio. London: ?1955. V. 53

GAMES of Skill, and Conjuring, Including Draughts, Dominoes, Chess...Conjuring, Legerdemain, Tricks with Apparatus... London: 1861. V. 47

GAMGEE, SAMPSON
On the Treatment of Wounds and Fractures: Clinical Lectures. London: 1883. V. 51

GAMMAGE, WASHINGTON LAFAYETTE
The Camp, the Bivouac and the Battle Field. Little Rock: 1958. V. 49

GAMMAR Gurton's Garland of Nursery Songs and Toby Tickle's Collection or Riddles. Glasgow: 1820's. V. 51

GAMMEL, H. P. N.
The Laws of Texas, 1822-1897. Austin: 1898. V. 47

A GAMUT, or Scale of Music. To Which is Added, Blank Lines for Favorite Music. London: 1816. V. 52

GANDEE, B. F.
The Artist, or Young Ladies' Instructor in Ornamental Painting, Drawing, &c... London: 1835. V. 47; 49; 53; 54

GANDHI, MAHATMA
For Pacifists. Ahmedabad: 1949. V. 51

GANDHI, MOHANDAS
The Story of My Experiences With Truth. Ahmedabad: 1927-29. V. 47; 52

GANDON, YVES
The Last White Man. London, et al: 1948. V. 53

GANNON, JACK
Jack of All Trades and Master of One. San Francisco: 1987. V. 47; 52
Poems. San Francisco: 1930. V. 54

GANNON, NICHOLAS J.
The O'Donoghue of the Lakes and Other Poems. London: 1858. V. 53

GANS, C.
Biology of Reptilia. London, New York: 1969-70. V. 52
Biology of the Reptilia. Volume 13. Physiological Ecology. London: 1982. V. 50
Biology of the Reptilia. Volumes 1-5. London and New York: 1969-76. V. 51

GANS-RUEDIN, E.
Caucasian Carpets. New York: 1986. V. 51
Modern Oriental Carpets. London: 1971. V. 50

GANT, ROLAND
Steps to the River. London: 1994. V. 50
Steps to the River. Andoversford: 1995. V. 53
Steps to the River. Lower Marston, Risbury: 1995. V. 52

GANTILLON, MAYA
Paraphrased into English by Birginia and Frank Vernon. Waltham St. Lawrence: 1930. V. 47

GANTILLON, SIMON
Maya. Waltham Saint Lawrence: 1930. V. 50

GANTT, E. W.
Address to the People of Arkansas. Philadelphia: 1863. V. 48

GANTT, W. H.
A Medical Review of Soviet Russia. London: 1928. V. 50; 52

GANVILLE-BARKER, HARLEY
Three Plays: The Marrying of Ann Leete: the Voysey Inheritance; Waste. London: 1909. V. 50

GANZ, PAUL
The Paintings of Hans Holbein. London: 1950. V. 50
The Paintings of Hans Holbein. London: 1956. V. 51

GARABETT, EDWARD LACY
Rudimentary Treatise on the Principles of Design in Architecture as Deducible from Nature and Exemplified in the works of the Greek and Gothic Architects. London: 1850. V. 50

GARAD, WAYNE
The Great Buffalo Hunt. New York: 1959. V. 50

GARAT, DOMINIQUE JOSEPH
Memoirs of the Revolution; or, an Apology for My Conduct, in the Public Employments Which I Have Held... Edinburgh: 1797. V. 47

GARATTINI, S.
Psychotropic Drugs. Amsterdam: 1957. V. 47

GARAVAGLIA
Firearms of the American West 1866-1894. Albuquerque: 1985. V. 51

GARBERI, MERCEDES PERCERUTTI
Frescoes from Ventian Villas. London: 1971. V. 51; 53

GARCES, FRANCISCO
On the Trail of a Spanish Pioneer The Diary and Itinerary of Francisco Garces... New York: 1900. V. 53

GARCIA, ANDREW
Tough Trip through Paradise 1878-79. Boston: 1967. V. 51

GARCIA, CHRISTINA
Dreaming in Cuban. New York: 1992. V. 52

GARCIA-BALLESTER, LUIS
Classics in Modern Otology. Granada: 1978. V. 50

GARCIA CUBAS, ANTONIO
The Republic of Mexico in 1876. Mexico: 1876. V. 48

GARCIA LORCA, FEDERICO
Ballad of the Little Square. 1983. V. 54
From Lorca's Theatre. Five Plays. New York: 1941. V. 52
Lament for the Death of a Bullfighter and other Poems. London: 1937. V. 49; 51
The Lieutenant Colonel and the Gypsy. Garden City: 1971. V. 52
Mariana Pineda. Madrid: 1928. V. 49
Poems. London: 1939. V. 49

GARCIA LORCA, FEDERICO
Poems. New York: 1939. V. 52; 53

GARCIA LORCA, FEDERICO
The Poet in New York and Other Poems. New York: 1940. V. 52
Poeta en Nueva York. Mexico City: 1940. V. 51; 54
Romance de la Guardia Civil Espanola./The Ballad of the Spanish Civil Guard. 1974. V. 52

GARCIA LORCA, FEDERICO continued
Songs of Childhood. Roslyn: 1994. V. 52
Sonnets of Dark Love. 1989. V. 54
Three Tragedies. New York: 1947. V. 52

GARCIA MARQUEZ, GABRIEL
El Amor en Los Tiempos del Colera. Bogota: 1985. V. 51
The Autumn of the Patriarch. London: 1977. V. 51
Chronicle of a Death Foretold. New York: 1982. V. 49
Cien Anos de Soledad. Buenos Aires: 1967. V. 49; 53
El General en Su Laberinto. Mexico City: 1989. V. 53
The General in His Labyrinth. V. 52
The General In His Labyrinth. New York: 1980. V. 50
The General in His Labyrinth. New York: 1990. V. 47; 50; 52; 53
The General in His Labyrinth. New York: 1993. V. 53
In Evil Hour. New York: 1979. V. 49; 52
Innocent Erendira and Other Stories. New York: 1978. V. 53
Leaf Storm and Other Stories. London: 1972. V. 52
Leaf Storm and Other Stories. New York: 1972. V. 49; 51; 52; 53; 54
Love in the Time of Cholera. New York: 1988. V. 47; 48; 49; 50; 51; 52; 53
La Mala Hora. Madrid: 1962. V. 52
No One Writes the Colonel and Other Stories. New York: 1968. V. 47; 50; 52
No One Writes to the Colonel. London: 1971. V. 49; 53
One Hundred Years of Solitude. London: 1970. V. 47; 50; 52; 53
One Hundred Years of Solitude. New York & Evanston: 1970. V. 47; 48; 49; 50; 51; 52; 53
One Hundred Years of Solitude. Lunenburg: 1982. V. 48
One Hundred Years of Solitude. New York: 1982. V. 48; 54
The Solitude of Latin America. New York: 1984. V. 54
The Story of a Shipwrecked Sailor. New York: 1986. V. 49; 51; 53

GARCIA VILLA, JOSE
Footnote to Youth. New York: 1933. V. 48

GARCIE, ARCHIBALD
The Truth About the Titanic. London: 1913. V. 47

GARCILASO DE LA VEGA, EL INCA
Histoire des Yncas Rois Du Perou Depuis le Premier Ynca Manco Capac... L'Historie de la Conquete de la Floride. Amsterdam: 1737. V. 48; 52

GARCILASSO DE LA VEGA, EL INCA
The Works, with a Life of the Author... London: 1823. V. 50

GARD, WAYNE
The Chisholm Trail. Norman: 1954. V. 50
The Great Buffalo Hunt. New York: 1959. V. 50
Sam Bass. Boston: 1936. V. 49; 53
Sam Bass. New York: 1936. V. 53

THE GARDEN. A Visual Meditation on Man and Nature. New York: 1993. V. 51

GARDEN, ALEXANDER
The Genius of Erin, Columbia's Freedom, Flights of Fancy, Lucinda, &c. Charleston: 1836. V. 54

GARDEN Amusements, for Improving the Minds of Little Children. New York: 1814. V. 47

THE GARDEN of America: The Salt River Valley, Maricopa County, Arizona. Chicago: 1885. V. 49

THE GARDEN of Caresses. Waltham St. Lawrence: 1934. V. 53

THE GARDEN of the Night - Twenty-six Sufi Poems. Andoversford: 1979. V. 48; 52

GARDENIER, ANDREW
Hand-Book of Ready Reference. Springfield: 1897. V. 52

GARDENS Old and New. The Country House and Its Garden Environment. London: 1910. V. 48

GARDENSTONE, FRANCIS GARDEN, LORD
Miscellanies in Prose and Verse.... Edinburgh: 1791. V. 48

GARDI, R.
African Crafts and Craftsmen. New York: 1969. V. 51
Indigenous African Architecture. New York: 1974. V. 48; 50; 51; 53; 54

GARDINAR, WREY
This Living Stone: The Grey Walls Anthology of New Poems. Billericay: 1941. V. 47

GARDINER, A. L.
Narrative of a Journey to the Zoolu Country in South Africa. London: 1836. V. 49

GARDINER, ALAN H.
Ancient Egyptian Onomastica. London: 1947. V. 51
Egyptian Letters to the Dead, Mainly from the Old and Middle Kingdoms... London: 1928. V. 49; 51
Egyptian Letters to the Dead, Mainly From the Old and Middle Kingdoms... London: 1975. V. 49
The Inscriptions of Sinai. London: 1952-55. V. 49; 51
The Library of A. Chester Beatty. Description of a Hieratic Papyrus with a Mythological Story, Love-songs and Other Miscellaneous Texts. London: 1931. V. 49
The Ramesseum Papyri: Plates. Oxford: 1955. V. 51
The Royal Canon of Turin. Oxford: 1959. V. 49; 51
Supplement to Gardiner's Egyptian Grammar. Neuilly-sur-Seine: 1935. V. 51
The Temple of King Sethos I at Abydos... London & Chicago: 1933-58. V. 49; 51
The Tomb of Amenemhet. London: 1915. V. 51
A Topographical Catalogue of the Private Tombs of Thebes. London & Le Caire: 1913-24. V. 49; 51

GARDINER, ALLEN F.
Narrative of a Journey to the Zoolu Country, in South Africa. London: 1836. V. 47; 48; 50; 51; 52; 54
A Visit to the Indians on the Frontiers of Chili. London: 1841. V. 48

GARDINER, DOROTHY KEMPE
English Girlhood at School. London: 1929. V. 51

GARDINER, E. NORMAN
Olympia: its History and Remains. Oxford: 1925. V. 50

GARDINER, HOWARD C.
In Pursuit of the Golden Dream. San Francisco: 1970. V. 53
In Pursuit of the Golden Dream. Stoughton: 1970. V. 47; 48; 50; 51; 54

GARDINER, J. STANLEY
The Fauna and Geography of the Maldive and Laccadive Archipelagoes. London: 1901-06. V. 49
The Fauna and Geography of the Maldive and Laccadive Archipelagoes. Cambridge: 1903-06. V. 50; 53
The Natural History of Wicken Fen. Cambridge: 1923. V. 48

GARDINER, JAMES T.
Special Report of the New York State Survey on the Preservation of the Scenery of Niagara Falls. Albany: 1880. V. 52

GARDINER, JOHN
The Art of Living and Other Stories. New York: 1981. V. 53
An Inquiry into the Nature, Cause and Cure of the Gout and of Some of the Diseases With Which it Is Connected. Edinburgh: 1792. V. 48; 50; 53

GARDINER, JOHN SMALLMAN
The Art and Pleasures of Hare-Hunting. In Six Letters to a Person of Quality. London: 1750. V. 47; 48

GARDINER, JOHN SYLVESTER
An Epistle to Zenas. Boston: 1786. V. 47

GARDINER, RICHARD
A Letter to Thomas William Coke, Esq. of Holham. London: 1778. V. 53
Remarks on the Letter to John Buxton, Esq. London: 1768. V. 48

GARDINER, ROBERT BARLOW
The Registers of Wadham College, Oxford. London: 1889-95. V. 49; 50

GARDINER, S. R.
History of England, from the Accession of James I to the Outbreak of the Civil War 1603-1642. London: 1899-1901. V. 52
History of the Commonwealth and Protectorate 1649-56. London: 1894-1901. V. 53
History of the Commonwealth and Protectorate 1649-56. London: 1903. V. 52
History of the Great Civil War 1642-1649. London: 1886-91. V. 53
History of the Great Civil War 1642-1649. London: 1894. V. 52
Letters and Papers Relating to the First Dutch Wars 1652-1654. London: 1894-1930. V. 52
Oliver Cromwell. London: 1899. V. 48

GARDINER, STEPHEN
De Vera Obedientia, Oratio. Strasbourg: 1536. V. 48; 50; 51

GARDINER, WILLIAM
The Music of Nature; or an Attempt to Prove That What Is Passionate and Pleasing in the Art of Singing, Speaking and Performing on Musical Instruments... London: 1832. V. 47; 49
The Royal Present of Princess Corolina, Orphan Daughter of Sampoo Noureddin, Monarch of the Most Powerful Kingdom of the East. London. V. 48
The Shepherd's Boy of Snowdon Hill... London: 1823. V. 49

GARDNER, ARTHUR
Alabaster Tombs of the Pre-Reformation Period in England. Cambridge: 1940. V. 50; 54

GARDNER, BENJAMIN FRANKLIN
Black. Caldwell: 1933. V. 53

GARDNER, DANIEL
A New System of Indian Doctoring. Windsor: 1839. V. 53

GARDNER, DANIEL PEREIRA
The Farmer's Dictionary: a Vocabulary of The Technical Terms Recently Introduced Into Agriculture and Horticulture from Various Sciences, and also a Compendium of Practical Farming... New York: 1846. V. 52

GARDNER, E. C.
Homes & How to Make Them. Boston: 1874. V. 48

GARDNER, ERLE STANLEY
The Case of the Backward Mule. New York: 1946. V. 52
The Case of the Cautious Coquette. New York: 1949. V. 51
The Case of the Fan-Dancer's Horse. New York: 1947. V. 50
The Case of the Nervous Accomplice. New York: 1955. V. 51
The Case of the One-Eyed Witness. New York: 1950. V. 51; 54
The Case of the Perjured Parrot. London: 1939. V. 53
The Case of the Rolling Bones. New York: 1939. V. 51
The Case of the Silent Partner. 1940. V. 53
The Case of the Silent Partner. New York: 1940. V. 49
The Case of the Stuttering Bishop. New York: 1936. V. 51

GARDNER, ERLE STANLEY continued
The D. A. Cooks a Goose. New York: 1942. V. 53
The D. A. Draws a Circle. New York: 1939. V. 49; 52
Neighborhood Frontiers. New York: 1954. V. 50; 52; 53
Off the Beaten Track in Baja. New York: 1967. V. 53

GARDNER, ERNEST ARTHUR
Ancient Athens. London: 1902. V. 54
A Catalogue of the Greek Vases in the Fitzwilliam Museum, Cambridge. Cambridge: 1897. V. 50; 52

GARDNER, EUGENE CLARENCE
Illustrated Homes: a Series of Papers Describing Real Houses and Real People. (with) *Home Interiors.* Boston: 1875/78. V. 48

GARDNER, GEORGE
Travels in the Interior of Brazil, Principally through the Northern Provinces and the Gold and Diamond Districts, During the Years 1836-1841. London: 1846. V. 48

GARDNER, HERBERT
American Duck Shotting. New York: 1901. V. 47

GARDNER, ISABELLA STEWART
A Choice of Books from the Library of Isabella Stewart Gardner, Fenway Court. Boston: 1906. V. 50
A Choice of Manuscripts and Bookbindings from the Library. Boston: 1922. V. 50
That Was Then. Brockport: 1979. V. 52

GARDNER, JOHN
The Canon's Yoeman's Prologue and Tale: an Interpretation. London: 1967. V. 47
The Forms of Fiction. New York: 1962. V. 49; 50; 51; 52; 53
Frankenstein. Dallas: 1979. V. 50
Frankenstein. USA: 1979. V. 53
The Gawain-Poet. Lincoln: 1967. V. 53
Grendel. New York: 1971. V. 47; 50; 52; 53
Household Medicine... London: 1863. V. 51
In the Suicide Mountains. New York: 1977. V. 53
Jason and Medeia. New York: 1973. V. 53
Licence Renewed. London: 1981. V. 53
Nickel Mountain. New York: 1973. V. 51
Nickel Mountain. New York: 1974. V. 50
Nickel Mountain. New York: 1983. V. 53
October Light. New York: 1976. V. 54
On Becoming a Novelist.. New York: 1983. V. 52
On Moral Fiction. New York: 1978. V. 51; 52
The Poetry of Chaucer. Carbondale: 1977. V. 53
The Resurrection. New York: 1966. V. 47; 48; 49; 50; 51; 52; 53; 54
Review of Art and Tradition in Sir Gawain & the Green Knight. 1966. V. 47
Rumpelstiltskin. Dallas: 1978. V. 49
Rumpelstiltskin. Dallas: 1979. V. 50; 52
Rumpelstiltskin. USA: 1979. V. 53
The Sunlight Dialogues. New York: 1972. V. 53
The Temptation Game. 1980. V. 52; 54
Vlemk the Box-Painter. Northridge: 1979. V. 49; 50; 53; 54
William Wilson. Dallas: 1979. V. 50; 52
William Wilson. USA: 1979. V. 53
The Wreckage of Agathon. New York: 1970. V. 47; 48; 50; 51; 52; 54

GARDNER, KEITH S.
Sir William Russell Flint 1880-1969. 1986. V. 52
Sir William Russell Flint 1880-1969. Bristol: 1986. V. 51
Sir William Russell Flint 1880-1969. A Comparative Review of the Artist's Signed Limited Edition Prints. London: 1986. V. 50

GARDNER, ROBERT W.
The Parthenon. Its Science of Forms. 1925. V. 47

GARDNER, ROY
Hellcatraz, the Rock of Despair. 1939. V. 51

GARDNER, THOMAS
A Pocket-Guide to the English Traveller... London: 1718. V. 53

GARDNER, W. H.
Gerard Manley Hopkins (1844-1889). A Study of Poetic Idiosyncrasy in Relation to Poetic Tradition. London: 1958. V. 49

GARDNER, WINIFRED A. H.
The Life of James First Duke of Ormonde, 1610-1688. London: 1912. V. 51

THE GARDYNERS Passeatunce. London: 1985. V. 48

GARFIELD, BRIAN
Death Wish. New York: 1972. V. 50

GARFIELD, VIOLA E.
Tsimshian Clan and Society. Seattle: 1939. V. 54

GARFIELDE, SELUCIUS
Climates of the Northwest: Being Condensed Notes of A Lecture Delivered by Hon. S. Garfielde. Philadelphia: 1872. V. 47

GARGAZ, PIERRE ANDRE
A Project of Universal and Perpetual Peace. New York: 1922. V. 52

GARGIAREUS, JOANNES BAPTISTA
Tractatus Varii. Bononiae: 1643. V. 48

GARIMBERTO, GIROLAMO
Concetti...Raccolti...per Scriuere & Ragionar Familiarmente. Venice: 1575. V. 49

GARIS, HOWARD R.
Uncle Wiggily's Friends. New York: 1939. V. 53

A GARLAND for Jake Zeitlin. Los Angeles: 1967. V. 52

A GARLAND for the Laureate. Poems Presented to Sir John Betjeman on His 75th Birthday. Stratford-upon-Avon: 1981. V. 49

GARLAND, HAMLIN
Back-Trailers from the Middle Border. New York: 1928. V. 54
The Book of the American Indian. New York and London: 1923. V. 50; 51; 52
The Book of the American Indian. New York: 1927. V. 47
The Captain of the Gray-Horse Troop. New York: 1902. V. 53; 54
Main Travelled Roads... Boston: 1891. V. 51
Main Travelled Roads. Cambridge & Chicago: 1893. V. 54
Prairie Folks. Chicago: 1893. V. 49
Prairie Songs. Cambridge: 1893. V. 51
A Son of the Middle Border. New York: 1917. V. 51; 53; 54
Wayside Courtships. New York: 1897. V. 48

GARLAND, JAMES
The Private Stable. Boston: 1903. V. 51

A GARLAND of Elizabethan Sonnets. London: 1923. V. 54

A GARLAND of New Songs. London: 1800. V. 52
A GARLAND of New Songs. Newcastle-upon-Tyne: 1800. V. 49; 51
A GARLAND of New Songs. Newcastle-upon-Tyne: 1802. V. 50
A GARLAND of New Songs. Newcastle-upon-Tyne: 1805. V. 50

GARLICK, THEODATUS
A Treatise on the Artificial Propagation of Certain Kinds of Fish, with the Description and Habits of Such Kinds as Are the Most Suitable Kinds for Pisciculture... Cleveland: 1857. V. 52

GARNER, ALAN
The Moon of Gomrath. London: 1963. V. 50
The Weirdstone of Brisingamen - a Tale of Alderley. London: 1960. V. 50

GARNER, ELVIRA
Ezekiel Travels. New York: 1938. V. 47

GARNER, H. M.
Chinese Art in Three-Dimensional Colour. Portland: 1969. V. 49

GARNER, HUGH
Waste No Tears. Toronto: 1950. V. 50

GARNER, R. L.
Gorillas and Chimpanzees. London: 1896. V. 48; 52

GARNER, THOMAS
The Domestic Architecture of England During the Tudor Period. London: 1911. V. 48; 51
The Domestic Architecture of England During the Tudor Period. New York: 1929. V. 47; 49

GARNET, HENRY HIGHLAND
A Memorial Discourse, Delivered in the Hall of the House of Representatives, Washington City, D.C. on Sabbath, February 12, 1865. Philadelphia: 1865. V. 53

GARNET, J. ROS
Wildflowers of South-Eastern Australia. London: 1974. V. 52

GARNETT, DAVID
Aspects of Love. London: 1955. V. 52
Go She Must!. London: 1927. V. 52; 54
The Grasshoppers. London: 1931. V. 53
The Grasshoppers Come. London: 1931. V. 53
Lady into Fox. London: 1922. V. 54
A Man in the Zoo by... London: 1924. V. 49
Never Be a Bookseller. New York: 1929. V. 52
No Love. London: 1929. V. 51; 52; 53
A Rabbit in the Air; Notes from a Diary Kept While Learning to Handle an Aeroplane. London: 1932. V. 53

GARNETT, EDWARD
Papa's War and Other Satires. London: 1918. V. 47
The Paradox Club. London: 1888. V. 51

GARNETT, FRANK W.
Westmorland Agriculture 1800-1900. Kendal: 1912. V. 50; 52

GARNETT, J.
Guide to the Highways of the Lake District of England. Windermere: 1891. V. 50

GARNETT, JAMES M.
Seven Lectures on Female Education. Richmond: 1824. V. 47

GARNETT, LOUISE AYRES
The Muffin Shop. Chicago: 1908. V. 48; 52
The Muffin Shop. Chicago: 1910. V. 49
The Rhyming Ring. Chicago: 1910. V. 53

GARNETT, LUCY M. J.
Greek Folk Poesy: Annotated Translations from the Whole Cycle of Romaic Folk-Verse and Folk-Prose. Guildford: 1896. V. 47
Ottoman Wonder Tales. London: 1915. V. 50; 51
The Women of Turkey and Their Folklore. London: 1890-91. V. 53; 54
The Women of Turkey and their Folklore, with Concluding Chapters of Matriarchy by John S. Stuart-Glennie. London: 1891. V. 48

GARNETT, M. R. H.
The Union, Past and Future: How it Works, and How to Save It. Charleston: 1850. V. 49

GARNETT, P.
Stately Homes of California. Boston: 1915. V. 48; 50; 51; 53; 54

GARNETT, PORTER
A Documentary Account of the Beginnings of the Laboratory Press, Carnegie Institute of Technology. Pittsburgh: 1927. V. 51
The Grove Plays of the Bohemian Club. San Francisco: 1918. V. 50
Porter Garnett: Philosophical Writings on the Ideal Book. San Francisco: 1994. V. 52

GARNETT, RICHARD
English Literature, an Illustrated Record. London: 1903. V. 51
The International Library of Famous Literature: Selections from the World's great Writers, Ancient, Medieval and Modern... London: 1900. V. 49
Iphigenia in Delphi. London: 1890. V. 52
Poems from the German. London: 1862. V. 50; 54
Relics of Shelley. London: 1862. V. 47
The Twilight of the Gods and Other Tales. London: 1924. V. 48; 53
The Twilight of the Gods and Other Tales. London: 1925. V. 50
William Blake, Painter and Poet. London: 1895. V. 47

GARNETT, THOMAS
Observations on a Tour through the Highlands and Part of the Western Isles of Scotland. London: 1800. V. 47; 48; 49
Popular Lectures on Zoonomia, or the Laws of Animal Life in Health and Disease... London: 1804. V. 47; 54

GARNIER, TONY
Une Cite Industrielle. Paris: 1932. V. 48; 50

GARRARD, LEWIS H.
Wah-To-Yah, and the Taos Trail. Cincinnati: 1850. V. 47; 49; 54
Wah-To-Yah and the Taos Trail. Glendale: 1938. V. 50; 53
Wah-To-Yah. The Taos Trail. Prairie Travel and Scalp Dances, with a Look at Los Rancheros from Muleback and the Rocky Mountain Campfire. San Francisco: 1936. V. 54

GARRARD, PHILLIS
Running Away with Nebby. Philadelphia: 1944. V. 52

GARRARD, THOMAS
Edward Colston, the Philanthropist, His Life and Times. Bristol: 1852. V. 53

GARRATT, ALFRED
Guide for Using Medical Batteries. Philadelphia: 1867. V. 47

GARRATT, JOHN
The World Encyclopedia of Model Soldiers. 1981. V. 50

GARRET, WILLIAM
A Collection of Papers, Speeches &c, &c. Delivered at the Durham County Election, in 1820. Newcastle-upon-Tyne: 1820. V. 48

GARRETT, EDMUND N.
Victorian Songs. Boston: 1895. V. 48

GARRETT, FLORENCE ROME
Japanese Sketches. Bridgewater: 1975. V. 48
The Mill and Us. Bridgewater: 1975. V. 48
The Mill and Us. Bridgewater: 1978. V. 51

GARRETT, GEORGE
The Magic Striptease. New York: 1973. V. 47
Poison Pen; or Live Now and Pay Later. 1986. V. 51

GARRETT, PATRICK FLOYD
The Authentic Life of Billy the Kid. Albuquerque: 1964. V. 53
Pat F. Garrett's Authentic Life of Billy the Kid. New York: 1927. V. 53

GARRETT, R.
Too Many Magicians. New York: 1967. V. 49

GARRICK, DAVID
Bon Ton or High Life above Stairs. London: 1775. V. 49
A Catalogue of the Library, Splendid Books of Prints, Poetical and Historical Tracts of David Garrick. London: 1823. V. 48
The Diary of David Garick. New York: 1928. V. 53
The Farmer's Return from London. London: 1762. V. 47
The Fribbleriad. London: 1761. V. 47; 52
Lethe; a Dramatic Satire...As It is Performed at the Theatre-Royal in Drury Lane, by His Majesty's Servants. London: 1749. V. 52
Letters of David Garrick and Georgina Countess Spencer 1759-1779. Cambridge: 1960. V. 54
A New Dramatic Entertainment, Called A Christmas Tale. London: 1774. V. 50
The Poetical Works... London: 1785. V. 50; 52
Some Unpublished Correspondence. Boston: 1907. V. 53
Three Plays. New York: 1926. V. 53
To Mr. Gray, on His Odes. Strawberry Hill: 1790. V. 48

GARRICK, T. W.
The Story of Wigton (Cumberland)... Carlisle: 1949. V. 52

GARRIOCH, A. C.
The Correction Line. Winnipeg: 1933. V. 47; 50; 52

GARRISON, FIELDING
An Introduction to the History of Medicine. Philadelphia: 1914. V. 50; 52
Introduction to the History of Medicine. Philadelphia: 1929. V. 51; 52
A Medical Bibliography. London: 1943-83. V. 49
Morton's Medical Bibliography. Aldershort: 1991. V. 49
The Principles of Anatomic Illustration Before Vesalius: an Inquiry into the Rationale of Artistic Anatomy. New York: 1926. V. 50
Texts Illustrating the History of Medicine in the Library of the Surgeon General's Office, U.S. Army. Washington: 1912. V. 53

GARRISON, GEORGE P.
Diplomatic Correspondence of the Republic of Texas. Washington: 1908. V. 47
Diplomatic Correspondence of the Republic of Texas. Washington: 1908/11. V. 52

GARRISON, JIM
A Heritage of Stone. New York: 1970. V. 53

GARRISON, LLOYD MC KIM
An Illustrated History of the Hasty Pudding Club Theatricals... Cambridge: 1897. V. 48

GARRISON, W. P.
The New Gulliver. Jamaica: 1898. V. 50
William Lloyd Garrison 1805-1879. The Story of His Life Told by His Children. New York: 1885-89. V. 54

GARRISON, WILLIAM LLOYD
Selections from the Writings and Speeches of... Boston: 1852. V. 54
Sonnets and Other Poems. Boston: 1843. V. 47; 52
Thoughts on African Colonization; or an Impartial Exhibition of the Doctrines, Principles and Purposes of the American Colonization Society... Boston: 1832. V. 48

GARROD, ARCHIBALD
Diseases of Children by Various Authors. London: 1913. V. 53
Garrod's Inborn Errors of Metabolism. London: 1963. V. 50
The Inborn Factors in Disease, an Essay. Oxford: 1931. V. 53

GARSAULT, F. A. P. DE
L'Art de la Lingere. Paris: 1771. V. 47
Art Du Perruquier... Paris: 1767. V. 47

GARSTANG, JOHN
El Arabah: a Cemetery of the Middle Kingdom: Survey of the Old Kingdom Temenos: Graffiti from the Temple of Sety. London: 1901. V. 49; 51
The Geography of the Hittite Empire. London: 1959. V. 49
Mahasna and Bet Khallaf. London: 1902. V. 49; 51
Prehistoric Mersin: Humuk Tepe in Southern Turkey. Oxford: 1953. V. 49; 51
Tombs of the Third Egyptian Dynasty at Reqaqnah and Bet Khhallaf. Report of the Excavations at Reqaqnah 1901-02. Westminster: 1904. V. 49; 51

GARSTIN, WILLIAM
Report Upon the Basin of the Upper Nile with Proposals for the Improvement of that River... Cairo: 1904. V. 48; 54

GARTH, SAMUEL
The Dispensary: a Poem. London: 1699. V. 50
The Dispensary. A Poem in Six Cantos. (with) A Complete Key. London: 1741/34. V. 47; 49
The Works. 1769. V. 47
The Works. Dublin: 1769. V. 50

GARTHWAIT, HENRY
The Evangelicall Harmonie, Reducing the Foure Evangelists Into One Continued Context... Cambridge: 1634. V. 49

GARTON, J.
The Practical Gardener and Gentleman's Directory, for Every Month in the Year.. London: 1769. V. 48

GARTON, RAY
The New Neighbor. 1991. V. 54
The New Neighbor. Lynbrook: 1991. V. 48
Trade Secrets. Shingletown: 1990. V. 50

GARTSIDE, M.
An Essay on a New Theory of Colours and on Composition in General... London: 1808. V. 48

GARVEY, ELEANOR
The Artist and the Book 1860-1960. Boston & Cambridge: 1962. V. 49

GARY, MADELEINE SOPHIE
Vignettes of the Beam in a Nigger's Eye. New York: 1970. V. 54

GARZONI, TOMMASO
Piazza Universale: Das Ist: Allgemeiner Schawplatz Harackt und Zusammenkunfft Aller Professionen... Franckfurt am Mayn: 1659. V. 53

GASC, F. E. A.
The Smallest French and English Dictionary in the World. Glasgow: 1896. V. 52

GASCOIGNE, GEORGE
The Posies. London: 1979. V. 51
The Queen's Majesty's Entertainment at Woodstock, 1575, from a Unique Fragment of the Edition of 1585... Oxford: 1903/10. V. 47

GASCOIGNE, MISS
The Handbook of Turning. London: 1842. V. 48
The Handbook of Turning. London: 1846. V. 52
The Handbook of Turning. London: 1852. V. 52
The Handbook of Turning. London: 1859. V. 52

GASCOYNE, DAVID
Holderlin's Madness. London: 1983. V. 51; 53
Journal 1936-1937. London: 1980. V. 51
The Magnetic Fields. London: 1985. V. 47
Man's Life Is This Meat. London: 1936. V. 50; 53
Night Thoughts. London: 1956. V. 54
Novalis: Hymn to Night. London: 1989. V. 53
Poems. London: 1943. V. 52
Roman Balcony and other Poems. London: 1932. V. 51
Selected Poems. London: 1994. V. 53
A Short Survey of Surrealism. London: 1935. V. 50; 51; 53; 54
The Sun at Midnight. London: 1970. V. 48
A Vagrant and Other Poems. London: 1950. V. 51

GASH, JONATHAN
Gold by Gemini. New York: 1978. V. 50
Gold from Gemini. London: 1978. V. 50
The Judas Pair. London: 1977. V. 49; 50
The Lies of Fair Ladies. 1981. V. 54
The Lies of Fair Ladies. Bristol: 1991. V. 52
Pontiff. London: 1971. V. 50
The Sleepers of Erin. New York: 1983. V. 50
Streetwalker. New York: 1960. V. 50
The Trail Tree. London: 1979. V. 50
The Vatican Rip. London: 1981. V. 48; 49; 50

GASK, NORMAN
Old Silver Spoons of England. London: 1926. V. 54

GASKELL, CATHERINE MILNES
Lady Ann's Fairy Tales. London: 1914. V. 48

GASKELL, ELIZABETH CLEGHORN
Cranford. London: 1853. V. 47; 51; 52; 54
Cranford. New York: 1855. V. 54
Cranford. London: 1867. V. 50
Cranford. London: 1891. V. 52; 54
Cranford. London: 1898. V. 54
Cranford. London: 1904. V. 53
Cranford. London: 1906. V. 51
Cranford. London: 1923. V. 53
Cranford. London: 1927. V. 47
Cranford. London: 1940. V. 49; 51
The Letters of... Manchester: 1966. V. 54
The Letters of... Cambridge: 1967. V. 52
The Life of Charlotte Bronte. Leipzig: 1857. V. 53
Life of Charlotte Bronte. London: 1857. V. 48; 49; 50; 52; 54
The Life of Charlotte Bronte. New York: 1857. V. 47; 52; 54
The Life of Charlotte Bronte. London: 1858. V. 48; 52; 54
Life of Charlotte Bronte. London: 1860. V. 52
Mary Barton, a Tale of Manchester Life. Leipzig: 1849. V. 54
The Moorland Cottage. London: 1850. V. 50
My Diary. London: 1923. V. 50
My Lady Ludlow, and Other Tales... London: 1861. V. 50
North and South. Leipzig: 1855. V. 49
North and South. London: 1855. V. 47; 48; 50; 54
Novels and Tales. London: 1881-83. V. 49
Novels and Tales. London: 1882-85. V. 50
Novels and Tales. London: 1889-93.. V. 51
The Pocket Edition of Mrs. Gaskell's Works. London: 1891. V. 54
Right at Last and Other Tales. London: 1860. V. 50
Right at Last and Other Tales. New York: 1860. V. 52; 54
Round the Sofa. London: 1859. V. 50; 54
Ruth. London: 1853. V. 47; 48; 50; 52; 54
Sylvia's Lovers. Leipzig: 1863. V. 51
Wives and Daughters. London: 1866. V. 47
Wives and Daughters. New York: 1866. V. 51; 54
The Works. London: 1880's. V. 49
The Works. London: 1890-93. V. 54
The Works. London: 1890's. V. 54
The Works. London: 1892-94. V. 51
The Works. London: 1925. V. 54

GASKELL, ERNEST
Lancashire Leaders: Social and Political. V. 53
Lancashire Leaders: Social and Political. London. V. 54

GASKELL, J.
Strange Evil. 1957. V. 48; 50; 52

GASKELL, P.
Artisans and Machinery: the Moral and Physical Condition of the Manufacturing Population Considered with Reference to Mechanical Substitutes for Human Labour. London: 1836. V. 50
John Baskerville. A Bibliography. Cambridge: 1959. V. 47

GASKELL, WALTER HOLBROOK
The Involuntary Nervous System. London: 1916. V. 53

GASKELL, WILLIAM
The Involuntary Nervous System. London: 1920. V. 47; 48

GASKIN, A. J.
A Book of Nursery Songs and Rhymes. London: 1895. V. 50

GASKIN, ARTHUR, MRS.
ABC: an Alphabet. London. V. 48

GASKIN, L. J. P.
A Bibliography of African Art. London: 1965. V. 54

GASPARONI, FRANCESCO
Sugli Obelischi Torlonia Nella Villa Nomentana. Rome: 1842. V. 53

GASPEY, THOMAS
The History of England: Under the Reign of George III, George IV, William IV and Queen Victoria. London: 1852-59. V. 54
The Lollards: a Tale, Founded on the Persecutions Which Marked the Early Part of the Fifteenth Century. New York: 1822. V. 47
Takings; or, the Life of a Collegian: a Poem. London: 1821. V. 48

GASPEY, W.
Tallis's Illustrated London: in Commemoration of the Great Exhibition Of All Nations in 1851... London: 1851?. V. 52

GASPRETTI, J.
The Snakes of Arabia. Basel. V. 50

GASQUET, ABBOT
The Greater Abbeys of England. London: 1908. V. 49; 51

GASS, PATRICK
Gass's Journal of the Lewis and Clark Expedition. Chicago: 1904. V. 48; 49
A Journal of the Voyages and Travels of a Corps of Discovery Under the Command of Captain Lewis and Captain Clarke of the Army of the United States from the Mouth of the River Missouri through the Interior Parts of North America to the Pacific Ocean... Minneapolis: 1958. V. 52
Voyage des Capitaines Lewis et Clarke. Paris: 1810. V. 52

GASS, WILLIAM H.
Culp. New York: 1985. V. 52; 53; 54
Fiction and the Figures of Life. New York: 1970. V. 51
The First Winter of My Married Life. Northridge: 1979. V. 51; 52; 54
In the Heart of the Heart of the Country. New York: 1968. V. 47; 49; 51; 52; 53; 54
Omensetter's Luck. New York: 1966. V. 47; 48; 49; 50; 51; 52; 53; 54
Omensetter's Luck. London: 1967. V. 47; 49; 51; 52; 53
On Being Blue. Boston: 1975. V. 47; 51; 53; 54
On Being Blue. 1977. V. 48; 51
On Being Blue. London: 1977. V. 54
The Tunnel. New York: 1995. V. 52; 53
Willie Masters' Lonesome Wife. 1968. V. 48; 53
Willie Masters' Lonesome Wife. Evanston: 1968. V. 47
Willie Master's Lonesome Wife. New York: 1971. V. 51
The World Within the Word. New York: 1976. V. 54
The World Within the Word. New York: 1978. V. 51

GASSENDI, PIERRE
Institutio Astronomica, Juxta Hypotheses Tam Veterum Quam Recentiorum. London: 1653. V. 47; 48; 50
Institutio Astronomica, Juxta Hypothesis Tam Veterum, Quam Copernici & Tychonis, Dictata a Petro Gassendo... London: 1675. V. 47
The Mirrour of True Nobility and Gentility. London: 1657. V. 47

GASSET, JOSE ORTEGA Y
Invertebrate Spain. London: 1937. V. 47

GASSIER, PIERRE
The Drawings of Goya. New York: 1975. V. 50; 51
Francisco Goya: the Drawings. London: 1973-75. V. 50
The Life and Complete Work of Francisco Goya. New York: 1971. V. 50; 51

GAST, JOHN
The History of Greece. Dublin: 1793. V. 50

GASTER, MOSES
The Ketubah in Historical Background. Berlin & London: 1923. V. 47; 48; 53

GASTINEAU, HENRY
Wales Illustrated. London: 1830. V. 47; 53

GASTIUS, JOANNES
De Virginitatis Custodia, Stupri Vindicta, Uxorum in Viros Pietate & Perfidia, de Scortationis Scelere, & Eius Poena, de Moribus ac Uirtutibus Uariarum Gentium... Basel: 1544. V. 52

GASTON, H. A.
The Little Lawyer or the Farmers', Mechanics', Miners', Laborers', and Business Men's Adviser and Legal help. San Francisco: 1881. V. 49

GAT, MOSHE
Moshe Gat. Tel Aviv: 1969. V. 54

GATE, DANIEL
Gate's Shepherd's Guide for Cumberland, Westmoreland, and Lancashire. Cockermouth: 1879. V. 50

GATENBY, GREG
52 Pickup 76. Toronto: 1977. V. 47

GATES, JOSEPHINE SCRIBNER
The Story of Live Dolls... Indianapolis: 1901. V. 50

GATES, R. R.
A Botanist in the Amazon Valley, an Account of the Flora and fauna in the Land of Floods. London: 1927. V. 52; 53

GATES, THEOPHILUS R.
The Trials, Experience, Exercises of Mind and First Travels, of Theophilus R. Gates. Poughkeepsie: 1810. V. 53

GATES, WILLIAM
The Dresden Codex. Reproduced From Tracings of the Original. Baltimore: 1932. V. 48

GATES, WILLIAM G.
City of Portsmouth: Record of the Corporation, 1835-(1945). Portsmouth: 1928-65. V. 49
Illustrated History of Portsmouth. Portsmouth: 1900. V. 52

GATEWOOD, CHARLES
Side-Tripping. New York: 1975. V. 48

GATHORNE-HARDY, A. E.
Autumns in Argyleshire with Rod and Gun. London: 1900. V. 48

GATHORNE-HARDY, GATHORNE
The Diary 1866-1892: Political Selections. London: 1981. V. 52

GATHORNE-HARDY, ROBERT
Darian: a Poem. 1928. V. 52
A Month of Years. 1956. V. 49; 52; 54
Recollections of Logan Pearsall Smith - The Story of a Friendship. London: 1949. V. 51
Seven Poems Written in War-Time. London: 1947. V. 51

GATKE, H.
Heligoland as an Ornithological Observatory, the Result of Fifty Years' Experience. Edinburgh: 1895. V. 52

GATSCHET, ALBERT SAMUEL
The Karankawa Indians, The Coast People of Texas. Cambridge: 1891. V. 48; 53
The Klamath Indians of Southwestern Oregon. Washington: 1890. V. 52
A Migration Legend of the Creek Indians with a Linguistic, Historic and Ethnographic Introduction. Philadelphia: 1884. V. 47; 50

GATTUSO, JOHN
A Circle of Nations. Voices and Visions of American Indians. Hillsboro: 1993. V. 50

GATTY, ALFRED
A Life at One Living. London: 1884. V. 53

GATTY, MARGARET SCOTT
The Book of Sun-Dials. London: 1872. V. 50
The Book of Sun-Dials. London: 1889. V. 50; 53
British Sea Weeds. London: 1872. V. 48; 50; 51; 52; 53
The Fairy Godmother and Other Tales. London: 1851. V. 50; 51
Parables from Nature with Notes on the Natural History. London: 1861. V. 49; 50
Parables from Nature with Notes on the Natural History, Third and Fourth Series. London: 1865. V. 49

GAUCHET, PAUL
Marionettes. Zurich: 1949. V. 50

GAUCI, W.
Windsor and Eton. London: 1828. V. 47; 49

GAUDEN, JOHN
A Discourse of Artificial Beauty, in Point of Conscience Between Two Ladies. London: 1662. V. 50; 51; 53
A Discourse of Artificial Beauty, in Point of Conscience Between Two Ladies. London: 1692. V. 50; 51; 53

GAUDET, PLACIDE
Acadian Genealogies and Documents Concerning the Expulsion of the Acadians in Report...Archives...1905. Volume II. Ottawa: 1906. V. 53

GAUGER, N.
Fires Improv'd: Being a New method of Building Chimneys... London: 1715. V. 48; 50

GAUGUIN, PAUL
Letters to Ambroise Vollard and Andre Fontainas. San Francisco: 1943. V. 47
Noa Noa, Voyage and Tahiti. Stockholm: 1947. V. 49

GAUL, ALBRO
The Complete Book of Space Travel. Cleveland: 1956. V. 54

GAULTER, P. JACOB
Tabula Chronographica Status Ecclesiae a Catholicae Christo Nato AD annum MDCXIV... Cologne: 1616. V. 49

GAULTIER, LEONARD
Bible Illustrations. Paris: 1576-80. V. 54

GAUNT, MARY
A Woman in China. London. V. 50

GAUNT, WILLIAM
The Etchings of Frank Brangwyn, R.A. A Catalogue Raisonne. London: 1926. V. 49; 50; 51; 52; 53
Etty and the Nude. The Art and Life of William Etty, R.A. 1787-1849. Essex: 1943. V. 51
London Promenade. London: 1903. V. 49
William De Morgan: Pre-Raphaelite Ceramics. Greenwich: 1971. V. 53

THE GAUNTLET 2. Baltimore: 1991. V. 49

GAUSS, KARL FRIEDRICH
Disquisitiones Arithmeticae. Leipzig: 1801. V. 47

GAUSSEN, ALICE C. C.
A Woman of Wit and Wisdom. A Memoir of Elizabeth Carter One of the 'Bas Bleu' Society. London: 1906. V. 49; 51

GAUTHIER, HENRI
Le Livre des Rois d'Egypte. (with) Repertoire Pharaonique Pur Servir d'Index au "Livre des Rois d'Egypte.". Le Caire: 1907-17/18. V. 51

GAUTIER, JUDITH
Album de Poemes Tires du Lvire de Jade. 1911. V. 50

GAUTIER, THEOPHILE
Constantinople of Today. London: 1854. V. 54
King Candaules. Paris: 1920's. V. 47
Mademoiselle de Maupin. 1927. V. 54
Mademoiselle de Maupin. Berkshire: 1938. V. 48
Mademoiselle de Maupin. Waltham St. Lawrence: 1938. V. 50
Mademoiselle de Maupin. 1943. V. 48
Mademoiselle de Maupin. New York: 1943. V. 51; 53; 54
Mademoiselle de Maupin. New York: 1945. V. 54
Mademoiselle de Maupin. London: 1948. V. 49
One of Cleopatra's Nights and Other Fantastic Romances. New York: 1882. V. 48
The Works of Theophile Gautier. 1901-02. V. 49

GAUTIER D'AGOTY, JACQUES FABIAN
Anatomie de la Tete, en Tableaux Imprimes...D'Apres les Pieces Dissequees et Preparees par M. Duverney. Paris: 1748. V. 49

GAUTIER-HION, A.
A Primate Radiation, Evolutionary Biology of the African Guenons. 1988. V. 50

GAUTIUS, FRIGEUILLAEUS
Palma Christlana, Seu Speculum Veri Status Ecclesiastici... London: 1593. V. 47; 54

GAUTRUCHE, PIERRE
The Poetical History: Being a Compleat Collection of all the Stories Necessary for a Perfect Understanding of the Greek and Latine Poets... London: 1678. V. 48; 54

GAVIN, ANTONIO
A Short History of Monastical Orders, In Which the Primitive Institution of Monks, Their Tempers, Habits, Rules and the Condition They Are In at Present, Are Treated Of. London: 1693. V. 51

GAVIN, G. M.
Royal Yachts. London: 1932. V. 52

GAVORSE, JOSEPH
The Story of Phaethon, Son of Apollo. New York: 1932. V. 49

GAWAIN AND THE GRENE KNIGHT
Sir Gawain and the Green Knight. London: 1899. V. 53
Sir Gawain and the Green Knight. Oxford: 1925. V. 48; 49; 52
Sir Gawain and the Green Knight. Oxford: 1930. V. 51
Sir Gawain and the Green Knight. London: 1952. V. 48
Sir Gawain and the Green Knight... London: 1956. V. 54
Sir Gawain and the Green Knight. New York: 1971. V. 52; 53; 54
Sir Gawain and the Green Knight, Pearl and Sir Orfeo. 1975. V. 52

GAWSWORTH, JOHN
Above the River. London: 1931. V. 54
Annotations on Some Minor Writings of "T.E. Lawrence". London: 1935. V. 47; 50; 54
Apes, Japes and Hitlerism. A Study and Bibliography. Toronto: 1971. V. 54
Collected Poems. London: 1948. V. 47
Confessions - Verses. 1931. V. 47
Fifteen Poems Three Friends. 1931. V. 47
Geburtslied. 1932. V. 51
Kingcup: Suite Sentimentale: Poems. London: 1932. V. 51
Legacy to Love - Selected Poems 1931-1941. London: 1943. V. 47
Mishka and Madeleine. London: 1932. V. 47
New Poems. London: 1939. V. 54
Snow and Sand - Poems from the Mediterranean 1942-1944. Calcutta: 1945. V. 47
Song for Nancy. 1932. V. 51

THE GAY ABC. New York: 1939. V. 49; 53

GAY, BEATRICE G.
Into the Setting Sun, a History of Coleman County. Santa Ana. V. 54

GAY, CARLO
Mezcala - Ancient Stone Sculpture from Guerrero, Mexico. Geneva: 1992. V. 47

GAY, FRANCIS
The Friendship Book of Francis Gay. London: 1939-94. V. 50

GAY, J. DREW
From Pall Mall to the Punjaub; or, With the Prince in India. London: 1876. V. 49

GAY, JOHN
Achilles. London: 1733. V. 47; 48; 52; 53; 54
The Beggar's Opera. London: 1728. V. 47; 49; 53; 54
The Beggar's Opera. London: 1728/29. V. 51
The Beggar's Opera. London: 1742. V. 47; 52
The Beggar's Opera. London: 1777. V. 52
The Beggar's Opera. London: 1921. V. 47; 52
The Beggar's Opera. Paris: 1937. V. 51; 54
The Distress'd Wife. London: 1743. V. 49; 52
Fables. London: 1727/38. V. 53
Fables. London: 1729. V. 47
Fables. London: 1733. V. 49
Fables. London: 1736. V. 53
Fables. London: 1746/51. V. 50
Fables. Glasgow: 1752. V. 54
Fables. London: 1757. V. 48; 49
Fables. Newcastle-upon-Tyne: 1765. V. 48
Fables. Gloucester: 1783. V. 54
Fables. London: 1792. V. 52; 54
Fables. London: 1793. V. 47; 48; 49; 50; 51; 52; 53; 54
Fables. London: 1796. V. 54
Fables. London: 1801. V. 51
The Fables. London: 1806. V. 52
The Fables. York: 1810. V. 53
The Fables. York: 1811. V. 53
Fables. Havant: 1816. V. 50
The Fryar and the Nun. London: 1710-15. V. 47
Miscellaneous Works. London: 1773. V. 47
The Petticoat: an Heroi-Comical Poem. London: 1716. V. 50
Plays. London: 1760. V. 50
The Poems. Chiswick: 1820. V. 47; 49; 52; 54
Poems on Several Occasions. London: 1720. V. 51; 53
Poems on Several Occasions. London: 1731. V. 51
Poems on Several Occasions. London: 1745. V. 50
Poems On Several Occasions. London: 1753. V. 51
Polly: an Opera. London: 1729. V. 47; 48; 49
Polly: an Opera. London: 1923. V. 48; 49; 52; 53
Rural Sports, Together with the Birth of the Squire and the Hound and the Huntsman. New York: 1930. V. 47
The Shepherd's Week. London: 1714. V. 48; 49; 50
Trivia; or, the Art of Walking the Streets of London. London: 1716. V. 47; 48; 49; 50; 51; 52; 53
Two Epistles; One, to the Right Honourable Richard Earl of Burlington; the Other to a Lady. London: 1717. V. 52
The What D'Ye Call It: a Tragi-Comi-Pastoral Farce. London: 1715. V. 47; 52
The What D'ye Call It: A Tragi-Comi-Pastoral Farce. London: 1736. V. 49

GAY, MARY ANN HARRIS
The Pastor's Story and Other Pieces; or Prose and Poetry. Nashville: 1861. V. 52

GAY, NICHOLAS
Strictures on the Proposed Union Between Great Britain and Ireland: with Occasional Remarks. London: 1799. V. 54

GAY, THERESA
James W. Marshall, the Discoverer of California Gold: a Biography. Georgetown: 1967. V. 47; 50; 54

GAY, ZHENYA
The Shire Colt. New York: 1931. V. 48

GAYA, LOUIS DE
Traite des Armes, de Machines de Guerre, des Feux d'Artifice, des Enseignes & des Instrumens Militaries Anciens & Modernes... Paris: 1678. V. 48

GAYARRE, CHARLES
Louisiana: Its Colonial History and Romance. New York: 1851. V. 52
Louisiana: Its History as a French Colony. New York: 1852. V. 52

GAYER, ALFRED EDWARD
The Catholic Layman. Dublin: 1852-58. V. 47

GAYER, ARTHUR EDWARD
The Catholic Layman. Dublin: 1852-58-62. V. 50; 52

GAYFERE, THOMAS
Gephryalogia. An Historical Account of Bridges, Antient and Modern, from the Most Early Mention of Them by Authors, Down to the Present Time. London: 1751. V. 51

GAYLE, ADDISON
Oak and Ivy: a Biography of Paul Laurence Dunbar. Garden City: 1971. V. 54

GAYLTON, EDMUND
Pleasant Notes Upon Don Quixot. London: 1654. V. 47

GAYNAM, JOHN
G——e and D——y; or the Injur'd Ghost. London: 1743. V. 47

GAYTON, EDMUND
Festivous Notes on the History and Adventures of the Renowned Don Quixote. London: 1771. V. 51
Pleasant Notes Upon Don Quixot. London: 1654. V. 48; 49; 51; 53

GAZA, THEODORUS
In Hoc Volumine Haec Insunt. Theodori Introductiuae Gra(m)matices Libri Quatuor. Venice: 1495. V. 51

GAZE, HAROLD
The Merry Piper or the Magical Trip of the Sugar Bowl Ship. London: 1925. V. 49

THE GAZETTEER Of Sikhim. New Delhi: 1972. V. 48

GEALE, HAMILTON
Notes of a Two Years' Residence in Italy. Dublin: 1848. V. 49

GEAR, H. L.
A Treatise on the Law of Landlord and Tenant with Special Reference to the American Law. San Francisco: 1888. V. 51

GEBHARD, DAVID
The Richfield Building 1928-1968. 1968. V. 53; 54

GEBHARDT, R. H.
The Allure of the Cat. London: 1992. V. 50

GEBOW, JOSEPH A.
A Vocabulary of the Snake, Or Sho-Sho-Nay Dialect... Green River City: 1868. V. 52

GEDDES, ALEXANDER
Letter to the Rev. Dr. Priestley; in Which the Author Attempts to Prove, by One Prescriptive Argument that the Divinity of Jesus Chrsit was a Primitive Tenet of Christianity. London: 1787. V. 51

GEDDES, MICHAEL
The Life of Maria de Jesus of Agreda, a Late Famous Spanish Nun. (with) A Tract Proving the Adoration of Images... London: 1714/14. V. 52
Miscellaneous Tracts. (and) Several Tracts Against Popery. London: 1730/15. V. 47
Miscellaneous Tracts: viz. I. The History of the Expulsion of the Moriscoes Out of Spain, in the Reign of Philip III. II. The History of the Wars of the Commons of Castile... III. A View of the Spanish Cortes... IV An Account of the Manuscripts... London: 1702. V. 51

GEDDIE, JOHN
The Lake Regions of Central Africa: a Record of Modern Discovery. London: 1883. V. 47

GEDNEY, C. W.
Angling Holidays. In Pursuit of Salmon, Trout and Pike. Bromley, Kent: 1896. V. 49; 53

GEE, ERNEST R.
The Sportsman's Library. 1940. V. 49
The Sportsman's Library. London: 1940. V. 47
The Sportsman's Library, Being a Descriptive List of the Most Important Books on Sport. New York: 1940. V. 47

GEE, GEORGE E.
The Hall-marking of Jewellery Practically Considered... London: 1882. V. 53

GEE, JOSHUA
The Trade and Navigation of Great Britain Considered... London: 1731. V. 54
The Trade and Navigation of Great Britain Considered... London: 1767. V. 50; 54

GEE, N. G.
A Key to the Birds of the Lower Yangtse Valley... Shanghai: 1917. V. 54

GEE of Freshford and London. London: 1916. V. 50

GEELHAAR, CHRISTIAN
Paul Klee. New York: 1952. V. 54
Paul Klee and the Bauhaus. 1973. V. 47; 50; 51; 53
Paul Klee and the Bauhaus. Greenwich: 1973. V. 47; 48; 52

GEEN, PHILIP
What I Have Seen While Fishing and How I Have Caught My Fish. 1905. V. 47
What I Have Seen While Fishing and How I Have Caught My Fish. London: 1905. V. 53
What I Have Seen While Fishing and How I Have Caught My Fish. Richmond: 1905. V. 54
What I Have Seen While Fishing and How I Have Caught My Fish. London: 1924. V. 47

GEERLINGS, G. K.
Metal Crafts in Architecture; Bronze, Brass, Cast Iron, Etc. New York: 1929. V. 54
Wrought Iron in Architecture. New York, London: 1929. V. 54

GEESTERANUS, R. A. M.
Mycenas of the Northern Hemisphere. Amsterdam: 1992. V. 52

GEFFS, MARY L.
Under 10 Flags, History of Weld County Colorado. Greeley: 1938. V. 50

GEGENBAUR, CARL
Elements of Comparative Anatomy. London: 1878. V. 48

GEGG, FRANK M.
The Founding of a Nation. Cleveland: 1915. V. 48; 50

GEHEIME Figuren der Rosenkreuzer aus Dem 16ten und 17ten Fahrhundert. (The Secret Symbols of the Rosicrucians in the 16th and 17th Centuries). Ultona: 1785. V. 47

THE GEHENNA Press: the Work of Fifty Years 1942-1992. Dallas & Northampton: 1992. V. 48; 51

GEHRTS, M.
A Camera Actress in the Wilds of Togoland. London: 1915. V. 50

GEIGER, JOHN LEWIS
A Peep at Mexico: Narrative of a Journey Across the Republic from the Pacific to the Gulf in December 1873 and Janaury 1874. London: 1874. V. 53

GEIGER, MALACHIAS
Kelegraphia, sive Descriptio Herniarum cum Earundem Curationibus Iam Medicis Quam Chirurgicis... Munich: 1631. V. 47

GEIGER, MAYNARD J.
The Life and Times of Fray Junipera Serra or the Man Who Never Turned Back. Washington: 1959. V. 48; 50; 51; 52; 54
The Serra Trail in Picture and Story. Santa Barbara: 1960. V. 54

GEIKIE, ARCHIBALD
The Ancient Volcanoes of Great Britain. London: 1897. V. 47; 48; 49; 50; 53
Annals of the Royal Society Club: the Record of a London Dining-club in the Eighteenth and Nineteenth Centuries. London: 1917. V. 50; 54
The Story of a Boulder, or Gleanings from the Note-Book of a Field Geologist. Edinburgh: 1858. V. 54
Text-Book of Geology. London: 1882. V. 48; 52; 53; 54
Text-Book of Geology. London: 1903. V. 48

GEIKIE, JAMES
The Great Ice Age and Its Relation to the Antiquity of Man. London: 1874. V. 54
Prehistoric Europe, a Geological Sketch. London: 1881. V. 48; 52

GEIKIE, WALTER
Etchings Illustrative of Scottish Character and Scenery, Executed After His Own Designs... Edinburgh: 1841. V. 48

GEIL, WILLIAM EDGAR
A Yankee in Pigmy Land. London: 1905. V. 54

GEISBERG, MAX
The German Single-Leaf Woodcut: 1500-1550. New York: 1974. V. 49

GEISEL, THEODORE SEUSS
The 500 Hats of Bartholomew Cubbins. New York: 1938. V. 47; 49
And To Think I Saw It On Mulberry Street. New York: 1937. V. 54
Boners by Those Who Pulled Them. New York: 1931. V. 48
The Butter Battle Book. New York: 1984. V. 49
The Cat in the Hat Comes Back. New York: 1958. V. 48; 54
The Cat's Quizzer. New York: 1976. V. 52; 53
Dr. Seuss's Sleep Book. New York: 1962. V. 50
Horton Hears a Who!. New York: 1954. V. 49; 52
More Boners. New York. V. 49
One Fish, Two Fish, Red Fish, Blue Fish. New York: 1960. V. 49
The Seven Lady Godivas. New York: 1939. V. 47; 48; 49
The Seven Lady Godivas. New York: 1967. V. 48
The Sneetches and Other Stories. New York: 1961. V. 51; 52
You're Only Old Once!. New York: 1986. V. 54

GEISER, SAMUEL WOOD
Horticulture and Horticulturists in Early Texas. Dallas: 1945. V. 50

GEIST und Weltlicher Staat Von Gross-Britannien und Irrland Unter der Regierung Georgii II. Leipzig: 1728. V. 54

GEKOSKI, R. A.
William Golding. A Bibliography 1934-1993. 1994. V. 52
William Golding. A Bibliography 1934-1993. London: 1994. V. 53

GELB, IGNACE J.
Inscriptions from Alishar and Vicinity. Chicago: 1935. V. 49

GELDART, E. M.
Folk-Lore of Modern Greece: The Tales of the People. London: 1884. V. 49

GELDART, ERNEST
The Art of Garnishing Churches at Christmas and Other Times. London: 1882. V. 52

GELDEREN, D. M. VAN
Rhododendrons. London: 1992. V. 49

GELL, A.
Wrapping in Images. Tattooing in Polynesia. Oxford: 1993. V. 54

GELL, WILLIAM
The Geography and Antiquities of Ithaca. London: 1807. V. 48; 52; 54
The Itinerary of Greece... London: 1819. V. 47
Pompeiana. London: 1817-19/32. V. 51
Pompeiana. London: 1824. V. 51; 54
Pompeiana. London: 1832. V. 47; 49; 50; 51
Pompeiana... London: 1835. V. 54
The Topography of Rome and its Vicinity. London: 1834. V. 48
The Topography of Rome and its Vicinity. London: 1846. V. 49; 50; 52
The Topography of Troy and Its Vicinity. London: 1804. V. 49

GELLERT, CHRISTIAN FURCHTEGOTT
The History of the Swedish Countess of G.* London: 1752. V. 54

GELLERT, CHRISTLIEB EHREGOTT
Metallurgic Chymistry. London: 1776. V. 52; 54

GELLERT, HUGO
Aesop Said So. New York: 1936. V. 47
Comrade Gulliver. New York: 1935. V. 47

GELLI, GIOVANNI BATISTA
La Circe. Firenze: 1549. V. 52
La Circe. Florence: 1550. V. 48

GELLIUS, AULUS
The Attic Nights. Amsterdam: 1665. V. 47
Luculentissimi Scriptoris Noctes Atticae. Paris: 1584. V. 48
Noctes Atticae. Amsterdam: 1651. V. 49; 51

THE GEM. London: 1832. V. 50

GEMINUS, THOMAS
Compendiosa Totius Anatomie Delineatio... London: 1545. V. 47
Compendiosa Totius Anatomie Delineatio. London: 1959. V. 47; 48; 50; 53

GEMMA, CORNELIUS
De Naturae Characterismis; Seu Rares et Admirandis Spectaculis, Causis, Indiciis, Proprietatibus Rerum in Partibus Singulis Universi Libri II. Antwerp: 1575. V. 50

GEMMA FRISIUS, REINERUS
Arithmetica Practicae Methodus Facilis. Leipzig: 1607. V. 49; 50

GEMS for Gentlemen: a Collection of Amatory Tales and Adventures. London: 1850. V. 48

GEMS from the Poets. London: 1885. V. 47

GENARD, FRANCOIS
The School of Man. London: 1753. V. 47; 48; 52

GENAUER, EMILY
Chagall at the 'Met'. New York: 1971. V. 47; 49; 50; 51; 53
Rufino Tamayo. New York. V. 47; 48; 52

A GENEALOGICAL Deduction of the Family of Rose of Kilravock. Edinburgh: 1848. V. 49

THE GENEALOGIST. London: 1877-91. V. 52

THE GENEALOGIST'S Pocket Library. London: 1908-10. V. 52

THE GENEALOGY and Chronological History of the Illustrious Family of Guelph or Welph; one of the Sons of Isenberd,...the Renown'd Ancestors of Our Sovereaign Lord George... London: 1716?. V. 53

GENERAL and Commercial Directory of Blackpool and the Fylde. Preston: 1938. V. 48

A GENERAL And Descriptive History of the Ancient and Present State of the Town of Liverpool... Liverpool: 1795. V. 53

A GENERAL Collection of Treatys, Declarations of War, Manifestos and Other Publick Papers, Relating to Peace and War. London: 1732. V. 54

A GENERAL Description of All Trades, Digested in Alphabetical Order: by Which Parents, Guardians and Trustees, May, with Greater Ease and Certainty, Make Choice of Trades Agreeable to the Capacity, Education, Inclination...of the Youth... London: 1747. V. 53

A GENERAL Description of the Model of the Ancient City of Jerusalem, Now To Be Seen At No. 7 Park Row, a Few Doors from Broadway, on a State, Twelve by Twenty Feet, Composed of Wood, and Arranged So As to Given an Idea of the Situation of that City, &c. New York?: 1820's. V. 50

THE GENERAL Grant Memorial. Vicksburg, Miss., August 8th, 1885. Vicksburg: 1885. V. 47

GENERAL Jackson Vetoed; Being a Review of the Veto Message of the Bank of the United States. 1832. V. 52

GENERAL Observations Upon the Probable Effects of Any Measures Which Have for Their Objects the Increase of the Regular Army... Edinburgh: 1807. V. 50

A GENERAL, or, No General Over the Present Army of the Common-Wealth, in Twenty Two Queries Briefly Handled. London: 1659. V. 53

GENERAL Orders, Department of the Cumberland, 1862, Remaining in Force, Oct. 1, 1863. Nashville: 1863. V. 49

GENERAL Regulations and Instructions for the Ten Troops of Wiltshire Yeomanry. London: 1798. V. 48

GENERAL Regulations for Inspection and Control Of All Prisons, Together with the Rules, Orders and Bye Laws, for the Government of the Gaol and Penitentiary House for the County of Gloucester.... Glocester: 1790. V. 50

GENERAL Stevenson. Cambridge: 1864. V. 52; 53

THE GENERAL Stud Book Containing Pedigrees of English Race Horses from the Earliest Accounts to the Year 1831...Inclusive. Baltimore: 1834. V. 54

THE GENERAL Stud Book Containing Pedigrees of Race Horses...from the Earliest Accounts to the Year 1821 Inclusive. London: 1820/22. V. 50

GENERAL Washington and General Jackson on Negro Soldiers. Philadelphia: 1863. V. 48; 49; 54

GENET, EDMOND C.
The Correspondence Between Citizen Genet, Minister of the French Republic to the United States of North America, and the Officers of the Federal Government... Philadelphia: 1793. V. 54

GENET, JEAN
Le Balcon. Paris: 1956. V. 47
The Blacks: a Clown Show. New York: 1960. V. 53
Funeral Rites. New York: 1969. V. 54
Miracle of the Rose. New York: 1965. V. 54
Notre Dame des Fleurs - Roman. Monte Carlo: 1945. V. 48
Poems. Lyon: 1948. V. 48
The Thief's Journal. New York: 1964. V. 54

GENGA, BERNARDINO
Anatomy Improved and Illustrated. V. 51

GENLIS, STEPHANIE FELICITE DUCREST DE ST. AUBIN, COMTESSE DE
Adelaide and Theodore; or Letters on Education... London: 1784. V. 47
Adelaide and Theodore; or Letters on Education... London: 1788. V. 52
Belisarius. Baltimore: 1810. V. 53; 54
Lessons of a Governess to Her Pupils. Dublin: 1793. V. 47; 53
New Moral Tales. New York: 1825. V. 54
Petrarch and Laura. London: 1820. V. 54
Sainclair, or the Victim to the Arts and Sciences. Georgetown: 1813. V. 54
Tales of the Castle or Stories of Instruction and Delight. Glasgow: 1824. V. 50
Theatre of Education. London: 1781. V. 53
The Theatre of Education. London: 1787. V. 47; 49

GENNARO, GAETANO
Gaetano de Gennaro: Pastels and Paintings. Dublin: 1945. V. 51

GENT, PETER
North Dallas Forty. New York: 1973. V. 53

GENT, THOMAS
Annales Regioduni Hullini; or the Hissotry of the Royal and Beautiful Town of Kingston-upon-Hull. London: 1735. V. 49; 54
The Antient and Modern History of the Famous City of York. London: 1730. V. 47; 53
The Antient and Modern History of the Famous City of York. York: 1730. V. 47; 48; 51
The Antient and Modern History of the Loyal Town of Rippon. York: 1733. V. 47; 48
Gent's History of Hull... Hull: 1869. V. 50
The Life of Mr. Thomas Gent, Printer, of York. London: 1832. V. 47; 48; 50; 52
Poems. London: 1828. V. 48; 51; 54
Poems. London: 1829. V. 49

GENTHE, ARNOLD
As I Remember. New York: 1936. V. 47; 48; 52; 54
The Book of the Dance. New York: 1914. V. 48; 51; 52
The Book of the Dance. Boston: 1920. V. 50
Impressions of Old New Orleans: A Book of Pictures... New York: 1926. V. 47; 48
Isadora Duncan. New York: 1929. V. 47; 49; 52; 53
Old Chinatown. New York: 1913. V. 47; 50
Old Chinatown. Oakland: 1946. V. 54
Pictures of Old Chinatown. New York: 1908. V. 47
Twenty-Four Studies. New York & London: 1929. V. 47

GENTIL, F.
Le Jardinier Solitaire, the solitary or Carthusian Gard'ner...also the Compleat Florist, Newly Done into English. London: 1706. V. 49

GENTILCORE, R. LOUIS
Ontario's History in Maps. Toronto: 1984. V. 50

GENTILLET, INNOCENT
Commentariorvm De Regno Recte Administrando, Libri Tres. Utopia: 1655. V. 51
Discours, Svr Les Moyens de Bien Governer et Maintenir en Bonne Paix vn Royaume ou Autre Principaute. Geneva: 1576. V. 51; 52

GENTLE, RUPERT
English Domestic Brass 1680-1810 and the History of Its Origin. London: 1975. V. 51

THE GENTLEMAN Angler. London: 1736. V. 47
THE GENTLEMAN Angler. London: 1786. V. 49; 52

GENTLEMAN, DAVID
Bridges on the Backs; a Series of Drawings. 1961. V. 52; 54

GENTLEMAN, FRANCIS
The Theatres. London: 1772. V. 52

GENTLEMAN OF ELVAS
The Discovery of Florida, Being a True Relation of the Vicissitudes that Attended the Governor Don Hernando de Soto and Some Nobles of Portugal in the Discovery of Florida. San Francisco: 1946. V. 49; 52
A Relation of the Invasion and Conquest of Florida by the Spaniards, Under the Command of Fernando de Soto... London: 1686. V. 48

THE GENTLEMAN'S Assistant, Tradesman's Lawyer and Country-Man's Friend. London: 1720. V. 53

THE GENTLEMAN'S Recreation. London: 1721. V. 52

THE GENTLEMAN'S Toilet. London: 1845. V. 50

GENTRY, HELEN
Tom of Bedlam's Song. San Francisco: 1931. V. 54

GENTZ, FRIEDRICH VON
On the State of Europe Before and After the French Revolution... London: 1803. V. 51

A GENUINE Account of the Late Grand Expedition to the Coast of France, Under the Conduct of the Admirals Hawke, Knowles and Broderick, General Mordaunt, &c. London: 1757. V. 50

A GENUINE Account of the Life and Actions of James Maclean, Highwayman to the Time of His Trial and Receiving Sentence at the Old-Bailey. London: 1750. V. 50

GENUINE Letters to a Young Lady, of Family, Figure and Fortune: Previous to Her Intended Espousals. London: 1762. V. 47

THE GENUINE Memoirs of Miss Faulkner; Otherwise Mrs. D***l**n; or, Countess of H*****x, in Expetancy. London: 1770. V. 48

A GENUINE Narrative of the Life and Surprising Adventures of William Page. London: 1758. V. 50

THE GENUINE Rejected Addresses, Presented to the Committee...for Drury Lane Theatre; Preceded by that Written by Lord Byron and Adopted by the Committee. London: 1812. V. 52

GEOFFREY Gambaldo; or, a Simple Remedy for Hypochondriacism and Melancholy Splenetic Humours by a Humorist Physician. London: 1850. V. 48

GEOGHEGAN, EDWARD
A Commentary on the Treatment of Ruptures, Particularly in a State of Strangulation. London: 1810. V. 52

GEOGRAPHICAL Description of the State of Texas... Philadelphia: 1846. V. 50

THE GEOGRAPHICAL Guide; a Poetical Nautical Trip Round the Island of Great Britain... London: 1805. V. 48

A GEOGRAPHICAL Present; Being Descriptions of the Several Countries of Europe...with Representations of the Various Inhabitants in their Respective Costumes. New York: 1831. V. 51

A GEOGRAPHICAL Table Shewing All the Intermediate and Respective Distances Between the Principal Towns in France, Holland, Flanders, on the Rhine in Switzerland and Savoy... Dublin: 1780. V. 47

THE GEOGRAPHY and History of England: Done in the Manner of Gordon's and Salmon's Geographical and Historical Grammars. London: 1765. V. 47; 49

GEOLOGICAL SOCIETY OF LONDON
Geological Literature Added to the Geological Society's Library, 1894-1900; 1901-1906. London: 1895-1907. V. 53

GEOLOGY of the County of Cape May, State of New Jersey. Trenton,: 1857. V. 47; 49; 51

GEOPONICA
Constantini Caesaris Selectarum Praeceptionum, de Agricultura Libri Uiginti. Basle: 1540. V. 52

GEORGE & CO.
Trade Catalogue for George & Co. London: 1928. V. 52

GEORGE, A.
The Bankisias. London: 1982. V. 49

GEORGE and His Hatchet. Greenfield: 1847. V. 52

GEORGE, ANDREW L.
A Texas Prisoner. Charlotte: 1895. V. 52

GEORGE, DANIEL
The Modern Dunciad, Virgil in London and Other Poems. London: 1835. V. 52

GEORGE Eliot. Moralist and Thinker. Edinburgh: 1884. V. 53

GEORGE, ELIZABETH
Missing Joseph. London: 1992. V. 52
Well-Schooled in Murder. New York: 1990. V. 52

GEORGE, ERNEST
Etchings of Old London. London: 1884. V. 47; 50; 52

GEORGE, GERTRUDE A.
Eight Months with the Women's Royal Air Force - (Immobile). 1920. V. 52

GEORGE, H.
Genealogical Tables Illustrative of Modern History. Oxford: 1875. V. 54
The Oberland and Its Glaciers: Explored and Illustrated with Ice-Axe and Camera. 1866. V. 53
The Oberland and Its Glaciers: Explored and Illustrated with Ice-Axe and Camera. London: 1866. V. 47; 52

GEORGE, HENRY
History of the 3d, 7th, 8th and 12th Kentucky, C.S.A. Louisville: 1911. V. 49
Progress and Poverty: an Enquiry into the Cause of Industrial Depressions, and of Increase of Want with Increase of Wealth - the Reedy... San Francisco: 1879. V. 53
Protection of Free Trade... New York: 1886. V. 50; 53
The Science of Political Economy. Toronto: 1898. V. 53

GEORGE, JOHN B.
Shots Fired in Anger. Plantersville: 1947. V. 54

GEORGE, JOHN NIGEL
English Guns and Rifles. Plantersville: 1947. V. 52; 54
English Pistols and Revolvers. London: 1938. V. 52

GEORGE, SAINT
The Life of St. George. London: 1919. V. 48

GEORGE The Third His Court, and Family. London: 1820. V. 54

GEORGE Washington Bridge Across the Hudson River at New York, New York. New York: 1933. V. 51

GEORGE I, KING OF GREAT BRITAIN
Message from the Late King to the Pr. of Wales, with the Answers. London: 1737?. V. 47

GEORGE II, KING OF GREAT BRITAIN
Letters, in the Original, with Translations and Messages, that Passed Between the King, Queen, Prince and Princess of Wales; on Occasion of the Birth of the Young Princess. London: 1737. V. 51

GEORGE III, KING OF GREAT BRITAIN
A Selection from the Papers of King George III, Preserved at Windsor Castle, from November 1781 to December 1783. London: 1927. V. 49
A Selection From the Papers of King George III Preserved in the Royal Archives at Windsor Castle. Cambridge: 1927. V. 48

GEORGE IV, KING OF GREAT BRITAIN
The Correspondence of George, Prince of Wales 1770-1812. London: 1963-71. V. 52

GEORGETOWN COLLEGE
Laws for the Government of Georgetown College, Georgetown, Ky. September, 1839. Georgetown: 1839. V. 54

GEORGI, CHRISTIAN SIEGISMUND
Wittenbergische Jubel-Geschichte... Wittenberg: 1756. V. 52; 54

GEORGI, J. P.
Russia: or, A Compleat Historical Account of All the Nations Which Compose that Empire. London: 1770. V. 52

GEORGIA. (COLONY). LAWS, STATUTES, ETC.
Acts Passed by the General Assembly of the Colony of Georgia 1755-1774. Wormsloe: 1881. V. 52

GEORGIA. GENERAL ASSEMBLY
Acts of the General Assembly of the State of Georgia, Passed in Milledgeville...1863; Also, Extra Session of 1864. Milledgeville: 1864. V. 49
Report On the Address of a Portion of the members of the General Assembly of Georgia. Charleston: 1860. V. 49

GEORGIA. LAWS, STATUTES, ETC.
Acts of a Public And General Character of the General Assembly of the State of Georgia, Passed at the Biennial Session of 1853 & 1854. Milledgeville: 1854. V. 48

GEORGIA MISSISSIPPI COMPANY
Grant to the Georgia Mississippi Company, the Constitution Thereof... Augusta: 1795. V. 48

THE GEORGIAN Bay and Thirty Thousand Islands. Views Representative of the Wonderful Beauty and Picturesque Scenery to be Found in the Georgian Bay District. Owen Sound: 1926. V. 53

THE GEORGIAN Era: Memoirs of the Most Eminent Persons, Who Have Flourished in Great Britain, From the Accession of George the First to the Demise of George the Fourth. London: 1832-34. V. 50

GEORGIAN Poetry 1911-1922. London: 1912-22. V. 48

GEORGIAN SOCIETY
Records of Eighteenth Century Domestic Architecture and Decoration in Dublin and Georgian Mansions in Ireland. Dublin: 1909-15. V. 47
Records of the 18th Century Domestic Architecture & Decoration in Dublin. Volume II. London: 1910. V. 52
Records of the 18th Century Domestic Architecture & Decoration in Dublin. Volume V. London: 1913. V. 52

THE GEORGIAN Society Records of Eighteenth-Century Architecture and Decoration in Dublin. Dublin: 1909-13. V. 50

GEORGIAN Stories 1925. New York: 1925. V. 53

GEORGIANA, PSEUD.
Algernon Hall. Oxford and London: 1866. V. 49

GEORGICK Papers for 1809, Consisting of Letters and Extracts Communicated to the Masschusetts Society for Promoting Agriculture. Boston: 1809. V. 51

GEORGII, AUGUSTUS
A Biographical Sketch of the Swedish Poet and Gymnasiarch, Peter Henry Ling. London: 1854. V. 54

GEORGIUS RAGUSAEUS
Epistolarum Mathematicarum Seu de Divinatione, Libri Duo. Paris: 1623. V. 50

GEORGYEVSKY, G.
Old Russian Miniatures. Moscow: 1934. V. 47; 49; 50

GERADUS DE ZUTPHANIA
Tractatus de Spiritualibus Ascensionibus. Strassburg: 1488-93. V. 53

GERALDINUS, ANTONIUS
Oratio in Obsequio Nomine Ferdinandi et Elisabeth Innocentio VIII Exhibito, 19, Sept. 1486. Rome: 1488-91. V. 47

GERARD, ALEXANDER
An Essay on Taste...With Three Dissertations on the Same Subject. London: 1759. V. 51; 53

GERARD, CECILE JULES EDUARD
The Adventures of Gerard, the Lion Killer, Comprising a History of His Ten Years' Campaign Among the Wild Animals of Northern Africa. New York: 1856. V. 47

GERARD, FRANCES
Picturesque Dublin, Old and New. London: 1898. V. 52; 53

GERARD, JOHN
Catalogus Arborum, Fruticum ac Plantarum tam Indigenarum Quam Exoticarum in Horto Johannis Gerardi... London: 1599. V. 47
The Herbal, or General History of Plants... London: 1975. V. 48; 52
The Herbal or General Historie of Plantes... London: 1633. V. 47; 48; 50; 51; 52; 53; 54
The Herball or General Historie Of Plantes. London: 1636. V. 47; 51; 53
Twelve Songs Set to Music. London: 1783. V. 49

GERARD, JOSEPH
Causes and Treatment of Sterility in Both Sexes. Boston: 1891. V. 50

GERARD, JULES BASILE
The Adventures of Gerard, the Lion Killer (of Algeria), Comprising His Ten years' Campaign Among Wild Animals of Northern Africa. New York: 1856. V. 48

GERARD, M.
Dali. New York: 1968. V. 47; 50; 51; 53; 54

GERARD, MONTAGU
Leaves from the Diaries of a Soldier and Sportsman, During Twenty Years Service in India, Afghanistan, Egypt and Other Countries. 1865-1885. 1903. V. 52; 54

GERARD, VALLERY C. O.
His Life and His Art. London: 1897. V. 51

GERARD DE NERVAL, GERARD LABRUNIE, KNOWN AS
Sylvie. Paris: 1886. V. 54

GERBER, HELMUT E.
Annotated Secondary Bibliography of Thomas Hardy. 1973. V. 52

GERBER, MORRIS
Old Albany. Albany: 1961. V. 53

GERDTS, WILLIAM H.
American Impressionism. New York: 1984. V. 47
American Still Life Painting. New York: 1971. V. 47; 47; 48; 49; 50; 51; 53; 54

GERE, CHARLOTTE
Victorian Jewellery Design. Chicago: 1973. V. 50

GERE, J. A.
Taddeo Zuccaro, His Development Studied in His Drawings. London: 1969. V. 49; 52

GERETSEGGER, H.
Otto Wagner 1841-1918: The Expanding City - The Beginning of Modern Architecture. London: 1970. V. 54

GERHARD, W. W.
Lectures on the Diagnosis, Pathology and Treatment of the Diseases of the Chest. Philadelphia: 1842. V. 48

GERHARDI, WILLIAM
Jazz and Jasper - the Story of Adams and Eva. London: 1928. V. 53

GERHARDIE, WILLIAM
The Vanity Bag. London: 1927. V. 49

GERIN, PHILIPPE
La Pratique de l'Arithmetique Vulgaire. Contenant les Computations Necessaires au Trafficq de Marchandise, & a Toutes Autres Affaires en General. Reims: 1614. V. 47

GERISH, WILLIAM BLYTH
Sir Henry Chauncey....a Biography. London: 1907. V. 52; 54

GERLACH, MARTIN
Industrial Monograms. Vienna: 1881. V. 53

THE GERM. Portland: 1898. V. 49

THE GERM: Thoughts Toward Nature in Poetry, Literature and Art, No. 2. Feb. 1850. London: 1850. V. 51

THE GERM: Thoughts Toward Nature in Poetry, Literature and Art. Portland: 1898. V. 48; 49

GERMAN Aviation Medicine, World War II. Washington: 1950. V. 50

GERMAN Medals and Decorations. 1943. V. 50

THE GERMAN Spy; or, Familiar Letters From a Gentleman on His Travels thro' Germany, to His Friend in England... London: 1740. V. 48

THE GERMAN Theatre. London: 1801. V. 47

GERMAN-REED, T.
Bibliographical Notes on T. E. Lawrence's Seven Pillars of Wisdom and Revolt in the Desert. London: 1928. V. 53; 54

GERNIN, J. J. VON
A Picturesque Tour Along the Rhine from Mentz to Cologne.... London: 1820. V. 48; 50; 52; 54

GERNSHEIM, HELMUT
Alvin Langdon Coburn, Photographer. London: 1966. V. 52
The History of Photography from the Camera Obscura to the Beginning of the Modern Era. London: 1969. V. 49
The History of Photography from the Camera Obscura to the Beginning of the Modern Era. New York: 1969. V. 47; 54
The History of Photography, From the Earliest Use of the Camera Obscura in the Eleventh Century Up to 1914. London: 1955. V. 47
Julia Margaret Cameron, Her Life and Photographic Work. London: 1948. V. 48; 52
Lewis Carroll, Photographer. New York: 1949. V. 47; 54
Queen Victoria. A Biography in Word and Picture. London: 1959. V. 48

GERRARD, SAMUEL
Prize Essay. On the Mode of Managing Arms in Ireland, Under 40 Statute Acres but Applicable to Farms of Any Size. Dublin: 1865. V. 50

GERRARE, W.
Phantasms. 1895. V. 47; 52

GERRING, CHARLES
Notes on Book Binding. Nottingham: 1899. V. 53; 54

GERRISH, ANDREW
A Synopsis on the Prevention and Cure of Disease. Boston: 1841. V. 48

GERRY, VANCE
Pochoir. Practical Stencilling for the Modern Craftsman as Applied to Illustrations and Designs for Books &c. Los Angeles: 1991. V. 48
Pochoir, Practical Stencilling for the Modern Craftsman as Applied to Illustrations and Designs for Books &c. Pasadena: 1991. V. 47
Twenty-Five Years of the Weather Bird Press. Pasadena: 1963. V. 54

GERSAINT, M.
A Catalogue and Description of the Etchings of Rembrandt Van-Rhyn... London: 1752. V. 50

GERSHE, LEONARD
Butterflies are Free. New York: 1969. V. 50

GERSHWIN, GEORGE
The George and Ira Gershwin Song Book. New York: 1960. V. 47; 54
George Gershwin's Song Book. New York: 1932. V. 49; 51
George Gershwin's Song Book. New York: 1941. V. 52
George Gershwin's Song Book. New York: 1952. V. 53
Porgy and Bess. New York: 1935. V. 47; 48; 51; 52

GERSHWIN, IRA
Lyrics on Several Occasions: a Selection of Stage and Screen Lyrics Written for Sundry Situations. New York: 1959. V. 50; 53

GERSON, JEAN CHARLIER DE
De Passionibus Anime. Paris: 1500-10. V. 49

GERSON, JOHANNES
Opera. Strassburg: 1514. V. 50
Secunda Pars Operum. Strassburg: 1488. V. 49; 50; 53

GERSON, VIRGINIA
Little Dignity: Pictures and Rhymes of Olden Times. New York: 1881. V. 51

GERSTAECKER, FRIEDRICH WILHELM CHRISTIAN
Gerstacker's Travels. London: 1854. V. 52
Narrative of a Journey Around the World. New York: 1853. V. 54
Narrative of a Journey Round the World. New York: 1854. V. 49
Travels. Rio de Janeiro - Buenos Ayres - Ride through the Pampas - Winter Journey Across the Cordilleras - Chili- Valparaiso - California and the Gold Fields. London: 1854. V. 48
Western Lands and Western Waters. London: 1864. V. 48; 52

GERSTELL, RICHARD
The Steel Trap in North America, the Illustrated Story of Its Design, Production and Use with Furbearing and Predatory Animals, from Its Colorful Past to the Present Controversy. Harrisburg: 1985. V. 54

GERSTENBERG, ALICE
Alice in Wonderland. Chicago: 1915. V. 53

GERSTER, ARPAD
The Rules of Aseptic and Antiseptic Surgery. New York: 1890. V. 51; 53
The Rules of Aseptic and Antiseptic Surgery. New York: 1891. V. 51

GERVASUTTI, G.
Gervasutti's Climbs. 1957. V. 53

GESAMTKATALOG der Wiegendrucke. Herausgegeben von der Kommission fur den Gesamtkatalog der Wiegendrucke. Volumes 1-8. Leipzig & Stuggart: 1925-78. V. 47

GESCHICKTER, C.
Diseases of the Breast. Philadelphia: 1943. V. 53
Tumors of the Bone. New York: 1931. V. 53

GESENIUS, WILLIAM
A Hebrew and English Lexicon of the Old Testament, Including the Biblical Chaldee. Boston: 1844. V. 49

GESNER, ABRAHAM
New Brunswick: With Notes for Emigrants... London: 1847. V. 53
A Practical Treatise on Coal, Petroleum and other Distilled Oils. New York: 1865. V. 48; 51

GESNER, KONRAD
Conradi Gesneri Histori Plantarum. Zurich: 1972-80. V. 53
Historiae Animalium Lib I de Quadrupedibus Viviparis. Zurich: 1551. V. 54
Historiae Animalium Liber IV... (with) Historiae Animalium Liber V. Frankfurt: 1620/21. V. 49
On the Admiration of Mountains... San Francisco: 1937. V. 47; 48
Physicarum Meditationum. Zurich: 1586. V. 47; 50; 53

GESSI, BERLINGIERO
La Spada di Honore. Osservazioni Cavaleresche. Milan: 1672. V. 51

GESSNER, SOLOMON
The Death of Abel. London: 1763. V. 48; 49
The Death of Abel. London: 1797. V. 53
Mort d'Abel, Poeme... Paris: 1793. V. 47; 49
New Idylles... London: 1776. V. 48; 52; 53
Rural Poems. London: 1762. V. 54
The Works. Liverpool: 1802. V. 48

GESVRES, FRANCOIS JOACHIM BERNARD POTIER, DUC DE
The Case of Impotency Debated, in the Late Famous Tryal at Paris... London: 1714. V. 47; 49

GETLEIN, FRANK
Chaim Cross. New York: 1974. V. 47; 48; 49; 50; 52
Jack Levine. New York. V. 47; 48; 49; 50; 52
Jack Levine. New York: 1966. V. 50

GETTY, ALICE
Ganesa: A Monograph on the Elephant Faced God. Oxford: 1936. V. 49

GETTY, EDMUND
Notices of Chinese Seals Found in Ireland, Read Before the Belfast Literary Society, May 1850. Dublin & Belfast: 1850. V. 50; 54

GETTY, J. PAUL
How to Be A Successful Executive. London: 1973. V. 49

GETZENDANER, W. H.
A Brief and Condensed History of Parsons' Texas Cavalry Brigade Composed of Twelfth, Nineteenth, Twenty-First, Morgan's Battalion, and Pratt's Battery of Artillery of the Confederate States Together with a Roster of the Several Commands as Far as... Waxahachie: 1892. V. 49

GEVARTIUS, CASPERIUS
Pompa Introitus Honori Serenissimi Principis Ferdinandi Austriaci Hispaniarum Infantis... Antwerp: 1642. V. 47

GHALIOUNGUI, PAUL
The Physicians of Pharaonic Egypt. Cairo: 1983. V. 49; 51

GHENT, W. J.
The Road to Oregon. London, New York: 1929. V. 54

GHIBOTA, A.
150 Years of Chicago Architecture, 1833-1983. Paris: 1985. V. 51

GHIKA, ELENA
Switzerland the Pioneer of the Reformation; or La Suisse Allemande. London & Edinburgh: 1858. V. 47

GHIRSHMAN, ROMAN
The Arts of Ancient Iran from Its Origin to the Time of Alexander the Great. New York: 1964. V. 54

GHOSE, SUDHIN N.
Folk Tales and Fairy Stories from India. London: 1961. V. 48
Folk Tales and Fairy Stories from India. Waltham St. Lawrence: 1961. V. 50; 51; 53

GHOSH, D. P.
Designs from Orissan Temples. 1950. V. 48

GHOSTLY Visitors: a Series of Authentic Narratives. London: 1882. V. 48

GIACOMINI TEBALDUCCI MALESPINI, LORENZO
Oratione e Discorsi. Florence: 1597. V. 51

GIAFFERRI, PAUL LOUIS DE
The History of Feminine Costume of the World. New York: 1926-27. V. 54
The History of Feminine Costume of the World from 5318 BC to Our Century. Paris: 1922-23. V. 50
The History of French Masculine Costume... From Gaul to the Second Empire. Paris: 1927. V. 50

GIANOLIO, FERRANTE
Regole et Ordini della Disciplina Militare. Padua: 1634. V. 50

GIARRE, GAETANO
Alfabeto di Lettere Iniziali Adorno di Animali e Proseguito da Vaga Serie di Caratteri. Firenze: 1797. V. 52

GIBBINGS, ROBERT
The 7th Man. 1930. V. 47
The 7th Man. A True Cannibal Tale of the South Sea Islands. Waltham St. Lawrence: 1930. V. 50; 51
Coming Down the Seine. 1953. V. 54
Coming Down the Seine. London: 1953. V. 47; 53
Fourteen Wood Engravings by...From Drawings made on Orient Line Cruises. Waltham St. Lawrence: 1932. V. 49
Iorana!. Boston: 1932. V. 48; 54
Iorana!. London: 1932. V. 51
Over the Reefs. 1948. V. 54
Over the Reefs. London: 1948. V. 49
Samson and Delilah. London: 1925. V. 50
Samson and Delilah. Waltham St. Lawrence: 1925. V. 52
Sweet Cork of Thee. London: 1951. V. 48; 51; 52
Twelve Woodcuts. London: 1923. V. 51
The Wood Engravings of... London: 1959. V. 48; 49

GIBBON, CHARLES
By Mead and Stream. London: 1884. V. 47
Fancy Free and Other Stories. London: 1884. V. 54
Heart's Delight. London: 1885. V. 49

GIBBON, CHARLES continued
In Love and War. London: 1877. V. 51

GIBBON, EDWARD
The Decline and Fall of the Roman Empire. London: 1817. V. 48
An Essay on the Study of Literature. London: 1764. V. 48; 49
Gibbon's History of the Decline and Fall of the Roman Empire... London: 1826. V. 48
Gibbon's Journey from Geneva to Rome. London: 1961. V. 47
Histoire de la decadence et de la Chute de l'Empire Romain... Paris: 1786. V. 52
The History of the Decline and Fall of the Roman Empire. London. V. 54
The History of the Decline and Fall of the Roman Empire. Philadelphia. V. 51
The History of the Decline and Fall of the Roman Empire. London: 1776-88. V. 47; 48; 51
The History of the Decline and Fall of the Roman Empire. London: 1777-81-88. V. 49
The History of the Decline and Fall of the Roman Empire. London: 1781-88. V. 51
The History of the Decline and Fall of the Roman Empire. London: 1783-90. V. 47
The History of the Decline and Fall of the Roman Empire. London: 1787-89. V. 52
The History of the Decline and Fall of the Roman Empire. London: 1787/81-88. V. 50
The History of the Decline and Fall of the Roman Empire. London: 1788/90. V. 50
The History of the Decline and Fall of the Roman Empire. London: 1789-88-96. V. 48
The History of the Decline and Fall of the Roman Empire. London: 1797. V. 52
The History of the Decline and Fall of the Roman Empire. London: 1817. V. 48
The History of the Decline and Fall of the Roman Empire. London: 1819. V. 48; 49; 50
The History of the Decline and Fall of the Roman Empire. London: 1825. V. 47; 48
The History of the Decline and Fall of the Roman Empire. London: 1828. V. 47
The History of the Decline and Fall of the Roman Empire. Edinburgh: 1832. V. 48
The History of the Decline and Fall of the Roman Empire. London: 1838. V. 48; 54
History of the Decline and Fall of the Roman Empire. New York: 1844. V. 50; 53
The History of the Decline and Fall of the Roman Empire. London: 1848. V. 50; 54
The History of the Decline and Fall of the Roman Empire. Boston: 1850. V. 51
The History of the Decline and Fall of the Roman Empire. London: 1862. V. 48; 51
History of the Decline and Fall of the Roman Empire. London: 1875. V. 50
The History of the Decline and Fall of the Roman Empire. London: 1887. V. 50; 53
The History of the Decline and Fall of the Roman Empire. London: 1896. V. 51
The History of the Decline and Fall of the Roman Empire. New York & London: 1900. V. 50; 51
The History of the Decline and Fall of the Roman Empire. London: 1909-14. V. 49; 51
The History of the Decline and Fall of the Roman Empire. London: 1929. V. 51
The History of the Decline and Fall of the Roman Empire. New York: 1946. V. 51; 54
The History of the Decline and Fall of the Roman Empire. New York: 1974. V. 51
The Letters of... London: 1956. V. 51
The Life of Edward Gibbon, Esq. London: 1839. V. 49
Memoires Litteraires de la Grande Bretagne, Pour l'an 1768. Londres: 1769. V. 48
Miscellaneous Works. Dublin: 1796. V. 50; 51; 53
Miscellaneous Works. London: 1796. V. 47; 51; 52
Miscellaneous Works. London: 1796-1815. V. 47; 48; 52; 53; 54
Private Letters of...(1753-1794). (in Two Volumes) (with) The Autobiographies of...Printed Verbati from Hitherto Unpublished Mss. London: 1896/97. V. 48
Roman Empire. London: 1836. V. 48
A Vindication of Some Passages in the Fifteenth and Sixteenth Chapters of the History of the Decline and Fall of the Roman Empire. London: 1779. V. 53

GIBBON, J. M.
The True Annals of Fairyland, the Reign of King Cole. London: 1901. V. 49

GIBBON, MONK
The Branch of Hawthorn Tree: Poems. London: 1927. V. 49; 51
The Tremulous String: Poems. London: 1926. V. 51

GIBBONS, A. R.
The Recollections of a Old Confederate Soldier. Shelbyville. V. 51

GIBBONS, ABBY HOPPER
Life of...Told Chiefly through Her Correspondence. New York & London: 1897. V. 49

GIBBONS, F.
The Red Napoleon. 1929. V. 47; 49
The Red Napoleon. London: 1929. V. 54

GIBBONS, FELTON
Catalogue of Italian Drawings in the Art Museum, Princeton University. Princeton: 1977. V. 53

GIBBONS, J. J.
In the San Juan, Colorado, Sketches. 1898. V. 54

GIBBONS, J. S.
The Banks of New York, Their Dealers, the Clearing House and the Panic of 1857. New York: 1859. V. 47

GIBBONS, KAYE
Birth of a Baby, so Lovely. Chapel Hill: 1990. V. 54
Ellen Foster. Chapel Hill: 1987. V. 48; 49; 50; 51; 53; 54
Ellen Foster. London: 1988. V. 51
Frost and Flower. Decatur: 1995. V. 54
A Virtuous Woman. Chapel Hill: 1989. V. 51; 53

GIBBONS, S. H.
Africa. From South to North through Marotseland. London: 1904. V. 48

GIBBONS, THOMAS
Memoirs of Eminently Pious Women. London: 1777. V. 48

Rhetoric; or, a View of Its Principal Tropes and Figures, in Their Origin and Powers... London: 1767. V. 47
The Tears of Friendship. London: 1759. V. 48

GIBBONS, WILLIAM
An Exposition of Modern Scepticism, in a Letter, Addressed to the Editors of the Free Enquirer. Wilmington: 1829. V. 49
A Reply to Sir Lucius O'Brien, Bart. Bristol: 1785. V. 52; 54

GIBBS, CHARLES
Confession of Charles Gibbs the Pirate. To Be Executed the 22nd of April, 1831. New York: 1831. V. 48

GIBBS, GEORGE
A Dictionary of the Chinook Jargon, or Trade Language of Oregon. Washington: 1863. V. 47; 53
Memoirs of the Administrations of Washington and John Adams. New York: 1846. V. 47

GIBBS, HENRY HUCKS
A Colloquy on Currency. London: 1893. V. 54

GIBBS, JAMES
A Book of Architecture, Containing Designs of Buildings and Ornaments. London: 1728. V. 53
A Book of Architecture, Containing Designs of Buildings and Ornaments. London: 1739. V. 47
Rules for Drawing the Several Parts of Architecture, in a More Exact and Easy Manner than Has Been Heretofore Practised. London: 1732. V. 48; 53; 54
Rules for Drawing the Several Parts of Architecture in a More Exact and Easy manner than Has Been Heretofore Practised. London: 1738. V. 47
Rules for Drawing the Several parts of Architecture the Several parts of Architecture. London: 1753. V. 50

GIBBS, JAMES GUIGUARD
Who Burnt Columbia?. Newberry: 1902. V. 50

GIBBS, JOHN
English Gothic Architecture; or Suggestions Relative to the Designing of Domestic Buildings, Ornaments, Church-Yard memorials, Chimney Pieces and Alphabets. Manchester: 1855. V. 47

GIBBS, JOSIAH F.
The Mountain Meadows Massacre. Salt Lake City: 1910. V. 54

GIBBS, MAY
The Complete Adventures of Snugglepot and Cuddlepie. London: 1949. V. 51

GIBBS, R. DARNLEY
Chemotaxonomy of Flowering Plants. Montreal: 1974. V. 53

GIBBS, WOLCOTT
Bird Life at the Pole. New York: 1931. V. 54

GIBBSON, A. R.
The Recollections of an Old Confederate Solider. Shelbyville. V. 53

GIBBS-SMITH, C. H.
Balloons. 1956. V. 52

GIBERNE, AGNES
A Lady of England. The Life and Letters of Charlotte Maria Tucker. London: 1895. V. 53

GIBNEY, VIRGIL
The Hip and Its Diseases. New York: 1884. V. 48; 53

GIBRALTAR GARRISON LIBRARY
Index to the Catalogue of Books in the Gibraltar Garrison Library, Established in 1793, With the Fundamental and By-Laws. Gibraltar: 1828. V. 50

GIBRAN, KAHLIL
The Prophet. New York: 1936. V. 49
The Prophet. New York: 1963. V. 48
Sand and Foam. New York: 1926. V. 48

GIBSON, ALEXANDER CRAIG
The Old Man; or Ravings and Ramblings Round Conistone. London: 1849. V. 50

GIBSON, ARTHUR HOPKIN
Robert Hopkin, Master Marine and Language Painter. 1962. V. 54

GIBSON, CHARLES DANA
Americans. New York & London: 1900. V. 50
Drawings. New York: 1894. V. 48
The Education of Mr. Pipp. New York: 1899. V. 50; 52
Eight Drawings Including the Weaker Sex. New York: 1903. V. 48
The Gibson Book: a Collection of the Published Works. New York: 1907. V. 53

GIBSON, CHARLES R.
Wireless Telegraphy and Telephony Without Wires. London: 1914. V. 50

GIBSON, EDMUND
Codex Iuris Ecclesiastici Anglicani; or, the Statutes, Constitutions, Canons, Rubricks and Articles of the Church of England. London: 1713. V. 48; 50; 51
Codex Juris Ecclesiastici Anglicani: or, the Statutes, Constitutions, Canons, Rubricks and Articles. Oxford: 1761. V. 48; 49
Observations Upon the Conduct and Behaviour of a Certain Sect, Usually Distinguished by the Name of Methodists. London: 1740. V. 52

GIBSON, FRANK
The Art of Henri Fantin-Latour: His Life and Works. London. V. 49; 51
The Art of Henri Fantin-Latour, His Life and Works. London: 1910. V. 50

GIBSON, FRANK continued
Charles Conder - His Life and Work, with a Catalogo of the Lithographs and Etchings by Campbell Dodgson, M.A. London: 1914. V. 47; 50; 52; 53

GIBSON, G. A.
Diseases of the Heart and Aorta. Edinburgh: 1898. V. 53

GIBSON, G. S.
The Flora of Essex. London: 1862. V. 50

GIBSON, GEORGE RUTLEDGE
Journal of a Soldier Under Kearny and Doniphan, 1846-1847. Glendale: 1935. V. 50

GIBSON, J. T.
History of the Seventy-Eighth Pennsylvania Volunteer Infantry. Pittsburgh: 1905. V. 48; 50; 52

GIBSON, J. W.
Recollections of a Pioneer. St. Joseph: 1912. V. 53

GIBSON, JAMES
The Bibliography of Robert Burns with Biographical and Bibliographical Notes and Sketches of Burns Clubs, Monuments and Statues. Kilmarnock: 1881. V. 51
Dr. Bodo Otto and the Medical Background of the American Revolution. Springfield: 1937. V. 52

GIBSON, JOHN
The History of Glasgow, From the Earliest Accounts to the Present Time; With an Account of the Rise, Progress and Present State, of the Different Branches of Commerce and Manufactures Now Carried On in the City of Glasgow. Glasgow: 1777. V. 48
Reminiscences of Sir Walter Scott. Edinburgh: 1871. V. 48

GIBSON, JOHN MASON
A Condensation of Matter Upon Anatomy, Surgical Operations and Treatment of Diseases of the Eye... Baltimore: 1832. V. 48; 51

GIBSON, R. W.
Francis Bacon. A Bibliography of His Work and of Baconiana to the Year 1750. Oxford: 1950-59. V. 48; 51; 54
Francis Bacon: A Bibliography of His Works and of Baconiana to the Year 1750. (with) Supplement. Oxford: 1950. V. 47; 49; 50
St. Thomas More: a Preliminary Bibliography of His Works and of Moreana to the Year 1750, with a Bibliography of Utopiana. New Haven and London: 1961. V. 48; 50; 52

GIBSON, ROBERT
A Treatise Of Practical Surveying: Which is Demonstrated From its First Principles. New York: 1803. V. 50

GIBSON, S.
Early Oxford Bindings. 1903. V. 50

GIBSON, THOMAS
The Anatomy of Humane Bodies Epitomized. London: 1682. V. 48; 49; 50
The Anatomy of Humane Bodies Epitomized. London: 1684. V. 53
Legends and Historical Notes on Places in the East and West Wards, Westmorland. Climate &c. Manchester: 1877. V. 52
Legends and Historical Notes on Places Of North Westmoreland. London: 1887. V. 50; 52

GIBSON, W. B.
The Book of Secrets. 1927. V. 48; 50
Mona Lisa Overdrive. London: 1988. V. 48
The New Magician's Manual. 1936. V. 54

GIBSON, W. HAMILTON
Our Edible Toadstools and Mushrooms and How to Distinguish Them. New York: 1895. V. 47; 49

GIBSON, WILFRID WILSON
The Golden Helm and Other Verse. London: 1903. V. 48
Home. A Book of Poems. London: 1920. V. 47; 51
The Web of Life. A Book of Poems. Cranleigh, Surrey: 1908. V. 53

GIBSON, WILLIAM
Count Zero. London: 1986. V. 47; 53
The Farrier's Dispensataory. London: 1734. V. 51; 53
The Farrier's New Guide. London: 1727. V. 47
The Institutes and Practice of Surgery. Philadelphia: 1832. V. 52
The Institutes and Practice of Surgery. Philadelphia: 1838. V. 53
Neuromancer. London: 1984. V. 49; 53; 54
A New Treatise on the Diseases of Horses, Wherein What is Necessary to the Knowledge of a Horse, the Cure of His Diseases... London: 1751. V. 47
The Seesaw Log. New York: 1959. V. 54
Virtual Light. New York and Northridge: 1993. V. 49; 50; 51

GIBSON, WILLIAM SIDNEY
A Descriptive and Historical Guide to Tynemouth:...the Monastery, the Church and the Castle... North Shields: 1849. V. 52
Dilston Hall, Bamburgh Castle. London: 1850. V. 53

GIBSON-CRAIG, W.
Facsimiles of National Manuscripts of Scotland. Southampton: 1867-72. V. 47

GIDDINGS, LUTHER
Sketches of the Campaign in Northern Mexico in Eighteen Hundred Forty-Six and Seven. New York: 1853. V. 47

GIDE, ANDRE
Un Esprit non Prevenu. Paris: 1929. V. 51
If It Die. New York: 1935. V. 49
Journal 1889-1939. Paris: 1940. V. 51
The Journals of Andre Gide. New York: 1947. V. 53
Montaigne. London and New York: 1929. V. 49; 50; 51; 52
Oscar Wilde: a Study. London: 1905. V. 53
Oscar Wilde a Study. Oxford: 1905. V. 49

GIEDION, SIEGFRIED
Mechanization Takes Command, a Contribution to Anonymous History. New York: 1948. V. 49
Walter Gropius, Work and Team-Work. New York: 1954. V. 51

GIEDION-WELCKER, CAROLA
Constantin Brancusi. Basel/Stuttgart: 1958. V. 50; 54
Constantin Brancusi. New York: 1959. V. 47; 48; 50; 52
Contemporary Sculpture: an Evolution in Volume and Space. New York: 1960. V. 54
In Memoriam James Joyce. Zurich: 1941. V. 47; 50; 54
Jean Arp. London: 1957. V. 50; 54

GIEDION-WELKER, CAROLA
Paul Klee. New York: 1952. V. 50

GIES, WILLIAM J.
Dental Education in the United States and Canada. New York: 1926. V. 52

GIEURE, MAURICE
G. Braque. Paris: 1956. V. 49; 51

GIFFARD, A. H.
Edward Giffard: Who Was My Grandfather? A Biographical Sketch. 1865. V. 49; 50; 54

GIFFARD, EDWARD
A Short Visit to the Ionian Islands, Athens and the Morea. London: 1837. V. 47; 49

GIFFEN, GEORGE
With Bat and Ball. London: 1898. V. 51; 54

GIFFORD, BARRY
No Enemy of Horses. 1970. V. 52

GIFFORD, EDWARD W.
Californian Indian Nights Entertainment. Glendale: 1930. V. 47

GIFFORD, G.
History of the Wars Occasioned by the French Revolution, from the Commencement of the Hostilities in 1792 to the end of the Year 1816... London: 1817. V. 48; 51

GIFFORD, ISABELLA
The Marine Botanist. London: 1848. V. 51
The Marine Botanist: an Introduction to the Study of Algology... London. V. 48

GIFFORD, JOHN
A History of the Political Life of the Righ Honourable William Pitt... London: 1809. V. 48; 49; 50; 51; 52; 53
A Residence in France, During the Years 1792, 1793, 1794 and 1795;. London: 1797. V. 52

GIFFORD, WILLIAM
The Baviad, a Parapharastic Imitation of the First Satire of Persius. London: 1791. V. 48; 52; 54
The Baviad and Maeviad. London: 1797. V. 48; 51
The Baviad and Maeviad. London: 1811. V. 52

GIFFORD & BEACH, NEW YORK
Illustrated Catalogue of Goods Used by Carriage and Sleigh Manufacturers, Manufactured and Furnished by Gifford and Beach. New York: 1874. V. 47

THE GIFT. Philadelphia: 1835. V. 48
THE GIFT. Philadelphia: 1838. V. 52
THE GIFT. Philadelphia: 1839. V. 47; 48; 52; 53
THE GIFT. Philadelphia: 1842. V. 48; 51
THE GIFT. Philadelphia: 1843. V. 52
THE GIFT. Philadelphia: 1844. V. 49
THE GIFT. Philadelphia: 1845. V. 48

GIGER, H. R.
Necronomicon. London: 1978. V. 48

GIGUERE, ROLAND
Eight Poems. Iroquois Falls: 1955. V. 47

GILBART, JAMES WILLIAM
Lectures on the History and Principles of Ancient Commerce. London: 1847. V. 50; 54
Logic for the Million, a Familiar Exposition of the Art of Reasoning by a Fellow of the Royal Society. London: 1851. V. 52
The Logic of Banking... London: 1859. V. 54
The Moral and Religious Duties of Public Companies. London: 1846. V. 53
The Moral and Religious Duties of Public Companies. London: 1856. V. 54
The Works of James William Gilbart, F.R.S. London: 1865-66. V. 54

GILBERT, BENNETT
A Leaf from the Letters of Saint Jerome, First Printed by Sixtus Reissinger, Rome c. 1466-1467. Los Angeles & London: 1981. V. 49; 54

GILBERT, CHRISTOPHER
The Life and Work of Thomas Chippendale. London: 1978. V. 54

GILBERT, DAVIES
The Parochial History of Cornwall... London: 1838. V. 47; 51; 53

GILBERT, FRANK T.
Historic Sketches of Walla Walla, Whitman, Columbia and Garfield Counties, Washington Territory and Umatilla County, Oregon. Portland: 1882. V. 52

GILBERT, G.
Report on the Geology of the Henry Mountains. Washington: 1880. V. 53

GILBERT, GEOFFREY
An Abstract of Mr. Locke's Essay on Human Understanding. Dublin: 1752. V. 48
Cases in Law and Equity...with Two Treatises, the One on the Action of Debt, the Other on the Constitution of England. London: 1760. V. 51
The History and Practice of the High Corut of Chancery. London: 1758. V. 52; 54
The Law and Practice of Ejectments. London: 1734. V. 49
The Law and Practice of Ejectments: Being a Compendious Treatise of the Common and Statute Law Relating Thereto... London: 1741. V. 52
The Law of Disstesses and Replevins, Delineated. London: 1757. V. 50
The Law of Evidence. London: 1760. V. 52
The Law of Evidence. London: 1769. V. 49; 53
The Law of Evidence. London: 1777. V. 47
The Law of Evidence. Philadelphia: 1788. V. 52
The Law of Uses and Trusts... London: 1811. V. 52
A Treatise on Tenures. Dublin: 1754. V. 54
A Treatise on the Court of Exchequer (etc.). London: 1758. V. 52

GILBERT, GEORGE
Cathedral Cities of England. London: 1905. V. 50

GILBERT, GERRY
White Lunch. Vancouver: 1964. V. 47

GILBERT, HUMPHREY
The Voyages and Colonising Enterprises of Sir Humphrey Gilbert. London: 1940. V. 47

GILBERT, J.
The Dolomite Mountains. London: 1864. V. 47; 52
Six Letters Relating to Travel, 1865-1869. 1954. V. 53

GILBERT, JACK
Kochan. Syracuse: 1984. V. 53
Love: a Diptych. Asheville: 1994. V. 53; 54
Poetry Selections from Views of Jeopardy. Storrs: 1964. V. 52; 53

GILBERT, JOHN
Playing at Settlers... London: 1855. V. 51

GILBERT, JOHN T.
Historic and Municipal Documents of Ireland 1172-1320 from the Archives of the City of Dublin. 1870. V. 54
Historic and Municipal Documents of Ireland 1172-1320 from the Archives of the City of Dublin, etc.,. London: 1870. V. 49; 50; 51
Register of the Abbey of St. Thomas, Dublin. London: 1889. V. 52; 53

GILBERT, JUDSON
Disease and Destiny: a Bibliography of Medical References to the Famous. London: 1962. V. 52

GILBERT, KARL GROVE
Lake Bonneville. Washington: 1890. V. 51

GILBERT, LINNEY
India Illustrated; an Historical and Descriptive Account of that Important and Interesting Country. London: 1860. V. 50
Russia Illustrated; an Historical and Descriptive Account of that Immense Empire... London. V. 48; 54

GILBERT, LORD BISHOP OF SARUM
A Discourse of the Pastoral Care. London: 1713. V. 48; 49

GILBERT, MERCEDES
Aunt Sara's Wooden God. Boston: 1938. V. 52

GILBERT, MICHAEL
The Road to Damascus. Helsinki. V. 48

GILBERT, STUART
The Wanderings of Ulysses. V. 47

GILBERT, THOMAS
Voyage from New South Wales to Canton, in the Year 1788, with Views of the Islands Discovered. London: 1789. V. 50

GILBERT, WILLIAM
De Magnete, Magneticisque Corporibus, et de Magno Tellure; Physiologia Nova, Plurimis & Arugmentis, & Experimentis Demonstrata. London: 1600. V. 47
De Mundo Nostro Sublunari Philosophia Nova. Amsterdam: 1651. V. 47
The Inquisitor: or, The Struggle in Ferrara. London: 1870. V. 54
The Magic Mirror. A Round of Tales for Young and Old. London: 1866. V. 53
On the Loadstone and Magnetic Bodies, and on the Great Magnet of the Earth... New York: 1893. V. 48

GILBERT, WILLIAM SCHWENCK
The Bab Ballads. London: 1869. V. 48; 53; 54
The Bab Ballads. London: 1908. V. 47
The Bab Ballads and More Bab Ballads. V. 54
The Bab Ballads and Songs of a Savoyard. London: 1926. V. 54
Comedy & Tragedy. London: 1884. V. 47
Fifty "Bab" Ballads. London. V. 52
Fifty "Bab" Ballads. London: 1900. V. 53
Gretchen. London: 1879. V. 53
The Mikado, or The Town of Titipu. London: 1928. V. 49
More "Bab" Ballads. Much sound and Little Sense. London: 1873. V. 47
Original Plays. London: 1876. V. 49
The Pinafore Picture Book. London: 1908. V. 54
The Savoy Operas. London: 1909. V. 54
Selections from the Aesthetic Opera Patience, or Bunthorne's Bride. New York: 1882. V. 53
Songs of...Savoyard. London: 1890. V. 47
Songs of...Savoyard. London: 1891. V. 53
The Story of the Mikado. London: 1921. V. 47; 49; 50
Sweethearts. London and New York: 1875. V. 52
A Topsy-Turvy Adventure. London: 1931. V. 48

GILBEY, WALTER
Animal Painters of England from the Year 1650. London: 1900. V. 47
George Morland: His Life and Works. London: 1907. V. 54

GILBRETH, FRANK B.
Motion Study: a Method for Increasing the Efficiency of the Workman. New York: 1911. V. 54

GILCHRIST, ALEXANDER
Life of William Blake. London: 1863. V. 47
Life of William Blake... London: 1880. V. 48; 49; 50; 51; 52; 53
Life of William Etty, R.A. London: 1855. V. 50; 51

GILCHRIST, ELLEN
In the Land of Dreamy Dreams. Fayetteville: 1981. V. 47; 48; 49; 50; 51; 53; 54
In the Land of Dreamy Dreams. London: 1982. V. 47
The Land Surveyor's Daughter. Fayetteville: 1979. V. 47; 51; 52
Two Stories. New York: 1988. V. 54
Victory Over Japan: A Book of Short Stories. Boston: 1984. V. 53

GILCHRIST, OCTAVIUS GRAHAM
Rhymes. London: 1805. V. 50; 52

GILCHRIST, ROBERT C.
Confederate Defence of Morris Island, Charleston Harbor, by the troops of South Carolina, Georgia and North Carolina, in the Late War Between the States. Charleston: 1884. V. 49

GILCRIST, JAMES P.
A Brief Display of the Origin and History of Ordeals; Trials by Battle; Courts of Chivalry or Honour... London: 1821. V. 48

GILDAS
Opvs Novvm...de Calamitate Excidio, & Conquestu Britanniae. Antwerp?: 1525?. V. 52

GILDER, WILLIAM H.
Ice Pack and Tundra; An Account of the Search for the Jeannette and a Sledge Journey through Siberia. New York: 1883. V. 48

GILDON, CHARLES
The Complete Art of Poetry. London: 1718. V. 47
The Life of Mr. Thomas Betterton, the Late Eminent Tragedian. London: 1710. V. 47; 52; 54
Miscellaneous Letters and Essays, on Several Subjects. London: 1694. V. 54
The New Metamorphosis; or, the Pleasant Transformation... London: 1794/95. V. 47
The Patriot, or the Italian Conspiracy. London: 1703. V. 47
The Post-Man Robb'd of His Mail: or, the Packet Broke Open. London: 1719. V. 50

GILDZEN, ALEX
Six Poems/Seven Prints. Kent: 1971. V. 48

GILES, HERBERT A.
A Chinese Biographical Dictionary. Taiwan: 1962. V. 50

GILES, L. B.
Terry's Texas Rangers. Austin: 1911. V. 52

GILES, L. H.
Color Me Brown. 1963. V. 50

GILES, LAURENCE
Goat Cottage Dream Poems. Mt. Horeb: 1978. V. 51

GILES, P.
The True Source of the Mississippi. Buffalo: 1887. V. 53

GILES, WILLIAM
The Guide to Domestic Happiness. London: 1781. V. 53

GILFILLAN, GEORGE
First and Second Galleries of Literary Portraits. Edinburgh: 1851. V. 52

GILGAMESH
Gilgamesh. Avon: 1974. V. 53

GILHAM, WILLIAM
Manual of Instruction for the Volunteers and Militia of the State of Texas. Galveston: 1861. V. 48
Manual of Instructions for the Volunteers and Militia of the Confederate States. Richmond: 1861. V. 49

GILKERSON, WILLIAM
American Whalers in the Western Arctic. Fairhaven: 1983. V. 53

GILL, BRENDAN
Death in April and Other Poems. Windham: 1935. V. 54
Wooings. Verona: 1980. V. 47; 48; 49; 50; 54

GILL, DAVID
Report on the Boundary Survey Between British Bechuanaland and German S.W. Africa Executed by Lieutenant-Colonel Laffan...and Lieutenant Wettstein. Berlin: 1906. V. 47

GILL, ERIC
And Who Wants Peace?. San Francisco: 1948. V. 51
Art & Love. Bristol: 1927. V. 47; 50
Art and Manufacture. 1929. V. 54; 54
Art and Prudence - an Essay. Waltham St. Lawrence: 1928. V. 48; 51; 53
Art Nonsense and Other Essays. London: 1929. V. 48; 51; 53
Clothes: an Essay Upon the Nature and Significance of the Natural and Artificial Integuments Worn by Men and Women. London: 1931. V. 47; 48; 50; 51; 53
Clothing Without Cloth. Berkshire: 1931. V. 48
Clothing Without Cloth: an Essay on the Nude. Waltham St. Lawrence: 1931. V. 51
Drawings from Life. London: 1940. V. 53
Engravings 1928-1933. London: 1934. V. 47; 52
The Engravings of Eric Gill. Wellingborough: 1983. V. 47; 48; 51; 53
An Essay on Typography. London: 1931. V. 47; 48; 49; 51
First Nudes. London: 1954. V. 49
The Future of Sculpture. London: 1928. V. 52
Id Quod Visum Placet. A Practical Test of the Beautiful. Waltham St. Lawrence: 1926. V. 49
The Lord's Song. London: 1934. V. 50; 53
The Lord's Song. Waltham St. Lawrence: 1934. V. 47; 49; 50; 51; 53; 54
The Passion of Our Lord According to the Four Evangelists. 1934. V. 51
Sculpture. Ditchling: 1918. V. 52
Sculpture. Ditchling: 1923. V. 49
Sculpture. Ditchling, Sussex: 1924. V. 48; 49; 50
Sculpture on Machine-Made Buildings - a Lecture Delivered to the Birmingham and Five Counties Architectural Association in the Royal Birmingham Society of Artists Galleries, Nov. 1936. Birmingham: 1937. V. 52
Songs Without Clothes. Ditchling: 1921. V. 48; 49; 52; 53
Twenty-Five Nudes. High Wycombe: 1938. V. 52
Twenty-Five Nudes. London: 1938. V. 51
War Memorial. Ditchling: 1923. V. 50
Wood Engravings: Being a Selection of Eric Gill's Engravings on Wood. Ditchling: 1924. V. 48; 50; 53

GILL, EVAN R.
Bibliography of Eric Gill. London: 1953. V. 48; 49

GILL, ISOBEL, LADY
Six Months in Ascension. London: 1878. V. 50; 53

GILL, JOHN
Perserverance. A Poem. London: 1755. V. 53

GILL, THOMAS
A Brief Sketch of the Coinage and Paper Currency of South Australia. Adelaide: 1912. V. 48
Report of the Dinner Given to Charles Dickens in Boston, February 1, 1842. Boston: 1842. V. 47

GILL, WILFRED AUSTIN
Edward Cracorft Lefroy, His Life and Poems... London: 1897. V. 48

GILL, WILLIAM
California Letters of William Gill Written in 1850 to His Wife Harriet Tarleton in Kentucky. New York: 1922. V. 47; 50
Gems from the Coral Islands. Philadelphia: 1855. V. 50; 54
Gems from the Coral Islands. Philadelphia: 1860's. V. 47
Gems of the Coral Islands. London: 1856. V. 52

GILL, WILLIAM F.
The Life of Edgar Allan Poe. New York: 1877. V. 48
The Life of Edgar Allan Poe. London: 1878. V. 49
The Life of Edgar Allan Poe... New York: 1878. V. 48

GILLE, JOSEPH GASPARD
Choix de Nouvelles Vignettes de la Founderie de Gille Fils, a Paris, Rue Jean-de-Beauvis, No. 28. Paris: 1808/10. V. 53

GILLENSON, LEWIS W.
Esquire's World of Jazz. New York: 1962. V. 47

GILLER, J. U.
Rhymes of Boyhood. Philadelphia: 1836. V. 54

GILLES, HAROLD D.
Plastic Surgery of the Face Based on Selected Cases of War Injuries of the Face Including Burns with Original Illustrations... London: 1920. V. 54

GILLES, PIERRE
Antiquities of Constantinople... London: 1729. V. 52

GILLES, ROBERT PEARSE
Tales of a Voyager to the Arctic Ocean. London: 1826. V. 48; 51; 53

GILLESPIE, ALEX
An Historical Review of the Royal Marine Corps, from Its Original Institution Down to the Present Era. Birmingham: 1803. V. 48; 53

GILLESPIE, CHARLES COULSTON
Dictionary of Scientific Biography. New York: 1970-76. V. 52
Monuments of Egypt: the Napoleonic Expedition. Princeton: 1987. V. 51

GILLESPIE, W. M.
A Manual of the Principles and Practice of Road-Making. New York: 1847. V. 52

Rome: As Seen by a New-Yorker in 1843-44. New York & London: 1845. V. 49

GILLET, HENRI
Decorative Medallions in French Taste. Modern French Ornamental Art. Paris: 1922. V. 47

GILLETT, CHARLES RIPLEY
Catalogue of the McAlpin Collection of British History and Theology. New York: 1927-30. V. 54

GILLETT, JAMES B.
Six Years With the Texas Rangers. Austin: 1921. V. 47; 50; 53
Six Years with the Texas Rangers 1875 to 1881. Yale: 1925. V. 49

GILLIAM, ALBERT M.
Travels Over the Table Lands and Cordilleras of Mexico 1843-44. Philadelphia: 1846. V. 50

GILLIAM MANUFACTURING CO.
Catalogue No. 12. Canton: 1897. V. 49

GILLIARD, E. T.
Birds of Paradise and Bower Birds. London: 1969. V. 49; 52; 53

GILLIES, HAROLD
Plastic Surgery of the Face, Based On Selected Cases of War Injuries of the Face, Including Burns... London: 1920. V. 54

GILLIES, JOHN
An Inquiry, Whether the Study of the Ancient Languages Be a Necessary Branch of Modern Education?. Edinburgh: 1769. V. 53
A View of the Reign of Frederick II of Prussia; with a Parallel Between That Prince and Philip II of Macedon. London: 1789. V. 52

GILLILAND, MAUDE T.
Rincon, Remote Dwelling Place, a Story of tthe Life on a South Texas Ranch at the Turn of the Century. Brownsville: 1964. V. 52
Wilson County Texas Rangers 1837-1977. 1977. V. 52

GILLING, ISAAC
A Sermon Preach'd at Lyme Regis in the County of Dorset, at a Quarterly lecture... London: 1705. V. 52

GILLINGHAM, JAMES
Artificial Limbs, Surgical Appliances, etc. with Illustrations of Remarkable Cases, Together with a Series of Articles on Psychology. Exeter: 1888. V. 51

GILLINGHAM, ROBERT CAMERON
The Rancho San Pedro: The Story of a Famous Rancho in Los Angeles County and Of Its Owners the Dominguez Family. Los Angeles: 1961. V. 47

GILLINGWATER, E.
An Historical and Descriptive Account of St. Edmund's Bury. St. Edmund's Bury: 1804. V. 53

GILLIS, STEVE
Mark Twain and the Old Enterprise Gang. San Francisco: 1940. V. 54
Memories of Mark Twain and Steve Gillis. Sonora: 1924. V. 53

GILLISS, JAMES MELVILLE
A Catalogue of 16,748 Southern Stars, Deduced by the United States Naval Observatory from the Zone Observations Made at Santiago de Chile by the U.S. Naval Astronomical Expedition to the Southern Hemisphere During the Years 1849-50-52. Washington: 1895. V. 50

GILLMAN, ALEXANDER W.
The Gillmans of Highgate with Letters from Samuel Taylor Coleridge. London: 1895. V. 48

GILLMOR, CLOTWORTHY
Jessie of Boulogne; or The History of a Few Minutes. London: 1877. V. 54

GILLMOR, FRANCES
Windsinger, an Idyll of the Navajos. New York: 1930. V. 52

GILLMORE, PARKER
A Hunter's Adventures in the Great West. London: 1871. V. 49
The Hunter's Arcadia. London: 1860. V. 50
The Hunter's Arcadia. London: 1886. V. 47; 49; 54
Lone Life: a Year in the Wilderness. London: 1875. V. 49
On Duty. A Ride through Hostile Africa. London: 1880. V. 49
Prairie and Forest: a Description of the Game of North America... London: 1874. V. 50; 53
Prairie Farms and Prairie Folk. London: 1872. V. 51

GILLUM, WILLIAM
Miscellaneous Poems, ...To Which is Added a Farce, Called What Will the World Say?. London: 1787. V. 47

GILLY, DAVID
Handbuch der Land-Bau-Kunst. Anweisung zur Landwirthschaftlichen Baukunst. Braunschweig: 1800/1798/1811. V. 50

GILLY, WILLIAM O. S.
Narratives of Shipwrecks of the Royal Navy. London: 1850. V. 51

GILLY, WILLIAM STEPHEN
Memoir of Felix Neff, Pastor of the High Alps... London: 1832. V. 54

GILMAN, CAROLINE HOWARD
The Lady's Annual Register and Housewife's Memorandum-Book for 1838. Boston: 1837. V. 50
Recollections of a Housekeeper. New York: 1834. V. 49; 50

GILMAN, CHANDLER ROBBINS
Life on the Lakes... New York: 1836. V. 54

GILMAN, CHARLOTTE PERKINS
Concerning Children. Boston: 1901. V. 50; 51
The Crux, a Novel. New York: 1911. V. 54
The Home, Its Work and Influence. New York: 1903. V. 54
Human Work. New York: 1904. V. 49
In This Our World and Other Poems. San Francisco: 1895. V. 49; 50
The Living of Charlotte Perkins Gilman. An Autobiograpphy. New York: 1935. V. 54
Moving the Mountain. New York: 1911. V. 54
The Yellow Wall Paper. Boston: 1899. V. 47

GILMAN, DANIEL
The Launching of a University and Other Papers. New York: 1906. V. 52

GILMER, ALBERT H.
When A Soldier Spoke Effectively: "Lafayette We Are Here!". V. 47

GILMER, JOHN H.
Letter Addressed to Hon. Wm. C. Rives. Richmond: 1864. V. 49

GILMOR, HARRY
Four Years in the Saddle. New York: 1866. V. 49; 51; 53

GILPIN, LAURA
The Enduring Navaho. Austin: 1968. V. 50; 51; 52; 53
The Pueblos - a Camera Chronicle. New York: 1941. V. 47; 54
The Rio Grande, River of Destiny. 1949. V. 48; 54
The Rio Grande: River of Destiny. New York: 1949. V. 47; 48; 52
Temples in Yucatan. New York: 1948. V. 47; 51
Winning Health in the Pikes Peak Region. Colorado Springs: 1923. V. 47

GILPIN, SIDNEY
The Songs and Ballads of Cumberland, to which are added Dialect and Other Poems. London: 1866. V. 52

GILPIN, WILLIAM
The Central Gold Region. Philadelphia: 1860. V. 47
An Essay on Prints. London: 1768. V. 48; 49; 51; 52
An Essay on Prints. London: 1781. V. 51; 53; 54
An Essay on Prints. London: 1792. V. 47; 48; 49; 50
Gilpin's Forest Scenery. London: 1879. V. 54
The Last Work Published of the Rev. William Gilpin, M.A.... London: 1810/11. V. 50; 52
Lectures on the Catechism of the Church of England. London: 1779. V. 48
The Life of Hugh Latimer, Bishop of Worcester. (with) The Life of Bernard Gilpin. London: 1755. V. 54
Moral Contrasts: or, the Power of Religion Exemplified Under Different Characters. Lymington: 1798. V. 48
Observations, on Several Parts of England, Particularly the Mountains and Lakes of Cumberland and Westmoreland. London: 1808. V. 50
Observations on Several Parts of the Counties of Cambridge, Norfolk, Suffolk, and Essex. London: 1809. V. 50
Observations on Several Parts of the Counties of Cambridge, Norfolk, Suffolk and Essex. (with) Observations on the Coasts of Hampshire, Sussex and Kent.. London: 1809/04. V. 49
Observations on the Coasts of Hampshire, Sussex and Kent, Relative Chiefly to Picturesque Beauty... London: 1804. V. 49
Observations on the River Wye. London: 1792. V. 47; 53
Observations on the River Wye and Several Parts of South Wales. London: 1789. V. 47; 48; 49
Observations on the River Wye and Several Parts of South Wales... London: 1800. V. 47
Observations on the Western Parts of England, Relative Chiefly to Picturesque Beauty. London: 1798. V. 47; 48; 49; 51; 53; 54
Observations on the Western Parts of England, Relative Chiefly to Picturesque Beauty... London: 1808. V. 50
Observations Relative Chiefly to Picturesque Beauty. London: 1786. V. 48
Observations Relative Chiefly to Picturesque Beauty. London: 1788. V. 47; 52
Observations Relative Chiefly to Picturesque Beauty. London: 1788-92. V. 49
Observations Relative Chiefly to Picturesque Beauty. London: 1792. V. 48
Observations Relative Chiefly to Picturesque Beauty Made in the Year 1772, on Several Parts of England. London: 1808. V. 54
Observations Relative Chiefly to Picturesque Beauty Made in the Year 1776 on Several Parts of Great Britain, Particularly the High Lands of Scotland. London: 1789. V. 48; 54
The Parks of Colorado. San Luis de Calebra: 1866. V. 49
Practical Hints Upon Landscape Gardening... London: 1835. V. 47
Remarks on Forest Scenery, and Other Woodland Views... London: 1791. V. 48; 49
Remarks on Forest Scenery, and Other Woodland Views... London: 1794. V. 47; 48; 54
Remarks on Forest Scenery, and Other Woodland Views... London: 1808. V. 52
Remarks on Forest Scenery, and Other Woodland Views. Edinburgh: 1834. V. 47
Six Landscapes. London: 1794. V. 47
Spoken at the "British Association of Science" Sept. 26th 1870. London: 1871. V. 48
Three Dialogues on the Amusements of Clergymen. London: 1796. V. 48; 52
Three Essays: On Picturesque Beauty - On Picturesque Travel; and on Sketching Landscape. London: 1794. V. 51
Three Essays: On Picturesque Beauty; On Picturesque Travel; and On Sketching Landscape. London: 1792. V. 49; 50; 54
Three Essays: on Picturesque Beauty; on Picturesque Travel; and On Sketching Landscape; with a Poem on Landscape Painting. London: 1808. V. 54
Voyage en Differentes Parties de l'Angleterre, et Particulierements Dans les Motagnes & Sur les Lacs du Cumberland & du Westmoreland. Paris...a Londres: 1789. V. 48; 50; 54

GILROY, CLINTON G.
The History of Silk, Cotton, Linen, Wool and Other Fibrous Substances: Including Observations on Spinning, Dyeing and Weaving... New York: 1845. V. 48

GILROY, FRANK D.
Private. New York: 1970. V. 54

GIMBEL, R.
Thomas Paine: a Bibliographical Check List of Common Sense with an Account of Its Publication. New Haven: 1956. V. 52

GIMBUTAS, MARIJA
Bronze Age Cultures in Cental and Eastern Europe. The Hague: 1965. V. 49; 51; 53

GINGER Beer; a Grand Pindaric, in Honour of the Radicals and Whigs; Humbly Dedicated to Those Great Northern Allies. Leeds: 1819. V. 52

GINSBERG, ALLEN
Angkor Wat. London: 1968. V. 49; 50; 51; 52; 53; 54
Bixby Canyon Ocean Path Word Breeze. New York: 1972. V. 47; 48; 51; 52
Careless Love. Madison: 1978. V. 52; 53; 54
Chicago Trial Testimony. San Francisco: 1975. V. 51
Collected Poems 1947-1980. New York: 1984. V. 47
Entering Kansas City High. Kansas: 1967. V. 47
First Blues: Rags, Ballads and Harmonium Songs 1971-74. New York: 1975. V. 49
The Gates of Wrath: Rhymed Poems, 1948-1952. Bolinas: 1972. V. 49; 52
Howl. San Francisco: 1971. V. 53
Howl. New York: 1986. V. 51
Iron Horse. Toronto: 1972. V. 52
Iron Horse. Toronto: 1973. V. 47; 53
Kaddish and Other Poems 1958-1960. San Francisco: 1961. V. 53; 54
Kaddish for Naomi Ginsberg, 1894-1956. San Francisco: 1992. V. 53
Kaddish...With Two Other Related Poems: White Shroud and Black Shroud. 1992. V. 52; 54
The Moments Return. San Francisco: 1970. V. 51
Mostly Sitting Haiku. Paterson: 1978. V. 50
New Year Blues. New York: 1972. V. 54
Open Head. Melbourne: 1972. V. 47
Planet News 1961-1967. California: 1968. V. 50; 52
Poems All Over the Place - Mostly 'Seventies. 1978. V. 47
Returning to the Country for a Brief Visit. 1973. V. 48
Scrap Leaves. Tasty Scribbles. New York: 1968. V. 52
To Eberhart from Ginsberg. Lincoln: 1976. V. 49
Wales — a Visitation, July 29th 1967. London: 1968. V. 52; 53
Wales Visitation. Hereford: 1979. V. 50
What's Dead. 1980. V. 48
White Shroud. Poems 1980-1985. New York: 1986. V. 48; 54

GIOIA, DANA
Formal Introductions: an Investigative Anthology. West Chester: 1994. V. 54
Journeys in Sunlight. 1986. V. 52; 54
Journeys in Sunlight. Cottondale: 1987. V. 54
Planting a Sequoia. Poems. West Chester: 1991. V. 54
Summer Poems. 1983. V. 52; 54

GIORNO, JOHN
Cancer in My Left Ball: Poems 1970-1972. West Glover: 1973. V. 54

GIOVANNI, NIKKI
Night Comes Softly-Anthology of Black Female Voices. 1970. V. 53
Spin a Soft Black Song: Poems for Children. New York: 1971. V. 53

GIOVIO, PAOLO, BP. OF NOCERA
Commentario de le Cose de Turchi. Venice: 1540. V. 49
Commentario de le Cose de Turchi. Venice: 1541. V. 49
Commentario de le Cose de Turchi. Venice: 1544. V. 49
Illustrium virorum Vitae. Florence: 1549. V. 49
Illustrium Virorum Vitae. Florentiae: 1551. V. 47
Novocomensis Episcopi Nucerini, Historiarum Sui Temporis... Paris: 1553-54. V. 49

THE GIPSIES: Dedicated, By Permission, to James Crabb, The Gipsies' Friend. London: 1842. V. 48

GIPSON, FRED
The Cow Killers. Austin: 1956. V. 47; 49; 50

GIPSON, LAWRENCE HENRY
The British Empire Before the American Revolution. Caldwell: 1939-56. V. 47

GIPSON, MORRELL
City Country ABC. New York: 1946. V. 51

GIRADOUX, JEAN
Ondine. New York: 1954. V. 50

GIRAFFI, ALEXANDRO
An Exact History of the Late Revolutions in Naples... London: 1664-63. V. 49

GIRALDI, GIGLIO GREGORIO
Dialogo Duo de Poetis Nostrorum Temporum. Florentiae: 1551. V. 47
Syntagma de Musis. Strassburg: 1512. V. 50

GIRALDUS CAMBRENSIS
The Itinerary of Archbishop Baldwin through Wales. London: 1806. V. 54
Opera. London: 1861-91. V. 49; 52

GIRARD, ALFRED C.
A Sketch of the Official Career of Colonel Edward Perry Vollum, Chief Medical Purveyor, U.S. Army. Fort Sheridan: 1891. V. 52

GIRARD, GUILLAUME
The History of the Life of the Duke of Espernon, the Great Favorite of France. London: 1670. V. 49; 51

GIRARD, PIERRE SIMON
Traite Analytique de la Resistance des Solides, et des Solides d'Egale Resistance. Paris: 1798. V. 49

GIRARD DE VILLETHIERRY, JEAN, ABBE
La Vie des Veuves, ou, les Devoirs et les Obligations des Veuves Chretiennes. Paris: 1697. V. 53; 54

GIRARDIN, R. L.
An Essay on Landscape; or, On the Means of Improving and Embellishing the country round Our Habitations. London: 1783. V. 52

GIRAUD, E. I.
The Flowers of Shakespeare. London: 1845. V. 47

GIRAUD, J. P.
The Birds of Long Island. New York: 1844. V. 54

GIRAUD, JANE ELIZABETH
The Flowers of Milton. London: 1846. V. 51

GIRAUD, P. F. F. J.
The Campaigns of Paris in 1814 and 1815. London: 1816. V. 50

GIRAUD, S. LOUIS
1, 2, 3 Figure Book With Living Models. London: 1937. V. 49
Bookano Stories. London: 1944. V. 48
Bookano Stories. London: 1946. V. 48
Bookano Stories. London: 1947. V. 54
Bookano Stories. London: 1950. V. 49
The Story of Jesus. London: 1930. V. 49

GIRAUDOUX, JEAN
Rues et Visages de Berlin. Paris: 1930. V. 52
Suzanne et le Pacifique. Paris: 1927. V. 47

GIRDLESTONE, A.
The High Alps Without Guides. 1970. V. 53

GIRDLESTONE, THOMAS
Facts Tending to Prove That General Lee, Was Never Absent from This Country, for Any Length of Time During the Years 1767, 1768, 1769, 1770, 1771, 1772 and that he was the author of Junius. London: 1813. V. 47

THE GIRL Who Wouldn't Mind Getting Married. 1887. V. 48; 50

THE GIRLHOOD of Queen Victoria. London: 1912. V. 53; 54

THE GIRL'S and Boy's Own Book of Sports. Philadelphia: 1850's. V. 49

THE GIRL'S Realm. May 1903. V. 51

LE GIROFFLIER Aux Dames Ensemble le Dit des Sibiles. Paris: 1860. V. 47

GIROUARD, MARK
Robert Smythson and the Architecture of the Elizabethan Era. London: 1966. V. 49; 51; 53

GIROUD, FRANCOISE
Dior: Christian Dior 1905-1957. New York: 1987. V. 54

GIRVAN, I. WAVENEY
A Bibliography and a Critical Survey of the Works of Henry Williamson. Chipping Campden: 1931. V. 53

GIRVIN, BRENDA
Alice and the White Rabbitt. Their Trips Round About London. London. V. 52
Round Fairyland with Alice and the White Rabbit. 1916. V. 48

GISBORNE, THOMAS
An Enquiry into the Duties of the Female Sex. London: 1797. V. 47; 49; 51; 53; 54
An Enquiry Into the Duties of the Female Sex. Philadelphia: 1798. V. 50
An Enquiry Into the Duties of the Female Sex. London: 1801. V. 52
A Familiar Survey of the Christian Religion, and of History... London: 1799. V. 49
A Familiar Survey of the Christian Religion, and of History as Connected with the Introduction of Christianity, and With Its Progress to the Present Time. London: 1801. V. 52
Observations on the Plan for the Training the People to the Use of Arms, With Reference to the Subject of Sunday Drilling. London: 1806. V. 50
Remarks on the Late Decision of the House of Commons Respecting the Abolition of the Slave Trade. London: 1792. V. 51
Walks in a Forest; or, Poems Descriptive of Scenery and Incidents Characteristic of a Forest at Different Seasons of the Year. London: 1794. V. 49; 54
Walks in a Forest; or, Poems Descriptive of Scenery and Incidents Characteristic of a Forest, at Different Seasons of the Year... London: 1796. V. 54

GISLA SAGA SURSSONAR
The Saga of Gisli. New York: 1936. V. 47; 54

GISSING, ALGERNON
At Society's Expense. London: 1894. V. 54
A Masquerader. London: 1892. V. 54
The Scholar of Bygate. London: 1897. V. 53
A Village Hampden. London: 1890. V. 54

GISSING, GEORGE ROBERT
Critical Studies of the Works of Charles Dickens. New York: 1924. V. 49; 51
The Crown of Life. London: 1899. V. 54
Demos: a Story of English Socialism. London: 1886. V. 54
The Emancipated. London: 1890. V. 48; 50; 54
Human Odds and Ends: Stories and Sketches. London: 1898. V. 53
In the Year of Jubilee. London: 1894. V. 51
In the Year of Jubilee. New York: 1895. V. 48
The Nether World. London: 1889. V. 54
New Grub Street, a Novel. London: 1891. V. 47; 52; 54
Our Friend the Charlatan. London: 1901. V. 53
The Paying Guest. London: 1895. V. 48; 50
The Private Papers of Henry Ryecroft. Toronto. V. 53
The Private Papers of Henry Ryecroft. London: 1903. V. 50
The Private Papers of Henry Ryecroft. Westminster: 1903. V. 52; 53
Sleeping Fires. New York: 1896. V. 48
Thyrza, a Tale. London: 1886. V. 51
The Town Traveller. New York: 1898. V. 48; 51
The Whirlpool. London: 1897. V. 51
Will Warburton. London: 1905. V. 51
Workers in the Dawn. Garden City: 1935. V. 48

GISSING, T. W.
Materials for a Flora of Wakfield and Its Neighbourhood. London: 1867. V. 54

GITTINGS, ROBERT
Famous Meeting: Poems Narrative and Lyric. London: 1953. V. 47; 48; 49

GIUDICI, CESARE
L'Ostreria Magra. Padua: 1692. V. 51

GIULIO romano L'Entree de l'Empereur Sigismond a Mantoue...Grave d'apres une Longue Frise... Paris: 1675. V. 53

GIUSTINIAN, LEONARDO
Strambotti e Canzonette d'Amore. 1945. V. 52; 54

GIUSTINIANI, FABIAN
Index Universalis Alphabeticus Materias in Omni Facultate Consulto Pertractatas, Earumq. Scriptores & Locos Designans. Rome: 1612. V. 47

GIVEON, RAPHAEL
Egyptian Scarabs from Western Asia from the Collections of the British Museum. Freiburg: 1985. V. 49; 51

GJERSTAD, EINAR
Early Rome. Lund: 1953-66. V. 50
Early Rome. Lund: 1953-73. V. 52

GLADDING, MC BEAN & CO.
Latin Tiles. Oakland: 1923. V. 48

GLADKY, SERGE
Motifs Decoratifs, Six Planches en Couleurs. Paris. V. 52

THE GLADSTONE ABC. London: 1882. V. 48

GLADSTONE, GEORGE, MRS.
Gold and Tinsel. London: 1885. V. 49

GLADSTONE, HUGH S.
The Birds of Dumfriesshire. London: 1910. V. 48; 49
A Catalogue of the Vertebrate Fauna of Dumfriesshire. Dumfries: 1912. V. 48; 52; 54

GLADSTONE, THOMAS
The Englishman in Kansas. New York: 1857. V. 53
Kansas or, Squatter Life and Border Warfare in the Far East. London: 1857. V. 47

GLADSTONE, WILLIAM EWART
Church Principles Considered In Their Results. London: 1840. V. 50
The State In Its Relations with the Church... London: 1841. V. 50
Studies on Homer and the Homeric Age. Oxford: 1858. V. 49; 50

GLADWIN, FRANCIS
The History of Hindostan, During the Reigns of Jehangir, Shahjehan, and Aurungzebe. Calcutta: 1778. V. 47

GLAISHER, JAMES
Travels in the Air... London: 1871. V. 47; 49; 51

GLANVILL, E.
De Legibus et Consuetudinibus Regni Angliae. New Haven: 1932. V. 50

GLANVILL, JOSEPH
A Blow at Modern Sadducism in Some Philosophical Considerations About Witchcraft. London: 1668. V. 47
Essays on Several Important Subjects in Philosophy and Religion. London: 1676. V. 48; 52
Lux Orientalis, or an Enquiry into the Opinion of the Eastern Sages, Concerning the Praeexistence of Souls... London: 1662. V. 50
Scepsis Scientifica; or, Confest Ignorance, the Way to Science... London: 1665. V. 48
Two Choice and Useful Treatises: the One Lux Orientalis, or an enquiry into the Opinion of the Eastern Sages Concerning the Praeexistence of Souls. London: 1682. V. 48; 52

GLANVILLA, RANULPHO DE
Tractatus de Legibus & Consuetudinibus Regni Angliae, Tempore Rgis Henrici Secundi Compositus, Iusticiae Gubernacula Tenente Illustri Viro Ranulpho de Glanvilla... London: 1604. V. 47

GLANVILLE, JOHN
Reports of Certain Cases, Determined and Adjudged by the Commons in Parliament... London: 1775. V. 48; 51

GLANVILLE, S. R. K.
Catalogue of Demotic Papyri in the British Museum. Volume II: The Instructions of 'Onchsheshonqy... London: 1955. V. 49
Catalogue of Egyptian Antiquities in the British Museum II: Wooden Model Boats. London: 1972. V. 49

GLAPTHORNE, HENRY
The Plays and Poems... London: 1874. V. 53

GLASCOCK, WILLIAM N.
Land Sharks and Sea Gulls. London: 1838. V. 49
Sailors and Saints; or, Martrimonial Manoeuvres. London: 1835. V. 51

GLASER, CHRISTOPHER
The Compleat Chymist, or, a Treatise of Chemistry... London: 1677. V. 50
Trait de la Chymie. Paris: 1663. V. 54

GLASER, LYNN
Engraved America, Iconography of America Through 1800. Philadelphia: 1970. V. 48

GLASER, MILTON
Graphic Design. 1973. V. 51
Graphic Design. Woodstock: 1973. V. 53

GLASER, R.
Denkbuch uber Die Anweisenheit Ihrer K. K. Majestaten Franz des Ersten und Caroline Auguste in bohmen im Jahre 1833. Prague: 1836. V. 53

GLASGOW, ELLEN
The Descendant. New York: 1897. V. 47; 48; 51; 53
The Miller of Old Church. Garden City: 1911. V. 54
Phases of an Inferior Planet. New York: 1898. V. 51
Works. New York: 1938. V. 49

GLASGOW. ROYAL COLLEGE OF SCIENCE & TECHNOLOGY
Bibliotheca Chemica... Glasgow: 1906. V. 48
Bibliotheca Chemica. London: 1954. V. 47; 49; 52; 54
Bibliotheca Chemica: a Catalogue of the Alchemical, Chemical and Pharmaceutical books in the Collection of the Late James Young of Kelly and Durris. Hildesheim: 1974. V. 50

GLASPELL, SUSAN
A Jury of Her Peers. London: 1927. V. 49

GLASS, E. L. N.
The History of the Tenth Cavalry, 1866-1921. Tucson: 1921. V. 49

GLASS, FRANCIS
A Life of George Washington, in Latin Prose. New York: 1835. V. 53

GLASS, JOHN
An Address Delivered at the Annual meeting of the Etherley Mechanic's Institue, December 31st, 1849. Darlington: 1850. V. 49

GLASS, MARK
Ancient Song. New York: 1980. V. 52; 53; 54

GLASS, SAMUEL
An Essay on Magnesia Alba. Oxford: 1764. V. 48; 51

GLASS, THOMAS
A Letter from Dr. Glass to Dr. Baker, on the Means of Procuring a Distinct and Favourable Kind of Small Pox. London: 1767. V. 50
Twelve Commentaries on Fevers. London: 1752. V. 47; 50

GLASS, WILLISON
The Caledonian Parnassus, a Museum of Original Scottish Songs. Glasgow: 1814. V. 50

GLASSCOCK, C. B.
The Death Valley Chuch-Walla. Greenwood: 1907. V. 47

GLASSE, DR.
The Magistrate's Assistant; or, a Summary of Those Laws, Which Immediately Respect the Conduct of a Justice of the Peace... Glocester: 1784. V. 49

GLASSE, HANNAH
The Art of Cookery, Made Plain and Easy. London: 1751. V. 48; 51
The Art of Cookery, Made Plain and Easy. London: 1760. V. 47; 51
The Art of Cookery, Made Plain and Easy. London: 1770. V. 52
The Art of Cookery, Made Plain and Easy. London: 1788. V. 50
The Art of Cookery Made Plain and Easy. Alexandria: 1805. V. 47

GLASSER, OTTO
Wilhelm Conrad Roentgen and the Early History of the Roentgen Rays. Springfield: 1934. V. 50

GLASSGOLD, PETER
Hwaet!. Perry Township: 1987. V. 49

GLAUBER, JOHANN RUDOLPH
Opera Chymica. Frankfurt am Main: 1658-59. V. 47; 53
Operis Mineralis. (with) *Furni Novi Philosophici.* Amsterdam: 1659/51-64. V. 50

GLEADALL, ELIZA EVE
The Beauties of Flora, With Botanic and Poetic Illustrations. London: 1834/36. V. 48

GLEANINGS from Books on Agriculture. London: 1801. V. 48

GLEANINGS from Books on Agriculture and Gardening. London: 1802. V. 48

GLEANINGS from the Most Celebrated Books on Husbandry, Gardening and Rural Affairs. Philadelphia: 1803. V. 51; 52

GLEANINGS Of a Wanderer, in Various Parts of England, Scotland and North Wales. London: 1805. V. 51

GLEASON, HENRY
New Britton and Brown Illustrated Flora of the Northeastern United States and Adjacent Canada. New York: 1952. V. 54

GLEASON, JOE DUNCAN
Islands of California: Their History, Romance and Physical Characteristics. Los Angeles: 1951. V. 47

GLEDITSCH, JOHANN GOTTLIEB
Methodus Fungorum Exhibens Genera, Species et Varietates cum Charactere, Differentia Specifica... Berlin: 1753. V. 49; 52

GLEED, CHARLES E.
From River to Sea. A Tourist's and Miner's Guide from the Missouri River to the Pacific Ocean. Chicago: 1882. V. 51

GLEED, CHARLES SUMNER
The Kansas Memorial, a Report of the Old Settler's Meeting, Held at Bismarck Grove, Kansas, Sept. 15th and 16th, 1879. Kansas City: 1880. V. 54
Rand, McNally & Company's Overland Guide from the Missouri River to the Pacific Ocean Via Kansas, Colorado, New Mexico, Arizona and California. Chicago: 1885. V. 54

GLEESON, JOHN
History of the Ely O'Carroll Territory, or, Ancient Ormonde Situated in Northern Tipperary and North Western King's County. London: 1915. V. 47; 53

GLEICHEN, ALEXANDER
The Theory of Modern Optical Instruments: a Reference Book for Physicists, Manufacturers of Optical Intruments, and for Officers in the Army and Navy. London: 1918. V. 51

GLEICHEN-RUSSWORM, WILHELM FRIEDRICH, FREIHERR VON
Histoire de la Mouche Commune de nos Appartemens. Nurnberg?: 1766. V. 47

GLEIG, G. R.
The Campaigns of the British Army at Washington and New Orleans, in the Years 1814-185. London: 1836. V. 50
The Chelsea Pensioners. London: 1829. V. 52
The Country Curate. London: 1830. V. 51
The History of the British Empire in India. London: 1830-35. V. 54
The History of the British Empire in India. London: 1835. V. 53; 54
The Life of Major-General Sir Thomas Munro, Bart. London: 1830. V. 52
A Narrative of the Campaigns of the British Army at Washington and New Orleans... London: 1821. V. 50; 54
A Narrative of the Campaigns of the British Army at Washington and New Orleans... London: 1826. V. 47
The Soldier's Help to the Knowledge of Divine Truth. London: 1835. V. 51; 52; 54
A Subaltern in America... Philadelphia: 1833. V. 48

GLEIM, BETTY
Erziehung und Unterricht des Weiblichen Geschlechts. Ein Buch fur Eltern und Erzieher... Leipzig: 1810. V. 53

GLEN, A. R.
Under the Pole Star. London: 1937. V. 54

GLEN, JAMES
A Description of South Carolina... London: 1761. V. 48

GLEN, W. CUNNINGHAM
A Treatise On the Law of Highways. London: 1860. V. 53

GLENDINNING, ROBERT
Description of Elvaston Gardens (Derbyshire). London: 1849. V. 49

GLENN, EDWIN F.
Reports of Explorations in the Territory of Alaska (Cooks Inlet, Sushitna, Copper and Tanana Riers), 1898. Washington: 1899. V. 50; 52

GLENN, THOMAS ALLEN
Some Colonial Mansions and Those Who Lived in Them. Philadelphia: 1899-1900. V. 52

GLIMCHER, ARNOLD B.
Louise Nevelson. New York and Washington: 1972. V. 54

GLIMPSES Along the Canadian Pacific Railway. Indian Series A. 1890. V. 52

GLISAN, RODNEY
Journal of Army Life. San Francisco: 1874. V. 47; 50

GLOAG, JOHN
A History of Cast Iron In Architecture. London: 1948. V. 50

GLOBUS, SEPTIMUS
Der Freischutz Travestie. London: 1824. V. 50

GLOREZ, ANDREAS
Volstaendige Hauss-und Land-Bibliothec. Regenspurg: 1699-1702. V. 53

GLOSSOGRAPHIA Anglicana Nova; or, a Dictionary, Interpreting Such Hard Words of Whatever Language, As Are at Present Used in the English Tongue... London: 1707. V. 53

THE GLOUCESTER Tragedy; or, the True Lover's Downfal. V. 47

GLOVER, J. W.
St. Patrick at Tara; a National Oratorio. V. 52

GLOVER, MARY BAKER EDDY
Science and Health. Boston: 1875. V. 47; 51
Science and Health. Boston: 1886. V. 51

GLOVER, MARY BAKER EDDY continued
Science and Health. Jerusalem: 1924. V. 51
Science and Health. Boston: 1934. V. 51

GLOVER, P.
An Enquiry Concerning Virtue and Hapiness. London: 1751. V. 48

GLOVER, RICHARD
Admiral Hosier's Ghost. London: 1740. V. 54
The Athenaid. London: 1787. V. 53
The Atheniad, a Poem. Dublin: 1788. V. 49
Leonidas, a Poem. London: 1737. V. 47; 48; 50; 51
Leonidas, a Poem. London: 1770. V. 49; 54
Medea. A Tragedy. London: 1761. V. 50

GLOVER, ROBERT
Nobilitas Politica vel Civilis Personas Scilicet Distinguendi, et ab Origine inter Gentes, ex Principum Gratia Nobilitandi Forma. London: 1608. V. 47; 52

GLOVER, WILLIAM
History of Ashton-Under-Lyne and the Surrounding District. Ashton-under-Lune: 1884. V. 48

GLUCK, LOUISE
Firstborn. Middlesex: 1969. V. 48

GLUECK, NELSON
Explorations in Eastern Palestine, I-IV. New Haven: 1934-51. V. 49; 51
Explorations in Eastern Palestine. Volume I. New York: 1934. V. 51
Explorations in Eastern Palestine. Volume II. New Haven: 1935. V. 51
Explorations in Eastern Palestine. Volume IV. New Haven: 1951. V. 51

GLYN, RICHARD H.
Bull Terriers and How to Breed Them. Dealing Fully with Both White and Coloured Bull Terriers. Oxford: 1950. V. 49

GLYNN, JOSEPH
Rudimentary Treatise on the Construction of Cranes and Machinery for Raising Heavy Bodies for the Erection of Building and for Hoisting Goods. London: 1849. V. 49
Rudimentary Treatise on the Power of Water. London: 1853. V. 49

GMELIN, LEOPOLD
Hand-Book of Chemistry. 1848-61. V. 54

GNAW-Wood: or New England Life in a Village. New York: 1868. V. 53

GNUDI, CESARE
Giotto. Milan: 1959. V. 53

GNUDI, MARTHA T.
The Life and Times of Gaspare Tagliacozzi, Surgeon of Bologna, 1545-1599. New York: 1950. V. 52

GO Ahead. No. 2. The Crockett Almanac. Nashville: 1840. V. 47

GO Ahead! Davy Crockett's 1838 Almanack of Wild Sports in the West, Life in the Backwoods, Skethces of Texas and Rows on the Mississippi. Nashville: 1837. V. 49

GO Ahead! The Crockett Almanac 1840. Nashville: 1839. V. 47

GOAD, CHARLES E.
Insurance Plan of Leeds Carriers' Warehouses 1896, 1899, 1908, 1928. V. 50

GOADBY, ROBERT
The King of the Beggars; or, the Surprising Adventures of Bamfylde Moore Carew... London: 1825?. V. 52
The Life, Voyages and Adventures of Bampfylde-Moore Carew... London: 1790. V. 53

GOARD, JOHN
Astro-Meteorologia Sana. London: 1690. V. 50

GOBAT, SAMUEL
Journal of a Three Years' Residence in Abyssinia, in Furtherance of the Objects of the Church Missionary Society... London: 1834. V. 53
Journal of Three Years' Residence in Abyssinia... New York: 1850. V. 50

GOBINEAU, JOSEPH ARTHUR, COMTE
Essai sur l'Inegalite des Races Humaines. Paris: 1853-55. V. 52; 54

GOBIUS, JOHANNES
Scala Coeli. Ulm: 1480. V. 52

GOBLE, WARWICK
The Book of Fairy Poetry. London: 1920. V. 52

GOBLET, EUGENE
The Migration of Symbols. London: 1894. V. 54

THE GOBLIN Spider. Tokyo: 1899. V. 48

GOCHER, W. H.
Trotalong. Pacealong. Racealong. Hartford: 1928. V. 51

GOCLENIUS, RUDOLPH
Physiologia Crepitvs Ventris et Risvs, Recognita Explanata, et Iterato Edita, a D. Rodolpho Goclenio. 1607. V. 51

GODCHAUX, ELMA
Stubborn Roots. New York: 1936. V. 53

GODDARD, DWIGHT
Eminent Engineers. New York: 1906. V. 50

GODDARD, FREDERICK B.
Where to Emigrate and Why. 1869. V. 53
Where to Emigrate and Why. Philadelphia/Cincinnati: 1869. V. 47

GODDARD, PAUL E.
The Anatomy, Physiology, and Pathology of the Human Teeth... Philadelphia: 1844. V. 54
The Morphology of the Hupa Language. 1905. V. 51

GODDARD, ROBERT H.
The Papers of Robert H. Goddard. New York: 1970. V. 54
Rocket Development: Liquid-Fuel Rockt Research, 1929-1941. New York: 1948. V. 52

GODDARD, T.
The Military Costume of Europe Exhibited in a Series of Highly Finished Military Figures in the Uniform of Their Several Corps with a Concise Description and Historical Anecdotes. London: 1822. V. 48

GODDARD, THOMAS
Plato's Demon; or, the State-Physician Unmaskt; Being a Discourse in Answer to a Book Call'd Plato Redivivus. London: 1684. V. 48

GODDARD, WILLIAM
An Extract from the Sessions-Rolls of the County of Somerset. London: 1765. V. 47

GODDARD, WILLIAM G.
An Address to the People of Rhode-Island, Delivered in Newport, on Wednesday, May 3, 1843, in Presence of the General Assembly, on the Occasion of the Change, in the Civil Government of Rhode Island... Providence: 1843. V. 54

GODDARD, WILLIAM H. D.
The Government Models. Lincoln: 1988. V. 51

GODDEN, GEOFFREY A.
Stevengraphs and Other Victorian Silk Pictures. New Jersey: 1971. V. 50

GODDEN, RUMER
A Candle for St. Jude. New York: 1948. V. 54
In Noah's Ark. New York: 1949. V. 54

GODDING, W. W.
Two Hard Cases. Sketches from a Physician's Portfolio. Boston: 1882. V. 50

GODEFROY, FREDERIC
Dictionnaire de l'Ancienne Langue Francaise et de Tous ses Dialectes du IXe au XVe Siecle. (with) Lexique de l'Ancien Francais. Paris: 1937-38/1901. V. 49

GODEFROY, JACQUES
The History of the United Provinces of Achaia. London: 1673. V. 52

GODEY'S Lady's Book and Magazine. Philadelphia: 1851/54. V. 52

GODFRED, EDWARD SETTLE
The Field Diary of Lt. Edward Settle Godfrey, Commanding Encounter at the Battle of the Little Big Horn. Portland: 1957. V. 53

GODFREY, BOYLE
Miscellanea Vere Utilia; or Miscellaneous Experiments and Observations on Various Subjects, in Three Parts. London: 1735. V. 48

GODFREY, DAVE
Death Goes Better with Coca-Cola. Toronto: 1967. V. 47; 50

GODFREY, E. L. B.
History of Medical Profession of Camden County, N.J., Including a Brief Review of the Charitable Institutions Within the County. Philadelphia: 1896. V. 51

GODFREY, M. J.
Monograph and Iconograph of Native British Orchidaceae. Cambridge: 1933. V. 52; 53

GODFREY, MICHAEL
A Short Account of the Bank of England. 1695?. V. 53

GODFREY, THOMAS
Juvenile Poems on Various Subjects. Philadelphia: 1765. V. 47; 54

GODFRIDUS
The Knowledge of Things Unknown. London: 1679. V. 54

GODINE, DAVID
Lyric Verse, a Printer's Choice. 1966. V. 52; 54

GODKIN, G. S.
The Monastery of San Marco. Florence: 1885. V. 50
The Monastery of San Marco. Florence: 1887. V. 52

GODLEE, RICKMAN JOHN
An Atlas of Human Anatomy Illustrating Most of the Ordinary Dissections and Many Not Usually Practised by the Student...Plates Volume. London: 1880. V. 48

GODLEY, JOHN ROBERT
Extracts from Letters of John Robert Godley to C. B. Adderley. London: 1863. V. 51
Letters from America. London: 1844. V. 47; 48

GODMAN, ERNEST
Norman Architecture in Essex. London: 1905. V. 51

GODMAN, F. DU CANE
Biologia Central-Americana... London: 1906. V. 51
A Monograph of the Petrels (Order Tubinares). London: 1907-10. V. 51; 52
Natural History of Azores, or Western Islands. London: 1870. V. 48; 50

GODMAN, JOHN D.
American Natural History. Philadelphia: 1826. V. 53

GODMAN, JOHN D. continued
American Natural History. Part 1 Mastology. Philadelphia: 1826-28. V. 49

GODOLPHIN, JOHN
Repertorium Canonicum; or an Abridgment of the Ecclesiastical Laws of the Realm, Consistent with the Temporal... London: 1680. V. 48; 52

GODON, JULIEN
Painted Tapestry and Its Application to Interior Decoration. 1879. V. 50
Painted Tapestry and Its Application to Interior Decoration: Practical Lessons in Tapestry Painting with Liquid Colour. London: 1879. V. 48

GOD'S Late Mercy to England, in Discovering of Three Damnable Plots by the Treacherous Papists and Jesuits in England and Wales, and Many Other Places. London: 1641. V. 49

GODWIN, ALBERT
Chris Beetles Gallery. London: 1982. V. 48

GODWIN, BENJAMIN
The Substance of a Course of Lectures on British Colonial Slavery, Delivered at Bradford, York and Scarborough. London: 1830. V. 48; 52

GODWIN, FRANCIS
Episcopi de Praesulibus Angliae Commentarius... Cambridge: 1743. V. 47
Rerum Anglicarum Henrico VIII, Edwardo VI et Maria Regnantibus Annales. London: 1628. V. 47; 52
The Strange Voyage and Adventures of Domingo Gonsales to the World in the Moon. London: 1768. V. 47

GODWIN, G. N.
The Civil War in Hampshire (1642-45). Southampton: 1904. V. 49; 53
The Geology, Botany and Natural History of the Maltese Islands. Valetta: 1880. V. 52

GODWIN, GAIL
Anna Margarita's Will. Concord: 1984. V. 48
The Perfectionists. New York: 1970. V. 53; 54

GODWIN, GEORGE
The Churches of London: a History and Description of the Eclesiastical Edifices of the Metropolis. London: 1838. V. 50

GODWIN, P.
A Biography of William Cullen Bryant. New York: 1883. V. 53

GODWIN, PARKE
Vala: a Mythological Tale. New York: 1851. V. 47

GODWIN, TED
Lower Bow: a Celebration of Wilderness Art and Fishing. Calgary: 1991. V. 53

GODWIN, THOMAS
Moses and Aaron. London: 1625. V. 49

GODWIN, WILLIAM
Adopted in the Charter-House School. The Pantheon: Or Ancient History of the Gods of Greece and Rome. London: 1809. V. 47
Cloudesley: a Tale. London: 1830. V. 50
Considerations on Lord Grenville's and Mr. Pitt's Bills, Concerning Treasonable and Seditious Practices and Unlawful Assemblies. London: 1795. V. 52
The Enquirer. Dublin: 1797. V. 49
The Enquirer. London: 1797. V. 48; 50; 51; 54
An Enquiry Concerning Political Justice, and Its Influence on General Virtue and Happiness. Dublin: 1793. V. 50; 52; 53
An Enquiry Concerning Political Justice and its Influence on General Virtue and Happiness. London: 1793. V. 48
Enquiry Concerning Political Justice and its Influence On Morals and Happiness. London: 1796. V. 48; 49; 53
Essay on Sepulchres: or, a Proposal for Erecting Some Memorial of the Illustrious Dead in all Ages on the spot Where Their Remains Have Been Interred. London: 1809. V. 48; 49; 51
Essay on Sepulchres; or, a Proposal for Erecting Some Memorial of the Illustrious Dead In All Ages on the Spot Where Their Remains Have Been Interred. New York: 1809. V. 49
Faulkener; a Tragedy. London: 1807. V. 48
Fleetwood; or the New Man of Feeling. London: 1805. V. 54
Fleetwood; or, the New Man or Feeling. New York: 1805. V. 49
History of the Commonwealth of England... London: 1824. V. 48; 51
History of the Commonwealth of England. London: 1824-28. V. 50; 51; 53
The History of the Life of William Pitt, Earl of Chatham. Dublin: 1783. V. 48; 52
The History of the Life of William Pitt, Earl of Chatham. London: 1783. V. 52
Life of Geoffrey Chaucer, the Early English Poet... London: 1803. V. 50; 51; 52
The Lives of the Necromancers... London: 1834. V. 50
Mandeville. Edinburgh: 1817. V. 47; 49; 51
Mandeville. New York: 1818. V. 49
Memoirs of Mary Wollstonecraft Godwin... Philadelphia: 1799. V. 48
Memoirs of the Author of a Vindication of the Rights of Woman. London: 1798. V. 48; 53
St. Leon: a Tale of the Sixteenth Century. London: 1799. V. 48
Things As They Are; or, The Adventures of Caleb Williams. London: 1796. V. 48; 51; 52; 53; 54
Things as they Are; or, the Adventures of Caleb Williams. London: 1816. V. 50
Thoughts on Man, His Nature, Productions and Discoveries. London: 1831. V. 48; 49; 53
Tragical Consequences; or, a Disaster at Deal, Being an Unpublished Letter of William Godwin dated Wed. Nov. 18th, 1789 and Remarks Thereon by Edmund Blunden. London: 1931. V. 53
Transfusion; or, the Orphans of Unwalden. New York: 1836. V. 54

GODWYN, T.
Moses and Aaron. Civil and Ecclesiastical Rites, Used by the Ancient Hebrews... London: 1655. V. 48

GODWYN, THOMAS
...An English Expostion of the Roman Antiquities: Wherein Many Roman and English Offices are Parallel'd and Divers Obscure Phrases Explained. London: 1674. V. 49
Romanae Historiae Anthologia... 1625. V. 47
Romanae Historiae Anthologia. London: 1668. V. 52

GOEDAERDT, JOHANNES
De Insectis, in Methodum Redactus. Londini: 1685. V. 53
Johannes Godartius of Insects. York: 1682. V. 53

GOEDART, JOANNES
Metamorphosis et Historia Naturalis Insectorum. Middleburgh: 1662-67. V. 54

GOEDE, C. A. G.
The Stranger in England; or Travels in Great Britain. London: 1807. V. 52

GOEDICKE, HANS
Re-Used Blocks from the Pyramid of Amenemhet I at Lisht. New York: 1971. V. 49; 51
The Report About the Dispute of a Man with His Ba: Papyrus Berlin 3024. Baltimore & London: 1970. V. 49

GOELL, MILTON J.
The Wall that is My Skin: Poems Inspired by the Negro's Flight for Democratic Rights. New York: 1945. V. 52

GOENIGK, ADOLPH
Pioneer History of Kansas. Lincoln: 1933. V. 49

GOERTZ, MAX
Zwei Novellen. Weimar: 1928/29. V. 47

GOETGHEBUER, PIERRE JACQUES
Choix des Monumens, Edifices et Maisons les plus Remarquables du Royaume des Pays-Bas. Ghent: 1827. V. 47; 48; 53

GOETHE, JOHANN WOLFGANG VON
Auserlesene Lieder, Gedichte und Balladen, Ein Strauss. Hammersmith: 1916. V. 49; 50; 51
Fancies Bizarreries & Ornamented Grotesques. Leeds: 1989. V. 52
Faust. London: 1825. V. 53
Faust. Paris: 1828. V. 47
Faust. London: 1877. V. 52
Faust. Paris: 1880. V. 51
Faust. London: 1890. V. 54
Faust. 1906. V. 49; 52; 54
Faust. Boston & New York: 1906. V. 48
Faust. London: 1906. V. 47; 50; 51
Faust. Hammersmith: 1906-10. V. 47
Faust. London: 1908. V. 47; 51
Faust. Berlin: 1925. V. 49
Faust. London: 1925. V. 47; 48; 50; 52; 53; 54
Faust... New York: 1925. V. 47; 48
Faust. New York: 1930. V. 50
Faust. London: 1951. V. 54
Goethe's Theory of Colours... London: 1840. V. 54
Goethe's Werke. Stuttgart und Tubingen: 1827-1834. V. 48
Herman and Dorothea. London: 1801. V. 54
Herman and Dorothea. Richmond: 1805. V. 50
Iphigenie auf Tauris: Ein Schauspiel. 1912. V. 52; 54
Italian Journey. Collins: 1962. V. 54
Italian Journey. London: 1962. V. 48; 52
Die Leiden des Jungen Werther. 1911. V. 49; 51; 52
Promethee. Paris: 1950. V. 53
Reynard the Fox. London: 1853. V. 47
Reynard the Fox. New York: 1860. V. 48
The Sorrows of Werter. Dublin: 1780. V. 48
The Sorrows of Werter. London: 1780. V. 49; 52
The Sorrows of Werter. London: 1784. V. 48; 50; 51
The Sorrows of Werter. London: 1929. V. 54
The Story of Reynard the Fox. New York: 1954. V. 47; 51; 52; 53
Versuch die Metamorphose der Pflanzen zu Erklaren. Gotha: 1790. V. 47; 50
West-Ostlicher Divan. Stuttgart: 1819. V. 48
West-Ostlicher Divan. (West-East Divan). Northampton: 1970. V. 53
Wilhelm Meister's Apprenticeship. Edinburgh: 1824. V. 52
Wilhelm Meister's Apprenticeship. Philadelphia: 1840. V. 51
Wilhelm Meister's Apprenticeship. New York: 1959. V. 53; 54

GOETSCHY, GUSTAVE
Les Jeunes Peintres Militaires: des Neuville, Detaille, Dupray. Paris: 1878. V. 50

GOETZ, DELIA
The Book of the People: Popul Vuh, the National Book of the Ancient Quiche Maya. Los Angeles: 1954. V. 50

GOETZ, RUTH
The Immoralist. New York: 1954. V. 54

GOETZMANN, WILLIAM H.
Army Exploration in the American West 1803-1863. New Haven: 1959. V. 54
Exploration and Empire. New York: 1966. V. 49; 51; 53; 54

GOFF, BRUCE
Architecture. Billings: 1978. V. 53; 54

GOFF, FREDERICK RICHMOND
Incunabula in American Libraries. New York: 1964. V. 50; 52

Incunabula in American Libraries. A Third Census of 15th Century Books Recorded in North American Collections... Millwood: 1973. V. 47; 50; 51

Incunabula in American Libraries. A Third Census of 15th Century Books Recorded in North American Collections. New York: 1973. V. 53

GOFF, G. L.
Historical Records of the 91st Argyllshire Highlanders, Now the 1st Battalion Princess Louise's Argyll and Sutherland Highlanders. London: 1891. V. 50

GOFF, HARRIET NEWELL
Other Fools and Their Doings, or, Life Among the Freedmen. New York: 1880. V. 47

GOGARTY, OLIVER ST. JOHN
Collected Poems. New York: 1954. V. 47
Elbow Room. 1939. V. 49; 50; 51; 54
Elbow Room. Dublin: 1939. V. 48; 53
Going Native. New York: 1940. V. 53
I Follow St. Patrick. London: 1938. V. 53
Mad Grandeur. New York: 1941. V. 53
An Offering of Swans. 1924. V. 48
An Offering of Swans. London: 1924. V. 52
Perennial Volume One. Baltimore: 1944. V. 53
Selected Poems. New York: 1933. V. 54

GOGH, VINCENT VAN
The Complete Letters of Vincent Van Gogh. 1958. V. 50
The Letters of Vincent Van Gogh to His Brother 1872-1886. (with) Further Letters to His Brother 1886-1889. London: 1927/29. V. 54
Letters to an Artist - from Vincent Van Gogh to Anton Van Rappard. London: 1936. V. 53
The Rijksmuseum Vincent van Gogh. Amsterdam: 1987. V. 49

GOGOL, NIKOLAI
Chichikov's Journey's (Dead Souls). 1944. V. 48; 51
Chichikov's Journeys (Dead Souls). New York: 1944. V. 51; 54
Dead Souls. Paris: 1885. V. 54
Dead Souls. New York: 1923. V. 51
(Dead Souls). Chichiknov's Journeys... Providence: 1944. V. 53; 54
The Diary of a Madman. London: 1929. V. 53
The Gamblers and Marriage. New York: 1927. V. 54
The Overcoat. 1975. V. 52; 54
The Overcoat. Verona: 1975. V. 47; 48; 49; 50
The Overcoat. Westport: 1976. V. 48; 53

GOGUET, ANTOINE YVES
The Origin of Laws, Arts and Sciences and their Progress Among the Most Ancient Nations. Edinburgh: 1775. V. 49

GOHS, C.
Ed Quigley, Western Artist. 1971. V. 50; 51; 53

GOLBORNE, JOHN
The Report of John Golborne, Engineer, Concerning the Drainiage of the North Level of the fens, and the Outfall of the Wisbeach River. London: 1769. V. 49

GOLD and Silver Mining in Sonora, Mexico. Proposed Purchase of the San Juan del Rio Mines & Lands Belonging to the Cincinnati and Sonora Mining Association. Cincinnati: 1867. V. 48

GOLD, CHARLES
Oriental Drawings: Sketched Between the Years 1791 and 1798. London: 1806. V. 48

GOLD Dust. How to Find It and How to Mine It. An Elementary Treatise on the Methods and Appliances Used by Miners on the Frontier, with Other Useful Information. Vancouver: 1898. V. 50

GOLD, MICHAEL
The Damned Agitator and Other Stories. Chicago: 1924?. V. 47
Life of John Brown. Girard: 1924. V. 49; 50

GOLD MINING CO.
Charter and By-Laws of the Gold Mining Company. Washington: 1886. V. 52

GOLD Stories of '49 by a Californian. Boston: 1896. V. 49

THE GOLD Stripe. A Tribute to the British Columbia Men Who Have Been Killed, Crippled and Wounded in the Great War. Vancouver: 1918. V. 53

GOLD, THOMAS D.
History of Clarke County Virginia and Its Connection with the War Between the States. Berryville: 1914. V. 49

GOLDAST AB HAIMINSFELD, MELCHIOR
Suevicarum Rerum Scriptores Aliquot Veteres. Frankfurt: 1605. V. 47; 52

GOLDBERG, NORMAN L.
John Chrome the Elder. New York: 1978. V. 51; 52

GOLDBERG, RUBE
Rube Goldberg vs. the Machine Age, a Retrospective Exhibition of His Work with Memoirs and Annotations. New York: 1968. V. 49

GOLDBORNE, SOPHIA, PSEUD.
Hartly House, Calcutta. Calcutta: 1908. V. 54

GOLDEN ABC. London: 1860. V. 51

THE GOLDEN Banquet and Other Functions During the Reception of President Roosevelt. San Francisco: 1903. V. 47

GOLDEN Cariboo. Ashcroft to Barkerville by Stage Route. 1906. V. 47

THE GOLDEN Cockerel Greek Anthology. London: 1937. V. 51

THE GOLDEN Fairy Book. London. V. 54

THE GOLDEN Gate Bridge. Report of the Chief Engineer to the Board of Directors of the Golden Gate Bridge and Highway District, California. San Francisco: 1970. V. 52

GOLDEN, HARRY
Carl Sandburg. Cleveland: 1961. V. 53

GOLDEN, MARITA
Wild Women Don't Wear No blues: Black Women Writers on Love, Men and Sex. New York: 1993. V. 53
A Woman's Place. New York: 1986. V. 51

THE GOLDEN Pomegranate, a Selection from the Poetry of the Mogul Empire in India 1526-1858. Bombay: 1957. V. 53

GOLDEN, RICHARD L.
Sir William Osler. An Annotated Bibliography. London: 1819. V. 47
Sir William Osler: an Annotated Bibliography with Illustrations. San Francisco: 1988. V. 47; 50; 51; 52; 54

GOLDEN Sands Mining Company of Cape Nome. New York: 1900. V. 48

GOLDEN Years. A Sonnet Sequence. Mount Vernon: 1924. V. 54

GOLDER, F. A.
Bering's Voyages. An Account of the Efforts of the Russians to Determine the Relation of Asia and America. New York: 1935. V. 48
Bering's Voyages...an Account of the Efforts of the Russians to Determine the Relation of Asia and America. New York: 1922. V. 53

GOLDFARB, THELMA
Echoes of Palestine. Brooklyn: 1929. V. 53

THE GOLDFINCH, or New Modern Songster. Glasgow: 1785. V. 47

GOLDICUTT, JOHN
Specimens of Ancient Decorations from Pompeii. London: 1825. V. 53

GOLDIE, JOHN
Diary of a Journey through Upper Canada and some of the New England States. 1819. Toronto: 1897. V. 53

GOLDILOCKS and the Three Bears. New York: 1934. V. 49

GOLDING, ARTHUR
A Moral Fable Talk. San Francisco: 1987. V. 48; 49; 53

GOLDING, HARRY
The Motor Boy. London. V. 52
Willie Winkle, the Tale of a Wooden Horse. London. V. 51
Zoo Days. London: 1919. V. 54

GOLDING, J.
Catalogue of the Valuable Collection of Pictures, Marbles, Bronzes, the Celebrated Musical Instruments, Ornamental Furniture, China and Ancient Glass. 1857. V. 47
The Song of Sion or Pictures in Paradise, a Sacred Ode. Middle Hill: 1838. V. 54

GOLDING, LOUIS
Poems Drunk and Drowsy. London: 1934. V. 51
Terrace in Capri. London: 1934. V. 53

GOLDING, WILLIAM
The Brass Butterfly. Chicago. V. 47
The Brass Butterfly. London: 1958. V. 49; 50; 52; 53; 54
Close Quarters. London: 1987. V. 53
Fire Down Below. London: 1989. V. 54
Free Fall. London: 1959. V. 47; 50; 53
The Hot Gates and Other Occasional Pieces. London: 1965. V. 47; 52; 53
The Inheritors. London: 1940. V. 53
The Inheritors. London: 1955. V. 47; 49; 51; 52; 53
The Inheritors. London: 1959. V. 47
The Ladder and the Tree. 1961. V. 51
Lord of the Flies. London: 1954. V. 47; 48; 49; 50; 53
Lord of the Flies. New York: 1955. V. 47; 50; 51; 53; 54
Nobel Lecture. Leamington Spa: 1983. V. 50
Nobel Lecture: 7 December 1983. Leamington Spa: 1984. V. 51; 52; 53
The Paper Man. London: 1984. V. 51; 53
Pincher Martin. London: 1956. V. 47; 49; 53
Pincher Martin. London: 1959. V. 47
The Pyramid. London: 1967. V. 48; 49; 51; 53
Sa Majeste des Mouches. (Lord of the Flies). Paris: 1956. V. 53
The Scorpion God - Three Short Novels. London: 1971. V. 51; 52; 53
Sometime, Never. London: 1956. V. 51
The Spire. London: 1964. V. 48; 49; 52; 53
To the Ends of the Earth. London: 1991. V. 49; 51; 53; 54
The Two Deaths of Christopher Martin. 1956. V. 50
Yes and No and For Whom the Bell Chimes. London: 1983. V. 50

GOLDMAN, EMMA
Anarchism and Other Essays. New York: 1911. V. 52

GOLDMAN, EMMA continued
A Fragment of the Prison Experiences. New York: 1919. V. 51
Living My Life. New York: 1921. V. 48
Living My Life. New York: 1931. V. 47
My Disillusionment in Russia. London: 1925. V. 54
The Psychology of Political Violence. New York: 1911. V. 52
The Social Significance of the Modern Drama. Boston: 1914. V. 51

GOLDMAN, HETTY
Excavations at Eutresis in Boestia. Cambridge: 1931. V. 50; 52

GOLDMAN, JAMES
Follies. New York: 1971. V. 50

GOLDMAN, WILLIAM
Boys and Girls Together. New York: 1964. V. 54
The Chamber, a Screenplay. New York: 1994. V. 53
No Way to Treat a Lady. V. 53
The Princess Bride. New York: 1973. V. 47; 49; 50; 52; 53
The Season: A Candid Look at Broadway. New York: 1969. V. 52
Soldier in the Rain. New York: 1960. V. 52; 53
The Temple of Gold. New York: 1957. V. 48; 50; 53
The Thing Of it Is... New York: 1967. V. 53

GOLDMARK, JOSEPHINE
Fatigue and Efficiency, a Study in Industry.... New York: 1912. V. 53

GOLDONI, CARLO
Commedie Scelte di Carlo Goldoni Avvocato Veneto. London: 1777. V. 54
The Gold Humoured Ladies. London: 1922. V. 49; 52

GOLDSBOROUGH, CHARLES W.
The United States' Naval Chronicle. Washington: 1824. V. 48

GOLDSBOROUGH, WILLIAM WORTHINGTON
The Maryland Line in the Confederate States Army. Baltimore: 1869. V. 48

GOLDSCHMIDT, ADOLPH
German Illumination. Florence: 1928. V. 50

GOLDSCHMIDT, E. P.
The First Cambridge Press In Its European Setting. Cambridge: 1954. V. 50
Gothic & Renaissance Bookbindings Exemplified and Illustrated from the Author's Collection. London: 1928. V. 47; 48
Gothic and Renaissance Bookbindings. Amsterdam: 1967. V. 48; 50; 51; 54
The Printed Book of the Renaissance. 1950. V. 52
The Printed Book of the Renaissance. Cambridge: 1950. V. 47; 51

GOLDSCHMIDT, LUCIEN
The Truthful Lens. New York: 1980. V. 47; 54

GOLDSCHMIDT, RICHARD
The Mechanism and Physiology of Sex Determination. London: 1923. V. 52; 53
Physiological Genetics. New York: 1938. V. 48; 53

GOLDSMID, EDMUND
A Bibliographical Sketch of the Aldine Press at Venice, Forming a Catalogue of All Works Issued by Aldus and His Successors, from 1494 to 1597 and a List of All Known Forgeries or Imitations... Edinburgh: 1887. V. 48
Collectanea Adamantaea. Edinburgh: 1884-88. V. 53
A Complete Catalogue of All the Publications of the Elzevier Presses at Leyden, Amsterdam, The Hague and Utrecht... Edinburgh: 1885-1888. V. 53

GOLDSMITH, J.
A Grammar of Geography for the Use of Schools and Young Persons. London: 1859. V. 50
The Natural and Artificial Wonders of the United Kingdom. London: 1825. V. 52

GOLDSMITH, JOHN
An Almanack for the Year of Our Lord 1701. London: 1701. V. 52

GOLDSMITH, JOHN BOROUGH
Fugitive Pieces: Chiefly Written Whilst the Author Was on Service in Egypt, and a Prisoner of War, in France. Derby: 1815. V. 49

GOLDSMITH, OLIVER
The Beauties of English Poesy. London: 1767. V. 47; 48; 51; 52
The Bee. London: 1760's. V. 50
The Citizen of the World... London: 1762. V. 47; 50; 52
The Citizen of the World... London: 1782. V. 52
The Citizen of the World; or, Letters from a Chinese Philosopher, Residing in London, to His Friends in the East. London: 1809. V. 50
The Collected Letters of Oliver Goldsmith. London: 1928. V. 49
Compendio della Storia Greca... Naples: 1816. V. 47
Le Cure de Wakefield. Dublin: 1797. V. 48
Dalziel's Illustrated Goldsmith... London: 1870. V. 51
The Deserted Village. Dublin: 1770. V. 48
The Deserted Village. London: 1770. V. 47; 52; 53; 54
The Deserted Village. Middlebury: 1819. V. 50
The Deserted Village. East Aurora: 1898. V. 47; 54
The Deserted Village. Campden: 1904. V. 48; 49; 50; 51; 52; 53
The Deserted Village. London & New York: 1904. V. 48
The Deserted Village. London: 1909. V. 51
The Deserted Village. Boston: 1912. V. 51; 52
The Deserted Village. San Francisco: 1926. V. 48; 53
An Enquiry into the Present State of Polite Learning in Europe. London: 1774. V. 54

Essays. London: 1765. V. 48; 51; 53
Essays of Oliver Goldsmith. Boston: 1928. V. 47
The Good Natur'd Man. London: 1768. V. 47; 48; 49
The History of England from the Earliest Times to the Death of George 11. London: 1790. V. 49
The History of England from the Earliest Times to the Death of George II. London: 1774. V. 50
An History of England, in a Series for Letters from a Nobleman to His Son. London: 1764. V. 49; 54
An History of England, In a Series of letters from a Nobleman to His Son. London: 1772. V. 50
A History of England in a Series of Letters, from a Nobleman to His Son. London: 1787. V. 48; 51
The History of Little Goody Twoshoes; Otherwise Called Mrs. Margery Twoshoes... Worcester: 1787. V. 47; 51
A History of Man and Quadrupeds. London: 1838. V. 54
A History of the Earth and Animated Nature. London and New York. V. 52
An History of the Earth, and Animated Nature. London: 1774. V. 50; 52
A History of the Earth and Animated Nature. London: 1779. V. 53
A History of the Earth and Animated Nature. London: 1816. V. 54
A History of the Earth and Animated Nature. Glasgow: 1832. V. 54
History of the Earth and Animated Nature. London: 1853. V. 50; 52
A History of the Earth and Animated Nature. London: 1855. V. 52
A History of the Earth and Animated Nature. London: 1859. V. 50
A History of the Earth and Animated Nature. London: 1862. V. 54
An History of the Lives, Actions, Travels, Sufferings and Deaths of the Most Eminent Martyrs...Adorned with Variety of Copper-plate Cuts. London: 1764. V. 50
The Life of Richard Nash of Bath. London: 1762. V. 47; 49; 51
Le Ministre de Wakefield, Histoire. Londres: 1767. V. 51
The Miscellaneous Works. Perth: 1792. V. 52
The Miscellaneous Works. London: 1812. V. 47; 51
The Miscellaneous Works. 1817. V. 54
The Miscellaneous Works. London: 1823. V. 53
The Miscellaneous Works. Paris: 1825. V. 47; 51
The Miscellaneous Works. London: 1837. V. 50
The Miscellaneous Works. New York: 1850. V. 47; 48
Overland in Forty-Nine. The Recollections of a Wolverine ranger after a Lapse of Forty-Seven Years. Detroit: 1896. V. 50
Poems. London: 1795. V. 47; 50; 53
The Poems. London: 1800. V. 52
Poems. London: 1804. V. 53
The Poems. London: 1859. V. 49; 52
Poems and Plays. Dublin: 1777. V. 51
The Poems and Plays. London: 1889. V. 52
Poems by Goldsmith and Parnell. London: 1795. V. 47; 50
Poems by Goldsmith and Parnell. London: 1804. V. 49
Poems for Young Ladies. London. V. 50
Poems for Young Ladies. London: 1785. V. 49; 51
The Poetical and Dramatic Works... London: 1780. V. 49; 52; 54
The Poetical Works. London: 1760. V. 51
The Poetical Works. Hereford: 1794. V. 51
The Poetical Works. London: 1811. V. 47; 52; 54
The Poetical Works. London: 1820. V. 51
The Poetical Works. London: 1865. V. 54
The Poetical Works. London: 1866. V. 51
The Poetical Works. New York: 1889. V. 47
A Pretty Book of Pictures for Little Masters and Misses, or, Tommy Trip's History of Beasts and Birds... London: 1867. V. 50
The Roman History, from the Foundation of the City of Rome, to the Destruction of the Western Empire. London: 1769. V. 51
The Roman History, from the Foundation of the City of Rome, to the Destruction of the Western Empire. London: 1770. V. 48
The Roman History, From the Foundation of the City of Rome, to the Destruction of the Western Empire. Dublin: 1771. V. 48; 54
The Roman History, from the Foundation of the City of Rome, to the Destruction of the Western Empire... London: 1786. V. 47
She Stoops to Conquer; or, Mistakes of a Night. Dublin: 1773. V. 49
She Stoops to Conquer or the Mistakes of a Night. London: 1912. V. 47; 49; 50; 54
She Stoops to Conquer or the Mistakes of a Night. New York: 1964. V. 47; 53
She Stoops to Conquer, or the Mistakes of a Night. 1978. V. 47
A Survey of Experimental Philosophy, Considered in Its Present State of Improvement. London: 1776. V. 47
The Traveller. London: 1765. V. 52
The Traveller. London: 1770. V. 47; 51; 52
The Traveller. London: 1851. V. 54
The Traveller. London: 1860's. V. 51
The Traveller and the Deserted Village. Chelsea: 1929. V. 49
Le Vicaire de Wakefield. Paris: 1838. V. 48
The Vicar of Wakefield. London: 1766. V. 47; 48; 51
The Vicar of Wakefield. Salisbury: 1766. V. 47; 48; 49; 51; 52; 53; 54
The Vicar of Wakefield. Philadelphia: 1772. V. 49; 50; 53
The Vicar of Wakefield. Paris: 1800. V. 54
The Vicar of Wakefield. London: 1817. V. 49
The Vicar of Wakefield. London: 1819. V. 48
The Vicar of Wakefield. Knoxville: 1831. V. 51
The Vicar of Wakefield. London: 1875. V. 50
The Vicar of Wakefield. London & New York: 1890. V. 53

GOLDSMITH, OLIVER continued
The Vicar of Wakefield. London: 1900. V. 50
The Vicar of Wakefield. Bedford Park, Chiswick: 1903. V. 47
The Vicar of Wakefield. London: 1903. V. 54
The Vicar of Wakefield. London: 1904. V. 53
The Vicar of Wakefield. London: 1914. V. 51
The Vicar of Wakefield. London: 1929. V. 47; 48; 49; 50; 51; 52; 54
The Vicar of Wakefield. Philadelphia: 1929. V. 47; 48; 52; 54
The Works. London: 1854. V. 47; 48; 49; 52
The Works. New York: 1881. V. 51
Works. New York & London: 1908. V. 50

GOLDSTEIN, SIDNEY M.
Pre Roman and Early Roman Glass in the Corning Museum of Glass. Corning: 1979. V. 49; 50; 51; 52

GOLDSTHWAIT, EZEKIEL
Rules and Regulations of the Salem Artillery; Organized October 16, 1786... Salem: 1810. V. 48

GOLDSTON, WILL
Secrets of Famous Illusionists. London: 1933. V. 51
Sensational Tales of Mystery Men. London: 1929. V. 51

GOLDSTONE, ADRIAN
A Bibliography of Arthur Machen. Austin: 1965. V. 50

GOLDWATER, R.
Catalogue of the Robert Goldwater Library of Primitive Art. Boston: 1982. V. 51
Rufino Tamayo. 1947. V. 48
Senufo Sculpture from West Africa. New York: 1964. V. 54

GOLENBOCK, PETER
BUMS. An Oral History of the Brooklyn Dodgers. V. 51; 52

GOLL, CLAIRE
Love Poems. New York: 1947. V. 52

GOLL, YVAN
Four Poems of the Occult. Kentfield: 1962. V. 47; 49; 54
Jean Sans Terre. New York: 1958. V. 49
Lackawanna Elegy. Fremont: 1970. V. 52
Der Neue Orpheus: Eine Dithyrambe, Dazu Sieben Orphische Hymnen. 1989. V. 52

GOLLANCZ, V.
The Betrayal of the Left. An Examination and Refutation of Communist Policy from October 1939 to January 1941... London: 1941. V. 49

GOLLY "I Squeak". London: 1940. V. 48

GOLOVIN, P. N.
The End of Russian America, Captain P.N. Golovin's Last Report, 1862. Portland: 1979. V. 54

GOLTRA, JOHN
Preventive Medicine in the Home. Chicago: 1912. V. 47

GOLTZ, FRIEDRICH L.
Beitrage zur Lehre von den Functionen der Nervencentren des Frosches. Berlin: 1869. V. 47; 48; 49

GOLTZ, HUBERT
Icones Imperatorum romanorum, Ex Priscis Numismatibus ad Viuum Delineatae & Breui Narratione Historica Illustratae... Antwerp: 1645. V. 49; 51; 53
Lebendige Bilder Gar Nach Aller Keysern... Antwerp: 1557. V. 50
Le Vive Imagini di Tutti Quasi Gl'Imperatori da C. Iulio Caesare, in Sino a Carlo. Antwerp: 1560. V. 52; 54

GOMBERVILLE, MARIN LE ROY, SIEUR DE
The Doctrine of Morality; or, a View of Human Life According to the Stoick Philosophy. London: 1721. V. 54

GOMBROWICZ, WITOLD
Ferdydurke. New York: 1961. V. 52

GOMEZ, ISAAC
Selections of a Father for the Use of His Children. New York: 1820. V. 53

GOMME, GEORGE LAURENCE
Folklore as an Historical Science. London: 1908. V. 50

GOMPERTZ, BENJAMIN
The Principles and Application of Imaginary Quantities. London: 1817-18. V. 54

GOMRINGER, EUGEN
Josef Albers. His Work as Contribution to Visual Articulation in the Twentieth Century. New York: 1968. V. 48; 49

GONCALEZ DAVILA, GIL
Entrada que Hizo en la Corte del Rey de les Espanas Don Felipe Quatro el Serenissimo Don Carlos Principe de Gales. Madrid: 1623. V. 47; 52

GONCALVES DOS SANTOS, LUIZ
Memorias Para Servir a Historia do Reino do Brazil...Escriptas na Corte do Rio de Janeiro no Anno de 1821. Lisbon: 1825. V. 48

GONCALVES VIANNA, DOMINGOS JOZE
Report of the trial of an Action, Viana v. Pratt, in the Court of King's Bench, Guildhall, London, on Monday, October 15, 1827, Before Lord Tenterden and a Special Jury. London: 1827. V. 50

GONCHAROV, IVAN
Oblomov. New York: 1915. V. 54

GONCOURT, EDMOND
Les Freres Zemganno. Paris: 1879. V. 52
Le Saint-Huberty d'Apres sa Correspondance et ses Papiers de Famille. Paris: 1882. V. 47
Salon de 1852. Paris: 1852. V. 52

GONGORA Y ARGOTE, LUIS DE
Todas las Obras de Don Luis de Gongora, en Varios Poemas. Madrid: 1654. V. 53

GONSALVIUS, REGINALDUS
Der Heiligen Hispanischen Inquisition, Etiche Entdeckte, und Offentliche an Tag Gebrachte Ranck und Praticken... Heidelberg: 1569. V. 53

GONZALES, AMBROSE ELLIOT
With Aesop Among the Black Border. Columbia: 1924. V. 48

GONZALEZ DE MENDOZA, JUAN
Dell'Historia della China. Venice: 1588. V. 49; 53

GONZALEZ-GERTH, MIGUEL
The Infinite Absence. Iowa City: 1964. V. 51

GOOCH, C. W.
Military Laws... Richmond: 1820. V. 54

GOOCH, ELIZABETH SARAH VILLA-REAL
The Contrast: a Novel. Wilmington: 1796. V. 52

GOOCH, G. P.
Before the War: Studies in Diplomacy. London: 1936 & 38. V. 48

GOOCH, RICHARD
Nuts to Crack, or Quips, Quirks, Anecdotes and Faceitae of Oxford and Cambridge Scholars. London: 1835. V. 47

GOOCH, ROBERT
An Account of Some of the Most Important Diseases Peculiar to Women. London: 1829. V. 51

GOOD and Joyful Newes Out of Buckinghamshire, Being an Exact and True Relation of a Battell, Stricken Betwixt Prince Robert and sir William Balfore... London: 1642. V. 51

THE GOOD Child or, Sweet Home. London: 1830. V. 49

THE GOOD Child's Coloured Book. London. V. 48

GOOD Company for Every Day of the Year. Boston: 1866. V. 52; 53

GOOD English: or, Certain Reasons Pointing Out the Safest Way of Settlement In This Kingdom; Drawne from the Nature of the Aims and Interests of the Several Parties Ingaged; and as the Case Now Stands, This Second Day of May. 1648. London: 1648. V. 53

THE GOOD Girl's Aviary. London: 1825. V. 47

GOOD Health: 1870. Boston: 1870. V. 48; 50; 52; 53

GOOD, JOHN BOOTH
A Vocabulary and Outlines of Grammar of the Nitlakapamuk, or Thompson Tongue... Victoria: 1880. V. 49

GOOD, JOHN MASON
Song of Songs or Sacred Idyls. London: 1803. V. 51

GOOD, PETER P.
The Family Flora and Materia Medica Botanica... Elizabethtown: 1851?. V. 53; 54

GOOD, THOMAS
The True Principles of Scientific Cutting Defined and Illustrated... London: 1842-43. V. 47; 53

THE GOOD Wine. Thetford: 1965. V. 53

GOODALE, GEORGE L.
The Wild Flowers of America. Boston: 1886. V. 47; 50

GOODALL, ARMITAGE
Place-Names of South-West Yorkshire. Cambridge: 1913. V. 53

GOODALL, D. W.
Arid-Land Ecosystems: Structure, Functioning and Management. Cambridge: 1979-81. V. 53

GOODALL, WALTER
An Examination of the Letters Said to Be Written by Mary Queen of Scots to James Earl of Bothwell... Edinburgh: 1754. V. 49
An Introduction to the History and Antiquities of Scotland. London: 1769. V. 47; 53

GOODCHILD, CECIL WRAY
California Milestones. Los Angeles: 1931. V. 51

GOODE, D.
Cyads of Africa. Cape Town: 1989. V. 47; 48; 51; 52

GOODE, GEORGE BROWN
Fisheries and Fishery Industries of the United States, Section 1. Natural History of Useful Aquatic Animals. Washington: 1884. V. 50; 52
A Memorial of George Brown Goode, Together with a Selection of His Papers on Museums and On the History of Science in America. Washington: 1901. V. 48
Oceanic Ichthyology. Washington: 1895. V. 47; 49; 52
The Smithsonian Institution 1846-1946. The History of Its First Half Century. Washington: 1897. V. 50; 52

GOODELL, WILLIAM
Forty Years in the Turkish Empire; or, Memoirs... New York: 1876. V. 49
The Old and the New; or, the Changes of Thirty Years in the East... New York: 1853. V. 54

GOODEN, C. M.
Conflict in Spain, 1920-1937. London: 1937. V. 49

GOODEN, STEPHEN
An Iconography of the Engravings of Stephen Gooden. London: 1944. V. 48; 50

GOODENOW, STERLING
A Brief Topographical and Statistical Manual of the State of New York. Albany: 1811. V. 47

GOODERS, J.
Birds of the World. London: 1969-71. V. 49
Birds of the World. London: 197-. V. 54

GOODHART, WILLIAM
Generation. Garden City: 1966. V. 49

GOODHUE, BERTRAM GROSVENOR
Book Decorations. New York: 1931. V. 50
A Book of Architectural and Decorative Drawings. New York: 1924. V. 48

GOODIN, SAMUEL H.
Plan for the Construction of the Direct Railroad South, Connecting Cincinnati with the Southern System of Railroads. Cincinnati: 1868. V. 54

GOODING, MEL
Knife Edge Texts. London: 1992. V. 52

GOODINGE, THOMAS
The Law Against Bankrupts; or, a Treatise Wherein the Statutes Against Bankrupts are Explained, by Several Cases, Resolutions, Judgments and Decrees... London: 1694. V. 53

GOODIS, DAVID
Behold This Woman. New York: 1947. V. 49
Black Friday. New York: 1954. V. 49
The Burgler. New York: 1953. V. 49
The Dark Chase. New York: 1953. V. 49
Dark Passage. New York: 1946. V. 49; 52
Fire in the Flesh. New York: 1957. V. 49
Nightfall. New York: 1947. V. 49
Of Missing Persons. New York: 1950. V. 49; 51; 52
Of Tender Sin. New York: 1952. V. 48; 51
Retreat from Oblivion. New York: 1939. V. 49; 51; 52

GOODISSON, WILLIAM
A Historical and Topographical Essay Upon the Islands of Corfu, Leucadia, Cephalonia, Ithaca and Zante. London: 1822. V. 47

GOODLAKE, THOMAS
The Courser's Manual or Studbook. London: 1828. V. 47

GOODLAND, ROGER
A Bibliography of Sex Rites and Custom: an Annotated Record of Books, Articles and Illustrations in all Languages. London: 1931. V. 48; 52

GOODLANDER, CHARLES W.
Early Days of Fort Scott, from 1858 to 1870, Covering the Time Prior to the Advent of the Railroad and During the Days of the Ox-team and Stage Transportation. Fort Scott: 1899. V. 48

GOODMAN, EDWARD J.
The Best Tour in Norway. London: 1892. V. 47

GOODMAN, PAUL
The Dead of Spring. Glen Gardner: 1950. V. 54

GOODMAN, RICHARD MERLE
Atlas of the Face in Genetic Disorders. St. Louis: 1977. V. 54

GOODMAN, S. M.
The Birds of Egypt. Oxford: 1989. V. 49; 50

GOODMAN, W. M.
Souvenir History of Knoxville, the Marble City and Great Southern Jobbing Market. Knoxville: 1907. V. 48

GOODMAN, WALTER
The Keeleys On the Stage and at Home. London: 1895. V. 48

GOODNIGHT, CHARLES
Pioneer Days in the Southwest 1850-1879. 1909. V. 47
Pioneer Days in the Southwest 1850-1879. Guthrie: 1909. V. 50; 53; 54

GOODRICH & CO.
Goodrich & Co.'s Circulating Library, Book and Stationary Store, No. 124 Broadway... New York: 1817. V. 54

GOODRICH, CHARLES
History of the United States of America, On a Plan Adapted to the Capacity of Youth, and Designed to Aid the Memory by Systematic Arrangement... Boston: 1853. V. 50
A New Family Encyclopedia; or Compendium of Universal Knowledge. Philadelphia: 1831. V. 51

GOODRICH, FRANCES
The Diary of Anne Frank. (Dramatized by Frances Goodrich and Albert Hackett). New York: 1956. V. 53

GOODRICH, FRANCES LOUISA
Mountain Homespun. New Haven: 1931. V. 51

GOODRICH, LLOYD
Edward Hopper. New York: 1971. V. 47; 48; 49; 50; 52
Edward Hopper. New York: 1978. V. 47; 51
Georgia O'Keefe. New York: 1970. V. 50
Georgia O'Keefe. 1971. V. 54
Max Weber. New York: 1949. V. 48; 50; 54
Raphael Soyer. New York. V. 47; 48
Reginald Marsh. New York. V. 47; 48; 49; 50; 52
Reginald Marsh. New York: 1972. V. 47; 52

GOODRICH, S. E.
What to Do and How to Do It, or, Morals and Manners Taught by Examples. London: 1845. V. 49

GOODRICH, SAMUEL GRISWOLD
The Manners, Customs and Antiquities of the Indians of North and South America. Boston: 1844. V. 47
Manners, Customs and Antiquities of the Indians of North and South America. New York: 1844. V. 52
Peter Parley's Method of Telling About Geography to Children. Boston: 1830. V. 54
Peter Parley's Story of Little Marion. Boston: 1830. V. 49
The Tales of Peter Parley About America. Boston: 1829. V. 51

GOODRICH, W.
The Organ in France. Boston: 1917. V. 49

GOODRIDGE, CHARLES MEDYETT
Narrative of a Voyage to the South Seas, and the Shipwreck of the Princess of Wales Cutter... Exeter: 1843. V. 47; 50

GOODSIR, JOHN
On the Supra-Renal, Thymus and Thyroid Bodies. London: 1846. V. 50

GOODSIR, ROBERT A.
An Arctic Voyage to Baffin's Bay and Lancaster Sound in Search of Friends of Sir John Franklin. London: 1850. V. 49

GOODSPEED, E. J.
History of the Great Fires of Chicago and the West. New York & Chicago: 1871. V. 50; 53

GOODWIN, ARTHUR
Two Letters of Great Consequence to the House of Commons: the One from Alisbury in Buckinghamshire Dated March 22, 1642... London: 1642. V. 52

GOODWIN, CARDINAL LEONIDAS
The Establishment of State Government in California 1846-1850. New York: 1914. V. 54

GOODWIN, CHARLES CARROLL
As I Remember Them. Salt Lake City: 1913. V. 54
The Comstock Club. Salt Lake City: 1891. V. 52
The Wedge of Gold. Salt Lake City: 1893. V. 47

GOODWIN, D.
Crows of the World... London: 1986. V. 49
Pigeons and Doves of the World... London: 1983. V. 49

GOODWIN, FRANCIS
Domestic Architecture. London: 1833. V. 52
Domestic Architecture... London: 1850. V. 47

GOODWIN, GORDON
British Mezzotinters, Thomas Watson, James Watason and Elizabeth Judkins. London: 1904. V. 50

GOODWIN, GRENVILLE
Myths and Tales of the White Mountain Apache. New York: 1939. V. 48; 51
The Social Organization of the Western Apache. Chicago: 1942. V. 54

GOODWIN, H. M.
The Suggestve Method. Chicago: 1850. V. 51

GOODWIN, HOWARD T.
The Magnificent Library of...to be sold...Oct. 22-Oct. 14, 1903. Catalogue No. 900. Parts 1-3. Philadelphia: 1903. V. 50

GOODWIN, ISAAC
Town Officer; or, Laws of Massachusetts Relative to the Duties of Municipal Officers... Worcester: 1825. V. 51

GOODWIN, JOHN
A Candle to See the Sunne: or a Further Cleering Up of Some Passages Mis-apprehended by Some in a Treatise Lately Published by Authoritie, Intituled Hagiomastix, &c. 1647. V. 47; 54
Hagionmastix, or the Scourge of Saints Displayed in His Colours of Ignorance & Blood... 1646. V. 47
Sion-Colledge Visited. 1648. V. 47
Sion-Colledge Visited. London: 1648. V. 50

GOODWIN, MAUD WILDER
Head of a Hundred in the Colony of Virginia 1622. Boston: 1900. V. 49

GOODWIN, THOMAS
An Account of the Neutral Saline Waters Recently Discovered at Hampstead. London: 1804. V. 50; 52; 54

GOODY *Two Shoes Series: Henry Brown, Tom Tearabut, Valentine and Orson and Two Brothers.* New York: 1860's. V. 48

GOODY Two-Shoes. London: 1881. V. 51

GOODYEAR, CHARLES
A Centennial Volume of the Writings of Charles Goodyear and Thomas Hancock... Boston: 1939. V. 49

GOODYEAR, WATSON ANDREWS
The Coal Mines of the Western Coast of the United States. San Francisco: 1877. V. 49; 52

GOOGE, BARNABY
The Whole Art and Trade of Hvsbandry. London: 1614. V. 49

GOOLRICK, JOHN T.
The Life of General Hugh Mercer. New York & Washington: 1906. V. 48

GOOSE, EDMUND
Silhouettes. London: 1925. V. 54

GORDAN, JOHN D.
Edgar Allan Poe and Exhibition on the Cetenary of His Death October 7, 1849. New York: 1949. V. 48

GORDIMER, NADINE
Burger's Daughter. London: 1979. V. 54
Burger's Daughter. New York: 1979. V. 49; 52
The Conservationist. New York: 1975. V. 52
A Correspondence Course and Other Stories. 1986. V. 52
A Correspondence Course and other Stories. Helsinki: 1986. V. 49
Face to Face. Johannesburg: 1949. V. 50; 51
Lifetimes: Under Apartheid. New York: 1986. V. 53
Livingstone's Companion. London: 1972. V. 47
The Lying Days. London: 1953. V. 54
My Son's Story. London: 1990. V. 52
Occasion for Loving. London: 1963. V. 52
On the Mines. Cape Town: 1973. V. 52
Selected Stories. London: 1975. V. 48; 51
Selected Stories. New York: 1976. V. 49; 52
Six Feet of the Country: Short Stories. London: 1956. V. 53
The Soft Voice of the Serpent. New York: 1952. V. 47; 50; 51
The Soft Voice of the Serpent and Other Stories. London: 1953. V. 49
Town and Country Lovers. Los Angeles: 1980. V. 49; 51; 53
A World of Strangers. New York: 1958. V. 51

GORDON a Tale. A Poetical Review of Don Juan. London: 1821. V. 53; 54

GORDON, ADAM LINDSAY
Bush Ballads and Galloping Rhymes. Melbourne: 1876. V. 47; 50; 52
Poems. Melbourne: 1880?. V. 54
Poems. London: 1905. V. 49

GORDON, ALEXANDER
Itinerarium Septentrionale; or, a Journey Thro' Most of the Counties of Scotland... London: 1727. V. 49
The Lives of Pope Alexander VI and His son Caesar Borgia. London: 1729. V. 52
A Treatise Upon Elemental Locomotion and Interior Communication, Wherein are Explained and Illustrated the History, Practice and Prospects of Steam Carriages; and the Comparative Value of Turnpike Roads, Railways and Canals. London: 1834. V. 54

GORDON, ALVIN J.
Of Vines and Missions. Flagstaff: 1971. V. 48

GORDON, ANTOINETTE K.
The Iconography of Tibetan Lamaism. Rutland: 1959. V. 48

GORDON, BENJAMIN LEE
Medicine Throughout Antiquity. Philadelphia: 1949. V. 54

GORDON, C. G.
The Journals of Major Gen. C. G. Gordon at Kartoum. London: 1885. V. 54

GORDON, CAROLINE
Aleck Maury Sportsman. New York: 1934. V. 53
The Forest of the South. New York: 1945. V. 48; 51; 52; 53
The Garden of Adonis. New York: 1937. V. 47; 50; 52
The House of Fiction: an Anthology of the Short Story with Commentary. New York: 1950. V. 52; 54
How to Read a Novel. New York: 1957. V. 50
The Malefactors. New York: 1956. V. 50
Penhally. New York: 1931. V. 54
The Strange Children. New York: 1951. V. 50; 51; 52; 53
The Women on the Porch. New York: 1944. V. 53

GORDON, CHARLES
Old Time Aldwych, Kingsway, and Neighbourhood. London. V. 48

GORDON, CHARLES ALEXANDER
Life on the Coast. London: 1874. V. 50
Our Trip to Burmah... London: 1877. V. 53

GORDON, COSMO
Life and Genius of Lord Byron. London: 1824-25. V. 49

GORDON, CYRUS H.
Ugaritic Handbook I-III. Roma: 1947. V. 51

GORDON, DANIEL M.
Mountain and Prairie: a Journey From Victoria to Winnipeg, Via Peace River Pass. Montreal: 1880. V. 48

GORDON, DAVID
Ernst Ludwig Kirchner. 1969. V. 50

GORDON, DONALD E.
Ernst Ludwig Kirchner. Cambridge: 1968. V. 47; 48; 50; 52; 53

GORDON, ELIZABETH
Bird Children. Chicago: 1912. V. 47
Mother Earth's Children. Chicago: 1914. V. 47
The Tale of Johnny Mouse. Chicago: 1920. V. 54

GORDON, G. B.
Notes on the Western Eskimo. Philadelphia: 1906. V. 53

GORDON, GEORGE
The Annals of Europe for the Year 1739. London: 1740. V. 52
The History of Our National Debts and Taxes, from the Year MDCLXXXVIII to the Present Year MDCCLI. London: 1751. V. 49
An Introduction to Geography, Astronomy, and Dialling... London: 1729. V. 53
An Introduction to Geography, Astronomy and Dialling. London: 1890. V. 47

GORDON, GEORGE BYRON
Examples of Maya Pottery in the Museum and Other Collections. Parts I-III. Philadelphia: 1925-43. V. 52
Researches in the Uloa Valley, Honduras. Report on Explorations by the Museum, 1896-97. (and) Caverns of Copan, Honduras. Cambridge: 1898. V. 50

GORDON, HAMPDEN
Rhymes of the Red Triangle. London. V. 49; 53

GORDON, HENRY FRANCIS
Love at Jerusalem, Divine and Human. London: 1896. V. 54

GORDON, HOME
Cricket Form at a Glance. London: 1902. V. 51

GORDON, JAMES
A Request to Roman Catholicks to Answer the Queries Upon These Their Following Tenets... London: 1687. V. 53
Terraquea; or, a New System of Geography and Modern History. Dublin: 1790/93/95/98. V. 53

GORDON, JAMES BENTLEY
History of the Rebellion in Ireland, in the Year 1798, &c. Dublin: 1801. V. 47

GORDON, JOHN
Memoirs of the Life of John Gordon, of Glencat, in the County of Aberdeen in Scotland... London: 1734. V. 53
A Probationary Surgical Essay, on the Dislocations of the Thigh Bone. Edinburgh: 1808. V. 52

GORDON, JOHN BROWN
Reminiscences of the Civil War. New York: 1903. V. 49

GORDON, JOSEPH
The Emigrant Barque; with Some Traits of Australian Life and Character in Prose and Verse. Edinburgh: 1871. V. 50

GORDON, JULIEN
Painted Tapestry and Its Application to Interior Decoration. London: 1879. V. 52

GORDON, L.
White Cargo. 1925. V. 50

GORDON, MARGARET MARIA
The Home Life of Sir David Brewster, by His Daughter. Edinburgh: 1869. V. 54

GORDON, MRS.
Christopher North. Edinburgh: 1862. V. 50
Christopher North, a Memoir of John Wilson. Edinburgh: 1863. V. 53

GORDON, RICHARD
Meta Photographs. 1978. V. 52

GORDON, ROBERT
A Catalogue of the Singular and Curious Library, Origianlly Formed Between 1610 and 1650, by Sir Robert Gordon, of Gordonstoun, One of the Gentleman of the Bedchamber to King James I and King Charles I... Weybridge, Surrey: 1816. V. 48; 51

GORDON, S.
Recollections of Old Milestown. Miles City: 1928. V. 54

GORDON, SETON
Amid Snowy Wastes. London: 1922. V. 50

GORDON, THOMAS
A Collection of Papers All Written, Some of Them Published, During the Late Rebellion. Dublin: 1748. V. 48
The Humourist: Being Essays on Several Subjects... London: 1724/25. V. 54
The Humourist: Being Essays on Several Subjects, viz. News Writers. Enthusiasm. The Spleen. Country Entertainments. Love. The History of Miss Manage. Ambition and pride...Prejudice. Witchcraft. Ghosts and Apparations. The Weather. London: 1725. V. 50
Principles of Naval Architecture. London: 1784. V. 48

GORDON, THOMAS CROUTHER
David Allan of Alloa...the Scottish Hogarth. Alva: 1951. V. 53

GORDON, THOMAS EDWARD
A Varied Life. London: 1906. V. 54

GORDON, THOMAS F.
A Gazetteer of the State of New Jersey...Together with a Topographical and Statistical account of its Counties, Towns, Villages, Canals, Rail Roads &c. (with) The History of New Jersey, From Its Discovery by Europeans to the Adoption of the Federal... Trenton: 1834. V. 50

The History of New Jersey, From its Discovery by Europeans, to the Adoption of the Federal Constitution. (with) A Gazetteer of the State of New Jersey. Trenton: 1834. V. 51

GORDON, W. J.
Round About the North Pole. London: 1907. V. 52

GORDON, WILLIAM
The History of the Rise, Progress and Establishment of the Independence of the United States of America... London: 1788. V. 51; 54

The History of the Rise, Progress and Establishment of the Independence of the United States of America. New York: 1794. V. 47

The Separation of the Jewish Tribes After the Death of Solomon, Accounted for and Applied to the Present Day in a Sermon Prached Before the General Court, on Friday July the 4th, 1777. Being the Anniversary of the Declaration of Independency. Boston: 1777. V. 51; 53

GORDON-CUMMING, CONSTANCE FREDERICA
Fire Fountains. The Kingdom of Hawaii. London: 1883. V. 47; 48
Memories. London: 1904. V. 50; 51
Two Happy Years in Ceylon. London: 1892. V. 50; 51
Two Happy Years in Ceylon. New York: 1892. V. 50; 51
Wanderings in China. London: 1886. V. 54
Wanderings in China. Edinburgh: 1888. V. 50; 51

GORDON-CUMMING, ROUALEYN GEORGE
Five Year's Hunting Adventures in South Africa... London: 1892. V. 47
Five Years of a Hunter's Life in...South Africa. London: 1850. V. 49; 52
Five Years of a Hunter's Life in...South Africa. New York: 1850. V. 47
A Hunter's Life Among Lion's, Elephants and Other Wild Animals of South Africa. New York: 1857. V. 47
The Lion Hunter in South Africa. London: 1855. V. 48

GORE, CATHERINE
Agathonia. London: 1844. V. 47
The Ambassador's Wife. London: 1842. V. 47
Hungarian Tales. London: 1829. V. 50
The Inundation: or, Pardon and Peace. Boston: 1840. V. 54
The Inundation; or, Pardon and Peace... London: 1860. V. 49; 50
Mrs. Armytage; or, Female Domination. London: 1836. V. 50
Mothers and Daughters: a Novel. London: 1834. V. 50
New Year's Day, A Winter's Tale. 1846. V. 53
New Year's Day, a Winter's Tale. London: 1846. V. 49; 50
Paris in 1841. London: 1842. V. 53
Quid Pro Quo; or, the Day of the Dupes. London: 1844. V. 50
The Snow Storm: a Christmas Story. London. V. 52
Stokeshill Place; or the Man of Business. London: 1837. V. 48; 52
The Tuileries. London: 1831. V. 50

GORE-BOOTH, EVA
The Buried Life of Deirdre. 1930. V. 48

GORER, EDGAR
Chinese Porcelain and Hard Stones. London: 1911. V. 48; 50; 52; 53

GOREY, EDWARD
Amphigorey Also. New York: 1983. V. 51
The Blue Aspic. New York: 1968. V. 51
The Broken Spoke. New York: 1976. V. 49; 51
The Bug Book. New York: 1959. V. 49; 52
The Bug Book. New York: 1960. V. 51
Dancing Cats & Neglected Murderesses. New York: 1980. V. 51
Dogear Wryde Postcards: Interpretive Series. 1979. V. 51
The Doubtful Guest. Garden City: 1957. V. 51; 52
Dracula - a Toy Theatre - The Sets and Costumes of the Broadway Production of the Play Designed by Edward Gorey. London: 1979. V. 47
The Dwindling Party. New York: 1982. V. 51
Les Echanges Malandreux. Worcester: 1989. V. 54
The Eclectic Abecedarium. Boston: 1983. V. 49; 51
The Epipletic Bicycle. New York: 1969. V. 51
The Fatal Lozenge. New York: 1960. V. 51
F.M.R.A. New York: 1980. V. 49
The Gilded Bat. New York: 1966. V. 47; 51
The Glorious Nosebleed Fifth Alphabet. New York: 1974. V. 53
The Gorey Alphabet. London: 1961. V. 51
A Gorey Festival. New York. V. 51
The Green Beads. New York: 1978. V. 51; 54
The Hapless Child. New York: 1961. V. 51
The Improvable Landscape. New York: 1986. V. 51
Leaves from a Mislaid Album. New York: 1972. V. 51
A Limerick. 1973. V. 49; 52
The Listing Attic. New York: 1954. V. 50; 51; 52
The Loathsome Couple. New York: 1977. V. 51
The Nursery Frieze. 1964. V. 51
The Object-Lesson. Garden City: 1958. V. 49; 50; 51

Les Passementeries Horribles. New York: 1971. V. 54
Les Passementeries Horribles. New York: 1976. V. 51
The Prune People. New York: 1983. V. 51; 54
The Prune People II. New York: 1985. V. 51
The Prune People: The Prune People II. New York: 1983/85. V. 49
Q.R.V. Boston: 1989. V. 49; 51
The Raging Tide; or, the Black Doll's Imbroglio. New York: 1987. V. 49; 51
The Remembered Visit. New York: 1965. V. 51
The Secrets: Volume One. The Other Statue. New York: 1968. V. 51
The Sopping Thursday. New York: 1970. V. 51
Story for Sara: What Happened to a Little Girl. New York: 1971. V. 54
Three Books from the Fantod Press: The Deranged Cousins. The Eleventh Episode. The Untitled Book. 1971. V. 51
Three Books from the Fantold Press: Three Chinese Obelisks. Fourth Alphabet. The Osbick Bird. Donald Has a Difficulty. 1970. V. 51
The Unstrung Harp; or, Mr. Earbrass Writes a Novel. New York: 1953. V. 49; 50; 51
Les Urnes Utiles. Cambridge: 1980. V. 51
The Vinegar Works. New York: 1963. V. 51
The Water Flowers. New York: 1982. V. 51
The Wuggy Ump. Philadelphia: 1963. V. 51

GORGAS, JOSIAH
The Civil War Diary of General Josiah Gorgas. University: 1947. V. 52

GORHAM, G. C.
Memoirs of John Martyn, F.R.S. and of Thomas Martyn...Professors of Botany in the University of Cambridge. London: 1830. V. 54

GORHAM, GEORGE C.
The Story of the Attempted Assassination of Justice Field by a Former Associate on the Supreme Bench of California. Washington: 1889. V. 49

GORHAM, GEORGE CORNELIUS
The History and Antiquities of Eynesbury and St. Neot's in Huntingdonshire and of St. Neot's in the County of Cornwall. London: 1820-24. V. 52

GORHAM, JOHN
Inaugural address, Delivered in the Chapel of the University of Cambridge, December 11, 1816. Boston: 1817. V. 50

GORHAM MANUFACTURING CO.
Gorham Silver. Trade Catalogue. Providence: 1930's. V. 52

GORHAM, MAURICE
The Local Colour. London: 1939. V. 50; 52; 53

GORHAM, THELMA THURSTON
Meeting the Challenge of Change...60 Year History: St. Stephen Baptist Church, Kansas City, Mo. Kansas City: 1962. V. 53

GORING, C. R.
Micrographia: Containing Practical Essays, on Reflecting Solar, Oxy-Hydrogen Gas Microscopies... London: 1837. V. 52

GORING, CHARLES B.
The English Convict. London: 1913. V. 51

GORKI, MAXIM
Bystander. New York: 1930. V. 54
Reminiscences of Leond Andreyev. New York: 1928. V. 52
Reminiscences of My Youth. London: 1924. V. 51

GORKY, MAXIM
Reminiscences of Leo Nicolayevitch Tolstoi. Richmond: 1920. V. 49

GORMAN, H.
The Place Called Dagon. 1927. V. 48

GORMAN, HERBERT S.
James Joyce - a Definitive Biography. London: 1941. V. 47
James Joyce His First Forty Years. New York: 1924. V. 51; 53

GOROSTIZA, MANUEL EDUARDO DE
Gorostiza Pamphlet. Washington: 1838. V. 49

GORRINGE, HENRY H.
Egyptian Obelisks. New York: 1882. V. 48; 51

GORRIS, JEAN DE
Definitionum Medicarum Libri XXIII. Frankfort: 1601. V. 53

GORST, GILPIN
A Narrative of an Excursion to Ireland by the Deputy Governor, Two members of the Court and the Assistant Secretary of the Honorable Irish Society London, 1825. London: 1825. V. 50; 51

GOSDEN, THOMAS
Impressions of a Series of Animals, Birds &c. Illustrative of British Field Sports: From a Set of Silver Buttons. London: 1821. V. 47

GOSLING, W. G.
Labrador: Its Discovery, Exploration and Development. London: 1910. V. 53

GOSS, FRED
Memories of a Stag Harbourer. A Record of Twenty-Eight Years with the Devon and Somerset Stag Hounds, 1894-1921. London: 1931. V. 47

GOSS, HELEN ROCCA
The Life and Death of a Quicksilver Mine. Los Angeles: 1958. V. 52

GOSS, N. S.
History of the Birds of Kansas. Topeka: 1891. V. 51

GOSS, WARREN
The Soldier's Story of His Captivity at Andersonville, Belle Isle and other Rebel Prisons. Boston: 1866. V. 50

GOSSE, EDMUND
The Allies' Fairy book. London: 1916. V. 49
A Critical Essay on the Life and Works of George Tinworth. London: 1883. V. 53
Father and Son: a Study of Two Temperaments. London: 1907. V. 51
Gossip in a Library. London: 1892. V. 52
Gray. London: 1882. V. 52
The Life of Philip Henry Gosse by His Son. London: 1890. V. 54
On Viol and Flute: Selected Poems. New York: 1883. V. 54
Swinburne. An Essay Written in 1875 and Now First Printed. Edinburgh: 1925. V. 51; 54

GOSSE, HELEN
Gathered Together. Chelsea: 1927. V. 49

GOSSE, PHILIP
Rest Billets. London: 1927. V. 53
Sir John Hawkins. London: 1930. V. 52

GOSSE, PHILIP HENRY
Actinologia Britannica. London: 1860. V. 48; 50; 51; 52; 54
The Aquarium; an Unveiling of the Wonders of the Deep Sea. London: 1854. V. 48; 54
The Birds of Jamaica. London: 1847. V. 54
The Canadian Naturalist. London: 1840. V. 47; 48; 53; 54
Evenings at the Microscope. London: 1859. V. 54
A Handbook to the Marine Aquarium. London: 1856. V. 54
A History of the British Sea-Anemones and Corals. London: 1860. V. 48
Illustrations of the Birds of Jamaica. London: 1849. V. 49
Land and Sea. London: 1879. V. 54
Letters from Alabama, (U.S.) Chiefly Relating to Natural History. London: 1859. V. 47; 48; 54
Life In Its Lower, Intermediate and Higher Forms... London: 1857. V. 54
A Manual of Marine Zoology for the British Isles. London: 1855-56. V. 54
A Memorial of the Last Days on Earth of Emily Gosse. London: 1857. V. 50
The Monuments of Ancient Egypt. London: 1847. V. 54
A Naturalist's Rambles on the Devonshire Coast. London: 1853. V. 47; 48; 49; 50; 54
A Naturalist's Sojurn in Jamaica. London: 1851. V. 49; 54
The Ocean. London: 1845. V. 50
The Ocean. London: 1854. V. 54
Omphalos: an Attempt to Untie the Geological Knot. London: 1857. V. 48; 49
Popular British Ornithology... London: 1849. V. 48
Popular British Ornithology. London: 1853. V. 51; 54
The Romance of Natural History. Second Series. London: 1862. V. 54
Tenby: a Sea-Side Holiday. London: 1856. V. 47; 48; 52; 54
Wanderings through the Conservatories at Kew. London: 1856. V. 54
A Year at the Shore. London: 1865. V. 47; 48; 49; 50; 51; 52; 53; 54
A Year at the Shore. London: 1870. V. 48; 54
A Year at the Shore. London: 1873. V. 49

GOSTLING, WILLIAM
A Walk in And About the City of Canterbury, With Many Observations Not to Be Found in Any Description Hitherto Published. Canterbury: 1774. V. 47; 48
A Walk In and About the City of Canterbury, With Many Observations Not to Be Found in any Description Hitherto Published. Canterbury: 1777. V. 50

GOSTWICK, JOSEPH
English Poets: Twelve Essays. New York: 1875. V. 47
German Culture and Christianity: Their Controversy in the Time 1770-1880. London: 1882. V. 49

GOSWAMI, A.
Orissan Sculpture and Architecture. Calcutta: 1956. V. 48

GOTCH, J. ALFRED
Architecture of Renaissance in England... London: 1894. V. 51
Early Renaissance Architecture in England. London: 1901. V. 52

GOTHAM BOOK MART
Catalogue 42: We Moderns, 1920-1940. New York: 1940. V. 51; 53

GOTHEIN, MARIE LUISE
A History of Garden Art. London & Toronto: 1928. V. 51; 54
A History of Garden Art. New York: 1928. V. 47

GOTO, SEIKICHIRO
Japanese Hand-Made Paper and Papermaking. Tokyo: 1958/60. V. 47

GOTTFREDSON, PETER
History of Indian Depredations in Utah. Salt Lake City: 1919. V. 49; 51; 53

GOTTLIEB, GERALD
Early Children's Books and Their Illustration. New York: 1975. V. 52

GOTTSCHALK, LILLIAN
American Toy Cars and Trucks 1894-1942. New York: 1986. V. 50

GOTTSCHALK, PAUL
The Earliest Diplomatic Documents on America: The Papal Bulls of 1493 and the Treaty of Tordesillas Reproduced and Translated with Historical Introduction and Explanatory Notes. Berlin: 1927. V. 49; 51

THE GOUDHURST Coronation Book. Turnbridge Wells: 1937. V. 52

THE GOUDHURST Jubilee Book. Turnbridge Wells: 1935. V. 52

GOUDY, FREDERIC WILLIAM
The Alphabet. New York: 1918. V. 53
The Alphabet. New York: 1922. V. 48
The Alphabet and Elements of Lettering. Berkeley: 1942. V. 48; 50
Ars Typographica. New York: 1918-34. V. 48; 50
Goudy Greek. Easthampton: 1976. V. 53
A Half-Century of Type Design and Typography 1895-1945. New York: 1945. V. 48; 50
Type Design for the Scholarly Book: an Address Given Before the Pasadena Library Club, Wednesday Evening, October 30, 1940 in Celebration of the Five Hundredth Anniversary of Printing. La Mesa: 1968. V. 51
Typologia. Berkeley and Los Angeles: 1940. V. 51; 52

GOUFFE, JULES
The Royal Cookery Book. London: 1869. V. 47; 49

GOUGE, THOMAS
A Word to Sinners, and a Word to Saints... London: 1691. V. 54
The Works.. London: 1706. V. 47

GOUGE, WILLIAM M.
A Short History of Paper Money and Banking in the United States... Philadelphia: 1833. V. 48

GOUGER, HENRY
A Personal Narrative of Two Years' Imprisonment in Burmah. London. V. 54
Personal Narrative of Two Years' Imprisonment in Burmah. London: 1862. V. 47

GOUGH, HUBERT
The Fifth Army. London: 1931. V. 47

GOUGH, JAMES
Memoirs of the Life, Religious Experiences and Labours in the Gospel of James Gough, Late of the City of Dublin. Deceased. Dublin: 1781. V. 49

GOUGH, JOHN
The Topographer and Genealogist. London: 1846-58. V. 53

GOUGH, RICHARD
A Catalogue of the Entire and Valuable Library (with the Exception of the Department of British Topography, Bequeathed to the Bodleian Library) of the Eminent Antiquary, Richard Gough, Esq. Deceased.... London: 1810. V. 48
Sepulchral Monuments in Great Britain. London: 1786-1796. V. 53

GOULARD, THOMAS
A Treatise on the Effects and Various Preparations of Lead, Particularly of the Extract of Saturn. London: 1772. V. 48
A Treatise on the Effects and Various Preparations Of Lead, Particularly of the Extract of Saturn... London: 1773. V. 51

GOULART, SIMON
Morum Philosophia Historica... 1594. V. 47

GOULBURN, EDWARD
Frederick de Montford. London: 1811. V. 48; 51; 54

GOULBURN, EDWARD MEYRICK
The Ancient Sculptures in the Roof of Norwich Cathedral. London: 1876. V. 47; 53

GOULD, A. A.
Report on the Invertebrata of Massachusetts. Cambridge: 1841. V. 49; 52; 53
Report on the Invertebrata of Massachusetts. Boston: 1870. V. 48; 49; 54
A System of Natural History... Brattleboro: 1834. V. 50; 52

GOULD, CHARLES
Mythical Monsters. London: 1886. V. 54

GOULD, CHARLES L.
An Nation United. Baltimore: 1940. V. 51

GOULD, CHESTER
Dick Tracy and Dick Tracy, Jr. and How They Captured Stooge Viller. New York: 1933. V. 53

GOULD, E. P.
Anne Gilchrist and Walt Whitman. Philadelphia: 1900. V. 51

GOULD, E. R. L.
The Gothenburg System of Liquor Traffic. Washington: 1893. V. 49; 51; 52

GOULD, EMERSON W.
Fifty Years on the Mississippi; or...A History of the Introduction of Steam as a Propelling Power... Columbus: 1951. V. 49

GOULD, F. J.
Pages for Young Socialists. London: 1913. V. 47

GOULD, GEORGE
The American Year-Book of Medicine and Surgery... Philadelphia: 1896-99. V. 50; 52
Anomalies and Curiosities of Medicine Being an Encyclopedic Collection of Rare and Extraordinary Cases... Philadelphia: 1901. V. 54
Biographic Clinics. Philadelphia: 1903-09. V. 48

GOULD, HANNAH
Gathered Leaves, or, Miscellaneous Papers. Boston: 1846. V. 47
New Poems. Boston: 1850. V. 54

GOULD, JOHN
The Birds of Asia. Volume 7. London: 1992. V. 49; 50; 54
The Birds of Australia. Melbourne: 1972-75. V. 49; 52
The Birds of Australia. London: 1992. V. 54
The Birds of Australia. London: 1993. V. 54
The Birds of Australia. London: 1994. V. 54
The Birds of Australia, Supplement. London: 1990. V. 49; 50
The Birds of Australia. Volume 1: Falconidae and Strigidae. London: 1992. V. 49; 50
The Birds of Australia. Volume 2. London: 1993. V. 50
The Birds of Australia. Volume 3. Robins, Wrens and Finches. London: 1991. V. 49; 50
The Birds of Australia. Volume 5. Parrots, Pigeons and Quails. London: 1989. V. 49; 50
Birds of Europe. Birds of Australia. Birds of Asia. Birds of New Guinea. Birds of South America. London: 1966-72. V. 53
The Birds of Great Britain. London: 1862-73. V. 54
The Birds of Great Britain. London: 1980. V. 47
The Birds of Great Britain. Volume 1, Birds of Prey. London: 1990. V. 49
The Birds of New Guinea. London: 1993. V. 54
The Birds of New Guinea and the Adjacent Papuan Islands. London: 1875-88. V. 48
The Birds of New Guinea. Volume 1, Birds of Paradise and Birds of Prey. London: 1988. V. 49; 50
The Birds of New Guinea. Volume 2. London: 1993. V. 50
The Birds of New Guinea. Volume 5, Parrots and Pigeons. London: 1991. V. 49; 50
An Introduction to the Birds of Australia. London: 1848. V. 52
An Introduction to the Birds of Great Britain. London: 1873. V. 53; 54
John Gould: The Drawn Image. Selected Works 1959-1979. Toronto: 1979. V. 50
Mr. Gould's Tropical Birds. London: 1955. V. 49; 54
A Monograph of the Odontophorinae, or Partridges of America. London: 1844-50. V. 47
Monograph of the Pittidae. London: 1989. V. 49; 50
Monograph of the Toucans. London: 1989. V. 49; 50
A Monograph of the Trochilidae or Family of Humming Birds. London: 1994. V. 54
A Monograph of the Trogonidae or Family of the Trogons. London: 1858-75. V. 48; 51

GOULD, ROBERT
Poems, Chiefly Consisting of Satyrs and Satyrical Epistles. London: 1689. V. 47
The Twelve of Hearts. Boston: 1982. V. 52

GOULD, ROBERT FREKE
The History of Freemasonry: its Antiquities, Symbols, Constitutions, Customs, etc. New York: 1884. V. 48; 54
The History of Freemasonry: Its Antiquities, Symbols, Constitutions, Customs, etc. Edinburgh: 1885. V. 51

GOULD, ROLAND F.
The Life of Gould, an Ex-Man-of-War's Man, with Indicents on Sea and Shore... Claremont: 1867. V. 47; 53

GOULD, RUPERT T.
The Marine Chronometer, Its History and Development. London: 1923. V. 53

GOULD, WILLIAM
An Account of English Ants; Which Contains. I. their Different Species and Mechanisms. II. Their Manner of Government....III. The Production of Their Eggs...IV. The Incessant Labours of the Workers of Common Ants. London: 1747. V. 48; 52

GOULDEN, SHIRLEY
Tales from Japan. London: 1961. V. 50

GOULDER, WILLIAM A.
Reminiscences, Incidents in the Life of a Pioneer in Oregon and Idaho... Boise: 1909. V. 47; 49; 54

GOULDING, FRANCIS ROBERT
Marooner's Island; or, Dr. Gordon in Search of His Children. Philadelphia: 1869. V. 47; 54
Sal-O-Quah: or Boy-Life Among the Cherokees. Philadelphia: 1870. V. 54

GOULDING, RICHARD W.
The Welbeck Abbey Miniatures. London: 1914-15. V. 53

GOULDSBURY, C. E.
Life in the Indian Police. 1912. V. 54

GOURLAY, J. L.
History of the Ottawa Valley: a Collection of Facts, Events and Reminiscences for Over Half a Century. Ottawa: 1896. V. 48; 53

GOURMONT, REMY DE
The Natural Philosophy of Love. 1926. V. 49
The Natural Philosophy of Love. London: 1926. V. 48

GOVE, JESSE A.
The Utah Expedition 1857-1858. Letters of Capt. Jesse A. Gove...to Mrs. Gove, and Special Correspondence of the New York Herald. Concord: 1928. V. 53

GOW, JAMES
Tomorrow the World. New York: 1943. V. 50

GOWANLOCK, THERESA
Two Months in the Camp of Big Bear. Parkdale: 1885. V. 49

GOWANS, ALAN
Building Canada: an Architectural History of Canadian Life. Toronto: 1966. V. 47

GOWANS, WILLIAM
The Phenix; a Collection of Old and Rare Fragments; viz The Morals of Confucius the Chinese Philosopher; the Oracles of Zoroaster... New York: 1835. V. 52

GOWEN, HERBERT H.
Church Work in British Columbia: Being a memoir of the Episcopate of Acton Windeyer Sillitoe... London: 1899. V. 49

GOWER, FRANCIS LEVENSON
The Mill. A Moravian Tale. London: 1826. V. 54

GOWER, JOHN
De Confessione Amantis. London: 1554. V. 49

GOWER, RONALD SUTHERLAND
Sir Thomas Lawrence. London: 1900. V. 50; 53

GOWERS, W. R.
Diagnosis of Diseases of the Brain and of the Spinal Cord. New York: 1885. V. 47; 48; 50; 52; 53; 54
Diagnosis of Diseases of the Spinal Cord. Philadelphia: 1881. V. 53
Epilepsy and Other Chronic Convulsive Diseases: Their Causes, Symptoms and Treatment. New York: 1885. V. 50; 53
Epilepsy and Other Chronic Convulsive Diseases: Their Causes, Symptoms and Treatment. London: 1901. V. 47
Lectures on the Diagnosis of Diseases of the Brain. London: 1885. V. 51; 53
Lectures on the Diagnosis of Diseases of the Brain Delivered at University College Hospital. Philadelphia: 1887. V. 50; 53
A Manual of Diseases of the Nervous System. London: 1886-88. V. 51
A Manual of Diseases of the Nervous System. Philadelphia: 1893. V. 49
A Manual of Diseases of the Nervous System. Darien: 1970. V. 47

GOYEN, WILLIAM
Come, the Restorer. Garden City: 1974. V. 47
The House of Breath. New York: 1950. V. 47
The House of Breath. London: 1951. V. 47; 50; 52; 53
Precious Door. New York: 1981. V. 52; 53; 54

GOZAK, A.
Ivan Leonidov. 1988. V. 48; 49; 50; 54; 54

GOZZI, CARLO
The Memoirs of Count Carlo Gozzi. London: 1890. V. 53

GRAAF, REINIER DE
De Virorum Organis Generationi Inservientibus, De Clysteribus et de Usu Syphonis in Antomia. Leiden: 1668. V. 49
Opera Omnia. Leiden: 1678. V. 47

GRABBE, EUGENE M.
Handbook of Automation, Computation and Control. New York: 1958-61. V. 54

GRABENHORST, GEORG
Zero Hour. London: 1929. V. 49

GRABER, H. W.
The Life Record of H. W. Graber: a Terry Texas Ranger, 1861-1865. Dallas: 1916. V. 49

GRABHORN, EDWIN
An Original Leaf From the Polycornoicon Printed by William Caxton at Westminster in the Year 1482. The Life and Works of William Caxton..an Appreciation of William Caxaton by Edwin Grabhorn. San Francisco: 1938. V. 50

GRABHORN, JANE
A California Gold Rush, Miscellany Comprising the Original Journal of Alexander Barrington... San Francisco: 1934. V. 47; 49; 54
The Compleat Jane Grabhorn. San Francisco: 1968. V. 54

GRABHORN, MARJORIE
Figure Prints of Old Japan. A Pictorial Pageant of Actors and Courtesans of the Eighteenth Century, Reproduced from Prints in the Collection of Marjorie and Edwin Grabhorn. San Francisco: 1959. V. 47

GRABHORN PRESS
Catalogue of Some Five Hundred Examples of the Printing of Edwin and Robert Grabhorn 1917-1960. Two Gentlemen from Indiana Now Resident in California. San Francisco: 1961. V. 47; 54
Nineteenth Century Type Displayed in 18 Fonts Cast by United States Founders Now in the Cases of the Grabhorn Press. San Francisco: 1959. V. 48; 54
Pages from Various Books Printed at the Grabhorn Press, San Francisco, 1928-1940. San Francisco: 1941. V. 54

GRABHORN, ROBERT
A Commonplace Book of Cookery. San Francisco: 1975. V. 48; 54
A Short Account of the Life and Work of Wynkyn de Worde. With a Leaf from the Golden Legend printed by Him at the Sign of the Sun in Fleet Street, London the Year 1527. San Francisco: 1949. V. 54

GRACE, FREDERICK R.
Archaic Sculpture in Boeotia. Cambrdige: 1939. V. 50; 52

GRACE, G. A.
Ornamental Turning Design... 1923. V. 52

GRACE, WILLIAM GILBERT
Cricket. Bristol & London: 1891. V. 48; 50; 51
Cricketing Reminiscences and Personal Recollections. London: 1899. V. 50

THE GRACES; *a Poetical Epistle from a Gentleman to His Son.* London: 1774. V. 54

GRACIAN Y MORALES, BALTASAR
The Courtiers Manual Oracle, or, the Art of Prudence. London: 1685. V. 52

GRACY, DAVID B.
Moses Austin, His Life. San Antonio: 1987. V. 47

GRAD, BONNIE
Milton Avery. Royal Oak: 1981. V. 50

GRADLE, H.
Bacteria and the Germ Theory of Disease. Chicago: 1883. V. 48

GRADUS ad Parnassum; Sive, Novus Synonymorum, Epithetorum, Phrasium Poeticarum, ac Versuum Thesaurus... Londini: 1700. V. 50

GRAEME, BRUCE
The Story of Buckinghamshire Palace: an Unconventional Study of the Palace from the Earliest Times, Together With Some Account of the Anecdotes and Vivid Personalities Connected With It. London: 1928. V. 53

GRAEME, ELLIOTT
A Novel with Two Heroes. London: 1872. V. 54

GRAEME, JAMES
Poems on Several Occasions. Edinburgh: 1773. V. 53; 54

GRAETZ, H.
History of the Jews. Philadelphia: 1891. V. 48
History of the Jews. Philadelphia: 1891-92. V. 52
History of the Jews. London: 1901. V. 48

GRAF, A. B.
Exotica 3. Rutherford: 1963. V. 51
Exotica 3. 1968. V. 47
Exotica, Series 3. 1976. V. 51
Hortica, Color Cyclopedia of Garden Flora in all Climates and Exotic Plants Indoors. Rutherford: 1992. V. 51
Tropica. East Rutherford: 1978. V. 47; 51
Tropica, Colour Cyclopedia of Exotic Plants and Trees from the Tropics and Sub-Tropics. Rutherford: 1992. V. 51

GRAF, OSKAR MARIA
Ua-Pua!. Regensburg: 1921. V. 52

GRAFER, JOHN
A Descriptive Catalogue of Upwards of Eleven Hundred Species and Varities of Herbaceous or Perenial Plants... London: 1794. V. 52

GRAFSTROM, A.
Une Annee en Suede, ou Tableaux des Costumes, Moeurs et Usages des Paysans... Stockholm: 1829-36. V. 53
Ett ar I Sverige, Taflor af Svenska Almogens Kladedragt... Stockholm: 1864. V. 53

GRAFTON, RICHARD
A Chronicle at Large and Meere History of Affayres of Englande, and Kinges of the Same... London: 1569. V. 47
Grafton's Chronicle; or, History of England. London: 1809. V. 47; 51; 53

GRAFTON, SUE
A is For Alibi. New York: 1982. V. 47; 49; 50; 52; 53
A is for Alibi. London: 1986. V. 50; 52; 54
B is for Burglar. New York: 1985. V. 48; 49; 51; 52; 53
C is for Corpse. New York: 1986. V. 48; 49; 50; 51; 52; 53
D is for Deadbeat. New York: 1987. V. 48; 49; 50; 52; 53
D is for Deadbeat. New York: 1988. V. 53
E is for Evidence. New York: 1988. V. 50; 51; 52; 53; 54
F is for Fugitive. New York: 1989. V. 53
K is for Killer. New York: 1994. V. 51
Keziah Dane. New York: 1967. V. 49; 50; 53; 54
Kinsey and Me. A Collection of Short Stories. Santa Barbara: 1991. V. 49; 52
Mark, I Love You. Los Angeles: 1980. V. 52
Sex and the Single Parent. New York: 1979. V. 52

GRAGLIA, G.
The New Pocket Dictionary of the Italian and English Languages... London: 1795. V. 52

GRAHAM, A.
Molluscs: Prosobranch and Pyramidellid Gasaatropods. Leiden: 1988. V. 50

GRAHAM, ALEXANDER OTONABEE
Leisure Hour Musings. Peterborough: 1874. V. 47

GRAHAM, ANDREW
Andrew Graham's Observations on Hudson's Bay 1767-91. London: 1969. V. 47; 48

GRAHAM, CAROLINE
The Killings at Badger's Drift. London: 1987. V. 47

GRAHAM, CATHARINE MACAULAY
The History of England from the Accession of James I (to the Revolution). (with) The History of England from the Revolution to the Present Time. Bath: 1766-83,. V. 50

GRAHAM, CHARLES
Miscellaneous Pieces, in Prose and Verse. Kendal: 1778. V. 50
Miscellaneous Pieces in Prose and Verse... Liverpool: 1793. V. 50

GRAHAM, CHARLES ALEXANDER
Travels in Tunisia... London: 1887. V. 50

GRAHAM, DOROTHY
Chinese Gardens. London: 1940. V. 48

GRAHAM, DOUGLAS
A Practical Treatise on Massage: Its History, Mode of Application and Effects, Indications and Contra-Indications with Results in Over Fourteen Hundred Cases. New York: 1884. V. 47

GRAHAM, E.
Aunt Liza's "Praisin' Gate". 1916. V. 50

GRAHAM, ELIZABETH S.
Voyage to Locuta; a Fragment; With Etchings and Notes of Illustrations... London: 1818. V. 48

GRAHAM, EVARTS AMBROSE
Some Fundamental Considerations in the Treatment of Empyema Thoracis. St. Louis: 1925. V. 49

GRAHAM, FREDERIK U.
Notes of a Sporting Expedition in the Far West of Canada, 1847. London: 1898. V. 52

GRAHAM, G. F.
An Account of the First Edinburgh Musical Festival, held...November, 1815. Edinburgh: 1816. V. 47
An Essay on the Theory and Practice of Musical Composition... Edinburgh: 1838. V. 48

GRAHAM, GEORGE
Telemachus, a Mask. London: 1763. V. 50

GRAHAM, HENRY
The Annals of the Yeomanry Cavalry of Wiltshire. Liverpool: 1886/1908. V. 50

GRAHAM, HENRY DAVENPORT
The Birds of Iona and Mull, 1852-1770...; with a Memoir of the Author. Edinburgh: 1890. V. 49

GRAHAM, JAMES
Corn and Currency; in an Address to the Land Owners. London: 1827. V. 48
The Life of General Daniel Morgan, of the Virginia Line of the Army of the United States, with Portions of His Correspondence. New York: 1856. V. 47
A Sketch: or Short Description of Dr. Graham's Medical Apparatus, &c. Erected About the Beginning of the Year 1780, in His House, on the Royal Terrace, Adelphi. London: 1780. V. 49

GRAHAM, JAMES D.
Report of the Secretary of War, Communiating...the Report of Lieutenant Colonel Graham on the Subject of the Boundary Line Between the United States and Mexico. Washington: 1852. V. 47; 48; 49; 52

GRAHAM, JOHN
Derriana: Consisting of a History of the Siege of Londonderry and Defence of Enniskillen in 1688 and 1689 with Historical Poetry and Biographical Notes &c. Toronto: 1851. V. 47
The Farmer's and Mechanic's Assistant and Companion; or a New System of Decimal Arithmetic... Eaton: 1824. V. 54
Ireland Preserved; or the Siege of Londonderry and the Battle of Aughrim. Dublin: 1841. V. 48
Poems, Chiefly Historical. Belfast: 1829. V. 51; 54

GRAHAM, JOHN W.
Britain and America - the Merttens Lecture 1930. London: 1930. V. 49
Conscription and Conscience - a History 1916-1916. London: 1922. V. 49
Neaera: a Tale of Ancient Rome. London: 1886. V. 54

GRAHAM, JOSEPH A.
Sporting Dog. New York: 1904. V. 53

GRAHAM, LORENZ
How God Fix Jonah. New York: 1946. V. 53
South Town. Chicago: 1958. V. 53

GRAHAM, MALCOLM
Cup and Saucer Land. London: 1908. V. 54

GRAHAM, MARIA
Journal of a Residence in India. Edinburgh: 1813. V. 50
Three Months Passed in the Mountains East of Rome, During the Year 1819... London: 1820. V. 49
Voyage of the H.M.S. Blonde to the Sandwich Islands, in the Years 1824-1825. London: 1826. V. 50; 52

GRAHAM, MARY WASHINGTON
Reminiscences of the Farmington Hunt Club. Crozet: 1970. V. 53

GRAHAM, PATRICK
Essay on the Authenticity of the Poems of Ossian. Edinburgh: 1807. V. 54

GRAHAM, RIGBY
Holt Mill Papers. Santa Cruz: 1994. V. 52
Imbroglio. Leicester: 1938. V. 49
Sketchbook Drawing. Oxford: 1989. V. 51

GRAHAM, ROBERT BONTINE CUNNINGHAME
The District of Menteith. Stirling: 1930. V. 47; 53
The Dream of the Magi. 1923. V. 54
Redeemed and Other Sketches. London: 1927. V. 48

GRAHAM, SHIRLEY
Jean Baptiste Pointe Desable. New York: 1953. V. 47

GRAHAM, SYLVESTER
Lectures on the Science of Human Life. Battle Creek: 1872. V. 54

GRAHAM, THOMAS
On the Diseases of Females; a Treatise... London: 1841. V. 48; 50; 52

GRAHAM, W. S.
Collected Poems - 1942-1977. London: 1979. V. 50
The Nightfishing. London: 1955. V. 50; 51; 53
Second Poems. London: 1945. V. 48; 50
The Seven Journeys. Glasgow: 1944. V. 47; 49

GRAHAM, WILLIAM
A Collection of Epitaphs and Monumental Inscriptions, Ancient and Modern. Carlisle: 1821. V. 49
Idealism: an Essay, Metaphysical and Critical. London: 1872. V. 50

GRAHAM, WILLIAM A.
The Official Record of a Court of Inquiry Convened at Chicago, Illinois, Jan. 13, 1879, by the President of the United States Upon the Request of major Marcus A. Reno, 7th U.S. Cavalry... Pacific Palisades: 1951. V. 53
Revolutionary History of North Carolina, In Three Lectures... Raleigh: 1853. V. 48
The Story of the Little Big Horn. New York: 1926. V. 53

GRAHAME, KENNETH
Dream Days. London: 1899. V. 48; 54
Dream Days. London: 1902. V. 51
Dream Days. London: 1930. V. 48; 50; 51
The Golden Age. London: 1895. V. 54
The Golden Age. 1900. V. 49; 54
The Golden Age. London & New York: 1900. V. 47; 48; 49; 50; 51
The Golden Age. New York: 1914. V. 49
The Golden Age. London: 1928. V. 51
The Headswoman. London & New York: 1898. V. 47
The Headswoman. London: 1921. V. 47; 48; 53
Pagan Papers. London: 1894. V. 47; 48; 54
The Reluctant Dragon. New York: 1983. V. 47
The Wind in the Willows. London: 1908. V. 48; 49; 51; 52
The Wind in the Willows. New York: 1908. V. 48; 50; 52; 53
Wind in the Willows. New York: 1913. V. 52; 53
The Wind in the Willows. London: 1927. V. 51
The Wind in the Willows. London: 1931. V. 47; 53
The Wind in the Willows. New York: 1940. V. 47; 49; 50; 51; 52; 53; 54
The Wind in the Willows. London: 1950. V. 50; 54
The Wind in the Willows. Cleveland: 1966. V. 54
The Wind in the Willows. London: 1971. V. 47; 52
The Wind in the Willows. London: 1986. V. 49

GRAHAME, THOMAS
A Letter to the Traders and Carriers on the Navigations Connecting Liverpool and Manchester, Showing the Easy Means they Possess of Establishing, on the Navigations Between These Towns, an Elegant and Comfortable Conveyance for Passengers... Glasgaow: 1833. V. 54

GRAHAM-WHITE, CLAUDE
Learning to Fly, a Practical Manual for Beginners. London: 1916. V. 50

GRAINGE, WILLIAM
The Battles and Battle Fields of Yorkshire; From the Earliest Times to the End of the Great Civil War. York: 1854. V. 54
The Castles and Abbeys of Yorkshire: a Historical and Descriptive Account of the Most Celebrated Ruins in the County. York: 1855. V. 47; 53
The History and Topography of Harrogate, with Notices of Birstwith, Blubberhouses, Castley, Clint, Dunkeswick... London: 1882. V. 47

GRAINGER, FRANCIS
The Register and Records of Holm Cultram. Kendal: 1929. V. 52

GRAINGER, JAMES
The Sugar-Cane: a Poem. London: 1764. V. 47

GRAINGER, LYDIA
Modern Amours. London: 1733. V. 47; 50; 52

GRAINGER, M. A.
Woodsmen of the Wst. London: 1908. V. 50

GRAM, HANS
The Massachusetts Compiler of Theoretical and Practical Elements of Sacred Vocal Music... Boston: 1795. V. 52

GRAMAYE, JOANNES BAPTISTA DE
Asia, sive Historia...Asiaticarum Gentium (etc.). Antwerp: 1604. V. 49; 53

A GRAMMAR of the English Tongue, With the Arts of Logick, Rhetorick, Poetry, etc. London: 1721. V. 49; 53

GRAMMONT, JUSTIN
The League of the Merrimack. Mysteries of Manchester. Manchester: 1848. V. 54

GRAMMONT, SIEUR DE
Heartsease and Honesty, Being the Pastimes of the Sieur de Grammont, Steward to the Duc de Richelieu in Touraine. Waltham St. Lawrence: 1935. V. 47; 52; 53

THE GRAND Canyon of Arizona: Being a Book of Words from Many Pens. Chicago: 1902. V. 47

THE GRAND Case of England, So Fiercely Now Disputed by Fire and Sword, Epitomized. London: 1642 i.e. 1643. V. 52

GRAND, GORDON
The Banshee Shadow Flies. Toronto. V. 47
Colonel Weatherford's Young Entry. New York: 1935. V. 47
A Horse for Christmas Morning. Millbrook: 1939. V. 47
Old Man and Other Colonel Weatherford Stories. New York: 1934. V. 47
Redmond C. Stewart, Foxhunter and Gentleman of Maryland. New York: 1938. V. 47; 48; 52; 54
Sail Ho! Windjammer Sketches Alow and Aloft. New York: 1931. V. 47
The Silver Horn. New York: 1932. V. 47; 53
The Silver Horn. Montreal: 1935. V. 47
The Southborough Fox. New York: 1939. V. 48

GRAND Musical Festival, in Westminster Abbey. Third Performance, June the 2d, 1787. London: 1787. V. 49

GRAND Musical Festival, in Westminster-Abbey. Fourth Performance, June the 8th, 1786. London: 1786. V. 47

GRAND New Balloon, to Be Called the Vauxhall Royal Balloon, Which Will When Inflated with Coal Gas, Ascend with From Eight to Ten Persons... Balne: 1836. V. 47

GRAND, PIERRE J. H.
A Parisian Pastor's Glance at America. Boston: 1854. V. 49

GRAND, SARAH, PSEUD.
Babs the Impossible. London: 1901. V. 50
The Beth Book. New York: 1897. V. 48; 50; 51
A Domestic Experiment. Edinburgh: 1891. V. 50
The Heavenly Twins. London: 1893. V. 50
The Heavenly Twins. London: 1950. V. 49
Ideala. London: 1893. V. 50
Ideala. New York: 1893. V. 50

GRAND Trunk Pacific Railway. Winnipeg: 1906?. V. 50

GRAND TRUNK PACIFIC RAILWAY
Bread Book. a Few Terse Stories of Success and Why Failures are Unheard of Along that Line of Railway through the Most Fertile Districts of Western Canada. Winnipeg: 1911. V. 52

GRAND TRUNK RAILWAY CO.
Official Time Table: the Great International Route Between the East and West; the Favorite Route To...Montreal, Chicago, Detroit and all Principal Points in Canada and the United States. Toronto: 1885. V. 50

GRAND, W. JOSEPH
Illustrated History of the Union Stock Yards. Chicago: 1901. V. 51; 53

GRANDE Enciclopedia Portuguesa a e Brasileira. Lisbon. V. 47

LES GRANDES Merveilles d'Amour. France?. V. 52

GRANDIDIER, A.
Histoire Physique, Naturelle et Politique de Madagascar: Atlas des Plantes (Phanerogames). Paris: 1886-1903. V. 51
Histoire Physique, Naturelle et Politique de Madagascar: Oiseaux. Paris: 1876-1937. V. 51; 54
Historie Physique, Naturelle et Politique de Madagascar: Mammiferes. Paris: 1875-97. V. 51

GRANDMAMMA Easy's Account of the Public Buildings of London. London: 1855. V. 50

GRANDMAMMA Easy's Merry Multiplication. London: 1860. V. 51

GRANDMA'S Nursery Rhymes. New York: 1870. V. 49

GRANDVILLE, J. J.
Un Auatre Monde. Paris: 1844. V. 53

GRANDVILLE, JEAN IGNACE ISIDORE GERARD
Les Fleurs Animees. Paris: 1847. V. 48; 49

GRANGE Over Sands. With Excursions Therefrom. Windermere: 1884. V. 50; 52

GRANGER, ALFRED HOYT
Charles Follen McKim. A Study of His Life and Work. Boston and New York: 1913. V. 50

GRANGER, JAMES
A Biographical History of England, from Egbert the Great to the Revolution... London: 1775-79. V. 50
A Biographical History of England, from Egbert the Great to the Revolution... London: 1824. V. 52
Letters Between the Rev. James Granger and Many of the Most Eminent Literary Men of His Time. London: 1805. V. 48; 50

GRANGER, WILLIAM
The New Wonderful Museum, and Extraordinary Magazine... London: 1803-05. V. 48

GRANIT, RAGNAR
Receptors and Sensory Perception. New Haven: 1956. V. 52

GRANNAN, JOSEPH C.
Grannan's Warning Against Fraud and Valuable Information. Akron: 1891. V. 50

GRANNIE'S Little Rhyme Book. London: 1912. V. 47

GRANNISS, RUTH S.
A Descriptive Catalogue of the First Editions in Book Form of the Writings of Percy Bysshe Shelley. Based on a Memorial Exhibition Held at the Grolier Club from April 20 to May 20, 1922. New York: 1923. V. 54
A Garland of Poppies, Gathered By... V. 47

GRANT, A. C.
Bush Land in Queensland or John West's Colonial Experiences. Edinburgh: 1882. V. 48

GRANT, ALEXANDER
The Story of the University of Edinburgh During Its First Three Hundred Years. London: 1884. V. 53; 54

GRANT, ALEXANDER HENLEY
The Literature and Curiosites of Dreams. London: 1865. V. 51

GRANT, ANNE MAC VICAR
Essays On the Superstitions of the Highlanders of Scotland... London: 1811. V. 47; 50; 52; 54
Letters from the Mountains: Being the Real Correspondence of a Lady Between the Years 1773 and 1807... Boston: 1809. V. 47; 49; 50; 51
Memoirs of an American Lady... London: 1808. V. 48; 49; 50; 51; 53; 54
Memoirs of an American Lady... New York: 1809. V. 48; 50; 51; 53
Memoirs of an American Lady. New York: 1909. V. 50
Poems on Various Subjects. Edinburgh: 1803. V. 47; 49; 50; 51; 54

GRANT, ASAHEL
The Nestorians; or, The Lost Tribes. New York: 1841. V. 47

GRANT, BLANCHE C.
Kit Carson's Own Story of His Life. Taos: 1926. V. 53
Taos Today. Taos: 1925. V. 54
When Old Trails Were New. The Story of Taos. New York: 1934. V. 49

GRANT, CAMPBELL
Rock Art of Baja California. Los Angeles: 1974. V. 50

GRANT, DONALD M.
Talbot Mundy: Messenger of Destiny. West Kingston: 1983. V. 51

GRANT, DUNCAN
Duncan Grant. London: 1924. V. 54
Duncan Grant. Watercolors and Drawings. Exhibition 25 April-19 May, 1972. London: 1972. V. 49

GRANT, ELIHU
Rumeileh: Being Ain Shems Excavations (Palestine). Part III. Haverford: 1934. V. 51

GRANT, FRANCIS
The Smelting of Copper in the Swansea District of South Wales, from the Time of Eliabeth to the Present Day. London: 1881. V. 54

GRANT, G.
An Essay on the Science of the Art of Acting. London: 1828. V. 47

GRANT, GEORGE MONRO
Ocean to Ocean - Sandford Fleming's Expedition through Canada in 1872. New York: 1877. V. 54
Ocean to Ocean: Sanford Fleming's Expedition through Canada in 1872... Toronto/London: 1873. V. 49; 50; 51; 53; 54
Our Picturesque Northern Neighbor. Chicago: 1899. V. 49
Picturesque Canada. London. V. 51
Picturesque Canada. Toronto: 1882. V. 47; 51
Picturesque Canada. Toronto: 1882-85. V. 50; 52

GRANT, GORDON
Greasy Luck. A Whaling Sketchbook. New York: 1932. V. 50

GRANT, J.
Winged Pharaoh. 1937. V. 49; 54

GRANT, J. P.
Memoir and Correspondence of Mrs. Grant of Laggan. London: 1844. V. 47

GRANT, JAMES
British Battles on Land and Sea. London: 1875. V. 50
Great Metropolis. New York: 1837. V. 54
History of the Burgh Schools of Scotland. London: 1876. V. 52
The Life of a Literary Man. London: 1843. V. 51
The Narrative of a Voyage of Discovery, Performed in His Majesty's Vessel the Lady Nelson of Sixty Tons Burthen with Sliding Keels in the Years 1800, 1801 and 1802. to New South Wales. Melbourne. V. 52
The Narrative of a Voyage of Discovery, Performed in His Majesty's Vessel the Lady Nelson, of Sixty Tons Burthen, with Sliding Keels in the Years 1800, 1801 and 1802 to New South Wales. London: 1803. V. 50; 52
Sketches of London. Philadelphia: 1839. V. 54

GRANT, JAMES B.
Inaugural Address of His Excellency, James B. Grant, Governor of Colorado, to the Fourth General Assembly of the State of Colorado. Denver: 1883. V. 48

GRANT, JAMES GREGOR
Madonna Pia and Other Poems. London: 1848. V. 50

GRANT, JOHN
The Penny Wedding. London: 1836. V. 47

GRANT, KENNETH
Aleister Crowley and the Hidden God. 1973. V. 52
Cults of Shadow. 1975. V. 47

GRANT, MARIA M.
Artiste. London: 1871. V. 47; 49

GRANT, MAURICE HAROLD
A Chronological History of the Old English Landscape Painters (in Oil) from the XVIth to the XIXth Century. London: 1926/47. V. 50; 54

GRANT, MAXWELL
The Shadow Laughs. New York: 1931. V. 47

GRANT, RICHARD
A Dissertation on the Chief Obstacles to the Improvement of Land, and Introducing Better Methods of Agriculture Throughout Scotland. Aberdeen: 1760. V. 47

GRANT, ROBERT
The Expediency Maintained of Continuing the System by Which the Trade and Government of India are Now Regulated. London: 1813. V. 52
History of Physical Astronomy, From the Earliest Ages to the Middle of the Nineteenth Century... London: 1852. V. 54
Jack Hall or the School Days of an American Boy. Boston: 1888. V. 54

GRANT, ROLAND
Mountains in the Mind. Andoversford: 1987. V. 47
Steps to the River. London: 1994. V. 50

GRANT, ULYSSES S.
Personal Memoirs of U.S. Grant. New York: 1885. V. 48; 50; 52

GRANT, ULYSSES SIMPSON
Personal Memoirs of U.S. Grant. New York: 1885-86. V. 53

GRANT, WILLIAM W.
A Quarter Century of the Arapahoe Hunt. 1954. V. 47

GRANTHAM, JOHN
Iron as a Material for Ship-Building; Being a Communication to the Polytechnic Society of Liverpool. London: 1842. V. 54

GRANTHAM, THOMAS
An Historical Account of Some Memorable Actions, Particularly in Virginia... Richmond: 1882. V. 48

GRANT-RENNICK, R.
Coursing: The Pursuit of Game With Gazehounds. Saul: 1976. V. 48

GRANVILLE, A.
The Fallen Race. 1892. V. 47; 52

GRANVILLE, A. B.
An Historical and Practical Treatise on the Internal Use of Hydro-Cynaic (Prussic) Acid in Pulmonary Consumption and Other Diseases of the Chest. London: 1820. V. 54
St. Petersburgh. A Journal of Travels to and from that Capital... London: 1828. V. 53
Spas of England, and Principal Sea-Bathing Places. Bath: 1971. V. 50; 52
The Spas of Germany. London: 1837. V. 49

GRAPALDUS, FRANCISCUS MARIUS
De Partibus Aedium. Parma: 1516. V. 47

GRAPES and Grape Vines of California. San Francisco: 1980. V. 47
GRAPES and Grape Vines of California. 1981. V. 47; 49; 50; 50; 51; 54

GRAPEWIN, CHARLEY
The Town Pump: an American Comedy. Los Angeles: 1933. V. 54

GRAPHEUS, CORNILLE
De Seer Wonderlucke Schoone Triumphelijck Incompst, Van...Prince Philips, Prince Van Spaignen...Inde Stadt Van Antwerpen, Anno MCCCCCXLIX. Antwerp: 1550. V. 49; 50

GRAPPA, PSEUD.
Cicalamenti del Grappa Intorno al Sonetto "Poi che Mia Speme e Lunga a Venir Troppe". Dove si'Cialia Allungo delle Lodi delle Donne et del Mal Francioso. Mantua: 1545. V. 47

GRASECCIUS, GEORGIUS
Examen (Greek) tou Mikrokosmou Theatrou in quo Ceu Viva Imagine Fabrica Humani... Strassburg: 1605. V. 54

GRASS, GUNTER
Cat and Mouse. New York: 1963. V. 53
Dog Years. New York: 1965. V. 53
Drawings and Words 1954-1977. London: 1983. V. 50
The Flounder. New York: 1985. V. 47; 48; 51; 52; 54
Headbirths or the Germans are Dying Out. New York: 1982. V. 53
Kinderlied. Northridge: 1982. V. 48
Local Anaesthetic. New York: 1970. V. 53
Max. New York: 1972. V. 50

GRASSE, P.
Traite de Zoologie. Paris: 1949-89. V. 48; 50
Traite de Zoologie, volume 16 Parts 1-7. Paris: 1967-82. V. 50

GRASSET, EUGENE
La Platne et ses Applications Ornamentales. Paris: 1897. V. 47

GRASSI, GIUNIO PAOLO
Medici Antiqui Graeci: Aretaeus, Palladius, Ruffus, Theophilus... Basilaeae: 1581. V. 47; 48; 49; 50

GRASSINEAU, JAMES
A Musical Dictionary... London: 1740. V. 48

GRASSUS, BENEVENTIUS
De Oculis Eorumque Egritudinibus et Curis. Stanford: 1929. V. 50; 52

GRASTORF, DENNIS J.
Wood type of the Angelica Press. New York: 1975. V. 47

GRATARALO, GUGLIELMO
Alchemiae, Quam Vocant, Artisque Metallicae, doctrina Certusque Modus, Scriptis Tum Novis, Tum Veteribus, duobus His Voluminibus Comprehensus... Basle: 1572. V. 48

GRATIANUS
Decretum Gratiani, Seu Verius Decretorum Canonicorum Collectanea... Paris: 1550. V. 52; 53

GRATTAN, HENRY
The Speeches of the Rt. Hon. Henry Grattan in the Irish and Imperial Parliament. 1822. V. 48
The Speeches of the Rt. Hon. Henry Grattan in the Irish and Imperial Parliament. London: 1822. V. 52

GRATTAN, THOMAS COLLEY
Civilized America. London: 1859. V. 47; 53
The Heiress of Bruges; a Tale of the Year Sixteen Hundred. London: 1830. V. 52
Highways and By-Ways; or, Tales of the Road-Side Picked Up in the French Provinces, by a Walking Gentleman. London: 1833. V. 51
The History of Switzerland, from the Conquest of Caesar to the Abdication of Buonaparte. London: 1825. V. 53
Jacqueline of Holland. London: 1831. V. 49; 53
Legends of the Rhine and of the Low Countries. London: 1832. V. 51; 54

GRATTEN, J. H. G.
Anglo-Saxon Magic and Medicine. London: 1952. V. 52

GRATTON, JOHN
A Journal of the Life of that Ancient Servant of Christ, John Gratton... London: 1779. V. 49; 54

GRATULATIO Academiae Cantabrigiensis Auspicatissimas George III. Magnae Britanniae Regis, et Serenissimae Charlottae Principis de Mecklenburgh-Strelitz Nuptias Celebrantis. Cambridge: 1761. V. 48; 50

GRATULATIO Academiae Cantabrigiensis de Pace Annae Auspiciis Feliciter Constituta Anno 1713. Cantabrigiae: 1713. V. 52

GRATULATIO Solennis Universitatis Oxoniensis ob Celsissimum Georgium Fred. Aug. Walliae principem Georgio II et Charlottae Reginae Auspicatissime Natum. Oxonii: 1762. V. 50; 52

GRAU, SHIRLEY ANN
The Condor Passes. New York: 1971. V. 47
Evidence of Love. Franklin Center: 1977. V. 47; 48
The Keepers of the House. Franklin Center: 1977. V. 47

GRAULICH, MICHEL
Rediscovered Masterpieces of Mesoamerica. 1985. V. 47

GRAVATT, W.
A Letter on Steam Gun-Boats of Shallow Draft and High Speed. London: 1854. V. 54

GRAVES, A. J., MRS.
Woman in America. New York: 1842. V. 50
Woman in America: Being an Examination Into the Moral and Intellectual Condition of American Female Society. New York: 1844. V. 50

GRAVES, ALFRED P.
Father O'Flynn, and other Irish Lyrics. London: 1889. V. 48
The Irish Fairy Book. London: 1909?. V. 49; 50
To Return to All That - An Autobiography. London: 1930. V. 54

GRAVES, ALGERNON
A Century of Loan Exhibitions 1813-1912. London: 1913. V. 50

GRAVES, CHARLES L.
Mr. Punch's History of Modern England. London: 1921. V. 53

GRAVES, GEORGE
British Ornithology: Being the History with a Coloured Representation of Every Known Species of British Birds. London: 1811. V. 52
Hortus Medicus, or Figures and Descriptions of the More Important Plants Used in Medicine... Edinburgh: 1834. V. 53
The Naturalist's Companion... London: 1824. V. 52
The Naturalist's Pocket-Book or Tourist's Companion. London: 1818. V. 54

GRAVES, HENRY LEA
A Confederate Marine: a Sketch of the Life of Henry Lea Graves with Excerpts from the Graves Family Correspondence 1861-1865. Tuscaloosa: 1963. V. 49

GRAVES, IDA
Epithalamion. 1934. V. 54
Epithalamium. Higham, Colchester: 1934. V. 47; 49; 51

GRAVES, JAMES
Roll of the Proceedings of the Kings Council in Ireland, AD 1392/3. 1877. V. 49

GRAVES, JOHN
Goodbye to a River. New York: 1960. V. 48
Goodbye to a River. Austin: 1989. V. 50
The Last Running. Austin: 1974. V. 50; 53
Self-Portrait with Birds: Some Semi-ornithological Recollections. Dallas: 1991. V. 47

GRAVES, JOSEPH A.
The History of the Bedford Light Artillery. Bedford: 1903. V. 49

GRAVES, R. P.
Life of Sir William Rowan Hamilton. London: 1882/85. V. 47; 52

GRAVES, RICHARD
Euphrosyne; or Amusements on the Road of Life. London: 1776. V. 52
Euphrosyne; or, Amusements on the Road of Life. London: 1780. V. 51
The Festoon: a Collection of Epigrams, Ancient and Modern. London: 1766. V. 48; 53
The Festoon: a Collection of Epigrams, Ancient and Modern. London: 1766/65. V. 52
The Festoon: a Collection of Epigrams, Ancient and Modern. London: 1767. V. 48
Lucubrations: Consisting of Essays, Reveries, &c. in Prose and Verse (and) Recollections of Some Particulars in the Life of the Late William Shenstone. London: 1876/88. V. 47
The Spiritual Quixote. London: 1773. V. 49
The Spiritual Quixote. London: 1774. V. 52
The Spiritual Quixote... London: 1783. V. 48

GRAVES, ROBERT
Across the Gulf. Deja, Mallorca: 1992. V. 50; 52; 53
Across the Gulf... Mallorca: 1993. V. 48
Across the Gulf; Late Poems. Deya: 1994. V. 52
Adam's Rib and Other Anomalous Elements in the Hebrew Creation of Myth. London: 1955. V. 50; 53
Another Future of Poetry. London: 1926. V. 50; 51
Antigua, Penny, Puce. London: 1936. V. 48; 53
Antigua Penny Puce. Majorca: 1936. V. 51; 52; 54
The Antigua Stamp. New York: 1937. V. 47; 48; 49; 51; 52; 54
At the Gate. Hatfield: 1974. V. 51
At the Gate. London: 1974. V. 47; 48; 50; 51
Beyond Giving. London: 1969. V. 47; 48; 49
The Big Green Book. 1962. V. 49
But It Still Goes On. London: 1930. V. 47; 48; 50; 51
Claudius the God. London: 1934. V. 49
Collected Poems. New York: 1938. V. 48; 51
Collected Poems - 1965. London: 1965. V. 54
Collected Poems (1914-1926). Garden City: 1929. V. 48; 51
Collected Poems (1914-1947). London: 1948. V. 50; 53
Collected Short Stories. London: 1965. V. 48; 51; 53
Colophon to Love Respelt. London: 1967. V. 47; 48; 49; 50; 51; 54
Contemporary Techniques of Poetry. London: 1925. V. 50; 52; 54
Count Belisarius. London: 1938. V. 51
Country Sentiment: Poems. London: 1920. V. 48; 49
The Cross and the Sword. Bloomington: 1954. V. 49
English and Scottish Ballads. London: 1957. V. 54
The English Ballad. London: 1927. V. 48; 50; 51
Fairies and Fusiliers. London: 1917. V. 47; 48; 50; 52
The Feather Bed. London: 1923. V. 51
George Sand in Majorca. Deia, Mallorca: 1986. V. 49
Goliath and David. London: 1916. V. 49
Good-Bye to All That. London: 1929. V. 47; 49; 50; 51; 53
Good-Bye to All That. London: 1957. V. 47
Greek Myths. London: 1958. V. 50
The Green Sailed Vessel Poems. Hatfield: 1971. V. 48
The Green Sailed Vessel. Poems. London: 1971. V. 47; 49; 50; 51
Hebrew Myths. London: 1964. V. 47; 50
A Historical Perspective. London: 1957. V. 47
I, Claudius. 1934. V. 50
Ich, Claudius - Kaiser und Gott. Leipzig: 1934. V. 52
Impenetrability or the Proper Habit of English. London: 1926. V. 50
John Kemp's Wager. A Ballad Opera. Oxford: 1925. V. 49; 50; 51
Lars Porsena or the Future of Swearing. 1927. V. 54
Lars Porsena or the Future of Swearing and Improper Language. London: 1927. V. 50
Lars Porsena or the Future of Swearing and Improper Language. London: 1972. V. 50
Lawrence and the Arabian Adventure. Garden City: 1928. V. 50
Lawrence and the Arabs. London: 1927. V. 50
Life of the Poet Gnaeus Robertulus Gravesa. Deia, Mallorca: 1990. V. 49; 53
The Long Week End: A Social History of Great Britain 1918-1939. New York: 1941. V. 48
Love Respelt. 1965. V. 48; 50; 51; 54
Love Respelt Again. New York: 1969. V. 51; 52
Mammon and the Black Goddess. London: 1965. V. 48; 50; 51
Man Does, Woman Is. 1964. V. 54
The Marmosite's Miscellany. London: 1925. V. 53
The Meaning of Dreams. Oxford: 1924. V. 50
Mrs. Fisher: or The Future of Humor. London: 1928. V. 48; 49; 50
Mock Beggar Hall. London: 1924. V. 50; 51; 52; 54
The More Deserving Cases. 1962. V. 48; 51; 52; 54
More Deserving Cases: Eighteen Old Poems for Reconsideration. Marlborough: 1962. V. 48
My Head! My Head!. London: 1925. V. 50; 51; 54
The Nazarene Gospel Restored. London: 1953. V. 49
The Nazarene Gospel Restored. Garden City: 1954. V. 50
Nine Hundred Iron Chariots. Cambridge: 1963. V. 49; 50
No Decency Left. London: 1932. V. 54
No More Ghosts: Selected Poems. London: 1940. V. 54
Old Soldier Sahib. London: 1936. V. 51
Old Soldier Sahib. New York: 1936. V. 50
On English Poetry. 1922. V. 54
On English Poetry. London: 1922. V. 48; 50; 51; 52

GRAVES, ROBERT continued
On English Poetry. New York: 1922. V. 47; 48; 49; 51; 52
On Poetry: Collected Talks and Essays. New York: 1969. V. 50
Over the Brazier. London: 1916. V. 48; 49; 51
Over the Brazier. London: 1920. V. 47; 50
A Pamphlet Against Anthologies. London: 1928. V. 48
The Penny Fiddle. London: 1960. V. 48; 51
Poems. New York: 1980. V. 47; 48; 50; 51
Poems 1914-1926. London: 1927. V. 49; 50; 51; 53
Poems 1914-1927. London: 1927. V. 52
Poems 1926-1930. London: 1931. V. 47; 48; 49; 50
Poems 1929. London: 1929. V. 50
Poems 1930-1933. London: 1933. V. 47; 49; 50
Poems 1938-1945. New York: 1946. V. 50
Poems 1953. London: 1953. V. 50; 51; 52
Poems for Shakespeare. 1972. V. 50
Poetic Unreason. London: 1925. V. 47; 48; 50; 51; 54
Proceed, Sergeant Lamb. London: 1941. V. 48; 51
Proceed, Sergeant Lamb. London: 1946. V. 49
The Real David Copperfield. London: 1933. V. 49; 50; 52
Sergeant Lamb of the Ninth. London: 1940. V. 49; 50
Sergeant Lamb's America. New York: 1940. V. 49; 51; 52
Seven Days in New Crete - a Novel. London: 1949. V. 51
Seventeen Poems Missing from Love Respelt. London: 1966. V. 50; 51; 53; 54
The Shout. London: 1929. V. 47; 48; 49; 50; 51; 52; 53
A Survey of Modernist Poetry. London: 1927. V. 50; 51
Ten Poems. Paris: 1930. V. 48
Ten Poems More. Paris: 1930. V. 47; 50; 53
Timeless Meeting. 1973. V. 54
Timeless Meeting. London: 1973. V. 47; 49; 50; 51
To Whom Else. Deya, Majorca: 1931. V. 47; 48; 49; 50; 51; 52
Treasure Box. London: 1919. V. 49; 52
Watch the Northwind Rise. New York: 1949. V. 47
Welchman's Hose. London: 1925. V. 47; 48; 49; 50; 51; 53
Whipperginny. London: 1923. V. 49; 50; 53
The White Goddess. London: 1948. V. 50
The White Goddess. New York: 1948. V. 48; 50
Work in Hand. London: 1942. V. 50

GRAVES, ROBERT JAMES
Clinical Lectures. Philadelphia: 1842. V. 48; 51
Clinical Lectures on the Practice of Medicine. London: 1884. V. 48; 53
A System of Clinical Medicine. Dublin: 1843. V. 52

GRAVES, W. W.
Life and Letters of Fathers Ponziglione, Schoemakers and Other Early Jesuits at Osage Mission. St. Paul: 1916. V. 54

GRAVES, WILLIAM
Some Account of Admiral Lord (Thomas) Graves. London: 1795?. V. 48

GRAVESANDE, WILLEM JACOB VAN S'
The Elements of Universal Mathematics, or Algebra... London: 1728. V. 48
An Explanation of Newtonian Philosophy, in Lectures Read to the Youth of the University of Leyden. London: 1735. V. 47; 50; 54

GRAVESANDE, WILLEM JACOB VAN 'S
Mathematical Elements of Natural Philosophy... 1720-21. V. 54

GRAVIER, YVES
Descriptions des Beautes de Genes. Genoa: 1781. V. 49

GRAY, A. STUART
Edwardian Architecture. Iowa City: 1986. V. 50

GRAY, ALASDAIR
1982, Janine. London: 1984. V. 47; 53
Lanark. Edinburgh: 1981. V. 50; 51
Poor Things. London: 1992. V. 50

GRAY, ANDREW
Explanation of the Engravings of the Most Important Implements of Scottish Husbandry, from Drawings Prepared for the Board of Agriculture. Edinburgh: 1814. V. 54

GRAY, ANDREW BELCHER
Report of the Secretary of Interior...Communicating a Report and Map of A. B. Gray, Relative to the Mexican Boundary. Washington: 1855. V. 47; 49

GRAY, ARTHUR
The Town of Cambridge. A History. (and) Cambridge University an Episodic History. Cambridge: 1925/26. V. 48

GRAY, ASA
Characters of Some New Genera and Species of Plants of the Natural Order Compositae. Boston: 1845. V. 52
Flora of North America. New York: 1838-40. V. 48
Genera Florae Americae Boreali-Orientalis Illustrata. The Genera of the Plants of the United States. New York: 1848-49. V. 48
Genera Florae Americae Boreali-Orientalis Illustrata. The Genera of the Plants of the United States. New York: 1849. V. 50
Letters of Asa Gray. Boston: 1893. V. 47; 48; 52
Manual of Botany of the Northern U. S. from New England to Wisconsin and South to Ohio and Pennsylvania Inclusive. Boston: 1848. V. 48; 52
Manual of the Botany of the Northern United States. New York: 1856. V. 48
Plantae Wrightianae Texano-Neo-Mexicanae, Account of a Collection of Plants Made by Charles Wright. Washington: 1852-53. V. 48; 51; 52
Plates Prepared Between the Years 1849 and 1859 to Accompany a Report on the Forest Trees of North America. Washington: 1891. V. 47; 48
Scientific Papers of Asa Gray... Boston and New York: 1889. V. 47
Scientific Papers of Asa Gray. London: 1889. V. 48; 52

GRAY, BARRY
Ale in Prose and Verse. New York: 1866. V. 47

GRAY, BASIL
Treasures of Asia, Persian Painting. Paris: 1961. V. 49

GRAY, C.
Hans Richter. London: 1971. V. 51
Murder in Millennium VI. 1951. V. 48

GRAY, CAMILLA
The Great Experiment: Russian Art 1863-1922. New York: 1962. V. 47; 50; 51

GRAY, CECIL
Gilles de Rais - a Play. London: 1941. V. 52

GRAY, CHRISTOPHER
A Catalogue of Trees, Shrubs, Plants and Flowers, Which are Propagated for Sale by Christopher Gray, Nurseryman, at Fulham, in Middlesex. London: 1755. V. 47
The Great Experiment: Russian Art 1863-1922. New York: 1961. V. 54
The Great Experiment: Russian Art 1863-1922. New York: 1962. V. 53
Sculpture and Ceramics of Paul Gaugin. Baltimore: 1963. V. 50; 53; 54

GRAY, DAVID
Gallops I: Gallops II: Mr. Carteret. New York: 1929. V. 47

GRAY, ELIZABETH
Tour to the Sepulchres of Etruria, in 1839. London: 1840. V. 47

GRAY, FRANK S.
For Love of Bears. A Description of a Recent Hunting Trip with a Romantic Finale... Chicago: 1886. V. 53

GRAY, G.
The Earlier Cambridge Stationers and Bookbinders and the First Cambridge Printer. Oxford: 1904. V. 50

GRAY, GEORGE G.
A Bibliography of the Works of Sir Isaac Newton... Cambridge: 1907. V. 49; 51

GRAY, GEORGE J.
The Earlier Cambridge Stationers and Bookbinders and First Cambridge Printer. Oxford: 1904. V. 50

GRAY, GEORGE ROBERT
Erebus and Terror Voyage 1839-43. Birds. London: 1846-75. V. 54
A Fasciculus of the Birds of China. London: 1871. V. 50
The Genera of Birds. London: 1844-49. V. 48; 50; 51
The Genera of Birds. London: 1849. V. 51
Hand-list of Genera and Species of Birds... London: 1869-71. V. 51
List of the Specimens of Birds in the Collection of the British Museum. London: 1844-67. V. 51

GRAY, HAROLD
Little Orphan Annie. New York: 1930. V. 53
Little Orphan Annie and Jumbo, the Circus Elephant. Chicago: 1935. V. 54
Little Orphan Annie Bucking the World. New York: 1929. V. 49

GRAY, HENRY
Anatomy, Descriptive and Surgical. Philadelphia: 1862. V. 53
Anatomy, Descriptive and Surgical. Philadelphia: 1865. V. 50; 51
On the Structure and Use of the Spleen. London: 1854. V. 48; 53

GRAY, HORACE
The Power of the Legislature to Create and Abolish Courts of Justice. Boston: 1858. V. 50

GRAY, HUGH
Letters from Canada, Written During a Residence There in the Years 1806, 1807 and 1808... London: 1809. V. 47; 51; 53; 54

GRAY, ISAAC MC KINLEY
My Observations of Europe and the Middle East. Baltimore: 1953. V. 54

GRAY, J. E.
Catalogue of Shield Reptiles in the Collection of the British Museum. London: 1855-72. V. 49
Spicilegia Zoologica, Conclusion. London: 1924. V. 48
Synopsis of the Species of Whales and Dolphins in the Collection of the British Museum. London: 1868. V. 54

GRAY, JOHN
The Country Attorney's Practice in Conducting Actions in the Superior Courts of Law at Westminster. London: 1836. V. 50
Emilio Montanaro. In the Garden of Citrons. London: 1892. V. 48
The Essential Principles of the Wealth of Nations, Illustrated, in Opposition to Some False Doctrines of Dr. Adam Smith, and Others. London: 1797. V. 54
Lectures on the Nature and Use of Money. Delivered Before the Members of the "Edinburgh Philosophical Institution" During the Months of Feb. and March 1848. Edinburgh: 1848. V. 49; 50
The Long Road. London: 1926. V. 47
The Nymphidia and the Muses Elizium. London: 1896. V. 49

GRAY, JOHN continued
Poems on Several Occasions. London: 1745. V. 48
Silverpoints. London: 1893. V. 47; 49; 51; 54
Spiritual Poems, Chiefly Done Out of Several Languages. London: 1896. V. 51

GRAY, JOHN CHIPMAN
Essays: Agricultural and Literary. Boston: 1856. V. 52
War Letters, 1862-1865. Boston and New York: 1927. V. 50; 53

GRAY, JOHN EDWARD
A Second Letter to the Earl of Ellesmere, on the Management of the Library of printed Books in the British Museum. London: 1849. V. 50

GRAY, JOHN HAMILTON
Autobiography of a Scotch Country Gentleman, the Rev. John Hamilton Gray of Carntyne. Edinburgh: 1868. V. 48

GRAY, JOHN HENRY
China: a History of the Laws, manners and Customs of the People. London: 1878. V. 49; 53

GRAY, JOHN S.
Centennial Campaign. The Sioux Indian War of 1876. Fort Collins: 1976. V. 52

GRAY, LANDON CARTER
A Treatise on Nervous and Mental Diseases for Students and Practitioners of Medicine. Philadelphia: 1895. V. 47; 48

GRAY, MAXWELL
The Last Sentence. London: 1893. V. 50; 53

GRAY, N.
Lettering on Buildings. London: 1960. V. 50
Nineteenth Century Ornamented Types and Title Pages. London: 1938. V. 53

GRAY, P.
The Microtomist's Formulary and Guide. New York: 1975. V. 50

GRAY, P. L.
Gray's Doniphan County History, a Record of the Happenings of Half a Hundred Years. Bandera: 1905. V. 51; 53

GRAY, PRENTISS N.
Africa Game-Lands. Missoula: 1995. V. 53
North American Big Game. Bridgeport: 1934. V. 47

GRAY, ROBERT
The Birds of the West of Scotland... Glasgow: 1871. V. 50; 52; 54
Letters During the Course of a Tour through Germany, Switzerland and Italy, in the Years MDCCXCI and MDCCXCII with Reflections on the Manners, Literature and Religion of Those Countries. London: 1794. V. 47
Observations on the Automaton Chess Player, Now Exhibited in London at 4, Spring Gardens. London: 1819. V. 52

GRAY, SIMON
Wise Child. London: 1968. V. 54

GRAY, THOMAS
The Correspondence... Oxford: 1971. V. 52
The Correspondence of Thomas Gray and William Mason, To Which are Added Some Letters Addressed by Gray to the Rev. James Brown, D.D. London: 1853. V. 48
Designs by Mr. R. Bentley, for Six Poems by Mr. T. Gray. London: 1753. V. 47; 48; 51
Designs by Mr. R. Bentley, for Six Poems by Mr. T. Gray. London: 1766. V. 47
Elegy. London & New York: 1846. V. 47; 49; 50
Elegy. Baltimore: 1950. V. 49
An Elegy Written in a Country Churchyard. London: 1751. V. 47; 49
An Elegy Written in a Country Churchyard. London: 1763. V. 54
Elegy Written in a Country Churchyard. London: 1839. V. 48
An Elegy Written in a Country Churchyard. London: 1861. V. 52
Elegy Written in a Country Churchyard. London: 1900. V. 52
Elegy Written in a Country Churchyard. 1901. V. 53
Elegy Written in a Country Churchyard. London: 1901. V. 48; 50
Elegy Written in a Country Churchyard. London: 1938. V. 48; 51; 52; 54
Elegy Written in a Country Churchyard. New York: 1938. V. 54
Elegy Written in a Country Churchyard. Waltham St. Lawrence: 1946. V. 51
Elegy Written in a Country Churchyard. New York: 1951. V. 49; 51
Elegy Written in a Country Churchyard. Norwalk: 1951. V. 52
Elegy Written in a Country Churchyard. Worcester: 1960. V. 52
An Elegy Written in a Country Churchyard. Market Drayton: 1995. V. 54
Gray's Elegy. London: 1866. V. 50
Ode on the Pleasure Arising from Vicissitude. San Francisco: 1933. V. 53
Ode Performed in the Senate-House at Cambridge, July 1, 1769, at the Installation of His Grace Augustus-Henry Fitzroy, Duke of Grafton, Chancellor of the University. Cambridge: 1769. V. 54
Odes. Strawberry Hill: 1757. V. 47; 48; 50; 52; 54
Poems. Glasgow: 1768. V. 47
Poems. London: 1768. V. 47; 48; 49; 51; 52
Poems. Dublin: 1775. V. 47
The Poems... London: 1775. V. 50; 52
The Poems. York: 1775. V. 54
The Poems. York: 1778. V. 47
Poems. Parma: 1793. V. 47
Poems. London: 1887. V. 49
Poems. 1894. V. 54
Poems. London: 1902. V. 51
Poems and Letters. London: 1867. V. 47; 51; 52

Poems and Letters. 1879. V. 48; 54
Poems and Letters. London: 1879. V. 49; 51
Poesies de Gray. Paris: 1798. V. 47
The Poetical Works... London: 1797. V. 47
Poetical Works. London: 1799. V. 49
A Sermon, Delivered in Boston, Before the African Society, on the 14th Day of July 1818, the Anniversary of the Abolition of the Slave Trade. Boston: 1818. V. 53
Stanzas. 1790. V. 52
The Value of Life and Charitable Institutions. Boston: 1805. V. 52
The Works... London: 1807. V. 47
Works. London: 1836. V. 47

GRAY, WILLIAM
Travels in Western Africa in the Years 1818, 19, 20 and 21... London: 1825. V. 47; 51; 53; 54

GRAYBILL, FLORENCE CURTIS
Visions of a Vanishing Race. New York: 1976. V. 54

GRAYDON, ALEXANDER
Memoirs of a Life, Chiefly Passed in Pennsylvania. Harrisburg: 1811. V. 53

GRAYDON, WILLIAM
The Justices and Constables Assistant... Harrisburg: 1805. V. 49

GRAYSON, A. J.
Birds of the Pacific Slope. San Francisco: 1986. V. 52

GRAYSON, CHARLES
The Sportsman's Hornbook. New York: 1933. V. 54

GRAYSON, DAVID
Adventures in Contentment. Garden City: 1907. V. 48

GRAYSON, WILLIAM J.
The Hireling and the Slave, Chicora, and Other Poems. Charleston: 1856. V. 47

GRAZEBROOK, HENRY
Lights Along the Line. Liverpool: 1855. V. 49

GRAZEBROOK, O. F.
Studies in Sherlock Holmes. London: 1951. V. 49

GRAZER, FREDERICK MARTEL
Body Image: a Surgical Perspective... St. Louis: 1980. V. 54

GRAZIANO, ROCKY
Somebody Up There Likes Me. New York: 1955. V. 53

GRAZZINI, ANTONIO FRANCESCO, CALLED IL LASCA
The Story of Doctor Manente. Florence: 1919. V. 53
The Story of Dr. Manente. Florence: 1929. V. 50; 53

GREACEN, ROBERT
The World of C. P. Snow. London: 1962. V. 51

GREARD, VALLERY
Meissonier. His Life and His Art. New York: 1897. V. 54
Meissonier. His Life and His Art. New York: 1907. V. 48

THE GREAT Ages of World Architecture. New York: 1963-63. V. 53

THE GREAT Bastard, Protector of the Little One. Cologne: 1689. V. 50; 52

GREAT BRITAIN
Copies or Extracts of any Despatches that Have Been Received by Her Majesty's Secretary of State for the Colonies, on the Subject of the Establishment of a Representative Assembly at Vancouver's Island. London: 1857. V. 54

GREAT BRITAIN. ARMY - 1822
General Regulations and Orders for the Army. London: 1822. V. 53

GREAT BRITAIN. BOARD OF AGRICULTURE - 1816
Agricultural State of the Kingdom, in February, March and April, 1816... London: 1816. V. 50

GREAT BRITAIN. COLONIAL OFFICE - 1863
Vancouver Island...Copies or Extracts of Correspondence Between Mr. Langford and the Colonial Department, Relative to Alleged Abuses in the Government of Vancouver's Island... London: 1863. V. 52

GREAT BRITAIN. CONSULAR SERVICE - 1907
General Instructions for His Majesty's Consular Officers, October 1907. London: 1907. V. 49

GREAT BRITAIN. COURT OF STAR CHAMBER - 1633
A Decree lately Made in the High Court of Starre-Chamber...(13 November 1633, Concerning Grain, Bread Prices, etc.)...And Also a Confirmation of that Decree by His Sacred Maiestie... London: 1633. V. 52

GREAT BRITAIN. COURT OF STAR CHAMBER - 1637
A Decree of Starre-Chamber, Concerning Printing... London: 1637. V. 50; 51

GREAT BRITAIN. COURT OF STAR CHAMBER - 1884
A Decree of Star Chamber Concerning Printing, Made July 11, 1637. New York: 1884. V. 52

GREAT BRITAIN. LAWS, STATUTES, ETC. - 1543
In This Volume are Contened the Stautes Made...from the Time of Kyng Henry the Thirde, vnto the Fyrste yere of...Henry the VIII. London: 1543. V. 49; 53

GREAT BRITAIN. LAWS, STATUTES, ETC. - 1551
The Second Volume Conteyinying Those Statutes Whiche Haue ben made in the Tyme of the Most Vicctoriouse Reigne of Kyng Henrie the Eight. London: 1551. V. 49; 53

GREAT BRITAIN. LAWS, STATUTES, ETC. - 1556
Magna Charta, cum Statutis Quae Antiqua Vocantur, Iam Recens Excusa & Summa Fide Emendata, Iuxta Vetusta Exemplatiae ad Parliamenti Rotulos Examinata... London: 1556. V. 47; 52

GREAT BRITAIN. LAWS, STATUTES, ETC. - 1606
Statutes. An. Regni Iacobi, 3...at the Second Session of Parliament Begun the Fifth Day of Nouvember...and...Continued vntill the 27 of May. London: 1606. V. 51

GREAT BRITAIN. LAWS, STATUTES, ETC. - 1607
Statutes. An. Regni Iacobi...At the Parliament Begun...the 18. day of Nouember (1606) ...and...Continued Vntil the 4. Day of Iuly 1607... London: 1607. V. 48; 51

GREAT BRITAIN. LAWS, STATUTES, ETC. - 1610
Anno Regni Iacobi...at the Fourth Session of Parliament Begun...the IX Day of February...Continued Vntill ...July...1610. London: 1610. V. 48; 52

GREAT BRITAIN. LAWS, STATUTES, ETC. - 1643
An Ordinance by the Lords and Commons Assembled in Parliament for the Preservation and Keeping Together for Publique Use, Such Books, Evidences, Records and Writings Sequestered or Taken by Distresse or Otherwise as are Fit to be so Preserved. London: 1643. V. 47

An Ordinance of the Lords and Commons (on the Scottish Army) Assembled in Parliament Declaring the Cases, Wherefore After the Refusall of Many Remonstrances, Declarations and Treaties Had Been Sent by the Kingdome of Scotland... London: 1643. V. 52

GREAT BRITAIN. LAWS, STATUTES, ETC. - 1644
An Ordinance of the Lords and Commons Assembled in Parliament, for Providing of Drught-Horses for Carriages of the Traine of Artillery to the Army Under the Command of Sir Thomas Farifax. And for Paying of Coat and Conduct Money. London: 1644. V. 52

Two Ordinances of the Lords and Commons...for the Speedy Demolishing of All Orangs, Images and All Manner of Superstitious Monuments in all Cathedrall Parish-Churches and Chappels, Throughout the Kingdom of England and Dominion of Wales... London: 1644. V. 51

GREAT BRITAIN. LAWS, STATUTES, ETC. - 1647
An Ordinance of the Lords and Commons Assembled in Parliament, for the Prohibiting the Transportation Out of the Kingdom of England, Ireland and Dominion of Wales... London: 1647/48. V. 51

GREAT BRITAIN. LAWS, STATUTES, ETC. - 1650
An Act for Making Ships and Merchandizes Taken, or to be Taken from the King of Portugal Or any of His Subjects, to be Prize. London: 1650. V. 47

An Act for Settled Convoys for Securing the Trade of This Nation. 1650. V. 47

An Act for Taking Away the Fee of Damage Cleere. London: 1650. V. 48

An Act Prohibiting Trade with the Barbada's, Virginia, Bermuda's and Antego. London: 1650. V. 51

GREAT BRITAIN. LAWS, STATUTES, ETC. - 1651
An Act Concerning the New Invention of Melting Down Iron and Other Metals with Stone-Coal and Other Coals, Without Charking Thereof. London: 1651. V. 48

GREAT BRITAIN. LAWS, STATUTES, ETC. - 1652
An Act for Making Salt-Petre. London: 1652. V. 47

GREAT BRITAIN. LAWS, STATUTES, ETC. - 1653
An Act for Continuing the Powers of Commissioners for Compounding &c. Advance of Money; and for.... London: 1653. V. 47

GREAT BRITAIN. LAWS, STATUTES, ETC. - 1661
Anno Regni Caroli II. Regis Angliae, Scotiae, Franciae & Hiberniae, Vicesimo Secundo & Vicesimo Tertio. At the Parliament Begun at Westminster the Eighth Day of May, Anno Dom. 1661...and Prorogued to the 16th Day of April...1672. London: 1671. V. 47

GREAT BRITAIN. LAWS, STATUTES, ETC. - 1662
An Act for Preventing the Frequent Abuses in Printing, Seditious, Treasonable, and Unlicensed Books and Pamphlets; and for Regulating of Printing and Printing Presses. London: 1662. V. 54

GREAT BRITAIN. LAWS, STATUTES, ETC. - 1671
Anno Regni Caroli II. regis Angliae, Scotiae, Franciae & Hibernaie, Vicesimo Secundo & Vicesimo Tertio. At the Parliament Begun at Westminster the Eighth Day of May Anno Dom. 1661...and prorogued to the 16th Day of April 1672. London: 1671. V. 50

GREAT BRITAIN. LAWS, STATUTES, ETC. - 1680
Magna Charta, Made in the Ninth Year of K. Henry the Third, and confirmed by K. Edward the First, in the Twenty-Eighth Year of His Reign. London: 1680. V. 50; 53

GREAT BRITAIN. LAWS, STATUTES, ETC. - 1692
An Act for Continuing the Acts for Prohibiting All Trade and Commerce with France, and for the Encouragement of Privateers. London: 1692. V. 50

GREAT BRITAIN. LAWS, STATUTES, ETC. - 1696
An Act That the Solemn Affirmation and Declaration of the People Called Quakers, Shall be Accepted, Instead of an Oath in the Usual Form. London: 1696. V. 47

GREAT BRITAIN. LAWS, STATUTES, ETC. - 1714
An Act to Make the River Kennet Navigable, from Reading to Newbury, in the County of Berks. (and) An Act for Enlarging the Time Granted for Making the River Kennet Navigable. 1714/21. V. 50

GREAT BRITAIN. LAWS, STATUTES, ETC. - 1725
An Act for Laying Certain Duties Upon Hides and Skins, Tanned, Tawed or Dressed and Upon Vellum and Parchment. London: 1725. V. 54

GREAT BRITAIN. LAWS, STATUTES, ETC. - 1729
An Act for Establishing an Agreement with Seven of the Lords Proprietors of Carolina, for the Surrender of Their Title and Interest in that Province to His Majesty. London: 1729. V. 54

GREAT BRITAIN. LAWS, STATUTES, ETC. - 1754
Anno Regni Georgii II...Vicesimo Primo (et Secundo). at the Parliament...the Tenth Day of November...1747 (etc.). Edinburgh: 1754. V. 50

GREAT BRITAIN. LAWS, STATUTES, ETC. - 1760
The Act for Permitting the Free Importation of Cattle from Ireland, Considered with a View to the Interests of Both Kingdoms. London: 1760. V. 52

GREAT BRITAIN. LAWS, STATUTES, ETC. - 1765
An Act to Amend and Render More Effectual, In His Majesty's Dominions in America, an Act Passed in This Present Session of Parliament, Intituled, an Act for Punishing Mutiny and Desertion and for the Better Payment of the Army and Their Quarters. London: 1765. V. 50

GREAT BRITAIN. LAWS, STATUTES, ETC. - 1817
Acts for Making Provision for the Effectual Performance of Quarantine; with Orders in Council. London: 1817. V. 50

GREAT BRITAIN. LAWS, STATUTES, ETC. - 1820
An Act to Deprive Her Majesty Queen Caroline Amelia Elizabeth of the Title, Prerogatives, Rights, Privileges and Exemptions of Queen Consort of this Realm, and to Dissolve the Marriage Between His Majesty and the Said Caroline Amelia Elizabeth... London: 1820. V. 53

GREAT BRITAIN. LAWS, STATUTES, ETC. - 1821
An Act for Regulating the Fur Trade, and Establishing a Criminal and Civil Jurisdiction Within Certain Parts of North America. London: 1821. V. 47

GREAT BRITAIN. LAWS, STATUTES, ETC. - 1845
The Harrogate Improvement Act, Being an Act for Improving Certain Parts of the Township of Bilton with Harrogate, and Pannal, Called High and Low Harrogate, for Protecting the Mineral Springs, and for Other Purposes Therein Mentioned. Harrogate: 1845. V. 53

GREAT BRITAIN. LAWS, STATUTES, ETC. - 1858
An Act to Provide for the Government of British Columbia (2d August 1858). London: 1858. V. 53

GREAT BRITAIN. LAWS, STATUTES, ETC. - 1863
An Act to Define the Boundaries of the Colony of British Columbia, and to Continue an Act to Provide for the Government of the Said Colony (28th July 1863). London: 1863. V. 53

GREAT BRITAIN. LAWS, STATUTES, ETC. - 1869
The Statutes of Henry VII. London: 1869. V. 51

GREAT BRITAIN. LAWS, STATUTES, ETC. - 1870
An Act to Make Further Provision for the Government of British Columbia (9th August 1870). London: 1870. V. 53

GREAT BRITAIN. LAWS, STATUTES, ETC. - 1946
Coal Industry Nationalization Act, 1946. London: 1946. V. 52

GREAT BRITAIN. PARLIAMENT - 1626
The Order and Manner of the Sitting of the Lords Spirituall and Temporall, as Peerees of the Realme, in the Higher House of Parliament,... and Also the Names of the Knights for the Counties, Citizens, Burgesses for the Boroughs and Baron for the Ports.. London: 1626. V. 47

GREAT BRITAIN. PARLIAMENT - 1640
The Priviledges and Practice of Parliaments in England. London: 1640. V. 53

GREAT BRITAIN. PARLIAMENT - 1642
The Answer of Both Houses of Parliament, Presented to His Majestie at York, the Ninth of May 1642. To Two Messages...Concerning Sir John Hothams Refusall to Give His Majestie Entrance Into His Town of Hull. London: 1642. V. 50; 53

The Declaration and Votes of the Lords and Commons Assembled in Parliament. Concerning the Treaty of Peace in Yorkshire. London: 1642. V. 50; 53

A Declaration of the Lords and Commons Assembled in Parliament for the Preservation and Safety of the Kingdom and Town of Hull. London: 1642. V. 50

Instructions Agreed Upon by the Lords and Commons Assembled in Parliament, for Sir William Brereton Barronet...and for Sir George Booth...and the Rest of the Deputie Lieutenants of the Citie and Countie of Chester. London: 1642. V. 53

The Votes of Both Houses of Parliament the 20th of Maii, 1642. With the Humble Petititon of the Lords and Commons in Parliament Assembled to the Kings Most Excellent Majestie at Yorke... London: 1642. V. 47

GREAT BRITAIN. PARLIAMENT - 1643
An Exact Collection of all Remonstrances, Declarations, Votes, Orders, Ordinances, Proclamations, Petitions, Messages, Answers and Other Remarkable Passages Betweene the Kings Most Excellent Majesty... London: 1643. V. 47

An Ordinance of the Lords and Commons (On the Scottish Army) Assembled in Parliament Declaring the Causes, Wehrefore After the Refusall of Many Remonstrances, Declarations, and Treaties, Had and Sent by the Kingdome of Scotland... London: 1643. V. 50

GREAT BRITAIN. PARLIAMENT - 1644
An Ordinance of Lords and Commons, Assembled in Parliament for the Making of Salt-Peter Within the Kingdom of England, and...Wales, for the Preservation and Safety of the Kingdom. London: 1644. V. 53

GREAT BRITAIN. PARLIAMENT - 1645
An Ordinance of the Lords and Commons,...for the Speedy Raising and Impresting of Men, for the Recruiting of the Forces Under the Command of Sir Thomas Fairfax, in the Defence of the Kingdome. London: 1645. V. 53

GREAT BRITAIN. PARLIAMENT - 1646
A Collection of All the Publicke Orders, Ordinances and Declarations of Both Houses of Parliament, from the Ninth of March 1642. Until December 1646. Together with Severall of His Majesties Proclamations and Other Papers. London: 1646. V. 48

GREAT BRITAIN. PARLIAMENT - 1648
A Declaration of the Parliament of England, Expressing the Grounds of Their late Proceedings and of Setling the Present Government in the Way of a Free State. London: 1648. V. 53

GREAT BRITAIN. PARLIAMENT - 1650
Two Orders of Parliament Concerning the Apprehending of Thieves. Die Veneris 10 Januarii, 1650. London: 1650. V. 47

GREAT BRITAIN. PARLIAMENT - 1652
Votes of Parliament for Setting Apart a Day of Publique Fasting and Humiliation. Wednesday the Ninth of February, 1652. London: 1652. V. 47

GREAT BRITAIN. PARLIAMENT - 1671
Anno Regni Caroli II...at the Parliament Begun at Westminster the Eighth Day of May, Anno Dom. 1661...and Prorogued to the 16th Day of April...1672. London: 1671. V. 54

GREAT BRITAIN. PARLIAMENT - 1685
Anno Regni Jacobi II, Regis Angliae, Scotiae, Franciae & Hiberniae, Primo. London: 1685. V. 53

GREAT BRITAIN. PARLIAMENT - 1689
An Exact Collection of the Debates of the House of Commons, Held at Westminster,... 1680. London: 1689. V. 51

GREAT BRITAIN. PARLIAMENT - 1695
The Debate At Large, Between the House of Lords and House of Commons,...Relating to the Word, Abdicated, and the Vacancy of the Throne. London: 1695. V. 50; 51

GREAT BRITAIN. PARLIAMENT - 1729
A Report from the Committee Appointed to Enquire into the State of the Goals of this Kingdom: Relating to the Fleet Prison. London: 1729. V. 48

GREAT BRITAIN. PARLIAMENT - 1753
A Bill, with the Amendments, for the Amendment and Preservation of the Public Roads of This Kingdom; and for the More Effectual Execution of the Laws Relating Thereto. London: 1753. V. 52

GREAT BRITAIN. PARLIAMENT - 1786
Report of the Select Committee, To Whom it Was Referred to Examine the State of Several Accounts, and Other Papers, Presented to the House in This Session of Parliament, Relating to the Public Income and Expenditure... London: 1786. V. 47; 49

GREAT BRITAIN. PARLIAMENT - 1811
Report from the Committee Upon the Roads Between Carlisle and Port Patrick. London: 1811. V. 51

GREAT BRITAIN. PARLIAMENT - 1842
Report from the Select Committee on Ventilation of the New Houses of Parliament; with the Minutes of Evidence. (1842). London: 1842. V. 53

GREAT BRITAIN. PARLIAMENT - 1851
Minutes of Evidence Taken Before the Select Committee on the Metropolis Water Bill; with an Index. London: 1851. V. 51

GREAT BRITAIN. PARLIAMENT - 1852
Second Report from the Select Committee on Ventilation and Lighting of the House; Together with the Proceedings of the Committee, Minutes of Evidence, Appendix and Index. London: 1852. V. 53

GREAT BRITAIN. PARLIAMENT - 1855
Report from the Select Committee on Downing Street Public Offices Extension Bill; Togethr with the Minutes of Evidence, Proceedings of the Committee and Appendix. London: 1855. V. 52

GREAT BRITAIN. PARLIAMENT - 1866
Report on the Present State of Trade Between Great Britain and Russia. London: 1866. V. 47

GREAT BRITAIN. PARLIAMENT - 1875
Correspondence Relating to the Complaints of the Mercantile Community in Hong Kong Against the Action of Chinese Revenue Cruizers in the Neighbourhood of the Colony. London: 1875. V. 47

GREAT BRITAIN. PARLIAMENT - 1894
Correspondence Relative to the Outbreak of Bubonic Plague at Hong Kong. (with) Further Correspondence Relative to the Outbreak of Bubonic Plague at Hong Kong. London: 1894. V. 49

GREAT BRITAIN. PARLIAMENT - 1966
Report from the Select (Parliamentary) Committee on Aborigines (British Settlements). Cape Town: 1966. V. 52

GREAT BRITAIN. PARLIAMENT. HOUSE OF COMMONS - 1680
A True Copy of the Journal-Book of the Last Parliament, Begun at Westminster the Sixth Day of march 1678... London: 1680. V. 52

GREAT BRITAIN. PARLIAMENT. HOUSE OF COMMONS - 1686
Debates and Speeches (on the Army) Made in the Honourable House of Commons - Assembled in Parliament: from the 9 to the 20th day of November, 1686. London: 1686. V. 47

GREAT BRITAIN. PARLIAMENT. HOUSE OF COMMONS - 1711
The Humble Representation of the House of Commons to the Queen with Her Majesty's Most Gracious Answer Thereunto. London: 1711. V. 53

GREAT BRITAIN. PARLIAMENT. HOUSE OF COMMONS - 1792
The Debate On a Motion for the Abolition of the Slave Trade in the House of Commons, on Monday the Second of April, 1792, Reported in Detail. London: 1792. V. 50

GREAT BRITAIN. PARLIAMENT. HOUSE OF COMMONS - 1795
Proceedings of the House of Commons Respecting the High Price of Corn. 1795. V. 51

GREAT BRITAIN. PARLIAMENT. HOUSE OF COMMONS - 1796
The First Report from the Select Committee of the Honourable House of Commons, Appointed to Take into Consideration the means of Promoting the Cultivation and Improvement of the Waste, Undisclosed and Unproductive lands of the Kingdom. London: 1796. V. 51

GREAT BRITAIN. PARLIAMENT. HOUSE OF COMMONS - 1810
First (and Second) Report from the Committee on Holyhead Roads and Harbour. London: 1810. V. 54

Report, Together with Minutes of Evidence and Accounts from the Select Committee on the High Price of Gold Bullion. London: 1810. V. 53; 54

GREAT BRITAIN. PARLIAMENT. HOUSE OF COMMONS - 1817
Report from the Committee of the Honourable House of Commons on the Employment of Boys in Sweeping of Chimneys Together With the Minutes of the Evidence Taken Before the Committe and an Appendix. London: 1817. V. 47

GREAT BRITAIN. PARLIAMENT. HOUSE OF COMMONS - 1819
Report from the Select Committee on the Highways of the Kingom, Together with the Minutes of Evidence Taken Before Them. London: 1819. V. 54

GREAT BRITAIN. PARLIAMENT. HOUSE OF COMMONS - 1821
Report from the Committee on the State of London Bridge. (with) Minutes taken Before the Select Committee, Appointed in Session 1820, to Inquire Into the State of London Bridge; and to Consider if Any, and What, Alterations or Improvements are... London: 1821. V. 51

Report from the Select Committee on the Existing Regulations Relative to the Making and Sale of Bread. London: 1821. V. 51

GREAT BRITAIN. PARLIAMENT. HOUSE OF COMMONS - 1823
Report from Select Committee on Mr. McAdam's Petition, Relating to His Improved System of Constructing and Repairing the Public Roads of the Kingdom. London: 1823. V. 51

GREAT BRITAIN. PARLIAMENT. HOUSE OF COMMONS - 1825
Report from the Select Committee on Metropolis Turnpike Trusts (Appointed to Inquire into the Receipts, Expenditure and Management of the Several Turnpike Trusts within Ten Miles of London). London: 1825. V. 51; 54

GREAT BRITAIN. PARLIAMENT. HOUSE OF COMMONS - 1828
Report from the Select Committe on the Supply of Water to the Metropolis. London: 1828. V. 51

GREAT BRITAIN. PARLIAMENT. HOUSE OF COMMONS - 1832
Report On Steam Carriages. By a Select Comittee of the House of Comons of Great Britain. Washington: 1832. V. 48

GREAT BRITAIN. PARLIAMENT. HOUSE OF COMMONS - 1836
Report(s) from the Secret Committee on Joint Stock Banks, together with the Minutes of Evidence and Appendix. London: 1836/15 July. V. 48; 53

Third Report from the Select Committee (of the Commons) Appointed to Inquire Into the State of Agriculture; with the Minutes of Evidence, Appendix and Index. London: 1836. V. 48; 50; 52

GREAT BRITAIN. PARLIAMENT. HOUSE OF COMMONS - 1839
Report from the Select Committee on the Caledonian and Crinian Canals together with the Minutes of Evidence and Appendix. London: 1839. V. 51

GREAT BRITAIN. PARLIAMENT. HOUSE OF COMMONS - 1846
Report from the Select Committee on Metropolitan Sewage Manure. London: 1846. V. 53

GREAT BRITAIN. PARLIAMENT. HOUSE OF COMMONS - 1851
Report from the Select Committee on the Kafir Tribes; Together with the Proceedings of the Committee, Minutes of Evidence... London: 1851. V. 49

GREAT BRITAIN. PARLIAMENT. HOUSE OF COMMONS - 1854
Report from the Select Committee on Poor Removal; Together with the Proceedings of the Committee, Minutes of Evidence, Appendix and Index. London: 1854. V. 51

GREAT BRITAIN. PARLIAMENT. HOUSE OF COMMONS - 1855
Report from the Select Committee on Metropolitan Communications; Together with the Proceedings of the Committee, Minutes of Evidence and Appendix. London: 1855. V. 52

GREAT BRITAIN. PARLIAMENT. HOUSE OF COMMONS - 1857
Report from the Select Committee on Banks of Issue; Together with the Proceedings of the Committee, Minutes of Evidence and Appendix. London: 1875. V. 53

GREAT BRITAIN. PARLIAMENT. HOUSE OF COMMONS - 1887
Verbatim Report of the Proceedings Before the Select Committe on Railway Bills (Group 4) in the House of Commons March, 1887. Ambleside: 1887. V. 50

GREAT BRITAIN. PARLIAMENT. HOUSE OF LORDS - 1695
The Humble Address of the Right Honourable the Lords Spiritual and Temporal in Parliament Assembled, Presented to His Majesty on the Sixteenth of Dec. 1695. London: 1695. V. 53

GREAT BRITAIN. PARLIAMENT. HOUSE OF LORDS - 1703
An Account of the Proceedings of the Lords...In Relation to the Bill, Intitutled, An Act for Preventing Occasional Conformity. London: 1703. V. 53

GREAT BRITAIN. PARLIAMENT. HOUSE OF LORDS - 1820
Select Committee Appointed...Foreign Trade of the Country. London: 1820-24. V. 53

GREAT BRITAIN. PARLIAMENT. HOUSE OF LORDS - 1828
Report from the Select Committe of the House of Lords, Appointed to Take into Consideration the State of the British Wool Trade, and to Report to the House... London: 1828. V. 49

GREAT BRITAIN. PARLIAMENT. HOUSE OF LORDS - 1835
Reports from the Select Committee of the House of Lords Appointed to Inquire Into the Present State of the Several Gaols and Houses of Correction in England and Wales.... London: 1835. V. 51

GREAT BRITAIN. PARLIAMENT. HOUSE OF LORDS - 1854
Report from the Select Committee of the House of Lords Appointed to Inquire Into the Possibily of Improving the Ventilation and the Lighting of the House, and the Contiguous Chambers, Galleries and Passages... London: 1854. V. 53

Report From the Select Committee of the House of Lords, Appointed to Inquire Into the Practical Working of All the System of National Education in Ireland... London: 1854. V. 50

GREAT BRITAIN. PARLIAMENT. HOUSE OF LORDS - 1857
Copies of or Extracts from Any Papers Connected with the Confinement of Chinese Prisoners at Hong Kong, and with the Trial of a Baker and Others on the Charge of Poisoning. London: 1857. V. 47

Papers Relating to the Colony of Hong Kong, &c. Comprising Report on Hong Kong; Report on Chusan; and Minute on the British Position and Prospects in China... London: 1857. V. 47; 49

Papers Relating to the Opium Trade in China. 1842-1856. London: 1857. V. 47

GREAT BRITAIN. PRIVY COUNCIL - 1870
Copy of Order in Council. Friday, June 24th 1870. London: 1870?. V. 50

GREAT BRITAIN. PRIVY COUNCIL - 1926
Forts and Trading Posts in Labrador Peninsula and Adjoining Territory. Ottawa: 1926. V. 50

GREAT BRITAIN. ROYAL COMM. FOR METROPOLITAN IMPROVEMENTS
First Report of the Commissioners Appointed by Her Majesty to Inquire Into and consider the Most Effectual Means of Improving the Metropolis, and of Provided Increased Facilities of Communication Within the Same. London: 1844. V. 52

GREAT BRITAIN. ROYAL COMMISSION ON ANCIENT & HISTORICAL
MONUMENTS - 1972 Inventory of the Historical Monuments in the City of York. Volume III. South-West of the Ouse. London: 1972. V. 53

GREAT BRITAIN. ROYAL COMMISSION ON CANALS & WATERWAYS
Reports...on the Canals and Inland Navigations of the United Kingdom. London: 1906-11. V. 53

GREAT BRITAIN. ROYAL COMMISSION ON COAST EROSION - 1907
First (Second, Third) Report on Certain Questions Affecting Coast Erosion, the Reclamation of Tidal Lands and Afforestation in the United Kingdom. London: 1907-11. V. 53

GREAT BRITAIN. ROYAL COMMISSION ON HISTORICAL MONUMENTS
An Inventory of the Historical Monuments in Buckinghamshire. London: 1912-13. V. 51
An Inventory of the Historical Monuments in Essex. London: 1916-23. V. 51
An Inventory of the Historical Monuments in London. London: 1924-30. V. 54
An Inventory of the Historical Monuments in the City of Cambridge. London: 1959. V. 50
An Inventory of the Historical Monuments in Westmorland. London: 1936. V. 50; 51

GREAT BRITAIN. SOVEREIGNS, ETC. - 1599
Injunctions Given by the Queenes Maiestie. London: 1599. V. 49

GREAT BRITAIN. SOVEREIGNS, ETC. - 1639
A Large Declaration Concerning the Late Tumults in Scotland, from their First Originals. London: 1639. V. 53

GREAT BRITAIN. SOVEREIGNS, ETC. - 1640
His Majesties Declaration, Concerning His proceedings with His Subjects of Scotland, Since the Pacification in the Camp Neere Berwick. London: 1640. V. 49

GREAT BRITAIN. SOVEREIGNS, ETC. - 1642
His Majesties Declaration to All His Loving Subjects of His True Intentions in Advancing Lately to Brainceford. Oxford: 1642. V. 53
His Majesties Instructions to His Commissioners of Array, for the Several Counties of England, and the Principality of Wales and to be Observed by All Sheriffs, Maiors, Justices of the Peace, Bayliffs, Head-boroughs, Constables... London: 1642. V. 52
His Majesties Proclamation and Declaration to All His Loving Subjects, Occasioned by a False and Scandalous Impuration...of Raising or Leavying War Against His Parliament. Oxford: 1642. V. 51

GREAT BRITAIN. SOVEREIGNS, ETC. - 1648
The Declaration of His Highnesse Prince Charles, to all His Majesties Loving Subjects, Concerning the Grounds and Ends of His Present Engagement Upon the Fleet in the Downes. London: 1648. V. 53

GREAT BRITAIN. SOVEREIGNS, ETC. - 1660
A Proclamation for the Suppressing of Disorderly and Unseasonable Meetings, in Taverns and Tipling-Houses and Also Forbidding Footmen to Wear Swords, or Other Weapons, Within London... London: 1660. V. 50

GREAT BRITAIN. SOVEREIGNS, ETC. - 1674
By the King. A Proclamation to Restrain the Spreading of False News and Licentious talking of Matters of State and Government. London: 1674. V. 47

GREAT BRITAIN. SOVEREIGNS, ETC. - 1685
The Royal Charter of Confirmation Granted by His Most Excellent Majesty King James II to the Trinity-House of Deptford-Strond; for the Government and Encrease of the Navigataion of Engalnd, and the Relief of Poor Mariners, Their Widdows and Orphans etc. London: 1685. V. 49

GREAT BRITAIN. SOVEREIGNS, ETC. - 1688
By the King, a Proclamation to Restrain the Spreading of False News...Given at Our Court at Whitehall the 26th Day of October, 1688. London: 1688. V. 47

GREAT BRITAIN. TREATIES, ETC. - 1667
Articles of Peace and Alliance, Between...Charles II...and...The States General of the United Netherlands, Concluded the 21/31 day of July, 1667. London: 1667. V. 53
Articles of Peace, Commerce & Alliance Between the Crowns of Great Britain and Spain. London: 1667. V. 47
Articuli Pacis, Inter...Carolvm...Secundum Magnae Britanniae Regem...& Celsos...Dominos Ordines Generales Foederatarum Belgii Provinciarium. (with) Articuli Pacis, Inter...Carolum..Secundum...& Celsos...Dominos Ordines Generales Foederati Belgii ... The Hague: 1667-74. V. 50

GREAT BRITAIN. TREATIES ETC. - 1679
A Collection of All the Acts, Memorials and letters, That Pass'd in the negotiation of the Peace; With the Treaties Concluded at Nimegven. London: 1679. V. 48

GREAT BRITAIN. TREATIES, ETC. - 1686
Treaty of Peace, Good Correspondence and Neutrality in America, Between the Most Serene and Mighty Prince James II. By the Grace of God. King of Great Britain, France and Ireland, Defender of the Faith... London: 1686. V. 48

GREAT BRITAIN. TREATIES, ETC. - 1739
The Convention Between the Crowns of Great Britain and Spain, Concluded at the Pardo on the 14th of January 1739. London: 1739. V. 48

GREAT BRITAIN. TREATIES, ETC. - 1762
Preliminary Articles of Peace, Between His Brittanick Majesty, the Most Christian King, and the Catholick King. London: 1762. V. 47

GREAT BRITAIN. TREATIES, ETC. - 1783
Authentic Copies of the Provisional and Preliminary Articles of Peace Signed Between Great Britain, France, Spain and the United States of America. London: 1783. V. 53
The Definitive Treaty Between Great Britain and the United States of America, Signed at Paris, the 3rd Day of September 1783. Paris: 1783. V. 47

GREAT BRITAIN. TREATIES, ETC. - 1792
Extracts from the Treaties Between Great Britain and Other Kingdoms and States of Such Articles as Relate to the Duty and Conduct of the Commanders of His Majesty's Ships of War. London: 1792. V. 47

GREAT BRITAIN. TREATIES, ETC. - 1795
Treaty of Amity, Commerce and Naigation, Between His Britannic Majesty and the United States of America, by Their President...Ratified...June 24, 1795. Philadelphia: 1795. V. 53

GREAT BRITAIN. TREATIES, ETC. - 1810
Treaty of Amity, Commerce, and Navigation, Between His Britannic Majesty and His Royal Higness the Prince Regent of Portugal; signed at Rio de Janeiro, the 19th of Feb. 1810. London: 1810. V. 48

GREAT BRITAIN. TREATIES, ETC. - 1919
The Treaty of Peace Between the Allied and Associated Powers and Germany, the Protocol Annexed Thereto, The Agreement Respecting the Military Occupation of the Territories of the Rhine, and the Treaty Between France and Great Britain Respecting Assistance... London: 1919. V. 50

GREAT BRITAIN. UNIVERSITIES COMMISSION - 1874
Report of the Commissioners Appointed to Inquire Into the Property and Income of the Universities of Oxford and Cambridge and of the Colleges and Halls Therein. London: 1874. V. 51

GREAT BRITAIN. WAR DEPARTMENT - 1858
Schedule(s) of Contract for (Artisan's) Work for the Service of the War Department, at ---- in the South-west and Sussex District. London: 1858. V. 47

GREAT BRITAIN. WAR OFFICE - 1912
Memorandum on Naval and Military Aviation. London: 1912. V. 53

GREAT Britain's Memorial (With: The Second Part)... London: 1741-42. V. 48

THE GREAT Encyclopaedia of Paeonies and Tree Paeonies. Tokyo: 1990. V. 50

GREAT Georgian Houses of America. New York: 1933/37. V. 48

THE GREAT Metropolis; or Guide to New York for 1846. New York: 1845. V. 53

THE GREAT Mysteries Now Revealed for the First Time. How to Escape from Handcuffs, Iron Boiler, Mail bag... Boston: 1909. V. 47

A GREAT National Exhibition of the Religious, Regal and Civic Solemnities, Public Amusements, Scientific Meetings and Commercial Scenes of the British Capital. London: 1841-44. V. 50

THE GREAT Northwest a Guide-Book and Itinerary for the Use of Tourist and Travelers Over the Lines of the Northern Pacific Railroad... St. Paul: 1889. V. 47

GREAT Ones of Ancient Egypt. New York: 1930. V. 53

THE GREAT Polyglot Bibles: Including a Leaf from the First: The Complutensian of Acala, 1514-17. San Francisco: 1976. V. 51

THE GREAT Register of Los Angeles County, State of California. Los Angeles: 1886. V. 54

GREAT Rivers of the World. London: 1984. V. 53

GREAT SOUTHERN RAILWAY
A Trunk Line, Between the North and the Tropics. New York: 1878. V. 47

THE GREAT Streets of the World. New York: 1892. V. 54

GREAT Toronto Illustrated. Toronto: 1909. V. 52

GREAT WESTERN TYPE FOUNDRY
Barnhart's Big Blue Book Containing specimens of Superior Copper-Mixed Type, Borders, Ornaments, Rule, Etc.... Chicago: 1890's. V. 50

THE GREATEST Burglary On Record. Robbery of the Northampton National Bank. Northampton: 1876. V. 54

THE GREATEST Plague in Life, or the Adventures of a Lady in Search of a Good Servant. London: 1847. V. 50; 54

GREATREX, CHARLES BUTLER
Whittlings from the West; With Some Account of Butternut Castle. Edinburgh: 1854. V. 49

GREAVES, EDWIN
Kashi, the City Illustrious, or, Benares. 1909. V. 50
Kashi, the City Illustrious, or Benares. Allahabad: 1909. V. 52

GREBAN, ARNOUL
Mystere des Actes des Apostres. Paris: 1541. V. 48

THE GRECIAN Astrologer, or the Calendar of Destiny. London: 1831. V. 53

GRECOURT, JEAN BAPTISTE JOSEPH
Oeuvres Completes. Paris: 1796. V. 52; 54

THE GREEK Portrait. London: 1934. V. 47; 51; 53; 54

THE GREEKS: A Poem... London: 1817. V. 49

THE GREEKS: Being the Jeremiad of an Exiled Greek; A Poem "Venu de France d'une Maniere Inconnue;" and dedicated to all the Legs!... London: 1817. V. 49

GREELEY, HORACE
Mr. Greeley's Letters from Texas and the Lower Mississippi... New York: 1871. V. 54

GREELEY, HORACE continued
An Overland Journey, From New York to San Francisco, in the Summer of 1859. New York: 1860. V. 47

GREELMANN, HEINRICH MORITZ GOTTLIEB
Dissertation on the Gipsies, Being an Historical Enquiry, Concerning the Manner of Life, Oeconomy, Customs and Conditions of These People in Europe, and Their Origin. London: 1787. V. 53

GREELY, ADOLPHUS W.
The Greeley Arctic Expedition as Fully Narrated by Lieut. A. W. Greeley, U.S.A. and Other Survivors. Philadelphia: 1884. V. 50
Reminiscences of Adventure and Service. A Record of Sixty-Five Years. New York, London: 1927. V. 49
Report on the Proceedings of the United States Expedition to Lady Franklin Bay, Grinnell Land. Washington: 1888. V. 49
Three Years of Arctic Service. London: 1886. V. 49
Three Years of Arctic Service. New York: 1886. V. 47; 49; 51

GREEN, ANNA KATHARINE
The Amethyst Box. Indianapolis: 1905. V. 51
The Circular Study. New York: 1900. V. 47; 49
The Filigree Ball. Indianapolis: 1903. V. 47
Hand and Ring. New York: 1883. V. 47; 48
Marked "Personal". New York: 1893. V. 47
The Woman in the Alcove. Indianapolis: 1906. V. 47

GREEN, BEN K.
Back to Back. Austin: 1970. V. 52; 53
Ben Green Tales. Flagstaff: 1974. V. 51; 52; 53
Ben K. Green Back to Back. Texas Cow Horses and the Vermont Maid; Mr. Undertaker and the Cleveland Bay Horse. Austin: 1970. V. 53
Biography of the Tennessee Walking Horse. Nashville: 1960. V. 54
Horse Conformation as to Soundness. 1963. V. 48
Horse Conformation as to Soundness. Greenville: 1969. V. 48
The Last Trail Drive through Downtown Dallas. Flagstaff: 1971. V. 53
The Shield Mares. Austin: 1967. V. 48; 54
A Thousand Miles of Mustangin'. Flagstaff: 1972. V. 47; 48; 52; 53
The Village Horse Doctor: West of the Pecos. New York: 1971. V. 54
Wild Cow Tales. New York: 1969. V. 51; 52

GREEN, BERIAH
Four Sermons Preached in the Chapel of the Western Reserve College. Cleveland: 1833. V. 54

GREEN, CALVIN
A Summary View of the Millenial Church, or United Society of Believers (Commonly Called Shakers). Albany: 1823. V. 47; 50

GREEN, CHARLES E.
Encyclopaedia of Agriculture. Edinburgh and London: 1908-09. V. 54

GREEN, CHARLES RANSLEY
A Historical Pamphlet. Wakeman Ohio. Lives of the Volunteers in the Civil War. The 'Minor' Family as Pioneers in Wakeman. Olathe: 1914. V. 50; 54

GREEN, D.
Gardener to Queen Anne. Henry Wise (1653-1738). London: 1956. V. 54

GREEN, D. M.
Amphibian Cytogenetics and Evolution. New York: 1991. V. 52

GREEN, DAVID
Blenheim Palace. London: 1951. V. 49
Grinling Gibbons, His Work as Carver and Statuary 1648-1721. London: 1964. V. 53

GREEN, DUFF
Facts and Suggestions Relative to Finance and Currency Addressed to the President of the Confederate States. Augusta: 1864. V. 49

GREEN, E. R. R.
The Industrial Archaeology of County Down. 1963. V. 54

GREEN, FLORIDA
Some Personal Recollections of Lillie Hitchcock Coit - 5. San Francisco: 1935. V. 47; 48; 54

GREEN, FRANCES H.
Biography of Mrs. Semantha Mettle, the Clairvoyant; Being a History of Spiritual Development and Containing an Account of the Wonderful Cures Performed through Her Agency. New York: 1853. V. 53

GREEN, G.
In the Royal Irish Constabulary. 1903. V. 50

GREEN, G. G., CO.
Home of August Flower and German Syrup. Woodbury: 1889. V. 53

GREEN, GEORGE
Mathematical Papers of the Late George Green... Cambridge: 1871. V. 48

GREEN, HANNAH
I Never Promised You a Rose Garden. New York: 1964. V. 49

GREEN, HARRY CLINTON
The Pioneer Mothers of America, a Record of the More Notable Women of the Early Days of the country, and Particularly of the Colonial and Revolutionary Periods. New York: 1912. V. 51

GREEN, HENRY
Back. London: 1946. V. 48; 49; 51; 53
Blindness. London: 1926. V. 49
Caught. London: 1943. V. 53
Concluding. London: 1948. V. 48; 49; 52
Doting. London: 1952. V. 48; 53
The Four Fountains of the Emblems of Alciat. London: 1870. V. 54
Living. New York: 1929. V. 49; 52
Loving. London: 1945. V. 53
Nothing. London: 1950. V. 47; 48; 52; 53
Pack My Bag: a Self Portrait. London: 1940. V. 51; 53
Party Going. London: 1939. V. 48; 53
Shakespeare and the Emblem Writers: an Exposition of their Similarities of Thought and Expression. London: 1870. V. 54
The Wooden Walls of Old England. Portsmouth: 1773. V. 49

GREEN, HORACE
Report On the Use and Effect of Applications of Nitrate of Silver to the Throat, Either in Local or General Disease. New York: 1856. V. 50
A Treatise on the Diseases of the Air Passages... New York: 1858. V. 48

GREEN, J.
Poetical Sketches of Scarborough. London: 1813. V. 48

GREEN, J. R.
History of the English People. London: 1890. V. 49
A Short History of the English People. London: 1874. V. 48
A Short History of the English People. London: 1892-94. V. 53
A Short History of the English People. London: 1898. V. 54

GREEN, JACOB
Advantages of Chemistry; or, an Introductory Address, Delivered in the Chemical Theatre of Jefferson Medical College, at the Opening of the Session of 1834-35. Philadelphia: 1834. V. 50
An Epitome of Electricity and Galvanism, by Two Gentlemen of Philadelphia. Philadelphia: 1809. V. 50; 53
A Small Help, Offered to Heads of Families, for Instructing Children and Servants. Morris-Town: 1814. V. 51

GREEN, JAMES K.
Grand Prairie. Dallas: 1935. V. 53

GREEN, JOHN
Casper Hauser, or the Power of External Cirumstances Exhibited in Forming the Human Character, with Remarks. Manchester: 1840?. V. 53
Considerations on the Expediency of Making and the Manner of Conducting the Late Regulations at Cambridge. London: 1751. V. 48
A New General Collection of Voyages and Travels: Consisting of the Most Esteemed Relations...in Its Kind in Europe, Asia, Africa, America. London: 1745. V. 47
The Priviledges of the Lord Mayor and Alderman of the City. The Advantages of the Freeman Thereof...The Usage of the Mayors Court, the Orphans Court, and all the Other Courts. London: 1722. V. 50

GREEN, JOHN PUGH
The Tour of the "Gentlemen of Philadelphia" in Great Britain in 1884. Philadelphia: 1897. V. 47

GREEN, JOHN RICHARDS
A Narrative of the Transactions Personally Relating to the Unfortunate Lewis the Sixteenth, King of France and Navarre... London: 1795. V. 49

GREEN, JONATHAN
Camera Work: A Critical Anthology. Millerton: 1973. V. 47

GREEN, JULIAN
Christine and other Stories. London: 1931. V. 50
The Dreamer. London: 1934. V. 50
The Pilgrim on the Earth. London: 1929. V. 47; 48; 49; 50; 53
The Pilgrim On the Earth. New York: 1929. V. 50

GREEN, MATTHEW
The Spleen. London: 1738. V. 47; 53
The Spleen, and Other Poems. London: 1796. V. 50

GREEN, N. E.
Practical Lessons in Watercolour Painting...in Six Parts... London: 1865. V. 54

GREEN, PAUL
In Abraham's Bosom. London: 1929. V. 51
Johnny Johnson. New York: 1937. V. 49
Lonesome Road. Six Plays for the Negro Theatre. New York: 1926. V. 54
The Lord's Will and Other Carolina Plays. New York: 1925. V. 51
The Lost Colony. Chapel Hill: 1937. V. 47

GREEN, PHILIP JAMES
Sketches of the War in Greece... London: 1828. V. 49

GREEN, R.
Illustrations of Perspective, Being a Popular Explantion of the Science and its Application to Design Generally. London: 1840. V. 49

GREEN, RALPH
The Iron Hand Press in America. Rowayton: 1948. V. 48

GREEN, RENA MAVERICK
Samuel Maverick Texan: 1803-1870 - A Collection of Letters, Jounrals, Memoirs. 1952. V. 51

GREEN, RICHARD
The Works of John and Charles Welsey. A Bibliography... London: 1896. V. 48; 49; 52; 53

GREEN, ROBERT M.
History of the Hundred and Twenty-Fourth Regiment Pennsylvania Volunteers in the War of the Rebellion 1862-63. Philadelphia: 1907. V. 49

GREEN, ROGER
Max Papart. New York: 1984. V. 48

GREEN, SAMUEL G.
French Pictures Drawn with Pen and Pencil. London. V. 54

GREEN, SARAH
Mental Improvement for a Young Lady, on Her Entrance Into the World. London: 1793. V. 49

GREEN, STANLEY
Starring Fred Astaire. New York: 1973. V. 52

GREEN, THOMAS
The Case of Capt. Tho. Green, Commander of the Ship Worcester and His Crew, Tried and Condemned for Pyracy & Murther, in the High Court of Admiralty of Scotland. London: 1705. V. 52
Extracts from the Diary of a Lover of Literature. Ipswich: 1810. V. 47; 50; 51
Some Cursory Remarks on a Late Printed Paper, Called, the Last Speeches and Dying Words of Capt. Thomas Green, Commander of the Ship Worcester; and of Capt. John Madder, Chief Mate of the Said Ship &c... Edinburgh: 1705. V. 52
The Universal Herbal; or, Botanical, Medical and Agricultural Dictionary. London: 1824. V. 48; 49

GREEN, THOMAS HILL
Works. London: 1885. V. 48

GREEN, THOMAS J.
Reply of Gen. Thomas J. Green, to the Speech of General Sam Houston, in the Senate of the United States, August 1, 1854. Washington: 1855. V. 52

GREEN, THOMAS MARSHALL
Historic Families of Kentucky. Cincinnati: 1889. V. 51

GREEN, WILLIAM
A Description of a Series of Sixty Small Prints, Etched by... 1814. V. 52
Portraits of the Late and Present Administration, Faithfully Drawn from the Criterion of Their Abilities, Their Integrity and Their Confidence with the Nation. London: 1807. V. 50
The Tourist's New Guide, Containing a Description of the Lakes, Mountains and Scenery, in Cumberland, Westmorland and Lancashire... Kendal: 1819. V. 50; 52

GREEN, WILLIAM SPOTSWOOD
Among the Selkirk Glaciers, Being the Account of a Rough Survey in the Rocky Mountain Regions of British Columbia. London: 1890. V. 47

GREENAN, EDITH
Of Una Jeffers. Los Angeles: 1939. V. 54

GREENAWAY, KATE
Almanack and Diary for 1897. London: 1896. V. 54
Almanack and Diary for 1929. London: 1929. V. 48
Almanack for 1883. London: 1882. V. 47; 53
Almanack for 1883. London: 1883. V. 48; 49
Almanack for 1884. London. V. 48; 51
Almanack for 1884. London: 1883. V. 47; 48; 54
Almanack for 1884. London: 1884. V. 49; 50
Almanack for 1885. London: V. 47; 48
Almanack for 1885. London: 1884. V. 52; 54
Almanack for 1885. London: 1885. V. 48
Almanack for 1886. London. V. 47; 48
Almanack for 1886. London: 1885. V. 47; 54
Almanack for 1887. London: V. 48; 52
Almanack for 1887. London: 1886. V. 47; 54
Almanack for 1888. London. V. 48
Almanack for 1888. London: 1887. V. 54
Almanack for 1889. London. V. 48
Almanack for 1889. London: 1888. V. 47
Almanack for 1890. London. V. 52
Almanack for 1890. London: 1889. V. 47
Almanack for 1891. London. V. 48
Almanack for 1892. London. V. 48
Almanack for 1893. London. V. 48
Almanack for 1894. London. V. 47; 48; 52; 53
Almanack for 1894. London: 1893. V. 47; 54
Almanack for 1895. London. V. 48
Almanack for 1895. London: 1894. V. 54
Almanack for 1924. London: 1924. V. 47; 48; 54
Almanack for 1925. London: 1925. V. 48; 50
Almanack for 1926. London: 1926. V. 48; 54
Almanack for 1927. London: 1927. V. 48
Almanacks 1883-1895. London: 1883-95. V. 50
Apple Pie. London: 1886. V. 51; 53
Birthday Book. London: 1880. V. 49
Calendar of the Seasons: 1882. London. V. 47
Dame Wiggins of Lee and Her Seven Wonderful Cats. London: 1885. V. 53
A Day in a Child's Life. London: 1881. V. 47; 51; 52
Flowers and Fancies. London: 1883. V. 49
Kate Greenaway Pictures from Originals Presented by Her to John Ruskin and Other Personal Friends... London: 1921. V. 48; 50; 51
Kate Greenaway's Almanack 1884. London: 1884. V. 48; 49; 50; 51
Kate Greenaway's Almanack for 1891. London: 1890. V. 47
Kate Greenaway's Alphabet. London & New York. V. 50
Kate Greenaway's Alphabet. London: 1885. V. 49; 51; 54
Kate Greenaway's Birthday Book for Children. London: 1880. V. 48; 51; 54
Kate Greenaway's Book of Games. London: 1889. V. 51
Kate Greenaway's Pictures. London: 1921. V. 53
The Language of Flowers. London: 1880. V. 53
Language of Flowers. London: 1884. V. 50; 51
The Little Folks Painting Book. London: 1879. V. 49; 52
Marigold Garden. London: 1885. V. 47; 51; 54
Marigold Garden. London: 1910. V. 51
The Quiver of Love. London: 1876. V. 51
Sixteen Examples in Colour of the Artist's Work. London: 1910. V. 50
Under the Window. London. V. 48
Under the Window. London: 1878. V. 51
Under the Window. New York: 1878-80. V. 53
Under the Window. London: 1879. V. 51; 52

GREENBAUM & LEVI
Catalogue of the Excelsior Jewelry, the Very Best Medium and Low Priced Jewelry Manufactured. New York: 1884. V. 47

GREENBERG, CLEMENT
Joan Miro. New York: 1948. V. 50
Mid-Century Modern: Furniture of the 1950's. New York. V. 54

GREENBURG, DAN W.
Sixty Years. A Brief Review. The Cattle Industry in Wyoming, its Organization and Present Status and Data Concerning the Wyoming Stock Grower's Association. Cheyenne: 1932. V. 53

GREENE, A. C.
The Last Captive. The Lives of Herman Lehmann, Who Was Taken by the Indians as a Boy From His Texas Home and Adopted by Them... Austin: 1972. V. 48; 49

GREENE, ALBERT
Recollections of the Jersey Prison-Ship. Providence: 1829. V. 51

GREENE, ASA
Travels in America. New York: 1833. V. 47; 53

GREENE, CHARLES W.
A Sketch of Kingston and Its Surroundings. Kingston: 1883. V. 49

GREENE, E. L.
Landmarks of Botanical History. Washington: 1909. V. 53
Landmarks of Botanical History. Stanford: 1983. V. 48; 52; 53

GREENE, EDWARD BURNABY
Corsica, an Ode. London: 1768. V. 54

GREENE, FRANCIS VINTON
General Greene. New York: 1893. V. 47

GREENE, GRAHAM
L'Agent Secret. (Confidential Agent). Paris: 1948. V. 47; 48; 49
Babbling April. Oxford: 1925. V. 53
The Basement Room and Other Stories. London: 1935. V. 47; 49; 51; 53; 54
The Bear Fell Free. London: 1935. V. 48; 51; 53; 54
Brighton Rock. London: 1938. V. 48; 53
Brighton Rock. New York: 1938. V. 47; 49; 51; 53
A Burnt Out Case. London: 1961. V. 48; 49; 50; 53
Carving a Statue. London: 1964. V. 50
Collected Essays. London: 1969. V. 47; 50
Collected Stories. London: 1972. V. 51
The Comedians. London: 1966. V. 48; 49; 50; 53; 54
The Comedians. New York: 1966. V. 47; 52
The Complaisant Lover. London: 1959. V. 48; 49; 51; 53
The Complaisant Lover. London: 1971. V. 53
The Confidential Agent. London: 1939. V. 51
Dear David, Dear Graham, a Bibliographic Correspondence. Oxford: 1989. V. 48; 50
Doctor Fischer of Geneva or the Bomb Party. New York: 1962. V. 51
Doctor Fischer of Geneva or the Bomb Party. London: 1980. V. 50; 52
Doctor Fischer of Geneva or the Bomb Party. New York: 1980. V. 47; 48; 49; 51; 52; 53
The End of the Affair. London: 1951. V. 49; 50; 51; 53; 54
England Made Me. London: 1935. V. 50
The Great Jowett. London: 1981. V. 47; 48; 51; 53; 54
A Gun for Sale. Melbourne: 1944. V. 51
L'Homme et Lui-Meme. Paris: 1931. V. 49
The Honorary Consul. New York: 1973. V. 48; 51
The Honorary Counsul. London: 1974. V. 53
How Father Quixote Became a Monsignor. Los Angeles: 1980. V. 47; 48; 51; 53
The Human Factor. Pennsylvania: 1978. V. 47
In Search of a Character. New York: 1962. V. 47; 48; 50; 51
It's a Battlefield. Garden City: 1934. V. 49
It's a Battlefield. London: 1934. V. 50; 51; 52; 54
J'Accuse: the Dark Side of Nice. London: 1982. V. 51
Journey Without Maps. Garden City: 1936. V. 50
Journey Without Maps. London: 1936. V. 51; 54

GREENE, GRAHAM continued
Journey Without Maps. New York: 1936. V. 51
The Labyrinthine Ways. New York: 1940. V. 47; 50
The Lawless Roads. London: 1939. V. 47; 49
The Little Fire Engine. London: 1950. V. 49; 53
The Little Horse Bus. London: 1952. V. 48; 52; 53; 54
The Little Horse Bus; The Little Fire Engine; The Little Train; and The Little Steamroller. London: 1973-74. V. 52
The Little Train. London: 1957. V. 50
The Little Train. The Little Fire Engine. The Little Steamroller. The Little Horse Bus. London: 1973-74. V. 47
The Living Room. London: 1953. V. 48; 51; 52
Loser Takes All. London: 1955. V. 51; 53
The Lost Childhood. London: 1951. V. 48; 49; 50; 51; 53
The Man Within. Garden City: 1929. V. 50; 51
The Man Within. London: 1929. V. 47; 48; 50; 53; 54
The Man Within. New York: 1929. V. 51
May We Borrow Your Husband?. London: 1967. V. 47; 49; 50; 52; 54
May We Borrow Your Husband?. 1981. V. 51
Mr. Visconti. London: 1969. V. 50
Monsignor Quixote. London: 1982. V. 50
Monsignor Quixote. New York: 1982. V. 50; 51; 52; 54
Monsignor Quixote. Toronto: 1982. V. 50
The Monster of Capri. Helsinki: 1985. V. 48; 53
The Name of Action. London: 1930. V. 50; 51
The Name of Action. New York: 1931. V. 47
Nineteen Stories. London: 1947. V. 48; 50; 54
The Old School. Essays by Divers Hands. London: 1934. V. 50
Our Man in Havana. London: 1958. V. 47; 48; 49; 51; 53
Our Man in Havana. New York: 1958. V. 51
The Potting Shed - a Play in Three Acts. London: 1958. V. 50
The Power and the Glory. London: 1940. V. 49; 50; 51; 52; 54
A Quick Look Behind. Los Angeles: 1982. V. 51
A Quick Look Behind. Los Angeles: 1983. V. 47; 48; 53
The Quiet American. London: 1955. V. 49; 51; 52; 53
Reflections on Travels with My Aunt. New York: 1989. V. 47; 48; 49; 50; 51; 52; 53; 54
The Return of A. J. Raffles. London: 1975. V. 50
The Revenge. London: 1963. V. 50; 54
Rumour at Nightfall. London: 1931. V. 50; 51
A Sense of Reality. London: 1963. V. 47; 48; 50
Shakespeare-Preise 1968 und 1969. Hamburg: 1969. V. 50
The Spy's Bedside Book. London: 1957. V. 50
Stamboul Train. London: 1932. V. 48; 49; 50
Stamboul Train. Sydney: 1944. V. 51
The Tenth Man. London: 1985. V. 47
The Third Man. New York: 1950. V. 47; 53
The Third Man. Helsinki: 1988. V. 48; 49; 50; 53
The Third Man and The Fallen Idol. London: 1950. V. 47; 51; 52; 53
This Gun for Hire. Garden City: 1936. V. 52
To Beg I Am Ashamed. New York: 1938. V. 48
Travels with My Aunt. London: 1969. V. 50
Travels With My Aunt. London: 1972. V. 53
The Virtue of Disloyalty. London: 1972. V. 49; 50; 51
A Visit to Morin. London: 1959. V. 47; 49; 50; 51; 52
A Visit to Morin. London: 1960. V. 48
Ways of Escape. 1980. V. 53
A Wedding Among the Owls. London: 1977. V. 49; 50; 53
A Weed Among the Flowers. Los Angeles: 1990. V. 47; 48; 51
Why the Epigraph?. London: 1989. V. 49; 54
Yes and No. Helsinki: 1983. V. 47; 49; 50
Yes and No. Helsinki: 1984. V. 48; 53
Yes and No and For Whom the Bell Chimes. London: 1983. V. 47; 48; 50; 51; 53

GREENE, HARVEY B.
Wild Flowers from Palestine. Lowell: 1895. V. 47

GREENE, HERBERT
Secret Agent in Spain. London: 1938. V. 49

GREENE, HON. MRS.
The Grey House on the Hill. London. V. 47
The Grey House on the Hill. London: 1903. V. 48

GREENE, MAX
The Kansas Region; Incidents of Travel on the Western Plains and in the Rocky Mountains... New York: 1856. V. 47; 49

GREENE, RICHARD WILSON
A Report of the Trial of James Forbes, William Graham, George Graham, Mathew Handwich, Henry Handwich and William Brownlow, for a Conspiracy to Create a Riot, and to Insult and Assault His Excellency the Lord Lieutenant, in the Theatre to Insult and... Dublin: 1823. V. 49; 51

GREENE, ROBERT
The Dramatic Works. London: 1831. V. 47; 49; 50; 53
Pandosto, or the Historie of Dorastus and Fawnia. New Rochelle: 1902. V. 53
The Plays and Poems. London: 1905. V. 53
The Principles of the Philosophy of the Expansive and Contractive Forces... Cambridge: 1727. V. 48

GREENE, TALBOT
American Nights' Entertainments. Jonesborough: 1860. V. 53; 54

GREENE, W. B.
The Doctrine of the Trinity, Briefly and Impartially Examined in the light of History and Philosophy. West Brookfield: 1847. V. 53

GREENE, W. T.
Parrots in Captivity. London: 1884-87. V. 51

GREENER, W. W.
The Breech-Loader and How to Use It. London: 1892. V. 48
The Gun and Its Development. London: 1896. V. 49
The Gun and Its Development. London: 1910. V. 49; 54
Gunnery in 1858: Being a Treatise on Rifles, Cannon and Sporting Arms... London: 1858. V. 48
Modern Breech-Loaders: Sporting and Military. London: 1871. V. 48
The Science of Gunnery as Applied to the Use and Construction of Fire Arms. London: 1841. V. 47; 51; 52

GREENEWALT, CRAWFORD H.
Humming Birds. Garden City: 1960. V. 49; 54
Humming Birds. London: 1960. V. 50; 52; 53
Humming Birds. New York: 1960. V. 49; 52; 53

GREENFIELD, J. GODWIN
The Cerebro-Spinal Fluid in Clinical Diagnosis. London: 1925. V. 47

GREENFIELD, JEFF
Television: the First Fifty Years. New York: 1977. V. 52

GREENHALGH, THOMAS
The Vicissitudes of Commerce. London: 1852.. V. 53

GREENHAM, GEORGE H.
Our Trip to America 1897-1898. London?: 1898?. V. 53

GREENHILL, ELIZABETH
Bookbinder. A Catalogue Raisonne. London: 1986. V. 50
Elizabeth Greenhill Bookbinder. 1986. V. 48; 50; 52

GREENHILL, THOMAS
Nekpokhaeia, or the Art of Embalming, Wherein Is Shewn the Right of Burial, the Funeral Ceremonies and the Several Ways of Preserving Dead Bodies in Most Nations of the World. London: 1705. V. 51

GREENHOUSE Favourites. London: 1880. V. 48

GREENHOUSE Favourties. London: 1840. V. 48

GREENHOW, E. HEADLAM
On Chronic Bronchitis Especially as Connected With Gout, Emphyema & Diseases of the Heart. Philadlephia: 1868. V. 48

GREENHOW, EDWARD
On Addison's Disease, Being the Croonian Lectures for 1875. Philadlephia: 1875. V. 48; 53

GREENHOW, ROBERT
The History of Oregon and California, and Other Territories. Boston: 1845. V. 51; 53
The History of Oregon and California, and the Other Territories on the North-West Coast of North America; from Their Discovery to the Present Day. Boston: 1847. V. 47

GREENING, C. E.
The Greening Pictorial System of Landscape Gardening... Monroe: 1910. V. 47

GREENLEAF, ABNER
An Address Delivered at Jefferson-Hall, Portsmouth, N.H. Jan. 8, 1828 Being the 13th Anniversary of Jackson's Victory at New Orleans. Portsmouth: 1828. V. 52

GREENLEE, WILLIAM B.
A Catalogue of the William B. Greenlee Collection of Portuguese History and Literature and the Portuguese Materials in the Newberry Library. Chicago: 1953. V. 47

GREENLY, ALBERT HARRY
A Selective Bibliography of Important Books, Pamphlets and Broadsides Relating to Michigan History. Lunenburg: 1958. V. 49

GREENOUGH, SARAH
Alfred Stieglitz. Photographs and Writings. New York: 1983. V. 49
Paul Strand: an American Vision. New York: 1990. V. 53

GREEN'S Almanack and Register, for the State of Connecticut; for the Year of Our Lord, 1798... New London: 1798. V. 47

GREENSTED, FRANCES
Fugitive Pieces. Maidstone: 1796. V. 54

GREENWAY, JOHN
Bibliography of the Australian Aborigines and the Native Peoples of Torres Strait to 1959. Sydney: 1963. V. 50

GREENWELL, G. C.
A Practical Treatise on Mine Engineering. London: 1869. V. 48; 49

GREENWELL, GRAHAM
An Infant in Arms - The Letters of a Company Officer 1914-1918. London: 1935. V. 53

GREENWELL, WILLIAM
British Barrows. Oxford: 1877. V. 51; 54

GREENWICH HOSPITAL
Commission. London: 1695. V. 50

GREENWICH HOSPITAL continued
Report of the Commissioners Appointed to Inquire into Greenwich Hosptial... London: 1860. V. 50

GREENWOOD, CHARLES
Atlas of the Counties of England, from Actual Surveys Made from the Years 1817 to 1833. London: 1834. V. 54

GREENWOOD, JAMES
Curiosities of Savage Life. London: 1863. V. 52; 54
An Essay Towards a Practical English Grammar. London: 1722. V. 52
The Hatchet Throwers. London: 1866. V. 49; 51; 53
Legends of Savage Life. London: 1867. V. 49; 52; 53; 54
The London Vocabulary, English and Latin. London: 1791. V. 51
The London Vocabulary, English and Latin... London: 1797. V. 51; 52
The London Vocabulary, English and Latin. London: 1802. V. 53
The London Vocabulary, English and Latin Put into a New Method... London: 1807. V. 48; 50; 51
The Philadelphia Vocabulary, English and Latin. Philadelphia: 1787. V. 53
The Purgatory of Peter the Cruel. London: 1868. V. 48; 52; 53
The Wilds of London. London: 1874. V. 49

GREENWOOD, JEREMY
The Wood Engravings of John Nash... Liverpool: 1987. V. 47; 50

GREENWOOD, ROBERT
California Imprints 1833-1862. Los Gatos: 1961. V. 49
The California Outlaw, Tiburcio Vasquez. Los Gatos: 1960. V. 48; 53; 54

GREENWOOD, THOMAS
Free Public Libraries, Their Organisation, Uses and Management. London: 1886. V. 50; 52

GREENWOOD, W. E.
The Villa Madama, Rome. London: 1928. V. 49; 51; 53

GREENWOOD, WILL
A Practical Demonstration of County Judicatures. London: 1675. V. 50

GREENWOOD'S Picture of Hull. Hull & London: 1835. V. 50; 52

GREER, GEORGEANNA H.
The Meyer Family: Master Potters of Texas. San Antonio: 1971. V. 52

GREER, JAMES
The Windings of the Moy with Skreen & Tireragh. 1920. V. 50

GREER, JAMES KIMMINS
Bois D'Arc to Barb'd Wire: Ken Carey: Southwestern Frontier Born. Dallas: 1936. V. 53; 54

GREER, JOHN JAMES
Beyond the Lines; or, a Yankee Prisoner Loose in Dixie. Philadelphia: 1864. V. 49

GREET, DORA VICTOIRE
Mrs. Greet's Story of the Golden Owl. 1892-93. V. 54
Mrs. Greet's Story of the Golden Owl. London: 1892-93. V. 50

GREEVER, WILLIAM S.
Arid Domain, The Santa Fe Railway and its Western Land Grant. Stanford: 1954. V. 48

GREEY, EDWARD
Young Americans in Japan or the Adventures of the Jewett Family... Boston: 1882. V. 48

GREG, PERCY
Errant. A Life-Story of Latter-Day Chivalry. London: 1880. V. 51

GREG, RICHARD
Memoria Technica; or, a New Method of Artificial memory, Applied to and Exemplified in Chronology, History, Geography, Astronomy. London: 1730. V. 52

GREG, WALTER WILSON
A Bibliography of the English Printed Drama to the Restoration. London: 1939-59. V. 48; 53
A Bibliography of the English Printed Drama to the Restoration. London: 1951-70. V. 51
A List of English Plays Written Before 1643 and Printed before 1700. London: 1900-2. V. 48

GREGER, DEBORA
Blank Country. 1985. V. 52
Blank Country. San Francisco: 1985. V. 54
Cartography. Poems. Lisbon: 1980. V. 54
Provisional Landscapes: Picture Postcards. Lisbon: 1974. V. 54

GREGG, FRANK M.
The Founding of a Nation. Cleveland: 1915. V. 52

GREGG, JOSIAH
Commerce of the Prairies... New York: 1844. V. 47; 48; 49; 52; 54
Commerce of the Prairies. New York: 1845. V. 49; 52
Commerce of the Prairies. New York: 1845/44. V. 53
Commerce of the Prairies. Philadelphia: 1851. V. 50
Diaries and Letters of Josiah Gregg. Norman: 1941/44. V. 49; 50
Diary and Letters of Josiah Gregg. Norman: 1941. V. 47
Diary and Letters of Josiah Gregg. Norman: 1941/44/58. V. 47

GREGG, LINDA
Eight Poems. Port Townsend: 1982. V. 54

GREGG, THOMAS
The Prophet of Palmyra. Mormonism Reviewed. New York: 1890. V. 50

GREGG, WILLIAM
Speech of William Gregg of Edgefield on a Bill to Amend an Act Entitled 'An Act to Authorize Aid to the Blue Ridge Railroad Company in South Carolina...1856. Columbia: 1857. V. 50

GREGO, JOSEPH
A History of Parliamentary Elections and Electioneering... London: 1892. V. 48
Pictorial Pickwickiana: Charles Dickens and His Illustrators. London: 1899. V. 49; 54
Thomas Rowlandson, the Caricaturist. New York: 1971. V. 54

GREGOIRE, HENRI
An Enquiry Concerning the Intellectual and Moral Faculties and Literature of Negroes... Brooklyn: 1810. V. 48; 50; 51; 53

GREGOR, JOSEPH
Masks of the World. London: 1936-37. V. 54

GREGORIE, JOHN
The Works of the Reverend and Learned Mr. John Gregorie. London: 1684. V. 47; 48; 49

GREGORIUS I
Homiliae. Venice: 1493. V. 47; 49
Pasataorale, Sive Regula Pastoralis. Cologne: 1482. V. 54

GREGOROVIUS, FERDINAND
History of the City of Rome in the Middle Ages. London: 1894. V. 48; 52
History of the City of Rome in the Middle Ages. London: 1894-1902. V. 47; 49
History of the City of Rome in the Middle Ages. London: 1900. V. 52
History of the City of Rome in the Middle Ages. London: 1909. V. 48
Wanderings in Corsica: Its History and Heroes. London: 1855. V. 49

GREGORY, ALYSE
King Log and Lady Lea. London: 1929. V. 53

GREGORY, DAVID
David Gregory, Isaac Newton and Their Circle. Extracts from David Gregory's Memoranda 1677-1708. Oxford: 1937. V. 54
Exercitatio Geometrica de Dimensione Figurarum Sive Specimen Methodi Generalis... Edinburgh: 1684. V. 48
A Treatise of Practical Geometry. Edinburgh: 1745. V. 52

GREGORY, G.
A New and Complete Dictionary of Arts and Sciences... London: 1807. V. 49; 52

GREGORY, GEORGE
The Elements of Polite Education; Carefully Selected from the Letters of the Late Right Hon. Philip Dormer Stanhope, Earl of Chesterfield, to His Son. Dublin: 1802. V. 47
Elements On the Theory and Practice of Physic. Philadelphia: 1831. V. 53
Lectures on the Eruptive Fevers. London: 1843. V. 51; 53
The Life of Thomas Chatterton, with Criticisms on His Genius and Writings... London: 1789. V. 48; 50; 53

GREGORY, HERBERT E.
Geology of the Navajo Country. Washington: 1917. V. 54

GREGORY, HORACE
D. H. Lawrence, Pilgrim of the Apocalypse, a Critical Study. New York: 1957. V. 52

GREGORY, I. B.
Gregorii Magni Episcopi Romani, De Cura Pastorali... London: 1629. V. 49

GREGORY, ISABELLA AUGUSTA PERSE
Alice Granger, a Tale of the West. Cincinnati: 1852. V. 47
A Book of Saints and Wonders Put Down Here By Lady Gregory According to the Old Writings and Memory of the People of Ireland. Dundrum: 1906. V. 51
Coole. 1971. V. 47
Cuchulain of Muirthemne. London: 1902. V. 49; 51
The Full Moon. Dublin: 1911. V. 47
Gods and Fighting Men. 1904. V. 52
The Golden Apple. London: 1916. V. 54
The Image. Dublin: 1910. V. 51
The Kiltartan Poetry Book. Dundrum, Dublin: 1918. V. 49
The Kiltartan Wonder Book. London: 1910. V. 47; 53
Kincora, a Drama in Three Acts. New York: 1905. V. 52
Mr. Gregory's Letter-Box, 1813-1830. London: 1898. V. 47; 53
My First Play. London: 1930. V. 51
Poets and Dreamers: Studies and Translations from the Irish. 1903. V. 48
Spreading the New, a Play in One Act. New York: 1904. V. 52
Three Last Plays. London: 1928. V. 48
Visions and Beliefs in the West of Ireland. New York: 1920. V. 47
The White Cockade: a Comedy and the Travelling Man: a Miracle Play. New York: 1905. V. 48

GREGORY, J. W.
To the Alps of Chinese Tibet. 1923. V. 54

GREGORY, JAMES
Conspectus Medicinae Theoreticae; or a View of the Theory of Medicine ... Edinburgh: 1833. V. 54
Dissertatio Medica Inauguralis, De Morbis Coeli Mutatione Medendis... Edinburgh: 1774. V. 47; 48; 49; 50
James Gregory Tercentenary Memorial Volume. London: 1939. V. 54

GREGORY, JAMES M.
Frederick Douglass, the Orator. Springfield: 1893. V. 51; 54

GREGORY, JOHN
A Comparative View of the State & Faculties of Man With Those of the Animal World. London: 1765. V. 48
A Comparative View of the State & Faculties of Man with Those of the Animal World. London: 1774. V. 48
A Comparative View of the State & Faculties of Man with Those of the Animal World. London: 1785. V. 54
A Father's Legacy to His Daughters. London: 1795. V. 47
Gregorii Posthuma; or, Certain Learned Tracts. Together with a Short Account of the Author's Life... London: 1650. V. 48; 51
The Works... London: 1671. V. 48; 52
The Works. London: 1672. V. 48
The Works... London: 1684. V. 49

GREGORY, JOHN WALTER
Australasia. London: 1907-08. V. 50

GREGORY, JOSEPH
Masks of the World. London: 1936-37. V. 50

GREGORY, OLINTHUS
Mathematics for Practical Men... London: 1825. V. 50

GREGORY, SAINT, THE GREAT
Operum Gregorii Nazianzeni. Basel: 1571. V. 51
St. Libri Dialogorum. Basel: 1496. V. 47; 52

GREGORY, W. K.
Evolution Emerging: Survey of Changing Patterns from Primeval Life to man. New York: 1951. V. 48
On the Structure and Relations of Northarctus, an American Eocene Primate. New York: 1920. V. 51
Our Face from Fish to Man... New York: 1929. V. 54

GREGORY, WILLIAM HENRY
Paddiana; or, Scraps and Sketches of Irish Life, Present and Past. London: 1847. V. 48

GREGORY I, SAINT
Works. Sancti Gregorii Magni Papae primi Opera, Sixti V. Pont, Max. Issu, Diligentisime Emendata... Paris: 1619. V. 48

GREGORY IX, POPE
Decretales d'ni Pape Gregorii noni Accurata Diligentia Nuper Emendate... Paris: 1516. V. 49

GREGORY OF NYSSA
Libri Octo. De Homine...De Providentia. Strasbourg: 1512. V. 49
Opera Omnia Quae Reperiri Potuerunt, Graece & latine Nunc Primum ex Mnss.... Paris: 1615. V. 50

GREGORY XIV
Breve...Confirmationis, Extensionis, ac Communicationis Privilegiorum Cisterciensis Ordinis & Eius Congregationum. Rome: 1591. V. 47
Literae Facultatum et Privilegium...Capellanorum. Rome: 1592. V. 49; 53

GREGSON, MATTHEW
History of Lancashire. Liverpool: 1817. V. 53
History of Lancashire. Liverpool: 1817-24. V. 48; 53
Portfolio. Liverpool: 1824. V. 51
Portfolio of Fragments Relative to the History and Antiquities of the County Palatine and Duchy of Lancaster. Liverpool: 1817. V. 47

GREIF, M.
Depression Modern: the 30's Style in America. New York: 1975. V. 54

GREIVE, CHRISTOPHER MURRAY
A Drunk Man Looks at the Thistle: Poems. Edinburgh & London: 1926. V. 53

GRELLMANN, HEINRICH MORITZ GOTTLIEB
Dissertation on the Gipsies. London: 1787. V. 49

GRENARD, F.
Tibet and Tibetans; or the Country and Its Inhabitants. London: 1904. V. 54

GRENFELL, BERNARD P.
The Oxyrhynchus Papyri. London: 1898-1904. V. 51

GRENFELL PRESS
The Grenfell Press Typefaces &c. New York: 1980. V. 54

GRENFELL, WILFRED T.
Down North on the Labrador. New York: 1911. V. 54
Labrador Looks at the Orient. Boston: 1928. V. 52
Tales of the Labrador. Boston: 1926. V. 50; 52

GRENVILLE, GEORGE
An Ode Upon the Present Period of Time; with a Letter to the Right Honourable Grenville. London: 1769. V. 54
The Speech of a Right Honourable Gentleman, on the Motion for Expelling Mr. Wilkes, Friday, February 3, 1769. London: 1769. V. 48; 53

GRENVILLE, LORD
Oxford and Locke. London: 1829. V. 51

GRENVILLE MURRAY, E. C.
The Roving Englishman in Turkey: Sketches from Life. London: 1855. V. 54

GREPPO, J. G. HONORE
Essay on the Hieroglyphic System of M. Champollion, Jun. and on the Advantages Which It Offers to Sacred Criticism. Boston: 1830. V. 50

GRESHAM, WILLIAM LINDSAY
Nightmare Alley. New York: 1946. V. 50

GRESSENT, V. A.
Growth and Manufacture of Silk. Washington: 1828. V. 54

GRESSET, JEAN BAPTISTE LOUIS
Oeuvres de M. Gresset de l'Academie Francoise... Londres: 1748. V. 51

GRESSIT, J. L.
Biogeography and Ecology of New Guinea. London: 1981. V. 48; 52

GRESWELL, WILLIAM PARR
Annals of Parisian Typography... London: 1818. V. 47; 48; 50; 52
Memoirs of Angelus Politianus, Joannes Picus of Mirandula, Actius Sincerus Sannazarius, Petrus Bembus, Hieronymus Fracastorius, Marcus Antonius Flaminius, and the Amalthei... Manchester: 1805. V. 47
The Monastery of Saint Werburgh: a Poem With Illustrative Notes. Manchester: 1823. V. 48; 54
A View of the Early Parisian Greek Press... Oxford: 1833. V. 50
A View of the Early Parisian Greek Press, Including the Lives of the Stephani or Estiennes... London: 1840. V. 47

GRETTIS SAGA
The Story of Grettir the Strong. London: 1901. V. 51

GRETTON, R. H.
The Burford Records. A Study in Minor Town Government. Oxford: 1920. V. 48

GREUB, SUZANNE
Authority and Ornament. Art of the Sepik River, Papua, New Guinea. Basel: 1985-88. V. 52

GREVILLE, CHARLES CAVENDISH FULKE
The Greville Memoirs - The Reigns of George IV, William IV. The Reign of Queen Victoria. London: 1885-87. V. 51
Greville Memoirs. 1814-1860. London: 1938. V. 52
The Greville Memoirs: a Journal of the Reigns of King George IV and King William IV. (and) A Journal of the Reign of Queen Victoria. London: 1874-87. V. 48; 49; 51; 52; 54
A Journal of the Reign of Queen Victoria from 1837 to 1852. London: 1885. V. 48; 52
A Journal of the Reigns of King George IV and King William IV. New York: 1975. V. 47

GREVILLE, FULKE
Maxims, Character and Refelctions, Critical, Satyrical and Moral. London: 1756. V. 47; 51
Selected Poems. London: 1968. V. 54

GREVILLE, ROBERT KAYE
Flora Edinensis; or, a Description of Plants Growing Near Edinburgh... Edinburgh: 1824. V. 49
Scottish Cryptogamic Flora... Edinburgh: 1823-28. V. 52; 53
Scottish Cryptogamic Flora, or Coloured Figures and Descriptions of Cryptogamic Plants... Edinburgh: 1923-28. V. 49

GREW, E. S.
Field-Marshal Lord Kitchener - His Life and Work for the Empire. London: 1916. V. 47

GREW, J. C.
Sport and Travel in the Far East. 1910. V. 52
Sport and Travel in the Far East. Boston: 1910. V. 47

GREW, NEHEMIAH
The Anatomy of Plants. London: 1682. V. 47; 48; 50; 53
Cosmologia Sacra; or a Discourse of the Universe As It Is in the Creature and Kingdom of God. London: 1701. V. 53
Musaeum Regalis Societatis or a Catalogue and Description of the Natural and Artificial Rarities Belonging to the Royal Society... London: 1681. V. 49; 51; 52; 53

GREY, C.
The Early Years of His Royal Highness the Prince Consort... New York: 1867. V. 51

GREY, C. H.
Hardy Bulbs, Including Half Hardy Bulbs and Tuberous and Fibrous Rooted Plants. London: 1937-38. V. 48
Hardy Bulbs. Volume 2. Amaryllidaceae, Commelinaceae, Haemodoraceae, Orchidaceae. London: 1938. V. 49; 54
Hardy Bulbs. Volume I. Iridaceae. London: 1937. V. 49; 54

GREY, EDWARD GREY, 1ST VISCOUNT
The Charm of Birds. London: 1927. V. 51
Fallodon Papers. London: 1926. V. 52
Fly Fishing. London: 1899. V. 53
Fly Fishing. London: 1930. V. 51; 54
Fly Fishing. London: 1947. V. 53

GREY, ELIZABETH CAROLINE
Hyacinthe; or, the Contrast. London: 1835. V. 54

GREY, F.
Tales Of Our Grandfather or India Since 1856. London: 1912. V. 50

GREY, GEORGE
Journals of Two Expeditions of Discovery in Northwest and Western Australia During the Years 1837, 1838 and 1839. London: 1841. V. 48; 53
Polynesian Mythology and Ancient Traditional History of the New Zealand Race, as Furnished by Their Priests and Chiefs. Auckland: 1885. V. 47

GREY, HARRY
The Hoods. New York: 1952. V. 54

GREY, HERACLITUS
Playing Trades. London: 1870. V. 48

GREY, JANE
The Literary Remains of Lady Jane Grey, with Memoir of Her Life. London: 1825. V. 52

GREY, JOHN
A Letter Addressed by Lieutenant Colonel John Grey, to a Member of the House of Commons, on the Subject of the Libility of the Pay of the Officers of the Navy and Army to the Tax Upon Property. London: 1810. V. 50

GREY, RICHARD
Memoria Technica: or, a New Method of Artificial memory... London: 1732. V. 47; 49; 51
A System of English Ecclesiastical Law. London: 1735. V. 52

GREY, ROMER
The Cruise of the 'Fisherman': Adventures in Southern Seas. New York: 1929. V. 49; 53
The Fisherman Under the Southern Cross: a Story of Adventure in New Zealand. New York: 1930. V. 47

GREY, THOMAS DE
The Compleat Horseman and Expert Farrier. London: 1639. V. 47
The Compleat Horseman and Expert Farrier. London: 1670. V. 54

GREY, WILLIAM
A Picture of Pioneer Times in California. San Francisco: 1881. V. 47

GREY, ZANE
The Adventures of Finspot. San Bernardino: 1974. V. 48
Arizona Ames. New York: 1932. V. 47
The Arizona Clan. New York: 1958. V. 51
Betty Zane. New York: 1903. V. 49; 54
Bonefish Brigade. 1922. V. 53
The Border Legion. New York: 1930. V. 51
The Call of the Canyon. New York: 1924. V. 53
Captives of the Desert. New York: 1952. V. 48
The Deer Stalker. New York: 1949. V. 51
Desert Gold: a Romance of the Border. New York: 1913. V. 52; 53
Desert Gold: a Romance of the Border. New York: 1913/14. V. 48
Desert Gold: A Romance of the Border. London: 1926. V. 52
The Desert of Wheat. New York: 1919. V. 50
Don: the Story of a Lion Dog. New York: 1928. V. 50; 53
Fighting Caravans. New York & London: 1929. V. 48; 49; 50
Forlorn River: a Romance. New York: 1927. V. 48
The Fugitive Trail. New York: 1957. V. 51
Great Game Fishing at Catalina. Catalina: 1919. V. 50; 53
The Hash Knife Outfit. New York: 1933. V. 49
The Heritage of the Desert. New York: 1924/10. V. 54
Ken Ward in the Jungle: Thrilling Adventures in Tropical Wilds. New York: 1912. V. 48; 49; 50
Knights of the Range. New York: 1939. V. 49
The Last of the Plainsmen. New York: 1908. V. 49
The Last of the Plainsmen. New York: 1920's. V. 51
Lost Pueblo. New York: 1954. V. 51
The Lost Wagon Train. New York & London: 1936. V. 49; 52
Majesty's Rancho. New York: 1938. V. 49; 52
The Man and His Work: An Auobiographical Sketch, Critical Appreciations and Bibliography. New York: 1928. V. 51
The Man of the Forest. New York: 1924. V. 54
The Mysterious Rider. New York: 1921. V. 53
Nevada: a Romance of the West. New York: 1928. V. 51
Raiders of Spanish Peaks. New York: 1938. V. 48; 49
The Rainbow Trail: A Romance. New York: 1915. V. 48
The Rainbow Trail: a Romance. London: 1925. V. 52
The Rainbow Trail: a Romance. New York: 1925. V. 48
The Ranger: and Other Stories. New York: 1960. V. 48
Riders of the Purple Sage. New York: 1912, 1920. V. 48; 49
Riders of the Purple Sage. London: 1926. V. 49
The Roaring U.P. Trail. London: 1920. V. 54
Rogue River Feud. New York: 1948. V. 51
Shadow on the Trail. New York: 1946. V. 51
The Shepherd of Guadaloupe. New York: 1930. V. 52; 54
Stairs of Sand. London: 1943. V. 49
Stairs of Sand. New York: 1943. V. 49
Stranger from the Tonto. New York: 1956. V. 51
Tales from a Fisherman's Log. Auckland: 1978. V. 51
Tales of Fishing Virgin Seas. New York: 1925. V. 52
Tales of Fresh-Water Fishing. New York: 1928. V. 49; 50; 51; 53
Tales of Lonely Trails. New York: 1922. V. 49
Tales of Southern Rivers. London: 1924. V. 53
Tales of Southern Rivers. New York: 1924. V. 47; 53
Tales of Swordfish and Tuna. London: 1927. V. 51; 53
Tales of Swordfish and Tuna. New York: 1930. V. 54
Tales of Tahitian Waters. New York: 1931. V. 53
Tales of the Angler's Eldorado New Zealand. New York & London: 1926. V. 50; 51; 52; 53
Tappan's Burro. New York: 1923. V. 47; 49; 51; 53
Thunder Mountain. New York. V. 53; 54
Thunder Mountain. New York: 1935. V. 49; 53
The Thundering Herd. New York: 1925. V. 47; 49; 53
The Trail Driver. New York: 1936. V. 49; 50
The Trail Driver. New York: 1937. V. 49
Twin Sombreros. New York: 1940. V. 47; 49
Under the Tonto Rim. London: 1925. V. 54
Under the Tonto Rim. New York: 1926. V. 48; 49; 50; 53; 54
The U.P. Trail. New York: 1918. V. 51
Valley of Wild Horses. New York: 1947. V. 51
Wanderer of the Wasteland. New York: 1923. V. 47
West of the Pecos. New York: 1937. V. 48; 49
Western Union. New York: 1939. V. 49; 51
Wild Horse Mesa. New York: 1928. V. 53
Wilderness Trek: a Novel of Australia. New York: 1944. V. 51
Works. 1990. V. 54
The Young Forester. 1910. V. 53
Zane Grey Fishing Library. 1990-91. V. 51
Zane Grey Fishing Library. New York: 1990-91. V. 48; 54

GRIBBLE, F.
The Early Mountaineers. 1899. V. 53
The Early Mountaineers. London: 1899. V. 52

GRIBBLE, SAMUEL
A Treatise on Deportment, Fencing, &c., Including the Science of Horsemanship... Derby: 1829. V. 47; 54

GRIDLEY, MARION E.
Indians of Yesterday. Chicago: 1940. V. 47

GRIER, ELDON
A Friction of Lights. Toronto: 1963. V. 47

GRIER, THOMAS G.
Pueblo Indians, More Particularly the Pueblo of Laguna and Few Incidents. 1912. V. 51

GRIER, WALTER
The Animals' Conference. London: 1955. V. 49

GRIER'S Southern Almanac for the States of Georgia, South Carolina, Alabama and Tennessee for the Year of Our Lord 1862. Augusta: 1861. V. 49

GRIER'S Southern Almanac For the States of Georgia, South Carolina, Mississippi, Louisiana, Alabama, Tennessee, for the Year of Our Lord 1863... Augusta: 1862. V. 49

GRIERSON, FLORA
Haunting Edinburgh. London: 1929. V. 49; 51

GRIERSON, JAMES
Delineations of St. Andrews. Cupar: 1823. V. 47

GRIERSON, JAMES MONCREIFF
Records of the Scottish Volunteer Force, 1859-1908. Edinburgh: 1909. V. 50
Records of the Scottish Volunteer Force, 1859-1908. London: 1972. V. 50

GRIERSON, PHILIP
Byzantine Coins. Berkley & London: 1982. V. 48

GRIESINGER, WILHELM
Mental Pathology and Therapeutics. New York: 1882. V. 47; 52
Die Pathologie und Therapie der Psychischen Krankheiten, fur Arzte und Studirende. Stuttgart: 1845. V. 52

GRIEVE, CHRISTOPHER MURRAY
Complete Poems - 1920-1976. London: 1978. V. 53
Direadh I, II and III; Poems. 1974. V. 54
A Drunk Man Looks at the Thistle. London: 1926. V. 47; 51
A Drunk Man Looks at the Thistle. Edinburgh: 1956. V. 51
Early Lyrics. Lancashire: 1968. V. 54
The Fire of the Spirit. Glasgow: 1965. V. 54
In Memoriam James Joyce. Glasglow: 1955. V. 50
The Kind of Poetry I Want. Edinburgh: 1961. V. 47; 52; 54
A Kist of Whistles - New Poems. Glasgow: 1947. V. 54
O Wha's Been Here Afore Me, Lass. London: 1931. V. 53
Penny Wheep. 1926. V. 49
Penny Wheep. Edinburgh & London: 1926. V. 47
Sangschaw. 1925. V. 49
Sangschaw. Edinburgh: 1925. V. 47; 48
Scottish Scene or the Intelligent Man's Guide to Albyn. London: 1934. V. 49
Selected Lyrics. 1977. V. 47
Selected Lyrics. London: 1977. V. 50
Selected Lyrics. Verona: 1977. V. 48; 52; 54
Selected Poems of Hugh MacDiarmid. Glasgow: 1944. V. 49
Song of the Seraphim. A Poem. London: 1973. V. 48; 53
Stony Limits - and Other Poems. London: 1934. V. 49
To Circumjack Cencrastus. 1930. V. 49
To Circumjack Cencrastus, or the Curly Snake: a Long Poem. Edinburgh & London: 1930. V. 53

GRIEVE, M.
A Modern Herbal: The Medicinal, Culinary, Cosmetic and Economic Properties, Cultivation and Folk-Lore of Herbs, Grasses, Fungi, Shrubs and Trees With All Their Modern Scientific Uses. London: 1931. V. 50
A Modern Herbal, the Medicinal, Culinary, Cosmetic and Economic Properties, Cultivation and Folk-Lore of Herbs, Grasses, Fungi, Shrubs and Trees, with All Their Modern Scientific Uses. New York: 1931. V. 52

GRIEVE, S.
The Great Auk, or Garefow... London: 1885. V. 54

GRIFFIN, A. P. C.
Bibliography of the Philippines Islands. 1903. V. 54

GRIFFIN, ERNEST F.
Westchester County and Its People. New York: 1946. V. 49

GRIFFIN, GEORGE BUTLER
Documents from the Sutro Collection. Los Angeles: 1891. V. 48

GRIFFIN, GERALD
The Collegians. London: 1829. V. 47; 51; 53

GRIFFIN, H. H.
Cycles and Cycling. London: 1890. V. 49

GRIFFIN, JAMES B.
Archaeology of Eastern United States. Chicago: 1952. V. 54
Archeology of Eastern United States. Chicago & London: 1966. V. 52
For Ancient Aspect- Its Cultural and Chronological Position in Mississippi Valley Archaeology. Ann Arbor: 1943. V. 47; 50

GRIFFIN, JOHN HOWARD
Black Like Me. Boston: 1961. V. 48; 50
The Devil Rides Outside. 1952. V. 51

GRIFFIN, JOHN JOSEPH
Chemical Handicraft: a Classified and Descriptive Catalogue of Chemical Apparatus... London: 1877. V. 50

GRIFFIN, JOHNNIE HARRY
A Man Without a Country Since Prohibition. New Orleans. V. 54

GRIFFIN, L. E.
The Anatomy of Nautilus Pompilius. Washington: 1900. V. 52

GRIFFIN, MARY SANDS
Old Facts and Modern Incidents, Supplementary to Impressions of Germany. Dresden: 1868. V. 49

GRIFFIN, RALPH
A List of Monumental Brasses Remaining in the County of Kent in 1922. Ashford & London: 1923. V. 52

GRIFFIN, SUSAN
Let Them Be Said. Oakland: 1973. V. 52

GRIFFIS, W. E.
The New Japan Primer, Number One: Introductory to the New Japan Readers. San Francisco: 1872. V. 47

GRIFFITH, CHARLES
The Present State and Prospects of the Port Phillip District of New South Wales. Dublin: 1845. V. 54

GRIFFITH, D. W.
The Birth of a Nation: The Most Stupendous and Fascinating Motion Picture Drama Created in the U.S. New York: 1915. V. 47

GRIFFITH, EDWARD
General and Particular Descriptions of the Vertebrated Animals. Order Quadrumana. London: 1821. V. 49

GRIFFITH, ELIZABETH
The Morality of Shakespeare's Drama Illustrated. London: 1775. V. 48; 49; 50; 52; 54
A Series of Genuine Letters Between Henry and Frances. London: 1767-70. V. 50
The Times, a Comedy. London: 1780. V. 49

GRIFFITH, F. L. L.
Catalogue of the Demotic Papyri in the John Rylands Library Manchester with Facsimiles and Complete Transactions. Manchester: 1909. V. 49; 51
A Collection of Hieroglyphs: a Contribution to the History of Egyptian Writing. London: 1898. V. 49; 51
The Demotic Magical Papyrus of London and Leiden. London: 1904-09. V. 49; 51
The Inscriptions of Siut and Der Riefh. London: 1889. V. 49

GRIFFITH, G.
The Gold-Finder. 1898. V. 52

GRIFFITH, GEORGE
The Free Schools and Endowments of Staffordshire, and Their Fulfilment. 1860. V. 49; 52
The Free Schools and Endowments of Staffordshire, and Their Fulfilment. Stafford: 1860. V. 51
The Free Schools of Worcestershire, and their Fulfilment. London: 1852. V. 52
Going to Markets and Grammar Schools... London: 1870. V. 53
The Outlaws of the Air. London: 1897. V. 48
Reminiscences and Records During Ten Years' Residence in the Midland Counties, from 1869 to 1880. 1880. V. 53

GRIFFITH, GEORGE CHETWYND
Valdar the Oft-Born: a Saga of Seven Ages. London: 1895. V. 48; 51; 54

GRIFFITH, HARRISON PASATILLO
Variosa a Collection of Sketches, Essays and Verses. 1911. V. 52; 54

GRIFFITH, J. W.
The Micrographic Dictionary. London: 1856. V. 48; 51
The Micrographic Dictionary. London: 1875. V. 52
The Micrographic Dictionary. London: 1883. V. 54

GRIFFITH, JOHN
A Journal of the Life, Travels and Labours in the Work of the Ministry. London: 1779. V. 49
A Journal of the Life, Travels and Labours...(with) Some Brief Remarks Upon Sundry Important Subjects... Philadelphia: 1780/81. V. 54

GRIFFITH, LLEWELLYN
Up to Mamet. London: 1931. V. 47

GRIFFITH, MATTHEW
A Patheticall Persuasion to Pray for Public Peace: Propounded in a Sermon Preached in the Cathedral Church of Saint Paul, Octob. 2, 1642. London: 1642. V. 47

GRIFFITH, PEGGY
The New Klondike: a Story of a Southern Baseball Training Camp. New York: 1926. V. 52

GRIFFITH, R. EGLESFELD
Medical Botany; or Description of the More Important Plants Used in Medicine, with their History, Properties and Mode of Administration. Philadelphia: 1847. V. 47; 51
A Universal Formulary: Containing the Methods of Preparing and Adminstering Official and Other Medicines. Philadelphia: 1850. V. 48; 53

GRIFFITH, R. H.
Alexander Pope, a Bibliography. Austin: 1922-27. V. 51

GRIFFITH, RICHARD
Facts and Arguments Respecting the Great Utility of an Extensive Plan of Inland Navigation in Ireland. Dublin: 1800. V. 54
Geological and Mining Survey of the Connaught Coal District in Ireland. London: 1818. V. 47
The Triumvirate; or, the Authentic Memoirs of A.B. and C. London: 1764. V. 52
Yoricks Nachgelatzne Werke. Leipzig: 1771. V. 54

GRIFFITH, THOMAS W.
Sketches of the Early History of Maryland. Baltimore: 1821. V. 47

GRIFFITH, WILLIAM
Itinerary Notes of Plants Collected in the Khasyah and Bootan Mountains 1837-38, in Afghanistan... Calcutta: 1848. V. 49
A Treatise on the Jurisdiction and Proceedings of Justices of the Peace in Civil Suits. Burlington: 1796. V. 54

GRIFFITH, WILLIAM PETTIT
Ancient Gothic Churches, Their Proportions and Chromatics. London: 1847. V. 48

GRIFFITHS, ACTON FREDERICK
Bibliotheca Anglo-Poetica, or a Descriptive Catalogue of a Rare And Rich Collection of Early English Poetry. London: 1815. V. 50; 53

GRIFFITHS, ARTHUR
Memorials of Millbank and Chapters in Prison History. London: 1875. V. 51
Mysteries of Police and Crime. London: 1901-02. V. 47
Secrets of the Prison-House or Gaol Studies and Sketches. London: 1894. V. 47

GRIFFITHS, BILL
The Nine Herbs Charm. 1981. V. 54

GRIFFITHS, JOHN
Travels in Europe, Asia Minor and Arabia. London & Edinburgh: 1805. V. 47; 49

GRIFFITHS, JULIA
Autographs for Freedom. Auburn: 1854. V. 53

GRIFFITHS, RALPH
Ascanius; or the Young Adventurer, a True History. London: 1746. V. 49

GRIFFITHS, ROGER
An Essay to Prove that the Jurisdiction and Conservacy of the River Thames, Etc., is Committed to the Lord Mayor and City of London... London: 1746. V. 47

GRIFFITHS, S. Y.
New Historical Description of Cheltenham and Its Vicinity. Cheltenham: 1826. V. 47; 49

GRIFFITHS, SAMUEL
Griffith's Guide to the Iron Trade of Great Britain... London: 1873. V. 49; 50

GRIGG, E. R. N.
The Trail of the Invisible Light. Springfield: 1965. V. 50; 52; 53

GRIGG, G.
Kangaroos, Wallabies and Rat Kangaroos. Chipping Norton: 1990. V. 48; 50

GRIGG, JOHN
Grigg's Southern and Western Songster. Philadelphia: 1829. V. 53

GRIGGS, F. L.
The Engraved Work of F. L. Griggs, A.R.A., R.E. Etchings and Dry-Points 1912-1928. Stratford-upon-Avon: 1928. V. 53

GRIGGS, GEORGE
History of Messilla Valley Or the Gadsden Purchase Known to Mexico as the Treaty of Mesilla. Messila: 1930. V. 47

GRIGGS, NATHAN K.
Lyrics of the Lariat. Chicago: 1893. V. 54
Lyrics of the Lariat. New York: 1893. V. 49; 53

GRIGG'S *Southern and Western Songster.* Philadelphia: 1829. V. 53

GRIGGS COUNTY PROGRESS CLUB, COPPERSTOWN, NORTH DAKOTA
Griggs County, North Dakota. Minneapolis: 1911. V. 54

GRIGSBY, HUGH BLAIR
Letters by a South Carolinan. Norfolk: 1827. V. 48

GRIGSON, GEOFFREY
The Arts To-Day. London: 1935. V. 53
The Englishman's Flora. London: 1955. V. 54
John Craxton: Paintings and Drawings. London: 1948. V. 53
A Master Of Our Time - A Study of Wyndham Lewis. London: 1951. V. 54
Samuel Palmer: the Visionary Years. London: 1947. V. 49
Visionary Poems and Passages, or the Poet's Eye. London: 1944. V. 51

GRILLI, ELISE
The Art of the Japanese Screen. New York and Tokyo: 1970. V. 48; 51; 54

GRIMALDI, JOSEPH
Memoirs of Joseph Grimaldi. London: 1838. V. 47; 49; 51; 53; 54
Memoirs of Joseph Grimaldi. Philadelphia: 1838. V. 53; 54

GRIMALDI, STACEY
The Foliet. London: 1850. V. 51
Origines Genealogicae; or the Sources Whence English Genealogies May be Traced from the Conquest to the Present Time. London: 1828. V. 47; 50
A Suit of Armour for Youth. London: 1824. V. 50; 54
The Toilet. London. V. 49; 52

GRIMBLE, A.
Deer Stalking. London: 1886. V. 48
Deer Stalking. 1888. V. 54
Highland Sport. London: 1894. V. 50
More Leaves from My Game Book. 1917. V. 52
Shooting and Salmon Fishing. London: 1892. V. 47; 49

GRIMES, J. STANLEY
Compend of the Phreno-Philosophy of Human Nature. Boston: 1853. V. 50

GRIMES, MARTHA
The Anodyne Necklace. Boston: 1983. V. 47; 51; 52
The Deer Leap. Boston: 1985. V. 52
The Dirty Duck. Boston: 1984. V. 52
The Five Bells and Bladebone. Boston: 1987. V. 52
Help the Poor Struggler. Boston: 1985. V. 52
I Am the Only Running Footman. Boston: 1986. V. 52
Jerusalem Inn. Boston: 1984. V. 52
The Man with a Load of Mischief. Boston: 1981. V. 52; 53
The Old Fox Deceiv'd. Boston: 1982. V. 47; 48; 51; 52
The Old Fox Deceiv'd. Boston: 1983. V. 51

GRIMES, ROY
300 Years in Victoria County. 1968. V. 52

GRIMESTON, EDWARD
A Generall Historie of the Netherlands. London: 1609. V. 53

GRIMKE, JOHN FAUCHERAUD
The Duty of Executors and Administrators...According to the Laws of South Carolina. New York: 1797. V. 48

GRIMKE, THOMAS SMITH
Address on the Power and Value of the Sunday School System in Evangelizing Heathen and Reconstructing Christian Communities... Philadelphia: 1834. V. 51
Mr. Grimke's Letter, to a Friend in Albany, on Temperance. Charlestown: 1833. V. 51; 53
Oration on the Advantages, to Be Derived From the Introduction to the Bible, and of Sacred Literature, as Essential Parts of all Education, in a Literary Point of View... New Haven: 1830. V. 51

GRIMM, HERMAN
Life of Michaelangelo. Boston. V. 50
The Life of Michaelangelo. Boston: 1906. V. 53

GRIMM, JACOB
Teutonic Mythology. London: 1900-1883-88. V. 49

GRIMM, THE BROTHERS
The Fairy Ring. London: 1847. V. 52
Fairy Tales. London: 1909. V. 47; 48; 51
The Fairy Tales... New York: 1909. V. 48; 54
Fairy Tales. New York: 1931. V. 51
Fairy Tales. London: 1943. V. 52
German Popular Stories. London: 1823-26. V. 49; 52; 53
German Popular Stories. London: 1825-26. V. 48
German Popular Stories. London: 1875. V. 54
Grimm's Fairy Tales. London & New York: 1888. V. 51; 52
Grimm's Fairy Tales. London: 1910. V. 54
Grimm's Fairy Tales. London: 1920. V. 52
Grimm's Fairy Tales. London: 1929. V. 49
Grimm's Fairy Tales. London: 1930. V. 51
Grimm's Fairy Tales. New York: 1962. V. 54
Grimm's Fairy Tales. New York: 1962-63. V. 50
Grimm's Fairy Tales Complete. 1962-63. V. 51
Grimm's Goblins. German Popular Stories. London: 1877. V. 47
Grimm's Household Fairy Tales. New York: 1890. V. 49
Grimm's Other Tales. Waltham St. Lawrence: 1956. V. 48; 50; 51; 52; 53; 54
Hansel and Gretel. Rochester: 1916. V. 53
Hansel and Gretel. London: 1925. V. 47; 50
Hansel and Gretel. New York: 1925. V. 47; 53
Hansel and Gretel. Zurich: 1944. V. 52
Household Stories. London: 1882. V. 51; 52; 53; 54
Household Tales. London: 1946. V. 49; 50
The Juniper Tree and other Tales from Grimm. 1973. V. 51
The Juniper Tree and Other Tales From Grimm. New York: 1973. V. 47; 52
King Grisly-Beard. New York: 1973. V. 53
Little Brother and Little Sister. London: 1917. V. 48; 53
Little Brother and Little Sister. New York: 1917. V. 51
Ein Marchen, Aufgeschrieben von Philipp Otto Runge: Van den Machandelboom. Hamburg: 1982. V. 50
Rumpelstiltskin. New York: 1973. V. 51
Six Fairy Tales. London: 1970. V. 50
Snow White and the Seven Dwarfs. New York: 1938. V. 52
Tales by the Brothers Grimm. New York: 1931. V. 53
Tales from the Brothers Grimm. London: 1930. V. 48
Three Gay Tales From Grimm. New York: 1943. V. 49; 51
The Wolfe and the Seven Kids. London: 1966. V. 53

GRIMMELSHAUSEN, JOHANN VON
The Adventures of Simplicissimus. New York: 1981. V. 51; 53; 54

GRIMSHAW, ANNE
The Horse: a Bibliography of British Books 1851-1976... London: 1982. V. 49

GRIMSHAW, BEATRICE
From Fiji to the Cannibal Islands. London: 1907. V. 50; 51

GRIMSLEY, DANIEL A.
Battles in Culpeper County, Virginia 1861-1865 and other Articles. Culpeper: 1900. V. 49; 50; 52; 54

GRIMSTON, CHARLOTTE
The History of Gorhambury. London: 1821. V. 52

GRIMWOOD, ETHEL ST. CLAIR
My Three Years in Manipur and Escape from the Recent Mutiny. London: 1891. V. 52
My Three Years in Manipur and Escape from the Recent Mutiny. London: 1892. V. 50; 51

GRINDALY, ROBERT MELVILLE
Scenery, Costumes and Architecture, Chiefly on the Western Side of India. London: 1826/30. V. 49

GRINDE, DONALD A.
The Iroquois and the Founding of the American Nation. San Francisco: 1977. V. 50

GRINDON, LEO H.
The Shakespeare Flora, a Guide to All the Principal Passages In Which Mention is Made of Trees, Plants, Flowers and Vegetable Prouctions... Manchester: 1883. V. 50

GRINNELL, GEORGE BIRD
American Big Game in Its Haunts: The Book of the Boone and Crockett Club. New York: 1904. V. 47
American Duck Shooting. New York: 1901. V. 52
Bent's Old Fort and the Builders. V. 54
Blackfoot Lodge tales: The Story of a Prairie People. New York: 1892. V. 49
The Cheyenne Indians, Their History and Way of Life. New Haven: 1923. V. 49; 53; 54
The Fighting Cheyennes. New York: 1915. V. 53
Hunting and Conservation. New Haven: 1925. V. 47; 49
Hunting Trails on Three Continents. New York: 1933. V. 47; 49
The Indians of To-day. Chicago and New York: 1900. V. 47
Pawnee Hero Stories and Folk Tales with Notes on the Origin, Customs and Character of the Pawnee People. New York: 1893. V. 49
Trail and Camp-Fire. The Book of the Boone and Crockett Club. New York: 1897. V. 47
Two Great Scouts and Their Pawnee Battalion... Cleveland: 1928. V. 47
Two Great Scouts and Their Pawnee Battalion. Cleveland: 1929. V. 50
When Buffalo Ran. New Haven: 1920. V. 49; 54

GRINNELL, JOSEPH
Animal Life in Yosemite... Berkeley: 1924. V. 48; 54
Fur-Bearing Mammals of California: Their Natural History, Systematic Status and Relations to Man. Berkeley: 1937. V. 52

GRIPPER, CHARLES F.
Railway Tunnelling in Heavy Ground. London: 1879. V. 49

GRISCOM, JOHN H.
The Uses and Abuses of Air... New York: 1854. V. 51

GRISCOM, L.
The Distribution of Bird-Life in Guatemala, A Contribution to a Study of the Origin of Central American Bird Life. 1932. V. 48
The Warblers of North America. New York: 1957. V. 52; 53

GRISHAM, JOHN
The Chamber. New York: 1994. V. 51; 52; 53; 54
The Client. New York: 1993. V. 53; 54
The Firm. New York: 1991. V. 50; 51; 52; 53; 54
The Pelican Brief. New York: 1992. V. 50; 54
A Time to Kill. New York: 1989. V. 50; 51

GRISONE, FEDERIGO
Gli Ordini di Davalcare. Naples: 1550. V. 54

GRISSOM, MARY ALLEN
The Negro Sings a New Heaven. Chapel Hill: 1930. V. 48

GRISWOLD, ANNA
Colonel Griswold. Boston?: 1866. V. 49

GRISWOLD, FRANK GRAY
After Thoughts. 1936. V. 47
Big and Little Fishes. 1927. V. 47
The Cascapedia Club. 1920. V. 47
The Horse and Buggy Days. 1936. V. 47
The International Polo Cup. New York: 1928. V. 47; 50
The Life History of the Atlantic and Pacific Salmon of Canada. New York: 1930. V. 47
The Life-History of the Canadian Salmon Salmo Salar. 1929. V. 47
The Memoirs of a Salmon. 1931. V. 47
Observations on a Salmon River. 1921. V. 47
Observations on a Salmon River. 1922. V. 47
Observations on a Salmon River. 1925. V. 47
A Salmon River. New York: 1928. V. 47
Salmon Score of F. Gray Griswold for Ten Seasons 1920-1929. 1930. V. 47
Sport on Land and Water, Recollections of Frank Gray Griswold. 1913-31. V. 47
The Tarpon. New York: 1922. V. 47

GRISWOLD, M.
The Golden Age of American Gardens, Proud Owners, Private Estates 1890-1940. New York: 1992. V. 50

GRISWOLD, NORMAN W.
Beauties of California. San Francisco: 1883. V. 52
Beauties of California. San Francisco: 1884. V. 47; 52

GRISWOLD, RUFUS W.
The Female Poets of America. Philadelphia: 1863. V. 51
Gift-Leaves of American Poetry. New York: 1849. V. 48
Passages from the Correspondence and Other Papers of Rufus W. Griswold. Cambridge: 1898. V. 48
The Poetry of the Sentiments. New York. V. 48
The Poets and Poetry of America. Philadelphia: 1842. V. 48; 49
The Prose Writers of America. Philadelphia: 1847. V. 48; 54
The Prose Writers of America. Philadelphia: 1856. V. 49
The Republican Court of American Society in the Days of Washington. New York: 1855. V. 51; 53
The Republican Court of American Society in the Days of Washington. New York: 1856. V. 48
Statement of the Relations of Rufus W. Griswold with Charlotte Myers (Called Cahrlotte Griswold)... Philadelphia: 1856. V. 48

GRISWOLD, WAYNE
Kansas Her Resources and Developments. Cincinnati: 1871. V. 49

GRITSCH, JOHANN
Quadragesimale vna cum Registro Sermonum de Tempore & de Sanctis per Circulum Anni. Venice: 1495. V. 51

GROBER, KARL
Children's Toys of Bygone Days. New York: 1928. V. 51

GROCE, GEORGE E.
The New York Historical Society's Dictionary of Artists in America 1564-1860. New Haven: 1957. V. 48

THE GROCER'S Guide: Being a Directory for Making and Managing All Kinds of Foreign Liquors and Domestic Compounds... New York: 1820. V. 54

GRODDECK, GEORG
The Book of the It. New York: 1928. V. 51

GRODECKI, LOUIS
Gothic Architecture. New York: 1977. V. 53

GROENVELT, JAN
The Rudiments of Physick... London: 1753. V. 51

GROGAN, EWART S.
From the Cape to Cairo: the First Traverse of Africa from Cape to Cairo. London: 1915. V. 54

GROHMANN, WILL
The Art of Henry Moore. New York. V. 47; 48; 50; 52
The Art of Henry Moore. New York: 1960. V. 49
The Art of Henry Moore. London: 1966. V. 50
The Drawings of Paul Klee. New York: 1944. V. 47; 48; 50; 52; 54
Paul Klee. New York: 1954. V. 50
Paul Klee. New York: 1955. V. 49
Paul Klee. New York: 1965. V. 48; 53
Wassily Kandinsky: Life and Work. New York. V. 47; 48; 50; 52
Willi Baumeister: Life and Work. New York. V. 47; 48; 50; 52

GROLIER, JEAN
Bookbindings from the Library of Jean Grolier. A Loan Exhibition. London: 1965. V. 50

GROLIER CLUB, NEW YORK
Catalogue of an Exhibition Illustrative of a Centenary of Artistic Lithography: 1796-1896. New York: 1896. V. 53
Catalogue of an Exhibition of the Works of Charles Dickens. New York: 1913. V. 47; 51
The Catalogue of Books from the Libraries of Collections of Celebrated Bibliophiles and Illustrious Persons of the Past with Arms of Devices Upon the Bindings Exhibited at the Grolier Club in the Month of January 1895. New York: 1895. V. 48; 49; 51; 53
Catalogue of Original and Early Editions of Some of the Poetical and Prose Works of English Writers from Langland to Wither. (&)...From Wither to Prior. New York: 1893-1905. V. 51
Catalogue of Original and Early Editions of Some of the Poetical and Prose Works of English Writers from Wither to Prior... New York: 1905. V. 50; 52
Catalogue of Original and Early Editions of Some of the Poetical and Prose Works of English Writers from Wither to Prior (and, from Langland to Wither). New York: 1963. V. 52
Catalogue of the Works of Rudyard Kipling Exhibited at the Grolier Club, Februrary - March 1929. New York: 1930. V. 51; 52
Description of Early Printed Books Owned by The Grolier Club, With a Brief Account of Their Printers and the History of Typography in the Fifteenth Century. New York: 1895. V. 48
Fifty-Five Books Printed Before 1525, Representing the Works of England's First Printers. New York: 1968. V. 52
Grolier 75: A Bibliographical Retrospective to Celebrate the Seventy-Fifth Anniversary of the Grolier Club. New York: 1959. V. 47; 48; 52
The Grolier Club 1884-1984: Its Library, Exhibitions and Publications. New York: 1984. V. 52
One Hundred Books Famous in English Literature. (and) Bibliographical Notes on One Hundred Books Famous in English Literature. New York: 1902-03. V. 49
One Hundred Influential American Books. New York: 1947. V. 49; 51; 53
Printers' Choice, a Selection of American Press Books, 1968-1978, Catalogue of an Exhibition Held at the Grolier Club, New York, December 19, 1978-February 3, 1979. Austin: 1983. V. 47; 51; 52
Transactions. New York: 1885-1921. V. 51

GROLLMAN, ARTHUR
The Cardiac Output of Man in Health and Disease. Springfield: 1932. V. 48; 53

GRONBECH, WILHELM
The Culture of the Teutons. Copenhagen & London: 1931. V. 49

GRONNIOSAW, JAMES ALBERT UKAWSAW
Wonderous Grace Display'd in the Life and Conversion of James Albert Ukawsaw Gronniosaw, an African Prince. Leeds: 1790. V. 53

GRONOVIUS, JOHAN FREDERICK
Flora Orientalis Siv Recensio Plantarum Quas Botanicorum Coryphaeus Leonhardus Rauwolffus, Medicus Augustanus, Annis 1573 1574 and 1575. Leiden: 1755. V. 49; 52
Flora Virginica... Leyden: 1762. V. 48

GRONOW, REES HOWELL
The Reminiscences and Recollections of Captain Gronow... London: 1889. V. 50
The Reminiscences and Recollections of Captain Gronow. London: 1892. V. 48; 51; 53
The Reminiscences and Recollections of Captain Gronow. London: 1900. V. 50
Reminiscences of Captain Gronow, Formerly of the Grenadier Guards, and M.P. for Stafford. London: 1862. V. 52

GROOM, C. LAURENCE
The Singing Sword. Lees: 1927. V. 52

GROOM, WINSTON
Better Times Than These. New York: 1978. V. 50
Forrest Gump. Garden City: 1986. V. 52; 54
Forrest Gump. New York: 1986. V. 52; 53

GROOME, FRANCIS H.
Ordnance Gazetteer of Scotland: a Survey of Scottish Topography. Edinburgh: 1884-85. V. 47; 53
Ordnance Gazetteer of Scotland: a Survey of Scottish Topography. Edinburgh: 1886. V. 47
Ordnance Gazetteer of Scotland: a Survey of Scottish Topography. London: 1893-95. V. 49
Ordnance Gazetteer of Scotland: A Survey of Scottish Topography. Edinburgh & Glasgow: 1895. V. 52
Two Suffolk Friends. Edinburgh: 1895. V. 49

GROOME, H. C.
Fauquier During the Proprietorship. Richmond: 1927. V. 54

GROPIUS, WALTER
Katsura, Tradition and Creation in Japanese Architecture. Tokyo: 1960. V. 50
The New Architecture and the Bauhaus. Boston. V. 52
The New Architecture and the Bauhaus... New York: 1936. V. 48
The Theater of the Bauhas. Middletown: 1961. V. 54
Town Plan for the Town of Selb. Cambridge: 1969. V. 52

GROPPER, WILLIAM
Your Brother's Blood Cries Out. New York: 1943. V. 53

GROSBOIS, CHARLES
Shuhga: Images of Spring. Essay on Erotic Elements in Japanese Art. Geneva: 1966. V. 53

GROSCH, HENRIK AUGUST
Haandbog til Brodering of Tegning... Copenhagen: 1794. V. 52

GROSE, D.
The Flora of Wiltshire. London: 1957-75. V. 52

GROSE, FRANCIS
The Antiquities of England and Wales... London: 1772-75. V. 47
The Antiquities of England and Wales. London: 1773. V. 54
The Antiquities Of England and Wales. London: 1773-73-75-76. V. 51
The Antiquities of England and Wales. London: 1783-87. V. 48; 49
The Antiquities of England and Wales. London: 1783-97. V. 47; 52
The Antiquities of England and Wales. London: 1784-87. V. 49
The Antiquities of England and Wales. (with) The Antiquities of Scotland. (with) The Antiquities of Ireland. London: 1789-91-97. V. 50

GROSE, FRANCIS continued
The Antiquities of Ireland. London: 1791-95. V. 47
The Antiquities of Ireland. Kilkenny: 1982. V. 48; 50
The Antiquities of Scotland. London: 1789. V. 48
The Antiquities of Scotland. London: 1797. V. 47; 49; 51; 53
A Classical Dictionary of the Vulgar Tongue. London: 1796. V. 52
Lexicon Balatronicum. London: 1811. V. 52
Military Antiquities Respecting a History of the English Army. London: 1786-88. V. 50
Military Antiquities Respecting a History of the English Army. London: 1801. V. 50; 54
Military Antiquities Respecting a History of the English Army. London: 1812. V. 48; 50; 51; 53
The Olio. London: 1792. V. 47; 51; 52
The Olio: Being a Collection of Essays, Dialogues, Letters, Biographical Sketches... London: 1796. V. 48; 50; 54
A Provincial Glossary, with a Collection of Local Proverbs and Popular Superstitions. London: 1787. V. 52
A Provincial Glossary: with a Collection of Local Proverbs and Popular Superstitions. London: 1790. V. 48; 51; 52
A Provincial Glossary: With a Collection of Local Proverbs and Popular Superstitions. London: 1811. V. 47; 51; 52
Rules for Drawing Caricatures: with an Essay on Comic Painting. London: 1788. V. 54
A Treatise on Ancient Armour and Weapons... London: 1785. V. 47
A Treatise on Ancient Armour and Weapons. London: 1812. V. 49

GROSE, JOHN HENRY
A Voyage to the East Indies, with Observations on Varaious Parts There. London: 1757. V. 53

GROSE, S. W.
Catalogue of the McClean Collection of Greek Coins. Chicago: 1979. V. 48

GROSER, HORACE G.
Little Folks'-Land. London: 1895. V. 49

GROSE SMITH, H.
Rhopalocera Exotica. London: 1887-94. V. 54

GROSJEAN, PAUL
A Catalogue of Incunabula in the Library at Milltown Park, Dublin. Dublin: 1932. V. 51

GROSLEY, PIERRE JEAN
A Tour to London; or, New Observations on England and Its Inhabitants. London: 1772. V. 48

GROSS, C.
Bibliography of English History to 1485. Oxford: 1970-79. V. 48

GROSS, C. W. F.
Descriptive Catalogue of Books Contained in the Lending Library. London: 1901. V. 48

GROSS, CHAIM
The Sculpture Reliefs of the Ten Commandments: at International Synagogue. Jamaica: 1973. V. 47

GROSS, LOUIS
The Blood Supply to the Heart in Its Anatomical and Clinical Apsects. New York: 1921. V. 49; 53
The Blood Supply to the Heart In Its Anatomical and Clinical Aspects. Springfield: 1932. V. 53

GROSS, ROBERT E.
The Surgery of Infancy and Childhood. Philadelphia: 1953. V. 54

GROSS, SAMUEL D.
The Anatomy, Physiology and Diseases of the Bones and Joints. Philadelphia: 1830. V. 53
Autobiography of Samuel D. Gross, M.D. Philadelphia: 1887. V. 49
Elements of Pathological Anatomy. Philadelphia: 1845. V. 48; 53
History of American Medical Literature from 1776 to the Present Time. Philadelphia: 1876. V. 52
A Practical Treatise on Foreign Bodies in the Air Passages. Philadelphia: 1854. V. 48
A System of Surgery. Philadelphia: 1859. V. 48; 51
A System of Surgery. Philadelphia: 1872. V. 52
A System of Surgery. Philadelphia: 1882. V. 48

GROSS, SAMUEL W.
A Practical Treatise on Tumors of the Mammary Gland: Embracing Their Histology, Pathology, Diagnosis and Treatment. New York: 1880. V. 48

GROSSE, ALEXANDER
A Fiery Pillar of Heavenly Truth: Shewing the Way to a Blessed Life... London: 1652. V. 49

GROSSE, HENNING
Magica de Spectris et Apparitionibus Spiritm, de Vaticiniis, Divinationibus &c. Leiden: 1656. V. 50; 54

GROSSETESTE, ROBERT
The Castle of Love, a Poem. Brixton Hill: 1849. V. 49
De Cessatione Legalium. London: 1658. V. 53

GROSSINGER, RICHARD
Book of the Earth and The Sky: Book I and II. Los Angeles: 1971. V. 54

GROSSMITH, GEORGE
The Diary of a Nobody. Bristol: 1892. V. 47; 54
The Diary of a Nobody. Bristol & London: 1911. V. 51

GROSVENOR, BENJAMIN
Health, an Essay on Its Nature, Value, Uncertainty, Preservation and Best Improvement. London: 1748. V. 47; 48; 49

GROSVENOR, EDWIN A.
Constantinople. Boston: 1895. V. 53

GROSZ, GEORGE
Ecce Homo. Berlin: 1923. V. 51
Ecce Homo. New York: 1966. V. 50; 52
Interregnum. New York: 1936. V. 54

GROTE, GEORGE
Fragments on Ethical Subjects. London: 1876. V. 49
A History of Greece. London: 1846-56. V. 54
A History of Greece. London: 1851. V. 49
History of Greece. London: 1851-57. V. 48
History of Greece. New York: 1856. V. 49
A History of Greece. London: 1862. V. 49; 51; 52
A History of Greece. London: 1884. V. 50
History of Greece. London: 1888. V. 48
The Minor Works of George Grote. London: 1873. V. 54
Poems...1815-1823. London: 1872. V. 51
Seven Letters on the Recent Politics in Switzerland. 1847. V. 49

GROTE, HARRIET
Collected Papers. London: 1862. V. 54

GROTE, JOHN
An Examination of the Utilitarian Philosophy... Cambridge: 1870. V. 52
Exploratio Philosophica: Rough Notes on Modern Intellectual Science. Cambridge: 1865. V. 49

GROTE, MRS.
The Philosophical Radicals of 1832. London: 1866. V. 51

GROTH, JOHN
John Groth's World of Sport. New York: 1970. V. 47; 48
Studio: Asia. Cleveland: 1952. V. 47
Studio: Europe. New York: 1945. V. 47

GROTIUS, HUGO
De Jure Belli Ac Pacis. Amsterdam: 1712. V. 48
De Jure Belli ac Pacis Libri Tres. Amsterdami: 1642. V. 47
De Jure Belli ac Pacis Libri Tres. Amsterdami: 1646. V. 49
Florum Sparsio ad Ius Justinianeum. Amstelodami: 1643. V. 47
His Three Books Treating of the Rights of War and Peace. London: 1682. V. 51; 54
Poemata, Collecta Olim a Fratre Ejus Guil Grotio & Per Eundem Edita... Londini: 1639. V. 48; 50

GROTO, LUIGI
Le Orationi Volgari. Venice: 1593. V. 48
Trofeo Della Vittoria Sacra, Ottenuta Dalla Christianiss... Venice: 1572. V. 51

THE GROUNDS and Rudiments of Law and Equity... London: 1751. V. 54

GROUT, A. J.
Moss Flora of North America. Newfane: 1928-40. V. 53
Moss Flora of North America. Newfane: 1936-39. V. 54

GROVE, GEORGE
A Dictionary of Music and Musicians. London: 1936. V. 49
Grove's Dictionary of Music and Musicians. London: 1922. V. 48
Grove's Dictionary of Music and Musicians. London: 1954-61. V. 49

GROVE, HARRIET
The Calendar of Nature or the Seasons of England, by the Honble. Mrs. (E. Grove) Cradock. London: 1851. V. 49

GROVE, HENRY
A System of Moral Philosophy... London: 1749. V. 48

GROVE, RICHARD ANDREW
Views of the Principal Seats and Marine and Landscape Scenery, in the Neighbourhood of Lymington (Hampshire). Lymington: 1832. V. 52

GROVES, J.
The British Charophyta. London: 1920-24. V. 48
The British Charophyta. London: 1920-25. V. 49

GROVES, J. P.
Sketches of Adventure and Sport. 1885. V. 48; 52; 54

GROVES, NAOMI JACKSON
A. Y.'s Canada. Toronto: 1968. V. 53

GROVES, PERCY
History of the 21st Royal Scots Fusiliers, (Formerly the 21st Royal North British Fusiliers, etc.), 1678-1895. Johnston, Edinburgh: 1895. V. 51
History of the 79th Queen's Own Cameron Highlanders, Now the First Battalion...1794-1893. Edinburgh: 1893. V. 51

GROWOLL, ADOLPH
Book Trade Bibliography in the United States. New York: 1939. V. 50
Three Centuries of English Booktrade Bibliography. New York: 1903. V. 50

GRUBB, DAVIS
The Night of the Hunter. New York: 1953. V. 47; 51; 52

GRUBB, DAVIS continued
The Night of the Hunter. London: 1954. V. 47
Twelve Tales of Suspense and the Supernatural. New York: 1964. V. 48; 50; 51

GRUBB, SARAH
Some Account of the Life and Religious Labours of... Dublin: 1792. V. 48; 52
Some Account of the Life and Religious Labours of... Trenton: 1795. V. 53
Some Acocunt of the Life and Religious Labours of... London: 1796. V. 54

GRUBE, ERNST J.
Islamic Paintings From the 11th to the 18th Century in the Collection of Hans P. Kraus. New York. V. 52

GRUBER, F.
Illustrated Guide and Catalogue of Woodwards Gardens Located on Mission Street. San Francisco: 1879. V. 54

GRUBER, FRANZ
Stille Nacht Heilige Hacht: A Christmas Song. New York: 1933. V. 48

GRUEBER, H. A.
Coins of the Roman Republic in the British Museum. London: 1970. V. 48

GRUEL, LEON
Manuel Historique et Bibliographiqe de l'Amateur de Reliures. Paris: 1887/1905. V. 49

GRUELLE, JOHNNY
Beloved Belindy. Chicago: 1926. V. 49
Eddie Elephant. Chicago: 1921. V. 54
Johnny Gruelle's Golden Book. Chicago: 1946. V. 47
The Little Brown Bear. Chicago: 1920. V. 54
Little Sunny Stories. Joliet: 1919. V. 54
Marcella: a Raggedy Ann Story. Joliet: 1929. V. 47
Raggedy Ann's Magical Wishes. New York: 1928. V. 47; 52
Raggedy Ann's Sunny Songs. New York: 1930. V. 54

GRUELLE, R. B.
Notes Critical and Biographical. Indianapolis: 1895. V. 48

GRUEN, J.
Menotti. New York: 1952. V. 49

GRUFFYDD, W. J.
Caniadau. 1932. V. 48
Caniadau. Newtown: 1932. V. 52; 54

GRUGER, HERIBERT
The Sing Song Picture Book. Philadelphia: 1931. V. 49; 54

GRUMBACH, DORIS
Chamber Music. New York: 1979. V. 54
The Spoil of the Flowers. New York: 1962. V. 48; 51

GRUNDTLICHER vnd Warhaffter Bericht/ von Erobergun der Statt S. Quintin/ Durch ein Namhafften aub dem Leger Geschriben (sic). 1557. V. 53

GRUNDY, C. R.
Catalogue of the Paintings and Drawings in the Collection of Frederick John Nettleford. London: 1933-38. V. 50

GRUNDY, GEORGE
Hunting Journal. London: 1913-55. V. 47

GRUNER, LEWIS
Decorations and Stuccos of Churches and Palaces in Italy. London: 1854. V. 52
The Decorations of the Garden Pavilion, in the Grounds of Buckingham Palace. London: 1846. V. 52; 53
Fresco Decorations and Stuccoes of Churches and Palaces in Italy During the Fifteenth and Sixteenth Centuries. London: 1854. V. 53
The Good Shunammite. London: 1847. V. 51; 54

GRUNER, OSKAR CAMERON
The Biology of the Blood-Cells with a Glossary of Hematological Terms. New York: 1914. V. 48; 53
Descriptive Catalogue of the Medical Museum of McGill University... Oxford: 1915. V. 53
A Treatise on the Canon of Medicine of Avicenna, Incorporating a Translation of the First Book. London: 1930. V. 50; 52

GRUNER, WILHELM HEINRICH LUDWIG
Specimens of Ornamental Art, Selected From the Best Models of the Classical Epochs. London: 1850. V. 51

GRUSHENKA. Three Times a Woman. Paris: 1933. V. 54

GRUSHKIN, P. D.
The Art of Rock; Posters from Presley to Punk. New York: 1987. V. 47

GRUYTRODE, JACOBUS DE
Lavarcrum Conscientie. 1505?. V. 51

GRYNAUS, SIMON
Novus Orbis Regionum Ac Insularum Veteribus Incognitarum... Basel: 1532. V. 51

GRZIMEK, BERNHARD
Grzimek's Animal Life Encyclopedia. New York: 1972-75. V. 50; 54
Grzimek's Animal Life Encyclopedia. Birds. New York: 1972-73. V. 50
Grzimek's Animal Life Encyclopedia. Volume 7-9, Birds. London: 1972-73. V. 50
Grzimek's Encyclopaedia of Mammals. London: 1990. V. 50

GSELL-FELS, THEODOR
Switzerland: Its Scenery and People. London: 1881. V. 47; 52

GUADALUPE ISLAND COMPANY INC.
Prospectus of the Guadalupe Island Company, Incorporated Jan. 25, 1873. San Francisco: 1873. V. 47

GUALDO PRIORATO, GALEAZZO
The History of France. London: 1676. V. 54

THE GUARDS. London: 1827. V. 48; 50; 51

GUARE, JOHN
Six Degrees of Separation. New York: 1990. V. 51; 52

GUARINI, GIOVANNI BATTISTA
Il Pastor Fido. London: 1676. V. 49
Il Pastor Fido. Londra: 1728. V. 49
Il Pastor Fido. Glasgua: 1763. V. 48; 54
Il Segretario. Dialogo... Venice: 1600. V. 47

GUAZZO, FRANCESCO MARIA, BROTHER
Compendium Maleficarum Collected in 3 Books from Many Sources by... London: 1929. V. 50

GUAZZO, STEFANO
Lettere. Venice: 1596. V. 48

GUBBINS, MARTIN RICHARD
An Account of the Mutinies of Oudh, and of the Siege of the Lucknow Residency... London: 1858. V. 53

GUBELIN, E. J.
Photoatlas of Inclusions in Gemstones. London: 1992. V. 54

GUDLAUGSON, MAGNUS G.
Three Times a Pioneer by Magnus G. Gudlaugson, a Peace River Pioneer. Winnipeg: 1959. V. 48

GUEDALLA, PHILIP
Ignes Fatui. (with) Metri Gratia: Verse and Prose. Oxford: 1911/11. V. 49

GUELLETTE, T. S.
Peruvian Tales, related in One Thousand and One Hours, By One of the Select Virgins of Cusco, to the Ynca of Peru... London: 1734/39/45. V. 50

GUENON, M. FRANCIS
A Treatise on Milch Cows, Whereby the Quality and Quantity of Milk Which Any Cow Will Give May be Accurately Determined by Observing Natural Marks on External Indications Alone... New York: 1854. V. 54

GUERBER, HELENE ADELINE
Myths of the Norsemen, from the Eddas and Sagas. London: 1911. V. 52; 54

GUERIN, JULES
Water Colour Rendering Suggestions by Jules Guerin & Maxfield Parrish. Cleveland: 1905-10. V. 48

GUERIN, MARCEL
L'Oeuvre Grave de Gauguin. Paris: 1927. V. 50
L'Oeuvre Grave de Gauguin. San Francisco: 1980. V. 49

GUERIN, MAURICE DE
The Centaur and The Bacchante. 1899. V. 47
The Centaur and the Bacchante. London: 1899. V. 49; 50; 53
Poemes en Prose. Verona: 1954. V. 50

GUERINI, V.
A History of Denistry from the Most Ancient Times Until the End of the Eighteenth Century. Philadelphia: 1909. V. 48; 49; 50; 51; 52; 53

GUERINOT, J. V.
Pamphlet Attacks On Alexander Pope 1711-1744, a Descriptive Bibliography. New York: 1969. V. 48

GUERLAC, HENRY A.
History of Science: a Bibliography for a Core Collection. Ann Arbor: 1968. V. 54
Science and War in the Old Regime. Cambridge: 1941. V. 54

GUERNSEY, COUNTESS
Most Important and Interesting Pamphlet, Being a New and Genuine edition of the Death Bed Confessions of the Late Countess of Guernsey to Lady Anne H(arrington) Developing a Series of Mysterious Transactions... London: 1822. V. 50; 51

GUERNSEY, HENRY N.
The Application of the Principles and Practice of Homoeopathy to Obstetrics and the Disorders Peculiar to Women and Young Children. New York: 1874. V. 53

GUERNSEY, ORRIN
History of Rock County, and Transactions of the Rock County Agricultural Society and Mecahnics' Inst. Janesville: 1856. V. 52

GUERRA, FRANCISCO
American Medical Bibliography 1639-1783. New York: 1962. V. 50; 52

GUESS, PSEUD.
Scenes from the Life of Nickleby Married. London: 1840. V. 49; 54

THE GUEST. Author Unknown. 17th Century Christ Church Manuscript. With Woodcuts by Helen Siegel. Vermont: 1976. V. 51

GUEST, BARBARA
Goodnough. Paris: 1962. V. 47

GUEST, GRACE DUNHAM
Shiraz Painting in the Sixteenth Century. Washington: 1949. V. 48

GUEST, JOHN
Relics and Records of Men and Manufactures At Or in the Neighbourhood of Rotherham, in the County of York. Rotherham: 1866. V. 50; 51; 53

GUEULETTE, THOMAS SIMON
Chinese Tales; or the Wonderful Adventures of the Mandarin Fum-Hoam. London: 1817. V. 49

GUEULLETTE, THOMAS SIMON
Chinese Tales: Or, the Wonderful Adventures of the Mandarin Fum-Hoam. London: 1745. V. 53
Tartarian Tales: or, a Thousand and One Quarter of Hours. London: 1759. V. 47; 48; 52; 53

GUEVARA, ANTONIO DE
The Dial of Princes... London: 1582. V. 47; 51; 52; 53
(Greek title), or, The Diall of Princes... London: 1619. V. 52
The Mount of Caluraie. London: 1595. V. 47; 49
The Praise and Happinesse of the Countrie-Life. Newtown: 1938. V. 47; 52; 54

GUEVARA, LAVARO
St. George at Silene. Paris: 1928. V. 50

GUEVARA, LUIS VELEZ DE
Ines Reigned in Death. Lexington: 1988. V. 51

GUGGENHEIM, PEGGY
Out of This Century. New York: 1946. V. 49

GUGLIELMINI, DOMENICO
Della Natura de'Fiumi Trattato Fisico-Matematico. Bologna: 1697. V. 52
Della Natura de'Fiumi Trattato Fisico-Matematico Nuova Edizione con Le Annotazioni di Eustachio Manfredi... Bologna: 1739. V. 50

GUGLIELMO DA SALICETO
Summa Conservationis et Curationis. (and) Chirurgia. Venice: 1502. V. 47

GUIA de Forasteros en Las Islas Filipinas, Para el Ano de 1842. Manila: 1844. V. 53

GUIART, JEAN
The Arts of the South Pacific. New York: 1963. V. 48; 50; 52; 54

GUICCIARDINI, FRANCESCO
Aphorismes Civill and Militarie: Amplified with Authorities and Exemplified with Historie... London: 1613. V. 53
Della Istoria d'Italia. Friburgo: 1775-76. V. 47
La Historia d'Italia. 1565. V. 47
The Historie of Guicciardin... London: 1599. V. 51; 52
The Historie of Guicciardin... London: 1618. V. 47; 48; 52

GUICCIARDINI, LODOVICO
Commentarii di...delle Cose Piu Memorabili Seguite in Europa: Specialmente in Questi Paesi Bassi; Dalla Pace di Cambrai, del CMXXIX... 1565. V. 47
Detti et Fatti Piacevoli et Gravi di Diversi Principi Filosofi, et Cortiginai... Venice: 1565. V. 47
Les Heures de Recreation et Apresdisnees... Paris: 1573. V. 48

GUICCIARDINI, LUDOVICO
Les Heures de Recreation et Apresdisnees... Paris: 1571. V. 53

GUICHARD, K.
British Etchers 1850-1940. London: 1977. V. 47

GUICHARD, KENNETH M.
British Etchers 1850-1940. London: 1977. V. 53

GUIDE Book and Atlas of Muskoka and Parry Sound Districts. Toronto: 1879. V. 50

GUIDE of Berlin, Potsdam and Environs. Berlin. V. 47

A GUIDE to Capitalists and Emigrants: Being a Statistical and Descriptive Account of the Several counties of the State of North Carolina. Raleigh: 1869. V. 49

GUIDE to Knole House. Sevenoaks: 1874. V. 47

GUIDE to the City and County of Perth. London: 1820. V. 52

A GUIDE to the City of York, Being the Best Concise Historical Description of All the Public Buildings, Antiquities &c. of that Ancient City. York: 1848. V. 51

A GUIDE to the English Lake District, Intended Principally for the Use of Pedestrians. Windermere: 1863. V. 47

A GUIDE to the English Lake District Intended Principally for the Use of Pedestrians. London: 1865. V. 52

A GUIDE to the Lions of Philadelphia. Philadelphia: 1837. V. 51

GUIDE to the National Museum of Ethnology. Osaka: 1992. V. 54

GUIDE to the Province of British Columbia for 1877-8. Victoria: 1877. V. 49

GUIDO DE MONTE ROCHEN
Manipulis Curatlorum. Strassburg: 1487. V. 53
Manipulus Curaltorum. London: 1500. V. 53

GUIDOL, JOBE
Goya 1746-1828: Biography, analytical Study and Catalogue of His Paintings. Barcelona: 1985. V. 47

GUIDONI, E.
Primitive Architecture. Milan: 1975. V. 51

GUIDOTT, THOMAS
A Collection of Treatises Relating to the City and Waters of Bath. London: 1725. V. 52
De Thermis Britannicis Tractatus, Accesserunt Observationes Hydrostaticae, Chromaticae, & Miscellaneae... London: 1691. V. 48

GUIGO THE CARTHUSIAN
On the Solitary Life. 1977. V. 48; 49

GUILD, GEORGE B.
A Brief Narrative of the Fourth Tennessee Cavalry Regiment... Nashville: 1913. V. 49

GUILDAY, PETER
The Life and Times of John England, First Bishop of Charleston (1786-1842). New York: 1927. V. 48

GUILELMUS, ABP. OF TYRE
The History of Goedefrey of Boloyne and of the Conquest of Iherusalem. Hammersmith: 1893. V. 48

GUILEVILLE, GUILLAUME DE
The Ancient Poem... (with) The Booke of the Pylgrymage of the Sowle... London: 1858/59. V. 54

GUILFORD, FRANCIS NORTH, 1ST BARON
A Philosophical Essay of Musick Directed to a Friend. London: 1677. V. 47

GUILHOU, E.
Catalogue of a Collection of Ancient Rings Formed by the Late E. Guilhou. V. 53

GUILLAM, JOHN
A Display of Heraldrie... London: 1611. V. 47

GUILLAUME, GEORGE
Architectural Views and Details of Netley Abbey (Southampton), Partly Shown As It Originally Existed... Southampton: 1848. V. 48

GUILLAUME, P.
Primitive Negro of Sculpture. New York: 1926. V. 47; 48; 50; 51; 53; 54

GUILLEMARD, ARTHUR G.
Over Land and Sea. London: 1875. V. 53

GUILLEMARD, F. H. H.
The Cruise of the Marchesa to Kamschatka and New Guinea. London: 1886. V. 48; 50; 51
The Cruise of the Marchesa to Kamschatka and New Guinea. London: 1889. V. 54

GUILLERMUS PARISIENSIS
Dialogus de Septem Sacramentis. Mainz: 1492. V. 47; 49; 50
Postilla, Super Epistolas et Evangelia. Basel: 1500. V. 47; 49
Rhetorica Divina. Basel: 1492. V. 52

GUILLET, EDWIN C.
Toronto: from Trading Post to Great City. Toronto: 1934. V. 50

GUILLET, PETER
Timber Merchant's Guide. Baltimore: 1823. V. 50; 54

GUILLET DE SAINT-GEORGE, GEORGES
The Gentleman's Dictionary. London: 1705. V. 48; 52

GUILLIE, SEBASTIEN
Essai Sur L'Instruction des Aveugle. Paris: 1817. V. 52; 54
An Essay on the Instruction and Amusements of the Blind. London: 1894. V. 50

GUILLIM, JOHN
A Display of Heraldrie... London: 1632. V. 54
A Display of Heraldrie: Manifesting a More Easie Accesse to the Knowledge Thereof... London: 1638. V. 47
A Display of Heraldrie: Manifesting a More Easie Accesse to the Knowledge Thereof... London: 1660. V. 52; 54
A Display of Heraldry... London: 1679. V. 49
A Display of Heraldry. London: 1724. V. 47; 48; 50; 53

GUINESS, ALEC
Blessings in Disguise. London: 1985. V. 50

GUINEY, LOUISE IMOGEN
Lover's Saint Ruth's and Three Other Tales. Boston: 1895. V. 49

GUINN, JAMES MILLER
Historical and Biographical Record of Southern California. Chicago: 1902. V. 47
A History of California and an Extended History Of its Southern Coast Counties. Los Angeles: 1907. V. 47
A History of California and an Extended History of Los Angeles and Environs. Los Angeles: 1915. V. 49; 52

THE GUINNESS Book of Superlatives. New York: 1956. V. 48; 51

GUINNESS, MARY GERALDINE
In the Far East. London: 1901. V. 50
The Story of the China Indland Mission. London: 1893-4. V. 52
The Story of the China Inland Mission. London: 1894. V. 53

GUINNESS Scrapbook. London: 1937. V. 54

GUINOT, M. EUGENE
A Summer at Baden-Baden. London: 1853. V. 53

GUISE, HENRI, DUKE OF
Memoires...Relating to His Passage to Naples, and Heading There the Second Revolt of that People. London: 1669. V. 48; 50; 54

GUITRY, SACHA
Deburau. 1925. V. 52

GUIZOT, M.
History of Oliver Cromwell, and the English Commonwealth, from the Execution of Charles I to the Death of Cromwell. London: 1854. V. 49

GUIZOT, MME.
L'Ecolier u Raoul & Victor. Paris: 1846. V. 50

GULLAND, W. G.
Chinese Porcelain. London: 1902. V. 51

GULLIVERIANA: or, a Fourth Volume of Miscellanies. London: 1728. V. 54

GULSTON, ALAN JAMES
Warren Knowles: a Novel. London: 1885. V. 54

GUMBLE, THOMAS
The Life of General Monck, Duke of Albemarle &c. with Remarks Upon His Actions... London: 1671. V. 49

GUMILLA, JOSEPH
El Orinoco Ilustrado, y Defendido, Historia Natural, Civil y Geographica de Este Gran Rio, y de sus Caudalosas Vertientes... Mardird: 1745. V. 48

GUMMER, ELLIS N.
Dickens' Works in Germany 1837-1937. Oxford: 1940. V. 49

THE GUN At Home and Abroad. London: 1912. V. 49
THE GUN At Home and Abroad. London: 1912-15. V. 48

THE GUN At Home and Abroad. British Deer & Ground Game, Dogs, Guns & Rifles. London: 1913. V. 48

THE GUN at Home and Abroad: The British Game of Asia and North America. 1915. V. 54

GUN, NERIN E.
Red Roses from Texas. London: 1964. V. 51; 54

GUNN, ALEXANDER
The Hermitage-Zoar Note-Book and Journal of Travel and Letters. New York: 1902. V. 47

GUNN, DONALD
History of Manitoba From the Earliest Settlement to 1835, by the Late Hon. Donald Gunn, and From 1835 to the Admission of the Province Into the Dominion, by Charles R. Tuttle. Ottawa: 1880. V. 49

GUNN, DOUGLAS
Picturesque San Diego. Chicago: 1887. V. 50; 51; 54

GUNN, GEORGE W.
The Adventures of Rufus Rastus Brown in Darktown. Chicago: 1906. V. 53

GUNN, JOHN
Memorials of John Gunn. Norwich: 1891. V. 48

GUNN, JOHN C.
Gunn's Domestic Medicine, or Poor Man's Friend. Madisonville: 1837. V. 48
Gunn's Domestic Medicine, or Poor Man's Friend. Xenia: 1838. V. 50
Gunn's Domestic Medicine, or Poor Man's Friend. New York: 1842. V. 50
Gunn's Domestic Medicine, or Poor Man's Friend. New York: 1849. V. 52
Gunn's New Domestic Physician; Or, Home Book of Health. Cincinnati: 1864. V. 48

GUNN, LEWIS
Records of a California Family, Journals and Letters. San Diego: 1928. V. 49

GUNN, M.
Botanical Exploration of Southern Africa. Rotterdam: 1981. V. 49; 52

GUNN, N.
Highland River. 1937. V. 50

GUNN, NEIL M.
The Lost Glen. Edinburgh: 1932. V. 51

GUNN, TH0M
Unsought Intimacies: Poems of 1991. Berkeley: 1993. V. 52

GUNN, THOM
At the Barriers. New York: 1989. V. 54
Collected Poems. London: 1993. V. 51; 53
The Explorers. Devon: 1969. V. 52; 53; 54
Fighting Terms. Eynsham: 1954. V. 47
Fighting Terms. New York: 1958. V. 49
Games of Chance. Omaha: 1979. V. 52
A Geography. Iowa City: 1966. V. 53; 54
Jack Straw's Castle. London: 1976. V. 53
Mandrakes. London: 1973. V. 48; 52; 53; 54
The Menace. San Francisco: 1982. V. 53
The Missed Beat. Newark: 1976. V. 52; 53; 54
Moly: Poems. London. V. 47; 49; 53
My Sad Captains and other Poems. London: 1961. V. 47; 49; 50; 53
Positives. London: 1964. V. 54
Songbook. New York: 1973. V. 52; 54
Sunlight. New York: 1969. V. 54
Touch. London: 1967. V. 54
Undesirables. Durham: 1988. V. 54

GUNN, THOMAS
The Sense of Movement. Chicago: 1957. V. 48

GUNNING, GEORGE
Documents on the Gunning Family. Cheltenham: 1834. V. 53

GUNNING, HENRY
Reminiscences of the University, Town and County of Cambridge, From the Year 1780. London: 1854. V. 53

GUNNISON, JOHN W.
The Mormons; or Latter-Day Saints, in the Valley of the Great Salt Lake. Philadelphia: 1852. V. 47; 49
The Mormons; or, Latter-Day Saints, in the Valley of the Great Salt Lake. Philadelphia: 1856. V. 49; 51

GUNPOWDER-TREASON: With a Discourse of the Manner of Its Discovery. London: 1679. V. 51

GUNTER, A. C.
Mr. Potter of Texas. New York: 1888. V. 51
My Japanese Prince. New York: 1904. V. 47; 52

GUNTER, EDMUND
The Description and Use of the Sector, the Crosse-Staffe and Other Instruments. London: 1636. V. 54
The Works. London: 1662. V. 51
The Works of... London: 1673. V. 48; 49; 52

GUNTHER, A. C.
Catalogue of the Batrachia Salientia in the...British Museum. London: 1858. V. 48; 50
The Reptiles of British India. London: 1864. V. 47

GUNTHER, JOHN
The Golden Fleece. New York: 1959. V. 54

GUNTHER, R. T.
The Herbal of Apuleius Barbarus from the Early 12th Century Manuscript Formerly in the Abbey of Bury St. Edmunds. Oxford: 1925. V. 54
The Life and Work of Robert Hooke. Oxford: 1930-38. V. 51

GUNTHER, R. W.
Early Science at Oxford. London: 1923-67. V. 53

GUNTHER, ROBERT T.
The Astrolabes of the World. London: 1976. V. 53

GUNTON, SYMON
The History of the Church of Peterburgh: Wherein the Most Remarkable Things Concerning that Place, from the First Foundation Thereof... London: 1686. V. 51

GUR-ARIE, MEIR
The Pioneers, Silhouettes of Image, Patches of Songs of the Pioneers. Jerusalem: 1924. V. 50; 53

GURDIJIAN, E. S.
Mechanisms, Diagnosis and Management of Head Injuries. Boston: 1958. V. 52

GURDIJIEFF, G. I.
Scenario of the Ballet - the Struggle of the Magicians. Cape Town: 1957. V. 50

GURDJIEFF, GEORGE
The Herald of Coming Good, First Appeal to Contemporary Humanity. Paris: 1933. V. 48

GURGANUS, ALLAN
Breathing Lessons. 1981. V. 51; 53
Oldest Living Confederate Widow Tells All. New York: 1989. V. 48; 49; 51; 53
White People. New York: 1991. V. 49; 51

GURNEY, EDMUND
Phantasms of the Living. London: 1886. V. 48

GURNEY, GOLDSWORTHY
Account of the Steam-Jet, or Blast... London: 1859. V. 50
First (-third) Report of Mr. Goldsworthy Gurney on the Ventilation of the New House of Commons. London: 1852. V. 53

GURNEY, IVOR
Poems. London: 1954. V. 49

GURNEY, J. H.
The Gannet. London: 1913. V. 50; 51; 52; 53

GURNEY, JOSEPH JOHN
Familiar Sketch of the Late William Wilberforce. Norwich: 1838. V. 49
Notes On a Visit made to Some of the Prisons in Scotland and England, in Company with Elizabeth Fry... London: 1819. V. 50; 51
A Winter in the West Indies. London: 1840. V. 47; 51; 52
A Winter in the West Indies. London: 1841. V. 49

GURNEY, R.
The British Freshwater Copedoda. London: 1931-33. V. 48

GURNEY, SAMUEL
London and its Environs Described. London: 1761. V. 49

GURNEY, WILLIAM
The Nosegay. London: 1830. V. 52

GURNEY, WILLIAM BRODIE
Trial of Pedro De Zuleta, Jun., in the Central Criminal Court of the City of London, on the 27th, 28th and 30th of Oc. 1843, on a Charge of Slave-Trading... London: 1844. V. 53

GUROWSKI, A. DE, COUNT
Russia As It Is. New York: 1854. V. 50

GUSSOW, ALAN
A Sense of Place: the Artist and the American Land. San Francisco: 1975. V. 53

GUSTAFSON, RALPH
Alfred the Great. London: 1937. V. 47
The Brazen Tower. Tillsonburg: 1974. V. 50
Flight into Darkness. New York: 1944. V. 47
The Golden Chalice. London: 1935. V. 47
Rocky Mountain Poems. Vancouver: 1960. V. 47
Twleve Landscapes. Toronto: 1985. V. 47

GUSTAFSSON, G. V.
Observations on the Steam-Navy of the Great Britain, & the Horse-Power of Marine-Engines, Being a Practical Solution...(with) A Letter to the Editor of the Practical Mechanic...(with) Practical Observations on the Present State of the Steam-Engine... London: 1847/47/47. V. 54

GUSTAVUS, C. DOANE
Report of Lieutenant Gustavus C. Doane, Upon the So-Called Yellowstone Expedition of 1870. Washington: 1873. V. 48

GUTCH, JOHN
Collectanea Curiosa; or Miscellaneous Tracts Relating to the History and Antiquities of England and Ireland... Oxford: 1781. V. 52

GUTCH, JOHN MATHEW
Caraboo. Bristol: 1817. V. 47

GUTCH, JOHN MATTHEW
A Lytell Geste of Robin Hode, With Other Ancient and Modern Ballads and Songs Relating to This Celebrated Yeoman, To Which is Prefixed His History and Character... London: 1847. V. 50

GUTERSON, DAVID
The Country Ahead of Us, The Country Behind. New York: 1989. V. 53

GUTHE, CARL E.
Pueblo Pottery Making, a Study at the Village of San Ildefonso. Andover: 1925. V. 52
Pueblo Pottery Making: a Study at the Village of San Ildefonso. New Haven: 1925. V. 51

GUTHRIE, A. B.
The Big Sky. London: 1947. V. 50
The Big Sky. New York: 1947. V. 51; 52; 54
Big Sky, Fair Land: the Environmental Essays. 1988. V. 50; 51
Big Sky, Fair Land: the Environmental Essays. Northland: 1988. V. 54
Once Upon a Pond. Missoula: 1973. V. 53
These Thousand Hills. Boston: 1956. V. 54
The Way West. New York: 1949. V. 53

GUTHRIE, GEORGE
Commentaries On the Surgery of the War in Portugal, Spain, France and the Netherlands, From the Battle of Rolica, in 1808... Philadelphia: 1862. V. 47; 48
Directions to Army Surgeons on the Field of battle. New York: 1861. V. 48
On Wounds and Injuries of the Abdomen and Pelvis. London: 1847. V. 53

GUTHRIE, JAMES
An Album of Drawings. London: 1900. V. 47; 49
The Book Craftsman, a Technical Journal for Printers and Collectors of Fine Editions. Flansham: 1934-35. V. 51
Divine Discontent. 1913. V. 49
The Elf: a Little Book. First Series Nos. 1-4. London: 1899-1900. V. 48
The Elf. Winter Number. London: 1904. V. 53
From a Sussex Village. Flansham: 1951. V. 49
A Little Anthology of Hietherto Uncollected Poems by Modern Writers. Bognor: 1922. V. 51
A Second Book of Drawings. Edinburgh: 1907. V. 51
The Wild Garden. Verses for Children. Flansham: 1924. V. 50

GUTHRIE, K. S.
A Romance of Two Centuries. 1919. V. 49; 54

GUTHRIE, KEITH
History of San Patricio County. Austin: 1986. V. 54

GUTHRIE, MARIA
A Tour Performed in the Years 1795-6, through the Taurida or Crimea. London: 1802. V. 48; 50

GUTHRIE, RAMON
Trobar Clus. Northampton: 1923. V. 47; 54

GUTHRIE, THOMAS
Autobiography of Thomas Guthrie, D.D. and Memoir by His Sons. London: 1875-76. V. 54

GUTHRIE, WOODY
American Folksong. New York: 1947. V. 52
Bound for Glory. New York: 1943. V. 47

GUTIERREZ DE GUALBA, JEAN
Arte Breve y Provechoso de Cuenta Castellana y Arithmetica Donde se Muestran los Cinco Reglas de Guarismo por la Cuenta Castellana, y Reglas de Memoria. Saragossa: 1555. V. 49; 53

GUTMAN, R. E.
American Diner. New York: 1979. V. 51

GUTTERSON, DAVID
The Country Ahead of Us, the Country Behind. Stories. New York: 1989. V. 54
Snow Falling on Cedars. New York: 1994. V. 54

GUTTIEREZ, VALENTIN LLANOS
Don Esteban; or Memoirs of a Spaniard. London: 1825. V. 47

GUY, ROSA
Bird at My Window. Philadelphia & New York: 1966. V. 52; 53

GUY, THOMAS
A True Copy of the Last Will and Testament of Thomas Guy, Esq... London: 1725. V. 48

GUY, WILLIAM
Principles of Forensic Medicine. New York: 1845. V. 48; 53

GUY, WILLIAM AUGUSTUS
The Factors of the Unsound Mind with Special Reference to the Plea of Insanity in Criminal Cases and the Amendment of the Law. London: 1881. V. 48; 52

GUYER, I. D.
History of Chicago; Its Commercial and Manufacturing Interests and Industry... Chicago: 1862. V. 52

GUY OF WARWICK
The Romances of Sir Guy of Warwick and Rembrun His Son. Edinburgh: 1840. V. 49

GUYON, JEANNE MARIE BOUVIER DE LA MOTTE
Poems. Newport-Pagnel: 1801. V. 48

GUYONNEAU DE PAMBOUR, FRANCOIS MARIE, COMTE
A Practical Treatise on Locomotive Engines Upon Railways... 1836. V. 54
A Practical Treatise on Locomotive Engines Upon Railways. London: 1836. V. 48
A Practical Treatise on Locomotive Engines Upon Railways. Philadelphia: 1836. V. 49
A Practical Treatise on Locomotive Engines Upon Railways. London: 1840. V. 49

GUYOT, ANTOINE PATRICE
Cours Complet de Paysage. Paris: 1818-19. V. 53

GUYS, P. A. DE
A Sentimental Journey through Greece. London: 1772. V. 54

GUYTON DE MORVEAU, LOUIS BERNARD
Methode de Nomenclature Chimique... Paris: 1787. V. 48; 52

GUZMAN, JOSE M.
Breve Noticia que da al Supremo Gobierno del Actual Estado del Territorio de la Alta California... Mexico: 1833. V. 49; 54

GWILLIAM, JOHN
The Battles of the Danube and Barrosa. London: 1811. V. 48; 54

GWILT, JOSEPH
Rudiments of a Grammar of the Anglo-Saxon Tongue. London: 1829. V. 50
Sciography; or, Examples of Shadows and Rules for Their Projection... London: 1824. V. 54
A Treatise on the Equilibrium of Arches, In Which the Theory is Demonstrated Upon Familiar Mathematical Principles. London: 1839. V. 50

GWIN, LAURA MC CLANAHAN
Miscellaneous Poems. Greenville: 1860. V. 54

GWIN, WILLIAM M.
Arguments of the Hon. William M. Gwin on the Subject of the Pacific Railroad, Before the Senate of the United States. Washington: 1860. V. 47

GWINNETT, AMBROSE
The Life and Adventures of Ambrose Gwinnett, Apprentice to an Attorney at law, Who for a Murder Which He Never Committed, Was tried, Condemned, Executed and Hung in Chains, in Old England... Boston: 1800. V. 54

GWYNN, AUBREY
Mediaeval Religious Houses Ireland. 1970. V. 50
Mediaeval Religious Houses Ireland. 1988. V. 48

GWYNN, JOHN
An Essay on Design, Including Proposals for Erecting a Public Academy to be Supported by Voluntary Subscription... London: 1749. V. 47; 52
London and Westminster Improved, Illustrated by Plans. London: 1766. V. 50; 52; 53

GWYNN, STEPHEN
River to River. London: 1937. V. 49
Scattering Branches. Tributes to the Memory of W. B. Yeats. London: 1940. V. 51

GWYNNE, C. W.
Monograph on the Manufacture of Wire and Tinsel in the United Provinces... Allahabad: 1910. V. 50

THE GYPSY. London: 1915-16. V. 52

GYSIN, BRION
Brion Gysin Let the Mice In. West Glover: 1973. V. 50
The Process. London: 1969. V. 50
To Master - a Long Goodnight - The Story of Uncle Tom, a Historical Narrative. New York: 1946. V. 50

GYSIUS, JOHANNES
Origo & Historia Belgicorum Tumultuum Immanissimaeque Crudelitatis per Cliviam & Westphaliam Patratae... Leiden: 1619. V. 52

GZOWSKI, CASIMIR STANISLAUS
Description of the International bridge, constructed Over the Niagara River, Near Fort Erie, Canada, and Buffalo... Toronto: 1873. V. 47; 51

H

H., E. W.
Little Annie and Her Sisters. London: 1839. V. 50

H., J.
Notes on a Trip to the West Coast Sounds of New Zealand. Timaru: 1878. V. 49

H., N.
The Ladies Dictionary; Being a General Entertainment for the Fair Sex... London: 1694. V. 48

H. P. M. Harold Patrick McGrath. Easthampton: 1991. V. 52

H., R.
The Angler's Sure Guide: or, Angling Improved and methodically Digested. London: 1706. V. 49
Edwin and Henry; or, the Week's Holidays... London: 1818. V. 47

H., T.
A Short Way to Know the World; or the Rudiments of Geography. London: 1712. V. 53

HA, SPURR
A Cockney in Arcadia. London: 1899. V. 54

HAAB, O.
Atlas and Eptiome of Operative Opthalmology... Philadelphia, New York: 1905. V. 49

HAAGENSEN, C. D.
Diseases of the Breast. Philadelphia: 1956. V. 48

HAAGNER, ALWIN
Sketches of South African Bird Life. V. 47

HAAK, BOB
Rembrandt: His Life, His Work, His Time. New York. V. 51
Rembrandt: His Life, His Work, His Time. New York: 1969. V. 48

HAAK, THEODORE
The Dutch Annotations Upon the Whole Bible: or, All the Holy Canonical Scriptures of the Old and New Testament. London: 1657. V. 51

HAARADT, G. M.
Across the Sahara by Motor Car. London: 1924. V. 54

HAAS, IRVIN
Bibliography of Modern American Presses. Chicago: 1935. V. 52
Bruce Rogers: A Bibliography. New York: 1936. V. 48

HAAS, ROBERT BARTLETT
A Primer for the Gradual Understanding of Gertrude Stein. Los Angeles: 1971. V. 51
William Grant Still and the Fusion of Cultures in American Music. Santa Barbara: 1972. V. 49

HABBERTON, JOHN
Helen's Babies. Boston: 1876. V. 52

HABER, HEINZ
The Walt Disney Story of Our Friend the Atom. New York: 1956. V. 49

HABERDASHERS Company: a Present for an Apprentice; or, a Sure Guide to Gain Both Esteem and Estate, with Rules for His Conduct to His Master... London: 1841. V. 47

HABERHSAM, WILLIAM G.
Records of Old London. Vanished and Vanishing. London. V. 48

HABERLY, LOYD
Anne Boleyn and Other Poems. Newtown: 1934. V. 51; 54
The Antiquary: a Poem Written in Waterperry Church... Long Crendon: 1933. V. 52
Artemis, a Forest Tale. St. Louis: 1942. V. 49
The Boy and the Bird. Long Crendon: 1932. V. 51; 52; 54
The City of the Sainted King and Other Poems. Cambridge: 1939. V. 49
The City of the Sainted King and Other Poems. St. Louis: 1941. V. 52
The Copper Coloured Cupid or the Cutting of the Cake. Long Crendon: 1931. V. 51; 54
The Crowning Year and Other Poems. Dorset: 1937. V. 49
Daneway. Long Crendon: 1929. V. 52
Echo and Other Poems. Long Crendon, Bucks: 1935. V. 47; 54
John Apostate an Idyll of the Quays. Long Crendon: 1927. V. 51; 54
The Keeper of the Doves. A Tale of Notley Abbey... Long Crendon, Bucks: 1933. V. 47; 51
Mediaeval English Pavingtiles. Oxford: 1937. V. 49; 50; 52
Poems. 1930. V. 51; 52
Poems. Long Crendon: 1930. V. 54
Silent Fame. St. Louis: 1944. V. 48

HABINGTON, WILLIAM
The Historie of Edward the Fourth, King of England. London: 1640. V. 47; 54
The Queene of Arragon. London: 1640. V. 54

HACHISUKA, M. U.
The Birds of the Philippine Islands. London: 1931-35. V. 48; 51
Contributions to the Birds of the Philippines. Tokyo: 1929-30. V. 48
The Dodo and Kindred Birds, or the Extinct Birds of the Mascarene Islands. London: 1953. V. 52
A Handbook of the Birds of Iceland. London: 1927. V. 49

HACHIYA, MICHIHIKO
Hiroshima Diary: the Journal of a Japanese Physician, August 6-September 30, 1945. Chapel Hill: 1955. V. 50; 52

HACK, MARIA BARTON
Harry Beaufoy, or the Pupil of Nature. London: 1821. V. 49
Winter Evenings or, Tales of Travellers. London: 1818/19. V. 49
Winter Evenings or, Tales of Travellers. London: 1818/19/24. V. 51

HACKENBROCH, YVONNE
English and Other Needlework, Tapestries and Textiles. Cambridge: 1960. V. 52

HACKER, LILIAN PRICE
Susan. London: 1912. V. 47; 54

HACKET, JOHN
Scrinia Reserata: a Memorial Offer'd to the Great Deservings of John Williams, D.D. Who Some Time Held the Places of the Great Seal of England, Ld. Bishop of Lincoln and Ld. Archbishop of York... London: 1693. V. 47

HACKETT, C.
Edible Horticultural Crops. London: 1982. V. 52

HACKETT, CHARLES WILSON
Historical Documents Relating to New Mexico, Nueva Vizcaya and Approaches Thereto to 1773. Washington: 1923/26/37. V. 52
Revolt of the Pueblo Indians of New Mexico and Otermin's Attempted Reconquest 1680-1682. Albuquerque: 1970. V. 52

HACKETT, J.
A History of the Orthodox Church of Cyprus from the Coming of the Apostles Paul and Barnabas to the Commencement of the British Occupation (Ad 45-Ad 1878). London: 1901. V. 49

HACKETT, JOHN
Select and Remarkable Epigraphs on Illustrious and Other Persons, in Several Parts of Europe. London: 1757. V. 48

HACKETT, MARIA
A Brief Account of Cathedral and Collegiate Schools; with an Abstract of their Statautes and Endownments. London: 1827. V. 52

HACKIN, J.
Asiatic Mythology. New York: 1932. V. 51

HACKLE, PALMER
Hints on Angling...In France and Belgium. London: 1846. V. 49; 50; 53

HACKMACK, ADOLF
Chinese Carpets and Rugs. Tientsin-Peking: 1924. V. 48

HACKMAN, JAMES
The Case and Memoirs of the Late Rev. Mr. James Hackman and of His Acquaintance with the Late Miss Martha Reay. London: 1779. V. 48; 53

HACOBIAN, M. P.
The Armenian Church - History, Ritual and Communion Service. Sydney: 1947. V. 52

HACQUET, B.
Plantae Alpinae Carniolicae. Vienna: 1782. V. 48; 49

HADDOCK, J. A.
Mr. Haddock's Narrataive of His Hazardous and Exciting Voyage in the Baloon Atlantic... Philadelphia: 1872. V. 48

HADDON, A. C.
Reports of the Cambridge Anthropological Expedition to Torres Straits. Volume V: Sociology, Magic and Religion of the Western Islands. Cambridge: 1904. V. 51

HADDON, WALTER
Lucubrationes. London: 1567. V. 49; 53

HADDOW, A.
Biological Hazards of Atomic Energy. Oxford: 1952. V. 53

HADELN, DETLEV, BARON VON
Titian's Drawings. London: 1927. V. 51; 53; 54

HADEN, SEYMOUR
About Etching. London: 1879. V. 50; 54

HADFIELD, JOHN
Elizabethan Love Songs. London: 1955. V. 50
Georgian Love Songs. Hertfordshire: 1949. V. 48; 49
Georgian Love Songs. London: 1949. V. 49; 50; 52
Restoration Love Songs. London: 1950. V. 50

HADFIELD, WILLIAM
Brazil and the River Plate in 1868. London: 1869. V. 47
Brazil, the River Plate, and the Falkland Islands... London: 1854. V. 47; 51; 54

HADIDI, ADNAN
Studies in the History and Archaeology of Jordan I-III. Amman: 1982-87. V. 49

HADLEY, D.
Stories Told in Winter. Forest Grove: 1976. V. 54

HADLEY, GEORGE
Introductory Grammatical Remarks on the Persian Language. Bath: 1776. V. 48
A New and Complete History of the Town and County...of Kingston-upon-Hull... Hull: 1788. V. 51

HADLEY, HENRY
The Atonement of Pan a Music Drama. San Francisco: 1912. V. 51

HAEBLER, KONRAD
The Early Printers of Spain and Portugal. London: 1897. V. 47; 48

HAECKEL, ERNST
Das System der Medusen. Jena: 1879-81. V. 50

HAECKEL, ERNST HEINRICH
A Visit to Ceylon. London: 1883. V. 48

HAEFTEN, BENEDICTUS VAN
Regia Via Crucis. Antwerp: 1728. V. 50

HAEMSTEDE, A. C.
Historien der Vromer Martelaren. Dordrecht: 1644. V. 52

HAESAERTS, PAUL
James Ensor. London: 1957. V. 50; 54
James Ensor. New York: 1959. V. 50

HAFEN, LEROY R.
Broken Hand. The Life Story...Thomas Fitzpatrick... Denver: 1931. V. 48; 49; 50; 51; 54
Broken Hand: The Life...Thomas Fitzpatrick... Denver: 1973. V. 52
Colorado and Its People. New York: 1948. V. 51
Colorado Gold Rush: Contemporary Letters and Reports, 1858-59. Glendale: 1941. V. 50; 53
The Far West and the Rockies 1820-1875. Glendale: 1954-61. V. 52; 54
Fort Laramie and the Pageant of the West, 1834-1890. Glendale: 1938. V. 47; 50; 54
Fremont's Fourth Expedition. Glendale: 1960. V. 48; 50; 52; 53
The Mountain Men and the Fur Trade... Glendale: 1964-72. V. 50
The Mountain Men and the Fur Trade... Glendale: 1965-66. V. 50
The Mountain Men and the Fur Trade. Glendale: 1965-72. V. 49; 50; 52
The Mountain Men and the Fur Trade... Glendale: 1972. V. 51
Old Spanish Trail Sante Fe to Los Angeles...Diaries of Antonio Armijo and Orvell Pratt. Glendale: 1954. V. 52
The Overland Mail, 1849-18... 1926. V. 48
The Overland Mail, 1849-1869. Cleveland: 1926. V. 50; 52; 53; 54
Overland Routes to the Gold Fields, 1859 from Contemporary Diaries. Glendale: 1942. V. 53
Pike's Peak Gold Rush Guide Books of 1859... Glendale: 1941. V. 47; 50; 53
The Utah Expedition, 1857-1858... Glendale: 1958. V. 50

HAFEN, LYMAN
Edward Abbey: an Interview at Pack Creek Ranch. Santa Fe: 1991. V. 48; 51

HAFEN, MARY ANN
Recollections of a Handcart Pioneer of 1860. Denver: 1938. V. 47; 49; 52

HAFER, ERMINIE SCHAEFFER
A Century of Vehicle Craftsmanship. A One Hundred years History of the Pennsylvania Dutch Transportation Heritage of Berks County... Boyertown: 1972. V. 49

HAFIZ, 14TH CENTURY
Hafiz of Shiraz: Selections from His Poems. London: 1875. V. 48
Odes From the Divan of Hafiz. New York: 1903. V. 49; 51; 54
Poems from the Divan of Hafiz. London: 1897. V. 49

HAFTMANN, WERNER
Emil Nolde. New York: 1959. V. 47; 48; 50; 52
Marc Chagall. New York: 1972. V. 53

HAGA
Comitis Illustrata; of Het Verheerlykt en Verligt 's Gravenhage: Bestaende in eene Naeuwkerige Verzameling...Afbeeldingen...ter Geleegenheid der Allerheughelykste Verkiezinge, Proclamatie en Installatie van... The Hague: 1751. V. 50

HAGEDORN, HERMANN
Leonard Wood, a Biography. New York: 1931. V. 53
The Rough Riders. New York: 1927. V. 47

HAGEK, THADDAUS
Aphorismorum Metascopicorum Libellus Unus. Frankfurt: 1584. V. 49

HAGELBERG, W.
The Children's Natural History. Bath: 1887. V. 54
The Children's Natural History. London: 1887. V. 54

HAGELIN, OVE
The Byrth of Mankynde Otherwyse Named the womans booke: Embryology, Obstetrics, Gynaecology, through Four Centuries. Stockholm: 1990. V. 52
Rare and Important Medical Books in the Library of the Karolinska Institute... Stockholm: 1992. V. 50; 52

HAGELSTEIN, GEORGE CARLTON
Courts of the Order of the Alamo: 1960-1975. V. 49

HAGEMAN, JOHN F.
History of Princeton and Its Institutions. Philadelphia: 1879. V. 51

HAGEN, TONI
Mount Everest, Formation, Population and Exploration of the Everest Region. London: 1963. V. 51

HAGER, EVERETT GORDON
The Zamorano Index to History of California. Los Angeles: 1985. V. 50; 54

HAGER, GIUSEPPE
An Explanation of the Elementary Characters of the Chinese... London: 1801. V. 48; 50

HAGER, JEAN
The Grandfather Medicine. New York: 1989. V. 53

HAGERTY, DONALD J.
Maynard Dixon. San Francisco: 1981. V. 53

HAGGADAH
Haggadah. Offenbach: 1722. V. 51
Haggadah for Passover. Paris: 1966. V. 51
Maaleh Beth Chorin (Ascent of the House of Freedom). Seder Haggadah Shel Pesach. Vienna: 1823. V. 53
A Song of David. Verona: 1987. V. 54

HAGGARD, ELLA
Myra; or the Rose of the East. London: 1857. V. 52
Myra; or the Rose of the East. London: 1857/78. V. 50

HAGGARD, HENRY RIDER
Allan Quartermain. 1887. V. 47; 52
Allan Quartermain. London: 1887. V. 48; 51; 53
Allan Quartermain. New York: 1887. V. 49; 54
Allan Quartermain. Toronto: 1887. V. 53
Allan the Hunter. A Tale of Three Lions. Boston: 1989. V. 53
Allan's Wife... 1889. V. 49
Allan's Wife. London: 1889. V. 48; 53
Allan's Wife. London: 1891. V. 53
The Ancient Allan. London: 1920. V. 53
Ayesha, the Return of She. London: 1905. V. 47; 53
Ayesha, the Return of She. New York: 1905. V. 53
Beatrice. 1890. V. 54
Beatrice. London: 1890. V. 49; 50; 53
Benita. London: 1906. V. 49; 52; 53
Benita. Toronto: 1906. V. 53
Black Heart and White Heart and Other Stories. London: 1900. V. 50; 53
The Brethren. 1904. V. 48
The Brethren. London: 1904. V. 53
Cetywayo and His White Neighbors. London: 1882. V. 47; 52; 53; 54
Child of Storm. London: 1913. V. 53
Child of Storm. New York: 1913. V. 53
Cleopatra. London: 1889. V. 48; 50; 52; 53; 54
Cleopatra. Toronto: 1889. V. 53
Colonel Quaritch. London & New York: 1888. V. 47; 48; 53; 54
Colonel Quaritch. Toronto: 1888. V. 53
Colonel Quaritch... 1889. V. 54
Colonel Quaritch... London: 1889. V. 49; 53
Colonel Quaritch... New York: 1889. V. 53
Dawn. 1887. V. 49
Dawn. London: 1887. V. 53
Dawn. New York: 1887. V. 53; 54
The Days of My Life. London: 1926. V. 48; 50; 52; 53
Doctor Therne. 1898. V. 51
Doctor Therne. London: 1898. V. 53
Elissa the Doom of Zimbabwe/Black Heart and white Heart A Zulu Idyll. New York: 1900. V. 53
Eric Brighteyes. 1891. V. 54
Eric Brighteyes. London: 1891. V. 50; 53
A Farmer's Year. 1899. V. 54
A Farmer's Year. London: 1899. V. 53
Finished. 1917. V. 49
Finished. London: 1917. V. 53
A Gardener's Year. London: 1905. V. 48
The Ghost Kings. London: 1908. V. 52; 53
Heart of the World. 1895. V. 51; 53
Heart of the World. New York: 1895. V. 50
Heart of the World. London: 1896. V. 51
Heu-Heu or the Monster. 1924. V. 49; 53
Heu-Heu or the Monster. Garden City: 1924. V. 53
A History of Transvaal. New York: 1899. V. 53
The Holy Flower. 1915. V. 49
The Holy Flower. London: 1915. V. 53
The Ivory Child. London: 1916. V. 49; 53
Jess. New York. V. 53
Jess. Chicago: 1887. V. 53
Jess. London: 1887. V. 48; 51; 52; 53
Jess. New York: 1887. V. 53
Joan Haste. London: 1895. V. 53
Joan Haste. New York: 1895. V. 53
King Solomon's Mines. London: 1885. V. 47; 48; 51
King Solomon's Mines. London: 1886. V. 53

HAGGARD, HENRY RIDER continued
King Solomon's Mines. London: 1905. V. 48
The Lady of Blossholme. London: 1909. V. 50; 51
The Lady of the Heavens. 1908. V. 49
Love Eternal. New York: 1918. V. 53
Lysbeth. London: 1901. V. 53
The Mahatma and the Hare. 1911. V. 53
The Mahatma and the Hare... London and elsewhere: 1911. V. 48; 53
The Mahatma and the Hare. New York: 1911. V. 52
Maiwa's Revenge. 1865. V. 54
Maiwa's Revenge. London: 1888. V. 47; 53; 54
Maiwa's Revenge. New York: 1888. V. 51; 53
Maiwa's Revenge... London & New York: 1891. V. 48
Maiwa's Revenge. 1895. V. 54
Marion Isle. 1929. V. 48
Mary of Marion Isle. London: 1929. V. 53
Mr. Meeson's Will. London: 1881. V. 48
Mr. Meeson's Will. 1888. V. 47; 50; 51
Mr. Meeson's Will. London: 1888. V. 48; 53
Montezuma's Daughter. London: 1893. V. 47; 53
Montezuma's Daughter. New York: 1893. V. 53
Montezuma's Daughter. London: 1898. V. 53
Morning Star. 1910. V. 54
Morning Star. London: 1910. V. 49; 53
Nada the Lily. 1892. V. 54
Nada the Lily. London: 1892. V. 53
Novels. London: 1901-05. V. 48
Pearl Maiden. London: 1903. V. 51; 53
Pearl Maiden. New York: 1903. V. 53
The People of the Mist. 1894. V. 51
The People of the Mist. London: 1894. V. 53
The People of the Mist. New York: 1894. V. 54
Queen of the Dawn. New York: 1925. V. 51; 53
Queen of the Dawn. Toronto: 1925. V. 53
Queen Sheba's Ring. 1910. V. 54
Queen Sheba's Ring. Toronto: 1910. V. 53
Red Eve. London: 1911. V. 50; 51
Red Eve. Garden City: 1912. V. 53
She. 1887. V. 48; 50
She. London: 1887. V. 47; 48; 51; 52; 53
She. New York: 1887. V. 54
She and Allan. Toronto: 192-?. V. 53
She and Allan. 1921. V. 51; 53
Smith and the Pharaohs and Other Tales. Bristol & London: 1920. V. 48
The Spirit of Bambatse. New York: 1906. V. 53
Stella Fregelius. New York: 1903. V. 50; 53
Stella Fregelius. London: 1904. V. 53
Swallow. London: 1899. V. 48; 50; 52; 53
The Treasure of the Lake. Toronto: 192-?. V. 53
The Wanderer's Necklace. London: 1914. V. 51
The Way of the Spirit. London: 1906. V. 49
The Way of the Spirit. Toronto: 1906. V. 53
When the World Shook. London: 1919. V. 53
A Winter Pilgrimage. London: 1901. V. 50; 51
Wisdom's Daughter. Toronto: 1923. V. 53
The Witch's Head. Leipzig: 1887. V. 52
The Witch's Head. London: 1887. V. 53
The Wizard. New York: 1896. V. 50; 53
Works. New York. V. 51
The World's Desire. London: 1890. V. 51; 53
The Yellow God. London: 1909. V. 53

HAGGIN, J. B.
Catalogue of the First Annual Sale of the Rancho del Paso Yearlings, the Property of Mr. J. B. Haggin, Rancho del Paso, California, Comprising: Seventy-Two Colts and Fillies...to be sold by Auction without reserve...at Madison Squre Garden... New York: 1888. V. 47

HAGHE, LOUIS
Haghe's Portfolio of Sketches. London: 1850. V. 47

HAGOOD, JOHNSON
Memoirs of the War of Secession. Columbia: 1910. V. 49

HAGREEN, PHILIP
Our Lady of the Rosary. Ditchling, Sussex: 1930?. V. 48

HAGUE & GILL LIMITED
Type Designed by Eric Gill and printed by Hague & Gill Ltd. High Wycombe. 1937/38. V. 52

HAGUE, ARNOLD
Atlas...Geology of the Yellowstone National Park. Washington: 1904. V. 47; 48

HAGUE, E.
Latin American Music Past and Present. Santa Ana: 1934. V. 49

HAGUE, MICHAEL
A Child's First Book of Prayers. New York: 1985. V. 49

HAGUE, PARTHENIA A. V.
A Blockaded Family: Life in Southern Alabama During the War. Boston & New York: 1888. V. 47

HAGUE, RENE
The Death of Hector. Wellingborough: 1973. V. 52

HAHN, J. E.
The Intelligence Service Within the Canadian Corps 1914-18. Toronto: 1930. V. 50

HAHNEMANN, SAMUEL
The Chronic Diseases: Their Specific Nature and Homoeopathic Treatment... New York: 1845-46. V. 50
The Lesser Writings of Samuel Hahnemann. New York: 1852. V. 50
Organon of Homoeopapthic Medicine. Allentown: 1836. V. 52; 53
Organon of the Art of Healing. Philadelphia: 1875. V. 50

HAIG, ALEXANDER M.
Caveat: Realism, Reagan and Foreign Policy. New York: 1984. V. 50

HAIG, DOUGLAS, 1ST EARL OF
Sir Douglas Haig's Despatches (December 1915-April 1919). London: 1919. V. 49

HAIG, JAMES
A Topographical and Historical Account of the Town of Kelso, and of the Town and Castle of Roxburgh... Edinburgh: 1825. V. 53

HAIG-BROWN, RODERICK
Bright Waters, Bright Fish: An Examination of Angling in Canada. Vancouver: 1980. V. 49
A Primer of Fly-Fishing. New York: 1964. V. 48; 49
A River Never Sleeps. Toronto: 1946. V. 50
The Western Angler: an Account of Pacific Salmon and Western Trout. 1991. V. 50
The Western Angler: an Account of Pacific Salmon and Western Trout. New York: 1991. V. 48

HAIGH, JAMES
The Dyer's Assistant in the Art of Dying Wool and Woollen Goods. York: 1787. V. 47

HAIGHT, SARAH
Letters from the Old World. New York: 1840. V. 49

HAILE, BERARD, FATHER
Beautyway. A Navajo Ceremonial. New York: 1957. V. 50; 52
Emergence Myth, Accourind to the Hanelthnayhe or Upward-Reaching Rite. Santa Fe: 1949. V. 52
Learning Navajo. Arizona: 1941/42/47. V. 52
Prayer Stick Cuttings in a Five Night Navajo Ceremonial of the Male Branch of Shootingway. Chicago: 1947. V. 52

HAILES, DAVID DALRYMPLE, LORD
A Catalogue of the Lords of Session, from the Institution of the College of Justice, in the Year 1532. Edinburgh: 1767. V. 50
Proposals for Carrying on a Certain Public Work in the City of Edinburgh. Edinburgh: 1752. V. 47

HAILEY, ARTHUR
Flight Into Danger. 1958. V. 53
Flight Into Danger. London: 1958. V. 52

HAILEY, JOHN
The History of Idaho. Boise: 1910. V. 53

HAILSTONE, EDWARD
Portraits of Yorkshire Worthies. London: 1869. V. 53

HAILSTONE, LILLA
Illustrated Catalogue of Ancient Framed Needlework Pictures, Both Formed By and in the Possession of... London: 1897. V. 53

HAILSTONE, SAMUEL
A Dose for the Doctor, or, a Bitter Pill for George Mossman. (with) The Dose Repeated, or Another Pill for George Mossman. London: 1796. V. 48; 53

HAIMAN, G.
Nicholas Kis. A Hungarian Punch-Cutter and printer, 1650-1702, the Creator of the 'Janson' Type. San Francisco: 1983. V. 50

HAINES, ALANSON A.
Ancestry of the Haines, Sharp, Collins, Wills, Gardiner, Prickitt, Eves, Evans, Moore, Troth, Borton and Engle Families. Camden: 1902. V. 49
History of the Fifteenth Regiment, New Jersey Volunteers. New York: 1883. V. 51

HAINES, CHARLES G.
Considerations on the Great Western Canal, from the Hudson to Lake Erie... Brooklyn: 1818. V. 47; 54

HAINES, CHARLES R.
A Complete Memoir of Richard Haines (1633-85) a Forgotten Sussex Worthy... London: 1899. V. 49

HAINES, ELIJAH M.
The American Indian. Chicago: 1888. V. 48

HAINES, FRANCIS
Red Eagles of the Northwest. Portland: 1939. V. 54

HAINES, HELEN
History of New Mexico, from the Spanish Conquest to the Present Time 1530-1980... New York: 1891. V. 53

HAINES, HERBERT
Manual of Monumental Brasses Comprising an Introduction to the Study of These Memorials and a List of Those Remaining in the British Isles. Oxford and London: 1861. V. 49; 52

HAINES, JENNIE DAY
Christmasse Tyde: Being a Collection of Seasonable Quotations. San Francisco: 1907. V. 51

HAINES, JONES & CADBURY CO., PHILADELPHIA
Illustrated Catalogue E. Porcelain Lines and Iron Baths, Washout Closets and Hoppers (&c.). Philadelphia: 1890. V. 54

HAINES, RICHARD
Ancestry of the Haines, Sharp, Collins, Wills, Gardiner, Prickitt, Eves, Evans, Moore, Troth, Borton and Engle Families. Camden: 1902. V. 47
Genealogy of the Stokes Family, Descended from Thomas and Mary Stokes Who Settled in Burlington County, N.J. Camden: 1903. V. 47; 49

HAINES, WILLIAM P.
History of the Men of Co. F., with Description of the Marches and Battles of the 12th New Jersey Vols. Mickleton: 1897. V. 49; 51

HAINES, WILLIAM WISTER
Command Decision. New York: 1948. V. 50

HAINING, PETER
Movable Books. An Illustrated History. 1979. V. 52

HAIR, JAMES T.
Iowa State Gazetteer Embracing Description and Historical Sketches... Chicago: 1865. V. 54

HAIR, T. H.
Sketches of the Coal Mines in Northumberland and Durham. New York: 1969. V. 50

HAKE, A. EGMONT
Paris Originals. London: 1878. V. 52

HAKE, LUCY
Something New on Men and Manners, a Critique on the Follies and Vices of the Age, Interspersed with Amusing Anecdotes, Biographical Sketches, and Useful Suggestions on various Interesting topics. Hailsham: 1828. V. 52

HAKE, THOMAS GORDON
Legends of the Morrow. London: 1879. V. 49
Parables and Tales. London: 1872. V. 51; 54

HAKEWEILL, GEORGE
An Apologie or Declaration of the Power and Providence of God in the Government of the World. Oxford: 1630. V. 48; 51
An Apologie or Declaration of the Power and Providence of God in the Government of the World... Oxford: 1635. V. 48

HAKEWILL, JAMES
A Picturesque Tour of the Island of Jamaica (1825)... Kingston: 1990. V. 49; 50

HAKEWILL, WILLIAM
The Manner How Statutes are Enacted in Parliament by Passing Bills. London: 1641. V. 53

HAKLUYT, RICHARD
The Principal Navigations, Voiages...Discoveries of... London: 1589. V. 50
The Principal Navigations, Voiages...Discoveries of... London: 1598-1600. V. 50
The Principal Navigations, Voiages...Discoveries of... Glasgow: 1903. V. 47
The Principal Navigations, Voiages...Discoveries of... London: 1927. V. 53
The Principal Navigations, Voiages...Discoveries of... London & Toronto: 1927/28. V. 48; 49; 50; 52; 54
The Principal Navigations, Voiages...Discoveries of... Cambridge: 1965. V. 50
The Principal Navigations, Voiages...Discoveries of... London: 1965. V. 50

HAKOLA, JOHN W.
Frontier Omnibus. Helena: 1962. V. 50; 52

HALBERT, HENRY S.
The Creek War of 1813 and 1814. Chicago: 1895. V. 54

HALDANE, DUNCAN
Islamic Bookbindings in the Victoria and Albert Museum. London: 1983. V. 50; 53; 54

HALDANE, J. W. C.
3800 Miles Across Canada. London: 1900. V. 51

HALDANE, JOHN SCOTT
Report...on the Health of Cornish Miners. London: 1904. V. 50
Respiration. New Haven: 1922. V. 49
Respiration. New Haven: 1927. V. 53

HALDE, JEAN BAPTISTE
The General History of China. London: 1736. V. 48

HALDEMAN, J.
War Year. 1972. V. 50; 51

HALE, ALBERT
Old Newburyport Houses. Boston: 1912. V. 49

HALE, EDWARD E.
Kanzas and Nebraska, The History, Geographical and Physical Characteristics, and Political Position of Those Territories. Boston: 1854. V. 48; 50; 52; 53
Life and Letters. Boston: 1917. V. 51

HALE, EDWARD EVERETT
The Fortunes of Rachel. New York & London: 1884. V. 54
The Man Without a Country. New York: 1936. V. 54

HALE, EDWIN M.
A Systematic Treatise on Abortion. Chicago: 1866. V. 49; 51; 53
A Systematic Treatise on Abortion... Chicago: 1868. V. 50

HALE, ENOCH
Boylston Medical Prize Dissertations for the Years 1819 and 1821. Boston: 1821. V. 51
Observations on the Typhoid Fever of New England. Boston: 1839. V. 51

HALE, JANET CAMPBELL
The Owl's Song. New York: 1974. V. 50

HALE, JOHN PETER
Trans Allegheny Pioneers. Cincinnati: 1886. V. 47; 50; 52

HALE, KATHERINE
Canadian Cities of Romance. Toronto: 1933. V. 48

HALE, KATHLEEN
Henrietta the Faithful Hen. London: 1943. V. 51
Henrietta's Magic Egg. London: 1973. V. 54
Orlando - a Seaside Holiday. London: 1952. V. 48; 53
Orlando - His Silver Wedding. London: 1944. V. 50
Orlando and the Three Graces. London: 1965. V. 54
Orlando and the Water Cats. London: 1972. V. 48; 52
Orlando Keeps a Dog. London: 1949. V. 48; 50
Orlando the Marmalade Cat. London: 1938. V. 47; 50
Orlando the Marmalade Cat Becomes a Doctor. London: 1944. V. 48
Puss in Boots. London: 1950. V. 48

HALE, LUCRETIA P.
The Peterkin Papers. Boston: 1880. V. 50

HALE, M.
Spring Water, Versus River Water, for Supplying the City of New York. New York: 1835. V. 52; 53

HALE, MATTHEW
Historia Placitorum Coronae... London: 1736. V. 49; 53
Historia Placitorum Coronae. Dublin: 1778. V. 50
The History of the Common Law... London: 1713. V. 47
The History of the Common Law... London: 1759. V. 48
The History of the Common Law. London: 1794. V. 52; 54
History of the Pleas of the Crown. London: 1778. V. 52
The Judgement of the Late Lord Chief Justice Sir Matthew Hale, of the Nature of True Religion, the Causes of its Corruption and the Churches Calamity, by mens Additions and Violences... London: 1684. V. 50
Pleas of the Crown; or, a Methodical Summary of the Principal Matters Relating to that Subject. London: 1685. V. 51
The Primitive Origination of Mankind, Considered and Examined According to the Light of Nature. London: 1677. V. 47
The Primitive Origination of Mankind, Considered and Examined According to the Light of Nature. London: 1710. V. 52
A Short Treatise Touching Sheriffs Accompts...to Which is added, a Tryal of Witches at the Assizes Held at Bury St. Edmonds...on the 10th of March 1664...(and) A Discourse Touching Provision for the Poor. London: 1716. V. 53

HALE, NATHAN
Remarks on the Practicability and Expediency of Rail Roads from Boston to the Hudson Rivert and From Boston to Providence. Boston: 1829. V. 53

HALE, NATHAN CABOT
Embrace of Life: the Sculpture... 1968. V. 51
Embrace of Life: the Sculpture... New York: 1968. V. 48; 50; 52; 53; 54

HALE, SARAH JOSEPHA BUELL
The Countries of Europe and the Manners and Customs of Its Various Nations. New York: 1842. V. 54
The Genius of Oblivion; and Other Original Poems by a Lady of New Hampshire. Concord: 1823. V. 49; 50
The Lectures; or Woman's Sphere. Boston: 1839. V. 48
Northwood: a Tale of New England. Boston: 1827. V. 47
Woman's Record; or, Sketches of all Distinguished Women... New York: 1853. V. 47
Woman's Record; or Sketches of All Distinguished Women... New York: 1854. V. 50

HALE, THOMAS
A Compleat Body of Husbandry. 1756. V. 52
A Compleat Body of Husbandry... London: 1756. V. 51
Social Harmony. London: 1763. V. 48

HALEN, WIDAR
Christopher Dresser. Oxford: 1990. V. 50

HALES, J. H. M.
The Astrologer; or the Eve of San Sebastian; a Romance. London: 1820. V. 49

HALES, JOHN
A Discourse of the Several Dignities and Corruptions of Man's Nature, Since the Fall... London: 1720. V. 48
A Tract Concerning the Sin Against the Holy Ghost. London: 1677. V. 53

HALES, JOHN W.
Bishop Percy's Folio Manuscript Ballads and Romances. London: 1867/8. V. 53

HALES, ROBERT
Memoirs of Robert Hales, the English Quaker Giant and His Wife the Quaker Giantess, the Tallest and Largest Pair In the World. New York: 1849. V. 53

HALES, STEPHEN
An Account of Some Experiments and Observations on Tar-Water. London: 1745. V. 49
Statical Essays... London: 1731. V. 49
Statical Essays. London: 1731-33. V. 52; 53
Statical Essays. London: 1769. V. 48; 53
Vegetable Staticks; or, An Account of Some Statical Experiments on the Sap in Vegetables... London: 1727. V. 49; 50; 53

HALEY, ALEX
A Different Kind of Christmas. New York: 1988. V. 48; 54
Roots. Garden City: 1976. V. 47; 48; 49; 50; 51; 52; 53; 54
Roots. New York: 1976. V. 47; 48; 49; 50; 51; 53
Roots. London: 1977. V. 53
Roots. Victoria: 1977. V. 54

HALEY, JAMES EVETTS
And So It Must Be...at Christmas...on the Ranges of Grass. Amarillo: 1952. V. 49
Charles Goodnight, Cowman & Plainsman. Boston: 1936. V. 51; 52; 53; 54
Charles Schreiner, General Merchandise, the Story of a Country Store.. Austin: 1944. V. 52
Christmas at the Hancock House. Amarillo: 1953. V. 49
Earl Vandale on the Trail of Texas Books. Canyon: 1965. V. 48; 49; 52; 53
F. Reaugh: Man and Artist. El Paso: 1960. V. 48
Fort Concho and the Texas Frontier. 1952. V. 52
Fort Concho and the Texas Frontier. San Angelo: 1952. V. 49; 51; 52; 53
George W. Littlefield, Texan. Norman: 1943. V. 54
The Heraldry of the Range: Some Southwestern Brands. Canyon: 1949. V. 48
Jeff Milton, a Good Man with a Gun. Norman: 1948. V. 52; 53
John Bouldin's First Christmas on the Plains. Amarillo: 1950. V. 49
Life of the Texan Range. Austin: 1952. V. 47; 49; 50; 53
Some Southwestern Trails. El Paso: 1948. V. 48; 49
The XIT Ranch of Texas. Chicago: 1929. V. 52; 53; 54

HALEY, WILLIAM
Plays of Three Acts: Written for a Private Theatre. London: 1784. V. 48

HALF Hours in the Wide West: Over Mountains, Rivers and Prairies. London: 1878. V. 47

HALF-FAIRY Tales and Dreamy Memories (of Romantic Nooks and Corners Admidst the Woods and Rocks of Croft Lodge, Windermere, and of the Curious Cryptogramic Growths Which Sometimes Spring in Them). Croydon: 1875?. V. 49

HALFER, JOSEPH
The Progress of the Marbling Art from Technical Scientific Principles. Buffalo: 1893. V. 50

HALFMOON, CHARLES
A Collection of Hymns in Muncey and English. Toronto: 1874. V. 48

HALFORD, FREDERIC M.
Dry Fly Entomology... London: 1897. V. 52; 53
Dry Fly Entomology... London: 1902. V. 48
Dry Fly Fishing in Theory and Practice. London: 1889. V. 48; 53
Dry Fly Fishing in Theory and Practice. London: 1902. V. 48
The Dry Fly Man's Handbook. London: 1913. V. 48; 52; 54
Floating Flies and How to Dress Them. London: 1886. V. 48; 51
Making a Fishery. London: 1895. V. 47; 51; 52; 53
Making a Fishery. 1902. V. 52
Making a Fishery. London: 1902. V. 47; 51; 52
Modern Development of the Dry Fly. London: 1910. V. 47; 48; 49; 52; 53
Modern Development of the Dry Fly. New York: 1910. V. 48
Modern Development of the Dry Fly... London: 1913. V. 52
Modern Development of the Dry Fly... London: 1923. V. 47

HALFORD, HENRY
Essays and Orations, Read and Delivered at the Royal College of Physicians... London: 1831. V. 49
Essays and Orations, Read and Delivered at the Royal College of Physicians... London: 1833. V. 53

HALFORD, W. C.
The Mechanic's Own Book... London: 1840. V. 47; 54

HALFPENNY, JOHN
The Gentleman's Jockey and Approved Farrier. London: 1687. V. 47; 48

HALFPENNY, JOSEPH
Fragmenta Vetusta or the Remains of Ancient Buildings in York. York: 1807. V. 54
Gothic Ornaments in the Cathedral Church of York. London: 1795. V. 47
Gothic Ornaments in the Cathedral Church of York. York: 1800. V. 48; 51
A Selection of the Gothic Ornaments in the Cathedral Church of York. York: 1831. V. 51

HALFPENNY, WILLIAM
Chinese and Gothic Architecture Properly Ornamented. London: 1752. V. 47
The Modern Builder's Assistant; or, a concise Epitome of the Whole System of Architecture... London: 1757. V. 51
A New and Compleat System of Architecture Delineated, in a Variety of Plans and Elevations of Designs for Convenient and Decorated Houses. London: 1749,. V. 54
Rural Architecture in the Gothick Taste. London: 1752. V. 50

HALHED, NATHANIEL B.
A Letter to Governor Johnstone, &c. &c. on Indian Affairs. London: 1783. V. 47

HALIBURTON, RICHARD
The Clockmaker: or, the Sayings and Doings of Samuel Slick of Slickville. Second Series. Philadelphia: 1838. V. 53
New Worlds to Conquer. Indianapolis: 1929. V. 49
The Royal Road to Romance. Indianapolis: 1925. V. 50

HALIBURTON, THOMAS CHANDLER
The Americans at Home; or, Byeways, Backwoods, and Prairies. London: 1854. V. 52
The Bubbles of Canada. London: 1839. V. 51; 54
The Clockmaker. London: 1838. V. 47
The Clockmaker. Philadelphia: 1839-40. V. 53; 54
The Clockmaker... Paris: 1841. V. 47
The English in America. London: 1851. V. 49
An Historical and Statistical Account of Nova Scotia. Halifax: 1829. V. 50; 53
The Letter Bag of the Great Western; or, Life in a Steamer. London: 1840. V. 49; 50
Nature and Human Nature. London: 1855. V. 54
Rule and Misrule of the English in America. London: 1851. V. 53
Sam Slick's Wise Saws and Modern Instances; or, What He Said, Did or Invented. London: 1853. V. 52
Sam Slick's Wise Saws and Modern Instances; or, What He Said, Did, or Invented. London: 1953. V. 50

HALIFAX, CHARLES MONTAGUE, EARL OF
Some Observations Upon Discourses Lately Published on the Publick Revenues, and On the Trade of England. London: 1698. V. 50
The Works and Life of...The History of His Lordship's Times. London: 1715. V. 49; 54

HALIFAX, GEORGE SAVILE, 1ST MARQUIS OF
The Lady's New-years Gift; or, Advice to a Daughter, Under These Following Heads... London: 1688. V. 48; 52
The Life and Letters... London: 1898. V. 49
Miscellanies... London: 1704. V. 48; 50; 51; 54

HALIFAX Nova Scotia and Its Attractions. V. 47; 54

HALIFAX The Garrison City. Toronto: 1903. V. 47

HALIFAX, WILLIAM SAVILE, 2ND MARQUIS OF
Miscellanies...Viz. I. Advice to a Daughter. II. The Character of a Trimmer. III. The Anatomy of an Equivalent. IV. A Letter to a Dissenter. V. Cautions for Choice of Parliament Men. VI. A Rough Draught of a New Model at Sea. VII. Maxims of State. 1704. V. 47

HALKETT, JOHN
Historical Notes Respecting the Indians of North America. London & Edinburgh: 1825. V. 47

HALKETT, SAMUEL
Dictionary of Anonymous and Pseudonymous English Literature. London: 1926-34. V. 50
Dictionary of Anonymous and Pseudonymous English Literature. Edinburgh: 1926-56. V. 48
Dictionary of Anonymous and Pseudonymous English Literature. Edinburgh: 1926-62. V. 51
Dictionary of Anonymous and Pseudonymous English Literature... 1971. V. 54
Dictionary of Anonymous and Pseudonymous English Literature. New York: 1971. V. 48

HALL, A. D.
The Genus Tulipa. London: 1940. V. 49; 51

HALL, A. OAKLEY
The Congressman's Christmas Dream and the Lobby Member's Happy New Year. New York: 1870-71. V. 47; 50

HALL, ANNA MARIA FIELDING
The Book of Royalty. London: 1839. V. 48; 51; 53
Chronicles of a School Room. Boston: 1830. V. 53
The Hartopp Jubilee, or, Profit from Play. 1839. V. 50
Sketches of Irish Character. London: 1842. V. 54
Stories of the Irish Peasantry. Edinburgh: 1855. V. 50

HALL, B. M.
The Life of Rev. John Clark... New York: 1856. V. 49; 54

HALL, B. P.
An Atlas of Speciation in African Passerine Birds. London: 1970. V. 49

HALL, BASIL
Account of a Voyage of Discovery to the West Coast of Corea. London: 1818. V. 47; 48
Extracts from a Journal, Written on the Coasts of Chili, Peru and Mexico, in the Year 1820, 1821, 1822. Edinburgh: 1824. V. 47; 49; 52; 53
Forty Etchings from Sketches Made with the Camera Lucida, in North America 1827 and 1828 of Arable and Pasture Grounds. Edinburgh: 1829. V. 47; 48; 52; 54
Fragments of Voyages and Travels... Edinburgh: 1832-33. V. 51
Fragments of Voyages and Travels... London: 1833. V. 54
The Great Polyglot Bibles. San Francisco: 1966. V. 48; 49; 51; 52
Travels in North America, in the Years 1827 and 1828. Edinburgh: 1829. V. 47; 52
Travels in North America, in the Years 1827 and 1828. Philadelphia: 1829. V. 53
Travels in North America, in the Years 1827 and 1828. Edinburgh: 1830. V. 52; 53
Travels in North America, in the Years 1827 and 1828. Paris: 1834. V. 53

HALL, BAYNARD
The New Purchase; or, Seven and a Half Years in the Far West. New York: 1843. V. 54

HALL, BRET
Roundup Years Old Muddy to Black Hills. Kennebec: 1956. V. 50; 54

HALL, CARROLL D.
Bierce and the Poe Hoax. San Francisco: 1934. V. 50; 52
Donner Miscellany. 41 Diaries and Documents. San Francisco: 1947. V. 48; 51
Heraldry of New Helvetia. San Francisco: 1945. V. 48; 49; 50; 53

HALL, CHARLES B.
Military Records of General Officers of the Confederate States of America 1861-1865... Austin: 1963. V. 52

HALL, CHARLES FRANCIS
Arctic Researches... New York: 1865. V. 53
Arctic Researches... New York: 1866. V. 52
Life with the Esquimaux: a Narrative of Arctic Experience In Search of Survivors of Sir John Franklin's Expedition. London: 1865. V. 49
Life with the Esquimaux: the Narrative of Captain Charles Francis Hall of the Whaling Barque 'George Henry' From the 29th May, 1860, to the 13th September 1862. London: 1864. V. 48
Narrative of the North Polar Expedition, U.S. Ship Polaris, Captain Charles Francis Hall Commanding. Washington: 1876. V. 50
Narrative of the Second Arctic Expedition Made by Charles F. Hall... Washington: 1879. V. 51

HALL, DAVID
A Mite Into the Treausry Etc. Philadelphia: 1758. V. 48
Some Brief Memoirs of the Life of David Hall... London: 1799. V. 49

HALL, DAVID C.
Return Trip Ticket. New York: 1992. V. 49

HALL, DONALD
As the Eye Moves. New York: 1973. V. 54
Brief Lives. Concord: 1983. V. 48
Brief Lives. Ewert: 1983. V. 50
The Dark Houses... New York: 1958. V. 47
The Dark Houses. USA: 1958. V. 53
Exile. Oxford: 1952. V. 47
Kicking the Leaves. Mt. Horeb: 1976. V. 53; 54
A Roof of Tiger Lilies - Poems. London: 1964. V. 47; 48
String Too Short to be Saved. New York: 1960. V. 52
The Toy Bone. Brockport: 1979. V. 51

HALL, E. HEPPLE
Lands of Plenty: British North America for Health, Sport and Profit: A Book for All Travellers and Settlers. London: 1879. V. 47; 49

HALL, E. R.
The Mammals of North America. New York: 1959. V. 50
Mammals of North America. New York: 1981. V. 52

HALL, EDNA CLARKE
Facets. A Book of Poems and Six Illustrations. London: 1930. V. 51

HALL, EDWARD
Chronicle, Containing the History of England During the Reign of Henry IV, and the Succeeding Monarchs to the End of the Reign of Henry VIII. London: 1809. V. 47; 50; 51

HALL, EDWARD H.
The Great West: a Guide for Emigrants, Travellers, and Miners... London: 1870. V. 54

HALL, EDWIN
Sweynheym and Pannartz and the Origins of Printing in Italy... 1991. V. 47
Sweynheym and Pannartz and the Origins of Printing in Italy... McMinnville: 1991. V. 47; 48; 51; 52; 54

HALL, EMMA SWAN
Antiquities from the Collection of Christos G. Bastis. New York: 1987. V. 49; 50; 51; 52
Mendes I-II. Cairo: 1980-76. V. 51

HALL, EVERARD
A Digested Index to the Virginia Reports...From Washington to Second Randolph Inclusive (etc.). Richmond: 1825. V. 49

HALL, FRANCES
Narrative of the Capture and Providential Escape of Misses Frances and Almira Hall.. St. Louis: 1832. V. 48

HALL, FRANCIS
Travels in Canada, and the United States in 1816 and 1817. Boston: 1818. V. 47; 50; 52; 53
Travels in Canada and the United States, in 1816 and 1817. London: 1818. V. 53

HALL, FRANK
History of the State of Colorado. Chicago: 1889/90. V. 51

HALL, FREDERIC
The History of San Jose and Surroundings with Biographical Sketches of Early Settlers. San Francisco: 1871. V. 52

HALL, FREDERICK
History of the Bank of Ireland. London: 1949. V. 53
Letters from East and the West. Washington City: 1840. V. 54

HALL, FREDERICK G.
The Bank of Ireland, 1783-1946. Dublin: 1949. V. 48; 50; 52

HALL, GEORGE
The History of Chesterfield, and Its Charities; With an Account of the Chapelries and Hamlets in the Parish... Chesterfield: 1823. V. 50
The Triumphs of Rome Over Despised Protestancie. London: 1655. V. 49

HALL, GRANVILLE STANLEY
Adolescence: Its Psychology and its Relations to Physiology, Anthropology, Sociology, Sex, Crime, Religion and Education. New York, London: 1904. V. 48; 49; 54
Aspects of German Culture. Boston: 1881. V. 47

HALL, H. B.
The Sportsman and His Dog, or Hints on Sporting. London: 1850. V. 51; 52

HALL, H. R.
Al-'Ubaid: a Report on the Work Carried Out at al-'Ubaid for the British Museum in 1919 and the Joint Expedition in 1922-23. Oxford: 1927. V. 49
Catalogue of Egyptian Scarabs, etc. in the British Museum. London: 1913. V. 49
A Season's Work at Ur: Al-Ubaid, Abu Shahrain (Eridu) and Elsewhere, Being an Unofficial Account of the British Museum Archaeological Mission to Babylonia, 1919. London: 1930. V. 54

HALL, HARRISON
Hall's Distiller, Containing...Full and Particular Directions for Mashing and Distilling All Kinds of Grain and Imitating Holland Gin and Irish Whisky... Philadelphia: 1813. V. 48; 52; 54

HALL, HENRY
The Tribune Book of Open-Air Sports. New York: 1887. V. 50

HALL, J. J.
The Crystal Bowl. London: 1921. V. 48

HALL, J. K.
One Hundred Years of American Psychiatry. New York: 1944. V. 47; 52

HALL, J. M.
The Beginning of Tulsa. 1933. V. 49; 54

HALL, J. N.
Tales of Pioneer Practice. Denver: 1937. V. 54

HALL, J. SPARKES
The Book of the Feet, a History of Boots and Shoes, with Illustrations of the Fashions of the Egyptians, Hebrews, Persians, Greeks and Romans... New York: 1847. V. 53

HALL, JAMES
An Account of a Series of Experiments Shewing the Effects of Compression in Modifying the Action of Heat. Edinburgh: 1805. V. 48
Account of a Series of Experiments Shewing the Effects of Compression in Modifying the Action of Heat... Edinburgh: 1812. V. 54
Eight Engravings of the Ruins Occasioned by the Great Fires in Edinburgh, on the 15th, 16th and 17th Novr. 1824. Edinburgh: 1825. V. 48
Experiments on Whinstone and Lava. Edinburgh: 1805. V. 47
Memorial of the Citizens of Cincinnati, to the Congress of the United States, Relative to the Navigation of the Ohio and Mississippi Rivers. Cincinnati: 1844. V. 48
Palaeontology of New York. Albany: 1847-52. V. 47
Palaeontology of New York. Volume 5. Part 1. Lamellibranchiata. Albany: 1883. V. 52
Palaeontology of New York. Volume 5, Part 2. Gasteropoda, Pteropoda and Cephalopoda. New York: 1879. V. 50
Palaeontology of New York. Volume 8. Genera of Palaeozoic Brachiopoda. Part 1. Albany: 1892. V. 50
The Soldier's Bride and Other Tales. Philadelphia: 1833. V. 47
The Wilderness and the War Path. New York: 1846. V. 48; 50

HALL, JAMES NORMAN
High Adventure. Boston: 1918. V. 54

HALL, JOHN E.
The Journal of Jurisprudence: a New Series of the American Law Journal. Philadelphia: 1821. V. 49; 51
Poems by the Late Doctor John Shaw. Philadelphia & Baltimore: 1810. V. 51

HALL, JOHN F.
The Daily Union History of Atlantic City and County. Atlantic City: 1900. V. 47; 49; 51

HALL, JOHN LINVILLE
Around the Horn in '49. The Journal of the Hartford Union Mining and Trading Company, December 1848 to September 1849. San Francisco: 1928. V. 47; 48

HALL, JOSEPH
The Balm of Gilead: or, Comforsts for the Distretsed (sic); Both Moral and Divine. London: 1655. V. 50
Cases of Conscience Practically Resolved... London: 1654. V. 49
Christian Moderation. London: 1640. V. 49
Contemplations Upon the Remarkable Passages in the Life of the Holy Jesus. London: 1679. V. 49
Episcopacie by Divine Right. London: 1640. V. 49; 54
An Humble Remonstrace to the High Covrt Of Parliament, by a Dutifull Sonne of the Chvrch. London: 1640. V. 49; 54
King Horn - a Middle English Romance. London: 1901. V. 54
Virgidemiarum. Oxford: 1753. V. 51
Virgidemiarum... London: 1825. V. 54
The Works... London: 1738. V. 47
The Works... Oxford: 1837. V. 51

HALL, JOSEPH, BP. OF NORWICH
The Great Mysterie of Godliness, Laid Fort by Way of Affectuous and Feeling Meditation. London: 1652. V. 52
Mundus Alter et Idem, Sive Terra Australis Antehac Semper Incognita... Amsterdam: 1643. V. 48
Mundus Alter et Idem, Sive Terra Australis Antehac Semper Incognita... Utrecht: 1643. V. 52
A Recollection of Such Treatises as Have Been Heretofore Seuerally Published and are Now Reuised... London: 1617. V. 48

HALL, KERMIT L.
A Comprehensive Bibliography of American Constitutional and Legal History 1896-1979. (with) Supplement 1980-87. Millwood: 1984-91. V. 53

HALL, LOWIE
Fifty-Six Waterloo Cups. London: 1922. V. 47

HALL, MADELINE
Miss Browne, the Story of a Superior Mouse. London: 1900. V. 54

HALL, MANLY PALMER
An Encyclopedic Outline of Masonic, Hermetic, Qabbalistic &... 1928. V. 54
An Encyclopedic Outline of Masonic, Hermetic, Qabbalistic &... San Francisco: 1928. V. 50
An Encyclopedic Outline of Masonic, Hermetic, Qabbalistic &... 1988. V. 47

HALL, MARSHALL
A Critical and Experimental Essay on the Circulation of the Blood... Philadelphia: 1835. V. 47
A Critical and Experimental Essay on the Circulation Of the Blood. London: 1837. V. 53
A Descriptive, Diagnostic and Practical Essay on Disorders of the Digestive Organs and General Health and Particularly Of Their Numerous forms and Complications, Contrasted with Some Acute and Insidious Diseases. Keen: 1823. V. 48; 53
Lectures on the Nervous System and Its Diseases. Philadelphia: 1836. V. 47
Memoirs of Marshall Hall, M.D., F.R.S.... London: 1861. V. 49

HALL, MARTIN HARDWICK
The Confederate Army of New Mexico. Austin: 1978. V. 50; 52

HALL, MARVIN HARWICK
Sibley's New Mexico Campaign. Austin: 1960. V. 49

HALL, MARY
A Woman in the Antipodes and in the Far East. London: 1914. V. 50; 51

HALL, PETER
Tekmhpia Metpika. Symptoms of Rhyme, Original and Translated. London: 1824. V. 48; 49

HALL, RADCLYFFE
The Forgotten Island. London: 1915. V. 54
The Master of the House. London: 1932. V. 53
Master of the House. New York: 1932. V. 53
Poems of the Past and Present. London: 1910. V. 54
The Sixth Beatitude. London: 1936. V. 47; 48; 49; 51
'Twixt Earth and Stars. London: 1906. V. 51
The Unlit Lamp. London: 1924. V. 51
The Well of Loneliness. New York: 1928. V. 49
The Well of Loneliness. New York: 1929. V. 51; 53
The Well of Loneliness. New York: 1932. V. 54

HALL, ROBERT
The History of Galashiels. Galashiels: 1898. V. 52
A Reply to a Review in the Christian Guardian, Jan. 1822 of 'An Apology for the Freedom of the Press, and for General Liberty, &c'. London: 1822. V. 51

HALL, SAMUEL
...Address to the British Association, Explanatory of the Injustice Done to His Improvements on Steam Engines by Dr. Lardner. Liverpool: 1837. V. 50

HALL, SAMUEL CARTER
The Baronial Halls and Ancient Picturesque Edifices of England. London: 1858. V. 52; 53
The Baronial Halls and Ancient Picturesque Edifices of England. London: 1881. V. 47; 49; 50
The Book of British Ballads. (First) and Second Series. London: 1842-44. V. 49; 53
The Book of Gems... London: 1836-37. V. 52
The Book of Gems. London: 1848. V. 48
The Book of Gems. London: 1853. V. 54
A Book of Memoirs of Great Men and Women of the Age, from Personal Acquaintance. London: 1871. V. 51
The Book of the Thames, From Its Rise to Its Fall. London: 1859. V. 47; 51
The Book of the Thames, from Its Rise to Its Fall. London: 1898. V. 52
Hand Books for Ireland: "Dublin & Wickow" "The North and the Giant's Causeway" "The South & Killarney" "The West & Connemara". London: 1853. V. 47
Ireland: Its Scenery, Character, &c. London: 1841-43. V. 47
Ireland: Its Scenery, Character &c. London: 1846. V. 49; 53
Retrospect of a Long Life: from 1815 to 1883. London: 1883. V. 51
Rhymes in Council. Aphorisms Versified. London: 1881. V. 51

HALL, SHARLOT M.
Cactus and Pine: Songs of the Southwest. Boston: 1911. V. 48

HALL, T. B.
A Floral of Liverpool. London: 1839. V. 54

HALL, THOMAS
The Fortunes and Adventures of Raby Rattler and His Man Floss... London: 1846. V. 48
The Fortunes and Adventures of Raby Rattler and His Man Floss. London: 1864. V. 51

HALL, TREVOR H.
A Bibliography of Books on Conjuring in English from 1580 to 1850. Lepton: 1957. V. 51
Old Conjuring Books. London: 1972. V. 52
Some Printers and Publishers of Conjuring Books and Other Ephemera, 1800-1850. Leeds: 1976. V. 48

HALL, WILLIAM
A Biography of David Cox, With Remarks on His Works and Genius. London, Paris, New York: 1881. V. 50; 54
Irrigation Development, History, Customs, Laws and Administrative Systes...in France, Italy and Spain. Sacramento: 1886. V. 52

HALL, WILLIAM E.
A Treatise on International Law. Oxford: 1884. V. 52

HALL, WILLIAM HENRY
The New Encyclopaedia; or Modern Universal Dictionary of Arts and Sciences... 1802. V. 52
The New Royal Encyclopaedia; or, Complete Modern Dictionary of Arts and Sciences. London: 1788-91. V. 49

HALL, WILLIAM HUTCHESON
Narrative of the Voyages and Services of the Nemesis, from 1840 to 1843... London: 1844. V. 47; 54

HALL, WILLIAM M.
Speech of William M. Hall, of New York in Favor of a National Railroad to the Pacific, at the Great Chicago Convention, July 7, 1847... New York: 1853. V. 47

HALLAM, ARTHUR HENRY
Oration, on the Influence of Italian Works of Imagination on the Same Class of Compositions in England. Cambridge: 1832. V. 51
Poems. London: 1830. V. 50

HALLAM, HENRY
The Constitutional History of England from the Accession of Henry VII to the Death of George II. Paris: 1827. V. 54
The Constitutional History of England from the Accession of Henry VII to the Death of George II. London: 1829. V. 53
The Constitutional History of England from the Accession of Henry VII to the Death of George II. London: 1850. V. 50
Introduction to the Literature of Europe in the Fifteenth, Sixteenth and Seventeenth Centuries. Paris: 1839. V. 51; 54
Introduction to the Literature of Europe in the Fifteenth, Sixteenth and Seventeenth Centuries. London: 1854. V. 49
View of the State of Europe During the Middle Ages. London: 1822. V. 53
View of the State of Europe During the Middle Ages. London: 1841. V. 54
View of the State of Europe During the Middle Ages... London: 1841-43. V. 47
View of the State of Europe During the Middle Ages. London: 1856. V. 51

HALLE, BERNARD
A Manual of Navaho Grammar. St. Michael's: 1926. V. 51

HALLECK, FITZ-GREENE
Alnwick Castle, With Other Poems. New York: 1827. V. 50; 53; 54
Fanny. New York: 1819. V. 54
The Poetical Writings... New York: 1869. V. 47; 48; 51
Poetical Writings. New York: 1873. V. 48

HALLENBECK, CLEVE
Alvar Nunez Cabeza de Vaca: The Journey and Route of the First European to Cross the Continent of North America 1534-1536. Glendale: 1940. V. 52; 53
The Journey of Fray Marcos de Niza. Dallas: 1949. V. 47; 49; 52; 53; 54
Legends of the Spanish Southwest. 1938. V. 48
Legends of the Spanish Southwest. Glendale: 1938. V. 49
Spanish Missions of the Old Southwest. Garden City: 1926. V. 50
Spanish Missions of the Old Southwest. New York: 1926. V. 48

HALLER, ALBRECHT VON
Deux Memoires sur Le Mouvemenet Du Sang, et Sur Les Effets de la Saignee: Fonde's Sur Ses Experiences Faites sur Des Animaux. Lausanne: 1756. V. 48; 53
Elementa Physiologiae Corporis Humani. Lausanne: 1757-69/77-78. V. 47
Opuscula Pathologica Partim Recusa Partim Inedita.... Lausanne: 1755. V. 53
Sur La Formation Du Coeur Dans Le Poulet Sur L'Oeil; Sur La Structure Du Jaune &c. Premier Memoire Exposed des Faits. Lausanne: 1758. V. 47; 48

HALLER ALBRECHT VON
Usong, an Oriental History in Four Books. London: 1773. V. 49

HALLETT, HOLT S.
A Thousand Miles on an Elephant in the Shan States. Edinburgh: 1890. V. 54

HALLEY, ANNE
Between Wars and Other Poems. Northampton: 1965. V. 50; 52

HALLEY, ROBERT
Lancashire: Its Puritanism and Nonconformity. Manchester: 1869. V. 47
Lancashire: Its Puritanism and Nonconformity. Manchester: 1872. V. 53

HALLEY, WILLIAM
The Centennial Year Book of Alameda County. Oakland: 1876. V. 54

HALLIDAY, ANDREW
The Savage-Club Papers. (with) The Savage Club Papers for 1868. London: 1868. V. 49
Town and Country Sketches. London: 1866. V. 54

HALLIDAY, BRETT
Blood on the Black Market. New York: 1943. V. 52
Bodies Are Where You Find Them. New York: 1941. V. 52
Michael Shayne's 50th Case. New York: 1964. V. 52

HALLIDAY, R.
The Talaings. Rangoon: 1917. V. 54

HALLIDAY, SAMUEL B.
The Lost and Found; or Life Among the Poor. New York: 1860. V. 51; 53

HALLIDAY, W. M.
Potlatch and Totem. London & Toronto: 1935. V. 53

HALLIFAX, CHARLES
Familiar Letters on Various Subjects of Business and Amusement... London: 1755. V. 52

HALLIWELL-PHILLIPPS, JAMES ORCHARD
An Account of the Only Known Manuscript of Shakespear's Plays... London: 1843. V. 51
A Dictionary of Archaic and Provincial Words... London: 1855. V. 52
A Dictionary of Archaic and Provincial Words... London: 1889. V. 54
A List of Works Illustrative of the Life and Writings of Shakespeare. London: 1867. V. 54
The Nursery Rhymes of England. London: 1843. V. 51
The Nursery Rhymes of England. London: 1844. V. 48
Outlines of the Life of Shakespeare. London: 1885. V. 49
Palatine Anthology... London: 1850. V. 48; 53
Popular Rhymes and Nursery Tales. London: 1849. V. 48
The Private Diary of Dr. John Dee. London: 1842. V. 50

HALLOCK, CHARLES
Camp Life in Florida: a Handbook for Sportsmen and Settlers. New York: 1876. V. 47
The Fishing Tourist: Angler's Guide and Reference Book. New York: 1873. V. 48
The Sportsman's Gazetteer and General Guide. New York: 1877. V. 47

HALLOWELL, ANNA DAVIS
James and Lucretia Mott. Life and Letters. Boston: 1884. V. 52

HALLYWELL, HENRY
Melampronoea; or a Discourse of the Polity and Kingdom of Darkness. (with) The Sacred Method of Saving Humane Souls by Jesus Christ. London: 1681/77. V. 47

HALM, PHILIPP MARIA
Erasmus Grasser. Augsburg: 1928. V. 53

HALPER, ALBERT
The Foundry. New York: 1934. V. 53
Union Square. New York: 1933. V. 53

HALPERN, JUDITH
Mickey Marcus. New York: 1949. V. 49

HALPERN, PAUL G.
The Keyes Papers Selections from the Private and Official Correspondence of Admiral of the Fleet Baron Keyes of Zeebrugge. London: 1972/80/81. V. 51

HALPERT, SAM
When We Talk About Raymond Carver. Layton: 1991. V. 49

HALPINE, CHARLES GRAHAM
The Life and Adventures, Songs, Services and Speeches of Private Miles O'Reilly. New York: 1864. V. 54

HALSE, GEORGE F.
Queen Loeta and the Mistletoe. London: 1857. V. 54

HALSELL, H. H.
My Autobiography. Fort Worth: 1948. V. 53

HALSEY, DON P.
A Sketch of the Life of Capt. Don P. Halsey of the Confederate States Army. Richmond: 1904. V. 49

HALSEY, HARLAN PAGE
Macon Moore, the Southern Detective. New York: 1881. V. 47; 51; 52
Phil Scott, the Indian Detective: a Tale of Startling Mysteries. New York: 1882. V. 49; 52

HALSEY, R. T. H.
The Homes of Our Ancestors. Garden City: 1925. V. 51
Pictures of Early New York on Dark Blue Staffordshire pottery. New York: 1899. V. 51

HALSEY, RICHARD T.
The Boston Port Bill as Pictured by a Contemporary London Cartoonist. New York: 1904. V. 47; 51

HALSEY, ROSALIE V.
Forgotten Books of the American Nursery. A History of the Development of the American Story Book. Boston: 1911. V. 50

HALSMAN, PHILIPPE
Dali's Mustache. New York: 1954. V. 49
Jump Book. New York: 1959. V. 48
Piccoli: a Fairy Tale. New York: 1953. V. 51

HALSTEAD, B. W.
Poisonous and Venomous Marine Animals of the World. Washington: 1965-67. V. 52
Poisonous and Venomous Marine Animals of the World. Washington: 1965-67-70. V. 53
Poisonous and Venomous Marine Animals of the World. Washington: 1965-70. V. 52
Poisonous and Venomous Marine Animals of the World. Princeton: 1988. V. 48

HALSTED, BRYAN DAVID
Barn Plans and Outbuildings. New York: 1882. V. 50

HALSTED, CAROLINE
Richard III. London: 1844. V. 50

HALSTED, EDWARD PELLEW
The Navy Unarmed Still. Westminster: 1865. V. 52

HALSTED, WILLIAM
A Clinical and Histological Study of Certain Adenocarcinomata of the Breast. 1898. V. 48; 53
The Employment of Fine Silk in Preference to Catgut and the Advantages of Transfixing Tissues and Vessels in Controlling Hemorrhage, also an Account of the Introduction of Gloves, Gutta-Percha Tissue and Silver Foil. 1913. V. 52
An Experimental Study of the Thyroid Gland of Dogs, with Especial Consideration of Hyperthrophy of This Gland. 1896. V. 48; 53
The Radical Cure of Inguinal Hernia in the Male. 1893. V. 53
Surgical Papers by William Stewart Halsted. Baltimore: 1924. V. 49; 52
Surgical Papers by William Stewart Halsted. Baltimore: 1952. V. 50; 52

HALY, R. STANDISH
An Impressment: Attempt to Prove, Why It Should and How It Could Be Abolished. Poole: 1822. V. 53

HALYBURTON, JAMES D.
Decisions of Hon. James D. Halyburton, Judge of the Confederate States District Court for the Eastern District of Virginia, in the Cases of John B. Lane and John H. Leftwich, in Relation to Their Exemption, as Mail Contractors, from the Performance... Richmond: 1864. V. 49

HAM, GEORGE H.
The New West Extending from the Great Lakes Across the Plain and Mountain to the Golden shores of the Pacific... Winnipeg: 1888. V. 48; 52

HAMADY, MARY
An Everday Celebration. Mt. Horeb: 1971. V. 51; 53; 54
Selected Poems 1973-1980. Springfield: 1982. V. 51; 54

HAMADY, WALTER
1985; a Collaboration. 1992. V. 54
Book No 68. Mt. Horeb: 1974. V. 51
The Chair; a Poem for my Jidu. Mt. Horeb: 1970. V. 51
Eyes Touch and Change (or) Weather Conditions at Other Locations: Three Poems. Mt. Horeb: 1986. V. 54
For the Hundredth Time, Gabberjab Number Five. Minor Confluence: 1981. V. 54
Hand Papermaking: Papermaking by Hand... Minor Confluence: 1982. V. 54
In Sight of Blue Mounds. Mt. Horeb: 1972. V. 51; 54
Neopostmodernism or, Gabberjab Number 6. Mt. Horeb: 1988. V. 54
One Day to Sintra and Back. Mt. Horeb: 1970. V. 51; 54
Plumfoot Poems. Madison: 1967. V. 49
The Plumfoot Poems. Mt. Horeb: 1967. V. 54
The Quartz Crystal History of Perry Township Since the Earliest Creation of Life. Mt. Horeb: 1979. V. 51
Seeds and Chairs. Mt. Horeb: 1979. V. 47; 49; 54
Since Mary. Mt. Horeb: 1969. V. 51; 54
Since Mary... Springdale: 1969. V. 52
These Chairs. Mt. Horeb: 1971. V. 51; 54
Thumbnailing the Hilex. Another (3) Interminable Gabberjabs. Mt. Horeb: 1974. V. 54
Voltaire the Hamadeh. Interminable Gabberjabbs. (with) Hunkering in Wisconsin. (with) Thumbnailing the Hilex. Gabberjabb Number 3. (with) The Interminable Gabberjabb Volume One (&) Number Four. Mt. Horeb: 1973-81. V. 52

HAMBERG, GUSTAF
Studies in Roman Imperial Art with Special Reference to State Reliefs of the Second Century. Uppsala: 1945. V. 50

HAMBLETON, CHALKLEY J.
A Gold Hunter's Experience. Chicago: 1848. V. 53
A Gold Hunter's Experience... Chicago: 1898. V. 47; 54

HAMBLETON, RONALD
Unit of Five. Toronto: 1944. V. 52

HAMBLY, W. D.
Serpent Worship in Africa, and The Ovimbundu of Angola and Culture Areas of Nigeria. New York: 1968. V. 54

HAMBURGER, MICHAEL
In Suffolk. Hereford: 1982. V. 47
Orpheus Street, London, S.E.5. 1967. V. 50
Trees. Llangynog: 1988. V. 54

HAMCONIUS, MARTIN
Frisia Seu De Viris Rebusqe Illustribus Libri Duo. Franeker: 1620. V. 53

HAMDAN Stables Stud Book of Arabian Horses. Volume I. Cairo: 1969. V. 53

HAMEL, MAURICE
Corot and His Work. Glasgow: 1905. V. 49; 50; 51; 52

HAMER, F.
Orchids of Central American, an Illustrated Field Guide. Selbyana: 1988-91. V. 52
Orchids of Nicaragua. Sarasota: 1982-85. V. 52

HAMER, S. H.
The Jungle School of Dr. Jibber-Jabber Burchall's Academy. London: 1903. V. 51
The Little Folks Picture Album in Color. London: 1904. V. 47; 49

HAMERTON, PHILIP GILBERT
Chapters on Animals. London: 1881. V. 47
Drawing and Engraving. A Brief Exposition of Technical principles and Practice... London: 1892. V. 49; 50
The Etcher's Handbook. London: 1881. V. 49
Etching and Etchers. Boston: 1876. V. 47
Etching and Etchers. London: 1876. V. 48; 52
Etching and Etchers. London: 1880. V. 48; 50
Imagination in Landscape Painting. London: 1887. V. 51; 54
Landscape, With Original Etchings and Many Illustrations... London: 1885. V. 51

HAMERTON, PHILIP GILBERT continued
The Portfolio: an Artistic Periodical. London: 1881-93. V. 48; 50
Wenderholme. London & Edinburgh: 1869. V. 48; 51; 53

HAMILIN, A. C.
The Tourmaline. Boston: 1873. V. 53

HAMILTON, ADRIAN
The Infamous Essay on Woman or John Wilkes Seated Between Vice and Virtue. London: 1972. V. 51

HAMILTON, ALEXANDER
Alexander Hamilton's Report on the Subject of Manufactures, Made in His Capacity of Secretary of the Treasury on the Fifth of December, 1791. Philadelphia: 1827. V. 47
The Family Female Physician; or, a Treatise on the Management of Female Complaints and of Children in Early Infancy. Worcester: 1793. V. 48
A New Account of the East Indies. London: 1744. V. 52
A New Account of the East Indies... London: 1930. V. 47; 49; 51
Outlines of the Theory and Practice of Mid-Wifery. London: 1796. V. 53
A Treatise on the Management of Female Complaints... New York: 1792. V. 48; 50; 51; 53
A Treatise On the Management of Female Complaints... New York: 1795. V. 53
The Works. New York: 1810. V. 47; 50; 51
The Works... New York: 1851. V. 52
The Works... New York: 1903. V. 54
The Works. New York: 1904. V. 47; 50

HAMILTON, ALLAN
Nervous Diseases: Their Description and Treatment. Philadelphia: 1878. V. 47

HAMILTON, ANGUS
Afghanistan. London: 1906. V. 51
Afghanistan. Boston and Tokyo: 1910. V. 54
Korea Its History, Its People and Its Commerce. Boston and Tokyo: 1910. V. 54

HAMILTON, ANNE
The Epics of the Ton; or, the Glories of the Great World: a Poem in Two Books... London: 1807. V. 47
Secret History of the Court of England, from the Accession of George the Third to the Death of George the Fourth. London: 1832. V. 51

HAMILTON, ANTHONY
Fairy Tales and Romances. London: 1849. V. 49
Grammont's Memoirs of the Court of Charles II. London: 1906. V. 53; 54
Memoirs of Count Grammont. London: 1793. V. 47
Memoirs of Count Grammont. London: 1811. V. 53
Memoirs of Count Grammont... London: 1876. V. 50
Memoirs of Count Grammont. Philadelphia: 1889. V. 51
Memoirs of the Count De Grammont. London: 1928. V. 53

HAMILTON, AUGUSTA
Marriage Rites, Customs and Ceremonies of all Nations of the Universe. London: 1822. V. 48; 50; 52

HAMILTON, AUGUSTUS
The Art and Workmanship of the Maori Race in New Zealand. Dunedin: 1896. V. 50; 52
The Art and Workmanship of the Maori Race in New Zealand. Dunedin: 1896-1901. V. 48

HAMILTON, CHARLES
Lincoln in Photographs: an Album of Very Known Pose. Norman: 1963. V. 54
The Patriot, a Tragedy. London: 1784. V. 48; 51

HAMILTON, CLAYTON
On The Trail of Stevenson. New York: 1915. V. 51

HAMILTON, DAVID
David Hamilton's Private Collection. New York: 1976. V. 54

HAMILTON, DUKE OF
Catalogue of the Collection of Pictures, Works of Art and Decorative Objects, the Property of His Grace the Duke of Hamilton...Saturday June 17 and Monday June 19, 1882. London: 1882. V. 47

HAMILTON, E.
The Haunted Stars. 1960. V. 48; 52
The Metal Giants. 1932. V. 47; 51

HAMILTON, EDITH
The Greek Way. New York: 1930. V. 47
The Greek Way. (and) The Roman Way. New York: 1930/32. V. 51

HAMILTON, EDMOND
The Best of Edmond Hamilton. 1977. V. 49; 54

HAMILTON, EDWARD
Recollections of Fly Fishing for Salmon, Trout and Grayling... London: 1884. V. 48
Recollections of Fly Fishing for Salmon, Trout and Grayling... New York: 1885. V. 47

HAMILTON, EDWARD JOHN
The Human Mind: a Treatise in Mental Philosophy. New York: 1883. V. 47; 49

HAMILTON, ELIZABETH
The Cottagers of Glenburnie... Edinburgh: 1808. V. 51; 53
Letters Addressed to the Daughter of a Nobleman, on the Formation of Religious and Moral Principle. London: 1806. V. 47; 50; 51; 53
Letters Addressed to the Daughter of a Nobleman, on the Formation of Religious and Moral Principle. Salem: 1821. V. 50; 51
Letters on Education. Dublin: 1801. V. 49
Letters on the Elementary Principles of Education. Bath: 1801-02. V. 52
Letters on the Elementary Principles of Education. London: 1801-02. V. 50
Letters on the Elementary Principles of Education. London: 1803. V. 49
Memoirs of Modern Philosophers. Bath: 1800. V. 50
Memoirs of Modern Philosophers. Dublin: 1800. V. 47
A Series of Popular Essays, Illustrative of the Principles Essentially Connected with the Improvement of the Understanding, the Imagination and the Heart. Edinburgh: 1813. V. 54
Translation of the Letters of a Hindoo Rajah... London: 1796. V. 49; 54
Translation of the Letters of a Hindoo Rajah... London: 1801. V. 50; 54
Translation of the Letters of a Hindoo Rajah... London: 1811. V. 50

HAMILTON, F.
An Account of the Fishes Found in the River Ganges and Its Branches. Edinburgh: 1822. V. 47
An Account of the Fishes Found in the River Ganges and Its Branches. London: 1822. V. 52

HAMILTON, FRANK HASTINGS
A Practical Treatise on Military Surgery. New York: 1861. V. 51; 54
A Treatise on Military Surgery and Hygiene. New York: 1865. V. 48

HAMILTON, GEORGE
The Elements of Drawing... London: 1812. V. 49
The Elements of Drawing... London: 1827. V. 50
The Telegraph: a Consolatory Epistle (in Verse) From Thomas Muir, Esq., of Botany Bay, to the Hon. Henry Erskine, Late Dean of Faculty. Edinburgh: 1796. V. 50; 54
A Voyage Round the World, In His Majesty's Frigate Pandora. Berwick: 1793. V. 50

HAMILTON, GEORGE ROSTREVOR
The Greek Portrait. London: 1934. V. 53
The Latin Portrait: an Anthology Made By... London: 1929. V. 48

HAMILTON, GERALD
Mr. Norris and I: an Autobiographical Sketch. London: 1956. V. 48

HAMILTON, GUSTAVUS
The Elements of Gymnastics for Boy and of Calisthenics for Young Ladies. London: 1838. V. 53

HAMILTON, H. P.
An Analytical System of Conic Sections. Cambridge: 1828. V. 47; 51

HAMILTON, HENRY RAYMOND
Foot Prints. Chicago: 1927. V. 49

HAMILTON, IAIN
Variations on an Original Theme for Strings. Op. 1. London: 1953. V. 52

HAMILTON, IAN
J. D. Salinger... 1986. V. 50
J. D. Salinger... New York: 1986. V. 47; 53
A Staff Officer's Scrap-Book During the Russo-Japanese War. London: 1906. V. 54

HAMILTON, JAMES
The Gospel of St. John Adapted to the Hamiltonian System, by an Analytical and Interlineary Translation. London: 1824. V. 52
Observations on the Use and Abuse of Mercurial Medicines in Various Diseases. Edinburgh: 1819. V. 51
Observations on the Utility and the Administration of Purgative Medicines in Several Diseases. Philadelphia: 1809. V. 48; 53
Observations on the Utility and the Administration of Purgative Medicines in Several Diseases. Philadelphia: 1829. V. 50
Outlines of Midwifery, for the Use of Students. Edinburgh: 1826. V. 48; 52
Wanderings in North Africa. London: 1856. V. 51; 54

HAMILTON, JAMES CLELAND
The Georgian Bay: an Account of its Position, Inhabitants, Mineral Interests, Fish, Timber and Other Resources. Toronto: 1893. V. 54
Osgoode Hall. Reminiscences of the Bench and Bar. Toronto: 1904. V. 51

HAMILTON, JAMES, MARQUESS OF
His Majesties Proclamation in Scotland; with an Explanation of the Meaning of the Oath and Covenant. London: 1639. V. 47

HAMILTON, JANE
The Book of Ruth. Boston: 1938. V. 54
The Book of Ruth. 1988. V. 54
The Book of Ruth. New York: 1988. V. 51; 52; 53; 54

HAMILTON, JOHN P.
Reminiscences of an Old Sportsman. London: 1860. V. 47
Travels through the Interior Provinces of Colombia. London: 1827. V. 47; 49; 51; 54

HAMILTON, JOHN R.
New Brunswick and It's Scenery. Saint John: 1874. V. 48; 49; 51; 53

HAMILTON, JOSEPH
The Only Approved Guide through all the Stages of a Quarrel... London: 1829. V. 51
Some Short and Useful Reflections Upon Duelling, Which Should Be In the Hands of Every Person Who is Liable to Receive a Challenge... Dublin: 1823. V. 51

HAMILTON, JOSEPH GREGOIRE DE ROULHAC
Reconstruction in North Carolina. Raleigh: 1906. V. 52; 54

HAMILTON, MARY WALKER
Le Village de Munster. Paris: 1811. V. 54

HAMILTON, PATRICK
Gaslight. London: 1939. V. 51

HAMILTON, PATRICK continued
Hangover Square. New York: 1942. V. 54
Impromptu in Moribundia. London: 1939. V. 51
The Resources of Arizona. Prescott: 1881. V. 52
The Resources of Arizona. San Francisco: 1883. V. 52
The Resources of Arizona. San Francisco: 1884. V. 47; 48; 52
The Slaves of Solitude. London: 1947. V. 51; 53
Twopence Coloured. Boston: 1928. V. 51
The West Pier. London: 1951. V. 51

HAMILTON, RICHARD
Amphibious Carnivora Including Walrus & Seals, also the Herbivorous Cetacea. Edinburgh: 1843. V. 51
Game In Southern India. Ootacamund: 1876. V. 48
Game in Southern India. Madras: 1881. V. 48
Mammalia. Whales, etc. Edinburgh. V. 51

HAMILTON, RICHARD VESEY
Letters and Papers of Sir Thos. Byam Martin. London: 1903-1898. V. 52

HAMILTON, ROBERT
Rules for Recovering Persons Recently Drowned: In a Letter to the Rev. George Rogers, A.M. Rector of Spraughton, in Suffolk. London: 1794. V. 54

HAMILTON, S. B.
A Qualitative Study of Some Buildings in the London Area. London: 1964. V. 52

HAMILTON, SINCLAIR
Early American Book Illustrators and Wood Engravers 1670-1870. Princeton: 1968. V. 47; 48; 52
Early American Book Illustrators and Wood Engravers 1670-1870. Princeton: 1970. V. 52

HAMILTON, TERRICK
Antar: a Bedoueen Romance. London: 1820. V. 48

HAMILTON, THOMAS
Annals of the Peninsular Campaigns. London: 1849. V. 50
Men and Manners in America. Edinburgh: 1833. V. 49; 50; 53
Men and Manners in America. Philadelphia: 1833. V. 49
Men and Manners in America. Edinburgh & London: 1834. V. 52; 53
Men and Manners in America. Edinburgh and London: 1843. V. 53
The Youth and Manhood of Cyril Thornton. Edinburgh: 1827. V. 48; 49; 50; 52; 53

HAMILTON, VIRGINIA
In the Beginning. San Diego, New York, London: 1988. V. 53
Paul Robeson: the Life and Times of a Free Black. New York: 1974. V. 54
W.E.B. DuBois: a Biography. V. 52
W.E.B. Dubois: a Biography. New York: 1972. V. 54

HAMILTON, WALTER
The Aesthetic Movement in England. London: 1882. V. 51
Dated Bookplates. London: 1895. V. 49
Dated Bookplates (Ex-Libris), with a Treatise On their Origin and Development. London: 1895. V. 47; 48
French Bookplates. London: 1896. V. 49
A Hand-Book; or Concise Dictionary of Terms Used in the Arts and Sciences. London: 1825. V. 52

HAMILTON, WESTON G.
A Compend of Domestic Medicine and Household Remedies with the Treatment of Diseases of Adult and Infant. Greensboro: 1887. V. 52

HAMILTON, WILLIAM
The Exemplary Life of James Bonnell, Esq... London: 1704. V. 49; 50; 51; 54
The Exemplary Life...of James Bonnell, Esq. London: 1707. V. 49; 50; 51; 54
Lectures on Metaphysics and Logic. London: 1860-70. V. 50
Letters Concerning the Northern Coast of the County of Antrim. Dublin: 1790. V. 48
Observations on Mount Vesuvius, Mount Etna, and Other Volcanos... London: 1773. V. 48
Outlines from the Figures and Compositions Upon the Greek, Roman, and Etruscan Vases of... London: 1814. V. 50
Poems on Several Occasions. Edinburgh: 1760. V. 50

HAMILTON, WILLIAM GERARD
Parliamentary Logick. London: 1808. V. 47; 49; 50; 51

HAMILTON, WILLIAM RICHARD
Memorandum on the Subject of the Earl of Elgin's Pursuits in Greece. London: 1811. V. 49
Remarks On Several Parts of Turkey. London: 1809-10. V. 50

HAMILTON, WILLIAM ROWAN
Elements of Quaternions. London: 1866. V. 47; 50
Elements of Quaternions. London: 1899-1901. V. 53

HAMILTON, WILLIAM T.
Address on the Importance of Knowledge; Delivered Before the Eroscophic Society of the University of Alabama at Tuscaloosa. Tuscaloosa: 1841. V. 52
My Sixty Years on the Plains. New York: 1905. V. 47; 52

HAMLEY, EDWARD BRUCE
Lady Lee's Widowhood. Edinburgh: 1854. V. 51; 53

HAMLIN, AUGUSTUS CHOATE
The Battle of Chancellorsville. Bangor: 1896. V. 49

HAMLIN, B. NASON
In Sunshine and Shade: Stories of Various Entertaining Incidents. Dedham: 1946. V. 47

HAMMACHER, A. M.
Marino Marini: Sculpture, Painting, Drawing. New York. V. 47; 48; 50

HAMMER, ARMAND
The Armand Hammer Collection. Five Centuries of Masterpieces. New York: 1980. V. 49

HAMMER, CAROLYN
Notes on the Two-Color Initials of Victor Hammer. Lexington: 1966. V. 47
Victor Hammer: Artist and Printer. Lexington: 1981. V. 47

HAMMER CREEK PRESS
Type Specimen Book. New York: 1954. V. 52

HAMMER, KENNETH
Biographies of the 7th Cavalry. June 25, 1876. Ft. Collins: 1972. V. 52

HAMMER, LAURA V.
Light n'Hitch. A Collection of Historical Writing Depicting Life on the High Plains. Dallas: 1958. V. 51

HAMMER, VICTOR
Chapters on Writing and Printing. Lexington: 1963. V. 50
Concern for the Art of Civilized man. Lexington: 1963. V. 48
De Quatuor Evangelistis: Ex Libro Primo Operis Paschalis Vulgati c. 434 A.D. Kentucky: 1955. V. 48
Memory and Her Nine Daughters/The Muses/A Pretext for Printing Cast Into the Mould of a Dialogue in Four Chapters. New York: 1957. V. 50
Victor Hammer. Raleigh: 1965. V. 51

HAMMER, WILLIAM
Radium and Other Radio-Active Substances; Polonium, Actinium, and Thorium, with a Consideration of Phosphorescent and Fluorescent Substances... New York: 1903. V. 48; 52; 53; 54

HAMMERSTEIN, OSCAR
Lyrics. New York: 1949. V. 48
Oklahoma!. New York: 1943. V. 51

HAMMERTON, J. A.
Wonders of the Past, The Romance of Antiquity and Its Splendors. New York and London: 1923/24/24/24. V. 54

HAMMERTON, JOHN
The Great War...I Was There! Undying Memories of 1914-1918. London: 1938-39. V. 47
The Second Great War: a Standard History. London: 1939-46. V. 54

HAMMETT, DASHIELL
$106,000 Blood Money. New York: 1943. V. 48; 53
The Battle of the Aleutians. Alaska: 1944. V. 50
The Battle of the Aleutians. San Francisco: 1944. V. 51; 52
The Dain Curse. New York: 1929. V. 50
The Dashiell Hammett Omnibus. 1950. V. 51
The Dashiell Hammett Omnibus... London: 1950. V. 50; 53
Dead Yellow Women. New York: 1947. V. 51; 52
The Glass Key. New York: 1931. V. 53
Hammett Homicides. New York: 1946. V. 53
The Maltese Falcon. New York: 1930. V. 53
The Maltese Falcon. New York: 1944. V. 49
The Maltese Falcon. San Francisco: 1983. V. 53; 54
The Maltese Falcon. San Francisco: 1984. V. 47
Modern Tales of Horror. London: 1932. V. 50
Nightmare Town. New York: 1948. V. 51
Red Harvest. New York & London: 1929. V. 51; 52; 53; 54
The Return of the Continental Op. New York: 1945. V. 53
The Thin Man. New York: 1924. V. 54
The Thin Man. New York: 1934. V. 50; 51; 52

HAMMETT, MARY JANE
The Crusader. Sherman Oaks: 1980. V. 49

HAMMON, HENRY J.
The Architectural Antiquities and Present State of Crosby Place, London, as Lately Restored by John Davies, Esq.... London: 1844. V. 50; 54

HAMMOND, CHARLES
View of General Jackson's Domestic Relations, in Reference to His Fitness for the presidency. Washington?: 1828. V. 48

HAMMOND, GEORGE PETER
Don Juan de Onate: Colonizer of New Mexico 1595-1628. Albuquerque: 1953. V. 52
The Larkin Papers for the History of California, Personal Business and Official Correspondence of Thomas Oliver Larkin, Merchant... Berkeley: 1951. V. 51
The Larkin Papers for the History of California, Personal Business and Official Correspondence of Thomas Oliver Larkin, Merchant... Berkeley: 1951-64. V. 48
The Larkin Papers for the History of California, Personal Business and Official Correspondence of Thomas Oliver Larkin, Merchant... Berkeley: 1951/52/53/55/. V. 53
Narratives of the Coronado Expedition 1540-1542. Albuquerque: 1940. V. 52
New Spain and the Anglo-American West: Historical Contributions Presented to Herbert Eugene Bolton. Los Angeles: 1932. V. 49
Noticias de California: First Report of the Occupation by the Portola Expedition, 1770. San Francisco: 1958. V. 47
On the Ambitious Projects of Russia in Regard to North West America... San Francisco: 1955. V. 47; 53
Overland to California on the Southwest Trail 1849. Berkeley & Los Angeles: 1950. V. 50
The Treaty of Guadalupe Hidalgo, February Second 1848. Berkeley: 1949. V. 52

HAMMOND, H.
A Practical Catechism. London: 1700. V. 49

HAMMOND, ISAAC B.
Reminiscences of Frontier Life. Portland: 1904. V. 49; 50

HAMMOND, J. L.
Gladstone and the Irish Nation. London: 1938. V. 49

HAMMOND, JABEZ D.
Life and Times of Silas Wright, Late Governor of the State of New York. Syracuse: 1848. V. 54

HAMMOND, JAMES
Love Elegies. London: 1743. V. 49

HAMMOND, JOHN
The Practical Surveyor: Shewing, Ready and Certain Methods for Measuring, Mapping and Adorning All Sorts of Lands and Waters... London: 1731. V. 49

HAMMOND, JOHN MARTIN
Quaint and Historic Forts of North America. Philadelphia & London: 1915. V. 51

HAMMOND, N.
Twentieth Century Wildlife Artists. London: 1986. V. 52; 53

HAMMOND, NATALIE HAYS
Anthology of Pattern. New York: 1949. V. 47

HAMMOND, NATHANIEL
The Elements of Algebra, to Which is Prefixed an Introduction Containing a Succinct History of This Science... London: 1764. V. 52

HAMMOND, OTIS
The Utah Expedition 1857-1858. Letters of Capt. Jesse Gove, 10th Infantry USA. Concord: 1928. V. 47

HAMMOND, R. A.
The Life and Writings of Charles Dickens: a Memorial Volume. Toronto: 1871. V. 49; 54

HAMMOND, ROBERT
The Electric Light in Our Homes. London: 1884. V. 53

HAMMOND, S. H.
Hills, Lakes and Forest Streams: or a Tramp in the Chateaugay Woods. New York: 1854. V. 54

HAMMOND, T. W.
Nottingham Past and Present. Nottingham: 1926. V. 51

HAMMOND, WAYNE G.
J.R.R. Tolkien: a Descriptive Bibliography. Winchester: 1993. V. 53

HAMMOND, WILLIAM
Masonic Emblems and Jewels: Treasures at Freemasons' Hall, London. London: 1917. V. 48

HAMMOND, WILLIAM ALEXANDER
Cerebral Hyperaemia the Result of Mental Strain or Emotional Disturbance. New York: 1878. V. 50; 52; 53
Insanity in its Medico-Legal Relations... New York: 1866. V. 47
Insanity in Its Medico-Legal Relations. New York: 1867. V. 48
Physics and Physiology of Spiritualism. New York: 1871. V. 50; 52; 53
Sexual Impotence in the Male. New York: 1883. V. 50; 52; 53
Sexual Impotence in the Male and Female. Detroit: 1887. V. 47
Sleep and Its Derangements. Philadelphia: 1880. V. 53
Sleep, Sleeplessness and the Derangements of Sleep or the Hygiene of the Night. London: 1892. V. 53
Spiritualism and Allied Causes and Conditions of Nervous Derangement. New York: 1876. V. 50
A Treatise on Diseases of the Nervous System. New York: 1872. V. 53
A Treatise on Diseases of the Nervous System. New York: 1874. V. 50
A Treatise on Insanity In Its Medical Relations. New York: 1883. V. 47; 50; 52; 53

HAMNER, LAURA V.
Light n'Hitch, a Collection of Historical Writing Depicting Life on the High Plains. Dallas: 1958. V. 53

HAMNETT, NINA
Is She a Lady? A Problem in autobiography. 1955. V. 49
Is She a Lady? A Problem in Autobiography. London: 1955. V. 47; 52; 54
The People's Album of London Statues. London: 1928. V. 53

HAMOD, SAM
After the Funeral of Assam Hamady. Mt. Horeb: 1971. V. 51
The Famous Blue Mounds Scrapbook. Mt. Horeb: 1972. V. 51

HAMPER, WILLIAM
The Life, Diary and Correspondence of Sir William Dugdale. Harding: 1827. V. 53

HAMPSON, ALFRED LEETE
Emily Dickinson - a Bibliography. Northampton: 1930. V. 51

HAMPSON, G. F.
Catalogue of the Lepidoptera Palaenae in the British Museum. London: 1898-1920. V. 49

HAMPSON, JOHN
Man About the House. London: 1935. V. 47; 53
Memoirs of the Late Rev. John Wesley, A.M. With a Review of His Life and Writings, and a History of Methodism... Sunderland: 1791. V. 48
O Providence. London: 1932. V. 47; 51; 53
Saturday Night at the Greyhound. London: 1931. V. 51; 53
Strip Jack Naked. London: 1934. V. 48; 50; 51
Two Stories. London: 1931. V. 48

THE HAMPSTEAD Annual. London: 1897 1907. V. 48; 52

HAMPSTEAD ANTIQUARIAN & HISTORICAL SOCIETY
Transactions for the Year(s) 1898, 1899, 1900, 1901 and 1902-03. Hampstead: 1898-1905. V. 54

HAMPSTON, CELWYN E.
History of the Twenty-First U.S. Infantry from 1812 to 1863. Columbus: 1911. V. 54

HAMPTON, CHRISTOPHER
Poems for Shakespeare. London: 1972. V. 51

HAMSUN, KNUT
Look Back on Happiness. New York: 1940. V. 51

THE HAMWOOD Papers of the Ladies of Llangollen and Caroline Hamilton. London: 1930. V. 53; 54

HANAFORD, PHOEBE ANN COFFIN
Our Martyred President. Boston: 1865. V. 52
Women of the Century. Boston: 1877. V. 48

HANAGHAN, JONATHAN
Eve's Moods Unveiled: Poems. Dublin: 1957. V. 49

HANBIDGE, WILLIAM
The Memories of William Hanbidge. 1939. V. 50; 54

HANBURY & CARVEY
Tierra Perfecta, the Perfect Land of the Mission Fathers Lower California the Peninsula Now Open to Colonists... San Francisco: 1887. V. 47

HANBURY, D.
Science Papers, Chiefly Pharmacological and Botanical. London: 1876. V. 54

HANBURY, DAVID T.
Sport and Travel in the Northland of Canada. London: 1904. V. 48
Sport and Travel in the Northland of Canada. New York: 1904. V. 53

HANBURY, F. J.
Flora of Kent. London: 1899. V. 50; 51

HANBURY WILLIAMS, CHARLES
The Works. London: 1822. V. 50

HANCARVILLE, PIERRE FRANCOIS HUGUES, CALLED D'
Antiquites Etrusques, Grecques et Romaines Gravees par F. A. David. Paris: 1785-88. V. 49

HANCHANT W. L.
Charles' Wain. A Miscellany of Short Stories. London: 1933. V. 51

HANCOCK, ALMIRA RUSSELL
Reminiscences of Winfield Scott Hancock. New York: 1887. V. 47; 53

HANCOCK, B. F.
The Law, Without the Advice of an Attorney... Norristown: 1831. V. 47

HANCOCK, H. IRVING
Japanese Physical Training. New York: 1904. V. 47
Jiu-Jitsu Combat Tricks. London: 1904. V. 48

HANCOCK, JOHN
A Fasciculous of Eight Drawings on Stone of Groups of Birds. London: 1853. V. 50; 52; 53
The Herons of the World. London: 1978. V. 48; 52
Storks, Ibises and Spoonbills of the World. London: 1992. V. 48; 50

HANCOCK, THOMAS
Essay on Instinct and Its Physical and Moral Relations. London: 1824. V. 52; 53
Personal Narrative of the Origin and Progress of the Caoutchouc of India-Rubber Manufacture in England... London: 1857. V. 47
The Principles of Peace Exemplified in the Conduct of the Society of Friends in Ireland, During the Rebellion of the Year 1798... 1825. V. 47
The Principles of Peace Exemplified in the Conduct of the society of Friends in Ireland, During the Rebellion of the Year 1798... London: 1825. V. 50

HANCOCK, WILLIAM NEILSON
An Introductory Lecture on Political Economy... Dublin: 1849. V. 47
Is the Competition Between Large and Small shops Injurious to the Community?. Dublin: 1851. V. 53

HANCOX, ALAN
Poems for Alan Hancox. Herefordshire: 1993. V. 51

HAND, WILLIAM
The House Surgeon and Physician: Designed to Assist Heads of Families, Travelers and Sea Faring People. New Haven: 1820. V. 48; 53

THE HAND-BOOK of Carving; with Hints on the Etiquette of the Dinner Table. Boston: 1840. V. 53

HAND-BOOK of the Mines and Mining Companies of Cripple Creek... Denver: 1899. V. 54

HAND-BOOK of the Mines and Mining Companies of Cripple Creek... Jan. 1899. V. 53

THE HAND-Book of Useful and Ornamental Amusements and Accomplishments... London: 1845. V. 54

HAND-BOOK to the Cathedral Church, With Some Account of the Monastic Buildings, Etc. Ely: 1887. V. 47

HAND-BOOK to the Cathedral Church, With Some Account of the Monastic Buildings, etc... London: 1891. V. 54

HANDASYDE
The Four Gardens. London: 1912. V. 48

HANDBOOK of Australian, New Zealand and Antarctic Birds. London: 1990. V. 49; 50

HANDBOOK of Calistoga Springs, or, Little Geysers, Its Mineral Waters, Climate, Amusements, Baths, Drives, Scenery, the Celebrated Great Geysers and Petrified Forest and the Clear Lake Country. San Francisco: 1871. V. 52

THE HANDBOOK of New Zealand Mines. Wellington: 1887. V. 50

HANDBOOK of the Birds of the World. Volume I: Ostrich to Ducks. London: 1992. V. 50

HANDCOCK, A. G.
The Siege of Delhi in 1857. Allahabad: 1899. V. 51

HANDEL, GEORGE FREDERICK
Israel in Babylon. London: 1768?. V. 47
The Sacred Oratorios. London: 1799. V. 47
Six Concertos for Harpsicord or Organ. London: 1750. V. 47

HANDFORTH, THOMAS
Faraway Meadow. New York: 1939. V. 52

HANDLER, HANS
The Spanish Riding School. New York: 1972. V. 48; 52; 54

HANDLEY, JAMES
Mechanical Essays on the Animal Oeconomy...Animal Secretion...Sensation... London: 1721. V. 53

HANDLEY-READ, CHARLES
The Art of Wyndham Lewis. London: 1951. V. 50; 53; 54

HANDLEY-TAYLOR, G.
A Bibliography of the Poet Laureate. Chicago: 1968. V. 48

HANDLIN, W. W.
American Politics, A Moral and Political Work, Treating of the Causes of the Civil War, the Nature of Government and the Necessity for Reform. New Orleans: 1864. V. 49; 50

HANDS, A. W.
Common Greek Coins.../Coins of Magna Graecia.../Italo-Greek Coins of Southern Italy. London: 1907/09/12. V. 48

HANDSON, LEVETT
An Accurate Historical Account of All the Orders of Knighthood at Present Existing in Europe. London: 1802. V. 53

HANDYSIDE, ANDREW, & CO.
Works in Iron. London: 1868. V. 52

HANDYSIDE, HENRY
A Treatise on an Improved Method for Overcoming Steep gradients on Railways, Read before the British Association in 1875, at Bristol. Bristol: 1875. V. 49

HANELY, JAMES
Stoker Bush. New York: 1935. V. 53

HANES, BARBARA
Tales of the North American Indians and Adventures of the Early Settlers in America. London. V. 49

HANFORD, ALBERT
Albert Hanford's Texas State Register for 1879. Galveston: 1879. V. 54
Texas State Register for... Galveston: 1868. V. 48; 49

HANFORD, GEORGE
Directory of Chenango County, New York. Elmira: 1902. V. 49; 50

HANFORD, PHEBE A.
The Life and Writings of Charles Dickens... Augusta: 1871. V. 49

HANGER, GEORGE
The Life, Adventures and Opinions of... London: 1801. V. 47; 49
Military Reflections on the Attack and Defence of the City of London. London: 1795. V. 54
To All Sportsmen, and Particularly to Farmers and Gamekeepers. London: 1814. V. 49

HANHAM, F.
Natural Illustrations of the British Grasses. Bath: 1846. V. 47; 52

HANKEN, J.
The Skull. Chicago: 1993. V. 50

HANKEY, THOMSON
The Principles of Banking... London: 1867. V. 52

HANKINS, MARIE LOUISE
Women of New York. New York: 1861. V. 47; 50

HANKINS, SAMUEL W.
Simple Story of a Soldier. Nashville: 1912. V. 52; 54

HANKINSON, A.
Camera on the Crags. 1975. V. 53

HANKS, HENRY G.
Report on the Borax Deposits of California and Nevada. Sacramento: 1883. V. 48

HANLEY, JAMES
Aria and Finale. 1932. V. 53
Aria and Finale. London: 1932. V. 51
At Bay. London: 1935. V. 51
Boy. London: 1931. V. 49; 50; 51
Boy. New York: 1932. V. 51
Broken Water; an Autobiographical Excursion. London: 1937. V. 51
Captain Bottell. London: 1933. V. 51; 53
Drift. London: 1930. V. 51
Drift. London: 1932. V. 51
Ebb and Flood. London: 1932. V. 51; 53
The Furys. London: 1935. V. 51
The German Prisoner. London. V. 51
The German Prisoner. London: 1920. V. 49
The German Prisoner. London: 1930. V. 47; 49; 51; 53
Grey Children; a Study in Humbug and Misery. London: 1937. V. 51
Half an Eye; Sea Stories. London: 1937. V. 51
Hollow Sea. London: 1938. V. 49; 51
The Last Voyage. London: 1931. V. 51; 53
Men in Darkness. London: 1931. V. 51; 53
Men in Darkness... New York: 1932. V. 51; 53
Our Time is Gone. London: 1940. V. 51; 53
A Passion Before Death. London: 1930. V. 51
Quartermaster Clausen. London: 1934. V. 47; 48; 51
Resurrexit Dominus. London: 1934. V. 50; 51
Say Nothing. London: 1962. V. 51; 53
The Secret Journey. London: 1936. V. 51; 53
Stoker Bush. New York: 1935. V. 51
Stoker Haslett. 1932. V. 53
Stoker Haslett. London: 1932. V. 47; 49; 51; 53
The Welsh Sonata: Variations on a Theme. London: 1954. V. 53

HANMER, JOHN
Fra Cipolla, and Other Poems. (with) *Sonnets.* London: 1839/40. V. 51

HANMER, JONATHAN
Archaioskopia, of a View of Antiquity, Presented in a Short but Sufficient Account of some of the Fathers... London: 1677. V. 53

HANNA, CHARLES A.
The Wilderness Trail. New York: 1911. V. 47; 51

HANNA, PHIL TOWNSEND
Libros Californianos or Five Feet of California Books. Los Angeles: 1931. V. 51

HANNA, WILLIAM
Memoirs of... Thomas Chalmers. Edinburgh & London: 1849-52. V. 47
Memoirs of Thomas Chalmers. Edinburgh: 1854. V. 51; 52; 53; 54

HANNAFORD, D. R.
Spanish Colonial or Adobe Architecture of California, 1800-1850. New York: 1931. V. 48; 50; 54

HANNAGAN, MARGARET
Londubh and Chairn. London: 1927. V. 47

HANNAH, BARRY
Airships. New York: 1978. V. 47
Black Butterfly. 1981. V. 48; 49; 51
Black Butterfly. 1982. V. 53
Geronimo Rex. New York: 1972. V. 47; 49; 50; 51; 53
Neighborhood. 1981. V. 53
Night-Watchmen. New York: 1973. V. 47; 49; 50; 51; 53; 54
Power and Light. 1983. V. 50; 53
Power and Light. Winston Salem: 1983. V. 47

HANNAH Duston. San Francisco: 1987. V. 51

HANNAY, JAMES
Satire and Satirists. Six Lectures. London: 1854. V. 52

HANNEFORD-SMITH, W.
The Architectural Work of Sir Banister Fletcher. London: 1934. V. 48

HANNEMAN, AUDRE
A Comprehensive Bibliography. Princeton: 1969/75. V. 52
Ernest Hemingway, a Comprehensive Bibliography. Princeton: 1967. V. 53; 54

HANNIBAL Not at Our Gates; or, an Enquiry Into the Grounds of Our Present Fears of Popery and the Pre-der: in a Dialogue Between My Lord Panick and George Steady Esq. London: 1714. V. 52; 53

HANNIGHEN, FRANK C.
Nothing but Danger. Thrilling Adventures of Ten Newspaper Correspondents in the Spanish War. London: 1940. V. 49

HANNINGTON, C. F.
Journal of Mr. C. F. Hanington, from Quesnelle through the Rocky Mountains During the Winter of 1874-75. Ottawa: 1888. V. 52

HANNON, MICHAEL
Fables: Thirteen Poems. 1989. V. 54

HANNOVER, EMIL
Pottery and Porcelain, a Handbook for Collectors. London: 1925. V. 49

HANOTAUX, GABRIEL
Contemporary France (1870-82). London: 1903-09. V. 49; 52

HANS, FRED
The Great Sioux Nation. Chicago: 1907. V. 51

HANSARD, GEORGE AGAR
The Book of Archery. London: 1840. V. 47
The Book of Archery. London: 1841. V. 52; 54

HANSARD, LUKE
The Auto-Biography of Luke Hansard, Written in 1817. Wakefield: 1991. V. 47; 49; 50
Remarks in Relation to an Appeal Now Before Parliament for the Suppression of an Intolerable Nuisance, Which Has Long Afflicted the Community by Tending to the destruction of Their Best Interests and Truest Happiness. London: 1844. V. 49

HANSBERRY, LORRAINE
Les Blancs: the Collected Last Plays of Lorraine Hansberry. New York: 1972. V. 54
A Raisin in the Sun. New York: 1959. V. 52; 53
The Sign in Sidney Brustein's Window. New York: 1965. V. 49; 53

HANSCOMB, BRIAN
Cornwall. 1992. V. 47
Cornwall... Herefordshire: 1992. V. 51
Cornwall. London: 1992. V. 47; 50
Cornwall... Lower Marston: 1992. V. 48; 49
Sun, Sea and Earth. 1989. V. 47

HANSEN, HANS JURGEN
Art and the Seafarer: A Historical Survey of the Arts and Crafts of Sailors and Shipwrights. New York: 1968. V. 50
European Folk Art in Europe and the Americas. New York: 1968. V. 54

HANSEN, JOSEPH
Fadeout. New York: 1970. V. 52

HANSEN, RON
Desperadoes. New York: 1979. V. 52; 53; 54

HANSHAL, J. H.
The History of the County Palatine of Chester. Chester: 1823. V. 48

HANSKI, I.
Dung Beetle Ecology. London: 1991. V. 50

HANSON, ANNE COFFIN
Jacopo Della Quercia's Fonte Gais. Oxford: 1965. V. 52

HANSON, CHARLES H.
The Land of Greece Described and Illustrated. London: 1886. V. 47; 49

HANSON, H. J.
Off the Irish Coast: Ianthe II, 1933. 1933. V. 50

HANSON, J. A.
Spirits in the Art, from the Plains and Southwest Cultures. Kansas City. V. 51

HANSON, JOHN
The Dissection of Owenism Dissected; or a Socialist's Answer to Mr. Frederic R. Lee's Pamphlet, Entitled "A Calm Examination of the Fundamental Principles of Robert Owen's Misnamed Rational System". Leeds: 1838. V. 53

HANSON, JOHN ARTHUR
Roman Theater-Temples. Princeton: 1959. V. 52

HANSON, JOSEPH MILLS
The Conquest of The Missouri Being the Story of the Life and Exploits of Captain Grant Marsh. Chicago: 1909. V. 52; 54

HANSON, LEVETT
An Accurate Historical Account of All the Orders of Knighthood at Present Existing in Europe. London: 1802. V. 47

HANSON, T. W.
Edwards of Halifax. A Family of Book Sellers, Collectors and Book-Binders. London: 1912. V. 50

HANSTROM, B.
South African Animal Life. Stockholm: 1955-73. V. 48; 50; 51

HANWAY, JONAS
An Historical Account of the British Trade Over the Caspian Sea... London: 1753. V. 52
A Journal of Eight Days Journey from Portsmouth to Kingston Upon Thames... London: 1756. V. 48; 52
A Journal of Eight Days Journey from Portsmouth to Kingston upon Thames... London: 1757. V. 53
Midnight the Signal. London: 1799. V. 49
The Soldier's Faithful Friend... London: 1766. V. 47
Soldier's faithful Friend... London: 1780. V. 52
Virtue in Humble Life. London: 1774. V. 54
Virtue in Humble Life... London: 1777. V. 48

HANWAY, MARY ANN
Ellinor; or the World As It Is. London: 1798. V. 54
A Journey to the Highlands of Scotland. London: 1777. V. 52

HANZELET LORRAIN, JEAN APPIER
La Pyrotechnie de Hanzelet Lorrain Ou Sont Representez les Plus Rare & Plus Appreuuez Secrets des Machines & des Feux Artificiels. Pont-a-Mousson: 1630. V. 53

HANZLICEK, C. G.
Living In It. Iowa City: 1971. V. 54

HANZLIK, P. J.
Actions and Uses of the Salicylates and Cinchophen. Baltimore: 1927. V. 48; 53

HAPGOOD, HUTCHINS
Types From City Streets. New York: 1910. V. 50

HAPPOLD, D. C. D.
The Mammals of Nigeria. Oxford: 1987. V. 50; 51

HAPPY Birthday, Kurt Vonnegut. New York: 1982. V. 48; 49

THE HAPPY Child. 1790-1800. V. 47

HAPPY Families and Their Tales. London: 1890. V. 49

THE HAPPY Negro; Being a True Account of an Extraordinary Negro in North America, and of an Interesting Conversation He Had with Very Respectable Gentleman From England. Coppergate York: 1830. V. 50

THE HAPPY Sequel, or the History of Isabella Mordaunt. London: 1814. V. 48; 50

HARA, HIROSHI
Catalogue of the Works of Dr. Hiroshi Hara. Tokyo: 1991. V. 50; 52

HARABIN, GEORGE
The Hereditary Right of the Crown of England Asserted... London: 1713. V. 51

HARADA, BIZAN
The Pageant of Chinese Painting. 1959. V. 50

HARADA, JIRO
Examples of Japanese Art in the Imperial Household Museum. Tokyo: 1934. V. 47

AN HARANGUE to the King. By a Minister of the French Church in the Savoy, the Nineteenth of October, 1681. London: 1681. V. 47

HARASZTHY, AGOSTON
Grape Culture, Wines and Wine Making. New York: 1862. V. 50; 54

HARAUCOURT, EDMOND
L'Effort. Paris: 1894. V. 54

HARBEN, HENRY A.
A Dictionary of London. London: 1918. V. 50

HARBER, G. B.
Report of Lieut. G. B. Harber, U.S.N., Concerning the Search for the Missing Persons Of the Jeannette Expedition, and the Transportation of the Remains of Lieutenant-Commander De Long and Companions to the United States. Washington: 1884. V. 50

HARBIN, GEORGE
The Hereditary Right of the Crown of England Asserted... London: 1713. V. 50; 54

THE HARBINGER: a May Gift. Boston: 1833. V. 50

HARBISON, MASSY
A Narrative of the Suffering of Massy Harbison, from Indian Barbarity, giving an Account of Her Captivity... Pittsburgh: 1825. V. 54
A Narrative of the Suffering of Massy Harbison, From Indian Barbarity, Giving an Account of Her Captivity... Pittsburgh: 1828. V. 51; 53

THE HARBOR Plan of Chicago. Chicago: 1927. V. 48

HARBOR AND RIVER CONVENTION, CHICAGO, 1847.
Proceedings of the Harbor and River Convention Held at Chicago, July 5th 1847... Chicago: 1847. V. 48

HARC, AUGUSTUS J. C.
The Life and Letters of Maria Edgeworth. Boston: 1895. V. 50

HARCLIFFE, JOHN
A Treatise of Moral and Intellectual Virtues... London: 1691. V. 47

HARCOURT, A. F. P.
The Himalayan Districts of Kooloo, Lahoul and Spiti. London: 1871. V. 47

HARCOURT, LEWIS VERNON
The Doctrine of the Deluge... London: 1838. V. 47; 51
An Eton Bibliography. London: 1898. V. 51

HARCOURT, SEYMOUR
The Gaming Calendar, to Which are Added, Annals of Gaming and Prefixed a Letter to Sir Robert Baker... London: 1820. V. 51

HARCOURT-SMITH, SIMON
A Catalogue of Various Clocks, Watches, Automata and Other Miscellaneous Objects of European Workmanship Dating from the XVIIIth and the Early XIXth Centuries in the Palace Museum and the Wu Ying Tien, Peiping. 1933. V. 53
The Last of Uptake or the Estranged Sisters. London: 1942. V. 49; 51
The Last of Uptake or the Estranged Sisters. London: 1944. V. 54

HARD, ABNER
History of the Eighth Cavalry Regiment, Illinois Volunteers, During the Great Rebellion. Aurora: 1868. V. 47

HARD, JOHAN LUDVIG
The Military, Historical and Political Memoirs of the Count de Hordt, a Swedish Nobleman and Lieutenant General in the Service of the King of Prussia. London: 1806. V. 47

HARDAKER, ALFRED
A Brief History of Pawnbroking. London: 1892. V. 50; 52

HARDAKER, JOSEPH
The Bridal of Tomar and Other Poems. Keighley: 1831. V. 54

HARDCASTLE, LUCY
An Introduction to the Elements of the Linneaen System of Botany for Young Persons. Derby: 1830. V. 54

HARDCASTLE, MARY SCARLETT
Life of John Lord Campbell. London: 1881. V. 52

HARDEE, WILLIAM JOSEPH
Rifle and Infantry Tactics. Raleigh: 1862. V. 49
Rifle and Infantry Tactics, Revised and Improved by Maj. Gen. W. J. Hardee, C. S. Army. Mobile: 1863. V. 49

HARDEN, DONALD B.
Catalogue of Greek and Roman Glass in the British Musem. Volume I (only): Core and Rod Formed Vessels and Pendants and Mycenaean Cast Objects. London: 1981. V. 50; 52
Roman Glass from Karanis Found by the University of Michigan Archaeological Expedition in Egypt, 1924-29. Ann Arbor: 1936. V. 50

HARDENBERG, J. R.
Answer of J. R. Hardenberg, U.s. Surveyor General for California, to the Charges Preferred Against Him by W. S. Chapman, Jesse D. Carr and Willis Drummond, Commissioner U.S. Land Office. San Francisco: 1874. V. 49

HARDIE, JAMES
An Account of the Malignant Fever, Lately Prevalent in the City of New York. New York: 1799. V. 52
The Description of the City of New York, Containing Its Population, Institutions, Commerce, Manufactures, Public Buildings, Courts of Justice, Places of Amusement &c. New York: 1827. V. 47
A Dictionary of the Most Uncommon Wonders of the Works of Art and Nature. New York: 1819. V. 54

HARDIE, MARTIN
English Coloured Books. London: 1906. V. 51
The Etched Work of W. Lee-Hankey, R.E. from 1904-1920. London: 1920. V. 52; 54
Frederick Goulding, Master of Copper Plates. Stirling: 1910. V. 49
War Posters Issued by Belligerent and Neutral Nations 1914-1919. London: 1920. V. 52
Water-Colour Painting in Britain. London. V. 47
Water-Colour Painting in Britain. London: 1966. V. 48
Water-colour Painting in Britain. London: 1966-68. V. 49; 50

HARDIE, R. P.
The Roads of Mediaeval Lauderdale. London: 1942. V. 52

HARDIMAN, JAMES
The History of...Galway...to the Present Time. 1926. V. 54
The History of...Galway...to the Present Time. Galway: 1958. V. 48; 51
Irish Minstrelsy. London: 1831. V. 50

HARDIN, JOHN WESLEY
The Life of... 1896. V. 48
The Life of John Wesley Hardin. Sequin: 1896. V. 50; 52; 53

HARDING, ANNE RAIKES
Correction, a Novel. Philadelphia: 1818. V. 54

HARDING, CHESTER
My Egoistigraphy. Cambridge: 1866. V. 52; 53

HARDING, COLIN
In Remotest Barotseland: Being an Account of a Journey of Over 8000 Miles through the Wildest and Remotest Parts of Lewanika's Empire. London: 1905. V. 54

HARDING, E.
The Biographical Mirror. London: 1795-98. V. 51
Portraits of the Whole of the Royal Family. London: 1806. V. 49

HARDING, E. W.
The Flyfisher and the Trout's Point of View... London: 1831. V. 53
The Flyfisher and the Trouts Point of View. London: 1931. V. 48; 53

HARDING, EDWARD
Costumes of the Russian Empire. London: 1811. V. 49; 50

HARDING, GEORGE L.
Don Agustin V. Zamorano: Statesman, Soldier, Craftsman and California's First Printer. Los Angeles: 1934. V. 47; 51; 52; 54

HARDING, GEORGE R.
The Acts and Orders Relating to Joint Stock Companies. Brisbane: 1887. V. 49; 52

HARDING, GUNNAR
The Fabulous Life of Guillaume Apollinaire. Iowa City: 1970. V. 54

HARDING, PHILIP M.
Harlem Interior, 3 Poems. Teaneck: 1947?. V. 47

HARDING, S.
The Biographical Mirrour: Comprising a Series of Ancient and Modern English Portraits... London: 1795-c. 1814. V. 47

HARDING, WILLIAM EDGAR
History of the Prize Ring, with Lives of Paddy Ryan and John L. Sullivan. New York: 1882. V. 47

HARDINGE, SARAH ANN LILLIE
Views of Texas: 1852-1856. V. 49
Views of Texas 1852-1856... Ft. Worth: 1988. V. 51

HARDOUIN, JAN
Opera Selecta. Amsterdam: 1709. V. 54

HARDRES, THOMAS
Reports of Cases Adjudged in the Court of Exchequer, in the Years 1655, 1656, 1657, 1659 and 1660. London: 1693. V. 47

HARDWICH, T. FREDERICK
A Manual of Photographic Chemistry, Including the Practice of the Collodion Process. London: 1857. V. 54

HARDWICK, CHARLES
History of the Borough of Preston and its Environs in the County of Lancaster. Preston: 1857. V. 51; 53
Traditions, Superstitions and Folklore. Manchester: 1872. V. 53

HARDWICK, ELIZABETH
The Ghostly Lover. New York: 1945. V. 50; 53
View of My Own. New York: 1962. V. 49

HARDWICKE, EARL OF
Athenian Letters or, The Epistolary Correspondence of the King of Persia, Residing at Athens During the Peloponnesian War. London: 1810. V. 47

HARDWICKE, PHILIP YORKE, 2ND EARL OF
Miscellaneous State Papers, from 1501 to 1726. London: 1778. V. 49

HARDY, CAMPBELL
Forest Life in Acadie. London: 1869. V. 47; 51; 53
Forest Life in Acadie... New York: 1869. V. 49
Sporting Adventures in the New World... London: 1855. V. 48; 49; 51; 52; 54

HARDY, CHARLES FREDERICK
The Hardys of Barabon and Some other Westmorland Statesman: Their Kith, Kin and Children. London: 1913. V. 50; 52

HARDY, DERMONT
Historical Review of South-East Texas and the Founders, Leaders and Representative Men Of Its Commerce, Industry and Civic Affairs. Chicago: 1910. V. 53

HARDY, ELIZABETH
Owen Glendower; or, the Prince in Wales. London: 1849. V. 50

HARDY, FLORENCE EMILY
All Change Here. The Story of a Seaside Trip. London: 1915. V. 52
The Early Life of Thomas Hardy 1840-1891... London: 1928/30. V. 49

HARDY, FRANCIS
Memoirs of the Political and Private Life of James Caulfield, Earl of Charlemont. London: 1810. V. 53

HARDY, FREDERICK
The Bijou Book of In-Door Amusements. London: 1868. V. 47

HARDY, GODFREY HAROLD
Collected Papers...Including Joint Papers with J. E. Littlewood and Others. Oxford: 1966-79. V. 47

HARDY, GRAHAME
American Locomotive, 1871-81. Oakland: 1950. V. 48

HARDY, H. F. H.
Good Gun Dogs. London: 1930. V. 48

HARDY, JOSEPH
A Picturesque and Descriptive Tour in the Mountains of the High Pyrenees...with some Account of the Bathing Establishments... London: 1825. V. 47; 48; 49; 52

HARDY, RENE
Bitter Victory. Garden City: 1956. V. 48; 51

HARDY, ROBERT WILLIAM HALE
Travels in the Interior of Mexico, in 1825, 1826, 1827 and 1828. London: 1829. V. 47; 50; 54

HARDY, T.
The Poetry of William Barnes. London: 1979. V. 54

HARDY, THOMAS
Autobiography: The Early Life, 1840-1891 (and) The Later Years, 1892-1928. London: 1928-30. V. 49
A Catalogue of the Library of Thomas Hardy O.M. with Books and Autograph Letters the property of the Late Mrs. Thomas Hardy Removed from Max Gate, Dorchester... London: 1938. V. 48
A Changed Man. London: 1913. V. 48; 50; 51; 52; 53
A Changed Man... New York: 1913. V. 53
Collected Poems. London: 1923. V. 47
The Duke's Reappearance. New York: 1927. V. 48
The Dynasts. London: 1903-08. V. 47; 49; 53
The Dynasts. London: 1904-06-08. V. 51; 52
The Dynasts... London: 1904-08. V. 48; 49
The Dynasts. London: 1927. V. 47; 48; 49; 50; 51; 52; 53; 54
The Famous Tragedy of the Queen of Cornwall. London: 1923. V. 49; 51; 53

HARDY, THOMAS continued
Far From the Madding Crowd. London: 1874. V. 53
Far from the Madding Crowd. 1958. V. 51
Far From the Madding Crowd. Cambridge: 1958. V. 51; 52; 54
Far From the Madding Crowd. London: 1958. V. 49
Far from the Madding Crowd. New York: 1958. V. 52
A Group of Noble Dames. London: 1891. V. 47; 48; 49; 51; 52; 53
A Group of Noble Dames. New York: 1891. V. 51
The Hand of Ethelberta. London: 1875. V. 49
The Hand of Ethelberta. London: 1876. V. 51
Human Shows Far Phantasies. London: 1925. V. 47; 48; 52; 53; 54
Human Shows Far Phantasies. New York: 1925. V. 51; 53; 54
In Time of "The Breaking of Nations.". V. 52
An Indiscretion in the Life of an Heiress. London: 1934. V. 52; 54
An Indiscretion in the Life of an Heiress... Baltimore: 1935. V. 53
Jude the Obscure. V. 49
Jude the Obscure. 1896. V. 50
Jude the Obscure. London: 1896. V. 49; 51; 52; 53; 54
Jude the Obscure. New York: 1896. V. 51; 54
Jude the Obscure. New York: 1969. V. 48; 51; 54
A Laodicean. London: 1881. V. 48; 51
Late Lyrics and Earlier. London: 1922. V. 47; 48; 51; 51; 53; 54
Life's Little Ironies. 1894. V. 54
Life's Little Ironies. London: 1894. V. 47; 48; 50; 51; 52; 53; 54
Life's Little Ironies. New York: 1894. V. 48; 53
The Mayor of Casterbridge. London: 1886. V. 51; 52
The Mayor of Casterbridge. London: 1964. V. 49
The Mayor of Casterbridge. New York: 1964. V. 47; 48; 52; 53; 54
The Mayor of Casterbridge. New York: 1965. V. 51
Moments of Vision. London: 1917. V. 52; 53
Old Mrs. Chundle... New York: 1929. V. 49
Old Mrs. Chundle. New York: 1930. V. 48
The Oxen. Hove: 1915. V. 47
A Pair of Blue Eyes. London: 1873. V. 48
A Pair of Blue Eyes. New York: 1873. V. 51
The Return of the Native. London: 1878. V. 47; 50; 51; 54
The Return of the Native. London: 1929. V. 52
The Return of the Native. New York: 1942. V. 52
Satires of Circumstance. London: 1914,. V. 53
Selected Poems. 1921. V. 54
Selected Poems. London: 1921. V. 48; 50; 51
The Short Stories. London: 1928. V. 53
Tess of the D'Urbervilles. London: 1891. V. 49; 51; 52; 54
Tess of the D'Urbervilles. London: 1892. V. 47; 51; 52; 53; 54
Tess of the D'Urbervilles. New York: 1892. V. 47; 53; 54
Tess of the d'Urbervilles. London: 1926. V. 47; 49; 51; 53
Tess of the D'Urbervilles. London: 1956. V. 49
Tess of the D'Urbervilles. New York: 1958. V. 51; 54
Tess-of the D'Urbervilles. New York: 1956. V. 47; 48; 51; 53; 54
Thomas Hardy's Works. London and New York: 1895-1900. V. 53; 54
The Three Wayfarers. New York: 1930. V. 47; 48; 49; 50; 52
The Three Wayfarers. New York: 1943. V. 53
The Three Wayfarers. Market Drayton: 1990-92. V. 52
The Three Wayfarers. Market Drayton: 1991. V. 50
Time's Laughingstocks and Other Verses. London: 1909. V. 49
The Trumpet Major. London: 1880. V. 47; 51
The Trumpet Major. London: 1893. V. 48
Two On a Tower. London: 1882. V. 48; 50; 51
Under the Greenwood Tree. London: 1872. V. 50; 51
Under the Greenwood Tree. New York: 1873. V. 53
Under the Greenwood Tree. London: 1940. V. 49; 53
The Vineyards and Wine Cellars of California. San Francisco: 1994. V. 52; 54
The Well Beloved. London: 1897. V. 47; 48; 49; 51; 52; 53
The Well Beloved. New York: 1897. V. 53
The Wessex Novels. London: 1923-25. V. 51
Wessex Poems and Other Verses. 1898. V. 51; 52
Wessex Poems and Other Verses. London and New York: 1898. V. 47; 49; 50; 53; 54
Wessex Poems and Other Verses. 1908. V. 54
Wessex Tales Strange, Lively and Commonplace... London & New York: 1888. V. 47; 48; 50; 54
Winter Words. 1928. V. 54
Winter Words. London: 1928. V. 47; 48; 50; 51
Winter Words... New York: 1928. V. 48; 53
The Woodlanders. London & New York: 1887. V. 48; 49; 50; 51; 52; 54
The Woodlanders. London: 1897. V. 49
The Works. New York: 1899. V. 51
The Works. London: 1912. V. 49
The Works. London: 1914-26. V. 48
The Works. London: 1919. V. 49
The Works. London: 1919-20. V. 48; 51
Works... London: 1992. V. 53
The Writings. New York: 1911. V. 53
The Writings... New York: 1920. V. 47
Yuletide in a Younger World. London: 1927. V. 50
Yuletide in a Younger World. New York: 1927. V. 48; 49

HARDY, THOMAS DUFUS
Descriptive Catalogue of Materials Relating to the History of Great Britain and Ireland to the End of the Reign of Henry VII. London: 1862-71. V. 49
Hegistrum Palatinum Dunelmense: the Register of Richard de Kellawe, Lord Palatine and Bishop of Durham, 1311-1316. London: 1873-78. V. 49

HARDY, W.
Life and Electricity in Health and Disease. Harrogate: 1865/62. V. 51

HARDYNG, JOHN
The Chronicle of John Hardyng. London: 1812. V. 47; 51

HARDYNGE, HAL
Cheltenham Lyrcis, Lays of a Modern Troubadour and Other Poems. Cheltenham: 1830. V. 50; 54

HARE, AMORY
Tristram and Iseult. Gaylordsville: 1930. V. 53

HARE, AUGUSTUS J. C.
Life and letters of Frances Bunsen, Baroness. London: 1879. V. 49; 52
The Life and Letters of Maria Edgeworth. London: 1894. V. 53; 54
The Story of My Life. London: 1896. V. 52
The Story of Two Noble Lives, Being Memorials of Charlotte, Countess Canning and Louisa, Marchioness of Waterford. London: 1893. V. 52; 53; 54

HARE, CYRIL
He Should Have Died Hereafter. London: 1958. V. 50

HARE, FRANCIS
The Conduct of the Duke of Marlborough During the Present War. London: 1712. V. 52

HARE, KENNETH
Roads and Vagabonds. London: 1930. V. 48

HARE, LLOYD C. M.
Lucretia Mott, the Greatest American Woman. New York: 1937. V. 54

HARE, W. LOFTUS
The Court of the Printers' Guild. London: 1914. V. 49
The Court of the Printer's Guild. San Francisco: 1975. V. 49

HARENBERG, JOHANN CHRISTOPH
Pragmatische geschichte des Ordens der Jesuiten, Seit Ihrem Ursprunge bis auf Gegenwartige Zeit. Halle & Helmstedt: 1760. V. 50

HARFORD, JOHN S.
The Life of Michael Angelo Buonarroti: With Translations of Many of His Poems and Letters, also, Memoirs of Savonarola, Raphael and Vittoria Colonna. London: 1857. V. 52

HARGITT, E.
Catalogue of the Picariae in the Collection of the British Museum. Scansores, Containing the Family Picidae. London: 1890. V. 47

HARGRAVE, CARRIE GUERPHAN
African Primitve Life as I Saw It in Sierra Leone British West Africa. Wilmington: 1944. V. 50

HARGRAVE, CATHERINE PERRY
A History of Playing Cards and a Bibliography of Cards and Gaming. Boston & New York: 1930. V. 47; 48; 51; 52

HARGRAVE, FRANCIS
Collectanea Jurdica Consisting of Tracts Relative to the Law and Constitution of England. London: 1791-92. V. 54
A Collection of Tracts Relative to the Law of England, from Manuscripts. Dublin: 1787. V. 52
A Collection of Tracts Relative to the Law of England, from Manuscripts.. London: 1787. V. 52

HARGRAVE, JOSEPH JAMES
Red River. Montreal: 1871. V. 48; 53

HARGREAVE, CHARLES JAMES
An Essay on the Resolution of Algebraic Equations. Dublin: 1866. V. 53

HARGROVE, E.
Anecdotes of Archery from the Earliest Ages to the Year 1791. London: 1845. V. 52
Anecdotes of Archery from the Earliest Ages to the Year 1791. York: 1845. V. 54
The History of the Castle, Town and Forest of Knaresborough with Harrogate and Its Medicinal Waters. York: 1789. V. 52
The Yorkkshire Gazetteer, or, a Dictionary of the Towns, Villages and Hamlets, Monasteries and Castles... Knaresborough: 1812. V. 51; 53

HARGROVE, WILLIAM
History and Description of the Ancient City of York... London: 1818. V. 50; 51

HARINGTON, DONALD
Lightning Bug. New York: 1970. V. 51

HARINGTON, JOHN
The Metamorphosis of Ajax... Chiswick: 1814. V. 47
The Metamorphosis of Ajax. London: 1927. V. 52
Nugae Antiquae: Being a Miscellaneous Collections of Original Papers, in Prose and Verse Written During the Reigns of Henry VIII, Edward VI, Queen Mary, Elizabeth and King James... London: 1804. V. 51

HARJO, JOY
In Mad Love and War. Middletown: 1990. V. 51

HARKE, KATHLEEN
Billy & Angelina. London. V. 47

HARKER, BAILY J.
Historical Account of the Cistercian Abbey of Salley in Craven, Yorkshire, Founded Ad 1147. London: 1853. V. 47

HARKEY, DEE
Mean as Hell. Albuquerque: 1948. V. 49; 51; 52; 53

HARKNESS, WILLIAM HALE
Ho Hum the Fisherman. New York: 1939. V. 51

HARLAN, JACOB
California '46 to '88. San Francisco: 1888. V. 49; 54

HARLAN, RICHARD
Fauna Americana: Being a Description of the Mammiferous Animals Inhabiting North America. Philadelphia: 1825. V. 52

HARLAN, ROBERT D.
At the Sign of the Lark: William Doxey's Publishing Venture. San Francisco: 1983. V. 54
Bibliography of the Grabhorn Press, 1957-1966 and Grabhorn Hoyem, 1966-1973. San Francisco: 1977. V. 48; 49
The Two Hundredth Book: a Bibliography of the Books Published by the Book Club of California, 1958-1993. 1993. V. 51
The Two Hundredth Book. A Bibliography of the Books Published by the Book Club of California, 1958-1993. San Francisco: 1993. V. 50

HARLAND, HENRY
The Cardinal's Snuff-Box. London: 1903. V. 51

HARLAND, JOHN
Ancient Charters and Other Muniments of the Borough of Clithero, in the County of Palatine of Lancaster. Manchester: 1851. V. 53
Historical Account of the Cistercian Abbey of Salley in Craven, Yorkshire, Founded AD 1147. London: 1853. V. 53
Mamecestre: Being Chapters from the Early Recorded History of the Barony; the Lordship or Manor; the VII, Borough, or Towns of Manchester. Manchester: 1851-62. V. 48

THE HARLEIAN Miscellany... London: 1744-46. V. 53; 54
THE HARLEIAN Miscellany... London: 1808. V. 53

THE HARLEIAN Miscellany. London: 1808-13. V. 48; 49; 50

HARLEQUIN Premier: a Farce, As It Is Daily Acted. 1769. V. 53

HARLEQUIN Skeleton. London: 1772. V. 47

HARLESTON, EDWARD NATHANIEL
The Toiler's Life. Philadelphia: 1907. V. 53

HARLEY, GEORGE
A Treatise on Diseases of the Liver, With and Without Jaundice. London: 1883. V. 48; 51

HARLEY, GEORGE DAVIES
Poems. London: 1796. V. 49

HARLEY, TIMOTHY
Lunar Science: Ancient and Modern. London: 1886. V. 50

HARLEY, WILLIAM
The Harleian Diary System. London: 1829. V. 54

HARLOW, ALVIN F.
Old Post Bags. The Story of the Sending of a Letter in Ancient and Modern Times. New York: 1928. V. 53
Old Towpaths. The Story of the American Canal Era. New York and London: 1926. V. 49; 53
Old Waybills. The Romance of the Express Companies. New York: 1934. V. 47; 51; 52; 53

HARLOW, NEAL
Maps and Surveys of the Pueblo Lands of Los Angeles. Los Angeles: 1976. V. 48; 51; 52; 54
The Maps of San Francisco Bay from the Spanish Discovery in 1769 to the American Occupation. San Francisco: 1950. V. 48; 51; 54
Maps of the Pueblo Lands of San Diego 1602-1874. Los Angeles: 1987. V. 47; 48; 50; 54

HARLOW, W. S.
Duties of Sheriffs and Constables, as Defined by the Laws and Interpreted by the Supreme Court, of the State of California. San Francisco: 1884. V. 50

HARLTEY, DAVID
The Budget. London: 1764. V. 48

HARLTEY, L. P.
The Go-Between. London: 1971. V. 50

HARMAN, APPLETON MILO
The Journal of Appleton Milo Harman. Glendale: 1946. V. 48; 50

HARMAN, JOHN N.
Harman Genealogy (Southern Branch) with Biographical Sketches 1700-1924. Richmond: 1925. V. 52; 54

HARMAN, SAMUEL W.
Hell on the Border. Fort Smith. V. 50; 51; 53
Hell on the Border: He Hanged Eighty-Eight Men. Fort Smith: 1898. V. 53; 54

HARMER, S. F.
The Cambridge Natural History. London: 1902-13. V. 48
Cambridge Natural History. London: 1920-23. V. 49

HARMER, THOMAS
Observations on Various Passages of Scripture Originally Compiled by... Charlestown: 1815-17. V. 47

HARMETZ, ALJEAN
The Making of the Wizard of Oz. New York: 1977. V. 51; 52

THE HARMONICON. A Journal of Music. London: 1823. V. 47

HARMSEN, DOROTHY
Harmsen's Western Americana: a Collection of One Hundred Western Paintings with Biographical Profiles of the Artists. Flagstaff: 1971. V. 53

HARMSWORTH, ALFRED C.
Motor and Motor-Driving. London: 1902. V. 53

HARMSWORTH, R. L.
A Short Title Catalogue of the printed books in the Library...to the Year 1640. 1925. V. 50

HARMSWORTH'S Universal Enccyclopedia... London: 1925. V. 49

THE HARNESSING Of Niagara. London: 1899. V. 50

HARNEY, GEORGE E.
Stables, Outbuildings and Fences. New York: 1870. V. 52

HARNEY, W. D.
Art Work of Seattle and Alaska. Racine: 1907. V. 50

HAROLD, EDMOND, BARON DE
Poems Of Ossian Lately Discovered. Dusseldorf: 1787. V. 49

HAROLD Patrick McGrath. 1991. V. 52; 54

HARPENDING, ASBURY
The Great Diamond Hoax and Other Stirring Incidents in the Life of Asbury Harpending. San Francisco: 1913. V. 53

HARPER, CHARLES G.
The Brighton Road. London: 1892. V. 47
Half-Hours with the Highwaymen. London: 1908. V. 53
The Hastings Road and the "Happy Springs of Tunbridge". London: 1906. V. 52
The Holyhead Road: the Mail Coach Road to Dublin. London: 1902. V. 51
The Manchester and Glasgow Road. London: 1907. V. 47; 49
The Newmarket, Bury, Thetford and Cromer Road Sport and History. London: 1904. V. 54
The Old Inns of Old England. London: 1906. V. 52; 53
The Oxford, Gloucester and Milford Haven Road. London: 1905. V. 49; 52; 53; 54
Revolted Woman, Past, Present and To Come. London: 1894. V. 47; 48; 50; 51
The Smugglers. London: 1909. V. 53
Stage-Coach and Mail in Days of Yore. London: 1903. V. 53
Thames Valley Villages. London: 1910. V. 53

HARPER, FRANCIS E. W.
Iola Leroy, or Shadows Uplifted. Boston: 1895. V. 53

HARPER, HARRIET WADSWORTH
Around the World in Eighty Years on a Side Saddle. New York: 1966. V. 51

HARPER, IDA HUSTED
The Life and Work of Susan B. Anthony... Kansas City: 1898/99. V. 53
The Life and Work of Susan B. Anthony. Indianapolis & Kansas: 1899. V. 47; 48

HARPER, J. RUSSELL
Painting in Canada: a History. Toronto: 1969. V. 50
Paul Kane's Frontier... Austin: 1971. V. 47
Paul Kane's Frontier. Ft. Worth: 1971. V. 48; 54
Paul Kane's Frontier. Toronto: 1971. V. 50; 51
Portrait of a Period: a Collection of Notman Photographs 1856 to 1915. Montreal: 1967. V. 47; 48; 49; 52

HARPER, LATHROP
A Selection of Incunabula from Over 150 Presses...Part I (-Part V with index) ... for Sale by Lathrop C. Harper. New York: 1927-30. V. 52

HARPER, MICHAEL S.
History is Your Own Heartbeat. Urbana: 1971. V. 47
Song: I Want a Witness. Pittsburgh: 1972. V. 53; 54

HARPER, ROBERT GOODLOE
Observations on the Dispute Between the United States and France. London: 1798. V. 48
Reflexoens Sobre a Questao Entre os Estados Unidos, e a Franca Offerecidas... aos seus Constituintes, em Maio de 1797... London: 1798. V. 48

HARPER, WILLIAM
The Antiquity, Innocence and Pleasure of Gardening. London: 1732. V. 54

HARPUR, JOSEPH
An Essay on the Principles of Philosophical Criticism, Applied to Poetry. London: 1810. V. 54

HARRAP, GEORGE G.
Love Lyrics from Five Centuries. London: 1932. V. 47

HARRER, HEINRICH
The White Spider. London: 1960. V. 54

HARRILD & SONS
Catalogue of Printing Machinery and Materials with Selected Type specimens. London: 1895. V. 51

HARRILL, LAWSON
Reminiscences 1861-1865, Lawson Harrill Captain Company I, 56th Regiment North Carolina Troops General M. W. Ransom's Brigade. Statesville: 1910. V. 50

HARRIMAN ALASKA EXPEDITION
Harriman Alaska Expedition. Volume IX, Insects: Part 2. Washington: 1904. V. 53
Harriman Alaska Expedition. Volume V. Cryptogamic Botany. Washington: 1910. V. 53
Harriman Alaska Expedition. Volume XI. Nemerteans. Bryozoans. Washington: 1904. V. 53
Harriman Alaska Expedition. Volume XIV. Monograph of the Shallow-Water Starfishes of the North Pacific Coast fromt he Arctic Ocean to California. Washington: 1914. V. 53

HARRIMAN-BROWNE, ALICE
Chaperoning Adrienne, a Tale of the Yellowstone National Park. Seattle: 1907. V. 53

HARRING, HARRO
Dolores: a Novel of South America. New York: 1846. V. 52

HARRINGTON, ALAN
Life in the Crystal Palace. New York: 1959. V. 47
The Revelations of Dr. Modesto. New York: 1955. V. 50

HARRINGTON, CHARLES E.
Summering in Colorado. Denver: 1874. V. 50; 52

HARRINGTON, GRANT W.
Historic Spots or Mile-Stones in the Progress of Wyandotte County, Kansas. Merriam: 1935. V. 53

HARRINGTON, H. NAZEBY
The Engraved Work of Sir Francis Seymour Haden, P.R.E. Liverpool: 1910. V. 48; 49; 52; 54

HARRINGTON, JAMES
The Art of Law-Giving: in III Books. London: 1659. V. 54
The Censure of the Rota Upon Mr. Milton's Book, Entitled the Ready and Easie Way to Establish a Free Common-wealth. London: 1660. V. 49
The Common-Wealth of Oceana. London: 1656. V. 47; 50
The Oceana...Other Works... London: 1700. V. 50
The Oceana...Other Works. London: 1737. V. 53
The Oceana...Other Works.. London: 1747. V. 50
The Oceana...Other Works.. London: 1771. V. 49; 50
The Rota; or, a Model of a Free-State, or Equall Common-Wealth... London: 1660. V. 49; 52

HARRINGTON, JOHN P.
Exploration of the Burton Mound at Santa Barbara Social and Religious Beliefs and Usages of the Chickasaw Indians, Uses of Plants by the Chippewa Indians. Washington: 1928. V. 52

HARRINGTON, JOHN W.
The Jumping Kangaroo and the Apple Butter Cat. New York: 1900. V. 48

HARRINGTON, M. R.
Cherokee and Earlier Remains On Upper Tennessee River. V. 54

HARRINGTON, MARK W.
Notes on the Climate and Meteorology of Death Valley, California. Washington: 1892. V. 53

HARRINGTON, MISS
Narrative of the Barbarous Treatment of Two Unfortunate Females, Natives of the Parish of Concordia, Louisiana, Whose Husband and Parent Were Inhumanely Murdered by Two Runaway Blacks. New York: 1842. V. 50

HARRIS, A. C.
Alaska and the Klondike Gold Fields... Philadelphia?: 1897. V. 52

HARRIS, ALBERT W.
The Blood of the Arab. Chicago: 1941. V. 47; 48; 52
The Cruise of a Schooner. Chicago: 1911. V. 47; 53

HARRIS, ALEX
A World Unsuspected: Portraits of Southern Childhood. Chapel Hill: 1987. V. 48

HARRIS, BESS
Lawren Harris. Toronto: 1969. V. 50

HARRIS, BURTON
John Colter: His Years in the Rockies. New York: 1952. V. 54

HARRIS, C. FISKE
Catalogue of American Poetry, Compriing Duplicates from the Collection of the Late... Providence: 1883. V. 52

HARRIS, C. R. S.
The Heart and the Vascular System in Ancient Greek Medicine from Alcmaeon to Galen. Oxford: 1973. V. 50

HARRIS, CLIVE
The History of the Birmingham Gun-Barrel Proof House. Birmingham: 1946. V. 54

HARRIS, DEAN
By Path and Trail. Chicago: 1908. V. 49
By Path and Trail. Chicago: 1909. V. 49; 54

HARRIS, EILEEN
British Architectural Books and Writers 1556-1785. Cambridge: 1990. V. 53

HARRIS, ELIZABETH M.
The Art of Medal Engraving: a Curious Chapter in the Development fo the 19th Century Printing Processes. Newtown: 1991. V. 49; 50

HARRIS, FRANK
Bernard Shaw. An Unauthorized Biography Based on First Hand Information. New York: 1931. V. 48
Joan La Romee. London: 1926. V. 48
My Life and Loves. Paris: 1922-27. V. 49; 54
My Reminiscences as a Cowboy. New York: 1930. V. 53
New Preface to "The Life and Confessions of Oscar Wilde". London: 1925. V. 47; 48; 49
The Veils of Isis and Other Stories. New York: 1915. V. 49

HARRIS, GEORGE WASHINGTON
Sut Lovingood. Yarns Spun bya "Nat'ral Born Durn'd Fool". Warped and Wove for Public Wear. New York: 1867. V. 54

HARRIS, GERTRUDE
A Tale of Men Who Knew Not Fear. San Antonio: 1935. V. 54

HARRIS, HELENA J.
Southern Sketches. New Orleans: 1866. V. 49

HARRIS, HENRY
California's Medical Story. San Francisco: 1932. V. 49
California's Medical Story. Springfield: 1932. V. 50; 52

HARRIS, J.
Inigo Jones: Complete Architectual Drawings. London: 1989. V. 53; 54

HARRIS, J. ARTHUR
A Biometric Study of Basal Metabolism in Man. Washington: 1919. V. 48; 53

HARRIS, J. H.
A Romance in Radium. 1906. V. 51

HARRIS, J. R.
Lexicographical Studies in Ancient Egyptian Minerals. Berlin: 1961. V. 49

HARRIS, J. RENDEL
Letters from the Scenes of the Recent Massacres in Armenia. London: 1897. V. 47

HARRIS, JAMES
Hermes or a Philosophical Inquiry Concerning Universal Grammar. London: 1794. V. 52
Miscellanies. London: 1785. V. 50
Philological Inquiries in Three Parts. London: 1781. V. 50
Philosophical Arrangements. London: 1775. V. 49
Three Treatises. The First Concerning Art. The Second Concerning Music, Painting and Poetry. London: 1744. V. 47; 48; 49; 52
Three Treatises. The First Concerning Art. The Second Concerning Music, Painting and Poetry... London: 1765. V. 53
Three Treatises. The First Concerning Art, the Second Concerning Music, Painting and Poetry... London: 1772. V. 48

HARRIS, JOEL CHANDLER
Aaron in the Wildwoods. Boston & New York: 1897. V. 54
Balaam and His Master and Other Sketches and Stories. Boston & New York: 1891. V. 51; 54
The Chronicles of Aunt Minervy Ann. New York: 1899. V. 53; 54
Daddy Jake, the Runaway. New York: 1889. V. 48; 53
Evening Tales. New York: 1893. V. 48; 51
Free Joe and Other Georgian Sketches. New York: 1887. V. 48; 51; 54
Gabriel Tolliver. New York: 1902. V. 53
Joel Chandler Harris, Editor and Essayist. Miscellaneous Literary, Political and Social Writings. Chapel Hill: 1931. V. 54
A Little Union Scout. New York: 1904. V. 48; 51
Mingo and Other Sketches in Black and White. Boston: 1884. V. 54
Mr. Rabbit at Home. Boston and New York: 1896. V. 52; 53
Nights with Uncle Remus. Boston: 1883. V. 47; 48; 49; 54
Nights with Uncle Remus. Boston: 1885. V. 47
On the Plantation. New York: 1892. V. 53
On the Wing of Occasions. New York: 1900. V. 54
Plantation Pageants. Boston: 1899. V. 51
The Runaway and Short Stories Told After Dark by "Uncle Remus". New York: 1889. V. 47
The Story of Aaron (So Named) the Son of Ben Ali Told by His Friends and Acquaintances. Boston: 1896. V. 53; 54
Tales of the Home Folks in Peace and War. Boston & New York: 1898. V. 54
The Tar Baby and Other Rhymes of Uncle Remus. New York: 1904. V. 48; 49
Uncle Remus... London: 1881. V. 47
Uncle Remus. New York: 1881. V. 48; 49
Uncle Remus. New York: 1906. V. 51
Uncle Remus and His Friends. Boston & New York: 1892. V. 51; 53
Uncle Remus, His Songs and His Sayings. 1881. V. 49
Uncle Remus, His Songs and His Sayings. New York: 1881. V. 47; 48; 49; 50; 51; 53; 54
Uncle Remus, His Songs and His Sayings. New York: 1895. V. 51
Uncle Remus, His Songs and His Sayings. New York: 1896. V. 52
Uncle Remus, His Songs and His Sayings. New York: 1905. V. 53
Uncle Remus, His Songs and His Sayings. New York: 1906. V. 51
Uncle Remus: His Songs and His Sayings. New York: 1957. V. 51; 53
Wally Wanderoon and His Story-Telling Machine. New York: 1903. V. 54

HARRIS, JOHN
A Catalogue of British Drawings for Architecture, Decoration, Sculpture and Landscape Gardening, 1500-1900 in American Collections. Upper Saddle River: 1971. V. 51
Essays and Orations, Read and Delivered at the Royal College of Physicians. London: 1833. V. 53
Gardens of Delight. London: 1978. V. 50
The History of Kent. London: 1719. V. 47; 53
Hofer, The Tyrolese. London: 1824. V. 52
Navigantium Atque Itinerantium Bibliotheca. London: 1744. V. 47; 48
Navigantium Atque Itinerantium Bibliotheca... London: 1764. V. 49; 50
Sir William Chambers Knight of the Polar Star. 1970. V. 51

HARRIS, JOHN continued
A Visit to the Bazaar. London: 1818. V. 54

HARRIS, JOHN H.
Dawn in Darkest Africa. London: 1912. V. 47

HARRIS, JOSEPH
The Description and Use of the Globes and the Orrery. London: 1740. V. 48

HARRIS, LAURA
The Animated Noah's Ark. New York: 1945. V. 49
Animated Noah's Ark. New York: 1956. V. 49
The Happy Little Choo-Choo. New York: 1944. V. 48

HARRIS, LAWREN
The Story of the Group of Seven. Toronto: 1964. V. 50

HARRIS, M.
Pathway of Mattie Howard (To and From Prison). 1937. V. 50

HARRIS, MARK
Bang the Drum Slowly. New York: 1956. V. 47; 50
Something about a Soldier. New York: 1957. V. 54

HARRIS, MARTHA DOUGLAS
History and Folklore of the Cowichan Indians. Victoria: 1901. V. 50

HARRIS, MEL
Naked Hollywood. London: 1953. V. 47

HARRIS, MOSES
The Aurelian. London: 1840. V. 49
An Exposition of English Insects... London: 1782. V. 47; 48; 49; 50; 52; 53
An Exposition of English Insects... London: 1782. V. 54
An Exposition of English Insects. London: 1786. V. 49

HARRIS, N. SAYRE
Journal of a Tour in the 'Indian Territory', Performed by Order of the Domestic Committee of the Board of Missions of the Protestant Episcopal Church... New York: 1844. V. 52

HARRIS, R. C.
Report to the Civic Transportation Committee on Radial Railway Entrances and Rapid Transit for the City of Toronto. Toronto: 1915. V. 52

HARRIS, R. G.
50 Years of Yeomanry Uniforms. 1972. V. 50

HARRIS, RICHARD
Hints on Advocacy, Intended for Practice in Any of the Courts, with suggestions as to Opening a Case, Examination, Re Examination (etc.). St. Louis: 1880. V. 49

HARRIS, ROBERT
South Africa. Port Elizabeth: 1888. V. 50

HARRIS, SARAH HOLLISTER
An Unwritten Chapter of Salt Lake 1851-1901. New York: 1901. V. 47; 50; 52

HARRIS, STANLEY
The Coaching Age. London: 1885. V. 47
Old Coaching Days. London: 1882. V. 47
Playing the Game. New York: 1925. V. 47

HARRIS, T. M.
Assassination of Lincoln - a History of the Great Conspiracy... Boston: 1892. V. 49; 50

HARRIS, THADDEUS MASON
Constitutions of the Ancient and Honorable Fraternity of Free and Accepted Masons... Worcester: 1798. V. 52
Discourses...Illustrating the Principles, Displaying the Tendency and Vindicating the Design of Free Masonry. Charlestown: (1801). V. 52
The Minor Encyclopedia, or Cabinet of General Knowledge. Boston: 1803. V. 52
A Sermon Preached at Wrentham, Oct. 10th, 1798, Before the Grand Lodge of Free and Accepted Masons...on the Occasion of the Consecration of Montgomery Lodge (of Franklin). Wrentham: 1799. V. 54

HARRIS, THADDEUS WILLIAM
A Treatise on Some of the Insects Injurious to Vegetation. Boston: 1862. V. 48; 50
A Treatise on Some of the Insects Injurious to Vegetation. New York: 1883. V. 49

HARRIS, THEODORE
Negro Frontiersman, The Western Memoirs of Henry O. Flipper: 1878-1916. El Paso: 1963. V. 48

HARRIS, THOMAS
Black Sunday. New York: 1975. V. 53; 54
A Lyric of the Morning Land. New York: 1854. V. 48

HARRIS, THOMAS LAKE
God's Breath in Man and In Humane Society. Fountain Grove, Santa Rosa: 1891. V. 48
The Wisdom of the Adepts. Esoteric Science in Human History. Fountain Grove, Santa Rosa: 1884. V. 48

HARRIS, VALERIE
Celebration With Anais Nin. Riverside: 1973. V. 53

HARRIS, W. R.
History of the Early Missions in Western Canada. Toronto: 1893. V. 51

HARRIS, WALTER
De Morbis Acutis Infantum. London: 1689. V. 50; 54
Hibernica; or, Some Ancient Pieces Relating to Ireland. Dublin: 1770. V. 47

HARRIS, WALTER B.
A Journey through Yemen and Some General Remarks Upon that Country. Edinburgh: 1893. V. 47

HARRIS, WILFRED
Neuritis and Neuralgia. London: 1926. V. 47

HARRIS, WILLIAM
An Historical and Critical Account of the Life and Writings of Charles I, King of Great Britain. London: 1758. V. 50
An Historical and Critical Account of the Life of Oliver Cromwell... London: 1762. V. 51; 53
Outlines of Geography, Natural, Civil, and Political... Carlisle: 1808. V. 53
Rambles About Dudley Castle. Halesowen: 1845. V. 54

HARRIS, WILLIAM CORNWALLIS
Adventures in Africa; During a Tour of Two Years through that Country. Philadelphia. V. 52
The Angler's Guide Book and Tourist's Gazetteer of the Fishing Waters of the United States and Canada. New York: 1885. V. 47
The Highlands of Ethiopia... London: 1844. V. 48
The Highlands of Ethiopia. New York: 1844. V. 50
Narrative of an Expedition into Southern Africa During 1830 and 1837, from Cape of Good Hope through Territories of Chief Moselekatse to Tropic of Capricorn. Bombay: 1838. V. 54
Portraits of the Game and Wild Animals of Southern Africa. London: 1840. V. 50; 53
Portraits of the Game and Wild Animals of Southern Africa. Cape Town: 1969. V. 48; 52
Shrikes of Southern Africa. Cape Town: 1988. V. 53
The Wild Sports of Southern Africa... London: 1839. V. 47; 51; 54
The Wild Sports of Southern Africa... London: 1844. V. 47

HARRIS, WILLIAM R.
The Catholic Church in Utah 1776-1909. Salt Lake City: 1909. V. 49

HARRIS, WILSON
Palace of the Peacock. London: 1960. V. 53
Tradition, the Writer and Society: Critical Essays. London: 1967. V. 53

THE HARRISON Almanac 1841. New York: 1840. V. 52

HARRISON, BENJAMIN
Speeches of... New York: 1892. V. 54

HARRISON, BIRGE
Landscape Painting. New York: 1909. V. 53

HARRISON, CANON FREDERICK
Treasures of Illumination: English Manuscripts of the Fourteenth Century. London: 1937. V. 49

HARRISON, CHARLES
Ancient Warriors of the North Pacific: the Haidas, their Laws, Customs and Legends, with Some Historical Account of the Queen Charlotte Islands. London: 1925. V. 54
A Treatise on the Culture and Management of Fruit Trees,. London: 1823. V. 53
A Treatise on the Culture and Management of Fruit Trees. Sheffield: 1823. V. 48

HARRISON, CHARLES YALE
Generals Die in Bed. London: 1930. V. 49

HARRISON, CLIFFORD
Stray Records, or Personal and Professional Notes. London: 1892. V. 47

HARRISON, CONSTANCE CARY
Bric-a-Brac Stories. New York: 1885. V. 47; 49; 50
Folk and Fairy Tales. London: 1885. V. 48
Woman's Handiwork in Modern Homes. New York: 1881. V. 49; 51

HARRISON, D. L.
The Mammals of Arabia. London: 1991. V. 49

HARRISON, DAVID
The Melancholy Narrative of the Distressful Voyage and Miraculous Deliverance of Captain David Harrison, of the Sloop, Peggy of New York, on His Voyage from Fyal on of the Western Islands, to New York, Who Having Lost All his Sails in a Long Series... London: 1766. V. 47

HARRISON, EVELYN B.
Archaic and Archaistic Sculpture. Princeton: 1965. V. 52
Portrait Sculpture. Princeton: 1953. V. 50; 52

HARRISON, FAIRFAX
The Belair Stud 1747-1761. Richmond: 1929. V. 51
The John's Island Stud Book 1750-1788. Richmond: 1931. V. 48; 50; 51
Landmarks of Old Prince William: a Study of Origins in Northern Virginia... Richmond: 1924. V. 52
The Roanoke Stud 1795-1833. Richmond: 1930. V. 47; 51

HARRISON, FLORENCE
The Rhyme of a Fun and Other Verse. London: 1907. V. 47

HARRISON, FRANCES S.
The Forest of Bourg-Marie. London: 1898. V. 48; 53

HARRISON, FREDERIC
Annals of an Old Manor-House. Guildford: 1893. V. 52
Annals of an Old Manor-House... London: 1893. V. 49
Annals of an Old Manor-House... London: 1899. V. 52

HARRISON, GEORGE
Fifty Years Adrift. London: 1984. V. 52

HARRISON, GODFREY
A Specimen Book of John Whatman Handmade paper. Maidstone: 1931. V. 51; 54

HARRISON, H.
Bill, the Galactic Hero. New York: 1965. V. 48; 52
Make Room! Make Room!. New York: 1966. V. 48; 52

HARRISON, J. B.
The Latest Studies on Indian Reservation. Philadelphia: 1887. V. 50

HARRISON, J. C.
Birds of Prey of the British Islands. London: 1980. V. 51

HARRISON, J. E.
Greek Vase Paintings. London: 1894. V. 50

HARRISON, J. M.
The Birds of Kent. London: 1953. V. 48; 50; 51; 52; 53
A Handlist of the Birds of Sevenoaks or Western District of Kent. London: 1942. V. 48

HARRISON, JACK
Famous Saddle Horses and Distinguished Horsemen a Historical Narrative and Personal Reminiscences. Shrewsbury: 1952. V. 54

HARRISON, JAMES
The Biographical Cabinet. London: 1823. V. 52
Bristow and the Hastings Rarities Affair. London: 1968. V. 50
How to Sing Plain Chant. Ditchling: 1920. V. 51; 53
Life and Letters of Edgar Allan Poe. New York: 1903. V. 48
Plain Song. New York: 1965. V. 47; 51

HARRISON, JANE ELLEN
Reminiscences of a Student's Life. London: 1925. V. 51

HARRISON, JIM
Dalva. New York: 1988. V. 54
Farmer. New York: 1976. V. 50; 51; 52; 53; 54
Farmer. New York: 1979. V. 52
A Good Day to Die. New York: 1973. V. 47; 50; 52
A Good Day to Die. London: 1975. V. 48; 54
Julip. Boston. V. 51; 53
Julip. Boston: 1994. V. 52
Julip. New York: 1994. V. 51
Just Before Dark. Livingston: 1991. V. 47; 48; 49; 50; 51; 52; 53; 54
Legends of the Fall... New York: 1978/79/79. V. 54
Legends of the Fall. New York: 1979. V. 50; 51; 52; 53; 54
Legends of the Fall. London: 1980. V. 54
Letters to Yesenin. Freemont: 1973. V. 50; 51; 53
Letters to Yesenin... Fremont: 1979. V. 54
Locations. New York: 1968. V. 47; 49; 51
Natural World. Barrytown: 1982. V. 48
New and Selected Poems 1961-1981. New York: 1982. V. 52
Outlyer and Ghazals. New York: 1971. V. 51
Outlyer and Ghazals. New York: 1973. V. 47
The Raw and the Cooked. New York: 1992. V. 47; 48; 49; 50; 51; 52; 53
Returning to Earth. 1977. V. 51
Returning to Earth. Berkeley: 1977. V. 53; 54
Returning to Earth. Ithaca: 1977. V. 50; 51
Selected and New Poems... Ann Arbor: 1981. V. 54
Selected and New Poems. New York: 1982. V. 48; 50; 51; 52; 53; 54
Sundog. New York: 1984. V. 47; 53; 54
The Theory and Practice of Rivers. Seattle: 1986. V. 48; 49; 51; 52; 53
Walking. Cambridge: 1967. V. 51; 54
Warlock. New York: 1981. V. 47; 48; 50; 51; 52; 53; 54
Wolf. New York: 1971. V. 49; 50; 52; 53; 54
The Woman Lit by Fireflies. Boston: 1990. V. 48; 49; 51

HARRISON, JOHN
Essay Towards a Correct Theory of the Nervous System. Philadelphia: 1844. V. 51; 53; 54
The Library of Isaac Newton. Cambridge, London: 1978. V. 54
Principles of Mr. Harrison's Time-Keeper, with Plates of the Same. London: 1767. V. 53; 54
Survey of the Manor of Sheffield. London: 1908. V. 47; 53

HARRISON, JOHN W., MRS.
A. M. Mackay, Pioneer Missionary of the Church Missionary Society to Uganda. London: 1890. V. 52

HARRISON, JOSEPH
The Accomplish'd Practiser in the High Court of Chancery... London: 1790. V. 52
The English Florist's Cabinet, Containing a Series of Original and Interesting Articles on Every Branch of Floriculture... London: 1846. V. 48

HARRISON, LOU
Jargon's Christmas in 1960. 1960. V. 54

HARRISON, MARY ST. LEGER KINGSLEY
The Wages of Sin. London: 1891. V. 47

HARRISON Melodies. Boston: 1840. V. 52

HARRISON OF PARIS
A Typographical Commonplace-Book. New York: 1932. V. 47

HARRISON, REGINALD
Clinical Lectures on Stricture of the Urethra and Other Disorders of the Urinary Organs. London: 1878. V. 53

HARRISON, REX
If Love Be Love. London: 1979. V. 48

HARRISON, ROBERT A.
The New Municipal Manual for Upper Canada, Containing Notes of Decided Cases and a Full Analytical Index. Toronto: 1859. V. 53

HARRISON, SUSANNA
Songs in the Night. Ipswich: 1788. V. 54

HARRISON, THOMAS
VI Greek Myths. London: 1879. V. 47

HARRISON, TOM
Borneo Jungle: an Account of the Oxford Expedition to Sarawak. 1938. V. 54

HARRISON, TONY
Anno Forty Two - Seven New Poems. London: 1987. V. 50
Bo Down. London: 1977. V. 52
A Cold Coming, Poems. London: 1991. V. 49
Dramatic Verse 1973-1985. Newcastle-upon-Tyne: 1985. V. 53
Earthworks. 1964. V. 50
Earthworks. Leeds: 1964. V. 49; 52
Earthworks. London: 1964. V. 53
The Fire Gap. 1985. V. 51
A Kumquat for John Keats. Newcastle-upon-Tyne: 1981. V. 52
The Loiners. London: 1907. V. 48
The Loiners. London: 1970. V. 47; 49; 52
Losing Touch - In memoriam George Cukor, Died 24.1.83. London: 1990. V. 50
Palladas: Poems - a Selection. London: 1975. V. 53
Phaedra Britannica. London: 1976. V. 53
Ten Poems from the School of Eloquence. London: 1976. V. 49

HARRISON, W. H.
The Tourist in Portugal. London: 1832. V. 48

HARRISON, WALTER
A New and Universal History, Description and Survey of the Cities of London and Westminster. London: 1775. V. 52

HARRISON, WILLIAM HENRY
The Humourist, a Companion for the Christmas Fireside. London: 1831. V. 50

HARRISON, WILLIAM RANDLE
Suggestions for Illuminating, with a Series of Alphabets and Designs for Initial letters, Borders, &c. London: 1863. V. 50; 53

HARRISS, WILL
The Bay Psalm Book Murder. New York: 1983. V. 49

HARRISSE, HENRY
Bibliotheca Americana Vetustissima: a Description of Works Relating to America Published Between the Years 1492 and 1551. New York: 1866. V. 54
Bibliotheca Americana Vetustissima, a Description of Works Relating to America Published Between the Years 1492 and 1551. (with) Additions. New York: 1872. V. 47
Christopher Columbus and the Bank of Saint George. New York: 1888. V. 52; 54
The Discovery of North America... Amsterdam: 1969. V. 48
Fernand Colomb: sa Vie, ses Oeuvres. Essai Critique par l'Auteur de la Bibliotheca Americana Vetustissima. Paris: 1872. V. 54

HARROD, HENRY
Gleanings Around the Castles and Convents of Norfolk. Norwich: 1857. V. 49; 54

HARROD, R. F.
Towards a Dynamic Economics. London: 1948. V. 50

HARROD, W.
The History of Mansfield. The History of Mansfield and it's (sic) Environs. Mansfield: 1801. V. 51; 52; 53

HARROD, WILLIAM
Sevenoke. A Poem. London: 1753. V. 47

HARRO-HARRING, PAUL
Dolores; a Novel of South America... New York: 1846. V. 47

HARROP, DOROTHY A.
A History of the Gregynog Press. 1980. V. 54
A History of the Gregynog Press. London: 1980. V. 48; 54
A History of the Gregynog Press. Newtown: 1980. V. 47

HARROWER, HENRY R.
Practical Hormone Therapy. London: 1914. V. 48
Practical Hormone Therapy. New York: 1916. V. 49

HARROWER, MOLLY
I Don't Mix Much With Fairies. London: 1928. V. 49

HARRSEN, META
Central European Manuscripts in the Pierpont Morgan Library. New York: 1958. V. 47; 48

HARRY & Lucy's Trip to Brighton; Being a Pleasing Description of This Fashionable Watering Place, Intended as a "Present from Brighton" for Little Boys and Girls at Home. Brighton: 1828. V. 53

HARRY Bluff. Hail Columbia! Hard Times. Blue-Ey'd Mary. 1824. V. 48

HARRYHAUSEN, RAY
Film Fantasy Scrapbook. South Brunswick: 1974. V. 53

HARRY'S Little Lessons. Philadelphia: 1850. V. 48

HARSDOEFFER, GEORG PHILIP
Porticus Serenissimo Atque Celsissimo Principi, Augusto Bruncvicensium Atque Luneburgensium. Nuremberg: 1646. V. 47

HARSHBERGER, JOHN W.
The Vegetation of the New Jersey Pine-Barrens. Philadelphia: 1916. V. 47; 49; 51

HART, A.
Funeral Sermon on the Death of Maj. Jos. W. Anderson, with an Obituary. Richmond: 1863. V. 54

HART, ALBERT BUSHNELL
The Varick Court of Inquiry to Investigate the Implication of Colonel Varick in the Arnold Treason. Boston: 1907. V. 47

HART, CHARLES HENRY
Memoirs of the Life and Works of Jean Antoine Houdon, the Sculptor of Voltaire and of Washington. Philadelphia: 1911. V. 50; 51

HART, D. BERRY
Atlas of the Female Pelvic Anatomy. Edinburgh: 1884. V. 51

HART, FRED H.
The Sazerac Lying Club. A Nevada Book. San Francisco: 1878. V. 49

HART, GEORGE
The Violin: Its Famous Makers and Their Imitators. London: 1885. V. 54

HART, GEORGE O.
George O. "Pop" Hart: 24 Selections from His Work. New York: 1928. V. 53

HART, HENRY
The Writer in a Changing World. London: 1937. V. 49

HART, HENRY CHICHESTER
Some Account of the Fauna and Flora of Sinai, Petra and Wady 'Arabah. London: 1891. V. 50

HART, HORACE
Notes On a Century of Typography at the University Press. Oxford, 1693-1794. Oxford: 1900. V. 51
Notes on a Century of Typography at the University Press Oxford, 1693-1794. Oxford: 1970. V. 47

HART, J. COLEMAN
Designs for Parish Churches, in the Three Styles of English Architecture. New York: 1857. V. 52

HART, JAMES D.
Fine Printing in California. Berkeley: 1960. V. 48; 51; 52; 54
John Steinbeck: His Language. Aptos: 1970. V. 48
An Original Leaf from the First Edition of Alexander Barclay's English Translation of Sebastian Brant's "Ship of Fools", Printed by Richard Pynson in 1059. With an Essay by... San Francisco: 1938. V. 48; 52

HART, JAMES S.
Scoop. Boston: 1930. V. 54

HART, JOHN
The Trial of John Hart, Esq. Alderman of London, for Adultery and Cruelty (etc.). London: 1780. V. 47

HART, JOHN S.
A Brief Exposition of the Constitution of the United States, for the Use of Common Schools. Philadelphia: 1848. V. 50
The Female Prose Writers of America. Philadelphia: 1855. V. 51
The Iris, an Illuminated Souvenir for 1852. Philadelphia: 1852. V. 49

HART, JOHN W.
External Plumbing Work. A Treatise on Lead Work for Roofs. London: 1902. V. 48

HART, JULIA C.
Tonnewonte, or the Adopted Son of America. Exeter: 1831. V. 49; 52

HART, LIDELL
T. E. Lawrence in Arabia and After. London: 1934. V. 49

HART, LOCKYER WILLIS
The Character and Costume of Afghaunistan. London: 1843. V. 53

HART, MABEL
In Cupid's College. London: 1894. V. 47

HART MANUFACTURING CO. SADDLERY
Catalog 2. Memphis: 1901. V. 50

HART, MISS
Letters from the Bahama Islands. Written in 1823-24. Philadelphia: 1827. V. 47; 51; 54

HART, MOSS
Once in a Lifetime. New York: 1930. V. 50

HART, NATHANIEL C.
Documents Relative to the House of Refuge. New York: 1832. V. 50; 51

HART, ROBERT
Foreign Customs Establishment in China. London: 1865. V. 47; 49

HART, SCOTT
The Moon is Waning. New York?: 1939. V. 50

HART, WILLIAM H.
Cartularium Monasterii de Rameseia. London: 1884-93. V. 49
Historia et Cartularium Monasterii S. Petri Gloucestriae. London: 1863-67. V. 52

HART, WILLIAM S.
Hoofbeats. New York: 1933. V. 48
The Law on Horseback and Other Stories. 1935. V. 50
The Law on Horseback and Other Stories. Los Angeles: 1935. V. 53
My Life East and West. Boston: 1929. V. 52
My Life East and West. New York: 1929. V. 52
The Order of Chanta Sutas. A Ritual. Hollywood: 1925. V. 49; 52
Pinto Ben: and Other Stories. New York: 1918. V. 48
Pinto Ben: and Other Stories. New York: 1919. V. 49

HART-DAVIS, RUPERT
A Catalogue of the Caricatures of Max Beerbohm. London: 1972. V. 50
Edmund Blunden - 1896-1974 - an Address. London: 1974. V. 52

HARTE, BRET
The Adventure of Padre Vicentio: a Legend of San Francisco:. Berkeley: 1939. V. 47; 51; 53
The Argonauts of North Liberty. Toronto: 1888. V. 53
Clarence. London: 1895. V. 51; 54
Colonel Starbottle's Client and Some Other People. London: 1892. V. 51; 54
Concerning "Condensed Novels.". Stanford: 1929. V. 47
Condensed Novels and Other Papers. New York: 1867. V. 54
Cressy. London: 1889. V. 49; 51; 54
The Crusade of the "Excelsior". London: 1888. V. 51; 54
Dickens in Camp. San Francisco: 1923. V. 54
East and West. London: 1871. V. 49
Echoes of the Foot-Hills. Boston: 1875. V. 51
Excelsior Presented by Enoch Morgan's Sons Co., New York. New York: 1877. V. 48; 50; 54
Fac-Simile of the Original Manuscript of the Heathen Chinee, as Written for the Overland Monthly... San Francisco: 1871. V. 52
Gabriel Conroy. Hartford: 1876. V. 49; 51; 54
The Heathen Chinee. Chicago: 1870. V. 48; 51
Heathen Chinee. 1895. V. 50
The Heathen Chinee. San Francisco: 1924. V. 51
The Heathen Chinee. San Francisco: 1936. V. 49
The Heritage of Dedlow Marsh and Other Tales. London: 1889. V. 49; 51; 54
How Santa Claus Came to Simpson's Bar. 1941. V. 47
How Santa Claus Came to Simpson's Bar. Los Angeles: 1941. V. 54
In a Hollow of the Hills. London: 1895. V. 51; 54
In the Carquinez Woods/ On the Frontier/ By Shore and Sedge. London: 1893. V. 53; 54
The Lectures of... Brooklyn: 1909. V. 51
The Lost Galleon and Other Tales. San Francisco: 1867. V. 48; 49
Lothaw, or the Adventures of a Young Gentleman in Search of a Religion. London: 1871. V. 49
The Luck of Roaring Camp... Boston: 1870. V. 47; 48; 50; 53; 54
The Luck of Roaring Camp... Boston: 1872. V. 48; 50; 51; 52
The Luck of Roaring Camp. San Francisco: 1948. V. 53
The Luck of Roaring Camp. San Francisco: 1958. V. 49
Maruja. London: 1885. V. 51; 54
A Millionaire of Rough and Ready. Boston: 1887. V. 48; 51
A Millionaire of Rough and Ready. Kentfield: 1955. V. 49; 52
Mr. Jack Hamilin's Mediation and Other Stories. London: 1899. V. 50; 51; 54
Mrs. Skagg's Husbands, and Other Sketches. Boston: 1873. V. 49
On the Frontier. Boston: 1884. V. 53; 54
On the Frontier... London: 1884. V. 54
Outcroppings: Being Selections of California Verse. San Francisco: 1866. V. 51; 52
The Pliocene Skull. Washington: 1871. V. 49; 53; 54
Poems. Boston: 1871. V. 47
The Poetical Works. Boston: 1872. V. 51
The Poetical Works... London: 1872. V. 47; 51
The Queen of the Pirate Isle. London: 1886. V. 47; 48; 51; 52; 53; 54
The Queen of the Pirate Isle. Boston and New York: 1887. V. 48; 50
The Queen of the Pirate Isle. London: 1890. V. 51
The Right Eye of the Commander. Berkeley: 1937. V. 51; 53; 54
San Francisco in 1866. San Francisco: 1951. V. 47; 51; 53
A Sappho of Green Springs. London: 1891. V. 51; 54
Sketches of the Sixties. San Francisco: 1926. V. 47
Sketches of the Sixties. San Francisco: 1927. V. 47; 50
Tales of the Argonauts and Other Sketches. Boston: 1875. V. 47; 51
Tales of the Gold Rush. New York: 1944. V. 51
Tennessee's Partner. San Francisco: 1907. V. 54
Trent's Trust and Other Stories. London: 1903. V. 53; 54
The Twins of Table Mountain. London: 1879. V. 48
Two Men of Sandy Bar. Boston: 1876. V. 48
A Waif of the Plains. London: 1890. V. 49; 54
West Point Tic Tacs. New York: 1878. V. 47
The Wild West. 1930. V. 52
The Wild West. Argenteuil: 1930. V. 51
The Wild West. Paris: 1930. V. 51; 53

HARTE, BRET continued
The Wild West. Paris: 1936. V. 48
The Works... London: 1880-81. V. 53
The Works. 1882-1907. V. 48
The Works... Boston: 1883. V. 49
The Writings. Boston & New York: 1896-1914. V. 50
The Writings... Boston & New York: 1899. V. 54

HARTE, GLYNN BOYD
Temples of Power... Burford, Oxon: 1979. V. 50; 52
Temples of Power. Oxfordshire: 1979. V. 54

HARTE, WALTER
The Amaranth; or, Religious Poems... London: 1767. V. 48
An Essay on Reason. London: 1735. V. 47; 48; 50
Essays on Husbandry. 1764. V. 49
Essays on Husbandry. London: 1764. V. 52
Essays on Husbandry. London: 1770. V. 50; 52; 54
The History...Gustavus Adolphus, King of Sweden... London: 1759. V. 51; 54
The History...Gustavus Adolphus, King of Sweden... London: 1767. V. 52
The History...Gustavus Adolphus, King of Sweden. London: 1807. V. 47
Poems on Several Occasions. London: 1727. V. 47; 48; 52

HARTER, HARRY
East Texas Oil Parade: a Story About Land, Oil, Politics and People Concerned with the World's Greatest Oil Field in East Texas. San Antonio: 1934. V. 48

HARTHAN, JOHN
The History of the Illustrated Book. London: 1981. V. 49

HARTING, JAMES EDMUND
The Birds of Shakespeare Critically Examined, Explained and Illustrated. London: 1871. V. 51; 54
British Animals Extinct Within Historic Times with Some Account of British Wild White Cattle. London: 1880. V. 49
Hints on the Management of Hawks. London: 1898. V. 54

HARTLEY, BENJAMIN
A Guide to Collodio-Etching. New York: 1881. V. 48

HARTLEY, DAVID
Argument on the French Revolution. Bath: 1794. V. 51
Observations on Man, His Frame, His Duty and His Expectations. London: 1791. V. 48; 49
The State of the Nation, with a Preliminary Defence of the Budget. London: 1765. V. 49; 54

HARTLEY, FLORENCE
The Ladies' Hand Book of Fancy and Ornamental Work... Philadelphia: 1860. V. 50

HARTLEY, JOHN
The Original Illuminated Clock Almanack, in the Yorkshire Dialect. Halifax and Wakefield: 1872-94. V. 53

HARTLEY, JOSEPH
The Wholesale and Retail Wine and Spirit Merchant's Companion. London: 1835. V. 47

HARTLEY, L. P.
The Boat. London: 1949. V. 48
The Collections. London: 1972. V. 52
The Eustace and Hilda... London: 1944-47. V. 48; 49; 51
Eustace and Hilda. 1947. V. 53
The Hireling. New York: 1958. V. 54
My Fellow Devils. London: 1951. V. 49; 50
Night Fears and Other Stories. 1924. V. 49
Simonetta Perkins. London: 1925. V. 48; 49
The Sixth Heaven. London: 1946. V. 49; 54
The Travelling Grave and Other Stories. Sauk City: 1948. V. 51
The Travelling Grave and Other Stories. London: 1951. V. 50; 54
Two for the River. London: 1961. V. 54

HARTLEY, LEONARD LAWRIE
Sale Catalogue (First-Third Portions). London: 1886. V. 51; 54

HARTLEY, LODWICK
Katherine Anne Porter. Athens: 1969. V. 49

HARTLEY, MARSDEN
Adventures in the Arts. Informal Chapters on Painters Vaudeveille and Poets. New York: 1921. V. 47
Adventures in the Arts: Informal Chapters on Painters Vaudeville and Poets. New York: 1921. V. 48
Twenty-Five Poems. Paris: 1923. V. 48; 51

HARTLEY, THOMAS
A Discourse on Mistakes Concerning Religion, Enthusiasm, Experiences &c. Germantown: 1759. V. 49
A Discourse on Mistakes Concerning Religion, Enthusiasm, Experiences &c. London: 1759. V. 54

HARTLEY, W.
In a London Suburb. London: 1885. V. 47

HARTLIB, SAMUEL
Considerations Tending to the Happy Accomplishment of Englands Reformation in Church and State. 1647. V. 52

HARTMAN, FRANK
Hepatitis Frontiers. Boston: 957. V. 53

HARTMANN, FRANZ
Cosmology, or Universal Science. Boston: 1888. V. 48
Secret Symbols of the Rosicrucians of the 16th and 17th Centuries. Chicago: 1935. V. 47

HARTMANN, GEORGE
Wooed by a Sphinx of Aztlan: the Romance of a Hero of Our Late Spanish-American War. Prescott: 1907. V. 50; 53

HARTMANN, J.
Officina Sanitatis, Sive Praxis Chymiatirca Plane Aurea... Nuremberg: 1677. V. 47

HARTMANN, KARL ROBERT EDUARD VON
Philosophy of the Unconscious: Speculative Results According to the Inductive method of Physical Science. New York: 1884. V. 47

HARTMANN, L.
Le Texas Ou Notice Historique Sur Le Champ d'Aisle, comprenant Tout Ce Qui S'est Passe Depuis la Formation Jusqu'a La Dissolution de Cette Colonie. Paris: 1819. V. 49

HARTMANN, NICOLAI
Ethics. Volume I: Moral Phenomena. Volume II. Moral Values. Volume III: Moral Freedom. London: 1932. V. 47

HARTMANN, SADAKICHI
Conversations with Walt Whitman. New York: 1895. V. 50
Landscape and Figure Composition. New York: 1910. V. 47

HARTMAN STOCK FARM, COLUMBUS, OHIO.
Pure Arabians/Americo-Arabs. Columbus: 1908. V. 50

HARTNOLL, PHYLLIS
The Grecian Enchanted. London: 1952. V. 48
The Grecian Enchanted. Waltham St. Lawrence: 1952. V. 47; 50; 52

HARTOG, W. G.
The Kiss in English Poetry. London: 1923. V. 48

HARTOPP, HENRY
Geneaology of the Brampton Family of Brampton Bryan in the County of Hereford, Ludlow, Shropshire, Cold Ashby Northants, Leicester, Birmingham, Sutton Coldfield, etc. London: 1924. V. 53

HARTREE, D. R.
Numerical Analysis. Oxford: 1952. V. 53

HARTSHORNE, ALBERT
Hanging in Chains. London: 1891. V. 53
Old English Glasses. London & New York: 1897. V. 50; 52

HARTSHORNE, CHARLES HENRY
The Book Rarities in the University of Cambridge. London: 1829. V. 51; 53; 54

HARTSHORNE, HENRY
Ancient Metrical Tables: printed Chiefly from Original Sources. London. V. 53

HARTSON, HALL
Youth. A Poem. London: 1773. V. 47

HARTT, FREDERICK
Donatello, Prophet of Modern Vision. New York. V. 50; 51

HARTY, WILLIAM
Observations on the Simple Dysentery and its Combinations, Containing a Review of the Most Celebrated Authors Who Have Written on this Subject.... London: 1805. V. 50; 51

HARTZ, S. L.
The Elseviers and Their Contemporaries. Amsterdam: 1955. V. 54

HARTZENBUSCH, JUAN EUGENIO
The Lovers of Teruel. 1938. V. 50
The Lovers of Teruel. London: 1938. V. 52
The Lovers of Teruel... Newtown: 1938. V. 48; 54

THE HARVARD Medical School, 1782-1906. Boston: 1906. V. 52

HARVARD University Baseball Club. Cambridge: 1903. V. 50

HARVARD UNIVERSITY. KRESS LIBRARY
Catalogue...through 1777-1817. Cambridge: 1993. V. 54
The Kress Library of Business and Economics Giving Data Upon Cognate Items in Other Harvard Libraries. Cambridge: 1964-93. V. 53

HARVARD UNIVERSITY. LAW SCHOOL
A Catalogue of the Law School of the University at Cambridge for the Academical Year 1853-54. Cambridge: 1854. V. 52

HARVARD UNIVERSITY. LIBRARY
Catalogue of Books and Manuscripts. Part I: French 16th Century Books. Cambridge: 1964. V. 47; 50; 52
Catalogue of Books and Manuscripts. Part II: Italian 16th Century Books. Cambridge: 1974. V. 47; 48; 50
A Catalogue of the Fifteenth-Century Printed Books in the Harvard University Library. New York: 1991-93. V. 50

HARVARD UNIVERSITY. LIBRARY. HOUGHTON LIBRARY
The Houghton Library 1942-1967. A Selection of Books and Manuscripts in Harvard Collections. Cambridge: 1967. V. 50; 51; 52

HARVEY, ALFRED SPALDING
Alfred Spalding Harvey. 1840-1905. Contributions to Magazines, Speeches, Etc. London: 1907. V. 54

HARVEY, CHARLES T.
General Statements Concerning the Construction of "Harvey-Roads". New York: 1866. V. 53

HARVEY, CORNELIUS BURNHAM
Genealogical History of Hudson and Bergen Counties, New Jersey. London: 1900. V. 47; 49; 51

HARVEY Cushing's Seventieth Birthday Party. April 8, 1939. Springfield: 1939. V. 47

HARVEY, E. G.
Mullyon: its History, Scenery and Antiquities. London: 1875. V. 47

HARVEY, E. NEWTON
A History of Luminescence, from the Earliest Times Until 1900. Philadelphia: 1957. V. 54

HARVEY, ELLWOOD
Valedictory Address to the Graduating Class of the Female Medical College of Pennsylvania. Philadelphia: 1854. V. 48; 50; 52; 53

HARVEY, FRED
First Families of the Southwest. Kansas City: 1900's. V. 52

HARVEY, GABRIELL
Pierce's Supererogation; or, a New Praise of the Old Ass... London: 1815. V. 50

HARVEY, GIDEON
The City Remembrancer: Being Historical Narratives of the Great Plague at London, 1665, Great Fire, 1666; and Great Storm, 1703... London: 1769. V. 47; 50
The Family Physician, and House Apothecary... London: 1776. V. 49
An Historical Narrative of the Great Plague at London 1665; with an Abstract of the Most Common Opinions concerning the Causes, Symptoms and Cure of that Fatal Disorder. London: 1769. V. 49
The Third Edition of the Vanities of Philosophy and Physick; Enlarg'd to More than Double the Number of the Sheets. London: 1702. V. 48
The Vanities of Philosophy and Physick; together with Directions and Medicines. London: 1700. V. 53

HARVEY, HENRY
History of the Shawnee Indians, From the Year 1681 to 1854, Inclusive. Cincinnati: 1855. V. 47

HARVEY, JAMES
Praesagium Medicum, or, the Best Prognostick Signs of Acute Diseases... London: 1706. V. 47; 48; 53

HARVEY, JOHN
English Mediaeval Architects. London: 1954. V. 54
The Life of Robert Bruce, King of Scots. Edinburgh: 1729. V. 49; 50

HARVEY, M.
The Dragon of Lung Wang. 1934. V. 48

HARVEY, MADISON
Love's Rosary. A Garland of Verses from the Garden of the Poet's Heart. Chicago: 1912. V. 48

HARVEY, MICHAEL
Reynolds Stone: Engraved Lettering in Wood. 1992. V. 47
Reynolds Stone: Engraved Lettering in Wood. London: 1992. V. 50; 52

HARVEY, MOSES
Newfoundland in 1897; Being Queen Victoria's Diamond Jubilee Year and the Four Hundredth Anniversary of the Discovery of the Island by John Cabot. London: 1897. V. 52; 54

HARVEY, MRS.
Turkish Harems and Circassian Homes. London: 1871. V. 47

HARVEY, W.
Strange Conquest. 1934. V. 48; 52
The Tlower Menagerie. London: 1829. V. 53

HARVEY, W. C.
Sensibility, the Stranger and Other Poems. London: 1818. V. 54

HARVEY, W. H.
A Manual of the British Marine Algae. London: 1849. V. 49; 54
Nereis Boreali Americana. Washington: 1851-57. V. 47; 51
Phyclogia Britannica: or, a History of British Sea-Weeds. London: 1846-51. V. 50; 51; 54

HARVEY, WILLIAM
The Anatomical Exercises. London: 1928. V. 47; 48; 49; 50; 51; 52; 54
The Anatomical Exercises... London: 1953. V. 52
Anatomical Exercitations, Concerning the Generation of Living Creatures. London: 1653. V. 54
The Anatomical Lectures of William Harvey. Edinburgh: 1964. V. 53
Bibliotheca Anatomica, Medica, Chirurgica &c. London: 1714. V. 47; 49
The Circulation of the Bood, Two Anatomical Essays Together with Nine Letters Written By (William Harvey). Oxford: 1958. V. 53
De Motu Locali Animalium, 1627. Cambridge: 1959. V. 50
Exercitationes Anatomicae, De Mot Cordis & Sanguinis Circulatione. Roterdami: 1671. V. 48; 52
Exercitationes de Generatione Animalium. Amstelodami: 1651. V. 49; 54
Exercitationes de Generatione Animalium. London: 1651. V. 53; 54
Exercitationes de Generatione Animalium. Amsterdam: 1662. V. 49
On Excision of the Enlarged Tonsil and Its Consequences in Cases of Deafness. London: 1850. V. 48; 51
Portraits of Dr. William Harvey. Oxford: 1913. V. 48; 49; 54
Prelectiones Anatomiae Universalis. London: 1886. V. 53
The Works of William Harvey, M.D. London: 1847. V. 48; 49; 50; 52

HARVEY, WILLIAM FRYER
The Arm of Mrs. Egan. New York: 1952. V. 51; 53
The Beast With Five Fingers. New York: 1947. V. 51; 53

HARVEY DARTON, F. J.
The Good Fairy. London: 1922. V. 50

HARVIE-BROWN, J. A.
The Capercaillie in Scotland. Edinburgh: 1879. V. 47
A Fauna of the North-West Highlands and Skye. Edinburgh: 1904. V. 54
A Fauna of the Tay Basin and Strath More. London: 1906. V. 50; 52; 53
The History of the Squirrel in Great Britain. Edinburgh: 1881. V. 48

HARWELL, H. I.
The Domestic Manual; or Family Directory. New London: 1816. V. 48

HARWELL, RICHARD BARKSDALE
In Tall Cotton the 200 Most Important Confederate Books for the Reader, Researcher and Collector. Austin: 1978. V. 53

HARWOOD, EDUARD
Populorum et Urbium, Selecta Numismata Graeca Ex Aere; Descripta, et Figuris Illustrata... Londini: 1812. V. 48

HARWOOD, EDWARD
Biographia Classica: the Lives and Characters of the Greek and Roman Classics. London: 1778. V. 50

HARWOOD, ISABELLA
Kathleen. London: 1869. V. 50

HARWOOD, J.
Harwood's Views of the Lakes. London: 1852. V. 52
Illustrations of the Lakes. London: 1852. V. 50; 52

HARWOOD, JOHN BERWICK
Falconbeck Hall. London: 1854. V. 54

HARWOOD, JOHN EDMUND
Select Poems. London: 1793. V. 50; 51

HARWOOD, JOHN JAMES
History and Description of the Thirlmer Water Scheme. Manchester: 1893. V. 48

HARWOOD, T. EUSTACE
Windsor Old and New. London: 1929. V. 50

HARWOOD, THOMAS
History of New Mexico Spanish and English Missions of the Methodist Episcopal Church from 1850 to 1910. Albuquerque: 1908/10. V. 52

HARWOOD, WILLIAM
On the Curative Influence of the Southern Coast of England... London: 1828. V. 47; 48; 53; 54

HARZBERG, HILER
Slapstick and Dumbbell. New York: 1924. V. 47; 52

HASEK, JAROSLAV
The Good Soldier Schweik. London: 1930. V. 47

HASELDEN, THOMAS
The Seaman's Daily Assistant, Being a Short, Easy, and Plain Method of Keeping A Journal At Sea... London: 1764. V. 52
The Seaman's Daily Assistant, Being a Short, Easy and Plain Method of Keeping a Journal at Sea... London: 1780. V. 52

HASELER, H.
A Series of Views of Sidmouth and Its Neighbourhood, Drawn From Nature and On Stone. 1825. V. 51
A Series of Views of Sidmouth and Its Neighbourhood, Drawn from Nature and on Stone. Sidmouth: 1825. V. 52

HASKEL, DANIEL
A Complete Descriptive and Statistical Gazetteer of the United States of America... New York: 1843. V. 54

HASKELL, ARNOLD
Diaghileff: His Artistic and Private Life. London: 1935. V. 53

HASKELL, WILLIAM B.
Two Years in the Klondike and Alaskan Gold-Fields; a Thrilling Narrative. Hartford: 1898. V. 48

HASKINS, DAVID GREENE
Ralph Waldo Emerson. Boston: 1887. V. 54

HASKINS, J.
James Van Der Zee: the Picture-Takin' Man. New York: 1979. V. 52

HASKOLL, W. DAVIS
Railway Construction: from the Setting Out of the Centre Line to the Completion of the Works... London: 1857. V. 53

HASLAM, C. J.
The Evils of Private Property, Being an Answer to a Letter by the Rev. J. Barker. Manchester: 1838. V. 53

HASLAM, JOHN
A Letter to the Governors of Bethlem Hospital Containing an Account of Their management of that Insitution for the Last Twenty Years... London: 1818. V. 52
Observations on Madness and Melancholy; Including Remarks on Those Diseases...(with) Illustrations of Madness; Exhibiting a Singular Case of Insanity, and a No Less Remarkable Difference in Medical Opinion... London: 1809/1810. V. 52

HASLEM, JOHN
The Old Derby China Factory and The Workmen and Their Productions. London: 1876. V. 49; 52

HASLER, P. W.
The House of Commons, 1558-1603. London: 1981. V. 52

HASLEWOOD, JOSEPH
The Secret History of the Green Room... London: 1792. V. 48

HASLUCK, F. W.
Athos and Its Monasteries. London: 1924. V. 47
Cyzicus: Being Some Account of the History and Antiquities of that City and of the District Adjacent to It, with the Towns of Apollonia ad Rhyndacum, Miletupolis, Hadrianutherae, Priapus, Zeleia, etc. Cambridge: 1910. V. 52

HASLUCK, PAUL N.
Glass Working by Heat and by Abrasion. London: 1899. V. 50

HASS, HANS
Diving to Adventure. The Daredevil Story of Hunters Under the Sea. New York: 1951. V. 47; 50

HASSALL, A. G.
Treasures From the Bodleian Library. New York: 1976. V. 50

HASSALL, ARTHUR HILL
Food and Its Adulterations; Comprising the Reports of the Analytical Sanitary Commission of "The Lancet" for the Years 1851 to 1854 Inclusive... London: 1855. V. 49
A History of the British Freshwater Algae... London: 1845. V. 49; 54
The Microscopic Anatomy of the Human Body, in Health and Disease. London: 1849. V. 52

HASSALL, JOAN
Dearest Sydney: Joan Hassall's Letters to Sydney Cockerell from Italy and France, April-May, 1950. 1991. V. 54
Dearest Sydney: Joan Hassall's Letters to Sydney Cockerell from Italy and France, April-May 1950. London: 1991. V. 52
The Wood Engravings of Joan Hassall. London: 1960. V. 47

HASSALL, JOHN
The John Hassall Way. London: 1920. V. 53

HASSALL, W. O.
Holkham Bible Picture Book. 1954. V. 53
The Holkham Library. 1970. V. 53
Illuminations and Illustrations in the Manuscript Library of the Earl of Leicester. Oxford: 1970. V. 53

HASSAM, CHILDE
Catalogue of the Etchings and Dry-Points of Childe Hassam, N.A. New York & London: 1925. V. 50

HASSAN, SELIM
Excavations at Giza. Season 1936-37-38. Volume IX: The Mastabas of the Eighth Season and Their Description;. Cairo: 1960. V. 49
The Sphinx: its History in the Light of Recent Excavations. Cairo: 1949. V. 51

HASSAN, THOMAS V., & CO.
Hassan's American and European Distance Tables, or Strangers Pocket Companion. Philadelphia: 1872. V. 54

HASSAN ALI, MEER, MRS.
Observations on the Musselmauns of India: Descriptive of Their Manners, Customs, Habits and Religious Opinions. London: 1832. V. 47

HASSAUREK, F.
The Secret of the Andes: a Romance. 1879. V. 51

HASSE, C.
An Anatomical Description of the Diseases of the Organs of Circulation and Respiration. London: 1846. V. 53

HASSELL, JOHN
Aqua Pictura. London: 1818. V. 48; 50; 51; 52
Beauties of Antiquity; or, Remanants of Feudal Splendor and Monastic Times. London: 1807. V. 47
Graphic Delineation. London: 1826. V. 52
Graphic Delineation. London: 1827. V. 50; 52
Picturesque Rides and Walks with Excursions by Water... London: 1817-18. V. 49; 51; 52; 54
A Series of Original Specimens, Exhibiting the Works of the Most approved Water Color Draftsmen... London: 1818. V. 51
Tour of the Grand Junction... London: 1819. V. 48; 51; 54
Tour of the Isle of Wight. London: 1790. V. 48

HASSELQUIST, FREDERICK
Voyages and Travels in the Levant; in the Years 1749, 50, 51, 52... London: 1766. V. 50

HASSELT, ANDRE VAN
Ceremonies et Fetes qui ont eu Lieu a Bruxelles du 21, au 23 Juillet 1856, a l'Occasion du XXVe Anniversaire de l'Inauguration de Sa Majeste le Roi Leopold Ier... Brussels: 1856. V. 47

HASSLER, EDGAR W.
Old Westmoreland: a History of Western Pennsylvania During the Revolution. Pittsburgh: 1900. V. 49

HASSLER, JON
Four Miles to Pinecone. New York: 1977. V. 51
Staggerford. New York: 1977. V. 50; 53

HASSRICK, PETER
Frederic Remington. New York: 1973. V. 48; 52

HASTAIN, E.
Hastain's Township Plats of the Creek Nation. Muskogee: 1910. V. 47; 50

HASTED, EDWARD
The History and Topographical Survey of the County of Kent. Canterbury: 1778-99. V. 47; 53
The History of the Ancient and Metropolitical City of Canterbury, Civil and Ecclesiastical. Canterbury: 1801. V. 47; 50; 53

HASTINGS, A. C. G.
Nigerian Days. London: 1925. V. 53

HASTINGS, FRANCIS RAWDON, MARQUIS OF
Summary of the Administration of the Indian Government, from October 1813 to January 1823. Malta: 1824. V. 49

HASTINGS, FRANK S.
A Ranchman's Recollections. Chicago: 1921. V. 47; 49; 50; 53

HASTINGS, JAMES
A Dictionary of Christ and the Gospels. New York: 1924. V. 54
A Dictionary of the Bible Dealing With its Language, Literature and Contents... Edinbrugh: 1910. V. 49; 51
Encyclopaedia of Religion and Ethics. Edinburgh: 1908-21. V. 49

HASTINGS, JOHN
Lectures on Yellow Fever. Philadelphia: 1848. V. 50; 51

HASTINGS, MICHAEL
The Handsomest Young Man in England. London: 1967. V. 52

HASTINGS, SALLY
Poems on Different Subjects. Lancaster: 1808. V. 47; 48; 49; 50; 51; 53

HASTINGS, SUSAN WILLARD JOHNSON
A Narrative of the Captivity of... Windsor: 1814. V. 50

HASTINGS, THOMAS
Dissertation on Musical Taste; or, General Principles of Taste Applied to the Art of Music. Albany: 1822. V. 49

HASTINGS, VISCOUNT
The Golden Octopus. New York: 1920. V. 51

HASTINGS, WARREN
The Means of Guarding Dwelling Houses, by Their Construction, Against Accidents by Fire. London: 1816. V. 52
Memoirs Relative to the State of India... London: 1786. V. 47
A Short Account of the Resignation of Warren Hastings, Esq. Governor General of Bengal in the Year MDCCLXXV, with Remarks. London: 1781. V. 49; 51; 52

HASTSELL, JOHN
Precedents of Proceedings in the House of Commons, with Observations. London: 1796. V. 48

HASWELL, ANTHONY
Memoirs and Adventures of Captain Matthew Phelps... Bennington: 1802. V. 47

HASWELL, J. F.
The Registers of Cliburn 1565-1812. Penrith: 1932. V. 52
The Registers of Newbiggen (Westmorland) 1571-1812. Penrith: 1927. V. 52

HASWELL, JAMES C.
The Man of His Time. London: 1871. V. 49

HATCH, FREDERICK H.
The Gold Mines of the Rand Being a Description of the Mining Industry of Witwatersand South African Republic. London: 1895. V. 49; 53

HATCH, WALTER M.
The Moral Philosophy of Aristotle: Consisting of a Translation of the Nichomachean ethics and of the Paraphrase Attributed to Andronicus of Rhodes... London: 1879. V. 49

HATCHER, J. B.
The Ceratopsia. Washington: 1907. V. 53

HATCHER, MATTIE AUSTIN
Letters of an Early American Traveller; Mary Austin Holley, Her Life and Her Works, 1784-1846. Dallas: 1933. V. 48

HATCHER, ROBERT
The Pharmacopoeia and the Physician... Chicago: 1908. V. 48; 50; 52; 53

HATFIELD, CHARLES WILLIAM
Catalogue of the Bonnell Collection in the Bronte Parsonage Museum. 1932. V. 54
Historical Notices of Doncaster. Second Series. Doncaster: 1868. V. 50
Historical Notices of Doncaster. Third Series. Doncaster: 1870. V. 50

HATFIELD, EDWARD F.
St. Helena and the Cape of Good Hope; or, Incidents in the Missionary Life of the Rev. James M'Gregor Bertram... New York: 1852. V. 50

HATFIELD, EDWIN A.
History of Elizabeth, New Jersey, Including the Early History of Union County. New York: 1868. V. 47; 49; 51

HATFIELD, EDWIN F.
Freedom's Lyre; or, Psalms, Hymns and Sacred Songs for the Slave and His Friends. New York: 1840. V. 54

HATFIELD, R. G.
The American House-Carpenter: a Treatise On the Art of Building, and the Strength of Materials. New York: 1857. V. 50

HATFIELD, ROBERT A.
The Work and Position of the Metallurgical Chemist, also, References to Sheffield and Its Place in Mettallurgy. London: 1922. V. 53

HATFIELD, S.
She Lives in Hopes; or Caroline, a Narration Founded Upon Facts. London. V. 53

HATFIELD'S Local Addenda; or Companion to the Almanack for 1830. Cambridge: 1830. V. 47

HATHAWAY, ANN
Muskoka Memories: Sketches from Real Life. Toronto: 1904. V. 50

HATHAWAY, ELLA C.
Battle of the Big Hole in August, 1877, Retold by T. C. Sherrill, a Volunteer member of General Gibbon's Command Which Was So Nearly Wiped Out on that Occasion. 1919. V. 53

HATHAWAY, JAMES ROBERT BENT
The North Carolina Historical and Genealogical Register. Edenton: 1900-03. V. 48

HATHCOCK, ROY
Ancient Indian Pottery of the Mississippi River Valley. Camden: 1976. V. 50

HATIM TAI
The Adventures...A Romance. London: 1830. V. 53

HATIN, JULIUS
A Manual of Practical Obstetrics...with an Appendix. Philadelphia: 1828. V. 53

HATSELL, JOHN
Precedents of Proceedings in the House of Commons... London: 1796. V. 50

HATTERAS, OWEN, PSEUD.
Pistols for Two. New York: 1917. V. 53

HATTON, ANN CURTIS
Poetic Trifles, by Ann of Swansea. Waterford: 1811. V. 53

HATTON, EDWARD
An Intire System of Arithmetic: or Arithmetic In All Its Parts. London: 1731. V. 50
A New View of London; or, An Ample Account of that City, in Two Volumes, or Eight Sections. London: 1708. V. 50

HATTON, JOSEPH
Cruel London: a Novel. London: 1878. V. 54
Newfoundland: ...History Its Present Condition and Its Prospects in the Future. Boston: 1883. V. 47
Newfoundland: ...History, Its Present Condition and Its Prospects in the Future. London: 1888. V. 53

HATTON, RICHARD G.
The Craftsman's Plant Book. London: 1909. V. 48; 49
Design. An Expisition of the Principles and Practice of the Making of Patterns. London: 1914. V. 51

HATTON, THOMAS
A Bibliography of the Periodical Works of Charles Dickens. London: 1933. V. 49; 51; 54
A Bibliography of the Periodical Works of Charles Dickens. Cambridge: 1992. V. 54
A Bibliography of the Periodical Works of Charles Dickens. London: 1992. V. 47
An Introduction to the Mechanical Part of Clock and Watch Work. London: 1773. V. 48

HATZFELD, JOHN CONRAD FRANCIS DE
The Case of the Learned Represented According to the Merit of the Ill Progress Hitherto Made in Arts and Sciences... London: 1724. V. 52

HAUDICQUER DE BLANCOURT, FRANCOIS
The Art of Glass. London: 1699. V. 47

HAUDICQUER DE BLANCOURT, JEAN
De L'Art de La Verrerie. Paris: 1697. V. 50

HAUGHTON, S.
Sport and Travel. Dublin: 1916. V. 48

HAULTAIN, T. ARNOLD
The War in the Soudan... Toronto: 1885. V. 50

HAUPT, HERMAN
A Consideration of the Plans Proposed for the Improvement of the Ohio River. Philadelphia: 1855. V. 50
General Theory of Bridge Construction... New York: 1853. V. 51
The Military Bridges: With Suggestions of new Expedients and Constructions for Crossing Streams and Chasms. New York: 1864. V. 47
Street Railway Motors; with Descriptions and Cost of Plants and Operation of the Various Systems in Use or Proposed for Motive Power on Street Railways. Philadelphia: 1893. V. 54

HAUPTMANN, CARL
Eva-Maria. Berlin: 1920's. V. 53

HAUSCHNER, AUGUSTE
Der Tod des Lowen. Leipzig & Prague: 1922. V. 50; 53

HAUSER, ARNOLD
The Social History of Art. London: 1951. V. 54

HAUSER, HEINRICH
Bitter Water. London: 1930. V. 47

HAUSSET, MADAME DU
The Private Memoirs of Louis XV from the Memoirs of Madame du Hausset Lady's Maid to Madame de Pompadour. Philadelphia: 1900. V. 54

HAUY, R. J.
Traite de Mineralogie. London: 1801. V. 47

HAUY, VALENTIN
Essai sur l'Education des Aveugles, ou Expose de Differens Moyens... Paris: 1786. V. 49

HAVELL, E. B.
A Handbook of Indian Art. London: 1927. V. 49

HAVEN, ALICE BRADLEY
All's Not Gold that Glitters; or the Young Californian. New York: 1853. V. 47; 53

HAVEN, CHARLES C.
Washington and His Army During Their March Through and Return to New Jersey in December 1776 and January 1777. Trenton: 1856. V. 49; 51

HAVEN, CHARLES T.
A History of the Colt Revolver... New York: 1940. V. 49; 51

HAVENS, MUNSON ALDRICH
Horace Walpole and the Strawberry Hill Press: 1757-1789. Canton: 1901. V. 49

HAVERFORDWEST UNION SOCIETY
Rules and Orders to be Observed and Kept by an Union Society of Tradesman, Artists, Etc. Held at the House of Mr. Joseph Perkins, at the Black Horse Inn, In Bridge-Street, in the Town and County of Haverfordwest, first Instituted on the 6th March 1772. Carmarthen: 1786. V. 52

HAVERGAL, FRANCES RIDLEY
Life Chords. London: 1880. V. 53
Swiss Letters and Alpine Poems. London: 1882. V. 50

HAVERKAMP-BEGEMANN, EGBERT
Drawings from the Clark Art Institute, A Catalogue Raisonne of the Robert Sterling Clark Collection of European and American Drawings, Sixteenth through Nineteenth Centuries. New Haven/London: 1964. V. 49; 50

HAVERLY, CHARLES E.
Klondyke and Fortune, the Experience of a Miner Who Has Acquired a Fortune in the Yukon Valley. London: 1898. V. 47

HAVERSCHMIDT, F.
Birds of Surinam. Edinburgh: 1968. V. 54
Birds of Surinam. London: 1968. V. 49

HAVERSHAM, LORD
Reflections on a Late Speech by the Lord Haversham, in So Far As it Relates to the Affairs of Scotland. London: 1704. V. 48; 51

HAVERTY, MARTIN
The History of Ireland, from the Earliest Period to the Present Time, Derived from Native Annals and the Researches of Dr. O'Donovan, Professor Eugene Curry, the Rev. C. P. Meehan, Dr. R. R. Madden... New York: 1867. V. 51

HAVILAND, VIRGINIA
Yankee Doodle's Literary Sampler of Prose, Poetry and Pictures. New York: 1974. V. 50

HAWAII. CONSTITUTION
Constitution of the Republic of Hawaii. Promulgated July 4th, a.D. 1894. 1894. V. 48

HAWARDEN, EDWARD
Charity and Truth; or Catholicks not Uncharitable in Saying That None are Sav'd Out of the Catholick Communion, Because the Rule is Not Universal. London: 1728. V. 47

HAWEIS, MARY ELIZA
The Art of Beauty. New York: 1878. V. 52
The Art of Beauty. Piccadilly: 1883. V. 50
Chaucer for Children: a Golden Key. London: 1882/87. V. 48

HAWES, CHARLES H.
In the Uttermost East. 1904. V. 50
In the Uttermost East. New York: 1904. V. 51

HAWES, DUNCAN
Merchant Fleets in Profile. 1978-89. V. 54
Merchant Fleets in Profile. London: 1978-89. V. 53

HAWES, LLOYD E.
The Dedham Pottery and the Earlier Robertson's Chelsea Potteries. Dedham: 1968. V. 51

HAWES, WILLIAM POST
Sporting Scenes and Sundry Sketches. New York: 1842. V. 52

HAWK, GEORGE J.
History of the S. S. St. Louis, Also Known as U. S. S. Louisville, 1895-1919. V. 49

HAWKE, JESSICA
Follow My Dust!. London: 1957. V. 49

HAWKE, M. B. E.
The Epwell Hunt; or, Black Collars in the Rear. V. 47

HAWKE, MICHAEL
The Grounds of the Lawes of England. London: 1657. V. 48
Killing is Murder and No Murder, or an Exercitation Concerning a Scurrilous Pamphlet of One William Allen, a Jesuitical Impostor... London: 1657. V. 49; 54

HAWKER, PETER
The Diary 1802-1853. London: 1893. V. 48; 49; 52; 54
Instructions to Young Sportsmen In All that Relates to Guns and Shooting. London: 1824. V. 47; 49; 52
Instructions to Young Sportsmen in All that Relates to Guns and Shooting. London: 1826. V. 47; 48; 51
Instructions to Young Sportsmen in All that Relates to Guns and Shooting. London: 1830. V. 49
Instructions to Young Sportsmen in all that Relates to Guns and Shooting. London: 1833. V. 50; 54
Instructions to Young Sportsmen In All that Relates to Guns and Shooting. London: 1854. V. 49
Instructions to Young Sportsmen, on the Choice, Care and Management of Guns... 1816. V. 54
The Sportsman's Pocket Companion. Rugby, Warks: 1980. V. 49

HAWKER, ROBERT
Lectures on the Person, Godhead and Ministry of the Holy Ghost... Plymouth: 1817. V. 47

HAWKER, ROBERT STEPHEN
Ecclesia: a Volume of Poems. Oxford: 1840. V. 50; 52
Echoes from Old Cornwall. London: 1846. V. 50
Poems: Containing the Second Series of Records of the Western Shore. and Pompeii. Stratton: 1836. V. 48
The Prose Works. London: 1893. V. 54

HAWKES, E. W.
The Inviting-In Feast of the Alaskan Eskimo. Ottawa: 1913. V. 51

HAWKES, F. L.
Narrative of the Expedition of an American Squadron to the China Seas and Japan Under the Command of Commodore Perry. New York: 1857. V. 49

HAWKES, JOHN
The Beetle Leg. 1951. V. 49; 53
The Beetle Leg. New York: 1951. V. 48; 49
The Cannibal. Norfolk: 1949. V. 48; 49; 51; 54
Fiasco Hall. Cambridge: 1943. V. 51
Innocence in Extremis. 1985. V. 52; 54
Innocence in Extremis. New York: 1985. V. 52; 54
The Innocent Party. New York: 1966. V. 50
The Lime Twig. 1961. V. 49; 54
The Lime Twig. New York: 1961. V. 53
Lunar Landscapes. New York: 1969. V. 49; 52
The Meynellian Science; or, Fox-Hunting Upon system. London: 1926. V. 47
The Passion Artist. New York: 1979. V. 48
Virginie, Her Two Lives. 1982. V. 54

HAWKESWORTH, JOHN
An Account of the Voyages Undertaken by Order of His Present Majesty for Making Discoveries in the Southern Hemisphere... London: 1773. V. 47; 50; 51; 54
An Account of the Voyages Undertaken by Order of His Present Majesty for Making Discoveries in the Southern Hemisphere. London: 1785. V. 50
The Adventurer. Volume the First (Second). London: 1753-54. V. 49
Almoran and Hamet: an Oriental Tale. London: 1761. V. 47; 48; 49
Almoran et Hamet, Anecdote Orientale... Londres: 1763. V. 47
A Letter to Mr. David Hume, on the Tragedy of Douglas, It's (sic) Analysis. And the Charge Against Mr. Garrick. London: 1757. V. 50
Relation des Voyages Entrepris Par Ordre de Sa Majeste Britannique... Paris: 1774. V. 50

HAWKING, STEPHEN W.
A Brief History of Time. New York: 1988. V. 53

HAWKINS, ABRAHAM
Kingsbridge and Salcombe, with the Intermediate Estuary, Historically and Topographically Depicted. Kingsbridge: 1819. V. 49

HAWKINS, ANTHONY HOPE
Comedies of Courtship. New York: 1896. V. 52
The Dolly Dialogues. 1894. V. 50
The Dolly Dialogues. London: 1894. V. 51
The God in the Car. London: 1895. V. 47
The King's Mirror. London: 1899. V. 48
The Prisoner of Zenda. Bristol: 1894. V. 51; 53
The Prisoner of Zenda. New York: 1894. V. 52
The Prisoner of Zenda. New York: 1966. V. 53

HAWKINS, BENJAMIN
Letter from the Principal Agent for Indian Affairs, South of the Ohio. Philadelphia: 1801. V. 52
A Sketch of the Creek Country in the Years 1798 and 1799. Savannah: 1848. V. 47

HAWKINS, BENJAMIN WATERHOUSE
A Comparative View of the Human and Animal Frame. London: 1859. V. 47; 48; 49; 50; 51; 54

HAWKINS, CHARLES HALFORD
Noctes Shakesperianae - a Series of Papears by Late and Present Members. 1887. V. 53

HAWKINS, EDWARD
Medallic Illustrations of the History of Great Britain and Ireland. London: 1979. V. 48
The Silver Coins of England Arranged and Described with Remarks on British Money Previous to the Saxon Dynasties. London: 1841. V. 48; 54

HAWKINS, EDWARDS COMERFORD
A Short Account of the Church and Parish of St. Bride, Fleet Street. London: 1883. V. 50

HAWKINS, FREDERICK
Annals of the French Stage, from Its Origin to the Death of Racine. London: 1884. V. 52

HAWKINS, J.
Spiritual Quixote, Geoffry (sic) Wildgoose, in Cheltenham... Cheltenham: 1830. V. 54

HAWKINS, JOHN
An Essay on the Law of Celibacy Imposed on the Clergy of the Roman Catholic Church and Observed in All the Religious Orders Abroad... Worcester: 1782. V. 48
A General History of Music, from the Earliest Times to the Present. London: 1819. V. 49
A General History of the Science and Practice of Music. London: 1776. V. 48
The Life of Samuel Johnson. Dublin: 1787. V. 47; 48; 54
The Life of Samuel Johnson. London: 1787. V. 47; 48; 49; 52

HAWKINS, JOSEPH
A History of A Voyage to the Coast of Africa, and Travels into the Interior of that Country. Troy: 1797. V. 50; 54

HAWKINS, LAETITIA MATILDA
Anecdotes, Biographical Sketches and Memoirs: Collected by.... London: 1822. V. 54
The Countess and Gertrude. London: 1811. V. 50
Heraline; or, Opposite Proceedings. London: 1821. V. 50
Memoirs, Anecdotes, Facts and Opinions, Collected and Preserved. London: 1824. V. 47; 50
Rosanne; or, a Father's Labour Lost. London: 1814. V. 47; 50

HAWKINS, R. N. P.
A Dictionary of Makers of British Metallic Tickets, Checks, Medalets, Tallies and Counters, 1788-1910. London: 1989. V. 48

HAWKINS, RICHARD
The Observations of Sir John Hawkins Knight, In His Voiage into the South Sea. London: 1622. V. 50; 52

HAWKINS, SHEILA
Appleby John - the Miller's Lad. London: 1938. V. 50

HAWKINS, THOMAS
The Lost Angel, and the History of the Old Adamites, Found Written on the Pillars of Seth. London: 1840. V. 50
The Origin of the English Drama. Oxford: 1773. V. 48; 50

HAWKINS, THOMAS S.
Some Recollections of a Busy Life. San Francisco: 1913. V. 47

HAWKINS, WALLACE
Case of John C. Watrous, United States Judge for Texas. Dallas: 1950. V. 48
El Sal Del Rey. Austin: 1947. V. 48; 49

HAWKINS, WALTER EVERETT
Chords and Discords. Washington: 1909. V. 53; 54

HAWKINS, WILLIAM
A Treatise of the Pleas of the Crown. London: 1739. V. 48
A Treatise of the Pleas of the Crown... London: 1762. V. 54
A Treatise of the Pleas of the Crown... London: 1771. V. 47; 48

HAWKS, FRANCIS LISTER
The Monuments of Egypt; or, Egypt a Witness for the Bible. New York: 1850. V. 48
Narrative of the Expedition of An American Squadron to the China Seas and Japan, Performed in the Years 1852, 1853, and 1854... Washington: 1856. V. 53
Uncle Philip's Conversations with the Young People About the Whale Fishery, and Polar Regions. London: 1837. V. 50

HAWLES, JOHN
The Englishman's Right... London: 1771. V. 48; 52
Hamilton's Juryman's Guide; or, the Englishman's Right Containing the Antiquity, Use, Duty and Just Privileges of Juries, by the Laws of England. London: 1794. V. 48
Remarks Upon the Tryals of Edward Fitzharris, Stephen Colledge, Count Coningsmark, the Lord Russel, Colonel Sidney, Henry Cornish and Charles Bateman. London: 1689. V. 52

HAWLEY, JOSEPH HENRY
Catalogue of the Library at Leybourne Grange. London: 1868. V. 48

HAWORTH, MARTIN E.
Road Scrapings: Coaches and Coaching. London: 1882. V. 47; 50; 52

HAWTHORN, AUDREY
The Art of Kwakiutl Indians and Other Northwest Coast Tribes. Vancouver/Seattle: 1967. V. 48; 49; 54

HAWTHORNE, JULIAN
Hawthorne and His Circle. New York: 1903. V. 52
Nathaniel Hawthorne and His Wife. Cambridge: 1884. V. 51; 52
Section 558 or the Fatal Letter. From the Diary of Inspector Byrnes. London: 1888. V. 53

HAWTHORNE, NATHANIEL
Astoria; or, Enterprises Beyond the Rocky Mountains. London: 1836. V. 49
The Blithedale Romance. Boston: 1852. V. 47; 49; 52; 53; 54
The Blithedale Romance. Boston: 1862. V. 49
The Complete Literary Prose Works. Boston: 1865-66. V. 53

HAWTHORNE, NATHANIEL continued
The Complete Works of Nathaniel Hawthorne. Boston: 1891. V. 54
Complete Writings. Boston: 1900. V. 51
Contes du Minotaure. Tours: 1954. V. 53
Doctor Grimshawe's Secret. Boston: 1882. V. 48
Doctor Grimshawe's Secret. Boston: 1883. V. 51; 52; 53
Doctor Grimshawe's Secret. Cambridge: 1883. V. 52
Famous Old People. Boston: 1841. V. 48; 53
The Gentle Boy. Boston: 1839. V. 47; 50; 51
Grandfather's Chair: a History for Youth. Boston: 1841. V. 48; 53
Grandfather's Chair: a History for Youth. Boston: 1842. V. 52
The House of the Seven Gables. Boston: 1851. V. 47; 48; 49; 50; 51; 52; 53; 54
The House of the Seven Gables. London: 1851. V. 49
The House of the Seven Gables... Boston: 1857. V. 49
The House of the Seven Gables. Boston & New York: 1899. V. 52; 54
The House of the Seven Gables. New York: 1935. V. 48; 49; 52; 54
Legends of the Province House. Boston: 1877. V. 51; 52
Letters of Hawthorne to William D. Ticknor. Newark: 1910. V. 47; 49
Life of Franklin Pierce. Boston: 1852. V. 49; 51; 52; 53
The Marble Faun. Boston: 1860. V. 47; 49; 50; 51; 52; 53; 54
The Marble Faun. Boston: 1889. V. 51
The Marble Faun. Zurich: 1931. V. 54
Mosses from an Old Manse. New York: 1846. V. 49; 50; 51; 52; 53; 54
Mosses from an Old Manse. Boston: 1854. V. 49
Our Old Home. Boston: 1863. V. 47; 48; 49; 51; 52; 53; 54
Our Old Home. Cambridge: 1891. V. 51
Pansie: a Fragment. London: 1864. V. 49
Passages from the American Note-Books. London: 1849. V. 53
Passages from the American Note-Books. Boston: 1861. V. 53
Passages from the American Note-Books. Boston: 1868. V. 47; 48; 49; 50; 51; 52; 53
Passages from the English Note-Books of Nathaniel Hawthorne. Boston: 1870. V. 47; 48; 50; 52; 53
Passages from the French and Italian Note-Books. London: 1871. V. 47; 54
Passages from the French and Italian Note-Books... Boston: 1872. V. 47; 50; 52; 53
Rappaccini's Daughter. Greenbrae: 1991. V. 54
The Scarlet Letter. London: 1841. V. 50
The Scarlet Letter. 1850. V. 50
The Scarlet Letter. Boston: 1850. V. 47; 49; 50; 52; 53; 54
The Scarlet Letter. London: 1851. V. 49
The Scarlet Letter. Boston: 1860. V. 49
The Scarlet Letter. New York: 1904. V. 52; 53
The Scarlet Letter. London: 1920. V. 47; 49
The Scarlet Letter. New York: 1928. V. 49
The Scarlet Letter. New York: 1941. V. 52; 54
The Scarlet Letter. West Hatfield: 1984. V. 48; 52; 54
Septimius Felton. Berlin: 1872. V. 52
Septimius Felton... Boston: 1872. V. 48; 50; 52; 53; 54
Sights from a Steeple. New York and Bremen: 1988. V. 51
The Snow Image... Boston: 1852. V. 49; 52
The Snow Image... Boston: 1861. V. 49
The Snow Image... New York: 1864. V. 47; 50; 52; 54
The Snow Image. London: 1865. V. 51
Tanglewood Tales... Boston: 1853. V. 51; 52
Tanglewood Tales... Boston: 1887. V. 50
Tanglewood Tales. Philadelphia: 1921. V. 49
Transformation; or, the Romance of Monte Beni. Leipzig: 1860. V. 49; 50; 51
Transformation: or, The Romance of Monte Beni. London: 1860. V. 51; 54
True Stories from History and Biography. Boston: 1851. V. 52; 53
Twice-Told Tales. Boston: 1837. V. 47; 49; 52; 53
Twice-Told Tales. Boston: 1842. V. 49; 51; 52
Twice-Told Tales. Boston: 1851. V. 49
Twice-Told Tales. New York: 1966. V. 52; 54
A Virtuoso's Collection and other Tales. Boston: 1877. V. 49
A Visit to the Celestial City. Philadelphia: 1845?. V. 54
A Wonder Book. London. V. 48; 51
A Wonder Book... Boston: 1852. V. 47; 49; 50; 52; 53
A Wonder Book... 1892. V. 51
A Wonder Book... London: 1892. V. 48; 52
A Wonder Book... Boston: 1893. V. 50
A Wonder Book. New York: 1908. V. 51
A Wonder Book... 1910. V. 47
A Wonder Book... London: 1910. V. 54
A Wonder Book... New York: 1910. V. 49; 50; 52; 53; 54
The Wonder Book. London: 1922. V. 48; 51; 52; 54
The Works. Cambridge: 1883. V. 50; 52

HAWTHORNE, SOPHIA AMELIA PEABODY
Notes... England and Italy. New York: 1869. V. 50
Notes... England and Italy. New York: 1875. V. 53

HAWTREY, GEORGE P.
Chester Historical Pageant, July 18th to 23rd, 1910: Book of Words. Chester: 1910. V. 52

HAXTHAUSEN, AUGUST VON
The Russian Empire, Its People, Institutions, and Resources. London: 1856. V. 53

HAY, ALEXANDER
The History of Chichester. Chichester: 1804. V. 52

HAY, DAVID RAMSAY
The Laws of Harmonious Colouring Adapted to Interior Decorations... London: 1838. V. 50
The Laws of Harmonious Colouring Adapted to Interior Decorations. London: 1844. V. 47
The Laws of Harmonious Colouring Adapted to Interior Decorations... Edinburgh: 1847. V. 48; 51
A Nomenclature of Colours Applicable to the Arts and Natural Sciences to Manufactures and Other Purposes of General Utility. London: 1846. V. 50
Original Geometrical Diaper Designs, Accompanied by an Attempt to Develope (sic) and Elucidate the True Principals of Ornamental Design... London: 1844. V. 52
The Principles of Beauty in Colouring Systemised. London: 1845. V. 48

HAY, GEORGE
A Memorial to the Public, in Behalf of the Roman Catholics of Edinburgh and Glasgow... London: 1779. V. 50; 54
The Necronomicon. 1798. V. 52

HAY, HELEN
Verses for Jock and Joan. New York: 1905. V. 49

HAY, JAMES
Mrs. Marden's Ordeal. Boston: 1918. V. 51

HAY, JOHN
The Bread-Winners. New York: 1884. V. 50
Castilian Days. Boston: 1871. V. 53
Jim Bludso... Boston: 1871. V. 47; 48; 54
Johnson - His Characteristics and Aphorisms. London: 1884. V. 48; 53
The Pike County Ballads. Boston: 1912. V. 49; 54
The Pike County Ballads. New York: 1982. V. 54
The Platform of Anarchy. Cleveland: 1896. V. 54
Poems. Boston: 1890. V. 47

HAY, MARIE
Mas-Aniello, a Neopolitan Tragedy. London: 1913. V. 53

HAY, MARY CECIL
Old Myddleton's Money. London: 1874. V. 54

HAY, R.
The Dictionary of Garden Plants in Colour. London: 1970. V. 54

HAY, THOMAS ROBSON
Hood's Tennessee Campaign. New York: 1929. V. 49

HAY, W. D.
An Elementary Text-Book of British Fungi. London: 1887. V. 49

HAY, WILLIAM
The Immortality of the Soul. London: 1754. V. 48
Mount Caburn. A Poem. London: 1730. V. 47; 52
Religio Philosophi: Or, the Principles of Morality and Christianity... London: 1753. V. 49; 54
The Works... London: 1794. V. 48; 49

HAYCRAFT, HOWARD
The Art of the Mystery Story: a Collection of Critical Essays. New York: 1946. V. 51

HAYDEN, ARTHUR
Spode and His Successors. London & New York: 1925. V. 48; 50; 51

HAYDEN, FERDINAND VANDIVEER
Geological and Geographical Atlas of Colorado and Portions of Adjacent Territory. Washington: 1881. V. 49
Geological Report of the Exploration of the Yellowstone and Missouri Rivers. Washington: 1869. V. 47
The Great West: its Attractions and Resources. Philadelphia: 1880. V. 50
Sun Pictures of Rocky Mountain Scenery... New York: 1870. V. 48; 50; 53; 54

HAYDEN, HORACE EDWIN
A Refutation of the Charges Made Against the Confederate States of America... Richmond: 1879. V. 49

HAYDEN, HORACE H.
Geological Essays; or, an Enquiry into Some of the Geological Phenomena to be Found in Various Parts of American and Elsewhere. Baltimore: 1820. V. 54

HAYDEN, ROBERT
Kaleiodoscope: Poems by American Negro Poets. New York: 1967. V. 53

HAYDEN, ROBERT E.
Heart-Shape in the Dust. Detroit: 1940. V. 54

HAYDON, BENJAMIN ROBERT
The Autobiography and Memoirs of Benjamin Robert Haydon (1786-1846). London: 1926. V. 52
The Diary. Cambridge: 1960-63. V. 51
Lectures on Painting and Design: Origin of the Arat - Anatomy the Basis of Drawing... London: 1844. V. 48
New Churches; Considered with Respect to the Opportunities They Offer for the Encouragement of Painting. London: 1818. V. 47

HAYDON, G. H.
Five Years' Experience in Australia Felix, Comprising a Short Account of its Early Settlement. London: 1846. V. 50

HAYELY, WILLIAM
The Life and Posthumous Writings of William Cowper, Esq. Chichester: 1803-04-06. V. 54

HAYES, ALICE
The Horsewoman. London: 1910. V. 51

HAYES, BENJAMIN
Pioneer Notes from the Diaries of Judge... Los Angeles: 1925. V. 53
Pioneer Notes from the Diaries of Judge... Los Angeles: 1929. V. 48; 50; 54

HAYES, CHARLES WELLS
Galveston: History of the Island and the City. Austin: 1974. V. 48; 53
A Long Journey. Portland: 1876. V. 49; 50; 54
William Wells of Southold and His Descendants, A.D. 1638 to 1878. Buffalo: 1878. V. 49; 51

HAYES, HARRY
Anthology of Plastic Surgery. Rockville: 1986. V. 52

HAYES, ISAAC ISRAEL
The Open Polar Sea. London: 1867. V. 50; 52
The Open Polar Sea. New York: 1867. V. 48; 52; 53

HAYES, JOHN
The Drawings of Thomas Gainsborough. London: 1970. V. 54
Rural Poems. Carlisle: 1807. V. 49

HAYES, JOHN W.
Roman and Pre-Roman Glass in the Royal Ontario Museum: a Catalogue. Toronto: 1975. V. 50; 52
Roman Pottery in the Royal Ontario Museum: a Catalogue. Toronto: 1976. V. 50; 52

HAYES, RICHARD
Biographical Dictionary of Irishmen in France. Dublin: 1949. V. 49
An Estimate of Places for Life... London: 1728. V. 50; 54
Irish Swordsmen of France. 1941. V. 54
Irish Swordsmen of France. London: 1941. V. 51
The Last Invasion of Ireland. 1937. V. 54
The Last Invasion of Ireland. London: 1937. V. 47; 51
The Negociator's Magazine of Monies and Exchanges. London: 1730. V. 48

HAYES, SAMUEL
Prayer. Cambridge: 1777. V. 49; 51; 52
Verses on His Majesty's Recovery. London: 1789. V. 49; 54

HAYES, WILLIAM C.
Royal Sarcophagi of the XVIII Dynasty. Princeton: 1935. V. 51

HAYLEY, WILLIAM
Ballads...Founded on Anecdotes Relating to Animals, with Prints, Designed and Engraved by William Blake. Chichester: 1805. V. 47
Douglas D'Arcy; Some Passages in the Life of an Adventurer. London: 1834. V. 47
An Elegy on the Ancient Greek Model. Cambridge: 1779. V. 52
An Essay on History; in Three Epistles to Edward Gibbon, Esq. London: 1780. V. 48; 52; 54
An Essay on Painting, in a Poetical Epistle to an Eminent Painter. (with) *An Essay on History in Three Epistles to Edward of Temper.* (with) *The Triumphs of Temper.* Dublin: 1781. V. 48
The Life of George Romeny, Esq. Chichester: 1809. V. 47; 50; 52
The Life of Milton. London: 1796. V. 48; 50; 54
The Life of... Milton. Basil: 1799. V. 49; 54
Occasional Stanzas, Written at the Request of the Revolution Society and Recited on Their Anniversary, Nov. 4, 1788. London: 1788. V. 54
A Philosophical, Historical and Moral Essay on Old Maids. London: 1785. V. 48; 49
A Philosophical, Historical and Moral Essay on Old Maids. London: 1786. V. 48; 54
A Philosophical, Historical and Moral Essay on Old Maids. London: 1793. V. 50
Plays of Three Acts; Written for a Private Theatre. London: 1784. V. 53
Poems and Plays. London: 1785. V. 50
A Poetical Epistle to an Eminent Painter. London: 1778. V. 54
The Triumph of Music; a Poem; in Six Cantos. Chichester: 1804. V. 47
The Triumphs of Temper... London: 1781. V. 47; 51; 52; 54
The Triumphs of Temper... Newburyport: 1781. V. 49
The Triumphs of Temper... London: 1788. V. 48
The Triumphs of Temper... London: 1795. V. 48; 49
The Triumphs of Temper. Chichester: 1803. V. 47; 54
The Triumphs of Temper. London: 1803. V. 49; 51
The Triumphs of Temper... Chichester: 1830. V. 48
The Young Widow; or, the History of Cornelia Sedley, in a Series of Letters. London: 1789. V. 47

HAYMAKER, WEBB
Peripheral Nerve Injuries, Principles of Diagnosis. Philadelphia: 1953. V. 47

HAYMAN, SAMUEL
Unpublished Geraldine Documents. London: 1870-81. V. 47

HAYNE, JOSEPH E.
The Negro in Sacred History, or Ham and His Immediate Descendants. Charleston: 1887. V. 50

HAYNE, M. H. E.
The Pioneers of the Klondyke: Being an Account of Two Years Police Service on the Yukon. London: 1897. V. 47; 48

HAYNE, PAUL HAMILTON
Poems. Boston. V. 47
Poems. Boston: 1855. V. 47

HAYNES, ALFRED E.
Man-Hunting in the Desert, Being a Narrative of the Palmer Search Expedition. London: 1894. V. 53

HAYNES, C. D.
Eleanor; or the Spectre of St. Michael's. London: 1821. V. 54

HAYNES, CHARLES
A Treatise of Fluxions; or an Introduction to Mathematical Philosophy. London: 1704. V. 52

HAYNES, DRAUGHTON
Field Diary of a Confederate Soldier... Darien: 1963. V. 53

HAYNES, ELIZABETH ROSS
The Black Boy of Atlanta. Boston: 1952. V. 52; 54

HAYNES, JAMES B.
History of the Trans-Mississippi and International Exposition of 1898. 1910. V. 54

HAYNES, JOSEPH E.
The Black Man; or the Natural History of the Hametic Race. Raleigh: 1894. V. 54

HAYNES, LEMUEL
Universal Salvation, a Very Ancient Doctrine, with Some Account of the Life and Character of its Author, a Sermon, Delivered at Rutland West Parish, Vermont, in the Year 1805. Concord: 1814. V. 50

HAYNES, MARTIN A.
A Minor War History. Lakeport: 1916. V. 49

HAYNES, SYBILLE
Etruscan Bronzes. London: 1985. V. 50; 52

HAYNES, THOMAS
A Treatise on the Improved Culture of the Strawberry, Raspberry, Gooseberry and Currant. London: 1823. V. 50

HAYS, GILBERT ADAMS
Life and Letters of Alexander Hays, Brevet Colonel United States Army, Brigadier General and Brevet Major General, United States Volunteers. Pittsburgh: 1919. V. 49

HAYS, JOHN
Observations on the Existing Corn Laws. London: 1824. V. 50

HAYS, MARY
Memoirs of Emma Courtney. London: 1796. V. 49

HAYTER, CHARLES
An Introduction to Perspective, Drawing and Painting, in a Series of Pleasing and Familiar Dialogues... Kingsbury: 1825. V. 50

HAYTER, STANLEY WILLIAM
New Ways of Gravure. London: 1949. V. 48

HAYTI
The Commission of Enquiry and Verification, Instituted by a Resolution of the president of the Republic on the 21st March 1903. Port-au-Prince: 1904. V. 51

HAYWARD,
The Adventive Flora of Tweedside. Arbroath: 1919. V. 53

HAYWARD, ABRAHAM
The Art of Dining; Gastronomy and Gastronomers. London: 1852. V. 52; 54
Verses of Other Days. London: 1847. V. 52

HAYWARD, HELENA
William and John Linnell, Eighteenth Century London Furniture Makers. London: 1980. V. 50; 54
World Furniture. London: 1967. V. 51

HAYWARD, J.
English Poetry: an Illustrated Catalogue. 1950. V. 50

HAYWARD, J. F.
Silver Bindings from the J. R. Abbey Collection. V. 50

HAYWARD, JOHN
The Columbian Traveller and Statistical Register. Boston: 1833. V. 47
The First Part of the Life and Raigne of King Henrie... 1599. V. 47
The First Part of the Life and Raigne of King Henrie... London: 1599. V. 49
The First Part of the Life and Raigne of King Henrie... London: 1638?. V. 53
The Lives of the III Normans, Kings of England: William I, William II, Henri I... London: 1613. V. 50
The Lives of the III Normans, Kings of England: William I, William II, Henri I... London: 1613/30. V. 51
The Science of Horticulture, Including a Practical System for the Management of Fruit Trees... London: 1818. V. 47; 49

HAYWARD, K. J.
Genera et Species Animalium Argentinorum, Lepidoptera (Rhopalocera). Buenos Aires: 1948-67. V. 49

HAYWARD, P. J.
The Marine Fauna of the British Isles. London: 1990. V. 48; 50

HAYWARD, THOMAS
The British Muse, of a Collection of Thoughts Moral, Natural and Sublime, of Our English Poets; Who Flourished in the Sixteenth and Seventeenth Centuries. London: 1738. V. 47

HAYWOOD, CHESTER D.
Negro Combat Troops in the World Ward: The Story of the 371st Infantry. Worcester: 1928. V. 53

HAYWOOD, ELIZA FOWLER
The History of Miss Betsy Thoughtless. London: 1772. V. 48
The Husband. London: 1756. V. 47; 48; 52
Memoirs of a Certain Island Adjacent to the Kingdom of Utopia. London: 1725-26. V. 47
Memoirs of the Court of Lilliput. London: 1727. V. 52
Secret Memoirs of the Late Mr. Duncan Campbell, the Famous Deaf and Dumb Gentleman. London: 1732. V. 54
The Wife. London: 1773. V. 51

HAYWOOD, FRANCIS
An Analysis of Kant's Critick of Pure Reason. London: 1844. V. 52

HAYWOOD, GAR ANTHONY
Not Long for this World. 1990. V. 54

HAYWOOD, JOHN
The Duty and Office of Justices of the Peace, and of Sheriffs, Coroners, Constables &c.... Halifax: 1800. V. 48
A Manual of the Laws of North Carolina, Arranged Under Distinct Heads, in Alphabetical Order. Raleigh: 1839. V. 48

HAZARD, NATHAN
Observations On the Peculiar Case of the Whig Merchants, Indebted to Great-Britain at the Commencement of the Late War... New York: 1785. V. 51

HAZARD, ROWLAND G.
Language: Its Connection with the Present Condition and Future. Providence: 1836. V. 49; 54
Two Letters on Causation and Freedom in Willing, Addressed to John Stuart Mill. Boston: 1869. V. 50

HAZARD, SAMUEL
Cuba With Pen and Pencil. London: 1873. V. 52

HAZARD, THOMAS R.
Report On the Poor and Insane in Rhode Island; Made to the General Assembly At its January Session, 1851. Providence: 1851. V. 47; 48; 50

HAZART, CORNELIUS
Kirchen Geschichte, Das Ist Catholisches Christenthum Durch Die Ganze Welt Ausgebreittet. Wien: 1678-84. V. 50

HAZELIUS, ERNEST LEWIS
The Life of John Henry Stilling, Doctor of Medicine and Philosophy. Gettysburg: 1831. V. 52

HAZELTON, J. M.
History and Handbook of Hereford Cattle and Hereford Bull Index. Kansas City: 1925. V. 54

HAZEN, ALLEN T.
A Bibliography of the Strawberry Hill Press... New Haven: 1942. V. 47; 48; 52
A Bibliography of the Strawberry Hill Press. London: 1973. V. 54
A Catalogue of Horace Walpole's Library. New Haven and London: 1969. V. 48; 49

HAZEN, EDWARD
Popular Technology; or, Professions and Trades. New York: 1841. V. 50

HAZEN, HENRY
Skin Cancer. St. Louis: 1916. V. 48

HAZEN, W. B.
A Narrative of Military Service. Boston: 1885. V. 47

HAZLITT, WILLIAM
The Character of W. Cobbett, M.P. to Which is Added Several Interesting Paraticulars of Mr. Cobbett's Life and Writings. London: 1835. V. 48
Characteristics; in the Manner of Rochefoucault's Maxims. London: 1837. V. 51
Characters of Shakespeare's Plays. London: 1817. V. 47; 49; 51; 52
Characters of Shakespeare's Plays. London: 1818. V. 48; 50
Characters of Shakespeare's Plays... London: 1903. V. 50
Conversations of James Northcote, Esq., R.A. London: 1830. V. 49; 53
Essays On the Principles of Human Action: On the Systems of Hartley and Helvetius: and on Abstract ideas. London: 1836. V. 49
Lectures Chiefly on the Dramatic Literature of The Age of Elizabeth. London: 1820. V. 48; 50
Lectures on the Dramatic Literature in the Age of Elizabeth. New York: 1845. V. 48
Lectures on the English Comic Writers. London: 1819. V. 49; 51
Lectures on the English Poets. London: 1818. V. 48; 51
Liber Amoris... London: 1823. V. 50
Liber Amoris... London: 1893. V. 47
The Life of Napoleon... London: 1830. V. 47
The Life of Napoleon. London: 1900. V. 50
Literary Remains. London: 1836. V. 52
The Plain Speaker. London: 1826. V. 47; 49; 52; 53; 54
Political Essays, with Sketches of Public Characters. London: 1819. V. 52
A Reply to the Essay on Population by the Rev. T. R. Malthus. London: 1807. V. 52
The Round Table; a Collection of Essays. Edinburgh: 1817. V. 47; 49; 51; 54
The Spirit of Monarchy. London: 1835?. V. 48
The Spirit of the Age; or Contemporary Portraits. London: 1825. V. 47
Table Talk: Opinions on Books, Men and Things. Second Series. New York: 1845. V. 48
Table Talk or Original Essays on Men and Manners. London: 1824. V. 51; 52; 54
A View of the English Stage: or, A Series of Dramatic Criticisms. London: 1818. V. 47; 49
Winterslow: Essays and Characters Written There. London: 1850. V. 52

HAZLITT, WILLIAM CAREW
British Columbia and Vancouver Island... London: 1858. V. 47; 53
Fairy Tales; Legends and Romances Illustrating Shakespeare and Other Early English Writers. London: 1875. V. 50
The Great Gold Fields of Cariboo... London: 1862. V. 53
Handbook to the Popular, Poetical and Dramatic Literature of Great Britain... (with) Bibliographical Collections and Notes on Early English Literature 1474-1700... (with) A Genral Index... London: 1867-1903. V. 47
The Livery Companies of the City of London. London: 1892. V. 49
Memoirs of William Hazlitt. London: 1867. V. 49; 50

HDRLICKA, ALES
Physiological and Medical Observations Among the Indians of Southwestern United States and Northern Mexico. Washington: 1908. V. 48; 52

HEACOX, CECIL E.
The Compleat Brown Trout. U.S.A: 1983. V. 51; 52

HEAD, BARCLAY V.
A Guide to the Principal Gold and Silver Coins of the Ancients From Circa B.C. 700 to A.D. 1. London: 1881. V. 48

HEAD, EDWARD FRANCIS
Poltroonius: a Tragic Farace. Boston: 1856. V. 49

HEAD, FRANCIS BOND
Descriptive Essays Contributed to the Quarterly Review. London: 1857. V. 53
The Emigrant. London: 1846. V. 48; 49; 51
The Life of Bruce, the African Traveller. London: 1838. V. 54
A Narrative. London: 1839. V. 47; 49; 50; 51; 52; 53
Rough Notes Taken During Some Rapid Journeys Across the Pampas and Among the Andes... London: 1826. V. 47; 49; 54
Rough Notes Taken During Some Rapid Journeys Across the Pampas, and Among the Andes. London: 1828. V. 48
The Royal Engineer. London: 1869. V. 50
Stokers and Pokers: or the London and North-Western Railway... London. V. 49

HEAD, GEORGE
Forest Scenes and Incidents, in the Wilds of North America... London: 1829. V. 51
A Home Tour Through the Manufacturing Districts of England, in the Summer of 1835. London: 1836. V. 51

HEAD, H. NUGENT
The Hoghunters' Annual. Allahabad: 1928. V. 51

HEAD, HENRY
Aphasia and Kindred Disorders of Speech. Cambridge: 1926. V. 54
Aphasia and Kindred Disorders of Speech. New York: 1926. V. 53; 54
Studies in Neurology. London: 1920. V. 47; 50
Studies in Neurology. Oxford: 1920. V. 49; 50; 51; 53; 54

HEAD, HERBERT
A World Within a War. London: 1943. V. 47

HEAD, RICHARD
The English Rogue...Witty Extravagant. London: 1666. V. 50
The English Rogue...Witty Extravagant... London: 1672/71. V. 47
The English Rogue...Witty Extravagant... London: 1688. V. 50
Proteus Redivivus: or the Art of Wheedling, or Insinuation... London: 1675. V. 47
Proteus Redivivus: the Art of Wheedling or Insinuation, in General and Particular Conversations and Trades... London: 1684. V. 48; 50

HEAD, THOMAS ANTHONY
Campaigns and Battles of the Sixteenth Regiment, Tennessee Volunteers, in the War Between the States. Nashville: 1885. V. 49

HEADLAM, CUTHBERT
History of the Guards Division in the Great War. 1914-1918. London: 1924. V. 47
The Three Northern Counties of England. Gateshead: 1939. V. 52; 53

HEADLAND, FREDERICK WILLIAM
The Action of Medicines in the System. Philadelphia: 1853. V. 53
The Action of Medicines in the System. Philadelphia: 1863. V. 47; 48

HEADLEY, HENRY
Poems and Other Pieces. London: 1786. V. 54
Select Beauties of Ancient English Poetry. London: 1787. V. 48; 50

HEADLEY, JOEL TYLER
The Achievements of Stanley and Other African Explorers. Philadelphia: 1878. V. 53
The Adirondack; or Life in the Woods. New York: 1849. V. 50
The Keepsake. New York: 1857?. V. 54
The Second War with England. New York: 1853. V. 51; 54

HEAGERTY, JOHN J.
Four Centuries of Medical History in Canada and a Sketch of the Medical History of Newfoundland. Toronto: 1928. V. 53

HEAL, AMBROSE
The English Writing-Masters and Their Copy-Books 1570-1800. Hildesheim: 1962. V. 51; 54
The London Furniture Makers from the Restoration to the Victorian Era 1660-1840. London: 1953. V. 50; 53; 54
The London Goldsmiths 1200-1800. Cambridge: 1935. V. 49
London Tradesmen's Cards... London: 1925. V. 47; 48; 49
London Tradesmen's Cards. New York: 1925. V. 50; 53; 54
The Signboards of Old London Shops. London: 1947. V. 49

HEAL, J. G. B.
Eighteenth Century British Books, a Subject Catalogue Extracted From the British Museum General Catalogue of Printed Books. Folkestone: 1979. V. 48; 49

HEALD, W. M.
The Advantages of Friendly Societies. Wakefield: 1805. V. 50

HEALES, ALFRED
The Records of Merton Priory in the County of Surrey. London: 1898. V. 49

HEALEY, EDWARD
A Series of Picturesque Views of Castles and Country Houses in Yorkshire. Bradford: 1885. V. 53

HEALEY, J. C.
Hare Hunting in the Pennines. Rochdale: 1910. V. 49

THE HEALING Art; or, Chapters Upon Medicine, Diseases, Remedies and Physicians, Historical, Biographical and Descriptive. London: 1887. V. 50; 52

HEALTH and Wealth a Description of the Garden Spot of Colorado...Sunny San Luis Valley. Alamosa: 1907. V. 54

HEALTH Science Books, 1876-1982. New York: 1982. V. 52

HEALY, JEREMIAH
Blunt Darts. 1984. V. 52; 53
Blunt Darts. New York: 1984. V. 53; 54

HEALY, MICHAEL AUGUSTINE
Report of the Revenue Marine Steamer Corwin in the Arctic... Washington: 1887. V. 49; 52; 53
Report... of the Revenue Marine Steamer Corwin in the Arctic...1884. Washington: 1889. V. 53

HEAMAN, PETER
Report of the Trial of Peter Heaman and Francois Gautiez or Gautier, for the Crimes of Piracy and Murder, Before the High Court of Admiralty, Held at Edinburgh, etc. Edinburgh: 1821. V. 47

HEANEY, HOWELL J.
Thirty Years of Bird and Bull: a Bibliography 1958-1988. 1988. V. 52
Thirty Years of Bird and Bull, a Bibliography 1958-1988. Newtown: 1988. V. 48; 50; 54

HEANEY, SEAMUS
After Summer. Old Deerfield: 1978. V. 52; 53
A Boy Driving His Father to Confession. Farnham, Surrey: 1970. V. 52; 53
The Cure at Troy. 1990. V. 51
The Cure at Troy. Derry: 1990. V. 50; 51
De Rugwaartse Blik. 1981. V. 50
The Death of a Naturalist. 1966. V. 49; 50
Death of a Naturalist. London: 1966. V. 47; 51; 52; 53
Death of a Naturalist. New York: 1969. V. 53
Door Into the Dark. 1969. V. 49; 54
Door into the Dark. London: 1969. V. 47; 48; 49; 50; 52; 53; 54
Eleven Poems. 1965. V. 50
Eleven Poems. Belfast: 1965. V. 48; 49; 52
Field Work. London: 1979. V. 47; 52; 54
Field Work. New York: 1979. V. 48; 50; 51; 52; 54
Glanmore Sonnets von Seamus Heaney. Mit Pastellen von Cecil King. Hamburg: 1977. V. 48
The Government of the Tongue. New York: 1989. V. 54
The Gravel Walks. Hickory: 1992. V. 52
Gravities: a Collection of Poems and Drawings. New Castle upon Tyne: 1979. V. 52
Hailstones. Dublin: 1984. V. 50; 53
The Haw Lantern. New York: 1987. V. 47; 49; 50; 52; 53; 54
Hedge School. Sonnets from Glanmore. Newark: 1979. V. 52; 53; 54
In Their Element. Belfast: 1977. V. 53
In Their Element... Northern Ireland: 1977. V. 52
Keeping Going... Cambridge: 1993. V. 53
Keeping Going. Concord: 1993. V. 49; 53
A Lough Neagh Sequence. Didsbury, Manchester: 1969. V. 47; 49
The New Lantern. New York: 1987. V. 53
New Selected Poems 1966-1987. London: 1990. V. 47; 48
North. London: 1975. V. 50; 51; 52; 53
North. New York: 1975. V. 54
An Open Letter. Derry: 1983. V. 50
The Place of Writing. Georgia. V. 48; 50
The Place of Writing. Georgia: 1988. V. 50
The Place of Writing. Atlanta: 1989. V. 50
Poems 1965-1975. New York: 1980. V. 47; 50
Poems and a Memoir. New York: 1982. V. 47; 48; 49; 52; 53
Preoccupations - Selected Prose 1968-1978. London: 1980. V. 47; 50
Preoccupations. Selected Prose 1968-1978. New York: 1980. V. 50
Responses. Great Britain: 1971. V. 52; 53
A Rich Hour. Loughcrew: 1988. V. 54
Seeing Things. London: 1991. V. 47; 48; 49; 50; 53; 54
Seeing Things. New York: 1991. V. 50
Selected Poems 1965-1965. London: 1980. V. 52
Selected Poems 1966-1987. New York: 1990. V. 48; 51; 52; 53
Soundings 72 - An Annual Anthology of New Irish Poetry. Belfast: 1972. V. 49; 50
The Sounds of Rain. Atlanta: 1988. V. 47; 52
The Spirit Level. London: 1966. V. 54
Station Island. London: 1984. V. 50
Stations. Belfast: 1975. V. 49; 52; 53
Sweeney Astray. 1983. V. 54
Sweeney Astray. Derry: 1983. V. 48; 50; 52; 54
Sweeney Astray. Now York: 1983. V. 49; 53
Sweeney Astray. New York: 1984. V. 47; 48; 49; 50; 52; 53
Sweeney Praises the Trees. New York: 1981. V. 52; 53
The Tree Clock. Belfast: 1990. V. 49; 50; 53
Verses for a Fordham Commencement. Nadja: 1982. V. 48
Verses for a Fordham Commencement. New York: 1984. V. 47; 50; 53; 54
Wintering Out. London: 1972. V. 47; 52
Wintering Out. New York: 1973. V. 48; 53

HEAP, GWINN HARRIS
Central Route to the Pacific From the Valley of the Mississippi to California: Journal of the Expedition of E. F. Beale, Superintendent of Indian Affairs in California, and Gwinn Harris Heap from Missouri to California 1853. Philadelphia: 1854. V. 52
Central Route to the Pacific: With Related Material on Railroad Explorations and Indian Affairs... Glendale: 1957. V. 50; 52; 54

HEAPHY, THOMAS
A Wonderful Ghost Story. London: 1882. V. 54

HEARD, JAMES
A Practical Grammar of the Russian Language. St. Petersburg: 1827. V. 49; 50; 52

HEARD, NATHAN
Howard Street. New York: 1968. V. 54

HEARN, LAFCADIO
Appreciations of Poetry. New York: 1916. V. 47
Buddha. Neue Geschichten und Studien Aus Japan. Frankfurt am Main: 1921. V. 47
Chin Chin Kobakama. Tokyo: 1895. V. 53
Chita: a Memory of Last Island. New York: 1889. V. 47
Complete Lectures: On Art, Literature and Philosophy. Kanda, Tokyo: 1932. V. 47
Creole Sketches. Boston: 1924. V. 47
La Cuisine Creole. New York: 1885. V. 47
A Drop of Dew. Tokyo: 1950. V. 52
Editorials. Boston & New York: 1926. V. 47; 49
En Glanant dans les Champs de Bouddha. Paris: 1925. V. 47
Essays in European and Oriental Literature. New York: 1923. V. 47
Exotics and Retrospectives. Boston: 1898. V. 47
Gibbetted: Execution of a Youthful Murderer, Shocking Tragedy at Dayton, a Broken Rope and a Double Hanging, Sickening Scenes Behind the Saffold-Screen... Los Angeles: 1933. V. 47
Gleanings in Buddha Fields. Boston: 1897. V. 47; 49; 52
Glimpses of Unfamiliar Japan. Boston and New York: 1894. V. 52; 53
Glimpses of Unfamiliar Japan. Cambridge, Boston: 1900. V. 54
The Goblin Spider. Tokyo: 1899. V. 49
Gombo Zhebes: Little Dictionary of Creole Proverbs. New York: 1885. V. 47; 50; 53
Historical Sketch Book and Guide to New Orleans and Environs... New York: 1885. V. 47
In Ghostly Japan. Boston: 1899. V. 48; 52; 54
Insects and Greek Poetry. New York: 1926. V. 48
Interpretation of Literature. New York: 1915. V. 47
Interpretations of Literature. London: 1916. V. 54
Interpretations of Literature. New York: 1916. V. 47
Japan an Attempt at Interpretation. New York: 1904. V. 47; 48; 49; 51; 52; 53; 54
Japanese Fairy Tales. Philadelphia: 1931. V. 50
The Japanese Letters of Lafacadio Hearn. Boston & New York: 1910. V. 47
Japanese Lyrics. Boston: 1915. V. 47; 48
A Japanese Miscellany. Boston: 1901. V. 47; 48; 52; 54
Karma. New York: 1918. V. 47
Kokoro. Tokyo: 1921. V. 47
Kotto. New York & London: 1902. V. 47; 50; 52; 53; 54
Kwaidan: Stories and Studies of Strange Things. Boston: 1904. V. 47
Kwaidan: Stories and Studies of Strange Things. London: 1904. V. 49
Kwaidan: Stories and Studies of Strange Things. Tokyo: 1932. V. 49; 53
Kyushu. Traume und Studien aus dem Neuen Japan. Frankfurt am Main: 1921. V. 47
Leaves From the Diary of an Impressionist. Boston & New York: 1911. V. 47; 54
Letters From the Raven. New York: 1907. V. 47
Letters to a Poem. Detroit: 1933. V. 49
Lettres Japonaises 1890-1893. Paris: 1928. V. 47
Life and Literature ... New York: 1917. V. 47
Life and Literature. London: 1922. V. 47
Miscellanies. London: 1924. V. 53
Occidental Gleanings. London: 1925. V. 53
Occidental Gleanings... New York: 1925. V. 47; 48
Out of the East Reveries and Studies in New Japan. Boston & New York: 1895. V. 47; 49; 54
The Romance of the Milky Way and Other Studies and Stories. Boston and New York: 1905. V. 47; 54
Shadowings. Boston: 1900. V. 47; 53; 54
Some Chinese Ghosts. Boston: 1887. V. 47; 48; 50; 53; 54
Stray Leaves From Strange Literature. Boston: 1884. V. 47; 48; 50; 52
Two Years in the French West Indies. New York: 1890. V. 51; 54
Un Voyage d'Ete aux Tropiques. Paris: 1931. V. 47
The Writings. Boston: 1922. V. 47; 53
Youma. Roman Martiniquais. Paris: 1923. V. 47

HEARN, WILLIAM EDWARD
Plutology; or the Theory of the Efforts to Satisfy Human Wants. Melbourne and Sydney: 1863. V. 54

HEARNE, MARY
The Lover's Week; or, the Six Days Adventures of Philander and Amarylis. London: 1718. V. 49

HEARNE, SAMUEL
A Journey from Prince of Wales's Fort in Hudson's Bay to the Northern Ocean. London: 1795. V. 47; 49; 52
A Journey from Prince of Wales's Fort in Hudson's Bay to the Northern Ocean... Amsterdam: 1968. V. 47; 50
A Journey from Prince of Wales's Fort in Hudson's Bay to the Northern Ocean. Edmonton: 1971. V. 50

HEARNE, THOMAS
A Collection of Curious Discourses... Oxford: 1720. V. 47
A Collection of Curious Discourses... London: 1771. V. 50; 53
A Collection of Curious Discourses... London: 1773. V. 48
Reliquiae Hearnianae: The Remains of Thomas Hearne, M.A... Oxford: 1857. V. 47; 49
The Remains of Thomas Hearne, M.A. London: 1869. V. 47; 48; 50
Remarks and Collections. London: 1885-1921. V. 53
Remarks and Collections... Oxford: 1885-1921/91. V. 48

HEARST, WILLIAM RANDOLPH, MRS.
The Horses of San Simeon. Paintings by Sam Savitt. San Simeon: 1985. V. 49

THE HEART of Man, Either a Temple of God, or a Habitation of Satan. Harrisburg: 1853. V. 52; 54

HEARTMAN, CHARLES FRANCIS
American Primers, Indian Primers, Royal Primers, & 37 Other Types of Non-New England Primers Issued Prior to 1830. Highland Park: 1935. V. 47; 50
A Bibliographical Check-list of First Editions of Edgar Allan Poe. Metuchen: 1932. V. 47; 49
A Census of First Editions and Source Materials by Edgar Allan Poe... 1932. V. 48
A Census of First Editions and Source Materials by Edgar Allan Poe. Metuchen: 1932. V. 47
Checklist of Printers in the U.S. from Stephen Daye to the Close of the War of Independence. New York: 1915. V. 48; 51
The Cradle of the United States, 1765-1789. Metuchen: 1922-23. V. 50
The Cradle of the United States, 1765-1789... Metuchen: 1923. V. 47
New-England primer Issued Prior to 1830: a Bibliographical Check-List... New York: 1934. V. 47
Poe Bibiliography. Hattiesburg: 1940. V. 53
Poe Bibliography. Hattiesburg: 1943. V. 53

THE HEARTY Old Boy, Who Looked Always the Same. London: 1866. V. 52

HEATH, AMBROSE
Good Drinks. London: 1939. V. 51
Good Food - Month by Month Recipes. London: 1932. V. 51

HEATH, BENJAMIN
A Catalogue of Books in the Various Branches of Literature, Which Lately formed the Library of a Distinguished Collector, and were sold by Auction, by Mr. Jeffery, of Pall-Mall... London: 1811. V. 50

HEATH, CHARLES
The Excursion Down the Wye from Ross to Monmouth, Comprehending Historical and Descriptive accounts of Wilton and Goodrich Castles, also of Court Field, the Nursery of King Henry the Fifth... Monmouth: 1803?. V. 50
Pickwickian Illustrations. London. V. 52; 54
Pickwickian Illustrations. London: 1837. V. 49
The Shakespeare Gallery. London: 1836-37. V. 53
The Waverley Gallery of the Principal Female Characters in Sir Walter Scott's Romances. 1858. V. 53

HEATH, CHRISTOPHER
A Manual of Minor Surgery and Bandaging for House Surgeons, Dressers and Junior Practioners. London: 1883. V. 50; 54

HEATH, EDWARD
Music: a Joy for Life. London: 1976. V. 50

HEATH, FRANCIS
The English Peasantry. London: 1874. V. 47; 49; 52

HEATH, GEORGE W.
Southern Refugees, or the South During the War. Haverhill: 1872. V. 49

HEATH, HENRY
The Book of Etiquette. London: 1830. V. 48
Nautical Dictionary. London: 1840. V. 50
Old Way's & New Way's. London: 1829. V. 53
Omnium Gatherum. London: 1830?. V. 53

HEATH, JOHN BENJAMIN
Some Account of the Worshipful Company of Grocers of the City of London. London: 1854. V. 50
Some Account of the Worshipful Company of Grocers of the City of London. London: 1869. V. 47

HEATH, LABAN
Heath's Greatly Improved and Enlarged Infallible Government Counterfeit Deetector... Boston & Washington: 1866. V. 47; 50
Infallible Counterfeit Detector. Boston: 1864. V. 47; 50; 53

HEATH, THOMAS
Aristarachus of Samos, the Ancient Copernicus. Oxford: 1913. V. 48; 49; 54
A History of Greek Mathemtics. Oxford: 1965. V. 54
Mathematics in Aristotle. Oxford: 1949. V. 54

HEATH, W. ROBINSON
Railway Ribaldry. London: 1935. V. 48

HEATH, WILLIAM
Memoirs... Boston: 1798. V. 49
Studies from the Stage, or, the Vicissitudes... London: 1822-23. V. 51
Studies from the Stage, or, the Vicissitudes. London: 1823. V. 51

HEATHCOTE, J. M.
Tennis. London: 1890. V. 54

HEATHCOTE, N.
St. Kilda. London: 1900. V. 51

HEATHCOTE, RALPH
Sylva; or, The Wood; Being a Collection of Anecdotes, Dissertations, Characters, Apophthegms, Original Letters, Bon Mots, and Other Little Things. London: 1786. V. 49; 51; 52

HEATHERINGTON, A.
A Practical Guide for Tourists, Miners and Investors and All Persons Interested in the Development of the Gold Fields of Nova Scotia. Montreal: 1868. V. 47

HEATH'S Book of Beauty. 1840. London: 1839. V. 48

HEAT MOON, WILLIAM LEAST
Blue Highways: a Journey into America. Boston: 1982. V. 53

HEATON, CHARLES, MRS.
Masterpieces of Flemish Art Including Examples of the Early German and Dutch Schools. London: 1869. V. 52

HEATON, JAMES
The Demon; or A Case of Extraordinary Affliction, and Gracious Relief, the Effects of Spiritual Agency... (with) Farther Observations on Demoniac Possession and Animadversions on Some of the Curious Arts of Superstition, &c. London: 1822/22. V. 51

HEAVEN, LOUIS PALMER
A Youth's History of California From the Earliest Period Of Its Discovery to the Present Time. San Francisco: 1867. V. 49

HEAVISIDES, M.
The History of the First Public Railway (Stockton & Darlington) the Opening Day and What Followed. Stockton-on-Tees: 1912. V. 49

HEAVYSEGE, CHARLES
The Advocate: a Novel. Montreal: 1865. V. 51

HEAWOOD, EDWARD
Watermarks Mainly of the 17th and 18th Centuries. Hilversum: 1950. V. 48

HEBARD, GRACE RAYMOND
The Bozeman Trail... Cleveland: 1922. V. 53
The Bozeman Trail... Glendale: 1922. V. 49
The Bozeman Trail... Cleveland: 1960. V. 50
The Bozeman Trail. Glendale: 1960. V. 53
The Pathbreakers from River to Ocean: the Story of the Great West From the Time of Coronado to the Present. Glendale: 1932. V. 51
The Pathbreakers from River to Ocean; The Story of the Great West from the Time of Coronado to the Present. Glendale: 1940. V. 50
Sacajawea. Glendale: 1957. V. 48
Sacajawea... Glendale: 1967. V. 53
Washakie. An Account of Indian Resistance of the Covered Wagon and Union Pacific Railroad Invasions of Their Territory. Cleveland: 1930. V. 50; 54

HEBBEL, FRIEDRICH
Die Nibelungen. Mit 44 Original-Radierungen Von Alois Kolb. Leipzig: 1924. V. 47

HEBER, AMELIA
The Life of Reginal Heber...By His Widow. London: 1830. V. 48; 49

HEBER, REGINALD
A Ballad. Chester: 1830?:. V. 50
The Life of the Right Rev. Jeremy Taylor, D. D. London: 1824. V. 52
Narrative of a Journey through the Upper Provinces of India... London: 1828. V. 47; 48; 50; 51; 53; 54
Narrative of a Journey through the Upper Provinces of India... Philadelphia: 1828. V. 50
Narrative of a Journey through the Upper Provinces of India... London: 1892. V. 52
Palestine. London: 1809. V. 54
Poems and Translations. London: 1812. V. 50

HEBER, RICHARD
Bibliotheca Heberiana. London: 1834-37. V. 52

HEBERDEN, WILLIAM
Commentaries On the History and Cure of Diseases. London: 1806. V. 48; 50
Commentaries on the History and Cure of Diseases. London: 1816. V. 53
Commentaries on the History and Cure of Diseases. Boston: 1818. V. 53
An Introduction to the Study Physic. New York: 1929. V. 48; 50; 53

HEBER PERCY, ALGERNON
Moab, Ammon and Gilead. London: 1896. V. 54

HEBER-PERCY, ALGERNON
Moab, Ammon and Gilead. Market Drayton: 1896. V. 53

HEBERT, LUKE
The Engineer's and Mechanic's Encyclopaedia... London: 1849-36. V. 48

HEBERT, R. L.
Barbizon Revisited; Essay and Catalogue. San Francisco: 1963. V. 51

HEBERT, THOMAS
Some Years Travels into Divers Parts of Africa, and Asia the Great. London: 1677. V. 52

HEBERT J. A.
Schools of Illumination, Reproductions from Manuscripts in the British Museum. London: 1914-26. V. 48

HEBRAND, JACQUES
Recherches sur la Theorie de la Demonstration. Warsaw: 1930. V. 47

HECHT, ANTHONY
Aesopic. Northampton: 1967. V. 48; 54
A Love for Four Voices: Homage to Franz Joseph Haydn. 1983. V. 50
Presumptions of Death. Northampton: 1995. V. 54
The Seven Deadly Sins. Northampton: 1958. V. 49; 54
A Summoning of Stones. New York: 1954. V. 49
The Venetian Vespers. Boston: 1979. V. 48; 49; 51; 53; 54

HECHT, BEN
1001 Afternoons in New York. New York: 1941. V. 51
Actor's Blood. New York: 1936. V. 47
The Bewitched Tailor. New York: 1941. V. 50
A Book of Miracles. New York: 1939. V. 47
Christmas Eve: a Morality Play. New York: 1928. V. 54
Cutie. A Warm Mamma. Chicago: 1924. V. 50
Fantazius Mallare. 1922. V. 48; 50; 52
Gargoyles. New York: 1922. V. 49
The Hero of Santa Maria. New York: 1920. V. 48; 51
The Kingdom of Evil. 1924. V. 48
The Kingdom of Evil. Chicago: 1924. V. 48; 51; 54
The Sensualists. New York: 1959. V. 54

HECHT, HANS
The Electrophysiology of the Heart. New York: 1957. V. 48

HECHT, JEAN
Bibliographical Handbooks on British History. 1968-87. V. 49

HECKER, J. F. C.
The Epidemics of the Middle Ages. London: 1846. V. 50; 51; 52

HECKER, JOHANN
Motuum Caelestium Ephemerides ab Anno ae. V. MDCLXVI ad MDCLXXX. Ex Observationibus Correctis Nobilissim. Danzig: 1662. V. 47

HECKETHORN, CHARLES WILLIAM
The Secret Societies of All Ages and Countries. London: 1875. V. 52
The Secret Societies of All Ages and Countries... London: 1897. V. 50; 53

HECKEWELDER, J.
History, Manners and Customs of the Indian Nations Who Once Inhabited Pennsylvania and the Neighbouring States. Philadelphia: 1876. V. 54

HECKMAN, MARLIN L.
Overland on the California Trail, 1846-1859. Glendale: 1984. V. 53

HECKSCHER, WILLIAM S.
Rembrandt's Anatomy of Dr. Nicolaas Tulp: an Iconological Study. New York: 1958. V. 51

HECTOR, JAMES
Notice of the Indians Seen by the Exploring Expediton Under the Command of Captain Palliser. London: 1861. V. 54

HEDEVIND, BERTIL
The Dialect of Dentdale in the West Riding of Yorkshire. Uppsala: 1967. V. 47

HEDGE, JOHN
Trout Fishing. Sydney: 1968. V. 48

HEDGE, LEVI
Elements of Logick; or a Summary of the General Principles and Different Modes of Reasoning. Cambridge: 1816. V. 50

HEDGECOE, JOHN
Henry Moore. New York: 1968. V. 47; 48; 50; 51; 52; 53; 54

HEDGES, ISAAC A.
Sugar Canes and Their Products Culture and Manufacture... St. Louis: 1879. V. 52

HEDGES, PHINEHAS
Strictures on the Elementa Medicinae of Doctor Brown. Goshen: 1795. V. 47
Strictures on the Elementa Medicinae of Doctor Brown. New York: 1795. V. 49

HEDGPETH, DON
New Western Images, the Hillin Collection of the Cowboy Artists of America. Flagstaff: 1978. V. 47

HEDGPETH, J. W.
Treatise of Marine Ecology and Paleoecology. 1957. V. 52
Treatise of Marine Ecology and Paleoecology. London: 1957. V. 48

HEDIARD, GERAIN
Fantin-Latour Catalogue de l'Oeuvre Lithographieque de Maitre. Paris: 1906. V. 49

HEDIN, SVEN
Adventures in Tibet. London: 1904. V. 52; 54
Big Horse's Flight. London: 1936. V. 48
Central Asia and Tibet. London: 1903. V. 50; 51; 52; 53; 54
A Conquest of Tibet. New York: 1934. V. 52
A Conquest of Tibet. London: 1935. V. 48
From Pole to Pole. London: 1912. V. 53
Overland to India. London: 1910. V. 50
The Silk Road. London: 1938. V. 48
Southern Tibet. Discoveries in Former Times Compared with My Own Reaserches in 1906-1908. 1917-22. V. 47
Through Asia. New York: 1899. V. 48
Trans-Himalaya, Discoveries and Adventures in Tibet. 1909. V. 54
Trans-Himalaya: Discoveries and Adventures in Tibet. London: 1909. V. 50
Trans-Himalaya. Discoveries and Adventures in Tibet. New York: 1909. V. 49
Trans-Himalaya. Discoveries and Adventures in Tibet. New York: 1909-13. V. 52
The Wandering Lake. New York: 1940. V. 50; 54

HEDIN, THOMAS
The Sculpture of Gaspard and Balthazard Marsy. Columbia: 1983. V. 49; 52; 54

HEDINGER, J. M.
A Short Description of Castleton... 1820. V. 47
A Short Description of Castleton... 1822. V. 47

HEDLEY, JAMES
Canada and Her Commerce and the Official History of the Dominion Commercial Travellers' association. Montreal: 1894. V. 50

HEDLEY, W. S.
Therapeutic Electricity and Practical Muscle Testing. London: 1899. V. 47

HEDRICK, ULYSSES P.
The Cherries of New York. Albany: 1915. V. 50; 51
The Grapes of New York. Albany: 1908. V. 48; 50; 51
The Peaches of New York. Albany: 1917. V. 50; 51; 52; 54
The Pears of New York. Albany: 1921. V. 53
The Plums of New York. Albany: 1911. V. 50; 52; 54
The Vegetables of New York. Albany: 1928-31-34-37. V. 50; 52; 54

HEDWIG, JOHANN
Fundamentum Historiae Naturalis Muscorum Frondosorum Concernens Eorum Flores, Fructus, Seminalem Propagationem... Leipzig: 1782. V. 47
Species Muscorum Frondosorum... (with) Supplementum Primum. Leipzig: 1801-16. V. 50
Theoria Genrationis et Fructificationis Plantarum Cryptogamicarum. Petropoli: 1784. V. 50; 52

HEEDLESS Harry. London: 1850. V. 49

HEELY, JOSEPH
A Description of Hagley, Envil and the Leasowes, Wherein All the Latin Inscriptions are Translated, and every Particular Beauty Described. Birmingham: 1775. V. 47

HEERE, H.
The Genera of the Mesembryanthemaceae. Cape Town: 1971. V. 50

HEEREN, ARNOLD H. L.
Historical Researches into the Politics, Intercourse and Trade of the Principal Nations of Antiquity; Asiatic Nations. Oxford: 1833. V. 48; 51; 53
Reflections of the Politics of Ancient Greece. Boston: 1824. V. 51

HEFELE, CHARLES JOSEPH
A History of the Christian Councils, from the Original Documents to the Close of the Council of Nicea, A.D. 325...(later volumes to the Close of the Second Council of Nicea, A.D. 787). Edinburgh: 1871-6-83-95-6. V. 52

HEFFERNAN, MICHAEL
Father Tom and the Pope; or, a Night at the Vatican. Philadelphia: 1861. V. 53

HEFFRON, RODERICK
Pneumonia With Special Reference to Pneumococcus Lobar Pneumonia. New York: 1939. V. 53

HEFNER, HUGH
That Toddlin' Town. Chicago: 1951. V. 50

HEFNER-ALTENECK, I. H. DE
Serrurie ou les Ouvrages en fer Force du Moyen-Age et de la Renaissance... Paris: 1870. V. 54

HEG, HANS CHRISTIAN
The Civil War Letters of Colonel Hans Christian Heg. Northfield: 1936. V. 49

HEGAN, ALICE CALDWELL
Mrs. Wiggs of the Cabbage patch. New York: 1901. V. 53

HEGEMANN, WERNER
City Planning Housing. Volume III: a Graphic Review of City Art 1922-37. New York: 1938. V. 53
Report On a City Plan for the Municipalities of Oakland and Berkeley. Berkeley: 1915. V. 50; 51

HEGESIPPUS
De Rebus a Judaeorum Principibus...Excidio Hierosolymorum. Cologne: 1525. V. 51

HEGETSCHWEILER, JOHANN
Sammlung von Schweizer Pflanzen, nach der Natur und auf Stein Gezeichnet von J.D. Labram. Zurich: 1826-34. V. 47

HEGGEN, THOMAS
Mister Roberts. New York: 1948. V. 53

HEGI, G.
Illustrierte Flora von Mitteleuropa... Munich: 1908-31. V. 51

HEHN, VICTOR
The Wanderings Of Plants and Animals from their First Home. London: 1885. V. 50; 52; 53

HEIBERG, NEILS
White-Ear and Peter. London: 1912. V. 49

HEIDEGGER, MARTIN
Sein und Zeit. Halle: 1927. V. 51
Zur Sache des Denkens. Tubingen: 1969. V. 52

HEIDEN, JAN VAN DER
Beschryving der Nieuwlyks Uitgevonden en Geoctrojeerde Slang-Brand-Spuiten... Amsterdam: 1735. V. 49

HEILNER, VAN CAMPEN
Duck Shooting. London: 1951. V. 49
Our American Game Birds. New York: 1941. V. 50; 51
Salt Water Fishing. New York: 1953. V. 54

HEILPRIN, ANGELO
Mont Pelee and the Tragedy of Martinique. Philadelphia and London: 1903. V. 54

HEINE, HEINRICH
Atta Troll. New York: 1914. V. 50
Florentine Nights. London: 1927. V. 54
Poems. New York: 1957. V. 52; 54
The Prose and Poetical Works. New York: 1920. V. 51
Der Rabbi von Bacherach. Berlin: 1921. V. 47
Der Rabbi von Bacherach. Berlin: 1923. V. 50; 53

HEINECKEN, ROBERT
Heinecken. Carmel: 1980. V. 47

HEINELEIN, ROBERT
Job. New York: 1984. V. 49

HEINEMANN, LARRY
Close Quarters. New York: 1977. V. 48; 50; 51; 52
Paco's Story. New York: 1986. V. 53

HEINEMANN, WILLIAM
The Hardships of Publishing. 1893. V. 50

HEINLEIN, ROBERT ANSON
Assignment in Eternity. 1953. V. 47; 49; 50; 51; 53; 54
Assignment in Eternity... Reading: 1953. V. 52
Between Planets. New York: 1951. V. 47; 49
Beyond the Horizon. 1948. V. 47; 49; 51; 54
Beyond This Horizon. Reading: 1948. V. 48; 51
The Cat Who Walks through Walls. 1985. V. 51
The Cat Who Walks Through Walls. New York: 1985. V. 47; 50; 52
Citizen of the Galaxy. New York: 1957. V. 47; 48; 49; 51
The Discovery of the Future. 1941. V. 47; 51; 53
Double Star. Garden City: 1956. V. 52
Double Star. New York: 1956. V. 48; 50; 51; 52; 53
Double Star. 1958. V. 48; 49
Double Star. London: 1958. V. 52; 53; 54
Farmer in the Sky. New York: 1950. V. 51
Farnham's Freehold. 1964. V. 49; 51; 54
Farnham's Freehold. New York: 1964. V. 47; 51
Friday. 1982. V. 47; 51; 52
Friday. New York: 1982. V. 50
Glory Road. 1963. V. 49
The Green Hills of Earth. 1951. V. 48; 52
The Green Hills of Earth. Chicago: 1951. V. 47; 49; 51; 53
Green Hills of Earth. London: 1954. V. 48; 53
Have Space Suit - Will Travel. New York: 1958. V. 52
I Will Fear No Evil. New York: 1970. V. 50
I Will Fear No Evil. 1971. V. 49; 54
Job: a Comedy of Justice. New York: 1984. V. 50; 53
The Man Who Sold the Moon. 1950. V. 47; 48; 49; 51; 52
The Man Who Sold the Moon. Chicago: 1950. V. 48; 51; 53
The Man Who Sold the Moon. 1952. V. 52
The Menace from Earth. 1959. V. 51
The Menace from Earth. 1966. V. 48; 52
Methuselah's Children. 1958. V. 48; 51; 52
The Moon is a Harsh Mistress. 1967. V. 51
The Moon is a Harsh Mistress. London: 1967. V. 53
The Number of the Beast. 1980. V. 51
Orphans of the Sky. London: 1963. V. 47; 49; 51; 52; 54
Orphans of the Sky. 1964. V. 52
Orphans of the Sky. New York: 1964. V. 47; 48
The Past Through Tomorrow. London: 1967. V. 48
The Past Through Tomorrow. New York: 1967. V. 49
Podkayne of Mars: Her Life and Times. New York: 1963. V. 50; 51; 53
The Puppet Masters. New York: 1951. V. 49
The Puppet Masters. 1953. V. 47; 51
Red Planet. London: 1963. V. 48
Rocket Ship Galileo. New York: 1947. V. 48; 51; 51
The Rolling Stones. New York: 1952. V. 51
Sixth Column. 1949. V. 52
Sixth Column. New York: 1949. V. 52
Space Cadet. New York: 1948. V. 51; 53
The Star Beast. New York: 1954. V. 47; 48; 52
Starman Jones. New York: 1953. V. 47; 48; 52
Starship Troopers. 1959. V. 50; 52; 53
Starship Troopers. New York: 1959. V. 48
Stranger in a Strange Land. 1961. V. 54
Stranger in a Strange Land. New York: 1961. V. 47; 51; 52; 54
Stranger in a Strange Land. 1975. V. 48; 50; 52
Time Enough for Love. 1973. V. 49; 52; 53; 54
Time Enough for Love. New York: 1973. V. 50; 51
Time for the Stars. New York: 1956. V. 47
Tunnel in the Sky. New York: 1955. V. 48; 52
Universe. New York: 1951. V. 54
The Unpleasant Profession of Jonathan Hoag. Hicksville: 1959. V. 49
Waldo & Magic, Inc. Garden City: 1950. V. 48; 54
Waldo & Magic, Inc. New York: 1950. V. 48; 49; 52

HEINROTH, K.
Oiseaux. Paris. V. 51

HEINS, H. H.
A Golden Anniversary Bibliography of Edgar Rice Burroughs. 1964. V. 48

HEINSIUS, DANIEL
D. Heynsii Crepundia Siliana (Being Notes on Silius Italicus De Bello Punico). Cambridge: 1646. V. 53

HEINTZELMAN, ARTHUR WILLIAM
H. de Toulouse-Lautrec. One Hundred and Ten Unpublished Drawings. Boston: 1955. V. 54

HEINZELMANN, FRIEDRICH
Reisebilder Und Skizzen Aus der Pyrenaeischen Halbinsel Nebst Blicken Auf Die Laender des Mejicanischen Golfes und Californien. Leipzig: 1851. V. 47; 54

HEIRS Of Hippocrates. 1990. V. 50

HEIRS of Hippocrates. Iowa: 1990. V. 48; 49; 51; 53
HEIRS of Hippocrates. Iowa City: 1990. V. 47; 50; 51
HEIRS of Hippocrates. Iowa City: 1991. V. 49

HEISTER, LORENZ
Compendium Anatomicum Totam rem Anatomicam... Nuremberg: 1741. V. 50
A Compendium of Anatomy. London: 1752. V. 50
A General System of Surgery, in Three Parts. London: 1768. V. 52; 54
Institutiones Chirurgicae. Amsterdam: 1739. V. 52
Medical, Chirurgical and Anatomical Cases and Observations... London: 1755. V. 51

HEITMAN, FRANCIS B.
Historical Register and Dictionary of the U.S. Army 1789-193. Urbana: 1965. V. 53

HEITON, JOHN
The Castes of Edinburgh:. Edinburgh: 1859. V. 54

HEKETHORN, CHARLES WILLIAM
Lincoln's Inn Fields and the Localities Adjacent: Their Historical and Topographical Associations. London: 1896. V. 50

HELCK, WOLFGANG
Lexikon der Agyptologie. Wiesbaden: 1975-86. V. 51

HELD, G. J.
The Papuas of Waropen. The Hague: 1957. V. 48

HELD, JOHN
The Gods Were Promiscuous. New York: 1937. V. 51

HELD, JULIUS S.
Rembrandt and the Book of Tobit. Northampton: 1964. V. 49
Rembrandt's Aristotle and Other Rembrandt Studies. Princeton: 1969. V. 54
Rubens Selected Drawings. London: 1959. V. 49; 52; 54

HELENA BOARD OF TRADE
Constitution of the Helena Board of Trade of Helena, Montana. Helena: 1890. V. 48

HELICZER, PIERO
The Soap Opera. London: 1967. V. 53

HELIODORUS
Historia Ethiopica. Antwerp: 1554. V. 53

HELLAS.. Boston: 1969. V. 54

HELLE, ANDRE
Big Beasts and Little Beasts. New York: 1924. V. 50

HELLER, ELINOR RASS
Bibliography of the Grabhorn Press, 1915-1940. San Francisco: 1940. V. 48
Bibliography of the Grabhorn Press 1915-1956. San Francisco: 1975. V. 48; 51

HELLER, HELEN WEST
Migratory Urge: Wood-Cut Poems. Chicago: 1928. V. 47

HELLER, JOSEPH
Catch-22. New York: 1961. V. 47; 48; 49; 50; 51; 52; 53; 54
Catch-22. London: 1962. V. 47; 48; 52
Catch-22. New York: 1973. V. 47; 52
Catch-22. 1978. V. 49
Catch-22. Franklin Center: 1978. V. 50
Closing Time. Franklin Center: 1994. V. 53
God Knows. New York: 1984. V. 48; 49; 51; 52; 54
Good as Gold. New York: 1979. V. 54
Picture This. New York: 1988. V. 51
Something Happened. New York: 1974. V. 47; 48; 49; 51; 53
We Bombed in New Haven. New York: 1968. V. 49

HELLER, JULES
Papermaking: The White Art. Scottsdale: 1980. V. 47

HELLER, MICHAEL
Figures of Speaking. Mt. Horeb: 1977. V. 49
Two Poems. Mt. Horeb: 1970. V. 51

HELLEU, PAUL CESAR
A Gallery of Portraits. London: 1907. V. 51

HELLINGA, WYTZE
Copy and Print in the Netherlands. An Atlas of Historical Bibliography. Amsterdam: 1962. V. 52

HELLINGA, WYTZE & LOTTE
The Fifteenth Century Types of the Low Countries. Amsterdam: 1966. V. 48

HELLMAN, C. DORIS
The Comet of 1577; Its Place in the History of Astronomy. New York: 1944. V. 54

HELLMAN, LILLIAN
The Autumn Garden. Boston: 1951. V. 51; 54
The Children's Hour. New York: 1934. V. 47; 48; 51
Days to Come. New York: 1936. V. 47; 51; 54
The Little Foxes. New York: 1939. V. 47
The North Star. New York: 1943. V. 49
Pentimento. Boston: 1973. V. 51
Soundrel Time. Boston: 1976. V. 53
Three. Boston: 1979. V. 53
Toys in the Attic. New York: 1960. V. 49; 53
Una Donna Segreta. Rome: 1982. V. 47
Watch on the Rhine. 1942. V. 47
Watch on the Rhine. London: 1942. V. 52
Watch on the Rhine. New York: 1942. V. 48

HELLMANN, ELLEN
Problems of Urban Bantu Youth. Johannesburg: 1940. V. 54

HELLMUTH, N. M.
Surface of the Underwaterworld. Culver City: 1987. V. 54

HELLOT, M.
L'Art De la Teinture des Laines et des Etoffes de Laine, en Gran et Petit Teint. Paris: 1750. V. 50

HELLSTROM, PONTUS
Rock Drawings. Including the Results of the Gordon Memorial College Expedition to Abka Under the Direction of Oliver Myers. Denmark: 1970. V. 49

HELLWIG, CHRISTOPH VON
Der Curieuse und Vernunfftige Zauber-Artzt Welcher Lehret und Zeiget, Wie Man Nicht Alleine ex Triplici Regno Curieuse Artzeneyen Verfertigen, Sondern Auch per Sympathiam et Antipathiam, Transplantationem, Amuleta et Magiam Naturalem... Franckfurt und Leipzig: 1725. V. 47; 51; 52

HELLYER, SAMUEL STEVENS
The Plumber and Sanitary Houses. London: 1877. V. 50; 53

HELM, F.
Between the Two Forces. 1894. V. 51

HELM, H. T.
American Roadsters and Trotting Horses. Chicago: 1878. V. 51; 54

HELM, KATHERINE
The True Story of Mary, Wife of Lincoln... New York: 1928. V. 54

HELM, MACKINLEY
Angel Mo and Her Son, Roland Hayes. Boston: 1942. V. 53

HELM, MARY
Scraps of Early Texas History. Austin: 1884. V. 53

HELM, THOMAS B.
History of Delaware County, Indiana... Chicago: 1881. V. 50

HELME, ELIZABETH
Instructive Rambles in London and the Adjacent Villages. London: 1812. V. 50
Louisa or the Cottage on the Moor. Paris: 1807. V. 50

HELMHOLTZ, HERMANN L. F. VON
On the Sensations of Tone as a Physiological Basis for The Theory of Music. London: 1885. V. 47
On the Sensations of Tone as a Physiological Basis for the Theory of Music. London: 1912. V. 53
On the Sensations of Tone as a Physiological Basis for the Theory of Music. London: 1930. V. 53
Treatise on Physiological Optics. 1924. V. 53
Treatise on Physiological Optics. Menasha: 1924. V. 49
Treatise on Physiological Optics. New York: 1924. V. 53
Treatise on Physiological Optics. New York: 1962. V. 49

HELMONT, FRANCISCUS MERCURIUS VAN
Alphabeti Vere Naturalis Hebraici Brevissima Delineatio. Sulzbaci: 1667. V. 48

HELMONT, JOHANNES BAPTISTA VAN
Opera Omnia. Frankfurt: 1682. V. 53
Ortus medicinae. Id est, Initia Physicae in Audita. Progressus Medicinae Novus, In Morborum Ultionem, ad Vitam Longam. Amsterdam: 1652. V. 49; 50
Ortus Medicinae. (with) Opuscula Medica Inaudita. Amsterdam: 1648. V. 47; 53

HELMS, ANTHONY ZACHARIAH
Travels from Buenos Ayres, by Potosi, to Lima. London: 1807. V. 47; 49; 51; 54

HELMUTH, J. HENRY C.
A Short Account of the Yellow Fever in Philadelphia for the Reflecting Christian. Philadelphia: 1794. V. 54

A HELP to Elocution. Containing Three Essays. 1. On Reading and Declamation...II. On the Marks and Characters of the Different Passions...III. On Composition... London: 1780. V. 52

HELPER, HINTON BROWN
The Three Americas Railway. An International and Intercontinental Enterprise... St. Louis: 1881. V. 47

HELPER, HINTON ROWAN
The Impending Crisis of the South: How to Meet It. New York: 1857. V. 50
Land of Gold. Reality Versus Fiction. Baltimore: 1855. V. 47; 49

HELPRIN, MARK
A Dove of the East. New York: 1975. V. 47; 49; 50; 51; 52; 53
Ellis Island and Other Stories. New York: 1981. V. 48
A Soldier of the Great War. New York: 1991. V. 52; 54
Winter's Tale. 1983. V. 53

HELPS, ARTHUR
Casimir Maremma. London: 1870. V. 52; 54
The Claims of Labour. London: 1844. V. 50; 54
Companions of My Solitude. London: 1851. V. 51
The Conquerors of the New World and Their Bondsmen: Being a Narrative of the Principal Events Which Led to Negro Slavery in the West Indies and America. London: 1848-52. V. 54
Life and Labours of Mr. Brassey 1805-1870. London: 1872. V. 52
The Life of Las Casas: "The Apostle of the Indies". London: 1868. V. 48
Oulita the Serf. London: 1858. V. 48; 51; 54
The Spanish Conquest in America and Its Relation to the History of Slavery and to the Government of Colonies. London: 1855-61. V. 47; 49
Thoughts Upon Government. London: 1872. V. 52

HELSHAM, R.
A Course of Lectures in Natural Philosophy. London: 1743. V. 47; 48; 50

HELVELIUS, JAN
The Star Atlas. Tashkent: 1978. V. 50

HELVETIUS, CLAUDE ADRIEN
De L'Esprit. Paris: 1758. V. 49; 53
De L'Esprit... London: 1759. V. 50; 54
Oeuvres Completes. London: 1777. V. 51

HELVETIUS, JOHANN FRIEDRICH
Microscopium Physiognomiae Medicum. Amstelodami: 1676. V. 49

HELVICUS, CHRISTOPHORUS
Theatrum Historicum et Chronologicum... Oxford: 1662. V. 49

HELWICH, CHRISTOPHER
Theatrum Historicum Chronologicum... Francofurti: 1666. V. 51

HELY-HUTCHINSON, JOHN
The Commercial Restraints of Ireland Considered. Dublin: 1779. V. 49; 52

HEMANS, FELICIA DOROTHEA BROWNE
Domestic Affections and Other Poems. London: 1812. V. 53
The Forest Sanctuary and Other Poems. London: 1725. V. 50
The Forest Sanctuary and other Poems. London: 1825. V. 47; 49
Hymns On the Works of Mature, for the Use of Children. Boston: 1827. V. 49
The Legend of the Alps, the Siege of Valencia, The Vespers of Palermo and Other Poems. Boston: 1826. V. 49; 50
Poems. Liverpool: 1808. V. 50
The Poetical Works. Edinburgh: 1853. V. 50
Records of Woman; with Other Poems. Edinburgh: 1828. V. 54
The Sceptic: a Poem. London: 1820. V. 50
The Works. Edinburgh: 1839. V. 50; 52; 54
The Works... Edinburgh and London: 1841-46. V. 54
The Works of...With a Memoir by His Sister (H. Hughes).... 1842. V. 47

HEMENWAY, ABBY MARIA
Vermont Historical Gazetteer: a Magazine Embracing a History of Each Town, Civil, Ecclesiastical, Biographical and Military. Burlington: 1867/71/77/82. V. 50

HEMINGWAY, ERNEST MILLAR
88 Poems. New York: 1979. V. 49
Across the River and Into the Trees. London: 1950. V. 47; 49; 50; 53
Across the River and Into the Trees. New York: 1950. V. 49; 50; 51; 52; 53
L'Adieu aux Armes. (A Farewell to Arms). Paris: 1931. V. 49; 53
Al Receives Another Letter. 1968. V. 50
By-Line: Ernest Hemingway. New York: 1967. V. 53
By-Line: Ernest Hemingway. London: 1968. V. 50
The Complete Short Stories of Ernest Hemingway. New York: 1987. V. 49
The Dangerous Summer. New York: 1985. V. 49; 51
Death in the Afternoon. London: 1932. V. 49; 51
Death in the Afternoon. New York: 1932. V. 47; 48; 49; 50; 52; 53; 54
A Divine Gesture. New York: 1974. V. 49; 52; 53
Ernest Hemingway Selected Letters: 1917-1961. New York: 1981. V. 48; 53
The Faithful Bull. London: 1980. V. 48; 51; 53
A Farewell to Arms. New York: 1926. V. 51
A Farewell to Arms. London: 1929. V. 47
A Farewell to Arms. New York: 1929. V. 47; 48; 50; 51; 52; 53; 54
A Farewell to Arms. New York: 1948. V. 50
Fiesta. (The Sun Also Rises). Manner. (Men Without Women). Berlin: 1928/29. V. 53
The Fifth Column. New York: 1940. V. 48; 49; 53
The Fifth Column and Four Stories of the Spanish Civil War. New York: 1969. V. 48; 53
The Fifth Column and the First 49 Stories. New York: 1938. V. 47; 48; 49; 50; 51; 52; 53; 54
The Fifth Column and the First 49 Stories. London: 1939. V. 49; 50
For Whom the Bell Tolls. New York: 1940. V. 47; 48; 49; 50; 51; 52; 53; 54
For Whom the Bell Tolls. London: 1941. V. 47; 48; 49; 50; 52
For Whom the Bell Tolls. 1942. V. 52
For Whom the Bell Tolls. New York: 1942. V. 49; 54
For Whom the Bell Tolls. Princeton: 1942. V. 51
Gattorno. Havana: 1935. V. 53
God Rest You Merry Gentlemen. New York: 1933. V. 49; 54
Green Hills of Africa. New York & London: 1935. V. 47; 50; 52; 53; 54
Green Hills of Africa. London: 1936. V. 47; 54
Hemingway. New York: 1944. V. 49
High on the Wild With Hemingway. 1969. V. 53
Hokum. Wellesley Hills: 1978. V. 47; 48; 49; 50; 51
In Einem Andern Land. (A Farewell to Arms). Berlin: 1930. V. 51
In Our Time. Paris: 1924. V. 48; 50; 51; 53
In Our Time. New York: 1925. V. 53
In Our Time. London: 1926. V. 49; 50; 53
In Our Time. New York: 1930. V. 49; 50; 51; 52
In Our Time... Bloomfield Hills: 1977. V. 50
Islands in the Stream. New York: 1970. V. 47
Men At War. New York: 1942. V. 51
Men Without Women. New York: 1927. V. 49; 50; 51; 54
Men Without Women. New York: 1928. V. 53
Mort dans l'Apres-Midi. Paris: 1958. V. 47
A Moveable Feast. 1964. V. 53
A Moveable Feast. London: 1964. V. 50; 53
A Moveable Feast. New York: 1964. V. 53
The Nick Adams Stories. New York: 1972. V. 52; 53; 54
The Old Man and the Sea. New York: 1951. V. 50
The Old Man and the Sea. London: 1952. V. 47; 49; 50; 53
The Old Man and the Sea. New York: 1952. V. 47; 49; 50; 51; 53; 54
The Old Man and the Sea. New York: 1960. V. 49
Selected Letters 1917-1961. New York. V. 50
Selected Letters 1917-1961. New York: 1981. V. 48; 54
The Spanish Earth. Cleveland: 1938. V. 48; 50; 51; 53
The Spanish War. London: 1938. V. 49; 51
The Sun Also Rises. New York: 1926. V. 47; 50
The Sun Also Rises. New York: 1929. V. 51
The Sun Also Rises. New York: 1930. V. 54
The Sun Also Rises. Detroit: 1990. V. 47; 48; 51
Three Stories and Ten Poems. Paris: 1923. V. 48; 51; 52; 53; 54
To Have and Have Not. New York: 1937. V. 47; 48; 49; 50; 52; 53
To Have and Have Not. New York: 1939. V. 53
Today is Friday. Englewood: 1926. V. 47
Today Is Friday. Englewood: 1962. V. 52
The Torrents of Spring. New York: 1926. V. 51
The Torrents of Spring. New York: 1926. V. 48; 50; 51; 53; 54
The Torrents of Spring. 1931. V. 50
The Torrents of Spring. London: 1932. V. 53
The Torrents of Spring. Paris: 1932. V. 49; 52; 54
The Torrents of Spring. London: 1933. V. 47; 50; 53
Winner Take Nothing. New York: 1932. V. 51
Winner Take Nothing. New York & London: 1933. V. 47; 48; 49; 50; 51; 53; 54
Winner Take Nothing. London: 1934. V. 49; 53
(Yiddish Title): The Old Man and the Sea. London, New York: 1958. V. 52

HEMINGWAY, G. H.
Heritage...for My Children. 1974. V. 53

HEMINGWAY, J.
History of the City of Chester, from Its Foundation to the Present Time... Chester: 1831. V. 48; 53

HEMINGWAY, PERCY
The Happy Wanderer. Chicago: 1896. V. 49

HEMMERLIN, FELIX
Opuscula et Tractatis. Strassburg: 1497. V. 47

HEMMETER, JOHN
Diseases of the Stomach. Philadelphia: 1898. V. 48; 53

HEMPEL, CHARLES
Complete Repertory of the Homoeopathic Materia Medica. New York: 1853. V. 48; 53

THE HEMPFIELD Rail Road and the Bonds of Ohio County, Virginia, and Washington County, Pennsylvania. Philadelphia: 1852. V. 54

HENAULT, CHARLES JEAN FRANCOIS
Nouvel Abrege Chronologique de l'Histoire de France. Paris: 1768. V. 48; 53

HENCKEL, C.
Nautical and Commercial Pocket Dictionary and Dialogue Book for Navigators, Merchants and Travellers, in Eight Languages. Aberdeen: 1840. V. 50

HENCKEN, HUGH
Tarquinia, Villanovans and Early Etruscans. Cambridge: 1968. V. 50

HENDERSON, ANDREW
The Practical Grazier, or, a Treatise on the Proper Selection and Management of Live-Stock... Edinburgh: 1826. V. 54
Scottish Proverbs Collected and Arranged. Edinburgh: 1832. V. 48; 51

HENDERSON, ARCHIBALD
Mark Twain. New York. V. 51
Mark Twain. New York: 1911. V. 47; 48; 53
Old Homes and Gardens of North Carolina. Chapel Hill: 1939. V. 52

HENDERSON, DAVID
De Mayor of Harlem. New York: 1970. V. 52
Felix of the Silent Forest. New York: 1967. V. 52

HENDERSON, E. PRIOLEAU
Autobiography of Arab. Columbia: 1901. V. 49

HENDERSON, EBENEZER
Iceland, or the Journal of a Residence in that Island, During the 1814 and 1815. Edinburgh: 1818. V. 47
Iceland, or the Journal of a Residence in that Island, During the Years 1814 and 1815. Edinburgh: 1819. V. 49; 52; 53
Life of James Ferguson, the Astronomer, in a Brief Autobiographical Account and Further Extended memoir... Edinburgh: 1867. V. 51

HENDERSON, ELLIOTT BLAINE
The Soliloquy of Satan and Other Poems. Springfield: 1907. V. 52; 54

HENDERSON, GEORGE
Lahore to Yarkand. London: 1873. V. 49; 50; 51; 52; 54

HENDERSON, GEORGE F. R.
Stonewall Jackson and the American Civil War. London & New York: 1898. V. 49

HENDERSON, GEORGE F.R.
Stonewall Jackson and the American Civil War. London: 1905. V. 48

HENDERSON, GEORGE WYLIE
Jule. New York: 1946. V. 52
Ollie Miss. New York: 1935. V. 52; 53; 54

HENDERSON, HAMISH
Ballads of World War Two. Glasgow. V. 47
Elegies for the Dead in Cyrenaica. London: 1948. V. 48

HENDERSON, HAROLD G.
The Surviving Works of Sharaku. New York: 1939. V. 47; 51; 54

HENDERSON, JAMES
A History of Brazil, Comprising Its Geography, Commerce, Colonization, Aboriginal Inhabitants, &c, &c, &c. London: 1821. V. 47; 53

HENDERSON, JAMES D.
Lilliputian Newspapers. Worcester: 1936. V. 49

HENDERSON, JOHN
Letters and Poems, by the Late... London: 1786. V. 47; 50; 51; 54
The West Indies. London: 1905. V. 49; 50

HENDERSON, M.
Malayan Orchid Hybrids. Singapore: 1956. V. 51

HENDERSON, PAUL C.
Landmarks On the Oregon Trail. New York: 1953. V. 48; 52

HENDERSON, ROBERT
The Arraignment of the Whole Creature at the Barre of Religion, Reason and Experience... London: 1631. V. 53
A Treatise on the Breeding of Swine, and Curing of Bacon; with Hints on Agricultural Subjects. Leith: 1811. V. 47

HENDERSON, ROBERT W.
Early American Sport. New York: 1937. V. 47

HENDERSON, WILLIAM
Homoeopathy Fairly Represented. Philadelphia: 1854. V. 52

HENDERSON, WILLIAM continued
Letter to John Forbes, M.D...on His Article Entitled "Homoeopathy, Allopathy and Young Physic". New York: 1846. V. 51
My Life as an Angler. London: 1879. V. 52
Notes and Reminiscences of My Life as an Angler. London: 1876. V. 47; 54

HENDERSON, WILLIAM AUGUSTUS
The Housekeeper's Instructor. London. V. 49
The Housekeeper's Instructor... London: 1790. V. 47
The Housekeeper's Instructor... London: 1790-91. V. 51
The Housekeeper's Instructor... London: 1800. V. 47
The Housekeeper's Instructor... London: 1803. V. 47
The Housekeeper's Instructor... London: 1850. V. 52

HENDERSON, YANDELL
Adventures in Respiration: Modes of Asphyxiation and Methods of Resuscitation. Baltimore: 1938. V. 53

HENDERSON, ZENNA
Pilgrimage: The Book of the People. Garden City: 1961. V. 49

HENDERSON'S Prince Rupert City Directory, 1911-12... Vancouver: 1911. V. 48

HENDLEY, T. H.
Memorials of the Jeypore Exhibition 1883. London: 1884. V. 48

HENDRICK, A. F.
Hand-Woven Carpets, Oriental and European. London: 1922. V. 47

HENDRICK, BURTON J.
The Life of Andrew Carnegie. Garden City: 1932. V. 47

HENDRICKS, GORDON
Albert Bierstadt: Painter of the American West. New York: 1973. V. 53
The Life and Work of Thomas Eakins. New York: 1974. V. 47; 49; 51
The Life and Work of Winslow Homer. New York: 1979. V. 49; 53
The Photographs of Thomas Eakins. New York: 1972. V. 47

HENDRICKS, ROSE ELLEN
Chit Chat. London: 1849. V. 50

HENDRICKS, W. C.
Bundle of Troubles and Other Tarheel Tales, by Workers of the Writers' Program of the Work Projects Administration in the State of North Carolina. Durham: 1943. V. 51
Governmental Roster, 1889. State and Country Governments of California. Executive, Judicial and Legislative Departments. Sacramento: 1889. V. 50

HENDRICKSON, JAMES E.
Journals of the Colonial Legislatures of the Colonies of Vancouver Island and British Columbia, 1851-1871. Victoria: 1980. V. 53

HENDRICKSON, JOHN
Trial of...for the Murder of His Wife Maria, by Poisoning, at Bethlehem, Albany County New York, March 6th, 1853... Albany: 1853. V. 50

HENDRIKS, ROSE ELLEN
The Wild Rose. London: 1847. V. 50

HENEGAN, RICHARD D.
Seven Years' Campaigning in the Peninsula. London: 1848. V. 50

HENIG, MARTIN
A Corpus of Roman Engraved Gemstones from British Sites. Oxford: 1978. V. 49

HENING, WILLIAM WALLER
The New Virginia Justice, Comprising the Office and Authority of a Justice of the Peace, in the Commonwealth of Virginia. Richmond: 1795. V. 49

HENKEL, FRIEDRICH
Die Romischen Fingerringe der Rheinlande und der Benachbarten Gebiete. Berlin: 1913. V. 50

HENLEY. A Poem. London: 1827. V. 48

HENLEY, BETH
The Debutante Ball. Jackson: 1991. V. 48; 50; 54

HENLEY, C. D.
A Man from Mars. 1891. V. 51

HENLEY, JOHN
The Primitive Liturgy: for the Use of the Oratory. Part I. London: 1726. V. 50

HENLEY, WILLIAM ERNEST
A Book of Verses. London: 1888. V. 47; 51; 54
Collected Works. London: 1908. V. 47; 51
Hawthorn and Lavender. New York & London: 1901. V. 47
A London Garland. London & New York: 1895. V. 54
London Types. London: 1888. V. 47
Poems. London: 1913. V. 54
Views and Reviews: Essays in Appreciation. London: 1890. V. 54

HENNEBERG, ALFRED, FREIHERR VON
The Art and Craft of Old Lace. New York: 1931. V. 51

HENNELL, MARY
An Outline of the Various Social Sytems and Communities Which Have Been Founded on the Principle of Co-operation. London: 1844. V. 53

HENNELL, THOMAS
Poems. 1936. V. 52
Six Poems. 1947. V. 49
Six Poems. Tunbridge Wells: 1947. V. 52

HENNEN, JOHN
Observations on Some Important Points in the Practice of Military Surgery... Edinburgh: 1818. V. 50; 54

HENNEPIN, LOUIS
Description de la Louisiane, Nouvellement Decouverte au Sud Ouest de la Nouvelle France... Paris: 1683. V. 48
A New Discovery of a Vast Country in America. Chicago: 1903. V. 53
Nouvelle Decouverte d'un Tres Grand Pays Situe dans l'Amerique, entre Le Nouveau Mexique, et La Mer Glaciale, Avec les Carates & Les Figures Necessaires... Utrecht: 1697. V. 53

HENNES, ALOYS
Therese Hennes and Her Musical Education... London: 1877. V. 49

HENNESSEY, ESME F.
The Slipper Orchids. V. 50

HENNESSY, J. B.
Stephania: a Middle and Late Bronze-Age Cemetery in Cyprus. London: 1985. V. 50; 52

HENNESSY, W. B.
History of North Dakota, Embracing a Relation of the History of the State from the Earliest Times Down to the Present Day, Including the Biographies of the Builders of the Commonwealth. Bismarck: 1910. V. 50

HENNI, J. M.
Ein Blick in's Thal des Ohio Oder Briefe Uber den Kampf und das Wiederaufleben der Katholischen Kirch im Fernen Westen der Vereinigten Staaten Nordamerika's. Munich: 1836. V. 48; 50

HENNIKER, FLORENCE
In Scarlet and Grey. Boston: 1896. V. 48; 53

HENNIKER, FREDERICK
Notes During a Visit to Egypt, Nubia, the Oasis Boeris, Mount Sinai and Jerusalem. London: 1824. V. 49

HENNIKER, JOHN
Two Letters on the Origin, Antiquity and History of Norman Tiles, Stained with Armorial Bearings. London: 1794. V. 53

HENNING, FRED
Fights for the Championship. The Men and Their Times. London: 1890. V. 54

HENNING, S. F.
The Charaxinae Butterflies of Africa. Johannesburg: 1989. V. 48; 50; 52

HENNING, WILLIAM W.
Reports of Cases...in the Supreme Court of Appeals of Virginia... Flatbush: 1809. V. 51

HENNINGO, M.
Memoriae Philosophorum, Oratorum, Poetarum, Historicorum... Francofurti: 1677. V. 50

HENNINGSEN, CHARLES FRANCIS
The Last of the Sophis. London: 1831. V. 54

HENOCH, EDWARD
Lectures on Diseases of Children. New York: 1882. V. 50

HENREY, BLANCHE
British Botanical and Horticultural Literature Before 1800... London: 1975. V. 47; 49; 50; 51; 52; 53; 54
British Botanical and Horticultural Literature Before 1800. Oxford: 1975. V. 47

HENREY, MATTHEW
The Communicant's Companion. Boston: 1716. V. 53

HENRI, ADRIAN
Tonight at Noon. London: 1968. V. 54

HENRICUS DE SEGUSIOS
Summa Super Titulis Decretalium. Venice: 1487. V. 51

HENRY, ALEXANDER
Travels and Adventures in Canada and the Indian Territories Between 1760 and 1776. New York: 1809. V. 53
Travels and Adventures in Canada and the Indian Territories between 1760 and 1776. Boston: 1901. V. 49
Travels and Adventures in Canada and the Indian Territories Between 1760 and 1776. Toronto: 1901. V. 53

HENRY, DAVID
An Historical Account of All the Voyages Round the World, Performed by English Navigators... London: 1774/73. V. 52
An Historical Account of All Voyages Round the World, Performed by English Navigators... London: 1774. V. 48

HENRY, E. R.
Classification and Uses of Finger Prints. London: 1900. V. 50

HENRY, FRANCOISE
Irish Art... London: 1940. V. 51
Irish Art... London: 1965-67-70. V. 51
Irish Art... 1965/70. V. 48
Irish Art. London: 1965/70. V. 47
Irish Art... London: 1967. V. 47

HENRY, FREDERICK
Founders' Week Memorial Volume Containing Histories of (Philadelphia's) Principal, Scientific Institutions, Medical Colleges, Hospitals, Etc. Philadelphia: 1909. V. 50; 52

HENRY, G. M.
Coloured Plates of the Birds of Ceylon. Colombo: 1927. V. 53
Coloured Plates of the Birds of Ceylon. Ceylon: 1927-35. V. 48; 50

HENRY, G. W.
Trials and Triumphs (for Half a Century) In the Life of G. W. Henry. New York: 1853. V. 50

HENRY, H. S.
De-Luxe Illustrated Catalogue of Paintings by 'the men of 1830' from the Private Collection of... New York: 1907. V. 47

HENRY, JAMES
An Account of the Proceedings of the Government Metropolitan Police in the City of Canton. Dublin: 1840. V. 49
My Book. Dresden: 1853. V. 52
Poems Chiefly Philosophical, in Continuation of My Book and a Half Year's Poems. Dresden: 1856. V. 52

HENRY, JAMES P.
Resources of the State of Arkansas with Description and the Counties, Railroads, Mines and the City of Little Rock. 1873. V. 52

HENRY, JOHN JOSEPH
An Accurate and Interesting Account of the Hardships and Sufferings of that Band of Heroes, Who Traversed the Wilderness in the Campaign Against Quebec in 1775. Lancaster: 1812. V. 47; 52

HENRY, MATTHEW
The Communicant's Companion; or, Instructions and Helps for Receiving of the Lord's Supper. Boston: 1716. V. 54

HENRY Miller: a Bibliography of Primary Sources. Ann Arbor: 1993. V. 49

HENRY, ROBERT MITCHELL
The History of Sinn Fein. Dublin: 1920. V. 49

HENRY, ROBERT SELPH
The Story of Reconstruction. Indianapolis: 1938. V. 47

HENRY, STUART OLIVER
Conquering Our Great American Plains. A Historical Development. New York: 1930. V. 53; 54

HENRY, THOMAS CHARLTON
Letters to an Anxious Inquirier, Designed to Relieve the Difficulties of a Friend, Under Serious Impressions. Charleston: 1827. V. 48

HENRY, WILL
The Big Pasture. Boston: 1955. V. 53

HENRY, WILLIAM CHARLES
Memoirs of the Life and Scientific Researches of John Dalton. 1854. V. 54
Memoirs of the Life and Scientific Researches of John Dalton. London: 1854. V. 50; 51; 52

HENRY G. W.
Shouting: Genuine and Spurious... Oneida: 1859. V. 50

HENRY III, KING OF FRANCE & POLAND
Code Dv Roy. Lyons: 1594. V. 48

HENRY IV, KING OF FRANCE
Anecdotes of Henry IV of France, Shewing the Great Encouragement He Gave to Literature. London: 1787. V. 53

HENRYSON, ROBERT
Poems and Fables. Edinburgh: 1865. V. 47; 53

HENRY VIII, KING OF GREAT BRITAIN
Assertio Septem Sacramentorum Adversus Martinum Lutherum. 17--?. V. 50; 51
Assertio Septem Sacramentorum Adversus Martinum Lutherum. 176-?. V. 53
Love-Letters from King Henry VIII to Anne Boleyn, some in French and Some in English. London: 1714. V. 49
Miscellaneous Writings... Waltham St. Lawrence: 1924. V. 47
A Necesary Doctrine and Ervdition for any Christen Man, Set Furthe by the Kynges Maiestie of Englande &c. London: 1543. V. 48; 52

HENSHALL, JAMES A.
Bass, Pike, Perch and Others. New York: 1903. V. 47
Book of the Black Bass Comprising Its Complete Scientific and Life History Together with a Practical Treatise on Angling and Fly-Fishing and a Full Description of Tools, Tackle and Implements. Cincinnati: 1889. V. 51; 52

HENSHALL, SAMUEL
Domesday; or, an Actual Survey of South Britain by the Commissioners of William the Conqueror, Completed in the Year 1086. London: 1799. V. 47; 53

HENSHAW, DAVID
Letters on the Internal Improvements and Commerce of the West. Boston: 1839. V. 53

HENSHAW, H. W.
Report Upon the Ornithological Collections Made in Portions of Nevada, Utah, California, Colorado, New Mexico and Arizona. Washington: 1875. V. 50

HENSHAW, J. W.
Mountain Wild Flowers of America, a Simple and Popular Guide to the Names and Descriptions of the Flowers That Bloom Above the Clouds. Boston: 1906. V. 52
Mountain Wild Flowers of Canada. Toronto: 1906. V. 47; 48; 51; 52

HENSHAW, S.
Some Chinese Vertebrates (Arnold Arboretum Expedtion, 1907-08). Cambridge: 1912. V. 49

HENSLOW, J. S.
Report on the Diseases of Wheat, London, 1841: an Address to Landlords on the Advantages...of a Spade Tenantry, Hadleigh and London, 1845; Suggestions Towards an Enquiry Into...the Labouring Population of Suffolk, Hadleigh, etc., (1844).... London: 1841-45. V. 51

HENSLOW, T. G. W.
Ye Sundial Booke. London: 1935. V. 53

HENSMAN, HOWARD
The Afghan War of 1879-80. London: 1881. V. 54

HENSMAN, MARY
Dante Map. London: 1892. V. 51

HENSON, MATTHEW
A Negro Explorer at the North Pole. New York: 1912. V. 53

HEN-TOH, BERTRAM WALKER
Tales of the Bark Lodges. Oklahoma City: 1919. V. 49

HENTY, GEORGE ALFRED
At Agincourt. London: 1897. V. 51
At the Point of the Bayonet. London: 1902. V. 52
Battles of the 19th Century. London: 1896. V. 51
Battles of the 19th Century. London: 1896/1902. V. 52
Beric the Briton. London: 1893. V. 53
Bonnie Prince Charlie. London: 1888. V. 52
Both Sides of the Border. London: 1899. V. 53
The Brahmins' Treasure. Philadelphia: 1900. V. 52
Brains and Bravery. 1903. V. 52
Brains and Bravery. London: 1903. V. 47; 51
Brains and Bravery. New York: 1903. V. 53
The Bravest of the Brave. London: 1887. V. 51; 52; 53
By England's Aid. London: 1891. V. 52
By Pike and Dyke. V. 53
By Pike and Dyke. London: 1890. V. 52
By Right of Conquest. V. 53
By Right of Conquest. London: 1891. V. 51; 52
By Sheer Pluck. London: 1884. V. 52
A Chapter of Adventures. London: 1891. V. 52
Colonel Thorndyke's Secret. London: 1899. V. 52
Condemned as a Nihilist. London: 1893. V. 52
Curse of Carne's Hold. V. 52
Cuthbert Hartington. V. 52
Cuthbert Hartington. London: V. 51; 53
The Dash for Khartoum. London: 1892. V. 51; 53
The Dragon and the Raven. London: 1886. V. 51; 52
Facing Death. London: 1883. V. 52
The Fall of Sebastopol. V. 52
The Fall of Sebastopol. Boston: V. 51
Fighting the Saracens. V. 52
For Name and Fame. London: 1887. V. 52
For Name and Fame. London: 1888. V. 51
For the Temple. London: 1888. V. 51; 52
Friends Though Divided. 1883. V. 51; 52; 53
A Girl of the Commune. New York. V. 53
A Girl of the Commune. 1895. V. 52
Hazard and Heroism. 1904. V. 53
Held Fast for England. London: 1892. V. 52
In Battle and Breeze. London. V. 51
In the Hands of the Cave Dwellers. London: 1900. V. 51
In the Hands of the Cave Dwellers. New York: 1900. V. 52; 53
In the Hands of the Malays. London: 1889. V. 51
In the Hands of the Malays. London: 1905. V. 53
In the Heart of the Rockies. London: 1895. V. 52
In the Irish Brigade. London: 1901. V. 51
In the Reign of Terror. London: 1888. V. 52
Jack Archer. 1884. V. 52
Jack Archer. Boston: 1884. V. 51
A Jacobite Exile: Being the Adventures of a Young Englishman in the Service of Charles XII, of Sweden. London: 1894. V. 54
A Knight of the White Cross. London: 1896. V. 51; 52
The Lion of St. Mark. London: 1889. V. 51; 52
The Lion of the North. London: 1886. V. 52
The Lost Heir. New York. V. 51
Maori and Settler. London: 1891. V. 52
A March in London - Being a Story of Wat Tyler's Insurrection. London: 1898. V. 51; 53
March to Coomassie. 1874. V. 51
March to Coomassie. London: 1874. V. 52
March to Magdala. 1868. V. 51
March to Magdala. London: 1868. V. 48; 52
On the Irrawaddy. London: 1897. V. 52
Orange and Green. London: 1888. V. 51; 52
Out of the Pampas. London: 1871. V. 52

HENTY, GEORGE ALFRED continued
Out with Garibaldi. London: 1901. V. 52
Peril and Prowess. New York. V. 52
The Point of the Bayonet. London: 1902. V. 51
The Queen's Cup. London: 1897. V. 51; 52
The Queen's Cup. New York: 1898. V. 51; 53
Redskin and Cowboy. London: 1892. V. 52
A Roving Commission. London: 1900. V. 48; 52
Rujub the Juggler. London: 1893. V. 51; 52
Rujub the Juggler. London: 1894. V. 51
Rujub the Juggler. London: 1899. V. 52
St. Bartholomew's Eve. London: 1894. V. 52
St. George for England. London: 1885. V. 52
A Search for a Secret, Gall and Inglis. V. 52
Seaside Maidens. London: 1880. V. 51
Steady and Strong. 1905. V. 52
Stirring Adventures Afloat and Ashore. London. V. 51
Stories of Adventure and Heroism. London. V. 51
Stories of History. London. V. 51
Stories of Sea and Land. London. V. 51
Stories of Sea and Land. London: 1891. V. 51
A Tale of Waterloo. V. 51; 52
Those Other Animals. V. 52
Those Other Animals. London: 1891. V. 51
Through the Sikh War. A Tale of the Conquest of the Punjaub. London: 1912. V. 52
The Tiger of Mysore. London: 1896. V. 49; 51; 52; 53
To Herat and Cabul. London: 1902. V. 50; 51
The Treasure of the Incas. London Glasgow & Dublin: 1903. V. 53
True to the Old Flag. London: 1885. V. 52
Two Sieges. V. 52
Under Drake's Flag. London: 1883. V. 52
Under Wellington's Command. London: 1899. V. 51; 52; 53
Venture and Valour. London: 1900. V. 52
With Butler in Natal. London Glasgow & Dublin: 1901. V. 48; 51; 53
With Clive in India. London: 1884. V. 51; 52
With Cochrane the Dauntless. London: 1897. V. 51
With Frederick the Great. London: 1898. V. 52
With Kitchener in the Soudan. London: 1903. V. 50; 51
With Lee in Virginia. London: 1890. V. 52
With Moore at Corunna. London: 1898. V. 51; 52; 53
With Roberts to Pretoria. London: 1902. V. 51
With the British Legion. London: 1903. V. 51
With Wolfe in Canada. London: 1887. V. 52
With Wolfe in Canada. New York: 1887. V. 51
A Woman of the Commune. 1895. V. 52
A Woman of the Commune. London: 1895. V. 51
A Woman of the Commune. London: 1897. V. 53
Won by the Sword. London: 1900. V. 50; 51
Wulf the Saxon. London: 1895. V. 48; 52
Yarns on the Beach. London: 1886. V. 52
The Young Buglers. London: 1880. V. 51
The Young Carthaginian. London: 1887. V. 51; 52
The Young Carthaginian. New York: 1887. V. 51
The Young Colonists. London: 1885. V. 51; 53

HENTZE, C.
Chinese Tomb Figures. London: 1928. V. 47; 50; 54

HENTZNER, PAUL
Itinerarium Germaniae, Galliae: Angliae; Italiae... Norinbergae: 1612. V. 51
A Journey Into England in the Year 1598. London: 1757. V. 54
A Journey into England...in the Year 1598. Strawberry Hill: 1757. V. 51

HEPBURN, A. BARTON
The Story of an Outing. New York: 1913. V. 47; 52

HEPBURN, H. P.
Reports of Cases Argued and Determined in the Supreme Court of the State of California in the Year 1852. Volume II. Philadelphia: 1854. V. 52

HEPBURN, KATHARINE
Me. Stories of My Life. New York: 1991. V. 52

HEPHAESTION, ALEXANDRINUS
(Greek: Hephaistionis Alexandreos Encheiridion peri metron kai Poiemation. Eis to Auto Scholia). Paris: 1553. V. 47

HEPPLEWHITE, ALICE
The Cabinet-Maker and Upholsterer's Guide. London: 1789. V. 54

HEPWORTH, BARBARA
Carvings and Drawings. London: 1952. V. 48; 49; 50
Stones. London: 1972. V. 54

HER Majesty's Theatre Grand Christmas Pantomime, Little Red Riding Hood; or, the Wizard and the Wolf. London: 1883. V. 50

THE HERALDIC Visitation of Westmoreland, made in the Year 1615 by Sir Richard St. George, Knt., Norroy King at Arms. London: 1853. V. 50; 52; 54

THE HERALDRY of Nature; or, Instructions for the King at Arms... London: 1785. V. 47

HERAPATH, JOHN
The Railway Magazine and Annals of Science... London: 1837. V. 49

(HERBARIUS Latinus). Speier: 1484. V. 52

HERBER, R. L.
Barbizon Revisited: Essay and Catalogue. San Francisco: 1963. V. 54

HERBERSTAIN, SIGISMUND
Rerum Moscoviticarum Commentarii... Basel/Vienna: 1556/1560. V. 50
Rervm Moscoviticarvm Commentarij. Basle: 1571. V. 49; 52

HERBERT, A. P.
The Bomber Gipsy and Other Poems. London: 1918. V. 54
Misleading Cases in the Common Law. (with) More Misleading Cases. London: 1927/30. V. 50
Poor Poems and Rotten Rhymes. Winchester: 1910. V. 47
The Secret Battle. London: 1919. V. 47

HERBERT, A. S.
Historical Catalogue of Printed Editions of the English Bible, 1525-1961. London: 1968. V. 51
Historical Catalogue of Printed Editions of the English Bible, 1525-1961. 1973. V. 53

HERBERT, AGNES
Casuals. 1912. V. 52
Casuals in the Caucasus: the Diary of a Sporting Holiday. London: 1912. V. 54
Two Dianas in Alaska. London, New York: 1909. V. 50

HERBERT, ANNE
The Tomb of the Kings. Toronto: 1967. V. 47

HERBERT, CHARLES
Italy and italian Literature. London: 1835. V. 53

HERBERT, DAVID
Fish and Fisheries. Edinburgh: 1883. V. 50; 53
Fish and Fisheries... London: 1894. V. 48

HERBERT, DOROTHEA
Retrospections of Dorothea Herbert 1770-1789. (with) Retrospections of Dorothea Hebert 1789-1806. London: 1929/30. V. 53

HERBERT, EDWARD HERBERT, BARON
The Autobiography. Newtown: 1928. V. 47; 48; 50; 51; 53; 54
Expeditio in Ream Insulam, Quam Publici Juris Fecit Timotheus Bladuinus. London: 1656. V. 53

HERBERT, EDWARD, HERBERT, BARON
The Life... London: 1770. V. 48; 51

HERBERT, EDWARD HERBERT, BARON
The Life... London: 1826. V. 54
The Life...Cherbury... Dublin: 1771. V. 52
The Life...Cherbury... London: 1792. V. 47
The Life...Henry the Eighth... London: 1649. V. 47; 54
The Life...Henry the Eighth... London: 1672. V. 50
The Life...Henry the Eighth... London: 1683. V. 54
Occasional Verses of Edward Lord Herbert, Baron of Cherbery (sic) and Castle-Island. London: 1665. V. 47
A Short Account of the Authorities in Law, Upon Which Judgement Was Given in Sir Edw. Hales His Case,. London: 1688. V. 52

HERBERT, FRANK
40 years Prospecting and Mining in the Black Hills of South Dakota. Rapid City: 1921. V. 47
Chapterhouse Dune. London: 1985. V. 47; 51
Chapterhouse: Dune. New York: 1985. V. 51; 53; 54
Children of Dune. 1976. V. 49; 52; 54
Children of Dune. New York: 1976. V. 51
The Dragon in the Sea. New York: 1956. V. 47; 51
The Dragon in the Sea. London: 1960. V. 51
Dune. 1965. V. 47; 51; 53
Dune. Philadelphia/New York: 1965. V. 51
Dune. London: 1966. V. 48; 50; 52
Dune. London: 1984. V. 47; 51
Dune Messiah. V. 54
Dune Messiah. 1969. V. 47; 49
Eye. 1985. V. 48
The Eyes of Heisenberg. 1975. V. 47
God Emperor of Dune. 1981. V. 47; 51
God Emperor of Dune. New York: 1981. V. 47; 51
God Emperor of Dune... 1981/84/85. V. 48; 52
The Green Brain. 1979. V. 47
Heretics of Dune. London: 1984. V. 47; 51
Heretics of Dune. New York: 1984. V. 54
Whipping Star. 1970. V. 48; 51; 52

HERBERT, GEORGE
The English Works of George Herbert. Boston and New York: 1905. V. 48; 50; 54
Herbert's Remains. London: 1652. V. 50; 51
Poems. Newtown: 1923. V. 47; 50
The Poetical Works. London: 1856. V. 50

HERBERT, GEORGE continued
The Poetical Works. London: 1857. V. 47
A Priest to the Temple. London: 1671. V. 50
A Priest to the Temple. London: 1675. V. 47; 48; 49; 53
Remains of Sundry Pieces of that Sweet Singer of Songs of the Temple. (with) Jacula Prudentum or Outlandish Proverbs, Sentences, Etc. London: 1652/51. V. 48
The Remains of that Sweet Singer of the Temple. London: 1841-44. V. 48
The Temple. Sacred Poems and Private Ejaculations... Cambridge: 1633. V. 48; 49
The Temple, Sacred Poems and Private Ejaculations. London: 1850. V. 48; 50
The Temple: Sacred Poems and Private Ejaculations. London: 1927. V. 47; 51; 52; 53; 54
Works... Prose and Verse. London: 1846. V. 52
Works...Prose and Verse. London: 1853. V. 48; 51; 52

HERBERT, HENRY WILLIAM
American Game In its Seasons. New York: 1853. V. 51
Cromwell. An Historical Novel. New York: 1838. V. 54
Field Sports of the United States and British Provinces of North America. New York: 1852. V. 51
Frank Forester's Field Sports of the United States and British Provinces... New York. V. 51
Frank Forester's Field Sports of the United States and British Provinces... New York: 1849. V. 47; 48; 51
Frank Forester's Field Sports of the United States and British Provinces... New York: 1858. V. 54
Frank Forester's Fish and Fishing of the United States and British provinces of North America. New York: 1855. V. 50
Frank Forester's Fugitive Sporting Sketches... Westfield: 1879. V. 47; 51
Frank Forester's Horsemanship of the United States and British Provinces of North America. New York: 1857. V. 54
The Horse of America. New York: 1857. V. 52
Life and Writings of Frank Forester. New York: 1882. V. 54
My Shooting Box by Frank Forester, Author of the Warwick Woodlands... Philadelphia: 1850. V. 47
The Quorndon Hounds; or a Virginian at Melton Mowbray. Philadelphia: 1852. V. 54
The Sporting Novels of Frank Forester. New York: 1930. V. 47
The Sportsman's Vade Mecum... New York: 1850. V. 47
The Sportsman's Vade Mecum. New York: 1853. V. 47
Supplement to Frank Forester's Fish and Fishing of the United States and British Provinces of North America. New York: 1850. V. 47
Trouting Along the Catasauqua. New York: 1927. V. 48
The Two Brothers. New York: 1835. V. 49
The Warwick Woodlands... Philadelphia: 1845. V. 50
The Warwick Woodlands... New York: 1851. V. 51
The Warwick Woodlands... Worcester: 1924. V. 47
The Warwick Woodlands. New York: 1934. V. 53

HERBERT, HERNY HOWARD MOLYNEAUX
Recollections of the Druses of the Lebanon. London: 1860. V. 47

HERBERT, J.
Fluke. 1979. V. 47
Lair. 1797. V. 48
The Spear. 1978. V. 48; 52

HERBERT, JAMES
The Magic Cottage. London: 1986. V. 49

HERBERT, R. L.
Barbizon Revisited: Essay & Catalogue. San Francisco: 1963. V. 47; 50; 53

HERBERT, REGINALD
When Diamonds Were Trumps. London: 1908. V. 47

HERBERT, ROBERT
Worthies of Thomond. 3 Series. London: 1944/46. V. 47

HERBERT, ROBERT L.
Georges Seurat 1859-1891. New York: 1991. V. 54

HERBERT, THOMAS
A Relation of Some Yeares Travaile, Begunne Anno 1626. London: 1634. V. 53
Som Yeares Travels Into Divers Famous Empires the Persian and Great Mogull: Eaved with the History of These Later Times. London: 1638. V. 51
Some Years Travels into Divers Parts... Asia and Afrique. London: 1638. V. 49
Some Years Travels into Divers Parts of Africa, and Asia the Great. London: 1677. V. 48

HERBERT, THOMAS MARTIN
The Realistic Assumptions of Modern Science Examined. London: 1879. V. 49

HERBERT, WILLIAM
Amaryllidaceae... London: 1837. V. 49
Antiquities of the Inns of Court and Chancery (etc.). London: 1804. V. 52
Helga. A Poem. London: 1815. V. 48; 54
The History of the Twelve Great Livery Companies of London... London: 1833-1837. V. 53
Lambeth Palace. London: 1806. V. 51
Syr Reginalde; or, the Black Tower. London: 1803. V. 48

HERBERT, WILLIAM V.
The Defence of Plevna 1877. London: 1895. V. 47

HERBERTS, K.
Oriental Lacquer: Art and Technique. New York. V. 54
Oriental Lacquer: Art and Technique. New York: 1963. V. 48; 49

HERBERTSON, AGNES
Teddy and Trots in Wonderland. New York. V. 47

HERBETIUS, JOHANNES
De Oratore Libri Quinque. Paris: 1574. V. 48

HERBINIUS, JOHANNES
Dissertationes Academicae de Admirandis Mundi Cataractis Supra & Subterraneis, Earumq: Principio Elementorum Circulatione, Ubi Eadem Occasaione Aestus Maris Reflui Vera ac Genuina Causa Asseritur, Nec Non Terrestri ac Primigenio Paradiso Locus Situsq... Copenhagen: 1670. V. 49

HERBS, Spices and Medicinal Plants, Recent Advances in Botany, Horticulture and Pharmacology. London: 1986-90. V. 50; 54

HERBST, JOSEPHINE
Rope of Gold. New York: 1939. V. 50

HERD, DAVID
Ancient and Modern Scottish Songs, Heroic Ballads, etc. Edinburgh: 1776. V. 50; 53

HERD, JOHN
Historia Quator Regum Angliae... London: 1868. V. 51

HERD, RICHARD
Scraps of Poetry. Kirkby Lonsdale: 1837. V. 48
Scraps of Poetry. Sedbergh: 1900. V. 52

HERDER, J. G.
The Spirit of Hebrew Poetry. Burlington: 1833. V. 54

HERDMAN, WILLIAM GAWIN
Pictorial Relics of Ancient Liverpool. Liverpool: 1856. V. 47
Pictorial Relics of Ancient Liverpool. London: 1856. V. 50
Pictorial Relics of Ancient Liverpool. Liverpool: 1878. V. 48; 50
Picturesque Views in Liverpool. Liverpool: 1864. V. 52
A Treatise on the Curvilinear Perspective of Nature and Its Applicability to Art. London: 1853. V. 54
Views of Fleetwood on Wyre. Manchester: 1838. V. 47

HERDMAN, WILLIAM GAWN
Views of Modern Liverpool in Chromo-lithography. Liverpool: 1864. V. 47

HERE, H.
The Genera of the Mesembryanthemaceae. Cape Town: 1971. V. 52

HERE Then is Love: Ballads of the XVI Century. East Aurora: 1897. V. 48

HEREFORD, CHARLES J.A.
The History of France, from the First Establishment of that Monarchy to the Present Revolution. London: 1790. V. 50; 53
The History of Spain, from the Establishment of the Colony of Gades by the Phoenicians, to the Death of Ferdinand, Surnamed the Sage. London: 1793. V. 50; 53; 54

HERFORD, OLIVER
An Alphabet of Celebrities. Boston: 1899. V. 47
Artful Anticks. New York: 1894. V. 53
The Herford Aesop. Boston: 1921. V. 47; 50
The Laughing Willow. New York: 1918. V. 47
More Animals. New York: 1901. V. 51
The Mythological Zoo. New York: 1912. V. 47
Overheard in a Garden. New York: 1900. V. 47

HERGESHEIMER, JOSEPH
Berlin. New York: 1932. V. 49; 53; 54
From an Old House. New York: 1925. V. 51
The Lay Anthony. New York: 1914. V. 48
The Presbyterian Child. London: 1924. V. 54
Tampico. New York: 1926. V. 50
The Three Black Pennys. New York: 1917. V. 54
The Three Black Pennys. New York: 1930. V. 47; 48
Triall by Armes. London: 1929. V. 48; 52

HERICK, E.
Folk-Toys/Les Jouets Populaires. Prague: 1951. V. 53

HERING, CONSTANTINE
The Homoeopathist, or Dometic Physician. Allentown: 1835-38. V. 52

HERING, OSWALD C.
Concrete and Stucco Houses. New York: 1912. V. 50

HERIOT, GEORGE
Travels through the Canadas... London: 1807. V. 50; 54
Travels through the Canadas... Rutland: 1971. V. 50

HERITAGE Of Music. Oxford: 1989. V. 49

THE HERITAGE Of the Desert. Pioche: 1923. V. 53

HERIVEL, JOHN
The Background to Newton's Principia; A Study of Newton's Dynamical Researches in the Years 1664-84. Oxford: 1965. V. 54

HERIZ, PATRICK DE
Le Belle O'Morphi, a Brief Biography. Waltham St. Lawrence: 1947. V. 47

HERKOMER, HUBERT
Etching and Mezzotint Engraving. London: 1892. V. 47

HERLE, CHARLES
Ahab's Fall by His Prophets Flatteries: Being the Substance of Three Sermons... London: 1644. V. 48; 49

HERLIHY, JAMES LEO
Blue Denim. New York: 1958. V. 54
Midnight Cowboy. New York: 1965. V. 51; 53; 54

HERMAN, LEON
The Practice of Urology. Philadelphia & London: 1938. V. 49

HERMAN, TOM
River Veins. Old Going On. Champaign: 1972. V. 49

HERMAN, WILLIAM
The Dance of Death. San Francisco: 1877. V. 53

HERMENEGILDO DE SAN PABLO, FR.
Defensa por la Religion Geronyma de Espana, y Su Antiguedad; En Que Se Responde a un Tratado, Que el Autor de la Poblacion Eclesiastaica Imprimio en su Quarta Parte... Zaragoza: 1672. V. 53

HERMES, WILLIAM
A Collection of 30 Lithograph Plates of Cottage and Landscape Scenery. Berlin and London?: 1845. V. 52
Studies of Trees. London: 1860?. V. 47

HERMINGHAUSEN, F. W.
A Tragedy of the Platte Valley. Kansas City: 1915. V. 48

THE HERMIT of the Chesapeake; or, Lessons of a Lifetime. Philadelphia: 1869. V. 54

THE HERMIT; or the Unparalled Sufferings and Adventures of Philip Quarll, an Englishman... Exeter: 1795. V. 47

HERMITAGE MUSEUM.
French Painting. Second Half of the 19th to the Early 20th Century. New York: 1975. V. 51

HERMOGENES OF TARSUS
HERMOGENIS Tarsensis Rhetoris-Acutissimi, De Dicendi Generibus sive Formis Orationum Libri II. Strassburg: 1571. V. 51

HERNANDEZ DE CORDOBA, FRANCISCO
The Discovery of Yucatan.. Berkeley: 1942. V. 54

HERNDON, DALLAS T.
Letters of David O. Dodd with Biographical Sketch. Little Rock?: 1917. V. 47

HERNDON, SARAH RAYMOND
Days on the Road, Crossing the Plains in 1865. New York: 1902. V. 47; 49; 50; 51; 53; 54

HERNDON, WILLIAM H.
The True Story of a Great Life. The History and Personal Recollections of Abraham Lincoln. Chicago: 1889. V. 52

HERNDON, WILLIAM LEWIS
Exploration of the Valley of the Amazon... Washington: 1853/54. V. 49
Exploration of the Valley of the Amazon. Washington: 1854. V. 47; 54

HERO et Leandre, Poeme Nouveau en Trois Chants, Traduit du Grec. Paris: 1801. V. 50

HERODIAN
De Romanorum Imperatorum Vita ac Rebus Gestis Libri VIII, Graece & Latine... Basel: 1563. V. 52
(Greek title) Herodiani Histor. Lib. VIII. cum Angeli Politiani Interpretatione... Geneva: 1581. V. 48
(Greek Title) Histor(iarum) Lib(ri) VIII. Lvgduni: 1611. V. 48; 49; 50; 53
Herodian of Alexandria His Imeriall History of Twenty Roman Caesars and Emperours of His Time. London: 1652. V. 52
Historia de Imperio Post Marcum. Bologna: 1493. V. 48
Historiarum Libri VIII. Basle: 1535?. V. 53
The History of Herodian, a Greeke Authour... London: 1556. V. 47; 49

HERODOTUS
Herodoti Halicarnassei Historiae Lib. IX. & De Vita Homeri Libellus. Geneva: 1566. V. 51
Herodotus...Epika. Venice: 1502. V. 47
Herodotus, Translated from the Greek, with Notes... London: 1812. V. 47; 50
His Historie of Twenty Roman Caesars and Emperors (of His Time). Together with the Most Solemne Deification of the Roman Emperors and Empresses. London: 1635. V. 51
Historiae Libri VIIII Musarum Nominibus Inscripti...De Genere Vitaque Homeri Libellus. Lyons: 1558. V. 54
Historiarum Libri IX. Londini: 1679. V. 49
Historico Delle Guerre de Greci, et de Persi. Venetia: 1565. V. 52
The Histories of... Haarlem: 1958. V. 52; 54
The History. London: 1858-60. V. 48
The History. New York: 1861-66. V. 50
The History... New York: 1875. V. 54
The History... Bloomsbury: 1935. V. 50; 54
History. London: 1935. V. 47; 48; 50; 51; 52; 54
Musae, Sive Historiarum Librix IX. London: 1824. V. 48
Opera Graece & Latine. Edinburgh: 1806. V. 48
Pyramids. London: 1995. V. 52; 54

AN HEROIC Epistle to Mr. Winsor, the Patentee of the Hydro-Carbonic Gas Lights, and Founder of the National Light and Heat Company. London: 1808. V. 54

HERON, ROBERT
The Comforts of Human Life; or Smiles and Laughter of Charles Chearful and Martin Merryfellow. London: 1807. V. 48; 50; 51; 52; 53

HERON-ALLEN, E.
The Foraminifera of the Kerimba Archipelago. London: 1914-15. V. 50
Violin Making, As It Was and Is. London, Melbourne: 1885. V. 47; 52

HERONDAS
The Mimiambs of Herondas. London. V. 52
The Mimiambs of Herondas. London: 1926. V. 48; 50

HERPORT, BUAT
An Essay on Truths of Importance to the Happiness of Mankind. London: 1768. V. 48

HERR, MICHAEL
Dispaches. New York: 1977. V. 47; 48; 51; 53

HERRE, H.
The Genera of the Mesembryanthemaceae. Cape Town: 1971. V. 48; 49; 51

HERRERA Y TORDESILLAS, ANTONIO DE
The General History of the Vast Continent and Islands of America. London: 1725-26. V. 47; 52
Prima (Secunda, Tercera) Parte de la Historia General del Mundo. Valladolid: 1606/12. V. 51

HERRESHOFF, L. FRANCIS
The Common Sense of Yacht Design. New York: 1946. V. 54
The Common Sense of Yacht Design. New York: 1948. V. 52

HERRICK, CHEESMAN A.
White Servitude in Pennsylvania, Indentured and Redemption Labor in Colony and Commonwealth. Philadelphia: 1926. V. 54

HERRICK, F. H.
Natural History of the American Lobster. Washington: 1911. V. 53

HERRICK, H. W.
Water Color Painting: Description of Materials with Directions for Their Use in Elementary Practice. New York: 1882. V. 50

HERRICK, JAMES
A Short History of Cardiology. Springfield: 1942. V. 50; 52

HERRICK, ROBERT
The Complete Poems of Robert Herrick. London: 1876. V. 53
Delighted Earth. London: 1927. V. 48
Hesperides... London: 1846. V. 50
Hesperides... London: 1897. V. 47; 51
Love's Dilemmas. Chicago: 1898. V. 52; 53
One Hundred and Eleven Poems. London: 1955. V. 48; 49; 53
One Hundred and Eleven Poems... Waltham St. Lawrence: 1955. V. 47
Poems Chosen Out of the Works. Hammersmith: 1895. V. 47; 49
The Poems of Robert Herrick. London: 1935. V. 54
Poetical Works. London: 1900. V. 50; 52
Poetical Works. London: 1928. V. 47; 48; 52
A Posy of Verses from Herrick. London: 1903. V. 49
Select Poems from the Hesperides, or Works Both Human and Divine... Bristol: 1810. V. 50
The Works. Edinburgh: 1823. V. 50

HERRICK, WILLIAM
Life and Deeds of William Herrick, Hermit of Minnehaha Falls: a Tale of the Wild West... Minneapolis: 1903. V. 47

HERRIES, JOHN MAXWELL, LORD
Historical Memoirs of the Reign of Mary Queen of Scots and a Portion of the Reign of King James the Sixth. Edinburgh: 1836. V. 48

HERRIES, ROBERT
A Letter from a Member of the House of Commons to His Constituents, on the Great Constitutional Questions Lately Agitated in Parliament. London: 1784. V. 52

HERRIMAN, GEORGE
Krazy Kat. New York: 1946. V. 53

HERRING, J. H.
Thames Bridges from London to Hampton Court. London: 1884. V. 47

HERRING, JAMES
National Portrait Gallery of Distinguished Americans. New York: 1834-39. V. 47; 52

HERRING, PHILLIP F.
Joyce's Ulysses Notesheets in British Museum. Charlottesville: 1972. V. 47

HERRING, RICHARD
Paper and Paper Making, Ancient and Modern. London: 1855. V. 48
Paper and Paper Making, Ancient and Modern. London: 1856. V. 48; 51; 54

HERRING, ROBERT
Adam and Evelyn at Kew. London: 1930. V. 48
The Impecunious Captain or Love as Liv'd - a Play on the Lives of George Farquhar and Anne Oldfield. London: 1944. V. 50

HERRING, THOMAS
A Sermon Preach'd at the Cathedral Church of York, September 22d, 1745... York: 1745. V. 47

HERRINGTON, W. D.
The Deserter's Daughter. Raleigh: 1865. V. 53

HERRIOT, EDOUARD
Madame Recamier. London: 1926. V. 50

HERRLINGER, ROBERT
History of Medical Illustration... London: 1970. V. 49
History of Medical Illustration. New York: 1970. V. 54

HERRMANN, GOTTFRIED
De Metris Poetarum Graecorum et Romanorum Libri III. Leipzig: 1796. V. 52

HERRMANN, JOHN
The Salesman. New York: 1939. V. 51

HERROD-HEMPSALL, W.
Bee-Keeping New and Old Described with Pen and Camera. London: 1930. V. 54
Bee-Keeping New and Old Described with Pen and Camera. London: 1930-37. V. 54

HERSAK, D.
Songye Masks and Figure Sculpture. London: 1986. V. 54

HERSCHEL, CAROLINE
Memoir and Correspondence of Caroline Herschel. London: 1876. V. 52

HERSCHEL, CLEMENS
The Two Books On the Water Supply of the City of Rome of Sextus Julius Frontinus. New York: 1913. V. 50

HERSCHEL, JOHN FREDERICK WILLIAM
Essays from the Edinburgh and Quarterly Reviews... London: 1857. V. 47; 49; 54
Physical Geography of the Globe. Edinburgh: 1867. V. 50
A Preliminary Discourse on the Study of Natural Philosophy. London: 1831. V. 49
A Preliminary Discourse on the Study of Natural Philosophy. London: 1832. V. 52
A Treatise on Astronomy. London: 1833. V. 48; 51

HERSEY, GEORGE L.
Alfonso II and the Artistic Renewal of Naples, 1485-1495. New Haven & London: 1969. V. 51

HERSEY, JOHN
A Bell for Adano. New York: 1944. V. 54
Hiroshima. 1983. V. 52; 54
Hiroshima. New York: 1983. V. 47; 49; 50; 53
Into the Valley. New York: 1943. V. 54
The Wall. New York: 1957. V. 54

HERSHBERGER, H. R.
The Horseman. New York: 1844. V. 47

HERTEL, A. W.
Sammlung von Landhausern und Landlichen Wohngebauden im Englischen Schweizer Italienischen, Franzosischen... Weimar: 1862. V. 53

HERTFELDER, BERNHARD
Basilica S. S. Udalrici et Afrae...Historice Descripta... Augsburg: 1653. V. 53

HERTRICH, W.
Camellias in the Huntington Gardens. San Marino: 1954-59. V. 48; 52

HERTSLET, EVELYN M.
Ranch Life in California, Extracted from the Home Correspondence of E. M. H. London: 1886. V. 47

HERTTWIG, CHRISTOPH
Neues Und Vookommenes Berg-Buch. Dresden und Leipzig: 1734. V. 49

HERTY, THOMAS
A Digest of the Laws of the United States of America. Baltimore: 1800. V. 52

HERTZ, HEINRICH
The Principles of Mechanics Presented in a New Form.. London: 1899. V. 48

HERTZ, JOHN
The Racing Memoirs of...As Told to Evan Shipman. Chicago: 1954. V. 47

HERTZLER, ARTHUR
Surgical Pathology of the Mammary Gland. Philadelphia: 1933. V. 48; 53
A Treatise on Tumors. Philadelphia: 1912. V. 48; 53

HERTZOG, CARL
Swinburnian Conincidences. El Paso: 1960. V. 49

HERVEY, ELIZABETH
Amabel; or, Memoirs of a Woman of Fashion. London: 1814. V. 50
The History of Ned Evans. London: 1797. V. 54
Melissa and Marcia; or the Sisters: a Novel. London: 1788. V. 54

HERVEY, JAMES
The Beauties of Hervey; or Descriptive, Picturesque and Instructive Passages... Wilmington: 1796. V. 50
The Beauties of Hervey; or Descriptive, Picturesque and Instructive Passages. Wilmington: 1797. V. 53
The Life of Danger, and the Means of Safety; to Which is Added, the Way of Holiness. London: 1757. V. 49

HERVEY, JOHN
The American Trotter. A History fo the Standard Bred Horse. New York: 1947. V. 50
Lady Suffolk the Old Grey Mare of Long Island. New York: 1936. V. 47
Memoirs of the Reign of George the Second... London: 1848. V. 47; 50; 52; 53
Memoirs of the Reign of King George II. London: 1931. V. 50; 54
Messenger. The Great Progenitor. New York: 1935. V. 50; 51
Miscellaneous Thoughts on the Present Posture Both of Our Foreign and Domestic Affairs. London: 1742. V. 48
Observations On the Writings of the Craftsman. London: 1730. V. 48
The Patriots Are Come; or, a New Doctor for a Crazy Constitution. London: 1742. V. 49
Racing In America 1665-1865. New York: 1944. V. 51

HERVEY, THOMAS KIBBLE
Australia; with Other Poems. London: 1824. V. 47; 52
The Poetical Sketch-Book... London: 1829. V. 54

HERVEY, WILLIAM
The Visitation of Sufolke, Made by William Hervye, Clarenceux King of Arms, 1561. Lowestoft & London: 1866. V. 51

HERVIEU, PAUL
Flirt. New York: 1890. V. 48
Flirt. Paris: 1890. V. 54

HERVIEUX DE CHANTELOUP, J. C.
A New Treatise of Canary Birds. London: 1718. V. 47

HERWIG, H. M.
The Art of Curing sympatheically, or Magnetically...With a Discourse Concerning the Cure of Madness... London: 1700. V. 49

HERZOG, JOHANN JAKOB
The New Schaff-Herzog Encyclopedia of Religious Knowledge... New York and London: 1908-12. V. 49

HES, LEX
The Leopards of Londolozi. V. 50
The Leopards of Londolozi. 1991. V. 54
The Leopards of Londolozi. London: 1991. V. 52

HESELTINE, G. C.
The Kalendar and Compost of Shepherds. 1930. V. 54

HESIOD
Opera et Dies. Lyons: 1550. V. 48
Poemata, Quae Extant Omnia Graece, cum Varia Interpretatione Latine. 1574. V. 47
Quae Exstant. Amstelodami: 1701. V. 48
The Works. London: 1728. V. 48
The Works. London: 1811. V. 51

HESLOP, OLIVER
Northumberland Words. London: 1892-94. V. 50

HESS, ALFRED
Collected Writings. Springfield: 1936. V. 53
Rickets Including Osteomalacia and Tetany. Philadelphia: 1929. V. 53

HESS, HANS
Lyonel Feininger. New York: 1961. V. 47; 48; 49; 50; 52

HESS, THOMAS B.
Willem de Koening Drawings. London: 1972. V. 49; 52

HESSE, ALICE, GRAND DUCHESS OF
Biographical Sketch and Letters. London: 1884. V. 52; 53

HESSE, HERMANN
Antworten. 1958. V. 48
Demian. Berlin: 1919. V. 52
Demian. New York: 1923. V. 49; 51
Demian. New York: 1948. V. 49; 51
Eine Stunde Hinter Mitternacht. Leipzig: 1899. V. 52
Das Glasperlenspiel. Zurich: 1943. V. 53
Goldmund. London: 1959. V. 51; 52
In Sight of Chaos. Zurich: 1923. V. 53
The Officina Bodoni in Montagnola. Verona: 1976. V. 52
Peter Camenzind...Neunundzwanzige Auflage.ons... Berlin: 1906. V. 48; 52
Poems by Hermann Hesse. New York: 1970. V. 51
Steppenwolf. Connecticut: 1977. V. 47

HESSELS, JEAN
Tractatus Pro Invocatione Sanctorum Contra Ioanne(m) Monheimiu(m) & Eius Defensorum Henricum Artopaeum. Louvain: 1562. V. 47; 48; 50

HESTON, ALFRED M.
Absegami: Annals of Eyren Haven and Atlantic City, 1609-1904. Atlantic City: 1904. V. 47
Heston's Hand-Book. 1902. V. 51
South Jersey. A History, 1664-1924. New York: 1924. V. 47; 49; 51

HESYCHIUS, ALEXANDRINUS
(Lexikon). Hesychii Dictionarum. Florence: 1520. V. 51

HETHERINGTON, A. L.
The Early Ceramic Wares of China. London: 1922. V. 52

HETHERINGTON, W. M.
History of the Church of Scotland, from the Introduction of Christianity to the Meetings of the Commission of the General Assembly in August 1841. Edinburgh: 1842. V. 54
National Education in Scotland, Viewed In Its Present Condition, Its Principles, and Its Possibilities. Edinburgh: 1850. V. 53

HETHERINGTON, WILLIAM
Branthwaite Hall, Canto III. And Other Poems. Cockermouth: 1850. V. 50; 52

HETLEY, THOMAS
Reports and Cases Taken in the Third (-) Seventh Years of the Late King Charles...at the Common Pleas Barre (etc). London: 1657. V. 50; 52

HETTINGER, PHILIPPE
Travaile et Progres au XXeme Siecle. Paris: 1907. V. 53

HETTNER, HERMANN
Athens and the Peloponnese with Sketches of Northern Greece. Edinburgh: 1854. V. 49

HEUDE, WILLIAM
Voyage de la Cote de Malabar a Constantinople, pal le Golfe Persique, l'Arabie, la Mesopotamie, le Kourdistan et la Turquie d'Asie... Paris: 1820. V. 47

HEULAND, JOHN HENRY
Minerals. A Catalogue of a Collection of About Two Hundred Lots, of British and Exotic Minerals, Generally in Fine Condition, Including some New Specimens and Many of Considerable rarity... London: 1825. V. 49

HEURNIUS, OTTO
Babylonica, Indica, Aegyptia &c. Leyden: 1619. V. 49

HEUSTIS, DANIEL D.
A Narrative of the Adventures and Sufferings of Captain Daniel D. Heustis and His Companions in Canada and Van Dieman's Land, During a Long Captivity with Travel in California and Voyages at Sea. Boston: 1848. V. 49; 54

HEVELIUS, JOHANNES
Selenographia: Sive, Lunae Descriptio... Danzig: 1647. V. 50

HEVESY, GEORGE
A Manual of Radioactivity. London: 1926. V. 50

HEWARD, CONSTANCE
Grandpa and the Tiger. London: 1924. V. 51
Mr. Pickles and the Party. London: 1926. V. 49

HEWARD, S. L.
Pillow Stories. London: 1901. V. 48

HEWAT, ALEXANDER
Historical Account of the Rise and Progress of the Colonies of South Carolina and Georgia. London: 1779. V. 48

HEWELETT, MAURICE HENRY
The Life and Death of Richard Yea-and-Nay. Toronto: 1900. V. 53

HEWES, GEORGE R. T.
A Retrospect of the Boston Tea Party, with a Memoir. New York: 1834. V. 50

HEWETSON, W. B.
History of Napoleon Bonaparte, and Wars of Europe. London: 1815. V. 50

HEWETT, EDGAR L.
The Fiesta Book. Papers of the School of American Research. Santa Fe: 1925. V. 52
Indians of the Rio Grande Valley. Albuquerque: 1937. V. 48; 51

HEWETT, SARAH
The Peasant Speech of Devon with Other Matters Connected Therewith. London: 1892. V. 52

HEWISON, JAMES KING
The Romance of Bewcastle Cross. Glasgow: 1923. V. 52

HEWITSON, A.
Our Country Churches and Chapels. London: 1872. V. 54

HEWITSON, WILLIAM C.
British Oology. Newcastle-upon-Tyne: 1831-38. V. 50; 52; 53
British Zoology. Newcastle: 1831-38. V. 47
Coloured Illustrations of the Eggs of British Birds. London: 1856-46. V. 50
Illustrations of New Species of Exotic Butterflies. London: 1851-76. V. 54

HEWITT, EDWARD RINGWOOD
Secrets of the Salmon. New York: 1922. V. 48
A Trout and Salmon Fisherman for Seventy-Five Years. New York: 1948. V. 52
Trout Raising and Stocking. 1935. V. 47

HEWITT, GIART
Minnesota: Its Advantages to Settlers. St. Paul: 1868. V. 48

HEWITT, GRAILY
Lettering. London: 1930. V. 49
The Pen and Type Design. London: 1928. V. 50; 52

HEWITT, J. N. B.
Journal of Rudolph Friederick Kurz. An Account of His Experiences Among Fur Traders and American Indians on the Mississippi and the Upper Missouri Rivers During the Years 1846-1852. Washington: 1937. V. 49

HEWITT, JOHN
No Rebel Word - Poems. London: 1948. V. 50
A Treatise Upon Money, Coins, and Exchange, In Regard Both to Theory and Practice. London: 1755. V. 54

HEWITT, JOHN H.
Shadows on the Wall, or Glimpses of the Past. Baltimore: 1877. V. 48

HEWITT, MARY ELIZABETH MOORE
Poems: Sacred, Passionate and Legendary. New York: 1854. V. 54

HEWITT, RANDALL H.
Across the Plains and Over the Divide a Mule Train Journey from East to West in 1862. New York: 1906. V. 47; 50

HEWLETT, ESTHER
The Old Man's Head; or Youthful Recollections. London: 1824. V. 51

HEWLETT, J. T.
Peter Priggins, the College Scout. London: 1841. V. 49

HEWLETT, MAURICE HENRY
Bendish: a study in Prodigality. London: 1905. V. 48
The Life and Death of Richard Yea-and-Nay. Toronto: 1900. V. 48
A Masque of Dead Florentines. London: 1895. V. 49; 54
Pan and the Young Shepherd. London: 1898. V. 48; 53
Quattrocentisteria: How Sandro Botticelli Saw Simonetta in the Spring. New York: 1921. V. 52; 54
Quattrocentisteria, How Sandro Botticelli Saw Simonetta in the Spring. New York: 1937. V. 54
Saint Gervase of Plessy: a Mystery. 1900. V. 48
The Wreath - 1894-1914. London: 1914. V. 49

HEWLETT, PIA
Grandmother's Fairy Tales. London: 1915. V. 47

HEWSON, JAMES
Every man His Own Lawyer, or, The Several Modes of Commencing and Conducting Actions in the Court for the Trial of Small Causes... Newark: 1841. V. 50

HEWSON, WILLIAM
The Works of William Hewson, F.R.S. London: 1846. V. 48; 50; 53

HEXHAM, LIONEL J. F.
Harry Roughton; or, Reminiscences of a Revenue Officer. London: 1859. V. 51

HEY, JOHN
Discourses on the Malevolent Sentiments. Newport-Pagnell: 1801. V. 51

HEY, REBECCA
The Moral of Flowers. London: 1836. V. 50
The Spirit of the Woods. London: 1837. V. 49
Sylvan Musings, or the Spirit of the Woods. London: 1849. V. 47

HEY, WILLIAM
Practical Observations in Surgery, Illustrated by Cases. London: 1814. V. 47

HEYDEN, DORIS
Pre-Columbian Architecture of Messoamerica. New York: 1975. V. 50; 52

HEYDEN, HERMAN VAN DER
Speedy Help for Rich and Poor. London: 1653. V. 52

HEYDEN, JAN VAN DER
Beschryvinge der Nieuwlyks Uitgevonden en Geoctrojeerd Slang-Brands-Spuiten, en Haare Wyze Van Brand-Blussen, Tengenwoordig Binnen Amsterdam in Gebruik Zijnde... Amsterdam: 1735. V. 50

HEYDON, CHRISTOPHER
A Defence of Judiciall Astrologie, in Answer to a Treatise Lately Published by M. John Chamber. Cambridge: 1603. V. 50
The New Astrology; or, the Art of Predicting, or Foretelling Future Events, by the Aspects, Positions and Influences of the Heavenly Bodies. London: 1786. V. 53

HEYECK, ROBIN
Marbling at the Heyeck Press. 1986. V. 52
Marbling at the Heyeck Press. California: 1986. V. 52
Marbling at the Heyeck Press. Woodside: 1986. V. 54

HEYER, GEORGETTE
An Infamous Army. London: 1937. V. 51

HEYERDAHL, THOR
American Indians in the Pacific. London: 1952. V. 52; 54
The Art of Easter Island. Garden City: 1975. V. 47; 52; 54
The Art of Easter Island. London: 1976. V. 50

HEYGATE, WILLIAM EDWARD
Holy Matrimony; or, the Wedding Gift, a Devotional Manual for the Married... London: 1850. V. 49

HEYL, EDITH STOWE GODFREY
Bermuda through the Camera of James B. Heyl 1868-1897. Hamilton: 1951. V. 54

HEYLYN, PETER
A Briefe Relation of the Death and Sufferings of the Most Reverend and Renowned Prelate the L. Archbishop of Canterbury. London: 1644. V. 48
A Briefe Relation of the Death and Sufferings of the Most Reverend and Renowned Prelate the L. Archbishop of Canterbury... Oxford: 1644. V. 50
Cosmographie, in Foure Bookes. London: 1652. V. 52
Cosmographie, in Foure Books. London: 1673-74. V. 50
Cyprianus Anglicus: or the History of the Life and Death of the Most Reverned and Reknowned Prelate William...(Laud). London: 1671. V. 47
Ecclesia Restaurata. London: 1674. V. 47
A Full Relation of Two Journeys: the One into the Main Land of France. London: 1656. V. 48
A Help to English History. London: 1670. V. 47
A Help to English History... London: 1680. V. 48
A Help to English History... London: 1709. V. 50
Mikrokosmos (in Greek). Oxford: 1629. V. 48
Mikrokosmos (in Greek Letters)... London: 1625. V. 48

HEYLYN, PETER continued
Respondet Petrus; or the Answer of Peter Heylin D.D. to So Much of Dr. Bernard's Book Entituled the Judgement of the Late Primate of Ireland... London: 1658. V. 54

HEYMAN, MAX L.
Prudent Soldier, a Biography of Major General E.R.S. Canby 1817-1873. Glendale: 1959. V. 52

HEYRICH, ELIZABETH
Immediate, Not Gradual Abolition; or, An Inquiry into the Shortest, Safest and Most Effectual Means of Getting Rid of West Indian Slavery. London: 1825. V. 47

HEYSHAM, JOHN
An Account of the Jail Fever, or Thyphus Carcerum: as It Appeared at Carlisle in the Year 1781. London: 1782. V. 48

HEYWARD, DUBOSE
Angel. New York: 1926. V. 50; 53
Brass Ankle. New York: 1931. V. 47
Carolina Chansons Legends of the Low Country. New York: 1922. V. 53
The Half Pint Flask. New York: 1929. V. 47; 53; 54
Jasbo Brown and Selected Poems. New York: 1931. V. 52
Mamba's Daughters. New York: 1939. V. 47; 48; 49; 53
Porgy. New York: 1925. V. 53
Porgy and Bess. New York: 1935. V. 48
The Theatre Guild Presents Porgy and Bess. New York: 1935. V. 48

HEYWOOD, E. H.
Free Speech: Report of Ezra H. Heywood's Defense...Together with Judge Nelson's Charge to the Jury, Notes of Anthony Comstock's Career...social Evolution and Other Interesting Matter. Princeton: 1883. V. 51

HEYWOOD, E. W.
Uncivil Liberty: an Essay to Show the Injustice and Impolicy of Ruling Woman Without Her Consent. Princeton: 1870. V. 50

HEYWOOD, GERALD G. P.
Charles Cotton and His River. Manchester: 1928. V. 47; 53

HEYWOOD, JAMES
Illustrations of the Principal English Universities. London: 1840's/last. V. 52
Illustrations of the Principal English Universities. 1863. V. 51

HEYWOOD, ROBERT
A Journey to America in 1834. Cambridge: 1919. V. 53

HEYWOOD, SAMUEL
A Digest of the Law Respecting County Elections. London: 1790. V. 47

HEYWOOD, THOMAS
The Earls of Derby and The Verse Writers and Poets of the 16th and 17th Centuries. Manchester: 1825. V. 53
Englands Elisabeth: Her Life and Troubles During Her Minoritie, from the Cradle to the Crown. Cambridge: 1632. V. 50
The Hierarchie of the Blessed Angells... London: 1635. V. 47; 50; 54
The Hierarchie of the Blessed Angells... London: 1973. V. 51
The Life of Merlin, Sirnamed Ambrosius. London: 1641. V. 52; 53; 54
Troia Britanica; or, Great Britaines Troy. London: 1974. V. 51
Tunaikeion; or, Nine Bookes of Various History Concerning Women... London: 1624. V. 48; 50; 51; 52; 54

HEYWOOD, V. H.
The Biology and Chemistry of the Umbelliferae. London: 1971. V. 48
The Biology and Chemistry of the Umbelliferae. London: 1972. V. 52

HIAASEN, CARL
A Death in China. 1984. V. 51
A Death in China. New York: 1984. V. 52; 53
Double Whammy. New York: 1987. V. 51; 52; 53; 54
Native Tongue. New York: 1991. V. 53
Powder Burn. New York: 1981. V. 49; 52; 53
Skin Trade. New York: 1989. V. 53
Stormy Weather. 1996. V. 54
Stormy Weather. London: 1996. V. 53
Tourist Season. New York: 1986. V. 50; 51; 52; 53; 54
Trap Line. New York: 1982. V. 48; 49; 50; 53

HIATT, CHARLES
Picture Posters. London: 1895. V. 49
Picture Posters... London: 1896. V. 48

HIBBERD, SHIRLEY
The Amateur's Greenhouse and Conservatory. London: 1875. V. 53
Floral World and Garden Guide 1871. London: 1871. V. 51
History of the Extinct Volcanos of the Basin of Neuwied on the Lower Rhine. Edinburgh: 1832. V. 47
New and Rare Beautiful Leaved Plants. London: 1870. V. 49; 51; 52
Rustic Adornments For Homes of Taste. London: 1895. V. 49

HIBBERT, E. H. R.
The Log of the Valhalla. London: 1894. V. 51

HIBBERT, GEORGE
A Catalogue of the Library of George Hibbert. London: 1829. V. 48
Tales of the Cordelier Metamorphosed, as Narrated in a Manuscript from the Borromeo Collection; and in the Cofdelier Cheval of M. Piron. London: 1821. V. 47

HIBBERT, SAMUEL
Sketches of Philosophy of Apparitions; or, an Attempt to Trace Such Illusions to Their Physical Causes. Edinburgh: 1824. V. 51

THE HIBERIAN
Patriot: *Being a Collection of the Drapier's Letters to the People of Ireland, Concerning Mr. Wood's Brass Half-Pence.* London: 1730. V. 50

HICHENS, ROBERT
The Garden of Allah. New York: 1936. V. 54
The Green Carnation. London: 1894. V. 53
The Holy Land. London: 1913. V. 53

HICKERINGILL, EDMUND
The Black Non-Conformist, Discover'd in More Naked Truth... London: 1682. V. 48; 49
Essays Concerning I. Excommunications in Times of Popery. II. Canon-Lawas & Ecclesiastical Tyranny. III. Excommunications in These Times. IV. The Writ De Excommunicato Capiendo. V. Sacrilege, Consecrating Churches & Baptizing Bells. VI. Absolutions... London: 1682?. V. 50
The Test or, Tryal of the Goodness and Value of Spiritual Courts. London: 1683. V. 52

HICKERSON, THOMAS FELIX
Happy Valley History and Genealogy. Chapel Hil: 1940. V. 48

HICKES, GEORGE
Apologetical Vindication of the Church of England, in Answer to those Who Reproach Her with the English Heresies and Schisms, or Suspect Her Not to Be a Catholic. London: 1687. V. 53
A Word to the Wavering: or An Answer to the Enquiry into the Present State of Affairs... London: 1689. V. 53

HICKEY, HARDEN, BARON
Euthanasia the Aesthetics of Suicide. New York: 1894. V. 53

HICKEY, J. J.
Peregrine Falcon Populations. Madison: 1969. V. 49

HICKEY, M.
100 Families of Flowering Plants. London: 1988. V. 50

HICKEY, WILLIAM
The Works of Martin Doyle. Dublin: 1831. V. 53
The Works of Martin Doyle... Dublin: 1836. V. 50

HICKLIN, JOHN
The Handbook of Llandudno and Its Vicinity, Including Conway and Pemmaenmawr. London: 1866. V. 54
The Illustrated Hand-Book of North Wales... London: 1851. V. 54
The Ladies of Llangollen as Sketched by Many Hands, With Notices of Other Objects of Interest in "That Sweetest of Vales". Chester: 1860. V. 53

HICKMAN, BILL
Brigham's Destroying Angel: Being the Life, Confession and Startling Disclosures of the Notorious Bill Hickman, the Danite Chief of Utah. New York: 1872. V. 49

HICKMAN, WILLIAM
A Treatise on the Law and Practice of Naval Courts-Martial. London: 1851. V. 53

HICKOK, LAURENS PERSEUS
Empirical Psychology, or, the Human Mind As Given In Consciousness. 1854. V. 51
Empirical Psychology; or, The Human Mind as Given in Consciousness. Schenectady: 1854. V. 49
A System of Moral Science. Schenectady: 1853. V. 48

HICKS, EDWARD
Sir Thomas Malory - His Turbulent Career - a Biography. Cambridge: 1928. V. 52

HICKS, F. C.
Forty Years Among the Wild Animals of India From Mysore to the Himalayas. Allahabad: 1910. V. 48

HICKS, GRANVILLE
One Of Us. The Story of John Reed. New York: 1935. V. 49

HICKS, HENRY
The Poll for Knights of the Shire to Represent the County of Kent...Taken at Maidstone, on Wednesday and Thursday the 15th and 16th of May, 1734. London: 1734. V. 47

HICKS, J.
Wanderings by the Lochs and Streams of Assynt: and the North Highlands of Scotland. London: 1855. V. 47

HICKSON, SYDNEY J.
A Naturalist in North Celebes. London: 1889. V. 52

HIDE And Seek Stories. London: 1909. V. 50

HIEB, LOUIS A.
Charles Bowden: a Bibliography. Santa Fe: 1994. V. 51
Collecting Tony Hillerman. Santa Fe: 1992. V. 48; 52

HIERN, W. P.
Catalogue of the African Plants, Collected by Dr. Friedrich Welwitsch in 1853-61. London: 1896-1901. V. 48
A Monograph of Ebenaceae. Cambridge: 1873. V. 51

HIERO-MASTIX, a Satire, Occasioned by Publications Which Have Recently Appeared in Connection with the Apocrypha Controversy. Edinburgh: 1828. V. 54

HIEROCLES
Commentarius in Aurea Pythagoreorum Carmina. Paris: 1583. V. 52
Hierocles Upon the Golden Verses of the Pythagoreans... Glasgow: 1761. V. 48

HIERONYMUS, SAINT
Aureola ex Floribus. Milan: 1475. V. 47; 49
Certaine Selected Epistles of S. Hierome, as Also the Lives of Saint Paul the Hermite, of Saint Hilarion the First Monke of Syria and of S. Malchus. St. Omer: 1630. V. 50
Commentary on the Prophets. Lugdunl: 1530. V. 54
De Viris Illustribus. Augsburg: 1472. V. 47; 49
Epistolae. Rome: 1740. V. 50
Epistolae Selectae. Paris: 1602. V. 52; 54
Vitae Sanctorum Patrum, Sive Vitas Patrum. Ulm: 1478-80. V. 51; 53
Vitae Sanctorum Patrum, Sive Vitas Patrum. Venice: 1483/84. V. 52; 54
Vitae Sanctorum Patrum, Sive Vitas Patrum. Venice: 1843/84. V. 53
Vitas Patrum. Lyons: 1512. V. 53

HIGBEE, ELIAS
"Latter-Day Saints", Alias Mormons. Washington: 1840. V. 49; 50

HIGDEN, HENRY
A Modern Essay on the Tenth Satyr of Juvena. London: 1687. V. 48

HIGDEN, RALPH
Polychonicon. London: 1865-86. V. 49; 52

HIGGINS, AIDAN
Balcony of Europe. London: 1972. V. 54

HIGGINS, AILEEN CLEVELAND
Dream Blocks. New York: 1908. V. 47

HIGGINS, BRYAN
Experiments and Observations with the View of Improving the Art of composing and Applying Calcareous Cements, and of Preparing Quick-Lime... London: 1780. V. 52

HIGGINS, C. A.
New Guide to the Pacific Coast Santa Fe Route. Chicago and New York: 1894. V. 52

HIGGINS, DICK
Pattern Poetry. Albany: 1987. V. 53

HIGGINS, F. R.
Arable Holdings. 1933. V. 48; 50; 54
Progress in Irish Printing. Dublin: 1936. V. 52

HIGGINS, GEORGE
The King of Counties. Miami County, Her Towns, Villages and Business, Timber, Water, Land Agricultural Resources.... Paola: 1877. V. 52

HIGGINS, GEORGE V.
The Friends of Eddie Coyle. New York: 1972. V. 49; 52

HIGGINS, GODFREY
Anacalypsis... London: 1833. V. 51
Anacalypsis... London: 1836. V. 47; 51
Anacalypsis... New York: 1927. V. 48
Anacalypsis... New York: 1965. V. 47
An Apology for the Life and Character of the Celebrated Prophet of Arabia, Called Mohamed, or the Illustrious. London: 1829. V. 47
The Celtic Druids. London: 1827. V. 51
The Celtic Druids... London: 1829. V. 52

HIGGINS, JACK
The Savage Day. London: 1972. V. 50
Seven Pillars to Hell. London & New York: 1963. V. 50

HIGGINS, R. A.
Catalogue of the Terracottas in the Department of Greek and Roman Antiquities, British Museum. Volume II (only). London: 1959. V. 52

HIGGINS, SOPHIA E. BERNARD
The Bernards of Abington and Nether Winchendon, a Family History. London: 1903-04. V. 49

HIGGINS, WILLIAM MULLINGER
The House Painter; or Decorator's Companion... London: 1841. V. 50; 54
An Introductory Treatise on the Nature and Properties of Light. London: 1829. V. 50

HIGGINSON, A. HENRY
British and American Sporting Authors... Berryville: 1949. V. 51
British and American Sporting Authors. London: 1951. V. 47; 50; 51
The Hunts of the United States and Canada. Boston: 1908. V. 47; 48; 54
Letters from an Old Sportsman to a Young One. Garden City: 1929. V. 47; 51; 52
Letters From an Old Sportsman to a Young One. New York: 1929. V. 49
Try Back, a Huntsman's Reminiscences. New York: 1931. V. 48

HIGGINSON, THOMAS
The Poetical Works. (bound with, as issued) The Literary Works of T. H. Higginson. Vanleek Hill: 1888. V. 49

HIGGINSON, THOMAS WENTWORTH
Oldport Days. Boston: 1873. V. 53
Women and Men. New York: 1888. V. 53

HIGGONS, BEVILL
Historical and Critical Remarks on BP. Burnet's History of His Own Time. London: 1725. V. 47
A Short View of the English History... Hague i.e. London?: 1727. V. 47

HIGGS, HENRY
Bibliography of Economics 1751-1775. London: 1990. V. 49; 50
Palgrave's Dictionary of Political Economy. London: 1925-26. V. 54

HIGGS, J. FULLER
The Silver Wedding: a Sketch of the Lives of the Prince and Princess of Wales. London: 1888. V. 54

THE HIGH German Fortune-Teller Laying Down True Rules and Directions, By Which Both Men and Women May Know Their Good and Bad Fortune. London: 1805. V. 54

THE HIGH History of the Holy Graal. London: 1898. V. 54

HIGH, JAMES L.
Treatise on Extraordinary Legal Remedies. Chicago: 1874. V. 49
A Treatise on the Law of Receivers. Chicago: 1876. V. 54

HIGH Life, a Novel. London: 1827. V. 47

HIGH RIVER PIONEER'S AND OLD TIMER'S ASSOCIATION
Leaves from the Medicine Tree. Lethbridge: 1960. V. 50

HIGH-WAYS and By-ways; or Tales of the Roadside; Picked Up in French Provinces, by a Walking Gentleman (and) Second Series. London and Paris: 1824/25. V. 51

HIGHLAND SOCIETY OF SCOTLAND
Report of the Committee of the Highland Society of Scotland, To Whom the Subject of Shetland Wool Was Referred. Edinburgh: 1790. V. 53

HIGHSMITH, DAVID
Poison in the System. San Francisco: 1979. V. 51

HIGHSMITH, PATRICIA
The Blunderer. New York: 1954. V. 47; 49
The Blunderer. New York: 1954. V. 47
The Blunderer. 1956. V. 53
The Blunderer. London: 1956. V. 49
The Man Who Wrote Books In His Head. Helsinki: 1986. V. 48
Mermaids on the Golf Course. New York: 1988. V. 48
Miranda the Panda is On the Veranda. New York: 1958. V. 48
Ripley Under Water. London: 1991. V. 53
Strangers On a Train. New York: 1950. V. 47; 51
The Talented Mr. Ripley. 1955. V. 50
The Talented Mr. Ripley. New York: 1955. V. 48; 51
The Talented Mr. Ripley. London: 1957. V. 53
The Two Faces of January. London: 1964. V. 53
Where the Action Is. Helsinki: 1991. V. 48

HIGHT, G. A.
Richard Wagner, a Critical Biography. London: 1925. V. 49

HIGHTOWER, JAMES
Happy Hunting Grounds. Colorado Springs: 1910. V. 54

HIGHTOWER, JOHN
Pheasant Hunting. New York: 1946. V. 48

HIGHWATER, JAMAKE
Anpao. An American Indian Odyssey. Philadelphia: 1977. V. 50
The Ceremony of Innocence. New York: 1985. V. 50
Ritual of the Wind. New York: 1977. V. 50
Song from the Earth: American Indian Painting. Boston: 1976. V. 50

HIGSON, DANIEL
Seafowl Shooting Sketches. 1909. V. 51
Seafowl, Shooting sketches. Preston, Lancs: 1909. V. 52; 54

HIJUELOS, OSCAR
The Mambo Kings Play Songs of Love. New York: 1989. V. 51; 53; 54
Mr. Ives' Christmas. New York: 1995. V. 52
Our House in the Last World. New York: 1983. V. 52; 53; 54

HILDBURGH, W. L.
Medieval Spanish Enamels and Their Relation to the Origin and Development of Copper Champleve Enamels of the 12th and 13th Centuries. London: 1936. V. 54

HILDEBURN, CHARLES
A Century of Printing: The Issues of the Press in Pennsylvania 1685-1784. Philadelphia: 1885. V. 47

HILDEBURN, CHARLES R.
Sketches of Printers and Printing in Colonial New York. New York: 1895. V. 48; 51; 54

HILDEN, WILHELM
Quaestionum et Commentariorum in Organon Aristotelis. Berlin: 1586. V. 48

HILDENBRAND, JOHANN
Treatise on the Nature, Cause and Treatment of Contagious Typhus. New York: 1829. V. 48

HILDRETH, CHARLES LORIN
OO Adventures in Orbelo Land. New York: 1889. V. 54

HILDRETH, RICHARD
The Slave... Boston: 1836. V. 50
The Slave... Boston: 1840. V. 52
The White Slave; or, Memoirs of a Fugitive. Boston: 1852. V. 54
The White Slave; or, Negro Life in the Slave States of America. London: 1850's?. V. 49

HILER, HILAIRE
From Nudity to Rainment... London: 1929. V. 54

HILER, HILAIRE continued
From Nudity to Rainment. New York: 1930. V. 49; 54

HILER, HILAIRE & MEYER
Bibliography of Costume: a Dictionary Catalogue of About Eight Thousand Books and Periodicals. New York: 1939. V. 54

HILL, ABRAHAM
Familiar Letters Which Passed Between Abraham Hill, Esq...and Several Eminent and Ingenious Persons of the Last Century. London: 1767. V. 47

HILL, ALFRED J.
History of Company E of the Sixth Minnesota Regiment of Volunteer Infantry. St. Paul: 1899. V. 48

HILL, ANTHONY
Directions in Art, Theory and Aesthetics. London: 1968. V. 49; 51

HILL, BENSON EARLE
Home Service; or, Scenes and Characters from Life, At Out and Head Quarters. London: 1839. V. 47
Playing About: or Theatrical Anecdotes and Adventures, with Scenes of General Nature from the Life; in England, Scotland and Ireland. London: 1840. V. 48

HILL, BERT HODGE
Corinth. Volume I. Part VI: The springs, Peirene, Sacred Spring, Glauke. Princeton: 1964. V. 52
The Temple of Zeus at Nemea. Princeton: 1966. V. 50; 52

HILL, BRIAN
Henry and Acasto. London: 1798. V. 54

HILL, CONSTANCE
Jane Austen: Her Home and Her Friends. London: 1902. V. 52; 54

HILL, DANIEL HARVEY
Bethel to Sharpsburg. Raleigh: 1926. V. 47; 51

HILL, DEAN
Football Thru the Years. New York: 1940. V. 52

HILL, EDWIN
Principles of Currency. London: 1856. V. 50; 52

HILL, EDWIN D.
The Northern Banking Company Limited. Belfast: 1925. V. 54

HILL, FRANCIS
Travels in Canada and the United States in 1816 and 1817. London: 1818. V. 53

HILL, FRANK PIERCE
Books, Pamphlets and Newspapers Printed at Newark, New Jersey, 1776-1900. 1902. V. 48; 53

HILL, FREDERICK
A Letter to the Earl of Falmouth on the Present State of the Stannary Courts of Cornwall, and on the Expediency of Reviving and Extending their Jurisdiction. Helston: 1835. V. 54

HILL, G. F.
Pisanello. London: 1905. V. 48

HILL, G. K.
Life and Recollections of Yankee (G.H.) Hill Together with Anecdotes & Incidents of His Travels. New York: 1850. V. 47

HILL, GEOFFREY
Collected Poems. London: 1985. V. 52
English Dioceses: a History of Their Limits from the Earliest Times to the Present Day. London: 1900. V. 49
Fantasy Poets No. 11. Eynsham: 1952. V. 49
For the Unfallen: Poems 1952-1958. London: 1959. V. 47; 52; 53; 54
King Log. London: 1968. V. 47; 49; 53
The Lords of Limit - Essays on Literature and Ideas. New York: 1984. V. 51
Mercian Hymns. London: 1971. V. 50
Mercian Hymns. London: 1976. V. 52
The Mystery of the Charity of Charles Peguy. London: 1983. V. 52; 53
The Mystery of the Charity of Charles Peguy. New York: 1984. V. 51
(Poems). Fantasy Poets Number Eleven. Swinford: 1952. V. 47
Preghiere. Leeds: 1964. V. 49; 51; 52
Somewhere Is Such a Kingdom. Boston: 1975. V. 50; 52
Somewhere is Such a Kingdom... New York: 1975. V. 48
Tenebrae. London: 1978. V. 50
Tenebrae. Boston: 1979. V. 51

HILL, GEORGE
A History of Cyprus. Volume IV. The Ottoman province. The British Colony. 1571-1948. Cambridge: 1952. V. 49
Medals of the Renaissance, Revised and Enlarged by Graham Pollard. London: 1978. V. 49; 52

HILL, GEORGE BIRKBECK NORMAN
Colonel Gordon in Central Africa 1874-1879. London: 1881. V. 51; 54
Footsteps of Dr. Johnson. (Scotland). Manchester. V. 48
Footsteps of Dr. Johnson (Scotland). London: 1890. V. 48; 49; 50; 53
Johnsonian Miscellanies. 1897. V. 50
Johnsonian Miscellanies. London: 1897. V. 54
Johnsonian Miscellanies. Oxford: 1897. V. 50
Select Essays of Dr. Johnson. London: 1889. V. 49

HILL, GEORGE FRANCIS
Coins of Ancient Sicily. Westminster: 1903. V. 48
Corolla Numismatica: Numismatic Essays in Honour of Barclay V. Head. London: 1906. V. 48
A Corpus of Italian Medals of the Renaissance Before Cellini. London: 1930. V. 49; 52
Drawings by Pisanello. Paris & Brussels: 1929. V. 50; 54
Historical Greek Coins. London: 1906. V. 48
Medals of the Renaissance. London: 1978. V. 49; 52; 54
Pisanello. London: 1905. V. 48
Portrait Medals of Italian Artists of the Renaissance. London: 1912. V. 48
Renaissance Medals From the Samuel H. Kress Collection at the National Gallery of Art Based on the Catalogue of Renaissance Medals in the Gustave Dreyfus Collection. London: 1967. V. 48

HILL, GEORGIANA
A History of English Dress, from the Saxon Period to the Present Day. London: 1893. V. 50

HILL, IRA
Antiquities of America Explained. Hagers-town: 1831. V. 50

HILL, J. B.
The Geology of Falmouth and Truro and of the Mining District of Camborne and Redruth. London: 1906. V. 47; 48; 50; 51

HILL, JAMES
The Following is an Authentic Copy of a Letter Sent by James Hill to His Brother in Manchester. 1782. V. 52

HILL, JAMES EWING
Historical Polk County, Texas Companies and Soldiers Organized in and Enrolled from Said County in Confederate States Army and Navy - 1861-1865. Organization of Ike Turner Camp, U.C.V. Unveiling, Etc. Livingston. V. 49

HILL, JASPER S.
The Letters of a Young Miner. San Francisco: 1964. V. 48

HILL, JEROME
Trip to Greece. New York: 1936. V. 47

HILL, JOHN
The Actor. London: 1750. V. 48; 50; 52; 53
Arithmetick, Both in the Theory and Practice, Made Plain and Easy in All the Common and Useful Rules, Both in whole Numbers and Fractions... London: 1733. V. 49
The British Herbal: an History of Plants and Trees, Natives of Britain, Cultivated for Use, or raised for Beauty. London: 1756. V. 52
Cautions Against the Immoderate Use of Snuff. London: 1761. V. 54
A Compleat Body of Husbandry. London: 1756. V. 51
The Conduct of Married Life... V. 48
The Conduct of Married Life. London: 1753. V. 48; 49
A Decade of Curious Insects: some of Them Not Describ'd Before... London: 1773. V. 53
Exotic Botany Illustrated, in Thirty-Five Figures of Curious and Elegant Plants... London: 1759. V. 47
The Family Herbal. Bungay: 1805. V. 50
The Family Herbal... Bungay: 1810. V. 48; 51
The Family Herbal... London: 1835. V. 47; 48; 50
A General Natural History... London: 1748-52. V. 49
A General Natural History... London: 1751. V. 47; 48
A General Natural History... London: 1751-52. V. 48
The History of a Woman of Quality; or, the Adventures of Lady Frail. London: 1751. V. 52
The Inspector. London: 1753. V. 49
Lucina Sine Concubitu. 1750. V. 54
Lucina Sine Concubitu. London: 1750. V. 48
Lucina Sine concubitu... Waltham St. Lawrence: 1930. V. 47; 50; 52; 53; 54
Observations on the Greek and Roman Classics in a Series of Letters to a Young Nobleman, Now Published for the Use of Gentleman at the University... London: 1973. V. 49
Observations on the Importance and Use of Theatres; Their Present Regulation, and Possible Improvements. London: 1759. V. 47; 54
A Review of the Works of the Royal Society of London... London: 1751. V. 47; 48; 49
A Series of Progressive Lessons, Intended to Elucidate the Art of Flower Painting in Water colours. Philadelphia: 1818. V. 52
A Series of Progressive Lessons, Intended to Elucidate the Art of Flower Painting in Water Colours. Philadelphia: 1836. V. 47; 53
The Story of Elizabeth Canning Considered. London: 1753. V. 49; 53; 54
The Young Secretary's Guide; or, a Speedy Help to Learning. London: 1724. V. 47

HILL, JOHN A.
Stories of the Railroad. New York: 1899. V. 51

HILL, JOHN H.
Princess Malah. Washington: 1933. V. 52; 53

HILL, JOHN HARWOOD
The History of Market Harborough with the Hundred of Gartreeee... Leicester: 1875. V. 54

HILL, JOSEPH J.
The History of Warner's Ranch and Its Environs. Los Angeles: 1927. V. 47; 50; 52

HILL, LESLIE PINCKNEY
Toussaint L'Ouverture: a Dramatic History. Boston: 1928. V. 53

HILL, LUCILLE E.
Athletics and Out-Door Sports for Women. New York and London: 1903. V. 49

HILL, M. O.
Atlas of the Bryophytes of Britain and Ireland. Colchester: 1991-92. V. 49

HILL, M. O. continued
Atlas of the Bryophytes of Britain and Ireland. Colchester: 1991-94. V. 52

HILL, MABEL B.
The Most Popular Mother Goose Songs. London: 1915. V. 50

HILL, MATTHEW DAVENPORT
Suggestions for the Repression of Crime, Contained in Charges Delivered to Grand Juries of Birmingham... London: 1857. V. 49; 52

HILL, MILDRED MARTIN
A Traipsin' Heart. New York: 1942. V. 53

HILL, NAPOLEON
The Master-Key to Riches. Los Angeles: 1945. V. 52

HILL, NATHANIEL
The Ancient Poem of Guillaume de Guileville Entitled Le Pelerinage de l'Homme... London: 1858. V. 52

HILL, OLIVER
English Country Houses Caroline 1625-1685. London: 1966. V. 53
The Garden of Adonis. London: 1923. V. 52
Pam's Garden. London: 1928. V. 53

HILL, R. T.
The Geology and Physical Geography of Jamaica: Study of a Type of Antillean Development... 1899. V. 53

HILL, REGINALD
Pictures of Perfection. 1993. V. 54
Pictures of Perfection. London: 1993. V. 53
Pictures of Perfection. Bristol: 1994. V. 52
Recalled to Life. 1992. V. 54
Recalled to Life. Bristol: 1992. V. 51; 52
Recalled to Life. London: 1992. V. 53
The Wood Beyond. 1996. V. 54
The Wood Beyond. London: 1996. V. 53

HILL, RICHARD
An Address to Persons of Fashion Relating to Balls... Shrewsbury: 1771. V. 51
The Blessings of Polygamy Displayed in an Affectionate Address to the Rev. Martin Madan... London: 1781. V. 53

HILL, ROWLAND
Journal through the North of England and Parts of Scotland. (and) Extract of a Journal of a Second Tour from London through the Highlands of Scotland and the Northern Western Parts of England. London: 1799/1800. V. 51; 52
The Life of Sir Rowland Hill and the History of Penny Postage. London: 1880. V. 47; 52

HILL, ROY L.
Booker T.'s Child: the Life and Times of Portia Marshal Washington Pittman. Newark: 1974. V. 52
Rhetoric of Racial Hope. Buffalo: 1976. V. 53

HILL, S. S.
The Dominions of the Pope and Sultan, or, Impressions of Travel and Observations,, in the Roman States and Turkey. London: 1870. V. 48; 53

HILL, THEOPHILUS HUNTER
Hesper, and Other Poems. Raleigh: 1861. V. 49; 53

HILL, THOMAS
Marmion Travestied; a Tale of Modern Times. London: 1809. V. 53

HILL Towns and Cities of Northern Italy. New York: 1932. V. 47

HILL, VERNON
Ballads Weird and Wonderful. London: 1912. V. 50; 51

HILL, W. B.
A New Earth and a New Heaven. 1936. V. 51

HILL, W. C. OSMAN
The Elephant in East Central Africa, a Monograph. London: 1953. V. 48; 51
Primates, Comparative Anatomy and Taxonomy. Edinburgh: 1953-60. V. 50
Primates, Comparative Anatomy and Taxonomy. Edinburgh: 1953-66. V. 52
Primates, Comparative Anatomy and Taxonomy. Edinburgh: 1953-74. V. 52
Primates, Comparative Anatomy and Taxonomy. Edinburgh: 1960-62. V. 49

HILL, W. E.
Among Us Cats. New York: 1926. V. 50

HILL, WILLIAM
Grammaticarum in Dionysii...cum Commentario Critico & Geographico... London: 1688. V. 50
Organization of the Territory of Oklahoma. Washington: 1684. V. 49

HILL, WILLIAM HENRY
Antonio Stradivari, His Life and Work. London: 1902. V. 48; 49
The Violin-Makers of the Guarneri Family (1626-1762). 1931. V. 50; 52
The Violin-Makers of the Guarneri Family (1626-1762). London: 1931. V. 47; 48; 49

HILLARD, ELIAS BREWSTER
The Last Men of the Revolution: a Photograph of Each from Life, Together with Views of their Homes Printed in Colors. Hartford: 1864. V. 50

HILLARD, GEORGE STILLMAN
Six Months in Italy. London: 1853. V. 49
Six Months in Italy. Boston: 1854. V. 52

HILLARD, KATHARINE
My Mother's Journal. Boston: 1900. V. 51

HILLARY, WILLIAM
An Appeal to the British Nation, On the Humanity and Policy of Forming a National Institution for the Preservation of Lives and Property from Shipwreck. London: 1823. V. 49; 52
Observations on the Changes of the Air and the Concomitant Epidemical Diseases, in the Island of Barbadoes. London: 1766. V. 49; 50; 54
A Rational and Mechanical Essay on the Small Pox, Wherein the Cause, Nature and Diathesis of that Disease, Its Symptoms, Their Causes and Manner of Production... London: 1735. V. 48

HILLEBRAND, KARL
Six Lectures on the History of German Thought. London: 1880. V. 47

HILLEBRAND, W.
Flora of Hawaiian Islands. Heidelberg: 1888. V. 48; 51; 54

HILLER, LEJAREN A.
Surgery through the Ages: A Pictorial Chronical. New York: 1944. V. 47

HILLER, O. PRESCOTT
American National Lyrics and Sonnets. Boston: 1860. V. 54

HILLERMAN, TONY
The Blessing Way. New York Evanston & London: 1970. V. 47; 50; 52; 53; 54
The Blessing Way. New York: 1989. V. 51
The Blessing Way. New York: 1990. V. 51
The Boy Who Made Dragonfly. New York: 1972. V. 47; 50; 51; 52; 53
Coyote Waits. New York: 1990. V. 50; 51; 52; 53
Dance Hall of the Dead. London: 1973. V. 49; 50
The Dance Hall of the Dead. New York: 1973. V. 50; 51; 52; 54
Dance Hall of the Dead. London: 1985. V. 51
Dance Hall of the Dead. New York: 1991. V. 51; 54
The Dark Wind. New York: 1982. V. 47; 48; 51; 52; 53
Finding Moon. New York: 1995. V. 53; 54
The Fly on the Wall. New York: 1971. V. 48; 49; 51; 52; 53
The Fly on the Wall. New York: 1990. V. 51
The Ghostway. New York: 1984. V. 53
The Ghostway. San Diego: 1984. V. 49; 51
The Ghostway. London: 1985. V. 51
The Ghostway. New York: 1985. V. 49; 51; 53; 54
The Great Taos Bank Robbery. 1972. V. 47
The Great Taos Bank Robbery. Albuquerque: 1973. V. 51; 53
Hillerman Country. New York: 1991. V. 48; 50; 51; 52; 53; 54
Hillerman Country: a Journey through the Southwest with Tony Hillerman. New York: 1991. V. 51
Indian Country: America's Sacred Land. Flagstaff: 1987. V. 47
Jim Chee Mysteries. New York: 1990. V. 51
The Joe Leaphorn Mysteries. New York: 1989. V. 51
Listening Woman. New York: 1978. V. 48; 51; 52
Listening Woman. London: 1979. V. 50; 51; 53; 54
Listening Woman. New York: 1994. V. 51; 52
New Mexico. Portland: 1974. V. 49; 51; 52
New Mexico... Portland: 1992. V. 51
People of Darkness. New York: 1980. V. 51; 53
People of Darkness. New York: 1994. V. 51
Rio Grande. Portland: 1975. V. 51; 52
Sacred Clowns. 1993. V. 50; 54
Sacred Clowns. New York: 1993. V. 50; 51; 52; 53
Skinwalkers. New York: 1986. V. 47; 50; 51
The Spell of New Mexico. Albuquerque: 1976. V. 47; 50; 51; 52; 53
Talking God. New York: 1989. V. 51; 52; 53; 54
Talking Mysteries. Albuquerque: 1991. V. 51; 53
A Thief of Time. New York: 1988. V. 51; 52; 53; 54
Words, Weather and Wolfman. 1989. V. 51
Words, Weather and Wolfmen. Gallup: 1989. V. 50; 51; 53; 54

HILLERNE, WILHELMINE VON
The Hour Will Come: a Tale of an Alpine Cloister. London: 1879. V. 54
The Hour Will Come, a Tale of an Alpine Cloister... London: 1880. V. 53

HILLES, FREDERICK W.
Johnson on Dr. Arbuthnot. 1957. V. 54

HILLHOUSE, JAMES A.
Dramas, Discourses and Other Pieces. Boston: 1839. V. 49

HILLHOUSE, MARY
German Songs in English Rhyme. Hartford: 1871. V. 47

HILLIAM, WILLIAM H.
Old Fort Edward Before 1800: An Account of the Historic Ground Now Occupied by the Village of Fort Edward, New York. Fort Edward: 1929. V. 51

HILLIAR, ANTHONY
A Brief and Merry History of Great Britain... London: 1730. V. 52

HILLIARD, FRANCIS
The Elements of Law; Being a Comprehensive Summary of American Civil Jurispurdence. Boston: 1835. V. 49

HILLIARD, JOHN NORTHERN
Greater Magic, a Practical Treatise on Modern Magic. Minneapolis: 1938. V. 50
Greater Magic, a Practical Treatise on Modern Magic. Minneapolis: 1945. V. 48

HILLIER, GEORGE
A Narrative of the Attempted Escapes of Charles the First from Carisbrook Castle, and of His Detention in the Isle of Wight, from November 1647 to the Seizure of His Person by the Army, at Newport, in Nov. 1648... London: 1852. V. 54

HILLIER, JACK
Catalogue of the Japanese Paintings and Prints in the Collection of Mr. and mrs. Richard Gale. London: 1970. V. 52
Hokusai. Paintings, Drawings and Woodcuts. London: 1955. V. 49
Japanese Prints and Drawings from the Vever Collection. London: 1976. V. 50; 51
Suzuki Harunobu. An Exhibition of the Colour Prints and Illustrated Books on the Bicentenary of His Death in 1770. Philadelphia: 1970. V. 50; 54
The Uninhibited Brush. London: 1974. V. 50; 54

HILLMAN, BRENDA
Coffee, 3 A.M. Poems. Lisbon: 1981. V. 52; 54

HILLS, CHESTER
The Builder's Guide; or a Practical Treatise on the Several Orders of Grecian and Roman Architecture... Hartford: 1834. V. 49; 50

HILLS, FRED
The Official Manual of the Cripple Creek District, Colorado, U.S.A. Volume I, A.D. 1900. Colorado Springs: 1900. V. 47

HILLS, JOHN WALLER
A History of Fly Fishing for Trout. London: 1921. V. 53
River Keeper, the Life of William James Lunn. London: 1934. V. 53
A Summer on the Test. London: 1924. V. 49; 53

HILLS, MRS.
Fair Faces and True Hearts, a Novel. London: 1882. V. 47

HILLS, OSBORN C.
Saint Mary Stratford Bow. London: 1900. V. 47

HILLS, S. S.
The Dominions of the Pope and Sultan, or, Impressions of Travel and Observations on Character, in the Roman States and Turkey. London: 1870. V. 50

HILL-TOUT, CHARLES
The Native Races of the British Empire: British North America: The Far West, The Home of the Salish and Dene. London: 1907. V. 52

HILLYER, ROBERT
The Death of Captain Nemo. New York: 1949. V. 54
The Relic and Other Poems. New York: 1957. V. 54
Sonnets and Other Lyrics. Cambridge: 1917. V. 54

HILPRECHT, HERMAN V.
The Excavations in Assyria and Babylonia. Philadelphia: 1904. V. 49
Exploration in Bible Lands During the 19th Century. Edinburgh: 1903. V. 51
Explorations in Bible Lands During the 19th Century. Philadelphia: 1903. V. 51; 53

HILSOP, HERBERT R.
An Englishman's Arizona. Tucson: 1965. V. 52; 53

HILTON, CONRAD N.
Inspirations of an Inn-Keeper. Los Angeles: 1963. V. 48

HILTON, HAROLD H.
The Royal and Ancient Game of Golf. London: 1912. V. 47

HILTON, JAMES
The Dawn of Reckoning. 1925. V. 53
The Dawn of Reckoning. London: 1925. V. 48; 54
Good-Bye, Mr. Chips. Boston: 1934. V. 50; 52; 53
Good-Bye Mr. Chips. London: 1934. V. 48; 51; 53
Lost Horizon. London: 1933. V. 47; 48
Lost Horizon. New York: 1936. V. 50
Lost Horizon. New York: 1936/33. V. 48
The Meadows of the Moon. Boston: 1927. V. 49
Nothing So Strange. Boston: 1947. V. 48
Random Harvest. London: 1941. V. 50; 54
To Your Mr. Chips. London: 1938. V. 48
Twilight of the Wise. London: 1949. V. 53
We Are Not Alone. V. 50
We Are Not Alone. London: 1937. V. 50
Without Armor. New York: 1934. V. 48; 51

HILTON, JOHN
Notes on Some of the Development and Functional Relations of Certain Portions of the Cranium... London: 1855. V. 53; 54
Random Harvest. London: 1941. V. 50

HILTON, JOHN HOWARD
The History and Topography of the United States...Brought Down from the Earliest period... Boston: 1852. V. 49

HILTON-SIMPSON, M. W.
Land and Peoples of Kasai. Being a Narrative of Two Years' Journey Among the Canibals of the Equatorial Forest and Other Savage Tribes of the South-Western Congo. Chicago: 1912. V. 51

HILZINGER, JOHN GEORGE
Treasure Land. A Story. Tucson: 1897. V. 51; 52

HIMES, CHARLES F.
Leaf Prints: or Glimpses at Photography. Philadelphia: 1868. V. 47

HIMES, CHESTER
Une Affaire de Viol. (Case of Rape). Paris: 1963. V. 52
The Big Gold Dream. New York: 1960. V. 51
Blind Man with a Pistol. New York: 1969. V. 54
A Case of Rape. New York: 1980. V. 53; 54
Cast the First Stone. New York: 1952. V. 47; 52
La Croisade De Lee Gordon. Paris: 1952. V. 52
For Love of Imabelle. New York: 1957. V. 51
The Heat's On. New York: 1966. V. 52
If He Hollers Let Him go. Garden City: 1945. V. 50; 52
If He Hollers Let Him Go. New York: 1945. V. 47
If He Hollers Let Him Go. London: 1947. V. 51
Lonely Crusade. New York: 1947. V. 47; 52; 53
Mamie Mason, ou Un Exercise de la Bonne Volante. Paris: 1962. V. 52
Le Manteau du Reve. Paris: 1982. V. 52
My Life of Absurdity. Garden City: 1976. V. 53
Pinktoes. Paris: 1961. V. 51
Pinktoes. New York: 1965. V. 48; 51; 53
The Primitive. New York: 1956. V. 52
The Quality of Hurt. Garden City: 1972. V. 49; 51; 52
Tout Pour Plaire. (Big Gold Dream). 1959. V. 52

HIMES, JOSHUA V.
The Advent Harp: Designed for Believers in the Speedy Coming of Christ. Boston: 1849. V. 47
Millennial Harp Designed for Meetings on the Second Coming of Christ. Boston: 1846. V. 47
Views of the Prophecies and Prophetic Chronology. Boston: 1841. V. 47; 49
Views of the Prophecies and Prophetic Chronology... Boston: 1849. V. 47

HIMLISCHES Freuden-Wahl der Kinder Gottes auf Erden. Luneburg: 1761. V. 50

HINCHCLIFF, THOMAS W.
Summer Months Among the Alps: with the Ascent of Monte Rosa. London: 1857. V. 51

HINCHMAN, WALTER
Sketches and Poems, 1845-1920. 1920. V. 47; 50

HINCKS, THOMAS
A History of the British Hydroid Zoophytes. London: 1868. V. 52

HIND, ARTHUR MAYGER
Catalogue of Early Italian Engravings Preserved in the Department of Prints and Drawings in the British Museum. London: 1909-10. V. 50
Catalogue of Rembrandt's Etchings. London: 1923. V. 50
The Drawings of Claude Lorrain. London: 1925. V. 53
Engraving in England in the Sixteenth and Seventeenth Centuries. Cambridge: 1955. V. 48; 51
The Etchings of D. Y. Cameron. London: 1924. V. 51
A History of Engraving and Etching. Boston & New York: 1923. V. 53
History of Engraving and Etching... New York: 1927. V. 48
An Introduction to a History of Woodcut. Boston: 1935. V. 49
Rembrandt's Etchings, an Essay and a Catalogue. London: 1912. V. 49
Wenceslaus Hollar and His Views of London and Windsor in the Seventeenth Century. London: 1922. V. 49; 52; 53

HIND, CHARLES LEWIS
Authors and I. New York: 1921. V. 52
Hercules Brabazon, 1821-1906. London: 1912. V. 49
More Author's and I. New York: 1922. V. 52
The Uncollected Work of Aubrey Beardsley. London: 1925. V. 53

HIND, G. W.
A Series of Twenty Plates Illustrating the Causes of Displacement in the Various Factures of the Bones of the Extremities. V. 47

HIND, HENRY YOULE
British North America. Reports on Progress. Together with a Preliminary and General Report of the Assinniboine and Saskatchewan Exploring Expedition. London: 1860. V. 52
Eighty Years' Progress of British North America... Toronto: 1863. V. 48
Explorations in the Interior of the Labrador Peninsula the Country of the Montagnais and Nasquapee Indians. London: 1863. V. 53
Narrative of the Canadian Red River Exploring Expedition of 1857 and of the Assinniboine and Saskatchewan exploring Expedition of 1858. London: 1860. V. 47; 48; 49; 50; 51
North-West Territory. Report of Progress...On the Assinboine and Saskatchewan Exploring Expedition. Toronto: 1859. V. 48; 52; 53
Report of the Sherbrooke Gold District Together with a Paper on the Gneisses of Nova Scotia and an Abstract of a Paper on Gold Mining in Nova Scotia. Halifax: 1870. V. 47
Territoire du Nord-Ouest. Rapports de Progres; Aussi, un Rapport Preliminaire et un Rapport General sur l'Expedition d'Exploration de l'Assiniboine et de la Saskatchewan... Toronto: 1859. V. 48

HIND, JAMES
The Declaration of Captain James Hind (Close Prisoner in Newgate) and His Acknowledgment, Protestation and Full Confession at His Examination Before the Councel of State... London: 1651. V. 47; 50
The Declaration of Captain James Hind (Close Prisoner in Newgate) and His Acknowledgment, Protestation and Full Confession at His Examination Before the Councel of State... London: 1820. V. 53

HIND, W.
A Monograph of the British Carboniferous Lamellibranchiata. London: 1896-1905. V. 49; 52

HIND, W. M.
The Flora of Suffolk. London: 1899. V. 51

HINDERER, ANNA
Seventeen Years in the Yoruba Country. London: 1873. V. 48; 50; 52

HINDERWELL, THOMAS
The History and Antiquities of Scarborough and the Vicinity. York: 1811. V. 54

HINDLEY, CHARLES
A Collection of Readable Reprints of Literary Rarities... London: 1876. V. 51
Curiosities of Street Literature... London: 1871. V. 49
The History of the Catnach Press at Berwick-upon-Tweed, Alnwick and Newcastle-upon-Tyne, Northumberland. London: 1886. V. 51
A History of the Cries of London. London: 1884. V. 49
The Life and Times of James Catnach, (Late of Seven Dials), Ballad Monger... London: 1878. V. 52
The Old Book Collector's Miscellany; or, a Collection of Readable Reprints of Literary Rarities... London: 1871-73. V. 48; 49
The Roxburghe Ballads. London: 1873. V. 48

HINDS, JAMES PITCAIRN
Bibliotheca Jacksoniana. Kendal: 1909. V. 52

HINDS, JOHN
The Groom's Oracle and Pocket Stable-Directory. London: 1829. V. 49

HINDS, WILLIAM ALFRED
American Communities: Brief Sketches of Economy, Zoar, Bethel, Aurora, Amana, Icaria, the Shakers, Oneida, Wallingford and the Brotherhood of the New Life. Oneida: 1878. V. 49

HINDUS, MILTON
A World at Twilight: a Portrait of the Jewish Communities of Eastern Europe before the Holocaust. New York: 1971. V. 49

HINE, C. G.
The New York and Albany Post Road. Albany: 1905. V. 48

HINE, DARYL
The Carnal and the Crane. Montreal: 1957. V. 47
The Prince of Darkness and Co. New York: 1961. V. 54

HINE, E. CURTISS
The Signal; or, the King of the Blue Isle. Boston: 1848. V. 49; 52; 53

HINE, REGINALD L.
The History of Hitchin. London: 1927-29. V. 49

HINES, D.
Who's Who in Music and Darama. New York: 1914. V. 49

HINES, EDWARD
Amateur's Turning Lathes and Accessories of the Workshop. Norwich: 1892. V. 52

HINES, GORDON
Alfalfa Bill, an Intimate Biography. Oklahoma City: 1932. V. 49; 52; 53
True Tales of the Old 101 Ranch. Oklahoma: 1953. V. 50

HINES, GUSTAVUS
Life on the Plains of the Pacific, Oregon: Its History, Condition and Prospects... Buffalo: 1851. V. 50
A Voyage Around the World, with a History of the ORegon Mission and Notes of Several Years Residence on the Plains. Buffalo: 1850. V. 51; 53

HINGESTON-RANDOLPH, F. C.
Royal and Historical Letters During the Reign of Henry the Fourth, King of England and France and Lord of Ireland. London: 1860-1965. V. 49
Royal and Historical Letters During the Reign of Henry the Fourth, King of England and France, and Lord of Ireland. London: 1965. V. 52

HINKS, PETER
Nineteenth Century Jewellery. London: 1975. V. 47
Twentieth Century British Jewellery 1900-1980. London: 1983. V. 50

HINKSON, H. A.
Dublin Verse of Trinity College. London: 1895. V. 50

HINKSON, KATHARINE TYNAN
Cuckoo Songs. London: 1894. V. 49; 52
Innocencies: a Book of Verse. London: 1905. V. 49
A Little Book of Courtesies. London: 1906. V. 49
Shamrocks. London: 1st edition. V. 52
Twenty-One Poems. Dundrum: 1907. V. 53

HINTON, MILTON
Bass Line: The Stories and Photographs of Milt Hinton. Philadelphia: 1988. V. 54

HINTON, RICHARD J.
The Hand-Book to Arizona: Its Resources, History, Towns, Mines, Ruins and Scenery. San Francisco: 1878. V. 47
Rebel Invasion of Missouri and Kansas and the Campaign of the Army of the Border Against General Sterling Price in Oct. and Nov. 1864. Chicago: 1865. V. 47

HINTON, S. S.
That Was Then, This is Now. New York: 1971. V. 48

HINTS Addressed to Radical Reformers. Glasgow: 1819. V. 54

HINTS and Directions for Authors in Writing, Printing and Publishing Their Works. London: 1842. V. 51

HINTS to Farmers on the Nature, Purchase and Application of Peruvian, Bolivian and African Guano: with a Series of Authenticated Experiments, Proving It to Be a Most Potent Manure. London: 1844. V. 50

HINTS to Unmarried Ladies, in a Letter from Ephraim Blenkinsop to His Ward Miss Lydia Languish. (with) Important Advice to Married Men. Manchester: 1830-31. V. 54

HIORT, JOHN WILLIAM
A Practical Treatise on the Construction of Chimneys. London: 1826. V. 51; 53

HIPKINS, A. J.
Musical Instruments: Historic, Rare and Unique. Edinburgh: 1888. V. 48; 49; 54
Musical Instruments, Historic, Rare and Unique. London: 1921. V. 49

HIPKINS, W. E.
The Wire Rope and Its Applications. Birmingham: 1896. V. 50

HIPPISLEY, JOHN
A Dissertation on Comedy, in Which the Rise and Progress of that Species of the Drama is Particularly Consider'd and Deduc'd from the Earliest to the Present Age. London: 1750. V. 49

HIPPOCRATES
Aphorismi...Graece et Latine, Una Cum Galen Commentarijs. Lyon: 1549. V. 47; 48; 49
De Aere, Aquis & Locis Libellus Eiusdem, de Flatibus Graece & Latine. Basileae: 1529. V. 51
De Flatibus. Paris: 1557. V. 47; 48; 49; 50; 51; 52; 53
The Genuine Works of Hippocrates. London: 1849. V. 50; 52
The Genuine Works of Hippocrates. New York: 1886. V. 50
Hippocrates Coi Medicorvm Omnivm Facile Principis Opera... Venetiis: 1575. V. 47
Octoginta Volumnia...Nunc Tandem per M. Fabium Calvum Rhavennatem... 1525. V. 49
On Intercourse and Pregnancy. New York: 1952. V. 50; 52
Opera. Basileae: 1554. V. 47; 50; 53
Opera Omnia Quae Extant...Oeconomia Hippocratis Alphabeti Serie Distincta... Geneva: 1657-62. V. 51; 52; 53
Prognostica (latin). In Magni Hippocratis prognostica iacobii Antonii Phrygii Ticinensis medici Collegiati... Ticini (Pavia): 1608. V. 50
The Writings of Hippocrates and Galen Epitomised from the Original Translations. Philadelphia: 1846. V. 54

HIROHITO, EMPEROR OF JAPAN
The Hydroids of Sagami Bay. Tokyo: 1988. V. 50

HIRSCH, AUGUST
Handbook of Geographical and Histological Pathology. London: 1883-86. V. 52

HIRSCHFELD, ALBERT
Art and Recollections From Eight Decades. New York: 1991. V. 48
The World of Hirschfeld. New York: 1969. V. 52

HIRSCHFELDER, ARTHUR
Diseases of the Heart and Aorta. Philadelphia: 1910. V. 53

HIRSCHFIELD, ALBERT
The American Theatre As Seen by Hirshfeld. New York: 1961. V. 48; 50

HIRSCHMAN, JACK
A Correspondence of Americans. Bloomington: 1960. V. 48; 51

HIRST, BARTON COOKE
Human Monstrosities. Philadelphia: 1891-93. V. 52
A System of Obstetrics. Philadelphia: 1888. V. 48; 53

HIRST, HENRY
The Coming of the Mammoth, the Funeral of Time, And Other Poems. Boston: 1845. V. 53

HIRST, L. FABIAN
The Conquest of Plague. Oxford: 1953. V. 53

HIRTZLER, VICTOR
Hotel St. Francis Book of Recipes and Model Menus. San Francisco: 1910. V. 48
The Hotel St. Francis Cook Book. Chicago: 1919. V. 48

HIS Catholic Majesty's Most Christian Manifesto, and Reasons for Not Paying the Ninety-Five Thousand Pounds... London: 1739. V. 47

HIS Imperial Highness the Grand Duke Alexis in the United States of America During the Winter of 1871-1872. Cambridge: 1872. V. 49

HIS Majesties Commission to All the Lords, and Others of the Prive Counsell, Touching the Creation of Baronets, Whereunto are Annexed Diuers Instructions, and His Majesties Letters Patents Containing the Forme of the Said Creation. London: 1611. V. 51

HIS Majesties Speech to the Gentlemen of Yorkshire, on Thursday the Fourth of August, 1642. London: 1642. V. 50

HISCOX, GARDNER D.
Mechanical Movements, Powers and Devices. (with) Mechanical Appliances, Mechanical Movements and Novelties of Construction... New York: 1907/10. V. 54

HISLOP, ALEXANDER
The Two Babylons; or, the Papal Worship Proved to Be Worship of Nimrod and His Wife with Sixty-One Woodcut Illustrations from Nineveh, Babylon, Egypt, Pompeii, &c. Edinburgh: 1842. V. 51

HISLOP, HERBERT R.
An Englishman's Arizona. Tucson: 1965. V. 50; 52; 53

HISPANIOLA, Hayti, Saint Domingo. London: 1851. V. 54

HISSEY, JAMES JOHN
Across England in a Dog-Cart from London to St. Davids and Back. London: 1891. V. 47

HISTOIRE des Revolutions de la Haute Allemagne. Zurich: 1766. V. 53

HISTOIRE Entiere & Veritable Dv Procez de Charles Stuart, Roy D' Angleterre. Londres: 1650. V. 49

HISTORIAE Romanae Autores Varii. Lyons: 1552. V. 54

THE HISTORIANS Guide In Two Parts. London: 1676. V. 48

AN HISTORIC Epistle from Omiah to the Queen of Otaheite; being His Remarks on the English Nation. London: 1775. V. 52

HISTORIC Houses of the United Kingdom: Descriptive, Historical, Pictorial. London: 1892. V. 51; 54

HISTORIC Interiors in Colour. New York: 1929. V. 53

HISTORICAL & Descriptive Guide to Carlisle and District. Carlisle: 1881. V. 52

AN HISTORICAL Account of All the Tryals and Attainders of High-Treason, From the Beginning of the Reign of King Charles the First...Acts of Attainder...Dying speeches, or Papers. London: 1716. V. 49

AN HISTORICAL Account of the Battle of Waterloo, Fought on the 18th of June 1815... London: 1817. V. 53

HISTORICAL Account of the Grand Tragic Ballet, Called Medea and Jason, as It is Performed with Uncommon Applause... London: 1781. V. 50

AN HISTORICAL Account of the Ten Tribes Settled Beyond the River Sambatyon, in the East... London & Philadelphia: 1835?. V. 48

HISTORICAL Accounting Literature. London: 1979. V. 54

HISTORICAL and Biographical Atlas of the New Jersey Coast. Philadelphia: 1878. V. 49

A HISTORICAL and Biographical Record of the Territory of Arizona Illustrated. Chicago: 1896. V. 49

HISTORICAL and Descriptive Review of the Industries of Houston, 1884-85. Houston: 1885. V. 49

THE HISTORICAL and Local New Bath Guide. Bath. V. 48; 49; 53

HISTORICAL and Scientific Sketches of Michigan... Detroit: 1834. V. 49

HISTORICAL Anecdotes of Old Prison Days. Yuma. V. 53

AN HISTORICAL, Antiquarian and Picturesque Account of Kirkstall Abbey... London & Leeds: 1827. V. 50

HISTORICAL Atlas Map of Sonoma County, California. Oakland: 1877. V. 50; 53

HISTORICAL Collections; or, a brief account of the Most Remarkable Transactions of the Two Last Parliaments... London: 1681. V. 48; 52

HISTORICAL Collections; or, a Brief Account Of the Most Remarkable Transactions of the Two Last Parliaments. London: 1685. V. 50; 51

AN HISTORICAL, Genealogical and Classical Dictionary. London: 1743. V. 50

HISTORICAL Memoranda Relative to the Discovery of Etherization and to the Connection With It of the Late Dr. William T. G. Morton. Boston: 1871. V. 50; 52

HISTORICAL MONUMENTS COMMISSION
An Inventory of the Historical Monuments in Buckinghamshire. London: 1912-13. V. 49

HISTORICAL Monuments in the County of Dorset. London: 1970. V. 48

HISTORICAL Monuments of Islam in the USSR. Tashkent: 1950's. V. 48

THE HISTORICAL Pocket Library; or, Biographical Vade-Mecum. London: 1790. V. 50

HISTORICAL Record of the First or Royal Regiment of Foot, Containing an Account of the Origin of the Regiment in the Reign of King James VI of Scotland and Of its Subsequent Services to 1838. London: 1838. V. 50

HISTORICAL Records of the 79th Queen's Own Cameron Highlanders, Compiled from the Orderly Room Records. Devonport: 1887. V. 50

HISTORICAL Records of the Cameron Highlanders. Volume VII. London: 1962. V. 50

HISTORICAL Sketch of Armenia and the Armenians in Ancient and Modern Times with Special Reference to the Present Crisis. London: 1896. V. 54

AN HISTORICAL Sketch of the Municipal Constitution of the City of Edinburgh. An Historical Account of the Blue Blanket. Edinburgh: 1826. V. 51; 54

HISTORICAL SOCIETY OF MONTANA
Contributions to the Historical Society of Montana. Volume 1. Helena: 1902. V. 52
Contributions to the Historical Society of Montana. Volume II. Helena: 1896. V. 52
Contributions to the Historical Society of Montana. Volume III. Helena: 1900. V. 52
Contributions to the Historical Society of Montana. Volume IV. Helena: 1903. V. 52
Contributions to the Historical Society of Montana. Volume V. Helena: 1904. V. 52

HISTORICAL Souvenir of San Francisco, California. San Francisco: 1887. V. 47

THE HISTORY And Adventures of Little Henry. London: 1830. V. 50

THE HISTORY and Antiquities of the University of Cambridge. London: 1721. V. 54

THE HISTORY and Description of Colchester. Colchester: 1803. V. 52

A HISTORY and Description of the Royal Abbaye of Saint Denis, with an Account of the Tombs of the Kings and Queens of France... London: 1795. V. 52

HISTORY and Description of Woburn and Its Abbey. Woburn: 1845. V. 50

HISTORY and Medical Description of the Two-Headed Girl, sold by Her Agents. Buffalo: 1869. V. 48

HISTORY and Memoir of the 33rd Battalion Machine Gun Corps, and of the 19th, 98th, 100th and 248th M.G. Companies. London: 1919. V. 50

THE HISTORY and Mystery of Puffing; or a few Fragrant Whiffs of the Weed, Evolving Sundry Pleasant, Pithy and Profitable Hints Touching the Poetry of Smoking... New York: 1844. V. 50

HISTORY and Roster of Maryland Volunteers, War of 1861-5. Baltimore: 1898-99. V. 54

THE HISTORY and Topography of Ashbourn, the Valley of the Dove and the Adjacent Villages... Ashbourn: 1839. V. 47; 50

HISTORY of 124th Machine Gun Battalion - 66th Brigade, 33rd Division - A.E.F. 1919. V. 52

THE HISTORY of a Goldfinch Intended to Excite in the Minds of Youth, Humanity Towards the Brute Creation. London: 1823. V. 51

HISTORY of Alameda County, California. Oakland: 1883. V. 48; 50; 52

THE HISTORY of an Apple Pie. London: 1835. V. 47

THE HISTORY of Arizona Territory. Flagstaff: 1964. V. 48

THE HISTORY of Blue Beard and Fatima. New Haven: 1824. V. 48

THE HISTORY Of Cass and Bates Counties, Missouri, Containing a History of These Counties, Their Cities, Towns, etc. St. Joseph: 1883. V. 54

THE HISTORY Of Cheshire: Containing King's Vale-Royal Entire, Together with Considerable Extracts from Sir Peter Leycester's Antiquites of Cheshire... Chester: 1778. V. 50

THE HISTORY of Commodore Anson's Voyage Round the World, at the Commencement of the Late Spanish War. London: 1769. V. 54

HISTORY of Company A and the 22d Regiment N.G.N.Y. New York: 1901. V. 52

THE HISTORY of Discoveries and Inventions, Chiefly Intended for the Entertainment and Instruction of Young Persons... London: 1808. V. 52; 53

HISTORY of Dixon and Lee County, Chronological Record, Showing the Current Events and Many Interesting Reminiscences in the History of Dixon and Lee County, from the Earliest White Settlement to the Present. 1880. V. 54

HISTORY of Egypt: Chaldea, Syria, Babylonia, and Assyria. London: 1904-06. V. 53

HISTORY of Eliza Musgrove. London: 1769. V. 50; 54

THE HISTORY of Eliza Warwick. London: 1791. V. 49; 54

THE HISTORY of England from Julius Caesar to George III. London: 1802. V. 49

HISTORY of Erie County, Pennsylvania. Chicago: 1884. V. 48

THE HISTORY of Helyas, Knight of the Swan. New York: 1901. V. 47; 51

HISTORY of Henry County, Indiana... Chicago: 1884. V. 50

HISTORY Of Hillsdale County, Michigan, with Illustrations and Biographical Sketches. Philadelphia: 1897. V. 49

THE HISTORY of How Ned Nimble Built His Cottage. London: 1861. V. 47

THE HISTORY of Ink, Including Its Etymology, Chemistry and Bibliography. New York: 1860. V. 51

THE HISTORY of Jackson County, Missouri. Kansas City: 1881. V. 49; 51

THE HISTORY of Jane Grey, Queen of England. London: 1792. V. 48

THE HISTORY of Little Charles and His Friend Frank Wilful. Litchfield: 1808. V. 50

THE HISTORY of Little Dame Crump and Her White Pig. London: 1840. V. 52

THE HISTORY of Little Fanny... Philadelphia: 1825. V. 50

HISTORY of Little Fanny. London: 1830. V. 51

THE HISTORY of Little Goody Two-Shoes: Otherwise Called Mrs. Margery Two-shoes. London: 1796. V. 52

THE HISTORY of Little Miss Pig. London: 1864. V. 49

THE HISTORY of Little Tom Tucker. York: 1840. V. 49

HISTORY of Livingston Co., Michigan. Philadelphia: 1880. V. 49

HISTORY of Medicine and Surgery and Physicians and Surgeons of Chicago. Chicago: 1922. V. 50; 52

THE HISTORY of Miss Sally Johnson, or, the Unfortuante Magdalen. London. V. 47

THE HISTORY of Miss Sally Johnson, or, the Unfortunate Magdalen. London: 1790. V. 47

THE HISTORY of More Persons Than One, or, Entertaining and Instructive Anecdotes for Youth. London: 1823. V. 48

A HISTORY of Morris County, New Jersey. Embracing Upwards of Two Centuries, 1710-1913. New York: 1914. V. 49; 51

HISTORY of Morris County, New Jersey with Illustrations and Biographical Sketches of Prominent Citizens and Pioneers. New York: 1882. V. 49; 51

THE HISTORY of Mother Tongue and Her Children. London: 1850. V. 50

THE HISTORY of Napoleon Buonoparte. London. V. 54

HISTORY of Nevada County, California, 1880. Berkeley: 1970. V. 54

THE HISTORY of Preston, in Lancashire: Together with the Guild Merchant and Some Account of the Duchy and County Palatine of Lancaster. London: 1822. V. 48; 53

THE HISTORY of Prince Mirabel's Infancy, Rise and Disgrace... London: 1712. V. 47; 48; 49

THE HISTORY of Printing from Its Beginnings to 1930; The Subject Catalogue of the American Type Founders Company Library in the Columbia University Libraries. Millwood: 1980. V. 48

THE HISTORY of Punch and Judy. London: 1835. V. 54

HISTORY of San Luis Obispo County, California, With Illustrations and Biographical Sketches of Its Prominent Men and Pioneers. Berkeley: 1966. V. 54

HISTORY of Southeastern, Its Settlement and Growth, Geological and Physical Features. Sioux City: 1881. V. 52

A HISTORY of Technology. New York: 1954-58. V. 51

HISTORY of Texas Together with a Biographical History of the Cities of Houston and Galveston. Chicago: 1895. V. 53; 54

HISTORY Of the 127th Regiment Pennsylvania Volunteers Familiarly Known as the "Dauphin County Regiment". Lebanon: 1902. V. 52

THE HISTORY Of the 14 Field Regiment, Royal Canadian Artillery, 1940-45. Amsterdam: 1945. V. 50

HISTORY of the Arkansas Valley, Colorado. Chicago: 1881. V. 50

HISTORY of the Baldwin Locomotive Works, 1923. Philadelphia: 1924. V. 53

HISTORY of the Bible. Albany: 1822. V. 49
HISTORY of the Bible. Albany: 1828. V. 49
HISTORY of the Bible. New London: 1850. V. 49
HISTORY of the Bible. Auburn: 1851. V. 49
HISTORY of the Bible. Buffalo: 1865. V. 47

THE HISTORY of the Brazier; or Reciprocal Gratitude. Derby: 1820. V. 50

THE HISTORY of the Castle, Town and Forest of Knaresbrough, with Harrogate, and Its Medicinal Waters. York: 1798. V. 50

HISTORY of the Cattlemen of Texas. Austin. V. 53
HISTORY of the Cattlemen of Texas. Austin: 1991. V. 49

HISTORY Of the Celebration of the Fiftieth Anniversary of the Taking Possession of California and Raising the American Flag at Monterey, California. Oakland: 1896. V. 49

THE HISTORY Of the Church of Crosthwaite. Cumberland. London: 1853. V. 50; 52

A HISTORY of the City of Newark, New Jersey, Embracing Practically Two and a Half Centuries, 1666-1913. New York: 1913. V. 47; 49; 51

HISTORY of the Connecticut Valley in Massachusetts. Philadelphia: 1879. V. 53

HISTORY of the Crusades. Philadelphia. V. 54

HISTORY of the Foundations in Manchester of Christ's College, Chetham's Hospital, and the Free Grammar School. London: 1828-33. V. 52

THE HISTORY of the House That Jack Built. London: 1850. V. 52

A HISTORY of the Japanese Arts. Tokyo: 1913. V. 47; 50

A HISTORY Of the Kings and Queens of France, With Engravings Representing Them in Their Costumes. Boston: 1828. V. 49

THE HISTORY of the Lives and Bloody Exploits of the Most Noted Pirates. Hartford: 1836. V. 52

THE HISTORY of the Mitre and Purse. London: 1714. V. 53

HISTORY of the Pequot War; the Contemporary Accounts of Mason, Underhill, Vincent and Gardener. Cleveland: 1897. V. 47; 53

HISTORY of the Police Department of Newark. Newark: 1893. V. 49; 51

THE HISTORY of the Press-Yard; or, a Brief Account of the Customs and Occurrences That Are Put in Practice and to Be Met with in that Antient Repository of Living Bodies, Called, His majesty's Gaol of Newgate in London. London: 1717. V. 50

THE HISTORY of the Prince Renardo and the Lady Goosiana. London: 1833. V. 47

THE HISTORY of the Proceedings in the Case of Peg, Only Lawful Sister to John Bull, Esq. London: 1761. V. 48

THE HISTORY of the Regin of Queen Anne, Digested Into Annals. London: 1704. V. 54

THE HISTORY of the Rise and Progress of the Judicial or Adawlut System, as Established for the Administration of Justice Under the Presidency of Bengal. London: 1820. V. 49; 51; 52

THE HISTORY of the Rise and Progress of the Judicial or Adawlut System. Part II. An Inquiry into the Supposed Existence of Trial by Jury in India. London: 1822. V. 52

HISTORY of the State of Rhode Island. Philadelphia: 1878. V. 49

THE HISTORY of the Times. London: 1935-52. V. 52; 53

HISTORY of the War. London: 1914-20. V. 47

THE HISTORY of the Whiggish-Plot: or, A Brief Historical Account of the Charge and Defence of William Lord Ruffel, Capt. Tho. Walcot, John Rouse, William Hone, Captain Blague, Algernon Sidney, Esq... London: 1684. V. 52

THE HISTORY of Three Brothers; a Moral and Entertaining Tale, Founded on Fact. New York: 1794. V. 54

THE HISTORY of Tom Jones the Foundling, In His Married State. London: 1750. V. 48; 49

A HISTORY of Trenton, 1679-1929: Two Hundred and Fifty Years of a Notable Town with Links in Four Centuries. Princeton: 1929. V. 49; 51

THE HISTORY of Tuscarawas County, Ohio... Chicago: 1884. V. 49

HISTORY Of Woman Suffrage. Rochester: 1887-1922. V. 54

HISTORY of Wyoming County, New York. New York: 1880. V. 54

THE HISTORY...of Little Fanny. London: 1810. V. 50

HITCHCOCK, C. H.
Outline of the Geology of the Globe, and of the United States in Particular. Boston: 1853. V. 47

HITCHCOCK, C. L.
Vascular Plants of the Pacific Northwest. Seattle: 1964/61/59/55. V. 48

HITCHCOCK, E.
Outline of the Geology of the Globe, and of the United States in Particular... Boston: 1856. V. 54

HITCHCOCK, EDWARD
Ichnology of New England. Boston: 1858. V. 48

HITCHCOCK, ENOS
Memoirs of the Bloomsgrove Family. Boston: 1790. V. 47; 49; 50; 51; 54

HITCHCOCK, ETHAN ALLEN
Fifty Years in Camp and Field, Diary of Major General Ethan Allen Hitchcock, U.S.A. New York: 1909. V. 49
Remarks Upon Alchemy and the Alchemists, Indicating a Method of Discovering the True Nature of Hermetic Philosophy... New York: 1865. V. 48
A Traveler in Indian Territory. The Journal of Ethan Allen Hitchcock, Late Major-General in the United States Army. Cedar Rapids: 1930. V. 51

HITCHCOCK, F. R. M.
The Midland Septs and the Pale. 1908. V. 47

HITCHCOCK, FRANK
Thrilling Chase and Capture of Frank Rande. Peoria: 1897. V. 48; 50

HITCHCOCK, HENRY RUSSELL
American Architectural Books: a List of Books, Portfolios and Pamphlets on Architecture & Related Subjects. Minneapolis: 1962. V. 48; 50; 51
Early Victorian Architecture in America. London: 1954. V. 50; 52
In the Nature of Materials. The Buildings of Frank Lloyd Wright 1887-1941. New York: 1942. V. 50
The International Architecture Since 1922. New York: 1932. V. 48; 50; 51; 53
Philip Johnson: Architecture, 1949-1965. New York: 1967. V. 48; 49; 50

HITCHCOCK, J. R. W.
Etching in America. New York: 1886. V. 47; 48; 50

HITCHCOCK, R.
American Architectural Books: a List of Books, Portfolios and Pamphlets on Architecture and Related Subjects... Minneapolis: 1962. V. 50

HITCHCOCK, RIPLEY
Important New Etchings by American Artists. New York: 1888. V. 54
Noteable Etchings by American Artists. New York: 1886. V. 49

HITCHENS, JAMES
A Short Account of the Death of Thomas Hichens. London: 1751. V. 53

HITCHIN, W. E.
Surrey at the Opening of the Twentieth Century... Brighton: 1906. V. 49; 54

HITCHMAN, FRANCIS
Richard F. Burton, K.C.M.G.: His Early, Private and Public Life with an Account of His Travels and Explorations. London: 1887. V. 53

HITCHMAN, WILLIAM
The Young Astronomer's Assistant and Countryman's Daily Companion. Cirencester: 1755. V. 47; 49

HITCHOCK, ALFRED M.
Over Japan Way. New York: 1917. V. 53

HITLER, ADOLF
Mein Kampf. Munich: 1932-33. V. 50
Mein Kampf. Munich: 1939. V. 51

HITT, THOMAS
The Modern Gardener; or, Universal Kalendar. London: 1771. V. 51

HITT, THOMAS continued
A Treatise of Fruit Trees. London: 1768. V. 53

HITTELL, JOHN S.
Hittell's Hand-Book of Pacific Coast Travel. San Francisco: 1887. V. 47

HITTELL, THEODORE H.
The Adventures of James Capen Adams, Mountaineer and Grizzly Bear Hunter, of California. Boston: 1860. V. 47
History of California. San Francisco: 1885-97. V. 53
History of California. San Francisco: 1885-98. V. 49
History of California. San Francisco: 1897. V. 50
History of California. San Francisco: 1897-98. V. 50
El Triunfo de la Cruz - a Description of the Building by Father Juan Ugarte of the First ship Made in California. San Francisco: 1930. V. 52

THE HIVE of Ancient and Modern Literature: a Collection of Essays, Narratives, Allegories and Instructive Compositions. Newcastle: 1806. V. 50

HIXON, ADRIETTA APPLEGATE
On to Oregon! A True Story of a Young Girl's Journey into the West (in 1852). Weiser: 1947. V. 47

HJORTSBERG, WILLIAM
Alp. New York: 1969. V. 53
Falling Angel. 1978. V. 53
Falling Angel. New York: 1978. V. 49; 50; 53
Gray Matters. New York: 1971. V. 52; 53
Gray Matters. New York: 1974. V. 53
Symbiography. Fremont: 1973. V. 53
Tales and Fables. Los Angeles: 1985. V. 47; 48; 51
Toro! Toro! Toro!. New York: 1974. V. 53

HOADLY, BENJAMIN
The Original and Institution of Civil Government, Discuss'd. London: 1710. V. 50; 52

HOAG, JOHN D.
Islamic Architecture. New York: 1977. V. 54

HOAGLAND, EDWARD
African Calliope. A Journey to the Sudan. New York: 1979. V. 52
The Circle Home. New York: 1960. V. 51; 53
Notes from the Century Before. New York: 1969. V. 52
Red Wolves and Black Bears. New York: 1976. V. 53

HOARE, CLEMENT
A Practical Treatise on the Cultivation of the Grape Vine on Open Walls. London: 1837. V. 50

HOARE, J. DOUGLAS
Arctic Exploration. London: 1906. V. 50

HOARE, LOUISA GURNEY
Hints for the Improvement of Early Education and Nursery Discipline. London: 1822. V. 48

HOARE, PRINCE
An Inquiry Into the Requisite Cultivation and Present State of the Arts of Design in England. London: 1806. V. 50; 52

HOARE, RICHARD COLT
A Classical Tour through Italy and Sicily... London: 1819. V. 49; 52
Hints on the Topography of Wiltshire. Salisbury: 1818. V. 47
Hints to Travellers in Italy. London: 1815. V. 54
The History of Modern Wiltshire. London: 1824. V. 50
The Itinerary of Archibisohp Baldwin through Wales... London: 1806. V. 51
Journal of a Tour in Ireland, A.D. 1806. London: 1807. V. 48; 51
A Journal of the Shrievalty in the Years 1740-41. Bath: 1815. V. 50
Modern History of South Wiltshire. London: 1822-44. V. 48
A Tour Through the Island of Elba. London: 1814. V. 52

HOBAN, RUSSELL
Riddley Walker. London: 1980. V. 48; 51
Riddley Walker. New York: 1980. V. 48

HOBART-HAMPDEN AUGUSTUS CHARLES
Never Caught. London: 1867. V. 49

HOBART, HENRY
The Reports...Lord Chief Justice of His Majesties Court of Common Pleas. London: 1658. V. 47
The Reports...Lord Chief Justice of His Majesties Court of Common Pleas... London: 1671. V. 52
The Reports...Lord Chief Justice of His Majesties Court of Common Pleas... London: 1678. V. 53

HOBART, T. D.
White Deer Lands in the Panhandle of Texas. Pampa: 1905. V. 49

HOBART, VERE HENRY
On Capital Punishment for Murder: an Essay. London: 1861. V. 53

HOBBES, E. W.
Reminiscences of Seventy Years' Life, Travel and Adventure: Military and Civil: Scientiic and Literary. London: 1893. V. 50

HOBBES, R. G.
Reminiscences and Notes of Seventy Years' Life Travel and Adventure: Military and Civil; Scientific and Literary. London: 1895. V. 52

HOBBES, THOMAS
An Answer to a Book Published by Dr. Bramhall...Called the Catching the Leviathan. London: 1682. V. 50
The Art of Rhetoric, with a Discourse of the Laws of England. London: 1681. V. 47
A Brief View and Survey of the Dangerous and Pernicious Errors to Church and State in Mr. Hobbes's Book, Entitled Levithan. Oxford: 1676. V. 48
Considerations Upon the Reputation, Loyalty, Manners & Religion. London: 1680. V. 48
The Correspondence. London: 1994. V. 52
De Mirabilis Pecci: Being the Wonders of the Peak in Darby-Shire, Commonly Called the Devil's Arse of Peak. London: 1678. V. 50
Decameron Physiologicum; or Ten Dialogues of Natural Philosophy... London: 1678. V. 52
The History of the Civil Wars of England from the Year 1640 to 1660. London: 1679. V. 54
Hobbe's Tripos, in Three Discourses... London: 1684. V. 47; 50; 54
Hobbe's Tripos, in Three Discourses... London: 1840. V. 48
Leviathan. London: 1651. V. 47; 48; 51; 52; 53; 54
Leviathan, or the Matter, Forme & Power of a Common-wealth Ecclesiastaicall and Civill. London: 1651. V. 48
Philosophicall Rudiments Concerning Government and Society. London: 1651. V. 47
The Treatise on Human Nature and That on Liberty and Necessity. London: 1812. V. 52

HOBBS, JAMES
Wild Life in the Far West; Personal Adventures of a Border Mountain Man. Hartford: 1872. V. 49
Wild Life in the Far West; Personal Adventures of a Border Mountain Man. Hartford: 1873. V. 47; 48; 49; 50

HOBBY, WILLIAM
An Inquiry Into the Itinerancy and the Conduct of the Rev. Mr. George Whitefield, an Itinerant Preacher. Boston: 1745. V. 54

HOBBY, WILLIAM J.
Remarks Upon Slavery; Occasioned by Attempts Made to Circulate Improper Publications in the Southern States. Augusta: 1835. V. 50

HOBHOUSE, JOHN CAM
Historical Illustrations of the Fourth Canto of Childe Harold... London: 1818. V. 51
Imitations and Translations from the Ancient and Modern Classics, Together with Original Poems Never Before Published. London: 1809. V. 47; 48; 53; 54
A Journey through Albania and other Provinces of Turkey in Europe and Asia. London: 1813. V. 49
A Journey Through Albania and Other Provinces of Turkey in Europe and Asia... London: 1833. V. 51; 52; 54
The Substance of Some Letters...During the Last Reign of the Emperor Napoleon... London: 1816. V. 47
The Substance of Some Letters...During the Last Reign of the Emperor Napoleon... London: 1817. V. 49

HOBKIRK, CHARLES P.
Huddersfield: Its History and Natural History. Huddersfield: 1868. V. 47

HOBLER, FRANCIS
Records of Roman History, from Caneus Pompeius to Tiberius Constantinus, as Exhibited on the Roman Coins Collected by Francis Hobler. Westminster: 1860. V. 48

HOBLEY, C. W.
Bantu Beliefs and Magic, with Particular Reference to the Kikuyu and Kamba Tribes of Kenya Colony... London: 1922. V. 47

HOBSON, ANTHONY
Apollo and Pegasus: an Enquiry Into the Formation and Dispersal of a Renaissance Library. Amsterdam: 1975. V. 50
Great Libraries. London: 1970. V. 47; 53; 54
Great Libraries. New York: 1970. V. 50
Humanists and Bookbinders. The Origins and Diffusion of the Humanistic Bookbinding 1459-1559... Cambridge: 1989. V. 50

HOBSON, BULMER
The Gate Theatre Dublin. Dublin: 1934. V. 50; 54

HOBSON, C. D.
Maioli, Canevari and others. London: 1926. V. 49

HOBSON, E. C., MRS.
A Report Concerning the Colored Women of the south. Baltimore: 1896. V. 51

HOBSON, E. W.
The Theory of Functions of a Real Variable and the Theory of Fourier's Series. Cambridge: 1927-(26). V. 49

HOBSON, ELIZABETH CHRISTOPHER KIMBALL
Recollections of a Happy Life. New York: 1914. V. 50

HOBSON, GEOFFREY DUDLEY
Bindings in Cambridge Libraries... Cambridge: 1929. V. 48; 50
Bindings in Cambridge Libraries. London: 1929. V. 53
English Binding Before 1500. Cambridge: 1929. V. 50
English Bindings 1490-1940 in the Library of J. R. Abbey. London: 1940. V. 50; 53
English Bookbinding Before 1500. 1929. V. 48
Maioli, Canevari and Others. London: 1926. V. 50
Thirty Bindings. London: 1926. V. 48; 50

HOBSON, JOHN A.
Confessions of an Economic Heretic. London: 1938. V. 49
The Industrial System. London: 1910. V. 54
John Ruskin Social Reformer. London: 1898. V. 47
The Social Problem: Life and Work. London: 1902. V. 48; 50

HOBSON, RICHARD
Charles Waterton: His Home, Habits and Handiwork. London: 1867. V. 51

HOBSON, ROBERT LOCKHART
Catalogue of the Collection of English Porcelain in the Department of British and Mediaeval Antiquities and Ethnography of the British Museum. London: 1905. V. 48
Catalogue of the Collection of English Pottery in the Department of British and Mediaeval Antiquities and Ethnography of the British Museum. London: 1903. V. 48
Catalogue of the Frank Lloyd Collection of Worcester Porcelain of the Wall Period Presented by Mr. and Mrs. Frank Lloyd in 1921 to the Department of Ceramics and Ethnography in the British Museum. London: 1923. V. 48
Chinese Ceramics in Private Collections. London: 1931. V. 52
Chinese Porcelain and Wedgewood Pottery With Other Works of Ceramic Art. London: 1928. V. 53
Chinese Pottery and Porcelain. London: 1915. V. 51
The George Eumorfopoulos Collection: Catalogue of the Chinese, Corean and Persian Pottery and Porcelain. London: 1925. V. 52
The Later Ceramic Wares of China, Being the Blue and White, Famille Verte, Famille Rose... London: 1925. V. 49; 53
The Wares of the Ming Dynasty. London: 1923. V. 52; 53

HOBSON, W.
American Jazz Music. New York: 1939. V. 49

HOBY, EDWARD
A Counter-Snarle for Ishamel Rabshacheh, A Cecropidan Lycaonite. London: 1613. V. 49; 53

HOCH, EDWARD D.
The Spy Who Read Latin. Eurographica: 1990. V. 48

HOCHST, LUCIUS & BRUNING
The Coal Tar Colours of the Farbwerke Vorm Meister Lucius & Bruning Hochst on the main, Germany. Main: 1896. V. 47; 49; 52

HOCHSTETTER, FERDINAND VON
New Zealand. Stuttgart: 1867. V. 50

HOCHWALT, A. F.
The Pointer and Setter in America. Cincinnati: 1911. V. 47

HOCKEN, EDWARD OCTAVIUS
A Treatise on Amaurosis. Philadelphia: 1842. V. 47; 49; 50; 51; 53; 54

HOCKEN, T. M.
Catalogue of the Hocken Library, Dunedin. Dunedin: 1912. V. 53

HOCKING, CHARLES
Dictionary of Disasters at Sea During the Age of Steam. London: 1969. V. 48

HOCKING, WILLIAM JOHN
Catalogue of the Coins, Tokens, Dies and Seals in the Museum of the Royal Mint. London: 1906-10. V. 48

HOCKLEY, WILLIAM BROWNE
The English in India. And Other Sketches. London: 1835. V. 52

HOCKNEY, DAVID
72 Drawings by David Hockney. London: 1971. V. 50
The Blue Guitar. London and New York: 1977. V. 51
David Hockney... London: 1970. V. 54
David Hockney. London: 1976. V. 50
David Hockney... Los Angeles: 1988. V. 53
Hockney's Alphabet. V. 50
Hockney's Alphabet. London. V. 50
Hockney's Alphabet. London: 1991. V. 47; 51
Martha's Vineyard & Other Places. My Third Sketchbook from the Summer of 1982. New York: 1985. V. 47; 49; 53

HODDER, EDWIN
George Fife Angas: Father and Founder of South Australia. London: 1891. V. 48; 50
The Life and Work of the Earl of Shaftesbury. London: 1886. V. 53

HODDER, W. R.
The Daughter of the Dawn. 1903. V. 48; 52

HODGE, ARTHUR
A Report of the Trial of Arthur Hodge...for the Murder Of His Negro Man Slave Named Prosper. Middletown: 1812. V. 53

HODGE, FREDERICK WEBB
Handbook of American Indians North of Mexico. Washington: 1911. V. 51
Handbook of American Indians North of Mexico. Washington: 1912. V. 47; 53
Handbook of the Indians of Canada. Ottawa: 1913. V. 49
History of Hawiku, New Mexico, One of the So Called Cities of Cibola. Los Angeles: 1937. V. 49; 51; 52
Original Narrative of Early American History, Spanish Explorers in the Southern United States 1528-1543. New York: 1907. V. 54
Spanish Explorers in the Southern United States 1528-1543. New York: 1907. V. 54

HODGE, GENE MEANY
The Kachinas are Coming... Los Angeles: 1936. V. 48; 49
The Kachinas are Coming. Flagstaff: 1967. V. 50; 54

HODGE, HIRAM C.
Arizona As It Is; or, the Coming Country. New York: 1877. V. 47; 49; 52; 53

HODGE, TOM, PSEUD.
The History of Four Kings, Their Queens and Daughters, Kings of Canterbury, Colchester, Cornwall & Cumberland. London: 1760. V. 47

HODGES, C. WALTER
The Globe Restored - a Study of Elizabethan Theatre. London: 1953. V. 53

HODGES, CHARLES CLEMENT
Ecclesia Hagustaldensis, the Abbey of St. Andrew Hexham. London: 1888. V. 50

HODGES, CYRIL
Seeing Voice Welsh Heart. Paris: 1965. V. 47

HODGES, GEORGE W.
My Souvenirs. New York: 1951. V. 53

HODGES, GREGG
A Music. Iowa City: 1990. V. 54

HODGES, J.
The Abbey of St. Andrew, Hexham. London: 1888. V. 47; 53

HODGES, NATHANIEL
(Greek title, then) Sive Pestis Nuperae Apud Populum Londinensem Grassantis Narratio Historica. London: 1672. V. 48
Loimologia; or, an Historical Account of the Plague in London in 1665. London: 1720. V. 50; 52; 53
Loimologia: or, an Historical Account of the Plague in London in 1665. London: 1721. V. 48; 53

HODGES, RICHARD
On the Nature, Pathology and Treatment of Puerperal Convulsions. London: 1864. V. 47

HODGES, WILLIAM
Humble Proposals for the Relief, Encouragement, Security and Happiness of the Loyal Courageous Seamen of England, in Their Lives and Payment, in the Service of Our Most Gracious King William and the Defense of These Nations. 1695. V. 53
Travels in India, During the Years 1780, 1781, 1782 and 1783. London: 1793. V. 50; 53

HODGES, WILLIAM ROMAINE
Carl Wimar, a Biography. Galveston: 1908. V. 49; 54

HODGINS, J. GEORGE
The Establishment of Schools and Colleges in Ontario, 1792-1910. Toronto: 1910. V. 47

HODGINS, JACK
Beginnings. Toronto: 1983. V. 50

HODGKIN, JOHN ELIOT
Rariora. London. V. 50; 52
Rariora. London: 1900-02. V. 49; 50
Rariora. London: 1902. V. 49; 54

HODGKIN, L. V.
A Book of Quaker Saints. London & Edinburgh: 1917. V. 54

HODGKIN, THOMAS
Italy and Her Invaders. 1892-99. V. 49
Italy and Her Invaders. Oxford: 1892-99. V. 50; 52
On the Anatomical Characters of Some Adventitious Structures, Being an Attempt to Point Out the Relation Between the Microscopic Characters and those Which are Discernible by the Naked Eye. 1843. V. 48

HODGKINSON, CLEMENT
Australia, from Port MacQuarie to Moreton Bay. London: 1845. V. 50; 52

HODGSON, ADAM
Letters From North America. London: 1824. V. 48
Remarks During a Journey Through North America in the Years 1819, 1820 and 1821. New York: 1823. V. 49

HODGSON, FRANCIS
Saeculomastix; or, the Lash of the Age We Live In: a Poem. London: 1819. V. 51

HODGSON, HENRY W.
A Bibliography of the History and Topography of Cumberland and Westmorland. Carlisle: 1968. V. 52
A Topographical and Historical Description of the County of Westmoreland... London: 1820. V. 50; 52

HODGSON, HERBERT
Printer: Work for T. E. Lawrence & at Gregynog. Wakefield: 1989. V. 50
Work for T. E. Lawrence and At Gregynog. London: 1989. V. 54

HODGSON, J. F.
The Churches of Austin Canons. London. V. 49

HODGSON, JAMES
The Doctrine of Fluxions, Founded on Sir Isaac Newton's Method... London: 1758. V. 50; 54
The Valuation of Annuities Upon Lives, Deduced from the London Bills of Mortality. London: 1747. V. 50

HODGSON, JOHN
History of Northumberland. Volume 4: Roman Wall, Haydon Bridge, Haltwhistle. Newcastle-upon-Tyne: 1974. V. 53

HODGSON, JOHN EDMUND
The History of Aeronautics in Great Britain. Oxford: 1924. V. 50

HODGSON, P. L., & SON
The Measurer: Particularly Adapted to Timber and Building... Dublin: 1801. V. 51

HODGSON, RALPH
The Last Blackbird and other Lines. London: 1907. V. 47; 48
The Muse and the Mastiff. Minerva: 1942. V. 54
Poets Remembered. Cleveland: 1967. V. 48
The Skylark and other Poems. London: 1958. V. 49
The Song of Honour. London: 1913. V. 54
Songs to Our Surnames. Cerne Abbas: 1960. V. 54

HODGSON, W.
Captain Gault. 1917. V. 48
The Nightland. 1972. V. 49

HODGSON, WILLIAM
Flora of Cumberland. Carlisle: 1898. V. 50; 54

HODGSON, WILLIAM BROWN
Notes on Northern Africa, The Sahara and Soudan, in Relation to the Ethnography, Languages, History, Political and Social Condition of the Nations of Those Countries. New York: 1844. V. 50

HODGSON, WILLIAM HOPE
Carnacki the Ghost-Finder. Sauk City: 1947. V. 51
The House on the Borderland. Sauk City: 1946. V. 47; 48; 51; 52

HODIN, J. P.
Barbara Hepworth. Boston: 1961. V. 47; 48; 50
John Milne: Sculptor - Life and Work. London: 1977. V. 52

HODING, SARAH
The Land Logbook. London: 1836. V. 52

HODSKINSON, JOSEPH
The Report of Joseph Hodskinson, Engineer, on the Probable Effect Which a New Cut, Now in Contemplation from Eau-Brink to a Little Above Lynn... London: 1793. V. 48; 53

HODSON, A. W.
Trekking the Great Thirst. London: 1913. V. 52

HODSON, ARNOLD
Where Lion Reign, an Account of Lion Hunting and Exploration in S.W. Abyssinia. London: 1929. V. 49

HODSON, JAMES
Dame Partlet's Farm. London: 1845. V. 48

HODSON, JAMES LANSDALE
Grey Dawn - Red Night. London: 1929. V. 47

HODSON, T. C.
The Naga Tribes of Manipur. London: 1911. V. 53

HODSON, THOMAS
The Accomplished Tutor, or Complete System of Liberal Education. London: 1806. V. 48

HODSON, WILLIAM
Zoraida: a Tragedy. London: 1780. V. 48

HODSON, WILLIAM S. R.
Twelve Years of a Soldier's Life in India. London: 1859. V. 49; 52

HOE, ROBERT
Catalogue of the Library of Robert Hoe of York. New York: 1912. V. 52
A Lecture on Bookbinding as a Fine Art, Delivered Before the Grolier Club, Feb. 26, 1885. New York: 1886. V. 50; 53

HOELTER, H. H.
Portfolio of Hopi Kachinas. Los Angeles: 1969. V. 54

HOFER, PHILIP
Baroque Book Illustration. A Short Survey from the Collection in the Department of Graphic Arts Harvard College Library. Cambridge: 1970. V. 51

HOFF, EBBE CURTIS
A Bibliographic Sourcebook of Compressed Air, Diving and Submarine Medicine. Washington: 1948/54/66. V. 52; 53

HOFFMAN, A.
Problematic Fossil Taxa. Oxford: 1987. V. 50

HOFFMAN, ABBIE
Revolution for the Hell Of It. New York: 1968. V. 50; 52
Square Dancing in the Ice Age: Underground Writings. New York: 1982. V. 48

HOFFMAN, ALICE
Property Of. New York: 1977. V. 49; 50; 51; 54

HOFFMAN, BARRY
Gauntlet 2. Baltimore: 1991. V. 49

HOFFMAN, BERNARD G.
Cabot to Cartier: Sources for a Historical Ethnography of Northeastern North America, 1497-1550. Toronto: 1961. V. 53

HOFFMAN, BRIAN
Electrophysiology of the Heart. New York: 1960. V. 53

HOFFMAN, CHARLES FENNO
The New-York Book of Poetry. New York: 1837. V. 51
A Winter in the West...By a New Yorker. New York: 1835. V. 53

HOFFMAN, HERBERT
Early Cretan Armorers. Mainz: 1972. V. 52
Modern Lettering, Design and Application. New York: 1935?. V. 47
Tarentine Rhyta. Mainz: 1966. V. 52

HOFFMAN, WERNER
Art in the Nineteenth century. London: 1961. V. 52

HOFFMAN, WILLIAM DAWSON
The Canyon of No Return. Chicago: 1932. V. 49

HOFFMANN, ANGELO JOHN
More Magic. Philadelphia: 1900. V. 47

HOFFMANN, DETLEF
The Playing Card. An Illustrated History. Greenwich: 1973. V. 48

HOFFMANN, ERNST THEODOR AMADEUS
Nutcracker. London: 1984. V. 48
The Nutcracker. New York: 1984. V. 49; 51
Tales of ... London: 1932. V. 48; 49; 52; 53
Tales of... New York: 1932. V. 54
The Tales of... 1943. V. 48
The Tales of... New York: 1943. V. 52; 54

HOFFMANN, GEORG FRANZ
Memoires, Couronnees en l'Annee 1786, par l'Academie des Sciences, Belles Lettres et Arts de Lyon, sur l'Utilite des Lichens... Lyon: 1787. V. 47

HOFFMANN-DONNER, HEINRICH
The English Struwwelpeter. London: 1897. V. 47
Exhibition International. Paris: 1937. V. 47
King Nutcracker or the Dream of Poor Reinhold. Leipzig: 1854. V. 53; 54
King Nutcracker or the Dream of Poor Reinhold. Leipzig: 1855. V. 48
Shock-Headed Peter and Other Funny Stories. London: 1900. V. 53
Slovenly Peter... Philadelphia: 1920's. V. 50
Slovenly Peter. New York: 1935. V. 48; 51; 52; 53
Struwwelpeter. London: 1914. V. 48
Struwwelpeter. London: 1925. V. 48

HOFFMEISTER, WERNER
Travels in Ceylon and Continental India... Edinburgh: 1848. V. 53

HOFFNUNG, GERARD
Ho Ho Hoffnung. London: 1959. V. 50

HOFLAND, BARBARA WREAKS HOOLE
Africa Described, In Its Ancient and Present State; Including Accounts from Bruce, Ledyard, Lucas, Horneman, Park, Salt, Jackson, Sir F. Henniker, Belzoni, the Portuguese Missionaries, and Others, Down to the Recent Discoveries by Major Denham... London: 1828. V. 54
Alfred Campbell, the Young Pilgrim: Containing the Travels in Egypt and Holy Land. London: 1825. V. 48
The Bond Farmer and His Children. London: 1819. V. 49
Daniel Dennison, and the Cumberland Statesman. London: 1848. V. 50
A Descriptive Account of the Mansion and Gardens of White-Knights... London: 1819. V. 52
The Good Grandmother and Her Offspring. London: 1817. V. 50
The Good Grandmother and Her Offspring. London: 1828. V. 50
The History of a Merchant's Widow and Her Young Family. London: 1818. V. 49
The History of a Merchant's Widow and Her Young Family. London: 1823. V. 49
Poems. Sheffield: 1805. V. 47
Says She to her Neighbour, What?. London: 1812. V. 50
The Son of Genius: a Tale for the Use of Youth. London: 1816. V. 48
The Son of Genius: a Tale for the Use of Youth. London: 1817. V. 49
The Young Cadet; or, Henry Delamere's Voyage to India, His Travels in Hindostan, His Account of the Burmese War, and Wonders of Elora. New York: 1828. V. 52
The Young Crusoe, or, the Shipwrecked Boy. London: 1829. V. 50
The Young Northern Traveller; or, the Invalid Restored. London: 1830. V. 51
The Young Pilgrim, or Alfred Campbell's Return to the East; and His Travels in Egypt, Nubia, Asia Minor, Arabia Petraea, &c. New York: 1828. V. 49

HOFLAND, T. C.
The British Angler's Manual; or, the Art of Angling... London: 1839. V. 47; 49

HOFMAN, B.
1000 Years of Jews in Pinsk. New York: 1941. V. 53

HOFMANN, HANS
Hans Hofmann. New York. V. 52
Search for the Real and Other Essays. 1948. V. 54

HOFMANN, WERNER
Art in the Nineteenth Century. London: 1961. V. 49; 52
The Sculpture of Henri Laurens. New York: 1970. V. 47; 48; 49; 50; 52

HOFMANNSTAHL, HUGO VON
Der Tod Des Tizian, Bruchstuck. 1928. V. 52

HOFSTADTER, DOUGLAS R.
Godel, Escher, Bach: an Eternal Golden Braid. New York: 1979. V. 53

HOFSTATTER, HANS H.
Gustav Klimt: Erotic Drawings. London: 1980. V. 49
Gustave Klimt: Erotic Drawings. New York: 1980. V. 51

HOFSTEDE DE GROOT, CORNELIUS
A Catalogue Raisonne of the Works of the Most Eminent Dutch Painters of the Seventeenth Century. London: 1908-27. V. 54

HOFTIJZER, J.
Aramaic Texts from Deir 'Alla. Leiden: 1976. V. 49

HOGAN, CLIO D.
Index to Stakes Winners 1865-1967. Solvang. V. 52

HOGAN, EDMUND
The Description of Ireland and the State Thereof As It Is At This Present in Anno 1598. 1878. V. 48

HOGAN, J. SHERIDAN
Canada: an Essay To Which is Awarded the First Prize by the Paris Exhibition Committee of Canada. Montreal: 1855. V. 48

HOGAN, LINDA
Savings. Minneapolis: 1988. V. 50
That Horse. Acomita: 1985. V. 53

HOGAN-MOGANIDES: or, the Dutch Hudibras. London: 1674. V. 48; 51

HOGART, RON CHARLES
Alchemy, a Comprehensive Bibliography of "The Manly P. Hall" Collection of Books and Manuscripts... Los Angeles: 1986. V. 47

HOGARTH, B.
The Golden Age of Tarzan: 1939-1942. New York: 1977. V. 53

HOGARTH, DAVID GEORGE
Excavations at Ephesus: the Archaic Artemisia. London: 1908. V. 50
Hittite Seals with Particular Reference to the Ashmolean Collection. Oxford: 1920. V. 49
Life of Charles Doughty. 1928. V. 54
The Penetration of Arabia. London: 1905. V. 50
A Wandering Scholar... London: 1896. V. 49
The Wandering Scholar. 1925. V. 50

THE HOGARTH Essays. New York: 1928. V. 47; 48; 49

HOGARTH, T. W.
The Bull-Terrier. Manchester: 1936. V. 49

HOGARTH, WILLIAM
The Analysis of Beauty. London. V. 49
The Analysis of Beauty. London: 1753. V. 48; 51; 53
Anecdotes of Mr. Hogarth, and Explantory Descriptions of the Plates of Hogarth Restored... London: 1803. V. 54
Biographical Anecdotes of William Hogarth, with A Catalogue of His Works Chronologically Arranged and Occasional Remarks. London: 1782. V. 49
The Complete Works... London. V. 53
The Complete Works... London: 1860. V. 48
The Complete Works. London: 1870. V. 54
The Genuine Works... London: 1808. V. 50
The Genuine Works. London: 1808-17. V. 47
Hogarth Moralized. London: 1768. V. 50
Hogarth Moralized. London: 1832. V. 48
Hogarth's Works. London. V. 50
A Poetical Description of Mr. Hogarth's Election Prints: In Four Cantos. London: 1759. V. 48
Die Werke des Hrn. Willm. Hogarth in Kupferstichen Moralisch und Satyrisch Erlautert. Hamburg & Leipzig: 1769. V. 48
Works... London: 1822. V. 49
The Works... London: 1833. V. 51; 52
The Works... London: 1850. V. 51
The Works... Philadelphia: 1900. V. 50; 52; 54

HOGG, EDWARD
Visit to Alexandria, Damascus and Jerusalem, During the Successful Campaign of Ibrahim Pasha. London: 1835. V. 49

HOGG, JABEZ
The Microscope: its History, Construction and Applications. London: 1856. V. 49

HOGG, JAMES
A Boys Song. Market Drayton: 1994. V. 52
Familiar Anecdotes of Sir Walter Scott. New York: 1834. V. 53
The Jacobite Relics of Scotland. Edinburgh: 1819. V. 48; 49
The Jacobite Relics of Scotland... Edinburgh: 1819-21. V. 47; 48; 49; 51; 53
The Mountain Baird... Edinburgh: 1807. V. 53; 54
The Mountain Baird... Edinburgh: 1821. V. 47
The Pilgrims of the Sun. London: 1815. V. 49; 54
The Poetical Works of... Edinburgh: 1822. V. 49; 51
The Private Memoirs and Confessions of a Justified Sinner. London: 1834. V. 52
The Queen's Wake: a Legendary Poem. Edinburgh: 1819. V. 51
The Shepherd's Calendar. Edinburgh: 1829. V. 47
The Shepherd's Guide: Being a Pratical Treatise on the Diseases of Sheep, Their Causes and the Best Means of Preventing Them... Edinburgh: 1807. V. 47
Songs and Poems of the Ettrick Shepherd. London: 1912. V. 52
Tales of the Ettrick Shepherd. London: 1900. V. 49
The Three Perils of Man; or, War, Women and Witchcraft. London: 1822. V. 47; 49
Winter Evening Tales, Collected Among the Cottagers in the South of Scotland. Edinburgh: 1820. V. 48; 52
The Works of the Ettrick Shepherd. London: 1869. V. 51

HOGG, JAMES STEPHEN
Speeches and State Papers of James Stephen Hogg, Ex-Governor of Texas, With a Sketch of His Life. Austin: 1905. V. 48

HOGG, R.
A Selection of the Eatable Funguses of Great Britain. London: 1866. V. 49

HOGG, THOMAS
A Concise and Practical Treatise on the Growth and Culture of the Carnation... London: 1822. V. 47
A Concise and Practical Treatise on the Growth and Culture of the Carnation... 1824. V. 47
A Concise and Practical Treatise On the Growth and Culture of the Carnation... London: 1830. V. 49
A Practical Treatise on the Culture of the Carnation, Pink, Auricula, Polyanthus, Ranunculus, Tulip, Hyacinth, Rose and Other Flowers. London: 1839. V. 51; 54

HOGG, THOMAS JEFFERSON
The Athenians. Waltham St. Lawrence: 1943. V. 48; 49
Harriet and Mary. London: 1944. V. 48
The Life of Percy Bysshe Shelley. London: 1858. V. 53
Shelley at Oxford: the Early Correspondence of P.B. Shelley with His Friend T. J. Hogg, Together with Letters of Mary Shelly and T.L... Waltham St. Lawrence: 1944. V. 54

HOGREWE, J. L.
Beschreibung der in England seit 1759 Angelegten, und Jetzt Grosstenteils, Vollenete Schiffbaren Kanale, zur Inneren Gemeinschaft der Vornehmsten Handelsstadte. Hannover: 1780. V. 54

HOGUE, C. L.
Latin American Insects and Entomology. London: 1993. V. 50

HOHL, REINHOLD
Alberto Giacometti. New York: 1971. V. 47; 48; 50; 52

HOHLWEIN, LUDWIG
Ludwig Hohlwein. Berlin: 1926. V. 47

HOHMAN, ELMO PAUL
The American Whaleman: A Study of Life and Labour in the Whaling Industry. New York: 1928. V. 51

HOHNEL, LUDWIG VON
Discovery of Lakes Rudolf and Stefanie. London: 1894. V. 50

HOLBACH, PAUL HEINRICH DIETRICH, BARON D'
Systeme de la Nature. Londres: 1770. V. 54

HOLBACH, PAUL HENRI THIRY, BARON D'
Systeme Social... London: 1773. V. 47
Systeme Social. Londres: 1774. V. 53

HOLBEIN, HANS
The Dance of Death. London: 1816. V. 53
The Dances of Death, through the Various Stages of Human Life... London: 1803. V. 50; 52; 53
Holbein's Dance of Death. London: 1858. V. 50
Icones Veteris Testamenti. London: 1830. V. 52
The Images of the Old Testament. Buenos Aires: 1947. V. 51
Imagines Mortis. Coloniae: 1572. V. 47

HOLBERG, LUDVIG, BARON
An Introduction to Universal History. London: 1755. V. 47
An Introduction to Universal History. London: 1758. V. 50; 52
A Journey to the World Under-Ground. London: 1742. V. 47; 49; 50; 52

HOLBERTON, WAKEMAN
The Art of Angling. How and Where to Catch Fish. New York: 1887. V. 47

HOLBROOK & CO.
Holbrook and Company's Catalogue of New and Useful Inventions, with Descriptions of a Variety of Novelties and Desirable Goods... Boston: 1870. V. 54

HOLBROOK, AMELIA WEED
One of the McIntyres. Chicago: 1896. V. 51

HOLBROOK, J.
Ten Years Among the Mail Bags; or, Notes from the Diary of a Special Agent of the Post-Office Department. Philadelphia: 1855. V. 50

HOLBROOK, JOHN EDWARD
Ichthyology of South Carolina. Charleston: 1860. V. 47; 48
North American Herpetology; or, a Description of the Reptiles Inhabiting the United States. Philadelphia: 1836-38. V. 48
North American Herpetology; or, a Description of the Reptiles Inhabiting the United States. Philadelphia: 1842. V. 49

HOLBROOK, JOSIAH
Description and Text Book, for Holbrook's Scientific Apparatus, Manufactured at the Lyceum Village, Berea, Ohio. Berea: 1847. V. 53
A Familiar Treatise on the Fine Arts... Boston: 1834. V. 53
A Familiar Treatise on the Fine Arts... Boston: 1840. V. 49

HOLBROOK'S Newark City and Buisness Directory for the Year Ending May 1, 1891... Newark: 1890. V. 51

HOLBROOK'S Newark City and Business Directory for the Year Ending April 1, 1884. Newark: 1883. V. 49; 51

HOLBROOK'S Newark City and Business Directory for the Year Ending May 1, 1888. Newark: 1887. V. 49; 51

HOLBROOK'S Newark City and Business Directory for the Year Ending May 1, 1889. Newark: 1888. V. 49; 51

HOLBROOK'S Newark City and Business Directory...for the Year Ending May 1, 1891. Newark: 1890. V. 49; 51

HOLBROOK'S Newark City and Business Directory...for the Year Ending May 1, 1892. Newark: 1891. V. 49

HOLBROOK'S Newark City Directory, for the Year Ending...1877. Newark: 1876. V. 49; 51

HOLCOMBE, HENRY
Sermon, Occasioned by the Death of Lieutenant-General George Washington, Late President of the United States of America...First Delivered in the Baptist Church, Savannah, Georgia, Jan. 19th, 1800 and Now Published at the Request... Savannah: 1800. V. 50

HOLCOMBE, RETURN IRA
An Account of the Battle of Wilson's Creek, or Oak Hills. Springfield: 1883. V. 49

HOLCOT, ROBERT
Super Sapientia Salomonis. Reutlingen: 1489. V. 53

HOLCROFT, THOMAS
A Catalogue of the Library of Books of Mr. Thomas Holcroft. London: 1807. V. 48
A Letter to the Right Honourable William Windham on the Intemperance and Dangerous Tendency of His Public Conduct. London: 1795. V. 47
The Life of Thomas Holcroft. London: 1925. V. 53
A Narrative of Facts, Relating to a Prosecution for High Treason; Including the Address to the Jury. London: 1795. V. 48; 52
The Theatrical Recorder. London: 1805/06. V. 53
Travels from Hamburg, through Westphalia, Holland and the Netherlands, to Paris. London: 1804. V. 47

HOLDEN, AUSTIN WELLS
A History of the Town of Queensbury, in the State of New York... Albany: 1874. V. 54

HOLDEN, CURRY
Hill of the Rooster. New York: 1956. V. 54

HOLDEN, EDGAR
The Sphygmograph: its Physiological and Pathological Indications. Philadelphia: 1874. V. 49

HOLDEN, EDITH
The Country Diary and the Nature Notes of an Edwardian Lady. London: 1989. V. 54

HOLDEN, EDWARD S.
Catalogue of Earthquakes on the Pacific Coast 1769 to 1897. 1898. V. 52

HOLDEN, EDWIN BABCOCK
Catalogue of the Very Important Collection of Rare Americana and Fine Engravings formed by the Late Edwin Babcock Holden. New York: 1910. V. 54

HOLDEN, GEORGE H.
Canaries and Cage-Birds. New York, Boston: 1883. V. 53
Canaries and Cage-Birds. Boston: 1888. V. 49

HOLDEN, JOHN
An Essay Towards a Rational System of Music. Glasgow: 1770. V. 47

HOLDEN, RAYMOND
It Is Earlier Than You Think. 1959. V. 49
It Is Earlier than You Think. New Hampshire: 1959. V. 47; 48
It Is Earlier Than You Think. New Hampshire: 1959. V. 48

HOLDEN, W. CLIFFORD
British Rule in South Africa: Illustrated in the Story of Kama and His Tribe and of the War in Zululand. London: 1879. V. 52; 54

HOLDEN, WILLIAM CURRY
Alkail Trails or Social and Economic Movements of the Texas Frontier 1846-1900. Dallas: 1930. V. 50
Rollie Burns Or an Account of the Ranching Industry On the South Plains. Dallas: 1932. V. 48; 50; 52; 53
The Spur Ranch: a Study of the Inclosed Ranch Phaase of the Cattle Industry in Texas. Boston: 1934. V. 52; 53

HOLDER & JACKSON
The Sunny Pecos Valley of New Mexico. The Place To Go and Buy Land. Lake Arthur: 1908. V. 50

HOLDER, CHARLES FREDERICK
All About Pasadena and Its Vicinity. Boston: 1889. V. 48
Big Game at Sea. New York: 1908. V. 50; 52
The Boy Anglers... New York: 1904. V. 50
The Game Fishes of the World. London: 1913. V. 48
Life in the Open: Sport With Rod, Gun, Horse and House in Southern California. New York: 1906. V. 48
Recreations of a Sportsman on the Pacific Coast. New York: 1910. V. 47
Southern California: Its Climate, Trails, Mountains, Canyons, Watering Places, Fruits, Flowers and Game, A Guide Book. Los Angeles: 1888. V. 48

HOLDER, WILLIAM
A Discourse Concerning Time, with Application of the Natural Day, and Lunar Month and Solar Year, as Natural... London: 1701. V. 48
A Treatise of the Natural Grounds and Principles of Harmony. London: 1694. V. 52

HOLDERLIN, FRIEDRICH
Patmos. 1978. V. 52; 54

HOLDERLIN, JOHANN CHRISTIAN FRIEDRICH
Fragmente des Pindar. Lexington: 1935. V. 49
Gedichte, Entwurfe zu Gedichten und Bruchstucke aus den Jahren MDCCXCVI-MDCCCIV. Aurora, New York: 1946-49. V. 50

HOLDERNESS, MARY
New Russia. London: 1823. V. 48

HOLDICH, T. HUNGERFORD
The Indian Borderland 1880-1900. London: 1901. V. 54

HOLDICH, THOMAS
Tibet, the Mysterious. London: 1904. V. 50
Tibet, the Mysterious... London: 1906. V. 48; 50

HOLDSWORTH, E.
Muscipula; or, the Mouse-Trap; a Poem in Latin and English. London: 1720. V. 48

HOLDSWORTH, WILLIAM
Natural Shorthand, Wherein the Nature of Speech and the manner of Pronunciation are Briefly Explained and a Natural Reason Assigned From Thence for the Particular Form of Every Stroke... London: 1766. V. 47

HOLE, JAMES
National Railways: an Argument for State Purchase... London Paris & Melbourne: 1895. V. 54

HOLE, RICHARD
Remarks on the Arabian Nights' Entertainments... London: 1797. V. 48; 49; 54

HOLE, S. REYNOLDS
A Little Tour in America. London & New York: 1895. V. 53; 54
Our Gardens. London: 1901. V. 52

HOLEHOUSE, SAMUEL
Catalogue of Furniture...Telescopes...Medallions...Coins...Harp, Guitar and Fine Violins... London: 1853. V. 53

HOLFORD, CHRISTOPHER
A Chat About the Broderers' Company. London: 1910. V. 47; 49

HOLFORD, G.
Observations on the Necessity of Introducing a Sufficient Number of Respectable Clergyman into Our Colonies in the West Indies... London: 1807. V. 50; 54

HOLFORD, GEORGE
The Holford Collection. London: 1924. V. 47
The Holford Library...forming Part of the Collection at Dorchester House, Park Lane... 1927-28. V. 53
The Holford Library...Forming Part of the Collection at Dorchester House, Park Lane... London: 1927-29. V. 54

HOLFORD, GEORGE PETER
The Destruction of Jerusalem, an Absolute and Irresistible Proof of the Divine Origin of Chrisitianity... Frankford: 1812. V. 50
The Storm; a Drama, in Three Acts. (with) The Cave of Neptune. London: 1801. V. 51

HOLFORD, MARGARET
Wallace; or, the Flight of Falkirk; a Metrical Romance. London: 1809. V. 49; 53

HOLIDAY, GILBERT
Horses and Soldiers. London: 1938. V. 47

HOLIDAY, JOHN
The Life of William Late Earl of Mansfield. London: 1797. V. 51

THE HOLIDAY Visit, and Other Tales: Being Sketches of Childhood, Designed for Juvenile Readers. London: 1826. V. 51

HOLINGS, J. F.
Sketches in Leicestershire, from Original Drawings; with Historical and Descriptive Notices. Leicester: 1846. V. 47

HOLINSHED, RAPHAEL
The First (-Laste) Volume of the Chronicles of England, Scotlande and Irelande. London: 1577. V. 49
Holinshed's Chronicles of England, Scotland and Ireland. 1807-08. V. 49
Holinshed's Chronicles of England, Scotland and Ireland. London: 1807-08. V. 47; 51; 54
Holinshed's Irish Chronicle. Dublin: 1979. V. 54

HOLITSCHER, ARTHUR
Amerika. Berlin: 1922. V. 53
Frans Masareel. Berlin: 1923. V. 49

THE HOLKHAM Bible Picture Book. London: 1954. V. 48

HOLLAN, F. R.
Arkansas Pass Light Station: a History. 1976. V. 54

HOLLAND: a Jaunt to the Principal Places in That Country. London: 1775. V. 49; 53

HOLLAND, CLIVE
Arctic Exploration and Development c. 500 B.C. to 1915. New York: 1994. V. 53

HOLLAND, FREDERICK WEST
Sinai and Jerusalem... London: 1870. V. 53
Sinai and Jerusalem... London: 1880. V. 47

HOLLAND, G. A.
History of Parker County and the Double Log Cabin.... Weatherford: 1937. V. 48; 49

HOLLAND, HENRY
Resolutions of the Associated Architects... London: 1793. V. 52
Travels in the Ionian isles, Albania, Thessaly, Macedonia &c. London: 1815. V. 47; 51

HOLLAND, HENRY RICHARD VASSALL FOX, 3RD BARON
A Dream. London: 1818. V. 52
Some Account of the Life and Writings of Lope Felix de Vega Carpio. London: 1806. V. 47
Some Account of the Lives and Writings of Lope Felix de Vega Carpio... London: 1817. V. 47; 53

HOLLAND, JOHN
The History and Description of Fossil Fuel... London: 1835. V. 49
The History and Description of Fossil Fuel... London: 1841. V. 49
The History, Antiquities and Description of the Town and Parish of Worksop. Sheffield: 1826. V. 48; 52

HOLLAND, LORD
Eve's Legend. London: 1928. V. 48

HOLLAND, MARY
Our Army Nurses: Interesting Sketches and Photographs of Over 100 of the Nobel Women Who Served in Hospitals and On Battle Fields During Our Late Civil War, 1861-1865. Boston: 1897. V. 48

HOLLAND, PATRICK
A Plan for Manning the Navy without Impressing, or Expence to Government. London: 1809. V. 53

HOLLAND, PHILIP H.
A Report of the Trial and Acquital of Mary Hunter, for the Alleged Murder of Her Husband by Arsenic, with Arguments in Proof of Her Innocence, and Strictures Upon Some Parts of the Medical Jurisprudence of this Country. Manchester: 1843. V. 48

HOLLAND, RAY P.
Bird Dogs. New York: 1948. V. 52
Shotgunning in the Lowlands. Hartford: 1945. V. 47

HOLLAND, ROBERT E.
The Song of Tekakwitha: the Lily of the Mohawks. New York: 1942. V. 52

HOLLAND, THOMAS
Select Titles from the Digest of Justinian. Oxford: 1881. V. 51

HOLLAND, TREVENEN J.
Record of the Expedition to Abyssinia. London: 1870. V. 50

HOLLAND, VYVYAN
Hand Coloured Fashion Plates 1770 to 1899. London: 1955. V. 54

HOLLAND, W.
History of West Cork and the Diocese of Ross. London: 1949. V. 52

HOLLAND, W. J.
The Butterfly Book... Toronto: 1898. V. 53

HOLLANDER, BERNARD
In Search of the Soul and the mechanism of Thought, Emotion and Conduct. London: 1916. V. 50
The Mental Functions of the Brain: an Investigation into their Localisation and Their Manifestation in Health and Disease. New York: 1901. V. 54

HOLLANDER, JACOB H.
The Economic Library of Jacob H. Hollander, Ph.D. Baltimore: 1937. V. 53

HOLLANDER, JOHN
A Crackling of Thorns. New Haven: 1958. V. 54
Dal Vero. New York: 1983. V. 49
Types of Shape. New York: 1969. V. 48

HOLLAND'S Fond Du Lac City Directory, for the Years 1880-84. Chicago: 1880. V. 52

HOLLAR, W.
Th Dance of Death, from the Original Designs of Hans Holbein. London: 1816. V. 54

HOLLDOBLER, B.
The Ants. Cambridge: 1990. V. 49; 50

HOLLES, DENZIL, BARON
The Case Stated of the Jurisdiction of the House of Lords in the Point of Impositions. London: 1676. V. 49; 51
The Grand Question Concerning the Judicature of the House of Peers States and Argued. London: 1669. V. 48
A Letter of a Gentleman to His Friend, Shewing that the Bishops Are Not to be Judges in Parliament in Cases Capital. London: 1679. V. 48
Memoirs...from the Year 1641 to 1648. London: 1699. V. 51

HOLLEY, HORACE
A Discourse Occasioned by the Death of Col. James Morrison, delivered in the Episcopal Church, Lexington, Kentucky, May 19th, 1893. Lexington: 1823. V. 51

HOLLEY, MARY AUSTIN
Texas... Baltimore: 1833. V. 49
Texas. Lexington: 1836. V. 47; 48; 54

HOLLEY, ORVILLE LUTHER
Address Delivered at the Request of the Mount Moriah Lodge at Palmyra, on the 24th of June, A.L. 5822, It Being the Anniversary of St. John the Baptist. Palmyra: 1822. V. 51

HOLLIDAY, CHARLES W.
The Valley of Youth. Caldwell: 1948. V. 49

HOLLIDAY, FRANCIS
An Easy Introduction to Practical Gunnery; or, Art of Engineering. London: 1756. V. 49

HOLLING, HOLLING CLANCY
Pagoo. Boston: 1957. V. 49

HOLLINGHURST, ALAN
Confidential Chats with Boys. Oxford: 1082. V. 50
The Swimming Pool Library. London: 1988. V. 50; 54

HOLLINGSHEAD, JOHN
The Story of Leicester Square. London: 1892. V. 52

HOLLINGSWORTH, JOHN MCHENRY
Journal of John McHenry Hollingsworth of the First New York Volunteers, Sept. 1846-Aug. 1849. San Francisco: 1923. V. 51; 53
The Journal of John McHenry Hollingsworth of the First New York Volunteers (Stevenson's Regiment). San Francisco: 1924. V. 49

HOLLINGSWORTH, NATHANIEL JOHN
Fleurs. A Poem. Newcastle: 1821. V. 51; 54

HOLLINGWORTH, RICHARD
Vindiciae Carolinae; or, a Defence of Eikon Basilike (Greek), the Portraicture of His Sacred Majesty in His Solitudes and Sufferings... London: 1692. V. 54

HOLLIS, THOMAS
Memoirs. London: 1780. V. 48

HOLLISTER, ISAAC
A Brief Narration of the Captivity of Isaac Hollister, Who Was Taken by the Indians, Anno Domini, 1763. Townsend: 1855. V. 54

HOLLISTER, OVANDO
The Mines of Colorado. Springfield: 1867. V. 49

HOLLISTER, URIAH S.
The Navajo and His Blanket. Denver: 1903. V. 47

HOLLO, ANSELM
Maya: Works 1959-1969. London: 1970. V. 50

HOLLOWAY, LAURA C.
An Hour with Charlotte Bronte; or, Flowers from a Yorkshire Moor. New York: 1883. V. 50
The Mothers of Great Men and Women and Some Wives of Great Men. New York: 1883. V. 48

HOLLOWAY, W.
The British Museum; or, Elegant Repository of Natural History: Volume III. Fishes-Insects. London: 1804. V. 54

HOLLOWAY, W. L.
Wild Life on the Plains an Horrors of Indian Warfare by a Corps of Competent Authors and Artists. St. Louis: 1891. V. 52

HOLLOWAY, W. R.
Indianapolis. A Historical and Statistical Sketch of the Railroad City, a Chronicle of Its Social, Municipal, Commercial and Manufacturing Progress, with Full Statistical Tables. Indianapolis: 1870. V. 54

HOLLOWAY, WILLIAM
A General Dictionary of Provincialisms... Lewes: 1839. V. 47; 49
The Minor Minstrel; or, Poetical Pieces, Chiefly Familiar and Descriptive. London: 1808. V. 50
The Peasant's Fate: a Rural Poem. Boston: 1802. V. 47; 52
The Peasants Fate; a Rural Poem. London: 1802. V. 54
Scenes of Youth or Rural Recollections; with Other Poems. London: 1803. V. 50

HOLLOWELL, J. M.
War-time Reminiscences and Other Selections. Goldsboro: 1939. V. 49

HOLLOWAY, JAMES A.
The Free and Voluntary Confession and Narrative of...(Addressed to His Majesty) Written with His Own Hand, and Delivered by Himself to Mr. Secretary Jenkins... 1684. V. 47

HOLLY Berries. London: 1880. V. 54

HOLLY, HENRY HUDSON
Holly's Country Seats... New York: 1863. V. 48; 50
Modern Dwellings in Town and Country... New York: 1878. V. 48; 50

HOLLYBAND, CLAUDIUS
The Elizabethan Home: Discovered in 2 Dialogues. London: 1925. V. 48

HOLM, E.
Fruit Chafers of Southern Africa (Scarabaeidae: Cetoniini). Hartebeesport: 1992. V. 52

HOLM, NORA
The Runner's Bible. Boston: 1915. V. 51

HOLMAN, BOB
Cupid's Cashbox. Poems. 1988. V. 54

HOLMAN, DAVID
Buckskin and Homespun. Austin: 1979. V. 48; 49; 52
Letters of Hard Times in Texas, 1840-1890. Austin: 1974. V. 49; 52

HOLMAN, FREDRICK V.
Dr. John McLoughlin, the Father of Oregon. Cleveland: 1907. V. 49

HOLMAN, JAMES
A Voyage Round the World, Including the Travels in Africa, Asia, Australasia, America, etc., etc. from MDCCCXXVII to MDCCCXXXII. London: 1834-35. V. 50

HOLMAN, JOHN P.
Sheep and Bear Trails. New York: 1933. V. 47; 48; 53

HOLMAN, LOUIS
The Graphic Processes: (Intaglio, Relief, Planographic). Boston: 1926. V. 50

HOLMAN, WILLIAM R.
Library Publications. 1965. V. 53
Library Publications. San Francisco: 1965. V. 47; 48; 51; 54

HOLMBERG, ERIK J.
The Swedish Excavations at Asea in Arcadia. Lund: 1944. V. 50; 52

HOLMBOE, J.
Studies on the Vegetation of Cyprus, Based Upon Researches During the Spring and Summer of 1905. Bergen: 1914. V. 51

HOLMDEN, H. R.
Catalogue of Maps, Plans and Charts in the Map Room of the Dominion Archives. Ottawa: 1912. V. 50

HOLME, BENJAMIN
A Collection of the Epistles and Works of Benjamin Holme. London: 1753. V. 48; 49; 54

HOLME, C. GEOFFREY
Children's Toys of Yesterday. London: 1932. V. 50
Decorative Art 1930. London: 1930. V. 52
Modern Book Illustrators and Their Work. London: 1914. V. 47
Modern Photography 1934-35. London. V. 53

HOLME, CHARLES
The Art of the Book. London: 1914. V. 48; 50
The Art-Revival in Austria. London: 1906. V. 48; 50; 51; 53; 54
Colour Photography: and Other Recent Developments of the Art of the Camera. London Paris & New York: 1908. V. 54
English Water-Colour. London: 1902. V. 48; 50
Modern Pen Drawings: European and American. London: 1901. V. 47; 49; 50; 54
The Old Water-Colour Society 1804-1904. London: 1905. V. 49
Representative Art of Our Time. London: 1903. V. 54
The War Depicted by Distinguished Artists. London: 1918. V. 47

HOLME, GEOFFREY
Industrial Design and the Future. London: 1934. V. 50

HOLMES, ABIEL
American Annals; or a Chronological History of America From Its Discovery in MCCCCXCII to MDCCCIV. Cambridge: 1805. V. 53

HOLMES, BAYARD
The Surgery of the Head. New York: 1903. V. 47

HOLMES BOOK CO.
Descriptive and Priced Catalogue of Books, (etc.)... Relating to California and the Far West...The Collection of Thomas Wayne Norris. Oakland: 1948. V. 48

HOLMES, BURTON
The Traveler's Russia. New York: 1934. V. 47

HOLMES, C. J.
Constable and His Influence on Landscape Painting. London: 1902. V. 54

HOLMES, CHRISTIAN R., MRS.
Selected Ancient Chinese Bronzes from the Collection of Mrs. Christian R. Holmes. New York. V. 51; 53

HOLMES, CLELLON
Go. New York: 1952. V. 51

HOLMES, E.
Report of an Exploration and Survey of the Territory of the Aroostook River, During the Spring and Autumn of 1836. Augusta: 1839. V. 54

HOLMES, EUGENIA K.
Adolph Sutro. San Francisco: 1895. V. 52

HOLMES, FRANCIS S.
Southern Farmer and Market Gardener; Being a Compilation of Useful Articles on these Subjects... Charleston: 1842. V. 49

HOLMES, G.
Sketches of Some of...Southern Counties of Ireland Collected During a Tour in the Autumn of 1797. 1801. V. 49; 50; 54
Sketches of Some of...Southern Counties of Ireland Collected During a Tour in the Autumn of 1797. London: 1801. V. 51

HOLMES, J. H.
In Primitive New Guinea. New York: 1924. V. 51

HOLMES, J. H. H.
A Treatise on the Coal Mines of Durham and Northumberland... London: 1816. V. 47; 48; 49; 52

HOLMES, JOHN
The Art of Rhetoric Made Easy; or, the Elements of Oratory Briefly Stated, and Fitted for the Practice of the Studious Youth of Great Britain and Ireland... London: 1739. V. 52
Historical Sketches of the Missions of the United Brethren for Propagating the Gospel Among Heathen, from Their Commencement to the Present Time. Dublin: 1818. V. 49

HOLMES, JOHN CLELLON
Go. New York: 1952. V. 47; 49; 52; 53
The Horn. New York: 1958. V. 47

HOLMES, KENNETH
Covered Wagon Women... 198-93. V. 51

HOLMES, KENNETH L.
Covered Wagon Women. Glendale: 1983. V. 49
Covered Wagon Women. Glendale and Spokane: 1983-91. V. 48
Covered Wagon Women... 1983-93. V. 48; 50; 51
Covered Wagon Women... Glendale & Spokane: 1983-93. V. 50; 52; 53

HOLMES, LOUIS A.
Fort McPherson, Nebraska. Guardian of the Tracks and Trails. Lincoln: 1963. V. 52

HOLMES, OLIVER WENDELL
Astraea: the Balance of Illusions. Boston: 1850. V. 47; 49; 51; 52; 54
The Autocrat of the Breakfast Table. Boston: 1853. V. 47
The Autocrat of the Breakfast Table. Boston: 1858. V. 47; 49; 50; 51; 52; 53
The Autocrat of the Breakfast Table. Boston: 1859. V. 47; 50; 52; 54
The Autocrat of the Breakfast Table. Edinburgh: 1859. V. 50
The Autocrat of the Breakfast Table. Boston: 1860. V. 54
The Autocrat of the Breakfast Table. London: 1893. V. 48
The Autocrat of the Breakfast Table. New Haven: 1955. V. 53
Benjamin Pierce: Astronomer, Mathematician, 1809-1880. 1880. V. 48
Benjamin Pierce: Astronomer, Mathematician, 1809-1880. Boston: 1880. V. 47
Border Lines of Knowledge in Some Provinces of Medical Science. Boston: 1862. V. 49; 50; 51; 52
Boylston Prize Dissertation for the Years 1836 and 1837. Boston: 1838. V. 47; 48; 49; 50; 51; 53
The Brave Old South. 1879. V. 47; 48
The Brave Old South. Boston: 1879. V. 47
Collected Legal Papers. London: 1920. V. 54
The Common Law. Boston: 1881. V. 49; 51; 52; 53; 54
The Complete Writings. Boston & New York: 1892. V. 47
Currents and Counter-Currents in Medical Science. Boston: 1861. V. 48; 49; 50; 52
Dorothy Q. Boston/New York: 1893. V. 48
Elsie Veneer. Boston: 1861. V. 47; 48; 49; 50; 51; 53; 54
Elsie Venner... Boston & New York: 1888. V. 51
Grandmother's Story of Bunker Hill Battle. New York: 1883. V. 47
Holmes Birthday Book. Boston & New York: 1889. V. 50
Holmes-Laski Letters The Correspondence of Mr. Justice Holmes and Harold J. Laski 1916-1935. Cambridge: 1953. V. 48; 54
Homoeopathy, and Its Kindred Delusions. Boston: 1842. V. 51; 52; 53; 54
Humorous Poems. Boston: 1865. V. 53
The Iron Gate, and Other Poems. Boston: 1880. V. 50
John Lothrop Motley. Boston: 1879. V. 50
Library of Practical Medicine... Boston: 1836. V. 50
Mechanism in Thought and Morals. Boston: 1871. V. 47; 49; 50; 52; 54
One Hundred Days in Europe. Boston and New York: 1887. V. 53; 54
The One-Hoss Shay. Boston: 1892. V. 54
The One-Hoss Shay... Boston: 1905. V. 48; 50; 51
Oration Delivered Before the City Authorities of Boston on the Fourth of July. Boston: 1863. V. 51
Our Hundred Days in Europe. Boston & New York: 1887. V. 54
Over the Teacups. Boston & New York: 1891. V. 54
Poems. Boston & New York: 1836. V. 47; 49; 50; 52; 54
Poems. London: 1846. V. 49; 50; 51; 52; 54
Poems. Boston: 1849. V. 47; 53
Poems. Boston: 1881. V. 48
Poems. Boston: 1890. V. 53
The Poet at the Breakfast Table. Boston: 1872. V. 47; 50; 52; 53
Practical Views on Medical Education. Boston: 1805. V. 49
Practical Views on Medical Education. Boston: 1850. V. 51
The Professor at the Breakfast Table; With the Story of Iris. Boston: 1860. V. 47; 48; 49; 50
Puerperal Fever as a Private Pestilence. Boston: 1855. V. 53; 54
Songs in Many Keys. Boston: 1862. V. 47; 50; 52
Soundings from the Atlantic. Boston: 1864. V. 47
Speeches. Boston: 1891. V. 52
Speeches. Boston: 1896. V. 51
Urania: a Rhymed Lesson. Boston: 1846. V. 47; 51; 54
The Vision of Sir Launfal. Cambridge: 1848. V. 47; 49
The Vision of Sir Launfal. Cambridge: 1948. V. 47
Wit and Humour. Poems by the Autocrat of the Breakfast-Table. London: 1867. V. 49
Works. Boston: 1892-1896. V. 48
The Works... Boston and New York: 1892-1907. V. 54
The Writings... Boston: 1891. V. 50
The Writings. Cambridge: 1891. V. 51; 52; 54

HOLMES, RICHARD RIVINGTON
Queen Victoria. London & Paris: 1897. V. 48; 51; 52; 54
Specimens of Royal Fine and Historical Bookbinding... London: 1893. V. 47; 50; 54
Trophies and Personal Relics of British Heroes. London: 1896. V. 50

HOLMES, ROBERTA EVELYN
The Southern Mines of California: Early Devleopment of the Sonora Mining Region. San Francisco: 1930. V. 47

HOLMES, SAMUEL J.
A Bibliography of Eugenics. Berkeley: 1924. V. 49

HOLMES, T. R. E.
A History of the Indian Mutiny, and of the Disturbances Which Accompanied It Among the Civil Population. London: 1883. V. 54

HOLMES, T. RICE
The Roman Republic and the Founder of the Empire. London: 1923. V. 48

HOLMES, THOMAS JAMES
Cotton Mather: a Bibliography of His Works. Cambridge: 1940. V. 48; 52
Increase Mather...His Works. Cleveland: 1930. V. 48; 52
Increase Mather...His Works. Cleveland: 1931. V. 48; 52

HOLMES, TIMOTHY
A Treatise on Surgery. Philadelphia: 1876. V. 51

HOLMES, WILLIAM H.
Aboriginal Pottery of the Eastern United States. 1903. V. 47; 54
Archaeological Studies Among the Ancient Cities of Mexico. Chicago: 1895-97. V. 50

HOLSTEIN, ANNA
Three Years in Field Hospitals of the Army of the Potomac. Philadelphia: 1867. V. 52

HOLSTENIUS, LUCAS
Porphyrii Philosophi Liber de Vita Pythagorae. Romae: 1630. V. 54

HOLT, ARDERN
Fancy Dresses Described; or, What to Wear at Fancy Balls. London: 1884. V. 50
Fancy Dresses Described; or, What to Wear at Fancy Balls. London: 1887. V. 49

HOLT, CHARLES
A Short Account of the Yellow Fever, As It Appeared in New-London, In August, September, October, 1798... New London: 1798. V. 49

HOLT, DAVID
A Lay of Hero Worship and Other Poems. London: 1850. V. 49

HOLT, E. EMMETT
The Diseases of Infancy and Childhood. New York: 1897. V. 47; 48; 49
The Diseases of Infancy and Childhood. New York: 1898. V. 50; 54
The Diseases of Infancy and Childhood. New York: 1899. V. 54

HOLT, EMILY SARAH
Memoirs of Royal Ladies. London: 1861. V. 48; 54

HOLT, GAVIN
Green for Danger. London: 1939. V. 48

HOLT, GUY
Jurgen and the Law, A Statement with Exhibits, Including the Court's Opinion and the Brief for the Defendants on Motion to Direct and Acquittal. New York: 1923. V. 48

HOLT, JOHN
An Attempt to Rescue that Aunciente English Poet, and Play Wrighte, Maister Williaume Shakespeare... London: 1749. V. 47
General View of the Agriculture of the County of Lancaster... London: 1795. V. 47; 49; 50; 51

HOLT, O. M.
Dakota. Chicago: 1885. V. 50; 54

HOLT, RACKHAM
George Washington Carver: an American Biography. Garden City: 1943. V. 53

HOLT, RICHARD
A Short Treatise of Artificial Stone, as Tis Now Made, and Converted in to all Manner of Curious Embellishments... London: 1730. V. 47

HOLT, ROSA BELLE
Rugs: Oriental and Occidental Antique and Modern: a Handbook for Ready Reference. Chicago: 1901. V. 54

HOLTBY, WINIFRED
Virginia Woolf. London: 1932. V. 51

HOLTEDAHL, O.
Report of the Scientific Results of the Norwegian Expedition to Novaya Zemlya 1921. Oslo: 1924-30. V. 48; 51

HOLTEN, E.
The Circumpolar Plants. Stockholm. V. 51

HOLTHAUS, P. D.
Wanderings of a Journeyman Tailor through Europe and the East During the Years 1824 to 1840. London: 1844. V. 48; 51

HOLTHOER, ROSTISLAV
New Kingdom Pharaonic Sites: The Pottery. New York: 1977. V. 49; 51

HOLTON, DAVID P.
Winslow Memorial. Family Records of Winslows and Their Descendants in America, with the English Ancestry as Far As it Is Known. New York: 1877-88. V. 47; 53

HOLTON, EDWARD H.
Travels with Jottings. From Midland to the Pacific. Milwaukee: 1880. V. 47

HOLTON, ISAAC F.
New Granada: Twenty Months in the Andes. New York: 1857. V. 47; 50; 51; 54

HOLTZAPFFEL, C.
Turning and Mechanical Manipulation. London: 1846-1904. V. 52

HOLUB, EMIL
Seven Years in South Africa: Travels, Researches and Hunting Adventures, Between the Diamond Fields and the Zambesi. Boston: 1881. V. 47; 51; 54

HOLWAY, JOHN
Voices from the Great Black Baseball Leagues. New York: 1975. V. 50

HOLWELL, JOHN ZEPHANIAH
A Genuine Narrative of the Deplorable Deaths of the English Gentlemen and Others, Who Were Suffocated in the Black Hole in Fort William, at Calcutta in the Kingdom of Bengal... London: 1758. V. 48; 52
Interesting Historical Events...Provinces of Bengal, and the Empire of Indostan. London: 1766/67. V. 54
Interesting Historical Events...Provinces of Bengal, and the Empire of Indostan. London: 1766/67-71. V. 54

HOLY Songs and Sonnets. Groningen: 1985. V. 52; 54

HOLYOAKE, GEORGE JACOB
The History of Co-Operation in England: Its Literature and its Advocates from 1812 to 1878. London: 1875-79. V. 47
Sixty Years of an Agitator's Life. London: 1892. V. 54
Working-Class Representation: its Conditions and Consequences. Birmingham: 1868. V. 54

HOLYROYD, ABRAHAM
A Garland of Poetry: By Various Authors. Saltaire: 1873. V. 53

HOLZWORTH, JOHN M.
The Wild Grizzlies of Alaska. New York London: 1930. V. 49; 50

HOMAGE To Redon. Northampton: 1959. V. 49

HOMANS, JOHN
A Textbook of Surgery. Springfield: 1931. V. 54

HOME, A. J.
Tables Showing the Relative Value of Government Securities and of Bank and Other Stocks Yielding Various Rates of Interest - Purchased at Different Rates of Discount and Premium. Maddras: 1847. V. 50

HOME Book of the Picturesque. New York: 1852. V. 47

HOME, EVERARD
A Dissertation on the Properties of Pus... London: 1788. V. 50; 54
Practical. Philadelphia: 1811. V. 48
Practical Observations on the Treatment of Strictures in the Urethra and the Esophagus. London: 1805-21. V. 48; 53
Practical Observations on the Treatment of the Diseases of the Prostate Gland. London: 1811. V. 50
Practical Observations on the Treatment of the Diseases of the Prostate Gland. London: 1811-18. V. 47; 49
A Short Tract on the Formation of Tumours. London: 1830. V. 47; 51

HOME, FERGUS
Madame Midas: Realistic and Sensational Story of Australian Mining Life. London: 1888. V. 47

HOME, FRANCIS
Principia Medicinae. Edinburgh: 1770. V. 51
The Principles of Agriculture and Vegetation. Edinburgh: 1759. V. 52

HOME, JOHN
Alonzo, a Tragedy. London: 1773. V. 50; 54
Douglas: a Tragedy. Edinburgh: 1757. V. 50
The History of the Rebellion in the Year 1745. London: 1802. V. 50; 54

HOME Kindness. London. V. 49
HOME Kindness. London: 1900. V. 47

THE HOME of the Emigrant from Everywhere. St. Louis: 1876. V. 52

HOME, or a Short Account of Charles Grafton. Boston: 1816. V. 47

HOME, ROBERT
Select Views in Mysore, the Country of Tippoo Sultan; from Drawings Taken on the spot... London: 1794. V. 53

HOMER, HENRY SACHEVERELL
An Enquiry Into the Means of Preserving and Improving the Publick Roads of This Kingdom. Oxford: 1767. V. 52

HOMER, PHILIP BRACEBRIDGE
The Garland: a Collection of Poems. Oxford: 1788. V. 53

HOMER, WINSLOW
Eventful History of Three Little Men and How They Became Blind. Boston: 1858. V. 47

HOMERUS
The First Book of Homer's Iliad. London: 1715. V. 48
Homeri Ilias & Odyssea... Amsterdam: 1655-56. V. 51
Homeri Ilias & Odyssea... Cambridge: 1711. V. 49
Homeri Odysseae Libri VIII, Francisco Florido Sabino Interprete, Ad Franciscvm Valesivm, Galliarum Regem Christianissimum. Paris: 1545. V. 47
Homeri Poetae Clarissimi Ilias. Coloniae: 1522. V. 53
The Homeric Hymn to Aphrodite. 1948. V. 47
The Homeric Hymn to Aphrodite. Waltham St. Lawrence: 1948. V. 47; 48; 50; 51; 52; 54
Homeric Hymn to Aphrodite. Waltham St. Lawrence: 1948. V. 51
Homerii Ilias Graece et Latinae. London: 1815. V. 54
Homer's Odyssee. Munchen: 1926. V. 53
Homers Werke von Johann H. Voss. 1814. V. 47
Hymns to Aphrodite. San Francisco: 1917. V. 49
The Iliad. Coloniae: 1522. V. 47; 49; 53
The Iliad... London: 1715-20. V. 49
Iliad... London: 1736. V. 54
The Iliad... London: 1763. V. 48

HOMERUS continued
The Iliad. Edinburgh: 1771. V. 50
The Iliad... London: 1808. V. 51
The Iliad... New York: 1808. V. 50
Iliad. London: 1841. V. 51
The Iliad... London: 1864. V. 54
The Iliad... Boston: 1870. V. 49
The Iliad... London: 1871. V. 50
The Iliad... London: 1898. V. 52
Iliad. Munich: 1923. V. 52
The Iliad. London: 1928. V. 49
The Iliad. London: 1931. V. 51
The Iliad and Odyssey. London: 1791. V. 47; 48; 52
The Iliad and Odyssey... Dublin: 1792. V. 54
The Iliad and Odyssey. Oxford: 1801. V. 47
The Iliad and Odyssey. London: 1833. V. 47
The Iliad and Odyssey... Munich: 1923-24. V. 50
The Iliad and Odyssey. Haarlem: 1931. V. 52
The Iliad and Odyssey. London: 1931. V. 48; 50
The Iliad (in Greek and Latin). Geneva: 1570. V. 54
The Iliad...Odyssey... London: 1743/25-26. V. 48
The Iliad...Odyssey... London: 1801. V. 51
The Iliad...Odyssey... London: 1805. V. 48
Iliad...Odyssey. London: 1824. V. 51
Ilias Graece et Lataine. Annotationes in Usum Serenissimi Principis Gulielmi Augusti... London: 1754. V. 47
Odyssea. London: 1831. V. 54
The Odyssey... London: 1725-26. V. 48
The Odyssey. London: 1745. V. 53
The Odyssey. London: 1752. V. 54
The Odyssey. Glasgow: 1758. V. 52
The Odyssey. London: 1763. V. 49
The Odyssey. London: 1771. V. 54
The Odyssey... Edinburgh: 1778. V. 50
The Odyssey... London: 1887. V. 51
The Odyssey... London: 1900. V. 52
The Odyssey... London: 1924. V. 49; 52; 54
The Odyssey. 1929. V. 51
The Odyssey. Cambridge: 1929. V. 47; 50
The Odyssey... 1932. V. 48
The Odyssey. London: 1932. V. 47; 48; 50; 51; 52
The Odyssey. London: 1935. V. 52
The Odyssey... New York: 1940. V. 54
The Odyssey. 1981. V. 47; 51; 52
The Odyssey. New York: 1981. V. 53; 54
The Odyssey and Iliad. London: 1808-11. V. 54
The Odyssey...Iliad... New York: 1931. V. 51
The Odyssey...Iliad. London: 1974/75. V. 51
Pages from the Iliad. Iowa City: 1976. V. 51; 53; 54
Patrocleia: Book XVI of Homer's Iliad. London: 1962. V. 48
Pax: From Book XIX of the Iliad. London: 1967. V. 48
Poetarum Omnium Seculorum Longe Principis Homeri Illias... Paris: 1545. V. 48
(The Odyssey and Iliad in Greek). Glasgow: 1956-58. V. 51
La Ulyxea. Antwerp: 1556. V. 48
The Whole Works of Homer; Prince of Poets in His Iliads and Odysses. London: 1616?. V. 49
Works. London: 1794. V. 53
(Works, Greek). Basilea: 1551. V. 50
The Works of Homer... London: 1780. V. 47; 49; 52; 54

HOMES, GEOFFREY
Forty Whacks. New York: 1931. V. 49

HOMES in Texas on the Line of the International & Great Northern R.R. 1880-'81. Buffalo: 1880. V. 52

HOMES of American Authors. New York & London: 1853. V. 50; 51; 52; 53; 54
HOMES of American Authors. New York: 1855. V. 53

HOMES of American Statesmen: With Anecdotal, Personal and Descriptive Sketches. New York: 1854. V. 47; 50

HOMMAIRE DE HELL, XAVIER
Travels in the Steppes of the Caspian Sea, The Crimea, The Caucasus,... London: 1847. V. 49; 50

HOMMEL, RUDOLF P.
China at Work, an Illustrated Record of the Primitive Industries of China's Masses... New York: 1937. V. 51

HONCE, CHARLES
Books and Ghosts. New York: 1948. V. 49
For Loving a Book. New York: 1945. V. 49
A Sherlock Holmes Birthday. New York: 1938. V. 49
Tales From a Beekman Hill Library. New York: 1952. V. 49

HONDIVS, HENRICUS
Instrvction en La Science de Perspective. The Hague: 1625. V. 49

HONE, ETHEL
Rington Priory. London: 1864. V. 50

HONE, J. M.
Bishop Berkeley - His Life, Writings and Philosophy. London: 1931. V. 52
Pilgrimage in the West. London: 1933. V. 51

HONE, JOSEPH
The Love Story of Thomas Davis Told in the Letters of Annie Hutton. 1945. V. 52

HONE, PERCY F.
Southern Rhodesia. London: 1909. V. 54

HONE, WILLIAM
Ancient Mysteries Described, Especially the English Miracle Plays... London: 1823. V. 47; 49; 50; 54
The Divine Right of the Kings to Govern Wrong. London: 1821. V. 50; 52
Don John, or Don Juan Unmasked. London: 1819. V. 53; 54
The First Trial of William Hone. (with) The Second Trial. (with) The Third Trial. London: 1817/1818. V. 49
HONE'S Interesting History of the Memorable Blood Conspiracy, Carried on By S. MacDaniel, J. Berry, J. Egan and J. Salmon, Thief-Takers and Their Trials and Sentences in 1756... London: 1816. V. 51
Hone's Popular Political Tracts... London: 1822. V. 49
A Sketch from Public Life: a Poem, Founded Upon Recent Domestic Circumstances. London: 1816. V. 53; 54
The Three Trials of William Hone for Publishing Three Parodies... London: 1818. V. 47; 52; 54
Yearbook of Daily Recreation and Information, Concerning Remarkable Men and Manners... London: 1832. V. 50
The Yearbook of Daily Recreation and Information, Concerning Remarkable Men and Manners... London: 1832/26/33/33. V. 52

HONEYMAN, A. VAN DOREN
History of Union County, New Jersey 1664-1923. New York: 1923. V. 47; 49; 51
Northwestern New Jersey. A History of Somerset, Morris, Hunterdon, Warren and Sussex Counties. New York: 1927. V. 47; 49

HONEYMAN, ROBERT
The Honeyman Collection of Scientific Books and Manuscripts. London: 1978-81. V. 47; 49; 53

HONEYWOOD, ST. JOHN
Poems...With Some Pieces in Prose. New York: 1801. V. 54

HONIG, LOUIS O.
James Bridger. The Pathfinder of the West. Kansas City: 1951. V. 51; 52
Westport, Gateway to the Early West. Kansas City: 1950. V. 49

HONIG, P.
Science and Scientists in the Netherlands Indies. New York: 1945. V. 48; 50

HONISCH, DIETER
Uecker. New York: 1986. V. 50; 54

THE HONOUR and Prerogative of the Queen's Majesty Vindicated and Defended Against...the Guardian: In a Letter from a Country Whig to Mr. Steele. London: 1713. V. 50

HOOD, B. H., MRS.
Records and Reminiscences of Confederate Soldiers in Terrell County. Dawson: 1914. V. 49

HOOD, DIANA H.
The Haskell F. Norman Library of Science and Medicine. San Francisco: 1991. V. 50; 51

HOOD, JOHN
Australia and the East; Being a Journal Narrative of a Voyage to New South Wales in an Emigrant Ship... London: 1843. V. 52

HOOD, JOHN BELL
Advance and Retreat. New Orleans: 1880. V. 48; 49; 50; 54

HOOD, T. H.
Notes of a Cruise in H.M.S. "Fawn" in the Western Pacific in the Year 1862. Edinburgh: 1863. V. 50

HOOD, THEODORE
Jack Brag (a Novel). London: 1837. V. 49

HOOD, THEODORE EDWARD
Maxwell. London: 1830. V. 49; 52

HOOD, THOMAS
The Comic Annual. London: 1830-42. V. 49
The Daughters of King Daher. London: 1861. V. 49
The Epping Hunt. London: 1830. V. 51
The Epping Hunt. New York: 1930. V. 47
Fairy Land or Recreation for the Rising Generation. London: 1866. V. 50
Hood's Own. London: 1838. V. 51
Hood's Own... London: 1862. V. 51
Jingles and Jokes for the Little Folks. London: 1865. V. 48
The Loves of Tom Tucker and Little Bo-Peep. London: 1863. V. 52; 54
Miss Kilmansegg and Her Precious Leg... London: 1870. V. 51; 54
Miss Kilmansegg and Her Precious Leg. Chipping Camden: 1904. V. 47; 52
National Tales. London: 1827. V. 51
Odes and Addresses to Great People. London: 1825. V. 52; 54
The Plea of the Midsummer Fairies. London: 1827. V. 51; 53
Poems. London: 1846. V. 51
Poems... London: 1846-54. V. 51
The Poems... New York: 1870. V. 52

HOOD, THOMAS continued
Poems... London: 1871. V. 52
Poems... London: 1871/72. V. 51
Poems. London: 1872. V. 49
Poems. London: 1881. V. 52
The Poetical Works of... Boston: 1861. V. 50
The Serious Poems of Thomas Hood. London: 1901. V. 47
Up the Rhine. London: 1840. V. 51
Whims and Oddities, in Prose and Verse. London: 1826/27. V. 51
Whims and Oddities, in Prose and Verse... London: 1827/29. V. 47; 52
The Works... London: 1862. V. 51
The Works... London: 1862-63. V. 51
The Works... London: 1862-69. V. 51
The Works. London: 1869-73. V. 47
Works... London: 1895. V. 49

HOOD, W. CHARLES
Suggestions for the Future Provision of Criminal Lunatics. London: 1854. V. 50

HOOD, WHARTON
On Bone-Setting (So Called), and Its Relation to the Treatment of Joints Crippled by Injury, Rheumatism, Inflammation, &c. London: 1871. V. 53

HOOD'S CANAL LAND & IMPROVEMENT CO.
Union City, Its Resources and Prospects. Port Towsend: 1890. V. 52

HOOGHE, ROMEYN DE
Hieroglyphica of Merkbeelden der Oude Volkeren: Namentyk Egyptenaren, Chaldeeuwen, Feniciers, Joden, Grieken, Romeynen. Amsterdam: 1735. V. 48
Schouburgh Der Nederlandse Veranderingen, Geopent in Ses Tooneelen... Amsterdam: 1674. V. 50

HOOK, JAMES
Guida di Musica Being a Complete Book of Instructions for Beginners on the Harpsichord or Pianoforte. London: 1790. V. 47; 54
Pen Owen. Edinburgh: 1822. V. 47; 48; 51
Pen Owen. London: 1822. V. 54

HOOK, THEODORE EDWARD
Gilbert Gurney. London: 1836. V. 48
Gilbert Gurney. London: 1841. V. 47
Gurney Married: a Sequel to Gilbert Burney. Philadelphia: 1839. V. 47
Sayings and Doings. London: 1836-38. V. 47; 50
The Soldier's Return; or, What Can Beauty Do?. London: 1805. V. 52
The Trial by Jury: a Comic Piece, in Two Acts. New York: 1811. V. 50

HOOKE, ANDREW
An Essay On the National Debt, and National Capital... London: 1750. V. 52
An Essay On the National Debt, and National Capital... London: 1751. V. 48

HOOKE, NATHANIEL
An Account of the Conduct of the Dowager Duchess of Marlborough, from Her First Coming to Court to the Year 1710. London: 1742. V. 47; 49; 50; 51
The Roman History, From the Building of Rome to the Ruin of the Commonwealth. Dublin: 1767-72. V. 48
The Roman History, from the Building of Rome to the Ruin of the Commonwealth. London: 1818. V. 54
The Roman History: From the Building of Rome to the Ruin of the Commonwealth. London: 1825. V. 53
The Secret History of Colonel Hooke's Negotiations in Scotland, in Favour of the Pretender in 1707. London: 1760. V. 50; 53

HOOKE, ROBERT
Micrographia; or Some Physiological Descritpions of Minute Bodies Made by Magnifying Glasses. V. 51
Philosophical Collections... London: 1679/81. V. 51
Philosophical Experiments and Observations of the Late Eminent Dr. Robert Hooke...and Other Eminent Virtuoso's in His Time. London: 1726. V. 47

HOOKER, JOHN
Some Reminiscences of a Long Life.... Hartford: 1899. V. 50; 51; 53

HOOKER, JOHN DALTON
A Century of Indian Orchids Selected from Drawings in the Herbarium of the Botanic Garden, Calcuta. Lehre: 1967. V. 52
The Flora of British India. London: 1954-61. V. 47

HOOKER, JOSEPH DALTON
Flora Antarctica: the Botany of the Antarctic Voyage of HM Discovery Ships Erebus and Terror, in the Years 1839-43 Under the Command of Captain Sir James Clark Ross. Part I. London: 1844-47. V. 49
Flora of British India. New Delhi. V. 49; 52
Flora of British India. London: 1875-97. V. 51
Handbook of the New Zealand Flora. London: 1864-67. V. 49; 54
Himalayan Journals. London: 1855. V. 48; 53
Himalayan Journals. London: 1891. V. 53
A Journal of a Tour in Morocco and the Grave Atlas. London: 1878. V. 50; 54
On the Flora of Australia, Its Origin, Affinities and Distribution... London: 1859. V. 49; 50

HOOKER, RICHARD
The Lawes of Ecclesiastaical Politie. London: 1622. V. 48; 49
Of the Lawes of Ecclesiastical Politie... London: 1617-16. V. 52
Of the Lawes of Ecclesiastical Politie... London: 1617-16-18. V. 47
Of the Lawes of Ecclesiastical Politie. London: 1622. V. 51
Of the Lawes of Ecclesiastical Politie. London: 1632-36. V. 47
Of the Lawes of Ecclesiastical Politie... London: 1639. V. 54
Of the Lawes of Ecclesiastical Politie... London: 1676. V. 47; 49
The Works... Dublin: 1721. V. 49
The Works... Oxford: 1807. V. 49

HOOKER, W.
Lessons from the History of Medical Delusions. New York: 1850. V. 50

HOOKER, WILLIAM DAWSON
Notes on Norway; or a Brief Journal of a Tour Made to the Northern Parts of Norway in the Summer of 1836. Glasgow: 1839. V. 47

HOOKER, WILLIAM JACKSON
The British Ferns. London: 1861. V. 50; 51; 52
British Jungermanniae. London: 1816. V. 49; 52
A Century of Orchidaceous Plants Selected from Curtis's Botanical Magazine. London: 1849. V. 52
Description of Victoria Regia, or Great Water Lily of south America. London: 1847. V. 49
Exotic Flora. Edinburgh: 1822-Dec. 1824. V. 52
Exotic Flora... Edinburgh: 1823-27. V. 54
Genera Filicum; or Illustrations of the Genera of Ferns... London: 1838-42. V. 48
Icones Plantarum. London: 1836. V. 51
Journal of a Tour in Iceland in the Summer of 1809. London: 1811. V. 51; 52
Journal of a Tour in Iceland in the Summer of 1809. Yarmouth: 1811. V. 54
Journal of a Tour in Iceland, in the Summer of 1809. London: 1813. V. 47; 48
Journal of a Tour in Iceland in the Summer of 1809. Yarmouth: 1813. V. 50
The Journal of Botany, Being a Second Series of the Botanical Miscellany. London: 1834-42. V. 52
Musci Exotici. London: 1818-20. V. 49
Niger Flora, or an Enumeration of the Plants of Western Tropica Africa Collected by T. Vogel... London: 1849. V. 51
Species Filicum... London: 1846-64. V. 48
Species Filicum. London: 1970. V. 50
Synopsis Filicum. London: 1868. V. 49; 51; 53; 54
Synopsis Filicum... London: 1874. V. 48
Synopsis Filicum... London: 1883. V. 50; 52; 53

HOOKS, NATHANIEL
Town on Trail. New York: 1959. V. 53

HOOLE, CHARLES
An Easie Entrance to the Latine Tongue... London: 1649. V. 52

HOOLE, ELIJAH
Madras, Mysore, and the South of India... London: 1844. V. 47

HOOLE, JOHN
Journal Narrative Relative to Doctor Johnson's Last Illness Three Weeks Before His Death. Iowa City: 1972. V. 53; 54

HOOLE, SAMUEL
Aurelia; or, the Contest: an Heroi-Comic Poem in Four Cantos. London: 1783. V. 51; 54

HOOPER, CHARLES E.
The Country House. London: 1906. V. 51

HOOPER, E. EDEN
The Stock Exchange in the Year 1900. London: 1900. V. 49

HOOPER, GEORGE
Down the River. New York: 1874. V. 50; 54
Waterloo: the Downfall of the First Napoleon: a History of the Campaign of 1815. London: 1862. V. 52

HOOPER, HENRY
Wash. Boltor, M.D.; or, the Life of an Orator. London: 1872. V. 49

HOOPER, JACOB
An Impartial History of the Rebellion and Civil Wars in England During the Reign of King Charles the First. London: 1738. V. 47; 50; 54

HOOPER, JOHN
A Comentarie or Cleare Confession of the Christian Faith... London: 1583. V. 49
An Ouersighte and Deliberacion Vppon the Holy Prophet Jonas. London: 1550 or 1560. V. 50

HOOPER, JOHNSON JONES
Dog and Gun; A Few Loose Chapters on Shooting. New York. V. 47

HOOPER, LUCY
The Lady's Book of Flowers and Poetry. New York: 1842. V. 50

HOOPER, ROBERT
Lexicon Medicum: or Medical Dictionary. New York: 1835. V. 50

HOOPER, W. EDEN
The British Empire in the First Year of the Twentieth Century and the Last of the Victorian Reign... London: 1900. V. 47
The Central Criminal Court of London. London: 1909. V. 50
Stock Exchange Sayings in Black and White. London: 1899?. V. 53

HOOPER, W. H.
Ten Months Among the Tents of the Tuski. London: 1853. V. 54

HOOPER, WILLIAM
Fifty Years Since: an Address, Delivered Before the Alumni of the University of North Carolina, on the 7th of June, 1859. Chapel Hill: 1861. V. 49

HOOPER, WILLIAM continued
Rational Recretations, In Which the Principles of Numbers and Natural Philosophy are Clearly and Copiously Elucidated by a Series of Easy, Entertaining, Interesting Experiments. London: 1783-82. V. 47

HOOPER, WILLIAM H.
Vindication of the People of Utah. Remarks Of Hon. William H. Hooper, of Utah, in Reply to the Charges of Hon. W. H. Clagett, of Montana on the 28th and 29th of January, 1873... Washington: 1873. V. 51

HOOPES, GULILEMA M.
Memoirs and Letters of Gulielma M. Hoopes. Philadelphia: 1862. V. 50

HOOPES, PENROSE R.
Connecticut Clockmakers of the Eighteenth Century. Hartford: 1930. V. 48

HOOTON, CHARLES
St. Louis' Isle, or Texiana; With Additional Observations Made in the United States and In Canada. London: 1847. V. 48; 49; 52

HOOTON, EARNEST ALBERT
The Indians of Pecos Pueblo: a Study of Their Skeletal Remains. New Haven: 1930. V. 52

HOOVER, HERBERT CLARK
Addresses Upon the American Road 1933-1938. New York: 1938. V. 54
American Individualism. New York: 1922. V. 47
America's First Crusade. New York: 1942. V. 47
The Challenge to Liberty. New York: 1934. V. 47; 51; 53; 54
The Challenge to Liberty. New York: 1935. V. 51
Fishing For Fun — And to Wash Your Soul. New York: 1963. V. 48
The Herbert Clark Hoover Collection of Mining and Metallurgy - Bibliotheca De Re Metallica. Claremont: 1980. V. 49
On Growing Up. New York: 1962. V. 54
A Remedy for Disappearing Game Fishes. New York: 1930. V. 48; 49; 53

HOOVER, J. EDGAR
Masters of Deceit: the Story of Communism in America and How to Fight It. New York: 1958. V. 47

HOPE, ALEXANDER JAMES BERESFORD
Poems. London: 1843. V. 51

HOPE, BOB
They Got Me Covered. Hollywood: 1941. V. 53

HOPE, EDWARD
Alice in the Delighted States. New York: 1928. V. 53

HOPE, JOHN
A Letter to Francis Jeffrey, Esq. Editor of the Edinburgh Review. Edinburgh: 1811. V. 48
Occasional Attempts at Sentimental Poetry, by a Man In Business... London: 1769. V. 47
Thoughts, in Prose and Verse, Started in His Walks... Stockton: 1780. V. 53; 54

HOPE, LAURENCE
The Garden of Kama. London: 1902. V. 48
Indian Love. London: 1925. V. 48
India's Love Lyrics. New York: 1906. V. 48
India's Love Lyrics. New York: 1923. V. 48

HOPE, MARGARET
Flowers From an Indian Garden. Dusseldorf: 1846. V. 50

HOPE, STANLEY
A New Godiva. London: 1876. V. 54

HOPE, THOMAS
Anastasius: or, Memoirs of a Greek. London: 1819. V. 50; 51
Costume of the Ancients. London: 1809. V. 49
An Essay on the Origin and Propsects of Man. London: 1831. V. 53

HOPE, THOMAS CHARLES
Experiments and Observations Upon the Contraction of Water by Heat at Low Temperatures. Edinburgh: 1805. V. 52

HOPE, WILLIAM H. ST. JOHN
The Abbey of St. Mary in Furness, Lancashire. 1902. V. 47
The Abbey of St. Mary in Furness, Lancashire. Kendal: 1902. V. 52
Architectural Description of Kirkstall Abbey. Leeds: 1907. V. 47; 53
The Architectural History of the Cathedral Church and Monastery of St. Andrew at Rochester. London: 1900. V. 49
Cowdray and Easebourne Priory in the County of Sussex. London: 1919. V. 52
Windsor Castle, an Architectural History. London: 1913. V. 49

HOPE NICHOLSON, WILLIAM
An Entertainment for Lady-Dayes: Eikonokosmesis or the Dressing of Images. London: 1925. V. 50

HOPEWEL-SMITH, ARTHUR
An Introduction to Dental Anatomy and Physiology, Descriptive and Applied. London: 1913. V. 49

HOPING, JOHANN A. J.
Chiromantia Harmonica... Jena: 1673. V. 52

HOPKINS, A. I.
In the Isles of King Solomon. Philadelphia: 1925. V. 50

HOPKINS, ALBERT
A Dickens Atlas, Including Twelve Walks in London with Charles Dickens. New York: 1923. V. 54

HOPKINS, ALBERT A.
Magic: Stage Illusions and Scientific Diversions, Including Trick Photography. New York: 1901. V. 47
Magic Stage: Illusions and Scientific Diversions, Including Trick Photography. New York: 1911. V. 47

HOPKINS, CHARLES
Boadicea Queen of Britain. London: 1696. V. 47
Boadicea, Queen of Britain. London: 1697. V. 48
Friendship Improved: Or, The Female Warriour. London: 1700. V. 48; 49
Pyrrhus King of Epirus. London: 1695. V. 47

HOPKINS, EDWARD J.
The Organ, Its History and Construction...(with) A New History of the Organ... London: 1877. V. 50

HOPKINS, G. H. E.
An Illustrated Catalogue of the Rothschild Collection of Fleas... London: 1953-81. V. 49; 50

HOPKINS, G. M.
Atlas of Westchester County, New York. Philadelphia: 1929-31. V. 49
Combined Atlas of the State of New Jersey and the County of Hudson, from Actual Survey (sic) Official Records & Private Plans, by... Philadelphia: 1873. V. 49
Complete Set of Surveys and Plats of Properties in the City of Kansas, Missouri. Philadelphia: 1886. V. 49

HOPKINS, GARLAND EVANS
The First Battle of Modern Naval History. Richmond: 1943. V. 49

HOPKINS, GERARD MANLEY
Hawaii: The Past, Present and Future of Its Island Kingdom. London: 1866. V. 47; 51; 54
Pied Beauty. A Selection of Poems. London: 1994. V. 52
Poems. 1930. V. 50
Poems of Gerard Manley Hopkins Now First Published. London: 1918. V. 53
Selected Poems. London: 1954. V. 47; 49; 50; 51; 52
A View of the Mermaids. London: 1929. V. 47; 50

HOPKINS, HENRY CLAYTON
The Moon Boat and Other Verse. Philadelphia: 1918. V. 47

HOPKINS, JAMES
Chopin: the Man and His Music. New York: 1926. V. 47

HOPKINS, JOHN HENRY
Essay on Gothic Architecture, with Various Plans and Drawings for Churches... Burlington: 1836. V. 53

HOPKINS, JOSEPH R.
Hamiltoniad; or, the Efects of Discord. Philadelphia: 1804. V. 52
Report of the Case of Trespass & Assault and Battery, Wherein John Evans Was Plaintif...Tried at a Court of Nisi Prius for the City and County of Philadelphia, Before the Hon. H. H. Brackenridge, and a Special Jury. Philadelphia: 1810. V. 48

HOPKINS, KENNETH
She Is My Bright and Smiling and Shy Dear. Easthampton: 1985. V. 49; 52
Six Sonnets. Bournemouth: 1938. V. 48

HOPKINS, SAMUEL
Historical Memoirs, Relating to the Housatunnuk Indians; or, an Account of the Methods Used and Pains Taken for the Propagation of the Gospel Among the Heathenish-tribe, and the Success Thereof, Under th Ministry of the Late. Rev. Mr. John Sergeant... Boston: 1753. V. 52

HOPKINS, SARAH WINNEMUCCA
Life Among the Piutes. Boston/New York: 1883. V. 47; 50; 54

HOPKINS, THOMAS SMITH
Colonial Furniture of West New Jersey. Haddonfield: 1936. V. 47; 49; 51

HOPKINSON, TOM
Down the Long Slide. London: 1949. V. 52
The Transitory Venus - Nine Stories. London: 1948. V. 52

HOPKIRK, THOMAS
Flora Glottiana: a Catalogue of the Indigenous Plants on the banks of the River Clyde, and in the Neighbourhood to the City of Glasgow. Glasgow: 1813. V. 51

HOPPE, A. J.
A Bibliography of the Writings of Samuel Butler... London: 1925. V. 52

HOPPE, E. O.
The Book of Fair Women. New York: 1922. V. 47
In Gipsy Camp and Royal Palace. New York: 1924. V. 48; 52
Picturesque Great Britain: the Architecture and the Landscape Wasmuth. Berlin: 1926. V. 52

HOPPIN, JOSEPH CLARK
Euthymides and His Fellows. Cambridge: 1917. V. 50; 52
A Handbook of Attic Red-Figured Vases Signed by or Attributed to the Various Masters of the Sixth and Fifth Centuries B.C. Cambridge: 1919. V. 50; 52

HOPPUS, EDWARD
the Gentleman's and Builder's Repository; or, Architecture Display'd. London: 1737. V. 49
Practical Measuring...to the Meanest Capacity... London: 1765. V. 50
Practical Measuring...to the Meanest Capacity... York: 1806. V. 48

HOPTON, ARTHUR
A Concordancy of Yeares. London: 1615. V. 52

HORACE Wells, Dentist. Father of Surgical Anesthesia. 1948. V. 52; 53

HORACE Wells, Dentist, Father of Surgical Anesthesia. Hartford: 1948. V. 50; 52

HORAN, JAMES D.
The Gunfighters: The Authentic Wild West. New York: 1976. V. 47
The Life and Art of Charles Schreyvogel. New York: 1969. V. 49; 53
The McKenney-Hall Portrait Gallery of American Indians. New York: 1972. V. 52; 54

HORATIUS FLACCUS, QUINTUS
Ab Omni Obscoenitate Purgatus. Dilingae: 1585. V. 51
Arte Poetica Commentarius. Venice: 1554. V. 53
Carmina Alcaica. 1903. V. 49
Carmina Alcaica. Chelsea: 1903. V. 47; 50; 51; 54
Carmina Sapphica. Chelsea: 1903. V. 50; 52
Carmina Sapphica. Boston: 1983. V. 47
Carmininum Libri Quator. Birmingham: 1770. V. 50
Eclogae, una Cum Scholiis Perpetuis, tam Veteribus Quam Novis, Praecipue Vero Antiquorum Grammaticorum Helenii Acronis Pomponiique Porphyrionis... London: 1701. V. 50
Emblemata. Antverpiae: 1612. V. 53
Epistolae ad Pisones, et Augustum. Cambridge: 1757. V. 48
Epistolae Ad Pisones, et Augustum. London: 1766. V. 48; 53
Horace's Satires, Epistles and Art of Poetry... London: 1729. V. 51
Horatius in Quo Quidem Praeter M. Antonii Mureti Scholia. Venice: 1570. V. 51
Lyric Works of Horace... Philadelphia: 1786. V. 48; 54
Odes... 1638. V. 47
Odes... Paris: 1939-58. V. 49
Odes. 1990. V. 54
Odes and Epodes... Boston: 1901-03. V. 51
Odes and Epodes. Boston: 1901-04. V. 49; 50
Odes and Epodes. New York: 1961. V. 52; 54
The Odes and Satyres... 1715. V. 49
The Odes and Satyrs... London: 1721. V. 54
The Odes and Satyrs... London: 1730. V. 49; 54
The Odes, Epodes and Carmen Seculare. (with) The Satires, Epistles and Art of Poetry. London: 1793-97. V. 48
The Odes, Epodes and Satires of Horace. Edinburgh & London: 1870. V. 47
Opera... Venice: 1481. V. 47; 51
Opera. Florence: 1482. V. 48
Opera. Venice: 1495-96. V. 48; 54
Opera. Venetijs: 1566. V. 53
(Opera). Leiden: 1629. V. 52; 54
Opera. Leyden & Rotterdam: 1670. V. 52
Opera. London: 1699. V. 51
Opera. Paris: 1733. V. 47
Opera. London: 1733-37. V. 47; 48; 49; 50; 51; 52; 53; 54
(Opera). Glasguae: 1750. V. 51; 53
Opera. Glasgow: 1756. V. 51
Opera. Birmingham: 1770. V. 53
Opera. Birmingham: 1777. V. 52; 54
Opera. London: 1784. V. 51
Opera. Parma: 1791. V. 51
Opera. London: 1792-93. V. 50
Opera. Parma: 1793. V. 50
Opera. London: 1820. V. 51
Opera. London: 1824. V. 50
Opera. London: 1824-28. V. 51
Opera. London: 1826. V. 50; 53
Opera. London: 1829. V. 51
Opera Omnia. Paris: 1828. V. 51; 52
(Opera) Quae Supersunt Recensuit et Notulis Instruxit Gilbertus Wakefield. London: 1794. V. 52
Poemata. Geneve: 1588. V. 51
Poemata. Amsterdam: 1676. V. 48
Poemata. Orleans: 1767. V. 48
Poemata Omnia. Venice: 1519. V. 51
The Poems... London: 1666. V. 47
The Poems... London: 1671. V. 47; 48; 49; 51
A Poetical Translation of the Odes of Horace... London: 1750/49/50. V. 48
A Poetical Translation of the Works of Horace. London: 1756. V. 53
A Poetical Translation of the Works of Horace. London: 1765. V. 49
A Poetical Translation of the Works of Horace. London: 1778. V. 48
Q. Horatii Flacci, Quae Supersunt Recensuit et Notulis... Londini: 1794. V. 47
Q. Horatii Flaccus, Ex Fide Atque Auctoriate Decem Librorum Manuscriptorum Opera Dionysii Lambini Monstroliensis. Venice: 1566. V. 51
Quinti Horatii Flacci, Opera. Edinburgh: 1731. V. 51
Quinti Horatii Flacci Opera. Londini: 1733. V. 49
Quintus Horatius Flacci... London: 1820. V. 47
Quintus Horatius Flaccus (Opera). Birmingham: 1762. V. 51
Quintus Horatius Flaccus (Opera). London: 1826 or later. V. 49
A Thousand Horation Quotations. Boston: 1904. V. 51
Works. Florence: 1482. V. 54
The Works. London: 1760. V. 48
The Works... London: 1767. V. 52
Works. Birmingham: 1770. V. 48; 51
Works. London: 1820. V. 50
The Works... London: 1849. V. 48; 49

HORBLIT, HARRISON D.
One Hundred Books famous in Science. 1964. V. 48

HORDEN, JOHN
A Grammar of the Cree Language, as Spoken by The Cree Indians of North America. London: 1881. V. 52; 53

HORDT, JOHAN LUDVIG
The Military, Historical and Political Memoirs of the Count de Hordt, a Swedish Nobleman and Lieutenant General in the Service of the King of Prussia. London: 1806. V. 50

HORE, EDWARD COODE
Tanganyika: Eleven Years in Central Africa. London: 1892. V. 47; 50; 51; 54

HORE, J. P.
The History of Newmarket and the Annals of the Turf... London: 1886. V. 47; 48
Sporting and Rural Records of the Chevely Estate. Newmarket: 1899. V. 50

HOREJS, A.
Antonin Dvorak: the Composer's Life & Work in Pictures. Prague: 1955. V. 49

HORENMAN, FREDERICK
The Journal of Frederick Horneman's Travels From Cairo to Mourzouk, the Capital of the Kingdom of Fezzan, in Africa. London: 1802. V. 50

HORFIELD, T. W.
The History and Antiquities of Lewes and Its Vicinity. Lewes: 1824-27. V. 48

HORGAN, PAUL
The Fault of Angels. New York: 1933. V. 51
Great River: the Rio Grande in North American History. 1954. V. 49; 52
Great River: The Rio Grande in North American History. New York: 1954. V. 51; 52; 54
Lamy of Santa Fe. New York: 1975. V. 48; 51
Men of Arms. Philadelphia: 1931. V. 47; 48
The Return of the Weed. New York: 1936. V. 50; 53
The Return of the Weed. Flagstaff: 1980. V. 50
Rome Eternal. 1959. V. 50; 51

HORKA-FOLLICK, LORAYNE A.
Los Hermanos Penitentes. Los Angeles: 1969. V. 48

HORLACHER, JAMES LEVI
A Year in the Oil Fields. Lexington: 1929. V. 48

HORLOCK, KNIGHTLEY WILLIAM
On the Management of Hounds. London: 1852. V. 54
Recollections of a Fox-Hunter. London: 1861. V. 47

HORMAN, WILLIAM
Vulgaria. Oxford: 1926. V. 48

HORN, HOSEA B.
Horn's Overland Guide from the U. S. Indian Sub-Agency, Council Bluffs...to the City of Sacramento. New York: 1851. V. 47

HORN, SARAH ANN
A Narrative of the Captivity of Mrs. Horn and Her Two Children, with Mrs. Harris, by the Camanche Indians, After They Had Murdered Their Husbands and Traveling Companions... St. Louis: 1839. V. 48

HORN, SUSAN G.
The Next World. London: 1890. V. 54

HORN, TOM
Life of Tom Horn, Government Scout and Interpreter. Denver: 1904. V. 53

HORN, W. F.
The Horn Papers; Early Western Movement on the Monongahela and Upper Ohio, 1765-1795. Scottdale: 1945. V. 52

HORN, WALLACE
Union Army Operations in the Southwest and Confederate Victories - In the Southwest. Albuquerque: 1962. V. 48

HORN, WALTER
The Plan of St. Gall: a Study of the Architecture & Economy Of, and Life in a Paradigmatic Carolingian Monastery. Berkeley: 1979. V. 47; 50
The Plan of St. Gall: a Study of the Architecture and Economy of, and Life in a Paradigmatic Carolingian Monastery. Berkeley: 1979. V. 47

HORNADAY, WILLIAM T.
Camp-Fires in the Canadian Rockies. New York: 1906. V. 53; 54
Camp-Fires in the Canadian Rockies. London: 1907. V. 53
Camp-Fires in the Canadian Rockies. New York: 1907. V. 50
Camp-Fires on Desert and Lava. New York: 1908. V. 49
Camp-Fires on Desert and Lava. London: 1910. V. 48; 52
Old Fashioned Verses. New York: 1919. V. 53
Taxidermy and Zoological Collecting. 1892. V. 49
Taxidermy and Zoological Collecting. U.S.A. 1892. V. 47

HORNBEIN, THOMAS F.
Everest: The West Ridge. 1964. V. 49
Everest: the West Ridge. San Francisco: 1965. V. 47; 48; 53; 54

HORNBY, BEATRIX
The Children's Garden: a Memory of the Old Porch House. 1913. V. 54

HORNBY, C. H. ST. JOHN
A Descriptive Bibliography of the Books printed at the Ashendene Press. San Francisco: 1976. V. 48; 51

HORNBY, EDWARD THOMAS STANLEY
Childhood, a Poem. London: 1821. V. 49

HORNBY, LADY
Constantinople During the Crimean War. London: 1863. V. 53

HORNE, BERNARD S.
The Compleat Angler 1653-1967. Pittsburgh: 1970. V. 51

HORNE, GEORGE
Letters on Infidelity. (with) A Letter to Adam Smith, LL.D. on the Life, Death and Philosophy of His friend David Hume Esq. Oxford: 1784/84. V. 49

HORNE, HENRY
Essays Concerning Iron and Steel. London: 1773. V. 52

HORNE, HERBERT P.
The Binding of Books. An Essay in the History of Gold Tooled Bindings. London: 1894. V. 49; 50

HORNE, JOHN
Alonzo, a Tragedy in Five Acts. London: 1773. V. 48
The Diversions of Purley. London: 1798. V. 48

HORNE, RICHARD HENRY HENGIST
Australian Facts and Prospects: To Which is Prefixed the Author's Australian Autobiography. London: 1859. V. 48; 49
Exposition of the False Medium and Barriers Excluding Men of Genius from the Public. London: 1833. V. 50; 52
Galatea Secunda, an Odaic Cantata, Addressed to H. R. H. Prince Alfred Duke of Edinburgh, on His First Arrival in the Colony of Victoria. Melborune: 1867. V. 47; 49; 50
The Great Peace Maker: a Sub-marine Dialogue. London: 1872. V. 48
The History of Napoleon. London: 1840. V. 50
A New Spirit of the Age. New York: 1844. V. 47
Orion: an Epic. London: 1843. V. 47; 48; 49; 53
Orion: an Epic... Melbourne: 1854. V. 47

HORNE, THOMAS HARTWELL
A Catalogue of the Library of the College of St. Margaret & St. Bernard, Commonly Called Queen's College in the University of Cambridge. London: 1827. V. 52
An Illustrated Record of Important Events in the Annals of Europe, During the last four Years. London: 1816. V. 48
The Lakes of Lancashire, Westmorland and Cumberland... London: 1816. V. 51
Landscape Illustrations of the Bible. London: 1836. V. 48; 53

HORNE, WILLIAM
Ancient Mysteries Described, Especially the English Miracle Plays Founded on Apocryphal New Testament Story. London: 1823. V. 51

HORNELL, JAMES
British Coracles and Irish Curraghs. 1938. V. 50
British Coracles and Irish Curraghs. London: 1938. V. 49; 51; 54
Fishing in Many Waters. Cambridge: 1950. V. 52

HORNEMAN, FREDERICK
The Journal of Frederick Horneman's Travels from Cairo to Marzouk, the Capital of the Kingdom of Fezzan in Africa, in the Years 1797-8. London: 1802. V. 54

HORNER, FRANCIS
Memoirs and Correspondence. London: 1843. V. 47; 53

HORNER, GEORGE R. B.
Medical Topography of Brazil and Uruguay with Incidental Remarks. Philadelphia: 1845. V. 50; 54

HORNER, J. M.
The Modern Emigrant; or Love of Liberty: Being a Discourse Delivered in the City of New York. New York: 1832. V. 53

HORNER, JOHN
The Linen Trade of Europe During the Spinning Wheel Period. Belfast: 1920. V. 52

HORNER, JOSHUA
Letters from an Artist Sojourning on the Continent. Halifax: 1841. V. 47

HORNEY, KAREN
The Neurotic Personality of Our Time. New York: 1937. V. 47

HORNOR, THOMAS
Prospectus. View of London, and the Surrounding country, Taken with Mathematical Accuracy from an Observatory Purposely Erected Over the Cross of St. Paul's Cathedral; to be published in four engravings. London: 1823. V. 51

HORNOR, WILLIAM S.
...This Old Monmouth of Ours. History, Tradition, Biography, Genalogy, Anecdotes. Freehold: 1932. V. 49; 51

HORNSBY, HENRY H.
The Trey of Sevens. Dallas: 1946. V. 48

HORNUNG, CLARENCE P.
Handbook of Early Advertising Art, Mainly from American Sources. New York: 1956. V. 51
Treasury of American Design. New York: 1976. V. 49; 50; 52

HORNUNG, E. W.
The Amateur Cracksman. Toronto: 1899. V. 48
The Camera Fiend. London: 1911. V. 52
Mr. Justice Raffles. London: 1909. V. 54
A Thief in the Night. London: 1905. V. 49

HORNUNG, ERIK
The Tomb of Pharoah Seti I... Zurich and Munchen: 1991. V. 51

HORNYOLD, HENRY
Genealogical Memoirs of the Family of Strickland of Sizergh. Kendal: 1928. V. 48; 52; 54

HORODISCH, ABRAHAM
Picasso as a Book Artist. Cleveland and New York: 1962. V. 54

HOROVITZ, MICHAEL
Midsummer Morning Jog Log. Hereford: 1986. V. 51

HORR, N. T.
A Bibliography of Card-Games and of the History of the Playing Card. Cleveland: 1892. V. 52

HORRAX, GILBERT
Neurosurgery - an Historical Sketch. Springfield: 1952. V. 48; 49; 50

HORREBOW, NIELS
The Natural History of Iceland... London: 1758. V. 47

HORREBOW, PEDER NIELS
Consilii de Nova methodo Paschali Particulam. Copenhagen: 1737-38. V. 54

HORRID Massacre at Dartmoor Prison England. Where the Unarmed American Prisoners of War Were Wantonly Fired Upon by the Guard, Under the Command of the Prison Turn-Key, the Blood Thirty Shortland; Seven Were Killed and About Fifty Wounded... Boston: 1815. V. 48

HORSBRUGH, B. R.
The Game-Birds & Water-Fowl of South Africa. London: 1912. V. 49; 52

THE HORSE. His Beauties and Defects. London: 1866. V. 49; 51

THE HORSE; With a Treatise on Draught; and a Copious Index. London: 1831. V. 47

THE HORSEMEN of the Americas. Austin: 1968. V. 48

HORSFALL, J. G.
Plant Disease, an Advance Treatise. London: 1977-78. V. 49

HORSFALL, T. C.
Proceedings of the Conference on Education Under Healthy Conditions. Manchester & London: 1885. V. 52

HORSFALL, THOMAS
Notes on the Manor of Well and Snape in the North Riding of the County of York. Leeds: 1912. V. 47; 53

HORSFALL, W. J.
Plant Disease, an Advanced Treatise. London: 1977-78. V. 50

HORSFIELD, T.
Catalogue of Birds in the Museum of the Hon. East India Company. London: 1856-58. V. 51
A Catalogue of the Mammalia in the Museum of the Hon. East-India Company. London: 1851. V. 51
Zoological Researches in Java and the Neighbouring Islands. London: 1991. V. 52

HORSFIELD, THOMAS WALKER
The History and Antiquities of Lewes and its Vicinity. Lewes: 1824-27. V. 49
The History, Antiquities and Topography of the County of Sussex. Lewes: 1835. V. 54

HORSHAM: Its History and Antiquities. London: 1868. V. 49

HORSLEY, J. SHELTON
Surgery Of the Blood Vessels. St. Louis: 1915. V. 48

HORSLEY, JOHN
Britannia Romana; or the Roman Antiquities of Britain. London: 1732. V. 47; 53

HORSLEY, SAMUEL
A Catalogue of the Entire and Very Valuable Library of the Late Right Rev. Samuel Horsley, Lord Bishop of St. Asaph. London: 1807. V. 48
The Speeches in Parliament of Samuel Horsley, LL.D... Dundee: 1813. V. 54

HORSLEY, VICTOR
Alcohol and the Human Body: an Introduction to the Study of the Subject, and a Contribution to National Health. London: 1908. V. 53
The Structure and Function of the Brain and Spinal Cord. London: 1892. V. 52
The Structure and Functions of the Cerebellum Examined by a New Method. London: 1908. V. 51; 52

HORSLEY, WILLIAM
A Treatise on Maritime Affairs; or a Comparison Between the Commerce and Naval Power of England and France. London: 1744. V. 52

HORSMAN, GILBERT
Precedents in Conveyancing Settled and Approved. London: 1768. V. 54

HORST, TILEMAN VAN DER
Theatrum Machinarum Universale; of Keurige Verzameling van Verscheide Groote en Zeer Fraaie Waterwerken, Schutsluizen, Waterkeringen, Ophaal- en Draaibruggen. Amsterdam: 1774. V. 51; 52

HORSTER, MARITA
Andrea Del Castagno... Ithaca: 1980. V. 51; 53
Andrea Del Castagno. London: 1980. V. 50; 54

HORT, JOHN JOSIAH
The Horse Guards, By the Two Mounted Sentries. London: 1850. V. 49; 50; 51

HORT, RICHARD
Abyssinia and Its People; or, Life in the Land of Prester John. London: 1868. V. 51
The Embroidered Banner and other Marvels. London: 1850. V. 51; 54
The Horse Guards, by the Two Mounted Sentries. London: 1850. V. 51
The Man Who Eloped With His Own Wife. London: 1850. V. 51
Penelope Wedgebone: the Supposed Heiress. London: 1850. V. 51

HORTENSIUS, PSEUD.
Deinology; or, the Union of Reason and Elegance; Being Instructions to a Young Barriester. London: 1789. V. 48

HORTICULTURAL SOCIETY OF LONDON
The Horticultural Society Journal. London: 1846. V. 51
The Horticultural Society Journal. London: 1847. V. 51
Transactions. London: 1820-24. V. 51
Transactions: First Series. London: 1820-30. V. 47; 51

THE HORTICULTURIST and Journal of Rural Art and Rural Taste. New York: 1858. V. 52

HORTON, HARRY HOWELLS
Birmingham: a Poem. Birmingham: 1853. V. 50; 51
Community the Only Salvation for Man, a Lecture Delivered in the Social Institution, Salford, on Sunday Morning, Sept. 16th 1838. London: 1838. V. 53

HORTON, LYDIARD HENEAGE WALTER
Dream Problem and the Mechanism of Thought Viewed from the Biological Standpoint. Philadelphia: 1926. V. 49; 54

HORTON, SAMUEL DANA
The Silver Pound and England's Monetary Policy Since the Restoration Together with the History of the Guinea. London: 1887. V. 50; 54

HORTON, WILLIAM THOMAS
A Book of Images. London: 1898. V. 50; 53
William Thomas Horton (1864-1919) - a Selection of His Work. London. V. 50

HORTUS Sanitatis. Mainz: 1491. V. 51

HORWITZ, B.
Chess Studies and End-Games, Systematically Arranged... London: 1884. V. 50

HORWOOD, A. R.
The Flora of Leicestershire and Rutland. London: 1933. V. 47

HORWOOD, ALFRED J.
Year Books of the Reign of Edward the First, Years 20 and 21, 21 and 22, 30 and 31, 32 and 33. London: 1866. V. 49

HORWOOD, J. W.
The Sei Whale, Population Biology, Ecology and Management. London: 1987. V. 51

HORWOOD, MURRAY
Public Health Surveys: What They Are, How to Make Them, How to Use Them. New York: 1921. V. 48; 50; 52; 53

HOSACK, DAVID
A Discourse Introductory to the Course of Lectures on the Theory and Practice of Medicine. 1814. V. 54
Lectures On the Theory and Practice of Physic. Philadelphia: 1838. V. 48; 53
Memoir of De Witt Clinton. New York: 1829. V. 51; 53; 54
Observation on Febrile Contagion, and on the Means of Improving the Medical Police of the City of New-York. New York: 1820. V. 51
Syllabus of the Course of Lectures, on Botany, Delivered in Columbia College. New York: 1795. V. 50; 53

HOSE, CHARLES
Natural Man: a Record from Borneo. London: 1926. V. 54
The Pagan Tribes of Borneo. London: 1912. V. 50; 54

HOSEMANN, T.
A Laughter Book for Little Folk from the German... London: 1850. V. 49

HOSIE, ALEXANDER
Manchuria Its People, Resources and Recent History. Boston and Tokyo: 1910. V. 54
Three Years in Western China; in a Narrative of Three Journeys in Ssu-Ch'an, Kuei-Chow and Yun-nan. London: 1890. V. 50

HOSKING, ERIC
Eric Hosking's Classic Birds. London: 1993. V. 50

HOSKING, WILLIAM
Treatises on Architecture, Building, Masonry, Joinery and Carpentry. Edinburgh: 1846. V. 52

HOSKINS, G. A.
Travels in Ethiopia. London: 1835. V. 49; 52
Visit to the Great Oasis of the Libyan Desert... London: 1837. V. 52

HOSKINS, GEORGE GORDON
An Hour with a Sewer Rat; or a Few Plain Hints on House Drainage and Sewer Gas. London: 1879. V. 53

HOSKINS, J. CASTELL
Canada: an Encyclopedia of the Country, the Canadian Dominion Considered In Its Historic Relations, Its Natural Resources, its Material Progress and its Natural Development. Toronto: 1898/99. V. 51

HOSKINS, JOSEPH
Hymns on Select Texts of Scripture, and Occasional Subjects. Bristol: 1789. V. 49

HOSKYNS, CHARLES WREN
Talpa: or the Chronicles of a Clay Farm. London: 1852. V. 49

HOSMER, JAMES KENDALL
The Color-guard: Being a Corporal's Notes of Military Service in the 19th Army Corps. Boston: 1864. V. 47; 48

HOSMER, WILLIAM
Autobiography of Rev. Alvin Torry, First Missionary to the Six Nations and the Northwestern Tribes of British North America. Auburn: 1862. V. 53

HOSOE, ELKAH
Man and Woman. Tokyo: 1961. V. 54

HOSPINIAN, RUDOLF
De Origine, Progressu, Ceremoniis et Ritibus Festorum Dierum Judaeorum, Graecorum, romanum & Turcarum...(with) Festa Christianorum... Geneva: 1592/93. V. 51

HOST, N. T.
Synopsis Plantarum in Austria. Vienna: 1797. V. 52

HOSTE, P. PAUL
A Treatise on Naval Tactics. Edinburgh: 1834. V. 54

HOSTETTER, G. L.
It's a Racket. 1929. V. 53

HOT and Healing Springs of Virginia. Chicago: 1891. V. 54

HOT Springs, Arkanasas, the Carlsbad of America. St. Louis: 1894. V. 54

THE HOT Springs of Kambu. Gangtok: 1919. V. 53

HOTCHKISS, JEDIDIAH
The Virginias...Volume VI. Staunton: 1885. V. 47

HOTEL Del Coronado. Coronado Beach, San Diego County, California. Its Attractions as a Health and Pleasure Resort... Oakland: 1895. V. 47

HOTMAN, FRANCOIS
Brutum Fulmen. Leyden?: 1585. V. 48; 52
Francogallia. Geneva: 1573. V. 48
Francogallia. Frankfurt: 1586. V. 51; 53
Francogallia:... London: 1711. V. 51; 52

HOTMAN, JEAN, SIEUR DE VILLIERS
L'Ambassadevr. 1603. V. 53

HOTSON, J. LESLIE
The Death of Christopher Marlowe. London: 1925. V. 51

HOTTEN, JOHN CAMDEN
Abyssinia... 1868. V. 47
Abyssinia... London: 1868. V. 48; 50; 53
The Book of Vagabonds and Beggars... London: 1860. V. 49
Charles Dickens the Story of His Life. London: 1870. V. 54
A Dictionary of Modern Slang, Cant and Vulgar Words... London: 1859. V. 52
A Dictionary of Modern Slang, Cant, and Vulgar Words. London: 1860. V. 48; 49; 53
A Hand-Book to the Topography and Family History of England and Wales... London: 1863. V. 49
The Slang Dictionary; or, the Vulgar Words, Street Phrases and 'Fast' Expressions of High and Low Society. London: 1865. V. 49
Thackeray the Humourist and the Man of Letters. London: 1864. V. 49; 53

HOUBIGANT, A. G.
Moeurs et Costumes des Russes. Paris: 1817. V. 51

HOUCK, LOUIS
A History of Missouri. Chicago: 1908. V. 49; 51

HOUDAR DE LA MOTTE, ANTOINE
One Hundred New Court Fables... London: 1721. V. 48

HOUDIN, J. P.
Barbara Hepworth. Boston: 1961. V. 52

HOUDIN, ROBERT
Life of Robert Houdin, the King of Conjurers. Philadelphia: 1890. V. 54
Memoirs of Robert-Houdin: Ambassador, Author and Conjurer. Philadelphia: 1859. V. 48; 54

HOUDINI, HARRY
Houdini Exposes the Tricks Used by Boston Medium "Margery". New York: 1924. V. 47
Magical Rope Ties and Escapes... London: 1921. V. 49; 51
A Magician Among the Spirits. New York: 1924. V. 48; 49; 54
Miracle Mongers and their Methods... New York: 1920. V. 51
The Unmasking of Robert Houdin. New York: 1908. V. 49; 51; 53; 54

HOUGH, A.
Samoan Phrase Book. Samoa: 1924. V. 52

HOUGH, EMERSON
The Covered Wagon. New York: 1922. V. 47; 53
The Story of the Cowboy. New York: 1897. V. 53; 54
The Story of the Outlaw. New York: 1907. V. 51; 53
The Web. Chicago: 1919. V. 54

HOUGH, R. B.
The American Woods, Exhibited by Actual Specimens and With Copious Explanatory Text. Lowville: 1894-1928. V. 47

HOUGH, WALTER
The Moki Snake Dance. Santa Fe: 1900. V. 48

HOUGHTON, ARTHUR A.
Collection of Miniature Books Formed by Arthur A. Houghton, Jr. London: 1979. V. 52

HOUGHTON, JOHN
A Collection of Letters for the Improvement of Husbandry and Trade... London: 1681. V. 54
Husbandry and Trade Improv'd...Collection of many Valuable Materials Relating to Corn, Cattle... London: 1717. V. 49
Husbandry and Trade Improv'd...Collection of Many Valuable Materials Relating to Corn, Cattle... London: 1727. V. 47

HOUGHTON, MARY
The Border Chieftains; or, Love and Chivalry. London: 1813. V. 54

HOUGHTON, MIFFLIN & CO.
A Portrait Catalogue of the Books Published by Houghton, Mifflin & Co. Boston, New York, Chicago: 1905-06. V. 50

HOUGHTON, RICHARD MONCKTON MILNES, 1ST BARON
Good Night and Good Morning. London: 1870. V. 49; 53
The Life, Letters and Friendships of Richard Monckton Milnes. London: 1890. V. 47
Memorials Of a Tour in Some Parts of Greece: Chiefly Poetical. London: 1834. V. 51
Palm Leaves: Memorials of Many Scenes. London: 1844. V. 48; 53
Selections From the Poetical Works. London: 1863. V. 48
Some Writings and Speeches...In the Last Year of His Life... London: 1888. V. 48; 49

HOUGHTON, STANLEY
The Works. London: 1914. V. 53

HOUGHTON, WALTER E.
The Wellesley Index to Victorian Periodicals 1824-1900. Toronto: 1966-79. V. 51

HOUGHTON, WILLIAM
British Fresh-Water Fishes. London: 1879. V. 49; 53
British Fresh-Water Fishes. London: 1880. V. 53
Sea-Side Walks of a Naturalist and His Children. London: 1880. V. 54

HOUGHTON, WILLIAM ROBERT
Two Boys in the Civil War and After. Montgomery: 1912. V. 49

HOULDBROOKE,
A Short Address to the People of Scotland, on the Subject of the Slave Trade. Edinburgh: 1792. V. 53

HOULT, NORAH
Time Gentlemen! Time!. London: 1930. V. 47

HOUNSELL, BERNARD
Coach Drives from London. 1892. V. 54

HOURST, LIEUT.
French Enterprise in Africa, the Personal Narrataive of Lieut. Hourst of His Exploration of the Niger. London: 1989. V. 51

HOUSATONUC BOOKSHOP
T. S. Eliot. Salisbury: 1938. V. 54

THE HOUSE Annual. London: 1902. V. 50

HOUSE, EDWARD J.
A Hunter's Camp-Fires. 1909. V. 54

HOUSE, HOMER D.
Wild Flowers of New York. Albany: 1918. V. 50
Wild Flowers of New York. Albany: 1923. V. 49; 50

THE HOUSE of Peeresses: or, Female Oratory. London: 1779. V. 50; 54

THE HOUSE That Jack Built. London: 1860. V. 52
THE HOUSE That Jack Built. Philadelphia: 1860. V. 49

THE HOUSE that Jack Built Wedding Book. San Francisco & Santa: 1909. V. 49

HOUSEHOLD, GEOFFREY
The Third Hour. Boston: 1938. V. 48; 52

HOUSEHOLD Manual and Practical Cook Book, Embracing Many Hundreds of Valuable Recipes... Waco: 1888. V. 47

HOUSEHOLDER, BOB
Grand Slam of North American Wild Sheep. Phoenix: 1974. V. 53

THE HOUSEKEEPER'S Scrap Book. Cleveland: 1907. V. 48

HOUSMAN, ALFRED EDWARD
The Collected Poems. London: 1939. V. 53
Fifteen Letters to Walter Asburner. 1976. V. 54
Last Poems. London: 1922. V. 47; 48; 51; 52; 54
Last Poems. New York: 1922. V. 48
The Parallelogram: The Amphisbaena: The Crocodile. Los Angeles: 1941. V. 48
Princess Badoura...Arabian Nights. London: 1913. V. 53
A Shropshire Lad. London: 1896. V. 47; 48; 49; 53
A Shropshire Lad. London: 1914. V. 48; 49; 50; 51
A Shropshire Lad... London: 1922/29. V. 53
A Shropshire Lad... Chipping Campden: 1929. V. 47
A Shropshire Lad... London: 1929. V. 53
A Shropshire Lad. New York & London: 1935. V. 47; 48; 52
A Shropshire Lad. Market Drayton: 1990. V. 50

Six Poems from "A Shropshire Lad" and "Last Poems". 1937. V. 51
When I Was One and Twenty. Fullerton: 1986. V. 51

HOUSMAN, CLEMENCE
The Werewolf. 1896. V. 47
The Werewolf. London: 1896. V. 47; 49; 51; 54

HOUSMAN, JOHN
A Descriptive Tour and Guide to the Lakes, Caves, Mountains and Other Natural Curiosities in Cumberland, Westmoreland, Lancashire... Carlisle: 1800. V. 50; 52
A Descriptive Tour And Guide to the Lakes, Caves, Mountains and Other Natural Curiosities in Cumberland, Westmoreland, Lancashire... Carlisle: 1812. V. 50; 52
A Descriptive Tour and Guide to the Lakes, Caves, Mountains and Other Natural Curiosities in Cumberland, Westmoreland, Lancashire... Carlisle: 1814. V. 52
A Descriptive Tour and Guide to the Lakes, Caves, Mountains and Other Natural Curiosities in Cumberland, Westmorland, Lancashire... Carlisle: 1802. V. 47
A Topographical Description of Cumberland, Westmoreland, Lancashire and a Part of the West Riding of Yorkshire... Carlisle: 1800. V. 54

HOUSMAN, LAURENCE
A. E. H. Some Poems, Some Letters and a Personal Memoir by His Brother. London: 1937. V. 54
Bethlehem. A Nativity Play. London: 1902. V. 47
The Blue Moon. London: 1904. V. 48; 51
Dethronements. Imaginary Portraits of Political Characters, Done in Dialogue. London: 1922. V. 50
False Premises: Five One-Act Play. Stratford-upon-Avon: 1922. V. 52; 54
A Farm In Fairyland. New York: 1894. V. 51
Field of Clover. London: 1898. V. 51
The Field of Clover. New York: 1902. V. 47; 50
The House of Joy. London: 1895. V. 49
Mendicant Rhymes. Chipping Camden: 1906. V. 50
A Modern Antaeus. New York: 1901. V. 49
Palace Scenes. More Plays of Queen Victoria. London: 1937. V. 50
Princess Badoura... London. V. 47
Princess Badoura. London: 1913. V. 54
Rue. London: 1899. V. 48
Stories from the Arabian Nights. London: 1907. V. 48; 53; 54
Stories from the Arabian Nights... New York: 1907. V. 49
Stories from the Arabian Nights. London: 1935. V. 49
The Story of the Seven Young Goslings. London: 1899. V. 52; 54
The Venture. London: 1903/05. V. 50

HOUSSER, F. B.
A Canadian Art Movement. Toronto: 1926. V. 47; 50; 51; 53; 54

HOUSTON & TEXAS CENTRAL RAILWAY CO.
Houston and Texas Central Through Route to Texas, the Field of Agriculture and Commerce. Chicago: 1878. V. 53

HOUSTON, MATILDA CHARLOTTE JESSE FRASER
The Poor of the Period. London: 1884. V. 54

HOUSTON, PAM
Cowboys are My Weakness. 1992. V. 54
Cowboys Are My Weakness. New York & London: 1992. V. 50; 51; 52; 53; 54
Women on Hunting. New York: 1994. V. 54

HOUSTON Post Almanac 1896. Houston: 1895. V. 53

HOUSTON, SAM
Governor's Message and Accompanying Documents. Austin: 1861. V. 49
Nebraska Bill - Indian Tribes. Speech of Hon. Sam Houston of Texas, Delivered in the Senate Feb. 14 and 15, 1854, in Favor of Maintaining the Public Faith with the Indian Tribes. Washington: 1854. V. 53
Speeches of Hon. Sam Houston, of Texas, on the Pacific Railroad Bill: and in Reply to Hon. A. Iverson of Georgia. Washington: 1859. V. 47
Speeches of Sam Houston, of Texas, on the Subject of an Increase of the Army, and the Indian Policy of the Government, Delivered in the Senate... Washington: 1855. V. 54
The Writings of Sam Houston... Austin: 1938-41. V. 47; 48
The Writings of Sam Houston. Austin: 1940. V. 48

HOUSTON (TEXAS). CHAMBER OF COMMERCE
Illustrated City Book of Houston Containing Annual Message of Ben Campbell, Mayor with Reports of all Departments of the City. Houston: 1915. V. 49

HOUSTOUN, MATILDA
Texas and the Gulf of Mexico; or, Yachting in the New World. London: 1844. V. 48
Texas and the Gulf of Mexico: or, Yachting in the New World. Philadelphia: 1845. V. 48; 53

HOUTCHENS, CAROLYN WASHBURN
The English Romantic Poets and Essayists - A Review of Research and Criticism. New York: 1957. V. 52

HOUTEN, HENDRIK VAN
Verhandelinge van de Grontregelen der Door-Zigtkunde of Tekenkonst. Amsterdam: 1705. V. 53

HOUTTUYN, MARTINUS
Hotkunde, Behelzende de Afbeeldingen van Meest Alle Bekund, in-en Uitlandsche Houten. Amsterdam: 1773-91. V. 52

HOVEY, CHARLES MASON
The Fruits of America... Boston: 1852-56. V. 48; 50; 51; 52; 54

HOVEY, HENRIETTA RUSSELL
Yawning. New York: 1896. V. 50; 51

HOVHANESS, ALAN
The Burning House: Opus 185. New York: 1960. V. 52
Magnificat for Soli, Chorus and Ochestra. New York: 1961. V. 52

HOW, G. E. P.
English and Scottish Silver Spoons. London: 1952. V. 50

HOW
Gambler's Win; or, the Secrets of Advantage Playing Exposed. New York: 1868. V. 47

HOW
the People's Constitution Was Made for Rhode-Island, Without the Aid of the Law or Of the Legislature. Providence?: 1843. V. 51

HOW
To Amuse an Evening Party. New York: 1869. V. 51

HOW
to Arrange the Hair; or, Golden Rules for the Fair Sex. London: 1857. V. 53

HOW
to Be Happy or Fairy Gifts... London: 1828. V. 49

HOW
to Make Doll's Furniture and Furnish a Doll's House. London: 1871. V. 48

HOWARD, B. DOUGLAS
Life with Trans-Siberian Savages. London: 1893. V. 54

HOWARD, BARBARA
Twenty-Eight Drawings. Toronto: 1970. V. 50

HOWARD, BEN
Father of Waters, Poems 1965-1976. Omaha: 1979. V. 47

HOWARD, BENJAMIN C.
Report of the Decision...in the Case of Dred Scott. Washington: 1857. V. 48

HOWARD, BRIAN
God Save the King. Paris: 1930. V. 51

HOWARD, CHARLES
Historical Anecdotes...the Howard Family. London: 1769. V. 52; 54

HOWARD, E. G. G.
Memoirs of Admiral Sir Sydney Smith, KCB &c. London: 1839. V. 48

HOWARD, EDWARD
Jack Ashore. London: 1840. V. 51
Poems, and Essays: with a Paraphrase on Cicero's Laelius, or, Of Friendship. London: 1674. V. 50

HOWARD, EDWIN L.
Gazebos and Garden Houses. Westport: 1935. V. 49

HOWARD, ELIZABETH JANE
The Long View. London: 1956. V. 53

HOWARD, F. E.
English Church Woodwork... London: 1900. V. 53
English Church Woodwork. London: 1933. V. 50

HOWARD, FRANK
The Art of Dress; or Guide to the Toilette... London: 1839. V. 50
Colour As a Means of Art... London: 1838. V. 47; 48; 50; 51; 53
Colour as a Means of Art. London: 1849. V. 47; 48; 49
The Spirit of the Plays of Shakespeare, Exhibited in A Series of Outline Plates... London: 1833. V. 53

HOWARD, GEORGE
Lady Jane Grey and her Times. London: 1822. V. 48; 51; 53

HOWARD, H. R.
The History of Virgil A. Stewart and His Adventures in Capturing and Exposing the Great Western Land Pirate. New York: 1836. V. 47; 49; 53
The History of Virgil A. Stewart and His Adventures....and the Execution of Five Professional Gamblers by the Citizens of Vicksburg, on the 6th of July 1835. New York: 1842. V. 52; 53
The Life and Adventures of Joseph T. Hare, the Bold Robber and Highwayman, with Sixteen Elegant Illustrative Engravings. New York: 1847. V. 50

HOWARD, HENRY
A Course of Lectures on Painting, Delivered at the Royal Academy of Fine Arts. 1848. V. 47
A Defensatiue Against the Poyson of Supposed Prophesies. London: 1583. V. 53
Memorials of the Howard Family. London: 1834. V. 48

HOWARD, HENRY ELIOT
The British Warblers: A History with Problems of Their Lives. London: 1907-14. V. 47; 48; 51
An Introduction to the Study of Bird Behaviour. London: 1929. V. 50; 52; 53

HOWARD, JAMES
Continental Farming and Peasantry. London: 1870. V. 50; 52

HOWARD, JAMES H. W.
Bond and Free; a True Tale of Slave Times. Harrisburg: 1886. V. 47; 52; 53

HOWARD, JOHN
An Account of the Principal Lazarettos in Europe. London: 1791. V. 48
An Account of the Principal Lazarettos in Europe. Warrington: 1879. V. 54
The Life of the Late John Howard, Esq. London: 1790. V. 53
The State of the Prisons in England and Wales... Warrington: 1777. V. 52; 53
The State of the Prisons in England and Wales... Warrington: 1777-80. V. 54
The State of the Prisons in England and Wales... Warrington: 1784. V. 50; 54
The State of the Prisons in England and Wales. London: 1792. V. 49; 50
The Works of John Howard, Esq. London: 1791-92. V. 48

HOWARD, JOHN E.
North American Big Game Hunting in the 1800s. 1982. V. 48

HOWARD, JOSEPH JACKSON
Vicitation of England and Wales. London: 1903-11. V. 52
The Wardour Press Series of Armorial bookplates. Baronets. From the Collections of Joseph Jackson Howard. London: 1895. V. 48

HOWARD, LELAND O.
The Insect Book. Toronto: 1901. V. 54

HOWARD, LUKE
Barometrographia: Twenty Years' Variation of the Barometer in the Climate of Great Britain... London: 1847. V. 53

HOWARD, MC HENRY
Recollections of a Maryland Confederate Soldier and Staff Officer. Baltimore: 1914. V. 49

HOWARD, MRS.
Reminiscences for My Children. London: 1836. V. 52

HOWARD, OLIVER OTIS
Autobiography of... New York: 1907. V. 54
Autobiography of... New York: 1908. V. 49
Famous Indian Chiefs I Have Known. New York: 1908. V. 50; 54
My Life and Experiences Among Our Hostile Indians. Hartford: 1907. V. 51; 54
Report of...Commanding Department of the Columbia, September 18, 1880. Vermont Barracks: 1880. V. 54
Views of Denver, Colorado, 1889. Denver. V. 54

HOWARD, ROBERT
The Great Favourite, or, the Duke of Lerma. London: 1668. V. 47
Historical Observations Upon the Reigns of Edward I. II. III. and Richrd II. With Remarks Upon Their Faithful Counsellors and False Favourites. London: 1689. V. 47
The Life and Reign of King Richard the Second. London: 1681. V. 49; 54
Poems. London: 1660. V. 47

HOWARD, ROBERT E.
Always Comes Evening. The Collected Poems. Sauk City: 1957. V. 50
The Coming of Conan. New York: 1953. V. 53
The Complete Conan Series. New York: 1950-57. V. 48
Conan the Barbarian. 1954. V. 49; 54
Conan the Barbarian. New York: 1954. V. 53
Conan the Conqueror. 1950. V. 54
Conan the Conqueror. New York: 1950. V. 51
Conan the Conqueror... 1950-55. V. 52
The Dark Man and Others. Sauk City: 1963. V. 52; 54
The Devil in Iron. West Kingston: 1976. V. 52; 53
The Garden of Fear and Other Stories of the Bizarre and Fantastic. Los Angeles: 1945. V. 52
A Gent From Bear Creek. West Kingston: 1965. V. 52
King Conan. New York: 1953. V. 52; 53
The People of the Black Circle. West Kingston: 1974. V. 53
Queen of the Black Coast. West Kingston: 1978. V. 52; 53
Red Nails. West Kingston: 1975. V. 52; 53
Red Shadows. 1968. V. 47
Rogues in the House. West Kingston: 1976. V. 52; 53
Singers in the Shadows. 1970. V. 47; 51
Singers in the Shadows. Kingston: 1970. V. 51
Skull Face and Others. Sauk City: 1946. V. 48; 51; 52
The Sword of Conan. 1952. V. 49
The Sword of Conan. New York: 1952. V. 51
The Sword of Conan. New York: 1962. V. 54
The Tower of the Elephant. West Kingston: 1975. V. 52; 53
A Witch Shall be Born. West Kingston: 1975. V. 52; 53

HOWARD, ROBERT MILTON
Reminiscences. Columbus: 1912. V. 49

HOWARD, SIDNEY
GWTH: The Screenplay. New York: 1980. V. 51
Half Gods. New York: 1930. V. 50

HOWARD, THOMAS
On the Loss of Teeth; and On the Best Means of Restoring Them. London: 1837. V. 49
On the Loss of Teeth: and on the Best Means of Restoring Them. London: 1857. V. 48; 51; 53

HOWARD, WILLIAM TRAVIS
Public Health Administration and the Natural History of Disease in Baltimore, Maryland 1797-1920. Washington: 1924. V. 49

HOWARD-BURY, C. K.
Mount Everest. The Reconnaissance, 1921. 1922. V. 53
Mount Everest, the Reconnaissance, 1921. New York: 1922. V. 48
Mount Everest. The Reconnaissance, 1922. London: 1921. V. 52
The Reconnaissance, 1921. London: 1922. V. 53

HOWARD-HILL, TREVOR HOWARD
British Literary Bibliography and Textual Criticism. Oxford: 1979-87. V. 47

HOWARD'S
Large and Small Round Text Copies with New Rules for Learners. Newburyport: 1805. V. 47

HOWARTH, E.
Catalogue of the Bateman Collection of Antiquites in the Sheffield Public Museum. London: 1899. V. 49

HOWARTH, EDWARD G.
West Ham. A Study in Social and Industrial Problems, Being the Report of the Outer London Inquiry Committee. London: 1907. V. 49

HOWARTH, THOMAS
Charles Rennie Mackintosh and the Modern Movement. London: 1925. V. 47
Charles Rennie Mackintosh and the Modern Movement. 1952. V. 48
Charles Rennie MacKintosh and the Modern Movement. London: 1952. V. 53
Charles Rennie MacKintosh and the Modern Movement. London: 1977. V. 48; 50; 51; 53; 54

HOWAY, FREDERIC W.
British Columbia From the Earliest Times to the Present. Vancouver: 1914. V. 49
The Early History of the Fraser River Mines. Victoria: 1926. V. 53
Voyages of the "Columbia" to the Northwest Coast 17a87-1790 and 1790-1793. Boston: 1941. V. 50; 54
The Work of the Royal Engineers in British Columbia, 1858 to 1863. Victoria: 1910. V. 48; 50; 53

HOWBERT, ABRAHAM R.
Reminiscences of the War. Springfield: 1884. V. 52; 54

HOWE, E. W.
The Mystery of the Locks. Boston: 1885. V. 51
The Story of a Country Town. Atchison: 1883. V. 51

HOWE, EDGAR F.
The Story of the First Decade in Imperial Valley California. Imperial: 1910. V. 50

HOWE, ELLIC
A List of London Bookbinders, 1648-1815. London: 1950. V. 52
The London Bookbinders - 1780-1806. London: 1950. V. 47; 50
The London Compositor. London: 1947. V. 48

HOWE, GEORGE
An Appeal to the Young Men of the Presbyterian Church in the Synod of South Carolina and Georgia. Columbia: 1836. V. 47

HOWE, HENRY
Historical Collections of Virginia... Charleston: 1845. V. 50
Historical Collections of Virginia. Charleston: 1856. V. 54
The Travels and Adventures of Celebrated Travelers in the Principal Countries of the Globe. Cincinnati: 1861. V. 48; 50; 52

HOWE, JAMES VIRGIL
The Modern Gunsmith... New York: 1934-41. V. 50
The Modern Gunsmith. London: 1944. V. 54

HOWE, JOHN
Address Occasioned by the Death of Aaron Bean, Esq...Delivered in the Presence and at the Request of St. Paul's Royal Arch Chapter, Boston. Boston: 1820. V. 54
The Christian's Pocket Companion. Enfield: 1826. V. 50
Some Consideration of a Preface to an Enquiry, Concerning the Occasional Conformity of Dissenters, &c. London: 1701. V. 53

HOWE, JULIA WARD
Is Polite Society Polite? And Other Essays. Boston/New York: 1900. V. 52
Passion Flowers. Boston: 1854. V. 47; 49

HOWE, OCTAVIUS THORNDIKE
American Clipper Ships 1833-1858. Salem: 1926-27. V. 54
Argonauts of '49; History and Adventures of the Emigrant Companies from Massachusetts 1849-50. Cambridge: 1923. V. 48

HOWE, PAUL STURTEVANT
Mayflower Pilgrim Descendants in Cape May County, New Jersey...1620-1920: a Record of the Pilgrim Descendants Who Early In its History Settled in Cape May County and some of Their Children Throughout the Several States of the Union at the Present Time. Cape May: 1921. V. 47; 49; 51

HOWE, SAMUEL GRIDLEY
An Historical Sketch of the Greek Revolution. New York: 1828. V. 47
The Journals and Letters of Samuel Gridley Howe. Boston: 1909. V. 50

HOWE, SUSAN
The Conformist's Memorial. New York: 1992. V. 53
Incloser. An Essay. Santa Fe: 1992. V. 53
The Nonconformist's Memorial. New York: 1992. V. 54

HOWE, W. E.
A History of the Metropolitan Museum of Art... New York: 1913. V. 47
A History of the Metropolitan Museum of Art. (with) Vol. 2: Problems and Principles in a Period of Expansion (1905-1941). New York: 1913/46. V. 50

HOWELL, FRANCIS
The Characters of Heophrastus. London: 1824. V. 47

HOWELL, FREDERICK W. W.
Icelandic Pictures Drawn with Pen and Pencil. London: 1893. V. 54

HOWELL, GEORGE
The Conflicts of Capital and Labour Historically and Economically Considered... London: 1878. V. 52

HOWELL, JAMES
Certain Letters, Selected from the Familiar Letters Published Between 1645 and 1655. New York: 1928. V. 48
Dendrologia (in Greek). Dodona's Grove. London: 1640. V. 47; 51
Dodona's Grove. London: 1640. V. 48; 49
Dodona's Grove... Cambridge: 1645. V. 49
Epistolae Ho-Elianae. Familiar Letters Domestic and Forren... London: 1645. V. 52; 53
Epistolae Ho-Elianae. Familiar Letters Domestic and Forren. London: 1655. V. 51
Florus Hungaricus: or the History of Hungaria and Transylvania Deduced from the Original of that Nation, and Their Settling in Europe in the Year of Our Lord 461... London: 1664. V. 49
(Greek, then) A Discourse Concerning the Precedency of Kings: Wherein the Reasons and Arguments of the Three Greatest Monarks of Christendom... London: 1668?. V. 54
Instructions for Forreine Travel. London: 1642. V. 54
Lexicon Teraglotton, an English-French-Italian-Spanish Dictionary... London: 1660/59/59. V. 54
Lexicon Tetraglotton, an English-French-Italian-Spanish Dictionary... London: 1660. V. 47; 50
Londinopolis: an Historical Discourse or Perlustration of the City of London. London: 1657. V. 50
Lustra Ludovici, or the Life of the Late Victorious King of France, Lewis the XIII. London: 1616. V. 51
Lustra Ludovici, or the Life of the Late Victorious King of France, Lewis the XIII. London: 1646. V. 47; 50
Proedria-Basiliki (Graece): A Discourse Concerning the Precedency of Kings... London: 1664. V. 53
S.P.Q.V. A Survay of the Signorie of Venice. London: 1651. V. 54
Therologia (Graece). The Parly of Beasts; or Morphandra Queen of the Inchanted Land: Wherein Men Were Found, Who Being Transmuted to Beasts... London: 1660. V. 53

HOWELL, JOHN M.
John Gardner: a Bibliographical Profile. Carbondale: 1980. V. 54

HOWELL, LAURENCE
The Orthodox Communicant, by Way of Meditation of the Order for the Administration of the Lord's Supper, or Holy Communion... London: 1721. V. 47

HOWELL, ROBERT
The Early Baptists of Virginia. Philadelphia: 1857. V. 54

HOWELL, SAMUEL
Fourteen Lithographic Views of Knaresborough, in Yorkshire, Sketched From Nature and Drawn on Stone by Samuel Howell... London: 1838. V. 48

HOWELL, WILLIAM
Medulla Historiae Anglicanae. London: 1719. V. 52

HOWELLS, JOHN MEAD
The Architectural Heritage of the Piscataqua. New York: 1937. V. 51
The Architectural Heritage of the Piscataqua. London: 1965. V. 48
Lost Examples of Colonial Architecture. New York: 1931. V. 47; 51

HOWELLS, MILDRED
A Little Girl Among the Old Masters. Boston: 1884. V. 54

HOWELLS, WILLIAM DEAN
Annie Kilburn. New York: 1889. V. 53
Between the Dark and the Daylight. New York and London: 1907. V. 52; 53
A Boy's Town. New York: 1890. V. 47; 48; 52; 53; 54
Buying a Horse. Boston & New York: 1916. V. 51
A Counterfeit Presentment. Boston: 1877. V. 47
Fennel and Rue. New York: 1908. V. 53
The Flight of Pony Baker. New York: 1902. V. 51
A Hazard of New Fortunes. New York: 1890. V. 53; 54
Imaginary Interviews. New York: 1910. V. 47; 48
Indian Summer. Boston: 1886. V. 52
The Lady of the Aroostook. Boston: 1879. V. 52
Letters Home. New York: 1903. V. 52; 54
Literary Acquaintances: Personal Retrospect of American Authorship. New York: 1900. V. 51
A Little Girl Among the Old Masters. Boston: 1884. V. 52
Mrs. Farrell. New York: 1921. V. 53
The Mouse-Trap. New York: 1889. V. 52
No Love Lost, A Romance of Travel. New York: 1869. V. 50
Poems. Boston: 1873. V. 48; 52
The Rise of Silas Lapham. Boston: 1885. V. 47; 48; 52; 53; 54
Seven English Cities. New York: 1909. V. 47
The Shadow of a Dream. New York: 1890. V. 54
Stops of Various Quills. New York: 1895. V. 54
Suburban Sketches. New York: 1871. V. 54
Suburban Sketches. Boston: 1875. V. 52
Their Silver Wedding Journey. New York: 1899. V. 53
Their Wedding Journey. Boston: 1872. V. 52; 53
Their Wedding Journey. Cambridge: 1895. V. 52
The Undiscovered Country. Boston: 1880. V. 51; 52
Venetian Life. New York: 1866. V. 51; 52
Venetian Life. Boston and New York: 1892. V. 48; 50; 54
Venetian Life. Cambridge: 1892. V. 52
Venetian Life. 1907. V. 52
Venetian Life. Boston: 1907. V. 51
Venetian Life. Cambridge: 1907. V. 47; 53; 54
Years of My Youth. New York: 1916. V. 53

HOWES, BARBARA
The Undersea Farmer. Pawlet: 1948. V. 54

HOWES, WRIGHT
U.S. Howes Iana 1700-1950. New York: 1954. V. 52

HOWGILL, FRANCIS
The Fiery Darts of the Divel Quenched; or, Something in Answer to a Book Called, A Second Beacon Fired... London: 1654. V. 53

HOWISON, JOHN
Foreign Scenes and Travelling Recreations. Edinburgh: 1825. V. 47; 51
Foreign Scenes and Travelling Recreations. Edinburgh: 1834. V. 47
Foreign Scenes and Travelling Recreations. London: 1834. V. 47
Sketches of Upper Canada, Domestic, Local and Characteristic... Edinburgh: 1821. V. 51; 52; 53

HOWISON, NEIL M.
Oregon. Report of Lieut. Neil M. Howison, United States navy, to the Commander of the Pacific Squadron... Washington: 1848. V. 47; 48; 50

HOWISON, ROBERT R.
A History of Virginia... Philadelphia/Richmond: 1846/48. V. 50; 54

HOWITH, HARRY
Total War. Toronto: 1966. V. 47

HOWITT, A. W.
Native Tribes of South East Australia. London: 1904. V. 50

HOWITT, ANNA MARY
An Art-Student in Munich. London: 1853. V. 48

HOWITT, EMANUEL
Selections from Letters Written During a Tour through the United States, in the Summer and Autumn of 1819. Nottingham: 1820. V. 47

HOWITT, MARY
An Autobiography. London: 1889. V. 50; 51; 52; 54
Biographical Sketches of the Queens of England from the Norman Conquest to the Reign of Victoria...etc. London: 1865. V. 50
Birds and Flowers and Other Country Things. Boston: 1839. V. 51
The Children's Year. London: 1847. V. 48; 52
Illustrated Library for the Young. London: 1856. V. 52
Pictures from Nature. London: 1870. V. 47
The Seven Temptations. London: 1834. V. 51
Tales in Verse for the Young. London: 1836. V. 52
Twelve Months with Fredrika Bremer in Sweden. London: 1866. V. 50
Wood Leighton; or, a year in the Country. London: 1836. V. 47; 49

HOWITT, S.
The Angler's manual; or Concise Lessons of Experience. Liverpool: 1808. V. 49
British Preserve, with Etchings from Drawings by... London: 1824. V. 48

HOWITT, WILLIAM
A Boy's Adventures in the Wilds of Australia; or, Herbert's Notebook. London: 1855. V. 49
Colonization and Christianity; a Popular History of the Treatment of the Natives by the Europeans in All Their Colonies. London: 1838. V. 47
The History of the Supernatural in All Ages and Nations and In All Churches, Christian and Pagan. London: 1863. V. 49; 51
Homes and Haunts of the Most Eminent British Poets. London: 1847. V. 47; 50; 54
Homes and Haunts of the Most Eminent British Poets. London: 1849. V. 51
Land, Labor & Gold, or, Two Years in Victoria: with Visits to Sydney & Van Diemen's Land. Boston: 1855. V. 48
Land, Labour and Gold; or, Two Years in Victoria; with Visits to Sydney and Van Diemen's Land. London: 1855. V. 48
The Northern Heights of London of Historical Associations of Hampstead, Highgate, Muswell Hill, Hornsey and Islington. London: 1869. V. 49
Ruined Abbeys and Castles of Great Britain. London: 1862. V. 48; 51
Ruined Abbeys and Castles of Great Britain... London: 1862/64. V. 53
Ruined Abbeys and Castles of Great Britian... 1864. V. 54
Ruined Abbeys and Castles of Great Britian... London: 1864. V. 53; 54
The Rural Life of England. London: 1838. V. 51
The Rural Life of England. (with) Homes and Haunts of the Most Eminent British Poets. London: 1840/47. V. 50; 51
The Student Life of Germany. London: 1841. V. 52
Visits to Remarkable Places... London: 1840. V. 54
Visits to Remarkable Places... London: 1840-42. V. 51; 53
Visits to Remarkable Places... London: 1856. V. 50; 51
Visits to Remarkable Places. London: 1900. V. 51

HOWLAND, ARTHUR
Materials Toward a History of Witchcraft Collected by Henry Charles Lea. Philadelphia: 1939. V. 47; 50

HOWLAND, RICHARD HUBBARD
The Architecture of Baltimore. Baltimore: 1953. V. 48; 52
Greek Lamps and their Survivals. Princeton: 1958. V. 50; 52

HOWLETT, BARTHOLOMEW
A Selection of Views in the County of Lincoln... London: 1805. V. 47; 50; 52

HOWLETT, RICHARD
Chronicles of the Reigns of Stephen, Henry II and Richard I. London: 1884-89. V. 49

HOWLETT, ROBERT
The Anglers Sure Guide: or, Angling Improved and Methodically Digested. London: 1706. V. 47; 51
The Royal Pastime of Cock-Fighting. London: 1899. V. 49
The School of Recreation; or, a Guide to the Most Ingenious Exercises of Hunting, Riding, Racing. London: 1732. V. 48

HOWLETT, W. J.
Life of the Right Reverend Joseph P. Machebeuf... Pueblo: 1908. V. 51

HOWMAN, K.
Pheasants of the World, Their Breeding and Management. Washington: 1903. V. 51
Pheasants of the World, Their Breeding and Management. Blaine: 1993. V. 50

HOWSHIP, JOHN
Practical Observations on the Symptoms, Discrimination, and Treatment, Of some of the Most Important Diseases of the Lower Intestines and Anus. Philadelphia: 1821. V. 53

HOWTITT, WILLIAM
The Year-Book of the Country; or, the Field, the Forest and the Fireside. London: 1850. V. 54

HOY, PATRICK C.
A Brief History of Bradford's Battery, Confederate Guards Artillery. Pontotoc: 1932. V. 49

HOYEM, ANDREW
Picture/Poems. San Francisco: 1975. V. 48; 51; 54

HOYER, M. A.
The Tale of a Dog. London: 1890. V. 52

HOYLAND, FRANCIS
Poems and Translations. London: 1763. V. 52; 54

HOYLAND, JOHN
A Historical Survey of the Customs, Habits & Present State of the Gypsies. York: 1816. V. 47; 53; 54

HOYLAND, ROSEMARY
Ethelbert Under the Sea. London: 1956. V. 52

HOYLE, EDMOND
Hoyle's Games Improved. London: 1778. V. 49
HOYLE'S Games Improved... London: 1788. V. 50
Hoyle's Games Improved. London: 1790. V. 49; 52
Hoyle's Games Improved... London: 1826. V. 51
HOYLE'S Games Improved... London: 1835. V. 54
Mr. Hoyle's Games of Whist, Quadrille, Piquet, Chess and Back-Gammon Complete. London: 1750. V. 51
A Short Treatise on the Game of Whist. (with) A Short Treatise on the Game of Quadrille. London: 1750/46. V. 54

HOYLE, JOHN
A Complete Dictionary of Music. London: 1791. V. 48; 52
Dictionarium Musica, Being a Complete Dictionary; or, Treasury of Music. London: 1770. V. 47

HOYLE, RAFAEL LARCO
Checan: Essay on Erotic Elements in Peruvian Art. Geneva: 1965. V. 53

HOYLE, WILLIAM
Crime in England and Wales in the Nineteenth Century. London: 1876. V. 52

HOYME, CHARLES, COMTE DE
Catalogus Librorum Bibliothecae Illustrissimi Viri Caroli Henrici Comitis de Hoym. Paris: 1738. V. 48

HOYNINGEN-HUENE, GEORGE
African Mirage: the Record of a Journey. New York: 1938. V. 50
Baalbek Palmyra. New York: 1946. V. 50; 51; 52
Egypt. New York: 1943. V. 50
Mexican Heritage. Mexico City: 1946. V. 53

HOYOS-SPRINZENSTEIN, E.
With a Rifle in Mongolia. Long Beach: 1986. V. 48

HOYT, HENRY FRANKLIN
A Frontier Doctor. Boston: 1929. V. 48; 53

HOYT, WILLIAM HENRY
The Mecklenburg Declaration of Independence: a Study of Evidence Showing That the Alleged Early Declaration of Independence by Mencklenburg County, North Carolina, on May 20th 1775 is Spurious. New York: 1907. V. 47

HOZIER, H. M.
The Franco-Prussian War: Its Causes, Incidents and Consequences. London: 1872. V. 49
The Franco-Prussian War: its Causes, Incidents and Consequences, with the Topography and History of the Rhine Valley.... London: 1880. V. 51
The Russo-Turkish War... London. V. 48
The Russo-Turkish War... London: 1877. V. 52

HRDLICKA, ALES
Children Who Run On All Fours and Other Animal-Like Behaviours in the Human Child. New York: 1913. V. 54
Early Man in South America. Washington: 1912. V. 50; 53; 54
Physiological and Medical Observations: Among the Indians of... Washington: 1908. V. 48; 50; 51; 53

HRISTOV, HRISTO
The Rila Monastery; History, Architecture, Frescoes, Wood Carvings. Sofia: 1959. V. 51

HRUBIN, F.
The Enchanted Forest. Prague: 1954. V. 50

HUARTE DE SAN JUAN, JUAN
Essame de gli Ingegni de gl'Huomini, per Apprendrer le Scienze... Venetia: 1586. V. 54
Examen de Ingenios... London: 1594. V. 52
Examen de Ingenios... London: 1596. V. 52
Examen de Ingenios. London: 1616. V. 49; 52
Examen de Ingenios... London: 1698. V. 49; 53

HUBBACK, J. H.
Jane Austen's Sailor Brothers. London: 1906. V. 52; 54

HUBBACK, T.
Ten Thousand Miles to Alaska for Moose and Sheep... Denver: 1921. V. 48
To Far Western Alaska for Big Game. London: 1929. V. 48

HUBBARD, ALICE
An American Bible. East Aurora: 1912. V. 49
Life Lessons. East Aurora: 1909. V. 53
Woman's Work: Being an Inquiry and an Assumption. East Aurora: 1908. V. 48; 50

HUBBARD, CHARLES EUSTIS
The Campaign of the Forty Fifth Regiment Massachussetts Volunteer Militia. Boston: 1882. V. 49

HUBBARD, ELBERT
An American Bible. Aurora: 1912. V. 53
The Complete Writings of Elbert Hubbard. East Aurora: 1908-15. V. 50
Contemplations. 1902. V. 47; 49
The Doctors. A Satire in Four Seizures. 1909. V. 49
Little Journeys to the Homes of English Authors, Robert Southey. East Aurora: 1900. V. 49; 53
Little Journeys to the Homes of Great Lovers. East Aurora: 1906. V. 54
A Message to Garcia. East Aurora: 1899. V. 53
A Message to Garcia and Thirteen Other Things. East Aurora: 1901. V. 48; 51; 53
The Olympians: a Tribute to "Tall Sun-Crowned Men". East Aurora: 1921. V. 50
Respectability Its Rise and Remedy. East Aurora: 1905. V. 48
Selected Writings of Elbert Hubbard. East Aurora: 1928. V. 47; 48; 50
This Then is a William Morris Book Being a Little Journey by Elbert Hubbard... New York: 1907. V. 50; 54
Thomas Jefferson: a Little Journey...and an Address. East Aurora: 1906. V. 51

HUBBARD, GARDINER GREENE
Catalog of the Gardiner Greene Hubbard Collection of Engravings. Washington: 1905. V. 47

HUBBARD, GURDON SALTONSTALL
Autobiography of ...Pa-Pa-Ma-Ta-Be, "The Swift Walker.". Chicago: 1911. V. 48; 53
Incidents and Events....Collected From Personal Narrations and Other Sources... Chicago: 1888. V. 48

HUBBARD, JEREMIAH
Forty Years Among the Indians. Miami: 1913. V. 48

HUBBARD, JOHN C.
A Brief Political History of the Rise an Fall of the Free Institutions of the United States of America. Hudson: 1873. V. 53

HUBBARD, JOHN N.
Sketches of Border Adventures, in the Life and Times of Major Moses Van Campen, a Surviving Soldier of the Revolution. Bath: 1842. V. 50

HUBBARD, L. RON
Battlefield Earth. A Saga of the Year 3000. New York: 1982. V. 47
Buckskin Brigades. 1937. V. 49; 54
The Creation of Human Ability. Phoenix: 1955. V. 50
Death Quest. 1985. V. 51
Death's Deputy. 1948. V. 47; 51
Dianetics. 1950. V. 49; 52; 53; 54
Dianetics. New York: 1950. V. 48; 49; 50; 54
Final Blackout. 1948. V. 48; 52
Final Blackout. Providence: 1948. V. 52
Fortune of Fear. 1986. V. 49; 53; 54
The Invaders Plan. 1985. V. 49; 54
The Kingslayer. 1949. V. 49; 54
Lives You Wished to Lead but Never Dared. 1978. V. 47; 51
Slaves of Sleep. 1948. V. 48; 52
Slaves of Sleep. Chicago: 1948. V. 48; 49; 51; 53
Triton. 1949. V. 48; 52
Typewriter in the Sky & Fear. 1951. V. 47; 49; 54
Typewriter in the Sky & Fear. New York: 1951. V. 47; 51; 54
Voyage Vengenance. 1985. V. 51

HUBBARD, LEONIDAS, MRS.
A Woman's Way through Unknown Labrador an Account of the Exploration of the Nascaupee and George Rivers. London: 1908. V. 54

HUBBARD, LUCIUS L.
Contributions Towards a Bibliography of Gulliver's Travels... Chicago: 1922. V. 48

HUBBARD, R. B.
Oration of Gov. R. B. Hubbard of Texas, Delivered at Philadelphia at the United States Centennial Exposition. St. Louis: 1876. V. 49

HUBBARD, T. O'B.
Tomorrow is a New Day. London: 1934. V. 47

HUBBARD, WILLIAM
The History of the Indian Wars in New England From the First Settlement to the Termination of the War with King Philip, in 1677. Roxbury: 1865. V. 47
A Narrative of the Indian Wars in New England... Danburgy: 1803. V. 47
A Narrative of the Indian Wars in New England... Brattleborough: 1814. V. 53

HUBBELL, ALVIN
The Development of Ophthalmology in America 1800-1870. Chicago: 1908. V. 50; 52

HUBBLE, EDWIN POWELL
The Observational Approach to Cosmology. Oxford: 1937. V. 53; 54

HUBER, JEAN PIERRE
The Natural History of Ants. London: 1820. V. 48; 49; 52

HUBER, VICTOR AIME
The English Universities. London: 1843. V. 50; 54

HUBERT, HENRI
The Rise of the Celts and The Greatness and Decline of the Celts. London: 1934. V. 48

HUBIN, ALLEN J.
Crime Fiction, 1749-1980: a Comprehensive Bibliography. New York: 1984. V. 48

HUBLEY, BERNARD
The History of the American Revolution, Including the Most Important Events and Resolutions of the Honourable Continental Congress During that Period... Northumberland: 1805. V. 50

THE HUBS *Vocabulary of Vehicles.* New York: 1892. V. 50

HUC, EVARISTE REGIS
The Chinese Empire: Forming a Sequel to the Work Entitled "Recollections of a Journey through Tartary and Thibet". London: 1855. V. 54
Christianity in China, Tartary, and Thibet. London: 1857-58. V. 52
A Journey through the Chinese Empire. New York: 1855. V. 51
A Journey through the Chinese Empire. New York: 1878. V. 52
Travels in Tartary, Thibet and China, During the Years 1844-5-6. London. V. 50
Travels in Tartary, Thibet and China, During the Years 1844-5-6. London: 1852. V. 51; 53

HUCKELL, JOHN
Avon. A Poem. Birmingham: 1758. V. 47; 52

HUDDART, JOSEPH
The Oriental Navigataor; or, New Directions for Sailing to and from the East Indies... Philadelphia: 1801. V. 50

HUDDESFORD, GEORGE
The Poems. London: 1801. V. 48; 50; 52
A Proper Reply to a Pamphlet, Entitled, A Defence of the Rector and Fellows of Exeter College &c. Oxford: 1755. V. 53
Salmagundi: a Miscellaneous Combination of Original Poetry...(with) Topsy Turvy; With Anecdotes and Observations Illustrataive of the Leading Characters in the Present Government of France. London: 1793/93. V. 52
The Wiccamical Chaplet, A Selection of Original Poetry. London: 1804. V. 51; 52; 54

HUDDLES, JOHN
Tales for Youth; in Thirty Poems: to Which are Annexed, Historical Remarks and Moral Applications in Prose. London: 1794. V. 50

HUDDLESTON, G. C., MRS.
Bluebell. London: 1875. V. 54

THE HUDDY *and Duval Prints, Being Hand-Coloured Facsimiles of the Uniform Plates Representing the Volunteers of the U.S.A...* New York: 1955. V. 50

HUDLESTON, C. ROY
Cumberland Familes and Heraldry With a Supplement to an Armorial for Westmorland and Lonsdale. Kendal: 1978. V. 53
The Registers of Morland. Part I: 1538-1742. London: 1957. V. 52

HUDSON, C. T.
The Rotifera; or Wheel-Animalcules. London: 1886. V. 47
The Rotifera; or Wheel-Animalcules. London: 1886-89. V. 50; 51; 52

HUDSON, CHARLES
History of the Town of Lexington, Middlesex County...from Its First Settlement to 1868. Boston: 1913. V. 54
Where There's a Will There's a Way: an Ascent of Mont Blanc. London: 1856. V. 51; 52

HUDSON, DAVID
History of Jemima Wilkinson, a Preacheress of the Eighteenth Century. Geneva: 1821. V. 51

HUDSON, DEREK
Arthur Rackham: His Life and Work. London: 1960. V. 50; 52

HUDSON, ELIZABETH
A Bibliography of the First Editions of the Works of E. Oe. Soemrville and Martin Ross. New York: 1942. V. 52

HUDSON, JOHN
A Complete Guide to the Lakes... Kendal: 1843. V. 50
Photographs of Killarney with Descriptive Letterpress. Glasgow London & Dublin: 1867. V. 52

HUDSON, JOSEPH
Remarks Upon the History of the Landed and Commercial Policy of England, from the Invasion of the Romans to the Accession of James the First. London: 1785. V. 48

HUDSON, JOSHUA HILARY
Sketches and Reminiscences. Columbia: 1903. V. 50

HUDSON, MARIANNE SPENCER STANHOPE
Almack's. London: 1026. V. 47; 51
Almack's... London: 1826/27. V. 51
Almack's... London: 1887. V. 51

HUDSON, MARY W.
Esther the Gentile. Topeka: 1888. V. 47; 50

HUDSON, MIKE
As Dead as the Proverbial... Katoomba: 1989. V. 54

HUDSON, PETER
The French Scholar's Guide; or, an Easy Help for Translating French into English. London: 1780. V. 54

HUDSON RIVER ICE YACHT CLUB
Constitution By-Laws Sailing Regulations, &c. of the... Poughkeepsie: 1908. V. 47

HUDSON, STEPHEN
Tony. London: 1924. V. 48

HUDSON, WILLIAM
Flora Anglica; Exhibens Plantas per Regnum Britanniae Sponte Crescentes, Distributas Secundum Systema Sexuale... London: 1778. V. 49

HUDSON, WILLIAM HENRY
153 Letters from W. H. Hudson. London: 1923. V. 51
Birds and Man. London: 1901. V. 47; 49
Birds and Man. London: 1915. V. 47; 53
Birds in a Village. London: 1893. V. 47; 54
Birds in London. London: 1898. V. 51; 52; 53
Birds of La Plata. London & Toronto: 1920. V. 48; 49; 50; 52; 53; 54
British Birds. London: 1895. V. 47; 53
The Collected Works. London: 1922-23. V. 49; 50; 51
A Crystal Age. London: 1887. V. 48
A Crystal Age. London: 1906. V. 53
Dead Man's Plack and Old Thorn. London: 1920. V. 49; 50; 54
Far Away and Long Ago. London & Toronto: 1918. V. 49; 52
Far Away and Long Ago. New York: 1918. V. 48
Far Away and Long Ago. London: 1931. V. 50
Far Away and Long Ago... Buenos Aires: 1943. V. 51; 52; 53
Green Mansions. London: 1904. V. 47; 50; 51; 52; 53; 54
Green Mansions. London: 1911. V. 47
Green Mansions... London: 1926. V. 48; 51
Green Mansions. Philadelphia: 1935. V. 49; 53; 54
Green Mansions. New York: 1943. V. 52
Idle Days in Patagonia. London: 1893. V. 47; 49; 51
Letters from William Henry Hudson. London: 1923. V. 52
The Man Napoleon. New York: 1914. V. 50
Nature in Downland. London: 1900. V. 53
Nature in Downland. London: 1906. V. 48
El Ombu. London: 1902. V. 49
The Purple Land: Being the Narrative of One Richard Lamb's Adventures in the Banda Oriental, in South America, as Told by Himself. London: 1904. V. 54
The Purple Land: Being the Narrative of One Richard Lamb's Adventures in the Banda Oriental, in South America, as Told by Himself. London: 1911. V. 47
A Shepherd's Life. 1977. V. 49
A Shepherd's Life. Tisbury, Wiltshire: 1977. V. 53
W. H. Hudson's Letters to R. B. Cunninghame-Graham. Waltham St. Lawrence: 1941. V. 47; 52
Works. London: 1923. V. 48

HUDSON'S BAY CO.
Confidential. Correspondence Relating to Disturbances at Red River, 1869-70. London: 1875. V. 50
Copy-Book Letters Outward &c Begins 29th May, 1680 Ends 5 July 1687.. London: 1948. V. 52
Copy-Book of Letters Outward &c. Begins 29th May, 1608; Ends 5 July 1687. Toronto: 1948. V. 51
Correspodence Between Her Majesty's Government and the Hudson's Bay Company. London: 1869. V. 50
Correspondence with the Colonial Office. London: 1868. V. 50
Cumberland and Hudson House Journals: 1775-82. London: 1951/52. V. 54
Cumberland House Journals and Inland Journal 1775-82. London: 1951-52. V. 51; 54
Cumberland House Journals and Inland Journal 1775-82: First Series, 1775-79. London: 1951. V. 51
Cumberland House Journals and Inland Journals 1775-82: Second Series 1779-82. London: 1952. V. 51
The History of the Hudson's Bay Company, 1670-1870. London: 1958-59. V. 51
The History of the Hudson's Bay Company: 1670-1870. London: 1958/59. V. 47; 51
Hudson's Bay Company, 1670-1870. Toronto: 1960. V. 54
Hudson's Bay Company. 1670-1870. New York: 1961. V. 54
Hudson's Bay Copy Booke of Letters. Commissions, Instructions Outward 1688-1696. London: 1957. V. 50; 51
John Rae's Correspondence with the Hudson's Bay Company on Arct Exploration 1844-1855. London: 1953. V. 51
Letter from the Colonial Office to the Governor of the Hudson's Bay Co., dated March 9th, 1869. London: 1869. V. 50
The Letters of Charles John Brydges, Hudson's Bay Company Land Commissioner, 1879-89. Winnipeg: 1977-81. V. 51
London Correspondence Inward from Eden Colville 1849-1852. London: 1956. V. 51
Minutes of the Hudson's Bay Company 1671-1674. London: 1942. V. 52
Minutes of the Hudson's Bay Company, 1671-1674. Toronto: 1942. V. 51
Minutes of the Hudson's Bay Company, 1679-1684. First Part. 1945. V. 49
Minutes of the Hudson's Bay Company, 1679-1684. First Part 1679-1682. London: 1945. V. 52
Minutes of the Hudson's Bay Company, 1679-1684. First Part 1679-82. Toronto: 1945. V. 51
Minutes of the Hudson's Bay Company, 1679-1684. Second Part, 1682-84. Toronto: 1946. V. 51
Moose Fort Journals 1783-1785. London: 1954. V. 47; 48; 51; 52
Northern Quebec and Labrador Journals and Correspondence, 1819-35. London: 1963. V. 51
Report by the Secretary on Matters Relating to the Company's Landed Property. Confidential. London: 1882. V. 49
Saskatchewan Journals and Correspondence: Edmonton House, 1795-1800: Chesterfield House, 1800-1802. London: 1967. V. 47; 49

HUEFFER, FORD M.
Ford Madox Brown. A Record of His Life and Work. London: 1896. V. 51

HUEFFER, FRANZ
Richard Wagner and the Music of the Future. London: 1874. V. 49

HUELSENBECK, RICHARD
Schalaben, Schalabai, Schalamegomai. Zurich: 1916. V. 53

HUEPPE, FERDINAND
The Methods of Bacteriological Investigation. New York: 1886. V. 51; 53

HUES, ROBERT
A Learned Treatise of Globes Both Celestial and Terrestriall... London: 1639. V. 54
Traicte des Globes, et de levr vsage. Paris: 1618. V. 49

HUET, PIERRE DANIEL
Catalogue des Livres de la Bibliotheque de la Maison Professe des ci-devant soi-disans Jesuites. Paris: 1763. V. 52
Diana de Castro; a Novel. London: 1730. V. 47
A Treatise of the Situation of Paradise... London: 1694. V. 52

HUFELAND, OTTO
Westchester County During the American Revolution 1775-1783. 1926. V. 50

HUFFMAN, EUGENE HENRY
Now I Am Civilized. Los Angeles: 1930. V. 52

HUFHAM, JAMES D.
Memoir of Rev. John L. Prichard. Raleigh: 1867. V. 50

HUGGINS, JOHN RICHARD DESBOROUS
Hugginiana; or, Huggins' Fantasy. New York: 1808. V. 51

HUGGINS, M. L.
Gio. Paolo Maggini, His Life and Work. London: 1892. V. 49

HUGGINS, NATHAN IRVIN
Harlem Reinaissance. New York: 1971. V. 47; 50

HUG-HELLMUTH, HERMINE VON
A Study of the Mental Life of the Child. Washington: 1919. V. 51

HUGHES, A. D.
A History of Durham Cathedral Library. Durham: 1925. V. 49

HUGHES, DANIEL LAWRENCE
The Divine Covenant Fulfilled in the Ancestral Family History of the Lawrence-Hughes and Eldredge Generations of Cape May County, New Jersey. Cape May City: 1891. V. 49

HUGHES, GEORGE B.
English, Scottish and Irish Table Glass, from the Sixteenth Century to 1820. London: 1956. V. 50

HUGHES, GRAHAM
Modern Jewelry. An International Survey, 1890-1963. New York: 1963. V. 49

HUGHES, GRIFFITHS
The Natural History of Barbados. London: 1750. V. 49

HUGHES, H. D.
A History of Durham Cathedral Library. Durham: 1925. V. 50; 53

HUGHES, HENRY MARSHALL
A Clinical Introduction to the Practice of Auscultation and Other Modes of Physical Diagnosis... Philadelphia: 1846. V. 52

HUGHES, HUBERT
The Joyce Book. 1933. V. 52

HUGHES, J. E.
Eighteen Years On Lake Bangweulu. London: 1932. V. 53

HUGHES, JOHN
The Ectasy. An Ode. London: 1720. V. 54
An Essay, on the Ancient and Present State of the Welsh Language... London: 1822. V. 51
An Itinerary of Provence and the Rhone, Made During the Year 1819.... London: 1822. V. 52
A Lecture on the Antecedent Causes of the Irish Famine in 1847, Delivered Under the Auspices of the General Committee for the Relief of the Sufferings... New York: 1847. V. 53
An Ode to the Creator of the World. London: 1713. V. 54
Poems on Several Occasions. London: 1735. V. 47; 49; 54

HUGHES, JOHN CEIRIOG
Caneuon Ceiriog: Detholiad. Newtown: 1925. V. 47

HUGHES, JOHN T.
Doniphan's Expedition... Cincinnati: 1847. V. 52
Doniphan's Expedition... Cincinnati: 1848. V. 47; 49; 51; 53; 54
Doniphan's Expedition... Cincinnati: 1854. V. 51

HUGHES, JOSEPH
The History of the Townships of Meltham, Near Huddersfield in the West Riding of the County of York. Huddersfield: 1866. V. 51

HUGHES, JOSIAH
Australia Revisited in 1890, and Excursions in Egypt, Tasmania and New Zealand, Being Extracts from the Diary of a Trip Round the World. London & Bangor: 1891. V. 48; 52

HUGHES, LANGSTON
Ask Your Mama. New York: 1961. V. 49; 50; 53; 54
The Big Sea. New York: 1940. V. 49; 53
The Big Sea. New York: 1945. V. 49
Black Magic... Englewood Cliffs: 1967. V. 48; 54
Black Magic. New York: 1967. V. 51
The Book of Negro Humor. New York: 1966. V. 52
Famous American Negro Music Makers. New York: 1955. V. 52; 54
Fields of Wonder. New York: 1947. V. 48; 49; 51; 54
Fight for Freedom: The Story of the NAACP. New York: 1962. V. 53
Fine Clothes to the Jew. New York: 1927. V. 48; 49; 54
The First Book of Rhythms. New York: 1954. V. 51
Five Plays. 1963. V. 50
Freedom's Plow. New York: 1943. V. 48
Jim Crow's Last Stand. New York: 1943. V. 53
Laughing to Keep from Crying. New York: 1952. V. 53
Montage of a Dream Deferred. New York: 1951. V. 54
Moon-Faced, Starry-Eyed. New York: 1947. V. 47
The Negro Mother and Other Dramatic Recitations. New York: 1931. V. 48; 51
The Negro Speaks of Rivers. New York: 1942. V. 53
New Negro Poets U.S.A. Bloomington: 1964. V. 48
Not Without Laughter. New York: 1930. V. 49; 51
One Way Ticket. New York: 1949. V. 47; 49
A Pictorial History of the Negro in America. New York: 1956. V. 51; 53
Shakespeare in Harlem. New York: 1942. V. 47; 48; 49; 50
Simple Speaks His Mind. New York: 1950. V. 54
Simple Stakes a Claim. New York: 1957. V. 49; 50; 51
Simple Takes a Wife. New York: 1953. V. 50; 52
Simple's Uncle Sam. New York: 1965. V. 52
Songs to the Dark Virgin. New York: 1941. V. 53
The Sweet Flypaper of Life. New York: 1955. V. 50; 53
Tambourines to Glory. London: 1958. V. 52
Tambourines to Glory. New York: 1958. V. 47; 50; 53; 54
The Ways of White Folks. New York: 1944. V. 54
The Weary Blues. New York: 1926. V. 51

HUGHES, MARION
Oklahoma Charlie, Miner, Cowboy, Corn Doctor, Indian Scout... St. Louis: 1910. V. 47

HUGHES, MARY
Pleasing and Instructive Stories: for Young Children. London: 1821. V. 48; 52

HUGHES, RICHARD
Burial and the Dark Child. London: 1930. V. 53
Confessio Juvenis: Collected Poems. London: 1926. V. 48
Gipsy-Night and Other Poems. Waltham St. Lawrence: 1922. V. 50; 54
A High Wind in Jamaica. 1929. V. 54
A High Wind in Jamaica. London: 1929. V. 48; 49; 51; 53
In Hazard. London: 1938. V. 50
The Innocent Voyage. Brattleboro: 1944. V. 53; 54
The Innocent Voyage. New York: 1944. V. 48; 52; 53; 54
The Spider's Palace and Other Stories. London: 1931. V. 47; 51; 52

HUGHES, RICHARD B.
Pioneer Years in the Black Hills. Glendale: 1957. V. 50; 52; 54

HUGHES, ROBERT
The Shock of the New. New York: 1981. V. 50

HUGHES, SUKEY
Washi, the World of Japanese Paper. Tokyo, San Francisco: 1978. V. 47; 51
Washi: The World of Japanese Paper. Tokyo: 1982. V. 49

HUGHES, T. HAROLD
Towns and Town Planning, Ancient and Modern. Oxford: 1923. V. 52

HUGHES, T. S.
The History of England, from the Accession of George III, 1760 to the Accession of Queen Victoria, 1837. London: 1846. V. 50

HUGHES, TED
Adam and the Sacred Nine. London: 1978. V. 54
Animal Poems. 1967. V. 48
The Burning of the Brothel. London: 1966. V. 52
Capriccio. Northampton: 1990. V. 47; 50; 53
The Cat and the Cuckoo. V. 49; 54
The Cat and the Cukoo. Winchester: 1987. V. 48
Cave Birds. London: 1975. V. 51
Cave Birds... London: 1978. V. 47; 49; 53
Chiasmadon. Baltimore: 1977. V. 52; 53
The Coming of the Kings and Other Plays. London: 1970. V. 52
Cows. London: 1981. V. 47
Crow. 1970. V. 49
Crow. London: 1970. V. 47; 50; 51; 52
Crow... New York: 1971. V. 52
Crow... London: 1973. V. 47; 49
Crow Wakes. Essex: 1971. V. 52
Crow Wakes... Woodford Green: 1971. V. 53
Earth Moon. 1976. V. 54
Earth Moon. London: 1976. V. 49; 54
The Earth-Owl and other Moon People: Poems. London: 1963. V. 47; 49; 52
Earthmoon. London: 1976. V. 54
Eat Crow. London: 1971. V. 48; 49
Eat Crow. London: 1978. V. 54
A Few Crows. 1970. V. 54
A Few Crows. Exeter: 1970. V. 52; 53
Five Autumn Songs for Children's Voices. 1968. V. 48; 49; 54
Five Autumn Songs for Children's Voices. Bow, Near Crediton, Devon: 1968. V. 47
Five Autumn Songs for Children's Voices. Gilbertson: 1968. V. 47
Flowers and Insects. Some Birds and a Pair of Spiders. New York: 1986. V. 48; 51
Four Crow Poems. 1978. V. 48
Gravestones. 1967. V. 48
The Hawk in the Rain. 1957. V. 49; 54
The Hawk in the Rain. London: 1957. V. 47; 51; 52; 53
The Hawk in the Rain. New York: 1957. V. 48; 49; 51; 52
Henry Williamson. A Tribute. London: 1979. V. 50
Lupercal. London: 1959. V. 47; 53
Lupercal. London: 1960. V. 47; 49; 52; 53
The Martyrdom of Bishop Farrar. Bow, Crediton, Devon: 1970. V. 52; 53
Meet My Folks!. London: 1961. V. 52; 53
Mokomaki. Leeds: 1985. V. 49; 54
Moortown. New York: 1980. V. 51
Moortown Elegies. London: 1978. V. 54
Nessie the Mannerless Monster. London: 1964. V. 53
Orts. London: 1978. V. 49; 50; 52; 54
Poems. London: 1971. V. 48; 50
Poetry Is. Garden City: 1970. V. 52
A Primer of Birds. 1981. V. 47
Prometheus on His Crag. London. V. 48; 50
Prometheus On His Crag. 21 Poems. London: 1973. V. 54
Rain-Charm for the Duchy, and other Laureate Poems. London: 1992. V. 48; 50; 52
Remains of Elmet. London: 1979. V. 49; 50; 54
Seneca's Oedipus. Adapted by Ted Hughes. London: 1969. V. 52
Spring, Summer, Autumn, Winter. 1973. V. 54
Spring, Summer, Autumn, Winter. London: 1973. V. 49; 52; 53
T. S. Eliot: a Tribute. London: 1987. V. 47; 51
The Threshold. London: 1979. V. 51
Wodwo... London: 1967. V. 47; 49; 53
Wodwo. New York: 1967. V. 50

HUGHES, THOMAS
David Livingstone. London: 1897. V. 54
Early Memories for the Children by the author of "Tom Brown's Schooldays". London: 1899. V. 53
Fifty Years Ago. A Layman's Address to Rugby School, Quinquagesima Sunday, 1891. London: 1891. V. 52
G.T.T. Gone to Texas: Letters from Our Boys. London: 1884. V. 53
G.T.T. Gone to Texas: Letters from Our Boys. New York: 1884. V. 53
Mental Furniture; or, the Adaption of Knowledge for Man. London: 1857. V. 48; 52
The Scouring of the White Horse. Cambridge & London: 1859. V. 47; 48; 49; 50; 51; 52; 53; 54
Tom Brown at Oxford. Cambridge & London: 1861. V. 47; 49
Tom Brown at Oxford. Boston: 1862-63. V. 54
Tom Brown's School Days. Cambridge: 1857. V. 48; 51
Tom Brown's School Days. London: 1857. V. 51

HUGHES, THOMAS E.
Hanes Cymry Minnesota, Forston a Lime Springs, Ia. Mankato: 1895. V. 50

HUGHES, WILLIAM
The American Physitian; or, a Treatise of the Roots, Plants, Trees, Shrubs, Fruit, Herbs &c. London: 1672. V. 47
An Atlas of Classical Geography... Philadelphia: 1857. V. 49
An Exact Abridgement in English of the Cases Reported by Sr. Francis More, Serjeant at Law. London: 1665. V. 51
The Practical Angler. London: 1842. V. 47

HUGHES, WILLIAM EDGAR
Journal of a Grandfather. St. Louis: 1912. V. 48; 49

HUGHES, WILLIAM R.
A Week's Tramp in Dickens-Land. London: 1891. V. 54

HUGHES-STANTON, BLAIR
Catalogue of an Exhibition of Recent Wood and Coloured Wood Engravings, February 14 - March 7, 1935. 1935. V. 48
The Wood Engravings of Blair Hughes-Stanton. 1991. V. 47

HUGHES STANTON, BLAIR
The Wood Engravings of Blair Hughes-Stanton. Pinner: 1991. V. 50

HUGHSON, D.
The New Family Receipt-book: or Universal Repository of Domestic Economy... London: 1817. V. 50

HUGHSON, DAVID
A History and Description of London, Westminster and Southwark. London: 182-?. V. 54
Walks through London. London: 1817. V. 50; 52

HUGO, HERMANN
De Prima Scribendi Oritine et Universa Rei Literariae Antiquitate. Antverpiae: 1617. V. 51
Pia Desideria... Antwerp: 1628. V. 52
Pia Desideria... London: 1712. V. 54
The Siege of Breda... Ghent: 1627. V. 48

HUGO, RICHARD
Death and the Good Life. New York: 1981. V. 51; 52; 53
A Fun of Jacks. Minneapolis: 1961. V. 53
Good Luck in Cracked Italian. New York & Cleveland: 1969. V. 53
The Lady in Kicking Horse Reservoir. New York: 1973. V. 53
Poems. Portland: 1959. V. 53
Sea lanes Out. Langley: 1983. V. 52
What Thou Lovest Well, Remains American. New York: 1975. V. 51; 53

HUGO, THOMAS
The Bewick Collector. London: 1866-68. V. 50; 51
The Bewick Collector. New York: 1970. V. 49; 51
The History of Mynchin, Buckland Priory and Preceptory, in the County of Somerset. London: 1861. V. 54

HUGO, VICTOR
L'Art d'Etre Grand-Pere. Paris: 1877. V. 48
The Battle of Waterloo. Connecticut: 1977. V. 47; 48
Hans of Iceland. London: 1825. V. 50; 51
Hernani, Drame en Cinq Actes. Paris: 1890. V. 49
The Hunchback of Notre Dame. London: 1833. V. 51
The Hunchback...of Notre Dame. London: 1840. V. 54
The Last Days of a Condemned. London: 1840. V. 53; 54
Les Miserables. Bruxelles: 1862. V. 52
Les Miserables. New York: 1862. V. 50; 52
Les Miserables. Boston: 1888. V. 49
Les Miserables. New York: 1938. V. 47; 48
Notre-Dame de Paris. Paris: 1831. V. 48
Notre-Dame de Paris. New York: 1930. V. 54
Notre-Dame de Paris. Paris: 1930. V. 47; 48; 52; 53; 54
Notre-Dame...Toilers of the Sea, Ninety-Three and By Order of the King. London: 1890. V. 54
Odes et Poesies Diverses. Paris: 1822. V. 50
Ruy Blas. Paris: 1838. V. 47; 49
Ruy Blas... Paris: 1889. V. 49
Ruy Blas. Boston: 1894. V. 49
Toilers of the Sea. London: 1866. V. 50; 53
The Toilers of the Sea. New York: 1960. V. 48
The Toilers of the Sea. Paris: 1960. V. 52
The Toilers of the Sea. Verona: 1960. V. 54
Works. Boston. V. 52
The Works... Philadelphia: 1894-97. V. 51

HUGUET, GENERAL
Britain and the War - a French Indictment. London: 1928. V. 47

HUIE, WILLIAM
Mud On the Stars. New York: 1942. V. 50

HUIE, WILLIAM BRADFORD
The Revolt of Mamie Stover. New York: 1951. V. 48

HUISH, MARCUS B.
The American Pilgrim's Way in England to Homes and Memorials of the Founders of Virginia, the New England States... 1907. V. 51; 52
The American Pilgrim's Way in England, to Homes and Memorials of the Founders of Virginia, the New England States... London: 1907. V. 52
British Water-Colour Art in the First Year of the Reign of King Edward the Seventh, and During the Century Covered by the Life of the Royal Society of Painters in Water Colours. 1904. V. 52
British Water-colour Art in the First Year of the Reign of King Edward the Seventh, and During the Century Covered by the Life of the Royal Society of Painters in Water Colours. London: 1904. V. 48
Happy England. London: 1903. V. 49; 50
Happy England. London: 1909. V. 54
Japan and Its Art. London: 1889. V. 52

HUISH, ROBERT
Edwin and Henry: or the Week's Holidays... Derby: 1815. V. 50
Edwin and Henry; or, the Week's Holidays. London: 1815. V. 48
The Female's Friend, and General Domestic Adviser... London: 1830. V. 50
The Last Voyage of Capt. Sir John Ross, Knt. R.N. to the Arctic Regions... London: 1835. V. 49; 54
The Life of James Greenacre, Who Was Executed at the Old Bailey for the Brutal Murder of Mrs. Hannah Brown. London: 1837. V. 47
Memoirs of George the Fourth, Descriptive of the Most Interesting Scenes of His Private and Public Life... London: 1830. V. 48; 52
Memoirs of Her Late Royal Highness Charlotte Augusta, Princess of Wales... London: 1818. V. 47; 50; 51; 53
A Treatise on the Nature, Economy and Practical Management of Bees. London: 1817. V. 51; 54

HULANISKI, F. J.
The History of Contra Costa County California. Berkeley: 1917. V. 49

HULBERT, ARCHER B.
Historic Highways of America. Cleveland: 1902-05. V. 51

HULBERT, CHARLES
The African Traveller; or, Select Lives, Voyages and Travels, Carefully Abridged from the Original Publications of Bruce, Barrow, Campbell and Park... Shrewsbury: 1817. V. 50
The History and Description of the County of Salop, Comprising Original Historical and Topographical Notices of the Hundreds, Towns, Parishes and Villages... Providence Grove,: 1837. V. 52

HULBERT, CHARLES AUGUSTUS
Annals of the Church and Parish of Almondbury, Yorkshire. London: 1882. V. 47; 53

HULL, ALFRED J.
Surgery in War. London: 1916. V. 47

HULL, DENISON B.
Thoughts on American Fox Hunting. London: 1958. V. 47; 49

HULL, E.
The Northmen in Britain. 1912. V. 47

HULL, EDWARD
The Coal Fields of Great Britain: Their History, Structure and Resources. London: 1861. V. 48
Contributions to the Physical History of the British Isles, with a Dissertation. London: 1882. V. 54

HULL, JOHN
The British Flora, or a Linnaean Arrangement of British Plants. Manchester: 1799. V. 53
The British Flora, or a Systematic Arrangement of British Plants. Manchester: 1808. V. 53
Elements of Botany. Manchester: 1800. V. 49; 54

HULL MECHANICS' INSTITUTE
Catalogue of Books Belonging to the Library of the Mechanics' Inst. Established in Hull, June 1, 1825; with the Laws and Regulations... Hull: 1829. V. 53

HULL, WILLIAM
Defence of Brigadier General W. Hull Delivered Before the General Court Martial, of Which Major General Dearaborn was President, March 1814. Boston: 1814. V. 54
The History of The Glove Trade, with the Customs Connected with the Glove. London: 1834. V. 52; 53
Report of the Trial of Brig. General William Hull: Commanding the North-Western Army of the United States. New York: 1814. V. 50

HULLMANDEL, CHARLES
The Art of Drawing on Stone. London: 1824. V. 53

HULLS *Managing of the Kingdoms Cause; or, a Brief Historicall Relation of the Several Plots and Attempts Against Kingston Upon Hull.* London: 1644. V. 50

HULME, F. EDWARD
Familiar Wild Flowers. London. V. 49
Familiar Wild Flowers... London Paris & New York: 1875. V. 47; 48
Familiar Wild Flowers... London: 1890's. V. 50
Familiar Wild Flowers. London: 1910. V. 50
Principles of Ornamental Art. London: 1875. V. 50; 52
A Series of Sketches from Nature of Plant Form. London: 1868. V. 54
Suggestions in Floral Design. London: 1878. V. 51
Suggestions in Floral Design. London: 1878-79. V. 50; 52

HULSE, ELIZABETH
A Dictionary of Toronto Printers, Publishers, Booksellers and the Allied Trade, 1798-1900. Toronto: 1982. V. 52

HULSIUS, LEVINUS
XII Primorum Caesarum et LXIIII Ipsorum Uxorum et Parentum ex Antiquis Numismatibus... Frankfurt A:M: 1597. V. 47; 50

HULTEN, E.
Flora of Alaska and Neighboring Territories. Stanford: 1968. V. 52
Flora of Alaska and Neighboring Territories. Stanford: 1990. V. 50

HULTEN, K. G. PONTUS
Brancusi and the Concept of Sculpture. London: 1988. V. 49; 51
Italian Art 1900-1945. New York: 1989. V. 52; 53
Jean Tinguely: "Meta". Boston: 1975. V. 48; 50; 52
The Machine As Seen at the End of the Mechanical Age. New York: 1968. V. 47; 51; 52; 53

HULTON, E.
Flora of the Aleutian Islands and Westernmost Alaska Peninsula with Notes on the Flora of Commander Islands. Stockholm: 1958. V. 51

HULTON, PAUL HOPE
The American Drawings of John White, 1577-1590. London: 1964. V. 48

HULTON, PAUL HOPE continued
Work of Jacques Le Moyne de Morgues, a Huguenot Artist in France, Florida and England. 1977. V. 47
The Work of Jacques Le Moyne de Morgues, a Huguenot Artist in France, Florida and England. London: 1977. V. 48; 51; 52

HUMANIORA. Essays in Literature, Folklore and Bibliography Honoring Archer Taylor, On His Seventieth Birthday. Locust Valley: 1960. V. 52

HUMANITY in Algiers; or, the Story of Azem. Troy: 1801. V. 50; 54

HUMASON, W. L.
From the Atlantic Surf to the Golden Gate. Hartford: 1869. V. 47; 50

HUMBER, WILLIAM
A Comprehensive Treatise on the Water Supply of Cities and Towns... London: 1876. V. 48; 51
A Practical Treatise on Cast and Wrought Iron Bridges and Girders, as Applied to Railway Structures, and to Buildings Generally, with Numerous Examples... London: 1857. V. 52
A Record of the Progress of Modern Engineering: Comprising Civil, Mechanical, Marine, Hydraulic, Railway, bridge and Other Engineering Works. London: 1863. V. 52

HUMBERT, ANTOINE DE QUEYRAS
Alexandre et Isabelle. Histoire Tragi-Comiqve. Paris: 1626. V. 51

HUMBLE Address of the Archbishop, President of the Convocation of the Province of Canterbury; and of the Bishops and Clergy of the Same Province, in Convocation Assembled; Presented to His Majesty at St. James's on Sat. 23rd of Feb. 1716. London: 1716. V. 48; 49

THE HUMBLE Petition and Address of the Right Honourable the Lord Mayor, Alderman and Commons of... London: 1681. V. 47

THE HUMBLE Petition and Representation of the Gentry Ministers and Others of the Counties of Cumberland and Westmorland, to His Sacred Majestie.... London: 1642. V. 51; 52

THE HUMBLE Petition of Many Thousand Citizens and Inhabitants in and About the City of London. London: 1658. V. 52

THE HUMBLE Petition of the Gentry and Inhabitants of Holderness; with His Majesties Answer July 6, 1642. London: 1642. V. 50

THE HUMBLE Petition of the Right Honourable the Lord Mayor, Aldermen and Commons of the City of London, in Common-Council Assembled on 13 Jan. 1680. London: 1680. V. 52; 53

HUMBLE, WILLIAM
Dictionary of Geology and Mineralogy... London: 1860. V. 54

HUMBOLDT, FRIEDRICH HEINRICH ALEXANDER, BARON VON
Cosmos: a Sketch of a Physical Description of the Universe. London: 1849-58. V. 49; 51; 52
Cosmos: a Sketch of a Physical Description of the Universe. New York: 1851. V. 48
Cosmos: a Sketch of a Physical Description of the Universe. London: 1949-68. V. 52
Personal Narrative of Travels to the Equinoctial Regions of America 1799-1804. London: 1871-76. V. 54
Personal Narrative of Travels to the Equinoctial Regions of America During the Years 1799-1804. London: 1890. V. 53
Personal Narrative of Travels to the Quinoctial Regions of the New Continent During the Years 1799-1804. (with) Reseraches, Concerning the Institutions and Monuments of the Ancient Inhabitants of America... London: 1814-29/1814. V. 51
Political Essay of the Kingdom of New Spain. London: 1822. V. 47
Researches, Concerning the Institutions and Monuments of the Ancient Inhabitants of America. London: 1814. V. 48; 52
Travels in the South of Europe and in Brazil. London: 1849. V. 49
Views of Nature. London: 1850. V. 54

HUMBUG, HUMPHREY, PSEUD.
The Life and Confessions of Humphrey Humbug, with a Brief Account of His Family... London: 1835. V. 51

HUME, A.
The Learned Societies and Printing Clubs of the United Kingdom. London: 1853. V. 53

HUME, ALAN OCTAVIAN
Contributions to Indian Ornithology, No. 1 Cashmere, Ladak, Yarkand. London: 1873. V. 51; 52
The Game Birds of India, Burmah and Ceylon. Calcutta: 1879-81. V. 48; 49; 51; 52
Nests and Eggs of Indian Birds. London: 1889-90. V. 50; 51

HUME, CYRIL
Cruel Fellowship. New York: 1925. V. 47; 49

HUME, D. C. H.
Nursairy Rhymes. 1919. V. 52

HUME, DAVID
Dialogues Concerning Natural Religion. London: 1779. V. 48; 52
Essays and Treatises on Several Subjects... London and Edinburgh: 1767. V. 51
Essays and Treatises on Several Subjects. London: 1770. V. 54
Essays and Treatises on Several Subjects. Dublin: 1779. V. 47
Essays and Treatises on Several Subjects. 1788. V. 47
Essays and Treatises on Several Subjects. London: 1788. V. 48; 52; 53
Essays and Treatises on Several Subjects. London: 1817. V. 50; 54
Essays and Treatises on Several Subjects. Edinburgh: 1825. V. 49
Essays, Moral and Political. London: 1748. V. 47; 50
Essays on Suicide and the Immortality of the Soul...(and) Two Letters on Suicide, from Rousseau's Eloisa. London: 1783. V. 54
The History of England... London: 1759. V. 49
The History of England... London: 1762/59. V. 48; 52; 54
The History of England... London: 1773. V. 48; 52; 54
The History of England... London: 1786. V. 47
The History of England. London: 1788. V. 52; 53; 54
The History of England... London: 1796. V. 48
The History of England... London: 1810. V. 49; 50
The History of England. London: 1823. V. 51
The History of England... London: 1860. V. 52
The History of England... London: 1864. V. 53
The History of Great Britain....(The History of England...). Edinburgh: 1754/1757-62. V. 51
The History of the Proceedings in the Case of Peg, Only Lawful Sister to John Bull, Esq. London: 1761. V. 47
The Letters. Oxford: 1969. V. 52
Letters...to William Strahan. Oxford: 1888. V. 48
My Own Life. Stanford Dingley: 1927. V. 54
Oeuvres Philosophiques. Londres: 1788. V. 49
The Philosophical Works... Edinburgh: 1854. V. 49
Political Discourses. Edinburgh: 1752. V. 47; 48; 52
Private Correspondence...with Several Distinguished Persons Between the Years 1761 and 1776. London: 1820. V. 49; 54
A Treatise on Human Nature... London: 1739/40. V. 53
A Treatise on Human Nature Being an Attempt to Introduce the Experimental method of Reasoning into Moral Subjects and Dialogues Concerning Natural Religion. London: 1874. V. 52

HUME, FERGUS W.
The Black Carnation. (with) The Chinese Jar, a Mystery. (with) The Mystery of a Hansom Cab. London: 1892/93/c.1888. V. 49
The Island of Fantasy. London: 1892. V. 53
The Mystery of a Hansom Cab...and a Startling and Realistic Story and Social Life. New York and Chicago: 1888. V. 51
When I Lived in Bohemia. Bristol: 1892. V. 51
When I Lived in Bohemia. New York: 1892. V. 48

HUME, JAMES
Traite de la Trigonometrie, Pour Resoudre Tous Triangles Rectilignes et Spheriques. Paris: 1636. V. 47

HUME, JOSEPH BURNLEY
Poems of Early Years, in Nine Chaplets. London: 1851. V. 50; 53

HUME, MR.
Observataions on the Origin and Treatment of Internal and External Diseases and Management of Children. Dublin: 1802. V. 51; 53

HUME, SOPHIA
Exhortation to the Inhabitants of the Province of South Carolina... Philadelphia: 1748. V. 49; 50
An Exhortation to the Inhabitants of the Province of South Carolina... London: 1752. V. 48
An Exhortation to the Inhabitants of the Province of South Carolina... Philadelphia: 1752. V. 53
An Exhortation to the Inhabitants of the Province of South Carolina... Dublin: 1784. V. 51

HUME, W. F.
Terrestrial Theories, a Digest of Various Views as to the Origin and Development of the Earth and their Bearing on the Geology of Egypt. Cairo: 1948. V. 49; 53

HUMELBERGIUS SECUNDUS, DICK, PSEUD.
Apician Morsels; or, Tales of the Table Kitchen and Larder... New York: 1829. V. 51; 54

HUMES, THOMAS WILLIAM
The Loyal Mountaineers of Tennessee. Knoxville: 1888. V. 48

HUMFREVILLE, JAMES LEE
Twenty Years Among Our Savage Indians. Hartford: 1897. V. 47

HUMFREY, LAWRENCE
Ioannis Iuelli Angli Vita et Mors. London: 1573. V. 51

HUMFREY, THOMAS
A True Narrative of God's Gracious Dealings with the Soul of Shalome Ben Shalomoh a Jew. London: 1700. V. 47

HUMMEL, CHARLES F.
With Hammer in Hand: The Dominy Craftsmen of East Hampton, New York. Charlottesville: 1968. V. 48

HUMOROUS Tales: (viz) The Strolling Player. The Cheese Present. The Newspaper Editor. Poetry. Watty and Meg. Tam O'Shanter. Newcastle-upon-Tyne: 1804. V. 51

THE HUMOURIST. London: 1892. V. 52

HUMPFREY, LAURENCE
Ionnis Iuelli Angli, Episcopi Sarisburiensis Vita and Mors..... Londini: 1573. V. 53

HUMPHREY, HEMAN
The Shining Path. Northampton: 1849. V. 50

HUMPHREY, HUBERT H.
The Education of a Public Man: My Life and Politics. Garden City: 1976. V. 53; 54

HUMPHREY, LILLIE MUSE
Aggie. New York: 1955. V. 54

HUMPHREY, LIZBETH
Child Life. Boston: 1890. V. 49

HUMPHREY, MABEL
The Book of the Child. New York: 1903. V. 47

HUMPHREY, MARY ANNE VANCE
The Squatter Sovereign, or Kansas in the '50's. Chicago: 1883. V. 50

HUMPHREY, MAUD
Baby's Record. New York: 1898. V. 47
The Bride's Book. New York: 1900. V. 47
Little Rosebuds. New York: 1898. V. 52

HUMPHREY, OZIAS
The Life and Work of Ozias Humphrey, R.A. London: 1928. V. 47

HUMPHREY, WILLIAM
The Last Husband and Other Stories. New York: 1953. V. 47; 48

HUMPHREYS, A. A.
Letter to the Hon. Wm. M. Gwin in Relation to the Railroad to the Pacific by the Thirty-Fifth and Thirty Second Parallels. Washington: 1858. V. 47
Report Upon the Physics and Hydraulics of the Mississippi River. Philadelphia: 1861. V. 47
Report Upon the Physics and Hydraulics of the Mississippi River. Washington: 1876. V. 47

HUMPHREYS, ARTHUR L.
Old Decorative Maps and Charts. London: 1926. V. 51

HUMPHREYS, DAVID
An Historical Account of the Incorporated Society for the Propagation of the Gospel in Foreign Parts. London: 1730. V. 47
The Miscellaneous Works. New York: 1790. V. 51; 52
A Poem on Industry. Philadelphia: 1794. V. 52

HUMPHREYS, H. D.
An Address Delivered Before the Western Literary Society of Wabash College, July 12, 1836. Crawfordsville: 1836. V. 52

HUMPHREYS, HENRY NOEL
Ancient Coins and Medals... London: 1850. V. 47
Ancient Coins and Medals... London: 1850/49. V. 48
Ancient Coins and Medals... London: 1851. V. 52
The Art of Illumination and Missal Painting. London: 1849. V. 51
British Butterflies and Their Transformations... London: 1841-45. V. 53
British Butterflies and Their Transformations. London: 1848. V. 51
British Butterflies and Their Transformations. London: 1849. V. 53
British Moths and Their Transformations. London: 1843. V. 50; 52; 53
British Moths and Their Transformations. London: 1845. V. 53
The Coinage of the British Empire. London: 1855. V. 52
The Genera and Species of British Butterflies. London: 1859. V. 52
The Genera of British Moths. London: 1858. V. 51
The Genera of British Moths. London: 1859-60. V. 52
The Gold, Silver and Cooper Coins of England. Exhibited in a Series of Fac-similes of the Most Interesting Coins of Each Successive Period; Printed in Gold, Silver and Cooper. London: 1849. V. 48
A History of the Art of Printing...to the Middle of the Sixteenth Century. London: 1868. V. 48; 51; 54
The Illuminated Books of the Middle Ages. London: 1849. V. 47
The Illuminated Calendar and Home Diary. London: 1845. V. 47
Insect Changes. An Illuminated Present for Youth... London: 1847. V. 50
Masterpieces of the Early Printers and Engravers. London: 1870. V. 51
Maxims and Precepts of the Saviour. London: 1848. V. 48; 51
The Miracles of Our Lord. London: 1848. V. 51
The Origin and Progress of the Art of Writing. London: 1853. V. 54
The Origin and Progress of the Art of Writing. London: 1855. V. 48; 49
The Parables of Our Lord. London: 1847. V. 49
A Record of the Black Prince. London: 1849. V. 52; 54
Sentiments and Similes of William Shakespeare. London: 1857. V. 54
Sentiments and Similes of William Shakespeare... London: 1864?. V. 51

HUMPHREYS, JOHN S.
Bermuda Houses. Boston: 1923. V. 50

HUMPHREYS, JOSEPHINE
Dreams of Sleep. New York: 1984. V. 53

HUMPHREYS, MILTON W.
A History of the Lynchburg Campaign by Milton W. Humphreys... Charlottesville: 1924. V. 50

HUMPHREYS, RICHARD F.
Index to Irish Statutory Instruments 1922-1986. 1987. V. 49

HUMPHRIES, ARTHUR L.
The Wisdom of the Foolish. London: 1913. V. 48

HUMPHRIES, BARRY
A Garland for Stephen Spender. 1991. V. 51

HUMPHRIES, RICHARD
The Memoirs of John Scroggins, the Pugilistic Hero, Otherwise John Palmer. London: 1827. V. 50

HUMPHRIES, ROLFE
...And Spain Sings: Fifty Loyalist Ballads adapted by American Poets. New York: 1937. V. 49

HUMPHRY, GEORGE M.
The Human Foot and the Human Hand. Cambridge & London: 1861. V. 50

HUNCKE, HERBERT
Elsie John and Joey Martinez. New York: 1979. V. 50
Huncke's Journal. New York: 1965. V. 50

HUNDERTPFUND, LIBERAT
The Art of Painting Restored To Its Simplest and Surest Principles. London: 1849. V. 47

HUNGARIAN Architecture (Until the End of the 19th Century). Budapest: 1954. V. 48; 50; 51; 53; 54

HUNGERFORD, EDWARD
The Story of the Baltimore and Ohio Railroad 1827-1927. New York: 1928. V. 49

HUNGERFORD, MARGARET WOLFE HAMILTON
Phyllis. London: 1877. V. 48; 51
Under-Currents. London: 1888. V. 50

HUNNEWELL, JAMES F.
Elegies and Epitaphs 1677-1717. Boston: 1896. V. 48

HUNNISETT, BASIL
Illustrated Dictionary of British Steel Engravings. London: 1989. V. 54

HUNT, A. B.
Houseboats and Houseboating. New York: 1905. V. 50; 51

HUNT, AURORA
The Army of the Pacific. Glendale: 1951. V. 50; 54

HUNT, BENJAMIN PETER
Why Colored People in Philadelphia are Excluded from the Street Cars. Philadelphia: 1866. V. 54

HUNT, CHARLES HAVENS
Life of Edward Livingston. New York: 1864. V. 53

HUNT, CORNELIUS E.
The Shenandoah; or the Last Confederate Cruiser. New York: 1867. V. 49

HUNT, D. C.
Karl Bodmer's America. Omaha: 1993. V. 51

HUNT, EDWARD EYRE
Scientific Management Since Taylor: a Collection of Authoritative Papers. New York: 1924. V. 48

HUNT, F. KNIGHT
The Fourth Estate... London: 1850. V. 48

HUNT, G. H.
Outram & Havelock's Persian Campaign... London: 1858. V. 53

HUNT, HENRY
An Atlas of the Differential Diagnosis of the Diseases of the Nervous System... Troy: 1913. V. 47
Orator, a Most Splendid Procession, This Day at 12 O'Clock, to Introduce Henry Hunt, Esq. Triumphantly into London... London: 1822. V. 47

HUNT, JOHN
Religious Thought in England from the Reformation to the End of Last Century. London: 1870-73. V. 49

HUNT, LEIGH
A Book for a Corner; or Selections in Prose and Verse From Authors The Best Suited to that Mode of Enjoyment. London: 1849. V. 47; 48
Captain Sword and Captain Pen. London: 1835. V. 52
The Companion. London: 1828. V. 51
Foliage; or Poems Original and Translated. London: 1818. V. 48; 49; 50; 51
The Indicator, and the Companion, a Miscellany for the Fields and the Fire-side. London: 1834. V. 51; 52
A Jar of Honey from Mount Hybla. London: 1847. V. 54
A Jar of Honey from Mount Hybla. London: 1848. V. 47; 48; 49; 50; 51; 52; 54
Juvenilia: or, a Collection of Poems. London: 1801. V. 47; 49
Juvenilia; or, a Collection of Poems. London: 1802. V. 47; 52; 53
Lord Byron and Some of His Contemporaries... London: 1828. V. 53; 54
Men, Women and Books... London: 1847. V. 47; 54
Men, Women and Books. New York: 1847. V. 47; 51
The Months, a Descriptive of the Succesive Beauties of the Year. London: 1821. V. 48
The Old Court Suburb: or, Memorials of Kensington, Regal, Critical and Anecdotal. London: 1855. V. 53
The Old Court Suburb, or, Memorials of Kensington, Regal, Critical and Anecdotal. London: 1902. V. 48; 49; 53
The Poetical Works. London: 1821. V. 48
The Poetical Works... London: 1832. V. 50
The Rebellion of the Beasts: or, the Ass is Dead!. London: 1825. V. 50
The Story of Rimini, a Poem. London: 1816. V. 52
Table-Talk. London: 1851. V. 48; 51; 54
A Tale for a Chimney Corner, and other Essays...From the "Indicator", 1819-1821. London: 1869. V. 49
The Town: Its Memorable Characters and Events. London: 1818. V. 51
The Town: its Memorable Characters and Events. London: 1848. V. 48

HUNT, LYNN BOGUE
An Artist's Game Bag. New York: 1936. V. 52
Game Birds of America. New York: 1944. V. 47

HUNT, MARGARET RAINE
Our Grandmother's Gowns. London: 1884. V. 53; 54

HUNT, PETER
Murder Among the Nudists. New York: 1934. V. 52

HUNT, RACHEL MC MASTERS MILLER
Catalogue of Botanical Books in the Collection. Pittsburgh. V. 47
Catalogue of Botanical Books in the Collection... London: 1958-61. V. 49
Catalogue of Botanical Books in the Collection... Pittsburgh: 1958-61. V. 47; 48; 51; 52; 53; 54
Catalogue of Botanical Books in the Collection. New York: 199-?. V. 50
Catalogue of Botanical Books in the Collection. New York: 1991. V. 47; 48; 49; 50; 51; 53; 54

HUNT, ROBERT
British Mining. A Treatise on the History, Discovery, Practical Development and Future Prospects of Metalliferous Mines in the United Kingdom. London: 1887. V. 49
A Manual of Photography. London and Glasgow: 1854. V. 54
Panthea, the Spirit of Nature. London: 1849. V. 47
Popular Romances of the West of England; or, the Drolls, Traditions and Superstitions of Old Cornwall. London: 1865. V. 49
Researches On Light In Its Chemical Relations. London: 1854. V. 48; 49; 50; 52
Ure's Dictionary of Arts, Manufactures and Mines... London: 1867. V. 54

HUNT, ROCKWELL D.
California and the Californians. Chicago: 1932. V. 47
John Bidwell, Prince of California Pioneers. Caldwell: 1942. V. 51

HUNT, THOMAS FREDERICK
Half a Dozen Hints on Picturesque Domestic Architecture. London: 1841. V. 49; 50; 51

HUNT, THOMAS STERRY
Report Of...on the Gold Region of Nova Scotia. Ottawa: 1868. V. 49

HUNT, VIOLET
The Desirable Alien at Home in Germany. London: 1913. V. 53

HUNT, WILLIAM GIBBES
An Address, Delivered at Nashville, Tennessee, April 6, 1831, at the Request of the Literary Society of the University of Nashville. Nashville: 1831. V. 47

HUNT, WILLIAM HOLMAN
Pre-Raphaelitism and the Pre-Raphaelite Brotherhood. London: 1905. V. 49; 50
Pre-Raphaelitism and the Pre-Raphaelite Brotherhood. London: 1913. V. 49

HUNT, WILLIAM POWELL
Rare Books, Manuscripts and Illustrative Works, Relating to the County of Suffolk. Ipswich: 1873. V. 47

HUNTEN, FRANZ
F. Hunten's Instructions for the Piano-Forte. Richmond: 1863. V. 54

HUNTER, ADAM
An Essay on Two Mineral Springs, Recently Discovered at Harogate; and on the Springs of Thorp-Arch and Ilkley... London: 1819. V. 50

HUNTER, ALEXANDER
The Buxton Manual: or, a Treatise on the Nature and Virtues of the Waters of Buxton. London: 1793. V. 51
Culina Famulatrix Medicinae; or, Receipts in Cookery. York: 1804. V. 47; 48; 53; 54
Georgical Essays: In Which the Food of Plants Is Particularly Considered. London: 1769. V. 48; 50; 52
Georgical Essays: In Which the Food of Plants is Particularly Considered... London: 1773. V. 54
Outlines of Agriculture, Addressed to Sir John Sinclair, Bart, President of the Board of Agriculture. York: 1797. V. 52
The Women of the Debatable Land. Washington: 1912. V. 50

HUNTER, ANOLE
Let's Ride to Hounds. New York: 1929. V. 51

HUNTER ARCHAEOLOGICAL SOCIETY
Transactions. Sheffield: 1918-50. V. 53

HUNTER, DARD
Chinese Ceremonial Paper. A Monograph Relating to the Fabrication of Paper and Tinfoil and the Use of Paper in Chinese Rites and Religious Ceremonies. Chillicothe: 1937. V. 53
Laid and Wove. Washington: 1923. V. 52
The Life and Work of Dard Hunter. Chillicothe: 1981-83. V. 49
The Life Work of Dard Hunter. Chillicothe: 1981. V. 53
The Life Work of Dard Hunter. Chillicothe: 1981-85. V. 49
The Life Work of Dard Hunter. Chillicothe: 1981/83. V. 51
The Literature of Papermaking 1390-1800. Chillicothe: 1925. V. 48; 53; 54
The Making of Books. Chillicothe: 1987. V. 49
My Life with Paper. New York: 1958. V. 47; 49; 50; 51; 52
Old Papermaking. Chillicothe: 1923. V. 50
Old Papermaking in China and Japan. Chillicothe: 1932. V. 53
Paper-making in the Classroom. Peoria: 1931. V. 52
Papermaking by Hand in America. Chillicothe: 1950. V. 47; 48; 50; 54
Papermaking by Hand in India. New York: 1939. V. 47; 48; 49; 52; 54
Papermaking in Indo-China. Chillicothe: 1947; 48; 53
Papermaking in Pioneer America. Philadelphia: 1952. V. 48; 50; 52
Papermaking in Southern Siam. Chillicothe: 1936. V. 53
A Papermaking Pilgrimage to Japan, Korea and China. New York: 1936. V. 48; 53
Papermaking: The History and Technique of an Ancient Craft. New York: 1943. V. 49; 50
Papermaking: The History and Technique of an Ancient Craft. New York: 1947. V. 52
Papermaking: The History and Technique of an Ancient Craft. New York: 1957. V. 48
Papermaking through Eighteen Centuries. New York: 1930. V. 48; 52
Primitive Papermaking. Chillicothe: 1927. V. 48; 53
The Romance of Watermarks, a Discourse on the Origin and Motive of These Mystic Symbols Which First Appeared in Italy Near the End of the 13th Century... Cincinnati: 1938. V. 52
A Specimen of Type. Cambridge: 1940. V. 52

HUNTER, EVAN
The Blackboard Jungle. New York: 1954. V. 50
Mothers and Daughters. New York: 1961. V. 54

HUNTER, GEORGE
Reminiscences of an Old Timer. San Francisco: 1887. V. 50; 53
Reminiscences of an Old Timer. Battle Creek: 1888. V. 53

HUNTER, GEORGE LELAND
Decorative Furniture. Philadelphia: 1923. V. 51
Decorative Textiles. Grand Rapids: 1918. V. 50
Decorative Textiles. Philadelphia & London: 1918. V. 47
Tapestries. New York: 1913. V. 51

HUNTER, HENRY
The History of London and Its Envrions... London: 1811. V. 51

HUNTER, J.
Antiquarian Notices of Lupset, the Heath, Sharlston and Ackton, in the County of York. London: 1851. V. 47; 53

HUNTER, JANE EDNA
A Nickel and a Prayer. Cleveland: 1940. V. 54

HUNTER, JOHN
Essays and Observations on Natural History, Anatomy, Physiology, Psychology and Geology... London: 1861. V. 52
An Historical Journal of the Transactions at Port Jackson and Norfolk Island.... London: 1793. V. 47; 48; 50; 51; 54
The Natural History of the Human Teeth. (with) A Practical Treatise on the Diseases of the Teeth... London: 1778/78. V. 53
Observations On Certain Parts of the Animal Oeconomy. London: 1786. V. 49
A Treatise on the Blood, Inflammation and Gun-Shot Wounds... London: 1794. V. 47; 48; 49; 50; 51; 52; 53
A Treatise on the Blood, Inflammation and Gun-Shot Wounds. London: 1812. V. 52
A Treatise on the Blood, Inflammation and Gun-Shot Wounds. Philadelphia: 1817. V. 48
Treatise on the Natural History and Diseases of the Human Teeth: Explaining their Structure, Use, Formation, Growth and Diseases. Philadelphia: 1839. V. 49
A Treatise on the Veneral Disease. Philadelphia: 1841. V. 51; 53
A Treatise on the Venereal Disease. Philadelphia: 1859. V. 51
A Tribute to the Manes of Unfortunate Poets; in Four Cantos. London: 1798. V. 52
The Works of John Hunter, F.R.S. with Notes. London: 1835-37. V. 47

HUNTER, JOHN DUNN
Manners and Customs of Several Indian Tribes Located West of Mississippi. Philadelphia: 1823. V. 47; 49; 50
Memoirs of a Captivity Among the Indians of North America. London: 1823. V. 47; 51
Memoirs of a Captivity Among the Indians of North America... London: 1824. V. 47; 53
Memoirs of a Captivity Among the Indians of North America... London: 183. V. 54
Memoirs of a Captivity Among the Indians of North America... London: 1923. V. 50

HUNTER, JOHN MARVIN
The Album of Gunfighters. 1951. V. 48; 54
The Album of Gunfighters. Bandera: 1951. V. 52; 53
The Album of Gunfighters. Bandera: 1976. V. 52
Frontier Times. 1932-33. V. 50
The Trail Drivers of Texas. San Antonio: 1920-23. V. 49
The Trail Drivers of Texas. Nashville: 1925. V. 47; 48; 49; 52; 53; 54
The Trail Drivers of Texas. New York: 1963. V. 48; 50; 51; 52

HUNTER, JOSEPH
The Hallamshire Glossary... London: 1829. V. 47

HUNTER, KRISTIN
The Landlord. New York: 1966. V. 52

HUNTER, MARTHA TALIAFERRO
A Memoir of Robert M. T. Hunter. Washington: 1903. V. 49

HUNTER, MARTIN
The Making of the Book of Common Prayer. 1990. V. 54
The Making of the Book of Common Prayer of 1928. 1991. V. 48

HUNTER, NORMAN
The Incredible Adventures of Professor Branestawm. London: 1933. V. 47; 49

HUNTER, RACHEL
Letters from Mrs. Palmerstone to Her Daughter; Inculcating Morality by Entertaining Narratives. London: 1810. V. 47

HUNTER, RICHARD
Three Hundred Years of Psychiatry, 1535-1860... London: 1964. V. 47; 48
Three Hundred Years of Psychiatry, 1535-1860. London: 1970. V. 50
Three Hundred Years of Psychiatry, 1535-1860. Hartsdale: 1982. V. 47; 49; 52

HUNTER, ROBERT MERCER TALIAFERRO
Observations on the History of Virginia. Washington: 1855. V. 53

HUNTER, SAM
Isamu Noguchi. 1978. V. 47

HUNTER, SAM continued
Isamu Nogushi. New York: 1980's. V. 53
Larry Rivers. New York: 1970. V. 47; 48; 49; 50; 52
The Museum of Modern Art, New York: The History and the Collection. London: 1984. V. 49

HUNTER, THOMAS
Reflections Critical and Moral on the Letters of the Earl of Chesterfield. London: 1776. V. 49

HUNTER, WILLIAM
The Anatomy of the Human Gravid Uterus. London: 1842?. V. 47
The Anatomy of the Human Gravid Uterus. London: 1851. V. 49; 52; 54
Medical Commentaries. Part 1. Containing a Plain and Direct Answer to Professor Monro Jun. Interspersed with Remarks on the Structure, Functions and Diseases of Several Parts of the Human Body. London: 1762. V. 47
Pernicious Anaemia: Its Pathology, Septic Origin, Symptoms, Diagnosis and Treatment Based Upon Original Investigations. London: 1901. V. 53
Uteri Humani Gravidi Tabulis Illustrata. The Anatamony of the Human Gravid UTerus Exhibited in Figures. London: 1851. V. 54

HUNTER, WILLIAM S.
Chisholm's Panoramic Guide from Niagara Falls to Quebec. Montreal: 1868. V. 52
Hunter's Eastern Townships Scenery, Canada, East. Montreal: 1860. V. 53
Hunter's Ottawa Scenery in the Vicinity of Ottawa City, Canada. Ottawa: 1855. V. 51

HUNTER, WILLIAM W.
The Annals of Rural Bengal. London: 1868. V. 50; 53
The Indian Empire: Its People, History and Products. London: 1893. V. 48
Life of Brian Houghton Hodgson: British Resident at the Court of Nepal. London: 1896. V. 54

THE HUNTER'S and Trapper's Complete Guide, A Manual of Instruction in the Art of Hunting, Trapping and Fishing... New York: 1875. V. 50

HUNTING.. London: 1926. V. 54

HUNTINGDON, SELINA HASTINGS, COUNTESS OF
A Select Collection of Hymns, to be Universally Sung in all the Countess of Huntingdon's Chapels... London: 1780. V. 51

HUNTINGTON, ARCHER M.
A Note-Book in Northern Spain. New York: 1898. V. 47

HUNTINGTON, D. B.
Vocabulary of the Utah and Sho-Sho-ne or Snake Dialects, With Indian Legends and Traditions... Salt Lake City: 1872. V. 53; 54

HUNTINGTON, D. W.
Big Game. London: 1904. V. 49

HUNTINGTON, DAVID C.
The Landscapes of Frederic Edwin Church. New York: 1966. V. 47; 50

HUNTINGTON, ELLSWORTH
The Climatic Factor as Illustrated in Arid America. Washington: 1914. V. 50

HUNTINGTON, EMILY
The Kitchen Garden; or, Object Lessons in Household Work. New York: 1878. V. 53

HUNTINGTON, GEORGE
Robber and Hero. The Story of the Raid On the First National Bank of Northfield, Minnesota... Northfield: 1895. V. 47; 53

HUNTINGTON, JONATHAN
Classical Sacred Musick. Boston: 1812. V. 51

HUNTINGTON, RANDOLPH
General Grant's Arabian Horses, Leopard and Linden Tree and their Sons Beagle and Hegira. Philadelphia: 1885. V. 49; 51
History in Brief of Leopard and Linden, General Grant's Arabian Stallions, Presented to Him by the Sultan of Turkey in 1879... Philadelphia: 1885. V. 47

HUNTLEY, HENRY VANE
Peregrine Scramble, or, Thirty Years' Adventures of a Blue Jacket. London: 1849. V. 54

HUNTON, ADDIE W.
Two Colored Women with the American Expeditionary Forces. Brooklyn: 1920. V. 53

HUNTON, DOROTHY
Alpheaus Hunton: the Unsung Valiant. New York: 1986. V. 53

HUNTON, PHILIP
A Treatise of Monarchy, Containing Two Parts. London: 1680. V. 49

HUNTON, W. GORDON
English Decorative Textiles: Tapestry and Chintz, Their Design and Development from the Earliest Times to the Nineteenth Century. 1930. V. 52

HUNT'S Universal Yacht List 1909. London. V. 51

HUNT'S Universal Yacht List 1913. London. V. 51

HUNT'S Universal Yacht List 1914. London. V. 51

HURD, PETER
Peter Hurd Sketch Book. Chicago: 1971. V. 47; 49; 52

HURD, RICHARD
Dialogues on the Uses of Foreign Travel... London: 1764. V. 47; 49; 52
Dialogues on the Uses of Foreign Travel... London: 1764/62. V. 52
Letters on Chivalry and Romance. Cambridge: 1762. V. 50
Moral and Political Dialogues: Being the Substance of Several Conversations Between Divers Eminent Persons of the Past and Present Age. London: 1759. V. 47; 50

HURD, WILLIAM
A New Universal History of the Religious Rites, Ceremonies and Customs of the Whole World. London: 1785. V. 53
A New Universal History of the Religious Rites, Ceremonies and Customs of the Whole World... London: 1788. V. 49
A New Universal History of the Religious Rites, Ceremonies and Customs of the Whole World. London: 1799?. V. 49

HURDIS, JAMES
The Favorite Village. A Poem. Bishopstone, Sussex: 1800. V. 48
The Favourite Village, with an Additional Poem... London: 1810. V. 48
Poems. Oxford: 1808. V. 50
The Village Curate, a Poem. London: 1790. V. 48
The Village Curate, and Other Poems... London: 1810. V. 52

HURD-MEAD, KATE CAMPBELL
A History of Women in Medicine from the Earliest Times to the Beginning of the Nineteenth Century. Haddam: 1938. V. 49; 51
Medical Women of America: a Short History of the Pioneer Medical Women of America and a Few of Their Colleagues in England. 1933. V. 52

HURLBERT, J. BEAUFORT
Physical Atlas with Coloured Maps, Showing the geographical Distribution of Plants Yielding Food... Montreal?: 1880. V. 50

HURLBURT, J. B.
Britain and Her Colonies. London: 1865. V. 48

HURLBUTT, FRANK
Bow Porcelain. London: 1926. V. 50; 51

HURLEY, FRANK
Pearls and Savages. Adventures in the Air, on Land and Sea - in New Guinea. New York, London: 1924. V. 48; 49; 50; 51

HURLEY, WILSON
Wilson Hurley, an Exhibition of Oil Paintings. Kansas City: 1977. V. 47

HURRELL, GEORGE
Hurrell Style...Hollywood. New York: 1976. V. 51; 53

HURRELL, JOHN WEYMOUTH
Measured Drawings of Old Oak English Furniture also of Some Remains of Architectural Woodwork, Platerwork, Metalwork, Glazing Etc. London: 1902. V. 49

HURRY, IVES, MRS.
Artless Tales. London: 1808. V. 50

HURRY, JAMIESON
Imhotep: the Vizier and Physician of King Zoser and Afterwards the Egyptian God of Medicine. London: 1928. V. 52

HURST, ALEX A.
Square-Riggers the Final Epoch. Sussex: 1972. V. 54

HURST, FANNIE
Lummox. New York: 1923. V. 47; 48; 49; 52
Mannequin. New York: 1926. V. 52

HURST, JOHN
Sale Catalogue of Books, etc. London?: 1826. V. 54

HURST, JOHN F.
Indika the Country and People of India and Ceylon. New York: 1891. V. 52

HURST, SAMUEL H.
Journal History of the Seventy-Third Ohio Volunteer Infantry. Chillicothe: 1866. V. 54

HURSTON, ZORA NEALE
Dust Tracks on a Road. Philadelphia: 1942. V. 53; 54
Jonah's Gourd Vine. Philadelphia: 1934. V. 54
Moses: Man of the Mountain. Philadelphia: 1939. V. 50; 51; 53
Mules and Men. Philadelphia: 1935. V. 48; 53
Seraph on the Suwanee. New York: 1948. V. 50; 52; 53; 54
Tell My Horse. Philadelphia/New York: 1938. V. 52; 54
Their Eyes Were Watching God. Philadelphia: 1937. V. 54

HURTADO DE MENDOZA, DIEGO
The Life and Adventures of that Witty and Ingenious Spaniard, Lazarillo de Tormes... Edinburgh (sic). V. 49

HURTLEY, THOMAS
A Concise Account of Some Natural Curiosities, in the Environs of Malham, in Craven, Yorkshire. London: 1786. V. 47; 48; 52; 53

HURWITZ, ALFRED
Milestones in Modern Surgery. New York: 1958. V. 49; 52

HUSBAND Hunting; or, the Mothers and Daughters. London: 1825. V. 51

HUSE, CALEB
The Supplies for the Confederate Army How They Were Obtained in Europe and How Paid for Personal Reminiscences and Unpublished History. Boston: 1904. V. 48; 49

HUSENBETH, F. C.
The History of Sedgley Park School, Staffordshire. London: 1856. V. 52

HUSK, WILLIAM HENRY
Songs of the Nativity; Being Christmas Carols, Ancient and Modern. London: 1868. V. 49

HUSKISSON, WILLIAM
The Speeches of the Right Honourable William Huskisson... London: 1831. V. 53

HUSMANN, GEORGE
American Grape Growing and Wine Making. New York: 1881. V. 47

HUSON, HOBART
Captain Phillip Dimmitt's Commandancy of Goliad, 1835-1836... Austin: 1974. V. 48; 50
Dr. J. H. Barnard's Journal, Dec. 1835-June 1836. 1950. V. 48
Refugio: a Comprehensive History of Refugio County from Aboriginal Times to 1953. Woodsboro: 1953. V. 48
Refugio: a Comprehensive History of Refugio County from Aboriginal Times to 1953. Woodsboro: 1953-55. V. 53
Refugio. A Comprehensive History of Refugio County from Aboriginal Times to 1955. Woodsboro: 1955. V. 53

HUSON, HOBERT
Capt. Phillip Dimmitt's Commandancy of Goliad...1835-1836. Austin: 1974. V. 50

HUSON, THOMAS
Round About Helvellyn. London: 1895. V. 50; 52

HUSSERL, EDMUND
L'Origine de la Geometrie. Paris: 1962. V. 52

HUSSEY, A. M.
Illustrations of British Mycology. London: 1847. V. 52; 53
Illustrations of British Mycology. London: 1847-55. V. 50; 52

HUSSEY, ARTHUR
Notes on the Churches in the Counties of Kent, Sussex, and Surrey, Mentioned in Domesday Book... London: 1852. V. 51

HUSSEY, CHRISTOPHER
English Country Houses... London: 1955. V. 51; 53
English Country Houses... London: 1955-58. V. 51
English Country Houses. London: 1955-67-58. V. 47
English Country Houses... London: 1955/56/58. V. 53
English Country Houses... London: 1967/66/70. V. 48
English Gardens and Landscapes 1700-1750. New York: 1967. V. 47
The Life of Sir Edwin Lutyens. London: 1953. V. 50; 54
Tait McKenzie: a Sculptor of Youth. London: 1929. V. 50

HUSSEY, GEORGE A.
History of the Ninth Regiment N.Y.S.M. - N.G.S.N.Y. (Eighty-Third N.Y. Volunteers). New York: 1889. V. 47

HUSSEY, JOHN ADAM
The History of Fort Vancouver and Its Physical Structure. Washington: 1957. V. 50
Preliminary Survey of the History and Physical Structure of Fort Vancouver. Portland?: 1945?. V. 48

HUSSON, A. M.
The Mammals of uriname. Leiden: 1978. V. 49

HUSTED'S
Oakland, Alameda, Berkeley and Alameda County Directory. San Francisco: 1894. V. 47

HUSTON, JOHN
Frankie and Johnny. New York: 1930. V. 48
An Open Book. New York: 1980. V. 52

HUTCHESON, FRANCIS
Considerations on Patronages. Glasgow: 1774. V. 48
An Essay on the Nature and Conduct of the Passions and Affections. Dublin: 1728. V. 50
An Essay on the Nature and Conduct of the Passions and Affections. London: 1742. V. 48; 52
An Inquiry Into the Original of Our Ideas of Beauty and Virtue... London: 1729. V. 47; 48
A Short Introduction to Moral Philosophy, in Three Books... Glasgow: 1764. V. 49
A System of Moral Philosophy, in Three Books. Glasgow: 1755. V. 48; 49

HUTCHINGS, JAMES MASON
In the Heart of the Sierras: the Yo Semite Valley. Yo Semite Valley & Oakland: 1886. V. 48; 51; 54
Scenes of Wonder and Curiosity in California. San Francisco: 1860. V. 54

HUTCHINS, B. L.
The Working Life of Women, Fabian Women's Group Series No. 1. London: 1911. V. 53

HUTCHINS, E. R.
The War of the Sixties. New York: 1912. V. 47

HUTCHINS, JOHN
The History and Antiquities of the County of Dorset... Westminster: 1861. V. 51
The History and Antiquities of the County of Dorset. London: 1861-70. V. 48

HUTCHINS, PATRICIA
James Joyce's World. London: 1957. V. 47

HUTCHINS, THOMAS
A Topographical Description of Virginia, Pennsylvania, Maryland and North Carolina Comprehending the Rivers Ohio, Kenhawa, Sioto, Cherokee, Wabash, Illinois, Mississippi, &c. London: 1778. V. 48

HUTCHINS, WELLS A.
Water Rights Laws in the Nineteen Western States. Washington: 1971. V. 52

HUTCHINSON, BENJAMIN
Cases of Tic Douloureux Successfully Treated. London: 1820. V. 54

HUTCHINSON, C. C.
Resources of Kansas Fifteen Years Experience. Topeka: 1871. V. 48; 50

HUTCHINSON, E.
Battles of Mexico: Containing an Authentic Account of All the Battles Fought... New York: 1848. V. 48; 49

HUTCHINSON, EDWARD
Girder-Making and the Practice of Bridge Building in Wrought Iron. London: 1879. V. 52

HUTCHINSON, FRANCIS
An Historical Essay Concerning Witchcraft. London: 1718. V. 48; 50; 51; 54
An Historical Essay Concerning Witchcraft. London: 1720. V. 49; 50

HUTCHINSON, H. D.
The Campaign in Tirah 1897-1898. London: 1898. V. 47; 50

HUTCHINSON, HORACE G.
Big Game Shooting. 1905. V. 54
Big Game Shooting. London: 1905. V. 48
The Book of Golf and Golfers. London: 1900. V. 51
British Golf Links. London: 1897. V. 47; 52
Cricketing Saws and Stories. London: 1889. V. 51
Golf. London: 1890. V. 50; 53; 54
Golf. London: 1898. V. 48
Shooting. London: 1903. V. 49

HUTCHINSON, J.
A Botanist in Southern Africa. London: 1946. V. 49; 52; 53
Flora of West Tropical Africa. London: 1927-36. V. 51

HUTCHINSON, JOHN
Hutchinson's Tour through the High Peak of Derbyshire. Macclesfield: 1809. V. 51; 52

HUTCHINSON, JONATHAN
Illustrations of Clinical Surgery.... London: 1878. V. 53; 54
On Leprosy and Fish-Eating: a Statement of Facts and Explanations. London: 1906. V. 54
The Pedigree of Disease... London: 1884. V. 47; 49
The Surgical Treatment of Facial Neuralgia. New York: 1905. V. 54
Syphilis. London: 1887. V. 51

HUTCHINSON, LUCY
Memoirs of the Life of Colonel Hutchinson, Governor of Nottingham Castle and Town... London: 1806. V. 53
Memoirs of the Life of Colonel (John) Hutchinson, Governor of Nottingham... London: 1808. V. 49

HUTCHINSON, R. C.
Elephant & Castle. London: 1949. V. 52

HUTCHINSON, THOMAS
The History of the Colony of Massachusetts Bay, from the First Settlement Thereof in 1628... Boston. V. 47
The History of the Colony of Massachusetts Bay, from the First Settlement Thereof in 1628... Boston: 1764/67/69/. V. 50
The History of the Colony of Massachusetts Bay, from the First Settlement Thereof in 1628.... London: 1765/67/1828. V. 50
The History of the Colony of Massachusetts Bay, from the First Settlement Thereof in 1628... London: 1765/78. V. 49
The History of the Province of Massachusetts Bay from 1749-1774, Comprising a Detailed Narrative of the Origin and Early Stages of the American Revolution. London: 1828. V. 50
The Hutchinson Papers: a Collection of Original Papers Relative to the History of the Colony of Massachusetts Bay. Albany: 1865. V. 47
The Natural History of the Frog Fish of Surinam... York: 1796. V. 48

HUTCHINSON, THOMAS JOSEPH
Impressions of Western Africa, With Remarks on the Diseases of the Climate and Report on the Peculiarities of Trade Up the Rivers... London: 1858. V. 50
Narrative of the Niger, Tshadda & Binue Exploration. London: 1855. V. 53
Ten Years Wanderings Among the Ethiopians... London: 1861. V. 48; 49; 50

HUTCHINSON, WALTER
Hutchinson's Dog Encyclopaedia. London. V. 48

HUTCHINSON, WILLIAM
An Excursion to the Lakes in Westmoreland and Cumberland... London: 1774. V. 48; 52
An Excursion to the Lakes in Westmoreland and Cumberland... London: 1776. V. 48; 51; 52; 54
The History of the County of Cumberland. London: 1974. V. 52
The Spirit of Masonry; in Moral and Elucidatory Lectures. London: 1775. V. 53
The Spirit of Masonry; in Moral and Elucidatory Lectures. London/Edinburgh: 1815. V. 53
A Treatise on Practical Steamanship; with Hints and Remarks Relating Thereto... Liverpool: 1777. V. 49

HUTCHISON, C. S.
Geological Evolution of South-East Asia. Oxford: 1989. V. 50; 51

HUTCHISON, ISABEL WYLIE
Stepping Stones from Alaska to Asia. London: 1937. V. 50

HUTCHISON, LT. COL.
History and Memoirs of the 33rd Battalion Machine Gun Corps of the 19th, 9th and 100th and 248th M.G. Companies. London: 1919. V. 47

HUTH, ALFRED HENRY
A Catalogue of the Woodcuts and Engravings in the Huth Library. London: 1910. V. 47; 50; 53

HUTH, F. H.
Works on Horses and Equitation. London: 1887. V. 47

HUTLEY, FRANK
Pearls and Savages. New York: 1924. V. 48

HUTSMITH, GEORGE W.
The Wyoming Lynching of Cattle Kate. Glendo: 1993. V. 50

HUTT, HENRY
Rosebuds. 1912. V. 52

HUTTO, JOHN
Howard County in the Making: Personalities, Business Institutions and Other Contributing Factors in the Development of a Progressive West Texas Community from Open Frontier. Big Spring: 1938. V. 53

HUTTON, CHARLES
A Course of Mathematics... London: 1799-98. V. 48; 52; 54
A Course of Mathematics. New York: 1816. V. 48
Elements of Conic Sections; with Select Exercises in Various Branches of Mathematics and Philosophy. London: 1787. V. 50; 54
A Key to the Course of Mathematics Composed for the Use of the Royal Military Academy, Woolwick, with an Appendix... London: 1824. V. 50
A Mathematical and Philosophical Dictionary... London: 1795. V. 47
A Mathematical and Philosophical Dictionary. London: 1796. V. 50
A Mathematical and Philosophical Dictionary. London: 1796-95. V. 53
On the Mean Density of the Earth... V. 54
Tracts on Mathematical and Philosophical Subjects... London: 1812. V. 49
A Treatise on Mensuration, Both in Theory and Practice... Newcastle-upon-Tyne: 1770. V. 47; 48; 49; 51

HUTTON, EDWARD
The Pageant of Venice. London: 1922. V. 48

HUTTON, J.
Central Asia, from the Aryan to the Cossack. London: 1875. V. 50

HUTTON, JOHN
A Tour to the Caves in the Environs of Ingleborough and Settle, in the West Riding of Yorkshire. London: 1781. V. 47; 50

HUTTON, LAURENCE
From the Books of... London: 1892. V. 48

HUTTON, R. N.
Five Years in the East. London: 1847. V. 50

HUTTON, SAMUEL KING
Among the Eskimos of Labrador. London: 1912. V. 53

HUTTON, W.
The Battle of Bosworth Field Between Richard the Third and Henry, Earl of Richmond, August 22, 1485... London: 1813. V. 48

HUTTON, WILLIAM
The Beetham Repository. Kendal: 1906. V. 52
History of Derby, from the Remote Ages of Antiquity to 1791. London: 1791. V. 50
The History of the Roman Wall, Which Crosses the Island of Britain, from the German Ocean to the Irish Sea. London: 1802. V. 47
A Journey from Birmingham to London. Birmingham: 1785. V. 48; 51; 52
The Life of William Hutton, F.A.S.S.... London and Birmingham: 1817. V. 51
A Tour to Scarborough in 1803... London: 1817. V. 54
A Trip to Coatham, a Watering Place in the North Extremity of Yorkshire. London: 1810. V. 51; 53; 54

HUTTON, WILLIAM R.
The Washington Bridge Over the Harlem River, at 181st St., New York City. New York: 1889. V. 49

HUTYRA, FRANZ
Special Pathology and Therapeutics of the Diseases of Domestic Animals. Chicago: 1926. V. 52

HUXELY, ALDOUS LEONARD
Texts and Pretexts: an Anthology with Commentaries. London: 1932. V. 48

HUXHAM, JOHN
An Essay on Fevers and Their Various Kinds, as Depending on Different Constitutions on the Blood. London: 1750. V. 51; 53
An Essay on Fevers, To Which is Now Added, A Dissertation on the Malignant, Ulcerious Sore-Throat. London: 1764. V. 50; 54

HUXLEY, ALDOUS LEONARD
Adonis and the Alphabet, and Other Essays. London: 1956. V. 50
After Many a Summer. London: 1939. V. 49; 51
Along the Road. London: 1925. V. 48; 52; 53
Along the Road... New York: 1925. V. 53; 54
Antic Hay. London: 1923. V. 50; 52
Apennine. Gaylordsville: 1930. V. 48; 51; 53
Beyond the Mexique Bay. London: 1934. V. 51; 53; 54
Brave New World. 1932. V. 48; 49; 52; 53; 54
Brave New World. Garden City: 1932. V. 54
Brave New World. London: 1932. V. 47; 48; 49; 50; 51; 52; 53; 54
Brave New World. New York: 1932. V. 52; 54
Brave New World. New York: 1932. V. 54
Brave New World. London: 1952. V. 48
Brave New World. Avon: 1974. V. 48; 51; 53
Brave New World. Connecticut: 1974. V. 47
Brave New World. New York: 1974. V. 52; 53; 54
Brief Candles. London: 1930. V. 47; 48; 49; 53; 54
Brief Candles. New York: 1930. V. 48; 50; 53; 54
The Burning Wheel. Oxford: 1916. V. 51; 52
The Cicadas and Other Poems. London: 1931. V. 47; 51; 54
The Defeat of Youth and Other Poems. 1918. V. 53
The Defeat of Youth and other Poems. London: 1918. V. 51
The Defeat of Youth and Other Poems. Oxford: 1918. V. 48; 49; 52; 53
The Devils of Loudun. London: 1952. V. 51
The Discovery...a Comedy in Five Acts. 1924. V. 50
The Discovery...a Comedy in Five Acts. London: 1924. V. 52
Do What You Will. London: 1929. V. 48; 49; 53; 54
The Doors of Perception. London: 1954. V. 47
The Doors of Perception. New York: 1954. V. 50; 52
An Encyclopedia of Pacifism. London: 1937. V. 48; 51
Ends and Means. London: 1937. V. 48; 51; 53
Essays New and Old. London: 1926. V. 47; 54
Eyeless in Gaza. London: 1936. V. 49; 50; 51
Eyeless in Gaza. Toronto: 1936. V. 48
Heaven and Hell. London: 1956. V. 52
Holy Face. London: 1929. V. 50; 51; 53
Island. London: 1962. V. 51; 52
Jonah. Oxford: 1917. V. 48
Leda. 1929. V. 50
Limbo. London: 1920. V. 49; 50; 53
Little Mexican & Other Stories. London: 1924. V. 47; 50; 51; 52; 54
Mortal Coils. London: 1922. V. 49; 52
Music At Night and Other Essays. New York and London: 1931. V. 48; 50; 51; 54
The Olive Tree. London: 1936. V. 48; 51; 53; 54
On the Margin. London: 1923. V. 48; 51; 52; 53
Point Counter Point. London: 1928. V. 47; 52; 53; 54
Proper Studies. London: 1927. V. 49; 53
Proper Studies. Garden City: 1928. V. 48; 51
Selected Poems. New York: 1925. V. 50
Selected Poems. Oxford: 1926. V. 48; 52
Texts and Pretexts, an Anthology with Commentaries. London: 1932. V. 47; 48; 53
Themes and Variations. London: 1950. V. 47
Themes and Variations. New York: 1950. V. 52
Those Barren Leaves. London: 1925. V. 47; 49; 52
Those Barren Leaves. New York: 1925. V. 48; 53
Two or Three Graces and Other Stories. London: 1926. V. 48; 49; 50; 52; 53
Two or Three Graces and Other Stories. Toronto: 1926. V. 48
What Are You Going to Do About It?. London: 1936. V. 48; 51
Words and Their Meanings. Los Angeles: 1940. V. 48
The World of Light. London: 1931. V. 53

HUXLEY, C. R.
Ant-Plant Interactions. London: 1991. V. 50

HUXLEY, JULIAN
Official Guide to the Gardens and Aquarium of the Zoological Society of London. London: 1936. V. 47

HUXLEY, LEONARD
The Life and Letters of Thomas Henry Huxley. London: 1900. V. 51; 52; 53; 54
Life and Letters of Thomas Henry Huxley. New York: 1901. V. 53

HUXLEY, THOMAS HENRY
Critiques and Addresses. London: 1873. V. 52
Diary of the Voyage of H.M.S. Rattlesnake. London: 1935. V. 54
Evidence as to Man's Place in Nature. 1863. V. 54
Evidence As to Man's Place in Nature. London: 1863. V. 48; 49
An Introduction to the Classification of Animals. London: 1869. V. 49
Lay Sermons, Addresses and Reviews. London: 1870. V. 47
Lectures On the Elements of Comparative Anatomy... London: 1864. V. 52
A Manual of the Anatomy of Invertebrated Animals. London: 1877. V. 53
The Monkey. Northampton: 1959. V. 52
The Oceanic Hydrozoa...Observed During the Voyage of H.M.S. 'Rattlesnake'. London: 1859. V. 49
On Our Knowledge of the Causes of the Phenomena of Organic Nature. London: 1862. V. 49
On Our Knowledge of the Causes of the Phenomena of Organic Nature. London: 1863. V. 48; 49; 52; 53
On the Origin of Species. New York: 1869. V. 51
The Scientific Memoirs of Thomas Henry Huxley. London: 1898-1902. V. 48
Yoga: Hindu Delusions, With Its Explanations. London & Madras: 1902. V. 48

HUYGENS, CHRISTIAAN
The Celestial World Discover'd: or, Conjectures Concerning the Inhabitants, Plants and Productions of the Worlds in the Planets. London: 1697. V. 49
Cosmotheoros, Sive De Terris Coelestibus, Earumque Ornatu, Conjecturae. The Hague: 1698. V. 49; 50; 54
Opera Reliqua. Amsterdam: 1728. V. 54

HUYGHE, RENE
Delacroix. London: 1963. V. 50

HUYSHE, GEORGE L.
The Red River Expedition. London: 1871. V. 51; 53; 54

HUYSMANS, JORIS KARL
Against the Grain. 1922. V. 48; 50; 52
Against the Grain. New York: 1922. V. 51
Down There. (La Bas). 1924. V. 47; 50; 51
Down There (La Bas). New York: 1924. V. 52
Les Soeurs Vatard. Paris: 1909. V. 51

HUYSUM, JAN VAN
Jan Van Huysum 1682-1749, Including a Catalogue Raisonne of the Artist's Fruit and Flower Paintings. Leigh-on-Sea: 1954. V. 48

HYAMS, E.
The Orchard and Fruit Garden. London: 1961. V. 50; 51; 52; 54

HYAMS, EDWARD S.
The Wings of the Morning. London: 1939. V. 49

HYATT, H. S.
Manufacturing, Agricultural and Industrial Resources of Iowa. Des Moines: 1872/73. V. 53; 54

HYATT, THADDEUS
The Prayer of Thaddeus Hyatt to James Buchanan...in Behalf of Kansas, Asking for a Postponement of All the Land Sales in that Territory... Washington: 1860. V. 49; 52

HYATT, THEODORE
The Dragon-Fly, or Reactive Passive Locomotion. London: 1882. V. 47

HYDE, C. W. G.
History of the Great Northwest. Minneapolis: 1901. V. 52

HYDE, CATHERINE
Secret Memoirs of the Royal Family of France During the Revolution. London: 1895. V. 52

HYDE, DOUGLAS
Beside the Fire. London: 1890. V. 50
The Children of Lir. Dublin: 1940. V. 48
The Children of Tuireann. Dublin: 1941. V. 48; 50
The Three Sorrows of Storytelling and Ballads of St. Columkille. 1895. V. 52

HYDE, E. BELCHER
Atlas of the Borough of Brooklyn...Newly Constructed and Based Upon Official Maps and Plans on File. Brooklyn: 1903. V. 49
Atlas of the Rural Country District North of New York City, Embracing the Entire Westchester County, New York, also a Portion of Connecticut, Greenwich, Stamford, New Canaan, Darien, Wilton & Ridgefield. Philadelphia: 1908. V. 49

HYDE, GEORGE E.
The Early Blackfeet and Their Neighbors. Denver: 1933. V. 50
Rangers and Regulars. Denver: 1933. V. 50
Red Cloud's Folk - a History of the Ogalla Sioux. Norman: 1937. V. 54

HYDE, J. A. LLOYD
Oriental Lowestoft, with Special Reference to the Trade With China and the Porcelain Decorated for the American Market. New York: 1936. V. 52

HYDE, LAURENCE
Southern Cross: a Novel of the south Seas. Los Angeles: 1951. V. 51

HYDE, NANCY MARIA
The Writings of Nancy Maria Hyde of Norwich, Connecticut. Norwich: 1816. V. 53

HYDE Nugent. *A Tale of a Fashionable Life.* London: 1827. V. 51

HYDE, THOMAS
De Ludis Orientalibus Libri Duo. Oxonii: 1694. V. 47
Historia Religionis Veterum Persarum, Eorumque Magorum... Oxford: 1700. V. 47

HYETT, FRANCIS ADAMS
The Bibliographer's Manual of Gloucestershire Literature. Gloucester: 1895-97. V. 50; 51; 54

HYGINUS, GAIUS JULIUS
Poetica Astronomica. Venice: 1482. V. 48
The Poeticon Astronomicon. 1985. V. 52; 54
The Poeticon Astronomicon. Greenbrae: 1985. V. 47

HYMAN, A.
The Failing Heart of Middle Life: The Myocardiosis Syndrome, Coronary Thrombosis and Angina Pectoris with a Section Upon the Medico-Legal Aspects of Sudden Death from Heart Disease. Philadelphia: 1933. V. 53

HYMAN, COLEMAN P.
An Account of the Coins, Coinages and Currency of Australasia. Sydney: 1893. V. 54

HYMAN, L.
The Invertebrates. New York: 1940-55. V. 53

HYMAN, S.
Edward Lear's Birds. London: 1980. V. 49

HYMEN'S Praeludia; or, Love's Mafter-Piece. Being that So-Much-Admired Romance Intituled, Cleopatra, in Twelve Parts. London: 1687. V. 49

HYMERS, JOHN
The Elements of the Theory of Astronomy. Cambridge: 1840. V. 54
A Treatise on Differential Equations, and on the Calculus of Finite Differences. Cambridge: 1839. V. 47

A HYMN to the Chair: or, Lucubrations, Serious and Comical, On the Use of Chairs, Benches, Forms, Joint-Stools, Three-Legged Stools, and Ducking Stools. 1732. V. 50; 54

THE HYMNARY. A Book of Church Song. London: 1872. V. 50; 52; 54

HYMNS and Prayers for Use at the Marriage of Michael Hornby and Nicolette Ward at St. Margaret's Church Westminster. November XV. MCMXXVIII. Shelley House, Chelsea: 1928. V. 51

HYMNS Composed by Different Authors, at the Request of the General Convention of Universalists of the New England States and Others... Charleston: 1810. V. 53

HYMNS on Select Passages of Scripture... Chambersburg: 1811. V. 53

HYNDMAN, HENRY MAYERS
The Economics of Socialism: Being a Series of Seven Lectures on Political Economy. London: 1896. V. 52
The Record of an Adventurous Life. (with) Further Reminiscences. London: 1911-12. V. 49; 52

HYNE, C. C.
The New Eden. 1892. V. 52

HYNEMAN, LEON
The Universal Masonic Record: or, Links in the Golden Chain of Brotherhood... Philadelphia: 1857. V. 51

HYNES, MICHAEL J.
The Mission of Rinuccini, Nuncio Extraordinary to Ireland, 1645-1649. Dublin: 1932. V. 51

HYNES, W. J.
Catalogue of Architectural Relief Decorations in Staff, Cements, Etc. Toronto: 1920. V. 48

I

THE I CHING or Book of Changes. New York: 1950. V. 49

IBANEZ, VICENTE BLASCO
The Four Horsemen of the Apocalypse. London: 1919. V. 50

IBBETSON, J.
A Picturesque Guide to Bath, Bristol, Hot-Wells. London: 1793. V. 48

IBBETSON, J. H.
Specimens in Eccentric Circular Turning... London: 1838. V. 52

IBBETSON, JULIUS CAESAR
An Accidence, or Gamut of Painting in Oil and Watercolours. London: 1803. V. 47

IBBETT, VERA
Flowers in Heraldry. Vancouver: 1977. V. 47

IBBETT, W. J.
Ibbett's Jessie. Flansham, Sussex: 1923. V. 48
Ten Lyrics. Taunton: 1924. V. 51

IBBOT, BENJAMIN
A Course of Sermons Preach'd for the Lecture Founded by the Honourable Robert Boyle Esq.... London: 1727. V. 47; 48

IBN KHALDUN
The Muqaddimah. An Introduction to History. New York: 1958. V. 48

IBSEN, HENRIK
Brand, a Dramatic Poem... London: 1891. V. 53
A Doll's House. London: 1889. V. 47
The Doll's House. New York: 1889. V. 51; 52
Hedda Gabler. Kobenhavn: 1890. V. 47; 49; 52; 53
John Gabriel Borkman. Copenhagen: 1896. V. 47
Lyrical Poems. London: 1902. V. 47
The Master Builder. London: 1893. V. 51
Peer Gynt. Kjobenhavn: 1867. V. 47
Peer Gynt. New York: 1929. V. 50; 54
Peer Gynt. London: 1936. V. 48; 51; 52
Peer Gynt. Philadelphia: 1936. V. 51
The Pillars of Society, and Other Plays. London: 1888. V. 51
Poems. New York: 1988. V. 50; 54
Three Plays. Oslo: 1964. V. 52
The Works. New York: 1911. V. 49
The Works... New York: 1917. V. 48; 50

IBY TUFAYL, MUHAMMUD IBN ABD AL-MALIK
The Improvement of Human Reason, Exhibited in the Life of Hai Ebn Yokdhan: Written in Arabick above 500 Years Ago... London: 1711. V. 52

ICEBERG SLIM
Pimp. The Story of My Life. Los Angeles: 1967. V. 54

ICELANDIC Sagas and Other Historical Documents Relating to the Settlements and Descents of the Northmen on the British Isles. London: 1887-94. V. 52

ICONES Roxburghianae or Drawings of Indian Plants. Fascicles 2-8. Calcutta: 19678-78. V. 50

IDDESLEIGH, EARL OF
Charms - Or an Old World Sensation. London: 1905. V. 49

IDE, SIMEON
A Biographical Sketch of the Life of William B. Ide: with a Minute and Interesting Account of One of the Largest Emigrating Companies. Claremont: 1880. V. 47

IDEAS for Rustic Furniture Proper for Garden Seats, Summer Houses, Hermitages, Cottages, &c. London: 1795. V. 48

IDEAS for Rustic Furniture Proper for Garden Seats, Summer Houses, Hermitages, Cottages, &c. London: 1838. V. 47

IDES, E. YSBRANDT
Three Years Travels from Moscow Over-Land to China...an Exact and Particular Description of the Extent and Limits of Those Countries and the Customs of the Barbarous Inhabitants... London: 1706. V. 52

IF it Happened Otherwise. 1931. V. 47; 53

IGNATIUS, SAINT OF ANTIOCH
Epistolae Undecim. Item Una...Polycarpi...Epistola. Basle: 1520. V. 49

IGNATOW, DAVID
Rescue the Dead. Brockport: 1979. V. 51
Ten Poems. New York: 1981. V. 52

IGNOTUS, PSEUD.
Poems. By Ignotus. Cork: 1870. V. 49
Purgatorial Purification of Irish Convicts; Being Remarks on a Pamphlet Entitled the Purgatory of Prisoners, Etc. by the Rev. Orby Shipley. London: 1858. V. 48

IKIN, ARTHUR
Texian Immigrant Guides. Waco: 1963. V. 47

ILCHESTER, EARL OF
Letters to Henry Fox Lord Holland, with a Few Addressed to His Brother Stephen, Earl of Ilchester. London: 1915. V. 51

ILIC, J.
CSIRO Atlas of Hardwoods. East Melbourne: 1991. V. 50

ILION, HERKIMER CO.
Price List 1877. Ilion: 1877. V. 51

I'LL Take My Stand by Twelve Southerners. New York: 1930. V. 51

THE ILLEGAL Marriage; or, the Adventures of a Young Lady of Fortune; Who Was Seduced from Her Parents by a Military Officer; and, with Her Children Perished in the Forests of America. Portsea: 1810. V. 48

ILLINGWORTH, A. HOLDEN
More Reminiscences. 1936. V. 52
More Reminiscences. Bradford: 1936. V. 51; 52
More Reminiscences. London: 1936. V. 51; 54
Reminiscences. London: 1932. V. 50; 53

ILLINGWORTH, CAYLEY
A Topographical Account of the Parish of Scampton in the County of Lincoln, and of the Roman Antiquities Lately Discovered There. London: 1810. V. 50; 52

ILLINGWORTH, WILLIAM
Placitorum In Domo Capitulari Westmonasteriensi Asservatorum Abbreviatio. London: 1811. V. 51

ILLINOIS
The Constitution of the State of Illinois, Adopted in Convention, at Kaskaskia on the Twenty-Sixth Day of August, in the Year of Our Lord, One Thousand Eight Hundred and Eighteen... Kaskaskia: 1818. V. 51

ILLINOIS CENTRAL RAILROAD CO.
Annual Report. 1908-1916. V. 54
A Guide to the Illinois Central Railroad Lands. Chicago: 1859. V. 49
The Illinois Central Railroad Company Offers for Sale Over 1,500,000 Acres Selected Farming and Wood Lands... Boston: 1857. V. 49

ILLINOIS. LAWS, STATUTES, ETC.
Private Laws of the State of Illinois. Springfield: 1863. V. 49
Public Laws of the State of Illinois Passed at the 21st Session of the General Assembly, 1859. Chicago: 1859. V. 49

ILLINOIS, MISSOURI & TEXAS RAILWAY CO.
Prospectus, Reports and Other Documents. St. Louis: 1873. V. 47

ILLINOIS SUNDAY SCHOOL UNION
Proceedings of the Fourth Annual Meeting of the Illinois Sunday School Union, Held at the State House in Vandalia, Dec. 4, 1833. Rock Spring: 1834. V. 52

ILLINOIS UNIVERSITY. LIBRARY
The Mereness Calendar: Federal Documents on the Upper Mississippi Valley 1780-1890. Boston: 1971. V. 53

ILLUSIONS of Sentiment, a Descriptive and Historical Novel. London: 1788. V. 49

THE ILLUSTRATED Atlas and History of Yolo County, California. San Francisco: 1879. V. 48

AN ILLUSTRATED Catalogue of Microscopes and Optical Instruments. Philadelphia: 1880. V. 53

ILLUSTRATED Ditties of the Olden Time. London: 1854. V. 48; 50; 52

THE ILLUSTRATED Exhibitor, a Tribute to the World's Industrial Jubilee; Comprising Sketches by Pen and Pencil of the Principal Objects of the Great Exhibition...1851. London: 1851. V. 48

ILLUSTRATED Guide to the Senate and House of Commons Canada. Ottawa: 1886. V. 53

THE ILLUSTRATED Guide to the Shootings of Scotland. 1905. V. 54

AN ILLUSTRATED History of Sonoma County, California. Chicago: 1889. V. 49

AN ILLUSTRATED Itinerary of the County of Lancaster. London: 1842. V. 53

ILLUSTRATED Songs and Hymns for the Little Ones. London: 1858. V. 49

ILLUSTRATED Souvenir Book Showing a Few Pasadena Homes, Schools, Churches etc. Pasadena: 1903. V. 54

AN ILLUSTRATION of Osbourne's Pictorial Alphabet. London: 1835. V. 47

ILLUSTRATIONS of Egyptian Antiquities. Bath: 1822. V. 50

ILLUSTRATIONS of Japanese Aquatic Plants and Animals. Tokyo: 1935. V. 52

ILLUSTRATIONS of Japanese Life. Tokyo: 1896. V. 47

ILLUSTRATIONS of Northern Antiquities, from the Earlier Teutonic and Scandinavian Romances... Edinburgh: 1814. V. 47; 54

ILLUSTRATIONS of Northern Antiquities, from the Earlier Teutonic and Scandinavian Romances. Edinburgh: 1848. V. 52

ILLUSTRATIONS of the Isle of Wight; from Original Drawings by Leitch, Clint, Cooke, Barry, &c. Ryde: 1858. V. 48

ILLUSTRATIONS of the Landscape and Coast Scenery of Ireland. Dublin: 1843. V. 54

ILLUSTRATIVE Cloud Forms, for the Guidance of Observers in the Classification of Clouds. Washington: 1897. V. 51; 53

IM Zoologischen Garten. Eklingen: 1890. V. 48

IMAGE DU MONDE
Mirroure of the Worlde. Oxford: 1980. V. 48

THE IMAGE of the Malignants peace: Or a Respresentation of the Seditious Carriages of the London Cavaliers, in Their First Endeavours for the Saccage and Plunder of the City, Under the Specious Vizor of a Petition for Peace and Accomodation. London: 1642. V. 49

IMAGE, SELWYN
Art, Morals and the War. London: 1914. V. 50

IMAGIST Anthology 1930. New York: 1930. V. 53

IMBERDIS, S. J.
Papyrus, or the Craft of Paper. Hilversum: 1952. V. 48
Papyrus or the Craft of Paper. North Hills: 1961. V. 54

IMITATIO CHRISTI
The Christians Pattern...Imitation of Christ. London: 1654. V. 51
The Christians Pattern...Imitation of Christ. London: 1677. V. 54
The Christians Pattern...Imitation of...Christ. London: 1707. V. 51
Counsels Selected from the Imitation of Christ. London: 1866. V. 53
De Imitatione Christi Libri Quatuor. Parma: 1793. V. 52
L'Imitation de Jesus Christ... Paris: 1643. V. 48
L'Imitation de Jesus Christ. Rouen: 1651. V. 49
L'Imitation de Jesus Christ. Paris: 1856-58. V. 47; 50; 52; 53; 54
The Imitation of Christ. London. V. 52
The Imitation of Christ. London: 1893. V. 49; 50
The Imitation of Christ. Oxford: 1900. V. 51
Of the Imitation of Christ. Philadelphia: 1783. V. 50; 53
Of the Imitation of Christ. London: 1825. V. 48
Of the Imitation of Christ. London: 1890. V. 48
Of the Imitation of Christ. London: 1898. V. 48
Of the Imitation of Christ. Boston: 1899. V. 50; 54
Of the Imitation of Christ. London: 1902. V. 50
Of the Imitation of Christ. London: 1908. V. 51
Of the Imitation of...Christ. London: 1828. V. 49; 51

IMLAH, JOHN
May Flowers. Poems and Songs: Some in the Scottish Dialect. London: 1827. V. 54

IMLAY, GILBERT
A Topographical Description of the Western Territory of North America... London: 1792. V. 48
A Topographical Description of the Western Territory of North America. London: 1797. V. 47

IMMERWAHR, HENRY R.
Attic Script: a Survey. Oxford: 1990. V. 50

IMMERWAHR, SARA ANDERSON
The Neolithic and Bronze Ages. Princeton: 1971. V. 52

IMMIGRATION AND DEVELOPMENT ASSOCIATION
Harris County Houston, Texas Home Seekers Journal. Houston: 1888. V. 52

IMMIGRATION ASSOCIATION OF CALIFORNIA
Resources of the Sacramento Valley and Tributary Country, California. San Francisco: 1884. V. 54
Resources of the Southern San Joaquin Valley, California. Fresno. Tulare and Kern Counties. San Francisco: 1885. V. 50

IMMORTELLES From Charles Dickens. London: 1856. V. 50

AN IMPARTIAL Account of the Horrid and Detestable Conspiracy to Assassinate His Sacred Majesty King William, Raise a Rebellion in England, Scotland and Ireland, and to Encourage an Invasion from France. London: 1695. V. 53

AN IMPARTIAL Account, of the Nature and Tendency, of the Late Addresses; in a Letter to a Gentleman in the Countrey. London: 1681. V. 52

AN IMPARTIAL History of the War in America Between Great Britain and Her Colonies, From Its Commencement to the End of the Year 1779. London: 1780. V. 54

IMPEY, ELIJAH BARWELL
Poems. London: 1811. V. 54

IMPEY, JOHN
The Office of Sheriff, Shewing its History and Antiquity. London: 1786. V. 48
The Office of Sheriff, Shewing its History and Antiquity... Dublin: 1797. V. 50
The Practice of the Office of Sheriff and Under Sheriff... London: 1817. V. 50

THE IMPORTANCE Of Sunday Schools at the Present Crisis... Canterbury: 1794. V. 48

IMPORTANT Communication, from the Highest Authortiy, to Those Who Are Embracing Arms in Defence of Their Country; as Well as to All Military Men. London: 1804. V. 52

IMPRENTA REAL
Muestras de Los Punzones y Matrices de la letra Que Se Funde en el Obrador. Madrid: 1799. V. 48

IMPRESSIONS De Voyages Promenades Pittoresques en France. Paris. V. 48

THE IMPRINT. 1913. V. 52
THE IMPRINT. London: 1913. V. 51
THE IMPRINT. London: 1913-Nov. 1913. V. 51

THE IMPROVED Reading and Spelling Made Easy. Dublin: 1840. V. 48; 50; 52

IM THURN, EVERARD F.
Birds of Marlborough... Marlborough: 1870. V. 51

IN DEFENCE of Woman. Waltham St. Lawrence: 1960. V. 54

IN Memoriam 1899-1977. New York: 1977. V. 48

IN Memoriam Dora Sigerson 1918-1923. Died January 6th, 1918. 1923. V. 50

IN Memoriam. Funeral Services of Phineas Taylor Barnum. April 10th, 1891. 1891. V. 48

IN Memoriam of John Rylands Born February 7, 1801. Died December 11, 1888. Manchester: 1889. V. 51

IN PETRA: Being a Sequel to 'Nisi Dominius'. Ditchling: 1923. V. 49

IN Principio. Hammersmith: 1911. V. 51

IN REMEMBRANCE of the Midwinter International Exposition. San Francisco, California, 1894. San Francisco. V. 51

IN THE LAND of Burns. London: 1896. V. 51; 54

IN the Matter of the Mission of St. James at Vancouver, Washington, Under the Act of August 14, 1848. Hopkins, Murphy and Hopkins, Attorneys. 189-. V. 48

INAN, JALE
Roman and Early Byzantine Portrait Sculpture in Asia Minor. London: 1970. V. 52

INATULLA
Tales (the "Baar Danesh"). London: 1768. V. 53

THE INAUGURATION of the Eudora Welty Chair in Southern Studies. Jackson: 1982. V. 49

INCHBALD, ELIZABETH
Nature and Art. London: 1797. V. 54
Simple Histoire. Paris: 1795. V. 50
A Simple Story. Dublin: 1791. V. 48
A Simple Story. London: 1791. V. 47; 48

INCIDENT on the Bark Columbia. Cummington: 1941. V. 52

INCIDENTS and Sketches Connected with the Early History and Settlement of the West. Cincinnati: 1847. V. 52

INDEX Expurgatorius Librorum Qui Hoc Saeculo Prodierunt, Vel Doctrinae Non Sanae Erroribus Inspersis, Vel Inutilis & Offensivae Maledictentiae Fellibus Permixitis...In Belgia Concinnatus Anno MDLXXI... Strassburg: 1599. V. 47

INDEX Kewensis, an Enumeration of the Genera and Species of Flowering Plants from the Time of Linnaeus to 1885. London: 1893-95. V. 53

INDIA. CONGRESS
Proceedings of the First Indian National Congress, Held at Bombay on the 28th, 29th and 30th December, 1885. Bombay: 1885. V. 47

INDIA HOUSE
A Descriptive Catalogue of the Marine Collection to be Found at India House. 1935. V. 54

INDIAN Antiquities: or, Dissertations, Relative to the Ancient Geographical Divisions, the Pure System of Primeval Theology, the Grand Code of Civil Laws, the Original Form of Government... London: 1800. V. 51

INDIAN Basket Weaving by the Navajo School of Indian Basketry. Los Angeles: 1903. V. 52

THE INDIAN Fairy Book, from the Original Legends. New York: 1856. V. 54

INDIAN Population in the United States and Alaska 1910. Washington: 1915. V. 52

INDIAN TERRITORY
The Eighth Annual Report of the Superintendent and Agents of the Central Indian Superintendency... Lawrence: 1876. V. 52
Journal of the Fifth (&) Sixth Annual Session of the General Council of the Indian Territory, Composed of Delegates Duly Elected From the Indian Tribes Legally Resident Therein, Assembled in Council at Okmulgee, Indian Territory. Lawrence: 1874/75. V. 48
Journal of the Fifth Annual Session of the General Council of the Indian Territory, Composed of Delegates Duly Elected from the Indian Tribes Legally Resident Therein, Assembled in Council at Okmulgee, Indian Territory, from the 4th to 14th of May 1874. Lawrence: 1874. V. 52
Journal of the Sixth Annual Session of the General Council of the Indian Territory, Composed of Delegates Duly Elected from the Indian Tribes Legally Resident Therein, Assembled in Council on Okmulgee, Indian Territory from 3rd to 15th May, 1875. Lawrence: 1875. V. 52

INDIAN Tribal Series. Phoenix: 1971-76. V. 53

INDIANA. LAWS, STATUTES, ETC.
The Revised Laws of Indiana, in Which are Comprised All Such Acts of a General Nature As Are in Force in Said State; Adopted and Enacted by the General Assembly at their Fifteenth Session. Indianapolis: 1831. V. 52

INDICE de Las Ordenes y Decretos Espedidos por el Honorable Congeso de Este Estado, Desde el Ano de 1824, Hasta fin de el de 1828. Leona Vicario: 1829. V. 48

INDUSTRIAL Great Britain, A Commercial Review of leading Firms Selected From Important Towns of England. London: 1894. V. 50

INDUSTRIES of New Jersey. Part V. Essex County, Including City of Newark, the Oranges, Montclair, Bloomfield and Belleville. New York: 1882. V. 49

INETT, JOHN
Origines Anglicanae; or, a History of the English Church. London: 1710. V. 47

AN INFALLIBLE Remedy for the High Prices of Provisions. Together With a Scheme for Laying Open the Trade to the East-Indies; with an Address to the Electors of Great Britain. London: 1768. V. 51; 52

INFANCY.. New York: 1817. V. 48

INFANTE, G. CABRERA
Three Trapped Tigers. New York: 1971. V. 53
View of Dawn in the Tropics. New York: 1974. V. 53

INFANTINE Complaints; or, Rather, Complaints of Infants, and Hints to Mothers. London: 1842. V. 47

INFANTRY Exercise of the United States Army Abridged for the Use of the Militia of the United States. Poughkeepsie: 1817. V. 50

THE INFANT'S Grammar, or a Pic-nic Party of the Parts of Speech. London: 1822. V. 52

THE INFANT'S Grammar; or A Pic-nic Party of the Parts of Speech. London: 1850. V. 50

THE INFANT'S Library. Book 1. London: 1800. V. 49
THE INFANT'S Library. Book 10. London: 1800. V. 49
THE INFANT'S Library. Book 11. London: 1800. V. 49
THE INFANT'S Library. Book 12. London: 1800. V. 49
THE INFANT'S Library. Book 13. London: 1800. V. 49
THE INFANT'S Library. Book 14. London: 1800. V. 49
THE INFANT'S Library. Book 15. London: 1800. V. 49
THE INFANT'S Library. Book 16. London: 1800. V. 49
THE INFANT'S Library. Book 2. London: 1800. V. 49
THE INFANT'S Library. Book 3. London: 1800. V. 49
THE INFANT'S Library. Book 5. London: 1800. V. 49
THE INFANT'S Library. Book 6. London: 1800. V. 49
THE INFANT'S Library. Book 7. London: 1800. V. 49
THE INFANT'S Library. Book 8. London: 1800. V. 49
THE INFANT'S Library. Book 9. London: 1800. V. 49

INFIDELITY and Abolitionism. An Open Letter to the Friends of Religion, Morality and the American Union. Washington: 1856. V. 48

ING, JANET
Johann Gutenberg and His Bible. A Historical Study. New York: 1988. V. 50

INGALL, ELFRIC DREW
Report On Mines and Mining on Lake Superior. Montreal: 1888. V. 53

INGALLS, RACHEL
Binstead's Safari. London: 1983. V. 54
Black Diamond. London: 1992. V. 54
Mrs. Caliban. London: 1982. V. 50; 54
Theft. London: 1970. V. 50; 54

INGATE, EDMOND
Maximes of Reason, or the Reason of the Common Law of England. London: 1658. V. 50

INGE, WILLIAM
Bus Stop. New York: 1955. V. 53
Come Back Little Sheba. New York: 1950. V. 52; 53
The Dark at the Top of the Stairs. New York: 1958. V. 54
Good Luck Miss Wyckoff. Boston: 1970. V. 48; 53
A Loss of Roses. New York: 1960. V. 54
Natural Affection. New York: 1963. V. 54
Summer Brave and Eleven Short Plays. New York: 1962. V. 54
Where's Daddy?. New York: 1966. V. 54

INGEGNERI, ANGELO
Del Buon Segretario Libri Tre. 1594. V. 47

L'INGEGNERIA
a Venzia dell' Ultimo Ventennio. Venice: 1887. V. 53

INGELEFIELD, JOHN NICHOLSON
Capt. Inglefield's Narrative, Concerning the Loss of H.M.S. the Centaur of Seventy-Four Guns... London: 1783. V. 52

INGELOW, JEAN
A Story of Doom and Other Poems. London: 1867. V. 53

INGERSOLL, CHARLES J.
Inchiquin, the Jesuit's Letters, During a Late Residence in the United States of America... New York: 1810. V. 47

INGERSOLL, LUTHER A.
Ingersoll's Century History. Los Angeles: 1908. V. 54

INGERSOLL, ROBERT H.
The Works. New York: 1902. V. 51

INGHAM, ALFRED
Cheshire, Its Traditions and History. Edinburgh: 1920. V. 53

INGHIRAMI, FRANCESCO
Monumenti Etruschi o di Etrusco Nome. Badia Fiesolana: 1821-26. V. 53

INGHOLT, HARALD
Gandharan Art in Pakistan. New York: 1957. V. 48; 52

INGHRAM, J. H.
Alice, May and Bruising Bill. Boston: 1845. V. 51

INGLE, R.
Larval Stages of North East Atlantic Crabs, an Illustrated key. London: 1991. V. 48; 50; 52

INGLEBY, LEONARD CRESSWELL
Oscar Wilde. London: 1907. V. 51

INGLEDEW, C. J. DAVISON
The History and Antiquities of North Allerton, in the County of York. London: 1858. V. 50

INGLEFIELD, JOHN NICHOLSON
Capt. Inglefield's Narrative, Concerning the Loss of H.M.S. The Centaur, of Seventy-Four Guns... London: 1783. V. 51

INGLETON, GEOFFREY C.
Catalogue of Select Books from the Ingleton Collection. Sydney: 1971-77. V. 47

INGLIS, HENRY DAVID
The Channel Islands. London: 1834. V. 49
Ireland in 1834. A Journey Throughout Ireland, During the Spring, Summer and Autumn of 1834. London: 1834. V. 48; 50; 53
Rambles in the Footsteps of Don Quixote. London: 1837. V. 48; 53

INGLIS, J.
Illustrated Ditties of Ye Olden Time with Steel Engravings. London. V. 54

INGLIS, JAMES
Tent Life in Tigerland... 1892. V. 54
Thoughts on John XVII with a Revised Version from a Critical Greek Text and the Authorized Version. New York: 1871. V. 51

INGLIS, JOHN
Commerce As It Was, Is and Ought to Be. London: 1811. V. 50; 54
An Examination of Mr. Dugald Stewart's Pamphlet, Relative to the Late Election of a Mathemataical Professor in the University of Edinburgh. Edinburgh: 1805. V. 52

INGMIRE, FRANCES
Texas Rangers: Frontier Battalion, Minute Men, Commanding Officers,, 1847-1900. St. Louis: 1982. V. 53

INGPEN, ARTHUR ROBERT
Master Worsley's Book. London: 1910. V. 50; 53

INGPEN, ROGER
William Thomas Horton - a Selection of His Work. London: 1920?. V. 48

INGRAHAM, HENRY ANDREWS
American Trout Streams. New York: 1926. V. 51; 53

INGRAHAM, JOSEPH HOLT
The Clipper-Yacht; or Moloch, the Money Lender!. Boston: 1845. V. 51; 52
Edward Austin: or, the Hunting Flask. Boston: 1845. V. 48
Joseph Ingraham's Journal of the Britantine Hope on a Voyage to the Northwest Coast of North America 1790-92. Barre: 1971. V. 52; 54
Kyd the Buccanier; or, the Wizard of the Sea. London: 1839. V. 53
The Seven Knights; or Tales of Many Lands. Boston: 1845. V. 51
The South-West. New York: 1835. V. 51; 52; 53
The Treason of Arnold. Jonesville: 1847. V. 49

INGRAM, BRUCE
Three Sea Journals of Stuart Times. London: 1936. V. 50

INGRAM, DALE
Practical Cases and Observations in Surgery with Remarks Highly Proper... London: 1751. V. 52; 53

INGRAM, GEORGE W.
Civil War Letters of George W. and Martha F. Ingram, 1861-65. College Station: 1973. V. 49

INGRAM, HENRY
Matilda, a Tale of the Crusades, a Poem in Six Books. London: 1830. V. 54

INGRAM, J.
Flora Symbolica: or, the Language and Sentiment of Flowers with Original Illustrations Printed in Colours by Terry. London. V. 53

INGRAM, JAMES
Memorials of Oxford. Oxford: 1837. V. 48; 49; 50; 51; 52; 54

INGRAM, JOHN H.
Edgar Allan Poe: His Life, Letters and Opinions. London: 1880. V. 47; 48
Edgar Allan Poe: His Life, Letters and Opinions. London: 1891. V. 48
Oliver Madox Brown. A Biographical Sketch. London: 1883. V. 49
The Raven by Edgar Allan Poe with Literary and Historical Commentary by John H. Ingram. London: 1885. V. 48

INGRAM, JOHN K.
A History of Political Economy. Edinburgh: 1888. V. 53

INGRAM, THOMAS L.
So My Thoughts: a Selection of Verse and prose. Vienna: 1948. V. 48

THE INHABITANTS
of the Deep, Being the Natural History of the Most Remarkable Fishes. London: 1818. V. 54

INMAN, HENRY
Buffalo Jones' Forty Years of Adventure. London: 1899. V. 52
Buffalo Jones' Forty Years of Adventure. Topeka: 1899. V. 47; 48; 53
The Great Salt Lake Trail. New York: 1898. V. 47
The Old Santa Fe Trail: the Story of a Great Highway. New York: 1897. V. 52

INMAN, THOMAS
Ancient Faiths Emboidied in Ancient Names... London: 1872-69. V. 53

INMAN, W. S.
Report of the Committee of the House of Commons, On Ventialtion, Warming and Transmission of Sound... London: 1836. V. 53

INN, H.
Chinese Houses and Gardens. New York: 1950. V. 51; 54

INNERLEITHEN ALPINE CLUB
Principal Excursions of the Innerleithen Alpine Club During the Years 1889-94. 1895. V. 53
Principal Excursions of the Innerleithen Alpine Club During the Years 1889-94. London: 1895. V. 52

INNES, ANNE
Sam's Annual Peerage of the British Empire. London: 1827. V. 47

INNES, COSMO
Lectures on Scotch Legal Antiquities. Edinburgh: 1872. V. 49; 52

INNES, GEORGE
The Works of George Innes: an Illustrated Catalogue Raisonne. Austin: 1965. V. 50; 52; 53

INNES, HAMMOND
The Conquistadors. London: 1969. V. 52

INNES, JOHN
Eight Anatomical Tables of the Human Body... Edinburgh: 1776. V. 54

INNES, MICHAEL
A Night of Errors. London: 1948. V. 54
Three Came Both Mist and Snow. London: 1940. V. 51

INNES, P. R.
The History of the Bengal European Regiment, Now the Royal Munster Fusiliers and How It Helped to Win India. London: 1885. V. 47

INNES, THOMAS
An Excursion in the Levant. Aberdeen: 1904. V. 54

INNIS, HAROLD A.
The Fur Trade in Canada: an Introduction to Canadian Economic History. New Haven: 1930. V. 50; 51; 52
Peter Pond. Fur Trader and Adventurer. Toronto: 1930. V. 50; 54

THE INNKEEPERS
Opinion of the Triennial Act. London: 1716. V. 53

INNOCENCE
Betrayed, and Infamy Avowed: Being the History of Miss Maria Thornhill, Contained in a Genuine Account of Her Seduction and the Barbarous Treatment She Afterwards met with from Mr. Sprightly. London: 1771. V. 47

THE INNOCENT
Epicure; or, The Art of Angling. London: 1697. V. 47

INNOMINATUS
In the Light of the Twentieth Century. London: 1886. V. 54

INNYS, WILLIAM
A Catalogue of Books Printer for and Sold by...at the West End of St. Paul's. London: 1742. V. 54

INOUE, MUNEKAZU
Castles of Japan. Tokyo: 1960. V. 48

AN INQUIRY Into the Fitness of Attending Parliament: in a Letter from a member to His Friend, Who Has Absented. London: 1739. V. 48

AN INQUIRY Into the Original Production of Insects in Human Bodies, Especially of the Seminal Animalcula. London: 1727. V. 51

AN INQUIRY Into the Rights of Free Subjects; in Which the Cases of the British Sailors and Common Soldiers are Distinctly Consider'd and Compar'd. London: 1749. V. 52

INQUISITIONS and Assessments Relating to Feudal Aids. London: 1899-1920. V. 52

INSCRIPTIONS on the Great Picture at Appleby Castle, Painted for the Right Honourable George Clifford, Third Earl of Cumberland. Appleby: 1877. V. 52

INSECTS Of Australia. London: 1992. V. 48; 50

INSIDE Sebastopol and Experiences in Camp. London: 1856. V. 54

THE INSIDE Story of the 1937 Studebaker: a Manual for the Use of Studebaker Salesmen. Chicago: 1936?. V. 53

INSTITORIS, HENRICUS KRAMER, CALLED
Malleus Maleficarum. Bungay: 1928. V. 51

INSTITUT DE FRANCE
Dictionnaire de l'Academie Francaise. Paris: 1835. V. 51

THE INSTITUTION of the Society of the Cincinnati. Formed by the Officers of the Army of the United States, for the Laudable Purposes Therein Mentioned. Boston: 1801. V. 48

INSTRUCTION for Heavy Artillery: Prepared by a Board of Officers, for the Use of the Army of the United States. Richmond: 1862. V. 49

INSTRUCTIONS for Officers and Non-Commissioned Officers On Outpost and Patrol Duty and Troops in Campaign. Washington: 1863. V. 52

INSTRUCTIONS For Such Merchants and Others Who Shall Have Commissions, or Letters of Marque, or Commissions for Private Men of War Against Against the French King His Subjects...Given at Our Court at Whitehal the 2d Day of May 1693... 1693. V. 52

INSTRUCTIONS for Surgeons Under the Commissioners for Conducting His Majesty's Transport Service, for Taking Care of Sick and Wounded Seamen, and for the Care and Custody of Prisoners of War... London: 1809. V. 51; 53

INSTRUCTIONS for the Commanders of Merchant Ships...Who Shall Have Letters of Marque and Reprizals...Against the Countries Stiling Themselves the Liguarian and italian Republicks... London: 1803. V. 51

THE INSTRUCTIVE Picture Book. Lessons From the Geographical Distribution of Animals, or the Natural History of the Quadrupeds which Characterise the Principal Divisions of the Globe. Edinburgh: 1867. V. 47

THE INTELLECTUAL Observer; Review of Natural History, Microscopic Research and Recreative Science. London: 1862-68. V. 54

INTER-STATE CONVENTION OF CATTLEMEN
Papers Relating to a Proposed System of Bureaus for Information and Statistics in Live Stock... 1892. V. 50

INTERCONTINENTAL RAILWAY COMMISSION, WASHINGTON, D. C.
Transactions of the Commission and of the Surveys and Explorations Of Its Engineers in Central and South America, 1891-1898. Washington: 1895-1898. V. 47

THE INTEREST of Great Britain Considered with Regard to her Colonies and the Acquisitions of Canada and Guadaloupe... Boston: 1760. V. 48

THE INTEREST of Great Britain Considered With Regard to Her Colonies and The Acquisitions of Canada and Guadaloupe. London: 1760. V. 53

THE INTERESTING and Affecting History of Prince Lee Boo, a Native of the Pelew Islands, Brought to England by Capt. Wilson. London: 1789. V. 51

THE INTERESTING History of the Princess de Ponthieu. Hartford: 1801. V. 54

THE INTERESTING Life, Travels, Voyages and Daring Engagements, of the Celebrated and Justly Notorious Pirate, Paul Jones... New York: 1807. V. 53

INTERESTING Particulars of the Glorious Victory, Obtained Over the Batavian Fleet, on the 11th of October, 1797, by the British Fleet, Under the Command of Admiral Duncan. Gosport: 1797. V. 54

INTERESTING State Papers, from President Washington, M. Fauchet and M. Adet, the Late and Present Ambassadors From the French Convention to the United States of America. London: 1796. V. 49

The **INTERESTING** Story of Cinderella and Her Glass Slipper. Banbury: 1820. V. 50

INTERNAL IMPROVEMENT CONVENTION, WHITE SULPHUR SPRINGS.
Proceedings of the Internal Improvement Convention, Held at the White Sulphur Springs on the 24, 25 and 26 August 1854... Richmond: 1855. V. 54

INTERNATIONAL & GREAT NORTHERN RAILROAD
Homes in Texas On the Line of the International and Great Northern R.R. 1880-81. Buffalo: 1880. V. 51

INTERNATIONAL BOUNDARY COMMISSION
Joint Report Upon the Survey and Demarcation of the Boundary Between the United States and Canada from the Western Terminus of the Land Boundary... Washington: 1921. V. 49
Joint Report Upon the Survey and Demarcation of the International Boundary Between the United States and Canada Along the 141st Meridian from the Arctic Ocean to Mount St. Elias. Washington: 1918. V. 50; 51

THE INTERNATIONAL Competition for a New Administration Building for the Chicago Tribune 1922... V. 50; 51; 53

INTERNATIONAL CONGRESS OF CLASSICAL ARCHAEOLOGY
The Proceedings of the Xth International Congress of Classical Archaeology, Ankara - Izmir 23-30/IX/1973. Ankara: 1978. V. 52

INTERNATIONAL HARNESS MACHINERY CO.
Improved Harness Machinery. Cincinnati. V. 54

INTERNATIONAL LABOUR OFFICE
Occupation and Health. Encyclopediae of Hygiene, Pathology and Social Welfare. Geneva: 1930-34. V. 53

INTERNATIONALE Ausstellung Neuer Theater-Technik... Vienna: 1924. V. 50

INTRATIONUM Excellentissimus Liber per Quem Necessarius Annibus Legis Hominibus.. London: 1510. V. 53

THE INTRIGUING Courtiers; or, The Modish Gallants...Wherein the Secret Histories of Several Persons are...Represented. London: 1732. V. 52

INTRODUCTION 7. Stories by New Writers. London: 1981. V. 48

INTRODUCTION to American Indian Art, to Accompany the First Exhibition of American Indian Art Selected Entirely with Consideration of Esthetic Value. 1931. V. 52

AN INTRODUCTION to the Art of Playing the Bassoon. Philadelphia: 1826. V. 53

INVENTORY of the Contents of Mount Vernon, 1810. Cambridge: 1909. V. 48

INVENTORY of the Historical in the City of Cambridge. London: 1959. V. 50

INVESTIGATION by the City Council of Salt Lake City of Rumors Affecting the Peace, Reputation and Welfare of the City and Its Inhabitants. Salt Lake City: 1885. V. 49

AN INVESTIGATION into the Affairs of the Delaware & Raritan Canal and Camden & Amboy Rail Road Companies, in Reference to Certain Charges by 'A Citizen of Burlington', December, 1848. Newark: 1849. V. 47

AN INVESTIGATION of the Native Rights of British Subjects. London: 1784. V. 48

IOBST, RICHARD W.
The Bloody Sixth the Sixth North Carolina Regiment Confederate States of America. Durham: 1964. V. 53
The Bloody Sixth the Sixth North Carolina Regiment Confederate States of America. Durham: 1965. V. 50

IONESCO, EUGENE
Double Act. 1992. V. 53; 54
Journeys Among the Dead. 1987. V. 47; 48; 49; 52
Pierre Alechinsky. Paintings and Writings. Paris: 1977. V. 54
Rhinoceros; the Chairs; the Lesson. Harmondsworth: 1974. V. 54
Le Roi Se Meurt. Paris: 1963. V. 47
Story Number 1, 2 and 3 for Children Under Three Years of Age. New York: 1968-70. V. 52

IOWA
The Code of Iowa, Passed at the Session of the General Assembly of 1850-1, and Approved 5th Feburary, 1851. Iowa City: 1851. V. 50

IOWA. BOARD OF IMMIGRATION
Iowa: the Home for Immigrants, Being a Treatise on the Resources of Iowa... Des Moines: 1870. V. 53; 54

IOWA. LEGISLATURE. HOUSE OF REPRESENTATIVES
Journal of...of the 11th General Assembly of the State of Iowa. Des Moines: 1866. V. 49

IPSEN, LUDVIG SANDOE
The Book-Plates of Ludvig Sandoe Ipsen. Boston: 1904. V. 49

IQBAL
Iqbal Poet of the East. 1962. V. 52

IRBY, L. HOWARD
The Ornithology of the Straits of Gibraltar. 1895. V. 52
The Ornithology of the Straits of Gibraltar... London: 1895. V. 47; 49; 52

IRBY, RICHARD
Historical Sketch of the Nottoway Grays, Afterwards Company G, Eighteenth Virginia Regiment, Army Of Northern Virginia... Richmond: 1878. V. 49

IRCASTRENSIS
Love and Horror; an Imitation of the Present, and a Model for All Future Romance. London: 1815. V. 53; 54

IREDALE, TOM
Birds of New Guinea. Melbourne: 1956. V. 48; 49; 52
Birds of Paradise. Melbourne: 1950. V. 48; 49; 52; 53

IREDELL, JAMES
Laws of the State of North Carolina. Edenton: 1791. V. 51

IRELAND, ALEXANDER
The Book-Lover's Enchiridion. Boston: 1883. V. 47
The Book-Lover's Enchiridion. London: 1888. V. 53
The Book-Lover's Enchiridion. London and New York: 1894. V. 52
Emerson: His Life, Genius and Writings. London: 1882. V. 52; 53
In Memoriam. Ralph Waldo Emerson: Recollections of His Visits to England in 1833, 1847-8, 1872-3... London: 1882. V. 48

IRELAND. ARMY MEDICAL BOARD
Instructions...to Regimental Surgeons and Assistant Surgeons. Dublin: 1803. V. 47

IRELAND, GORDON
Boundaries, Possessions and Conflicts in Central and North America and the Caribbean. (with) Boundaries, Possessions and Conflicts in South America. Cambridge: 1941/38. V. 53

IRELAND Illustrated, in a Series of Views. London: 1829. V. 53

IRELAND, JILL
Life Wish. Boston: 1987. V. 53

IRELAND, JOHN
Hogarth. London: 179-98. V. 47
Hogarth... London: 1791-98. V. 49

IRELAND, JOHN B.
Wall-Street to Cashmere. A Journal of Five Years in Asia, Africa, and Europe... New York: 1859. V. 53

IRELAND. LAWS, STATUTES, ETC.
The Statutes at Large Passed in the Parliaments Held in Ireland. Dublin: 1786-1801. V. 54

IRELAND, M. W.
The Medical Department of the U.S. Army in the World War. Washington: 1921-29. V. 52

IRELAND, SAMUEL
Graphic Illustrations of Hogarth from Pictures, Drawings and Scarce Prints in the Possession of Samuel Ireland. London: 1794. V. 48; 50
A Picturesque Tour through Holland, Brabant, and Part of France... London: 1790. V. 48
A Picturesque Tour through Holland, Brabant, and Part of France... 1796. V. 51
A Picturesque Tour through Holland, Brabant, and Part of France. Whitehall: 1796. V. 53
Picturesque Views of the Severn with Historical and Topographical Illustrations by Thomas Harral. London: 1824. V. 54
Picturesque Views on the River Medway. London: 1793. V. 49; 52
Picturesque Views on the River Thames...with Observations on the Public Buildings and Other Works of Art in Its Vicinity. London: 1792. V. 49
Picturesque Views on the River Wye... London: 1797. V. 52
Picturesque Views on the Upper, or Warwickshire Avon, from Its Source at Naseby to Its Junction with the Severn at Jewkesbury... London: 1795. V. 50; 54
Picturesque Views, with an Historial Account of the Inns of Court, in London and Westminster. London: 1800. V. 50; 52
Picturesque Views, With an Historical Account of the Inns of Court, in London and Westminster. London: 1809. V. 51

IRELAND, WILLIAM HENRY
Chalcographimania; or the Portrait Collector and Printsellers Chronicle, With Infatuations of Every Description. London: 1814. V. 49; 51; 54
The Confessions... London: 1805. V. 48; 51; 54
The Cottage-Girl. London: 1810. V. 51
The Life of Napoleon Bonaparte. London: 1828. V. 51; 52
Sribbleomania; or, The Printer's Devil's Polichronicon. London: 1815. V. 47; 51; 52
Stultifera Navis... London: 1807. V. 48; 51
Vortigern: an Historical Play: with an Original Preface... London: 1832. V. 47; 48

IRELAND, WILLIAM WOTHERSPOON
The Mental Affections of Children: Idiocy, Imbecility and Insanity. Philadelphia: 1900. V. 52

IREMONGER, VALENTIN
Reservations. Poems. Dublin: 1950. V. 51

THE IRISH Compendium or, Rudiments of Honour. 1756. V. 48; 52

IRISH Eloquence. The Speeches of the Celebrated Irish Orators Philips, Curran and Grattan to Which is Added the Powerful Appeal of Robert Emmett, at the Close of His Trial for High Treason. Philadelphia: 1836. V. 51

IRISH Fairy Tales, Folklore and Legends. London: 1904. V. 54

IRISH Folk Tales. Avon: 1973. V. 50

IRISH Law Times. Dublin: 1991. V. 49

THE IRISH Register; or a List of the Dowager Duchesses, Countesses, Widow Ladies, Maiden Ladies, Widows and Misses of Large Fortunes in England, as Register'd by the Dublin Society, for the Use of Their Members... Dublin: 1742. V. 47

IRISH, WILLIAM
The Dancing Detective. Philadelphia/New York: 1946. V. 51
You'll Never See Me Again. New York. V. 49

IRISH INTERNATIONAL EXHIBITION, 1907
Irish Rural Life and Industry. Dublin: 1907. V. 53

THE IRISHMAN'S Friend... Limerick: 1836. V. 50

IRON BRIDGE ASSOCIATION
General Descriptive Treatise on Iron Bridges Applied to Roads and Railways, Together With a Full Description of the Radiating, Parallel Inclined... London: 1857. V. 52

IRRAHIM-HILMY, PRINCE
The Literature of Egypt and the Soudan from the Earliest Times to the Year 1885 Inclusive. New York: 1923. V. 53

IRVINE, F. R.
The Fishes and Fisheries of the Gold Coast. London: 1947. V. 53

IRVINE, LYN L.
Ten Letter Writers. London: 1932. V. 48

IRVINE, WILLIAM FERGUSSON
A Short History of the Township of Rivington in the Township of Lancaster. Edinburgh: 1904. V. 48

IRVING, B. A.
The Commerce of India. Bombay: 1850. V. 53

IRVING, C.
Daughter of Egypt. 1937. V. 48; 52

IRVING, CHRISTOPHER
Catechism of Universal History, Containing a Concise Account of the Most Striking Events from the Earliest Period to the Present Time. Montreal: 1839. V. 54

IRVING, CONSTANCE
A Child's Book of Hours. London: 1921. V. 48

IRVING, DAVID
Lives of Scottish Authors; viz. Fergusson, Falconer and Russell. Edinburgh: 1801. V. 48

IRVING, HELEN
The Ladies Wreath: an Illustrated Annual. New York: 1852. V. 51

IRVING, HENRY
The Drama: Addresses. New York: 1893. V. 47; 48

IRVING, JOHN
The 158-Pound Marriage. New York: 1974. V. 47; 51; 52; 53
The Cider House Rules. 1985. V. 47
The Cider House Rules. Franklin Center: 1985. V. 52; 54
Cider House Rules. New York: 1985. V. 48; 51; 52; 53; 54
The Hotel New Hampshire. London: 1981. V. 52
The Hotel New Hampshire. New York: 1981. V. 47; 48; 48; 51; 52; 53; 54
The Hotel New Hampshire. New York: 1982. V. 52
The Pension Grillparzer. Logan: 1980. V. 52; 54
A Prayer for Owen Meany. New York: 1989. V. 49; 50; 51; 52
Setting Free the Bears. New York: 1968. V. 47; 50; 51
A Son of the Circus. London: 1994. V. 53
The Water Method Man. New York: 1972. V. 48; 49; 50; 51; 52; 53; 54
The World According to Garp. London: 1978. V. 52
The World According to Garp. New York: 1978. V. 47; 48; 51; 52; 53; 54

IRVING, JOHN B.
South Carolina Jockey Club. Charleston: 1857. V. 47; 50

IRVING, JOHN TREAT
Indian Sketches Taken During an Expedition to the Pawnee... London: 1835. V. 47; 50; 51
Indian Sketches Taken During an Expedition to the Pawnee... Philadelphia: 1835. V. 47; 50; 51

IRVING, L. H.
Sketches of Gibraltar... Edinburgh: 1853. V. 53

THE IRVING Offering: a Token of Affection, for 1851. New York: 1851. V. 48

IRVING, PIERRE M.
The Life and Letters of Washington Irving. New York: 1862. V. 54
The Life and Letters of Washington Irving. New York: 1862-64. V. 47; 48
The Life and Letters of Washington Irving. London: 1864. V. 49; 54
The Life and Letters of Washington Irving. New York: 1864. V. 49

IRVING, THEODORE
The Conquest of Florida by Hernando De Soto. Philadelphia: 1835. V. 47

IRVING, W. WILLIAM
The Case of the Merchants Considered. Washington?: 1811-12. V. 49

IRVING, WASHINGTON
Abbotsford and Newstead Abbey. Philadelphia: 1835. V. 53; 54
Abu Hassan and The Wild Huntsman. Boston: 1924. V. 49; 54
Adventures of Captain Bonneville... London: 1837. V. 47
Adventures of Captain Bonneville. London: 1840?. V. 49
The Alhambra. London: 1832. V. 48; 51
The Alhambra... Philadelphia: 1832. V. 50; 54
The Alhambra. New York: 1969. V. 53
Astoria...Enterprise Beyond the Rocky Mountains. London: 1836. V. 47
Astoria...Enterprise Beyond the Rocky Mountains. Paris: 1836. V. 48
Astoria...Enterprise Beyond the Rocky Mountains. Philadelphia: 1836. V. 47; 49; 50; 52; 52
Astoria...Enterprise Beyond the Rocky Mountains. New York: 1897. V. 52
Bracebridge Hall... London: 1822. V. 48; 49; 50; 51
Bracebridge Hall. London: 1877. V. 53
Bracebridge Hall. London & New York: 1896. V. 48; 50
The Child's Rip Van Winkle. New York: 1908. V. 47; 49
A Chronicle of the Conquest of Granada. London: 1829. V. 50; 51; 52; 54
A Chronicle of the Conquest of Granada. Philadelphia: 1829. V. 53
Collected Set of Irving's Works. Philadelphia: 1869-72. V. 54
The Crayon Miscellany. Philadelphia: 1835. V. 53; 54
The Discovery and Conquest of the New World. Cleveland: 1892. V. 50
The Gentleman in Black and Tales of Other Days. London: 1840. V. 52
A History of New York... New York: 1809. V. 48; 51; 52; 54
A History of New York. New York: 1812. V. 53; 54
A History of New York... Glasgow: 1821. V. 49
A History of New York... London: 1821. V. 52

IRVING, WASHINGTON continued
A History of the Life and Voyages of Christopher Columbus. London: 1828. V. 48; 51; 53; 54
A History of the Life and Voyages of Christopher Columbus. New York: 1828. V. 47
A History of the Life and Voyages of Christopher Columbus. Paris: 1828. V. 51; 54
A Humorous History of New York... London: 1821. V. 48
The Keeping of Christmas at Bracebridge Hall. London and New York: 1906. V. 49
Knickerbocker's History of New York. New York: 1894. V. 52
Knickerbocker's History of New York. New York: 1903. V. 50
Knickerbocker's History of New York. Garden City: 1930. V. 53
The Legend of Sleep Hollow. London: 1928. V. 48; 49; 50; 54
The Legend of Sleepy Hollow. Philadelphia: 1928. V. 47; 48; 50; 51; 53
The Legend of Sleepy Hollow. Philadelphia: 1929. V. 48
The Legend of Sleepy Hollow. New York: 1951. V. 54
The Legend of Sleepy Hollow. Hyattsville: 1983. V. 52
Legends of the Conquest of Spain. Philadelphia: 1835. V. 54
Letters of Jonathan Oldstyle, Gent. New York: 1824. V. 47
The Life and Voyages of Christopher Columbus. Boston: 1839. V. 51
The Life of George Washington. New York. V. 51
The Life Of George Washington. New York: 1855-59. V. 47; 54
Lives of Mahomet and His Successors. London: 1850. V. 47; 48; 52
Old Christmas. London: 1876. V. 49; 53
Old Christmas... London: 1882. V. 50
Old Christmas. London: 1908. V. 48
Old Christmas. London: 1925. V. 52
Oliver Goldsmith. New York: 1849. V. 49; 53
Oliver Goldsmith. Philadelphia: 1872. V. 52
Rip Van Winkle... 1850. V. 49
Rip Van Winkle. New York: 1870. V. 48
Rip Van Winkle... London: 1893. V. 49
Rip Van Winkle. New York: 1897. V. 47
Rip Van Winkle. 1905. V. 49
Rip Van Winkle. London: 1905. V. 47; 49; 50; 53
Rip Van Winkle. New York: 1905. V. 51
Rip Van Winkle. Stockholm: 1905. V. 53
Rip Van Winkle. London: 1908. V. 50; 54
Rip Van Winkle. London: 1909. V. 48
Rip Van Winkle. London: 1915. V. 49; 51
Rip Van Winkle. London: 1917. V. 50
Rip Van Winkle. 1921. V. 52; 53
Rip Van Winkle. Philadelphia: 1921. V. 49
Rip Van Winkle. New York: 1930. V. 48; 50; 53; 54
Rip Van Winkle... New York: 1970. V. 52
Rip Van Winkle... West Hatfield: 1985. V. 48; 52; 54
The Rocky Mountains... Philadelphia: 1836. V. 53
The Rocky Mountains... Philadelphia: 1837. V. 50; 52
The Rocky Mountains. Philadelphia: 1843. V. 47
Salmagundi. London: 1811-11. V. 49; 53
Schetsen en Portretten, in Engeland en Amerika Naar Het Leven Geteekend Door Geoffrey Crayon... Leeuwarden: 1823. V. 47
The Sketch-Book. New York: 1819-20. V. 54
Sketch-Book. Philadelphia: 1882. V. 52; 53
The Sketch-Book. London & New York: 1895. V. 48; 51
The Sketch-Book. New York: 1895/94. V. 48
The Sketch-Book... London: 1902. V. 48
The Sketchbook. New York: 1819. V. 49
Tales of a Traveller. London: 1824. V. 49; 52; 53
Tales of a Traveller. London: 1825. V. 49
Tales of a Traveller. London: 1895. V. 48
Tales of a Traveller. New York: 1895. V. 48; 51
Three Choice Sketches by Geoffrey Crayon, Gent... San Mateo: 1941. V. 48
A Tour on the Prairies. London: 1835. V. 48; 49; 50; 51
A Tour on the Prairies. Philadelphia: 1835. V. 52; 53; 54
A Tour on the Prairies. London: 1838. V. 49
Two Tales: Rip Van Winkle and The Legend of Sleepy Hollow. New York: 1984. V. 52
Voyage to the Eastern Part of Terra Firma or the Spanish Main, in South America. New York: 1806. V. 53
Voyages and Discoveries of the Companions of Columbus. London: 1831. V. 49
Voyages and Discoveries of the Companions of Columbus. Philadelphia: 1831. V. 47; 50; 51
Voyages and Discoveries of the Companions of Columbus. New York: 1929. V. 48
Washington's Earlier Years. New York: 1857. V. 53
Wolfert's Roost, and Other Papers. New York: 1855. V. 47; 48; 51; 52; 54
Wolfert's Roost: and Other Papers... New York: 1855/54. V. 48
The Works... London: 1850. V. 51
Works. London: 1857-63. V. 49
The Works... Garden City: 1859-60. V. 52; 53
Works. London: 1866. V. 51
Works. London: 1868-77. V. 48
The Works... Philadelphia: 1869-71. V. 51
The Writings of Washington Irving. New York: 1897. V. 53

IRVINGIANA: a Memorial of Washington Irving. New York: 1860. V. 52

IRWIN, DAVID
English Neoclassical Art Studies in Inspiration and Taste. London: 1966. V. 49
Scottish Painters at Home and Abroad 1700-1900. London: 1975. V. 49; 52; 54

IRWIN, EYLES
A Series of Adventures in the Course of a Voyage Up the Red Sea, on the Coasts of Arabia and Egypt... London: 1780. V. 48; 49
The Triumph of Innocence; an Ode. London: 1796. V. 50; 54

IRWIN, FRANCIS
Stonyhurst War Record. London: 1927. V. 54

IRWIN, GODFRED
American Tramp and Underworld Slang... London: 1931. V. 53

IRWIN, JOHN
Origins of Chintz: With a Catalogue of Indo-European Cotton-Paintings in the Victoria and Albert Museum, London and the Royal Ontario Museum, Toronto. London: 1970. V. 53

IRWIN, MABEL MAC COY
Whitman: the Poet Liberator of Woman. New York: 1905. V. 53

IRWIN, WILL
Pictures of Old Chinatown. New York: 1908. V. 52

ISAAC, FRANK
English & Scottish Printing Types 1501-25... London: 1940-42. V. 48
English & Scottish Printing Types 1501-35... London: 1930/32. V. 49
*English & Scottish Printing Types 1501-35 * 1508-41...* Oxford: 1930. V. 50
*English & Scottish Printing Types 1535-58 * 1552-58.* Oxford: 1932. V. 50

ISAAC, ISAAC S.
Friday Night. A Selection of Tales Illustrating Hebrew Life. New York: 1870-5630. V. 52

ISAAC, PETER
William Bulmer, 1757-1830. The Fine Printer in Context. London: 1993. V. 52
William Bulmer, 1757-1830. The Fine Printer in Context. 1995. V. 54

ISAACS, EDITH
The Negro in the American Theatre. New York: 1947. V. 49

ISAACS, JUDD
The Story of an Ostrich. Boston: 1903. V. 47

ISAACS, NATHANIEL
Travels and Adventures in Eastern Africa. London: 1836. V. 53
Travels and Adventures in Eastern Africa... Cape Town: 1970. V. 47

ISAACSON, HENRY
Saturni Ephemerides sive Tabula Historico Chronolgica. London: 1633. V. 51; 53; 54

ISAACSON, R. T.
The Garden Center of Greater Cleveland: Flowering Plant Index of Illustration and Information 1979-1981. Boston: 1982. V. 47

ISABELLA.. London: 1823. V. 54

ISE, JOHN
The United States Oil Policy. New Haven: 1928. V. 49

ISENBART, HANS HEINRICH
The Imperial Horse. The Saga of the Lipizzaners. New York: 1986. V. 52; 54
The Imperial Horse. The Saga of the Lipizzaners. Newton Abbott: 1986. V. 54

ISHAM, ASA BRAINERD
Prisoners of War and Military Prisons Personal Narratives of Experience in the Prisons at Richmond, Danville, Macon, Andersonville, Savannah, Millen, Charleston and Columbia... Cincinnati: 1890. V. 52

ISHAM, CHARLES
The Fishery Question: its Origin, History and Present Situation... New York/London: 1887. V. 53

ISHAM, JAMES
James Isham's Observations on Hudsons Bay...Notes and Observations on a Book Entitled, a Voyage to Hudsons Bay in the Dobbs... London: 1949. V. 47; 49; 51; 52; 53
James Isham's Observations on Hudsons Bay...Notes and Observations on a Book Entitled, a Voyage to Hudsons Bay in the Dobbs... Toronto: 1949. V. 51

ISHAM, NORMAN M.
Early Connecticut Houses... Providence: 1900. V. 50
A History of the Fabric. The Meeting House of the First Baptist Church in Providence. Providence: 1925. V. 51
In Praise of Antiquaries. Boston: 1931. V. 51; 53

ISHAM, RALPH HEYWARD
The Private Papers of James Boswell from Malahide Castle in the Collection of Lt.-Colonel Ralph Heyward Isham. A Catalogue. London & New York: 1931. V. 47

ISHERWOOD, CHRISTOPHER
All the Conspirators. London: 1928. V. 49
Berlin Stories. New York: 1945. V. 49; 51; 52
Christopher and His Kind. Los Angeles: 1976. V. 51
Christopher and His Kind. New York: 1976. V. 53
Down There On a Visit. New York: 1962. V. 49
Goodbye to Berlin. London: 1939. V. 49; 53
Lions and Shadows... London: 1938. V. 51
Lions and Shadows. Norfolk: 1947. V. 51
The Memorial. London: 1932. V. 48; 50; 51; 53
My Guru and His Disciple. New York: 1980. V. 53
October. Los Angeles: 1981. V. 53
Prater Violet. New York: 1945. V. 47; 49; 51

ISHERWOOD, CHRISTOPHER continued
Prater Violet. London: 1946. V. 53
Sally Bowles. London: 1937.. V. 52; 53
A Single Man. New York: 1964. V. 49
A Single Man. London: 1980. V. 50
The World in the Evening. London: 1954. V. 49

ISHIGURO, KAZUO
An Artist of the Floating World. London: 1986. V. 49; 50; 51; 52; 53
An Artist of the Floating World. New York: 1986. V. 53; 54
A Pale View of Hills. London: 1982. V. 51; 53
A Pale View of Hills. New York: 1982. V. 49; 52; 53; 54
The Remains of the Day. London: 1989. V. 49; 52; 54
The Remains of the Day. New York: 1989. V. 53; 54
The Unconsoled. London: 1995. V. 53
The Unconsoled. New York: 1995. V. 53

ISHILL, JOSEPH
Elisee and Elie Reclus - in Memoriam... Berkeley Heights: 1927. V. 53

ISHIZU, R.
The Mineral Springs of Japan, with Tables of Analyses, Radio-Activity, Notes on Prominent Spas and List of the Seaside Resorts and Summer Retreats Specially Edited for the Panama Pacific International Exposition. Tokyo: 1915. V. 50

ISLA, JOSE FRANCISCO DE
The History of the Famous Preacher Friar Gerund de Campazas: otherwise Gerund Zotes. London: 1772. V. 51

ISLE of Wight. In a series of Views Printed in Oil Colours. London: 1860-70. V. 49; 52

ISLER, M. L.
The Tanagers, Natural History, Distribution and Identification. Washington: 1987. V. 48

ISMAN, FELIX
Weber and Fields: Their Triumphs and Their Associates. New York: 1924. V. 52

ISMENE and Ismenias, a Novel. London: 1788. V. 49; 54

ISOCRATES
(Greek title) *Isocratis Orationes et Epistole.* Geneva: 1593. V. 52
Opera. Basel: 1594. V. 53
Orationes Tres. Venice: 1555. V. 52
Scripta, Quae Quidem Nunc Extant. Basle: 1570. V. 51

ISSAVERDENTZ, HAGOPOS
The Island of San Lazzaro, or the Armenian Monastery Near Venice. Venice: 1879. V. 51

ISUMBRAS
Syr Ysambrace. Hammersmith: 1897. V. 50; 52

ISVARAKRISHNA
The Sankhya Karika, or Memorial Verses of the Sankhya Philosophy. Oxford: 1837. V. 50; 53

ITALIAN Furniture, Interiors and Decoration... New York. V. 52

THE ITALIAN Opera in 1839. London: 1840. V. 50

ITALIC Quartet: a Record of the Collaboration Between Harry Kessler, Edward Johnston, Emery Walker and Edward Prince in Making the Cranch Press italic, by John Dreyfus. Cambridge: 1966. V. 53

ITHACA & OWEGO RAILROAD CO.
Report of the President and Directors to the Stockholders of the Ithaca and Owego Railroad Co. Ithaca: 1833. V. 53

ITOH, TEIJI
The Elegant Japanese House. New York: 1969. V. 52
The Essential Japanese House. New York & London: 1967. V. 48; 49; 50; 53
Imperial Gardens of Japan. New York and Tokyo: 1970. V. 51; 54

ITTEN, J.
The Art of Color: the Subjective Experience and Objective Rationale of Color. New York: 1973. V. 47

IU-KIAO-LI; or, the Two Fair Cousins. London: 1827. V. 47

IVENS, W. G.
Melanesians of the South-East Solomon Islands. London: 1927. V. 50

IVERNOIS, FRANCIS D'
A Cursory View of the Assignats; and Remaining Resources of French Finance (September 6, 1795). London: 1795. V. 54

IVES, EDWARD
A Voyage from England to India, in the Year MDCCLIV. (also) A Journey from Persia to England, by an Unusual Route. London: 1773. V. 53

IVES, GEORGE
A Bibliography of Oliver Wendell Holmes. Boston: 1907. V. 50

IVES, J. D.
Arctic and Alpine Environments. London: 1974. V. 53

IVES, JOSEPH CHRISTMAS
Report Upon the Colorado River of the West. Washington: 1861. V. 47; 50; 51; 53

IVES, MARGUERITE
Seventeen Famous Outdoorsmen Known to Marguerite Ives. Chicago: 1929. V. 52

IVES, SIDNEY
The Parkman Dexter Howe Library... Gainesville: 1983-87. V. 51
The Trial of Mrs. Leigh Perrot, Wife of James Leigh Perrot, Esq... London: 1980. V. 52; 54

IVORY, JAMES
On the Attractions of Homogeneous Ellipsoids. London: 1809. V. 49

IVY, R.
Poems from a Campaign. Thorpe Bay. V. 47

IYER, K. BHARATHA
Art and Thought. London: 1947. V. 52; 54

IZACKE, RICHARD
Remarkable Antiquities of the City of Exeter. London: 1681. V. 48; 54
Remarkable Antiquities of the City of Exeter. London: 1723. V. 48

IZENOUR, GEORGE C.
Roofed Theaters of Classical Antiquity. New Haven and London: 1992. V. 52
Theater Design. New York: 1917. V. 53
Theater Design. New York: 1977. V. 54

IZETELLY, HENRY
Four Months Among the Gold-finders In Alta California Being the Diary of an Expedition From San Francisco to the Gold Districts. London: 1849. V. 48

IZETT, JAMES
The Traditions of the Maori People. Wellington: 1904. V. 51

IZLAR, WILLIAM VALMORE
A Sketch of the War Record of the Edisto Rifles, 1861-1865. Columbia: 1914. V. 49

J

J., A.
An Apology for Camp=Meetings, Illustrative of Their Good Effects and Answering the Principal Objections Urged Against Them. New York: 1810. V. 49

J., E.
A New Answer to a Speech Lately Made by a Noble Peer of This Realm. 1681?. V. 47

JAASTAD, BEN
Man of the West, Reminiscences of George Washington Oakes, 1840-1917. Tucson: 1956. V. 52

JABES, EDMOND
A Share of Ink. London: 1979. V. 51

JABLONSKI, N. G.
Theropithecus. Rise and Fall of a Primate Genus. Cambridge: 1993. V. 51

JACK and the Bean-Stalk. London: 1830's. V. 51

JACK and the Beanstalk. London: 1854. V. 49
JACK and the Beanstalk. New York: 1944. V. 49

JACK, GEORGE S.
History of Roanoke County (and) History of Roanoke City and History of the Norfolk & Western Railway Co. Roanoke: 1912. V. 54

JACK Jingle and Sucky Shingle. York: 1840. V. 49

JACK Kerouac. Paris: 1971. V. 50

JACK London: A Sketch of His Life and Work. New York: 1905. V. 53

JACK, R. L.
The Geology and Palaeontology of Queensland and New Guinea. Brisbane: 1892. V. 49

JACK, ROBERT L.
History of the National Association for the Advancement of Colored People. Boston: 1943. V. 52

JACK the Giant Killer. London: 1888. V. 51
JACK the Giant Killer. London: 1914. V. 51
JACK the Giant Killer. 1973. V. 51

JACKMAN, JOSEPH
The Sham-Robbery, Committed by Elijah Putnam Goodridge, on His Own Person...and His Trial with Mr. Ebenezer Pearson, Whom He Maliciously Arrested for Robbery. Also the Trial of Levi & Laban Kenniston. Concord: 1819. V. 48; 52

JACKMAN, W. J.
Flying Machines: Construction and Operation. Chicago: 1910. V. 52

JACKO'S Merry Method of Learning (of the Pence Table). London: 1843. V. 47

JACKSON, A. E.
Dot's Visit to the Gnomes. London: 1907. V. 50

JACKSON, A. L.
When Shiloh Came. 1899. V. 52

JACKSON, A. P.
Oklahoma Politically and Topographically Described. History and Guide to the Indian Territory. Kansas City: 1885. V. 49

JACKSON, A. T.
Picture Writing of Texas Indians. 1938. V. 54
Picture Writing of Texas Indians. Austin: 1938. V. 49; 53

JACKSON, A. V. WILLIAMS
History of India. London: 1906-07. V. 47; 51; 54

JACKSON, A. W.
A Sure Foundation and a Sketch of Negro Life in Texas. Houston: 1942. V. 54

JACKSON, A. Y.
A Painter's Country: The Autobiography of A. Y. Jackson. Toronto: 1958. V. 47

JACKSON and a Standing Army. Philadelphia: 1828. V. 48

JACKSON, ANDREW
Annual Messages, Veto Messages, Protest, &c of Andrew Jackson, President of the United States. Baltimore: 1835. V. 47
Official Record from the War Department, of the Proceedings of the Court Martial Which Tried, and the Orders of General Jackson for Shooting the Six Militia Men...Showing that These American Citizens Were Inhumanly and Illegally Massacred. Concord: 1828. V. 47
The Presidential Election, Written for the Benefit of the People of the United States... Louisville: 1823. V. 48
Robert O'Hara Burke and the Australian Exploring Expedition of 1860. London: 1862. V. 52

JACKSON, AURILDA
Untangled. New York: 1956. V. 53

JACKSON, C. E.
Bird Illustrators, Some Artists in Early Lithography. London: 1975. V. 52

JACKSON, C. F. W.
Bull Dog Pegirees...Complete to 1st Dec. 1897. Bath: 1892-98. V. 49

JACKSON, CATHERINE HANNAH CHARLOTTE, LADY
Fair Lusitania. London: 1874. V. 53
Old Paris: Its Court and Literary Salons. London: 1878. V. 49
Works (On French History). London: 1899. V. 52; 54

JACKSON, CHARLES
The Fall of Valor. New York: 1946. V. 49
The Lost Weekend. New York: 1944. V. 48; 54
A Second Hand Life. New York: 1967. V. 54

JACKSON, CHARLES JAMES
English Goldsmiths and Their Marks. London: 1905. V. 51
English Goldsmiths and Their Marks... London: 1921. V. 50; 51
An Illustrated History of English Plate... London: 1911. V. 51
An Illustrated History of English Plate Ecclesiastical and Secular, in Which the Development of Form and Decoration in the Silver and Gold Work of the British Isles... London: 1967. V. 49

JACKSON, CHARLES T.
A Manual of Etherization.... Boston: 1861. V. 51
Report on the Geological and Agricultural Survey of the State of Rhode-Island. Providence: 1840. V. 48
Report to the House of Representatives of the United States of America, Vindicating the Rights of Charles T. Jackson to the Discovery of Anaesthetic Effects of Ether Vapor and Disproving the Claims of W. T. G. Morton to that Discovery. Washington: 1852. V. 47

JACKSON, CHEVALIER
Diseases of the Air and Food Passages of Foreign Body Origin. Philadelphia: 1937. V. 48; 53

JACKSON, CLARENCE S.
Pageant of Pioneers - The William Henry Jackson, Picture Maker of the Old West. Minden: 1958. V. 54
Picture Maker of the Old West: William H. Jackson. New York: 1947. V. 50

JACKSON, DAVID K.
Poe and the Southern Literary Messenger. Richmond: 1934. V. 48

JACKSON, DONALD
The Expeditions of John Charles Fremont. Urbana, Chicago: 1970. V. 54
The Expeditions of John Charles Fremont. Urbana: 1970/73. V. 54
Johann Amerbach. Iowa City: 1956. V. 52
Letters of the Lewis and Clark Expedition with Related Documents 1783-1854. Urbana: 1962. V. 50
Letters of the Lewis and Clark Expedition with Related Documents 1783-1854. Urbana: 1978. V. 50

JACKSON, EDGAR ALLAN
Letters of Edgar Allan Jackson, September 7, 1860-April 15, 1863. Franklin: 1939. V. 49
Three Rebels Write Home, Including the Letters of Edgar Allan Jackson, James Fenton Bryant, Irvin Cross Wills and Miscellaneous Items. Franklin: 1955. V. 49; 52; 54

JACKSON, EMILY
A History of Hand-Made Lace Dealing with the Origin Of the Great Lace Centers...the Care of Various Kinds of Lace. London & New York: 1900. V. 47; 48; 50
The History of Silhouettes. London: 1911. V. 48; 51

JACKSON, F. J.
Birds of Kenya Colony and the Uganda Proectorate. London: 1938. V. 49
Notes on the Game Birds of Kenya and Uganda. London: 1926. V. 48; 50; 51; 52

JACKSON, FREDERICK G.
A Thousand Days in the Arctic. New York, London: 1899. V. 49

JACKSON, GEORGE
Sixty Years in Texas. 1908. V. 48; 49
Sixty Years in Texas. Dallas: 1908. V. 49

JACKSON, GEORGE A.
Jackson's Diary of 59'. Idaho Springs: 1929. V. 52; 54

JACKSON, HELEN
My Lady's Carriage. London: 1900. V. 47

JACKSON, HELEN HUNT
Bits of Travel. Boston: 1872. V. 48
A Century of Dishonor: A Sketch of the United States Government's Dealings with Some of the Indian Tribes. New York: 1881. V. 47; 48; 49; 50; 51
Poems. Boston: 1892. V. 50
Ramona. 1884. V. 48; 49; 50
Ramona. Boston: 1884. V. 53
Ramona. New York: 1884. V. 51
Ramona. Boston: 1900. V. 53
Ramona. Los Angeles: 1959. V. 49; 52; 53
Verses. Boston: 1870. V. 49

JACKSON, HENRY C.
Osman Digna. London: 1926. V. 48; 50; 53

JACKSON, HENRY R.
Tallulah and Other Poems. Savannah: 1850. V. 52

JACKSON, HERBERT J.
European Hand Firearms of the Sixteenth, Seventeenth, & Eighteenth Centuries. London: 1923. V. 47

JACKSON, HOLBROOK
The Anatomy of Bibliomania. London: 1930. V. 47; 48
Bernard Shaw. London: 1907. V. 51
A Cross-Section of English Printing: the Curwen Press 1918-1934. London: 1935. V. 48; 52
The Early History of the Double Crown Club - Fiftieth Dinner Address delivered by the President Holbrook Jackson at the Cafe Royal Ninth October Nineteen Thirtyfive. London: 1935. V. 52
The Eighteen-Nineties. London: 1913. V. 52; 53
Maxims of Books and Reading. London: 1924. V. 53

JACKSON, ISAAC R.
The Life of William Henry Harrison, the People's Candidate. Philadelphia: 1840. V. 52

JACKSON, J. R.
Observations on Lakes, Being an Attempt to Explain the Laws of Nature Regarding Them... London: 1833. V. 50

JACKSON, JAMES
Another Letter to a Young Physician: To Which Are Appended Some Other Medical Papers. Boston: 1861. V. 48
Cases of Cholera Collected at Paris. Boston: 1832. V. 48
Consumption: How to Prevent It and How to Cure It. Boston: 1862. V. 48
Diptheria: its Causes, Treatment and Cure. Dansville: 1864. V. 50
Letters to a Young Physician Just Entering Upon Practice. Boston: 1855. V. 48; 50; 52
A Memoir of James Jackson Jr., M.D. Boston: 1835. V. 53
A Report on Spasmodic Cholera. Boston: 1832. V. 48; 50; 51; 52; 53
A Syllabus of the Lectures Delivered in the Massachusetts Medical College to the Medical Students of Harvard University. Boston: 1816. V. 51; 52

JACKSON, JAMES GREY
An Account of the Empire of Morocco, and the Districts of Suse and Tafilelt...Etc. London: 1814. V. 50

JACKSON, JESSE
The Sickest Don't Always Die the Quickest. Garden City: 1971. V. 53

JACKSON, JOHN
A Defense of Human Liberty, in Answer to the Principal Arguments Which Have Been Alledged Against It. London: 1725. V. 52
The History of the Scottish Stage, from Its First Establishment to the Present Time. Edinburgh: 1793. V. 47
Hunting Songs and Other Memorabilia. Bury, Lancashire: 1902. V. 49
Hunting Songs and Other Memorabilia. London: 1902. V. 47
Journey from India, Towards England, in the Year 1797. London: 1799. V. 51; 52
Rational Amusements for Winter Evenings; Or a Collection of Above 200 Curious and Interesting Puzzles and Paradoxes Relating to Arithmetic, Geometry, Geography &c. London: 1821. V. 48
Remarks on the Miscellaneous Poems Published by Thomas Pierson of Stockton in the Year 1786. Stockton: 1786. V. 50; 52
A Treatise on Wood Engraving, Historical, and Practical. London: 1839. V. 49; 53
A Treatise on Wood Engraving, Historical and Practical. London: 1861. V. 48
A Vindication of Humane Liberty; in Answer to a Dissertation on Liberty and Necessity, Written by A. C. Esq. London: 1730. V. 52

JACKSON, JOHN BAPTIST
An Essay on the Invention of Engraving and Printing in Chiaro Oscuro as Practised by Albert Durer, Hugo de Carpi etc. and the Application Of it to the Making of Paper Hangings of Taste, Duration and Elegance. London: 1754. V. 47; 53

JACKSON, JOHN GEORGE
Illustrations of Bishop West's Chapel. London: 1825. V. 47

JACKSON, JOHN HUGHLINGS
Selected Writings of... London: 1931. V. 53

JACKSON, JOHN, OF TANFIELD MILL
The Practical Fly-Fisher; More particularly for Grayling or Umber. London: 1854. V. 48
The Practical Fly-Fisher, More Particularly for Grayling or Umber... London: 1899. V. 51

JACKSON, JOHN P.
The Ammergau Passion Play: Descriptive Guide to the Scenes and Tableaux. Frankfort-on-the-Main: 1871. V. 47

JACKSON, JON A.
The Blind Pig. New York: 1978. V. 50
The Diehard. New York: 1977. V. 52

JACKSON, JOSEPH
English Notes. New York: 1920. V. 48

JACKSON, JOSEPH HENRY
Bad Company - The Story of California's Legendary and Actual Stage-Robbers, Bandits, Highwaymen and Outlaws from the Fifties to the Eighties. New York: 1949. V. 52

JACKSON, KENNETH
Studies in Early Celtic Nature Poetry. Cambridge: 1935. V. 49

JACKSON, LUCRETIA E.
The Health Reformer's Cook Book; or How to Prepare Food from Grains, Fruits and Vegetables. Dansville: 1874. V. 49

JACKSON, MARIA ELIZABETH
Botanical Diagloues, Between Hortensia and Her Four Children. London: 1797. V. 54
The Florists Manual, or, Hints for the Construction of a Gay Flower-garden... London: 1822. V. 47; 48; 53
The Florist's Manual, or, Hints for the Construction of a Gay Flower-Garden... London: 1827. V. 51; 53

JACKSON, MARY ANNA
Life and Letters of General Thomas J. Jackson (Stonewall Jackson). New York: 1892. V. 49
Memoirs of Stonewall Jackson by His Widow. Louisville: 1895. V. 47

JACKSON, MARY E.
The Life of Nellie C. Bailey or a Romance of the West. Topeka: 1885. V. 49; 52; 54

JACKSON, MASON
The Pictorial Press; its Origin and Progress. London: 1885. V. 53

JACKSON, MICHAEL
Moon Walk. New York: 1988. V. 53

JACKSON, NAOMI
A. Y.'s Canada. Toronto: 1968. V. 54

JACKSON, R. T.
Phylogeny of the Echini... Boston: 1912. V. 48; 50; 52; 53

JACKSON, RICHARD
An Historical Review of the Constitution and Government of Pennsylvania, From Its Origin; so Far As Regards the Several Points of Controversy... London: 1759. V. 47; 48
Literatura Graeca...to Which is Prefixed, an Essay on the Study of the Greek Language... London: 1769. V. 47

JACKSON, ROBERT
A Systematic View of the Formation, Discipline and Economy of Armies. London: 1804. V. 48; 50; 51; 53
A Treatise on the Fevers of Jamaica, with Some Observations on the Intermitting Fever of America, and an Appendix, Containing Some Hints on the Means of Preserving the Health of Soldiers in Hot Climates. Philadelphia: 1795. V. 47; 50; 51

JACKSON, ROGER
Henry Miller: a Bibliography of Primary Sources (1919-1992). Paris: 1992. V. 48

JACKSON, ROWLAND
The History of the Town and Township of Barnsley, in Yorkshire, from an Early Period. London: 1858. V. 53

JACKSON, SAMUEL
The Principles of Medicine Founded on the Stricture and Functions of Animal Organism. Philadelphia: 1832. V. 48; 53

JACKSON, SHEILA
Ballet in England. London and New York: 1945. V. 54

JACKSON, SHELDON
Alaska and Missions on the North Pacific Coast. New York: 1880. V. 53

JACKSON, SHIRLEY
9 Magic Wishes. 1963. V. 52
The Bad Children. Chicago: 1959. V. 49
The Bird's Nest. New York: 1954. V. 52; 53; 54
Hangsaman. New York: 1951. V. 49; 53
The Haunting of Hill House. New York: 1959. V. 47; 49; 52; 53
The Haunting of Hill House. 1960. V. 52
The Haunting of Hill House. London: 1960. V. 50
Life Among the Savages. New York: 1958. V. 48
The Lottery. 1949. V. 48; 50
The Lottery. New York: 1949. V. 51
Nine Magic Wishes. New York: 1963. V. 49
Raising Demons. New York: 1957. V. 47
The Road through the Wall. 1948. V. 53
The Road through the Wall. New York: 1948. V. 47; 51; 54
The Sundial. New York: 1958. V. 48; 50; 51; 52; 53; 54
We Have Always Lived in the Castle. New York: 1962. V. 48; 50; 52
The Witchcraft of Salem Village. New York: 1956. V. 52

JACKSON, THOMAS
Tropical Medicine with Special Reference to the West Indies, Central America, Hawaii and the Philippines. Philadelphia: 1907. V. 48

JACKSON, THOMAS GRAHAM
Byzantine and Romanesque Architecture. 1920. V. 50
The Church of St. Mary the Virgin, Oxford. Oxford: 1897. V. 47
The Renaissance of Roman Architecture: Italy; England; France. Cambridge: 1921-23. V. 53

JACKSON, W.
An Abstract of the Several Deeds and Muniments that Relate to Or Concern the, Charitable Donations Belonging to the Parish of Hampton, in the County of Middlesex. London: 1816. V. 49
Papers and Pedigrees Mainly Relating to Cumberland and Westmorland. London: 1892. V. 50

JACKSON, W. H.
The Canons of Colorado from Photographs By... Denver: 1900. V. 52
The White City. Chicago: 1894. V. 53

JACKSON, WILLIAM
Book-Keeping, in the True Italian Form of Debtor and Creditor by Way of Double Entry; or, Practical Book-Keeping... New York: 1804. V. 48
The Four Ages; Together with Essays on Various Subjects. London: 1798. V. 47
Observations on the Present State of Music, in London. London: 1791. V. 47
Papers and Pedigrees Mainly Relating to Cumberland and Westmorland. London: 1892. V. 52; 54
Thirty Letters on Various Subjects. London: 1783. V. 47; 54

JACKSON, WILLIAM ALEXANDER
Annotated List of the Publications of the Reverend Thomas Frognall Dibdin, D.D. Cambridge: 1965. V. 48; 51

JACKSON, WILLIAM HENRY
Time Exposure. New York: 1940. V. 47; 48

JACKSON, Z.
Shakespeare's Genius Justified. 1819. V. 48

JACOB, ALEXANDER
A Complete English Peerage. London: 1766-69-67. V. 48

JACOB, E. F.
The Register of Henry Chichele, Archbishop of Canterbury, 1414-1443. Oxford: 1938-43-45-47. V. 48

JACOB, EDWARD
The History of the Town and Port of Faversham, in the County of Kent. London: 1774. V. 47
Plantae Favreshamienses, a Catalogue of...Plants Growing Spontaneously About Faversham....Kent. London: 1777. V. 54

JACOB, GILES
The Clerk's Remembrancer. London: 1714. V. 50
The Compleat Court-Keeper; or, Land-Steard's Assistant. London: 1724. V. 52
The Complete Parish-Officer... London: 1720. V. 47
The Complete Parish-Officer... London: 1731. V. 48
The Complete Parish-Officer. London: 1754. V. 53
Every Man His Own Lawyer... London: 1740. V. 47
The General Laws of Estates; or, Freeholder's Companion... London: 1740. V. 49
An Historical Account of the Lives and Writings of Our Most Considerable English Poets, Whether Epick, Lyrick, Elegiack, Epigrammatists. London: 1720. V. 51
The Law Dictionary... London: 1809. V. 50
The Law-Dictionary... London: 1797. V. 52
Lex Constitutionis; or, the Gentleman's Law Being a Compleat Treatise of all the Laws and Statutes Relating to the King and the Prerogative of the Crown; the Nobility and House of Lords; House of Commons; Officers of State, the Exchequer and Treasury... London: 1719. V. 47
Memoirs of the Life of the Right Honourable Joseph Addison, Esq., Late One of His Majesty's Principal Secretaries of State. London: 1719. V. 53
A New Dictionary. London: 1782. V. 54
The New Law-Dictionary. London: 1750. V. 54
The Poetical Register; or, the Lives and Characters of all the English Poets. London: 1723. V. 52
The Rape of the Smock. London: 1717. V. 47
The Statute-Law Common-Plac'd; or, a General Table to the Statutes. London: 1739. V. 49
The Statute-Law Common-plac'd: or, a General Table to the Statutes... London: 1748. V. 50; 54
The Statute-Law Common-Plac'd; or, a Second General Table to the Statutes. London: 1719. V. 48

JACOB, JOHN G.
The Life and Times of Patrick Gass, Now the Sole Survivor of the Overland Expedition to the Pacific Under Lewis and Clark, 1804-05-06. Wellsburg: 1859. V. 50

JACOB, JOHN JEREMIAH
Biographical Sketch of the Life of the Late Captain Michael Cresap. Cincinnati: 1866. V. 47

JACOB, NED
National Cowboy Hall of Fame and Western Heritage Center, Mar 4-May 14, 1972. 1972. V. 47; 50

JACOB, S. S.
Jeypore Enamels. London: 1886. V. 52

JACOBACCI, VINCENZO
A Giambatista Bodoni, Che Gli fe Dono Dell Orazio Stampato Co'Suoi Caratteri. Parma: 1791. V. 54

JACOBAEUS, HOLGER
Museum Regium seu Catalogus Rerum tam Naturalium, Quam Artificialium... Copenhagen: 1696. V. 47

JACOBI, ABRAHAM
The Intestinal Diseases of Infancy and Childhood. Detroit: 1887. V. 48; 53
Therapeutics of Infancy and Childhood. Philadelphia: 1896. V. 48; 51
A Treatise on Diphtheria. New York: 1880. V. 52; 53

JACOBI, CARL
Revelations in Black. Sauk City: 1947. V. 51; 54

JACOBI, CHARLES T.
Gesta Typographica or a Medley for Printers and Others. London: 1897. V. 48

JACOBI, EDWARD
Portfolio of Dermochromes. New York: 1903. V. 48

JACOBI, LOTTE
Lotte Jacobi. Danbury: 1978. V. 47

JACOBI, MARY PUTNAM
Essays on Hysteria, Brain-Tumor and Other Cases of Nervous Diseases. New York: 1888. V. 47; 48; 49
On the Use of the Cold Pack Followed by Massage in the Treatment of Anaemia. New York: 1880. V. 48
A Pathfinder in Medicine with Selections from Her Writings and a Complete Biography. New York: 1925. V. 51

JACOBITE Miscellany. Eight Original Papers on the Rising of 1745-46. Oxford: 1948. V. 50

JACOBS, JIM
Grease. New York: 1972. V. 50

JACOBS, JOSEPH
The Book of Job. London: 1896. V. 47
The Book of Wonder Voyages. New York: 1896. V. 50
Celtic Fairy Tales. London: 1892. V. 52
English Fairy Tales. London: 1890. V. 52
Indian Fairy Tales. London: 1892. V. 52
More Celtic Fairy Tales. London: 1894. V. 49; 51

JACOBS, MELVILLE
Northwest Sahaptin Texas. New York: 1934. V. 50

JACOBS, ORANGE
The Memoirs of Orange Jacobs; Written by Himself. Seattle: 1908. V. 47; 53

JACOBS, THOMAS JEFFERSON
Scenes, Incidents and Adventures in the Pacific Ocean. New York: 1856. V. 53

JACOBS, W. W.
Deep Waters. 1919. V. 53
The Lady of the Barge. New York: 1902. V. 53
Many Cargoes. London: 1898. V. 53
A Master of Craft. London: 1900. V. 47; 49; 50
Ship's Company. London: 1911. V. 51
Short Cruises. London: 1907. V. 50

JACOBSEN, H.
A Handbook of Succulent Plants. London: 1960. V. 54

JACOBSEN, THORKILD
Sennacherib's Aqueduct et Jerwan. Chicago: 1935. V. 51

JACOBSON & CO.
The General Catalogue. New York: 1924. V. 51; 53; 54

JACOBSON, HARRY P.
Fungous Diseases, a Clinico-Mycological Text... Springfield and Baltimore: 1932. V. 51

JACOBSON, OSCAR BROUSSE
Kiowa Indian Art. Santa Fe: 1979. V. 50

JACOBSTHAL, PAUL
Ornamente Griechischer Vasen. Berlin: 1927. V. 52

JACOBUS, MAGDALIUS GAUDENSIS
Passio Magistralis Dni Nri Jesu Christi... Cologne: 1505. V. 53

JACOBUS DE GRUYTRODE
Lavacrum Conscientiae. Augsburg: 1492. V. 47; 49
Lavacrum Conscientiae. Leipzig: 1497. V. 47; 49
Lavacrum Conscientiae. Augsburg: 1498. V. 47; 49

JACOBUS DE VARAGINE
The Golden Legend of Master William Caxton Done Anew. Hammersmith: 1892. V. 49; 51
Historiae Plurimorum Sanctorum. Louvain: 1485. V. 51; 52; 53
In the State of Innocensye. Beckenham, Kent: 1988. V. 47
Legenda Aurea, or Golden Legened. London: 1521. V. 52

JACOLLIOT, M. LOUIS
The Bible in India, Hindoo Origin of Hebrew and Christian Revelation. London: 1870. V. 50

JACQUES, HENRY
Sous le Signe Du Rossignol. Paris: 1923. V. 51

JACQUIN, NICOLAUS JOSEPH VON
Collectanea ad Botanicam, Chemiam, et Historiam Naturalem Spectantia, cum Figuris. Vindobonae: Wappler 1786-96. Vienna: 1786-96. V. 49
Dreyhundert Auserlesene Amerikanische Gewachse Nach Linneischer Ordnung. Nurnberg: 1785-87. V. 53
Florae Austriacae Sive Plantarum Selectarum in Austriae Archiducatu Sponte Crescentium, Icones, ad Vivum Coloratae... Vienna: 1773-78. V. 47
Icones Plantarum Rariorum. Vienna: 1781-93. V. 49
Miscellanea Austraica ad Botanicam, Chemiam et Historiam Naturlem Spectantia. Vienna: 1778-81. V. 49; 52
Observationum Botanicarum. Vienna: 1764-71. V. 49

JAEGER, BENEDICT
The Life of North American Insects... Providence: 1854. V. 52

JAESCHKE, HEINRICH AUGUST
Romanized Tibetan and English Dictionary. Kyelang in British Lahoul: 1866. V. 49

JAFFE, IRMA B.
John Trumbull: Patriot-Artist of the American Revolution. Boston: 1975. V. 53

JAFFE, MICHAEL
Van Dyck's Antwerp Sketchbook. London: 1966. V. 50; 51; 52

JAFFE, SHERRIL
Scars Made Your Body More Interesting. Los Angeles: 1975. V. 48; 51

JAGGARD, WILLIAM
Shakespeare Bibliography: a Dictionary of every Known Issue of the Writings of Our national Poet and of Recorded Opinion Thereon in the English Language. Stratford-on-Avon: 1911. V. 50; 52

JAGGER, CEDRIC
Paul Philip Barraud: a Study of a Fine Chronometer Maker and of His Relatives, Associates and Successors in the family Business, 1750-1929. London: 1968. V. 53

JAGO, F. W. P.
An English-Cornish Dictionary. London: 1887. V. 52

JAGO, RICHARD
Edge-Hill, or, the Rural Prospect Delineated and Moralized. London: 1767. V. 52
Poems, Moral and Descriptive. London: 1784. V. 48

JAGO, WILLIAM
A Text-Book of the Science and Art of Bread-Making... London: 1895. V. 50; 51

JAGOR, FEODOR
Travels in the Philippines. London: 1875. V. 53

JAHSS, BETTY
Inro and Other Miniature Forms of Japanese Lacquer Art. Rutland: 1971. V. 50; 52; 53

JAKOB, CHRISTFIELD
Atlas of the Nervous System. Philadelphia: 1901. V. 47

JAKSCH, RUDOLF VON
Clinical Diagnosis: The Bacteriological Chemical and Mircoscopical Evidence of Disease. London: 1890. V. 48; 51; 53

JALOVEC, KAREL
German and Austrian Violin makers. London: 1967. V. 49
Italian Violin Makers. New York. V. 49
Italian Violin Makers. London: 1964. V. 51

JAMA, STEPHEN
Currently. Santa Cruz: 1974. V. 53

JAMAICA. ASSEMBLY
The Proceedings of the Governor and Assembly of Jamaica, in Regard to the Maroon Negroes... London: 1796. V. 50

JAMAICA. LAWS, STATUTES, ETC.
The Laws of Jamaica Passed in the Fourth Year of the Reign of Queen Victoria. Jamaica: 1841. V. 48
The Laws of Jamaica. To Which is Added the State of Jamaica, As It Is Now. London: 1684. V. 53; 54

JAMAIN, H.
Les Roses, Histoire, Culture, Description. Paris: 1873. V. 48

JAMBLICHUS, OF CHALCIS
De Mysteriis Liber. Oxford: 1678. V. 48
Iamblichi Chalcidensis Ex Coele-Syria. de Mysteriis Liber. Praemittitur Epistola Porphyrii ad Anebonem Aegyptium, Eodem Argumento. Oxford: 1678. V. 52
Iamblichus on the Mysteries of the Egyptians, Chaldeans & Assyrians. Chiswick: 1821. V. 51
Iamblichus On the Mysteries of the Egyptians, Chaldeans & Assyrians. London: 1895. V. 48
Iamblichvs de Mysteriis Aegyptiorum, Chaldaeorum, Assyriorum... 1516. V. 50

JAMBON, JEAN
Our Trip to Blunderland. Edinburgh: 1877. V. 49
Our Trip to Blunderland. London: 1877. V. 48

JAMES, ALICE
Mississippi Verse. Chapel Hill: 1934. V. 48

JAMES, ANNA
Memoirs of the Beauties of the Court of Charles II. London: 1851. V. 48

JAMES, ARTHUR C.
Songs of Sixpenny and Pupilroom Rippings etc. London: 1899. V. 51

JAMES, ARTHUR E.
The Potters and Potterires of Chester County, Pennsylvania. West Chester: 1945. V. 49

JAMES, BEAUREGARD, PSEUD.
The Road to Birmingham. New York: 1964. V. 53

JAMES, BERTHA TEN EYCK
Zodiac. 1963. V. 53

JAMES, C. L. R.
Beyond a Boundary. London: 1963. V. 49
The Black Jacobins: Toussaint L'Ouverture and the San Domingo Revolution. London: 1938. V. 54
The Black Jacobins: Toussaint L'Ouverture and the San Domingo Revolution. New York: 1938. V. 54
The Black Jacobins: Toussaint L'Ouverture and the San Domingo Revolution. New York: 1939. V. 52
The Case for West-Indian Self Government. New York & Detroit: 1967. V. 47
A History of Negro Revolt. London: 1938. V. 53
History of the French Revolution. Chicago: 1902. V. 50
Lecture on Federation (West Indies and British Guiana). Demerara: 1958. V. 47
Mariners, Renegades, and Castaways - The Story of Herman Melville and the World We Live In. New York: 1953. V. 52
Marxism and the Intellectuals. Detroit: 1962. V. 53
Why Negroes Should Oppose the War. New York. V. 47
Wilson Harris - a Philosophical Approach. Trinidad. V. 47
World Revolution 1917-1936. The Rise and Fall of the Communist International. London: 1937. V. 49

JAMES, CHARLES
A New and Enlarged Military Dictionary, or Alphabetical Explanation of Technical Terms... London: 1802. V. 53
Poems by the Author of Hints to Lord Raawdon on Some Military Abuses. London: 1792. V. 54

JAMES, CHARLES THOMAS CLEMENT
Honours Easy. London: 1892. V. 54
One Virtue a Fiction. London: 1893. V. 53

JAMES, EDWARD
La Belle au Bois Dormant and Other Poems. London: 1933. V. 48
The Bones of My Hand Including La Belle au Bois Dormant, etc. London: 1938. V. 48
Carina Amico, Opus Quintum. 1932. V. 47
Carmina Amico. Verona: 1932. V. 48; 49
The Next Volume. London: 1932. V. 48
Reading Into the Picture. London: 1934. V. 47; 50
Rich Man, Poor Man, Beggerman, Wop... London: 1937-38. V. 47
The Venetian Glass Omnibus - Peace Propaganda for Grown-up Children and Sophisticated Tots. London: 1933. V. 52

JAMES, EDWIN
Account of an Expedition from Pittsburgh to the Rocky Mountains, Performed in the Years 1819, 1820. London: 1823. V. 47
Account of an Expedition from Pittsburgh to the Rocky Mountains, Performed in the Years 1819 and '20... Philadelphia: 1823. V. 47; 49
A Narrative of the Captivity of John Tanner...During Thirty Years Residence Among the Indians in the Interior of North America. New York: 1830. V. 47; 49

JAMES *Forbes; a Tale.* London: 1824. V. 51

JAMES, FRANK LINSLY
The Unknown Horn of Africa. London: 1888. V. 48; 50; 51
The Wild Tribes of the Soudan. London: 1883. V. 50; 52
The Wild Tribes of the Soudan. 1884. V. 54
The Wild Tribes of the Soudan. London: 1884. V. 48; 52

JAMES, FRED J.
Completion Report of Camp Abraham Eustis, School of Railway Artillery Fire. Lee Hall: 1919. V. 49

JAMES, GEORGE PAYNE RAINSFORD
Adra, or the Peruvians; the Ruined City, &c. London: 1829. V. 47; 48
Adrian; or the Clouds of the Mind. New York: 1852. V. 48
The Ancient Regime. London: 1844. V. 51
Arabella Stuart. London: 1847. V. 51
Charles Tyrrel, or, The Bitter Blood. London: 1839. V. 51
The Convict. London: 1847. V. 51
Corse De Leon; or, the Brigand. London: 1841. V. 51
De L'Orme. New York: 1830. V. 52
The Desultory Man. London: 1836. V. 51
The False Heir. London: 1847. V. 51
Forest Days. London: 1843. V. 51
The Gentleman of the Old School. London: 1839. V. 51
Heidelberg. London: 1846. V. 51
Henry Masterton; or the Adventures of a Young Cavalier. London: 1832. V. 51
The History of Chivalry. London: 1830. V. 50; 52
A History of the Life of Edward the Black Prince. London: 1836. V. 49; 53
The Huguenot. London: 1839. V. 51
The Jacquerie; or, The Lady and the Page. London: 1844. V. 51
The Last of the Fairies. London: 1848. V. 53
Letters Illustrative of the Reign of William III from 1696 to 1708. London: 1841. V. 48; 50
The Life and Adventures of John Marston Hall. London: 1844. V. 51
The Life and Times of Louis the Fourteenth. London: 1838. V. 49
The Life of Henry the Fourth King of France and Navarre. New York: 1847. V. 48
The Man at Arms; or, Henri De Cerons. London: 1840. V. 51
Mary of Burgundy; or, the Revolt of Ghent. London: 1833. V. 48
Morley Ernstein, or The Tenants of the Heart. London: 1842. V. 51
Richelieu. London: 1831. V. 51
Rose D'Abret; or, Troublous Times. London: 1847. V. 51
Sir Theodore Broughton; or, Laurel Walter. London: 1848. V. 51
The Step-Mother. London: 1846. V. 51

JAMES, GEORGE WHARTON
The 1910 Trip of the H.M.M.B.A. to California and the Pacific Coast. San Francisco: 1911. V. 47
Arizona, the Wonderland. Boston: 1917. V. 52; 53
California, Romantic and Beautiful. Boston: 1914. V. 52; 54
The Grand Canyon of Arizona. Boston: 1910. V. 47
Indian Basketry. New York: 1901. V. 48; 51; 54
Indian Blankets and Their Makers. Chicago: 1920. V. 51; 53
Indian Blankets and Their Makers. New York: 1937. V. 52
The Land of Delight Makers. Boston: 1920. V. 51
Mark Twain, an Appreciation of His Pioneer Writings on Fasting and Health. Pasadena: 1919. V. 53
Practical Basket Making. Pasadena: 1910. V. 50; 54
The Wonders of the Colorado Desert (Southern California). Boston: 1906. V. 53

JAMES, GRACE
Green Willow and Other Japanese Fairy Tales. London: 1910. V. 47; 49; 50; 54

JAMES, H. E. M.
Extracts from Pedigrees of James of Barrock. Exeter: 1913. V. 50; 52
The Long White Mountain. London: 1888. V. 47
Pedigrees of the Family of James of Culgarth, West Auckland and Barrock and Their Kinsfolk. Exeter: 1913. V. 52

JAMES, HENRY
The Ambassadors. London: 1903. V. 47
The Ambassadors. New York: 1903. V. 47; 50; 52; 53; 54
Ambassadors. New York and London: 1904. V. 51
The Ambassadors. New York: 1930. V. 54
The American. Boston: 1877. V. 51; 53
The American. London: 1879. V. 49; 50
The American Scene. London: 1907. V. 48; 51; 53
The American Scene. New York: 1907. V. 47
The Aspern Papers/ Louisa Pallant/ The Modern Warning. London, New York: 1888. V. 49; 53
The Author of Beltraffio. Boston: 1885. V. 50; 54
The Awkward Age. London: 1899. V. 51
The Awkward Age. New York: 1899. V. 53
The Beast in the Jungle. Kentfield: 1963. V. 49; 53
The Bostonians. London & New York: 1886. V. 50; 54
A Bundle of Letters. Boston: 1880. V. 50; 51; 52; 53
Charles W. Eliot. Boston: 1930. V. 48
Christianity the Logic of Creation. London: 1857. V. 49
The Complete Plays of Henry James. London: 1949. V. 54
Confidence. London: 1879. V. 48
Confidence. Boston: 1880. V. 47; 48; 49; 50; 51
Confidence. London: 1880. V. 48; 49; 50; 53
Confidence. New York: 1880. V. 52
Daisy Miller. New York: 1878. V. 47
Daisy Miller. Boston: 1883. V. 49; 50; 53
Daisy Miller. New York: 1892. V. 51
Daisy Miller. Cambridge: 1969. V. 47; 48; 52; 54
Daisy Miller and an International Episode. New York: 1892. V. 48
The Diary of a Man of Fifty and A Bundle of Letters... New York: 1880. V. 47; 52
Domesday Book or the Great Survey of England of William the Conqueror, A.D. MLXXXVI. Southampton: 1861. V. 54
Embarrassments. New York: 1896. V. 48
English Hours. Boston: 1905. V. 48; 49; 51; 53
English Hours. Cambridge: 1905. V. 52; 53
Essays in London and Elsewhere. London: 1893. V. 54
The Europeans. London: 1878. V. 52; 54
The Europeans. Boston: 1879. V. 47; 50; 53
The Europeans. London: 1879. V. 49
Facsimile of the Black-Letter Prayer Book of 1636, Showing the Manuscript Alterations Made in 1661, and Authorized by the Act of Uniformity, 13 and 14 Car. II., A.D. 1662. Southampton: 1870. V. 54
The Finer Grain: Stories. London: 1910. V. 48; 53
French Poets and Novelists. London: 1878. V. 47; 53; 54
Gabrielle de Bergerac. New York: 1918. V. 50
The Golden Bowl. New York: 1904. V. 48; 50
The Golden Bowl. London: 1905. V. 48; 50; 51
Hawthorne. London: 1879. V. 50; 53
Hawthorne. New York: 1880. V. 47; 52
In the Cage. Chicago & New York: 1898. V. 47; 50; 51
In the Cage. London: 1898. V. 47; 48; 50; 53
An International Episode. New York: 1879. V. 50
Italian Hours. Boston & New York: 1909. V. 47; 48; 49; 50; 52; 54
Italian Hours. London: 1909. V. 50
The Ivory Tower. New York: 1917. V. 50

JAMES, HENRY continued
Julia Bride. New York and London: 1909. V. 48; 51; 53; 54
The Lesson of the Master. London: 1892. V. 50; 53
The Lesson of the Master. New York: 1892. V. 54
The Letters. London: 1920. V. 53
The Letters. New York: 1920. V. 50
Letters. Cambridge: 1974. V. 51
Letters of Henry James to Walter Berry. Paris: 1928. V. 47
Letters to A. C. Benson and Auguste Monod: Now First Published, and Edited... London: 1930. V. 52
The Literary Remains of Henry James. Boston: 1885. V. 47
A Little Tour in France. Boston: 1885. V. 51
A Little Tour in France. Boston: 1900. V. 50; 54
A Little Tour in France. Cambridge: 1900. V. 48; 49; 52; 54
A Little Tour in France. London: 1900. V. 50
A London Life. New York: 1957. V. 52
A London Life. The Patagonia. The Liar. Mrs. Temperly. London: 1889. V. 49
The Madonna of the Future. London: 1879. V. 47
The Madonna of the Future and Other Tales. London: 1880. V. 51
Master Eustace. New York: 1920. V. 49; 50; 53; 54
The Middle Years. London: 1917. V. 47; 49; 50
The Middle Years. New York: 1917. V. 50
A Most Unholy Trade. Cambridge: 1923. V. 48; 50; 51
A Most Unholy Trade Being Letters on the Drama... New York: 1923. V. 50
The Notebooks of Henry James. London: 1955. V. 52
Notes and Reviews. Cambridge: 1921. V. 53
Notes of a Son and Brother. London: 1914. V. 47; 53
Notes on Novelists. London: 1914. V. 53
The Novels and Tales. New York: 1907-09. V. 52
The Novels and Tales. New York: 1907-13. V. 53
The Novels and Tales of Henry James. London: 1908-09. V. 47
The Other House. London: 1896. V. 47; 49; 50; 51
The Other House. New York: 1896. V. 50
The Other House. London: 1897. V. 54
The Outcry. London: 1911. V. 47; 50
Partial Portraits. London: 1888. V. 53
Passionate Pilgrim. Boston: 1875. V. 47; 48; 49; 51; 52; 54
Picture and Text. New York: 1893. V. 47; 49; 50
The Portrait of a Lady. London: 1881. V. 48; 49; 50; 54
The Portrait of a Lady. Boston: 1882. V. 47; 49; 51
The Portrait of a Lady. London: 1882. V. 53
The Portrait of a Lady. Boston: 1882/81. V. 48
The Portrait of a Lady. London: 1883. V. 49
The Portrait of a Lady. New York: 1967. V. 48
Portraits of Places. London: 1883. V. 47; 53
Portraits of Places. Boston: 1884. V. 47; 50; 53
Portraits of Places. Boston: 1884/83. V. 48
The Princess Casamassima. London & New York: 1886. V. 50; 53; 54
The Princess Casamassima. London: 1887. V. 49
The Private Life. London: 1893. V. 47; 51; 53
The Question of Our Speech the Lesson of Balzac. Boston & New York: 1905. V. 48; 50; 52; 53; 54
The Real Thing and Other Tales. London: 1893. V. 47; 51; 53
The Reverberator. London: 1888. V. 47; 50; 52; 53
Roderick Hudson. Boston: 1876. V. 53
Roderick Hudson. London: 1880. V. 47
The Sacred Fount. London: 1901. V. 50
The Secret of Swedenborg: Being an Elucidation of His Doctrine of the Divine Natural Humanity. Boston: 1869. V. 49
The Sense of the Past. London: 1917. V. 51; 54
The Sense of the Past. New York: 1917. V. 49; 50; 51
The Siege of London. The Pension Beaurepas, and The Point of View. Boston: 1883/82. V. 54
A Small Boy and Others. London: 1913. V. 48; 53
A Small Boy and Others. New York: 1913. V. 47; 50
The Social Significance of Our Institutions. Boston: 1861. V. 47; 49
The Soft Side. London: 1900. V. 47; 53
The Soft Side. New York: 1900. V. 48
The Spoils of Poynton. Boston & New York: 1897. V. 54
The Spoils of Poynton. London: 1897. V. 47; 49; 50; 51
Stories Revived in Three Volumes. London: 1885. V. 52; 53
Tales of Three Cities. Boston: 1884. V. 49
Tales of Three Cities. London: 1884. V. 48
Terminations. London: 1895. V. 47; 54
Terminations. New York: 1895. V. 50; 51; 53; 54
Theatricals - Second Series - The Album - The Reprobate. 1895. V. 52
Theatricals - Two Comedies. London: 1894. V. 47; 49; 50
Theatricals. Second Series. London: 1895. V. 49; 51; 52; 53
The Tragic Muse. Boston: 1890. V. 47; 50; 51; 53
The Tragic Muse. London: 1890. V. 47; 48; 49
Transatlantic Sketches. Boston: 1875. V. 47; 48; 49; 50; 52; 53
Transatlantic Sketches. New York: 1875. V. 52
The Turn of the Screw. London: 1940. V. 47
The Two Magics, The Turn of the Screw, Covering End. London: 1898. V. 47; 54
The Two Magics, The Turn of the Screw, Covering End. New York: 1898. V. 49; 54

Views and Reviews. Boston: 1908. V. 53
Washington Square. London: 1881. V. 47; 49; 50
Washington Square. New York: 1881. V. 47; 49; 51; 52; 54
Washington Square. New York: 1971. V. 53
Watch and Ward. Boston: 1878. V. 47; 48; 50; 51
What Maisie Knew. Chicago & New York: 1897. V. 47; 49; 50; 54
The Wheel of Time/Collaboration/Owen Wingrave. New York: 1893. V. 49; 50
William Wetmore Story and His Friends. Boston: 1903. V. 48; 51
William Wetmore Story and His Friends. Edinburgh and London: 1903. V. 53
William Wetmore Story and His Friends. New York: 1903. V. 50
The Wings of the Dove. London: 1902. V. 49; 50
The Wings of the Dove. New York: 1902. V. 50

JAMES, HENRY, COLONEL
Instructions for Taking Meteorological Observations... London: 1860. V. 50

JAMES, HENRY FIELD
Abolitionism Unveiled! Hypocrisy Unmasked! and Knavery Scourged! Luminously Portraying the Formal Hocusses, Whining Philanthropists, Moral Coquets, Practical Atheists and Hollow-Hearted Swindlers of Labor... New York: 1850. V. 54

JAMES, J. T.
The Flemish, Dutch and German Schools Of Painting. London: 1822. V. 50
The Italian Schools of Painting, With Observations on the Present State of the Art. London: 1820. V. 50
Journal of a Tour in Germany, Sweden, Russia, Poland in 1813-14. London: 1819. V. 51; 54

JAMES, JASON W.
Memories and Viewpoints. Roswell: 1928. V. 49; 52; 53; 54

JAMES, JAY
The Book of Spurs...A Catalogue of (The collection of) Jay James. London: 1855?. V. 51

JAMES, JESSE
Jesse James: the Life and Daring Adventures of this Bold Highwayman and Bank Robber and His No Less Celebrated Brother, Frank James; Together with the Thrilling Exploits of the Younger Boys. Philadelphia: 1882. V. 54

JAMES, JOSEPH
A System of Exchange with Almost All Parts of the World. New York: 1800. V. 50; 53

JAMES, KATE
Momotaro, or Little Peachling. Tokyo: 1890. V. 51

JAMES, M. E.
How to Decorate Our Ceilings, Walls and Floors. London: 1883. V. 52

JAMES, MARIA A. W.
I Remember. San Antonio: 1938. V. 48

JAMES, MARQUIS
The Cherokee Strip: an Oklahoma Boyhood. New York: 1945. V. 49

JAMES, MONTAGUE RHODES
The Apocalypse in Latin. Ms. 10 in the Collection of Dyson Perrins. Oxford: 1927. V. 52
The Collected Ghost Stories. London: 1931. V. 48; 49; 50
A Descriptive Catalogue of the Manuscripts in the Fitzwilliam Museum. Cambridge: 1895. V. 52
A Descriptive Catalogue of the Manuscripts in the Library of Eton College. 1895. V. 51
A Descriptive Catalogue of the Manuscripts in the Library of Lambeth Palace. Cambridge: 1930-32. V. 52
A Descriptive Catalogue of the Manuscripts in the Library of Peterhouse... Cambridge: 1899. V. 52
A Descriptive Catalogue of the Manuscripts in the Library of St. John's College Cambridge. 1913. V. 48; 51
A Descriptive Catalogue of the Manuscripts in the Library of Sidney Sussex College, Cambridge. Cambridge: 1895. V. 52
A Descriptive Catalogue of the Manuscripts in the Library of Trinity Hall. 1907. V. 51
A Descriptive Catalogue of the Manuscripts Other than Oriental in the Library of King's College, Cambridge. Cambridge: 1895. V. 51; 54
Fasciculus Ioanni Willis Clark Dicatus. Cambridge: 1909. V. 50
The Five Jars. London: 1922. V. 50; 51
The Frescoes in the Chapel at Eton College. 1907. V. 54
Ghost Stories of an Antiquary. London: 1904. V. 48
Ghost Stories of an Antiquary. New York: 1905. V. 51
Ghost Stories of an Antiquary. New York: 1950. V. 51
Some Remarks on Ghost Stories. Edinburgh: 1985. V. 54
A Thin Ghost and Others. London: 1919. V. 53
Wailing Well. 1928. V. 53

JAMES, NORAH C.
Sleeveless Errand. Paris: 1929. V. 48

JAMES, P. D.
The Black Tower. London: 1975. V. 53
The Black Tower. New York: 1975. V. 52
Cover Her Face. New York: 1966. V. 54
Death of an Expert Witness. London: 1977. V. 48
Death of an Expert Witness. New York: 1977. V. 47
Innocent Blood. London: 1980. V. 51
The Maul and the Pear Tree. London: 1971. V. 52
A Mind to Murder. London: 1963. V. 51
A Mind to Murder. New York: 1963. V. 48; 52
Shroud for a Nightingale. London: 1971. V. 50
Shroud for a Nightingale. New York: 1971. V. 52

JAMES, P. D. *continued*
The Skull Beneath the Skin. London: 1982. V. 48; 49
Unnatural Causes. New York: 1967. V. 52; 54
An Unsuitable Job for a Woman. 1972. V. 54
An Unsuitable Job for a Woman. London: 1972. V. 49; 50
An Unsuitable Job for a Woman. New York: 1972. V. 50

JAMES, PHILLIP
Henry Moore on Sculpture. London: 1966. V. 52; 54

JAMES, ROBERT
Dictionnaire Universel de Medicine... Paris: 1746-48. V. 47
A Treatise on Canine Madness. London: 1760. V. 48; 53; 54

JAMES, S. P.
A Monograph of the Anopheline Mosquitoes of India. Calcutta: 1911. V. 52

JAMES Sprunt: a Tribute From the City of Wilmington. Raleigh: 1925. V. 48; 49

JAMES, T. G. H.
Corpus of Hieroglyphic Inscriptions in the Brooklyn Museum. Brooklyn: 1974. V. 49
Hieroglyphic Texts from Egyptian Stelae, etc. Part 1. London: 1961. V. 51

JAMES, T. H., MRS.
The Hare of Inaba. London: 1888. V. 48
The Hare of Inaba. London: 1900. V. 53
The Prince's Fire-Flash and Fire-Fade. London: 1900. V. 53

JAMES, THOMAS
The History of the Herculean Straits. London: 1771. V. 48; 49; 54
The Jesuit's Downfall, Threatened Against Them by the Secular Priests for Their Wicked Lives... Oxford: 1612. V. 49; 50; 53
Three Years Among the Indians and Mexicans. St. Louis: 1916. V. 49

JAMES, THOMAS ANDREW
Count Cagliostro; or the Charlatan; a Tale of the Reign of Louis XVI. London: 1838. V. 48; 51

JAMES, VINTON LEE
Frontier and Pioneer Recollections of Early Days in San Antonio and West Texas. 1938. V. 49
Frontier and Pioneer Recollections of Early Days in San Antonio and West Texas. San Antonio: 1950. V. 49

JAMES, W. S.
Cow-Boy Life in Texas or 27 Years a Mavrick. Chicago: 1893. V. 50; 52; 53
Cow-boy Life in Texas: or, 27 Years a Mavrick (sic). Chicago: 1898. V. 53

JAMES, WILL
Cow Country. New York: 1927. V. 51
Cowboys North and South. New York: 1924. V. 51; 53
Cowboys North and South. New York: 1925. V. 54
Cowboys, North and South. New York: 1926. V. 47
The Drifting Cowboy. New York: 1925. V. 51; 53
Horses I Have Known. New York: 1940. V. 49
My First Horse. New York: 1940. V. 50
Scorpion. A Good Bad Horse. New York: 1936. V. 47
Smoky. The Cow Horse. 1929. V. 47
The Three Mustangers. New York: 1933. V. 53

JAMES, WILLIAM
A Full and Correct Account of the Chief Naval Occurrences of the Late War Between Great Britain and the United States of America... London: 1817. V. 47
A Full and Correct Account of the Military Occurrences of the Late War Between Great Britain and the United States of America. London: 1818. V. 49
The Literary Remains of Henry James. Boston: 1885. V. 49
The Naval History of Great Britain, from the Declaration of War by France in 1793, to the Accession of George IV... London: 1837. V. 51; 52
A Pluralistic Universe: Hibbert Lectures at Manchester College on the Present Situation. London: 1909. V. 47
The Principles of Psychology. New York: 1890. V. 47; 49
The Varieties of Religious Experience: a Study in Human Nature. New York: 1902. V. 49
What Is An Emotion?. 1884. V. 52

JAMES, WILLIAM DOBEIN
A Sketch of the Life of Brig. Gen. Francis Marion, and a History of His Brigade, From Its Rise in June 1780, Until Disbanded in December 1782... Charleston: 1821. V. 48

JAMES, WILLIAM F.
History of San Jose. San Jose: 1933. V. 52
Saint Patrick of England. San Francisco: 1955. V. 47

JAMES, WILLIAM WARWICK
Inquiries of the Jaws and Face; with Special Reference to War Casualties. London: 1940. V. 54

JAMES I, KING OF GREAT BRITAIN
Apologia pro Juramento Fidelitatis. London: 1609. V. 50; 53
An Apologie for the Oath of Allegiance: First Set Forth Without a Name, and Now Acknowledged by the Author... London: 1609. V. 47; 50
Basilikon Doron (graece). Or His Maiesties Instructions to His Dearest Sonne, Henry the Prince...Felix Kyngston, for John Norton, According to the Copie Printed at Edenburgh. London: 1603. V. 47; 48
Basilikon Doron (graece); or His Maiestys Instructions to His Dearest Sonne, Henry the Prince... London: 1887. V. 53
Dissertatio Politica, De Ivre Monarchiae Liberae. 1615. V. 52
His Maiesties Declaration, Touching His Proceedings in the Late Assemblie and Conuention of Parliament. London: 1621. V. 48; 50
His Maiesties Speach in the Starre-Chamber, The XX. Of Ivne...1616. London: 1616. V. 47; 48; 50
His Majesties Speach in This Last Session of Parliament, as Neere His very Words as Could be Gathered at the Instant. London: 1605. V. 47; 48; 50
His Majesties Speach to Both the Houses of Parliament...the Day of the Adjournment of the Last Session... London: 1607. V. 50
The Kings Maiesties Speech to the Lords and Commons of This Present Parliament at Whitehall, on Wednesday the XXI. of March, Anno Dom. 1609. London: 1609. V. 47
The Political Works... 1918. V. 52
A Proclamation Declaring His Maiesties Pleasure Concerning the Dissoluing of the Present Conuention of Parliament. London: 1621. V. 48; 50
A Publication of His Majesties Edict and Severe Censure against Private Combats and Combatants... London: 1613. V. 48; 50
A Remonstrance...for the Right of Kings, and the Independence of Their Crownes. Cambridge: 1616. V. 48
The Workes of the Most High and Mightly Prince, James, by the Grace of God King of Great Brittaine, France & Ireland. London: 1616. V. 47; 49

JAMES I, KING OF GREAT BRITIAN
Opera. Frankfurt: 16389. V. 51

JAMES I, KING OF SCOTLAND
The King's Quair. 1815. V. 54
The King's Quair. 1903. V. 52; 54
Poetical Remains. Edinburgh: 1783. V. 51

JAMESON, ANNA BROWNELL MURPHY
The Beauties of the Court of King Charles the Second. London: 1833. V. 49
Characteristics of Women, Moral, Poetical and Historical. London: 1833. V. 50
Characteristics of Women, Moral, Poetical and Historical. Philadelphia: 1833. V. 48; 50; 51
Characteristics of Women, Moral, Poetical and Historical. New York: 1837. V. 50
Characteristics of Women, Moral, Poetical and Historical. Philadelphia: 1883. V. 53
A Commonplace Book of Thoughts, Memories, and Fancies. London: 1855. V. 50
Companion to the Most Celebrated Private Galleries of Art in London. London: 1844. V. 50; 53
Legends of the Madonna. London: 1890. V. 47
Legends of the Monasatic Orders. London: 1891. V. 48
Legends of the Monastic Orders. London: 1850. V. 50; 52
Legends of the Monastic Orders. London: 1863. V. 50
Memoirs and Essays Illustrative of Art, Literature and Social Morals. London: 1846. V. 50
Memoirs of Celebrated Female Sovereigns. London: 1831. V. 53; 54
Memoirs of Celebrated Female Sovereigns. London: 1840. V. 50
Memoirs of the Beauties of the Court of Charles II. London: 1851. V. 47; 49; 52; 54
Sacred and Legendary Art. London: 1848-57. V. 51
Sacred and Legendary Art. London: 1857/57/52. V. 51
Sacred and Legendary Art. London: 1891. V. 48
Shakespeare's Heroines. London: 1900. V. 51
Sisters of Charity, Catholic and Protestant and the Communion of Labor. Boston: 1857. V. 51
Sketches in Canada and Rambles Among the Red men. London: 1852. V. 49
Visits and Sketches at Home and Abroad. London: 1835. V. 52; 53
Winter Studies and Summer Rambles in Canada. London: 1838. V. 54
Winter Studies and Summer Rambles in Canada. New York: 1839. V. 53

JAMESON, HORATIO GATES
A Treatise on Epidemic Cholera. Philadelphia: 1855. V. 49; 50

JAMESON, JAMES S.
Story of the Rear Column of the Emin Pasha Relief Expedition. London: 1890. V. 48; 51

JAMESON, R. G.
New Zealand, South Australia and New South Wales: a Record of Recent Travels in These Colonies... London: 1842. V. 50

JAMESON, ROBERT
Historical Record of the Seventy-Ninth Regiment of Foot or Cameron Highlanders. Edinburgh: 1863. V. 51
A Trip to London; or, the Humours of a Berwick Smack. Edinburgh: 1815. V. 53

JAMESON, THOMAS
Essays on the Changes of the Human Body, At its Different Ages; The Diseases to Which It Is Predisposed in Each period of Life... London: 1811. V. 48; 54

JAMI
Salaman and Absal. London: 1856. V. 50

JAMIESON, ALEXANDER
A Dictionary of Mechanical Science, Arts, Manufactures and Miscellaneous Knowledge. London: 1829. V. 50

JAMIESON, FRANCES THURTLE
Ashford Rectory or, the Spoiled Child Reformed. London: 1820. V. 49; 52
Stories from Spanish History, for the Amusement of Children. London: 1820. V. 53

JAMIESON, JOHN
An Etymological Dictionary of the Scottish Language... Edinburgh: 1818. V. 52; 54
An Etymological Dictionary of the Scottish Language... 1878-82. V. 48

JAMIESON, ROBERT
Popular Ballads and Songs, from Tradition, Manuscripts and Scarce Editions. Edinburgh: 1806. V. 50

JAMINET, ALPHONSE
Physical Effects of Compressed Air, and of the Causes of Pathological Symptoms Produced on Man, by Increased Atmospheric Pressure Employed for the sinking of Piers, in the Construction of the Illinois and St. Louis Bridge over the Mississippi... St. Louis: 1871. V. 53

JAMISON, DAVID FLAVEL
The Life and Times of Bertrand Du Guesclin: A History of the Fourteenth Century. Charleston: 1864. V. 48; 50

JAMISON, JAMES CARSON
With Walker in Nicaragua of Reminiscences of an Officer of the American Phalanx. Columbia: 1909. V. 48; 50

JAMISON, MATTHEW H.
Recollections of Pioneer and Army Life. Kansas City: 1911. V. 47

JAMMES, ANDRE
La Reforme de la Typographie Royale Sous Louis SIV le Grandjean. Etude Accompagnee de CX Cuivres Originaux Conserves a l'Imprimerie Nationale. Paris: 1961. V. 48

JAMMES, FRANCIS
Le Tombeau de Jean de la Fontaine by Francis Jammes. Paris: 1921. V. 47

JAMOT, FREDERIC
Varia Poemata Graeca et Latine. Antwerp: 1593. V. 51

JANE, CECIL
Select Documents Illustrating the Four Voyages of Columbus Including Those Contained in R. H. Major's Select Letters of Christopher Columbus. London: 1930/33. V. 49
A Spanish Voyage to Vancouver and the North-West Coast of America Being the Narrative of the Voyage Made in the Year 1792 by the Schooner Sutil and Mexicana to Explore the Strait of Fuca. London: 1930. V. 47; 49; 52
The Voyages of Christopher Columbus... London: 1930. V. 51

JANE, FRED T.
Blake of the 'Rattlesnake' or the Man who saved England. London: 1895. V. 52
The Imperial Russian Navy. London: 1899. V. 48
Jane's Fighting Ships. 1944-45 and 1946-47. London: 1946/47. V. 51
The World's Warships. London: 1915. V. 51

JANE'S All the World's Aircraft 1941. New York: 1942. V. 48

JANE'S All the World's Aircraft 1942. London: 1943. V. 48

JANE'S All the World's Aircraft 1943-44. New York: 1945. V. 48

JANE'S All the World's Fighting Ships. London: 1899. V. 48

JANES, EMILY
The Englishwoman's Year Book and Directory. London: 1900/02-14/16. V. 53

JANE'S Fighting Ships. London: 1938. V. 52
JANE'S Fighting Ships. London: 1940. V. 54
JANE'S Fighting Ships. London: 1944/45. V. 52
JANE'S Fighting Ships. 1906-07. London: 1906. V. 54
JANES Fighting Ships 1907. London: 1907. V. 53
JANE'S Fighting Ships. 1939. London: 1939. V. 54
JANES' Fighting Ships, 1941. London: 1942. V. 48

JANES, THOMAS
The Beauties of the Poets: Being a Collection of Moral and Sacred Poetry, From the Most Eminent Authors. London: 1777?. V. 47
The Beauties of the Poets; Being a Collection of Moral and Sacred Poetry, from the Most Eminent Authors. London: 1800?. V. 52

JANET, PIERRE
The Major Symptoms of Hysteria: Fifteen Lectures Given in the Medical School of Harvard University. New York: 1907. V. 47; 52
Mental State of Hystericals: a Study of Mental Stigmata and Mental Accidents. New York: 1901. V. 52
Psychological Healing: a Historical and Clinical Study. New York: 1925. V. 52

JANIN, JULES GABRIEL
The American in Paris During the Summer. London: 1844. V. 48

JANIS, CHARLES G.
Barbed Boredom. Irvington: 1950. V. 54

JANIS, EUGENIA PARRY
Degas Monotypes. Essay, Catalogue and Checklist. Fogg Art Museum, Harvard University April-June 1968. Greenwich. V. 54

JANIS, HARRIET
Picasso: The Recent Years, 1939-1946. Garden City: 1947. V. 51
Picasso, the Recent Years 1939-46. New York: 1947. V. 51; 53; 54

JANIS, SIDNEY
Abstract and Surrealist Art in America. New York: 1944. V. 50
They Taught Themselves: American Primitive Painters of the 20th Century. New York: 1942. V. 47

JANKA, GYULA
Advises (sic) for Collectors of Miniature Books. Budapest: 1971. V. 52

JANNEAU, GUILLAUME
Le Luminaire et les Moyens d'Eclairages Nouveaux. Paris: 1926/29. V. 48

JANOUCH, GUSTAV
Heckmeck: Ein Prager Nachstuck. 1974. V. 52; 54

JANSEN, MURK
Feebleness of Growth and Congenital Dwarfism With Special Reference to Dysostosis Cleido-Cranialias. New York: 1921. V. 48; 53

JANSON; A Definitive Collection. San Francisco: 1954. V. 48; 52

JANSON, CHARLES WILLIAM
The Stranger in America... London: 1807. V. 47; 48; 50; 51; 52; 53; 54

JANSON, H. W.
The Sculpture of Donatello by... Princeton: 1957. V. 50

JANSSON, TOVE
Who Will Comfort Toffle?. London: 1960. V. 52

JANVIER, CHARLES
Practical Ceramics for Students. London: 1880. V. 50

JANVIER, THOMAS ALLIBONE
Color Studies. New York: 1885. V. 48; 49
In Great Waters. New York: 1901. V. 51
In Old New York. New York: 1894. V. 47; 48
The Uncle of an Angel and Other Stories. New York: 1891. V. 54

JANZEN, D. H.
Costa Rican Natural History. Chicago: 1983. V. 53

JAPAN, Ancient Buddhist Paintings. 1959. V. 48

JAPAN: Her Strength and Her Beauty. New York: 1904. V. 48

JAPAN. SUPREME COURT
Judgment Upon Case of Translation and Publication of Lady Chatterly's Lover and Article 175 of the Penal Code. Tokyo: 1958. V. 51

JAPANESE Children. Tokyo: 1930's. V. 53

JAPANESE Paper Balloon Bombs: the First ICBM. North Hills: 1982. V. 54

JAPP, ALEXANDER HAY
Robert Louis Stevenson, a Record, an Estimate, a Memorial. London: 1905. V. 47
Thoreau: His Life and Aims, a Study. Boston: 1877. V. 51

JAQUES, F. P.
Francis Lee Jaques, Artist of the Wilderness World. Garden City: 1973. V. 50

JAQUES, JOHN
Croquet: the Laws and Regulations of the Game, with a Descritpion of the Implements, Etc., Etc. London: 1867. V. 49

JAQUET, EUGENE
Technique and History of the Swiss Watch. Olten: 1953. V. 47; 52; 53

JARAMILLO, CLEOFAS M.
Shadows of the Past/Sombras del Pasado. Santa Fe: 1941. V. 51

JARDI, ENRIC
Torres Garcia. Barcelona: 1974. V. 47; 49; 52

JARDINE, ALEXANDER
Letter from Barbary, France, Spain, Portugal, &c. London: 1788. V. 52; 53

JARDINE, DAVID
A Narrative of the Gunpowder Plot. London: 1857. V. 51

JARDINE, GEORGE
Outlines of Philosophical Education, Illustrated by the Method of Teaching the Logic, or First Class of Philosophy, in the University of Glasgow. Glasgow: 1818. V. 47; 50

JARDINE, WILLIAM
Birds of Great Britain and Ireland. Part I. Birds of Prey. Edinburgh: 1838. V. 50
British Salmonidae. London: 1979. V. 50; 52; 53; 54
Gallinaceous Birds. Edinburgh: 1834. V. 48
Jardine's Naturalist's Library. Ichthyology. Edinburgh: 1835-43. V. 54
Jardine's Naturalist's Library. Ornithology. Edinburgh: 1845. V. 49
Magazine of Zoology and Botany. Edinburgh: 1837-38. V. 47
Mammalia. Ruminantia. Edinburgh: 1843. V. 49
Memoirs of Hugh Edwin Strickland (and reprints of His Papers). London: 1858. V. 53
The Natural History of Fishes of the Perch Family. Edinburgh: 1835. V. 48; 53
The Natural History of Gallinaceous Birds. London: 1836. V. 48
The Natural History of Humming Birds. Edinburgh: 1833-34. V. 54
The Natural History of the Felinae. Edinburgh: 1834. V. 54
The Natural History of the Ordinary Cetacea or Whales. Edinburgh: 1837. V. 54
The Natural History of the Pachydermes, or Thick Skinned Quadrupeds. Edinburgh: 1836. V. 48; 53
The Naturalist's Library. Edinburgh: 1833-43. V. 49; 52; 54
The Naturalist's Library. Edinburgh: 1839-58. V. 51
The Naturalist's Library. Edinburgh: 1840. V. 53
The Naturalist's Library. Edinburgh: 1845. V. 48
The Naturalist's Library: Ichthyology. Edinburgh: 1853. V. 50

JARMAN, THOMAS
A Treatise on Wills. Jersey City: 1880. V. 50

JARMAN, WILLIAM
U.S.A., Uncle Sam's Abscess, or Hell Upon Earth for U.S. Uncle Sam. Exeter: 1884. V. 49; 50; 52

JARRATT, RIE
Gutierrez de Lara: Mexican Texan, the Story of a Creole Hero. Austin: 1949. V. 48; 52

JARRELL, RANDALL
The Animal Family. New York: 1965. V. 52; 53
Blood for a Stranger. New York: 1942. V. 47; 48; 49; 51; 52; 53; 54
The Death of the Ball Turret Gunner. New York: 1969. V. 49
The Gingerbread Rabbit. New York: 1964. V. 52
Little Friend, Little Friend. New York: 1945. V. 47; 48; 51; 52; 53; 54
Losses. New York: 1948. V. 47; 48; 50; 52; 53
The Lost World. New York: 1965. V. 48; 51; 52; 53
Pictures from an Institution. New York: 1954. V. 47; 50; 51; 52; 53
Poetry and the Age. New York: 1953. V. 52; 53
A Sad Heart at the Supermarket. New York: 1962. V. 51; 53
Selected Poems. New York: 1955. V. 52
The Seven-League Crutches. New York: 1951. V. 47; 48; 51; 52; 53; 54
The Woman at the Washington Zoo. New York: 1960. V. 51; 53

JARRIGE, PIERRE
A Further Discovery of the Mystery of Jesuitisme. London: 1658. V. 53

JARRIN, W. A.
The Italian Confectioner; or, Complete Economy of Desserts, According to the Most Modern and Approved Practice. London: 1844. V. 48; 51

JARRY, ALFRED
Cesar Antechrist. Paris: 1895. V. 51
Mesaline. Paris: 1901. V. 54
Le Moutardier du Pape. 1907. V. 52

JARVES, JAMES JACKSON
A Glimpse at the Art of Japan. New York: 1876. V. 48
History of the Hawaiian or Sandwich Islands... Boston: 1843. V. 47; 49; 52; 54
Italian Sights and Papal Principles, Seen through American Spectacles. New York: 1856. V. 49
Kiana: a Tradition of Hawaii. Boston: 1857. V. 50

JARVIS, RUPERT C.
The Jacobite Risings of 1715 and 1745. Carlisle: 1954. V. 51; 54

JARVIS, T. M.
Accredited Ghost Stories. London: 1823. V. 48; 51

JASPER National Park. Montreal?: 1927. V. 50

JASPERT, W. PINCUS
The Encyclopaedia of Type Faces. New York: 1970. V. 51

THE JATAKA or Stories of the Buddha's former Births. 1895-1907. V. 50; 53

JAUFFRET, LOUIS FRANCOIS
The Travels of Rolando: Containing, In a Supposed Tour Round the World, Authentic Descriptions of the Geography, Natural History, Manners and Antiquities of Various Countries. London: 1823. V. 49

JAUME SAINT-HILAIRE, J. H.
La Flore et la Pomone Francaises. London: 1828-35. V. 49

JAY, CHARLES W.
My New Home in Northern Michigan, and Other Tales. Trenton: 1874. V. 49; 54

JAY, CORNELIA
Diary of Cornelia Jay (1861 to 1873), Rye, Westchester, N.Y. New York: 1924. V. 49

JAY, RICKY
Learned Pigs and Fireproof Women. New York: 1986. V. 53

JAY, WILLIAM
The Life of John Jay, With Selections from His Correspondence and Miscellaneous Papers. New York: 1833. V. 47
A Review of the Causes and Consequences of the Mexican War. Boston: 1849. V. 50

JAYNE, WALTER ADDISON
The Healing Gods of Ancient Civilizations. New Haven: 1925. V. 51; 52

JEAFFRESON, J. C.
The Life of Robert Stephenson, F.R.S. London: 1864. V. 54

JEAN, ELSIE
Singing As We Go. New York: 1925. V. 50

JEAN, MARCEL
The Autobiography of Surrealism. New York: 1980. V. 50
The History of Surrealist Painting. New York: 1967. V. 50; 51; 53; 54

JEAN-AUBREY, G.
Joseph Conrad, Life and Letters. New York: 1927. V. 53; 54
Life and Letters of Joseph Conrad. London: 1927. V. 53

JEAN-AUBRY, G.
Eugene Boudin. Greenwich: 1968. V. 49; 51
Eugene Boudin. London: 1969. V. 54
Joseph Conrad in the Congo. London: 1926. V. 52
Twenty Letters to Joseph Conrad. 1926. V. 52; 54

JEANCON, J. A.
Pathological Anatomy, Pathology and Physical Diagnosis. Cincinnati: 1883. V. 48
Pathological Anatomy, Pathology and Physical Diagnosis. Cincinnatti: 1885. V. 54

JEANNERET-GRIS, CHARLES EDOUARD
Aircraft. London: 1935. V. 53; 54
The Chapel at Ronchamp. New York: 1957. V. 49
The City of Tomorrow and Its Planning. London: 1929. V. 49; 52
Des Canons, des Munitions? Merci! Des Logis... Boulogne: 1938. V. 48
The Marseilles Block. London: 1953. V. 50; 51; 53; 54
My Work. London: 1960. V. 49

JEANS, J. S.
Jubilee Memorial of the Railway System. London: 1875. V. 49
Notes on Northern Industries. London: 1878. V. 53

JEANS, JAMES
Problems of Cosmogony and Stellar Dynamics, Being an Essay to Which the Adams Prize of the University of Cambridge for the Year 1917 was Adjudged. Cambridge: 1919. V. 52

JEANS, THOMAS
The Tommiebeg Shootings; or, a Moor in Scotland. London: 1860. V. 47

JEANSON, MARCEL
The Library of Marcel Jeanson. - Hunting. London: 1987. V. 47; 49

JEBB, BERTHA
A Strange Career: Life and Adventures of John Gladwyn Jebb. Boston: 1895. V. 51
A Strange Career...Life and Adventures of John Gladwyn Jebb. London: 1894. V. 47; 51

JEBB, J.
A Practical Treatise On Strengthening and Defending Outposts Villages, Houses, Bridges &c... (with) A Practical Treatise on the Attack of Military Posts, Villages, Intrenchments &c. Chatham: 1837. V. 50

JEBB, JOHN
Remarks Upon the Present Mode of Education in the University of Cambridge; To Which is Added a Proposal for its Improvement. Cambridge: 1773. V. 48
Select Cases of the Disorder Commonly Termed the Paralysis of the Lower Extremities. London: 1783. V. 47

JEBB, SAMUEL
The Life of Robert Earl of Leicester, The Favourite of Queen Elizabeth. London: 1727. V. 48; 50; 52

JEBSEN, HARRY
Centennial History of the Dallas, Texas Park System, 1876-1976. Lubbock: 1976. V. 47

JEFERIES, RICHARD
Hodge and His Masters. London: 1880. V. 48

JEFFCOCK, JOHN THOMAS
Parkin Jeffcock, Civil and Mining Engineer. London: 1867. V. 49

JEFFCOTT, P. R.
Nooksack Tales and Trails. Ferndale: 1949. V. 54

JEFFERIES, RICHARD
After London; or, Wild England. London: 1884. V. 52
After London, or Wild England. London: 1885. V. 47; 54
Amaryllis at the Fair. London: 1887. V. 47; 48; 49
The Amateur Poacher. London: 1879. V. 53
Bevis: the Story of a Boy. London: 1882. V. 52; 54
Country Vignettes. 1991. V. 50
The Dewy Morn. London: 1884. V. 48; 51; 54
Field and Hedgerow. London: 1889. V. 49
Field and Hedgerow... London: 1892. V. 54
The Gamekeeper at Home. Sketches of Natural History and Rural Life. London: 1878. V. 48; 50
Greene Ferne Farm. London: 1880. V. 48; 50; 51
Hodge and His Masters. London: 1880. V. 47; 48; 49; 51; 52; 54
Jefferies' Land. A History of Swindon and Its Environs. London: 1896. V. 51
The Life of the Fields. London: 1884. V. 53
The Nature Diaries and Note-Books of Richard Jefferies. Billericay, Essex: 1941. V. 54
Nature Near London. London: 1883. V. 53; 54
The Open Air. London: 1885. V. 47; 48
Red Deer. London: 1884. V. 50; 51
A Rook Book. Shropshire: 1988. V. 51; 52
Round About a Great Estate. London: 1880. V. 50; 52
Selections of His Work. London: 1937. V. 50
The Toilers of the Field. London: 1892. V. 48; 51; 54
Wild Life in a Southern County. London: 1879. V. 51; 52
Wild Life in a Southern County. London: 1937. V. 50
Wild Life in a Southern County. London: 1979. V. 48
Wood Magic. London: 1881. V. 48; 51; 52; 54
Wood Magic. London: 1882. V. 50

JEFFERIES RICHARD
After London or Wild England. London: 1885. V. 51

JEFFERS, ROBINSON
All the Corn in One Barn. San Francisco: 1926. V. 47
The Alpine Christ and Other Poems. 1973. V. 53
The Alpine Christ and Other Poems. 1974. V. 51
Apology for Bad Dreams. Paris: 1930. V. 54
An Artist. Austin: 1928. V. 47
Ave Vale. San Francisco: 1962. V. 51
Be Angry at the Sun. New York: 1941. V. 47; 48; 50; 51; 52; 53
The Beaks of Eagles: an Unpublished Poem By... San Francisco: 1936. V. 49; 52
Brides of the South Wind: Poems 1917-1922. 1974. V. 52
Brides of the South Wind, Poems 1917-1922... Santa Barbara: 1974. V. 48; 49

JEFFERS, ROBINSON continued
Californians. New York: 1916. V. 48; 51; 52; 53
Californians. New York: 1928. V. 53
Cawdor. New York: 1928. V. 47; 48; 49; 52; 53; 54
Cawdor. London: 1929. V. 51
Cawdor. 1983. V. 48; 49; 52; 54
Dear Judas. New York: 1929. V. 48; 49; 50; 51; 53; 54
Dear Judas. New York: 1937. V. 53
Descent to the Dead. New York: 1930. V. 53
Descent to the Dead. New York: 1931. V. 48; 49; 50; 51; 52; 53; 54
The Double Axe and Other Poems. New York: 1948. V. 48; 51; 53; 54
Flagons and Apples. Los Angeles: 1912. V. 47; 48; 51; 53
Give Your Heart to the Hawks and Other Poems. New York: 1933. V. 48; 51; 52; 53; 54
Hungerfield and Other Poems. New York: 1954. V. 53
The Inscriptions at Tor House and Hawk Tower. Los Angeles: 1988. V. 48
Light and Shadows from the Lantern. San Francisco: 1926. V. 51; 52
The Loving Shepherdess. New York: 1956. V. 48; 51
Medea. New York: 1946. V. 50; 51; 52
Not Man Apart: Photographs of the Big Sur Coast. San Francisco: 1965. V. 47; 48
The Ocean's Tribute. 1958. V. 51
Poems. San Francisco: 1928. V. 47; 51; 52
Poetry, Gongorism and a Thousand Years. Los Angeles: 1949. V. 48
Return: an Unpublished Poem. San Francisco: 1934. V. 47; 48; 51; 52
Roan Stallion, Tamar and Other Poems. New York: 1925. V. 51; 53
Roan Stallion, Tamar and Other Poems. New York: 1935. V. 49
The Selected Poetry. New York: 1938. V. 48; 52; 53
Solstice and Other Poems. New York: 1935. V. 47; 51; 52; 53; 54
Songs and Heroes. Los Angeles: 1988. V. 47; 48; 49; 51; 52; 53; 54
Stars. Pasadena: 1930. V. 54
Such Counsels You Gave Me and Other Poems. New York: 1937. V. 48; 49; 50; 51; 52; 53; 54
Tamar and Other Poems. New York: 1924. V. 48; 53
Themes in My Poems. New York: 1936. V. 53
Themes in My Poems. San Francisco: 1956. V. 48; 51
Thurso's Landing and Other Poems. New York: 1932. V. 48; 49; 52; 53; 54
Tragedy Has Obligations. Santa Cruz: 1973. V. 53
Two Consolations. San Mateo: 1940. V. 48; 49; 51
The Women at Point Sur. New York: 1927. V. 48; 49; 50; 51; 53; 54

JEFFERS, UNA
Visits to Ireland; Travel-Diaries of Una Jeffers. Los Angeles: 1954. V. 49; 54

JEFFERSON, FRANCIS G.
Best Advice to Youg (sic) Ladies and Gentlemen Before they Get Married. Montreal: 1890?. V. 53

JEFFERSON, GEOFFREY
Selected Papers. London: 1960. V. 52

JEFFERSON, ISAAC
Memoirs of a Monticello Slave. Charlottesville: 1951. V. 53

JEFFERSON, J. B.
The History of Thirsk; Including an Account of Its Once Celebrated Castle, Topcliffe, Byland and Rievalx Abbeys, &c. &c. London: 1821. V. 50

JEFFERSON, JOSEPH
The Autobiography of Joseph Jefferson. London: 1890. V. 53

JEFFERSON, ROBERT L.
A New Ride to Khiva. New York: 1900. V. 53

JEFFERSON, SAMUEL
The History and Antiquites of Leath Ward in the County of Cumberland. Carlisle: 1840. V. 50
The History and Antiquities of Allerdale Ward, Above Derwent, in the County of Cumberland. Carlisle: 1842. V. 50; 52
The History and Antiquities of Carlisle; with an Account of the Castles, Gentlemen's Seats and Antiquities in the Vicinity... Carlisle: 1838. V. 50; 52
The History and Antiquities of Leath Ward, in the County of Cumberland. Carlisle: 1840. V. 50; 52
The Trial and Life of Thomas Cappoch, (The Rebel-Bishop of Carlisle). Carlisle: 1839. V. 50; 52

JEFFERSON, THOMAS
Catalogue of the Library of... Washington: 1952. V. 53
Catalogue of the Library of Thomas Jefferson. Washington: 1952-59. V. 48; 52
The Life and Morals of Jesus of Nazareth. Washington: 1904. V. 51
Memoir, Correspondence and Miscellanies, from the Papers of Thomas Jefferson. Charlottesville: 1829. V. 53; 54
Notes on the State of Virginia. London: 1787. V. 48; 50; 52
Notes on the State of Virginia. Philadelphia: 1788. V. 54
Notes on the State of Virginia. Philadelphia: 1794. V. 50
Notes, On the State of Virginia. Baltimore: 1800. V. 47; 48
Notes on the State of Virginia. New York: 1801. V. 53
Notes on the State of Virginia. Richmond: 1853. V. 51
Observations sur La Virginie. (Notes on Virginia). Paris: 1786. V. 52; 54
The Writings of... Lunenberg: 1967. V. 53

JEFFERSON, WILLIAM
A Selection of Curiosities of Literature, Consisting of Wonders of Nature and Art. York: 1795. V. 47; 48

JEFFERYS, CHARLES
A Price List of British and Foreign Bird-Eggs and Skins, Shells, Crustaceans, Echinoderms, Lepidoptera, Cabinets, Store Boxes & Apparatus of All Kinds. Weston-super-Mare: 1890. V. 54

JEFFERYS, CHARLES W.
Dramatic Episodes in Canada's Story. Toronto: 1930. V. 54

JEFFERYS, THOMAS
The Natural and Civil History of the French Dominions in North and South America. London: 1760. V. 47; 50

JEFFRESS, J. MURRAY
Ritual of the Grand United Order of Moses Incorporated... Charlotte: 1930. V. 52

JEFFREY, F.
Contributions to the Edinburgh Review. London: 1846. V. 47; 54

JEFFREY, J. K.
The Territory of Wyoming: Its History, Soil, Climate, Resources. Laramie: 1874. V. 48

JEFFREYS, ELIZABETH
The Whole Tryal of John Swann and Elizabeth Jeffreys, at Walthamstow, in Essex on the Third Day of July 1751, at the Assizes Held at Chelmsford in Essex, on Wednesday the 11th of March, 1752. London: 1752. V. 50

JEFFREYS, GEORGE
Edwin: a Tragedy. London: 1724. V. 51
An Exact Account of the Trial Between Sr. William Pritchard... and Thomas Papillon...in an Action Upon the Case...Before Sir George Jefferies. London: 1689. V. 50
Miscellanies in Verse and Prose. London: 1754. V. 52
The Proceedings at the Sessions of the Peace Held a Hicks-Hall, for the County of Middlesex...with...Sir William Smith's Speech to the Grand Jury... London: 1682. V. 50

JEFFREYS, GEORGE WASHINGTON
A Series of Essays on Agricultural & Rural Affairs. Raleigh: 1819. V. 48

JEFFREYS, HAROLD
Theory of Probability. Oxford: 1939. V. 50

JEFFREYS, J. G.
British Conchology. London: 1862-69. V. 54
British Conchology. London: 1904, 1862-69. V. 52

JEFFRIES, DAVID
A Treatise on Diamonds and Pearls... London: 1851. V. 50

JEFFRIES, EWEL
Short Biography of John Leeth. Cleveland: 1904. V. 52

JEFFRIES, JOHN
A Narrative of the Two Aerial Voyages of Doctor Jeffries with Mons. Blanchard; with Meteorological Observations and Remarks... 1941. V. 48; 52; 54

JEFFRIES, RICHARD
By the Brook. London: 1981. V. 48

JEHL, FRANCIS
Menlo Park Reminiscences. Dearborn: 1936-41. V. 49; 51

JEKYLL: a Political Eclogue. London: 1788. V. 48

JEKYLL, GERTRUDE
Garden Ornament. London: 1927. V. 47; 48; 51
A Gardener's Testament. London: 1937. V. 54
Gardens for Small Country Houses. London: 1913. V. 48; 50; 53
Gardens for Small Country Houses. London: 1920. V. 51; 54
Gardens for Small Country Houses. London: 1927. V. 48; 49
Old West Surrey. London: 1904. V. 51
Roses for English Gardens. London: 1902. V. 51
Some English Gardens. London: 1904. V. 48
Some English Gardens. London: 1920. V. 48
Wall and Water Gardens. London: 1901. V. 52
Wall and Water Gardens. New York: 1901. V. 51
Wood and Garden. London: 1899. V. 52; 53

JELEN, NICOLETTE
A Dog's Story. New York: 1987. V. 49; 50; 52

JELENSKI, CONSTANTIN
Lenor Fini. New York: 1968. V. 47; 52

JELITTO, L. W.
Hardy Herbaceous Perennials. London: 1990. V. 49
Hardy Herbaceous Perennials. Portland: 1990. V. 47; 51

JELLETT, MAINIE
The Artist's Vision: Lectures and Essays on Art. Dundalk: 1958. V. 54

JELLICOE, JOHN, VISCOUNT
The Grand Fleet 1914-1916.... London: 1919. V. 50

JEMMAT, CATHERINE
Miscellanies, in Prose and Verse. London: 1766. V. 53

JEMMY STRING. New York: 1880. V. 52

JENCKS, CHARLES
Post-Modernism: the New Classicism in Art and Architecture. New York: 1987. V. 50

JENKINS, A. O.
Olive's Last Roundup. Loup City. V. 53
Olive's Last Roundup. Loup City: 1920. V. 47

JENKINS, C. E., MRS.
Evenings at Haddon Hall. London: 1848. V. 54

JENKINS, C. FRANCIS
Animated Pictures: an Exposition of the Historical Development of Chrono-Photography... Washington: 1898. V. 47
The Boyhood of an Inventor. Washington: 1931. V. 48; 53
Radiomovies, Radiovision, Television. Washington: 1929. V. 48; 51; 53
Vision by Radio, Radio Photographs, Radio Photograms. Washington: 1925. V. 48; 50; 52; 53; 54

JENKINS, CATHERINE MINNA
Sport and Travel in Both Tibets. London: 1909. V. 53; 54

JENKINS, DAN
The Dogged Victims of Inexorable Fate. Boston: 1970. V. 50
Semi-Tough. New York: 1972. V. 52

JENKINS, DAVID
Eight Centuries of Reports, Or Eight Hundred Cases Solemnly adjudged in the Exchequer-Chamber, or Upon Writs of Error. London: 1734. V. 52
Jenkinsius Redivivus; or the Works of...Judge Jenkins. London: 1681. V. 48
The King's Prerogative, and Subjects Privileges Asserted According to Law and Reason. London: 1680. V. 49
The Works of that Grave and Learned Lawyer, Judge Jenkins, Prisoner in Newgate. London: 1648. V. 50; 53

JENKINS, G. K.
Ancient Greek Coins. New York: 1972. V. 48

JENKINS, J. T.
History of the Whale Fisheries From the Basque Fisheries of the Tenth Century to the Hunting of the Finner Whale at the Present Date. London: 1921. V. 50
Whales and Modern Whaling. London: 1932. V. 51

JENKINS, JAMES
The Martial Achievements of Great Britain and Her Allies: From 1799 to 1815. London: 1814-15. V. 50
The Martial Achievements of Great Britain and Her Allies, from 1799 to 1815. London: 1815-16. V. 52

JENKINS, JEFF
the Northern Tier, or Life Among the Homestead Settlers. Topeka: 1880. V. 47

JENKINS, JOHN
The Art of Writing. Cambridge: 1813. V. 48; 49; 51; 52; 53
Naval Achievements of Great Britain, from the Year 1793 to 1817. London. V. 52

JENKINS, JOHN EDWARD
Ginx's Baby: His Birth and Other Misfortunes. London: 1870. V. 51
Lord Bantam. London: 1872. V. 51

JENKINS, JOHN H.
Basic Texas Books. Austin: 1983. V. 54
Cracker Barrel Chronicles. Austin: 1965. V. 48; 50; 52; 53
I'm Frank Hamer, the Life of a Texas Peace Officer. Austin: 1968. V. 52
The Papers of the Texas Revolution, 1835-1836. Austin: 1973. V. 52

JENKINS, JOSEPH
The Right Improvement of Divine Judgements. Wrexham: 1772. V. 49

JENKINS, PAUL
Anatomy of a Cloud. New York: 1983. V. 50

JENKINS, PAUL B.
The Battle of Westport. Kansas City: 1906. V. 49

JENKINS, RHYS
Collected Papers, Links In the History of Technology from Tudor Times. Cambridge: 1936. V. 49

JENKINS, ROBERT
Spanish Insolence Corrected by English Bravery.... London: 1739. V. 51

JENKINS, SIMON
Images of Hampstead. Narrative: Simon Jenkins, Catalogue: Johnathan Ditchburn, Gallery of Prints: Harriet and Peter George. Richmond-upon-Thames: 1982. V. 50

JENKINS, WELBORN VICTOR
The Incident at Monroe. Atlanta: 1948. V. 53

JENKINS, WELLBORN VICTOR
We Also Serve: The Story of a Colored Boy Who Stood Single-Handed Against the World and Played the Part of a Hero. 1934. V. 52

JENKINSON, CHARLES
A Discourse on the Conduct of the Government of Great Britian in Respect to Neutral Nations. London: 1794. V. 53

JENKINSON, HENRY IRWIN
Practical Guide to Carlisle, Gilshand, Roman Wall and Neighbourhood. London: 1875. V. 52
Practical Guide to the English Lake District. London: 1876. V. 52

JENKINSON, HILARY
The Later Court Hands in England from the 15th to the 17th Century. Cambridge: 1927. V. 50; 51; 53
The Later Court Hands in England. From the Fifteenth to the Seventeenth Century. New York: 1969. V. 48; 50
Mediaeval Tallies, Public and Private. London: 1925. V. 54

JENKS, A. E.
The Bontoc Igorot. Manila: 1905. V. 54

JENKS, FRANCIS
Mr. Francis Jenk's (sic) Speech Spoken in a Common Hall, the 24th of June 1679. London: 1679. V. 52

JENKS, JAMES
The Complete Cook: Teaching the Art of Cookery In All Its Branches... London: 1768. V. 47

JENKS, SILVESTER
A Contrite and Humble Heart with Motives and Considerations to Prepare It. 1693. V. 50

JENNER, CHARLES
The Destruction of Niniveh: a Poem. Cambridge: 1768. V. 52
Letters from Altamont in the Capital, to His Friends in the Country. London: 1767. V. 52
Louisa: A Tale (in Verse). London: 1774. V. 48
The Placid Man; or, Memoirs of Sir Charles Belville. London: 1770. V. 54
Town Eclogues. London: 1773. V. 50

JENNER, E.
A Flora of Tunbridge Wells. Tunbridge Wells: 1845. V. 54

JENNER, EDWARD
An Inquiry Into the Causes and Effects of the Variolae Vaccinae...Known by the Name of the Cow Pox. 1923. V. 52

JENNES, CHARLES
Messiah; an Oratorio. London: 1767. V. 48; 53

JENNESS, DIAMOND
Eskimo String Figures. Ottawa: 1924. V. 53
The Life of the Copper Eskimos. Ottawa: 1922. V. 51

JENNINGS, BRENDAN
Michael O'Cleirig, Chief of the Four Masters and His Associates. London: 1936. V. 53

JENNINGS, DAVID
An Introduction to the Knowledge of Medals. Birmingham: 1775. V. 52

JENNINGS, EDITH
The Everlasting Animals and Other Stories. London: 1898. V. 52

JENNINGS, ELIZABETH
Poems. Swinford: 1953. V. 48; 49
Winter Wind. 1979. V. 52

JENNINGS, GEORGE HENRY
An Anecdotal History of the British Parliament, From the Earliest Periods to the Present Time. London: 180. V. 48

JENNINGS, HARGRAVE
Phallic Miscellanies: Facts and Phases of Ancient and Modern Sex Worship... 1881. V. 48
Phallic Objects Monuments and Remains... 1889. V. 48

JENNINGS, HENRY CONSTANTINE
An Endeavour to Prove the Reason is Alone Sufficent to the Firm Establishment of Religion, Which Must on Principles of Faith be Ever Precarious. Chelmsford: 1785. V. 53
Summary and Free Reflections, In Which the Great Outline Only, and Principal Features, of the Following Subjects are Impartially Traced and Candidly Examined. Chelmsford: 1783. V. 52

JENNINGS, HERBERT SPENCER
Behavior of the Lower Organisms. New York: 1906. V. 49

JENNINGS, ISAAC
Medical Reform: a Treatise on Man's Physical Being and Disorders, Embracing an Outline of a Theory of Human Life and a Theory of Disease... Oberlin: 1847. V. 53

JENNINGS, JAMES
The Family Cyclopaedia, or Manual of Useful and Necessary Information... London: 1822. V. 48; 50; 52
Observations On Some of the Dialects in the West of England. London: 1825. V. 52
Observations on Some of the Dialects in the West of England, Particularly Somersetshire. London: 1869. V. 52

JENNINGS, JOHN
Two Discourses: The First, of Preaching Christ; the Second, of Particular and Experimental Preaching. Boston: 1740. V. 48

JENNINGS, JOHN J.
Theatrical and Circus Life... St. Louis: 1883. V. 52
Theatrical and Circus Life, or, Secrets of the Stage, Green-Room and Sawdust Arena, Embracing a History of the Theatre, Exposition of the Mysteries of the Stage, Origin and Growth of Negro Minstrelsy... Chicago: 1893. V. 52

JENNINGS, LOUIS JOHN
The Millionaire. Edinburgh and London: 1883. V. 54
The Philadelphian. London: 1891. V. 54

JENNINGS, N. A.
A Texas Ranger. New York: 1898. V. 51
A Texas Ranger. New York: 1899. V. 53

JENNINGS, O. E.
Wild Flowers of Western Pennsylvania and the Upper Ohio Basin. Pittsburgh: 1953. V. 47; 50; 51; 52; 53

JENNINGS, OBADIAH
Debate on Campbellism; Held at Nashville, Tennessee. In Which the principles of Alexander Campbell Are Confuted and His Conduct Examined. Pittsburgh: 1832. V. 49

JENNINGS, PAUL
A Colored Man's Reminiscences of James Madison. Brooklyn: 1865. V. 54

JENNINGS, PAYNE
Summer Holidays in North East England. London: 189-?. V. 54
Sun Pictures of the Norfolk Broads. London: 1892. V. 51

JENNINGS, SAMUEL KENNEDY
The Married Lady's Companion, or Poor Man's Friend. New York: 1808. V. 50

JENNINGS, W. T.
Report Of...On Routes to the Yukon. Ottawa: 1898. V. 47; 50

JENNISON, WILLIAM
An Outline of Political Economy. Philadelphia: 1828. V. 48

JENNY to Jockey. 1752. V. 47

JENSEN, J. MARINUS
History of Provo, Utah. Provo: 1924. V. 51

JENSEN, JORGEN
Design Guide to Orbital Flight. New York: 1962. V. 50

JENSEN, LAURA
Anxiety and Ashes. Poems. Lisbon: 1976. V. 53; 54
A Sky Empty of Orion. San Francisco: 1985. V. 54
Tapwater. Port Townsend: 1978. V. 47; 53

JENYNS, R. SOAME
Chinese Art: the Minor Arts. 1963-65. V. 52

JENYNS, SOAME
Disquisitions on Several Subjects. London: 1782. V. 48; 52; 53
A Free Inquiry Into the Nature and Origin of Evil. London: 1757. V. 51
Lectures Delivered by Soame Jenyns... New York: 1791. V. 48
Miscellaneous Pieces in Two Volumes. London: 1761. V. 50
Miscellaneous Pieces, in Verse and Prose. London: 1770. V. 50; 52; 54
Poems. London: 1752. V. 47; 48; 50; 52; 54
Thoughts on the Causes and Consequences of the Present High-Price of Provisions. London: 1767. V. 52; 53
A View of the Internal Evidence of the Christian Religion. Boston: 1793. V. 49; 52
The Works. London: 1790. V. 47; 48
The Works. Dublin: 1790-91. V. 48
The Works. London: 1793. V. 48

JEPERSEN, ANDERS
Report on Watermills. Volume Three - Scale Drawings. 1957. V. 51

JEPHSON, R. H.
Observations on the Outdoor Relief Systems in England and Wales. Dublin: 1881. V. 52

JEPHSON, RICHARD MOUNTENEY
The Red Rag. London: 1880. V. 54

JEPHSON, ROBERT
Braganza. London: 1775. V. 51

JEPSEN, JORGEN GRUNNET
Jazz Records 1942-1965. Holte, Denmark: 1963-70. V. 47

JEPSON, EDGAR
Memoirs of a Victorian. London: 1933. V. 47

JEPSON, W. L.
The Jepson Manual: Higher Plants of California. London: 1993. V. 50

JEQUIER, GUSTAVE
L'Architecture et la decoration dans l'Ancienne egypte. Paris: 1920-24. V. 49
Le Monument Funeraire de Pepi II. Le Caire: 1936-40. V. 51

JERDAN, WILLIAM
The Autobiography. London: 1852-53. V. 50
National Portrait Gallery of Illustrious and Eminent Personages of the Nineteenth Century. London: 1830's. V. 52

JERDON, T. C.
The Mammals of India. London: 1874. V. 49

JEREMIE, NICOLAS
Twenty Years of York Factory 1694-1714. Ottawa: 1926. V. 53

JEREMY, HENRY
The Law of Carriers, Inn-Keepers, Warehousemen and Other Depositories of Goods for Hire. New York: 1816. V. 52

JERMAINE, JOHN
The Tryal Between Henry Duke of Norfolk, Plaintiff, and John Jermaine Defendant, in an Action of Trepass on the Case at the Court of Kings-Bench at Westmisnter, on the 24th of November, 1692. London: 1692. V. 47

JERMY, A. C.
The Island of Mull, a Survey of Its Flora and Environment by the Dept. of Botany, British Museum. London: 1978. V. 52

JERMYN, JAMES
Book of English Epithets, Litera and Figurative, with Elementary Remarks and Minute References to Abudant Authorities. London: 1849. V. 52

JERNIGAN, T. R.
China's Business Methods and Policy. Shanghai: 1904. V. 54

JERNINGHAM, EDWARD
The Magdalens: an Elegy. London: 1763. V. 54
The Nun: an Elegy. London: 1764. V. 54
The Nunnery. London: 1762?. V. 54
Poems. London: 1774. V. 47
Poems. London: 1779. V. 50; 51
Poems. London: 1786. V. 48; 51; 54
Yarico to Inkle, an Epistle. London: 1766. V. 54

JEROME, CHAUNCEY
History of the American Clock Business for the Past Sixty Years and Life of Chauncey Jerome... New Haven: 1860. V. 47; 50; 53

JEROME, JEROME K.
They and I. London: 1909. V. 52
Three Men in a Boat. Bristol: 1889. V. 47; 51; 52
Three Men in a Boat. Ipswich: 1975. V. 47; 48
Three Men on Wheels. New York: 1900. V. 52
Told After Supper. London: 1891. V. 54

JEROME, JOSEPH
Montague Summers - a Memoir. London: 1965. V. 50

JEROME, JUDSON
Serenade. Berkeley: 1967. V. 47

JEROME, WILLIAM
The Substance of a Sermon, on the Mode of Baptism: Preached at the Presbyterian Meeting House, in Jerseyville, Jersey County, Illinois, Oct. 8th, 1843. Alton: 1843. V. 54

JERRARD, PAUL
The Floral Offering. London: 1852. V. 48
Flower Painting in Twelve Progressive Lessons. London: 1852. V. 52

JERRETT, HERMAN DANIEL
California's El Dorado Yesterday and Today. Sacramento: 1915. V. 47; 49

JERROLD, BLANCHARD
A Brage-Beaker With the Swedes: or, Notes from the North in 1852. London: 1854. V. 52
The Life and Remains of Douglas Jerrold. London: 1859. V. 54
The Life of George Cruikshank. London: 1882. V. 49; 51; 54
London: a Pilgrimage. London: 1872. V. 47; 52

JERROLD, DOUGLAS WILLIAM
The Big Book of Fairy Tales. London: 1911. V. 51
The Catspaw, a Comedy. London: 1850. V. 47
Fireside Saints. London: 1904. V. 49
A Man Made of Money. London: 1849. V. 49; 52
Men of Character. London: 1838. V. 48
Mrs. Caudle's Curtain Lectures. London: 1866. V. 48; 49; 51
Punch's Complete Letter Writer. London: 1845. V. 50
The Story of a Feather. London: 1844. V. 48
The Works of Douglas Jerrold. London: 1855. V. 52

JERROLD, MAUD F.
Francesco Petrarca Poet and Humanist. London: 1909. V. 53

JERROLD, WALTER
The Big Book of Fables. New York: 1912. V. 48
The Big Book of Fables. London: 1913. V. 54
The Big Book of Fairy Tales. London: 1938. V. 52
The Big Book of Nursery Rhymes. London: 1940. V. 51
Bon-Mots of the Eighteenth Century. London: 1897. V. 52
Douglas Jerrold. Dramatist and Wit. London: 1914. V. 54
Thomas Hood: His Life and Times. London: 1907. V. 51
The True Annals of Fairyland, The Reign of King Oberon. London: 1902. V. 49

JERSEY, COUNTESS OF
Maurice or the Red Jar. 1894. V. 47; 51

JERSEY. LAWS, STATUTES, ETC.
A Code of Law for the Island of Jersey. St. Helier: 1771. V. 49

JERSEY, WILLIAM VILLIERS, EARL OF
A Letter to Miss (Ann) F(or)d (later Thicknesse). London: 1761. V. 53

JERVIS, H.
Narrative of a Journey to the Falls of the Cavery... London: 1834. V. 49

JERVIS, THOMAS BEST
Records of Ancient Science, Exemplified and Authenticated in the Primitive Universal Standard of Weights and Measures. Calcutta: 1835. V. 48; 51

JERVOISE, E.
The Ancient Bridges of England and Wales. London: 1930-36. V. 48

JESSE, EDWARD
Anecdotes of Dogs. London: 1870. V. 47
Angler's Rambles. London: 1836. V. 53
Gleanings in Natural History... London: 1832-34. V. 51; 54

JESSE, EDWARD continued
Gleanings in Natural History. London: 1834-35. V. 54
Gleanings in Natural History. London: 1838. V. 49; 51; 52

JESSE, F. TENNYSON
The City Curious. London: 1920. V. 51

JESSE, G. R.
Researches Into the History of the British Dog... London: 1866. V. 47; 49

JESSE, J. HENEAGE
Historical Memoirs Complete. London: 1901. V. 49
Literary and Historical Memorials of London. London: 1847. V. 50; 52
London and its Celebrities. London: 1850. V. 50
London: Its Celebrated Characters and Remarkable Places. London: 1871. V. 47; 52; 53
Memoirs of the Life and Reign of King George III. London: 1867. V. 49

JESSE, WILLIAM
The Life of George Brummell, Esq. Commonly Called Beau Brummel. London: 1886. V. 48; 53

JESSEL, FREDERIC
A Bibliography of Works in English on Playing Cards and Gaming. London: 1905. V. 51; 54

JESSEN, B. H.
W. N. McMillan's Expeditions and Big Game Hunting in sudan, Abyssinia, and British East Africa. London: 1906. V. 48

JESSOP, J. P.
Flora of South Australia. Canberra: 1991. V. 50

JESSOP, T. E.
Bibliography of David Hume and of Scottish Philosophy. New York: 1983. V. 53

JESSOP, THOMAS
The Jesuites Ghostly Wayes to Draw other Persons Over to Their Damanable Principle of the Meritoriousness of Destroying Princes... London: 1679. V. 48; 49

JESSOP, WILLIAM
River Severn. To the Noblemen and Gentlemen Owners of Land on the Banks of the Severn. Newark-upon-Trent: 1786. V. 54

JESSUP, HENRY H.
Fifty Three Years in Syria. New York: 1910. V. 47

JESUIT Letters. *Litterae Annvae Societatis Iesv anni MDCI.* Antwerp: 1618. V. 53

THE JESUIT'S *Justification, Proving they Died as Innocent as the Child Unborn.* 1679. V. 47

JET Propulsion: a Reference Text. 1946. V. 52

JETTE, JULES S.
Canotle Rannaga Kelekak. Delochet Roka. Winnipeg: 1904. V. 48

JEVONS, MARY ANNE ROSCOE
Poems for Youth. London: 1820. V. 50

JEVONS, WILLIAM STANLEY
Method of Social Reform and Other Parts. London: 1883. V. 50
Money and the Mechanism of Exchange. New York: 1875. V. 50
The Principles of Science: a Treatise on Logic and Scientific Method. London: 1874. V. 52
The Principles of Science; a Treatise on Logic and Scientific Method. London: 1905. V. 48; 52; 54
The State in Relation to Labour. London: 1882. V. 54

JEWEL, JOHN
Apologia Ecclesiae Anglicanae. London: 1581. V. 49
A Defense of the Apologie of the Churche of Englande. London: 1570. V. 47
An Exposition Vpon the Two Epistles of the Apostle Saint Paul to the Thessalonians. London: 1594. V. 50
The Tourist's Companion, or the History and Antiquities of Harewood in Yorkshire... Leeds: 1822. V. 47
The True Copies of the Letters Betwene the Reverend Father in God John Bishop of Sarum and D. Cole, Upon Occasion of a Sermon that the Said Bishop Preched Before the Quenes Majestie, and hyr Most Honorable Counsayle. 1560. London: 1560. V. 52
The Workes... London: 1609. V. 51
The Workes... London: 1611. V. 49

THE JEWELERS' Circular-Keystone, Philadelphia. *Sterling Flat-Ware Pattern* index. 1958. V. 52

JEWELL, P. A.
The Biology of Large African Mammals in Their Environment. Oxford: 1989. V. 50

JEWERS, ARTHUR J.
Wells Cathedral: its Monumental Inscriptions and Heraldry. London: 1892. V. 48; 50; 53

JEWETT, PAUL
The New-England Farrier: or A Compendium of Farriery... Exeter: 1822. V. 47

JEWETT, SARAH ORNE
Betty Leicester, a Story for Girls. Boston: 1890. V. 53
Country By-Ways. Boston: 1881. V. 51
Country By-Ways. Boston: 1886. V. 50
A Country Doctor. Boston & New York: 1884. V. 49; 50; 51
The Country of the Pointed Firs. Boston: 1896. V. 49; 54
The Country of the Pointed Firs. Boston: 1899. V. 50
Deephaven. Cambridge: 1874. V. 50
Deephaven. 1877. V. 53
Deephaven. Boston: 1877. V. 48; 50; 51; 54
Deephaven. Cambridge: 1894. V. 50; 53
A House Party. Boston: 1901. V. 49
The Life of Nancy. Boston & New York: 1895. V. 51; 53; 54
A Marsh Island. Boston: 1885. V. 47; 50, 54
A Native of Winby, and Other Tales. Boston: 1893. V. 51
A Native of Winby and Other Tales. Boston & New York: 1894. V. 54
Old Friends and New. Boston: 1879. V. 49
The Queen's Twin and Other Stories. Boston and New York: 1899. V. 48; 54
Strangers and Wayfarers. Boston and New York: 1890. V. 49
Tales of New England. Boston: 1895. V. 51
The Tory Lover. Boston and New York: 1901. V. 49
A White Heron and Other Stories. Boston & New York: 1886. V. 54

JEWISH Emancipation a Christian Duty. London: 1853. V. 54

JEWISH PUBLICATION SOCIETY
Constitution and By-Laws of the American Jewish Publication Society. Philadelphia: 1845. V. 50; 53

JEWITT, JOHN R.
The Adventures of John Jewitt. London: 1896. V. 48
Narrative fo the Adventures and Sufferigns (sic) of John R. Jewitt. Ithaca: 1851. V. 47
A Narrative of the Adventures and Sufferings of John R. Jewitt; Only Survivor of the Crew of the Ship Boston During a Captivity of Nearly 3 Years Among the Savages of Nootka Sound. Middletown: 1815. V. 48

JEWITT, LLEWELLYNN
The Ceramic Art of Great Britain. London: 1883. V. 51
The Corporation Plate and Insignia of Office of the Cities and Towns of England and Wales. London: 1895. V. 52
The Life and Works of Jacob Thompson. London: 1882. V. 48

JEWKES, JOHN
An Industrial Survey of Cumberland and Furness. Manchester: 19133. V. 52

JEWS. LITURGY & RITUAL. HAGADAH
The Haggadah. Jerusalem. V. 52
The Haggadah for Passover. Paris: 1965. V. 49
Haggadah for Passover. 1966. V. 52
Haggadah for Passover. Paris: 1966. V. 48

JEWSBURY, GERALDINE
The Half Sisters. London: 1848. V. 50
Marian Withers. London: 1851. V. 54
The Sorrows of Gentility. London: 1856. V. 50

JEZREEL, JAMES J.
Extracts from the Flying Roll: Being a Series of Sermons Compiled for the Gentile Churches of All Sects and Denominations. 1879. V. 52

JHABVALA, RUTH PRAWER
Esmond in India. London: 1958. V. 51; 52
Heat and Dust. London: 1975. V. 47
The Householder. London: 1960. V. 51
The Nature of Passion. London: 1956. V. 51; 52
To Whom She Will. London: 1955. V. 51; 52

JICHENG, L.
The Realm of Tibetan Buddhism. San Francisco: 1985. V. 51

JOAN, NATALIE
Cosy-Time Tales. London. V. 51
The Glad Book. London: 1920. V. 49
In the Garden. London. V. 49
The Joyous Book. London: 1920. V. 49
Little Mothers. V. 49
The Pleasant Book. London: 1920. V. 49

JOANNIDES, PAUL
The Drawings of Raphael, with a Complete Catalogue. Oxford: 1983. V. 50

JOAO DOS PRAZERES, F.
Abecedario Real, e Regia Instruccam de Principes Lustianos... Lisbon: 1692. V. 48

JOAQUIN Murieta, the Brigand Chief of California. San Francisco: 1932. V. 49; 52

JOBE, JOSEPH
Great Tapestries, The Web of History from the 12th to the 20th Century. Lausanne: 1965. V. 47

JOBLIN, MAURICE
Cincinnati, Past and Present, or, Its Industrial History, as Exhibited in the Life-Labors of Its Leading Men. Cincinnati: 1872. V. 54

JOBSON, RICHARD
The Golden Trade: or, a Discovery of the River Gambra, and the Golden Trade of the Aethiopians. London: 1623. V. 50

JOCELYN, ARTHUR
Awards of Honour: the Orders, Decorations, Medals and Awards of Great Britian and the Commonwealth from Edward III to Elizabeth II. London: 1956. V. 50

JOCELYN, ROBERT
Six Months with the Chinese Expedition; or Leaves from a Soldier's Note Book. London: 1841. V. 54

JOCELYN, SIMEON S.
College for Colored Youth. An Account of the New-Haven City Meeting and Resolutions, with Recommendations of the College and Strictures Upon the Doings of New Haven. New York: 1831. V. 49

JOCELYN, STEPHEN PERRY
Mostly Alkali. Caldwell: 1953. V. 47; 48; 49; 52; 53; 54

JOE Miller's Jests; or, the Wits Vade-Mecum... London: 1750. V. 47

JOE Miller's Jests; or, the Wits Vade-Mecum. London: 1775. V. 48

JOE Miller's Jests, or, Wit's Merry Companion. London: 1790. V. 47

JOEL-PETER Witkin. Paris: 1989. V. 53

JOESTING, EDWARD
The Islands of Hawaii. Honolulu: 1958. V. 51

JOHANKNECHT, SUSAN
Salt Flower. 1977. V. 54

JOHANNES, ALBERT
The House of Beadle and Adams and Its Dime and Nickel Novels. Norman: 1950-62. V. 47

JOHANNES DE JANDUNO
Quaestiones Super Libros Aristotelis de Anima. Venice: 1480. V. 50

JOHANNES DE LAPIDE
Resolutorium Dubiorum Circa Celebrationem Missarum Occurrentium. Strassburg. V. 47; 49

JOHANNES DE SANCTO GEMINIANO
Opusculum de Quibusdam Materijs Predicabilibus de Operibus Sex Dieuorum Predicatum. Paris: 1512. V. 53

JOHANNES DE VERDENA
Sermones Dormi Secure de Tempore. Basel: 1484. V. 52

JOHANNES GALLENSIS
Summa Collationum, Sive Communiloquium. Venice: 1496. V. 51

JOHANNES VERCELLENSES
Sermones Vademecum de Tempore idem Sanctis per Figures Utiles. Strassburg: 1488-93. V. 47; 49

JOHANNSEN, ALBERT
Phiz. Illustrations from the Novels of Charles Dickens. Chicago: 1956. V. 54

JOHANSEN, A. C.
Randers Fjords Naturhistorie. Copenhagen: 1918. V. 51

JOHANSEN, HJALMAR
With Nansen in the North. A Record of the Fram Expedition in 1893-96. London: 1899. V. 50

JOHN, AUGUSTUS
Augustus John. London: 1944. V. 53
Fifty-Two Drawings. London: 1957. V. 48; 50; 54

JOHN Betjeman - a Celebration - October 29 - December 8. 1984. V. 49

JOHN Buchan. 1847-1911. Peebles: 1912. V. 49; 54

JOHN Bull's New Budget of Mirth. London: 1828. V. 47

JOHN Cheap the Chapman's Library: The Scottish Chap Literature of the Last Century, Classified. With Life of Dougal Graham. London: 1877-88. V. 48

JOHN Chipman Gray. Boston: 1917. V. 54

JOHN Davies; Memories and Appreciations. Newtown: 1938. V. 52

THE JOHN Donkey. Philadelphia and New York: 1848. V. 48

JOHN, E.
Sixty Years of Canadian Cricket. Toronto: 1895. V. 51

JOHN, E. B.
Camp Travis and its Part in the World War. New York: 1919. V. 52

JOHN, EDMOND
The Flute of the Sardonyx. 1991. V. 52

JOHN Fitzgerald Kennedy Memorial. Dallas. V. 48

JOHN Keats Unpublished Poem to His Sister Fanny, April, 1818. Boston: 1909. V. 53

JOHN, OF SALISBURY, BP. OF CHARTRES
Policrataicus...Libri Octo. Lugduni Batavorum: 1639. V. 50; 51; 52
Policraticvs. Leyden: 1595. V. 48; 50

JOHN Paul Jones - Commemoration at Annapolis April 24, 1906. Washington: 1907. V. 47

JOHN, RERESBY
Memoirs...Containing Several Private and Remarkable Transactions, from the Restoration to the Revolution Inclusively. London: 1735. V. 47

JOHN, SAMUEL
A Journey to the Western Islands of Scotland. London: 1775. V. 48

JOHN, W. D.
Pontypool and Usk Japanned Wares: with the Early History of the Iron and Tinplate Industries at Ponypool. Newport: 1953. V. 52
William Gillingsley (1758-1828) the Outstanding Achievements as an Artist and Porcelain Maker. Newport: 1968. V. 52

JOHN CHRYSOSTOM, SAINT
(Greek title, then) In Omnes Pauli Apostoli Epistolas Accuratissima, Vereque Aurea et Divina Interpretartio. Verona: 1529. V. 54

JOHN OF THE CROSS, SAINT
Poems of St. John of the Cross. London: 1951. V. 50
The Song of the Soul. Capel-y-Ffin, Abergavenny: 1927. V. 48

JOHNS, C. A.
British Birds in their Haunts. London: 1862. V. 51; 54
Flora Sacra; or the Knowledge of the Works of Nature. London: 1840. V. 54
A Ramble in Spring (Summer, Autumn): a Winter Ramble in the Country. London: 1847/50?/52/47. V. 54

JOHNS, JASPER
Drawings 1954-1984. New York: 1984. V. 48; 49
Technics and Creativity. New York: 1971. V. 51
Technics and Creativity II: Gemini Gel. New York: 1971. V. 52

JOHNS, ORRICK
Asphalt and other Poems. New York: 1917. V. 47; 48; 49

JOHNS, W. E.
Biggles Flies West. 1937. V. 48
Biggles of the Camel Squadron. London: 1934. V. 48
The Camels Are Coming. London: 1934. V. 48

JOHNSON, A. E.
Below Zero A Travesty of Winter Sport. London: 1918.. V. 53
The Russian Ballet. London: 1913. V. 49; 51

JOHNSON, A. F.
Type Designs: Their History and Development. London: 1934. V. 52

JOHNSON, A. J.
Johnson's New Illustrated...Family Atlas, with Descriptions, Geographical, Statistical and Historical. New York: 1862. V. 50

JOHNSON, A. S.
Cattle Raising in South Central and South West Kansas. Leavenworth: 1881. V. 48

JOHNSON, A. W.
The Birds of Chile and Adjacent Regions of Argentina. Buenos Aires: 1965-67. V. 48
The Birds of Chile and Adjacent Regions of Argentina, Bolivia and Peru. Buenos Aires: 1965-67-72. V. 54

JOHNSON, ADAM R.
The Partisan Rangers of the Confederate States Army... Louisville: 1904. V. 47

JOHNSON, ALEXANDER
Ten - and Out! The Complete Story of the Prize Ring in America. New York: 1927. V. 50

JOHNSON, ALEXANDER B.
An Inquiry into the Nature of Value and Capital and Into the Operation of Government Loans, Banking Institutions and Private Credit. New York: 1813. V. 48; 53

JOHNSON, ALFRED
The Golden Playbook, Comprising the Golden Alphabet, Dorothy's Dolls and Red Riding Hood's Party. London: 1886. V. 49

JOHNSON, ALFRED FORBES
A Catalogue of Engraved and Etched English Title-Pages... London: 1933. V. 48
A Catalogue of Engraved and Etched English Title-Pages... London: 1934. V. 48
A Catalogue of Engraved and Etched English Title-Pages... Oxford: 1934. V. 48
Decorative Initial Letters, Collected and Arranged... London: 1931. V. 47; 52
German Renaissance Title-Borders. London: 1929. V. 48
German Renaissance Title-Borders. Oxford: 1929. V. 50
One Hundred Title-Pages, 1500-1800. London: 1928. V. 49
Selected Essays on Books and Printing. Amsterdam: 1970. V. 47
Selected Essays on Books and Printing. Amsterdam: 1971. V. 48

JOHNSON, ALGERNON SYDNEY
Memoirs of a Nullifier. Columbia: 1832. V. 49

JOHNSON, AMANDUS
The Swedish Settlements on the Delaware: Their History and Relation to the Indians, Dutch and English, 1638-1664. Philadelphia: 1911. V. 47; 49; 51

JOHNSON, ANDREW
Trial of Andrew Johnson...on Impeachment by the House of Representatives for High Crimes and Misdeameanors. Published by Order of the Senate. Washington: 1868. V. 47

JOHNSON, ANNA
Shakespeare's Heroines. London and New York: 1900. V. 49

JOHNSON, B. S.
Albert Angelo. London: 1964. V. 49; 50; 51
House Mother Normal - a Geriatric Comedy. London: 1971. V. 50; 53
Poems. 1964. V. 51
Street Children. London: 1964. V. 50
Travelling People. London: 1963. V. 49; 51; 53
Trawl. London: 1966. V. 51
The Unfortunates. London: 1969. V. 49; 50; 51

JOHNSON, BRADLEY TYLER
A Memoir of the Life and Public Service of E. Johnston, Once the Quartermaster General of the Army of the United States and a General in the Army of the confederate States of America. Baltimore: 1891. V. 49; 51

JOHNSON, BRITA ELIZABETH
Maher-Shalal-Hash-Baz or Rural Life in Old Virginia. Claremont: 1923. V. 50

JOHNSON, BURGES
Pleasant Tragedies of Childhood. New York: 1905. V. 49

JOHNSON, C.
British Poisonous Plants. London: 1856. V. 51; 52; 53; 54

JOHNSON, CECIL
A Printer's Garland. San Francisco: 1935. V. 48; 50

JOHNSON, CHARLES
English Court Hand, A.D. 1066 to 1500... Oxford: 1915. V. 48; 50; 51; 53
English Court Hand, A.D. 1066 to 1500. New York: 1967. V. 48; 50
A General History of the Lives and Adventures of the Most Famous Highwaymen, Murderers, Street Robbers, Etc. London: 1734. V. 49; 50
A General History of the Pyrates, from Their First Rise and Settlement, in the Island of Providence, to the Present Time. London: 1724. V. 47
A General History of the Robberies and Murders of the Most Notorious Pirates... London: 1926. V. 50
Middle Passage. New York: 1990. V. 48; 52; 53; 54
The Sorcerer's Apprentice. New York: 1986. V. 48; 53
The Village Opera. London: 1729. V. 52
The Wife's Relief; or, the Husband's Cure. London: 1712. V. 47

JOHNSON, CHARLES E.
An Address Delivered Before the Medical Society of North Carolina, At Its Second Annual Meeting, in Raleigh, May, 1851. Raleigh: 1854. V. 50

JOHNSON, CHARLES P.
Hints to Collectors of Original Editions of the Work of Charles Dickens. London: 1885. V. 50; 51; 54

JOHNSON, CHARLES R.
Being and Race: Black Writing Since 1970. Bloomington: 1988. V. 53
Black Humor. Chicago: 1970. V. 51; 54

JOHNSON, CHRISTOPHER TURNER
A Practical Essay on Cancer; Being the Substance of Observations to Which the Annual Prize for 1808 was Adjudged by the Royal College of Surgeons of London. Philadelphia: 1811. V. 51

JOHNSON, CLIVE W.
With Memsaab on Safari. Los Angeles: 1956. V. 47

JOHNSON, CUTHBERT WILLIAM
The Life of Sir Edward Coke. London: 1837. V. 53
On Guano as a Fertilizer. London: 1843. V. 50
On Increasing the Demand for Agricultural Labour. London: 1841. V. 49; 53
On Rendering Manures More Portable and Applicable by the Drill. London: 1841. V. 50

JOHNSON, D.
Palms for Human Needs in Asia: Palm Utilization and Conservation in India, Indonesia, Malaysia and the Philippines. London: 1991. V. 50
Palms for Human Needs in Asia; Palm Utilization and Conservation in india, Indonesia, Malaysia and the Philippines. Rotterdam: 1991. V. 52; 54

JOHNSON, DANIEL
Sketches of Field Sports as Followed By the Natives of India. London: 1822. V. 52
Sketches of Indian Field Sports. London: 1827. V. 51

JOHNSON, DENIS
Angels. New York: 1983. V. 53
Fiskadoro. New York: 1985. V. 49; 53
The Incognito Lounge and Other Poems. New York: 1982. V. 53
Inner Weather. Port Towsend: 1976. V. 54
The Man Among the Seals. Iowa City: 1969. V. 51; 54

JOHNSON, DIANA L.
Fantastic Illustration and Design in Britain 1850-1930. 1979. V. 54

JOHNSON, DIANE CHALMERS
American Art Nouveau. New York: 1979. V. 51

JOHNSON, EARVIN
My Life. New York: 1992. V. 54

JOHNSON, EDGAR
Charles Dickens - His Tragedy and Triumph. London: 1953. V. 53

JOHNSON, EDWARD A.
History of Negro Soldiers in the Spanish American War. Raleigh: 1899. V. 48; 49; 51

JOHNSON, EDWIN F.
Railroad to the Pacific. Northern Route. Its General Character, Relative Merits, etc. New York: 1854. V. 47

JOHNSON, ELDRIDGE REEVES
Tarpomania and Buck Fever. 1928. V. 47

JOHNSON, F. W.
History of Texas and Texans. Chicago: 1914. V. 53
History of Texas and Texans. Chicago: 1916. V. 53
Texas and Texans. Chicago & New York: 1914. V. 48

JOHNSON, FENTON
Visions in the Dusk. New York: 1915. V. 53

JOHNSON, FRANKLIN P.
The Farwell Collection. Cambridge: 1953. V. 50; 52

JOHNSON, G. W.
The Cottage Gardener; or, Amateur and Cottager's Guide to Out-Door Gardening and Spade Cultivation. London: 1849. V. 47; 51; 54
The Cottage Gardeners' Dictionary... London: 1852. V. 50
The Cottage Gardeners' Dictionary. London: 1860. V. 53
A History of English Gardening. London: 1829. V. 54

JOHNSON, GEORGE
Johnson's Graphic Statistics. Ottawa: 1887. V. 49

JOHNSON,, GUION GRIFFIS
Ante-Bellum North Carolina: a Social History. Chapel Hill: 1937. V. 51

JOHNSON, HARISON
Johnson's History of Nebraska. Omaha: 1880. V. 48

JOHNSON, HENRY
An Introduction to Logography, or the Art of Arranging and Composing for Printing with Words Intire (sic!), Their Radices and Terminations Instead of Single Letters... London: 1783. V. 49

JOHNSON, HENRY LEWIS
Gutenberg and the Book of Books with Bibliographical Notes, Reproductions of Specimen Pages... New York: 1932. V. 48; 49; 51
Historic Design in Printing. Boston: 1923. V. 51

JOHNSON, HERBERT CLARK
Poems from Flat Creek. Francistown: 1943. V. 54

JOHNSON, HOMER URI
From Dixie to Canada Romances and Realities of the Underground Railroad. Buffalo: 1894. V. 50

JOHNSON, HONOR
Herbal: Poems. Woodside: 1980. V. 54

JOHNSON, J.
A View of the Jurisprudence of the Isle of Man... Edinburgh: 1811. V. 52

JOHNSON, J. B.
The Theory and Practice of Modern Framed Structures. New York: 1895. V. 50

JOHNSON, JACK
Jack Johnson- In the Ring and Out. Chicago: 1927. V. 51; 52

JOHNSON, JAMES
An Account of a Voyage to India, China &c. in His Majesty's Ship Caroline, Performed in the Years 1803-04-05... London: 1806. V. 50
Change of Air, or the Philosophy of Travelling... New York: 1831. V. 47; 50; 52; 53
Change of Air or the Pursuit of Health and Recreation Through France, Switzerland and Italy... London: 1832. V. 48
The Influence of Tropical Climates on European Constitutions... London and Portsmouth: 1818. V. 53
Transactions of the Corporation of the Poor, in the City of Brisol, During a Period of 126 Years. Bristol: 1826. V. 53

JOHNSON, JAMES RAWLINS
A Treatise on the Medicinal Leech. London: 1816. V. 48

JOHNSON, JAMES WELDON
Along This Way. The Autobiography of James Weldon Johnson. New York: 1933. V. 47
The Autobiography of an Ex-Colored Man. Boston: 1912. V. 53
Black Manhattan. New York: 1930. V. 49; 50; 53; 54
The Book of American Negro Poetry. New York: 1922. V. 47
The Book of American Negro Poetry. New York: 1931. V. 51
Fifty Years and Other Poems. Boston: 1917. V. 47
God's Trombone. New York: 1928. V. 52; 53
God's Trombones, Seven Negro Sermons in Verse. New York: 1927. V. 49
Lynching, America's National Disgrace. New York: 1924. V. 48
Saint Peter Relates an Incident. New York: 1935. V. 48; 54
Saint Peter Relates and Incident. New York: 1935. V. 48
The Second Book of Negro Spirituals. London: 1927. V. 47
The Shining Life. Nashville: 1932. V. 47; 50

JOHNSON, JESSE J.
Roots of Two Black Marine Sergeants Major-Sergeant Majors Edgar R. Hugg and Gilbert H. "Hashmark" Johnson. Hampton: 1978. V. 54

JOHNSON, JOHN
Print and Privilege at Oxford to the Year 1700. London: 1946. V. 51
Typographia, or the Printer's Instructor. London: 1824. V. 48; 49; 50; 51; 53
The Unbloody Sacrifice and Altar, Unvail'd and Supported. London: 1724. V. 47

JOHNSON, JOHN EVERETT
Regulations for Governing the Province of the Californias...1781. San Francisco: 1929. V. 47

JOHNSON, JOHN J.
Directions for Using the Patent Excelsior Tanning Process. Russell: 1865. V. 53

JOHNSON, JOHN L.
University Memorial Biographical Sketches of Alumni of the University of Virginia Who Fell in the Confederate War. Baltimore: 1871. V. 50

JOHNSON, JOHN, LT. COLONEL
A Journey from India to England, through Persia, Georgia, Russia, Poland and Prussia in the Year 1817. 1818. V. 54

JOHNSON, JOSEPH FORSYTH
The Natural Principles of Landscape Gardening: or, the Adornment of Land for Perpetual Beauty. Belfast: 1874. V. 49; 53

JOHNSON, K.
Aerial California: an Account of Early Flight in Nothern and Southern California 1849 to World War I. Los Angeles: 1961. V. 53

JOHNSON, KENNETH M.
San Francisco As It Is: Gleanings from the Picayune. Georgetown: 1964. V. 47
The Sting of the Wasp. San Francisco: 1967. V. 47

JOHNSON, L.
A Manual of the Medical Botany of North America. New York: 1884. V. 54

JOHNSON, LADY BIRD
A White House Diary. New York: 1970. V. 54
Wildflowers Across America. New York: 1988. V. 48

JOHNSON, LAURA WINTHROP
Eight Hundred Miles in an Ambulance. Philadelphia: 1889. V. 52; 54

JOHNSON, LAURENCE
A Manual of the Medical Botany of North America. New York: 1884. V. 48; 53

JOHNSON, LEE
The Paintings of Eugene Delacroix. Oxford: 1981-89. V. 49; 51
The Paintings of Eugene Delacroix. A Critical Catalogue. Oxford: 1987-89. V. 48

JOHNSON, LESLIE L.
Notes on U.S. Cavalry, 1865-1890. Little Rock: 1960. V. 50

JOHNSON, LIONEL
The Art of Thomas Hardy. London: 1894. V. 54
Poems. London and Boston: 1895. V. 47; 53
Poetry and Fiction. 1982. V. 54
The Religious Poems of Lionel Johnson. London: 1916. V. 47; 49
Three Poems. London: 1928. V. 49
Twenty-One Poems. Dundrum: 1904. V. 48

JOHNSON, LORENZO D.
Martha Washingtonianism, or, a History of the Ladies' Tempeprance Benevolent Societies. New York: 1843. V. 54

JOHNSON, LYNDON BAINES
No Retreat From tomorrow. Washington: 1967. V. 49
This America. New York: 1966. V. 53
To Heal and to Build. New York: 1968. V. 50
The Vantage Point. New York: 1971. V. 48; 49; 52; 53; 54

JOHNSON, M. L.
Intensely Interesting Little Volume of True History of the Struggles with Hostile Indians on the Frontier of Texas... Dallas: 1923. V. 47
Trail Blazing. Dallas: 1835. V. 51

JOHNSON, MERLE
American First Editions. New York: 1929. V. 51
American First Editions. New York: 1932. V. 51
A Bibliography of the Works of Mark Twain. New York: 1910. V. 47
A Bibliography of the Works of Mark Twain. New York: 1935. V. 53; 54
High Spots of American Literature. New York: 1929. V. 47; 49; 51
Howard Pyle's Book of the American Spirit. New York: 1923. V. 49
You Know These Lines! A Bibliography of the Most Quoted Verses in American Poetry. New York: 1935. V. 53

JOHNSON, NORA
The World of Henry Orient. New York: 1963. V. 47; 49

JOHNSON, OVERTON
Route Across the Rocky Mountains, with a Description of Oregon and California; Their Geographical Features, Their Resources, Soil, Climate, Productions, etc. Lafayette: 1846. V. 52

JOHNSON, PERCY ERNEST
The Truth: A Social Problem Play in Three Acts. Atlanta: 1930. V. 54

JOHNSON, PHIL
Life on the Plains. Chicago: 1888. V. 49; 52

JOHNSON, PHILIP
Writings. New York: 1979. V. 49; 51

JOHNSON, R. BRIMLEY
Famous Reviews Selected and Edited with Introductory Notes. London: 1914. V. 54
Fanny Burney and the Burneys. London: 1926. V. 48

JOHNSON, R. W.
The River Tyne, Its Trade and Facilities, an Official Handbook... Newcastle-upon-Tyne: 1925-30-40. V. 48

JOHNSON, RAY
The Paper Snake. New York: 1965. V. 53

JOHNSON, REVERDY
Sir, the Friends of General Jackson in Baltimore, Have Appointed the Undersigned a Committee of Arrangement, for the Approaching Jackson Convention... Baltimore: 1828. V. 48

JOHNSON, RICHARD
The Blossoms of Morality. London: 1789. V. 48
The Blossoms of Morality. London: 1801. V. 50
The Children in the Wood Restored. Banbury: 1814. V. 48
The Children in the Wood, Restored. Banbury: 1820. V. 48
The Drawing School for Little Masters and Misses, Containing the Most Easy and Concise Rules or Learning to Draw by Master Michael Angelo. London: 1777. V. 49
The History of North America. London: 1789. V. 52
The History of South America. London: 1789. V. 52
The History of the Seven Champions of Christendom. London: 1810. V. 52
The Juvenile Biographer; Containing the Lives of Little Masters and Misses... Worcester: 1787. V. 47
A New History of the Grecian States, from the Earliest Period to Their Extinction by the Ottomans. London: 1786. V. 47; 49
A New Theatrical Dictionary. London: 1792. V. 47
The Picture Exhibition: Containing the Original Drawings of Eighteen Disciples. Worcester: 1788. V. 51
The Toy-Shop; or, Sentimental Preceptor, Containing some Choice Trifles for the Instruction and Amusement of Every Little Miss and Master. Swaftham: 1830. V. 48

JOHNSON, RICHARD Z.
The Idaho Test Oath. Salt Lake City: 1888. V. 50

JOHNSON, ROBERT C.
Commons Debates 1628. New Haven: 1977-78. V. 53

JOHNSON, ROBERT J.
Specimens of Early French Architecture. Newcastle-upon-Tyne: 1864. V. 52

JOHNSON, ROBERT UNDERWOOD
Battles and Leaders of the Civil War. New York: 1884. V. 52
Battles and Leaders of the Civil War. New York: 1884-88. V. 52
Battles and Leaders of the Civil War. New York: 1887. V. 49
Battles and Leaders of the Civil War. New York: 1887-88. V. 54
Battles and Leaders of the Civil War. New York: 1956. V. 49
Battles and Leaders of the Civil War. South Brunswick: 1956. V. 54
Poems of Fifty Years: 1880-1930. New York: 1931. V. 54

JOHNSON, RONALD
A Line of Poetry, a Row of Trees. Highlands: 1964. V. 54
The Spirit Walks, the Rocks Will Talke. New York and Penland: 1969. V. 54
Sports and Divertissements. Urbana: 1969. V. 52; 54

JOHNSON, ROSSITER
Author's Digest. 1908. V. 47
Little Classics. Boston: 1875. V. 47
Little Classics. Boston: 1876-77. V. 53

JOHNSON, RUTH
Bookman's Holiday. Meriden: 1971. V. 48

JOHNSON, SAMUEL
An Account of the Life of Dr. Samuel Johnson... London: 1805. V. 48
An Account of the Life of Dr. Samuel Johnson From His Birth to His Eleventh Year. London: 1984. V. 48; 53
An Account of the Life of Mr. Richard Savage, son of the Earl Rivers. London: 1748. V. 48
The Adventurer. London: 1777. V. 48
The Beauties of Johnson... London: 1781. V. 48
The Beauties of Johnson... Dublin: 1782. V. 48
The Beauties of Johnson. London: 1782. V. 48; 52
The Beauties of Johnson... London: 1787. V. 48; 53
The Beauties of Johnson... London: 1792. V. 48; 53
The Beauties of Johnson. London: 1804. V. 48; 53
The Celebrated Letter to Philip Dormer Stanhope, Earl of Chesterfield. 1927. V. 47
A Compleat Introduction to the Art of Writing Letters Universally Adapted to All Classes and Conditions of Life. London: 1758. V. 52
Debates in Parliament. London: 1787. V. 48
Debates in Parliament. London: 1811. V. 47; 48; 53
Diaries, Prayers and Annals. New Haven: 1958. V. 53
A Diary of a Journey into North Wales in the Year 1774. London: 1816. V. 47; 48; 53; 54
A Dictionary of the English Language. London: 1755. V. 47; 49; 50; 51; 52; 53; 54
A Dictionary of the English Language. London: 1755-56. V. 52
A Dictionary of the English Language. London: 1756. V. 50; 52
A Dictionary of the English Language. London: 1760. V. 47; 48; 52
A Dictionary of the English Language. London: 1765. V. 54
A Dictionary of the English Language. London: 1766. V. 48; 52
A Dictionary of the English Language... London: 1770. V. 47; 52
A Dictionary of the English Language. London: 1773. V. 47; 51; 52
A Dictionary of the English Language. Dublin: 1775. V. 52
A Dictionary of the English Language... London: 1778. V. 48
Dictionary of the English Language. London: 1783. V. 47; 48
A Dictionary of the English Language. London: 1785. V. 47; 52; 54
A Dictionary of the English Language. London: 1786. V. 52
A Dictionary of the English Language. London: 1792. V. 48; 52
A Dictionary of the English Language. Dublin: 1798. V. 53
A Dictionary of the English Language. London: 1799. V. 48; 50; 52

JOHNSON, SAMUEL continued
A Dictionary of the English Language... London: 1805. V. 48
A Dictionary of the English Language... Philadelphia: 1805. V. 50; 51; 52
A Dictionary of the English Language. London: 1806. V. 48; 54
A Dictionary of the English Language. London: 1810. V. 48
A Dictionary of the English Language... London: 1818. V. 51; 52; 54
A Dictionary of the English Language... Philadelphia: 1818. V. 51; 53
A Dictionary of the English Language. Philadelphia: 1818-19. V. 48
A Dictionary of the English Language... Philadelphia: 1819. V. 49; 50; 53; 54
A Dictionary of the English Language. London: 1822. V. 47; 48; 50; 52
A Dictionary of the English Language. London: 1824. V. 53
A Dictionary of the English Language. London: 1826. V. 48
A Dictionary of the English Language... London: 1832. V. 50
A Dictionary of the English Language. London: 1843. V. 52
Dictionary of the English Language. London: 1849. V. 48
Dictionary of the English Language. London: 1881. V. 53
A Dictionary of the English Language. Lebanon: 1978. V. 52
A Dictionary of the English Language. London: 1979. V. 54
A Dictionary of the English Language. London: 1990. V. 47
Dictionary of the English Language in Miniature. Montrose: 1803. V. 50
Elementa Philosophica... Philadelphia: 1752. V. 48; 49; 53
The False Alarm. London: 1770. V. 48; 53
The Fountains. Brisbane: 1984. V. 48; 53
The Harleian Miscellany... London: 1753/ 1744-46. V. 49
A History and Defence of Magna Charta.. London: 1772. V. 50; 53
The History of Rasselas, Prince of Abyssinia. London: 1801. V. 53
The History of Rasselas, Prince of Abyssinia. London: 1807. V. 54
The History of Rasselas, Prince of Abyssinia. London: 1817. V. 51
The History of Rasselas, Prince of Abyssinia. London: 1818. V. 54
The History of Rasselas Prince of Abyssinia. London and New York: 1926. V. 54
The History of the Yorubas. From the Earliest Time to the Beginning of the British Protectorate. London: 1921. V. 52
Hurlothrumbo: or, the Super-Natural. London: 1729. V. 47; 50
The Idler. London: 1761. V. 49; 52
The Idler. London: 1767. V. 47; 48; 50; 52
The Idler. London: 1790. V. 50; 51
The Idler. Newburyport: 1803. V. 48
The Idler and the Adventurer. New Haven: 1970. V. 53
Irene. London: 1749. V. 48; 53
Johnsoniana; or, Supplement to Boswell: Being Anecdotes and Sayings of Dr. Johnson. London: 1836. V. 48; 49; 53
Johnson's Dictionary of the English Language, in Miniature. Boston: 1804. V. 49
Johnson's English Dictionary, as Improved by Todd and Abridged by Chalmers... Boston: 1828. V. 47; 52
Johnson's Proposals for His Edition of Shakespeare 1756, Printed in Type Facsimile. 1923. V. 51
Johsoniana, Anecdotes of the Late Samuel Johnson, LL.D. London: 1884.. V. 54
The Journal of a Tour to the Hebrides with Samuel Johnson. Dublin: 1785. V. 54
A Journey to the Western Islands of Scotland. Dublin: 1775. V. 48; 49; 53
A Journey to the Western Islands of Scotland. London: 1775. V. 47; 48; 49; 51; 52; 53; 54
A Journey to the Western Islands of Scotland. London: 1785. V. 47; 48; 49; 51; 52; 53
A Journey to the Western Islands of Scotland. Edinburgh: 1798. V. 48
A Journey to the Western Islands of Scotland. Baltimore, Boston, Albany: 1810. V. 48; 50
A Journey to the Western Isles of Scotland. Glasgow: 1817. V. 48; 52
Know Thyself. Kingston: 1992. V. 49; 52
A Letter to Mr. Jonathan Dickinson... Boston: 1747. V. 49
The Letters of Samuel Johnson. Oxford: 1892. V. 48; 49; 53
The Letters of Samuel Johnson. Oxford: 1952. V. 48; 53; 54
The Letters of Samuel Johnson. Oxford: 1992. V. 48
The Letters of Samuel Johnson, 1731-1784. Oxford: 1992/94. V. 53
Letters to and from the Late Samuel Johnson, LL.D. Dublin: 1688. V. 48
Letters to and From the Late Samuel Johnson, LL.D.... Dublin: 1788. V. 48; 53
Letters to and From the Late Samuel Johnson, LL.D. London: 1788. V. 47; 48; 49; 51; 52; 54
The Life of Samuel Johnson, LL.D.... (with) The Poetical Works... London: 1785/85. V. 52
The Lives of the English Poets. Dublin: 1779. V. 50
The Lives of the English Poets; and A Criticism of Their Works. Dublin: 1781. V. 48; 50; 54
The Lives of the English Poets, With Critical Observations of Their Works. London: 1820. V. 53
The Lives of the Most Eminent English Poets. Dublin: 1779-81. V. 54
The Lives of the Most Eminent English Poets... London: 1781. V. 47; 51; 52; 53; 54
The Lives of the Most Eminent English Poets. Bathurst: 1783. V. 48
The Lives of the Most Eminent English Poets. London: 1783. V. 47; 49; 50
The Lives of the Most Eminent English Poets. London: 1790-91. V. 49
The Lives of the Most Eminent English Poets... London: 1790-91. V. 47; 50
The Lives of the Most Eminent English Poets. London: 1794. V. 47; 53
The Lives of the Most Eminent English Poets. London: 1800-01. V. 52
The Lives of the Most Eminent English Poets... London: 1800/01. V. 48
The Lives of the Most Eminent English Poets. London: 1806. V. 48
The Lives of the Most Eminent English Poets... London: 1821. V. 53
The Lives of the Most Eminent English Poets. London: 1822. V. 48
The Lives of the Most Eminent English Poets. London: 1825. V. 48; 53
The Lives of the Most Eminent English Poets. London: 1883. V. 51
Lives of the Most Eminent Poets... London: 1854. V. 51; 52
The Lives of the Poets. London: 1816. V. 52

London: a Poem and the Vanity of Human Wishes. London: 1930. V. 49; 52; 54
London: a Poem, in Imitation of the Third Satire of Juvenal. London: 1738. V. 48
The Matrimonial Preceptor. London: 1755. V. 53
The Matrimonial Preceptor... London: 1759. V. 53
The Matrimonial Preceptor. London: 1765. V. 53
Memoirs of Charles Frederick, King of Prussia... London: 1786. V. 47; 49; 51; 52; 54
Miscellaneous and Fugitive Pieces: Consisting of Essays, Dissertations, Prefaces, Reviews, Lives, Etc. Sheffield: 1804. V. 48
Mr. Johnson's Preface to His Edition of Shakespeare's Plays. London: 1765. V. 48; 52
A New and General Biographical Dictionary... London: 1798-1810. V. 47
The New London Letter Writer. London: 1948. V. 54
The New London Letter Writer... Waltham St. Lawrence: 1948. V. 48; 52
A Pastoral Ballad in Four Parts: Admiration, Hope, Disappointment, Success. London: 1774. V. 54
The Plan of a Dictionary of the English Language: Addressed to the Right Honourable Philip Dormer, Earl of Chesterfield, One of His majesty's Principal Secretaries of State. London: 1747. V. 48
The Poetical Works. Dublin: 1785. V. 48; 50; 52; 53
The Poetical Works. London: 1785. V. 47; 48; 49; 50; 54
The Poetical Works. London: 1789. V. 48
The Poetical Works of Samuel Johnson, LL.D. Burlington: 1816. V. 50
Political Tracts. London: 1776. V. 48; 49; 50; 52
Political Tracts... Dublin: 1777. V. 48
Prayers and Meditations. London: 1785. V. 47; 48; 49; 51; 52
Prayers and Meditations. London: 1796. V. 47
Prayers and Meditations. London: 1807. V. 48; 51; 52; 54
The Prayers of Dr. Samuel Johnson. New York: 1902. V. 48
Prefaces, Biographical and Critical to the Works of the English Poets. London: 1779-81. V. 53; 54
The Prince of Abbisinia. Dublin: 1759. V. 49
The Prince of Abissinia. London: 1759. V. 48; 50; 52; 53; 54
The Prince of Abissinia. London: 1760. V. 48
The Prince of Abissinia. London: 1775. V. 51
The Prince of Abissinia. London: 1783. V. 51
The Prince of Abissinia. London: 1786. V. 48; 53
The Prince of Abissinia. London: 1790. V. 48; 52
The Rambler. Edinburgh: 1750/51/53. V. 53
The Rambler. London: 1751. V. 48
The Rambler... London: 1752. V. 47
The Rambler. London: 1779. V. 48
The Rambler. London: 1794. V. 51; 52; 54
The Rambler. London: 1798. V. 48
The Rambler. London: 1806-10. V. 50
The Rambler. London: 1822. V. 54
The Rambler. New Haven: 1969. V. 53
Rasselas. London: 1798. V. 47
Rasselas. Hartford: 1803. V. 52
Rasselas. Banbury: 1804. V. 47; 49
Rasselas... Frederick-Town: 1810. V. 50
Rasselas. London: 1819. V. 48; 49; 51; 54
Rasselas. Paris: 1849. V. 48
Rasselas. Birmingham: 1898. V. 49; 50
Rasselas. London: 1942. V. 52
Samuel Johnson's Prologue Spoken at the Opening of the Theatre in Drury-Lane in 1747, with Garrick's Epilogue. New York: 1902. V. 52
Sermons... 1835. V. 53
Sermons by Samuel Johnson, LL.D. Ripon: 1835. V. 48; 50
Some Unpublished Letters. London: 1915. V. 50
Taxation No Tyranny, an Answer to the Resolutions and Address of the American Congress. London: 1775. V. 53
Thoughts on the Late Transactions Respecting Falkland's Islands. London: 1771. V. 48; 49
The Vanity of Human Wishes. London: 1749. V. 48; 53
The Vanity of Human Wishes. London: 1984. V. 53
A Voyage to Abissinia. New Haven: 1985. V. 53
The Works... London: 1777. V. 48
The Works. London: 1787. V. 49
The Works. London: 1787-88. V. 52
The Works. Dublin: 1793. V. 49; 50; 52; 54
The Works. London: 1801. V. 47; 48; 50
The Works... Edinburgh: 1806. V. 48
The Works. Boston: 1809/11/12. V. 54
Works. London: 1810. V. 49; 51
The Works. London: 1816. V. 50
Works. London: 1823. V. 50
Works. London: 1824. V. 50
The Works. London: 1825. V. 51; 54
The Works. Oxford: 1825. V. 48; 49; 50; 51; 52; 54
The Works. Philadelphia: 1825. V. 50
The Works. New York: 1835. V. 54
The Works. New York: 1836-40. V. 50
Works. London: 1850. V. 49; 52
The Works. New Haven: 1958. V. 48
The Works. New Haven: 1968. V. 48
The Works. New Haven: 1969. V. 48
The Works of the English Poets. London. V. 50
The Works of the English Poets. London: 1779-81. V. 49; 53

JOHNSON, SAMUEL continued
The Works of the English Poets. London: 1790. V. 53

JOHNSON, SIDNEY SMITH
Texans Who Wore the Gray. Tyler: 1907. V. 47; 49; 50

JOHNSON, STEPHEN
The History of Cardiac Surgery 1896-1955. Baltimore: 1970. V. 50; 52

JOHNSON, T. BROADWOOD
Tramps Round the Mountains of the Moon... London: 1908. V. 50
Tramps Round the Mountains of the Moon. London: 1912. V. 54

JOHNSON, THEODORE T.
California and Oregon; or Signs in the Gold Region and Scenes by the Way. Philadelphia: 1851. V. 47
Sights in the Gold Region, and Scenes by the Way. New York: 1849. V. 53
Sights in the Gold Region, and Scenes by the Way. Dublin: 1850. V. 47
Sights In the Gold Region, and Scenes by the Way. New York: 1850. V. 51

JOHNSON, THOMAS
Chippendale's Ornaments and Interior Decorations, in the Old French Style. London: 1834. V. 48; 50; 53

JOHNSON, THOMAS BURGELAND
The Gamekeeper's Directory, and Complete Vermin Destroyer... London: 1830. V. 54
The Hunting Directory... London: 1826. V. 47
The Hunting Directory... London: 1830. V. 47
The Shooter's Companion... 1819. V. 54
The Shooter's Companion... London: 1819. V. 47
The Shooter's Companion; a Description of Pointers and Setters... London: 1823. V. 47; 51; 52
The Shooter's Guide; or, Complete Sportsman's Companion. London: 1814. V. 47
The Shooter's Guide; or, Complete Sportsman's Companion... London: 1824. V. 47
The Shooter's Guide; or, Complete Sportsman's Companion... London: 1832. V. 51
The Shooter's Preceptor. London: 1838. V. 51; 52

JOHNSON, THOMAS M.
Collecting the Edged Weapons of the Third Reich. Columbia: 1975-81. V. 47

JOHNSON, UWE
An Absence. London: 1970. V. 52
Anniversaries: from the Life of Gesine Gresspahl. New York: 1975. V. 52
Specualtions About Jakob. New York: 1963. V. 51
The Third Book About Achim. New York: 1967. V. 51

JOHNSON, W. R.
Anno Domini. 1970. V. 52
Easter. Philadelphia: 1970. V. 52; 53; 54
Flowering Time. 1976. V. 52
Lilac Wind. 1983. V. 52
Narcissus. 1990. V. 52
Narcissus. Newark: 1990. V. 52
The Town at Dusk. Newark: 1980. V. 53

JOHNSON, WALTER
The Morbid Emotions of Women; Their Origin, Tendencies and Treatment. London: 1850. V. 53

JOHNSON, WILLIAM
Deus Nobiscum. London: 1664. V. 47
A Letter to Joshua Spencer, Esq., on an Union. London: 1789. V. 54
Lexicon Chymicum cum Obscuriorum Verborum, et Rerum Hermeticarum... Frankfurt & Leipzig: 1652-53. V. 49
Lexicon Chymicum Cum Obscuriorum Verborum, et Rerum Hermeticarum... London: 1652-53. V. 49; 53
The Practical Draughtsman's Book of Industrial Design. London. V. 53

JOHNSON, WILLIAM SAVAGE
An Account of a Summer's Pilgrimage. Meriden: 1972. V. 50

JOHNSON'S New Illustrated Family Atlas of the World... New York: 1868. V. 54

JOHNSON'S New Illustrated (Steel-Plate) Family Atlas... New York: 1863. V. 52

JOHNSTON, ALASTAIR
Muted Hawks. Berkeley: 1995. V. 53
New Dryads. Berkeley: 1980. V. 50

JOHNSTON, ALEXANDER KEITH
Atlas to Alison's History of Europe. Edinburgh & London: 1848. V. 50; 52
The Physical Atlas. A Series of Maps and Notes Illustrating the Geographical Distribution of Natural Phenomena... 1848. V. 54
The Physical Atlas of Natural Phenomena. London: 1850. V. 52; 53
School Atlas of Astronomy, Comprising, in Twenty-One Plates, a Complete Series of Illustrations of the Heavenly Bodies... Edinburgh: 1877. V. 50

JOHNSTON, ANDREW
50 Years in the Saddle. Dickson: 1963/65. V. 49

JOHNSTON, ANNIE FELLOWS
In League with Israel. Cincinnati: 1896. V. 54

JOHNSTON, ARCHIBALD
Diary (1632-1639, 1650-1660). Edinburgh: 1911-40. V. 51

JOHNSTON, ARTHUR
Paraphrasis Poetica Psalmorum Davidis. London: 1657. V. 53

JOHNSTON, CHARLES
Ireland, Historic and Picturesque. Philadelphia: 1902. V. 47
A Narrative of the Incidents Attending the Capture, Detention and Ransom of Charles Johnston of Botetourt, Virginia, Who Was Made Prisoner by the Indians, on the River Ohio, in the Year 1790... New York: 1827. V. 47; 50

JOHNSTON, DAVID CLAYPOOL
Phrenology Exemplified and Illustrated Upwards of Forty Etchings: Being Scraps No. 7 for the Year 1837. Boston: 1836. V. 50

JOHNSTON, DENIS
The Brazen Horn. Dublin: 1976. V. 49

JOHNSTON, ELIZA GRIFFIN
Texas Wild Flowers. Austin: 1972. V. 53

JOHNSTON, F.
Memorials of Old Virginia Clerks. Lynchburg: 1888. V. 54

JOHNSTON, FRANCES B.
The Early Architecture of North Carolina, a Pictorial Survey. Chapel Hill: 1947. V. 47; 51
Plantations of the Carolina Low Country. Charleston: 1938. V. 47

JOHNSTON, FREDERICK
Terracina Cloud: Poems. Verona: 1936. V. 54

JOHNSTON, G. P.
Catalouge of the Rare and Most Interesting Books and Manuscripts in the Library at Drummond Castle. Edinburgh: 1910. V. 52

JOHNSTON, GEORGE
A History of British Sponges and Lithophytes. Edinburgh: 1842. V. 49; 50; 54
A History of British Zoophytes. London: 1847. V. 49; 50; 51; 52; 53; 54
An Introduction to Chonchology. London: 1850. V. 50; 54

JOHNSTON, HARRY H.
British Central Africa. London: 1897. V. 53
British Central Africa. New York: 1897. V. 47; 51; 54
British Central Africa. London: 1906. V. 50
Liberia. London: 1906. V. 49; 50; 52
Livingstone and the Exploration of Central Africa. London: 1891. V. 47
The Negro in New World. London: 1910. V. 48; 50
The Uganda Protectorate. London: 1902. V. 48; 49
The Uganda Protectorate. New York: 1904. V. 47; 51; 54

JOHNSTON, HARRY V.
My Home on the Range. Frontier Life in the Bad Lands. St. Paul: 1942. V. 53

JOHNSTON, ISAAC N.
Four Months in Libby and the Campaign against Atlanta. Cincinnati: 1864. V. 48; 49

JOHNSTON, J. STODDARD
First Explorations of Kentucky. Louisville: 1898. V. 53

JOHNSTON, JAMES
Reality Versus Romance in South Central Africa. London: 1893. V. 47

JOHNSTON, JAMES A.
Prison Life is Different. Boston: 1937. V. 47; 53

JOHNSTON, JAMES C.
Atlas of Venereal and Skin Diseases... New York: 1900. V. 53

JOHNSTON, JAMES F. W.
Experimental Agriculture, Being the Result of Past, and Suggestions for Future Experiments. Edinburgh: 1849. V. 48
Lectures on Agricultural Chemistry and Geology. Edinburgh: 1844. V. 50; 52
Lectures on Agricultural Chemistry and Geology. London: 1847. V. 53
Notes on North America, Agricultural, Economical and Social. Edinburgh and London: 1851. V. 52; 54
What Can Be Done for English Agriculture?. Edinburgh & London: 1842. V. 53

JOHNSTON, JENNIFER
The Christmas Tree. London: 1981. V. 52

JOHNSTON, JOHN
Diary Notes of a Visit to Walt Whitman. Manchester: 1898. V. 50
Thaumatographia Naturalis. Amstelodami: 1665. V. 47

JOHNSTON, JOHN W.
Speech of Hon. John W. Johnston, of Virginia in the Senate of the United States, June 5, 1878, Contrasting the Plan of a Genuine Southern Transcontinental Railroad, as Laid Down in S. Bill 1186, with the Scheme of Col. T. A. Scott to Extend the ... Washington: 1878. V. 47

JOHNSTON, JOSEPH EGGLESTON
Narrative of Military Operations. New York: 1873. V. 49
Narrative of Military Operations. New York: 1874. V. 49; 54
Reports of the Secretary of War, with Reconnaisances of Routes from San Antonio to El Paso. Washington: 1850. V. 47
Southern Boundary Line of Kansas...The Report of Colonel Johnston's Survey of the Southern Boundary Line of Kansas...With the Accompanying Paper and Map. Washington: 1858. V. 47; 49

JOHNSTON, KEITH
A Physical, Historical, Political and Descriptive Geography. London: 1880. V. 53

JOHNSTON, MARY
Sir Mortimer. New York: 1904. V. 49
To Have and to Hold. Boston: 1900. V. 48

JOHNSTON, NATHANIEL
The Assurance of Abby and Other Church-Lands in England to the Possessors, Cleared from the Doubts and Arguments Raised About Danger of Resumption. London: 1687. V. 52; 54

JOHNSTON, PRISCILLA
The Mill Book. Ditchling and Hammersmith: 1917. V. 52

JOHNSTON, R.
From Peking to Mandalay, a Journey from North China to Burma through Tibetan Ssuch'uan and Yunnan. London: 1908. V. 48

JOHNSTON, R. F.
The Chinese Drama: With Six Illustrations Reproduced from the Original Paintings by C. F. Winzer. Shanghai: 1921. V. 50

JOHNSTON, RICHARD MALCOLM
Dukesborough Tales. Baltimore: 1871. V. 50; 54
Pearce Amerson's Will. Chicago: 1898. V. 47

JOHNSTON, RICHARD W.
Follow Me: The Story of the Second Marine Division in World War II. New York: 1948. V. 50; 52

JOHNSTON, ROBERT
Historia Rerum Britannicarum et Multarum Gallicarum, Belgicarum & Germanicarum...ab 1572 ad 1628. Amsterdam: 1655. V. 47

JOHNSTON, S. H.
The Cleveland Herbal, Botanical and Horticultural Collections. Kent: 1992. V. 49

JOHNSTON, SAMUEL B.
Letters Written During a Residence of Three Years in Chili, Containing an Account of the Most Remarkable Events in the Revolutionary Struggles of that Province... Erie: 1816. V. 48

JOHNSTON, STANLEY H.
The Cleveland Herbal, Botanical and Horticultural Collections. 1992. V. 53

JOHNSTON, T. B.
Historical Geography of the Clans of Scotland. Edinburgh: 1899. V. 50

JOHNSTON, VERLE B.
Legions of Babel. The International Brigades in the Spanish Civil War. University Park & London: 1967. V. 49

JOHNSTON, WILLIAM
History of the County of Perth from 1825 to 1902. Stratford: 1903. V. 54

JOHNSTON, WILLIAM G.
Experiences of a Forty-Niner. Pittsburgh: 1892. V. 47; 48; 50

JOHNSTON, WILLIAM PRESTON
The Life of Gen. Albert Sidney Johnston...In the Armies of the U.S., The Republic of Texas, and the Confederate States. New York: 1878. V. 47; 49; 50
The Life of Gen. Albert Sidney Johnston...in the Armies of the U.S., the Republic of Texas, and the Confederate States. New York: 1879. V. 50

JOHNSTONE, CHARLES
Chrysal. London: 1767-71. V. 47; 52
Chrysal. London: 1771/67-71. V. 48
Chrysal: or, The Adventures of a Guinea. London: 1785. V. 48
Chrysal; or, the Adventures of a Guinea... London: 1794. V. 53; 54
Chrysal; or the Adventures of a Guinea. London: 1821. V. 49; 51
The History of Arsaces, Prince of Betlis. London: 1774. V. 52; 54
The History of Arsaces, Prince of Betlis. Dublin: 1775/4. V. 49; 54
The Reverie: or, a Flight to the Paradise of Fools. London: 1763/62. V. 48
The Reverie: or, a Flight to the Paradise of Fools. London: 1767. V. 54

JOHNSTONE, CHEVALIER DE
Memoirs of the Rebellion in 1745 and 1746. London: 1822. V. 52; 54

JOHNSTONE, CHRISTIAN ISOBEL
Clan-Albin: a National Tale... London: 1815. V. 50
The Edinburgh Tales. London: 1850. V. 50
The Wars of the Jews As Related by Josephus, Adapted to the Capacities of Young Persons. London: 1823. V. 54

JOHNSTONE, G. H.
Asiataic Magnolias in Cultivation. London: 1955. V. 47; 48; 49; 50; 51; 52; 53

JOHNSTONE, JAMES
Antiquitates Celto-Normannicae. (with) Antiquitates Celto-Scandicae. Copenhagen: 1786. V. 53
Historical and Descriptive Account of George Heriot's Hospital. Edinburgh: 1827. V. 52

JOHNSTONE, JAMES FOWLER KELLAS
Bibliographia Aberdonensis. Aberdeen: 1929-30. V. 48; 50; 52

JOHNSTONE, JOHN
An Account of the Mode of Draining Land... London: 1808. V. 53
An Account of the Most Approved Mode of Draining Land... 1800. V. 53
A Systematic Treatise On the Theory and Practice of Draining Land.... Edinburgh: 1834. V. 51

JOHNSTONE, NANCY
Hotel in Spain. London: 1937. V. 49

JOHNSTONE, WILLIAM
The Table Talker or Brief Essays on Society and Literature. London: 1840. V. 53

JOHNSTONE, WILLIAM GROSART
The Nature Printed British Sea Weeds. London: 1859. V. 49; 50; 54
The Nature Printed British Sea-Weeds. London: 1859-60. V. 47; 50; 52; 53; 54

JOHNSTON'S Stroot and Street Railway Guide of Toronto. Toronto: 1910. V. 54

JOINVILLE, JEAN
The History of Saint Louis. Newtown: 1937. V. 47; 50; 51
Memoirs of John Lord de Joinville... London: 1807. V. 47

JOLAS, EUGENE
Transition - Numbers 1-12. Paris: 1927-28. V. 47
Transition Stories. New York: 1929. V. 50; 53
Vertical. Paris. V. 50
Vertical, a Yearbook for Romantic - Mystic Ascensions. New York: 1941. V. 47; 48; 49; 50
Vertical: a Yearbook for Romantic Mystic Acensions. New York: 1947. V. 48

JOLLEY, JOHN
The Head-Constable's Assistant; or, a Mize - Book for the County - Palatine of Cheshire... London: 1726. V. 53

JOLLIE, F.
Jollie's Cumberland Guide and Directory... Carlisle: 1811. V. 52

JOLLIFFE, T. R.
Letters From Palestine, Descriptive of a Tour through Galilee and Judaea, with Some Account of the Dead Sea, and of the Present State of Jerusalem. (with) Letters from Egypt. London: 1820. V. 48

JOLLY, ELIZABETH
The Newspaper of Claremont Street. Freemantle: 1981. V. 54

THE JOLLY Old Man, Who Sings Down, Derry Down. London: 1866. V. 52

JOLY, GUY
Memoirs of Guy Joli, Private Secretary to Cardinal de Retz... London: 1775. V. 48

JOMINI, ANTOINE HENRI DE
The Art of War. Philadelphia: 1862. V. 47
Life of Napoleon. New York: 1864. V. 50

JONATHAN Rogers. Vancouver: 1948?. V. 51

JONCQUET, DENIS
Hortus, sive Index Onomasticus Plantarum, Quas Excoleabate Parisiis Annis 1658 & 1659. Paris: 1659. V. 49

JONES & CO.
Jones' Views of the Seats, Mansions, Castles, &c...In England, Wales, Scotland and Ireland... London: 1829. V. 49

JONES, A.
The Art of Playing Skittles; or, the Laws of Nine-Pins Displayed. London: 1773. V. 48; 50

JONES, A. H. M.
The Cities of the Eastern Roman Provinces. Oxford: 1971. V. 50

JONES, ABNER
Memoirs of the Life and Experience, Travels and Preaching of Abner Jones. Exeter: 1807. V. 53

JONES, ALFRED T.
The Secret. New York: 1958. V. 54

JONES, AMANDA THEODOSIA
A Prairie Idyl and Other Poems. Chicago: 1882. V. 48; 50

JONES, ARTHUR
Cellulose Lacquers, Finishes and Cements: Their History, Chemistry, Manufacture, Analysis and Testing Industrial Uses and Applications with Some Notes on Synthetic Resin Lacquers. London: 1937. V. 50

JONES, BARBARA
Follies and Grottoes. London: 1953. V. 49

JONES, BEN
Speech of Ben Jones, of East Tennessee, on November 20, 1863. New York: 1863. V. 48

JONES, BENCE
The Life and Letters of Michael Faraday. London: 1870. V. 48; 50; 51; 52; 54

JONES, BERNARD E.
Cassell's Cyclopaedia of Photography. London: 1911. V. 54
Cassell's Reinforced Concrete. London: 1920. V. 50

JONES, BUEHRING
The Sunny Land; or, Prison Prose and Poetry. Baltimore: 1868. V. 50

JONES, C. W.
In Prison at Point Lookout. Martinsville: 1890. V. 48; 49

JONES, CHARLES C.
Antiquities of the Southern Indians Particularly of the Georgia Tribes. New York: 1873. V. 47; 50
Biographical Sketches of the Delegates from Georgia to the Continental Congress. Boston & New York: 1891. V. 50
General Sherman's March from Atlanta to the Coast. Augusta: 1884. V. 49
Historical Sketch of the Chatham Artillery During the Confederate Struggle for Independence. Albany: 1867. V. 49
The Life and Services of Commodore Josiah Tattnall. Savannah: 1878. V. 50
Monumental Remains of Georgia. Savannah: 1861. V. 48; 49

JONES, CHARLES C. continued
The Siege of Savannah in December, 1864 and the Confederate Operations in georgia...During General Sherman's March from Atlanta to the Sea. Albany: 1874. V. 50

JONES, CHARLES COLCOCK
Report of Charles C. Jones, Jr., Mayor of the City of Savannah, for the Year Ending September 30th 1861. Savannah: 1861. V. 49

JONES, CHARLES WILLIAMS
A Series of Lectures On the Most Approved Principles and Practice of Modern Surgery... Boston: 1823. V. 50

JONES, D. CARADOG
The Social Survey of Merseyside. Liverpool: 1934. V. 49; 52

JONES, DAN BURNE
The Prints of Rockwell Kent: a Catalogue Raisonne. Chicago: 1975. V. 48; 49; 50; 52

JONES, DAVID
The Anathemata. London: 1952. V. 47; 48; 49; 53
The Anathemata. London: 1955. V. 49
Anathemata. 1963. V. 51
Diary with Dominican Calendar and XII Wood-Engravings. Ditchling: 1928. V. 49
The Engravings. London: 1981. V. 47; 51
The Fatigue. 1965. V. 53; 54
The History of the Most Serene House of Brunswick-Lunenburgh... London: 1715. V. 49
In Parenthesis. London: 1937. V. 47; 49; 51; 52; 53
In Parenthesis. London: 1955. V. 49
In Parenthesis. London: 1961. V. 48; 53
In Parenthesis. New York: 1961. V. 52
An Introduction to the Rime of the Ancient Mariner. London: 1972. V. 51; 52
On the Value of Annuities and Reversionary Payments. London: 1943. V. 48; 54
The Secret History of Whitehall, from the Restoration of Charles II. London: 1697. V. 48
The Secret History of Whitehall, from the Restoration of Charles II. London: 1717. V. 48
The Sleeping Lord. London: 1974. V. 48; 49
The Tragical History of the Stuarts. London: 1697. V. 48; 49
The Tribune's Visitation. London: 1969. V. 48; 49; 54
A Voice from Our Penal Settlements; or Garrotting, Its Causes and Cure. London: 1863. V. 53

JONES, E. ALFRED
The Loyalists of New Jersey. Newark: 1927. V. 47; 49; 51
The Old Plate of the Cambridge Colleges. Cambridge: 1910. V. 50
The Old Silver of American Churches. Letchworth: 1913. V. 47; 49; 50

JONES, E. GWYNNE
A Bibliography of the Dog. Books Published in the English Language 1570-1965. London: 1971. V. 54

JONES, EBENEZER
Studies of Sensation and Event: Poems. London: 1843. V. 47; 53
Studies of Sensation and Event. Poems. London: 1879. V. 49; 50

JONES, EDWARD
Index to Records Called, the Originalia and the Memoranda on the Lord Treasurer's Remembrancer's Side of the Exchequer. London: 1793-95. V. 47; 53

JONES, EDWARD ARTHUR
8-Endake Ehen or Old Huronia. Toronto: 1909. V. 54

JONES, EDWARD S.
Flag of the Free. San Francisco: 1917. V. 53
The Sylvan Cabin. Boston: 1911. V. 51

JONES, ERNEST
The Elements of Figure Skating. London: 1931. V. 51
The Life and Work of Sigmund Freud. New York: 1953/55/57. V. 51
Sigmund Ernest. New York: 1953. V. 48

JONES, EVAN ROWLAND
The Emigrant's Friend: Containing Information and Advice for Persons Intending to Emigrate to the United States. London: 1880. V. 52

JONES, FRED R.
An Uneventful Tramp. 1975. V. 52

JONES, FREDERIC WOOD
The Matrix of the Mind. London: 1929. V. 51

JONES, GEORGE
Excursions to Cairo, Jerusalem, Damascus and Balbec, from the United States Ship Delaware, During Her Recent Cruise. New York: 1836. V. 49
Sketches of Naval Life, with Notices of Men, Manners and Scenery On the Shore of the Mediterranean, in a Series of Letters from the Brandywine and Constitution Frigates. New Haven: 1829. V. 49; 53

JONES, GEORGE HENRY
Account of the Murder of the Late Mr. William Weare, of Lyon's Inn, London, Including the Cirumstances Which First Led to the Discovery of the Murder and the Detection of the Murderers, the Depositions Taken Before the Magistrates... London: 1824. V. 52

JONES, GEORGE W.
Catalogue of the Library of George W. Jones at the Sign of the Dolphin next to Dr. Johnson's House in Gough Square. London: 1938. V. 52
Nicolas Jenson, Printer at Venice, 1470-1480. London: 1930's. V. 54

JONES, GLYN
The Story of Heledd. 1994. V. 52

JONES, GWYN
The Green Island. London: 1946. V. 48
The Green Island. Waltham St. Lawrence: 1946. V. 49; 52

JONES, HANNAH MARIA
The Gipsey Girl; or the Heir of Hazel dell. London & New York: 1840. V. 49
The Gipsy Mother; or the Miseries of Enforced Marriage: a Tale of Mystery. London: 1835?. V. 47; 49
The Gipsy Mother, or the Miseries of Enforced Marriages. London: 1840. V. 51

JONES, HAROLD R.
Broadway and Other Poems. Montclair: 1932. V. 53

JONES, HARRIET
Belmont Lodge. London: 1799. V. 54

JONES, HARRY LONGUEVILLE
Illustrations of the Natural Scenery of Snowdonian Mountains... London: 1829. V. 49

JONES, HENRY
The Bird Paintings of Henry Jones. London: 1976. V. 48
The Isle of Wight, a Poem. Isle of Wight: 1782. V. 51; 54
The Scriptures Searched; or Christ's second Coming and Kingdom at Hand. New York: 1839. V. 47
The Wildfowl Paintings of Henry Jones. London: 1987. V. 48; 50; 51

JONES, HENRY ARTHUR
Michael and His Lost Angel. London: 1895. V. 48
What is Capital?. London: 1925. V. 53

JONES, HENRY FESTING
Samuel Butler, author of Erewhon (1835-1902). London: 1919. V. 52
Samuel Butler, Author of Erewhon (1835-1902). London: 1920. V. 52
The Samuel Butler Collection at Saint John's College Cambridge: a Catalogue and Commentary. Cambridge: 1921. V. 52

JONES, HERSCHEL V.
Adventures in Americana, 1492-1897. New York: 1928. V. 47; 49; 51
Adventures in Americana 1492-1897.....Books from the Library of Herschel V. Jones, Minneapolis, Minnesota. New York: 1964. V. 54

JONES, HORACE
The Story of Early Rice County. Wichita: 1928. V. 52

JONES, INIGO
Facsimile of Sketch-Book. London: 1831. V. 47

JONES, ISAAC H.
Equilibrium and Vertigo. Philadelphia: 1918. V. 47
Flying Vistas: the Human Being, as seen through the Eyes of the Flight Surgeon. Philadelphia: 1937. V. 49

JONES, J. LEVERING
Chronicle of the Union League of Philadelphia, 1862-1902. Philadelphia: 1902. V. 48

JONES, J. P.
Flora Devoniensis. London: 1829. V. 52

JONES, JAMES
From Here to Eternity. New York: 1951. V. 47; 48; 49; 50; 51; 52; 53; 54
From Here to Eternity. London: 1952. V. 50; 53
The Pistol. New York: 1958. V. 54
Sepulchrorum Inscriptiones: or a Curious Collection of Above 900 of the Most Remarkable Epitaphs, Antient and Modern, Serious and Merry, in the Kingdoms of Great Britain, Ireland, etc. in english Verse... Westminster: 1727. V. 49
Some Came Running. New York: 1957. V. 50
A Touch of Danger. Garden City: 1973. V. 54
Viet Journal. New York: 1974. V. 51
Whistle: a Work in Progress. Bloomfield Hills: 1974. V. 54

JONES, JAMES ATHEARN
Reft Rob; or, the Witch of Scot-Muir, Commonly Called Madge the Snoover. London: 1817. V. 49
The Refugee: a Romance. New York: 1825. V. 51

JONES, JAMES DUKE
Songs of the Wye, and Poems... London: 1859. V. 47

JONES, JENKIN
Hobby Horses, a Poetic Allegory, in Five Parts. London: 1797. V. 48

JONES, JENKIN LLOYD
An Artilleryman's Diary. Madison: 1914. V. 50

JONES, JOHN BEAUCHAMP
A Rebel War Clerk's Diary at the Confederate States Capital. Philadelphia: 1866. V. 50

JONES, JOHN D.
Life and Adventure in the South Pacific by a Roving Printer. New York: 1861. V. 50

JONES, JOHN FREDERICK DRAKE
A Treatise on the Process Employed by Nature in Suppressing the Hemorrhage from Divided and Punctured Arteries, and on the Use of the Ligature... Philadelphia: 1811. V. 48; 52

JONES, JOHN MATTHEW
The Naturalist in Bermuda: a Sketch of the Geology, Zoology and Botany, of the Remarkable Groups of Islands... London: 1859. V. 48

JONES, JOHN P.
Borger, The Little Oklahoma, Read It and Weep. V. 47

JONES, JOHN PAUL
Life and Correspondence of John Paul Jones, Including His Narrative. New York: 1830. V. 47; 52
The Life, Travels, Voyages and Daring Engagements of Paul Jones... Albany: 1809. V. 47
Memoirs of Rear Admiral Paul Jones. Edinburgh: 1830. V. 49

JONES, JOHN THOMAS
Account of the War in Spain and Portugal, and In the South of France, from 1808 to 1814, Inclusive. London: 1818. V. 52; 54

JONES, JOHN WILLIAM
Christ in the Camp or Religion in Lee's Army. Richmond: 1887. V. 51
Christ in the Camp; or Religion in Lee's Army. Waco: 1887. V. 49
The Davis Memorial Volume; or Our Dead President, Jefferson Davis and the World's Tribute to His Memory. Richmond: 1890. V. 49
Life and Letters of Robert E. Lee Soldier and Man. New York and Washington: 1906. V. 50; 52
Personal Reminiscences, Anecdotes and Letters of Gen. Robert E. Lee. New York: 1875. V. 53

JONES, JONATHAN H.
A Condensed History of the Apache and Comanche Indian Tribes for Amusements and General Knowledge. San Antonio: 1899. V. 54

JONES, JOSEPH
Agricultural Resources of Georgia. Augusta: 1861. V. 49
Observations On Some of the Physical, Chemical, Physiological and Pathological Phenomena of Malarial Fever. Philadelphia: 1859. V. 48; 51

JONES, JUSTIN
The Nun of St. Ursula, or the Burning of the Convent. Boston: 1845. V. 51
Yankee Jack; or, the Perils of a Privateersman. New York: 1852. V. 49

JONES, KENNETH
Stone Soup. Portland: 1985. V. 52

JONES, L. T.
An Historical Journal of the British Campaign on the Continent, in the Year 1794. Birmingham: 1797. V. 50

JONES, LESLIE W.
The Miniatures of the Manuscripts of Terence Prior to the 13th Century. Princeton: 1931. V. 48; 50; 52; 54

JONES, LLOYD
Life and Adventure of Harry Tracy, "The Modern Dick Turpin". Chicago: 1902. V. 53

JONES, LUCY
Original Rhymes, Accompanying an Historical Chart of the Borough of Nottingham. Nottingham: 1844. V. 53

JONES, MADISON
The Innocent. New York: 1957. V. 48; 51
Season of the Strangler. New York: 1982. V. 49

JONES, MARGARET BELLE
Bastrop: a Compilation of Material Relating to the History of the Town of Bastrop with Letters Written by Terry's Rangers. Bastrop: 1936. V. 48; 49

JONES, MARY EIRWEN
The Romance of Lace. London and New York: 1951. V. 54

JONES, O. A.
Biology and Geology of Coral Reefs. London: 1973. V. 50; 51

JONES, OWEN
Examples of Chinese Ornament Selected from Objects in the South Kensington Museum and Other Collections. London: 1867. V. 47; 51
The Grammar of Ornament. London: 1856. V. 47; 51; 52
The Grammar of Ornament. London: 1865. V. 53
The Grammar of Ornament. London: 1868. V. 50; 54
The Grammar of Ornament. London: 1910. V. 52
The Grammar of Ornament. London: 1910/28. V. 48
The Myvryian Archaiology of Wales... Denbigh: 1870. V. 48
One Thousand and One Initial Letters. London: 1864. V. 48; 49
Rock-Climbing in the English Lake District. London: 1897. V. 51; 52; 53
Rock-Climbing in the English Lake District. Keswick: 1900. V. 54
Scenes from the Winter's Tale. London: 1866. V. 49; 52
Winged Thoughts. London: 1851. V. 47

JONES, P. MANSELL
Emile Verhaeren - a Study in the Development of His Art and Ideas. Cardiff and London: 1926. V. 54

JONES, PAUL
Flora Magnifica. London: 1976. V. 48; 50
Flora Superba. 1971. V. 52

JONES, RAYMOND F.
This Island Earth. Chicago: 1952. V. 52
The Year When Stardust Fell. Philadelphia: 1958. V. 51

JONES, REUBEN
A History of the Virginia Portsmouth Baptist Association... Raleigh: 1881. V. 51

JONES, RICHARD
An Essay on the Distribution of Wealth, and on the Sources of Taxation. London: 1831. V. 52

JONES, ROBERT
The Muses Gardin for Delights 1610; or the Fift Booke ot Ayres Composed by Robert Jones. Oxford: 1901. V. 48
Orthopaedic Surgery of Injuries by Various Authors. London: 1921. V. 53
Orthopedic Surgery. New York: 1923. V. 52
Orthopedic Surgery. New York: 1924. V. 53

JONES, ROBERT EDMOND
Drawings for the Theater. New York: 1925. V. 50

JONES, ROBERT T.
Down the Fairway. London: 1928. V. 48

JONES, SAMUEL A.
Pertaining to Thoreau. Detroit: 1901. V. 52

JONES, SARAH L.
Life in the South: from the Commencement of the War by a Blockaded British Subject. London: 1863. V. 54

JONES, SHERIDAN R.
Black Bass and Bass Craft: tthe Life Habits of the Two Bass and Successful Angling Strategy. New York: 1924. V. 52

JONES, SHIRLEY
Backgrounds. South Croydon: 1979. V. 47
A Dark Side of the Sun. London: 1985. V. 48
Falls the Shadow: Six Essays. 1995. V. 54
For Gladstone. 1988. V. 52; 54
For Gladstone. South Croydon: 1988. V. 52
Impressions; Eight Aquatints to Accompany Eight Poems and Prose Pieces. 1984. V. 52; 54
The Same Sun: Nine Poems and Nine Etchings. 1978. V. 54
Scop Hwillum Sang. London: 1983. V. 50
Two Moons. London: 1991. V. 51

JONES, STEPHEN
A General Pronouncing and Explanatory Dictionary of English Language for the Use of Schools, Foreigners, etc. on the Plan of Mr. Sheridan. London: 1813. V. 48
The History of Poland, from Its Origin as a Nation to the Commencement of the Year 1795. Dublin: 1795. V. 47; 50; 53
The Natural History of Birds. London: 1793. V. 54
A Natural History of Fishes and of Reptiles, Insects, Waters, Earths, Fossils, Minerals and Vegetables. London: 1795. V. 54
A New Biographical Dictionary. London: 1811. V. 51
A Pronouncing Dictionary of the English Language... London: 1796. V. 52
Sheridan Improved. London: 1804. V. 52
Sheridan Improved. London: 1806. V. 52
Sheridan Improved. London: 1812. V. 52
Sheridan Improved. 1835. V. 52

JONES, SYDNEY R.
Old Houses in Holland. London: 1913. V. 53
Posters and Their Designers. London: 1924. V. 47; 53

JONES, T. E.
Leaves from an Argonaut's Note Book. San Francisco: 1905. V. 50

JONES, T. GWYNN
Detholiad o Ganiadau. Newtown: 1926. V. 52

JONES, T. L.
From the Gold Mine to the Pulpit the Story of Reverend T. L. Jones, Backwoods Methodist Preacher in the Pacific Northwest. Cincinnati: 1904. V. 49

JONES, T. W.
The Principles and Practice of Ophthalmi Medicine and Surgery. Philadelphia: 1847. V. 53

JONES, THEOPHILUS
A History of the Country of Brecknock. Brecknock: 1909. V. 51

JONES, THOM
The Pugilist at Rest. Boston: 1993. V. 50; 51; 53; 54

JONES, THOMAS
The Gregynog Press, a Paper Read to the Double Crown Club on 7 april 1954. Oxford: 1954. V. 48
History of New York During the Revolutionary War. New York: 1879. V. 49

JONES, THOMAS GOODE
Last Days of the Army of Northern Virginia. Richmond?: 1893. V. 49; 53; 54

JONES, THOMAS H.
Experience and Personal Narrative of Uncle Tom Jones: Who Was for Forty Years a Slave. New York: 1854. V. 48

JONES, VIRGIL CARRINGTON
The Civil War at Sea. New York: 1960-62. V. 48; 50

JONES, W. B.
The History and Antiquities of Saint Davids (Cathedral). London and Tenby: 1856. V. 54

JONES, W. H.
Bradford-on-Avon: a History and Description. Bradford-on-Avon: 1907. V. 54

JONES, W. NORTHEY
The History of St. Peter's Church in Perth Amboy...from Its Organization in 1698 to the Year of Our Lord 1923... Perth Amboy: 1924. V. 49; 51

JONES, WILLIAM
Clavis Campanalogia or a Key to the Art of Ringing. 1788. V. 54
Clavis Campanalogia or a Key to the Art of Ringing. London: 1788. V. 50
An Essay on the First Principles of Natural Philosophy... Oxford: 1762. V. 47; 53
An Essay on the Law of Bailments. London: 1781. V. 52
A Grammar of the Persian Language. London: 1775. V. 47; 49
A Grammar of the Persian Language. London: 1823. V. 48
The History of the Life of Nader Shah, King of Persia. London: 1773. V. 50; 51
Institutes of Hindu Law... Calcutta: 1794. V. 54
Letters from a Tutor to His Pupils. London: 1780. V. 53
Memoirs of the Life, Writings and Correspondence of Sir William Jones. London: 1804. V. 50; 54
Memoirs of the Life, Writings and Correspondence of Sir William Jones. London: 1806. V. 53
Physiological Disquisitions; or, Discourses on the Natural History of the Elements. London: 1781.. V. 53
Poems, Consisting Chiefly of Translations from the Asiatick Languages. London: 1777. V. 51; 54
Poikilographia. London: 1830. V. 48; 51
Remarks on the Proposed Breakwater at Cape Henlopen. Philadelphia: 1825. V. 54
The Works of Sir William Jones. London: 1799. V. 48
The Works of Sir William Jones. London: 1799-1802. V. 51
The Works...with the Life of the Author... London: 1807. V. 49; 51

JONES, WILLIAM A.
Report Upon the Reconnaissance of Northwestern Wyoming. Washington: 1875. V. 47

JONES, WILLIAM CAREY
In the Supreme Court of the United States. Argument in the Case of Cruz Cervantes vs. the United States an Appeal from the District...for the Northern District of California. Washington: 1854. V. 50

JONES, WILLIAM TODD
Authentic Detail of an Affair of Honour, Between William Todd Jones Esq. and Sir Richard Musgrave. Dublin: 1802. V. 49; 52

JONES & WILLIS, LTD.
A Book of Designs of Ecclesiastaical Art by Jones and Willis Ltd. London: 1910. V. 52

JONG, ERICA
At the Edge of the Body. New York: 1979. V. 51
Fear of Flying. New York: 1973. V. 51
Fruits and Vegetables. New York: 1971. V. 51
Half-Lives. New York: 1973. V. 51
How to Save Your Own Life. New York: 1977. V. 51
The Poetry of Erica Jong. New York: 1971-75. V. 51

JONGHE, ADRIAEN DE
Emblemata, ad D. Arnoldum Cobelium, Ejusdem Aenigmatum Libellus, ad D. Arnoldum Rosenbergum. Antwerp: 1565. V. 47

JONSON, BEN
Ben Jonson's Jests; or the Wit's Pocket Companion. London: 1762. V. 51
Catiline His Conspiracy. London: 1616. V. 49
Catiline His Conspiracy. London: 1669. V. 52
A Croppe of Kisses, Selected Lyrics, Chosen and with an Appreciation by John Wallis. Waltham St. Lawrence: 1937. V. 47; 50; 51
The Masque of Queenes. London: 1930. V. 48; 50
The Poems of Ben Jonson. Oxford: 1936. V. 52; 54
The Sad Shepherd; or, a Tale of Robin Hood, a Fragment. London: 1783. V. 51
Songs: a Selection from the Plays, Masques and Poems, with the Earliest Known Settings of a Certain Numbers. Hammersmith: 1906. V. 47; 48
Volpone. London: 1898. V. 48; 50; 51; 53
Volpone. Berlin: 1910. V. 49; 50; 54
Volpone or the Fox. Oxford: 1952. V. 47; 48; 49; 52; 54
The Workes. London: 1616/40. V. 53
The Workes. London: 1640/1631-40. V. 48; 51; 52; 54
The Works. London: 1692. V. 49
The Works. London: 1716. V. 52
The Works. London: 1716-17. V. 50
The Works. London: 1756. V. 49
The Works. London: 1816. V. 47; 51; 53
The Works. London: 1875. V. 48

JONSTONIUS, JOANNES
Inscriptiones Historicae Regum Scotorum (in verse)... Amsteldami: 1602. V. 48
Thaumatographia Naturalis in Decem Classes Distincta, in Quibus Admiranda I. Coeli II. Elementorum III. Meteororum IV. Fossilium V. Plantarum VI. Avium. VII. Quadrupedum. VIII. Exanguium IX. Piscium X. Hominis. Amsterdam: 1665. V. 47
Theatrvm Vniversale de Avibvs. Heilbronn: 1756. V. 53
Theatrvm Vniversale Omnivm Animalivm Insectorvm. (and) Historiae Natvralis de Serpentibvs. Heilbronn: 1757. V. 53
Theatrvm Vniversale Omnivm Animalivm Qvadrvpedvm. Heilbronn: 1755. V. 53

JONVEAUX, EMILE
Two Years in East Africa: Adventures in Abyssinia and Nubia, with a Journey to the Sources of the Nile. London: 1876. V. 48

JOPLING, CHARLES M.
Sketch of Furness and Cartmel, Comprising the Hundred of Lonsdale North of the Sands. London: 1843. V. 50; 52

JOPLING, JOSEPH
The Practice of Isometrical Perspective. London: 1834. V. 54

JOPPIEN, R.
The Art of Captain Cook's Voyages. New Haven: 1985-88. V. 48; 51
The Art of Captain Cook's Voyages. New York, London: 1985/88. V. 49

JORAY, M.
Vasarely. Neuchatel: 1954. V. 54

JORDAN & DAVIESON
Descriptive Catalogue of the Museum of Anatomy, Science and Art. No. 807 Chestnut Street, Philadelphia. Philadelphia: 1870. V. 53

JORDAN, CHARLES EDWARD
A Letter from Charles Edward Jordan to His Family and Friends. Charlottesville: 1932. V. 49

JORDAN, CORNELIA JANE MATTHEWS
Flowers of Hope and Memory: a Collection of Poems. Richmond: 1861. V. 54

JORDAN, DAVID STARR
American Food and Game Fishes. New York: 1902. V. 54
American Food and Game Fishes. New York: 1903. V. 47
The Aquatic Resources of the Hawaiian Islands. Washington: 1905-06. V. 48
The Aquatic Resources of the Hawaiian Islands. Part I the Shore Fishes. Washington: 1905. V. 49
A Catalogue of the Fishes of Japan. Tokyo: 1913. V. 48
The Days of a Man. New York: 1922. V. 53
The Days of a Man. Yonkers-on-Hudson: 1922. V. 48; 50; 52
Fishes. New York: 1907. V. 49
Fur Seals and Fur Seal Islands of the North Pacific Ocean. Washington: 1898-99. V. 51; 54
The Genera of Fishes and a Classification of Fishes. Stanford: 1917-23. V. 52

JORDAN, EDWIN
The Newer Knowledge of Bacteriology and Immunology. Chicago: 1928. V. 51; 53

JORDAN, GREEN & ETTINGER
Historic Homes and Institutions and Genealogical and Personal Memoirs of the Lehigh Valley. New York: 1905. V. 53

JORDAN, JIM M.
The Paintings of Arshile Gorky: a Critical Catalogue. New York: 1982. V. 47; 49; 50; 52

JORDAN, JOHN W.
Colonial and Revolutionary Families of Pennsylvania: Genealogical and Personal Memoirs. New York: 1911. V. 52

JORDAN, JUNE
Some Changes. New York: 1971. V. 53
Who Look at Me. New York: 1969. V. 54

JORDAN, MILDRED
I Won't Said the King or the Purple Flannel Underwear. New York: 1945. V. 54

JORDAN, NEIL
Night in Tunisia. London: 1976. V. 47
Night in Tunisia. London: 1979. V. 51
Night in Tunisia. New York: 1980. V. 50
The Past. London: 1980. V. 47

JORDAN, ROBERT
The Dragon Reborn. New York: 1991. V. 51
The Fires of Heaven. New York: 1993. V. 51

JORDAN, THOMAS
A Speech Made to the Lord General Monck, at Clotheworkers Hall in London the 13. of March 1659, at Which Time He Was there Entertained by that Worthie Companie. 1659. V. 47

JORDANUS DE NEMORE
Arithmetica Decem Libris... 1496. V. 49

JORTIN, JOHN
The Life of Erasmus. London: 1758. V. 47
The Life of Erasmus. London: 1758-60. V. 47; 49; 54
Tracts, Philological, Critical, and Miscellaneous. London: 1790. V. 49

JOSE Clemente Orozco. New York: 1932. V. 48

JOSEPH Delteil. Essays in Tribute. London: 1962. V. 51

JOSEPH, F. J.
Amateurs in Arms. London: 1938. V. 49

JOSEPH, GEORGE
The Editor Regrets. London: 1937. V. 47

JOSEPH, H. S.
Memoirs of Convicted Prisoners; Accompanied by Remarks on the Causes and Prevention of Crime. London: 1853. V. 48; 49; 53

JOSEPH, JACQUES
Rhinoplasty and Facial Plastic Surgery with a Supplement on Mammalplasty and Other Operations in the Field of Plastic Surgery of the Body. Phoenix: 1987. V. 51

JOSEPH BEN DAVID IBN YAHYA
Torah-Or. Bologna: 1538. V. 51; 52

JOSEPHINE County As It Is! Climate and Resources. Portland: 1887. V. 52

JOSEPHUS, FLAVIUS
Di Flavio Giuseppe, Della Guerra de Gudei. Libri VII... In Venegia: 1581. V. 50
The Famous and Memorable Workes of Josephus. London: 1609. V. 51; 52; 53
The Famous and Memorable Works... London: 1640. V. 52
The Famous and Memorable Works. London: 1655. V. 51
Flavii Iosephi Hebraei, Historiogrpahi Clariss. Opera, Ad Multorum Codicum Latinorum, Eorundemq... Cologne: 1524. V. 47
The Genuine Works of Flavius Josephus, the Jewish Historian... Boston: 1849. V. 47; 50
(Opera). Antiquitatus Ac De bello Judaico. Venice: 1502. V. 47; 50
Les Sept Livres de Flavius Josephus de La Guerre et Captivite des Juifz,.. Paris: 1557. V. 47; 50
The Whole Genuine and Complete Works of Flavius Josephus, the Learned and Authentic Jewish Historian and Celebrated Warrior... New York: 1792-94. V. 52
The Whole Genuine Works of... Glasgow: 1818. V. 48
The Works. London: 1701. V. 51
The Works... London: 1725. V. 53
The Works. London: 1738. V. 47
Works. London: 1818. V. 49
The Works. London: 1841. V. 48
The Works. London: 1856. V. 50
The Works. New York: 1890. V. 50
Zweyntzig Bucher von Den Alten Geschichten...(The Works). 1535. V. 47

JOSEPHY, ALVIN M.
The Nez Perce Indians and Opening of the Northwest. New Haven: 1965. V. 51

JOSI, CHRISTIAN
A Catalogue of a Collection of the Engravings, Etchings and Original Drawings and Books of Prints of Christian Josi, Esq., Deceased....Which Will Be Sold by Mr. Christie at His Great Room in King Street. London: 1829. V. 50

JOSSELYN, CHARLES
The True Napoleon: a Cyclopedia of His Life. New York: 1902. V. 50

JOSSELYN, JOHN
New-England's Rarities. Boston: 1865. V. 51

JOSTES, BARBARA DONOHOE
John Parrott, Consul, 1811-1884. Selected Papers of a Western Pioneer. San Francisco: 1972. V. 52; 54

JOUBERT, LAURENT
Paradoxorum decas Prima Atque Altera... Lyon: 1566. V. 49; 50; 52

JOUBERT DE L'HIBERDERIE, M.
Le Dessinateur, Pour Les Fabriques d'Etoffes d'Or, D'Argent et de Soie... Paris: 1774. V. 47

JOUFFREAU DE LAZARIE, ABBE DE
Le Joujou des Demoiselles. Paris: 1750?. V. 48

JOUFFROY, ALAIN
Miro Sculpture. New York: 1974. V. 50; 52

JOUHANDEAU, MARCEL
Descente aux Enfers. Paris: 1961. V. 51
Petit Bestiaire. Paris: 1944. V. 50

JOURDAIN, F. C. R.
The Eggs of European Birds. London: 1906-09. V. 50

JOURDAIN, H. F. N.
A History of the Mess Plate of the 88th Connaught Rangers. 1904. V. 49

JOURDAIN, MARGARET
Decoration in England from 1660-1770. London: 1914. V. 49
English Decoration and Furniture of the Early Renaissance 1500-1650. London: 1924. V. 49
English Decoration and Furniture of the Later XVIIIth Century, 1760-1820. London: 1922. V. 49
English Decorative Plasterwork of the Renaissance. London: 1926. V. 50; 54
English Decorative Plasterwork of the Renaissance. London: 1933. V. 48
English Furniture: the Georgian Period (1750-1830). London: 1953. V. 54
English Interior Decoration 1500 to 1830. London: 1950. V. 50; 54
English Interiors in Smaller Houses. London: 1923. V. 53
English Interiors in Smaller Houses. New York: 1923. V. 51
Furniture in England from 1660 to 1760. London: 1914. V. 54
The Work of William Kent, Artist, Painter, Designer and Landscape Gardener. London: 1948. V. 48; 53

JOURNAL de L'Academie D'Horticulture Manuel, Periodique, Pratique et Progressif, Indispensable Aux Jardiniers et Amateurs de Jardins. Paris: 1831-35. V. 47

JOURNAL of a Tour and Residence in Great Britain, During the Years 1810 and 1811, by a French Traveller... Edinburgh: 1815. V. 53

JOURNAL of Herpetology. 1968-89. V. 52

JOURNAL of History of Medicine and Allied Scienés. 1946-58. V. 47

THE JOURNAL of Horticulture, Cottage Gardener, and Country Gentleman... London: 1861-62. V. 47; 51

JOURNAL of Korean Plant Taxonomy. Seoul: 1969-90. V. 47; 51; 52

THE JOURNAL of the Economic and Social History Society of Ireland. Belfast: 1974-92. V. 51

A JOURNAL of the Siege of Mentz, Under the Command of His Serene Highness, The Duke of Lorrain and the Confederate Princes. London: 1689. V. 47; 50

A JOURNEY From London to Scarborough, In Several Letters...With A List of the Nobility, Quality and Gentry at Scarborough...in...1733. London: 1734. V. 50

A JOURNEY Round the World. London: 1889. V. 52

A JOURNEY through the Head of a Modern Poet, Being the Susbstance of a Dream, Occasioned by Reading the Sixth Book of Virgil. London: 1750. V. 52

JOUSSE, JOHN
Arcana Musicae; or, a Variety of Curious and Entertaining Musical Problems, with Their Solutions... London: 1818. V. 47

JOUSSE, MATHURIN
Le Theatre de l'Art de Charpentier, Enrichi de Diverses Figures, avec l'Interpretation d'Icelles. La Fleche: 1650. V. 52

JOUTEL, HENRI
Journal Historique du Dernier Voyage Que feu M. de la Sale fit Dans le Golfe de Mexique... Paris: 1713. V. 50; 54

JOUTEL, HENRY
Joutel's Journal of La Salle's Last Voyage. Chicago: 1896. V. 47
Joutel's Journal of Lasalle's Last Voyage 1684-87. Albany: 1906. V. 47

JOUY, VICTOR JOSEPH ETIENNE DE
The Hermit in Italy, or Observations on the Manner and Customs of Italy. London: 1825. V. 47

JOVII, PAULI
Pauli Jovii Novocomensis Episcopi Nucerini Elogia Virorum Bellica Virtute Illustruim. Basil: 1575-77. V. 51

JOY, N. H.
A Practical Handbook of British Beetles. London: 1976. V. 50

JOYCE, J.
A System of Practical Arithmetic, Applicable to the Present State of Trade and Money Transactions... London: 1828. V. 48

JOYCE, JAMES
Anna Livia Plurabelle. New York: 1928. V. 47; 49; 50; 51; 52
Anna Livia Plurabelle. London: 1930. V. 47; 49; 51; 53
The Cat and the Devil. London: 1965. V. 47; 52
Chamber Music. Boston. V. 47; 48
Chamber Music. London: 1907. V. 47; 49
Chamber Music. Boston: 1918. V. 48; 49; 51; 53
Chamber Music. London: 1927. V. 52
Collected Poems. New York: 1936. V. 47; 50; 51; 52
Collected Poems. New York: 1937. V. 47; 48
Dedalus - Portrait de l'Artiste Jeune par Lui-meme. Paris: 1924. V. 47
Dublin-Novelelr (Dubliners). Stockholm: 1931. V. 47
Dubliners. London: 1922. V. 52
Epiphanies. New York: 1988. V. 47; 50; 52
Exiles. New York. V. 47
Exiles. London: 1918. V. 49; 50; 52; 53
Exiles. New York: 1918. V. 49; 53; 54
Exiles. London: 1921. V. 47; 52
Exiles. New York: 1951. V. 47; 48; 49
Finnegans Wake. London: 1939. V. 47; 48; 49; 50; 51; 53
Gens de Dublin. Lausanne: 1941. V. 47
Giacomo Joyce. New York: 1968. V. 47; 54
Giacomo Joyce. New York: 1989. V. 50; 52
Haveth Childers Everywhere. Paris, New York: 1930. V. 47; 48; 49; 50; 51; 52; 53
Haveth Childers Everywhere. London: 1931. V. 47; 49; 51; 54
The Joyce Book. London: 1933. V. 48; 51
Letters. London: 1957. V. 47
Letters. New York: 1957-66. V. 52
Letters. New York: 1966. V. 48; 50; 52
Letters. New York: 1966-67. V. 54
Mime of Mick, Nick and the Maggies. The Hague: 1933. V. 47; 48
The Mime of Mick, Nick and the Maggies. 1934. V. 54
The Mime of Mick, Nick and the Maggies. The Hague/New York: 1934. V. 50; 51; 53
Poems Penyeach. Paris: 1927. V. 47; 49; 50; 51; 52
Pomes Penyeach/Pometti da un Soldo. Verona: 1991. V. 47
A Portrait of the Artist as a Young Man. London: 1916. V. 52; 53
A Portrait of the Artist as a Young Man. London: 1917. V. 48; 51
Portrait of the Artist as a Young Man. New York: 1917. V. 54
A Portrait of the Artist as a Young Man. London: 1918. V. 50
A Portrait of the Artist as a Young Man. London: 1921. V. 48; 53
A Portrait of the Artist as a Young Man. London: 1965. V. 47
Portrait of the Artist as a Young Man. New York: 1968. V. 49; 50; 53
A Shorter Finnegans Wake. London: 1966. V. 47; 50
Stephen Hero. London: 1944. V. 47; 53
Stephen Hero. New York: 1944. V. 47; 48; 49; 50; 54
Stephen Hero. New York: 1955. V. 53
Storiella As She Is Syung. London: 1937. V. 49; 53
Tales Told of Shem and Shaun. Paris: 1929. V. 47; 49; 50; 51; 53
Topf!. London: 1976. V. 47
Trois Lettres a Leon-Paul Fargue (Juin-Juillet 1925). France: 1986. V. 47

JOYCE, JAMES continued
Two Tales of Shem and Shaun. 1932. V. 54
Two Tales of Shem and Shaun. London: 1932. V. 51; 52
Ulysses. London: 1922. V. 47; 48; 51; 53
Ulysses. Paris: 1922. V. 47; 48; 49; 50; 51; 53; 54
Ulysses. Paris: 1925. V. 48
Ulysses. Paris: 1926. V. 47
Ulysses. Basel: 1927. V. 51
Ulysses. Paris: 1927. V. 51
Ulysses. Paris: 1930. V. 47
Ulysses. Zurich: 1930. V. 47
Ulysses. Hamburg, Paris, Bologna: 1932. V. 47; 48; 49; 51; 53
Ulysses. Hamburg: 1933. V. 48; 53
Ulysses. New York: 1934. V. 50
Ulysses. 1935. V. 54
Ulysses. Hamburg: 1935. V. 47
Ulysses. New York: 1935. V. 47; 48; 49; 51; 52; 53; 54
Ulysses. London: 1936. V. 47; 49; 50; 51; 53
Ulysses. London: 1937. V. 47; 49; 50; 51; 52
Ulysses. London: 1941. V. 47
Ulysses. New York: 1949. V. 54
Ulysses, a Critical and Synoptic Edition. New York & London: 1984. V. 47; 49
Verbannte (Exiles). Schauspiel in Drei Akten. Zurich: 1919. V. 52

JOYCE, JAMES GERALD
The Fairford Windows, a Monograph. London: 1872. V. 52

JOYCE, JOHN A.
Jewels of Memory. Washington: 1895. V. 52; 53; 54

JOYCE, P. W.
English as We Speak It In Ireland. London: 1910. V. 54
Old Irish Folk Music and Songs: a Collection of 842 Irish Aris and Songs Hitherto Unpublished.. 1909. V. 50
The Origin and History of Irish Names of Places. London. V. 49; 53
The Origin and History of Irish Names of Places. 1910/2/3. V. 54
A Social History of Ancient Ireland. 1903. V. 49
A Social History of Ancient Ireland. London: 1920. V. 53

JOYCE, R. V.
Dreams Wherein are Contained a Few Morals for the Consideration of Fishermen... Wakefield. V. 47

JOYCE, ROBERT D.
Deirdre. Boston: 1877. V. 54

JOYCE, STANISLAUS
Le Journal de Dublin. Paris: 1967. V. 53
My Brother's Keeper: James Joyce's Early Years. New York: 1958. V. 52; 53
Recollections of James Joyce by His Brother. New York: 1950. V. 49

JOYCE, T. ATHOL
Women of All Nations. London: 1908. V. 50; 51; 53

JOYCE, WILLIAM J.
Life of W. J. Joyce, Written by Himself.... San Marcos: 1913. V. 50

JOYFULL
Newes From the King. Or, The True Proceedings of His Maties Armie at Nottingham, Lichfield, Tamworth, Warwick, Coventry, Medingham... London: 1642. V. 49; 54

JUAN, DON GEORGE
A Voyage to South America. London: 1760. V. 53
A Voyage to South America. London: 1806. V. 54
A Voyage to South America. London: 1807. V. 49

JUCHEREAU DE SAINT DENIS, ANTOINE DE
Revolutions de Constantinople en 1807 et 1808. Paris: 1819. V. 47

JUDAH, SAMUEL B. H.
Gotham and Gothamites, a Medley. New York: 1823. V. 52; 54
The Rose of Aragon. New York: 1822. V. 47; 53
A Tale of Lexington; a National Comedy. New York: 1823. V. 51

JUDD, NEIL M.
Architecture of Pueblo Bonito. Washington: 1964. V. 47
Material Culture of Pueblo Bonito. Washington: 1954. V. 47; 52
Pueblo Del Arroyo, Chaco Canyon, New Mexico. Washington: 1959. V. 52

JUDD, SILAS
A Sketch of the Life and Voyages of Captain Alvah Dewey. New York: 1838. V. 47

JUDGES, A. V.
The Elizabethan Underworld - a Collection of Tudor and Early Stuart Tracts and Ballads Telling of the Lives and Misdoings of Vagabonds, Thieves, Rogues and Cozeners, and Giving Account of the Operation of the Criminal Law. London: 1930. V. 52

THE JUDGMENT
of Whole Kingdoms and Nations, Concerning the Rights, Power and Prerogative of Kings and the Rights, Priviledges and Properties of the People. London: 1710. V. 51; 53

JUDSON, E. Z. C.
The Black Avenger of the Spanish Maine; or, the Fiend of Blood. Boston: 1847. V. 49
The Mysteries and Miseries of New York: a Story of Real Life. New York: 1848. V. 52
The Mysteries and Miseries of New York: a Story of Real Life. Dublin: 1849. V. 51; 53

JUDSON, R. RICHARD
The Drawings of Jacob de Gheyn II. Northampton: 1972. V. 48; 49

JUETTNER, OTTO
Daniel Drake and His Followers. Cincinnati: 1898. V. 53
Daniel Drake and His Followers. Cincinnati: 1909. V. 51; 52

JUGAKU, BUNSHO
Paper-Making by Hand in Japan. Tokyo: 1959. V. 47; 48; 52

JUKES, JOSEPH BEETE
Excursions in and About Newfoundland. London: 1842. V. 50
Letters and Extracts from the Addresses and Occasional Writings of J. Beete Jukes... London: 1871. V. 54
Narrative of the Surveying Voyage of H.M.S. Fly, Commanded by Captain F. P. Blackwood, R.N. in Torres Strait, New Guinea... London: 1847. V. 48; 49; 50; 52
On the Mode of Formation of Some of the River Valleys in the South of Ireland. London: 1862. V. 48

JULIA
; or the Pilgrim, in Two Cantos. London: 1825. V. 50

JULIA
Stanley: a Novel. Dublin: 1780. V. 54

JULIAN, HUBERT
Black Eagle. London: 1964. V. 54

JULIAN, JOHN
A Dictionary of Hymnology, Setting Forth the Origin and History of Christian Hymns of all Ages and Nations. London: 1892. V. 49

JULIAN, PHILIPPE
The Orientalists. European Painters of Eastern Scenes. Oxford: 1977. V. 54

JULIAN
Symons at 80: a Tribute. Helsinki: 1992. V. 49

JULIEN, EDOUARD
The Posters of Toulouse-Lautrec. 1966. V. 51

JULIUS,
or the Deaf and Dumb Orphan: A Tale for the Youth of Both Sexes: Founded on the Popular Play of Deaf and Dumb. London: 1801. V. 47

JULIUS II, POPE
Bulla Contra Johannem Bentiuolum in Ciuitate Bononiensis... Rome: 1506. V. 50
Bulla Indulgentiarum Apostolica p Fabrica Scti. Milan?: 1507-08. V. 50
Bulla Reformationis Officialium Ro. Curie. Rome: 1512. V. 50; 53
Julii Secundi Pontificis Max. Decretum Sanctissimum, in Quinta Sessione Sacri Conciliii Lateranenum. De Cretione Summi Pont. Approbatum. Rome: 1513. V. 48

JULLIEN, ANDRE
The Topography of All the Known Vineyards. London: 1824. V. 53

JUNCKER, J.
Dissertationes Duae De Viribus Medicatis Olei Animalis in Epilepsia, Aliisque Affectibus Convulsivis. London: 1732. V. 47

JUNCKHAUSEN, BARTOLDT
New Kunstlich Obst Garten Buchlein, Darinnen Ordentlich Begrieffen, Wie Man Auss Rechtem Grund der Natur, Jedes Lands Art Boden, Und Gelegenheit Nach, Mit Geburlicher Arbeit.. Brandenburg?: 1619. V. 49

JUNG, CARL GUSTAV
Collected Papers on Analytical Psychology. London: 1917. V. 48
The Integration of the Personality. New York: 1939. V. 53
Psychology and Alchemy. New York: 1953. V. 52
Studies in Word Association. London: 1918. V. 52
Studies in Word Association. New York: 1919. V. 53
Wandlungen und Symbole der Libido: Beitrage zur Entwicklungsgeschichte des Denkens. Leipzig und Wien: 1912. V. 49; 51
Zur Psychologie und Pathologie Sogenannter Occulter Pha. Leipzig: 1902. V. 53

JUNGE, CARL S.
Ex Libris. New York: 1935. V. 52

JUNGER, ERNST
Copse 125 - a Chronicle from the Trench Warfare of 1918. London: 1930. V. 52
The Storm of Steel. London: 1929. V. 54

JUNG-STILLING, JOHANN HEIRNICH
Theory of Pneumatology, in Reply to the Question, What Ought to Be Believed or Disbelieved, Concerning Presentiments, Visions, Apparitions, According to Nature, Reason and Scripture... New York: 1851. V. 47

JUNIUS, FRANCISCUS
Etymologicum Anglicanum. Oxonii: 1743. V. 50; 54

JUNIUS, HADRIANUS
Batavia. Dordrecht: 1652. V. 47
Emblemata. Antverpiae: 1565. V. 49; 50
Hadriani Junii Medici Emblemata. (with) Aenigmatum Libellus... Antwerp: 1565. V. 47; 52

JUNIUS, PSEUD.
The Genuine Letters of Junius, To which are Prefixed Anecdotes of the Author. London: 1771. V. 54
Junius: Including Letters by the Same Writer, Under Other Signatures... 1812. V. 47
Junius: Including Letters by the Same Writer, Under Other Signatures. London: 1812. V. 50
Junius: Including Letters by the Same Writer, Under Other Signatures... London: 1814. V. 51
The Letters. London: 1772. V. 47
The Letters. Philadelphia: 1791. V. 49
Letters. London: 1799. V. 53

JUNIUS, PSEUD. continued
The Letters. London: 1801. V. 48; 53; 54
The Letters. London: 1805. V. 48; 49; 51; 54
The Letters. Philadelphia: 1007. V. 51
Letters. London: 1814. V. 53
Letters. Paris: 1819. V. 50
The Letters. London: 1820. V. 48
Stat Nominis Umbra. London: 1772. V. 51
Stat Nominis Umbra. London: 1799. V. 48
Stat Nominis Umbra. London: 1801. V. 50; 51
Stat Nominis Umbra. London: 1805. V. 51
Stat Umbra. London: 1797. V. 52
Stat Umbra. London: 1797/94. V. 49

JUPP, E. B.
An Historical Account of the Worshipful Company of Carpenters of the City of London... (with Genealogical Memoranda Relating to Richard Wyatt)...Citizen and Carpenter of London... V. 47

JURIN, JAMES
An Account of the Success of Inoculating the Small Pox in Great Britain, for the Year 1724. London: 1725. V. 48
Geometry No Friend to Infidelity; or, a Defence of Sir Isaac Newton and the British Matematicians, in a Letter to the Author of the Analyst. London: 1734. V. 48; 51; 52

JUSSERAND, JEAN ADRIEN ANTOINE JULES
The English Novel in the Time of Shakespeare. London: 1890. V. 49
English Wayfaring Life in the Middle Ages (XIVTH Century). London: 1889. V. 48; 50

JUSSIEU, ANTOINE LAURENT DE
Genera Plantarum, Secundum Ordines Naturales Disposita. Paris: 1789. V. 51
Genera Plantarum Secundum Ordines Naturales Disposita, Juxta Methodum in Horto Regio Parisiensi Exaratam. Paris: 1879. V. 53

A JUST Narrative of the Hellish New Counter-Plots of the Papists, to Cast the Odium of Their Horrid Treasons Upon the Presbyterians... London: 1679. V. 52

JUST, WARD
A Soldier of the Revolution. New York: 1970. V. 53

JUSTICE, ALEXANDER
A General Treatise of the Dominion of the Sea... London: 1707?. V. 48

THE JUSTICE and Necessity of Taxing the American Colonies, Demonstrated, Together with a Vindication of the Authority of Parliament. London: 1766. V. 48; 52

JUSTICE, DONALD
Departures. Iowa City: 1973. V. 48; 51; 53; 54
From a Notebook. Iowa City: 1972. V. 51; 53
L'Homme Qui Se Ferme. (The Man Closing Up). Iowa City: 1973. V. 54
Sixteen Poems. Iowa City: 1970. V. 48; 51; 52; 54

JUSTICE, JEAN
Dictionary of Marks and Monograms of Delft Pottery. London: 1930. V. 51

JUSTINUS, MARCUS JUNIANUS
Codicis D. N. Justiniani Sacratiss... Paris: 1548. V. 52
Corpus Juris Civilis, Pandectis ad Florentinum Archetypum Expressis, Institutionibus, Codice et Novellis...cum Notis Integris, Repetitae Quintum Praelectionis, Dionysii Gothofredi. Amsterdam: 1663. V. 50
Historiae Philippicae. Lugduni Batavorum: 1760. V. 48; 49
The History of the Warres of the Emperour Justinian in Eight Books. London: 1653. V. 48
History of the World... London: 1719. V. 54
In Trogi Pompeii Historias Libri Quadragintaquatuor... Paris: 1538. V. 48
The Institutes of Justinian. Oxford: 1889. V. 50
Institutionum Libri IIII. Paris: 1534. V. 48
Justini Ex Trogi Pompeii Historia Libri XLIII. Antwerp: 1552. V. 52
Justini Historiae Philippicae, Ex Recensione Joannis Georgii Graevii. Amsterdam: 1722. V. 48; 50
Justin's History of the World, from the Assyrian Monarchy. London: 1702. V. 47; 49
Justinus Historicus. Venice: 1497. V. 48; 54
Trogi Pompeii Historiarum Philippicarum Epitoma: Ex manuscriptis codicibus Emenadatior... Paris: 1581. V. 52

JUSTINUS, SAINT
Opera. Paris: 1551. V. 50; 53
Opera... Paris: 1565. V. 49

JUVENALIS, DECIMUS JUNIUS
Juvenal's Sixteen Satyrs... London: 1647. V. 47; 48; 49
Mores Hominum. London: 1660. V. 49; 52
A New Translation (by John Duer) with Notes, of The Third Satire of Juvenal. New York: 1806. V. 47
Nobility, a Poem. London: 1811. V. 51
Paraphrasi Nella Sesta Satira di Givvenale. Venice: 1538. V. 52
The Satires. London: 1693. V. 50
The Satires. London: 1785. V. 48
Satires. Paris: 1796. V. 49
The Satires. London: 1802. V. 51
The Satires. London: 1807. V. 49
Satyrae... Venice: 1488. V. 47
Satyrae. Venice: 1492. V. 51; 52
Satyrae. London: 1612. V. 49
Satyrae. Dublin: 1728. V. 47
Satyrae. Birmingham: 1761. V. 48; 52; 53
The Third Satire of Juvenal. New York: 1806. V. 51

THE JUVENILE Library, Including a Complete Course of Instruction on Every Useful Subjects... London: 1800-03. V. 47

THE JUVENILE Party. London: 1866. V. 53

THE JUVENILE Rambler; or, Sketches and Anecdotes of the People of Various Countries. London: 1845. V. 52

K

K., C.
Art's Masterpiece; or, a Companion for the Ingenious, of Either Sex. London: 1721. V. 51

KAAS, P.
Monograph of the Living Chitons. Leiden: 1985-90. V. 50

KABAT, ELVIN
Experimental Immunochemistry. Springfield: 1948. V. 53

KABERRY, C. J.
Our Little Neighbours. Animals of the Farmyard and the Woodland. London: 1921. V. 47; 48; 50

KABERRY, PHYLLIS M.
Aboriginal Woman. London: 1939. V. 50

KABOTIE, FRED
Designs from Ancient Mimbrenos with a Hopi Interpretation by Fred Kabotie. San Francisco: 1949. V. 49; 51
Fred Kabotie, Hopi Indian Artist. Flagstaff: 1977. V. 53

KACHI-Kachi Mountain. London: 1900. V. 53

KAEMPFER, ENGELBERT
The History of Japan, Giving An Account of the Ancient and Present State and Government of the Empire... Tokyo: 1977. V. 48

KAFKA, FRANZ
Amerika. Munich: 1927. V. 47
Amerika. London: 1938. V. 50; 53
Amerika. Norfolk: 1940. V. 48
Beim Bau der Chinesischen Mauer. Del Mar: 1975. V. 47
Betrachtung. 1990. V. 51; 52; 54
The Castle. New York: 1930. V. 54
Conversation with the Supplicant. West Burke: 1971. V. 51
The Country Doctor. Oxford: 1945. V. 51
A Country Doctor. Philadelphia: 1962. V. 54
A Franz Kafka Miscellany... New York: 1940. V. 51
The Great Wall of China. London: 1933. V. 54
The Great Wall of China. New York: 1946. V. 48; 51
Der Heizer. (The Stocker). Leipzig: 1913. V. 53
In der Strafkolonie. (In the Penal Colony). Leipzig: 1919. V. 53
In the Penal Colony. 1987. V. 48; 49; 51; 52; 54
In the Penal Colony. New York: 1987. V. 47; 50
Der Kubelreiter... 1972. V. 52
Der Kubelreiter... Newark: 1972. V. 51
Ein Landarzt. Munich: 1919. V. 49; 51
Ein Landarzt... 1962. V. 52
The Metamorphosis. London: 1937. V. 48; 50; 51; 53; 54
Metamorphosis. New York: 1984. V. 47; 48; 52
Parables and Pieces. New York: 1990. V. 50; 52
The Trial. London: 1937. V. 49
The Trial. 1975. V. 48; 49
The Trial. Avon: 1975. V. 48; 49; 51; 52
The Trial. Connecticut: 1975. V. 47
Die Verwandlung. Leipzig: 1915. V. 49
Die Verwandlung. Leipzig: 1916. V. 47; 52; 54

KAFTAL, GEORGE
Iconography of the Saints in the Painting of North East Italy. Florence: 1978. V. 50; 54
Iconography of the Saints in Tuscan Painting. Florence: 1952. V. 49; 50
Iconography of the Saints in Tuscan Painting. Sansoni: 1952. V. 54

KAGAN, SOLOMON
Jewish Contributions to Medicine in America (1656-1934) with Medical Chronology, Bibliography and 69 Illustrations. Boston: 1934. V. 47
Jewish Contributions to Medicine in America from Colonial Times to the Present. Boston: 1939. V. 52

KAHN, DOUGLAS
John Heartfield: Art and Mass Media. New York: 1985. V. 51

KAHN, ELY JACQUES
Design in Art and Industry. New York: 1935. V. 50; 51; 53

KAHN, GORDON
Hollywood on Trial. New York: 1948. V. 53

KAHN, MORITZ
The Design and Construction of Industrial Buildings. London: 1917. V. 52

KAHN, ROGER
The Boys of Summer. New York: 1972. V. 51; 52

KAHNWEILER, DANIEL HENRY
Juan Gris: His Life and Work. London: 1947. V. 49; 51
Juan Gris: His Life and Work. London: 1969. V. 47; 54
Juan Gris: His Life and Work. New York: 1969. V. 47; 48; 50; 51; 52; 53
The Sculptures of Picasso. London: 1948(1949). V. 52
The Sculptures of Picasso. London: 1949. V. 54

KAHRL, WILLIAM L.
The California Water Atlas. 1979. V. 54
The California Water Atlas. Sacramento: 1979. V. 47; 50

KAIN, SAUL
The Daffodil Murderer. London: 1913. V. 49

KAINEN, JACOB
John Baptist Jackson: 18th Century Master of the Color Woodcut. Washington: 1962. V. 51

KAISER, HENRY J.
Twenty-Six Addresses Delivered During the War Years by Henry J. Kaiser. San Francisco: 1945. V. 52

KAISER, THOMAS E.
Historic Sketches of Oshawa. Oshawa: 1921. V. 54

KALADLIT Assilialiait, or Woodcuts Drawn and Engraved by Greenlanders. Godthaab in South Greenland: 1860. V. 47

KALASHNIKOV, ANATOLII
War and Peace: a Suite of Wood-Engravings. 1991. V. 52
War and Peace: a Suite of Wood-Engravings... London: 1991. V. 50

KALDEWEY, GUNNAR A.
California Time. 1987. V. 54
California Time. New York: 1987. V. 47
Clouds. 1982. V. 54
Clouds. Dusseldorf, New York: 1982. V. 47
Trees. 1988. V. 54
Trees. Postenkill: 1988. V. 47

KALER, JAMES OTIS
Toby Tyler or Ten Weeks with a Circus. New York: 1881. V. 49

KALIDASA
A Circle of Seasons. Waltham St. Lawrence: 1929. V. 51; 53
The Megha Duta; or, Cloud Messenger: a Poem in the Sanscrit Language. Calcutta: 1813. V. 49
Sakoontala; or the Lost Ring; An Indian Drama. Hertford: 1855. V. 49; 50; 53
Sakuntala; or, Sakuntala Recognised by the Ring, a Sanscrit Drama, in Seven Acts... Hertford: 1853. V. 50; 54

KALISH, MAX
Labor Sculpture. New York: 1938. V. 54

KALKAR, GEORGE
The Green Fidler. London: 1920. V. 49

KALLIR, JANE
Egon Schiele, the Complete Works with a Catalogue Raisonne of the Paintings, Watercolours, Drawings, Sketchbooks and Prints. London: 1990. V. 49

KALLIR, OTTO
Grandma Moses. New York: 1973. V. 47; 50; 51; 53; 54

KALM, PETER
Peter Kalm's Travels in North America. New York: 1937. V. 53
Travels Into North America... Warrington: 1770. V. 50; 52
Travels Into North America... Warrington and London: 1770-71. V. 51; 53; 54
Travels into North America. London: 1772. V. 47

KALTENBORN, H. V.
Kaltenborn Edits the News. Europe - Asia - America. New York: 1937. V. 49

KAMENSKY, ALEXANDER
Chagall: the Russian Years, 1907-1922. London: 1989. V. 49

KAMES, HENRY HOME, LORD
The Gentleman Farmer. Edinburgh: 1779. V. 52
Introduction to the Art of Thinking. Edinburgh: 1789. V. 54
Sketches of the History of Man. Edinburgh: 1774. V. 48; 50
Sketches of the History of Man. Dublin: 1775. V. 47
Sketches of the History of Man. Dublin: 1779. V. 48; 53
Sketches of the History of Man. Edinburgh: 1813. V. 48

KAMINSKY, STUART M.
Murder on the Yellow Brick Road. New York: 1977. V. 50

KAMPH, JAMIE
A Collector's Guide to Book-binding. New Castle: 1982. V. 50

KANAVEL, ALLEN B.
Infections of the Hand... Philadelphia and New York: 1912. V. 51
Infections of the Hand... New York: 1914. V. 51

KANDINSKY, WASSILY
The Art of Spiritual Harmony. London: 1914. V. 47
Point and Line to Plane. New York: 1947. V. 50; 51; 53
Wassily Kandinsky. Anvers: 1933. V. 50

KANE, ELISHA KENT
Arctic Explorations. Philadelphia: 1856. V. 49; 50; 51; 52; 54
Arctic Explorations... Philadelphia: 1857. V. 49; 50; 54
Arctic Explorations... Philadelphia: 1858. V. 48
Arctic Explorations... London: 1885. V. 53
The U.S. Grinnell Expedition in Search of Sir John Franklin. New York: 1854. V. 47; 49; 50
The U.S. Grinnell Expedition in Search of Sir John Franklin... Boston: 1857. V. 53

KANE, PAUL
Paul Kane's Frontier - Including Wanderings of an Artist Among the Indians of North America. Austin: 1971. V. 54
Wanderings of an Artist Among the Indians of North America... London: 1859. V. 50; 53
Wanderings Of an Artist Among the Indians of North America... Toronto: 1925. V. 53

KANE, ROBERT
The Industrial Resources of Ireland. Dublin: 1845. V. 49; 53

KANE, THOMAS LEIPER
Alaska and the Polar Regions. Lecture of...Before the American Geographical Society, in New York City, Thursday Evening May 7, 1868. New York: 1868. V. 52

KANGRA Valley Painting. Calcutta: 1954. V. 52

KANIN, FAY
Rashomon. New York: 1959. V. 54

KANIN, GARSON
Born Yesterday. New York: 1946. V. 50
Moviola. New York: 1979. V. 48
The Smile of the World. New York: 1949. V. 48; 49

KANN, ALPHONSE
The Alphonse Kann Collection Sold by His Order. New York: 1927. V. 49; 51

KANN, RODOLPHE
Catalogue of the Collection. Paris: 1907-07. V. 47

KANNER, LEO
Child Psychiatry. Springfield: 1937. V. 47

KANPPE, KARL ADOLF
Durer: The Complete Engravings, Etchings and Woodcuts. New York: 1965. V. 50

KANSAS City, Illustrated. 1876-1877. Kansas City: 1877?. V. 50

THE KANSAS Home Cook-Book. Leavenworth: 1888. V. 49

KANSAS. LAWS, STATUTES, ETC.
General Laws of the State of Kansas Passed at the Third Session of the Legislature. Lawrence: 1863. V. 49

KANSAS PACIFIC RAILROAD
Opening Excursion. Kansas Pacific Railway. St. Louis to Denver. August 30-September 10, 1870. Denver: 1870. V. 52
The Union Pacific Railway, (Eastern Division), (Kansas Pacific Railway). Economy to the Government. Washington: 1868. V. 47

KANSAS STATE AGRICULTURAL SOCIETY
Premium List of the Kansas State Agricultural Society, for 1871. Fair at Topeka... Topeka: 1871. V. 49

KANSAS. STATE BOARD OF AGRICULTURE
Rules and Regulations and List of Premiums of the Kansas State Board of Agriculture for the Ninth Annual Exhibition... Topeka: 1873. V. 49
Rules and Regulations and List of Premiums of the Kansas State Board of Agriculture for the Tenth Annual Exhibition, to be Held in Leavenworth... Topeka: 1874. V. 49

KANSAS STATE FAIR ASSOCIATION
Premium List and Rules of the Second Annual Fair of the Kansas State Fair Association...to be Held September 11th to 16th 1882 at Topeka, Kansas. Topeka: 1882. V. 49

KANT, IMMANUEL
Critick of Pure Reason. London: 1838. V. 48
Gedanken von der Wahren Schatzung der Lebendigen Krafte. Konigsberg: 1746. V. 53
Grundlegung zur Metaphysik der Sitten...Zweyte Auflage. (with) Metaphysische Anfangsgruende der Naturwissenschaft...Zweyte Auflage. (with) Ueber Eine Entdeckung Nach der alle Neue Critik der Reinen Vernunft Durch Eine Aeltere Entbehrlich Gemacht ... Riga: 1786/87/90. V. 50
Kritik of Judgment. London: 1892. V. 47; 52
Die Metaphysik der Sitten. Konigsburg: 1797. V. 48
Religion Within the Boundary of Pure Reason. Edinburgh: 1838. V. 47; 52
Text-Book to Kant. The Critique of Pure Reason: Aesthetic, Categories, Schematism. Edinburgh: 1881. V. 49
Werke Sorgfaltig Reviderte Gesammtausgabe in Zehn Banden. Leipzig: 1838-39. V. 52

KANTNER, H. W. B.
Information of Denver, Colorado. Denver: 1892. V. 48

KANTOR, HELENE J.
The Aegean and the Orient in the Second Millennium B.C. Bloomington: 1947. V. 52

KANTOR, MACKINLAY
Andersonville. Cleveland & New York: 1955. V. 49; 50; 53
Andersonville. Cleveland: 1965. V. 49
Divorcey. New York: 1928. V. 51; 52
Here Lies Holly Springs. New York: 1938. V. 47; 48; 50
Long Remember. New York: 1934. V. 51
The Work of Saint Francis. Cleveland: 1958. V. 54

KAPLAN, MAUREEN F.
The Origin and Distribution of Tell el Yahudiyeh Ware. Goteborg: 1980. V. 49; 51

KAPLAN, SIDNEY
The Black Presence in the Era of the American Revolution. Washington: 1973. V. 48

KAPLAN, STUART R.
The Encyclopedia of Tarot. New York: 1985-86. V. 54

KAPPEL, A. W.
British and European Butterflies and Moths... London. V. 47
British and European Butterflies and Moths... London: 1895. V. 54
British and European Butterflies and Moths. London: 1896. V. 50

KAPPERS, C. U.
Comparative Anatomy of the Nervous System of Vertebrates, Including Man. New York: 1936. V. 47

KAPPLER, CHARLES J.
Indian Treaties 1778-1883. New York: 1972. V. 50

KAPROW, ALLAN
Assemblage, Environments & Happenings. New York: 1966. V. 48; 51

KARAGEORGHIS, VASSOS
Excavations at Kition. Volume I: The Tombs. Nicosia: 1974. V. 50; 52
Excavations in the Necropolis of Salamis IV. Nicosia: 1978. V. 50
Sculptures from Salamis I-II. Nicosia: 1964-66. V. 50

KARALUS, K. E.
The Owls of North America (North of Mexico).. Garden City: 1974. V. 54

KARAMSIN, NICOLAI
Travels from Moscow, Through Prussia, Germany, Switzerland, France and England. London: 1803. V. 50

KARIGAL, HAIJIM ISAAC
A Sermon Preached at the Synagogue, in Newport, Rhode-Island, Called, "The Salvation of Israel". Newport: 1773. V. 54

KARLSTRON, PAUL J.
Louis Michel Eilshemius. New York: 1978. V. 52

KARO, GEORGE
Greek Personality in Archaic Sculpture. Cambridge: 1948. V. 52

KAROLIK, M.
M. & M. Karolik Collection of American Water Colors & Drawings 1800-1875. Boston: 1962. V. 48; 49

KAROUZOU, SEMNI
The Amasis Painter. Oxford: 1956. V. 50; 52

KARP, ABRAHAM
Beginnings. Early American Judaica. Philadelphia: 1975. V. 50

KARPINSKI, L. C.
Contributions to the History of Science. Ann Arbor: 1930. V. 49

KARPMAN, BENJAMIN
Case Studies in the Psychopathology of Crime: a Reference Source for Research in Criminal Material. Washington: 1933/47/47/48. V. 52

KARPOVICH, PETER
Adventures in Artificial Respiration. New York: 1953. V. 52

KARSH, YOUSUF
Faces of Our Time. Toronto: 1971. V. 53
Karsh: a Fifty-Year Retrospective. Boston: 1983. V. 47
Karsh Portraits. Boston: 1976. V. 50; 51
Karsh Portraits. Boston: 1979. V. 52
Portraits of Greatness. New York: 1960. V. 50

KARSHAN, DONALD
Archipenko: The Sculpture and Graphic Art, Including a Printed Catalogue Raisonne. Boulder: 1975. V. 50

KARSLAKE, FRANK
Notes from Sotheby's, Being a Compilation of 2032 Notes from Catalogues of Book-Sales Which Have Taken Place in the Rooms of Messrs. Sotheby, Wilkinson & Hodge, Between the Years 1895-1909. London: 1909. V. 51; 52

KARTESZ, J. T.
A Synonymized Checklist of the Vascular Flora of the United States, Canada and Greenland. Portland: 1994. V. 50

KASPARE Cohn. A Commemorative Tribute to the Founder and First President of Union Bank. Los Angeles: 1964. V. 48

KASSABIAN, MIRHAN
Rontgen Rays and Electro-Therapeutics with Chapters On Radium and Phototherapy. Philadelphia: 1907. V. 48; 53

KASSNER, THEODORE
My Journey from Rhodesia to Egypt Including an Ascent of Ruwenzori and a Short Account of the Route from Cape Town to Broken Hill and Lado to Alexandria. London: 1911. V. 48; 50

KASSON, GRACIA
Tin Tan Tales. London: 1890. V. 50
Tin Tan Tales. London: 1912. V. 47

KASTNER, ERICH
Puss in the Boots. London: 1967. V. 53

KATACHI, A Picture-Book of Traditional Japanese Workmanship. 1962. V. 49

KATER, HENRY
A Treatise on Mechanics. Philadelphia: 1835. V. 50

KATES, GEORGE N.
Chinese Household Furniture... New York: 1948. V. 51; 53; 54

KATHERINE Dunham and Her Dance Company. Hollywood: 1940. V. 54

KATON, SEYMOUR
Charles Dickens Rare Print Collections. Philadelphia: 1900. V. 49

KATRAK, SORAB K. H.
Through Amanullah's Afghanistan. A Book of Travel. Karachi: 1929. V. 51

KATZ, OTTO
The Nazi Conspiracy in Spain. London: 1937. V. 49

KATZ, VINCENT
A Tremor in the Morning. New York: 1986. V. 51

KATZ, WILLIAM
Stamped Indelibly: a Collection of Rubberstamp Prints. New York: 1967. V. 51

KATZENELLENBAUM, S. S.
Russian Currency and Banking 1914-1924. London: 1925. V. 50

KATZENELLENBOGEN, ADOLF
The Sculptural Programs of Chartres Cathedral: Christ-Mary-Ecclesia. Baltimore: 1959. V. 50

KAUFFER, E. MC KNIGHT
The Art of the Poster. New York: 1925. V. 47

KAUFFMAN, ANGELICA
Angelica's Ladies Library; or, Parents and Guardians Present. London: 1794. V. 53
The Life and Works Of... London: 1924. V. 50

KAUFFMAN, C. H.
The Agaricaceae of Michigan. Lansing: 1918. V. 47; 49; 52
The Dictionary of Merchandise, and Nomenclature in All Languages... London: 1803. V. 52
The Dictionary of Merchandise, and Nomenclature In All Languages... Philadelphia: 1805. V. 50

KAUFFMAN, S. A.
The Origins of Order, Self Organization and Selection in Evolution. London: 1993. V. 50

KAUFMAN, ALICE
The Navajo Weaving Tradition 1650 to the Present. New York: 1987. V. 52

KAUFMAN, GEORGE S.
The American Way. New York: 1939. V. 49
Beggar on Horseback. New York: 1924. V. 49; 54
The Royal Family. New York, London: 1929. V. 48

KAUFMAN, MARGARET
Aunt Sallie's Lament. West Burke: 1988. V. 51; 54
Praise Basted In: a Friendship Quilt for Aunt Sallie. Vermont: 1995. V. 54

KAUFMANN, ARTHUR
Old Canvas, New Varnish. The Hague: 1963. V. 50

KAUFMANN, MORITZ
Utopias; or, Schemes of Social Improvement. London: 1879. V. 54

KAUKOL, MARIA JOSEPH CLEMENT
Christlicher Seelen-Schatz Ausserlesener Gebetter. Bonn: 1729. V. 49

KAULBACH, WILLIAM
Schiller-Gallery. (and) Goethe-Gallery. New York. V. 47

KAUS, GINA
Luxury Liner. New York: 1932. V. 48

KAVANAGH, JAMES W.
Mixed Educuation. Dublin: 1859. V. 47

KAVANAGH, JULIA
English Women of Letters: Biographical Sketches. London: 1863. V. 47
French Women of Letters: Biographical Sketches. London: 1862. V. 53
Seven Years, and Other Tales. London: 1860. V. 54
A Summer and Winter in the Two Sicilies. London: 1858. V. 50
Woman in France During the Eighteenth Century. New York and London: 1893. V. 54

KAVANAGH, MORGAN
Origin of Language and Myths. London: 1871. V. 48

KAVANAGH, P. J.
The Perfect Stranger. London: 1966. V. 53

KAVANAGH, PATRICK
By Night Unstarred - An Autobiographical Novel. New York: 1978. V. 50
The Great Hunger. Dublin: 1942. V. 53; 54
The Green Fool. New York: 1939. V. 53
Self Portrait. Dublin: 1964. V. 52
A Soul for Sale. London: 1947. V. 48; 50; 53
Tarry Flynn. London: 1948. V. 51

KAVANAUGH, DAN
Duffy. London: 1980. V. 50

KAVENEY, ROZ
Tales from the Forbidden Planet. London: 1987. V. 49

KAWAMURA, S.
Icones of Japanese Fungi. Tokyo: 1954-55. V. 52

KAY County, Oklahoma. Ponca City: 1919. V. 51; 53

KAY, GERTRUDE ALICE
The Friends of Jimmy. New York: 1926. V. 47

KAY, HENRY CASSELS
Yaman. Its Early Mediaeval History... London: 1892. V. 49

KAY, HUGH R.
Battery Action! The Story of the 43rd Battery - C.F.A. Toronto: 1920. V. 54

KAY, JOSEPH
Free Trade in Land... London: 1879. V. 54

KAY, R.
The New Preceptor, or, Young Lady's & Gentleman's True Instructor in the Rudiments of the English Tongue. Newcastle-upon-Tyne: 1801. V. 52

KAY, TERRY
The Year the Lights Came On. Boston: 1976. V. 50; 52

KAY, ULYSSES
Symphony. 1967. V. 52

KAYE, JOHN WILLIAMS
History of the War in Afghanistan. London: 1878. V. 54
Lives of Indian Officers, Illustrative of the History of the Civil and Military Services of India. London: 1867. V. 53

KAYE, WALTER J.
Records of Harrogate Including the Register of Christ Church (1748-1812) with Supplementary Extracts from Knaresborough (1560-1753)... Leeds: 1922. V. 53

KAYE-SMITH, SHEILA
The Tramping Methodist. London: 1908. V. 51

KAY-SHUTTLEWORTH, JAMES PHILLIPS
Scarsdale; or, Life on the Lancashire and Yorkshire Border, Thirty Years Ago. London: 1860. V. 48; 51

KAZANJIAN, V. H.
Surgical Treatment of Facial Injuries. Baltimore: 1974. V. 48

KAZANTZAKIS, NIKOS
Christopher Columbus. Kentfield: 1972. V. 51
The Odyssey. A Modern Sequel. Athens: 1958. V. 49
Zorba the Greek. London: 1952. V. 49; 50; 53
Zorba the Greek. New York: 1953. V. 49; 53

KAZIMIERZ, MICHALOWSKI
Art of Ancient Egypt. New York. V. 47

KEACH, BENJAMIN
The Travels of True Godliness. London: 1733. V. 49
War with the Devil: or the Young Man's Conflict with the Powers of Darkness. London: 1673. V. 49

KEAN, B. H.
Tropical Medicine and Parasitology: Classic Investigations. Ithaca: 1978. V. 50; 51

KEANE, A. H.
Africa. London: 1895. V. 50

KEANE, J. F.
On Blue Water. London: 1883. V. 49

KEARLSEY, G.
Kearsley's Traveller's Entertaining Guide through Great Britain; or, a Description of the Great and Principal Cross-Roads... London: 1801. V. 49

KEARNEY, PATRICK J.
The Private Case. An Annotated Bibliography of the Private Case Erotica Collection in the British (Museum) Library. London: 1981. V. 50

KEARNY, PHILIP
Service With the French Troops in Africa. 1888. V. 49
Service With the French Troops in Africa. New York: 1888. V. 47; 51

KEARNY, THOMAS
General Philip Kearny. New York: 1937. V. 54

KEARSLEY, C.
Kearsley's Stranger's Guide, or Companion through London and Westminster and the Country Round... London: 1800. V. 50

KEARTON, A. C.
Kearton's Nature Pictures. London: 1910. V. 50; 52

KEARTON, CHERRY
Wild Life Across the World. London. V. 47

KEARY, ELIZA
At Home Again. London: 1881. V. 49
The Magic Valley. London: 1877. V. 49

KEATE, GEORGE
An Account of the Pelew Islands. Dublin: 1788. V. 47; 50
An Account of the Pelew Islands. London: 1788. V. 47; 50; 51; 52; 53
An Account of the Pelew Islands... Basil: 1789. V. 51
An Account of the Pelew Islands... London: 1789. V. 52
An Account of the Pelew Islands... Boston: 1796. V. 50; 53
The Alps. London: 1763. V. 48
Ancient and Modern Rome. London: 1760. V. 47
An Epistle from Lady Jane Grey to Lord Guildford Dudley. London: 1762. V. 54
The Monument in Arcadia: a Dramatic Poem, in Two Acts. London: 1773. V. 49; 52
Narrative of the Shipwreck of the Antelope East-India Pacquet, on the Pelew Islands, Situated on the Western Part of the Pacific Ocean, in August 1783. Perth: 1788. V. 50
The Poetical Works. London: 1781. V. 48
Sketches from Nature; Taken and Coloured in a Journey to Margate. London: 1779. V. 47; 53

KEATE, THOMAS
Observations on the Fifth Report of the Commissioners of Military Enquiry; and More Particularly on Those Parts of It Which Relate to the Surgeon General. London: 1808. V. 51

KEATING, C. A.
Keating and Forbes Families: and Reminiscences of C. A. Keating, A.D. 1758-1920. Dallas: 1920. V. 47

KEATING, GEOFFREY
The General History of Ireland. Dublin: 1841. V. 53
Tri Bior-Ghaoithe an Bhais. (The Three Shafts of Death). Dublin: 1890. V. 54

KEATING, GEORGE T.
A Conrad Memorial Library... Garden City: 1929. V. 54
A Conrad Memorial Library. New York: 1929. V. 49; 51

KEATING, H. R. F.
Inspector Ghote and Some Others. Helsinki: 1991. V. 48

KEATING, J. M.
A History of the Yellow Fever. The Yellow Fever Epidemic of 1878, in Memphis, Tennessee. Memphis: 1879. V. 47; 51; 53

KEATING, W. H., MRS.
Captain Anthony Somersall Van Crosen Forbes. Dallas: 1899. V. 47

KEATING, WILLIAM H.
Narrative of an Expedition to the Source of St. Peter's River, Lake Winnepeek, Lake of the Woods... Philadelphia: 1824. V. 47; 48; 50; 53; 54
Narrative of an Expedition to the Source of St. Peter's River, Lake Winnepeek, Lake of the Woods... London: 1825. V. 47; 48; 51; 52; 53; 54

KEATS, JOHN
Endymion. London: 1818. V. 48; 50; 51; 52; 54
Endymion. New Rochelle: 1902. V. 48; 53
Endymion... London: 1943-47. V. 53
Endymion. Waltham St. Lawrence: 1947. V. 48
Eve of St. Agnes. London: 1885. V. 49
The Eve of St. Agnes. 1900. V. 51
The Eve of St. Agnes. London: 1904. V. 49
Isabella and the Eve of St. Agnes. Boston. V. 48
Lamia, Isabella, the Eve of St. Agnes and Other Poems. London: 1820. V. 48; 50; 51; 52
Lamia, Isabella, the Eve of St. Agnes and Other Poems. Waltham St. Lawrence: 1928. V. 51
The Letters. 1931. V. 47
Letters of John Keats to Fanny Brawne. London: 1878. V. 47; 51
Letters of John Keats to Fanny Brawne. New York: 1878. V. 47
Life, Letters and Literary Remains. London: 1848. V. 47; 48; 49; 51
Life, Letters and Literary Remains. New York: 1848. V. 53
A Love Letter from John Keats. 1981. V. 48
Ode on a Grecian Urn. Bronxville: 1952. V. 48
Odes. Bussum: 1927. V. 51; 53
On the Eve of St. Agnes. London: 1901. V. 52
The Poems... London. V. 48
Poems... London: 1817. V. 47; 48; 49; 51; 54
The Poems... London: 1851. V. 48
The Poems... Hammersmith: 1894. V. 49; 50; 51
Poems. London: 1897. V. 52
The Poems... London: 1898. V. 48
Poems. Hammersmith: 1914. V. 51
The Poems... Cambridge: 1966. V. 48
The Poems... New York: 1966. V. 48
The Poetical Works... London: 1854. V. 51; 54
The Poetical Works. London: 1884. V. 50
The Poetical Works... London: 1888. V. 54
The Poetical Works. London: 1910. V. 47
The Poetical Works. 1912. V. 48

KEATS, JOHN continued
The Poetical Works... London: 1926. V. 48; 54
The Poetical Works... London: 1937. V. 48
The Poetical Works... New York: 1938. V. 49
The Poetical Works... Oxford: 1939. V. 47
Selections from the Poems of John Keats. Florence: 1906. V. 47
To Autumn. Hingham: 1951. V. 49
Two Odes: On Melancholy, On Autumn. Providence: 1989. V. 51
Unpublished Poem: To His Sister Fanny. Boston: 1909. V. 53

KEBES
The Picture of Kebes the Theban. Campden Gloucestershire: 1906. V. 51

KEBLE, JOHN
The Christian Year: Thoughts in Verse for the Sundays and Holydays throughout the Year. Oxford: 1827. V. 48; 51; 53
Letters of Spiritual Counsel and Guidance... Oxford and London: 1875. V. 49

KEBLE, JOSEPH
The Statutes at Large, in Paragraphs and Sections or Numbers, from Magna Charta Until This Time.... London: 1684. V. 47; 53

KEEBLE, JOHN
The Theory of Harmonics; or, an Illustration of the Grecian Harmonica. London: 1784. V. 48

KEEBLE, SAMUEL E.
Industrial Day-Dreams: Studies in Industrial Ethics and Economics. London: 1896. V. 52

KEEFE, CHARLES S.
The American House, Being a Collection of Illustrations and Plans of the Best Country & Suburban Houses Built in U.S... New York: 1922. V. 48; 50; 54

KEELE, K. D.
Leonardo da Vinci on Movement of the Heart and Blood. London: 1952. V. 47
Leonardo da Vinci on Movement of the Heart and Blood. Philadelphia: 1952. V. 53

KEELE, W. C.
The Provincial Justice, or Magistrate's Manual. Toronto: 1851. V. 53

KEELER, S.
The Mechanics (and Kinematics) of Web - Work Plot Construction with Diagrams. 1955. V. 47

KEELEY, GERTRUDE
An Alphabet of Birds. Chicago: 1901. V. 49

KEELY, ROBERT NEFF
In Arctic Seas. The Voyage of the 'Kite' with the Peary Expedition Together with a Transcript of the Log of the 'Kite'... Philadelphia: 1892. V. 49; 50

KEEN, WILLIAM
An American Text-Book of Surgery. Philadelphia: 1892. V. 47
American Text-Book of Surgery. Philadelphia: 1894. V. 51; 53
The Surgical Complications and Sequels of Typhoid Fever. Philadelphia: 1898. V. 51; 53

KEENE, CAROLYN
The Quest of the Missing Map. New York: 1942. V. 50

KEENE, DONALD
Bunraku. The Art of the Japanese Puppet Theatre. Tokyo: 1965. V. 48; 49
No, the Classical Theatre of Japan. Tokyo: 1966. V. 48

KEENE, H. G.
Persian Fables. London: 1838. V. 47

KEENE, J. HARRINGTON
Fly-Fishing and Fly-Making for Trout, Etc. New York: 1887. V. 48; 51

KEENS, WILLIAM
Dear Anyone. Poems. Lisbon: 1976. V. 54

THE KEEPSAKE for 1829. London. V. 51
THE KEEPSAKE for 1829. London: 1828. V. 47; 54

THE KEEPSAKE for 1830. London: 1828. V. 54

THE KEEPSAKE for 1831. London: 1830. V. 47; 50
THE KEEPSAKE for 1831. London: 1831. V. 50; 51

THE KEEPSAKE for 1831, 1832, 1833 & 1835. London. V. 52

THE KEEPSAKE for 1834. London: 1834. V. 50; 51

A KEEPSAKE for Alfred A. Knopf. New York: 1965. V. 49; 52; 54

KEES, WELDON
The Collected Poems of Weldon Kees. Iowa City: 1960. V. 53; 54
The Fall of the Magicians. New York: 1947. V. 53
Fall Quarter. Brownsville: 1990. V. 54
Non Verbal Communication: Notes on the Visual Perception of Human Relations. Berkeley: 1956. V. 48; 51
Poems 1947-1954. San Francisco: 1954. V. 53
Two Prose Sketches. West Chester: 1984. V. 47; 49

KEETON, WILLIAM
The Practical Cask Gauger; Designed for the Use of Excise Officers, Distillers, Rectifiers, Spirit Merchants, Wine Merchants, Oil Merchants, Drysalters, Common Brewers, Victaullers, &c. &c. 1836. V. 51

KEEVER, KIM
Yes and No. Dusseldorf - New York: 1982. V. 47

KEFFER, FRANK M.
History of San Fernando Valley. Glendale: 1934. V. 47

KEHR, HANS
Introduction to the Differential Diagnosis of the Separate Forms of Gallstone Disease Based Upon His Own Experience Gained In 433 Laparotomies for Gallstones. Philadelphia: 1901. V. 53

KEIGHTLEY, THOMAS
An Account of the Life, Opinions and Writings of John Milton. London: 1855. V. 49; 50; 54
The Shakespeare-Expositor, an Aid to the Perfect Understanding of Shakespeare's Plays. London: 1867. V. 48

KEILIN, DAVID
The History of Cell Respiration and Cytochrome. Cambridge: 1966. V. 52

KEILL, JOHN
Introductio ad Veram Astronomiam, Seu Lectiones Astronomicae Habitae in Schola Astronomica Academiae Oxoniensis. London: 1721. V. 51
An Introduction to Natural Philosophy; or, Philosophical Lectures Read in the University of Oxford, Anno Dom. 1700. London: 1720. V. 53
An Introduction to Natural Philosophy; or, Philosophical Lectures Read in the University of Oxford, Anno Dom. 1700.... London: 1726. V. 47
An Introduction to the True Astronomy; or, Astronomical Lectures... London: 1769. V. 53
An Introduction to the True Astronomy; or, Astronomical Lectures.... Dublin: 1793. V. 49

KEILWAY, ROBERT
Reports D'Ascuns Cases (Qui ont Events Aux Temps du Roy Henry le Septieme de Tres Heureuse Memoire, & du Tres Illustre Roy Henry le Huitesme)... London: 1688. V. 47

KEIM, DE B. RANDOLPH
Sheridan's Troopers on the Borders: a Winter Campaign On the Plains. Philadelphia: 1870. V. 51

KEIR, JAMES
An Account of the Life and Writings of Thomas Day, Esq. London: 1791. V. 47
The First Part of a Dictionary of Chemistry. Birmingham: 1789. V. 48; 54

KEITH, ARTHUR
Menders of the Maimed. London: 1919. V. 52

KEITH, CHARLES
Provincial Councillors of Pennsylvania Who Held Office Between 1733 and 1776... Philadelphia: 1883. V. 47

KEITH, CONWAY
Taming a Shrew. London: 1863. V. 54

KEITH, E. C.
A Countryman's Creed. London: 1938. V. 48

KEITH, ELMER
Big Game Rifles and Cartridges. 1936. V. 53
Elmer Keith's Big Game Hunting. Boston: 1948. V. 53
Guns and Ammo for Big Game Hunting. Los Angeles: 1965. V. 51; 52; 53
Hell, I Was There!. Los Angeles. V. 54
Keith's Rifles for Large Game. Huntington: 1946. V. 51
Safari. 1968. V. 53
Shotguns by Keith. Harrisburg: 1950. V. 52
Sixgun Cartridges and Loads. Onslow County: 1936. V. 53
Sixguns by Keith. Harrisburg: 1955. V. 51; 53

KEITH, GEORGE
The Way to the City of God Described, or a Plain Declaration How Any Man May...Pass Out of the Unrighteous, Into the Righteous State... Aberdeen: 1678. V. 50

KEITH, JAMES
Addresses on Several Occasions. Richmond: 1917. V. 49
The Volunteer's Guide, in To Parts. London: 1803. V. 50

KEITH, NOEL
Brites of Capote. Fort Worth: 1950. V. 53

KEITH, ROBERT
The History of the Affairs of the Church and State of Scotland, from the Beginning of the Reformation in the Reign of King James V. Edinburgh: 1734. V. 51

KEITH, THOMAS
An Introduction to the Theory and Practice of Plane and Spherical Trigonometry, and the Orthographic and Stereographic Projections of the Sphere... London: 1801. V. 50; 54
A New Treatise on the Use of the Globes; or, a Philosophical View of the Earth and Heavens... New York: 1811. V. 47
A New Treatise on the Use of the Globes, or a Philosophical View of the Earth and Heavens... New York: 1826. V. 49
Struggles of Capt. Thomas Keith in America, Including the Manner In Which He, His Wife and Child Were Decoyed by the Indians; Their Temporary Captivity and Happy Deliverance... London: 1808?. V. 48

KEITH, WILLIAM
The History of the British Plantations in America. London: 1738. V. 50
Keith, Old Master of California. New York & Berkeley: 1942/57. V. 48
Keith, Old Master of California. Fresno: 1956. V. 48

KELAART, E. F.
Prodromus faunae Zeylanicae. London: 1852. V. 50

KELD, CHRISTOPHER
An Essay On the Polity of England; with a View to Discover the True Principles of the Government, What Remedies Might by Likely to Cure the Grievances Complained Of, and Why the Several provisions Made by the Legislature... London: 1785. V. 48

KELEHER, JULIA
The Padre of Isleta. Santa Fe: 1940. V. 54

KELEHER, WILLIAM A.
The Fabulous Frontier. Santa Fe: 1945. V. 51; 53
Maxwell Land Grant, a New Mexico Item. Santa Fe: 1942. V. 51; 53
Turmoil in New Mexico, 1846-68. Santa Fe: 1952. V. 48
Violence in Lincoln County, 1869-1881. Albuquerque: 1957. V. 47; 52; 53; 54

KELEMAN, PAL
Medieval American Art. 1943. V. 54

KELEMEN, PAL
Medieval American Art. London: 1943. V. 50
Medieval American Art. New York: 1943. V. 47; 49; 51; 52; 53
Medieval American Art. New York: 1944. V. 51

KELHAM, ROBERT
A Dictionary of the Norman or Old French Language... London: 1779. V. 50

KELLAND, CLARENCE BUDINGTON
The Cosmic Jest: a Grove Play... San Francisco: 1949. V. 47
Not Their Breed and the Forgotten Man. 1938. V. 51

KELLAND, PHILIP
Introduction to Quaternions, With Numerous Examples. London: 1873. V. 48

KELLEHER, D. L.
An Anthology of Christmas Prose and Verse. London: 1928. V. 47

KELLER, D.
The Homunculus. 1949. V. 48
Popular Medicine. 1934-35. V. 48; 52

KELLER, ELIZABETH LEAVITT
Walt Whitman in Mickle Street. New York: 1921. V. 54

KELLER, FRANZ
The Amazon and Madeira Rivers. London: 1874. V. 48

KELLER, GOTTFRIED
A Village Romeo and Juliet - a Tale. London: 1915. V. 52

KELLER, HELEN
The History of Banking. Boston: 1852. V. 54
Our Duties to the Blind. Boston: 1904. V. 47; 48; 49; 51
The Song of the Stone Wall. New York: 1910. V. 52
The Story of My Life... Garden City: 1954. V. 51

KELLER, JAMES EDWARD
Photographs of Nebulae and Clusters, Made with the Crossley Reflector. Sacramento: 1908. V. 53

KELLER, M. J.
Album of Oakland, California Comprising a Bird's Eye View of the City, Views of Prominent Business Blocks, Hotels, City and County Buildings, Public Schools, Churches, Residences, Etc. and a Description of Oakland by the President of the Board of Trade. Oakland: 1893. V. 48

KELLER, W. B.
A Catalogue of the Cary Collection of Playing Cards in the Yale University Library. New Haven: 1981. V. 50

KELLERMAN, JONATHAN
When the Bough Breaks. 1985. V. 51

KELLERMANN, MICHEL
Paintings by Andre Derain. Paris: 1992. V. 49; 52

KELLETT, JOSEPHINE
That Friend of Mine. A Memoir of Magueritte McArthur. London: 1920. V. 47

KELLEY, CHARLES FABENS
Chinese Bronzes from Buckingham Collection. Chicago: 1946. V. 49

KELLEY, HALL JACKSON
A Narrative of Events and Difficulties in the Colonization of Oregon and the Settlement of California. Boston: 1852. V. 50

KELLEY, ISABEL
The Archaeology of the Autlan-Tuxcacuesco Area of jalisco. Berkeley: 1945-49. V. 50

KELLEY, JOSEPH
Thirteen Years in the Oregon Penitentiary. Portland: 1908. V. 48
Thirteen Years in the Oregon Penitentiary. Portland: 1918. V. 50; 52

KELLEY, ROBERT
Racing in America 1937-1959. New York: 1960. V. 54

KELLEY, ROBERT L.
Gold vs. Grain. Glendale: 1959. V. 47; 50; 52; 54

KELLEY, WILLIAM D.
The New Northwest: an Address on the Northern Pacific Railway. Philadelphia: 1871. V. 47
Why Colored People in Philadelphia are Excluded from the Street Cars. Philadelphia: 1866. V. 53

KELLEY, WILLIAM MELVIN
A Different Drummer. Garden City: 1962. V. 54

KELLOGG, DAVID
The Nature, Obligation and Importance of Christian Compassion... Boston: 1796. V. 54

KELLOGG, HARRIET S.
Life of Mrs. Emily J. Harwood. Albuquerque: 1903. V. 52

KELLOGG, J. H.
Rational Hydrotherapy. Philadelphia: 1903. V. 50

KELLOGG, LOUISE PHELPS
The British Regime in Wisconsin and the Northwest. Madison: 1935. V. 52

KELLY & CO.
Post Office Directory of Hampshire, Wiltshire and Dorsetshire. London: 1859. V. 54

KELLY, BERNARD
The Mind and Poetry of Gerard Manley Hopkins. Ditchling: 1935. V. 48; 54

KELLY, CELSUS
La Australia Del Espiritu Santo. Cambridge: 1966. V. 52

KELLY, CHARLES
Miles Goodyear First Citizen of Utah. Salt Lake City: 1937. V. 50
Old Greenwood. Salt Lake City: 1936. V. 50; 52
Old Greenwood... Georgetown: 1965. V. 52; 54
Outlaw Trail, a History of Butch Cassidy and His Wild Bunch. Salt Lake City: 1938. V. 51; 53
Salt Desert Trails. Salt Lake City: 1930. V. 48; 50; 52; 53

KELLY, CHRISTOPHER
A Full and Circumstantial Account of the Memorable Battle of Waterloo... London: 1836. V. 50
History of the French Revolution, and of the Wars Produced by that Memorable Event... London: 1817. V. 50

KELLY, EBENEZER
An Autobiography. Norwich: 1856. V. 51

KELLY, EMERSON C.
Medical Classics. Baltimore: 1936-41. V. 54

KELLY, FANNY
Narrative of My Captivity Among the Sioux Indians. Hartford: 1872. V. 53

KELLY, FRANCIS M.
A Short History of Costume and Armour Chiefly in England 1066-1800. London & New York: 1931. V. 50

KELLY, FRED C.
One Thing Leads to Another. Boston: 1935. V. 48; 51
One Thing Leads to Another... Boston and New York: 1936. V. 52

KELLY, GEORGE
Reflected Glory. New York: 1937. V. 54

KELLY, HOWARD ATWOOD
Medical Gynecology. New York: 1908. V. 48; 51; 53
Operative Gynecology. New York: 1899. V. 48
Operative Gynecology. New York: 1899/98. V. 51
Operative Gynecology. New York: 1902. V. 53
Operative Gynecology. New York: 1992. V. 50
Snakes of Maryland. Baltimore: 1936. V. 52
Some American Medical Botanists Commemorated in Our Botanical Nomenclature. Troy: 1914. V. 52
The Vermiform Appendix and Its Diseases. Philadelphia and London: 1905. V. 48; 51
Walter Reed and Yellow Fever. Baltimore: 1923. V. 51

KELLY, HUGH
Memoirs of a Magdalen, or the History of Louisa Mildmay. London: 1785. V. 49; 50; 51; 53
Thespis; or, a Critical Examination...the Principal Performers Belonging Drury-Lane Theatre. London: 1766. V. 47; 48
Thespis: or, a Critical Examination...the Principal Performers Belonging to Drury-Lane Theatre. Dublin: 1767. V. 53
The Works...To Which Is Prefixed the Life of the Author. London: 1778. V. 48

KELLY, ISABEL
The Archaeology of the Autlan-Tuxcacuesco Area of Jalisco I-II. Berkeley and Los Angeles: 1945-49. V. 50; 52

KELLY, JAMES
A Complete Collection of Scottish Proverbs. London: 1721. V. 49; 50; 52; 53

KELLY, JOHN
Pamela's Conduct in High Life. (with) Pamela's Conduct in Hight Life, to the Time of Her Death;. London: 1741. V. 47

KELLY, LEROY VICTOR
The Range Men, The Story of the Ranchers and Indians of Alberta. Toronto: 1913. V. 53
The Range Men, The Story of the Ranchers and Indians of Alberta. New York: 1965. V. 47

KELLY, LIORIH J. Y.
Fockleyr Manninagh as Baarlagh. Douglas: 1866. V. 49

KELLY, LUTHER SAGE
Yellowstone Kelly: the Memoirs of Luther S. Kelly. New Haven: 1926. V. 48; 50; 52

KELLY, MATTHEW
Apologia Pro Hibernia Adversus Cambri Calumnias. Dublin: 1849. V. 48
Dissertations Chiefly on Irish Church History. Dublin: 1864. V. 50; 52

KELLY, MICHAEL
Reminiscences of Michael Kelly of the King's Theatre, and Theatre Royal Drury Lane, Includes a Period of Half a Century. London: 1826. V. 49; 52

KELLY, PATRICK
The Universal Cambist and Commercial Instructor... London: 1821. V. 52
The Universal Cambist and Commercial Instructor... London: 1835. V. 52

KELLY, R. TALBOT
Burma, Painted and Described. 1905. V. 54
Burma, Painted and Described. London: 1905. V. 48; 52
Burma the Land and the People. Boston and Tokyo: 1910. V. 54
Egypt, Painted and Described. London: 1902. V. 53
Egypt, Painted and Described. London: 1904. V. 48

KELLY, ROBERT
Armed Descent. New York: 1961. V. 52
Axon Dendron. New York: 1967. V. 53
The Book of Persephone. New York: 1978. V. 49
The Common Shore: Books I-V. Los Angeles: 1969. V. 54
Finding the Measure. 1968. V. 47; 48; 49
Songs I-XXX. Cambridge: 1968. V. 49
Sonnets. Los Angeles: 1968. V. 49
Statement. 1968. V. 47; 48; 49
Twenty Poems. New York: 1967. V. 53
Under Words. Santa Barbara: 1983. V. 48

KELLY, ROBERT N.
In Arctic Seas - The Voyage of the "Kite". Philadelphia: 1892. V. 53

KELLY, S.
Eucalypts. New York: 1983. V. 50

KELLY, THOMAS
Kelly's Practical Builder's Price Book, or Safe Guide to the Valuation of All Kinds of Artificer's Work... London: 1857. V. 50; 52
Practical Masonry, Bricklaying and Plastering, Both Plain and Ornamental. London: 1837. V. 53

KELLY, W.
The Glob. New York: 1952. V. 48; 50; 52

KELLY, WALT
The Incomplete Pogo. New York: 1954. V. 53
Pogo: Prisoner of Love. New York: 1969. V. 53
Songs of the Pogo. New York: 1956. V. 51
Ten Ever-Lovin' Blue-Eyed Years with Pogo. New York: 1959. V. 51

KELLY, WILLIAM
Excursion to California Over Prairie. London: 1851. V. 47; 53
A Stroll through the Diggings of California. London: 1852. V. 47

KELLY'S Directory of Birmingham (Including the Suburbs and the Borough of Smethwick). London: 1919. V. 53

KELLY'S Directory of Bristol and Suburbs. London: 1937. V. 52

KELLY'S Directory of Cheshire. 1939. London: 1939. V. 48

KELLY'S Directory of Cumberland. 1897. V. 52
KELLY'S Directory of Cumberland. London: 1910. V. 52

KELLY'S Directory of Cumberland and Westmorland. London: 1894. V. 50; 52
KELLY'S Directory of Cumberland and Westmorland. London: 1906. V. 50
KELLY'S Directory of Cumberland and Westmorland. London: 1910. V. 50; 54
KELLY'S Directory of Cumberland and Westmorland. London: 1925. V. 50; 52
KELLY'S Directory of Cumberland and Westmorland. London: 1929. V. 50
KELLY'S Directory of Cumberland and Westmorland. London: 1934. V. 50; 52

KELLY'S Directory of Devonshire. 1893. V. 51

KELLY'S Directory of Essex. London: 1937. V. 48

KELLY'S Directory of Essex, Hertfordshire and Middlesex. London: 1908. V. 50

KELLY'S Directory of Hertfordshire. 1937. London: 1937. V. 48

KELLY'S Directory of Leicestershire and Rutland. London: 1932. V. 53

KELLY'S Directory of Lincolnshire. London: 1900. V. 51
KELLY'S Directory of Lincolnshire. London: 1909. V. 53
KELLY'S Directory of Lincolnshire. London: 1913. V. 51

KELLY'S Directory of Sheffield, and Rotheram and Suburbs. London: 1951. V. 51; 53

KELLY'S Directory of Suffolk. London: 1929. V. 52

KELLY'S Directory of the Counties of Cambridge, Norfolk and Suffolk. London: 1937. V. 48

KELMAN, JAMES
The Busconductor Hines. Edinburgh: 1984. V. 51
A Chancer. Edinburgh: 1985. V. 51
A Disaffection. London: 1989. V. 51
Greyhound for Breakfast. London: 1987. V. 51

KELMAN, JOHN
From Damascus to Palmyra. London: 1908. V. 48
The Holy Land. London: 1902. V. 49

KELMO, F.
Watch-Repairer's Hand-Book... Boston: 1869. V. 49

KELSALL, CHARLES
Classical Excursion From Rome to Arpino. Geneva: 1820. V. 49; 50
Classical Excursion from Rome to Arpino. London: 1821. V. 49

KELSALL, J. E.
The Birds of Hampshire and the Isle of Wight. London: 1905. V. 50

KELSEY, ALBERT WARREN
Autobiographical Notes and Memoranda... Baltimore: 1911. V. 49

KELSEY, CHARLES
Diseases Of the Rectum and Anus. New York: 1890. V. 53

KELSEY, HENRY
The Kelsey Papers,. Ottawa: 1929. V. 47; 50; 52; 54

KELSEY, SALLEY
Gusta: a Story of the Virgin Islands. New York: 1944. V. 53

KELSEY-WOOD, D.
The Atlas of Cats of the World. London: 1989. V. 51

KELSON, GEORGE M.
The Land and Water Salmon Flies 1886-1902. 1970. V. 54
The Salmon Fly: How to Dress It and How to Use It. London: 1895. V. 47; 52; 54
The Salmon Fly: How to Dress it and How to Use It. Goshen: 1979. V. 48

KELTIE, JOHN S.
A History of the Scottish Highlands, Highland Clans and Highland Regiments. London. V. 52
A History of the Scottish Highlands,, Highland Clans and Highland Regiments. Edinburgh & London: 1875. V. 48
History of the Scottish Highlands, Highland Clans and Highland Regiments. London: 1886. V. 50
The Partition of Africa. London: 1893. V. 53

KELTON, C. G.
The New England Collection of Hymns and Spiritual Songs... Montpelier: 1829. V. 50

KELTON, ELMER
The Day the Cowboys Quit. Garden City: 1971. V. 53
The Good Old Boys. New York: 1978. V. 53

KELTY, MARY ANNE
The Favourite of Nature. London: 1821. V. 47; 49; 50; 54
The Favourite of Nature. London: 1822. V. 50
Osmond, a Tale. London: 1822. V. 50
Reminiscences of Thought and Feeling. London: 1852. V. 50
Trials, a Tale. London: 1824. V. 50

KELVIN, WILLIAM THOMSON, 1ST BARON
Notes of Lectures on Molecular Dynamics and the Wave Theory of Light. Baltimore: 1884. V. 47; 54
Reprint of Papers on Electrostatics and Magnetism. London: 1872. V. 50

KEMBLE, EDWARD W.
Comical Coons. London: 1898. V. 47

KEMBLE, FRANCES ANNE
Francis the First, an Historic Drama. London: 1832. V. 49
Journal. Philadelphia: 1835. V. 50; 51; 53; 54
Journal of a Residence on a Georgia Plantation in 1838-1839. London: 1863. V. 47; 49; 51
Journal of a Residence on a Georgian Plantation in 1838-1839. New York: 1863. V. 47; 50; 51; 53
Poems. London: 1844. V. 47; 51; 53; 54
Record of Girlhood. London: 1878. V. 47
Records of Later Life... London: 1882. V. 48
The Star of Seville. London: 1837. V. 47; 49

KEMBLE, JOHN HASKELL
Journal of a Cruise to California and the Sandwich Islands in the United States Sloop-of-War Cyane by William H. Meyers, Gunner, U.S.N. 1841-1844. San Francisco: 1955. V. 48
The Panama Route 1849-1869. Berkeley & Los Angeles: 1943. V. 52; 54

KEMBLE, JOHN PHILIP
An Authentic Narrative of Mr. Kemble's Retirement from the Stage... London: 1817. V. 47; 51
Fugitive Pieces. York: 1780. V. 52
Macbeth and King Richard the Third: an Essay, In Answer to Remarks on Some of the Characters of Shakespeare. London: 1817. V. 47; 53

KEMP, A.
The Birds of Southern Africa. Johannesburg: 1982. V. 51

KEMP, BARRY J.
Minoan Pottery in Second Millenium Egypt. Mainz am Rheim: 1980. V. 51

KEMP, DIXON
A Manual of Yacht and Boat Sailing. London: 1880. V. 50
A Manual of Yacht and Boat Sailing. London: 1886. V. 54
A Manual of Yacht and Boat Sailing. London: 1891. V. 51
Manual of Yacht and Boat Sailing. London: 1904. V. 51
A Manual of Yacht and Boat Sailing... London: 1913. V. 54

KEMP, DONALD
Happy Valley - A Promoter's Paradise-Being an Historical Sketch of Eldora, Colorado and Its Environs. Denver: 1945. V. 52

KEMP, LOUIS W.
Signers of the Texas Declaration of Independence. Houston: 1944. V. 53
Signers of the Texas Declaration of Independence. Salado: 1959. V. 51

KEMP, T. S.
Mammal-Like Reptiles and the Origin of Mammals. London: 1982. V. 50
The Owls of Southern Africa. Cape Town: 1987. V. 50

KEMPFERHAUSEN, PHILIP
Letters from the Lakes. Ambleside: 1889. V. 51

THE KEMPTON-Wace Letters. 1903. V. 54

KENDALL, EDWARD AUGUSTUS
Burford Cottage, and Its Robin-Red-Breast. London: 1835. V. 49
Keeper's Travels in Search of His Master... London: 1809. V. 48
Letters to a Friend, On the State of Ireland, the Roman Catholic Question, and the Merits of Constitutional Religious Distinctions. London: 1826. V. 50
Travels through the Northern Parts of the United States in the Years 1807 and 1808. New York: 1809. V. 50; 53

KENDALL, GEORGE WILKINS
Narrative of the Texan Santa Fe Expedition. New York. V. 47
Narrative of the Texan Santa Fe Expedition. New York: 1844. V. 47; 48; 50; 52
Narrative of the Texan Santa Fe Expedition. New York: 1846. V. 50
Narrative of the Texan Santa Fe Expedition... New York: 1847. V. 48; 50
Narrative of the Texan Santa Fe Expedition. New York: 1856. V. 47; 48; 49; 53

KENDALL, HENRY EDWARD
Designs for Schools and School Houses, Parochial and National. London: 1847. V. 52

KENDALL, JANE
Pride and Prejudice. A Romantic Comedy in 3 Acts Adapted From the Novel. Chicago: 1942. V. 52; 54

KENDALL, KATHARINE
The Interior Castle. Worcester: 1968. V. 53

KENDALL, N. C.
Reminiscences of the Closing Scenes of the Great American Rebellion, and the Part Taken Toward the Consummation of the Same by the Third Michigan Volunteer Infantry. Texas: 1866. V. 49

KENDALL, PAUL GREEN
Polo Ponies. New York: 1933. V. 47

KENDALL, PERCY FRY
Geology of Yorkshire. London: 1924. V. 47; 48; 49; 51; 52; 53; 54

KENDALL, W. H.
The Registers of the Parish Church of Tunstall. Wigan: 1911. V. 48; 53

KENDALL, WILLIAM
Poems. 1791. V. 54
Poems. Exeter: 1793. V. 54

KENDERDINE, T. F.
A California Tramp and Later Footprints or Life on the Plains and in the Golden State Thirty Years Ago. Newtown: 1888. V. 49; 54

KENDERDINE, THADDEUS S.
A California Tramp and Later Footprints. Newtown: 1888. V. 47; 51

KENDRICK, A. F.
English Embroidery. London. V. 47
Hand-Woven Carpets Oriental and European. London: 1922. V. 47; 52

KENEALLY, THOMAS
The Chant of Jimmie Blacksmith. New York: 1972. V. 51
A Dutiful Daughter. London: 1971. V. 53
The Place at Whitton. New York: 1965. V. 53
Schindler's Ark. London: 1982. V. 50; 51; 52; 53; 54
Schindler's List. New York: 1982. V. 50; 51; 52; 53
To Asmara. New York: 1989. V. 51

KENEALY, ARABELLA
Feminism and Sex-Extinction. London: 1920. V. 50

KENEALY, EDWARD VAUGHAN HYDE
Brallaghan, or the Deipnosophists. London: 1845. V. 48; 51
Edward Wortley Montagu. London: 1869. V. 54

KENILWORTH Illustrated; or, The History of the Castle, Priory and Church of Kenilworth. Chiswick: 1821. V. 48

KENLEY, JOHN R.
Memoirs of a Maryland Volunteer, War with Mexico in the years 1846-7-8. Philadelphia: 1873. V. 47

KENNA, V. E. G.
Cretan Seals, with a Catalogue of the Minoan Gems in the Ashmolean Museum. Oxford: 1960. V. 52

KENNAN, GEORGE
Siberia and the Exile System. New York: 1891. V. 48; 51; 53

KENNARD, JOSEPH SPENCER
The Italian Theatre: from its Beginning to the Close of the Seventeenth Century. New York: 1932. V. 52

KENNARD, NINA H.
Lafacadio Hearn. London: 1912. V. 48

KENNE, JOHN HARRINGTON
Fly-Fishing and Fly-Making for Trout. New York: 1887. V. 47
Fly-Fishing and Fly-Making for Trout... New York: 1891. V. 50

KENNEDY & CO.
The Orville Gold and Copper Mining Co. Burlington: 1899. V. 48

KENNEDY, ADMIRAL
Sporting Sketches in South America. London: 1892. V. 49

KENNEDY, ALEXANDER
The End of a Holiday, 1914. London: 1914. V. 49
Petra: Its History and Monuments. London: 1827. V. 48
Petra: Its History and Monuments. London: 1925. V. 48

KENNEDY, ARTHUR CLARK
Erotica. London: 1894. V. 48

KENNEDY, DAVID
Kennedy's Colonial Travel. Edinburgh: 1876. V. 48

KENNEDY, E. B.
Thirty Seasons in Scandinavia. London: 1908. V. 52

KENNEDY, EDWARD
Partial Denture Construction,... Brooklyn: 1928. V. 51

KENNEDY, G. W.
The Pioneer Campfire in Four Parts. Portland: 1914. V. 47

KENNEDY, GRACE
Anna Ross in Turkish. Malta: 1829. V. 54
Dunallan; or, Know What You Judge... Edinburgh: 1825. V. 49; 50
Dunallan; or, Know What You Judge... Edinburgh: 1826. V. 50; 53; 54
Dunallan; or, Know What You Judge. New York: 1828. V. 54
Dunallan; or, Know What You Judge... Edinburgh: 1836. V. 54
Willoughby; or Reformation. London: 1823. V. 50

KENNEDY, HARRY
Jingleman Jack. New York: 1901. V. 49

KENNEDY, JAMES
Conversations on Religion, with Lord Byron and Others, Held on Cephalonia, a Short Time Previous to His Lordship's Death. London: 1830. V. 53; 54
A Description of the Antiquities and Curiosities in Wilton-House. Salisbury: 1769. V. 50
Dictionary of Anonymous and Pseudonymous English Literature. New York: 1971. V. 51

KENNEDY, JOHN
A Complete System of Astronomical Chronology, Unfolding the Scriptures. London: 1762. V. 49
The History of Steam Navigation. Liverpool: 1903. V. 50
The History of Steam Navigation. Liverpool: 1905. V. 53
A New Method of Stating and Explaining the Scripture Chronology, Upon Mosaic Astronomical Principles, Mediums and Data, as Laid Down in the Pentateuch. London: 1751. V. 52
A Treatise Upon Planting, Gardening and the Management of the Hot-House... Dublin: 1784. V. 49; 53

KENNEDY, JOHN FITZGERALD
As We Remember Joe. Cambridge: 1945. V. 51
The Burden and the Glory. New York: 1964. V. 52
Profiles in Courage. New York: 1956. V. 48; 49; 50; 52; 53
Profiles in Courage. New York: 1964. V. 52
Sam Houston and the Senate. Austin: 1970. V. 51
The Strategy of Peace. New York: 1960. V. 48; 53
Why England Slept. London: 1940. V. 48; 51; 53
Why England Slept. New York: 1940. V. 47

KENNEDY, JOHN PENDLETON
The Border States, Their Power and Duty in the Present Disordered Condition of the Country. Baltimore?: 1860. V. 49
The Border States. Their Power and Duty in the Present Disordered Condition of the Country. Baltimore?: 1861?. V. 52
Memoirs of the Life of William Wirt, Attorney General of the United States. Philadelphia: 1850. V. 52; 53
Rob of the Bowl: a Legend of St. Inigoe's. Philadelphia: 1838. V. 54
Swallow Barn. Philadelphia: 1832. V. 51; 52

KENNEDY, KEVIN
Idiot's Delight. Madison: 1979. V. 51

KENNEDY, MARGARET
Dewdrops. London: 1928. V. 52; 54

KENNEDY, MARK
The Pecking Order. New York: 1953. V. 53

KENNEDY, MICHAEL S.
The Red Man's West: True Stories of the Frontier Indians from Montana, the Magazine of Western History. New York: 1965. V. 49

KENNEDY, P.
The Birds of Ireland. Edinburgh: 1954. V. 48

KENNEDY, PATRICK
The Banks of the Boro: A Chronicle of County Wexford. London: 1867. V. 53

KENNEDY, ROBERT F.
The Pursuit of Justice. New York, Evanston, London: 1964. V. 52

KENNEDY, RUTH WEDGWOOD
Four Portrait Busts by Francesco Laurana. Northampton: 1962. V. 48; 51

KENNEDY, S. J.
Celebrations After the Death of John Brennan. Lincoln: 1974. V. 51

KENNEDY, THOMAS FRANCIS
Letters Chiefly Connected with the Affairs of Scotland, from Henry Cockburn Solicitor General Under Early Grey's Government... London: 1874. V. 54

KENNEDY, VANS
A Useful Collection of Translations viz, of the Persian Moonshee, of the New Articles of War, and two Court Martials... Bombay: 1847. V. 49

KENNEDY, W. R.
Sporting Adventures in the Pacific, Whilst in command of the 'Reindeer'. London: 1876. V. 47

KENNEDY, WILLIAM
Billy Phelan's Greatest Game. New York: 1978. V. 47; 48; 49; 50; 51; 52; 53; 54
Charlie Malarky and the Belly-Button Machine. London: 1987. V. 49
The Cotton Club. Astoria: 1982. V. 53
The Ink Truck. New York: 1969. V. 49; 51; 53
The Ink Truck. London: 1970. V. 47; 50
Ironweed. New York: 1983. V. 48; 49; 50; 51; 52; 53; 54
Legs. London: 1975. V. 48; 51
Legs. New York: 1975. V. 49; 50; 51
O Albany!. New York: 1983. V. 47; 54
Quinn's Book. New York: 1988. V. 49
Texas: Its Geography, Natural History and Topography. New York: 1844. V. 49

KENNELLY, BRENDAN
Love Cry. Dublin: 1972. V. 48; 50
Moloney Up and At It. Dublin/Cork: 1984. V. 48; 50

KENNER, HUGH
Paradox in Chesterton. London: 1948. V. 48; 51; 53

KENNET, EDWARD HILTON YOUNG, BARON
A Bird in the Bush. London: 1936. V. 48

KENNETH-BROWN, K.
Two Boys in a Gyrocar. 1911. V. 47; 51

KENNETT, BASIL
The Lives and Characters of the Ancient Grecian Poets. London: 1697. V. 48
Romae Antiqua Notitia; or the Antiquities of Rome. London: 1699. V. 48
Romae Antiquae Notitia; or the Antiquities of Rome. London: 1721. V. 51

KENNETT, WHITE
The Case of Impropriations, and of the Augmentation of Vicarages and Other Insignificant Cures... London: 1704. V. 54
A Complete History of England: With the Lives of all the Kings and Queens Thereof... London: 1719. V. 47
Parochial Antiquities. Oxford: 1695. V. 52
Parochial Antiquities... Oxford: 1818. V. 48

KENNEY, C. E.
Catalogue of the Celebrated Collection...of C. E. Kenney. London: 1965-68. V. 49

KENNEY, JAMES F.
The Sources of the Early History of Ireland.. New York: 1966. V. 51

KENNEY, LOUIS A.
Catalogue of the Rare Astronomical Books in the San Diego State University Library. San Diego: 1988. V. 50; 54

KENNEY'S. *Twenty Poems for a Lost Tavern.* Iowa City: 1970. V. 54

KENNINGTON, ERIC
Tanks and Tank Men. London: 1944. V. 47

KENNION, EDWARD
An Essay on Trees in Landscape: or, an Attempt to Shew the Propriety and Importance of Characteristic Expression in this Branch of Art, and the Means of Producing It... London: 1844. V. 54

KENNION, ROGER LLOYD
By Mountain Lake and Plain, Being Sketches of a Sport in Eastern Persia. 1911. V. 54
By Mountain Lake and Plain, Being Sketches of a Sport in Eastern Persia. Edinburgh: 1911. V. 49; 54
Sport and Life in the Further Himalaya. 1910. V. 54
Sport and Life in the Further Himalaya. Edinburgh: 1910. V. 47; 53

KENNY, WILLIAM STOPFORD
Practical Chess Exercises... London: 1818. V. 47
Practical Chess Grammar; or, an Introduction to the Royal Game of Chess, in a Series of Plates. London: 1818. V. 50

KENRICK, JOHN
Horrors of Slavery. Cambridge: 1817. V. 50
Phoenicia. London: 1855. V. 50

KENRICK, WILLIAM
Annual Catalogue of Fruit and Hardy Ornamental Trees, Shrubs, Herbaceous Plants &c... Boston: 1833/34. V. 51
Descriptive Catalogue. Nursery of William Kenrick, Nonantum Hill, in Newton, (Near Boston). 1843. V. 51
The New American Orchardist... Boston: 1833. V. 47
The New American Orchardist... Boston: 1844. V. 50; 51; 52; 54
Nursery of William Kenrick, Nonantum Hill in Newton, Near Boston. Annual Catalogue of Fruit and Hardy Ornamental Shrubs, Herbaceous Plants, &c. Boston: 1835. V. 51
Poems; Ludicrous, Satirical and Moral. London: 1768. V. 51; 52

KENT, ALEXANDER
Command a King's Ship. London: 1973. V. 51
The Flag Captain. London: 1971. V. 51
Signal-Close Action!. London: 1974. V. 51

KENT ARCHAEOLOGICAL SOCIETY
Transactions of the Kent Archaeological Society. London: 1920-39/46-80. V. 47

KENT, AUSTIN
Free Love; or a Philosophical Demonstration of the Non-Exclusive Nature of Connubial Love... Hopkinton: 1857. V. 53

KENT, C. H.
Texas. The Future Home of the Emigrant. Iowa: 1878. V. 49

KENT, CHARLES
The Book of the Poet Centenary. Charlottesville: 1909. V. 48
The Humour and Pathos of Charles Dickens. London: 1884. V. 54

KENT, CHARLES N.
History of the Seventeenth Regiment, New Hampshire Volunteer Infantry. Concord: 1898. V. 52

KENT, CHARLES W.
The Unveiling of the Bust of Edgar Allan Poe in the Library of the University of Viriginia. Lynchburg: 1901. V. 48

KENT, ELIZABETH
Flora Domestica, or the Portable Flower Garden... London: 1823. V. 47; 48; 50
Flora Domestica, or, the Portable Flower Garden... London: 1825. V. 48

KENT, ELIZABETH TALBOT GREY, COUNTESS OF
A Choice Manuall of Rare and Select Secrets in Physick and Chirurgery...(with) A True Gentlewomans Delight. London: 1653. V. 47

KENT, HENRY BRAINARD
Graphic Sketches of the West. Chicago: 1890. V. 53

KENT, HENRY W.
Bibliographical Notes on One Hundred Books Famous in English Literature. New York: 1903. V. 52; 53
One Hundred Books Famous in English Literature with Facsimiles of the Titlepages. New York: 1902/03. V. 48

KENT, J. P. C.
Roman Coins. New York: 1978. V. 48; 52

KENT, JAMES
An Address Delivered at New Haven, Before the Phi Beta Kappa Society, September 13, 1831. New Haven: 1831. V. 54
Commentaries on American Law. Boston: 1884. V. 51
A Course of Reading Drawn Up by the Hon. James Kent (late Chancellor of the State of New York). New York: 1840. V. 50
An Introductory Lecture to a Course of Law Lectures, Delivered Nov. 17, 1794. New York: 1794. V. 52
Lectures on Homoeopathic Philosophy. Lancaster: 1900. V. 52

KENT, JOHN
Racking Life of Lord George Cavendish Bentick, and Other Reminiscences. London & Edinburgh: 1892. V. 51

KENT, NATHANIEL
General View of the Agriculture of the County of Norfolk... 1796. V. 53
General View of the Agriculture of the County of Norfolk... London: 1796. V. 47
General View of the Agriculture of the County of Norfolk... Norwich: 1796. V. 49; 50
General View of the Agriculture to the County of Norfolk... London: 1796/97. V. 52
Hints to Gentlemen of Landed Property. London: 1776. V. 47; 48
Hints to Gentlemen of Landed Property. London: 1793. V. 51

KENT, NORMAN
The Book of Edward A. Wilson: a Survey of His Work 1916-1948. New York: 1948. V. 50

KENT, ROCKWELL
Americana Esoterica. 1927. V. 49
Architec-Tonics. New York: 1914. V. 49; 52
A Birthday Book. New York: 1931. V. 47; 50; 53; 54
The Bookplates and Marks of... New York: 1929. V. 48; 49; 51; 52
Elmer Adler. New York: 1929. V. 48
Greenland Journal. New York: 1962. V. 47; 49; 53
How I Make a Wood Cut. Pasadena: 1934. V. 54
It's Me O Lord. New York: 1955. V. 50; 52
The Jewel - a Romance of Fairyland. Portland: 1990. V. 48
Later Bookplates and Marks. New York: 1937. V. 49; 51
The Mad Hermit. 1955. V. 54
N by E. New York: 1930. V. 47; 48; 50; 54

KENT, ROCKWELL continued
Of Men and Mountains, Being an Account of the European Travels of the Author and His Wife, Sally... Ausable Forks: 1959. V. 52
Rockwell Kent: an Anthology of His Work. New York: 1982. V. 47; 48; 50
Rockwellkentiana. New York: 1933. V. 49; 50; 52; 54
Rockwellkentiana... New York: 1935. V. 49
Salamina. New York: 1935. V. 47; 48; 49; 50; 52
This Is My Own. New York: 1940. V. 53; 54
To Thee! A Toast in Celebration of a Century of Opportunity and Accomplishment in America, 1847-1947. Manitowac: 1946. V. 48
Voyaging: Southward from the Strait of Magellan. New York & London: 1924. V. 48; 50; 54
What is an American?. Los Angeles: 1936. V. 52
Wilderness... V. 52; 54
Wilderness. Los Angeles: 1970. V. 51
World-Famous Paintings. New York: 1939. V. 49
World-Famous Paintings. New York: 1947. V. 54

KENT, S. H.
Within the Arctic Circle. Experiences of Travel through Norway to the North Cape, Sweden and Lapland. London: 1877. V. 48; 50

KENT, SAMUEL
The Grammar of Heraldry; or, Gentleman's Vade Mecum... London: 1718. V. 49

KENT, W. W.
Rare Hooked Rugs, and Others Both Antique and Modern From Cooperative Sources. Springfield: 1941. V. 54

KENT, WILLIAM
Reminiscences of Outdoor Life. San Francisco: 1929. V. 50; 54

KENT, WILLIAM SAVILLE
The Great Barrier Reef of Australia... London: 1893. V. 47; 54
A Manual of the Infusoria... London: 1880-82. V. 47; 48; 49; 50
A Manual of the Infusoria. London: 1881-82. V. 48; 50; 54
The Naturalist in Australia. London: 1897. V. 51; 53

KENTISH, BASIL LEONARD
The Chronicles of an Ancient Yorkshire Family. 1963. V. 53
The Chronicles of an Ancient Yorkshire Family. Kelvedon: 1963. V. 54

KENTISH, MRS.
The Maid of the Village; or, the Farmer's Daughter of the Woodlands. London: 1835. V. 49

KENT'S Original London Directory. London: 1814. V. 52

KENTUCKY. BOARD OF INTERNAL IMPROVEMENT
Report of the Board of Internal Improvement. Frankfort: 1836. V. 50

KENTUCKY. LAWS, STATUTES, ETC.
Acts Passed at the First Session of the Eighteenth General Assembly for the Commonwealth of Kentucky, Begun and Held in the Capitol, in the Town of Frankfort...1809. Frankfort: 1810. V. 50

KENYON, FREDERIC G.
Ancient Books and Modern Discoveries. Chicago: 1927. V. 47; 48

KENYON, JOHN
Rhymed Plea for Tolerance. London: 1839. V. 53

KENYON, KATHLEEN M.
Excavations at Jericho. London: 1965. V. 49
Excavations at Jericho. Volume II. London: 1965. V. 51

KENYON, R.
By Mountain Lake and Plain (Sport in Eastern Persia). London: 1911. V. 50

KEOWN, ERIC
The Tale Of an Old Tweed Jacket. London. V. 53
The Tale of an Old Tweed Jacket. London: 1955. V. 52

KEPLER, JOHANNES
Epitome Astronomiae Copernicanae. Frankfurt: 1635. V. 49
Narratio de Observationis a se Quatuor Iovis Staellitibus Erronibus, Quos Galialaeus Galilaeus Mathematicus Florentinus Iure Inventionis Medicaea Sidera Nuncupavit. Frankfurt: 1611 (Oct.1610). V. 47

KEPPEL, GEORGE THOMAS
Narrative of a Journey Across the Balcan, by the Two Passes of Selimmno and Pravadi... London: 1831. V. 48; 51; 54
Personal Narrative of a Journey from India to England... London: 1827. V. 47; 53; 54

KEPPEL, HENRY
The Expedition to Borneo of H.M.S. Dido for the Supression of Piracy. London: 1846. V. 48; 54

KEPPEL, THOMAS
The Life of Augustus Viscount Keppel, Admiral of the White and First Lord of the Admiralty in 1782-83. London: 1842. V. 50; 51

KER, CHARLES HENRY BELLENDEN
Icones Plantarum Sponte China Nascentium; e Bibliotheca Braamiana Excerptae. London: 1821. V. 47

KER, HENRY
Travels through the Western Interior of the United States, from the Year 1808 Up to the Year 1816. Elizabethtown: 1816. V. 47; 49; 53

KER, JOHN
The Memoirs of John Ker of Kersland in North Britain, Esq... London: 1726. V. 50

KER, NEIL R.
English Manuscripts In the Century After the Norman Conquest. Oxford: 1960. V. 48
Fragments of Medieval Manuscripts Used as Pastedowns in Oxford Bindings With a Survey of Oxford Binding c. 1515-1620. London: 1954. V. 51; 53
The Parochial Libraries of the Church of England. London: 1959. V. 52
Pastedowns in Oxford Bindings with a Survey of Oxford Binding c. 1515-1620. Oxford: 1954. V. 50

KERCHEVAL, SAMUEL
A History of the Valley of Virginia. Winchester: 1833. V. 54

KERENYI, CHARLES
Asklepios: Archetypal Image of the Physician's Existence. London: 1960. V. 47; 50; 52

KERFOOT, J. B.
American Pewter. Boston: 1924. V. 47

KERKUT, G. A.
Comprehensive Insect Physiology, Biochemistry and Pharmacology. 1985. V. 49
Comprehensive Insect Physiology, Biochemistry and Pharmacology. London: 1985. V. 52; 53
Comprehensive Insect Physiology, Biochemistry and Pharmacology. New York: 1985. V. 50

KERN, G. M.
Practical Landscape Gardening... Cincinnati: 1855. V. 47

KERN, JEROME
The Library of Jerome Kern. New York: 1929. V. 47; 54

KERNER, JUSTINUS
The Seeress of Prevorst, being Revelations Concerning the Inner-Life of Man, and the Inter-Diffusion of a World of Spirits in the One We Inhabit. London: 1845. V. 50

KERNER VON MARILAUN, A.
The Natural History of Plants, Their Forms, Growth, Reproduction and Distribution. London: 1894-95. V. 48

KERN INSTITUTE, LEIDEN
Annual Bibliography of Indian Archaeology. Leiden: 1930-72. V. 54

KEROUAC, JACK
Big Sur. New York: 1962. V. 47; 49; 51; 53; 54
Big Sur. London: 1963. V. 50
The Dharma Bums. New York: 1958. V. 47; 49; 50; 51
The Dharma Bums. London: 1959. V. 50; 53
Doctor Sax. New York: 1959. V. 49; 51
Excerpts from Visions of Cody. New York: 1959. V. 48; 51; 52
Excerpts from Visions of Cody. Norfolk: 1959. V. 47
Excerpts from Visions of Cody. 1960. V. 49
Four Chorus Poems. Verona: 1981. V. 47
The History of Bop. New York: 1993. V. 52
Home at Christmas. 1973. V. 51
Hymn. New York: 1959. V. 48
Lonesome Traveler. New York: 1960. V. 51; 53
Mexico City Blues. New York: 1959. V. 48
On the Road. New York: 1957. V. 47; 49; 50; 51; 53; 54
Poem. New York: 1962. V. 47
Pull My Daisy. New York: 1959. V. 51
Pull My Daisy. 1961. V. 53
Pull My Daisy. New York: 1961. V. 50
Rimbaud. San Francisco: 1960. V. 53
Satori in Paris. New York: 1966. V. 48; 50; 51; 52
Someday You'll Be Lying. Pleasant Valley: 1968. V. 47
The Subterraneans. New York: 1958. V. 49
The Subterraneans. London: 1960. V. 50; 51; 53; 54
Take Care of My Ghost, Ghost. 1977. V. 52
The Town and the City. New York: 1950. V. 47; 48; 49; 50; 51; 52; 53; 54
The Town and the City. London: 1951. V. 47
Two Early Stories. London: 1973. V. 50
Two Early Stories. New York: 1973. V. 50
Uncollected Writings. New York: 1972. V. 48
Vanity of Duluoz. New York: 1968. V. 48; 50; 51
Visions of America. Sudbury: 1992. V. 47
Visions of Cody. New York: 1960. V. 50
Visions of Cody. New York: 1972. V. 49; 50; 51
Visions of Cody. London: 1973. V. 53
Visions of Gerard. New York: 1963. V. 48; 50; 51

KERR, ANNE
Adeline St. Julian; or the Midnight Hour. London: 1800. V. 54

KERR, J. H.
Glimpses of Life in Victoria. Edinburgh: 1872. V. 49

KERR, J. M. MUNRO
Historical Review of British Obstetrics and Gynaecology 1800-1950. Edinburgh: 1954. V. 52

KERR, JACOB
The Several Trials of the Reverend David Barclay, Before the Presbytery of New-Brunswick... Elizabeth-Town: 1814. V. 47

KERR, JOHN
Curling in Canada and the United States: a Record of the Tour of the Scottish Team, 1902-3, and of the Game in the Dominion and the Republic. Edinburgh: 1904. V. 53

KERR, PHILIP
A German Requiem. London: 1991. V. 51

KERR, R.
Memoirs of the Life, Writings and Correspondence of William Smellie. Edinburgh: 1811 V. 52

KERR, ROBERT
The Gentleman's House; or, How to Plan English Residences. London: 1864. V. 51

KERR, W. H.
The Address of the Hon. John Thorn, to the Free and Enlightened Electors of Splashville Centre as Originally Composed and Written. 1867?. V. 49

KERR, WALTER MONTAGU
The Far Interior: a Narrative of Travel and Adventure from the Cape of Good Hope Across the Zambesi to the Lake Regions of Central Africa. London: 1886. V. 54

KERR, WILLIAM J.
The Genealogical Tree of the Family of Jarrett of Orange Valley, Jamaica and Camerton Court, Somerset. Southampton: 1896. V. 49; 52

KERRIDGE, PHILIP MARKHAM
An Address on Angling Literature, Including Some Mysteries and Personal Observations as Well as Some Comments on Piscatoria Californiana and Hints for Collectors of Angling. Fullerton: 1970. V. 47; 54

KERRIGAN, THOMAS
The Young Navigator's Guide to the Sidereal and Planetary Parts of Nautical Astronomy... London: 1828. V. 49

KERRISON, ROBERT MASTERS
Observations and Reflections on the Bill Now in Progress through the House of Commons, for 'Better Regulating the Medical Profession as Far as Regards Apothecaries;'... London: 1815. V. 50; 54

KERRUISH, J. D.
Babylonian Nights' Entertainments. 1934. V. 48; 52

KERRY, A. J.
The History of the Corps of Royal Canadian Engineers 1749-1939 and 1936-1946. Ottawa: 1962. V. 54

KERSHAW, ALISTER
Richard Aldington - an Intimate Portrait. Carbondale & Edwardsville: 1965. V. 51; 52
Salute to Roy Campbell. Francestown: 1984. V. 53

KERSTING, RUDOLF
The White World: Life and Adventures Within the Arctic Circle Portrayed by Famous Living Explorers. New York: 1902. V. 47

KERTESZ, ANDRE
Andre Kertesz: a Lifetime of Perception. New York: 1982. V. 51
Andre Kertesz: Sixty Years of Photography 1912-1972. New York: 1972. V. 49
Day of Paris. New York: 1945. V. 47; 51
Distortions. New York: 1976. V. 47; 49; 51; 54
From My Window. Boston: 1981. V. 50
J'Aime Paris: Photographs Since the Twenties. London: 1974. V. 51
J'Aime Paris: Photographs Since the Twenties. New York: 1974. V. 47; 50
The Manchester Collection. 1984. V. 50
Of New York. New York: 1976. V. 50

KERY, PATRICIA FRANTZ
Great Magazine Covers of the World. New York: 1982. V. 52; 53

KESEY, KEN
The Day After Superman Died. Northridge: 1980. V. 49; 53
Kesey. 1977. V. 50
Kesey's Garage Sale. New York: 1973. V. 48; 50; 51; 52; 53; 54
One Flew Over the Cuckoo's Nest. London: 1962. V. 48; 52; 54
One Flew Over the Cuckoo's Nest. New York: 1962. V. 49; 50; 51; 52; 53; 54
Sailor Song. New York: 1992. V. 50
Sometimes a Great Notion. New York: 1962. V. 53
Sometimes a Great Notion. New York: 1964. V. 51; 52; 53; 54
Sometimes a Great Notion. London: 1966. V. 52

KESHAVARZ, FATEME
A Descriptive and Analytical Catalogue of Persian Manuscripts in the Library of the Wellcome Institute for the History of Medicine. London: 1986. V. 50; 52

KESSEL, JOSEPH
Kisling. New York: 1971. V. 47; 48; 50; 52

KESSELL, JOHN L.
Kiva, Cross and Crown. The Pecos Indians and New Mexico, 1540-1840. Washington: 1979. V. 54

KESTEN, HERMANN
Children of Gernika. London: 1939. V. 49

KESTER, JESSE Y.
The American Shooter's Manual. Philadelphia: 1827. V. 47; 48; 50; 52
The American Shooter's Manual... New York: 1928. V. 47

KETCHUM, WILLIAM
Authentic and Comprehensive History of Buffalo. Buffalo: 1864-65. V. 47

KETCHUM, WILLIAM C.
Western Memorabilia, Collectibles of the Old West. New York: 1980. V. 48

KETHAM, JOHANNES DE
Fasciculus Medicinae. Venice: 1500. V. 49

KETT, HENRY
Emily, a Moral Tale, Including Letters from a Father to His Daughter Upon the Most Important Subjects. London: 1809. V. 50

KETTELL, RUSSELL HAWES
Early American Rooms, 1650-1858. Portland: 1936. V. 51

KETTELL, SAMUEL
Manual of the Practical Naturalist; or, Directions for Collecting, Preparing and Preserving Subjects of Natural History. Boston: 1831. V. 52
Specimens of American Poetry. Boston: 1829. V. 47; 49; 51; 52; 53

KETTELL, THOMAS PRENTICE
Southern Wealth and Northern Profits. New York: 1860. V. 49

KETTILBY, MARY
A Collection of Above Three Hundred Recipes in Cookery, Physick and Surgery, for the Use of all Good Wives, Tender Mothers and Careful Nurses. London: 1719. V. 47

KETTLE, DANIEL
Pens, Ink and Papers. 1885. V. 51

KETTON-CREMER, ROBERT WYNDHAM
The Early Life and Diaires of William Wyndham. London: 1930. V. 49

KEULEMANS, J. G.
A Natural History of Cage Birds. London: 1871. V. 51
Onze Vogels in Huis en Tuin. Leiden: 1869-76. V. 51

KEULEMANS, TONY
Feathers to Brush. The Victorian Bird Artist John Gerrard Keulemans. Australia: 1982. V. 50

KEVILL-DAVIES, ALBERT
Miss Blanchard of Chicago. London: 1892. V. 49

KEY, ASTLEY COOPER
A Narrative of the Recovery of H.M.S. Gorgon (Charles Hotham, Esq., Captain) Stranded in the Bay of Monte Video, May 10th, 1844. London: 1847. V. 51

KEY, FRANCIS SCOTT
Poems of the Late Francis Scott Key. New York: 1857. V. 53

KEY, HOBART
Of Money and Men, a Brief History of Early Banking In Texas, and the First National Bank, Marshall, Texas. Marshall: 1965. V. 49

KEY, THOMAS
Key and Elphinstone's Compendium of Precedents, in Conveyancing. London: 1890. V. 49

KEY to "Almack's" Reprinted from the Literary Gazette of December 9, 1826. London: 1827. V. 51

A **KEY** to the Business of the Present S(essio)n: Viz I. His H(ighness)s (i.e. William Augustus, Duke of Cumberland, or Perhaps Robert Walpole) Speech to His Life-Guard of Switzers, at Their General Rendevous in D(ownin)g S(tree)t. II. Certaine Important... London: 1742. V. 47

A **KEY** to the Present Politicks of the Principal Powers of Europe. London: 1743. V. 53

KEYES, ANGELA M.
The Five Senes. New York: 1911. V. 48; 54

KEYES, CHARLES ROLLIN
Paleontology of Missouri. Jefferson City: 1894. V. 53

KEYES, DANIEL
The Fith Sally. Boston: 1980. V. 53
Flowers for Algernon. 1966. V. 47
Flowers for Algernon. New York: 1966. V. 53

KEYES, EDWARD L.
Lewis Atterbury Stimson, M.D. New York: 1918. V. 49
The Tonic Treatment of Syphilis. New York: 1877. V. 48; 51; 53

KEYES, LORD
Amphibious Warfare and Combined Operations. Cambridge: 1943. V. 52

KEYES, ROGER
The Art of Surimono. Dublin: 1985. V. 52
The Art of Surimono. London: 1985. V. 48

KEYNES, FLORENCE ADA
Gathering Up the Threads. Cambridge: 1950. V. 49

KEYNES, GEOFFREY
A Bibliography of Dr. Robert Hooke. London: 1960. V. 49
A Bibliography of Dr. Robert Hooke. Oxford: 1960. V. 48; 51; 52; 53
A Bibliography of Sir Thomas Browne... 1924. V. 47
A Bibliography of Sir Thomas Browne... 1968. V. 49; 51
A Bibliography of Sir Thomas Browne. Oxford: 1968. V. 47; 48; 50; 51; 52; 53
A Bibliography of Sir William Petty... London: 1971. V. 47
A Bibliography of Sir William Petty... Oxford: 1971. V. 52
Bibliography of the Works of Dr. John Donne. Cambridge: 1914. V. 47; 48; 49
A Bibliography of the Writings of William Harvey. Cambridge: 1953. V. 47; 48; 49; 50; 51; 53; 54
A Bibliography of William Blake. New York: 1921. V. 53
Bibliography of William Hazlitt. London: 1931. V. 48; 52; 54

KEYNES, GEOFFREY continued
Bibliotheca Bibliographici. A Catalogue of the Library Formed by Geoffrey Keynes. London: 1964. V. 48; 51; 53; 54
Blake Studies Essays on His Life and Work. Oxford: 1971. V. 50; 54
Blood Transfusion. Baltimore: 1949. V. 52
Engravings by William Blake, the Separate Plates. A Catalogue Raisonne. Dublin: 1956. V. 52
Jane Austen. A Bibliography. London: 1929. V. 47; 49; 50; 51; 52; 53; 54
John Ray, a Bibliography. London: 1951. V. 48; 49; 51; 52; 54
Pencil Drawings by William Blake. 1927. V. 51
The Portraiture of William Harvey... London: 1949. V. 54
The Portraiture of William Harvey... London: 1985. V. 54
A Study of the Illuminated Books of William Blake... 1964. V. 54
A Study of the Illuminated Books of William Blake... London: 1964. V. 47; 48; 49; 50
A Study of the Illuminated Books of William Blake. New York: 1964. V. 50
William Blake Essays in Honour of Sir Geoffrey Keynes. Oxford: 1973. V. 50
William Blake's Illuminated Books: a Census. New York: 1953. V. 53
William Blake's Laocoon. A Last Testament. With Related Works: on Homers' Poetry and on Virgil, The Ghost of Abel. London: 1976. V. 48
William Pickering Publisher. A Memoir and a Check-List of His Publications. London: 1969. V. 47; 52
William Pickering, Publisher. A Memoir and a Hand-List of His Editions. London: 1924. V. 47; 50; 52

KEYNES, JOHN MAYNARD, 1ST BARON
The Collected Writings. Cambridge: 1971. V. 53
The Economic Consequences of the Peace. London: 1919. V. 48; 50
Economic History. London: 1926-40. V. 49
The End of Laissez-Faire. London: 1926. V. 52
Essays in Biography. London: 1933. V. 48; 54
Essays in Persuasion. London: 1931. V. 53
General Theory of Employment, Interest and Money. London: 1936. V. 47; 48; 49; 51; 54
Indian Currency and Finance. London: 1913. V. 50; 52; 53; 54
Laissez-Faire and Communism. 1926. V. 50
The Means of Prosperity. London: 1933. V. 48; 49; 53
A Revision of the Treaty. London: 1922. V. 47
A Tract on Monetary Reform. London: 1923. V. 48; 49; 50; 54
A Treatise on Money. London: 1930. V. 49; 53
A Treatise on Probability. London: 1921. V. 48; 50

KEYNES, JOHN NEVILLE
Studies and Exercises in Formal Logic. London: 1894. V. 54

KEYNES, RICHARD
Juvenilia; or Essays on Various Subjects composed by the Pupils of Blandford Academy, and in Part Recited at Their Annual Midsummer Examination, 1822. Blandford: 1822. V. 47

KEYS, THOMAS E.
The History of Surgical Anesthesia. New York: 1945. V. 49

KEYSLER, JOHANN GEORGE
Travels through Germany, Bohemia, Hungary, Switzerland, Italy, and Lorrain. London: 1756-57.. V. 49; 50

KEYSTONE TYPE FOUNDRY
Abridged Specimen Book: Type. Philadelphia: 1906. V. 49

KHAN, GEOFFREY
Arabic Legal and Administrative Documents in the Cambridge Genizah Collections. Cambridge: 1993. V. 51

KHAN, S. M.
Life of Abdur Rahman (Amir of Afghanistan). London: 1900. V. 50

KHANDALAVALA, KARL J.
New Documents of Indian Painting - a Reappraisal. Bombay: 1969. V. 54

KHATCHATRIANZ, I.
Armenian Folk Tales. 1946. V. 52

KHERDIAN, DAVID
Homage to Adana. 1970. V. 50
Homage to Adana. Mt. Horeb: 1970. V. 51; 54

KHORY, RUSTOMJEE N.
The Bombay Materia Medica and their Therapeutics. Bombay: 1887. V. 51; 53

KHUEN, J. C.
Magnus in Ortu. Munich: 1727. V. 53; 54

KHULLAR, S. P.
An Illustrated Fern Flora of West Himalaya. Dehra Dun: 1994. V. 52

KIDD, BENJAMIN
Social Evolution. London: 1894. V. 52

KIDD, DUDLEY
The Essential Kafir. London: 1925. V. 48
Savage Childhood a Study of Kafir Children. London: 1906. V. 53

KIDD, J. H.
Personal Recollections of a Cavalryman. Ionia: 1908. V. 54

KIDD, JOHN
On the Adaptation of External Nature of the Physical Condition of Man, Principally with Reference to the Supply of His Wants and the Exercise of His Intellectual Faculties. London: 1833. V. 47; 49; 54

KIDD, ROBERT
The Yorkshire Volunteers. (with) A Poem, on the Glorious Victory Obtained in the 1st and 2d. of August 1798 by Rear Admiral Sir Horatio Nelson, K.B. Settle: 1799. V. 51

KIDD, SAMUEL
China, or, Illustrations of the Symbols, Philosophy, Antiquities, Customs, Superstitions, Laws, Government, Education and Literature of the Chinese. London. V. 52
China, or, Illustrations of the Symbols, Philosophy, Antiquities, Customs, Superstitions, Laws, Government, Education and Literature of the Chinese. London: 1841. V. 49

KIDD, THOMAS
History of Lulu Island and Occasional Poems. Vancouver: 1927. V. 49
History of Lulu island and Occasional Poems. Vancouver: 1937. V. 51

KIDDER, ALFRED VINCENT
The Artifacts of the Pecos. New Haven: 1932. V. 48; 49; 52
The Artifacts of Uaxactun Guatemala. Washington: 1947. V. 50
Excavations at Kaminaljuyu, Guatemala. Washington: 1946. V. 50
An Introduction to the Study of Southwestern Archaeology... New Haven: 1924. V. 48; 49; 52; 54
Pecos, New Mexico: Archaeological Notes. Andover: 1958. V. 52
Pottery of the Pecos - Volume II - The Glaze Paint Culinary and Other Wares - The Technology of Pecos Pottery. New Haven: 1936. V. 47

KIDDER, DANIEL PARISH
Brazil and the Brazilians, Portrayed in Historical and Descriptive Sketches. Philadelphia: 1857. V. 49
Mormonism and the Mormons: a Historical View of the Rise and Progress of the Sect Self-Styled Latter-Day Saints. New York: 1842. V. 51; 53; 54
Sketches of Residence and Travels in Brazil, Embracing Historical and Geographical Notices of the Empire and Its Several Provinces. Philadelphia/London: 1845. V. 52; 54

KIDDER, EDWARD
E. Kidder's Receipts of Pastry and Cookery, for the Use of His Scholars. London: 1720. V. 48; 54

KIDDER, FREDERIC
The Expeditions of Capt. John Lovewell, and His Encounters with the Indians. Boston: 1865. V. 47

KIDDER, J. EDWARD
Japanese Temples... Tokyo. V. 50
Japanese Temples. London: 1964. V. 49
Japanese Temples... New York: 1964. V. 49
Japanese Temples... Tokyo and Amsterdam: 1964. V. 49; 54
Japanese Temples... Tokyo: 1968. V. 53
Masterpieces of Japanese Sculpture. Tokyo/Rutland: 1961. V. 54

KIDDER, TRACY
The Road to Yuba City: a Journey Into the Juan Corona Murders. Garden City: 1974. V. 47
The Road to Yuba City: a Journey Into the Juan Corona Murders. New York: 1974. V. 51

KIDGELL, JOHN
The Card. London: 1755. V. 47; 50
A Genuine And Succinct Narrative of a Scandalous, Obscence and Exceedingly Profane Libel, Entitled, an Essay on Woman, as Also of Other Poetical Pieces... London: 1763. V. 53

KIDWELL, JONATHAN
The Alpha and Omega. 1843-44. V. 49

KIELLAND, ALEXANDER LANGE
Skipper Worse. London: 1885. V. 49

KIERKEGAARD, SOREN
Journals and Papers. 1967-78. V. 48

KIERNAN, JOHN
Hints on Horse-Shoeing: Being an Exposition of the Dunbar System, Taught to the Farriers of the United States Army. Washington: 1871. V. 48

KIESTER, J. A.
History of Faribault County Minnesota, From Its First Settlement to the Close of the Year 1879. Minneapolis: 1896. V. 48

KIFFE, H. H., CO.
Fishing Tackle and Hunting Outfits. New York: 1907. V. 53

KIJEWSKI, KAREN
Katapult. 1990. V. 51; 54
Katwalk. 1989. V. 54
Katwalk. London: 1989. V. 53

KIKUCHI, SADAO
A Treasury of Japanese Wood Block Prints: Ukiyo-e. New York: 1968. V. 51
A Treasury of Japanese Wood Block Prints: Ukiyo-e. New York: 1969. V. 54

KILBOURNE, DAVID W.
Strictures, On Dr. I. Galland's Pamphlet, Entitled "Villainy Exposed," with Some Account of His Transactions in Lands of the Sac and Fox Reservation... Fort Madison: 1850. V. 48; 52

KILBURN, S. S.
Specimen of Designing and Engraving on Wood. Boston: 1872. V. 47

KILBURNE, RICHARD
Choice Precedents Upon All Acts of Parliament. London: 1694. V. 47; 52
Choice Precedents Upon All Acts of Parliament... London: 1715. V. 48
A Topographie, or Survey of the County Of Kent. London: 1659. V. 47; 48; 51

KILBY, T.
Original Designs and Sketches from Life by an Amateur. Southampton: 1838. V. 53

KILDARE, MARQUIS OF
Earls of Kildare and their Ancestors from 1057-1773. 1864. V. 48

KILDUFFE, ROBERT
The Blood Bank and the Technique and Therapeutics of Transfusions. St. Louis: 1942. V. 48; 53

KILGORE, D. E.
A Texas Ranger. Austin: 1973. V. 52

KILIANO, WOLFGANG
Genealogia Serenissimorum Boiariae Ducum et Quorundam Genuiae Effigies. Augsburg: 1620. V. 54

KILLEBREW, J. B.
Introduction to the Resources of Tennessee. Nashville: 1874. V. 47
Mineral and Agricultural Reources of the Portion of the Tennessee Along the Cincinnati Southern and Knoxville and Ohio Railroads. Nashville: 1876. V. 47
Oil Region of Tennessee with Some Account of Its Other Resources and Capabilities. Nashville: 1877. V. 47

KILLENS, JOHN OLIVER
Black Man's Burden. New York: 1965. V. 53
A Man Ain't Nothin' But a Man: the Adventures of John Henry. Boston: 1975. V. 53
Youngblood. New York: 1954. V. 48; 51; 52; 54
Youngblood. London: 1956. V. 51

KILLIGREW, HENRY
The Conspiracy. London: 1638. V. 47

KILLIGREW, THOMAS
Miscellanea Aurea: Or the Golden Medley. London: 1720. V. 49; 54

KILLIGREW, WILLIAM
Three Plays. London: 1665. V. 53

KILLINGTON, F. J.
A Monograph of the British Neuroptera. London: 1936. V. 54
A Monograph of the British Neuroptera. London: 1936-37. V. 48; 50; 51

KILLION, TOM
Fortress Marin: an Aesthetic and Historical Description of the Coastal Fortifications of Southern Marin County. Santa Cruz: 1977. V. 54
Walls: a Journey Across Three Continents. Santa Cruz: 1990. V. 52; 54

KILLMISTER, A. K.
The Shooter's Handbook. Edinburgh: 1842. V. 49

KILMAN, AUGUST FRIEDRICH CHRISTOPH
An Essay on Musical Harmony, According to the Nature of that Science and the Principles of the Greatest Musical Authors. (with) An Essay on Practical Musical Composition... London: 1796/99. V. 48

KILMAN, ED
Texas Musketters: Stories of Early Texas Battles and Their Heroes. Richmond: 1935. V. 48

KILMER, JOYCE
The Circus and Other Essays. New York: 1916. V. 53; 54
Main Street and Other Poems. New York: 1917. V. 49; 51
Summer of Love. New York: 1911. V. 50
Trees... New York: 1914. V. 49; 50; 52; 53

KILNER, DOROTHY
The Adventures of Hackney Coach. London: 1781. V. 48
The Holyday Present. London: 1788. V. 47
Letters from a Mother to Her Children, on Various Important Subects. London: 1780?. V. 48; 52; 54

KILNER, MARY ANN
A Course of Lectures for Sunday Evenings. London: 1793. V. 48
Memoirs of a Peg-Top. London: 1790. V. 54
Memoirs of a Peg-Top. London: 1790's. V. 48

KILPATRICK, JACK FREDERICK
Sequoyah of Earth and Intellect. Austin: 1965. V. 48; 50

THE KILPECK Anthology. 1981. V. 54

KILVERT, FRANCIS
The Curate of Clyro: Extracts from the Diary of the Reverend Francis Kilvert. Newtown: 1983. V. 50
Diary. London: 1977. V. 50
Kilvert's Diary, Selections fromt he Diary of Rev. Francis Kilvert. 1 January 1870-13 March, 1879. London: 1969. V. 51
Memoirs of the Life and Writings of the Rev. Richard Hurd. Durham: 1860. V. 50
Selections from His Dairy, 1870-1879. London: 1938-40. V. 49
A View of Kilvert: Passages from the Diary of Reverend Francis Kilvert. Glasgow: 1979. V. 53; 54

KIM, CHEWON
The Arts of Korea - Ceramics, Sculpture, Gold, Bronze and Lacquer. London: 1966. V. 50

KIM, RANDOLPH H.
The Gettysburg Campaign. Richmond: 1915. V. 50

KIMBALL, CHARLES P.
The San Francisco City Directory. September 1, 1850. San Francisco: 1850. V. 47
The San Francisco City Directory. September 1, 1850. San Francisco: 1890. V. 50

KIMBALL, HENRIETTA
Witchcraft Illustrated; Witchcraft to Be Understood. Boston: 1892. V. 47

KIMBALL, J. P.
Laws and Decrees of the State of Coahuila and Texas, in Spanish and English, to Which is Added the Constitution of Said State.... Houston: 1839. V. 49

KIMBALL, MARIA BRACE
My Eighty Years. 1934. V. 47
A Soldier - Doctor of Our Army James P. Kimball. Boston: 1917. V. 54

KIMBALL, SOLOMON F.
Life of David P. Kimball and Other Sketches. Salt Lake City: 1918. V. 54

KIMBER, EDWARD
The Generous Briton; or, the Authentic Memoirs of William Goldsmith, Esq. London: 1765. V. 54
The Peerage of Ireland: a Genealogical and Historical Account. 1768. V. 54

KIMBER, ISAAC
The Life of Oliver Cromwell. London: 1724. V. 47; 48
The Life of Oliver Cromwell. London: 1755. V. 52

KIMBERLY, W. B.
History of West Australia. Melbourne: 1897. V. 50

KIMCHI, DAVID
Commentarii...in Haggaevm. Paris: 1557. V. 48

KIMES, VALENTINE
An Autobiography: April 17. 1811-November 25, 1892. Mariposa: 1981. V. 48

KIMES, WILLIAM F.
John Muir: A Reading Bibliography. Palo Alto: 1977. V. 47; 51
John Muir: a Reading Bibliography. Fresno: 1986. V. 48

KIMSEY, L. S.
The Chrysidid Wasps of the World. Oxford: 1990. V. 50

KIMURA, K.
Japanese Medicinal Plants. 1958-60. V. 48

KIMURA, S.
Description of the Fishes Collected from The Yangtze-Kiang, China. 1934. V. 50

KINCAID, J.
Adventures in the Rifle Brigade, in the Peninsula, France and the Netherlands from 1809 to 1815. London: 1847. V. 53

KINCAID, JAMAICA
Annie Gwen, Lilly, Pam and Tulip. New York: 1986. V. 53

KINCAID-SMITH, PRISCILLA
The Kidney, a Clinico-Pathological Study. Oxford: 1975. V. 53

THE KIND Uncle and His Dog Ganges, or, a Visit to Covent Garden. London: 1830. V. 47

KINDERSLEY, DAVID
Mr. Eric Gill - Recollections. San Francisco: 1967. V. 52; 53
Twelve Alphabetick Images in Colour. Linton: 1983. V. 48

KINDERSLEY, N. E.
Specimens of Hindoo Literature... London: 1794. V. 52

KINDIG, JOE
Thought on the Kentucky Rifle In Its Golden Age. Wilmington: 1960. V. 54

KINDIG, R. H.
Pictorial Supplement to Denver South Park and Pacific. Denver: 1959. V. 51

KING, A. S.
Form and Function in Birds. London: 1978-81. V. 50
Form and Function in Birds. Volume 3. London: 1985. V. 50

KING, ALEXANDER
Gospel of the Goat. Paris: 1927. V. 51
An Interpretation, a Credo and Ten Drawings by Alexander King. New York: 1928. V. 51
Peace Is Hell. New York: 1934. V. 51

KING, ALEXANDER WILLIAM
An Aubrey Beardsley Lecture... London: 1924. V. 49; 51

KING, ALICE
Fettered Yet Free. London: 1883. V. 50

KING, CHARLES
The British Merchant, or Commerce Preserv'd. London: 1721. V. 48; 50; 52
Campaigning with Crook and Stories of Army Life. New York: 1880. V. 53
The Colonel's Daughter or Winning His Spurs. Philadelphia: 1883. V. 51
A Daughter of the Sioux. New York: 1903. V. 47
The Fifth Cavalry in the Sioux War of 1876. Milwaukee: 1880. V. 51
Sunset Pass or Running the Gauntlet through Apache Lande. New York: 1890. V. 51

KING, CLARENCE
Clarence King Memoirs. New York: 1904. V. 53
Geological Exploration of the Fortieth Parallel. Washington: 1877-78. V. 51; 52; 53; 54
Mountaineering in the Sierra Nevada. Boston: 1872. V. 51; 53
Mountaineering in the Sierra Nevada. London: 1947. V. 48
United States Geological Exploration of the Fortieth Parallel. Washington: 1878-80. V. 47
United States Geological Exploration of the Fortieth Parallel, Volume 1, Systematic Geology. Washington: 1878. V. 48
United States Geological Exploration of the Fortieth Parallel. Volume II. Descriptive Geology. Washington: 1877. V. 48; 50
United States Mining Laws and Regulations Thereunder, and State and Territorial Mining Laws, to Which are Appended Local Mining Rules and Regulations. Washington: 1885. V. 50

KING, CONSTANCE EILEEN
The Collector's History of Dolls' Houses, Doll's House Dolls and Miniatures. London: 1983. V. 49

KING, CORETTA SCOTT
My Life With Martin Luther King, Jr. New York: 1969. V. 54

KING, DANIEL
The Cathedrall and Conventuall Churches of England and Wales... London: 1656. V. 53
The Vale Royall of England, or, The County Palatine of Chester Illustrated. London: 1656. V. 49; 52; 54

KING, DOROTHY N.
Find the Animals. New York: 1945. V. 53
Fix the Toys. Pennsylvania: 1950. V. 49
Help the Farmer. 1949. V. 49
Set the Clock. 1946. V. 49

KING, EDWARD
An Essay on the English Constitution and Government. London: 1767. V. 47
An Essay on the English Constitution and Government. London: 1771. V. 48
Hymns to the Supreme Being. London: 1798. V. 48
Joseph Zalmonah. Boston: 1893. V. 53
Monumenta Antiqua; or Observations on Ancient Castles. London: 1799-1805. V. 47
The Southern States of North America... Glasgow & Edinburgh: 1875. V. 53
Vestiges of Oxford Castle. London: 1796. V. 50; 53; 54

KING, ELIZABETH
Lord Kelvin's Early Home. London: 1909. V. 50

KING, FRANCES ELIZABETH
The Rector's Memorandum Book, Being the Memoirs of a Family in the North. London: 1819?. V. 49

KING, FRANCIS
To the Dark Tower. London. V. 49

KING, FRANK M.
Longhorn Trail Days - Being a True Story of the Cattle Drives of Long Ago. 1940. V. 54
Longhorn Trail Drivers. King: 1940. V. 47
Longhorn Trail Drivers... Los Angeles: 1940. V. 50; 53
Longhorn Trail Drivers. Vanity: 1940. V. 50
Wranglin' the Past... Los Angeles: 1935. V. 51; 53
Wranglin' the Past. 1946. V. 52
Wranglin' the Past. Pasadena: 1946. V. 52

KING, G.
The Orchids of the Sikkim-Himalaya. Lehre: 1967. V. 48; 51; 52

KING, GEORGE GORDON
The Library of George Gordon King. Newport: 1885. V. 48

KING, GRACE
New Orleans: the Place and the People. New York: 1904. V. 47

KING *Harry the Ninth's Speech to Both Houses of P----t, the 31st Day of November, 1647.* V. 47

KING, HENRY
Poems of Bishop Henry King. London: 1925. V. 51

KING, HENRY C.
Geared to the Stars; the Evolution of Planetariums, Orreries, and Astronomical Clocks. Toronto: 1978. V. 49; 53
The History of the Telescope. London or Cambridge: 1955. V. 49

KING *Henry the Eighth's Scheme of Bishopricks with Illustrations of His Assumption of Church Property, Its Amount and Appropriation and Some Notices of the State of Popular Education at the Period of the Reformation, Now First Published...* London: 1838. V. 50

KING, J. ANTHONY
Twenty-Four Years in the Argentine Republic... London: 1846. V. 53

KING, J. C. H.
Artificial Curiosities from the Northwest Coast of America... London: 1981. V. 48; 54

KING, JEFF
Where the Two Came to Their Father. A Navaho War Ceremonial. New York: 1943. V. 54
Where the Two Came to Their Father. A Navaho War Ceremonial. Princeton: 1969. V. 47; 51

KING, JESSE M.
Kirkcudbright. A Royal Burgh. London/Glasgow: 1934. V. 50

KING, JESSIE M.
Budding Life - A Book of Flowers. London: 1907. V. 47
The City of the West. London: 1911. V. 54
Mummy's Bedtime Story Book. London: 1915. V. 47
Mummy's Bedtime Story Book. London: 1929. V. 54

KING, JOHN
Lectvres Vpon Ionas, Delivered at Yorke. Oxford: 1597. V. 47; 49
Thoughts on the Difficulties and Distresses in which the Peace of 1783, has involved the People of England on the Present Disposition of the English Scots and Irish to Emigrate to America... London: 1783. V. 51
Urological Dictionary. Cincinnati: 1878. V. 48
Vitis Palatina. A Sermon Appointed to Be Preached at Whitehall...After the Mariage of the Ladie Elizabeth... London: 1614. V. 50; 53

KING, JOHN H.
Three Hundred Days in a Yankee prison. Kennasaw: 1959. V. 48

KING, KATHERINE
The Bubble Reputation. London: 1878. V. 54
Ethel Mildmay's Follies. London: 1872. V. 50; 54

KING, L. W.
Chronicles Concerning Early Bablyonian Kings. Including Records of Early History of the Kassites and the Country of the Sea. London: 1907. V. 51

KING, LARRY L.
The One-Eyed Man. New York: 1966. V. 53

KING, LAURIE R.
A Grave Talent. 1993. V. 54

KING *Luckieboy's Picture Book.* London. V. 48

KING, MARTIN LUTHER
Declaration of Independence from the War in Vietnam. V. 48
Nobel Lecture by the Reverend Dr. Martin Luther King, Jr. Recipient of the 1964 Nobel Peace Prize. Oslo, Norway, December 11, 1964. New York: 1964. V. 51
Stride Towards Freedom. New York: 1958. V. 50; 54
Stride Towards Freedom. London: 1959. V. 53
Where Do We Go From Here. 1967. V. 50
Where Do We Go From Here... New York: 1967. V. 48; 50; 52; 53

KING, MONIQUE
European Textiles in the Keir Collection 400 BC to 1800 A.D. London: 1990. V. 50

THE KING *of the Beggars; or, The History of Bamfylde Moore Carew; Who Was the Son of a Gentleman Nar Plymouth, and Ran Away from His Father and Joined a Gang of Gipsies, Detailing the Numerous Tricks and Impositions Practised by Him in Various Disguises.* Derby: 1840. V. 47

KING, PETER
An Enquiry Into the Constitution, Discipline, Unity and Worship fo the Primitive Church... London: 1691. V. 47; 50
The Life of John Locke... London: 1803. V. 52
Life of John Locke... London: 1829. V. 47
A Selection from the Speeches and Writing of the late Lord King. London: 1844. V. 50; 54

KING, PHILLIP PARKER
Narrative of a Survey of the Intertropical and Western Coasts of Australia. London: 1827. V. 48; 49; 50; 52

KING, RICHARD
The Book of Fair Women. London: 1922. V. 50

KING, RICHARD J.
Handbook to the Cathedrals of England. London: 1861-61-62-64. V. 54

KING, ROBERT
Cries of Tyneside. Tynemouth: 1924. V. 53
A Memoir Introductory to the Early History of the Primacy of Armagh. Armagh: 1854. V. 51; 54

KING, ROBERT MOSS, MRS.
Diary of a Civilian's Wife in India 1877-1882. London: 1884. V. 53

KING, RONALD
The White Alphabet. 1984. V. 47
The White Alphabet. Surry: 1984. V. 52

KING, RUFUS
The Case of the Dowager's Etchings. New York: 1944. V. 53

KING, STEPHEN
The Bachman Books. 1985. V. 48; 50
Bare Bones: Conversations on Terror with Stephen King. Los Angeles: 1988. V. 48; 51
The Breathing Method. 1984. V. 47
Carrie. Garden City: 1974. V. 49; 50; 51; 52; 53
Christine. New York: 1983. V. 54
Christine. West Kingston: 1983. V. 51; 52
Cujo. New York: 1981. V. 47; 49; 50; 51
Cycle of the Werewolf. 1983. V. 51
Cycle of the Werewolf. Westland: 1983. V. 47; 50; 54
Danse Macabre. 1981. V. 54
Danse Macabre. New York: 1981. V. 49; 51
The Dark Half. New York: 1989. V. 47; 48; 51
The Dark Tower II: the Drawing of the Three. 1987. V. 49; 54
Dark Tower III: The Waste Land. 1991. V. 47; 48

KING, STEPHEN *continued*
Dark Tower III: The Waste Land. Hampton Falls: 1991. V. 52; 53
The Dark Tower: The Gunslinger. 1982. V. 47; 48; 51; 52
The Dark Tower: The Gunslinger. West Kingston: 1982. V. 48; 51; 54
The Dark Tower: the Gunslinger. West Kingston: 1984. V. 51
The Dead Zone. London: 1979. V. 47; 48; 51
The Dead Zone. New York: 1979. V. 54
Different Seasons. New York: 1982. V. 47; 49; 52
Dolan's Cadillac. Northridge: 1988. V. 48
Dolan's Cadillac. 1989. V. 47; 51
Dolan's Cadillac. Northridge: 1989. V. 49; 53
Dolores Claiborne. London: 1992. V. 54
Dolores Claiborne. New York: 1992. V. 48
The Drawing of the Three. 1987. V. 51; 52
The Drawing of the Three. 1989. V. 48; 50
The Eyes of the Dragon. 1984. V. 49; 53; 54
The Eyes of the Dragon. Bangor: 1984. V. 48; 51
The Eyes of the Dragon. New York: 1987. V. 48; 51
Firestarter. New York: 1980. V. 48
Firestarter. New York: 1982. V. 48
Four Past Midnight. New York: 1990. V. 47; 52; 54
Gerald's Game. 1992. V. 48
Gerald's Game. New York: 1992. V. 47; 49; 51; 52; 53; 54
The Ideal Genuine Man. 1987. V. 54
Insomnia. London: 1994. V. 51; 52
Insomnia. New York: 1994. V. 50; 51; 52
It. New York: 1986. V. 49; 51; 52; 54
Letters from Hell. Northridge: 1988. V. 48
Misery. 1987. V. 47; 51; 53
Misery. New York: 1987. V. 49; 51
My Pretty Pony. New York: 1988. V. 48; 53
My Pretty Pony. 1989. V. 48; 50; 52
My Pretty Pony. New York: 1989. V. 49
Needful Things. 1991. V. 48
Needful Things. New York: 1991. V. 51; 52; 54
Night Shift. Garden City: 1978. V. 47; 48
Night Shift. London: 1978. V. 51
Night Shift. New York: 1978. V. 54
Nightmares and Dreamscapes. New York: 1993. V. 49
The Plant. 1983. V. 49; 50; 54
The Plant. Part Two. Maine: 1983. V. 51
Prime Evil. West Kingston: 1988. V. 47
Rare Bones: Conversations On Terror with Stephen King. Los Angeles: 1988. V. 48
Salem's Lot. 1975. V. 48; 50; 52; 53
Salem's Lot. Garden City: 1975. V. 50; 51; 52
The Shining. Garden City: 1977. V. 49
The Shining. London: 1977. V. 48; 51
The Shining. New York: 1977. V. 51; 52; 54
Skeleton Crew. 1985. V. 49; 50; 51; 53
Skeleton Crew. London: 1985. V. 47
Skeleton Crew. Santa Cruz: 1985. V. 52; 53
The Stand. Garden City: 1978. V. 48
The Stand. New York: 1978. V. 47; 48; 50; 51; 52; 53
The Stand. 1979. V. 47
The Stand. London: 1979. V. 51; 53
The Stand. New York: 1990. V. 47; 48; 50; 51; 52
The Talisman. New York: 1984. V. 47; 49; 50; 51; 53; 54
Thinner. 1984. V. 54
The Tommyknockers. New York: 1987. V. 48; 51; 52
The Waste Lands. London: 1991. V. 50
Whispers: Stephen King Issue. 1982. V. 52

KING, THOMAS BUTLER
California: the Wonder of the Age. New York: 1850. V. 49
Correspondence on the Subject of Appraisements... Washington: 1852. V. 49
Report of Hon. T. Butler King, on California. Washington: 1850. V. 49

KING, THOMAS H.
The Study-Book of Mediaeval Architecture and Art. London: 1890. V. 48

KING, THOMAS STARR
The White Hills: Their Legends, Landscape and Poetry. Boston: 1869. V. 47

KING, WILLIAM
The Art of Cookery. London: 1708. V. 48; 49; 54
The Art of Cookery. London: 1709. V. 49
The Art of Love. 1708. V. 47
The Art of Love. London: 1708. V. 50; 53
The Art of Love. London: 1709. V. 49; 51; 52
Chelsea Porcelain. London: 1922. V. 49
De Origine Mali. London: 1702. V. 47
Divine Predestination and Fore-Knowledge, Consistent with the Freedom of Man's Will. Dublin: 1709. V. 48
Divine Predestination and Fore-Knowledge, Consistent with the Freedom of Man's Will. 1710. V. 50
Doctor King's Apology; or, Vindication of Himself from the Several Matters Charged On Him by the Society of Informers. Oxford: 1755. V. 53
The Dreamer. London: 1754. V. 48; 52
An Historical Account of the Heathen Gods and Heroes... London: 1727. V. 47
History of Homeopathy and its Institutions in America. New York: 1905. V. 50
Letter from the Secretary of War Transmitting a copy of the Proceedings of a Court Martial, for the Trial of (Col. William King). Washington: 1820. V. 52
Miltoni Epistola ad Pollionem... Londini: 1738. V. 54
Miscellanies in Prose and Verse. London: 1709. V. 47; 49
The Old Cheese; an Original Tale, Recited by Mr. Fawcett, at Covent-Garden Theatre. London: 1798. V. 48
Opera. Oxford: 1763. V. 50
The Original Works. London: 1776. V. 50
Poetical and Literary Anecdotes of His Own Times. London: 1819. V. 52
Political and Literary Anecdotes of His Own Times. London: 1818. V. 53
Templum Libertatis. Liber Primus (Secundus). Londini: 1742-43. V. 54
Useful Miscellanies... London: 1712. V. 49
Useful Transactions in Philosophy and Other Sorts of Learning, for the Months of January and February, 1708/9. (and The Months of March and April, 1709.) (and) The Months of May, June, July, August and September 1709. London: 1709. V. 49

KING, WILLIAM, ABP. OF DUBLIN
The State of the Protestants of Ireland... London: 1691. V. 47; 48
The State of the Protestants of Ireland Under the Late King James's Government... London: 1692. V. 48

KING, WILLIAM, PRINCIPAL OF ST. MARY HALL, OXFORD
Elogium Famae Inserviens Jacci Etonensis, sive Gigantis; or, the Praises of Jack of Eton, Commonly Called Jack the Giant... Oxford: 1750. V. 48; 49
A New Speech From the Old Trumpeter of Liberty Hall; in English, with a few Gentle Animadversions. London: 1756. V. 49
A Poetical Abridgement, Both in Latin and English, of the Reverend Mr. Tutor Bentham's Letter to a Young Gentleman of Oxford. London: 1749. V. 49

KING, WILLIAM ROSS
The Sportsman and Naturalist in Canada, or Notes on the Natural History of the Game, Game Birds and Fish of that Country. London: 1866. V. 47; 49; 53

KINGDON, JONATHAN
East African Mammals. London: 1971-82. V. 53
East African Mammals... London: 1971-84. V. 49; 54

KINGDON-WARD, FRANCIS
Assam Adventure. London: 1941. V. 54
Burma's Icy Mountains. London: 1949. V. 54

KINGDON WARD, FRANCIS
Field Notes of Rhododendrons and other Plants Collected by Kingdom Ward in 1927/28. London: 1929. V. 52
A Plant Hunter in Tibet. London: 1934. V. 49; 50; 52

KINGDON-WARD, FRANCIS
Plant Hunting on the Edge of the World. London: 1930. V. 54

KINGDON WARD, FRANCIS
Return to the Irrawaddy. London: 1956. V. 49

KINGDON-WARD, FRANCIS
The Riddle of the Tsangpo Gorges. London: 1926. V. 50

KINGHAM, W. R.
London Gunners, The Story of the H.A.C. Seige Battery in Action. London: 1919. V. 47

KINGLAKE, ALEXANDER WILLIAM
Eothen...Traces of Travel Brought Home from the East. Philadelphia. V. 53
Eothen...Traces of Travel Brought Home from the East. London: 1844. V. 49
The Invasion of the Crimea; Its Origin and an Account of Its Progress Down to the Death of Lord Raglan. London & Edinburgh: 1863. V. 48; 51; 52
The Invasion of the Crimea; Its Origin and An Account of Its Progress Down to the Death of Lord Raglan. Edinburgh & London: 1863-87. V. 47; 51
The Invasion of the Crimea: Its Origin and an Account of Its Progress Down to the Death of Lord Raglan. New York: 1888. V. 47
Origin of the Crimean War. London: 1874. V. 50

KINGLAKE, ROBERT
A Dissertation on Gout. London: 1804. V. 48

KINGMAN, DONG
The Water Colors of Dong Kingman: And How the Artist Works. New York: 1958. V. 48

KINGMAN, RALPH CLARKE
New England Georgian Architecture. New York: 1913. V. 51

KINGS of the Rod, Rifle and Gun. London: 1901. V. 53

KINGSBURY, BENJAMIN
A Treatise of Razors; in Which the Weight, Shape and Temper of a Razor, the Means of Keeping it In order and the Manner of Using It, are Particularly Considered, and in Which It Its Intended to Convey a Knowledge of All that is Necessary on this Subject. London: 1830. V. 52

KINGSBURY, GAINES P.
Colonel Dodge's Journal...A Report of the Expedition of the Dragoons, Under the Command of Colonel Dodge, to the Rocky Mountains. Washington: 1836. V. 47; 50

KINGSBURY, GEORGE
History of Dakota Territory, South Dakota and Its People. Chicago: 1915. V. 54

KINGSBURY, JEROME
Portfolio of Dermochromes. New York: 1913. V. 48

KINGSFORD, ANNA
Astrology Theologized: the Spiritual Hermeneutics of Astrology and Holy Writ. London: 1886. V. 47

KINGSFORD, EDWARD
The Claims of Abolitionism Upon the Church of Christ, Candidly Examined. Harrisburg: 1838. V. 48

KINGSFORD, WILLIAM
Canadian Canals: Their History and Cost with an Inquiry into the Policy Necessary to Advance the Well-Being of the Province. Toronto: 1865. V. 48; 51; 54
The History of Canada. Toronto: 1887-98. V. 53

KINGSLEY, ADRIEL
A Bold Arraignment of the Medical Profession for the Practice of False Theories, False Pretenses, Fraudulent Claims for a False Science and for Their Determined Purpose to Oppose the Cold Bath in All Fevers... Indianapolis: 1890. V. 52

KINGSLEY, AMIS
Bright November. London: 1947. V. 53
A Frame of Mind. 1953. V. 53
Lucky Jim. London: 1953. V. 53

KINGSLEY, CHARLES
Alton Locke, Tailor and Poet. London: 1850. V. 50; 51
At Last: a Christmas in the West Indies. New York: 1871. V. 52; 54
Charles Kingsley: His Letters and His Life. London: 1883. V. 52
Glaucus; or, the Wonders of the Shore. Cambridge: 1855. V. 51; 52; 53
Glaucus; or, the Wonders of the Shore. London: 1855. V. 49
Glaucus; or, the Wonders of the Shore. Cambridge: 1858. V. 51
Hereward the Wake, "Last of the English.". London: 1866. V. 49
Hereward the Wake, "Last of the English". London: 1867. V. 48; 50; 52
The Heroes...Greek Fairy Tales for My Children. London: 1856. V. 47; 50
The Heroes...Greek Fairy Tales for My Children. London: 1912. V. 48; 49; 52
Hypatia; or, New Foes with an Old Face. London: 1853. V. 47
Kingsley's Novels. London and New York: 1889. V. 54
The Life and Works of... London: 1901-03. V. 51; 54
Novels. London: 1881. V. 53
Poems. 1856. V. 49
Poems. USA: 1856. V. 53
Poems. London: 1897. V. 49
Poems. London: 1907. V. 54
Politics for the People. London: 1848. V. 54
The Saint's Tragedy; or, the True Story of Elizabeth of Hungary. V. 51
The Saint's Tragedy; or, the True Story of Elizabeth of Hungary. London: 1848. V. 47; 48; 49
Town Geology. London: 1872. V. 47; 50; 52; 53
Two Years Ago. Boston: 1857. V. 52; 53
Two Years Ago. Cambridge: 1857. V. 51
The Water-Babies. London. V. 49
The Water-Babies... London: 1864. V. 51
The Water-Babies. London: 1869. V. 51
The Water-Babies. London: 1882. V. 49; 52
The Water-Babies. London: 1885. V. 52
The Water-Babies... London: 1886. V. 50
The Water-Babies. London: 1900. V. 48
The Water-Babies. London: 1907. V. 49
The Water-Babies. London: 1908. V. 49
The Water-Babies. London: 1909. V. 49; 54
The Water-Babies. London: 1914. V. 52
The Water-Babies. London: 1915. V. 53
The Water-Babies. New York, Nottingham, London: 1916. V. 47; 49; 52; 54
The Water-Babies. London: 1922. V. 54
The Water-Babies. London: 1924. V. 53; 54
The Water-Babies. London: 1925. V. 47; 49
The Water-Babies. London: 1935. V. 52
Westward Ho!. Boston: 1855. V. 49
Westward Ho!. Cambridge: 1855. V. 51; 53
Westward Ho!. London: 1855. V. 47
Westward Ho!. London: 1903. V. 54
Westward Ho!. New York: 1920. V. 50
Westward Ho!. Philadelphia: 1920. V. 49
Westward Ho!. New York: 1928. V. 48; 49
Works. London: 1881. V. 47; 49
Yeast: a Problem. London: 1851. V. 51

KINGSLEY, HENRY
Tales of Old Travel. London: 1869. V. 47; 53
Valentin. London: 1872. V. 47; 48; 51

KINGSLEY, JOHN STERLING
Nature's Wonderland or Short Talks on Natural History for Young and Old. New York: 1894. V. 52
The Standard Natural History. Boston: 1885. V. 54

KINGSLEY, MARY H.
Travels in West Africa. London: 1897. V. 48; 54
Travels in West Africa. London: 1898. V. 50; 51

KINGSLEY, SIDNEY
Dead End. New York: 1936. V. 47

KINGSLEY, VINE W.
Reconstruction in America. New York: 1865. V. 47

KINGSLEY, ZEPHANIAH
A Treatise on the Patriarchal, or Co-Operative System of Society As it Exists in some Governments, and Colonies in America, and in the United States, Under the Name of Slavery, with Its Neccessity and Advantages. Tallahassee: 1829. V. 49; 50

KINGSMILL, JOSEPH
Chapters on Prisons and Prisoners. London: 1852. V. 48; 52

KINGSMILL, WILLIAM
The Greenwood Tragedy: Three Addresses Delivered to the Prisoners in Toronto Gaol Soon After the Suicide of William Greenwood... Guelph: 1864. V. 53

KINGSOLVER, BARBARA
Another America. Otra America. Seattle: 1992. V. 53
The Bean Trees. New York: 1988. V. 50; 51; 52; 53; 54
The Bean Trees. London: 1989. V. 50; 52
High Tide in Tucson. New York: 1995. V. 54
Holding the Line. Ithaca: 1989. V. 51; 53
Homeland. New York: 1989. V. 50; 51; 53

THE KINGSTON Literary Wreath, a Quarterly Magazine of the Belles Lettres, etc., etc. Hull: 1838-39. V. 47

KINGSTON, MAXINE HONG
The Woman Warrior. New York: 1976. V. 50; 52

KINGSTON, PETER
Foxie Tails. Sydney: 1989. V. 47
Mountain Relief. Sydney: 1990. V. 47
A to Z. Sydney: 1991. V. 48
Wheel of Fortune. Sydney: 1989. V. 51

KINGSTON, RICHARD
A True History of the Several Designs and Conspiracies Against His Majesties Sacred Person and Government... London: 1698. V. 48; 54

KINGSTON, WILLIAM HENRY GILES
Western Wanderings, or, a Pleasure Tour in the Canadas. London: 1856. V. 53
The Western World. London: 1884. V. 49

KINGSTON Wit, Humour and Satire, an Impartial record of the Spirit of Party as Evinced at the General Election and Scrutiny Which Took Place at Kingston-upon-Hul in June and July 1818... Hull. V. 51

KINKEAD, A. S.
Landscapes of Corsica and Ireland. London: 1921. V. 49

KINKLE, ROGER D.
The Complete Encyclopedia of Popular Music and Jazz 1900-1950. New Rochelle: 1974. V. 47

KINLOCH, ALEXANDER A. A.
Large Game Shooting in Thibet and the North West. 1869-76. V. 54
Large Game Shooting in Thibet and the North West. London: 1869-76. V. 48; 53
Large Game Shooting in Thibet, the Himalayas, Northern and Central India. Calcutta: 1892. V. 52

KINLOCH, ARCHIBALD GORDON
The Trial of Sir..., of Gilmerton, Bart. For the Murder of Sir Francis Kinloch, Bart, His Brother-German... Edinburgh: 1795. V. 47

KINNAIRD, LAWRENCE
Spain in the Mississippi Valley, 1765-1794... Washington: 1949. V. 50; 53

KINNE, O.
Marine Ecology. London: 1970-75. V. 50; 51
Marine Ecology... New York: 1982-84. V. 52

KINNEAR, JOHN GARDINER
Cairo, Petra and Damascus, in 1839. London: 1841. V. 48; 49; 51

KINNEIR, JOHN MAC DONALD
A Geographical Memoir of the Persian Empire. London: 1813. V. 47

KINNELL, GALWAY
The Auction. A Poem. Ewert: 1989. V. 50
Black Light. Boston: 1966. V. 47
Body Rags. London: 1969. V. 48
Fergus Falling. Newark: 1979. V. 50; 54
First Poems 1946-1954. Mt. Horeb: 1970. V. 49; 50; 51; 53; 54
Flower Herding on Mount Monadnock. Boston: 1964. V. 51
The Last Hiding Places of Snow. Madison: 1980. V. 52; 53; 54
Poems of Night. London: 1967. V. 47; 49; 54
Saint Francis and the Sow. Evanston: 1976. V. 47
The Seekonic Woods. Concord: 1985. V. 47
Selected Poems. Boston: 1982. V. 47
The Shoes of Wandering. Mt. Horeb: 1971. V. 53; 54
Three Poems. New York: 1976. V. 54
Two Poems. 1979. V. 54
Two Poems. Newark: 1979. V. 52
Two Poems. Vermont: 1979. V. 51
Two Poems. New York: 1981. V. 52; 54
What a Kingdom It Was. Boston: 1960. V. 47; 48; 49

KINNEY, ARTHUR E.
The Birds and Beasts of Shakespeare. Easthampton: 1990. V. 47; 50

KINNEY, ELIZABTH C.
Felicita: a Motrical Romance. New York: 1855. V. 51

KINNEY, HANNAH
A Review of the Principal Events of the Last Ten Years in the Life of... Boston: 1841. V. 50; 51

KINNEY, JAMES R.
How to Raise a Dog. New York: 1938. V. 48

KINNEY, TROY
The Etchings of Troy Kinney. Garden City: 1929. V. 47; 50; 53

KINNS, SAMUEL
Moses and Geology; or, the Harmony of the Bible with Science. London: 1882. V. 49

KINO, EUSEBIO FRANCISCO
Kino's Historical Memoir of Pimeria Alta. Cleveland: 1919. V. 53
Kino's Historical Memoir of Pimeria Alta. Berkeley: 1948. V. 47; 50; 54

KINSELLA, THOMAS
Another September. Dublin: 1958. V. 53
Another September. Dublin: 1966. V. 47
Butcher's Dozen. Dublin: 1972. V. 48; 50; 52
Downstream. Dublin: 1962. V. 48
Fifteen Dead (with) One and Other Poems. Dublin: 1979. V. 47
Finistere. Dublin: 1972. V. 47
The Good Flight. 1973. V. 47; 50
The Messenger. Dublin: 1978. V. 53
Moralities. Dublin: 1960. V. 53
Nightwalker. Dublin: 1967. V. 47; 53
Nightwalker... 1968. V. 48
Notes from the Land of the Dead. Dublin: 1972. V. 47; 51; 54
One. Dublin: 1974. V. 47; 51
One Fond Embrace. Old Deerfield & Dublin: 1981. V. 54
Poems and Translations. New York: 1961. V. 54
A Selected Life. Dublin: 1972. V. 47; 50; 53
Selected Poems. Helsinki: 1989. V. 48
Song of the Night and Other Poems. V. 47; 48
Song of the Night and Other Poems. Dublin: 1978. V. 47; 53
The Sons of Usnech. Dublin: 1960. V. 48
Tear. Cambridge: 1969. V. 47; 48; 50
Tear. Massachusetts: 1969. V. 48
A Technical Supplement. Dublin: 1976. V. 47; 53
Vertical Man: A Sequel to a Selected Life. Dublin: 1972. V. 47

KINSELLA, W. P.
Born Indian. Canada: 1981. V. 52
The Dixon Cornbelt League. Toronto: 1993. V. 52
The First and Last Annual Six Towns Area Old Timers' Baseball Game. Minneapolis: 1991. V. 47; 53; 54
Five Stories. Vancouver: 1986. V. 48; 49
The Moccasin Telegraph. Ontario: 1983. V. 50
Scars. 1978. V. 50
Scars. Canada: 1978. V. 53
Shoeless Joe. Boston: 1982. V. 47; 48; 49; 50; 51; 52; 53; 54
Shoeless Joe. London: 1982. V. 50
The Thrill of the Grass. London: 1984. V. 52

KINSEY, ALFRED C.
Sexual Behavior in the Human Female. Philadelphia & London: 1953. V. 50
Sexual Behavior in the Human Male. Philadelphia & London: 1948. V. 50

KINSKI, KLAUS
All I Need Is Love. New York: 1988. V. 52

KINZIE, JULIETTE A.
Wau-Bun, the 'Early Day' in the North-West. New York: 1856. V. 50

KIP, FREDERIC ELLSWORTH
History of the Kip Family in America. Montclair: 1928. V. 49; 51

KIP, JOHANNES
Britannia Illustrata, or Views of Several of the Queen's Palaces, as Also of the Principal Seats of the Nobility and Gentry of Great Britain. London: 1714-17. V. 49; 50
Nouveau Theatare de la Grande Bretagne: ou Description Exacte Des Palais du Roy, et des Maisons les Plus Considerables des Seigneurs & des Gentilhommes de la Grande Bretagne. Londres: 1716. V. 51

KIP, L.
Hannibal's Man and Other Tales. 1878. V. 48; 52

KIP, LAWRENCE
Army Life on the Pacific; a Journal of the Expedition Against the Northern Indians. New York: 1859. V. 47; 53

KIPLING, JOHN LOCKWOOD
Beast and Man in India. London: 1904. V. 54

KIPLING, RUDYARD
Abaft the Funnel. New York: 1909. V. 51; 53
The Absent Minded Beggar. London: 1899. V. 47; 48; 49
An Almanac of Twelve Sports... London: 1898/97. V. 48
The Army of a Dream. New York: 1904. V. 53
Ballads and Barrack-Room Ballads. New York: 1892. V. 48; 53
Barrack-Room Ballads... London: 1892. V. 51
Barrack-Room Ballads. London: 1899. V. 53
The Bombay Edition of the Works of Rudyard Kipling. London: 1913-20. V. 50
The Brushwood Boy. New York: 1899. V. 50
Captains Courageous. London: 1897. V. 47; 48; 50; 51; 52; 53
Captains Courageous. New York: 1897. V. 47; 53; 54
The Cat That Walked by Himself. New York: 1947. V. 49
Certain Maxims of Hafiz. 1898. V. 50
Chartres Windows: a Poem. Garden City: 1925. V. 53
Chartres Windows: a Poem. New York: 1925. V. 47
A Choice of Songs. Garden City: 1925. V. 48; 53
A Choice of Songs... London: 1925. V. 51
The City of Dreadful Night. New York: 1899. V. 47
Collected Verse... New York: 1910. V. 48
Collected Verse. London: 1912. V. 50
Collected Works. London: 1910-12. V. 48
The Collected Works... New York: 1941. V. 49
The Collected Works... U.S.A.: 1941. V. 51
The Complete Stalky & Co. London: 1929. V. 49; 53
The Complete Works... New York: 1916. V. 54
The Complete Works... London: 1937-39. V. 47; 48
The Complete Works... New York: 1941. V. 48
The Day of the Dead. Garden City: 1930. V. 48; 49; 51
The Day of the Dead. Garden City: 1939. V. 48
The Day's Work. Toronto and New York: 1898. V. 53
Debits and Credits. Garden City: 1926. V. 51; 53
Debits and Credits. London: 1926. V. 52; 54
Debits and Credits. Toronto: 1926. V. 53
Departmental Ditties... Calcutta: 1888. V. 49
Departmental Ditties... New York: 1890. V. 51
Departmental Ditties... London: 1897. V. 47; 49
Destroyers at Jutland. Garden City: 1916. V. 49; 51
Destroyers at Jutland. New York: 1916. V. 54
Different Seasons. New York: 1982. V. 49
A Diversity of Creatures. London: 1917. V. 48; 49; 53
Doctors. An Address Delivered to the Students of the Medical School at the Middlesex Hospital, 1st Oct. 1908. London: 1908. V. 49
Elfandel. Berlin: 1922. V. 50
The Eyes of Asia. Garden City: 1918. V. 53
The Feet of the Young Men. New York: 1920. V. 53
The Five Nations. London: 1903. V. 48; 52; 53; 54
The Flag. London: 1908. V. 50
A Fleet in Being. London: 1898. V. 50; 51
France at War. Garden City: 1915. V. 48; 52
France at War. London: 1915. V. 50
France at War. New York: 1915. V. 50
The Fringes of the Fleet. Garden City: 1915. V. 48; 49; 51
From Sea to Sea. New York: 1899. V. 53; 54
The Greek National Anthem. Garden City: 1918. V. 48
L'Habitation Forcee. Paris: 1921. V. 47; 50
Ham and the Porcupine. Garden City: 1935. V. 48; 49; 51
Healing by the Stars. Garden City: 1928. V. 53
The Holy War. Garden City: 1917. V. 48; 49; 53
How Shakespeare Came to Write "The Tempest". New York: 1916. V. 47; 49; 50
How the Camel Got His Lump. Garden City: 1942. V. 49
In Black and White. 1888. V. 49; 51; 52; 54
Independence. Garden City: 1923. V. 48; 49
Indian Tales. New York: 1899. V. 48
The Irish Guards. Garden City: 1918. V. 48; 53
The Irish Guards in the Great War. London: 1923. V. 47; 52; 53; 54
The Irish Guards in the Great War. New York: 1923. V. 47
The Jungle Book. London: 1894. V. 49; 53
The Jungle Book. New York: 1894. V. 52; 53
The Jungle Book. New York: 1897. V. 52
The Jungle Book. London: 1910. V. 53
The Jungle Book. New York: 1913. V. 52
The Jungle Book. Luxenburg: 1968. V. 52; 54
The Jungle Books. London: 1968. V. 49
The Jungle Book...Second Jungle Book. London: 1894. V. 48
The Jungle Book...Second Jungle Book. London and New York: 1894/95. V. 47; 48; 49; 50; 51; 52; 53; 54
The Jungle Book...Second Jungle Book. London: 1895. V. 48
The Jungle Book...Second Jungle Book. London: 1896. V. 51
The Jungle Book...Second Jungle Book. London: 1899. V. 49
The Jungle Book...Second Jungle Book. London: 1959/56. V. 50
The Just So Song Book. London: 1903. V. 53
Just So Stories. London: 1902. V. 47; 48; 49; 50; 51; 52; 54
Justice. Garden City: 1918. V. 48; 53
Kim. London: 1900. V. 49
Kim. London: 1901. V. 49; 50; 51; 52
Kim. New York: 1901. V. 54

KIPLING, RUDYARD continued
Kim. Garden City: 1935. V. 52
Kim. New York: 1962. V. 48
The King's Pilgrimage. Garden City: 1922. V. 48; 49
Land and Sea Tales for Scouts and Guides. London: 1923. V. 51; 54
Letters of Marque. Allahabad: 1891. V. 47; 49; 53; 54
Letters of Travels (1892-1913). London: 1920. V. 47; 48
The Light that Failed. London: 1891. V. 52; 54
Le Livre De La Jungle. Paris: 1910?. V. 47; 48
The Maltese Cat. London: 1936. V. 53
The Maltese Cat... New York: 1936. V. 50
Mesopotamia. Garden City: 1917. V. 48; 53
The Naulahka. London: 1892. V. 49; 52
Neighbours. Garden City: 1932. V. 48; 49; 51
The Nerve That Conquers. Garden City: 1928. V. 48; 53
The Neutral. Garden City: 1916. V. 51
The New Army; Fringes of the Fleet; The Neutral. New York: 1914-16. V. 51
On Dry Cow Fishing as a Fine Art. Cleveland: 1926. V. 48; 50
Our Lady fo the Sack-Cloth. Garden City: 1935. V. 48; 49
Out of India. New York: 1895. V. 51
Plain Tales from the Hills. Calcutta: 1888. V. 49; 51
Les Plus Beaux Contes de Kipling. Paris: 1926. V. 51
Poems 1886-1929. London: 1929. V. 51; 52
Poems 1886-1929. New York: 1930. V. 47; 54
Puck of Pook's Hill. London: 1906. V. 47
Puck of Pook's Hill. New York: 1906. V. 47; 49; 50; 51; 52
Puck of Pook's Hill. New York: 1913. V. 49
A Rector's Memory. Garden City: 1926. V. 53
Rewards and Fairies. 1910. V. 52
Rewards and Fairies. London: 1910. V. 48
Rudyard Kipling's Verse. London: 1919. V. 53; 54
The Scholars. Garden City: 1919. V. 53
Sea and Sussex. Garden City: 1926. V. 49
Sea and Sussex. London: 1926. V. 51; 52
Sea and Sussex. New York: 1926. V. 50; 51; 53
Sea Warfare. London: 1916. V. 48; 52
The Second Jungle Book. London: 1895. V. 48; 49; 50; 51; 53
The Seven Seas. London: 1896. V. 49; 50
The Seven Seas. New York: 1899. V. 48
The Seven Seas. London: 1913. V. 49; 52
The Shipping Industry. Garden City: 1925. V. 48
The Sin of Witchcraft. London: 1901. V. 50
Soldier Tales. London: 1896. V. 48; 53; 54
A Song of the English. 1909. V. 47
A Song of the English. London: 1909. V. 51
A Song of the English. London: 1913. V. 53
A Song of the English. London: 1915. V. 52; 53; 54
The Song of the Lathes. Garden City: 1918. V. 48
Songs from Books. London: 1913. V. 49
Songs of the Sea... Garden City: 1927. V. 48
Songs of the Sea. London: 1927. V. 51; 53
Songs of the Sea. New York: 1927. V. 54
Stalky & Co. London: 1899. V. 48
A Story of the English. London: 1909. V. 48
The Story of the Gadsbys. Allahabad & London: 1890. V. 47; 50; 54
The Story of the Gadsbys... 1891. V. 50
Tales of "The Trade". Garden City: 1916. V. 48; 49
Tales of East and West. Avon: 1973. V. 53
They. London: 1905. V. 47; 48; 49; 50; 51; 53; 54
Traffics and Discoveries. London: 1904. V. 47; 48
Two Forewords. Garden City: 1935. V. 52
The Two Jungle Books. New York: 1930. V. 53
Under the Deodars. Allahabad: 1888. V. 51
The War in the Mountains. (Parts I-V). Garden City: 1917. V. 51
With the Night Mail. New York: 1909. V. 51; 53
The Works. London: 1913-. V. 52
Works. London: 1913-27. V. 49; 51
Works. London: 1913-38. V. 48; 50
Works. London: 1925-32. V. 50
The Writings in Prose and Verse. New York: 1897-99. V. 54
The Writings in Prose and Verse... New York: 1913-19. V. 48; 49
The Years Between. London: 1919. V. 47; 48; 49; 52; 53; 54

KIPLING, THOMAS
Codex Theodori Bezae Cantabrigiensis. Cambridge: 1793. V. 48

KIPNISS, LEVIN
Aleph-Bet. Berlin: 1923. V. 47; 50

KIPPIS, ANDREW
Biographical Britannica: or, the Lives of the Most Eminent Persons Who Have Flourished in Great Britain and Ireland... London: 1778-93. V. 47; 48; 49
The Life of Captain James Cook. Basil: 1788. V. 50; 52
The Life of Captain James Cook. Dublin: 1788. V. 50; 53
The Life of Captain James Cook. London: 1788. V. 49; 52
A Narrative of the Voyages Round the World Performed by Captain James Cook... London: 1814. V. 50
A Narrative of the Voyages Round the World Performed by Captain James Cook... London: 1826. V. 52

KIR, T.
The Forest Flora of New Zealand. Wellington: 1889. V. 51

KIRA, T.
Shells of the Western Pacific in Color. Osaka: 1964-68. V. 50

KIRBY, JOHN
An Historical Account of the Twelve Prints of Monasteries, castles, Antient Churches and Monuments, in the Country of Suffolk... Ipswich: 1748. V. 49
The Suffolk Traveller... Ipswich: 1735. V. 50; 52; 54
The Suffolk Traveller... London: 1764. V. 52
The Suffolk Traveller... Woodbridge: 1820. V. 48
A Topographical and Historical Description of the County of Suffolk. London: 1829. V. 51

KIRBY, JOSHUA
The Perspective of Architecture in Two Parts, A Work Entirely New... London: 1761. V. 47

KIRBY, M.
Birds of Gay Plumage: Sun Birds &c. London: 1875. V. 50; 52; 53

KIRBY, R. S.
Kirby's Wonderful and Eccentric Museum; or, Magazine of Remarkable Characters. London: 1803-20. V. 49

KIRBY, S. WOODBURN
The History of the Second World War the War Against Japan. London: 1958-65. V. 54

KIRBY, W. F.
The Butterflies and Moths of Europe. London: 1903. V. 51
European Butterflies and Moths. London: 1882. V. 52; 54

KIRBY, WILLIAM
An Introduction to Entomology... London: 1815-26. V. 54
An Introduction to Entomology... London: 1816/17/26. V. 47
An Introduction to Entomology. London: 1828. V. 49
Monographia Apum Angliae; or, an Attempt to Divide Into Their Natural Genera and Families, Such Species of the Linnean Genus Apis as Have Been Discovered in England. Ipswich: 1802. V. 47; 53
On the Power, Wisdom and Goodness of God as Manifested in the Creation of Animals and Their History, Habits and Instincts. London: 1835. V. 51
The U. E. a Tale of Upper Canada. Niagara: 1859. V. 48; 53

KIRCHENHOFFER, H.
The Book of Fate, Formerly in the Possession of Napoleon, Late Emperor of France... London: 1824. V. 54

KIRCHER, ATHANASIUS
Arithmologia sive de Abditis Numerorum Mysteriis... Rome: 1665. V. 48
Ars Magna Lucis et Umbrae... Rome: 1646. V. 48
Iter Extaticum Coeleste... Wurzburg: 1660. V. 54
Iter Extaticum II. Qui & Mundi Subterranei Prodromus Dicitur...In III. Dialogos Distinctum. Rome: 1657. V. 50
Itinerarium Exstaticum Quo Mundi Opificium... Rome: 1656. V. 50
Magnes, sive de Arte Magnetica. Rome: 1641. V. 47
Magnes Sive de Arte Magnetica, Opus Tripartitum, Quo Praeterquam Quod Universa Magnetis Natura... Cologne: 1643. V. 48
Mundus Subterraneus, in XII Libros Digestus. Amstelodami: 1678. V. 50
Obelisci Aegyptiaci Nuper Inter Isaei romani Rudera Effossi Interpretatio Hieroglyphica. Rome: 1666. V. 50
Obeliscus Pamphilius, Hoc Est, Interpretatio Nova & Hucusque Intentata Obelisci Hieroglyphici... Romae: 1650. V. 50; 51
Phonurgia Nova. Campidonae: 1673. V. 50
Prodromus Coptus sive Aegyptiacus...In Quo Cum Lingaue Coptae, Siave Aegyptiacae, Quondam Pharaonicae... Rome: 1636. V. 50
Scrutinium Physico-Medicum Contagiosae Luis, Quae Dicitur Pestis Quo Origo, Caussae, Signa, Prognostica Pestis nec Non Insolentes... Leipzig: 1659. V. 49; 50

KIRCHMANN, JOHANN
De Annulis Liber singularis. Schleswig: 1657. V. 51

KIRICHENKO, E.
Moscow Architectural Monuments of the 1830-1910's. Moscow: 1977. V. 53; 54

KIRK, J. A.
Kirk's Map of Trail Creek Mining Camp, British Columbia 1897. Rossland: 1897. V. 49

KIRK, JOHN FOSTER
History of Charles the Bold, Duke of Burgundy. London: 1863-68. V. 53

KIRK, ROBERT C.
Twelve Months in Klondike. London: 1899. V. 47

KIRK, T.
The Forest Flora of New Zealand. London: 1889. V. 47; 48; 50
The Forest Flora of New Zealand. Wellington: 1889. V. 48; 52; 54

KIRKALDY, WILLIAM G.
Illustrations of David Kirkaldy's System of Mechanical Testing as Originated and Carried on By Him During a Quarter of a Century. London: 1891. V. 49; 54
Memoirs and Adventures of Sir William Kirkaldy. Edinburgh: 1849. V. 54

KIRKBRIDE, THOMAS S.
On the Construction, Orgranization an General Arrangements of Hospitals for the Insane. Philadelphia/London: 1880. V. 52

KIRKCONNELL, WATSON
The Flying Bull and Other Tales. London: 1940. V. 47

KIRKER, H.
California's Architectural Frontier: Style & Tradition in the 19th Century. San Marino: 1960. V. 48

KIRKLAND, CAROLINE MATILDA STANSBURY
The Evening Book; or, Fireside Talk on Morals and Manners, with Sketches of Western Life. New York: 1852. V. 54
Forest Life. New York: 1842. V. 53
A New Home-Who'll Follow?. New York: 1840. V. 54
Western Clearings. London: 1846. V. 53

KIRKLAND, ELIZABETH S.
Six Little Cooks; or Aunt Jane's Cooking Class. Chicago: 1877. V. 52

KIRKLAND, FORREST
The Rock Art of Texas Indians. Austin: 1967. V. 53
The Rock Art of Texas Indians. (with) *Indian Pictographs in Texas.* Austin: 1967/43. V. 48

KIRKLAND, FREDERIC R.
Letters on the American Revlution in the Library at 'Karolfred'. Philadelphia: 1941. V. 49

KIRKMAN, F. B.
The British Bird Book. London: 1911-13. V. 49; 52; 54
How Lotys Had Tea with a Lion. London: 1921. V. 49

KIRKMAN, MARSHALL M.
Classical Portfolio of Primitive Carriers...(with) 1500 Engravings Portraying the Primitive People of the World and Their Method of Carriage in Every Age and Quarter of the Globe. Chicago: 1895. V. 47

KIRKPATRICK
Alpine Days and Nights. 1932. V. 52
Dim Trails. A Collection of Poems. Brownwood: 1938. V. 51

KIRKPATRICK, BROWNLEE
A Bibliography of Edmund Blunden. London: 1979. V. 53

KIRKPATRICK, CYNTHIA
Poems for the Times. Parkersburg: 1865. V. 51

KIRKPATRICK, JAMES
The Sea-Piece a Narrative, Philosophical and Descriptive Poem. London: 1750. V. 47; 54

KIRKPATRICK, WILLIAM
Select Letters of Tippoo Sultan to Various Public Functionaries, Including His Principal Military Commanders... London: 1811. V. 53

KIRKPATRICK B. J.
A Bibliography of E. M. Forster. London: 1968. V. 52
A Bibliography of Virginia Woolf. Oxford: 1980. V. 49

KIRKWOOD, A.
The Undeveloped Lands in Northern and Western Ontario. Toronto: 1878. V. 54

KIRKWOOD, JAMES
A Copy of a Letter Anent a Project, for Erecting a Library, in Every Presbytry, or a Least County in the Highlands. Edinbrugh: 1702. V. 47
Good Times/Bad Times. New York: 1968. V. 51
An Overture for Founding and Maintaining of Bibliothecks in Every Paroch Through-Out This Kingdom: Humbly Offered to the Consideration of this Present Assembly. Edinburgh: 1699. V. 47
Proposals Made by Rev. James Kirkwood in 1699, to Found PUblic Libraries in Scotland. London: 1889. V. 52
Proposals Made by Rev. James Kirkwood...in 1699, to Found Public Libraries in Scotland. London: 1899. V. 47
P.S. Your Cat is Dead. New York: 1972. V. 51

KIRKWOOD, JIM
There Must Be a Pony!. Boston: 1960. V. 51

KIRKWOOD, ROBERT
The Journal and Order Book of Captain Robert Kirkwood of the Delaware Regiment of the Continental Line. Wilmington: 1910. V. 50

KIRMSE, MARGUERITE
Dogs. New York: 1930. V. 48
Dogs in the Field. 1935. V. 51
Dogs in the Field. New York: 1935. V. 47

KIRN, WALTER
My Hard Bargain. New York: 1990. V. 50

KIRSCHSTEIN, S.
Juedische Graphiker aus der Zeit von 1624-1825. Berlin: 1918. V. 53

KIRSTEIN, LINCOLN
Elie Nadleman. New York: 1973. V. 49
For My Brother. London: 1943. V. 48; 50; 51
The New York City Ballet. New York: 1973. V. 52
Paul Cadmus. New York: 1984. V. 51
Walker Evans: American Photographs. New York: 1938. V. 52

KIRTIKAR, K. R.
Indian Medicinal Plants. 1984. V. 47
Indian Medicinal Plants. Dehra Dun: 1986. V. 49

KIRTON, JOHN WILLIAM
Buy Your Own Ghosts. London: 1869. V. 49
The Gin Shop. London: 1869. V. 49

KIRWAN, RICHARD
Elements of Mineralogy. London: 1784. V. 49
An Essay on the Analysis of Mineral Waters. London: 1799. V. 50
An Estimate of the Temperature of Different Latitudes. London: 1787. V. 50; 54
Logick; or, an Essay on the Elements, Principles and Different Modes of Reasoning. London: 1807. V. 48
The Manures Most Advantageously Applicable to the Various Sorts of Soils, and the Causes of Their Beneficial Effects in Each Particular Instance. London: 1796. V. 53

KISCH, BRUNO
Electron Microscopic Histology of the Heart. New York: 1951. V. 53

KISSAM, RICHARD S.
The Nurse's Manual and Young Mother's Guide: Containing Advice to the Management of Infants and Conduct to be Observed by the Mother Before and After Child-Birth. Hartford: 1834. V. 54

THE KIT Book for Soldiers, Sailors and Marines. Chicago: 1942. V. 49
THE KIT Book for Soldiers, Sailors and Marines. Chicago: 1943. V. 48; 50; 51; 52

KIT-CAT Club: Memoirs of the Celebrated Persons Composing the Kit-Cat Club; with a Prefatory Account of the Origin of the Association. London: 1821. V. 51

KITAJ, R. B.
R. B. Kitaj: a Retrospective. London: 1994. V. 51

KITAZUME, EITARO
W. H. Davies. Tokyo: 1934. V. 50

KITCHEN, D. C.
Record of the Wyoming Artillerists. Tunkhannock: 1874. V. 49

THE KITCHEN Directory, and American Housewife: Containing the Most Valuable and Original Receipts, In All the Various Branches of Cookery... New York: 1841. V. 48

KITCHENER, WILLIAM
A Companion to the Telescope. London: 1811. V. 50

KITCHIN, C. H. B.
Streamers Waving. London: 1925. V. 52

KITCHIN, JOHN
Le Court Leete et Court Baron Collect per Iohn Kitchin de Greies Inne..Ouesque Diuers Nouel Additions, Come Court de Marshalsey, Auncient, Demesne Court de Pipowders, Essoines, Imparlance & Diuers Auter Matters. London: 1598. V. 52
Jurisdictions: or, the Lawful Authority of Courts Leet, Courts Baron, Court of Marshalseyes, Court of Pypowder, and Ancient Demesne. London: 1653. V. 52

KITCHINER, JOHN
The Horse and Carriage Oracle; or, Rules for Purchasing and Keeping, or Jobbing Horses and Carriages... London: 1828. V. 47

KITCHINER, WILLIAM
The Cook's Oracle... Boston: 1822. V. 51
The Cook's Oracle... London: 1823. V. 50
The Cook's Oracle... New York: 1830. V. 48; 52
The Cook's Oracle... New York: 1831. V. 51
The Cook's Oracle... New York: 1838. V. 47
The Economy of the Eyes... London: 1824. V. 53; 54

KITCHING, ARTHUR LEONARD
On the Backwaters of the Nile. London: 1912. V. 50; 52

KITE, OLIVER
A Fisherman's Diary. London: 1969. V. 53

KITMAS, K. K.
Country Poems. Pownal: 1969. V. 49

KITSON, ARTHUR
Captain James Cook, R.N., f.R.S. "The Circumnavigator". New York: 1907. V. 48

KITSON, SYDNEY D.
The Life of John Sell Cotman. London: 1937. V. 53

THE KITTEN Who Listened. New York: 1950. V. 53

KITTENBERGER, KALMAN
Big Game Hunting and Collecting in East Africa 1903-1926. New York: 1929. V. 47

KITTLITZ, FRIEDRICH HEINRICH VON
Twenty-Four Views of the Vegetation of the Coasts and Islands of the Pacific... London: 1861. V. 51

KITTON, FREDERIC GEORGE
Dickens and His Ilustrators: Cruikshank, Seymour, Buss, "Phiz", Cattermole, Leech, Doyle, Stanfield, Maclise, Tenniel, Frank Stone, Ladseer, Palmer, Topham, marcus Stone and Luke Fildes. London: 1899. V. 49; 54
Dickens Illustrations. London: 1900. V. 54
Dickensiana, a Bibliography of the Literature Relating to Charles Dickens and His Writings. London: 1886. V. 51
John Leech, Artist and Humourist... London: 1883. V. 48
The Novels of Charles Dickens: a Bibliography and Sketch. (with) *The Minor Writings of Charles Dickens.* London: 1897-1900. V. 49
Phiz: a memoir. London: 1872. V. 51

KITTREDGE, WILLIAM
Hole in the Sky. New York: 1992. V. 53; 54
Lost Cowboys (but Not Forgotten). New York: 1992. V. 51; 53; 54
We Are Not In This Together. Port Townsend: 1984. V. 53

KITTY Dan; a Poem. Leicester: 1808. V. 54

KIYOOKA, ROY
Kyoto Airs. Vancouver: 1964. V. 47
Nevertheless These Eyes. Toronto: 1967. V. 47

KIYOSU, YUKIYASU
The Birds of Japan. Tokyo: 1952. V. 48

KIZER, CAROLYN
Ungrateful Garden. Bloomington: 1961. V. 47; 51; 53

KJELLMAN, F. R.
The Algae of the Arctic Sea, a Survey of the Species, Together With an Exposition of the General Characters and Development of the Flora... Stockholm: 1883. V. 48

KLADO, NICOLAS
The Battle of the Sea of Japan. London: 1906. V. 48

KLAH, HASTEEN
Navajo Creation Myth. Santa Fe: 1942. V. 49; 53

KLAPP, H. MINOR
Krider's Sporting Anecdotes, Illustrative of the Habits of Certain Varieties of American Game. Philadelphia: 1853. V. 50; 51

KLASNER, LILY
My Girlhood Among Outlaws. Tucson: 1972. V. 52

KLAUBER, LAURENCE M.
A Herpetological Review of the Hopi Snake Dance. 1932. V. 54
Rattlesnakes. Their Habits, Life Histories and Influence on Mankind. 1956. V. 50
Rattlesnakes: Their Habits, Life Histories and Influence On Mankind. Berkeley: 1956. V. 52

KLEE, PAUL
The Diaries of Paul Klee 1898-1918. London: 1965. V. 49; 54
The Inward Vision: Watercolors, Drawings, Writings. New York: 1959. V. 47; 50; 51; 53; 54
Notebooks. Vol. I: The Thinking Eye: Volume II: The Nature of Nature. New York: 1961/73. V. 47
Notebooks. Volume I: The Thinking Eye. Volume II: The Nature of Nature. London: 1973. V. 48; 49; 50; 52
The Thinking Eye: the Notebooks... 1961. V. 47
The Thinking Eye: The Notebooks. Wittenborn: 1961. V. 50

KLEECK, MARY
Women in the Bookbinding Trade. New York: 1913. V. 48

KLEIN, A. M.
The Hitleriad. New York: 1944. V. 51
The Rocking Chair. Toronto: 1948. V. 54

KLEIN, ADRIAN BERNARD
Colour-Music: the Art of Light. London: 1926. V. 48; 51

KLEIN, AUGUSTA
Among the Gods. Edinburgh & London: 1895. V. 49

KLEIN, EDWARD E.
Studies in Bacteriology and Etiology of Oriental Plague. London: 1906. V. 50

KLEIN, HERMANN J.
Star Atlas, Containing Maps of All the Stars from 1 to 6.5 Magnitude Between the North Pole.... London: 1888. V. 49

KLEIN, JACOB THEODOR
Ova Avium Plurimarum ad Naturalem Magnitudinem Delineata et Genuinis Coloribus Picta. Leipzig: 1766. V. 47
Stemmata Avivm. Lipsiae: 1759. V. 49; 53

KLEIN, WILLIAM
Mr. Freedom. Paris: 1970. V. 54
Moscow. New York: 1964. V. 47; 48
Photogrpahs. 1981. V. 52
Rome: The City and Its People. New York: 1959. V. 47; 49; 50

KLEINER, ROBERT W. L.
An Exhibition of Chinese Snuff Bottles from the Collection of Mary and George Boch at the Galleries of Sydney L. Moss, Ltd. London: 1987. V. 49

KLEINER, SOLOMON
Representation Au Naturel des Chateaux de Weissenstein au Dessus De Pommersfeld et...Geubach. Augusburg: 1728. V. 48

KLEINHOLZ, FRANK
Frank Kleinholz: a Self Portrait. New York: 1964. V. 52
Kleinholz Graphics: Catalogue Raisonne 1940-1975. Miami: 1975. V. 50

KLEINSCHMIDT, BEDA
Die Basilika San Francisco in Assisi. Berlin: 1915/26/28. V. 49

KLEYKAMP, JAN
The Jan Kleykamp Collection, Chinese and Japanese Paintings. New York: 1925. V. 51

KLIMT, GUSTAV
Erotic Drawings. London: 1980. V. 47
Erotic Drawings. New York: 1980. V. 51
Twenty-Five Drawings Selected and Interpreted by Alice Strobl. Vienna: 1964. V. 52

KLINE, OTIS ADELBERT
The Plant of Peril. 1929. V. 48

KLINEFELTER, WALTER
A Bibliographical Check-List of Christmas Books. Portland: 1937. V. 48

KLINGER, FRIEDRICH MAXIMILIAN VON
Travels Before the Flood. London: 1796. V. 49
Travels Before the Flood... London: 1797. V. 54

KLINGER, JULIUS
Das Weib Im Modernen Ornament. Leipzig: 1902. V. 47

KLINGER, MAX
Amor und Psyche. Munchen: 1881. V. 49; 53

KLIPPART, JOHN H.
The Wheat Plant: Its Origin, Culture, Growth, Development, Composition, Varities, Diseases, etc. Cincinnati: 1860. V. 47; 50; 52

KLIPSTEIN, A.
Kathe Kollwitz: Verzeichnis des Graphischen Werkes. Bern: 1955. V. 53; 54

KLIX, F.
Human Memory and Cognitive Abilities: Mechanisms and Performances. Amsterdam: 1986. V. 54

KLONDIKE & BOSTON GOLD MINING & MANUFACTURING CO.
Placer Gold. Concerning the Klondike & Boston Gold Mining and Manufacturing Company's Rich Palcer Mines in Willow Creek, Southern Alaska. Boston: 1902-03. V. 52

KLONDIKE: The Chicago Record's Book for Gold Seekers. Chicago: 1897. V. 48; 49

KLONDYKE and Yukon Guide. Alaska and Northwest Territory gold Fields. Seattle: 1898. V. 50

KLONDYKE Souvenir. Drayton: 1901. V. 53

KLOPSTOCK, FRIEDRICH
Memoirs of Frederick and Margaret Klopstock. Bath: 1808. V. 52

KLOPSTOCK, FRIEDRICH GOTTLIEB
Klopstock and His Friends. London: 1814. V. 49; 51
The Messiah. London: 1770. V. 53

KLOSS, B. C.
In the Andamans and Nicobars...in the schooner "Terrapin" with Notices of the Islands, Their Fauna, Ethnology, Etc. London: 1903. V. 48

KLOSS, GEORG FRANZ BURKHARD
Catalogue of the Library of Dr. Kloss... 1835. V. 47
Catalogue of the Library of Dr. Kloss... London: 1835. V. 48; 54

KLUCKER, CHRISTIAN
Adventures of an Alpine Guide. 1932. V. 53
Adventures Of An Alpine Guide. London: 1932. V. 50

KLUCKHORN, CLYDE
To the Foot of the Rainbow: A Tale of Twenty-Five Hundred Miles of Wandering on Horseback... New York: 1927. V. 47

KNAB, MICHAEL
Hortipomolegium, Das ist Ein Sehr Liebreich und Ausserlesen Obstgarten und Peltzbuch... Nurnberg: 1620. V. 49

KNAPP, ANDREW
The Newgate Calendar. Liverpool: 1809-10. V. 54
The Newgate Calendar Improved... London: 1826. V. 47; 49

KNAPP, F. H.
The Botanical Chart of British Flowering Plants and Ferns. Bath: 1846. V. 50

KNAPP, HERMANN
Cocaine and Its Use in Ophthalmic and General Surgery... New York: 1885. V. 47; 51

KNAPP, JOHN LEONARD
The Journal of a Naturalist. London: 1829. V. 52
The Journal of a Naturalist. London: 1838. V. 51

KNAPP, OSWALD G.
The Intimate Letters of Hester Piozzi and Penelope Pennington 1788-1821. London: 1914. V. 54

KNAPP, SAMUEL LORENZO
Biographical Sketches of Eminent Lawyers, Statesmen and Men of Letters. Boston: 1821. V. 51
Extracts from a Journal of Travels in North America.... Boston: 1818. V. 51; 54
Female Biography... Philadelphia: 1865. V. 53
Letters of Shacoolen, a Hindu Philosopher Residing in Philadelphia... Boston: 1802. V. 50; 54

KNAPP, WILLIAM I.
Life, Writings and Correspondence of George Borrow. London: 1899. V. 51

KNAPPE, KARL ADOLF
Durer: The Complete Engravings, Etchings and Woodcuts. New York: 1965. V. 51

KNATCHBULL-HUGESSEN, C. M.
The Poetical Evolution of the Hungarian Nation. London: 1908. V. 49

KNAUSS, WILLIAM H.
The Story of Camp Chase a History of the Prison and Its Cemetery, Together With Other Cemeteries Where Confederate Prisoners are Buried, Etc. Nashville: 1906. V. 54

KNEALE, W.
Kneale's Guide to the Isle of Man, Comprising an Account of the Island, Historical, Physical, Archaeological and Topographical... Douglas: 1855. V. 53

KNECHT, R.
The Voyage of Sir Nicholas Carewe... Cambridge: 1959. V. 47; 54

KNEELAND, ABNER
The Antitheistical Catechism, Being a Complete Refutation of Both Ancient & Modern Theology. Boston: 1831. V. 49
An Appeal to Univeralists, on the Subject of Excommunication, or the Withdrawing of Fellowship, on Account of Diversity of Opinion. New York: 1829. V. 53
National Hymns, Original and Selected: for the Use of Those Who are "Slaves to No Sect". Boston: 1832. V. 53

KNEELAND, SAMUEL
The Wonders of the Yosemite Valley and of California. Boston and New York: 1872. V. 47; 48; 51; 53

KNEEN, J. J.
The Place-Names of the Isle of Man. London: 1970. V. 54

KNEIPP, SEBASTIAN
Plant-Atlas to "My Water-Cure" Containing Sixty Nine Pictorial Representations of All the Medicinal Plants Mentioned as Well as Some Others in General Use Among the People. Kempten: 1891. V. 51

KNELLER, GODFREY
The Kit-Cat Club Done from the Original Paintings of Sr. Godfrey Kneller by Mr. Faber. London: 1735. V. 47

KNEWSTUB, JOHN
The Lectures of John Knewstub, Upon the Twentith (sic) Chapter of Exodus, and Certeine Other Places of Scripture. London: 1578. V. 49

KNIBBS, HENRY HERBERT
First Poems. Rochester. V. 49

KNIBBS, S. G. C.
The Savage Solomons as They Were and Are. London: 1929. V. 50

KNIGGE, ADOLF FRANZ
Practical Philosophy of Social Life; or, the Art of Conversing With Men, After the German of Baron Knigge by P. Will. Lansingburgh: 1805. V. 48

KNIGHT & SLOVER
Indian Atrocities. Narratives of the Perils and Sufferings of...Among the Indians, During the Revolutionary War... Cincinnati: 1867. V. 53

KNIGHT, ANN
Poetic Gleanings, from Modern Writers... London: 1827. V. 49
Poetic Gleanings, from Modern Writers... London: 1833. V. 48

KNIGHT, C. MORLEY
Hints of Driving. London: 1911. V. 47

KNIGHT, CHARLES
An Address to the Subscribers to the Windsor and Eton Public Library, Delivered in the Town-Hall Windsor on the 29th October 1833. London: 1833. V. 50
The Bridal of the Isles; a Mask. London: 1817. V. 52
Cyclopaedia of London. London: 1851. V. 51
Half-Hours with the Best Authors. London. V. 51
History of England. London: 1862. V. 50
Knight's Cyclopaedia of the Industry of All Nations, 1851. London: 1851. V. 50
The Land We Live In. London: 1854-56. V. 49
London... London: 1841. V. 54
London. London: 1841-43. V. 47
London. London: 1841-44. V. 53
Old England: a Pictorial Museum... London. V. 51
Old England: a Pictorial Museum... London: 1844. V. 48; 50
Old England, A Pictorial Museum... London: 1845-46. V. 49
Old England: a Pictorial Museum... London: 1845-47. V. 51
Old England: a Pictorial Museum. London: 1860. V. 48; 51; 52
Old England: a Pictorial Museum... London: 1865. V. 53
The Old Printer and the Modern Press. London: 1854. V. 52
Passages of a Working Life During Half a Century... London: 1864. V. 54
Penny Cyclopaedia. London: 1833-43. V. 51
The Popular History of England... London: 1856. V. 54
The Popular History of England. London: 1856-62. V. 48; 51; 53
The Popular History of England... London: 1870. V. 51
The Popular History of England. London: 1888. V. 47; 48
The Struggles of a Book Against Excessive Taxation. London: 1850. V. 51

KNIGHT, CLIFFORD
The Affair of the Skiing Clown. New York: 1941. V. 52; 53

KNIGHT, EDWARD FREDERICK
The Cruise of the "Falcon": a Voyage to South America. London: 1906. V. 54
Turkey the Awakening of Turkey the Turkish Revolution of 1908. Boston and Tokyo: 1910. V. 54

KNIGHT, ELLIS CORNELIA
A Description of Latium or La Campagna di Roma. London: 1805. V. 47
Dinarbas: a Tale... London: 1779. V. 47
Dinarbas; a Tale. London: 1790. V. 48; 50; 54
Dinarbas: a Tale. London: 1792. V. 48
Dinarbas, a Tale. London: 1793. V. 50; 51
Marcus Flaminius. An Historical Novel. London: 1795. V. 47

KNIGHT, ERIC
Lassie Come Home. Chicago: 1940. V. 50

KNIGHT, FREDERICK
Modern and Antique Gems. London: 1828. V. 54
Vases and Ornaments Designed for the Use of Architects, Silversmiths, Jewellers, Modellers, Chasers. London: 1833. V. 51

KNIGHT, HENRY COGSWELL
The Cypriad in Two Cantos; with Other Poems and Translations. Boston: 1809. V. 48
Letters From the South and West. Boston: 1824. V. 48

KNIGHT, HENRY GALLY
Ilderim: a Syrian Tale. (with) Phrosyne: a Grecian Tale. Alashtar: an Arabian Tale. London: 1817/16-17. V. 54

KNIGHT, HERBERT BILLINGSHURST FINLAY
A Girl With a Temper. A Romance of the Wills Act. London: 1892. V. 53

KNIGHT, J. H.
Light Moter Cars and Voiturettes. London: 1902. V. 47

KNIGHT, JOHN
Narratives of the Perils and Sufferings of Dr. Knight and John Slover, Among the Indians, During the Revolutionary War, With Short Memoirs of Col. Crawford and John Slover, and a Letter From H. Brackenridge on the Rights of the Indians, Etc. Cincinnati: 1867. V. 48

KNIGHT, JOHN ALDEN
Woodcock. New York: 1944. V. 47

KNIGHT, JOSEPH
David Garrick. London: 1894. V. 52

KNIGHT, LAURA
A Book of Drawings. London: 1923. V. 49
A Proper Circus Omie. London: 1962. V. 53

KNIGHT, RICHARD PAYNE
An Analytical Inquiry Into the Principles of Taste. London: 1805. V. 47; 49
The Landscape, a Didactic Poem. London: 1794. V. 48
A Monody on the Death of the Right Honourable Charles James Fox. London: 1806-07. V. 50; 54
The Progress of Civil Society. London: 1796. V. 48

KNIGHT, S. G., MRS.
Minnie Maverick; or, Man's Wrongs and Woman's Foibles. New York: 1870. V. 53

KNIGHT, SAMUEL
The Life of Dr. John Colet, Dean of St. Paul's...Founder of St. Paul's School... London: 1724. V. 50
The Life of Dr. John Colet, Dean of St. Paul's...Founder of St. Paul's School. Oxford: 1823. V. 53

KNIGHT, SARAH K.
The Journals of Madam Knight and Rev. Mr. Buckingham. New York: 1825. V. 52

KNIGHT, T., & SON
Suggestions for House Decoration. London: 1880. V. 50

KNIGHT, THOMAS ANDREW
A Selection from the Physiological and Horticultural Papers... London: 1841. V. 53

KNIGHT, TITUS
An Elegy on the Death of the Late Revd. Mr. George Whitefield, A.M. and Chaplain to the Right Honourable the Countess of Huntington. Halifax: 1771. V. 48

KNIGHT, WILLIAM
Principal Shairp and His Friends. London: 1888. V. 54

KNIGHT, WILLIAM A.
The Life of William Wordsworth. 1889. V. 47
The Life of William Wordsworth. Edinburgh: 1889. V. 50
Wordsworthiana - a Selection from Papers Read to the Wordsworth Society. London: 1889. V. 50

KNIGHT, WILLIAM HENRY
Diary of a Pedestrian in Cashmere and Thibet. London: 1863. V. 48; 50; 53

KNIGHTLEY, PHILLIP
The Secret Lives of Lawrence of Arabia. London: 1969. V. 51

KNIGHTON, HENRY
Chronicon Henrici Knighton, vel Critthon, Monachi Leycestrensis. London: 1889-95. V. 49; 52

KNIGHTON, WILLIAM
Forest Life in Ceylon. London: 1854. V. 51
The History of Ceylon: From the Earliest Period to the Present Time... London: 1845. V. 51
Memoirs of Sir William Knighton, Bart., G. C. H., Keeper of the Privy Purse During the Reign of...George the Fourth. London: 1838. V. 48; 50; 53

THE KNIGHTS of the Frozen Sea. London: 1868. V. 50

KNIPE, WILLIAM
Criminal Chronology of York Castle, with a Register of the Criminals Capitally Convicted and Executed at the County Assizes, from 1379 to the Present Time. York: 1867. V. 53

KNISTER, RAYMOND
My Star Predominant. Toronto: 1934. V. 50

KNITL, KASPAR
Cosmographia Elementaris Propositionibus Physico-Mathematicis Proposita... Nuremberg: 1674. V. 47

KNOCKER, DOUGLAS
Accidents in Their Medico-Legal Aspect by Leading Medical and Surgical Authorities. London: 1912. V. 53

KNOLLES, RICHARD
The General Historie of the Turkes, from the First Beginning of that Nation... London: 1638. V. 52
The Turkish History, Comprehending the Origin of that Nation and the Growth of the Othoman Empire. London: 1704. V. 47

KNOOP, JOHANN HERMANN
Pomologia, das is Beschryvingen en Afbeeldingen van de Beste Soorten van Appels en Peeren... (with) Fructologia, of Beschryving der Vrugtbomen en Vrugten die men in de Hoeven...(with) Dendrologia, of Beschryving der Plantagie-Gewassen, die men in de... Leeuwarden: 1763. V. 47

KNOPF, ALFRED A.
Portrait of a Publisher. New York: 1965. V. 47; 48; 50; 54

KNORR, GEORG WOLFGANG
Thesaurus Rei Herbariae Hortenisque Universalis, Exhibens Figuras Florum, Herbarum, Arborum, Fruticum, Aliarumque Plantarum Prorsus Novas et ad Ipsos Delineatas Depictasque... Nurnberg: 1750-70-71. V. 49

KNOTT, CARGILL GILSTON
Life and Scientific Work of Peter Guthrie Tait... Cambridge: 1911. V. 48
Napier Tercentenary Memorial Volume. London: 1915. V. 47; 50; 51; 52; 54

KNOTT, FREDERICK
Dial "M" for Murder. New York: 1953. V. 52

KNOTT, J. FORTUNE
Wild Animals, Photographed and Described. London: 1886. V. 47

KNOTTS, BENJAMIN
Pennsylvania German Designs, a Portfolio of Silk Screen Prints. 1943. V. 48

KNOW NOTHING PARTY
Address: by the President of the State Council of Arkansas... Little Rock: 1855. V. 48
The American's Text-Book: Being a Series of Letters. Nashville: 1855. V. 48
Facts For the People! Read Before You Vote!! Americans Should Govern America!!. 1855. V. 48
The Satanic Plot, or Awful Crimes of Popery in High and Low Places. Boston: 1855. V. 48
Startling Facts For Native Americans Called "Know Nothings", or a Vivid Presentation of the Dangers to American Liberty to be Apprehended from Foreign Influence. New York: 1855. V. 48

KNOWLE Estate (Cranleigh, Surrey) Particulars. London: 1878. V. 52

KNOWLER, WILLIAM
The Earl of Strafforde's Letters and Dispatches, With an Essay Towards His Life... Dublin: 1740. V. 47

KNOWLES, DAVID
Monastic Sites from the Air. Cambridge: 1952. V. 49

KNOWLES, E. H.
The Castle of Kenilworth, a Hand-Book for Visitors. Warwick: 1872. V. 52

KNOWLES, G. B.
The Floral Cabinet and Magazine of Exotic Botany. London: 1837. V. 49

KNOWLES, JAMES
A Pronouncing and Explanatory Dictionary of the English Language. London: 1835. V. 52
A Vocabulary of the Greek, Latin and Scripture Proper Names, with Their Classical Pronunciation Correctly Marked. London: 1835. V. 52

KNOWLES, JAMES SHERIDAN
The Beggar's Daughter of Bethnal Green. London: 1828. V. 52
The Dramatic Works. London: 1841. V. 53
The Dramatic Works... London: 1841-43. V. 48
The Dramatic Works... London: 1843. V. 47

KNOWLES, JOHN
Morning in Antibes. London: 1962. V. 52; 53; 54
A Separate Peace. London: 1959. V. 54
A Separate Peace. New York: 1960. V. 49

KNOWLES, JOHN A.
Essays in the History of the York School of Glass Painting. London: 1936. V. 53

KNOWLES, PATRICK
Cloud's Hill - Dorset "An Handful with Quietness" - T. E. Lawrence: a Final and Important Eye-Witness Account. Dorset. V. 53

KNOWLSON, J.
A Journal of Becket Studies. 1976-85. V. 54

KNOWLSON, JOHN C.
The Yorkshire Cattle-Doctor and Farrier. Otley: 1864. V. 54

KNOWLSON, SAMUEL
Samuel Beckett: an Exhibition - Held at Reading University Library, May to July 1971 - also Held at the Institute of Contemprary Arts and the National Book League, August 10 to September 1971 - The University of East Anglia, Oct. to Dec. 1971. London: 1971. V. 54

KNOWLTON, CHARLES
Elements of Modern Materialism... Adams: 1829. V. 49

KNOWN Fables. New York: 1964. V. 49

KNOX, A. E.
Autumns on the Spey. London: 1872. V. 47
Game Birds and Wild Fowl: The Friends and Their Foes. London: 1850. V. 51
Ornithological Rambles in Sussex... London: 1849. V. 53

KNOX, ALEXANDER
The Climate of the Continent of Africa. Cambridge: 1911. V. 48

KNOX, CHARLES H.
Harry Mowbray. London: 1843. V. 51

KNOX, E. BLAKE
Buller's Campaign with Field Force of 1900. London: 1902. V. 54

KNOX, GEORGE
Giambattista and Domenico Tiepolo. 1980. V. 49
Giambattista and Domenico Tiepolo. A Study and Catalogue Raisonne of the Chalk Drawings. Oxford: 1980. V. 54

KNOX, JOHN
An Historical Journal of the Campaigns in North-America, for the Years 1757, 1758, 1759 and 1760. London: 1769. V. 53; 54
The Historie of the Reformation of Religion Within the Realm of Scotland...Together with the Life of John Knoxe the author... Edinburgh: 1732. V. 51
The Historie of the Reformation of the Church of Scotland... Edinburgh: 1644. V. 48
Knox's Investors' Guide, Topeka, Kansas Real Estate Mortgage Loans. Topeka: 1885. V. 52
A Tour through the Highlands of Scotland and the Hebride Isles in 1786. London: 1787. V. 47; 49

KNOX, JOHN P.
A Historical Account of St. Thomas, W.I., with its Rise...in Commerce...Climate...Natural History and Botany and Incidental Notices of St. Croix and St. Johns... New York: 1852. V. 50; 54

KNOX, NORTHRUP R.
To. B. A. and Back...Again. 1966. V. 49

KNOX, R.
Memories of the Future - Being Memoirs of the Years 1915-1972 Written in the Year of Grace 1988... 1923. V. 49

KNOX, ROBERT
The Races of Men: a Fragment. London: 1850. V. 53

KNOX, RONALD ARBUTHNOTT
Juxta Salices. Oxford: 1910. V. 50
A Selection from the Occasional Sermons of the Right Reverend Monsignor Ronald Knox... London: 1949. V. 48
Sermons. London: 1949. V. 49

KNOX, SEYMOUR H.
Polo Tales and Other Tales 1921-1971. V. 47

KNOX, THOMAS W.
Camp-Fire and Cotton-Field; Southern Adventures in the Time of War. New York: 1865. V. 52
The Travels of Marco Polo for Boys and Girls. New York: 1885. V. 48

KNOX, VICESIMUS
Liberal Education; or, a Practical Treatise on the Methods of Acquiring Useful and Polite Learning. Dublin: 1781. V. 47
Liberal Education; or, a Practical Treatise on the Methods of Acquiring Useful and Polite Learning. London: 1782. V. 53
Liberal Education; or, a Practical Treatise on the Methods of Acquiring Useful and Polite Learning. London: 1783. V. 47
Liberal Education; or, a Practical Treatise on the Methods of Acquiring Useful and Polite Learning. London: 1789. V. 47
The Spirit of Despotism. London: 1795. V. 53
The Spirit of Despotism. London: 1822. V. 50

KNUTTEL, GERARD
The Letter as a Work of Art. Amsterdam: 1951. V. 49; 50

KNUTTEL, W. P. C.
Catalogus Van de Pamfletten-Verzameling Berustende in De Koninklijke Bibliotheek. Utrecht: 1978. V. 48

KOBAYASHI, K.
Catalogue of Japanese Birds and Eggs (Including Formosan Birds). Yokohama: 1910. V. 48
The Eggs of Japanese Birds. Kobe: 1932-40. V. 48

KOBAYASHI, T.
Geology and Palaeontology of Southeast Asia. Tokyo: 1964-66. V. 54

KOBBE, G.
Opera Singers: a Pictorial Souvenir. Boston: 1906. V. 49

KOBEL, JACOB
Astrolabii Declaratio, Eivsdemqve Usus Mire Iucundus, Non Modo Astrologis, Medicis, Geographis, Caeterisque Literarum Cultoribus Multum Utilis ac Necessarius... Paris: 1550. V. 52

KOBER, GEORGE M.
Diseases of Occupation and Vocational Hygiene. Philadelphia: 1916. V. 47; 48; 53

KOBER, GEORGE M. continued
Reminiscences of George Martin Kober, M.D., LL.D. Washington: 1930. V. 48

KOCH, ALBERT
Description of the Missourium, or Missouri Leviathan... Louisville: 1841. V. 48

KOCH, CHARLES R. E.
History of Dental Surgery. Fort Wayne: 1910. V. 48; 49; 50; 51

KOCH, FREDERICK H.
Carolina Folk-Plays. (Second Series). New York: 1924. V. 53
The Return of Buck Gavin, the Tragedy of a Mountain Outlaw. 1924. V. 50

KOCH, KENNETH
Nell Blaine - Prints: Kenneth Koch - Poems. New York: 1952. V. 53
Poems from 1952-1953. 1968. V. 47; 48; 49
Quinevere, or the Death of the Kangaroo. New York: 1961. V. 52
When the Sun Tries to Go On. Los Angeles: 1969. V. 47; 51; 52

KOCH, ROBERT
Bacteriological Diagnosis of Cholera, Water-filtration in Cholera, and the Cholera in Germany During the winter of 1892-93. Edinburgh: 1894. V. 51; 53
Investigations into the Etiology of Traumatic Infective Diseases. London: 1880. V. 51; 53
Louis C. Tiffany. New York: 1976. V. 53

KOCH, RUDOLF
Das Blumentbuch. Darmstadt: 1929-30. V. 47
The Typefoundry in Silhouette. San Francisco: 1982. V. 48

KOCHER, FRANZ
Die Babylonisch-Assyrische Medizin in Texten und Untersuchungen. Berlin: 1963-80. V. 49

KOCHER, THEODOR
Operative Surgery. New York: 1894. V. 47
Text-Book of Operative Surgery. London: 1911. V. 47
Text-Book of Operative Surgery. New York: 1911. V. 47; 48; 49; 50; 54

KOCIEJOWSKI, MARIUS
The Testament of Charlotte B. 1988. V. 47
The Testament of Charlotte B. London: 1988. V. 50
The Testament of Charlotte B. Wiltshire: 1988. V. 53

KOCK, CHARLES PAUL DE
The Barber of Paris... Paris: 1839. V. 47
The Barber of Paris... Boston, Paris, London: 1903. V. 47
The Barber of Paris. New York: 1903. V. 53
The Gogo Family. Boston: 1903. V. 48
A Queer Legacy. New York: 1906. V. 50
The Works. Boston: 1902. V. 48

KOEBEL, W. H.
The Romance of the River Plate. London: 1914. V. 48

KOECHLIN, R.
Oriental Art: Ceramics, Fabrics, Carpets. New York: 1920's. V. 54
Oriental Art. Ceramics, Fabrics, Carpets. New York: 1930. V. 48

KOECKER, LEONARD
An Essay on Diseases of the Jaws, and Their Treatment... London: 1847. V. 50

KOEHLER, S. R.
Catalogue of the Engraved and Lithographed Work of John Cheney and Seth Wells Cheney. Boston: 1891. V. 54

KOEHN, ALFRED
The Art of Japanese Flower Arrangement (Ikebana). Kobe: 1933. V. 54

KOELLIKER, ALBERT VON
Observationes de prima Insectorum Genesi Adiecta Articulatorum Evolutionis cum Vertebratorum Comparationi... Zurich: 1842. V. 49

KOENIG, A. F.
Avifauna Spitzbergensis. Bonn: 1911. V. 51
Reisen und Forschungen in Algerien, 1. London: 1895-96. V. 51

KOENIG, ARTHUR
Authentic History of the Indian Campaign Which Culminated in Custer's Last Battle June 25, 1876. St. Louis. V. 49; 54

KOENIG, EBERHARD
The 1462 Fust & Schoeffer Bible. Austin: 1993. V. 51; 52

KOENIGSMARACK, H. VON
The Markhor, Sport in Cashmere. London: 1910. V. 48

KOEPPEN, ADOLPHUS LOUIS
Historico-Geographical Atlas of the Middle Ages Containing a Series of Six General Maps; Delineating the Migrations of the Northern and Eastern Nations, Together with the States Arising from Their Fusion with the Ancient Roman Empire... New York & London: 1855. V. 51

KOESTER, AUGUST
Ship Models of the Seventeenth to the Nineteenth Centuries. New York: 1926. V. 47

KOESTER, F.
Under the Desert Stars. 1923. V. 48; 52

KOESTLER, ARTHUR
The Age of Longing. New York: 1951. V. 48; 50; 51; 54
Darkness at Noon. London: 1940. V. 53
Darkness at Noon. 1979. V. 49
Spanish Testament. London: 1937. V. 47
The Spanish Testament. London: 1938. V. 51
Thieves in the Night. New York: 1947. V. 48
The Trial of the Dinosaur. New York: 1955. V. 50

KOFOID, C. A.
The Plankton of the Illinois River, 1894-1899. Urbana: 1903-08. V. 53

KOHL, JOHANN GEORG
Austria. Vienna, Prague, Hungary, Bohemia and the Danube; Galicia, Styria, Moravia. London: 1843. V. 53
A History of the Discovery of the ...Coast of Maine, from the Northmen in 990 to the Charter of Gilbert in 1578. Portland: 1869. V. 51
Russia. St. Petersburg, Moscow, Kharkoff, Riga, Odessa, the German Provinces of the Baltic, the Steppes, the Crimea and the Interior of the Empire. London: 1842. V. 53
Wanderings Round Lake Surperior. London: 1860. V. 48; 52; 54

KOHLHANS, JOHANN CHRISTOPH
Cometa Generalis cum Speciali, Oder Cometen-Konig, Welcher im 1664 und 1665 Jahr am Himmel Erschienen... Nurnberg: 1665. V. 50; 54

KOHN, DAVID
Internal Improvement in South Carolina, 1817-1828. Washington: 1938. V. 50

KOHN, FERDINAND
Iron and Steel Manufacture. London: 1869. V. 53

KOHNER, FREDERICK
Gidget. New York: 1957. V. 53

KOKINMEIBUTSU Ruishu. (Collection of Special Products, Ancient and Present Cloths.). Tokyo: 1791. V. 52

KOKOSCHKA, OSKAR
Oskar Kokoschka October-November 1966. New York: 1966. V. 47

KOLB BROTHERS
The Grand Canyon of Arizona. Grand Canyon: 1914. V. 47

KOLDEWEY, KARL
The German Arctic Expedition of 1869-70, and Narrative of the Wreck of the "Hansa" in the Ice... London: 1874. V. 48; 49; 51; 52

KOLLE, FREDERICK STRANGE
Plastic and Cosmetic Surgery. New York and London: 1911. V. 47; 51; 54

KOLLMANN, AUGUST FRIEDRICH CHRISTOPH
Remarks on What Mr. J. B. Logier Calls His New System of Musical Education; with a Sequel. London: 1824. V. 49

KOLLMANN, PAUL
The Victoria Nyanza. London: 1899. V. 47; 50; 51

KOLLNER, AUGUSTUS
Public Buildings and Statuary of the Government: The Public Buildings and Architectural Ornaments of the Capitol of the United States at the City of Washington. Washington: 1839. V. 47

KOLLWITZ, KAETHE
The Diaries and Letters. Chicago: 1955. V. 50; 53

KOLODNY, ANATOLE
Bone Sarcoma: the Primary Malignant Tumors of Bone and Giant Cell tumor. Chicago: 1927. V. 53

KOLPACOFF, VICTOR
The Prisoners of Quai Dong. London: 1967. V. 49

KOLTHOFF, KJELL
Studies on Birds in the Chinese Provinces of Kianxu and Anhwei 1921-1922. Gothenburg: 1932. V. 53

KOMENSKY, JOHN AMOS
The Labyrinth of the World and the Paradise of the Heart. London: 1950. V. 48
The Labyrinth of the World and the Paradise of the Heart. Waltham St. Lawrence: 1950. V. 48; 52

KOMROFF, MANUEL
The Voice of Fire. Paris: 1927. V. 47

KONDOLEON, HARRY
The Cote d'Azur Triangle. New York: 1985. V. 50; 52

KONG, W. S.
The Plant Geography of Korea With an Emphasis on the Alpine Zones. Dordrecht: 1993. V. 50

KONKLE, BURTON
Standard History of the Medical Profession of Philadelphia. New York: 1977. V. 50; 52

KONSTAM, GERTRUDE A. M.
The May Pole. London: 1882. V. 48; 51

KONSTANTINOS o Sinaitis, Patriarchis Kon/Poleos: Constantiniade ou Description de Constantinople Ancienne et Moderne. Constantinople: 1846. V. 49

KONTOPOULOS, N.
A Lexikon Modern Greek-English and English-Modern Greek. Smyrna: 1867. V. 49

KOONTZ, DEAN R.
After the Last Race. New York: 1974. V. 49

KOONTZ, DEAN R. continued
Blood Risk. Indianapolis: 1973. V. 51
Chase. New York: 1972. V. 51; 52; 54
Dragon Tears. New York: 1993. V. 52; 53
Dragonfly. New York: 1975. V. 49; 50; 51; 52; 54
Dragonfly. 1977. V. 54
The Face of Fear. 1977. V. 48; 50
Hanging On. 1973. V. 48; 50; 52
Hanging On. New York: 1973. V. 48; 49; 51; 52
Hideaway. New York: 1992. V. 48; 51
The House of Thunder. 1988. V. 49; 51; 52; 53
The House of Thunder. Arlington Heights: 1988. V. 51; 52
How to Write Best Selling Fiction. Cincinnati: 1981. V. 49
The Mask. London: 1980. V. 52
Mr. Murder. New York: 1993. V. 51; 52; 53
Night Chills. 1976. V. 48
Night Chills. New York: 1976. V. 50; 51; 52; 53
Nightmare Journey. New York: 1975. V. 49; 50; 51; 52
Phantoms. New York: 1983. V. 47
Prison of Ice. Philadelphia: 1976. V. 48; 50
The Servants of Twilight. 1984. V. 52; 53
The Servants of Twilight. 1988. V. 48; 49; 51
The Servants of Twilight. Arlington Heights: 1988. V. 51; 52
Shattered. 1973. V. 47
Shattered. New York: 1973. V. 49; 52
The Vision. 1977. V. 48
The Vision. New York: 1977. V. 51
The Wall of Masks. Indianapolis: 1975. V. 51; 52
Whispers. New York: 1980. V. 51
Winter Moon. London: 1994. V. 51; 52
Writing Popular Fiction. Cincinnati: 1972. V. 50

KOONTZ, LOUIS KNOTT
Robert Dinwiddie: His Career in American Colonial Government and Westward Expansion. Glendale: 1941. V. 50

KOOP, ALBERT J.
Early Chinese Bronzes. London: 1924. V. 50; 52

KOOPMAN, HARRY LYMAN
Miniature Books. Los Angeles: 1968. V. 49

KOOPS, MATTHIAS
Historical Account of the Substances Which Have Been Used to Describe Events... London: 1801. V. 47; 48; 51; 52

KOOTENAY-CARIBOO MINING & INVESTMENT CO., LTD.
Prospectus. Traffic and Transportation. Toronto: 1898. V. 53

KOOY, J. M. J.
Ballistics of the Future: With Special Reference to the Dynamical and Physical theory of the Rocket Weapons. New York: 1946. V. 52

KORAN
L'Alcoran de Mahomet. Paris: 1647. V. 53
L'Alcoran de Mahomet. Amsterdam: 1649. V. 51; 52; 53
The Alcoran of Mahomet. London: 1649. V. 50
The Alcoran of Mahomet. London: 1688. V. 51
The Koran: Commonly called the Alcoran of Mahammed. London. V. 52
The Koran, Commonly Called the Alcoran of Mahomet. Springfield: 1806. V. 48; 50; 51
The Koran, Commonly called the Alcoran of Mohammed... Philadelphia: 1833. V. 51
The Koran. Selected Suras Translated from the Arabic by Arthur Jeffery. 1958. V. 50
Selected Sutras. New York: 1958. V. 48

KORESH
The Cellular Cosmogony or-Earth a Concave Sphere... 1905. V. 52

KORETSKY, ELAINE
The Gold-Beaters of Mandalay, an Account of Hand Papermaking in Burma Today. Brookline: 1991. V. 48

KORMAN, EZRA
Yidishe Dikhterins: Antologye. Detroit: 1928. V. 50

KORN, ERIC
Lepidoptera Fantastica. Leeds: 1993. V. 52
Lepidoptera Fantastica. Northampton: 1994. V. 51

KORN, GRANINO A.
Electronic Analog Computers. New York: 1952. V. 50; 52; 54

KORNBLUTH, C. M.
Not This August. New York: 1953. V. 54
Not This August. Garden City: 1955. V. 51
Takeoff. New York: 1952. V. 48

KORNMANN, HEINRICH
De Virginitatis Ivre Tractatvs Novvs et Ivcvndvs... Frankfurt: 1631. V. 48

KORNS, J. RODERIC
West from Fort Bridger. The Pioneering of the Immigrant Trails Across Utah, 1846-1850. Salt Lake City: 1951. V. 54

KORNWOLF, JAMES D.
M. H. Baillie Scott and the Arts and Crafts Movement. Pioneers of Modern Design. Baltimore and London: 1972. V. 49; 51

KORSMO, E.
Weed Seeds: Ugressfor: Unkrautsamen. Oslo: 1935. V. 54

KORTRIGHT, FRANCIS H.
The Ducks, Geese and Swans of North America. Washington: 1942. V. 47

KOSINSKI, JERZY
The Art of the Self: Essays A Propos "Steps". New York: 1968. V. 54
Being There. New York: 1970. V. 53
Blind Date. Boston: 1971. V. 48
Blind Date. Boston: 1977. V. 47; 51
Cockpit. Boston: 1975. V. 49
The Devil Tree. New York: 1973. V. 48
The Future Is Ours, Comrade. Garden City: 1960. V. 47; 51
The Future is Ours, Comrade. New York: 1960. V. 50
The Hermit of 69th Street. New York: 1988. V. 53
No Third Path. New York: 1962. V. 50
Notes of the Author on the Painted Bird. London: 1967. V. 47
The Painted Bird. Boston: 1965. V. 49; 51; 53
The Painted Bird. London: 1966. V. 48; 50
The Painted Bird. New York: 1970. V. 53
Passion Play. New York: 1979. V. 48; 49; 53

KOSMOPOULOS, LESLIE WALKER
The Prehistoric Inhabitation of Corinth. Munich: 1948. V. 52

KOSOWER, E. M.
Molecular Mechanisms for Sensory Signals, Recognition and Transformation. Princeton: 1991. V. 52

KOSSAK-SZCZUCKA, Z.
The Troubles of a Gnome. London: 1928. V. 50

KOSTABI, MARK
Sadness Because the Video Rental Store Was Closed. New York: 1988. V. 53

KOSTER, HENRY
Travels in Brazil. London: 1817. V. 47

KOTELIANSKY, S. S.
the Life and Letters of Anton Tchekhov. London: 1925. V. 53

KOTZ, SAMUEL
Encyclopedia of Statistical Sciences. New York: 1982-89. V. 47

KOTZEBUE, AUGUSTUS VON
The Constant Lover; or, William and Jeanette, a Tale. London: 1799. V. 49; 54
The Dramatic Works. New York: 1801. V. 54
Travels from Berlin, through Switzerland, to Paris, in the Year 1804. London: 1806. V. 49

KOTZEBUE, MORITZ VON
Narrative of a Journey into Persia, in the Suite of the Imperial Russian Embassy, in the Year 1817. Philadelphia: 1820. V. 49

KOTZEBUE, OTTO VON
A New Voyage Round the World in the Years 1823, 24, 25 and 26. London: 1830. V. 53
A New Voyage Round the world, in the Years 1823, 24, 25 and 26. Amsterdam/New York: 1967. V. 47; 52
Reise um die Welt, in den Jahren 1823, 24, 25, und 26. Weimar: 1830. V. 47
Rolla; or, the Peruvian Hero. London: 1799. V. 47
Voyage of Discovery into the South Sea, and Bering Straits... London: 1821. V. 47; 49; 50
A Voyage of Discovery into the South Sea, and Bering Straits... Amsterdam: 1967. V. 49

KOTZWINKLE, WILLIAM
Swimmer in the Secret Sea. London: 1976. V. 51

KOUDELKA, JOSEF
Gypsies. Millerton: 1975. V. 54

KOVACS, ERNIE
Zoomar. Garden City: 1957. V. 50; 53

KOVALEVSKY, SOPHIA
Vera Barantzova. London: 1895. V. 47

KOVIC, RON
Born on the Fourth of July. New York: 1976. V. 48

KOYEN, KENNETH
The Fourth Armored Division from Beach to Bavaria. Germany: 1946. V. 54

KOZAKIEWICZ, STEFAN
Bernardo Bellotto. London: 1972. V. 49; 53

KOZISEK, JOSEF
The Magic Flutes. New York: 1929. V. 54

KOZLOWSKI, T. T.
Fire and Ecosystems. New York: 1974. V. 53
Seed Biology. New York: 1972. V. 48

KRAAY, COLIN M.
Greek Coins. New York: 1966. V. 48; 52

KRAELING, CARL H.
Gerasa, City of the Decapolis: an Account Emboyding the Record of a Joint Excavation conducted by Yale University and the British School of Archaeology in Jerusalem (1928-1930) and Yale University and the American Schools of Oriental Research ... New Haven: 1938. V. 52
Ptolemais, City of the Libyan Pentapolis. Chicago: 1967. V. 50; 52
The Synagogue. New Haven: 1956. V. 49

KRAELING, EMIL G.
The Brooklyn Museum Aramaic Papyri; New Documents of the Fifth Century B.C. from the Jewish Colony at Elephantine. New Haven: 1953. V. 49

KRAEPELIN, EMIL
Clinical Psychiatry: a Text Book for Students and Physicians Abstracted and Adapted from the Seventh German Edition of Kraepelin's "Lehrbuch der Psychiatrie"... New York: 1902. V. 52
Dementia Praecox and Paraphrenia. Edinburgh: 1919. V. 52; 54
General Paresis. Nervous and Mental Disease Monograph Series No. 14. New York: 1913. V. 54
Lectures on Clinical Psychiatry. New York: 1913. V. 52
Manic-Depressive Insanity and Paranoia. Edinburgh: 1921. V. 54
Psychologische Arbeiten. Leipzig: 1896-1928. V. 52

KRAFFT, GEORGE WOLFFGANG
Wahrhaffte und Umstandliche Beschreibung und Abbildung des im Monath Januarius 1740 in St. Petersburg Aufgerichteten Merckwurdigen Hauses on Eiss... St. Petersburg: 1741. V. 53

KRAFFT, J. C.
Plans, Coupes et Elevations de Diverses Productions de l'Art de la Charpente Executees Tant en France que Dans les Pays. Paris: 1805. V. 52

KRAFFT-EBING, RICHARD, FREIHERR VON
Psychopathia Sexualis with Especial Reference to Contrary Sexual Instinct. Philadelphia: 1892. V. 48; 52
Text-Book of Insanity Based on Clinical Observations for Practioners and Students of Medicine. Philadelphia: 1904. V. 47; 52

KRAFT, WILLIAM
The Dream Tunnel: a Magical Journey through the Music of America: for Narrator and Orchestr. 1976. V. 52

KRAITSIR, CHARLES
Glossology: Being a Treatise on the Nature of Language and on the Language of Nature. New York: 1852. V. 54

KRAKEL, DEAN
James Boren - a Study in Discipline. Flagstaff: 1968. V. 47; 50; 54
The Saga of Tom Horn. Laramie: 1954. V. 50; 52; 53
The Sketchbook of Byron B. Wolfe. Kansas City: 1972. V. 47
Tom Ryan: A Painter in Four Sixes Country. Flagstaff: 1971. V. 47

KRAMER, HILTON
Richard Lindner. 1975. V. 51; 53; 54
Richard Lindner. Boston: 1975. V. 52
Richard Lindner. London: 1975. V. 50; 54

KRAMER, SIDNEY
A History of Stone and Kimball and Herbert S. Stone & Co., with a Bibliography of Their Publications, 1893-1905. Chicago: 1940. V. 49

KRAMM, JOSEPH
The Shrike. New York: 1952. V. 54

KRAMRISCH, S.
Persephone's Quest.... New Haven: 1986. V. 49

KRAMRISCH, S,
A Survey of Painting in the Deccan. 1937. V. 52

KRANS, HORATIO SHEAFE
The Lincoln Tribute Book. New York: 1909. V. 47; 51; 54

KRANTZ, ALBERT
Regnorum Aquilonarium Daniae, Sueciae, Norvagiae, Chronica...Wandalia. De Wandalorum Vera Origine. Frankfurt: 1580/80. V. 53
Regnorum Aquilonarium Daniae, Sueciae, Norvagiae, Chronica...Wandalia. De Wandalorum Vera Origine. Frankfurt: 1583/80. V. 50
Rerum Germanicarum, Historici. Frankfurt: 1590/80. V. 53
Rerum Germanicarum, Historici... Francofurti: 1621. V. 47

KRAPF, JOHANN LUDWIG
Travels, Researches, and Missionary Labours, During an Eighteen Years' Residence in Eastern Africa. London: 1860. V. 50

KRASHENINNIKOV, STEPAN PETROVICH
The History of Kamtschatka, and the Kurilski Islands, with the Countries Adjacent. Gloucester: 1764. V. 47; 49; 51
The History of Kamtschatka, and the Kurilski Islands, With the Countries Adjacent. London: 1764. V. 47

KRASNA, NORMAN
Dear Ruth: a Comedy. New York: 1945. V. 48
Kind Sir. New York: 1954. V. 54
Small Miracle: a Play in Three Acts. New York: 1935. V. 48

KRAUS, HANS P.
The Nineteenth Catalogue. New York. V. 47
A Rare Book Saga. London: 1979. V. 53
Sir Francis Drake. Amsterdam: 1970. V. 48

KRAUS, KARL
Die Demolierte Litteratur. Vienna: 1897. V. 49

KRAUSE, ERNST
Erasmus Darwin. London: 1879. V. 49

KRAUSE, FEDOR
Surgery of the Brain and Spinal Cord Based on Personal Experiences. New York: 1909-12. V. 49; 51

KRAUSE, GEORG A. J.
Oologia Universalia Palaearctica. London: 1905-13. V. 48
Oologia Universalia Palaearctica. Stuttgart: 1905-13. V. 53; 54

KRAUSE, GREGOR
Borneo. 1920. V. 48

KRAUSS, ROSALIND E.
Terminal Iron Works: The Sculpture of David Smith. Cambridge: 1971. V. 48; 50; 51; 52

KRAUSS, RUTH
Charlotte and the White Horse. New York: 1955. V. 49
A Hole Is to Dig. New York: 1952. V. 49; 53
I'll Be You and You Be Me. New York: 1954. V. 49
Somebody Else's Nut Tree. New York: 1958. V. 50
Somebody Else's Nut Tree... Lenox: 1971. V. 49

KRAUTHEIMER, R.
Lorenzo Ghiberti. Princeton: 1956. V. 48
Lorenzo Ghiberti. Princeton: 1970. V. 47

KREDEL, FRITZ
Dolls and Puppets of the Eighteenth Century. Lexington: 1958. V. 53

KREHBIEL, HENRY EDWARD
Afro-American Folksongs: a Study in Racial and National Music. New York and London: 1914. V. 48; 52

KREIDER, CLAUDE M.
The Bamboo Rod and How to Build It. New York: 1941. V. 53

KRENEK, ERNST
Horizons Circled. Berkeley: 1974. V. 49
Johannes Ockeghem. London: 1953. V. 49
Music Here and Now. New York: 1939. V. 49

KRENKEL, E.
Camping at the Pole. Moscow: 1939. V. 53

KRESS LIBRARY
The Kress Library of Business and Economics 1473-1848. Boston/Cambridge: 1940-67/ 1993. V. 49
The Kress Library of Business and Economics. Catalogue Covering material Published through 1776. (with) 1777-1817. 1993. V. 52
The Kress Library of Business and Economics. Giving Data Upon Cognate Items in Other Harvard Libraries. Cambridge: 1957-67. V. 49

KRESS, N.
Beggars in Spain. 1991. V. 48; 52

KREUGER, MILES
Showboat, the Story of a Classic American Musical. New York: 1977. V. 53

KREYMBORG, ALFRED
Funnybone Alley. New York: 1927. V. 47; 50; 52
Love and Life and Other Studies. New York: 1908. V. 54
Others: an Anthology of the New Verse. New York: 1916. V. 49
Others, an Anthology of the New Verse. New York: 1917. V. 50
Others for 1919, An Anthology of New Verse. New York: 1920. V. 50

KRIEG, ROBERT
Atlas of Diseases of the Nose. Stuttgart-Enke: 1901. V. 54

KRIEGER, ALEX D.
Culture Compleses and Chronology in Northern Texas. Austin: 1946. V. 52; 53

KRIMS, LES
The Incredible Case of the Stack O'Wheats Murders. Buffalo: 1972. V. 50
Target: the Deerslayers. Buffalo: 1972. V. 50

KRISHNAMURTI, G.
The Eighteen-Nineties: a Literary Exhibition, September 1973. London: 1975. V. 53
Women Writers of the 1890's. London: 1991. V. 49; 50; 54

KRIST, GUSTAV
Alone through the Forbidden Land. Journeys in Disguise through Soviet Central Asia. London: 1938. V. 50

KRISTELLER, PAUL
Early Florentine Woodcuts. London: 1897. V. 47
Early Florentine Woodcuts. London: 1968. V. 51; 53; 54

KRIVINE, J.
Juke Box Saturday Night. London: 1977. V. 49

KRIVITSKY, W. G.
I Was Stalin's Agent. London: 1939. V. 49

KROEBER, A. L.
Archaeological Explorations in Peru. Chicago: 1926-30. V. 50; 52

KROEBER, A. L. continued
Handbook of the Indians of California. Washington: 1925. V. 48; 49; 50; 54

KROEBER, THEODORA
The Inland Whale. Covelo: 1987. V. 48

KROGH, AUGUST
The Anatomy and Physiology of Capillaries. New Haven: 1922. V. 49

KROHN, J. A.
The Walk of Colonial Jack. Kenne: 1910. V. 50

KROMBEIN, K. V.
Catalogue of Hymenoptera in America North of Mexico. Washington: 1979. V. 49

KROMER, TOM
Waiting for Nothing. New York: 1935. V. 52

KRON, KARL
Ten Thousand Miles on a Bicycle. New York: 1887. V. 53

KRONFELD, MARION
Designs Cut for Plantin Press Calendars 1941-46. Fallbrook: 1980. V. 48

KROODSMA, D. E.
Acoustic Communication in Birds. New York: 1982. V. 54

KROPOTKIN, PETER ALEXEIVICH
Anarchism: Its Philosophy and Ideal. London: 1908. V. 53
Ideals and Realities in Russian Literature. London: 1903. V. 50
Modern Science and Anarchism. London: 1912. V. 50

KRUEGER, M.
Pioneer Life in Texas. V. 48
Pioneer Life in Texas. 1930. V. 52
Pioneer Life in Texas... San Antonio: 1930. V. 52

KRUMGOLD, JOSEPH
Sweeny's Adventure. New York: 1942. V. 50

KRUSEN, FRANK
Physical Medicine: the Employment of Physical Agents for Diagnosis and Therapy. Philadelphia: 1941. V. 53

KRUSENSTERN, ADAM JOHANN VON
Voyage Round the World, in the Years 1803, 1804... London: 1813. V. 50; 52
Voyage Round the World, in the Years 1803, 1804... Amsterdam: 1968. V. 47

KRUSI, HERMANN
Handbook of Perspective Drawing. New York: 1874. V. 53

KRUSKEMPER, H. L.
Anabolic Steroids. New York: 1968. V. 53

KRUSSMANN, G.
Manual of Cultivated Broad Leaved Trees and Shrubs. Portland: 1984-86. V. 52
Manual of Cultivated Broad-Leaved Trees and Shrubs. London: 1985-86. V. 49
Manual of Cultivated Conifers. London: 1985. V. 49

KRUTCH, JOSEPH WOOD
Edgar Allan Poe A Study in Genius. New York: 1926. V. 48; 49
Samuel Johnson. New York: 1944. V. 50; 52

KU KLUX KLAN
Constitution of the Women of the Ku Klux Klan Accepted and Adopted June 2nd, 1923... Little Rock: 1924?. V. 50
Papers Read at the Meeting of Grand Dragons, Knights of the Ku Klux Klan, at Their First Annual Meeting Held at Asheville, North Carolina, July 1923, Together with Other Articles of Interest to Klansmen. Asheville: 1923. V. 47

KUBASTA, V.
Tournament. London: 1961. V. 54

KUBLER, GEORGE
The Religious Architecture of New Mexico in the Colonial Period and Since American Occupation. Colorado Springs: 1940. V. 47; 54

KUBRICK, STANLEY
Stanley Kubrick's Clockwork Orange. New York: 1972. V. 54

KUCHENMEISTER, F.
On Animal and Vegetable Parasites of the Human Body. London: 1857. V. 51

KUETTNER, CARL GOTTLOB
Travels through Denmark, Sweden, Austria and Part of italy in 1798 & 1799. London: 1805. V. 50

KUGLER, FRANCIS
The Pictorial History of Germany, During the Reign of Frederick the Great... London: 1845. V. 48

KUHLER, OTTO
My Iron Journey. An Autobiography of a Life with Steam and Steel. Denver: 1967. V. 54

KUHLMAN, CHARLES
Gen. George A. Custer: a Lost Trail and the Gall Saga... Billings: 1940. V. 53
Legend Into History. Harrisburg: 1952. V. 53

KUHN, A. L.
Report Of a Journey through the Khanate of Khiva During the Expedition of 1873. Calcutta: 1874. V. 49

KUHN, FRITZ
Compositions of Black and White. Paris: 1959. V. 52

KUHNEL, ERNST
Cairene Rugs and Others Technically Related, 15th Century - 17th Century. Washington: 1957. V. 52
The Textile Museum: Catalogue of Dated Tiraz Fabrics: Umayyad, Abbasid, FAtimid. Washington: 1952. V. 47; 54

KUHNERT, WILHELM
Animal Portraiture. London: 1912. V. 49

KULL, IRVING S.
New Jersey. A History. New York: 1930. V. 47; 49; 51

KULTERMANN, UDO
Trova. New York: 1978. V. 50

KUMAR, SATISH
Learning by Heart. 1986. V. 49

KUME, YASUO
Tesuki Washi Shuho. Fine Handmade Papers of Japan. Tokyo: 1980. V. 48; 49

KUMIN, MAXINE
The Microscope. New York: 1984. V. 49

KUMM, H. KARL W.
From Hausland to Egypt. Through the Sudan. London: 1910. V. 47; 49; 50
Khnot-Hon-Nofer. The Lands of Ethiopia. London: 1910. V. 52
The Sudan. London: 1907. V. 51

KUNCKEL, JOHANN
Collegium Physico-Chymicum Experimentale, Oder Laboratorium Chymicum. Hamburg & Leipzig: 1716. V. 48; 50; 54

KUNDERA, MILAN
The Book of Laughter and Forgetting. New York: 1980. V. 51
The Book of Laughter and Forgetting. London: 1982. V. 54
The Farewell Party. New York: 1976. V. 54
The Joke. London: 1969. V. 50; 53
The Joke. New York: 1969. V. 50; 51; 52
The Joke. New York: 1982. V. 49
Laughable Loves. New York: 1974. V. 50; 51

KUNDIG, JACOB
Dictionarium Affinitatis. Basel: 1546. V. 52

KUNHARDT, DOROTHY
Junket is Nice. New York: 1933. V. 47
Tiny Nonsense Stories. Roger Mouse's Wish. Mrs. Sheep's Little Lamb. Wonderful Silly Picnic. Naughty Little Guest. Uncle Quack. Cowboy Kitten. April Fool. Easter Bunny. Happy Valentine. Two Snowbulls. Little Squirrel's Santa Claus. Poor Frightened Mr... New York: 1949. V. 53

KUNISAKE, JIHEI
Kamiskuki Chohoki. Berkeley: 1948. V. 53

KUNITZ, STANLEY J.
The Coat Without a Seam. Northampton: 1974. V. 50; 51; 53
Intellectual Things. New York: 1930. V. 54
Twentieth-Century Authors. New York: 1942/55. V. 51

KUNO, MEYER
Cath Finntraga. 1885. V. 54

KUNO, TAKESHI
A Guide to Japanese Sculpture. Tokyo: 1963. V. 52

KUNSTADTER, P.
Southeast Asian Tribes, Minorities and Nations. Princeton: 1967. V. 51

KUNSTLERGABE Zum XII. Zionisten-Kongress Karlsbad 1921. Berlin: 1921. V. 50; 53

KUNZ, GEORGE FREDERICK
The Book of the Pearl. New York: 1908. V. 47; 50
The Curious Lore of Precious Stones... Philadelphia & London: 1913. V. 47; 50; 52
Gems and Precious Stones of North America. New York: 1890. V. 47; 50; 53
The History, Art, Science and Industry of the Queen of Gems. New York: 1908. V. 50
Ivory and the Elephant in Art, in Archaeology and in Science. Garden City: 1916. V. 47
Ivory and the Elephant in Art, In Archaeology and in Science. New York: 1916. V. 50
The Magic of Jewels and Charms. Philadelphia and London: 1915. V. 50
Rings for the Finger. Philadelphia and London: 1917. V. 50
Shakespeare and Precious Stones. Philadelphia: 1916. V. 50; 51

KUNZEL, HEINRICH
Obercalifornien. Eine Geographische Schilderung fur den Zwek Deutscher Auwanderung und Ansiedlung. Darmstadt: 1848. V. 48

KURETSKY, SUSAN DONAHUE
The Paintings of Jacob Ochtervelt (1634-1682). (with Catalogue Raisonne). Oxford: 1979. V. 50; 54

KURLAND, PHILIP B.
The Founders' Constitution. Chicago: 1987. V. 51

KURODA, N.
A Bibliography of the Duck Tribe, Anatidae, Mostly From 1926 to 1940, Exclusive of that in Dr. Phillips' Work. Tokyo: 1942. V. 48

KURODA, N. continued
Birds in Life Colours. Tokyo: 1933-39. V. 49
Birds in Life Colours. Tokyo: 1936-39. V. 48
Birds of Fujiyama. Tokyo: 1926. V. 48
Birds of the Island of Java. Tokyo: 1933-36. V. 48
A Contribution to the Knowledge to the Avifauna of the Riu Kiu Islands and the Vicinity. Tokyo: 1925. V. 48
Geese and Ducks of the World. Tokyo: 1985. V. 48
A Monograph of the Charabriidae (Plovers and Snipes). Tokyo: 1918. V. 48
A Monograph of the Pheasants of Japan, Including Korea and Formosa. London: 1926. V. 48

KURODA, T.
Check List and Bibliography of the Recent Marine Mollusca of Japan. Tokyo: 1952. V. 53
The Sea Shells of Sagami Bay Collected by H.M. The Emperor of Japan. Tokyo: 1971. V. 50

KUROSAWA, REIKICHI
Imperial Chinese Art. Shanghai: 1917. V. 53

KURR, JOHANN GOTTLOB
The Mineral Kingdom. Edinburgh: 1859. V. 53; 54

KURTEN, B.
Pleistocene Mammals of North America. New York: 1980. V. 50

KURTZ, BENJAMIN P.
An Original leaf from the Polychronicon Printed by William Caxton at Westminster in the Year 1482. San Francisco: 1938. V. 48; 52

KURTZ, DONNA CAROL
The Berlin Painter. Oxford: 1983. V. 50; 52

KURTZ, O. H.
Official Route Book of Ringling Brothers' World's Greatest Railroad Shows. Season of 1892. Buffalo: 1892. V. 52

KURZ, O.
Bolognese Drawings of the XVII and XVII Centuries. London: 1955. V. 54

KUSANO, NOBUO
Atomic Bomb Injuries. Tokyo: 1953. V. 48

KUSSMAUL, ADOLF
Disturbances of Speech. An Attempt in the Pathology of Speech. New York: 1877. V. 47

KUTTNER, HENRY
Ahead of Time. New York: 1953. V. 48; 51

KUTZ, M. JENNIE
Wab-Ah-See, a Legend of the Sleeping Dew; and other Poems. Chicago: 1868. V. 48

KUTZING, F. T.
Tabulae Phycologicae. Nordhausen: 1845-71. V. 50

KUYKENDALL, IVAN LEE
Ghost Riders of the Mogollon. San Antonio: 1954. V. 52; 53

KUYKENDALL, WILLIAM L.
Frontier Days. A True Narrative of Striking Events on the Western Frontier. 1917. V. 53

KWEN, F. S.
Descriptive Catalogue of Ancient and Genuine Chinese Paintings... New York & Shanghai: 1918. V. 49; 53

KYAN, JOHN HOWARD
On the Elements of Light and Their Identity with Those of Matter Radiant and Fixed. London: 1838. V. 49

KYD, STEWART
A Treatise on the Law of Bills of Exchange and Promissory Notes. Albany: 1800. V. 53

KYD, THOMAS
The Tragedy of Solimon and Perseda. London: 1599. V. 51

KYLE, D. BRADEN
A Text-Book of Diseases of the Nose and Throat. Philadelphia: 1899. V. 51

KYLE, THOMAS
A Treatise on the Management on the Management of Peach and Nectarine Trees; Either in Forcing-Houses, or On Hot and Common Walls... Edinburgh: 1787. V. 53

KYNE, PETER B.
The Book I Never Wrote. San Francisco: 1942. V. 48
Outlaws of Eden. New York: 1930. V. 48

KYNNERSLEY, T. C.
Pratt's Law of Highways...with an Introduction, Explanatory of the Whole Law Upon the Subject. London: 1865. V. 52

KYNOCH PRESS
The Kynoch Press Book of Type Specimens. Birmingham: 1927. V. 51
Specimens of Types In Use at the Kynoch Press. Corrected to January 1934. (with) Supplement No. 1...showing Types Added During 1934. 1934. V. 52

KYSEL, MELCHIOR
Icones Biblicae Veteris et Novi Testamenti. Figuren Biblischer Historien Alten und Neuen Testaments. 1679. V. 48

KYSTER, ANKER
Bookbindings in the Public Collections of Denmark. Copenhagen: 1938. V. 53

L

L., D.
The Plain Case of Great Britain, Fairly Stated, in a Letter to a Member of the...House of Commons... Edinburgh?: 1712. V. 53
The Scots Scouts Discoveries: by Their London Intelligences And Presented to the Lords of the Covenant of Scotland. London: 1642. V. 53

L., J.
Poems. London: 1854. V. 52; 54

L., W. E. P.
Tetford Club. A Poem. Horncastle: 1812. V. 54

LA LIVE D'EPINAY, LOUISE FLORENCE PETRONILLE DE
The Conversations of Emily. London: 1815. V. 52

LA TOUR LANDRY
The Book of the Knight of... 1930. V. 47

LAAR, G. VAN
Magazijn Van Tuin-Sieraden. Zalt-Bommel: 1814. V. 48

LABARTE, JULES
Handbook of the Arts of the Middle Ages and Renaissance, as Applied to the Decoration of Furniture, Arms, Jewels... London: 1855. V. 51

LABAT, GASTON
Regional Anesthesia. Philadelphia: 1922. V. 47; 54
Regional Anesthesia... Philadelphia and London: 1923. V. 51

LABAUME, EUGENE
A Circumstantial Narrative of the Campaign in Russia... London: 1815. V. 54

LABAW, GEORGE WARNE
A Genealogy of the Warne Family in America, Principally the Descendants of Thomas Warne, Born 1652, Died 1722... New York: 1911. V. 47; 49; 51
Preakness and the Preakness Reformed Church, Passaic County, New Jersey. A History, 1695-1902. New York: 1902. V. 51

LA BEAUMELLE, LAURENT ANGLIVIEL DE
The Life of Madam de Maintenon. London: 1753-60. V. 47
Memoirs For the History of Madame de Mainenon and the Last Age. London: 1757. V. 48

LABELS: Beautiful Designs for Wines and Liquors... San Francisco: 1941. V. 47

LABELYE, CHARLES
The Present State of Westminster Bridge. London: 1743. V. 51
The Result of a View of the Great Level fo the Fens, Taken at the Desire of His Grace the Duke of Bedford &c., Governor and the Gentlemen of the Corporation of the Fens, in July 1745. London: 1745. V. 51
A Short Account of the Methods Made Use Of in Laying the Foundation of the Piers of Westminster-Bridge. London: 1739. V. 51

LA BERAUDIERE, MARC DE
Le Combat De Seul a Seul en Camp Clos... Paris: 1608. V. 48

LABILLARDIERE, JACQUES JULIEN HOUTEN DE
Relation du Voyage a la Recherche de La Perouse, fait par Ordre de l'Assemblee Constituante, Pendant les Annees 1791, 1792, et Pendant la Lere et la 2de Annee de la Replubique Francoise. Paris: 1800. V. 50; 51
Voyage in Search of La Perouse. London: 1800. V. 47; 51

LABORDE, LEON DE
Journey through Arabia Petraea, to Mount Sinai and the Excavated City of Petra, the Edom of the Prophecies. London: 1836. V. 52; 54
Journey through Arabia Petraea, to Mount Sinai and the Excavated City of Petra, the Edom of the Prophecies. London: 1838. V. 47; 48; 51

LABOUCHERE, H.
Diary of the Besieged Resident in Paris. London: 1871. V. 52

LABOUCHERE, NORNA
Ladies' Book-Plates, an Illustrated Handbook for Collectors and Book-Lovers. London & New York: 1895. V. 49; 51; 53

LABOULAYE, EDOUARD
Laboulaye's Fairy Book. New York and London: 1920. V. 54

LA BRANCHE, GEORGE M. L.
The Dry Fly and Fast Water: Fishing with the Floating Fly on American Trout Streams. New York: 1914. V. 53

LA BREE, BENJAMIN
Camp Fires of the Confederacy. Louisville: 1898. V. 54
The Confederate Soldier in the Civil War, 1861-1865... Louisville: 1895. V. 54

LA BRUNE, JEAN DE
The Life of That Most Illustrious Prince, Charles V. Lake Duke of Lorrain and Bar, Generalissimo of the Imperial Armies. London: 1691. V. 54

LA BRUYERE, JEAN DE
The Characters of... London: 1885. V. 54

LABYRINTE de Versailles. Amsterdam: 1682. V. 49; 53

LACAITA, J. P.
Catalogue of the Library at Chatsworth. London: 1879. V. 48; 54

LA CALPRENEDE, GAULTIER DE COSTE
Cassandra: the Fam'd Romance. London: 1652. V. 47
Cassandra: the Fam'd Romance. London: 1667. V. 50
Hymen's Praeludia: or Love's Master-piece. London: 1663. V. 50
Pharamond: or the History of France. London: 1662. V. 54

LACEY, JAMES D., & CO.
The Tensas Delta of Louisiana. Chicago?: 1900. V. 50

LA CHAMBRE, MARTIN CUREAU DE
The Art How to Know Men. London: 1665. V. 52; 53
Discours sur les Causes du Desbordement du Nil. Paris: 1665. V. 51

LACHEMAN, ERNEST R.
Miscellaneous Texts from Nuzi. Part II. The Palace and Temple Archives. Cambridge: 1950. V. 49; 51

LACHLAN, ELIZABETH
Leonora; or, the Presentation At Court. London: 1829. V. 47; 49

LACH-SZYRMA, KRYSTYN
Letters, Literary and Political, on Poland... Edinburgh: 1823. V. 47

LACINIUS, JANUS
Pretiosa Margarita Novella De Thesauro, ac Pretiosissimo Philosophorum Lapide... Venice: 1546. V. 48; 54
Pretiosa Margarita Novella de Thesauro, ac Pretiosissimo Philosophorum Lapide. Venice: 1564. V. 53

LACKINGTON, JAMES
The Confessions of J. Lackington, Late Bookseller, at the Temple of the Muses, in a Series of Letters to a Friend. London: 1804. V. 50; 51
The Confessions of J. Lackington, Late Bookseller, at the Temple of the Muses, in a Series of Letters to a Friend. New York: 1808. V. 50; 52
Memoirs of...James Lackington... London: 1791. V. 48; 51
Memoirs of...James Lackington... London: 1792. V. 47; 54
Memoirs of...James Lackington... London: 1794. V. 49
Memoirs of...James Lackington... London: 1795. V. 50
Memoirs of...James Lackington... London: 1796. V. 48
Memoirs of...James Lackington... Newburgh: 1796. V. 53
Memoirs of...James Lackington... London: 1800. V. 48

LACLOS, PIERRE AMBROISE FRANCOIS CHODERLOS DE
Les Liaisons Dangereuses. Paris: 1929. V. 48; 51
Les Liaisons Dangereuses. Paris: 1934. V. 51; 52

LACOMBE, JEAN DE
A Compendium of the East Being an account of Voyages to the Grand Indies. London: 1937. V. 47; 50

LA CONDAMINE, CHARLES MARIE DE
A Succint Abridgement of a Voyage Made in the Inland Parts of South America; from the Coasts of the South Sea, to the Coasts of Brazil and Guiana, Down the River Amazon. London: 1747. V. 48

LA CROIX, A PHEROTTE DE
Of the Mechanism of the Motions of Floating Bodies... London: 1746. V. 53

LA CROIX, D. D.
Connubia Florum Latino Carmine Demonstrata... Bath: 1791. V. 47; 54

LACROIX, JEAN FRANCOIS
Dictionnaire Portrait des Femmes Celebres, Contenant l'Histoire des Femmes Savantes, des Actrices & Generalement des Dames Qui se Sont Rendues Fameuses Dans Tous les Siecles, par Leurs Aventure, Les Talens, L'Esprit & Le Courage. Paris: 1788. V. 48

LA CROIX, M. B.
The Married woman's Private Medical Companion. Albany: 1870. V. 52

LACROIX, PAUL
The Arts in the Middle Ages, and At the Period of the Renaissance. New York: 1875. V. 51
The Arts in the Middle Ages, and at the Period of the Renaissance. London: 1875-78. V. 48
The Arts in the Middle Ages and the Renaissance. London: 1880. V. 52

LA CROIX, PAUL
History of Prostitution Among All the Peoples of the World, From the Most Remote Antiquity to the Present Day. Chicago: 1926. V. 48

LACROIX, PAUL
Military and Religious Life in the Middle Ages and at the Period of the Renaissance. London: 1874. V. 53
Military and Religious Life in the Middle Ages and at the Period of the Renaissance. London: 1878. V. 47
Le Moyen Age et la Renaissance. Paris: 1848-51. V. 54
The XVIIIth Century. Its Institutions, Customs and Costumes. France 1700-1789. London: 1876. V. 48

LACRYMAE Cantabrigienses in Obitum Serenissimae Reginae Mariae. Cantabrigiae: 1694/95. V. 48

LACTANTIUS, LUCIUS COELIUS FIRMIANUS
De Divinis Institutionibus. Venice: 1479. V. 48; 54
De Divinis Institutionibus. (Opera). Venice: 1497. V. 54
Divinaru(m) Institutionu(m). Lyon: 1587. V. 52
Divinarvm Institvtionvm Libri Septem (and other works). Venetiis: 1535. V. 47; 49; 52
Opera. Venice: 1490. V. 51
Opera. Lyons: 1594. V. 52
Opera, Quae Extant. Oxonii: 1684. V. 48

LACY, CHARLES DE LACY
The History of the Spur. London. V. 54

LACY, GEORGE
Pictures of Travel, Sport and Adventure. London: 1899. V. 48; 52

LACY, JOHN
The Dramatic Works. Edinburgh & London: 1875. V. 51

LACY, THOMAS
Home Sketches on Both Sides of the Channel (i.e. the Irish Sea). 1852. V. 48
Home Sketches on Both Sides of the Channel (i.e. the Irish Sea). London: 1852. V. 51

LADA, JOSEF
Purrkin the Talking Cat. London: 1966. V. 53

LADA-MOCARSKI, VALERIAN
Bibliography of Books on Alaska Published Before 1868. New Haven: 1969. V. 47; 50; 54

LADBROOKE, R.
Views of the Churches in Norfolk, Illustrative of Blomefield's History of that County, From Original Drawings. Norwich: 1823. V. 47

LADD, JOHN
A Succinct Description of the New-Invented Patent Chain and Wheel... London: 1759. V. 50

LADD, RUSSELL
The History of Albert and Eliza. Philadelphia: 1812. V. 50; 54

LADD, WILLIAM E.
Abdominal Surgery of Infancy and Childhood. Philadelphia: 1941. V. 51

LADER, LAWRENCE
The Margaret Sanger Story and the Fight for Birth control. Garden City: 1955. V. 50

LADER, OCTAVIANUS
Historia and Wunderzaichen dess...Sacraments. Augsburg: 1625. V. 47; 50; 53; 54

THE LADIES Charity School-House Roll of Highgate; or a Subscription of Many Noble, Well Disposed Ladies for the Easie Carrying Of It On. London: 1670. V. 52

THE LADIES' Companion, Containing First, Politeness of Manners and Behavior... Brookfield: 1826. V. 50

THE LADIES' Companion for Visiting the Poor; Consisting of Familiar Addresses, Adapted to Particular Occassions. London: 1820. V. 53

THE LADIES Delight. London: 1732. V. 49

THE LADIES' Hand-book of Haberdashery and Hosiery. London: 1844. V. 53

LADIES' Indispensable Assistant. New York: 1853. V. 48; 49

THE LADIES Library. London: 1714. V. 51

THE LADIES' Pocket Book of Etiquette. Waltham St. Lawrence: 1928. V. 51; 53

LADIES SOCIETY, NEW YORK.
Constitution of the Ladies Society, Established in New York for the Relief of Poor Widows with Small Children. New York: 1800. V. 50

L'ADMIRAL, JACOB
Naauwkeurige Waarneemingen Omtrent de Veranderingen van Delle Insekten of Gekorvene Diertjes, Die in Omtrent Vyftig Jaaren... Amsterdam: 1774. V. 47

LADY, A.
Flora and Thalia. London: 1835. V. 53

THE LADY'S Toilet. London: 1845. V. 50

LAENNEC, R. T. H.
De L'Ausculation Mediate Ou Traite Du Diagnostic des Maladies des Poumons et Du Coeur. Paris: 1819. V. 48; 54
A Treatise on Medite Auscultation, and on Diseases of the Heart and Lungs. London: 1846. V. 54
A Treatise on the Diseases of the Chest... Philadelphia: 1823. V. 48
A Treatise on the Diseases of the Chest and on Mediate Ausculation... Philadelphia: 1835. V. 48
A Treatise on the Diseases of the Chest, and on Mediate Ausculation. New York: 1838. V. 49; 51; 52; 53; 54

LAET, IOANNE DE
Novus Orbis Seu Discriptionis Indiae Occidentalis... Leiden: 1633. V. 48

LA FAILLE, J. B.
The Works of Vincent Van Gogh. New York: 1970. V. 50

LAFARGE, MARIE FORTUNEE POUCHE
Memoirs... London: 1841. V. 51

LA FARGE, OLIVER
As Long As the Grass Shall Grow. New York and Toronto: 1940. V. 51; 54
Laughing Boy. Boston: 1929. V. 49; 53

LAFAYETTE, MARIE JOSEPH PAUL YVES ROCH GILBERT DU MOTIER
Memoirs of General Lafayette... Hartford: 1825. V. 54

LA FAYETTE, MARIE MADELEINE PLOCHE DE LA VERGNE, COMTESSE DE
The Death of Madame. Paris: 1931. V. 48; 50; 51

LAFAYETTE, MARIE MADELEINE PLOCHE DE LA VERGNE, COMTESSE DE
The Princess of Cleves. London: 1679. V. 52; 53; 54
La Princesse de Cleves. Paris: 1741. V. 52
La Princesse de Cleves. Paris: 1925. V. 53

LA FEUILLE, DANIEL DE
Devises et Emblemes Anciennes et Modernes, Tirees des Plus Celebres Auteurs... Amsterdam: 1693. V. 47

LAFEVER, MINARD
The Modern Builders' Guide. New York: 1833. V. 47; 49

LAFITAU, JOSEPH FRANCOIS
Customs of the American Indians Compared with the Customs of Primitive Times. Toronto: 1974/77. V. 50
Moeurs des Sauvages Ameriquains, Comparees Aux Moeures des Premiers Temps... Paris: 1724. V. 47; 48; 49; 54

LA FONT, DON
Rugged Life in the Rockies. Casper: 1951. V. 51

LAFONTAINE, AUGUSTE HEINRICH JULIUS
The Family of Halden; a Novel. London: 1799. V. 51

LA FONTAINE, JEAN DE
Les Amours de Psiche et de Cupidon. La Haye: 1700. V. 51
Les Amours de Psyche et de Cupidon. Paris: 1791. V. 49; 50; 53
The Amours of Cupid and Psyche. London: 1749. V. 52
Cassell's Illustrated Book of Fables. London: 1870. V. 47
Contes et Nouvelles en Vers. Amsterdam: 1762. V. 48; 51
Fables. Paris: 1811. V. 52; 54
Fables... Boston: 1841. V. 47
Fables... New York: 1865. V. 53
The Fables... London and New York: 1867. V. 49
Fables... Paris: 1906. V. 53
The Fables. New York: 1930. V. 52; 54
The Fables. London: 1931. V. 47; 50; 53
The Fables. New York: 1954. V. 48; 51; 53; 54
Fables. Paris: 1966. V. 52
Fables Choisies. Paris: 1755-59. V. 47; 50; 54
La Fontaine. A Present For the Young. Boston: 1839. V. 49
La Fontaine's Fables. Paris: 1806. V. 47; 51
La Fontaine's Fables. London: 1905. V. 51
La Fontaine's Tales: Imitated in English Verse. London: 1814. V. 47; 49; 51
Forty-Two Fables of La Fontaine. London: 1924. V. 47; 48; 49; 50; 51
A Hundred Fables. London: 1900. V. 48
The Loves of Cupid and Psyche: in Verse and Prose. London: 1744. V. 49
Oeuvres Complettes... Paris: 1814. V. 47; 52
Poeme du Quinquina, et Autres Ourages en Vers. Paris: 1682. V. 52
Selected Fables... New York: 1948. V. 48
Selected Fables. New York: 1957. V. 48
Tales and Novels and Verse. London: 1735. V. 52
Tales and Novels in Verse. Paris: 1884. V. 50; 52

LAFORGUE, RENE
The Defeat of Baudelaire - a Psycho-Analytical Study of the Neurosis of Charles Baudelaire. London: 1932. V. 53

LA FRAMBOISIERE, NICHOLAS ABRAHAM
Consvltationvm Medicinalivm Libri tres. Paris: 1595. V. 54

LA FRENTZ, F. W.
Cowboy Stuff. New York: 1927. V. 51

LAFUENTE, ENRIQUE FERRARI
El Greco. The Expressionism of His Final Years. London: 1969. V. 47

LAGARDE, FRANCOIS
The Three Minds. Paris: 1978. V. 47

LAGDEN, GODFREY
The Basutos. The Mountaineers and Their Country. London: 1909. V. 50

LAGERBERG, LARS DE
New Jersey Architecture. Colonial & Federal. Springfield: 1956. V. 49

LAGERKVIST, PAR
Barrabbas. New York: 1951. V. 54
The Death of Ahasuerus. New York: 1964. V. 54
The Eternal Smile and Other Stories. New York: 1954. V. 54
Herod and Marianne. New York: 1968. V. 54
The Holy Land. New York: 1966. V. 54
The Sibyl. New York: 1958. V. 54

LA GRANGE, HELEN
Clipper Ships of America and Great Britain 1833-1869. New York: 1936. V. 47; 49

LAGRANGE, JOSEPH LOUIS
De La Resolution des Equations Numeriques de Touts les Degres. Paris: 1798. V. 47
Mechanique Analitique. Paris: 1788. V. 54

LA GRONE, OLIVER
Footfalls: Poetry from America's Becoming. Detroit: 1949. V. 54

LA GUERINIERE, FRANCOIS ROBICHON DE
Ecole de Cavalerie Contenant la Connoissance, l'Instruction, et la Conversation du Cheval. Paris: 1733. V. 47

LA HARPE, JEAN FRANCOIS DE
Abrege de l'Histoire General des Voyages... Paris: 1780-1804. V. 49

Del Fanatismo en la Lengua Revolucionaria o de la Persecucion Suscitada Contra la Religion Christiana y sus Ministros por los Barbaros del Siglo ... Guatemala: 1825. V. 48

LA HIRE, M. DE
L'Art de Charpenterie de Mathurin Jousse, Architects & Ingenieur de la Ville de la Fleche. Paris: 1751. V. 52

LA HIRE, PHILIPPE DE
Sectiones Conicae in Novem Libros Distributae... Paris: 1685. V. 48

LAHONTAN, LOUIS ARMAND, BARON DE
Lanhontan's Voyages. Ottawa: 1932. V. 51
New Voyages to North-America... Chicago: 1905. V. 54
Nouveaux Voyages de Mr. Le Baron de Lahontan Dans l'Amerique Septentrionale. La Haye: 1709. V. 49
Voyages Du Baron de La Hontan Dans L'Amerique Septentrionale. Memoires. Hague: 1706. V. 51

LAINEZ, MANUEL MUJICA
Cantata de Bomarzo. 1981. V. 52; 54

LAING, ALASTAIR
Francois Boucher 1703-1770. New York: 1986. V. 50

LAING, ALEXANDER GORDON
Travels in Western Africa in the Timannee, Kooranko and Soolina Countries. London: 1825. V. 48

LAING, ALLAN M.
More Prayers and Graces. London: 1957. V. 51; 53
Prayers and Graces. London: 1944. V. 51; 53

LAING, D.
Hints for Dwellings; Consisting of Original Designs for Cottages, Farmhouses, Villas, &c. London: 1804. V. 47

LAING, G. BLAIR
Memoirs of an Art Dealer. Toronto: 1979. V. 53
Memoirs of an Art Dealer 2. Toronto: 1982. V. 50

LAING, MALCOLM
The Historie and Life of King James the Sext, Written Towards the Latter Part of the 16th Century. Edinburgh: 1804. V. 50

LAING, R. D.
The Politics of Experience. New York: 1967. V. 53
The Self & Others. London: 1961. V. 51

LAING, R. M.
Plants of New Zeland. 1907. V. 49

LAING, S.
Prehistoric Remains of Caithness... London: 1866. V. 52

LAING, SAMUEL
Observations on the Social and Political State of the European People in 1848 and 1849. London: 1850. V. 52
A Tour in Sweden in 1838; Comprising Observations on the Moral, Political and Economical State of the Swedish Nation. London: 1839. V. 47

LAING, SETON
The Great City Frauds of Cole, Davidson and Gordon, Fully Exposed. London: 1856. V. 50; 52

LAIRD, MAC GREGOR
Narrative of an Expedition Into the Interior of Africa, by the River Niger in the Steam-Vessels Quorra and Alburkah, in 1832, 1833 and 1834. London: 1837. V. 47

LAIRD, MARY
The Eggplant Skin Pants and Poems. Mt. Horeb: 1973. V. 51
Wind/Call Yourself Nothing. Poems and Drawings. Madison: 1985. V. 51

LAIRESSE, GERARD DE
The Art of Painting... London: 1778. V. 49
The Art of Painting...Demonstrated by Discourses and Plates... S. Vandenbergh: 1778. V. 47

LAKE CITY MINING & SMELTING CO.
Prospectus, Articles of Incorporation, and By-Laws of the Lake City Mining and Smelting Co., San Juan. New Haven: 1876. V. 48

LAKE, EDWARD
Journals of the Sieges of the Madras Army in the Years 1817, 1818, and 1819 with Observations on the System... London: 1825. V. 50
Memoranda: Touching the Oath Ex Officio, Pretended Self-Accusation, and Canonical Purgation. London: 1662. V. 51

LAKE, JAMES WINTER
A Catalogue of genuine and Extensive Collection of Engraved Prints, Portraits, Illustrated Books, Books of Prints, Atlases, and British Topography... London: 1808. V. 48

LAKE, STUART N.
Wyatt Earp, Frontier Marshal. New York: 1931. V. 52

LAKE Superior Region. 1888?. V. 53

LAKEMAN, STEPHEN
What I Saw in Kaffir-Land. Edinburgh: 1880. V. 51

LAKES, ARTHUR
Prospecting for Gold and Silver in North America. Scranton: 1896. V. 48

LAKING, GUY FRANCIS
The Armoury of Windsor Castle. European Section. London: 1904. V. 47

LAL, MOHAN
Life of the Amir Dost Mohammed Khan of Kabul; with His Political Proceedings Towards the English, Russian and Persian Governments... London: 1846. V. 52; 53

LALAMANT, JEAN
Exterarvm Fere Omnivm Et Praecipvarvm Centivm Anni Ratio & Cum Romano Collatio: Rara & Exquisita Rerum Scitu Dignissimarum Cognitione... Geneva: 1571. V. 53

LA LANDE, J. J. L. DE
Astronomie. Paris: 1764. V. 47

LALANDE, JOSEPH JEROME DE
The Art of Paper Making. Ireland: 1976. V. 51

LALANDE, JOSEPH JEROME LE FRANCAIS DE
Des Canaux de Navigation, et Specialement du Canal de Languedoc Paris. 1778. V. 54

LALLEMAND, FRANCOIS
Le Hachych. Paris: 1843. V. 48

LALLEMAND, HENRI DOMINIQUE
A Complete Treatise Upon Artillery. New York: 1819/20. V. 51

LALLY TOLLENDAL, THOMAS ARTHUR, COMTE
Memoirs of Count Lally, from His Embarking for the East Indies, as Commander of the French Forces in that Country to His Being Sent Prisoner of War to England.. London: 1766. V. 47

LA LOUPE, VINCENT DE
In Cornelii Taciti Annalium Libros XVI. Paris: 1556. V. 52

LAMA, GIUSEPPE DE
Vita del Cavaliere Giambattista Bodoni, Tipografo Italiano: E Catalogo Cronologico Delle Sue Edizioni. Parma: 1816. V. 51

LA MAMYE CLAIRAC, LOUIS A. DE
The Field Engineer of M. le Chevalier de Clairac. 1773. V. 47
The Field Engineer of Mle. Chevalier de Clairac. London: 1773. V. 50

LAMANTIA, PHILIP
Ekstasis. San Francisco: 1959. V. 47
Touch of the Marvelous. 1966. V. 53; 54

LAMAR, MIRABEAU B.
Calendar of Lamar Papers. Austin: 1914. V. 52

LAMARCK, JEAN BAPTISTE ANTOINE DE MONET DE
Philosophie Zoologique ou Exposition des Considerations Relatives a l'Histoire Naturelle des Animaux... Paris: 1822. V. 47
Zoological Philosophy, an Exposition with Regard to the Natural History of Animals. London: 1914. V. 48; 50

LAMARTINE, A. DE
Graziella. London: 1921. V. 50

LA MARTINIERE, PIERRE MARTIN DE
A New Voyage into the Northern Countries, Describing the Manners, Customs, Superstititon, Buildings and Habits of the Norwegians, Laponians, Kilops, Borandians, Siberians, Samojedes, Zemblians and Islanders. London: 1674. V. 47
Voyage Des Pais Septentionaux. Paris: 1671. V. 50

LAMB, CAROLINE
Glenarvon. London: 1816. V. 47; 48; 51; 52; 53
Graham Hamilton. London: 1822. V. 48; 51

LAMB, CHARLES
The Adventures of Ulysses. London: 1808. V. 48
The Adventures of Ulysses. London: 1819. V. 53
Adventures of Ulysses. London: 1839. V. 53
Album Verses, with a Few Others. London: 1830. V. 48; 49; 52; 54
Beauty and the Beast. London: 1886. V. 49
Bon-Mots of Charles Lamb and Douglas Jerrold. London: 1893. V. 52
A Book Explaining the Ranks and Dignities of British Society. London: 1809. V. 51
The Child Angle: a Dream. London: 1910. V. 47
The Complete Letters of Charles and Mary Lamb. London: 1935. V. 47
A Dissertation Upon Roast Pig. London. V. 50; 51
A Dissertation Upon Roast Pig. Concord: 1902. V. 48; 50
A Dissertation Upon Roast Pig. New York: 1932. V. 48
Elia and the Last Essays of Elia. Newtown: 1923-30. V. 47; 50
Elia and the Last Essays of Elia. Newtown: 1931. V. 48; 54
Elia. Essays Which Have Appeared Under that Signature in the London Magazine... Philadelphia: 1828. V. 47; 50
Elia. Essays Which Have Appeared Under that Signature in the London Magazine... London: 1833. V. 50
Elia. Essays Which Have Appeared Under that Signature in the London Magazine. (with) Last Essays of Elia. London: 1823. V. 47; 49
Essays of Elia. New York: 1883. V. 51
The Essays of Elia... London: 1902. V. 50
The Essays of Elia. London: 1932. V. 49
Final Memorials...Consisting Chiefly of His Letters Not Before Published... London: 1848. V. 47; 52
John Woodvil. London: 1802. V. 47
The King and Queen of Hearts; with the Rogueries of the Knave Who Stole the Queen's Pies. London: 1900. V. 52
The Laughing Philosopher... London: 1825. V. 47
The Letters of Charles Lamb... Boston: 1905. V. 52; 53
The Letters of Charles Lamb To Which are Added Those of His Sister Mary Lamb. London: 1935. V. 50; 53
The Letters of Charles Lamb, With a Sketch of His Life. London: 1837. V. 47; 50; 52
The Letters... (with) The Essays of Elia. (with) Poems, Plays and Miscellaneous Essays. London: 1888/91/88. V. 53
The Life and Works... New York: 1899. V. 51
The Life and Works... London: 1899-1900. V. 47; 49; 50
The Life, Letters and Writings. London: 1876. V. 48; 54
The Life, Letters and Writings. 1890. V. 53
The Life, Letters and Writings... London: 1892. V. 49
The Life, Letters and Writings... London: 1900. V. 47
The Life, Letters and Writings... London: 1924. V. 47; 49
A Masque of Days. London: 1901. V. 48; 50; 54
Mr. H.; or Beware a Bad Name. Philadelphia: 1825. V. 54
Original Letters &c. of Sir John Falstaff and His Friends... London: 1796. V. 48; 52
Original Letters, &c. Of Sir John Falstaff, Selected From Genuine Manuscripts, Which Have Been in the Possession of Dame Quickly and Her Descendants, Near Four Hundred Years... Philadelphia: 1813. V. 48
Poetry for Children... Boston: 1812. V. 51; 53
Poetry for Children. London: 1872. V. 49
Prince Dorus; or Flattery Put Out of Countenance. London: 1889. V. 48
Satan in Search of a Wife: With the Whole Process of His Courtship and Marriage, and Who Danced at the Wedding. London: 1831. V. 52
Specimens of English Dramatic Poets Who Lived About the Time of Shakespeare... London: 1808. V. 53
Specimens of English Dramatic Poets Who Lived About the Time of Shakespeare... London: 1893. V. 52
Tales from Shakespeare. London: 1807. V. 47; 51
Tales from Shakespeare... London: 1816. V. 49
Tales from Shakespeare. London: 1903. V. 51
Tales from Shakespeare. London: 1905. V. 47; 52
Tales from Shakespeare. London: 1909. V. 47; 50; 51; 52; 53
Tales from Shakespeare. London: 1972. V. 50
The Works... London: 1818. V. 47; 48; 50; 52; 54
The Works... London: 1850. V. 54
The Works. New York: 1871. V. 50
The Works... London: 1900. V. 52
Works. London: 1903. V. 49; 52
The Works. London: 1903-05. V. 52
Works. London: 1904. V. 52
The Works... London: 1914-16. V. 50; 52

LAMB, DANA S.
Bright Salmon and Brown Trout. Barre: 1964. V. 50
Wood-Smoke and Water Cress. Barre: 1965. V. 50

LAMB, JAMES BLAND
The Birth and Triumph of Love. London: 1823. V. 54

LAMB, MABEL
Some Annals of the Lambs: a Border Family. London: 1926. V. 50

LAMB, MARTHA J.
History of the City of New York. New York: 1877-80. V. 48; 49; 52
The Homes of America. New York: 1879. V. 50; 51

LAMB, MARY
The Letters. London: 1935. V. 51
Mrs. Leicester's School; or the History of Several Young Ladies... London: 1810. V. 54
Mrs. Leicester's School; or the History of Several Young Ladies... London: 1820. V. 53

LAMB, R. H.
Lamb's Sherherd's Guide. Penrith: 1937. V. 51

LAMB, W.
The World Ends. 1937. V. 48
The World Ends. London: 1937. V. 52

LAMB, WILLIAM
The Battle of Fort Fisher North Carolina. Wilmington: 1900. V. 49

LAMBARDE, WILLIAM
Archeion, or, A Discourse Upon the High Courts of Justice in England. London: 1635. V. 50; 52
Dictionarium Angliae Topographicum & Historicum. London: 1730. V. 49
The Duties of Constables, Borsholders, Tythingmen and Such Other Lovve Ministers of the Peace... London: 1594. V. 51
Eirenarcha; or, of the Office of the Justices of Peace. London: 1581. V. 50
Eirenarcha: or of the Office of the Justices of Peace... London: 1582. V. 48
A Perambulation of Kent: Conteining the Description, Hystorie and Cutomes of that Shyre. London: 1596. V. 52

LAMBART, W. HUBERTO
The Ghost of Dunboy Castle. London: 1889. V. 48

LAMBE, DAVIES
Practical Observations on the Culture of Lucerne, Turnips, Burnet, Timothy Grass and Fowl meadow Grass. London: 1766. V. 48

LAMBE, JOHN
Briefe Description of the Notorious Life of Ion Lambe. London: 1880. V. 48

LAMBE, JOHN LAWRENCE
To Theodore Watts-Dunton. Sonnets 1912-1914. Tiptree, Esssex: 1915. V. 51; 54
Twelve Months of Travel. Manchester: 1888. V. 47

LAMBE, ROBERT
An Exact and Circumstantial History of the Battle of Floddon. Berwick-upon-Tweed: 1774. V. 47

LAMBERT & GERMAN NAVAL ARCHITECTS
Floating Equipment. Montreal: 1932. V. 52

LAMBERT, ANNE THERESE, MARCHIONESS DE
The Works... London: 1769. V. 51

LAMBERT, AYLMER BOURKE
A Description of the Genus Pinus. London: 1832. V. 48; 49; 50

LAMBERT, B.
The History and Survey of London and Its Environs. London: 1806. V. 50

LAMBERT, C. E.
The Bar-Sinister, or Memoirs of an Illegitimate. London: 1836. V. 50

LAMBERT, FRANCOIS
In Divi Lucae Evangelium Commentarii. Nuremburg: 1524. V. 47

LAMBERT, JOHAN HEINRICH
Pyrometrie Oder Vom Maasse des Feuers und der Warme. Berlin: 1779. V. 48; 50; 54

LAMBERT, JOHN
Travels through Canada and the United States of North America in the Years 1806, 1807 and 1808. London: 1816. V. 49; 52

LAMBERT, JOSEPH I.
One Hundred Years with the Second Cavalry. Topeka: 1939. V. 48

LAMBERT, M.
Little Henry. New York: 1825. V. 53

LAMBERT, MISS
The Hand-Book of Needlework. New York: 1842. V. 50

LAMBERT, W. G.
Babylonian Wisdom Literature. Oxford: 1960. V. 49

LAMBERT, WILL
Report of the Ceremonies of the Laying of the corner Stone of the Capitol of Texas. Austin: 1885. V. 49

LAMBERT, WILLIAM HARRISON
George Henry Thomas Oration Before the Society of the Army of the Cumberland. Cincinnati: 1885. V. 53; 54

LAMBETH, JOSEPH A.
Lambeth Method of Cake Decoration. London: 1937. V. 48

LAMBETH Palace Illustrated By a Series of Views Representing its Most Interesting Antiquities in Buildings, Portraits, Stained, Glass &c. London: 1805. V. 49

LAMBETH, WILLIAM ALEXANDER
Thomas Jefferson As an Architect and a Designer of Landscapes. Boston: 1913. V. 49

LAMESLE, CLAUDE
Epreuves Generales des Caracteres qui se Trouvent chez Claude Lamesle Fondeur de Caracteres d'Imprimerie. Paris: 1742. V. 47; 48

LA METTRIE, JULIEN OFFRAY DE
Oeuvres Philosophiques. Amsterdam: 1752. V. 49

LAMI, EUGENE
Voyage en Angleterre. Paris: 1829-30. V. 52

LAMINGTON, ALEXANDER BAILLIE COCHRANE, LORD
Poems. London: 1838. V. 51

LAMM, CARL JOHAN
Cotton in Mediaeval Textiles of the Near East. Paris: 1937. V. 48; 52

LAMOND, H.
The Sea Trout. London: 1916. V. 49; 51; 52; 53

LAMONT, JAMES
Seasons with the Sea-Horses; or, Sporting Adventures in the Northern Seas. London: 1861. V. 49
Seasons with the Sea-Horses: or, Sporting Adventures in the Northern Seas. New York: 1861. V. 48
Yachting in the Arctic Seas...Sport and Discovery in the Neighbourhood of spitzbergen and Novaya Zemlya. London: 1876. V. 48

LA MOTTE, ANTOINE HOUDART DE
Fables Nouvelles, Dediees au Roy... Paris: 1719. V. 49

LA MOTTE FOUQUE, FRIEDRICH HEINRICH KARL, FREIHERR DE
The Four Seasons; Minstrel Love; Wild Love; Magic Ring; Thiodolf; Romantic Fiction. London: 1843-46. V. 50
Undine... Leipzig: 1867. V. 52
Undine. London: 1909. V. 48; 50; 51; 52; 54
Undine. Paris: 1912. V. 51
Undine. London: 1919. V. 47
Undine. New York: 1919. V. 51
Undine. New York: 1930. V. 53; 54

L'AMOUR, LOUIS A.
Bendigo Shafter. New York: 1979. V. 48
The Californios. New York: 1974. V. 52
La Conquete de l'Ouest. (How the West Was Won). Paris: 1962. V. 48
Fair Blows the Wind. New York: 1978. V. 47; 50, 54
Frontier. New York: 1984. V. 51
Heller With Gun: A Gold Medal Original. Greenwich: 1958/55. V. 48
Hopalong Cassidy and the Rustlers of West Fork. London: 1951. V. 52
Hopalong Cassidy, Trouble-Shooter. London: 1953. V. 52
Jubal Sackett. New York: 1985. V. 54
Last of the Breed. New York: 1986. V. 51
The Lonesome Gods. New York: 1983. V. 53
Milkenny. 1978. V. 50
Over on the Dry Side. New York: 1975. V. 51; 52; 53
Rivers West. New York: 1975. V. 53
Smoke From This Altar. Oklahoma City: 1939. V. 48
To the Far Blue Mountain. New York: 1975. V. 49
The Walking Drum. New York: 1984. V. 52

LAMPMAN, ARCHBALD
Among the Millet and Other Poems. Ottawa: 1888. V. 54

LAMPRECHT, KURT
Regiment Reichstag - The Fight for Berlin, 1919. London: 1932. V. 50

LAMSON, J.
Round Cape Horn. Voyage of the Passenger Ship James W. Paige, From Maine to California in the Year 1852. Bangor: 1878. V. 47; 48

LAMY, BERNARD
The Art of Speaking: Written in French by Messieurs du Port Royal... London: 1676. V. 47

LANA TERZI, FRANCESCO
Prodromo Overo Saggio di Alcune Inventioni Nuove Premesso all'Arate Maestra... Brescia: 1670. V. 53

LANCASHIRE Leaders. Social and Political. Exeter: 1895. V. 53; 54

LANCASTER, BRUCE
The Scarlet Patch. Boston: 1947. V. 48

LANCASTER, CLAY
The Japanese Influence in America. New York: 1963. V. 53

LANCASTER, I.
The Soaring Birds. Chicago?: 1900. V. 54

LANCASTER, JOSEPH
British System of Education... Washington: 1812. V. 49
Improvements in Education, As It Respects the Industrious Classes of the Community... London: 1803. V. 52
Improvements in Education as It Respects the Industrious Classes of the Community... London: 1805. V. 52
The Lancasterian System of Education, with Improvements. Baltimore: 1821. V. 51
Letters on National Subjects, Auxiliary to Universal Education and Scientific Knowledge... Washington City: 1820. V. 49

LANCASTER, OSBERT
All Done from Memory. London: 1953. V. 47
Assorted Sizes. London: 1944. V. 50
Classical Landscape with Figures. London: 1947. V. 48
The Letters of Mercurius. London: 1970. V. 52
The Pleasure Garden. London: 1977. V. 47
Sailing to Byzantium - an Architectural Companion. London: 1969. V. 52
With an Eye to the Future. London: 1967. V. 49

LANCASTER, ROBERT A.
Historic Virginia Homes and Churches. Philadelphia: 1915. V. 47; 51

LANCELOT, CLAUDE
A New Method of Learning with Facility the Greek Tongue... London: 1777. V. 54

LANCEREAUX, ETIENNE
A Treatise on Syphilis Historical and Practical. London: 1868. V. 51
A Treatise on Syphilis Historical and Practical. London: 1868-69. V. 48; 49; 50; 51; 53

LANCEY, P. A.
The Birds of Natal and Zululand. London: 1964. V. 50

LANCHESTER, F. W.
Aerodynamics... London: 1907-08. V. 50
Aircraft in Warfare - the Dawn of the Fourth Arm. London: 1916. V. 47

LAND, ANDREW
Angling Sketches. London & New York: 1891. V. 50

THE LAND Grant of the Northern Pacific Railroad, as Described in Debate in the Senate of the United States and the House of Representatives by Those Who Felt Constrained to Vote Against Its Increase. Cambridge: 1870. V. 47

THE LAND of Enchantment. London: 1907. V. 48; 51

THE LAND We Live In, A Pictorial Sketch-Book. London: 1880. V. 51

THE LAND-LEVIATHAN; or, Modern Hydra: in Burlesque Verse, By the Way of Letter to a Friend. London: 1712. V. 49

LANDA, FRIAR DIEGO DE
Yucatan: Before and After the Conquest. Baltimore: 1937. V. 47

LANDACRE, PAUL
California Hills and Other Wood Engravings. Los Angeles: 1931. V. 50; 54

LANDAU, HORACE DE, BARON
Catalogue of Very Important Manuscripts and Printed Books... 1948. V. 52
Catalogue of Very Important Manuscripts and Printed Books... London: 1948. V. 51

LANDAU, JACOB
Kingdom of Dreams. New York: 1969. V. 47

LANDAUER, BELLA C.
Early American Trade Cards from the Collection of Bella C. Landauer. New York: 1927. V. 48
Some Aeronautical Music from the Collection of Bella C. Landauer. Paris: 1933. V. 49

LANDE, LAWRENCE
The Compleat Moralist and Bagatelle Poems. Montreal: 1972. V. 54
The Lawrence Lande Collection of Canadiana in the Redpath Library of McGill University. Montreal: 1965. V. 48

LANDECK, PHILIP
The Floating Opera. A Screenplay. New York: 1970. V. 53

LANDELLS, EBENEZER
The Boy's Own Toy-Maker: a Practical Illustrated Guide to the Useful Employment of leisure Hours. New York: 1860. V. 51

LANDEN, JOHN
The Residual Analysis; a New Branch of the Algebraic Art of Very Extensive Use, Both in Pure Mathematics and Natural Philosophy. (with) A Discourse Concerning the Residual Analysis. London: 1764/58. V. 52; 54

LANDER, FREDERICK W.
Additional Estimate for Fort Kearney, South Pass and Honey Lake Wagon Road. Washington: 1861. V. 47
Practicability of Railroads through South Pass. Washington: 1858. V. 47
Synopsis of a Report of the Reconnaissance of a Railroad Route from Puget Sound via South Pass to the Mississippi River. Washington: 1856. V. 47

LANDER, GEORGE
Bleak House; or, Poor 'Jo'. A Drama in Four Acts. London: 1883. V. 49
The Old Curiosity Shop. A Drama in Four Acts. London: 1883. V. 54

LANDER, RICHARD
Journal of an Expedition to Explore the Course and Termination of the Niger... 1832. V. 47
Journal of an Expedition to Explore the Course and Termination of the Niger... London: 1845. V. 52
Records of Captain Clapperton's Last Expedition to Africa... London: 1830. V. 49

LANDER, SAMUEL
Our Own Primary Arithmetic. Greensboro: 1863. V. 49; 50
Our Own School Arithmetic. Greensboro: 1863. V. 49; 52

LANDERHOLM, CARL
Notices and Voyages of the Famed Quebec Mission to the Pacific Northwest... Portland: 1956. V. 50

LANDIS, CHARLES K.
Carabajal, the Jew. A Legend of Monterey. Vineland: 1894. V. 47; 51

LANDMANN, ISAAC
The Principles of Fortification, Reduced Into Questions and Answers, for the Use of the Royal Military Academy at Woolwich. London: 1801. V. 50

LANDON, H. C. ROBBINS
Haydn: Chronicle and Works. London: 1976-80. V. 50

LANDON, JAMES TIMOTHY BAINBRIDGE
Eureka: a Sequel to Lord John Russell's Post Bag. (with) Eureka No. II. A Sequel to a Sequel. Oxford: 1851/53. V. 54
The Rime of the New Made Baccalare. Oxford: 1841. V. 51

LANDON, JOSEPH
Angel of Attack. Garden City: 1952. V. 48

LANDON, LAETITIA ELIZABETH
Complete Works. Boston: 1854. V. 52
The Fate of Adelaide, a Swiss Romantic Tale; and Other Poems. London: 1821. V. 52
The Golden Violet, with its Tales of Romance and Chivalry; and Other Poems. London: 1827. V. 50
The Improvisatrice and Other Poems. London: 1824. V. 52

LANDON, MELVILLE
Eli Perkins (At Large): His Sayings and Doings. New York: 1875. V. 51

LANDON, PERCEVAL
Lhasa. An Account of the Country and People of Central Tibet and of the Progress of the Mission Sent There by the English Government in the Year 1903-04. London: 1905. V. 50
Nepal. London: 1928. V. 53

LANDOR, ARNOLD HENRY SAVAGE
Across Coveted Lands or, a Journey from Flushing (Holland) to Calcutta. London: 1902. V. 50
Across the Unknown South America. London: 1913. V. 48; 51; 52; 54
Across Widest Africa. London: 1907. V. 47; 52
Alone with the Hairy Anu; or, 3800 Miles on a Pack Saddle and a Cruise to the Kurile Islands. London: 1893. V. 54
China and Allies. London: 1901. V. 47; 51; 52
China and Allies. New York: 1901. V. 49; 54
The Gems of the East. London: 1904. V. 49
In the Forbidden Land. London: 1898. V. 53
In the Forbidden Land. New York and London: 1899. V. 47; 49; 51; 52
Tibet and Nepal. 1905. V. 54
Tibet and Nepal... London: 1905. V. 49; 50

LANDOR, ROBERT EYRES
Selections from His Poetry and Prose... London: 1927. V. 54

LANDOR, WALTER SAVAGE
Andrea of Hungary, and Giovanna of Naples. London: 1839. V. 48; 51
The Complete Works of... London: 1927-36. V. 49
Epicurus, Leontion and Ternissa. 1896. V. 47; 49
Epicurus, Leontion and Ternissa. England: 1896. V. 47
Epicurus, Leontion and Ternissa. London: 1896. V. 48; 50; 51; 52
Gebir; a Poem, in Seven Books. London: 1798. V. 50
Gebir, Count Julian, and Other Poems. London: 1831. V. 48; 49; 52; 54
Heroic Idyls, with Additional Poems. London: 1863. V. 54
Imaginary Conversations. London: 1891. V. 51
Imaginary Conversations. New York: 1936. V. 54
Imaginary Conversations. Verona: 1936. V. 49; 52
The Last Fruit off an Old Tree. London: 1853. V. 47
Letters of an American, Mainly on Russia and Revolution. London: 1854. V. 47
Literary Hours: by Various Friends. Liverpool: 1837. V. 54
Pericles and Aspasia. London: 1836. V. 47; 49; 52; 53
Poems from the Arabic and Persian... Warwick: 1800. V. 52
The Works of... London: 1846. V. 47

LANDRE, CHRISTOPHE
Hauss Artzney. Augspurg: 1578. V. 47; 50; 53

LANDRIANI, PAOLO
Osservazioni Sui Difetti Prodotti Nei Teatari Dalla Cattiva Cost-Ruzione del Palco Scenico e su Alcune Inavvertenze Nel Dipingere le Decorazioni...(with) Aggiunta Alle Osservazioni Sui Teatrie Sulle Decorazioni... Milano: 1815/18. V. 48

LANDRIN, M. H. C.
A Treatise on Steel, Comprising the Theory, Metallurgy, Properties, Practical Working and Use. Philadelphia: 1868. V. 50

LANDRUM, GRAHAM
An Illustrated History of Grayson County, Texas. Fort Worth: 1960. V. 52

LANDRUM, J.
Colonial and Revolutionary History of Upper South Carolina. Greenville: 1897. V. 53

LANDRUM, J. B. O.
History of Spartanburg County... Atlanta: 1900. V. 50

LANDSBOROUGH, DAVID
Arran: Its Topography, Natural History and Antiquities. 1875. V. 49

LANDSCAPE *Illustrations of the Waverley Novels.* London: 1832. V. 52

LANDSEER, EDWIN
The Landseer Gallery. London: 1873. V. 50
The Landseer Series of Picture Books... London: 1882. V. 51; 52

LANDSEER, JOHN
A Descriptive, Explanatory and Critical, Catalogue of Fifty of the Earliest Pictures Contained in the National Gallery of Great Britain. London: 1834. V. 47
Lectures on the Art of Engraving, Deliverd at the Royal Institution of Great Britain. London: 1807. V. 48; 52
Sabaean Researches, In a Series of Essays, Addressed to Distinguished Antiquaries and Including the Substance of a Course of Lectures Delivered at the Royal Institution of Great Britain on the Engraved Hieroglyphics of Chaldea, Egypt & Canaan... London: 1823. V. 51

LANDSEER, THOMAS
Life and Letters of William Bewick. London: 1871. V. 47
Monkeyana. London: 1827. V. 47; 54

LANDSELL, HENRY
Through Siberia. London: 1882. V. 49

LANDSTEINER, KARL
The Specificity of Seriological Reactions. Springfield: 1936. V. 51; 53; 54

LANDSTROM, BJORN
Ships of the Pharaohs: 4000 Years of Egyptian Shipbuilding. Garden City: 1970. V. 49; 51

LANDWEHR, JOHN
Romeyn de Hooghe (1645-1708) as Book Illustrator, a Bibliography. Amsterdam: 1970. V. 47
Studies in Dutch Books with Coloured Plates Published 1662-1875. The Hague: 1976. V. 52
VOC A Bibliography of Publications Relating to the Dutch East India Company 1602-1800... Utrecht: 1991. V. 51

LANE, ALLEN STANLEY
Emperor Norton, the Mad Monarch of America. Caldwell: 1939. V. 47; 54

LANE, ARCHIBALD
A Rational and Speedy Method of Attaining to the Latin Tongue. London: 1695. V. 54

LANE, C. G.
Adventures in the Big Bush in the Haunts of the Aboriginal. London: 1920. V. 48; 50

LANE, CHARLES
Sporting Aquatints and Their Engravers 1775-1900. London: 1978-79. V. 54

LANE, DAVID
A Soldier's Diary. The Story of a Volunteer, 1862-1865. Jackson?: 1905?. V. 54

LANE, LEVI COOPER
The Surgery of the Head and Neck. San Francisco: 1896. V. 51
The Surgery of the Head and Neck. Philadelphia: 1898. V. 47; 49; 51; 54

LANE, MARK
Rush to Judgment. New York: 1966. V. 54

LANE, PATRICK
Letters from the Savage Mind. Vancouver: 1966. V. 47

LANE, RICHARD
Reports in the Court of Exchequer, Beinning in the Third and Ending in the Ninth Year of the Reign of the Late King James, etc. London: 1657. V. 51

LANE, SAMUEL A.
Fifty Years and Over of Akron and Summit County... Akron: 1892. V. 47

LANE, THOMAS
The Student's Guide through Lincoln's Inn. London: 1805. V. 50
The Student's Guide through Lincoln's Inn... London: 1814. V. 50

LANE, W. ARBUTHNOT
Cleft Palate and Hare Lip. (with) Operative Treatment of Chronic Constipation. London: 1905. V. 50
Cleft Palate and Hare Lip. (with) Operative Treatment of Chronic Constipation. London: 1905/04. V. 51
The Operative Treatment of Chronic Constipation. (with) The Kink of the Ileum in Chronic Intestinal Statis. London: 1909/10. V. 51

LANE, WILLIAM
A Few Clusters of the Seventy-Fifth Vintage: Consisting of Poems, on Various Subjects... Wycombe: 1819. V. 54
Poems on the Following Subjects: Abram and Lot... Reading: 1798. V. 51; 52; 54

LANE, YOTI
African Folk Tales. London: 1946. V. 52

LANEHAM, ROBERT
A Letter; Whearin Part of the Entertainment Untoo the Queenz Majesty, at Killingwoorth Castl in Warwick Sheer, in This Sommerz Progrest 1575 iz Signified... Warwick: 1784. V. 47; 52; 53

LANE-POOLE, STANLEY
Social Life in Egypt, a Description of the Country and Its People. London: 1884?. V. 52

LANES, SELMA G.
The Art of Maurice Sendak. New York: 1980. V. 47; 53
The Art of Maurice Sendak. London: 1981. V. 49; 53; 54

LANG, ANDREW
Angling Sketches. London: 1891. V. 48; 53
The Animal Story Book. London: 1896. V. 48; 51; 53; 54
Ballads and Lyrics of Old France: With Other Poems. London: 1872. V. 47; 48
The Blue Fairy Book. London: 1889. V. 47; 48; 54
The Blue Fairy Book. London: 1892. V. 52
The Blue Poetry Book. London: 1891. V. 53
The Book of Dreams and Ghosts. London: 1897. V. 52
The Book of Princes and Princesses by Mrs. Lang. New York: 1908. V. 54
The Book of Romance. London & New York: 1902. V. 48; 49; 50; 51; 54
A Book of Saints and Heroes. London: 1912. V. 49
The Brown Fairy Book. London: 1904. V. 49; 51
The Brown Fairy Book. New York: 1904. V. 52
The Crimson Fairy Book. London: 1903. V. 53
Grass of Parnassus, Rhymes Old and New. London: 1888. V. 47
The Green Fairy Book. Philadelphia. V. 49
The Green Fairy Book. London: 1892. V. 47; 48; 49
The Green Fairy Book. London: 1893. V. 52
The Grey Fairy Book. London: 1900. V. 48
A History of Scotland from the Roman Occupation. Edinburgh: 1900-07. V. 51
A History of Scotland from the Roman Occupation. London: 1907. V. 49; 52
The Life and Letters of John Gibson Lockhart. New York: 1897. V. 47; 48
The Lilac Fairy Book. London: 1910. V. 48
The Lilac Fairy Book. London: 1914. V. 52
The Mark of Cain. 1886. V. 48; 50
Old Friends. London: 1890. V. 54
The Olive Fairy Book. London: 1907. V. 51
The Orange Fairy Book. London: 1906. V. 47; 48; 52
Oxford: Brief Historical and Descriptive Notes. London: 1880. V. 50
The Pink Fairy Book. London: 1897. V. 50
Prince Charles Edward. Edinburgh: 1900. V. 50
Prince Charles Edward. London: 1900. V. 54
Prince Charles Edward. Paris: 1900. V. 47
Prince Ricardo of Pantouflia. London: 1893. V. 52
Princes and Princesses. London: 1908. V. 49
The Red Book of Animal Stories. London: 1899. V. 48; 54
The Red Book of Heroes. London: 1909. V. 47; 51; 54
The Red Fairy Book. London: 1890. V. 48; 50
The Red Fairy Book. London: 1891. V. 52
The Red Fairy Book. Philadelphia: 1924. V. 49
The Red Romance Book. London: 1905. V. 49
The Red Story Book. London: 1895. V. 48
St. Andrews. London: 1893. V. 52
The Secret of the Totem. London: 1905. V. 48; 50
Tales of a Fairy Court. London: 1905. V. 51
Tales of Troy and Greece. London: 1907. V. 51
The Violet Fairy Book. London: 1901. V. 51
XXII Ballades in Blue China. London: 1880. V. 48
The Yellow Fairy Book. London: 1894. V. 48; 52

LANG, D.
Hints for Dwellings: Consisting of Original designs for Cottages, Farmhouses, Villas &c. Plain and Ornamental... London: 1804. V. 49

LANG, G. BLAIR
Memoirs of an Art Dealer. Toronto: 1979. V. 47

LANG, H. C.
Rhopalocera Europae Descrita et Delineata. The Butterflies of Europe Described and Figured. London: 1884. V. 52

LANG, JOHN DUNMORE
Freedom and Independence for the Golden Lands of Australia. London: 1852. V. 49
An Historical and Statistical Account of New South Wales... London: 1837. V. 52
An Historical and Statistical Account of New South Wales... London: 1852. V. 54
Report of a Visit to Some of the Tribes of Indians, Located West of the Mississippi River. New York: 1843. V. 47

LANG, LEONORA BLANCHE
The All Sorts of Stories Book. London: 1911. V. 51; 54

LANG, LINCOLN A.
Ranching with Roosevelt. Philadelphia: 1926. V. 54

LANG, R. HAMILTON
Cyprus: Its History, Its Present Resources and Future Prospects. London: 1878. V. 49

LANG, W.
History of Seneca County, from the Close of the Revolutionary War to July, 1880. Springfield: 1880. V. 50

LANG, W. H.
Australia. London: 1900. V. 54

LANG, W. W.
A Paper on the Resources and Capabilities of Texas. Austin: 1881. V. 50

LANG, WILLIAM
Animal Magnetism, or, Mesmerism. New York: 1844. V. 48

LANGBAINE, GERARD
An Account of the English Dramatick Poets. Oxford: 1691. V. 47; 49; 50; 54
The Lives and Characters of the English Dramatic Poets. London: 1698. V. 50; 51; 53
The Lives and Characters of the English Dramatic Poets... London: 1699. V. 49; 50; 54

LANGDALE, THOMAS
The History of North Allerton, in the County of York. Northallerton: 1791. V. 50; 54

LANGDON, CHARLES W.
Treatise on the Civil and Criminal Jurisdiction of Justices of the Peace and Duties of Sheriffs and Constables, Especially Adapted to the Pacific States and Territories. San Francisco: 1870. V. 50

LANGDON, JOHN E.
Candian Silversmiths 1700-1900. Toronto: 1966. V. 50

LANGDON, STEPHEN
Excavations at Kish. The Hebert Weld (for the University of Oxford) and the Field Museum of natural History (Chicago). Paris: 1924-34. V. 49

LANGDON, WILLIAM B.
A Descriptive Catalogue of the Chinese Collection, Now Exhibiting at St. George's Place, Hyde Park Corner, London, with Condensed Accounts of the Genius, Government, History, Literature, Agriculture, Arts, Trade, Manners, Customs and Social Life... London: 1842. V. 49

LANGDON-DAVIES, JOHN
Behind the Spanish Barricades. London: 1936. V. 47; 49
Behind the Spanish Barricades. New York: 1937. V. 49

LANGE, DOROTHEA
An American Exodus: a Record of Human Erosion. New York: 1939. V. 47

LANGE, FRED W.
History of Baseball in California and Pacific Coast Leagues, 1847-1938. Oakland: 1938. V. 50; 52

LANGE, J. E.
Flora Agaricina Danica. Copenhagen: 1935-40. V. 50; 51; 54

LANGE, M.
Reconstruction Surgery and Traumatology... Basel & New York: 1953-56. V. 54

LANGEVIN, H. L.
British Columbia. Report of the Hon. H. L. Langevin, C.B., Minister of Public Works. Ottawa: 1872. V. 48

LANGFIELD, WILLIAM
Washington Irving, a Bibliography. New York: 1933. V. 51

LANGFORD, NATHANIEL PITT
Diary of the Washburn Expedition to the Yellowstone and Firehole Rivers in the Year 1870. 1905. V. 52

LANGFORD, R.
An Introduction to Trade and Business. London: 1830. V. 50; 52

LANGFORD, T.
Plain and Full Instructions to raise All Sorts of Fruit Trees that Prosper in England... London: 1681. V. 51
Plain and Full Instructions to Raise All Sorts of Fruit Trees that Prosper in England... London: 1696. V. 52; 54

LANGHAM, WILLIAM
The Garden of Health: Containing the Sundry Rare and Hidden Vertues and Properties of all Kindes of Simples and Plants. London: 1633. V. 52

LANGHANS, EDWARD A.
Eighteenth Century British and Irish Promptbooks. A Descriptive Bibliography. New York: 1987. V. 51

LANGHORNE, JOHN
The Fables of Flora. London: 1771. V. 50
The Fables of Flora. London: 1794. V. 48
Frederic and Pharamond, or the Consolations of Human Life. London: 1769. V. 52; 54
A Hymn to Hope. London: 1761. V. 54
Poetical Works. London: 1766. V. 47; 48; 50
Solyman and Almena. London: 1762. V. 48; 53
The Tears of Music. London: 1760. V. 47; 54

LANGHORNE, RICHARD
Considerations Touching the Great Question of the King's Right in Dispensing with the Penal Laws. London: 1687. V. 49; 51; 52

LANGLAND, WILLIAM
The Vision and Creed of Piers Ploughman. London: 1842. V. 51; 54
The Vision and Creed of Piers Ploughman. London: 1856. V. 48; 51
The Vision of Pierce Plowman, Newlye Imprynted After the Authours Olde Copy, with a Brefe Summary of the Principall Matters Set Before Very Part Called Passus. London: 1561. V. 47
The Vision of William Concerning Piers the Plowman. New Rochelle: 1901. V. 50
The Vision of William Concerning Piers the Plowman. New York: 1901. V. 48

THE LANGLEY Aerodrome. Washington: 1901. V. 51

LANGLEY, BATTY
The Builders Compleat Assistant. London: 1766. V. 53
The Builder's Director, or Bench-Mate. London: 1763. V. 48
The Builder's Jewel... London: 1746. V. 52
The Builder's Jewel... London: 1763. V. 49
The Builder's Jewel... Haddington: 1805. V. 52
The City and County Builder's and Workman's Treasury of Designs... London: 1750. V. 51
Gothic Architecture, Improved by Rules and Proportions... London: 1793. V. 50
Gothic Architecture, Improved by Rules and Proportions... London: 1797. V. 52
New Principles of Gardening, or, The Laying Out and Planting Parterres, Groves, Wildernesses, Labyrinths, Avenues, Parks, Etc. London: 1728. V. 52
Pomoma; or, the Fruit Garden Illustrated. London: 1729/28. V. 48; 50
Practical Geometry Applied to the Useful Arts of Building, Surveying, Gardening and mensuration... London: 1726. V. 52
A Survey of Westminster Bridge, as 'tis Now Sinking into Rain. London: 1748. V. 51

LANGLEY, HENRY G.
A Map and Street Directory of San Francisco. San Francisco: 1872. V. 52

LANGLEY, JIM A.
The Peanut Special: an Inaugural Commemoration. Atlanta: 1977. V. 50

LANGLEY, SAMUEL PIERPONT
Langley Memoir on Mechanical Flight. Washington: 1911. V. 48; 49; 54
Researches on Solar Heat and Its Absorption by the Earth's Atmosphere... Washington: 1884. V. 48

LANGLOIS
The Transmigration of the Seven Brahamans. New York: 1931. V. 50

LANGLOIS DE MOTTEVILLE, FRANCOISE
Memoirs for the History of Anne of Austria, Wife to Lewis XIII of France... London: 1726/25. V. 47

LANGLOTZ, ERNST
The Art of Magna Graecia: Greek Art in Southern Italy and Sicily. London: 1965. V. 48; 52
The Art of Magna Graecia: Greek Art in Southern Italy and Sicily. New York: 1965. V. 52

LANGMAN, I. K.
A Selected Guide to the Literature on the Flowering Plants of Mexico. Philadelphia: 1964. V. 47; 48; 51; 52; 53; 54

LANGMUIR, IRVING
The Collected Works. London: 1960-62. V. 49

LANGREN, MICHEL FLORENTZ VAN
Obeservation Astronomique du Comete Commence au Mois de Decembre en l'an MDCLII. Brussels?: 1653. V. 47

LANGSDORFF, GEORGE H. VON
Bermerkungen auf Einer Reise um die Welt in de Jahren 1803 bis 1807. Frankfurt: 1812. V. 47
Langsdorff's Narrative of the Rezanov Voyage to Nueva California in 1806... San Francisco: 1927. V. 47
Voyages and Travels in Various Parts of the World, ... 1803, 1804, 1805, 1806 & 1807. London: 1813. V. 47; 52
Voyages and Travels in Various Parts of the World, ... 1803, 1804, 1805, 1806 & 1807. Amsterdam: 1968. V. 51

LANGSHAW, JAMES
A Letter to the Reverend Mr. R. Houseman. Lancaster: 1787. V. 54

LANG-SIMS, L.
Canterbury Cathedral: Mother Church of Holy Trinity. London: 1979. V. 49

LANGTOFT, PIERRE DE
The Chronicle. London: 1866. V. 52

LANGTON, JANE
The Transcendental Murder. New York: 1964. V. 49; 50

LANGTON, N.
The Cat in Ancient Egypt, Illustrated from the Collection of Cat and Other Egyptian Figures formed by N. & B. Langton. Cambridge: 1940. V. 51

LANGTON, ROBERT
The Childhood and Youth of Charles Dickens. London: 1891. V. 49; 54

THE LANGUAGE of Flowers, Poetically Expressed, Being a Complete Flora's Album. New York: 1853. V. 47

THE LANGUAGE of Flowers, With Illustrative Poetry: to Which are Now Added the Calendar of Flowers and the Dial of Flowers. London: 1846. V. 50

THE LANGUAGE of the Walls; and a Voice from the Shop Windows. Manchester: 1855. V. 47

LANGUET, HUBERT
De La Pvissance Legitime Dv Prince svr le Pevple, et du Peuple sur Le prince. 1581. V. 48; 51; 53
Vindiciae, Contra Tyrannos; Sive De Principis In Populum, Populique in Principem... Edinburgh: 1579. V. 51; 53

LANGWORTHY, EDWARD
Memoirs of the Life of the Late Charles Lee, Esq., Lieutenant Colonel of the Forty Fourth Regiment... Dublin: 1792. V. 47

LANGWORTHY, FRANKLIN
Scenery of the Plains, Mountain and Mines. Ogdensburgh: 1855. V. 47; 52

LANHAM, EDWIN M.
Sailors Don't Care. Paris: 1929. V. 48

LANIER, HENRY WYSHAM
A. B. Frost: the American Sportsman's Artist. New York: 1933. V. 49; 50
Greenwich Village: Today and Yesterday. New York: 1949. V. 47

LANIER, NICOLAS
Prove Prime Fatti a l'Aquaforte da N. Lanier a l'Eta Sua Giovenile di Sessanta Otto Anni. 1656. V. 53
Prove Prime Fatti a l'Aquaforte da N. Lanier a l'Eta Sua Giovenile di Sessanta Otto Anni. London: 1656. V. 49

LANIER, SIDNEY
Florida: Its Scenery, Climate and History. Philadelphia: 1881. V. 47; 48
Letters: Sidney Lanier to Col. John G. James. Austin: 1942. V. 48; 52
Poems. Philadelphia & London: 1877. V. 51; 53; 54
The Science of English Verse. New York: 1880. V. 48

LANIER, STERLING E.
The Peculiar Exploits of Brigadier Ffellowes. New York: 1971. V. 53

LANIGAN, ERNEST J.
The Baseball Cyclopedia. (with) First Supplement (1922), and Third Supplement (1924). New York: 1922/22/24. V. 47

LANIGAN, JOHN
An Ecclesiastical History of Ireland. 1822. V. 49; 50; 54

LANKESTER, E. RAY
Monograph of the Okapi. London: 1910. V. 48; 51; 53
A Treatise on Zoology. London: 1900-09. V. 48; 52

LANKESTER, EDWIN
An Account of Askern and Its Mineral Springs. Together with a Sketch of the Natural History and Brief Topography of the Immediate Neighbourhood. London: 1842. V. 53
Hayden's Dictionary of Popular Medicine and Hygiene. London: 1875. V. 54
Vegetable Substances Used for the Food of Man. London: 1846. V. 49

LANMAN, CHARLES
Adventures in the Wilds of North America. London: 1854. V. 51
Adventures in the Wilds of the United States... Philadelphia: 1856. V. 47
Adventures of an Angler in Canada, Nova Scotia and the United States. London: 1848. V. 52; 53
Farthest North; or Life and Explorations of Lieutenant James Booth Lockwood of the Greely Expedition. New York: 1885. V. 48; 52

LANNING, G.
Wild Life in China, or Chats on Chinese Birds and Beasts. Shanghai: 1911. V. 53

LA NOUE, FRANCOIS DE
Discovrs Politiqves et Militaires du Seigneur de la Noue. Basle: 1587. V. 54
The Politicke and Militarie Discourses of the Lord de la Nowe. London: 1588. V. 50

LANSDALE, JOE R.
The Magic Wagon. New York: 1986. V. 54
Mr. Weed-Eater. Huntington Beach: 1993. V. 51

LANSDELL, HENRY
Chinese Central Asia: a Ride to Little Tibet. New York: 1894. V. 49

LANSDOWNE, GEORGE GRANVILLE, BARON
The British Enchanters; or, No Magic Like Love. London: 1706. V. 48
The Genuine Works in Verse and Prose... London: 1736. V. 48
Heroick Love: a Tragedy... London: 1698. V. 48; 50
Poems Upon Several Occasions. London: 1712. V. 50; 51; 54
The She-Gallants: a Comedy. London: 1696. V. 48
Three Plays, viz. The She-Gallants, a Comedy. Heroick Love, a Tragedy. The Jew of Venice, a Comedy. London: 1713. V. 47; 48

LANSDOWNE, HENRY WILLIAM PETTY FITZMAURICE, 6TH MARQUIS OF
Catalogue of the Celebrated Collection of Ancient Marbles, the Property of the Most Honourable the Marquess of Lansdowne, M.V.O., D.S.O....March 5, 1930. London: 1930. V. 52
The Queeney Letters. New York: 1934. V. 52

LANSDOWNE, J. FENWICK
Birds of the Eastern Forest. Boston: 1968-70. V. 50
Birds of the Eastern Forest. Toronto: 1968/70. V. 48
Birds of the Northern Forest (Canada). Toronto: 1966. V. 49
Birds of the West Coast. Boston: 1976. V. 48
Birds of the West Coast. Toronto: 1976. V. 47
Birds of the West Coast. Boston: 1976-80. V. 49
Birds of the West Coast. Toronto: 1976-80. V. 48; 52; 54

THE LANTHORN Book. New York: 1898. V. 47; 49; 53

LANYON, ANDREW
Peter Lanyon, 1918-1964. 1990. V. 52

LANZ, PHILIPPE LOUIS
Analytical Essay on the Construction of machines. London: 1820. V. 48

LANZONE, RIDOLFO VITTORIS
Dizionario di Mitologia Egizia. Torino & Amsterdam: 1881-86/75. V. 49

LAPE, ESTHER
American Medicine: Expert Testimony Out of Court. New York: 1937. V. 52

LA PEROUSE, JEAN FRANCOIS GALAUP DE
Voyage de La Perouse Autour du Monde, Publie Conformement au Decret du 22 Avril 1791, et Redige... Paris: 1797. V. 50
The Voyage of La Perouse Round the World, in the Years 1785, 1786, 1787 and 1788... London: 1798. V. 47
A Voyage Round the World, Performed In the Years 1785, 1786, 1787 and 1788 by the Boussole and Astrolabe. London: 1799. V. 50
A Voyage Round the World, Performed in the Years 1785, 1786, 1787 and 1788 by the Boussole and Astrolabe, Under the command of J. F. B. de La Perouse... Amsterdam/New York: 1968. V. 47

LAPHAM, INCREASE A.
The Antiquities of Wisconsin, as Surveyed and Described...on Behalf of the American Antiquarian Society... Washington: 1855. V. 47
Wisconsin: Its Geography and Topography, History, Geology and Mineralogy... Milwaukee: 1846. V. 47

LAPIDE, JOHAN DE
Decisiones Casvvm Qvi Sacerdotibvs in Missaravm Celebratione Contingere Solent (etc). Konstanz: 1598. V. 51

LAPINE, JAMES
Sunday in the Park with George. New York: 1986. V. 47; 51; 54

LAPINER, ALAN
Pre-Columbian Art of South America. New York: 1976. V. 52

LA PLACE, PIERRE DE
Politiqve Discourses, Treating of the Differences and Inequalities of Vocations... London: 1578. V. 47

LAPLACE, PIERRE SIMON
Exposition du Systeme du Monde. Paris: 1796. V. 50
Mecanique Celeste. Boston: 1829-39. V. 47; 50; 51
Oeuvres Completes. Paris: 1843-47. V. 53
The System of the World. London: 1809. V. 54

LA PLANCHE, REGNIER DE
A Legendarie Conteining an Ample Discovrse of the Life and Behaviour of Charles Cardinal of Lorraine and His Brethren, of the House of Guise. 1577. V. 50

LAPOINTE, PAUL MARIE
Six Poems. Iroquois Falls: 1955. V. 47

LAPORTE, JOHN
The Progress of a Water-Coloured Drawing,... London: 1801. V. 49
The Progress of a Water-Coloured Drawing... London: 1802. V. 47; 48; 53
The Progress of a Water-Coloured Drawing... London: 1808. V. 48
Progressive Lessons Sketched from Nature. Parts I-IV. London: 1798-99. V. 49

LA PRIMAUDAYE, PIERRE DE
The French Academie. London: 1618. V. 49; 52

LA QUINTINYE, JEAN DE
The Compleat Gard'ner. London: 1699. V. 51
The Complete Gard'ner; or, Directions for Cultivating and Right Ordering of Fruit Gardens and Kichen-Gardens. London: 1710. V. 50; 51
Instruction Pour les Jardins, Fruitiers et Potagers, avec un Traite des Orangers, et des Reflexions sur l'Agriculture. Paris: 1746-56. V. 47

LARAMIE, WYOMING.
Revised Ordinances and Charter of the City of Laramie, Wyoming. Laramie: 1900. V. 54

LARBAUD, VALERY
200 Chambres, 200 Sales de Bains. La Haye: 1927. V. 54
Rues et Visages de Paris. Paris: 1926. V. 48; 51

LARCOM, HENRY
Distressing Narrative of the Loss of the Ship Margaret of Salem. 1810. V. 50

LARCOM, LUCY
Childhood Songs. Boston: 1875. V. 49
Poems. Boston: 1869. V. 54
The Unseen Friend. Boston: 1892. V. 54

LARDEN, W.
Recollection of an Old Mountaineer. 1910. V. 53
Recollections of an Old Mountaineer. London: 1910. V. 52

LARDEN, WALTER
Inscriptions from Swiss Chalets. Oxford: 1913. V. 54

LARDNER, DIONYSIUS
An Analytical Treatise on Plane and Spherical Trigonometry, and the Analysis of Angular Sections. London: 1826. V. 49
Lectures on the Steam Engine, In Which Its Construction and Operation are Familiarly Explained... London: 1832. V. 50
The Museum of Science and Art. London: 1854-56. V. 49
Railway Economy: a Treatise on the New Art of Transport, Its Management, Prospects and Relations... London: 1850. V. 49
A Rudimentary Treatise on the Steam Engine: for the Use of Beginners. London: 1859. V. 50
The Steam Engine Familiarly Explained and Illustrated... London: 1836. V. 50
A Treatise on Algebra, from the Encyclopedia Metropolitana. London: 1838. V. 47

LARDNER, RING W.
Bib Ballads. Chicago & New York: 1915. V. 47; 48; 49; 51; 52; 54
The Big Town. Indianapolis: 1921. V. 51
The Big Town. New York: 1925. V. 52
First and Last. New York: 1934. V. 51
The Golden Honeymoon and Haircut. 1926. V. 50
How to Write Short Stories (With Samples). New York: 1924. V. 48
June Moon. New York: 1930. V. 49; 54
Lose With a Smile. New York: 1933. V. 48; 54
The Love Nest and Other Stories. New York: 1926. V. 50; 51; 53
Own Your Own Home. Indianapolis: 1919. V. 51
Say It With Oil. A Few Remarks About Wives. New York: 1923. V. 47; 48
Symptoms of Being 35. Indianapolis: 1921. V. 51
You Know me Al. New York: 1960. V. 51

LARDNER, W. B.
A History of Placer and Nevada Counties California LA Historic Company 1924. Los Angeles: 1924. V. 51

LAREN, A. J. VAN
Cactus. Los Angeles: 1935. V. 47; 51; 52

LARISON, CORNELIUS W.
The Clas Abrod. A Descipshun ov the Tenting Tur Mad bi the Techerz and Students ov the Academi ov Siens and Art at Ringos, N.J. 1877. Ringoes: 1888. V. 49; 51
The Larisun Famili: A Biografic Scetch ov the Descendants ov Jon Larisun the Dan, thru hiz Sun Jamz Larisun and Hiz Grandsun Andru Laraisun. Ringoes: 1888. V. 47; 49; 51
Silvia Dubois, (Now 116 Yers Old). A Biografy ov the Slav Who Whipt her Mistres and Gand her Fredom. Ringoes: 1883. V. 47; 53
The Tenting School: a Description of the Tours Taken and of the Field Work Done...in the Academy of Science and Art at Ringos, N.J. During the Year 1882. Ringoes: 1883. V. 47; 49; 51

THE LARK: a Collection of Choice Scots Songs Together with a Few Songs for the Bottle. Edinburgh: 1768. V. 48

LARKIN, EDWARD
Speculum Patrum: A Looking-Glasse of the Fathers, Wherein... London: 1659. V. 50

LARKIN, PHILIP
All What Jazz. London: 1970. V. 50; 52; 53
Aubade. Salem: 1980. V. 47; 48; 49; 52; 54
The Fantasy Poets - Number Twenty-One. Swinford, Eynsham: 1954. V. 52
A Girl in winter. London: 1947. V. 50; 51
A Girl in Winter. New York: 1962. V. 51
High Windows. London: 1974. V. 47; 49; 51; 53
High Windows. New York: 1974. V. 50; 51; 53
High Windows. London: 1976. V. 50
Jill. London: 1946. V. 53
Jill. London: 1964. V. 49; 51
The Less Deceived. 1955. V. 47
The Less Deceived. Hessle, East Yorkshire: 1955. V. 50; 51; 53
The Less Deceived... London: 1955. V. 52
The Less Deceived. 1956. V. 49
The Less Deceived. New York: 1960. V. 50
The North Ship. London: 1945. V. 47; 50; 53; 54
The North Ship. London: 1965. V. 49; 50
The North Ship. London: 1966. V. 51
The Whitsun Weddings. London: 1964. V. 47; 48; 49; 51; 52; 54

LARKIN, PHILIP continued
The Whitsun Weddings: Poems. New York: 1964. V. 53

LARKIN, THOMAS OLIVER
The Larkin Papers: Personal, Business and Official Correspondence of Thomas Oliver Larkin.. Berkeley: 1951-64. V. 54
The Larkin Papers: Personal, Business and Official Correspondence of Thomas Oliver Larkin...Volume I. 1822-42. Berkeley: 1951. V. 54
The Larkin Papers: Personal Business and Official Correspondence of Thomas Oliver Larkin...Volume II. 1843-1844. Berkeley: 1952. V. 54
The Larkin Papers: Personal, Business and Official Correspondence of Thomas Oliver Larkin...Volume III, 1845. Berkeley: 1952. V. 54
The Larkin Papers: Personal, Business and Official Correspondence of Thomas Oliver Larkin...Volume IV, 1845-46. Berkeley: 1953. V. 54
The Larkin Papers: Personal, Business and Official Correspondence of Thomas Oliver Larkin...Volume VII, 1847-48. Berkeley: 1960. V. 54

LARMINE, MARGARET RIVERS
Soames Green. London: 1925. V. 48

LARMOR, JOSEPH
Mathematical and Physical Papers. Cambridge: 1929. V. 53
Memoir & Scientific Correspondence of the Late Sir George Gabriel Stokes. 1907. V. 49; 50

L'ARMOUR, LOUIS
Rivers West. New York: 1975. V. 49

LARNER, E. T.
Practical Television. 1928. V. 54
Practical Television. London: 1928. V. 53

LA ROCHE, F.
En Route to the Klondike. A Practical Guide. Chicago: 1897. V. 52

LA ROCHE, RENE
Pneumonia: its Supposed Connection, Pathological and Etiological with Autumnal Fevers... Philadelphia: 1854. V. 48; 51; 54
Yellow Fever, Considered In its Historical, Pathological, Etiological and Therapeutical Relations. Philadelphia: 1855. V. 51; 52

LA ROCHEFOUCAULD, FRANCOIS, DUC DE
Maximes... Paris: 1827. V. 50
Maximes. London: 1902. V. 54
Moral Maxims. London: 1749. V. 48
Moral Maxims. Waltham St. Lawrence: 1924. V. 53

LA ROCHE-GUILHEM,
The History of Female Favourites. London: 1772. V. 49

LA ROCHE-GUILHEM, ANNE DE
Zingis: a Tartarian History. London: 1692. V. 47

LAROCHEJAQUELEIN, MARCHIONESS DE
Memoirs of the Marchioness De Larochejaquelein. Edinburgh: 1816. V. 52

LA ROQUE, J. DE
A Voyage to Arabia the Happy, by Way of the Eastern Ocean, and the Streights of the Red Sea: Perform'd by the French for the First Time, A.D., 1708, 1709, 1710. London: 1726. V. 47; 49

LARRABEE, E.
Knoll Design. New York: 1981. V. 50; 51; 53; 54

LARRANCE, ISAAC
Larrance's Post Office Chart, and Maps of Ten States, Showing the Locality of the Counties and County Seats in a Moment by Figures... Cincinnati: 1866. V. 51

LARREY, D. J.
Surgical Memoirs of the Campaigns of Russia, Germany and France. Philadelphia: 1832. V. 48; 49

LARROQUE, MATTHIEU DE
The History of the Eucharist Divided into Three Parts. London: 1684. V. 49

LARSEN, ELLOUISE BAKER
American Historical Views of Staffordshire China. Garden City: 1950. V. 51

LARSEN, HENNING
An Old Icelandic Medical Miscellany. Oslo: 1931. V. 50

LARSEN, JACK LENOR
The Dyer's Art. New York: 1976. V. 48

LARSEN, K.
Tropical Botany, Proceedings of a Symposium Held August 10-12, 1978. 1979. V. 52

LARSEN, NELLA
Passing. New York: 1929. V. 54

LARSEN, SOFUS
Danish Eighteenth Century Bindings 1730-1780. Copenhagen: 1930. V. 50

LARSEN, T.
The Butterflies of Kenya and Their Natural History. London: 1991. V. 49; 52

LARSON, P. S.
Tobacco: Experimental and Clinical Studies. Baltimore: 1961. V. 48

LARSON, ROGER KEITH
Controversial James. An Essay on the Life and Work of Geoge Wharton James. San Francisco: 1991. V. 47; 52; 54

LARSSON, CARL
Larssons. Stockholm: 1902. V. 53

LART, C. E.
Jacobite Extracts of Births, Marriages and Deaths with Notes and Appendices. The Parochial Registers of Saint Germain-en Laye, Volume 1, 1689-1702. London: 1910. V. 54

LARTIGUE, JACQUES HENRI
Boyhood Photos...the Family Album of a Gilded Age. 1966. V. 52
Boyhood Photos...the Family Album of a Gilded Age. Lausanne: 1966. V. 47; 49; 52
Diary of a Century. New York: 1970. V. 47; 52
Les Femmes. New York: 1974. V. 54

LA RUE, MABEL GUINNIP
Cats for the Tooseys. New York: 1939. V. 51

LARWOOD, JACOB
The History of Signboards, from the Earliest Times to the Present Day. London: 1866. V. 48
The Story of the London Parks. London: 1872. V. 50

LA SAGE, ALAIN RENE
The Adventures of Gil Blas De Santillane. London: 1819. V. 51

LASATER, LAURENCE M.
The Lasater Philosophy of Cattle Raising. El Paso: 1972. V. 48

LASCARIS, CONSTANTINE
In Hoc Libro Haec Continentur...de Octo Partibus Or(ati)onis Lib. I...de Constructione Liber Secundus... Venice: 1515?. V. 47

LAS CASES, EMMANUEL, COMTE DE
Journal of the Private Life and Conversations of the Emperor Napoleon at Saint Helena. London: 1824. V. 52

LASCELLES, EDWARD, PSEUD.
Scenes from the Life of Edward Lascelles, Gent. Dublin: 1837. V. 50; 52

LA SERRE, JEAN PUGET, SIEUR DE
The Secretary in Fashion; or, an Elegant and Compendious Way of Writing All Manner of Letters. London: 1654. V. 48
The Secretary in Fashion: or, an Elegant and Compendious Way of Writing All Manner of Letters. London: 1683. V. 47; 49

LASHLEY, KARL SPENCER
Brain Mechanisms and Intelligence: a Quantitative Study of Injuries to the Brain. Chicago: 1929. V. 50

LASINIO, CARLO
Ornati Presi da Graffiti e Pitture Antiche Esistenti in Firezne. Florence: 1789. V. 53

LASKEY, J. C.
A Description of the Series of Medals Struck at the National Medal Mint by Order of Napoleon Bonaparte... London: 1818. V. 51; 53

LASKI, HAROLD
Parliamentary Government in England. London: 1938. V. 54
The State in Theory and Practice. New York: 1935. V. 54

LASNER, MARK SAMUELS
A Selective Checklist of the Published Work of Aubrey Beardsley. Boston: 1995. V. 53

LASSAIGNE, JACQUES
The Ballet. 1969. V. 54
Chagall. Paris: 1957. V. 52
Flemish Painting. Geneva: 1957-58. V. 53
Flemish Painting... London: 1957-58. V. 49
Marc Chagall: Drawings & Watercolors for "The Ballet". New York: 1969. V. 47; 52
Marc Chagall, the Ceiling of the Paris Opera. New York: 1966. V. 48

LASSELS, RICHARD
An Italian Voyage, or, a Compleat Journey through Italy. London: 1698. V. 47; 50
The Voyage of Italy, or a Compleat Journey through Italy. London: 1670. V. 47; 49
The Voyage of Italy, Or a Compleat Journey through Italy. Paris;: 1670. V. 50

LASSEPAS, ULISES URBANO
De La Colonizacion de La Baja California y Decreto de 10 Marzo de 1857. Mexico City: 1859. V. 47

LASSUS, JEAN
Antioch On-the-Orontes V (only): Les Portiques d'Antioche. Princeton: 1972. V. 50

LASSWEL, MARY
Suds in Your Eye. Boston: 1945. V. 51

LASSWELL, MAY
John Henry Kirby. Austin: 1967. V. 48; 49

THE LAST Blow; or, An Unanswerable Vindication of the Society of Exeter College. London: 1755. V. 53

LAST, JEF
The Spanish Tragedy. London: 1939. V. 49; 50

THE LAST of the Buffalo. Cincinnati: 1909. V. 50

THE LAST of the Garayes and Other Poems by an Englishwoman. Dinan,: 1868. V. 47

THE LAST WORDS of Polly Goold. 1790-1800. V. 47

LAST Words on the History of the (Early) Title-Page; With Notes on some Colophons. London: 1891. V. 48

THE LAST Years of Mary Queen of Scots. London: 1990. V. 50

LASTEYRIE, CHARLES PHILIBERT, COMTE DE
Lettres Autographes et Inedites de Henry IV... Paris: 1816. V. 53; 54
Typographie Economique ou l'Art de l'Imprimerie mis a la Portee de Tous, et Applicable aux Differens Besoins Sociaux. Paris: 1837. V. 50; 54

LA SUZE, HENRIETTE DE COLIGNY, COMTESSE DE
Recueil de Pieces Galantes, en Prose et en Vers de Madame la Comtesse de La Suze,... A Lyon: 1695. V. 53; 54

LASZLO, P. A. DE
Selections from the Work of P.A. de Laszlo, Represented By... London: 1921. V. 53

LATCH, JEAN
Plusieurs Tres-Bons Cases, Come Ils Estoyent Adjudgees es trois Premiers ans du Raign du Feu Roy Charles le Premier en La Court de Bank le Roy, Non Encore Pubilees per Aucum Autre (etc.). London: 1661. V. 47; 51; 53

THE LATE Contemplated Insurrection in Charleston, S.C., with the Execution of Thirty-Six of the Patriots: the Death of William Irving, the Provoked Husband; and Joe Devaul, for Refusing to be the Slave of Mr. Roach.... New York: 1850. V. 48

THE LATE Gallant Exploits of a Famous Balancing Captain: a New Song. London: 1741. V. 54

THE LATE Insurrection in Demerara, and Riot in Barbados. 1823. V. 47; 51

LATERRIERE, PIERRE DE SALES
A Political and Historical Account of Lower Canada; with Remarks on the Present Situation of the People, as Regards Their Manners, Character, Religion, Etc. London: 1830. V. 48

LATHAM, CHARLES
The Gardens of Italy. London: 1905. V. 47
In English Homes. London: 1904. V. 54
In English Homes. Covent Garden: 1908-09. V. 50

LATHAM, GEORGE
The History of Stydd Chapel and Preceptory, Near Ribchester, Lancashire. London: 1853. V. 48; 53

LATHAM, HENRY
Black and White a Journal of a Three Months' Tour in the United States. London: 1867. V. 47; 50

LATHAM, J.
An Essay on the Tracheae or Windpipes of Various Kinds of Birds. London: 1798. V. 51

LATHAM, PETER M.
The Collected Works of Dr. P. M. Latham. London: 1876-78. V. 48; 50; 52; 54
Lectures On Subjects Connected with Clinical Medicine, Comprising Diseases of the Heart. London: 1846. V. 54
Lectures on Subjects Connected with Clinical Medicine; Comprising Diseases of the Heart. Philadelphia: 1847. V. 48

LATHAM, PHILIP
Missing Men of Saturn. New York: 1953. V. 51; 53

LATHAM, ROBERT GORDON
A Dictionary of the English Language. London: 1872. V. 48
A Dictionary of the English Language. London: 1990. V. 48
Elements of Comparative Philogy. London: 1862. V. 48
The Ethnology of the British Colonies and Dependencies. London: 1851. V. 48; 54
The Nationalities of Europe. London: 1863. V. 50

LATHAM, SIMON
Falconry or the Faulcons Lure and Cure in Two Books. (and) New and Second Booke of Faulconry. London: 1633. V. 48; 50; 53

LATHAM, WILFRID
The States of the River Plate... London: 1866. V. 47; 49; 54
The States of the River Plate. London: 1868. V. 47; 52

LATH BURY, THOMAS
A History of the Nonjurors; their Controversies and Writings... London: 1845. V. 52

LATHEN, EMMA
Banking On Death. New York: 1961. V. 50

LATHERBURY, MARY A.
Idyls of the Months. Poems and Drawings. New York: 1885. V. 54

LATHOM, FRANCIS
Men and Manners, a Novel. London: 1799-1800. V. 54

LATHROP, DOROTHY
The Fairy Circus. New York: 1942. V. 49
Puppies for Keeps. New York: 1943. V. 50

LATHROP, GEORGE
Some Pioneer Recollections Being the Autobiogrpahy of George Lathrop. Philadelphia: 1927. V. 51

LATHROP, GEORGE PARSONS
A Masque of Poets. Boston: 1878. V. 48
A Study of Hawthorne. Boston: 1876. V. 52; 53

LATHROP, JOHN
Compendious Treatise on the Use of the Globes and of Maps. Boston: 1812. V. 53
An Oration, Pronounced July 4, 1796, at the Request of the Inhabitants of the Town of Boston, in Commemoration of the Anniversary of American Independence. Boston: 1796. V. 48

LATHROP, JOSEPH
A Miscellaneous Collection of Original Pieces: Political, Moral and Entertaining in One Volume. Springfield: 1786. V. 49

LATHROP, L. E.
The Farmer's Library, or Essays Designed to Encourage the Pursuits and promote the Science of Agriculture. Rutland: 1825. V. 48

LATHY, THOMAS PIKE
The Angler: a Poem, in Ten Cantos, with Proper Instructions in the Art...By Picasso. London: 1819. V. 47
Pike the Angler; a Poem. London: 1822. V. 47

LATILLA, EUGENIO
Cartoons in Outline Illustrative of the Gospels with Illuminated Text. Florence: 1848. V. 47

LATIMER, HUGH
Frvitfvll Sermons. London: 1596. V. 47; 49
Frvitfvll Sermons... 1635. V. 47
Frvitfvll Sermons. London: 1635. V. 50

LATIMER, JONATHAN
Black in the Fashion for Dying. New York: 1959. V. 51
The Mink Lined Coffin. London: 1960. V. 48
Red Gardenias. Garden City: 1939. V. 48; 49
The Search for My Great Uncle's Head. Garden City: 1937. V. 48; 52
Sinners and Shrouds. New York: 1955. V. 51
Solomon's Vineyard. Santa Barbara: 1982. V. 48; 49; 51; 53

LATIMER, PHILIP
The Village on the Forth, and Other Poems. London: 1868. V. 49

LATIMORE, SARAH BRIGGS
Arthur Rackham: a Bibliography. Los Angeles: 1936. V. 47; 48; 50; 54

LA TOUCHE, J. D. D.
A Handbook of the Birds of Eastern China. London: 1925-34. V. 49

LATOUCHE, JOHN
Travels In Portugal. London: 1875. V. 53

LA TOUCHE, T. H.
A Bibliography of Indian Geology and Physical Geography. Calcutta: 1917-26. V. 47

LA TOURETTE, STOCKWELL
Dublin Theatres and Theatre Customs, 1637-1820. Kingsport: 1938. V. 49

LA TOUR LANDRY, GEOFFREY DE
The Book of the Knight of La Tour Landry. London: 1930. V. 52

LATROBE, BENJAMIN HENRY
Anniversary Oration, Pronounced Before the Society of Artists of the United States. Philadelphia: 1811. V. 49
The Virginia Journals of Benjamin Henry Latrobe 1795-1798. New Haven: 1977. V. 52

LATROBE, BENJAMIN HENRY BONEVAL
Characteristic Anecdotes and Miscellaneous Authentic Papers, Tending to Illustrate the Character of Frederic II, Late King of Prussia... London: 1788. V. 51

LATROBE, CHARLES JOSEPH
The Rambler in Mexico. London: 1836. V. 51; 52; 53; 54
The Rambler in North America. London: 1835. V. 53
The Rambler in North America... New York: 1835. V. 53
The Solace of Song. London: 1837. V. 52

LATROBE, CHRISTIAN IGNATIUS
Journal of a Visit to South Africa in 1815, and 1816. London: 1818. V. 47; 49; 52; 53
Journal of a Visit to South Africa, in 1815 and 1816. New York: 1818. V. 54
Journal of a Visit to South Africa, With some Account of the Missionary Settlements of the United Brethren, Near the Cape of Good Hope. London: 1821. V. 47; 52; 54

LATROBE, JOHN H. B.
The History Mason and Dixon's Line. Philadelphia: 1855. V. 47
Reminiscences of West Point from September 1818 to March 1882. East Saginaw: 1887. V. 52

LATTA, FRANK F.
California Indian Folklore as Told to F. F. Latta. Shafter: 1936. V. 54
Handbook of Yokuts Indians. Oildale: 1949. V. 47; 51

LATTA, M. L.
The History of My Life and Work. Raleigh: 1903. V. 54

LATTA, ROBERT R.
Reminiscences of Pioneer Life. Kansas City: 1912. V. 51; 53

LATTIMORE, O.
Desert Road to Turkestan. Boston: 1929. V. 50

LAU, ROBERT JULIUS
Old Bablonian Temple Records. New York: 1906. V. 51

LAU, T.
Greek Vases: Their System of Form and Decoration. Boston: 1879. V. 48

LAUBER, PATRICIA
Cowboys and Cattle Ranching Yesterday and Today. New York: 1973. V. 52

LAUCK, REX
John L. Lewis and the International Union...United Mine Workers of America...The Story from 1917 to 1952. 1952. V. 53

LAUD, WILLIAM
The History of Troubles and Tryal... London: 1695. V. 54
A Relation of the Conference Between William Laud, Late Lord Archbishop of Canterbury, and Mr. Fisher the Jesuit... London: 1686. V. 50
A Summarie of Devotions, Compiled and Used by Dr. William Laud... Oxford: 1667. V. 47

LAUDER, THOMAS DICK
The Great Floods of August 1829 in the Province of Moray and Adjoining Districts... Elgin: 1873. V. 50
Lochandhu, Histoire du XVIIIe Siecle... Paris: 1828. V. 49
Memorial of the Royal Progress in Scotland. Edinburgh: 1843. V. 50; 53
The Miscellany of Natural History. Volume I. Parrots. Edinburgh: 1833. V. 52

LAUDER, WILLIAM
An Essay on Milton's Use and Imitation of the Moderns, in His Paradise Lost. London: 1750. V. 48; 49; 52; 54

LAUDERDALE, JAMES MAITLAND, 8TH EARL OF
An Inquiry Into the Nature and Origin of Public Wealth, and Into the means and Causes of its Increase. Edinburgh: 1819. V. 50
Letters to the Peers of Scotland. London: 1794. V. 53
Observations by the Earl of Lauderdale on the Review of His Inquiry into the Nature and Origin of Public Wealth... Edinburgh: 1804. V. 50

LAUDERDALE, R. J.
Life On the Range and On the Trail. San Antonio: 1936. V. 48; 49

LAUER, JEAN PHILIPPE
Saqqara. The Royal Cemetery of Memphis: Excavations and Discoveries Since 1850. New York: 1976. V. 51

LAUGH and Be Fat, or, The Merry Companion... London: 1765?. V. 47

LAUGHALIN, CLARENCE JOHN
Ghosts Along the Mississippi. New York: 1948. V. 48

LAUGHLIN, JAMES
Angelica. Fragment from an Autobiography. New York: 1993. V. 54
Ezra. New York: 1994. V. 51
Gists and Piths. Iowa City: 1982. V. 52; 53; 54
The House of Light. New York: 1986. V. 54
The House of Light... Newtown: 1986. V. 52
The Pig. Mt. Horeb: 1970. V. 51; 54
The River. Norfolk: 1938. V. 47; 49; 52
Stolen and Contaminated Poems. Isla Vista: 1985. V. 48
Tabellae. New York: 1986. V. 54

LAUGHLIN, LEDLIE IRWIN
Pewter in America: Its Makers and Their Marks. Boston: 1940. V. 48; 51

LAUGHTON, BRUCE
The Euston Road School. 1986. V. 52; 54
The Euston Road School. London: 1986. V. 49
Philip Wilson Steer 1860-1942. Oxford: 1971. V. 49; 52; 54

LAUGHTON, GEORGE
The History of Ancient Egypt, as Extant in the Greek Historians, Poets and Others... London: 1774. V. 50

LAUGHTON, JAMES KNOX
Memoirs of the Life and Correspondence of Henry Reeve. London: 1898. V. 54

LAUGHTON, L. G. CARR
Old Ship Figure-Heads and Sterns... London. V. 52; 53
Old Ship Figure-Heads and Sterns... London: 1925. V. 47

LAUMER, K.
Retief: Ambassador to Space. New York: 1969. V. 48

LAUN, HENRI VAN
The Characters of Jean De La Bruyere. London: 1885. V. 51; 54

LAURANA, FRANCESCO
Four Portrait Busts. Northampton: 1962. V. 49

LAURA'S Pride. London: 1868. V. 52

LAUREL, Archic, Rude. A Collection of Poems Presented to Yvor Winters on His Retirement by the Stanford English Department. Stanford: 1966. V. 54

LAURENCE, DAN H.
Bernard Shaw: a Bibliography. London: 1983. V. 53

LAURENCE, EDWARD
A Dissertation on Estates Upon Lives and Years, Whether in Lay or Church-hands. London: 1730. V. 47
The Duty of a Steward to His Lord. London: 1727. V. 53

LAURENCE, JOHN
The Clergy-Man's Recreation... (with) The Gentleman's Recreation, and The Fruit Garden Kalendar. London: 1717-18. V. 51
The Fruit-Garden Kalendar; or, a Summary of the Art of Managing the Fruit-Garden. London: 1718. V. 47
A New System of Agriculture, Being a Complete Body of Husbandry and Gardening... London: 1726. V. 51; 54

LAURENCE, MARGARET
The Stone Angel. Toronto: 1964. V. 51

LAURENCIN, MARIE
Petit Bestiaire. Paris: 1926. V. 54

LAURENS, HENRY
The Physiological Effects of Radiant Energy. New York: 1933. V. 48; 54

LAURENS, JOHN
The Army Correspondence of Colonel John Laurens in the Years 1777-8. New York: 1867. V. 53

LAURENT, JEAN
Abrege Pour les Arbres Nains et Autres... Paris: 1675. V. 53

LAURENT, PETER EDMUND
Recollections of a Classical Tour through Various parts of Greece, Turkey and Italy, Made in the Years 1818 and 1819. London: 1822. V. 49

LAURENTS, ARTHUR
Gypsy. New York: 1960. V. 53
West Side Story. London: 1959. V. 48

LAURIDSEN, PETER
Russian Explorations, 1725-1743. Chicago: 1889. V. 48

LAURIE, A. P.
The Brushwork of Rembrandt and His School. London: 1932. V. 50

LAURIE, J. S.
Sketches of Political Economy. London: 1864. V. 53

LAURIE, ROBERT
Laurie and Whittle's New Traveller's Companion... London: 1811. V. 51

LAURIE, THOMAS
Dr. Grant and Mountain Nestorians. Boston: 1853. V. 51

LAURIE, WILLIAM F. B.
Ashe Pyee, The Superior Country; or, the Great Attractions of Burma to British Enterprise and Commerce. London: 1882. V. 47
Pegu, Being a Narrative of Events During the Second Burmese War, from August 1852 to Its Conclusion in June 1853, with a Succinct Continuation Down to February 1854. London: 1854. V. 47

LAUT, AGNES C.
The Blazed Trail of the Old Frontier. New York: 1926. V. 54
Cadillac. Indianapolis: 1931. V. 52
The Conquest of the Great Northwest. New York: 1908. V. 49; 54
The Fur Trade of America. New York: 1921. V. 50

LAUTERBACH, ANN
Book One. New York: 1975. V. 52
A Clown, Some Colors, a Doll, Her Stories, A Song, A Moonlit Cove. New York: 1995. V. 54
Later that Evening. New York: 1981. V. 52; 54
Sacred Weather. New York: 1984. V. 52; 54

LAUTREC
Lautrec by Lautrec. New York: 1964. V. 48

LAUTS, JAN
Carpaccio: Paintings and Drawings. London: 1962. V. 49; 51; 54

LA VALLEE, JOSEPH
The Negro Equaled (sic) by Few Europeans. Dublin: 1791. V. 50

LAVALLEE, JOSEPH
The Negro Equaled by Few Europeans.... Philadelphia: 1801. V. 48; 49

LAVALLEYE, JACQUES
Bruegel and Lucas Van Leyden. London: 1967. V. 48

LA VALLIERE, LOUIS CESAR
Catalogue des Livres de la Bibliotheque de feu M. Le Duc de la Valliere... Paris: 1783. V. 48; 50

LAVANTE
The Poets and Poetry of America a Satire by Lavante. New York: 1887. V. 48

LAVARDIN, JACQUES DE
Histoire de Georges Castriot Surnomme Scanderbeg, Roy d'Albanie. La Rochelle: 1593. V. 47
The Historie of George Castriot, Surnamed Scanderbeg, King of Albanie. London: 1596. V. 48

LAVATER, JOHANN CASPAR
Aphorisms on Man. London: 1789. V. 48; 53
Essays on Physiognomy... London: 1789. V. 47; 50; 52
Essays on Physiognomy... London: 1789-98. V. 50
Essays on Physiognomy... London: 1789-98/1802. V. 53
Essays on Physiognomy... London: 1804. V. 53
Essays on Physiognomy. London: 1840. V. 47

LAVATER, JOHANN HEINRICH
Introduction to the Study of the Anatomy of the Human Body... London: 1824. V. 48

LAVATER, LUDWIG
De Spectris, Lemuribus et Magnis Atque Insolitis Fragoribus, Variisque Praesagitionibus, Quae Plerunque Obitum Hominum, Magnas Clades, Mutationesque Imperiorum Praecedunt, Libert Unus. Geneva: 1580. V. 50

LAVELEYE, EMILE DE
The Elements of Political Economy... London: 1884. V. 52

LAVELLE, P.
The Irish Landlord Since the Revolution. 1870. V. 49

LAVENDER, DAVID
The American Heritage History of the Great American West. New York: 1965. V. 52

LAVER, JAMES
A History of British and American Etching. London: 1929. V. 50
The House of Haig. London: 1958. V. 50
Ladies' Mistakes. Bloomsbury: 1933. V. 48; 49
A Stitch in Time; or Pride Prevents a Fall. London: 1927. V. 54

LAVERACK, EDWARD
The Setter: with Notices of the Most Eminent Breeds now Extant... London: 1872. V. 47; 49

LAVERAN, CHARLES L. A.
Paludism. London: 1893. V. 48; 51; 54
Trypanosomes and Trypanosomiases. London: 1907. V. 49

LAVERY, D. A.
Road Traffic Law in Northern Ireland. Belfast: 1989. V. 49

LAVIN, IRVING
Studies...Medieval and Renaissance Painting in Honour of Millard Meiss... 1977. V. 49
Studies...Medieval Renaissance Painting in Honour of Millard Meiss. New York: 1977. V. 52

LAVIN, MARY
The Great Wave. New York: 1961. V. 53
The Patriot Son, and Other Stories. London: 1956. V. 50
The Second-Best Children in the World. London: 1972. V. 53

LAVIN, S. R.
Cambodian spring. Deerfield: 1973. V. 48

LAVOISIER, ANTOINE LAURENT
Elements of Chemistry in a New Systematic Order... Edinburgh: 1796. V. 48
Elements of Chemistry in a New Systematic Order.. Edinburgh: 1799. V. 54
Elements of Chemistry in a New Systematic Order... New York: 1806. V. 47
Essays on the Effects Produced by Various Processes on Atmospheric Air, with a Particular View to an Investigation of the Constitution of the Acids. Warrington: 1783. V. 47
Essays Physical and Chemical... London: 1776. V. 51

THE LAVVES Resolutions of Womens Rights; or the Lavves Provision of Woemen. London: 1632. V. 53

LAW, ALICE
Emily Jane Bronte and the Authorship of Wurthering Heights. Accrington: 1928. V. 52; 54

THE LAW and Lawyers Laid Open, in Twelve Visions. To Which is Added, Plain Truth, in Three Dialogues, Between Truman, Skinall, Dryboots, Three Attorneys and Season a Bencher. London: 1737. V. 47

LAW, ANDREW
Harmonic Companion, and Guide to Social Worship: Being a Choice Selection of Tunes...Together with the Principles of Music and Easy Lessons for Learners. Philadelphia: 1810. V. 48

LAW, ERNEST
The History of Hampton Court Palace. London: 1888. V. 51
The Royal Gallery of Hampton Court Illustrated. London: 1898. V. 47

LAW, GEORGE
A Sketch of Events in the Life of George Law, Published in Advance of His Autobiography. New York: 1855. V. 50

LAW, HENRY
The Construction of Roads and Streets. London: 1890. V. 51
The Rudiments of Civil Engineering for the Use of Beginners. London: 1848/49. V. 49

THE LAW Instructor, or Farmer's & Mechanic's Guide... Bridgeton: 1824. V. 47

LAW, JOHN
Address Delivered Before the Vincennes Historical and Antiquarian Society, February 22, 1839. Louisville: 1839. V. 49
A Full and Impartial Account of the Company of Mississippi, Otherwise Called the French East-India-Company, Projected and Settled by Mr. Law. London: 1720. V. 49

THE LAW of Arrests in Both Civil and Criminal Cases... London: 1742. V. 48

THE LAW of Commons and Commoners. London: 1698. V. 52

THE LAW of Ejectments, or, a Treatise Shewing the Nature of Ejectione Firme. London: 1700. V. 53

LAW Quibbles, or, a Treatise of the Evasions, Tricks, Turns and Quibbles, Commonly Used in the Profession of the Law, to the Prejudice of Clents and Others... London: 1724. V. 48

LAW Quibbles: or, a Treatise of the Evasions, Tricks, Turns and Quibbles Commonly Used in the Profession of the Law, to the Prejudice of Clients and Others... London: 1736. V. 49; 52

LAW, SAMUEL
A Domestic Winter-Piece; or, a Poem, Exhibiting a Full View of the Author's Dwelling Place in the Winter Season. Leeds: 1772. V. 50

LAW, T. PARKENHAM
Report of the Trials of Alexander M. Sullivan & Richard Pigott for Seditious Libel. 1868. V. 48

LAW, WILLIAM
An Appeal to all that Doubt, or Disbelieve the Truths of the Gospel, Whether They Be Deists, Arians, Socinians, or Nominal Christians... London: 1742. V. 51
The Bishop of Bangor's (Hoadly) Late Sermon, and His Letter to Dr. Snape in Defence of It, Answer'd. 1717. V. 47
A Forest Ramble. London: 1818. V. 54
An Humble, Earnest, and Affectionate Address to the Clergy. Exeter: 1830. V. 54
A Practical Treatise Upon Christian Perfection... London: 1728. V. 51; 52
A Serious Call to a Devout and Holy Life. London: 1729. V. 49; 52; 53
The Way to Divine Knowledge; Being Several Dialogues Between Humanus, Academicus, Rusticus and Theophilus. London: 1752. V. 47
The Works. Brockenhurst: 1892-93. V. 52; 54

THE LAW-French Dictionary Alphabetically Digested.... London: 1718. V. 48

LAWARENCE, JOHN
The Modern Land Steward.. London: 1801. V. 53

LAWES, W. G.
Grammar and Vocabulary of Language Spoken by Motu Tribe (New Guinea). Sydney: 1888. V. 48; 52

LAWFORD, LOUISA
Every Girl's Book. London: 1862. V. 51

THE LAWFULNESSE Of Our Expedition into England Manifested. Edinburgh: 1640. V. 52

LAWLER, RAY
Summer of the Seventeenth Doll. New York: 1957. V. 54

LAWLESS, EMILY
A Chelsea Householder. London: 1882. V. 48
Grania: The Story of an Island. London: 1892. V. 47; 49; 50; 51
Maelcho, a Sixteenth Century Narrative. London: 1894. V. 48

LAWLESS, JOHN
A Compendium of the History of Ireland, from the Earliest Period to the Reign of George I. Edinburgh: 1823. V. 53

LAWLOR, P. A.
The Mystery of Maata - a Katherine Mansfield Novel. Wellington: 1946. V. 51

LAWRENCE, A. B.
A History of Texas, or the Emigrant's Guide to the New Republic... New York: 1844. V. 48; 51; 52; 54
Texas in 1840, or the Emigrant's Guide to the New Republic. New York: 1840. V. 49

LAWRENCE, A. W.
T. E. Lawrence - By His Friends. London: 1937. V. 54

LAWRENCE, ADA
Early Life of D. H. Lawrence - Together with Hitherto Unpublished Letters and Articles. London: 1932. V. 54
Young Lorenzo. Florence: 1931. V. 49
Young Lorenzo... Florence: 1932. V. 48; 49; 51

LAWRENCE, CHARLES
History of the Philadelphia Almshouses and Hospitals from the Beginning of the Eighteenth to the Ending of the Nineteenth Centuries... Philadelphia: 1905. V. 50

LAWRENCE, DAVID HERBERT
Aaron's Rod. London: 1922. V. 52; 53
Aaron's Rod. New York: 1922. V. 48; 52; 53
Amores. London: 1916. V. 48; 49; 54
Amores. New York: 1916. V. 48; 49; 52
Apocalypse. Florence: 1931. V. 47; 48; 49; 54
El Arco Iris. (The Rainbow). Mexico: 1948. V. 49
Assorted Articles. London: 1930. V. 53
Assorted Articles. New York: 1930. V. 48; 51
Bay. London: 1919. V. 47
Bay... Westminster: 1919. V. 49
Birds, Beasts and Flowers. London: 1923. V. 47; 50
Birds, Beasts and Flowers. New York: 1923. V. 47; 48; 50
Birds, Beasts and Flowers. London: 1930. V. 52; 54
Collected Poems. New York: 1925. V. 50
The Collected Poems... London: 1928. V. 47
The Collected Poems... London: 1932. V. 49
Complete Poems. New York: 1964. V. 51
David: a Play. London: 1926. V. 53
David: a Play. New York: 1926. V. 52; 53
Death of a Porcupine and Other Essays. Philadelphia: 1925. V. 48
England My England. New York: 1922. V. 49; 52
England, My England. London: 1924. V. 49; 52; 53
The Escaped Cock. Paris: 1929. V. 53
Fantasia of the Unconscious. London: 1923. V. 47; 49; 52
Fire and Other Poems. San Francisco: 1940. V. 49; 53
Glad Ghosts. London: 1926. V. 50
Hijos Y Amantes. (Sons and Lovers). Buenos Aires: 1933. V. 49
Kangaroo. London: 1923. V. 48; 49; 52
Kangaroo. New York: 1923. V. 48
Lady Chatterley. Paris: 1946. V. 52
Lady Chatterley's Lover. 1928. V. 47; 51
Lady Chatterley's Lover. Florence: 1928. V. 47; 48; 49; 52; 53

LAWRENCE, DAVID HERBERT continued
Lady Chatterley's Lover. 1929. V. 47
Lady Chatterley's Lover. London: 1929. V. 48; 49
Lady Chatterley's Lover... Paris: 1929. V. 51
Lady Chatterley's Lover. 1930. V. 47
Lady Chatterley's Lover. London: 1932. V. 50
Lady Chatterley's Lover. Harmondsworth: 1960. V. 53
Last Poems. Florence: 1932. V. 48; 49; 50; 51; 53
The Letters of D. H. Lawrence. London: 1932. V. 48; 49; 51; 53
Letters...to Martin Secker, 1911-1930. London: 1970. V. 53
Life. St. Ives: 1954. V. 48
Look! We Have Come Through!. London: 1917. V. 47; 53
The Lost Girl. London: 1920. V. 49; 53; 54
Love Among the Haystacks. London: 1930. V. 47; 48; 49; 50; 52; 53; 54
Love Among the Haystacks... New York: 1933. V. 48
Love Poems and Others. London: 1913. V. 47; 50; 51; 53; 54
Love Poems and Others. New York: 1915. V. 51
The Lovely Lady. London: 1932. V. 53
The Man Who Died. London: 1931. V. 48; 52; 53
The Man Who Died. Cambridge: 1935. V. 49
The Man Who Died. London: 1935. V. 49; 51; 52; 53
Movements in European History. London. V. 53
La Mujer Perida. (The Lost Girl). Buenos Aires: 1943. V. 49
La Mujer Y La Bestia. (St. Mawr). Santiago de Chile: 1933. V. 49
My Skirmish with Jolly Roger. New York: 1929. V. 47; 53
Nettles. London: 1930. V. 50
New Poems. London: 1918. V. 47; 49; 52
An Original Poem. London: 1934. V. 47
The Paintings of D. H. Lawrence. London: 1929. V. 49; 52
Pansies. 1929. V. 54
Pansies. London: 1929. V. 47; 49; 50; 51; 52; 53
Pansies... New York: 1929. V. 47
El Pavo Real Blanco. (The Peacock). Mexico: 1949. V. 49
Phoenix: the Posthumous Papers of... London: 1936. V. 49
A Propos of Lady Chatterley's Lover... London: 1930. V. 49
The Prussian Officer. London: 1914. V. 49; 50; 51; 53; 54
Psychoanalysis and the Unconscious. New York: 1921. V. 50; 52
Psychoanalysis and the Unconscious. London: 1923. V. 47
The Rainbow. London: 1915. V. 54
The Rainbow. New York: 1916. V. 51; 52
Rawdon's Roof. London: 1928. V. 47; 48; 51; 53
Reflections on the Death of a Porcupine. Philadelphia: 1925. V. 47; 49; 50; 51; 53
Reports of Cases in Equity, Argued and Decreed in the Courts of Chancery and Exchequer, Chiefly in the Reign of King George I... London: 1734. V. 50
St. Mawr, Together with the Princess. London: 1925. V. 51; 52; 53; 54
Sea and Sardinia. New York: 1921. V. 53
Sea and Sardinia. London: 1923. V. 49
Selected Literary Criticism. London: 1955. V. 53
Selected Poems. 1980. V. 49
Sex Locked Out. London: 1928. V. 49; 53
The Ship of Death and Other Poems. London: 1933. V. 47
Sons and Lovers. London: 1913. V. 51; 54
Sons and Lovers. New York: 1913. V. 48; 50; 52
Sons and Lovers. Avon: 1975. V. 52; 53; 54
The Spirit of Place. London: 1935. V. 52
Studies in Classic American Literature. New York: 1923. V. 47; 50; 53
Studies in Classic American Literature. London: 1924. V. 53
Tortoises. New York: 1921. V. 47; 48; 49; 50; 52
Tortoises. Williamsburg: 1983. V. 47; 49; 50; 52
Touch and Go. London: 1920. V. 47; 53; 54
Touch and Go. New York: 1920. V. 48; 51
The Trespasser. London: 1912. V. 49; 50; 53
The Triumph of the Machine. London: 1930. V. 47; 48; 53
Twilight in Italy. London: 1916. V. 47; 49; 50
The Virgin and the Gipsy. Florence: 1930. V. 47; 48; 50; 51; 52; 53; 54
The Virgin and the Gipsy. London: 1930. V. 47; 48; 49; 52; 53
The Virgin and the Gipsy. New York: 1930. V. 51
We Need One Another. New York: 1933. V. 50
The White Peacock. London: 1911. V. 47; 49; 51; 53
The White Peacock. New York: 1911. V. 47; 48; 49
The Widowing of Mrs. Holroyd. New York: 1914. V. 48; 49; 52; 53
The Woman Who Rode Away and Other Stories. New York: 1928. V. 51
Women in Love. New York: 1920. V. 47; 48; 52; 53; 54
Women in Love. London: 1921. V. 51; 54

LAWRENCE, E.
It May Happen Yet: a Tale of Bonaparte's Invasion of England. 1899. V. 52

LAWRENCE, FREDERICK
The Lawyer's Companion, Diary and London and Provincial Law Directory for 1868, containing Scales of Costs, Legal Time Tables, etc. London: 1868. V. 47

LAWRENCE, FRIEDA
Not I, But the Wind.... Santa Fe: 1934. V. 48; 51; 53

LAWRENCE, GEORGE ALFRED
Border and Bastille. New York: 1863. V. 53
Brakespeare; or, The Fortunes of a Free Lance. London: 1868. V. 47
Guy Livingstone; or 'Through'. London: 1857. V. 49

LAWRENCE, HERBERT
The Life and Adventures of Common Sense; an Historical Allegory. London: 1769. V. 47
The Passions Personify'd, in Familiar Fables. London: 1773. V. 49

LAWRENCE, J.
Man in the Moon Stories Told Over the Radio-Phone. 1922. V. 48
Man In the Moon Stories Told Over the Radio-Phone. London: 1922. V. 50

LAWRENCE, J. M.
A Functional Biology of Echinoderms. Baltimore: 1987. V. 51

LAWRENCE, JACOB
The Great Migration: an American Story. New York: 1993. V. 52

LAWRENCE, JEROME
Auntie Mame. New York: 1957. V. 53
The Gang's All Here. Cleveland: 1960. V. 49; 50
Mame. New York: 1967. V. 48; 49

LAWRENCE, JOHN
British Field Sports... 1818. V. 53
British Field Sports: Embracing Practical Instructions in Shooting - Hunting - Coursing - Racing - Cocking - Fishing, Etc. London: 1818. V. 47; 48
British Field Sports: Embracing Practical Instructions in Shooting - Hunting - Coursing - Racing - Cocking - Fishing, Etc. London: 1820. V. 49
The Clergy-man's Recreation... London: 1717. V. 49
The History and Delineation of the Horse, In All His Varieties, Comprehending the Appropriate Uses... 1809. V. 47; 48
The History and Delineation of the Horse, In All His Varities, Comprehending the Appropriate Uses... London: 1809. V. 50; 52
Inherit the Wind. New York: 1955. V. 53
John Lawrence's Handbook of Cricket in Ireland and Record of Athletic Sports, Football &c. Dublin: 1879. V. 48; 51
The New Farmer's Calendar... London: 1800. V. 51; 52; 54
The New Farmer's Calendar... London: 1801. V. 49; 50; 53
A Philosophical and Practical Treatise on Horses, and the Moral Duties of man Towards the Brute Creation. London: 1796. V. 47
The Sportsman's Repository, or, a Correct Delienation of the Horse and Dog. London: 1820. V. 49

LAWRENCE, RICHARD
The Complete Farrier, and British Sportsman... London: 1816. V. 54
The Interest of Ireland In Its Trade and Wealth Stated. Dublin: 1682. V. 48; 50

LAWRENCE, RICHARD HOE
History of the Society of Iconophiles of the City of New York: MDCCCXCV, MCMXXX and Catalogue of Its Publications with Historical and Biographical Notes, Etc. New York: 1930. V. 53

LAWRENCE, ROBERT
Primitive Psycho-Therapy and Quackery. London: 1910. V. 52

LAWRENCE, SIDNEY
Roger Brown. New York: 1987. V. 50

LAWRENCE, SIMON
Forty-Five Wood-Engravers. 1982. V. 47
Forty-Five Wood-Engravers. London: 1982. V. 50

LAWRENCE, THOMAS
Works of... London: 1837. V. 51

LAWRENCE, THOMAS EDWARD
(40) Letters from T. E. Shaw to Bruce Rogers and (13) More Letters. New Fairfield: 1933/36. V. 48
A Brief Record of the Advance of the Egyptian Expeditionary Force - Under the Command of Gen. Sir Edmund H. H. Allenby... Cairo: 1919. V. 47; 49
A Brief Record of the Advance of the Egyptian Expeditionary Force Under the Command of General Sir Edmund H. H. Allenby... London: 1919. V. 47; 48; 52
Cats and Landladies' Husbands: T. E. Lawrence in Bridlington. London: 1995. V. 53
Crusader Castles. London: 1936. V. 47; 50; 52
Crusader Castles. Waltham St. Lawrence: 1936. V. 47; 48; 51; 52
The Diary of T. E. Lawrence, 1911. London: 1937. V. 48; 53; 54
From a Letter of T. E. Lawrence. 1959. V. 51; 52
The Frontier: a Miscellany... Peshewar: 1955. V. 53
The Home Letters of T. E. Lawrence and His Brothers. New York: 1954. V. 47
The Home Letters of T. E. Lawrence and His Brothers. Oxford: 1954. V. 52
The Letters of T. E. Lawrence. London: 1938. V. 49; 51; 53
The Letters of T. E. Lawrence. New York: 1939. V. 48; 51
Men in Print: Essays in Literary Criticism. London: 1940. V. 54
Men in Print: Essays in Literary Criticism. Waltham St. Lawrence: 1940. V. 48; 49; 50; 51; 52
Minorities. London: 1971. V. 52
The Mint. Garden City: 1955. V. 48; 51; 54
The Mint. London: 1955. V. 47; 49; 51; 52; 53
The Mint. Garden City: 1957. V. 47
Oriental Assembly. 1939. V. 48
Oriental Assembly. London: 1939. V. 47
Revolt in the Desert. London: 1927. V. 47; 50; 51; 52; 53; 54
Revolt in the Desert. New York: 1927. V. 47; 49; 53
The Sayings and Doings of T. E. Lawrence. Wakefield: 1994. V. 51
Secret Despatches from Arabia. Waltham St. Lawrence. V. 52

LAWRENCE, THOMAS EDWARD continued
Secret Despatches from Arabia. Waltham St. Lawrence: 1939. V. 49; 50; 51; 53
Seven Pillars of Wisdom... London: 1926. V. 54
Seven Pillars of Wisdom. Garden City: 1935. V. 47; 48; 49; 51; 53
Seven Pillars of Wisdom. London & Toronto: 1935. V. 47; 48; 49; 50; 51; 52; 53; 54
Seven Pillars of Wisdom. New York: 1935. V. 47; 48; 50
Shaw-Ede....Letters to H.S. Ede 1927-1935. London: 1942. V. 47; 53
Shaw-Ede...Letters to H.S. Ede 1927-1935. Waltham St. Lawrence: 1942. V. 49; 50; 51; 52
Die Sieben Saulen der Weisheit. (Seven Pillars). Leipzig: 1936. V. 48
The Suppressed Introductory Chapter (of Seven Pillars of Wisdom). Totnes: 1977. V. 53
T. E. Lawrence: Letters to E. T. Leeds. 1988. V. 47
T. E. Lawrence: Letters to E. T. Leeds. Andoversford: 1988. V. 47; 49; 53; 54
T. E. Lawrence: Letters to E. T. Leeds. Gloucestershire: 1988. V. 49
T. E. Lawrence: Letters to E. T. Leeds. London: 1988. V. 50; 53
T. E. Lawrence to His Biographer, Liddell Hart. (and) T. E. Lawrence to His Biographer, Robert Graves. London: 1938. V. 51; 53; 54
T. E. Lawrence to His Biographers... New York: 1938. V. 53
T. E. Lawrence to His Biographers. Garden City: 1963. V. 50

LAWRENCE, W. J.
The Elizabethan Playhouse and Other Studies. London: 1912. V. 51
The Elizabethan Playhouse and Other Studies. Stratford-upon-Avon: 1912-13. V. 50

LAWRENCE, WILLIAM
Lectures on Physiology, Zoology and the Natural History of Man... London: 1819. V. 49; 52
Lectures on Physiology, Zoology and the Natural History of Man... London: 1822. V. 47
Lectures on Physiology, Zoology and the Natural History of Man. Salem: 1828. V. 48; 50; 54
A Treatise on Diseases of the Eye. London: 1833. V. 53

LAWRENCE, WILLIAM BEACH
Disabilities of American Women Married Abroad. New York: 1871. V. 48; 50; 51

THE LAWS and Constitutions of the Master, Wardens and Commonalty of Watermen and Lightermen of the River Thames. London: 1858. V. 52

THE LAWS and Customs, Rights, Liberties and Privileges, of the City of London... London: 1765. V. 48

LAWS and Ordinances Relating to the Baltimore and Ohio Rail Road. Baltimore: 1850. V. 52

LAWS Concerning the Election of Members of Parliament; with Determinations of the House of Commons Thereon, and All Their Incidents: Contuned...to the Present... London: 1774. V. 50; 51; 52

LAWS, Documents and Judicial Decisions, Relating to the Baltimore and Fredericktown, York and Reisterstown, Cumberland and Boonsborough, Turnpike Road Companies. Baltimore: 1841. V. 50

LAWS of the United States, Resolutions of Congress...Treaties, Proclamations and Other Documents, Having Operation and Respect to the Public Lands... Washington: 1817. V. 47

THE LAWS Respecting Women, as They Regard Their Natural Rights, Or Their Connections and Conduct... London: 1777. V. 54

LAWSON, A.
The Modern Farrier... London: 1841. V. 50

LAWSON, ALEXANDER
The Compositor as Artist, Craftsman and Tradesman. Athens: 1990. V. 48

LAWSON, G. W.
The Marine Algae and Coastal Environment of Tropical West Africa. 1987. V. 50

LAWSON, HENRY
A Paper on the Arrangement of an Observatory for Practical Astronomy and Meterology. Bath: 1844. V. 54
The Stories of Henry Lawson. Sydney: 1965. V. 51

LAWSON, J. A.
Wanderings in New Guinea. London: 1875. V. 53

LAWSON, JOHN
Childhood Valley the Favourite Songs of Childhood with New Pictures in Color by John Lawson. London: 1880. V. 54
Lectures Concerning Oratory... 1758. V. 54
Lectures Concerning Oratory. Dublin: 1759. V. 48; 51; 53
A New Voyage to Carolina: Containing the Exact Description and natural History of that Country; Together with the Present State Thereof. London: 1709. V. 48
A Synopsis of All the Data for Construction of Triangles, from Which Geometrical Solutions Have Hitherto Been in Print. Rochester: 1773. V. 49

LAWSON, JOHN D.
American State Trials, with Notes and Annotations. Volume VIII. St. Louis: 1917. V. 51

LAWSON, JOHN PARKER
The Book of Perth: an Illustration of the Moral and Ecclesiasatical State of Scotland Before and After the Reformation. Edinburgh: 1847. V. 52; 54

LAWSON, L. M.
A Practical Treatise on Phthisis Pulmonalis: Embracing Its Pathology, Causes, Symptoms and Treatment. Cincinnati: 1861. V. 48

LAWSON, RICHARD
A History of Flixton, Urmston and Davyhulme. Urmston: 1898. V. 54

LAWSON, ROBERT
Ben and Me. 1939. V. 52; 53
Ben and Me. Boston: 1939. V. 47
The Fabulous Flight. Boston: 1949. V. 49
I Discover Columbus. Boston: 1941. V. 49
Mr. Revere and I. Boston: 1953. V. 49; 51; 52
Rabbit Hill. New York: 1944. V. 49
They Were Strong and Good. New York: 1940. V. 47

LAWSON, WILLIAM
A New Orchard and Garden... London: 1638. V. 50

LAWTON, EDWARD
Lectures on Science, Politics, Morals and Society. St. Louis: 1862. V. 54

LAWTON, GEORGE
Collections Relative to Churches and Chapels Within the Diocese of York. London: 1842. V. 49; 53

LAWTON, MARY
A Lifetime with Mark Twain. New York: 1925. V. 54

THE LAWYER'S and Magistrate's Magazine...Volume I for the Year MDCCXC. Dublin: 1792. V. 52

LAX, ROBERT
The Circus of the Sun. New York: 1959. V. 51

LAXNESS, HALLDOR
A Place of Safety. Helsinki: 1986. V. 48

LAXTON, HENRY
Examples of Building Construction, Intended as an Aide-Memoire for the Professional Man and the Operative... London: 1859-60/61-67. V. 52

LAY, GEORGE TRADESCANT
The Chinese As They Are: Their Moral, Social and Literary Character: a New Analysis of the Language... London: 1841. V. 51; 53

LAY, WILLIAM
A Narrative of the Mutiny on Board the Ship Globe, of Nantucket, in the Pacific Ocean, Jan. 1824. New London: 1828. V. 50; 51; 52; 54

LAYARD, AUSTEN HENRY
Discoveries in the Ruins of Nineveh and Babylon.... London: 1853. V. 47; 50; 51; 53
Discoveries In the Ruins of Nineveh and Babylon... New York: 1853. V. 47; 52
Nineveh and Its Remains... London: 1849. V. 49; 52
Nineveh and Its Remains. New York: 1849. V. 48; 50
Nineveh and Its Remains. London: 1850. V. 54
Nineveh and its Remains... London: 1850-53. V. 47; 53
Nineveh and Its Remains... New York: 1853. V. 52
A Popular Account of Discoveries at Nineveh. London: 1854. V. 54
Sir A. Henry Layard: Autobiography and letters from His Childhood Until His Appointment as H. M. Ambassador at Madrid. London: 1903. V. 51

LAYARD, E. L.
The Birds of South Africa. London: 1875-84. V. 49; 50; 51; 52; 53

LAYARD, GEORGE SOMES
Catalogue Raisonne of Engraved British Portraits from Altered Plates. London: 1927. V. 54
Mrs. Lynn Linton: Her Life, Letters and Opinions. London: 1901. V. 50
Suppressed Plates Wood Engravings, &c. Together with Other Curiosities Germane Thereto. London: 1907. V. 47
Tennyson and His Pre-Rapahelite Illustrators. London: 1894. V. 49; 51

LAYARD, JOHN
Stone men of Malekula, athe Small Island of Vao. London: 1942. V. 52

LAYCOCK, THOMAS
An Essay on Hysteria: Being an Analysis of its Irregular and Aggravated Forms... Philadelphia: 1840. V. 52
Mind and Brain: or, the Correlations of Consciousness and Organization... Edinburgh: 1860. V. 54

LAYNE, J. GREGG
Annals of Los Angeles from the Arrival of the First White Men to the Civil War, 1769-1861. San Francisco: 1935. V. 48; 50; 52; 54
Books of the Los Angeles District. Los Angeles: 1950. V. 54

LAYNG, HENRY
The Rod, a Poem. Oxford: 1754. V. 48; 50

LAYS of the Belvoir Hunt. Grantham: 1866. V. 47

LAYS of the Minnesingers of German Troubadours. London: 1825. V. 50

LAYS of the Western World. New York: 1848. V. 49

LAYTON, IRVING
Balls for a One-Armed Juggler. Toronto: 1963. V. 47
Dance with Desire. Toronto: 1992. V. 48
The Improved Binoculars. Highlands: 1956. V. 47; 54
Kingdom of Absence. Toronto: 1967. V. 47
The Laughing Rooster. Toronto & Montreal: 1964. V. 47
A Laughter in the Mind. Highlands: 1958. V. 54
The Long Pea-Shooter. Montreal: 1954. V. 54
The Love Poems of Irving Layton. Toronto: 1973. V. 47
The Love Poems of Irving Layton. Toronto: 1978. V. 47; 51
Nail Polish. Toronto & Montreal: 1971. V. 47

LAYTON, IRVING continued
Now is the Place. Montreal: 1948. V. 47
Periods of the Moon. Toronto & Montreal: 1967. V. 47
A Red Carpet for the Sun. Highlands: 1959. V. 47
The Shattered Plinths. Toronto & Montreal: 1968. V. 47
The Uncollected Poems...1936-1959. Oakville & Ottawa: 1976. V. 47
The Whole Bloody Bird (Obs, Aphs and Pomes). Toronto & Madrid: 1969. V. 47
Wiggle to the Laundromat. Toronto & Chicago: 1970. V. 47

LAZARE DE BAIF
...De Re Navali Commentarius, in L. II. de Captivis & Postlimino Reversis... Basel: 1537. V. 51

LAZARILLO DE TORMES
The Life and Adventures of Lazarillo de Tormes. London: 1726. V. 54

LAZARUS, EMMA
Admetus and Other Poems. New York: 1871. V. 47
The Poems. (with) Selections from Her Poetry and Prose. Boston and New York: 1888/1944. V. 52; 54
Songs of a Semite: the Dance to Death, and Other Poems. New York: 1882. V. 47; 50

LAZIUS, WOLFGANG
De Gentium Aliquot Migrationibus....Linguarumque...ac Dialectis, Libri XII. Frankfurt: 1600. V. 50

LAZY Bones or Funny Rhymes with Funny Pictures. London: 1860. V. 54

THE LAZY Ladye of 1851. London: 1851. V. 50

LAZZARO, C.
The Italian Renaissance Garden from the Conventions of Planting, Design and Ornament to the Grand Gardens of Sixteenth Century Central Italy. New Haven: 1990. V. 51

LE PAGE DU PRATZ
The History of Louisiana, or of the Western Parts of Virginia and Carolina... London: 1763. V. 48

LEA, HENRY
An Historical Sketch of Sacerdotal Celibacy. Philadelphia: 1867. V. 54
An Historical Sketch of Sacerdotal Celibacy... Boston: 1884. V. 48

LEA, HENRY CHARLES
Materials Toward a History of Witchcraft. Philadelphia: 1939. V. 52

LEA, ISSAC
Contributions to Geology. Philadelphia: 1833. V. 51

LEA, TOM
The Brave Bulls. Boston: 1949. V. 53; 54
Calendar of Twelve Travelers through the Pass of the North. El Paso. V. 48
Calendar of Twelve Travelers through the Pass of the North. El Paso: 1946. V. 48
Calendar of Twelve Travelers through the Pass of the North. El Paso: 1947. V. 48
Eighty-seven Paintings & Drawings by Tom Lea. El Paso: 1971. V. 48
Fort Bliss. 100th Anniversary. Fort Bliss: 1948. V. 48
Grizzly from the Coral Sea, Conversation and Pictures by Lea. El Paso: 1944. V. 47
The Hands of Cantu. Boston & Toronto: 1964. V. 47; 48; 52
In the Crucible of the Sun. Kingsville: 1974. V. 49
In the Crucible of the Sun. Meridan: 1974. V. 52; 54
The King Ranch. V. 52
The King Ranch. Boston: 1957. V. 47; 48; 49; 50; 51; 52; 54
The King Ranch. Kingsville: 1957. V. 47; 48; 52; 53
Old Mount Franklin. El Paso: 1968. V. 48
Pelelliu Landing. El Paso: 1945. V. 48
A Picture Gallery. Boston: 1968. V. 47; 48; 50; 51; 52
Selection of Paintings and Drawings from the Nineteen Sixties. 1969. V. 51; 52; 54
Tom Lea, A Selection of Paintings and Drawings from the Nineteen-Sixites. San Antonio: 1970. V. 49
Western Beef Cattle. Austin: 1967. V. 48; 51; 52

LEACH, A. J.
Early Day Stories. Norfolk: 1916. V. 47; 48
A History of Antelope County Nebraska from Its First Settlement in 1868 to the Close of the Year 1883. Chicago: 1909. V. 51

LEACH, BERNARD
Drawings. Verse and Belief. London: 1973. V. 50; 51
A Potter's Portfolio, a Selection of Fine Pots. New York: 1951. V. 49

LEACH, D. G.
Rhododendrons of the World and How to Grow Them. New York: 1961. V. 51; 52
Rhododendrons of the World and How to Grow Them. London: 1962. V. 50

LEACH, EDMUND
A Treatise of Universal Inland Navigations, and the Use of All Sorts of Mines... London: 1790. V. 54

LEACH, ISAAC
A New Enquiry of the Earth's Motion. London: 1731. V. 53

LEACH, J.
Rough Sketches of the Life of an Old Soldier; During a Service in the West Indies; at the Siege of Copenhagen in 1807... London: 1831. V. 53

LEACH, JOSIAH GRANVILLE
Genealogical and Biographical Memorials fo the Reading, Howell, Yerkes, Watts, Latham and Elkins Families. Philadelphia: 1898. V. 47; 49; 51

LEACH, LINDA YORK
Indian Miniature Paintings and Drawings. Catalogue of Oriental Art. Cleveland: 1986. V. 49; 51; 53

LEACH, THOMAS
Modern Reports; or, Select Cases Adjudged in the Courts of King's Bench, Chancery, Common Pleas and Exchequer. London: 1793. V. 52

LEACH, W. E.
The Zoological Miscellany. London: 1814-17. V. 48; 54

LEACOCK, STEPHEN
Literary Lapses: a Book of Sketches. Montreal: 1910. V. 47; 48; 49
Moonbeams from the Larger Lunacy. Toronto: 1915. V. 50
Over the Footlights. Toronto: 1923. V. 48; 51
Winsome Winnie and Other New Nonsense Novels. Toronto: 1920. V. 50

LEACROFT, EDWARD BECHER
To Mr. Blore, on His Elaborate History of Winfield. 1794. V. 48; 54

LEAD, JANE
The Revelation of Revelations Particularly as an Essay Towards the Unsealing, Opening and Discovering the Seven Seals, the Seven Thunders and the New Jerusalem State. London: 1683. V. 49

LEADABRAND, RUSS
The California Deserts: Their People, Their History and Their Legends. Los Angeles: 1964. V. 53

LEADBEATER, MARY
Biographical Notices of Members of the Society of Friends Who Were Resident in Ireland. 1823. V. 47
Cottages Dialogues Among the Irish Peasantry. London: 1811. V. 52
Memoirs and Letters of Richard and Elizabeth Shackleton. London: 1849. V. 47; 53
Poems... Dublin: 1808. V. 49

LEADBETTER, J.
The Gentleman and Tradesman's Compleat Assistant... London: 1770. V. 48

LEADBITTER, MIKE
Blues Records 1943-1966. London and New York: 1968. V. 52

LEADER, ALFRED
Through Jamaica With a Kodak. Bristol: 1907. V. 50

A LEAF From the First Edition of the First Complete Bible in English, the Coverdale Bible, 1535. San Francisco: 1974. V. 47; 49; 52

A LEAF From the Letters of St. Jerome, First Printed by Sixtus Reissinger, Rome, ca. 1466-1467. Los Angeles: 1981. V. 51

LEAF, MUNRO
Geography Can Be Fun. Philadelphia: 1951. V. 52
Listen Little Girl. New York: 1938. V. 50
Noodle. New York: 1937. V. 49
The Story of Ferdinand the Bull. New York: 1936. V. 53
The Story of Ferdinand the Bull. London: 1937. V. 52
The Story of Ferdinand the Bull. New York: 1938. V. 52
The Story of Simpson and Sampson. New York: 1941. V. 52
Wee Gillis. New York: 1938. V. 48; 49; 51; 52

LEAFLETS of Memory: an Illuminated Annual for MDCCCL. Philadelphia: 1850. V. 48

LEAHY, JOHN
The Art of Swimming in the Eton Style. Nottingham: 1875. V. 52

LEAHY, MICHAEL
The Land that Time Forgot. New York: 1937. V. 50

LEAKE, ISAAC Q.
Memoir of the Life and Times of General John Lamb, an Officer of the Revolution...and His Correspondence with Washington, Clinton, Patrick Henry, and Other Distinguished men of His Time. Albany: 1857. V. 51

LEAKE, STEPHEN MARTIN
Heraldo Memoriale, or Memoirs of the College of Arms from 1727 to 1744. 1881. V. 48
An Historical Account of English Money, from the Conquest to the Present Time. London: 1745. V. 50
An Historical Account of English Money, From the Conquest to the Present Time... London: 1793. V. 49; 50; 51

LEAKE, WILLIAM MARTIN
Journal of a Tour in Asia Minor, with Compartive Remarks on the Ancient and Modern Geography of that Country. London: 1824. V. 47
The Topography of Athens, with Some Remarks on Its Antiquities. London: 1821. V. 47; 48; 49
Travels in the Morea. London: 1830. V. 53

LEAKEY, CAROLINE
The Broad Arrow: Being Passages from the History of Maida Gwynnham, a Lifer. Hobart Town & Launceston: 1860. V. 48

LEAKEY, JOHN
Grandad and I Memories of a Pioneer and His Grandson. Leakey: 1951. V. 49

LEAKEY, L. S. B.
Olduvai Gorge. Cambridge: 1965-71. V. 49
Olduvai Gorge. Cambridge: 1967. V. 50
Olduvai Gorge. 1967-71. V. 50

LEALAND, JOHN
The Itinerary 1535-1543. 1964. V. 52

LEAMING, JAMES R.
Contributions to the Study of the Heart and Lungs. New York: 1890. V. 51

LEAMING, JEREMIAH
A Defence of the Episcopal Government of the Church... New York: 1766. V. 47

LEAN, FLORENCE MARRYAT CHURCH
Facing the Footlights. Leipzig: 1883. V. 49
Life and Letters of Captain Marryat. London: 1872. V. 51
Tom Tiddler's Ground. London: 1886. V. 53

LEAPOR, MARY
Poems Upon Several Occasions. London: 1748. V. 48

LEAR, EDWARD
The Birds of Edward Lear... London: 1975. V. 47; 48; 50
The Book of Nonsense. London. V. 48
A Book of Nonsense. London: 1862. V. 48; 52
The Book of Nonsense. London: 1899. V. 48
The Book of Nonsense. London: 1903. V. 50; 52
Book of Nonsense and More Nonsense. London & New York: 1920. V. 51; 54
The Complete Nonsense of Edward Lear. London: 1947. V. 52
Edward Lear on My Shelves. London: 1933. V. 50
Illustrations of the Family of Psittachidae, or Parrots... London and New York: 1978. V. 48; 52; 53; 54
Journal of a Landscape Painter in Corsica. London: 1870. V. 47; 51; 52; 53; 54
Journals of a Landscape Painter in Albania &c. London: 1851. V. 48; 51; 52
Journals of a Landscape Painter in Southern Calbria. London: 1852. V. 51
Journals of a Landscape Painter. (with) Journals of a Landscape Painter in Albania. London: 1852/51. V. 52
The Jumblies. New York: 1968. V. 53
The Jumblies. 1991. V. 52
Later Letters...to Chichester Fortescue (Lord Carlingford), Frances Countess Waldegrave and Others. London: 1911. V. 52
Laughable Lyrics. London: 1877. V. 50; 53
A Lear Song. 1977. V. 47
Letters of...(and) Later Letters of Edward Lear to Chichester Fortescue (Lord Carlingford) and Frances Countess Waldegrave and Others. London: 1907-11. V. 48; 51
More Nonsense... London: 1872. V. 52
More Nonsense. London: 1888. V. 48
The New Vestments. Portland: 1978. V. 52
Nonsense Songs... Boston: 1871. V. 47; 53
Nonsense Songs. London: 1900. V. 48; 52
Nonsense Songs. London: 1920's. V. 49
The Owl and the Pussy Cat and The Ducke and the kangaroo. London: 1889. V. 48
The Pelican Chorus and Other Nonsense Verses. London: 1900. V. 51
The Story of the Four Little Children Who Went Round the World and The History of the Seven Families of the Lake Pipple-Popple; Nonsense Stories. 1990. V. 52; 54
Views in Rome and Its Environs. Haymarket: 1841. V. 53
Views in the Seven Ionian Islands. Oldham: 1979. V. 49
Views in the Seven Ionian Islands. 1980. V. 47

LEARED, ARTHUR
Marocco and the Moors: Being an Account of Travels... London: 1891. V. 51

LEARNED, WILLIAM LAW
The Fancy Ball; a Letter, Lost from the Portfolio of a Young Lady of Albany. Albany: 1846. V. 52

LEARNER, ALAN JAY
Brigadoon. New York: 1947. V. 51

LEARNING by Heart. Devon: 1986. V. 47

LEAR'S Corfu: an Anthology Drawn from the Painter's Letters. Corfu: 1965. V. 47

LEARY, TIMOTHY
Interpersonal Diagnosis of Personality. New York: 1957. V. 53

LEATHAM, A. E.
Sport in Five Continents. London: 1912. V. 48

THE LEATHER Bottel. Concord: 1902. V. 48

LEATHER, GEORGE
Reports of George Leather, Esq. Civil Engineer, With other Documents, Relative to a Project for a Canal from the River Tees, to the Coal District Contiguous to West-Auckland Presented to a Meeting of the Inhabitants of Stockton, on the 9th of July, 1818. Stockton: 1818. V. 54

LEATHERMAN, LEROY
Martha Graham Portrait of the Lady as an Artist. New York: 1966. V. 54

LEATHERWOOD, S.
The Bottlenose Dolphin. London: 1990. V. 48; 50

LEAVES From the Annals of the Sisters of Mercy By a member of the Order. New York: 1895. V. 49

LEAVES from the Medicine Tree. Lethrbridge, Alberta. V. 50

LEAVES From the Medicine Tree. Alberta: 1960. V. 50

LEAVIS, F. R.
For Continuity. Cambridge: 1933. V. 54
Two Cultures? The Significance of C. P. Snow. New York: 1963. V. 50

LEAVITT, DAVID
Family Dancing. New York: 1984. V. 51; 53
While England Sleeps. 1993. V. 53
While England Sleeps. New York: 1993. V. 51; 53

LEAVITT, DUDLEY
Leavitt's Farmer's Almanack and Miscellaneous Year Book for the Year of Our Lord 1854... Franklin: 1854. V. 49

LEAVITT, JOHN MC DOWELL
Kings of Capital and Knights of Labor. New York: 1885. V. 52

LEAVITT, JONATHAN
A Concise View of the Covenant; The Church's Duty; and of Divine Appointment, or Decrees. Northampton: 1801. V. 51
A Summary of the Laws of Massachusetts, Relative to the Settlement, Support, Employment and Removal of Paupers. Greenfield: 1810. V. 50; 52

LEAVITT, JOSHUA
An Essay on the Best Way of Developing Improved Political and Commercial Relations Between Great Britain and America. London: 1869. V. 53

LEAVITT, RICHARD F.
The World of Tennessee Williams. New York: 1978. V. 48; 50

LEAVITT, THAD W. H.
History of Leeds and Grenville, Ontario, from 1749 to 1879... Brockville: 1879. V. 48

LEBEAUD, M.
Principles of the Art of Modern Horsemanship, For Ladies and Gentlemen; In Which All Late Improvements Are Applied to Practice. Philadelphia: 1833. V. 48

LEBEDEV, VALENTIN
Diary of a Cosmonaut: 211 Days in Space. College Station: 1988. V. 53

LEBEL, ROBERT
Marcel Duchamp. London: 1959. V. 52
Marcel Duchamp. New York: 1959. V. 50; 54

LE BERTHON, J. L.
An Illustrated Souvenir Directory of Southern California. Los Angeles: 1903. V. 52

LE BLANC, H.
The Art of Tying the Cravat... London: 1828. V. 52
The Art of Tying the Cravat: Demonstrated in Sixteen Lessons, Including Thirty-Two Different Styles, Forming a Pocket Manual. New York: 1829. V. 51

LE BLANC, JEAN BERNARD
Letters On the English and French Nations... London: 1747. V. 53

LE BLANC, M.
The Engineer and Machinist's Drawing Book. Glasgow: 1855. V. 52
The Engineer and Machinist's Drawing Book. London: 1864. V. 53

LE BLANC, MAURICE
Arsene Lupin, Super Sleuth. New York: 1927. V. 50

LE BLOND, ELIZABETH ALICE FRANCES HAWKINS WHITSHED
Adventures on the Roof of the World. London: 1904. V. 53
High Life and Towers of Silence. London: 1886. V. 51

LE BLOND, JEAN
Deux Exemples des Cinq Ordres de l'Architecture Antique, et des Quatre plus Excelens Autheurs Qui en Ont Traitte... Paris: 1683. V. 50

LE BOSSU, RENE
Monsieur Bossu's Treatise of the Epick Poem... London: 1695. V. 50
Treatise of the Epick Poem: Containing Many Curious Reflexions, Very Useful and Necessary for the Right Understanding and Juding of the Excellencies of Homer and Virgil. 1719. V. 47

LE BROOY, PAUL JAMES
Michelangelo Models Formerly in the Paul Von Praun Collection. Vancouver: 1972. V. 50; 51; 53

LEBRUN, RICO
Drawings for Dante's Inferno by Rico Lebrun. 1963. V. 47; 50; 52

LE CAMUS, ANTOINE
Abdeker: or, the Art of Preserving Beauty. London: 1754. V. 48

LE CARRE, JOHN
Call for the Dead. London: 1961. V. 52
Call for the Dead. 1962. V. 54
The Clandestine Muse. Portland. V. 52
The Clandestine Muse. 1986. V. 53
The Clandestine Muse. Newark: 1986. V. 51; 53; 54
The Clandestine Muse. Portland: 1986. V. 48; 49
The Honourable Schoolboy. Franklin Center: 1977. V. 51; 52
The Honourable Schoolboy. London: 1977. V. 51; 53
The Little Drummer Girl. London: 1983. V. 50
The Little Drummer Girl. New York: 1983. V. 48; 49; 50; 52; 53
The Looking-Glass War. London: 1965. V. 48; 51; 52; 53
The Looking-Glass War. London: 1985. V. 51
A Murder of Quality. London: 1962. V. 48
A Murder of Quality. New York: 1963. V. 47
The Naive and Sentimental Lover. London: 1971. V. 48; 50; 51; 52

LE CARRE, JOHN continued
The Night Manager. New York: 1933. V. 49
Our Game. New York: 1995. V. 51; 53
A Perfect Spy. 1986. V. 54
A Perfect Spy. London: 1986. V. 51
A Perfect Spy. New York: 1986. V. 48; 50; 52
The Russia House. 1989. V. 54
The Russia House. London: 1989. V. 49; 51; 53
The Russia House. London: 1991. V. 48
The Secret Pilgrim. London: 1991. V. 51
The Secret Pilgrim. New York: 1991. V. 49; 52; 53
A Small Town in Germany. 1968. V. 50
A Small Town in Germany. London: 1968. V. 48; 50
A Small Town in Germany. New York: 1968. V. 48; 52; 53
Smiley's People. London: 1980. V. 50; 53; 54
Smiley's People. New York: 1980. V. 52
The Spy Who Came In from the Cold. London: 1963. V. 47; 48; 49; 50; 51; 52; 53
Tinker, Tailor, Soldier, Spy. London: 1974. V. 50; 51; 53
Tinker, Tailor, Soldier, Spy. New York: 1974. V. 48; 51; 52

LECHFORD, THOMAS
Plain Dealing: or, Newes from New England. London: 1642. V. 48
Plain Dealing: or, Newes from New England. Boston: 1867. V. 49

LECHLER, PROFESSOR
John Wiclif and His English Precursors. London: 1878. V. 51

LECHMERE, EDMUND
A Disputation of the Church Wherein the Old Religion Is Maintained. Douai: 1640. V. 50

LECKENBY, CHARLES H.
The Tread of Pioneers. Steamboat Springs: 1944. V. 47; 52
The Tread of the Pioneers. Steamboat Springs: 1945. V. 52; 53

LECKIE, GOULD FRANCIS
An Historical Research Into the Nature of the Balance of Power... London: 1817. V. 50

LECKY, HALTON STIRLING
The King's Ships. London: 1913-14. V. 50

LECKY, PETER
Peter Lecky By Himself. New York: 1936. V. 48

LECKY, S.
Hand in Hand in Children's Land. London. V. 48

LECKY, S. T. S.
Wrinkles in Practical Navigation. London: 1894. V. 53

LECKY, WILLIAM
Tentamen Medicum Inaugurale, Quaedam Complectens de Morbis ex Graviditate Pendentibus. Edinburgh: 1787. V. 52; 54

LECKY, WILLIAM EDWARD HARTPOOLE
A History of England in the Eighteen Century. London: 1883-90. V. 53
A History of England in the Eighteenth Century. London: 1878-90. V. 47; 49
A History of England in the Eighteenth Century. New York: 1888-90. V. 52
History of European Morals from Augustus to Charlemagne. London: 1869. V. 48; 52
A History of Ireland in the Eighteenth Century. London: 1892. V. 49; 50
History of the Rise and Influence of the Spirit of Rationalism in Europe. London: 1865. V. 52
History of the Rise and Influence of the Spirit of Rationalism in Europe. London: 1866. V. 48
History of the Rise and Influence of the Spirit of Rationalism in Europe. London: 1872. V. 52
Leaders of Public Opinion in Ireland. London: 1903. V. 49; 50

LE CLERC, CHARLES GABRIEL
The Compeat Surgeon: or, The Whole Art of Surgery... London: 1714. V. 51
The Compeat Surgeon: or, the Whole Art of Surgery... London: 1727. V. 51

LE CLERC, DANIEL
Historia Naturalis et Medica Latorum Lumbricorum, Intra Hominem & Alia Animalia... Geneva: 1715. V. 51

LECLERC, FREDERIC
Texas and Its Revolution. Houston: 1950. V. 49; 52; 53

LE CLERC, JEAN
Historia Ecclesiastica Duorum Primorum a Christo Nato Saeculorum, e Veteribus Monumentis Depromta... Amstelodami: 1716. V. 48; 49
The Life of the Famous Cardinal-Duke de Richelieu, Principal Minister of State to Lewis XIII, King of France and Navarr. London: 1695. V. 47
Memoirs of Emeric Count Teckely... London: 1693. V. 49
Mr. Le Clerc's Judgment and Censure of Dr. Bentley's Horace... London: 1713. V. 49

LE CLERC, NICHOLAS
Histoire Physique, Morale, Civile et Politique de la Russie Ancienne. Paris: 1783-94. V. 49

LE CLERC, SEBASTIEN
Practical Geometry; or, A New and Easy Method of Treating that Art... London: 1727. V. 50
Practical Geometry; or, A New and Easy Method of Treating that Art. London: 1742. V. 48; 52; 54

L'ECLUSE, CHARLES DE
Rariorum Plantarum Historia. Antwerp: 1601. V. 51

LE COMPTE, LOUIS
Memoirs and Observations... London: 1697. V. 53; 54
Memoirs and Observations... London: 1698. V. 48

LE CONTE, JOSEPH
Evolution, Its Nature, Its Evidences and Its Relation to Religious Thought. London: 1898. V. 49
A Journal of Ramblings through the High Sierra of California by the University of Excursion Party. San Francisco: 1960. V. 54

LE CONTE, MICHEL
Les Trophees de l'Amour Divin au Tres-Sainct Sacrement de l'Autel. Charleville: 1645. V. 52; 54

LE CORBEAU, ADRIEN
The Forest Giant. London: 1924. V. 50
The Forest Giant. New York: 1924. V. 48; 49; 50

LECOUNT, PETER
A Practical Treatise on Railways, Explaining Their Construction and Management... Edinburgh: 1839. V. 48; 49; 52

LECOUVREUR, FRANK
From East Prussia to the Golden Gate. Letters and Diary of the California Pioneer. New York: 1906. V. 47; 52

LECTIONES ad Matutinum Offici Defunctorum... Ditchling: 1925. V. 47

LECTIUS, JACOBUS
Poetae Graeci Veteres Carminis Heroici Scriptores Qui Extant, Omnes. Aureliae Allobrogum: 1606. V. 52

LECTURES Delivered in a Course Before the Lowell Institute...On Subjects Relating to the Early History of Massachusetts. Boston: 1869. V. 53

LEDAY, JAY
The Melville Log. New York: 1951. V. 51

LEDFORD, PRESTON LAFAYETTE
Reminiscences of the Civil War, 1861-1865. Thomasville: 1909. V. 54

LEDGER, EDWARD
The Era Almanack and Annual 1868-98. London: 1868-98. V. 53

LEDGER, HENRY
Dramatic Poems. London: 1843. V. 52

LEDIARD, THOMAS
The Life of John, Duke of Marlborough. London: 1736. V. 47; 48; 49; 51; 52
The Life of John, Duke of Marlborough... London: 1743. V. 50
The Naval History of England... London: 1735. V. 50

LEDOUX, LOUIS V.
The Art of Japan. New York: 1927. V. 50
Japanese Prints of the Primitive Period in the Collection of Louis V. Ledoux. New York: 1942. V. 54

LEDWICH, EDWARD
Antiquities of Ireland. Dublin: 1790. V. 53

LEDWIDGE, FRANCIS
Last Songs. London: 1918. V. 47
Songs of the Fields. 1916. V. 54

LEDYARD, LAURA
Tutti-Frutti, a Book of Child Songs. New York: 1881. V. 54

LEE, ALBERT
The History of the Tenth Foot. 1911. V. 48

LEE, AMY FREEMAN
Hobby Horses. New York: 1940. V. 52; 53

LEE, ANDREW
The Indifferent Children. New York: 1947. V. 53

LEE, ANNA MARIA
Memoirs of Eminent Female Writers of All Ages and Countries. Philadelphia: 1827. V. 53; 54

LEE, ARTHUR
An Appeal to the Justice and Interests of the People of Great Britain, in the Present Dispute with America. London: 1775. V. 53
An Appeal to the Justice and Interests of the People of Great Britain, in the Present Dispute with America. New York: 1775. V. 47
A Second Appeal to the Justice and Interests of the People, on the Measures Respecting America. London: 1775. V. 47

LEE, AUSTIN
Miss Hogg and the Squash Club Murder. London: 1957. V. 51

LEE, BOURKE
Death Valley Men. New York: 1932. V. 47; 48

LEE, BRIAN NORTH
The Bookplate Designs of Rex Whistler. 1973. V. 54
Bookplates by Simon Brett. 1989. V. 47
Bookplates by Simon Brett. London: 1989. V. 50
British Royal Bookplates and Ex-Libros of Related Families. London: 1992. V. 48

LEE, CHARLES
Memoirs of the Life of the Late Charles Lee, Esq. New York: 1792. V. 47

LEE, CHARLES CARTER
Virginia Georgics, Written for the Hole and Corner Club. Richmond: 1858. V. 49

LEE, CHARLES H.
The Judge Advocate's Vade Mecum... Richmond: 1863. V. 49

LEE, CHAUNCEY
The American Accomptant; Being a Plain, Practical and Systematic Compendium of Federal Arithmetic. Lansingburgh: 1797. V. 49; 50

LEE, CHRISTOPHER
Poems. London: 1937. V. 51

LEE, CLARENCE
The Instrumental Detection of Deception, the Lie Test. Springfield: 1953. V. 54

LEE, EDGAR
Black Beauty in Words of One Syllable. Akron: 1905. V. 50

LEE, EDMUND
The Story of a Sister's Love. London: 1891. V. 54

LEE, EDWIN
Hydropathy and Homoeopathy, Impartially Appreciated, with an Appendix of Notes Illustrative of the Influence of the Mind on the Body. New York: 1848. V. 51
The Watering Places of England... London: 1859. V. 51

LEE, F. D.
Historical Record of the City of Savannah. Savannah: 1869. V. 49

LEE, FITZHUGH
Chancellorsville... Richmond: 1879. V. 54
Chancellorsville. Richmond: 1884. V. 49
General Lee. New York: 1894. V. 50

LEE, FRANCIS BAZLEY
Genealogical and Memorial History of the State of New Jersey. New York: 1910. V. 47; 49; 51
Genealogical and Personal Memorial of Mercer County, New Jersey. New York: 1907. V. 47; 49; 51
History of Trenton, New Jersey. Trenton: 1895. V. 47; 49; 51

LEE, FREDERICK GEORGE
The Other World, or, Glimpses of the Supernatural. London: 1875. V. 52

LEE, G. HERBERT
A Historical Sketch of the First Fifty Years of the Church of England in the Province of New Brunswick (1783-1833). St. John: 1880. V. 47

LEE, GEORGE
History of Ceylon Presented by Captain John Ribeye to the King of Portugal in 1685... Ceylon: 1847. V. 53

LEE, GEORGE W.
Beale Street: Where the Blues Began. New York: 1934. V. 52
River George. New York: 1937. V. 53

LEE, GYPSY ROSE
The G-String Murders. New York: 1941. V. 48
Mother Finds a Body. New York: 1942. V. 49; 50

LEE, H.
The Campaign of 1781 in the Carolinas; With Remarks Historical and Critical on Johnson's Life of Greene... Philadelphia: 1824. V. 49

LEE, HANNAH FARNHAM
The Contrast; or Modes of Education. Boston: 1837. V. 49
The Huguenots in France and America. Cambridge: 1843. V. 49; 50

LEE, HARPER
To Kill a Mockingbird. V. 54
To Kill a Mockingbird. London, Melbourne, Toronto: 1960. V. 47; 48; 49; 50; 51; 53
To Kill a Mockingbird. New York: 1991. V. 53

LEE, HENRY
Memoirs of the War in the Southern Department of the United States. Washington: 1827. V. 49
Memoirs of the War in the Southern Department of the United States. New York: 1869. V. 49

LEE, J. FRANCIS
What You Gwine to Do Wid Ham?. Norfolk: 1905. V. 47

LEE, J. J.
Biology of Foraminifera. London: 1991. V. 50

LEE, J. R.
A History of Market Drayton, With Some Account of Ashley, Betton, Norton, Cheswardine and Other Villages. 1861. V. 50

LEE, JAMES
An Introduction to Botany. London: 1765. V. 54
An Introduction to Botany. London: 1776. V. 53
An Introduction to Botany. London: 1794. V. 49; 54

LEE, JAMES W.
The Romance of Palestine: a History. Atlanta: 1897. V. 52

LEE, JOHN
Memorial for the Bible Societies in Scotland... Edinburgh: 1824. V. 47
Wrestling in the North Country. Consett: 1953. V. 53

LEE, JOHN D.
A Mormon Chronicle: The Diaries of... San Marino: 1955. V. 47; 48; 52
Mormonism Unveiled or the Life and Confessions of the Late Mormon Bishop John D. Lee. St. Louis: 1877. V. 54

LEE, L. P.
History of the Spirit Lake Massacre!. New Britain: 1857. V. 52

LEE, LAURIE
Cider with Rosie. London: 1959. V. 47; 48; 50; 53
The Firstborn. London: 1964. V. 51
I Can't Stay Long. London: 1975. V. 51
Peasant's Priest. Canterbury: 1947. V. 51
A Rose for Winter - Travels in Andalusia. London: 1955. V. 51
The Sun My Monument. London: 1944. V. 51
The Voyage of Magellan. 1948. V. 54
The Voyage of Magellan. London: 1948. V. 47; 48; 50; 54

LEE, LAWRENCE
A Hawk from Cuckoo Tavern. Gaylordsville: 1930. V. 54

LEE, MARGUERITE D.
Virginia Ghosts and Others. Richmond: 1932. V. 49

LEE, MARSHALL
Erte at Ninety-five: the Complete New Graphics. New York: 1987. V. 50

LEE, NATHANIEL
Caesar Borgia, A Son of Pope Alexander the Sixth. London: 1680. V. 48; 49; 53
Constantine the Great: a Tragedy. London: 1684. V. 48; 50
Gloriana, or the Court of Augustus Caesar. London: 1676. V. 47; 48
Lucius Junius Brutus; Father of His Country. London: 1681. V. 47; 48
The Massacre of Paris... London: 1690. V. 48
The Rival Queens, or the Death of Alexander the Great. London: 1684. V. 47
Sophinisba; or, Hannibal's Overthrow. London: 1681. V. 47

LEE, NELSON
The Royal Acting Punch and Judy as Played Before the Queen. New York: 1880. V. 49

LEE, NORMAN
The Journal of Norman Lee, 1898, Which is the Account of the Cattle Drive from Chilcotin country to Teslin Lake by the Telegraph Trail. Vancouver: 1959. V. 47; 50; 53

LEE, QUONG
The Song Book of Quong Lee of Limehouse. London: 1920. V. 48

LEE, RICHARD
Political Curiosities, Including an Account of the State of Political Affairs in Europe. Philadelphia: 1796. V. 50

LEE, ROBERT
The Family and Its Duties, with Other Essays and Discourses for Sunday Reading. London: 1863. V. 49

LEE, ROBERT M.
China Safari. 1986. V. 48; 53
China Safari. Clinton: 1986. V. 49

LEE, RONALD A.
The First Twelve Years of the English Pendulum Clock or the Fromanteel Family and Their Contemporaries 1658-1670. London: 1969. V. 53
The Knibb Family of Clockmakers. Surrey: 1964. V. 53

LEE, SAMUEL PHILLIPS
Reports and Charts of the Cruise of the U.S. Brig Dolphin. Washington: 1854. V. 47

LEE, SARAH WALLIS BOWDICH
Playing at Settlers; or the Faggot House. London: 1855. V. 49
Stories of Strange Lands; and Fragments from the Notes of a Traveller. London: 1835. V. 54
Taxidermy: or, the Art of Collecting, Preparing and Mounting Objects of Natural History... London: 1843. V. 54
Trees, Plants and Flowers... London: 1854. V. 50
Trees, Plants and Flowers... London: 1859. V. 54

LEE, SIDNEY
Shakespeare's England. An Account of the Life and Manners of His Age. London: 1916. V. 51

LEE, SOPHIA
The Recess; or, a Tale of the Times. London: 1785. V. 48; 49

LEE, SPIKE
Spike Lee's Gotta Have It: Inside Guerilla Filmmaking. New York: 1987. V. 48

LEE, STEPHEN DILL
Campaign of Generals Grant and Sherman Against Vicksburg in December 1862...Known As the "Chickasaw Bayou Campaign". 1901. V. 49

LEE, W.
Concerts of Ancient Music...as Performed at the New Rooms, Tottenham-Street, MDCCLXXXVIII. London: 1788. V. 47

LEE, WEYMAN
An Essay to Ascertain the Value of Leases and Annuities for Years and Lives, and to Estimate the Chances of the Duration of Lives. London: 1738. V. 49

LEE, WILLIAM
A Chronological Catalogue of the Works of Daniel Defoe. London: 1869. V. 51; 54
Daniel Defoe: His Life, and Recently Discovered Writings: Extending from 1716 to 1729. London: 1869. V. 49
The Plan of the Boxes at the King's Theatre, Hay-Market. London: 1806. V. 54

LEECH, A. B.
Irish Riflemen in America. 1875. V. 50; 54
Irish Riflemen in America. London: 1875. V. 49; 51

LEECH, BOSDIN
History of the Manchester Ship Canal From Its Inception to Its Completion. Manchester & London: 1907. V. 48

LEECH, CARLYLE
Hide and Seek Riddle Book. New York: 1943. V. 49

LEECH, J. H.
Butterflies from China, Japan and Corea. London: 1892-94. V. 49

LEECH, JOHN
Mr. Briggs and His Doings (Fishing). London: 1860. V. 48
Pictures of Life and Character from the Collection of 'Mr. Punch'. London: 1887. V. 50
Portraits of Children of the Mobility. London: 1841. V. 47
Portraits of Children of the Mobility. London: 1875. V. 54

LEECH, SAMUEL
Thirty Years From Home, or a Voice from the Main Deck, Being the Experience of Samuel Leech, Who Was for Six Years in the British American Navies... Boston: 1844. V. 51

LEECH, SAMUEL VANDERLIP
The Raid of John Brown at Harper's Ferry As I Saw It. Washington: 1909. V. 50

LEEDS, LEWIS W.
Lectures on Ventilation: Being a Course Delivered in the Franklin Institute of Philadelphia During the Winter of 1866-67. New York: 1868. V. 53

LEEDS LIBRARY
Catalogue of the Leeds Library with a Short History of the Library, The Rules at Present in Force... Leeds: 1889. V. 51

LEEDS, W. H.
Rudimentary Architecture: for the Use of Beginners. London: 1843. V. 50

LEE-HAMILTON, EUGENE
Mimma Bella. London: 1909. V. 53

LEEKEY, WILLIAM
A Discourse on the Use of the Pen. London: 1750. V. 49

LEEMING, HENRY
The General and Quarter Sessions of the peace: Their Jurisdiction and Practice in Other than Criminal Matters. London: 1858. V. 51

LEEPER, DAVID ROHRER
The Argonauts of Forty-Nine. 1894. V. 54
The Argonauts of 'Forty-Nine. South Bend: 1894. V. 47; 52

LEES, F. A.
A Flora of West Yorkshire. London: 1888. V. 47; 48; 50; 53
The Flora of West Yorkshire... London: 1888/1941. V. 53

LEES, G. ROBINSON
Life and Adventure Beyond Jordan. London: 1906. V. 48; 53

LEESBERG, ARNOLD C. M.
Comparative Philology. A Comparison Between Semitic and American languages with a Map and Illustrations. Leyden: 1903. V. 49

LEESE, JACOB P.
Historical Outline of Lower California. New York: 1865. V. 52

LEESER, ISAAC
The Forms of Prayers According to the Custom of the Spanish and Portuguese Jews. Volume First. Philadelphia: 1846. V. 49

LEES-MILNE, JAMES
The Age of Adam. London: 1947. V. 54
The Age of Inigo Jones. London: 1953. V. 53
Diaries. London: 1975/85. V. 49
English Country Houses, Baroque 1685-1715. London: 1970. V. 50; 53

LEET, FRANK R.
The Clowns' Acrobatic Alphabet. Cleveland: 1928. V. 47

LEEUWENHOEK, ANTON VAN
Anatomia et Contemplatio Nonnullorum Naturae Invisibilium Secretorum comprehensorum Epistolis Quibusdam Scriptis ad Illustre... Leiden: 1685. V. 47
The Leeuwenhoek Letter. Baltimore: 1937. V. 47
Selected Works... London: 1800-07. V. 51

LEFANU, ALICIA
The India Voyage. London: 1804. V. 50

LE FANU, ALICIA
Memoirs of the Life and Writings of Mrs. Frances Sheridan... London: 1824. V. 52

LEFANU, ALICIA
Rosara's Chain; or, the Choice of Life. London: 1812. V. 50

LE FANU, ALICIA
Strathallan. London: 1817. V. 49

LE FANU, JOSEPH SHERIDAN
All in the Dark. London: 1866. V. 48
Checkmate. London: 1899. V. 48; 51
The Evil Guest. London: 1895. V. 48; 51; 52
Guy Deverell. London: 1865. V. 53
In a Glass Darkly. London: 1929. V. 51
The Poems of Joseph Sheridan Le Fanu. 1896. V. 48
The Rose and the Key. London: 1871. V. 48
A Stable for Nightmares. New Amsterdam: 1896. V. 48; 50; 52
Uncle Silas. London: 1865. V. 47; 51
The Watcher and Other Weird Stories. London: 1894. V. 48

LE FANU, W. R.
Seventy Years of Irish Life Being Anecdotes and Reminiscences. London: 1893. V. 52

LEFEVRE, G. SHAW
English and Irish Land Questions. 1881. V. 54

LEFEVRE, GEORGE WILLIAM
An Apology for the Nerves: or, their Influence and Importance in Health and Disease. London: 1844. V. 50; 53

LE FEVRE, JULES
Sir Lionel D'Arquenay. Paris: 1834. V. 54

LEFEVRE, LEON
Architectural Pottery. London: 1900. V. 53

LEFEVRE, RAOUL
The Recuyell of the Historyes of Troye. 1892. V. 54
The Recuyell of the Historyes of Troye. London: 1892. V. 50; 54

LEFFERTS, CHARLES M.
Uniforms of the Armies in the War of the American Revolution 1775-1783. New York: 1926. V. 50

LEFFINGWELL, WILLIAM B.
The Happy Hunting Grounds, Also Fishing, of the South... Chicago: 1895. V. 50
Wild Fowl Shooting. Chicago: 1890. V. 52

LEFLON, JEAN
Eugene De Mazenod: Bishop of Marseille, Founder of the Oblates of Mary Immaculate, 1782-1861. New York: 1961/66/68/70. V. 51; 54

LE FLORS, JOE
Wyoming Peace Officer... Autobiography... Laramie: 1953. V. 51; 52

LE FORS, JOE
Wyoming Peace Officer... Autobiography. Laramie: 1954. V. 48; 52

LE FRERE, JEAN
La Vraye et Entiere Histoire Des Trovbles et Gverres Civiles, Advenves de Nostre Temps. Paris: 1578. V. 52

LEFROY, ANNA AUSTEN
Jane Austen's Sanditon: a Continuation by Her Niece, Together with Reminiscences of Aunt Jane. Chicago: 1983. V. 54

LEFROY, W. CHAMBERS
The Ruined Abbeys of Yorkshire. London: 1883. V. 47; 53

LEFT to Their Own Devices. New York: 1937. V. 48; 52

LEFTWICH, NINA
Two Hundred Years at Muscle Shoals Being an Authentic History of Colbert County 1700-1900 With Special Emphasis on the Stirring Events of the Early Times. Tuscumbia: 1935. V. 50

A LEGACY of Affection, Advice and Instruction, from a Retired Governess, to the Present Pupils of an Establishment Near London for Female Education, Which She Conducted Upward of 40 Years. London: 1872. V. 52

LE GAL, EUGENE
The School of the Guides, for the Use of the Army of the Confederate States, With Questions. Griffin: 1861. V. 49

LE GALLIENNE, RICHARD
English Poems. London: 1892. V. 49; 54
George Meredith - Some Characteristics. London: 1890. V. 47
The Love-Letters of the King, Or, the Life Romantic. Boston: 1901. V. 48
The Maker of Rainbows and Other Fairy Tales and Fables. New York: 1912. V. 51
An Old Country House. New York: 1902. V. 49
Prose Fancies. London: 1894. V. 49
The Quest of the Golden Girl. London & New York: 1896. V. 54
The Religion of a Literary Man. London: 1893. V. 47; 49; 52; 53
The Romance of Perfume. New York & Paris: 1928. V. 49; 50; 53
Volumes in Folio. London: 1889. V. 47; 48; 49

LEGALLOIS, JULIEN
Experiments on the Principle of Life and Particularly on the Principle of the Motions of the heart, and on the Seat of this Principle. Philadelphia: 1813. V. 47; 48

LE GALLOIS, PIERRE
A Critical and Historical Account of All the Celebrated Libraraies in Foreign Countries, as Well Ancient as Modern and Particularly the Vatican. London: 1740. V. 48

LEGARD, JAMES DIGBY
The Legards of Anlaby & Ganton: Their Neighbours & Neighbourhood. London: 1926. V. 47; 48; 53; 54

THE LEGEND Of Saint Ursula. London: 1869. V. 49; 50

LEGENDRE, ADRIENNE MARIE
Exercices de Calcul Integral sur Divers Ordres de Transcendantes et sur les Quadratures. Paris: 1811-17-16. V. 50

LEGENDRE, ADRIENNE MARIE continued
Nouvelles Methodes Pour la Determination des Orbites des Cometes. Paris: 1805. V. 47

LEGENDS from Fairyland. London: 1907. V. 53

LEGER, ALEXIS SAINT-LEGER
Anabasis. London: 1930. V. 47; 48; 49; 50; 52; 53
Anabasis. London: 1937. V. 48; 54
Anabasis. New York: 1938. V. 48; 51
Anabasis. New York: 1949. V. 51
Anabasis. London: 1959. V. 53
Chronique. New York: 1961. V. 51
Eloges and Other Poems. New York: 1956. V. 51
Exile and Other Poems. New York: 1949. V. 51
Winds. New York: 1953. V. 51

LEGG, J. WICKHAM
On the Bible Jaundice and Bilious Diseases. London: 1870. V. 54

LEGG, LEOPOLD G. WICKHAM
English Coronation Records. London: 1901. V. 52

LEGGE, CHARLES
Report of Exploration From Deep River to the Georgian Bay. Montreal: 1874. V. 50

LEGGE, THOMAS
Industrial Maladies. Oxford: 1934. V. 54

LEGGE, W. V.
A History of the Birds of Ceylon. London: 1878-80. V. 51; 52
A History of the Birds of Ceylon. Dehiwala, Siri Lanka: 1983. V. 51

LEGGE, WILLOW
An African Folktale. 1979. V. 47

LEGGETT, WILLIAM
Leisure Hours at Sea: Being a Few Miscellaneous Poems by a Midshipman. New York: 1825. V. 48
Tales and Sketches. New York: 1829. V. 47

THE LEGION Book. London: 1929. V. 49; 53

LEGLER, HENRY
Walt Whitman: Yesterday and Today. Chicago: 1916. V. 52

LE GONIDEC, JEAN FRANCOIS
Dictionnaire Francais-Breton. (and) Breton-Francais. Saint Brieue: 1847/50. V. 54

LEGRAIN, LEON
Terra Cottas From Nippur. Philadelphia: 1930. V. 48

LE GRAND, ANTOINE
Dissertation de Carentia Sensus & Cognitionis in Brutis. London: 1675. V. 52

LE GRAND, LOUIS
The Military Hand-book, and Soldier's Manual of Information. New York: 1862. V. 49; 52

LE GRAND, M.
Fabliaux, or Tales, Abridged from French Manuscripts of the XIIth and XIIIth Centuries. London: 1796. V. 50
Fabliaux, or Tales, Abridged from French Manuscripts of the XIIth and XIIIth Centuries. London: 1796/1800. V. 47

LEGRAND, M.
Fabliaux or Tales, Abridged from French Manuscripts of the XIIth and XIIIth Centuries. London: 1815. V. 53

LE GUIN, URSULA K.
Always Coming Home. 1985. V. 49; 54
The Dispossessed. 1974. V. 52
The Dispossessed. New York: 1974. V. 49
The Farthest Shore. 1972. V. 49

LEGUIN, URSULA K.
The Farthest Shore. New York: 1972. V. 51

LE GUIN, URSULA K.
Findings. 1992. V. 52
From Elfland to Poughkeepsie. Portland: 1973. V. 49
Gwilan's Harp. Northridge: 1981. V. 49
The Lathe of Heaven. New York: 1971. V. 53
The Left Hand of Darkness. 1969. V. 47
The Left Hand of Darkness. London: 1969. V. 49; 54
Tehanu. 1990. V. 49; 54
The Tombs of Atuan. 1971. V. 52
A Wizard of Earthsea. 1968. V. 52
The Wizard of Earthsea. Berkeley: 1968. V. 51; 53

LEGUIN, URSULA K.
The Word for World is Forest. New York: 1976. V. 49

LEHMAN, AMBROSE E.
Report of the Water Supply, Source and Upper Waters of the St. Louis River. Philadelphia: 1894. V. 54

LEHMAN, ANTHONY L.
Paul Landacre: a Life and Legacy. Los Angeles: 1983. V. 51
A Paul Landacre Bookplate. Los Angeles: 1986. V. 48
A Visit With William Everson. Los Angeles: 1987. V. 50

LEHMAN, ROBERT
The Philip Lehman Collection, New York: Paintings. Paris: 1928. V. 53

LEHMANN, CHARLES
The Noise of History. London: 1934. V. 51

LEHMANN, ERNST A.
The Zeppelins. New York: 1927. V. 49

LEHMANN, GEOFFREY
A Voyage of Lions and Other Poems. Sydney: 1968. V. 50

LEHMANN, HERMAN
Nine Years Among the Indians, 1870-1879. 1927. V. 52
Nine Years Among the Indians, 1870-1879... Austin: 1927. V. 47; 48; 54

LEHMANN, JOHN
Down River - Danubian Study. London: 1939. V. 52
Evil Was Abroad. London: 1938. V. 48
In My Own Time - Memoirs of a Literary Life. Boston and Toronto: 1969. V. 54
New Writing. London: 1936-Sum. 1938. V. 51
The Noise of History. London: 1934. V. 47
Poets of Tomorrow - Second Selection - Cambridge Poetry 1940. London: 1940. V. 49
Ralph Fox. A Writer in Arms. London: 1937. V. 49

LEHMANN, KARL
Samothrace: Excavations Conducted by the Institute of Fine Arts, New York University... New York: 1960. V. 54
Samothrae: Excavations Conducted by the Institute of Fine Arts, New York University, Karl Lehmann and Phyllis Williams Lehmann, Editors. New York: 1962-64. V. 54

LEHMANN, PHYLLIS WILLIAMS
The Hiernon, Samthrace. London: 1969. V. 48

LEHMANN, ROSAMOND
Dusty Answer. London: 1927. V. 54
A Note in Music. London: 1930. V. 51

LEHMANN-HAUPT, HELLMUT
Two Essays on the Decretum of Gratian...Together with an Original Leaf Printed on Vellum by Peter Schoeffer at Mainz in 1492. Los Angeles/San Francisco: 1971. V. 47; 51

LEHNER, JOSEPH
Neue Dekorations-Malereien im Modernen Stil. Vienna: 1899. V. 47

LEHNER, MARK
The Pyramid Tomb of Hetep=Heres and the Satellite Pyramid of Khufu. Mainz am Rhein: 1985. V. 49

LEHRER, WARREN
Versations: a Setting for Eight Conversations. Mattapoinset: 1980. V. 47

LEIBER, FRITZ
Gather, Darkness. New York: 1950. V. 48; 49
The Ghost Light. New York: 1984. V. 52
Night's Black Agents. Sauk City: 1947. V. 47; 49; 51; 53; 54
The Saga of Fafhrd and the Gray Mouser Being Swords and Deviltry, Swords Against Death, Swords in the Mist, Swords Against Wizardry, the Swords of Lankhmar and Swords and Ice Magic. 1977. V. 47
The Secret Songs. 1968. V. 48; 52
The Swords of Lankhmar. 1969. V. 49; 54
Two Sought Adventure. 1957. V. 47; 52
The Wanderer. 1967. V. 48; 52

LEIBNITZ, GOTTFRIED WILHELM VON
Collectanea Etymologica... Hanover: 1717. V. 50
Commercium Philosophicum et Mathematicum. Lausanne and Geneva: 1745. V. 50; 54
Opera Omnia... Geneva: 1768. V. 49; 52; 54

LEICESTER, EARLS OF. LIBRARY. (HOLKHAM HALL)
The Holkham Library. Illuminations and Illustrations in the Manuscript Library of the Earl of Leicester. Oxford: 1970. V. 50; 54

LEICESTER, ROBERT DUDLEY, EARL OF
The Perfect Picture of a Favourite; or Secret Memoirs of... London: 1708. V. 49
Secret Memoirs of Robert Dudley, Earl of Leicester. London: 1706. V. 52

LEICHHARDT, LUDWIG
Journal of an Overland Expedition in Australia from Moreton Bay to Port Essington, a Distance of Upwards of 3000 Miles During the Years 1844-45. London: 1847. V. 50; 52

LEIDY, J.
Fresh-water Rhizopods fo North America. Washington: 1879. V. 49; 54
Memoir on the Extinct Species of American Ox: The Ancient Fauna of Nebraska... Washington: 1852-65. V. 47

LEIDY, JOSEPH
An Elementary Treatise on Human Anatomy. Philadelphia: 1861. V. 48

LEIFCHILD, JOHN R.
Cornwall: Its Mines and Miners, with Sketches of Scenery Designed as a Popular Introduction to Metallic Mines. (with) Our Coal and Our Coal Pits: the People in Them... London: 1855. V. 50; 54

LEIGH, AUSTEN
Recollections of the Early Days of the Vine and Hunt and of its Founder William John Chute, Esq., M.P. of the Vine. London: 1865. V. 47

LEIGH, CHANDOS, 1ST BARON
Poems, Now First Collected. London: 1839. V. 50

LEIGH, CHANDOS, 1ST BARON continued
Sylva: Poems on Several Occasions. London: 1823. V. 48
The View, and other Poems. London: 1820. V. 50

LEIGH, CHARLES
The Natural History of Lancashire, Cheshire, and the Peak in Derbyshire... Oxford: 1700. V. 53; 54

LEIGH, CHARLES W. E.
Catalogue of the Christie Collection Comprising the Printed Books and Manuscripts Bequeathed to the Library of the University of Manchester by the Late Richard Copley Christie. 1915. V. 50; 52

LEIGH, EDWARD
England Described; or, the Several Counties and Shires Thereof Briefly Handled. London: 1659. V. 50; 51
Select and Choice Observations Concerning the Roman and Greek Emperors. London: 1670. V. 51

LEIGH, EGERTON
Considerations on Certain Political Transactions of the Province of South Carolina... London: 1774. V. 47

LEIGH, FELIX
London Town. London: 1883. V. 53
London Town. London: 1890. V. 49

LEIGH, GEORGE
The Leigh Peerage. London: 1834. V. 47; 50; 53
Mary Grainger. London: 1874. V. 54

LEIGH, HENRY SAMBROOKE
Carols of Cockayne. London: 1869. V. 49

LEIGH, HOWARD
Planes of the Great War... London. V. 47
Planes of the Great War. London: 1934. V. 54

LEIGH, J. E. AUSTEN
A Memoir of Jane Austen. London: 1879. V. 54

LEIGH, M. A.
Leigh's Guide to the Lakes and Mountains of Cumberland, Westmorland, and Lancashire... London: 1843. V. 52

LEIGH, PERCIVAL
The Comic Latin Grammar. London: 1840. V. 48
Manners and Customs of ye Englyshe, Drawn from ye Quick by Rychard Doyle. London: 1849. V. 47
Paul Prendergast; or the Comic Schoolmaster... London: 1859. V. 50

LEIGH, SAMUEL
Leigh's New Pocket Road-Book of England and Wales... London: 1835. V. 50; 52
New Pocket Road-Book of Ireland. 1827. V. 50; 54
New Pocket Road-Book of Ireland. London: 1827. V. 51

LEIGH, W. H.
Reconnoitering Voyages, Travels and Adventures in the New Colonies of South Australia. London: 1840. V. 50

LEIGH, WILLIAM R.
The Western Pony. New York: 1933. V. 48; 50

LEIGH FERMOR, PATRICK
Between the Woods and the Water. London: 1986. V. 50
Mani. London: 1958. V. 52

LEIGHLEY, JOHN
California as an Island. San Francisco: 1972. V. 48; 52; 54

LEIGHTON, CLARE
Country Matters. New York: 1937. V. 49
Four Hedges. London: 1935. V. 48; 49; 51; 54
Four Hedges. New York: 1935. V. 47; 48; 49; 54
Give Us This Day. New York: 1943. V. 54
Growing New Roots - an Essay with Fourteen Wood Engravings. San Francisco: 1976. V. 52; 53
The Musical Box. London: 1936. V. 49
Southern Harvest. London: 1943. V. 51
Tempestuous Petticoat: The Story of an Invincible Edwardian. New York: 1947. V. 52
Where Land Meets Sea - The Tide Line of Cape Cod. New York and Toronto: 1954. V. 49; 52; 54
The Wood that Came Back. Poughkeepsie: 1935. V. 49
Wood-Engraving and Woodcuts. London: 1932. V. 53
Woodcuts. Examples of the Work of Clare Leighton. London: 1930. V. 51; 52; 53

LEIGHTON, FRANCIS
The Muse's Blossoms: or, Juvenile Poems. London: 1769. V. 54

LEIGHTON, J. & J.
A Catalogue of Books in Fine Bindings or in Fine Original State Offered for Sale by J. & J. London: 1899. V. 50

LEIGHTON, JOHN
Madre Natura Versus the Moloch of Fashion. London: 1874. V. 51; 54
Money: How Old Brown Made It, and How Young Brown Spent It. London: 1851. V. 47
Suggestions in Design. London: 1853. V. 50; 53; 54
Suggestions in Design... 1880. V. 50
Suggestions in Design... London: 1880. V. 51
Suggestions in Design. New York: 1881. V. 51

LEIGHTON, ROBERT
The Whole Works...to Which is Prefixed a Life of the Author... London: 1830. V. 53

LEIGHTON, W. A.
A Flora of Shropshire. London: 1841. V. 47
A Flora of Shropshire. Shrewsbury: 1841. V. 50; 51
The Lichen-Flora of Great Britain, Ireland and the Channel Islands. Shrewsbury: 1879. V. 49; 52; 54

LEINSTEIN, MADAME
Punctuation in Verse; or, the Good Child's Book of Stops. Philadelphia: 1835. V. 47

LEINSTER, MURRAY
Operation: Outer Space. 1954. V. 48; 52
Operation: Outer Space. Reading: 1954. V. 50

LEIPNIK, F. L.
History of French Etching from the 16th Century to Present. London: 1924. V. 48; 53

LEIRIS, MICHEL
African Art. New York: 1968. V. 51; 52; 54
Andre Masson and His Universe. London/Paris: 1947. V. 50
Francis Bacon. Full Face and in Profile. New York: 1983. V. 49; 50; 51
Joan Miro Lithographs. New York: 1972/75. V. 50
Joan Miro Lithographs. 1972/75/77. V. 50
Joan Miro Lithographs. Volume I. New York: 1972. V. 47; 50
Joan Miro Lithographs. Volume II. New York: 1975. V. 47

LEISENRING, JAMES E.
The Art of Tying The Wet Fly...As Told to V. S. Hidy. New York: 1943. V. 47

LEISHER, J. J.
The Decline and Fall of Samuel Sawbones, M.D. On the Klondike. New York: 1900. V. 49; 54

LEISTIKOW, DANKWART
Ten Centuries of European Hospital Architecture. Ingelheim am Rhein: 1967. V. 50

THE LEISURE of a Lady Employed in Extraction from the best Authors Pieces in Prose and Verse, for the Amusement and Instruction of Her Own Children. London: 182. V. 48

LEITH, WILLIAM FORBES
Memoirs of Scottish Catholics During the SVIIth and XVIIIth Centuries... London: 1909. V. 49

LEIVICK, HALPER
Two Poems. Providence: 1995. V. 53

LEJARD, ANDRE
The Art of the French Book From Early Manuscripts to the Present Time. Elek. V. 48

LE JEUNE, J. M.
Okanagan Manual, or, Prayers and Hymns and Catechism in the Okanagan Language. Kamloops: 1897. V. 53
Prayers Before and After Holy Communion in Several Languages of the Natives of British Columbia, in the Diocese of Vancouver... Kamloops: 1925. V. 48
Prayers Before and After Holy Communion in Several Languages of the Natives of British Columbia, in the Diocese of Vancouver... Liege: 1925. V. 52
The WaWa Shorthand Instructor; or, the Duployan Stenography, Adapted to English... Kamloops: 1896. V. 48

LEJEUNE, RITA
The Legend of Roland in the Middle Ages. London: 1971. V. 50

LEKAGUL, B.
Mammals of Thailand. Bangkok: 1989. V. 50; 51

LELAND, CHARLES GODFREY
The English Gipsies and Their Language. London: 1893. V. 49
Etruscan Roman Remains. London: 1892. V. 53
Etruscan Roman Remains. New York: 1892. V. 49
A Gypsy Sorcery & Fortune Telling Illustrated by Numerous Incantations, Specimens of Medical Magic, Anecdotes & Tales. London: 1901. V. 48
Hans Breitmann's Ballads. Philadelphia: 1880. V. 52
Pidgin-English Sing-Song, or Songs and Stories in the China-English Dialect. London: 1876. V. 52
The Union Pacific Railway, Eastern Division Or Three Thousand Miles in a Railway Car. Philadelphia: 1867. V. 50
Ye Book of Copperheads. Philadelphia: 1863. V. 52

LELAND, JOHN
De Rebus Britannicis Collectanea. Cum Tnomae Hearnii Praefatione... London: 1774. V. 48
Genethliacon Illustrissimi Eaduerdi Principis Cambriae... London: 1543. V. 51
The Itinerary... Oxford: 1745. V. 49
Itinerary. Oxford: 1770. V. 50
The Itinerary... Oxford: 1770/69. V. 53
A View of the Principal Deistical Writers That Have Appeared in England in the Last and Present Country...In Several Letters to a Friend. London: 1757. V. 49

LELAND, THOMAS
A Dissertation on the Principles of Human Eloquence... 1765. V. 47
The History of Ireland From the Invasion of Henry II. London: 1773,. V. 48; 51
The History of Ireland from the Invasion of Henry II... Dublin: 1814. V. 51
The History of the Life and Reign of Philip, King of Macedon... London: 1775. V. 48
The History of the Life and Reign of Philip, King of Macedon... London: 1806. V. 47; 53

LELAND, THOMAS continued
Longsword, Earl of Salisbury. London: 1762. V. 47; 49

LELIEVRE, J. F.
Nouveau Jardinier de la Louisiane, Contenant les Instructions Necessaires aux Personnes Qui s'Occupent de Jardinage. New Orleans: 1838. V. 53

LE LORRAIN DE VALLEMONT, PIERRE
Curiosities of Nature and Art in Husbandry and Gardening. London: 1707. V. 51

LE LOYER, PIERRE, SIEUR DE LA BROSSE
A Treatise of Specters or Straunge Sights, Visions and Apparitions, Appearing Sensibly Unto Men. London: 1605. V. 52; 53; 54

LEM, F. H.
Sudanese Sculpture. Paris: 1949. V. 54

LE MAIR, H. WILLEBEEK
Baby's Little Rhyme Book. London: 1920. V. 51

LE MAIRE DE BELGES, JEAN
L'Epistre du Roy a Hector de Troye. Paris: 1513. V. 48

LEMAIRE DE BELGES, JEAN
Les Illvstrations de Bavlle, et Singvlaritez de Troye...Auec Plusieurs Autres Additions... Paris: 1548-49. V. 51

LEMAISTRE, JOHN GUSTAVUS
Frederic Latimer; or, The History of a Young Man of Fashion. London: 1799. V. 48
A Rough Sketch of Modern Paris; or, Letters on Society, Manners, Public Curiosities and Amusements in that Capital. London: 1803. V. 53

LEMANT, ALBERT
Bebetes. Bulan: 1991. V. 54

LE MARIE, JOSEPH JEAN FRANCOIS
Le Dentiste des Dames... Paris: 1818. V. 48; 50

LE MASSENA, ROBERT A.
Rio Grande...to the Pacific. Denver: 1974. V. 54

LEMAY, ALAN
The Searchers. New York: 1954. V. 52; 53

LEMERY, LOUIS
A Treatise of All Sorts of Food, Both Animal and Vegetable; Also of Drinkables... London: 1745. V. 48; 49; 50; 54

LEMERY, NICHOLAS
An Appendix to a Course of Chymistry. London: 1680. V. 47
A Course of Chymistry. London: 1677. V. 47
Dictionaire ou Traite Universel des Drogues Simples. Rotterdam: 1727. V. 47
Vollstandiges Materialien-Lexicon. Leipzig: 1721. V. 47; 53

LEMNIUS, LEVINUS
De Miraculis Occultis Naturae: Four Books in One. Frankfurt: 1598. V. 47
De Miraculis Occultis Naturae, Libri III. (with) Similitudinum a Parabolarum Quae in Biblis ex Herbis Atque Arboribus Desumuntur, Dilucida Expliatio. Frankfurt: 1591. V. 50
Les Occultes Merveilles et Secretz de Nature. Paris: 1574. V. 50
Similitudinum Ac Parabolarum Quae in Biblis Ex herbis Atque Arboribus. Antverpiae: 1568. V. 48; 50
Von Den Wunderbarlichen Geheimnissen der Natur. Leipzig: 1588. V. 47

LEMOINE, HENRY
History, Origin and Progress of the Art of Printing, From Its First Invention in Germany to the End of the Seventeenth Century. London: 1797. V. 52
Modern Manhood; or, the Art and Practice of English Boxing. London: 1788. V. 49
Origin and History of the Art of printing, Foreign and Domestic... London: 1813. V. 48
Typographical Antiquities... 1797. V. 53
Typographical Antiquities. London: 1797. V. 48; 54

LEMOISNE, P. A.
Gothic Painting in France 14th and 15th Centuries. Florence: 1931. V. 50

LEMON, MARK
The Chimes. London: 1845. V. 54
The Enchanted Doll. London: 1899. V. 52
Fairy Tales. London: 1868. V. 50
Legends of Number Nip. London: 1864. V. 47; 49
The New Table Book. London: 1867. V. 50
Up and Down the London Streets. London: 1867. V. 54

LEMON, ROBERT
Catalogue of a Collection of printed Broadsides in the Possession of the Society of Antiquaries of London... London: 1866. V. 47

LEMONNIER, CAMILLE
Birds and Beasts. London: 1911. V. 48; 49

LE MONNIER, PIERRE CHARLES
Institutions Astronomiques, ou Lecons Elementaires d'Astronomie, Pour Servir d'Introduction a la Physique Celeste, & a La Science des Longitudes... Paris: 1746. V. 47

LEMORE, CLARA
Penhala; a Wayside Wizard. London: 1895. V. 54

LE MOYNE, JACQUES
The Work of Jacques Le Moye de Morgues. London: 1977. V. 54

LEMOYNE, LOUIS VALCOULON
Country Residences in Europe and America. New York & London: 1921. V. 48

LE MOYNE, PIERRE
De L'Art Des Devises. Paris: 1666 V 49

L'EMPEREUR CONSTANT
The Tale of the Emperor Coustans and Of over Sea. 1894. V. 49
The Tale of The Emperor Coustans and Of Over Sea. Hammersmith: 1894. V. 48
The Tale of the Emperor Coustans and of Over Sea. London: 1894. V. 47

LEMPRIERE, JOHN
Bibliotheca Classica: or, a Classical Dictionary.... Reading: 1788. V. 48; 52
Bibliotheca Classica; or, a Classical Dictionary,... London: 1797. V. 52
Univeral Biography. New York: 1810. V. 47; 49; 52

LEMPRIERE, WILLIAM
A Tour from Gibraltar to Tanger, Sallee, Mogodore, Santa Cruz, Tarudant... London: 1791. V. 50; 53; 54

LE NAIN DE TILLEMONT, LOUIS SEBASTIAN
An Account of the Life of Apollonius Tyaneus... London: 1702. V. 47

LE NESTOUR, PATRICK
The Mystery of Things: Evocations of the Japanese Supernatural. New York & Tokyo: 1972. V. 50; 52

LE NEVE, JOHN
Monumenta Anglicana: Being Inscriptions on the Monuments of Several Eminent Persons Deceased in or Since the Year 1700, to the End of the Year 1715...(together with) Monumenta Anglicana:...In Our Since the Year 1650, to the end of the Year 1718... London: 1717/19. V. 48

LENG, KYRLE
Juvenilia. 1931. V. 48

L'ENGLE, MADELEINE
Camilla Dickinson. New York: 1951. V. 50
The Small Rain. New York: 1943. V. 52
The Small Rain. New York: 1945. V. 50
A Wind in the Door. New York: 1973. V. 49
A Wrinkle in Time. New York: 1962. V. 49
A Wrinkle in Time. New York: 1987. V. 53

LENGLET-DUFRESNOY, NICOLAS
Histoire de la Philosophie Hermetique... La Haye: 1742. V. 49

LENGLET DUFRESNOY, NICOLAS
Histoire de la Philosophie Hermetique. Paris: 1742. V. 52; 54

LENIN, VLADIMIR IL'ICH
The Letters of Lenin. London: 1937. V. 52
The Proletarian Revolution and Kautsky the Renegade. London: 1920. V. 48

LENNART, ISOBEL
Funny Girl. New York: 1964. V. 50; 51

LENNON, JOHN
Skywriting by Word of Mouth. New York: 1986. V. 52
A Spaniard in the Works. London: 1965. V. 51

LENNOX, CHARLOTTE RAMSEY
The Female Quixote:... London: 1752. V. 51
The Female Quixote... Dublin: 1763. V. 52; 54
Henriette. Lausanne: 1760. V. 47
The Life of Harriot Stuart. London: 1751. V. 48
Shakespear Illustrated: or the Novels and Histories, On Which the Plays of Shakespear are Founded, Collected and Translated... London: 1753-54. V. 48; 50

LENNOX, WILLIAM
Pictures of Sporting Life and Character. London: 1860. V. 47

LENNOX, WILLIAM PITT
The Story of My Life. London: 1857. V. 54

LENOIR, ALEXANDER
Museum of French Monuments; or, an Historical and Chronological Description of the Monuments in Marble, Bronze and Bas-Relief Collected in the Museum at Paris... Paris: 1803. V. 47; 53

LE NORMAND, VICTORINE
The Unerring Fortune-Teller: Containing the Celebrated Oracle of Human Destiny... New York: 1866. V. 52

LENOX, EDWARD H.
Overland to Oregon in the Tracks of Lewis and Clark. Oakland: 1904. V. 47

LENSKI, LOIS
Indian Captive - the Story of Mary Jemison. New York: 1941. V. 52
Songs of Mr. Small. New York: 1954. V. 52
Two Brothers and Their Baby Sister. New York: 1930. V. 51

LENTULUS, CYRIACUS
Princeps Absolutus....Politicus in Annalium Taciti Commentarius. Herborn: 1663. V. 52

LENTZ, T. W.
Reise Nach Saint Louis Am Mississippi, Nebst Meinen, Wahrend Eines Vierzehmonatlichen Aufenthaltes I.D. J. 1836 und 1837... Weimar: 1838. V. 48; 52

LENYGON, FRANCIS
Decoration in England from 1660 to 1770. London: 1920. V. 53

LEO AFRICANUS, JOHN
A Geographical Historie of Africa, Written in Arabicke and Italian by John leo a More, Borne in Granad, and Brought Up in Barbarie. London: 1600. V. 50

LEO I, THE GREAT, SAINT, POPE
D Leonis Papae Huius Nominis Primi,, Qui Merito Summo Magni Cognome Iam Olim Obtinet... Cologne: 1548. V. 48
Le Veritable Enchiridion. Ancona: 1667. V. 48

LEON & BROTHER
First Editions of American Authors. New York: 1885. V. 52

LEON, GOTTLIEB VON
Rabbinische Legenden. 1913. V. 52; 54

LEONARD, AGNES
The Colorado Blue Book. Denver: 1892. V. 52

LEONARD, CHARLES C.
The History of Pithole. Pithole City: 1867. V. 50

LEONARD, ELIZA LUCY
The Ruby Ring; or, the Transformations. London: 1816. V. 47

LEONARD, ELMORE
The Big Bounce. 1989. V. 53
The Bounty Hunters. New York: 1954.. V. 53
Cat Chaser. New York: 1982. V. 52
Dutch Treat. New York: 1977. V. 48; 52
Fifty-Two Pick Up. 1974. V. 53
Fifty-Two Pick Up. London: 1974. V. 52
Fifty-Two Pick Up. New York: 1974. V. 50; 53
Gold Coast. London: 1982. V. 52; 53
Hombre. 1988. V. 53
Hombre. 1989. V. 50
Lawless River. London: 1959. V. 51
The Moonshine War. Garden City: 1969. V. 50; 54
The Moonshine War. New York: 1969. V. 50; 51
Notebooks. Northridge: 1990. V. 48
Split Images. New York: 1981. V. 52
Stick. New York: 1983. V. 52
Swag. New York: 1976. V. 47; 48; 49; 50; 51; 52; 53
The Switch. London: 1979. V. 52; 53
Unknown Man No. 89. V. 49
Unknown Man No. 89. London: 1977. V. 52
Unknown Man No. 89. New York: 1993. V. 54

LEONARD, FRED E.
Guide to the History of Physical Education. Philadelphia: 1947. V. 48

LEONARD, IRVING
Spanish Approach to Pensacola, 1689-1693. 1967. V. 50

LEONARD, THOMAS H.
From Indian Trail to Electric Rail. Atlantic Highlands: 1923. V. 47; 49; 51

LEONARD, WILLIAM
Reports of Cases of Law; Argued and Adjudged in the Courts of Law... London: 1658. V. 52

LEONARD, WILLIAM ELLERY
Gilgamesh. Avon: 1974. V. 49
Gilgamesh. Connecticut: 1974. V. 47
Two Lives. New York: 1925. V. 51
Two Lives... New York: 1929. V. 49

LEONARD, ZENAS
Leonard's Narrative Adventures of Zenas Leonard, Fur Trader and Trapper, 1831-1836. Cleveland: 1904. V. 54

LEONARDO, RICHARD A.
History of Gynecology. New York: 1944. V. 50
History of Surgery. New York: 1943. V. 53

LEONARDO DA VINCI
Leonardo Da Vinci. New York: 1956. V. 53
The Madrid Codices. New York: 1976. V. 47; 48; 49
The Notebooks... London: 1938. V. 50; 51
The Notebooks... New York: 1938. V. 52
The Notebooks... London: 1948. V. 50
El Tratado la Pintura...Traducidos e Illustrados Con Algunas Notas Por Don Diego Antonia Rejon de Silva. Madrid: 1784. V. 47
A Treatise of Painting. London: 1721. V. 51; 54
A Treatise on Painting... London: 1796. V. 52

LEONCE, G.
Etude d'Oiseaux. Paris: 1900. V. 47

LEON PINELO, ANTONI RODRIGUEZ DE
Tratado de Confirmaciones Reales de Encomiendas, Oficios i Casos, en Que se Reuieren Para las Indias Occidentales. Madrid: 1630. V. 47

LEONTIEF, ESTELLE
Whatever Happens. 1975. V. 52

Whatever Happens. West Burke: 1975. V. 54

LEOPOLD, ALDO
Game Management. 1933. V. 54
Report On a Game Survey of the North General States. Madison: 1931. V. 49
Round River: From the Journals of Aldo Leopold. New York: 1953. V. 51
A Sand County Almanac. New York: 1949. V. 52

LEOPOLD, RUDOLF
Egon Schiele. London: 1972. V. 50

LEO X, POPE
Bulla Cene Domini. Wittenberg: 1527. V. 53

LE PAGE DU PRATZ
The History of Louisiana, or of the Western Parts of Virginia and Carolina. London: 1763. V. 53

LE PAULMIER DE GRENTEMESNIL, JACQUES
Lapis Philosophicus Dogmaticorum. Paris: 1609. V. 48

LE PAUTRE, JEAN
Chaires De Predicateurs. Paris: 1659. V. 51

LE PICHON, Y.
The World of Henri Rousseau. New York: 1982. V. 53; 54

LE PLONGEON, AUGUSTUS
Sacred Mysteries Among the Mayas and the Quiches. New York: 1909. V. 52

LEPPER, JOHN HERON
History of the Grand Lodge of Free and Accepted Masons of Ireland. London: 1925. V. 53

LEPSIUS, C. R.
Standard Alphabet for Reducing Unwritten Languages and Foreign Graphic Systems to a Uniform Orthography in European Letters. London: 1863. V. 52

LEPSIUS, RICHARD
Discoveries in Egypt, Ethiopia and the Peninsula of Sinai in the Years 1842-45. London: 1852. V. 53
Letters from Egypt, Ethiopia, and the Peninsula of Sinai. London: 1853. V. 47; 52

LE QUEUX, WILLIAM
The Maker of Secrets. London: 1914. V. 48; 49
The Man from Downing Street: a Mystery. London: 1904. V. 48

LERCH, P.
Khiva or Kharizm: Its Historical and Geographical Relations. Calcutta: 1873. V. 49
Russian Toorkestan: Its People and External Relations. Calcutta: 1874. V. 49

LE REVRE, RAOUL
The Recuyell of the Historyes of Troye. 1892. V. 53

LERMA, JOSE LARIOS, DUKE OF
Combat Over Spain. Memoirs of a Nationalist Fighter Pilot 1936-39. London: 1966. V. 49

LERMONTOV, MIKHAIL YUREVICH
A Hero of Our Own Times. London: 1854. V. 50
A Song About Tsar Ivan Vasilyevitch, His Young Body-Guard, and the Valiant Merchant Kalashnikov. Kensington: 1929. V. 50; 52
The Song of Czar Ivan Vasilievich, the Young Oprichnik and the Brave Merchant Kalashnikov. Moscow: 1943. V. 53

LERNER, ALAN JAY
Camelot. New York: 1961. V. 47; 50
My Fair Lady. New York: 1955. V. 53
My Fair Lady. New York: 1956. V. 51

LEROUX, GASTON
The Mystery of Yellow Room. New York: 1908. V. 51
The Phantom of the Opera. 1911. V. 47
The Phantom of the Opera. New York: 1911. V. 51
The Phantom of the Opera. 1925. V. 52; 53
The Phantom of the Opera. London: 1925. V. 54

LE ROUX, HUGUES
Acrobats and Mountebanks. London: 1890. V. 47; 50

LEROY, L. ARCHIER
Wagner's Music Drama of the Ring. London: 1925. V. 51; 54

LEROY, LOUIS
La Vicissitvdine O Mvtabile Varieta Delle Cose.Vicissitvdine. In Vinetia: 1585. V. 53

LE SAGE, ALAIN RENE
The Adventures of Gil Blas... London: 1766. V. 53
The Adventures of Gil Blas... London: 1771. V. 53
The Adventures of Gil Blas... London: 1773. V. 51
The Adventures of Gil Blas... Glasgow: 1790. V. 49
The Adventures of Gil Blas... London: 1819. V. 47; 51; 52; 54
The Adventures of Gil Blas... London: 1822. V. 49
The Adventures of Gil Blas... London: 1833. V. 48; 51
The Adventures of Gil Blas... Edinburgh: 1886. V. 51; 52; 53
The Adventures of Gil Blas... London: 1910. V. 52
The Adventures of Gil Blas... Oxford: 1937. V. 52; 53; 54
Asmodeus; Or The Devil on Two Sticks. London: 1841. V. 49
Les Avantures de Monsieur Robert Chevalier, it de Beauchene, Captaine de Flibustiers dans la Nouvelle France. Paris: 1732. V. 48

LE SAGE, ALAIN RENE continued
Le Diable Boiteux; Or, the Devil Upon Two Sticks. London: 1708. V. 53
Histoire de Gil blas de Santillane. A Londres: 1809. V. 53

LESCARBOT, MARC
The Theatre of Neptune in New France. Boston: 1927. V. 52; 53

LESCARBOURA, AUSTIN C.
Behind the Motion-Picture Screen. London: 1920. V. 49

LE SCENE-DES-MAISONS, JACQUES
Contrat Conjugal, Ou Loix du Mariage de la Repudiation et du Divorce. Paris?: 1781. V. 48

LESLEY, CRAIG
Talking Leaves, Contemporary Native American Short Stories. New York: 1991. V. 51
Winterkill. Boston: 1984. V. 50

LESLEY, LEWIS B.
Uncle Sam's Camels. Cambridge: 1929. V. 49

LESLIE, A. S.
The Grouse in Health and Disease. London: 1911. V. 54

LESLIE, AMY
Some Players: Personal Sketches. Chicago: 1899. V. 50; 51; 53; 54

LESLIE, CHARLES
The History of Sin and Heresie Attempted, From the First War that They Rais'd in Heaven. London: 1698. V. 53; 54
A Letter from a Gentleman in the City to His Friend in the Country, Concerning the Threaten'd Prosecution of the Rehearsal, Put Into the News-Papers (drop title). 1708. V. 47
The New Association of Those Called, Moderate-Church Men, with the Modern-Whigs and Fanaticks to Under-Mine and Blow-up the Present Church and Government. (with) The New Association. Part II. London: 1702-03. V. 53
A View of the Times, Their Principles and Practices: in the First Volume of the Rehearsals. London: 1708. V. 49

LESLIE, CHARLES ROBERT
Autobiographical Recollections. London: 1860. V. 50
A Hand-Book for Young Painters. London: 1855. V. 50
Memoirs of the Life of John Constable... London: 1845. V. 49
Memoirs of the Life of John Constable... London: 1937. V. 51; 53

LESLIE, ELIZA
The Girl's Book of Diversions, or, Occupation for Play Hours. London: 1835. V. 50
New Recipts for Cooking. Philadelphia: 1854. V. 47

LESLIE, FRANK
Frank Leslie's Illustrated History of the Civil War. New York: 1895. V. 48
Historical Register of the United States Centennial Exposition, 1876. New York: 1877. V. 53

LESLIE, GEORGE D.
Our River. London: 1881. V. 53

LESLIE, JAMES
Dictionary of the Synonymous Words and Technical Terms in the English Language. Edinburgh: 1806. V. 47

LESLIE, JAMES B.
Ferns Clergy and Parishes... Dublin: 1936. V. 51

LESLIE, JOHN
De Origine Moribus & Rebus Gestis Scotorum. Romae: 1675. V. 49; 53
Discovery and Adventure in the Polar Seas and Regions. 1851. V. 50
Elements of Natural Philosophy. Edinburgh: 1823. V. 50
Narrative of Discovery and Adventures in the Polar Seas with an Account of the Whale Fisheries. New York: 1844. V. 52
The Philosophy of Arithmetic: Exhibiting a Progressive View of the Theory and Practice of Calculation, with Tables. Edinburgh: 1820. V. 49
A Short Account of Experiments and Instruments Depending On the Relations of Air to Heat and Moisture. 1813. V. 49
A Short Account of Experiments and Instruments, Depending On the Relations of Air to Heat and Moisture. Edinburgh: 1813. V. 51; 52

LESLIE, MARY
The Cromaboo Mail Carrier. A Canadian Love Story. Guelph: 1878. V. 54

LESLIE, SHANE
The Armagh Hymnal. Dublin: 1912. V. 48
A Ghost in the Isle of Wight. London: 1929. V. 47
The Greek Anthology. London: 1929. V. 50
Mark Sykes: His Life and Letters. London: 1923. V. 50
Verses in Peace and War. New York: 1917. V. 54

LESLIE, THOMAS EDWARD CLIFFE
Essays in Political and Moral Philosophy. Dublin: 1879. V. 50

LE SOUEF, A. S.
The Wild Animals of Australia: Embracing the Mammals of New Guinea and the Nearer Pacific Islands. London: 1926. V. 49

LESSEPS, FERDINAND DE
Percement de l'Isthme de Suez. Paris: 1855. V. 54

LESSING, DORIS
Canopus in Argos: Archives. New York: 1979-82. V. 53
Canopus in Argos: Archives. New York: 1979-83. V. 48
Documents Relating to the Sentimental Agents in Volyen Empire. London: 1983. V. 52
The Four-Gated City. London: 1968. V. 49
Fourteen Poems. London: 1959. V. 52
Fourteen Poems. Northwood, Middlesex: 1959. V. 50
The Golden Notebook. London: 1962. V. 51
The Golden Notebook. New York: 1962. V. 51; 52; 53
The Grass is Singing. London: 1950. V. 47; 50
The Grass is Singing. New York: 1950. V. 50
The Habit of Loving. London: 1957. V. 53
In Pursuit of the English. London: 1960. V. 53
Landlocked. London: 1965. V. 48; 49
A Man and Two Women. London: 1963. V. 49
The Marriages Between Zones Three, Four and Five. London: 1980. V. 51; 54
Martha Quest. London: 1952. V. 50; 51
A Proper Marriage. London: 1954. V. 51
A Small Personal Voice: Essays, Reviews, Interviews. New York: 1974. V. 54
The Story of a Non-Marrying Man and Other Stories. London: 1972. V. 52
The Summer Before Dark. New York: 1973. V. 53
The Temptation of Jack Orkney... New York: 1972. V. 53
The Temptation of Jack Orkney. London: 1978. V. 50
This Was the Old Chief's Country. New York. V. 52
This Was the Old Chief's Country. 1951. V. 50
This Was the Old Chief's Country. London: 1951. V. 47
Three Stories. Helsinki: 1988. V. 48
Under My Skin: Volume One of My Autobiography to 1949. New York: 1994. V. 52

LESSING, GOTTHOLD EPHRAIM
Fabeln: Drey Bucher 1759-1777 und Anhang. 1920. V. 51

LESSING, JULES
Die Gewebe-Sammlung des Koniglichen Kunstgewerbe-Museums zu Berlin. Berlin: 1900-13. V. 51

LESSIUS, LEONARDUS
Hygiasticon; or, the Right Course of Preserving Life and Health unto Extream old Age... Cambridge: 1634. V. 52

LESSONS of Thrift, Published for General Benefit by a Member of the Save All Club. London: 1820. V. 51; 53

LESTER, CHARLES EDWARD
The Glory and Shame of England. London: 1841. V. 54
The Glory and Shame of England. New York: 1841. V. 53
The Glory and Shame of England. New York: 1866. V. 54
The Life of Sam Houston. New York: 1855. V. 48

LESTER, GARY
Australians at the Olympics. A Definitive History. Melbourne: 1984. V. 49

LESTER, GEORGE
In Sunny Isles: Chapters Treating Chiefly of the Bahama Islands and Cuba. London and Rochdale: 1897. V. 53; 54

LESTER, HORACE FRANCIS
Queen of the Hamlet. London: 1894. V. 51

LESTER, JOHN HENRY
Bat v. Ball... 1900. V. 52
Bat v Ball. London: 1900. V. 51

LESTER, W. W.
A Digest of the Military and Naval Laws of the Confederate States. Columbia: 1864. V. 49

LESTERMAN, JOHN
The Adventures of a Trafalgar Lad - a Tale of the Sea. London: 1926. V. 52

L'ESTRANGE, A. G.
The Life of Mary Russell Mitford. London: 1870. V. 52; 53

L'ESTRANGE, HAMON
The Alliance of Divine Offices, Exhibiting All the Liturgies of the Church of England Since the Reformation... London: 1690. V. 50

L'ESTRANGE, HENRY
Platonia. A tale of Other Worlds. Bristol: 1893. V. 47

L'ESTRANGE, M.
Heligoland; or, Reminiscences of Childhood. London: 1850. V. 48

L'ESTRANGE, ROGER
A Brief History of the Times, &c. London: 1687/88/88. V. 54
A Brief History of the Times, etc. London: 1687. V. 52
The Character of a Papist in a Masquerade. London: 1681. V. 47
Fables of Aesop and other Eminent Mythologists; With Morals and Reflections... London: 1704/1699. V. 51
Fables of Aesop and Other Eminent Mythologists: with Morals and Reflections. London: 1714. V. 49
A Fox and a Sick Lion. Bloomington: 1944. V. 51
A Further Discovery of the Plot: Dedicated to Dr. Titus Oates. London: 1680. V. 47
Interest Mistaken, or the Holy Cheat. London: 1661. V. 52

L'ESTRANGE, W. D.
Under Fourteen Flags, Being the Life and Adventures of Brigadier-General MacIver, a Soldier of Fortune. London: 1884. V. 54

LETAROUILLY, PAUL
Le Vatican et la Basilique de Saint-Pierre de Rome. Paris: 1882. V. 52

LETCHER, OWEN
Big Game Hunting in North-Eastern Rhodesia. London: 1911. V. 49
The Bonds of Africa. 1913. V. 54

LETCHIOT, REV.
The Southampton Guide; or an Account of the Antient and Present State of that Town. Southampton: 1768. V. 52

LETCHWORTH, WILLIAM PRYOR
The Insane in Foreign Countries. New York/London: 1889. V. 52

LETH, ANDRIES DE
De Vechtstroom, van Utrecht tot Muiden, Verheerlykt Door Honderd Gezichten... Amsterdam: 1790. V. 50

LETHABY, W. R.
The Church of Sancta Sophia Constantinople. London: 1894. V. 50

LETI, BRUNO
Found. Milano: 1991. V. 54
Promontory Visions. 1995. V. 54
Studio Emblems: Twenty Lithographs. Melbourne: 1994. V. 54

LETI, GREGORIO
Il Cardinalismo de Santa Chiesa; or the History of the Cardinals of the Roman Church... London: 1670. V. 47; 52

LET'S Have a Party. 1960's. V. 49

LETTER Addressed to the Legislators of the Several States, Composing the Federal Union; Recommending an Uniform Continental Currency. New York: 1795. V. 54

A **LETTER** Concerning Libels, Warrants, and the Seizure of Papers... London: 1764. V. 52

A **LETTER** from a Gentleman in the West of England to His Friend in London. London?: 1754. V. 50

A **LETTER** From a Gentleman in Town to His Friend in the Country, Recommending the Necessity of Frugality. London: 1750. V. 53

A **LETTER** From a Member of Parliament to His Friend in the Country, Upon the Motion to Address His Majesty to Settle 100,000 1. per annum on...the Prince of Wales &c. London: 1736. V. 53

A **LETTER** from a Merchant in the City of London, to the R--t H---ble W-- P---- Esq; Upon the Affairs and Commerce of North America, and the West Indies; Our African Trade. London: 1757. V. 47

A **LETTER** from a Physician in Town to His Friend in the Country, Concerning the Disputes at Present Subsisting Between the Fellows and Licentiates of the College of Physicians in London. London: 1753. V. 53

A **LETTER** From an English Gentleman, to a Member of Parliament: Shewing, the Hardships, Cruelties... With Which the Irish Nation Has Been Treated. London: 1751. V. 50

A **LETTER** From an Officer at Madras, to a Friend Formerly in the Service, Now in England: Exhibiting an Unbiased Account and Supported by Authentic Documents, of the Late Rise, Progress and Actual State... London: 1810. V. 50

A **LETTER** from an Officer in the Army to the People of Great-Britain, Relative to the Late Secret Expedition. London: 1757. V. 50

A **LETTER** from Ernest Barlach. Northampton: 1957. V. 54

A **LETTER** from One of the Society of Friends, Relative to the Consientious Scrupulousness of Its Members to Bear Arms. Philadelphia?: 1795. V. 51

A **LETTER** On the True Principles of Advantageous Exportation. In Refutation of Certain Popular Notions On that Subject. London: 1818. V. 50

A **LETTER** or and Epistle to All Well-Minded Men in England, Wales and Ireland, in Special to the Parliament and Army... 1649. V. 50; 53

A **LETTER** Sent from the Inhabitants of Hull to the Right Worshipfull the High Sheriffe, and the Rest of the Gentry in the County of Yorke... London: 1642. V. 48; 50

A **LETTER** to a Friend in Suffolk, Occasion'd by a Report of Repealing the Triennial Act. London: 1716. V. 53

A **LETTER** to a Friend in the Country, Concerning the Use of Instrumental Musick in the Worship of God; in Answer to Mr. Newte's Sermon Preach'd at Tiverton in Devon, on the Occasion of an Organ Being Erected in the Parish-Church. London: 1698. V. 52

A **LETTER** to a Friend Upon Occasion of the Death of His Intimate Friend: by the Learned Sir Browne, Knight Doctor of Physick, Late of Norwich. Boston: 1971. V. 53

A **LETTER** to a Member of Parliament, Relating to the bill for the Opening of a Trade to and From Persia through Russia. London: 1741. V. 52

A **LETTER** To a Member of the Convention of the States of Scotland. Edinburgh?: 1689. V. 47

A **LETTER** to a member of the Late Parliament, Concerning the Debts of the Nation. London: 1700. V. 49

A **LETTER** to a Member of the Late Parliament, Concerning the Debts of the Nation. London: 1701. V. 49

A **LETTER** to a Member of the October-Club; Shewing that to Yield spain to the Duke of Anjou by a Peace, Would Be the Ruin of Great Britain. London: 1711. V. 53

A **LETTER** To a Noble Lord, Occasioned by the Proceedings Against Dr. Henry Sacheverell. London: 1710. V. 53

LETTER to a Proprietor of the East-India Company. London: 1750. V. 47

A **LETTER** to Dr. Sangrado, in Answer to Thomsonus Redivius. London: 1746. V. 47

LETTER to His Grace the Duke of Newcastle, K.G. H.M.'s Secretary of State for the Colonies. Relative to the Petition of the Inhabitants of Malta by Four Elected Members of the Council of Government. Malta: 1864. V. 49

A **LETTER** to Mr. John Gay, Concerning His Late Farce, Entitled, a Comedy. London: 1717. V. 53

A **LETTER** to the Author of a Pamphlet Entitled, Some Thoughts On the Nature of Paper Credit. Dublin: 1760. V. 51

A **LETTER** to the Examiner Suggesting Proper Heads, for Vindicating His Masters. London: 1714. V. 50

A **LETTER** to the Merchants of the Portugal Committee, from a Lisbon Trader. London: 1754. V. 52

A **LETTER** to the New Parliament; with Hints of Some Regulations Which the Nation Hopes and Expects from Them. London: 1780. V. 50

A **LETTER** to the Right Honourable J---- P----, Speker of the House of Commons in Ireland. London: 1767. V. 47

A **LETTER** to the Right Honourable the Earl of Buckinghamshire, President of the Board of Commissioners for the Affairs of India, on the Subject of an Open Trade to India. London: 1813. V. 51

A **LETTER** to the Secret Committee. Containing Extraordinary Practices of the Late M-----r, Intended to Have Been Laid Before Them in a Private Manner and Now Submitted to Their Publick Consideration. London: 1742. V. 48

A **LETTER** to Viscount Milton, M.P. By One of His Constituents... London: 1827. V. 48

A **LETTER** Without Any Superscription, Intercepted in the Way to London. 1643. V. 52

A **LETTER** Without any Superscription, Intercepted in the Way to London. London: 1643. V. 50

THE LETTER Writ by the Last Assembly General of the Clergy of France to the Protestants, Inviting Them to Return to Their Communion. London: 1683. V. 50

A **LETTER** Written To One of the Members of Parliament, About the State of This Present War. London: 1692. V. 52

LETTERE Annve d'Etiopia, Malabar, Brasil e Goa. Dall'Anno 1620 fin'al 1624 (etc). Rome: 1627. V. 51

LETTERS & Papers on Agriculture and Planting &c. Selected from the Correspondence-Book of the Society Instituted at Bath for the Encouragement of Agriculture, Arts, Manufactures and Commerce... Bath: 1783. V. 50; 54

LETTERS from a Moor at London to His friend at Tunis. London: 1736. V. 50; 54

LETTERS from an Irish Student in England to His Father in Ireland. London: 1809. V. 51

LETTERS From Ireland, 1886. 1887. V. 49; 50

LETTERS From Old Friends. Cheyenne: 1923. V. 53

LETTERS from Several Parts of Europe and the East. Written in the Years 1750, &c. London: 1753. V. 52; 54

LETTERS From the Irish Highlands of Cunnemarra. London: 1825. V. 51

LETTERS from the Living to the Living, Relating to the Present Transactions Both Publick and Private. London: 1703. V. 49

LETTERS of Religion and Vertue, to Several Gentlemen and Ladies. London: 1695. V. 49; 51; 52

LETTERS of Wit, Politicks and Morality. London: 1701. V. 53

LETTERS on Courtship and Marriage. Trenton: 1813. V. 48

LETTERS Patent, Establishing a Supreme Court of Judicature, at Fort-William, in Bengal, Bearing Date the Twenty-Sixth Day of March, in the Fourteenth Year of the reign of George III. London: 1774. V. 49; 51; 52

LETTERS to a Young Nobleman. London: 1762. V. 47; 49; 54
LETTERS to a Young Nobleman. Dublin: 1763. V. 48

LETTERS to Conrad. London: 1926. V. 47; 49

LETTICE, JOHN
A Plan for the Safe Removal of Inhabitants, Not Military, From Towns and Villages on the Coasts of Great Britain and Ireland, In the Case of the Threatened Invasion... London: 1803. V. 50

LETTS, J. M.
California Illustrated: Including a Description of the Panama and Nicaragua Routes, by a Returned Californian. New York: 1852. V. 47

LETTSOM, JOHN COAKLEY
Hints Designed to promote Beneficence, Temperance & Medical Science. London: 1801, 1802. V. 47
Hints for Promoting a Bee Society. London: 1796. V. 54
History of Some of the Effects of Hard Drinking. London: 1789. V. 53
The Naturalist's and Traveller's Companion... London: 1774. V. 49; 51
The Naturalist's and Traveller's Companion. London: 1799. V. 48; 49; 52

LETTY, C.
Wild Flowers of the Transvaal. Pretoria: 1962. V. 47; 52

LEUCHARS, ROBERT B.
A Practical Treatise on the Construction, Heating and Ventilation of Hot-Houses... Boston: 1851. V. 52

LEUCHT, CHRISTIAN LEONARD
Augusti Corona Augustissima Augustae Coronatae. (with) *Austria S.R. Conjux.* (with) *Verzeichnis Aller Fursten und Vertreter der Stande auf dem Augsburger Reichstag.* Augsburg: 1690. V. 53

LEUPOLD, JACOB
Theatrum Machinarium, Oder: Schauplatz der Heb-Zeuge. Leipzig: 1725. V. 52
Theatrum Pontificiale, Oder Schau-Platz der Brucken und Brucken-Baues. Leipzig: 1726. V. 52

LEURECHON, JEAN
Mathematicall Recreations. Or, Collection of Many Problems, Extracted Out of the Ancient and Modern Philosophers, as Secrets and Experiments in Arithmetick, Geometry, Cosmographie, Horologiographie, Astronomy, Navigation, Musick, Opticks... London: 1653. V. 52

LEUSCHNER, A. O.
Research Surveys of the Orbits and Perturbations of Minor Planets 1 to 1091. From 1801.0 to 1929.5. Berkeley: 1935. V. 53

LEUSDEN, JOHANNES
Philologus Hebraeo-Mixtus. (with) *Philologus Hebraeus.* (with) *Catalogus Hebraicus et Latinus Sexcentorum et Tredecum Praeceptorum.* Utrecht: 1663/57. V. 53

LEUTZE, E.
Washington Crossing the Delaware. New York: 1853. V. 52

LEUWIS, DIONYSIUS DE
D. Dionysii Carthusianai, in Quatuor Evangelistas Enarrationes...Praeclarae Admodum & Ab Eruditiss. Cologne: 1543. V. 53

LEVAILLANT, FRANCOIS
Histoire Naturelle des Perroquets... Paris: 1801-05. V. 49
Travels from the Cape of Good Hope, Into the Interior Parts of Africa... London: 1790. V. 47
Travels into the Interior Parts of Africa. (with) *New Travels Into the Interior Parts of Africa...in the Years 1783, 84, and 85...* London: 1796/96. V. 53

LE VAYER DE BOUTIGNY, ROLAND
The Famous Romance of Tarsis and Zelie Digested Into Ten Books. London: 1685. V. 47

LEVAYER DE BOUTIGNY, ROLAND
Tarsis et Zelie. Paris: 1774. V. 50

THE LEVELLERS *New Remonstrance or Declaration Sent to His Excellencie the Lord General Fairfax, Concerning Their Present Proceedings, and Making Choice of a Glorious King, and Heavenly Protector...* London: 1649. V. 50

THE LEVELLERS *Remonstrance, Concerning the Parliament and Army...With Their Present Design Touching the Cities of London, York, Bristol, Chester...* London: 1649. V. 50

LEVENS, HENRY C.
A History of Cooper County, Missouri, from the First Visit by White Men, in February 1804 to the 5th Day of July, 1876. St. Louis: 1876. V. 50

LEVER, CHARLES JAMES
Arthur O'Leary. London: 1845. V. 49; 50; 51; 52
Barrington. London: 1862-63. V. 52
Barrington. London: 1863. V. 50; 51; 53; 54
Charles O'Malley, the Irish Dragoon. Dublin: 1841. V. 47; 50; 51
Confessions of Con Cregan; the Irish Gil Blas. London: 1849. V. 49
The Confessions of Harry Lorrequer. Dublin: 1839. V. 47; 53; 54
The Daltons, or Three Roads in Life. London: 1852. V. 51; 54
Davenport Dunn. London: 1857-59. V. 49; 52
Davenport Dunn... London: 1859. V. 51
A Day's Ride: a Life's Romance. London: 1863. V. 54
The Dodd Family Abroad. London: 1852-54. V. 52
The Fortunes of Glencore. London: 1587. V. 54
The Fortunes of Glencore. London: 1857. V. 51; 52
The Fortunes of Glencore. London: 1862. V. 51
Jack Hinton. London: 1842. V. 51
Jack Hinton... Philadelphia: 1843. V. 51
The Knight of Gwynne: a Tale of the Time of the Union. London: 1847. V. 54
The Knight of Gwynne: a Tale of the Time of the Union. London: 1851. V. 47; 49
Lord Kilgobbin. New York: 1872. V. 53
Luttrell of Arran. London: 1865. V. 50; 51
The Martin's of Cro' Martin. London: 1854-56. V. 48; 52
The Martins of Cro' Martin. London: 1856. V. 50
Military Novels. V. 50; 54
Novels. London: 1872-73. V. 51
The O'Donoghue; a Tale of Ireland Fifty Years Ago. Dublin: 1845. V. 51
Our Mess. Dublin: 1843-44. V. 47; 50; 51
Paul Gosslett's Confessions in Love, Law and the Civil Service. London: 1868. V. 53
Roland Cashel. London: 1850. V. 51
St. Patrick's Eve. London: 1845. V. 51; 54

LEVER, DARCY
The Young Sea-Officers Sheet Anchor or a Key to the Leading of the Rigging and to Practical Seamanship. London: 1819. V. 49
The Young Sea-Officers Sheet Anchor; or a key to the Leading of the Rigging and to Practical Seamanship. Philadelphia: 1819. V. 50
The Young Sea-Officers Sheet Anchor or a key to the Leading of the Rigging and to Practical Seamanship. New York: 1853. V. 49; 53

LE VERN, JEAN LOUIS
Blackfoot Catechism and Prayers. Calgary: 1920. V. 51

LEVERTOV, DENISE
5 Poems. 1958. V. 52; 53
The Cold Spring and Other Poems. 1968. V. 51; 53
The Cold Spring and Other Poems. Norfolk: 1968. V. 47
The Double Image. London: 1946. V. 47; 48; 52
Embroideries. Los Angeles: 1969. V. 47
Here and Now. San Francisco: 1957. V. 47; 52
In the Night. New York: 1968. V. 47; 52; 54
Life in the Forest. New York: 1978. V. 49; 54
A Marigold from North Viet Nam. New York: 1968. V. 52; 53; 54
Mass for the Day of St. Thomas Didymus. Concord: 1981. V. 47; 52
The Menaced World. Concord: 1985. V. 47
Modulations for Solo Voice. San Francisco: 1977. V. 47; 52
A New Year's Garland for My Students (MIT 1969-70). Mt. Horeb: 1970. V. 51; 53; 54
Overland to the Islands. Highlands: 1958. V. 47; 54
El Salvador: Requiem and Invocation. Boston: 1983. V. 47
El Salvador: Requiem and Invocation. 1984. V. 47
Summer Poems. Berkeley: 1970. V. 47; 52; 54
Three Poems. Mt. Horeb: 1968. V. 47; 51; 54
A Tree Telling of Orpheus. Los Angeles: 1968. V. 52
Two Poems. Concord: 1983. V. 47; 52
Wanderer's Daysong. 1981. V. 52; 54

LEVESON, HENRY ASTBURY
Camp Life and Its Requirements for Soldiers, Travellers and Sportsmen. London: 1872. V. 48
The Forest and the Field. London: 1867. V. 52

LEVESQUE, RODRIGUES
History of Micronesia. A Collection of Source Documents. Gatineau: 1992. V. 52

LEVI, CARLO
The Watch. London: 1952. V. 54

LEVI, DORO
Antioch Mosaic Pavements. Princeton: 1947. V. 52

LEVI, LEONE
On Taxation: How It Is Raised and How It Is Expended. London: 1860. V. 48; 50; 52

LEVI, PETER
The Gravel Ponds. London: 1960. V. 50; 53
The Light Garden of the Angel King. London: 1972. V. 51
Pancakes for the Queen of Babylon. Northwood: 1968. V. 51; 53
Ruined Abbeys. Northwood: 1968. V. 51; 53

LEVI, PRIMO
If This Is a Man. New York: 1959. V. 48; 50
The Periodic Table. New York: 1984. V. 49

LEVIEN, J. R.
John Andrew Levien's Family Quotations. Enkuizen: 1970. V. 47
The Tower of Babel: Enkhuizen; Smart Cat; Book of Doom; Get Well Enkhuizen. 1971. V. 53

LEVIGNE, RICHARD G. A.
Jottings for the Early History of the Levigne Family. Part I. Dublin: 1873. V. 47; 53

LEVIN, IRA
Rosemary's Baby. New York: 1967. V. 53

LEVIN, MARTIN
Five Boyhoods. Garen City: 1962. V. 54

LEVIN, MEYER
Compulsion. New York: 1959. V. 54
Reporter. New York: 1929. V. 48; 51

LEVINE, ALBERT NORMAN
Myssium. Toronto: 1948. V. 47

LEVINE, BERNARD R.
Knifemakers of Old San Francisco. San Francisco: 1978. V. 54

LEVINE, DAVID
Pens and Needles. Boston: 1969. V. 47; 49

LEVINE, MARK
Capital: Eight Poems. Iowa City: 1991. V. 54

LEVINE, PHILIP
5 Detroits. Santa Barbara: 1970. V. 53
Ashes. Poems New and Old. Port Townsend: 1979. V. 53; 54
The Names of the Lost. Poems. Iowa City: 1976. V. 49; 53; 54
New Season. Port Townsend: 1975. V. 51; 53; 54
Not This Pig. Middletown: 1968. V. 53
On the Edge. Iowa City: 1963. V. 51; 54
One for the Rose. New York: 1981. V. 53

LEVINE, PHILIP continued
Pili's Wall. Santa Barbara: 1971. V. 51; 53
Red Dust. Santa Cruz: 1971. V. 51; 53
They Feed They Lion. New York: 1972. V. 51; 53
Thistles. London: 1970. V. 49; 53

LEVINE, SAMUEL ALBERT
Clinical Heart Disease. Philadelphia: 1936. V. 51
Coronary Thrombosis: its Various Clinical Features. Baltimore: 1931. V. 48; 54

LEVINGE, RICHARD GEORGE AUGUSTUS, BART.
Echoes from the Backwoods, or Sketches of Transatlantic Life. London: 1843. V. 53
Historical Records of the Forty-Third Regiment, Monmouthshire Light Infantry... London: 1868. V. 50

LEVINREW, WILL
Murder on the Palisades. London: 1930. V. 48

LEVINSON, ABRAHAM
Pioneers of Pediatrics. New York: 1936. V. 52
Pioneers of Pediatrics. New York: 1943. V. 50

LEVINSON, ANDRE
Baskt, the Story of the Artist's Life. London: 1923. V. 47

LEVINSON, ISAAC BEER
Efes Dammim. A Series of Conversations at Jerusalem Between a Patriarch of the Greek Church and a Chief Rabbi of the Jews, Concerning the Malicious Charge Against the Jews of Using Christian Blood. London: 1841. V. 47

LEVINSON, ORDE
John Piper. The Complete Graphic Works. London: 1987. V. 54

LEVIS, HOWARD C.
Baziliologia. A Booke of Kings. New York: 1913. V. 50; 53
Catalogue of Engraved Portraits, Views, Etc. Connected with the Name of Levis. London: 1914. V. 51
A Descriptive Bibliography of the Most Important Books in the English Language Relating to the Art and History of Engraving and The Collecting or Prints...(with) Supplement & Index. London: 1912-13. V. 51
Notes on the Early British Engraved Royal Portraits 1521 to the End of the Eighteenth Century. London: 1917. V. 53

LEVIS, LARRY
The Afterlife. Iowa City: 1977. V. 51; 54
The Rain's Witness. Iowa City: 1975. V. 51

LEVISON, SARAH RACHEL
The Extraordinary Life and Trial of Madame Rachel at the Central Criminal Court, Old Bailey,.. London: 1868. V. 48

LEVITT, HELEN
A Way of Seeing. New York: 1965. V. 49

LEVITT, M. P.
Bloomsday - an Interpretation of James Joyce's Ulysses. 1972. V. 53

LEVY, AMY
A Ballad of Religion and Marriage. V. 50; 51

LEVY, ESTHER
Jewish Cookery Book, on Principles of Economy, Adapted for Jewish Housekeepers... Philadelphia: 1871. V. 51

LEVY, FERDINAND
Flashes from the Dark. Dublin: 1941. V. 52

LEVY, JONAS P.
Claim of Capt. Jonas P. Levy, vs. United States, as Trustee for the Government of Mexico. Washington: 1860. V. 49
The Memorial of Captain Jonas P. Levy. To the Honorable, The Senate and House of Representatives in Congress Assembled. New York: 1882. V. 48; 49

LEVY, JULIAN
Surrealism. New York: 1936. V. 47
Surrealism. 1968. V. 54

LEVY, SAMUEL YATES
The Italian Bride. Savannah: 1856. V. 49

LEWER, H. W.
A Book of Simples. London: 1910. V. 47

LEWES, C. L., MRS.
Dr. Southwood Smith: a Retrospect. Edinburgh: 1898. V. 49

LEWES, CHARLES LEE
Memoirs...Containing Anecdotes, Historical and Biographical of the English and Scottish Stages, During a Period of Forty Years. London: 1805. V. 53

LEWES, GEORGE HENRY
Aristotle: a Chapter from the History of Science, Including Analyses of Aristotle's Scientific Writings. London: 1864. V. 49
The Biographical History of Philosophy, From Its Origin in Greece Down to the Present Day. London: 1857. V. 48; 49
Comte's Philosophy of the Sciences: Being an Exposition of the Cours de Philosophies Positive of Auguste Comte. London: 1853. V. 47; 49
The Life of Goethe. London: 1864. V. 53
On Actors and Acting. London: 1875. V. 51
The Physical Basis of Mind. London: 1877. V. 51
The Physiology of Common Life. New York: 1860. V. 49
Sea-Side Studies at Infracombe, Tenby, the Scilly Isles & Jersey. London: 1858. V. 51

LEWIN, FREDERICK
An ABC Book for Good Boys and Girls. Bristol: 1911. V. 53
Rhymes of Ye Olde Sign Boards. Bristol: 1911. V. 53

LEWIN, J. W.
A Natural History of the Birds of New South Wales. Melbourne: 1978. V. 50; 51; 54

LEWIN, LOUIS
The Incidental Effects of Drugs, a Pharmacological and Clinical Hand-Book. New York: 1882. V. 48; 54

LEWIN, W.
Climbs. 1932. V. 53

LEWINE, J.
Bibliography of Eighteenth Century Art and Illustrated Books... London: 1898. V. 54

LEWIS, ALETHEA BRERETON
Isabella. London: 1823. V. 50
Isabella. London: 1851. V. 54
Rhoda. London: 1816. V. 48; 50
Things by Their Right Names; a Novel. London: 1812. V. 50

LEWIS, ALFRED HENRY
Faro Nell & Her Friends. New York: 1913. V. 48

LEWIS, ALICE BRADBURY
The Valley of San Fernando. 1924. V. 50

LEWIS, ALUN
Ha! Ha! Among the Trumpets. London: 1945. V. 49; 54
The Last Inspection - and other Stories. London: 1942. V. 50

LEWIS, ANDREW
The Orderly Book of That Portion of the American Army Stationed At or Near Williamsburg, Va., Under the Command of General Andrew Lewis, From March 18th, 1776 to August 28th, 1776. Richmond: 1860. V. 48

LEWIS, ANGELO JOHN
Conjurer Dick; or, the Adventures of a Young Wizard. London and New York: 1885. V. 54
Drawing-Room Conjuring. London: 1887. V. 53
Magic at Home. London: 1891. V. 51
Modern Magic... London: 1889. V. 48
Modern Magic... Philadelphia: 1900. V. 47
More Magic. Philadelphia: 1900. V. 54
More Magic... Philadelphia: 1920. V. 51
Puzzles Old and New. London: 1893. V. 51
Tricks with Cards. London: 1889. V. 51

LEWIS, BENJAMIN
Riding. New York: 1936. V. 47

LEWIS Carroll's The Hunting of the Snark Illustrated by Henry Holiday. Los Altos: 1981. V. 50

LEWIS, CECIL
Sagittarius Rising. London: 1936. V. 47

LEWIS, CECIL ARTHUR
Broadcasting from Within. London: 1924. V. 53

LEWIS, CHARLES THOMAS COURTNEY
George Baxter Colour Printer His Life and Work. London: 1908. V. 48; 50; 51; 53
George Baxter the Picture Printer. London: 1924. V. 48; 51
The Picture Printer of the 19th Century, George Baxter 1804-1867. London: 1911. V. 48; 50
The Story of Picture Printing in England During the XIXth Century... London: 1928. V. 51; 54
The Story of Picture Printing in England During the XIXth Century. Forty Years of Wood and Stone. London: 1930. V. 52

LEWIS, CLIVE STAPES
The Discarded Image - an Introduction to Medieval and Renaissance Literature. Cambridge: 1963. V. 47

LEWIS, CLIVE STAPLES
Beyond Personality: The Christian Idea of God. London: 1944. V. 52
Beyond the Bright Blur. New York: 1963. V. 51
Broadcast Talks: Reprinted with Some Alterations From Two Series of Broadcast Talks...Given in 1941 and 1942. London: 1942. V. 52
Christian Behavior. London: 1943. V. 54
The Chronicles of Narina. 1994. V. 51
Dymer. A Poem. New York: 1926. V. 50
English Literature in the 16th Century. 1954. V. 53
English Literature in the 16th Century. New York: 1954. V. 53
The Great Divorce. London: 1945. V. 50; 51; 53
A Grief Observed. London: 1961. V. 49; 50; 54
The Horse and His Boy. 1954. V. 52
The Horse and His Boy. London: 1954. V. 48; 49; 50; 51
The Horse and His Boy. New York: 1954. V. 53
The Last Battle. 1956. V. 52
The Last Battle... London: 1956. V. 47; 51
The Lion, The Witch, and the Wardrobe. London: 1950. V. 47; 49; 52
The Magician's Nephew. London: 1935. V. 53
The Magician's Nephew. London: 1955. V. 47; 52

LEWIS, CLIVE STAPLES continued
Miracles: a Preliminary Study. London: 1947. V. 47; 50
Miserable Offenders - an Interpretation of Prayer Book Language. Cincinnati. V. 54
Porelandra. 1942. V. 52
Perelandra. 1943. V. 52; 53
Perelandra. London: 1943. V. 53
Perelandra. London: 1944. V. 50
Perelandra. New York: 1944. V. 51; 53; 54
The Pilgrim's Regress: an Allegorical Apology for Christianity Reason and Romanticism. 1935. V. 51
The Pilgrim's Regress: An Allegorical Apology for Christianity Reason and Romanticism. London: 1943. V. 50
A Preface to Paradise Lost. London: 1942. V. 51
Prince Caspian... 1951. V. 54
Prince Caspian. London: 1951. V. 49; 50
Rehabilitations and Other Essays. London: 1939. V. 54
The Screwtape Letters. London: 1942. V. 49
The Screwtape Letters. 1943. V. 52
The Screwtape Letters. 1947. V. 54
The Silver Chair. 1953. V. 52
The Silver Chair. New York: 1953. V. 48
Surprised by Joy: The Shape of My Early Life. London: 1955. V. 51; 54
That Hideous Strength. New York: 1946. V. 48
Till We Have Faces. 1956. V. 49; 53; 54
Till We Have Faces. London: 1956. V. 51

LEWIS, DAVID
Miscellaneous Poems by Several Hands. London: 1726. V. 53
Miscellaneous Poems by Several Hands. London: 1726-30. V. 52

LEWIS, DIO
Gypsies, or Why We Went Gypsying in the Sierras. Boston: 1881. V. 47

LEWIS, EDWARD
The Patriot King Displayed, in the Life and Reign of Henry VIII. Dublin: 1769. V. 49

LEWIS, EDWIN
Duty, not Decay. London: 1902. V. 47

LEWIS, ELISHA J.
The American Sportsman: Containing Hints to Sportsmen, Notes on Shooting... Philadelphia: 1885. V. 48
Hints to Sportsmen, Containing Notes on Shooting; the Habits of the Game Birds... Philadelphia: 1851. V. 47

LEWIS, F. C.
Scenery of the River Dart, Being a Series of Thirty-Five Views. London: 1821. V. 47; 49; 52

LEWIS, FLORENCE
China Painting. V. 50
China Painting. London: 1883. V. 52; 53
China Painting. London: 1884. V. 50

LEWIS, G. R.
The Ancient Church of Shobdon, Herefordshire... London: 1852. V. 51

LEWIS, GEORGE
A Series of Groups, Illustrating the Physiognomy, Manners and Character of the People of France and Germany. London: 1823. V. 47

LEWIS, GEORGE CORNEWALL
An Essay On the Government of Dependencies. London: 1841. V. 48; 49
An Essay On the Influence of Authority in Matters of Opinion. London: 1849. V. 52
An Inquiry into the Credibility of the Early Roman History. London: 1855. V. 48

LEWIS, GEORGE E.
The Indiana Company, 1763-1798. Glendale: 1941. V. 51; 53

LEWIS, HARRY
Pulsars. Mt. Horeb: 1974. V. 54

LEWIS, HENRY
The Valley of the Mississippi Illustrated. St. Paul: 1967. V. 48

LEWIS, HENRY C.
Papers and Notes on the Glacial Geology of G. B. and Ireland. 1894. V. 48; 52

LEWIS, J. VANCE
Out of the Ditch: a True Story of an Ex-Slave. Houston: 1910. V. 53

LEWIS, JAMES HENRY
The Test of Teachers; or, Questions to Detect Impostors in the Art of Writing. London: 1820. V. 52

LEWIS, JAMES OTTO
The American Indian Portfolio. An Eyewitness History. 1823-28. Kent: 1980. V. 51

LEWIS, JANET
The Earth-Bound, 1924-1944. Aurora: 1946. V. 48; 54
The Wife of Martin Guerre. San Francisco: 1941. V. 49; 53; 54

LEWIS, JOHN
A Complete History of the Several translations of the Holy Bible... London: 1739. V. 51
Graphic Design with Special Reference to Lettering, Typography and Illustration. London: 1954. V. 51
The History and Antiquities, as Well Ecclesiastical as Civil, of the Isle of Tenet, in Kent. London: 1736. V. 47; 50
The History and Antiquities of the Abbey and Church of Faversham in Kent; of the Adjoining Priory of Davington and Maison-Dieu of Ospringe and Parish of Bocton... London: 1727. V. 47
John Nash, the Painter as Illustrator. Godalming, Surrey: 1978. V. 53
The Twentieth Century Book - Its Illustration and Design. London: 1967. V. 53
Young Kate, or, the Rescue; a Tale of the Great Kanawha. New York: 1844. V. 53

LEWIS, JOHN ANGELO
Modern Magic: a Practical Treatise on the Art of Conjuring by Professor Hoffmann. Philadelphia: 1910. V. 50

LEWIS, JOHN FREDERICK
Lewis's Sketches and Drawings of the Alhambra... London: 1835. V. 49; 52

LEWIS, JOHN W.
The Life, Labors and Travels of Elder Charles Bowles of the Free Will Baptist Denomination Together with an Essay on the Character and Conditions of the African Race. Watertown: 1852. V. 50; 53

LEWIS, JOSEPH N.
Old Things and New; or, Ancient Fables and Modern Men. Baltimore: 1835. V. 54

LEWIS, LEON
The Facts Concerning the Eight Condemned Leaders. Greenport: 1887. V. 52

LEWIS, LUNSFORD LOMAX
A Brief Narrative Written for His Grandchildren. Richmond: 1915. V. 50

LEWIS, M. D. S.
Antique Paste Jewellery. Boston: 1970. V. 48

LEWIS, M. J. T.
Temples in Roman Britain. Cambridge: 1966. V. 50; 52

LEWIS, MARGARET
What I Have Saved From the Writings of My Husband, Thomas B. Lewis. San Francisco: 1874. V. 49

LEWIS, MATTHEW GREGORY
Ambrosio, or the Monk: a Romance. London: 1798. V. 47
The Castle Spectre: a Drama. Dublin: 1799. V. 47
Feudal Tyrants; or, the Counts of Carlsheim and Sargans. London: 1806. V. 53
Journal of a West India Propreitor, Kept During a Residence in the Island Of Jamaica. London: 1834. V. 49; 52; 54
Koenigsmark the Robber, or, the Terror of Bohemia... London: 1808. V. 51
The Life and Correspondence of M. G. Lewis. London: 1839. V. 47; 48
The Monk. London: 1797. V. 48; 51
The Monk. Paris: 1807. V. 53
The Monk... London: 1913. V. 48
Poems. London: 1812. V. 47; 48; 54
Romantic Tales. London: 1808. V. 49
Tales of Terror and Wonder. London: 1887. V. 49; 53; 54
Tales of Wonder. V. 53
Tales of Wonder. Dublin: 1801. V. 48; 49; 54
Tales of Wonder. London: 1801. V. 47; 48; 50; 51; 52
Twelve Ballads, The Words and Music by M.G. Lewis... London: 1808. V. 53

LEWIS, MERIWETHER
History of the Expedition...Lewis and Clark... Philadelphia: 1814. V. 47; 49; 52
History of the Expedition...Lewis and Clark... New York: 1844. V. 53
History of the Expedition...Lewis and Clark... Chicago: 1902. V. 47
The Journals of the Expedition Under the Command of Capt. Lewis and Clark... 1962. V. 48
The Journals of the Expedition Under the Command of Capts. Lewis and Clark... New York: 1962. V. 48; 53
Journals of the Expedition Under the Command of Capts. Lewis and Clark... New York: 1967. V. 47; 48
Original Journals of the Lewis and Clark Expedition, 1804-06. 1969. V. 49
Original Journals of the Lewis and Clark Expedition, 1804-06. New York: 1969. V. 47; 49; 51; 53
Travels to the Source of the Missouri River and Across the American Continent to the Pacific Ocean. London: 1814. V. 51; 53; 54

LEWIS, N. LAWSON
The Sculpture of Max Kalish. Cleveland: 1933. V. 52

LEWIS, NAOMI
Hans Christian Andersen The Snow Queen, a New Adapted Version. New York: 1979. V. 49

LEWIS, NORMAN
Sand and Sea. London: 1938. V. 50
Spanish Adventure. London: 1935. V. 49

LEWIS, OSCAR
The Big Four. The Story of Huntington, Stanford, Hopkins and Crocker and of the Building of the Central Pacific. New York: 1938. V. 52
California in 1846. San Francisco: 1934. V. 47
Hearn and His Biographers. San Francisco: 1930. V. 48; 53; 54
Lola Montez. San Francisco: 1938. V. 51; 53
The Origin of the Celebrated Jumping Frog of Calaveras County. San Francisco: 1931. V. 47; 52
The Quest for Wual-A-Wa-Loo (Humbolt Bay). San Francisco: 1943. V. 53
The Wonderful City of Carrie Van Wie. San Francisco: 1963. V. 47; 48

LEWIS, R. B.
Light and Truth: Collected from the Bible and Ancient and Modern History... Boston: 1844. V. 52

LEWIS, RALPH
Sir William Russell Flint, R.A. 1880-1969. London: 1989. V. 47

LEWIS, RICHARD
History of the Life-Boat and It's Work. London: 1874. V. 54

LEWIS, SAMUEL
An Atlas, Comprising Maps of the Several Counties (of England and Wales) and of the Islands of Guernsey, Jersey and Man. London: 1842. V. 50
Atlas to the Topographical Dictionaries of England and Wales. London: 1844. V. 51
Lewis's Atlas Comprising the Counties of Ireland... London: 1846. V. 49; 51
A Topographical Dictionary of England (Ireland, Wales and Scotland). London: 1842-46. V. 53
Topographical Dictionary of Ireland. London: 1837. V. 52
Topographical Dictionary of Scotland... London: 1851. V. 49

LEWIS, SAMUEL E.
The Treatment of Prisoners-of-War 1861-65. Richmond: 1910. V. 50

LEWIS, SARAH
Woman's Mission. Boston: 1840. V. 50; 51; 53

LEWIS, SINCLAIR
Ann Vickers. Garden City: 1933. V. 47; 49; 53
Ann Vickers. London: 1933. V. 54
Arrowsmith. New York: 1925. V. 49; 51
Arrowsmith. Paris: 1931. V. 47
Babbit. New York: 1922. V. 47; 51; 53; 54
Bethel Merriday. New York: 1940. V. 51
Cass Timberlane. 1945. V. 50
Cass Timberlane. New York: 1945. V. 47
Dodsworth. New York: 1929. V. 49; 52
Elmer Gantry. New York: 1927. V. 49; 50; 53; 54
Hike and the Aeroplane. New York: 1912. V. 51
The Innocents. New York: 1917. V. 48; 50
It Can't Happen Here. Garden City: 1935. V. 49
It Can't Happen Here. New York: 1938. V. 52
Jayhawker: a Play in Three Acts. Garden City: 1935. V. 49
Keep Out of the Kitchen. New York: 1929. V. 47; 51
Kingsblood Royal. New York: 1947. V. 47; 48; 49; 50; 51; 52; 54
Main Street. V. 50
Main Street. New York: 1920. V. 48; 49; 52; 54
Main Street. Chicago: 1937. V. 49; 53; 54
Main Street. New York: 1937. V. 47; 48
The Man Who Knew Coolidge. 1928. V. 50
The Man Who Know Coolidge. New York: 1928. V. 48
Mantrap. New York: 1925. V. 50
Our Mr. Wrenn. New York: 1914. V. 49; 52; 54
The Prodigal Parents. Garden City: 1938. V. 52
The Trail of the Hawk. New York: 1915. V. 48
The Trail of the Hawk. New York: 1930. V. 49
Work of Art. Garden City: 1934. V. 49; 53

LEWIS, SUZANNE
The Art of Matthew Paris in the Chronica Majora. Berkeley: 1987. V. 53

LEWIS, T. C.
From the East and From the West. London: 1908. V. 47; 54

LEWIS, T. PERCY
The Book of Cakes. London: 1903. V. 50

LEWIS, TAYLER
State Rights: a Photograph from the Ruins of Ancient Greece, with...the Ideas of Nationality of sovereignty and the Right of Revolution. Albany: 1865. V. 49

LEWIS, THOMAS
Clinical Disorders of the Heartbeat. London: 1912. V. 48
Clinical Disorders of the Heartbeat. London: 1913. V. 51
Clinical Disorders of the Heartbeat. 1914. V. 54
Clinical Electrocardiography. London: 1913. V. 48
Clinical Electrocardiography. New York: 1919. V. 54
Lectures on the Heart. New York: 1915. V. 51
The Mechanism and Graphic Registration of the Heart Beat. London: 1925. V. 48
The Scorge: in Vindication of the Church of England. London: 1720. V. 50; 54
Seasonable Considerations on the Indecent and Dangerous Custom of Burying in Churches and Church-Yards. London: 1721. V. 53
The Soldier's Heart and the Effort Syndrome. London: 1940. V. 54

LEWIS, TIMOTHY
The Laws of Howel Dda. London: 1912. V. 50

LEWIS, WILLIAM
The Book of the Japanese Bazaar. Bath: 1882. V. 51
Elements of the Game of Chess, or a New Method of Instruction in that Celebrated Game... New York: 1827. V. 47; 50
The New Dispensatory... London: 1753. V. 52
The New Dispensatory... London: 1765. V. 51
The New Dispensatory... London: 1770. V. 51
The New Dispensatory... Dublin: 1778. V. 49

LEWIS, WILLIAM BEVAN
The Human Brain: Histological and Coarse Methods of Research. London: 1882. V. 53
Text-Book of Mental Diseases... Philadelphia: 1890. V. 53
Text-Book of Mental Diseases... Philadelphia: 1899. V. 53

LEWIS, WILLIAM DRAPER
Great American Lawyers: The Lies and Influence of Judges and Lawyers Who Have Acquired Permanent National Reputation and have developed the Jurisprudence of the United States. Philadelphia: 1907. V. 49; 50

LEWIS, WILLIAM S.
Ranald MacDonald - the Narrative of His Early Life on the Columbia Under the Hudson's Bay Company's Regime; of His Experiences in the Pacific Whale Fishery; and of His Great Adventure to Japan; With a Sketch of his Later Life on the Western Frontier... Spokane: 1923. V. 53

LEWIS, WYNDHAM
America and Cosmic Man. London: 1948. V. 48; 50; 51
America, I Presume. New York: 1940. V. 50; 53
The Apes of God. London: 1930. V. 47; 48; 50; 51; 52; 54
The Apes of God. London: 1931. V. 50; 52
The Apes of God. New York: 1932. V. 51
The Apes of God. London: 1955. V. 50
The Art of Being Ruled. London: 1926. V. 49; 50; 51; 54
The Art of Being Ruled. New York: 1926. V. 52
The Art of Wyndham Lewis. London: 1951. V. 51; 53
Blasting & Bombardiering. London: 1937. V. 47; 48; 49; 50; 51
The Caliph's Design... London: 1719. V. 48
The Caliph's Design. London: 1919. V. 47; 50; 51
The Childermass. London: 1928. V. 48; 50; 51; 52; 53
Count Your Dead: They Are Alive!. London: 1937. V. 49; 50
The Diabolical Principle and the Dithyrambic Spectator. London: 1931. V. 50
Doom of Youth. London: 1932. V. 50
The Enemy of the Stars. London: 1932. V. 47; 50; 51; 53
Engine Fight Talk. The Song of the Militant Romance. If So The Man You Are. One-Way Song. Envoy. 1933. V. 54
Fifteen Drawings. London: 1920. V. 50
Filibusters in Barbary. London: 1932. V. 50
Filibusters in Barbary. New York: 1932. V. 47; 48; 51; 53
Filibusters in Barbary. USA: 1932. V. 50
Harold Gilman. An Appreciation. London: 1919. V. 50
Hitler. London: 1931. V. 50
The Hitler Cult. London: 1939. V. 50
The Human Age. Book 2 and 3. London: 1955. V. 50
The Human Age: Childermass, Nonstre Gai and Malighn Fiesta. London: 1955-56. V. 48
The Ideal Giant: the Code of a Herdsman. London: 1917. V. 50
The Jews: Are They Human?. London: 1939. V. 50; 52; 53; 54
Left Wings Over Europe. London: 1936. V. 50
The Lion and the Fox. London: 1927. V. 50
The Lion and the Fox. New York: 1927. V. 50; 53
Men Without Art. London: 1934. V. 47; 50; 53
The Mysterious Mr. Bull. London: 1938. V. 50
The Old Gang and the New. London: 1933. V. 47; 50; 52
One Way Song. London: 1933. V. 47; 50; 51; 54
One Way Song... New York: 1933. V. 51
Paleface. London: 1929. V. 50; 51
The Red Priest. London: 1956. V. 52; 53
The Revenge of Love. London: 1937. V. 50
The Roaring Queen. Bristol: 1973. V. 53
The Roaring Queen. London: 1973. V. 50; 51; 53
Rotting Hill. London: 1951. V. 50
Rude Assignment. London: 1950. V. 50
Satire and Fiction. London: 1930. V. 51
Self Condemned. London: 1954. V. 49; 50; 51; 52; 53
The Slade. A Collection of Drawings and Some Pictures Done by Past and Present Students of the London Slade School of Art 1893-1907. London: 1907. V. 48
Snooty Baronet. London: 1932. V. 50
Tarr. London: 1918. V. 50; 51; 53
Tarr. New York: 1918. V. 49; 50; 51
Tarr. London: 1928. V. 47
Thirty Personalities and a Self Portrait. London: 1932. V. 48; 50; 54
Time and Western Man. London: 1927. V. 50; 51; 53
Time and Western Man. New York: 1928. V. 52
The Vulgar Streak. London: 1941. V. 50
The Wild Body. London: 1927. V. 48; 50
The Writer and the Absolute. London: 1952. V. 50
Wyndham Lewis the Artist, from "Blast" to Burlington House. 1939. V. 54
Wyndham Lewis the Artist from "Blast" to Burlington House. London: 1939. V. 54

LEWIS BROS. LTD., MONTREAL.
Catalogue No. 70 Wholesale Hardware. Montreal: 1937. V. 53

LEWISOHN, LUDWIG
The Case of Mr. Crump. Paris: 1926. V. 48; 51
The Last Days of Shylock. New York: 1931. V. 49; 51

LEWIS-RANSOM, SIDNEY
The Flame. A Book of Poems. London. V. 54

LE WRIGHT, J.
Two Proposals Becoming England as This Juncture to Undertake. London: 1706. V. 53

LEWTON, VAL
Rasputin and the Empress. New York: 1933. V. 54

LEX Londinensis; or, the City Law. London: 1680. V. 53

LEY, WILLY
Rockets. The Future of Travel Beyond the Stratosphere. New York: 1944. V. 48; 49

LEYBOURE, THOMAS
The Mathematical Questions, Proposed in the Ladies' Diary, and Their Original Answers. Together with Some New Solutions, from Its Commencement in the Year 1704 to 1816. London: 1817. V. 52; 54

LEYBOURN, WILLIAM
The Art of Dialling, Performed Geoemtrically, by Scale and Compasses... London: 1669. V. 53; 54
The Compleat Surveyor: Containing The Whole Art of Surveying... London: 1653. V. 51
Cursus Mathematicus. Mathematical Sciences in Nine Books... London: 1690. V. 48
Dialling: Plain, Concave, Convex, Projetive, Reflective, Refractve, Shewing How to Make All Such Dials. 1682. V. 54

LEYDA, JAY
The Years and Hours of Emily Dickinson. New Haven: 1960. V. 50

LEYDEN, JOHN
A Historical and Philosophical Sketch of the Discoveries and Settlements of the Europeans in Northern and Western Africa, at the Close of the 18th Century. Edinburgh: 1799. V. 54
Scenes of Infancy: Descriptive of Teviotdale... Edinburgh: 1803. V. 50; 51; 53

LEYDEN, LUCAS VAN
La Passion De Notre Seigneur. Antwerp: 1911. V. 53; 54

LEYLAND, FRANCIS A.
The Bronte Family... London: 1886. V. 50; 52
The Bronte Family... Manchester: 1973. V. 54

LEYLAND, FREDERICK RICHARDS
Sale Catalogue of the Very Valuable Collection of Ancient and Modern Pictures of F. R. Leyland, to be Sold at Auction by Christie, Manson & Woods, May 28th, 1892. V. 49

LEYLAND, JOHN
Contemporary Medical Men and Their Professional Work... Leicester: 1888. V. 47; 50; 52
The Yorkshire Coast and Cleveland Hills and Dales. London: 1892. V. 47; 53

LEYLAND, R. W.
A Holiday in South Africa. 1882. V. 54
A Holiday in South Africa. London: 1882. V. 48; 52

LEYMARIE, JEAN
Balthus. New York: 1979. V. 47; 48; 50; 52
The Graphic Works of the Impressionists: Manet, Pissarro, Renoir, Cezanne, Sisley. New York: 1972. V. 54
The Jerusalem Windows. New York: 1962. V. 47
Marc Chagall Monotypes 1966-1975. Geneva: 1966. V. 49; 51; 53
Marc Chagall: the Jerusalem Windows. New York: 1962. V. 47; 48

LEZAMIS, JOSE DE
Vida del Apostol Santiago el Mayor...Unico y Singular Patron de Espana con Alguans Antiguedades y Excelencias de Espana... Mexico City: 1699. V. 54

L'HERITIER, LOUIS FRANCOIS
Le Champ-d'Asile, Tableau Topographique et Historique du Texas... Paris: 1819. V. 49

L'HERITIER DE BRUTELLE, CHARLES LOUIS
Sertum Anglicum 1788. Pittsburgh: 1963. V. 50

L'HOPITAL, WINEFRIDE DE
Westminster Cathedral and Its Architect. London: 1919. V. 52

L'HOSPITAL, GUILLAUME FRANCOIS ANTOINE, MARQUIS DE
An Analytick Treatise of Conick Sections, and Their Use for Revolving of Equations in Determinant and Indeterminate Problems. London: 1723. V. 48

L'HOSTE, JEAN
Epipolimerie ou Art de Mesurer Toutes Superficies. Verdun: 1619. V. 47

LHUYD, EDWARD
Archaeologia Britannica, Giving Some Account Additional to What Has Been Hithero Publish'd of the Languages, Histories and Customs of the Original Inhabitants of Great Britain. Oxford: 1707. V. 53

LHUYD, HUMFREY
The Breviary of Britayne. London: 1573. V. 54

LI, CHUAN-SHIH
All Men Are Brothers. V. 47
All Men are Brothers. New York: 1948. V. 51; 52; 53; 54

LI, HSIAO-FANG
Bibliography of Chinese Geology. Bibliography of Geology and Geography of Sinkiang. Nanking: 1947. V. 47

LI, PO
Poems. Lexington: 1983. V. 51

LIARDET, FRANCIS
Professional Recollections On Points of Seamanship, Discipline, Etc. Portsea: 1849. V. 49

LIARDET, FREDERICK
Tales of a Barrister. London: 1847. V. 53; 54

LIBANUS Press: Daylight Jobbery. (Ephemera to 1985 by the Libanus Press). Marlborough: 1986. V. 51

LIBAVIUS, ANDREAS
Singularium. Frankfurt: 1599. V. 50

LIBBEY, WILLIAM
The Jordan Valley and Petra. New York: 1905. V. 47

LIBBY, O. G.
The Arikara Narrative of the Campagin Against the Hostile Dakotas, June 1876. Bismarck: 1920. V. 52; 54
The Arikara Narrative of the Campaign Against the Hostile Sioux in 1876. Bismarck: 1970. V. 49

LIBBY, WILLARD F.
Radiocarbon Dating. Chicago: 1952. V. 53; 54

LIBELLUS Lapidum. 1924. V. 54

LIBER Chronicarum. Nurnberg: 1493. V. 53

LIBER Vacetiarum, Being a Collection of Curious and Interesting Anecdotes. Newcastle-upon-Tyne: 1809. V. 50

LIBERACE
Liberace Cooks!. Garden City: 1970. V. 52; 53

THE LIBERAL Preacher. Keene: 1828-30. V. 48

THE LIBERAL. Verse and Prose from the South. London: 1822-23. V. 54

LIBERMAN, ALEXANDER
The Art and Technique of Color Photography. New York: 1951. V. 47
The Artist in His Studio. New York: 1960. V. 47; 48

LIBERMAN, M. M.
Maggot and Worm and Eight Other Stories. West Branch: 1969. V. 52; 54

LIBERTY & CO., LONDON.
Modern Silver Designed and Made by Liberty & Co. Trade Catalogue. London: 1924-25. V. 52

LIBMAN, EMANUEL
Contributions to the Medical Sciences of Dr. Emanuel Libman by His Pupils, Friends and Colleagues. New York: 1932. V. 51

LIBRAIRIE DE LA CONSTRUCTION MODERNE
Garages et Salles d'Esposition. Paris: 1928. V. 49

LIBRARY Catalog of the International Museum of Photography at George Eastman House. Boston: 1982. V. 47

LIBRARY COMPANY OF PHILADELPHIA
Supplement to the Catalogue of Books, Belong to... Philadelphia: 1838. V. 47

THE LIBRARY of Congress Mural Paintings in the Colors of the Originals. Washington: 1902. V. 51

THE LIBRARY of Fiction, or Family Story-Teller, Consisting of Original Tales, Essays and Sketches of Character. London: 1836-37. V. 47; 54

LIBRI Censualis Vocati Domesday-Book. London: 1783. V. 49

LIBRI, GUGLIELMO
The Case of M. Libri. London: 1852. V. 54
Catalogue of the Choice Portion of the Magnificent Library...Unknown Blockbooks...Collection of Historical Bindings, Etc. 1859. V. 50
A Catalogue of the Choicer Portion of the Magnificent Library Formed by M. Guglielmo Libri. London: 1859. V. 54
Catalogue of the Extraordinary Collection of Splendid Manuscripts Chiefly Upon Vellum, in Various Languages of Europe and the East. London: 1859. V. 54

LIBRORUM Levitici et Numerorum, Versio Antiqua itala e Codice Perantiquo in Bibliotheca Ashburnhamiense Conservatio. Londini: 1868. V. 49

LIBURNIO, NICCOLO
Le Occorrenze Hvmane. Vinegia: 1546. V. 53
Le Selvette... Venice: 1513. V. 52

LICETI, FORTUNIO
De Lucernis Antiquorum Reconditis Libb. Quatuor: in Quibus Earum...Explicatais Diligenter Abditissimis Questionibus De Ignium Causis, Origine, Varietate... Venice: 1621. V. 49
De Monstris. Ex Recensione Geradi Blasii...Qui Monstra Quaedam Nova & Ariora ex Recentiorum Scriptis Addidit... Amsterdam: 1665. V. 49; 53
De Spontaneo Viventum Ortu Libb. Quatuor. Vicetiae: 1618. V. 49
Hieroglyphica, Sive Antiqua Schemata Gemmarum Anularium. Padua: 1653. V. 50

LICHT, KJELD DE FINE
The Rotunda in Rome: a Study of Hadrian's Pantheon. Copenhagen: 1968. V. 52

LICHTENSTEIN, ISAAC
Niggun. Paintings by Isaac Lichtenstein. New York: 1945. V. 53

LICHTENSTEIN, ROY
Mural with Brush Stroke. New York: 1987. V. 50

LICK OBSERVATORY
Studies of the Nebulae Made at the Lick Observatory, University of California at Mount Hamilton, California and Santiago, Chile. Berkeley: 1918. V. 54

LIDDELL, R. S.
The Memoirs of the Tenth Royal Hussars (Prince of Wales' Own); Historical and Social. London: 1891. V. 50

LIDDIE, BRUCE R.
I Buried Custer, the Diary of Pvt. Thomas W. Coleman, Only Enlisted Man's Account of of the Events Surrounding the Battle of Little Bighorn. V. 52

LIDDY, JAMES
Blue Mountain. 1968. V. 48
In a Blue Smoke. Dublin: 1964. V. 48

LIDELL, HENRY GEORGE
A Greek-English Lexicon. Oxford: 1901. V. 48

LIEBER, FRANCIS
Guerrilla Parties Considered with Reference to the Laws and Usages of War...August 1862. New York: 1862. V. 47
Letters to a Gentleman in Germany, Written After a trip from Philadelphia to Niagara. Philadelphia: 1834. V. 47

LIEBER, FRITZ
Gather, Darkness!. New York: 1950. V. 50

LIEBIG, G. A.
Practical Electricity in Medicine and Surgery. Philadelphia: 1890. V. 47; 49; 54

LIEBIG, JUSTUS VON
Animal Chemistry. Cambridge: 1842. V. 50; 52; 54
Animal Chemistry... London: 1842. V. 51; 52
Animal Chemistry... New York: 1842. V. 50
Chemistry In Its Applications to Agriculture and Physiology. London: 1842. V. 47
Chemistry in Its Applications to Agriculture and Physiology. London: 1843. V. 47; 49; 52
The Natural Laws of Husbandry. London: 1863. V. 50; 53
Organic Chemistry, In Its Application to Agriculture and Physiology. Cambridge: 1841. V. 50; 52
Die Organische Chemie in Ihrer Anwendung auf Physiologie und Pathologie. Braunschweig: 1842. V. 47; 49
Professor Liebig's Complete Works on Chemistry. Philadelphia: 1850. V. 50
Researches on the Chemistry of Food and the Motion of the Juices in the animal body. Lowell: 1848. V. 49; 51; 53; 54
Researches on the Motion of the Juices in the Animal body. London: 1848. V. 48; 50; 52; 54

LIEBLING, A. J.
Back Where I Came From. New York: 1938. V. 53

LIECHTENSTEIN, MARIA, PRINCESS
Holland House. London: 1874. V. 50; 52

LIENARD, PAUL
Specimens of the Decorative Art and Ornament of the XIXth Century. London: 1872. V. 50

LIENHARD, HEINRICH
A Pioneer at Sutter's fort, 1846-1850: The Adventures of Heinrich Lienhard. Los Angeles: 1941. V. 47; 50

LIESS, B.
Classical Swine Fever and Related Viral Infections. 1987. V. 52

LIETZE, ERNST
Modern Heliographic Processes... New York: 1888. V. 54

LIEUTAUD, JOSEPH
Synopsis of the Universal Practice of Medicine, Exhibiting a Concise View of All Diseases, Both Internal and External... Philadelphia: 1816. V. 51; 54

LIEVEN, DAR'IA KHRISTOFOROVNA BENCKENDORFF
Letters of Princess Lieven to Lady Holland, 1847-57. Oxford: 1956. V. 48; 50; 54

THE LIFE, Amours and Secret History of Francelia, Late D----ss if O-----h, Favourite Mistress to King Charles II. London: 1734. V. 52

LIFE and Adventures of Calamity Jane. 1896. V. 47

THE LIFE and Adventures of Capt. John Avery, the Famous English Pirate (Rais'd from a Cabbin-Boy, to a King) Now in Possession of Madagascar... London: 1709. V. 52

THE LIFE and Adventures of Matthew Bishop of Deddington in Oxfordshire. London: 1744. V. 49

LIFE and Adventures of Mr. Pig and Miss Crane. 1830?. V. 47

THE LIFE and Adventures of Mrs. Christian Davies, Commonly Call'd Mother Ross; Who, in Several Campaigns Under King William and the Late Duke of Marlborough, in the Quality of a Foot-soldier and Dragoon... London: 1740. V. 49

THE LIFE and Adventures of that Most Eccentric Character James Hirst. Knottingley: 1840. V. 52; 54

THE LIFE and Adventures of the Celebrated Walking Stewart: Including His Travels in The East Indies. London: 1822. V. 47

THE LIFE and Death of Gamaliel Ratsey, a Famous Thief of England, Executed at Bedford the 26th of March Last Past. 1605. London: 1935. V. 50

THE LIFE and Death of Jenny Wren. London: 1850. V. 53

THE LIFE and Death of John Carpenter, Alias Hell Fire Jack, the Noted Horse Stealer, Who Was Executed April 4, 1805; also the Particulars of Eliz. Barber, Alias Mrs. Daley, Hanged for Murder. To Which is Added the Trial of J. Dransfield... London: 1805. V. 47

THE LIFE and Death of Rich Mrs. Duck, a Notorious Glutton. New York: 1869. V. 52

THE LIFE and Explorations of David Livingstone. London: 1876. V. 54

THE LIFE and Public Services of Hon. Abraham Lincoln, of Illinois, and Hon. Hannibal Hamlin, of Maine. Boston: 1860. V. 48

LIFE and Remarkable Adventures of Israel R. Potter... Providence: 1824. V. 47; 50

THE LIFE and Singular Adventures of Jack Shepherd. London: 1787. V. 50

LIFE High and Low. London: 1819. V. 51

LIFE in the West: Back-wood Leaves and Prairie Flowers: Rough Sketches on the Borders of the Picturesque, the Sublime and Ridiculous. London: 1843. V. 48

THE LIFE of Admiral Lord Nelson... London: 1806. V. 53

THE LIFE of Captain James Cook, the Celebrated Circumnavigator, Compiled from the Most Authentic Sources. Dublin: 1831. V. 52

THE LIFE Of Christ. New York: 1951. V. 52

THE LIFE of Colonel Don Francisco. London: 1730?. V. 50

THE LIFE of James, Late Duke of Ormonde. London: 1747. V. 47

LIFE of John C. Calhoun. New York: 1843. V. 50

THE LIFE of John Metcalf, Commonly Called Blind Jack of Knaresborough. York: 1695. V. 50

THE LIFE of John Metcalf, Commonly Called Blind Jack of Knaresborough... York: 1795. V. 47

THE LIFE Of Miss Marion Smith. Boston: 1844. V. 47

THE LIFE of Mrs. Abington (formerly Miss Barton), Celebrated Comic Actress.... London: 1888. V. 54

THE LIFE of Napoleon Bonaparte, Late Emperor of the French, From His Birth in the Island of Corsice, to the Period of His Death at St. Helena... Newcastle-upon-Tyne: 1820. V. 51

THE LIFE of Paddy O'Flarrity, Who, From a Shoe Black, Has, By Perseverance and Good Conduct, Arrived to a Member of Congress, Interspersed with Many Curious Anecdotes... 1834. V. 48

THE LIFE of Pythagoras, With His Symbols and Golden Verses. London: 1707. V. 48

THE LIFE of St. George. London: 1919. V. 52

THE LIFE of Sir Robert Cochran. London: 1734. V. 53

LIFE of the Late John Howard, Esq. London: 1790. V. 48; 50

THE LIFE of the Rev. James Ireland. Winchester: 1819. V. 49

THE LIFE of the Russian General Suworow; with a Circumstantial Detail of His Surprising Victories; His Cruelty to the Turks at Ismail, and the Poles at Warsaw... London: 1800. V. 54

THE LIFE of William McKinley 1843-1901. New York: 1901. V. 50

THE LIFE, Travels, Voyages and Daring Engagements of Paul Jones...etc. To Which is Prefixed The Life and Adventures of Peter Williamson, Who Was Kidnapped When an Infant from His Native Place, Aberdeen, and sold for a Slave in America. Albany: 1809. V. 47

THE LIFE, Trial and Conviction of Captain John Brown, Known As "Old Brown of Ossawatomie", with a Full Account of the Attempted Insurrection at Harper's Ferry. New York: 1859. V. 49

THE LIFE, Trial, Condemnation and Dying Address of the Three Thayers!. Who Were Executed for the Murder of John Love, at Buffalo, New York, June 17th, 1825. Buffalo: 1825. V. 51

LIGHT, ALEXANDER
A Plan for the Amelioration of the Condition of the Poor of the U.K. London: 1830. V. 53

LIGHT, WILLIAM
Sicilian Scenery. London: 1823. V. 52; 54

LIGHTBOWN, RONALD
Donatello & Michelozzo. London: 1980. V. 51
Mantegna. Oxford: 1986. V. 49; 52
Sandro Botticelli Life and Work... London: 1978. V. 54

LIGHTFOOT, J. B.
The Apostolic Fathers. London: 1885-90. V. 50

LIGHTHALL, WILLIAM DOUW
Montreal after 250 Years. Montreal: 1892. V. 49
Songs of the Great Dominion; Voices from the Forests and Waters, The Settlements and Cities of Canada. London: 1889. V. 47; 48
The Young Seigneur... Montreal: 1888. V. 54

LIGHTMAN, ALAN
Einstein's Dreams. New York: 1993. V. 49

LIGHTON, NORMAN C. K.
The Paintings of Norman Lighton for Roberts Birds of South Africa. Capetown: 1977. V. 50; 52; 54

LIGNE, CHARLES JOSEPH, PRINCE DE
Letters and Reflections of the Austrian Field-Marshall Prince de Ligne... Philadelphia: 1809. V. 51
Mon Refuge: ou Satyre sur les Abus des Jardins Modernes... London: 1801. V. 53

LIGON, RICHARD
A True and Exact History of the Island of Barbadoes. London: 1673. V. 51; 54

LIKINS, J. W., MRS.
Six Years Experience as a Book Agent in California. 1992. V. 54

LILBURNE, JOHN
A Discourse Betwixt Lieutenant Colonel John Lilburn Close Prisoner in the Tower of London, and Mr. Hugh Peter. London: 1649. V. 50; 53
An Impeachment of High Treason Against Oliver Cromwel... London: 1649. V. 50
The Triall, of Lieut. Collonell John Lilburne, by a Extraordinry or Special Commission...the 24, 25, 26 of Octob. 1649. London: 1649. V. 50

LILFORD, THOMAS LITTLETON POWYS, 4TH BARON
Coloured Figures of the Birds of the British Islands. London: 1885-97. V. 47; 49; 51
Coloured Figures of the Birds of the British Islands. London: 1891-97. V. 51; 52
Notes on the Birds of Northamptonshire and Neighbourhood. London: 1893. V. 47
Notes on the Birds of Northamptonshire and Neighbourhood... London: 1895. V. 51; 54

LILIENTHAL, OTTO
Birdflight as the Basis of Aviation. London: 1911. V. 52; 54
Der Vogelflug als Grundlage der Fliegekunst. Berlin: 1889. V. 52; 54

LILIUOKALANI, QUEEN OF HAWAIIAN ISLANDS
Hawaii's Story by Hawaii's Queen. Boston: 1898. V. 50

LILIUS, ZACHARIAS
Orbis Breviarium... Paris: 1515. V. 48; 52

LILLIE, GORDON W.
Life Story of Pawnee Bill. 1916. V. 53

LILLINGSTON, LUKE
Reflections On Mr. Burchet's Memoirs...of Captain Wilmot's Expedition to the West Indies. London: 1704. V. 52

LILLO, GEORGE
The Dramatic Works. London: 1993. V. 51
The Works. London: 1775. V. 49; 52; 54

LILLY, ELI
Prehistoric Antiquities of Indiana. 1937. V. 51
Prehistoric Antiquities of Indiana... Indianapolis: 1937. V. 47; 53

LILLY, JOHN
A Collection of Modern Entries; or, Select Pleadings in the Court of King's Bench, Common Pleas and Exchequer...(with) a Collection of Writs... London: 1758. V. 52
Modern Entries: Being a Collection of Select Pleadings in the Courts of King's Bench, Common Pleas and Exchequer. London: 1741. V. 53

LILLY, JOHN K.
Man and Dolphin. Garden City: 1961. V. 53; 54

LILLY, OCTAVE
Cathedral in the Ghetto and Other Poems. New York: 1970. V. 53

LILLY, WILLIAM
Christian Astrology: Modestly Treated Of in Three Books. London: 1647. V. 47
An Introduction to Astrology...Being the Whole that Celebrated Author's Rules for the Practice of Horary Astrology, Divested of the Superstititions of the 17th Century. London: 1835. V. 48
Mr. William Lilly's History of His Life and Times, from the Year 1602 to 1681. London: 1715. V. 48; 50
The Starry Messenger; or, an Interpretation of that Strange Apparition of Three Suns Seen in London, 19 Novemb. 1644, Being the Birth Day of King Charles. London: 1645. V. 47
Strange News from the East, or, a Sober Account of the Comet or Blazing Star that Has Been Seen Several Mornings of late. London: 1677. V. 47
William Lilly's History of His Life and Times, from the Year 1602 to 1618. London: 1822. V. 54
The Worlds Catastrophe. London: 1647. V. 53

LILY, WILLIAM
A Short Introduction of Grammar... London: 1661/61. V. 51
A Short Introduction of Grammar... Oxford: 1699. V. 50

LIMA, E. DA CRUZ
Mammals of Amazonia. Rio de Janiero: 1945. V. 49; 52; 53

LIMA E MELLO BACELLAR, BERNARDO DE
Arte, e Diccionario do Commercio, e Economia Portugueza, Para que Todos Negoceem, e Governem os Seus bens Por Calculo... Lisbon: 1784. V. 48

LIMBORCH, PHILIP
The History of the Inquisition... London: 1731. V. 47

LIMBOUR, GEORGES
Andre Beaudin. London: 1961. V. 47; 48; 50; 52

LIMBOURG, JEAN PHILIPPE DE
New Amusements of the German Spa. London: 1764. V. 50

LIMITED EDITIONS CLUB
Quarto-Millenary... 1959. V. 52
Quarto-Millenary. New York: 1959. V. 47; 48; 51; 52; 53; 54

LIMMER, RAYMOND
Reminiscences of a Year's Captivity in the Hands of the Turks. Dorset. V. 47

LIMOUSIN, J. A.
Missouri, Oklahoma and Gulf Railway et Railroad. Angouleme: 1915. V. 54

LIN, TSAN-PIAO
Native Orchids of Taiwan. Taiwan: 1975-87. V. 50; 52

LINCK, JOANNES BERNARD
Annales Austrico-Clara-Vallenses. Vienna: 1723. V. 52

LINCOLN, ABRAHAM
Addresses of Abraham Lincoln. Kingsport: 1929. V. 49
The Collected Works of Abraham Lincoln. New Brunswick: 1953. V. 53
The Collected Works of Abraham Lincoln. New Brunswick: 1953-55. V. 50; 53
The Gettysburg Speech by Abraham Lincoln. New York: 1924. V. 50
The Life and Public Services of General Zachary Taylor. Boston: 1922. V. 52
Lincoln's Gettysburg Address. New York: 1950. V. 52
The Literary Works of... Menasha: 1942. V. 53; 54
Political Debates Between Hon. Abraham Lincoln and Hon. Stephen A. Douglas, in the Celebrated Campaign of 1858... Columbus: 1860. V. 49; 50; 52; 53
The Writings of Abraham Lincoln. New York: 1905. V. 54

LINCOLN, C. ERIC
The Black Muslims in America. Boston: 1961. V. 52

THE LINCOLN Catechism, Wherein the Eccentricities and Beauties of Despotism are Fully Set Forth. New York: 1864. V. 48

LINCOLN, ENOCH
The Village: a Poem. Portland: 1816. V. 50

LINCOLN Illustrated and Lincoln's Growth. Lincoln: 1887. V. 52; 54

LINCOLN, JOSEPH C.
Cape Cod Ballads and other Verse. Trenton: 1902. V. 48; 49; 51
Kekwan. A Poem. 1902. V. 49
Mr. Pratt. New York: 1906. V. 54

LINCOLN, MARY JOHNSON BAILEY
Carving and Serving. Boston: 1887. V. 50; 52
Frozen Dainties, Fifty Choice Receipts for Ice Creams, Frozen Fruits, Frozen Beverages, Sherberts and Water Ices. Nashua: 1889. V. 51

LINCOLN, REUBEN
Pecker the Super Bird or the Caves of Delight. 1948. V. 54

LINCOLN, SOLOMON
History of the Town of Hingham, Plymouth County, Massachusetts. Hingham: 1827. V. 51

LINCOLN, WILLIAM S.
Alton Trials: Of Winthrop S. Gilman...for the Crime of Riot...Also, the Trial of John Solomon... New York: 1838. V. 47

LINCOLN'S INN
Records of the Honourable Society of Lincoln's Inn. The Black Books. London: 1897-1968. V. 50; 53

LINCOLNSHIRE in 1836: Displayed in a Series of Nearly One Hundred Engravings on Steel and Wood... Lincoln: 1836. V. 50

LIND, JAMES
A Treatise on the Scurvy. London: 1757. V. 54
A Treatise on the Scurvy... London: 1772. V. 52

LIND, JOHN
An Answer to the Declaration of the American Congress. London: 1776. V. 48
Letters Concerning the Present State of Poland. London: 1773. V. 49

LIND, L. R.
Studies in Pre-Vesalian Anatomy. Philadelphia: 1975. V. 50; 52; 54

LINDA, LUCUS DE
Le Descrittioni Universali et Particolari Del Mondo & Della Republiche Tradotte, Osservate, & Accresiute da Maiolino Bisaccioni... Venice: 1660. V. 49; 50

LINDBERGH, ANNE MORROW
Earth Shine. New York: 1969. V. 51
North to the Orient. New York: 1935. V. 51
The Unicorn. New York: 1956. V. 51

LINDBERGH, CHARLES A.
Of Flight and Life. New York: 1948. V. 47
The Spirit of St. Louis. New York: 1953. V. 47; 49; 51; 54
The Spirit of St. Louis. New York: 1954. V. 48
We. New York, London: 1927. V. 48; 49; 51; 52; 53; 54

LINDBERGH, REEVE
John Apples. Mt. Horeb: 1995. V. 54

LINDE, A. VAN
The Haarlem Legend Of the Invention of Printing by Lourens Janszoon Coster, Critically Examined. London: 1871. V. 48

LINDEBOOM, G. A.
Boerhaave's Correspondence. Leiden: 1962-64. V. 50

LINDEBROG, FRIEDRICH
Codex Legum Antiquarum. Frankfurt: 1613. V. 47

LINDEMAN, M. H.
The Quarter Horse Breeder. Wichita Falls: 1959. V. 53

LINDEN, DIEDERICK WESSEL
A Treatise on Three Medicinal Mineral Waters at Landrindod, in Radnorshire, South Wales, with Some Remarks on Mineral and Fossil Mixtures, in Their Native Veins and Beds. London: 1756. V. 51

LINDEN, JOHANN ANTONIDES VAN DER
De Scriptis Medicis. Amstelredami: 1662. V. 47; 53
De Scriptis Medicis Libri Duo. Amsterdam: 1637. V. 47; 48
De Scriptis Medicis Libri Duo... Nuremberg: 1686. V. 49

LINDER, LESLIE
The Journal of Beatrix Potter from 1881 to 1897. London: 1966. V. 54

LINDER, USHER F.
Reminiscences of the Early Bench and Bar of Illinois. Chicago: 1879. V. 52

LINDERMAN, FRANK B.
Blackfeet Indians. St. Paul: 1935. V. 47; 50; 52; 54
Bunch-Grass and Blue-Joint. A Book of Verse. New York: 1924. V. 50
Indian Why Stories. Sparks from War Eagle's Lodge Fire. New York: 1915. V. 51
Out of the North, a Brief Historical Sketch of the Blackfeet Indian Tribe. St. Paul: 1940. V. 50

LINDLEY
The Lindley Library. Catalogue of Books, Pamphlets, Manuscripts and Drawings. London: 1927. V. 52

LINDLEY, AUGUSTUS F.
Ti-Ping Tien-Kwoh: The History of the Ti-Ping Revolution... London: 1866. V. 53

LINDLEY, CURTIS H.
A Treatise on the American Law Relating to Mines and Mineral lands Within the Public Land States and Territories. 1988. V. 50

LINDLEY, JOHN
Digitalium Monographia. London: 1821. V. 48; 50; 51
Ladies' Botany: or a Familiar Introduction to the Study of the Natural System of Botany. London: 1834. V. 53
Ladies' Botany: or, A familiar Introduction to the Study of the Natural System of Botany. London: 1837. V. 51
Ladies Botany: or a Familiar Introduction to the Study of the Natural System of Botany. London: 1839. V. 54
Ladies' Botany: or a Familiar Introduction to the Study of the Natural System of Botany. London: 1865. V. 51
Sertum Orchidaceum: Wreath of the Most Beautiful Orchidaceous Flowers. New York and Amsterdam: 1974. V. 51
The Theory of Horticulture. London: 1840. V. 54
The Vegetable Kingdom; or, the Structure, Classification and Uses of Plants Illustrated Upon the Natural System. London: 1846. V. 54

LINDLEY, KENNETH
Border Incidents. Hereford: 1982. V. 48

LINDLEY, THOMAS
Narrative of a Voyage to Brasil; Terminating in the Seizure of a British Vessel, and the Imprisonment of the Author and the Ship's Crew, by the Portuguese. London: 1805. V. 48

LINDMAN, M.
Snipp, Snapp, Snurr and the Gingerbread. Chicago: 1932. V. 49

LINDO, A. A.
A Retrospect of the Past, as Connected with and Preparatory to a Faithful Exposition Intended to be Given of the Divine Will and Dispensation Disclosed in the Sacred Books Received as Authority by Jews. Cincinnati: 1848. V. 47; 50

LINDROTH, C. H.
The Ground Beetles (Carabidae, Excl. Cicindelinae) of Canada and Alaska. Lund: 1961-69. V. 53

LINDSAY, DAVID
The Violet Apple. London: 1978. V. 52

LINDSAY, H.
Report of Proceedings on a Voyage to the Northern Ports of China in the Ship Lord Amherst. London: 1833. V. 52

LINDSAY, HOWARD
The Great Sabastians. New York: 1956. V. 54
Happy Hunting. New York: 1957. V. 54
Life with Father. New York: 1940. V. 54
State of the Union. New York: 1946. V. 50
Strip for Action. New York: 1943. V. 50

LINDSAY, IAN G.
Inverary and the Dukes of Argyll. Edinburgh: 1973. V. 52; 54

LINDSAY, J. MAURICE
Predicament - Thirteen Poems. Oxford: 1942. V. 51

LINDSAY, JACK
Dionysos. London: 1928. V. 48; 49; 50
Helen Comes of Age. London: 1927. V. 48
The London Aphrodite. London: 1929. V. 48
The Passionate Neathered. London: 1930. V. 54
Storm at Sea. London: 1935. V. 47
Storm at Sea. Waltham St. Lawrence: 1935. V. 53

LINDSAY, JOAN
Picnic at Hanging Rock. Melbourne: 1967. V. 48; 52

LINDSAY, JOHN
A View of the Coinage of Ireland, From the Invasion of the Danes to the Reign of George IV... Cork: 1839. V. 49

LINDSAY, NICHOLAS VACHEL
Collected Poems. London: 1923. V. 51
Collected Poems. New York: 1923. V. 50; 54
Collected Poems. New York: 1925. V. 51
Collected Poems. New York: 1927. V. 48; 51
The Congo and Other Poems. New York: 1914. V. 49
The Golden book of Springfield. New York: 1920. V. 49; 52; 53
The Golden Whales of California. New York: 1920. V. 47; 53; 54
Rhymes to Be Traded for Bread. 1912. V. 48; 51
Rhymes to be Traded for Bread... Springfield: 1912. V. 54

LINDSAY, NORMAN
Hyperborea: Two fantastic Travel Essays. 1928. V. 51
The Magic Pudding. London: 1936. V. 50
Pen Drawings. Sydney: 1931. V. 51

LINDSAY, OWEN
The Baldwinsville Homicide. Verbatim Report of the Trial of Owen Lindsay, for the Murder of Francis A. Colvin. Syracuse: 1875. V. 49

LINDSAY, PHILIP
An Account Biographical and Informative of the Later Days of Sir Henry Morgan Admiral of Sir Henry Morgan Admiral of Buccaneers... (etc.). London: 1930. V. 48
The Little Wench. London: 1935. V. 53
Morgan in Jamaica. London: 1930. V. 49

LINDSAY, WILLIAM LAUDER
Mind in the Lower Animals in Health and Disease. New York: 1880. V. 48; 49; 54

LINDSEY, THOMAS H.
Lindsey's Guide Book to Western North Carolina. Asheville: 1890. V. 48

LINDSEY, WILLIAM
Apples of Istakhar. Boston: 1895. V. 47
Cinder-Path Tales. Boston: 1896. V. 49

LINDSLEY, A. L.
Sketches of an Excursion to Southern Alaska. Portland?: 1880?. V. 48
Sketches of an Excursion to Southern Alaska. Portland: 1881?. V. 54

LINDSLEY, PHILIP
An Address Delivered at Nashville, Ten. Feb. 22, 1832, at the Request of Nashville and its Vicinity, on the Occasion of the Centennial Birth Day of George Washington. Nashville: 1832. V. 50
An Address, Delivered in Nashville, January 12, 1825, at the Inauguration of the President of Cumberland College. Nashville: 1825. V. 50
Cause of Education in Tennessee. An Address Delivered to the Young Gnetlemen Admitted to the Degree of Bachelor of Arts, at the First Commencement of the University of Nashville, October 4, 1826. Nashville: 1833. V. 50
A History of Greater Dallas and Vicinity. Chicago: 1909. V. 54

LINE Etchings. A Trip from the Missouri River to the Rocky Mountains Via the Kansas Pacific Railway. St. Louis: 1875. V. 52

LINE, LES
Some Birds and Mammals of North America. London: 1971. V. 49

LINEBARGER, P.
The Political Doctrines of Sun Yat-Sen. 1937. V. 51
The Political Doctrines of Sun Yat-sen. Baltimore: 1937. V. 47

LINEN, JAMES
The Golden Gate. San Francisco: 1869. V. 49

LINES Addressed to a Friend, Descriptive of a Visit to London in the Summer of 1825. Wisbech: 1825. V. 47

LINES Composed on the Death of General Washington. 1800. V. 48

LINES, KATHLEEN
Lavender's Blue. A Book of Nursery Rhymes. London: 1954. V. 53
Once in Royal David's City. 1956. V. 53

LING, NICHOLAS
Politeuphia, Wits Common-Wealth. London: 1602?. V. 52
Politeuphia, Wits Common-Wealth. London: 1647. V. 48
Politeuphia, Wits Common-Wealth... London: 1699. V. 54

LING, PRINCESS DER
Two Years in the Forbidden City. London & Leipsic: 1912. V. 51

LINGARD, JOHN
The History of England from the First Invasion by the Romans to the Accession of William and Mary in 1688. London: 1849. V. 50; 53
The History of England from the First Invasion by the Romans to the Accession of William and Mary in 1688. Dublin & London: 1878. V. 52
A History of England from the First Invasion by the Romans to the Revolution in 1688. London: 1819-30. V. 50
Remarks on the 'Saint Cuthbert' of the Rev. James Raine, M.A., &c. Newcastle: 1828. V. 50

LINGENFELTER, RICHARD E.
First through the Grand Canyon. Los Angeles: 1958. V. 54

LINGENFELTER, RICHARD E. continued
Presses of the Pacific Islands, 1817-1867. Los Angeles: 1967. V. 51; 52

LING ROTH, H.
The Aborigines of Tasmania. Tasmania. 1955. V. 53

LINGSTONE, ROWE
John Chinaman. London: 1890. V. 54

LINGUAE Latinae Liber Dictionarius Quadripartitus. London: 1678. V. 49

LINGUAE Romanae Dictionarium Luculentum Novum. A New Dictionary In Five Alphabets. Cambridge: 1693. V. 49

LINGUET, SIMON NICOLAS HENRI
Reflexions sur la Lumiere, ou Conjectures sur la Part qu'elle a au Mouvement des Corps Celestes. London: 1784. V. 47

LINK, MAE
Medical Support of the Army Air Forces in World War II. Washington: 1955. V. 50; 52

LINKLATER, ERIC
Sealskin Trousers and Other Stories. London: 1947. V. 48; 49
White Man's Saga. London: 1929. V. 53

LINN, CHARLES BLAIR
Valerian, a Narrative Poem... Philadelphia: 1805. V. 51

LINN, JOHN J.
Reminiscences of Fifty Years in Texas. New York: 1883. V. 53
Reminiscences of Fifty Years in Texas. Austin: 1986. V. 48; 52

LINN, LEWIS F.
Report On the...Committee of the Occupation of Oregon Territory. Washington: 1838. V. 47; 50

LINN, WILLIAM
Serious Considerations on the Election of a President; Addressed to the Citizens of the United States. New York: 1800. V. 47

LINNE, CARL VON
Amoenitates Academicae. Erlangen: 1785-90. V. 49
The Animal Kingdom, or Zoological System, of the Celebrated Sir Charles Linnaeus. London: 1792. V. 50; 54
A Catalogue of the Works... London: 1933. V. 49
A Catalogue of the Works... London: 1933-36. V. 49
Critica Botanica in Qua Nomina Plantarum Generica, Specifica, et Variantia Examin Subjiciuntur. Leiden: 1737. V. 52
A Disseratation on the Sexes of Plants. London: 1786. V. 48
The Elements of Botany... London: 1775. V. 49
Entomologia, Fauna Suecicae... Lugduni: 1789. V. 53
The Families of Plants. 1787. V. 51
The Families of Plants.... Litchfield: 1787. V. 49
Genera Plantarum Eorumque Characteres Naturales Secundum Numerum, Figuram, Situm & Proportionem Omnium Fructificationis Partium. Leiden: 1737. V. 52
A General System of Nature... London: 1802. V. 47; 49
A General System of Nature... London: 1802-06. V. 49
A General System of Nature. London and Swansea: 1806. V. 48; 54
A Generic and Specific Description of British Plants. Kendal: 1775. V. 53
A Generic and Specific Description of British Plants... London: 1775. V. 53
Hortus Cliffortianus... Amsterdam: 1737. V. 47
Hortus Cliffortianus. Amsterdam: 1737 i.e. 1738. V. 47
Lachesis Lapponica, Or A Tour in Lapland... London: 1811. V. 47; 48; 50; 54
Musa Cliffortiana Florens Hartecampi 1736 Prope Harlemum. Leiden: 1736. V. 47
Museum S(veci)ae R(egin)ae M(ajes)tis Ludovicae Ulricae Reginae Svecorum, Gothorum, Vandalorumque &c. (with) Museum...Adolphi Friderici Regis Svecorum... Stockholm: 1764. V. 47
Philosophia Botanica in Qua Explicantur Botanica. Stockholm: 1751. V. 48; 50
Species Plantarum. Stockholm: 1753. V. 48; 49
Species Plantarum... Stockholm: 1762-63. V. 52; 53
Species Plantarum. Berlin: 1797-1810. V. 48
System of Botany... London: 1777. V. 51
A System of Vegetables... Lichfield: 1783. V. 54
A System of Vegetables... Lichfield: 1783-83-85. V. 54
Systema Naturae... Stockholm: 1758-59. V. 49
Systema Naturae. Vienna: 1767-70. V. 53
Systeme Sexuel des Vegetaux. Paris: 1798. V. 49
Voyages and Travels in the Levant in the Years 1749-52. London: 1766. V. 49

LINNE, SIGVALD
Archaeological Researches at Teotihuacan, Mexico. Stockholm: 1934. V. 47
Mexican Highland Cultures: Archaeological Researches at Teotihuacan, Calpulalpan and Chalchicomula in 1934/35. Stockholm: 1942. V. 50; 52
Zapotecan Antiquities and the Paulson Collection in the Ethnographical Museum of Sweden. Stockholm: 1938. V. 50; 52

LINNEAN SOCIETY
Transactions. London: 1791-94. V. 48

LINNEAN SOCIETY OF LONDON
Catalogue of the Printed Books and Pamphlets in the Library. London: 1925. V. 52

LINNEAN SOCIETY OF NEW SOUTH WALES
Proceedings. Sydney: 1877-1952. V. 47

LINNEHAN, JOHN
The Driving Clubs of Greater Boston. Boston: 1914. V. 50

LINNELL, OLIVE
Autumn songs with Music from "Flower Fairies of the Autumn". London: 1925. V. 53
Spring Spongs with Music. London: 1925. V. 50

LINNERHJELM, JONAS CARL
Bref under Esor (-nya resor, -Senare Resor) i Sverige. Stockholm: 1816. V. 52

LINNEY, E. J.
A History of the Game of Bowls. London: 1933. V. 48

LINSLEY, D. C.
Morgan Horses. New York: 1857. V. 53

LINSLEY, JOHN S.
Jersey Cattle in America. New York: 1885. V. 52

LINSSEN, E. F.
Beetles of the British Isles. 1959. V. 54
Beetles of the British Isles. London: 1959. V. 51; 54

LINTON, ELIZA LYNN
The Lake Country. London: 1864. V. 51; 52
The One Too Many. London: 1894. V. 50
Realities. London: 1851. V. 51
The True History of Joshua Davidson. London: 1874. V. 53
Witch Stories. London: 1861. V. 50; 53; 54

LINTON, WILLIAM
The Scenery of Greece and its Islands. V. 47; 48

LINTON, WILLIAM JAMES
The Ferns of the English Lake Country... Windermere: 1865. V. 52
The House That Tweed Built. Cambridge: 1871. V. 52
The Masters of Wood Engraving. London: 1889. V. 48
Poems and Translations. London: 1889. V. 52
Poetry of America. London: 1887. V. 48

LINWOOD, MISS
Gallery of Pictures in Needlework, Leicester Square. London: 1810. V. 50

LION & WERTHEIMER
Manufacturer's Catalogue. New York: 1904. V. 49

THE LION and the Ox: an Old Arabian Tale. New York: 1932. V. 47

LIONARDI, ALESSANDRO
Dialogi...Della Inventione Poetica. Venetia: 1554. V. 50; 53

LION-GOLDSCHMIDT, DAISY
Chinese Art. Bronze, Jade, Sculpture, Ceramics. New York: 1960. V. 48

LION GOLDSCHMIDT, DAISY
Chinese Art: Bronze, Jade, Sculpture, Ceramics. New York: 1961. V. 54

LION-GOLDSCHMIDT, DAISY
Chinese Art: Bronzes, Jade, Sculpture, Ceramics. New York: 1966. V. 50

LIONNI, LEO
Frederick's Fables. New York: 1985. V. 49

THE LION'S Tail and Eyes. Madison: 1962. V. 49

LIPMAN, JEAN
Calder's Universe. New York: 1976. V. 47; 48; 49; 50; 52; 53

LI PO
Poems. Lexington: 1983. V. 54

LIPPARD, LUCY R.
Ad Reinhardt. New York: 1981. V. 47; 48; 49; 50; 52
The Graphic Work of Philip Evergood: Selected Drawings and Complete Prints. New York: 1966. V. 47

LIPPE, ADOLPHUS
Text Book of Materia Medica. Philadelphia: 1866. V. 54

LIPPINCOTT, BENJAMIN E.
From Fiji Through the Philippines with the Thirteenth Air Force. San Angelo: 1948. V. 49

LIPPINCOTT, J. GORDON
Design for Business. Chicago: 1947. V. 51

LIPPINCOTT, SARAH JANE
New Life in New Lands: Notes of Travel by Grace Greenwood. New York: 1873. V. 48

LIPPMAN, FRIEDERICH
Drawings by Sandro Botticelli for Dante's Divina Commedia. London: 1896. V. 51

LIPSCHITZ, JACQUES
Twelve Bronzes. New York: 1943. V. 48

LIPSCOMB, GEORGE
The History and Antiquities of the County of Buckingham. London: 1847. V. 48

LIPSCOMB, HARRY CARTER
History of Staindrop Church. London: 1852. V. 47
History of Staindrop Church... London: 1888. V. 53

LIPSCOMB, KEN
Duke Casanova. New York: 1958. V. 53

LIPSCOMB, WILLIAM
Poems. Oxford: 1784. V. 54

LIPSIUS, JUSTUS
A Discourse of Constancy, in two Books. London: 1670. V. 47

LISBON, ACADEMIA REAL DAS SCIENCIAS
Memorias de Litteratura Portugueza, Publicadas Pela... Lisbon: 1792-1814. V. 48

LISCOMB, HARRY F.
The Prince of Washington Square. New York: 1925. V. 52

LISIANSKY, UREY
A Voyage Round the World, in the Years 1803, 04, 05 and 06, Performed by Order of His Imperial Majesty Alexander the First, Emperor of Russia, in the Ship Neva. London: 1814. V. 47; 50
A Voyage Round the World, in the Years 1803, 4, 5, & 6; Performed, by Order of His Imperial Majesty Alexander the First, Emperor of Russia, in the Ship Neva. Amsterdam & New York: 1968. V. 47; 49; 51

THE LISLE Letters 1533-1540. Chicago: 1981. V. 52

L'ISLE-ADAM, VILLIERS DE
Olympe and Henriette. Sherman Oaks: 1992. V. 47

LISNEY, ARTHUR A.
A Bibliography of British Lepidoptera 1608-1799. London: 1960. V. 48; 50; 51; 53

LISSIM, SIMON
An Artist's Interpretation of Nature. New York: 1958. V. 50

LISSITZKY, EL
The Isms of Art. Erlenbach-Zurich: 1925. V. 47
El Lissitzusky: Life, Letters, Texts. London: 1980. V. 47

A LIST of Books on Travels and Voyages at the Toyo Bunko. Tokyo: 1963-64. V. 48

LIST of Etonians Who Fought in the Great War 1914-1919. London: 1921. V. 47

LIST of Field Officers, Regiments and Battalions in the Confederate States Army, 1861-1865. Washington: 1891. V. 49

A LIST of Officers Claiming to the Sixty Thousand Pounds, &c. Granted by His Sacred Majesty for the Relief of His Truly-Loyal and Indigent Party... London: 1663. V. 48

A LIST of the Country Banks of England and Wales, Private and Proprietary... London: 1838. V. 50

A LIST of the Names of the Long Parliament, Anno 1640...As Also of the Three Ensuing Parliaments...1653, 1654, 1656 (And of the Late Parliament, Dissolved...1659). London: 1659. V. 50

A LIST of Various Editions of the Bible, and the Parts Thereof, in English from the Year 1526 to 1776. From a Manuscript (No. 1140) in the Archiepiscopal Library at Lambeth, Much Enlarged and Improved. 1777. V. 53

LISTER, A.
Monograph of the Mycetozoa. London: 1925. V. 52; 54

LISTER Centenary Exhibition at the Wellcome Historical Medical Museum. Handbook. London: 1927. V. 51

LISTER, JOSEPH
The Collected Papers... London: 1909. V. 49
The Collected Papers. Oxford: 1909. V. 53
The Collected Papers. Birmingham: 1979. V. 50; 51; 54

LISTER, M.
Historia sive Synopsis Methodica Conchyliorum. Oxford: 1823. V. 53

LISTER, MARTIN
A Journey to Paris in the Year 1698. London: 1699. V. 48; 50; 51
Novae ac Curiosae Exercitationes & Descriptiones Thermarum ac Fontium Medicatorum Angliae... London: 1686. V. 52

LISTER, R. P.
Allotments. Andoversford: 1985. V. 51
Allotments. London: 1985. V. 53

LISTER, RAYMOND
Catalogue Raisonne of the Works of Samuel Palmer. 1988. V. 50; 54
Old Maps and Globes. London: 1797. V. 54
Samuel Palmer and His Etchings. London: 1969. V. 54

LISTER, THOMAS
The Rustic Wreath. Leeds: 1834. V. 54

LISTER, THOMAS HENRY
Arlington: a Novel. London: 1832. V. 47; 54
Granby. London: 1826. V. 47; 53

LISTON, ROBERT
Elements of Surgery. London: 1840. V. 47; 49
Elements of Surgery. Philadelphia: 1846. V. 52

LITCHFIELD, F.
Pottery and Porcelain. London: 1925. V. 47

LITCHFIELD, H. E.
Emma Darwin: Wife of Charles Darwin. Cambridge: 1904. V. 48

THE LITERARY Emporium, a Compendium of Religious, Literary and Philosophical Knowledge. New York: 1845. V. 51

LITERARY Ideals in Ireland. 1899. V. 48

LITHGOW, WILLIAM
The Totall Discourse, of the Rare Adventures, and Painefull Peregrinations of Long Nineteene Yeares Travailes from Scotland, to the Most Famous Kingdomes in Europe, Asia and Africa... London: 1640. V. 52; 53; 54

LITHO-MEDIA. A Demonstration of the Selling Power of Lithography. New York: 1939. V. 51

LITT, W.
Wrestliana; or an Historical Account of Ancient and Modern Wrestling. Whiteheaven: 1823. V. 54

LITTAUER, V. S.
Jumping the Horse. New York: 1931. V. 48

LITTELL, JOHN
Family Records: or Genealogies of the First Settlers of Passaic Valley... Feltville: 1852. V. 47; 51

LITTELL, WILLIAM
Cases Selected from the Decisions of the Court of Appeals of Kentucky, not Heretofore reported. Frankfurt: 1824. V. 51

LITTLE Ann and her Mamma. London. V. 52

LITTLE, ARCHIBALD, MRS.
Round About My Peking Garden. London: 1905. V. 50; 51

LITTLE Bo-Peep. Philadelphia: 1850. V. 52

LITTLE, BROWN & CO., BOSTON.
A Catalogue of Books, Ancient and Modern, Comprising Useful and Valuable Works in Every Class of Literature. Boston: 1857. V. 53

THE LITTLE Chimney-Sweep. Dublin: 1831. V. 52

LITTLE Dot and Her Friends and other Stories. London. V. 48

THE LITTLE Dutch Book. New York: 1909. V. 54

LITTLE Fables for Little Folks. London: 1870. V. 52

THE LITTLE Folks First Steps on the Ladder of Knowledge. New York: 1850's,. V. 50

LITTLE Folks in Tabbyland. London: 1910. V. 49; 50

LITTLE Folks Spice For All Who Are Nice. London: 1893. V. 49

THE LITTLE Frog's Lecture and Other Stories. New York: 1880-90. V. 52

LITTLE, G.
The Angler's Complete Guide and Companion. London: 1850. V. 53
The Angler's Complete Guide and Companion. London: 1882. V. 53

A LITTLE Garland of Christmas Verse. Portland: 1905. V. 48

LITTLE, GEORGE
A History of Lumsden's Battery, C.S.A. Tuskaloosa: 1905. V. 48; 49

THE LITTLE Gingerbread Man. London: 1880. V. 48

LITTLE Hydrogen, or, the Devil on Two Sticks in London. London: 1819. V. 51; 52

LITTLE Innocents - Childhood Reminiscences. London: 1932. V. 50

LITTLE Jack of All Trades; or Mechanical Arts Described... London: 1823. V. 48; 49; 52

LITTLE Jack's Primer. London: 1840. V. 47

LITTLE, JAMES A.
What I Saw on the Old Santa Fe Trail. Plainfield: 1904. V. 47; 49

LITTLE, JAMES STANLEY
My Royal Father: a Story for Women. London: 1886. V. 54

LITTLE, JANET
The Poetical Works of Janet Little, the Scotch Milkmaid. 1792. V. 47

THE LITTLE Learner's Toybook. London: 1880. V. 48

THE LITTLE London Directory of 1677. London: 1863. V. 49; 52

THE LITTLE Man and the Little Maid. Boston: 1849. V. 49

LITTLE Man's Family. Phoenix: 1940. V. 52

LITTLE Mary's Picture Riddles. London: 1850. V. 49

LITTLE Nancy, or, the Punishment of Greediness. A Moral Tale. Philadelphia: 1824. V. 49

LITTLE Nell, the Fisherman's Daughter. London: 1848. V. 51

LITTLE, NINA FLETCHER
The Abby Aldrich Rockefeller Folk Art Collection. London: 1957. V. 50; 54

LITTLE Orphan Annie: Bucking the World. New York: 1929. V. 47

LITTLE Red Cloak. Philadelphia: 1866. V. 49

LITTLE Red Riding Hood. 1840. V. 49; 51
LITTLE Red Riding Hood. London: 1900. V. 53

THE LITTLE Showman's Series No. 2: Spring. New York: 1884. V. 48

LITTLE Songs of Long Ago. London. V. 52

LITTLE Stories About Mark Twain. New York: 1911. V. 53; 54

LITTLE Tales, in Verse, for Little Folks. London: 1856. V. 47

LITTLE, THOMAS
The Poetical Works. London: 1814. V. 54

LITTLE, WILLIAM
The Easy Instructor; or, a New Method of Teaching Sacred Harmony. Utica: 1818. V. 48

LITTLE, WILLIAM JOHN KNOX
The Child of Stafferton. London: 1888. V. 54

THE LITTLE Woman and the Pedlar. London: 1830-35. V. 51

LITTLEHALES, L.
Pablo Caslas. New York: 1929. V. 49

LITTLEJOHN, DAVID
Dr. Johnson and Noah Webster: Two Men and Their Dictionaries... San Francisco: 1971. V. 49; 50

LITTLEJOHN, F. J.
Legends of Michigan and the Old North West... Allegan: 1875. V. 50

LITTLETON, ADAM
A Latin Dictionary. London: 1684. V. 47
Latin Dictionary in Four Parts. London: 1735. V. 48; 50
Linguae Latinae Liber Dictionarius Quadri-Partibus. London: 1678. V. 48; 49; 50; 51; 53
Linguae Romanae Dictionarium Luculentum Novum. Cambridge: 1693. V. 54

LITTLETON, EDWARD
A Project of a Descent Upon France. London: 1691. V. 53

LITTLETON, THOMAS
Littleton's Tenures in England, Lately Perused and Amended. London: 1612. V. 52
Les Tenures du Monsieur Littleton. London: 1581. V. 47
Les Tenures du Monsieur Littleton... Londini: 1604. V. 48
Tenures in Englishe. London: 1576. V. 54

LITTLEWOOD, LETTY
Our Nursery Rhyme Book. London: 1912. V. 54

LITTON, GASTON
History of Oklahoma at the Golden Anniversary of Statehood. New York: 1957. V. 49; 54

LITURGIA Britannica. London: 1845. V. 48

THE LITURGY of the Church of England Adorned with Historical Cuts. London: 1773. V. 47

THE LIVE Doll or Ellen's New Year's Gift. London. V. 48

LIVEING, EDWARD
On Megrim, Sick-Headache, and Some Allied Disorders; a Contribution to the Pathology of Nerve-Storms. London: 1873. V. 47; 53

LE LIVER des Assises & Plees del Corone, Moues & Dependauntz Deuaunt les Iustices, Sibien en Iour Circuitz Come Aylours, en Temps le Roy Edwarde le Tierce (etc.). Londini: 1580. V. 47

LIVERMORE, ABIEL ABBOT
The War with Mexico Reviewed. Boston: 1850. V. 48

LIVERMORE, DANIEL PARKER
Woman Suffrage Defended by Irrefutable Arguments, and All Objections to Woman's Enfranchisement Carefully Examined and Completely Answered. Boston: 1885. V. 51

LIVERMORE, GEORGE
The Souldier's Pocket Bible. Cambridge: 1861. V. 47

LIVERMORE, MARY A.
My Story of the War: a Woman's Narrative of Four Years Personal Experience as a Nurse in the Union Army... Hartford: 1888. V. 51
My Story of the War: a Woman's Narrative of Four Years Personal Experience as a Nurse in the Union Army... Hartford: 1890. V. 50; 52
What Shall We Do With Our Daughters?. New York: 1883. V. 48

LIVERPOOL, CHARLES JENKINSON, 1ST EARL OF
Representation of the Lords of the Committee of Council, Appointed for the Consideration of all Matters Relating to Trade and Foreign Plantations, Upon the Present State of the Laws for Regulating the Importation and Exportation of Corn. London: 1800. V. 53
A Treatise on the Coins of the Realm: in a Letter to the King. Oxford: 1805. V. 50

LIVERSIDGE, A.
The Minerals of New South Wales. London: 1888. V. 47; 49; 52

THE LIVERY-MAN; or, Plain Thoughts on Publick Affairs. London: 1740. V. 53

THE LIVES of Arthur Lord Balmerino, William Earl of Kilmarnock, George Earl of Croemrtie, Jenny Cameron and Simon Lord Lovat. London: 1746. V. 50

LIVES of Distinguished Shoemakers. Portland: 1849. V. 52

THE LIVES of Eminent and Remarkable Characters, Born or Long Resident in the Counties of Essex, Suffolk and Norfolk. London: 1820. V. 54
THE LIVES of Eminent and Remarkable Characters, Born or Long Resident in the Counties of Essex, Suffolk and Norfolk. London: 1830. V. 51

THE LIVES of the Ancient Philosophers, Containing an Account of Their Several Sects, Doctrines, Actions and Remarkable Sayings... London: 1702. V. 52

LIVES of the Most Eminent French Writers. Philadelphia: 1840. V. 50

LIVES Of The Most Eminent Literary and Scientific Men of Italy, Spain and Portugal. (with), Lives of the Most Eminent Literary and Scientific Men of France. London: 1835-38. V. 48

LIVES of the Most Remarkable Criminals Who Have Been Condemned and Executed for Murder, Highway Robberies, Housebreaking, Street Robberies, Coining, or Other Offences, from the Year 1720 to the Year 1735. London: 1873. V. 52

LIVESAY, DOROTHY
Signpost. Toronto: 1932. V. 50
The Unquiet Bed. Toronto: 1967. V. 47

LIVESEY, JAMES
Enchiridion Judicum; or Jehosophatas Charge to His Judges. London: 1657. V. 53

LIVING and Moving. London. V. 47; 49

LIVING English Poets MDCCCLXXXII. London: 1883. V. 51

A LIVING Theatre Setting Forth the Aims and Objects of the Movement and Showing Many Illustrations the City of Florence the Arena. Florence: 1913. V. 50

LIVINGS, HENRY
Eh?. London: 1965. V. 50

LIVINGSTON, EDWARD
Remarks on the Expediency of Abolishing the Punishment of Death. Philadelphia: 1831. V. 48

LIVINGSTON, FLORA V.
Bibliography of the Works of Rudyard Kipling. London: 1927. V. 50

LIVINGSTON, JOHN
The United States Law Magazine. New York: 1850-51. V. 49

LIVINGSTON, JOHN A.
Birds of the Eastern Forest. Toronto: 1968. V. 48
Birds of the Eastern Forest. Boston: 1968-70. V. 54
Birds of the Northern Forest (Canada). Toronto: 1966. V. 52

LIVINGSTON, JOHN H.
A Dissertation on the Marriage of a Man With His Sister in Law. New Brunswick: 1816. V. 52

LIVINGSTON, LIDA
Dali a Study of His Art-in-Jewels. Greenwich: 1959. V. 48; 52

LIVINGSTON, LUTHER S.
Franklin and His Press at Passy. New York: 1914. V. 54

LIVINGSTON, ROBERT R.
Essay on Sheep: Their Varieties-Account of the Merinoes...Reflections on the Best Method of Treating Them and Raising a Flock in the United States... Concord: 1813. V. 50
Examination of the Treaty of Amity, Commerce and Navigation, Between the United States and Great Britain in Several Numbers. New York: 1795. V. 52

LIVINGSTON, WILLIAM
A Funeral Elogium on the Reverend Mr. Aaron Burr, Late President of the College of New Jersey. New York: 1758. V. 47
The Papers of William Livingston. Trenton: 1979-87. V. 47; 49; 51

LIVINGSTONE, DAVID
Dr. Livingstone's Cambridge Lectures, Together with a Prefatory Letter by the Rev. Professor Sedgwick. Cambridge: 1858. V. 47; 48
The Last Journals of David Livingstone, in Central Africa. London: 1874. V. 47; 49; 52
The Last Journals of David Livingstone, in Central Africa... Hartford: 1875. V. 47; 48
The Last Journals of David Livingstone, in Central Africa... London: 1880. V. 49
The Life and Explorations of David Livingstone... London: 1880. V. 52
Livingstone's Travels and Researches in South Africa... Philadelphia: 1860. V. 52
Missionary Travels and Researches in South Africa... London: 1857. V. 47; 49; 51; 52; 53; 54
Missionary Travels and Researches in South Africa... New York: 1858. V. 50; 51; 52; 54
Narrative of an Expedition to the Zambesi... London: 1865. V. 47; 52; 54
Narrative of an Expedition to the Zambesi... New York: 1866. V. 48; 54

LIVRE des Livres. 1993. V. 54

LE LIVRE du Faucon des Dames. 1860. V. 47

LIVY
Histoire Romaine... 1810-12. V. 47
Historiae Romanae Decades. Milan: 1495. V. 48; 52
Historiarum Ab Urbe Condita, Libri Qui Extant XXX. Cum Universae Historiae Epitomis... Venice: 1566. V. 52
Historiarum Ab Urbe Condita Libri Qui Supersunt. Oxford: 1708. V. 52
Historiarum Ab Urbe Condita Libri Qvi Extant XXXV, cum Universae Epitomus. Venetiis: 1592. V. 47
Historiarum Quod Extat, Cum Perpetuis Gronovii et Variorum Notis. Amstelodami: 1665-64. V. 50
The History of Early Rome. Verona: 1970. V. 49; 52; 53; 54
The History of Rome. London: 1952-67. V. 48
The Roman History. London: 1686. V. 47; 53
The Romane Historie... London: 1600. V. 48; 49; 50
The Romane Historie... London: 1700. V. 51

LIVY continued
T. Livii Patavini, Historicorum Omnium Romanorum. Frankfurt: 1588. V. 53

LIZARS, K. M.
The Valley of the Humber, 1615-1913. Toronto: 1913. V. 50; 54

LIZARS, ROBINA
In the Days of the Canada Company 1825-1850. Toronto: 1896. V. 50; 51

LIZZY'S Poems and Pictures for Her Young Friends. London: 1857. V. 51

LLANOS, GUTIERREZ VALENTIN MARIA
Don Esteban: or, Memoirs of a Spaniard. London: 1825. V. 50; 51

LLEWELLYN, MARTIN
Men Miracles. Oxford: 1646. V. 48

LLEWELLYN, RICHARD
How Green Was My Valley. London: 1939. V. 47; 50; 51; 52
None But the Lonely Heart. London: 1943. V. 50
None But the Lonely Heart. New York: 1943. V. 54

LLLOYD, LLEWELLYN
Scandinavian Adventures, During a Residence of Upwards of Twenty Years. London: 1854. V. 48

LLLOYD-GEORGE, DAVID LLOYD GEORGE, 1ST EARL OF
War Memoirs 1914-1918. Boston: 1933-37. V. 48

LLOYD, ALBERT B.
Uganda to Khartoum. Life and Adventure on the Upper Nile. London: 1907. V. 47; 52
Uganda to Khartoum. Life and Adventure on the Upper Nile. London: 1911. V. 53

LLOYD, BARTHOLOMEW
An Elementary Treatise of Mechanical Philosophy, Written for the Use of the Undergraduate Students of the University of Dublin. Dublin: 1835. V. 50

LLOYD, CHARLES
Poems on Various Subjects. Carlisle: 1795. V. 47

LLOYD, CURTIS GATES
The Geastrae, The Tylostomeae, The Nidulariaceae, Synopsis of the Known Phalloids, Synopsis of the Genus Cladoderris... Cincinnati: 1902-19. V. 49; 52
Mycological Writings of C. G. Lloyd. Cincinnati: 1894-1925. V. 49

LLOYD, DAVID
Economy of Agriculture: Being a Series of Compendious Essays on Different Branches of Farming. Germantown: 1832. V. 47
The Legend of Captain Jones, Relating His Adventure to Sea... (with) The Legend of Captain Jones Continued. London: 1671/70. V. 48
State-worthies. Or, The Statesman and Favourites of England... London: 1670. V. 47
State-worthies; or, the Statesmen and Favourites of England... London: 1766. V. 49; 52
The States-Men and Favourites of England Since The Reformation... London: 1665. V. 48

LLOYD, EVAN
The Curate. London: 1766. V. 48
A Plain System of Geography. Edinburgh: 1797. V. 52

LLOYD, FRANCIS
Hampson Court; or, the Prophecy Fulfilled. London: 1844. V. 54

LLOYD, FREDERICK
Life of Viscount Nelson, Also of Sir R. Abercrombie and Marquis Cornwallis... Ormskirk: 1806. V. 54
Special Report on Indians at San Carlos Agency. San Carlos: 1883. V. 48

LLOYD, HENRY DEMAREST
A Country Without Strikes. New York: 1900. V. 50
Labor Copartnership. London and New York: 1898. V. 50

LLOYD, HENRY HUMPHREY
Introduction a l'Histoire de la Guerre en Allemagne en MDCCLVI entre le Roi de Prusse, et l'Imperatrice-Reine Avec ses Allies. Londres: 1784. V. 50

LLOYD, HUMPHREY
Elementary Treatise on the Wave-Theory of Light. London: 1873. V. 48; 52; 54

LLOYD, J. U.
The Chemistry of Medicines... Cincinnati: 1888. V. 49
Drugs and Medicines of North America... Cincinnati: 1884-86. V. 54
Elixirs: Their History, Formulae and Methods of Preparation... Cincinnati: 1883. V. 49; 54

LLOYD, JAMES T.
Lloyd's Steamboat Directory, and Disasters on the Western Waters. Cincinnati: 1856. V. 47

LLOYD, JEREMY
Captain Beaky. London: 1976. V. 54

LLOYD, JOHN
Thesaurus Ecclesiasticus... London: 1796. V. 47

LLOYD, JOHN URI
Etidorhpa or the End of the earth. Cincinnati: 1895. V. 52

LLOYD, LLEWELLYN
Field Sports of the North of Europe... London: 1830. V. 47
Field Sports of the North of Europe. London: 1831. V. 48
The Game Birds and Wild Fowl of Sweden and Norway; with an Account of the Seals and Salt Water Fishes of Those Countries. London: 1867. V. 47; 48; 49; 54

LLOYD, LODOWICK
A Brief Conference of Divers Lawes: Diuided into Certaine Regiments. London: 1602. V. 50; 53

LLOYD, NATHANIEL
A History of English Brickwork. Montgomery: 1934. V. 51; 54
A History of the English House from Primitive Times to the Victorian Period. London: 1931. V. 49
History of the English House From Primitive Times to the Victorian Period. London: 1949. V. 48
A History of the English House from Primitive Times to the Victorian Period. London: 1951. V. 51

LLOYD, ROBERT
The Actor. London: 1760. V. 47; 49
Poems. London: 1762. V. 47; 51
The Poetical Works of... London: 1774. V. 47; 54
Shakespeare: an Epistle (in verse) To Mr. Garrick; with the Ode to Genius. London: 1760. V. 47

LLOYD, SETON
Ancient Architecture: Mesopotamia, Egypt, Crete, Greece. New York: 1974. V. 52

LLOYD, WILLIAM
A Chronological Account of the Life of Pythagoras, and Of Other Famous men His contemporaries. London: 1699. V. 49
An Historical Account of Church-Government As It Was in Great Britain and Ireland... London: 1684. V. 49; 50; 51; 54
Narrative of a Journey from Caunpoor to the Boorendo Pass, in the Himalaya Mountains... London: 1846. V. 51
The Pretences of the French Invasion Examined. London: 1692. V. 47

LLOYD, WILLIAM WATKISS
Elijah Fenton: His Poetry and Friends. Hanley: 1894. V. 54
Elijah Fenton: His Poetry and Friends. London: 1894. V. 50

LLOYD, WILLIAM WHITELOCK
Union Jottings. London: 1894?. V. 50

LLOYD-GEORGE, DAVID LLOYD GEORGE, 1ST EARL OF
Our Part in the Great War. 1919. V. 54

LLOYDS, F.
Practical Guide to Scene Painting and Painting on Distemper. London: 1860. V. 53

LLOYD'S OF LONDON
Report of the Special Committee, Appointed on the 18th of May, 1824 by the Subscribers to Lloyd's for the Purpose of Opposing an Application to Parliament, to Repeal the Restrictions Contained in the Act of 6th Geo. I. Cap. 18, Presented at a General... London: 1824. V. 50

LLOYDS' Register of Yachts 1888. 1888. V. 51

LLOYD'S Sketches of Indian Life. London: 1890. V. 49

LLWYD, RICHARD
The Poetical Works of Richard Llwyd, the Bard of Snowdon. London: 1837. V. 54

LOANS by Private Individuals to Foreign States Entitled to Government Protection by the Fundamental Laws, As a Branch of Trade... London: 1842. V. 53

LOBB, THEOPHILUS
A Practical Treatise of Painful Distempers, With Some Effectual Methods of Curing Them, Exemplified in a Great Variety of Suitable Histories. London: 1739. V. 48; 52
A Treatise of the Small Pox. London: 1731. V. 48
A Treatise on Dissolvents of the Stone; and on Curing the Stone and Gout by Ailment. London: 1739. V. 50

LOBEIRA, VASCO
Amadis of Gaul. London: 1803. V. 50

LOBEL, ARNOLD
Days With Frog and Toad. New York: 1979. V. 49
On Market Street. New York: 1981. V. 49
A Treeful of Pigs. New York: 1979. V. 49

LOBENSTINE, WILLIAM C.
Extracts from the Diary of William C. Lobenstine December 31, 1851-1858. 1920. V. 47

LOBO, JERONYMO
A Short Relation of the River Nile of Its Overflowing the Campagnia of Aegypt... London: 1669. V. 50
A Short Relation of the River Nile...of its Overflowing the Campagnia of Aegypt... London: 1673. V. 48; 51
A Voyage to Abbyssinia. London: 1735. V. 48; 51; 53; 54
A Voyage to Abyssinia. London: 1789. V. 48; 53

LOBSTEIN, J. F. DANIEL
A Treatise on the Structure, Functions and Diseases of the Human Sympathetic Nerve. Philadelphia: 1831. V. 54
A Treatise Upon the Semeiology of the Eye, for the Use of Physicians. New York: 1830. V. 48; 51; 52

LOCH, C. S.
Charity and Social Life. London: 1910. V. 49

LOCH, HENRY BROUGHAM
Personal Narrative of Occurrences During Lord Elgin's Second Embasssy to China 1860. London: 1869. V. 50

LOCHEE, LEWIS
Elements of Field Fortification... London: 1783. V. 53
An Essay on Castrametation. London: 1778. V. 53; 54

LOCHER, G. W.
The Serpent in Kwakiutl Religion. A Study in Primitive Culture. Leiden: 1932. V. 51

LOCHER, J. L.
Escher: with a Complete Catalogue of Graphic Works... London: 1981. V. 52
Mark Boyle's Journey to the Surface of the Earth. Stuttgart/London: 1978. V. 49

LOCHNER, J. H.
Rariora Musei Besleriani. Nuremberg: 1716. V. 54

LOCK, A. G.
A Practical Treatise on the Manufacture of Sulphuric Acid. London: 1879. V. 52

LOCK, C. G. WARNFORD
Spon's Encyclopaedia of Industrial Arts, Manufactures... London: 1879-82. V. 49
Spon's Encyclopaedia of Industrial Arts, Manufactures... London: 1882. V. 49; 50

LOCK, MATTHIAS
A Collection of Ornamental Designs, Applicable to Furniture, Frames & the Decoration of Rooms in the Style of Louis XIV. London: 1840. V. 53

LOCKE, ALAIN
Negro Art: Past and Present. Washington: 1936. V. 54
The New Negro. New York: 1925. V. 51; 53; 54
Plays of Negro Life. New York: 1927. V. 50

LOCKE, DAVID ROSS
Hannah Jane. Boston: 1882. V. 53
Swinging Round the Cirkle. Boston: 1867. V. 50

LOCKE, E. W.
Three Years in Camp and Hospital. Boston: 1870. V. 49; 50; 52

LOCKE, EDWIN
Tuberculosis in Massachusetts. Boston: 1908. V. 50; 51

LOCKE, JOHN
An Abridgement of Mr. Locke's Essay Concerning Humane Understanding. London: 1700. V. 48; 53; 54
An Abridgment of Mr. Locke's Essay Concerning Human Understanding. London: 1737. V. 48
An Abridgment of Mr. Locke's Essay Concerning Human Understanding. Boston: 1794. V. 50
The Collected Works. London: 1801. V. 50
A Collection of Several Pieces Never Before Printed, or Not Exant in His Works. London: 1720. V. 48; 50
A Common-Place Book to the Holy Bible; or, the Scriptures Sufficiency Practically Demonstrated. London: 1697. V. 49; 54
An Essay Concerning Human Understanding. London: 1690. V. 48; 54
An Essay Concerning Human Understanding. London: 1695. V. 50
An Essay Concerning Human Understanding. London: 1700. V. 49; 50; 53
An Essay Concerning Human Understanding. London: 1721. V. 53
An Essay Concerning Human Understanding... London: 1726. V. 47
An Essay Concerning Human Understanding... London: 1795. V. 49; 53
An Essay Concerning Human Understanding... New York: 1818. V. 49
An Essay Concerning Human Understanding. London: 1819. V. 48
An Essay Concerning Human Understanding. London: 1824. V. 51
Letters Concerning Toleration. London: 1765. V. 48
Mr. Locke's Reply to the Right Reverend the Lord Bishop of Worcester's Answer to His Letter... London: 1697. V. 49
Philosophical Beauties. New York: 1828. V. 49
Philosophical Works. London: 1890. V. 48
Posthumous Works... London: 1706. V. 47
Some Familiar Letters Between Mr. Locke and Several of His Friends. London: 1708. V. 47
Some Thoughts Concerning Education. London: 1693. V. 53
Some Thoughts Concerning Education. London: 1699. V. 49; 50; 51; 52
Some Thoughts Concerning Education. London: 1705. V. 48
Some Thoughts Concerning Education... Dublin: 1738-38. V. 51
Some Thoughts Concerning Education. London: 1809. V. 49
Some Thoughts on the Conduct of the Understanding in the Search of Truth. 1741. V. 52
Two Treatises of Government: in the Former, the False Principles and Foundation of Sir Robert Filmer, and His Followers are Detailed and Overthrown. London: 1713. V. 52
The Works... London: 1714. V. 48; 50; 51; 54
The Works... London: 1727. V. 51; 53
Works. London: 1751. V. 53

LOCKER, EDWARD HAWKE
Memoirs of Celebrated Naval Commanders, Illustrated by Engravings from Original Pictures in the Naval Gallery of Greenwich Hospital. London: 1832. V. 54
Report on the State and Condition of the Roads and Mines, on the Estates of Greenwich Hospital, in the Counties of Cumberland, and Northumberland, with Suggestions for Their Improvement. London: 1823. V. 51

LOCKER-LAMPSON, FREDERICK
A Catalogue of the Printed Books, Manuscripts, Autograph Letters, Drawings and Pictures Collected by Frederick Locker-Lampson; A Catalogue of the Printed Books, Manuscripts, Autograph Letters, Etc. Collected Since the Printing of the First Catalogue... London: 1886-1900. V. 48
London Lyrics. London: 1857. V. 47
London Lyrics. London: 1868. V. 47; 51
London Lyrics. London: 1885. V. 51
London Lyrics. London: 1904. V. 52
Patchwork. Second Series.. Cleveland: 1927. V. 47
The Rowfant Library. (with) An Appendix... London: 1886-1900. V. 53
Rowfant Rhymes. Cleveland: 1895. V. 52
A Selection from the Works of Frederick Locker. London: 1865. V. 47

LOCKER-LAMPSON, GODFREY
An Appendix to the Rowfant Library. A Catalogue of the Printed Books, Manuscripts, Autograph Letters, Etc., Collected Since the Printing of the First Catalogue in 1886 by the Late Frederick Locker-Lampson. London: 1900. V. 48

LOCKETT, T. A.
Davenport China, Earthenware, Glass. London: 1989. V. 50

LOCKHART, GEORGE
Memoirs Concerning the Affairs of Scotland, From Queen Anne's Accession to the Throne, to the Commencement of the Union of the Two Kingdoms of Scotland and Engalnd, in May, 1707. London: 1714. V. 50; 51

LOCKHART, J.
Portraits of Nature. 1967. V. 49

LOCKHART, JOHN GIBSON
Ancient Spanish Ballads. London: 1841. V. 49
Ancient Spanish Ballads. London: 1842. V. 52
The History of Matthew Wald. Edinburgh: 1824. V. 52
Letter to the Right Hon. Lord Byron. London: 1821. V. 53; 54
The Life of Robert Burns. Liverpool: 1914. V. 53
Memoirs of the Life of Sir Walter Scott. Edinburgh: 1837-38. V. 50
Peter's Letters to His Kinsfolk. Edinburgh: 1819. V. 49; 50
Postscript to the Third Edition of Peter's Letters. Edinburgh: 1819. V. 54
Reginald Dalton. Edinburgh: 1823. V. 47
Reginald Dalton. London: 1823. V. 51; 53
Valerius. Edinburgh: 1821. V. 48; 49; 51

LOCKLEY, R. M.
Sea-Birds. London: 1954. V. 50; 52; 53

LOCKMAN, JOHN
Travels of the Jesuits, Into Various Parts of the World... London: 1743. V. 51
Travels of the Jesuits, Into Various Parts of the World... London: 1762. V. 47

LOCKRIDGE, RICHARD
Mr. and Mrs. North. New York: 1936. V. 47

THE LOCKS of the Oxford Canal: a Journey from Oxford to Coventry. Manor Farm, Andoversford: 1984. V. 51

LOCKSPEISER, E.
Debussy, His Life and Mind. London: 1965/66. V. 49

LOCKWOOD, ALICE G. B.
Gardens of Colony and State. New York: 1931. V. 49; 51
Gardens of Colony and State... New York: 1931-34. V. 51

LOCKWOOD, BELVA A.
Peace and the Outlook. Washington: 1899. V. 48

LOCKWOOD, CHARLES A.
Tragedy at Honda. Philadelphia: 1960. V. 54

LOCKWOOD, FRANK C.
The Apache Indians. New York: 1938. V. 49; 51
Arizona Characters. Los Angeles: 1928. V. 52; 53
The Frank Lockwood Sketch Book. London: 1898. V. 53
Pioneer Days in Arizona: from the Spanish Occupation to Statehood. New York: 1932. V. 48; 52; 53

LOCKWOOD, HENRY F.
The History and Antiquities of the Fortifications to the City of York. Doncaster: 1834. V. 53

LOCKWOOD, JAMES D.
Life and Adventures of a Drummer Boy or Seven Years a Soldier. Albany: 1893. V. 54
Life and Adventures of a Drummer boy or Seven Years a Soldier. New York: 1893. V. 49

LOCKWOOD, LUKE VINCENT
Colonial Furniture in America. New York: 1901. V. 51
Colonial Furniture in America. New York: 1913. V. 47; 48
Colonial Furniture in America. New York: 1926. V. 51

LOCKWOOD, M. S.
Art Embroidery. London: 1878. V. 51; 52

LOCKWOOD, MARGO
Bare Elegy. 1980. V. 54

LOCKWOOD, SARAH M.
Decoration - Past, Present and Future. New York: 19343. V. 49
New York. Not So Little and Not So Old. Garden City: 1926. V. 53

LOCKYER, JOSEPH NORMAN
The Chemistry of the Sun. London and New York: 1887. V. 50
The Meteoritic Hypothesis: a Statement of the Results of a Spectroscopic Inquiry Into the Origin of Cosmical Systems. London and New York: 1890. V. 50

LODDIGES, CONRAD
The Botanical Cabinet. London: 1817-24. V. 48

LODDIGES, CONRAD, & SONS
Catalogue of Plants, Which are Sold by Conrad Loddiges and Sons, Nurserymen, at Hackney, Near London. London: 1820. V. 47
Catalogue of Plants, Which are sold by Conrad Loddiges and Sons, Nurserymen, at Hackney, Near London. London: 1823. V. 47

LODER, ROBERT
The History of Framlingham in the County of Suffolk... Woodbridge: 1798. V. 47; 49

LODER-SYMONDS, F. C.
A History of the Old Berks Hunt from 1760 to 1904. London: 1905. V. 47

LODGE, DAVID
The British Museum is Falling Down. London: 1965. V. 47
Graham Greene. New York & London: 1966. V. 52
Paradise News. London: 1991. V. 54
The Picturegoers. London: 1960. V. 49; 53; 54

LODGE, EDMUND
The Peerage, Baronetage, Knightage & Companionage of the British Empire. London: 1905. V. 48
Portraits of Illustrious Personages of Great Britain... London: 1823-35. V. 53
Portraits of Illustrious Personages of Great Britain. London: 1824-34. V. 54
Portraits of Illustrious Personages of Great Britain. London: 1835. V. 47; 50; 53; 54
Portraits of Illustrious Personages of Great Britain. London: 1860. V. 48

LODGE, GEORGE EDWARD
George Edward Lodge: Unpublished Bird Paintings. London: 1982. V. 49
Memoirs of an Artist Naturalist. London. V. 48
Memoirs of an Artist Naturalist. London: 1946. V. 47; 48; 49; 50; 51; 52; 54
Unpublished Bird Paintings. London: 1983. V. 53

LODGE, JOHN
Introductory Sketches, Towards a Topographical History of the County of Hereford. Kingston: 1793. V. 50

LODGE Odes of the Independent Order UFFU Published by Authority, Under Dispensation 12347-001. And Odes of Dennis the Shoemaker. Olympia: 1868. V. 53

LODGE, R. B.
Bird Hunting through Wild Europe. London: 1908. V. 50; 51

LODOR, JOHN A.
In Memoriam. An Address Commemorative of Their Fraternal Dead of 1860; Delivered Before Halo Lodge, No. 5...December 27, 1860. Cahaba: 1861. V. 54
The Speculative Temple. An Address Delivered by Bro. John A. Lodor, of Cahaba, Before the Grand Lodge of the State of Alabama in the Masonic Hall, in the City of Montgomery, on Thursday Evening, Dec. 3, 1861. Montgomery: 1862. V. 54

LOEB, HANAU W.
Operative Surgery of the Nose, Throat and Ear for Laryngologists, Rhinologists, Otologists and Surgeons. St. Louis: 1914. V. 51

LOEB, JACQUES
Artificial Parthenogenesis and Fertilization. Chicago: 1913. V. 49; 54
Comparative Physiology of the Brain... New York: 1900. V. 51
Comparative Physiology of the Brain... London: 1901. V. 48
The Mechanistic Conception of Life: Biological Essays. Chicago: 1912. V. 49; 54
Regeneration from a Physico-Chemical Viewpoint. New York: 1924. V. 50
Studies in General Physiology. Chicago: 1905. V. 54

LOEB, THEOPHILUS
A Treatise of the Small Pox. London: 1731. V. 52

LOECHEL, WILLIAM
Medical Illustration: A Guide for the Doctor-Author and Exhibitor. Springfield: 1964. V. 49

LOEHR, MAX
Ancient Chinese Jades. From the Grenville L. Winthrop Collection in the Foog Art Museum, Harvard University. Cambridge: 1975. V. 53

LOEWY, RAYMOND
The Locomotive. London: 1937. V. 48
Never Leave Well Enough Alone. New York: 1951. V. 47

LOFFT, CAPEL
Eudosia; Or, a Poem on the Universe. London: 1781. V. 48
Laura: or an Anthology of Sonnets... and Elegiac Quatumorzains... London: 1814-13-14. V. 47; 48
Remarks on the Letter of the Rt. Hon. Edmund Burke, Concerning the Revolution in France, and On the Proceedings in Certain Societies in London, Relative to that Event. London: 1790. V. 51
Remarks on the Letter of the Rt. Hon. Edmund Burke, Concerning the Revolution in France, and on the Proceedings in Certain Societies in London, Relative to that Event. London: 1791. V. 48

LOFTIE, ARTHUR G.
The Rural Deanery of Gosforth, Diocese of Carlisle, Its Churches and Endowments. Kendal: 1889. V. 52

LOFTIE, W. J.
An Essay of Scarabs. London: 1884. V. 49
Kensington Picturesque & Historical. London: 1888. V. 50; 51; 52

LOFTING, HUGH
Doctor Dolittle's Garden. New York: 1927. V. 49
Doctor Doolittle and the Green Country. Philadelphia: 1950. V. 49
Doctor Doolittle in the Moon. New York: 1928. V. 52
Gub Gub's Book. An Encyclopedia of Food. London: 1932. V. 50
Noisy Nora. New York: 1929. V. 49
Porridge Poetry. New York: 1924. V. 49; 51; 54
Tommy, Tilly and Mrs. Tubbs. London: 1937. V. 51

LOFTUS, CHARLES
My Youth By Sea and Land From 1809 to 1816. London: 1876. V. 48

LOFTUS, WILLIAM R.
The Brewer: a Familiar Treatise on the Art of Brewing... London: 1856. V. 51; 52
The Brewer: a Familiar Treatise on the Art of Brewing. London: 1857. V. 48
The Maltster: a Compendious Treatise on the Art of Malting In All Its Branches. London: 1876. V. 53

LOG of the U.S. Gunboat Gloucester Commanded by Lt. Commander Richard Wainwright, and the Official Reports of the Principal events of Her Cruise During the Late War with Spain. Annapolis: 1899. V. 50

LOGAN, C. A.
Physics of the Infectious Diseases. Chicago: 1878. V. 51; 52

LOGAN, GEORGE
The Finishing Stroke; or, Mr. Ruddiman Self Condemned... Edinburgh: 1748. V. 48
A Treatise on Government; Shewing, That the Right of the Kings of Scotland to the Crown Was Not Strictly and Absolutely Hereditary. Edinburgh: 1746. V. 48

LOGAN, JAMES
The Clans of the Scottish Highlands. London: 1845-1847. V. 48
The Scottish Gael: Or, Celtic Manners, As Preserved Among the Highlanders... Inverness: 1876. V. 49

LOGAN, JOHN
The Bridge of Change. New York: 1978. V. 52
The House that Jack Built. Omaha: 1974. V. 51
Poems. London: 1781. V. 49; 51; 52

LOGAN, JOHN A.
The Volunteer Soldier of America. 1887. V. 54

LOGAN, JOSHUA
The Wisteria Trees. New York: 1950. V. 54

LOGAN, OLIVE
Apropos of Women and Theatres. New York: 1869. V. 50; 51; 52
The Mimic World, and Public Exhibitions. Their History, Their Morals and Effects. Philadelphia: 1871. V. 48

LOGAN, RAYFORD WHITTINGHAM
Two Bronze Titans: Frederick Douglass and William Edwarad Brughardt Du Bois. Washington: 1972. V. 54
What the Negro Wants. Chapel Hill: 1944. V. 54

LOGAN, W. E.
Notes on the Gold of Eastern Canada: Being a Reprint of Portions of Various Reports of the Geological Survey of Canada from 1848 to 1863. Montreal: 1864. V. 49
Remarks on the Mining Region of Lake Superior; and Report on Mining Locations Claimed on the Canadian Shores of the Lake... Montreal: 1847. V. 49

LOGAN, WALTER S.
Arizona and Some of Her Friends. The Toasts and Responses at a Complimentary Dinner Given by Walter S. Logan at the Marine Field Club, N.Y. Tuesday, July 28th, 1891 to Hon. John N. Irwin, Governor of Arizona and Herbert H. Logan of Phoenix, Arizona. 1891. V. 49

LOGAN, WILLIAM
The Deplorable Condition of Woman... 1840. V. 50

LOGAN, WILLIAM BARNETT
Dress of the Day - War and After Reminiscences of the British navy. London: 1930. V. 47

LOGGAN, DAVID
Cantabrigia Illustrata. Cambridge: 1905. V. 48; 51
Oxonia Illustrata, Sive Omnium Celeberrimae Istius Universitatis Collegiorum, Aularum, Bibliothecae Bodleianae, Scholarum Publicarum... Oxford: 1675. V. 53

LOGIER, JOHANN BERNHARD
A System of the Science of Music and Practical Composition. London: 1827. V. 48

LOGUE, CHRISTOPHER
The Girls. London: 1969. V. 52
The Man Who Told His Love. Northwood: 1958. V. 47
Pax, from Book XIX of the Iliad. London: 1967. V. 51
Red Bird... 1979. V. 47
Red Bird. London: 1979. V. 52
Wand and Quadrant. Paris: 1953. V. 52

LOGUEN, J. W.
The Rev. J. W. Loguen as a Slave and as a Freeman: a Narrative of Real Life. Syracuse: 1859. V. 53

LOHF, KENNETH A.
Season: Seven Poems. 1981. V. 52
Seasons: Seven Poems. Newark: 1981. V. 54

LOHNIS, F.
Studies Upon the Life Cycles of the Bacteria. Washington: 1921. V. 50; 51; 52; 54

LOLLIUS, ANTONIUS
Oratio Circumcisionis Dominicae Coram Innocentis VIII Habita. Rome: 1485. V. 52

LOLME, JEAN LOUIS DE
The Constitution of England, or an Account of the English Government... London: 1775. V. 48

LOMAS, H. M.
Staghunting Photographs. Richmond: 1901. V. 47

LOMAS, JOHN A.
Negro Folk songs as Sung By Lead Belly. New York: 1936. V. 50

LOMAS, THOMAS J.
Recollections of a Busy Life. Cresco: 1923. V. 47

LOMAX, JAMES
Diary of Otter Hunting. 1892. V. 49
Diary of Otter Hunting. Liverpool: 1892. V. 47
Diary of Otter Hunting. London: 1892. V. 47
Otter Hunting Diary... Blackburn: 1910. V. 48; 53
Otter Hunting Diary... London: 1910. V. 47; 49

LOMAX, JOHN A.
American Ballads and Folk Songs. New York: 1934. V. 48
Negro Folk Songs As Sung by Lead Belly. New York: 1936. V. 51; 53

LOMBARD, DANIEL
A Succinct History of Ancient and Modern Persecutions. London: 1747. V. 52

LOMMEL, A.
Masks, Their Meaning and Function. New York: 1972. V. 54

LONDESBOROUGH, ALBERT DENISON, 1ST BARON
Miscellanea Graphica: Representations of Ancient, Medieval and Renaissance Remains in the Possession of Lord Londesborough. London: 1856. V. 50
The Natural Son. London: 1835. V. 48

LONDINA Illustrata. Graphic and Historic Memorials of Monasteries, Churches, Chapels, Schools, Charitable Foundations, Palaces, Halls, Courts, Processions, Places of Early Amusement and Modern and Present Theatres in the Cities and Suburbs of London &... London: 1819-25. V. 50; 52

THE LONDON Almanack. London: 1779. V. 49

LONDON Almanack. London: 1823. V. 54

THE LONDON Almanack 1779. London. V. 48

LONDON Almanack...1774. London: 1773. V. 52

LONDON Almanack...1791. London: 1790. V. 51

LONDON Almanack...1794. London: 1793. V. 47; 51

LONDON Almanack...1858. London: 1857. V. 53

THE LONDON and Country Brewer, Containing the Whole Art of Brewing All Sorts of Malt-Liquors... London: 1758-59. V. 50

LONDON and Its Men of Affairs. London. V. 50

THE LONDON and Leith Smack and Steam Packet Guide... Leith: 1824. V. 54

THE LONDON Aphrodite. London: 1928-29. V. 49

LONDON, ARTHUR G.
Espagne... Paris: 1966. V. 49

LONDON CABINET MAKERS' UNION
The London Cabinet Makers' Union Book of Prices. (with) *The London Cabinet-Makers Book of Prices, for the Most Improved Extensible Dining Tables.* (with) *Designs of Ornaments for Cabinet Furniture with Prices.* London: 1824/21/21. V. 50

THE LONDON Carcanet. New York: 1831. V. 49

LONDON Catalogue of Books, Selected from the General Catalogue...and Including the Additions and Alterations to September MDCCXCI, Classed Under the Several Branches of Literature and Alphabetically Disposed Under Each Head... London: 1791/93. V. 50

LONDON, CHARMIAN
The Book of Jack London. New York: 1921. V. 50; 53
Jack London. London: 1921. V. 49
The Log of the Snark. New York: 1925. V. 50; 52
Our Hawaii. New York: 1917. V. 50; 53

LONDON. CHARTER
The Royal Charter of Confirmation Granted by King Charles II to the City of London. London: 1680. V. 52

LONDON. COMMON COUNCIL
An Act of Common Council for Regulating the Election of Sheriffs, and for Repealing the Treasonable and Disloyal Acts and Proceedings of that Court in the Time of the Late Rebellion. London: 1683. V. 52
An Act of Common Councill of the City of London (Made in the 1st and 2nd Years of the Reign of Philip and Mary) for Retrenching of the Expences of the Lord Mayor & Sheriffs, &c. London: 1680. V. 52; 53
A Brief Account of What Pass'd at the Common Council Held in London, on Fryday 13, May 1681. London: 1681. V. 52

LONDON. DEPARTMENT OF OVERSEAS TRADE
Reports on the Present Position and Tendencies of the Industrial Arts as Indicated at the Internation Exhibition of Modern Decorative and Industrial Arts, Paris, 1925. London: 1927. V. 48

LONDON, GEORGE
The Retir'd Gardener. London: 1717. V. 53

THE LONDON Guide and Stranger's Safeguard Against the Cheats, Swindlers, and Pickpockets... London: 1818. V. 50

THE LONDON Guide Describing the Public and Private Buildings of London. London: 1782. V. 49; 50

LONDON Horse and Carriage Repository, and Turf Betting Rooms... London: 1828. V. 47

LONDON in 1838. New York: 1839. V. 50

LONDON, JACK
The Abysmal Brute. New York: 1913. V. 48; 49; 53
The Abysmal Brute. Toronto: 1913. V. 50; 53
the Acorn Planter - a California Forest Play - Planned to Be Sung... London: 1916. V. 47
Adventure. 1911. V. 53
Adventure. New York: 1911. V. 48; 53
The Apostate. Girard: 1906. V. 53
The Apostate. Chicago: 1906?. V. 53
Before Adam. 1907. V. 50; 52
Before Adam. London: 1907. V. 48
Before Adam. New York: 1907. V. 47; 48; 49; 51; 53; 54
Burning Daylight. New York. V. 50
Burning Daylight. New York: 1910. V. 47; 50
The Call of the Wild. London: 1903. V. 49
The Call of the Wild. New York: 1903. V. 48; 49; 51; 52
The Call of the Wild. Los Angeles: 1960. V. 48
Children of the Frost. New York: 1902. V. 53
The Cruise of the Dazzler. New York: 1902. V. 52; 54
The Cruise of the Dazzler. London: 1906. V. 50
The Cruise of the Snark. New York: 1911. V. 48; 49; 51; 52; 53
Daughter of the Snows. Philadelphia: 1902. V. 49; 50; 53
The Dream of Debs. Chicago: 1912. V. 49; 51
Dutch Courage and Other Stories. New York: 1922. V. 53
The Faith of Men. New York: 1904. V. 47; 48; 51; 53
The Game. London: 1905. V. 50; 53
The Game. New York: 1905. V. 47; 53; 54
The Game. Toronto: 1905. V. 53
The God of His Fathers... New York: 1901. V. 51; 53
The God of His Fathers. 1902. V. 50
Hearts of Three. New York: 1912. V. 53
Hearts of Three. New York: 1920. V. 53; 54
The House of Pride... 1912. V. 50
The House of Pride... New York: 1912. V. 53
The Iron Heel. Girard: 1908. V. 51
The Iron Heel. London: 1908. V. 48; 52; 53
The Iron Heel. New York: 1908. V. 48
Jack London: a Sketch of His Life and Work. New York: 1905. V. 53; 54
Jack London as Seen by Himself. New York: 1913. V. 51; 53
Jack London as Seen by Himself. San Francisco: 1913. V. 51
The Jacket. 1915. V. 48; 52; 53
Jerry of the Islands. New York: 1917. V. 47; 48; 53; 54
John Barleycorn. New York: 1913. V. 47; 49; 51; 52; 53; 54
John Barleycorn... London: 1914. V. 50
A Klondike Trilogy: Three Uncollected Stories. Santa Barbara: 1983. V. 48; 51; 54
The Little Lady of the Big House. New York: 1916. V. 48; 49; 51
London's Essays Of Revolt. New York: 1926. V. 48; 53
Love of Life... 1907. V. 50
Love of Life. New York: 1907. V. 48; 50; 51; 53
Love of Life... New York: 1911. V. 53
Love of Life. London: 1946. V. 48; 51
Martin Eden. New York: 1909. V. 53
Martin Eden. London: 1910. V. 50
Michael, Brother of Jerry. New York: 1917. V. 48; 50; 53
Moon-Face. New York: 1906. V. 48; 51; 53
The Mutiny of the Elsinore. New York: 1914. V. 53; 54
The Night-Born. New York: 1913. V. 51
An Old Life Finally Nailed. Minneapolis: 1916. V. 51
On the Makaloa Mat. New York: 1918. V. 47; 48
On the Makaloa Mat. New York: 1919. V. 53
The People of the Abyss. London: 1903. V. 53
The People of the Abyss. New York: 1903. V. 47; 51; 53; 54
The People of the Abyss. Toronto: 1903. V. 49
The Red One. New York: 1918. V. 53
The Red One. 1919. V. 48; 50; 52
Revolution. Chicago: 1909. V. 53; 54
Revolution. New York: 1910. V. 48; 53
The Road. New York: 1907. V. 51
The Scab. Chicago: 1905. V. 53
The Scarlet Plague. 1915. V. 48; 50; 52
The Scarlet Plague. London: 1915. V. 48
The Scarlet Plague. New York: 1915. V. 48; 51; 53; 54
Scorn of Women. London: 1906. V. 48; 51; 53
Scorn of Women. New York: 1906. V. 53
The Sea Sprite and the Shooting Star. 1932. V. 53
The Sea-Wolf. London: 1904. V. 53
The Sea-Wolf. New York: 1904. V. 47; 50

LONDON, JACK continued
The Sea-Wolf. Hartford: 1961. V. 48
Smoke and Shorty. 1920. V. 50
Smoke Bellew. New York: 1912. V. 49; 51; 53
A Son of the Sun. Garden City: 1912. V. 53
The Son of the Wolf. Boston: 1900. V. 47; 48; 53
Star Rover. New York: 1915. V. 49; 53
The Strength of the Strong. Chicago: 1912. V. 47; 54
The Strength of the Strong. New York: 1914. V. 50
Tales of the Fish Patrol. London: 1906. V. 53
Theft. New York: 1910. V. 50; 52
The Turtles of Tasman. New York: 1916. V. 47; 53
The Valley of the Moon. London: 1914. V. 53
The War of the Classes. London: 1905. V. 51
War of the Classes. New York: 1905. V. 50; 51
War of the Classes. New York: 1906. V. 53
What Life Means to Me. Chicago: 1912. V. 51
White Fang. New York: 1906. V. 47; 53
White Fang. London: 1907. V. 53
White Fang. Lunenburg: 1973. V. 53
Wonder of Woman. 1912. V. 50
Wonder of Woman. New York: 1912. V. 50

LONDON MISSIONARY SOCIETY
A Missionary Voyage to the Southern Pacific Ocean, Performed in the Years 1796, 1797, 1798... London: 1799. V. 49; 50; 51; 52

LONDON: or, a Month at Stevens's... London: 1819. V. 51

LONDON. POLICE
Report from the Committe on the State of the Police of the Metropolis, 1816 (and) First (-third) Report on the State of the Police of the Metropolis, 1817-18. V. 52

THE LONDON Practice of Physic: Wherein the Definitions and Symptoms of Diseases With the Present method of Cure... London: 1773. V. 49

THE LONDON Practice of Physic: Wherein the Definitions and Symptoms of Diseases With the Present Method of Cure... London: 1779. V. 49

LONDON. ROYAL ACADEMY OF ARTS
A Commemorative Catalogue of the Exhibition of Italian Art Held in the Galleries of the Royal Academy, Burlington House, London, January-March, 1930. London: 1931. V. 47

LONDON. The Great Metropolis. London: 1836 & 1837. V. 50

LONDON. THE TATE GALLERY
The Pre-Raphaelites. 7 March-28 May 1984. V. 53

THE LONDON Universal Letter-Writer; or, Whole Art of Polite Correspondence... London: 1800. V. 47

THE LONDON Universal Letter-Writer; or, Whole Art of Polite Correspondence... London: 1802. V. 52

LONDON. UNIVERSITY LIBRARY
Catalogue of the Goldsmiths' Library of Economic Literature. London: 1982. V. 53
The Sterling Library. A Catalogue of the Printed Books and Literary Manuscripts: Collected by Sir Louis Sterling, and Presented by Him to the University of London. 1954. V. 48

LONDONDERRY, CHARLES WILLIAM STEWART VANE, 3RD MARQUIS OF
Recollections of a Tour in the North of Europe in 1836-37. London: 1838. V. 49; 51

LONDONDERRY, MARCHIONESS OF
A Catalogue of the Books, MSS. and prints... 1864. V. 50

LONDON'S Flames Reviv'd: or, an Account of the Several Informations Exhibited to a Committee Appointed by Parliament, Sept. the 25th 1666 to Enquire into the Burning of London... London: 1689. V. 50; 53

LONDON'S Gratitude: or, an Account of Such Pieces of Sculpture and Painting As Have Been Placed in Guildhall at the Expense of the City of London. London: 1783. V. 49

LONE, WOLF
Lone Wolf Guest Ranch and Club. Browning: 1932. V. 50

LONG, ARMISTEAD LINDSAY
Memoirs of Robert E. Lee: His Military and Personal History... London: 1886. V. 49

LONG, ARMISTEAD, LINDSAY
Memoirs of Robert E. Lee: His Military and Personal History... Philadelphia & Richmond: 1886. V. 47

LONG, BELKNAP
The Horror from the Hills. Sauk City: 1963. V. 53

LONG, C. CHAILLE
Central Africa: Naked Truths of Naked People. New York: 1877. V. 54

LONG, CATHERINE
Sir Roland Ashton: a Tale of the Times. London: 1844. V. 48; 51; 54

LONG, CHARLES EDWARD
Royal Descents: a Genealogical List of the Several Persons Entitled to Quarter the Arms... London: 1845. V. 49

LONG, EDWARD
The History of Jamaica. London: 1774. V. 54

LONG, ESMOND
A History of Pathology. Baltimore: 1928. V. 50; 52

LONG, F. B.
The Goblin Tower. 1935. V. 49; 54

LONG, FRANK BELKNAP
The Hounds of Tindalos. Sauk City: 1946. V. 48; 51; 52

LONG, GEORGE
The Decline of the Roman Republic. London: 1864-74. V. 48
The Mills of Man. London: 1931. V. 50
The Penny Cyclopaedia of The Society for the Diffusion of Useful Knowledge. London: 1833-43. V. 48; 50; 53

LONG, H. P.
My First Days in the White House. 1935. V. 50

LONG, HANIEL
French Soldier: Home from Being a War Prisoner. (with) Children, Students and a few Adults. Santa Fe: 1942/42. V. 53
Pittsburgh Memoranda. Santa Fe: 1935. V. 48; 54
Poems. New York: 1920. V. 53

LONG, JAMES L.
Land of the Nakoda the Story of the Assinboine Indians - from the Tales of the Old Ones Told to First Boy... Helena: 1942. V. 54

LONG, JOHN
Journal of the East India Association...The Eastern Question its Anglo-Indian Aspect. London. V. 49
A Treatise on Malting. Dublin: 1800. V. 51
Voyages and Travels of an Indian Interpreter and Trader... London: 1791. V. 48; 49; 50; 51; 52

LONG, JOHN ST. JOHN
A Critical Exposure of the Ignorance and Mal-Practice of Certain Medical Practioners, in Their Theory and Treatment of Disease... London: 1831. V. 54

LONG, JOSEPH W.
American Wild Fowl Shooting...Instructions Concerning Guns, Blinds, Boats and Decoys... New York: 1879. V. 49

LONG, MASON
The Life of Mason Long, the Converted Gambler, Being a Record of His Experiences as a White Slave, a Soldier in the Union Army...written by himself. Chicago: 1878. V. 47

LONG, PERRIN
The Clinical and Experimental Use of Sulfanilamide, Sulfapyridine and Allied Compounds. New York: 1939. V. 51

LONG, ROGER
The Music Speech, Spoken at the Public Commencement in Cambridge, July the 6th, 1714. London: 1714. V. 50

LONG, ROSE CAROL WASHTON
Kandinsky, the Development of an Abstract Style. 1980. V. 54

LONG, STEPHEN H.
Voyage in a Six-Oared Skiff to the Falls of Saint Anthony in 1817. Philadelphia: 1860. V. 48; 51

LONG, W. H.
Medals of the British Navy and How They Were Won. London: 1895. V. 48; 50; 52

LONG, WILLIAM
Stonehenge and Its Barrows. Devizes: 1876. V. 50

LONG, WILLIAM J.
Beasts of the Field. Boston and London: 1901. V. 47

LONGACRE, J. J.
Craniofacial Anomalies: Pathogenesis and Repair. Philadelphia: 1968. V. 47

LONGAKER, MARK
English Biography in the Eighteenth Century. Philadelphia: 1931. V. 52

LONGFELLOW, HENRY WADSWORTH
The Birds of Killingworth. Bremen & New York: 1974. V. 51
Collected Writings. London: 1892. V. 51
Coplas de Don Jorge Manrique. Boston: 1833. V. 50
The Courtship of Miles Standish... 1858. V. 47
The Courtship of Miles Standish. Boston: 1858. V. 47; 48; 49; 50; 51; 52; 53; 54
The Courtship of Miles Standish. London: 1858. V. 47; 49; 50; 51; 54
The Courtship of Miles Standish. London: 1920. V. 49
The Divine Tragedy. Boston: 1871. V. 52
The Estray. Boston: 1847. V. 50; 52; 53; 54
Evangeline, A Tale of Acadie. London: 1866. V. 54
Evangeline: a Tale of Acadie. London: 1882. V. 51
Evangeline: a Tale of Acadie. London: 1897. V. 50; 51
From My Arm-Chair to the Children of Cambridge, Who Presented to Me, on My Seventy-Second Birthday, February 27, 1879, This Chair Made from the Wood of the Village Blacksmith's Chestnut Tree. Cambridge: 1879. V. 53
The Golden Legend. Boston: 1851. V. 47; 50; 52; 53; 54
The Hanging of the Crane. Boston: 1875. V. 53; 54
Hiawatha. London: 1911. V. 49
Household Poems. Boston: 1865. V. 53
Hyperion. 1839. V. 50
Hyperion. New York: 1839. V. 47; 49; 50; 51; 52; 53; 54
Hyperion... Boston: 1848. V. 53
Hyperion... London: 1853. V. 49

LONGFELLOW, HENRY WADSWORTH continued
Hyperion... London: 1865. V. 47; 52
Kavanagh, a Tale. Boston: 1849. V. 54
Manuel de Proverbes Dramatiques. Boston: 1840. V. 54
The Masque of Pandora and Other Poems. Boston: 1875. V. 50
Miscellaneous Poems Selected from the United States Literary Gazette. Boston: 1826. V. 50; 51
Novelas Espanolas. Brunswick: 1831. V. 47
Nuremberg. Philadelphia: 1888. V. 47
Outre-Mer. Boston: 1833/34. V. 53; 54
Outre-Mer... New York: 1835. V. 50; 53
Poetical Works. London: 1865. V. 51
The Poetical Works. Boston: 1879/79. V. 53
The Poetical Works. Boston: 1881. V. 52
The Poetical Works. London: 1890. V. 51
The Poetical Works. London: 1914. V. 53
The Poets and Poetry of Europe. Philadelphia: 1845. V. 50; 54
Saggi De Novellieri Italian. Boston: 1832. V. 50; 54
The Seaside and the Fireside. Boston: 1850. V. 51; 52
The Seaside and the Fireside. Liverpool: 1850. V. 53; 54
The Song of Hiawatha. Boston: 1855. V. 47; 48; 49; 50; 51; 52; 53; 54
The Song of Hiawatha. London: 1855. V. 49; 51; 54
The Song of Hiawatha. London: 1856. V. 48; 49; 51
The Song of Hiawatha. Boston New York: 1891. V. 53
The Song of Hiawatha. Boston: 1892. V. 47
The Song of Hiawatha. Boston: 1911. V. 47
The Song of Hiawatha. Boston: 1991. V. 49
The Spanish Student. Cambridge: 1843. V. 53; 54
Tales of a Wayside Inn. 1863. V. 49
Tales of a Wayside Inn. Boston: 1863. V. 47; 50; 52; 53; 54
Tales of a Wayside Inn. USA: 1863. V. 53
Three Books of Song. Boston: 1872. V. 51
Voices of the Night. Cambridge: 1839. V. 50; 53
Voices of the Night. Cambridge: 1840. V. 47; 54
Voices of the Night. Boston: 1845. V. 54
The Waif: a Collection of Poems. Cambridge: 1845. V. 53
The Wreck of the Hesperus. Boston: 1845?. V. 51; 52
Writings of... Cambridge: 1886. V. 51; 54

LONGFELLOW, SAMUEL
A Few Verses of Many Years. Cambridge: 1887. V. 53
Life of Henry Wadsworth Longfellow. (with) Final Memorials of Henry Wadsworth Longfellow. Boston: 1886-67. V. 47; 50

LONGHI, ROBERTO
Piero Della Francesca. London: 1930. V. 50

LONGHURST, MARGARET H.
Catalogue of Carvings of Ivory. Part I: Up to the Thirteenth Century; Part II: Thirteenth Century to Present Day. London: 1927-29. V. 50
English Ivories. London: 1926. V. 48; 52

LONGINUS, CAESAR
Trinum magicum; Sive, Secretorum Magicorum Opus. Frankfurt: 1673. V. 50

LONGINUS, DIONYSIUS CASSIUS
De Sublimitate Commentarius. Londini: 1743. V. 53
De Sublimitate Commentarius, Quem Nova Versione. London: 1732. V. 49
Dionysii Longini de Sublimitate Libellus. Oxford: 1718. V. 52
Dyonysius Longinus on the Sublime... London: 1739. V. 52
The Works of Dionysius Longinus, on the Sublime... London: 1712. V. 49

LONGLEY, ELIAS
American Manual of Phonography: Being A Complete Guide to the Acquisition of Pitman's Phonetic Shorthand. Cincinnati: 1881. V. 47

LONGLEY, MICHAEL
The Echo Gate. Poems 1975-79. London: 1979. V. 50; 53
An Exploded View - Poems 1968-1972. London: 1973. V. 47
Lares. Essex: 1972. V. 50
No Continuing City. Dublin: 1969. V. 52
Ten Poems. Belfast: 1965. V. 52

LONGMAN, C. J.
Archery. London: 1894. V. 54

LONGMAN, E. D.
Pins and Pincushions. London: 1911. V. 49

LONGMAN, W.
Tokens of the Eighteenth Century Connected with Booksellers and Bookmakers. London: 1916. V. 50
Tokens of the Eighteenth Century Connected with Booksellers and Bookmakers. 1970. V. 50

LONGMAN, WILLIAM
The History of the Life and Times of Edward the Third. London: 1869. V. 47; 53; 54

LONGOLIUS, CHRISTOPHORUS
Orationes Duae Pro Defensione Sua (and other works). Florentiae: 1524. V. 47; 49

LONGRIDGE, C. NEPEAN
The Cutty Sark. London: 1933. V. 51

LONGRIDGE, JAMES A.
Longridge's Patent Locomotive. London: 1885. V. 53

LONGSTAFF, F. V.
The Book of the Machine Gun. London: 1917. V. 47

LONGSTAFF, GEORGE B.
Butterfly-Hunting in Many Lands, Notes of a Field Naturalist... London: 1912. V. 47; 52
The Langstaffs of Teesdale and Weardale. London: 1906. V. 49; 52

LONGSTAFF, S. F.
(Sale) Catalogue of the Extensive Library. 1894. V. 50

LONGSTAFFE, W. HYLTON DYER
The History and Antiquities of the Parish of Darlington in the Bishopric. Darlington: 1854. V. 47
The History and Antiquities of the Parish of Darlington in the Bishopric. London: 1909. V. 47; 53

LONGSTREET, AUGUSTUS BALDWIN
Letters on the Epistle of Paul to Philemon, or the Connection of Apostolical Christianity with Slavery. Charleston: 1845. V. 49
A Voice from the South... Baltimore: 1847. V. 48; 51

LONGSTREET, JAMES
From Manassas to Appomattox. Philadelphia: 1896. V. 50

LONGSWORTH, BASIL NELSON
Diary of...March 15, 1853 to January 22, 1854, Covering the Period of His Migration from Ohio to Oregon. Denver: 1927. V. 54

LONGUEVILLE, PETER
The Hermit; or, the Unparalleled Sufferings, and Surprizing Adventures of Philip Quarll, an Englishman. London: 1790. V. 52

LONGUS
Les Amours Pastorales de Daphnis et Chloe. Paris: 1745. V. 49
Les Amours Pastorales de Daphnis et Chloe. 1933. V. 48
Amours Pastorales de Daphnis et de Chloe. Paris: 1800. V. 50; 51
Daphnis and Chloe. London: 1890. V. 47
Daphnis and Chloe. London: 1893. V. 49
Daphnis and Chloe. New Rochelle: 1904. V. 53
Daphnis and Chloe. Waltham St. Lawrence: 1923. V. 47
Daphnis and Chloe. London: 1925. V. 48; 50; 53
Daphnis and Chloe. New York: 1977. V. 47; 48
Daphnis et Chloe. Paris: 1937. V. 48; 54
The Pastoral Loves of Daphnis and Chloe. London: 1924. V. 48
Les Pastorales de Longus, ou Daphnis et Chloe. Paris: 1926. V. 47; 48

LONGYEAR, JOHN M.
Copan Ceramics. Washington: 1952. V. 50

LONICERUS, PHILIPPUS
Chronicorum Turcicorum, in Quibus Turcoram Origo, Principes, Imperatores, Bella, Praelia, Caedes, Victoriae... Frankfurt: 1578. V. 47; 50

LONN, ELLA
Salt as a Factor in the Confederacy. New York: 1933. V. 47; 48

LONNEUX, MARTIN
The Graded Catechism in Innuit. Chaneliak,: 1951. V. 48

LONSDALE, HENRY
The Life and Works of Musgrave Lewthwaite Watson, Sculptor. London: 1866. V. 52; 54
The Life of John Heysham, M.D... London: 1870. V. 52; 54

LOOK Before You Leap: or, a Few Hints to Such Artizans, Mechanics, Labourers, Farmers and Husbandmen, As are Desirous of Emigrating to America... London: 1796. V. 53

THE LOOKING-GLASS for the Mind... London: 1794. V. 52
THE LOOKING-GLASS for the Mind... London: 1821. V. 52

LOOMER, L. S.
Print Techniques in Canadiana: A Background Survey of Methods and History in Pictorial Reproduction from 1575 (in 8 parts). Windsor: 1975/76. V. 53

LOOMIS, ALFRED
Lectures on Diseases of the Respiratory Organs, Heart and Kidneys. New York: 1878. V. 54

LOOMIS, LEANDER V.
A Journal of the Birmingham Emigration company. Salt Lake City: 1928. V. 50; 52; 54

LOOS, ANITA
But Gentlemen Marry Brunettes. New York: 1928. V. 49; 51; 54
Gentlemen Prefer Blondes. New York: 1925. V. 49
Gigi. New York: 1952. V. 53
Twice Over Lightly: New York Then and Now. New York: 1972. V. 54

LOPES DE CASTANHEDA, FERNAO
Chronica del Rey D. Ioam. I. de boa Memoria, e dos Reys de Portugal o Decimo. Primeira (-Terceira) Parte. Lisbon: 1644. V. 53
The First Booke of the Historie of the Discoverie and Conquest of the East Indias, Enterprised by the Portingales, in Their Dangerous Navigations, in the Time of King Don John, the Second of That Name. London: 1582. V. 50

LOPEZ, BARRY HOLSTUN
Arctic Dreams. New York: 1986. V. 54
Coyote Love. Portland: 1989. V. 50; 51; 54
Crow and Weasel. 1990. V. 54

LOPEZ, BARRY HOLSTUN continued
Crow and Weasel. San Francisco: 1990. V. 47; 48; 50
Desert Notes. Kansas City: 1976. V. 50; 51; 53
Desert Reservation. 1980. V. 54
Giving Birth to Thunder Sleeping With His Daughter. Kansas City: 1977. V. 51
Giving Birth to Thunder Sleeping with His Daughter. New York: 1977. V. 52
Giving Birth to Thunder Sleeping with His Daughter. Kansas City: 1978. V. 52
Of Wolves and Men. New York: 1978. V. 48; 51; 52; 53; 54
River Notes. 1979. V. 50; 54
River Notes. Kansas City: 1979. V. 53
Winter Count. New York: 1981. V. 51; 52

LOPEZ, KEN
Robert Stone: a Bibliography. V. 52
Robert Stone: a Bibliography. Hadley: 1992. V. 48; 49; 50; 51; 52; 53; 54

LOPEZ, RAFAEL
Utah's Greatest Man Hunt. Salt Lake City: 1913. V. 52

LOPEZ DE CORELLA, ALFONSO
Enchiridion Medicinae, in Quo Praecipua Theoricae & Practicae Iuxta Classicorum Authorum Dogmata Dilucidantur... Zaragoza: 1549. V. 53

LOPEZ MADERA, GREGORIO
Discursos de la Certidumbre de las Reliquias Descubiertas en Granada desde el Ano de 1588 Hasts el de 1598... Granada: 1601. V. 48
Excelencias de la Monarchia y Reyno de Espana. Valladolid: 1597. V. 53

LOPEZ-REY, JOSE
Velazquez, the Artist as Maker, With a Catalogue Raisonne of His Extant Works. Lausanne/Paris: 1979. V. 50; 54

LORAIN, JOHN
Nature and Reason Harmonized in the Practice of Husbandry. Philadelphia: 1825. V. 48

LORAINE, PETRE F.
Napoleon at Bay 1814. London: 1914. V. 50

L'ORANGE, H. P.
Likeness and Icon; Selected Studies in Classical and Early Mediaeval Art. Odense: 1973. V. 52

LORCA, FEDERICO GARCIA
Ballad of the Spanish Civil Guard/Romance De La Guardia Civil Espanola. Newark: 1974. V. 49
Lament for Ignacio Sanchez Mejias. Northampton: 1957. V. 48
Lament for the Death of a Bullfighter and Other Poems. London: 1937. V. 48
Lament for the Death of a Bullfighter and Other Poems. New York: 1937. V. 47; 49
Poems. London: 1939. V. 48

LORD, ALBERT B.
Russian Folk Tales. New York: 1970. V. 54

LORD Byron's Farewell to England; With Three Other Poems, Viz. Ode to St. Helena, To My Daughter, on the Morning of Her Birth, and to the Lily of France. London: 1816. V. 49

LORD, ELIOT
Comstock Mining and Miners. Washington: 1883. V. 52

LORD, ELIZABETH
Reminiscences of Eastern Oregon. Portland: 1903. V. 47; 52

LORD, F. W.
The Book of the London International Chess Congress 1899. London: 1900. V. 49

LORD, JAMES
Alberto Giacometti Drawings. Greenwich: 1971. V. 47; 48; 52

LORD, JOHN
Memoir of John Kay of Bury, County of Lancaster, Inventor of th Fly-Shuttle, Metal Reeds, etc. Rochdale: 1903. V. 48; 53; 54

LORD, JOHN KEAST
At Home in the Wilderness. What To Do There and How to Do It. A Handbook for Travelers and Emigrants. London: 1876. V. 54
The Naturalist in Vancouver Island and British Columbia. London: 1866. V. 47; 49

LORD, JOHN P.
The Maine Townsman, or Laws for the Regulation of Towns. Boston: 1844. V. 53

LORD John Sanger & Sons At Windsor by Royal Command. Glasgow: 1892. V. 49

LORD John Signatures. Northridge. V. 48
LORD John Signatures. Northridge: 1991. V. 48

LORD John Ten. 1988. V. 54
LORD John Ten. Northridge: 1988. V. 49; 53

LORD, JOSEPH L.
A Defense of Dr. Charles T. Jackson's Claims to the Discovery of Ether. Boston: 1848. V. 47; 50; 51; 52

LORD, LOUIS E.
A History of the American School of Classical Studies at Athens 1882-1942: an Intercollegiate Project. Cambridge: 1947. V. 52

LORDE, AUDRE
The First Cities. New York: 1968. V. 53

LORENTO'S Wizard's Guide; or, Magic Made Easy. New York: 1878. V. 47

LORENTZ, H. A.
The Theory of Electrons and Its Applications to the Phenomena of Light and Radical Heat. Leipzig: 1909. V. 50; 52

LORENZANA, FRANCISCO ANTONIO
Concilios Provinciales Primero, y Segundo Celebrados en la Muy Noble, y Muy leal Ciudad de Mexico... Mexico City: 1769. V. 54

LORENZEN, EIVIND
Technological Studies in Ancient Metrology I-II. Copenhagen: 1966-70. V. 49

LORENZINI, CARLO
The Adventures of Pinocchio. New York: 1929. V. 52
Pinocchio... Philadelphia and London: 1916. V. 53
Pinocchio. Philadelphia: 1920. V. 52
Pinocchio. New York: 1937. V. 48; 49; 51; 52; 53; 54
Pinocchio. New York: 1940. V. 51
Pinocchio. New York: 1946. V. 52
The Story of a Puppet or the Adventures of Pinocchio. 1892. V. 49
Walt Disney's Pinocchio. Boston: 1940. V. 53

LORIMER, H. L.
Homer and the Monuments. London: 1950. V. 52

LORIMER, JOHN
A Concise Essay on Magnetism... London: 1795. V. 50

LORIOT, L.
A New Short and Easy Method of Geography, French and English... Reading: 1797. V. 49

LORT, ROSS
All Creatures Great and Small. Verses and Linocut Illustrations. Vancouver: 1931. V. 53

LOS Angeles and Vicinity. New York: 1886. V. 47

LOS ANGELES. BOARD OF PUBLIC SERVICE COMMISSIONERS
Construction of the Los Angeles Aqueduct: Final Report. Los Angeles: 1916. V. 54

LOS ANGELES. CHAMBER OF COMMERCE
New Facts and Figures Concerning California: Including the Actual Experience of Individual Producers. Los Angeles: 1891. V. 47

LOS Angeles City Directory, 1891. Los Angeles: 1891. V. 52

LOS Angeles City Directory, 1907. Los Angeles: 1907. V. 52

LOS ANGELES COUNTRY CLUB
Officers, Constitution and Rules. Los Angeles: 1907. V. 50

LOS ANGELES COUNTY MUSEUM
Catalogue for the Retrospective Exhibition of the Walt Disney Medium Held at the Los Angeles County Museum. Los Angeles: 1940. V. 54

LOS ANGELES COUNTY MUSEUM OF ART
David Hockney. A Retrospective. New York: 1988. V. 53

LOS Angeles County Woman's Christian Temperance Union Historical Number 1884-1908. Los Angeles: 1908. V. 52

LOS ANGELES. DEPARTMENT OF PUBLIC SERVICE
Complete Report on Construction of the Los Angeles Aqueduct with Introductory Historical Sketch. Los Angeles: 1916. V. 47

LOSHAK, DAVID
The Art of Thomas Girtin. London: 1954. V. 50; 54

LOSKIEL, GEORGE HENRY
History of the Mission of the United Brethren Among the Indians in North America. London: 1794. V. 54

THE LOSS Of the Comet Steam Boat, Impartially Detailed; With a Brief Narrative of the Loss of the Catherine of Iona... Edinburgh: 1825. V. 47

LOSSING, BENSON JOHN
A Brief Catalogue of Books Illustrated with Engravings by Dr. Alexander Anderson; with a Biographical Sketch of the Artist. New York: 1885. V. 53
Harper's Encyclopeida of United States History from 458 A.D. to 1909. New York, London: 1905. V. 47
Harper's Popular Cyclopaedia of United States History...to 1876. New York: 1882. V. 48; 50
A History of the Civil War. New York: 1912. V. 49
The Hudson, from the Wilderness to the Sea. New York: 1866. V. 49
Our Country. New York: 1875-77?. V. 52
The Pictorial Field Book of the Civil War in the United States of America. Hartford: 1880. V. 51; 52
The Pictorial Field Book of the Revolution; or, Illustrations by Pen and Pencil, of the History... New York: 1855. V. 49; 53
Washington and the American Republic. New York: 1870. V. 53

LOSSIUS, KASPAR FRIEDRICH
Gamal and Lina; or, the African Children. London: 1817. V. 49

LOSSIUS, LUCAS
Arithmetices Erotemata Puerilia. 1560. V. 49

THE LOST Supper, and Other Stories, Interspersed with Moral and Religious Reflections. Yarmouth: 1835. V. 49

LOTHIAN, JAMES
Practical Hints on the Culture and General Management of Alpine rock Plants. Edinburgh: 1845. V. 48

LOTHIAN, MARQUESS OF
Illuminated Manuscripts, Incunabua, and Americana from the Famous Libraries of Marques of Lothian. New York: 1932. V. 49

LOTHIAN, WILLIAM
The History of the United Provinces of the Netherlands, from the Death of Philip II, King of Spain, to the Truce Made With Albert and Isabella. Dublin: 1780. V. 48

LOTHROP, ALONZO H.
The Beginning of the March from Atlanta to the Sea... Madison. V. 50

LOTHROP, SAMUEL KIRKLAND
An Archaeological Study of Ancient Remains on the Borders of Lake Atitlan, Guatemala. Washington: 1933. V. 50
Cocle: an Archaeological Study of Central Panama. Cambridge: 1937-42. V. 50
Metals from the Cenote of Sacrifice Chichen Itza, Yucatan. Cambridge: 1952. V. 50; 52
Treasures of Ancient America. The Arts of the Pre-Columbian Civilization from Mexico to Peru. Geneva: 1964. V. 47; 50; 52; 53
Zacualpa: a Study of Ancient Quiche Artifacts. Washington: 1936. V. 50

LOTI, PIERRE
Impressions. Westminster: 1898. V. 48; 49; 50
The Romance of a Child. Chicago and New York: 1891. V. 54

LOTT, EMMELINE
The English Governess in Egypt. Harem Life in Egypt and Constantinople. London: 1866. V. 48; 49; 50; 52; 53

LOTTINI, GIOVANFRANCESCO
Avvedimenti Civilis...al Serenissimo D. Francesco Medici. Florence: 1574. V. 53; 54

LOTTO, F.
Fayette County, Her History and Her People. Schulenburg: 1902. V. 50; 53

LOUBAT, ALPHONSE
The American Vine Dresser's Guide. New York: 1872. V. 51; 54

LOUBAT, J. F.
The Medallic History of the United States of America, 1776-1876. New Milford: 1967. V. 54

A LOUD Call to Repentance; or, God's Judgments Against the Despairing Sinner. London: 1758. V. 53

LOUD, GORDON
Khorsabad II: the Citadel and the Town. Chicago: 1938. V. 52
Megiddo II (only): Seasons of 1935-39. Chicago: 1948. V. 49
The Megiddo Ivories. Chicago: 1939. V. 52

LOUDON, JANE WEBB
British Wild Flowers. London: 1846. V. 48; 51; 52; 53
British Wild Flowers. London: 1849. V. 47; 49
British Wild Flowers. London: 1855. V. 48
British Wild Flowers. London: 1859. V. 52
The Entertaining Naturalist. London: 1850. V. 53
Instructions in Gardening for Ladies. London: 1840. V. 54
The Ladies' Companion to the Flower-Garden. London: 1846. V. 47
The Ladies' Flower-Garden of Ornamental Bulbous Plants. London: 1850. V. 48
The Ladies Flower-Garden of Ornamental Greenhouse Plants. London: 1848. V. 50
The Mummy!. London: 1827. V. 50
My Own Garden; or, the Young Gardener's Year Book. London: 1855. V. 54

LOUDON, JOHN CLAUDIUS
Arboretum et Fruiticetum Britannicum; or the Trees and Shrubs of Britain... London: 1838. V. 48
Arboretum et Fruiticetum Britannicum; or the Trees and Shrubs of Britain. London: 1844. V. 54
The Derby Arboretum. London: 1840. V. 51
The Different Modes of Cultivating the Pine-apple... London: 1822. V. 51
An Encyclopaedia of Agriculture... London: 1825. V. 54
An Encyclopaedia of Agriculture... London: 1826. V. 47
An Encyclopaedia of Agriculture. London: 1831. V. 52
An Encyclopaedia of Agriculture... London: 1857/44. V. 50
An Encyclopaedia of Gardening.. London: 1824. V. 52
An Encyclopaedia of Gardening... London: 1830. V. 51
An Encyclopaedia of Gardening... London: 1835. V. 47
An Encyclopaedia of Gardening. London: 1845. V. 52
An Encyclopaedia of Gardening... London: 1878. V. 47
An Encyclopaedia of Plants... London: 1829. V. 48; 49; 54
An Encyclopaedia of Plants... London: 1836. V. 48; 50; 53
An Encyclopaedia of Plants... London: 1841. V. 51; 53
An Encyclopaedia of Trees and Shrubs... London: 1869. V. 47; 50
The Green-House Companion... London: 1825. V. 49
The Green-House Companion... London: 1832. V. 48; 50
The Green-House Companion. London: 1932. V. 49
Loudon's Hortus Britannicus. London: 1850. V. 53
Observations on Laying Out Farms in the Scotch Style... London: 1812. V. 48; 49; 51; 53
Observations on the Formation and Management of Useful and Ornamental Plantations... London: 1804. V. 51
Self-Instruction for Young Gardeners. London: 1845. V. 51
The Suburban Gardener and Villa Companion. London: 1838. V. 53
A Treatise on Forming, Improving and Managing Country Residences... London: 1806. V. 47; 48; 49
The Villa Gardener... London: 1850. V. 47; 52

LOUGH, JOHN
Essays On the Enclopedie of Diderot and D'Alembert. London: 1968. V. 50

LOUGHBOROUGH, J. N.
Hand Book of Health; or, a Brief Treatise on Physiology and Hygiene, Comprising Practical Instruction on the Structure and Functions of the Human System, and Rules for the Preservation of the Health. Battle Creek: 1868. V. 53

LOUGHBOROUGH, JOHN
The Pacific Telegraph and Railway. Saint Louis: 1849. V. 48; 50

LOUGHBOROUGH, MARY ANN
My Cave Life in Vicksburg, With Letters of Trial and Travel. New York & London: 1864. V. 48; 50; 51; 53

LOUGHEED, VICTOR
Vehicles of the Air. Chicago: 1910. V. 50; 52; 54

LOUGHERY, E. H.
Personnel of the Texas State Government for 1885. Austin: 1885. V. 48
Texas State Government. A Volume of Biographical Sketches and Passing Comment. Austin: 1897. V. 53

LOUGHRIDGE, R. M.
English and Muskokee Dictionary Collected from Various Sources and Revised. St. Louis: 1890. V. 52

LOUIS, PIERRE
Anatomical, Pathological and Therapeutic Researches on the Yellow Fever of Gibraltar of 1828. Boston: 1839. V. 49; 51; 54
Anatomical, Pathological and Therapeutic Researches Upon the Disease Known Under the Name of Gastro-Enterite, Putrid, Adynamic, Ataxic, or typhoid Fever... Boston: 1836. V. 49; 51
Memoir on the Proper Method of Examining a Patient, and of Arriving at Facts of a General Nature,. 1838. V. 54
Pathological Researches on Phthisis. Boston: 1836. V. 47; 49; 51; 54

LOUIS XIV The Great Bastard, Protector of the Little One. London: 1702. V. 48

LOUISA; a Narrative of Facts Supposed to Throw Light on the Mysterious History of "The Lady of the Hay-Stack". London: 1801. V. 54

LOUISA: or, Virtue in Distress. London: 1760. V. 50

LOUISBOURG in 1745. The Anonymous Lettre d'un Habitant de Louisbourg (Cape Breton), Containing a Narrative by an Eye-Witness of the Siege in 1745. New York & Toronto: 1897. V. 47

LOUISIANA. BOARD OF STATE ENGINEERS
Report of the Board of State Engineers for the Year 1876. New Orleans: 1878. V. 47

LOUISIANA. (TERRITORY). LAWS, STATUTES, ETC.
The Laws of the Territory of Louisiana Comprising All Those Which are Now Actually in Force within the Same. St. Louis: 1808. V. 48

LOUIS XIV, KING OF FRANCE
Edict...Portant Novvelle Fabrication d'Especes d'Argent, Augmentation du Marc d'Argent. Paris: 1650. V. 48; 52

LOUIS XVI, KING OF FRANCE
The Accusation, Trial, Defence, Sentence, Execution and Last Will of Lewis XVI, Late King of France and Navarre. Edinburgh: 1793. V. 54

LOUKOMSKI, GEORGES
Charles Cameron (1740-1812). An Illustrated Monograph on His Life and Work in Russia... London: 1943. V. 54

THE LOUNGER. London: 1787. V. 47

LOUTHERBOURG, PHILLIPPE JACQUES DE
The Romantic and Picturesque Scenery of England and Wales. London: 1808. V. 51; 52
The Romantic and Picturesque Scenery of England and Wales... 1979. V. 48

LOUVAIN, BELGIUM. UNIVERSITY
Privilegia Academiae sive Studio Generali Lovaniensi... Louvain: 1644. V. 52

LOUVET DE COUVRAY, JEAN BAPTISTE
An Account of the Dangers to Which I Have Been Exposed, since the 31st of May, 1793. Perth: 1795. V. 53
Love and Patriotism!. New Haven: 1813. V. 50

LOUVET DE COUVRAY, JOHN BAPTISTE
The Amours of the Chevalier de Faublas. London: 1822. V. 48

LOUX, DUBOIS H.
Ongon. A Tale of Early Chicago. New York: 1902. V. 50

LOUYS, PIERRE
Aphrodite. London: 1926. V. 52
Aphrodite. London: 1928. V. 49
The Collected Tales of... Chicago: 1930. V. 50
Leda or In Praise of the Blessings of Darkness. Easthampton: 1985. V. 50; 51
Leda Ou La Louange des Bienheureuses Tenebres. Paris: 1898. V. 47
Satyrs and Women. New York: 1930. V. 48
The Songs of Bilitis. New York: 1926. V. 54
The Songs of Bilitis. 1928. V. 48
The Twilight of the Nymphs. 1928. V. 54
Woman and Puppet. A Spanish Romance. Philadelphia: 1927. V. 48

LOVAT, SIMON FRASER, BARON
Memoirs of the Life of Simon Lord Lovat: Written by Himself... London: 1797. V. 50

LOVE and Revenge; or, the vintner Outwitted: An Opera; as Acted at the New Theatre in the Hay-Market. London: 1729. V. 49

LOVE and War in Three Cantos. London: 1810. V. 50

LOVE, AUGUSTUS EDWARD HOUGH
A Treatise On the Mathematical Theory of Elasticity. Cambridge: 1906. V. 50

LOVE, B.
The Hand-Book of Manchester... Manchester: 1843. V. 48

LOVE, E. K.
History of the First African Baptist Church. Savannah: 1888. V. 52

LOVE, ELIZABETH
Summer Sunshine for Little Ones. New York & London. V. 48

LOVE In it's Extasie: or the Large Preogative. Ilkley: 1981. V. 48; 50; 54

LOVE is Green. San Francisco: 1962. V. 54

LOVE, JOHN
Geodaesia: or, the Art of Surveying and Measuring of Land Made Easie. London: 1715. V. 50; 52

THE LOVE, Joy and Distress of the Beautiful and Virtuous Miss Fanny Adams, That Was Trapan'd in a False Marriage, to Lord Whatley, His Base and Ungenerous Treatment of Her in Marrying another Lady, Who Afterwards Died; He Repents... London: 1760. V. 48; 50; 54

LOVE Letters of Mrs. Piozzi, Written When She Was Eightly to William Augustus Conway... London: 1843. V. 50

LOVECHILD, LAWRENCE
The Book of Nursery Rhymes, Tales and Fables. Philadelphia: 1859. V. 49

LOVECHILD, SOLOMON
Sketches of Little Boys. London: 1848. V. 47
Sketches of Little Girls. London: 1820. V. 54

LOVECHILD, SOLOMON, PSEUD.
Sketches of Little Girls... London: 1845. V. 48

LOVECRAFT, HOWARD PHILLIPS
At the Mountains of Madness. West Kingston: 1990. V. 51; 53
At the Mountains of Madness and Other Novels. London: 1966. V. 48; 50
Beyond the Wall of Sleep. Sauk City: 1943. V. 50
Collected Poems. Sauk City: 1963. V. 52; 53
Dagon and Other Macabre Tales. London: 1967. V. 50
The Dark Brotherhood and Other Pieces. Sauk City: 1966. V. 47
Dreams and Fancies. Sauk City: 1962. V. 47; 53
The Haunter of the Dark and Other Tales of Terror. London: 1951. V. 47; 52; 53
Lovecraft At Last... 1975. V. 52
Lovecraft at Last. Arlington: 1975. V. 47
The Lurker at the Threshold. Sauk City: 1945. V. 48; 52
The Outsider and Others. Sauk City: 1939. V. 48; 50; 52; 53; 54
Shadow of Innsmouth. 1936. V. 54
Shunned House. Sauk City: 1928. V. 48
The Shuttered Room and Other Pieces. Sauk City: 1959. V. 48
Something About Cats. Sauk City: 1949. V. 48; 51; 52; 53
Supernatural Horror in Literature. New York: 1945. V. 48
The Survivor and Others. Sauk City: 1957. V. 50; 51; 53
The Watchers Out of Time. Sauk City: 1974. V. 52

LOVEDAY, ROBERT
Loveday's Letters Domestick and Foreign. London: 1659. V. 50
Lovedays Letters Domestick and Foreign. London: 1684. V. 49

LOVEJOY, JOSEPH C.
Memoir of the Rev. Elijah P. Lovejoy; Who Was Murdered in Defence of the Liberty of the Press. New York: 1838. V. 53

LOVELACE, RICHARD
Lucasta. The Poems of Richard Lovelace. London: 1864. V. 53

LOVELAND, CYRUS C.
California Trail Herd: The 1850 Missouri-to-California Journal of... Los Gatos: 1961. V. 48

LOVELASS, PETER
The Law's Disposal of a Person's Estate Who Dies Without Will or Testament. London: 1790. V. 51
The Will Which the Law makes; or, How It Disposes of a Person's Estate, in Case He Dies Without Will or Testament... London: 1775. V. 52

LOVELING, BENJAMIN
Latin and English Poems. London: 1738. V. 49; 54
Latin and English Poems. London: 1741. V. 47; 48; 49; 50; 51; 54

LOVELL, JOHN
Lovell's Province of Ontario Directory for 1871. Montreal: 1871. V. 54

LOVELL, M. S.
The Edible Mollusks of Great Britain and Ireland. London: 1867. V. 50

LOVELL, ROBERT
Poems: Containing The Retrospect, Odes, Elegies, Sonnets, &c. Bath: 1795. V. 48

LOVELL, S.
The Recorder's Letter of Advice to the Lord Mayor of London, January 14, 1702. 1702. V. 47

LOVEMAN, SAMUEL
The Hermaphrodite. Athol: 1926. V. 51

LOVER, SAMUEL
Characteristic Sketches of Ireland and the Irish. Dublin: 1844. V. 51
The Collected Writings of... New York: 1901. V. 48
The Collected Writings of... Boston: 1901-02. V. 48; 49
The Flag is Half-Mast-High... London. V. 47
The Flag is Half-Mast-High. London: 1852. V. 52
Handy Andy: A Tale of Irish Life. London: 1842. V. 51
Handy Andy: a Tale of Irish Life. London: 1846. V. 51
Legends and Stories of Ireland. London: 1837. V. 51
The Life and Adventures of Rory O'More. London: 1850. V. 47
The Lyrics of Ireland. London: 1858. V. 54
Metrical Tales. London: 1860. V. 51
The Parson's Horn-Book. Dublin: 1831. V. 51
Songs and Ballads. London: 1839. V. 47; 53
Treasure Trove:...Accounts of Irish Heirs: Being a Romantic Tale of the Last Century. London: 1844. V. 54

LOVERING, ANNA TEMPLE
Hints in Domestic Practice and Home Nursing. Boston and Providence: 1896. V. 53

A LOVERS Progress. Waltham St. Lawrence: 1938. V. 52; 53

THE LOVES of Clitophon & Leucippe. London: 1923. V. 48

LOVESEY, PETER
The Last Detective. 1981. V. 54
The Last Detective. Bristol: 1991. V. 52
The Staring Man. Helsinki: 1988. V. 48
Wobble to Death. London: 1970. V. 50
Wobble to Death. New York: 1970. V. 49; 52

LOVETT, RICHARD
The Electrical Philosopher... Worcester: 1774. V. 53; 54
United States Pictures Drawn with Pen and Pencil. London: 1891. V. 54

LOVETT, ROBERT
The Treatment of Infantile Paralysis. Philadelphia: 1916. V. 47; 51; 54

LOVETT, WILLIAM
Elementary Anatomy. London: 1853. V. 47

LOVIBOND, EDWARD
Poems on Several Occasions. London: 1785. V. 47; 48; 50

LOVISINO, MARCO ANTONIO
Espositione Dell' XI. et XII. Cap. Del IIII. Lib. D'Esdra: Sopra Gli Accidenti Passati, Presenti, & Futuri Della Revolutione Del Grande & Tremendo Imperio Dell' Aquila... Venice: 1571. V. 50

LOW, ALBERT PETER
Report On the Dominion Government Expedition to Hudson Bay.... Ottawa: 1906. V. 48; 49; 51; 52; 54

LOW, CHARLES RATHBONE
Her Majesty's navy, Including Its Deeds and Battles. 1890-93. V. 47
Her Majesty's Navy Including Its Deeds and Battles. London: 1890-93. V. 52

LOW, FRANCES H.
Queen Victoria's Dolls. London: 1894. V. 48; 51; 52

LOW, FREDERIC F.
Some Reflections of an Early California. Sacramento: 1959. V. 47; 54

LOW, GEORGE
Fauna Orcadensis; or The Natural History of the Quadrupeds, Birds, Reptiles and Fishes of Orkney and Shetland. Edinburgh: 1813. V. 47; 53

LOW, J. G.
Plastic Sketches. Boston: 1887. V. 52

LOW, MARY
Red Spanish Notebook. London: 1937. V. 49

LOW, NATHANIEL
An Astronomical Diary...1796. Boston: 1796 (1795). V. 53

LOW, ROSEMARY
Amazon Parrots. London: 1983. V. 49; 52; 53; 54

LOWDERMILK, SUSAN
All My Relations. Eugene: 1993. V. 54
Interior Passage. Eugene: 1991. V. 54

LOWE, ALFRED
Six Cartoons. London: 1930. V. 47

LOWE, CONSTANCE
Little Folk's Fun. London: 1900. V. 52

LOWE, E. A.
Palaeographical Papers 1907-1965. Oxford: 1972. V. 52

LOWE, EDWARD JOSEPH
Beautiful Leaved Plants... London: 1861. V. 48; 54
Beautiful Leaved Plants... London: 1863. V. 47
Beautiful Leaved Plants. London: 1864. V. 53

LOWE, EDWARD JOSEPH continued
Beautiful Leaved Plants... London: 1865. V. 48; 53
Beautiful Leaved Plants. London: 1866. V. 51
Beautiful Leaved Plants. London: 1872. V. 49; 53
Beautiful Leaved Plants. London: 1891. V. 49; 51; 52
Ferns: British and Exotic. London: 1866-72. V. 50
Ferns: British and Exotic. London: 187. V. 54
Ferns: British and Exotic. London: 1872. V. 48; 51
A Natural History of British Grasses. London: 1868. V. 52
Natural History of New and Rare Ferns. London: 1862. V. 52
A Natural History of New and Rare Ferns... London: 1864. V. 49
A Natural History of New and Rare Ferns. London: 1871. V. 48
Our Native Ferns... London: 1865-67. V. 48
Our Native Ferns... London: 1867. V. 47; 51; 52; 53; 54
Our Native Ferns... London: 1867/69. V. 52
Our Native Ferns... London: 1874-76. V. 50
Our Native Ferns. London: 1874-80. V. 52; 53; 54
Our Native Ferns. London: 1880. V. 52

LOWE, F. A.
The Heron. London: 1954. V. 48

LOWE, J. M.
The National Old Trails Road: The Great Historic Highway of America. Kansas City: 1924. V. 50

LOWE, JOSEPH
The Present State of England in Regard to Agriculture, Trade and Finance. London: 1823. V. 49

LOWE, R. T.
A History of Fishes of Madeira. London: 1843-60. V. 54

LOWE, ROBERT W.
A Bibliographical Account of English Theatrical Literature From the Earliest Times to the Present Day. London: 1888. V. 49

LOWE, T. S. C.
The Air-Ship City of New York: a Full Description of the Air-Ship and the Apparatus to Be Employed in the Aerial Voyage to Europe... New York: 1859. V. 51

LOWE, WILLOUGBY P.
The Trail that is Always New. 1932. V. 52; 54

LOWE, WILLOUGHBY P.
The Trail that is Always New. London: 1932. V. 48

LOWELL, AMY
Ballads for Sale. Boston and New York: 1927. V. 53
Can Grande's Castle. New York: 1918. V. 47; 49
A Critical Fable. Boston and New York: 1922. V. 54
A Dome of Many-Coloured Glass. Boston and New York: 1912. V. 53
John Keats. Boston: 1925. V. 47; 50; 51; 53
Legends. Boston, New York: 1921. V. 48
Pictures of the Floating World. New York: 1919. V. 47; 48; 51
Some Imagist Poets - An Anthology. Boston & New York: 1915. V. 54
Sword Blades and Poppy Seed. New York: 1914. V. 53; 54

LOWELL, ANNA CABOT
Seed-Grain for Thought and Discussion. Boston: 1856. V. 52

LOWELL, GUY
American Gardens. Boston: 1902. V. 47; 51; 54
More Small Italian Villas and Farmhouses. New York: 1920. V. 48; 49; 53; 54
Smaller Italian Villas and Farmhouses. New York: 1916. V. 47; 48

LOWELL, JAMES H.
Poetical Works. Boston: 1863. V. 48

LOWELL, JAMES RUSSELL
Among My Books, Second Series. Boston: 1876. V. 51
The Anti-Slavery Papers of James Russell Lowell. Boston & New York: 1902. V. 47; 50; 52
The Biglow Papers. Cambridge: 1848. V. 51; 53
The Biglow Papers. London: 1859. V. 51; 54
The Biglow Papers. London: 1861. V. 49
The Biglow Papers... London: 1865. V. 49
The Biglow Papers. Montreal: 1866. V. 53
The Biglow Papers. Second Series. Boston: 1867. V. 49
Class Poem. Cambridge: 1838. V. 50
Conversation On Some of the Old Poets. Cambridge: 1845. V. 47; 52; 53; 54
Conversations on Some of the Old Poets. Cambridge: 1846. V. 47; 54
The Courtin'. Boston: 1874. V. 50; 52; 53
A Fable for Critics. New York: 1848. V. 53
A Fable for Critics. Boston: 1891. V. 48
A Fable for Critics. New York: 1948. V. 51
Fireside Travels. London: 1864. V. 49
Four Poems: The Ballad Of The Stranger, King Retro, The Royal Pedigree, and a Dream I Had. 1906. V. 52; 54
Heartsease and Rue. Boston: 1888. V. 50; 53
Impressions of Spain. Boston: 1899. V. 53
Latest Literary Essays and Addresses. New York: 1892. V. 53
Il Pescebalo. Cambridge: 1862. V. 53
Poems. Cambridge: 1844. V. 51; 52
Poems. London: 1844. V. 51
Poems. Boston: 1849. V. 50
Poems... London: 1912. V. 51; 54
The Poetical Works of James Russell Lowell. London: 1896. V. 54
Political Essays. Boston: 1888. V. 53; 54
Under the Willows and Other Poems. Boston: 1869. V. 54
The Vision of Sir Launfal. Cambridge: 1848. V. 48; 53; 54
The Vision of Sir Launfal. Boston: 1870. V. 52
The Writings... Cambridge: 1890-92. V. 50
A Year's Life. Boston: 1841. V. 48

LOWELL, JOHN
Peace Without Dishonour, War Without Hope. Boston: 1807. V. 52

LOWELL, MARIA
The Poems of Maria Lowell. Cambridge: 1907. V. 52; 54

LOWELL, MARIA WHITE
Letter of Maria White Lowell to Sophia Nawthorne. 1910. V. 53

THE LOWELL Offering. Lowell: 1844. V. 53

LOWELL, PERCIVAL
Mars as the Abode of Life. New York: 1908. V. 50

LOWELL, ROBERT
4 by Robert Lowell. Cambridge: 1967. V. 51
4 by Robert Lowell. Cambridge: 1969. V. 49; 51; 53; 54
For the Union Dead. New York: 1964. V. 47; 52
For the Union Dead. London: 1965. V. 47
Land of Unlikeness. Cummington: 1944. V. 49; 52; 53; 54
Life Studies. London: 1959. V. 47; 50; 51; 52
Life Studies. New York: 1959. V. 47; 48; 50; 51; 52
Lord Weary's Castle. 1946. V. 50
Lord Weary's Castle. New York: 1946. V. 47; 48; 49; 52; 53
The Mills of Kavanaughs. New York: 1951. V. 47; 48; 49; 50; 51; 52; 53; 54
Poems 1938-1949. London: 1950. V. 47; 52
Poems 1938-1949. London: 1964. V. 47
The Voyage and Other Versions of Poems by Baudelaire. 1968. V. 54
The Voyage and Other Versions of Poems by Baudelaire. London: 1968. V. 47; 53

LOWENFELS, WALTER
Finale of Seem: a Lyrical Narrative. London: 1929. V. 53

LOWER, MARK ANTHONY
The Curiosties of Heraldry. London: 1845. V. 49
The Worthies of Sussex... Lewes: 1865. V. 54

LOWER, WILLIAM
Relation en Forme de Journal du Voyage et Sejour Que...Charales II a fait en Hollande. Hague: 1660. V. 53

LOWER, WILLIAM E.
Roentgenographic Studies of the Urinary System. St. Louis: 1938. V. 51

LOWERY, G. H.
The Mammals of Louisiana and Its Adjacent Waters in the British Museum. Baton Rouge: 1974. V. 54

LOWES, JOHN LIVINGSTON
The Road ot Xanadu - a Study in the Ways of the Imagination. Boston and New York: 1927. V. 52

LOWES, WILLIAM LAIRD
The Royal Navy. London: 1897-1903. V. 47

LOWIE, R. H.
The Crow Indians. New York: 1935. V. 51

LOWINSKY, THOMAS
Modern Nymphs, Being a Series of Fourteen Fashion Plates by Thomas Lowinsky. London: 1930. V. 53

LOWLSEY, BARZILLAI
A Glossary of Berkshire Words and Phrases. London: 1888. V. 52

LOWLSEY, OSWALD SWINNEY
Clinical Urology. Baltimore: 1944. V. 51

LOWMAN, AL
Printer at the Pass: the Work of Carl Hertzog. San Antonio: 1972. V. 50
Printing Arts in Texas. Austin: 1975. V. 48; 51
Remembering Carl Hertzog, a Texas Printer and His Books. Dallas: 1985. V. 49; 50; 53
This Bitterly Beautiful Land: a Texas Commonplace Book. Austin: 1972. V. 48; 51

LOWNDES, HANNAH MARIA JONES
Rosaline Woodbridge; or the Midnight Visit. London: 1827. V. 51
The Strangers of the Glen; or, the Travellers Benighted. London: 1827. V. 53
Trials of Love; or Woman's Reward; a Romance of Real Life. London: 1849. V. 48

LOWNDES, MARIE BELLOC
The Chianti Flask. London: 1935. V. 49

LOWNDES, NIKOLAOS
A Modern Greek and English Lexicon, to Which is Prefixed an Epitome of Modern Greek Grammar. Corfu: 1837. V. 48; 49

LOWNDES, WILLIAM
A Report Containing an Essay for the Amendment of the Silver Coins. London: 1695. V. 50; 52

LOWNDES, WILLIAM THOMAS
The Bibliographer's Manual of English Literature. London: 1834. V. 47; 48; 49; 52; 53
The Bibliographer's Manual of English Literature. London: 1857-64. V. 50; 53
The Bibliographer's Manual of English Literature. London: 1857-65. V. 49
The Bibliographer's Manual of English Literature. London: 1864. V. 51
The Bibliographer's Manual of English Literature... London: 1865. V. 54
The Bibliographer's Manual of English Literature. London: 1869. V. 54
The Bibliographer's Manual of English Literature. London: 1885. V. 47; 51
The Bibliographer's Manual of English Literature... London: 1890. V. 47
The Bibliographer's Manual of English Literature... London: 1900. V. 51

LOWNE, B. THOMPSON
The Anatomy, Physiology, Morphology and Development of the Blow-Fly. London: 1890-95. V. 54

LOWREY, GROSVENOR P.
English Neutrality. Is the Alabama a British Pirate?. Philadelphia: 1863. V. 49

LOWRY, H. D.
Make Believe. London: 1896. V. 49

LOWRY, J. W.
Illustrations of Zoology... London: 1851. V. 54

LOWRY, L. S.
Drawings of L. S. Lowry. 1963. V. 49; 51

LOWRY, MALCOLM
Au Dessous du Volcano. Paris: 1949. V. 47
Au-Dessous Du Volcan. Paris: 1950. V. 51; 52
China and Kristbjotg's Story in the Black Hills. London: 1979. V. 51
Dark As the Grave Wherein My Friend is Laid. New York: 1968. V. 47; 49
Hear Us O Lord From Heaven Thy Dwelling Place. Philadelphia: 1961. V. 47; 51
Hear Us O Lord From Heaven Thy Dwelling Place. London: 1962. V. 49
Lunar Caustic. London: 1968. V. 52; 53
October Ferry to Gabriola. London: 1971. V. 47; 49
The Selected Letters of Malcolm Lowry. London: 1967. V. 49; 51
Ultramarine. 1933. V. 49
Ultramarine. London: 1933. V. 53
Ultramarine. Philadelphia & New York: 1962. V. 47; 49; 50; 51; 53
Ultramarine. London: 1963. V. 47; 49
Under the Volcano. 1947. V. 49
Under the Volcano. London: 1947. V. 47; 49; 52; 53
Under the Volcano. New York: 1947. V. 47; 48; 49; 51; 52; 53; 54

LOWRY, ROBERT
The Blaze Beyond the Town. Uomo: 1945. V. 51
Hutton Street. Cincinnati: 1940. V. 48; 51
Murder Pie. Cincinnati: 1939. V. 53; 54

LOWRY, WALKER
Wallace Lowry. 1974. V. 50

LOWSLEY, BARZILLAI
A Glossary of Berkshire Words and Phrases. London: 1888. V. 52

LOWSLEY, OSWALD SWINNEY
The Sexual Glans of the Male. New York, London: 1942. V. 51

LOWTH, ROBERT
Billesdon Coplow, a Poem on Foxhunting... London: 1833. V. 47
Billesdon Coplow. February 24th, 1800. London: 1828. V. 47
De Sacra Poesi Hebraeorum. Oxford: 1753. V. 49
Lectures on the Sacred Poetry of the Hebrews. Andover: 1829. V. 49
The Life of William of Wykeham, Bishop of Winchester. London: 1759. V. 52
A Short Introduction to English Grammar; with Critical Notes... London: 1767. V. 51
A Short Introduction to English Grammar; with Critical Notes. London: 1785. V. 48

LOY, MINA
The Last Lunar Baedeker. Highlands: 1982. V. 52; 53; 54
Lunar Baedecker. Paris: 1923. V. 52; 53
Lunar Baedeker... Highlands: 1958. V. 51; 54
Virgins Plus Curtains. Rochester: 1981. V. 47; 51

THE LOYAL FEAST Design'd to be Kept in Haberdashers-Hall, on Friday the 21st of April 1682. 1684. V. 47

LOYAU, GEORGE E.
Notable South Australians: or Colonists - Past and Present. Adelaide: 1885. V. 48

LOYOLA, IGNACIO DE, SAINT
Epistolae Undecim. Item una...Polycarpi...Epistola. Basle: 1520. V. 48
Vita Beati P. Ignatii Loiolae. Rome: 1609. V. 51

LOZANO DE IBDES, JUAN
Destierro y Azote del Libro del Duelo... Zaragoza: 1640. V. 48

LUARD, HENRY R.
Annales Monastici. London: 1864-69. V. 49; 52

LUBBOCK, BASIL
Adventures by Sea from Art of Old Time. London: 1925. V. 48
Bully Hayes, South Sea Pirate. Boston: 1921. V. 51
The China Clippers. Glasgow: 1914. V. 47
The Last of the Windjammers. Glasgow: 1927. V. 47; 50
The Last of the Windjammers. London: 1927. V. 51
The Last of the Windjammers. Glasgow: 1927/29. V. 51
The Last of the Windjammers. Glasgow: 1948/49. V. 54
The Last of the Windjammers. Glasgow: 1954. V. 52
Sail, the Romance of the Clipper Ships. London: 1927. V. 48; 51
Sail, the Romance of the Clipper Ships. New York: 1972. V. 52

LUBBOCK, FRANCIS RICHARD
Six Decades in Texas or Memoirs of... Austin: 1900. V. 50; 53; 54

LUBBOCK, J.
A Contribution to Our Knowledge of Seedlings. New York: 1892. V. 50; 51

LUBBOCK, JOHN
Pre-Historic Times, as Illustrated by Ancient Remains, and the Manners and Customs of Modern Savages. London: 1865. V. 49
Pre-Historic Times, as Illustrated by Ancient Remains, and the Manners and Customs of Modern Savages. 1869. V. 52

LUBBOCK, JOSEPH G.
Aspects of Art and Science. Leicester: 1969. V. 54
From Garden to Galaxy. London: 1980. V. 52
From the Snows to the Seas. 1986. V. 52; 54
From the Snows to the Seas. London: 1986. V. 49; 50; 51; 52
Landscapes of the Spirit. 1994. V. 52; 54
Light and the Mind's Eye. London: 1974. V. 48; 49
Love for the Death. Cambridge: 1990. V. 51
Love for the Earth. 1990. V. 52; 54
Love for the Earth. Cambridge: 1990. V. 52; 54
Love for the Earth. London: 1990. V. 47; 49; 50; 51; 54
Reflections from the Sea. Leicester: 1971. V. 48; 49
The Sphere of Rocks and Water. London: 1983. V. 50

LUBBOCK, R.
Observations On the Fauna of Norfolk. Norwich: 1848. V. 50
Observations On the Fauna of Norfolk. Norwich: 1879. V. 50; 51; 52

LUCA, MARK
Back to the Cave. San Francisco: 1956. V. 50; 53

LUCANUS, MARCUS ANNAEUS
De Bello Civili Libri Decem. Paris: 1545. V. 48; 50
...De Bello Civili Libri Decem. Lyon: 1547. V. 52
De Bello Civili Libri Decem. Lyon: 1561. V. 53
De Bello Civili Libri Decem... 15845. V. 47
Lucan's Pharsalia... London: 1627. V. 49
Lucan's Pharsalia. London: 1718. V. 48; 50; 53; 54
Lucan's Pharsalia. Dublin: 1719. V. 48; 50; 52
Lucan's Pharsalia. London: 1722. V. 54
Lucanus. Venice: 1502. V. 52
Lucanus. Venice: 1515. V. 52
Pharsalia, cum Notis Hugonis Grotii et Richardi Bentleii. Strawberry Hill: 1760. V. 48; 53
Pharsalia, sive de Bello Civili, Libri X. Glasgow: 1785. V. 50
Pharsaliae Libri X. Basileae: 1578. V. 49; 50

LUCAS, A.
Ancient Egyptian Materials and Industries. London: 1962. V. 49

LUCAS, ARTHUR
John Lucas, Portrait Painter, 1825-1874: a Memoir of His Life, Mainly Deduced from Correspondence of His sitters. London: 1910. V. 51

LUCAS, C. P.
Lord Durham's Report on the Affairs of British North America. London: 1912. V. 53

LUCAS, CHARLES
The Complaints of Dublin...In Behalf of Himself and the Rest of the Citizens and Inhabitants of the Said City. Dublin: 1748. V. 47
A Critical Review of the Liberties of British Subjects. London: 1750. V. 47
The Infernal Quixote. London: 1801. V. 54
The Old Serpentine Temple of the Druids, at Avebury, in North Wiltshire, a Poem. Marlborough: 1795. V. 54

LUCAS, CURTIS
Third Ward Newark. Chicago/New York: 1946. V. 53

LUCAS, EDWARD VERRALL
All the World Over. London: 1898. V. 52
Bernard Barton and His Friends: a Record of Quiet Lives. London: 1893. V. 47
The Book of Shops. London: 1899. V. 49
Edwin Austin Abbey... London: 1921. V. 52; 53
Edwin Austin Abbey. New York: 1921. V. 49; 50
Four and Twenty Toilers. London: 1900. V. 49; 51
Old Fashioned Tales. London: 1905. V. 51
The Open Road. London: 1926. V. 48
Playtime and Company. A Book for Children. London: 1925. V. 50; 52; 53

LUCAS, F. L.
Gilgamesh, King of Erech. Waltham St. Lawrence: 1948. V. 48
The Golden Cokcerel Greek Anthology. Waltham St. Lawrence: 1937. V. 52

LUCAS, FRED C.
An Historical Souvenir Diary of the City of Winnipeg, Canada. Winnipeg: 1923. V. 48; 52

LUCAS, FRED W.
Appendiculae Historicae; or, Shreds of History Hung on a Horn. London. 1891. V. 50

LUCAS, GEORGE
The Diary of George A. Lucas: an American Art Agent in Paris, 1857-1909. Princeton: 1979. V. 53

LUCAS, HENRY
Poems to Her Majesty; to which is Added a New Tragedy, Entitled, The Earl of Somerset... London: 1779. V. 48

LUCAS, JOHN
History of Warton Parish. Kendal: 1931. V. 54

LUCAS, KEITH
The Conduction of the Nervous Impulse. London: 1917. V. 53

LUCAS, MARGARET
An Account of the Convincement and Call to the Ministry Of...late of Leek in Staffordshire. Stanford: 1803. V. 53

LUCAS, MATTIE DAVIS
History of Grayston County, Texas. Sherman: 1936. V. 54

LUCAS, PIERRE HIPPOLYTE
Histoire Naturelle des Lepidopteres d'Europe. Paris: 1845. V. 53

LUCAS, RICHARD
An Enquiry After Happiness, in Several Parts. London: 1704-1696. V. 54
An Inquiry After Happiness. Edinburgh: 1754. V. 47

LUCAS, S.
In Praise of Toadstools. London: 1992. V. 49; 52

LUCAS, S. E.
The Catalogue of Sassoon Chinese Ivories. London: 1950. V. 52

LUCAS, THOMAS J.
Camp Life and Sport in South Africa... London: 1878. V. 47; 49; 52

LUCAS, W. J.
British Dragonflies (Odonata). London: 1900. V. 52; 53; 54

LUCAS-LUCAS, H. F.
The Fox Hunting Alphabet. London: 1910. V. 47
The Fox Hunting Alphabet. London: 1920. V. 53

LUCATT, EDWARD
Rovings in the Pacific, from 1837 to 1849... London: 1851. V. 47

LUCCHESE, SAM
A Lifetime with Boots. V. 53

LUCE, EDWARD S.
Keough, Comanche and Custer. Ashland: 1974. V. 49; 54

LUCE, G. H.
Poems. London: 1924. V. 49

LUCE, NANCY
Poor Little Hearts. Cottage City?: 1866. V. 49

LUCIANUS SAMOSATENSIS
Certaine Select Dialogues of Lucian; together With His True Historie. Oxford: 1634. V. 52; 53
Dialogorum Selectorum Libri Duo. Londini: 1709. V. 54
The Dialogues... London: 1930. V. 51
Dialogues. Paris: 1951. V. 47
Dialogues Des Courtisans. Paris. V. 51
I Dialoi Piacevoli, le Vere Narrationi, le Facete Epitole... Venice: 1541. V. 52
Lucian's Dialogues, and Other Greek Extracts, Literally Translated Into English. Albany: 1816. V. 52
Lucian's True History. London: 1894. V. 49
The Select Dialogues of Lucian. Philadelphia: 1789. V. 49
The True Historie of Lucian the Samosatenian. Waltham St. Lawrence: 1927. V. 47; 50; 51; 52
The Works of Lucian. London: 1780. V. 47

LUCIDUS, JOANNES
Opusculum de Emendationibus Temporum ab Orbe Conditio ad Usque Hanc Aetatem Nostram. Venice: 1537. V. 47; 48; 49; 50

LUCIO ESPINOSA Y MALO, FELIX DE
Declamaciones, Escarmientos Politicos, Y Morales... Madrid: 1674. V. 48

LUCK, BARBARA
Night Street. 1993. V. 52
Poems. 1993. V. 51

LUCKE, JEROME B.
History of the New Haven Grays from Sept. 13, 1816 to Sept. 13, 1876. New Haven: 1876. V. 47

LUCKENBACH, ABRAHAM
Forty-Six Select Scripture Narratives from the Old Testament. New York: 1838. V. 50

LUCKENBEILL, DANIEL DAVID
Ancient Records of Assyria and Babylonia. Chicago: 1926-27. V. 52

LUCKENBILL, DANIEL DAVID
The Annals of Sennacherib. Chicago: 1924. V. 52
Inscriptions from Adab. Chicago: 1930. V. 52

LUCKLAW, ELISABETH
Information of Elisabeth Lucklaw, Widow of Mr. John Cameron Minister of the Gospel, Dr. Thomas Cameron and Elisabeth Cameron, Spouse to Mr. David Watson...Against John Kennedy Chirurgeon in Edinburgh and Others... Edinburgh: 1732. V. 53

LUCKOCK, JAMES
Hints for Practical Economy, in the Management of Household Affairs, with Tables, Shewing Different Scales of Expences... Birmingham: 1834. V. 52

LUCKOMBE, PHILIP
The History and Art of Printing. In Two Parts. London: 1771. V. 47; 48

LUCRETIUS CARUS, TITUS
De La Nature des Choses. Parais: 1788. V. 50
De Rerum Natura. London: 1796-97. V. 53
De Rerum Natura. London: 1813. V. 54
De Rerum Natura... Los Angeles: 1957. V. 53; 54
De Rerum Natura Libri Sex... Antwerp: 1561. V. 48
De Rerum Natura Libri Sex. Paris: 1570. V. 52
De Rerum Natura Libri Sex. Frankfurt: 1583. V. 48; 49; 50
De Rerum Natura Libri Sex. Glasguae: 1749. V. 54
De Rerum Natura Libri Sex. Glasgow: 1759. V. 47; 52; 53
De Rerum Natura Libri Sex. Birmingham: 1772. V. 50; 52
De Rerum Natura Libri Sex... Londini: 1823. V. 53
De Rerum Natura Libri Sex. 1913. V. 51; 52; 54
De Rerum Natura Libri Sex. Chelsea: 1913. V. 47; 50
De Rerum Natura Sex. London: 1712. V. 49; 52; 54
The Nature of Things. London: 1813. V. 53
Of the Nature of Things. London: 1743. V. 50
Of the Nature of Things. Los Angeles: 1956. V. 52
Of the Nature of Things. London: 1957. V. 49
Of the Nature of Things. Los Angeles: 1957. V. 54
Titi Lucretii Cari De Rerum Natura... Birmingham: 1773. V. 52
Titus Lucretius Carus His Six Books of Epicurean Philosophy. London: 1683. V. 52; 54

LUCY, HENRY WILLIAM
East by West. A Journey in the Recess. London: 1885. V. 49

LUDERS, ALEXANDER
Reports of the Proceedings in Committees of the House of Commons, Upon Controverted Elections...During the Present Parliament. London: 1785-90. V. 49

LUDERS, THEODORIC
Traicte Mathematique, Contenant Les Principales Definitions...La Planimetrie et Stereometrie...La Perspective Militaire. (and) Traite d'Arithmetique, Contenant les Reigles Necassiares aux Marchands, Banquiers. Paris: 1680. V. 49

LUDLOW, EDMUND
Memoirs... London: 1751. V. 53; 54
Memoirs. London: 1771. V. 47; 50
The Memoirs... London: 1894. V. 49; 52
Memoirs. Vivay: 1968-69. V. 50

LUDLOW, FITZ HUGH
The Hasheesh Eater. New York: 1857. V. 51; 53
The Heart of the Continent: a Record of Travel Across the Plains and in Oregon. London: 1870. V. 49
The Heart of the Continent: a Record of Travel Across the Plains and in Oregon With an Examination of the Mormon Principle. New York: 1870. V. 51

LUDLOW, N. M.
Dramatic Life As I Found It A Record of the Rise and Progress of Drama in the West... St. Louis: 1880. V. 54

LUDLOW, WILLIAM
Report of a Reconaissance from Carroll, Montana Territory on the Upper Missouri, to the Yellowstone National Park and Return, Made in the Summer of 1875. Washington: 1876. V. 49; 50

LUDLUM, ROBERT
The Gemini Contenders. New York: 1976. V. 50
Osterman Weekend. New York: 1972. V. 48
The Road to Gandolfo. New York: 1975. V. 54
The Scarlatti Inheritance. New York: 1971. V. 47; 48
Trevayne. New York: 1973. V. 49; 53
Trevayne. London: 1974. V. 52

LUDOLPH, JOB
A New History of Ethiopia. London: 1682. V. 50

LUDOVICO DEGLI ARRIGHI, VINCENTINO
The Calligraphic Models of Ludovico Degli Arrighi Surnamedd Vicentino. Paris: 1926. V. 49

LUDWIG, EMIL
Lincoln. Boston: 1930. V. 49

LUER, C. A.
The Native Orchids of Florida. New York: 1972. V. 52; 54
The Native Orchids of the United States and Canada. New York: 1975. V. 52

LUFF, LORRY, PSEUD.
The Texan Captain and the Female Smuggler. New York: 1850. V. 52; 53

LUFFMAN, JOHN
The Chapters of London Complete; Also Magna Charta and the Bill of Rights... London: 1793. V. 49; 52

LUFFMAN, JOHN GEORG
A New Pocket Atlas and Geography of England and Wales. London: 1805. V. 51

LUGAR, ROBERT
The Country Gentleman's Architect... London: 1807. V. 47
The Country Gentleman's Architect... London: 1823. V. 48

LUGARD, FREDERICK JOHN D.
The Rise of Our East African Empire. Edinburgh and London: 1893. V. 47; 48; 50; 52; 53; 54

LUGRIN SHAW, N. DE B.
A Handbook of Vancouver Island. Victoria: 1918. V. 49

LUGS, JAROSLAV
Firearms Past and Present. London: 1973. V. 49

LUHAN, MABEL DODGE
Lorenzo in Taos. New York: 1932. V. 48; 50; 53
Movers and Shakers. New York: 1936. V. 51; 52
Taos and Its Artists. New York: 1947. V. 48; 50; 52
Winter in Taos. New York: 1935. V. 48; 51; 52; 54

LUIS DE GRANADA
Conciones Quae de Praecipuis Sanctorum Festis in Ecclesia Habentur, a Festo Sancti Andrae Usque ad Festum Beatae Mariae Magdalenae. Antwerp: 1593. V. 53
A Memorial of a Christian Life... Rouen: 1586. V. 48; 52
A Memorial of a Christian Life... London: 1688. V. 50

LUISINO, ALOYSIO
Aphrodisiacus, Sive de Lue Venera: in Duos Tomos Bipartitus... Leyden: 1728. V. 49; 50; 51; 52

LUKIN, JAMES
The Lathe and its Uses. London: 1868. V. 52
The Lathe and Its Uses. London: 1874. V. 48; 52
Turning Lathes... Colchester: 1894. V. 52

LUKINS, GEORGE
A Narrative of the Extraordinary Case of Geo. Lukins, of Yeatton, Somersetshire, Who was Possessed of Evil Spirits for Near Eighteen Years... Bristol: 1788. V. 48

LUKIS, PARDEY
Tropical Hygiene for Anglo-Indians and Indians. Calcutta: 1914. V. 49; 50; 51; 52; 54

LUKIS, W. C.
An Account of Church Bells... London: 1857. V. 48

LULL, EDWARD P.
History of the United States Navy-Yard at Gosport, Virginia. Washington: 1874. V. 50

LULL, RAMON
Libro de la Concepcion Virginal, por el Qual se Manifiesta por Racones Necessarias que la Virgen Purissima Madre de Dios fue Concebida fin Alguna mancha de Pecado Original. Brussels: 1664. V. 50

LULL, RAYMOND
Opera... Strassburg: 1609. V. 48

LULLIES, REINHARD
Greek Sculpture. New York: 1960. V. 52

LULLY, LOUIS
Zephire et Flore, Opera en Musique. Paris: 1688. V. 49

LUM, DYER
The Spiritual Delusion. Its Methods, Teachings and Effects. Philadelphia: 1873. V. 50; 54

LUMHOLTZ, CARL
Among Cannibals. London: 1889. V. 48
Among Cannibals. New York: 1889. V. 50
New Trails in Mexico. New York: 1912. V. 48; 53
Through Central Borneo, an Account of Two Years Travel in the Land of the Head-Hunters Between the Years 1913 and 1917. New York: 1920. V. 54
Unknown Mexico... New York: 1902. V. 50; 51; 52
Unknown Mexico. Glorieta: 1902/73. V. 50; 52
Unknown Mexico. London: 1903. V. 48; 51

LUMISDEN, ANDREW
Remarks on the Antiquities of Rome and Its Environs: Being a Classical and Topographical Survey of the Ruins of that Celebrated City. London: 1797. V. 49

LUMLEY, BENJAMIN
Reminiscences of the Opera. London: 1864. V. 47

LUMLEY, BRIAN
The Caller of the Black. Sauk City: 1971. V. 52

LUMLEY, THOMAS
Bribery: a Poem. London: 1765. V. 48

LUMLEY, WILLIAM GOLDEN
The Law of Parochial Assessments, Explained in a Practical Commentary on the Statute 6 and 7 W.4. Cap. 96. London: 1844. V. 53

LUMMIS,
Honour the Light Brigade. London: 1973. V. 50

LUMMIS, CHARLES FLETCHER
General Crook and the Apache Wars. Flagstaff: 1966. V. 47
The Home of Ramona: Photographs of Camulos, the Fine Old Spanish Estate... Los Angeles: 1888. V. 47
The Man Who Married the Moon and Other Pueblo Indian Folk-Stories. New York: 1894. V. 54
Mesa, Canon and Pueblo. New York: 1925. V. 50; 52; 53
A New Mexico David, and Other Stories and Sketches of the Southwest. New York: 1891. V. 50; 52

LUMMUS, AARON
The Life and Adventures of Dr. Caleb; Who Migrated from Egypt and Afterwards Practised Physic in the Land of Canaan and Elsewhere. Boston: 1822. V. 54

LUMPKIN, WILSON
The Removal of the Cherokee Indians From Georgia. Savannah: 1907. V. 48
The Removal of the Cherokee Indians from Georgia. Wormsloe: 1907. V. 48; 50

LUMSDEN, HARRY
The Records of the Trades House of Glasgow, 1605-1678. Glasgow: 1910. V. 52

LUMSDEN, J.
An Abridgment of the New Testament, or the Life, Miracles and Death of Our Lord & Saviour jesus Christ. Glasgow: 1814. V. 49
Fun Upon Fun; or the Humours of a Fair. London: 1815. V. 50

LUMSDEN, JAMES
American Memoranda, by a Mercantile Man, During A Short Tour in the Summer of 1843. Glasgow: 1844. V. 53

LUND, JOHANNES
Die Alten Judischen Heiligthumer...Des Levitschen Priesterthums... Hamburg: 1738. V. 52

LUNDE, KARL
Isabel Bishop. New York: 1975. V. 47

LUNDELL, C. L.
Flora of Texas. 1967-69-61. V. 48
Flora of Texas. Renner: 1967-69-61. V. 51

LUNDY, BENJAMIN
The Origin and True Causes of the Texas Insurrection Commenced in the Year 1835. Philadelphia: 1836. V. 48; 52
The War in Texas; a Review of Facts and Circumstances Showing that this Contest Is a Crusade Against Mexico, set on Foot and Supported by Slaveholders, Land-Speculators, etc. Philadelphia: 1837. V. 49

LUNETTES, HENRY
The American Gentleman's Guide to Politeness and Fashion. New York: 1857. V. 53

LUNEZ, L.
The Andes: Pathway of Encounters. Santiago: 1994. V. 54

LUNGE, GEORGE
Coalt-Tar and Ammonia. London: 1887. V. 54

LUNN, ARNOLD H. M.
Oxford Mountaineering Essays. London: 1912. V. 50; 53

LUNN, EDWIN
Divine Revelation Examined: a Lecture on the Nature and Attributes of the Deity, as Revealed to Us in the Scripture, or the Truth of the First Article of the Creed of the New Moral World. Manchester: 1840?. V. 53

LUNT, GEORGE
The Grave of Byron, With Other Poems. Boston: 1826. V. 49
Leisure Hours. Boston: 1826. V. 49
The Origin of the Late War: Traced from the Beginning of the Constitution to the Revolt of the Southern Sates. New York: 1866. V. 47
Radicalism in Religion, Philosophy and Social Life. Boston: 1858. V. 49

LUNT, WILLIAM E.
Accounts Rendered by Papal Collectors in England 1317-1378. Philadelphia: 1968. V. 49

LUOKOMSKI, GEORGES
Charles Cameron (1740-1812). London: 1943. V. 50

LUPOFF, RICHARD A.
Edgar Rice Burroughs: Master of Adventure. New York: 1965. V. 52

LUPOLDUS BAMBERGENSIS
Germanorum Veterum Principum Zelus et Fervor in Christianum Religionem Deique Ministros. Basel: 1497. V. 52

LUPTON, THOMAS
A Thousand Notable Things of Sundrie Sorts; Whereof Some are Wonderfull, Some Strange, Some Pleasant, Diuers Necessary, a Great Sort Profitable and Many Very Precious. London: 1631. V. 48

LURIE, ALISON
Foreign Affairs. Franklin Center: 1984. V. 52; 53
Love and Friendship. New York: 1962. V. 49; 50; 53
The Nowhere City. London: 1965. V. 53

LUSCOMBE, EDWARD THORNHILL
Practical Observations on the Means of Preserving the Health of Soldiers in Camp and in Quarters. Edinburgh: 1821. V. 54

LUSCOMBE, MICHAEL H. T.
The Pleasures of Society, a Poem. London: 1824. V. 50

LUSHINGTON, FRANK
The Gambardier. Giving Some Account of the Heavy and Siege Artillery in France 1914-1918. London: 1930. V. 47

LUSHINGTON, FRANKLIN
Memoir of Henry Fitzmaurice Hallam. London: 1850. V. 49

LUSHINGTON, HENRY
La Nation Boutiquiere, and Other Poems Chiefly Political... Cambridge: 1855. V. 48

LUSSAN, MARGUERITE DE
The Life of the Countess de Gondez. London: 1729. V. 47; 48

LUSSAN, RAVENEAU DE
Raveneau De Lussan, Buccaneer of the Spanish Main and Early French Filibuster of the Pacific. Cleveland: 1930. V. 51

LUST, BENEDICT
Universal Naturopathic Encyclopedia Directory and Buyers' Guide. Year-Book of Drugless Therapy for 1918-19. Butler: 1918. V. 48

LUST, HERBERT C.
The Complete Graphics and 15 Drawings. New York: 1970. V. 47; 50; 51; 53; 54

LUSTER, MARY R.
The Autobiography of Mary R. Luster, Springfield, Missouri. Springfield: 1935. V. 47

LUTHER, CLAIR FRANKLIN
The Hadley Chest. Hartford: 1935. V. 53

LUTHER, MARTIN
Acta. Leipzig: 1518. V. 48
Ain Kurtze Underrichtung Warauff Christus Seyne Kirchen Oder Gemain Gebawet Hab. Wittenberg: 1524. V. 50
Ain Sermon Von der Frucht Unnd Nutzbarkait des Hayligen Sacraments. Wittenberg: 1524. V. 53
Assertio Omnivm Articvlorvm M. Lutheri, per Bullam Leonis, X. Nouissimam Damnatorum. Wittenberg: 1520. V. 53
The Book of Vagabonds and Beggars; with A Vocabulary of Their Language. London: 1860. V. 48
A Commentaraie or Exposition Vpon the twoo Epistles Generall of Sainct Peter and That of Sainct Jude. London: 1581. V. 50
A Commentarie of M. Doctor Martin Luther Upon the Epistle of S. Paul to the Galatians. (with) A Commentarie Upon the Fifteene Psalmes, Called Pslami Graduum, that is Psalmes of Degrees... London: 1616/15. V. 48; 52
A Commentarie...Upon the Epistle of S. Paul to the Galathians... (with) A Commentarie Upon the XV Psalmes... London: 1637. V. 50
Commentary Upon St. Paul's Epistle to the Galatians: Together with Edwin, Bishop of London's Licence and Commendation of the Work... Wigan: 1791. V. 47
An Den Bock Zu Leyptzck. Wittenberg: 1521. V. 53
Dr. Martin Luther's Divine Discourses at His Table. London: 1652. V. 47; 48; 49; 54
Eine Heer Predigt Widder den Turcken. Wittenberg: 1529. V. 48; 49; 53
Evangelium Von Den Tzehen Auszsetzigen. Wittenberg: 1521. V. 53
Das Gloria in Excelsis Deo. Augsburg: 1524. V. 53
Haubpostilla. Oer Die Sontags und der Furnemesten Feste Evangelien/ Durchs Ganze Jar. Wittemberg: 1598. V. 48
In Cantica Canticorum, Breuis sed Admodum Dilucida Enarratio. Vvitenbergae: 1539. V. 49
Loci Communes... ... Excriptis Ipsius Latinis Forma Gnomologica & Aphoristica Collecti & in Quinque Classes Distributi... Magdeburg: 1594. V. 49
Ordenung Eyns Gemeynen Kastens. Wittenberg?: 1523. V. 53
An Die Pfarrherrn Wider de Wucher zu Predigen. Wittenberg: 1540. V. 52
Ein Sermon von den Siebe(n) Broten Gepredigt Im. Jar XXIII. Augsburg: 1523?. V. 48; 49
Special and Chosen Sermons. London: 1578. V. 50
Die Syben Bueszpsalmen. Strasbourg: 1519. V. 48
Tischreden Oder Colloquia. Eisleben: 1566. V. 50
Verantwortung der Auffgelegten Auffrur Von Hertzog Georgen. Wittenberg: 1533. V. 53
Vermanung an die Geistlichen Versamlet auff dem Reichstag zu Augsburg Anno 1530. Wittenberg: 1530. V. 48
Von Schem Hamphoras: Und Vom Geschlecht Christi. Wittenberg: 1543. V. 53
Vrsacb (sic) Vnd Anttwortt Das Iungkfrawen Kloster Gottlich Verlassen Mugen. Wittemburg: 1523. V. 53
The Way to Prayer. London: 1846. V. 52
Zwo Predig Auff die Epistel S. Pauli...Ueber der Leich des Churfuersten Hertzog Friedrichs zu Sachsen. Strasbourg: 1525?. V. 48

LUTHER, SETH
An Address to the Working Men of New England, on the State of Education, and on the Condition of the Producing Classes in Europe and America. Boston: 1832. V. 53

LUTTIG, JOHN C.
Journal of a Fur Trading Expedition on the Upper Missouri, 1812-1813. St. Louis: 1920. V. 52

LUTTINGER, ABIGAIL
Good Evening and Other Poems. Lisbon: 1979. V. 54

LUTTRELL, HENRY
Advice to Julia. A Letter in Rhyme. London: 1820. V. 54
Crockford House, A Rhapsody in Tow Cantos. (with) A Rhymer in Rome. London: 1827. V. 47; 52
Crockford's or Life in the West... London: 1828. V. 51

LUTTRELL, NARCISSUS
A Brief Historical Relation of State Affairs from September 1678 to April 1714. 1857. V. 53
A Brief Historical Relations of State Affairs from September 1678 to April 1714. London: 1857. V. 49

LUTWYCHE, EDWARD
Un Livre des Entries: Contenant Auxi un report des Resolutions Del Court Sur Diverse Exceptions Prises as Pleadings, et Sur Auters Matters en Ley (etc.). London: 1704. V. 47
The Reports and Entries of Sir Edward Lutwyche, Kt. Sergeant at Law and Late One of the Judges of the Court of Common Pleas... London: 1718. V. 52

LUTYENS, EDWIN
Fulbrook - A House You Will Love to Live In. Marlborough: 1989. V. 52

LUTZ, HENRY FREDERICK
Egyptian Statues and Statuettes in the Museum of Anthropology of the University of California. Leipzig: 1930. V. 51
Egyptian Tomb Steles and Offering Stones of the Museum of Anthropology and Ethnology of the University of California. Leipzig: 1927. V. 51

LUXBOROUGH, HENRIETTA KNIGHT, LADY
Letters to William Shenstone, Esq. London: 1775. V. 53; 54

LUXMOORE, H. E.
Some Views and Opinions of Sparrow on Housetops. Eton College: 1885. V. 52; 53

LUYKEN, JAN
Afbeelding der Menschelyke Bezighede, Bestaande in Hondert Onderscheiden Printverbeeldingen, Vertonende Allerhande Stantspersonen, zo van Regeeringe, Konsten, Wetenschappen, als Handwerken... Amsterdam: 1695. V. 48; 52; 54

LUYTS, JOANNIS
Introductio Ad Geographim. Trajecti ad Rhenum: 1692. V. 48

LYALL, ALFRED COMYN
Verses Written in India. London: 1889. V. 49

LYALL, EDNA
Donovan: a Novel. London: 1882. V. 50
A Hardy Norseman. London: 1890. V. 48
In the Golden Days. London: 1885. V. 54

LYALL, ROBERT
The Character of the Russians, and a Detailed History of Moscow... London: 1823. V. 50; 53

LYCOPHRON
Alexandra. (Partly Greek title). Geneva?: 1601. V. 50; 53
(Part Greek title) Alexandra cum Graecis Isaacii Tzetzis Commentarius. Oxonii: 1697. V. 49

LYCOPHRONIS CHALCIDENSIS
Cassandra. Romae: 1803. V. 52

LYCOSTHENES
Prodigiorum Ac Ostentorum Chronicon... Basel: 1557. V. 48

LYCOSTHENES, CONRADUS
Apophthegmata Ex optimis Utriusque Linguae Scriptoribus... Lyon: 1574. V. 52

LYDE, SAMUEL
The Ansyreeh and Ismaeleeh: a Visit to the Secret Sects of Northern Syria. London: 1853. V. 51

LYDEKEKR, RICHARD
A Hand-Book to the Marsupialia and Monotremata. London: 1894. V. 53

LYDEKKER, RICHARD
Animal Portraiture. London. V. 48; 50; 52; 53
Animal Portraiture... London: 1912. V. 54
Catalogue of the Fossil Mammalia in the British Museum. London: 1885-87. V. 50
Catalogue of the Fossil Reptilia and Amphibia in the British Museum. London: 1888-90. V. 48
Catalogue of the Ungulate Mammals. London: 1913-15. V. 47
Catalogue of the Ungulate Mammals... London: 1913-16. V. 48; 50; 54
The Game Animals of Africa. London: 1908. V. 48; 49
The Game Animals of India, Burma, Malaya and Tibet... London: 1907. V. 47
The Game Animals of India, Burma, Malaya and Tibet. London: 1924. V. 48; 49
Harmsworth Natural History. 1910. V. 52
Library of Natural History. New York and Chicago: 1901. V. 51
Notes on the Specimens of Wild Asses in English Collections. London: 1904. V. 51
The Royal Natural History. London & New York: 1893-94. V. 50; 52
The Royal Natural History. 1893-96. V. 52
The Royal Natural History. London: 1893-96. V. 47; 50; 51; 52; 53; 54
Royal Natural History. London: 1922. V. 49
The Sheep and Its Cousins. London: 1912. V. 49
Wild Life of the World. London: 1915. V. 48
Wild Life of the World. London: 1916. V. 51; 54

LYDGATE, JOHN
The Temple of Glass. Cambridge: 1905. V. 50

LYDIAT, THOMAS
De Variis Annorum Formis etc. London: 1605. V. 51

LYDON, A. F.
English Lake Scenery. London: 1880. V. 52; 54
Fairy Mary's Dream. London: 1870. V. 51
Scottish Loch Scenery. London: 1882. V. 52; 54

LYE, LEN
No Trouble. Deja, Majorca: 1930. V. 47

LYELL, CHARLES
Elements of Geology. London: 1838. V. 48; 50; 53

LYELL, CHARLES continued
Elements of Geology. Philadelphia: 1839. V. 51
Elements of Geology. Boston: 1841. V. 48; 54
Elements of Geology. London: 1841. V. 54
Elements of Geology... London: 1847. V. 48
Elements of Geology. London: 1865. V. 53
The Geological Evidence of the Antiquity of Man... London: 1863. V. 48; 49; 50; 53
The Geological Evidences of the Antiquity of Man. Philadelphia: 1863. V. 49; 50
A Manual of Elementary Geology... London: 1855. V. 54
A Manual of Elementary Geology. London: 1855-59. V. 53
A Manual of Elementary Geology. London: 1867-68. V. 50
Principles of Geology. London: 1830-33. V. 48; 53
Principles of Geology. London: 1832-33. V. 47; 49; 51
Principles of Geology... London: 1834. V. 53
Principles of Geology... London: 1835. V. 49; 53; 54
Principles of Geology... London: 1837. V. 51; 52; 53; 54
Principles of Geology... London: 1847. V. 47; 50; 54
Principles of Geology... London: 1850. V. 54
Principles of Geology. London: 1853. V. 51; 53
Principles of Geology. New York: 1860. V. 53
Principles of Geology... London: 1867-68. V. 47; 48; 50; 54
The Principles of Geology... London: 1867-78. V. 53
Principles of Geology. London: 1872. V. 53
Principles of Geology. New York: 1872. V. 54
Principles of Geology... London: 1872-68. V. 49
Principles of Geology... London: 1875. V. 47; 53
Principles of Geology. New York: 1877. V. 49
Principles of Geology... London: 1878-72. V. 52
A Second Visit to the United States of North America. London: 1849. V. 49; 54
A Second Visit to the United States of North America. New York: 1849. V. 53
Second Visit to the United States of North America. New York: 1850. V. 47; 48; 50
Second Visit to the United States of North America. New York: 1855. V. 48; 53
The Student's Elements of Geology. London: 1871. V. 53
Travels in North America. London: 1845. V. 47; 48; 53; 54
Travels in North America... New York: 1845. V. 54
Travels in North America... London: 1855. V. 48; 52

LYELL, DENIS D.
African Adventure. New York: 1935. V. 53
The Hunting and Spoor of Central African Game. Philadelphia: 1920. V. 52
The Hunting and Spoor of Central African Game. London: 1929. V. 49; 52; 53
The Hunting and Spoor of Central African Game. Philadelphia: 1929. V. 47
Hunting Trips in Northern Rhodesia. 1910. V. 54
Memories of an African Hunter. Boston: 1923. V. 47; 53
Memories of an African Hunter. London: 1924. V. 48
Wild Life in Central Africa. London: 1913. V. 48

LYELL, J. C.
Fancy Pigeons. London: 1887. V. 50

LYELL, J. P. R.
Early Book Illustration in Spain. London: 1926. V. 47; 49; 50; 51

LYFORD, WILLIAM GILMAN
The Western Address Directory... Baltimore: 1837. V. 49; 51; 54

LYLE, L.
Colonel and Mrs. Revel. London: 1883. V. 54

LYLE, R. C.
The Aga Khan's Hroses. London: 1938. V. 47

LYLE, ROYSTER
The Architecture of Historic Lexington. Charlottesville: 1977. V. 49

LYLY, JOHN
The Complete Works. 1902. V. 50
The Complete Works. Oxford: 1902. V. 53
Euphues. The Anatomie of Wit. London: 1636. V. 50; 53
Euphues. The Anatomy of Wit... London: 1868. V. 50
Euphues. The Anatomy of Wit. (with) Euphues and His England. London: 1623. V. 47
Sixe Covrt Comedies. London: 1632. V. 49

LYMAN, CHESTER S.
Around the Horn to the Sandwich Islands and Calfiornia 1845-1850. New Haven: 1924. V. 47; 49; 52

LYMAN, DARIUS
Leaven For Doughfaces; or, Threescore and Ten Parables Touching Slavery by a Former Resident of the South. Cincinnati: 1856. V. 48

LYMAN, GEORGE D.
John Marsh, Pioneer. New York: 1930. V. 52
The Scalpel Under Three Flags in California. San Francisco: 1925. V. 51

LYMAN, HENRY M.
Artificial Anaesthesia and Anaesthetics. New York: 1881. V. 50; 52; 54
Insomnia and Other Disorders of Sleep. Chicago: 1885. V. 54

LYMAN, JOSEPH B.
Cotton Culture. New York: 1868. V. 47; 50

LYMAN, THEODORE
A Short Account of the Hartford Convention, Taken from Official Documents and Addressed to the Fair Minded and Well Disposed to Which is Added an Attested Copy of the Secret Journal of that Body. Boston: 1823. V. 51

LYMBURNER, ADAM
The Paper Read at the Bar of the House of Commons, by Mr. Lymburner; Agent for the Subscribers to the Petitions from the Province of Quebec. Quebec: 1791. V. 47

LYMINGTON, LORD
Spring Song of Iscariot. Paris: 1929. V. 51

LYNAM, C. C.
Log of the Blue Dragon 1892-1904. London: 1907. V. 51
The Log of the Blue Dragon II in Orkney and Shetland 1909-1910. London: 1911. V. 51
To Norway and the North Cape in Blue Dragon II 1911-12. London: 1913. V. 48; 51

LYNCH, BERNARD
A Guide to Health through the Various Stages of Life. London: 1744. V. 48

LYNCH, BOHUN
A History of Caricature. London: 1926. V. 47; 48

LYNCH, GEORGE
In Many Wars by Many War Correspondents. Tokyo: 1904. V. 54
In Many Wars By Many War Correspondents. Tokyo: 1905?. V. 51

LYNCH, H. F. B.
Armenia Travels and Studies. Beirut: 1967. V. 49

LYNCH, JAMES D.
Bench and Bar of Texas. St. Louis: 1885. V. 53

LYNCH, JAMES J.
Box, Pit and Gallery - Stage and Society in Johnson's London. 1953. V. 52

LYNCH, JAMES K.
With Stevenson to California 1846. 1896. V. 52

LYNCH, JEREMIAH
Three Years in the Klondike. London: 1904. V. 49

LYNCH, JEROME
Tumors of the Colon & Rectum: Their Pathology, Diagnosis and Treatment. New York: 1925. V. 49; 54

LYNCH, JOHN R.
Facts of Reconstruction. New York: 1913. V. 47; 50; 53; 54

LYNCH, LAWRENCE L.
The Lost Witness or the Mystery of Leah Paget. London: 1890. V. 47

LYNCH, PATRICK
The Life of Saint Patrick... Dublin: 1810. V. 53

LYNCH, STANISLAUS
Rhymes of an Irish Huntsman. London & New York: 1937. V. 47; 48

LYNCH, THEODORA ELIZABETH
The Cotton-Tree; or, Emily, the Little West Indian. London: 1847. V. 50

LYNCH, THOMAS KERR
A Visit to the Suez Canal. London: 1866. V. 49; 51; 53; 54

LYNCH, WILLIAM FRANCIS
Narrative of the United States Expedition to the River Jordan and the Dead Sea. Philadelphia: 1849. V. 51

LYND, ROBERT
Rambles in Ireland. Boston: 1912. V. 51; 54

LYNDSAY, DAVID
The Poetical Works... London: 1806. V. 50; 52
The Poetical Works. Edinburgh: 1879. V. 50; 53

LYNDSTON, G. FRANK
Panama and the Sierras - a Doctors Wander Days. Chicago: 1900. V. 54

LYNE, MICHAEL
Horses, Hounds and Country. London: 1938. V. 47
A Parson's Son. London: 1974. V. 47; 49

LYNES, GEORGE PLATT
Ballet. 1985. V. 54

LYNES, H.
On the Birds of North and Central Darfur (Sudan). Ibis: 1924-26. V. 51

LYNK, M. V.
The Black Troopers, or the Daring Heroism of the Negro soldiers in the Spanish American War. Jackson: 1899. V. 53

LYNN CAMP CREEK OIL CO.
The Lynn Camp Creek Oil Company of West Virginia...Oil Territory. Two Tracts - 910 Acres - Fee Simple. Philadelphia: 1865. V. 50

THE LYNN *Magazine: or a Collection of Papers, Published During the Contest in that Town.* London: 1768. V. 48

LYNN, SAMUEL
A Short Narrative of the Case of Samuel Lynn, Esq. Late Muster Master General of the Late Marine Forces &c... London: 1720. V. 49; 51; 52

LYON, A. B.
Lyon Memorial. Massachusetts Families Including Descendants of the Immigrants William Lyon, of Roxbury, Peter Lyon, of Dorchester, George Lyon, of Dorchester with Introduction Treating of the English Ancestry of the American Families. Detroit: 1905. V. 47

LYON, C. J.
History of St. Andrews, Episcopal, Monastic, Adademic and Civil... Edinburgh: 1843. V. 47

LYON, DANNY
The Bikeriders. New York/London: 1968. V. 47; 53

LYON, GEORGE FRANCIS
A Brief Narrative of an Unsuccessful Attempt to Reach Repulse Bay, in His Majesty's Ship Griper, in the Year 1824. London: 1825. V. 47; 51; 52
Journal During the Recent Voyage of Discovery Under Captain Parry, 1821-23. Barre: 1970. V. 50
Journal of a Residence and Tour in the Republic of Mexico in the Year 1826 with Some Account of the Mines of that Country. London: 1828. V. 48; 51
A Narrative of the Travels in Northern Africa, in the Years 1818, 19 and 20... London: 1821. V. 50; 52; 53
The Private Journal of Captain G. F. Lyon of H.M.S. Hecla, During the Recent Voyage of Discovery Under Captain Parry. London: 1824. V. 47; 49; 52; 54
The Private Journal of Captain G. F. Lyon of H.M.S. Hecla During the Recent Voyage of Discovery Under Captain Parry. 1821-1823. Barre: 1970. V. 50; 52; 53; 54

LYON, H. M.
Sardonics. 1909. V. 48; 52

LYON, IRVING WHITALL
Colonial Furniture of New England. Boston & New York: 1925. V. 48

LYON, LILLIAN BOWES
Collected Poems. London: 1948. V. 52

LYON & HEALY, CHICAGO
Catalogue of Their Collection of Rare Old Violins: 1896-97 to Which Is Added a Historical Sketch of the Violin and Its Master Makers. Chicago: 1896. V. 49

LYONS, A. NEIL
Tom, Dick and Harriet. London: 1937. V. 47

LYONS, ARTHUR
The Dead are Discreet. New York: 1974. V. 52
The Second Coming: Satanism in America. New York: 1970. V. 50; 51

LYONS, CICELY
Salmon: Our Heritage. Vancouver: 1969. V. 48; 50

LYONS, H. G.
A Report on the Island and Temples of Philae... Cairo: 1896. V. 49

LYONS, NICK
Two Fish Tales. New York: 1991. V. 47
Two Fish Tales. Pine Plains. 1991. V. 47

LYONS, WILLIAM
Atlas of Peripheral Nerve Injuries. Philadelphia: 1949. V. 54

LYRA Germanica... London: 1861. V. 52
LYRA Germanica... London: 1864. V. 51

LYRA Germanica. London: 1868. V. 49; 52

LYRA Germanica... London: 1872-73. V. 54

LYRICAL Poetry from the Bible. (First and Second Series). London: 1895. V. 47

LYSAGHT, A. M.
The Book of Birds. London: 1975. V. 52; 53
Joseph Banks in Newfoundland and Labrador, 1766: His Diary, Manuscripts and Collections. London: 1971. V. 47

LYSAGHT, ELIZABETH J.
The Gold of Ophir. London: 1890. V. 51

LYSER, ALICE
Spain and Spanish America in the Libraries of the University of California: a Catalogue of Books. Berkeley: 1928-30. V. 49

LYSERUS, JOHANNES
Polygamia Triumphatrix, Id est Discursus Politicus de Polygamia... Lund: 1682. V. 52

LYSIAS
Eratosthenes, hoc Est, Brevis et Lvcvlenta Defensio Lysiae Praelectionibus Illustrata Andreae Dvnaei... Cambridge: 1593. V. 48; 52

LYSON'S Britannia: Berkshire Section complete. London: 1806. V. 47

LYSONS, DANIEL
The County Palatine of Cheshire. London: 1810. V. 48
The Environs of London. London: 1792-1811. V. 53
The Environs of London... London: 1800-11. V. 47; 50
History of the Origin and Progress of the Meeting of the Three Choirs of Gloucester, Worcester and Hereford and of the Charity Connected with It... Gloucester: 1812. V. 50
Magna Britannia. London: 1806-22. V. 49; 51; 53; 54
Magna Britannia... London: 1808. V. 49
Magna Britannia. London: 1816. V. 49; 50; 52; 54
Magna Britannia... London: 1817. V. 50
Magna Britannia... London: 1822. V. 50; 54
Practical Essays Upon Intermitting Fevers, Dropsies, Diseases of the Liver, the Epilepsy, the Colic, Dysentric Fluxes and the Operation of Calomel. Bath: 1772. V. 51

LYSONS, SAMUEL
An Account of the Remains of a Roman Villa Discovered at Bignor, in the County of Sussex, in the Year 1811 and the Four Following Years. London: 1815. V. 51
A Collection of Gloucestershire Antiquities. London: 1791-1804. V. 52
A Collection of Gloucestershire Antiquities. London: 1804. V. 51; 54
Remains of Two Roman Temples and of the Roman Antiquities Discovered at Bath. London: 1802. V. 47

LYTE, H. C. MAXWELL
A History of Eton College. 1440-1875. London: 1875. V. 48
A History of Eton College (1440-1910). London: 1911. V. 49; 52

LYTHGOE, ALBERT M.
The Predynastic Cemetery N 7000. Berkeley: 1965. V. 49; 51

LYTLE, ANDREW NELSON
At the Moon's Inn. Indianapolis/New York: 1941. V. 51
At the Moon's Inn. London: 1943. V. 52
Bedford Forrest... New York: 1931. V. 47; 50; 52; 53
Bedford Forrest. London: 1939. V. 52; 54
The Long Night. Indianapolis: 1936. V. 47
A Name for Evil. Indianapolis: 1947. V. 47; 48
A Name for Evil. New York: 1947. V. 47
The Velvet Horn. New York: 1957. V. 51

A LYTTEL Booke of Nonsense. 1925. V. 53

LYTTELTON, GEORGE LYTTELTON, 1ST BARON
The Court Secret: a Melancholy Truth. London: 1741. V. 47; 53
Dialogues of the Dead. London: 1760. V. 48; 49; 52; 54
Dialogues of the Dead. (bound with) New Dialogues of the Dead. London: 1760/62. V. 49
The History and Life of King Henry the Second and of the Age in Which He Lived. London: 1767-71. V. 47; 50; 53
Letters 1955-1962. London: 1978-84. V. 53
Letters from a Persian in England to His Friend at Ispahan. London: 1735. V. 49
The Works. London: 1774. V. 50

LYTTLETON, GEORGE COURTNEY
The History of England, from the Earliest Dawn of Authentic Record to the Commencement of Hostilities in the Year 1803... Stratford: 1808/03. V. 52

LYTTON, B., LADY
The School for Husbands' or, Moliere's Life and Times. 1852. V. 50

LYTTON, EDWARD GEORGE EARLE LYTTON BULWER-LYTTON, 1ST BARON
The Caxtons. Edinburgh & London: 1849. V. 47; 49; 50; 52
Devereux. London: 1829. V. 47; 49; 50; 51
The Disowned. London: 1829. V. 47; 50
England and the English. London: 1833. V. 49; 52
Eugen Aram. London: 1832. V. 47; 48; 50
Harold, the Last of the Saxon Kings. London: 1848. V. 51
Ishmael: An Oriental Tale, With Other Poems. London: 1820. V. 47; 49
Kenelm Chillingly, His Adventures and Opinions. London: 1873. V. 51; 53; 54
The Last Days of Pompeii. London: 1834. V. 51
The Last Days of Pompeii. Verona: 1954. V. 54
The Last Days of Pompeii. Verona: 1956. V. 51; 53; 54
The Last of the Barons. London: 1843. V. 49
Leila; or the Siege of Granada; and Calderon and Courtier... London: 1838. V. 49; 50
The Life of Edward Bulwer, First Lord Lytton. London: 1913. V. 49
My Novel. London: 1853. V. 51; 54
Night and Morning. London: 1841. V. 47
The Novels... London: 1862. V. 51
The Novels... London: 1877-78. V. 51
The Novels. Boston: 1891-92. V. 51; 54
Outlines of the Early History of the East... Royston: 1852. V. 49
The Parisians. Edinburgh: 1873. V. 51
The Parisians. London: 1873. V. 54
Paul Clifford. London: 1830. V. 48; 51
Pelham; or, the Adventures of a Gentleman... London: 1828. V. 50
The Rebel and Other Tales. New York: 1835. V. 50
St. Stephen's: a Poem. Edinburgh & London: 1860. V. 47; 48; 50; 53
The Siamese Twins. London: 1831. V. 49
The Student. London: 1835. V. 48; 51; 54
What Will He Do With It?. Edinburgh and London: 1859. V. 47; 50
Works. London: 1880. V. 51
Zanoni. London: 1842. V. 47; 49; 51

LYTTON, EDWARD ROBERT BULWER-LYTTON, 1ST EARL OF
Fables in Song. Edinburgh: 1874. V. 53
Fables in Song. London: 1874. V. 51
Glenaveril, or the Metamorphoses. London: 1885. V. 50
King Poppy. London: 1892. V. 49; 50; 51; 54
Lucile. London: 1860. V. 48
Lucile. Boston: 1873. V. 48
Poems. Boston: 1881. V. 52
Tannhauser: Or, The Battle of the Bards. A Poem. Mobile: 1863. V. 48

LYTTON, NEVILLE, MRS.
Toy Dogs and Their Ancestors, Including the History and Management of Toy Spaniels, Pekingese, Japanese and Pomeranians. London: 1911. V. 48

M

MAC ADAM, JOHN LOUDON
Remarks on the Present System of Road Making. London: 1820. V. 52; 53; 54
Remarks On the Present System of Road Making... London: 1822. V. 51; 54
Report from Select Committee on Mr. McAdam's Petition, Relating to His Improved System of Constructing and Repairing the Public Roads of the Kingdom. London: 1823. V. 54

MC ADAMS, FRANCIS MARION
Our Knapsack. Sketches for the Boys in Blue. Columbus: 1884. V. 50

MC ADIE, ALEXANDER
The Clouds and Fogs of San Francisco. San Francisco: 1912. V. 50; 54

MC ADOO, WILLIAM
William Henry Schuetz. 1903. V. 48

MC AFEE, JOSEPH B.
Official Military History of Kansas Regiments During the War for the Suppression of the Great Rebellion. Leavenworth: 1870. V. 49

MC AFEE, ROBERT BRECKINRIDGE
History of the Late War in the Western Country. Lexington;: 1816. V. 48

MC AFEE, THOMAS
My Confidant, Catullus. Mount Carmel. V. 53

MC ALDOWIE, A. M.
The Birds of Staffordshire, with Illustrations of Local Bird Haunts. Stroke on Trent: 1893. V. 47

MAC ALISTER, R. A. STEWART
The Excavation of Gezer 1902-1905 and 1907-1909. London: 1912. V. 52

MC ALLISTER, A.
A Dissertation on the Medical Properties and Injurious Effects of the Habitual Use of Tobacco... Boston: 1832. V. 53

MC ALLISTER, JAMES GRAY
Sketch of Captain Thompson McAllister. Petersburg: 1896. V. 49

MC ALMON, ROBERT
Being Geniuses Together. 1938. V. 50
Being Geniuses Together. London: 1938. V. 47; 51; 53
Being Geniuses Together. Garden City: 1968. V. 54
Contact Collection of Contemporary Writers. Paris: 1923. V. 53
Distinguished Air: Grim Fairy Tales. Paris: 1925. V. 52
Explorations. London: 1921. V. 51
A Hasty Bunch. Paris: 1922. V. 50; 51; 53
A Hasty Bunch. Paris: 1923. V. 47; 48
North America. Paris: 1929. V. 52
Post-Adolescence. Paris: 1923. V. 48; 50; 53
Village: as It Happened through a Fifteen Year Period. Paris: 1924. V. 53

MAC ALPINE, ARTHUR
Man in a Metal Cage. Easthampton: 1977. V. 48

MC ALPINE, D.
Life Histories of Plants. London: 1900. V. 48

MAC ALPINE, IDA
Schizophrenia 1677. London: 1956. V. 53

MC ALPINE, WALLACE
Heart and Coronary Arteries: an Anatomical Atlas for Clinical Diagnosis, Radiological Investigation and Surgical Treatment. New York: 1975. V. 54

MC ALPINE, WILLIAM HENRY
A Catalogue of the Law Library at Hartwell House, Buckinghamshire. London: 1865. V. 53

MAC ARTHUR, CHARLES G.
A Bug's-Eye View of the War. 1919. V. 48

MAC ARTHUR, DOUGLAS
Reminiscences. New York Toronto London: 1964. V. 47

MC ARTHUR, HARRIET NESMITH
Recollections of the Rickreall. Portland: 1930. V. 52; 54

M'ARTHUR, JOHN
The Antiquities of Arran. Edinburgh: 1873. V. 54

MC ARTHUR, JOHN
The Army and Navy Gentleman's Companion; or a New and Complete Treatise...of Fencing. London: 1784. V. 49; 54

MAC ARTHUR, JOHN
A Treatise of the Principles and Practice of Naval Courts-Martial, with an Appendix... 1792. V. 47

MC ARTHUR, JOHN W.
New Developments: Including the Grange, Anti-Monopoly, Farmers' Alliance, Co-operative Fire Insurance and the Economic Barn to which is Added an Account of Artificial Butter. Oneonta: 1886. V. 51

MAC ARTHUR, MILDRED YORBA
California-Spanish Proverbs. San Francisco: 1964. V. 50

MC ARTHUR, MOLLY
Tribute (Poems and Woodcuts). London: 1923. V. 48

MC ARTHUR, PETER
The Red Cow and Her Friends. Toronto: 1919. V. 50
The Red Cow and Her Friends. Toronto: 1949. V. 53

MAC ASKILL, WALLACE R.
Out of Halifax: a Collection of Sea Pictures. New York: 1937. V. 50; 52; 53; 54

MC AULEY, JAMES
Under Aldebaran. Carlton: 1946. V. 54

MC AULEY, JEREMIAH
Transformed, or, the History of a River Thief, Briefly Told. New York?: 1876. V. 48

MC AULIFFE, EUGENE
History of the Union Pacific Coal Mines 1868-1940. Omaha: 1940. V. 54

MAC AVOY, R. A.
Tea With a Black Dragon. 1987. V. 48; 49; 52; 54

MC BAIN, ED
The 87th Precinct. New York: 1959. V. 52
The 8th Squad. New York: 1960. V. 52
The Cop Hater. New York: 1989. V. 52
Find the Feathered Serpent. 1952. V. 51
Hail to the Chief. New York: 1973. V. 52
The Heckler. New York: 1960. V. 52
The Interview. Helskinki: 1986. V. 48
Let's Hear It For the Deaf Man. Garden City: 1973. V. 49
The Pusher. New York: 1990. V. 52
See Them Die. New York: 1960. V. 52
Shotgun. Garden City: 1969. V. 52
Ten Plus One. New York: 1963. V. 51; 52

M'BAIN, J.
The Merrick and the Neighbouring Hills. Ayr. V. 54
The Merrick and the Neighbouring Hills. Ayr: 1910. V. 52

MAC BEAN, ALEXANDER
A Dictionary of the Bible, or an Explanation of the Proper Names and Difficult Words... London: 1766. V. 48
A Dictionary of the Bible or an Explanation of the Proper Names and Difficult Words in the Old and New Testament. Worcester: 1798. V. 54

MAC BEAN, WILLIAM
The Constitution of Germany. London: 1743. V. 50

MAC BETH, GEORGE
A Form of Words. Eynsham: 1954. V. 47
The Humming Birds - a Monodrama. London: 1965. V. 54
A War Quartet. London: 1969. V. 47

MAC BRIDE, DAVID
Experimental Essays on Medical and Philosophical Subjects... London: 1767. V. 51; 52

MC BRIDE, JAMES
Symme's Theory of Concentric Spheres... Cincinnati: 1826. V. 48

MC BRIDE, JOHN R.
History of the Thirty-Third Indiana Veteran Volunteer Infantry. Indianapolis: 1900. V. 47

MC BRYDE, JAMES
The Story of a Troll-Hunt. 1904. V. 54

MC CABE, CYNTHIA JAFFEE
Fernando Botero. Washington: 1979. V. 47

MAC CABE, FREDERIC
The Art of Ventriloquism. London: 1875. V. 47

M'CABE, JOHN COLLINS
Scraps. Richmond: 1835. V. 52; 54

MAC CABE, JULIUS PATRICK B.
MacCabe's Directory of Drogheda, and its Environs... Drogheda: 1830. V. 53

MC CAFFERTY, W. PATRICK
Aquatic Entomology. Boston: 1981. V. 48

MC CAFFREY, A.
Cooking Out of This World. 1992. V. 48; 52
The Dolphins Bell. 1993. V. 52
Dragonflight. 1968. V. 52
Dragonquest. 1973. V. 52
Dragonsong. 1976. V. 48
The Year of the Lucy. 1986. V. 47

MAC CAFFREY, JAMES
The Black Book of Limerick. Dublin: 1907. V. 51

MAC CAIG, NORMAN
Riding Lights - Poems. London: 1955. V. 50
The Sinai Sort. London: 1957. V. 50

MC CAIN, C. W.
History of the SS Beaver. Vancouver: 1894. V. 49

MC CALEB, WALTER FLAVIUS
The Aaron Burr Conspiracy. New York: 1903. V. 52; 53

MC CALL, D.
Three Years in the Service. Record of the Doings of the 11th Reg. Missouri Volumes. Springfield: 1864. V. 50

MC CALL, GEORGE A.
Colonel McCall's Reports in Relation to New Mexico. Washington: 1851. V. 54
Report of the Secretary of War Communicating...Col. McCall's Reports, in Relation to New Mexico, 31st Congress, 2nd Sess. Ex Doc. 26. Washington: 1851. V. 47; 49; 54

M'CALL, H. B.
The Early History of Bedale in the North Riding of Yorkshire. London: 1907. V. 53
Richmondshire Churches. London: 1910. V. 53

MC CALL, JOHN C.
The Witch of New England: a romance. (and) Hobomok, a Tale of Early Times. Philadelphia: 1824. V. 51

MC CALLUM, D.
China to Chelsea. London: 1930. V. 54

M'CALLUM, HUGH
An Original Collection of the Poems of Ossian, Orrann, Ulin and Other Bards, Who Flourished in the Same Age. Montrose: 1816. V. 48; 50; 51

MAC CALLUM, WILLIAM
The Pathology of the Pneumonia in the United States Army Camps During the Winter of 1917-18. New York: 1919. V. 51

MC CALMONT, ROSE E.
Memoirs of the Binghams. London: 1915. V. 53

MC CAMMON, ROBERT
Baal. London: 1985. V. 51
Blue World. London: 1989. V. 50; 51
Mystery Walk. New York: 1983. V. 51
Swan Song. 1987. V. 51
Swan Song. Arlington Heights: 1989. V. 51
They Thirst. 1991. V. 51; 54

MC CANDLESS, BYRON
Flags of the World. Washington: 1917. V. 49

MC CANN, ANNA MARGUERITE
The Portraits of Septimius Severus (A.D. 193-211).. Roma: 1968. V. 52

MC CANN, EDSON
Preferred Risk. New York: 1955. V. 50

MC CANN, IRVING GOFF
With National Guard on the Border: Our National Military Problem. St. Louis: 1917. V. 49; 50

MAC CANN, WILLIAM
Two Thousand Miles' Ride through the Argentine Provinces... London: 1853. V. 48; 51

MC CARRISON, ROBERT
The Thyroid Gland in Health and Disease.. London: 1917. V. 54

MC CARRY, CHARLES
The Miernik Dossier. New York: 1973. V. 51

MAC CARTHY, B.
Codex Palatino-Vaticanus. London: 1892. V. 47; 53

MC CARTHY, CARLTON
Contributions to a History of the Richmond Howitzer Battalion. Richmond: 1883-6. V. 53; 54
Detailed Minutiae of Soldier Life in the Army of Northern Virginia 1861-1865. Richmond: 1882. V. 47
Detailed Minutiae of Soldier Life in the Army of Northern Virginia 1861-1865. Richmond: 1908. V. 50

MC CARTHY, CHARLOTTE
Justice and Reason, Faithful Guides to Truth. London: 1767. V. 52

MC CARTHY, CORMAC
All the Pretty Horses. New York: 1982. V. 52; 54
All the Pretty Horses. London: 1992. V. 51
All the Pretty Horses. New York: 1992. V. 47; 48; 49; 50; 51; 52; 53; 54
All The Pretty Horses. London: 1993. V. 51; 52; 53; 54
All the Pretty Horses. New York: 1993. V. 51
Blood Meridian. London: 1985. V. 53
Blood Meridian. New York: 1985. V. 49; 50; 51; 52; 53; 54
Blood Meridian or The Evening Redness in the West. London: 1989. V. 51; 53; 54
Child of God. New York: 1973. V. 48; 49; 50; 51; 52; 53; 54
Child of God. London: 1975. V. 53
The Crossing. London: 1994. V. 51; 52; 53
The Crossing. New York: 1994. V. 50; 51; 52; 53
The Orchard Keeper. New York: 1965. V. 49; 50; 51; 52; 54
The Orchard Keeper. London: 1966. V. 53
The Orchard Keeper. New York: 1969. V. 53
Outer Dark. New York: 1968. V. 49; 50; 51; 52; 53; 54
Outer Dark. London: 1970. V. 51; 52; 53
The Stonemason. Hopewell: 1994. V. 51; 52; 53; 54
The Stonemason. New York: 1994. V. 52; 54
Suttree. New York: 1979. V. 50; 51; 53; 54
Suttree. New York: 1986. V. 53

MAC CARTHY, DENIS FLORENCE
Shelley's Early Life from Original Sources. London: 1872. V. 49

MC CARTHY, E. T.
Incidents in the Life of a Mining Engineer. London: 1919. V. 54

MC CARTHY, JUSTIN
Charing Cross to St. Paul's. London: 1891. V. 50; 52
The Grey River. London: 1889. V. 50; 52; 54
A History of Our Own Times from the Accession of Queen Victoria to the Berlin Congress.... London: 1880-1905. V. 49
A History of Our Own Times from the Accession of Queen Victoria to the General Election of 1880. London: 1880. V. 53
The Right Honourable. London: 1886. V. 48
Violets. London: 1881. V. 54

MC CARTHY, LEE
Histopathology of Skin Diseases. St. Louis: 1931. V. 49

MAC CARTHY, THOMAS
Montalto; or the Heart Unveiled. London: 1819. V. 54

MAC CARTHY REAGH, J., COMTE DE
Catalogue des Livres Rares et Precieux de la Bibliotheque de feu M. Le Comte de Mac-Carthy Reagh. Paris: 1815. V. 47

MC CAUGHEY, PATRICK
Fred Williams. Sydney: 1980. V. 47

MC CAUL, JOHN
The Maple Leaf or Canadian Annual: a Literary Souvenir for 1848. Toronto: 1847. V. 47

MC CAULEY, EDWARD Y.
A Dictionary of Eygptian Language Transactions of the American Philosophical Society. Philadelphia: 1882. V. 51

MC CAULEY, JAMES E.
A Stove-Up Cowboys Story. Austin: 1942. V. 53
A Stove-Up Cowboy's Story. Austin: 1943. V. 47; 48

MC CAULEY, JAMES EMMET
A Stove-Up Cowboy's Story. Austin: 1943. V. 48

MC CAULEY, KIRBY
Dark Forces. New York: 1980. V. 51; 52

MC CAUSLAND, ELIZABETH
Changing New York; Photographs by Berenice Abbott. New York: 1939. V. 50; 51

MC CLATCHY, J. D.
Lantskip, Platan, Creatures Ramp'd: A Garden Bestiary. New York: 1983. V. 51; 53

MC CLELLAN, CARSWELL
Notes on the Personal Memoirs of P. H. Sheridan. St. Paul: 1889. V. 49

MC CLELLAN, ELISABETH
Historic Dress in America, 1607-1800 (&) Historic Dress in America 1800-1870. Philadelphia: 1904/10. V. 47

MC CLELLAN, GEORGE
Organization of the Army of the Potomac and Of Its Campaigns in Virginia and Maryland, from July 26, 1861 to November 7, 1862. Washington: 1864. V. 49; 50; 52

MAC CLELLAN, GEORGE B.
The Armies of Europe... Philadelphia: 1861. V. 53

MC CLELLAN, HENRY BRAINARD
Life and Campaigns of Major-General J.E.B. Stuart. Boston and New York: 1885. V. 49; 50

MC CLELLAND, J.
Geological Survey of India. Report 1848-49. Zillahs, Hazareebagh, Monghyr, Bhagulpore and Rajmahal. Calcutta: 1850. V. 51

MAC CLESFIELD, THOMAS, EARL OF
The Tryal of Thomas Earl of Macclesfield, in the House of Peers, for High Crimes and Misdeameanors; Upon an Impeachment (etc). London: 1725. V. 51

MC CLINTOCK, ALEXANDER
Best O'Luck. How a Fighting Kentuckian Won the Thanks of Britain's King. New York: 1917. V. 47

M'CLINTOCK, FRANCIS LEOPOLD
A Narrative of the Discovery of the Fate of Sir John Franklin and His Companions. London: 1859. V. 52
The Voyage of the 'Fox' in the Arctic Seas. London: 1859. V. 47; 49

MC CLINTOCK, JAMES H.
Arizona. Chicago: 1916. V. 50
Arizona With Particular Attention to Its Imperial County of Maricopa. Phoenix: 1901. V. 49
Mormon Settlement in Arizona. Phoenix: 1921. V. 52
Phoenix Arizona in the Great Salt River Valley. Phoenix: 1908. V. 52

MC CLINTOCK, JOHN S.
Pioneer Days in the Black Hills. Deadwood: 1939. V. 47; 53

MC CLINTOCK, SAMUEL
A Sermon Preached Before the Honorable the Council and the Honorable the Senate and House of Representatives, of the State of New Hampshire June 3, 1784. Portsmouth: 1784. V. 50

MC CLINTOCK, W.
The Old North Trail or Life, Legends and Religion of the Blackfeet Indians. London: 1910. V. 48

MC CLOSKEY, ROBERT
One Morning in Maine. New York: 1952. V. 51

MC CLUNG, JOHN A.
Sketches of Western Adventure. Cincinnati: 1839. V. 47

MC CLUNG, NELLIE
Clearing in the West. My Own Story. Toronto: 1935. V. 53
Flowers for the Living. Toronto: 1931. V. 50

MC CLURE, FLOYD ALONZO
Chinese Handmade Paper. Newtown: 1986. V. 49; 53

MAC CLURE, JAMES REID
Edison and His Inventions Including the Many Incidents, Anecdotes and Interesting Particulars Connected with the Life of the Great Inventor. Chicago: 1879. V. 54

MAC CLURE, MAC DONALD & CO.
Yacht Raching on the Clyde and Belfast Lough. Season 1898. Glasgow: 1899. V. 52

MC CLURE, MICHAEL
The Cherub. Los Angeles: 1970. V. 54
For Artaud. New York: 1959. V. 47

MAC CLURE, MICHAEL
Ghost Tantras. San Francisco: 1964. V. 47

MC CLURE, MICHAEL
Jaguar Skies. New York: 1975. V. 50

MAC CLURE, MICHAEL
Love Lion Book. San Francisco: 1966. V. 47

MC CLURE, MICHAEL
Ninety-nine Theses. Lawrence: 1972. V. 50
Passage. Big Sur: 1956. V. 47
Selected Poems. New York: 1986. V. 50
The Sermons of Jean Harlow and The Curses of Billy the Kid. San Francisco: 1968. V. 54

MAC CLURE, MICHAEL
Thirteen Mad Sonnets. Milan: 1964. V. 47

MC CLURE, MICHAEL
(Untitled - but known as Mandalas, Black Dot and Mantras and Prayers). San Francisco: 1966. V. 47; 50

MAC CLURE, MICHAEL
Untitled Broadside Poem. San Francisco: 1966. V. 47

MC CLURE, SAMUEL SIDNEY
My Autobiography. 1914. V. 50
My Autobiography. London: 1914. V. 53
My Autobiography. New York: 1914. V. 53; 54

MAC CLURE, V.
The Ark of the Covenant. 1924. V. 49
The Ark of the Covenant. New York: 1924. V. 54

MAC CLURE, WILLIAM
Observations on the Geology of the United States of America: With Some Remarks on the Effect Produced on the Nature and Fertility of Soils, by the Decomposition of the Different Classes of Rocks. Philadelphia: 1817. V. 47

M'COMBIE, THOMAS
Adventures of a Colonist; or, Godfrey Arabin the Settler. London: 1845. V. 47

M'COMBIE, WILLIAM
Memoirs of Alexander Bethune... Aberdeen: 1845. V. 52

MC CONATHAY, DALE
Hollywood Costume - Glamour! Glitter! Romance!. New York: 1976. V. 47; 48; 52

M'CONKEY, HARRIET E. BISHOP
Dakota War Whoop. Saint Paul: 1863. V. 48

MC CONKEY, HARRIET E. BISHOP
Dakota War Whoop. St. Paul: 1864. V. 52

MC CONKIE, BRUCE R.
Mormon Doctrine. Salt Lake City: 1958. V. 52

MC CONNELL, H. H.
Five Years a Cavalryman; or, Sketches of Regular Army Life on the Texas Frontier, Twenty Odd Years Ago. Jacksboro: 1889. V. 47; 48; 52

MC CONNELL, R. G.
Report of an Exploration in the Yukon and Mackenzie Basins, N.W.T. Montreal: 1891. V. 53
Report on An Exploration of the Finlay and Omenica Rivers. Ottawa: 1896. V. 51; 54
Report on the Cypress Hills Wood Mountain and Adjacent Country, Embracing that Portion of the District of Assinboia, Lying Between the International Boundary and the 51st Parallel and Extending from London... Montreal: 1885. V. 54

MC CONNELL, W. J.
Early History of Idaho. Caldwell: 1913. V. 48; 50

MC CONNELL, WILLIAM M.
Five Years a Cavalryman: or Sketches of Regular Army Life on the Texas Frontier, Twenty Odd Years Ago. Jackboro: 1889. V. 49

MC CONNOCHIE, A. I.
The Deer and Deer Forests of Scotland. Historical, Descriptive, Sporting. 1923. V. 54

MC CORD, DAVID
Alice in Botolphland. Boston: 1932. V. 51

MC CORKLE, JAMES
Incident on the Bark Columbia. Being Letters Received and Sent by Captain McCorkle and the Crew of His Whaler, 1860-1862. Cummington: 1941. V. 49; 52

MC CORKLE, JILL
The Cheer Leader. Chapel Hill. 1984. V. 51; 52; 53; 54
July 7th. Chapel Hill. 1984. V. 48; 51; 52; 53

MC CORKLE, JOHN
Three Years with Quantrell (sic)...Told by His Scout. Armstrong: 1914. V. 48

MC CORKLE, SAMUEL
Incident On the Bark Columbia: Being Letters Received & Sent by McCorkle and the Crew of His Whaler, 1860-62. Cummington: 1941. V. 48

MC CORKLE, WILLIAM ALEXANDER
The White Sulphur Springs: The Traditions, History and Social Life of the Greenbrief White Sulphur Springs. Charleston: 1924. V. 50

M'CORMAC, HENRY
On the Best Means of Improving the Moral and Physical Condition of the Working Classes Being an Address, Delivered on the Opening of the First Monthly Scientific Meetings of the Belfast Mechanic's Inst. London: 1830. V. 52

MAC CORMACK, WILLIAM
An Address of Welcome Delivered on the Occasion of the Centenary Festival of the Royal College of Surgeons of England. London: 1900. V. 51
Antiseptic Surgery: an Address Delivered at St. Thomas's Hospital with Subsequent Debate to Which are Added a Short Statement on the Theory of the Antiseptic Method... London: 1880. V. 51; 54

MAC CORMICK, CHARLES
The Secret History of the Court and reign of Charles the Second, by a Member of His Privy Council... London: 1792. V. 47

MC CORMICK, HARRIET HAMMOND
Landscape Art, Past and Present. New York: 1923. V. 47; 51; 54

MC CORMICK, HENRY
Across the Continent in 1865. Harrisburg: 1937. V. 47

MC CORMICK, J. B.
The History of Microscopes and Microscopical Technique. San Francisco: 1990. V. 49

MC CORMICK, RICHARD
Arizona: its Resources and Prospects. New York: 1865. V. 47; 49; 52; 54
A Visit to the Camp Before Sevastopol. New York: 1855. V. 47; 52

M'CORMICK, S. J.
Portland Directory for 1880. Portland: 1880. V. 54

MC COSH, J.
Realistic Philosophy Defended in a Philosophic Series. New York: 1887. V. 47; 49
The Religious Aspect of Evolution. New York: 1888. V. 53

MC COWAN, DAN
A Naturalist in Canada. Toronto: 1941. V. 47

MC COY, E.
Five California Arachitects: Maybeck, Irving, Gill, Charles/Henry Greene, R.M. Schnidler. New York: 1960. V. 54

MC COY, HORACE
Kiss Tomorrow Good-Bye. New York: 1948. V. 50
They Shoot Horses, Don't They?. London: 1935. V. 49
They Shoot Horses Don't They?. New York: 1935. V. 49; 51; 54
Walk Three Steps Down. Los Angeles: 1950. V. 49

MC COY, ISAAC
The Annual Register of Indian Affairs with the Indian (or Western) Territory. Shawonoe Mission: 1837. V. 47
The Annual Register of Indian Affairs within Indian (or Western) Territory (Numbers 1, 2, 3 and 4). Shawnoe Baptist Mission: 1835/36/37. V. 49
The Annual Register of Indian Affairs Within the Indian (or Western) Territory. No. 2. Shawonoe Baptist Mission: 1836. V. 47
Periodical Account of Baptist Missions Within the Indian Territory for the Year Ending Dec. 31, 1836. Shawonoe Baptist Mission: 1837. V. 48; 49
Remarks on the Practicability of Indian Reform, Embracing their Colonization. New York: 1829. V. 47; 48

MC COY, JOSEPH G.
Historic Sketches o the Cattle Trade of the West and Southwest. Glendale: 1940. V. 50
Historic Sketches of the Cattle Trade of the West and Southwest... Kansas City: 1874. V. 48; 50; 52
Historic Sketches of the Cattle Trade of the West and Southwest. Washington;: 1932. V. 54
Historic Sketches of the Cattle Trade of the West and Southwest. Columbus: 1951. V. 48; 53

MC COY, RALPH E.
Freedom of the Press, an Annotated Bibiliography, Second Supplement: 1978-1992. Carbondale: 1933. V. 53

MC CRACKEN, HAROLD
The Charles M. Russell Book: the Life and Work of the Cowboy Artist. Garden City: 1957. V. 50; 54

MC CRACKEN, HAROLD continued
Frederic Remington, Artist of the Old West. Philadelphia: 1947. V. 47; 53
The Frederic Remington Book. Garden City: 1966. V. 50; 52
George Catlin and the Old Frontier. New York: 1959. V. 54
The West of Buffalo Bill. New York: 1974. V. 52

MC CRACKIN, JOSEPHINE C.
The Woman Who Lost Him and Tales of the Army Frontier. Pasadena: 1913. V. 49; 53

MC CRADY, EDWARD
The History of South Carolina 1670-1783. New York: 1897-1902. V. 50

MC CRAE, HUGH
Colombine. Sydney: 1920. V. 48
Satyrs and Sunlight. London: 1928. V. 48; 50; 51

MC CRARY, GEORGE W.
El Paso Troubles in Texas. Letter from the Secretary of War. Washington: 1878. V. 49

MC CRAY, FLORINE THAYER
The Life Work of the Author of "Uncle Tom's Cabin". New York: 1889. V. 53

MC CREA, LOWRAIN E.
Clinical Cystoscopy; a Treatise on Cystoscopic Technic, Diagnosis, Procedures and Treatment. Philadelphia: 1945. V. 51

MC CREA, R. B.
Lost Amid the Fogs: Sketches of Life in Newfoundland England's Ancient Colony. London: 1869. V. 47

MC CREATH, ANDREW S.
The New River-Cripple Creek Mineral Region of Virginia. Harrisburg: 1887. V. 54

MC CREERY, JOHN
The Press, a Poem. Liverpool & London: 1803-27. V. 48; 52

MC CREIGHT, M. I.
Chief Flying Hawk's Tales. New York: 1936. V. 50

MC CRIE, T.
The Bass Rock, Its Civil and Ecclesiastic History, Geology, Martyrology, Zoology and Botany. Edinburgh: 1848. V. 54

MC CROSSAN, R. G.
Geological History of Western Canada. Calgary: 1964. V. 49

MC CULAGH, FRANCIS
In Franco's spain. London: 1937. V. 49

MAC CULLAGH, JAMES
The Collected Works. Dublin: 1880. V. 53

MC CULLAGH, W. TORRENS
Memoirs of the Right Honourable Richard Lalor Sheil. London: 1835. V. 54

MC CULLERS, CARSON
The Ballad of the Sad Cafe. Boston: 1951. V. 50; 51
Clock Without Hands. Boston: 1961. V. 49; 50; 51; 53; 54
The Heart is a Lonely Hunter. 1940. V. 50
The Heart is a Lonely Hunter. Boston: 1940. V. 51; 54
The Heart is a Lonely Hunter. London: 1943. V. 48; 50; 51
The Member of the Wedding. Boston: 1946. V. 50
Reflections in a Golden Eye. Boston: 1941. V. 48; 50
Reflections in a Golden Eye. Cambridge: 1941. V. 47; 51
The Square Root of Wonderful. Boston: 1958. V. 49; 51
Sweet as a Pickle and Clean as a Pig. Boston: 1964. V. 48; 52

MAC CULLOCH, DONALD B.
The Wondrous Isle of Staffa. Glasgow: 1934. V. 54

MC CULLOCH, J.
Urban Renewal: A Study of the City of Toronto. Toronto: 1956. V. 52

MAC CULLOCH, JOHN
An Essay on the Remittent and Intermittent Diseases Including Generically Marsh Fever and Neuralgia. Philadelphia: 1830. V. 49; 51

MC CULLOCH, JOHN RAMSAY
Descriptive and Statistical Account of the British Empire... London: 1847. V. 49
A Dictionary, Practical, Theoretical and Historical of Commerce and Commercial Navigation. London: 1832. V. 49
A Dictionary, Practical, Theoretical and Historical Of Commerce and Commercial Navitation. London: 1850. V. 52
The Literature of Political Economy... London: 1845. V. 51
The Literature of Political Economy: a Classified Catalogue of Select Publications in the Different Departments of the Science, with Historical, Critical and Biographical Notices. London: 1938. V. 50
The Principles of Political Economy: with Some Inquiries Respecting their Application and a Sketch of the Rise and Progress of the Science. Edinburgh: 1843. V. 48; 52
Statements Illustrative of the Policy and Probable Consequences of the Proposed Repeal of the Exisiting Corn Laws... London: 1841. V. 47; 49
A Statistical Account of the British Empire... London: 1837. V. 52
A Treatise on the Principles and Practical Influence of Taxation and the Funding System. London: 1845. V. 53
A Treatise on the Principles and Practical Influence of Taxation and the Funding System. London: 1852. V. 49

MC CULLOCH, WARREN STURGIS
Embodiments of Mind. Cambridge: 1965. V. 54

MC CULLOCH-WILLIAMS, MARTHA
Dishes and Beverages of the Old South. New York: 1913. V. 47

MC CULLOH, RICHARD S.
Memorial to the Congress of the United States, Requesting an Investigation and Legislation in Relation to the New Method for Refining Gold... Princeton: 1851. V. 47

MAC CURDY, JOHN T.
War Neuroses. Cambridge: 1918. V. 52

MC CURDY, MICHAEL
Face to Face. Great Barrington: 1985. V. 51
Genesis. Boston: 1965-66. V. 49

MC CUTCHEON, JOHN
John McCutcheon's Book. Chicago: 1948. V. 48

MC CUTCHEON, JOHN T.
In Africa. Hunting Adventures in the Big Game Country. Indianpolis: 1910. V. 47; 50

MC DADE, THOMAS M.
The Annals of Murder a Bibliography of Books and Pamphlets on American Murders from Colonial Times to 1900. Norman: 1961. V. 48; 53

MC DANIEL, JAMES
Reply of the Delegates of the Cherokee Nation to the Demands of the Commissioner of Indian Affairs. Washington: 1866. V. 48

MAC DERMONT, E. T.
The Devon and Somerset Staghounds, 1907-1936. London: 1936. V. 47

M'DERMONT, MARTIN
The Beauties of Modern Literature, in Verse and Prose... London: 1824. V. 47
A Philosophical Inquiry into the Source of the Pleasures Derived from Tragic Representations... London: 1824. V. 50; 52

MC DERMOTT, ALICE
A Bigamist's Daughter. New York: 1982. V. 50

MAC DERMOTT, P. L.
British East Africa, or Ibea. 1893. V. 47

MC DEVITT, ELIZABETH
Octopus. Berkeley: 1988. V. 51
Octopus. Berkeley: 1992. V. 51; 52; 53

MAC DONAGH, DONAGH
Happy As Larry. Dublin: 1946. V. 48; 51

MC DONAGH, J. E. R.
Salversan in Syphilis and Allied Diseases. London: 1912. V. 49

MC DONAGH, THOMAS
The Golden Joy. London: 1906. V. 48

MAC DONAGH, THOMAS
Last and Inspiring Address of Thomas MacDonagh. 1916. V. 48

M'DONALD, ALEXANDER
A Galick and English Vocabulary, with an Appendix of the Terms of Divinity in the Said Language. Edinburgh: 1741. V. 48

MAC DONALD, ARCHIBALD
Peace River. A Canoe Voyage from Hudson's Bay to Pacific, by the Late George Simpson... in 1828. Journal of the Late Chief Factor, Archibald MacDonald... Ottawa: 1872. V. 52

MAC DONALD, ARTHUR
Abnormal Man, Being Essays on Education and crime and Related Subjects, with Digests of Literature and a Bibliography. Washington: 1893. V. 48

MC DONALD, CORNELIA PEAKE
A Diary with Reminiscences of the War and Reuge Life in the Shenandoah Valley 1860-65. Nashville: 1935. V. 49

MAC DONALD, D. G. F.
Cattle, Sheep and Deer. London: 1872. V. 53

MC DONALD, DONALD
A History of Platinum from the Earliest Times to the Eighteen Eighties. London: 1960. V. 49

MAC DONALD, DUNCAN
The New London Family cook... London: 1808. V. 47

MAC DONALD, DUNCAN F. G.
British Columbia and Vancouver's Island Comprising a Description of These Dependencies... London: 1862. V. 47

MAC DONALD, EDWARD D.
A Bibliography of the Writings of D. H. Lawrence. Philadelphia: 1925. V. 48; 49; 50
A Bibliography of the Writings of Norman Douglas... Philadelphia: 1927. V. 49; 51

MAC DONALD, GEORGE
Adela Cathcart. Boston: 1864. V. 50
At the Back of the North Wind. London: 1871. V. 51
At the Back of the North Wind. Philadelphia: 1919. V. 51; 52; 53
At the Back of the North Wind. New York: 1924. V. 49
A Book of Strife in the Form of the Diary of an Old Soul. London: 1880. V. 50
Catalogue of Greek Coins in the Hunterian Collection, University of Glasgow. Bologna: 1975. V. 48
Cross Purposes. London: 1905. V. 52
David Elginbrod. Boston: 1863. V. 50
Donal Grant. Boston: 1883. V. 51

MAC DONALD, GEORGE continued
The Flight of the Shadow. New York: 1891. V. 51
Heather and Snow. London: 1893. V. 49
The Lost Princess or the Wise Woman. London: 1895. V. 49; 50
Phantastes. London: 1858. V. 47; 54
Phantastes. London: 1905. V. 47; 49
Poems. London: 1857. V. 48
The Poetical Works. London: 1893. V. 47
The Portent. Boston: 1864. V. 50
The Princess and Curdie. Philadelphia: 1908. V. 53
The Princess and Curdie. New York: 1927. V. 48
The Princess and Curdie. New York: 1951. V. 48
Robert Falconer. Boston: 1868. V. 50
The Roman Wall in Scotland. Glasgow: 1911. V. 53
A Threefold Cord, Poems by Three Friends. London: 1883. V. 48; 50
The Vicar's Daughter. Toronto: 1872. V. 53
Warlock O'Glenwarlock. Boston;: 1881. V. 48; 51; 53
Weighed and Wanting. London: 1882. V. 51
The Wise Woman, a Parable. London: 1875. V. 49; 50

MAC DONALD, GEORGE HEATH
Edmonton Fort- House - Factory. Edmonton: 1959. V. 47
Fort Augustus-Edmonton: Northwest Trails and Traffic. Edmonton: 1954. V. 47

MAC DONALD, GOLDEN
The Little Island. Garden City: 1946. V. 49

MAC DONALD, GREVILLE
The Magic Crook or the Stolen Baby. London: 1911. V. 51

MAC DONALD, HUGH
John Dryden. A Bibliography of Early Editions and of Drydeniana. Oxford: 1939. V. 47; 48
Thomas Hobbes a Bibliography. London: 1952. V. 48; 49

MAC DONALD, J. A.
Gun-Fire an Historical Narrative of the 4th Bde. C.F.A. in the Great War (1914-18). Toronto. V. 54

MAC DONALD, J. D.
Planet of the Dreamers. 1954. V. 47

MC DONALD, JAMES H.
The Poems and Prose Writings of Robert Southwell, S.J. A. Bibliographical Study. Oxford: 1937. V. 47; 54

MC DONALD, JOHN
Biographical Sketches of General Nathaniel Massie, General Duncan McArthur, Captain Willia Wells and General Simon Kenton... Cincinnati: 1838. V. 53

MAC DONALD, JOHN
Travels, in Various Parts of Europe, Asia and Africa, During a Series of Thirty Years and Upwards... Dublin: 1791. V. 47

MAC DONALD, JOHN D.
All These Condemned. 1954. V. 53
The Annex. Helsinki: 1987. V. 48
April Evil. New York: 1956. V. 52
Bright Orange for the Shroud. New York: 1972. V. 51
Bright Orange for the Shroud. Philadelphia: 1972. V. 53; 54
Cinnamon Skin. New York: 1982. V. 52
Condominium. New York: 1977. V. 53
The Crossroads. New York: 1959. V. 52
The Damned. 1952. V. 53
A Deadly Shade of Gold. London: 1965. V. 52
A Deadly Shade of Gold. New York: 1974. V. 47; 49; 51
A Deadly Shade of Gold. Philadelphia: 1974. V. 52; 53
The Deep Blue Good-by. 1964. V. 53
The Deep Blue Good-by. Philadelphia/New York: 1975. V. 47; 50
The Dreadful Lemon Sky. Philadlephia: 1974. V. 50
Dress Her in Indigo. Philadelphia/New York: 1971. V. 47; 50
The Executioners. New York: 1958. V. 50; 51
Free Fall in Crimson. New York: 1981. V. 52
The Girl in the Plain Brown Wrapper. Philadelphia: 1973. V. 53
The Good Old Stuff. New York: 1982. V. 52
The Green Ripper. New York: 1979. V. 52
The Last One Left. Garden City: 1967. V. 49
The Last One Left. New York: 1967. V. 48
The Long Lavender Look. London: 1972. V. 53
The Long Lavender Look. Philadelphia: 1972. V. 47; 50; 52; 53
Nightmare in Pink. Philadelphia/New York: 1976. V. 47; 50; 52
One Fearful Yellow Eye. New York: 1977. V. 50
One Fearful Yellow Eye. Philadelphia: 1977. V. 50; 53
Please Write for Details. New York: 1959. V. 51
A Purple Place for Dying. New York: 1976. V. 50
The Quick Red Fox. 1966. V. 53
The Scarlet Ruse. 1973. V. 53
The Scarlet Ruse. New York: 1980. V. 50; 52
The Scarlet Ruse. Philadelphia: 1980. V. 51; 53
Slam the Big Door. 1960. V. 53
A Tan and Sandy Silence. London: 1971. V. 52
A Tan and Sandy Silence. Philadelphia: 1972/79. V. 47
A Tan and Sandy Silence. 1973. V. 53
A Tan and Sandy Silence. Philadelphia: 1979. V. 50
Three for McGee. New York: 1967. V. 53
Weep For Me. 1951. V. 53
Wine of the Dreamers. New York: 1951. V. 47; 48; 49; 51

MAC DONALD, JOHN DENIS
Sound and Colour, Their Relations, Analogies & Harmonies. Gosport: 1869. V. 48
Sound and Colour, Their Relations, Analogies and Harmonies. London: 1869. V. 50

MAC DONALD, KENNETH
To the Arctic Circle and Beyond. Iverness: 1895. V. 50

MAC DONALD, PHILIP
The Link. Garden City: 1930. V. 49

MAC DONALD, R. J.
The History of Dress of the Royal Regiment of Artillery, 1625-1897. London: 1899. V. 50; 52; 54

MAC DONALD, ROBERT
The Romance of Canadian History. Calgary: 1974/78. V. 52

MAC DONALD, ROSS
The Barbarous Coast. New York: 1956. V. 47; 50; 53
The Barbarous Coast. London: 1957. V. 53
Black Money. New York: 1966. V. 47; 52; 53
Blue City. New York: 1947. V. 52
A Collection of Reviews. Northridge: 1979. V. 48
The Doomsters. London: 1958. V. 50
The Drowning Pool. New York: 1950. V. 52
The Drowning Pool. London: 1952. V. 54
Experience with Evil. London: 1954. V. 54
The Far Side of the Dollar. Columbia and Bloomfield: 1982. V. 53
Find a Victim. New York: 1954. V. 51
Find a Victim. London: 1955. V. 54
The Goodbye Look. New York: 1969. V. 49; 50
The Instant Enemy. New York: 1968. V. 49; 50
The Ivory Grin. New York: 1952. V. 47
The Ivory Grin. 1953. V. 53
Lew Archer Private Investigator. 1977. V. 53
Lew Archer, Private Investigator. New York: 1977. V. 51
The Name is Archer. New York: 1955. V. 47; 49; 50
On Crime Writing. Santa Barbara: 1973. V. 52
Self Portrait: Ceaselessly Into the Past. Santa Barbara: 1981. V. 47; 48; 51; 52
The Three Roads. New York: 1948. V. 52; 54
The Way Some People Die. New York: 1951. V. 48
The Way some People Die. 1953. V. 53
The Zebra-Striped Hearse. New York: 1962. V. 47; 49; 52

MC DONALD, STERLING B.
Color: How to Use It. Chicago: 1940. V. 51

MAC DONALD, THOREAU
A Year on the Farm, or the Woodchuck's Almanac Drawings By... Thornhill: 1934. V. 51

MAC DONALD, W. J.
Pioneer 1851. N.P: 1914. V. 53

MC DONALD, WILLIAM
A History of the Laurel Brigade. Baltimore: 1907. V. 49

MAC DONALD, WILLIAM
Poems. Edinburgh: 1809. V. 49; 54

MC DONALD, WILLIAM A.
The Political Meeting Places of the Greeks. Baltimore: 1943. V. 52

MC DONALD, WILLIAM NAYLOR
A History of the Laurel Brigade, Originally the Ashby Cavalry of the Army of Northern Virginia and Chew's Battery. Baltimore: 1907. V. 49

MAC DONALD, WILLIAM RUSSELL
First and Second Lessons for the Nursery, in Words of One and Two Syllables. London: 1838?. V. 48

MAC DONELL, A. G.
England Their England. London: 1933. V. 48

MAC DONNEL, DAVID EVANS
A Dictionary of Quotations, in Most Frequent Use. London: 1798. V. 49

MAC DONNELL, A. G.
The Crew of the Anconda. London: 1940. V. 48

MC DONNELL, ALEXANDER
A Letter to Thos. Fowell Buxton Esq. M.P. in Refutation of His Allegations Respecting the Decrease of the Slaves in the British West India Colonies. London: 1833. V. 53

M'DONNELL, ALEXANDER GREENFIELD
A Narrative of Transactions in the Red River Country... London: 1819. V. 52

MC DONNELL, JOSEPH
Gold Tooled Bookbindings Commissioned by Trinity College Dublin in the Eighteenth Century. London: 1987. V. 49; 53
Gold-Tooled Bookbindings Commissioned by Trinity College Dublin in the Eighteenth Century. 1987. V. 52

MAC DONNELL, R. WOGAN
Gabriel Laurance, Actor; and other Tales. Dublin: 1885. V. 49

MAC DONNELL, WILLIAM
Manita. a Poem... Lindsay?: 1880. V. 49

MC DONOGH, JOHN
The Last Will and Testament of John McDonogh, Late of Macdonoghville, State of Louisiana, Alos, His Memoranda of Instructions to His Executors, Relative to the Management of His Estate. New Orleans: 1851. V. 52

M'DONOUGH, FELIX
The Hermit Abroad. London: 1823. V. 49

MAC DOUGALL, ARTHUR R.
Dud Dean and His Country. New York: 1946. V. 47

MAC DOUGALL, ELISABETH B.
Fons Sapientiae, Renaissance Garden Fountains. Dumbarton Oaks: 1978. V. 50; 54

MAC DOUGALL, FRANCES
Might and Right: by a Rhode Islander. Providence: 1844. V. 54

MC DOUGALL, FRANCES HARRIET
Memoirs of Elleanor Eldridge. Providence: 1843. V. 47

M'DOUGALL, GEORGE F.
The Eventful Voyage of H.M. Discovery Ship 'Resolute' to the Arctic Regions in Search of Sir John Franklin and the Missing Crews of HM. Discovery Ships "Erebus" and "Terror" in 1852, 1853, 1854,... London: 1857. V. 49

MC DOUGALL, JOHN
George Millward McDougall, the Pioneer, Patriot and Missionary. Toronto: 1888. V. 48

MC DOUGALL, MARION GLEASON
Fugitive Slaves (1619-1865). Boston: 1891. V. 50

MC DOUGLAS, HENRY C.
Recollections 1844-1909. Kansas City: 1910. V. 52

MC DOWALL, WILLIAM
History of the Burgh of Dumfries, with Notices of Nithsdale, Annandale and the Western Border. Edinburgh: 1873. V. 54

MC DOWELL, J. R.
Henry Wallace; or the Victim of Lottery Gambling. New York: 1832. V. 48; 52; 54

M'DOWELL, JOHN
Church Manual for the Members of the First Presbyterian Church, Elizabeth-Town, New Jersey. Elizabeth-Town: 1824. V. 49; 51

MC DOWELL, WILLIAM A.
A Demonstration of the Curability of Pulmonary Consumption in All Its Stages. Louisville: 1843. V. 47

MAC DUFF, JOHN R.
The Hart and the Water-Brooks... London: 1860. V. 49

MC DUFFIE, GEORGE
Address to the People of the United States By the Convention of the People of South Carolina. Columbia: 1832. V. 48; 49

MC ELEROY, ROBERT
Jefferson Davis. New York & London: 1937. V. 47

MC ELRATH, CLIFFORD
On Santa Cruz Island: The Rancing Recollections of Clifford McElrath. Los Angeles: 1967. V. 48

MC ELRATH, JOSEPH R.
Frank Norris, a Descriptive Bibliography. Pittsburgh: 1992. V. 49

MC ELRATH, THOMSON P.
A Press Club Outing. New York: 1893. V. 52

MC ELROY, JOSEPH
Ancient History: a Paraphrase. New York: 1971. V. 53
Hind's Kidnap. New York: 1969. V. 52
Plus. New York: 1977. V. 53
Ship Rock: a Place. Concord: 1980. V. 52
A Smuggler's Bible. New York: 1919. V. 54
A Smuggler's Bible. New York: 1966. V. 48; 51; 52; 53; 54
A Smuggler's Bible. London: 1968. V. 47; 48; 49; 50; 51
Women and Men. New York: 1987. V. 49; 52; 53

MC ELWAINE, EUGENE
The Truth About Alaska. The Golden Land of the Midnight Sun. Chicago: 1901. V. 50

MC EWAN, CALVIN W.
Soundings at Tell Fakhariyah. Chicago: 1958. V. 49; 52

MC EWAN, IAN
Black Dogs. London: 1992. V. 48; 49
The Cement Garden. 1978. V. 50
The Child in Time. London: 1987. V. 47; 49
The Comfort of Strangers. London: 1981. V. 49; 51
First Love, Last Rites. London: 1975. V. 48; 49; 50; 51
First Love, Last Rites. New York: 1975. V. 49; 51; 53
The Imitation Game. London: 1981. V. 49
In Between the Sheets. London: 1978. V. 47; 48; 54

MAC EWEN, ALEXANDER R.
Life and Letters of John Cairns. London: 1895. V. 54

MAC EWEN, GWENDOLYN
The Drunken Clock. Toronto: 1961. V. 47
Marking Time. Toronto: 1991. V. 51

MC EWEN, JEAN
Les Iles Reunies. Montreal: 1975. V. 47

MAC EWEN, WILLIAM
Pyogenic Infective Diseases of the Brain and Spinal Cord. Glasgow: 1893. V. 47; 48; 49; 50; 51; 54

MC FADDEN, DAVID
The Poem Poem. Kitchener: 1967. V. 47

MAC FADDEN, HARRY A.
Rambles in the Far West. Hollidaysburg: 1906. V. 49

MC FALL, FRANCES ELIZABETH CLARK
The Beth Book. New York: 1897. V. 53
The Heavenly Twins. London: 1905. V. 47; 50; 51

MAC FALL, HALDANE
The Art of Hesketh Hubbard. London: 1924. V. 47
Aubrey Beardsley the Man and His Work. London: 1928. V. 47
The Book of Lovat Claud Fraser. London: 1923. V. 48; 49; 51; 53
A History of Painting. London. V. 48
Rouge. London: 1906. V. 50
The Spendid Wayfaring. London: 1913. V. 48; 52

MC FALL, HALDANE
The Wooings of Jezebel Pettyfer. London: 1898. V. 50

MAC FARLAN, ALLAN A.
American Indian Legends. Los Angeles: 1968. V. 53

MAC FARLAN, ROBERT
A New Alphabetical Vocabulary, Gailic and English... Edinburgh: 1795. V. 52
The Poems of Ossian. London: 1807. V. 48

MC FARLAND, LOUIS BURCHETTE
Memoirs and Addresses of L. B. McFarland. Memphis?: 192?. V. 49

MC FARLAND, MARVIN W.
The Papers of Wilbur and Orville Wright, Including the Chanute-Wright Letters and Other Papers of Octave Chanute. New York: 1953. V. 53

MC FARLAND, ROSS A.
Human Factors in Air Transport Design. New York: 1946. V. 48

MC FARLAND, WILLIAM LANDRAM
Salmon of the Atlantic. New York: 1925. V. 49

MAC FARLANE, CHARLES
The Armenians. London: 1830. V. 54
The Lives and Exploits of Banditti and Robbers in All Parts of the World. London: 1837. V. 48
The Lives of Banditti and Robbers in All Parts of the World. London: 1833. V. 48
Turkey and Its Destiny: The Result of Journeys Made in 1847 and 1848 to Examine Into the State of That Country. Philadlephia: 1850. V. 49

MAC FARLANE, JOHN
Antoine Verard. London: 1900. V. 50
A Trip to Parnassua; or, Pieces in Verse. Edinburgh: 1820. V. 54

MAC FARLANE, NIGEL
Hand-Made Papers of the Himalayas. Winchester: 1986. V. 47
Handmade Papers of India. Winchester: 1987. V. 47; 51; 53; 54

MAC FARLANE, WALTER
Genealogical Collections Concerning Families in Scotland, Made by Walter MacFarlane 1750-1751. Edinburgh: 1900. V. 51
Geographical Collections Relating to Scotland... Edinburgh: 1906-08. V. 51

MAC FARLANE, WALTER & CO.
Illustrated Catalogue of MacFarlane's Castings. Glasgow: 1880's. V. 52

MC FEE, WILLIAM
Born to Be Hanged. Gaylordsville: 1930. V. 51; 53
The Captain Macedonie Cocktail. 1930. V. 48
The Harbourmaster. Garden City: 1931. V. 54
The Harbourmaster. New York: 1931. V. 51; 53
Letters From an Ocean Tramp. London: 1908. V. 48; 53
North of Suez. New York: 1930. V. 51; 53
The Reflections of Marsyas. Gaylordsville: 1933. V. 50
A Six Hour Shift. New York: 1920. V. 51; 53

MAC FIE, MATHEW
Vancouver Island and British Columbia: Their History, Resources and Prospects. London: 1865. V. 52

MAC GAHAN, J. A.
Campaigning on the Oxus, and the Fall of Khiva. London: 1874. V. 49; 54
Campaigning on the Oxus and the Fall of Khiva. New York: 1874. V. 49; 54

MC GAHERN, JOHN
The Barracks. London: 1963. V. 47; 53

MC GAHERN, JOHN continued
The Dark. New York: 1966. V. 54
The Leavetaking. London: 1974. V. 50
Nightlines. London: 1970. V. 50
Nightlines. Boston: 1971. V. 47

MC GARRAHAN, WILLIAM
The History of the McGarrahan Claim As Written by Himself. San Francisco: 1875. V. 48

MC GARRELL, ANN
Flora. Mt. Horeb: 1990. V. 47; 53; 54

MAC GEE, THOMAS D'ARCY
The Poems of... 1869. V. 47
The Poems of... New York: 1869. V. 49; 50; 54

MAC GEOGHEGAN, JAMES
History of Ireland... Dublin: 1831-31-32. V. 53
The History of Ireland, Ancient and Modern. Dublin: 1844. V. 49

MAC GEORGE, A.
An Inquiry as to the Armorial Insignia of the City of Glasgow. Glasgow: 1866. V. 47; 50

M'GHEE, J. L.
How We Got to Pekin. London: 1862. V. 50

MC GHEE, REGINALD
The World of James Van Derzee: a Visual Record of Black Americans. New York: 1969. V. 47

MAC GIBBON, DAVID
The Castellated and Domestic Architecture of Scotland from the Twelfth to the Eighteenth Century. Edinburgh: 1887-92. V. 50
The Castellated and Domestic Architecture of Scotland from the Twelfth to the Eighteenth Century. Edinburgh: 1990. V. 51
The Ecclesiastical Architecture of Scotland, from the Earliest Christian Times to the Seventeenth Century. Edinburgh: 1991. V. 49; 50; 51

MAC GILL, PATRICK
The Diggers - The Australians in France. London: 1919. V. 47

MAC GILL, STEVENSON
Remarks on Prisons. Glasgow: 1810. V. 52

MC GILL UNIVERSITY. LIBRARY
THE Lawrence Lande Collection of Canadiana in the Redpath Library of McGill University. Montreal: 1965. V. 50; 51; 54

MC GILLIVARY, SIMON
A Narrative of Occurrences in the Indian Countries of North America... London: 1817. V. 53

M'GILLIVRAY, DUNCAN
The Journal of Duncan M'Gillivray of the North West Company at Fort George on the Saskatchewan. Toronto: 1929. V. 48

MAC GILLIVRAY, W.
Descriptions of the Rapacious Birds of Great Britain. London: 1836. V. 50
A History of British Birds, Indigenous and Migratory... London: 1837-52. V. 49
The Natural History of Dee Side and Braemar. London: 1855. V. 54
The Travels and Researches of Alexander Von Humboldt... New York: 1836. V. 48

MC GILLYCUDDY, JULIA B.
McGillycuddy Agent. Stanford: 1941. V. 54

MAC GILVRAY, JOHN
Poems. London: 1787. V. 54

MC GINLEY, PATRICK
Bogmail. London: 1978. V. 53

MC GINNISS, JOE
Fatal Vision. New York: 1983. V. 53

MC GIRT, JAMES E.
Avenging the Maine, a Drunken A.B. and Other Poems. Philadelphia: 1901. V. 53
For Your Sweet Sake. Philadelphia: 1909. V. 54

MC GIVERN, ED
Ed McGivern's Book on Fast and Fancy Revolver Shooting and Police Training. Springfield: 1938. V. 50

MC GIVERN, JAMES SABINE
Truly Canadian. Toronto: 1968-69. V. 54

MC GLASHAN, C. F.
History of the Donner Party. Sacramento. V. 48
History of the Donner Party. Truckee: 1879. V. 52; 54
History of the Donner Party. Sacramento: 1885. V. 53
History of the Donner Party. Sacramento: 1890. V. 50
History of the Donner Party. Sacramento: 1907. V. 47
History of the Donner Party. San Francisco: 1929. V. 50

MC GONAGALL, WILLIAM
The Autobiography and Poetical Works of William M'Gonagall. 1887. V. 47

MC GOWAN, EDWARD
Narrative of Edward McGowan, Including a Full Account of the Author's Adventures and Perils While Persecuted by the San Francisco Vigilance Committee of 1856. San Francisco: 1857. V. 47; 50
Narrative of Edward McGowan, Including a Full Account of the Author's Adventures and Perils While Persecuted by the San Francisco Vigilance Committee of 1856. San Francisco: 1917. V. 50; 52

MAC GOWAN, JOHN
Infernal Conference; or Dialogues of Devils. Lexington: 1804. V. 53
Priestcraft Defended. A Sermon, Occasioned by the Expulsion of Six Young Gentlemen from the University of Oxford... London: 1815. V. 47
Priestcraft Defended: A Sermon Occasioned by the Expulsion of Six Young Gentlemen from the University of Oxford, for Praying, Reading and Expounding the Scriptures... Boston: 1819. V. 53

MC GRANDLE, LEITH
Europe The Quest for Unity... London: 1975. V. 47; 49; 54

MC GRATH, DANIEL FRANCIS
Bookman's Price Index. Detroit: 1964-1983. V. 47

MAC GRATH, HAROLD
The Puppet Crown. Indianapolis: 1901. V. 49

MC GRATH, RAYMOND
Glass in Architecture and Decoration. London: 1937. V. 48; 54

MAC GRATH, RAYMOND
Glass in Architecture and Decoration. London: 1961. V. 50

MAC GREGOR, A. WALLACE
Fifty Years of Lawn Tennis in Scotland. Edinburgh: 1927. V. 47

MAC GREGOR, AUGUSTINE
The Story of Snips. London. V. 47
The Wonderful Bunnies and Silversuit. London: 1930. V. 47

MAC GREGOR, BARRINGTON
King Longbeard. London: 1898. V. 48; 49

MAC GREGOR, DUNCAN
A Narrative of the Loss of the "Kent" East Indiaman, by fire, In the Bay of Biscay, on the 1st of March 1825. Edinburgh: 1825. V. 53

M'GREGOR, JAMES
Medical Sketches of the Expedition to Egypt from India. London: 1804. V. 52

M'GREGOR, JOHN
British America. Edinburgh: 1832. V. 52; 54
British America. Edinburgh: 1833. V. 54

MAC GREGOR, JOHN
Commercial Statistics. A Digest of the Productive Resources, Commercial Legislation, Custom Tariffs, Navigation, Port and Quarantine Laws and Charges, Shipping, Imports and Exports and the Monies, Weights, and Measures of All Nations. London: 1844-47. V. 47; 49
Commercial Tariffs and Regulations, Resources and Trade of the Several States of Europe and America... London: 1847. V. 49; 51

MAC GREGOR, LADY
The Life and Opinions of General Sir C. M. MacGregor. London: 1888. V. 54

MAC GREGOR, MIRIAM
Predators in My Garden. Andoversford: 1993. V. 49
Predators in My Garden. London: 1993. V. 50
Whittington: Aspects of a Cotswold Village. 1991. V. 47
Whittington: Aspects of a Cotswold Village. London: 1991. V. 50

MAC GREGOR, PATRICK
The Genuine Remains of Ossian. London: 1841. V. 53

MC GREGOR, ROBERT
The Byron Gallery... New York: 1849. V. 51

MC GREGORY, CHARLES
History of the 15th Regiment, New Hampshire Volunteers 1862-63. 1900. V. 47

MC GREW, CHARLES B.
Italian Doorways. Measured Drawings and Photographs. Cleveland: 1929. V. 48

MC GROARTY, JOHN S.
Los Angeles from the Mountains to the Sea. Chicago: 1921. V. 54

MC GUANE, THOMAS
The Bushwhacked Piano. New York: 1971. V. 50; 51; 52; 54
In the Crazies. Seattle: 1985. V. 54
Keep the Change. Boston: 1989. V. 48; 49; 51; 52; 53
Ninety-Two in the Shade. New York: 1973. V. 48; 51; 52; 53; 54
Nobody's Angel. New York: 1981. V. 48
Nobody's Angel. New York: 1982. V. 50
Nothing But Blue Skies. Boston: 1992. V. 47; 48; 49; 51; 52; 53; 54
Panama. New York: 1978. V. 50; 51; 53
Sons. Northbridge: 1993. V. 48
The Sporting Club. New York: 1968. V. 47; 50; 51; 53; 54
The Sporting Club. New York: 1969. V. 51; 53
To Skin a Cat. New York: 1986. V. 52; 54
To Skin a Cat. London: 1987. V. 52
Untitled. Northridge. V. 48

MC GUFFEY, WILLIAM H.
McGuffey's New First Electric Reader. 1928. V. 53

MAC GUIRE, CATHAL
Amabel. London: 1893. V. 49

MC GUIRE, J. A.
The Alaska-Yukon Gamelands. 1921. V. 52
In the Alaska-Yukon Gamelands... Cincinnati: 1921. V. 47

MC GUIRE, JOSEPH D.
Pipes and Smoking Customs of the American Aborigines, Based on Material in the U.S. National Museum. Washington: 1898. V. 48

MC GUIRE, JUDITH WHITE BROCKENBROGH
Diary of a Southern Refugee, During the War By a Lady of Virginia. New York: 1867. V. 48; 50

M'GUIRE, S.
Beast or Man. 1930. V. 49

MC HARDY, JAMES
Half Hours with an Old Golfer. London: 1895. V. 50

M'HENRY, JAMES
The Jackson Wreath, or National Souvenir. Philadelphia: 1829. V. 52

M'HENRY, JOHN
The Ejectment Law of Maryland. Frederick-Town: 1822. V. 54

MC HENRY, LAWRENCE
Garrison's History of Neurology Revised and Enlarged with a Bibliography of Classical, Original and Standard Works in Neurology. Springfield: 1969. V. 52

MC ILHANY, EDWARD
Recollections of a '49er. A Quaint and Thrilling Narrative of a Trip Across the Plains. Kansas City: 1908. V. 47

MC ILHANY, HUGH MILTON
Some Virginia Families. Being Genealogies of the Kinney, Stribling, Trout, McIlhany, Milton, Rogers, Tate, Snickers, Taylor, McCormick and other Families of Virginia. Staunton: 1903. V. 47

MC ILHENNY, EDWARD A.
The Wild Turkey and Its Hunting. Garden City: 1914. V. 53

MC ILVAINE, C.
Toadstools, Mushrooms, Fungi, Edible and Poisonous One Thousand American Fungi. Indianapolis: 1900. V. 49; 52

MC ILVAINE, EILEEN
P. G. Wodehouse, a Comprehensive Bibliography and Checklist. New York: 1990. V. 49

M'ILVAINE, WILLIAM
Sketches of Scenery and Notes of Personal Adventure in California. San Francisco: 1951. V. 47; 48; 49; 50; 53

MC ILVANNEY, WILLIAM
Laidlaw. London: 1977. V. 50

MAC ILWAIN, G.
Memoirs of John Abernethy, F.R.S. London: 1853. V. 47; 52

MC INDOE, G.
Poems and Songs, Chiefly in the Scottish Dialect. Edinburgh;: 1805. V. 54

MC INNES, ALEX P.
Chronicles of the Cariboo Number One Being a True Story of the First Discovery of Gold in the Cariboo District on the Horsefly River... Lillooet: 1938. V. 50

MAC INNES, COLIN
England, Half English. London: 1961. V. 51
June in Her Spring. London: 1942. V. 53
June in Her Spring. London: 1952. V. 49; 51

MC INTOSH, ANGUS
Introduction to a Survey of Scottish Dialects. Edinburgh: 1961. V. 50

M'INTOSH, CHARLES
The New and Improved Practical Gardener and Modern Horticulturist... London: 1854. V. 51

MC INTOSH, DAVID GREGG
The Campaign of Chancellorsville. Richmond: 1915. V. 49; 52

MC INTOSH, JAMES
Syphilis from the Modern Standpoint. London: 1911. V. 51; 54

MC INTOSH, MARIA J.
Woman in America, Her Work and Her Reward. New York: 1850. V. 49; 50; 51; 53

MC INTOSH, W. C.
A Monograph of the British Marine Annelids. London. V. 49

MC INTYRE, A. R.
Curare, Its History, Nature and Clinical Use. Chicago: 1947. V. 51

MAC INTYRE, CARLYLE
The Brimming Cup and Potsherds. Pasadena: 1930. V. 54

MAC INTYRE, DONALD
Hindu-Koh: Wanderings and Wild Sport On and Beyond the Himalayas. London: 1889. V. 53; 54
Hindu-Koh: Wanderings and Wild Sport on and Beyond the Himalayas. 1891. V. 54
Hindu-Koh: Wanderings and Wild Sport on and Beyond the Himalayas. Edinburgh and London: 1891. V. 48; 50

MC INTYRE, JAMES
Musings on the Banks of Canadian Thames, Including Poems on Local, Canadian and British Subjects, and Lines on the Great Poets of England, Ireland, Scotland and America. Ingersoll: 1884. V. 54

MC INTYRE, PETER
Pacific. Wellington: 1966. V. 51

MC INTYRE, R. C.
Martin Johnson Heade, 1819-1904. New York: 1948. V. 47; 50; 51

MC INTYRE, V.
Dreamsnake. 1978. V. 49; 54

MAC ISAAC, F.
The Vanishing Professor. 1927. V. 47

MAC KAIL, DENIS
Romance to the Rescue. Boston and New York: 1921. V. 54

MAC KALL, LAWTON
Knife and Fork in New York. New York: 1949. V. 47

MAC KANESS, GEORGE
Admiral Arthur Phillip, Founder of New South Wales, 1738-1814. Sydney: 1937. V. 52

MAC KAY, ALEXANDER
Western India... London: 1853. V. 48
The Western World, or Travels in the United States in 1846-47... London: 1849. V. 52
The Western World; or, Travels in the United States in 1846-47... Philadelphia: 1849. V. 50; 53

MAC KAY, ANGUS M.
The Brontes. New York: 1897. V. 52

MC KAY, BARRY
Marbling Methods and Receipts from Four Centuries. Kidlington: 1990. V. 47; 51
Patterns and Pigments in English Marbled Papers. Kidlington: 1988. V. 47; 51

MAC KAY, CHARLES
The Gaelic Etymology of the Languages of Western Europe. London: 1877. V. 50
Life and Liberty in America. London: 1859. V. 54
Memoirs of Extraordinary Popular Delusions. London: 1841. V. 53
Memoirs of Extraordinary Popular Delusions and the Madness of Crowds. London. V. 51
Memoirs of Extraordinary Popular Delusions and the Madness of Crowds. London: 1852. V. 49
Memoirs of Extraordinary Popular Delusions and the Madness of Crowds. London: 1869. V. 50
The Scenery and Poetry of the English Lakes. London: 1846. V. 50; 52
The Thames and Its Tributaries; Or Rambles Among the Rivers... London: 1840. V. 49; 52; 53; 54
A Thousand and One Gems of English Poetry. London: 1877. V. 48

MAC KAY, CHARLES ROBERT
Life of Charles Bradlaugh, M.P. London: 1888. V. 49

MC KAY, CLAUDE
Banjo. New York: 1929. V. 49; 50; 52; 54
Harlem Shadows. New York: 1922. V. 48; 49
Home to Harlem. New York: 1928. V. 54
A Long Way from Home. New York: 1937. V. 53; 54
Selected Poems of Charles McKay. New York: 1953. V. 53
Songs of Jamaica. Kingston: 1912. V. 48
Spring in New Hampshire and Other Poems. London: 1920. V. 54

MAC KAY, DOUGLAS
The Honourable Company. Indianapolis: 1936. V. 50; 54

MAC KAY, ERIC
The Little Gods of Grub Street. London: 1896. V. 54
Love Letters of a Violinist. London: 1893. V. 54
Love Letters of a Violinist and Other Poems. New York: 1894. V. 48

MAC KAY, ERNEST
Report on the Excavation of the "A" Cemetery at Kish, Mesopotamia. (and) A Sumerian Palace and the "A" Cemetery at Kish, Mesopotamia (Part II). Chicago: 1925-29. V. 49; 52

MC KAY, GEORGE
American Book Auction Catalogues, 1713-1937. New York: 1937. V. 54
A Bibliography of Robert Bridges. New York and London: 1933. V. 54

MAC KAY, GEORGE HENRY
Shooting Journal of George Henry Mackay 1865-1922. Cambridge: 1929. V. 47

MAC KAY, HELEN
Stories for Pictures. New York: 1912. V. 48; 54

MAC KAY, J. T.
Flora Hibernica, Comprising the Flowering Plants, Ferns, Characeae, Musci, Hepaticae... Dublin: 1836. V. 52; 53

MAC KAY, JOHN
An Old Scots Brigade, Being a History of Mackay's Regiment Now Incoporated with the Royal Scots. Edinburgh/London: 1885. V. 50

MAC KAY, JOHN HENRY
The Anarchists. A Picture of Civilization at the Close of the 19th Century. Boston: 1891. V. 52

MAC KAY, MALCOLM S.
Cow Range and Hunting Trail. New York: 1925. V. 50

MC KAY, RICHARD C.
Some Famous Sailing Ships andd Their Builder Donald McKay, A Study of the American Sailing Packet and Clipper Eras. New York: 1928. V. 52

MC KAY, ROBERT H.
Little Pills, an Army Story. Pittsburgh: 1918. V. 49; 51

MC KAY, SETH SHEPARD
Debates in the Texas Constitutional Convention of 1875. Austin: 1930. V. 52

MAC KAY, WILLIAM
Ex-Soldier We Are Dead. London: 1930. V. 49

MC KAY, WILLIAM
John Hoppner, R.A. London: 1909. V. 49

MAC KAY, WILLIAM
Narrative of the Shipwreck of the Juno, on the Coast of Aracan, and of the Singular Preservation of Fourteen of Her Company on the Wreck... London: 1798. V. 47

MAC KAY BROWN, GEORGE
The Storm and Other Poems. 1954. V. 50
Twelve Poems. Belfast: 1967. V. 50

MAC KAYE, PERCY
The Mystery of Hamlet, King of Denmark... New York: 1950. V. 48; 50
Sanctuary, a Bird Masque. New York: 1914. V. 47

MAC KAY SMITH, ALEXANDER
The American Foxhound. 1747-1967. Milwood: 1968. V. 48; 54

MAC KAY-SMITH, ALEXANDER
The Race Horses of America 1832-1872. Portraits and Other Paintings by Edward Troye. Saratoga Springs: 1981. V. 53
The Songs of Foxhunting. Millwood: 1974. V. 47

MC KEAN, EMMA C.
Magic Fairy Tales... Springfield: 1943. V. 54

MC KEAN, H. F.
The Lost Treasures... Garden City: 1980. V. 54

M'KEAN, JOSEPH
Catalogue of the Library of the Rev. Joseph M'Kean, D.D., LL.D., Boylston Professor of Rhetoric and Oratory in the University of Cambridge. Boston: 1818. V. 52

MC KEE, JAMES COOPER
Narrative of the Surrender of a Command of US Forces at Fort Fillmore, New Mexico, in July 1861. Boston: 1886. V. 48

MC KEE, ROBERT E.
The Zia Company in Los Alamos. A History. El Paso: 1950. V. 50

MC KEEVER, HARRIET
The Nursery Treasury. Philadelphia: 1873. V. 53

MC KELL, C. M.
The Biology and Utlization of Shrubs. 1988. V. 52

MAC KELLAR, THOMAS
The American Printer, a Manual of Typography. Philadelphia: 1879. V. 51
The American Printer: a Manual of Typography. Philadelphia: 1882. V. 51

MC KELVEY, S. D.
Botanical Exploration of the Trans-Mississippi West, 1790-1850. Jamaica Plain: 1955. V. 47; 48; 51; 52; 53
The Lilac, a Monograph. London: 1928. V. 49; 52
The Lilac, a Monograph. New York: 1928. V. 48; 54

MC KELVIE, C. L.
Game Birds of the British Isles. V. 50
The Grouse, Studies in Words and Pictures. V. 50
The Grouse: Studies in Words and Pictures. London: 1992. V. 48; 49
The Partridge, Studies in Words and Pictures. London: 1993. V. 50
The Snipe, Studies in Words and Pictures. V. 50
The Snipe, Studies in Words and Pictures. London: 1989. V. 48; 49

MAC KENIE'S
Five Thousand Receipts in All the Useful and Domestic Arts: Constiuting a Complete Practical Library. Philadelphia: 1859. V. 47

MAC KENNA, F. SEVERNE
Chelsea Porcelain: The Red Anchor Wares. Leight on Sea: 1951. V. 52

MC KENNA, R.
Casey Agonistes and Other Science Fiction and Fantasy Stories. 1973. V. 49
Casey Agonistes and Other Science Fiction and Fantasy Stories. New York: 1973. V. 53; 54

MC KENNA, RICHARD
The Sand Pebbles. New York: 1962. V. 53

MC KENNA, ROLLIE
Letter to Loren: a Previously Unpublished Poem. 1993. V. 51
Rollie McKenna. A Life in Photography. New York: 1991. V. 53

M'KENNA, THEOBALD
Thoughts on the Civil Condition and Relations of the Roman Catholic Clergy, Religion and People, in Ireland. London: 1805. V. 52

MC KENNEY, THOMAS LORRAINE
History of the Indian Tribes of North America. Philadelphia: 1838-44. V. 47
History of the Indian Tribes of North America. Philadelphia: 1872. V. 48
History of the Indian Tribes of North America. Edinburgh: 1933. V. 47
History of the Indian Tribes of North America... Kent: 1978. V. 51
Indian Tribes of North America. Edinburgh: 1933. V. 47
The Indian Tribes of North America. Edinburgh: 1933-34. V. 51; 54
Memoirs, Official and Personal... New York: 1846. V. 48
Sketches of a Tour to the Lakes, of the Character and Customs of the Chippeway Indians... Baltimore: 1827. V. 50
Sketches of a Tour to the Lakes, of the Character and Customs of the Chippeway Indians... New York: 1827. V. 50; 53
Sketches of a Tour to the Lakes, of the Character and Customs of the Chippeway Indians. Barre: 1972. V. 48

MAC KENTOSH, JOHN
Receipts for the Cure of Most Diseases Incident to the Human Family. New York: 1827. V. 52

MAC KENZIE, ALEXANDER
Frequent Communion: or, the Advantages and Necessity Of It... London: 1780. V. 53
History of Macleods with Genealogies of the Principal Families of the Name. Inverness: 1889. V. 47
Voyages from Montreal on the River St. Laurence, through the Continent of North America... London: 1801. V. 47; 49; 50
Voyages from Montreal, On the River St. Laurence, Through the Continent of North America. London: 1802. V. 48
Voyages from Montreal on the River St. Laurence, Through the Continent of North America. New York: 1803. V. 50
Voyages from Montreal Through the Continent of North America to the Frozen and Pacific Oceans in 1789 & 1793. New York: 1902. V. 47

MAC KENZIE, ALEXANDER SLIDELL
The American in England. Paris: 1836. V. 54

MAC KENZIE, ANNA MARIA
Martin and Mansfeldt, or the Romance of Franconia. London: 1802. V. 50

MAC KENZIE, CECIL W.
Donald MacKenzie "King of the Northwest". Los Angeles: 1937. V. 52

MAC KENZIE, CHARLES
Notes on Haiti, Made During a Residence in that Republic. London: 1830. V. 50

MC KENZIE, CHARLES H.
The Religious Sentiments of Charles Dickens, Collected From His Writings. London: 1884. V. 49

MAC KENZIE, COLIN
A Family Library: or, Five Thousand Receipts in the Useful and Domestic Arts, Constituting a Practical Operative Cyclopaedia. London: 1836. V. 52
Five Thousand Receipts In All the Useful and Domestic Arts... London: 1829. V. 48
One Thousand Processes in Manufactures and Experiments in Chemistry... London: 1823. V. 48

MAC KENZIE, COMPTON
Gallipoli Memories. London: 1929. V. 53
Kensington Rhymes. London: 1912. V. 51
My Life and Times. Octave One (-Ten) 1883-1963. London: 1963-71. V. 50; 53
Poems. Oxford: 1907. V. 48; 49

MC KENZIE, D. F.
The Cambridge University Press 1696-1712. A Bibliographical Study. 1966. V. 51; 54

MAC KENZIE, D. R.
The Spirit-Ridden Konde A Record of the Interesting... London: 1925. V. 48; 51

MAC KENZIE, ENEAS
A Descriptive and Historical Account of the Town and County of Newcastle Upon Tyne. Newcastle: 1827. V. 47; 53
An Historical, Topographical and Descriptive View of the County of Northumberland and of Those Parts of the County of Durham Situated North of the River Tyne. Newcastle: 1825. V. 53

MAC KENZIE, FREDERICK ARTHUR
From Tokyo to Tiflis. London: 1900. V. 51

MAC KENZIE, GEORGE
The Institutions of the Law of Scotland. Edinburgh: 1688. V. 51
The Institutions of the Law of Scotland... London: 1694. V. 51
The Laws and Customs of Scotland, in Matters Criminal. Edinburgh: 1699. V. 49; 52
Memoirs of the Affairs of Scotland from the Restoration of King Charles II. Edinburgh: 1821. V. 52; 54
Observations Upon the Laws and Customs of Nations.... (with) Science of Herauldry (sic), Treated as a Part of the civil Law and Law of Nations... Edinburgh: 1680. V. 49
Pleadings, In Some Remarkable Cases Before the Supreme Courts of Scotland Since the Year 1661. Edinburgh: 1704. V. 52
The Science of Herauldry (sic), Treated as a Part of the Civil Law and Law of Nations... Edinburgh: 1680. V. 51

MAC KENZIE, GEORGE STEWART
Travels in the Island of Iceland, During the Summer of the Year 1810. Edinburgh: 1811. V. 48
Travels in the Island of Iceland During the Summer of the Year MDCCCX. Edinburgh: 1812. V. 51

MAC KENZIE, HELEN
Life in the Mission, the Camp and the Zenana; or Six Years in India. London: 1854. V. 49; 50

MAC KENZIE, HENRY
Julia de Roubigne, a Tale. London: 1777. V. 54
Julia de Roubigne, a Tale. London: 1782. V. 48
The Man of Feeling. London: 1778. V. 54
The Man of Feeling. London: 1794. V. 48
The Man of the World. London: 1773. V. 47
The Mirror, a Periodical Paper... London: 1809. V. 47
The Miscellaneous Works. London: 1819. V. 52
Works. With a Critical Dissertation on the Tales of the Author by John Galt. Edinburgh: 1824. V. 51

MAC KENZIE, J.
A Woolen Draper's Letter on the French Treaty, to His Friend's and Fellow Tradesmen all Over England. London: 1786. V. 50; 54

MAC KENZIE, J. B.
The Six-Nations Indians in Canada. Toronto: 1896. V. 48

MAC KENZIE, JAMES
Angina Pectoris. London: 1923. V. 51; 54
Diseases of the Heart. London: 1908. V. 51; 54
Diseases of the Heart. 1910. V. 54
Diseases of the Heart. London: 1910. V. 49
Diseases of the Heart. New York: 1910. V. 51
Diseases of the Heart. London: 1925. V. 51
The General Grievances and Oppressions of the Isles of Orkney and Shetland. Edinburgh: 1836. V. 52; 54
The History of Health and the Art of Preserving It; or, An Account of All That Has Been Recommended by Physicians and Philosophers Towards the Preservation of Health... Edinburgh: 1759. V. 47; 48; 49; 50
The Study of the Pulse: Arterial, Venous and Hepatic and Of the Movements of the Heart. Edinburgh: 1902. V. 49

MAC KENZIE, JAMES D.
The Castles of England; their Story and Structure. London: 1807. V. 50
The Castles of England: Their Story and Structure. New York: 1896. V. 47
The Castles of England: Their Story and Structure. London: 1897. V. 47

MAC KENZIE, JOHN
Austral Africa Losing It or Ruling It. London: 1887. V. 50; 54
Poems on...I. The Tithing System...II. The Two Rich Misers....III. An Ode to Liberty and the Rights of Man...IV. De Young and the Inquisition...V. Jack Tar's Petititon to the Temperance Societies...VI. The Leeching Lawauer and the Quack Doctor... Philadelphia: 1835. V. 49
Ten Years North of the Orange River. Edinburgh: 1871. V. 50; 52

MAC KENZIE, KENNETH
Orain Ghaidhealach, Ags Bearla air an Eadar-Theangacha le Coinneach Mac'Coinnich. Edinburgh: 1792. V. 54

MAC KENZIE, MARY JANE
Private Life; or, Varieties of Character and Opinion. London: 1829. V. 50

MAC KENZIE, MORELL
Diseases of the Pharynx, Larynx and Trachea. (with) Diseases of the Esophagus, Nose and Naso-Pharynx. New York: 1884. V. 54
Diseases of the Pharynx, Larynx and Trachea. (with) Diseases of the Oesophagus, Nose and Naso-Harynx. New York: 1880/84. V. 49
The Fatal Illness of Frederick the Noble. London: 1888. V. 53; 54
The Use of the Laryngoscope in Diseases of the Throat. Philadelphia: 1865. V. 49; 54

MAC KENZIE, PETER
The Life of Thomas Muir, Esq. Advocate Younger of Huntershill, near Glasgow... Glasgow: 1831. V. 49; 52

MAC KENZIE, R. SHELTON
Life of Charles Dickens. With Personal Recollections and Anecdotes... Philadelphia: 1870. V. 51

MAC KENZIE, RANALD S.
Ranald S. MacKenzie's Official Correspondence Relating to Texas 1871-1873 (and) 1873-1879. Lubbock: 1968. V. 50

MAC KENZIE, WILLIAM
The Physiology of Vision. London: 1841. V. 47

MAC KENZIE, WILLIAM LYON
The Caroline Almanack, and American Freeman's Chronicle for 1840. Rochester: 1840. V. 54
The Lives and Opinions of Benj'n Franklin Butler, United States District Attorney for the Southern District of New York; and Jesse Hoyt, Counsellor at Law, Formerly Collector of Customs for the Port of New York. Boston: 1845. V. 53; 54
Sketches of Canada and the United States. London: 1833. V. 54

MC KERROW, RONALD BRUNLEES
Printers' & Publishers' Devices in England and Scotland 1485-1640. London: 1949. V. 47; 48; 50; 54
Title-page Borders Used in England and Scotland. London: 1932. V. 48
Title-Page Borders Used in England and Scotland. Oxford: 1932. V. 50

MC KILLIP, P.
The Forgotten Beasts of Eld. 1974. V. 52
The Riddle Master of Hed, Heir of Sea and Fire & Harpist in the Wind. 1976/77/79. V. 47

MC KILLIP, PATRICIA A.
The Forgotten Beats of Eld. New York: 1966. V. 51
The Riddle-Master of hed. New York: 1976. V. 51

MC KIM, J. MILLER
The Freedmen of South Carolina. An Address...in Sansom Hall, July 9th, 1862. Together with a Letter...to Stephen Colwell... Philadelphia: 1862. V. 48

MC KIM, MEAD & WHITE
A Monograph of the Work of McKim, Mead & White 1879-1915. New York: 1915-17. V. 47; 48
A Monograph of the Work of McKim, Mead & White, 1879-1915. Volume IV. New York: 1915. V. 50

MC KIM, RANDOLPH HARRISON
The Motives and Aims of the Soliders of the South in the Civil War. Nashville: 1904. V. 49
The Soul of Lee. London: 1918. V. 49

MC KINLAY, JOHN
McKinlay's Journal of Exploration in the Interior of Australia (Burke Relief Expedtiion). Melbourne: 1861. V. 52

MC KINNEY, LOREN C.
Medical Illustrations in Medieval Manuscripts. London: 1965. V. 53

MC KINNON, BARRY
The Golden Daybreak Hair. Toronto: 1967. V. 47

MAC KINNON, JAMES
South African Traists. Edinburgh: 1887. V. 47

MAC KINNON, WILLIAM ALEXANDER
History of Civilisation and Public Opinion... London: 1849. V. 49; 52
On the Rise, Progress and Present State of Public Opinion. London: 1828. V. 49

MC KINSTRY, ELIZABETH
The Fairy Alphabet As Used by Merlin. New York: 1933. V. 50; 52

MAC KINTOSH, ALEXANDER
The Driffield Angler...to Which are added Instructions for Shooting... Gainsborough: 1806. V. 47
The Modern Fisher; or, Driffield Angler. Derby: 1821. V. 47; 49

MAC KINTOSH, CHARLES RENNIE
Haus Eines Kunstfreundes. Glasgow: 1991. V. 51
MacKintosh Watercolours. New York: 1978. V. 53

MAC KINTOSH, H. B.
The Inverness Shire Highlanders or 97th Regiment of Foot 1794-1796. Elgin: 1926. V. 50

MAC KINTOSH, JAMES
A Discourse On the Study of the Law of Nature and Nations... London: 1799. V. 49; 52
An Historical Sketch of the French Revolution from its Commencement to the Year 1792. Dublin: 1792. V. 50
The History of England. London: 1830-40?. V. 50
The History of England (from the Beginning to 1588). London: 1830-32. V. 53
History of the Revolution in England in 1688 Comprising a View of the Reign of James Ii... London: 1834. V. 52; 53
Memoirs of the Life of Sir James Mackintosh. London: 1836. V. 48; 53
Memoirs of the Life of the Right Honourable Sir James Mackintosh. London: 1835. V. 54
The Roman Law of Sale with Modern Illustrations. Edinburgh: 1892. V. 48; 50
Vindiciae Gallicae. Dublin: 1791. V. 53; 54
Vindiciae Gallicae. Defence of the French Revolution and Its English Admirers Against the Accusations of the Right Hon. Edmund Burke... London: 1791. V. 47; 51

MAC KINTOSH, N. A.
Southern Blue and Fin Whales. Cambridge: 1929. V. 50

MC KITTERICK, DAVID
Cambridge University Library, a History, the Eighteenth and Nineteenth Centuries. London: 1986. V. 49
A New Specimen Book of Curwen Pattern Papers. 1987. V. 47; 51
A New Specimen Book of Curwen Pattern Papers. Andoversford: 1987. V. 48; 50; 53
A New Specimen Book of Curwen Pattern Papers. Gloucestershire: 1987. V. 51
A New Specimen Book of Curwen Pattern Papers. London: 1987. V. 50
Wallpapers by Edward Bawden Printed at the Curwen Press. 1988. V. 47
Wallpapers by Edward Bawden printed at the Curwen Press. London: 1988. V. 50

MAC KNIGHT, THOMAS
The Right Honourable Benjamin Disraeli, M.P. London: 1854. V. 49

MC KUEN, ROD
And Autumn Came. New York: 1954. V. 48

M'LACHLAN, ALEXANDER
Lyrics. Toronto: 1858. V. 54
Poems. Toronto: 1856. V. 54

MC LACHLAN, R.
A Monographic Revision and Synopsis of the Trichoptera of the European Fauna... (and) First Additional Supplement. London: 1874-84. V. 54

MAC LAGAN, T. J.
The Germ Theory Applied to the Explanation of the Phenomena of Disease. The Specific Fevers. London: 1876. V. 51

MAC LAINE, ARCHIBALD
A Series of Letters, Addressed to Soame Jenyns, Esq; on Occasion of His View of the Internal Evidence of Christianity. London: 1777. V. 52

MAC LAREN, ARCHIBALD
The Fairy Family. London: 1857. V. 52

MAC LAREN, ARCHIBALD CAMPBELL
The Perfect Batsman: J. B. Hobbs in Action. London: 1926. V. 52

MAC LAREN, C.
A Sketch of the Geology of Fife and the Lothians... Edinburgh: 1866. V. 47

MAC LAREN, IAN
Beside the Bonnie Brier Bush. New York: 1896. V. 51

MC LAREN, JACK
Our Great Ones. Toronto: 1932. V. 50

MC LAREN, LOYALL
Shakespeare in Bohemia. Three Plays. 1961. V. 48

MC LAREN, MORAY
Corsica Boswell - Paoli, Johnson and Freedom. London: 1966. V. 52

MAC LAREN-ROSS, JULIAN
The Stuff to Give the Troops - Twenty Five Tales of Army Life. London: 1944. V. 47
Until the Day She Dies - A Tale of Terror. London: 1960. V. 47

M'LAUCHLAIN, THOMAS
The Dean of Lismore's Book. Edinburgh: 1862. V. 48

MC LAUGHLIN, J. FAIRFAX
The American Cyclops, the Hero of New Orleans, and Spoiler of Silver Spoons. Baltimore: 1868. V. 52; 53

MAC LAURIN, COLIN
An Account of Sir Isaac Newton's Philosophical Discoveries, in Four Books. London: 1748. V. 47; 48; 50; 51; 53
Geometria Oranica, Sive Descriptio Linearum Curvarum Universalis. London: 1720. V. 50
A Treatise of Algebra...To Which is Appended, an Appendix Concerning the General Properties of Geometrical Lines. London: 1779. V. 50

MC LEAN, ALEXANDER
History of Jersey City, N.J. A Record of its Early Settlement and Corporate Progress... Jersey City: 1895. V. 47; 49; 51

MAC LEAN, ALISTAIR
H.M.S. Ulysses. London: 1955. V. 54

MC LEAN, BRUCE
King for a Day and 999 Other Pieces/Works/Things, etc. London: 1972. V. 47

MAC LEAN, CHARLES
An Excursion in France, and Other Parts of the Continent of Europe... London: 1804. V. 52
Practical Illustrations of the Progress of Medical Improvement, for the Last Thirty Years... London: 1818. V. 49; 51

MC LEAN, GEORGE N.
The Rise and Fall of Anarchy in America. Chicago: 1888. V. 47

MAC LEAN, HECTOR
The Watermillock and Matterdale Parish Registers, The Registers of the Parish of Watermillock in the County of Cumberland, Baptisms, Burials and Marriages (1579-1812); The Registers of Matterdale Church 1634-1720. Kendal: 1908. V. 52

MAC LEAN, JAMES
A Genuine Account of the Life and Actions of James Maclean, Highwayman, To the Time of His Trial and Receiving Sentence at the Old Bailey. London: 1750. V. 48

MAC LEAN, JOHN
Canadian Savage Folk. The Native Tribes of Canada. Toronto: 1896. V. 48; 54

MC LEAN, JOHN
The Indians: Their Manners and Customs. Toronto: 1889. V. 53

M'LEAN, JOHN
Notes of a Twenty-Five Years' Service in the Hudson's Bay Territory. London: 1849. V. 54

MAC LEAN, JOHN
Parochial and Family History of the Deanery of Trigg Manor, in the County of Cornwall. London: 1873-79. V. 52

MAC LEAN, LACHAN
An Enquiry into the Nature, Causes and Cure of Hydrothorax... Hartford: 1814. V. 48; 54

MAC LEAN, NORMAN
A River Runs Through It. Chicago: 1976. V. 48; 49; 50; 51; 52; 53; 54
A River Runs Through it. Chicago: 1983. V. 49; 51
A River Runs Through It. West Hatfield: 1989. V. 48; 50; 51; 52; 53; 54
Young Men and Fire. Chicago: 1992. V. 51

MAC LEAN, O. J. P.
The Mound Builders; being an Account of a Remarkable People that Once Inhabited the Valleys of the Ohio and Mississippi, Together with an Investigation into the Archaeology of Butler County. Cincinnati: 1879. V. 51

MC LEAN, RUARI
Benjamin Fawcett, Engraver and Colour Printer. 1988. V. 47; 49
Joseph Cundall. A Victorian Publisher. 1976. V. 54
Motif: a Journal of Visual Arts. London: 1958-Winter1965. V. 51
Victorian Book Design and Colour printing. London: 1963. V. 47; 48; 50
Victorian Book Design and Colour Printing. Berkeley: 1972. V. 53
Victorian Book Design and Colour Printing. London: 1972. V. 48; 52; 54
Victorian Publisher's Book-Binding in Cloth and Leather. London: 1974. V. 47; 48; 49; 50; 51
Victorian Publishers' Book-Bindings in Paper. London: 1983. V. 52

MC LEARY, A. C.
Humorous Incidents of the Civil War. 1903. V. 49

MAC LEAY, KENNETH
Description of the Spar Cave, Lately Discovered in the Isle of Skye, with Some Geological Remarks Relative to that Island... Edinburgh: 1811. V. 51

MAC LEISH, ARCHIBALD
Art Education and the Creative Process. New York: 1954. V. 54
Dedication of the Carleton Library. Northfield: 1956. V. 54
Einstein. Paris: 1929. V. 53
An Evening's Journey to Conway Massachusetts. Northampton: 1967. V. 49
Frescoes for Mr. Rockefeller's City. New York: 1933. V. 47; 51; 54
The Happy Marriage and Other Poems. Boston & New York: 1924. V. 51; 54
The Human Season. Boston: 1972. V. 47
Land of the Free. New York: 1938. V. 47; 54
The Love of This Land. New York: V. 54
New Found Land. Boston: 1930. V. 51
New Found Land: Fourteen Poems. Paris: 1930. V. 54
On the Beaches of the Moon. Laguna Beach: 1978. V. 51; 54
The Pot of Earth. Boston: 1925. V. 51; 54
Remarks at the Dedication of the Wallace Library, Fitchburg, Massachusetts. Worcester: 1967. V. 47
Streets in the Moon. Boston: 1926. V. 51
Tower of Ivory. New Haven: 1917. V. 51

MC LELLAN, CHARLES ARTHUR
The Art of Shoeing and Balancing the Trotter. New York: 1927. V. 54

MC LELLAN, E.
History of American Costume 1607-1870. New York: 1904/37. V. 54

MAC LENNAN, HUGH
Two Solitudes. Toronto: 1945. V. 53

MAC LENNAN, MALCOLM
Peasant Life. Sketches of the Villagers and Field Labourers in Glenaldie. London: 1871. V. 52

M'LEOD, ALEXANDER
Negro Slavery Unjustifiable. New York: 1802. V. 54

MC LEOD, ALEXANDER
Pigtails and Gold Dust. Caldwell: 1947. V. 54

M'LEOD, ALEXANDER
Trial of Alexander M'Leod for the Murder of Amos Durfee; and as an Accomplice in the Burning of the Steamer Caroline, in the Niagara River... New York: 1841. V. 52

M'LEOD, DONALD
Brief Review of the Settlement of Upper Canada by the U.E. Loyalists & Scotch Highlanders, in 1783... Cleveland: 1841. V. 48

MAC LEOD, DONALD
Memoirs of Norman MacLeod, D.D. London: 1876. V. 54
Treatises On the Second Sight. Glasgow: 1819. V. 48

MAC LEOD, HENRY DUNNING
Bimetalism. London: 1893. V. 49

MAC LEOD, IAIN
One Nation: a Tory Approach to Social Problems. London: 1950. V. 52

MAC LEOD, JOHN
Carbohydrate Metabolism and Insulin. London: 1926. V. 49
Diabetes: Its Pathological Physiology. London: 1913. V. 49

M'LEOD, JOHN
Narrative of a Voyage in His Majesty's Ship 'Alceste' to the Yellow Sea Along the Coast of Corea...to the Island of Lewchew. London: 1817. V. 49

MC LEOD, JOHN
Voyage Of His Majesty's Ship Alceste, along the Coast of Corea, to the Island of Lewchew... London: 1818. V. 47; 48; 50

M'LEOD, JOHN
Voyage of His Majesty's Ship Alceste, to China, Corea, and the Island of Lewchew. London: 1819. V. 50; 54
Voyage of His Majesty's Ship Alceste, to China, Corea, and the Island of Lewchew, with an Account of Her Shipwreck. London: 1820. V. 47; 52

MAC LEOD, JOSEPH GORDON
The Ecliptic. London: 1930. V. 52

MC LEOD, MALCOLM
The Pacific Railway: Britannicus' Letters from the Ottawa Citizen. Ottawa: 1875. V. 50

MAC LEOD, MARY
The Book of King Arthur and His Noble Knights. London: 1900. V. 51

MAC LEOD, NORMAN
Dictionary of the Gaelic Language. 1. Gaelic and English. II. English and Gaelic. Edinburgh: 1909. V. 54
Good Cheer Being the Christmas Number of Good Words. London: 1867. V. 47
Simple Truth: Spoken to Working People. London: 1867. V. 49

MAC LEOD, R. C.
The MacLeods of Dunvegan from the Time of Leod to the End of the Seventeenth Century. London: 1927. V. 54

MAC LEOD, RODERICK
On Rheumatism In Its Various Forms and On the Affections of Internal Organs, More Especially the Heart and Brain, to Which it Gives Rise. London: 1842. V. 51; 54

MAC LISE, DANIEL
The Story of the Norman Conquest. London: 1866. V. 53

MAC LISE, JOSEPH
Surgical Anatomy. Philadelphia: 1851. V. 47

MC LOUGHLIN, JOHN
The Letters From Fort Vancouver to the Governor and Committee. Second Series, 1839-44. Toronto: 1943. V. 49; 51
The Letters of John McLoughlin From Fort Vancouver to the Governor and Committee. First Series. 1825-38. Toronto: 1941. V. 51
The Letters of John McLoughlin From Fort Vancouver to the Governor and Committee. Third Series. 1844-46. Toronto: 1944. V. 51

MC LUHAN, HERBERT MARSHALL
The Mechanical Bride. New York: 1951. V. 47; 48; 50; 51; 53; 54
Through the Vanishing Point - Space in Poetry and Painting. New York: 1968. V. 50

MC LUHAN, T. C.
Touch the Earth. Toronto: 1971. V. 50

MAC MAHON, A. RUXTON
Far Cathay and Farthest India. London: 1893. V. 54
The Karens of the Golden Chersonese. London: 1876. V. 54

MC MAHON, JO
Deenie Folks and Friends of Theirs. Joliet: 1925. V. 47

MAC MAHON, JOSEPH PARKYNS
Paris in Miniature: Taken from The Picture at Full Length... London: 1782. V. 54

MAC MAHON, T. W.
Cause and Contrast: an Essay on the American Crisis. Richmond: 1862. V. 49

MC MANUS, GEORGE
Bringing Up Father. New York: 1919. V. 47; 48; 50

MAC MANUS, S.
The Red Poocher. New York: 1903. V. 47
The Rocky Road to Dublin. New York: 1938. V. 47

MAC MANUS, SEAMUS
Donegal Fairy Stories. London: 1902. V. 50; 51; 54
Woman of Seven Sorrows. Dublin: 1905. V. 52

MAC MASTER, DONALD
The Seal Arbitration 1893. Montreal: 1894. V. 47

MC MASTER, J.
A History of the People of the United States from the Revolution to the civil War. New York: 1896-1910. V. 53

MC MASTER, S. W.
60 Years on the Upper Mississippi. My Life and Experiences. Rock Island: 1893. V. 50

MC MECHEN, EDGAR CARLISLE
The Moffat Tunnel of Colorado. Denver: 1927. V. 54

MC MECHEN, JAMES H.
Legends of the Ohio Valley; or Thrilling Incidents of Indian Warefare. Wheeling: 1887. V. 53

MAC MEEKEN, J. W.
History of the Scottish Metrical Psalms. Glasgow: 1872. V. 48

MC MERROW, RONALD B.
Printer's & Publishers' Devices in England and Scotland 1485-1640. London: 1949. V. 49

MC MICHAEL, JOHN
Circulation: Proceedings of the Harvey Tercentenary Congress. Springfield: 1958. V. 52; 54

MAC MICHAEL, WILLIAM
The Gold Headed Cane. London: 1827. V. 47; 52; 54
The Gold Headed Cane. London: 1828. V. 47; 48; 49; 50
The Gold Headed Cane. New York: 1915. V. 47; 49; 52
Journey from Moscow to Constantinople, in the Years 1817, 1818. London: 1819. V. 48; 54
Lives of British Physicians. London: 1830. V. 52

MAC MILLAN, ALEXANDER
A Night with the Yankees; a Lecture Delivered in the Town Hall, Cambridge on March 30, 1868. Ayr Scotland: 1868. V. 53

MC MILLAN, HENRY G.
The Inside of Mormonism, a Judicial Examination of the Endowment oaths Administered In All the Mormon Temples, by the United States District Court... Salt Lake City: 1903. V. 51

MC MILLAN, TERRY
Disappearing Acts. New York: 1989. V. 50; 51; 52; 53

MAC MILLAN, TERRY
Disappearning Acts. London: 1990. V. 51

MC MILLAN, TERRY
Mama. Boston: 1987. V. 48; 49; 50; 51; 52; 53; 54
Waiting to Exhale. New York: 1992. V. 47; 53
What We've Lost. Anaheim: 1992. V. 54

MAC MINN, GEORGE R.
The Theater of the Golden Era in California. Caldwell: 1914. V. 54

MC MORRIES, EDWARD YOUNG
History of the First Regiment, Alabama Volunteer Infantry, C.S.A. Montgomery: 1904. V. 49; 51; 54

MAC MULLEN, R. T.
Orion, or How I Came to Sail Alone in a 19-Ton Yacht. 1878. V. 47

MAC MUNN, G. F.
The Armies of India. London: 1911. V. 47; 51

MAC MUNN, GEORGE
Afghanistan from Darius to Amanullah. 1929. V. 51

MC MURRAY, MARK
Type Specimens of Caliban Press. On the Occasion of Its Sixth Anniversary. Montclair: 1991. V. 51; 52

MC MURRAY, WILLIAM J.
History of the Twentieth Tennessee Regiment Volunteer Infantry, C.S.A. Nashville: 1904. V. 49

MC MURTRIE, DOUGLAS C.
Alphabets: Manual of Letter Design, with Complete Alphabets of Varied Styles of Lettering. Pelham: 1926. V. 54
The Beginnings of Printing in Arizona. Chicago: 1937. V. 52
The Disabled Soldier. New York: 1919. V. 54
Early Printing in Colorado. Denver: 1935. V. 54
Early Printing in New Orleans 1764-1810. New Orleans: 1929. V. 54
Early Printing in Tennessee, with a Bibliography of the Issues of the Tennessee Press, 1793-1830. Chicago: 1933. V. 47; 48
Eighteenth Century North Carolina Imprints 1749-1800. Chapel Hill: 1938. V. 52; 54
The Establishment of the First Texas Newspaper with Some Excerpts from the "Texas Republican" Pioneer of Newspapers at Nacogdoches in 1819. El Paso: 1935. V. 47
The First Printers of Chicago with a Bibliography of the Issues of the Chicago Press 1836-1850. chicago: 1927. V. 52
The First Printing in New Mexico. Chicago: 1929. V. 49
A Forgotten Press of Kansas. Chicago: 1930. V. 52
A History of California Newspapers: Being a Contemporary Chronicle of Early Printing and Publishing on the Pacific Coast. New York: 1927. V. 52
Jotham Meeker. Pioneer Printer of Kansas with Bibliography of the Known Issues of the Baptist Mission Press at Shawanoe, Stockbridge and Ottawa, 1834-1854. Chicago: 1930. V. 51
Montana Imprints 1864-1880. Chicago: 1937. V. 52
Plantin's Index Chracterum of 1567. New York: 1924. V. 48
Two Georgia Printed Acts of 1757 and 1763. Chicago: 1933. V. 54

M'MURTRIE, HENRY
The Gentleman's Medical Vade-Mecum and Travelling Companion... Philadelphia: 1824. V. 48

MC MURTRY, LARRY
All My Friends Are Going to Be Strangers. New York: 1972. V. 50; 51; 54
Anything for Billy. New York: 1988. V. 47; 48; 49; 51; 52; 54
Booked Up: Permanent Want List. Washington. V. 48
Buffalo Girls. New York: 1990. V. 51
Cadillac Jack. New York: 1982. V. 48; 49; 51; 52; 53; 54
The Desert Rose. New York: 1983. V. 47; 48; 49; 50; 51; 52; 53
The Evening Star. New York: 1992. V. 52
Film Flam. New York: 1987. V. 48; 51
Horseman, Pass By. New York: 1961. V. 49; 50; 51; 52; 53
In a Narrow Grave. Austin: 1968. V. 49; 50; 51; 52; 53
It's Always We Rambled: an Essay on Rodeo. New York: 1974. V. 47; 50; 51; 52
The Last Picture Show. New York: 1966. V. 48; 50; 51; 52; 53; 54
Leaving Cheyenne. New York, Evanston, & London: 1963. V. 48; 52; 53
Lonesome Dove. New York: 1985. V. 47; 48; 49; 50; 51; 52; 53; 54
Moving On. New York: 1970. V. 47; 48; 50; 51; 52; 53
Pretty Boy Floyd. New York: 1994. V. 53
Some Can Whistle. New York: 1989. V. 51
Somebody's Darling. New York: 1978. V. 51; 52; 53
Terms of Endearment. New York: 1975. V. 47; 49; 50; 51; 52; 53; 54
Texasville. New York: 1987. V. 48; 51; 52
The Uncollected Fictional Works. Thaila: 1979. V. 50; 54

M'NAB, W.
Hints on the Planting and General Treatment of Hardy Evergreens in the Climate of Scotland. Edinburgh: 1831. V. 48
A Treatise on the Propagation, Cultivation and General Treatment of Cape Heaths. Edinburgh: 1832. V. 49; 52; 53

MC NABB, VINCENT
Geoffrey Chaucer: a Study in Genius and Ethics. London: 1934. V. 52
God's Book and Other Poems. Ditchling, Sussex: 1930. V. 52

MC NAIL, STANLEY
Something Breathing. Sauk City: 1965. V. 51

MAC NAIR, P.
The Geology and Scenery of the Grampians and the Valley of Strahmore. Glasgow: 1908. V. 49; 53

MC NALLY, LEONARD
The Rules of Evidence On Pleas of the Crown, Illustrated from Printed and Manuscript Trials and Cases. Philadelphia: 1804. V. 50

MAC NALLY, LEONARD
Sentimental Excursions to Windsor and Other Places, with Notes Critical and Illustrative and Explanatory... London: 1781. V. 50; 54

MAC NAMARA, JOHN
In Perils by Mine Own Countrymen Three Years on the Kansas Border. New York: 1856. V. 47

MAC NAMARA, M. H.
The Irish Ninth in Bivouac and Battle. Boston: 1867. V. 47

MC NAMEE, EOIN
The Last of Deeds. 1989. V. 54

MAC NAMEE, JAMES J.
History of the Diocese of Ardagh. 1954. V. 49; 50

MAC NAUGHT, MRS.
Through Distant Lands. Diary of a Tour Round the World in 1886-7. London?: 1887?. V. 53

MC NAUGHTON, ARNOLD
The Book of Kings. London: 1973. V. 48

MAC NAUGHTON, HUGH
Eton Letters 1915-1918. London: 1920. V. 54

MC NAUGHTON, JAMES H.
Onnalinda. A Romance. London: 1886. V. 48

MC NAUGHTON, MARGARET
Overland to Cariboo: an Eventful Journey of Canadian Pioneers to the Gold-Fields of British Columbia in 1862. Toronto: 1896. V. 47; 48; 49; 53

MAC NEICE, LOUIS
Autumn Journal. London: 1939. V. 49; 51
Autumn Sequel - a Rhetorical Poem in XXVI Cantos. London: 1954. V. 50
Blind Fireworks. London: 1929. V. 47; 50; 51; 53
Christopher Columbus - a Radio Play. London: 1944. V. 50
Collected Poems 1925-1948. London: 1949. V. 47; 53; 54
The Earth Compels. London: 1938. V. 54
Holes in the Sky: Poems, 1944-47. London: 1948. V. 54
Letters from Iceland. London: 1937. V. 49
Meet the U.S. Army. London: 1943. V. 51
Modern Poetry. London: 1938. V. 53
Out of the Picture: a Play in Two Acts. London: 1937. V. 54
Poems. London: 1935. V. 49; 54
Poems. New York: 1937. V. 47
Poems. New York: 1940. V. 54
Poems. New York: 1974. V. 51
The Poetry of W. B. Yeats. London: 1941. V. 53
The Revenant. Dublin: 1975. V. 48
Solstices. London: 1961. V. 48; 49; 50; 54
Springboard: Poems 1941-1944. London: 1944. V. 47; 52
Springboard Poems: 1941-44. London. V. 53
Ten Burnt Offerings. London: 1952. V. 47; 53

MC NEIL, MARION
The Blue Elephant and the Pink Pig. Akron: 1931. V. 52

MAC NEILL, ALYSON
Twenty-Three Wood-Engravings for The Song of the Forest. Llandago: 1987. V. 47

MC NEILL, GEORGE E.
Factory Children. Report Upon the Schooling and Hours of Labor of Children Employed in the Manufacturing and Mechanical Establishments of Massachusetts. Boston: 1875. V. 54

MAC NEILL, HECTOR
Bygane Times, and Late Come Changes; or, a Bridge Street Dialouge, in Scottish Verse. Edinburgh: 1811. V. 47; 52
The Poetical Works. London: 1801. V. 48

MAC NEISCH, R. S.
The Prehistory of the Tehuacan Valley. Austin/London: 1967-70. V. 54

MAC NENY, PATRICK
The Freedom of Commerce of the Subjects of the Austrian Nether-Lands, Asserted and Vindicated. Brussels: 1725. V. 54

MAC NICHOL, JOHN R.
A Review (of the) National Liberal-Conservative Convention Held at Winnipeg, Manitoba, October 10th to 12th 1927. Toronto: 1930. V. 48

MC NICKLE, D'ARCY
The Surrounded. New York: 1936. V. 50

M'NICOL, DONALD
Remarks on Dr. Samuel Johnson's Journey to the Hebrides. London: 1779. V. 50

MC NICOLL, DAVID
A Rational Enquiry Concerning the Operation of the Stage on the Morals of Society. Newcastle-upon-Tyne: 1823. V. 52

MAC NISH, ROBERT
The Philosophy of Sleep. Glasgow: 1830. V. 47; 48

MC NITT, FRANK
Richard Wetherill: Anasazi. Albuquerque: 1957. V. 48; 54

MC NUTT, G. W.
My Twenty-Three Experience as a Detective. Des Moines: 1923. V. 49

MAC NUTT, J. SCOTT
A Manual for Health Officers. New York: 1915. V. 49; 51; 54

MC PALMER, JOHN
History of the Twenty-Second United States Infantry, 1866-1922. 1922. V. 48

MC PHAIL, J.
The Gardener's Remembrancer Throughout the Year. London: 1807. V. 48

MC PHAIL, RODGER
Fishing Season, an Artist's Fishing Year. V. 50

MC PHEE, JOHN
Alaska. San Francisco: 1981. V. 52
Annals of the Former World. New York. V. 47; 49
Annals of the Former World. New York: 1983. V. 51; 52; 54
Annals of the Former World. (with) Basin and Range and In Suspect Terrain. New York: 1981. V. 53
Basin and Ranger. New York: 1981. V. 54
Coming Into the Country. New York: 1977. V. 52
Coming into the Country. London: 1978. V. 54
The Crofter and the Laird. London: 1970. V. 54
The Crofter and the Laird. New York: 1970. V. 49; 50; 51; 52; 54
The Curve of Binding Energy. New York: 1974. V. 49; 50; 51; 52; 54
The Deltoid Pumpkin Seed. New York: 1973. V. 49; 50; 51; 54
Encounters with the Archdruid. New York: 1971. V. 53
Giving Good Weight. New York: 1979. V. 54
The Headmaster. New York: 1966. V. 48; 49; 51; 52; 53; 54
In Suspect Terrain. New York: 1983. V. 54
Levels of the Game. New York: 1969. V. 51; 52
Oranges. New York: 1967. V. 49; 50; 51
Pieces of the Frame. New York: 1975. V. 48; 49; 52; 54
The Pine Barrens. New York: 1968. V. 50; 51; 52; 53; 54
La Place de la Concorde Suisse. New York: 1984. V. 47; 50; 52; 54
Riding the Boom Extension. Worcester: 1983. V. 54
Rising from the Plain. New York: 1986. V. 50; 51; 54
A Roomful of Hovings. New York: 1968. V. 49; 50; 51; 52; 54
A Sense of Where You Are: a Profile of Princeton's Bill Bradley. New York: 1965. V. 47; 49; 51; 54
The Survival of the Bark Canoe. New York: 1975. V. 49; 51; 52; 54
Table of Contents. New York: 1985. V. 47; 48; 51; 52; 53; 54
Wimbledon: a Celebration. New York: 1972. V. 51

MC PHERREN, IDA
Imprints on Pioneer Trails. Boston: 1950. V. 48

MC PHERSON, AIMEE SEMPLE
Give Me My Own God. New York: 1936. V. 47

MAC PHERSON, DAVID
Annals of Commerce, Manufacataures, Fisheries and Navigation, With Brief Notices of the Arts and Sciences Connected With Them. London: 1805. V. 51; 52

MAC PHERSON, GERALDINE
Memoirs of the Life of Anna Jameson. Boston: 1878. V. 50

MAC PHERSON, H. A.
The Birds of Cumberland. Carlisle: 1886. V. 51; 52
The Birds of Cumberland. London: 1886. V. 48
A History of Fowling. Edinburgh: 1897. V. 49; 52
Vertebrata Fauna of Lakeland Including Cumberland and Westmorland and Lancashire North of the Sands. Edinburgh: 1892. V. 48; 50; 52
A Vertebrate Fauna of Lakeland, Including Cumberland and Westmorland with Lancashire North of the Sands. Edinburgh: 1892. V. 47; 48; 50; 51

MAC PHERSON, J. F.
Tabasco-Land. Cincinnati: 1906. V. 52

MAC PHERSON, JAMES
Fingal, an Ancient Epic Poem, in Six Books... London: 1762. V. 48; 49; 52
Fragments of Ancient Poetry. Edinburgh: 1760. V. 48
Fragments of Ancient Poetry. Dublin: 1770. V. 50; 54
Die Gedichte Ossians Eines Alten Celtischen Dichters... Vienna: 1768-69. V. 51; 54
The History of Great Britain, from the Restoration to the Accession of the House of Hannover. London: 1775. V. 50; 53
The History of Great Britain, from the Restoration to the Accession of the House of Hannover. London: 1776. V. 48
Morison's Edition of the Poems of Ossian, the Song of Fingal. Perth: 1795. V. 50
An Original Collection of the Poems of Ossian, Orrann, Ulin and Other Bards... Montrose: 1816. V. 49; 52; 53
The Poems of Ossian. London: 1796. V. 48
The Poems of Ossian... Glasgow: 1799. V. 47
The Poems of Ossian. London: 1807. V. 51
The Poems of Ossian. London: 1905. V. 53
A Short History of the Opposition During the Last Session of Parliament. London: 1779. V. 48
Skaldestycken af Ossian. Uppsala: 1794-1800. V. 54
The Works of Ossian... London: 1765. V. 52

MC PHERSON, JAMES ALAN
Elbow Room. Boston: 1977. V. 47; 51; 53; 54

MC PHERSON, JAMES ALAN continued
Hue and Cry. Boston: 1969. V. 47; 49; 50; 51; 53
Railroad: Trains and Train People in American Culture. New York: 1976. V. 48; 51

MAC PHERSON, JAY
O Earth Return. Toronto: 1954. V. 47

MAC PHERSON, R. A.
The Birds of Cumberland Critically Studied, Including Some Notes on the Birds of Westmorland. Carlisle: 1886. V. 50

MC PHERSON, SANDRA
Designating Duet. West Burke: 1989. V. 52
Duet. 1989. V. 52
Floralia. Portland: 1985. V. 48; 53; 54
Floralia. Vermont: 1985. V. 51
Sensing. San Francisco: 1980. V. 54

MC PHERSON, WILLIAM
Homes in Los Angeles City and County and Description Thereof, with Sketches of the Four Adjacent Counties. Los Angeles: 1873. V. 51

M'PHUN, W. R.
The Merchant's Banker's Commercial Pocket Guide. Glasgow: 1840. V. 53

MAC QUEEN, DANIEL
Letters on Mr. Hume's History of Great Britain. Edinburgh: 1756. V. 50

MAC QUEEN, JOHN FRASER
Chief Points in the Laws of War and Neutrality, Search and Blockade... Richmond: 1863. V. 52

MC QUILL, T.
The Hudson River by Daylight. New York: 1878. V. 53

MAC QUIOD, PERCY
A History of English Furniture: the Age of Oak; the Age of Walnut; the Age of Mahogany; The Age of Satinwood. London: 1925-28. V. 49

MAC QUOID, KATHARINE
In the Adrennes. London: 1881. V. 52

MAC QUOID, PERCY
The Age of Oak, a History of English Furniture Series. London: 1904. V. 49
The Dictionary of English Furniture from the Middle Ages to the Late Georgian Period. London: 1953. V. 48
A History of English Furniture... London. V. 47; 52
A History of English Furniture. London: 1938. V. 47
A History of English Furniture from the Middle Ages to the Late Georgian Period. London: 1924-27. V. 48
A History of English Furniture: The Age of Oak; The Age of Walnut; The Age of Mahogany: The Age of Satinwood. London: 1925-28. V. 48; 51
A History of English Furniture: the Ages of Oak/Satinwood/Mahogany/Walnut. 1904. V. 54

MAC RAE, WENDELL
Wendell MacRae. Photos: 1927-1949. New York: 1980. V. 47

MC REYNOLDS, ROBERT
Thirty Years on the Frontier. Colorado Springs: 1906. V. 49

MC ROBBIE, KENNETH
Eyes Without a Face. Toronto: 1960. V. 47; 51

MC RUER, D. C.
Statements and Argument of D. C. McRuer in Behalf of the Citizens of San Francisco, Against the 'Goat Island Bill', Before the Committee on Military Affairs of the United States Senate. Friday Evening, January 31, 1873. Washington: 1873. V. 49

MC SHANE, CHARLES
The Locomotive Up to Date. Chicago: 1911. V. 53

MC SHINE, KYNASTON
Andy Warhol: A Retrospective. New York: 1989. V. 50

M'TAGGART, ANN
Constantia, a Tragedy, in Five Acts and Valville... London: 1824. V. 51

MAC TAGGART, JOHN
Three Years in Canada: An Account of the Actual State of the Country in 1826-27-28. London: 1829. V. 48

MC TAGGART, M. F.
From Colonel to Subaltern: Some Keys for Horse Owners. London: 1928. V. 47; 48; 50; 52

MAC TAVISH, NEWTON
The Fine Arts in Canada. Toronto: 1925. V. 53

MC TYEIRE, H. N.
Duties of Masters to Servants: Three Premium Essays. Charleston: 1851. V. 54

MC VAIL, JOHN
Vaccination Vindicated: Being an Answer to the Leading Anti-Vaccinators. London: 1887. V. 50; 51; 52

MAC VEAGH, CHARLES, MRS.
Fountains of Papal Rome. New York: 1915. V. 47

MC VEAN, DONALD N.
A Plant Communities of the Scottish Highlands. London: 1962. V. 54

MC VEY, J. P.
CRC Handbook of Mariculture. Volume I. Crustacean Aquaculture. Boca Raton: 1983. V. 53

MAC VICAR, JOHN G.
On the Beautiful, the Picturesque, the Sublime. London: 1837. V. 48; 50; 53

MC VICKAR, H. W.
Our Amateur Circus or a New York Season. New York: 1892. V. 53

MAC VITIE, WILLIAM
Whiskey, a Poem. Edinburgh: 1795. V. 48

MC VOY, J. P.
The Bam-Bam Clock. Chicago: 1920. V. 54

MC WATTERS, GEORGE S.
Detectives of Europe and America of Life in the Secret Service. Hartford: 1878. V. 51

MAC WHORTER, ALEXANDER
A Funeral Sermon, Preached in Newark, December 27, 1799...for the Universally Lamented, General Washington... Newark: 1800. V. 49

MC WHORTER, L. V.
The Border Settlers of Northwestern Virginia from 1768 to 1795... Hamilton: 1915. V. 50; 52
Hear Me My Chiefs, Nez Perce History and Legend. Caldwell: 1952. V. 47; 50; 53
Yellow Wolf: His Own Story. Caldwell: 1940. V. 49

MC WILLIAM, J. M.
The Birds of the Island of Brute. London: 1927. V. 51

MC WILLIAM, JAMES
Medical History of the Expedition to the Niger During the Years 1841-42 Comprising an Account of the Fever Which Led to Its Abrupt Termination. London: 1843. V. 49

MC WILLIAM, ROBERT
An Essay on the Origin and Operation of the Dry Rot, with a View to Its Prevention or Cure. London: 1818. V. 47

MC WILLIAMS, CAREY
Louis Adamic and Shadow America. Los Angeles: 1935. V. 54

MC WILLIAMS, JOHN
Recollections of John McWilliams. Princeton. V. 47; 50

M., A.
Cherrycomb & Silvertail: a Tragedy in 2 Acts... London: 1862. V. 47
The Reformed Gentleman; or, the Old English Morals Rescued from the Immoralities of the Present Age. London: 1693. V. 47

M., L.
A Short Narrative of the Life and Death of John Rhinholdt Count Patkul...Together with the Manner of His Execution... London: 1717. V. 47

M., R.
A General Survey of That Part of the Island of St. Christophers, Which Formerly Belonged to France.... London: 1722. V. 48

MAAS, WILLARD
Fire Testament. New York: 1935. V. 50

MAASKAMP, E.
Representations of Dresses, Morals and Customs, in the Kingdom of Holland, at the Beginning of the Nineteenth Century. Amsterdam: 1808. V. 48; 49
Vues Remarquables, Edifices, Monuments et Statues dans les Provinces Septentrionales du Royaume des Pays-Bas. Amsterdam: 1816. V. 47; 54

MABBERLEY, D. J.
Jupiter Botanicus: Robert Brown of the British Museum. Braunschweig: 1985. V. 49

MABBUT, GEORGE
Tables for Renewing and Purchasing of the Leases of Cathedral-Churches, and Colleges, According to Several Rates of Interest; with Their Construction and Use Explain'd... London: 1722. V. 47

MABERLY, J.
The Print Collector. New York: 1880. V. 53

MABIE, HAMILTON
Our New England. Here Nature Described by Hamilton Wright Mabie and s e of Her Familiar Scenes Illustrated. Boston: 1890. V. 51
Young Folks' Treasury. New York: 1909. V. 49

MABINOGION
Mabinogion. Waltham St. Lawrence: 1948. V. 51; 51; 54

MACARIUS, JOANNES
Abraxas, seu Apistopistus; Quae est Antiquaria de Gemmis Basilidianis Disquisitio. Antwerp: 1657. V. 53

MACARTNEY, ERVYN E.
The Practical Exemplar of Architecture. London: 1907-28. V. 48; 51

MACARTNEY, MERVYN E.
The Practical Exemplar of Architecture. London: 1910. V. 50

MACAULAY, AULAY
Polygraphy; or, Short-Hand Made Easy to the Meanest Capacity... London: 1747. V. 52

MACAULAY, CATHERINE
The History of England from the Accession of James I to the Elevation of the House of Hanover... London: 1766-71. V. 52
The History of England from the Revolution to the Present Time, in a Series of Letters to the Reverend Doctor Wilson. Bath: 1768. V. 47
Observations on a Pamphlet, Entitled, Thoughts on the Cause of the Present Discontents. London: 1770. V. 48

MACAULAY, JAMES
The Gothic Revival 1745-1845. London: 1975. V. 50
The Truth About Ireland: Tours of Observation in 1872 and 1875. London: 1876. V. 50

MACAULAY, JOHN
Verses Occasioned by the Death of the Late Unfortunate Lewis the Sixteenth. Dublin: 1793. V. 54

MACAULAY, KENNETH
The History of St. Kilda. London: 1764. V. 49; 50

MACAULAY, ROSE
Non-Combatants and Others. London: 1916. V. 50
Orphan Island. 1924. V. 48
The Writings of E. M. Forster. London: 1938. V. 48; 54

MACAULAY, THOMAS BABINGTON MACAULAY, 1ST BARON
The Complete Writings. Boston & New York: 1899. V. 50; 52
Critical and Historical Essays Contributed to the Edinburgh Review. London: 1843. V. 47; 50; 51
Critical and Historical Essays Contributed to the Edinburgh Review. London: 1858. V. 48; 50
Critical and Historical Essays Contributed to the Edinburgh Review. London: 1866. V. 51
Critical and Historical Essays Contributed to the Edinburgh Review. London: 1891. V. 54
History of England. New York: 1884. V. 49
The History of England. London: 1886. V. 53
The History of England from the Accession of James the Second. Philadelphia. V. 52
The History of England from the Accession of James the Second. London: 1849-55. V. 51
The History of England from the Accession of James the Second. London: 1849-61. V. 52
The History of England from the Accession of James the Second. London: 1855-61. V. 47; 51; 53
The History of England from the Accession of James the Second. New York: 1856-67. V. 54
The History of England from the Accession of James the Second. London: 1858. V. 51
The History of England from the Accession of James the Second. London: 1860-61. V. 54
The History of England From the Accession of James the Second. London: 1863/55/61. V. 50
The History of England. From the Accession of James the Second. London: 1871. V. 54
The History of England from the Accession of James the Second. London: 1877. V. 48
The History of England from the Accession of James the Second. London: 1913. V. 52
The History of England from the Accession of james the Second. (with) *Critical and Historical Essays Contributed to the edinburgh Review.* (with) *Miscellaneous Writings and Speeches.* London: 1867-71. V. 49
The History of England. (with) *Miscellaneous Writings and Speeches of...(and) Essays and Lays of Ancient Rome.* London: 1889-90. V. 50
Lays of Ancient Rome. London: 1842. V. 50; 51; 54
Lays of Ancient Rome. London: 1852. V. 48
Lays of Ancient Rome. London: 1865. V. 49; 51
The Miscellaneous Writings of Lord MacAulay. London: 1860. V. 53
Pompeii. Cambridge: 1819. V. 54
Two Essays on the Earl of Chatham. London: 1901. V. 54
The Works. London: 1844-61. V. 54
Works. London: 1867-71. V. 48

MACAULEY, ELIZABETH WRIGHT
Tales of Drama, Founded on the Tragedies of Shakspeare, Massinger, Shirley, Rowe, Murphy, Lillo and Moore... London: 1822. V. 54
The Wrongs of Her Royal Highness the Princess Olive of Cumberland... 1833. V. 50; 52

MACCARI, ENRICO
Saggi Di Architettura e Decorazione Italiana. Rome: 187?. V. 48

MACE, ARTHUR C.
The Tomb of Senebtisi at Lisht. New York: 1916. V. 49; 51
The Tomb of Senebtisi at Lisht. New York: 1973. V. 49; 51

MACEDO, JOAQUIM MANOEL DE
Notions on the Choreography of Brazil. Leipzig: 1873. V. 47
Um Passeio Pela Cidade do Rio de Janeiro...Primeira Serie. Rio de Janeiro: 1862. V. 48

MACEDO, JOSE DE
Antidoto da Lingua Portugueza... Amsterdam: 1710. V. 48

MACH, RUDOLF
Catalogue of Arabic Manuscripts (Yahuda Section) in the Garrett Collection Princeton University Library. Princeton: 1977. V. 51

MACHELL, HUGH
Some Records of the Annual Grasmere Sports. Carlisle: 1911. V. 50; 52

MACHEN, ARTHUR
The Anatomy of Tobacco. London: 1884. V. 47
The Autobiography of Arthur Machen. London: 1954. V. 48
Bridles and Spurs. Cleveland: 1951. V. 49; 52; 54
The Canning Wonder. London: 1925. V. 48
Dr. Stiggins: His Views and Principles. London: 1906. V. 47; 48; 49
Dog and Duck. London: 1924. V. 47; 51; 53
Fantastic Tales of the Way to Attain. Carbonnek: 1923. V. 51
Far Off Things. London: 1922. V. 47; 48; 49
The Fortunate Lovers. London: 1887. V. 47; 48; 49
The Green Round. Sauk City: 1968. V. 52; 53
Notes and Queries. London: 1926. V. 47; 48; 49
One Hundred Merrie and Delightsome Stories. Carbonnek: 1924. V. 47
Ornaments in Jade. New York: 1924. V. 51; 54
Precious Balms. London: 1924. V. 49
A Preface to Casanova's Escape from the Leads. 1925. V. 50
Strange Roads. London: 1924. V. 54
Things Near and Far. London: 1923. V. 54
The Three Imposters. London: 1895. V. 47; 49; 53
Tom O' Bedlam and His Song. London: 1930. V. 47
The Works. London: 1923. V. 54

MACHIAVELLI, NICCOLO
The Art of War... Albany: 1815. V. 48; 53
The Florentine Historie. London: 1595. V. 51
The Florentine History in VIII Books. London: 1674. V. 49; 52
Historiae Florentinae. Strasbourg: 1610. V. 52
Historie. (with) *Libro dell'Arte Della Guerra.* Venice: 1540/41. V. 52
The Prince. London: 1640. V. 53
The Prince. New York: 1954. V. 51
The Prince. London: 1970. V. 54
The Prince. Letter to Francesco Vettori, Dec. 10, 1513. Reports on the Affairs of France and Germany. Life of Castruccio Castracani. Rome & Milan: 1930. V. 47
Tutte le Opere di...Divise in V. Parti, et di Nuovo con Somma Accuratezza Ristampate. 1550. V. 47; 48; 51
The Works. London: 1675. V. 48; 49; 50; 51; 53
The Works. London: 1680. V. 47; 48; 49
The Works. London: 1720. V. 47; 50; 52; 53
The Works. Edinburgh: 1762. V. 48; 52
The Works. London: 1775. V. 47; 48; 49; 51; 52

MACIEL DA COSTA, JOAO SEVERIANO
Memoria Sobre a Necessidade de Abolir a Introducao dos Escravos Africanos no Brasil; Sobre o Modo e Condicois com Que Esta Abolicao se Deve Fazer... Coimbra: 1821. V. 48

MACK, CONNIE
Connie Mack's Baseball Book. New York: 1950. V. 53

MACK, EBENEZER
The Cat-Fight; a Mock Heroic Poem. New York: 1824. V. 52; 53

MACK, EFFIE MONA
The Indian Massacre of 1911 at Little High Rock Canyon Nevada. 1968. V. 52
The Indian Massacre of 1911 at Little High Rock Canyon, Nevada. Sparks: 1968. V. 53
Nevada - a History of the State fromt he Earliest Times through the Civil War. Glendale: 1936. V. 52

MACK, ROBERT ELLICE
All Round the Clock. New York: 1880. V. 47
All Round the Clock. London: 1886. V. 54
Old Father Christmas, His Picture Book. London: 1888. V. 54
Queen of the Meadow. New York: 1880's. V. 54
Round the Hearth. London: 1885. V. 54
The Talking Clock. London: 1885. V. 54
When All is Young. London: 1888. V. 54

MACKAIL, JOHN WILLIAM
Biblia Innocentium: Being the Story of God's Chosen People Before the Coming of Our Lord Jesus Christ Upon Earth. Hammersmith: 1892. V. 51; 53
The Life of William Morris. London: 1899. V. 48
The Life of William Morris. London: 1907. V. 51
William Morris: an Address Delivered the 11th November 1900 at Kelmscott House, Hammersmith Before the Hammersmith Socialist Society. Hammersmith: 1901. V. 49; 50; 51; 52; 53; 54
William Morris. An Address Delivered the XIth November MDCCCC at Kelmscott House Hamemrsmith Before Hammersmith Socialist Society. Hammersmith: 1902. V. 51

MACKALL, LAWTON
Knife and Fork in New York. New York: 1949. V. 50

MACKALL, WILLIAM W.
A Son's Recollections of His Father. New York: 1930. V. 49

MACKARNESS, MATILDA ANNE
Old Joliffe: Not a Goblin Story. London: 1850. V. 54

MACKE, AUGUST
August Macke, Tunisian Watercolours and Drawings. New York: 1959. V. 50; 54

MACKEN, WALTER
Seek the Fair Land. The Silent People. The Scorching Wind. 1959/62/64. V. 49

MACKERELL, BENJAMIN
A New Catalogue of the Books in the Publick Library of the City of Norwich in the Year 1732. Norwich: 1732. V. 48

MACKEY, FRANK
Forward March! Photographic Record of America in the World War and the Post War Social Upheaval. Chicago: 1934. V. 48

MACKEY, JAMES
Compositions in Verse: With an Essay in Feamle Education. Dublin: 1819. V. 47; 49

MACKLEY, GEORGE
Engraved in the Wood: a Collection of Wood Engravings... London: 1968. V. 48; 51
Monica Poole: Wood Engraver. 1984. V. 47; 54
Monica Poole: Wood Engraver. Biddenden, Kent: 1984. V. 51; 52
Monica Poole: Wood-Engraver. London: 1984. V. 50
Wood Engraving (Its History and Technique). 1948. V. 54

MACKLIN, CHARLES
The Man of the World. (and) Love A La Mode. London: 1793. V. 51

MACKLIN, W. R.
The Decorative Paintings in Christ's Hospital Chapel MCMXIII-MCMXXIII. Ditching, Sussex: 1925. V. 47

MACKWORTH, DIGBY
Diary of a Tour through Southern India, Egypt and Palestine in the years 1821 and 1822. London: 1823. V. 52

MACKWORTH-PRAED, CYRIL WINTHROP
African Handbook of Birds. Series 1 to 3. London: 1952-73. V. 51
Birds of Eastern and North Eastern Africa. London: 1980. V. 52
Birds of the Southern Third of Africa. London: 1962. V. 50; 52
Birds of the Southern Third of Africa. London: 1962-63. V. 50

MACKWORTH-PRAED, GRANT
Birds of Eastern and Northeastern Africa. London: 1952-55. V. 49

MACKWORTH PRAED, WINTHROP
Poems. Boston and New York: 1909. V. 54

MACKY, JOHN
A Journey through England. London: 1723-24. V. 50; 52
A Journey through England. London: 1724. V. 50
A Journey through England. London: 1732. V. 52
Memoirs of the Secret Services of John Macky, Esq... London: 1733. V. 49

MACLAGAN, T. J.
The Germ Theory Applied to the Explanation of the Phenomena of Disease, the specific Fevers. London: 1876. V. 54

MACLAY, ELISE
The Art of Bev Doolittle. New York: 1990. V. 53

MACLAY, WILLIAM
Sketches of Debate in the First Senate of the United States in 1789-90-91. Harrisburg: 1880. V. 51

MACLEHOSE, JAMES
The Glasgow University Press 1638-1931, with Some Notes on Scottish printing in the Last Three Hundred Years. Glasgow: 1931. V. 50

MACLELLAN, FRANCES
Sketches of Corfu, Historical and Domestic; Its Scenery and Natural Productions... London: 1835. V. 48

MACLISE, DANIEL
A Gallery of Illustrious Literary Characters. London: 1873. V. 48
The Story of the Norman Conquest. London: 1866. V. 52

MACLISE, J.
Surgical Anatomy. London: 1851. V. 52

MACLISE, JOSEPH
Surgical Anatomy. Philadelphia: 1851. V. 51
Surgical Anatomy. Philadelphia: 1866. V. 49

MACLURE, WILLIAM
Opinions on Various Subjects, Dedicated to the Industrious Producers. Indiana: 1831. V. 54
Opinions on Various Subjects, Dedicated to the Industrious Producers. New Harmony: 1831-37-38. V. 53

MACLURG, JAMES
Experiments Upon the Human Bile: and Reflections on the Biliary Secretion. London: 1772. V. 51

MACOMB, ALEXANDER
Treatise on Martial Law and Courts-Martial; as practised in the United States of America. Charleston: 1809. V. 50

MACOMB, JOHN N.
Report of the Exploring Expedition from Santa Fe, New Mexico to the Junction of the Grand and Green Rivers of the Great Colorado to the West, in 1859. Washington: 1876. V. 47; 49; 51

MACON, NATHANIEL
Letters to Chas. O'Conor. The Destruction of the Union is Emancipation. The Status of Slavery. The Rights of the States and Territories. 1860. V. 48; 49

MACONOCHIE, ALEXANDER
Report on the State of Prison Discipline In Van Diemen's Land, &c. London: 1838. V. 49

MACORLAN, P.
Rues et Visage de Londres. Paris: 1928. V. 48

MACOUN, JAMES M.
Report on the Peace River Region. Ottawa: 1904. V. 50

MACOUN, JOHN
Autobiography of John Macoun, M.A., Canadian Explorer and Naturalist... Ottawa: 1922. V. 53
Catalogue of Canadian Birds. (Parts I, II and III). Ottawa: 1900/03/04. V. 49
Report of Professor Macoun, Botanist to the Expedition Addressed to Alfred R. C. Selwyn...Director of the Geological Survey of Canada. Ottawa: 1876. V. 51

MACQUER, PIERRE JOSEPH
Elements of the Theory and Practice of Chymistry. London: 1775. V. 53

MACRAE, A.
Handbook of Deer-Stalking. 1880. V. 48

MACRAY, WILLIAM DUNN
Letters and Papers of Patrick Ruthven, Earl of Forth and Brentford and of His Family: AD 1615-AD 1662. London: 1868. V. 51

MACREADY, WILLIAM CHARLES
Macready's Reminiscences and Selections from His Diaries and Letters. London: 1875. V. 47; 48

MACRI, M. C.
Modern Greek Interpreter... 1825. V. 47

MACROBIUS, A. A. T.
In Somnium Scipionis Lib. II. Saturnaliorum, Lib. VII. Lyon: 1556. V. 49
Opera. Lug. Batav: 1597. V. 48; 51

MACY, O.
The History of Nantucket... Mansfield: 1880. V. 53

MAD Cow. London: 1994. V. 53

THE MAD Dog; a Romance. London: 1804. V. 47

MADAN, FALCONER
A Chart of Oxford Printing '1468'-1900, with Notes and Illustrations. Oxford: 1904. V. 51
The Daniel Press. Oxford: 1921. V. 48; 50; 51
Oxford Books', Comprising I. The Early Oxford Press. II. Oxford Literature 1450-1640 and 1641-1650. Oxford: 1895-1912. V. 49
Pulls from Formes in the Clarendon Press,. London: 1923. V. 50
Records of the Club at Oxford 1790-1917. Oxford: 1917. V. 53

MADAN, FRANCIS
A Chart of Oxford printing '1468'-1900 with Notes and Illustrations. London: 1903. V. 48

MADAN, FRANCIS F.
A New Bibliography of the Eikon Basilike of King Charles I. Oxford: 1950. V. 53

MADAN, M.
Thoughts on Executive Justice, With Respect to Our Criminal Laws, Particularly on the Circuits. London: 1775. V. 52

MADAN, MARTIN
Thelyphthora; or, a Treatise on Female Ruin... London: 1780-81. V. 49
Thelyphthora; or, a Treatise On Female Ruin, In Its Causes Effects, Consequences, Prevention and Remedy... London: 1780. V. 50; 51

MADARASZ, GYULA
Magyarorszag Madarai. Budapest: 1899-1903. V. 51

MADARIAGA, SALVADOR DE
Don Quixote: an Introductory Essay in Psychology. Newtown: 1934. V. 47; 50; 54
Elegia en La Muerta de Federico Garcia Lorca. New York: 1938. V. 47

MADAUS, HOWARD MICHAEL
The Battle Flags of the Confederate Army of Tennessee. Milwaukee: 1976. V. 53

MADDEN, B. J. G.
A History of the 6th Battalion of the Black Watch (Royal Highland Regiment) 1939-1945. Perth: 1948. V. 48

MADDEN, DANIEL OWEN
Ireland and Its Rulers Since 1829. London: 1844. V. 50

MADDEN, DAVID
Rediscoveries. New York: 1971. V. 50

MADDEN, FREDERIC W.
History of Jewish Coinage, and Of Money In the Old and New Testament. London: 1864. V. 48

MADDEN, HENRY MILLER
German Travelers in California. San Francisco: 1958. V. 48; 51

MADDEN, JEROME
The Lands of the Southern Pacific Railroad Company of California: With General Information on the Resources of Southern California. San Francisco: 1882. V. 47

MADDEN, RICHARD F.
The Island of Cuba: Its Resources, Progress and Prospects, Considered in Relation Especially to the Influence of Its Prosperity on the Interest of the British West India Colonies. 1853. V. 47

MADDEN, RICHARD ROBERT
The Connexion Between the Kingdom of Ireland and the Crown of England. Dublin: 1845. V. 49; 50
The History of the Penal Laws Inacted Against Roman Catholics; the Operation and Results of that System of Legalized Plunder, Persecution and Proscription... London: 1847. V. 53
The Literary Life and Correspondence of the Countess of Blessington. London: 1855. V. 47; 49; 50; 51; 53
The Shrines and Sepulchres of the Old and New World... London: 1831. V. 49
Travels in Turkey, Egypt, Nubia and Palestine, in 1824, 1825, 1826 and 1827. London: 1829. V. 52
The United Irishmen, Their Lives and Times. London: 1842-43. V. 53

MADDEN, SAMUEL
Reflections and Resolutions Proper for the Gentlemen of Ireland. Dublin: 1738. V. 47

MADDOCK, ALFRED BEAUMONT
Practical Observations on Mental and Nervous Disorders. London: 1857. V. 52

MADDOCK, JAMES
The Florist's Directory, a Treatise on the Culture of Flowers. London: 1810. V. 48; 51; 52

MADDOW, BEN
Edward Weston: Fifty Years. 1973. V. 52
Edward Weston: Fifty Years. Millerton: 1973. V. 50; 54
Edward Weston: Fifty Years. New York: 1973. V. 49
Edward Weston: His Life and Photographs. Millerton: 1979. V. 47; 50
Faces: a Narrative History of the Portrait in Photography. Boston: 1977. V. 54

MADDOX, WILLES
Views of Landsdown Tower, Bath... London: 1844. V. 52

MADEIRA, CRAWFORD CLARK
The Delaware and Raritan Canal: a History. East Orange: 1941. V. 49; 51

MADEIRA, PERCY C.
Hunting in British East Africa. Philadelphia: 1909. V. 47; 48

MADGE, CHARLES
The Disappearing Castle. London: 1937. V. 50

MADIS, GEORGE
The Winchester Book. Brownsboro: 1985. V. 50

MADISON: The Capital of Wisconsin, Its Progress, Capabilities and Destiny. Madison: 1855. V. 48

MADOX, THOMAS
Baronia Anglica. London: 1736. V. 47; 53
Firma Burgi, or an Historical Essay Concerning the Cities, Towns and Boroughs of England. London: 1726. V. 49
Formulare Anglicanum; or, a Collection of Ancient Charters and Instruments of Divers Kinds, etc. London: 1702. V. 50
The History and Antiquities of the Exchequer of the Kings of England, in Two Periods... London: 1711. V. 47; 50
The History and Antiquities of the Exchequer of the Kings of England, in Two Periods... London: 1759. V. 49
The History and Antiquities of The Exchequer of the Kings of England, in Two Periods... London: 1769. V. 52

THE MADRAS Almanac for the Year 1829, Calculated For the Meridian of Fort St. George. Madras: 1829. V. 49

MADRAZO, PEDRO DE
Catalogo de los Cuadros del Real Museo de Pintura y Escultura... Madrid: 1843. V. 53

MAETERLINCK, MAURICE
The Blue Bird: a Fairy Play in 6 Acts. New York: 1911. V. 49
Hours of Gladness. London: 1912. V. 48; 50; 51; 52; 54
News of Spring. New York: 1913. V. 48
The Treasure of the Humble. London: 1906. V. 51
Works. New York: 1901-16. V. 50

MAFFEI, FRANCESCO SCIPIONE
A Compleat History of Ancient Amphitheatres, More Peculiarly Regarding the Architecture of Those Buildings... London: 1735. V. 51
Museum Veronense hoc est Antiquarum Inscriptionum Atque Anaglyphorum... Veronae: 1749. V. 49

MAFFEI, JOHANNES PETRUS
Historiarvm Indicarvm Libri XVI...Selectaravm Epistolaravm ex India Libri Qvatvor. Venice: 1589-88. V. 48; 53

MAFFITT, EMMA MARTIN
The Life and Services of John Newland Maffitt. New York and Washington: 1906. V. 49

MAFOFFIN, SUSAN SHELBY
Down the Santa Fe Trail and Into Mexico. New Haven: 1926. V. 50

MAGALHAENS DE MENEZES, JOSE NARCISO DE
Ordens Instructivas, e Economicas Para o Primeiro Regimento de Infantaria, da Cidade do Porto, Sendo Chefe Deste Corpo... Porto: 1799. V. 48

MAGAREY, WILLIAM ASHLEY
Individualism: or Socialism?. Adelaide: 1895. V. 54

MAGDALEN HOSPITAL
The Rules and Regulations of the Magdalen-Charity, with Instructions to the Women Who are Admitted, and Prayers for Their Use. London: 1769. V. 48

MAGEE, DAVID
Catalogue of Some Five Hundred Examples of the Printing of Edwin and Robert Grabhorn 1917-1960. 1961. V. 52
Catalogue of Some Five Hundred Examples of the Printing of Edwin and Robert Grabhorn, 1917-1960... San Francisco: 1961. V. 48; 54
A Course in Correct Cataloguing or Notes to the Neophyte. (with) *The 2nd Course in Correct Cataloguing...* San Francisco: 1962. V. 49
The Hundredth Book: a Bibliography of the Publications of the Book Club of California, and a History of the Club. San Francisco: 1958. V. 48; 54
The Spider and the Flie. San Francisco: 1939. V. 50

MAGENDIE, FRANCOIS
An Elementary Compendium of Physiology; for the Use of Students. Edinburgh: 1823. V. 47; 49; 51
Formulary for the Preparation and Employment of Several New Remedies... Philadelphia: 1834. V. 49; 54
Formulary for the Preparation and Mode of Employing Several New Remedies. Philadelphia: 1824. V. 52
Summary of Physiology. Baltimore: 1822. V. 47

MAGGI, GIROLAMO
Anglarensis De Tintinnabulis Liber Postumus. (and) *Anglaraensis de Equuelo Liber Postumus.* (and, as part of the second work) *Appendix De Eculei Tormento, ex Signoii Gallonii & Jureti Scriptis.* Amstelodami: 1664. V. 53

MAGGS BROS.
The Art of Writing, 2800 B.C. to 1930 A.D. Illustrated in a Collection of Original Documents Written on Vellum, Paper, Papyrus, Silk, Linen, Bamboo or Inscribed on Clay, Marble, Steatite, Jasper &c. London: 1930. V. 50
Bibliotheca Aeronautica. A Descriptive Catalogue of Books and Engravings Illustrating the Evolution of the Airship and the Aeroplane. (Part I) Catalogue No. 387. (with) *Bibliotheca Aeronautica...Part II. Catalogue No. 435.* London: 1920/23. V. 50
Bibliotheca Aeronautica (Catalogs 387 and 435);. London: 1920-23. V. 49
Bibliotheca Brasiliensis. London: 1930. V. 47; 50
Book Bindings; Historical and Decorative. Catalogue No. 407. London: 1921. V. 50
Book Bindings: Historical and Decorative. Catalogue No. 489. London: 1927. V. 50
Bookbinding in Great Britain, Sixteenth to the Twentieth Century. Catalogue No. 893. London: 1964. V. 52
Bookbinding in the British Isles. Cat. 1075, Parts I and II. London: 1987. V. 48; 52; 54
Bookbindings of Great Britain, Sixteenth to the Twentieth Century. Catalogue No. 845. London: 1957. V. 52
Books Printed in Spain and Spanish Books printed in Other Countries. Catalogue No. 495. London: 1927. V. 47; 50; 51
Catalogue of a Unique Collection of Early Editions of Ronsard by Seymour De Ricci. London: 1927. V. 50; 52
Catalogue of Medical Works from the Library of Dr. Nicolaus Pol Born c. 1470; Court Physician to the Emperor Maximilian I. London: 1929. V. 47
A Collection of French XVIIIth Century Illustrated Books with Plates After le Jeune, Boucher, Choffard...etc. London: 1930. V. 50; 52
A Descriptive Catalogue of Books, Engravings and Medals Illustrating the Evolution of the Airship and the Aeroplane. Catalogue Number 545. London: 1930. V. 54
English Armorial and Decorative Bindings. Catalogue No. 665. London: 1938. V. 49; 50; 52
Historic and Artistic Bookbindings from the XIVth Century to the Present Time. Catalogue No. 324. London: 1914. V. 50
The History of Flight. A Descriptive Catalogue of Books, Engravings, and Airmail Stamps Illustrating the Evolution of the Airship and Aeroplane. Catalogue 619. London: 1936. V. 50; 54
Old Medicine. No. 485. London: 1926. V. 50; 52
One Hundred Spanish Books Selected from the Stock of Maggs Bros. London: 1929. V. 47
A Selection of Books, Manuscripts, Engravings and Autograph Letters Remarkable for Their Interest and Rarity, Being the Five Hundredth Catalogue. London: 1928. V. 52
Twenty-Two Spanish American Imprints. London: 1932. V. 47
Voyages and Travels in All Parts of the World. London: 1937-62. V. 53

MAGIC Fairy Tales: Goldilocks and the Three Bears. Springfield: 1943. V. 48

THE MAGIC Lantern. Its Construction and Use, by a Fellow of the Chemical Society. London: 1890. V. 53

MAGIC Tales. The Devil's Dice; The Magic Ring!; The Fatal Prediction; The Magic Mirror!; The Ocean Spirit; The Magic Dream!; The Three Witches!, also The Dwarf and Miller's Daughter; the Magic Car!; the Elfin Queen!; The Double Transformation... London: 1820. V. 52

THE MAGICIAN'S Own Book, or the Whole Art of Conjuring, Being a Complete Hand-Book of Parlor Magic Containing Over One Thousand Optical, Chemical, Mechanical, Magnetical and Magical Experiments. New York: 1857. V. 50

MAGID, BARRY
Father Louie: Photographs of Thomas Merton. New York: 1991. V. 51; 54

MAGILL, FRANK N.
Survey of Science Fiction Literature. Englewood Cliffs: 1979. V. 53

MAGINI, GIOVANNI ANTONIO
Ephemerides Coelestium Motuum...Ab Anno Domini 1581... Venice: 1582. V. 49
Novae Coelestium Orbium Theoricae Congruentes cum Observationibus. Venice: 1589. V. 47

MAGINN, WILLIAM
A Gallery of Illustrious Literary Characters (1830-1838) Drawn by the Late Daniel Mclise... London: 1873. V. 51
Homeric Ballads: with Translations and Notes by the Late William Maginn. London: 1850. V. 51
John Manesty, the Liverpool Merchant. London: 1844. V. 49
Maxims of Sir Morgan O'Doherty, Bart. Edinburgh & London: 1849. V. 51
Miscellanies: Prose and Verse. London: 1885. V. 51
Tales of Military Life. London: 1829. V. 51
Tales of Military Life. New York: 1829. V. 54

MAGIRUS, JOHANN
Physiologiae Peripateticae Libris Sex Cum commentariis... London: 1619. V. 51

MAGISTRIS, JOHANNES DE
Summularum Petri Hispani Glossulae. Venice: 1490. V. 49; 50; 53

MAGNA Carta and other Charters of English Liberties. London: 1938. V. 52

MAGNE DE MAROLLES, GERVAIS FRANCOIS
An Essay on Shooting: Containing the Various Methods of Forging, Boring and Dressing Gun Barrels... London: 1789. V. 54

MAGNER, D.
Magner's ABC Guide to Sensible Horse-shoeing. Akron: 1899. V. 53

LA MAGNIFICA et Triumphale Entrata del Christianiss Re di Francia Henrico Secondo. Lyon: 1549. V. 53

MAGNITSKII, LEONTII FILIPPOVICH
Arithmetika... Moscow: 1703. V. 50

MAGNOLIA CEMETERY CO., CHARLESTON
Magnolia Cemetery. The Proceedings at the Dedication of the Grounds. To Which are Appended the Rules, Regulations and Charter of the Company... Charleston: 1851. V. 50

MAGNUS, OLAUS
A Compendious History of the Goths, Swedes & Vandals and Other Northern Nations. London: 1658. V. 47; 54
Gentivm Septentrionalivm Historiae Breviarivm.. Leiden: 1652. V. 53

MAGNUSSON, EIRIKR
The Saga Library. London: 1891-1905. V. 53
Three Northern Love Stories, and other Tales. London: 1875. V. 49

MAGOFFIN, SUSAN SHELBY
Down the Santa Fe Trail and Into Mexico. New Haven: 1926. V. 48; 50

MAGOUN, F. ALEXANDER
The Frigate Constitution and Other Historic Ships. Salem: 1928. V. 51

MAGOUN, H. W.
Neurophysiology. Washington: 1959. V. 50

MAGRA, JAMES
A Journal of a Voyage Round the World, in His Majesty's Ship Endeavour, in the Years 1768, 1769, 1770 and 1771. London: 1771. V. 50; 52

MAGRATH, JOHN RICHARD
The Obituary Book of Queen's College, Oxford. Oxford: 1910. V. 48; 49; 54
The Queen's College. Oxford: 1921. V. 49

MAGRATH, THOMAS WILSON
Authentic Letters from Upper Canada... Dublin: 1833. V. 47

MAGRY, PIERRE
Decouvertes et Etablissments des Francais dans L'Ouest et dans le Sud de l'Amerique Septentrionale... Paris: 1879-88. V. 50

MAGUIRE, JOHN FRANCIS
The Industrial Movement in Ireland, as Illustrated by the National Exhibition of 1852. Cork: 1853. V. 52
The Irish in America. London: 1868. V. 48; 50

MAHAFFY, J. P.
Collection of the Works on Greek and Latin History and Culture. London: 1888-96. V. 48

MAHAM, D. H.
An Elementary Course of Civil Engineering. London: 1859. V. 48

MAHAN, ALFRED THAYER
The Embodiment of the Sea Power of Great Britain. London: 1899. V. 54
The Influence of Sea Power Upon History 1660-1783. London: 1890. V. 53
The Influence of Sea Power Upon the French Revolution and Empire 1793-1812. London: 1892. V. 52; 53; 54
The Influence of Sea Power Upon the French Revolution and Empire 1793-1812. Boston: 1894. V. 47
The Life of Nelson. Boston: 1897. V. 50; 54
The Life of Nelson. London: 1897. V. 50; 51; 52; 53; 54
The Life of Nelson. Boston: 1900. V. 48
Naval Strategy Compared and Contrasted with the Principles and Practices of Military Operations on Land. Boston: 1911. V. 52
Sea Power in It's Relation to the War of 1812. London: 1905. V. 52; 54
Types of Naval Officers Drawn from the History of the Britsh Navy. London: 1902. V. 54

MAHAN, ARTHUR THAYER
Great Commanders. Admiral Farragut. New York: 1892. V. 52
The Influence of Sea Power Upon the French Revolution and Empire, 1793-1812. London: 1900. V. 47
The Life of Nelson. The Embodiment of the Sea Power of Great Britain. Boston: 1897. V. 52

MAHAN, DENNIS HART
An Elementary Course of Civil Engineering, for the Use of the Cadets of the United States' Military Academy. New York: 1846. V. 49
Summary Of the Course of Permanent Fortification and of the Attack and Defence of Permanent Works. Charleston: 1862. V. 49
A Treatise on Field Fortification...On the Methods of Laying Out, Constructing, and Attacking Intrenchments... Richmond: 1862. V. 49

MAHOMET II, SULTAN OF TURKEY
Epistolae Magni Turci. Padua: 1475. V. 52

MAHON, DEREK
Twelve Poems. Belfast: 1965. V. 48

MAHONEY, BERTHA
Contemporary Illustrators of Children's Books. Boston: 1930. V. 50
Illustrators of Children's Books 1744-1945. Boston: 1947. V. 50

MAHONY, FRANCIS SYLVESTER
Facts and Figures from Italy... London: 1847. V. 49

MAHR, AUGUST C.
The Visit of the "Rurik" to San Francisco in 1816. Stanford: 1932. V. 54

THE MAID of Renmore or Platonic Love; a Mock Heroic Romance, in Verse... London: 1810. V. 52

MAIDEN HOSPITAL
The Rules and Constitutions for Governing and Managing the Maiden Hospital, Founded by the Company of Merchants, and Mary ERskine in Anno 1695. Edinbrugh: 1731. V. 47; 54

MAIDEN, J. H.
A Critical Revision of the Genus Eucalyptus. Sydney: 1903-33. V. 49; 50; 51; 54
The Flowering Plants and Ferns of New South Wales. Sydney: 1895-98. V. 48; 50; 51; 54
The Forest Flora of New South Wales. Sydney: 1904-24. V. 49; 52; 53
Sir Joseph Banks, the Autocrat of the Philosophers 1744-1820. Sydney: 1909. V. 49; 54

THE MAIDEN'S Hopes in the Lottery. 1760. V. 47

MAIDMENT, JAMES
A Book of Scotish Pasquils 1568-1715. Edinburgh: 1868. V. 50; 52; 54
The Court of Session Garland. Edinburgh: 1839. V. 52

MAIER, MICHAEL
Examen Fucorum Pseudo-Chymicorum Detectorum et in Gratiam Vertiatis Amantium Succincte Refutatorum. Frankfort: 1617. V. 48

MAILER, NORMAN
The 1974 Marilyn Monroe Datebook. 1973. V. 51
Advertisements for Myself. New York: 1959. V. 47; 48; 51; 54
Advertisements for Myself. London: 1961. V. 49
An American Dream. New York: 1965. V. 49; 53
Ancient Evenings. Boston: 1983. V. 48; 51; 52
The Armies of the Night. New York: 1968. V. 48; 51; 52
Barbary Shore. New York & Toronto: 1951. V. 47; 48; 49; 50; 51; 53; 54
The Bullfight, a Photographic Narrative. New York: 1967. V. 50; 51; 53
Cannibals and Christians. New York: 1966. V. 54
Deaths for the Ladies. New York: 1962. V. 48
Deer Park. New York: 1955. V. 48; 49; 51
The Deer Park. London: 1957. V. 51
The Faith of Graffiti. New York: 1974. V. 48; 50; 51; 52; 53; 54
The Flight. Boston: 1975. V. 54
A Fragment From Vietnam. New York: 1984. V. 48
A Fragment from Vietnam. Helsinki: 1985. V. 49
Harlot's Ghost. New York: 1991. V. 47; 48; 49; 51; 52; 53; 54
How the Wimp Won the War. Northridge: 1992. V. 48
Huckleberry Finn, Alive at 100. Montclair: 1985. V. 48; 51; 54
The Last Night. New York: 1984. V. 48; 49; 50; 51; 54
Marilyn. New York: 1973. V. 49; 51; 53
The Naked and the Dead. New York: 1947. V. 50
The Naked and the Dead. New York: 1948. V. 47; 48; 49; 50; 51; 52; 53; 54
The Naked and the Dead. London: 1949. V. 53
The Naked and the Dead. Franklin Center: 1979. V. 47; 49; 50
Of a Fire on the Moon. Boston: 1970. V. 48
Of a Small and Modest Malignancy, Wicked and Bristling with Dots. Northridge: 1980. V. 48; 54
Of Women and Their Elegance. New York: 1980. V. 50; 51
The Prisoner of Sex. 1971. V. 50
Tough Guys Don't Dance. New York: 1984. V. 47; 48; 49; 51
Why Are We in Vietnam?. New York: 1967. V. 51

MAILLARD, N. DORAN
History of Texas. London: 1842. V. 49; 50; 53

MAILLES, JACQUES DE
The Right Joyous and Pleasant History of the Feats, Gests and Prowesses of the Chevalier Bayard, the Good Knight without Fear and Without Defeat. London: 1825. V. 50

MAILLET, BENOIT DE
Telliamed: or, Discourses Between an Indian Philosopher and a French Missionary, on the Diminution of the Sea, The formation of the earth, The Origin of Men and Animals... London: 1750. V. 48
Telliamed; or, the World Explain'd. Baltimore: 1797. V. 49; 52

MAILLET, LOUIS
Les Figures du Temple et du Palais de Salomon. Paris: 1695. V. 53

MAILLY, LOUIS
Les Illustres des Fees. Contes Galans. La Haye: 1698. V. 51

MAILS, THOMAS E.
Dog Soldiers, Bear Men and Buffalo Women, a Study of the Societies and Cults of the Plains Indians. Englewood Cliffs: 1973. V. 48; 53
The Mystic Warriors of the Plains. Garden City: 1972. V. 52; 53; 54
The Pueblo Children of the Earth Mother. Garden City: 1983. V. 48
The Pueblo Children of the Earth Mother. New York: 1983. V. 47; 48; 50
Sundancing At Rosebud and Pine Ridge. Lake Mills: 1978. V. 51
Sundancing at Rosebud and Pine Ridge. Sioux Falls: 1978. V. 50

MAIMBOURG, LOUIS
The History of the Crusade. London: 1685. V. 54
The History of the League. London: 1684. V. 47; 48; 49

MAIN & WINCHESTER
Tanners of Harness, Skirting, Sole and Collar Leather, Manufacturers of Saddles, Bridles, Harness, Collars, Whips, etc. San Francisco: 1880's. V. 49

MAIN, JAMES
Popular Botany. London: 1835. V. 54
The Villa and Cottage Florist's Directory: Being a Familiar Treatise on Floriculture. London: 1830. V. 51; 53

MAIN, MRS.
Hints on Snow Photography. London: 1894. V. 47

MAINDRON, ERNEST
Les Affiches Illustrees (1886-1895) Ouvrage Orne de 64 Lithographies en Couleur. Paris: 1896. V. 50

MAINE, E. S.
Marchmont of Redlands. London: 1872. V. 49

MAINE, HENRY SUMNER
Ancient Law: Its Connection with the Early History of Society, and Its Relation to Modern Ideas. London: 1861. V. 49
Dissertations on Early Law and Custom, Chiefly Selected from Lectures Delivered at Oxford. London: 1891. V. 50
Lectures on the Early History of Institutions. London: 1875. V. 52
Popular Government, Four Essays. London: 1886. V. 54
Village-Communities in the East and West. London: 1871. V. 52
Village-Communities in the East and West... New York: 1876. V. 50

MAINGOT, RODNEY
Post-Graduate Surgery. New York: 1936. V. 51

MAINILLI, JACOMO
Villa Borghese Fuori di Porta Pinciana Descritta. Rome: 1650. V. 47

MAINS & Fitzgerald's Trenton, Chambersburg, Milham and Mercer County Directory. 1879. Trenton: 1879. V. 49; 51

MAINSTEIN, CHRISTOF HERMANN VON
Memoirs of Russia, Historical, Political and Military, from the Year MDCCXXVII, to MDCCXLIV. Dublin: 1770. V. 49

MAINTENON, FRANCOISE D'AUBIGNE, MARCHIONESS DE
Letters of Madame de Maintenon. London: 1772. V. 47
The Life of Madam de Maintenon. Dublin: 1753. V. 50

MAINWARING, A. J.
The Lost Manuscripts of a Blue Jacket. Newcastle: 1850. V. 54

MAINWARING, ARTHUR
Crown and Comapny: the Historical Records of the 2nd Batt. Royal Dublin Fusiliers, 1662-1911. London: 1911. V. 53

MAINWARING, HENRY
The Life and Works. London: 1920-22. V. 52

MAINWARING, JOHN
Memoirs of the Life of the Late George Frederic Handel. London: 1760. V. 54

MAINWARING, THOMAS
A Defence of Amicia, Daughter of Hugh Cyveliok, Wherein It is Proved That Sir Peter Leicester Baronet... London: 1673. V. 47; 52
A Reply to an Answer to the Defence of Amicia... London: 1673. V. 47

MAIOLO, SIMONE
Historiarum Totius Orbis, Omniumque Temporum Pro Defensione Sacrarum Imaginum Adversus Iconomachos Libri Seu Centuria Sexdecim. Rome: 1585. V. 50

MAIR, CHARLES
Dreamland and Other Poems. Montreal: 1868. V. 54
Through the Mackenzie Basin: a Narrative of the Athabasca and Peace River Treaty Expedition of 1899. Toronto: 1908. V. 47; 50

MAIRET, ETHEL
A Book on Vegetable Dyes. 1916. V. 54
Vegetable Dyes. Ditchling: 1924. V. 54

MAIS, CHARLES
The Surprising Case of Rachel Baker, Who Prays and Preaches in Her Sleep... New York: 1814. V. 52

MAISEY, J. G.
Santana Fossils. An Illustrated Atlas. New Jersey: 1991. V. 51

MAISON, K. E.
Honore Daumeir. Catalogue Raisonne of the Paintings, Watercolours and Drawings. Greenwich: 1968. V. 53

MAISSIN, EUGENE
The French in Mexico and Texas (1838-1839). Salado;: 1961. V. 49

MAISTRE, FRANCOIS XAVIER, COMTE DE
The Leper of Aost. Boston: 1825. V. 48; 52

MAITLAND CLUB
Catalogue of the Works Printed for the Maitland Club, Instituted March, MDCCCXXVIII. London: 1836. V. 48; 51; 54
Chronicon de Lanercost, 1201-1346, e Codice Cottoniano Nunc Primum Typis Mandatum. Edinburgi: 1839. V. 50

MAITLAND, F. L.
Narrative of the Surrender of Bonaparte and Of His Residence on Board H.M.s. Bellerophon... London: 1826. V. 49

MAITLAND, FREDERIC WILLIAM
The Charters of the Borough of Cambridge. Cambridge: 1901. V. 54

MAITLAND, FREDERICK WILLIAM
The Life and Letters of Leslie Stephen. London: 1906. V. 51; 53

MAITLAND, JOHN
Observations On the Impolicy or Permitting the Exploration of British Wool and of Preventing the Free Importation of Foreign Wool. London: 1818. V. 49; 51; 52

MAITLAND, SAMUEL ROFFEY
Eruvin: or, Miscellaneous Essays on Subjects Connected With the Nature, History and Destiny of Man. London: 1831. V. 50; 52

MAITLAND, THOMAS
The Devil's Due. A Letter to the Editor of "The Examiner". 1875. V. 51; 54

MAITLAND, WILLIAM
The History and Antiquities of Scotland, from the Earliest Account of Time to the Death of James the First, Anno 1437. London: 1757. V. 48
The History of London, from Its Foundation by the Romans to the Present Time. London: 1739. V. 52
The History of London From Its Foundation to the Present Time. London: 1756. V. 50

MAITTAIRE, MICHEL
Miscellanea Graecorum Aliquot Scriptorum Carmina, Cum Versione Latina et Notis. Londini: 1722. V. 48

MAITZ, DON
First Maitz: Selected Works by Don Maitz. Kansas City: 1988. V. 51

MAIUS, JUNIANUS
Liber de Verborum Priscorum Proprietate. Venice: 1490. V. 51
De Priscorum Proprietate Verborum. Venice: 1490. V. 50

MAJOR, CHARLES
When Knighthood Was in Flower or the Love Story of Charles Brandon and Mary Tudor. Indianapolis: 1898. V. 48

MAJOR, CLARENCE
No. New York: 1973. V. 47
Parking Lots. Mt. Horeb: 1992. V. 54

MAJOR Frank Wolcott Alias the Jack of Spades. 1886. V. 50

MAJOR, HARLAN
Salt Water Fishing Tackle. New York: 1939. V. 53

MAJOR, HENRY
Hollywood 1938. V. 50

MAJOR, HOWARD
The Domestic Architecture of the Early American Republic: The Greek Revival. Philadelhia & London: 1926. V. 49; 50; 54

MAJOR, JOHN
A Catalogue of Miscellaneous Books, Consisting of Valuable Library Works, and Articles of General Interest in Elegant and Useful Literature... London: 1822. V. 51
Historia Majoris Britanniae tam Angliae Quam Scotiae. Edinburgh: 1740. V. 47
Historia Majoris Britanniae, tam Anglie, Atque Scotie. Paris: 1521. V. 47; 49

MAJOR League Baseball Facts, Figures and Official Rules. Racine: 1943. V. 54

MAJOR, RALPH H.
Classic Descriptions of Disease, with Biographical Sketches of the Authors. Springfield: 1932. V. 49; 51; 54
A History of Medicine. Springfield: 1954. V. 47; 50; 51; 52; 54

MAJOR, RICHARD HENRY
India in the Fifteenth Century: Being a Collection of Narratives... London: 1857. V. 52

MAJORBANKS, ALEXANDER
Tour to the Loire and La Vendee, in 1835. Edinburgh: 1836. V. 50

MAJORS, ALEXANDER
Seventy Years on the Frontier. Denver: 1893. V. 47; 54
Seventy Years On the Old Frontier, Alexander Majors Memoirs. Chicago: 1893. V. 50; 53

MAJOR'S Alphabet. New York: 1890. V. 51

MAKAIL, JOHN WILLIAM
William Morris, an Address Delivered the XIth November MDCCCC at Kelmscott House Hammersmith, Before the Hammersmith Socialist Society. Hammersmith: 1901. V. 48

MAKEMSON, W. K.
Historical Sketch of First Settlement and Organization of Williamson County. Constitution of Old Settlers Association Organized Aug. 27th, 1904. Georgetown: 1904. V. 52

MAKINS, GEORGE
Surgical Experiences in South Africa 1899-1900. London: 1913. V. 52

MAKINSON, R. L.
Greene & Greene: Architecture as a Fine Art. Salt Lake City: 1977. V. 50; 51; 53; 54
Greene & Greene: Furniture and Related Designs. Santa Barbara: 1979. V. 50; 51; 53

MALAMUD, BERNARD
The Assistant. New York: 1957. V. 47; 49; 50; 52
Dubin's Lives. New York: 1979. V. 51; 54
The Fixer. New York: 1966. V. 52
God's Grace. New York. V. 52
God's Grace. New York: 1982. V. 48; 51; 53; 54
The Magic Barrel. New York: 1958. V. 47; 49
The Magic Barrel. Philadelphia: 1958. V. 51
The Natural. New York: 1952. V. 47; 48; 51; 52
The Natural. London: 1963. V. 49
Pictures of Fidelman. New York: 1968. V. 51
Rembrandt's Hat. New York: 1973. V. 52; 54
The Stories of Bernard Malamud. New York: 1979. V. 53
The Stories of Bernard Malamud. New York: 1983. V. 47; 48; 53; 54
The Tenants. New York: 1971. V. 52; 54

MALAMUD, BERNARD continued
Two Fables. 1978. V. 49; 51; 53; 54

MALCOLM, ALEXANDER
Malcolm's Treatise of Music, Speculative, Practical and Historical. London: 1776. V. 49; 51; 52
A New Treatise of Arithmetick and Book-Keeping... Edinburgh: 1718. V. 52; 54
A Treatise of Musick, Speculative, Practical and Historical. Edinburgh: 1721. V. 48

MALCOLM, HOWARD
Travels in South-Eastern Asia, Embracing Hindustan, Malaya, Siam and China. Boston: 1839. V. 47; 53

MALCOLM, JAMES PELLER
Anecdotes of the Manners and Customs of London During the Eighteenth Century... London: 1808. V. 52; 54
Anecdotes of the Manners and Customs of London During the Eighteenth Century. London: 1810. V. 48; 52
Anecdotes of the Manners and Customs of London From the Roman Invasion to the Year 1700... London: 1811. V. 51
First Impressions or Sketches from Art and Nature... London: 1807. V. 51
An Historical Sketch of the Art of Caricaturing. London: 1813. V. 47; 48; 51
Lives of Topographers and Antiquaries Who Have Written Concerning the Antiquities of England, with Portraits of the Authors... London: 1815. V. 54

MALCOLM, JOHN
The Buccaneer, and Other Poems. Edinburgh: 1824. V. 49
The History of Persia. London: 1815. V. 48
The History of Persia. London: 1829. V. 47; 50; 53
History of Persia. Lahore: 1888. V. 53
The Life of Robert, Lord Clive, Collected from the Family Papers Communicated by the Earl of Powis. London: 1836. V. 48; 54
A Memoir of Central India. London: 1823. V. 50
A Memoir of Central India, Including Malwa and Adjoining Provinces. London: 1823. V. 47; 53
Memoir of Central India, Including Malwa and Adjoining Provinces. London: 1824. V. 47
Miscellaneous Poems... Bombay: 1829. V. 52; 54
The Political History of India from 1784 to 1823. London: 1826. V. 54
Sketch of the Political History of India, from the Introduction of Mr. Pitt's Bill, A.D. 1784 to the Present Date. London: 1811. V. 49
Sketch of the Sikhs: a Singular Nation, Who Inhabit the Provinces of the Penjab, Situated Between the Rivers Jumna and Indus. London: 1812. V. 52; 54
Sketches of Persia, from the Journals of a Traveller in the East. London: 1827. V. 54
Sketches of Persia, from the Journals of a Traveller in the East. London: 1828. V. 47; 51

MALCOLM, S. B.
Biology and Conservation of the Monarch Butterfly. London: 1993. V. 50; 52

MALCOLM, SARAH
A True Copy of the Paper, Delivered the Night Before Her Execution by Sarah Malcolm, to the Rev. Mr. Piddington, Lecturer of St. Bartholomew the Great, March 6th, 1732-33. London: 1732;. V. 48

MALCOLM X
The Autobiography of Malcolm X. New York: 1964. V. 52
The Autobiography of Malcolm X. New York: 1965. V. 47; 54
The Autobiography of Malcolm X. New York: 1968. V. 54

MALDEN, H. F.
Victoria County History of Surrey. London: 1905-14. V. 50

MALDONADO, LORENZO FERRER
Viaggio Dal Mare Atlantico Al Pacifico per La Via Del Nordovest Fatta Dal Capitano Lorenzo Ferrer Maldonando L'Anno MDLXXXVIII... Bologna: 1812. V. 47

MALEBRANCHE, NICHOLAS
Father Malebranche His Treatise Concerning the Search After Truth... To which is Added The Author's treatise of Nature and Grace... London: 1700. V. 51

MALER, TEOBERT
Explorations of the Upper Usumatsintla and Adjacent Region. Cambridge: 1908. V. 50

MALESPINA, LEONARDO
In Epistolas M. Tullii Ciceronis ad Atticum, Brutum et Q. Fratrem,... Venice: 1563. V. 48

MALESPINI, LORENZO GIACOMINI TEBALDUCCI
Orationi E Discorsi. Florence: 1597. V. 48

MALET, HAROLD ESDAILE
Annals of the Road. London: 1876. V. 47; 54

MALET, HUGH POYNTZ
Lost Links in the Indian Mutiny. London: 1867. V. 53

MALET, RAWDON
When the Red Gods Call. 1934. V. 54
When the Red Gods Call. London: 1934. V. 49

MALGAIGNE, J. F.
Surgery and Ambroise Pare. Norman: 1965. V. 50; 52

MALHAM, JOHN
The Naval Gazeteer: or, Seamans Complete Guide. London: 1801. V. 48

MALIN, JAMES C.
John Brown and the Legend of Fifty-Six. Philadelphia: 1942. V. 50

MALINIAC, JACQUES W.
Plastic Surgery: Collected Papers 1924-1938. New York: 1938. V. 54
Rhinoplasty and Restoration of Facial Contour, with Special Reference to Trauma. Philadelphia: 1947. V. 54

MALIPIERO, GIROLAMO
Il Petrarcha Spirituale. Venice: 1538. V. 52

MALKIEL, THERESA
Woman and Freedom. New York. V. 52

MALKIN, ARTHUR THOMAS
The Portrait Gallery. London: 1853. V. 49

MALKIN, BENJAMIN HEATH
A Father's Memoirs of His Child. London: 1806. V. 50

MALL, THOMAS
A Cloud of Witnesses; or, The Sufferers Mirrour, Made Up of the Swanlike-Songs and Other Choice Passages of Several Martyrs and Confessors to the End of the Sixteenth Century, in Their Treatises, Speeches, Letters, Prayers, &c... London: 1665. V. 49
The History of the Martyrs Epitomised. Boston: 1747. V. 51; 52

MALLARME, STEPHANE
L'Apres-Midi d'un Faune. The Hague: 1956. V. 50
L'Apres-Midi d'un Faune. Waltham St. Lawrence: 1956. V. 51
A Throw of the Dice. Santa Cruz: 1990. V. 48

MALLERY, GARRICK
Study of Sign Langauge Among North American Indians. Washington: 1880. V. 50

MALLESON, F. A.
Wordsworth and the Duddon. Ulverston: 1890. V. 50

MALLESON, G. B.
The Decisive Battles of India, from 1746 to 1849 Inclusive. London: 1885. V. 54
An Historical Sketch of the Native States of India in Subsidiary Alliance with the British Government. London: 1875. V. 49
History of Afghanistan, from the Earliest Period to the Outbreak of the War of 1878. London: 1878. V. 51
The Indian Mutiny. London: 1891. V. 54

MALLESON, MILES
D Company and Black 'Ell - Two Plays. London: 1916. V. 47

MALLET, ALLAIN MANESSON
Les Travaux de Mars Ou la Fortification Nouvelle. Paris: 1671-72. V. 48; 51

MALLET, BERNARD
Mallet du Pan and the French Revolution. London: 1902. V. 47

MALLET, DAVID
Alfred; a Masque. London: 1751. V. 52
Amyntor and Theodora: or, the Hermit. London: 1747. V. 48
A Congratulatory Letter to Selim (i.e. Lytttelton) on Three Letters to the Whigs. London: 1748. V. 48
Edwin and Emma. Birmingham: 1760. V. 47; 48; 53
The Life of Francis Bacon, Lord Chancellor of England. London: 1740. V. 49; 52
Mustapha. London: 1739. V. 52
Poems on Several Occasions. London: 1762. V. 47; 48

MALLET, PAUL HENRI
Northern Antiquities: or, A Description of the Manners, Customs, Religion and Laws of the Ancient Danes... London: 1770. V. 50; 52

MALLET, ROBERT
Great Neapolitan Earthquake of 1857. London: 1862. V. 50; 54
On the Physical Conditions Involved in the Construction of Artillery... London: 1856. V. 52

MALLET DU PAN, JACQUES
The British Mercury, or, Historical and Critical Views of the Events of the Present Times. London: 1798-1800. V. 47; 48
Memoirs and Corresondence of Mallet du Pan, Illustrative of the History of the French Revolution. V. 49; 52

MALLEY, ERN
The Darkening Ecliptic. London: 1974. V. 53

MALLING, OVE
Great and Good Deeds of the Danes, Norwegians and Holsteinians... London: 1807. V. 50

MALLISON, WILLIAM HENRY
The Seaman's Friend. London. V. 51

MALLOCH, P. D.
Life History and Habits of Salmon, Sea Trout, Trout and Other Freshwater Fish. London: 1910. V. 48

MALLOCK, H.
Plates to Accompany the Report On Railway Telegraphs. Calcutta: 1874. V. 50

MALLOCK, WILLIAM HURRELL
The Heart of Life. London: 1895. V. 54
The New Republic: or, Culture, Faith and Philosophy in an English Country House. London: 1877. V. 48; 54
Property and Progress; or, a Brief Enquiry into Contemporary Social Agitation in England. London: 1884. V. 52

MALLOWAN, M. E. L.
Nimrud and Its Remains. New York: 1966. V. 52

MALLOWMAN, MAX
Furniture from SW.7 Fort Shalmaneser; Commentary, Catalogue and Plates. London: 1974. V. 52

MALMESBURY, JAMES HARRIS, 1ST EARL OF
Diaries and Correspondence. London: 1844. V. 53
Diaries and Correspondence of... London: 1844-45. V. 48

MALO, CHARLES
La Corbeille de Fruits. Paris: 1821. V. 51
Histoire des Roses. Paris: 1818. V. 53
Livre Mignard ou la Fleur des Fabliaux. Paris: 1820. V. 54

MALO, LEON
On Asphalt Roadways. London: 1886. V. 49

MALONE, DUMAS
Jefferson and His Time... Boston: 1949-81. V. 50

MALONE, EDMUND
A Biographical Memoir of the Late Right Honourable William Windham. London: 1810. V. 48
An Inquiry into the Authenticity of Certain Miscellaneous Papers and Legal Instruments... London: 1796. V. 47; 53

MALONE, JAMES H.
The Chickasaw Nation. Louisville: 1922. V. 49

MALONE, MICHAEL
The Delectable Mountains. New York: 1976. V. 53
Painting the Roses Red. New York: 1974. V. 47; 48; 53
Psychetypes. New York: 1977. V. 49

MALONEY, ALICE
Fur Brigade to the Bonaventura, John Work's California Expedition for the Hudson's Bay Company 1832-33. San Francisco: 1945. V. 49; 53

MALONEY, T. J.
A Pageant of Photography. 1940. V. 47

MALORITIE, C. S. DE
A Treatise on Topography, for Both Civil and Military Purposes. London: 1815. V. 51; 52

MALORY, THOMAS
The Birth, Life and Acts of King Arthur, of His Noble Knights of the Round Table. London: 1893. V. 47
The Birth, Life and Acts of King Arthur of His Noble Knights of the Round Table. London: 1893-94. V. 48; 50
The Birth, Life and Acts of King Arthur, of His Noble Knights of the Round Table. New York & London: 1909. V. 50; 51; 54
The Birth, Life and Acts of King Arthur of His Noble Knights of the Round Table.. London: 1927. V. 47; 50; 51
The Book of the Holy Grail, from the Morte D'Arthur. Birmingham: 1934. V. 51
The Byrth, Lyf and Actes of Kyng Arthur (i.e. Morte d'Arthur). London: 1817. V. 54
The Death of King Arthur, Being the 21st Book of Sir Thomas Malory's Book of King Arthur... London: 1928. V. 52
The History of the Renowned Prince Arthur, King of Britain... London: 1816. V. 49
Le Morte Arthur. London: 1864. V. 47
Le Morte D'Arthur. Boston. V. 51
Le Morte d'Arthur. London: 1893-94. V. 47
Le Morte D'Arthur. London: 1897-98. V. 49
Le Morte D'Arthur. London and New York: 1900. V. 54
Le Morte d'Arthur. London: 1909. V. 53
Le Morte D'Arthur. London: 1910-11. V. 49; 53
Le Morte d'Arthur. London: 1920. V. 47
Le Morte d'Arthur. London: 1927. V. 53
Le Morte d'Arthur. New York: 1927. V. 51
Le Morte d'Arthur. 1936. V. 51
Le Morte d'Arthur. London: 1936. V. 50; 53; 54
Le Morte d'Arthur. New York: 1936. V. 49; 53
Le Morte D'Arthur. Waltham St. Lawrence: 1936. V. 49
Le Morte D'Arthur. Ilkley: 1976. V. 49
The Most Ancient and Famous History of the Renowned Prince Arthur King of Britaine... London: 1634. V. 48
The Noble and Joyous Boke Entytled Le Morte D'Arthur. London: 1933. V. 50
The Romance of King Arthur and His Knights of the Round Table. London: 1917. V. 49; 50; 51; 54
The Romance of King Arthur and His Knights of the Round Table. New York: 1917. V. 48

MALOUF, DAVID
Bicycle and other Poems. Queensland: 1970. V. 51; 53
An Imaginary Life. New York: 1978. V. 53
Johnno. Queensland: 1975. V. 53
Johnno. St. Lucia: 1975. V. 48; 51
Remembering Babylon. London: 1993. V. 50; 51

MALOUIN, PAUL JACQUES
Description et Details des Arts du Meunier, du Vermicelier et du Boulenger... Paris: 1767. V. 49

MALPIGHI, MARCELLO
Discours Anatomique sur la Structure des Visceres, Scavoir du Foye du Derveau, des Reins de la Ratte, du Polype du Coeur, et des Poulmons. Paris: 1683. V. 47

MALRAUX, ANDRE
Anti-Memoires. Paris: 1967. V. 51
Israel. London: 1958. V. 54
The Metamorphosis of the Gods. Garden City: 1960. V. 49; 51
Psychologie de l'Art. Lausanne. V. 51
Psychologie de l'Art. 1948. V. 48
The Voices of Silence. Man and His Art. Garden City: 1953. V. 49

MALTA, par un Voyageur. Malta: 1791-91. V. 47

MALTBY, WILLIAM J.
Captain Jeff, or Frontier Life. Colorado: 1906. V. 50; 52

MALTE-BRUN, M. CONRAD
Universal Geography, or a Description of All the Parts of the World on a New Plan. Edinburgh: 1822-33. V. 47; 52; 53

MALTHUS, THOMAS ROBERT
Additions to the Fourth and Former Editions of An Essay on the Principle of Population. London: 1817. V. 51; 52; 54
Definitions in Political Economy, Preceded by an Inquiry into the Rules Which Ought to Guide Political Economists in the Definition and Use of their Terms. London: 1827. V. 51
Essai sur le Principe de Population, Ou Expose des Effets Passes et Presens... Paris: 1823. V. 47; 48; 49
An Essay on the Principle of Population; or, a View of Its Past and Present Effects on Human Happiness. London: 1803. V. 48; 50
An Essay on the Principle of Population; or, a View of its Past and Present Effects on Human Happiness... London: 1806. V. 47; 52
An Essay on the Principle of Population; or, a View of its Past and Present Effects on Human Happiness... London: 1807. V. 48; 50; 52; 54
An Essay on the Principle of Population; or, a View Of its Past and Present Effects on Human Happiness... (with) Additions to an Essay on the Principle of Population, &c. Washington City: 1809. V. 49; 51
An Essay on the Principle of Population; or, a View Of its Past and Present Effects on Human Happiness... (with) Principles of Political Economy Considered With a View to their Practical Application. London: 1826/36. V. 51; 53
The Grounds of an Opinion on the Policy of Restricting the Importation of Foreign Corn; Intended as an Appendix to "Observations on the Corn Laws". London: 1815. V. 47
An Inquiry into the Nature and Progress of Rent, and the Principles by Which It is Regulated. London: 1815. V. 47
Principles of Political Economy Considered with a View to Their Practical Application. London: 1820. V. 47; 53
Principles of Political Economy Considered with a View to Their Practical Application. London: 1836. V. 50; 51; 52

MALTON, JAMES
The Young Painter's Maulstick... London: 1800. V. 47; 48; 50; 52
The Young Painter's Maulstick... London: 1803. V. 48

MALTON, T.
Views of Oxford. London: 1810. V. 54
Views of Oxford (Feb. 24th-Dec. 31st 1802). London: 1805. V. 49

MALTZ, ALBERT
The Journey of Simon McKeever. Boston: 1949. V. 49

MALVEZZI, VIRGILIO
Il Davide Persequitato. David Persecuted. London: 1647. V. 52
Il Ritratto del Privato Politico Christiano... Bologna: 1635. V. 52

MAMA'S Pictures or the History of Fanny and Mary. London: 1825. V. 47

MAMET, DAVID
American Buffalo. New York: 1978. V. 49; 51
American Buffalo. San Francisco: 1992. V. 48
The Frog Prince. New York: 1984. V. 49; 50; 54

MAMIANI DELLA ROVERE, TERENZIO, COUNT
Rights of Nations or, the New Law of European States Applied to the Affairs of Italy... London: 1860. V. 49; 52

MAMMATT, E.
A Collection of Facts and Practical Observations... Ashby-de-la-Zouch: 1834. V. 54
A Collection of Facts and Practical Observations Intended to Elucidate the Formation of the Ashby Coal-Field, in the Parish of Ashby-de-la Zouch and the Neighbouring District. London: 1836. V. 47; 48; 50

MAMPEL, JOHAN CHRISTIAN
The Adventures of a Young Rifleman, in the French and English Armies, During the War in Spain and Portugal, from 1806 to 1816. London: 1826. V. 48

MAN, FELIX H.
Eight European Artists. New York: 1954. V. 47; 50

THE MAN in the Leather Helmet: A Souvenir Booklet of the Dallas Fire Department. Dallas: 1931. V. 47

MAN, JOHN
The History and Antiquities of the Borough of Reading. Reading: 1816. V. 50; 52

THE MAN Who... Bristol: 1992. V. 52; 53; 54

THE MAN Who. London: 1992. V. 50

MAN-Eaters and Other Denizens of the Indian Jungle. Calcutta & Simla: 1928. V. 47

MANARDO, GIOVANNI
Epistolarum Medicinalium Libri Duodeviginti. Basle: 1535. V. 47

MANARIN, LOUIS H.
North Carolina Troops 1861-1865: a Roster. Raleigh: 1966-85. V. 49

MANBY, CHARLES W.
Tom Racquet and His Three Maiden Aunts: with a Word or Two About the 'Whittleburys'. London: 1850. V. 51

MANCHESTER As it Is: or, Notices of the Institutions, Manutactures, Commerce, Railways, Etc. of the Metropolis of Manufactures... London: 1839. V. 50

THE MANCHESTER Athenaeum Album. Manchester: 1850. V. 54

MANCHESTER. CHAMBER OF COMMERCE
The Corn Laws. An Authentic Report of the Late Important Discussions in the Manchester Chamber of Commerce, on the Destructive Effects of the Corn Laws Upon the Trade and Manufactures of the Country. London: 1839. V. 53

MANCHESTER, DUKE OF
Court and Society from Elizabeth to Anne. London: 1864. V. 54

MANCHESTER, HENRY MONTAGU, 1ST EARL OF
Contemplatio Mortis, et Immortalitatis. London: 1631. V. 51

MANCHESTER, HERBERT
Four Centuries of Sport in America. New York: 1931. V. 47; 48

MANCHESTER LITERARY AND PHILOSOPHICAL SOCIETY
Memoirs. Warrington: 1785. V. 53

THE MANCHESTER Ship Canal. London: 1894. V. 49; 54

MANCHESTER UNIVERSITY. LIBRARY
Catalogue of Medical Books in Manchester University Library 1480-1700. Manchester: 1972. V. 50; 53; 54
A Descriptive Catalogue of the Latin Manuscripts in the John Rylands Library at Manchester. Manchester: 1921. V. 53

MANDAVILLE, J. P.
The Flora of Eastern Saudi Arabia. London: 1990. V. 52

MANDEL, ELI
Fuseli Poems. Toronto: 1960. V. 47

MANDEL, GEORGE
Flee the Angry Strangers. Indianapolis: 1952. V. 48; 53

MANDELBAUM, ALLAN
A Lied of Letterpress for Moser and McGrath. Northampton: 1980. V. 48

MANDELL, D. J.
The Adventures of Search for Life, a Bunyanic Narrative, as Detailed by Himself. Portland: 1838. V. 47

MANDELSLO, JOHN ALBERT DE
The Voyages and Travels Of the Ambassadors Sent by Frederick Duke of Holstein, to the Great Duke of Muscovy, and the King of Prussia. London: 1669. V. 50

MANDER, JAMES
The Derbyshire Miners' Glossary; or an Explantion of the Technical Terms of the Miners, Which are Used in the King's Field, in the Hundred of High Peak... Bakewell: 1824. V. 52

MANDER, RAYMOND
The Artist and the Theatre. London: 1955. V. 54

MANDEVILLE, BERNARD DE
An Enquiry into the Origin of Honour, and the Usefulness of Christianity in War. London: 1732. V. 48
The Fable of the Bees; or, Private Vices, Publick Benefits. London: 1723. V. 47; 51
The Fable of the Bees; or, Private Vices, Publick Benefits. London: 1724. V. 47; 48
The Fable of the Bees: or, Private Vices, Publick Benefits... London: 1725. V. 48; 54
The Fable of the Bees; or, Private Vices, Publick Benefits. London: 1729. V. 47
The Fable of the Bees; or, Private Vices, Publick Benefits. (with) Fable of the Bees Part II. London: 1724/29. V. 49
A Treatise of the Hypochondriack and Hysterick Diseases. London: 1730. V. 52

MANDEVILLE, JAMES H.
The Rights of American Inventors. Washington: 1879. V. 52

MANDEVILLE, JOHN
The Marvelous Adventures of... Westminster: 1895. V. 53
The Travels of Sir John Mandeville. London: 1900. V. 50; 52
Voiage and Travaile of Sir John Maundevile. New York: 1928. V. 50

MANDIARGUES, ANDRE PIEYRE DE
Chagall. New York: 1974. V. 50; 52

MANDOWSKY, ERNA
Pirro Ligorio's Roman Antiquities: The Drawings in MS XIII. B. in the National Library in Naples. London: 1963. V. 52

MANEKEN, CAROLUS
Formule Epistolaru. Strassburg: 1493. V. 53

MANENTE DA COCAGLIO, ANDREA
L'Impetrita Perfidia. Brescia: 1673. V. 47

MANETHO
Apotelesmaticorum Libri Sex. Leyden: 1698. V. 50

MANFRED, FREDERICK FEIKEMA
Boy Almighty. Saint Paul: 1945. V. 48; 51
The Golden Bowl. Saint Paul: 1944. V. 48; 51

MANFREDI, MUZIO
La Semiramis Boscareccia. Bergamo: 1593. V. 51

MANGAN, FRANK J.
Bordertown, The Life and Times of El Paso Del Norte. El Paso: 1964. V. 48

MANGAN, JAMES CLARENCE
Anthologia Germanica; or, a Garland from the German Poets, And Miscellaneous Poems... Dublin: 1884. V. 50
Prose Writings of James Clarence Mangan. London: 1904. V. 51

MANGAN, JERRY WILLIAM
Colorado on Glasss, Colorado's First Half Century as Seen by the Camera. Denver: 1980. V. 47

MANGET, JOHANNES JACOB
Bibliotheca Pharmacceutico Medico, Seu Rerum ad Pharmacia Galenico-Chymicam Spectantium Thesaurus Refertissimus... Genevae: 1703. V. 47; 48; 49; 50; 51; 53

MANGIN, A.
The Mysteries of the Ocean. London: 1874. V. 53; 54

MANGIN, EDWARD
Essays on the Sources of the Pleasures Received From Literary Compostions. London: 1809. V. 49
George the Third. London: 1807. V. 50; 54
The Life of C. G. Lamoignon Malesherbes, Formerly First President of the Court of Aids... Edinburgh: 1804. V. 51
Oddities and Outlines. London: 1806. V. 47
The Parlour Window; or, Anecdotes, Original Remarks on Books, etc. London: 1841. V. 51
Stories for Short Students; or, Light Lore for Little People. London: 1829. V. 48
Utopia Found: Being an Apology for Irish Absentees. Bath: 1813. V. 51

MANGIN, GEORGE
George the Third. London: 1807. V. 50

MANGLES, JAMES
The Floral Calendar, Monthly and Daily. London: 1839. V. 47
Papers and Despatches Relating to the Arctic Searching Expeditions of 1850-51-52. London: 1852. V. 48; 53

MANGO, CYRIL
Materials For the Study of the Mosaics of St. Sophia at Istanbul. Washington: 1962. V. 49

MANGUM, ADOLPHUS WILLIAMSON
Myrtle Leaves; Or, Tokens at the Tomb. Raleigh: 1864. V. 49

MANHOFF, BILL
The Owl and the Pussycat. Garden City: 1965. V. 54

MANHOOD, H. A.
Bread and Vinegar. London: 1931. V. 54

MANI, M. S.
Butterflies of the Himalaya. Amsterdam: 1986. V. 52

MANIFOLD-CRAIG, R.
The Weird of "The Silken Thomas". 1900. V. 47; 51

MANILIUS, MARCUS
The Five Books of M. Manilius, Containing a System of the Ancient Astronomy and Astrology: Together with The Philosophy of the Stoicks. London: 1697. V. 54

MANING, FREDERICK EDWARD
Old New Zealand. London: 1863. V. 52

MANKOWITZ, WOLF
Wedgwood. London: 1953. V. 51

MANLEY, MARY DE LA RIVIERE
The Adventures of Rivella; or, the History of the Author of the Atlantis. London: 1714. V. 49
Love Upon Tick; or, Implicit Gallantry Exemplified, in Some Merry Memoirs of the Rise and Progress of an Extraordinary and Occasional Amour. London: 1725. V. 54
The Power of Love: In Seven Novels. London: 1741. V. 48
Secret Memoirs and Manners of Several Persons of Quality, of Both Sexes. (with) Memoirs of Europe. London: 1709/10. V. 47
Secret Memoirs of Several Persons of Quality, of Both Sexes. London: 1709. V. 51
A True Relation of the Several Facts and Circumstances on the Intended Riot and Tumult on Queen Elizabeth's Birth-day. London: 1711. V. 54

MANLEY, WILLIAM LEWIS
Death Valley in '49. San Jose: 1894. V. 47; 48; 53

MANN, ALBERT W.
History of the Forty-Fifth Regiment, Massachusetts Volunteer Militia. Dept. of North Carolina. The Cadet Regiment. Boston: 1908. V. 47; 49

MANN, ALICE
Mann's Black Book of the British Aristocracy... London: 1848. V. 51

MANN, ARTHUR
The Jackie Robinson Story. New York: 1950. V. 47

MANN, EDWARD
A Manual of Psychological Medicine and Allied Nervous Diseses. Philadelphia: 1883. V. 47

MANN, ELIAS
The Northampton Collection of Sacred Harmony. Northampton: 1797. V. 50

MANN, ERIKA
A Gang of Ten. New York: 1942. V. 52

MANN, F. O.
A Garlande of Good Wille...to the Honour and Joyful Remembrance of Sir Stephenson Kent... London: 1919. V. 47; 50

MANN, HEINRICH
The Hill of Lies. New York: 1935. V. 48
In the Land of Cockaigne. New York: 1929. V. 48
The Royal Woman. New York: 1930. V. 49

MANN, HORACE
An Oration Delivered Before the Authorities of the City of Boston, July 4, 1842. Boston: 1842. V. 54

MANN, IDA
Developmental Abnormalities of the Eye. Cambridge: 1937. V. 47; 49; 54

MANN, J.
Maker of Shadows. 1938. V. 48
Medical Sketches of the Campaigns of 1812, 13, 14 to Which are Added Surgical Cases, Observations on Military Hospitals... Dedham: 1816. V. 47; 49
Nightmare Farm. 1937. V. 48

MANN, JAMES
Wallace Collection. European Arms and Armour. London: 1962. V. 51; 52

MANN, KLAUS
Heute und Morgen. Hamburg: 1927. V. 47

MANN, MARY E.
In Summer Shade. London: 1893. V. 47

MANN, MARY TYLER
Moral Culture of Infancy and Kindergarten Guide, with Music for the Plays. New York: 1869. V. 50

MANN, MATTHEW
A System of Gynecology by American Authors. Philadelphia: 1887. V. 49; 54

MANN, THOMAS
Bashan and I. New York: 1924. V. 54
Bekentnisse des Hochstaplers Felix Krull. Stuttgart: 1923. V. 51
The Beloved Returns. New York: 1940. V. 50; 51; 52; 53; 54
The Coming Victory of Democracy. New York: 1938. V. 51
Death in Venice. New York: 1925. V. 47
Death in Venice. New York: 1972. V. 53
Doktor Faustus. Stockholm: 1947. V. 47; 53
An Exchange of Letters. Stamford: 1938. V. 52
Goethe and Tolstoi. Aachen: 1923. V. 51
Joseph and His Brethern: I. The Tales of Jacob. London: 1934. V. 47
Joseph and His Brothers. New York: 1934. V. 47
Joseph in Egypt. New York: 1938. V. 47; 49
Joseph the Provider. New York: 1944. V. 47; 52
Joseph und Seine Bruder. Stockholm. V. 53
Joseph und Seine Bruder. Berlin: 1933-43. V. 52
Der Kleine Herr Friedemann. Berlin: 1898. V. 51
Konigliche Hoheit. Berlin: 1922. V. 51
Lotte in Weimar. Stockholm: 1939. V. 49
The Magic Mountain. New York: 1927. V. 47; 52
The Magic Mountain. New York: 1962. V. 47; 48; 49
Mario and the Magician. New York: 1931. V. 49
Nocturnes. New York: 1934. V. 48; 49; 51; 53
Novellen. Berlin: 1922. V. 51
Past Masters and Other Papers. New York: 1933. V. 49; 51; 54
Schopenhauer. Stockholm: 1938. V. 53
A Sketch of My Life. Paris: 1930. V. 47; 50; 51
Three Essays - Goethe and Tolstoy, Frederick the Great and the Grand Coalition, an Experience in the Occult. London: 1932. V. 49
Der Tod in Venedig. Berlin: 1913. V. 51
The Transposed Heads. New York: 1941. V. 48; 52
The Transposed Heads. Kentfield: 1977. V. 48; 53; 54
Young Joseph. New York: 1935. V. 47; 49; 51
Young Joseph. New York: 1939. V. 47
Der Zauberberg. (Magic Mountain). Berlin: 1924. V. 53

MANN, WILLIAM
Six Years' Residence in the Australian Provinces, Ending in 1839... London: 1839. V. 54

MANNERING, GEORGE EDWARD
With Axe and Rope in New Zealand Alps. London: 1891. V. 50; 53

MANNERS, CATHERINE REBECCA
Poems. London: 1794. V. 53
Review of Poetry, Ancient and Modern. London: 1799. V. 53; 54

THE MANNERS, Customs and Antiquities of the Indians of North and South America. Boston: 1844. V. 50

MANNERS, VICTORIA
Angelica Kauffmann, R.A. Her Life and Her Works. New York. V. 48
Angelica Kauffmann, R.A.: Her Life and Her Works. London: 1924. V. 51
Angelica Kauffmann, R.A. Her Life and Her Works. New York: 1924. V. 50
John Zoffany, R.A. His Life and Works, 1735-1810. London and New York: 1920. V. 54

MANNEX, P. J.
History, Gazetteer and Directory of Cumberland. Beverley: 1847. V. 52
History, Topography and Directory of Westmorland; and Lonsdale North of the Sands, in Lancashire... London: 1849. V. 50; 52; 54

MANNIN, ETHEL
Women and Revolution. London: 1938. V. 49

MANNING, ANNE
The Chronicle of Ehtelfled. London: 1861. V. 50
The Household of Sir Thomas More. London: 1890. V. 54
Poplar House Academy. London: 1859. V. 54
The Spanish Barber; a Tale. London: 1869. V. 52

MANNING, ETHEL F.
The Coming of Father Christmas. London. V. 47

MANNING, FREDERIC
Her Privates We. London: 1930. V. 47; 51; 52
The Middle Parts of Fortune. 1929. V. 52
The Middle Parts of Fortune. London: 1929. V. 47; 51
The Vigil of Brunhild - a Narrative Poems. London: 1907. V. 54

MANNING, G. T.
Rural Rhymes, Illustrative of Rustic Customs and Popular Superstitions... London: 1837. V. 47; 50

MANNING, HENRY
Modern Improvements in the Practice of Surgery. (with) Modern Improvements in the Practice of Physic. London: 1780. V. 51; 52; 53

MANNING, HUGO
Buenos Aires. Buenos Aires: 1942. V. 47
The Crown and the Fable. 1950. V. 51

MANNING, JAMES M.
Aviso. San Antonio de Bexar: 1838. V. 48

MANNING, LEAH
What I Saw in Spain. London: 1935. V. 49

MANNING, OLIVIA
The Danger Tree. The Battle Lost and Won. The Sum of Things. London: 1977-80. V. 54
A Different Face. London: 1953. V. 49
The Levant Trilogy. London: 1977/78/80. V. 52; 53
The Remarkable Expedition. London: 1947. V. 49; 50; 52
School for Love. London: 1951. V. 49; 54

MANNING, OWEN
The History and Antiquities of the County of Surrey... London: 1804-14. V. 47; 50; 51

MANNING, R.
Book of Fruits... Salem: 1838. V. 50; 51

MANNING, REV.
Palestine Illustrated. New York: 1890. V. 54

MANNING, ROBERT
A Plain and Rational Account of the Catholick Faith... (with) The Reform'd Churches Proved Destitute of a Lawful Ministry. Rouen: 1721/22. V. 52

MANNING, SAMUEL
American Pictures, Drawin with Pen and Pencil. London: 1876. V. 49; 51
Italian Pictures Drawan with Pen and Pencil. London. V. 53
Swiss Pictures, Drawn with Pen and Pencil. London: 1880's. V. 47; 48

MANNING, WILLIAM RAY
The Nootka Sound Controversy. Chicago: 1904. V. 48
The Nootka Sound Controversy. Washington: 1905. V. 48

MANNINGS, JOHN SPELMAN
Cromer, a Descriptive Poem. London: 1806. V. 50

MANNING-SANDERS, RUTH
Karn. Richmond: 1922. V. 49

MANNYNG, ROBERT
The Story of England to A.D. 1338. London: 1887. V. 49

MANRING, B. F.
The Conquest of the Coeur D'Alenes, Spokanes and Palouses. Spokane: 1912. V. 50

MANRIQUE, SEBASTIAN
The Travels Of...1629-1643. Oxford: 1926. V. 53

MAN'S Greatest Adventure. Selah: 1974. V. 49

MANSEL, HENRY LONGUEVILLE
Letters, Lectures and Reviews, Including the Phrontisterion, or, Oxford in the 19th Century... London: 1873. V. 52

MANSEL-PLEYDELL, J. C.
The Flora of Dorsetshire. Dorchester: 1895. V. 50; 51

MANSERGH, JAMES
The Thirlmere Water Scheme of the Manchester Corporation... London: 1878. V. 50; 52
The Water Supply of the City of Toronto, Canada, by... Westminster: 1896. V. 52

MANSFIELD, EDGAR
Modern Design in Bookbinding. The Works of Edgar Mansfield. London: 1966. V. 49

MANSFIELD, EDWARD
The Mexican War. History of Its Origin. New York: 1848. V. 47; 48

MANSFIELD, JARED
Essays, Mathematical and Physical. New Haven: 1800. V. 50
Essays, Mathematical and Physical... New Haven: 1801. V. 51; 52

MANSFIELD, JOHN
Interesting Collection of Curious Anecdotes, Scarce Pieces, and Genuine Letters... London: 1790. V. 52

MANSFIELD, KATHERINE
The Aloe. 1930. V. 54
The Aloe. New York: 1930. V. 49; 51; 53
Bliss. London: 1920. V. 53
Bliss. 1923. V. 54
The Doves' Nest and Other Stories. 1923. V. 54
The Dove's Nest and Other Stories. London: 1923. V. 50; 51; 53
The Garden Party. London: 1922. V. 47; 48; 50; 51; 54
The Garden Party: and other Stories. London: 1939. V. 48; 49; 50
In a German Pension. 1911. V. 54
In a German Pension. New York: 1926. V. 49; 50
Je ne Parle pas Francais. Hampstead: 1919 (1918). V. 53
The Journal of Katherine Mansfield. London: 1927. V. 54
The Letters of... London: 1928. V. 47; 48; 54
Novels and Novelists. London: 1930. V. 54
Poems. London: 1923. V. 51; 54
Poems. New York: 1924. V. 48
Prelude. Richmond: 1918. V. 53
To Stanislaw Wyspianski. London: 1938. V. 48

MANSFIELD, ROBERT BLACHFORD
School-Life at Winchester College; or, the Reminiscences of a Winchester Junior. London: 1866. V. 49; 50; 54

MANSION, HORACE
Old French Nursery Songs. London: 1920. V. 53

MANSION, J. E.
Harrap's New Standard French and English Dictionary. London: 1972-80. V. 51

MANSION, L.
Letters Upon the Art of Miniature Painting. London: 1823. V. 49

MANSON, J. B.
The Life and Work of Edgar Degas. London: 1927. V. 54

MANSON, OTIS
A Treatise on the Physiological and Therapeutic Action of the Sulphate of Quinine. Philadelphia: 1882. V. 49; 51; 54

MANSON, PATRICK
Tropical Diseases. A Manual of the Diseases of Warm Climates. London: 1898. V. 50; 54

MANSTEIN, C. H. DE
Memoirs of Russia. London: 1770. V. 52

MANT, ALICIA CATHARINE
The Canary Bird. London: 1817. V. 48; 54
Montague Newburgh: or, the Mother and Son. London: 1817. V. 50

MANT, FREDERICK WOODS
The Midshipman; or Twelve Years at Sea. London: 1854. V. 50

MANTELL, GIDEON ALGERNON
A Day's Ramble in and About the Ancient Town of Lewes. London: 1846. V. 47
The Fossils of the South Downs... London: 1822. V. 47; 52
Geological Excursions Round the Isle of Wight and Along the Adjacent Coast of Dorsetshire. London: 1847. V. 54
Geological Excursions Round the Isle of Wight, and Along the Adjacent Coast of Dorsetshire. London: 1854. V. 53; 54
The Geology of the South-East of England. London: 1833. V. 47
The Medals of Creation; or, First Lessons in Geology... London: 1844. V. 47
A Narrative of the Visit of Their Most Gracious Majesties William IV, and Queen Adelaide, to the Ancient Borough of Lewes, on the 22d. of October 1830. London: 1831. V. 47
Petrifcations and Their Teachings; or a Hand-Book to the Gallery of Organic Remains of the British Museum. London: 1851. V. 51; 54
A Pictorial Atlas of Fossil Remains, Consisting of Coloured Illustrations Selected from Parkinson's "Organic Remains of a Former World" and Artis's "Antediluvian Phytology". London: 1850. V. 47
Thoughts on a Pebble. London: 1849. V. 47
Thoughts on Animalcules, or a Glimpse of the Invisible World Revealed by Microscope. London: 1846. V. 47
The Wonders of Geology. London: 1838. V. 54
The Wonders of Geology. London: 1839. V. 54
The Wonders of Geology; or a Familiar Exposition of Geological Phenomena. London: 1848. V. 51
The Wonders of Geology; or, a Familiar Exposition of geological Phenomena. London: 1857/8. V. 47

MANTLE, MICKEY
All My Octobers. New York: 1994. V. 51; 54
My Favorite Summer 1956. New York: 1991. V. 54

THE MANUAL of the Knights of the Round Table Club (A.D. 1720) (Confirmed in the General Council...1927). 1927. V. 47

MANUAL Of the Police Department of the City of Buffalo. Buffalo: 1873. V. 48

MANUCCI, NICCOLAO
History of the Mogul Dynasty in India From Its Foundation by Tamerlane in the Year 1399 to the Accession of Aurengzebe, in the Year 1657. London: 1826. V. 50
Storia do Mogor or Mogul India, 1653-1708. London: 1907-08. V. 54

MANUEL, KING OF PORTUGAL
Early Portuguese Books 1489-1600 in the Library of His Majesty the King of Portugal. London: 1929-35. V. 47

MANUEL DE MELLO, FRANCISCO
Epanaphoras de Varia Historia Portugueza... Lisbon: 1660. V. 48

THE MANUFACTURER and Builder. New York: 1871. V. 49

MANUFACTURES of the United States in 1860. Washington: 1865. V. 54

MANUTIUS, ALDUS
Eleganze Insieme Con La Copia Della Lingua Toscana, E Latina, Scielte Da Aldo Manutio... Venice: 1570. V. 52
Orthographiae Ratio Ab Aldo. Manutio Pauli. F(ilio). Collecta Ex Libris Antiquis, Grammaticis, Etymolgoia... Venice: 1566. V. 52
Phrases Linguae Latinae...Nunc Primum in Ordinem Abecedarium Adductae, & in Anglicum Sermonem Conversae... London: 1636. V. 52

MANUZIO, ALDO PIO
Di Castruccio Castracane de Gli Antelminelli. Rome: 1590. V. 48
Eleganze, Insieme Con La Copia, Della Lingva Toscana e Latina. Venice: 1558. V. 48
Orthographiae Ratio. Venice: 1561. V. 53

MANUZIO, PAOLO
Epistolarum Pauli Manutii Libri V. Venice: 1561. V. 52
Epistolarum Pauli Manutii Libri XII. London: 1603. V. 52
In Epistolas Ciceronis ad Atticvm, Pavli Manvtii Commentarivs. Venetiis: 1553. V. 53

MANVILL, P. D., MRS.
Lucinda: or the Mountain Mourner. New York: 1807. V. 54
Lucinda; or the Mountain Mourner. Ballston Spa: 1810. V. 49; 52; 53
Lucinda; or, the Mountain Mourner. Ballston Spa: 1817. V. 47; 49; 50; 51; 52

MANZINI, CARLO ANTONIO
L'Occhiael all'Occhio Dioptrica Pratica. Bologna: 1660. V. 49

MANZINI, CESARE
Instruction Pour Elever, Nourir, Dresser, Instruire & Penser Toutes Sortes de Petis Oyseaux de Voliere, que l'on Tient en Cage Pour Entendre Chanter. Paris: 1674. V. 47

MANZONI, ALESSANDRO
The Betrothed. (I Promessi Sposi). Verona: 1952. V. 52; 54
The Betrothed Lovers: a Milanese Story of the Seventeenth Century. London: 1845. V. 50; 54
I Promessi Sposi. (The Betrothed). New York: 1951. V. 48
I Promessi Spossi (The Betrothed). Verona: 1951. V. 54
I Promessi Spossi (The Betrothel). Verona: 1951. V. 52

MAPLESON, T. W. GWILT
Lays of the Western World, Illuminated by T. W. Gwilt Mapleson, Esq. New York: 1848. V. 48; 54
Pearls of American Poetry. New York: 1853. V. 51

MAPLET, JOHN
A Greene Forest or a Naturall Historie... London: 1930. V. 53; 54

MAPPLETHORPE, ROBERT
Black Book. New York: 1986. V. 47; 54
Lady Lisa Lyon. New York: 1983. V. 47
Mapplethorpe. New York. V. 49
Photographs. Norfolk: 1978. V. 53
The Power of Theatrical Madness. London: 1986. V. 51
Some Women. London: 1989. V. 47

MAPS and Descriptions of Routes of Exploration in Alaska in 1898. Washington: 1899. V. 52

MAQUEST DE LA MOTTE, GUILLAUME
A General Treatise on Midwifery; Illustrated with Upward of Four Hundred Curious Observations and Reflexions Concerning the Art. London: 1746. V. 53

MARABET, MOHAMMED
The Beach Cafe and the Voice. Santa Barbara: 1980. V. 49

MARACHIAFAVA, E.
Two Monographs on Malaria and the Parasites of Malarial Fevers. London: 1894. V. 54

MARACK, JAN VAN DER
Lucio Fontana. Brussels: 1974. V. 50

MARAN, RENE
Batouala. New York: 1922. V. 53
Batouala. New York: 1932. V. 50; 52; 54

MARANA, GIOVANNI PAOLO
Letters Writ by a Turkish Spy, Who Liv'd Five and Forty Years Undiscover'd at Paris... London: 1753-54. V. 53
Letters Writ by a Turkish Spy, Who Lived Five and Forty Years, Undiscovered at Paris. London: 1770. V. 47; 48

MARANTA, BARTOLOMEO
Libri Duo, de Theriaca et Mithridatio... Frankfurt: 1576. V. 47; 50; 53

MARAT, JEAN PAUL
Les Chaines de L'Esclavage... Paris: 1792. V. 51; 52

MARATELLI, VINCENZIO
Rime. Lettere. Florence: 1563. V. 50

MARBAKER, THOMAS D.
History of the Eleventh New Jersey Volunteers From its Organization at Appomattox, to Which is Added, Experiences of Prison Life and Sketches of Individual members. Trenton: 1898. V. 47; 49; 51

MARBARGER, JOHN P.
Space Medicine: The Human Factor in Flights Beyond the Earth. Urbana: 1951. V. 54

MARBLE, MELINDA
Herna. Cambridge: 1993. V. 52

MARBURG, OTTO
Hydrocephalus Its Symptomatology, Pathology, Pathogenesis and Treatment. New York: 1940. V. 54

MARBURY, MARY ORVIS
Favorite Flies and Their Histories. Boston: 1896. V. 52

MARCEL, C. V. A.
Practical Method of Teaching the Living Languages, Applied to the French, In Which Several Defects of the Old Method Are Pointed Out... London: 1820. V. 47

MARCEL, VERTES
Variations. Greenwich: 1961. V. 48

MARCELIN, PIERRE
The Pencil of God. Boston: 1951. V. 49

MARCELLINUS, AMMIANUS
Rerum Gestarum, Qui de XXXI Supersunt, Libri XVIII, Ope MSS. Codicum Emendati ab Henrico Valesio... Paris: 1681. V. 51
The Roman Historie, Containing Such Acts and Occurents as Passed Under Constanius, Iulianus, Iovianus, Valentinianus, and Valens, Emperours. London: 1609. V. 47; 48

MARCET, JANE
Bertha's Visit to Her Uncle in England. London: 1830. V. 49
Conversations of Botany. London: 1831. V. 54
Conversations on Chemistry... London: 1813. V. 52
Conversations on Chemistry... New Haven: 1813. V. 48
Conversations on Chemistry... London: 1824. V. 48
Conversations on Chemistry... London: 1825. V. 54
Conversations on Political Economy; in Which the Elements of that Science are Familiarly Explained. London: 1817. V. 48
Conversations on Political Economy; In Which the Elements of that Science are Familiarly Explained. London: 1827. V. 49; 52
Conversations on Vegetable Physiology... Boston: 1830. V. 50; 51; 52
The Seasons. London: 1835-33. V. 51
Willy's Holidays or Conversations on Different Kinds of Governments Intended for Young Children. London: 1836. V. 49

MARCET, WILLIAM
On the Composition of Food and How It Is Adulterated, with Practical Directions for Its Analysis. London: 1856. V. 47

MARCH, D.
Night Scenes in the Bible. Philadelphia: 1870. V. 51

MARCH, DAVID N.
The History of Missouri. New York: 1967. V. 53

MARCH, EDGAR J.
Sailing Drifters. The Story of the Herring Luggers of England, Scotland and the Isle of man. London: 1969. V. 48
Sailing Trawlers. Newton Abbot: 1978. V. 53
Spritsail Barges of Thames and Medway. London: 1948. V. 54

MARCH, ELEANOR S.
Nature Children. A Flower Book for Little Folks. London: 1911. V. 47

MARCH, HARRY A.
Pro Football. Its "Ups" and "Downs". Albany: 1934. V. 47

MARCH, JOHN
The Jolly Angler or Waterside Companion &c. London: 1933. V. 51; 52

MARCH, JOSEPH MONCURE
The Set-Up. New York: 1928. V. 47

MARCH, WILLIAM
The Bad Seed. New York: 1954. V. 50; 53
Company K. New York: 1931. V. 51
Company K. 1933. V. 51
Company K. New York: 1933. V. 53

MARCHANT, JOHN
A Review of the Bloody Tribunal: or the Horrid Cruelties of the Inquisition, as Practised in Spain, Portugal, Italy and East and West Indies... Perth: 1770. V. 49

MARCHANT, N. G.
Flora of the Perth Region. Perth: 1987. V. 50

MARCHANT, S.
Handbook of Australian, New Zealand and Antarctic Birds. Melbourne: 1990. V. 54

MARCHIAFAVA, E.
Two Monographs on Malaria and the Parasites of Malarial Fevers. London: 1894. V. 49; 51

MARCHINI, G.
Italian Stained Glass Windows. New York: 1956. V. 52
Italian Stained Glass Windows. London: 1957. V. 51

MARCHISI, J. B.
Dr. Marchisi's Uterine Catholicon, Is Hereby Most Respectfully Dedicated to the Mothers and Daughters of Our Country, for Whose Benefit It Is Designed, and Whose Happiness It Will Promote. New York: 1851. V. 52; 53

MARCI, JACOB
Illustrium Hollandiae Vvestfrisiae Ordinvm Alma Academia Leidensis... Lvgdvni Batavorvm: 1614. V. 48

MARCI A KRONLAND, JOHANNES MARCUS
Liturgia Mentis Seu Disceptatio MEdica, Philosophica et Optica de Natura Epilepsiae Illius Ortu et Causis. Ratisbonae: 1678. V. 47; 53

MARCK, H. VAN DER
Bibliotheca Marckiana. The Hague: 1712. V. 48; 52

MARCK, JAN VAN DER
Lucio Fontana. Brussels: 1974. V. 47; 48

MARCONI INTERNATIONAL MARINE COMMUNICATION CO. LTD.
Marconi Telegraphy. A Short History of Its Invention, Revolution and Commercial Development. London: 1907. V. 51

MARCONI WIRELESS TELEGRAPH CO., LTD.
Copy of Agreement...With Regard to the Establishment of a Chain of Imperial Wireless Stations. London: 1913. V. 50
Reports From the Select Commitee on Marconi's Wireless Telegraph Co., Limited, Agreement. (with) Index and Digest of Evidence. London: 1913. V. 50

MARCUCCI, L.
Medieval Painting. London: 1960. V. 50

MARCUS, FRANK
The Killing of Sister George. New York: 1965. V. 50

MARCUS, MOSES
The Principle Motives and Circumstances That Induced Moses Marcus to Leave the Jewish, and Embrace the Christian Faith... London: 1724. V. 48

MARCUS, STANLEY
The Book Club of Texas. Dallas: 1898. V. 49

MARCY, L. J.
The Sciopticon Manual, Explaining Lantern Projections in General and the Sciopticon Apparatus in Particular... Philadelphia: 1877. V. 52

MARCY, RANDOLPH BARNES
Border Reminiscences. New York: 1872. V. 48
Exploration of the Red River of Louisiana in the Year 1852. Washington: 1853. V. 54
Exploration of the Red River of Louisiana in the Year 1852. Washington: 1854. V. 47; 48; 49; 52; 53; 54
Message of the President of the United States...Communicating...the Report and Maps of Captain Marcy of His Explorations of the Big Wichita and Head Waters of the Brazos Rivers. Washington: 1856. V. 47; 49; 52
The Prairie and Overland Traveller: a Companion for Emigrants, Traders and Travellers, Hunters and Soldiers Traversing Great Plains and Prairies. London: 1860. V. 48
The Prairie Traveler. New York: 1859. V. 47; 49; 52
The Prairie Traveler. London: 1863. V. 47
Route from Fort Smith to Santa Fe. Washington: 1850. V. 47; 49; 52
Thirty Years of Army Life on the Border Comprising Descriptions of the Indian Nomads of the Plains... New York: 1866. V. 47; 49

MARDEN, PHILIP SANFORD
Travels in Spain. Boston & New York: 1910. V. 54

MARDER, ARTHUR J.
From the Dreadnought to Scapa Flow, The royal Navy in the Fisher Era, 1904-1919. 1961-70. V. 53

MARDERSTEIG, GIOVANNI
The Making of a Book at the Officina Bodoni. Verona: 1973. V. 47; 48; 51; 52
Die Officina Bodoni. Verona: 1929. V. 49
The Officina Bodoni. Verona: 1980. V. 47; 49; 51; 52

MARDERSTEIG, HANS
Pastonchi. A Specimen of a New Letter for Use on the Monotype. Verona: 1928. V. 50

MARDIKIAN, GEORGE
Dinner at Omar Khayyam's. New York: 1944. V. 48

MARES, FREDERICK H.
Photographs of Dublin with Descriptive Letterpress. Glasgow: 1867. V. 52; 54
Sunny Memories of Ireland's Scenic Beauties: Killarney. Dublin: 1867. V. 47; 48; 52

MARESCOTTI, GIORGIO
Thesoro di Virtu...Tresor de Vertu...Stamapto Nuovamanete, Da Girogio Marescotti. Fiorenza: 1592. V. 50

MAREY, E. J.
Animal Mechanism: a Treatise on Terrestrial and Aerial Locomotion. London: 1874. V. 48
Animal Mechanism: a Treatise on Terrestrial and Aerial Locomotion. New York: 1874. V. 50; 54

MARGARET Mitchell and Her Novel Gone with the Wind. New York: 1936. V. 49; 50

MARGARET, RANEE OF SARAWAK
Good Morning and Good Night. London: 1934. V. 54
My Life in Sarawak. London: 1913. V. 54

MARGARITA Davitica, Seu Expositio Psalmorum. Augsburg: 1475. V. 51; 53

MARGARY, I. D.
Roman Ways in the Weald. London: 1948. V. 49

MARGERIE, PIERRE DE
Eloge de la Typographie. Weimar: 1931. V. 52

MARGERISON, SAMUEL
The Registers of the Parish Church of Calverley, in the West Riding of the County of York... Bradford: 1880-87. V. 53

MARGOLIOUTH, G.
A Catalogue of the Hebrew and Samaritan Manuscripts in the British Museum. London: 1899/1905. V. 53

MARGUERITE D'ANGOULEME, QUEEN OF NAVARRE
The Heptameron. London: 1855. V. 53
The Heptameron... 1886. V. 54
The Heptameron. London: 1894. V. 48; 52
The Heptameron... London: 1898. V. 50; 54
The Heptameron... London: 1904. V. 48
The Heptameron. London: 1922. V. 47; 49; 52

MARGUERITE DE VALOIS, QUEEN OF FRANCE
Les Memoires de la Roine Margverite. Paris: 1628. V. 54
The Memorialls of Margaret de Valoys. London: 1641. V. 51

MARIACHER, GIOVANNE
Italian Blown Glass from Ancient Rome to Venice. New York: 1961. V. 53

MARIANA, JUAN
Historiae de Rebus Hispaniae Libri XXX. Mainz: 1605-19. V. 48

MARIANI, ANGELO
Coca and Its Therapeutic Application. New York: 1890. V. 49; 54

MARIANI, FOSCO
Where Four Worlds Meets. New York: 1964. V. 54

MARIANI, PAUL
Timing Devices. Easthampton: 1977. V. 47; 48; 49; 51; 53
Timing Devices. 1978. V. 52; 54

MARIANI, VALERIO
Michelangelo the Painter. New York: 1964. V. 47; 48

MARIE, JANE
The Case of Jane Marie, Exhibiting the Cruelty and Barbarous Conduct of James Ross to a Defenceless Woman. Philadelphia: 1808. V. 52
The Case of Jane Marie, Exhibiting the Cruelty and Barbarous Conduct of James Ross, to a Defenseless Woman. Philadelphia: 1818. V. 51; 53

MARIE, PIERRE
Essays on Acromegaly. London: 1891. V. 50
Lectures on Diseases of the Spinal Cord. London: 1895. V. 48; 54

MARIE, QUEEN OF ROUMANIA
The Dreamer of Dreams. London: 1915. V. 53
The Story of Naughty Kildeen. New York: 1927. V. 54

MARILLIER, H. C.
Dante Gabriel Rossetti. London: 1899. V. 49

MARIN, JOHN
The Complete Etchings. Philadelphia: 1969. V. 53
Drawings and Watercolors. New York: 1950. V. 52
Letters of John Marin. New York: 1931. V. 52

MARIN, RENE
Batoula. New York: 1932. V. 47

MARINATOS, SPYRIDON
Crete and Mycenae. London: 1960. V. 48; 52; 54
Crete and Mycenae. New York: 1960. V. 50; 54

MARINELLI, GIOVANNI
Gli Ornamenti delle Donne. Venice: 1574. V. 52
La Prima (Seconda) Parte Della Copia delle Parole... Venice: 1562. V. 49

MARINER, WILLIAM
An Account of the Natives of the Tonga Islands... Boston: 1820. V. 48

MARINE SOCIETY, LONDON
The Bye-Laws and Regulations of the Marine Society, Incorporated in MDCCLXXII with Several Instructions, Forms of Indentures and Other Instruments Used By It. London: 1792. V. 47; 51

MARINHO DE AZEVEDO, LUIS
Apologeticos Discursos Offerecidos a Magestade del Rei Dom Ioam Nosso Senhor Quarto do Nome...em Deensa da Fama, e Boa memoria de Fernao d'Albuquerque do Seu Conselho... Lisbon: 1641. V. 48

MARINI, MARINO
Marino Marini: Graphic Work and Paintings. New York: 1960. V. 53

MARINO, GIAMBATTISTA
L'Adone. Poema. Paris: 1623. V. 54
L'Adone. Poema. Amsterdam: 1678. V. 49; 54
L'Adone. Poema. Con gli Argomenti del Conte Sanvitale e l'Allegorie di Don Lorenzo Scoto. Amsterodamo: 1679. V. 49

MARINO, JOSEF
Hi! Ho! Pinocchio! The American Boy. Chicago: 1940. V. 53; 54

MARINONI, GIOVANNI JACOPO
De Astronomica Specula Domestica et Organico Apparatu Astronomico Libri Duo. Vienna: 1745. V. 47

MARION, WILLIAM B.
The House that B— Built. San Bernardino: 1929. V. 52

MARIOTTE, EDME
Oeuvres; Divisees en Deux Tomes... Leide: 1717. V. 53

MARIS, ROGER
Slugger in Right. New York: 1963. V. 50

MARITAIN, RAISSA
Patriach Tree. Worcester: 1965. V. 47; 50; 51

MARITAL Frolics. Dover. V. 54

MARITIME Capture. Shall England Uphold the Capture of Private Property at Sea?. London: 1866. V. 51

A MARITIME History of New York. Garden City: 1941. V. 50

MARIUS, RICHARD
The Coming of Rain. London: 1969. V. 54
The Coming of Rain. New York: 1969. V. 49

MARIVAUX, PIERRE CARLET DE CHAMBLAIN DE
Le Jeu De L'Amour et du Hasard. Paris: 1905. V. 54

MARJORIBANKS, ALEXANDER
Travels in New Zealand. London: 1845. V. 47; 52
Travels in South and North America. London: 1853. V. 52

MARJORIBANKS, E.
The Life of Lord Carson. 1932-36. V. 54

MARK, ENID
An Afternoon et Les Collettes. Wallingford: 1988. V. 53

MARK, JOHN
Genealogy of the Family of Mark or Marke, Cumberland, Pedigree and Arms of the Bowscale Branch of the Family. Manchester: 1898. V. 52

MARK, MARY ELLEN
Ward 21. New York: 1979. V. 54

MARKEVITCH, MARIE ALEXANDRE
The Epicure in Imperial Russia. San Francisco: 1941. V. 50

MARKHAM, ALBERT HASTINGS
Great Frozen Sea: Aractic Expedition of 1875-76. London: 1878. V. 53
A Whaling Cruise to Baffin's Bay and the Gulf of Boothia. London: 1875. V. 54

MARKHAM, ALEXANDER
The Avenged Bride; a Tale of the Glens. Belfast: 1833. V. 49

MARKHAM, BERYL
West With the Night. Boston: 1942. V. 51; 52; 53

MARKHAM, CLEMENTS ROBERT
Cuzco...and Lima... London: 1856. V. 50
The Life and Acts of Don Alonzo Enriquez de Guzman (etc.). London: 1862. V. 48
Narratives of the Mission of George Bogle to Tibet; and of the Journey of Thomas Manning to Lhasa. London: 1876. V. 53; 54
Ollanta. London: 1871. V. 52
Peruvian Bark. London: 1880. V. 52; 54
Travels in Peru and India While Superintending the Collection of Chinchona Plants and Seeds in South America, and Their Introduction Into India. London: 1862. V. 51; 54

MARKHAM, EDWIN
California the Wonderful. New York: 1914. V. 54
The Man with the Hoe. New York: 1899. V. 53
The Man With the Hoe. San Francisco: 1899. V. 48
The Man With the Hoe. New York: 1900. V. 48
The Man With the Hoe. San Francisco: 1916. V. 54
Our Israfel in memory of Edgar Allan Poe. New York: 1925. V. 48

MARKHAM, FRANCIS
The Booke of Honovr. or, Five Decads of Epistles of Honovr. London: 1625. V. 47
Five Decades of Epistles of Warre. London: 1622. V. 51

MARKHAM, FRED
Shooting in the Himalayas. London: 1854. V. 54

MARKHAM, GERVASE
The Citizen and Countryman's Experienced Farrier... Baltimore: 1797. V. 48
The Citizen and Countryman's Experienced Farrier... Chambersburg: 1839. V. 47
Country Contentments...Hunting, Hawking, Coursing...Art of Angling of the Use of the Fighting Cocke. London: 1631. V. 49
The Farmouse Whore, or Noble Curtizan. London: 1868. V. 54

MARKHAM, GERVASE continued
The Inrichment of the Weald of Kent... London: 1636. V. 47; 49; 50; 51
The Inrichment of the Weald of Kent. London: 1653. V. 51
Markham's Farewell to Husbandry. London: 1638. V. 48
Markham's Farewell to Husbandry. London: 1656. V. 48
Markham's Farewell to Husbandry.... London: 1668. V. 54
Markham's Farewell to Husbandry... (with) The Enrichment of the Weald of Kent... London: 1660/60. V. 50
Markham's Maister-Peece: Containing All Knowledge Belonging to the Smith, Farrier, or Horse Leech. London: 1651. V. 47
Markham's Masterpiece.... London: 1717. V. 47
The Perfect Horse-man. London: 1684. V. 47

MARKHAM, PETER
Poison Detected: or Frightful Truths and Alarming to the British Metropolis. London: 1757. V. 51
Shyhoroc: or Considerations on the Ten Ingredients Used in the Adulteration of Bread-Flour, and Bread. London: 1758. V. 51

MARKHAM, ROSS JAMES
A Coming of Winter. Ontario: 1981. V. 47

MARKLAND, ABRAHAM
Pteryplegia; or, the Art of Shooting-Flying. London: 1727. V. 47; 49
Pteryplegia; or, The Art of Shooting-Flying, a Poem. London: 1735. V. 47
Pteryplegia: the Art of Shooting Flying. New York: 1931. V. 47

MARKLAND, JOHN
Typographia. An Ode on Printing... Roanoke: 1926. V. 51; 53

MARKLOVE, H.
Views of Berkeley Castle, Taken on the spot, and Drawn on Stone. Bristol, Gloucester: 1840. V. 52

MARKMAN, SIDNEY DAVID
Colonial Architecture of Antigua Guatemala. Philadelphia: 1966. V. 48

MARKOV, VLADIMIR
Russian Futurism, a History. London: 1969. V. 49; 52; 54

MARKS, A. A.
Manual of Artificial Limbs. New York: 1914. V. 50; 54

MARKS, CHRISTOPHER G.
Rackets in Canada and the Montreal Racket Club... Quebec: 1990. V. 47; 50

MARKS, DAVID
The Life of David Marks to the 26th Year of His Age. Limerick: 1831. V. 50
A Treatise on the Faith of the Freewill Baptists: with an Appendix... Dover: 1834. V. 51; 54

MARKS, JOHN GEORGE
Life and Letters of Frederick Walker, A.R.A. London: 1896. V. 54

MARKS, LILLIAN
Saul Marks and the Plantin Press: The Life and Work of a Singular Man. Los Angeles: 1980. V. 47

MARKS, MARILLA
Memoirs of the Life of David Marks, Minister of the Gospel. Dover: 1846. V. 49

MARKS, MARY
Five-Chimney Farm. London: 1877. V. 52

MARKS, ROBERT W.
The Dymaxion World of Buckminster Fuller. New York: 1960. V. 50

MARKS, SAUL
Christopher Plantin & the Officina Plantiana. Los Angeles: 1972. V. 54

MARKWICK, E.
The City of Gold. 1898. V. 54

MARLBOROUGH, 3RD DUKE OF
Gemmarum Antiquarum Delectus, Ex Praesentioribus Desumptus, Quae in Dactyliothecis Ducis Marlburiensis Conservantur... London: 1845. V. 53

MARLBOROUGH, GEORGE SPENCER, 4TH DUKE OF
Gemmarum Antiquarum Delectus...Choix de Pierres Antiques Gravees du Cabinet du duc de Marlborough. London: 1845. V. 48

MARLBOROUGH, JOHN CHURCHILL, 1ST DUKE OF
Letters and Despatches, from 1702 to (1712). London: 1845. V. 48
The Marlborough-Godolphin Correspondence. London: 1975. V. 49

MARLBOROUGH, JOHN, DUKE OF
Memoirs. London: 1820. V. 50

MARLBOROUGH, SARAH JENNINGS CHURCHILL, DUCHESS OF
An Account of the Conduct of...to 1710, in a Letter from Herself to My Lord ——. London: 1742. V. 50
The Opinions of Sarah Duchess-Dowager of Marlborough. Edinburgh: 1788. V. 47
A True Copy of the Last Will and Testament of Her Grace, Sarah, Late Duchess Dowager of Marlborough, with the Codicil Thereto Annexed. London: 1744. V. 47

MARLENE Dietrich: Ten Stills. New York: 1965. V. 54

MARLIANI, BARTHOLOMEO
Urbis Romae Topographia Accurate, tum Veterum tum Etiam Recentiorum Auctatum... Venice: 1588. V. 54

MARLIANUS, JOANNES FRANCISCUS
Jo. Francisci Marliani Mediolanensis: Magnifici Antonii Filii: Illustrissimi Ducis Mediolani Legati... Rome: 1485. V. 47

MARLIN FIRE ARMS CO.
Manufacturers of Marlin Repeating Rifles, Ballard Rifles, Standard Revolvers, Daley's Patent Handcuffs, Reloading Tools, Everlasting Shells, Sights &c. New Haven: 1885. V. 50

MARLORAT, AUGUSTIN
Remonstrance A La Royne Mere du Roy par Ceux Qui Sont Persecutez Pour la Parole de Dieu. 1561. V. 48

MARLOW, JEREMIAH
A Book of Cyphers Reverst. London: 1683. V. 48

MARLOW, JOHN
Letters to a Sick Friend, Containing Such Observations as May Render the Use of Remedies Effectual Towards the Removal of Sickness and Preservation of Health. London: 1682. V. 53

MARLOWE, CHRISTOPHER
Doctor Faustus. London: 1903. V. 53
Edward the Second. Kensington: 1929. V. 48; 51
Edward the Second. London: 1929. V. 54
Hero and Leander. London: 1894. V. 49; 53
Hero and Leander. Edinburgh: 1909. V. 48
The Tragical History of Doctor Faustus. London: 1903. V. 48; 49
The Tragicall History of Dr. Faustus. 1932. V. 53
The Works. 1826. V. 54
The Works. London: 1826. V. 48
The Works... London: 1850. V. 48

MARLOWE, G. S.
I Am Your Brother. London: 1935. V. 49

MARMADUKE Multiply's Merry Method of Making Minor Mathematicians. London: 1832. V. 47

MARMELSZADT, WILLARD
Musical Sons of Aesculapius. New York: 1946. V. 49; 50; 52; 54

MARMION, SHACKERLEY
The Dramtic Works. London: 1875. V. 49

MARMONT, AUGUSTE F. L.
The Present State of the Turkish Empire. London: 1839. V. 53
The Spirit of Military Institutions. Columbia: 1864. V. 49

MARMONTEL, JEAN FRANCOIS
Belisaire. London: 1767. V. 48; 51
Belisaire. Paris: 1767. V. 54
Belisarius. London: 1794. V. 52
The Incas; or, the Destruction of the Empire of Peru. London: 1777. V. 47; 52
Memoirs of Marmontel. London: 1805. V. 47
Moral Tales. London: 1766. V. 47; 48
Oeuvres Completes. Liege: 1777. V. 48

THE MARMOSITE'S Miscellany. Victoria: 1975. V. 50

MARNE, CLAUDE
Rerum Moscoviti-Carum Auctores Varii...Quibus & Gentis Historia... Frankfurt: 1600. V. 49

MARNY, SUZANNE
Tales of Old Toronto. Toronto: 1909. V. 53

MAROLLES, LEWIS DE
An Essay on Providence. London: 1790. V. 50; 54

MAROLLES, MICHEL DE
Tableaux du Temple des Muses; Tirez du Cabinet de feu Mr. Favereau. Amsterdam: 1676. V. 47

MARON, MARGARET
Bootlegger's Daughter. New York: 1992. V. 49

MAROON, FRED J.
The Egypt Story. Its Art, Its Monuments, Its People, Its History. New York: 1979. V. 53

MAROT, CLEMENT
Les Oeuvres. Lyon: 1548-47. V. 52
Les Oeuvres... 1596. V. 48

MAROT, JEAN
Receuil des Plus Beaux Edifices, et Frontispieces des Eglises de Paris. Paris: 1650. V. 50
Recueil des Plans, Profils et Elevations des Plusieurs Palais, Chasteaux, Eglises, Sepultures, Grotes et Hostels, Batis dans Paris et aux Environs... 1660. V. 54

MARQUAND, ERNEST DAVID
Flora of Guernsey and the Lesser Channel Islands; Namely Alderney, Sark, Herm, Jethou and the Adjacent islets. London: 1901. V. 52

MARQUAND, JOHN P.
Last Laugh, Mr. Moto. London: 1943. V. 50; 51
Mr. Moto is So Sorry. Boston: 1938. V. 52
Point of No Return. Boston: 1949. V. 53; 54
Prince and Boatswain. Greenfield: 1915. V. 51
So Little Time. Boston: 1943. V. 51
Think Fast, Mr. Moto. Boston: 1937. V. 52

MARQUAND, JOHN P. continued
Unspeakable Gentleman. New York: 1922. V. 53
Wickford Point. Boston: 1939. V. 48

MARQUES, SIMAO
Brasilia Pontificia, sive Speciales Facultates Pontificiae, Quae Brasiliae Episcopis conceduntur... Lisbon: 1749. V. 48

MARQUIS, DON
Archy and Mehitabel. New York: 1927. V. 49
Archy Does His Part. Garden City: 1935. V. 48; 51
Archy's Life of Mehitabel. Garden City: 1933. V. 48; 51
Archy's Life of Mehitabel. New York: 1933. V. 49
Danny's Own Story. 1912. V. 50
Danny's Own Story. Garden City: 1912. V. 48; 51
The Dark Hours: Five Scenes from a History. Garden City: 1924. V. 50
An Ode to Hollywood. 1929. V. 50
The Old Soak's History of the World. Garden City: 1924. V. 47
The Revolt of the Oyster. Garden City: 1922. V. 47

MARQUIS, F. DICKINSON
John Marshall, the Tribute of Massachusetts...in Commemoration of the One Hundredth Anniversary of His Elevation to the Bench as Chief Justice of the Supreme Court of the United States. Boston: 1901. V. 52

MARQUIS, THOMAS B.
Memoirs Of a White Crow Indian. New York: 1928. V. 51; 53
A Warrior Who Fought Custer. Minneapolis: 1934. V. 52

MARR, J. E.
The Geology of the Lake District and the Scenery as Influenced by Geological Structure. Cambridge: 1916. V. 51

MARRA, JOHN
Journal of the Resolution's Voyage in 1772, 1773, 1774 and 1775...(with) A Journal of the Adventure's Voyage in the Years 1772, 1773 and 1774. London: 1775. V. 49; 52

MARRIACHER, GIOVANNE
Italian Blown Glass from Ancient Rome to Venice. New York: 1961. V. 54

MARRIAGE & *Home.* London: 1873. V. 52

MARRIOTT, CHARLES
Laura Knight, A Book of Drawings. London: 1923. V. 48

MARRIOTT, JAMES
Poems Written Chiefly at the University of Cambridge... London: 1761. V. 48; 50; 52
Political Considerations: Being a few Thoughts on a Candid Man at the Present Crisis. London: 1762. V. 50

MARRIOTT, JOHN
A Short Account of John Marriott, Including Extracts from Some of His Letters. Doncaster: 1803. V. 50; 54

MARRIOTT, THOMAS
Female Conduct: Being an Essay on the Art of Pleasing. London: 1759. V. 48

MARRIOTT, WILLIAM
A Collection of English Miracle Plays or Mysteries. Basel: 1838. V. 51
The Country Gentleman's Lawyer; and the Farmer's Complete Law Library. London: 1811. V. 49

MARROT, H. V.
A Bibliography of the Works of John Galsworthy. London: 1928. V. 48; 53
Bulmer and Bensley, a Study in Transition. London: 1930. V. 50

MARRYAT, B.
A Diary in America. New York: 1939. V. 53

MARRYAT, FRANK
Borneo and the Indian Archipelago. London: 1848. V. 52; 54
Mountains and Molehills, or Recollections of a Burnt Journal. London: 1855. V. 49; 52

MARRYAT, FREDERICK
The Children of the New Forest. London: 1849. V. 51
A Diary in America. London: 1839. V. 50; 53; 54
The Handy Volume Marryat. London: 1890's. V. 50
Jack Ashore. London: 1840. V. 51
Jacob Faithful. London: 1834. V. 51
Jacob Faithful. London: 1837. V. 47
Japhet, in Search of a Father. London: 1836. V. 51
Joseph Rushbrook: or, the Poacher. London: 1841. V. 48; 53
The King's Own. London: 1830. V. 50; 51; 52; 53
The Little Savage. London: 1849. V. 47
Masterman Ready; or the Wreck of the Pacific. London: 1841. V. 50
Masterman Ready; or, the Wreck of the Pacific. London: 1841-1842. V. 47; 48; 50; 51
The Mission: or, Scenes in Africa. London: 1845. V. 50; 51
Mr. Midshipman Easy. London: 1836. V. 48; 51; 52; 54
The Naval Officer; or, Scenes and Adventures in the Life of Frank Mildmay. London: 1829. V. 51
Newton Forster; or, The Merchant Service. London: 1832. V. 51; 52
The Novels. London: 1896. V. 52
Olla Podrida. London: 1840. V. 49
Olla Podrida. Paris: 1841. V. 48; 53
The Pacha of Many Tales. London: 1835. V. 47; 51
Percival Keene... London: 1842. V. 50
Peter Simple. London: 1834. V. 47; 50; 51; 52
The Phantom Ship. London: 1839. V. 51; 52
The Phantom Ship. Boston: 1913. V. 51
The Pirate and the Three Cutters. London: 1836. V. 48; 51
The Pirate and The Three Cutters. London: 1854. V. 51
Poor Jack. London: 1840. V. 51
The Privateersman, One Hundred Years Ago. London: 1846. V. 49
Rattlin' the Reefer. London: 1836. V. 51
Rattlin' the Reefer. Philadelphia: 1836. V. 48; 53
The Settlers in Canada. London: 1844. V. 52
Snarleyyow, or the Dog Fiend. London: 1837. V. 50
Snarleyyow; or, the Dog Fiend. Philadelphia: 1837. V. 47
Valerie, an Autobiography. London: 1849. V. 49; 53

MARRYAT, JOSEPH
Collections Towards a History of Pottery and Porcelain in the 15th, 16th, 17th and 18th Centuries... London: 1850. V. 50
A History of Pottery and Porcelain, Medieval and Modern. London: 1868. V. 53
The Substance of a Speech Delivered in the House of Commons, On the 20th of February, 1810, Upon a Motion for a Select Committee to Consider of the Act of 6th Geo. I and of the means of Effecting Marine Insurances; also Observations on the Report of the... London: 1824. V. 51

MARRYAT, SAMUEL FRANCIS
Mountains and Molehills, or Recollections of a Burnt Journal. London: 1885. V. 50

MARS, G. C.
Brickwork in Italy. Chicago: 1925. V. 53

MARSDEN, B. A.
Genealogical Memoirs of the Family of Marsden, Their Ancestors and Descent Traced From Public Records, Wills and Other Documents and from Private Sources, of Information Hitherto Unrecorded. Birkenhead: 1914. V. 48

MARSDEN, J. B.
The History of the Early Puritans: from the Reformation to 1642. The Hitory of the Later Puritans: from 1642-1662. London: 1853-54. V. 53

MARSDEN, R. G.
Documents Relating to Law and Custom of the Sea. London: 1915/16. V. 53

MARSDEN, WILLIAM
The History of Sumatra Containing an Account of the Government, Laws, Customs and Manners of the Native Inhabitants. London: 1784. V. 48

MARSH, ANNE
Emilia Wyndham. London: 1846. V. 51

MARSH, CHARLES
The Clubs of London; with Anecdotes of Their Members, Sketches of Their Character and Conversations. London: 1828. V. 48

MARSH, E. A.
The Evolution of Automatic Machinery as Applied to the Manufacture of Watches at Waltham, Mass. by the American Waltham Watch Company. Chicago: 1896. V. 52

MARSH, ELSIE A. G.
The Econcomic Library of Jacob H. Hollander... Baltimore: 1937. V. 53

MARSH, GEORGE
Toilers of the Trails. Philadelphia: 1921. V. 53

MARSH, HERBERT
The History of the Politicks of Great Britain and France, From the Time of the Conference at Pillnitz, to the Declaration of War, Against Great Britain. London: 1800. V. 48; 52

MARSH, HIPPISLEY CUNLIFFE
A Ride Through Islam: Being a Journey through Persia and Afghanistan to India, via Meshed, Herat and Kandahar. London: 1877. V. 51

MARSH, HONORIA
Shades from Jane Austen. London: 1975. V. 52; 54

MARSH, J. B. T.
The Story of the Jubilee Singers, with their Songs. London: 1886. V. 49; 52

MARSH, JAMES B.
Four Years in the Rockies; or, the Adventures of Isaac P. Rose...Giving His Experience as a Hunter and Trapper... New Castle: 1884. V. 47

MARSH, JOHN FITCHETT
Annals of Chepstow Castle or Six Centuries of the Lords of Striguil from the Conquest to the Revolution. Exeter: 1883. V. 50; 53

MARSH, NGAIO
Colour Scheme. London: 1943. V. 53
Swing, Brother Swing. London: 1949. V. 48
Tied Up In Tinsel. London: 1972. V. 50

MARSH, OTHNIEL CHARLES
Dinocerata. Washington: 1884. V. 50
Dinocerata, a Monograph of an Extinct Order of Gigantic Mammals. Washington: 1886. V. 51
Odontornithes: a Monograph on the Extinct Toothed Birds of North America. New Haven: 1880. V. 50
Odontornithes, a Monograph on the Extinct Toothed Birds of North America. Washington: 1880. V. 50; 54

MARSH, R.
The Joss: a Reversion. 1901. V. 47; 51

MARSH, SAM
Hunting, Snowing and Chasing. London: 1930. V. 48

MARSHAL, ANDREW
The Morbid Anatomy of the Brain, In Mania and Hydrophobia... London: 1815. V. 54

MARSHALL, A. J.
Bower-Birds, Their Displays and Breeding Cycles. London: 1954. V. 49

MARSHALL, AGNES B.
Mrs. Marshall's Larger Cookery Book of Extra Recipes. London: 1902. V. 51

MARSHALL, ALFRED
Principles of Economics. London: 1890. V. 50; 53
Principles of Economics. London: 1895. V. 48; 50; 52

MARSHALL, C.
A Monograph of the Capitionidae or Scansorial Barbets. London: 1871. V. 49

MARSHALL, C. F. DENDY
The British Post Office, From Its Beginning to the End of 1925. London: 1926. V. 47; 48
Centenary History of the Liverpool & Manchester Railway. London: 1930. V. 49
A History of Railway Locomotives Down to the End of the Year 1831. London: 1953. V. 49
A History of the Southern Railway. London: 1936. V. 50
Two Essays in Early Locomotive History. London: 1928. V. 49

MARSHALL, CHARLES
An Introduction to the Knowledge and Practice of Gardening. London: 1798. V. 48

MARSHALL, CHARLES HENRY TILSON
A Monograph of the Capitonidae, or Scansorial Barbets. London: 1870-71. V. 50; 52

MARSHALL, CHARLES K.
The Colored Race Weighed In the Balance. Nashville: 1883. V. 50

MARSHALL, D. PORTER
Company "K", 155th Pa. Volunteer Zouaves, a Detailed History of its Organization and Service During the Civil War, from 1862 Until the Collapse of the Rebellion... 1888?. V. 48

MARSHALL, F. H.
Catalogue of the Finger Rings, Greek, Eturscan and Roman in the Department of Antiquities, British Museum. London: 1968. V. 50
Catalogue of the Jewellery, Greek, Etruscan and Roman, in the Department of Antiquities, British Museum. London: 1911. V. 50; 52

MARSHALL, G. F. L.
Birds Nesting in India. Calcutta: 1877. V. 53

MARSHALL, GEORGE
Epistles in Verse, Between Cynthio and Leonora, in Three Cantos... Newcastle-upon-Tyne: 1812. V. 53; 54
The Life of George Washington. Fredericksburg: 1926. V. 47
Marshall's Practical Marine Gunnery... Norfolk: 1822. V. 50

MARSHALL, HENRY
On the Enlisting, Discharging and Pensioning of Soldiers, with the Official Documents on These Branches of Military Duty. Edinburgh: 1839. V. 53

MARSHALL, HUMPHREY
The History of Kentucky. Frankfort: 1824. V. 47; 54

MARSHALL, J. D.
The Autobiography of William Stout of Lancaster, 1665-1752. Manchester: 1967. V. 54

MARSHALL, J. U.
The Times: or Chaos Has Come Again. Charleston: 1868. V. 49

MARSHALL, JOHN
Anatomy for Artists. London: 1883. V. 49
Atlas to Marshall's Life of Washington. New York?: 1832. V. 47
Atlas to Marshall's Life of Washington. Philadelphia: 1832. V. 50; 52
The Life of George Washington. Philadelphia: 1804. V. 47; 52
The Life of George Washington. Philadelphia: 1804-07. V. 47; 48; 50; 52; 53; 54
The Life of George Washington... Philadelphia: 1839. V. 52
The Life of George Washington, Commander in Chief of the American Forces... New York: 1925. V. 51
Mohenjo-Daro and the Indus Civilization. Delhi: 1973. V. 50
The Village Paedagogue, a Poem, and Other Lesser Pieces. Newcastle: 1810. V. 54

MARSHALL, JOSEPH
Travels through Holland, Flanders, Germany, Denmark, Sweden, Lapland, Russia, the Ukraine and Poland in the Years 1768, 1769 and 1770. London: 1773-76. V. 52

MARSHALL, JULIAN
Catalogue of the Musical Library of Julian Marshall, Esq. London: 1884. V. 47

MARSHALL, N. B.
Aspects of Marine Zoology. 1967. V. 52

MARSHALL, PAULE
Brown Girl, Brownstone. New York: 1959. V. 49; 50; 53; 54
The Chosen Place, The Timeless People. New York: 1969. V. 47; 52; 54
Daughters. New York: 1991. V. 53
Praisesong for the Widow. New York: 1983. V. 51; 53
Soul Clap Hands and Sing. New York: 1961. V. 47; 48; 54

MARSHALL, RICHARD
Robert Mapplethorpe. London: 1988. V. 53

MARSHALL, STEPHEN
A Vindication Of the Ansvver to the Hvmble Remonstrance... London: 1641. V. 49

MARSHALL, THOMAS
Lives of the Most Celebrated Actors and Actresses. London: 1847. V. 50

MARSHALL, THOMAS HAY
The History of Perth, from the Earliest Period to the Present Time. Perth: 1849. V. 54

MARSHALL, THOMAS MAITLAND
A History of the Western Boundary of the Lousiana Purchase, 1819-1841. Berkeley;: 1914. V. 48

MARSHALL, W.
Marshall's Views in London and Invirons. 1825. V. 54
Monsell Digby. London: 1880. V. 54

MARSHALL, W. E.
A Phrenologist Amongst the Todas, or the Study of a Primitive Tribe in South India... London: 1873. V. 52

MARSHALL, W. T.
Cactaceae. Pasadena: 1941. V. 47; 54

MARSHALL, WILLIAM
Memories of Four Fronts. London: 1929. V. 49
Minutes, Experiments, Observation, and General Remarks on Agriculture in the Southern Counties. London: 1799. V. 47; 53
On Planting and Rural Ornament. London: 1803. V. 49
On the Landed Property of England, and Elementary and Practical Treatise... London: 1804. V. 50
Planting and Ornamental Gardening. London: 1785. V. 47; 48; 49; 51; 53; 54
Planting and Rural Oranment. London: 1796. V. 47; 49
The Review and Abstract of the County Reports to the Board of Agriculture from Sevral Agricultural Departments of England. New York: 1968. V. 54
A Review of "The Landscape" (by Richard Payne Knight) also of "An Essay on the Picturesque" (by Uvedale Price); Together with Practical Remarks on Rural Ornaments. London: 1795. V. 52; 53
The Rural Economy of Glocestershire; Including Its Dairy, Together with the Dairy Management of North Wiltshire... Glocester: 1789. V. 47; 49
The Rural Economy of Gloucestershire, Including Its Dairy... London: 1796. V. 48; 50
The Rural Economy of the Midland Counties. London: 1790. V. 51
The Rural Economy of the Midland Counties. London: 1796. V. 47; 48; 49; 50; 51
The Rural Economy of the Southern Classics... London: 1798. V. 52
The Rural Economy of the West of England... London: 1796. V. 53
The Rural Economy of the West of England... Dublin: 1797. V. 51; 52; 53; 54
The Rural Economy of Yorkshire. London: 1788. V. 53; 54
The Rural Economy of Yorkshire Comprizing the Management of Landed Estates and the Present Practice of Husbandry in the Agricultural Districts. London: 1796. V. 48; 49

MARSHALL, WILLIAM E.
Travels Amongst the Todas or the Study of a Primitive Tribe in South India. London: 1873. V. 54

MARSHALL'S Chess 'Swindles'. New York: 1914. V. 50

MARSH-CALDWELL, ANNE
Mount Sorel; or, the Heiress of the De Veres. London: 1845. V. 47; 48; 54
Ravenscliffe. London: 1854. V. 48; 51; 54
Tales of the Woods and Fields. London: 1836. V. 50
Two Old Men's Tales. London: 1834. V. 50

MARSILIIS, HIPPOLYTUS DE
Mariana Hippolyti de Marsiliis... Venice: 1559. V. 52

MARSON, T. B.
The Scotch Shorthorn. Edinburgh: 1946. V. 54

MARSTON, ANNA LEE
Records of a California Family... San Diego: 1928. V. 54

MARSTON, EDWARD
By Meadow and Stream. Pleasant Memories of Pleasure Places. London: 1896. V. 47
Days in Clover by the Amateur Angler... London: 1892. V. 47
Frank's Ranche Or My Holiday in the Rockies. Boston: 1886. V. 47

MARSTON, JOHN
The Metamorphosis of Pigmalion's Image. Waltham St. Lawrence: 1926. V. 47; 50; 52; 53; 54
The Plays... London: 1934-8-9. V. 48; 53
The Works. London: 1887. V. 53

MARSTON, PHILIP BOURKE
Song-Tide, and other Poems. London: 1871. V. 49
Wind-Voices. London: 1863. V. 51

MARSTON, R. B.
By Meadown and Stream. London: 1896. V. 53

MARSTON, WESTLAND
Our Recent Actors: Being Recollections Critical and In Many Cases, Personal, of Late Distinguished Performers of Both Sexes. London: 1888. V. 54

MARTEAU, ROBERT
Stained-Glass Windows of Chagall, 1957-70. New York: 1973. V. 49

MARTELLI, C.
An Improved System of Fencing. London: 1819. V. 47

MARTELLI, VINCENZIO
Rime. Lettere. Florence: 1563. V. 53

MARTEMONT, C. MALORTI DE
The Theory of Field-Fortification. London: 1810. V. 53

MARTENS, G. F. VON
The Law of Nations, Founded on the Treaties and Customs of the Modern Nations of Europe, With the Science of National Law... London: 1803. V. 48
Summary of the Law of Nations, Founded on the Treaties and Customs of the Modern Nations of Europe. Philadelphia: 1795. V. 49

THE MARTIAL Achievements of Great Britain and Her Allies from 1799 to 1815. London: 1815. V. 53

A MARTIAL Medley - Fact and Fiction. London: 1931. V. 47; 51

MARTIAL D'AUVERGNE
Aresta Amorum, cum Erudita Benedicti Curtii Symphoriani... Paris: 1544. V. 52; 53
Aresta Amorum L.I. Lyon: 1546. V. 47

MARTIALIS, MARCUS VALERIUS
Epigrammata. Parma: 1480. V. 48; 54
Epigrammata. Venice: 1493. V. 47
Epigrammata. Venice: 1495. V. 48; 54
Epigrammaton Libros Omnes... Ingolstadt: 1611. V. 47
Select Epigrams of Martial. London: 1755. V. 47
Select Epigrams of Martial Englished. London: 1689. V. 52

MARTIN, ARCHER
The Hudson's Bay Company Land Tenures and the Occupation of Assinboia by Lord Seklkirk's Settlers... London: 1898. V. 53

MARTIN, BENJAMIN
Bibliotheca Philosphica: or, an Account of the Lives and Writings of the Most Eminent Philosophers and Mathematicians... London: 1763. V. 49
The Description and Use of Both the Globes. London: 1770. V. 48
An Essay on Visual Glasses (Vulgarly called Spectacles) Wherein Is Shewn from the Principles of Optics and the Nature of the Eye, and the Common Structure of Those Glasses is Contrary to the Rules of Art... London: 1760. V. 53
A New and Comprehensive System of Philology; or, A Treatise of the Literary Arts and Sciences... London: 1759. V. 48
New Elements of Optics; or, The Theory of the Aberrations, Dissipation and Colours of Light... London: 1759. V. 49
A Panegyrick On the Newtonian Philosophy, Shewing the Nature and Dignity of the Science... London: 1754. V. 49
The Philosophical Grammar; Being a View of the Present State of Experimental Physiology, or National Philosophy. London: 1778. V. 53
A Plain and Familiar Introduction to the Newtonian Experimental Philosophy. London: 1765. V. 53
A Plain and Familiar Introduction to the Newtonian Philosophy... London: 1754. V. 49
The Theory of Comets, Illustrated, in Four Parts. London: 1757. V. 49

MARTIN, C.
The Civil Costume of England. London: 1842. V. 53

MARTIN, CHARLES WYKEHAM
The History and Description of Leeds Castle, Kent. London: 1869. V. 47; 49; 53

MARTIN, CHESTER
Lord Selkirk's Work in Canada. Oxford: 1916. V. 50; 53

MARTIN, CORNEILLE
Les Genealogies et Anciennes Descentes, des Forestiers et Comtes de Flandre... Antwerp: 1598. V. 47

MARTIN, E. S.
Martin's System of Practical Penmanship Taught in 24 Lessons at His Writing and Book Keeping Academy. No. 182 Main Street, Worcester, Mass. Worcester: 1847 or 1848. V. 49

MARTIN, EDDIE OWENS
St. EOM in the Land of Pasaquan: the Life and Times and Art of Eddie Owens Martin. Winston-Salem: 1987. V. 54

MARTIN, EDWARD
E. M. A Long Imprisoned Malignant, His Humble Submission to the Covenant and Directory; With Some Reasons and Grounds of Use to Settle and Satisfie Tender Consciences. Presented in a Petition to the...Lords... London: 1647. V. 48

MARTIN, ERNEST
Project for the Construction of a Submarine Tunnel for a Railway Between England and France. Paris: 1869. V. 54

MARTIN, EUSTACE MEREDYTH
A Tour through India in Lord Canning's Time. London: 1881. V. 52

MARTIN, F. X.
Friar Nugent: a Study of Francis Lavalin Nugent, 1569-1635. Rome: 1962. V. 51
The History of Louisiana From the Earliest Period. New Orleans: 1827-29. V. 48

MARTIN, FRED
A Travel Book. San Francisco: 1976. V. 47; 51; 53

MARTIN, FREDERICK
The Life of John Clare. London: 1865. V. 50

MARTIN, G. R. R.
Dying of the Light. 1977. V. 47; 51
Dying of the Light. New York: 1977. V. 52
Songs the Dead Men Sing. Niles: 1983. V. 52; 53

Wild Cards - a Mosaic Novel. 1987-90. V. 51

MARTIN, GEOFFREY THORNDIKE
Corpus of Reliefs of the New Kingdom from Memphite Necropolis and Lowere Egypt. London: 1987. V. 49; 51
The Memphite Tomb of Horemheb, Commander-in Chief of Tut-ankhamun, I (only): The Reliefs, Inscriptions and Commentary. London: 1989. V. 51

MARTIN, GEORGE
The First Two Years of Kansas, or, Where and How the Missouri Bushwacker, the Missouri Train and Bank Robber...in the Name of Liberty, Were Sired and Reared. Topeka: 1907. V. 48

MARTIN, H. BRADLEY
Library of H. Bradley Martin. New York: 1989. V. 54
The Library of H. Bradley Martin. London: 1989-90. V. 49
The Library of H. Bradley Martin. New York: 1989-90. V. 48; 50; 51; 53

MARTIN, H. NEWELL
Physiological Papers. Baltimore: 1895. V. 49

MARTIN, HORACE
Pictorial Guide to the Mammoth Cave, Kentucky. New York: 1851. V. 53

MARTIN, HORACE T.
Castorologia, or the History and Traditions of the Canadian Beaver. London: 1892. V. 50; 51
Castorologia, or the History and Traditions of the Canadian Beaver. Montreal: 1892. V. 50; 54

MARTIN, J. L.
Circle: International Survey of Constructive Art. London: 1937. V. 51; 53

MARTIN, JAMES
The Influence of Tropical Climates on European Constitutions, Including Practical Observations on the Nature and Treatment of the Diseaes of Europeans on Their Return from Tropical Climates. London: 1856. V. 49; 51; 54
Memorandums (of an Escape by Australian Convicts 1791). Cambridge: 1937. V. 48
The Photographic Art: Its Theory and Practice Including Its Chemistry and Optics, Etc. London: 1859. V. 54

MARTIN, JAMES C.
Maps of Texas and the Southwest 1513-1900. Albuquerque: 1984. V. 50; 53

MARTIN, JAMES RANALD
Influence of Tropical Climates in Producing the Acute Endemic Diseases of Europeans... London: 1861. V. 54

MARTIN, JOHN
An Account of the Natives of the Tonga Islands, in the South Pacific Ocean. Edinburgh: 1827. V. 47
Bibliographical Catalogue of Privately Printed Books. 1854. V. 51
Bibliographical Catalogue of Privately Printed Books. London: 1854. V. 54
Bibliographical Catalogue of Privately Printed Books. London: 1865. V. 50
Biographical Catalogue of Privately Printed Books... London: 1854. V. 47
French Homonyms, or, a Collection of Words Similar in Sound, But Different in Meaning and Spelling. New York: 1807. V. 54
Mary Magdalen's Tears Wip't Off; or, the Voice of Peace to an Unquiet Conscience. London: 1676. V. 48; 49

MARTIN, JOHN RUPERT
The Illustration of the Heavenly Ladder of John Climacus. Princeton: 1954. V. 47

MARTIN, LADY
Our Maoris. London: 1884. V. 52

MARTIN, MARCUS J.
Wireless Transmission of Photographs. London: 1916. V. 53

MARTIN, MARTIN
A Late Voyage to St. Kilda, the Remotest of the Hebrides, or Western Isles of Scotland. London: 1698. V. 52

MARTIN, MARY EMMA
Her Debut. London: 1895. V. 50
Many a Year Ago. London: 1892. V. 54

MARTIN, MRS.
The Enchantress, or Where Shall I Find Her?. London: 1801. V. 54

MARTIN, P. J.
A Geological Memoir on a Part of Western Sussex; with Some Observations Upon Chalk Basins. London: 1828. V. 49

MARTIN, PETER
The Landsmen. Boston: 1952. V. 51

MARTIN, R. D.
Primate Origins and Evolution, a Phylogenetic Reconstruction. London: 1990. V. 50
Prosimian Biology. London: 1974. V. 50

MARTIN, ROBERT MONTGOMERY
China: Political, Commercial and Social... London: 1847. V. 50; 52
The Hudson's Bay Territories and Vancouver's Island, with an Exposition of the Chartered Rights, Conduct and Policy of the Honble Hudson's Bay Corporation. London: 1849. V. 48
The Indian Empire: History, Topography, Geology, Climate, Population, Chief Cities, and Provinces... London. V. 52
The Indian Empire: History, Topography, Geology, Climate, Population, Chief Cities, and Provinces... London: 1858-61. V. 50; 51
Ireland Before and After the Union. London: 1848. V. 53
Statistics of the Colonies of the British Empire in the West Indies, South America, North America, Asia, Austral-Asia, Africa and Europe. London: 1839. V. 48; 49; 52; 53; 54

MARTIN, SADIE
The Life and Professional Career of Emma Abbott (1850-1891). Minneapolis: 1891. V. 47; 52; 54

MARTIN, SAMUEL
An Essay Upon Plantership, Humbly Inscribed to His Excellency, George Thomas, Esq... Antigua: 1756. V. 50
An Essay Upon Plantership, Humbly Inscribed to His Excellency George Thomas, Esq. Antigua & London: 1765. V. 48
A Plan for Establishing and Disciplining a National Militia in Great Britain, Ireland and In all the British Dominions in America. London: 1745. V. 48

MARTIN, T. MOWER
Canada. London: 1907. V. 50

MARTIN, THEODORE
The Book of Ballads. Edinburgh & London: 1866. V. 48
Essays on the Drama. 1874. V. 49
The Life of His Royal Highness the Prince Consort. London: 1875-80. V. 47; 48; 49
The Life of the Prince Consort. London: 1879-78-80. V. 49; 53

MARTIN, THOMAS
The Circle of the Mechanical Arts... London: 1813. V. 54
The Conveyancers' Recital-Book: with Explanatory Introduction and Notes. London: 1834. V. 53
Historica Descriptio Complectens Vitam Guilielmi Wicami. Oxford: 1690. V. 50

MARTIN, VICTORIA CLAFLIN WOODHULL
Congressional Reports on Woman Suffrage. The Majority and Minority Repots of the Judiciary Committee of the House of Representatives on the Woodhull Memorial. New York: 1871. V. 53

MARTIN, W.
Outlines of an Attempt to Establish Knowledge of Extraneous Fossils on Scientific Principles. 1809. V. 51

MARTIN, W. A. P.
A Cycle of Cathay or China, South and North. London: 1896. V. 50

MARTIN, W. K.
The Concise British Flora in Colour. London. V. 53
The Concise British Flora in Colour. London: 1965. V. 48
Flora of Devon. London: 1939. V. 50; 51

MARTIN, WILLIAM
Diamond Cut Diamond. Newcastle upon Tyne: 1836. V. 50

MARTIN, WILLIAM MAXWELL
Lyrics and Sketches. Nashville: 1861. V. 53

MARTINDALE, ANDREW
Simone Martini. Oxford: 1988. V. 50; 54

MARTINDALE, THOMAS
Hunting in the Upper Yukon. Philadelphia: 1913. V. 53

MARTIN DU GARD, ROGER
The Postman. New York: 1955. V. 54

MARTINE, GEORGE
Essays Medical and Philosophical. London: 1740. V. 47; 49
Essays on the Construction and Graduation of Thermometers and on the Heating and Cooling of Bodies. Edinburgh: 1792. V. 54
Reliquae Divi Andreae, or the State of the Venerable and Primital See of St. Andrews... St. Andrews: 1797. V. 47

MARTINEAU, HARRIET
Autobiography. Boston: 1877. V. 50; 53
Autobiography. London: 1877. V. 50
Biographical Sketches. London: 1869. V. 50; 53
Complete Guide to the English Lakes. Windermere. V. 52
A Complete Guide to the English Lakes. Windermere: 1855. V. 50
A Complete Guide to the English Lakes. Windermere: 1855. V. 50; 51
A Complete Guide to the English Lakes... London: 1858. V. 50; 52
A Complete Guide to the English Lakes... London: 1866. V. 50
A Complete Guide to the Lake District of England. Windermere: 1885. V. 54
Dawn Island. Manchester: 1845.. V. 50
Deerbrook. London: 1839. V. 53
Deerbrook: a Novel. New York: 1839. V. 47; 49; 54
Eastern Life, Past and Present. London: 1848. V. 50; 51
England and Her Soldiers. London: 1859. V. 50
The Factory Controversy: a Warning Against Meddling Legislation. Manchester: 1855. V. 50
Feats on the Fiord: a Tale of Norway. (with) The Billow and the Rock. London: 1846. V. 50
Feats on the Fjord. London: 1899. V. 49
Guide to Windermere, with Tours to the Neighbouring Lakes and Other Interesting Places... Windermere: 1856. V. 52
The Hampdens: an Historiette. London: 1880. V. 50
Health, Husbandry and Handicraft. London: 1861. V. 50
The History of England During the Thirty Years' Peace: 1816-1846. London: 1849-50. V. 50
The History of England During the Thirty Years' Peace: 1816-1846. London: 1855. V. 50
Household Education. Philadelphia: 1849. V. 53
How to Observe. Morals and Manners. London: 1838. V. 52; 52
Illustrations of Political Economy. Boston: 1832. V. 54
Illustrations of Political Economy. London: 1832-34. V. 48; 50
Illustrations of Political Economy. London: 1845. V. 50
Illustrations of Political Economy. No. III. Brooke and Brooke Farm. A Tale. Boston: 1832. V. 54
Illustrations of Taxation. London: 1834. V. 50
Life in the Sick-Room. London: 1844. V. 50
A Manchester Strike. London: 1832. V. 47
The Martyr Age in the United States of America. New York: 1838. V. 50
Miscellanies. Boston: 1836. V. 50; 51; 53
Poor Laws and Paupers Illustrated. London: 1833-34. V. 50
Retrospect of Western Travel. London: 1838. V. 53; 54
Retrospect of Western Travel. New York: 1838. V. 50; 52; 53
The Scholars of Arneside. London: 1834. V. 47
Sketches from Life. London: 1856. V. 50; 52
Society in America. London: 1837. V. 50; 53
Society in America. New York: 1837. V. 49; 53; 54
Society in America. Paris: 1837. V. 49; 53
Suggestions Towards the Future Government of India. London: 1858. V. 49; 52
Traditions of Palestine. London: 1830. V. 50
Voyage au Etats-Unis, Ou Tableau de la Societe Americaine... Paris: 1839. V. 53

MARTINEAU, JOHN
The Life and Correspondence of Rt. Hon. Sir Henry Bartle Frere. London: 1895. V. 47

MARTINET, JOHANNES FLORENTIUS
The Catechism of Nature, for the Use of Children. Boston: 1793. V. 52
The Catechism of Nature for the Use of Children. Boston: 1795. V. 53
The Catechism of Nature, for the Use of Children. Boston: 1820. V. 53

MARTINEZ, JOSE LONGINOS
Journal of Jose Longinos Martinez Notes and Observations of the Naturalist of the Botanical Expedition in Old and New California and the South Coast 1791-1792. San Francisco: 1961. V. 48; 54

MARTINEZ CARO, RAMON
Verdadera Idea da la Primera Campana de Tejas. Mexico: 1837. V. 49

MARTINEZ DE ARAUJO, JUAN
Manual de Los Santos Sacramentos en el Idioma de Michuacan... Mexico: 1690. V. 47

MARTINI, PEDRO
(Hebrew title) That is a the Key of of the Holy Tongue. Amsterdam: 1650. V. 47

MARTINIERE, PIERRE MARTIN DE LA
A New Voyage to the North... London: 1706. V. 51

MARTIN'S Annals of Crime; or, New Newgate Calendar...Comprehending a history of the Most Notorious Murderers...Highwaymen, Pirates, Burglars, Pickpockets, Adulterers, Ravishers, Decoyers, Incendiaries, Poachers, Swindlers, etc. London: 1873-38. V. 52

MARTIUS, CARL FRIEDRICH PHILLIP VON
Historia Naturalis Palmarum... Leipzig: 1823-53. V. 49

THE MARTRIMONIAL Sketch Book; a Mirror for the Million. London: 1840?. V. 47

MARTUSCELLI, PASQUALE
Trattato di Calligrafia Analiticamente Esposto... Naples: 1840. V. 50; 53

MARTYN, BENJAMIN
An Impartial Enquiry Into the State and Utility of the Province of Georgia. London: 1741. V. 50

MARTYN, EDWARD
Mogante the lesser. London: 1890. V. 51

MARTYN, JOHN
The First Lecture of a Course of Botany; Being an Introduction to the Rest. London: 1729. V. 48

MARTYN, RICHARD
A Modest Representation of the Past and Present State of Great Britain, Occasion'd by the Late Change in the Administration. London: 1711. V. 53

MARTYN, THOMAS
A Chronological Series of Engravers From the Invention of the Art to the Beginning of the Present Century. Cambridge: 1770. V. 50
The English Connoisseur... London: 1766. V. 47
The English Entomologist Exhibiting all the Coleopterous Insects Found in England. London: 1792. V. 54
Flora Rustica; Exhibting Figures on Such Plants as Are Either Useful or Injurious in Husbandry. London: 1792-94. V. 53; 54
The Language of Botany: Being a Dictionary of the Terms Made Use of... London: 1793. V. 53
Letters on the Elements of Botany... London: 1796. V. 48; 51
Thirty-Eight Plates, with Explanations... London: 1788. V. 49; 51
Thirty-Eight Plates with Explanations... London: 1794. V. 54
The Universal Conchologist, Exhibiting the Figure of Very Known Shell, Accurately Drawn and Painted After Nature. London: 1784-89. V. 47

MARTYN, W. F.
A New Dictionary of Natural History. London: 1785. V. 54

MARTYN, WILLIAM
The Historie and Lives of the Kings of England. London: 1615. V. 47

MARTYROLOGIUM
Viola Sanctorum. Augsburg: 1482. V. 47; 49
Viola Sanctorum. Strassburg: 1487. V. 47; 49

A MARVEL Among Cities! Spokane Falls a Western Wonder Whose Whole History is Comprised Within Eight Years. Saint Paul: 1888. V. 52

MARVELL, ANDREW
The Complete Works in Verse and Prose. London: 1872-75. V. 54
Miscellaneous Poems. London: 1681. V. 47; 48; 52
Miscellaneous Poems. London: 1923. V. 47; 52
The Poems and Letters. Oxford: 1952. V. 53
The Rehearsal Transpos'd (and) The Rehearsal Transpos'd the Second Part. London: 1672/73. V. 48; 53
A Short Historical Essay Touching General Councils, Creeds and Impositions in Matters of Religion. London: 1680. V. 50
Three Poems. Los Angeles: 1932. V. 54

MARVELOUS Adventures and Rare Conceits of Master Tyll Owlglass. London: 1860. V. 53

THE MARVELOUS Musical Prodigy, Blind Tom, the Negro Boy Pianist....Anecdotes, songs, Sketches of the Life, Testimonials of Musicians and Savans...of Blind Tom. Baltimore: 1876?. V. 51

MARVIN, CHARLES
The Petroleum Question. London: 1887. V. 54
Reconnoitring Central Asia: Pioneering Adventures in the Region Lying Between Russia and India. London: 1886. V. 54
The Russians at the Gates of Herat. London: 1885. V. 51

MARVIN, EDWIN D.
The Fifth Regiment, Connecticut Volunteers. A History. Hartford: 1889. V. 48; 49

MARWICK, JAMES D.
The River Clyde and the Harbour of Glasgow. Glasgow: 1898. V. 49; 54

MARWIL, JOHN
Frederic Manning - an Unfinished Life. Durham: 1988. V. 53

MARX, CARL FRIEDRICH HEINRICH
On the Decrease of Disease Effected by the Progress of Civilization. London: 1844. V. 54

MARX, GROUCHO
Beds. 1930. V. 50
Many Happy Returns...Tax Guide. New York: 1942. V. 53

MARX, KARL
Capital. New York: 1889. V. 53
Das Kapital. Hamburg: 1890-85. V. 52
Manifesto of the Communist Party. New York: 1898. V. 53

MARY, PRINCESS
Princess Mary's Gift Book. London: 1915. V. 54

MARY Putnam Jacobi, M.D. A Pathfinder in Medicine with Selections from Her Writings and a Complete Bibliography. New York: 1925. V. 47

MARY, QUEEN OF SCOTS
L'Innocence de la Tresillvstre Tres-Chasate, et Debonnaire Princesse, Madame Marie Royne d'escosse... 1572. V. 48

MARY Roseberry; or, The Pretty Village Girl. 1841. V. 47

MARY, the Maid of the Inn; an Affecting Narrative; Detailing Her Unfortunate and Ill requited Attachment; Her Singular Courage, and teh Miraculous Manner in Which She Becomes the Instrument in the Discovery of a Murder. London: 1824. V. 47

MARYAN, WILLIAM
A Treatise Explaining the Impossibility of the Disease Termed Hydrophobia: Being caused by the Bite of Any Rabid Animal. London: 1809. V. 47

MARYLAND
The Report of and Testimony Taken Before the Joint Committee of the Senate and House of Delegates of Maryland To Which was Referred the Memorials of John B. Morris, Reverdy Johnson and Ohters... Annapolis: 1836. V. 52

MARYLAND. SENATE
Journal of the Proceedings of Senate of Maryland, Jan. Session, 1865. Annapolis: 1865. V. 52

MARY'S Scrapbook. London: 1838. V. 48

MARY THEODORE, SISTER
Heralds of Christ the King: Missionary Record of the North Pacific: 1837-1878. New York: 1939. V. 52

MARY THERESA LOUISA, PRINCESS DE LAMBALLE
Secret Memoirs of the Royal Family of France, During the Revolution... London: 1826. V. 49

MARZIALS, THEO
Pan Pipes, A Book of Old Songs. London: 1883. V. 50

MARZIO, PETER
The Democratic Art: Chromolithography 1840-1900. Boston: 1979. V. 53

MAS, ALPHONSE
Le Verger. Paris: 1873. V. 48

MASCAL, JOHN
The Government of Cattle. London: 1633. V. 47

MASCALL, L.
A Booke of the Arte and Manner How to Plant and Graffe. London: 1592. V. 52

MASCARDI, AUGUSTIN
An Historical Relation of the Conspiracy of John Lewis Count de Fieschi, Against the City and Republic of Genova, in the Year 1547. London: 1693. V. 47; 53

MASCOV, JOHN JACOB
The History of the Ancient Germans. London and Westminster: 1737-38. V. 48; 49

MASEFIELD, JOHN
The Battle of the Somme. London: 1919. V. 52; 53
The Box of Delights, or, When the Wolves Were Running. London: 1935. V. 50
The Country Scene. London: 1937. V. 47; 51; 54
Easter, a Play for Singers. New York: 1929. V. 53
The Faithful - a Tragedy in Three Acts. London: 1915. V. 52
John M. Synge: a Few Personal Recollections and Biographical Notes. Churchtown, Dundrum: 1915. V. 52; 54
Martin Hyde. The Duke's Messenger. London: 1910. V. 48
Midsummer Night and Other Tales in Verse. London: 1928. V. 52
Minnie Maylow's Story and Other Tales and Scenes. New York: 1931. V. 47
Philip the King. London: 1927. V. 54
Poems by... New York: 1925. V. 51
Recent Prose. London: 1924. V. 48
Reynard the Fox or the Ghost Heath Run. London: 1921. V. 47; 49
Right Royal. London: 1920. V. 53
Salt-Water Ballads. 1902. V. 49
Salt-Water Ballads. London: 1902. V. 53; 54
The Widow in the Bye Street. London: 1912. V. 53

MASENIUS, JACOB
Sarcotis, et Caroli V. Imp. Panegyris. Londini: 1771. V. 49; 54

MASEREEL, FRANS
Danse Macabre. New York: 1942. V. 48
My Book of Hours - 167 Designs Engraved on Wood. London: 1922. V. 49

MASERES, FRANCIS
Considerations on the Expediency of Admitting Representatives from the American Colonies into the English House of Commons. London: 1770. V. 48
Elements of Plane Trigonometry. London: 1760. V. 49
Occasional Essays on Various Subjects, Chiefly Political and Historical... London: 1809. V. 52
Select Tracts Relating to the Civil Wars in England in the Reign of Charles the First... London: 1815. V. 51
Tracts on the Resolution of Affected Algebraick Equations by Dr. Halley's, Mr. Raphson's and Sir Isaac Newton's methods of Approximation. London: 1800. V. 50

MASI, GIROLAMO
Teoria e Pratica di Architettura Civile. Rome: 1788. V. 49; 53

THE MASK: a Quarterly Illustrated Journal of the Art of the Theatre. Florence: 1909-10/11-12. V. 51

THE MASK: an Illustrated Quarterly of the Art of the Theatre. Florence: 1924-Dec. 1929. V. 53

MASKELL, WILLIAM
Monumenta Ritualia Ecclesiae Anglicanae: the Occasional Offices of the Church of England According to the Old Use of Salisbury, the Prymer in English, and Other Prayers and Forms. London: 1882. V. 50

MASKELYNE, NEVILLE
The Nautical Almanac and Astronomical Ephemeris for the Year 1767. London: 1766. V. 48
The Nautical Almanac and Astronomical Ephemeris for the Year 1771. London: 1769. V. 48
Tables Requisite to Be Used with the Nautical Ephemeris, for Finding the Latitude and Longitude at Sea. London: 1802. V. 50

MASLEN, T. J.
The Friend of Australia; or, a Plan for Exploring the Interior and for Carrying on a Survey of the Whole Continent of Australia. London: 1836. V. 52

MASON, A. J.
Poetical Essays. London: 1822. V. 48; 54

MASON, ALFRED EDWARD WOODLEY
At the Villa Rose. London: 1910. V. 48
Konigsmark. 1938. V. 54
A Romance of Wastdale. London: 1895. V. 49
The Witness for the Defence. London: 1911. V. 48; 52

MASON, AMELIA GERE
The Women of the French Salons. New York: 1891. V. 48

MASON AND DIXON LINE RESURVEY COMMISSION
Report on the Resurvey of the Maryland-Pennsylvania Boundary Part of the Mason and Dixon Line. Harrisburg: 1909. V. 54

MASON, BERNARD
Clock and Watchmaking in Colchester, England. London: 1969. V. 53

MASON, BOBBIE ANN
The Girl Sleuth. Old Westbury: 1975. V. 52; 53
Love Life. New York: 1989. V. 53
Nabokov's Garden. Ann Arbor: 1974. V. 48; 52
Shiloh and Other Stories. New York: 1982. V. 53
With Jazz. Monterey: 1994. V. 52; 53; 54

MASON, E.
Lincoln Campaign Songster. For the Use of Clubs. Philadelphia: 1864. V. 47; 50

MASON, F.
Burmah, Its People and Natural Productions...with Systematic Catalogues of the Known Mammals, Birds, Fish, Reptiles, Insects, Mollusks, Crustaceans... Rangoon: 1860. V. 48

MASON, G. FINCH
Flowers of the Hunt. London: 1889. V. 47
Sporting Sketches. Cambridge: 1882. V. 47

MASON, G. H.
Zululand. A Mission Tour in South Africa. London: 1862. V. 47

MASON, GEORGE
Ode On the Loss of the Steamship 'Pacific' November 4th 1875. Nanaimo: 1875. V. 50
Prize Poem. Lo! The Poor Indian!... Read Before the Mechanics' Literary Institute, Victoria, Thursday, October 28, 1875. Victoria: 1875. V. 49; 51
Supplement to Johnson's English Dictionary. London: 1801. V. 50
A Supplement to Johnson's English Dictionary. New York: 1803. V. 50; 54

MASON, GEORGE HENRY
The Costumes of China. (with) The Punishments of China. London: 1800. V. 49
The Punishments of China. London: 1804. V. 50

MASON, HENRY
The New Art of Lying, Covered by Jesuits Under the Vaile of Equivocation; Discovered and Disproved. London: 1634. V. 47

MASON, HENRY JOSEPH MONCK
Reasons and Authorities and Facts Afforded by the History of the Irish Society, Respecting the Dusty of Employing the Irish Language, as a More General Medium for Conveying Scriptural Instruction to the Native Peasantry of Ireland. Dublin: 1835. V. 52

MASON, J. A.
A Treatise on the Climate and Meteorolgy of Madeira... London: 1850. V. 48; 49; 52

MASON, J. ALDEN
Archaeology of Santa Marta Colombia: the Tairona Culture. Chicago: 1933-39. V. 50
Archaeology of Santa Marta Colombia; The Tairona Culture, Part I-II: 2. Chicago: 1931-39. V. 52

MASON, JAMES
The Public Life and Diplomatic Correspondence of James M. Mason with Some Personal History by His Daughter. Roanoke: 1903. V. 47

MASON, JESSE D.
History of Santa Barbara County, California, with Illustrations and Biographical Sketches of its Prominent Men and Pioneers. Oakland: 1883. V. 49

MASON, JOHN
An Essay on Elocution, or Pronunciation. London: 1751. V. 52
An Excellent Tragedy of Muleasses the Turke, and Borgias Governour of Florence. London: 1632. V. 50
Five Papers Hand Made at the Twelve by Eight Mill. Leicester: 1954. V. 52
More Papers Hand Made. London: 1966. V. 50
More Papers Hand Made. New York: 1966. V. 48
More Papers Hand Made. Leicester: 1967. V. 48; 50; 53
Paper Making as an Artistic Craft. London: 1959. V. 53
Paper Making as an Artistic Craft. Leicester: 1963. V. 47; 48; 49; 50; 52
Papermaking: Notes. Leicester: 1959. V. 52
Select Remains of the Reverend John Mason... Cork: 1755. V. 53
Some Papers Hand Made by John Mason. London: 1959. V. 52
The Student and Pastor, or Directions How to Attain to Eminence and Usefulness In those Respective Characters. Exeter: 1794. V. 52
Twelve Papers by John Mason. London: 1959. V. 48

MASON, MONCK
Account of the Late Aeronatucial Expedition from London to Weilburg, Accomplished by Robert Hollond, Esq., Monck Mason, Esq., and Charles Green, Aeronaut. London: 1836. V. 48

MASON, OTIS TUFTON
Aboriginal American Basketry: Studies in a Textile Art Without Machinery. Washington: 1904. V. 49
Basket-Work of the North American Aborigines. Washington: 1890. V. 54
Indian Basketry: Studies in a Textile Art Without Machinery... New York: 1904. V. 47
Primitive Travel and Transportation. Washington: 1896. V. 54

MASON, RICHARD
The Gentleman's New Pocket Companion, Comprising a General Description of the Noble and Useful Animal the Horse. Petersburg: 1811. V. 47
Gentleman's New Pocket Farrier, Comprising a General Description of the Noble and Useful Animal the Horse... Richmond: 1830. V. 48
A Manuell of the Arch-Confraternitie of the Cord of the Passion, Instituted in the Seraphicall Order of s. Francis. Doway: 1654. V. 48; 50

MASON, RICHARD LEE
Narrative of Richard Lee Mason in the Pioneer West, 1819. New York: 1915. V. 50

MASON, ROSEL H.
Military Essays and Recollections. Volume IV. Chicago: 1907. V. 47

MASON, STUART
Bibliography of Oscar Wilde. London: 1914. V. 50
A Bibliography of the Poems of Oscar Wilde. New York: 1908. V. 51; 53

MASON, WILLIAM
An Archaeological Epistle to...Jeremiah Milles, D.D... London: 1782. V. 49
Caractacus, a Dramatic Poem... London: 1759. V. 48
The English Garden: a Poem. London: 1772/77/79/81. V. 48
The English Garden: a Poem. York: 1777-81. V. 53
The English Garden: a Poem. Dublin: 1782. V. 49; 52
The English Garden: a Poem. York: 1783. V. 47; 54
The English Garden: a Poem. London: 1803. V. 49
Essays, Historical and Critical on English Church Music. York: 1795. V. 47
An Heroic Epistle to Sir William Chambers, Knight...(with) An Heroic Postscript to the Public, Occasioned by Their Favourable Reception of a Late Heroic Epistle to Sir William Chambers. London: 1773/74. V. 54
Isis. An Elegy. London: 1749. V. 48
Musaeus: a Monody to the Memory of Mr. Pope. London: 1747. V. 49; 54
Ode to Mr. Pinchbeck, Upon His Newly Invented Patent Candle-Snuffers. London: 1776. V. 48; 49
Odes. Cambridge: 1756. V. 48
Poems. London: 1764. V. 52
Poems. Glasgow: 1774. V. 49
Poems. York: 1774. V. 47; 50; 54

MASON, WILLIAM SHAW
A Statistical Account of Parochial Survey of Ireland, Drawn Up from the Communications of the Clery. 1814-16. V. 54

MASPERO, G.
History of Egypt, Chaldea, Syria, Babylonia and Assyria. London: 1903. V. 54
La Trouvaille de Deir-El-Bahari. Le Caire: 1881. V. 49

A MASQUE of Poets. Boston: 1878. V. 47; 49; 51; 52; 54

MASSACHUSETTS ASSN. OPPOSED...EXTENSION OF SUFFRAGE TO WOMEN
First Annual Report of te Massachusetts Association Opposed to the Extension of Suffrage to Women. 1896. V. 48

MASSACHUSETTS. BOARD OF HEALTH
First Annual Report of the State Board of Health, Lunacy, and Charity of Massachusetts, 1879. A Supplement Containing the Reports and Papers on Public Health. Boston: 1880. V. 51
Ninth (and Tenth) Annual Reports of the State Board of Health of Massachusetts. Boston: 1878/79. V. 51

MASSACHUSETTS. COLONY
The Charter Granted by their Majesties King William and Queen Mary to the Inhabitants of the Province of Massachusetts-Bay, in New England. Boston: 1726. V. 50

MASSACHUSETTS. CONSTITUTION
The Constitution of the State of Massachusetts, and That of the United States; The Declaration of Independence, with President Washington's Farewell Address. Brookfield: 1807. V. 48

MASSACHUSETTS. CONSTITUTIONAL CONVENTION
Journal of Debates and Proceedings in the Convention of Delegates, Chosen to Revise the Constitution of Massachusetts, Begun and Holden at Boston, November 15, 1820 and Continued by Adjournment to January 9, 1821. Boston: 1853. V. 48
Journal of the Constitutional Convention of the Commonwealth of Massachusetts, Begun and Held in Boston, on the Fourth Day of May, 1853. Boston: 1853. V. 50

MASSACHUSETTS GENERAL HOSPITAL
Neurological Clinic Reports: Cases Presented at Staff Meetings in the Neurological Service Massachusetts General Hospital 1933-1944. 1933-44. V. 47
Report of the Board of Trustees of the Massachusetts General Hospital Presented to the Corporation at Their Annual Meeting, January 26, 1848. Boston: 1848. V. 53

MASSACHUSETTS HISTORICAL SOCIETY
Proceedings of a Special Meeting of the Massachusetts Historical Society. Boston: 1874. V. 51

MASSACHUSETTS HORTICULTURAL SOCIETY
Catalogue of the Library of the Massachusetts Horticultural Society. Mansfield: 1994. V. 52; 53; 54
Catalogue of the Library of the Massachusetts Horticultural Society. Mansfield: 1995. V. 54

MASSACHUSETTS. LAWS, STATUTES, ETC.
An Act for Enquiring Into the Rateable Estates Within This Commonwealth. Boston: 1792. V. 51
Laws of the Commonwealth of Massachusetts. Boston: 1796-1802. V. 53

MASSACHUSETTS. LEGISLATURE
An Investigation Into Freemasonry by a Joint Committee of the Legislature of Massachusetts.... Boston: 1834. V. 48

MASSACHUSETTS MEDICAL SOCIETY
Acts of Incoporation and Acts Regulating the Practice of Physic and Surgery with the By-Laws and Orders of the Massachusetts Medical Society. Boston: 1826. V. 47; 48; 50; 51
Acts of Incorporation and Acts Regulating the Practice of Physic and Surgery, With the By-Laws and Orders. Boston: 1832. V. 48
A Report on Spasmodic Cholera, Prepared by a Committee Under the Direction of the Counsellors of the Massachusetts Medical Society. Boston: 1832. V. 51; 52

MASSACHUSETTS PEACE SOCIETY
Constitution of the Massachusetts Peace Society. Boston;: 1815. V. 50

MASSACHUSETTS SOCIETY FOR PROMOTING AGRICULTURE
Laws and Regulations of the Massachusetts Society for Promoting Agriculture. Boston: 1793. V. 51
Rules and Regulations of the Massachusetts Society for Promoting Agriculture... Boston: 1796. V. 51

MASSACHUSETTS. STATE ANTI-TEXAS COMMITTEE
Report of the Massachusetts Committee to Prevent the Admission of Texas as a Slave State. Boston: 1846. V. 48; 49

MASSACHUSETTS. STATE TEXAS COMMITTEE
How to Settle the Texas Question. Boston: 1845. V. 48

THE MASSACRE of Lieutenant Grattan and His Command by Indians. Glendale: 1983. V. 52

MASSARI, FRANCESCO
In Nonum Plini de Naturali Historia Librum Castigationes et Annotations. Basel: 1537. V. 47; 50; 53

MASSE, GERTRUDE C.
Walter Crane: a Bibliography of First Editions. 1923. V. 51

MASSEE, G.
British Fungus-Flora, A Classified Text-Book of Mycology. London: 1892-95. V. 49

MASSEY, GERALD
Caraigcrook Castle. London: 1856. V. 51

MASSEY, LINTON R.
Man Working 1919-1961. William Faulkner. A Catalogue of the William Faulkner Collections at the University of Virginia. Charlottesville: 1968. V. 49; 53

MASSEY, W. T.
How Jerusalem Was Won. London: 1919. V. 47

MASSEY, WILLIAM
The Origin and Progress of Letters. London: 1763. V. 48

MASSIE, J. C.
A Treatise on the Eclectic Southern Practice of Medicine. Philadelphia: 1854. V. 51

MASSIE, JAMES W.
America: the Origin of Her Present Conflict; Her Prospect for the Slave and Her Claim for Anti-Slavery Sympathy... London: 1864. V. 50; 53

MASSIE, SUZANNE
The Living Mirror: 5 Young Poets from Leningrad. Garden City: 1972. V. 54

MASSILLON, JEAN B.
Sermons "On the Duties of the Great". Dublin: 1770. V. 54

MASSINGER, PHILIP
The Dramatick Works of Philip Massinger Complete. London: 1779. V. 51
The Duke of Millaine. London: 1638. V. 47
The Excellent Comedy, Called the Old Law... London: 1656. V. 47
The Plays. London: 1805. V. 49; 50

MASSINGHAM, H. J.
Country Relics. Cambridge: 1939. V. 51

MASSMANN, ROBERT E.
A Dard Hunter Keepsake. New Britain: 1971. V. 50
Master Papermakers: Dard Hunter and Harrison Elliott. New Britain: 1980. V. 49

MASSON, ANDRE
Carnet de Croquis. Paris: 1950. V. 47

MASSON, CHARLES
Narrative of Various Journeys in Balochistan, Afghanistan and the Panjab... 1842. V. 54

MASSON, CHARLES FRANCOIS PHILIBERT
Secret Memoirs of the Court of Petersburg... London: 1800. V. 49

MASSON, DAVID
British Novelists and their Styles. Boston: 1859. V. 51; 54

MASSON, ELSIE R.
An Untamed Territory, the Northern Territory of Australia. London: 1915. V. 52

MASSON, F.
Stapellae Novae: or, a Collection of Several New Species of That Genus Discovered in the Interior Parts of Africa. London: 1796. V. 49

MASSON, FREDERIC
Cavaliers De Napoleon. 1895. V. 50
Napoleon at Home - the Daily Life of the Emperor at the Tuileries. London: 1894. V. 50

MASSON, GEORGINA
Italian Gardens. London: 1961. V. 53
Italian Gardens. New York: 1961. V. 47
Italian Villas and Palaces. London: 1959. V. 47; 49; 53

MASSON, IRVINE
The Mainz Psalters and Canon Missae 1457-1459. London: 1954. V. 48

MASSY, RICHARD TUTHILL
Analytical Ethnology: the Mixed Tribes in Great Britain and Ireland Examined, and the Political, Physical and Metaphysical Blunderings on the Celt and the Saxon Exposed. London: 1855. V. 50

MAST, ISAAC
The Gun, Rod and Saddle: or, Nine Months in California. Philadelphia: 1875. V. 49

MAST, P. P., & CO., SPRINGFIELD, OHIO
Grain Drills and Cider Mills. Buffalo: 1880's-90's?. V. 52

THE MASTABA of Mereuka. Parts I-II. Chicago: 1938. V. 49; 51

THE MASTER Passion Or, the History of Frederick Beaumont. London: 1808. V. 49

MASTER Peter Patelan. A Fifteenth Century Farce.. Iowa City: 1975. V. 54

MASTER Richard's Bestiary of Love and Response. Northampton 1985. V. 54

MASTER Speakers Letter Ordered by the Honorable House of Commons, to Be Sent to the High Sheriffe and Gentry of Yorkshire. London: 1641. V. 50

MASTEROFF, JOE
Cabaret. New York: 1967. V. 50

THE MASTERPIECES of the Centennial International Exhibiton. Philadelphia: 1875. V. 52

MASTERS, EDGAR LEE
Althea. 1907. V. 50
A Book of Verses. Chicago: 1898. V. 49
Gettysburg - Manila - Acoma. New York: 1930. V. 49; 53
Godbey: A Dramatic Poem. New York: 1931. V. 50
The Great Valley. New York: 1916. V. 54
Lincoln the Man. New York: 1931. V. 51; 54
Maximillan: a Play in Five Acts. Boston: 1902. V. 54
Mirage. New York: 1924. V. 50
Mitch Miller. New York: 1920. V. 53; 54
The New Spoon River. New York: 1924. V. 49; 50
The New Star Chamber and Other Essays. Chicago: 1904. V. 53
Poems of People. New York: 1936. V. 49
The Serpent in the Wilderness. New York: 1933. V. 50
Skeeters Kirby. New York: 1923. V. 50
Spoon River Anthology. New York: 1915. V. 47; 49; 50; 51; 53; 54
Spoon River Anthology. New York: 1919. V. 54
Spoon River Anthology. New York: 1942. V. 50; 52; 53; 54
Toward the Gulf. New York: 1918. V. 49
Whitman. New York: 1937. V. 49

MASTERS, JAMES E.
Shaftesbury: the Shaston of Thomas Hardy. Shaftesbury: 1932. V. 50; 52

MASTERS, M. T.
Vegetable Teratology, an Account of the Principal Deviations from the Usual Construction of Plants. London: 1869. V. 49; 50; 54

MASTERS, MARTIN
Progress of Love. Boston: 1808. V. 54

MASTERS, W.
Hortus Duroverni; or, a Tabular and Descriptive Catalogue of Perennial Flower Roots, Hardy Trees and Shrubs, Green-House and Hot-House Plants, Fruit Trees, Kitchen Garden and Flower Seeds, &c.... London: 1831. V. 47

MASTERSON, THOMAS
Masterson's Arithmetick, Shewing the Ingenious Inventions and Figurative Operations, to Calculate the True Solution or Answer of Arithmeticall Questions... London: 1634. V. 49; 52

MASTERSON, WILLIAM
The Authentic Confessions of William Masterson, the Cruel Murderer of His Father and Mother. Richmond: 1854. V. 48; 52; 53

MASTIN, J.
Through the Sun in an Airship. 1909. V. 47; 51

MASUCCIO
The Novellino of Masuccio. London: 1895. V. 52; 53; 54

MASUDA, H.
Coastal Fishes of Southern Japan. Tokyo: 1975. V. 50; 51
The Fishes of the Japanese Archipelago. Tokyo: 1984. V. 52

MASURY, JOHN W.
Automobile Color Schemes. New York & Chicago;: 1905. V. 54
A Popular Treatise on House-Painting: Plain and Decorative. New York: 1868. V. 48

MASURY, JOHN W., & SON
Superfine Coach Colors for Coach, Carriage and Car. New York & Chicago: 1893. V. 48

THE MATABELE GOLD REEFS & ESTATES COMPANY LIMITED Report and Statements of the Accounts for the Year Ending 31st December, 1897. London: 1898. V. 47

MATAGORDA. COUNTY CLERK'S OFFICE
Constitution of the Proprietors of the Town of Matagorda. V. 53

MATEAUX, C. L.
Old Proverbs with New Pictures. London: 1890. V. 47

THE MATERNAL Physician; a Treatise on the Nuture and Management of Infants from the Birth Until Two Years Old. New York: 1811. V. 53; 54

MATHER, COTTON
Essays to Do Good, Addressed to All Christians, Whether in Public or Private Capacities. Johnstown: 1815. V. 52
Essays To Do Good: Addressed to All Christians, Whether In Public or Private Capacities. London: 1816. V. 49
Magnalia Christi Americana; or, the Ecclesiastical History of New England From its First Planting in the Year 1620, Unto the Year of Our Lord 1698. London: 1702. V. 50
Memoirs of the Life of the Late Reverend Increase Mather, D. D. Who Died August 23, 1723. London: 1725. V. 49
Psalterium Americanum. Boston: 1718. V. 49; 52
Wonders of the Invisible World... Bostun (sic): 1693. V. 52
The Wonders of the Invisible World: Being an Account of the Tryals of Several Witches Lately Executed in New England... London: 1862. V. 47

MATHER, GEORGE MARSHALL
The Elements of Drawing... Edinburgh: 1830. V. 47

MATHER, INCREASE
A Further Account of the Tryals of the New-England Witches... London: 1693. V. 53
The Order of the Gospel, Professed and practised by the Churches of Christ, in New England, Justified by the Scripture, and by the Writings of Many Learned Men. Boston: 1700. V. 50
Practical Truths Tending to Promote the Power of Godliness... Boston: 1682. V. 50

MATHER, J. MARSHALL
Rambles Round Rossendale. Rawtenstall: 1894. V. 53

MATHER, JAMES
The Coal Mines: Their Dangers and Means of Safety. London: 1853. V. 53

MATHER Rambles Round Rossendale. (First Series). Rawtenstall: 1888. V. 54

MATHER, SAMUEL
All Men Will Not Be Saved Forever: or, An Attempt to Prove, That This is a Scripture Doctrine. Boston: 1782. V. 49
An Apology for the Liberties of the Churches in New England; to Which is Prefix'd, a Discourse Concerning Congregational Churches. Boston: 1738. V. 47
The Life of the Very Reverend and Learned Cotton Mather. Boston: 1729. V. 48
A Sermon Preached to the Ancient and Honourable Artillery Company, on June 4, 1739. Boston: 1739. V. 50

MATHER, W. W.
Elements of Geology, for the Use of Schools. Norwich: 1833. V. 54
Natural History of New York. Geology. Albany: 1843. V. 53

MATHERS, E. POWYS
Eastern Love. London: 1927-30. V. 48; 50
Eastern Love. New York: 1930. V. 51
Love Night. London: 1936. V. 47; 50
Love Night. Waltham St. Lawrence: 1936. V. 51; 53
Procreant Hymn. Waltham St. Lawrence: 1926. V. 47; 48; 49; 50; 51; 52; 54
Red Wise. 1926. V. 47
Red Wise. Waltham St. Lawrence: 1926. V. 48; 50; 52; 53

MATHERS, EDWARD P.
South Africa and How to Reach It by the Castle Line. London: 1889. V. 48

MATHERS, HELEN
Eyre's Acquittal. London: 1884. V. 50

MATHERS, JOHN, PSEUD.
The History of Mr. John Decastro and His Brother Bat, Commonly Called Old Crab. London: 1815. V. 49

MATHERS, S. L. MAC GREGOR
The Kabbalah Unveiled. (Kabbala Denudata). London: 1887. V. 47

MATHES, J. HARVEY
General Forrest. New York: 1902. V. 49
The Old Guard in Gray. Memphis: 1897. V. 54

MATHES, W. MICHAEL
Mexico on Stone: Lithography in Mexico, 1826-1900. San Francisco: 1984. V. 48; 50; 51; 52; 53

MATHESON, ELIZABETH
Blithe Air: Photographs from England, Wales and Ireland. Winston Salem: 1995. V. 54

MATHESON, JOHN
England to Delhi: a Narrative of Indian Travel. London: 1870. V. 54

MATHESON, RICHARD
The Beardless Warriors. Boston: 1960. V. 53
Bid Time Return. New York: 1975. V. 52; 53
Born of Man and Woman. 1954. V. 49; 54
Collected Stories. 1989. V. 47; 51; 52
Collected Stories. Los Angeles: 1989. V. 48; 51; 52
Hell House. New York: 1971. V. 47; 48; 49; 50; 52; 53; 54
I Am Legend. 1970. V. 48
I Am Legend. New York: 1970. V. 47
Scars. Los Angeles: 1987. V. 49
The Shrinking Man. London: 1973. V. 48
Somewhere in Time/What Dreams May Come. Los Angeles: 1991. V. 48; 51

MATHEW, DAVID
The Celtic Peoples and Renaissance Europe. 1933. V. 50; 54
The Celtic Peoples and Renaissance Europe. London: 1933. V. 51

MATHEW, JOHN
Captain Material and Useful Considerations About the Laws Positive and Laws of Necessity, Relating to the Unhappy Distractions of the Present Times. London: 1680. V. 54

MATHEW, RICHARD
The Unlearned Alchymist His Antidote. London: 1660. V. 50

MATHEWS, A. E.
Pencil Sketches of Colorado, its Cities, Principal Towns and Mountain Scenery. 1961. V. 48

MATHEWS, ANNE
Anecdotes of Actors: with Other Desultory Recollections. London: 1844. V. 50
A Continuation of the Memoirs of Charles Mathews, Comedian. Philadelphia: 1839. V. 49
Memoirs of Charles Mathews comedian (1776-1835). London: 1838. V. 49
Tea-Table Talk, Ennobled Actresses and Other Miscellanies. London: 1857. V. 52

MATHEWS, C.
The Annals of Mont Blanc. London: 1898. V. 48; 52; 53

MATHEWS, CHARLES
The London Mathews, Containing a Copious Narration of All the Celebrated Entertainments of the Inimitable Charles Mathews... London: 1820's. V. 48
Sketches of Mr. Mathews's Celebrated Trip to America. London: 1824?. V. 48

MATHEWS, G. M.
The Birds of Australia. London: 1910-27. V. 48; 50
Systema Avium Australasianarum... London: 1927-30. V. 50

MATHEWS, GEORGE
An Account of the Trial, on 14th June, 1703, Before the Court of Queen's Bench, Dublin, of the Rev. Thomas Emlyn, for a Publication Against the Doctrine of the Trinity, with a Sketch of His Associates, Predecessors and Successors. Belfast, Dublin: 1839. V. 53

MATHEWS, HARRY
The Conversions. New York: 1962. V. 53
The Long Way Home. New York: 1988. V. 54
Out of Bounds. Providence: 1989. V. 50; 53; 54
The Planisphere. Providence: 1974. V. 53
Selected Declarataions of Independence. Calais: 1977. V. 53
Singular Pleasures. 1988. V. 52; 54
Singular Pleasures. New York: 1988. V. 53; 54
The Sinking of Odradek Stadium and Other Novels. New York: 1975. V. 50; 53; 54
Tlooth. Garden City: 1966. V. 52; 53
Trial Impressions. Providence: 1977. V. 53
The Way Home. New York: 1988. V. 53; 54

MATHEWS, JOHN H.
A Treatise on the Doctrine of Presumption and Presumptive Evidence as Affecting the Title to Real and Personal Property. New York: 1830. V. 48

MATHEWS, JOHN JOSEPH
The Osages. Children of the Middle Waters. Norman: 1961. V. 50
Talking to the Moon. Chicago: 1945. V. 50

MATHEWS, JOSEPH
A Treatise on Diseases of the Rectum, Anus and Sigmoid Flexure. New York: 1897. V. 49; 54

MATHEWS, MARY MC NAIR
Ten Years in Nevada or, Life on the Pacific Caosat. Buffalo: 1880. V. 50; 51; 53

MATHEWS, MRS.
Memoirs of Charles Mathews, Comedian. London: 1839. V. 48

MATHEWS, THOMAS
...Account of the Action in the Mediterranean. London: 1745. V. 47
A Narrative of the Proceedings of His Majesty's Fleet in the Mediterranean, and the Combined Fleets of France and Spain, from the Year 1741 to March 1744... London: 1745. V. 48

MATHEWSON, A.
The Song of the Evening Stars. Boston: 1911. V. 49

MATHEWSON, CHRISTY
Won in the Ninth. New York: 1910. V. 50

MATHIAS, ANDREW
The Mercurial Disease. Philadelphia: 1811. V. 54

MATHIAS, THOMAS JAMES
Componimenti Lirici de Piu Illustri Poeti d'Italia. London: 1802. V. 48
The Political Dramatist, in November, 1795. London: 1795?. V. 52
The Pursuits of Literature. London: 1798. V. 50
The Pursuits of Literature: a Satirical Poem in Dialogue. London: 1797. V. 49; 52
The Pursuits of Literature. (with) A Translation of the Passages from Greek, Latin, Italian and French Writers, Quoted in the Prefaces and Notes to the Pursuit of Literature... London: 1799/98. V. 52
The Shade of Alexander Pope on the Banks of the Thames. London: 1799. V. 50; 51

MATHIESEN, KENNETH
How We Saw the Unites States of America. Edinburgh: 1883. V. 47

MATHIESON, THOMAS A.
Catalogue of the Library. Glasgow: 1891. V. 50; 54

MATHIEU, PIERRE
Gustave Moreau. Boston: 1976. V. 51
Gustave Moreau. London: 1977. V. 50
Gustave Moreau. Oxford: 1977. V. 54
The History of Lewis the Eleventh. Griemston: 1614. V. 54

MATHISON, GILBERT FARQUHAR
Narrative of a Visit to Brazil, Chile, Peru and the Sandwich Islands, During the Years 1821 and 1822. London: 1825. V. 47; 48
Notices Respecting Jamaica, in 1808-1809-1810. (with) A Short Review of the Reports of the African Institution... London: 1811/16. V. 50

MATICH, EDWARD M.
Reed, Pen and brush Alphabets for Writing and Lettering. Davenport: 1972. V. 50

MATISSE, HENRI
Catalogue of an Exhibition of Pictures by Henri Matisse and Sculpture by Maillol. London: 1919. V. 48; 50
Jazz. 1983. V. 47
Portraits by Matisse. Monte Carlo: 1955. V. 50
The Sculpture of Henri Matisse. New York: 1972. V. 47

MATLOCK, J. EUGENE
Gone Beyond the Law. Dallas: 1940. V. 49; 53

MATON, WILLIAM GEORGE
Observations Relative Chiefly to the Natural History, Picturesque Scenery and Antiquities of the Western Counties of England. Salisbury: 1797. V. 47; 49; 52

THE MATRIMONIAL Preceptor; or Instructive Hints to Those Who Are, And Those Who Are Like to Be Married. New York: 1829. V. 48

MATRIX. Andoversford: 1981-90. V. 48

MATRIX 4. London: 1984. V. 51

MATRIX 1. Andoversford: 1981. V. 53
MATRIX 1. 1985. V. 54

MATRIX 1-11. Andoversford: 1981-91. V. 47; 48

MATRIX 10. Andoversford: 1989. V. 51
MATRIX 10. 1990. V. 47; 54
MATRIX 10. Andoversford: 1990. V. 48; 51

MATRIX 11. 1991. V. 52; 53
MATRIX 11. London: 1991. V. 50

MATRIX 12. 1992. V. 52
MATRIX 12. Herefordshire: 1992. V. 52
MATRIX 12. London: 1992. V. 51; 53
MATRIX 12. London: 1992/93. V. 52
MATRIX 12. Risbury, Herefordshire: 1993. V. 48

MATRIX 13. Lower Marston Farm: 1990. V. 51

MATRIX 14. 1994. V. 52; 54
MATRIX 14. London: 1994. V. 52; 53

MATRIX 15. 1995. V. 54
MATRIX 15. London: 1995. V. 54

MATRIX 2. Andoversford: 1982. V. 53
MATRIX 2. Gloucestershire: 1982. V. 50
MATRIX 2. London: 1993. V. 52

MATRIX 3. Andoversford: 1983. V. 53

MATRIX 4. 1984. V. 54
MATRIX 4. Andoversford: 1984. V. 51; 53

MATRIX 5. 1985. V. 52; 54
MATRIX 5. London: 1985. V. 51

MATRIX 6. 1986. V. 54
MATRIX 6. Andoversford: 1986. V. 47; 51

MATRIX 7. 1987. V. 54
MATRIX 7. Andoversford: 1987. V. 47

MATRIX 8. 1988. V. 54
MATRIX 8. Andoversford: 1988. V. 47; 50; 51
MATRIX 8. London: 1988. V. 52

MATRIX 9. 1989. V. 47; 52; 54
MATRIX 9. Andoversford: 1989. V. 48; 51
MATRIX 9. Gloucestershire: 1989. V. 51
MATRIX 9. London: 1989. V. 53

MATSON, NEHEMIAH
Memories of Shaubena. With Incidents Relating to the Early Settlement of the West. Chicago: 1878. V. 50

MATSUSHITA, TAKAAKI
Japan: Ancient Buddhist Paintings. New York: 1959. V. 50

MATTAEI, R.
Goethe's Color Theory. 1971. V. 51

MATTERS of Great Consequence and Worthy of Note to all England... London: 1642. V. 51

MATTESON, THOMAS JEFFERSON
The Diary of Thomas Jefferson Matteson, Calaveras Pioneer. San Andreas: 1954. V. 54

MATTHA, GIRGIS
Demotic Ostraka from the Collections at Oxford, Paris, Berlin, Vienna and Cairo. Le Caire: 1945. V. 49; 51

MATTHAEUS WESTMONASTERIENSIS
Flores Historiarum... London: 1570. V. 51; 52; 53

MATTHES, FRANCOIS E.
Geologic History of the Yosemite Valley. Washington: 1930. V. 48

MATTHEW, JOHN
Eloisa in Deshabille: a Satirical Poem. London: 1819. V. 47

MATTHEWS, BRANDER
Actors and Actresses of Great Britain and the United States. London: 1886. V. 49; 53
Bookbindings, Old and New. Notes of a Book Lover, with an Account of the Grolier Club, New York. New York: 1895. V. 52

MATTHEWS, CHARLES GEORGE
The Microscope In the Brewery and Malt-House. London: 1889. V. 50

MATTHEWS, FRANKLIN
The New-Born Cuba. New York & London: 1899. V. 49

MATTHEWS, FREDERICK C.
American Merchant Ships 1850-1900. (and)....Second Series. Salem: 1930-31. V. 51

MATTHEWS, HENRY
The Diary of an Invalid. London: 1820. V. 49; 50; 51; 52; 54
The Diary of an Invalid. London: 1824. V. 52

MATTHEWS, JOHN N.
The Statutes at Large of the Provisional Government of the Confederate States of America...February 8, 1861, to...February 18, 1862. Richmond: 1864. V. 48

MATTHEWS, KEITH
Who Was Who of Families Engaged in the Fishery and Settlement of Newfoundland 1660-1840. St. John's: 1971. V. 54

MATTHEWS, LEONARD
A Long Life in Review. St. Louis?: 1927. V. 47

MATTHEWS, RICHARD F.
Poems. London: 1866. V. 53

MATTHEWS, ROBERT
The Prophet! A full and Accurate Report of the Judicial Proccedings in the Extraordianry and Highly interesting Case of Matthews, Alias Matthias, Charged with Having Swindled Mr. B. H. folger, of the City of New York... New York: 1834. V. 51; 53

MATTHEWS, SALLIE REYNOLDS
Interwoven, a Pioneer Chronicle. Houston: 1936. V. 48; 49
Interwoven, A Pioneer Chronicle. 1958. V. 49
Interwoven, a Pioneer Chronicle. El Paso: 1958. V. 47
Interwoven and Lambshead Before Interwoven. College Station: 1982. V. 51

MATTHEWS, THOMAS
Advice to the Young Whist Player. London: 1806. V. 52

MATTHEWS, W. H.
Mazes and Labyrinths. London: 1922. V. 51

MATTHEWS, WASHINGTON
The Night Chant, a Navaho Ceremony. 1902. V. 52

MATTHEWS, WILLIAM
Canadian Diaries and Autobiographies. Berkeley & Los Angeles: 1950. V. 53
A Collection of Affidavits and Certificates, Relative to the Wonderful Cure of Mrs. Ann Mattingly, Which Took Place in the City of Washington, D.C. on the Tenth of march 1824. City of Washington: 1824. V. 47
Hydraulia; an Historical and Descriptive Account of the Water Works of London... London: 1835. V. 49; 53; 54
Modern Bookbinding Practically Considered. New York: 1889. V. 49

MATTHIAE, AUGUSTUS
A Copious Greek Grammar. London: 1832. V. 52

MATTHIAS CORVINUS, KING OF HUNGARY
Bibliotheca Corviniana. 1969. V. 47

MATTHIESSEN, F. O.
Translation - an Elizabethan Art. Cambridge: 1931. V. 52

MATTHIESSEN, PETER
At Play in the Fields o the Lord. New York: 1965. V. 47; 48; 49; 50; 51; 52; 53; 54
Blue Meridian. The Search for the Great White Shark. New York: 1971. V. 51
The Cloud Forest. New York: 1961. V. 47; 48; 51; 53
The Cloud Forest. London: 1962. V. 52
Far Tortuga. New York: 1975. V. 52
In the Spirit of Crazy Horse. London: 1983. V. 54
In the Spirit of Crazy Horse. New York: 1983. V. 47; 48; 49; 50; 51; 52; 53; 54
Indian Country. New York: 1984. V. 50; 51; 52; 53
Killing Mr. Watson. New York: 1989. V. 51
Killing Mr. Watson. New York: 1990. V. 53
Men's Lives: Surfmen and Baymen of the South Fork. New York: 1986. V. 50; 52; 54
The Mountain Wall. New York: 1962. V. 51
On the River Styx. New York: 1988. V. 53
On the River Styx. New York: 1989. V. 51
Oomingmak. The Expedition to the Musk Ox Island in the Bering Sea. New York: 1967. V. 53
Partisans. New York: 1955. V. 50; 51; 52
Partisans. London: 1956. V. 53
Race Rock. New York: 1954. V. 48; 51; 52; 53
Raditzer. New York: 1961. V. 50; 53
Sal Si Puedes: Cesar Chavez and the New American Revolution. New York: 1969. V. 51
Sand Rivers. New York: 1981. V. 54
Seal Pool. Garden City: 1972. V. 49
The Shorebirds of North America. London: 1967. V. 48; 49; 50; 51; 52; 53; 54
The Shorebirds of North America. London: 1968. V. 50; 52; 53
The Snow Leopard. 1978. V. 48; 50

MATTHIESSEN, PETER continued
The Snow Leopard. Franklin Center: 1978. V. 50; 51; 52; 53; 54
The Snow Leopard. New York: 1978. V. 48; 51; 52; 53; 54
Under the Mountain Wall. New York: 1962. V. 50; 52
The Valley (working title). Sagaponack: 1972. V. 52
Wildlife in America. New York: 1959. V. 47; 48; 49; 50; 54
The Wind Birds. New York: 1973. V. 50

MATTHISON, FRIEDRICH VON
Letters Written from Various Parts of the Continent, Between the Years 1785 and 1794... London: 1799. V. 47; 50

MATTINGLY, HAROLD
The Coins of the Roman Empire in the British Museum. Augustus to Commodus. London: 1965-68. V. 49

MATTIOLI, PIETRO ANDREA
Apateka Domacy. Prazskem: 1595. V. 47; 53
Apologia Adversus Amathum Lusitanum, cum Censura in Eiusdem Enarrationes. Venice: 1558. V. 47
Commentaries svr les Six Livres de Ped. Dioscor. Anazarbeen de la Matiere Medicinale,... Lyon: 1579. V. 52
Commentarii, in Libros Sex...Dioscorides...de Medica Materia. Venetiis: 1554. V. 47; 49
Commentarii in Sex Libros Pedacii Dioscoridis. Venetiis: 1565. V. 47
Commentarii Secundo Aucti in Libros Sex Pedacii Dioscoridis. (with) Apologia Adversus Amathum Lusitantum. Venetiis: 1560/59. V. 47; 50; 53
Il Dioscoride Dell' Eccelent'e Dottor medico M.P. Andrea matthioli Da Siena... (with) Il Sesto Libro di Pedacio Diosc oride Anazarbeo... Venice: 1548. V. 54
Herbar Aneb Bylinar. Prague: 1596. V. 47; 53; 54
Kreutterbuch. Frankfurt: 1586. V. 47
Opera Omnia. Frankfurt: 1598. V. 51
Opvscvlvm de Simplicium Medicamentorum Facultatibus Secundum Locos & Genera. Venetiis: 1569. V. 47; 50; 53

MATTISON, SETH
The Retired Muse, or Forest Songster... Ithaca: 1825. V. 49

MATTOCKS, BREWER
Minnesota As a Home for Invalids. Philadelphia & St. Paul: 1871. V. 53

MATTY'S Hungry Missionary-Box and the Message It Brought. Toronto and Montreal: 1866. V. 47

MATULAY, LASZLO
Then and Now. New York: 1980. V. 49

MATURIN, CHARLES ROBERT
Fatal Revenge; or, the Family of Montorio. London: 1807. V. 49
Melmoth the Wanderer. London: 1892. V. 50
Women; or, Pour et Contre. Edinburgh: 1818. V. 48; 52

MAUBRAY, JOHN
The Female Physician, Containing All the Diseases Incident to that Sex, in Virgins, Wives and Widows... London: 1724. V. 47

MAUCLAIR, CAMILLE
J. M. W. Turner. London: 1939. V. 50

MAUDE, AYLMER
A Peculiar People. The Doukhobors. New York: 1904. V. 52

MAUDE, FRANCIS CORNWALLIS
Memories of the Mutiny... London: 1894. V. 47

MAUDE, FREDERIC PHILIP
A Compendium of the Law of Merchant Shipping... London: 1853. V. 54

MAUDE, THOMAS
The School Boy: a Poem. London: 1836. V. 50
Viator, a Poem; or a Journey from London to Scarborough. London: 1782. V. 51; 54
Wensley-Dale: or, Rural Contemplations: a Poem. London: 1780. V. 48
Wensleydale; or, Rural Contemplations: a Poem. Richmond: 1816. V. 53

MAUDSLAY, A. P.
Biologia Centrali-Americana; or, Contributions to the Knowledge of the Fauna and Flora of Mexico and Central America. New York: 1974. V. 50; 52

MAUDSLEY, HENRY
Body and Will: Being an Essay concerning Will in Its Metaphysical, Physiological, and Pathological Respects. New York: 1884. V. 47
The Physiology and Pathology of the Mind. New York: 1867. V. 52

MAUDUIT, ISRAEL
Remarks Upon Gen. Howe's Account of His Proceedings on Long Island, in the Extraordinary Gazette of October 10, 1776. London: 1778. V. 47

MAUGHAM, WILLIAM SOMERSET
Ah King. London: 1933. V. 47; 51; 52; 54
The Art of Fiction: an Introduction to Ten Novels and Their Authors. Garden City: 1955. V. 54
Ashenden; or the British Agent. Garden City: 1928. V. 49; 52
Ashenden or the British Agent. London: 1928. V. 51; 54
The Book Bag. Florence: 1932. V. 47; 51; 53; 54
Books and You. Garden City: 1940. V. 54
Books and You. London: 1940. V. 50
Cakes and Ale. London: 1930. V. 49; 50; 51; 52
Cakes and Ale. New York: 1930. V. 49
Cakes and Ale. London: 1953. V. 53
Cakes and Ale. London: 1954. V. 47; 48; 49
The Casuarina Tree. Six Stories. London: 1926. V. 51; 52
Catalina. Garden City: 1948. V. 49
Catalina. London: 1948. V. 54
Christmas Holiday. London: 1939. V. 50; 52
The Circle. London: 1921. V. 47; 48
The Constant Wife. New York: 1926. V. 51
Cosmopolitans. London: 1936. V. 47; 48
Creatures of Circumstance. Garden City: 1947. V. 54
Don Feranando or Variations on Some Spanish Themes. London: 1935. V. 47; 50; 51
The Explorer. London: 1908. V. 53
First Person Singular. London: 1931. V. 53
For Services Rendered - A Play in Three Acts. London: 1932. V. 47
France at War. Garden City: 1940. V. 54
Great Novelists and Their Novels. Philadelphia & Toronto: 1948. V. 51; 54
Here and There. London: 1948. V. 51; 52
The Hero. London: 1901. V. 52
Lady Frederick. London: 1912. V. 49; 53
The Land of the Blessed Virgin. London: 1905. V. 47; 49; 53; 54
The Letter. New York: 1925. V. 47; 48; 49; 50
The Letter. A Play. New York: 1927. V. 48; 53
Liza of Lambeth. London: 1897. V. 47; 48; 49; 51; 52; 53; 54
Liza of Lambeth. London: 1947. V. 51; 53; 54
The Magician. 1909. V. 48
The Magician. New York: 1909. V. 51
The Making of a Saint. Boston: 1898. V. 47; 53
The Making of a Saint. London: 1898. V. 48; 52; 53; 54
Maugham's Encore. Garden City: 1952. V. 54
The Mixture as Before. London: 1940. V. 47
The Moon and Sixpence. London: 1919. V. 47; 49; 51
The Moon and Sixpence. New York: 1919. V. 49; 53
The Narrow Corner. London: 1932. V. 47; 49; 50
Of Human Bondage. London: 1915. V. 48; 49
Of Human Bondage. New York: 1915. V. 48; 50
Of Human Bondage. Garden City: 1936. V. 47; 51
Of Human Bondage. New York: 1936. V. 48; 49
Of Human Bondage. New Haven: 1938. V. 47; 48; 50; 51; 52; 53; 54
Of Human Bondage. New York: 1938. V. 52
Of Human Bondage. London: 1956. V. 48
Of Human Bondage - With a Digression on the Art of Fiction - an Address. Washington: 1946. V. 48; 52
Orientations. London: 1889. V. 47; 51; 53; 54
The Painted Veil. London: 1925. V. 49; 52; 53
The Painted Veil. New York: 1934. V. 54
La Passe Dangereuse. (The Painted Veil). Paris: 1926. V. 50
Princess September. New York: 1969. V. 54
Princess September and the Nightingale. New York: 1939. V. 54
Purely for Pleasure. Garden City: 1963. V. 54
Quartet: Four Stories. Garden City: 1949. V. 54
The Razor's Edge. Garden City: 1944. V. 49
The Razor's Edge. London: 1944. V. 49; 51; 53; 54
The Selected Novels. London: 1953. V. 48
The Selected Novels... Melbourne: 1961. V. 53
Seventeen Lost Stories. Garden City: 1969. V. 54
Smith. New York: 1911. V. 49
Strictly Personal. Garden City: 1941. V. 48
Strictly Personal. New York: 1941. V. 48
The Summing Up. London: 1938. V. 47
The Summing Up. New York: 1938. V. 51
The Summing Up. Garden City: 1954. V. 53; 54
Theatre. London: 1937. V. 48; 52
Then and Now. Garden City: 1946. V. 54
Then and Now. London: 1946. V. 49
Trio. Garden City: 1950. V. 54
Trio. London: 1950. V. 53
The Unconquered. New York: 1944. V. 51
Up At the Villa. New York: 1941. V. 49
The Vagrant Mood, Six Essays. London: 1952. V. 48
The Vagrant Mood: Six Essays. Garden City: 1953. V. 54
A Writer's Notebook. Garden City: 1949. V. 48; 51; 54
A Writer's Notebook. London: 1949. V. 47; 54
A Writer's Notebook. New York: 1949. V. 48; 50; 51
The Writer's Point of View. London: 1951. V. 47

MAULDIN, BILL
Mud, Mules and Mountains. 1944. V. 51
A Sort of Saga. New York: 1949. V. 54

MAULSBY, ORLANDO W.
Rolling Stone: The Autobiography of O. W. Maulsby. Los Angeles: 1931. V. 47

MAUND, BENJAMIN
The Auctarium of the Botanic Garden. (with) The Floral Register. London: 1825-50. V. 50
The Botanic Garden... London: 1835-36. V. 51
The Botanic Garden. London: 1840. V. 51
The Botanist. London: 1837-1842. V. 48

MAUND, BENJAMIN continued
The Botanist. London: 1893. V. 49
The Fruitist: a Treatise on Orchard and Garden Fruits... London: 1843-50. V. 49

MAUNDE, JOHN
The Rural Philosopher: or, French Georgics. Newbern: 1804. V. 50

MAUNDEVILE, JOHN
The Travels. London: 1923. V. 51
The Voiage and Travaile of Sir John Maundevile, Kt. Which Treatheth of the Way to Hierusalem.... New York: 1928. V. 51

MAUNDRELL, HENRY
A Journey from Aleppo to Jerusalem at Easter, A.D. 1697... Oxford: 1708. V. 48; 51
A Journey from Aleppo to Jerusalem at Easter, A.D. 1697. Oxford: 1714. V. 47; 50
A Journey From Aleppo to Jerusalem; at Easter AD 1697. Oxford: 1749. V. 49
A Journey from Aleppo to Jerusalem, at Easter, A.D. 1697, Also a Journal from Grand Cairo to Mount Sinai and Back Again. London: 1810. V. 51

MAUNY, COUNT DE
The Gardens of Taprobane (Ceylon). London: 1937. V. 54

MAUNZIO, PAOLO
Commentarius in Epistolas M. Tulii Ciceronis ad T. Pomponium Atticum.. Francofurti: 1580. V. 51

MAUPASSANT, GUY DE
Boule de Suif. London: 1899. V. 53
Claire de Lune. Leipzig: 1916. V. 52; 54
The Odd Number. New York: 1889. V. 50
The Odd Number. London: 1891. V. 50
Saint Anthony and Other Stories. New York: 1924. V. 54
The Works. New York and London: 1903. V. 51
Wretch. Cazenovia: 1966. V. 47

MAUPERTUIS, PIERRE LOUIS MOREAU DE
The Figure of the Earth, Determined from Observations Made by Order of the French King, at the Polar Circle... London: 1738. V. 50; 54

MAURETTE, MARCELLE
Anastasia. New York: 1955. V. 54

MAURICE, ARTHUR BARTLETT
New York in Fiction. New York: 1901. V. 52

MAURICE, C.
Un Mois dans les Pyrenees. Paris: 1850. V. 48

MAURICE, F.
The History of the Scots Guards, from the Creation of the Regiment to the Eve of the Great War. London: 1934. V. 50

MAURICE, F. D.
The Epistles to the Hebrews. London: 1846. V. 51
Learning and Working. Cambridge: 1855. V. 51
The Life... London: 1884. V. 51
Social Morality. Twenty-One Lectures Delivered in the University of Cambridge. London and Cambridge: 1869. V. 52; 53

MAURICE, THE LEARNED
Monumentum Sepulcrale, ad Illustrissimi Celsissimique Principis ac Domini, Dn. Mauritii Hassiae Landgravij, Comitis Cattimoelibocorum Deciorum Zigenhainiae & Niddae... Cassellis: 1638. V. 51

MAURICE, THOMAS
The Crisis, or the British Muse to the British Minister and Nation. London: 1798. V. 50; 52; 54
A Dissertation on the Oriental Trinities. London: 1800. V. 50
An Elegiac and Historical Poem, Sacred to the Memory and Virtues of the Honourable Sir William Jones. London: 1795. V. 48; 52; 53
The History of Hindostan: Its Arts, and its Sciences, as Connected with the History of the Other great Empires of Asia, During the Most Ancient periods of the World. London: 1795-98. V. 49
Indian Antiquities; or, Dissertations, Relative to the Antient Geographical Divisions... London: 1806/1800/01. V. 52
The Modern History of Hindostan... London: 1802. V. 49
The Oxonian. Oxford: 1778. V. 48; 51
The School-Boy, a Poem. Oxford: 1775. V. 51
Westminster Abbey with Occasional Poems and a Free Translation of the Oedipus Tyrannus of Sophocles. London: 1813. V. 48; 51; 53

MAURICEAU, A. M.
The Married Woman's Private Medical Companion... New York: 1849. V. 50; 51
The Married Woman's Private Medical Companion. New York: 1850. V. 51; 53
The Married Woman's Private Medical Companion. New York: 1851. V. 50
The Married Woman's Private Medical Companion. New York: 1852. V. 48

MAURICEAU, FRANCOIS
The Diseases of Women with Child, and in Child-Bed... London: 1727. V. 53
Traite des Maladies des Femmes Grosses, et de Celles qui Sont Accouchees... Paris: 1681. V. 48; 51
Traite des Maladies des Femmes Grosses, et de Celles qui Sont Accouchees... Paris: 1740. V. 48; 49

MAUROIS, ANDRE
Ariel - a Shelley Romance. London: 1935. V. 53
Ariel. A Shelley Romance. 1935. V. 47
Aspects De La Biographie. 1928. V. 48
Byron. 1930. V. 50
Fatty Puffs and Thinifers. New York: 1940. V. 49; 52
The Silence of Colonel Bramble. London: 1919. V. 49; 51
A Voyage to the Island of the Articoles. New York: 1929. V. 51

MAUROLICO, FRANCESCO
Cosmographia. Venice: 1543. V. 50
Cosmographia, in Tres Dialogos Distincta. Paris: 1558. V. 50

MAURON, CHARLES
The Nature of Beauty in Art and Literature. London: 1927. V. 51

MAURY, DABNEY HERNDON
Recollections of a Virginian in the Mexican Civil and Indian Wars. New York: 1894. V. 48

MAURY, JEAN SIFFREIN
The Principles of Eloquence; Adapted to the Pulpit and the Bar. London: 1793. V. 47

MAURY, MATTHEW FONTAINE
The Physical Geography of the Sea. New York: 1855. V. 47; 53; 54
The Physical Geography of the Sea. New York: 1858. V. 51
The Physical Geography of the Sea. London: 1860. V. 50; 53
The Physical Geography of the Sea, and its Meteorology. London: 1874. V. 52
Physical Survey of Virginia. Her Resources, Climate and Productions. Richmond: 1878. V. 52

MAURY, RICHARD L.
The Battle of Williamsburg and the Charge of the 24th Virginia, of Early's Brigade. Richmond: 1880. V. 49

MAURY, SARAH MYTTON
The Statesmen of America in 1846. London: 1847. V. 48

MAVELOT, CHARLES
Nouveau Livre de Chiffres qui Contient en General Tous les Nomes et Surnoms... Paris: 1680. V. 49

MAVERICK, MARY ANN
Memoirs of Mary A. Maverick. San Antonio: 1921. V. 48; 52

MAVONIUS, RICHARD
Exercitationvm Lingvae Graecae, Liber Primus. Paris: 1599. V. 54

MAVOR, AUNT
St. Valentine's Day: or, the Conceited Goldfinch. London: 1860's-70's. V. 48

MAVOR, HENRY A.
On Public Lighting by Electricity. Glasgow: 1890. V. 53

MAVOR, W. F.
A New Description of Blenheim... Oxford: 1810. V. 50

MAVOR, WILLIAM
The British Tourists; or Traveler's Pocket Companion through england, Wales, Scotland and Ireland. London: 1798. V. 48
The Elements of Natural History... London: 1808. V. 48
The English Spelling Book. London: 1885. V. 48; 49; 52
Historical Account of the Most Celebrated Voyages, Travels and Discoveries From the Time of Columbus to the Present Period. London: 1796-97. V. 49
Miscellanies, in Two Parts. I. Prose: - II. Verse. Oxford: 1829. V. 50
A Tour in Wales, and through Several Counties of England, Including Both the Universities, Performed in the Summer of 1805. London: 1806. V. 52
Youth's Miscellany; or, a Father's Gift to His Children.... London: 1798. V. 49

MAW, S.
A Catalogue of Surgical Instruments, Appliances, Aseptic Hospital Furniture, Surgical Dressings, etc. 1925. V. 54

MAW, SON & SONS, LTD., LONDON
A Catalogue of Surgical Instruments, Appliances, Aseptic Hospital Furniture, Surgical Dressings, Etc. London: 1925. V. 50

MAWDESLEY, BRUCE
Song of the Scythe. 1983. V. 47

MAWE, JOHN
Familiar Lessons on Mineralogy and Geology... London: 1819. V. 54
Familiar Lessons on Mineralogy and Geology. London: 1825. V. 53
Familiar Lessons on Mineralogy and Geology.... London: 1828. V. 50
Familiar Lessons on Mineralogy and Geology... London: 1830. V. 53
The Linnean System of Conchology... London: 1823. V. 53; 54
The Mineralogy of Derbyshire. London: 1802. V. 53
Travels in the Interior of Brazil. London: 1812. V. 49; 54
Travels in the Interior of Brazil... London: 1823. V. 47
A Treatise on Diamonds and Precious Stones, Including Their History... London: 1813. V. 48; 53
A Treatise on Diamonds, and Precious Stones: Including Their History - Natural and Commercial to Which is Added, The Methods of Cutting and Polishing. London: 1823. V. 50; 52
The Voyager's Companion; or Shell Collector's Pilot. London: 1821. V. 54
Voyages dans l'Interieur du Bresil, Particulierement dans les Districts de l'or et du Diamant, faits Avec l'Autorisation du Prince Regent de Portugal, en 1809 et 1810... Paris: 1816. V. 50

MAWE, T.
The Universal Gardener and Botanist... London: 1778. V. 48

MAWE, THOMAS
Every Man His Own Gardener. London: 1769. V. 49

MAWE, THOMAS continued
Every Man His Own Gardener. London: 1787. V. 52
Every Man His Own Gardener. London: 1822. V. 47; 51
Every Man His Own Gardener, Being a New and Much More Complete Gardener's Calendar and General Directory... London: 1813. V. 50
The Universal Gardener and Botanist. London: 1778. V. 48; 49; 51; 52; 53; 54

MAWSON, DOUGLAS
Home of the Blizzard. Philadelphia/London. V. 49
The Home of the Blizzard. London: 1915. V. 49; 52; 54

MAWSON, JOHN
A Few Local Sketches. Calcutta: 1846. V. 49

MAWSON, THOMAS H.
Amounderness. London: 1937. V. 53
The Art and Craft of Garden Making. London: 1900. V. 47; 50; 52
The Art and Craft of Garden Making. Batsford: 1901. V. 48
The Art and Craft of Garden Making. London: 1901. V. 49
The Art and Craft of Garden Making. London: 1912. V. 52
The Art and Craft of Garden Making. London: 1926. V. 51; 54
Bolton As It is and As it Might Be. Bolton: 1916. V. 48

MAXFIELD, ARCHIBALD
Observations On Ulcers of the Legs, and Other Parts Shewing that the Most Obstinate and Intractable Cases May be Speedily Cured by Mild Methods of Treatment. London: 1842. V. 51

MAXIM, HIRAM S.
Artificial and Natural Flight. New York & London: 1908. V. 47
Artificial and Natural Flight. London: 1909. V. 48

MAXIMUS
Capitum Theologicorum Centuriae Quinque. Parisiis: 1560. V. 48
Sermones, e Graeca in Latinam Linguam Versi, Cosmo Paccio... Paris: 1554. V. 53

MAX MULLER, F.
Lectures on the Science of Language... London: 1866-68. V. 49

MAXWEL, H. M.
Los Angeles County Tract Directory: an Alphabetical List of All Tracts or Subdivisions and Grants of Land in Los Angeles County. Los Angeles: 1894. V. 48

MAXWELL, A. E.
Gatsby's Vineyard. Garden City: 1987. V. 54

MAXWELL, ANNA
Hampstead: Its Historic Houses, Its Literary and Artistic Associations. Hampstead: 1900. V. 53

MAXWELL, BENSON
Whom Shall We Hang? The Sebastopol Inquiry. London: 1855. V. 49

MAXWELL, CONSTANTIA
Dublin Under the Georges. London: 1936. V. 49

MAXWELL, HENRY
An Essay Towards a Union of Ireland With England. London: 1703. V. 48

MAXWELL, HERBERT
The Art of Love or New Lessons in Old Lore. Edinburgh: 1889. V. 54
The Chronicle of Lanercost 1272-1346. Glasgow: 1913. V. 50; 52
Chronicles of the Houghton Fishing Club 1822-1908. (and) Further Chronicles of the Houghton Fishing Club 1980-1931. London: 1932. V. 47
Fishing at Home and Abroad. London: 1913. V. 53; 54
The Lowland Scots Regiments, Their Origin, Character and Services Previous to the Great War of 1914. Glasgow: 1918. V. 50
Passages in the Life of Sir Lucian Elphin of Castle Weary. London: 1889. V. 54
Sixty Years a Queen. London: 1897. V. 48

MAXWELL, JAMES CLERK
An Elementary Treatise on Electricity... Oxford: 1881. V. 52; 54
The Life of James Clerk Maxwell... London: 1882. V. 48
On the Stability of the Motion of Saturn's Rings. Cambridge: 1859. V. 50
The Scientific Papers. Cambridge: 1890. V. 47; 48
A Treatise on Electricity and Magnetism. Oxford: 1881. V. 48
A Treatise on Electricity and Magnetism. Oxford: 1881-92. V. 49
A Treatise on Electricity and Magnetism. London: 1904. V. 48

MAXWELL, M.
Stalking Big Game with a Camera in Equatorial Africa with a Monograph on the African Elephant. London: 1925. V. 48; 50; 51

MAXWELL, MARY ELIZABETH BRADDON
All Along the River. London: 1893. V. 50; 53
The Captain of the Vulture; a Novel. London: 1886. V. 50
The Doctor's Wife: a Novel. London: 1886. V. 50
Gerard, or, the World, the Flesh, and the Devil. London: 1891. V. 50
The Golden Calf. London: 1883. V. 51
Hostages to Fortune: a Novel. London: 1884. V. 50
Lady Audley's Secret. London: 1862. V. 50
Run to Earth: a Novel. London: 1886. V. 50
Taken at the Flood: a Novel. London: 1884. V. 50
The Trail of the Serpent: a Novel. London: 1886. V. 50

MAXWELL, W. H.
The Dark Lady of Doona. London: 1834. V. 48
The Field Book; or, Sports and Pastimes fo the United Kingdom. London: 1833. V. 47
The Fortunes of Hector O'Halloran, and His Man Mark Anthony O'Toole. London: 1843. V. 51; 53
Highlands and Islands. London: 1852. V. 47
Hill-Side and Border Sketches. With Legends of the Cheviots and the Lammermuir. London: 1847. V. 49
History of the Irish Rebellion in 1798... London: 1845. V. 49
Life of Field-Marshal, His Grace the Duke of Wellington. London: 1839-41. V. 50
Wild Sports of the West. London: 1832. V. 53

MAXWELL, WILLIAM
All the Days and Nights: the Collected Stories of William Maxwell. New York: 1995. V. 53
Ancestors. New York: 1971. V. 54
The Chateau. New York: 1961. V. 52; 54
The Field Book: or, Sports and Pastimes of the United Kingdom. London: 1833. V. 48
The Folded Leaf. New York: 1945. V. 53
The Outermost Dream. New York: 1989. V. 53
Over by the River and Other Stories. New York: 1977. V. 53
Poems. Philadelphia: 1816. V. 49
So Long, See You Tomorrow. New York: 1980. V. 49; 50; 51; 52; 53; 54
Time Will Darken it. New York: 1948. V. 50; 52
The Virginia Historical Register. Richmond: 1848. V. 49
The Writer as Illusionist. New York: 1955. V. 47

MAXWELL, WILLIAM H.
The Removal and Disposal of Town Refuse. London: 1898. V. 51

MAXWELL-HYSLOP, K. R.
Western Asiatic Jewellery c. 3000-612 B.C. London: 1971. V. 52

MAXWELL-LYTE, H. C.
A History of Dunster and of the Families of Mohun and Luttrell. London: 1909. V. 52

MAY, BEULAH
Buccaneer's Gold: a Selection from the Poems of... Santa Ana: 1935. V. 47

THE MAY Flower for MDCCCXLVI. Boston: 1846. V. 48

MAY, FRANCES
Beyond the Argentine; or, Letters from Brazil. London: 1890. V. 54

MAY, GEORGE
A Descriptive History of the Town of Evesham, from the Foundation of Its Saxon Monastery... Evesham: 1845. V. 47

MAY, HANS
Plastic and Reconstructive Surgery. Philadelphia: 1971. V. 54
Reconstructive and Reparative Surgery. Philadelphia: 1947. V. 53

MAY, J.
Brede's Tale. 1982. V. 48; 52

MAY, J. B.
The Hawks of North America. New York: 1935. V. 49; 50; 52; 53

MAY, PERCY
The Chemistry of Synthetic Drugs. London: 1911. V. 54

MAY, PHIL
The Phil May Album. London: 1900. V. 51
The Phil May Folio or Caricature Drawings and Sketches in Line Block. London: 1910. V. 54
Phil May's Gutter-Snipes. London: 1896. V. 51

MAY, PHILIP
Love: the Reward. London: 1885. V. 54

MAY, THOMAS
A Breviary of the History of the Parliament of England. London: 1650. V. 50
A Discourse Concerning the Successe of Former Parliaments. London: 1642. V. 48
Historiae Parliamenti Angliae Breviarium. London: 1651. V. 48
The Roman Forts of Templeborough Near Rotherham. Rotherham: 1922. V. 53

MAY, W.
The Little Book of British Birds. London: 1835. V. 52
The Little Book of British Quadrupeds. London: 1835. V. 52
May's British Quadrupeds. London: 1835. V. 54

MAYAKOVSKY, VLADIMIR
Groznyi Smekh (A Terrible Laugh). Moscow: 1932. V. 47
Vladimir Mayakovsky Complete Oeuvre. Moscow: 1955-61. V. 50

MAYBANK, THOMAS
Mirth for Young and Old Alike. London: 1937. V. 47

MAYBERRY, DAVID F.
Trial of David F. Mayberry, for the Murder of Andrew Alger... Janesville: 1855. V. 51

MAYDON, H. C.
Big Game Shooting in Africa. London: 1951. V. 49
Simen, It's Heights and Abysses. London: 1925. V. 52

MAYER, A. G.
Medusae of the World. Washington: 1910. V. 53

MAYER, ALFRED M.
Sport with Gun and Rod in American Woods and Waters. Edinburgh: 1834. V. 50

MAYER, ALFRED M. continued
Sport with Gun and Rod in American Woods and Waters. New York: 1883. V. 49; 51; 52; 54

MAYER, AUGUST L.
Velazquez: A Catalogue Raisonne of the Pictures and Drawings. London: 1936. V. 49

MAYER, BRANTZ
Baltimore: Past and Present. Baltimore: 1871. V. 52
Mexico As It Was and As it Is. New York, London: 1844. V. 48; 50; 52; 53
Mexico, Aztec, Spanish and Republican: A Historical Geographical, Political, Statistical and Social Account. Hartford: 1853. V. 47
Mexico, Aztec, Spanish and Republican: a Historical, Geographical, Political...Social Account. Hartford: 1852. V. 52

MAYER, GERTRUDE TOWNSHEND
Women of Letters. London: 1894. V. 47; 53

MAYER, HENRY
The Adventures of a Japanese Doll. London: 1901. V. 51
Jumbo and His Family. London: 1910. V. 47

MAYER, J.
The Sportsman's Directory; and Park and Gamekepper's Companion. London: 1838. V. 49
The Sportsman's Directory; or Park and Gamekeeper's Companion... Colchester: 1817. V. 47
The Sportsman's Directory or Park and Gamekeeper's Companion. London: 1819. V. 51; 52
The Sportsman's Directory, or Park and Gamekeeper's Companion... London: 1823. V. 51; 52
The Sportsmen's Directory or Park and Gamekeeper's Companion... London: 1828. V. 49

MAYER, JOSEPH
Memoirs of Thomas Dodd, William Upcott and George Stubbs, R.A. Liverpool: 1879. V. 47
Vortrefflich-Hoch-Adeliches Controfee des Uralten Hauses von Lamberg... Vienna: 1709. V. 53

MAYER, L. A.
Eretz-Israel: Archaeological, Historical and Geographical Studies. Jerusalem: 1964. V. 49; 52

MAYER, LUIGI
Interesting Views in Turkey. London: 1819. V. 49
Views in Egypt from the Original Drawings in the Possession of Sir Robert Ainslie, Taken During His Embassy to Constantinople by Luigi Mayer... London: 1804. V. 54
Views in Eygpt, Palestine and the Ottoman Empire. (with) *Views in Palestine.* (with) *Vues dans l'Empire Ottoman.* London: 1803-05. V. 49; 54
Views in the Ottoman Empire. London: 1803. V. 49
Views in the Ottoman Empire, Chiefly in Caramania... (with) *Views in Palestine.* London: 1803-04. V. 47

MAYER, TOM
The Weary Falcon. Boston: 1971. V. 49; 51

MAYES, FRANCES
The Arts of Fire. Woodside: 1982. V. 47; 48

MAYFIELD, EUGENE
Fairy Tales of the Western Range and Other Tales. Lincoln: 1902. V. 50

MAYFIELD, JOHN S.
Mark Twain vs. the Street Railway Company. 1926. V. 47; 49; 50

MAYHALL, JOHN
The Annals of Yorkshire, from the Earliest Period to the Present Time. Leeds: 1861. V. 47; 53
The Annals of Yorkshire from the Earliest Period to the Present Time. Leeds: 1865-74. V. 54

MAYHEW, AUGUSTUS
Paved with Gold or The Romance and Reality of the London Streets. London: 1858. V. 48; 49; 50; 52

MAYHEW, EDWARD
The Horse's Mouth. London. V. 47; 49

MAYHEW, HENRY
1851; or, the Adventures of Mr. and Mrs. Sandboys and Family, who Came Up to London... London: 1851. V. 48; 49; 52
Acting Charades or Deeds not Words. London: 1850. V. 50; 54
The Comic Almanack. London: 1839-42/45-50. V. 52
The Criminal Prisons of London and Scenes of Prison Life. London: 1862. V. 48
German Life and Manners As Seen in Sacony in the Present Day. London: 1864. V. 49
London Labour and the London Poor...Those That Will Not Work... London: 1862. V. 48
The Lower Rhine and its Picturesque Scenery. London: 1860. V. 51
The Rhine and Its Picturesque Scenery. London: 1856. V. 52
The Upper Rhine: the Scenery of Its Banks and the Manners of Its People. London: 1858. V. 54
The Upper Rhine: the Scenery of Its Banks and the Manners of Its People. London: 1860. V. 51

MAYHEW, HORACE
Guy Faux. London. V. 47
Letters Left at the Pastrycook's: Being the Clandestine Correspondence Betwee Kitty Clover at School and Her "Dear, Dear Friend"... London: 1857. V. 47

MAYHEW, JONATHAN
A Dicourse Concerning Unlimited Submission and Non-Resistance to the Higher Powers... Boston: 1750. V. 48
A Discourse on Rev. XV. 3d, 4th. Occasioned by the Earthquakes in November 1755... Boston: 1755. V. 48
God's Hand and Providence to Be Religiously Acknowledged in Public Calamaties. A Sermon Occasioned by the Great Fire in Boston, New England, Thursday, March 20, 1760... Boston: 1760. V. 48

MAYHEW, THE BROTHERS
Acting Charades or Deeds Not Words, a Christmas Game. London: 1850. V. 53
The Greatest Plague in Life, or, The Adventures of a Lady in Search of a Good Servant. London: 1847. V. 48; 51; 53
The Image of His Father; Or One Boy is More Trouble Than a Dozen Girls... London: 1851.. V. 52
Whom to Marry and How to Get Married. London: 1848. V. 49; 51; 52

MAYLARD, A. ERNEST
Abdominal Tuberculosis. Philadelphia: 1908. V. 51

MAYNARD, C. J.
Butterflies of New England. Boston: 1886. V. 49
Eggs of North American Birds. Boston: 1890. V. 54
Handbook of the Sparrows, Finches, etc. of New England. Newtonville: 1896. V. 50

MAYNARD Dixon. *Images of the Native American.* San Francisco: 1981. V. 50

MAYNARD, FREDERIC W.
Descriptive Notice of the Drawings and Publications of the Arundel Society, from 1849 to 1868 Inclusive... London: 1869. V. 48

MAYNARD, HENRY N.
Handbook to the Crumlin Viaduct, Monmouthshire... Crumlin: 1862. V. 51; 54
The Viaduct Works' Handbook; Being a Collection of Examples from Actual Practice of Viadcuts, Bridges, Roofs, and Other Structures in Iron... London: 1868. V. 49; 52

MAYNARD, JOE
William S. Burroughs: a Bibliography, 1953-1973. Charlottesville: 1978. V. 50; 51

MAYNE, COLBURN
Strawberry Hill and Other Poems. London: 1868. V. 49

MAYNE, J. T.
Short Notes of Tours in America and India. Madras: 1869. V. 47

MAYNE, JASPER
The Citye Match. Oxford: 1639. V. 54

MAYNE, JOHN
Socius Mercatoris: or the Merchant's Companion: In Three Parts. London: 1674. V. 48

MAYNE, JONATHAN
Thomas Girtin. Leigh-on-Sea: 1949. V. 54

MAYNE, LEGER D.
What Shall We Do To-Night? or Social Amusements for Evening Parties. New York: 1873. V. 48; 51

MAYNE, R. C.
Four Years in British Columbia and Vancouver Island. London: 1862. V. 47; 48; 50; 52; 54

MAYNWARING, ARTHUR
The Life and Posthumous Works... London: 1715. V. 47; 54

MAYNWARING, ROGER
Religion and Allegiance: In Two Sermons Preached Before the Kings Maiestie: The One on the Fourth of Iuly, Anno 1627. At Oatlands. London: 1627. V. 49

MAYO, CHARLES H.
Collected Papers by the Staff of St. Mary's Hospital, Mayo Clinic. 1905-09. Philadelphia: 1911. V. 50; 54

MAYO, ELIZABETH
Lessons on Shells, as Given to Children Between the Ages of Eight and Ten in a Pestalozzian School, at Cheam, Surrey. London: 1832. V. 49

MAYO, HERBERT
A Course of Dissections for the Use of Students. London: 1827. V. 54
Observations on Injuries and Diseases of the Rectum. London: 1833. V. 54

MAYO, JOHN HORSLEY
Medals and Decorations of the British Army and Navy. London: 1897. V. 50

MAYO, ROBERT
Political Sketches of Eight Years in Washington; in Four Parts. Baltimore: 1839. V. 48; 49

MAYO, WILLIAM STARBUCK
Kaloolah, or Journeyings to the Djbel Kumri. New York: 1849. V. 48; 54

MAY'S Garden and Where the Flowers Went. London: 1873. V. 48

MAYS, WILLIE
Say Hey. New York: 1988. V. 51

MAZARIN, HORTENSE DE LA PORTE, DUCHESSE
The Memoirs of the Dutchess Mazarine. London: 1676. V. 47

MAZARIN, JULES, CARDINAL
Cardinal Mazarin's Letters to Lewis XIV, the Present King of France, On His Love to the Cardinal's Niece. London: 1691. V. 50

MAZRO, SOPHIA
Turkish Barbarity. Providence: 1828. V. 48

MAZUCHELLI, NINA ELIZABETH
The Indian Alps and How We Crossed Them. London: 1876. V. 50; 51

MAZYCK, ARTHUR
Guide to Charleston Illustrated. Charleston: 1875. V. 48

MAZZANOVICH, ANTON
Trailing Geronimo. Los Angeles: 1926. V. 49

MAZZE, CLEMENS
Vita di san Zenobio. Florence: 1487. V. 47; 49

MAZZEI, FILIPPO
Recherches Historiques et Politiques sur les Etats-Unis de l'Amerique Septentrionale... Paris: 1788. V. 50
Selected Writings and Correspondence (1765-1816). Prato: 1983. V. 49

MAZZINI, GIUSEPPE
The Duties of Man. London: 1862. V. 53

MAZZINI, JOSEPH
Royalty and Republicanism in Italy; or, Notes and Documents Realting to the Lombard Insurrection and to the Royal War of 1848. London: 1850. V. 50

MAZZOTTI, GIUSEPPE
Palladin and Other Venetian Villas. London: 1966. V. 51; 53

MEAD, CHARLES
Mississippian Scenery; a Poem. Philadelphia: 1819. V. 49; 50; 52

MEAD, ELWOOD
Report of Irrigation Investigataions in California. Washington: 1901. V. 47; 54

MEAD, F.
Leaves of Thought. Cincinnati: 1868. V. 52; 53

MEAD, HENRY
The Sepoy Revolt, it's Causes and Consequences. London: 1859. V. 50

MEAD, MARGARET
Childhood in Contemporary Cultures. Chicago: 1955. V. 52
People and Places. Cleveland: 1959. V. 52

MEAD, RICHARD
De Imperio solis ac Lunae in Corpore Humana et Morbis Inde Oriundis. Londini: 1704. V. 53
A Mechanical Account of Poisons. London: 1702. V. 47; 50; 54
A Mechanical Account of Poisons in Several Essays. London: 1708. V. 48
Medica Sacra: sive, De Morbis Insignioibvs, qvi in Bibliis Memorantvr, Commentarivs. London: 1759. V. 47; 48; 49; 53
The Medical Works. Edinburgh: 1765. V. 49
The Medical Works. Dublin: 1767. V. 51; 52
The Medical Works. Edinburgh: 1775. V. 52
Of the Power and Influence of the Sun and Moon on Humane Bodies: and of the Diseases That Rise From Thence. London: 1712. V. 48
A Short Discourse Concerning Pestilential Contagion... London: 1720. V. 53

MEADE CYCLE CO.
Wanderings Awheel. Chicago: 1898. V. 51

MEADE, GEORGE GORDON
With Meade at Gettysburg. Philadelphia: 1930. V. 50

MEADE, HERBERT
A Ride through the Disturbed Districts of New Zealand, Together with Some Account of the South Sea Islands. London: 1871. V. 47; 52

MEADE, L. T.
The Angel of Love. London: 1915. V. 53

MEADE, R. W.
A Treatise on Naval Architecture. Annapolis: 1868. V. 50

MEADE, WILLIAM
Sermon Preached by Bishop Meade at the Opening of the Convention of the Protestant Episcopal Church of Virginia... Richmond: 1861. V. 49

MEADOWS, DON
Orange County Under Spain, Mexico and the United States. Los Angeles: 1966. V. 50

MEADOWS, KENNY
Heads of the People. London: 1840. V. 50
Heads of the People. London: 1840-41. V. 48; 50
Heads of the People. London & New York: 1878. V. 53; 54
Home for the Holidays: a Pleasant Remembrance of My Early Days. London: 1859. V. 48

MEADOWS, THOMAS TAYLOR
The Chinese and Their Rebellions, Viewed in Connection With Their National Philosophy, Ethics, Legislation and Administration. London: 1856. V. 53

MEAGER, L.
The English Gardener; or, a Sure Guide to Young Planters and Gardeners in Three Parts... London: 1670. V. 51

MEAGER, LEONARD
The English Gardener. London: 1688. V. 47; 48

MEAGHER, THOMAS FRANCIS
Speeches on the Legislative Independence of Ireland. New York: 1853. V. 54

MEAKIN, BUDGETT
The Moors. London: 1902. V. 51; 52

MEAKIN, WALTER
The 5th North Staffords and the North Midland Territorials (the 46th and 59th Divisions) 1914-1919. London: 1920. V. 47

MEAN Streets: the Second Private Eye Writers of America Anthology. New York: 1986. V. 52

MEANS, JAMES
Epitome of the Aeronautical Annual. Boston: 1910. V. 49

MEANS, P. A.
Peruvian Textiles, Examples of the Pre-Incaic Period, with a Chronology of Early Peruvian Cultures. 1930. V. 54

MEANWELL, T.
On Common Swearing. To the Publisher of the Edinburgh Magazine. Edinburgh: c. 1783. V. 52

MEANY, EDMOND S.
Vancouver's Discovery of Puget Sound. New York: 1907. V. 51

MEARES, JOHN
Voyages Made in the Years 1788 & 1789, from China to the Northwest Coast of America. London: 1790. V. 47; 49; 50; 52
Voyages Made in the Years 1788 and 1789, From China to the North West Coast of America. Amsterdam: 1967. V. 53

MEASE, JAMES
An Inaugural Dissertation on the Disease Produced by the Bite of a Mad Dog, or Other Rabid Animal. Philadelphia: 1792. V. 54
Introductory Lecture to a Course of Lectures Upon Comparative Anatomy, and the Diseases of Domestic Animals. Philadelphia;: 1814. V. 50
The Picture of Philadelphia, Giving an Account of Its Origin, Increase and Improvements... Philadelphia: 1811. V. 53

MEASOM, GEORGE
The Official Illustrated Guide to the Great Northern Railway... Leicester: 1861. V. 50
The Official Illustrated Guide to the London and North-Western Railway...(...Lancaster and Carlisle, Edinburgh and Glasgow, and Caledonian Railways). London: 1859. V. 50

MEASOR, CHARLES PENNELL
Criminal Correction. Remarks and Suggestions Upon a Consistent and Uniform System of Punishment... London: 1864. V. 49; 52

MEAUZE, PIERRE
African Art: Sculpture. Cleveland: 1968. V. 53

MEBANE, LETTY CARTER
Child Life Ont he Old Plantation. Strasburg: 1920. V. 50

MECHAM, CLIFFORD HENRY
Sketches and Incidents of the Siege of Lucknow. London: 1858. V. 50; 51

MECHNIKOV, ILIA IL'ICH
Immunity in Infective Diseases. Cambridge: 1905. V. 47; 48; 49; 51; 54
Lectures on the Comparative Pathology of Inflammation. London: 1893. V. 49; 51; 54
The Nature of Man, Studies in Optimistic Philosophy. London: 1903. V. 50; 52

MECREDY, R. J.
The Motor Book. London: 1903. V. 47

MEDE, JOSEPH
The Works... London: 1677. V. 48

MEDHURST, G.
Calculations and Remarks...a Plan for the Rapid Conveyance of Goods and Passangers Upon an Iron Road through a Tube of 30 Feet in Area by the Power and Velocity of Air. London: 1812. V. 52

MEDHURST, WALTER HENRY
Pamphlets Issued by the Chinese Insurgents at Nan-King; to Which is Added a History of the Kwang-Se Rebellion, Gathered from public Documents... Shanghai: 1853. V. 49

MEDICAE Artis Principes, Post Hippocratem & Galenum. Geneva: 1567. V. 53

THE MEDICAL and Physical Journal. London: 1801-04. V. 52

THE MEDICAL and Surgical History of the War of the Rebellion. 1861-1865. Washington: 1870-88. V. 51

THE MEDICAL and Surgical Register: Consisting Chiefly of Cases in the New York Hospital by John Watts, Jun., Valentine Mott and Alexander H. Stevens. New York: 1818. V. 49

MEDICAL and Surgical Reports of the Episcopal Hospital. Philadelphia: 1913-30. V. 53

MEDICAL Botany; or History of Plants in the Materia Medica of the London, Edinburgh and Dublin Pharmacopoeias.... London: 1821-22. V. 53

MEDICAL Classics. Baltimore: 1936-41. V. 47; 52

MEDICAL Leaves. Chicago: 1937. V. 52
MEDICAL Leaves. Chicago: 1939. V. 52
MEDICAL Leaves. Chicago: 1943. V. 52

MEDICAL SOCIETY OF NEW JERSEY
The Rise, Minutes and Proceedings of the New Jersey Medical Society, Established 1766. Newark: 1881. V. 49; 51
Transactions, 1869 (1874-1876, 1878-1880, 1885-1888, 1890-1893, 1896-1903). 1869-1903. V. 47; 49

MEDICAL SOCIETY OF THE CITY & COUNTY OF NEW YORK
Report on the Epidemic Small Pox and Chicken Pox. Which Prevailed in New York During the Last Autumn and Winter, Explantory of the Causes of Supposed Failures of the Vaccine Disease. New York: 1816. V. 51

MEDICAL SOCIETY OF THE DISTRICT OF COLUMBIA
Constitution of the Medical Society of the District of Columbia, to Which is Prefixed the Act of Incorporation. Washington: 1820. V. 54

MEDICAL SOCIETY OF THE STATE OF NORTH CAROLINA
Provisional Record of Confederate Medical Officers, Offered by the Confederate Veterans Committee, Medical Society, N.C., for Corrections and Additions. N.P. V. 49; 52; 54

MEDICI, LORENZO DE
Poesi Volgari. Venice: 1554. V. 48; 49; 50; 52

MEDICINA Flagellata; or, the Doctor Scarified. London: 1721. V. 52

MEDICINA Flagellata: or, The Doctor Scarify'd. London: 1727. V. 49

MEDICINE In Modern Times or Discourses Delivered at a Meeting of the British Medical Association at Oxford. London: 1869. V. 52

MEDINA POMAR, DUKE DE
Who Is She? A Mystery of Mayfair. London: 1878. V. 54

MEDIZ, ANTONIO BOLIO
The Land of the Pheasant and the Deer: Folksong of the Maya. Mexico: 1935. V. 51

MEDLEY, JULIUS GEORGE
An Autumn tour in the United States and Canada. London: 1873. V. 53

MEDULLA Medicinae Universae; or, a New Compendious Dispensatory... London: 1761. V. 51

MEDWAY, LORD
The Birds of the Malay Peninsula. Volume 5. Conclusion and Survey of Every Species. London: 1976. V. 50; 51; 54

MEDWIN, THOMAS
Conversations of Lord Byron: Noted During a Residence with His Lordship at Pisa, in the Years 1821 and 1822. London: 1824. V. 52; 53
Conversations of Lord Byron with Thomas Medwin, Esq. London: 1832. V. 53
Journal of the Conversations of Lord Byron, Noted During a Residence with His Lordship at Pisa in the Years 1821 and 1822. New York: 1824. V. 48; 50
The Life of Percy Bysshe Shelley. London: 1847. V. 50
The Shelley Papers. A Memoir of Percy Bysshe Shelley. London: 1833. V. 47

MEE, ARTHUR
The Book of Knowledge, The Children's Encyclopedia. New York: 1911. V. 49
Durham. The King's England Series. London: 1952. V. 51
I See All. The World's First Picture Encyclopedia. London: 1928-30. V. 49

MEE, MARGARET
Flowers of the Brazilian Forests. London: 1968. V. 52

MEEHAN, CHARLES P.
The Fate and Fortunes of Hugh O'neill, Early of Tyrone and Rory O'Donel, Earl of Tyrconnel... Dublin: 1868. V. 53

MEEHAN, T.
Wayside Flowers. Philadelphia: 1881. V. 48; 51

MEEHAN, THOMAS
The American Handbook of Ornamental Trees. Philadelphia: 1853. V. 47; 52
The Native Flowers and Ferns of the United States in Their Botanical, Horticultural and Popular Aspects. Boston: 1878/80. V. 47; 53
The Native Flowers and Ferns of the United States in Their Botanical, Horticultural and Popular Aspects. Boston: 1879/80. V. 52
The Native Flowers and Ferns of the United States in Their Botanical, Horticultural and Popular Aspects. (with) The Native Flower and Ferns of the United States in Their Botanical, Horticultural and Popular Aspects. Series II. Boston: 1897. V. 49
Wayside Flowers. Philadelphia: 1881. V. 47; 53

MEEK, C. K.
A Sudanese Kingdom, an Ethnographical Study of the Jukun-Speaking Peoples of Nigeria. London: 1931. V. 51

MEEK, GEORGE
Evening Hours: a Collection of Original Poems. London: 1817. V. 54
George Meek: Bath Chair-Man. London: 1910. V. 54

MEEK, STEPHEN HALL
The Autobiography of a Mountain Man, 1805-1889. Pasadena: 1948. V. 52

MEEKER, EZRA
Pioneer Reminiscences of Puget Sound: The Tragedy of Leschi... Seattle: 1905. V. 50; 52; 54
Washington Territory West of the Cascade Mountains. Olympia: 1870. V. 48

MEEKER, I. DAY
The Improved American Family Physician; or, Sick Man's Guide to Health... New York: 1833. V. 51

MEEKS, CARROLL L. V.
Italian Architecture 1750-1914. New Haven: 1966. V. 50

MEEN, V. B.
Crown Jewels of Iran. Toronto: 1968. V. 50

MEERMAN, GERARD
Origines Typographicae. The Hague: 1765. V. 49

MEGGENDORFER, LOTHAR
Always Jolly!. London: 1898. V. 51
Im Stadtpark. Ein Bilderbuch Zum Kufftellen mit Ausgeschnittenen Figuren. Munich: 1892. V. 47
Schau Mich An!. Stuttgart: 1895. V. 47

MEGGERS, BETTY
Early Formative Period of Coastal Ecuador: the Valdivia and Machalila Phases. Washington: 1965. V. 50

MEGINNESS, JOHN F.
Biography of Frances Slocum, the Lost Sister of Wyoming. Williamsport: 1891. V. 48; 53

MEHEMET-MELEK-HANUM, WIFE OF KIBRIZLI-MEHEMET-PASHA
Thirty Years in the Harem; or, the Autobiography of... New York: 1872. V. 53

MEHRING, WALTER
No Road Back. New York: 1944. V. 51

MEHTA, NANALAL CHAMANLAI
Studies in Indian Painting. Bombay: 1926. V. 49; 52; 54

MEIBOMUS, JOAN HENRICUS
De Flagrorum Usu in re Veneria... London: 1757. V. 50

MEIER, AUGUST
Negro Thought in America, 1880-1915: Racial Ideoloies in the Age of Booker T. Washington. Ann Arbor: 1963. V. 52

MEIER, RICHARD
Richard Meier Architect: Buildings and Projects, 1966-1976. New York: 1976. V. 48

MEIER-GRAEFE, JULIUS
Cezanne. London: 1927. V. 51
Degas. London: 1923. V. 54
Felix Vallotton: Biographie De Cet Artiste...Avec Gravures Originales & Nouvelles. Paris & Berlin: 1898. V. 49
Modern Art. London: 1908. V. 49; 52
Vincent Van Gogh, a Biographical Study. London and Boston: 1926. V. 54

MEIGE, HENRY
Tics and Their Treatment. New York: 1907. V. 50

MEIGHAN, CLEMENT W.
Indian Art and History, The Testimony of Prehispanic Rock Paintings in Baja California. Los Angeles: 1969. V. 50

MEIGS, ARTHUR
A Study of the Human Blood-Vessels in Health and Disease. Philadelphia: 1907. V. 49; 54
A Study of the Human Blood-Vessels in Health and Disease. Philadelphia: 1971. V. 47

MEIGS, ARTHUR J.
An American Country House. The Property of Arthur E. Newbold, Jr., Esq.; Laverock, Pa. New York: 1925. V. 52

MEIGS, CHARLES D.
A Treatise on Acute and Chronic Diseases of the Neck of the Uterus... Phiadlephia: 1854. V. 48; 49

MEIGS, JOHN
The Cowboy in American Prints. Chicago: 1972. V. 47

MEIGS, PEVERIL
The Dominican Mission Frontier of Lower California. Berkeley: 1935. V. 48; 50; 54

MEIKLE, D.
Wild Flowers of Cyprus. London: 1973. V. 47

MEIKLE, JAMES
The Traveller; or, Meditations on Various Subjects. New York: 1811. V. 52

MEIKLE, R. D.
Flora of Cyprus. London: 1977-85. V. 50

MEIKLEHAM, ROBERT
On the History and Art of Warming and Ventilating Rooms and Buildings by Open Fires, Hypocausts, German, Dutch, Russian and Swedish Stoves, Steam, Hot Water, Heated Air, Heat of Animals and Other Methods... London: 1845. V. 50

MEIKLEJOHN, J. M. D.
The Golden Primer. London & Edinburgh: 1884-85. V. 47

MEINE, FRANKLIN J.
The Crockett Almanacs, Nashville Series 1835-1838. Chicago: 1955. V. 48; 51

MEINERTZHAGEN, FREDERICK
The Art of the Netsuke Carver. London: 1956. V. 50

MEINERTZHAGEN, R.
Army Diary 1899-1926. London: 1960. V. 50
Birds of Arabia. London: 1954. V. 49; 50; 51; 53
The Birds of Arabia. London: 1980. V. 48; 49; 50; 53
Kenya Diary 1902-1906. London: 1957. V. 54
The Life of a Boy - Daniel Meinertzhagen 1925-1944. London: 1947. V. 52
Nicholl's Birds of Egypt. London: 1930. V. 48
Pirates and Predators, the Piratical and Predatory Habits of Birds. London: 1959. V. 48

MEINHOLD, WILHELM
Sidonia the Sorceress. London: 1894. V. 53

MEINHOLD, WILLIAM
Mary Schweidler, the Amber Witch - the Most Interesting Trial for Witchcraft Ever Known. London: 1903. V. 48; 52

MEIR, JOSEPH BEN JOSHUA BEN
The Chronicles. London: 1836. V. 51

MEIRON-JONES, GWYN I.
The Vernacular Archtiecture of Brittany. Edinburgh: 1982. V. 48

MEISEL, LOUIS K.
Photo Realism. New York: 1981. V. 53

MEISEL, MAX
A Bibliography of American Natural History, the Pioneer Century 1769-1865. Mansfield: 1994. V. 52; 54

MEISS, MILLARD
De Artibus Opuscula XL. Essays in Honor of Erwin Panofsky. New York: 1961. V. 53
Essays in Honor of Erwin Panofsky. 1961. V. 52
French Painting in the Time of Jean de Berry. London & New York: 1967. V. 50
French Painting in the Time of Jean De Berry, the Boucicaut Master. London: 1968. V. 50
French Paintings in the Time of Jean De Berry - T Limbours and Their Contemporaries. London: 1974. V. 50
The Great Age of Fresco: Discoveries, Recoveries and Survivals. London: 1970. V. 50
Painting in Florence and Siena after the Black Death. Princeton: 1951. V. 50
The Visconti Hours. London: 1973. V. 49

MELA, POMPONIUS
De Situ Orbis, Libri III: cum Notis Integris Hermolai, Barbari, Olivarii, et al, Accedunt Petri Joannis Nunnesii et Jacobi Perizonii. Lugduni Batavorium: 1748. V. 47; 54

MELADY, THOMAS
Idi Amin Dada Hitler in Africa. Kansas City. V. 54

MELANCHTHON, PHILIPP
Loci Communes, Das ist fie Furnemesten Artikel Christlicher Lere... Wittemberg: 1538. V. 48
Omnivm Opervm...Pars Seunda. Wittebergae: 1562. V. 50
Oratio Vber der Leich des Ehrwirdigen Hern Martini Lutheri. Wittenberg: 1546. V. 48; 52
Testimonia D. Martini Luteri de Socio Laborum et Periculorum Suorum. Gorlitz: 1580. V. 48

MELAS, E. M.
The Islands of Karpathos, Saros and Kasos in the Neolithic and Bronze Age. Goteborg: 1985. V. 48

MELENDY, H. B.
The Governors of California: Peter H. Burnett to Edmund G. Brown. Georgetown: 1965. V. 50; 52; 54

MELINE, JAMES F.
Two Thousand Miles on Horseback. New York: 1867. V. 47; 50; 52

MELISH, JOHN
A Geographical Description of the United States, With...British and Spanish Possessions. Philadelphia: 1816. V. 48
Travels through the United States of America, in the Years 1806 and 1807 and 1809, 1810 and 1811... Belfast: 1818. V. 53

MELLADEW, H.
Sport and Travel Papers. London: 1909. V. 49

MELLEN, PETER
Jean Clouet. London: 1971. V. 51; 53
Landmarks of Canadian Art. Toronto: 1978. V. 50; 54

MELLICK, ANDREW D.
The Story of an Old Farm, or, Life in New Jersey in the Eighteenth Century. Somerville: 1889. V. 47; 49; 51

MELLIN, CHRISTOPH
Der Kinderartz... Kempten: 1781. V. 47

MELLIS, C. J.
Lion-Hunting in Somali-land, also An Account of 'Pigsticking' the African Wart-Hog. London: 1895. V. 51

MELLIS, J. C.
St. Helena: a Physical, Historical and Topographical Description of the Island... London: 1875. V. 51

MELLO, FRANCISCO MANUEL DE
Relics of Melodino. London: 1815. V. 54

MELLO FRANCO, FRANCISCO DE
Medicina Theologica, ou Supplica Humilde, Feita a Todos os Senhores Confessores e Directores, Sobre o Modo de Proceder com Seus Penitentes na Emenda Dos Peccados, Principalmente da Lascivia, Colera e Bebedice. Lisbon: 1794. V. 48
Reposta Segunda ao Filosofo Solitario, Por Hum Amigo dos Homens; Na Qual se Mostra Que Toda a Sua Obra Nao he Mais Que Huma Simplez Traduccao... Lisbon: 1787. V. 48
Tratado da Educacao Fysica dos Memninos, Para Uso da Nacao Portugueza... Lisbon: 1790. V. 48

MELLON, JAMES
African Hunter. New York: 1975. V. 48
African Hunter. 1990. V. 54

MELLON, PAUL
English Drawings and Watercolours 1550-1850 in the Collection of Mr. & Mrs. Paul Mellon. New York: 1972. V. 49

MELLOR MEIGS & HOWE
A Monograph of the Works of Mellor Meigs & Howe. New York: 1923. V. 48; 51; 52

MELLY, GEORGE
Khartoum, and the Blue and White Niles. London: 1851. V. 54

MELMOTH, HENRY
Sorrows of Memory, and Other Poems. London: 1807. V. 54

MELMOTH, WILLIAM
Of Active and Retired Life, an Epistle. London: 1735. V. 54
The Translator of Pliny's Letters (i.e. W. Melmoth) Vindicated from Certain Objections (of Jacob Bryant in His "Treatise Upon the Authenticity of the Scriptures") to his Remarks Respecting Trajan's Persecution of the Christians in Bithynia. Bath: 1793. V. 47; 53

MELOT, MICHEL
The Graphic Works of the Impressionists: Manet, Pissarro, Renoir, Cezanne, Sisley. London: 1972. V. 50

MELTON, HENRY
Hints on Hats. London: 1865. V. 49

MELTON, PHILIP
A Serious Address to the Frequenters of Play-Houses, or, RAther, Serious Motives to Draw People to a Just Consideration of the Folly, Sin and anger of Encouraging and Being Present... London?: 1746. V. 47

MELTZER, DAVID
The Clown, a Poem. Larkspur: 1960. V. 51
The Dark Continent. 1967. V. 54

MELTZER, MILTON
In Their Own Words: a History of the American Negro, 1916-1966. New York: 1967. V. 48

MELVILL, JAMES
The Diary of Mr. James Melvill 1556-1601. Edinburgh: 1829. V. 53

MELVILL, JOHN
Observations on the Nature and Properties of Fixible Air, and on the Salutary Effects of the Aqua Salubris, in Preserving Health and Preventing Diseases. London: 1789?. V. 48

MELVILLE, E. J.
The Arab's Ride to Cairo. London: 1855. V. 52

MELVILLE, ELIZABETH HELEN
A Residence at Sieera Leone. London: 1849. V. 47

MELVILLE, F. J.
Postage Stamps in the Making, a General Survey of the Practices and Processes Employed in the Manufacture of Postage Stamps. Volume I. London: 1916. V. 52

MELVILLE, HENRY, VISCOUNT
A Compendious Report of the Trial of Henry Viscount Melville, upon the Impeachment of the Commons of the United Kingdom of Great Britain and Ireland, in Parliament Assembled for High Treason and Misdemeanours. London: 1806. V. 54
The Trial by Impeachment, of Henry Lord Viscount Melville, for High Crimes and Misdemeanors, Before the House of Peers, in Westminster Hall (etc.). London: 1806. V. 47; 48

MELVILLE, HERMAN
Battle-Pieces and Aspects of the War. New York: 1866. V. 47; 49; 51; 52; 53; 54
Benito Cereno. London: 1926. V. 47; 48; 49; 50; 51; 52; 53; 54
Billy Budd & Beneto Cereno. 1965. V. 48
Billy Budd. Benito Cereno. New York: 1965. V. 53
Billy Budd Sailor. Mount Holly: 1987. V. 49; 52; 54
Collected Poems. Chicago: 1947. V. 51
The Confidence Man. New York: 1857. V. 50; 52
The Confidence Man. New York: 1957. V. 47
The Encantadas, or, Enchanted Isles. Burlingame: 1940. V. 49; 54
Israel Potter: His Fifty Years of Exile. New York: 1855. V. 49; 52; 53; 54
John Marr and Other Poems. Princeton: 1922. V. 54
Journal Up the Straits. New York: 1935. V. 54
The Life of William Makepeace Thackeray. Chicago: 1899. V. 51
Mardi. New York: 1849. V. 47; 48; 49; 50; 51; 52; 53; 54
Mardi. New York: 1855. V. 54
Moby Dick. New York: 1851. V. 48; 50; 51; 53; 54
Moby Dick. New York: 1863. V. 47
Moby Dick. Chicago: 1930. V. 47; 48; 49; 50; 51; 52; 53; 54
Moby Dick. London: 1930. V. 51
Moby Dick. New York: 1930. V. 47; 48; 49; 50; 51; 53
Moby Dick. 1943. V. 53
Moby Dick. London: 1952. V. 51
Moby Dick. New York: 1975. V. 48; 52
Moby Dick. San Francisco: 1979. V. 47; 48; 52
Moby Dick. West Hatfield: 1979. V. 48
Narrative of a Four Months' Residence Among the Natives of a Valley of the Marquesas Islands, or a Peep at Polynesian Life. London: 1846. V. 47; 50; 51; 54
Omoo. London: 1847. V. 49; 53; 54
Omoo. New York: 1847. V. 47; 49; 50; 52; 53; 54
Omoo. Oxford: 1961. V. 48
The Piazza Tales. New York: 1856. V. 47; 49; 51; 53
Pierre; or, the Ambiguities. New York: 1851. V. 47
Pierre; or, the Ambiguities. London: 1852. V. 49
Pierre; or, the Ambiguities. New York: 1852. V. 52; 53; 54
Pierre; or, the Ambiguities. New York: 1855. V. 52
Redburn: His First Voyage. New York: 1849. V. 50; 52; 53; 54

MELVILLE, HERMAN continued
Redburn: His First Voyage. New York: 1850. V. 47
Redburn: His First Voyage. Being the Confessions of a Sailor-Boy. London: 1853. V. 48
Rock Rodondo. New York: 1981. V. 47; 51; 52
Typee: a Peep at Polynesian Life. New York: 1846. V. 47; 54
Typee: a Peep at Polynesian Life. New York 1847. V. 47; 49; 51; 52
Typee: a Peep at Polynesian Life... New York: 1855. V. 52
Typee, a Romance of the South Seas. New York: 1935. V. 52; 53; 54
The Whale. London: 1851. V. 49; 50; 51; 52; 53
White Jacket; or the World in a Man of War. New York: 1850. V. 47; 49; 52; 53; 54
White Jacket; or the World in a Man of War. London: 1853. V. 49
White Jacket; or the World in a Man-of-War. New York: 1860. V. 51
White Jacket; or the World in a Man-of-War. New York: 1950. V. 47

MELVILLE, JAMES
Memoirs of His Own Life. Edinburgh: 1827. V. 54
The Memoirs of Sir James Melvil of Hal-Hil. London: 1683. V. 47

MELVILLE, JULIA
Old Memories. London: 1856. V. 54

MELVILLE, LEWIS
The Life and Letters of Tobias Smollett. Boston and New York: 1927. V. 52

MELVILLE, ROBERT
Henry Moore: Sculpture and Drawings 1921-1969. New York. V. 47; 48; 50; 52
Henry Moore Sculpture and Drawings 1921-1969. London: 1970. V. 50
Henry Moore. Sculpture and Drawings 1921-1969. New York: 1970. V. 52

A **MEMENTO** of the Quarter-Centenary Year of William Shakespeare 1564-1964. Worcester: 1964. V. 54

MEMES, JOHN SMYTH, MRS.
Precipitance: a Highland Tale. Edinburgh: 1823. V. 54

MEMMINGER, CHRISTOPHER GUSTAVUS
The Book of Nullification, by a Spectator of the Past. Charleston: 1830. V. 48; 49

MEMMO, ANDREA
Elementi d'Architettura Lodoliana. Zara and Milan: 1834. V. 47

A **MEMOIR** of Field-Marshal the Duke of Wellington... London. V. 48

MEMOIR of Frank Russell Firth. Boston: 1873. V. 47

A **MEMOIR** of Mary Ann. New York: 1961. V. 53

MEMOIR of Mr. and Mrs. Wood an Authentic Account...in the Lives of These Vocalists, Including the Marriage of Miss Paton to Lord William Lenox; and the Causes Which Led to Their Divorce: Her Marriage to Joseph Wood. Boston: 1840. V. 47; 52

A **MEMOIR** on the Subject of a Navigation Act, Including the Encouragement of the Manufactory of Boats and Sea Vessels, and the Protection of Mariners. Philadelphia: 1809. V. 47

MEMOIRES de Litterature, Tirez des Registres Academie Royale des Inscriptions et Belles Lettres. Paris: 1736-77. V. 51

MEMOIRS, British and Foreign, of the Lives and Families of the Most Illustrious Persons Who Dy'ed in the Year 1711. London: 1712. V. 51; 54

MEMOIRS Illustrative of the History and Antiquities of the County and City of Lincoln, Communicated to the Annual Meeting of the Archaeolgoical Institute of Great Britain and Ireland, Held at Lincoln July 1848. London: 1850. V. 54

MEMOIRS of a Stomach. 1876. V. 48

MEMOIRS of Eminent Men of Leeds. London: 1868. V. 47; 48

MEMOIRS of Frederica Sophia Wilhelmina, Princess Royal of Prussia, Margravine of Bareith, Sister of Frederick the Great. London: 1812. V. 50

MEMOIRS Of James the Second, King of England, &c. Colchester: 1821. V. 54

MEMOIRS of Jeremy Diddler the Younger. London: 1887. V. 54

MEMOIRS of Maitre Jacques of Savoy. London: 1779-83. V. 54

MEMOIRS of Sylvester Daggerwood, Comedian &c. Deceased: Including Many Years of Personal Vicissitudes, Interspersed with Genuine Anecdotes of Many Eminent Persons, and Several Deceased and Living Actors and Managers. London: 1807. V. 53

THE **MEMOIRS** of the Harcourt Family; a Tale for Young Ladies. London: 1816. V. 53

MEMOIRS of the Life of Eleanor Gwinn, a Celebrated Courtezan, in the Reign of King Charles II. and Mistress to that Monarch. London: 1752. V. 53

MEMOIRS of the Life of Mr. John Kettlewell...Vicar of Coleshill in Warwickshire (with) Some Account of the Transactions of His Time. London: 1718. V. 50

MEMOIRS of the Literary and Philosophical Society of Manchester. Warrington: 1785. V. 52

MEMOIRS of the Most Remarkable Enterprises and Actions of James Duke of York, albany and Ulster. London: 1681. V. 49

MEMOIRS of the Public and Private Life of Sir Richd. Phillips, Knight High Sheriff for the City of London and County of Middlesex. London: 1808. V. 52

MEMOIRS of the Secret Societies of the South of Italy, Particularly the Carbonari. London: 1821. V. 50; 51

MEMOIRS of the Society of Grub-Street. Volume I (II). London: 1737. V. 49

MEMORANDUM on the Subject of the Earl of Elgin's Pursuits in Greece. London: 1815. V. 47

MEMORANDUMS of a Residence in France, in the Winter of 1815-16, Including Remarks on French Manners and Society, with a Description of the Catacombs and Notices of Some Other Objects of Curiosity and Works of Art, Not Hitherto Described. London: 1816. V. 47

MEMORIAL and Biographical History of Dallas County, Texas. Chicago: 1892. V. 47

A **MEMORIAL** and Biographical History of the Coast Counties of Central California... Chicago: 1893. V. 49

MEMORIAL and Biographical History of the Counties of Fresno, Tulare, and Kern, California. Chicago: 1892?. V. 49

MEMORIAL and Biographical Record - and Illustrated Compendium of Biography. Chicago: 1899. V. 54

MEMORIAL and Genealogical Records of Southwest Texas. Chicago: 1894. V. 52

THE **MEMORIAL** History of Boston, Including Suffolk County Mass. 1630-1880. Boston: 1880. V. 50

MEMORIAL of a Convention of the Friends of National Industry. Washington: 1819. V. 53

A **MEMORIAL** of American Authors. 1885. V. 47; 49

MEMORIAL OF Charles Howard Esq., of Greystock and Miss Frances Howard, of the Family of Norfolk. London: 1763. V. 49

A **MEMORIAL** of George Brown Goode, Together with a Selection of His Papers on Museums and on the History of Science in America. Washington: 1901. V. 54

A **MEMORIAL** of John Greenleaf Whittier from His Native City, Haverhill, Massachusetts. Haverhill: 1893. V. 47

A **MEMORIAL** of the American Patriots Who Fell at the Battle of Bunker Hill June 17, 1775. Boston: 1889. V. 54

A **MEMORIAL** of the American Patriots Who Fell at the Battle of Bunker Hill, June 17, 1775. Boston: 1889. V. 52

MEMORIAL Presented by the Inhabitants of Lousiana to the Congress of the United States, In Seante and House of Representatives Convened. Washington: 1804. V. 50

MEMORIAL Record of the Northern Peninsula of Michigan. Chicago: 1895. V. 51; 53

MEMORIALS Concerning Several Ministers and Others, Decased, of the Religious Society of Friends; with Some of Their Last Expressions. New York: 1814. V. 49; 54

THE **MEMORIALS** of C. H. O. Daniel With a Bibliography of the Press 1845-1919. Oxford: 1921. V. 54

MEMORIALS of Charles John, King of Sweden and Norway: Illustrative of His Character; of His Relations With the Emperor Napoleon; and the Present State of His Kingdoms. London: 1829. V. 50

MEMORIALS of Rugbeians Who Fell in the Great War. 1916. V. 54

MEMORIALS of Shakespeare; or Sketches of His Character and Genius, by Various Writers, Now First Collected. London: 1828. V. 53

MEMORIES of Daly's Theatres with Passing Recollections of Others... 1897. V. 51

MEN of Mark. A Gallery of Contemporary Portraits of Men Distinguished by the Senate, the Church, In Science, Literature and Art, the Army, Navy, Law, Medicine, etc. London: 1876-77. V. 54

MEN of Mark. A Gallery of Contemporary Portraits of Men Distinguished in the Senate, the Church, in Science, Literature and Art, the Army, Navy, Law, Medicine, Etc. London: 1880. V. 48; 54

MEN of Texas: A Collection of Portraits of Men Who Deserve to Rank as Typical Representatives of...the State of Texas. Houston: 1903. V. 48

MEN Of the Period Selected From Centres of Commerce and Industry. London: 1900. V. 50

MENABONI, ATHOS
Menaboni's Birds. New York: 1950. V. 52

MENCE, RICHARD
The Mutual Rights of Husband and Wife; with the Draft of a Bill to Replace that of Mr. Serjeant Talfourd for the Custody of Infants. London: 1838. V. 54

MENCKEN, HENRY LOUIS
The American Language. New York: 1919. V. 51
The American Language. New York: 1960/61/61. V. 52
The Artist. Boston: 1912. V. 48; 49; 51; 53
A Book of Prefaces. London: 1922. V. 51
Christmas Story. New York: 1946. V. 47; 48; 51
Damn!. New York: 1918. V. 49
Europe After 8:15. New York: 1914. V. 47; 48; 49; 51
George Bernard Shaw: His Plays. Boston and London: 1905. V. 49; 50
The Gist of Nietzsche. Boston: 1910. V. 52; 53
Happy Days 1880-1892. New York: 1940. V. 48; 50; 51; 53; 54
Happy Days/ Newspaper Days/ Heathen Days. New York: 1940/41/43. V. 48; 51
Heathen Days, 1890-1936. New York: 1943. V. 50

MENCKEN, HENRY LOUIS continued
Heliogabalus. New York: 1920. V. 47; 48; 49; 51
In Defence of Women. London: 1923. V. 47
In Defense of Women. New York: 1918. V. 50
Letters of H. L. Mencken. New York: 1961. V. 54
Menckeniana. A Schimpflexion. New York: 1928. V. 47; 48; 51; 53
Menckeniana: a Selection from a Mencken Chrestomathy. New York: 1949. V. 51
Newspaper Days, 1899-1906. New York: 1941. V. 48; 50
Notes on Democracy. New York: 1926. V. 48; 49; 51
The Philosophy of Friedrich Nietzsche. Boston: 1908. V. 48; 49
Pistols for Two. New York: 1917. V. 51
Prejudices. Fifth Series. New York: 1926. V. 53
Prejudices, Fourth Series. New York: 1924. V. 52
Prejudices. Sixth Series. New York: 1927. V. 48; 49; 50; 53
Prejudices Third Series. New York: 1922. V. 50
Selected Prejudices. London: 1926. V. 47
Treatise on the Gods. New York: 1930. V. 47; 49; 50; 51
Vachel Lindsay. Washington: 1947. V. 49

MENCKEN, JOHANN BURCKHARD
The Charlantary of the Learned. New York: 1937. V. 49; 54

MENDALL, P. H., MRS.
The New Bedford Practical Receipt Book. New Bedford: 1862. V. 49

MENDEL, VERA
Brokenbrow, a Tragedy by Ernst Toller. London. V. 50

MENDELEEFF, D. I.
The Principles of Chemistry. St. Petersburg: 1889. V. 53
The Principles of Chemistry. London: 1897. V. 50; 52; 54

MENDELL, G. H.
Report on the Various Projects for the Water Supply of San Francisco, Cal. Made to the Mayor, the Auditor, and the District Attorney, Constituting the Board of Water Commissioners. San Francisco: 1877. V. 48

MENDELL, MISS
Notes of Travel and Life. New York: 1854. V. 50; 51

MENDELSOHN, ERIC
Three Lectures on Architecture. Berkeley: 1944. V. 48; 50; 51; 53

MENDELSSOHN, MOSES
Phaedon; or, the Death of Socrates. London: 1789. V. 52

MENDELSSOHN, SIDNEY
Mendelssohn's South African Bibliography. New York: 1993. V. 53
South African Bibliography. 1993. V. 49
South African Bibliography. Being the Catalogue Raisonne of the Mendelssohn Library of Works Relating to South Africa... Cambridge: 1993. V. 50; 54
A South African Bibliography to the Year 1925. London: 1979. V. 51

MENDES, CATULLE
Hesperus. Paris: 1904. V. 47; 49; 52
Petits Poemes Russes Mis en Vers Francais. Paris: 1893. V. 52

MENDES, PETER
Clandestine Erotic Fiction in English 1800-1930: a Bibliograpical Study. London: 1993. V. 53

MENDES PINTO, FERNAO
The Voyages and Adventures of Fernand Mendes Pinto, a Portugal: During His Travels for the Space of One and Twenty Years in the Kingdoms of Ethiopia, China, Tartaria, Cauchinchina, Calaminham, Siam, Pegu, Japan... London: 1653. V. 50

MENDEZ, MOSES
A Collection of the Most Esteemed Pieces of Poetry That Have Appeared for Several Years. London: 1770. V. 50

MENDHAM, JOSEPH
An Account of the Indexes, Both Prohibitory and Expurgatory, of the Church or Rome. London: 1826. V. 50

MENDIZABAL VILLALBA, ALFRED
The Martyrdom of Spain. London: 1938. V. 49

MENDO, ANDRES
Il Principe Perfetto e Ministri Adatti Documenti Politici e Morali Corredati d'Emblemi... Rome: 1816. V. 51; 52

MENDOZA, DANIEL
Memoirs of the Life of Daniel Mendoza... London: 1816. V. 50

MENDOZA RIOS, JOSEPH DE
A Complete Collection of Tables for Navigation and Nautical Astronomy...Particularly for Deducing the Longitude from Lunar Distances and the Latitude from Two Attitudes of the Sun... London: 1809. V. 49

MENEFEE, CAMPBELL A.
Historical and Descriptive Sketch Book of Napa, Sonoma, Lake and Mendocino... Napa City: 1873. V. 50

MENESTRIER, CLAUDE FRANCOIS
Traite des Tovrnois, Iovstes, Carrovsels, et Avtres Spectacles Pvblics. Lyon: 1669. V. 53
Traite des Tovrnois, Iovstes, Carrovsels, et Avtres Spectacles Pvblics. Lyon: 1674. V. 53

MENETRIES, E.
Monographie de la Famille des Myiotherinae...Extrait des Memoires de l'Academie Imperiale des Sciences. St. Petersburg: 1836. V. 47; 52

MENEZES, ESTEVAN DE, CONDE DE TAROUCA
Copia de las Cartas, Que Dexo Escritas en Castilla...en las Quales Declara la Razon de su Passaje, que es Cumplir com la Deuida Obligacion de Buscar el Servicio du su Legitimo Rey... Lisbon: 1663. V. 48

MENGHI, GIROLAMO
Compendio dell'Arte Essorcistica, et Possibilita Della Mirabili. Bologna: 1590. V. 50

MENGOUS, PETROS
Narrative of a Greek Soldier... New York: 1830. V. 49

MENGS, ANTHONY RAPHAEL
The Works of Anthony Raphael Mengs First Painter His Catholic Majesty Charles 111. London: 1796. V. 48; 52

MENIN Gate Pilgrimage. St. Barnabas 1927. 1927. V. 49

MENJOU, ADOLPHE
It Took Nine Tailors. New York: 1948. V. 51

MENKEN, ADAH ISAACS
Infelicia. London, Paris, New York: 1868. V. 49; 51; 52; 54
Infelicia. London, Paris, New York: 1869. V. 54

MENKES, HERMAN
Isidor Kaufmann. Vienna: 1926. V. 47; 48

MENNELL, JAMES B.
The Treatment of Fractures by Mobilisation and Massage. London: 1911. V. 51

MENNIE, DONALD
The Grandeur of the Gorges. Shanghai: 1926. V. 51
The Pageant of Peking. Shanghai: 1920. V. 48

MENNINGER, KARL A.
Man Against Himself. New York: 1938. V. 52

MENNIS, JOHN
Facetiae. Musarum Deliciae; or, The Muse's Recreation. Wit Restor'd. Wits Recreations. London: 1874. V. 51

MENOCAL, A. G.
Report of the U. S. Nicaragua Surveying Party, 1885. Washington: 1886. V. 50; 52

MENOTTI, GIAN-CARLO
Amahl and the Night Visitors. New York: 1952. V. 49

MENPES, DOROTHY
Venice. London: 1904. V. 53; 54

MENPES, MORTIMER
The Durbar... London: 1903. V. 48
Japan, A Record in Colour. London: 1905. V. 48; 49
War Impressions, Being a Record in Colour by Mortimer Menpes. London: 1901. V. 50
World's Children. London: 1903. V. 50

MENSING, A. W. M.
The Mensing Library. Catalogue of the Very Valuable and Important Library... London: 1936-37. V. 50; 53

MENTEITH, ROBERT
The History of the Troubles of Great Britain. London: 1735. V. 47; 53

MENTZ, A.
Billeder af Nordens Flora. Copenhagen: 1917-27. V. 51

MENZBIR, M.
(Russian): Game and Commercial Birds of European Russia and the Caucasus. Moscow: 1898-1902. V. 52

MENZEL, DOROTHY
The Paracas Pottery of ica: a Study in Style and Time. Berkeley: 1964. V. 50

MENZIES, ARCHIBALD
Menzies' Journal of Vancouver's Voyage, April to October, 1792. Victoria: 1923. V. 48; 49

MENZIES, JOHN W.
To the People of the Sixth Congressional District, Kentucky. Covington: 1863. V. 47

MENZIES, ROBERT
Winston Churchill - a Tribute Given on the Occasion of the State Funeral of Sir Winston Churchill - January 30, 1965. London: 1965. V. 49

MENZIES, WILLIAM
Catalogue of the Books and Manuscripts Forming the Private Library of William Menzies of New York. New York: 1875. V. 54
Forest Trees and Woodland Scenery, as Described in Ancient and Modern Poets. London: 1875. V. 47; 52
The History of Windsor Great Park and Windsor Forest. London: 1864. V. 47; 52

MEPISASHVILI, RUSUDAN
The Arts of Ancient Georgia. London: 1979. V. 54

MERA, H. P.
The Alfred I. Barton Collection of Southwestern Textiles. Santa Fe: 1949. V. 48
Pueblo Indian Embroidery. 1943. V. 52
The Rain Bird, a Study in Pueblo Design. Santa Fe: 1937. V. 48; 51; 54

THE MERCANTILE Penman, a Series of Commercial Letters to Qualify the Pupil for Mercantile Correspondence. London: 1851. V. 52

MERCATOR, GERARD
The Treatise of Gerard Mercator. Literarum Latinarum, Quas Italicas, Cursoriasque Vocant, Scribendarum Ratio. Antwerp: 1930. V. 50

MERCER, A. H. H.
The Late Captain Henry Mercer, of the Royal Artillery, who Was Killed by Undue and Useless Exposure at the Battle of Rangiriri, New Zealand, Nov. 1863... Toronto: 1865. V. 52

MERCER, ASA SHINN
The Banditti of the Plains. Cheyenne: 1894. V. 47; 48
Banditti of the Plains. Sheridan: 1930. V. 48; 50
The Banditti of the Plains. San Francisco: 1935. V. 52

MERCER, CAVALIE
Journal of the Waterloo Campaign, kept Throughout the Campaign of 1815. London: 1870. V. 50

MERCER, HENRY C.
The Bible in Iron, or Pictured Stoves and Stove Plates of the Pennsylvania Germans. Doylestown: 1941. V. 47

MERCER, JEROME J.
Mountains and Lakes of Switzerland and Italy. London: 1871. V. 51

MERCER, THOMAS
A Vocabulary, Latin and English... London: 1817. V. 51

MERCER, TONY
Mercer Chronometers: Radical Tom Mercer and the House He Founded. Kent: 1978. V. 53

MERCER, VAUDREY
The Frodshams: The Story of a Family of Chronometer Makers. 1981. V. 53
John Arnold and Son. 1972. V. 53
The Life and Letters of Edward John Dent, Chronometer Maker and some Account of His Successors. 1977. V. 53

MERCHANT Marine, 1453-1850. Athens: 1972. V. 47

MERCHANT, PAUL
Stones. Exeter: 1973. V. 48; 54

MERCIER, CHARLES ARTHUR
The Nervous System and the Mind: a Treatise on the Dynamics of the Human Organism. London: 1888. V. 53; 54

MERCIER, LOUIS SEBASTIEN
Fragments of Politics and History... London: 1795. V. 48
Memoirs of the Year Two Thousand Five Hundred. London: 1772. V. 49
Paris in Miniature; Taken from the French Picture at Full Length, Entituled Tableau de Paris. London: 1782. V. 51; 52

MERCIER, S. A. B.
The Tell El-Amarna Tablets. Toronto: 1939-51. V. 50

MERCURIALE, GIROLAMO
La Commare Oriccoglitrice...Divisa in tre Libri. Ristampata Correta et Accresciuta dall' Istesso Autore... Venice: 1601. V. 47
De Arte Gymnastica Libri Sex. Venice: 1573. V. 48
De Arte Gymnastica Libri Sex. Paris: 1577. V. 47
De Arte Gymnastica, Libri Sex... Amsterdam: 1672. V. 47

MERCURIO, GERONIMO SCIPION
Le Commare o Raccoglitrice Dell' Eccellentissimo Signor Scipion Mercurio Filososo, Medico e Cittadino Romano... Venetia: 1680. V. 49

MEREDITH, GEORGE
The Adventures of Harry Richmond. New York: 1900. V. 48
The Amazing Marriage. London: 1895. V. 48; 53; 54
Beauchamp's Career. London: 1876. V. 54
The Cheer. New York: 1980. V. 47
The Collected Works. London: 1912. V. 47
Diana of the Crossways. London: 1865. V. 48
Diana of the Crossways. London: 1885. V. 48; 54
The Egoist. London: 1879. V. 49
Emilia in England. London: 1864. V. 47; 51
An Essay on Comedy and the Uses of Comic Spirit. Westminster: 1897. V. 53
Evan Harrington. London: 1861. V. 51
The House on the Beach. New York: 1877. V. 48; 53
Jump to Glory Jane. London: 1892. V. 50
Letters of George Meredith. London: 1912. V. 53; 54
The Letters of George Meredith to Alice Meynell, with Annotations Thereto, 1896-1907. London: 1923. V. 47; 52; 54
Lord Ormont and His Aminta. London: 1894. V. 48; 52; 54
Modern Love. Portland: 1881. V. 52
Modern Love. London: 1892. V. 53
Modern Love and Poems of the English Roadside with Poems and Ballads. London: 1862. V. 51; 54
One of Our Conquerors. London: 1891. V. 47; 48; 50; 51; 52
The Ordeal of Richard Feverel. London: 1859. V. 47; 51
Poems. London: 1851. V. 50; 51
Rhoda Fleming. 1865. V. 50
Rhoda Fleming. London: 1865. V. 52
The Shaving of Shagpat: an Arabian Entertainment. London: 1856. V. 47; 51
The Tragic Comedians. London: 1880. V. 47
The Tragic Comedians. London: 1881. V. 48
Works of... London: 1910-20. V. 47; 51

MEREDITH, GRACE E.
Girl Captives of the Cheyennes - a True Story of the Capture and Rescue of Pioneer Girls. Los Angeles: 1927. V. 52; 54

MEREDITH, LOUISA ANNE TWAMLEY
Loved and Lost! The True Story of a Short Life. London: 1860. V. 54
My Home in Tasmania; or, Nine Years in Australia. New York: 1853. V. 53
Notes and Sketches of New South Wales, During a Residence in that Colony from 1839 to 1844. London: 1844. V. 54
Our Wild Flowers... London: 1843. V. 50; 54
The Romance of Nature; or, the Flower-Seasons Illustrated. London: 1839. V. 54
Tasmanian Friends and Foes, Feathered, Furred and Finned. London: 1881. V. 53

MEREDITH, ROY
Mr. Lincoln's Camera Man. Mathew B. Brady. New York: 1946. V. 53

MEREDITH, WILLIAM
Love Letters from and Impossible Land. New Haven: 1944. V. 47
Ships and Other Figures. Princeton: 1948. V. 47

MERES, JOHN
Information for Sir John Meres Against the York-Building Company. (with) Information for the Governor and Company of the York-Buildings; Against Sir John Meres. Edinburgh: 1730. V. 53

MERIAN, M. S.
De Europiche Insecten. Amsterdam: 1730. V. 53

MERIAN, MATTHIEU
La danse Des Morts, Comme Elle est Depeinte dans La Louable et Celebre Ville de Basle... Basel: 1756. V. 51

MERICKA, VACLAV
Orders and Decorations. London: 1967. V. 50

MERIGOT, JAMES
Promenade Ou Itineraire des Jardins d'Ermenonville... Paris: 1788. V. 50
A Select Collection of Views and Ruins in Rome and Its Vicinity. London. V. 54
A Select Collection of Views and Ruins in Rome and its Vicinity. London: 1815. V. 54
A Select Collection of Views and Ruins in Rome and its Vicinity... London: 1819. V. 51; 52; 54
A Select Collection of Views and Ruins in Rome and its Vicinity. London: 1827-28. V. 50; 53

MERIMEE, PROSPER
1572. A Chronicle of the Times of Charles the Ninth. New York: 1830. V. 50
Carmen. London: 1887. V. 47; 54
Carmen. Boston: 1896. V. 48
Carmen. Winchester: 1896. V. 49
Carmen. Paris: 1911. V. 48
Carmen. London: 1916. V. 53; 54
Carmen. New York: 1941. V. 47; 48; 49; 52
Carmen. New York: 1945. V. 50; 52; 54
Carmen and Letters from Spain. 1931. V. 48
Carmen and Letters from Spain. Paris: 1931. V. 52

MERINO DE JESUCRISTO, ANDRES
Escuela Paleographica, o de Leer Letras Antiguas, Desde la Entrada de Los Godos en Espana, Hasta Nuestros Tiempos... Madrid: 1780. V. 50; 53

MERITON, GEORGE
Land-Lords Law a Treatise Very Fit for the Perusal of All Gentlemen and Others. London: 1665. V. 48
Nomenclatura Clericalis; or, the Young Clerks Vocabulary, in English & Latine. London: 1685. V. 52
The Praise of York-shire Ale Wherein Is Enumerated Several Sorts of Drink... York: 1697. V. 49

MERIVALE, HERMAN
Lectures on Colonization and Colonies Delivered Before the University of Oxford in 1839, 1840 & 1841. London: 1861. V. 49; 51

MERIVALE, JOHN HERMAN
Orlando in Roncesvalles, a Poem, in Five Cantos. London: 1814. V. 51; 54

MERIWETHER, ELIZABETH AVERY
Facts and Falsehoods. Concerning the War On the South 1861-1865. Memphis: 1904. V. 48; 52

MERK, FREDERICK
Fur Trade and Empire, George Simpson's Journal. Cambridge: 1931. V. 54

MERKEN, JOHANN
Liber Artificiosus Alphabeti Maioris, Oder Neu Inventirtes Kunst - Schreib - und Zeichenbuch..., Erste (Anderer) Theil. Elberfield: 1785. V. 50; 53
Liber Artificiosvs Alphabeti Maioris, Oder: Neu Inventirtes Kunst-Schreig- und Zeichenbuch. Mulheim am Rhein: 1782-85. V. 53

MERKLEY, CHRISTOPHER
Biography of Christopher Merkley: Written by Himself... Salt Lake City: 1887. V. 47; 49

MERLE, JEAN TOUSSAINT
Description Historique et Pittoresque du Chateau de Chambord... Paris: 1821. V. 49

MERMAN, ETHEL
Merman. New York: 1978. V. 52

MERREM, B.
Avium Rariorum et Minus Cognitarum Icones et Descriptiones. Leipzig: 1786-87. V. 48

MERRETT, C.
Pinax Rerum Naturalium Britannicarum Continens Vegetabilia, Animalia et Fossilia, in hac Insula Reperta Inchoatus. London: 1667. V. 51

MERRIAM, C. HART
The Dawn of the World: Myths and Weird Tales Told by the Mewan Indians of California. Cleveland: 1910. V. 48

MERRICK, JAMES
The Destruction of Troy. Oxford: 1742?. V. 48; 52

MERRICK, JOHN
Heliocrene: a Poem in Latin and English, on the Chalybeate Well at Sunning-Hill in Windsor Forest. Reading: 1744. V. 47

MERRICK, LEONARD
Cynthia. A Daughter of the Philistines. London: 1896. V. 51
The Man Who Was Good: a Novel. London: 1892. V. 54
The Works. New York: 1919-27. V. 51

MERRIFIELD, MARY PHILADELPHIA
A Sketch of the Natural History of Brighton and Its Vicinity. Brighton: 1860. V. 49

MERRILL, ELMER D.
The Botany of Cook's Voyages and Its Unprecedented Significance in Relation to Anthropology, Biogeography and History. Waltham: 1954. V. 54

MERRILL, G. P.
Contributions to a History of American State Geological and Natural History Surveys. 1920. V. 53

MERRILL, HENRY A.
Alexander Gifford, or, Vi'let's Boy: A Story of Negro Life. Salem: 1905. V. 47

MERRILL, JAMES
Braving the Elements. New York: 1972. V. 51; 53
Bronze. New York: 1984. V. 47; 52; 53; 54
The Country of a Thousand years of Peace. New York: 1959. V. 48; 50; 53
David Jackson: Scenes from His Life. New York: 1994. V. 54
The (Diblos) Notebook. New York: 1965. V. 50
Divine Comedies. (and) Scripts for the Pageant. New York: 1976. V. 51; 53
First Poems. New York: 1951. V. 47; 48; 50; 51; 52
Five Inscriptions. Cambridge: 1974. V. 47
From the First Nine: Poems 1946-1976. New York: 1982. V. 53
Ideas, Etc. New York: 1980. V. 51; 53; 54
The Image Maker. New York: 1986. V. 47; 53; 54
Japan: Prose of Departure. New York: 1987. V. 54
Japan: Prose of Departure. New York: 1988. V. 47; 53; 54
Late Settings. New York: 1985. V. 51
Marbled Paper. Salem: 1972. V. 47
Marbled Paper. Salem: 1982. V. 51; 52; 53
The Medusa. Amherst: 1946. V. 53
Metamorphosis Of 741. 1977. V. 47; 50; 51; 53; 54
Mirabell: Books of Number. New York: 1978. V. 51; 53; 54
Nights and Days. New York: 1966. V. 53
Nine Lives. New York & Kripplebush: 1993. V. 54
Overdue Pilgrimage to Nova Scotia. New York: 1990. V. 49; 51; 52; 53; 54
Plays of Light. Ann Arbor: 1984. V. 47; 50; 53
Rendevous. 1984. V. 47
Samos. Los Angeles: 1980. V. 48; 51
Santorini: Stopping the Leak. Worcester: 1982. V. 54
Scripts for the Pageant. New York: 1980. V. 53
Selected Poems. London: 1961. V. 47
The Seraglio. New York: 1957. V. 47
Souvenirs. New York: 1984. V. 50; 53; 54
Violent Pastoral. 1965. V. 47
Water Street. New York: 1962. V. 51
Yannina. New York: 1973. V. 48; 52; 53; 54
The Yellow Pages. Cambridge: 1974. V. 47

MERRILL, MARION
The Animated Peter Rabbit. New York: 1945. V. 49

MERRILL, ORIN S.
Mysterious Scott, the Monte Cristo of Death Valley and Tracks of a Tenderfoot through the New Goldfields of Nevada. Chicago: 1906. V. 53

MERRILL, SAMUEL
The Seventieth Indiana Volunteer Infantry in the War of the Rebellion. Indianapolis: 1900. V. 52

MERRILL, SELAH
East of the Jordan: a Record of Travel and Observation in the Countries of Moab, Gilead and Bashan. London: 1881. V. 51
East of the Jordan. A Record of Travel and observation in the Countries of Moab, Gilead and Bashan During the Years 1875-77. New York: 1883. V. 49; 52

MERRIMAN, BRYAN
The Midnight Court. Dublin. V. 48; 50

MERRIMAN, NATHANIEL JAMES
The Kafir, the Hottentot and the Frontier Farmer, Passages of Missionary Life from the Journals... London: 1853. V. 47

MERRIMAN, ROGER BIGELOW
The Rise of the Spanish Empire in the Old World and the New. New York: 1918-34. V. 47

MERRITT, A.
Burn Witch Burn. London: 1955. V. 51
The Ship of Ishtar. 1926. V. 52
Three Lines of Old French. London. V. 47
Three Lines of Old French. 1937. V. 51

MERRITT, BENJAMIN DEAN
The Athenian Calendar in the Fifth Century Based on a Study of the Detailed Accounts of Money Borrowed by the Athenian State. Cambridge: 1928. V. 50; 52
Athenian Financial Documents of the Fifth Century. Ann Arbor: 1932. V. 50; 52
Documents on Athenian Tribute. Cambridge: 1937. V. 50

MERRITT, JOHN
Memoirs of the Life of Wm. Henry West Betty, Known by the Name of the Young Roscius, with a General Estimate of His Talents and a Critique on His Principal Characters. Liverpool: 1804. V. 49

MERRITT, PERCIVAL
Piozzi Marginalia... Cambridge: 1925. V. 53
The True Story of the So-Called Love Letters of Mrs. Piozzi. Cambridge: 1927. V. 54
The True Story of the So-Called Love Letters of Mrs. Piozzi. Cambridge: 1928. V. 48; 50; 52

THE MERRY Alphabet. New York: 1900. V. 53

THE MERRY Ballads of Oldentime. London: 1885. V. 50

MERRY Christmas!. New York: 1943. V. 52

THE MERRY Droll, or Pleasing Companion. London: 1769. V. 51

THE MERRY Frolics or the Comical Cheats of Swalpo; A Notorious Pickpocket and the Merry Pranks of Rogert the Clown. London: 1826. V. 48

MERRY Making, Holidays and Jolly Days. London: 1850. V. 47

MERRY, ROBERT
The Pains of Memory. London: 1796. V. 49; 50; 54

MERRY, THOMAS
The American Thoroughbred. Los Angeles: 1905. V. 54

MERRYMOUNT PRESS
A Selection of Type Ornaments - the Merrymount Press Collection of Daniel Berkeley Updike Now at the Bancroft Library. Berkeley: 1984. V. 52

MERRYTHOUGHT, MATTHEW, PSEUD.
The Comic Primer, or, Synonyms Explained to Children. London: 1830. V. 49

MERRYWEATHER, F. SOMNER
Bibliomania in the Middle Ages; or, Sketches of Bookworms - Collectors - Bible Students - Scribes and Illuminators... London: 1849. V. 53

MERRYWEATHER, GEORGE
A Lecture on Gold and Iron and Iron Ore, With Especial Reference to the Ironstone of the Vale of Esk... London: 1853. V. 51; 53

MERRYWEATHER, JAMES COMPTON
The Fire Brigade Handbook: a Manual of the Organization and Equipment of Fire Brigades. London: 1911. V. 53
Fire Protection for Mansions. London: 1886. V. 52

MERSHON, GRACE L. O.
My Folks. Story of the Forefathers of Oliver Francis Mershon, M.D. 1946. V. 49

MERSHON, W. B.
The Passenger Pigeon. New York: 1907. V. 51

MERTINS, LOUIS
The Intervals of Robert Frost: A Critical Bibliography. Berkeley: 1947. V. 48

MERTON, THOMAS
The Alaskan Journal of Thomas Merton with Sixteen Letters. Isla Vista: 1988. V. 52; 53
Boris Pasternak/Thomas Merton. Six Letters. Lexington: 1973. V. 48; 51
Bread in the Wilderness. New York: 1953. V. 53
The Christmas Sermons of Bl. Guerric of Igny. An Essay by Thomas Merton. Louisville: 1959. V. 48; 49; 51; 52; 53; 54
The Covenant. New York: 1980. V. 49
Early Poems 1940/1942. Lexington: 1971. V. 50; 53
Elected Silence. London: 1949. V. 48; 51
Encounter - Thomas Merton and D. T. Suzuki. Monterey: 1988. V. 48; 51
Father Louie. New York. V. 48
Father Louie. London: 1991. V. 47
Father Louie. New York: 1991. V. 49
Hagia Sophia. Lexington: 1962. V. 53
A Man in the Divided Sea. New York: 1946. V. 49; 52
Nativity Kerygma. 1958. V. 53
On the Solitary Life. 1977. V. 48; 51
Original Child Bomb. 1961. V. 50
Original Child Bomb. New York: 1961. V. 48
Original Child Bomb. New York: 1962. V. 50
Original Child Bomb. Norfolk: 1962. V. 53
Praying the Psalms. Collegeville: 1956. V. 51
Raids on the Unspeakable. New York: 1966. V. 49
Seeds of Contemplation. New York: 1949. V. 49
Seeds of Contemplation. Norfolk: 1949. V. 48; 49; 52

MERTON, THOMAS continued
The Seven Storey Mountain. New York: 1948. V. 49; 50; 52
The Sign of Jonas. London: 1953. V. 50
The Spirit of Simplicity. Gethsemani: 1948. V. 48; 51
The Strange Islands. Poems. Norfolk;: 1957. V. 47; 48
The Tears of the Blind Lions. New York: 1949. V. 49; 51
Thirty Poems. Norfolk: 1944. V. 48; 52; 53
The Tower of Babel. Norfolk: 1957. V. 53; 54
Waters of Silence. London: 1950. V. 48; 51
The Waters of Siloe. New York: 1949. V. 47; 48; 51
The Way of Chuang Tzu. New York: 1965. V. 50

MERULA, GAUDENTIUS
Memorabilium...Ultra Primam Editionem et Recognitum et Quator Libris Auctum Opus cum Emendatione et Scholiis. Lyon: 1556. V. 47; 48; 49; 50

MERVAULT, PETER
The Last Famous Siege of the city of Roche; Together with the Edict of Nantes. London: 1680. V. 52

MERWIN, RAYMOND
The Ruins of Holmul, Guatemala. Cambridge: 1932. V. 50

MERWIN, W. S.
Chinese Figures (Second Series). Mt. Horeb: 1971. V. 53; 54
The Dancing Bears. New Haven: 1954. V. 53
Feathers from the Hill. Iowa City: 1978. V. 54
Green with Beasts. London: 1956. V. 47; 48; 53
Green With Beasts. New York: 1956. V. 51
Koa. New York: 1988. V. 47; 54
Mary. New York: 1976. V. 53
A Mask for Janus. New Haven: 1952. V. 47; 48; 50; 51; 53
Signs. Iowa City: 1971. V. 53; 54
Three Poems. New York: 1968. V. 48; 54

MERYMAN, RICHARD
Andrew Wyeth. Boston: 1968. V. 47; 48; 49; 50; 52

MERZ, JOHN THEODORE
A History of European Thought in the Nineteenth Century. Edinburgh & London: 1923/28/30. V. 54

MERZBACHER, GOTTFRIED
Aus Den Hochregionen des Kaukasus. Leipzig: 1901. V. 54

MESENS, E. L. T.
Idolatry and Confusion. 1944. V. 50
Troisieme Front Poems de Guerre Suivi de Pieces Detachees.... 1944. V. 50

MESERVE, CHARLES F.
A Tour of Observations Among Indians and Indian Schools in Arizona, New Mexico, Oklahoma and Kansas. Philadelphia: 1894. V. 47

MESSIAH. A Sacred Eclogue, in Imitation of Virgil's Pollio. London: 1751. V. 53

MESSITER, CHARLES ALSTON
Sport and Adventures Among the North-American Indians. London: 1890. V. 47

MESSLER, ABRAHAM
Centennial History of Somerset County. Somerville: 1878. V. 47; 49; 51
First Things in Old Somerset. Somerville: 1899. V. 49

THE METALLURGIST Johann Conrad Fischer 1773-1854 and His Relations with Britain. Schaffhausen: 1947. V. 50

METCALF, JOHN
The Life of John Metcalf, Commonly Called Blind Jack of Knaresboro... Leeds: 1801. V. 51

METCALF, SAMUEL L.
A Collection of Some of the Most Interesting Narratives of Indian Warfarae in the West, Containing an Account of the Adventures of Colonel Daniel Boone, One of the First Settlers of Kentucky. Lexington: 1821. V. 47; 48

METCALF, THERON
Digest of the Cases Decided in the Supreme Judicial Court of...Massachusetts. Boston: 1825. V. 51
Digest of the Cases Decided in the Supreme Judicial Court of...Massachusetts. Cincinnati: 1884. V. 52

METCALFE, C. R.
Anatomy of Monocotyledons. Oxford: 1960-82. V. 50
Anatomy of Monocotyledons. Oxford: 1960-69. V. 54

METCALFE, FREDERICK
The Oxonian in Iceland: or, Notes of Travel in that Island in the Summer of 1860... London: 1861. V. 54
The Oxonian in Norway. London: 1856. V. 47; 53
The Oxonian in Norway; or, Notes of Excursions in that Country. London: 1857. V. 52

METCALFE, J.
The Feasting Dead. Sauk City: 1954. V. 52

METCALFE, SAMUEL L.
Caloric: Its Mechanical, Chemical and Vital Agencies in the Phenomena of Nature. London: 1843. V. 53

METCALFE, W. M.
Ancient Lives of Scottish Saints. Paisley: 1895. V. 54
A History of the County of Renfrew from the Earliest Times. Paisley: 1905. V. 49

METCHIM, B.
Wild West Poems. London: 1890?. V. 47

THE METEROR; or, General Censor: Comprising Satirical and Humourous Essays. London: 1816. V. 49

METEYARD, ELIZA
Choice Examples of Wedgwood Art. London: 1879. V. 47; 48; 51
The Doctor's Little Daughter. London: 1850. V. 47
The Lady Herbert's Gentlewomen. London: 1862. V. 47
The Life of Josiah Wedgwood, from His Private Correspondence and Family Papers in the Possession of Joseph Mayer, F. Wedgwood, C. Darwin... London: 1865. V. 47; 51; 52

METFESSEL, MILTON
Phonophotography In Folk Music: American Negro Songs in New Notation. Chapel Hill: 1928. V. 48

METHODISM Anatomiz'd: or an Alarm to Pennsylvania. Philadelphia: 1763. V. 54

METHUEN, H. H.
Life in the Wilderness, or Wanderings in South Africa. London: 1846. V. 48; 49; 52

METHVIN, JOHN J.
Andele, or the Mexican Kiowa Captive. Aranarko: 1899. V. 49
Andele or the Mexican-Kiowa Captive. Louisville: 1859. V. 53
Andele or the Mexican-Kiowa Captive. Louisville: 1899. V. 51

METLAKE, GEORGE
The Life and Writings of St. Columban, 542?-615. Philadelphia: 1914. V. 50; 51; 54

THE METRICAL History of Sir William Wallace, Knight of Ellerslie, by Henry, Commonly Called Blind Harry... Perth: 1790. V. 47

METRO International Directory of Contemporary Art, 1964. Milano: 1964. V. 54

METROPOLITAN Grievances: or, A Serio-Comic Glance at Minor Mischiefs in London and Its Vicinity, Including a Few Which Extend to the Country. London: 1812. V. 49

METROPOLITAN MUSEUM OF ART
The Architect and the Industrial Arts. An Exhibition of Contemporary American Design, Feb. 12 - March 24, 1929. V. 54
Mexico, Splendors of Thirty Centuries. Boston: 1990. V. 47
The Temple of Hibris in El Khargeh Oasis. New York: 1939-53. V. 51

METROPOLITAN OPERA GUILD
Opera Calvalcade: the Story of the Metropolitan. New York: 1938. V. 49

METROPOLITAN TELEPHONE & TELEGRAPH CO., NEW YORK
List of Subscribers, June 1st, 1893. New York: 1893. V. 47

METTLER, CECILIA
History of Medicine. Philadelphia: 1947. V. 47; 48; 50; 52

METTLER, FREDERICK ALBERT
Psychosurgical Problems. The Columbia Greystone Associates Second Group. London: 1952. V. 52
Selective Partial Ablation of the Frontal Cortex: a Correlative Study of its Effects on Human Psychotic Subjects. New York: 1949. V. 53

METZ, LEON C.
The Shooters. El Paso;: 1976. V. 50

METZ, PETER
The Golden Gospels of Echternach. Codex Aureus Epternacensis. New York: 1957. V. 50

METZDORF, ROBERT F.
The Tinker Library: a Bibliographical Catalogue of the Books and Manuscripts Collected by Chauncey Brewster Tinker. New Haven: 1959. V. 48

METZEROTT, W. G.
Our National Buildings! Views of Washington. Washington: 1845-50. V. 51

METZGAR, JUDSON D.
Adventures in Japanese Prints. Los Angeles: 1943. V. 52

MEUNIER, CHARLES
La Flore Ornamentale Appropriee aux Decors des Reliures. Paris: 1938. V. 50

MEUNIER, LOUIS
Veue du Palais, Jardins et Fontaine Darangouesse, Maison de Plaisance do Roy d'Espagne. Paris: 1665. V. 53

MEURDRAC, MARIE
La Chymie Charitable et Facile en Faveur des Dames, par Demoiselle M.M. Lyons: 1680. V. 47

MEURS, JAN DE
Criticvs Arnobianvs Tributus in Libros Septem. Lugduni Batavorum: 1599. V. 54

MEUTRA, RICHARD
Mystery and Realities of the Site. Scarsdale: 1951. V. 50

MEUVE, M. DE
Dictionaire Pharmaceutique ou Apparat de Medecine, Pharmacie et Chymie. Paris: 1689. V. 54

MEUZE, M.
African Art. Cleveland: 1968. V. 54

MEW, CHARLOTTE
The Farmer's Bride. London: 1921. V. 52

MEWBURN, FRANCIS
The Larchfield Dairy. London: 1876. V. 49

MEWBY, ERIC
A Short Walk in the Hindu Kush. London: 1958. V. 48

MEXIA, PEDRO
La Selva di Varia Lettione... Venice: 1558. V. 50

MEYENDORF, BARON VON
A Journey From Orenburg to Bokhara in the Year 1820. Calcutta: 1870. V. 49

MEYER, A. B.
The Birds of Celebes and the Neighbouring Islands. Berlin: 1898. V. 48

MEYER, A. J. P.
Oceanic Art. Cologne: 1995. V. 54

MEYER, AGNES E.
Chinese Painting, As Reflected in the Thought and Art of Li Lung-Mien 1070-1106. Duffield: 1923. V. 50
Chinese Painting as Reflected in the Thought and the Art of Li Lung-Mien 1070-1106. New York: 1923. V. 54

MEYER, ALFRED
Historical Aspects of Cerebral Anatomy. London: 1971. V. 52

MEYER, CARL
Bound for Sacramento. Travel-Pictures of a returned Wanderer. Claremont: 1938. V. 48

MEYER, F. J.
Steam Towing on Rivers and Canals, by means of a Submerged Cable. London: 1876. V. 54

MEYER, FRANZ
Chagall: His Graphic Work. New York: 1957. V. 53; 54
Marc Chagall. New York: 1963. V. 47; 50; 51; 53
Marc Chagall: Life and Work. New York. V. 47; 48; 50; 52
Marc Chagall: Life and Work. New York: 1964. V. 47; 50; 52

MEYER, G. F. W.
Flora des Konigreichs Hannover. Gottingen: 1842-54. V. 47; 49

MEYER, H. L.
Coloured Illustrations of British Birds and Their Eggs. London: 1853-57. V. 54

MEYER, HANS
Der Kilimandjaro. Reisen und Studien... Berlin: 1900. V. 48

MEYER, HENRY C.
Civil War Experiences Under Bayard, Gregg, Kilpatrick, Custer, Raulston, and Newberry, 1862, 63, 64. New York: 1911. V. 49

MEYER, HENRY LEONARD
Coloured Illustrations of British Birds and Their Eggs. London: 1842-50. V. 50; 53
Coloured Illustrations of British Birds and Their Eggs. London: 1853-57. V. 48
Illustrations of British Birds. London: 1835-50. V. 48; 49
Illustrations of British Birds. London: 1837-44. V. 48

MEYER, J. J.
The Deer - Smellers of Haunted Mountain. 1921. V. 47; 51

MEYER, KUNO
Cath Finntraga. London: 1885. V. 47; 51

MEYER, MICHAEL
Eight Oxford Poets. London: 1941. V. 47

MEYER, NICHOLAS
The West End Horror - a Posthumous Memoir of John H. Watson, M.D. New York: 1976. V. 54

MEYER, RUDOLF
Die Menschliche Sterblichkeit under Dem Titel Todten Tanz in LXI Original Kupfern, von Rudolf und Conrad Meyeren Beruhmten Kunstmahlern in Zurich... Hamburg und Leipzig: 1759. V. 52; 54

MEYER, RUSS
The Glamour Camera of Russ Meyer. Louisville: 1958. V. 51

MEYER, THOMAS
Ann Lee Leads the Way. 1974. V. 47
May. Champaign: 1983. V. 54
Monotypes & Tracings: German Romantics. London: 1994. V. 50; 51; 52
O Nathan. Vermont: 1973. V. 49
Sappho's Raft. Highlands: 1982. V. 54
The Umbrella of Aesculapius. Highlands: 1975. V. 48; 52; 54

MEYER, TOM
Poikilos. Urbana: 1971. V. 54

MEYER, WILLY
Cancer: Its Origin, Its Development, and Its Self-Perpetuation. New York: 1931. V. 49

MEYER DE SCHAUENSEE, R.
The Birds of China. Oxford: 1984. V. 52; 53
The Birds of the Republic of Colombia, Their Distribution and Keys for Their Indentification. Bogota: 1948-49. V. 54
A Guide to the Birds of South America. Wynnewood: 1970. V. 49; 51
A Guide to the Birds of Venezuela. Princeton: 1978. V. 49

The Species of Birds of South America and Their Distribution. Philadelphia: 1966. V. 51; 52; 54

MEYERS, ERIC M.
Excavations at Ancient Meiron, Upper Galilee, Israel 1971-72, 1974-75, 1977. Cambridge: 1981. V. 49; 52

MEYERS, WILLIAM E.
Sketches of California and Hawaii. 1970. V. 48

MEYERS, WILLIAM H.
Journal of a Cruise to California and the Sandwich Islands in the United States Sloop-of-War Cyane, 1841-1844. San Francisco: 1955. V. 47; 50; 53; 54
Naval Sketches of the War in California. New York: 1939. V. 47; 49; 50; 53; 54
Sketches of California and Hawaii by...., Gunner U.S.N. Aboard the United State Sloop-of-War-Cyane 1842-1843. San Francisco: 1970. V. 47; 49; 50; 53

MEYLER, WILLIAM
Poetical Amusement on the Journey of Life: Consisting of Various Pieces in Verse... Bath: 1806. V. 48; 54

MEYNELL, ALICE
Cere's Runaway and Other Essays. London: 1909. V. 47
The Children. London: 1897. V. 52; 53
Later Poems. London and New York: 1902. V. 54
London Impressions, Etchings and Pictures in Photogravures. Westminster: 1898. V. 50
Mary, the Mother of Jesus: an Essay. London: 1912. V. 54
The Poems of... London: 1923. V. 50

MEYNELL, FRANCIS
Nonesuch Century. An Appraisal, a Personal Note and a Bibliography of the First Hundred Books Issued by the Press 1923-1934. V. 48
The Poetry of Alice Meynell... 1971. V. 52; 54
Seventeen Poems. London: 1945. V. 53
Two Poems by Francis Meynell. 1961. V. 51
Typography, the Written Word and the Printed Word... London: 1923. V. 47; 52
The Week-End Book. London: 1939. V. 47

MEYNELL, GERARD T.
Pages from Books. (with) Pages from Books Set on the 'Monotype' Composing Machine and Published Mainly in London, 1928-1931. London: 1927-31. V. 47

MEYNELL, HUGO
Meynellian Science or Fox Hunting Upon System. 1926. V. 47

MEYNELL, KATHARINE
Eat Book. London: 1990. V. 52
Eat Book. 1991. V. 52
Seas of the Moon. London: 1988. V. 51; 53

MEYNELL, VIOLA
Friends of a Lifetime - Letters to Sydney Carlyle Cockerell. London: 1940. V. 54

MEYNELL, WILFRID
The Annual Register or A View of the History, Politics and Literature for the Year 1810. London: 1801. V. 47
The Child Set in the Midst. London: 1892. V. 50; 53

MEYNERT, THEODOR HERMANN
Psychiatry: a Clinical Treatise on Diseases of the Fore-Brain Based Upon a Study of Its Structure, Functions and Nutrition. New York/London: 1885. V. 52

MEYRICK, EDWIN
The Texian Grand March for the Piano Forte. New York: 1836. V. 52
The Texian Grand March for the Piano Forte. New York: 1847?. V. 47

MEYRICK, SAMUEL RUSH
Costume of the Original Inhabitants of the British Islands... London: 1821. V. 50
A Critical Enquiry Into Ancient Armour, as It Existed in Great Britain, from the Norman Conquest to the Reign of King Charles II. London: 1824. V. 48
A Critical Inquiry Into Antient Armour, from the Norman Conquest to the Reign of King Charles II. London: 1842. V. 50

MEYRICK, WILLIAM
The New Family Herbal; or, Domestic Physician... Birmingham: 1790. V. 49

MEYRINK, G.
The Golem. 1928. V. 48; 52; 53
The Golem. Boston: 1928. V. 49

MEZERAY, FRANCOIS
A General Chronological History of France... London: 1683. V. 47; 52

MEZZROW, MEZZ
Really the Blues. New York: 1946. V. 51

MIALL, L. C.
The Early Naturalists: Their Lives and Work (1530-1789). London: 1912. V. 53
The Life and Work of Charles Darwin, a Lecture delivered to the Leeds Philosophical and Literary Society. Leeds: 1883. V. 48

MICHAEL, A. D.
British Oribatidae. London: 1884-88. V. 54

MICHAEL, EMILE
Rembrandt: His Life, His Work and His Time. London: 1910. V. 47

MICHAEL, W.
Wyndham Lewis: Paintings and Drawings. Berkeley: 1971. V. 47

MICHAELIS, H. VON
Birds of the Gauntlet. London: 1952. V. 53

MICHALOWSKI, KAZIMIERZ
Art of Ancient Egypt. New York: 1968. V. 48; 51

MICHALS, DUANE
Album: the Portraits of Duane Michaels, 1958-1988. Pasadena: 1988. V. 50
Homage to Cavafy. Danbury: 1978. V. 47; 53
Real Dreams. Photo Studies by Duane Michals. Danbury: 1976. V. 47
Sequences. Garden City: 1970. V. 47

MICHAUD, JOSEF FRANCOIS
History of the Crusades. London: 1852. V. 51

MICHAUD, JOSEPH FRANCOIS
The History of the Crusades. New York: 1853. V. 54

MICHAUX, ANDRE
Flora Boreali-Americana, sistens Caracteres Plantarum Quas in America Septentrionali Collegit et Detexit. Paris & Strasbourg: 1803. V. 48

MICHAUX, FRANCOIS ANDRE
The North American Sylva, or a Description of the Forest Trees of the United States, Canada and Nova Scotia. Philadelphia: 1817. V. 51
The North American Sylva; or a Description of the Forest Trees of the United States, Canada and Nova Scotia... Philadelphia: 1855. V. 49
The North American Sylva, or a Description of the Forest Trees of the United States, Canada and Nova Scotia. Philadelphia: 1871. V. 49
Travels to the Westward of the Alleghany Mountains, in the States of the Ohio, Kentucky and Tennessee in the Year 1802. London: 1805. V. 47; 50

MICHAUX, HENRI
Ecuador. Paris: 1929. V. 54
Henri Michaux: the Poet of Supreme Solipsism. Birmingham: 1990. V. 53
Ideograms in China. New York: 1984. V. 50; 54

MICHAUX, RICHARD RANDOLPH
Sketches of Life in North Carolina. Culler: 1894. V. 48

MICHEAUX, OSCAR
The Masquerade. New York: 1947. V. 52
The Story of Dorothy Stanfield. New York: 1946. V. 49; 51; 52
The Wind from Nowhere. New York: 1943. V. 52
The Wind from Nowhere. New York: 1944. V. 47

MICHEL, A.
Reports of...On the Gold Region of Canada. Ottawa: 1866. V. 49

MICHEL, E.
Rembrandt, His Life, His Work and His Time. London: 1894. V. 48; 50; 51; 53
Rembrandt, His Life, His Work and His Time. London: 1895. V. 50
Rubens. His Life, His Work and His Time. London: 1899. V. 47

MICHEL, HENRI
Scientific Instruments in Art and History. New York: 1967. V. 54

MICHEL, PAUL HENRI
Romanesque Wall Paintings in France. London: 1950. V. 50

MICHEL, WALTER
Wyndham Lewis: Paintings and Drawings. 1971. V. 54
Wyndham Lewis. Paintings and Drawings. Berkeley: 1971. V. 49; 50; 52
Wyndham Lewis. Paintings and Drawings. London: 1971. V. 50

MICHELET, JULES
The Bird. New York: 1869. V. 51
The Bird. London: 1876. V. 53
The Insect. London: 1875. V. 51
The People. London: 1846. V. 52
The Sorceress: a Study in Middle Age Superstition. Paris: 1904. V. 50
La Sorciere: The Witch of the Middle Ages. London: 1863. V. 48

MICHELI, MARIO DE
Siqueiros. New York: 1968. V. 47; 48; 49; 50

MICHELL, JOHN
A Treatise of Artificial Magnets; in Which is Shewn an Easy and Expeditious Method of Making Them... Cambridge: 1750. V. 47
A Treatise of Artificial Magnets; In Which is Shewn an Easy and Expeditious Method of Making Them... Cambridge: 1751. V. 50

MICHELSON, ALBERT A.
Light Waves and their Uses. Chicago: 1903. V. 48

MICHENER, JAMES ALBERT
About Centennial. Some Notes on the Novel. New York: 1974. V. 49
Alaska. New York: 1988. V. 54
The Bridges at Toko Ri. New York: 1953. V. 53; 54
Caravans. New York: 1963. V. 50; 54
Caravans. London: 1964. V. 52
Caribbean. New York: 1989. V. 52; 54
Centennial. New York: 1974. V. 47; 50
Chesapeake. New York: 1978. V. 49
Collectors, Forgers - And a Writer: a Memoir. New York: 1983. V. 51; 54
The Covenant. New York: 1980. V. 48; 52; 53; 54
The Drifters. 1971. V. 50
The Drifters. New York: 1971. V. 53
The Eagle and the Raven. Austin: 1990. V. 53
Facing East. New York: 1970. V. 47; 49; 50; 51
The Fires of Spring. 1949. V. 53
Fires of Spring. New York: 1949. V. 48
The Floating World. 1954. V. 50
The Floating World. New York: 1954. V. 54
Hawaii. New York: 1959. V. 49; 53; 54
The Hokusai Sketch-Books. Rutland: 1958. V. 53
Iberia. New York: 1968. V. 48; 51; 53; 54
Japanese Prints. London: 1959. V. 50
Japanese Prints. From the Early Masters to the Modern. Rutland/Tokyo: 1959. V. 49; 53
Japanese Prints from the Early Masters to the Modern. 1960. V. 54
Legacy. New York: 1987. V. 48; 50; 54
Literary Reflections. Austin: 1993. V. 51; 52; 54
Literary Reflections. Houston: 1993. V. 51; 52; 53
Mexico. New York: 1992. V. 49; 51; 53; 54
Miracle in Seville. New York: 1995. V. 54
My Lost Mexico. Austin: 1992. V. 48; 51; 52; 54
Poland. New York: 1983. V. 49; 51; 52; 54
The Quality of Life. 1970. V. 48
Rascals. London: 1957. V. 52
Rascals in Paradise. 1957. V. 50
Rascals in Paradise. New York: 1957. V. 52; 53
Recessional. New York: 1994. V. 54
Report of the County Chairman. New York: 1961. V. 50
Return to Paradise. 1951. V. 53
Return to Paradise. New York: 1951. V. 50; 54
Sayonara. New York: 1954. V. 48; 53; 54
The Source. New York: 1965. V. 48; 50; 51
South Pacific. San Diego: 1992. V. 47
Space. New York: 1982. V. 48; 49; 51; 52; 53; 54
Tales of the South Pacific. 1947. V. 50
Tales of the South Pacific. New York: 1950. V. 48
Tales of the South Pacific. London: 1951. V. 47
Tales of the South Pacific. Sydney: 1951. V. 51
Tales of the South Pacific. New York: 1970. V. 50
Texas. New York: 1985. V. 48; 49; 50; 51; 53
Texas. Austin: 1986. V. 51; 52; 53
The Voice of Asia. New York: 1951. V. 50
The World is My Home. New York: 1992. V. 51

MICHIELS, ALFRED
Secret History of the Austrian Government and Of its Systematic Persecutions of Protestants. London: 1859. V. 49

MICHIGAN. ADJUTANT GENERAL
Annual Report of the Adjutant General of the State of Michigan for the Years 865-6. Lansing: 1866. V. 54

MICHIGAN. STATE BOARD OF HEALTH
Michigan, a Summer and Health Resort State. Lansing: 1898. V. 50

MICHIGAN. UNIVERSITY. CLEMENTS LIBRARY
Author/Title Catalogue of Americana 1493-1860 in the William L. Clements Library. Boston: 1970. V. 53

MICKELSON, MAE E.
Tales of the Seeds-Ke-Dee. Denver: 1963. V. 47

MICKLE, ISAAC
Reminiscences of Old Gloucester; or Incidents in the History of the Counties of Gloucester, Atlantic and Camden, New Jersey. Philadelphia: 1845. V. 47; 49; 51

MICKLE, WILLIAM ENGLISH
Well Known Confederate Veterans and Their War Records. New Orleans: 1907. V. 49; 52; 54

MICKLE, WILLIAM JULIUS
General Paralysis of the Insane. London: 1880. V. 52

MICKLEY, J.
Brief Account of Murders by the Indians, and the Cause Thereof, in Northampton County, Pennsylvania, Oct. 8th, 1763. Philadelphia: 1875. V. 53

MICKS, WILLIAM L.
History of the Congested Districts Board. London: 1925. V. 48

MICQUELLUS, JOHANNES LODOVICUS
Avreliae Vrbis Memorabilis ab Anglis Obsidio, Anno 1428. Paris: 1560. V. 48; 50; 53

THE MICROCOSM. London: 1825. V. 52

THE MICROCOSM of London, or London in Miniature. London: 1808-10. V. 54

THE MICROCOSM of London or London in Miniature. London: 1904. V. 54

MICROSCOPICAL SOCIETY
History, Constitution and Laws. London: 1840. V. 48; 49

MIDDENDORP, JACOB
Academiarum Celebrium Universi Terrarum Oribis Libri VIII. Cologne: 1602. V. 50

MIDDIMAN, SAMUEL
Select Views in Great Britain... London: 1813. V. 47; 49; 54

MIDDLE East Anthology. London: 1946. V. 47

MIDDLE HILL PRESS
The Middle Hill Press. A Short Catalogue of Some of sir Thomas Phillipps' Privately Printed Works. London: 1886. V. 53

THE MIDDLE States: a Handbook for Travellers. Boston: 1879. V. 47

MIDDLEBROOK, LOUIS F.
History of Maritime Connecticut During the American Revoution, 1775-1783. Salem: 1925. V. 52

MIDDLESEX County Directory. 1896. New Brunswick: 1896. V. 49; 51

MIDDLETON, BERNARD C.
Recollections: My Life in Bookbinding. Newtown: 1995. V. 54

MIDDLETON, CHARLES
The Architect and Builder's Miscellany; or Pocket Library. London: 1799. V. 47; 48; 51
Designs for Gates and Rails Suitable to Parks, Pleasure Grounds, Balconys, &c., Also Some Designs for Trellis Work on 27 Plates. London: 1799. V. 48
Picturesque And Archiectural Views for Cottages, Farm Houses and Country Villas. London: 1795. V. 49

MIDDLETON, CHARLES THEODORE
A New and Complete System of Geography... London: 1777-78. V. 48

MIDDLETON, CONYERS
Dissertation Concerning the Origin of Printing in England. Cambridge: 1735. V. 48; 51; 53; 54
The History of the Life of Marcus Tullius Cicero. Dublin: 1741. V. 50
The History of the Life of Marcus Tullius Cicero. London: 1757. V. 47; 48; 50
The Life of Maracus Tullius Cicero. London: 1741. V. 53
The Miscellaneous Works. London: 1755. V. 51

MIDDLETON, G. A. T.
Ornamental Details of the Italian Renaissance... London: 1900. V. 48

MIDDLETON, J. HENRY
The Engraved Gems of Classical Times with a Catalogue of the Gems in the Fitzwilliam Museum. Cambridge: 1891. V. 50; 52
The Remains of Ancient Rome. London: 1892. V. 47

MIDDLETON, JAMES
The Celestial Atlas Containing Maps Of All the Constellations Visible in Great Britain... London: 1840. V. 50

MIDDLETON, JESSE EDGAR
Toronto During the French Regime: the History of the Toronto Region from Brule to Simcoe, 1615-1793. Toronto: 1933. V. 54

MIDDLETON, JOHN
View of Agriculture of Middlesex; with Observations On the Means of its Improvement. London: 1798. V. 47; 50; 51; 52; 53; 54
View of the Agriculture of Middlesex. London: 1807. V. 47; 49; 52

MIDDLETON, JOSEPH
A Correct Book of Interest, Containing the Fullest Tables...that Have Yet Appeared...also... Dublin: 1778. V. 49

MIDDLETON, R. HUNTER
Greeting to Fritz Kredel Upon His First Visit to America. New York: 1938. V. 51

MIDDLETON, REGINALD E.
Triangulation and Measurements at the Forth Bridge. London: 1887. V. 49

MIDDLETON, RICHARD
Epigrams and Satyres: made by Richard Middleton of Yorke, Gentleman. Edinburgh: 1840. V. 47; 53
Letters to Henry Savage. London: 1929. V. 54

MIDDLETON, STANLEY
Holiday. London: 1974. V. 50

MIDDLETON, THOMAS
Michaelmas Terme. As it hath Beene Sundry Times Acted by the Children of Paules. London: 1630. V. 47; 50
A Tragi-Comodie Called the Witch Long Since Acted by His Ma(jes)ties Servants at the Black-Friers. London: 1778. V. 49; 52
Works. London: 1840. V. 52

MIDDLETON, W. E. KNOWLES
The History of the Barometer. Baltimore: 1964. V. 53

MIDGELEY, SAMUEL
Hallifax and its Gibbet-Law Placed in a True Light. Together With a Description of the Town; the Nature of the Soil, the Temper and Disposition of the People... London: 1708. V. 49

THE MIDGET London. 1901. V. 54

THE MIDLAND Counties' Railway Companion, with Topographical Descriptions of the Country through Which the Line Passes. Nottingham: 1840. V. 52

THE MIDNIGHT Spy, or, a View of the Transactions of London and Westminster, from the Hours of Ten in the Evening, Till Five in the Morning... London: 1766. V. 49; 50; 54

MIDOLLE, JEAN
Receuil ou Alphabet de Lettres, Initiales Historiques avec Bordures et Fleurons d'Apres le 14 et 15 Siecles. Gand: 1846. V. 49

MIDON, FRANCIS
The Remarkable History of the Rise and Fall of Masaniello, The Fisherman of Naples. London: 1756. V. 50

MIDSUMMER Holidays at Briar's Hall; or, Summer Mornings Improved. London: 1828. V. 48

MIDSUMMER Holydays; or, A Long Story. London: 1790. V. 47

MIEGE, GUY
The Great French Dictionary. London: 1688. V. 50; 53; 54
A Relation of Three Embassies from...Charales II to the Great Duke of Muscovie, The King of Sweden, and the King of Denmark. Performed by the...Earle of Carlisle in the Years 1663 and 1664. London: 1669. V. 52
A Short Dictionary, English and French. With Another French and English. London: 1684. V. 51
The Short French Dictionary, in Two Parts... Hague: 1691. V. 48; 50

MIERS, HENRY A.
Yukon. A Visit to the Yukon Gold-Fields. 1901. V. 52

MIGHELS, ELLA STERLING
Literary California. Poetry, Prose and Portraits.. San Francisco: 1918. V. 53

MIGNAN, ROBERT
Travels in Chaldea Including a Journey from Bussorah to Bagdad, Hillah and Babylon, Performed on Foot in 1827, with Observations on the Sites and Reamins of Babel, Seleucia and Ctesiphon. London: 1829. V. 48; 53

MIKEL, W. C.
City of Belleville History. Picton: 1943. V. 50

MIKKELSEN, EJNAR
Lost in Arctic. London: 1913. V. 49

MILBANK, KITTY
The Flightly Prince. New York: 1963. V. 47

MILBOURNE, LUKE
Notes on Dryden's Virgil. London: 1698. V. 50

THE MILD-White Thorn. London. V. 53

MILDENBERG, LEO
The Arthur S. Dewing Collection of Greek Coins. New York: 1985. V. 48
The Coinage of the Bar Kokhba War. Aarau: 1984. V. 48

MILDMAN, W.
The Method and Rule of Proceeding Upon All Elections, Polls and Scrutinies at Common Halls and Wardmotes Within the City of London. London: 1743. V. 54

MILDMAY, WILLIAM
An Account of the Southern Maritime Provinces of France... London: 1764. V. 52

MILES, ALFRED H.
The Poets and the Poetry of the Century. London: 1893. V. 49

MILES, BARRY
A Descriptive Catalogue of the William S. Burroughs Archive. London: 1973. V. 48; 49; 50

MILES, E.
An Epitome, Historical and Statistical, Descriptive of the Royal Naval Service of England... London: 1841. V. 51

MILES, EMMA BELLE
The Spirit of the Mountains. New York: 1905. V. 50

MILES, HENRY A.
Lowell, As It Was, and As It Is. Lowell: 1845. V. 48; 50; 51; 53; 54

MILES, NELSON APPLETON
Personal Recollections and Observations. Chicago: 1896. V. 47; 48; 49; 50; 53; 54
Personal Recollections and Observations of General Nelson A. Miles.. Chicago: 1897. V. 52; 53
Personal Recollections of... New York: 1896. V. 49
Report of Brig. General N. A. Miles...Commanding the Department of the Columbia, 1884. Vancouver Barracks: 1884. V. 48

MILES, PERRY L.
Fallen Leaves: Memories of an Old Soldier. Berkeley: 1961. V. 49

MILES, S. B.
The Countries and Tribes of the Persian Gulf. London: 1919. V. 49

MILES, W. J.
General Remarks on Stables and Examples of Stable Fittings. London: 1860. V. 51
General Remarks on Stables and Examples of Stable Fittings. London: 1864. V. 52
Modern Practical Farriery, a Complete Ssytem of the Veterinary Art... London: 1880. V. 47; 50; 52

MILFORD, JOHN
Norway, and Her Laplanders, in 1841: with a Few Hints to the Salmon Fisher. London: 1842. V. 49
Observations, Moral, Literary, and Antiquarian, Made During a Tour through the Pyrennes, South of France, Switzerland, the Whole of Italy and the Netherlands, in the Years 1814 and 1815. London: 1818. V. 54

MILHAUD, DARIUS
Notes Without Music. New York: 1953. V. 49

MILHOUS, KATHERINE
The Egg Tree. New York: 1950. V. 48

MILIONI, PIETRO
Vero e Facil Modo d'Imparare a Sonare et Accordare da se medesimo la Chittara Spagnuolo... Venice: 1690. V. 54

THE MILITARY Costume of Turkey. London: 1818. V. 47; 50; 54

A MILITARY Dictionary. Explaining All Difficult Terms in Martial Discipline, Fortification and Gunnery. London: 1704. V. 48

A MILITARY Dictionary Explaining All Difficult Terms in Military Discipline, Fortification and Gunnery. London: 1708. V. 53

MILITARY Essays and Recollections (on the Civil War): Papers Read Before the Commandry of the State of Illinois... Chicago: 1891. V. 47

MILITARY Expedition Against the Sioux Inddians. Washington: 1876. V. 48

MILITARY Orders and Instructions for the Wiltshire Battalion of Militia. Chelsea: 1772. V. 54

THE MILITARY Panorama or Officer's Companion, Embellished with Elegant and Correct Portraits of Distinguished Officers and Military Plans. 1812/13. V. 50

MILIZIA, FRANCESCO
Del Teatro. Venezia: 1773. V. 51
The Lives of Celebrated Architects, Ancient and Modern. London: 1862. V. 48

MILL, HUGH ROBERT
The English Lakes. London: 1895. V. 50; 52
The Life of Sir Ernest Shackleton. London: 1923. V. 50
The Siege of the South Pole. London: 1905. V. 48; 49; 51; 54

MILL, JAMES
Analysis of the Phenomena of the Human Mind. London: 1829. V. 49; 54
Elements of Political Economy. London: 1821. V. 52
Elements of Political Economy. London: 1824. V. 48
Elements of Political Economy. London: 1826. V. 53
Elements of Political Economy. London: 1844. V. 47; 49; 51
The History of British India. London: 1858. V. 53

MILL, JOHN
The Visit of the King of the Belgians. London: 1870. V. 48

MILL, JOHN STUART
L'Assujettissement des Femmes. Paris: 1869. V. 54
Autobiography. London: 1873. V. 48; 50; 51; 52; 53
Autobiography. New York: 1924. V. 48
Considerations on Representative Government. London: 1861. V. 51; 53
Considerations on Representative Government. New York: 1862. V. 48
Considerations on Representative Government. London: 1865. V. 48; 52; 53
Dissertations and Discussions, Political, Philosophical and Historical. London: 1859. V. 47; 50; 51
England and Ireland. London: 1868. V. 52
Essays on Some Unsettled Questions of Political Economy. London: 1844. V. 49; 52
An Examination of Sir William Hamilton's Philosophy and of the Principal Philosophical Question Discussed in His Writings. London: 1865. V. 48; 54
Inaugural Address Delivered to the University of St. Andrews Feb. 1st, 1867. London: 1867. V. 51; 52
Nature and Utility of Religion and Theism. London: 1874. V. 53
On Liberty... London: 1849. V. 47
On Liberty. London: 1859. V. 54
On Liberty. Boston: 1863. V. 47; 50
Principles of Political Economy With Some of Their Applications to Social Philosophy. London: 1848. V. 50; 52; 53
Principles of Political Economy, with Some of Their Applications to Social Philosophy. London: 1849. V. 47; 53
Principles of Political Economy with Some of Their Applications to Social Philosophy... London: 1852. V. 52
The Subjection of Women. London: 1869. V. 51; 52; 53
The Subjection of Women. New York: 1869. V. 50; 52
The Subjection of Women. Philadelphia: 1869. V. 47; 49; 50; 51
The Subjection of Women. New York: 1870. V. 50; 51; 53
The Subjection of Women. London: 1969. V. 53
A System of Logic, Ratiocinative and Inductive... London: 1846. V. 53
A System of Logic; Ratiocinative and Inductive. New York: 1848. V. 47
A System of Logic, Ratiocinative and Inductive. London: 1856. V. 47; 51
A System of Logic, Ratiocinative and Inductive, Being a Connected View of the Principles of Evidence and the Methods of Scientific Investigation. London: 1872. V. 48; 51
Thoughts on Parliamentary Reform... London: 1859. V. 53
Three Essays on Religion: Nature, the Utility of Religion and Theism. London: 1874. V. 53
The Utility of Religion; and Theism. (and) Autobiography. London: 1873-74. V. 47

MILL, W. H.
Forty Years at El Paso, 1858-1898. El Paso: 1962. V. 53

MILLAIS, JOHN EVERETT
Illustrations. A Collection of Drawing on Wood. London: 1866. V. 49
The Life and Letters of Sir John Everett Millais. London: 1899. V. 51

MILLAIS, JOHN GUILLE
A Breath from the Veldt. London: 1895. V. 47
A Breath from the Veldt. London: 1899. V. 49; 50; 52
British Deer and Their Horns. London: 1897. V. 47; 48; 49
British Deer and Their Horns. London: 1982. V. 48
British Diving Ducks.. London: 1913. V. 51
Far Away Up the Nile. London: 1924. V. 47; 49
Game Birds and Shooting Sketches. London: 1892. V. 47; 49; 50; 51; 52
The Gun at Home and Abroad. London: 1913. V. 47
The Life and Letters of Sir John Everett Millais. London: 1899. V. 48; 49

The Life and Letters of Sir John Everett Millais. New York: 1899. V. 49
Magnolias. London: 1927. V. 50; 51
The Mammals of Great Britain and Ireland. London: 1904. V. 47
The Mammals of Great Britain and Ireland. London: 1904-06. V. 47; 48; 49; 50; 52; 53; 54
The Natural History of British Game Birds. London: 1909. V. 47; 48; 49; 50
The Natural History of British Surface Feeding Ducks. London: 1902. V. 48; 49; 50; 51; 54
Newfoundland and its Untrodden Ways. London: 1907. V. 49; 50; 54
Rhododendrons: in Which is Set Forth an Account of All species of the Genus Rhododendron (Including Azaleas) and Various Hybrids (First Series). London: 1917. V. 52
The Wildfowler in Scotland. London: 1901. V. 47; 49; 51; 52; 53

MILLAR, ERIC GEORGE
English Illuminated Manuscripts of the X (-XV) Century. Paris and Brussels: 1926-28. V. 48
English Illuminated Manuscripts of the XIVth and XVth Centuries. Paris: 1928. V. 49

MILLAR, G. H.
A New Complete and Universal Body or System of Natural History. London: 1785. V. 49; 53; 54

MILLAR, H. R.
The Dreamland Express. 1927. V. 51
The Silver Fairy Book. London. V. 51

MILLAR, JOHN
A History of the Witches of Renfrewshire, Who Were Burned On the Gallowgreen of Paisley. Paisley: 1809. V. 49
Observations Concerning the Distinctions of Ranks in Society. London: 1773. V. 48; 49

MILLAR, KENNETH
Blue City. New York: 1947. V. 48
The Three Roads. New York: 1948. V. 51

MILLAR, MARGARET
Do Evil In Return. London: 1950's. V. 50
The Iron Gates. New York: 1945. V. 54
Wall of Eyes. New York: 1943. V. 53

MILLAR, OLIVER
Italian Drawings and Paintings in the Queen's Collection. London: 1965. V. 53
Later Georgian Pictures in the Collection of Her Majesty the Queen. London: 1969. V. 49; 52; 54

MILLAR, W.
Plastering Plain and Decorative. A Practical Treatise on the Art and Craft of Plastering and Modelling. London: 1897. V. 47

MILLAR, WILLIAM
The Fairy Minstrel, and Other Poems. Edinburgh: 1822. V. 50; 54

MILLARD, BAILEY
History of the San Francisco Bay Region. Chicago: 1924. V. 48; 53; 54

MILLARD, CHRISTOPHER
The Printed Work of Claud Lovat Fraser. London: 1923. V. 50

MILLARD, DAVID RALPH
Cleft Craft: the Evolution of Its Surgery. Boston: 1976-77. V. 54

MILLARD, HENRY
A Treatise on Bright's Disease of the Kidneys, Its Pathology, Diagnosis and Treatment. New York: 1884. V. 49

MILLAY, EDNA ST. VINCENT
Aria da Capo: a Play in One Act. New York: 1921. V. 51; 54
The Ballad of the Harp Weaver. New York: 1922. V. 50; 52
The Ballad of the Harp-Weaver. New York: 1927. V. 48
The Buck in the Snow and Other Poems. London: 1928. V. 47
The Buck in the Snow and Other Poems. New York: 1928. V. 47; 48; 49; 50; 51; 53; 54
The Buck in the Snow and Other Poems. London: 1938. V. 48
Conversation at Midnight. New York: 1937. V. 47; 48; 49; 51; 53
Conversation at Midnight. Los Angeles: 1964. V. 51
Fatal Interview. New York: 1931. V. 47; 48; 51; 52; 53
A Few Figs from Thistles. New York: 1922. V. 49
The Harp-Weaver and Other Poems. New York: 1923. V. 49
Huntsman, What Quarry?. New York: 1929. V. 54
Huntsman, What Quarry?. New York: 1939. V. 48; 49; 50; 51
The King's Henchman. New York: 1927. V. 47; 48; 49; 51; 52; 53; 54
The Lamp and the Bell. New York: 1921. V. 50
The Murder of Lidice. New York and London: 1942. V. 47; 54
Renascence and Other Poems. London: 1917. V. 48
Renascence and Other Poems. New York: 1917. V. 51; 53; 54
Second April. New York: 1921. V. 49
Two Slatterns and a King: a Moral Interlude. Cincinnati: 1921. V. 48
Wine From These Grapes. New York: 1934. V. 47; 48; 49; 51; 54

MILLE, E. D.
Modern Polo. London: 1902. V. 48

MILLER & RICHARD
Printing Type Specimens. London: 1932. V. 54
Specimens of Modern Old Style and Ornamental Type Cast on Point Bodies. Toronto: 1890. V. 51

MILLER, A. A.
Communion Tokens fo the Presbyterian Church in Ireland. London: 1920. V. 48

MILLER, A. E. H.
Military Drawings and Paintings. London: 1969/70. V. 52; 54
Military Drawings and Paintings in the Collection of Her Majesty the Queen. London: 1966. V. 50

MILLER, A. P.
Tom's Experience in Dakota. Minneapolis: 1883. V. 51

MILLER, ALFRED JACOB
The West of Alfred Jacob Miller (1837) from the Notes and Colors in the Walters Art Gallery with an Account of the Artist by Marvin C. Ross. Norman: 1951. V. 53
The West of Alfred Jacob Miller (1837) from the Notes and Water Colors in the Walters Art Gallery with an Account of the Artist by Marvin C. Ross. Norman: 1968. V. 54

MILLER, ANNA RIGGS
Letters from Italy, Describing the Manners, Customs, Antiquities, Paintings &c of that Country. London: 1777. V. 54
Poetical Amusements at a Villa Near Bath. Bath: 1775. V. 54

MILLER, ARTHUR
After the Fall. New York: 1964. V. 47; 48; 49; 50; 51; 52; 53; 54
The American Clock. New York: 1981. V. 49
Collected Plays. 1980. V. 49
The Crucible. New York: 1953. V. 48
Death of a Salesman. New York. V. 50
Death of a Salesman. London: 1949. V. 52
Death of a Salesman. New York: 1949. V. 47; 49; 51; 52; 53
Death of a Salesman. New York: 1981. V. 50; 52
Death of a Salesman. New York: 1984. V. 47; 48
Focus. New York: 1947. V. 51; 52
Homely Girl, a Life. New York: 1992. V. 53
The Misfits. New York: 1961. V. 47; 53; 54
On Social Plays. New York: 1955. V. 54
Situation Normal. New York: 1944. V. 49; 51; 52; 53
The Theater Essays. New York: 1978. V. 50

MILLER, ARTHUR G.
On the Edge of the Sea: Mural Painting at Tancah - Tulum, Quintana Roo, Mexico. Washington: 1982. V. 50

MILLER, BENJAMIN S.
Ranch Life in Southern Kansas and the Indian Territory. New York: 1896. V. 48
Ranching in the Southwest: Ranch Life in Southern Kansas and the Indian Territory. New York: 1896. V. 52

MILLER, C. WILLIAM
Benjamin Franklin's Philadelphia Printing, 1728-1766. A Descriptive Bibliography. Philadelphia: 1974. V. 47

MILLER, CHARLES A.
The Official and Political Manual of the State of Tennessee. Nashville: 1890. V. 47

MILLER, CHARLES CONRAD
Cosmetic Surgery. The Correction of Featural Imperfections. Philadelphia: 1924. V. 51

MILLER, E.
The City of Delight. 1908. V. 52

MILLER, E. H.
The Pacific Railroad. A Defense Against Its Enemies, with Report of the Supervisors of Placer County, and Report of Mr. Montanya, Made to the Supervisors of the City and County of San Francisco. Sacramento: 1864. V. 47

MILLER, EDMOND
A Friendly Letter to Dr. Bentley. Occasion'd By His New Edition of Paradise Lost. London: 1732. V. 49

MILLER, EDMUND
Financial History of Texas. Austin: 1916. V. 53

MILLER, EDWARD
Address Delivered, by Request, Before a Railroad Meeting of the Citizens of Cooper County, at Boonville, Mo., April 3, 1858. St. Louis: 1858. V. 53
The History and Antiquities of Doncaster and Its Vicinity, With Anecdotes of Eminent Men. Doncaster: 1804. V. 50
The Medical Works of Edward Miller, M.D. New York: 1814. V. 47; 48; 50

MILLER, EDWARD GEE
Captain Edward Gee Miller of the 20th Wisconsin: His War 1861-1865. Fayetteville: 1960. V. 47

MILLER, ELIZABETH SMITH
In the Kitchen. Boston: 1875. V. 47

MILLER, EMILY VAN DORN
A Soldier's Honor, With Reminiscences of Major-General Earl Van Dorn, by His Comrades. New York: 1902. V. 49

MILLER, FRANCIS TREVELYAN
The Photographic History of the Civil War. New York: 1911. V. 47; 53
The Photographic History of the Civil War. New York: 1912. V. 47; 48
The Photographic History of the Civil War. New York: 1957. V. 49
The World in the Air, the Story of Flying in Pictures. New York: 1930. V. 48; 49; 52

MILLER, FRED
The Training of a Craftsman. London: 1901. V. 50; 52

MILLER, G. S.
Catalogue of the Mammals of Western Europe. London: 1912. V. 54

MILLER, GEORGE
Latter Struggles in the Journey of Life; or the Afternoon of My Days... Edinburgh: 1833. V. 48; 50
Syllabus of Lectures on Modern History Delivered in Trinity College, Dublin, Part the First. Dublin: 1801. V. 52
The Trial of Frank James for Murder, with Confessions of Dick Liddil and Clarence Hite and History of the "James Gang". Kansas City: 1898. V. 53

MILLER, GEORGE C.
Blackburn: the Evolution of a Cotton Town. Blackburn: 1951. V. 48

MILLER, GEORGE J.
The Courts of Chancery in New Jersey 1684-1696. Perth Amboy: 1934. V. 49; 51

MILLER, H.
Footprints of the Creator or the Asterolepis of Stromness. London: 1849. V. 53

MILLER, HARRIET PARKS
Pioneer Colored Christians. Clarksville: 1911. V. 54

MILLER, HENRY
Account of a Tour of the California Missions 1856: The Journals and Drawings of... San Francisco: 1952. V. 47
The Air-Conditioned Nightmare. New York: 1945. V. 49
Aller Retour New York. Paris: 1935. V. 48; 51
Aller Retour New York. New York: 1946. V. 53
Big Sur and the Oranges of Hieronymus Bosch. New York: 1957. V. 49
Big Sur and the Oranges of Hieronymus Bosch. London: 1958. V. 50
Black Spring. Paris: 1936. V. 48; 51; 52; 53
Black Spring. Paris: 1938. V. 49
Blaise Cendrars. Paris: 1951. V. 52
The Books in My Life. London: 1952. V. 47
The Books in My Life. New York: 1952. V. 50; 51
The Cosmological Eye. 1939. V. 49; 53
The Cosmological Eye. Norfolk: 1939. V. 48; 53
The Cosmological Eye. London: 1945. V. 49
Echolalia: Reproductions of Water Colours by Henry Miller. Berkeley: 1945. V. 48
Gliding Into the Everglades. 1976. V. 49; 53
Gliding into the Everglades. Santa Barbara: 1977. V. 50
Hamlet. Paris: 1939. V. 49; 53
Hamlet I & II. London: 1962. V. 49; 53
Hamlet II. New York: 1941. V. 49; 53
Henry Miller Miscellanea. 1945. V. 53
Henry Miller's Book of Friends - a Tribute to Friends of Long Ago. Santa Barbara: 1976. V. 48; 49
Het Heelal van de Dood: Een Studie Over Lawrence, Proust en Joyce. (The Universe of Death). Holland: 1941. V. 48
Insomnia, or the Devil at Large. Albuquerque: 1970. V. 47
Insomnia or the Devil at Large. Garden City: 1974. V. 53
Into the Night Life. Berkeley: 1947. V. 48; 49; 50; 53
A Letter 12 Pages in Why Abstract?. New York: 1945. V. 48
Les Livres de Ma Vie. Paris: 1957. V. 48
Love Between the Sexes. New York: 1978. V. 49; 50
Maurizius Forever. 1946. V. 49; 53
Maurizius Forever. San Francisco: 1946. V. 48; 53
Maurizius Forever. Michigan: 1959. V. 47
Max and the White Phagocytes. Paris: 1938. V. 53
Max et les Phagocytes. Paris: 1947. V. 53
Men God Forgot. New York: 1946. V. 49; 53
The Michael Fraenkel-Henry Miller Correspondence Called Hamlet. London: 1962. V. 48
Money and How It Gets That Way. Paris: 1937. V. 48
Money and How It Gets That Way. Paris: 1938. V. 51; 53; 54
Mother, China and the World Beyond. Santa Barbara: 1977. V. 50
Murder the Murderer. Berkeley: 1944. V. 49
My Bike and Other Friends. 1978. V. 49; 53
My Bike and Other Friends. Santa Barbara: 1978. V. 47; 48
My Life and Times. New York: 1971. V. 49; 50; 51; 53
My Life and Times. New York: 1975. V. 48
The Nightmare Notebook. New York: 1975. V. 49; 53
Notes on Aaron's Rod. 1980. V. 49; 53
Notes on Aaron's Rod. Santa Barbara: 1980. V. 51; 53
Obscenity and the Law of Reflection. New York: 1945. V. 51
Order and Chaos. 1966. V. 49
Order and Chaos chez Hans Reichel. New Orleans: 1966. V. 50; 53
Order and Chaos Chez Hans Reichel. Tucson: 1966. V. 47; 51
Plexus. Paris: 1953. V. 47; 48; 49; 53
Preface to Tropic of Cancer. New York: 1947. V. 49; 53
The Red Notebook. Highland: 1958. V. 54
Reflections on the Death of Mishima. Santa Barbara: 1972. V. 49
Reflections on the Maurizius Case. 1974. V. 49; 53
Relfections. 1981. V. 49
Remember to Remember. New York: 1947. V. 49; 51; 53
Reunion in Barcelona. 1959. V. 53
The Rosy Crucifixion. Sexus. Nexus. Plexus. New York: 1965. V. 47; 51; 54
Scenario. Paris: 1937. V. 49; 53
Selected Prose. London: 1965. V. 51
Sexus. Paris: 1949. V. 47; 48; 53
The Smile at the Foot of the Ladder. 1955. V. 49; 53

MILLER, HENRY continued
Sunday After the War. Norfolk: 1944. V. 47; 50
Thirteen California Towns from the Original Drawings. San Francisco: 1947. V. 47
The Time of the Assassins. New York: 1956. V. 49
Tropic of Cancer. Paris: 1934. V. 47
Tropic of Cancer. Paris: 1938. V. 49; 53
Tropic of Cancer. New York: 1940. V. 49; 53
Tropic of Cancer. Paris: 1947. V. 49; 53
Tropic of Capricorn. Paris: 1939. V. 47; 48; 49; 50; 51; 52; 53
Tropic of Capricorn. New York: 1961. V. 54
Tropique du Capricorne. 1950. V. 52
Watercolors, Drawings and His Essay, "The Angel Is My Watermark!". New York: 1962. V. 51
The Waters Reglittered. 1950. V. 49; 53
The Waters Reglitterized. San Jose: 1950. V. 53
The Waters Reglitterized. 1973. V. 49; 53
The Waters Reglitterized. Santa Barbara: 1973. V. 47; 50
What Are You Going to Do About Alf?. Paris: 1938. V. 49; 53
The Wisdom of the Heart. 1941. V. 49
The World of Lawrence. A Passionate Appreciation. Santa Barbara: 1980. V. 48; 50
The World of Sex. New York: 1940. V. 51

MILLER, HUGH
Edinburgh and Its Neighbourhood Geological and Historical. Edinburgh: 1864. V. 47
The Old Red Sandstone; or New Walks in an Old Field. Edinburgh: 1841. V. 47; 49
The Works of Hugh Miller. London: 1874-77. V. 51

MILLER, J.
Botanicum Officinale... London: 1722. V. 52

MILLER, J. R.
The Home Beautiful, or the Wedded Life. London: 1900. V. 47

MILLER, J. ROSCOE
Childcraft. Chicago: 1954. V. 49

MILLER, JAMES
How to Get a Farm and Where to Find One. New York: 1864. V. 52
The Humours of Oxford, a Comedy. London: 1730. V. 47; 49; 54
The Man of Taste. London: 1735. V. 47
Of Politeness. London: 1738. V. 49; 54
The Practice of Surgery. Edinburgh: 1846. V. 54
The Practice of Surgery. Edinburgh: 1977. V. 50
St. Baldred of the Bass, a Pictish Legend. Edinburgh: 1824. V. 54

MILLER, JEFFREY
Paul Bowles: a Descriptive Bibliography. Santa Barbara: 1986. V. 52; 54

MILLER, JOAQUIN
'49 The Gold-Seeker of the Sierras. New York & London: 1884. V. 50; 54
The Building of the City Beautiful. Cambridge & Chicago: 1893. V. 48
Songs of the Sierras. 1871. V. 50
Songs of the Sierras. Boston: 1871. V. 47; 48
Specimens. Portland: 1868. V. 53
True Bear Stories. 1985. V. 49; 52; 54
Unwritten History: Life Amongst the Modocs. Hartford: 1874. V. 47; 49; 50

MILLER, JOE
Joe Miller's Jests; or, the Wits Vade-Mecum... London: 1739. V. 52

MILLER, JOHN
The Country Gentleman's Architect, in a Great Variety of New Designs... London: 1797. V. 53
Kansas, a Desirable Field for Emigration and Agricultural Enterprise... London: 1870. V. 50
The Miller's Guide... Dublin: 1820. V. 51

MILLER, JONATHAN P.
The Condition of Greece in 1827 and 1828...As Contained in His Journals, Kept by Order of the Executive Greek Committee of the City of New York... New York: 1828. V. 49

MILLER, KARL
Poetry from Cambridge 1952-54. Swinford: 1955. V. 52

MILLER, KELLY
The Everlasting Stain. Washington: 1924. V. 52; 53

MILLER, LEO
Woman and the Divine Republic. Buffalo: 1874. V. 50

MILLER, LEWIS B.
Saddles and Lariats. Boston: 1912. V. 49

MILLER, LINUS W.
Notes of an Exile to Van Diemen's Land... Fredonia: 1846. V. 47
Notes of an Exile to Van Diemen's Land... New York: 1846. V. 53

MILLER, MADELAINE HEMINGWAY
Ernie Hemingway's Sister "Sunny" Remembers. New York: 1975. V. 47

MILLER, MALCOLM
The Emperor of Massachusetts. Montreal: 1970. V. 47

MILLER, MERLE
What Happened. New York: 1972. V. 54

MILLER, NYLE
Why the West Was Wild, a Contemporary Look at Some Highly Publicized Kansas County Personalities. Topeka: 1963. V. 48; 50; 53

MILLER, OLIVE BEAUPRE
My Bookhouse. Chicago: 1920/25. V. 49
My Bookhouse. Chicago: 1925. V. 47
Whisk Away on a Sunbeam. New York: 1919. V. 47

MILLER, P. S.
The Titan. 1952. V. 48; 52
The Titan. Reading: 1952. V. 50

MILLER, PATRICK
Ana the Runner. Waltham St. Lawrence: 1937. V. 47
The Green Ship. Waltham St. Lawrence: 1936. V. 47; 51
The Natural Man. London: 1924. V. 47
Woman in Detail: a Scientific Survey. Waltham St. Lawrence: 1947. V. 52

MILLER, PETER
Meditation at Noon. Toronto: 1953. V. 47
The Serpent Ink. Montreal: 1956. V. 47
A Shifting Pattern. Toronto: 1962. V. 47
Sonata for Frog and Man. Toronto: 1959. V. 47

MILLER, PHILIP
The Abridgement of the Gardeners Dictionary. London: 1771. V. 54
The Gardener's and Botanist's Dictionary. London: 1795-1807. V. 52
The Gardener's Dictionary... London: 1743-39. V. 48
The Gardener's Dictionary. London: 1752. V. 47
The Gardener's Dictionary... London: 1759. V. 52
The Gardener's Kalendar. London: 1748. V. 51
The Gardeners Kalendar... London: 1762. V. 47
The Gardener's Kalendar. London: 1769. V. 53

MILLER, RICHARD L.
Travels Abroad: Embracing Holland, England, Belgium, France, Sandwich Islands, New Zealand, Australia &c... Lynchburg: 1891. V. 52

MILLER, ROY ANDREW
Japanese Ceramics. Tokyo: 1963. V. 53

MILLER, SAMUEL
Notes of Hospital Practice. Part I. Philadelphia Hospitals. Philadelphia: 1885. V. 49
A Sermon Delivered January 19, 1812 at the Request of a Number of Young Gentlemen of the City of New York. New York: 1812. V. 47; 52; 54

MILLER, SAMUEL H.
The Fenland. Past and Present. V. 54

MILLER, SLOSS & SCOTT
Tools, Brass Goods, Sporting Goods, Cutlery, Iron, Steel, Pipe, Etc. Illustrated Catalogue No. 7. San Francisco: 1890's. V. 52

MILLER, STEVE
Hurricane Lake. Madison: 1979. V. 52; 53; 54

MILLER, THEODORE W.
Theodore W. Miller, Rough Rider: His Diary as a Soldier Together with the Story of His Life. Akron: 1899. V. 49

MILLER, THOMAS
Common Wayside Flowers. London and New York: 1860. V. 47; 52
Elegy on the Death of Lord Byron's Mary. London: 1832. V. 54
Fair Rosamond; or the Days of King Henry II. London: 1839. V. 53
Gideon Giles the Roper. London: 1841. V. 51
Lady Jane Grey. London: 1840. V. 53
Royston Gower; or, the Days of King John. London: 1838. V. 53

MILLER, W. C.
Vignettes of Early St. Thomas. St. Thomas: 1967. V. 50

MILLER, WALTER
A Canticle for Leibowitz. Philadelphia: 1959. V. 51
A Canticle for Leibowitz. 1960. V. 49; 52; 53
A Canticle for Leibowitz. London: 1960. V. 51
A Canticle for Leibowitz. Philadelphia: 1960. V. 48; 51; 52
A View from the Stars. London: 1965. V. 47; 51; 52

MILLER, WILLIAM
Eighth Wonder of the World, of Milelr's Discovery of the World's Destruction by Fire, in 1843. Boston: 1843. V. 47
Evidence from Scripture and History of the Second Coming of Christ, About the Year 1843. Troy: 1828. V. 53
Evidence from Scripture and History of the Second Coming of Christ, About the year 1843. New York: 1836. V. 47
Evidence from Scripture and History of the Second Coming of Christ, About the Year 1843. Troy: 1836. V. 49; 53
Evidence from Scripture and History of the Second Coming of Christ, About the Year 1843. Troy: 1838. V. 49
Evidence from Scripture and History of the Second Coming of Christ, About the Year 1843... Boston: 1841. V. 47
Evidence from Scripture and History of the Second Coming of Christ, about the Year 1843... Boston: 1842. V. 47
Review of a Discourse, Delivered in the North Church, Neburyport, on the Last Evening of the Year, by L. F. Dimmick, Pastor of the Church. Boston: 1842. V. 49

MILLER, WILLIAM continued
Whistle-Binkie or the Piper of the Party Being a Collection of Songs for the Social Circle. Glasgow: 1878. V. 53

MILLERS, GEORGE
A Description of the Cathedral Church of Ely; with Some Account of the Conventual Building. London: 1807. V. 48

MILLER'S Planters' & Merchants' Almanac, for...1858. For the States of Carolina and Georgia. Charleston: 1857. V. 48

MILLES DE SOUVIGNY, JEAN
Praxis Criminis Perseqvendi, Elegantibvs Aliqvot Figvris Illvstrata. Parisiis: 1541. V. 47; 49; 50; 53

MILLET, J. F.
The Drawings. London: 1906. V. 53

MILLET, SAMUEL
A Whaling Voyage on the Bark 'Willis' 1849-1850. Boston: 1924. V. 50

MILLHOUSE, ROBERT
Sherwood Forest and Other Poems. London: 1827. V. 54
The Song of the Patriot, Sonnets and Songs. London: 1826. V. 54

MILLIEN, GASPARD T.
Travels in Africa, to the Sources of the Senegal and Gambia, in 1818. London: 1820. V. 47

MILLIER, A.
Millard Sheets. Los Angeles: 1935. V. 48; 50; 51

MILLIGAN, ROBERT H.
The Fetish Folk of West Africa. New York: 1912. V. 54

MILLIGAN, SPIKE
Silly Verse for Kids. London: 1959. V. 51

MILLIKEN, RALPH
The Plains Over the Reminiscences of William Jasper Stockton. Los Banos: 1939. V. 51

MILLIKIN, ROBERT
Historico-Masonic Tracts, Being a Concise History of Freemasonry. Cork: 1848. V. 54

MILLIN, AUBIN LOUIS
Antiquites Nationales. Paris: 1790-91-1802. V. 53

MILLIN, S. SHANNON
Additional Sidelights on Belfast History. London: 1938. V. 51

MILLINGEN, JAMES
Ancient Unedited Monuments. Painted Greek Vases; Statues, Busts, Bas-Relies, from Collections in Various Countries, Principally in Great Britain. London: 1822-26. V. 49; 53

MILLINGEN, JOHN GIDEON
The Passions; or Mind and Matter. London: 1848. V. 52

MILLIS, WALTER
Road to War - America 1914-1917. London: 1935. V. 52

MILLON, RENE
The Teotihuacan Map. Parts 1-2. Austin & London: 1973. V. 50; 52

MILLOT, CLAUDE F. X.
Elements of the History of France. London: 1771. V. 47
Elements of the History of France. Dublin: 1772. V. 53

MILLS, ALFRED
Biography of Eminent Persons, Alphabetically Arranged. London: 1814. V. 47
Natural History of 48 Birds. London: 1816. V. 54
Natural History of 48 Quadrupeds. London: 1815. V. 54
Pictures of Roman History, in Miniature. London: 1812. V. 52

MILLS, ALISON
Francisco. Berkeley: 1974. V. 53

MILLS, ANSON
My Story. Washington: 1918. V. 47; 49; 50

MILLS, CHARLES
The History of Chivalry, or Knighthood and its Times. London: 1824. V. 49
The History of Chivalry, or Knighthood and Its Times. London: 1826. V. 53
An History of Muhammedanism: Comprising the Life and Character of the Arabian Prophet and Succinct Accounts of the Empires Founded by the Muhammedan Arms... London: 1818. V. 53
The History of the Crusades. London: 1821. V. 51
History of the Crusades. London: 1822. V. 50
The Travels of Theodore Ducas, in Various Countries in Europe at the Revival of Letters and Art. Part the First, Italy. London: 1822. V. 47; 53
Tumors of the Cerebellum. New York: 1905. V. 52; 54
Tumors of the Cerebrum. Their Focus Diagnosis and Surgical Treatment. Philadelphia: 1906. V. 52

MILLS, CLIFFORD
Where the Rainbow Ends. London: 1920. V. 54

MILLS, FREDERICK WILLIAM
An Introduction to the Study of Diatomaceae, with a Bibliography. London: 1893. V. 48

MILLS, GEORGE
The Beggar's Benison; or, a Hero Without a Name, but With an Aim. London and New York: 1866. V. 54

MILLS, J. SAXON
David Lloyd George War Minister. London: 1924. V. 47

MILLS, J. TRAVIS
John Bright and the Quakers. London: 1935. V. 49; 54

MILLS, JAMES E.
Geological Report on the Mine La Motte Estate. The Property of Hon. Rowland Hazard Situated in Madison County, Missouri. New York: 1877. V. 47

MILLS, JOHN
D'Horsay; or, the Follies of the Day. London: 1844. V. 47; 48; 51; 54
The Flyers of the Hunt. London: 1859. V. 47; 51; 52
The Sportsman's Library. London: 1845. V. 47; 49
The Sportsman's Library. Philadelphia: 1846. V. 47
Stable Secrets; or, Puffy Doddles, His Sayings and Sympathies. London: 1863. V. 51; 52
The Stage Coach; or, the Road of Life. London: 1843. V. 47
Up in the Clouds, Gentlemen Please. New York: 1981. V. 51

MILLS, JOHN HENRY
Poetic Trifles. Baltimore;: 1808. V. 54

MILLS, LESTER
A Sagebrush Saga. Springville: 1956. V. 52

MILLS, ROBERT
Atlas of the State of South Carolina. Baltimore: 1826. V. 47
Memorial of Robert Mills, Respecting a New Route to the Pacific Ocean, with a Plan for the Transportation of Despatches to Astoria in Fifteen Days. Washington: 1848. V. 47
Memorial of Robert Mills, Submitting a New Plan of Roadway. Washington: 1846. V. 47

MILLS, W. JAY
Historic Houses of New Jersey. Philadelphia: 1903. V. 51

MILLS, W. W.
Forty Years at El Paso, 1858-1898. 1901. V. 48

MILLS, WEYMER
The Girl I Left Behind Me. New York: 1910. V. 54

MILLS, WILLIAM H.
Placer County; Its Resources and Advantages... 1885. V. 49

MILLSPAUGH, CHARLES F.
American Medicinal Plants... New York and: 1887. V. 47

MILMAN, H. H.
The Fall of Jerusalem: a Dramatic Poem. London: 1822. V. 47
History of Latin Christianity, Including that of the Popes tot he Pontificate of Nicholas V. London: 1854-55. V. 49
The History of the Jews. London: 1829. V. 54
The Life of Edward Gibbon, Esq. With Selections From His Correspondence and Illustrations. London: 1839. V. 48
The Martyr of Antioch: a Dramatic Poem. London: 1822. V. 48; 49; 54
Nala and Damayanti, and Other Poems... Oxford: 1835. V. 50

MILMINE, GEORGINE
The Life of Mary Baker G. Eddy and the History of Christian Science. New York: 1909. V. 50

MILNE, A. T.
Writings on British History. 1934-45. V. 48

MILNE, ALAN ALEXANDER
By Way of Introduction. London: 1929. V. 47; 49
By Way of Introduction. New York: 1929. V. 49; 50; 53
The Christopher Robin Birthday Book. London: 1930. V. 53
The Christopher Robin Story Book. London: 1929. V. 48; 50; 53
The Christopher Robin Verses - Being 'When We Were Very Young' and 'Now We Are Six'. London: 1932. V. 48
A Gallery of Children. London: 1925. V. 47; 48; 49; 51; 52; 53
The House at Pooh Corner. London: 1926. V. 52
The House at Pooh Corner. London: 1927. V. 52
The House at Pooh Corner. London: 1928. V. 47; 48; 49; 50; 51; 52; 53
The House at Pooh Corner. New York: 1928. V. 51; 53
The Hums of Pooh. London: 1929. V. 54
The Ivory Door. New York: 1928. V. 47; 48
The King's Breakfast. London: 1925. V. 49; 54
Lovers in London. London: 1905. V. 54
Michael and Mary. London: 1930. V. 53
Michael and Mary. London: 1950. V. 47
Miss Elizabeth Bennet. London: 1936. V. 49
More 'Very Young' Songs from "When We Were Very Young" and "Now We Are Six". London: 1928. V. 52
Now We Are Six. London: 1927. V. 47; 48; 49; 50; 51; 52; 53; 54
Now We Are Six. New York: 1927. V. 50
Now We Are Six. London: 1928. V. 48
Once On a Time. London: 1925. V. 49; 54
Once Upon a Time. London: 1917. V. 53
The Pooh. London: 1926. V. 51
The Pooh Calendar. London: 1930. V. 48
Pu Der Bar. (Winne-the-Pooh). Berlin: 1929. V. 53
The Red House Mystery. London: 1922. V. 49
Second Plays. London: 1921. V. 49
The Secret and Other Stories. New York: 1929. V. 47; 48; 49; 50; 53

MILNE, ALAN ALEXANDER continued
Songs From Now We Are Six. London: 1927. V. 52
Teddy Bear and Other songs from "When We Were Very Young". London: 1927. V. 48
Teddy Bear and Other Songs from When We Were Very Young. London: 1926. V. 52
Those Were the Days - The Day's Play. The Holiday Round. Once a Week. The Sunny Side. London: 1929. V. 47
Toad of Toad Hall. London: 1929. V. 47; 48; 49; 50; 53
Toad of Toad Hall. New York: 1929. V. 51
When We Were Very Young. London: 1924. V. 48; 50; 53
When We Were Very Young. New York: 1924. V. 52
When We Were Very Young. London: 1925. V. 51; 54
When We Were Very Young. London: 1928. V. 54
When We Were Very Young. London: 1930. V. 54
When We Were Very Young. Winnie the Pooh. Now We Are Six. The House at Pooh Corner. London: 1924-28. V. 48; 49; 50; 51; 53
When We Were Very Young. Winnie the Pooh. The House at Pooh Corner. And Now We Are Six. London: 1930. V. 53; 54
Winne-the-Pooh. London: 1926. V. 48; 49; 51; 53; 54
Winnie-the-Pooh. New York: 1926. V. 53; 54
Winnie-the-Pooh. London: 1927. V. 54
Winnie-the-Pooh. Leipzig: 1933. V. 54
Winnie-the-Pooh. London: 1933. V. 51
Winnie-the-Pooh. London: 1973. V. 48
Winnie-the-Pooh and the Bees. New York: 1952. V. 53
Winnie-the-Pooh and the Eeyore's Tail. New York: 1952. V. 53

MILNE, COLIN
A Botanical Dictionary... London: 1770. V. 54
A Botanical Dictionary (a supplement). London: 1770-78. V. 53
A Botanical Dictionary; or, Elements of Systematic and Philosophical Botany. London: 1805. V. 49; 51; 53

MILNE, EWART
Forty North Fifty West. Dublin: 1938. V. 49
Letter from Iceland. Dublin: 1940. V. 49

MILNE, J. G.
Catalogue of Alexandrian Coins. Oxford: 1933. V. 48

MILNE, JOHN
The Cruise of H.M.S. Galatea, Captain H.R.H. The Duke of Edinburgh, K.G. in 1867-1868. London: 1869. V. 54

MILNE-EDWARDS, A.
Notice sur Quelques Especes d'Oiseaux Actuellement Eteintes Qui Se Trouvent Representees dans les Collections du Museum d'Histoire Naturelle. Paris: 1893. V. 51; 52

MILNE-EDWARDS, H.
British Fossil Corals. London: 1850-54. V. 49; 51; 52; 53; 54
A Monograph of the British Fossil Corals. London: 1850. V. 50

MILNER, HENRY ERNEST
The Art and Practice of Landscape Gardening. London: 1890. V. 49; 54

MILNER, JOE
California Joe. Caldwell: 1935. V. 47; 48; 50; 54

MILNER, JOHN
The Cruise of the H. M. S. Galatea, Capt. HRH the Duke of Edinburgh, in 1867-1868. London: 1869. V. 47; 52; 54
The History Civil and Ecclesiastical and Survey of the Antiquities of Winchester. Winchester: 1809. V. 52
A View of the Dissertation Upon the Epistles of Phalaris, Themistocles, &c. Lately Publish'd by the Reverend Dr. Bentley. London: 1698. V. 49

MILNER, JOSEPH
Gibbon's Account of Christianity Considered; Together with some Strictures on Hume's Dialogues Concerning Natural Religion. York: 1781. V. 52
The History of the Church of Christ... London: 1824. V. 49; 51

MILNER, THOMAS
The Gallery of Geography: a Pictorial and Descriptive Tour of the World. Glasgow: 1872. V. 50
The Gallery of Nature. London: 1855. V. 48; 54
Russia; Its Rise and Progress, Tragedies and Revolutions. London: 1856. V. 53

MILNES, CHARLOTTE
The Loves of Hally and Sophy... London: 1795-96. V. 47

MILNES, JACOB
Sectionum Conicarum Elementa Nova methodo Demonstrata. Oxford: 1712. V. 48

MILNES, RICHARD, OF HORBURY
The Warning Voice of a Hermit Abroad, Who Has Been Compelled to write in His Justification, and He Hopes for the Good of Mankind... Wakefield: 1825. V. 51

MILNOR, WILLIAM
An Authentic Historical Memoir of the Schuylkill Fishing Company of the State in Schuykill... Philadelphia: 1830. V. 50
A History of the Schuykill Fishing Company of the State of Schuykill 1732-1888 and 1888-1932. Philadelphia: 1889/1932. V. 54
Memoirs of the Gloucester Fox Hunting Club Near Philadelphia. New York: 1927. V. 47; 49; 51

MILNS, WILLIAM
The Well-Bred Scholar, or Practical Essays on the Best methods of Improving the Taste, and Assisting the Exertions of Youth in Their Literary Pursuits. London: 1794. V. 48; 50

MILOSZ, CZESLAW
The Captive Mind. New York: 1953. V. 51; 53
The Captive Mind. New York: 1983. V. 48; 53
The Collected Poems. New York: 1988. V. 53
Native Realm. Garden City: 1968. V. 49
The Seizure of Power. New York: 1955. V. 53
Selected Poems. New York: 1973. V. 53
Selected Poems. Helsinki: 1989. V. 48

MILOSZ, O. V. DE L.
Fourteen Poems by O. V. de L. Milosz. San Francisco: 1952. V. 53

MILROY, JACK
Portraits of the Queen, the Stamp Collages of Jack Milroy. Dallas: 1979. V. 47

MILTON, JOHN
Accedence Commenc't Grammar, Supply'd with Suffcient Rules, for the Use of Such (Younger or Elder) as Are Desirous, Without More Trouble than Needs to Attain the Latin Tongue. London: 1669. V. 52
Aeropagitica. Cambridge: 1973. V. 47
L'Allegro and Il Penseroso... 1848. V. 53
L'Allegro and Il Penseroso. London: 1859. V. 53
L'Allegro and Il Penseroso. New Rochelle: 1903. V. 49
L'Allegro and Il Penseroso. New York: 1954. V. 52; 54
Angli Pro Populo Anglicano Defension. London: 1651. V. 53
Areopagitica. London: 1664. V. 52
Areopagitica. Hammersmith: 1903. V. 52
Areopagitica. 1904. V. 51
Areopagitica. 1907. V. 48; 49
Areopagitica. Hammersmith: 1907. V. 47; 51
Areopagitica. New York: 1927. V. 53
Areopagitica. Cambridge: 1973. V. 47; 48; 50; 51; 52; 53; 54
Coll Gwynfa Cyfieithiad gan Idrison. Llundain: 1819. V. 49
A Collection of Divine Hymns and Poems Upon Several Occasions. London: 1719. V. 49
A Common-Place Book. London: 1876. V. 49
A Complete Collection of the Historical, Political and Miscellaneous Works... Amsterdam: 1698. V. 47; 49; 50
A Complete Collection of the Historical, Political and Miscellaneous Works... London: 1738. V. 50
The Complete Poetical Works. Edinburgh: 1859. V. 49
The Complete Poetical Works. London: 1908. V. 50
Comus. London: 1738. V. 54
Comus. London: 1762. V. 48; 54
Comus. Dublin: 1764. V. 49
Comus. London: 1799. V. 54
Comus. Paris: 1812. V. 49
Comus. London: 1858. V. 49; 54
Comus. London: 1901. V. 49; 52; 54
Comus. 1902. V. 54
Comus. New Rochelle: 1902. V. 47; 51
Comus. New York: 1903. V. 54
Comus. New York: 1903. V. 49
Comus. New York and London: 1921. V. 47; 48; 49; 50; 51; 52
Comus. 1926. V. 52
Comus. London: 1926. V. 48; 49; 50; 53
Comus. Newtown: 1931. V. 50
De Doctrina Christiana Libri Duo Posthumi. Cantabrigiae: 1825. V. 49; 54
A Defence of the People of England. 1692. V. 48; 49; 50; 54
A Defence of the People of England. Amsterdam: 1692. V. 47; 50; 52; 53
A Defence of the People of England...in Answer to Salmasius's Defence of the King. London: 1692. V. 48
Defense Du Peuple Anglais. Valence: 1792. V. 50
Defensio Secunda...Accessit Alexandri Mori...Fides Publica Contra Calumnias Ioannis Miltoni Scurrae. Hagae-Comitvm: 1654. V. 49
The Doctrine and Discipline of Divorce... London: 1645. V. 49; 54
The Doctrine and Discipline of Divorce; In two Books... London: 1820. V. 47; 48
The Doctrine and Discipline of Divorce Restor'd to the Good of Both Sexes. London: 1643. V. 54
Early Poems. London: 1896. V. 54
Eikonoklastes. London: 1649. V. 49
Eikonoklastes. London: 1652. V. 49; 54
Eikonoklastes. Amsterdam: 1690. V. 48; 49; 54
Epistolarum Familiarum Liber Unus. London: 1674. V. 54
Facsimile of the Manuscript of Milton's Minor Poems, Preserved in the Library of Trinity College, Cambridge. Cambridge: 1899. V. 48
The First Edition of Paradise Lost. Urbana: 1945. V. 51
Four Poems. Newtown: 1933. V. 47; 48; 50
(Greek, then) In Answer to a Book Intitl'd (Greek), the Portrature of His Sacred Majesty in His Solitudes and Sufferings. London: 1649. V. 54
(Greek Title) Samson Agonistes Graeco Carmine Redditus cum Versione Latina. Oxonii: 1788. V. 53; 54
The History of Britain. London: 1670. V. 47; 49; 54
The History of Britain... London: 1677. V. 49; 54
The History of Britain... London: 1695. V. 49; 54
The History of Britain... London: 1818. V. 54

MILTON, JOHN *continued*
Hymn on the Morning of Christ's Nativity. London: 1903. V. 51
Hymn on the Morning of Christ's Nativity. Chelsea: 1928. V. 50
Ioannis Miltoni Angli Pro Populo Anglicano Defensio... Londini: 1652. V. 47
Latin and Italian Poems of Milton. Chichester: 1808. V. 54
Latin and Italian Poems of Milton. London: 1808. V. 52
Letters of State, Written by Mr. John Milton, To Most of the Sovereign Princes and Republicks of Europe. London: 1694. V. 47; 50
Licida. Monodia Per La Morte del Naufragato Eduardo King. Londra;: 1812. V. 54
The Life and Reigne of King Charles, or the Pseudo-Martyr Discovered. London: 1651. V. 54
Literae Pseudo-Senatus Anglicani Cromwelii. Brussels: 1676. V. 47
Literae Pseudo-Senatus Anglicani, Cromwelii, Reliquorumque Perduellium Nomine ac Jassu conscriptae a Joanne Miltono. 1676. V. 49; 50; 54
A Manifesto of the Lord Protector Of the Commonwealth of England, Scotland, Ireland, &c. London: 1738. V. 49; 54
The Mask of Comus. Bloomsbury: 1937. V. 47; 51; 52; 53; 54
The Masque of Comus. 1954. V. 48; 51
Milton's Italian Poems. London: 1776. V. 49; 54
Milton's Paradise Lost. London: 1802. V. 50; 54
Milton's Paradise Lost. New York & London: 1880. V. 54
Milton's Paradise Lost Illustrated with Texts of Scripture... London: 1793. V. 54
Milton's Paradise Lost. With Life of the Author. London: 1802. V. 54
The Minor Poems of John Milton. London: 1898. V. 52
Nova Solyma, the Ideal City, or Jerusalem Regained. New York: 1902. V. 53
Ode On the Morning of Christ's Nativity. Oxford: 1894. V. 49; 54
On the Morning of Christ's Nativity. London: 1896. V. 48
On the Morning of Christ's Nativity. Cambridge: 1923. V. 50
On the Morning of Christ's Nativity. Newtown: 1937. V. 54
On the Morning of Christ's Nativity. Andoversford: 1981. V. 48
On the Morning of Christ's Nativity. London: 1981. V. 47; 50
Opera Omnia Latina. Amsterdam: 1698. V. 50; 53
Original Letters and Papers of State, Addressed to Oliver Cromwell, Concerning the Affairs of Great Britain from the Year MDCXLIX to MDCLVIII. London: 1743. V. 49; 54
Le Paradis Perdu. Paris: 1792. V. 49; 52
Le Paradis Perdu De Milton. Paris: 1755. V. 49
Paradise Lost. London: 1668. V. 48
Paradise Lost. London: 1669. V. 47; 49; 50; 52; 54
Paradise Lost. London: 1674. V. 49; 54
Paradise Lost. London: 1678. V. 49; 52
Paradise Lost. London: 1688. V. 49; 51; 52; 53; 54
Paradise Lost. London: 1695. V. 48
Paradise Lost. London: 1705. V. 48
Paradise Lost. London: 1711. V. 49
Paradise Lost. London: 1719. V. 49
Paradise Lost... London: 1725. V. 49
Paradise Lost... London: 1727. V. 50
Paradise Lost... London: 1730. V. 54
Paradise Lost. London: 1732. V. 47; 49; 50; 54
Paradise Lost. London: 1741. V. 49
Paradise Lost... London: 1749. V. 49; 54
Paradise Lost... Dublin: 1751. V. 54
Paradise Lost. London: 1751. V. 49
Paradise Lost. Birmingham: 1759. V. 48; 49; 52
Paradise Lost. London: 1760. V. 47
Paradise Lost. London: 1763. V. 52; 54
Paradise Lost. Glasgow: 1770. V. 49; 52; 54
Paradise Lost. London: 1770. V. 48; 54
Paradise Lost. Glasgow: 1771. V. 49; 54
Paradise Lost. Dublin: 1773. V. 50
Paradise Lost. London: 1778. V. 54
Paradise Lost. London: 1790. V. 54
Paradise Lost. London: 1794. V. 51; 54
Paradise Lost. London: 1795. V. 48
Paradise Lost. London: 1799. V. 49
Paradise Lost. Washington: 1801. V. 49; 54
Paradise Lost. London: 1802. V. 54
Paradise Lost... London: 1808. V. 49; 54
Paradise Lost. London: 1825. V. 49
Paradise Lost. London: 1827. V. 54
Paradise Lost. London: 1833. V. 51
Paradise Lost. London: 1835. V. 49
The Paradise Lost. London: 1838. V. 48
The Paradise Lost. London: 1849. V. 52
The (sic) Paradise Lost. New York: 1850. V. 52
Paradise Lost. London: 1858. V. 47
Paradise Lost. London, Paris, & New York: 1873. V. 51; 52
Paradise Lost. Philadelphia: 1880. V. 52
Paradise Lost. Hammersmith: 1902. V. 53
Paradise Lost. London: 1937. V. 50; 54
Paradise Lost. Waltham St. Lawrence: 1937. V. 49; 54
Paradise Lost & Paradise Regained. London: 1795/96. V. 51
Paradise Lost and Paradise Regain'd. San Francisco: 1936. V. 52
Paradise Lost. (and) Paradise Regain'd A Poem in Four Books to Which is Added Samson Agonistes and Poems Upon Several Occasions. Birmingham: 1760. V. 51

Paradise Lost and Paradise Regain'd. To Which is Added Samson Agonistes: and Poems Upon Several Occasions. Birmingham: 1758. V. 47; 48; 49; 52; 54
Paradise Lost. Paradis Perdu. Paris: 1805. V. 51
Paradise Lost; Paradise Regain'd. Hammersmith: 1902/05. V. 51
Paradise Lost. Paradise Regain'd. A Poem in Four Books. To Which is added, Samson Agonistes; and Poems Upon Several Occasions. Birmingham: 1760. V. 49
Paradise Lost. Paradise Regained, Samson Agonistes, etc. London: 1816. V. 54
Paradise Lost. Paradise Regained...Miscellaneous Poems. London: 1795/96. V. 49
Paradise Lost. (with) Paradise Regain'd. A Poem in Four Books. To Which are added, Samson Agonistes; and Poems on Several Occasions. Philadelphia: 1777. V. 47
Paradise Lost. (with) Paradise Regain'd. A Poem. To Which is Added Samson Agonistes. London: 1688. V. 51
Paradise Lost. (with) Paradise Regain'd. To Which is added Samson Agonistes; and Poems Upon Several Occasions. London: 1754/62. V. 49
Paradise Lost. (with) Paradise Regain'd....Samson Agonistes. London: 1678/80. V. 49; 54
Paradise Lost. (with) Paradise Regain'd...Samson...Poems. London: 1753/53. V. 54
Paradise Lost. (with) Paradise regain'd...to which is added Samson agonistes; and Poems Upon Several Occasions... Birmingham: 1759. V. 50
Paradise Lost. (with) Paradise regain'd...to which is added Samson agonistes; and Poems Upon Several Occasions. London: 1763/66. V. 48
Paradise Lost. (with) Paradise Regained. London: 1931. V. 49
Paradise Lost. (with) Paradise Regained. A Poem, in Four Books. To Which is added Samson Agonistes: and Poems Upon Several Occasions. London: 1749/52. V. 48
Paradise Lost. (with) Paradise Regan'd...Saomson...Poems... Dublin: 1751/54. V. 54
Paradise Lost...Paradise Regain'd... Samson... Poems. Birmingham: 1759. V. 49; 52; 54
Paradise Lost...Paradise Regain'd...Samson...Poems. Birmingham: 1760. V. 49; 52; 54
Paradise Lost...(with) Paradise Regan'd...to Which is Added Samons Agonistes; and Poems Upon Several Occasions, with a Tractate of Education. London: 1753. V. 54
Le Paradise Perdu. La Haye: 1740. V. 54
Paradise Perdu. Paris: 1805. V. 54
Paradise Regain'd. London: 1680. V. 49
Paradise Regain'd... London: 1742. V. 49; 54
Paradise Regain'd... London: 1765. V. 54
Paradise Regain'd. A Poem in IV Books. To Which is Added Samson Agonistes. London: 1671. V. 47; 49; 52; 54
Paradise Regain'd. A Poem...Samson Agonistes. London: 1680. V. 49; 51; 54
Paradise Regain'd... Samson...Poems. London: 1766. V. 54
Paradise Regain'd. (with) Samson Agonistes. London: 1688. V. 47
Paradise Regain'd...Samson Agonistes. (with) Paradise Lost. London: 1678. V. 49
Paradise Regain'd...Samson Agonistes...Poems Upon Several Occasions. London: 1752. V. 49
Paradise Regain'd...Samson Agonistes...Poems...A Tractate. Glasgow: 1772. V. 49
Paradise Regain'd...Samson...Poems... London: 1725. V. 49
Paradise Regain'd...Samson...Poems... London: 1753. V. 54
Paradise Regain'd...Samson...Poems. Dublin: 1754. V. 49
Paradise Regain'd...Samson...Poems.... Dublin: 1754. V. 54
Paradise Regain'd...Samson...Poems. London: 1773. V. 54
Paradise Regain'd...Samson...Poems. London: 1785. V. 54
Paradise Regain'd...To Which are Added, Poems on Several Occasions. Philadelphia: 1791. V. 54
Paradise Regain'd...(with) Samson Agonistes; and Poems Upon Several Occasions with a Tractate of Education. London: 1743. V. 49
Paradise Regained. London: 1795-1800. V. 47
Paradise Regained. London: 1924. V. 54
Paradise Regained. London: 1932. V. 48
Paradise Regained, a Poem in Four Books, to Which are added Samson Agonistes and Poems Both English and Latin. Hammersmith: 1905. V. 54
Paradise Regained...Samson Agonistes...Poems... London: 1761. V. 52
Paradise Regained...Together with, Poems Upon Several Occasions in English and Latin. (with) A Small Tractae... London: 1725. V. 52
Il Paradiso Perduto Di Giovanni Milton. Londra: 1796. V. 54
Il Paradiso Perduto Poema Inglese Di Giovanni Milton... In Parigi, Verona: 1742. V. 49; 54
Paradisus Amissus. Poema Joannis Miltoni. Oxonii: 1750. V. 48
Paradisus Amissus. Poema Joannis Miltoni. Oxonii: 1750/53. V. 49; 54
Paradisus Amissus Poema Joannis Miltoni. Oxonii: 1855. V. 54
'T Paradys Verlooren. Te Haarlem: 1728. V. 49; 54
Het Paradys Verlooren. Te Amsterdam: 1730. V. 49
O Paraiso Perdido...Vertido do Original Inglez Para Verso Portuguez por Antonio Jose de Lima Leitao... Lisbon: 1840. V. 47; 49
Paraphrasis Poetica In Tria...Poemata, Viz, Paradisum Amissum Paradisum Recuperatum, Et Samsonem agonisten... Londini: 1690. V. 49; 54
The Poems. New York: 1925. V. 54
Poems. London: 1926. V. 52
Poems, &c. Upon Several Occasions... London: 1673. V. 51; 52; 54
Poems. Both English and Italian. London: 1645. V. 48
Poems in English. London. V. 47; 50
Poems in English. London: 1926. V. 47; 48; 52; 54
Poems of Mr. John Milton, Both English and Latin, Compos'd at Several Times. London: 1645. V. 49
Poems on Affairs of State. London: 1697. V. 54
Poems on Affairs of State: From the Time of Oliver Cromwell, to the Abdication of K. James the Second. London: 1702. V. 49
Poems Upon Several Occasions. London: 1785. V. 49; 54
Poems Upon Several Occasions, English, Italian and Latin. London: 1791. V. 48; 49; 50; 54
The Poetical Works. London: 1695. V. 54
The Poetical Works. London: 1707/05. V. 54
The Poetical Works. London: 1720. V. 49; 50; 54
The Poetical Works. Edinburgh: 1762. V. 54

MILTON, JOHN continued
Poetical Works. Edinburgh: 1767. V. 49
Poetical Works. London: 1794-97. V. 49; 51; 52; 53
The Poetical Works. Boston: 1796. V. 49; 54
The Poetical Works. London: 1801. V. 49; 53
The Poetical Works... London: 1809. V. 54
The Poetical Works. Oxford: 1824. V. 50
The Poetical Works. London: 1825. V. 48
The Poetical Works... London: 1826. V. 49; 54
The Poetical Works. London: 1834. V. 53
The Poetical Works. London: 1835. V. 54
The Poetical Works. London: 1843. V. 49
The Poetical Works. London: 1845. V. 54
The Poetical Works. London: 1853. V. 54
The Poetical Works. London: 1861. V. 49; 50; 54
The Poetical Works. London: 1890. V. 53
Poetical Works. Guildford: 1904. V. 52
The Poetical Works. London: 1904. V. 48
The Poetical Works. Boston: 1909. V. 53
Pro Populo Anglicano Defensio... Londini: 1651. V. 49; 50; 51; 54
Pro Populo Anglicano Defensio. Londini: 1652. V. 49; 50; 52; 54
A Reply to the Answer (Printed by His Majesties Command at Oxford) to a Printed Booke Intituled Observations Upon some of His Maiesties Late Answers and Expresses. London: 1642. V. 49; 54
Samson Agonistes. 1931. V. 52; 54
Samson Agonistes, a Dramatic Poem. New Rochelle: 1904. V. 47; 49; 52; 54
A Selection from the English Prose Works... Boston: 1826. V. 49
The Shorter Poems. London: 1889. V. 52
The Sonnets. London: 1883. V. 52
The Sonnets of Mr. John Milton, Both English and Italian. Maastricht: 1929. V. 49
Det Tabte Paradiis. Copenhagen: 1790. V. 49; 54
Tetrachordon: Exposition Upon the Foure Chief Places in Scripture, Which Treat of Mariage (sic) or Nullities in Mariage. London: 1645. V. 49; 54
A Treatise on Christian Doctrine. Cambridge: 1825. V. 49
Das Verlohrne Paradies. Altona: 1762-63. V. 49
The Works. London: 1697. V. 54
The Works. London: 1753. V. 54
The Works. London: 1851. V. 47
The Works. London: 1863. V. 50
The Works. New York: 1931. V. 47; 48; 54
The Works in Prose and Verse. London: 1863. V. 50
The Works in Prose and Verse. London: 1867. V. 51
The Works in Verse and Prose. London: 1851. V. 48

MILTON, WILLIAM FITZWILLIAM, VISCOUNT
The North-West Passage by Land. London: 1865. V. 47; 50; 51
The North-West Passage by Land. London: 1875. V. 50

MILTON, WILLIAM W. F.
A History of the San Juan Water Boundary Question, as Affecting the Division of Territory Between Great Britain and the United States. London: 1869. V. 48; 50

MILUNSKY, AUBREY
The Prenatal Diagnosis of Hereditary Disorders. Springfield: 1973. V. 54

MILWARD-OLIVER, EDWARD
Len Deighton, an Annotated Bibliography, 1954-1985. 1985. V. 51

MILWAUKEE LAKE SHORE & WESTERN RAILWAY
Gogebic and Other Resorts in Northern Michigan and Wisconsin Reached by the... Chicago: 1885. V. 54

MINADOI DA ROVIGO, GIOVANNI T.
Historia della Guerra fra Turchi et Persiani... Venice: 1588. V. 49
Historia della Guerra fra Turchi, et Persiani di...Con Una Descrittione di Tutte le Cose Pertinenti Alla Religione, Alle Forze... Venice: 1594. V. 48

MINASIAN, KHATCHIK
Five Poems. Mt. Horeb: 1971. V. 54
The Simple Songs of... San Francisco: 1950. V. 48; 51

MINCHIN, H.
Great Short Stories of the War - England, France, Germany, America. London: 1930. V. 47
The Legion Book. London: 1929. V. 47; 50

MINCHIN, JAMES G. C.
The Growth of Freedom in the Balkan Peninsula. London: 1886. V. 52

MINDERER, RAYMUND
Aloedarivm Marocostinvm. Avgvstae Findelicorum: 1622. V. 53

MINER, CHARLES
History of Wyoming. Philadelphia: 1845. V. 53

MINER, DOROTHY
The History of Bookbinding 525-1950 A.D. An Exhibition Held at the Baltimore Museum of Art Nov. 12, 1957 to Jan. 2, 1958... Baltimore: 1957. V. 54
Studies in Art and Literature for Belle Da Costa Greene. Princeton: 1954. V. 52

MINER, H. S.
Orchids, the Royal Family of Plants. Boston: 1885. V. 47; 48; 52; 54
Orchids, the Royal Family of Plants, with Illustrations from Nature. London: 1885. V. 52

THE MINER'S Own Book. San Francisco: 1949. V. 51

THE MINES of New Mexico. Inexhaustible Deposits of Gold and Silver Copper, Lead, Iron and Coal. Santa Fe: 1896. V. 52

MINGAUD, MONSIEUR
The Noble Game of Billiards Wherein are Exhibited Extraordinary and Surprising Strokes Which Have Excited the Admiration of Most of the Sovereigns of Europe. London: 1830. V. 47

MINGAZZINI, PAOLINO
Vasi della Cooezione Castellani. Roma: 1930. V. 50

MINGHETTI, MARCO
The Masters of Raffaello. London: 1882. V. 51

MINKOWSKI, HERMANN
Raum und Zeit. Leipzig & Berlin: 1909. V. 47

MINNESOTA in the Civil and Indian Waras 1861-1865. St. Paul: 1890-93. V. 50
MINNESOTA: Its Advantages to Settlers. St. Paul: 1867. V. 49
MINNESOTA: Its Advantages to Settlers. St. Paul: 1868. V. 54

MINNICH, J. W.
Inside of Rock Island Prison, from December 1863 to June 1865. Nashville: 1908. V. 50

MINNIGERODE, MEADE
Some Personal Letters of Herman Melville and a Bibliography. New York, New Haven: 1922. V. 49; 50; 51; 53

MINNION, W. J.
Topsy Turvy, Being Shreds and Patches of a Christmas Dream. London: 1913. V. 49

MINOR, DOROTHY
Studies in Art and Literature. 1954. V. 47

MINOR, H. A.
Dr. H. A. Minor's Account of Gen. Lee's Surrender at Appomatox at Appomatox Court House, Va. Some Reminiscences of a Surgeon of Mahone's Division. 1904?. V. 47

MINOR, RALEIGH C.
Notes on the Science of Government and the Relation of the States to the United States. Charlottesville: 1913. V. 49

MINOT, GEORGE RICHARDS
Continuation of the History of the Province of Massachusetts Bay, from the Year 1748. Boston: 1798/June 1803. V. 50
Continuation of the History of the Province of Massachusetts Bay from the Year 1748. Boston: 1803. V. 47
An Eulogy On George Washington. Boston: 1800. V. 50

MINOTAURE. Revue Artistique et Litteraire. Paris: 1933-39. V. 50; 52

MINSHULL, JOHN
A Comic Opera. Entitled Rural Felicity; with the Humour of Patrick and Marriage of Shelty. New York: 1801. V. 51; 52

MINTO, EARL OF
Lord Minto's Canadian Papers: a Selection of the Public and Private Papers of the Fourth Earl of Minto: 1898-1904. Toronto: 1981/83. V. 49

MINTO, GILBERT ELLIOT, 1ST EARL OF
The Speech of Lord Minto in the House of Peers, April 11, 1799 on a Motion...Respecting an Union Between Great Britain and Ireland. (with) The Speech of Lord Minto in the House of Peers, June 6th, 1803 on Certain Resolutions of Censure on the Conduct... London: 1799/1803. V. 52

MINTO, JOHN
Time Was Away. A Notebook of Corsica. London: 1948. V. 54

MINTO, WALTER
An Inaugural Oration, on the Progress and Importance of the Mathematical Sciences. Trenton: 1788. V. 53

MINTORN, JOHN
The Hand-Book for Modelling Wax Flowers. London: 1844. V. 49

MINTURN, ROBERT BROWNE
From New York to Delhi by Way of Rio de Janeiro, Australia and China. New York: 1858. V. 48; 50

MINTURNO, ANTONIO S.
L'Arte Poetica...Nella Quale si Contengono i Precetti Heroici, Tragici, Comici Satyrici, e d'Ogni Alta Poesia. 1564. V. 47

MINUCIUS FELIX, MARCUS
Minucius Felix, His Dialogne (sic) Called Octavius. Containing a Defence of Christian Religion. Oxford: 1636. V. 52
Those Two Excellent Monuments of Anicent Learning and Pietry, Minucius Felix's Octavius, and Tertullian's Apology for the Primitive Christians... London: 1708. V. 52

A MINUTE And Circumstantial Narrative of the Loss of the Steam-Packet Pulaski, Which Burst Her Boiler, and Sunk On the Coast of North Carolina, June 14, 1838. Providence: 1839. V. 48

MINUTES of Council Northern Department of Rupert Land. 1821-1831. Toronto: 1940. V. 51

MINUTES of the Proceedings at a Court-Martial, Assembled to Inquire Into the Cause of the Loss of His Majesty's Late ship Ardent. Taken by George Jackson, Esq. Judge-Advocate of His Majesty's Fleet... London: 1780. V. 52

MINUTOLI, WOLFRADINE VON WATZDORFF, FREIHERRRIN VON
Recollections of Egypt. Philadelphia: 1827. V. 53

MIOLNE, COLIN
Indigenous Botany; or Habitations of English Plants... London: 1793. V. 54

MIRABEAU, HONORE GABRIEL RIQUETI, COMTE DE
Avis Aux Hessois et Autres Peuples de L'Allemagne Vendus par Leurs Princes a l'Angleterre. Cleves: 1777. V. 52
Letters, During His Residence in England; with Anecdotes, Maxims &c. London: 1832. V. 51
Memoirs of the Courts of Berlin and St. Petersburg. New York: 1910. V. 50
Mirabeau's Letters During His Residence in England, with Anecdotes, Maxims, &c. London: 1832. V. 52
Mirabeau's Love-Letters. London: 1909. V. 48
The Secret History of the Court of Berlin. London: 1789. V. 51
Sur La Liberte de La Presse. London: 1788. V. 48

MIRABEAU, OCTAVE HENRI MARIE
Le Jardin des Supplices. Paris: 1899. V. 54
Mirabeau's Love Letters. London: 1909. V. 54

MIRABEAU, SIBYLLE GABRIELLE MARIE ANTOINETTE RIQUETI DE
Le Monde a Cote. Paris: 1884. V. 50

THE MIRACULOUS Power of Clothes, and Dignity of the Taylors; Being an Essay on the Words, Clothes Made Men. Philadelphia: 1772. V. 48; 53; 54

MIRANDA, MARTIM AFONSO
Discursos Historicos de la Vida, y Muerte de Don Antonio de Zuniga... Lisbon: 1618. V. 48

MIRANDA, or the Discovery. Norwich: 1800. V. 47; 49

MIR HASSAN ALI, B., MRS.
Observations on the Mussulmauns of India... London: 1832. V. 47; 50; 51; 53

MIRO, JOAN
Les Essencies De La Terra. Barcelona: 1968. V. 49
Joan Miro Lithographs. New York: 1972. V. 47; 51
Joan Miro Lithographs. New York and Paris: 1972/75/77/81. V. 47
Joan Miro Lithographs. New York: 1975. V. 47; 50; 51; 52; 53
Litografos I-III. Barcelona and Paris: 1972/75/77. V. 51
Miro. Saint Paul: 1968. V. 50
The Prints of Joan Miro. London: 1947. V. 49

MIRRLEES, HOPE
Paris. London: 1919. V. 47; 51
Paris a Poem. Richmond: 1919. V. 53

THE MIRROR of the Graces; or, the English Lady's Costume. London: 1811. V. 53

THE MIRROR of the Graces; or, the English Lady's Costume... Edinburgh: 1830. V. 51

MIRSKY, JEANETTE
To the North! The Story of Arctic Exploration from Earliest Times to the Present. New York: 1934. V. 50

MISCELLANEOUS Antiquitie; or, a Collection of Curious Papers; Either Republished from Scarce Tracts, or Now First Printed from Original Mss. Numbers I (II). Strawberry Hill: 1772. V. 47; 53

A MISCELLANEOUS Metaphysical Essay; or, An Hypothesis Concerning the Formation and Generation of Spiritual and Material Beings. London: 1748. V. 50

MISCELLANEOUS Pieces, Consisting of Select Poetry and Methods of Improvement in Husbandry, Gardening and Various Other Subjects, Useful to Families. 1752. V. 49

MISCELLANEOUS Pieces Relating to the Chinese. London: 1762. V. 53

MISCELLANEOUS Poems. Windsor: 1812. V. 54

MISCELLANEOUS Poems, by Several Hands. (with) Miscellaneous Poems, By Several Hands. London: 1726/30. V. 48; 54

MISCELLANEOUS Poems Selected from the Untied States Literary Gazette. Boston: 1826. V. 47

MISCELLANEOUS State Papers. From 1501 to 1726. London: 1778. V. 51

MISCELLANIES in Prose and Verse. The First (Second) Volume. London: 1727. V. 49

MISCELLANIES, Viz. I. The Time-Piece; or, an Honest Servant's Advice to His Master. II. Verses On the Month of May. III. An Affectionate Father's Dying Advice. Philadelphia: 1790. V. 50

A MISCELLANY of Rhimes. Glocester: 1782. V. 50

MISERDINE Estate. Particulars. London: 1874. V. 52

MISHIMA, YUKIO
Confessions of a Mask. Norfolk: 1958. V. 52
Five Modern No Plays. New York: 1957. V. 47
The Sailor Who Fell from Grace with the Sea. New York: 1965. V. 50; 51; 52
The Sea of Fertility Tetralogy. (Spring Snow, Runaway Horses, The Temple of Dawn, and The Decay of the Angel). New York: 1972-74. V. 53
The Sound of Waves. New York: 1956. V. 52
Sun and Steel. London: 1971. V. 53
The Temple of the Golden Pavilion. New York: 1959. V. 52
Twilight Sunflower: a Play in Four Acts. Tokyo: 1958. V. 53

MISONNE, LEONARD
Leonard Misonne. Vienna: 1939. V. 47

MISS, DAVID
A Report on the Boundaries of the Province of Ontario. Toronto: 1873. V. 54

MISSION Furniture: How to Make It. Chicago: 1909/10/12. V. 50

MISSION Scientifique du Cap Horn 1882-1883. London: 1885-91. V. 47

A MISSIONARY Present About Kaffir Children. 1871. V. 51

A MISSIONARY Present About the Children in British Guiana. V. 51

THE MISSIONARY'S Daughter: a Memoir of Lucy Goodale Thurston, of the Sandwich Islands. New York: 1842. V. 52

MISSISSIPPI & TENNESSEE RAILROAD
Report of the President, Treasurer and Chief Engineer of the Mississippi and Tennessee Railroad. Memphis: 1854. V. 47

MISSISSIPPI. CONSTITUTION
Constitution of the State of Mississippi, as Amended with the Orbinances (sic) and Resolutions Adopted by the Constitutional Convention August 1865. Jackson: 1865. V. 47; 54

MISSISSIPPI FRIENDS OF SOUTHERN RIGHTS
Address of the Committee Appointed by the Friends of Southern Rights to the People of Mississippi, December 10th, 1850. Jackson: 1850. V. 53

MISSISSIPPI. LAWS, STATUTES, ETC.
The Revised Code of the Laws of Mississippi, in Which are Comprised All Such Acts of the General Assembly of a Public Nature, As Were in Force at the End of the Year 1823. Natchez: 1824. V. 50
Statutes of the Mississippi Territory...the Ordinance for the Government of the Territory of the United States, North West of the River Ohio... Natchez: 1816. V. 47; 48; 50; 53

MISSON, HENRI M.
Misson's Memoirs and Observations in His Travels Over England. London: 1719. V. 50

MISSON DE VALBOURG, HENRI
Memoires et Observations Faites par un Voyageur en Angleterre. The Hague: 1698. V. 50; 54

MISSOURI, Kansas and Texas Railway Company. 1871. V. 50

MISSOURI. STATE CONVENTION
Journal and Proceedings of the Missouri State Convention, Held at Jefferson City and St. Louis, March 1861 (and) Journal of the Missouri State Convention, Held at the City of St. Louis, Print, January 6-April 10, 1865. St. Louis: 1861/65. V. 49

MISSOURI. STATE GEOLOGIST
First and Second Annual Reports of the Geological Surveys in Missouri. Jefferson City: 1855. V. 51

MISUGI, T.
Chinese Porcleain Collections in the Near East, Topkapi, and Ardebil... Hong Kong: 1981. V. 48; 49

MITCHEL, JOHN
Jail Journal; or, Five Years in British Prisons. Glasgow: 1876. V. 47

MITCHEL, MARTIN
History of the County of Fond du Lac, Wis(consin) From Its Earliest Settlement to the Present Time. Fond du Lac: 1854. V. 49

MITCHEL, O. W.
The Planetary and Stellar Worlds: a Popular Exposition of the Great Discoveries and Theories of Modern Astronomy. New York: 1848. V. 54

MITCHELL, ADRIAN
Out Loud. London: 1968. V. 47

MITCHELL, B. W.
Trail Life in the Canadian Rockies. New York: 1924. V. 53

MITCHELL, CLARENCE BLAIR
The ABC of Riding to Hounds. Princeton: 1916. V. 47

MITCHELL, DAVID W.
Ten Years in the United Sates: Being an Englishman's Views of Men and Things in the North and South. London: 1862. V. 49; 53

MITCHELL, DONALD GRANT
American Lands and Letters. New York: 1897/99. V. 54
American Lands and Letters. New York: 1901. V. 52
Dream Life: a Fable of the Seasons. New York: 1851. V. 54
English Lands, Letters and Kings. New York: 1904-07. V. 54
Fudge Doings: Being Tony Fudge's Record of the Same. New York: 1855. V. 48
Reveries of a Bachelor. New York: 1850. V. 53; 54
Reveries of a Bachelor. New York: 1896. V. 48

MITCHELL, F. S.
The Birds of Lancashire. London: 1885. V. 51; 53; 54

MITCHELL, FLORA H.
Vanishing Dublin. 1966. V. 54
Vanishing Dublin. London: 1966. V. 51

MITCHELL, FREDERICK SHAW
The Birds of Lancashire... London: 1892. V. 52

MITCHELL, GEORGE
A Catalogue of the Library of George Mitchell, Esq. 1869. V. 54
A Catalogue of the Library of George Mitchell Esquire. London: 1869. V. 48; 51

MITCHELL, GLADYS
Speedy Death. New York: 1929. V. 47
Watson's Choice - a Detective Story. London: 1955. V. 50

MITCHELL, ISAAC
The Asylum; or, Alonzo and Melissa, an American Tale. Poughkeepsie: 1811. V. 48; 54
A Short Account of the Courtship of Alonzo and Melissa... Plattsburgh: 1811. V. 49; 52

MITCHELL, JAMES
First Lines of Science. London: 1827. V. 52
The Portable Encyclopaedia: or, a Dictionary of the Arts and Sciences... London: 1828. V. 48; 52

MITCHELL, JOHN
A Full Account of the Proceedings in Relation to Capt. Kidd. London: 1701. V. 50
A Night on the Banks of Doon and Other Poems. Paisley: 1838. V. 54
Notes from Over Sea, Consisting of Observations Mad in Europe in the Years 1843 and 1844. New York: 1845. V. 52
Organized Labor. Philadelphia: 1903. V. 52
Treatise on the Falsifications of Food and the Chemical Means Employed to Detect Them. London: 1848. V. 49; 54

MITCHELL, JOHN KEARSLEY
Five Essays by John Kearsley Mitchell, M.D. Philadelphia: 1859. V. 47; 49; 50; 54

MITCHELL, JONATHAN
Nehemiah On the Wall in Troublesome Times... Cambridge: 1671. V. 47

MITCHELL, JOSEPH
The Bottom of the Harbor. Boston: 1959. V. 52
The Bottom of the Harbor. Boston: 1960. V. 49
The Highland Fair; or, Union of the Clans. London: 1731. V. 48
Joe Gould's Secret. New York: 1965. V. 50
Mc Sorley's Wonderful Saloon. New York: 1943. V. 53
My Ears Are Bent. New York: 1938. V. 50
Old Mr. Flood. New York: 1948. V. 47; 50; 52
Practical Suggestions for Relieving the Over-Crowded Throroughfares of London... London: 1857. V. 52
Up in the Old Hotel. New York: 1992. V. 50; 51; 52

MITCHELL, MAIRIN
Storm Over Spain. London: 1937. V. 49

MITCHELL, MARGARET
Gone With the Wind. New York: 1934. V. 54
Gone with the Wind. London: 1936. V. 51
Gone With the Wind. New York: 1936. V. 47; 48; 49; 51; 52; 53
Gone With the Wind. London: 1939. V. 51
Gone With the Wind. New York: 1939. V. 48; 49; 50
Gone with the Wind. New York: 1961. V. 48; 54
Gone With the Wind. New York: 1968. V. 48; 49
Gone With the wind. New York: 1986. V. 53

MITCHELL, PETER
Jan Van Os 1744-1808. Leigh-on-Sea: 1968. V. 50

MITCHELL, SALLY
The Dictionary of British Equestrian Artists. London: 1985. V. 48

MITCHELL, SAMUEL AUGUSTUS
An Accompaniment to Mitchell's Reference & Distance Map of the United States... Philadelphia: 1834. V. 50
Mitchell's New Travellers Guide through the United States...Together with the Railroad, Stage, Steamboat and Canal Routes. Philadelphia: 1849. V. 47
A New Map of Texas Oregon and California with the Regions Adjoining. Philadelphia: 1846. V. 52
A New Universal Atlas Containing maps of the Various Empires, Kingdoms, States, and Republics of the World... Philadelphia: 1853. V. 54
Parallaxes of 260 Stars, Derived from Photographs Made at the Leander McCormick observatory. New York: 1920. V. 50
A Route-Book Adapted to Mitchell's National Map of the American Repbulic... Philadelphia: 1847. V. 54

MITCHELL, SAMUEL CHILES
An Aftermath of Appomattox. Atlanta: 1954. V. 54

MITCHELL, SILAS WEIR
Books and the Man. Read to the Charaka Club of New York. March 4, 1905. V. 50
The Collected Poems. New York: 1896. V. 47
The Comfort of the Hills and Other Poems. New York: 1910. V. 49; 54
The Comfort of the Hills and Other Poems. New York: 1911. V. 47; 48; 49; 50; 52; 53; 54
A Contribution to the Study of the Effect Venom of Crotalus Adamanteus Upon the Blood of Man and Animals. Washington: 1898. V. 53
Doctor and Patient. Philadelphia: 1888. V. 49; 54
Fat and Blood: an Essay on the Treatment of Certain Forms of Neurasthenia and Hysteria. Philadelphia: 1884. V. 52
Fat and Blood: and How to Make Them. Philadelphia: 1878. V. 47
Hephzibah Guinness: Thee and You... Philadelphia: 1880. V. 47; 53
Lectures on Diseases of the Nervous System, Especially in Women. Philadelphia: 1881. V. 47
Lectures on Diseases of the Nervous System, Especially in Women. Philadelphia: 1885. V. 52
The Madeira Party. New York: 1895. V. 47
Researches Upon the Venom of the Rattlesnake (the Venoms of Poisonous Serpents). Washington: 1860-86. V. 47
Researches Upon the Venoms of Poisonous Serpents. Washington: 1886. V. 47; 48; 50; 53
Selections from Poems of S. Weir Mitchell. London: 1901. V. 47
Some Recently Discovered Letters of William Harvey with Other Miscellanea... Philadelphia: 1912. V. 47; 49; 50; 52
When All the Woods are Green. New York: 1894. V. 53; 54
The Works of W. Weir Mitchell. New York: 1905. V. 53

MITCHELL, SUSAN L.
Secret Springs of Dublin Song. London: 1918. V. 47

MITCHELL, T. L.
Journal of an Expedition into the Interior of Tropical Australia... London: 1848. V. 54
Three Expeditions into the Interior of Eastern Australia. London: 1838. V. 52; 53

MITCHELL, WALTER
Mechanical Philosophy: Including the Properties of Matter. London: 1856. V. 53

MITCHELL, WILLIAM ANDREW
An Essay on Capacity and Genius; to Prove that There is no Original Mental Superiority Between the Most Illiterate and Most Learned of Mankind and that No Genius, Whether Individual or National, is Innate, but Solely Produced by and Depedent on... London: 1821. V. 47
On the Pleasure and Utility of Angling; a Paper Read to the Waltonian Club of Newcastle on Tyne, July 27th, 1824. Newcastle on Tyne: 1824. V. 47

MITCHELL, WILLIAM SMITH
A History of Scottish Bookbinding 1432 to 1650. Edinburgh: 1955. V. 50

MITCHELL'S
Compendium of the Internal Improvements of the United States...Canals and Rail-Roads... Philadelphia: 1835. V. 53

MITCHIE, JOHN
The Vices of the Tavern Dissected; or, Drunkenness Laid Open. Edinburgh: 1816. V. 48; 54

MITCHILL, SAMUEL LATHAM
Catalogue of the Organic Remains, Which With Other Geological and some Mineral Articles were Presented to the New York Lyceum of Natural History. New York: 1826. V. 53
Devotional Somnium; or, a Collection of Prayers and Exhortations, Uttered by Miss Rachel Baker...During Her Abstracted and Unconscious State. New York: 1815. V. 54

MITCHINSON, ALEXANDER WILLIAM
The Expiring Continent: a Narrative of Travel in Senegambia. London: 1881. V. 51

MITCHISON, NAOMI
Beyond This Limit. London: 1935. V. 48; 49; 50; 51; 54

MITFORD, B.
Through the Zulu Country. London: 1883. V. 54
The Weird of Deadly Hollow. 1891. V. 48

MITFORD, JOHN
My Cousin in the Army; or Johnny Newcome on the Peace Establishment. London: 1922. V. 48

MITFORD, MARY RUSSELL
Atherton, and Other Tales. London: 1854. V. 50; 53
Belford Regis; or Sketches of a Country Town. London: 1835. V. 47; 50; 54
Christina, the Maid of the South Seas; Narrative Poems on the Female Character...; Our Village... London: 1811/13/24. V. 52
Country Stories. London: 1837. V. 50
Dramatic Scenes, Sonnets and Other Poems. London: 1827. V. 49
The Friendships of Mary Russell Mitford As Recorded in Letters from Her Literary Correspondents. London: 1882. V. 52
Letters Of...Second Series. London: 1872. V. 53
The Life of Mary Russell Mitford, Related in a Selection from Her Letters to Her Friends. London: 1870. V. 50; 53; 54
Lights and Shadows of American Life. London: 1832. V. 53
Our Village. London: 1824. V. 50
Our Village. London: 1824-32. V. 50
Our Village. London: 1893. V. 50; 51; 53; 54
Our Village. London: 1906. V. 53
Poems. London: 1810. V. 47
Recollections of a Literary Life. London: 1852. V. 48; 50; 52; 53
Recollections of a Literary Life. New York: 1852. V. 52
Recollections of a Literary Life. London: 1853. V. 52

MITFORD, NANCY
Christmas Pudding. London: 1932. V. 51
Don't Tell Alfred. London: 1960. V. 47
Noblesse Oblige. London: 1956. V. 51
The Pursuit of Love. London: 1945. V. 52

MITFORD, R. C. W.
To Caubul with the Cavalry Brigade. London: 1881. V. 53

MITFORD, WILLIAM
The History of Greece. London: 1814-20. V. 53
The History of Greece. London: 1822. V. 48
The History of Greece. London: 1829. V. 51
The History of Greece, from the Earliest Period to the Death of Agesilaus. London: 1835. V. 52
An Inquiry into the Principles of Harmony in Language, and of the Mechanism of Verse, Modern and Ancient. London: 1804. V. 51
Three Essays...a Defence or Vindication of the Women, Church Music, Ancient and Modern Music. London: 1788. V. 51

MITRA, RAJENDRALALA
Indoaryans... London: 1881. V. 48

MITTELHOLZER, EDGAR
Of Trees and the Sea. London: 1963. V. 50
Swarthy Boys. London: 1963. V. 50

MITTEN, DAVID GORDON
Classical Bronzes. Providence: 1975. V. 50; 52

MITTERMANN, HARALD
A Complete Concordance to the Novels of John Lyly. London: 1986. V. 51

MIURA, KERSTIN TINI
A Master's Bibliophile Bindings: Tini Miura, 1980-1990. Tokyo: 1991. V. 49
My World of Bibliophile Binding. Tokyo: 1980. V. 51
My World of Bibliophile Binding. 1984. V. 49; 51

MIVART, ST. G.
The Cat: an Introduction to the Study of Backboned Animals, Especially Mammals. London: 1881. V. 53
Dogs, Jackals, Wolves and Foxes... London: 1890. V. 51; 52; 54
A Monograph of the Lories, or Brush-Tongued Parrots... London: 1896. V. 49; 51; 54
A Monograph of the Lories, or Brush-Tongued Parrots, Comprising the Family Loriidae. London: 1896. V. 47; 52; 53; 54
A Monograph of the Lories, or Brush-Tongued Parrots, Comprising the Family Loriidae. Seibersbach: 1992. V. 51; 52

MIXSON, FRANK M.
Reminiscences of a Private. Columbia: 1910. V. 48; 49

MIYOSHI, M.
Pocket Atlas of Alpine Plants of Japan. Tokyo: 1906-07. V. 50

MIZAUD, ANTOINE
Le Mirouer du Temps, Autrement Dict, Ephemerides Perpetuelles de l'Air... Paris: 1547. V. 48
Neunhundert Gedachtnuszwurdige Geheimnusz und Wunderwerck, von Mancherley Kreutern, Metallen, Thieren, Vogeln und Andern Naturlichen Kunsten und Historien... Basle: 1574. V. 48

MIZNER, ADDISON
Florida Architecture. New York: 1928. V. 52; 53; 54

MIZUNO, K.
Manchurian Birds in Life Colours. Tokyo: 1940. V. 48

MIZWA, STEPHEN P.
Nicholas Copernicus 1543-1943. New York: 1943. V. 50

MJOBERG, ERIC
Forest Life and Adventures in the Malay Archipelago. London: 1930. V. 54

MO, TIMOTHY
The Monkey King. London: 1978. V. 47; 49; 50; 51; 54
The Redundancy of Courage. London: 1991. V. 49; 51
Sour Sweet. London: 1982. V. 50; 51

MOBERLY, WALTER
Early History of Canadian Pacific Railway. Vancouver: 1909. V. 52
The Rocks and Rivers of British Columbia. London: 1885. V. 51; 54
The Rocks and Rivers of British Columbia. Vienna: 1929. V. 53

MOBIUS, GOTTFRIED
Anatomia Camphorae. Jena: 1660. V. 47

MOCATTA, FREDERIC DAVID
Catalogue of the Printed Books and Manuscripts forming the Library of Frederic David Mocatta. London: 1904. V. 48; 51; 54

MOCHI, UGO
Hoofed Mammals of the World. New York: 1953. V. 53
Hoofed Mammals of the World. New York: 1954. V. 53

MOCK, ELIZABETH B.
The Architecture of Bridges. New York: 1949. V. 49

MOCK, HARRY
Industrial Medicine and Surgery. Philadelphia: 1921. V. 49; 54

MOCKET, RICHARD
God and the King: or, a Dialogue, Shewing, That our Soveraign Lord the King...Doth Rightly Claim Whatsoever Is Required by the Oath of Allegiance. London: 1663. V. 52

MOCKLER-FERRYMAN, A. F.
Up the Niger: Narrative of Major Claude MacDonald's Mission to the Niger and Benue Rivers, West Africa... London: 1892. V. 54

MOCQUET DE MEAUX, JEAN
Travels and Voyages into Africa, Asia and America, the East and West Indies; Syria, Jerusalem and the Holy Land. Newton: 1696. V. 47

THE MODEL Menagerie. London: 1890. V. 49

THE MODEL Menagerie with Natural History. London: 1895. V. 47

MODENA, LEO DE
Kerk-Zeeden en de Gewoonten, Die Huiden in Gebruik Zyn Onder de Jooden. Amsterdam: 1700. V. 53

MODERN Beauties in Prose and Verse, Selected from the Most Eminent Authors... Darlington: 1793. V. 50; 54

MODERN Book Production. London: 1928. V. 51

MODERN Bookbindings and Their Designers. London: 1899. V. 50

MODERN Design in Jewellery and Fans. London Paris & New York: 1901-02. V. 47

MODERN Fashions (A Poem Address'd to the Ladies). London: 1745. V. 48

MODERN Homes. The Perspective Views and Building Plans for Sensible Low Cost Houses. Philadelphia: 1889. V. 50

MODERN London. London: 1806. V. 54

THE MODERN Patriot. London?: 1757?. V. 53

MODERN Pen Drawings: European and American. London: 1901. V. 47

THE MODERN SONGSTER; or, Universal Banquet of vocal Music. Baltimore: 1805. V. 51

THE MODERN Story-Teller; Being a Collection of Merry, Polite, Grave, Moral, Entertaining and Improving Tales. Poughkeepsie: 1816. V. 52

THE MODERN Traveller. London: 1826. V. 52

A MODEST Apology in Defence of the Bakers. London: 1757. V. 51

A MODEST Enquiry Concerning the Election of the Sheriffs of London. London: 1682. V. 53

MODJESKI & MASTERS
Gateway Bridge, Clinton, Iowa over the Mississippi River. Fianl Report to City of Clinton Bridge Commission. Harrisburg: 1957. V. 51
Report on Pecos River Bridge, at High Bridge, Texas to Texas and New Orleans Railroad Company Houston, Texas. Harrisburg: 1945. V. 49

MODY, N. H. N.
A Collection of Japanese Clocks. London: 1932. V. 53

MOEBS, THOMAS T.
Black Soldiers-Black Sailors-Black Ink: Research Guide on African-Americans in U.S. Military History, 1526-1900. Chesapeake Bay and (sic): 1994. V. 51

MOELLER, MAX
The Violin-Makers of the Low Countries. (Belgium & Holland). Amsterdam: 1955. V. 49

MOENS, WILLIAM J. C.
English Travellers and Italian Brigands. London: 1866. V. 49
The Walloons and Their Church at Norwich; Their History and Registers, 1565-1832. Lymington: 1887-88. V. 49

MOESCH, JOHANNES
De Horis Canonicis Dicendis. Augsburg: 1489. V. 51

MOESCHLIN, ELSA
The Little Boy with the Big Apples. New York: 1937. V. 49

MOFFAT, A. S.
The Secrets of Angling. Edinburgh: 1865. V. 52

MOFFAT, ALFRED
Little Songs of Long Ago. Philadelphia: 1912. V. 52
Our Od Nursery Rhymes. Philadelphia: 1912. V. 52

MOFFAT, C. B.
Life and Letters of Alexander Goodman More... Dublin: 1898. V. 47
Life and Letters of Alexander Goodman More with Selections from His Zoological and Botanical Writings. 1898. V. 49; 50
Life and Letters of Alexander Goodman More with Selections from His Zoological and Botanical Writings. London: 1898. V. 51

MOFFAT, JOHN S.
The Lives of Robert and Mary Moffat. New York: 1886. V. 52

MOFFAT, ROBERT
Missionary Labours and Scenes in Southern Africa. London: 1842. V. 49; 51; 54
Missionary Labours and Scenes in Southern Africa. London: 1846. V. 54

MOFFETTE, JOSEPH F.
The Territories of Kansas and Nebraska. New York: 1856. V. 47

MOFFIT, A.
A Manual of Instruction for Attendants on Sick and Wounded in War. London: 1870. V. 52

MOGELON, ALEX
Miller Brittain: In Focus. Toronto: 1981. V. 54

MOGEY, WILLIAM, & SONS
Illustrated Catalogue of Astronomical and Terrestrial Telescopes 1882-1927. Plainfield. V. 48

MOGG, EDWARD
Paterson's Roads... London: 1831. V. 51

MOGGRIDGE, J. T.
Contributions to the Flora of Mentone, and to a Winter Flora of the Riviera. London: 1871. V. 52
Harvesting Ants and Trap-Door Spiders, Notes and Observations on Their Habits and Dwellings. London: 1873. V. 53
Harvesting Ants and Trap-Door Spiders, with Supplement. London: 1873-74. V. 48; 52

MOGRIDGE, GEORGE
The Moral Budget of My Uncle Newbury. London: 1835. V. 54
Points and Pickings of Information About the Chinese. London: 1844. V. 54

MOGRIDGE, GEORGE continued
Sergeant Bell, and His Raree-show. London: 1839. V. 49

MOHAN, LAL
Life of the Amir Dost Mohammed Khan, of Kabul. London. 1846. V. 50; 54

MOHANTY, BIJOY CHANDRA
Block Printing and Dyeing of Bagru, Rajasthan. Ahmedabad: 1983. V. 52
Natural Dyeing Processes of India. Ahmedabad: 1987. V. 52

MOHN, ISABELLA
Geraldine Hamilton; or, Self-Guidance. London: 1832. V. 50

MOHOLY, LUCIA
A Hundred Years of Photography, 1839-1939. Hammondsworth: 1939. V. 47
A Hundred Years of Photography, 1839-1939. Middlesex: 1939. V. 52

MOHOLY-NAGY, LASZLO
L. Moholy-Nagy: 60 Photos. Berlin: 1930. V. 47
The New Vision from Material to Architecture. New York: 1930. V. 48; 54
The New Vision: from Material to Architecture. New York: 1932. V. 49
The New Vision...and Abstract of an Artist. New York: 1947. V. 52
Portrait of Eton. London: 1949. V. 52
Sibyl Moholy-Nagy. A Biography. New York: 1950. V. 48
The Street Markets of London. London: 1936. V. 47
Vision in Motion. Chicago: 1947. V. 52

MOHOLY-NAGY, S.
Carlos Raul Villa-Nueva and the Architecture of Venezuela. New York: 1964. V. 48; 50; 51; 53; 54
Moholy-Nagy. Experiment in Totality. New York: 1950. V. 47

MOHR, EDWARD
To The Victoria Falls of the Zambesi. London: 1876. V. 54

MOHR, JOHN H.
Medical Guide in Treating All Internal and External Diseases of Horses, Mules and Neat Cattle. Reading: 1866. V. 50

MOHRINGER, KARL
The Bridges of the Rhine: Roman, Medieval, and Modern. Messkrich: 1931. V. 49

MOHYNHAN, B. G. A.
Duodenal Ulcer. Philadelphia: 1910. V. 53

MOINET, L.
Nouveau Traite General, Astronomique et Civil d'Horlogerie, Theorique et Pratique... Paris: 1848. V. 53; 54
Nouveau Traite General Elementaire, Pratique et Theorique d'Horlogerie... Paris: 1853. V. 53

MOIR, DAVID MAC BETH
Domestic Verses. Edinburgh: 1871. V. 48; 49; 52; 54

MOIR, GEORGE T.
Sinners and Saints. Victoria: 1948. V. 49

MOIR, J.
One Thing Needful; or Devout and Philosophical Exercises on Various Subjects of Superlative Importance in Theology and Morals. Walworth: 1799. V. 50

MOIR, JOHN
Gleanings; or, Fugitive Pieces... London: 1785?. V. 48

MOIR, JOHN S.
History of the Royal Canadian Corps of Signals 1903-196. Ottawa: 1962. V. 53

MOIVRE, ABRAHAM DE
Annuities Upon Lives. London: 1725. V. 49; 53

MOKLER, ALFRED J.
History of Natrona County, Wyoming 1888-1922. Chicago: 1923. V. 52; 53

MOLDENKE, CHARLES
The New York Obelisk, Cleopatra's Needle, with a Preliminary Sketch of the History, Erection, Uses and Signification of Obelisks. New York: 1891. V. 52

MOLDENKE, H. N.
Plants of the Bible. London: 1952. V. 53

MOLEMA, S. M.
The Bantu Past and Present. Edinburgh: 1920. V. 54

MOLESWORTH, MARY LOUISA STEWART
The Adventures of Herr Baby. London: 1881. V. 51
Five Minutes' Stories. London: 1888. V. 48
The Rectory Children. London: 1889. V. 53

MOLESWORTH, ROBERT MOLESWORTH, VISCOUNT
An Account of Denmark, As It Was in the Year 1692. London: 1694. V. 47; 50

MOLEVILLE, BERNARD DE
The Costume of the Hereditary States of the House of Austria. London: 1804. V. 54

MOLEVILLE, BERTRAND DE
Annals of the French Revolution; or a Chronological Account Of its Principal Events, with a Variety of Anecdotes and Character Hitherto Unpublished. London: 1813. V. 52

MOLIEN, G.
Travels in Africa to the Sources of the Senegal and Gambia in 1818. London: 1820. V. 47

MOLIERE, JEAN BAPTISTE POQUELIN DE
The Dramatic Works. Edinburgh: 1875. V. 51; 52
The Kiltartan Moliere. The Miser. The Doctor in Spite of Himself. The Rogueries of Scapin. London: 1910. V. 53
Le Malade Imaginaire. Paris: 1921. V. 51
The Misanthrope. London: 1973. V. 52
Oeuvres... Paris: 1773. V. 50
Select Comedies...in French and English. London: 1732. V. 49; 52
Tartuffe: or, the French Puritan. London: 1707. V. 48; 52
Tartuffe: or, the French Puritan. New York: 1963. V. 50
Tartuffe or the Hypocrite. Leipzig: 1930. V. 52; 53; 54
Theatre Choisi. Tours: 1878-79. V. 54
Theatre Complete de J. B. Poquelin de Moliere... Paris: 1876-81. V. 49
The Works. Paris: 1734. V. 51
The Works. London: 1739. V. 50
The Works. Paris: 1891-85. V. 53

MOLINA, GIOVANNI I.
The Geographical, Natural and Civil History of Chili. Middletown: 1808. V. 47; 52

MOLINEAUX, THOMAS
The Stenographical Copy-Book; or, Short-Hand Instructor. Macclesfield: 1824. V. 48

MOLINEUX, GISBORNE
Memoir of the Molineux Family. London: 1882. V. 47

MOLL, HERMAN
A Complete System of Geography. London: 1744. V. 50
A New Description of England and Wales, and with Adjacent Islands. London: 1724. V. 54
A Set of Fifty New and Correct Maps of England and Wales, &c. with the Great Roads and Principal Cross-Roads &c. London: 1724. V. 51
Thirty Two New and Accurate Maps of the Geography of the Ancients. London: 1726. V. 53

MOLLER, MAX
The Violin Makers of the Low Countries (Belgium and Holland). Amsterdam: 1955. V. 51

MOLLET, ANDRE
Le Jardin de Plaisir, Contenant Plusieurs Dessins de Jardiange Tant Parterres en Broderie, Compartiments de Gazon, que Bosquets et Autres. Stockholm: 1651. V. 47

MOLLHAUSEN, BALDWIN
Diary Of a Journey from the Mississippi to the Coasts of the Pacific. London: 1858. V. 48; 49; 52; 53; 54

MOLLIEN, GASPAR THEODORE, COMTE DE
Travels in the Interior of Africa, to the Sources of the Senegal and Gambia... London: 1820. V. 50; 52

MOLLOY, CHARLES
The Coquet; or, the English Chevalier. London: 1718. V. 47
De Jure Maritimo et Navali; or a Treatise of Affaires Martime, and of Commerce. London: 1677. V. 50

MOLLOY, E.
A Narrative of the Tungani Insurrection in Eastern Turkistan in 1863. Calcutta: 1874. V. 49

MOLLOY, J. FITZGERALD
The Life and Adventures of Peg Woffington. London: 1884. V. 51

MOLMENTI, P.
The Life and Works of Vittorio Cappaccio. London: 1907. V. 51; 53

MOLNAR, FERENC
The Plays of Ferenc Molnar. New York: 1929. V. 50; 52

MOLYNEAUX, PETER
The Romantic Story of Texas. New York & Dallas: 1936. V. 48

MOLYNEUX, WILLIAM
The Case of Ireland's Being Bound by Acts of Parliament in England, State. Dublin: 1698. V. 48; 52

MOMADAY, NATACHEE SCOTT
Before and Old Painting of Crucifixion. San Francisco: 1975. V. 50
Colorado. Chicago: 1973. V. 50; 53
House Made of Dawn. New York: 1968. V. 48; 50; 52; 53; 54
In the Presence of the Sun: a Gathering of Shields. Santa Fe: 1992. V. 48; 52
The Journey of Tai-Me. Santa Barbara: 1967. V. 50
Owl in the Cedar Tree. N.P: 1965. V. 50
The Way to Rainy Mountain. Albuquerque: 1969. V. 50; 53

MOMMSEN, THEODOR
The History of Rome. London: 1862-66. V. 48
The History of Rome. London: 1867. V. 51
The Provinces of the Roman Empire, From Caesar to Diocletian... London: 1886. V. 48; 50; 51

MOMUS; *or, the Fall of Britain.* London: 1789. V. 52

MONAGHAN, JAY
Lincoln Bibliography 1839-1939. Springfield: 1945. V. 53

MONAHAN, JOHN
Records Relating to the Dioceses of Ardagh and Clonmacnoise. London: 1886. V. 47

MONARDES, NICOLAS
Joyfull Newes Out of the New-found Worlde. London: 1596. V. 51; 53

MONARDES, NICOLAS continued
Joyfull News Out of the New Founde Worlde Written in Spanish... London: 1925. V. 49; 50; 52; 54

MONASTICON Hibernicum. London: 1722. V. 51

MONASTICON Hibernicum. Or the Monastical History of Ireland. 1722. V. 49; 50; 54

MONCK, CHARLES ATTICUS
An Address to the Agricultural Classes of Great Britain, on the Evils Which are the consequence of Restricting the Importation of Foreign Corn. London: 1833. V. 52

MONCONYS, B. DE
Voyages, ou Les Scavans Trouveront un Nombre Infini de Nouveautez, en Machines de Mathematique, Experiences Physiques, Raisonnemens de la Belle Philosophie, Curiositez de Chymie & Converstions des Illustres de ce Siecle. Paris: 1695. V. 50

MONCREIFF, FREDERICK
The Moncreiffs and the Moncreiffes: a History of the Moncreiff of that Ilk and Its Collateral Branches. Edinburgh: 1929. V. 53

MONCRIEF, WILLIAM THOMAS
The Pickwickians; or, the Peregrinations of Sam Weller. London: 1872?. V. 49

MONCRIEFF, A. R. HOPE
Bonnie Scotland. London: 1904. V. 54
London. London: 1916. V. 50

MONCRIEFF, WILLIAM T.
Monsieur Mallet; or, My Daughter's Letter... London: 1851. V. 50
The Pickwickians... London: 1872?. V. 49
Sam Weller, or, the Pickwickians. 1837. V. 54
The Spectre Bridegroom; or, a Ghost in Spite of Himself. New York: 1821. V. 51

MONCRIF, FRANCOIS AUGUSTIN PARADIS DE
Moncrif's Cats... London: 1961. V. 48; 49; 53

MOND, ROBERT
The Bucheum. London: 1934. V. 49; 51
Cemeteries of Armant I. London: 1937. V. 49; 51

MONDOR, HENRI
Doctors and Medicine in the Works of Daumier: Notes and Catalogue by Jean Adhemar. Boston: 1960. V. 52

MONETTE, JOHN W.
History of the Discovery and Settlement of the Valley of the Mississippi, by the Three Great European Powers, Spain, France and Great Britain. New York: 1848. V. 47

MONETTE, PAUL
Taking Care of Mrs. Carroll. Boston: 1978. V. 51

MONEY, EDWARD
Twelve Month with the Bashi-Bazouk. London: 1880. V. 54

MONEY, JOHN
The History of the Campaign of 1792. London: 1794. V. 53

MONEY, LIEUT. GENERAL
A Letter to the Right Hon. Wm. Windham, on the Defence of the Country, at the Present Crisis. Norwich: 1806. V. 50

MONEY, WILLIAM TAYLOR
Observations on the Expediency of Shipbuliding at Bombay, for the Service of His Majesty and of the East India Co. London: 1811. V. 53

MONGAN, AGNES
Drawings in the Fogg Museum of Art: a Critical Catalogue. Cambridge: 1946. V. 47; 50; 54

MONGOLIAN-English Dictionary. Berkeley & Los Angeles: 1960. V. 48

MONIER-WILLIAMS, MONIER
A Sanskrit-English Dictionary... London: 1964. V. 51

MONITOR & NORTHWESTERN SILVER MINING CO.
Prospectus and Charter of the Monitor and Northwestern Silver Mining Co.... Milwaukee: 1870. V. 54

MONK, J.
An Agricultural Dictionary, Consisting of Extracts from the Most Celebrated Authors. London: 1794. V. 49

MONK, MARY MOLESWORTH
Marinda. Poems and Translations Upon Several Occasions. London: 1716. V. 47

MONKHOUSE, ALLAN
The Rag. London: 1928. V. 48

MONKHOUSE, W.
The Churches of York. London: 1843. V. 47; 50

MONKHOUSE, WILLIAM COSMO
A Dream of Idleness, and Other Poems. London: 1865. V. 53
The Life and Works of Sir John Tenniel, R.I. London: 1901. V. 47
Pictures and Painters of the English School. New York. V. 53
The Works of Sir Edwin Landseer R.A. London: 1879. V. 48; 53

MONK'S Pond: Old Hermit Hai. Monterey: 1988. V. 54

MONMOUTH BAPTIST ASSOCIATION OF NEW JERSEY
Minutes of the Eighth (9th, 11th, 12th, 14th-16th, 24th) Meeting... Point Pleasant: 1906-22. V. 47

MONMOUTH, ROBERT CARY, 1ST EARL OF
Memoirs, Written by Himself. Edinburgh: 1808. V. 47; 53

MONNET, CHARLES
Etudes d'Anatomie a Lusage des Peintres. Paris: 1800. V. 54

MONNETT, HOWARD N.
Action Before Westport. Kansas City: 1964. V. 49; 52; 53

MONNETTE, ORRA EUGENE
First Settlers of ye Plantations of Piscataway and Woodbridge, Olde East New Jersey, 1664-1714. Los Angeles: 1930-35. V. 47; 49; 51

MONNIER, HENRY
Moeurs Administratives, Dessinees d'Apres Nature. Paris: 1828. V. 53
Recontres Parisiennes. Macedoine Pittoresque. Paris: 1820's. V. 47; 49; 53

MONOD, E.
L'Exposition Universelle de 1889. Paris: 1890. V. 51

MONOTYPE CORPORATION, LTD., LONDON.
Pastonchi. Verona: 1928. V. 53

MONRO, ALEXANDER
An Account of the Inoculation of Small Pox in Scotland. Edinburgh: 1765. V. 48; 51
The Anatomy of the Human Bones and Nerves, with a Description of the Human Lacteal Sac and Duct by.. Edinburgh: 1828. V. 54
The Anatomy of the Human Bones, Nerves and Lactaeral Sac and Duct. Edinburgh: 1782. V. 54
The Morbid Anatomy of the Human Gullet, Stomach and Intestines. Edinburgh: 1811. V. 49; 54
The Structure and Physiology of Fishes Explained and Compared with Those of Man and Other Animals. Edinburgh: 1785. V. 54

MONRO, DONALD
An Account of the Diseases Which Were Most Frequent in the British Military Hospitals in Germany, from January 1716 to the Return of the Troops to England in March 1763. London: 1764. V. 52
Praelectiones Medicae Ex Cronii Instituto, Annis 1774 et 1775, et Oratio Anniversaria ex Harveii Instituto die Octobris 18 anni 1775. London: 1776. V. 52; 53; 54
A Treatise on Medical and Pharmaceutical Chemistry, and the Materia Medica... London: 1788. V. 47; 52

MONRO, HAROLD
Collected Poems. London: 1933. V. 52
The Earth for Sale - Poems. London: 1928. V. 54
Elm Angel. London: 1930. V. 50
Trees. London: 1916. V. 54

MONROE, DONALD
A Treatise On Mineral Waters. London: 1770. V. 49

MONROE, HARRIET
Valeria and Other Poems. Chicago: 1891. V. 50

MONROE, JAMES
The Memoir of James Monroe, Esq., Relating to His Unsettled Claims Upon the People and Governemtn of the United States. Charlottesville: 1828. V. 50
A View of the Conduct of the Executive in Foreign Affairs, Etc. Philadelphia: 1797. V. 48

MONROE, JOHN
The American Botanist, and Family Physician... Wheelock: 1824. V. 51; 54

MONROE, MARILYN
My Story. 1974. V. 53

MONROE, PAUL
A Cyclopedia of Education. New York: 1911-13. V. 52

MONROE, ROBERT
His Expedition with the Worthy Scots Regiment. London: 1637. V. 48; 52
The Scotch Military Discipline Learned from the Valiant Swede, and Collected for the Use of All worthy Commanders Favouring the Laudable Profession of Armes. London: 1644. V. 47

MONROE, THOMAS
The Olla Podrida, a Periodical Work... London: 1788. V. 47
The Olla Podrida, a Periodical Work, in Forty-Four Numbers. Oxford: 1787-88. V. 48

MONSELL, JOHN S. B.
Simon the Cyrenian, and Other Poems. London: 1873. V. 50
Spiritual Songs... London: 1859. V. 47

MONSEY, MESSENGER
A Sketch of the Life and Character of the Late Dr. Monsey, Physician to the Royal Hospital at Chelsea... London: 1789. V. 47; 49

MONSTRELET, ENGUERRAND DE
Chronicles. London: 1853. V. 53
Chronicles Containing an Account of the Cruel Civil War Between the Houses of Orleans and Burgundy, etc., etc.... London: 1810. V. 47; 48
The Chronicles of Enguerrand de Monstrelet... London: 1809. V. 47; 51

MONTAGNANA, BARTHOLOMAEUS
Consilia Montagnane. Lyons: 1525. V. 48; 49; 50

MONTAGU, BARBARA
A Description of Millenium Hall and the Country Adjacent... London: 1762. V. 48; 51

MONTAGU, BASIL
Some Enquiries into the Effects of Fermented Liquors. London: 1818. V. 47

MONTAGU, BASIL continued
A Summary of the Law of Set-Off... Philadelphia: 1825. V. 49

MONTAGU, EDWARD WORTLEY
Genuine Memoirs...With Remarks on the Manners and Customs of the Oriental World... London: 1781. V. 48
Reflections on the Rise and Fall of the Antient Republicks. London: 1759. V. 48; 53
Reflections on the Rise and Fall of the Antient Republicks. London: 1769. V. 48; 50; 53; 54
Reflections ont he Rise and Fall of the Ancient Republicks. London: 1778. V. 49; 51; 52

MONTAGU, ELIZABETH ROBINSON
Elizabeth Montagu, The Queen of the Blue-Stockings: Her Correspondence from 1720-1761. London: 1906. V. 53
An Essay on the Writings and Genius of Shakespear... London: 1770. V. 47; 48; 50
An Essay On the Writings and Genius of Shakespear, Compared with the Greek and French Dramatic Poets. Dublin: 1769. V. 50; 52; 54
An Essay on The Writings and Genius of Shakespeare. London: 1772. V. 49
An Essay on the Writings and Genius of Shakespeare. London: 1777. V. 50
The Letters of...With Some of the Letters of Her Correspondents. Boston: 1825. V. 47; 49
Mrs. Montagu, Queen of the Blues. Her Letters and Friendships from 1762-1800. Boston: 1923. V. 48

MONTAGU, GEORGE
Ornithological Dictionary of British Birds. London: 1831. V. 50; 51
Ornithological Dictionary; or, Alphabetical Synopsis of British Birds. London: 1802/13. V. 50; 51

MONTAGU, H. I.
Scramble. London: 1870. V. 54

MONTAGU, J. A.
A Guide to the Study of Heraldry. London: 1840. V. 49; 50; 53

MONTAGU, LORD
The Art of Driving a Motor Car. London: 1906. V. 49

MONTAGU, MARY PIERREPONE WORTLEY, LADY
The Complete Letters. Oxford: 1966-67. V. 47
The Letters and Works. London: 1837. V. 47; 48; 50; 51; 53; 54
The Letters and Works. Paris: 1837. V. 51
The Letters During the Embassy to Constantinople...and from France and Italy. London: 1820. V. 53
Letters from the Levant During the Embassy to Constaninople 1716-18. London: 1838. V. 54
Letters of the Right Honorable Lady....(with) An Additional volume of Letters. London: 1763/67. V. 48; 51; 52
Letters of the Right Honourable Lady... London: 1777. V. 50; 52
Letters of the Right Honourble Lady.... London: 1779. V. 48
Letters Written During Her Travels in Europe, Asia and Africa to Persons of Distinction... London: 1767. V. 49
Letters Written During Her Travels in Europe, Asia and Africa, to Persons of Distinction, Men of Letters &c. In Different Parts of Europe. London: 1763/67. V. 49; 54
Lettres de Miladi Marie Wortley Montague, Ecrites Pendant ses Voyages en Europe... Rotterdam: 1763. V. 50
The Poetical Works of the Right Honourable Lady M—y W——y M——e. London: 1768. V. 49
Verses Address'd to the Imitator of the First Satire of the Second Book of Horace. London: 1733. V. 48; 53
The Works... London: 1803. V. 49; 50; 51; 52
The Works... London: 1817. V. 50
The Works of...Including Her Correspondence, Poems and Essays. London: 1805. V. 51

MONTAGU, RICHARD
Appello Caesarem. London: 1625. V. 50
Articles of Enquiry and Direction for the Diocese of Norwich, in the First Visitation to the Reverend Father in God, Richard Mountaigu Bishop of that Diocese, Anno Dom. 1638. London: 1638. V. 50

MONTAGU, WALTER
Miscellanea Spiritualia; or Devout Essaies. London: 1648-54. V. 52

MONTAGUE, C. E.
The Front Line. London: 1917. V. 47
A Hind Let Loose. London: 1910. V. 48
The Manchester Stage - 1880-1900. London: 1900. V. 47
Notes from Calais Base - and Pictures of Its many Activities. London: 1918. V. 47
Right Off the Map. London: 1927. V. 48
The Western Front - One Hundred Drawings. London: 1917. V. 47
A Writer's Notes on His Trade. London: 1930. V. 47

MONTAGUE, ELIZABETH
The Letters, with Some of the Letters of Her Corrspondents. Boston: 1825. V. 50

MONTAGUE, JOHN
The Bread God. 1968. V. 50
The Bread God. Dublin: 1968. V. 48
A Chosen Light. 1967. V. 50
A Chosen Light. London: 1967. V. 48
Death of a Chieftain and Other Stories. London: 1964. V. 50
Forms of Exile. Dublin: 1959. V. 54
Poisoned Lands and Other Poems. London: 1961. V. 48; 50
The Rough Field. 1974. V. 54
A Slow Dance. 1975. V. 54
Tides. Chicago: 1971. V. 48

MONTAGUE, PEREGRINE
The Family Pocket-Book: or Fountain of True and Useful Knowledge. London: 1765. V. 53

MONTAGUE, W.
The Youth's Encyclopaedia of Health with Games and Playground Amusements. London: 1838. V. 49

MONTAIGNE, MICHEL DE
Essais... Paris: 1587. V. 48
Les Essais. Paris: 1604. V. 51
Les Essais... Londres: 1724. V. 48
Essais. Paris: 1801. V. 51
The Essayes. London: 1603. V. 48; 50
Essayes. London: 1613. V. 47; 48; 53
The Essayes. London: 1632. V. 50
The Essayes. London: 1908. V. 51
Essays... London: 1693. V. 54
Essays. London: 1700. V. 52
The Essays... London: 1759. V. 51
The Essays. London: 1776. V. 49
Essays. Boston & New York: 1902-03-04. V. 47; 53
Essays. London: 1923. V. 48
Essays. London: 1931. V. 52
The Essays. New York: 1934. V. 48
The Essays. New York: 1946. V. 53; 54
Essays. New York: 1947. V. 47; 53
The Works of Michael de Montaigne. London: 1853. V. 51

MONTALE, EUGENIO
The Motets of Eugenio Montale. San Francisco;: 1973. V. 48; 50; 51; 54
Mottetti/Motets. Iowa City: 1981. V. 54
Poet in Our Time. New York: 1976. V. 49; 51
Xenia. Los Angeles: 1970. V. 50

MONTALEMBERT, CHARLES, COMTE DE
The Monks of the West from St. Benedict to St. Bernard. London: 1861-79. V. 47
The Monks of the West from St. Benedict to St. Bernard. London: 1896. V. 54

MONTANA
First Annual Report of the Bureau of Agriculture, Labor and Industry of Montana for the Year Ended Nov. 30, 1893. Helena: 1893. V. 52

MONTANA, a State Guide Book. New York: 1939. V. 53

MONTANA. CONSTITUTION
Constitution of the State of Montana, as Adopted by the Constitutional Convention Held at Helena, Montana, July 4, A.D. 1889 and Ending August 17, A.D. 1889. Helena: 1889. V. 50

MONTANA STOCK GROWERS' ASSOCIATION
Brand Book of the Montana Stock Growers' Association for 1886. Chicago: 1886. V. 47

MONTANA. (TERRITORY). LAWS, STATUTES, ETC.
Laws, Memorials and Resolutions of the Territory of Montana, Passed at the Sixth Session of the Legislative Assembly, Begun at Virginia City, Monday, Dec. 6, 1869, and Concluded January 7, 1870. Helena: 1870. V. 54
Laws of the Territory of Montana, Passed at the Third Session of the Legislature Beginning November 5, 1866 and Ending December 15 1866. Virginia City: 1866. V. 50
Organic Act of Montana Territory. Virginia City: 1867. V. 48

MONTANO, LORENZO
Bishop San Zeno. Patron of Verona. Verona: 1949. V. 49

MONTAUT, H. DE
Vertus & Qualites. Paris: 1850. V. 52

MONTE, GUIDOBALDO, MARCHESE DEL
Mechanicorum Liber. Pisa: 1577. V. 47

MONTEATH, ROBERT
The Forester's Guide and Profitable Planter... Edinburgh: 1824. V. 49

MONTECASHELL, MARGARET JANE MOORE, COUNTESS OF
A Grandmother's Advice to Young Mothers of the Physical Education of Children. London: 1835. V. 49

MONTECINO, MARCEL
The Crosskiller. New York: 1988. V. 52

MONTECRUCIS, RICOLDUS DE
Verlegung des Alcoran. Wittenberg: 1542. V. 53

MONTEIRO, JOACHIM JOHN
Angola and the River Congo. London: 1875. V. 50; 52

MONTEITH, ROBERT
Descriptions of the Islands of Orkney and Zetland. Edinburgh: 1845. V. 53

MONTELATICI, DOMENICO
Villa Borghese, Fuori di Porta Pincinana con l'Ornamenti... Rome: 1700. V. 53

MONTES, ANTONIO
To the Honorable Mexican and American Joint Commission... Washington: 1870. V. 48

MONTES DA OCA, R.
Humming Birds and Orchids of Mexico. Mexico: 1963. V. 54

MONTE SOCIO, CARLO, PSEUD.
The New Metamorphosis; or Pleasant Trans-formation of the Golden Ass of Lucius Apuleius... London: 1724. V. 54

MONTESPAN, FRANCOISE
Memoirs of Madame La Marquise de Montespan. London: 1895. V. 48

MONTESQUIEU, CHARLES LOUIS DE SECONDAT, BARON DE LA BREDE
Miscellaneous Pieces. London: 1759. V. 48; 53
Oeuvres... Londres: 1769. V. 50
Persian Letters. London: 1722. V. 54
Reflections on the Causes of the Grandeur and Declension of the Romans. London: 1734. V. 49; 53
The Spirit of Laws... London: 1750. V. 49
The Spirit of Laws. Edinburgh: 1762. V. 47
The Spirit of Laws. London: 1766. V. 48
The Spirit of Laws. London: 1773. V. 49
The Spirit of Laws. Glasgow: 1793. V. 53
The Spirit of Laws. Worcester: 1802. V. 51; 52
The Spirit of the Laws. New York: 1900. V. 48
Le Temple de Gnide, Suivi d'Arsace et Ismerie. Paris: 1796. V. 50

MONTESSORI, MARIA
Dr. Montessori's Own Handbook. New York: 1914. V. 54
Il Metodo della Pedagogia Scientifica applicato all Educazione Infantile Nelle Case dei Bambini. 1909. V. 47
The Montessori Method. London: 1912. V. 50
The Montessori Method. New York: 1912. V. 54

MONTEVAL, MARION
The Klan Inside Out. Claremore: 1924. V. 53

MONTFAUCON, BERNARD DE
A Collection of Regal and Ecclesiastical Antiquities of France. London: 1750. V. 47; 49; 50; 53

MONTFERRAND, AUGUSTE RICHARD DE
Eglise Cathedrale de Saint-Isaac. St. Petersburg: 1845. V. 52
Plans et Details de Monument Consacre a la Memoire de l'Empereur Alexandre... Paris: 1836. V. 49; 53

MONTFORD, CHARLES P.
Nomads of the Australian Desert. Rigby, Australia: 1976. V. 48

MONTFORT, EUGENE
La Belle Enfant Ou L'Amour a Quarante Ans. Paris: 1930. V. 52

MONTFORT, GUILLAUME
Traite Elementaire de l'Art d'Ecrire. Paris: 1800. V. 53

MONTGOMERY, BRIAN
The Montgomery Manuscripts. Belfast: 1830. V. 52

MONTGOMERY, CORA
Eagle Pass; or Life on the Border. 1852. V. 48
Eagle Pass, or Life on the Border. New York: 1852. V. 49; 53
The Queen of Islands and the King of Rivers. New York: 1850. V. 47

MONTGOMERY, D. J. X.
Cosmic Ray Physics, Based on Lectures Given by Marcel Schein at Princeton University... Princeton: 1949. V. 48

MONTGOMERY, DOUGLASS W.
Collected Writings of Douglass W. Montgomery, M.D. (1859-1941). San Francisco: 1943. V. 51

MONTGOMERY, F.
Textiles in America 1650-1870. New York: 1984. V. 53

MONTGOMERY, FLORENCE
A Very Simple Story: Being a Chronicle of the Thoughts and Feelings of a Child. London: 1867. V. 50

MONTGOMERY, GEORGE WASHINGTON
Bernardo del Carpio. New York: 1834. V. 52

MONTGOMERY, JAMES
The Chimney-Sweeper's Friend, and Climbing-Boy's Album. London: 1824. V. 48; 51; 52
The Chimney-Sweeper's Friend and Climbing-Boy's Album... London: 1825. V. 48; 51
Greenland, and Other Poems. 1819. V. 47
Greenland and Other Poems. London: 1819. V. 49; 50
Journal of Voyages and Travels by Rev. Daniel Tyerman and George Bennet, Esq. Deputed from the London Missionary Society, to visit Their Various Stations in the South Sea Islands, China, India &c. London: 1831. V. 48; 52
Lectures on Poetry and General Literature. London: 1833. V. 51
The Pelican Island and Other Poems. London: 1827. V. 54
Poems. London: 1860. V. 51
Poems on the Abolition of the Slave Trade. London: 1809. V. 49; 50
The Poetical Works of... Boston: 1825. V. 54
The Poetical Works of... London: 1855. V. 49
Poetical Works...With a Memoir of the Author by the Rev. Rufus W. Griswold. Philadelphia: 1846. V. 47
A Poet's Portfolio; or, Minor Poems: in Three Books. London: 1835. V. 51
Prose by a Poet. London: 1824. V. 51
Verses to the Memory of the Late Richard Reynolds, of Bristol. London: 1816. V. 50
The Wanderer of Switzerland and Other Poems. London: 1806. V. 51

MONTGOMERY, JOHN
Jack Kerouac: a Memoir in Which is Revealed Secret Lives and West Coast Whispers. Fresno: 1970. V. 54

MONTGOMERY, L. M.
Emily Climbs. New York: 1925. V. 54
Rilla of Ingleside. New York: 1921. V. 52

MONTGOMERY, MARION
Darrell. New York: 1964. V. 53

MONTGOMERY, ROBERT
The Age Reviewed: a Satire in Two Parts. London: 1827. V. 48
The Omniprescence of the Deity. (with) A Universal Prayer; Death; a Vision of Heaven; and a Vision of Hell. London: 1830/29. V. 53
Oxford, a Poem. Oxford: 1831. V. 50; 54
The Sacred Annual: Being the Messiah, a Poem in Six Books. London: 1834. V. 47

MONTGOMERY, RUTHERFORD G.
High Country. New York: 1938. V. 52

MONTGOMERY, ZACHARY
The Poison Fountain, or, Anti-Parental education, Essays and Discussions on the School Question. San Francisco: 1878. V. 47

MONTGOMERY OF ALAMEIN, BERNARD LAW MONTGOMERY, 1ST VISCOUNT
A History of Warfare. London: 1968. V. 49
Normandy to the Baltic. London: 1946. V. 52
Ten Chapters - 1942-1945. London: 1945. V. 47

MONTHAN, D.
R. C. Gorman: the Lithographs. Flagstaff: 1962. V. 50
R. C. Gorman: the Lithographs. Flagstaff: 1978. V. 47; 51; 53; 54

MONTHAN, GUY
Art and Indian Individualists, The Art of Seventeen Contemporary Southwestern Artists and Craftsmen. Flagstaff: 1975. V. 47; 48; 52

MONTHLY Chronicle of North-Country Lore and Legend. Newcastle-upon-Tyne: 1887-91. V. 54

THE MONTHLY Chronicle of North-Country Lore and Legend. London: 1888-91. V. 50; 52

MONTHOLON, COUNT
History of the Captivity of Napoleon at St. Helena. London: 1846-47. V. 49

MONTMORRES, HERVEY REDMOND MORRES, VISCOUNT
The Prodigal: or, Marriage A-La-Mode. London: 1794. V. 49

MONTOLIEU, ISABELLE POLIER, BARONNE DE
Caroline of Lichtfield. Dublin: 1786. V. 49
Caroline of Lichtfield. London: 1786. V. 48; 49

MONTORGUEIL, GEORGES
Paris Dansant. Paris: 1898. V. 47

MONTOTYPE CORPORATION LTD., LONDON
Pastonchi. A Specimen of a New Letter for Use on the "Monotype". Verona: 1928. V. 47

MONTOYA, JUAN DE
New Mexico in 1602. Juan de Montoya's Relation of the Discovery of New Mexico. Albuquerque: 1938. V. 49

MONTREAL MUSEUM OF FINE ARTS
Montreal Museum of Fine Arts, Formerly Art Association of Montreal: Spring Exhibitions 1880-1970. Toronto: 1988. V. 51

MONTSTRELET, ENGUERRAND DE
The Chronicles of... 1809. V. 52

MONTULE, EDUARD DE
A Voyage to North America, and the West Indies in 1817. London: 1821. V. 47

MONUMENTS Of Washington's Patriotism: Containing a Fac Simile of His Publick Accounts Kept During the Revolutionary War... Washington: 1838. V. 49

MONYPENNY, WILLIAM FLAVELLE
The Life of Benjamin Disraeli. London: 1910-20. V. 49
The Life of Benjamin Disraeli. New York: 1913. V. 50
The Life of Benjamin Disraeli. London: 1929. V. 49
The Life of Benjamin Disrareli. London: 1920. V. 48

MOODIE, DONALD
An Inquiry Into the Justice and Expediency of Completing the Publication of the Authentic Records of the Colony of the Cape of good Hope, Relative to the Aboriginal Tribes. Cape of Good Hope: 1841. V. 49

MOODIE, J. W. DUNBAR
Scenes and Adventures as a Soldier and Settler, During Half a Century. Montreal: 1866. V. 50

MOODIE, ROY L.
Roetgenologic Studies of Egyptian and Peruvian Mummies. Chicago: 1931. V. 51

MOODIE, SUSANNA STRICKLAND
Life in the Clearings Versus the Bush. London: 1853. V. 48
Life in the Clearings Versus the Bush. New York: 1854?. V. 54
Roughing It In the Bush... New York: 1852. V. 50
Roughing It in the Bush; or, Forest Life in Canada. Toronto: 1871. V. 50; 54

MOODY, JOSEPH LEDLIE
Letter of a Forty-Niner... San Francisco: 1941. V. 47

MOODY, R. A.
The Moody Lands Corn and Alfalfa Lands in the Rich Valley of the Canadian River, Adjoining Oklahoma in the Great Texas Panhandle... Kansas City: 1908. V. 49

MOODY, SARAH
The Palm Tree. London: 1864. V. 54

MOODY, T. W.
Queen's, Belfast, 1845-1949. The History of a University. London: 1959. V. 53

MOODY, WALTER D.
Wacker's Manual of the Plan of Chicago, Municipal Economy. Chicago: 1915. V. 52

MOODY, WILLIAM VAUGHN
The Masque of Judgment. Boston: 1900. V. 47

MOON, ANNA MARIA
Family Memorial. London: 1872. V. 48; 54
A Family Memorial. London: 1972. V. 53
In Memoriam. The Rev. W. Leeves, Author of the air of "Auld Robin Gray". 1873. V. 52; 54

MOON, GRACE P.
Indian Legends in Rhyme. New York: 1907. V. 52

MOON, KARL
Photographic Studies of Indians. Grand Canyon: 1910. V. 50

MOON, WILLIAM LEAST HEAT
Blue Highways. A Journey through America's Back Roads. Boston: 1982. V. 51

MOONEY, BOOTH
The Lyndon Johnson Story. New York: 1956. V. 52

MOONEY, THOMAS
Thomas J. Mooney, Petitioner, vs. Court Smith, Warden of San Quentin, State of California et al... Sacramento: 1937. V. 50

MOONSHINE, MAURITIUS, PSEUD.
The Battle of the Bards. London: 1800. V. 54

MOOR, ANN
An Account of the Extraordinary Abstience of Ann Moor, of Tutbury, Staffordshire, Who Has, for More than Three Years Lived Entirely without Food... Boston: 1811?. V. 50

MOOR, J. H.
Notices of the Indian Archipelago and Adjacent Countries... Singapore: 1837. V. 49

MOOR, JOHN FREWEN
The Birth-Place, Home, Churches and Other Places Connected with the Author of "The Christian Year". Winchester: 1867. V. 54

MOORAT, S. A. J.
Catalogue of Western Manuscripts on Medicine and Science in the Wellcome Historical Medical Library. London: 1962-73. V. 48; 51; 52

MOORCOCK, M.
The Stealer of Souls. 1963. V. 47; 51

MOORE, A.
The Annals of Gallantry; or, the Conjugal Monitor... London: 1814/14/15. V. 54

MOORE, A. R.
Scenes from Tulare County, California. Porterville: 190-?. V. 53

MOORE, ADA SMALL
A Study of Chinese Paintings in the Collection of Ada Small Moore. London: 1940. V. 47

MOORE, ALAN
Sailing Ships of War 1800-1860 Including the Transition to Steam. London: 1926. V. 48; 53

MOORE, ALISON
He Died Furious. Baton Rouge: 1983. V. 49

MOORE, ANN
A Full Exposure of Ann Moore the Pretended Fasting Woman of Tutbury. London: 1813. V. 50

MOORE, ANNE CARROLL
The Three Owls. A Book About Children's Books. New York: 1925. V. 47

MOORE, ARTHUR
Compendium of the Irish Poor Law: Containing the Acts for the Relief of the Destitute Poor in Ireland. Dublin: 1850. V. 50

MOORE, BRIAN
An Answer from Limbo. Boston: 1962. V. 52
The Black Robe. London: 1985. V. 50
Black Robe. New York: 1985. V. 47
The Feast of Lupercal. 1957. V. 47
I Am Mary Dunne. London: 1968. V. 49
Judith Hearne. London: 1955. V. 53
Lies of Silence. Bloomsbury: 1990. V. 47; 48; 49; 50; 51
The Luck of Ginger Coffey. 1960. V. 47
The Luck of Ginger Coffey. Boston: 1960. V. 51
Sailor's Leave. New York: 1953. V. 50
The Temptation of Eileen Hughes. New York: 1981. V. 53

MOORE, C.
Handbook of the Flora of New South Wales... Sydney: 1893. V. 49; 52; 53

MOORE, C. L.
Black God's Shadow. 1977. V. 52
Judgement Night. 1952. V. 49; 54
Shambleau and Others. New York: 1953. V. 47; 48; 52

MOORE, CHARLES
The Case of Charles Moore, Late Master Cooper of the Victualling Office. London: 1749. V. 50
Daniel H. Burnham: Architect, Planner of Cities. Boston: 1921. V. 47; 51
A Full Inquiry Into the Subject of Suicide. London: 1790. V. 48
The Improvement of the Park System of the District of Columbia. Washington: 1902. V. 47

MOORE, CLARA SOPHIA JESSUP
Keely and His Discoveries Aerial Navigation. London: 1893. V. 51
Social Ethics and Society Duties through Education of Girls for Wives and Mothers and for Professors. Boston: 1892. V. 51

MOORE, CLARENCE B.
Aboriginal Remains of the Northwest Florida Coast. Philadelphia: 1901. V. 51
Aboriginal Remains of the Northwest Florida Coast. Philadelphia: 1902. V. 51

MOORE, CLEMENT C.
Denslow's Night Before Christmas. Chicago: 1902. V. 47
Denslow's Night Before Christmas. New York: 1902. V. 49
The New York Book of Poetry. New York: 1837. V. 49
The Night Before Christmas. Worcester. V. 51
The Night Before Christmas. London: 1931. V. 49; 51
The Night Before Christmas. Philadelphia: 1931. V. 52
The Night Before Christmas. New York: 1937. V. 53; 54
The Night Before Christmas. London: 1939. V. 51
The Night Before Christmas. 1940's. V. 53
The Night Before Christmas. Arkansas: 1940's. V. 49
The Night Before Christmas. Racine: 1958. V. 53
The Night Before Christmas; or, Account of a Visit From St. Nicholas. Los Angeles: 1984. V. 48; 52
Observations Upon Certain Passages in Mr. Jefferson's Notes on Virginia, Which Appear to Have a Tendency to Subvert Religion and Establish a False Philosophy. New York: 1804. V. 52
A Plain Statement Addressed to the Proprietors of Real Estate, in the City and County of New York. New York: 1818. V. 52
A Sketch of Our Political Condition. New York: 1813. V. 51
A Visit from St. Nicholas. Boston;: 1921. V. 54

MOORE, CLEON
Epitome of the Life of "Ossawatomie" John Brown, Including the Story of His Attack on Harpers Ferry and His Capture, Trial and Execution. Point Pleasant: 1904. V. 48; 50

MOORE, DAVID
Concise Notices of British Grasses Best Suited for Agriculture, with Preserved Specimens of Each Kind. Dublin: 1851. V. 49
Contributions Towards a Cybele Hibernica. Dublin: 1866. V. 51
Contributions Towards a Cybele Hibernica. London: 1866. V. 53

MOORE, DUGALD
The African, a Tale; and other Poems. Glasgow: 1829. V. 50; 54

MOORE, E. A.
The Story of A Cannoneer Under Stonewall Jackson. Lynchburg: 1910. V. 54

MOORE, E. HAMILTON
Fifteen Roses Being Our Lady's Rosary in Verse. Oxford: 1926. V. 51

MOORE, EDWARD
Fables for Ladies. To Which are Added, Fables of Flora. Philadelphia: 1787. V. 50
Fables for the Female Sex. London: 1744. V. 47
Fables for the Female Sex. London: 1766. V. 48; 50
Fables For the Female Sex. London: 1771. V. 48
The Gamester. London: 1753. V. 48
The World. London: 1767. V. 51
The World. London: 1782. V. 52; 54

MOORE, EDWARD ALEXANDER
The Story of a Cannoneer Under Stonewall Jackson In Which is Told the Part taken by the Rockbridge Artillery in the Army of Northern Virginia. Lynchburg: 1910. V. 48; 50

MOORE, EDWARD MARTIN
Spoil of the North Wind. Chicago: 1900. V. 47; 49

MOORE, ELDON
The Magic Halibut. London. V. 49

MOORE, F. F.
The Secret of the Court. 1895. V. 48
The Secret of the Court. London: 1895. V. 52

MOORE, FRANCES
Historical Life of Joanna of Sicily, Queen of Sicily, Queen of Naples and Countess of Provence... London: 1824. V. 50; 51

MOORE, FRANCIS
Cases Collect and Report... London: 1663. V. 49
The History of Lady Julia Manderville. London: 1773. V. 47
Map and Description of Texas, Containing Its History, Geology, Geography and Statistics. Philadelphia: 1840. V. 49

MOORE, FRANCIS continued
Travels Into the Inland Parts of Africa... London: 1738. V. 50; 51; 52

MOORE, FRANK
The Portrait Gallery of the Ar, Civil, Military and Naval: a Biographical Record. New York: 1865. V. 52
Women of the War; Their Heroism and Self Sacrifice. Hartford: 1867. V. 49; 50; 52

MOORE, FREDERICK H.
Mistress Haselwode, a tale of the Reformation Oak. London: 1876. V. 49; 54

MOORE, GEORGE
An Anthology of Pure Poetry. New York: 1924. V. 48; 50
Aphrodite in Aulis. London: 1930. V. 47; 52
The Brook Kerith. 1916. V. 49; 50
The Brook Kerith. Edinburgh: 1916. V. 47
The Brook Kerith. London: 1929. V. 47; 54
The Brook Kerith. New York: 1929. V. 52; 54
The Coming of Gabrielle: a Comedy. London: 1920. V. 50
A Communication to My Friends. London: 1933. V. 50
Confessions of a Young Man. London: 1888. V. 48
Elizabeth Cooper. Dublin and London: 1913. V. 53
Epistles, Odes and other Poems. London: 1806. V. 51
Esther Waters. London: 1894. V. 51
Esther Waters. London: 1920. V. 50
Flowers of Passion. London: 1878. V. 52
Hail and Farewell. 1911-14. V. 52
Hail and Farewell. London: 1911-14. V. 53
Hail and Farewell. London: 1925. V. 47; 53
Heloise & Abelard. (with) *Fragments from Heloise.* London: 1921. V. 48
Heloise and Abelard. 1920-21. V. 50
Heloise and Abelard. New York: 1921. V. 48; 52
Heloise and Abelard. (with) *Fragments from Heloise.* London: 1921/21. V. 53
The History of Ireland. 1835-46. V. 53
Impressions and Opinions. London: 1891. V. 53
Journal of a Voyage Across the Atlantic: with Notes on Canada and the United States; and Return to Great Britain in 1844. London: 1845. V. 53
The Lake. London: 1905. V. 50
Lives of Cardinal Alberoni, the Duke of Ripperda, and Marquis of Pombal, Three Distinguished Political Adventurers of the Last Century. London: 1814. V. 51
The Making of an Immortal. New York: 1927. V. 51
Memoirs of My Dead Life. London: 1906. V. 52
Modern Painting. London: 1893. V. 48; 53
The Passing of the Essenes: a Drama in 3 Acts. New York: 1930. V. 48
Peronnik the Fool. London: 1933. V. 47
Sister Teresa. London: 1901. V. 48; 53
The Talking Pine. Paris: 1931. V. 49
Ulick and Soracha. London: 1926. V. 50; 51; 52
Ulick and Soracha. New York: 1926. V. 51
The Untilled Field. Philadlephia: 1903. V. 48
Vale. London: 1914. V. 54
The Works of George Moore. London: 1936. V. 47

MOORE, GEORGE EDWARD
Principia Ethica. 1903. V. 50; 53

MOORE, GEORGE H.
Notes on the History of Slavery in Massachusetts. New York: 1866. V. 49
The Treason of Charles Lee, Major General, Second in Command in the American Army of the Revolution. New York: 1860. V. 50
Washington as an Angler... New York: 1887. V. 49

MOORE, GEORGE W.
Bones: His Anecdotes and Goaks. London: 1868. V. 54

MOORE, H. KEATLEY
The Nursery Song Book. London. V. 51

MOORE, H. MILES
Coal Resources of Leavenworth, Kansas. Leavenworth: 1890. V. 48

MOORE, HENRY
Heads, Figures and Ideas. London: 1958. V. 47; 52
Henry Moore. New York: 1968. V. 48
Henry Moore. Catalogue of His Graphic Works. Geneva. V. 50
Henry Moore. Sculpture and Drawings. New York: 1944. V. 53
Henry Moore's Sheep Sketchbook. London: 1980. V. 54
Poems, Lyrical and Miscellaneous. London: 1803. V. 47; 52; 54
Sculpture and Drawings. London. V. 49
Shelter Sketch Book. London: 1940. V. 50; 52
Shelter Sketch Book. London: 1945. V. 47; 49

MOORE, HENRY CHARLES
Omnibuses and Cabs: Their Origin and History. 1902. V. 47

MOORE, IAN
Grass and Grasslands. London: 1966. V. 50

MOORE, J.
Tanganyika Problem, an Account of the Researches Undertaken concerning the Existence of Marine Animals in Central Africa. London: 1903. V. 48

MOORE, J. E. S.
The Tanganyika Problem. Account of the Researches Undertaken Concerning the Existence of Marine Animals in Central Africa. London: 1903. V. 50

MOORE, J. G.
Patent Office and Patent Laws; or, a Guide to Inventors and a Book of Reference for Judges, Lawyers, Magistrates and Others. Philadelphia: 1855. V. 48; 54

MOORE, J. HAMILTON
The Young Gentleman and Lady's Monitor and English Teacher's Assistant. New York: 1792. V. 52
The Young Gentleman and Lady's Monitor and English Teacher's Assistant... London: 1794. V. 53

MOORE, JAMES
Kilpatrick and Our Cavalry: Comprising a Sketch of the Life of General Kilpatrick, With an Account of the Cavalry Raids, Engagements, and Operations Under His Command... New York: 1865. V. 52
A List of the Principal Castles and Monasteries in Great Britain. London: 1798. V. 50
Modern Fortifications: or Elements of Military Architecture. London: 1673. V. 53

MOORE, JAMES CARRICK
A Narrative of the Campaign of the British Army in Spain, Commanded by His Excellency Lieut.-General Sir John Moore. London: 1809. V. 47; 52; 54

MOORE, JESSIE T.
Twenty Years in Assam, or Leaves from My Journal. Calcutta: 1901. V. 49

MOORE, JOHN
Brensham Village. London: 1946. V. 50
Edward. Various Views of Human Nature, Taken from Life and Manners, Chiefly in England. London: 1796. V. 48; 54
A Journal During a Residence in France, from the Beginng of August to the Middle of December, 1792... London: 1793. V. 51; 52
A Journal During a Residence in France, from the Beginning of August, to the Middle of December, 1792. London: 1794. V. 52
Medical Sketches. Providence: 1794. V. 49; 51
Mordaunt. Sketches of Life, Characters, and Manners, in Various Countries... London: 1800. V. 48; 51; 52
Mordaunt. Sketches of Life, Characters and Manners in Various Countries, Including the Memoirs of a French Lady of Quality. Dublin: 1800. V. 54
Various Views of Human Nature, Taken from Life and Manners, Chiefly in England. Mount Pleasant: 1798. V. 50
A View of Society and Manners in France, Switzerland, Germany and Italy... Philadelphia: 1783. V. 50; 54
A View of Society and Manners in Italy... Boston: 1792. V. 52
A View of the Causes and Progress of the French Revolution. Dublin: 1795. V. 50
Zeluco. Various Views of Human Nature, taken from Life and Manners, Foreign and Domestic. London: 1789. V. 48; 51

MOORE, JOHN BASSETT
Extradition. Washington?: 1890?. V. 50
History and Digest of the International Arbitrations to Which the United States Has Been a Party. Washington: 1898. V. 47

MOORE, JOHN CARRICK
A Narrative of the Campaign of the British Army in Spain Commanded by His Excellency Lieut. Gen. Sir John Moore. London: 1809. V. 53

MOORE, JOHN EDWARD SHOREC
The Tanganyika Problem. London: 1903. V. 54

MOORE, JOHN F.
The Providence Alamanc and Business Directory...for 1849. Providence: 1848. V. 48

MOORE, JOHN HAMILTON
The New Practical Navigator... Dublin: 1800. V. 49

MOORE, JOHN T.
Tom's Last Forage. Nashville: 1926. V. 48

MOORE, JOHN WHEELER
Roster of North Carolina Troops in the War Between the States. Raleigh: 1882. V. 49; 52

MOORE, JOSEPH
Eighteen Views Taken at and Near Rangoon. (with) *Views in the Birman Empire.* London. V. 49
Eighteen Views Taken at and Near Rangoon. (with) *Views in the Birman Empire.* London: 1825-26. V. 52
Penicillin in Syphilis. Springfield: 1946. V. 49; 51; 54

MOORE, JOSHUA
A Discourse, Delivered at the Council-House, Detroit, Before the Legislative Council of Michigan Territory, June 21, 1824. Detroit: 1824. V. 52

MOORE, JULIA A.
The Sentimental Song Book. Grand Rapids: 1876. V. 48

MOORE, LANGDON
Langdon Moore, His Own Story of His Eventful Life. Boston: 1893. V. 47

MOORE, LORRIE
Self-Help. New York: 1985. V. 54

MOORE, M. B.
The First Dixie Reader; to Succeed the Dixie Printer. Raleigh: 1863/64. V. 49
The Geographical Reader for the Dixie Children. Raleigh: 1863. V. 47
Primary Geography, Arranged as a Reading Book, with Questions and Answers Attached. Raleigh: 1864. V. 52

MOORE, MARIANNE
The Absentee. New York: 1962. V. 49
Collected Poems. New York: 1951. V. 48; 51
Collected Poems. New York: 1952. V. 49
The Complete Prose of Marianne Moore. London: 1987. V. 53
Eight Poems. New York: 1962. V. 48; 49; 51; 53
Eight Poems. New York: 1963. V. 49; 50; 53
Like a Bulwark. New York: 1956. V. 51; 54
Like a Bulwark. London: 1957. V. 51
A Marianne Moore Reader. New York: 1961. V. 49; 54
O to Be A Dragon. New York: 1959. V. 47; 49; 51; 52; 53; 54
Observations. New York: 1924. V. 49
The Pangolin and Other Verse. London: 1936. V. 53
Poems. London: 1921. V. 47; 48; 51; 53; 54
Predilections. New York: 1955. V. 51; 53
Predilections. London: 1956. V. 53
Selected Poems. New York: 1934. V. 51
Selected Poems. London: 1935. V. 51
Selected Poems. New York: 1935. V. 48
Tell Me, Tell Me, Granite, Steel and Other Topics (Poems). New York: 1966. V. 47; 49; 54
Tipoo's Tiger. New York: 1967. V. 54
What Are Years. New York: 1941. V. 47; 49; 50; 51

MOORE, MARK
The Memoirs and Adventures of Mark Moore, Late an Officer in the British Navy. London: 1795. V. 49

MOORE, MAURICE
Frauds and Swindles. London: 1933. V. 51

MOORE, MERRILL
Case Record from a Sonnetorium. New York: 1951. V. 51
Clinical Sonnets. New York: 1953. V. 51
Illegitimate Sonnets. New York: 1950. V. 47; 51
The Noise That Time Makes. New York: 1929. V. 50; 54
Six Sides to a Man. New York: 1935. V. 47; 48; 49
Sonnets from New Directions. Norfolk: 1938. V. 53
Sonnets from the Fugitive (1922-1926). Boston: 1937. V. 53

MOORE, MILCAH MARTHA HILL
Miscellanies, Moral and Instructive in Prose and Verse... Philadelphia: 1787. V. 47; 54

MOORE, NICHOLAS
The Glass Tower. London: 1944. V. 47
The Island and the Cattle - Poems. London: 1941. V. 49
A Wish in Season - Poems. London: 1941. V. 49

MOORE, NORMAN
The History of St. Bartholomew's Hospital. London: 1918. V. 49; 53
The History of the Study of Medicine In the British Isles. Oxford: 1908. V. 50; 52

MOORE, OLIVE
Fugue. London: 1932. V. 51; 53
Further Reflections on the Death of a Porcupine. London: 1932. V. 51

MOORE, R. C.
Treatise on Invertebrate Paleontology. New York & Lawrence: 1953-79. V. 48

MOORE, RICHARD
Important Notices of that Which Concerns the Pecuniary Credit of a State, and in Particular that of England. London: 1833. V. 53

MOORE, ROBIN
The French Connection. Boston: 1969. V. 52

MOORE, S. LE M.
The Phanerogamic Botany of the Matto Grosso Expedition, 1891-92. London: 1895. V. 48

MOORE, S. S.
The Traveller's Directory: or, a Pocket Companion, Shewing the Course of the Main Road from Philadelphia to New York... Philadelphia: 1804. V. 48

MOORE, SAMUEL
An Accurate System of Surveying...the Whole Being Performed Without the Use of Scale and Compasses, or a Table of Logarithms. Litchfield: 1796. V. 50; 53

MOORE, SUZANNE
A Blind Alphabet. Easthampton: 1986. V. 50

MOORE, TEX
The Official Cowboy Artist of Texas. 1935. V. 49

MOORE, THEOPHILUS
Marriage Customs and Ceremonies, and Modes of Courtship of the Various Nations of the Universe... New York: 1827. V. 50

MOORE, THOMAS
British Wild Flowers. London: 1867. V. 48; 50; 54
The Epicurean, a Tale. (and) Alciphron, a Poem. London: 1839. V. 54
Fables for the Holy Alliance; Rhymes for the Road. London: 1823. V. 47; 51; 54
The Ferns of Great Britain and Ireland... London: 1863. V. 49; 54
The Fudges in England. London: 1835. V. 53
The Fudges in England: Being a Sequel to the "Fudge Family in Paris". Paris: 1835. V. 48
Irish Melodies. London: 1821. V. 48
Irish Melodies. London: 1856. V. 51
Jack Randall's Diary of Proceedings at the House of Call for Genius. (with) Tom Crib's Memorial to congress. London: 1820/19. V. 50
Lalla Rookh. London: 1817. V. 50; 54
Lalla Rookh. London: 1826. V. 54
Lalla Rookh. London: 1858. V. 51
The Life and Death of Lord Edward Fitzgerald. Hamburg: 1831. V. 53
The Life and Death of Lord Edward Fitzgerald. London: 1831. V. 48; 51; 54
The Life and Death of Lord Edward Fitzgerald. London: 1832. V. 52; 54
The Life of Lord Byron, with His Letters and Journals. London: 1847. V. 52; 54
The Loves of the Angels, a Poem. London: 1823. V. 50
Memoirs of Captain Rock, the Celebrated Irish Chieftain with Some Account of His Ancestors. London: 1824. V. 51; 52
Memoirs of the Life of the Right Honourable Richard Brinsley Sheridan. London: 1825. V. 50; 52
Memoirs of the Life of the Rt. Hon. Richard Brinsley Sheridan. New York: 1866. V. 51
Moore's Irish Melodies. London: 1866. V. 54
Moore's Irish Melodies. London and New York: 1879. V. 54
M.P. or the Blue-Stocking, a Comic Opera, in Three Acts, first Performed at the English Opera, Theatre Royal, Lyceum, on Monday Sept. 8, 1811. London: 1811. V. 52
Nature Printed British Ferns. London: 1859. V. 54
The Nature Printed British Ferns. London: 1859-60. V. 48; 52
Nature Printed British Ferns. London: 1863. V. 50; 52; 53
The Octavo Nature Printed British Ferns. London: 1859-60. V. 50
Odes Upon Cash, Corn, Catholics and Other Matters. London: 1828. V. 50
Paradise and the Peri. London: 1860. V. 49; 50
Poetical Works. London. V. 47; 48; 49
The Poetical Works. London: 1801. V. 49
The Poetical Works... London: 1840-41. V. 54
Poetical Works. Paris: 1841. V. 51
The Poetical Works. London: 1843. V. 48
The Poetical Works. London: 1853. V. 50; 54
Poetical Works. New York: 1860. V. 49
The Poetical Works. London: 1861-68. V. 53
A Selection of Irish Melodies, with Symphones and Accompaniments... Dublin: 1807. V. 47
A Selection of Irish Melodies, with Symphonies and Accompaniments by Sir John Stevenson. 1810. V. 54
Spirit of Boccaccio's Decameron. London: 1812. V. 48; 51
Tom Crib's Memorial to Congress. London: 1819. V. 50; 52
Travels of an Irish Gentleman in Search of a Religion. London: 1833. V. 51

MOORE, THOMAS GEORGE
The Bachelor; a Novel in Three Volumes. London: 1809. V. 50; 54

MOORE, THOMAS STURGE
A Brief Account of the Origin of the Eragny Press & a Note on the Relation of the Printed Book as a Work of Art to Life. Hammersmith: 1903. V. 47
Danae. London: 1903. V. 47; 49; 50; 52
The Little School. London: 1905. V. 47; 49
The Passionate Pilgrim and the Songs in Shakespeare's Plays. 1896. V. 51
Passionate Pilgrim and the Songs in Shakespeare's Plays. London: 1896. V. 49
The Poems. London: 1931. V. 54
Roderigo of Bivar. New York: 1925. V. 54
The Vine Dresser. London: 1899. V. 48; 50; 51; 53
The Vinedresser. 1899. V. 49

MOORE, THOMAS VERNER
God Our Refuge and Strength In This War. Richmond: 1861. V. 49

MOORE, VIRGINIA
The Life and Eager Death of Emily Bronte. 1936. V. 54

MOORE, W. OSBORNE
The Cosmos and the Creeds: Elementary Notes on the Alleged Finality of the Christian Faith. London: 1903. V. 50

MOORE, WILLIAM
The Constitutional Requirements for Tropical Climates and Observations on the Sequel of Disease Contracted in India. London: 1890. V. 49; 51; 54

MOORE, WILLIAM V.
Indian Wars of the United States, From the Discovery to the Present Time... Philadelphia: 1860. V. 48

MOOREHEAD, ALAN
The White Nile. London: 1960. V. 54

MOOREHEAD, WARREN K.
Archaeology of the Arkansas River Valley. New Haven: 1931. V. 50; 51
Etowah Papers, Exploration of the Etowah Site in Georgia. New Haven: 1932. V. 51
Fort Ancient, the Great Prehistoric Earthwork of Wararen County, Ohio. Cincinnati: 1890. V. 47; 48
A Narrative of Explorations in New Mexico, Arizona, Indiana, Etc. Andover: 1906. V. 51
Prehistoric Implements, A Description of the Ornaments, Utensils and Implements of Pre-Columbian Man in America. Union City: 1968. V. 51
Prehistoric Implements, A Description of the Ornaments, Utensils and Implements of Pre-Columbian Man in America. Union City: 1972. V. 51
Prehistoric Implements. a Reference Book. A Description of the Ornaments, Utensils and Implements of Pre-Columbian Man in America. Cincinnati: 1900. V. 47; 52
A Report on the Archaeology of Maine Being a Narrative of Explorations in That State 1912-1920 Together with a Work at Lake Champlain in 1917. Andover: 1922. V. 47
The Stone Age in North America. Boston: 1910. V. 47; 50
Stone Ornaments Used by Indians In the United States and Canada. Andover: 1917. V. 47; 51; 54

MOORMAN, F. W.
The Place-Names of the West Ridig of Yorkshire. Leeds: 1910. V. 47
Yorkshire Dialect Poems (1673-1915)...Songs of the Ridings. London: 1919/18. V. 53

MOORMAN, JOHN JENNINGS
A Guide to the Virginia Springs: Giving, in addition to the Routes and Distances, a Description of the Springs and Also of the Natural Curiosities of the State. Staunton: 1851. V. 52
Mineral Springs of North America: How to Reach and How to Use Them. Philadelphia: 1873. V. 52; 53

MOORMAN, MADISON
The Journal of... 1850-1851. San Francisco: 1948. V. 49

MOORMAN, MARY
William Wordsworth - a Biography. The Early Years 1770-1803. Oxford: 1957. V. 50; 52
William Wordsworth - a Biography. The Later Years 1803-1850. Oxford: 1965. V. 50; 52

MOORS, JOHN FARWELL
History of the Fifty-Second Regiment Massachusetts Volunteers. Boston: 1893. V. 47

MOORSOM, W.
Letters from Nova Scotia Comprising Sketches of a Young Country. London: 1830. V. 48

MOORSOM, W. S.
Historical Record of the Fifty-Second Regiment (oxfordshire Light Infantry) from the Year 1755 to the Year 1856. London: 1860. V. 50

MOORTGAT, ANTON
The Art of Ancient Mesopotamia: the Classical Art of the Near East. London: 1969. V. 52

MOOSO, JOSIAH
The Life and Travels Of...a Life on the Frontier Among the Indians and Spaniards. Winfield: 1888. V. 47; 51; 53

MORA, CONSTANCIA DE LA
In Place of Splendour. The Autobiography of a Spanish Woman. London: 1940. V. 49

MORA, DOMENICO
Il Soldato di M. domenico Mora, Bolognese, Gentilhuomo Grisone, et nel Quale si Tratta di Tutto Quello, Che ad un Vero Soldato, et Nobile Cavaliere si Conviene Sapere... Venice: 1570 (1569). V. 53
Tre Questiti in Dialogo Sopra il Fare Batterie, Fortificare una Citta, et Ordinar Battaglia Quadrate... Venice: 1567. V. 50

MORA, JO
Californios: the Saga of the Hard-Riding Vaqueros, America's First Cowboys. Garden City: 1949. V. 50

MORAES, D.
Green is the Grass. Bombay & Calcutta: 1951. V. 52

MORAL Lectures, on the Following Subjects. Pride, Envy, Avarice, Anger, Hypocrisy, Charity, Generosity, Compassion, Ill-Humour, Good-Humour, Affectation, Truth, Falsehood, Education, Industry, Wisdom, Indolence, Application, Beauty, Advice, Company... London: 1769. V. 47

MORAL Recreations in Prose and Verse... London: 1830. V. 50

MORALES-ZAMORANO, FRANCISCO
Crossing Dreams. New York: 1995. V. 54
A Family Game. New York: 1993. V. 54
I Followed the Sun. New York: 1994. V. 54
My Rights...Your Rights. New York: 1994. V. 54
The Story of Blue. 1994. V. 54
William's Baggage. New York: 1994. V. 54

MORAN, JAMES
The Double Crown Club: a History of Fifty Years. London: 1974. V. 52
Heraldic Influence On Early Printers' Devices. Leeds: 1978. V. 47; 48; 49

MORAN, JONATHAN J.
A Defense of Edgar Allan Poe. Washington: 1885. V. 50

MORAN, LORD
Churchill: Taken from the Diaries of Lord Moran. Boston: 1966. V. 47; 48; 50

MORAN, PATRICK F.
The Analecta of David Rothe, Bishop of Ossory. 1884. V. 49; 50; 54
The Analecta of David Rothe, Bishop of Ossory. London: 1884. V. 51

MORAN, W. H. W.
From School-Room to Bar. Philadelphia: 1892. V. 50

MORAND, J.
Memoir on Acupuncturation, Embracing a Series of Cases. Philadelphia: 1825. V. 53; 54

MORAND, PAUL
Closed All Night. London: 1924. V. 53
Earth Girdled. London: 1928. V. 48
Earth Girdled. New York: 1928. V. 52
Open All Night. London: 1923. V. 53

MORANG, ALFRED
Adventure in Drawing. Denver: 1947. V. 48

MORANT, PHILIP
The History and Antiquities of the County of Essex. London: 1768. V. 49; 51; 53

MORAVIA, ALBERTO
The Conformist. London: 1952. V. 52

MORD, W.
The Four Champions of Great Britain and Ireland. London. V. 54

THE MORDAUNT Divorce Case. An Official Report...As Tried Before Lord Penzance, in the Divorce Court, February 16th and Following days. London: 1870. V. 49

MORDECAI, ALFRED
Military Commission to Europe, in 1855 and 1856. Washington: 1860. V. 49
Report of Experiments On Gunpowder, Made at Washington Arsenal, in 1843 and 1844. Washington: 1845. V. 50

MORDECAI, SAMUEL
Richmond in By-Gone Days: Being Reminiscences of an Old Citizen. Richmond: 1856. V. 48

MORDEN, WILLIAM J.
Across Asia's Snows and Deserts. New York: 1927. V. 53

MORE, ALEXANDER GOODMAN
Contributions to Cybele Hibernica. Dublin: 1898. V. 54
Contributions Towards a Cybele Hibernica... 1866. V. 54
Contributions Towards a Cybele Hibernica...Outlines of Geographical Distribution of Plants in Ireland. London: 1898. V. 48; 52
Life and Letters of Alexander Goodman More, F.R.S.E., F.L.S., M.R.I.A. 1898. V. 47
Life and Letters of Alexander Goodman More, F.R.S.E., F.L.S., M.R.I.A. Dublin: 1898. V. 54

MORE Broad Grins, or Mirth Versus Melancholy. London: 1819. V. 51

MORE, CRESACRE
The Life of Sir Thomas More, by His Great-Grandson... London: 1828. V. 47
The Life of Sir Thomas More, Kt. Lord High Chancellour of England Under K. Henry the Eighth... London: 1726. V. 48; 50; 52; 54

MORE, HANNAH
Christian Morals. London: 1813. V. 50; 53
Coelebs in Search of a Wife. London: 1800. V. 48
Coelebs In Search of a Wife. London: 1809. V. 49
Coelebs in Search of a Wife. New York: 1809. V. 54
Coelebs in Search of a Wife. London: 1826. V. 50
The Complete Works. New York: 1842. V. 51
The Complete Works Of... New York: 1855. V. 53
An Essay on the Character and Practical Writings of Saint Paul. London: 1815. V. 53
Essays on Various Subjects, Principally Designed for Young Ladies. London: 1777. V. 48
An Estimate of the Religion of the Fashionable World. London: 1791. V. 50
An Estimate of the Religion of the Fashionable World. (with) Thoughts on the Importance of the Manners of the Great to General Society. London: 1799. V. 50
Florio, A Tale... London: 1786. V. 49; 50; 51; 52
Hints Towards Forming the Character of a Young Princess. London: 1805. V. 47; 48; 50
Hints Towards Forming the Character of a Young Princess... London: 1819. V. 47; 49; 52
Memoirs of the Life and Correspondence of Mrs. Hannah More. London: 1834. V. 47
Memoirs of the Life and Correspondence of Mrs. Hannah More by William Roberts. London: 1835. V. 49
Moral Sketches of Prevailing Opinions and Manners, Foreign and Domestic: With Reflections on Prayer. London: 1819. V. 50
Patient Joe; or, the Newcastle Collier. 1800. V. 47
Percy, a Tragedy. London: 1778. V. 48
Poems. London: 1816. V. 51
Practical Piety; or, the Influence of the Religion of the Heart on the Conduct of Life. London: 1811. V. 50; 53
Remarks on the Speech of M. Dupont, Made in the Natinal Convention of France, on the Subjects of Religion and Public Education. London: 1793. V. 48
The Search After Happiness: a Pastoral Drama. Philadelphia: 1811. V. 48; 53
The Shepherd of Salisbury Plain. New Haven: 1810. V. 48; 53
Shorter Religious, Moral and Entertaining Tracts. London: 1850. V. 50
Sir Eldred of the Bower, and the Bleeding Rock. London: 1776. V. 48; 51
Stories for the Middle Ranks of Society, and tales for the Common People. London: 1818. V. 50
Strictures on the Modern System of Female Education. Dublin: 1797. V. 52
Strictures on the Modern System of Female Education. London: 1799. V. 47; 48
Strictures On the Modern System of Female Education... Charlestown: 1800. V. 50; 51; 53
Strictures on the Modern System of Female Education... Philadelphia: 1800. V. 48; 51; 52; 54
Strictures On the Modern System of Female Education. London: 1826. V. 52
The Works. London: 1801. V. 50
The Works of... Dublin: 1803. V. 47
The Works of... New York: 1835. V. 53
The Works of... London: 1853. V. 49

MORE, HENRY
An Antidote Against Atheism, or, an Appeal to the Natural Faculties of the Minde of Man, Whether There Be Or Not a God... London: 1655. V. 47
A Collection of Several Philosophical Writings of Dr. Henry More... London: 1662. V. 47
Conjectura Cabbalistica, or a Conjecturall Essay of Interpreting the Mind of Mose, According to a Threefold Cabbala. London: 1653. V. 47
Enchiridion Ethicum... Amstelodami: 1679. V. 51
An Explanation of the Grand Mystery of Godliness, or A True and Faithful Representation of the Ever Lasting Gospel... London: 1660. V. 48; 49; 50
Opera Theologica - Opera Omina. London: 1675-79. V. 48
The Theological Works...According to the Author's Improvements in His Latin Edition. London: 1708. V. 48

MORE Last Words of Dr. Johnson. London: 1787. V. 48

MORE Plots Found Out, and Plotters Apprehended. A True Relation of the Discovery of a Most Desparate and Dangerous Plot, for the Delivering Up... London: 1643. V. 52

MORE, THOMAS
The Common-Wealth of Utopia... London: 1639. V. 48
The Commonwealth of Utopia. Philadelphia: 1753. V. 47
De Optimo Reip. Satu Deque Nova Insula Utopia Libellus. Basel: 1518. V. 51; 52
De Optimo Reipublicae Statu, Deque Nova Insula Utopia. Hanover: 1613. V. 48
De Optimo Reipublicae Statu, Deque Nova Insula Utopia... Glasgow: 1750. V. 48
A Dialogue of Cumfort Against Tribulation, Made by the Right Vertuous wise and Learned Man, Sir Thomas More... Antwerpiae: 1573. V. 47
A Frutefull Pleasaunt, and Wittie Worke, of the Beste State of a Publique Weale & of the Neweyle Called Utopia. Berkshire: 1929. V. 47
A Most Pleasant, Fruitful and Witty Work or a Best State of a Public Weal, and of the New Isle Called Utopia. London: 1808. V. 48; 49
Utopia... London: 1624. V. 47; 50; 53
Utopia. Glasgow: 1743. V. 47; 49; 51
Utopia. Glasgow: 1762. V. 49
Utopia. London: 1808. V. 48; 49
Utopia. Boston: 1878. V. 47; 49
Utopia. Detroit: 1902. V. 49; 53
Utopia. London: 1903. V. 53
Utopia. Waltham St. Lawrence: 1929. V. 54
Utopia. New York: 1934. V. 47; 48; 50; 51; 52; 54
Utopia. 1935. V. 49
L'Utopie de Thomas Morus... Amsterdam: 1643. V. 51
L'Utopie de Thomas Morus... Leide: 1715. V. 47
The Workes. London: 1557. V. 47; 50
The Workes. London: 1978. V. 51
The XII Properties of Condicyons of a Lover by John Picus, Erle of Myrandula, a Grete Lord of Italy, Expressed in Balade by Sir Thomas More. Sussex: 1928. V. 47; 54

MOREAU, CESAR
Rise and Progress of the Silk Trade in England, from the Earliest Period to the Present Time (Feby. 1826) Founded on Official Documents. London: 1826. V. 49

MOREAU, F. J.
A Practical Treatise on Midwifery... Philadelphia: 1844. V. 48; 54

MOREAU, JULIAN
The Black Commandos. Atlanta: 1967. V. 52

MOREAU, P.
Description of the Rail Road from Liverpool to Manchester. Boston: 1833. V. 52

MOREAU, R. E.
The Bird Faunas of Africa and Its Islands. London: 1966. V. 49

MOREAU DE SAINT-MERY, MEDERIC LOUIS ELIE
Moreau de St. Mery's American Journey. Garden City: 1947. V. 47; 48
Opinion. Paris: 1789. V. 47

MORECAMP, ARTHUR THOMAS PILGRIM
Live Boys or Charley Nasho in Texas. Boston: 1879. V. 47; 49

MORELAND, F. A.
Practical Decorative Upholstery. Boston: 1890. V. 50

MORELAND, SINCLAIR
The Texas Women's Hall of Fame. Austin: 1917. V. 48

MORELAND Vale; or the Fair Fugitive. New York: 1801. V. 47

MORELY, JOHN
The Life of William Ewart Gladstone. New York & London: 1903. V. 52

MORENHOUT, JACQUES ANTOINE
The Inside Story of the Gold Rush. San Francisco: 1935. V. 49; 54

MORENO, J. L.
Who Shall Survive?. Beacon: 1953. V. 49

MORER, THOMAS
An Account of the Present Persecution of the Church in Scotland, in Several Letters. London: 1690. V. 47

MORERI, LOUIS
Le Grand Dictionnaire Historique ou le Melange Curieux de l'Histoire Sacree et Profane. Paris: 1759. V. 47
The Great Historical, Geographical and Poltical Dictionary... London: 1694. V. 47

MORES, EDWARD ROWE
A Dissertation Upon English Typographical Founders and Founderies. London: 1778. V. 49
A Dissertation Upon English Typographical Founders and Founderies. New York: 1924. V. 48; 50; 52

MORESBY, JOHN
Discoveries and Surveys in New Guinea and the D'Entrecasteaux Islands. London: 1876. V. 48; 52

MORETON, C. O.
The Auricula, Its History and Character. London: 1964. V. 49
Old Carnations and Pinks. London: 1955. V. 51; 52; 54

MORETON, JULIAN
Life and Work in Newfoundland; Reminiscences of Thirteen Years Spent There. London: 1863. V. 49

MORETTE, EDGAR
The Sturgis Wager. A Detective Story. New York: 1899. V. 54

MOREWOOD, SAMUEL
An Essay on the Inventions and Customs of Both Ancients and Moderns in the Use of Inebriating Liquors. London: 1824. V. 48; 50
A Philosophical and Statistical History of the Inventions and Customs of Ancient and Modern Nations in the Manufacture and Use of Inebriating Liquors. Dublin: 1838. V. 54

MOREY, FRANK
A Guide to the Natural History of the Isle of Wight. Newport: 1909. V. 49

MORFI, JUAN AGUSTIN
History of Texas: 1673-1779. Albuquerque: 1935. V. 50; 53

MORFI, JUAN AUGUSTIN
Memorias for the History of Texas (Indian Exceprts). San Antonio: 1932. V. 48

MORFORD, HENRY
John Jasper's Secret. Philadelphia: 1871. V. 47
Morford's Scenery and Sensation Hand-Book of the Pacific Railroads and California. London and New York: 1878. V. 50

MORGADO, MARTIN J.
Junipero Serra's Legacy. Pacific Grove: 1987. V. 54

MORGAGNI, GIOVANNI BATTISTA
De Sedibus, et Causis Morborum per Anatomen Indagatis Libri Quinque. Padua: 1765. V. 50; 54
De Sedibus et Causis Morborum per Anatomen Indagatis Libri Quinque. Helvetia: 1779. V. 51
The Seats and Causes of Diseases Investigated by Anatomy. New York: 1960. V. 48
The Seats and Causes of Diseases, Investigated by Anatomy: Containing a Great Variety of Dissections and Accompanied with Remarks. Boston: 1824. V. 49

MORGAN, ABEL
Anti-Paedo Rantism; or Samuel Finley's Charitable Plea for the Speechless Examined and Refuted... Philadelphia: 1747. V. 50
A Reply to Mr. Samuel Finley's Vindication of the Charitable Plea for the Speechless... Philadelphia: 1750. V. 49

MORGAN, ARTHUR
A Short Account of the Society for Equitable Assurances on Lives and Survivorships, Established by Deed, Inrolled in His Majesty's Court of King's Bench, at Westmisnter. London: 1836. V. 49

MORGAN, CHARLES
The Flashing Stream. London: 1938. V. 50; 52
The Gunroom. London: 1919. V. 53
Six Philosophical Dissertations on The Mechanical Powers. Elastic Bodies. Falling Bodies. The Cycloid. The Parabola. The Rain-Bow. Cambridge: 1770. V. 52

MORGAN, CHARLES H.
Corinth. Volume XI: The Byzantine Pottery. Cambridge: 1942. V. 52

MORGAN, CONWAY LLOYD
Animal Life and Intelligence. London: 1891. V. 54

MORGAN, DALE L.
In Pursuit of the Golden Dream. Stoughton: 1970. V. 53
Jedediah Smith and the Maps of the American West. San Francisco: 1954. V. 47; 54
Jedediah Smith and the Opening of the West. Indianapolis: 1953. V. 50; 52
Jedediah Smith and the Opening of the West. New York: 1953. V. 48; 51; 54
Overland in 1846. Diaries and Letters of the California-Oregon Trail. Georgetown: 1963. V. 47; 53; 54
The West of William Ashley...Recorded in the Diaries and Letters, 1822-38. Denver: 1964. V. 48; 49; 50; 51; 52; 53; 54

MORGAN, GEORGE
The New Complete Sportsman; or, the Town and Country Gentleman's Recreation. London. V. 49

MORGAN, GEORGE B.
The Identification of the Writer of the Anonymous Letter to Lord Monteagle in 1605. London: 1916. V. 53

MORGAN, HECTOR DAVIES
The Doctrine and Law of Marriage, Adultery and Divorce. Oxford: 1826. V. 48; 50; 51

MORGAN, HENRY J.
The Dominion Annual Register and Review for the Fourteenth and Fifteenth years of the Canadian Union, 1880-81. Montreal: 1882. V. 50
Sketches of Celebrated Canadians and Persons Connected With Canada, from the Eariest period in the History of the Province Down to the Present Time. Quebec: 1862. V. 54

MORGAN, J.
A Complete History of Algiers. London: 1731. V. 52
Phoenix Britannicus: Being a Miscellaneous Collection of Scarce and Curious Tracts... London: 1732. V. 49

MORGAN, JAMES MORRIS
Prince and Boatswain Sea Tales. Greenfield: 1915. V. 47
Recollections of a Rebel Reefer. Boston and New York: 1917. V. 47; 51

MORGAN, JOHN
A Discourse Upon the Institution of Medical Schools in America. Philadelphia: 1765. V. 49
The Life and Adventures of William Buckley; Thirty-Two Years a Wanderer Amongst the Aborigines of the Then Unexplored Country Round Port Phillip, Now the Province of Victoria. Tasmania: 1852. V. 52
New Guide to Bristol, Clifton, &c. Bristol: 1849. V. 54

MORGAN, JOHN E.
University Oars, Being a Critical Enquiry Into the After health of the men Who Rowed in the Oxford and Cambridge Boat-Race, From the Year 1829 to 1869... London: 1873. V. 49

MORGAN, JOHN MINTER
The Revolt of the Bees. London: 1830. V. 53

MORGAN, JOHN TYLER
Address of Hon. Jno. T. Morgan on the Unveiling of the Monuments to the Unknown Confederate Dead, Delivered at Winchester, Virginia, June 6th 1879. Washington: 1879. V. 49; 54

MORGAN, JULIA
How It Was: Four Years Among the Rebels. Nashville: 1892. V. 49

MORGAN, LEWIS H.
The American Beaver and His Works. Philadelphia: 1868. V. 49; 50; 52
Houses and House-Life of the American Aborigines. Washington: 1881. V. 53
League of the Ho-De-No-Sau-Nee or Iroquois. New York: 1901. V. 52
League of the Ho-De-No-Sau-Nee or Iroquois. New York: 1904. V. 50
League of the Hode-no-sau-nee, or, Iroquois. Rochester: 1851. V. 50
League of the So-De-No-Sau-nee or Iroquis. New York: 1922. V. 54

MORGAN, LOUISA
Baron Bruno; or the Unbelieving Philosopher. London: 1875. V. 48

MORGAN, M. D.
The Ecology of Mysidacea. The Hague: 1982. V. 52

MORGAN, MARY
A Tour to Milford Haven, in the Year 1791. London: 1795. V. 54

MORGAN, MISS
The Gaol of the City of Bristol Compared with What a Gaol Ought to Be. Bristol: 1815. V. 47; 50

MORGAN, OLGA
The Twins ABC. London. V. 54

MORGAN, OWEN
The Light of Britannia. Cardiff: 1893. V. 52

MORGAN, R. B.
Tales of Troy. London: 1915. V. 47

MORGAN, RICHARD WILLIAM
Raymond de Monthault, the Lrod Marcher: a Legend of the Welch Borders. London: 1853. V. 54

MORGAN, ROBERT
Red Owl. New York: 1972. V. 54
Zirconia Poems. Northwood Narrows: 1969. V. 52

MORGAN, ROBIN
Death Benefits. Port Townsend: 1981. V. 48

MORGAN, SETH
Dead Man Walkin'. New York: 1990. V. 51
Homeboy. New York: 1990. V. 49; 51; 54

MORGAN, SYDNEY OWENSON, LADY
Absenteeism. London: 1825. V. 51
The Book Without a Name. London: 1841. V. 47
Florence Macarthy. London: 1818. V. 47; 51
France. London: 1817. V. 47; 50
France in 1829-30. London: 1830. V. 50; 52
France in 1829-30. London: 1830. V. 47
Glorvina, ou la Jeune Irlandaise, Histoire Nationale. (The Wild Irish Girl). Paris: 1813. V. 47
Italy. London: 1821. V. 52
Italy. New York: 1821. V. 47; 49; 50
Lady Morgan's Memoirs: Autobiography, Diaries and Correspondence. London: 1862. V. 49; 51
The Lay of an Irish Harp; or Metrical Fragments. 1808. V. 47
The Lay of an Irish Harp; or Metrical Fragments. New York: 1808. V. 50
The Life and Times of Salvator Rosa. 1824. V. 47
The O'Briens and the O'Flahertys; a National Tale. London: 1827. V. 50
O'Donnell. London: 1814. V. 47; 50; 51; 54
Passages from My Autobiography. London: 1859. V. 51
The Princess; or the Begune. London: 1835. V. 50
The Wild Irish Girl... London: 1807. V. 51
The Wild Irish Girl. Philadelphia: 1807. V. 51
The Wild Irish Girl. London: 1846. V. 49

MORGAN, T.
The Mechanical Practice of Physick: in Which the Specifick Method is Examin'd and Exploded... London: 1735. V. 47; 48

MORGAN, T. J.
The Negro in America and the Ideal American Republic. Philadelphia: 1898. V. 48

MORGAN, THOMAS CHARLES
Sketches of Philosophy of Morals. London: 1822. V. 49; 52
Sketches of the Philosophy of Life... London: 1818. V. 50

MORGAN, THOMAS HUNT
A Critique of the Theory of Evolution. Princeton: 1916. V. 49
The Development of the Frog's Egg. New York: 1897. V. 49; 54
Evolution and Adaptation. New York: 1903. V. 49
Experimental Embryology. New York: 1927. V. 50
The Physical Basis of Heredity. Philadelphia: 1919. V. 49; 50; 52; 54
Sex-Linked Inheritance in Drosophila. Washington: 1916. V. 49
The Theory of the Gene. New Haven: 1926. V. 49; 52; 54

MORGAN, WILLIAM
The Homoeopathic Treatment of Indigestion, Constipation, and Haemorrhoids. Philadelphia: 1854. V. 49; 54
Illustrations of Masonry, by One of the Fraternity. New York: 1827. V. 50
Illustrations of Masonry, by One of the Fraternity. Cincinnati: 1867. V. 54
The Liver and Diseases, both Functional and Organic, Their History, Anatomy, Chemistry, Pathology, Physiology and Treatment. London: 1877. V. 54
More Light on Masonry, or Morgan Revived. Rochester: 1827. V. 50
A Narrative of the Facts and Circumstances Relating to the Kidnapping and Presumed Murder of William Morgan, and of Attempt to Carry Off David C. Miller and to Burn or Detsory the Printing Office of the Latter... Brookfield: 1827. V. 48; 53
A Narrative of the Facts and Circumstances Relating to the Kidnapping and Presumed Murder of William Morgan and of the Attempt to Carry Off David C. Miller and to Burn or Destroy the Printing Office of the Latter, or the Purpose of Preventing... Batavia: 1827. V. 50
The Trial of William Morgan, for the Murder of Miss Mary Jones, Daughter of William Jones, Esq.; of Nass in the County of Glocester, at the Assizes Held at Glocester, on Wednesday the 11th March, 1772... Glocester: 1772. V. 50

MORGAN, WILLIAM HENRY
Personal Reminiscences of the War of 1861-65, in Camp, en Bivouac, on the March,, on Pickt, On the Skirmish Line, on the Battlefield, and in Prison. Lynchburg: 1911. V. 49; 54

MORGANE, PETER J.
Anatomy of the Hypothalamus. Handbook of the Hypothalamus. Volume 1. New York: 1979. V. 50
Physiology of the Hypothalamus. Handbook of the Hypothalamus Volume 2. New York, Basel: 1980. V. 50

MORGANN, MAURICE
An Essay on the Dramatic Character of Sir John Falstaff. London: 1777. V. 47; 48; 53; 54

MORGARD, NOEL LEON
Le Manifeste et Prophetie de Morgard Speculateur es Causes Secondes. Lyon: 1619. V. 48

MORGENSTERN, CHRISTIAN
Das Mittags Mahl il Pranzo. Hamburg: 1991. V. 47
Das Mittagsmahl (Il Pranzo): Paraodie Auf Gabriele d'Annunzio (and other works). 1991. V. 52
Osterbuch. Berlin: 1910. V. 53

MORGULIS, SERGIUS
Fasting and Undernutrition: a Biological and Sociological Study of Inanitation. New York: 1923. V. 47; 49

MORHOF, DANIEL GEORG
De Metallorum Transmutatione... Hamburg: 1673. V. 48
Polyhistor, Literarius, Philosophicus et Practicus... Lubeck: 1747. V. 49

MORHOUS, HENRY C.
Reminiscences of the 123rd Regiment N.Y.S.U. Greenwich: 1870. V. 52

MORI, M.
Japans Schlangen. Tokyo: 1982-86. V. 50

MORIARTY, H. M.
Fifty Plates of Green-House Plants... London: 1807. V. 52

MORICAND, CONRAD
Portraits Astrologiques. Paris: 1933. V. 48

MORICE, A. G.
The History of the Northern Interior of British Columbia formerly New Caledonia (1660 to 1880). Toronto: 1904. V. 53
Primitive Tribes and Pioneer Traders. The History of the Northern Interior of British Columbia (Formerly New Caledonia) (1660 to 1880). London: 1905. V. 48

MORIER, JAMES JUSTINIAN
Abel Allnutt. London: 1837. V. 51
The Adventures of Hajii Baba or Ispahan. Paris: 1824. V. 47
The Adventures of Hajji Baba of Ispahan. London: 1824. V. 51
The Adventures of Hajji Baba, of Ispahan, in England. London: 1828. V. 51
The Adventures of Hajji Baba, of Ispahan, in England. New York: 1828. V. 53; 54
The Adventures of Hajji Babba of Ispahan. New York: 1947. V. 54
Ayesha, the Maid of Kars. London: 1834. V. 51
A Journey through Persia, Armenia and Asia Minor to Constantinople, in the Years 1808 and 1809. Journey. London: 1812. V. 49
The Mirza. London: 1841. V. 48; 49; 52
An Oriental Tale. Brighton: 1839. V. 51; 52
A Second Journey through Persia, Armenia and Asia Minor to Constantinople, Between the Years 1810 and 1816. London: 1818. V. 49
Zohrab the Hostage. London: 1833. V. 51

MORIGI, PAOLO
Histori dell' Origine di Tutte le Religioni. Venice: 1590. V. 48; 52
Sommario Cronologico Diviso in Sette Libri Ne' Quali con Ordinata Serie de Tempi, si Ha Notitia Delli Piu Gravi... Bergamo: 1601. V. 50

MORING, THOMAS
Fifty Book Plates Engraved On Copper. London: 1901. V. 49
One Hundred Book Plates Engraved On Wood. London. V. 49
One Hundred Book Plates Engraved on Wood. London: 1900. V. 48

MORING, THOMAS continued
One Hundred Book Plates Engraved on Wood by Thomas Moring. London: 1901. V. 51

MORISON, ALEXANDER
The Physiognomy of Mental Diseases. V. 51

MORISON, DOUGLAS
Views of Haddon Hall. London: 1842. V. 52

MORISON, JAMES
Morisoniana; or, Family Adviser of the British College of Health, Being A Collection of the Works of Mr. Morison, the Hygeist... London: 1833. V. 48

MORISON, JEANIE
Selections from the Poems. Edinburgh: 1890. V. 51

MORISON, ROBERT
Plantarum Umbelliferarum Distributio Nova, Per Tabulas Cognationis et Affinitatis ex Libro Naturae Observata & Detecta. Oxford: 1672. V. 52

MORISON, SAMUEL ELIOT
Journals and Other Documents on the Life and Voyages of Christopher Columbus. New York: 1963. V. 48; 52; 54
Journals and Other Documents on the Life and Voyages of Christopher Columbus. New York: 1965. V. 52; 54

MORISON, STANLEY
American Copybooks. An Outline of Their History from Colonial to Modern Times. Philadelphia: 1951. V. 52
The Art of the Printer: 250 Title and Text Pages Selected from Books Composed in the Roman Letter Printed from 1500 to 1900. London: 1925. V. 51
Black Letter Text. Cambridge: 1942. V. 52
The Calligraphic Models of Ludovico Degli Arrighi Sur-named Vicentino. Paris: 1926. V. 54
The English Newspaper. 1932. V. 54
The English Newspaper; Some Account of the Physical Development of Journals Printed in London Between 1622 and the Present Day. Cambridge: 1932. V. 47
English Prayer Books - an Introduction to the Literature of Christian Public Worship. Cambridge: 1943. V. 51
A Fifteenth Century Modus Scribendi from the Abbey of Melk. Cambridge: 1940. V. 52
The Fleuron: a Journal of Typography...No. VII. Cambridge: 1930. V. 49
Four Centuries of Printing. London: 1924. V. 52
Fra Luca de Pacioli. 1933. V. 48
Fra Luca de Pacioli of Borgo S. Sepolcro. New York: 1933. V. 47; 50; 52
German Incunabula in the British Museum. 1928. V. 47
German Incunabula in the British Museum. London: 1928. V. 49; 52
German Incunabula in the British Museum. London: 1975. V. 47
German Incunabula in the British Museum. New York: 1975. V. 52
The History of the Times. London: 1935-52. V. 52
The History of the Times. London: 1950-52. V. 51
Ichabod Dawks and His News-Letter, with An Account of the Dawks Family of Booksellers and Stationers, 1635-1731. Cambridge: 1931. V. 52
John Bell 1745-1831. Cambridge: 1930. V. 52; 54
John Bell 1745-1831. London: 1930. V. 48
John Fell, the University Press and the "Fell" Types. Oxford: 1967. V. 47; 48; 50; 51; 53
The Likeness of Thomas More: an Iconographical Survey of Three Centuries. New York: 1963. V. 50
Marcello Cervini Pope Marcellus II Bibliography's Patron Saint. London: 1962. V. 48
Modern Fine Printing, an Exhibit of Printing Issued in England, the United States of America, France, Germany, Italy, Switzerland, Czecho-Slovakia, Holland and Sweden... London: 1925. V. 47; 48; 50; 52
A Newly Discovered Treatise on Classic Letter Design Printed at parma by Damianus Moyllus Circa 1480 Reproduced in Facsimile. Paris: 1927. V. 48
Notes on the Development of Latin Script from Early to Modern Times. Cambridge: 1949. V. 50; 52
Notes Towards a Specimen of the Ancient Typographical Materials Principally Collected and Bequeated to the Unviersity of Oxford by Dr. John Fell d. 1686. Oxford: 1953-57. V. 52
On Type Faces. Examples of the Use of type For the Printing Of Books. London: 1923. V. 48; 50
Politics and Script. Oxford: 1972. V. 48; 52
Printing "The Times" since 1785. London: 1953. V. 52; 53
A Review of Recent Typography in England, the United States, France and Germany. London: 1927. V. 50
The Roman Italic and Black Letter Bequeathed to the University of Oxford by Dr. John Fell. Oxford: 1950. V. 53
Selected Essays on the History of Letterforms in Manuscript and Print. Cambridge: 1981. V. 53
A Specimen of the Roman, Italic, Black-letter, Greek, Exotic and Other Typographical material Principally Collected and Bequeathed to the University of Oxford by Dr John Fell d. 1686. London: 1953. V. 48
Splendour of Ornament. London: 1968. V. 49
Stanley Morison and D. B. Updike, Selected Correspondence. New York: 1979. V. 47
A Study of Fine Typography through Five Centuries: exhibited in Upwards of Three Hundred and Fifty Title and Text Pages Drawn From PResses Working in the European Tradition. Chicago: 1963. V. 47
Talbot Baines Reed: Author, Bibliographer, Typefounder. Cambridge: 1960. V. 47; 53
A Tally of Types Cut for Machine Composition and Introduced at the University Press, Cambridge 1922-1932. Cambridge: 1953. V. 50; 53
The Typographic Book, 1450-1935. Chicago: 1963. V. 47; 50; 51; 52; 54
The Typographic Book 1450-1935... London: 1963. V. 47; 48; 50; 52; 54
Typographic Design in Relation to Photographic Composition. San Francisco: 1959. V. 52; 53

MORISON, WILLIAM MAXWELL
The Decisions of the Court of Session, from Its Institution Until the Separation of the Court into Two Divisions in the Year 1808... Edinburgh: 1811-16. V. 54

MORISOT, BERTHE
The Correspondence of Berthe Morisot With Her Family and Her Friends... London: 1957. V. 48; 50; 52; 53

MORITZ, L. A.
Grain-Mills and Flour in Classical Antiquity. Oxford: 1958. V. 50

MORITZ, R. F. A.
Bees as Superorganisms. London: 1992. V. 50

MORLAND, SAMUEL
The History of the Evangelical Churches of the Valleys of Piedmont. London: 1658. V. 48

MORLAND, THOMAS HORNBY
The Genealogy of the English Race Horse. London: 1810. V. 47

MORLEY, CHRISTOPHER DARLINGTON
Born in a Beer Garden or She Troupes to Conquer. New York: 1930. V. 48
Don't Open Until Christmas. New York: 1931. V. 52
The Goldfish Under the Ice. London: 1929. V. 47; 53
The Haunted Bookshop. New York: 1919. V. 54
Kitty Foyle. Philadelphia, New York: 1939. V. 53
Mandarin in Manhattan. Garden City: 1933. V. 54
On Visiting Bookshops. USA: 1931. V. 53
The Palette Knife. Chelsea, New York: 1929. V. 50; 54
Parnassus on Wheels. Garden City: 1917. V. 49; 52; 53; 54
Plum Pudding, of Divers Ingedients, Discreetly Blended and Seasoned. New York: 1922. V. 54
Swiss Family Manhattan. Garden City: 1932. V. 52
Thunder on the Left. Garden City: 1925. V. 54
Travels in Philadelphia. Philadelphia: 1920. V. 49
Where the Blue Begins. New York: 1922. V. 48
Where the Blue Begins. Philadelphia: 1922. V. 53
Where the Blue Begins. London: 1925. V. 49

MORLEY, FRANCES TALBOT PARKER, COUNTESS OF
The Flying Burgermaster, a Legend of the Black Forest. London: 1832. V. 47

MORLEY, HENRY
Cornelius Agrippa. The Life of Henry Cornelius Agrippa von Nettesheim, Doctor and Knight... London: 1856. V. 47
Memoirs of Bartholomew Fair. London: 1880. V. 52
Oberon's Horn. London: 1861. V. 51; 52

MORLEY, JOHN
Diderot and the Encyclopaedists. London: 1878. V. 53
Edmund Burke: a Historical Study. London: 1867. V. 53
An Essay on the Nature and Cure of Scrophlous Disorders, vulgarly called the King's Evil Deduced from Observation and practice. London: 1770. V. 48
An Essay on the Nature and Cure of Scrophulous Disorders, Commonly Called the King's Evil... London: 1777. V. 48
The Life of William Ewart Gladstone. London: 1903. V. 52; 54
The Life of William Ewart Gladstone. London and New York: 1905-06. V. 54
Regency Design. Gardens, Buildings, Interiors, Furniture, 1790-1840. London: 1993. V. 51; 53
Rousseau. London: 1873. V. 53
Works. London: 1921. V. 50

MORLEY, SUSAN
Throstlethwaite. London: 1875. V. 50

MORLEY, SYLVANUS G.
Guide Book to the Ruins of Quirigua. Washington: 1935/47. V. 50; 52
The Inscriptions at Copan. Washington: 1920. V. 47
An Introduction to the Study of the Maya Hieroglyphs. Washington: 1915. V. 48

MORLEY, THOMAS
A Plain and Easy Introduction to Practical Music, Set Down in the Form of a Dialogue... London: 1771. V. 49
A Plaine and Easie Introduction to Practicall Musicke, Set Down in Form of a Dialogue. London: 1597. V. 51
A Plaine and Easie Introduction to Practicall Musicke, set downe in Forme of a Dialogue... London: 1608. V. 54

MORLEYANA; A Collection of Writings In Memoriam, Sylvanus Griswold Morley 1883-1948. Santa Fe: 1950. V. 52

MORNAY, PHILIPPE DE
Memoires. Le Forest-sur-Sevre: 1624-25. V. 53
A Worke Concerning the Trunesse of Christian Religion. London: 1604. V. 48; 50

MORNER, HJALMAR
Stockholmska Scener Tecknade och Lithografierarde. Stockholm: 1830. V. 49

A MORNING In Cork-Street: or, Raising the Wind!. London: 1822. V. 51

MORNING Prayer According to the Sepharaadic Custom. Venice: 1735. V. 53

MORNING Star Scrapbook. Occidental: 1973. V. 51

MORONI, LINO
Descrizione del Sacro Monte della Vernia... Florence: 1612. V. 49

MORPHIS, J. M.
History of Texas from Discovery...with a Description of Its Principal Cities and Counties...and Resources of the State. New York: 1875. V. 53

MORRAH, HERBERT A.
The Oxford Union 1823-1923. London: 1923. V. 53

MORRELL, BENJAMIN
A Narrative of Four Voyages, to the South Sea, North and South Pacific Ocean, Chinese Sea, Ethiopic and Southern Atlantic Ocean, Indian and Antarctic Ocean, from the Year 1822-1831. New York: 1832. V. 48; 52

MORRELL, CHARLES
The Tales of the Genii: or, the Delightful Lessons of Horam, The Son of Asmar. London: 1764. V. 49
The Tales of the Genii, or, the Delightful Lessons of Horam the Son os Asmar. London: 1805. V. 53

MORRELL, DAVID
First Blood. New York: 1972. V. 47; 54

MORRELL, E.
The Twenty-Fifth Man. Montclair: 1924. V. 54

MORRELL, J. D.
An Historical and Critical View of the Speculative Philosophy in Europe in the Nineteenth Century. New York: 1848. V. 49

MORRELL, JOHN REYNELL
Algeria: The Topography and History, Political, Social and Natural, of French Africa. London: 1854. V. 52

MORRELL, W. WILBERFOSS
The History and Antiquites of Selby in the West Riding of the County of York Containining Its Ancient and Present State, Ecclesiastical and Civil. Selby & London: 1867. V. 47; 48; 53

MORRELL, WILLIAM
New England Or a Brief Enarration of the Ayre, Earth, Water, Fish and Fowles of that Country...New. Boston: 1895. V. 48

MORRELL, Z. N.
Flowers and Fruits from the Wilderness. Boston: 1872. V. 52

MORRICE, ALEXANDER
A Treatise on Brewing... London: 1810. V. 53

MORRICE, BEZALEEL
Love and Resentment: a Pastoral. London: 1717. V. 47; 50

MORRIN, J.
Calendar of Patents and Close Rolls fo Chancery in Ireland. Dublin: 1861. V. 47; 49; 50

MORRIS, ALEXANDER
Nova Britannia; or, British North America, Its Extent and Future. Montreal: 1858. V. 53

MORRIS, ALICE TALWIN
Old Friends and New Friends. London: 1916. V. 48

MORRIS, ANN
Word Dreams I. Leicestershire: 1979. V. 52

MORRIS, BEVERLEY ROBINSON
British Game Birds and Wild Fowl. London: 1855. V. 52; 53
British Game Birds and Wildfowl. London: 1889. V. 47
British Game Birds and Wildfowl. London: 1891. V. 53
The Naturalist. London: 1851-58. V. 48

MORRIS, CASPER
Lectures on Scarlet Fever. Philadelphia: 1851. V. 51

MORRIS, CORBYN
An Essay Towards Fixing the True Standards of Wit, Humour, Raillery, Satire and Ridicule. London: 1744. V. 51
A Letter from a By-Stander to a Member of Parliament; Wherein is Examined What Necessity There Is for the Maintenance of a Large Regular Land-Force in This Island... London: 1742. V. 53
A Letter to the Mayor of ------ Wherein the Discouragement of the Seamen Employed in His Majesty's Navy and the Merits of the Bill Brought into Parliament in the Last Session... London: 1758. V. 52

MORRIS, D.
The Colony of British Honduras, Its Resources and Prospects... London: 1883. V. 48; 51

MORRIS, DRAKE
The Travels of Mr. Drake Morris, Merchant in London. London: 1755. V. 47; 49; 50

MORRIS, E.
Notes of a Tour through Turkey, Greece, Egypt and Arabia Petraea, to the Holy Land... London: 1843. V. 49
Notes of a Tour Through Turkey, Greece, Egypt and Arabia Petraea, to the Holy Land... Aberdeen: 1847. V. 48

MORRIS, EARL H.
Anasazi Basketry: Basket Maker II Through Pueblo III: A Study Based on Specimens From the San Juan Country. Washington: 1941. V. 48
Archaeological Studies in the La Plata District, Southwestern Colorado and Northwestern New Mexico. Washington: 1939. V. 50
The Temple of the Warriors at Chichen Itza, Yucatan. Washington: 1931. V. 53

MORRIS, EDMUND
Derrick and Drill, or an Insight into the Discovery, Development and Present Condition and Future Prospects of Petroleum, in New York, Pennsylvania, Ohio, West Virginia, &c. New York: 1865. V. 50

MORRIS, EDWARD
The Life of Henry Bell. Glasgow: 1844. V. 49

MORRIS, ELLWOOD
Treatise on the Improvement of the Ohio River. Pottsville: 1857. V. 48

MORRIS, F.
Our Wild Orchids, Trails and Portraits. New York: 1929. V. 51

MORRIS, FRANCIS ORPEN
Beautiful British Birds. London: 1860. V. 54
Bible Natural History: Book of Natural History. Manchester: 1852. V. 54
Book of Natural History. Manchester: 1852. V. 54
A History of British Birds. London: 1851-57. V. 49; 50
A History of British Birds. London: 1863-67. V. 48; 49; 51
A History of British Birds. London: 1866. V. 50
A History of British Birds. London: 1870-71. V. 53
A History of British Birds. London: 1888. V. 48; 51
A History of British Birds. London: 1903. V. 52; 53
A History of British Birds. (and) A Natural History of the Nests and Eggs of British Birds. London: 1870/67-79. V. 48
A History of British Birds. (with) A Natural History of the Nests and Eggs of British Birds. London: 1857-63/61. V. 51
A History of British Birds (with) A Natural History of the Nests and Eggs of British Birds. London: 1866. V. 51
A History of British Butterflies. London: 1853. V. 47
A History of British Butterflies. London: 1864. V. 50
A History of British Butterflies. London: 1865. V. 50
A History of British Butterflies. London: 1868. V. 48
A History of British Butterflies. London: 1870. V. 50; 51; 54
A History of British Butterflies. London: 1890. V. 49; 50
A History of British Butterflies. London: 1893. V. 47
A History of British Butterflies. London: 1895. V. 49
A History of British Moths. London: 1896. V. 49; 51; 52; 53; 54
A History of British Moths. London: 1903. V. 48; 50; 52
A Natural History of British Moths. Edinburgh: 1871. V. 49; 52
A Natural History of British Moths. London: 1872. V. 52
A Natural History of British Moths. London: 1894. V. 47
A Natural History of the Nests and Eggs of British Birds. London: 1875. V. 52; 53; 54
A Natural History of the Nests and Eggs of British Birds. London: 1879. V. 49
A Natural History of the Nests and Eggs of British Birds. London: 1894. V. 49
The Natural History of the Nests and Eggs of British Birds. London: 1896. V. 47; 49; 51
A Series of Picturesque Views of Seats of Noblemen and Gentlemen of Great Britain and Ireland. (with) Facsimile Autographs of Subscribers to the Picturesque Views of Seats of Noblemen... London: 1880/80. V. 49
A Series of Picturesque Views of Seats of the Noblemen and Gentlemen of Great Britain and Ireland. London: 1868-77. V. 53
A Series of Picturesque Views of Seats of the Noblemen and Gentlemen of Great Britain and Ireland. London: 188-?. V. 54

MORRIS, FRANCIS W. JARRETT
Elva's Revenge: a Lgendary Poem in Five Cantos. With Other Poems. London: 1834. V. 54

MORRIS, FRANK T.
Birds of Prey of Australia. Melbourne: 1973. V. 48
Impressions of Waterfowl of Australia. London: 1977. V. 50

MORRIS, GEORGE FORD
Portraitures of Horses. Shrewsbury: 1952. V. 51
The Saddle Horse of America nd the Morgan Horse. 1914. V. 53

MORRIS, GEORGE P.
The Deserted Bride, and Other Poems. New York: 1838. V. 49; 50; 52
The Little Frenchman and His Water Lots, with Other Sketches of the Times. Philadelphia: 1839. V. 52; 54

MORRIS, GOUVERNEUR
The Diary and Letters of Gouverneur Morris... 1970. V. 52
The Diary and Letters of Gouverneur Morris, U.S. Minister to France... New York: 1970. V. 49

MORRIS, H. J., MRS.
Founders and Patriots of the Repbulic of Texas: The Lineage of the Members of the DRT. Austin: 1963/74/85. V. 53

MORRIS, HARRISON
Commercial Directory and Gazetteer of the County of Cumberland. Nottingham: 1861. V. 50; 52

MORRIS, HARRY JOSEPH
Founders and Patriots of the Republic of Texas; the Lineages of the members of the Daughters of the Republic of Texas. Austin: 1963. V. 48

MORRIS, HENRY
Bird & Bull Number 13. North Hills: 1972. V. 47
Bird & Bull Pepper Pot. 1977. V. 52; 54
Bird & Bull Pepper Pot. North Hills: 1977. V. 48; 51; 53; 54
The Bird and Bull Commonplace Book. North Hills: 1971. V. 53
Bird and Bull Pepper Pot. North Hills: 1977. V. 51
Five on Paper. North Hills: 1963. V. 47

MORRIS, HENRY continued
Guilford & Green. North Hills: 1970. V. 48
Japonica: the Study and Appreciation of the Art of Japanese Paper. North Hills: 1981. V. 53
No. V-109. The Bibliography of a Printing Press. 1978. V. 48
No. V-109. The Biography of a Printing Press. Boston: 1978. V. 49
Omnibus. 1967. V. 48; 51; 54
Omnibus. North Hills: 1967. V. 48; 51
A Pair On Paper: Two Essays on Paper History and Related Matters. North Hills: 1976. V. 49
Pepper Pot. North Hills: 1977. V. 49
The Private Press-Man's Tale. Newtown: 1990. V. 50; 52
Surgical Diseases of the Kidney and Ureter Including Injuries, Malformations and Misplacements. London: 1901. V. 54
Trade Tokens of British and American Booksellers & Bookmakers. Newtown: 1989. V. 48; 50; 51; 53

MORRIS, J.
A Catalogue of British Fossils. London: 1854. V. 53

MORRIS, J. P.
A Glossary of the Words and Phrases of Furness (North Lancashire). London: 1869. V. 50; 52

MORRIS, JAN
A Machynlleth Triad. Newtown: 1993. V. 50

MORRIS, JOHN
From the Third Programme: a Ten Years' Anthology. London: 1956. V. 47; 50

MORRIS, JOHN BRANDE
Jesus the son of Mary or the Doctrine of the Catholic Church... London: 1851. V. 51; 54

MORRIS, JOSEPH
The German Air Raids on Great Britain, 1914-1918. London: 1925. V. 49

MORRIS, LEOPOLD
Pictorial History of Victoria and Victoria County. Victoria: 1953. V. 51
Pictorial History of Victoria and Victoria County. (with) *History of the County.* Clemens: 1953. V. 53

MORRIS, MAURICE O'CONNOR
Rambles in the Rocky Mountains. London: 1864. V. 47; 50; 53
Triviata, or Crossroad Chronicles...of Passages in Irish Hunting History... London: 1877. V. 47; 49

MORRIS, MAY
William Morris: Artist, Writer, Socialist. Oxford: 1936. V. 49

MORRIS, R. H.
Chester in the Plantagenet and Tudor Reigns. Chester. V. 48

MORRIS, RALPH
The Life and Astonishing Adventures of John Daniel. London: 1926. V. 49

MORRIS, RICHARD
Essays on Landscape Gardening and on Uniting Picturesque Effect with Rural Scenery. London: 1825. V. 47

MORRIS, ROBERT
The Architectural Remembrancer... London: 1751. V. 53
The Art of Architecture. London: 1742. V. 48

MORRIS, THOMAS B.
Report of the Chief Engineer of the Seattle and Walla Walla Railroad Co... Weattle: 1874. V. 50

MORRIS, THOMAS HOLLINGSWORTH
A.D. 1862, or The volunteer Zouave in Baltimore, by an Officer of the "Guards". Baltimore: 1862. V. 52

MORRIS, W. P.
The Records of Patterdale. Kendal: 1903. V. 50; 52

MORRIS, WILLIAM
An Address Delivered by William Morris at the Distribution of Prizes to Students of the Birmingham Municipal School of Art on Feb. 21, 1894. London: 1898. V. 47; 51; 54
Architecture and History, and Westminster Abbey. London: 1900. V. 49; 51; 54
Architecture, Industry and Wealth: Collected Papers. London: 1902. V. 47; 51
The Art and Craft of Printing. New Rochelle: 1902. V. 50; 52
Art and the Beauty of the Earth - a Lecture Delivered at Burslem Town Hall on October 13, 1881. London: 1898. V. 47; 49; 53; 54
A Book of Verse. London: 1980. V. 51
Child Christopher and Goldilind the Fair. 1895. V. 49
Collected Letters of William Morris, Volume I & II. Princeton: 1984/87. V. 49
The Collected Works of William Morris. London/New York/Bombay: 1910. V. 53
Communism: a Lecture. London: 1903. V. 50
The Defence of Guenevere, and Other Poems. London: 1858. V. 47
The Defence of Guenevere and Other Poems. London and New York: 1904. V. 47; 49; 52
The Defence of Guenevere and Other Poems. London: 1915. V. 51
A Dream of John Ball. East Aurora: 1898. V. 49
A Dream of John Ball. Portland: 1902. V. 48
A Dream of John Ball and a King's Lesson. London: 1888. V. 51
A Dream of John Ball and a King's Lesson. London: 1892. V. 51
Early Poems of William Morris. London: 1914. V. 47; 49; 51
The Earthly Paradise. London: 1868. V. 49
The Earthly Paradise. London: 1870. V. 50
The Earthly Paradise. 1896-97. V. 49; 51
Gothic Architecture: a Lecture for the Arts and Crafts Exhibition Society. London: 1893. V. 47; 48; 52
The Hollow Land and Other Contributions to the Oxford and Cambridge Magazine... London: 1903. V. 49
Hopes and Fears for Art. Boston: 1882. V. 50
Hopes and Fears for Art: Five Lectures. And Signs of Change: Seven Lectures. London: 1902. V. 48
Hopes and Fears for Art. Five Lectures... (with) Signs of Change. Seven Lectures. London: 1882/88. V. 51
The Inhabitants. New York: 1946. V. 50
Lectures on Art Delivered in Support of the Society for the Protection of Ancient Buildings. London: 1882. V. 47; 49
The Letters of William Morris to His Family and Friends. London: 1950. V. 54
The Life and Death of Jason. Boston: 1867. V. 49
The Life and Death Of Jason. London: 1882. V. 49
The Life and Death of Jason. Hammersmith: 1895. V. 50
Love is Enough. London: 1873 but 1872. V. 52
Love Is Enough; or, the Freeing of Pharamond. London: 1873. V. 47; 48; 53
Love Is Enough, or the Freeing of Pharamond: a Morality. 1897. V. 51; 52
Love Is Enough, or the Freeing of Pharamond: a Morality. Hammersmith: 1897. V. 47; 54
Love Is Enough, or the Freeing of Pharamond: a Morality. Hammersmith: 1897/98. V. 51; 52
News from Nowhere. London: 1891. V. 51
News from Nowhere. 1892. V. 51; 52
A Note by William Morris on His Aims in Founding the Kelmscott Press. 1898. V. 49
A Note by William Morris On His Aims in Founding the Kelmscott Press, together with a Short Description of the Press by S. C. Cockerell & an Annotated List of the Books Printed Thereat. Hammersmith: 1898. V. 54
Outlanders, Whence Come Ye Last?. New York: 1928. V. 50
The Pilgrims of Hope: a Poem in Thirteen Books. London: 1886. V. 52
Pre-Raphaelite Ballads. New York: 1900. V. 48; 49
The Roots of the Mountains. London: 1889. V. 54
The Roots of the Mountains. London: 1890. V. 47; 49
The Roots of the Mountains Wherein is Told Somewhat of the Lives of the Men of Burgdale. London: 1901. V. 51
The Saga of Hen Thorir. Cincinnati: 1903. V. 51
Signs of Change: Seven Lectures Delivered On Various Occasions. London: 1888. V. 52
Sir Galahad, a Christmas Mystery. New Rochelle: 1902. V. 49
Sir Galahad: a Christmas Mystery. New York: 1902. V. 48
Socialism, Its Growth and Outcome. London: 1893. V. 53
Socialist Diary. 1981. V. 52
Socialist Diary. Iowa City: 1981. V. 54
Some Hints on Pattern Designing. London: 1899. V. 47; 50; 51
The Story of Cupid and Psyche. London & Cambridge: 1974. V. 47
The Sundering Flood. Hammersmith: 1897. V. 51
A Tale of the House of the Wolfings and All the Kindreds of the Mark Written in Prose and In Verse. London: 1889. V. 53
A Tale of the House of Wolfings and All the Kindreds of the Mark Written in Prose and Verse by. London: 1901. V. 49; 51
Two Poems by William Morris. The Defense of Guenevere and Kign Arthur's Tomb. London: 1930. V. 51; 54
Under an Elm-Tree; or, Thoughts in the Countryside. Aberdeen: 1891. V. 49; 52
The Well at the World's End. London: 1896. V. 49; 51
The Wood Beyond the World. Hammersmith: 1894. V. 54
The Wood Beyond the World. Hammersmith: 1896. V. 54
The World of Romance. London: 1906. V. 52

MORRIS, WILLIAM, & CO.
Metal Casements, Stained Glass & Decorative Ironwork. Westminster: 1922. V. 52
Metal Casements, Stained Glass and Decorative Ironwork. 1922. V. 47

MORRIS, WILLIAM O'CONNOR
Letters on the Land Question of Ireland. London: 1870. V. 48; 50; 52

MORRIS, WILLIE
Homecomings. Jackson & London: 1989. V. 47
My Dog Skip. New York: 1995. V. 54

MORRIS, WRIGHT
About Fiction. New York: 1975. V. 51
The Cat's Meow. Los Angeles: 1975. V. 54
Collected Stories, 1948-1986. New York: 1986. V. 51
Fire Sermon. New York: 1971. V. 53
God's Country and My People. New York: 1968. V. 53
Here is Einbaum. 1973. V. 53
The Home Place. New York: 1948. V. 47; 48; 49; 51; 53
The Inhabitants. New York: 1946. V. 47; 48; 51; 52; 53; 54
The Man Who Was There. New York: 1945. V. 47; 48
The Origin of Sadness. Alabama: 1984. V. 53
Photographs and Words. Carmel: 1982. V. 53
War Games. 1972. V. 47; 48; 49; 53
War Games. Los Angeles: 1972. V. 48
War Games. 1973. V. 53
Will's Boy. New York: 1981. V. 51

MORRISON & Fourmby's General Directory of the City of Waco, 1886-87.
Galveston: 1886. V. 48

MORRISON, ALFRED
Catalogue of the Collection of Autograph Letters and Historical Documents Formed Between 1865 and 1882 by Alfred Morrison. London: 1883-92. V. 52

MORRISON, ALFRED continued
The Collection of Autograph Letters and Historial Documents: the Hamilton and Nelson Papers. 1893-94. V. 53

MORRISON, ANDREW
The City of San Antonio. St. Louis: 1891. V. 48

MORRISON, ARTHUR
A Child of the Jago. London: 1896. V. 53
Chronicles of Martin Hewitt Being the Second Series of the Adventures of Martin Hewitt: Investigation. London: 1895. V. 47; 53
The Green Diamond. Boston: 1904. V. 53; 54
Green Ginger. London: 1909. V. 51
The Painters of Japan. London: 1911. V. 50; 54
The Painters of Japan. New York: 1911. V. 52
Tales of Mean Streets. Boston: 1895. V. 49

MORRISON, CHARLES ROBERT
New Hampshire Town Officer: Containing the General Laws of 1878 (Other than School Laws) and Acts Since Passed Relating to Towns and Cities, with Decisions, Directions and Forms. Concord: 1886. V. 48

MORRISON, GOUVERNEUR
Bells: Their History and Romance. Santa Barbara: 1932. V. 53

MORRISON, HENRIETTA
My Summer in the Kitchen. Indianapolis: 1878. V. 50; 52

MORRISON, JAMES
The Elements of Book Keeping. London: 1818. V. 48
The Journal of James Morrison Boatswain's Mate of the Bounty. London: 1935. V. 52
The Journal of James Morrison Boatswain's Mate of the Bounty. Waltham St. Lawrence: 1935. V. 50

MORRISON, JIM
The Lords and the New Creatures. New York: 1970. V. 54

MORRISON, JOHN ROBERT
A Chinese Commercial Guide, Consisting of a Collection of Details and Regulations Respecting Foreign Trade with China... Macao: 1844. V. 47

MORRISON, LOIS
The Caterpillar Who is a Corps de Ballet. 1993/94. V. 53
Jardin de Guadalupe. 1994. V. 53
My Garden from Weeding Height. 1993. V. 53
Ste. Ostrich in Manhattan: the Visitations of a Martyr. Berkeley: 1990. V. 53

MORRISON, MABEL
The Quest of Joy - Fragments from Manuscripts. London: 1935. V. 52

MORRISON, RICHARD JAMES
The Grammar of Astrology. London: 1842. V. 47
The Grammar of Astrology, Containing All Things Necessary for Calculating a Nativity by Common Arithmetic. London: 1833. V. 48
The Horoscope.... Liverpool: 1834. V. 50

MORRISON, ROBERT
Horae Sinicae: Translations from the Popular Literature of the Chinese. London: 1812. V. 52
Plantarum Umbellieferarum Distributio Nova per Tabulas Cognationis et Affinitatis ex Libro Naturae Observata & Detecta. Oxford: 1672-80. V. 47

MORRISON, TONI
Beloved. New York: 1987. V. 50; 51; 52; 53
Beloved. New York: 1988. V. 53
The Bluest Eye. New York: 1970. V. 50; 53; 54
The Bluest Eye. London: 1979. V. 48; 49; 50; 51
Jazz. Franklin Center: 1992. V. 51; 53
Jazz. New York: 1992. V. 48; 49; 50; 51; 52; 53; 54
Playing in the Dark: Whiteness and the Literary Imagination. Cambridge: 1992. V. 53
Song of Solomon. New York: 1977. V. 47; 49; 50; 53; 54
Song of Solomon. London: 1978. V. 49
Sula. New York: 1972. V. 47
Sula. New York: 1973. V. 50; 54
Sula. New York: 1974. V. 49; 50; 51; 52; 53; 54
Tar Baby. London: 1981. V. 51
Tar Baby. New York: 1981. V. 47; 48; 49; 50; 51; 53; 54

MORRISON, WILLIAM B.
Military Posts and Camps in Oklahoma. Oklahoma City: 1936. V. 49

MORROW, BRADFORD
A Bestiary. New York: 1990. V. 54
A Bibliography of the Writings of Wyndham Lewis. Santa Barbara: 1978. V. 47; 50
Black Sparrow Press 1966-1978. A Bibliography. Santa Barbara: 1981. V. 50
Danae's Progress. 1982. V. 53
The New Gothic. New York: 1991. V. 51
Passing from the Provinces: Three Fragments. V. 49
Posthumes. Santa Barbara: 1982. V. 53

MORROW, FELIX
Revolution and Counter-Revolution in Spain. New York: 1938. V. 47

MORROW, PRINCE A.
Atlas of Skin and Venereal Diseases. New York: 1889. V. 51

MORROW, W. C.
A Man: His Mark. Philadelphia: 1900. V. 47

MORSE, CHARLES FESSENDEN
A Sketch of My Life Written for My Children and a Buffalo Hunt in Nebraska in 1871. Cambridge: 1927. V. 50

MORSE, EDWARD S.
Japanese Homes and Their Surroundings. Boston: 1886. V. 48; 49
Japanese Homes and Their Surroundings. New York: 1895. V. 52

MORSE, JEDIDIAH
The American Gazetteer, Exhibiting a Full Account of the Civil Divisions, Rivers, Harbors, Indian Tribes, &c. Boston: 1810. V. 53
The American Geography, or, a View of the Present Situation of the United States of America. Elizabeth Town: 1789. V. 47
The American Geography; or, a View of the Present Situation of the United States of America. London: 1792. V. 48; 51
Geography Made Easy Being an Abridgement of the American Universal Geography... Boston: 1816. V. 48; 49
A Report to the Secretary of War of the United States, On Indian Affairs, Comprising a Narrative of a Tour Performed in the Summer of 1820... New Haven: 1822. V. 48

MORSE, PETER
Jean Charlot's Prints. A Catalogue Raisonne. Honolulu: 1976. V. 47; 52
John Sloan's Prints. New Haven: 1969. V. 47; 50; 54
Popular Art: the Example of Jean Charlot. Santa Barbara: 1978. V. 47

MORSE, SAMUEL B.
Foreign Conspiracy Against the Liberties of the United States. New York: 1835. V. 54

MORSE, SAMUEL FRENCH
Time of Year, A First Book of Poems. Cummington: 1943. V. 54

MORSE, WILLARD
Howard Pyle, a Record of His Illustrations and Writings. Wilmington: 1921. V. 49

MORSE, WILLIAM INGLIS
Acadiensia Nova I and II. London: 1935. V. 53
Bliss Carman. Bibliography, Letters, Fugitive Verses and Other Data. Windham: 1941. V. 53
Catalogue of the William Inglis Morse Collection - Dalhousie University. Plaistow: 1938. V. 53
Gravestones of Acadie and Other Essays on Local History, Genealogy and Parish Records of Annapolis County, N.S. London: 1929. V. 47; 53
Nordic Trails: a Journey to Iceland, Norway, Sweden, Denmark, Germany and Czecho-slovakia. Boston: 1930. V. 53
Sicilian Days and Other Journeys Round the Mediterranean and Adriatic. Boston: 1927. V. 53

MORTENSEN, WILLIAM
Monsters and Madonas: a Book of Methods. San Francisco: 1936. V. 53

MORTIMER, ALFRED
Saint Mark's Church, Philadelphia. New York: 1909. V. 47

MORTIMER, FAVELL LEE, MRS.
The Peep of Day, Translated Into Tamil. Madras: 1852. V. 52

MORTIMER, GEORGE FERRIS W.
The Immediate Abolition of Slavery, Compatible with the Safety and Prosperity of the Colonies... Newcastle: 1833. V. 47

MORTIMER, J. R.
Forty Years' Researches in British & Saxon Burial Mounds of East Yorkshire Including Romano-British Discoveries and a Description of the Ancient Entrenchments on a Section of the Yorkshire Wolds. London & Hull: 1905. V. 47; 52; 53; 54

MORTIMER, JOHN
Answer Yes or No. London: 1950. V. 50; 52
Charade. London: 1947. V. 48; 52
Like Men Betrayed. London: 1953. V. 52
The Mail Robbers. Philadelphia: 1830. V. 50
The Narrowing Stream. London: 1954. V. 50
Regina V. Rumpole. Rumpole for the Defense and Rumple's Return. London: 1981. V. 53
Rumming Park. London: 1948. V. 52
Sketches From One to Another. London: 1960. V. 49
Will Shakespare. London: 1977. V. 52
With Love and Lizards. London: 1957. V. 48
The Wrong Side of the Park. London: 1960. V. 49; 54

MORTIMER, THOMAS
Every Man His Own Broker; or, a Guide to Exchange-Alley. London: 1762. V. 48
Every Man His Own Broker; or, a Guide to the Stock-Exchange. London: 1791. V. 51

MORTIMER, W. GOLDEN
Peru, History of Coca: "The Divine Plant" of the Incas. New York: 1901. V. 49; 52

MORTIMER, WILLIAM WILLIAMS
The History of the Hundred of Wirral, with a Sketch of the City and County of Chester. London: 1847. V. 47; 52

MORTON, A. C.
Report on the St. Lawrence and Atlantic Railroad, Its Influence on the Trade of the St. Lawrence and Statistics of the Cost and Traffic of the New York and Massachusetts Rail-Roads. Montreal: 1849. V. 52

MORTON, A. S.
Beyond the Palaeocrystic Sea or the Legend of Halfjord. Chicago: 1895. V. 48; 52

MORTON, ANNE DOUGLAS, COUNTESS OF
The Countess of Moreton's Daily Exercise; or, a Book of Prayers and Rules How to Spend Our Time in the Service and Pleasure of Almighty God. London: 1760. V. 48

MORTON, ARTHUR S.
A History of the Canadian West to 1870-1871. London. V. 53
A History of the Canadian West to 1870-71; Being a History of Rupert's Land... London: 1939. V. 48
Sir George Simpson, Overseas Governor of the Hudson's Bay Company, a Pen Picture of a man of Action. Portland: 1944. V. 51

MORTON, DESMOND
Telegrams of the North-West Campaign, 1885. Toronto: 1972. V. 52; 54

MORTON, H. V.
In the Steps of St. Paul. London: 1920. V. 50
In the Steps of the Master. London: 1934. V. 49

MORTON, JOHN
The Natural History of Northamptonshire: with Some Account of the Antiquities. London: 1712. V. 47; 48

MORTON, JOHN BINGHAM
1933 and Still Going Wrong?. 1932. V. 51

MORTON, JOHN LOCKHART
The Resources of Estates... 1858. V. 47
The Resources of Estates: Being a Treatise on the Agricultural Improvement and General Management of Landed Property. London: 1858. V. 54

MORTON, JOHN WATSON
The Artillery of Nathan Bedford Forrest's Cavalry. Nashville: 1909. V. 49

MORTON, LESLIE
Garrison and Morton's Medical Bibliography. New York: 1954. V. 51
A Medical Bibliography (Garrison & Morton). An Annotated Check-List of Texts Illustrating the History of Medicine. London: 1976. V. 51
Morton's Medical Bibliography. 1991. V. 48; 49; 50; 51; 53
Morton's Medical Bibliography. An Annotated Check-list of Texts Illustrating the History of Medicine. Aldershot: 1991. V. 47

MORTON, NATHANIEL
New England's memorial. Boston: 1826. V. 47; 50
The New England's Memorial; or, a Brief Relation of the Most Memorable and Remarkable Passaes of the Providence of God, Manifested to the Planters of New England in America... Plymouth: 1826. V. 50

MORTON, OHLAND
Teran and Texas. Austin: 1948. V. 53

MORTON, PETER
Fire Across the Desert; Woomera and the Anglo-Australian Joint Project 1946-1980. Canberra: 1989. V. 52

MORTON, RICHARD
Opera Medica, in Tres Tomos Distributa. Venice: 1696. V. 51
Phthisiologia Seu Exercitationes de Phthisi Tribus Libris Comprehendae. Londini: 1689. V. 47; 48; 49; 52
Phthisiologia Seu Exercitationes De Phthisi Tribus Libris Comprehensae. Frankfurt & Leipzig: 1691. V. 48

MORTON, RICHARD L.
The Negro in Virginia Politics, 1865-1902. Charlottesville: 1918. V. 48

MORTON, SAMUEL GEORGE
Brief Remarks on the Diversities of the Human Species, and on Some Kindred Subjects... Philadelphia: 1842. V. 50
Crania Americana: or, a Comparative View of the Skulls of Various Aboriginal Nations of North and South America... Philadelphia: 1839. V. 53
Illustrations of Pulmonary Consumption, Its Anatomical Characters, Causes, Symptoms and Treatment. Philadelphia: 1834. V. 48; 50; 54
Illustrations of Pulmonary Consumption, Its Anatomical Characters, Causes, Symptoms and Treatment... Philadelphia: 1837. V. 49
Letter to the Rev. John Bachman, D.D. on the Question of Hybridity in Animals, Considered in Reference to the Unity of the Human Species. Charleston: 1850. V. 50; 53

MORTON, THOMAS
Apologia Catholica ex meris Jesuitarum Contradictionibus Conflata (etc.). London: 1605. V. 50; 53
A Discharge of Five Imputations of Mis-Allegations, Falsely Charged Upon the Bishop of Duresme by an English Baron. London: 1633. V. 48
An Exact Account of Romish Doctrine in the Case of Conspiracy and Rebellion... London: 1679. V. 53
New English Canaan, or New Canaan. London: 1632?. V. 52

MORTON, THOMAS, BP. OF COVENTRY & LICHFIELD
Of the Institution of the Sacrament of the Blessed Bodie and Blood of Christ. London: 1631. V. 52

MORTON, THOMAS G.
The History of the Pennsylvania Hospital 1751-1895. Philadelphia: 1895. V. 50; 52

MORTON, WILLIAM T. G.
Sulphuric Ether. Thirtieth Congress - Second Session. Report No. 114. Washington: 1949. V. 52

THE MORTONS
of Bardon. A Lancashire Tale. London: 1863. V. 48; 53

MORVAN DE BELLEGARDE, JEAN BAPTISTE
Reflexions Upon Ridicule; or, What It Is that Makes a Man Ridiculous; and the Means to Avoid It. London: 1706. V. 47
Reflexions Upon Ridicule; or, What It Is That Makes a Man Ridiculous, and the means to Avoid It. London: 1717. V. 47; 49

MORYSON, FYNES
An Itinerary Containing His Ten Years Travel through the Twelve Dominions of Germany, bohmeriand, Switzerland, Netherland, Denmark, Poland, Italy, Turkey, Franco, England, Scotland and Ireland. London: 1617. V. 47; 48; 51
An Itinerary Containing His Ten Yeeres Travell through the Twelve Dominions of Germany, Bohmrland, Switzerland, Therland, Denmarke, Poland, Italy, Turkey... Glasgow: 1907-08. V. 48; 49

MOSAICS
of Haghia Sophia at Istanbul. Boston: 1950. V. 51

MOSBY, JOHN SINGLETON
The Memoirs of Colonel John S. Mosby. Boston: 1917. V. 48; 49
Mosby's War Reminiscences and Stuart's Cavalry Campaigns. Boston: 1887. V. 49
Mosby's War Reminiscences and Stuart's Cavalry Campaigns. New York: 1887. V. 49

MOSCARDO, LODOVICO
Note Overo Memorie del Museo di Lodovico Moscardo... Padua: 1656. V. 49

MOSCATI, SABATINO
Italy Before Rome. Milano: 1987. V. 50
The Phoenicians. Milan: 1988. V. 49; 52

MOSCHENI, CARLO
Brutes Turn'd Criticks, or mankind Moralized by Beasts. London: 1695. V. 47

MOSCHETTI, ALESSANDRO
Raccolta delle Principali Vedute di Roma Antica e Moderna. Rome: 1843. V. 53

MOSCHINI, VITTORIO
Canaletto. Milan: 1954. V. 51

MOSELEY, BENJAMIN
A Treatise on Sugar. London: 1800. V. 47
A Treatise on Tropical Diseases; and on the Climate of the West-Indies. London: 1788. V. 53

MOSELEY, HENRY N.
Notes by a Naturalist. New York/London: 1892. V. 47; 52; 53; 54

MOSELEY, SYDNEY A.
Television To-Day and Tomorrow. New York: 1930. V. 50; 52; 54

MOSELLY, EMILE
Charrue d'Erable. Paris: 1912. V. 50

MOSEMAN, C. M.
Illustrated Guide for Purchasers of Horse Furnishings, Goods, Novelties and Stable Appointments. New York: 1879. V. 54

MOSENTHAL, J. DE
Ostriches and Ostrich Farming. London: 1876. V. 47

MOSER, BARRY
An Alphabet. Northampton: 1986. V. 52
Death of the Narcissus: Delven Botanico-Erotic Etchings. Easthampton: 1970. V. 50
Eight Wood Engravings on a Theme of Pan. Northampton: 1980. V. 48
Engraving. Notes on the Craft. Northampton: 1979. V. 48
Fifty Wood-engravings. Northampton: 1978. V. 48; 51
Gold Rush. Twenty-Five Engravings. Los Angeles: 1985. V. 48
Goudy Greek. Easthampton: 1976. V. 48
Seven Flowers. Northampton: 1971. V. 50
Thirteen Botanical Wood Engravings. Northampton: 1974. V. 48
Twelve American Writers. Amherst: 1974. V. 51
Twelve Woodengravings of Cirsia & Various Thistles. Hancock: 1978. V. 48
The Wonderful Wizard of Oz. West Hatfield: 1985. V. 47; 51
Wood Engraving, Notes on the Craft. Northampton: 1979. V. 49

MOSER, GEORGE
A Family Letter Written in Nineteen Thirty-Two by George Moser to His Nephew Arthur Moser. Easthampton: 1979. V. 48; 51

MOSER, J. F.
The Salmon and Salmon Fisheries of Alaska. Washington: 1899. V. 50; 51
The Salmon and Salmon Fisheries of Alaska... Washington: 1902. V. 52

MOSER, JOSEPH
The Adventures of Timothy Twig, Esq. in a Series of Poetical Epistles. London: 1794. V. 47; 49

MOSER, LOUIS
The Caucasus and Its People, with a Brief History of Their Wars and a Sketch of the Achievements of the Renowned Chief Schamyl. London: 1856. V. 48

MOSES, ANNA MARY ROBERTSON
Grandma Moses. My Life's History. New York: 1952. V. 47; 49
My Life's History. New York: 1952. V. 50

MOSES, HENRY
A Collection of Antique Vases, Altars, Paterae, Tripods, Candelabra, Sarcophagi, &C., from Various Museums & Collections. London: 1814. V. 50
Designs of Modern Costume, &c. London: 1823. V. 51
Sketches in Outline. London: 1808. V. 54

MOSES, MICHAEL
Master Craftsmen of Newport: the Townsends and Godards. Tenafly: 1984. V. 47

MOSES, WILLIAM S.
Address Delivered Before the Fraternity of Free and Accepted Masons of Jacksonville, Oregon, June 24, 1859. Yreka: 1859. V. 53

MOSHEIM, JOHANN LORENZ
An Ecclesiastical History, Ancient and Modern, from the Birth of Christ to the Beginning of the Eighteenth Century. Edinburgh: 1819. V. 47; 50
An Ecclesiastical History, Ancient and Modern, From the Birth of Christ, to the Beginning of the Present Century... London: 1765. V. 47

MOSHER, HOWARD FRANK
Disapearances. New York: 1977. V. 51; 53
Marie Blythe. New York: 1983. V. 51
Where the Rivers Flow North. New York: 1978. V. 51

MOSHER PRESS
The Mosher Books. Portland: 1910. V. 48

MOSHER, THOMAS BIRD
The Bibleot. New York: 1925. V. 47
The Mosher Books. Portland: 1913. V. 54

MOSIN, VLADIMIR
Anchor Watermarks. Amsterdam: 1973. V. 53

MOSLEY, NICHOLAS
Catastrophe Practice. London: 1979. V. 48

MOSLEY, OSWALD
The Greater Britain. London: 1933. V. 53
The Natural History of Tutbury, Together with the Fauna and Flora of the District Surrounding Turbury and Hurton on Trent. London: 1863. V. 52

MOSLEY, SETH LISTER
A History of British Birds, Their Nests and Eggs. Huddersfield: 1881-92. V. 50

MOSLEY, WALTER
Devil in a Blue Dress. New York: 1990. V. 49; 51; 52; 53; 54
Devil in the Blue Dress/ A Red Earth/ White Butterfly. New York: 1990-92. V. 47
A Red Death. New York: 1991. V. 52; 53; 54
White Butterfly. New York: 1992. V. 51; 52; 53; 54

MOSS, ARTHUR B.
The Workman's Foe (and) Paul the Rebel. London: 1895. V. 51

MOSS, FLETCHER
Pilgrimages to Old Homes. Manchester: 1920. V. 53

MOSS, FREDERICK JOSEPH
A Month in Fiji. Melbourne: 1868. V. 49

MOSS, HOWARD
Instant Lives. New York: 1974. V. 49; 50; 51; 53

MOSS, JAMES A.
Memories of the Campaign of Santiago. San Francisco: 1899. V. 52

MOSS, ROSALIND
The Life After Death in Oceania and the Malay Archipelago. Oxford: 1925. V. 52

MOSS, THOMAS
The Imperfections of Human Enjoyments. London? Birmingham?: 1783. V. 50; 54
Poems on Several Occasions. Wolverhampton: 1769. V. 50; 54
A Treatise of Gauging. London: 1765. V. 48

MOSSE, A. H. E.
My Somali Book: a Record of Two Shooting Trips. London: 1913. V. 47; 54

MOSSMAN, SAMUEL
The Gold Regions of Australia: a Descriptive Account of New South Wales, Victoria and South Australia. London: 1852. V. 48

MOSSO, ANGELO
Fatigue. London: 1906. V. 47

MOSSOM, ROBERT
The King on His Throne; or a Discourse Maintaining the Dignity of a King, the Dusty of a Subject and the Unlawfulnesse of Rebellion. (with) A True Relation of the Queen's Majesties Return Out of Holland... York: 1642/43. V. 50

MOTELAMBERT, COUNT DE
The Monks of the West from St. Benedict to St. Bernard. 1861-79. V. 52

MOTHER GOOSE
Denslow's Mother Goose. London: 1902. V. 47
Denslow's Mother Goose A.B.C. Book. New York: 1904. V. 52; 54
The Fanny Cory Mother Goose. New York: 1913. V. 53
The Gay Mother Goose. New York: 1938. V. 49
Histories, or Tales of Past Times Told by Mother Goose, with Morals. London: 1925. V. 49
The Jessie Willcox Mother Goose. New York: 1914. V. 47
The Jolly Jump-Ups Mother Goose Book. Springfield: 1944. V. 49
The Little Mother Goose. New York: 1918. V. 50
Mother Goose. London: 1818. V. 54
Mother Goose. London: 1913. V. 49; 52
Mother Goose. Chicago: 1915. V. 47; 49
Mother Goose. Philadelphia: 1915. V. 49
Mother Goose. London: 1920. V. 49
Mother Goose. London: 1925. V. 49
Mother Goose. New York: 1928. V. 49
Mother Goose. London: 1930. V. 49
Mother Goose. Akron: 1933. V. 53
Mother Goose. New York: 1934. V. 54
Mother Goose. New York: 1938. V. 49
Mother Goose. Portland: 1987. V. 52
Mother Goose: A Unique Version. New York: 1942. V. 50
Mother Goose for Grown Folks. New York: 1860. V. 54
Mother Goose Gems Illustrated in Color by S. Noble Ives. New York: 1911. V. 50
Mother Goose: Her Best Known Rhymes. Akron: 1933. V. 49
Mother Goose in Hieroglyphics. Part First. Syracuse: 1853. V. 53
Mother Goose in Washington. Harrisburg: 1936. V. 51; 52
Mother Goose Melodies. Philadelphia: 1870. V. 50
Mother Goose Nursery Tales. London. V. 52
Mother Goose or the Old Nursery Rhymes. London. V. 51
Mother Goose or the Old Nursery Rhymes. London and New York: 1881. V. 47; 50
Mother Goose Rhymes. London: 1910. V. 49
Mother Goose Rhymes. New York: 1940. V. 49
Mother Goose Rhymes. Chicago: 1942. V. 50
Mother Goose Rhymnes, Chimes & Jingles. New York: 1901. V. 48
Mother Goose: Seventy-Seven Verses with Pictures by Tasha Tudor. New York: 1944. V. 49
Mother Goose The Old Nursery Rhymes. London: 1913. V. 47; 48; 49; 51; 53
Mother Goose. The Old Nursery Rhymes. London: 1949. V. 50
Mother Goose's ABC. New York: 1900. V. 53
Mother Goose's Bicycle Tour. Toronto: 1900. V. 50
Mother Goose's Chimes, Rhymes and Jingles. New York: 1880. V. 54
Mother Goose's Melodies. Philadelhia: 1870's. V. 50
Mother Goose's Nursery Rhymes. London: 1928. V. 50
Mother Goose's Nursery Rhymes. New York: 1930. V. 54
Mother Goose's Rag Book. London: 1920. V. 48; 49; 54
The Old Mother Goose Nursery Rhyme Book. New York: 1926. V. 53
Old Mother Goose's Rhymes and Tales. New York: 1889. V. 49
The Pop-Up Mother Goose. New York: 1934. V. 54
Willy Pogany's Mother Goose. New York: 1928. V. 47
Willy Pogany's Mother Goose. London: 1929. V. 48

MOTHER Hubbard and Her Dog. Edinburgh: 1870. V. 49

MOTHER Hubbard's Grand Party. London: 1873?. V. 52

MOTHERBY, G.
A New Medical Dictionary; or, General Repository of Physic. London: 1775. V. 50
A New Medical Dictionary; or, General Repository of Physic. London: 1785. V. 54

MOTHERHILL, JOHN
The Trial of John Motherhill, for Committing a Rape on the Body of Miss Catharine Wade. Tried at the Assize Holden at East Grinstead for the County of Sussex...Before the Hon. Sir William Henry Ashhurst (etc.). London: 1786. V. 47

MOTHERLY, MRS.
Nursery Poetry. London: 1859. V. 49

THE MOTHER'S Assistant and Young Lady's Friend. Boston: 1850. V. 48

THE MOTHER'S Hymn Book. New York: 1836. V. 51

MOTHER'S Little Rhyme Book. London. V. 47

MOTHERWELL, ROBERT
Dada Painters and Poets: an Anthology. 1951. V. 50
The Dada Painters and Poets: an Anthology. New York: 1951. V. 48
The Dada Painters and Poets: an Anthology. Boston: 1981. V. 50
From Baudelaire to Surrealism. 1950. V. 50
Reconciliation Elegy. Geneve: 1980. V. 51

MOTHERWELL, WILLIAM
Minstrelsy: Ancient and Modern, with an Historical Introduction and Notes. Glasgow: 1827. V. 48; 49; 50
Renfrewshire Characters and Scenery: a Poem... Paisley: 1824. V. 50; 54

MOTION, ANDREW
Goodnestone. London: 1972. V. 53

MOTLEY, JOHN LOTHROP
The Complete Works of John Lothrop Motley. New York: 1900. V. 47; 48; 50
History of the Netherlands. New York: 1861-68. V. 50
History of the Netherlands. (with) The Rise of the Dutch Republic. (with) John of Barneveld. New York: 1869-74. V. 50
History of the United Netherlands. New York: 1861-68. V. 54
History of the United Netherlands; from the Death of William the Silent to the Twelve Year's Truce - 1609. London: 1875. V. 54
The Rise of the Dutch Republic. New York. V. 48
The Rise of the Dutch Republic. London: 1856. V. 51
The Rise of the Dutch Republic. New York: 1856. V. 51; 53
The Rise of the Dutch Republic. New York: 1857. V. 50
The Rise of the Dutch Republic. New York: 1860. V. 49
The Rise of the Dutch Republic. London: 1886. V. 51
The Writings of John Lothrop Motley. New York: 1900. V. 49

MOTLEY, WILLARD
Let No Man White My Epitaph. New York: 1958. V. 50

MOTOR Mania. London: 1921. V. 53

MOTT, ABIGAIL FIELD
Narratives of Colored Americans. New York: 1875. V. 50
Narratives of Colored Americans. New York: 1882. V. 50

MOTT, FRANK LUTHER
A History of American Magazines 1741-1885. New York: 1938. V. 51; 54
A History of Amrican Magazines, 1741-1850 (1850-1865, 1865-1885). New York: 1930-38. V. 47

MOTT, FREDERICK
The Degeneration of the Neurone. London: 1900. V. 47

MOTT IRON WORKS
Stable Fittings, Cow House and Piggery Fittings, Catalogue S. of the J. L. Mott Iron Works, Fifth Ave. & 17th St., new York;. New York: 1910. V. 48; 52

MOTT, JAMES
Observations on the Education of Children; and Hints to Young people, on the Duties of Civil Life. New York printed: 1822. V. 48

MOTT, LAWRENCE
Jules of the Great Heart. London: 1905. V. 48

MOTT, LUCRETIA
A Sermon to th Medical Students...at Cherry Street Meeting, Philadelphia, on First-Day Evning, Second Month 11th, 1849. Philadelphia: 1849. V. 48

MOTT, VALENTINE
Eulogy on the Late John W. Francis, Being a Discourse on His Life and Character. New York: 1861. V. 52
Narrative of Privations and Sufferings of United States Officers and Soldiers While Prisoners of War in the Hands of the Rebel Authorities. Philadelphia: 1864. V. 52
Travels in Europe and the East. New York: 1842. V. 49; 50

MOTTELAY, PAUL FLEURY
Bibliographical History of Electricity and Magnetism Chronologically Arranged. New York: 1991. V. 49
Bibliographical History of Electricity and Magnetism...Researches into the Domain of the Early Sciences. New York: 1992. V. 50; 52; 54

MOTTEUX, PIERRE ANTOINE
Love's Triumph: an Opera. London: 1708. V. 48

MOTTLEY, JOHN
Joe Miller's Jests; or, the Wits Vade-Mecum... London: 1743. V. 50
A Survey of the Cities of London and Westminster, Borough of Southwark and Parts Adjacent... London: 1734-35. V. 50

MOTTRAM, J. C.
Fly-Fishing: Some New Arts and Mysteries. London: 1915. V. 53

MOTTRAM, RALPH HALE
The Crime at Vanderlynden's. London: 1926. V. 47; 50; 51
Journey to the Western Front - Twenty Years After. London: 1936. V. 52
Repose and Other Verses. London: 1907. V. 48
The Spanish Farm. London: 1924. V. 47
The Spanish Farm Trilogy - 1914-1918. London: 1927. V. 47
Strawberry Time and the Banquet. London: 1934. V. 47; 50
Strawberry Time and The Banquet. Waltham St. Lawrence: 1934. V. 51; 54

MOUAT, FREDERIC JOHN
Adventures and Researches Among the Andaman Islanders. London: 1863. V. 51

MOUBRAY, BONINGTON
A Practical Treatise on Breeding, Rearing and Fattening All Kinds of Domestic Poultry, Pheasants and Rabbits... London: 1816. V. 52
A Practical Treatise on Breeding, Rearing and Fattening All Kinds of Domestic Poultry, Pheasants, Pigeons and Rabbits... London: 1822. V. 50
A Practical Treatise on Breeding, Rearing and Fattening All Kinds of Domestic Poultry, Pheasants, Pigeons, and Rabbits... London: 1830. V. 50

MOUDGIL, K. R.
Architectural Design (Classic and Indian). Delhi: 1964. V. 49

MOUHOT, HENRI
Travels in the Central Parts of Indo-China (Siam), Cambodia and Laos During the Years 1858, 1859 and 1860. London: 1864. V. 54

MOULE, THOMAS
Bibliotheca Heraldica Magnae Britanniae. London: 1966. V. 49
Great Britain Illustrated. London: 1830. V. 53

MOULT, THOMAS
The Best Poems of 1935. New York: 1935. V. 51
The Best Poems of 1936. New York: 1936. V. 51

MOULTON, LOUISE CHANDLER
Arthur O'Shaughnessy. London: 1894. V. 49

MOULTRIE, JOHN
Poems... London: 1837. V. 47

MOULTRIE, WILLIAM
Memoirs of the American Revolution, So Far As Is Related to the States of North and South Carolina, and Georgia. New York: 1802. V. 48
The Moultrie-Montague Letters 1781. Walhalla: 1904. V. 48

MOUNSEY, GEORGE G.
Authentic Account of the Occupation of Carlisle in 1745 by Prince Charles Edward Stuart. London: 1846. V. 49; 50; 52; 53

MOUNTAGU, RICHARD
Appello Caesarem. A Just Appeale from Two Unjust Informers. London: 1625. V. 52

MOUNTAIN, GEORGE JEHOSHAPHAT
A Journal of Visitation to Parts of the Diocese of Quebec, by the Lord Bishop of Montreal in 1843 and 1844, Part II. (with) A Journal of Vistitation in a Portion of the Diocese of Quebec by the Lord Bishop of Montreal, Part III. London: 1845/47. V. 49
The Journey of the Bishop of Montreal, During a Visit to the Church Missionary Society's North West America Mission. London: 1845. V. 48; 53

MOUNTAIN, JAMES
The History of Selby, Ancient and Modern... York: 1800. V. 50; 54

MOUNTAINE, WILLIAM
The Seaman's Vade-Mecum and Defensive War by Sea... London: 1757. V. 52

MOUNTBATTEN, LOUIS MOUNTBATTEN, EARL OF
An Introduction to Polo. London: 1931. V. 47

MOUNT EDGCUMBE, RICHARD EDGCUMBE, EARL OF
Muscial Reminiscences, Containing an Account of the Italian Opera in England, from 1773. London: 1834. V. 52
Musical Reminiscences Chiefly Respecting the Italian Opera in England from the Year 1773 to the Present Time. London: 1828. V. 47
Musical Reminiscences of an Old Amateur Chiefly Respecting the Italian Opera in England for Fifty Years, from 1773 to 1823. London: 1827. V. 47

MOUNTENEY-JEPHSON, A. J.
Emin Pasha and the Rebellion at the Equator... London: 1890. V. 47; 50; 52
Emin Pasha and the Rebellion at the Equator. New York: 1890. V. 48; 52

MOUNTFORD, C.
Records of the American Australian Scientific Expedition to Arnhem Land. Melbourne: 1956-64. V. 48; 51

MOUNTFORD, CHARLES P.
Ayers Rock: Its People, Their Beliefs and Their Art. Sydney: 1965. V. 52
Nomads of the Australian Desert. Rigby: 1976. V. 52
The Tiwi Their Art, Myth and Ceremony. London: 1958. V. 52

MOUNTFORD, WILLIAM
Henry the Second, King of England; with the Death of Roasmund. London: 1693. V. 47
Martyria: a Legend. Boston: 1846. V. 48

MOUNTFORT, WILLIAM
Six Plays...To which is Prefix'd Some Memoirs of the Life of Mr. Mountfort. London: 1720. V. 54

MOUNTMORRES, HERVEY REDMOND MORRES, 2ND VISCOUNT
The Crisis. London: 1794. V. 51

MOUNTNORRIS, GEORGE ANNESLEY, 2ND EARL OF
Voyages and Travels to India, Ceylon, the Red Sea, Abyssinia, and Egypt, in the Years 1802, 1803, 1804, 1805 and 1806. London: 1809. V. 51

MOURELLE, DON FRANCISCO ANTONIO
Voyage of the Sonora in the Second Bucareli Expedition to Explore the Northwest Coast, Survey the Port of San Francisco and Found Franciscan Missions... San Francisco;: 1920. V. 49; 52; 54

MOURIKIS, DOULA
The Mosaics of the Nea Moni of Chios. Athens: 1985. V. 49

MOURLOT, FERNAND
Art in Posters. The Complete Original Posters of Braque, Chagall, dufy, Leger, Matisse, Miro, Picasso. Monte Carlo/New York: 1959. V. 50
Joan Miro: Litografo I. Barcelona: 1972. V. 50
The Lithographs of Chagall. Monte Carlo: 1960. V. 54
The Lithographs of Marc Chagall. Volume II: 1957-62. Monte Carlo: 1963. V. 50
The Lithographs of Marc Chagall. Volume III: 1962-1968. Boston: 1969. V. 50
Picasso Lithographs. Boston: 1970. V. 47

MOURNFUL Tragedy or, The Death of Jacob Webb, David Morrow, John Harris, Henry Lewis, David Hunt and Edward Lindsay, Six Militia Men Who Were Condemned... By Major General Jackson, and by His order the Whole Six Shot. Boston: 1828. V. 48

MOUSA, SULEIMAN
T. E. Lawrence: an Arab View. London: 1966. V. 53

THE MOUSE'S Wedding. Tokyo: 1888. V. 50
THE MOUSE'S Wedding. Tokyo: 1926. V. 53

MOUSSA, AHMED M.
The Tomb of Nefer and Ka-hey. Mainz am Rheim: 1971. V. 51

MOUTON, GABRIEL
Observations Diametrorum Solis et Lunae Apparentium Meridianarumque Aliquot Altitudinum Solis & Paucarum Fixarum. Lyons: 1670. V. 47

MOVING Picture Dolls. Chicago: 1907. V. 49

MOVING Picture Teddies. Chicago: 1907. V. 49

MOVIUS, HALLAM L.
the Irish Stone Age: Its Chronology, Development and Relationships. Cambridge: 1942. V. 47

MOWAT, FARLEY
Never Cry Wolf. Toronto: 1963. V. 47; 50; 52; 53
Wake of the Great Sealers. Toronto: 1973. V. 52; 53
A Whale for the Killing. Toronto: 1972. V. 52

MOWAT, J. L. G.
Alphita. Oxford: 1887. V. 49

MOWATT, ANNA CORA
Autobiography of an Actress, or, Eight Years on the Stage. Boston: 1854. V. 48

MOWER, ARTHUR
The White Cottage, a Tale. Edinburgh: 1817. V. 54
Zulneida: a Tale of Sicily. London: 1837. V. 47; 52

MOWRIS, JAMES A.
A History of the One Hundred and Seventeenth Regiment N.Y. Volunteers. (Fourth Oneida). Hartford: 1866. V. 47

MOWRY, SYLVESTER
Arizona and Sonora: the Geography, History and Resources of the Sivler Region of North America. New York: 1864. V. 53

MOXON, JOSEPH
Mechanick Exercises on the Whole Art of Printing (1683-84). Oxford: 1958. V. 52
Mechanick Exercises on the Whole Art of Printing (1683-84). London: 1962. V. 49
Mechanick Exercises, or the Doctrine of Handy Works. London: 1677-83. V. 54
Practical Perspective or Perspective Made Easie. London: 1670. V. 47; 49
A Tutor to Astronomy and Geographie... London: 1659. V. 50
A Tutor to Astronomy and Geography. London: 1674. V. 48
A Tutor to Astronomy and Geography. London: 1686. V. 54

MOYER, JOHN W.
Trophy Heads. New York: 1962. V. 48

MOYLLUS, DAMIANUS
A Newly Discovered Treatise on Classic Letter Design Printed at Parma by Damianus Moyllus Circa 1480. 1923. V. 52
A Newly Discovered Treatise on Classic Letter Design Printed at Parma by Daminaus Moyllus Circa 1480. 1927. V. 49; 51; 54

MOYNIHAN, B.
Duodenal Ulcer. Philadelphia: 1910. V. 54
The Spleen and Some of Its Diseases. London: 1921. V. 54

MOYNIHAN, BERKELEY
Abdominal Operations. Philadelphia: 1914. V. 54
Duodenal Ulcer. Philadelphia and London: 1910. V. 51

MOYSEY, ABEL
The Confederates: a Story. London: 1823. V. 50

MOZART, WOLFGANG AMADEUS
The Letters (1764-1791). London: 1865. V. 49
The Letters of Mozart and His Family. London: 1938. V. 50
The Letters of Mozart and His Family... London New York: 1966. V. 48

MOZEEN, THOMAS
Young Scarron. London: 1752. V. 54

MOZLEY, CHARLES
Concerning Ulysses and the Bodley Head. London: 1960. V. 51
Concerning Ulysses and the Bodley Head. London: 1961. V. 47

MOZLEY, HARRIET
The Lost Brooch, or the History of Another Month. London: 1841. V. 50

MOZLEY, JAMES B.
Essays Historical and Theological. London: 1878. V. 49

MPHAHLELE, EZEKIEL
The Wanderers. New York: 1971. V. 51

MR. *Campbell's Packet. For the Entertainment of Gentlemen and Ladies.* London: 1720. V. 48

MR. *Dyce Sombre's Refutation of the Charge of Lunacy Brought Against Him in the Court of Chancery.* Paris: 1849. V. 53

MRABET, MOHAMMED
The Beach Cafe and the Voice. Santa Barbara: 1980. V. 52
The Big Mirror. Santa Barbara: 1977. V. 48; 51; 53
The Boy Who Set the Fire. Los Angeles: 1974. V. 53
Harmless Poisons, Blameless sins. Santa Barbara: 1976. V. 48; 51; 52; 53
Love With a Few Hairs. London: 1967. V. 50; 53
Marriage with Papers. Bolinas: 1986. V. 51

MUCHA, J.
Alphonse Mucha, The Master of Art Nouveau. Prague: 1967. V. 50; 51

MUCKLE, HUGH
Tetecan: an Aztec Tragedy. San Francisco: 1950. V. 47; 49

MUDD, RICHARD D.
The Mudd Family of the United States. 1977. V. 54

MUDFORD, WILLIAM
A Critical Enquiry into the Moral Writings of Dr. Samuel Johnson. London: 1802. V. 54
The Five Nights of St. Albans. Edinburgh: 1829. V. 54
The Five Nights of St. Albans. London: 1835. V. 51
The Life and Adventures of Paul Plaintive, Esq. an Author. London: 1811. V. 51

MUDGE, THOMAS
A Description, with Plates, of the Time-Keeper Invented By the Late Mr. Thomas Mudge. London: 1799. V. 53

MUDIE, ALEXANDER
Scotiae Indiculum: or the Present State of Scotland, Together with Divers Reflections Upon the Antient State Thereof. London: 1682. V. 50

MUDIE, ROBERT
The Feathered Tribes of the British Islands. London: 1834. V. 47; 49
The Feathered Tribes of the British Islands. London: 1841. V. 47; 48; 51
The Feathered Tribes of the British Islands. London: 1853. V. 48; 52; 54
Glenfergus. Edinburgh: 1820. V. 50
Mental Philosophy: a Popular View of the Nature, Immortality, Phenomena, and Conduct of the Human Mind. London: 1838. V. 50
The Modern Athens: a Dissection and Demonstration of Men and Things in the Scotch Capital. London: 1825. V. 54
The Picture of Australia: Exhibiting New Holland, Van Dieman's Land, and All the Settlements from the First at Sydney to the Last at the Swan River. London: 1829. V. 54
The Seasons. London: 1837. V. 54
A Second Judgment of Babylon the Great; or More Men and Things in the British Capital. London: 1829. V. 50

MUDWINKLE, H. J.
A Study of Dinosaurs on the Comparative Method of Comparative Dionsaurs for Students, Amateurs and Breeders... Andoversford and Fullerton: 1988. V. 47

MUELLER, A. H.
Atlas of the City of Newark, New Jersey... Philadelphia: 1912. V. 49

MUELLER, F.
Facts and Arguments for Darwin. London: 1869. V. 50

MUELLER, F. VON
Iconography of Australian Species of Acacia and Cognate Gener. Melbourne: 1887-88. V. 47; 48
The Native Plants of Victoria, Succinctly Defined. Melbourne: 1879. V. 49

MUELLER, FRIEDRICH MAX
Suggestions for the Assitance of Officers in Learning the Languages of the Seat of the War in the East. London: 1854. V. 49

MUELLER, GERHARD FRIEDRICH
Voyages from Asia to America, for Completing the Discoveries of the North West Coast of America. London: 1761. V. 50

MUELLER, HANS ALEXANDER
Woodcuts and Wood Engravings: How I Make Them. New York: 1939. V. 47; 49; 53; 54

MUELLER, JOHANN SEBASTIEN
Illustratio Systematis Sexualis Linnaei... London: 1777. V. 48

MUENSCHER, W. C.
Garden Spice and Wild Pot-Herbs. Ithaca: 1954. V. 51; 52; 54

MUENSTER, SEBASTIAN
A Brief Collection and Compendious Extract of Strange and Memorable Things, Gathered Out of the Cosmographye of Sebastian Munster. London: 1574. V. 47
Der Horologien, Oder Sonnen Uhren, Kunstliche Beschreibung... Basel: 1579. V. 48; 52; 54

MUENTZ, J. H.
Encaustic: or, a Count Caylus's Method of Painting in the Manner of the Ancients. London: 1760. V. 47; 52

MUFFETT, THOMAS
Healths Improvement: or, Rules Comprizing and Discovering the Nature, Method and Manner of Preparing All Sorts of Food Used in this Nation. London: 1655. V. 49

MUGGE, THEODORE
Switzerland in 1847: and Its Condition, Political, Social, Moral and Physical, Before the War. London: 1848. V. 50

MUGGERIDGE, MALCOLM
The Thirties: 1930-40 in Great Britain 1940. London: 1940. V. 50

MUHAMMAD KHUDAVAND, KADIRI
The Tooti Nameh, or Tales of a Parrot, in the Persian Langauge... London: 1801. V. 48

MUHAMMED, ABDUL-QADER
The Development of the Funerary Beliefs and Practices Displayed in the Private Tombs of the New Kingdom at Thebes. Cairo: 1966. V. 49

MUHLBACH, LOUISA
Historical Romances. New York & London: 1898. V. 49; 50

MUILMAN, TERESA CONSTANTIA PHILLIPS
An Apology for the Conduct of Mrs. T. C. Phillips, More Particularly that Part of It Which Relates to Her Marriage to an Eminent Dutch Merchant. London: 1750. V. 48

MUIR, EDWIN
Collected Poem - 1921-1958. London: 1960. V. 50
First Poems. London: 1925. V. 50; 51; 52
Journeys and Places. London: 1937. V. 50
Latitudes. 1924. V. 49
The Marionette. London: 1927. V. 53
Selected Letters of Edwin Muir. London: 1974. V. 50
The Three Brothers. London: 1951. V. 52
We Moderns: Enigmas and Guesses. London: 1918. V. 47

MUIR, JOHN
Catalogue of Books in the Library of the Faculty of Procurators in Glasgow. (and) Supplement to the Catalogue of Books. Glasgow: 1903/23. V. 52
The Cruise of the Corwin. Boston: 1917. V. 47; 48; 50; 52; 53; 54

MUIR, JOHN continued
John of the Mountains: The Unpublished Journals of John Muir. Boston: 1938. V. 48
The Mountains of California. New York: 1913. V. 51
The Mountains of California. New York: 1917. V. 51
My First Summer in the Sierra. Boston: 1911. V. 48; 49; 54
My First Summer in the Sierra. Covelo: 1988. V. 47; 51
Our National Parks. Boston: 1901. V. 53
Picturesque California... New York and San Francisco: 1888. V. 47; 49; 53
Steep Trails. Boston: 1918. V. 51
Stickeen. Boston & New York: 1910. V. 53
A Thousand Mile Walk to the Gulf. Boston: 1916. V. 47; 48; 50
Travels in Alaska. Boston: 1915. V. 47
The Writings of John Muir. Boston & New York: 1916-24. V. 53
The Yosemite. New York: 1912. V. 53
Yosemite and the Sierra Nevada. Boston: 1948. V. 47

MUIR, M. M. PATTISON
The Elements of Thermal Chemistry... London: 1885. V. 50
A History of Chemical Theorie and Laws. New York: 1907. V. 49

MUIR, MARCIE
A Bibliography of Australian Children's Books. London: 1970/76. V. 49

MUIR, PERCY H.
Catnachery. San Francisco: 1955. V. 48; 51; 52
English Children's Books 1600 to 1900. London: 1954. V. 52; 54
English Children's Books 1600-1900. New York: 1954. V. 49; 51
Points 1874-1930. London: 1931. V. 47; 48; 50
Points 1874-1930, Being Extracts from a Bibliographer's Note-Book. Together with: Points Second Series 1866-1934. London: 1931/34. V. 49; 50
Points: Second Series 1866-1934. London: 1934. V. 47; 48; 50; 53
Victorian Illustrated Books. New York: 1971. V. 49

MUIR, R. CUTHBERTSON
The Early Political and Military History of Burford. Quebec: 1913. V. 53

MUIR, THOMAS
Contributions to the History of Determinants 1900-1920. London: 1930. V. 49
The Theory of Determinants in the Historical Order of Development (up to 1900). (and) Contributions to the History of Determinants 1900-1920. London: 1906-30. V. 49
The Theory of Determinants in the Historical Order of Its Development, Part I. London: 1906. V. 52
The Theory of Determinants in the Historical Order of Its Development. Volume II 1841-1860. London: 1911. V. 52

MUIR, WILLIAM
The Mameluke or Slave Dynasty of Egypt 1260-1517 A.D. London: 1896. V. 48

MUIRHEAD, ARNOLD
Grace Revere Osler. A Brief Memoir. 1931. V. 47; 49; 50; 52
Grace Revere Osler, a Brief Memoir. London: 1931. V. 48; 51; 52

MUIRHEAD, GEORGE
The Birds of Berwickshire, with Remarks on Their Local Distribution, Migration and Habits... Edinburgh: 1889. V. 49; 51; 52; 54
The Birds of Berwickshire with Remarks on Their Local Distribution, Migration and Habits and Also on the Folklore, Proverbs, Popular Rhymes and Sayings Connected With Them. London: 1889-95. V. 50

MUIRHEAD, JAMES FULLARTON
American the Land of Contrasts: a Briton's View of His American Kin. London: 1907. V. 47

MUIRHEAD, JAMES PATRICK
The Origin and Progress of the Mechanical Inventions of James Watt... London: 1854. V. 48; 54

MUKERJI, DHAN GOPAL
Gay-Neck; the Story of a Pigeon. New York: 1928. V. 52

MUKHERJEE, BHARATI
The Tiger's Daughter. Boston: 1971. V. 49; 50
Tiger's Daughter. Boston: 1972. V. 49; 51

MUKHOPADHYAYA, GIRANDRANATH
History of Indian Medicine... Calcutta: 1923-29. V. 49

MULAS, UGO
New York: the New Art Scene. New York: 1967. V. 51

MULBACH, LOUISA
Historical Romances. New York and London: 1898. V. 52

MULDER, G. J.
The Chemistry of Wine. London: 1857. V. 50

MULDOON, PAUL
Out of Siberia. 1982. V. 48; 50

MULERIUS, NICOLAUS
Tabulae Frisciae Lunae - Solares. Alkmaar: 1611. V. 50; 53

MULFORD, CLARENCE E.
Bar 20 Days. Chicago: 1911. V. 48
Black Buttes. Garden City: 1923. V. 51
The Coming of Cassidy. Chicago: 1913. V. 47
Hopalong Cassidy. Chicago: 1910. V. 52

MULFORD, ISAAC S.
A Civil and Political History of New Jersey... Philadelphia: 1851. V. 50

MULFORD, PRENTICE
Prentice Mulford's Story. Life By Land and Sea. New York: 1889. V. 49

MULGRAVE, CONSTANTINE JOHN PHIPPS, 2ND BARON
A Voyage Toards the North Pole. London: 1774. V. 47; 48; 49; 50; 52

MULHOLLAND, ROSA
A Fairy Tale. London: 1874. V. 51
The Little Flower Seekers. London: 1885. V. 48

MULINARI, STEFANO
Disegni Originali d'Eccelenti Pittori Esistenti Nella Real Galleria di Firenze... Florence: 1774. V. 49

MULJI, KARSANDAS
History of the Sect of Maha-ra'jas, or Vallabha 'Cha'ryas in Western India. London: 1865. V. 52

MULLALLA, JAMES
A View of Irish Affairs Since the Revolution of 1688, to the Close of the Parliamentary Session of 1795... Dublin: 1795. V. 48

MULLAN, JOHN
Miners and Travelers' Guide to Oregon, Washington, Idaho, Montana, Wyoming & Colorado. Via the Missouri and Columbia Rivers. New York: 1865. V. 47
Report on the Construction of Miliary Road from Fort Walla-Walla to Fort Benton. Washington: 1863. V. 47

MULLEN, STANLEY
Kinsmen of the Dragon. 1951. V. 47; 52
Kinsmen of the Dragon. Chicago: 1951. V. 47

MULLENS, W. H.
A Bibliography of British Ornithology, from the Earliest Times to the End of 1912. London: 1916-17. V. 49; 52; 53

MULLER, ALIX J.
History of the Police and Fire Departments of the Twin Cities. Minneapolis: 1889. V. 50

MULLER, DAN
My Life with Buffalo Bill. Chicago: 1948. V. 47

MULLER, H.
The Fertilisation of Flowers. London: 1883. V. 50

MULLER, JOHN
Indian Tables for the Conversion of Indian Mun Into Factory and Bazar Maunds, Madras and Bombay.... Calcutta: 1836. V. 51
A Treatise Containing the Elementary Part of Fortification, Regular and Irregular. London: 1746. V. 47
A Treatise Containing the Elementary Part of Fortification, Regular and Irregular. London: 1799. V. 48; 51

MULLER, JOSEPH EMILE
Petite Encyclopedie de L'Art. Klee (Picasso, Bonnard, Matisse). Paris: 1956-71. V. 52

MULLER, PRISCILLA E.
Jewels in Spain 1500-1800. New York: 1972. V. 49

MULLER, W. MAX
Egyptological Researches. Volume III: Bilingual Decrees of Philade. Washington: 1920. V. 49; 51

MULLGARADT, LOUIS CHRISTIAN
Monastery of the Visitation of the Blessed Virgin Mary. San Francisco: 1919. V. 51

MULLINGER, JAMES BASS
The University of Cambridge. London: 1873-1911. V. 47

MULSO, THOMAS
Callistus; or, the Man of Fashion. London: 1768. V. 47

MULTILINGUAL Illustrated Dictionary of Aquatic Animals and Plants. London: 1993. V. 50

THE MULTUM in Parvo Recipe Book. Albany: 1860. V. 54

MULVANEY, CHARLES PELHAM
The History of the North-West Rebellion of 1885. Toronto: 1885. V. 48
The History of the North-West Rebellion of 1885. Toronto: 1886. V. 50

MUMBY, FRANK
The Great World War, a History. London: 1920. V. 49

MUMBY, FRANK A.
Publishing and Bookselling. London: 1930. V. 47

MUMEY, NOLIE
The Black Ram of Dinwoody Creek. Denver: 1951. V. 53
Bloody Trails Along the Rio Grande... Denver: 1958. V. 48; 50
Calamity Jane. Denver: 1950. V. 50; 51; 54
Clark, Gruber and Company (1860-1865), a Pioneer Denver Mint. Denver: 1950. V. 53
History of the Early Settlements of Denver, 1599-1860... Glendale. V. 49
James Pierson Beckwourth, an Enigmatic Figure of the West 1856-1866. Denver: 1957. V. 47; 54
John Williams Gunnison. Denver: 1955. V. 47; 52; 53; 54
Legends of Images. Denver: 1980. V. 54
The Life of Jim Baker, 1818-1898. New York: 1972. V. 51; 53

MUMEY, NOLIE continued
March of the Dragoons: Ford Diary 1835. Denver: 1957. V. 52
Old Forts and Trading Posts of the West. Denver: 1956. V. 47
Pioneer Denver, Including Scenes from Central City, Colorado City and Nevada City. Denver: 1948. V. 49; 54
A Pioneer Denver Mint. Denver: 1950. V. 51
Poker Alice - Alice Ivers, Duffield, Tubbs, Hucker... Denver: 1951. V. 52
Reverend Thomas Thacher. A Biographical Sketch. Denver: 1937. V. 47; 48; 49; 50
Rocky Mountain Dick (Richard W. Rock). Stories of His Adventures in Capturing Wild Animals. Denver: 1953. V. 47
A Study of Rare Books; with Special Reference to Colophons, Press Devices and Title-pages of Interest to the Bibliophile and Student of Literature. Denver: 1930. V. 47
The Teton Mountains: Their History and Tradition with Any Account of the Early Fur Trade, Trappers... Denver: 1947. V. 52
Wyoming Bullwacker, Episodes in the Life of James Milton Sherrod from His Reminiscences 1815-1819. Denver: 1976. V. 49

MUMFORD, ERASMUS
A Letter to the Club at White's. London: 1750. V. 52

MUMFORD, JAMES
The Catholick-Scripturist. London: 1717. V. 51; 54
A Narrative of Medicine in America. Philadelphia: 1903. V. 50
Surgical Aspects of Digestive Disorders. New York: 1905. V. 54

MUMFORD, JOHN KIMBERLY
The Yerkes Collection of Oriental Carpets. V. 54

MUMFORD, LEWIS
Man as Interpreter. New York: 1951. V. 54

MUMMERY, A. F.
My Climbs in the Alps and Caucasus. London: 1895. V. 49; 50; 52; 53
My Climbs in the Alps and Caucasus. London: 1908. V. 54

MUNARI, BRUNO
Animals For Sale. Cleveland and New York: 1957. V. 49
The Birthday Present. New York: 1959. V. 54
Bruno Munari's Zoo. New York: 1963. V. 53
Circus in the Mist. New York: 1969. V. 49; 52
Tic, Tac and Toe. Cleveland: 1957. V. 54
Tic, Tac and Toe. New York: 1957. V. 49; 52
What I'd Like to Be. London: 1945. V. 53

MUNBY, A. N. L.
British Book Sale Catalogues 1676-1800: a Union List. London: 1977. V. 52
Phillipps Studies. 1951-60. V. 47
Phillipps Studies. Cambridge: 1951-60. V. 51
Phillipps Studies. London: 1951-60. V. 48
Phillipps Studies. 1971. V. 47
Phillipps Studies. (Nos. 1-5). Cambridge: 1951-60. V. 50
Some Caricatures of Book-Collectors, an Essay. London: 1948. V. 52

MUNBY, ARTHUR JOSEPH
Ann Morgan's Love. London: 1896. V. 47

MUNCASTER, MARTIN
The Wind in the Oak. 1978. V. 52
The Wind in the Oak. The Life, Work and Philosophy of the Marine and Landscape Artist Claude Muncaster. London: 1978. V. 50

MUNDAY, ALBERT H.
The Eyes of the Army and Navy: Pracitcal Aviation. New York: 1917. V. 51

MUNDAY, DON
The Unknown Mountains. London: 1948. V. 48; 53

MUNDAY, LUTA
A Mounty's Wife; Being the Life Story of One Attached to the Force But Not Of it. London: 1930. V. 49

MUNDEL, E. H.
Poe's 1843 the Murders in the Rue Morgue A Census of Known Copies. Portrage: 1974. V. 48

MUNDT, CLARA
Joseph II and His Court. An Historical Novel. Mobile: 1864. V. 49; 54

MUNDY, FRANCIS CLARKE
Poems. Oxford: 1768. V. 47; 48; 50; 54

MUNDY, GODFREY CHARLES
Our Antipodes: or, Residence and Rambles in the Australasian Colones with a Glimpse of the Gold Fields. London: 1852. V. 47; 52
Pen and Pencil Sketches, Being the Journal of a Tour in India. London: 1832. V. 50
Pen and Pencil Sketches Being the Journal of a Tour to India. 1833. V. 54

MUNDY, HENRY
Opera Omnia Medico-Physica Tractatibus Compresa, De Aere Vitali, de Esculentis, de Potulentis. Amsterdam: 1685. V. 47

MUNDY, P.
The Vultures of Africa. London: 1992. V. 50

MUNDY, RODNEY
H. M. S. "Hannibal" at Palermo and Naples During the Italian Revolution, 1859-61. London: 1863. V. 49; 53
Narrative of Events in Boreno and Celebes, Down to the Occupation of Labuan, from the Journals of James Brooke Esq. London: 1848. V. 47

MUNDY, TALBOT
Cock O'the North. 1929. V. 49
Jimgrim and Allah's Peace. New York & London: 1936. V. 51; 53; 54
The King in Check. 1934. V. 48
King of the Khyber Rifles. Indianapolis: 1916. V. 52
The Mystery of Khufu's Tomb. 1935. V. 48
Old Ugly-Face. New York: 1940. V. 48
Queen Cleopatra. 1929. V. 48; 52; 53
Queen Cleopatra. Indianapolis: 1929. V. 49; 51; 54

MUNFORD, WILLIAM
Poems, and Compositions in Prose on Several Occasions. Richmond: 1798. V. 50; 52

MUNILLA, MARTIN DE
His Journal and Other Documents Relating to the Voyages of Pedro Fernandez de Quiros to the south Sea (1605-1606) and the Franciscan Missnary Plan (1617-1627). Cambridge: 1966. V. 52

MUNIMENTA
Academica, or Documents Illustrative of Academical Life and Studies at Oxford. London: 1868. V. 50

MUNK, JOSEPH AMASA
Activities of a Lifetime. Los Angeles: 1924. V. 53
Arizona Sketches. New York: 1905. V. 47
Story of the Munk Library of Arizoniana. Los Angeles: 1927. V. 53

MUNK, WILLIAM
Euthanasia: or, Medical Treatment In Aid of an Easy Death. London: 1887. V. 49
The Roll of the Royal College of Physicians of London; Comprising Biographical Sketches. London: 1878-1968. V. 52
The Roll of the Royal College of Physicians of London; Comprising Biographical Sketches of All the Eminent Physicians...from 1518 to 1984. London: 1878-1984. V. 47; 49

MUNKACSI, MARTIN
Nudes by Munkacsi. New York: 1951. V. 47; 48; 51

MUNN, HENRY TOKE
Prairie Trails and Arctic By-Ways. London: 1932. V. 52

MUNN, WARNER
The Werewolf of Ponkert. Providence: 1958. V. 48

MUNNICKS, JOHANNES
De Re Anatomica Liber. Utrecht: 1697. V. 49

MUNNINGS, A. J.
Pictures of Horses and English Life. London: 1927. V. 51
Pictures of Horses and English Life. London: 1939. V. 49; 52

MUNNINGS, ALFRED
Autobiography. London: 1950-52. V. 49; 50; 52; 54
The Autobiography. London: 1951/52. V. 48

MUNNINGS, ALFRED JAMES
An Artist's Life; The Second Burst; The Finish. London: 1950-52. V. 47
Ballads and Poems. London: 1957. V. 50
Larkbarrow Farm, a Ballad of Exmoor. 1938. V. 47
Old Brandy and Cherry Bounce - A Ballad of Exmoor. London: 1943. V. 49
Pictures of Horses and English Life. London: 1927. V. 47; 54
Pictures of Horses and English Life. London: 1939. V. 47
The Tale of Anthony Bell, A Hunting Ballad. London: 1921. V. 47

MUNRO, AENEAS
Deaths in Childbed and Our Lying-In-Hospitals: Together with a Proposal for Establishing a Modern Maternity Institution for Affording Clinical Instruction and For Training Nurses. London: 1879. V. 50; 51

MUNRO, ALICE
The Beggar Maid. New York: 1979. V. 51
Dance of the Happy Shades. Toronto: 1958. V. 52
Dance of the Happy Shades. Toronto: 1968. V. 48; 51
Lives of Girls and Women. Toronto: 1971. V. 51; 52; 54
The Progress of Love. Toronto: 1986. V. 52; 54
Something I've been Meaning to Tell You. New York: 1974. V. 48; 51

MUNRO, HECTOR HUGH
Beasts and Super-Beasts. London: 1914. V. 47; 52; 53
The Chronicles of Clovis. London: 1912. V. 53
Reginald. London: 1904. V. 53; 54
Reginald in Russia and Other Sketches. London: 1910. V. 49; 50; 51; 53
The Rise of the Russian Empire. Boston/London: 1900. V. 48; 51; 54
The Square Egg and Other Sketches with Three Plays and Illustrations. London: 1924. V. 53
The Toys of Peace and Other Papers. London: 1910. V. 50
The Toys of Peace and Other Papers. London: 1919. V. 47; 50
The Unbearable Bassington. London: 1912. V. 47; 50; 53
The Westminster Alice. 1902. V. 49
The Westminster Alice. London: 1902. V. 48; 50; 51
When William Came. London: 1914. V. 53

MUNRO, J.
A Trip to Venus. 1897. V. 47; 51

MUNRO, MARGARET
Poems by Two Friends. London: 1905. V. 48; 53

MUNRO, NEIL
The Clyde. London: 1907. V. 49
John Splendid. The Tale of a Poor Gentleman and the Little Wars of Lorn. Edinburgh: 1898. V. 48

MUNRO, NEIL GORDON
Ainu Creed and Cult. London: 1962. V. 49

MUNRO, ROBERT
Ancient Scottish Lake-Dwellings or Crannogs... Edinburgh: 1882. V. 52
Palaeolithic Man in Terramara Settlements in Europe.a. New York: 1912. V. 51
Prehistoric Scotland and Its Place in European Civilisation. London: 1899. V. 54

MUNRO, WILLIAM BENNETT
Documents Relating to the Seigniorial Tenure in Canada: 1598-1854. Toronto: 1908. V. 47; 49; 51

MUNROE, DAVID HOADLEY
The Grand National, 1839-1930. New York: 1931. V. 48

MUNRO-FRASER, J. P.
History of Contra Costa County, California... San Francisco: 1882. V. 54
History of Marin County California. San Francisco: 1880. V. 49
History of Sonoma County, Including Its Geology, Topography, Mountains, Valleys and Streams... San Francisco: 1880. V. 47

MUNSELL, A. H.
A Grammar of Color. Mittineague: 1921. V. 53

MUNSELL, CHARLES
A Collection of Songs of the American Press, and Other Poems Relating to the Art of Printing. Albany: 1868. V. 51
Songs of the American Press and Other Poems Relating to the Art of Printing. Albany: 1868. V. 49

MUNSON, D.
Foundations of American Grape Culture. New York: 1909. V. 52

MUNSON, GORHAM B.
Waldo Frank: a Study. New York: 1923. V. 47

MUNSON, JOHN WILLIAM
Reminiscences of a Mosby Guerrila. New York: 1906. V. 49; 51

MUNSON, LAURA GORDON
Flowers from My Garden Sketches and Painted from Nature. New York: 1864. V. 54

MUNSTER, WILHELMINA FITZCLARENCE, COUNTESS OF
A Scotch Earl. London: 1891. V. 49

MUNTHE, AXEL
The Story of San Michele. London: 1929. V. 49

MUNTZ, EUGENE
Leonardo Da Vinci. Artist, Thinker and Man of Science. London: 1898. V. 50

MUNZ, LUDWIG
The Etchings of Rembrandt. London: 1952. V. 50; 51; 54

MURAI, GENSAI
Hana. A Daughter of Japan. Tokyo: 1904. V. 49

MURAKAMI, HARUKI
The Elephant Vanishes. New York: 1993. V. 52
A Wild Sheep Chase. New York: 1989. V. 51

MURASAKI, LADY
The Tale of Genji. London: 1925-33. V. 49

MURATOFF, PAUL
Thirty-Five Russian Primitives. Paris: 1931. V. 52

MURCH, JEROM
Mrs. Barbauld and Her Contemporaries: Sketches of Some Eminent Literary and Scientific Englishwomen. London: 1877. V. 53

MURCHIO, VINCENZO MARIA
Il Viaggio all'Indie Orientali...con le Osservationi, e Successi nel Medesimo, i Costumi, e Kiti di Variae Nationi & Reconditissimi Arcani d e'Gentili... Venice: 1678. V. 48

MURCHISON, CHARLES
Clinical Lectures on Diseases of the Liver, Jaundice and Abdominal Dropsy. New York: 1877. V. 49; 54
Clinical Lectures on Diseases of the Liver, Jaundice and Abdominal Dropsy. London: 1885. V. 49
On Functional Derangements of the Liver, Being the Croonian Lectures. London: 1874. V. 51
A Treatise on the Continued Fevers of Great Britain. London: 1873. V. 49; 51; 54

MURCHISON, R. I.
Address to the Royal Geographical Society of London Delivered at the Anniversary Meeting on the 24th May 1858 (23rd May 1864). London: 1858-64. V. 47; 48; 54
First Sketch of a Geological Map of Scotland. Edinburgh: 1861. V. 47
Outline of the Geology of the Neighbourhood of Cheltenham. London: 1845. V. 51; 52
Siluria. London: 1854. V. 47; 49; 53
Siluria. London: 1859. V. 47; 48; 54
Siluria. London: 1867. V. 53
Siluria. London: 1872. V. 48; 53; 54
The Silurian System, Founded on Geological Researches in the Counties of Salop, Hereford, Radnor, Montgomery, Caermarthen, Brecon, Pembroke, Monmouth, Gloucester, Worcester and Stafford. London: 1839. V. 51; 52; 53; 54

MURDOCH, BEAMISH
A History of Nova-Scotia or Acadie. Halifax: 1865-Feb.1867. V. 53

MURDOCH, IRIS
The Bell. London: 1958. V. 49; 52; 53
Existentialists and Mystics. London: 1994. V. 51
The Flight from the Enchanter. London: 1956. V. 48; 52
The One Alone: a Play. 1995. V. 54
Reynolds Stone: An Address Given by Iris Murdoch in St. James's Church Piccadilly London on 20 July 1979. London: 1981. V. 51
The Sandcastle. London: 1957. V. 48; 51; 53
Sartre. London: 1953. V. 47; 50
Sartre. New Haven: 1953. V. 51
A Severed Head. London: 1961. V. 49; 51
A Severed Head. London: 1964. V. 51
Something Special/ Four Poems and a Story. Helsinki: 1991. V. 48
Under the Net. London: 1954. V. 52; 53
The Unicorn. London: 1963. V. 53
An Unofficial Rose. London: 1962. V. 53
A Year of Birds. Tisbury, Wiltshire: 1978. V. 49; 50; 52; 53

MURDOCH, JOHN
The Dictionary of Distinctions, in Three Alphabets. London: 1811. V. 52
Ethnological Results of the Point Barrow Expedition. Washington: 1892. V. 50
Pictures of the Heart, Sentimentally Delineated by the Danger of the Passions... Dublin: 1783. V. 48

MURDOCK, HAROLD
Earl Percy Dines Abroad, a Boswellian Episode. Boston: 1924. V. 48; 50

MURDOCK, KENNETH B.
The Portraits of Increase Mather, with Some Notes on Thomas Johnson... Cleveland: 1924. V. 47

MURE, G. R. G.
Retreat from Truth. Oxford: 1958. V. 48

MURET, MARC ANTOINE
Oratio Habita Ad...Caradinales Ipso die Paschae...MDLXXXV. Rome: 1585. V. 48
...Orationum Volumina Duo, Quorum Primum Ante Aliquot Annos in Lucem Prodijt, Secundum Vero Recens est Editum... Cologne: 1595. V. 49
Variarum Lectionvm Libri XV. Antverpiae: 1586. V. 54

MURFREE, MARY NOAILLES
The Champion. Boston & New York: 1902. V. 53; 54
In the Tennessee Mountains. Boston: 1884. V. 54
The Phantoms of the Foot-Brigade and other Stories. New York: 1895. V. 53; 54

MURIE, J.
On the Anatomy of the Lemuroidea. London: 1869. V. 49

MURIETA, JOAQUIN
Joaquin Murieta: The Bandit Chief of California. San Francisco: 1932. V. 47

MURIHEAD, GEORGE
The Birds of Berwickshire. Edinburgh: 1889. V. 54

MURILLO, G.
Las Artes Populares en Mexico. Mexico: 1922. V. 47

MURPHY, ANN BROWNWELL
A First or Mother's Dictionary... London: 1815. V. 48

MURPHY, ARTHUR
The Desert Island. London: 1760. V. 52
An Essay on the Life and Genius of Samuel Johnson. London: 1792. V. 47
An Essay on the Life and Genius of Samuel Johnson, LL.D. London: 1793. V. 48
The Life of David Garrick, Esq. London: 1801. V. 47; 48; 49
The Orphan of China. Dublin: 1760-70. V. 49

MURPHY, CORNELIUS
A True and Exact Relation of the Death of Two Catholicks, Who Suffered for Their Religion at the Summer Assizes, Held at Lancaster in the Year 1628. London: 1737. V. 49

MURPHY, DENIS
The Annals of Clonmacnoise. London: 1896. V. 52

MURPHY, DERVIA
Muddling through in Madagascar. London: 1985. V. 52

MURPHY, ELIZABETH H. F.
The Levite; or, Scenes Two Hundred Years Ago. London: 1845. V. 48

MURPHY, J. L.
An Essay Towards a Science of Conciousness, More Particularly Illustrative of the Phenomena of Human Knowledge, Feeling and Action. London: 1838. V. 50

MURPHY, JAMES
Travels in Portugal...Consisting of Observations on the Manners, Customs, Tade, Public Buildings, Arts, Antiquities &c. London: 1795. V. 52

MURPHY, JOHN BENJAMIN
Resection of Arteries and Veins Injured in Continuity... New York: 1987. V. 53; 54

MURPHY, JOHN M'LEOD
Spars and Rigging from Nautical Routine. Providence: 1933. V. 54

MURPHY, JOHN MORTIMER
Sporting Adventures in the Far West. London: 1879. V. 48; 52
Sporting Adventures in the Far West. New York: 1880. V. 49; 52

MURPHY, JOHN NICHOLAS
Ireland: Industrial, Political and Social. London: 1870. V. 53
Terra Incognita or the Convents of the United Kingdom. London: 1873. V. 49

MURPHY, R. C.
Birds of Peru, the Record of a Sojourn on the West Coast. New York: 1925. V. 54
Oceanic Birds of South America. London: 1936. V. 48
Oceanic Birds of South America. New York: 1936. V. 48; 49; 50; 51; 53; 54
Oceanic Birds of South America. New York: 1948. V. 52; 53

MURPHY, RICHARD
The Archaeology of Love. Dublin: 1955. V. 47; 53
The Mirror Wall. Dublin: 1989. V. 48
Sailing to an Island. London: 1963. V. 47

MURPHY, T. D.
On Sunset Highways: A Book of Motor Rambles in California. Boston: 1915. V. 47

MURPHY, WILLIAM
Anemia in Practice, Pernicious Anemia. Philadelphia: 1939. V. 49; 54

MURPHY, WILLIAM S.
The Textiles Industries. London: 1911. V. 47; 49

MURRAY, A.
Botanical Expedition to Oregon... Edinburgh: 1853. V. 52

MURRAY, A. S.
Designs from Greek Vases in the British Museum. London: 1894. V. 48
Excavations in Cyprus (Bequest of Miss E.T. Turner to the British Museum). London: 1900. V. 50
Tasmanian Rivers, Lakes and Flowers... London: 1900. V. 48
Terracotta Sarcophagi: Greek and Etruscan in the British Museum. London: 1898. V. 50; 52
Twelve Hundred Miles on the River Murray. London: 1898. V. 48
Twelve Hundred Miles on the River Murray. Sydney: 1898. V. 51

MURRAY, A. W.
Missions in Western Polynesia: Being Historical Sketches of These Missions, from Their Commencement in 1839 to the Present Time. London: 1863. V. 52

MURRAY, ALBERT
The Omni-Americans: New Perspectives on Black Experience and American Culture. New York: 1970. V. 54
South to a Very Old Place. New York: 1971. V. 49; 54
Stomping the Blues. New York: 1976. V. 54

MURRAY, AMELIA MATILDA
Letters form the United States, Cuba and Canada. New York: 1856. V. 50; 52; 53

MURRAY, ANDREW
Geographical Distribution of Mammals. London: 1866. V. 49; 52; 53; 54
Ship-Building in Iron and Wood... London: 1863. V. 49
Ship-Building in Iron and Wood and Steamships by Robert Murray. Edinburgh: 1863. V. 53

MURRAY, ARCHIBALD K.
History of the Scottish Regiments in the British Army. Glagow: 1862. V. 50

MURRAY, CHARLES AUGUSTUS
The Prairie Bird. London: 1844. V. 47; 51; 52
The Prairie-Bird. London: 1854. V. 47
Travels In North America. London: 1839. V. 50; 52
Travels in North America During the Years 1834, 1835 and 1836. New York: 1839. V. 48

MURRAY, CHARLES FAIRFAX
Catalogue of a Collection of Early French Books in the Library of C. Fairfax Murray. London: 1961. V. 47
Catalogue of the Pictures Belonging to His Grace the Duke of Portland, at Welbeck Abbey, and in London MDCCCLXXXXIIII. London: 1894. V. 50

MURRAY, D. P.
South African Butterflies, a Monograph of the Lycaenidae. London: 1935. V. 53

MURRAY, D. R.
Seed Dispersal. London: 1987. V. 50; 51

MURRAY, DAVID CHRISTIE
Rainbow Gold. London: 1885. V. 54
The Way of the World. London: 1884. V. 49

MURRAY, EUSTACE GRENVILLE
Six Months in the Ranks; or the Gentleman Private. London: 1881. V. 52
Young Brown or the Law of Inheritance. London: 1874. V. 48

MURRAY, FLORENCE
The Negro Handbook 1944. New York: 1944. V. 52

MURRAY, FRANCIS EDWIN
A Bibliography of Austin Dobson Attempted by Francis Edwin Murray. Derby: 1900. V. 47
Rondeaux of Boyhood. London: 1923. V. 50

MURRAY, FRANCIS J.
The Theory of Mathematical Machines. New York: 1948. V. 54

MURRAY, G. W.
The Tweeddale Shooting Club. Edinburgh: 1945. V. 49

MURRAY, GEORGE GILBERT AIME
Greek Comic Verse. Oxford: 1886. V. 47; 49
Olympia. Carmen Latinum Cancellarii Praemio Donatum et in Theatro Sheldoniano Recitatum die Junii XXX MDXXXLXXXVI. Oxford: 1886. V. 49

MURRAY, GEORGE W.
A History of George W. Murray, and His Long Confinement at Andersonville, Ga.... Northampton: 1865?. V. 47

MURRAY, GILBERT
The Airplane Spider. London: 1921. V. 49

MURRAY, HENRY A.
Lands of the Slave and the Free; Or, Cuba, the United States, and Canada. London: 1855. V. 48

MURRAY, HILDA
Flower Legends for Children. London: 1901. V. 50

MURRAY, HUGH
Historical Account of Discoveries and Travels in Asia, from the Earliest Age to the Present Time. Edinburgh: 1820. V. 49; 51
Historical Account of Discoveries and Travels in North America. London: 1829. V. 48
An Historical and Descriptive Account of British America... Edinburgh: 1839. V. 48; 49; 53; 54
An Historical and Descriptive Account of China. Edinburgh: 1836. V. 50; 51
An Historical and Descriptive Account of China. Edinburgh: 1843. V. 52
History of British India, Continued to the Year 1856. London: 1863. V. 47
Narrative of Discovery and Adventure in Africa. Edinburgh: 1840. V. 54

MURRAY, J. A.
The Avifauna of the island of Ceylon. London: 1890. V. 51

MURRAY, J. OGDEN
The Immortal Six Hundred, a Story of Cruelty to Confederate Prisoners of War. Roanoke: 1911. V. 50

MURRAY, J. W.
Ecology and Palaeoecology of Benthic foraminifera. London: 1991. V. 48

MURRAY, JAMES
Antarctic Days. Sketches of the Homely Side of Polar Life... London: 1913. V. 50
An Impartial History of the Present War in America... London: 1778-79. V. 53
An Impartial History of the Present War in America... Newcastle Upon Tyne: 1780. V. 47
New Sermons to Asses. London: 1773. V. 54
Sermons to Asses. London: 1768. V. 48
The Travels of the Imagination; a True Jurney from Newcastle to London, in a Stage Coach. London: 1783. V. 47

MURRAY, JAMES A.
The Avifauna of British India. London: 1890. V. 52; 53
The Edible and Game Birds of British India with its Dependencies and Ceylon. 1889. V. 53

MURRAY, JAMES A. H.
A New English Dictionary of Historical Principles. Oxford: 1884. V. 51

MURRAY, JAMES ERSKINE
A Summer in the Pyrenees. London: 1837. V. 51

MURRAY, JOHN
An Author's Conduct to the Public, Stated in the Behaviour of Dr. William Cullen, His Majesty's Physician at Edinburgh. London: 1784. V. 48
Elements of Materia Medica and Pharmacy. Edinburgh: 1804. V. 48
A Handbook for Travellers in Greece: Describing the Ionian Islands... London: 1872. V. 48
A Memoir on the Diamond. London: 1831. V. 54
A Memoir on the Diamond, Including Its Economical and Political History. London: 1839. V. 54
Notes on Captain Medwin's Conversations of Lord Byron. London: 1824. V. 53
Practical Remarks on Modern Paper. North Hills: 1981. V. 47; 48; 49; 52
Report on Deep-Sea Deposits Based on the Specimens Collected During the Voyage of H. M. S. Challenger in the Years 1872 to 1876. London: 1891. V. 51
A Supplement of the First Edition of a System of Chemistry, Containing a View of the Recent Discoveries in the Science. Philadelphia: 1811. V. 48
A Treatise on Pulmonary Consumption; its Prevention and Remedy. London: 1831. V. 51

MURRAY, JOHN FISHER
The Chinese and the Ministry. London: 1840. V. 54
A Picturesque Tour of the River Thames in Its Western Course... London: 1845. V. 52
A Picturesque Tour of the River Thames In Its Western Course... London: 1853. V. 49

MURRAY, JOHN OGDEN
The Immortal Six Hundred. Winchester: 1905. V. 52; 54
The Immortal Six Hundred. Roanoke: 1911. V. 49

MURRAY, LADY
Memoirs of the Lives and Characters of the Right Honourable George Baillie of Jeerviswood, and of Lady Grisell Baillie by Their Daughter. Edinburgh: 1822. V. 50; 51; 53

MURRAY, LES A.
Equainimities. Copenhagen: 1982. V. 50
The Idyll Wheel - Cycle of a year at Bunyah, New South Wales, April 1986-April 1987. Canberra: 1989. V. 50
The Weatherboard Cathedral - Poems. Sydney: 1969. V. 50

MURRAY, LINDLEY
A Compendium of Religious Faith and Practice...(with) The Duty and Benefit of a daily Perusal of the Holy Scriptures in Families. York: 1815/17. V. 49
An English Grammar; Comprehending the Principles and Rules of the Language... York: 1809. V. 52
An English Grammar; Comprehending the Principles and the Rules of Language. York: 1824. V. 47; 49
The English Reader; or, Pieces in Prose and Poetry... Montreal: 1847. V. 50
Exercises, Adapted to Murray's English Grammar. Lexington: 1815. V. 50
Some Account of the Life and Religious Labours of Sarah Grubb. Trenton: 1795. V. 52

MURRAY, LOIS L.
Incidents of Frontier Life...Written From Personal Experience. Goshen: 1880. V. 48; 49

MURRAY, LORD GEORGE
A Particular Acocunt of the Battle of Culloden...In a Letter from an Officer of the Highland Army. London: 1749. V. 50

MURRAY, MARISCHAL
Union-Castle Chronicle 1853-1953. London: 1953. V. 50

MURRAY, MRS.
An Abridgement of the History of France, From the Origin of the Franks, to the Second Restoration of Louis XVIII, for the Use of Schools. London: 1818. V. 48

MURRAY, NICHOLAS
Notes, Historical and Biographical, Concerning Elizabeth-Town, Its Eminent Men, Churches and Ministers. Elizabeth Town: 1844. V. 47; 50; 51

MURRAY, PAULI
Dark Testament and Other Poems. Norwalk: 1970. V. 52

MURRAY, R. DUNDAS
The Cities and Wilds of Andalucia. London: 1850. V. 48

MURRAY, R. W.
South African Reminiscences: a Series of Sketches of Prominent Public Events in South Africa Within the Memory of the Author During the Forty Years Since 1854... Cape Town: 1894. V. 47

MURRAY, ROBERT
An Account of the Constitution and Security of the General Bank of Credit. London: 1683. V. 53
Rudimentary Treatise on Marine Engines and Steam Vessels... London: 1858. V. 50

MURRAY, S., MRS.
A Companion and Useful Guide to the Beauties of Scotland, to the Lakes...and to the District of Craven. London: 1799. V. 47

MURRAY, THOMAS
The Literary History of Galloway. Edinburgh: 1832. V. 54

MURRAY, THOMAS B.
Pitcairn: the Island, the People and the Pastor... (with) a Short Notice of the Original Settlement and Present Condition of Norfolk Island. 1860. V. 47

MURRAY, W. W.
The History of the 2nd Canadian Battalion (East. Ontario Regiment) Canadian Expeditonary Force in the Great War 1914-19. Ottawa: 1947. V. 53

MURRAY, WILLIAM
A Treatise on Emotional Disorders of the Sympathetic System of Nerves. London: 1866. V. 50

MURRAY, WILLIAM FITZGERALD JENKINS
Space Platform. Chicago: 1953. V. 51

MURRAY, WILLIAM H.
The Farewell and Occasional Addresses Delivered by W. H. Murray, Esq. in the Theatres Royal and Adelphi, Edinburgh... Edinburgh: 1851. V. 50

MURRAY, WILLIAM HENRY HARRISON
Adventures in the Wilderness; or, Camp-Life in the Adirondacks. Boston: 1869. V. 47
Daylight Land: Experiences, Incidents and Adventures, Humorous and Otherwise, Which Befel Judge John Doe, Tourist, of San Francisco... Boston: 1888. V. 48
The Perfect Horse: How To Know Him, How to Breed Him, How to Train Him, How to Shoe Him... Boston: 1873. V. 47

MURRELL, WILLIAM
Nitro-Glycerine as a Remedy for Angina Pectoris. Detroit: 1882. V. 54

MURRY, JOHN MIDDLETON
The Evolution of an Intellectual. London: 1920. V. 54
The Free Society. London: 1948. V. 48
The Life of Katherine Mansfield. London: 1933. V. 50

MURTADHA IBN AL-KHAFIF
The Egyptian History, Treating of the Pyramids, the Inundation of the Nile and Other Prodigies Of Egypt, According to the Opinions and Traditions of the Arabians. London: 1672. V. 48

MURTHA, E.
Paul Manship. New York: 1957. V. 47; 50; 51

MUSAE Etonenses: Sive Poematia in Duos Tomos Distributa... Londini: 1755. V. 49

MUSAE Seatonianae. London: 1772. V. 47

MUSAEUS
Hero and Leander. Waltham St. Lawrence: 1949. V. 48; 49
The Loves of Hero and Leander. London: 1747. V. 52
The Loves of Hero and Leander. London: 1797. V. 50
Musaei, Moschi & Bionis, Quae Extant Omnia; Quibus Accessere Quaedam Selectiora Theocriti Eidyllia. Autore Davide Whitfordo. Londini: 1655. V. 48

MUSARUM Anglicanarum Analecta. Volume I-III. Londini: 1714/17. V. 50

MUSARUM Anglicanarum Analecta...In Unum Volumen (Duo Volumina) Congesta. Oxon: 1692/99. V. 48

MUSAUS, JOHANN KARL AUGUST
Physiognomical Travels, Preceded by a Physiognomical Journal. London: 1800. V. 47

MUSCARELLA, OSCAR WHITE
Ancient Art: The Norbert Schimmel Collection. Mainz: 1974. V. 52

MUSCATINE, CHARLES
The Book of Geoffrey Chaucer: An Account of Publication of Geoffrey Chaucer's Works From the Fifteenth Century to Modern Times. San Francisco: 1963. V. 48
The Book of Geoffrey Chaucer: an Account of the Publication of Geoffrey Chaucer's Works from the Fifteenth Century to Modern Times. 1963. V. 52

MUSE Anthology of Poetry. New York: 1928. V. 48

MUSE, CLARENCE
Way Down South. Hollywood: 1932. V. 51

LE MUSEE Pour Rire Dessins par Tous les Caricaturistes de Paris. Paris: 1840. V. 54

MUSES, C. A.
Aspects of the Theory of Artificial Intelligence. New York: 1962. V. 52; 54

THE MUSES Farewel to Popery and Slavery, or, a Collection of Miscellany Poems, Satayrs, Songs, &c. Made by the Most Eminent Wits of the Nation...(and) A Supplement to the Collection of Miscellany Poems Against Popery and Slavery. London: 1689. V. 53

THE MUSES Library; or a Series of English Poetry. London: 1737. V. 47

THE MUSES Library; or, a Series of English Poetry. London: 1741. V. 54

THE MUSE'S Mirrour, Being a Collection of Poems. London: 1778. V. 51

THE MUSE'S Pocket Companion. A Collection of Poems. Carlisle: 1782. V. 48

THE MUSE'S Recreation, In Four Poems. London: 1762. V. 54

MUSEUM Criticum. Or, Cambridge Classical Researches. London: 1826. V. 48

MUSEUM Hermeticum Reformatum et Amplificatum... Frankfurt: 1678. V. 48

MUSEUM of Painting and Sculpture. London: 1829-34. V. 53

MUSEUM OF FINE ARTS, BOSTON
Illustrated Catalogue of a Special Loan Exhibition of Art Trearuers from Japan. Boston: 1936. V. 47
Tapestries of Europe and of Colonial Peru in the Museum of Fine Arts, Boston. Boston: 1967. V. 54
Zen Painting and Calligraphy: an Exhibition of Art Lent by Temples, Private Collectors and Public and Private Museums. London: 1970. V. 54

MUSEUM OF MODERN ART, NEW YORK
Drawings In the Collection of the Museum of Modern Art. New York: 1969. V. 50
First Loan Exhibition. New York: 1929. V. 51
The Machine. (Exhibition Catalogue). New York: 1968. V. 54

MUSGRAVE, GEORGE CLARK
To Kumassi with Scott. London: 1896. V. 54

MUSGRAVE, GEORGE MUSGRAVE
A Ramble through Normandy. London: 1855. V. 50

MUSGRAVE, PERCY
Collectanea Mustraviana, Notes on the Ancient Family of Musgrave of Musgrave, Westmorland and Its Various Branches in Cumberland, Yorkshire, Northumberland, Somerset etc. Leeds: 1911. V. 47
Notes on the Ancient Family of Musgrave of Musgrave, Westmorland and its Arious Branches in Cumberland, Yorkshire, Northumerland, Somerset, &c. Leeds: 1911. V. 50; 52; 54

MUSGRAVE, RICHARD
Memoirs of the Different Rebellions in Ireland, from the Arrival of the English... Dublin: 1801. V. 47; 50; 51; 52; 53; 54
Strictures Upon an Historical review of the State of Ireland. 1804. V. 49

MUSGRAVE, SAMUEL
Two Dissertations. I. On the Graecian Mythology. II. An Examination of Sir Isaac Newton's Objections to the Chronology of the Olympiads. London: 1782. V. 49; 53

MUSGRAVE, SUSAN
Becky Swan's Book. Erin: 1977. V. 47
I Do Not Know If Things That Happen Can Be Said to Come to Pass or Only Happen. Vancouver: 1930. V. 47
Songs of the Sea-Witch. Vancouver: 1970. V. 47

MUSHET, DAVID
Papers On Iron and STeel Practical and Experimental... London: 1840. V. 50

MUSIC Hall Memories. London: 1936. V. 53

MUSICAL Festival. The First Grand Selection: As Performed at the Church of the Holy Trinity, in Kingston-upon-Hull, Wednesdya, September 19, 1792, for the Benefit of the General Infirmary. Hull: 1792. V. 49

THE MUSICAL Miscellany: a Select Collection of Scots, English and irish Songs, Set to Music. Perth: 1786. V. 49; 54

THE MUSICAL Miscellany: Being a Collection of Choice Songs, set to the Violin and Flute, by the Most Eminent Masters. London: 1729-30-31. V. 47; 53

THE MUSICAL Repertory. A Selection of the Most Approved and Modern Songs. Hallowell: 1811. V. 48

MUSICAL Travels through England by the Late Joel Collier, Licentiate in Music. London: 1776. V. 48; 52

MUSICK, JOHN ROY
Hawaii...Our New Possessions. New York: 1898. V. 53

MUSIL, ALOIS
In the Arabian Desert. New York: 1930. V. 49

MUSIL, ROBERT
The Man of Many Qualities. London: 1953/54/60. V. 54
The Man Without Qualities. London: 1953/54/60. V. 49
Der Mann Ohne Eigenschaften. Berlin: 1930/33. V. 54
Nachlass zu Lebzeiten. Zurich: 1936. V. 53
Die Verwirrungen des Zoglings Torless. Wien: 1906. V. 53

MUSPRATT, SHERIDAN
Chemistry, Theoretical, Practical and Analytical, as Applied and Related to the Arts and Manufactures. London: 1860. V. 47

MUSSCHENBROEK, PETER VAN
Physicae Experimentales, et Geometricae, de Magnete, Tuborum Capillarium Viterorumque Speculorum Attractione, Magnitude Terrae, Cohaerentia Corporum Firmorum Disserationes... Leiden: 1729. V. 49; 50

MUSSET, ALFRED DE
Fantasio - A Comedy in Two Acts. London: 1929. V. 47

MUSSEY, R. D.
An Address Read to the Medical Class at Dartmouth College Dec. 1, 1818. Hanover: 1818. V. 51

MUSSO, CORNELIUS
Synodus Bituntina, Totam Fere Ecclesiasticam Disciplinam Sermonibus, Constitutionibus, Legibus Synodalibus, Complectens. Venice: 1579. V. 50

MUSTA'IDD KHAN, MUHAMMAD SAQI
The History of the First Ten Years of the Reign of Alemgeer. Calcutta: 1785. V. 49

MUSTERS, GEORGE C.
At Home with the Patagonians; A Year's Wanderings Over Untrodden Ground from the Straits of Magellan to the Rio Negro. London: 1871. V. 47

MUSURUS, MARCUS
Etymologicum Magnum Graecum... Venice: 1499. V. 49

MUTCH, NATHAN
Cocaine - Being a Paper Read Before Ye Sette of Odd Volumes - On April 24th, 1923, at Oddenino's Imperial Restaurant, by Nathan Mutch, M.D., F.R.C.P., Pessimist to Ye Sette. London: 1924. V. 52

MUTER, D. D., MRS.
Travels and Adventures of an Officer's Wife in India, China and New Zealand. London: 1864. V. 51; 54

MUTHER, R.
The History of Modern Painting. 1895-96. V. 54

MUTINELLI, FABIO
Dell'Avvenimento di S.M.I.R.A. Ferdinando I d'Austria in Venezia e delle Civiche Solennita d'allora. Venice: 1838. V. 47; 52

MUTSCHMANN, HEINRICH
A Phonology of the North-East Scotch Dialect. Bonn: 1909. V. 50

MUTUAL Criticism. Oneida: 1876. V. 51

MUTUKISNA, HENRY FRANCIS
A New Edition of the Thesawaleme, or the Laws and Customs on Jaffna. Together With the Decisions of the Various Courts on the Subject. Colombo: 1862?. V. 51

MUYBRIDGE, EADWEARD
Animals in Motion, An Electro-Photographic Investigation of Consecutive Phases of Muscular Actions. London: 1899. V. 49
Descriptive Zoopraxography or the Science of Animal Locomotion Made Popular. Chicago: 1893. V. 49
One City/Two Visions. San Francisco: 1878/1900. V. 47

MUYS, JOHANNES
Praxis Chirurgica Rationalis Seu Observationes Chirurgicae Secundum Solida Verae Philosophiae Fundamenta Resolutae... Leiden: 1685. V. 51; 53; 54

MUYUYAMA, JUNKICHI
Japanese Art in the West. Tokyo: 1966. V. 50

MUZEL, HEINRICH WILHELM
Verzeichniss Einer Sammlung Hauptsachlich zu des Alterthumern der Historie, den Schonen Kunsten... Berlin: 1783. V. 53

MY First Book. The Experiences of Rudyard Kipling, A. Conan Doyle, H. Rider Haggard, Bret Harte and others. London: 1894. V. 49

MY First Publication. San Francisco: 1961. V. 51

MY Goodness! My Gilbert and Sullivan!. London: 1961. V. 54

MY Lord Bag-O'-Rice. London: 1890. V. 50

MY New Toy Book. New York: 1880. V. 48

MY Own Fairy Tale Library. U.S.A: 1930. V. 49

MY Poetry Book. Philadelphia: 1934. V. 54

My Policy or, the New Gospel of Peace, According to St. Andy, the Apostate. Pittsburgh: 1866. V. 47

EN MYCKET Nyttig Och Forbattrad Trenchier-Bok, Hwar Uti Tilfinnandes ar Huruledes man... Stockholm: 1725. V. 54

MYDANS, CARL
More Than Meets the Eye. London: 1961. V. 51

MYDORGE, CLAUDE
Les Recretations Mathematiqves Avec l'Examen de ses Problemes en Arithmetique, Geometrie, Mecahnique, Cosmographie, Optique, Catoptrique &c... Paris: 1660. V. 49

MYER, ALBERT J.
A Manual of Signs for the Use of Signal Officer in the Field. Wasahington: 1897. V. 50

MYERS, ARTHUR B. R.
Life with the Hamran Arabs: an Account of a Sporting Tour of Some Officers of the Guards in the Soudan During the Winter of 1874-75. London: 1876. V. 54

MYERS, B. S.
The German Expressionists: a Generation in Revolt. New York: 1957. V. 47; 49; 50; 51; 53; 54

MYERS, CHARLES E.
Memoirs of a Hunter: a Story of Fifty-Eight Years of Hunting and Fishing. Davenport: 1948. V. 54

MYERS, DWIGHT
In Celebration of the Book. Literary New mexico. Albuquerque: 1982. V. 51

MYERS, F. W. H.
Human Personality and Its Survival of Bodily Death. London: 1920. V. 52

MYERS, FRED
Wieghorst, Dean of Western Painters. Tulsa: 1982. V. 51

MYERS, ISABEL BRIGGS
Give Me Death. London: 1935. V. 48

MYERS, J. ARTHUR
Fighters of Fate: a Story of Men and Women Who Have Achieved Greatly. Baltimore: 1927. V. 50; 52

MYERS, J. C.
Sketches on a Tour through the Northern and Eastern States, the Canadas and Nova Scotia. Harrisonburg: 1849. V. 47

MYERS, J. W.
The Aerial Atlas of Ancient Crete. Berkeley: 1992. V. 49

MYERS, JOAN
Along the Santa Fe Trail. Albuquerque: 1986. V. 50

MYERS, VIRGINIA
The Letters and Correspondence of Mrs. Virginia Myers... Philadelphia: 1847. V. 52

MYERS, WILLIAM H.
Through Wonderland to Alaska. Reading: 1895. V. 47

MYERS, WILLIAM STARR
The Story of New Jersey. New York: 1945. V. 47; 49; 51

MYERSON, JOEL
Ralph Waldo Emerson: a Descriptive Bibliography. Pittsburgh: 1982. V. 47

MYLIUS, ARNOLD
Principvm et Regvm Polonorvm Imagines ad Vivum Expressae... Cologne: 1594. V. 50; 53

MYLNE, ROBERT SCOTT
The Master Masons to the Crown of Scotland and Their Works. Edinburgh: 1893. V. 48; 52; 54

MYLONAS, GEORGE E.
Aghios Kosmas: an Early Bronze Age Settlement and Cemetery in Attica. Princeton: 1959. V. 52

MYNORS, R. A. B.
Durham Cathedral Manuscripts to the End of the Twelfth Century. Oxford: 1939. V. 47

MYNTER, HERMAN
Appendicitis and Its Surgical Treatament. Philadelphia: 1897. V. 54

MYRES, JOHN L.
Handbook of the Cesnola Collection of Antiquites from Cyprus. New York: 1914. V. 52

MYRES, SAMUEL D.
The Permian Basin - Petroleum Empire of the Southwest: Era of Discovery from the Beginning to the Depression. El Paso: 1973. V. 48; 54
The Permian Basin, Petroleum Empire of the Southwest. Era of Advancement, From the Depression to the Present. El Paso: 1977. V. 48

MYRICK, DAVID F.
Railroads of Nevada and Eastern California. Berkeley: 1962/63. V. 53
Railroads of Nevada and Eastern California. 1963. V. 48
Railroads of Nevada and Eastern California. Reno and Las Vegas: 1992. V. 48; 53

MYRICK, HERBERT
Cache la Poudre. The Romance of a Tenderfoot in the Days of Custer. New York: 1905. V. 47; 54

MYRICK, MILTON H.
Reports of Cases in the Probate Court of the City and County of San Francisco from Jan. 1, 1872 to Dec. 31, 1879. San Francisco: 1880. V. 51

MYRTON, HOPE
Round About Pictures. London: 1890. V. 49

LE MYSTERE De Saint Louis, Roi De France. Westminster: 1871. V. 48

THE MYSTERY of the Good Old Cause Briefly Unfolded. London: 1660. V. 50

THE MYSTIQUE of Vellum. Boston: 1984. V. 54

MYTHOLOGICAL Papyri. New York: 1957. V. 51

MYTTON, THOMAS
A Poem On the Pomfret Statues. Oxford: 1758. V. 48

N

N., E.
The Life of a Midshipman, a tale Founded on Facts and Intended to Correct an Injudicious Predilection in boys for the Life of a Sailor. London: 1829. V. 48

N., J.
Select Lessons in Prose and Verse, from Various Authors, Designed for the Improvement of Youth. Bristol: 1774. V. 54
Select Lessons in Prose and Verse, From Various Authors, Designed for the Improvement of Youth. Tamworth: 1798. V. 54

N., S.
Rawleigh Redivivus; or the Life and Death of the Right Honourable Anthony late Earl of Shaftesbury. London: 1683. V. 50

THE N-M-K-T Vestry; Alias Judge W-r Triumphant, or Justice Shallow Defeated. London: 1779. V. 47

NABBES, THOMAS
Microcosmus. London: 1637. V. 47

NABOD, VALENTIN
De Calculatoria Numerorumque Natura Sectiones Quatuor. Cologne: 1556. V. 50

NABOKOV, VLADIMIR
Bend Sinister. New York: 1947. V. 48; 49; 51; 54
Camera Obscura. London: 1935. V. 53
Camera Obscura. London: 1936. V. 51
Carrousel. Aartswoud, The Netherlands: 1987. V. 53
Chambre Obscure. Paris: 1934. V. 52
Conclusive Evidence. New York: 1951. V. 47; 50; 52; 53
Despair. London: 1966. V. 52; 54
Despair. New York: 1966. V. 48; 51; 52
The Eye. New York: 1965. V. 50; 51; 52
The Gift. London: 1963. V. 50
The Gift. New York: 1963. V. 48; 49; 51
Invitation to a Beheading. New York: 1959. V. 48; 49; 51; 52; 54
King, Queen, Knave. New York: 1968. V. 51
Laughter in the Dark. 1938. V. 50
Laughter in the Dark. Indianapolis & New York: 1938. V. 51; 53; 54
Lectures on Ulysses. Bloomfield Hills: 1980. V. 51
Lolita. New York: 1955. V. 47; 50
Lolita. Paris: 1955. V. 47; 49; 51; 52; 53
Lolita. London: 1959. V. 52; 53; 54
Lolita. 1960. V. 51; 52
Lolita. New York: 1967. V. 48; 51; 54
Lolita: a Screenplay. New York: 1974. V. 52
La Meprise. Paris: 1939. V. 47
Nabokov's Dozen. Garden City: 1958. V. 51
Nabokov's Dozen. London: 1959. V. 51
Nabokov's Quartet. New York: 1966. V. 51
Nikolai Gogol. 1944. V. 50
Nikolai Gogol. Norfolk: 1944. V. 48; 52; 54
Nikolai Gogol. London: 1947. V. 49
Nine Stories. Norfolk: 1947. V. 51
Pale Fire. 1962. V. 50
Pale Fire. London: 1962. V. 51
Pale Fire. New York: 1962. V. 48; 53; 54
Pale Fire. San Francisco: 1994. V. 51
Pnin. Garden City: 1957. V. 52
Pnin. Melbourne, London, Toronto: 1957. V. 47
Poems. Garden City: 1959. V. 47
Poems. New York: 1959. V. 48
The Real Life of Sebastian Knight. Norfolk: 1941. V. 47; 53
The Real Life of Sebastian Knight. London: 1945. V. 51; 54
The Return of Chorb: Stories and Poems. Berlin: 1930. V. 53
A Russian Beauty and Other Stories. New York: 1973. V. 51
The Song of Igor's Campaign. London: 1960. V. 51
Speak, Memory. London: 1951. V. 48; 51; 53
Speak, Memory. New York: 1966. V. 51
Speak Memory. London: 1967. V. 51
Three Russian Poets. Norfolk: 1944. V. 51
The Waltz Invention - a Play in Three Acts. New York: 1966. V. 47; 51

NACENTA, RAYMOND
School of Paris: The Painters and the Artistic Climate of Paris Since 1910. Greenwich: 1967. V. 48

NADAILLAC, MARQUIS DE
Manners and Monuments. New York & London: 1892. V. 52
Pre-Historic America. London: 1885. V. 50; 54
Prehistoric America. New York: 1899. V. 54

NADAL, GERONIMO
Adnotations et Meditations in Evangeli Quae in Sacrosancto Missae Sacrificio... Antverpiae: 1595. V. 51

NADASD, FRANCISCUS DE
Mausoleum Potentissimorum ac Gloriossimorum Regni Apostolici Regum & Primorum Militantis Ungariae Ducum... Nuremberg: 1664. V. 47

NADEAU, REMI A.
The Water Seekers. Garden City: 1950. V. 53

NAEGELE, FRANZ KARL
An Essay on the Mechanism of Parturition. London: 1829. V. 48
The Obliquely Contracted Pelvis Containing Also an Appendix of the Most Important Defects of the Female Pelvis. New York: 1939. V. 48; 53

NAGATY, H. F.
Medical Parasitology and Entomology. Cairo: 1963. V. 50

NAHUM, PETER
Monograms of Victorian and Edwardian Artists. 1976. V. 52

NAIL, LESLIE
Resurrection Ball. Tuscaloosa: 1982. V. 52; 53; 54

NAIPAUL, SHIVA
The Chip-Chip Gatherers. London: 1973. V. 49; 50; 52
Fireflies. London: 1970. V. 48; 51; 53
North and South. London: 1981. V. 47

NAIPAUL, VIDIADHAR SURAJPRSAD
An Area of Darkness. London: 1964. V. 53; 54
A Bend in the River. London: 1979. V. 47
A Congo Diary. Los Angeles: 1980. V. 49; 51
A Flag on the Island. London: 1967. V. 51
Guerrillas. London: 1975. V. 47
Guerrillas. New York: 1975. V. 49; 53
A House for Mr. Biswas. London: 1961. V. 49; 50; 52; 53
In a Free State. London: 1971. V. 49; 50; 53
In a Free State. New York: 1971. V. 53
India. London: 1990. V. 48; 49; 51; 53
The Loss of El Dorado. London: 1969. V. 53; 54
The Middle Passage. London: 1962. V. 53
Miguel Street. London: 1959. V. 50
Miguel Street. New York: 1959. V. 53
Miguel Street. 1960. V. 50
The Mimic Men. London: 1967. V. 48; 51
Mr. Stone and the Knights Companion. London: 1963. V. 47; 50
Mr. Stone and the Knights Companion. New York: 1963. V. 53
Mr. Stone and the Knights Companion. New York: 1964. V. 53
The Mystic Masseur. London: 1957. V. 48; 49
The Mystic Masseur. New York: 1957. V. 52
The Mystic Masseur. New York: 1959. V. 51
The Overcrowded Barracoon. London: 1972. V. 51; 53
The Suffrage of Elvira. London: 1958. V. 52; 53
A Turn in the South. 1989. V. 50
A Turn in the South. Franklin Center: 1989. V. 48; 49; 51; 52
A Way in the World. London: 1994. V. 51; 52; 53; 54
A Way in the World. New York: 1994. V. 50; 51; 53

NAIRN, A. E. M.
The Ocean Basins and Margins. New York: 1973-74-75. V. 53

NAIRNE, JAMES
The Trial (brought by) Lady Ramsay Against James Nairne, W.S. for Falsehood and Defamation... Edinburgh: 1833. V. 51

NAISMITH, JOHN
General View of the Agriculture of the county of Clydesdale. Edinburgh: 1798. V. 51; 52
General View of the Agriculture of the County of Clydesdale; with Observations on the Means Of its Improvement. London: 1806. V. 49; 52
Thoughts on Various Objects of Industry Pursued in Scotland, with a View to Enquire by What Means the Labour of the People May be Directed to Promote the Public Prosperity. Edinburgh: 1790. V. 48

NAITHANI, H. B.
Flowering Plants of India, Nepal and Bhutan. 1990. V. 51
Flowering Plants of India, Nepal and Bhutan (Not Recorded in Sir J. D. Hooker's Flora of British India). Dehra Dun: 1990. V. 48

NAITO, AIKIRA
Katsura a Princely Retreat. Tokyo: 1977,. V. 48

NAKHLAH, YA'KUB
New Manual of English and Arabic Conversation. Boulack nr. Cairo: 1874. V. 49

NALDRET, PERCY
Collected Magic Series. Numbers 1-8. Portsmouth: 1920-27. V. 52

NALL, G. H.
The Life of the Sea Trout, Especially in Scottish Waters... London: 1930. V. 52; 53

NALL, JOHN GREAVES
Great Yarmouth and Lowestoft, a Handbook for Visitors and Residents... London: 1866. V. 54

NALSON, J.
A True Copy of the Journal of the High Court of Justice, for the Tryal of K. Charles I, As It Was Read in the House of Commons, and Attested Under the Hand of Phelps, Clerk to that Infamous Court. London: 1684. V. 47

NALSON, JOHN
The Character of a Rebellion, and What England May Expect From One. London: 1681. V. 49
The Common Interest of King and People... London: 1678. V. 51

NAMES of the Streets, Lanes, and Alleys in the Town of Boston, with an Index, Directing to the Page Where the Streets, &c May Be Found. Boston: 1800. V. 49; 53

NAMIER, LEWIS B.
The House of Commons 1754-1790. London: 1964. V. 52

NANCE, JOSEPH M.
The Attack and Counter-Attack: the Texas-Mexican Frontier, 1842. Austin: 1964. V. 49

NANCE, ROBERT MORTON
Sailing-Ship Models. London: 1924. V. 47; 50; 52; 54

NANCREDE, JOSEPH
Proposals for Publishing, by Subscription, a New System of Geography, Ancient and Modern. Salem: 1802. V. 49

NANI, BATTISTA
The History of the Affairs of Europe in this Present Age, But More Particularly of the Republick of Venice. London: 1673. V. 49

NANKIEVELL, JOHN H.
History of the Military Organizations of the State of Colorado 1860-1935. Denver: 1935. V. 54

NANKING Memorial Hall of Taiping Tienkuo. The Arts of Taiping Tienkuo. 1959. V. 52

NANNI, GIOVANNI
Berosus Babilonicus de Antiquitatibus. Paris: 1509. V. 50; 53

NANSEN, FRIDTJOF
Adventure and Other Papers. London: 1927. V. 50
Farthest North. London: 1897. V. 47; 48; 49; 50; 51; 53; 54
Farthest North. New York: 1897. V. 47; 48; 50; 51
Farthest North. London: 1898. V. 47; 48; 49; 50; 54
Farthest North. London: 1904. V. 53
The First Crossing of Greenland. London: 1890. V. 49
The First Crossing of Greenland. London: 1910. V. 53
The Fram Expedition. San Francisco: 1897. V. 54
In Northern Mists. London: 1910. V. 49
In Northern Mists. London: 1911. V. 49; 50; 52; 54
In Northern Mists. Arctic Exploration in Early Times. New York: 1911. V. 49
The Norwegian North Polar Expedition 1893-1896 Scientific Results. New York: 1969. V. 52; 54
Through Siberia - The Land of the Future. London: 1914. V. 50; 53
Through Siberia, the Land of the Future. New York: 1914. V. 50; 53

NANSON, W.
Some Municipal Records of the City of Carlisle, viz, the Elizabethan Constitutions, Orders, Provisions, Articles and Rules from the Dormont Book, and Rules and Orders of the Eight Trading Guilds, Prefaced by Chapters on the Corp. Charters & Guilds... Carlisle: 1887. V. 52

NAOGEORGUS, THOMAS
The Popish Kindome or Reigne of Antichrist... London: 1880. V. 51

NAOUM, PHOKION P.
Nitroglycerine and Nitroglycerine Explosives. Baltimore: 1928. V. 54

NAPIER, CHARLES
An Account of the War in Portugal Between Don Pedro and Don Miguel. London: 1836. V. 47; 50

NAPIER, D. DEHANE
David Napier Engineer 1790-1869. Glasgow: 1912. V. 49

NAPIER, E.
Wild Sports in Europe, Asia and Africa. London: 1844. V. 49

NAPIER, FRANCIS
Notes of a Voyage from New South Wales to the North Coast of Australia. Glasgow: 1876. V. 52

NAPIER, JOHN
De Arte Logistica Joannis Naperi Merchistonii Baronis Libri Qui Supersunt. Edinburgi: 1839. V. 54

NAPIER, JOHN W.
John Thomson of Duddingston, Landscape Painter. Edinburgh: 1919. V. 47

NAPIER, MARK
Memoirs of John Napier of Merchiston, His Lineage, Life and Times... Edinburgh: 1834. V. 52; 54
Memorials and Letters Illustrative of the Life and Times of John Graham of Claverhouse, Viscount Dundee. Edinburgh: 1859. V. 52
Memorials and Letters Illustrative of the Life and Times of John Graham of Claverhouse, Viscount Dundee. Edinburgh: 1859-62. V. 49; 53

NAPIER, P. H.
Catalogue of Primates in the British Museum. London: 1976-90. V. 50

NAPIER, ROBERT W.
John Thomson of Duddingston, Landscape Painter, His Life and Work... Edinburgh/London: 1919. V. 54

NAPIER, WILLIAM FRANCIS PATRICK
History of the War in the Peninsula and in the South of France. London: 1851. V. 51
History of the War in the Peninsula and in the South of France from 1807 to 1814. Warne: 1900. V. 52
History of the War in the Peninsula, and in the South of France, from the Year 1807 to 1814... London: 1835-40. V. 50
History of the War in the Peninsula and In the South of France from the Year 1807 to the Year 1814. London: 1828-40. V. 52; 54
History of the War in the Peninsula and in the South of France, from the Year 1807 to the Year 1814. London: 1832-40. V. 50
History of the War in the Peninsula and in the South of France from the Year 1807 to the Year 1814. London: 1900. V. 53
Observations on the Corn Law...Addressed to Lord Ashley, Because His Perserving Efforts to Protect the Factory Children Given Him a Just title to the Respect of All Persons Who Acknowledge the Value of Justice and Benevolence in National Policy. London: 1841. V. 53

THE NAPOLEON Gallery; or, Illustrations of the Life and Times of the Emperor of France. London: 1837. V. 51

NAPOLEON, JOSEPH CHARLES PAUL, PRINCE
On the Conduct of the War in the East. London: 1855. V. 51; 52

NAPOLEON I, EMPEROR OF THE FRENCH
Copies of Original Letters from the Army of General Bonaparte in Egypt, Intercepted by the Fleet Under the Command of Admiral Lord Nelson. London: 1798-99. V. 50
Letters Written on Board His Majesty's Ship the Northumberland, and at Saint Helena... London: 1816. V. 50
Memoirs of the Public and Private Life... London: 1837. V. 49
Napoleon His Own Historian. London: 1818. V. 47
Napoleon's Memoirs. London: 1945. V. 50
Napoleon's Memoirs. Waltham St. Lawrence: 1945. V. 49; 50
Supper at Beaucaire. Waltham St. Lawrence: 1945. V. 47; 49

NAPOLEON III, EMPEROR OF THE FRENCH
History of Julius Caesar. (with) The History of Julius Caesar. Atlas. Maps to the Second Volume. New York: 1865. V. 47

NAPOLEONIS Reliquiae. A Poem in Six Cantos. London: 1841. V. 49

NAPTON, WILLIAM B.
Over the Santa Fe Trail 1857. Santa Fe: 1964. V. 52; 53

NARAMORE, EARL
Principles and Practice of Loading Ammunition. 1971. V. 54

NARASIMHACHAR, R.
The Kesava Temple at Bellur. Bangalore: 1979. V. 49

NARBOROUGH, JOHN
An Account of Several Late Voyages and Discoveries to the South and North. Walford: 1694. V. 50

NARDELLI, F.
The Rhinoceros, a Monograph. London: 1988. V. 49

NARDI, JACOPO
Le Historie Della Citta Di Fiorenza. Lyons: 1582. V. 48; 52
Vita Dantonio Giacomini Tebalducci Malespini. Florence: 1597. V. 48

NARES, EDWARD
Heraldic Anomalies. London: 1823. V. 50; 53
Heraldic Anomalies. London: 1824. V. 48
Heraldic Anomalies. London: 1832. V. 52
Memoirs of the Life and Administration of the Right Honourable William Cecil, Lord Burghley... London: 1828-30-31. V. 53
Sermons, Composed for Country Congregations. London: 1803. V. 47
Think's-I-To-Myself. London: 1811. V. 48
Thinks-I-To-Myself; a Serio-Ludicro, Tragico-Conico Tale... London: 1816. V. 51

NARES, GEORGE STRONG
Narrative of a Voyage to the Polar Sea During 1875-6 in H.M. Ships 'Alert' and 'Discovery'. London: 1878. V. 49

NARES, ROBERT
Illustrations of Difficult Words and Phrases Occurring in the English Writers of the Age of Elizabeth.. London: 1818. V. 52

NARES, ROBERT continued
Principles of Government Deduced from Reason, Supported by English Experience and Opposed to French Errors. London: 1792. V. 52

NARJOUX, FELIX
Notes and Sketches of an Architect: Taken During a Journey in the North-West of Europe. London: 1876. V. 48

NARKISS, BEZALEL
Hebrew Illuminated Manuscripts in the British Isles. London: 1982. V. 48

A **NARRATIVE** Of a Singular Imposition, Practised Upon the Benevolence of a Lady Residing in the Vicinity of the City of Bristol by a Young Woman of the Name of Mary Willcocks, Alias Baker, Alias Bakerstendht, Alias Caraboo, Princess of Javasu. Brisol: 1817. V. 50

A **NARRATIVE** of Five Youth from the Sandwich Islands, viz: Obookiah, Hopoo, Tennoe, Honoree and Prince Tamoree Now Receiving Education in This Country. New York: 1816. V. 47; 48

NARRATIVE of James Williams, an American Slave, Who Was for Several Years a Driver on a Cotton Plantation in Alabama. New York: 1838. V. 51

NARRATIVE of Privations and Sufferings of United States Officers and Soldiers...in the Hands of Rebel Authorities. Philadelphia: 1864. V. 50

A **NARRATIVE** of Procedure Before the Court of Session, and Circumstances Connected Therewith in the Trial of John Hay (etc.). Edinburgh: 1822. V. 50

A **NARRATIVE** of the Grand Festival, Given by the Inhabitants fo King's Lynn, on Friday the 22nd of July, 1814. Lynn Regis: 1814. V. 50; 52

NARRATIVE of the Loss of the Hon. East India Company's ship Duke of York, in the Bay of Bengal, on the 21st May, 1833. Edinburgh: 1834. V. 53

A **NARRATIVE** of the Loss of the Kent East India Man, by Fire, in the Bay of Biscay, on the 1st march, 1825, in a Letter to a Friend. Edinburgh: 1825. V. 51

NARRATIVE of the Loss of the Mary Rose at Spithead July 20th, 1545. Portsea: 1849. V. 48

A **NARRATIVE** of the Proceedings of His Majesty's Fleet in the Mediterranean and the Combined Fleets of France and Spain, from the Year 1741 to March 1744... London: 1745. V. 53

NARRATIVE of the Surveying Voyages of His Majesty's Ships Adventure and Beagle, Between the Years 1826 and 1836... London: 1839. V. 52

A **NARRATIVE** of the Voyages, Undertaken by Order of Prince Henry... London: 1790. V. 53

NARRATIVES of Shipwrecks: Loss of the Lady Hobart Packet; of the Hon. East India Company's Ship Cabalva; and of the Centaur and Litchfield Men-of-War. London: 1824. V. 53

NARRATIVES of the Wreck of the Whale-Ship Essex of Natucket Which Was Destroyed by a Whale in the Pacific Ocean in the Year 1819... Waltham St. Lawrence: 1935. V. 51

NARRAYAN, R. K.
An Astrologer's Day and Other Stories. London: 1947. V. 51
The Bachelor of Arts. London: 1937. V. 53
The English Teacher. London: 1945. V. 52; 53

NARRIEN, JOHN
An Historical Account of the Origin and Progress of Astronomy... London: 1850(1833). V. 52

NASATIR, A. P.
Before Lewis and Clark - Documents Illustrating the History of the Missouri, 1785-1804. St. Louis: 1952. V. 52; 54

NASH, CHARLES EDWARD
Biographical Sketches of Gen. Pat Cleburne and Gen. T. C. Hindman. Little Rock: 1898. V. 49

NASH, FREDERICK
Picturesque Views of the City of Paris and Its Environs. London: 1823. V. 52; 54
A Series of Views...of the Collegiate Chapel of St. London: 1805. V. 50

NASH, JOHN
Balise Hamlet. Bristol: 1826. V. 47
Happy New Lear. London: 1957. V. 49
Illustrations of Her Majesty's Palace at Brighton. London: 1838. V. 47
John Nash. Twenty One Engravings. Wakefield: 1993. V. 50; 51
Twenty One Wood Engravings. London: 1993. V. 49; 52

NASH, JOHN HENRY
Cobden-Sanderson and the Doves Press. San Francisco: 1929. V. 51

NASH, JOSEPH
The Mansions of England in the Olden Time. London: 1869-72. V. 48
The Mansions of England in the Olden Time. (with) Views of the Interior and Exterior of Windsor Castle. London: 1839-52. V. 50; 52

NASH, OGDEN
The Bad Parents' Garden of Verse. New York: 1936. V. 49; 50
The Cricket of Carador. Garden City: 1925. V. 49
Everyone But Thee and Me. Boston: 1962. V. 48
Family Reunion. Boston: 1951. V. 54
Four Prominent So and So's. New York: 1934. V. 48; 50; 51
Free Wheeling. New York: 1931. V. 48
Good Intentions. Boston: 1942. V. 48; 54
Happy Days. New York: 1933. V. 48
Hard Lines. New York: 1931. V. 48
I'm a Stranger Here Myself. 1938. V. 50
One Touch of Venus. Boston: 1944. V. 51
The Primrose Path. New York: 1935. V. 48
The Private Dining Room. Boston: 1952. V. 48
The Private Dining Room. Boston: 1953. V. 50; 53; 54
There's Always Another Windmill. Boston: 1968. V. 48
Versus. Boston: 1949. V. 54

NASH, PAUL
Aerial Flowers: an Essay. Oxford: 1946. V. 49
The Complete Graphic Work of Paul Nash. London: 1973. V. 49
Dear Mercia: Paul Nash Letters to Mercia Oakley 1909-18. London: 1909-18. V. 52
Dear Mercia: Paul Nash Letters to Mercia Oakley, 1909-18. 1991. V. 47; 54
Dear Mercia: Paul Nash Letters to Mercia Oakley, 1909-18. London: 1991. V. 50
Engravings on Wood 1919-1928. London: 1928. V. 52
Monster Field - a Discovery Recorded by Paul Nash. Oxford: 1946. V. 49; 52; 53
Paintings, Drawings and Illustrations. London: 1948. V. 48
Paul Nash. Harmondsworth: 1944. V. 52
Paul Nash - a Portfolio of Colour Plates. London: 1937. V. 48; 52; 53
Room and Book. London: 1932. V. 52
Room and Book. New York: 1932. V. 51

NASH, R.
Calligraphy and Printing in the Sixteenth Century. Antwerp: 1964. V. 52

NASH, THOMAS
Qvarternio or a Fovrefold Vvay to a Happie Life Set Fort in a Dialouge Betweene a Countryman and a Citizen, a Divine and a Lawyer. London: 1633. V. 49
The Returne of the Renowned Cavaliero Pasquill of England, from the Other Side of the Seas, and His Meeting with Marforius at London Upon the Royall Exchange. London: 1589. V. 47
A Spring Song. London: 1898. V. 50

NASH, WALLIS
Two Years in Oregon. New York: 1882. V. 53

NASHE, THOMAS
Summer's Last Will and Testament. London: 1946. V. 50
The Works. London: 1910. V. 51
The Works. Oxford: 1966. V. 48; 50

NASKAR, K.
Plant Wealth of the Lower Ganga Delta. Delhi: 1993. V. 50

NASMITH, JAMES
An Examination of the Statutes Now in Force Relating to the Assize of Bread... Wisbech: 1800. V. 51
Itineraria Symonis Simeonis et Willelmi de Worcestre Quibus Accedit Tractatus de Metro. Cambridge: 1778. V. 54

NASMYTH, JAMES
James Nasmyth, Engineer. London: 1885. V. 50
James Nasymth, Engineer. London: 1883. V. 51
The Moon: Considered as a Planet, a World and a Satellite. London: 1874. V. 50; 54
The Moon: Considered as a Planet, A World and a Satellite. New York: 1885. V. 47

NASR, SEYYED HOSSEIN
Islamic Science, an Illustrated Study. 1976. V. 50
Persia. Bridge of Turquoise. Boston: 1975. V. 52

NASSAU and Florida. New York: 1879. V. 48

NASSAU, ROBERT H.
Fetichism in West Africa: Forty Years' Observation of Native Customs and Superstitions. London: 1904. V. 54

NAST, THOMAS
Aunt Louisa's Gems of Kindness: Comprising Home Kindness, Santa Claus and Kindness to Animals. New York: 1870. V. 49
The Fight at Dame Europa's School. New York: 1871. V. 52

NASTI, MAURO
Schmied. Vicenza: 1991. V. 47

NATALIBUS, PETRUS DE
Catalogus Sanctorum et Gestorum Eorum ex Diversis Voluminibus Collectus. Vicenza: 1493. V. 53

NATES, ROBERT
A Glossary; or Collection of Works, Phrases, Names and Allusions to Custom Proverbs, etc. in the Works of English Authors. London: 1867. V. 51

NATHAN, ELIZA
Langreath, a Tale. London: 1822. V. 53

NATHAN, GEORGE JEAN
The Theatre of the Moment. New York: 1936. V. 47

NATHAN, LEONARD
The Matchmaker's Lament and Other Astonishments: Poems. Northampton: 1967. V. 48; 49; 52; 54

NATHAN, ROBERT
Autumn. New York: 1921. V. 51; 52
Portrait of Jennie. New York: 1940. V. 53

NATION, EARL F.
Student and Chief. The Osler-Camac Correspondence. Pasadena: 1980. V. 51

THE NATION: The Spirit of the Nation. Dublin: 1845. V. 48

NATIONAL Antarctic Expedition 1901-04 Natural History. London: 1901-12. V. 47

NATIONAL ASSOCIATION FOR THE ADVANCEMENT OF ART
Transactions. Liverpool Meeting, 1888. London: 1888. V. 50; 53

NATIONAL ASSOCIATION FOR THE PROMOTION OF SOCIAL SCIENCE
Transactions. 1862. V. 50
Transactions. Dublin: 1881. V. 50; 54

NATIONAL BISCUIT CO.
Trade Mark Litigation. Opinions, Orders, Injunctions and Decrees Relating to Unfair Competition and Infingement of Trade Marks. 1915. V. 50

THE NATIONAL Cyclopaedia of American Biography. New York: 1892. V. 47

THE NATIONAL Encyclopaedia. London: 1882. V. 51

THE NATIONAL Gallery of Pictures by the Great Masters; Purchased by Parliament for the nations, or Presented by Individuals. London: 1860. V. 47

THE NATIONAL Gazetteer: a Topographical Dictionary of the British Islands... London: 1868. V. 49

THE NATIONAL Geographic Society -- U.S. Army Air Corps Stratosphere Flight of 1935 in the Balloon "Explorer II". Washington: 1936. V. 53

NATIONAL HOME FOR DISABLED VOLUNTEER SOLDIERS
Report of the Board of Managers...for the Fiscal Year Ended 30, 1895-1905 (Lacking 1896). Washington: 1896-1906. V. 54

NATIONAL Iron and Steel, Coal and Coke Blue Book. Pittsburg: 1902. V. 49; 50

NATIONAL LEAGUE OF PROFESSIONAL BASEBALL CLUBS
Constitution and Playing Rules of the National League of Professional Base Ball Clubs, 1906. New York and Chicago: 1906. V. 49

NATIONAL LIVE STOCK ASSOCIATION
Proceedings of the Fourth Annual Convention, Salt Lake City. Salt Lake City: 1901. V. 49
Proceedings of the Second Annual Convention, Denver, Colorado... Denver: 1899. V. 49

NATIONAL MARITIME MUSEUM
Catalogue of the Library. London. V. 52
Catalogue of the Library. London: 1968-71. V. 47; 51

NATIONAL Nursery Rhymes and Nursery songs. London. V. 51

NATIONAL PALACE MUSEUM
Blue-White Ware of the Ming Dynasty. Hong Kong: 1963. V. 49

THE NATIONAL Tax Law of July 1st, 1862 and the Amended Act of March '63, Embracing, Also a Complete Alphabetical Summary of Articles Taxed and Rates Imposed. Springfield: 1863. V. 51

THE NATIONAL Temple: Containing a Complete History of the Battles Fought by the Navy of the United States. Boston: 1816. V. 50

NATIONAL Union Catalog of Pre-1956 Imprints. London: 1968-81. V. 47

NATIONAL UNION CONVENTION
Presidential Election, 1864. Proceedings of the National Union Convention Held in Baltimore, Md., June 7th and 18th, 1864. New York: 1864. V. 54

NATIONAL WOMAN SUFFRAGE & EDUCATIONAL COMMITTEE
An Appeal to the Women of the United States. Hartford: 1871. V. 50

NATIONAL GALLERY, LONDON
Report of the National Gallery Site Commission, Together with Minutes, Evidence, Appendix and Index. London: 1857. V. 52

THE NATIONS of the Earth. London: 1858. V. 54

THE NATIVE Tribes of South Australia. Adelaide: 1879. V. 52

NATKIN, MARCEL
Photography of the Nude. London: 1937. V. 47

NATTA, MARCO ANTONIO
Marci Antonii Nattae Astensis De Deo Libri XV. Venice: 1560. V. 52

NATTER, LAURENT
Traite de la Methode Antique de Graver en Pierres Fines, Comparee avec la methode Moderne... London: 1754. V. 52

NATTES, JOHN CLAUDE
Bath, Illustrated by a Series of Views from the Drawings of J. C. Nattes... London and Bristol: 1806. V. 47; 52
A Graphic and Descriptive Tour of the University of Oxford. London: 1805. V. 49; 52

NATURA Brevium Newly Corrected, in Englishe: with Divers Addicions. London: 1557. V. 51

The **NATURAL** History of Quadrupeds and Cetaceous Animals. London: 1821. V. 51

A **NATURAL** History of Singing Birds; and Particularly, That Species of Them Most Commonly Bred in Scotland, by a Lover Birds. Edinburgh: 1754. V. 54

THE NATURAL History of the Three Kingdoms. London: 1870. V. 49

THE NATURE and Making of Papyrus. Yorkshire: 1973. V. 49; 53

THE NATURE Book. A Popular Description by Pen and Camera of the Delights and Beauties of the Open Air. London: 1908/09. V. 48

NATUURLYK Toverboek, Behelzende de Verbaazendste Geheimen van Natuur en Konst, Opgehelderd met Plaaten. Amsterdam & Harlingen: 1791-94. V. 51

NAUBERT, CHRISTIANE BENEDICTE EUGENIE
Herman of Unna; a Series of Adventures of the Fifteenth Century, in Which the Proceedings of the Secret Tribunal Under the Emperors Winceslaus and Sigismond, are Delineated. London: 1794. V. 54
Walter de Monbary, Grand Master of Knights Templars. London: 1803. V. 54

NAUDE, GABRIEL
The History of Magic by Way of Apology... London: 1657. V. 48
Instructions Concerning Erecting a Library: Presented to My Lord the President De Mesme. Cambridge: 1903. V. 48; 54
Parisini Bibliographia Politica. 1642. V. 50

NAUMANN, EMIL
The History of Music. London. V. 48

NAUMANN, J. A.
Naturgesc hichte der vogel Mitteleuropas. Gera: 1897-1905. V. 54

NAUMANN, J. F.
Iconographie d'Oiseaux d'Europe et de Leurs Oeufs. Paris: 1910. V. 51; 52

NAUNY, B.
A Treatise on Cholelithiasis. London: 1896. V. 49; 54

NAVAJO SCHOOL OF BASKETRY
Indian Basket Weaving. Los Angeles: 1903. V. 51; 54

A NAVAL Alphabet. London: 1910. V. 53

NAVAL and Martial Biography: or Its Memoirs of Several Hundred Illustrious British Naval and Military Characters Who Have Distinguished Themselves Under the British Standard by their Achievements... Ormskirk: 1806. V. 51

THE NAVAL Record Containing Authentick memoirs of...Admiral Lord Nelson...Particularly His Engagements Fought at the Nile, Copenhagen and Trafalgar near Cadiz. Halifax: 1806. V. 51

NAVARI, LEONORA
Greece and the Levant. The Catalogue of the Henry Myron Blackmer Collection of Books and Manuscripts. London: 1989. V. 48

NAVARRETE, DOMINGO
The Travels and Controversies of Friar Domingo Navarrete, 1618-1686. Cambridge: 1962. V. 47; 50; 53

NAVIER, L. M. H.
Rapport A Monsieur Becquey...et Memoire sur Les Ponts Suspendus. Paris: 1823. V. 51

NAVILLE, EDOUARD
The Cemeteries of Abydos. London: 1913-14. V. 49; 51
The Temple of Deir el Bahari. London: 1894-1908. V. 51
The Temple of Deir El Bahari. London: 1895/96/98. V. 48
The XIth Dynasty Temple at Deir el-Bahari. London: 1907-13. V. 49

NAVIR, M.
Projet Pour l'Etablissement d'une gare a Choisy, Contenant l'Expose des Travaux Proposes ou Entrepris Jusqu'a Present a Paris Pour Mettre les Bateaux a l'Abri des debacles, Suivi d'une Notice Descriptive du Pont de Choisy, ou Sont Indiques... Paris: 1811. V. 51

NAVISTOKE HYDRAULIC GOLD MINING CO.
Prospectus. 1899?. V. 50

NAWAB, SARABHAI MANILAL
Oldest Rajasthani Paintings from Jain Bhandars. Ahmedabad: 1959. V. 51

NAXAGORAS, J. E. VON, PSEUD.
Chymischer Oder Alchymistischer Particular, Das Ist Treuer Unterricht Vom Goldund Silber-Machen. Rostock: 1706. V. 53

NAYLER, GEORGE
A Collection of Coats of Arms Borne by the Nobility and Gentry of the County of Glocester. London: 1792. V. 49; 51

NAYLOR, COLLIN
Contemporary Artists. London: 1989. V. 49

NAYLOR, FRANCIS HARE
The History of the Helvetic Republics. London: 1809. V. 50; 53

NAYLOR, G.
Bloomsbury: the Artists, Authors and Designers by Themselves. London: 1990. V. 52

NAYLOR, GLORIA
The Women of Brewster Place. New York: 1982. V. 47; 51; 52; 54
The Women of Brewster Place. London: 1983. V. 51

NAYLOR, ROBERT
From John O'Groats to Land's End or 1372 Miles on Foot. London: 1916. V. 54

NAYLOR, ROBERT A.
Across the Atlantic. London: 1894?. V. 53

NAZARI, GIOVANNI BATTISTA
Della Tramutione Metallica Sogni Tre... Brescia: 1599. V. 48

NEAGOE, PETER
Americans Abroad. The Hague,: 1932. V. 49; 51; 53
Storm. Paris: 1932. V. 52
What is Surrealism. Paris: 1932. V. 53

NEAL, AVON
Pigs and Eagles. North Brookfield: 1978. V. 47; 48

NEAL, D. A.
The Illinois Central Railroad. Its Position and Prospects. 1851. V. 48

NEAL, DANIEL
The History of New England. London: 1720. V. 47; 50
The History of the Puritans or Protest and Non-Coformists, from the Reformation Under King Henry VIII, to an Account of Their Principles... London: 1754. V. 49
The History of the Puritans or Protestant Non-Conformists, from the Reformation...to the Act of Toleration by King William and Queen Mary in the Year 1689. London: 1732-3-6-8. V. 54

NEAL, JOHN
Otho: a Tragedy, in Five Acts. Boston: 1819. V. 54
Our Country. Portland: 1830. V. 50

NEAL, JOSEPH C.
In Town and about of Pencillings and Pennings. Philadelphia: 1843. V. 49

NEAL, MARIE C.
In Honolulu Gardens. Honolulu: 1928. V. 52

NEAL, THOMAS
Commentarii...in Haggaevm. Paris: 1557. V. 50

NEAL, THOMAS ATWILL
Saint Vibiana's: Los Angeles Cathedral 1876-1950. Los Angeles: 1950. V. 48

NEAL, WILLIAM KEITH
Great British Gunmakers 1740-1760: The History of John Twigg and the Packington Guns. London: 1975. V. 50

NEALE, C. M.
An Index to Pickwick. London: 1897. V. 49

NEALE, CORNELIUS
Lyrical Dramas: With Dramatic Hours, A Miscellany of Odes and Songs. London: 1819. V. 51

NEALE, ERSKINE
Whychcotte of St. John's. Or, the court, the Camp, the Quarter-Deck, and the Cloister. London: 1833. V. 51

NEALE, HARRY
A Reply to Erroneous Statements and Unwarranted Reflections in a Publication Entitled Sketches of Algiers, by William Shaler, American Consul General for that Regency. Malta: 1826. V. 49

NEALE, JAMES
The Abbey Chruch of St. Ablans. London: 1878. V. 47; 49

NEALE, JOHN
The Elizabethan House of Commons. 1949. Elizabeth I and Her Parliaments 1559-1581. Elizabeth I and Her Parliaments 1584-1601. London: 1949-57. V. 52

NEALE, JOHN MASON
Good King Wenceslas: A Carol. Birmingham: 1895. V. 48; 51

NEALE, JOHN PRESTON
The History and Antiquities of the Abbey Church of St. Peter, Westminster... London: 1818/23. V. 54
The History and Antiquities of Westminster Abbey... London: 1856. V. 49
Views of the Most Interesting Collegiate and Paraochial Churches of Great Britain... London: 1824. V. 49

NEALE, WALTER
The Sovereignty of the States, an Oration Address to the Survivors of the Eighth Virginia Regiment. New York & Washington: 1910. V. 47; 50; 53

NEALE, WILLIAM JOHNSON
The Captain's Wife. London: 1842. V. 51
Cavendish; or, the Patrician at Sea. 1832. V. 47
The Flying Dutchman: a Legend of the High Seas. London: 1839. V. 51
Gentleman Jack. London: 1837. V. 51
Paul Periwinkle: or, the Pressgang. London: 1841. V. 53
Paul Periwinkle: or, the Pressgang. London: 1847. V. 51
The Priors of Prague. London: 1836. V. 51

NEALLY, AMY
Baby Days. Our Baby's History. New York: 1890. V. 53

NEANDER, MICHAEL
Opus Aureum et Scholasticum... Leipzig: 1577. V. 52

NEARING, SCOTT
Black America. New York: 1929. V. 54
Free Born. An Unpublishable Novel. New York: 1932. V. 52

NEASHAM, GEORGE
North Country Sketches. Durham: 1893. V. 47

NEBRASKA Brand Book 1906. V. 50

NEBRASKA Brand Book 1908. V. 50

NEBRIJA, ELIO ANTONIO DE
Introductiones in Latinam Grammaticen... Granada: 1540. V. 48
Rerum a Fernando et Elisabe Hispania & Felicissimis Regibus Gestarum Decades Duae, Necnon Belli Navariensis Libri Duo, Nunc Secundo Editi & Exactiore Vigilantia ad Prototypi Fidem Recogniti & Emendati. Granada: 1550. V. 52

A NECESSARY Doctrine and Erudition for Any Christen Man, Sette Forthe by the Kynges Maieste of England, &c. London: 1543. V. 49; 51

NECKER, JACQUES
Of the Importance of Religious Opinions. Boston: 1796. V. 50; 51; 53

NECKER, SUZANNE CURCHOD
The Importance of Religious Opinions. Boston: 1796. V. 50

THE NECKLACE. Newburyport: 1824. V. 53

NEED, THOMAS
Six Years in the Bush; or extracts from the Journal of a Settler in Upper Canada, 1832-1838. London: 1838. V. 52

NEEDHAM, JOSEPH
Biochemistry and Morphogenesis. Cambridge: 1942. V. 53
Heavenly Clockwork: The Great Astronomical Clocks of Medieval China. Cambridge: 1960. V. 53
A History of Embryology. London: 1959. V. 53
Science and Civilisation in China. Cambridge: 1965-71. V. 49
Science and Civilisation in China. Volume 2: History of Scientific Thought. Cambridge: 1956. V. 49
Science and Civilisation in China. Volume 3. Mathematics and the Sciences of the Heavens and the Earth. Cambridge: 1959. V. 49
Science and Civilisation in China. Volume 4: Physics and Physical Technology, Part II; mechanical Engineering. Cambridge: 1965. V. 49
Science and Civilization in China. Cambridge: 1959-71. V. 53
Science and Civilisation in China. Volume 4: Physics and Physical Technology, Part III: Civil Engineering and Nautics. Cambridge: 1971. V. 49

NEEDHAM, MARCHAMONT
A Pacquet of Advices and Animadversions, Sent from London to the Men of Shaftesbury. London: 1676. V. 50
A Pacquet of Advices and Animadversions Sent from London to the Men of Shaftesbury. (with) A Second Pacquet of Advices...Sent to the Men of Shaftesbury. London: 1676-77. V. 47

NEEDHAM, PAUL
Twelve Centuries of Bookbindings 400-1600. New York, London: 1979. V. 50; 51; 52

NEEDHAM, T. H.
The Complete Sportsman. London: 1817. V. 48

NEEDLER, HENRY
The Works... London: 1728. V. 48

NEEDLER, WINIFRED
Predynastic and Archaic Egypt in the Brooklyn Museum. Brooklyn: 1984. V. 49

NEEL, ALICE
Exhibition Catalogue. Atlanta: 1975. V. 51

NEELE, GEORGE P.
Railway Reminiscences. London: 1904. V. 49

NEELY, BARBARA
Blanche on the Lam. 1992. V. 54
Blanche on the Lam. New York: 1992. V. 50

NEESE, GEORGE MICHAEL
Three Years in the Confederate Horse Artillery, by a Gunner in Chew's Battery, Stuart's Horse Artillery Army of Northern Virginia. New York & Washington: 1911. V. 48; 49; 50

NEFF, WALLACE
Architecture of Southern California. Chicago: 1964. V. 48; 50

NEFTEL, WILLIAM
Galvano-Therapeutics. New York: 1873. V. 47; 49; 54

NEGI, J. SINGH B.
Himalayan Travels. 1920. V. 53

THE NEGOTIATORS. Or, Don Diego Brought to Reason. London: 1738. V. 47; 54

THE NEGRO Problem. New York: 1903. V. 51; 52; 54

THE NEGRO Question. Attitude of the Progressive Party Toward the Colored Race. Colonel Roosevelt's Reply to a Query at the Progressive National Convention: His Letter to Julian Harris of Atlanta and the Statement of All the Negro Delegates... New York: 1912. V. 54

NEGULESCO, JEAN
Things I Did...and Things I Think I Did. New York: 1984. V. 51

NEHLS, EDWARD
D. H. Lawrence: a Composite Biography. 1957/58/59. V. 51

NEHRU, JAWAHARLAL
Nehru on World History. New York: 1960. V. 47; 48; 49

NEIDHARD, C.
Diphtheria, As It Prevailed in the United States from 1860 to 1866, Preceded by an Historical Account of Its Phenomena, Its Nature and Homoeopathic Treatment. New York: 1867. V. 51

NEIHARDT, JOHN G.
The Divine Enchantment. New York: 1900. V. 53
Indian tales and Others. New York: 1926. V. 50
The Song of the Indian Wars. New York: 1925. V. 50; 51

NEIL, T. H.
Neil's Complete Angler. London: 1830. V. 47

NEILL, A. S.
The Problem Teacher. London: 1939. V. 47

NEILL, EDWARD D.
The Founders of Maryland as Portrayed in Manuscripts, Provincial Records and Early Documents. Albany: 1876. V. 53
History of Hennepin County and the City of Minneapolis, Including the Explorers and Pioneers of Minnesota...and Outlines of the History of Minnesota... Minneapolis: 1881. V. 48
History of the Virginia Company of London. Albany: 1869. V. 51; 54
History of Washington County and the St. Croix Valley, Including the Explorers and Pioneers of Minnesota. Minneapolis: 1881. V. 52
Virginia Carolorum: the Colony Under the Rule of Charles the First and Second. Albany: 1886. V. 54

NEILL, J. MARTIN BLADEN
Recollections of Four Years' Service in the East with H. M. Fortieth Regiment. London: 1846. V. 53

NEILL, J. R.
The Scalawagons of Oz. 1941. V. 47

NEILL, JOHN
Outlines of the Arteries: With Short Descriptions. Philadelphia: 1852. V. 49; 51; 54

NEILSON, GEORGE
Annals of the Solway Until A.D. 1307. Glasgow: 1899. V. 52

NEILSON, HARRY B.
Droll Doings. London: 1915. V. 50

NEILSON, WILLIAM
Mesmerism in Its Relation to Health and Disease and the Present State of Medicine. Edinburgh: 1855. V. 52

NEIMAN, LE ROY
Horses. New York: 1979. V. 51; 52

NEISON, EDMUND
The Moon and the Condition and Configurations of its Surface. London: 1876. V. 48; 54

NELIGAN, WILLIAM CHADWICK
A Brief Inscription of a Rare French Testament by the Doctors of Louvain, Printed at Paris 1662... Cork: 1861. V. 49

NELL, WILLIAM C.
The Colored Patriots of the American Revolution, with Sketches of Several Distinguished Colored Persons. Boston: 1855. V. 48; 50; 53

NELLES, ANNIE
Ravenia: or, The Outcast Redeemed. Topeka: 1872. V. 53

NELSON, ALICE RUTH MOORE DUNBAR
Give Us Each Day: The Diary of Alice Dunbar-Nelson. New York: 1984. V. 53
The Goodness of St. Rocque and Other Stories. New York: 1899. V. 53

NELSON, B.
The Sulidae, Gannets and Boobies. 1978. V. 52
The Sulidae. Gannets and Boobies. London: 1978. V. 50; 53

NELSON, C.
The Trees of Ireland, Native and Naturalized. London: 1993. V. 52

NELSON, DENNIS D.
The Integration of the Negro Into the U.S. Navy. New York: 1951. V. 53

NELSON, EDWARD
The Eskimo Bering Strait. Washington: 1899. V. 49; 50

NELSON, EDWARD W.
Lower California and Its Natural Resources. Washington: 1921. V. 53
Lower California and Its Natural Resources. Washington: 1922. V. 50
Report Upon Natural History Collection Made in Alaska Between the Years 1877 and 1881. Washington: 1887. V. 49; 52; 53; 54

NELSON, GEORGE
Annals of the Solway Until A.D. 1307. Glasgow: 1899. V. 50
Display. New York: 1953. V. 50; 51; 53
Living Spaces. New York: 1952. V. 51

NELSON, HAROLD HAYDEN
The Great Hypostyle Hall at Karnak. Chicago: 1981. V. 49; 51
Key Plans Showing Locations of Theban Temple Decorations. Chicago: 1929. V. 51

NELSON, HENRY LOOMIS
The Army of the United States. New York: 1895. V. 52

NELSON, HORATIO, VISCOUNT
The Dispatches and Letters of Vice Admiral Lord Viscount Nelson. London: 1845-44-46. V. 47
Nelson's Letters from the Leeward Islands and Other Original Documents in the Public Record Office and the British Museum. Waltham St. Lawrence: 1953. V. 47

NELSON, J. B.
The Sulidae, Gannets and Boobies. Oxford: 1978. V. 54

NELSON, J. S.
Fishes of the World. New York: 1984. V. 50; 51

NELSON, JOHN
The History, Topography, and Antiquities of the Parish of St. Mary Islington, In the County of Middlesex. London: 1811. V. 49

NELSON, JOHN R.
Twelve American Writers. Easthampton: 1974. V. 48

NELSON, MARY C.
The Legendary Artists of Taos. New York: 1980. V. 51

NELSON, OLIVER
The Cowman's Southwest: Being the Reminiscences of Oliver Nelson... Glendale: 1953. V. 51; 54

NELSON, PAUL
Cargo. Iowa City: 1972. V. 54

NELSON, PHILIP
Ancient Painted Glass in England 1170-1500. London: 1913. V. 50
The Coinage of Ireland in Copper, Tin and Pewter, 1460-1826. London: 1905. V. 47

NELSON, R.
Asiatic Cholera: its Origin and Spread in Asia, Africa and Europe, Introduction into America through Canada... New York: 1866. V. 51; 54

NELSON, ROBERT
An Address to Persons of Quality and Estate. London: 1715. V. 48; 49
The Life of Dr. George Bull, Late Lord Bishop of St. David's. London: 1714. V. 53
The Life of Dr. George Bull...with the History of Those Controversies in Which He Was Engaged. London: 1713. V. 49

NELSON, STEVE
The Volunteers. New York: 1953. V. 49

NELSON, T. H.
The Birds of Yorkshire. London: 1907. V. 47; 48; 52; 53

NELSON, W.
The Office and Authority of a Justice of Peace... London: 1724. V. 52

NELSON, WILLIAM
Fishing in Eden. London: 1922. V. 52
History of the City of Paterson and the County of Passaic, New Jersey. Paterson: 1901. V. 47
The Laws Concerning Game. London: 1753. V. 48; 50
The Laws Concerning Game, Of Hunting, Hawking, Fishing and Fowling &c. London: 1751. V. 52
The Laws of England Concerning the Game, of Hunting, Hawking, Fishing and Fowling, &c. London: 1736. V. 48
The New Jersey Coast in Three Centuries. New York: 1902. V. 49; 51
The Office and Authority of a Justice of the Peace. London: 1718. V. 48
The Office and Authority of a Justice of the Peace... London: 1729. V. 48
The Office and Authority of a Justice of the Peace. London: 1745. V. 48

NELTHORPE, GEORGE
Julia to Pollio. London: 1770. V. 48; 51; 54

NELVILLE, THOMAS
Imitations of Horace. London: 1758. V. 49

NEMEROV, HOWARD
Guide to the Ruins. New York: 1950. V. 51
The Image and the law. New York: 1947. V. 48
Journal of the Fictive Life. New Brunswick: 1963. V. 52
The Painter Dreaming in the Scholar's House. New York: 1968. V. 48
Stories, Fables and Other Diversions. Boston: 1971. V. 48

NEMES, SYLVESTER
Soft-Hackled Fly Imitations. Bozeman: 1991. V. 47

NEMESIUS
(Greek title) *Nemesis Episcopi et Philosophi, De Natura Hominis.* Antverpiae: 1565. V. 48

NEPOS, CORNELIUS
The Lives of Illustrious Men. London: 1685. V. 47

NEQUATEWA, EDMUND
Truth of a Hopi and Other Clan Stories of Shung-Opovi. Flagstaff: 1936. V. 47; 48

NERI, ANTONIO
L'Arte Vetratia Distinta in Libri Sette...Impressione Seconda, Ricorretta, ed Espurgata da Vari Errori. Florence: 1661. V. 50; 52

NERI, MARY ANNE
The Hour of Trial, a Tale. London: 1808. V. 54

NERNST, WALTER
Theoretical Chemistry From the Standpoint of Avogadro's Rule & Thermodynamics. London: 1895. V. 49; 54

NERSESSIAN, SIRARPIE DER
Armenian Manuscripts in the Freer Gallery of Art. Washington: 1963. V. 50; 54
Armenian Manuscripts in the Walters Art Gallery. Baltimore: 1973. V. 50; 54
The Chester Beatty Library. A Catalogue of the American Manuscripts with an Introduction on the History of Armenian Art. Dublin: 1958. V. 49; 51

NERUDA, PABLO
20 Poemas de Amor Y 1 Cancion Desesperada. 1989. V. 54
20 Poemas de Amor y Una Cancion Desperada. New York: 1989. V. 47
Bestiary/Bestiario. New York: 1965. V. 49; 50

NERUDA, PABLO continued
Canto General. Mexico: 1950. V. 47
The Elementary Odes of Pablo Neruda. New York: 1961. V. 52
The Heights of Macchu Picchu. New York: 1967. V. 52
Odas Elementales. Buenos Aires: 1954/55/57. V. 49
Ode to Typography. Torrance: 1977. V. 54
Selected Poems. Boston: 1971. V. 52
Selected Poems. New York: 1972. V. 52
Skystones. Easthampton: 1981. V. 47
Skystones. Los Angeles: 1990. V. 47
Still Another Day. Port Townsend: 1983. V. 51
We Are Many. London: 1967. V. 49; 51; 52
We Are Many. New York: 1968. V. 52

NESBIT, EDITH
The Complete History of the Bastable Family. London: 1928. V. 48
The Enchanted Castle. London: 1907. V. 48
Five Children and It. London: 1902. V. 49
Five of Us and Madeline. London: 1925. V. 49
Harding's Luck. London: 1909. V. 49
The House of Arden. London: 1908. V. 48; 54
The Magic World. London: 1912. V. 49
Oswald Bastable and Others. London: 1905. V. 48
The Phoenix and the Carpet. London: 1904. V. 47; 48; 54
The Phoenix and the Carpet. New York: 1904. V. 51
A Pomander of Verse. London: 1895. V. 49
A Pomander of Verse. London & Chicago: 1896. V. 54
The Railway Children. London: 1906. V. 49; 53
The Story of the Amulet. London: 1906. V. 47
The Story of the Amulet. 1907. V. 51
The Story of the Amulet. New York: 1907. V. 47
The Story of the Treasure Seekers. London: 1899. V. 47
To the Adventurous. London: 1923. V. 48
The Wouldbegoods Being the Further Adventures of the Treasure Seekers. London: 1901. V. 47

NESBIT, REED M.
Transurethral Prostatectomy. Springfield: 1943. V. 51

NESBITT, FRANCES E.
Algeria and Tunis. London: 1906. V. 53

NESBITT, PAUL H.
The Ancient Mimbrenos. Beloit: 1931. V. 52

NESFIELD, W. EDEN
Specimens of Mediaeval Architecture Chiefly Selected from Examples of the 12th and 13th Centuries in France and Italy. London: 1862. V. 48; 52

NESOM, S.
1000 Years of Japanese Gardens. Tokyo: 1953. V. 48

THE NETHERLAND-Historian. Amsterdam: 1675. V. 47; 49

NETHERSOLE-THOMPSON, D.
The Snow Bunting. London: 1966. V. 50

NETTER, FRANK
The Ciba Collection of Medical Illustrations. Summit: 1975. V. 54

NETTLE, RICHARD
The Salmon Fisheries of the St. Lawrence and Its Tributaries. Montreal: 1857. V. 54

NETTLEFOLD, F. J.
Catalogue of the Paintings and Drawings in the Collection of Frederick John Nettlefold. London: 1933-38. V. 49
The Collection of Bronzes and Castings in Brass and Ormolu Formed by Mr. F. J. Nettlefold. London: 1934. V. 49; 52; 54

NETTLESHIP, J. T.
Robert Browning - Essays and Thoughts. London: 1890. V. 49

NETTLETON, THOMAS
A Treatise on Virtue and Happiness. London: 1736. V. 48
A Treatise on Virtue and Happiness. London: 1751. V. 48

NETTO, J. F.
Die Kunst zu Stricken in Ihrem Ganzen Umfange, Oder Vollstandige und Grundliche Anweisung... Leipzig: 1800. V. 47

NEUBAUER, C.
A Guide to the Qualitatie and Quantitative Analysis of the Urine. London: 1863. V. 49; 54

NEUBERG, VICTOR B.
Songs of the Groves: Records of the Ancient World. Steyning: 1921. V. 47

NEUBERGER, MAX
History of Medicine. London: 1910. V. 48
History of Medicine. London: 1910/25. V. 47

NEUE Thierbilder. 1890. V. 52

NEUFELD, E.
The Hittite Laws. London: 1951. V. 52

NEUGEBAUER, O.
Astronomical Cuneiform Texts. Princeton. V. 49; 52
Astronomical Cuneiform Texts.... London: 1955. V. 50
Astronomical Cuneiform Texts, Babylon Ephemerids of the Seleucid Period for the Motion of the Sun, the Moon and the Planets. New York: 1983. V. 51
Mathematical Cuneiform Texts. New Haven: 1945. V. 49

NEUHAUS, E.
The Art of Treasure Island... Berkeley: 1939. V. 54
The History & Ideals of American Art. Stanford: 1931. V. 47; 50; 51; 53
William Keith, the Man and the Artist. Berkeley: 1938. V. 48; 50

NEUHOF, SELIAN
The Heart: its Physiology, Pathology and Clinical Aspects. Philadelphia: 1923. V. 51

NEUMANN, ARTHUR H.
Elephant Hunting in East Equatorial Africa. 1898. V. 54
Elephant-Hunting in East Equatorial Africa. London: 1898. V. 48
Elephant-Hunting in East Equatorial Africa: Being an Account of Three Years' Ivory-Hunting Under Mount Kenia... New York: 1966. V. 47

NEUMANN, CASPAR
The Chemical Works of Caspar Neumann, M.D.... London: 1759. V. 48; 52

NEUMANN, CHARLES F.
Translations from the Chinese and Armenian. London: 1831. V. 50; 53

NEUMANN, ERICH
The Great Mother. London: 1955. V. 50

NEURDENBURG, ELISABETH
Old Dutch Pottery and Tiles. New York: 1923. V. 47

NEUTRA, RICHARD
Buildings and Projects. Zurich: 1951. V. 48
Buildings and Projects. 1959. V. 54
Life and Human Habitat. Stuttgart: 1956. V. 48
Mystery and Realities of the Site. Scarsdale: 1951. V. 50; 51; 53
Survival Through Design. 1954. V. 50; 53
Survival through Design. New York: 1954. V. 51; 54

NEVADA: a Guide to the Silver State. Portland: 1940. V. 50

NEVADA Brand Book 1946. Reno: 1946. V. 54

NEVADA County Mining Review. Grass Valley: 1895. V. 50

NEVADA Historical Papers 1913-1916. Carson City: 1917. V. 51; 53

NEVADA HISTORICAL SOCIETY
State of Nevada. Second Biennial Report of the Nevada Historical Society, 1909-10. Carson City: 1911. V. 54

NEVADA. STATE BOARD OF STOCK COMMISSIONERS
The Nevada Brand Book and a Compilation of Laws Affecting Live Stock... Reno: 1924. V. 47
Official Brand Book of the State of Nevada. Reno: 1932. V. 47

NEVE, PHILIP
Cursory Remarks On Some of the Ancient English Poets, Particularly Milton. London: 1789. V. 49; 53; 54

NEVE, RICHARD
The City and Country Purchaser and Builder's Dictionary; or the Compleat Builders Guide... London: 1726. V. 48; 54

NEVERS, LE DUC DE
Le Parfait Coacher. Paris: 1744. V. 47

NEVILE, CHRISTOPHER
A Defence of Paley's Moral Philosophy, In Answer to the Objections of Mr. Whewell and Professor Sedgwick. London: 1839. V. 49

NEVILE, THOMAS
Imitations of Juvenal and Persius. London: 1769. V. 48

NEVILL, RALPH
British Military Prints. 1909. V. 54
Old English Sporting Books. London: 1924. V. 47; 49; 52; 53
Old English Sporting Prints and Their History. London: 1923. V. 47; 50; 52
Old French Line Engravings. London. V. 52

NEVILLE, A. W.
The History of Lamar County. Paris: 1937. V. 52
The Red River Valley: Then and Now. Paris: 1948. V. 48; 50; 54

NEVILLE, ALEXANDER
De Furoribus Norfolcensium Ketto Duce...Eiusdem Norvicus. London: 1575. V. 51

NEVILLE, EDITH, PSEUD.
The Smugglers. A Story of Puget Sound. V. 48

NEVILLE, HENRY
The Isle of Pines. Katoomba: 1991. V. 54
Plato Redivivus; or, a Dialogue Concerning Government... London: 1681. V. 52
Plato Redivivus, or a Dialogue Concerning Government. London: 1765. V. 48

NEVILLE, RICHARD CORNWALLIS
Saxon Obsequies Illustrated by Ornaments and Weapons. London: 1852. V. 53

NEVILLE, WILLIAM B.
On Insanity: Its Nature, Causes and Cure. London: 1837. V. 50

THE NEVILLES Of Garretstown: a Tale of 1760. London: 1860. V. 54

NEVIN, WILLIAM W.
The Westward March of Emigration in the United States. Considered In Its Bearing Upon the Future of Colorado and New Mexico. Lancaster: 1874. V. 47

NEVINS, ALLAN
History of the Bank of New York and Trust Company 1784 to 1934. New York: 19343. V. 49

NEVINS, IRIS
Varities of Spanish Marbling. Newtown: 1991. V. 49; 51

NEVINSON, C. R. W.
Modern War - Paintings by C. R. W. Nevinson. London: 1917. V. 47; 54
Paint and Prejudice. Autobiography. London: 1937. V. 49

NEVIUS, JOHN W.
The New Brunswick Collection of Sacred Music. New Brunswick: 1818. V. 53

THE NEW American Clerk's Magazine, and Complete Practical Conveyancer...Adapted to the use of the Citizens of the United States, and More Particularly to Those of the State of Maryland... Frederick-Town: 1806. V. 50

THE NEW American Clerk's Magazine, and Complete Practical Conveyancer... Hagers-Town: 1806. V. 47

A NEW and General Biographical Dictionary... London: 1761-67. V. 52
A NEW and General Biographical Dictionary... London: 1784. V. 47
A NEW and General Biographical Dictionary... London: 1798. V. 49; 52; 54

THE NEW Annual Register, or General Repository of History, Politics, and Literature for the Year 1791 to Which is Prefixed a Continuation of the History of Knowledge, Learning and Taste in Great Britain, During the Reign of Queen Elizabeth. London: 1792. V. 49

THE NEW Book of Nonsense, a Contribution to the Great Central Fair, Philadelphia Commission. Philadelphia: 1864. V. 50

A NEW Book of Sports. London: 1885. V. 54

NEW British Columbia: The Underdeveloped Areas of the Great Central and Northern Interior. Victoria: 1908. V. 51

THE NEW Brunsiwck City and Business Directory, 1888. York: 1888. V. 49; 51

NEW Brunswick City and Middlesex County Directory. 1891. New Brunswick: 1891. V. 49; 51

NEW Brunswick City Directory, 1886-87. New Brunswick: 1886. V. 47; 49; 51

NEW Brunswick City Directory, 1890. New Brunswick: 1890. V. 49

NEW Brunswick City Directory. 1893. New Brunswick: 1893. V. 49; 51

NEW Brunswick City Directory 1897. New Brunswick: 1897. V. 49; 51

NEW Brunswick Directory for 1872-73. New Brunswick: 1872. V. 49

NEW Brunswick Directory, for 1874-75. New Brunswick: 1874. V. 47; 49

NEW Brunswick Directory, for 1877-78. New Brunswick: 1877. V. 47; 49; 51

NEW Brunswick Directory for 1880-81. New Brunswick: 1880. V. 47; 49; 51

NEW Brunswick Directory for 1883-84. New Brunswick: 1883. V. 47; 49; 51

NEW BRUNSWICK. LEGISLATURE
Reports Relating to the Project of Constructing a Railway, and a Line of Electro-Magnetic Telegraph, through the Province of New Brunswick, from Halifax to Quebec. Fredericton: 1847. V. 50

THE NEW Cabinet of Entertainment and Instruction. London: 1835. V. 53

THE NEW Cambridge Modern History. 1957-79. V. 52

NEW, CHARLES
Life, Wanderings and Labours in Eastern Africa. London: 1874. V. 51

THE NEW Children's Friend; or, Pleasing Incitements to Wisdom and Virtue; Conveyed through the Medium of Anecdote, Tale and Adventure. London: 1797. V. 47

A NEW Child's Play. London: 1877. V. 52

NEW Clerk's Magazine, Containing All the Most Useful Forms, Which Occur in Business Transactions Between Man and Man. Boston: 1833. V. 52

A NEW Collection of Enigmas, Charades, Transpositions &c. London: 1791. V. 48

A NEW Collection of Enigmas, Charades, Transpositions, &c. London: 1806. V. 53

A NEW Collection of Poems Relating to State Affairs, from Oliver Cromwel, to His Present Time; By the Greatest Wits of the Age. London: 1705. V. 47; 53

A NEW Collection of the Most Easy and Approved Methods of Preparing Baths, Essences, Pomatums, Powders, Perfumes, Sweet Scented Waters and Opiates, for Preserving the Teeth and Gums, and Sweetening the Breath. London: 1787. V. 54

NEW Complete Guide to all Persons Who Have Any Trade or Concern with the City of London and Parts Adjacent... London: 1777. V. 52

A NEW Conductor Generalis: Being a Summary of the Law Relative to the Duty and Office of Justices of the Peace, Sheriffs, Coroners, Constables... Albany: 1803. V. 47; 50

NEW Country. London: 1933. V. 53

THE NEW Cries of London; or, Itinerant Trades of the British Metropolis with Characteristics Engravings. London: 1823. V. 50

A NEW Day for the Colored Women Worker: A Study of Colored Women in Industry in New York City. New York: 1919. V. 48

THE NEW Decameron. 1919. V. 50
THE NEW Decameron. New York: 1919. V. 48

A NEW Description of Paris. London: 1687. V. 51

NEW Directions 11. New York: 1949. V. 54

NEW Directions 12. New York: 1950. V. 54

NEW Directions 14. New York: 1953. V. 54

NEW Directions 16. New York: 1957. V. 54

NEW Directions in Prose & Poetry. New York: 1950. V. 50

A NEW Display of the Beauties of England; or A Description of the Most Elegant of Magnificent Public Edifices, Royal Palaces, Nobelman's and Gentlemen's Seats etc. London: 1776. V. 47

NEW EDINBURGH Dispensatory. Edinburgh: 1801. V. 48

THE NEW Encyclopaedia Britannica. London: 1974. V. 52

NEW ENGLAND ANTI-SLAVERY SOCIETY
First Annual Report of the Board of Managers of the New-England Anti-Slavery Society, Presented Jan. 9, 1833. Boston: 1833. V. 47

NEW England Anti-Masonic Alamanac for the Year of Our Lord 1832 (& 1835). Boston: 1831/34. V. 49; 51

NEW ENGLAND COMPANY
Report of the Proceedings of the New England Company, for the Civilization and Conversion of Indians, Blacks and Pagans, in the Dominion of Canada, South Africa and the West Indies, During the Two Years, 1871-1872. London: 1874. V. 47

NEW ENGLAND EMIGRANT AID COMPANY
Florida: the Advantages and Inducements Which It Offers to Immigrants. Boston: 1868. V. 54

NEW ENGLAND FREEDMEN'S AID SOCIETY
Second Annual Report of the New England Freedman's Aid Society.... Boston: 1864. V. 48

NEW England Lasses. 1790. V. 47

THE NEW England Primer. Hartford: 1850?. V. 49

THE NEW England Primer: Containing the Assembly's Cathechism; the Account of the Burning of John Rodgers... Worcester: 183?. V. 48

THE NEW England Primer, or an Easy and Pleasant Guide to the Art of Reading. New England: 1802? or 1803?. V. 50

THE NEW England Primer; To Which is Added, The Shorter Catechism of the Westminster Assembly of Divines. Pittsburg: 1830's. V. 47

A NEW English Dictionary of Historical Principles...(Together with) Introduction, Supplement and Bibliography. Oxford: 1888-1933. V. 52

NEW English Dramatists. Harmondsworth: 1959-70. V. 54

A NEW Essay Upon Tea Addressed to the Medical Profession. 1936. V. 53

A NEW Essay Upon Tea. Addressed to the Medical Profession. London: 1936. V. 49

THE NEW Family Receipt-Book, containing Eight Hundred Truly Valuable Receipts in Various Branches of Domestic Economy... New Haven: 1819. V. 50

THE NEW Farmer's Calendar, or Monthly Remembrancer, by a Farmer and Breeder. London: 1802. V. 48; 54

THE NEW FOREST, A Plan of His Majesty's Forest Called the New Forest in the County of Southampton, Laid Down from Surveys Taken by Thos. Richardson, Wm. King... London: 1789. V. 47

THE NEW Forget-Me-Not, a Calendar. London: 1929. V. 50

THE NEW Foundling Hospital for Wit. London: 1786. V. 53

A NEW General Collection of Voyages and Travels; Consisting of the Most Esteemed Relations, Which Have Been Hitherto Published in any Language.. London: 1745-47. V. 50; 52

THE NEW Guide for Strangers and Residents in the city of York, Being the Latest and the Best Concise Historical Description... York: 1838. V. 47

NEW Guide for the Hotel, Bar, Restaurant, Butler and Chef. London: 1885. V. 47

THE NEW Guide of the Conversation in English. London: 1884. V. 49

THE NEW Guide to Cheltenham: Being a Complete History and Description of That Celebrated Watering Place.... Cheltenham: 1825. V. 47

THE NEW Guide to Montreal and Its Environs. Montreal: 1851. V. 48

THE NEW Guide to Quebec and its Environs. Quebec: 1851. V. 48; 53

THE NEW Hampshire Book: Being Specimens of the Literature of the Granite State. Nashua: 1842. V. 52

NEW HAMPSHIRE. LAWS, STATUTES, ETC.
Acts and Laws of the State of New-Hampshire, in America. Printed at Exeter, in: 1780. V. 48

NEW HAMPSHIRE STATE AGRICULTURAL SOCIETY
Transactions of the New Hampshire State Agricultural Society for the Year 1856. Concord: 1857. V. 51

NEW Handbook of Texas. V. 53

A **NEW** History of England, or Picturesue, Biographical, Historical, Legendary and Antiquarian Sketches. London: 1838. V. 53

A **NEW** History of the Holy Bible. Ipswich. V. 52

NEW JERSEY
Journal of the Governor & Council. 1682-1775. Trenton: 1890-93. V. 47
Report of the Commissioners on the Controversy with the State of New York, Respecting the Eastern Boundary of the State of New-Jersey. Trenton: 1807. V. 51
Report of the Minority of the Committee of Enquiry, Relative to the Railroad at Trenton &c. Trenton: 1837. V. 51
Report on the Rail Road Controversy, Made by the Joint Committee of the Legislature of New Jersey, with the Correspondence Between the Treasurer, Attorney-General and the Companies. Read March 8th, 1841. Trenton: 1841. V. 51

NEW JERSEY. ADJUTANT GENERAL
Report...for the Year Ending October 31st, 1873, (1876, 1877, 1880-1882, 1884, 1885, 1890-1892, 1894, 1896-1911, 1913-1914, 1916-1918, 1918-1920, 1921-1932, 1934-1943). 1873-1943. V. 47

NEW JERSEY. ARCHIVES
Archives of the State of New Jersey. 1800-1949. V. 47
Archives of the State of New Jersey. Subset: Documents Relating to the Colonial History of the State of New Jersey, 1631-1776. Newark: 1880-86. V. 47
Archives of the State of New Jersey. Subset: Extracts from American Newspapers Relating to New Jersey 1704-1782. 1894-1923. V. 47
Archives of the State of New Jersey. Subset: Journal of the Governor and Council, 1682-1775. Trenton: 1890-93. V. 47
Calendar of New Jersey Wills, 1670-1760. Paterson: 1901-24. V. 47
Documents Relating to the Colonial History of the State of New Jersey...1631-1776. Newark: 1880-88. V. 47
Extracts from American Newspapers Relating to New Jersey 1704-1782. 1894-1923. V. 47

NEW JERSEY. ASSEMBLY
An Act to Incoporate the Washington Canal Company. Trenton: 1822. V. 51

NEW JERSEY. CHANCERY COURT
The Joint and Several Answers of Edwin A. Stevens, James Neilson and John R. Thomson, Defendants, to the Bill of Complaint of John D. Hager, Complainant. 1847. V. 47; 51

NEW JERSEY EDITORIAL ASSOCIATION
Minutes of the Twenty-Fifth (-29th, 31st-43rd, 45th-53rd) Annual Meeting... 1881-1909. V. 47

NEW JERSEY. GENERAL ASSEMBLY
Debates in the Eighty-Ninth General Assembly of the State of New Jersey, on the Bill to Ratify an Amendment to the Constitution of the United States. Trenton: 1865. V. 49; 51

NEW JERSEY. GEOLOGICAL SURVEY
First Annual Report of the Geological Survey of the State of New Jersey for the Year 1854. Trenton: 1855. V. 51

NEW JERSEY. LAWS, STATUTES, ETC.
An Act to Incorporate the Washington Canal Company. Trenton: 1822. V. 49
Acts of the Council and General Assembly of the State of New Jersey, from the Establishment of the Present Government and Declaration of Independence, to the End of...December 1783; with the Constitution Prefixed... Trenton: 1784. V. 51
The Acts of the General Assembly of the Province of New Jersey, from the Time of the Surrender of the Government of the Said Province, to the Fourth Year of the Reign of King George the Second... Philadelphia: 1732. V. 47; 48
Acts of the General Assembly of the Province of New-Jersey, from the Surrender of the Government to Queen Anne, on the 17th Day of April, in the Year of Our Lord 1702 to the 14th day of January 1776. Burlington: 1776. V. 51
Acts of the One Hundred and Twenty-Fifth (-One Hundred and Seventy-Third) Legislature of the State of New Jersey... Trenton: 1901-50. V. 47; 51
Acts Relative to the Delaware and Raritan Canal Company and camden and Amboy Rail Road and Transportation Co., Passed by the Legislature of the State of New Jersey. 1832. V. 47; 51
Acts Relative to the Delaware and Raritan Canal Company and Camden and Amboy Rail Road and Transportation Company.... Princeton: 1840. V. 47; 51
The Grants, Concessions and Original Constitutions of the Province of New Jersey. Philadelphia: 1758. V. 47; 48; 50; 51; 54
The Grants, Concessions, and Original Constitutions of the Province of New Jersey, the Acts Passed During the Proprietary Governments, and Other Material Transactions. Philadelphia: 1881. V. 47; 49
Laws of the State of New Jersey... New Brunswick: 1800. V. 47
Laws of the State of New Jersey... Newark: 1800. V. 51

THE NEW Jersey Register, for the Year Eighteen Hundred and Thirty Seven. Trenton: 1837. V. 49; 51

NEW JERSEY. STATE BOARD OF EDUCATION
Annual Report...1910-1920. 1911-21. V. 47

THE NEW Keepsake. London: 1931. V. 53

THE NEW Lion and the Unicorn Fighting for the Crown. London: 1845. V. 50

THE NEW London Spy; or, a Twenty-Four Hours Ramble Through the Bills of Mortality. London: 1771. V. 50

THE NEW Mexico Brand Book, Showing All the Brands on Cattle, Horse, Mules and Asses, Recorded Under the Provisions of the Act, Approved Feb. 16, 1899 and Other Brands Recorded Up to December 31, 1914. Albuquerque: 1915. V. 51

NEW MEXICO. TERRITORIAL BUREAU OF IMMIGRATION
Report as to Socorro Country...Prepared by M. Fischer and Antonio Y. A. Abeytia, Commissioners, Socorro, Socorro County. Socorro: 1881. V. 51

NEW MEXICO. (TERRITORY). LAWS, STATUTES, ETC.
1882 Acts of the Legislative Assembly of the Territory of New Mexico. Twenty-Fifth Session. Santa Fe: 1882. V. 54

A **NEW** Miscellany for the Year 1738. London: 1738. V. 48

THE NEW Native American Novel. Albuquerque: 1986. V. 51

THE NEW Navigation; or, Stroud-Water Triumphant: a Poem, in Two cantos. Stroud? Gloucester?: 1776. V. 48

THE NEW Newgate Calendar: Being Interesting Memoirs of Notorious Characters...Convicted of Outrages on the Laws of England...Chronologically Arranged... London: 1810. V. 49

NEW Paths - Verse, Prose, Pictures, 1917-1918. London: 1918. V. 53

THE NEW Pharmacopoeia of the Royal College of Physicians of London. London: 1788. V. 51

A **NEW** Pocket Companion for Oxford; or, Guide through the University. Oxford: 1794. V. 47

THE NEW Project Examin'd, or, The Design of the Faction to Deprive the Family of Honover, or the Power to Name Lords Justices, Anatomiz'd in a Letter... London: 1714. V. 53

NEW Puss in Boots or Marquis of Carabas. London: 1845. V. 47

NEW Puss in Boots with Transforming Pictures - Capable of Numerous Metamorphoses. London: 1877. V. 51; 53

NEW Remarks of London: or, a Survey of the Cities of London and Westminster, of Southwark and Part of Middlesex and Surrey, Within the Circumference of the Bills of Mortality... London: 1732. V. 50

A **NEW** Royal and Universal Dictionary of Arts and Sciences, or a Complete System of Human Knowledge. London: 1770/71. V. 53

NEW Standard Dictionary of the English Language...Also a Standard History of the World. New York & London: 1926. V. 48

THE NEW States. New York and Chicago: 1889. V. 54

THE NEW STATISTICAL Account of Scotland. By the Ministers of the Respective Parishes, Under the Superintendence of a Committee of the Society for the benefit of the Sons and Daughters of the Clergy. Edinburgh: 1837-45. V. 48

THE NEW Survey of London Life and Labour. London: 1930-35. V. 49

THE NEW Swing. Boston: 1839. V. 48

A **NEW** System of Agriculture; or, a Plain, Easy and Demonstrative Method of Speedily Growing Rich... Dublin: 1755. V. 48; 54

A **NEW** Theatrical Dictionary. London: 1792. V. 54

A **NEW** Years Gift for the High Church Clergy, Being an Account of the Sufferings of a Great Number of the Clergy of the Church of England. 1712. V. 51

NEW YORK & ERIE RAILROAD COMPANY
First Annual Report of the Directors of the New York and Erie Railroad Company Made to the Stockholders September 29, 1835. New York: 1835. V. 47; 48

NEW YORK ACADEMY OF MEDICINE
The New York Academy of Medicine Catalogue of an Exhibition of Early and Later medical Americana. New York: 1927. V. 51

NEW YORK AUTOMATIC HATCH COVER CO.
Fires and Conflagrations! Their Origin, Aids, Means of Prevention. New York: 1878. V. 54

NEW YORK CENTRAL & HUDSON RIVER RAILROAD CO.
Annual Report. 1905-16. V. 54

NEW YORK. (CITY)
Manual of the Corporation of the City of New York, 1863. New York: 1863. V. 51; 54
An Ordinance for the Better Regulation of the Firemen of the City of New York. Approved by the Mayor, December 31, 1864. New York: 1865. V. 50

NEW YORK. (CITY). AQUEDUCT COMMISSION
Report to the Aqueduct Commissioners by the President, James C. Duane... New York: 1895. V. 49

NEW YORK. (CITY). CHARTER
The Charter of the City of New York. New York: 1819. V. 49

NEW YORK. (CITY). MERCANTILE LIBRARY ASSOCIATION
New York City During the American Revolution. New York: 1861. V. 47

NEW YORK. (CITY). POLICE
Regulations for the Day and Night Police of the City of New York, with Instructions to the Legal Powers and Duties of Policeman. New York: 1845. V. 53

NEW YORK. (COLONY). EXECUTIVE COUNCIL
Minutes of the Executive Council of the Province of New York. Administration of Francis Lovelace, 1668-1673. Collateral & Illustrative Doucments 1-98. Albany: 1910. V. 49

NEW YORK. (COLONY). LAWS, STATUTES, ETC.
The Laws of New York, from the Year 1664 to the Revolution. Albany: 1894-96. V. 49
Laws of New York, from the Year 1691 to 1751. (with) Laws of New York from the 11th Nov. 1752, to 22d May 1762. New York: 1752/62. V. 48; 50; 53; 54

NEW YORK. (COLONY). LEGISLATIVE COUNCIL
Journal of the Legislative Council of the Colony of New York, 1691-1775. Albany: 1861. V. 48; 50; 53

NEW York Critics Theatre Reviews. New York: 1940-46. V. 49

THE NEW YORK Gardener, or Twelve Letters From a Farmer to His Son, In Which He Describes the Method of Laying Out and Managing the Kitchen Garden. White Creek: 1827. V. 48

NEW YORK HISTORICAL SOCIETY
Abstract of Wills Recorded in the Surrogate's Office of the City of New York, 1665-1800. New York: 1893-1908. V. 47

NEW YORK. HOUSE OF ASSEMBLY
Journal of the House of Assembly of the State of New York. The Second Meeting of the Thirteenth Session. New York: 1790. V. 47

NEW YORK. LEGISLATURE
Report of the Joint Committee of the Senate and the Assembly on the Application for the Relief of the Greeks. Albany: 1827. V. 47

NEW YORK NAUTICAL INSTITUTION & SHIPMASTERS' SOCIETY
Constitution and By-Laws, of the New York Nautical Instutiton and Shipmasters's Society. New York: 1821. V. 47; 48; 50

NEW YORK. PUBLIC LIBRARY
Portugal Brazil. The Age of Atlantic Discoveries. Catalogue of an Exhibition at New York Public Library, June 2 - September 1, 1990. Lisbon: 1990. V. 47

NEW YORK SOCIETY LIBRARY
A Catalouge of the Books Belonging to the New York Society Library... New York: 1813. V. 50

NEW YORK. (STATE)
Report of the Commissioners...to Revise the Laws for the Assessment and Collection of Taxes. Albany: 1871. V. 52

NEW YORK. (STATE). BOARD OF HEALTH
Annual Report(s) of the Metropolitan Board of Health of the State of New York. New York: 1866-69. V. 51

THE NEW York State Business Directory, 1874. Boston: 1874. V. 47

NEW York State Canals. Albany: 1860. V. 49

NEW YORK. (STATE). CENSUS
Census for 1865. Albany: 1867. V. 49
Census of the State of New York for 1835. Albany: 1836. V. 49
Census of the State of New York for 1855. Albany: 1857. V. 49

NEW YORK STATE CONFERENCE OF CHARITIES & CORRECTION
Proceedings. 2nd, 6th, 8th, 9th. For the Years 1901, 1905, 1907, 1908. 1902/06/06/10. V. 52

NEW YORK. (STATE). CONSTITUTION
Reports of the Proceedings and Debates of the Convention of 1821, Assembled for the Purpose of Amending the Constitution of the State of New York. Albany: 1821. V. 48

NEW YORK. (STATE). DEPARTMENT OF PUBLIC PARKS
Third General Report of the Board of Commissioners of the Department of Public Parks. New York: 1875. V. 53

NEW YORK. (STATE). LEGISLATURE
Manual for the Use of the Legislature of the State of New York, for the Year 1858. Albany: 1858. V. 51

NEW YORK. (STATE). LIBRARY
Catalogue of the Books on Bibliography, Typography and Engraving in the New York State Library. Albany: 1858. V. 53

NEW YORK. (STATE). METROPOLITAN BOARD OF HEALTH
Annual Reports of the Metropolitan Board of Health of the State of New York. New York: 1866-69. V. 53

NEW YORK. (STATE). SENATE
Report & Procedings of the Senate Committee Appointed to Investigate the Police Department of the City of New York:. New York: 1895. V. 48

NEW YORK. (STATE). STATE BOTANIST
Annual Report of the State Botanist. Albany: 1897. V. 52; 54
Annual Reports of the State Botanist. New York: 1895-1912. V. 53
Report of the State Botanist. New York for the Years 1900-12. Albany: 1901-13. V. 52
Report of the State Botanist on Edible Fungi of New York 1895-99. Albany: 1900. V. 52; 53

NEW ZEALAND ASSOCIATION
A Statement of the Objects of the New Zealand Association With some Particulars Concerning the Position, Extent, Soil and Climate, Natural Productions and Natives of New Zealand. London: 1837. V. 49

A NEW-Come Guest to the Towne. That Is, The Descriminant Oath Which the Earle of Newcastle Imposeth Upon the Countie and Citie of Yorke... London: 1644. V. 50

NEWALL, J. T.
Hog Hunting in the East and Other Sports. London: 1867. V. 48

THE NEWARK Anniversary Poems. New York: 1917. V. 48; 49; 51

NEWARK, N.J., Illustrated. A Souvenir of the City and its Numerous Industries... Newark: 1893. V. 51

NEWBERRY, ARTHUR ST. JOHN
A Fisherman's Paradise...An Excerpt from the Second Book of Arthur St. John Newberry Another Catch. Cleveland: 1914. V. 47

NEWBERRY, CLARE TURLAY
Cats: a Portfolio of Drawings by.... New York: 1943. V. 53

NEWBERRY, J. S.
Paleozoic Fishes of North America. Washington: 1889. V. 51; 53

The Paleozoic Fishes of North America. 1890. V. 53
The U. S. Sanitary Commission in the Valley of the Mississippi, During the War of the Rebellion, 1861-1866. Cleveland: 1971. V. 49

NEWBERRY LIBRARY
A Bibliographical Checklist of North and Middle American Indian Linguistics in the Edward E. Ayer Collection. Chicago: 1941. V. 52

NEWBERRY, PERCY E.
Ben Hasan I-IV. London: 1893-1900. V. 49; 51
El Bersheh with Plans and Measurements of the Tombs... London: 1895. V. 49; 51
Scarabs: an Introduction to the Study of Egyptian Seals and Signet Rings. London: 1908. V. 49

NEWBERY, JOHN
An Historical Account of the Curiosities of London and Westminster, in Three Parts. London: 1767. V. 50
Letters on the Most Common, As Well as Important Occasions in Life. Dublin: 1758. V. 47
Letters on the Most Common, as Well as Important Occasions in Life... London: 1758. V. 52
Newbery's Spelling Dictionary of the English Language, On a New Plan for the Use of Young Gentlemen, Ladies and Foreigners. London: 1798. V. 52
The Newtonian System of Philosophy Explained by Familiar Objects, in an Entertaining Manner, for the Use of Young Laides & Gentlement. Philadelphia: 1808. V. 48

NEWBIGGING, THOMAS
History of the Forest of Rossendale. London: 1868. V. 48
History of the Forest of Rossendale. 1893. V. 53

NEWBOLD, THOMAS JOHN
Political and Statistical Account of the British Settlements in the Straits of Malacca... London: 1839. V. 51

NEWBOLT, HENRY
Drake's Drum and Other Songs of the Sea. London. V. 48
Essays by Divers Hands. Oxford: 1921. V. 54

NEWBY, ERIC
The Last Grain Race. London: 1956. V. 52; 53
Love and War in the Appenines. London: 1971. V. 47
A Short Walk in the Hindu Kush. London: 1958. V. 47

NEWCASTLE, 7TH DUKE OF
The Clumber Library. Catalogue of the Magnificent Library...Removed from Clumber, Worksop. London: 1937-38. V. 52

NEWCASTLE, MARGARET LUCAS CAVENDISH, DUCHESS OF
Grounds of Natural Philosophy... London: 1668. V. 48

NEWCASTLE, THOMAS PELHAM HOLLES, 1ST DUKE OF
The Duke of Newcastle's Letter by His Majesty's Order to Monsieur Michell, the King of Prussia's Scretary of the Embassy, in Answer to the Memorial and Other Papers... London: 1753. V. 48; 49; 51; 52

NEWCASTLE UNION GAS LIGHT COMPANY
Deeds, Rules and Regulations, for the Settlement and Government of the Newcastle Upon Tyne and Gateshead Union Gas Light Company. Newcastle;: 1839. V. 49; 52

NEWCASTLE, WILLIAM CAVENDISH, DUKE OF
A New Method and Extraordinary Invention, to Dress Horses and Work Them According to Nature... London: 1667. V. 47

NEWCASTLE, WILLIAM CAVENDISH, MARQUIS OF
The Phanseys of William Cavendish Marquis of Newcastle Addressed to Margaret Lucas and Her Letters in Reply. London: 1956. V. 48

NEWCOMB, COVELLE
Cortez the Conqueror. New York: 1947. V. 49

NEWCOMB, F. J.
Navajo Omens and Taboos. Santa Fe: 1940. V. 52
Sandpaintings of the Navajo Shooting Chant. New York: 1937. V. 51; 54

NEWCOMB, R.
Architecture of the Old Northwest Territory. Chicago: 1950. V. 48; 54
The Colonial and Federal House: How to Build an Authentic Colonial House. Philadelphia: 1933. V. 53; 54
The Spanish House for America, Its Design, Furnishing and Garden. Philadelphia: 1927. V. 54

NEWCOMB, REXFORD
Architecture of the Old Northwest Territory. Chicago: 1950. V. 50
Mediterranean Domestic Architecture in the United States. Cleveland: 1928. V. 50
The Old Mission Churches and Historic Houses of California. Philadelphia: 1925. V. 50
Spanish Colonial Architecture in the United States. New York: 1937. V. 50
The Spanish House for America. Philadelphia: 1927. V. 51; 52

NEWCOMB, THOMAS
The Last Judgement of Men and Angels. London: 1723. V. 50
A Miscellaneous Collection of Original Poems... London: 1740. V. 47
A Supplement (In Verse) to One Thousand Seven Hundred Thirty-Eight. London: 1738. V. 48

NEWCOMBE, C. F.
The First Circumnavigation of Vancouver Island. Victoria: 1914. V. 50; 53; 54

NEWCOMBE, SAMUEL PROUT
Little Henry's Holiday at the Great Exhibition. London: 1851. V. 50

NEWCOME, PETER
The History of the Ancient and Royal Foundation Called the Abbey of St. Alban in the County of Hertford... London: 1795. V. 47; 49

NEWCOMEN Society for the Study of the History of Engineering and Technology
Transactions. London: 1956-66. V. 47

NEWDIGATE, B. H.
The Art of the Book. London: 1938. V. 47
Book Production Notes, Articles Contributed to the London Mercury 1920-1925. London: 1986. V. 50

NEWELL, C. M.
Kamehameha and the Conquering King. New York and London: 1885. V. 53

NEWELL, CHESTER
History of the Revolution in Texas, Particularly of the War of 1835 & 1836. New York: 1838. V. 47; 49

NEWELL, EDWARD T.
The Coinage of Demetrius Poliorcetes. London: 1927. V. 48
Reattribution of Certain Tetradrachms of Alexander the Great. New York: 1912. V. 48
Tyrus Rediviva. New York: 1923. V. 48

NEWELL, G. R.
The H. W. McCurdy Marine History of the Pacific Northwest.... Seattle: 1966. V. 48

NEWELL, GORDON
Pacific Coastal Liners. Seattle: 1959. V. 48

NEWELL, HARRIET
Memoirs of... London: 1815. V. 50; 51

NEWELL, PETER
Favorite Fairy Tales. New York and London: 1907. V. 54
The Hole Book. New York: 1908. V. 52; 54
Peter Newell's Pictures and Rhymes. New York: 1899. V. 47
The Rocket Book. New York: 1912. V. 54
The Slant Book. New York: 1910. V. 47; 49; 54
Topsy and Turvey. 1893. V. 50
Topsys & Turvys. New York: 1893. V. 47
Topsys and Turvys Number 2. New York: 1894. V. 47

NEWELL, R. H.
Letterwriters on the Scenery of Wales... London: 1821. V. 52

NEWELL, ROBERT
Robert Newell's Memoranda... Portland: 1959. V. 49
The Rocket Book. New York: 1912. V. 49

NEWELL, ROBERT HENRY
The Mystery of Mr. E. Drood. (with) The Orpheus C. Kerr papers... London: 1871/1866. V. 49
The Orpheus C. Kerr Papers. London: 1866. V. 51

NEWENHAM, THOMAS
View of the Natural, Political and Commercial Circumstances of Ireland. London: 1809. V. 47; 53

THE NEWEST Keepsake for 1840. Norwch (sic): 1840. V. 47

NEWFELD, E.
The Hittite Laws... London: 1951. V. 49; 52

NEWFIELD, W. EDEN
Specimens of Medieval Architecture Chiefly Selected from Examples of the 12th and 13th Centuries in France and Italy. London: 1862. V. 49

NEWHALL, BEAUMONT
Airborne Camera: the World from the Air and Outer Space. New York: 1969. V. 51
The Daguerreotype in American. 1961. V. 54
The History of Photography from 1839 to the Present Day. New York: 1949. V. 49

NEWHALL, EDWIN WHITE
Edwin White Newhall. San Francisco?: 1915. V. 49

NEWHALL, FREDERIC CUSHMAN
With General Sheridan in Lee's Last Campaign. Philadelphia: 1866. V. 52

NEWHALL, JOHN B.
Sketches of Iowa, or the Emigrant's Guide... With Sketches of Black Hawk and Others... New York: 1841. V. 50

NEWHALL, NANCY
Ansel Adams; the Eloquent Light. San Francisco: 1963. V. 49
The Daybooks of Edward Weston. 1973. V. 52
The Daybooks of Edward Weston: Volume I. Mexico/Volume II. California. New York: 1961/73. V. 47
P. H. Emerson: the Fight for Photography. 1972. V. 52
The Pageant of History...in Northern California. San Francisco: 1954. V. 54
This is the American Earth. San Francico: 1960. V. 54
Time in New England. New York: 1950. V. 47

NEWHALL, VIRGINIA WHITING
Edwin White Newhall. San Francisco: 1915. V. 47

NEWHOUSE, EDWARD
This Is Your Day. New York: 1937. V. 51

NEWHOUSE, S.
The Trapper's Guide; a Manual of Instructions for Capturing All Kings of Fur Bearing Animals... New York: 1869. V. 48

NEWLAND, HENRY
Forest Scenes from Norway and Sweden. London: 1855. V. 54
Forest Scenes in Norway and Sweden. London: 1854. V. 47

NEWLANDS, DAVID L.
Early Ontario Potters: Their Craft and Trade. Toronto: 1979. V. 52

NEWLANDS, JAMES
The Carpenter and Joiner's Assistant. Glasgow: 1860. V. 50; 52
The Carpenter and Joiner's Assistant. Glasgow: 1862. V. 52
The Carpenter and Joiner's Assistant. London: 1867. V. 53
The Carpenter and Joiner's Assistant... London: 1870. V. 50
The Carpenter and Joiner's Assistant... London: 1880. V. 52

NEWLANDS, JOHN A. R.
On the Discovery of the Periodic Law, and on Relations Among the Atomic Weights. London: 1884. V. 50

NEWLOVE, JOHN
Dreams Surround Us. Delta: 1977. V. 47
Elephants, Mothers and Others. Vancouver: 1963. V. 47
Grave Sirs. Vancouver: 1962. V. 47
Moving in Alone. Toronto: 1965. V. 47; 52

NEWMAN, ARTHUR
Pleasvres Vision; with Deserts Complaint; and a Short Dialogve of a Womans Properties Betweene and Old Man and a Young. Ryde: 1840. V. 49

NEWMAN, BERNARD
Spy and Counter-Spy. London: 1970. V. 49

NEWMAN, ERNEST
A Study of Wagner. London: 1899. V. 47

NEWMAN, FRANCES
The Short Story's Mutations, from Petronius to Paul Morand. New York: 1924. V. 53

NEWMAN, FRANCIS WILLIAM
Lectures on Political Economy. London: 1851. V. 52

NEWMAN, ISIDORA
Fairy Flowers. London. V. 49

NEWMAN, J.
The Giant Rat of Sumatra. Roanoke: 1973. V. 54
The Giant Rat of Sumatra. Edgewater: 1995. V. 54

NEWMAN, J. A.
The Autobiography of an Old-Fashioned Boy. Oklahoma City: 1923. V. 47; 50

NEWMAN, JEREMIAH WHITTAKER
The Lounger's Common-Place Book, or, Miscellaneous Anecdotes. London: 1796/98/99. V. 51

NEWMAN, JOHN B.
The Illustrated Botany. New York: 1846-47. V. 48

NEWMAN, JOHN HENRY, CARDINAL
Apologia pro Vita Sua. London: 1864. V. 47; 48; 49; 50; 52; 53; 54
Apologia Pro Vita Sua: Being a Reply to a Pamphlet Entitled "What, Then, Does Mr. Newman Mean?". London: 1973. V. 48
The Arians of the Fourth Century, Their Doctrine, Temper and Conduct... London: 1833. V. 49
Callista, a Sketch of The Third Century. London: 1856. V. 54
Discourses On the Scope and Nature of University Education. Dublin: 1852. V. 50
The Dream of Gerontius... London: 1909. V. 52
The Dream of Gerontius. London: 1976. V. 51
An Essay on the Development of Christian Doctrine. London: 1845. V. 48; 49; 53
Lectures on the History of the Turks in Its Relation to Christianity. Dublin: 1854. V. 54
Parochial and Plain Sermons. London: 1868/77. V. 49
Tract One. Thoughts on the Ministerial Commission, Respectfully Addressed to the Clergy. 1985. V. 53
Verses on Various Occasions. London: 1868. V. 48; 50; 53

NEWMAN, NEIL
Famous Horses of the American Turf... New York: 1931-33. V. 47

NEWMAN, T.
Newman's Tract Directory of Los Angeles County. Volume 2. Los Angeles: 1905. V. 48

NEWMAN, WILLIAM
The History of a Quartern Loaf. The History of a scuttle of Coals in Rhymes and Pictures. The History of a Cup of Tea in Rhymes and Pictures. London: 1860. V. 50

NEWMARK, HARRIS
Sixty Years in Southern California. 1853-1913. New York: 1916. V. 47; 48
Sixty Years in Southern California 1853-1913. Boston: 1930. V. 53
Sixty Years in Southern California, 1853-1913. Los Angeles: 1970. V. 53

NEWMARK, MAURICE H.
Census of the City and County of Los Angeles, California, for the Year 1850, Together with an Analysis and an Appendix. Los Angeles: 1929. V. 48

NEWMAYER, S. W.
Medical and Sanitary Inspections of Schools for the Health Officer and Physician, the Nurse and Teacher. Philadelphia: 1924. V. 54

NEWNAN, JOHN
The Tennessee Administration Advocate. Nashville: 1828. V. 48; 54

NEWNHAM, E. V., MRS.
Hurricanes and Tropical Revolving Storms. London: 1922. V. 48

NEWNHAM, WILLIAM
An Essay on Superstition; Being an Inquiry Into the Effects of Physical Influence on the Mind, in the Production of Dreams, Ghosts and Other Supernatural Appearances. London: 1830. V. 48; 49

Essay on Superstition; Being an Inquiry Into the Effects of Physical Influence on the Mind in the Production of Dreams, Visions, Ghosts and Other Supernatural Appearances. London. V. 52

Human Magnetism: Its Claims to Dispassioante Inquiry... London: 1845. V. 48

The Principles of Physical, Intellectual, Moral and Religious Education. London: 1827. V. 48

NEWPORT, MAURICE
Sereniss Principi Carolo Secundo Mag. Brit. Fran. et Hib. Regi Votum Candidum Vivat Rex. Editio Altera Emendatior. Londini: 1669. V. 52

NEWS from New England, Being a True and Last Account of the Bloody Wars Carried On Betwixt the Infidels, Natives... Boston: 1850. V. 53

NEWS from Prince Rupert. Whose Forces Being Discovered by the Earle of Denbigh. The Earle with His Forces Marched Against Them; and How Captaine Pinkney Left Prince Rupert, and Came in to the Earle of Denbigh with 100 Welchmen... London: 1644. V. 52

NEWS from Purgatory. Or, the Jesuits Legacy to all Countries. London: 1679?. V. 52

NEWSHOLME, ARTHUR
Public Health and Insurance: American Addresses. Baltimore: 1920. V. 49

NEWSOM, S.
1000 Years of Japanese Gardens. Tokyo: 1953. V. 50; 51

NEWSON, T. M.
Pen Pictures of St. Paul, Minnesota and Biographical Sketches of Old Settlers From the Earliest Settlement of the City, Up to and Including the Year 1857. St. Paul: 1886. V. 48; 53

NEWSTEAD, G. COULTHARD
Gleanings Towards the Annals of Aughton, Near Ormskirk. Liverpool: 1893. V. 48

NEWTE, JOHN
The Lawfulness and Use of Organs in the Christian Church of September 1696. London: 1696. V. 53

NEWTE, THOMAS
Prospects and Observations: On a Tour in England and Scotland: Natural, Economical and Literary. London: 1791. V. 52; 54

A Tour in England and Scotland in 1785. London: 1788. V. 52

NEWTON, A.
President's Address to the Norfolk and Norwich Naturalist's Society. Norwich: 1888. V. 52

NEWTON, ALFRED EDWARD
The Alfred Edward Newton Collection. New York: 1941. V. 47
The Amenities of Book Collecting and Other Affections. Boston: 1918. V. 49
The Book Collecting Game. Boston: 1928. V. 54
Derby Day and Other Adventures. Boston: 1934. V. 50; 51; 52; 54
End Papers, Literary Recreations. Boston: 1933. V. 48; 49; 51
The Format of the English Novel. Cleveland: 1928. V. 47; 48
The Greatest Book in the World and Other Papers. Boston: 1925. V. 48; 51
Mr. Strahan's Dinner Party. 1930. V. 52
Rare Books, Original Drawings, Autograph Letters and Manuscripts Collected by... New York: 1941. V. 47
A Thomas Hardy Memorial. Oak Knoll: 1931. V. 53
Thomas Hardy, Novelist or Poet. London: 1929. V. 51
Thomas Hardy, Novelist or Poet?. Philadelphia: 1929. V. 49; 50; 53

NEWTON, C. T.
Travels and Discoveries in the Levant. London: 1865. V. 49; 50; 52; 53

NEWTON, D.
Art Styles of the Papuan Gulf. 1861. V. 54

NEWTON, E. T.
The Chimaeroid Fishes of the British Cretaceous Rocks. London: 1878. V. 48

NEWTON, G. W.
Rural Sports, and How to Enjoy Them. London: 1867. V. 47

NEWTON, GRACE CLARKE
The A B C of Drag Hunting. New York: 1917. V. 50

NEWTON, HELMUT
Sleepless Nights. New York: 1978. V. 52
White Women. New York: 1976. V. 52

NEWTON, HENRY
Report of the Geology of the Black Hills of Dakota. Washington: 1880. V. 52

NEWTON, I.
Lifetime Reproduction in Birds. London: 1989. V. 50

NEWTON, ISAAC
Arithmetica Universalis; Sive de Compositione et Resolutione Arithmetica Liber. Cambridge: 1707. V. 47
Arithmetica Universalis; Sive de Compositione et Resolutione Arithmetica Liber. Leiden: 1732. V. 47
Arithmetique Universelle du Latin en Francais; avec des Notes Explicatives... Paris: 1802. V. 47
The Chronology of Ancient Kingdoms Amended. London: 1728. V. 49; 50; 51
The Correspondence of Isaac Newton. 1959. V. 49
The Mathematical Principles of Natural Philosophy... London: 1729. V. 53
The Mathematical Principles of Natural Philosophy. London: 1803. V. 50
Mathematicheskyiya Nachala Natural'noi Filosofii. Petrograd: 1915-16. V. 47
Mathematische Principien der Naturlehre. Berlin: 1872. V. 47
Mathematische Principien der Naturlehre. Shanghai: 1931. V. 47
The Method of Fluxions and Infinite Series: With Its Application to the Geometry of Curve-Lines. London: 1736. V. 47
Newton's Principia. New York: 1846. V. 47; 53
Newton's Principia. New York: 1848. V. 47
Newton's Principia. The Mathematical Principles of Natural Philosophy. New York. V. 49
Observations Upon the Prophecies of Daniel, and the Apocalypse of St. John. Dublin: 1733. V. 48
The Optical Papers of Isaac Newton. Cambridge: 1984. V. 54
Optice: sive De Reflexionibus, Refractionibus Inflexionibus et Coloribus Lucis, Libri Tres. London: 1706. V. 48
Optice: sive de Reflexionibus, Refractionibus Inflexionibus et Coloribus Lucis, Libri Tres. Lausanne and Geneva: 1740. V. 47
Optices Libri Tres... Padua: 1749. V. 47
Opticks; or, a Treatise of the Reflections, Refractins, Inflections and Colours of Light. London: 1721. V. 52
Opticks; or, a Treatise of the Reflections, Refractions, Inflections and Colours of Light. London: 1718. V. 47
Opticks; or, a Treatise of the Reflexions, Refractions, Inflections and Colours of Light. London: 1704. V. 47
Opticks; or, a Treatise of the Relfections, Refractions, Inflections and Colours of Light. London: 1730. V. 50
Opticks; or, a Treatise of the Relfexions, Refactions, Inflexions and Colours of Light... Bruxelles: 1966. V. 54
Optique... Paris: 1787. V. 50
Opuscula Mathematica, Philosophica et Philologica Collegit Partimque Latine... London: 1744. V. 48
Philosophiae Naturalis Principia Mathematica. London. V. 54
Philosophiae Naturalis Principia Mathematica. Londini: 1687. V. 47; 53
Philosophiae Naturalis Principia Mathematica... Amsterdam: 1723. V. 47; 48
Philosophiae Naturalis Principia Mathematica... London: 1726. V. 48; 52
Philosophiae Naturalis Principia Mathematica... Geneva: 1739. V. 48
Philosophiae Naturalis Principia Mathematica... Geneva: 1739-42. V. 50
Philosophiae Naturalis Principia Mathematica. 1760. V. 49
Philosophiae Naturalis Principia Mathematica... Glasgow: 1822. V. 54
Philosophiae Naturalis Principia Mathematica. Glasguae: 1833. V. 54
Philosophiae Naturalis Principia Mathematica. London: 1953. V. 48
Philosophiae Naturalis Principia Mathematica. Brussels: 1965. V. 48
Philosophiae Naturalis Principia Mathematica. Cambridge: 1972. V. 48; 54
Principes Mathematiques de la Philosophie Naturelle par Feue Madame la Marquise du Chastellet. Paris: 1759. V. 47
Principia. Glasgow: 1871. V. 47; 48
Traite d'Optique sur les Reflexions, Refractions, Inflexions, et les Couleurs, de la Lumiere... Paris: 1722. V. 47
A Treatise of the System of the World. London: 1728. V. 48; 52; 54
Universal Arithmetic... Dublin: 1769. V. 48
Universal Arithmetick: or, A Treatise of Arithmetical Composition and Resolution. London: 1720. V. 49

NEWTON, JAMES
A Compleat Herbal of the Late James Newton, M.D. London: 1752. V. 48; 49; 50
A Complete Herbal. London: 1805. V. 47; 49

NEWTON, JOHN MARSHALL
Memoirs of John Marshall Newton. Cambridge: 1913. V. 47

NEWTON, RICHARD
Pluralities Indefensible. A Treatise Humbly Offered to the Consideration of the Parliament of Great Britain. London: 1745. V. 52

NEWTON, WILLIAM
The History and Antiquities of Maidstone, the County-Town of Kent. London: 1741. V. 47
Twenty Years on the Saskatchewan, N.W. Canada. London: 1897. V. 47; 50

NEWTON, WILLIAM G.
The Work of Ernest Newton, R.A. London: 1925. V. 53

THE NEWTONIAN System of Philosophy: Explained by Familiar Objects, in an Entertaining Manner, for the Use of Young Ladies and Gentleman. London: 1798. V. 50

NEW YORK. (STATE). FOREST, FISH & GAME COMMISSION
Annual Reports of the Forest, Fish and Game Commissioner for New York State. 1904/05/06. V. 52
Eighth and Ninth Reports of the Forest, Fish and Game Commission. Albany: 1904. V. 50
Forest, Fish and Game Commission of the State of New York. Seventh Report. Albany: 1902. V. 52

NEZELOFF, PIERRE
Napoleon and His Son. New York: 1937. V. 50

THE NIAGARA Book, a Complete Souvenir of Niagara Falls Containing Sketches... Buffalo: 1893. V. 49; 51

NIALL, IAN
English Country Traditions. London: 1988. V. 50
Portrait of a Country Artist, Charles Tunnicliffe, 1901-1979. London: 1980. V. 49

NIATUM, DUANE
Ascending Red Cedar Moon. New York: 1973. V. 50
Carriers of the Dream Wheel. New York: 1975. V. 50
Taos Pueblo. Greenfield: 1973. V. 50

NIBBS, REV.
Reay Morden: a Novel... Edinburgh: 1829. V. 48

NIBBS, RICHARD HENRY
The Churches of Sussex. Brighton: 1851. V. 50; 53

NIBLACK, ALBERT P.
The Coast Indians of Southern Alaska and Northern British Columbia...In Connection with the Survey of Alaska in the Seasons of 1885, 1886 and 1887. Washington: 1890. V. 53

NICANDER
Alexipharmaca. Parisiis: 1549. V. 47; 50; 53
The Second Book of the Travels of Nicander Nucius of Coryra. London: 1841. V. 54

NICCOL, ROBERT
Essay on Sugar, and General Treatise on Sugar Refining, as Practised in the Clyde Refineries... Greenock: 1864. V. 47

NICHOL, B. P.
Aleph Unit. Toronto: 1973. V. 47
Craft Dinner: Stories and Texts 1966-76. Toronto: 1978. V. 47; 50
Cycles Etc. Cleveland: 1965. V. 49
Door to Oz. Toronto: 1979. V. 47
From My Window. Toronto: 1978. V. 47; 49
In England Now That spring... Toronto: 1979. V. 47
Love Affair. Toronto: 1979. V. 47
The Martyrology. Books I & II. Toronto: 1972. V. 47
Movies. Toronto: 1979. V. 47
The Rose and the Puritan. Fredericton: 1958. V. 47
Unit of Four. Toronto: 1973. V. 47

NICHOLAS, J. W.
At Midnight's Chime. Bristol: 1889. V. 47
The Two Crosses. Bristol: 1887. V. 47

NICHOLAS, JOHN L.
Narrative of a Voyage to New Zealand, Performed in the Years 1814 and 1815, in Company with the Rev. Samuel Marsden... London: 1817. V. 47; 52

NICHOLAS OF CUSA
Dialogue About the Hidden God. New York: 1989. V. 48; 51

NICHOLAS V, POPE
Tractatus de Iudeorum et Christianorum Comunione et Conversatione... (and) Commissio Data Fr. Iohanni De Capistrano Circa Conversionem Iudaeorum et Innovatonem et Confirmationem Ecclesiae De Iudaeis. Basel: 1474. V. 47; 50

NICHOLL, EDITH M.
Observations of a Ranchwoman in New Mexico. London: 1898. V. 54
Observations of a Ranchwoman in New Mexico. Cincinnati: 1901. V. 54

NICHOLL, JOHN
Some Account of the Worshipful Company of Ironmongers. London: 1866-1916. V. 52; 54

NICHOLL, ROBERT
Poems and Lyrics. Paisley: 1877. V. 54

NICHOLLS, CAPTAIN
English and Bristol Channels Ship Canal. Report of Captain Nicholls to the Committe of Management Dated 23d March, 1825. London: 1825. V. 51

NICHOLLS, H. G.
Iron Making in the Olden Times; as Instanced in the Ancient Mines, Forges and Furnaces of the Forest of Dean... London: 1866. V. 50

NICHOLLS, J. F.
Bristol Past and Present. Bristol: 1881/81/82. V. 50

NICHOLLS, W.
The History and Traditions of Ravenstonedale, Westmorland. Manchester: 1877. V. 50; 52
The History and Traditions of Ravenstonedale, Westmorland. Manchester: 1910. V. 50; 52

NICHOLLS, W. A.
The National Drawing Master. London: 1865. V. 50

NICHOLLS, W. H.
Orchids of Australia. Melbourne: 1951. V. 50
Orchids of Australia. Melbourne: 1969. V. 52

NICHOLLS, WILLIAM
The Duty of Inferiours Towards their Superiours, in Five Discourses. London: 1701. V. 54

NICHOLS, BROOKE
The Broadcasting Kookaburra. His Life and Adventures. London: 1933. V. 49

NICHOLS, D.
Peter Matthiessen: a Bibliography: 1951-1979. Canoga Park: 1979. V. 48

NICHOLS, DALE
The Mayan Mystery. Chicago: 1978. V. 48

NICHOLS, FREDERICK DOVETON
The Early Architecture of Georgia. Chapel Hill: 1957. V. 48; 51

NICHOLS, GEORGE WARD
Art Education Applied to Industry. New York: 1877. V. 50; 52
Pottery, How it is Made, its Shape and Decoration. London: 1878. V. 51; 52

NICHOLS, ISAAC T.
Historic Days in Cumberland County, New Jersey, 1855-1865. Political and War Time Reminiscences. 1907. V. 49; 51

NICHOLS, J.
A Select Collection of Poems: with Notes... London: 1780-82. V. 50

NICHOLS, J. B.
Account of the Royal Hospital and Collegiate Church of Saint Katharine, Near the Tower of London. London: 1824. V. 50; 52
The History of the Royal Hospital and Collegiate Church of St. Katharine, near the Tower of London, from its Foundation in the Year 1273 to the Present Time. London: 1782. V. 50; 52

NICHOLS, J. T.
The Fresh-Water Fishes of China. New York: 1943. V. 48

NICHOLS, JAMES WILSON
Now You Hear My Horn, the Journal of James Wilson Nichols, 1820-1887. Austin: 1967. V. 49

NICHOLS, JEANNETTE PADDOCK
Alaska, a History of Its Administration, Exploitation, and Industrial Development During Its First Half Century Under the Rule of the United States. Cleveland: 1924. V. 49; 50

NICHOLS, JOHN
Biographical Anecdotes of William Hogarth. London: 1781. V. 48
Biographical Anecdotes of William Hogarth... London: 1782. V. 48; 53
Biographical Anecdotes of William Hogarth. London: 1785. V. 51
A Collection of All the Wills Now Known to be Extant, of the Kings and Queens of England, Princes and Princesses of Wales, and Every Branch of the Blood Royal, from the Reign of William the Conqueror, to That of Henry the Seventh Exclusive. London: 1780. V. 48
A Fragile Beauty. John Nichols' Milagro Country. Salt Lake City: 1987. V. 51
A Ghost in the Music. New York: 1979. V. 53
The Last Beautiful Days of Autumn. New York: 1982. V. 51
Literary Anecdotes of the Eighteenth Century... London: 1812-15. V. 53
The Milagro Beanfield War. New York: 1974. V. 47; 49; 50; 53
Miscellaneous Tracts by the Late William Bowyer, Printer, F.S.A. and Several of His Learned Friends... Edinburgh: 1775. V. 52
The Nirvana Blues. New York: 1981. V. 53
A Select Collection of Poems with Notes Biographical and Historical. London: 1780-82. V. 47; 54
Six Old Plays On Which Shakespeare Founded His Measure for Measure, Comedy of Errors, Taming of the Shrew, King John, King Henry IV and King Henry V, King Lear. London: 1779. V. 53
Some Account of the Alien Priories, and Of Such Lands as They are Known to Have Possessed in England and Wales. London: 1779. V. 49
The Sterile Cuckoo. New York: 1965. V. 47; 49; 53
The Wizard of Loneliness. New York: 1966. V. 47; 49

NICHOLS, JOHN GOUGH
Autographs of Royal, Noble, Learned and Remarkable Personages Conspicious in English History, from the Reign of Richard II to that of Charles II... London: 1829. V. 53
Examples of Decorative Tiles, Sometimes Called Encaustic. London: 1845. V. 52
London Pageants. London: 1831. V. 50

NICHOLS, JOSEPH
Condensed History of the Consequences of the Construction of the Union Pacific Railway. Omaha: 1892. V. 47

NICHOL'S Library Edition of the British Poets. Edinburgh: 1861. V. 49

NICHOLS, MARY GOVE
Lectures to Ladies on Anatomy and Physiology. Boston: 1842. V. 48
Reminiscences of Edgar Allan Poe. New York: 1931. V. 48

NICHOLS, ROBERT
Aurellia and Other Poems. New York: 1920. V. 50
Invocation: War Poems and Others. London: 1915. V. 47
The Smile of the Sphinx. London: 1920. V. 49; 52; 53
A Year's Grain - 1920-1921. Tokyo: 1921. V. 47

NICHOLS, RUTH
Wings for Life. Philadelphia: 1957. V. 51

NICHOLS, T. L.
Esoteric Anthropology... New York: 1854. V. 51
Forty Years of American Life. London: 1864. V. 47
Supramundane Facts: In the Life of Rev. Jesse Babcock Ferguson: Including 20 Years Observation of Preternatural Phenomena. London: 1865. V. 52

NICHOLSON, ALFRED
Cimabue: a Critical Study. Princeton: 1932. V. 51; 53

NICHOLSON, ASENATH
Ireland's Welcome to the Stranger. New York: 1847. V. 52
Nature's Own Book. New York: 1835. V. 47; 49; 51; 54

NICHOLSON, B. D.
Brief Sketch of the Life of an Ex-Confederate Soldier and the Ups and Downs During Pioneer and Indian Warfare in Texas. Dallas: 1928. V. 54

NICHOLSON, BEN
Circle - International Survey of Constructive Art. London: 1937. V. 49
Joseph Wright of Derby; Painter of Light. London: 1968. V. 50
Paintings, Reliefs, Drawings... London: 1955. V. 48; 51
Recent Work. Zurich: 1966. V. 49

NICHOLSON, CHARLES
Aegyptiaca, Comprising a Catalogue of Egyptian Antiquities, Collected in the Years 1856, 1857 and Now Deposited in the Museum of the University of Sydney... London: 1891. V. 51

NICHOLSON, CORNELIUS
The Annals of Kendal... Kendal: 1832. V. 47; 49
The Annals of Kendal... London: 1861. V. 48; 50; 52

NICHOLSON, FRANCIS
The Practice of Drawing and Painting Landscape from Nature in Water Colours. London: 1820. V. 48
The Practice of Drawing and Painting Landscape from Nature in Water Colours. London: 1823. V. 47

NICHOLSON, G. W. L.
The Fighting Newfoundlander: a History of the Royal Newfoundland Regiment. 1963. V. 50

NICHOLSON, GEORGE
The Illustrated Dictionary of Gardening. London: 1881-88/1901. V. 48
The Illustrated Dictionary of Gardening. London: 1884-85. V. 54
The Illustrated Dictionary of Gardening... London: 1884-88. V. 49; 51
The Illustrated Dictionary of Gardening. London: 1885. V. 49; 50
The Illustrated Dictionary of Gardening. London and New York: 1887. V. 50
The Illustrated Dictionary of Gardening. London: 1890. V. 47
The Illustrated Dictionary of Gardening. New York & London: 1890. V. 51; 52

NICHOLSON, H. A.
An Essay on the Geology of Cumberland and Westmorland. Hardwicke & Ireland: 1868. V. 48
An Essay on the Geology of Cumberland and Westmorland. London: 1868. V. 48
A Manual of Palaeontology. London: 1879. V. 53
A Monograph of the Silurian Fossils of the Girvan Distrcit in Ayrshire. London: 1878-80. V. 49

NICHOLSON, HENRY D.
The Organ Manual, for the Use of Amateurs and Church Committees... Boston: 1866. V. 48

NICHOLSON, J.
The History and Antiquities of the Counties of Westmorland and Cumberland. London: 1777. V. 50; 52

NICHOLSON, JAMES B.
A Manual of the Art of Bookbinding... Philadelphia: 1856. V. 48; 49; 52
A Manual of the Art of Bookbinding... Philadelphia: 1871. V. 52
A Manual of the Art of Bookbinding... Philadelphia: 1878. V. 50; 52

NICHOLSON, JOHN
Martyrdom of Joseph Standing on the Murder of a Mormon Missionary. Salt Lake City. V. 49; 54
The Martyrdom of Joseph Standing; or, the Murder of a 'Mormon' Missionary. Salt Lake City: 1886. V. 49
The Millwright's Guide. London: 1830. V. 50
The Operative Mechanic, and British Machinist... London: 1830. V. 48

NICHOLSON, JOSEPH WALKER
Crosby Garrett, Westmorland. Kirkby Stephen: 1914. V. 52

NICHOLSON, M. A.
The Carpenter and Joiner's Companion, in the Geometrical Construction of Working Drawings, Required by Journeymen in the Progress of Building Comprehending a Complete System of Lines. London: 1826. V. 50
The Carpenter and Joiner's Companion, in the Geometrical Construction of Working Drawings, Required by Journeymen in the Progress of Building Comprehending a Complete System of Lines. London: 1843. V. 53

NICHOLSON, MR.
The Trial at Full Length of Maj. Gen. Sir Robt. Thomas Wilson, Michael Bruce, Esq. and Captain John Hely Hutchinson...for Aiding...the Escape of General Lavalette. 1816. V. 52

NICHOLSON, NORMAN
The Fire of the Lord. London: 1944. V. 51; 52
A Local Habitation. London: 1972. V. 48
A Match for the Devil. London: 1955. V. 52
Prophesy to the Wind. London: 1950. V. 51; 52
Rock Face. London: 1948. V. 49
Wednesday Early Closing. London: 1975. V. 52

NICHOLSON, PETER
The Builder's and Workman's New Director. London: 1864. V. 52
The Carpenter's New Guide: Being a Complete Book of Lines and Joinery... London: 1814. V. 47
Carpentry, Joinery and Cabinet-Making... London: 1837. V. 51
Encyclopedia of Architecture. London: 1852. V. 47; 48
The Guide to Railway Masonry Containing a Complete Treatise on the Oblique Arch in four Parts. London: 1846. V. 49
The New Practical Builder, and Workman's Companion... London: 1823. V. 51
The Practical Cabinet-Maker, Upholsterer, and Complete Decorator. London: 1843.. V. 52
Practical Carpentry, Joinery and Cabinet Making... London: 1839. V. 50
Practical Carpentry, Joinery and Cabinet Making. London: 1845. V. 47
Practical Carpentry, Joinery and Cabinet Making... London: 1854. V. 48
Practical Carpentry, Joinery and Cabinet-Making... London: 1847. V. 50
Practical Carpentry, Joinery and Cabinet-Making... London: 1856. V. 47
The Student's Instructor in Drawing and Working the Five Orders of Architecture. London: 1810. V. 52
The Student's Instructor in Drawing and Working the Five Orders of Architecture. London: 1823. V. 54

NICHOLSON, RENTON
Cockney Adventures and Tales of London Life. London: 1838. V. 54
Dombey and Daughter. London: 1847. V. 54

NICHOLSON, S.
Twenty-Six Lithographic Drawings in the Vicinity of Liverpool. Liverpool: 1821. V. 49; 52

NICHOLSON, WILLIAM
An Almanac of Twelve Sports. London: 1897. V. 51
An Almanac of Twelve Sports. London: 1898. V. 49
An Almanac of Twelve Sports. London: 1989. V. 47
An Almanac of Twelve Sports. (and) London Types. (with) William Nicholson's An Almanac of Twelve Sports and London Types, an Introduction tot he Reprint from the Original Woodblocks (by) Edward Craig. Andoversford: 1980. V. 47
An Alphabet. London: 1898. V. 47; 52
An Alphabet. New York: 1898. V. 49
An Alphabet. Andoversford: 1978. V. 54
The Book of Blokes. London: 1929. V. 49; 50; 51
Characters of Romance. London: 1900. V. 47; 53
Clever Bill. New York: 1926. V. 49
Clever Bill. London: 1929. V. 52; 53
A Collection of Papers Scatter'd Lately About the Town in the Daily-Fourant, St. James's Post, &c... London: 1717. V. 52
A Dictionary of Practical and Theoretical Chemistry, With Its Application to the Arts and Manufactures... London: 1808. V. 48; 52
An Introduction to Natural Philosophy. 1805. V. 54
A Journal of Natural Philosophy, Chemistry and the Arts. London: 1802. V. 54
London Types: Twelve Coloured Illustrations. London: 1898. V. 49; 51; 53
A Match for the Devil. London: 1955. V. 51
Oxford. London: 1905. V. 53
The Pirate Twins. London: 1929. V. 50
The Square Book of Animals. London: 1900. V. 52

NICHOLSON'S
New Carpenter's Guide. 1825. V. 49

NICK, AARON
Best Short Stories by Afro-American Writers. Boston: 1950. V. 47

NICKALLS, JAMES
The Statutes of the Province of Upper Canada; together with Such British Statutes, Ordinances of Quebec and Proclamations.... Kingston: 1831. V. 52

NICKELSON, B. C.
A Brief Sketch of the Life of an Ex-Confederate Soldier and the Ups and Downs During Pioneer and Indian Warfare in Texas. Dallas: 1928. V. 49

NICKERSON, ANSEL D.
A Raw Recruit's War Experiences. Providence: 1888. V. 54

NICKERSON, JOSEPH
Joseph Nickerson, Dealer in Ship Chandlery and Ship Stores, Nos. 46 and 47 Commercial Street, Boston... Boston: 1845. V. 54

NICKLIN, PHILIP H.
A Pleasant Peregrination through the Prettiest Parts of Pennsylvania. Philadelphia: 1836. V. 47

NICKSON, CHARLES
History of Runcorn; with an Account of the Ancient Village of Weston. Warrington: 1887. V. 48; 53

NICKSON, E. A.
The Lytham Century. London: 1982. V. 50; 53

NICKSON, G.
A Portrait of Salmon Fishing. London: 1976. V. 51; 52

NICLAES, HENRICK
A New Balade or Songe of the Lambes Feast. 1928. V. 51
A New Balade or Songe of the Lambes Feast. Long Crendon: 1928. V. 54

NICLOUX, MARIA LOUISA
A Week's Amusement. London: 1823. V. 53

NICOL, GEORGE
The Three Bears. London: 1837. V. 50

NICOL, J.
Guide to the Geology of Scotland... Edinburgh: 1844. V. 54

NICOL, J. A. C.
The Eyes of Fishes. Oxford: 1989. V. 51

NICOL, WALTER
The Gardeners Kalendar; or, Monthly Directory of Operations in Every Branch of Horticulture. London: 1812. V. 51; 52; 53; 54
The Practical Planter; or, a Treatise on Forest Planting... London: 1803. V. 51; 52

NICOLAS, HARRIS
A Treatise on the Law of Adulterine Bastardy, with a Report of the Banbury Case, and All Other Cases Bearing Upon the Subject. London: 1836. V. 49; 51; 52

NICOLAS, NICHOLAS HARRIS
The Dispatches and Letters of Vice Admiral Lord Viscount Nelson. London: 1844-46. V. 54
A History of the Royal Navy, From the Earliest Times to the Wars of the French Revolution. London: 1847. V. 49
Privy Purse Expenses of Elizabeth of York... London: 1830. V. 47; 51

NICOLAUS DE AUXIMO
Supplementum. Venice: 1474. V. 51; 52

NICOLAUS DE HANAPIS
Auctoritates Utriusque Testamenti. Strasburg: 1470-72. V. 50

NICOLAUS DE LYRA
Praeceptorium (Divinae Legis), Cum Additionibus det Tractatulis Pulcerrimus Multis... Cologne: 1502. V. 48

NICOLAY, C. G.
Notes on the Aborigines of Western Australia. London: 1886. V. 52
The Oregon Territory: a Geographical and Physical Account of that Country and Its Inhabitants; with Outlines of Its History and Discovery. London: 1846. V. 47; 48; 53; 54

NICOLAY, JOHN G.
Abraham Lincoln. A History. New York: 1909. V. 48; 50

NICOLAYSEN, N.
The Viking-Ship Discovered at Gokstad in Norway. Christiana: 1882. V. 52

NICOLET, C. C.
Death of a Bridge Expert. London: 1933. V. 48

NICOLL, ALLARDYCE
An Annual Survey of Shakespearian Study and Production. 1948-63. V. 51
A History of English Drama. 1927-65. V. 51

NICOLL, HENRY J.
C (100) Sonnets by C (100) Authors. Edinburgh: 1883. V. 47; 49

NICOLL, M. J.
Nicoll's Birds of Egypt. London: 1930. V. 49; 50; 51; 53

NICOLL, ROBERT
Poems and Lyrics. Paisley: 1877. V. 53

NICOLL, W. ROBERTSON
Literary Anecdotes of the Nineteenth Century. New York: 1894. V. 54
Literary Anecdotes of the Nineteenth Century... London: 1895. V. 47; 51; 53

NICOLLET, I.
Report Intended to Illustrate a Map of the Hydrographical Basin of the Upper Mississippi. Washington: 1843. V. 47
Report Intended to Illustrate a Map of the Hydrographical Basin of the Upper Mississippi River. Washington: 1845. V. 53

NICOLLET, JOSEPH N.
The Journals of Joseph N. Nicollet. St. Paul: 1970. V. 51

NICOLLIER, JEAN
Collecting Toy Soldiers. Rutland: 1967. V. 53

NICOLLS, JAMES A.
The Sportsman in South Africa. London: 1892. V. 48

NICOLS, THOMAS
A Lapidary: or, the History of Precious Stones... Cambridge: 1652. V. 53; 54

NICOLSON, BENEDICT
Joseph Wright of Derby, Painter of Light. London: 1968. V. 49; 50; 51; 52
Joseph Wright of Derby, Painter of Light. New Haven: 1971. V. 48

NICOLSON, HAROLD
Diaries and Letters 1930-1962. London: 1966-68. V. 49
Some People. London: 1927. V. 54
Sweet Waters. London: 1921. V. 47

NICOLSON, MARJORIE HOPE
The Correspondence of Anne, Viscountess Conway, Henry More and Their Friends, 1642-1684. 1930. V. 51

NICOLSON, PETER
The Carpenter's New Guide; or, The Book of Lines for Carpenters, Geometrically Explained... London: 1857. V. 47

NICOLSON, REYNOLD A.
A Literary History fo the Arabs. London: 1923. V. 48; 54

NICOLSON, WILLIAM
The English Historical Library. London: 1696. V. 50; 54
The English Historical Library. London: 1696/97/99. V. 51
The English Historical Library. London: 1697. V. 50; 54
The English Historical Library. London: 1714. V. 47; 49; 50; 51; 52
The English, Scotch and Irish Historical Libraries. London: 1736. V. 54
The English, Scotch and Irish Historical Libraries. London: 1776. V. 47; 53
Leges Marchiarum, or Border-Laws, Containing Several Original Articles and Treaties, Made and Agreed Upon by the Commissioners of the Respective Kings of England and Scotland... London: 1705. V. 54
Miscellany Accounts of the Diocese of Carlisle, with the Terriers Delivered In to Me at My Primary Visitation. London: 1877. V. 50

The Petition of Sir William Nicolson of Glenbervy, Baronet...(with) Information for Sir William Nicholson...Against Margaret, Marchioness of Lothian. Edinburgh: 1729. V. 53

NICONITIUS, FRANCISCUS
Bis Centum et Viginti Quatuor Rationes Dubitandi (etc.). Cracow: 1541. V. 51

NICOSIA, GERALD
Memory Babe. New York: 1983. V. 53

NIDER, JOHANNES
Consolatorium Timoratae Conscientiae. Cologne: 1473. V. 51; 53
De Morali Lepra. Cologne: 1479. V. 51; 53
Formicarius. Augsburg: 1484. V. 51; 52
Sermones de Tempore et de Sanctis cum Quadragesimali. Cologne: 1482. V. 51

NIEBAUER, ABBY
Three Windows; Poems. Woodside: 1980. V. 47; 52

NIEBUHR, BARTHOLD GEORG
The Greek Heroes. London: 1910. V. 51
History of Rome. London: 1837. V. 51

NIEBUHR, CARSTEN
Beschreibung von Arabien Aus Eigenen Beobachtungen und im Lande Selbst Gesammelten Nachrichten. Kopenhagen: 1772. V. 54
Descriptio de l'Arabie d'Apres les Observations et Recherches faites dans le Pays Meme. Copenhague: 1773. V. 52
Description de L'Arabie, Faites sur des Observations Propres et des Avis Recueillis dans Les Lieux Memes. Amsterdam: 1774. V. 53; 54
Voyage en Arabie. Amsterdam: 1776-80. V. 50

NIEDECKER, LORINE
The Collected Poems (1936-1966). Penland: 1968. V. 54
From This Condensery: the Complete Writing of Lorine Niedecker. Highlands: 1985. V. 47; 52; 53; 54
My Life by Water - Collected Poems 1936-1968. London: 1970. V. 48
North Central. London: 1968. V. 47; 48; 51; 53; 54

NIEDIECK, PAUL
With Rifle in Five Continents. London: 1908. V. 49; 54

NIELSEN, FREDERIK
The History of the Papacy in the XIXth Century. London: 1906. V. 49

NIELSON, HARRY B.
An Animal ABC. London: 1901. V. 52

NIEMANN, AUGUST
Ephraim; or, the Many and the Few. London: 1883. V. 49

NIEMEYER, A. H.
Travels on the Continent and in England. London: 1823. V. 52; 54

NIEMEYER, WILHELM
Nicola Tuldo und Santa Catarina Im Kerker Zu Siena. 1918-19. V. 51; 52; 54

NIENHUIS, P. H.
The Oosterschelde Estuary (The Netherlands). Dordrecht: 1994. V. 53

NIERENDORF, KARL
Paul Klee: Paintings, Watercolors, 1913 to 1939. New York: 1941. V. 47; 48; 50; 52

NIES, JAMES B.
Ur Dynasty Tablets: Texts Chiefly from Tello and Drehem Written During the Reigns of Dungi, Bur-Sin, Gimil-Sin and Ibi-Sin. Leipzig: 1920. V. 49; 52

NIETZSCHE, FRIEDRICH
The Antichrist of Nietzsche. London: 1928. V. 53
Goetzen-Daemmerung, Oder Wie Man Mit Dem Hammer Philosophint. Leipzig: 1889. V. 49
The Nietzsche-Wagner Correspondence. London: 1922. V. 53
Thus Spake Zarathustra. London: 1896. V. 54
Thus Spake Zarathustra. Edinburgh: 1909. V. 53

NIEUWENTIJT, BERNARD
The Regligious Philosopher, or the Right Use of Contemplating the Works of the Creator. London: 1724. V. 48

NIEWENHUIS, A. W.
Quer Durch Borneo. Ergebnisse Seiner Reisen in den Jahren 1894, 1896-97 und 1898-1900. Leiden: 1904. V. 50

NIFO Y CAGIGAL, FRANCISCO MARIANO
Estafeta de Londres. Obra Periodica, Repartida en Diferentes Cartas, en las Que se Declara el Proceder de la Inglaterra... Madrid: 1762. V. 48

NIGGUN. Paintings by Isaac Lichtenstein. New York: 1945. V. 50

THE NIGHT Before Christmas. New York: 1913. V. 53

THE NIGHT Before Christmas or a Visit of St. Nicholas. New York: 1896. V. 53

A NIGHT in Venice Belvedere California. 1899. V. 52

THE NIGHT Watch; or, Tales of the Sea. London: 1828. V. 47; 51

NIGHTINGALE, B.
The Ejected of 1662 in Cumberland and Westmorland. Manchester: 1911. V. 49; 50; 52
The Story of Lancashire Congregational Union 1806-1906. Manchester: 1906. V. 48; 49; 53

NIGHTINGALE, FLORENCE
Notes On Nursing: What It Is, and What It Is Not. London. V. 49

NIGHTINGALE, FLORENCE continued
Notes on Nursing: What It Is, and What it Is Not. London: 1859. V. 48; 51
Notes On Nursing: What It Is, and What It Is Not. Boston: 1860. V. 47; 48; 49; 50; 53; 54
Notes on Nursing: What It Is, and What It Is Not. Boston: 1860. V. 50; 53
Notes on Nursing: What It is and What It Is Not. New York: 1860. V. 48; 49; 50; 53
Notes on Nursing: What It Is, and What It Is Not. London: 1900. V. 51
Om Sjukskotsel: Hvad den ar, Och Hvad den Icke ar. Ofversattning fran Engelskan af E(mily) N(onne)n. (Notes on Nursing). Goteborg: 1861. V. 47
On Trained Nursing for the Sick Poor. London: 1881. V. 49

NIGHTINGALE, JOSEPH
English Topography; or, a Series of Historical and Statistical Descriptions. London: 1816, but later. V. 54
Memoirs of the Public and Private Life of Her Most Gracious Majesty Caroline, Queen of Great Britain and Consort of King George the Fourth. London: 1820. V. 47

NIL Mortalibus Arduum; or, a Vindication of the Disposal of the Puppet-Shew House. Edinburgh: 1767. V. 50

NIL Timeo. A Song Addressed to John Wilson Esq. Captain of the Windermere Sailing Club, Instituted 1808. 1810-20?. V. 47

NILES, JOHN M.
History of South America and Mexico. Hartford: 1837. V. 47; 53

NILSSON, JOHN R.
The Story of the Century. 1946. V. 53

NIMIS, P. L.
The Lichens of Italy, an Annotated Catalogue. Torino: 1993. V. 50

NIMMO, WILLIAM
History of Stirlingshire Corrected and Brought Down to the Present Time... London: 1817. V. 52; 54

NIMROD CO., CHICAGO
A Complete Line of High Grade Furnishings for Men, Women and Children. 1930's. V. 53

NIN, ANAIS
Children of the Albatross. New York: 1947. V. 53; 54
D. H. Lawrence: an Unprofessional Study. Paris: 1932. V. 49; 50; 51; 52
Delta of Venus: Erotica. New York: 1977. V. 53
The Diary of Anais Nin. 1934-1939. New York: 1967. V. 48
The Diary of Anais Nin. Volume 6, 1955-1966. New York: 1976. V. 53
The Diary of Anais Nin. Volume Three 1939-1944. New York: 1969. V. 53
The Four-Chambered Heart. New York: 1950. V. 50; 53
House of Incest. New York. V. 48; 49; 50
House of Incest. New York: 1947. V. 47; 51
House of Incest. London: 1958. V. 49; 52
Ladders to Fire. New York: 1946. V. 52; 53; 54
Solar Barque. London: 1958. V. 49; 52
A Spy in the House of Love. New York: 1954. V. 51; 53
This Hunger. New York: 1945. V. 47; 48; 50
Under a Glass Bell. New York: 1944. V. 53
Winter of Artifice. Paris: 1939. V. 47
Winter of Artifice. New York: 1942. V. 53

NINE Artists and a Press. Andoversford: 1988. V. 51

NINE Niggers More. New York: 1870. V. 53

NININGER, H. H.
The Nininger Collection of Meteorites, a Catalog and a History. Winslow: 1950. V. 51
Our Stone-Pelted Planet... Winslow: 1933. V. 54

NISBET, ALEXANDER
An Essay on the Ancient and Modern Use of Armories. Edinburgh: 1718. V. 52
A System of Heraldry. Edinburgh: 1804. V. 47; 53
A System of Heraldry, Speculative and Practical... Edinburgh: 1816. V. 49

NISBET, CHARLES
An Address to the Students of Dickinson College, Carlisle. Edinburgh: 1786. V. 53

NISBET, JAMES COOPER
Four Years on the Firing Line. Chattanooga: 1900. V. 49
Four Years on the Firing Line. Chattanooga: 1914. V. 48

NISBET, JOHN
Some Doubts and Questions, in the Law; Especially of Scotland...Also Some Decisions of the Lords of Council and Session. Edinburgh: 1698. V. 49

NISEI in Uniform.. Washington: 1944. V. 50

NISSER, WILHELM
Michael Dahl and the Contemporary School of Painting in England. London: 1927. V. 50

NISTER'S Holiday Annual for 1907. London: 1907. V. 52

NISTER'S Panorama Pictures. London: 1895. V. 49

NITSCHE, PAUL
The History of Prison Psychoses. New York: 1912. V. 48

NITZSCH, CHRISTIAN LUDWIG
Nitzsch's Pterylography. London: 1867. V. 50

NIVEN, L.
A Gift from the Earth. 1969. V. 48; 52
Inconstant Moon. London: 1973. V. 47; 51

Limits. London: 1986. V. 51
Lucifer's Hammer. 1977. V. 48
The Mote in God's Eye. 1974. V. 48; 52
Neutron Star. 1969. V. 49; 52
Neutron Star. London: 1969. V. 54
Ringworld. 1977. V. 54
World of Ptavvs. 1968. V. 47; 49; 51; 54
World of Ptavvs. 1969. V. 52

NIX, JOHN W.
The Tale of Two Schools Springtown-Parker Country. Ft. Worth: 1945. V. 49

NIX, NELLEKE LANGHOUT
1940-1945 Remembered: Translated and Retold From my Diary. Seattle: 1991. V. 53; 54
Papua New Guinea: Where She Invented Bow and Arrow. Mercer Island: 1996. V. 54

NIXON, CAPTAIN
The Ramble of Philo, and His Man Sturdy. Dublin: 1789. V. 54

NIXON, FRANCIS R.
The Cruise of the Beacon: A Narrative of a Visit to the Islands in Bass's Straits... London: 1856. V. 47

NIXON, HERMAN CLARENCE
Forty Acres and Steel Mules. Chapel Hill: 1938. V. 47; 49

NIXON, HOWARD MILLAR
British Bookbindings Presented by Kenneth H. Oldaker to the Chapter Library of Westminster Abbey. London: 1982. V. 52
Broxbourne Library. Styles and Designs of Bookbindings for the 12th to the 20th Century. London: 1956. V. 50; 51
Catalogue of the Pepys Library at Magdalene College Cambridge. Volume VI. Bindings. Cambridge: 1984. V. 50
English Restoration Bookbindings: Samuel Mearne and His Contemporaries. London: 1974. V. 49; 50; 51
Roger Powell & Peter Waters. 1965. V. 49
Sixteenth Century Gold-Tooled Bookbindings in the Pierpont Morgan Library. New York: 1971. V. 47; 50; 51; 52
Styles and Designs of Bookbinding from the Twelfth to the Twentieth Century. London: 1956. V. 47; 50
Twelve Books in Fine Bindings from the Library of J. W. Hely-Hutchinson. Oxford: 1953. V. 50; 52; 54

NIXON, MIMA
Royal Palaces and Gardens. London: 1916. V. 51; 53

NIXON, PAT IRELAND
A Century of Medicine in San Antonio: The Story of Medicine in Bexar County, Texas. San Antonio: 1936. V. 48
The Early Nixons of Texas... El Paso: 1956. V. 48; 52
In Memoriam Olive Read Nixon 1886-1964. San Antonio: 1965. V. 53
The Medical Story of Early Texas, 1528-1853. 1946. V. 48

NIXON, RICHARD MILHOUS
1999: Victory Without War. New York: 1988. V. 52
The Challenges We Face. New York: 1960. V. 51
In the Arena. New York: 1990. V. 49
Leaders. New York: 1982. V. 49; 53
The Memoirs of Richard Nixon. New York: 1978. V. 49; 51; 53; 54
No More Vietnams. New York: 1985. V. 52
The Real War. New York: 1980. V. 49
Seize the Moment. New York: 1992. V. 49
Six Crises. Garden City: 1962. V. 47; 51; 52; 53

NIXON, ROBERT
Nixon's Cheshire Prophecies. Manchester: 1878. V. 47
The Original Predictions or Prophecies of Robert Nixon, the Cheshire Prophet... London: 1810. V. 52

NIZAMI
The Poems of Nizami. London: 1928. V. 50; 52; 53

NIZER, LOUIS
The Implosion Conspiracy. Garden City: 1973. V. 49

NO Appeal. A Novel. London: 1870. V. 52

NO JEST Like a True Jest: Being a Compendious Record of the Merry Life, and Mad Exploits of Capt. James Hind the Great Rober (sic) of England. London: 1674. V. 48

NOAH, MORDECAI M.
The Fortress of Sorrento: a Petit Historical Drama. New York: 1808. V. 51; 53

NOAKES, AUBREY
Ben Marshall. Leigh-on-Sea: 1978. V. 50; 53

NOALL, CYRIL
Wreck and rescue Round the Cornish Coast. Truro: 1963-65. V. 51

NOBBES, ROBERT
The Compleat Troller, or, the Art of Trolling. London: 1682. V. 52

NOBBS, PERCY ERSKINE
Design: a Treatise on the Discovery of Form. London: 1937. V. 52

NOBEL, E.
The Nutrition of Healthy and Sick Infants and Children. Philadelphia: 1929. V. 49; 54

NOBEL, P. S.
Environmental Biology of Agaves and Cacti. London: 1988. V. 50

NOBILI, FLAMINIO
De Rebvs Gestis Stephani I Regis Poloniae... Rome: 1582. V. 52

NOBILITY, a Poem. In Imitation of the eight Satire of Juvenal. London: 1811. V. 49

NOBLE, ALDEN CHARLES
Scott Who Was Nine a Tale of the Joyous Universe. Chicago: 1901. V. 47

THE NOBLE and Renowned History of Guy, Earl of Warwick. London: 1821. V. 49

NOBLE, CELIA BRUNEL
The Brunels Father and Son. London: 1938. V. 49

NOBLE, CHARLES FREDERICK
A Voyage to the East Indies in 1747 and 1748. London: 1762. V. 53

NOBLE, DANIEL
The Brain and its Physiology: a Critical Disquisition On the Methods of Determining the Relations Subsisting Between the Structure and Functions of the Encephalon. London: 1846. V. 47; 49; 54

NOBLE, EDWARD
The Elements of Linear Perspective Demonstrated by Geometrical Principles... London: 1771. V. 47

NOBLE, JAMES ASHCROFT
The Sonnet in England and Other Essays. London: 1893. V. 54

NOBLE, JOHN
Descriptive Handbook of the Cape Colony; Its Condition and Resources. Cape Town: 1875. V. 47; 52

NOBLE, JOSEPH VEACH
The Techniques of Painted Attic Pottery. New York: 1988. V. 52

NOBLE, MARK
A History of the College of Arms. London: 1804. V. 53
A History of the College of Arms. London: 1805. V. 47
The Lives of the English Regicides and Other Commissioners of the Pretended Court of Justice... London: 1798. V. 51
Memoirs of the Protectorate-House of Cromwell. Birmingham: 1784. V. 47; 52
Memoirs of the Protectorate-House of Cromwell... Birmingham: 1787. V. 49
Two Dissertations Upon the Mint and Coins of the Episcopal Palatines of Durham. Birmingham: 1780. V. 50; 53

NOBLE, MARY E.
A History of the Parish of Bampton. Kendal: 1901. V. 52
Register of Births, Deaths and Marriages of the Parish of Bampton, in the County of Westmorland. From 1637 to 1812. Kendal: 1897. V. 48

NOBLE, PETER
The Negro in Films. London. V. 54

NOBLE, SAMUEL H.
Life and Adventures of Buckskin Sam. Rumford Falls: 1900. V. 49; 54

NOBLE, T.
City News, Notes and Queries. Manchester: 1878-86. V. 48
The Counties of Chester, Derby, Leicester, Lincoln and Rutland Illustrated. London: 1836. V. 48; 53

NOBLE, W. T.
A Guide to the Watering Places, on the Coast, Between the Exe and the Dart... Teignmouth: 1817. V. 51

NOBLES, WILLIAM H.
Speech of the Hon. Wm. H. Nobles, Together with Other Documents, Relative to an Emigrant Route to California and Oregon through Minnesota Territory... Saint Paul: 1854. V. 47

NOCQ, HENRY
Le Poincon de Paris: Repertoire des Maitres-Orfevres de la Juridiction de Paris Depuis le Moyen-Age Jusqu'a La Fin Du XVIII Siecle. Paris: 1931. V. 50

NODIN, JOHN
The British Duties of Customs, Excise &c. Containing an Account of the Net Sums Payable on All Goods Imported, Exported or Carried Coastwise. London: 1792. V. 48

NOEHDEN, GEORGE HENRY
Specimens of Ancient Coins, of Magna Graecia and Sicily... London: 1826. V. 48

NOEL, BAPTIST W.
Notes of a Tour in Switzerland in the Summer of 1847. London: 1848. V. 48

NOEL, GERALD T.
Arvendel; or, Sketches in Italy and Switzerland. London: 1826. V. 49

NOEL, JOHN BAPTIST LUCIUS
Through Tibet to Everest. London: 1927. V. 51

NOEL, RUTH S.
The Mythology of Middle Earth. Boston: 1977. V. 51

NOEL, THEOPHILUS
Autobiography and Reminiscences of Theophilus Noel. Chicago: 1904. V. 49
A Campaign from Santa Fe to the Mississippi, a History of the Old Sibley Brigade from Its First Organization to the Present Time. Houston: 1961. V. 54
A Campaign from Sante Fe to the Mississippi... Raleigh: 1961. V. 50

NOGALES, MANUEL CHAVES
And in the Distance a Light...?. London: 1938. V. 47

NOGUCHI, H.
Snake Venoms. Washington: 1909. V. 50

NOGUCHI, ISAMU
A Sculptor's World: an Autobiography. New York: 1968. V. 47; 50

NOGUCHI, YONE
Emperor Shomu and the Shosoin. Tokyo: 1941. V. 53
Harunobu. London: 1927. V. 47
Hiroshige. New York: 1921. V. 49; 50
Lafcadio Hearn in Japan. London & Yokohama: 1910. V. 50
Lafcadio Hearn in Japan. New York: 1911. V. 47
Through the Torii. Boston: 1922. V. 51
Utamoro... London: 1925. V. 49

NOHL, LUDWIG
Beethoven Depicted by His Contemporaries. London: 1880. V. 47
The Life of Mozart. London: 1877. V. 48

NOKES, WILLIAM
The Nature, Title and Evidence of Eternal Life Given in Jesus Christ by the Gosepl Briefly Stated. London: 1709. V. 53

NOLAN, L. E.
The Training of Cavalry Remount Horses, a New System. London: 1852. V. 48

NOLAN, SIDNEY
Sidney Nolan. London: 1961. V. 53

NOLAN, W.
The Ray Bradbury Companion. 1975. V. 47; 51
Ray Bradbury Review. San Diego: 1952. V. 54

NOLAN, WILLIAM F.
Logan's Run. New York: 1967. V. 51

NOLHAC, PIERRE DE
Marie Antoinette. London: 1905. V. 51
Versailles and the Trianons. London: 1906. V. 47

NOLLET, JEAN ANTOINE
L'Art des Experiences, Ou Avis Aux Amateurs de la Physique, sur le Choix la Construction et l'Usage des Instruments... Paris: 1770. V. 47
Lectures in Experimental Philosophy. London: 1752. V. 52
Lettres sur l'Electricite. Paris: 1767. V. 47

THE NOMENCLATURE of Diseases Drawn Up by a Joint Committee Appointed by the Royal College of Physicians of London. London: 1869. V. 49

THE NOMENCLATURE Of Diseases Drawn Up By a Joint Committee Appointed by the Royal College of Physicians of London... Philadelphia: 1869. V. 49

THE NONE-SUCH Charles His Character, Extracted Out of Divers Original Transactions... London: 1651. V. 49; 54

THE NONESUCH Century: an Appraisal, a Personal Note and a Bibliography of the First Hundred Books Issued by the PRess 1923-1934. London: 1936. V. 48

THE NONESUCH Century. The First 100 Books. London: 1929. V. 48

NONESUCH PRESS
The Nonesuch Century. London: 1936. V. 47; 53

NOON, JEFF
Vurt. 1993. V. 54

NOONAN, D. A.
Alaska, the Land of Now. Seattle: 1923. V. 52

NOORTHOUCK, JOHN
An Historical and Classical Dictionary...Lives and Characters of...Eminent and Learned Persons in Every Age and Nation... London: 1776. V. 54
An Historical and Classical Dictionary...Lives and Characters of...Eminent and Learned Persons in Every Age and Nation, from the Earliest Period to the Present Time. London: 1777. V. 49
A New History of London, Including Westminster and Southwark. London: 1773. V. 49; 50; 52

NOOTH, CHARLOTTE
Original Poems, and a Play. London: 1815. V. 48

NOPPEN, LEONARD VAN
The Challenge - War Chants of the Allies - Wise of Otherwise. London: 1919. V. 47

NORBURY, JOHN
The Box of Whistles. London: 1877. V. 50

NORCROSS, J.
The Proposed Constitution of Georgia. The Democracy - The Capital. Atlanta: 1877. V. 48

NORDAN, LEWIS
Welcome to the Arrow-Catcher Fair. Baton Rouge: 1983. V. 52; 53; 54

NORDEN, FREDERICK LEWIS
Travels in Egypt and Nubia. London: 1757. V. 52

NORDEN, JOHN
Speculi Britanniae Pars: a Topographical and Historical Description of Cornwall. London: 1728. V. 49

NORDEN, JOHN continued
Speculi Britanniae Pars: an Historical and Chorographical Description of the County of Essex, 1594. London: 1840. V. 50

NORDEN, MARIKA
The Gentle Men. Paris: 1935. V. 52

NORDENSKIOLD, GUSTAF ERIK ADOLF
The History of Biology, a Survey. London: 1929. V. 50; 54
Ruiner Af Klippboningar I Mesa Verde's Canons. Stockholm: 1893. V. 50

NORDENSKIOLD, NILS ADOLF ERIK
The Arctic Voyages, 1858-1879. London: 1879. V. 47
Periplus, an Essay on the Early History of Charts and Sailing Directions... New York: 1967. V. 51
The Voyage of the Vega Round Asia and Europe. London: 1881. V. 49

NORDHOFF, CHARLES BERNARD
Botany Bay. Boston: 1941. V. 50; 53
The Bounty Trilogy. Boston: 1940. V. 49; 52
California for Health, Pleasure and Residence. New York: 1872. V. 51; 52
California for Health, Pleasure and Residence. New York: 1875. V. 50
The Dark River. Boston: 1938. V. 50; 51
The Hurricane. Boston: 1936. V. 50
Mutiny on the Bounty. Boston: 1932. V. 48; 51; 52; 53; 54
Mutiny on the Bounty. New York: 1947. V. 50; 53
Northern California, Oregon and the Sandiwch Islands. New York: 1874. V. 53
Pitcairn's Island. Boston: 1934. V. 48; 51

NORDHOFF, WALTER
The Journey of the Flame. Boston: 1933. V. 50

NORDLUNDE, C. VOLMER
Sir Emery Walker and the Revival of Printing. Copenhagen: 1959. V. 53

NORDNESS, LEE
Art USA Now. Lucerne: 1962. V. 47; 50; 51; 53; 54

NORDOFF, CHARLES
Peninsula California. New York: 1888. V. 51

NORDSTROM, HANS-AKE
Neolithic and A-Group Sites. Copenghagen: 1972. V. 51

NORDWALL, ERIK
Afhandling Rorande Mechaniquen. Stockholm: 1800-1794. V. 53

NORFOLK, CHARLES HOWARD, DUKE OF
Historical Anecdotes of Some of the Howard Family. London: 1817. V. 53
Thoughts, Essays and Maxims, Chiefly Religious and Political. London: 1768. V. 50; 54

THE NORFOLK Congress: Or, A Full and True Account of Their Hunting, Feasting and Merrymaking; Being Singularly Delightful and Likewise Very Instructive to the Publick... London: 1728. V. 48; 50

NORFOLK, HORATIO EDWARD
Gleanings in Graveyards.. London: 1866. V. 54

NORFOLK, LAWRENCE
Lempriere's Dictionary. London: 1991. V. 49; 53; 54

NORGATE, THOMAS STARLING
Essays, Tales and Poems. Norwich: 1795. V. 49

NORIE, J. W.
Catalogue of the Latest and Most Approved Charts, Pilots and Navigation Books. 1818. V. 47
Plates, Descriptive of the Maritime Flags of All Nations... London: 1824. V. 49

NORMAN, BENJAMIN M.
Norman's New Orlenas and Environs... New Orleans: 1845. V. 53

NORMAN, CHARLES BERNARD
Mr. Oddity - Samuel Johnson LL.D. Drexel Hill: 1951. V. 52

NORMAN, DOROTHY
Dualities. New York: 1933. V. 47
Stieglitz Memorial Portfolio. 1864-1946. New York: 1947. V. 47

NORMAN, FRANCIS MARTIN
Martello Tower in China and the Pacific in H.M.S. "Tribune" 1856-60. London: 1902. V. 54

NORMAN, GEORGE WARDE
Papers on Various Subjects. London: 1869. V. 51

NORMAN, GURNEY
Crazy Quilt - A Novel in Progress. Monterey: 1990. V. 48

NORMAN, HENRY
The Peoples and Politics of the Far East. London: 1895. V. 50
Real. Lynn: 1897. V. 53

NORMAN, HOWARD
The Bird Artist. New York: 1994. V. 52; 53
Kiss in the Hotel Joseph Conrad. New York: 1989. V. 51; 52; 53; 54
The Northern Lights. New York: 1987. V. 52; 53; 54
The Owl-Scatterer. Boston: 1986. V. 52; 53

NORMAN, JEREMY M.
Morton's Medical Bibliography. Aldershot: 1991. V. 53

NORMAN, JOHN
The Town and Country Builder's Assistant; Absolutely Necessary to Be Understood, by Builders and Workmen... Boston: 1786. V. 51

NORMAN, SIDNEY
Northwest Mines Handbook: A Reference Work of the Mining Industry of Idaho, Washington, British Columbia, Western Montana and Oregon. Spokane: 1918. V. 47

NORMAN, W. M.
A Popular Guide to the Geology of the Isle of Wight. 1887. V. 51; 52; 53; 54

NORMANBY, CONSTANTINE HENRY PHIPPS, 1ST MARQUIS OF
The English In Italy. London: 1825. V. 49
A Voyage Towards the North Pole Undertaken by His Majesty's Command, 1773. London: 1774. V. 52
A Year of Revolution. From a Jouranl Kept in Paris in 1848. London: 1857. V. 49; 53

NORMAND, VICTORINE LE
The Oracle of Human Destiny. London: 1826. V. 48

NORMAN-NERUDA, L.
The Climbs of Norman-Neruda. 1899. V. 53
The Climbs of Norman-Neruda. London: 1899. V. 52

NORMANY, PHILIPPE DE
The Mysterie of Iniquitie... London: 1612. V. 49

NORMENT, MARY C.
The Lowrie History, As Acted in Part by Henry Berry Lowrie, the Great North Caolina Bandit... Lumberton: 1909. V. 50

NORRIS, FRANK
Blix. New York: 1899. V. 53
Collected Letters. 1986. V. 54
Collected Letters. San Francisco: 1986. V. 51; 52; 53
Collected Works of Frank Norris. New York: 1928. V. 51
A Deal in Wheat and Other Stories. New York: 1903. V. 49; 51; 54
Frank Norris of "The Wave". Stories & Sketches From the San Francisco Weekly, 1893 to 1897. San Francisco: 1931. V. 48
The Letters of Frank Norris. San Francisco: 1956. V. 47; 48; 50; 54
McTeague, a Story of San Francisco. New York: 1899. V. 53; 54
Moran of the Lady Letty. New York: 1898. V. 48; 51; 52; 53
The Octopus. New York: 1901. V. 48; 52; 54
The Pit. New York: 1903. V. 48; 49; 50; 51; 53; 54
The Pit. Toronto: 1903. V. 48

NORRIS, GEORGE
Blood-Pressure: Its Clinical Applications. Philadelphia: 1914. V. 54
Studies In Cardiac Pathology. Philadelphia: 1911. V. 54

NORRIS, J. A.
The First Afghan War 1838-1842. 1967. V. 51

NORRIS, JOAN
Banquet. Lincoln: 1978. V. 52

NORRIS, JOHN
A Collection of Miscellanies; Consisting of Poems, Essays, Discourses & Letters... London: 1699. V. 54
An Essay Towards the Theory of the Ideal or Intelligible World. London: 1701/04. V. 47
Letters Concerning the Love of God, Between the Author of the Proposal to the Ladies and Mr. John Norris... London: 1695. V. 50
The Theory and Regulation of Love. Oxford: 1688. V. 47

NORRIS, K. S.
Whales, Dolphins and Porpoises. Berkeley: 1966. V. 49

NORRIS, KATHLEEN
Dedications. Berkeley: 1936. V. 51

NORRIS, LESLIE
A Tree Sequence. Seattle: 1984. V. 52; 54

NORRIS, THADDEUS
American Fish Culture, Embracing All the Details of Artificial breeding and Rearing of Trout, The Culture of Salmon, Shad and Other Fishes. Philadelphia: 1868. V. 47; 50

NORRIS, THOMAS WAYNE
A Descriptive and Priced Catalogue of Books, Pamphlets and Maps Relating Directly or Indirectly to the History, Literature and Printing of California and the Far West... Oakland: 1948. V. 47; 53; 54

NORRIS, WILLIAM EDWARD
Adrian Vidal. London: 1885. V. 54
A Victim of Good Luck. London: 1894. V. 54

NORTH & SOUTH JUNCTION RAILWAY
(Prospectus). Junction of the North Sea, Irish Sea, Bristol Channel and English Channel by Railway (from drop title). 1839. V. 47

NORTH American Boundary. Part I. Correspondence Relating to the Boundary Between the British Possessions in North America and the United States of America, Under the Treaty of 1783. London: 1840. V. 53

NORTH AMERICAN MINING CO.
North American Mining Company, for Gold & Silver Mining in Nevada, and other Sections of the United States. Philadelphia: 1865. V. 49

NORTH AMERICAN TRANSPORTATION & TRADING CO.
To the Gold Fields of Alaska and Yukon Territory. 1900. V. 50

THE NORTH Briton. London: 1763. V. 48

NORTH, C. N. MC INTYRE
Leabhar Comunn Nam Fior Ghael: The Book of the Club of True Highanders. London: 1881. V. 51

NORTH CAROLINA. CONSTITUTION
Constitution of the State of North Carolina, Together with the Ordinances and Resolutions of the Constituional Convention, Assembled in the City of Raleigh, Jan. 14th, 1868. Raleigh: 1868. V. 54

THE NORTH Carolina Historical review. Raleigh: 1924-54. V. 51

NORTH CAROLINA. LAWS, STATUTES, ETC.
Laws of the State of North Carolina. Edenton;: 1791. V. 48
Laws of the State of North Carolina. Edenton: 1791-1800. V. 50
Ordinances of the State Convention Published in Pursuance of a Resolution of the General Assembly (Ratified 11th Feb. 1863). Raleigh: 1863. V. 50

NORTH Carolina Petroleum and Mining Company. Greensborog: 1866. V. 48

THE NORTH Country Angler; or the Art of Angling: as Practised in the Northern Counties of England. London: 1817. V. 49

NORTH Dakota, a Guide to the Northern Prairie State. Fargo: 1938. V. 51; 53; 54

NORTH EASTERN RAILROAD CO. OF SOUTH CAROLINA
Reports of the President and Chief Engineer of the North Eastern Rail Road Co. of South Carolina. Charleston: 1852. V. 49

NORTH, ELISHA
Outlines of the Science of Life... New York: 1829. V. 48
A Treatise on a Malignant Epidemic, Commonly Called Spotted Fever... New York: 1811. V. 51; 53

NORTH, ESCOTT
The Saga of the Cowboy - All About the Cattleman and the Part He Has Played in the Great Drama of the West. London. V. 54

NORTH, FRANCIS
The Kentish Barons: a Play, in Three Acts. Dublin: 1791. V. 47

NORTH, FRANCIS DUDLEY
A Narrative of Some Passages in or Relating to the Long Parliament. London: 1670. V. 53

NORTH, ISAAC WILLIAM
A Week in the Isles of Scilly. Penzance: 1850. V. 50

NORTH, JOSEPH
Men in the Ranks. New York: 1939. V. 49; 50; 51; 53
No Men are Strangers. New York: 1958. V. 49

NORTH, OLIVER
Rambles After Sport: or Travels and Adventures in the Americans and at Home. London: 1874. V. 52

NORTH, ROGER
The Autobiography of the Hon. Roger North. London: 1887. V. 54
A Discourse of Fish and Fish-Ponds. London: 1713. V. 47; 49
The History of Esculent Fish. London: 1794. V. 53
The Life of the Honourable Sir Dudley North. London: 1744. V. 49
The Lives of Francis North, Sir Dudley North and Dr. John North. London: 1826. V. 47; 49; 51
Memoirs of Musick... London: 1846. V. 47

NORTH, S. N. D.
Simeon North, First Official Pistol Maker of the United States. Concord: 1913. V. 47

NORTH, STERLING
The Pedro Gorino. Boston: 1929. V. 48
So Red the Nose. New York: 1935. V. 49

NORTH, THOMAS
Five Years in Texas; or, What You Did Not Hear During the War from January 1861 to January 1865. Cincinnati: 1870. V. 48; 50

NORTH-WESTERN RAILROAD
Hot Springs South Dakota. N.P: 1891. V. 52

NORTHALL, WILLIAM KNIGHT
Before and behind the Curtain or Fifteen Years' Observations Among the Theatres of New York. New York: 1851. V. 49

NORTHAMPTON Business Directory and General Advertiser, 1860-61. Northampton: 1860. V. 47

NORTHAMPTON, MARGARET, LADY
Irene, a Poem, in Six Cantos. Miscellaneous Poems. London: 1833. V. 51

NORTHCLIFFE, ALFRED CHARLES HARMSWORTH, VISCOUNT
Motor and Motor Driving. London: 1906. V. 54

NORTHCOTE, JAMES
Fables, Original and Selected. Second Series. London: 1833. V. 47; 53
The Life of Titian: With Anecdotes of the Distinguished Persons of His Time. London: 1830. V. 49
Northcote's Fables. London: 1833. V. 49
Northcote's Fables First Series. 1828. V. 49
One Hundred Fables. Original and Selected. London: 1828. V. 47; 48; 53

NORTHCOTT, W. HENRY
A Treatise on Lathes and Turning Simple, Mechanical and Ornamental. London: 1876. V. 50; 52

THE NORTHERN And Eastern Songster: A Choice Collection of Fashionable Songs. Boston: 1835. V. 53

NORTHERN Antiquities: or a Description of the Manners, Customs, Religion, and Laws of the Ancient Danes... Edinburgh: 1809. V. 48

NORTHERN MICHIGAN AGRICULTURAL & MECHANICAL SOCIETY
The Great Union Fair of Michigan, 1872. Grand Haven: 1872. V. 49

NORTHERN NAVIGATION CO.
N. N. Co. to the Alaska Gold Fields. San Francisco: 1909. V. 50

NORTHERN PACIFIC RAILROAD
Alaska. Chicago: 1891. V. 50
Annual Report. 1897-1904. V. 54
Annual Report of the Board of Directors of the Northern Pacific Railroad Co., to the Stockholders for the Year Ending June 30th, 1884. New York: 1884. V. 47
Memorial, &c. Northern Pacific Railroad. Washington: 1867. V. 47
Memorial of the Board of Direction of the Company. Communications from Lieut. Gen'l. Grant, Bevet Maj. Gen'l. Meigs, Q.M.G. and Brevet Maj. Gen'l. Ingalls, A.Q.M. and Report of the Engineer-in-Chief, November, 1867. Hartford: 1867. V. 47
The Northern Pacific Railroad: Its Route, Resources, Progress and Business. Philadelphia: 1871. V. 47
The Northern Pacific Tour. From the Lakes & Mississippi River to the Pacific. St. Paul: 1885. V. 47
The Pacific Northwest, Information for Settlers and Others. Oregon and Washington Territory. New York: 1883. V. 47
Report of Edwin F. Johnson, Engineer-in-Chief, to the Board of Directors, April, 1869 and Reports of Surveys Executed in 1867, by Gen. Ira Spaulding, Chief Engineer of the Minnesota Division, and Gen. James Tilton, Chief Engineer... Hartford: 1869. V. 47
Report of the Board of Directors to the Stockholders at their Annual Meeting, October 20th, 1892. New York: 1892. V. 47
Report of the President and Directors of the Northern Pacific Railroad Co. to the Stockholders, at the Annual Meeting, Sept. 27th, 1876. New York: 1876. V. 47
Report of the President to the Stockholders at Their Annual Meeting, September 20th, 1883. V. 47
Saint Paul and the Northern Pacific Grand Opening September 1883. St. Paul: 1883. V. 54
The Yellowstone National Park. Chicago: 1883. V. 52

NORTHERN Regions; or a Relation of Uncle Richard's Voyages for the Discovery of a North-West Passage, and an Account of the Overland Journies of Other Enterprizing Travellers. London: 1825. V. 48

THE NORTHERN Sheperd, Being a Report of a Committee...Upon the Diseases and Management of Sheep. Winthrop: 1835. V. 54

THE NORTHERN Traveller; Containing the Hudson River Guide, and Tour to the Springs... New York: 1844. V. 52

NORTH LEE, B.
Bookplates and Labels by Leo Wyatt. 1988. V. 47

NORTHLEIGH, JOHN
The Parallel: or, The New Specious Association an Old Rebellious Covenant. London: 1682. V. 47; 48
Topographical Descriptions: with Historico-Political and Medico-Physical Observations: made in Two Several Voyages, through Most Parts of Europe. London: 1702. V. 50

NORTHMORE, THOMAS
Washington of Liberty Restored: a Poem, in Ten Books. Baltimore: 1809. V. 53

NORTHROP, HENRY DAVENPORT
Lives of Harrison and Reid. 1892. V. 54

NORTHROP, JOHN
Crystalline Enzymes: the Chemistry of Pepsin, Trypsin and Bacteriophage. New York: 1939. V. 49; 54

NORTHROP, JOHN W.
Chronicles from the Diary of a War Prisoner in 1864. Wichita: 1904. V. 51

NORTHUMBERLAND, ELIZABETH PERCY, DUCHESS OF
A Short Tour Made in the Year One Thousand Seven Hundred Seventy One. London: 1775. V. 54

NORTHUP, SOLOMON
Twelve Years a Slave. Auburn: 1853. V. 51

NORTHWEST Review: Native American Poetry. Eugene: 1973. V. 50

NORTHWICK, LORD
Catalogue of the Late Lord Northwick's Extensive and Magnificent Collection. Cheltenham: 1859. V. 47
Catalogue of the Late Lord Northwick's Extensive and Magnificent Collection of Ancient and Modern Pictures, Cabinet of Miniatures and Enamels...at Thirlestane House, Cheltenham. London: 1859. V. 47

NORTON, ANDRE
The Day of the Ness. 1975. V. 54
Gryphon in Glory. 1981. V. 52
Huon of the Horn. New York: 1951. V. 51; 54
Lord of Thunder. 1962. V. 54
Merlin's Mirror. 1976. V. 52
Octagon Magic. 1967. V. 52
Ordeal in Otherwhere. 1964. V. 52
Shadow Hawk. 1960. V. 49
Shadow Hawk. New York: 1960. V. 51; 52
Stand to Horse. 1956. V. 47
Star Man's Son 2250 A.D. 1953. V. 52
Victory on Janus. 1966. V. 49

NORTON, ANDRE continued
Wolfshead. 1977. V. 52
The X Factor. 1965. V. 52

NORTON, ANDREWS
A Statement of Reasons for Not Believing the Doctrines of Trinitarians, Concerning the Nature of God, and the Person of Christ. Cambridge & Boston: 1833. V. 48

NORTON, ARCHIBALD
Dragon Magic. 1972. V. 48
Ordeal in Otherwhere. 1964. V. 48
Plague Ship. 1956. V. 48
Sargasso of Space. 1955. V. 48
The X Factor. 1965. V. 48

NORTON, CAROLINE
The Child of the Islands. London: 1845. V. 50
The Child of the Islands. London: 1846. V. 50
The Dream and Other Poems. London: 1840. V. 48
The Dream and Other Poems. London: 1841. V. 50
The Lady of La Garaye. Cambridge: 1862. V. 48; 49
Lost and Saved. London: 1864. V. 50
Stuart of Dunleath. A Story of Modern Times. London: 1851. V. 48
The Undying One, and Other Poems. London: 1830. V. 54

NORTON, CHARLES ELIOT
Considerations on Some Recent Social Theories. Boston: 1853. V. 47
A Leaf of Grass from Shady Hill. Cambridge: 1928. V. 54

NORTON, E.
The Fight for Everest: 1924. 1925. V. 53
The Flight for Everest: 1924. London: 1925. V. 52

NORTON, E. F.
The Fight for Everest. New York: 1925. V. 48

NORTON, F. J.
A Descriptive Catalogue of Printing in Spain and Portugal 1501-1520. 1978. V. 52
A Descriptive Catalogue of Printing in Spain and Portugal 1501-1520. Cambridge: 1978. V. 47; 50; 53
Italian Printers 1501-1520. 1958. V. 53
Printing in Spain 1501-1520. Cambridge: 1966. V. 50; 53

NORTON, FRANK H.
Frank Leslie's Historical Register of the United States Centennial Exposition, 1876. New York: 1877. V. 52

NORTON, GEORGE
Commentaries on the History, Constitution, and Chartered Franchises of the City of London. London: 1829. V. 53

NORTON, HARRY J.
Wonder-Land Illustrated; or, Horseback Rides through the Yellowstone National Park... Virginia City: 1873. V. 48; 50

NORTON, J. E.
A Bibliography of the Works of Edward Gibbon. London: 1940. V. 51

NORTON, JOHN
The Journal of Major John Norton, 1816. Toronto: 1970. V. 52

NORTON, JOHN PITKIN
Elements of Scientific Agriculture: a Prize Essay. Albany: 1850. V. 49; 50

NORTON, L. A.
Life and Adventures of Col. L. A. Norton. Oakland: 1887. V. 47; 50; 53

NORTON, ROSALEEN
The Art of Rosaleen Norton: With Poems by Gavin Greenlees. Sydney: 1952. V. 48

NORTON, THOMAS
An Addition Declaratorie to the Bulles, with a Searching of the Maze... London. V. 48

NORTON'S Literary Almanac...1852, and, Norton's Literary Register...1853 & 1854. New York: 1851/53/54. V. 48

NORVELL, LIPSCOMB, MRS.
King's Highway, The Great Strategic Military Highway of America, El Camino Real, the San Antonio Road. 1945. V. 53

NORWAY, ARTHUR H.
History of the Post-Office Packet Service Between the Years 1793-1815. London: 1895. V. 54

NORWOOD, C. W.
Sholes Georgia State Gazetteer and Business Directory. For 1879 & 1880. Atlanta: 1879. V. 52

NORWOOD, RICHARD
Norwood's Epitome: Being the Application of the Doctrine of Triangles...The Use of the Plain Sea Chart, and Meractor's Chart... London: 1690. V. 49; 52
The Sea-Mans Practice. London: 1676. V. 48; 53
Trigonometrie; or, the Doctrine of Triangles; the Mensuration of Right Linted Triangles and Second of Spherical, with the Grounds and Demonstrations Thereof. London: 1685. V. 47; 49
A Voyage to Virginia. V. 48

NORZI, RAPHAEL
Seah Soleth. Venice: 1579. V. 53

NOSHY, IBRAHIM
The Arts in Ptolemaic Egypt: a Study of Greek and Egyptian Influences in Ptolemaic Architecture and Sculpture. London: 1937. V. 49

NOSNHOJ, R. S.
A Novel Railroad Strike, One Hundred Thirty-Nine. Aurora: 1877. V. 53; 54

NOSTRADAMUS, MICHEL
The True Prophecies or Prognostications of Nostradamus... London: 1673. V. 53

THE NOT-Browne Mayd. London: 1905. V. 52

NOTABLE Lawyers of the West Including Members of the United States Supreme Court, Supreme Courts of Several States and Prominent Lawyers in the Western States. Chicago: 1902. V. 52

NOTES Of the Evidence Given Against the Lord Howard of Escrick to the Grand Inquest of the Hundred of Edmonton and Gore...Middlesex; Taken by Sir Charles Lee Their Foreman... London: 1681. V. 47

NOTICES and Illustrations of the Costume, Processions, Pageantry &c. Formerly Displayed by the Corporation of Norwich. Norwich: 1850. V. 47

NOTICES and Voyages of the Famed Quebec Mission to the Pacific Northwest: Being the Correspondence, Notices, Etc. of Fathers Blanchet and Demers... Portland: 1956. V. 52; 53; 54

NOTICIA Certa da Grande Batalha, Que Houve na America Entre os rancezes, e Ingleses, em Cujo Conflicto Forao Estes Derrotados; Refere-se o Numero dos Mortos, o dos Feridos, e o aos Prisioneiros... Lisbon: 1756. V. 48

NOTICIA Certa da Tomada, e Rendimento de Cabo-Berton (sic), Cuja Praca se Rendeo aos Inglezes, ficando Toda a Guarnicao Prizioneira de Guerra. Lisbon: 1758. V. 48

NOTMAN, WILLIAM
Portrait of a Period. Montreal: 1967. V. 50; 52; 53; 54
Portraits of British Americans, by...with Biographical Sketches by fennings Taylor. Montreal: 1865-67. V. 50

NOTMAN, WILLIAM, & SON
The King's Highway: On the Line of the Canadiana Pacific Ry. Montreal: 1900. V. 53

NOTT, J. C.
Types of Mankind: or, Ethnological Researches, Based Upon the Ancient Monuments, Paintings, Sculptures and Crania of Races, and Upon Their Natural, Geographical, Philological and Biblical History... Philadelphia: 1868. V. 47

NOTT, JOHN
Alonzo; or the Youthful Solitaire. London: 1772. V. 54

NOTT, JOSIAH
Types of Mankind: or, Ethnological Researches based Upon the Ancient Monuments, Paintings and Sculptures and Biblical History... Philadelphia: 1854. V. 50

NOTT, JOSIAH CLARK
Types of Mankind: or, Ethnological Researches, Based Upon the Ancient Monuments, Paintings, Sculptures and Crania or Races, and Upon Their Natural Geographical, Philological and Biblical History... Philadelphia: 1854. V. 49

NOTT, SAMUEL
Slavery and the Remedy; or, Principles and Suggestions for a Remedial Code. Boston: 1856. V. 50

NOTT, STANLEY CHARLES
Catalogue of Rare Chinese Jade Carvings. Palm Beach: 1940. V. 47; 53
Chinese Jade throughout the Ages. London: 1936. V. 47
Chinese Jade Throughout the Ages. New York: 1937. V. 47
Voices from the Flowery Kingdom: Being an Illustrated Descriptive Record of the Beginnings of Chinese Cultural Existence Incorporating a Complete Survey of the Numerous Emblematic Forces Selected from Nature by the Ritualistic Leaders... New York: 1947. V. 52; 54

NOTTAGE, CHARLES G.
In Search of a Climate. London: 1894. V. 47; 51; 52

NOTTINGHAM, HENEAGE FINCH, 1ST EARL OF
The Indictment, Arraignment, Tryal and Judgment...of Twenty-Nine Regicides The Murtherers of...King Charles the 1st...with a Summary of the Dark and Horrid Decrees of these Cabbalists...Their Speeches... London: 1724. V. 54

NOUET, JACQUES
An Answer to the Provinciall Letters Published by the Jansenists,, Under the Name of Lewis Montale, Against the Doctrine of the Jesuits and School-Divines... 1659. V. 48

NOUR, MOHAMMAD ZAKI
The Cheops Boat. Cairo: 1960. V. 49

NOURSE, J. E.
American Explorations in the Ice Zones. Boston: 1884. V. 54

NOUVEAU Dictionnaire d'Histoire Naturelle Appliquee Aux Arts, Principalement a l'Agriculture et a l'Economie Rurale et Domestique. Paris: 1803-04. V. 54

NOVA Britannia. Offering Most Excellent Fruits by Planting in Virginia... New York: 1867. V. 53

NOVA, CRAIG
The Geek. New York: 1975. V. 52

NOVA SCOTIA HISTORICAL SOCIETY
Collections. Volumes I-VIII, 1878-1895. Belleville: 1976-77. V. 50

NOVA Scotia Steel and Coal Company Limited and Its Subsidary The Eastern Car Company Limited. New Glasgow: 1916. V. 53

THE NOVA-Scotia Almanack for the Year of Our Lord 1834. Halifax: 1834. V. 53

NOVA SCOTIA. VICE-ADMIRALTY COURT, HALIFAX
Reports of Cases, Argued and Determined in the Court of Vice-Admiralty, at Halifax in Nova-Scotia, from the Commencement of the War, in 1803, to the End of the Year 1813, in the Time of Alexander Croke, LL.D.... London: 1814. V. 52

NOVELLE Scelte Rarissime, Stampate a Spese di XL Amatori. London: 1814. V. 51

NOVOTNY, FRITZ
Gustav Klimt. Salzburg: 1967. V. 48; 50
Gustav Klimt, with a Catalogue Raisonne of His Paintings. Boston: 1968. V. 49; 54
Gustav Klimt, with a Catalogue Raisonne of His paintings. New York: 1968. V. 47; 50; 53; 54

NOWELL, THOMAS S.
Art Work of Seattle and Alaska. Racine: 1907. V. 52

NOWELL-SMITH, SIMON
The Legend of the Master. London: 1947. V. 54

NOWELL-USTICKE, GORDON W.
The Distinguished Collection of Rembrandt Etchings Fromed by Gordon W. Nowell-Usticke. 1968. V. 50

NOWILL, SIDNEY EDWARD PAWN
The Mountains of My Life. Journeys in Turkey and the Alps. Edinburgh & London: 1954. V. 49

NOWLAN, ALDEN
A Darkness in the Earth. Eureka: 1959. V. 52
The Rose and the Puritan. Fredericton: 1958. V. 52
The Things Which Are. Toronto: 1962. V. 52
Wind in a Rocky Country. Toronto: 1960/61. V. 52

NOWLAND, JOHN
Leadville. A Silver Setting in a Sea of Silver, What it Accomplished in a Decade. Together with Expert Opinions of the permanency of its Mineral Deposits. Leadville: 1890. V. 48

NOWROJEE, JEHANGEER
Journal of a Residence of Two Years and a Half in Great Britain. London: 1841. V. 52

NOY, WILLIAM
The Principal Grounds and Maxims with an Analysis... London: 1821. V. 53

NOYCE, W.
South Col. 1954. V. 53

NOYES, A. J.
In the Land of Chinook, or the Story of Blaine County. Helena: 1917. V. 51; 53

NOYES, ALFRED
Mystery Ships (Trapping the "U" Boat). London: 1916. V. 50

NOYES, DAVID
The History of Norway... Norway: 1852. V. 48

NOYES, JOHN HUMPHREY
The Berean: a Manual for the help of Those Who Seek the Faith of the Primitive Church. Putney: 1847. V. 52
Hand-Book of the Oneida Community 1875. Oneida: 1875. V. 53
History of American Socialisms. Philadelphia: 1870. V. 52
Male Continence. Oneida: 1866. V. 50
Male Continence. Onedia: 1877. V. 50
Slavery and Marriage. 1850. V. 54

NOYES, ROBERT GALE
Ben Jonson on the English Stage 1660-1776. Cambridge: 1935. V. 52

NUCIUS, NICANDER
The Second Book of the Travels of...of Corcyra. London: 1841. V. 48

NUCKEL, OTTO
Destiny. A Novel in Pictures. New York: 1930. V. 49; 53

NUCLEAR Explosions and Their Effects. Delhi: 1958. V. 52

NUECES Valley Townsite Co. Pleasanton, Texas. 1913. San Antonio: 1913. V. 49

NUGENT, CHRISTOPHER
An Essay on Hydrophobia: to Which is Prefixed the Case of a Person Who Was Bit by a Made Dog... London: 1753. V. 53

NUGENT, GEORGE NUGENT GRENVILLE, BARON
Legends of the Library at Lilies. London: 1832. V. 48; 51

NUGENT, ROBERT CRAGGS
Considerations Upon a Reduction of the Land-Tax. London: 1749. V. 48

NUGENT, THOMAS
The Grand Tour; or, a Journey through the Netherlands, Germany, Italy and France... London: 1778. V. 50
The Life of Benvenuto Cellini, a Florentine Artist. London: 1771. V. 48
The Life of Benvenuto Cellini, a Florentine Artist. Dublin: 1772. V. 53
The New Pocket Dictionary of the French and English Languages. London: 1793. V. 52
The Primitives of the Greek Tongue. London: 1748. V. 49

NUIX, JUAN
Reflexiones Imparciales Sobre la Humanidad de los Espanoles en las Indias, Contra los Pretendiods Filosofos y Politicos. Madrid: 1782. V. 53

THE NUN: an Elegy. London: 1764. V. 54

NUNEZ CABECA DE VACA, ALVAR
Relation of Alvar Nunez Cabeca de Vaca. New York: 1871. V. 47
Relation That Alvar Nunez Cabeza De Vaca Gave of What Befel the Armament in the Indias Whither Pamphilo De Narvaez Went for Governor (from the Years 1527 to 1537). San Francisco: 1929. V. 53

NUNIS, DOYCE B.
Andrew Sublette, Rocky Moountain Prince, 1808-1853. Los Angeles: 1960. V. 53
The Letters of a Young Miner. San Francisco: 1964. V. 47
Women in the Life of Southern Calfiornia. 1941. V. 54

NUNN, ANCEL E.
Remnants of Change, a Sketchbook of Texas. Palestine: 1989. V. 48

NUNN, GEORGE E.
Origin of the Strait of Anian, Concept by... Philadelphia: 1929. V. 48

NUNN, JOHN J.
Mrs. Montague Jones' Dinner Party; or, Reminiscences of Cheltenham Life and Manners. London: 1872. V. 49

NUNO, R. BONIFAZ
The Art in the Great Temple. Mexico-Tenochtitlan. Mexico City: 1981. V. 54

NUOVA Racolta de Fontaine che si Vedano nel'Alma Citta di Roma, Tivoli e Frascati. Rome. V. 47; 53

NUOVI Avisi dell'Indie di Portogallo... Venice: 1568. V. 51

NURA
All Aboard We Are Off. New York: 1944. V. 49
The Buttermilk Tree. New York: 1934. V. 49
Nura's Children Go Visiting. New York: 1943. V. 49; 51; 52
Nura's Garden of Betty and Booth. New York: 1935. V. 49

THE NUREMBERG Chronicle. New York: 1966. V. 51

A NURSERY Rhyme Picture Book. London: 1910. V. 52

NURSERY Songs. London: 1871. V. 48

NURSERY Tales for Good Little Boys. London: 1860. V. 48; 53

NURSIE'S Little Rhyme Book. London. V. 47

NUTCHUK
Son of the Smoky Sea. New York: 1941. V. 50

NUTT, ALFRED
Studies on the Legend of the Holy Grail with Special Reference to the Hypothesis of Its Celtic Origin. London: 1888. V. 54

NUTT, THOMAS
Humanity to Honey Bees; or, Practical Directions for the Management of Honey Bees Upon an Improved and Humane Plan... Wisbech: 1845. V. 54
Humanity to Honey Bees, or Practical Directions for the Management of Honey Bees Upon an Improved and Humane Plan. London: 1945. V. 54

NUTTAL, ZELIA
The Fundamental Principles of Old and New World Civilizations... Cambridge: 1901. V. 47

NUTTALL, G. H. F.
Ticks, a Monograph of the Ixodoidea. London: 1908-26. V. 49; 50

NUTTALL, THOMAS
The Genera of North American Plants and a Catalogue of the Species to the Year 1817. Philadelphia: 1818. V. 50
A Manual of the Ornithology. Boston: 1834. V. 48
A Manual of the Ornithology of the United States and of Canada. The Land Birds. Boston: 1840. V. 49
A Popular Handbook of the Birds of Canada and the United States. Toronto: 1910. V. 54

NUTTING, M. ADELAIDE
A History of Nursing. New York: 1907-12. V. 50

NUTTING, WALLACE
Furniture of the Pilgrim Century. Boston: 1921. V. 51
Furniture of the Pilgrim Century. Framingham: 1921. V. 53
Furniture Treasury (Mostly of American Origin). New York: 1948-49. V. 49; 50
Furniture Treasury (Mostly Of American Origin)...Also American Hardware and Household utensils. Framingham: 1928. V. 51

NYBLOM, HELENA
Jolly Calle and Other Swedish Fairy Tales. London. V. 50
Jolly Calle and Other Swedish Fairy Tales. London: 1912. V. 49

NYE, ELWOOD I.
Marching With Custer, a Day-By-Day Evaluation of the Uses, Abuses and Conditions of the Animals of the Ill-Fated Custer Expedition of 1876. Glendale: 1964. V. 49

NYE, GIDEON
The Opium Question and the Northern Campaigns... Canton: 1875. V. 49

NYE, I. W. B.
The Generic Names of Moths of the World. London: 1975-91. V. 52

NYE, NELSON
The Complete Book of the Quarter Horse. New York: 1964. V. 53

NYENBORGH, JOHAN VAN
Toonneel der Ambachten: of Den Winckel der Handtwercken en Konsten. Groeningen: 1659-60. V. 53

NYLANDER, CARL
Ionians in Pasargadae: Studies in Old Persian Architecture. Uppsala: 1970. V. 52

NYREN, JOHN
The Young Cricketer's Tutor... London: 1948. V. 51

NYS, JOANNES
Vita et Miracula S. P. Dominici. Antwerp: 1611. V. 48

NYSTEL, OLE T.
Lost and Found, or Three Months with the Wild Indians a Brief Sketch of the Life of... Dallas: 1888. V. 47

O

O. HENRY Memorial Award Prize Stories, 1932. New York: 1932. V. 52; 53

OAK Hill Pictorial. Boston: 1854. V. 50

OAKES, CLIFFORD
The Birds of Lancashire. London: 1953. V. 50; 53; 54

OAKES, MAUD
Where the Two Came to their Father. Princeton: 1943. V. 50
Where the Two Came to their Father. London: 1969. V. 50

OAKES, WILLIAM
Scenery of the White Mountains; With Sixteen Plates, from the Drawings of Isaac Sprague. Boston: 1848. V. 48

OAKESHOTT, WALTER
The Mosaics of Rome. 1967. V. 50
The Mosaics of Rome. Greenwich: 1967. V. 47; 53; 54
Some Wood Cuts by Hans Burgmair Printed as an Appendix to the Fourth Part of Le Relationi Universali di Giovanni Botero 1618. Oxford: 1960. V. 47; 53; 54
The Two Winchester Bibles. Oxford: 1981. V. 48; 50

OAKLAND and Surroundings. Oakland: 1885. V. 49; 50; 51

OAKLAND COLLEGE
Constitution of Oakland College, Located in Claiborne County, Mississippi. Natchez: 1840. V. 54

OAKLEY, EDWARD
The Expedience, Utility and Necessity of a New Bridge at or near Blackfryars; all Objections Thereto Fully answered, and the Requisite Dispositions Exemplified. London: 1756. V. 51

OAKLY, OBADIAH
Expedition to Oregon. New York: 1914. V. 47; 51; 53

OASTLER, RICHARD
The Fleet Papers, Being Letters to Thomas Thornhill, Esq., from His Prisoner in the Fleet. London: 1841-43. V. 47
Richard Oastler's Reply to Richard Cobden's Speech at Leeds, 18th December 1849. London: 1850. V. 51

OATES, FRANK
Matabele Land and the Victoria Falls. London: 1889. V. 50; 52

OATES, JOYCE CAROL
All the Good People I've Left Behind. Santa Barbara: 1979. V. 50; 53
Angel Fire. Baton Rouge: 1973. V. 50
The Assignation. New York: 1988. V. 52
By the North Gate. New York: 1963. V. 49; 52; 53
Childwold. New York: 1976. V. 50
Cybele. Santa Barbara: 1979. V. 47; 53
Daisy. Santa Barbara: 1977. V. 49
Do With Me What You Will. New York: 1973. V. 50
A Garden of Earthly Delights. New York: 1967. V. 50
The Girl. Cambridge: 1974. V. 54
The Goddess and Other Women. New York: 1974. V. 52
Grenzuberschreitungen. (Crossing the Border). Stuttgart: 1978. V. 54
The Hostile Sun: The Poetry of D. H. Lawrence. Los Angeles: 1973. V. 50
The Lamb of Abyssinia. 1979. V. 50; 51; 53
Love and Its Derangements. Baton Rouge: 1970. V. 51
Love and Its Derangements and Other Poems. Greenwich: 1974. V. 50
Miracle Play. Los Angeles: 1974. V. 50
Nemesis. New York: 1990. V. 52
Night-Shade. New York: 1977. V. 50
Nightless Nights. 1981. V. 47
Nightless Nights. New Hampshire: 1981. V. 48; 50
The Poisoned Kiss and Other Stories From the Portuguese. New York: 1975. V. 50
Queen of the Night. Northridge: 1979. V. 50; 54
Scenes from American Life. New York: 1973. V. 50
The Seduction and Other Stories. Los Angeles: 1975. V. 50; 53
Small Avalanches. Helsinki: 1989. V. 48; 49
Son of the Morning. New York: 1978. V. 50; 54
Them. New York: 1969. V. 47; 50; 53
The Triumph of the Spider Monkey. Santa Barbara: 1976. V. 50; 51; 53
Unholy Loves. New York: 1979. V. 50; 52; 54
Upon the Sweeping Flood and Other Stories. New York: 1966. V. 49; 53
Upon the Sweeping Flood and Other Stories. London: 1973. V. 50; 53
The Wheel of Love. New York: 1967. V. 50
Where Are You Going, Where Have You Been?. Greenwich: 1974. V. 50
Will You Always Love Me?. Huntington Beach: 1994. V. 52
With Shuddering Fall. New York: 1964. V. 47; 49; 53
Women in Love and Other Poems. New York: 1968. V. 53; 54
Women Whose Lives are Food, Men Whose Lives are Money. Baton Rouge: 1978. V. 54
Wonderland. New York: 1971. V. 50

OATES, STEPHEN B.
Confederate Cavalry West of the River. Austin: 1961. V. 49; 50

OATES, TITUS
Eikon Basilike Dextera; or, the Picture of the Late King James further Drawn to the Life. London: 1697. V. 53
A Sermon Preached in an Anabaptist Meeting in Wapping, On Sunday the 19th of February, by the Reverend T.O.D.D. Upon This Text... London: 1699. V. 50

OATMAN, EDWARD L.
Diagnostics of the Fundus Oculi. Troy: 1913. V. 54
Diagnostics of the Fundus Oculi... Troy: 1920. V. 47

OATTS, L. B.
Proud Heritage, the Story of the Highland Light Infantry. Edinburgh & London: 1952/59. V. 50

OBACH, T.
The Channel Railroad Ferry for a Safe and Regular Steam Service Between England and the Continent. London: 1874. V. 51; 54

OBAID-E ZAKANI
The Pious Cat. London: 1986. V. 51

O'BANION, NANCE
Correspondence Course. Berkeley: 1993. V. 51; 53

O'BANLON, NANCE
Domestic Science: Pop-Up Icons. Domestic Science: Idioms. Berkeley: 1990. V. 51; 52; 53

O'BEIRNE, H. F.
Leaders and Leading Men of Indian Territory with Interesting Biographical Sketches... Chicago: 1891. V. 52

O'BEIRNE, SEAMUS
Paistidheacht. 1910. V. 54

OBERSTE, WILLIAM H.
History of Refugio Mission. Refugio: 1942. V. 48; 49
The Restless Friar: Venerable Fray Antonio Margil de Jesus, Missionary to the Americas--Apostle to Texas. Austin: 1970. V. 48

OBERT, PETER G.
Obert's System of Nature: or, Infidelity Exposed... New York: 1837. V. 54

OBERTH, HERMANN
The Moon Car... New York: 1959. V. 52; 54

AN OBJECT of Pity, or, The Man Haggard. A Romance by Many Competent Hands. Sydney: 1892. V. 53

OBOLER, ARCH
Night of the Auk: a Free Prose Play. New York: 1958. V. 50

O'BRADLEY, ARTHUR
The Gretna-Green Bolt-A, or, Young Ladies' Man-ual. London: 1853. V. 47
The Gretna-Green Bolt-a, or, Young Ladies' Man-ual. Paris: 1853. V. 52

OBREGON, MAURICIO
The Columbus Papers. The Barcelona Letter of 1493, the Landfall Controversy, and the Indian Guides. New York: 1991. V. 48

O'BRIAN, PATRICK
A Book of Voyages. London: 1947. V. 52
The Chian Wine and Other Stories. London: 1974. V. 54
Collected Short Stories. London: 1994. V. 54
The Commodore. 1994. V. 52
The Commodore. London: 1994. V. 54
Desolation Island. London: 1978. V. 54
Desolation Island. New York: 1979. V. 52; 53
Joseph Banks - a Life. London: 1987. V. 53
The Letter of Marque. London: 1988. V. 54
Master and Commander. Philadelphia: 1969. V. 50
Master and Commander. London: 1970. V. 54
The Mauritius Command. New York: 1978. V. 53
Pablo Ruiz Picasso - a Biography. London: 1976. V. 54
The Reverse of the Medal. London: 1986. V. 51
Richard Temple. London: 1962. V. 54
The Road to Samarcand. London: 1954. V. 52
Testimonies. London: 1994. V. 54
Three Bear Witness. London: 1952. V. 50

O'BRIEN, CHARLES
A Treatise on Calico Printing, Theoretical and Practical... London: 1792. V. 47

O'BRIEN, DONOUGH
History of the O'Briens from Brian Boroimhe, AD 1000 to AD 1945. London: 1949. V. 53

O'BRIEN, EDNA
James and Nora: Portrait of Joyce's Marriage. Northridge: 1981. V. 50
Mrs. Reinhardt and Other Stories. London: 1978. V. 48

O'BRIEN, EDWARD J.
The Best Short Stories of 1919 and the Yearbook of the American Short Story. Boston: 1920. V. 51
The Best Short Stories of 1922. Boston: 1923. V. 51
The Best Short Stories of 1923. Boston: 1924. V. 51

O'BRIEN, FLANN
At Swim-Two-Birds. London: 1909. V. 52
At Swim-Two-Birds. London: 1939. V. 51
At Swim-Two-Birds. New York: 1939. V. 47; 49
At Swim-Two-Birds. 1951. V. 51; 53
At Swim-Two-Birds. London: 1951. V. 47
An Beal Bocht. Dublin. V. 47
An Beal Boct. Baile ata Cliat: 1941. V. 52
The Dalkey Archive. London: 1964. V. 49; 50; 52; 53
The Dalkey Archive. New York: 1965. V. 49; 51
The Hard Life. London: 1961. V. 47; 51
The Hard Life. New York: 1962. V. 47
The Poor Mouth. (An Beal Bocht). London: 1973. V. 51; 53
The Third Policeman. London: 1967. V. 50; 51

O'BRIEN, GEORGE
The Economic History of Ireland in the Seventeenth Century. 1919. V. 50; 54
The Economic History of Ireland In...Seventeenth Century. London: 1919. V. 51

O'BRIEN, HENRY
The Round Towers of Ireland, or, The History of the Tuath-de-Danaans. London: 1898. V. 47; 51

O'BRIEN, JAMES
Irish Celts. Detroit: 1884. V. 50

O'BRIEN, JOHN
Folcoir Gaoidhilge-Sacs-Bheurla; or, an Irish English Dictionary. 1832. V. 54
Leaving Los Vegas. Wichita: 1990. V. 53; 54

O'BRIEN, M. D.
The Natural Right to Freedom. 1900. V. 47

O'BRIEN, PATRICK
Desolation Island. New York: 1978. V. 53

O'BRIEN, PHILIP M.
T. E. Lawrence: a Bibliography. 1988. V. 53

O'BRIEN, RICHARD BAPTIST
Jack Hazlitt, A.M. Dublin: 1875. V. 51

O'BRIEN, TIM
Going After Cacciato. London: 1978. V. 51; 52; 54
Going After Cacciato. New York: 1978. V. 48; 51; 52; 53
If I Die in a Combat Zone. London: 1973. V. 48; 49; 51; 52
If I Die in a Combat Zone. New York: 1973. V. 48; 49; 51; 52
In the Lake of the Woods. Boston/New York: 1994. V. 52; 53
Northern Lights. New York: 1975. V. 48; 49; 51; 52
Northern Lights. London: 1976. V. 51; 52
The Nuclear Age. Portland: 1981. V. 52
The Nuclear Age. New York: 1985. V. 51; 53
Speaking of Courage. Santa Barbara: 1980. V. 49; 50; 52; 53
The Things They Carried. Boston: 1990. V. 52; 53; 54
The Things They Carried. Franklin Center: 1990. V. 53

O'BRYEN, DENNIS
UTRUM Horum? The Government; or, The Country?. London: 1796. V. 47; 53

OBSERVATIONS and Remarks Upon the Lives and Reigns of King Henry VIII. King Edward VI. Queen Mary I. Queen Elizabeth and King James I. London: 1712. V. 49; 53

OBSERVATIONS on a Late Pamphlet, Entituled "Considerations Upon the Society or Order of the Cincinnati", Clearly Evincing the Innocence and Propriety of that Honourable and Respectable Institution. Philadelphia: 1783. V. 54

OBSERVATIONS on Mr. Gladstone's Denunciation of Certain Millowners of Lancashire, contained in a Speech Delivered by him at Newcastle, on the 7th of October, 1862. London: 1862. V. 49; 50

OBSERVATIONS on Mrs. Siddons, in the Following Characters: Margaret of Anjou, Belvidera, Jane Shore, Lady Randolph, Isabella, Zara, Euphrasia and Zara in the Mourning Bride. Dublin: 1784. V. 48

OBSERVATIONS on Professions, Literature, Manners and Emigration in the United States and Canada Made During a Residence There in 1832 by Rev. Isaac Fidler. New York: 1833. V. 48

OBSERVATIONS on the Bill Now Depending in Parliament for the Relief of Debtors, &c. in a series of Letters. London: 1780. V. 51

OBSERVATIONS on the Conduct of Great Britain with Regard to the Negociations and Other Transactions Abroad. Edinburgh: 1729. V. 47; 49; 50; 51; 52

OBSERVATIONS on the Late Increase of the Dividend On Bank Stock. London: 1788. V. 49

OBSERVATIONS on the Present State of Denmark, Russia and Switzerland. London: 1784. V. 47

OBSERVATIONS on the Real, Relative and Market Value of the Turnpike Stock of the State of New York. New York: 1806. V. 49

OBSERVATIONS On the Use of Vapour, Tepid and Other Baths; Shewing In What Cases They May Be Used With Advantage; and Where Recourse to Them May be Attended with Danger... London: 1814. V. 50

OBSERVATIONS, Rules and Orders, Collected Out of Divers Journals of the House of Commons. London: 1717. V. 50

OBSERVATIONS Upon Certain Passages in Mr. Jefferson's Notes on Virginia. New York: 1804. V. 51

OBSERVATIONS Upon the Act for the Redemption of the Land Tax: Showing the Benefits Likely to Arise. London: 1798. V. 49

OBSERVATIONS Upon the Administration of Justice in Bengal; Occasioned by Some Late Proceedings at Dacca. 1778. V. 50; 52; 54

OBSESSION.. Rockville: 1994. V. 53

OBSESSIONS.. Arlington Heights: 1991. V. 51; 52

OBSOLETE Ideas. In Six Letters, Addressed to Maria by a Friend. Sherborne: 1805. V. 50; 52

OBST, F. J.
The Completely Illustrated Atlas of Reptiles and Amphibians for the Terrarium. London: 1988. V. 48; 50

THE OBSTETRICAL Journal of Great Britain and Ireland Including Midwifery and the Diseases of Women and Children. London: 1873-79. V. 52

O'BYRNE, WILLIAM R.
A Naval Biographical Dictionary... London: 1849. V. 48; 50; 53

O'CALLAGHAN, E. B.
Documentary History of the State of New York... Albany: 1849-51. V. 48; 49; 50; 53
The Documentary History of the State of New York. Albany: 1850. V. 52
The Documentary History of the State of New York. Albany: 1850-51. V. 50; 52

O'CALLAGHAN, JOHN CORNELIUS
History of Irish Brigades in the Service of France, from the Revolution in Great Britain and Ireland Under James II, to the Revolution in France Under Louis XVI. Glasgow: 1870. V. 51; 54

O'CALLAGHAN, JULIE
Jasper the Lion Heart. London: 10. V. 53

OCAMPO, VICTORIA
338171 T. E. (Lawrence of Arabia). 1963. V. 54

O'CASEY, SEAN
Collected Plays. London: 1949. V. 53
Collected Plays. 1949-51. V. 54
Collected Plays. London: 1952. V. 48; 51
Oak Leaves and Lavender - or a World on Wallpaper. London: 1946. V. 49
The Plough and the Stars. London: 1926. V. 47; 48; 49
The Star Turns Red: a Play. London: 1940. V. 53
The Story of the Irish Citizen Army. 1919. V. 50; 54
The Story of the Irish Citizen Army. Dublin and London: 1919. V. 48; 49; 51; 52; 53; 54
Two Plays. Juno and the Paycock. The Shadow of a Gunman. London: 1925. V. 48; 49
Windfalls. London: 1934. V. 51; 52
Within the Gates. 1933. V. 49; 50

OCCASIONAL Reflections Upon Several Subjects. Whereto Is Premis'd a Discourse About Such Kind of Thoughts. London: 1665. V. 54

OCCOM, SANSOM
A Sermon Preached at the Execution of Moses Paul, an Indian Who Was Executed at new Haven, on the 2d of September 1772, for the Murder of Mr. Moses Cook, Late of Waterbury, on the 7th of December 1771. Preached at the Desire of Said Paul. New London: 1772. V. 48

THE OCEAN: a Description of Wonders and Important Products of the Sea. London: 1833. V. 49; 51
THE OCEAN: a Description of Wonders and Important Products of the Sea. London: 1835. V. 47

OCEAN Grove. Its Origin and Progress As Shown in the Annual Reports Presented by the President to Which are Added, Other Papers of Intent... Ocean Grove: 1874. V. 49; 51

OCHARTE, PEDRO
Cartilla Para Ensenar a Leer. Los Angeles: 1935. V. 54

OCHINUS, BERNARDINUS
The Cases of Polygamy, Concubinage, Adultery, Divorce, etc. by the Most Eminent Hands. London: 1732. V. 53
A Dialogue of Polygamy. London: 1657. V. 49; 53

OCHOA, C. M.
The Potatoes of South America, Boliva. London: 1991. V. 48

OCHSE, J. J.
Tropical and Subtropical Agriculture. New York: 1961. V. 52

OCHSNER, ALBERT
Clinical Surgery. Chicago: 1902. V. 54
The Organization, Construction and Management of Hospitals with Numerous Plans and Details. Chicago: 1907. V. 50; 52

O'CIANAIN, TADHG
The Flight of the Earls. 1916. V. 48; 52

OCKLAND, CHRISTOPHER
Anglorum Praelia ab Anno 1327...ad Annun 1558 (etc.). London: 1582. V. 50; 54

OCKLEY, SIMON
An Account of South-West Barbary... London: 1713. V. 54
The History of the Saracens... London: 1718. V. 48
The Improvement of Human Reason, Exhibited in the Life of Hai Ebn Yokdhan... London: 1708. V. 48
Sentences of Ali Son-in-Law of Mahomet and His Fourth Successor. London: 1717. V. 48; 51

O'CLERY, LUGHAIDH
Beatha...The Life of Hugh Roe O'Donnell, Prince of Tirconnell (1586-1602). Dublin: 1895. V. 50

O'CONNELL, CAROL
Killing Critics. London: 1996. V. 53; 54
Mallory's. London: 1994. V. 54

O'CONNELL, DANIEL
The Correspondence of Daniel O'Connell. London: 1972. V. 53
Letters...to the Minsters and Office-Bearers of the Wesleyan Methodist Societies in Manchester. Kingston: 1842. V. 53
A Memoir of Ireland Native and Saxon. Volume I 1172-1660. Dublin: 1843. V. 54
Observations on Corn Laws, on Political Pravity and Ingratitude... 1842. V. 47
Observations on Corn Laws, On Political Pravity and Ingratitude, and on Clerical and Personal Slander. Dublin: 1842. V. 50; 54
A Special Report of the Proceedings, in the Case of the Queen Against Daniel O'Connell, Esq., M.P. John O'Connell, Esq. M.P. (and Seven Others) In the Court of Queen's Bench, Ireland, Michaelmas Term, 1843. Dublin: 1844. V. 50

O'CONNELL, JAMES F.
A Residence of Eleven Years in New Holland and the Caroline Islands. Boston: 1841. V. 48

O'CONNELL, JOHN
An Argument for Ireland. Dublin: 1844. V. 49
The Taxation Injustice. Dublin: 1843. V. 49

O'CONNELL, MORGAN J., MRS.
Charles Bianconi: a biography, 1786-1875. London: 1878. V. 48; 51
The Last Colonel of the Irish Brigade. London: 1892. V. 47

O'CONNOR, ARTHUR
The Present State of Great Britain. Paris: 1804. V. 48

O'CONNOR, EDWIN
The Edge of Sadness. Boston: 1961. V. 52

O'CONNOR, ELLEN M.
Myrtilla Miner. A Memoir. Boston and New York: 1885. V. 54

O'CONNOR, F.
On the Frontier and Beyond. London: 1931. V. 49; 50

O'CONNOR, FLANNERY
Les Braves Gens Ne Courent Pas les Rules. (A Good Man Is Hard to Find). Paris: 1963. V. 51
The Complete Stories. New York: 1971. V. 47; 48; 52; 53
Et Ce sont les Violents Qui L'Emportent. (The Violent Bear It Away). Paris: 1965. V. 51
Everything that Rises Must Converge. New York: 1965. V. 47; 48; 49; 50; 51; 52; 53; 54
Everything That Rises Must Converge. London: 1966. V. 47
A Good Man Is Hard to Find. New York: 1952. V. 48
A Good Man Is Hard to Find. New York: 1955. V. 51; 53; 54
The Habit of Being. New York: 1978. V. 47; 49; 50
Mon Mal Vient De Plus Loin. (Everything That Rises Must Converge). Paris: 1969. V. 51
Mystery and Manners. New York: 1969. V. 49; 51; 52; 53
Le Sagesse dans le Sang. Paris: 1959. V. 48; 51
Some Aspects of the Grotesque in Southern Fiction. Macon: 1960. V. 50
The Violent Bear It Away. London: 1960. V. 49; 50; 51
The Violent Bear It Away. New York: 1960. V. 47; 50
Wise Blood. New York: 1952. V. 47; 51; 53
Wise Blood. London: 1955. V. 51

O'CONNOR, FRANCIS VALENTINE
Jackson Pollock. A Catalogue Raisonne of Paintings, Drawings and Other Works. New Haven: 1978. V. 50

O'CONNOR, FRANK
Bones of Contention and Other Stories. London: 1936. V. 47
The Complete Stories. New York: 1971. V. 52
The Fountain of Magic. London: 1939. V. 48; 50
Guests of the Nation. London: 1931. V. 47; 48; 51; 53
A Lament for Art O'Leary. Dublin: 1940. V. 51
The Little Monasteries. Dublin: 1963. V. 50
The Midnight Court. London: 1945. V. 49
A Picture Book. Dublin: 1943. V. 48
The Saint and Mary Kate. London: 1932. V. 51; 52

O'CONNOR, JACK
The Big Game Rifle. New York: 1952. V. 51; 53
Game in the Desert. New York: 1939. V. 47; 53
Game in the Desert Revisited. Clinton: 1977. V. 53
Horse and Buggy West. New York: 1969. V. 53
The Last Book. Clinton: 1984. V. 53
Sheep and Sheep Hunting. 1974. V. 53

O'CONNOR, JAMES
The Irish Justice of the Peace. A Treatise On the Powers and Duties of Justices of Peace in Ireland. Dublin: 1915. V. 50; 53

O'CONNOR, JAMES W.
Selections from the Work of James W. O'Connor, Architect, New York City. New York: 1930. V. 50

O'CONNOR, JEANNIE
The Wood Engravings of John O'Connor. 1989. V. 47
The Wood Engravings of John O'Connor. London: 1989. V. 50

O'CONNOR, JOHN
Ariel and Miranda. Blewbury: 1992. V. 53
Canals, Barges and People. London: 1950. V. 48
Dukes Village: a Suite of Wood Engravings by John O'Connor. Biddenden, Kent: 1988. V. 53
Knipton: A Leicestershire Village. Herefordshire: 1996. V. 54
Wood Engravings from La Vida Breve. Blewsbury. V. 51; 53
Wood-engravings. Andoversford: 1989. V. 48

O'CONNOR, ROBERT
Buffalo Soldiers. New York: 1993. V. 53

O'CONNOR, V. L.
A Book of Caricatures. Dundalk: 1916. V. 49

O'CONNOR, WILLIAM DOUGLAS
The Good Gray Poet. New York: 1866. V. 54
Three Tales. The Ghost. The Brazen Android. The Carpenter. Boston & New York: 1892. V. 47

O'CONOR, CHARLES
Dissertations On the History of Ireland... Dublin: 1812. V. 53
An Historical Address on the Calamities Occasioned by Foreign Influence in the Nomination of Bishops to Irish Sees. 1810-12. V. 52
An Historical Address on the Calamities Occasioned by Foreign Influence in the Nomination of Bishops to Irish Sees. London: 1810-12. V. 47

O'CONOR, MATHEW
The Irish Brigades; or, Memoirs of the Most Eminent Irish Military Commanders Who Distinguished Themselves in the Elizabethan and Williamite Wars in Their Own Country... Dublin: 1855. V. 48
Picturesque and Historical Recollections During a Tour through Belgium, Germany, France and Switzerland, in the Summer Vacation of 1835. London: 1837. V. 53

O'CURRY, EUGENE
Lectures on the Manuscript Materials of Ancient Irish History. Dublin: 1861. V. 49
Lectures On the Manuscript Materials of Ancient Irish History. Dublin: 1873. V. 50

O'DALY, JOHN
Fenian Poems. Second Series. Dublin: 1861. V. 48; 50
Laoithe Fiannuigheachta; or, Fenian Poems. London: 1859. V. 53
Laoithe Fiannuigheachta; or, Fenian Poems, Second Series. London: 1861. V. 53

O'DAY, EDWARD F.
An Appreciation of James Wood Coffroth, Written for His Son James W. Cofforth. San Francisco: 1926. V. 49

AN ODD Bestiary; or, a Compendium of Instructive and Entertaining Descriptions of Animals... Easthampton: 1982. V. 54

AN ODD Bestiary; or a Compendium of Instructive and Entertaining Descriptions of Animals, Culled from Five Centuries of Travelers' Accounts, Natural Histories, Zoologies, Etc. by Authors Famous and Obscure, Arranged as an Abecedary. Williamsburg: 1982. V. 47

ODDI, SFORZA DEGLI
L'Erofilomachia, Ouero il Dvello d'Amore, et D'Amicitia. Comedia Nvova (etc.). Venice: 1586. V. 51; 54

ODDICURIOUS, PSEUD.
The Oddest of All Oddities: Being an Odd Book Of All The Odd Sermons That Have Been Preached in the Fields, and Such Odd Chapels, in Every Odd Year, Odd Month, or Odd Day... London: 1804. V. 49

ODE to Lansdown-Hill, with Notes, Mostly Relative to the Granville Family; to Which are Added, Two Letters of Advice from George Lord Lansdown, anno MDCCXI, to William Henry Earl of Bath. London: 1785. V. 47

AN ODE to Mr. Handel. London: 1745. V. 47; 48

O'DEA, AGNES
Bibliography of Newfoundland. Toronto: 1986. V. 53

ODELL, JAMES
An Essay on the Elements, Accents & Prosody, of the English Language... London: 1806. V. 48

ODES to the Pillory. Supposed to Have Been Written by a K-t and His Lady. London: 1820?. V. 48; 54

ODETS, CLIFFORD
Golden Boy. New York. 1937. V. 53; 54
Night Music. New York: 1940. V. 53; 54
Paradise Lost. New York: 1936. V. 48
Rocket to the Moon. New York: 1939. V. 53
Waiting for Lefty and Till the Day I Die. New York: 1935. V. 52

O'DOGHERTY, WILLIAM
A Sketch of the History of Europe, from the Reign of Charlemagne to the Beginning of that of George III. Dublin: 1786. V. 53

ODOM, MARY MC CALEB
Lenare; a Story of the Southern Revolution, and Other Poems. New Orleans: 1866. V. 52

O'DONAGHUE, FREEMAN
A Catalogue of Engraved British Portraits Preserved in the Department of Prints and Drawings in the British Museum. London: 1908-25. V. 49

O'DONNEL, MATTHEW
The Second Addenda to the Analytical Digest of All the Reported Cases, etc. in the Several Courts of Equity in Ireland, and the House of Lords. Dublin: 1846. V. 49

O'DONNELL, E.
Dinevah the Beautiful. 1907. V. 48
Famous Curses. London: 1929. V. 52
The Sorcery Club. 1912. V. 48
Werewolves. London: 1912. V. 48

O'DONNELL, PEADAR
Adrigoole. London: 1929. V. 47
Adrigoole. New York: 1929. V. 47

O'DONNELL, PETER
Sabre Tooth - a Modesty Blaise Adventure. London: 1966. V. 47

O'DONNELL, T. C.
The Ladder of Rickety Rungs. Chicago: 1923. V. 49

O'DONOGHUE, D. J.
The Poets of Ireland. Dublin: 1912. V. 48
Prose Writings of James Clarence Mangan. 1904. V. 49; 50

O'DONOGHUE, FREEMAN
A Catalogue of Engraved British Portraits Preserved in the Department of Prints and Drawings in the British Museum. London: 1908-25. V. 53

O'DONOVAN, EDMOND
The Merv Oasis. Travels and Adventures East of the Caspian During the Years 1879-80-81... London: 1882. V. 48
The Merv Oasis: Travels and Adventures East of the Caspian During the Years 1879-80-81, Including Five Month's Residence Among the Tekkes of Merv. New York: 1883. V. 53

O'DONOVAN, EDMUND
The Merv Oasis, Travels and Adventures East of the Caspian During the Years 1879-80-81. 1882. V. 54

O'DONOVAN, JOHN
The Banquet of Dun Na n-Gedh and The Battle of Magh Rath. London: 1845. V. 53
Miscellany of the Celtic Society. London: 1849. V. 53
The Topographical Poems. Dublin: 1862. V. 48; 50

O'DRISCOL, JOHN
Views of Ireland, Moral, Political and Religious. 1823. V. 50; 54
Views of Ireland, Moral, Political and Religious. London: 1823. V. 49; 51

ODUM, HOWARD W.
Negro Workaday Songs. Chapel Hill: 1926. V. 47; 53
Wings On My Feet: Black Ulysses at the Wars. Indianapolis: 1929. V. 53; 54

OE, KENZABURO
Japan, the Ambiguous and Myself. Tokyo and New York: 1995. V. 53
A Personal Matter. New York: 1968. V. 52; 53
A Personal Matter. London: 1969. V. 53
The Silent Cry. Tokyo and New York: 1974. V. 53
Teach Us to Outgrow Our Madness. London: 1978. V. 53

THE OECUMENICAL Patriarchate. The Great Church of Christ. Athens: 1989. V. 49

OELSSNER, GOTTLIEB
Philosophisch-Moralische und Medizinische Betrachtung, Ueber mancherley zur Hoffart und Schönheit Hervorgesuchte... Breslau & Leipzig: 1754. V. 52

OERKE, ANDREW
Black Christ and Other Poems. 1970. V. 52

OERTEL, HORST
The Anatomic Histological Processes of Bright's Disease and Their relation to the Functional Changes. Philadelphia: 1910. V. 49; 54

OERTEL, W.
The Rhine. History and Legends of the Castles, Abbeys, Monasteries and Towns... Wiesbaden: 1868. V. 51

OF Garlands and Coronary or Garland Plants: Thomas Browne to John Evelyn Esq. F.R.S. Northampton: 1962. V. 54

OF the French Monarchy; and Absolute Power. And Also a Treatise of the Three Estates, And Their Power. London: 1680. V. 48

OF The Use of Tobacco, Tea, Coffee, Chocolate and Drams. London: 1722. V. 51

O'FAOLAIN, SEAN
Bird Alone. London: 1936. V. 48; 49
The Born Genius. Detroit: 1936. V. 51; 53; 54
Midsummer Night Madness and Other Stories. London: 1932. V. 47; 48; 49; 50; 51
A Nest of Simple Folk. London: 1933. V. 49; 51
A Purse of Coppers. London: 1937. V. 48
There's a Birdie in the Cage. London: 1935. V. 48

O'FERRALL, CHARLES T.
Forty Years of Active Service. New York & Washington: 1904. V. 49

OFFCUTS: The Campbell-Logan Bindery's Suggestions for Successful Book Binding. Minneapolis: 1985. V. 52

OFFENBACH, JACQUES
Offenbach in America. Notes of a Travelling Musician... New York: 1877. V. 49

THE OFFICE of the Clerk of Assize: Containing the Form and Method of the Proceedings at the Assizes, and General Gaol-Delivery, As Also on the Crown and Nisi Prius Side. London: 1682. V. 50

THE OFFICIAL Edition of the Revised Laws of Ping-Pong. London: 1902. V. 50

OFFICIAL Historical Atlas map of Fresno County, California. Tulare: 1891. V. 50

OFFICIAL History of the Great War. Veterinary Services. London: 1925. V. 47

THE OFFICIAL Manual of the Cripple Creek District, Colorado, USA. Colorado Springs: 1900. V. 49

OFFICIAL Report of the Battle of Chickamauga. Richmond: 1864. V. 49

OFFICINA BODONI, VERONA.
The Officina Bodoni: the Operation of a Hand-Press During the First Six Years Of Its Work. Paris & New York: 1929. V. 54

L'OFFICO di Maria Vergine. Vienna: 1672. V. 49

OFFNER, ELLIOT
The Granjon Arabesque, Thirty Arrangements of the Ornaments with Type and an Introduction. Northampton: 1969. V. 51

O'FLAHERTY, JOSEPH
An End and a Beginning and Those Powerful Years. Los Angeles: 1992. V. 49; 50

O'FLAHERTY, LIAM
Aranmen All. Tom O'Flaherty. Dublin: 1934. V. 47
The Assassin. 1928. V. 49; 50
The Assassin. London: 1928. V. 47; 48; 49; 51; 53
The Black Soul. London: 1924. V. 47; 48
The Child of God. 1926. V. 49
The Child of God. London: 1926. V. 47
Civil War. London: 1925. V. 47
Cliffman of the West. London: 1935. V. 47
A Cure for Unemployment. London: 1931. V. 47; 51; 53
The Cutting of Tom Bottle. V. 47
Darkness. A Tragedy in Three Acts. London: 1926. V. 47; 51
The Ecstasy of Angus. 1931. V. 48; 49
The Ecstasy of Angus. London: 1931. V. 47; 48; 49; 51; 53
The Fairy Goose and Two Other Stories. New York and London: 1927. V. 47; 48; 49
Famine. London: 1937. V. 47
His First Flight. V. 47
Hollywood Cemetery. London: 1935. V. 47
The House of Gold. London. V. 47
The House of Gold. 1929. V. 48; 52
The House of Gold. London: 1929. V. 47; 51; 53
I Went to Russia. London: 1931. V. 47
The Informer. London: 1925. V. 47; 49; 51; 52
Insurrection. London: 1950. V. 47
Joseph Conrad. An Appreciation. London: 1930. V. 47
Land. London: 1946. V. 47
The Life of Tim Healy. London: 1927. V. 47; 48
The Life of Tim Healy. New York: 1927. V. 47
The Martyr. London: 1933. V. 47
Match Making. 1923. V. 47
Mr. Gilhooley. London: 1926. V. 47
The Mountain Tavern. London: 1929. V. 47; 48; 51
The Pedlar's Revenge and Other Stories. Dublin: 1976. V. 47
The Puritan. London: 1932. V. 47; 51; 53
Red Barbara and Other Stories. London: 1928. V. 51
Red Barbara and Other Stories, The Mountain Tavern, Prey, The Oar. New York: 1928. V. 47; 48
A Red Petticoat. Tomorrow. Volume !. Number 1. 1924. V. 47
Return of the Brute. London: 1929. V. 47; 49; 51; 53
Shame the Devil. London: 1934. V. 47; 49
The Short Stories. London: 1937. V. 47
Skerrett. London: 1932. V. 47; 49; 51; 53
Spring Sowing. London: 1924. V. 47; 48; 49
Spring Sowing. New York: 1926. V. 47

O'FLAHERTY, LIAM continued
Der Stromer. 21 Erzahlungen aus Irland. Zurich: 1975. V. 47
The Tent. London: 1926. V. 47; 48; 49; 50; 51; 53
The Terrorist. 1926. V. 49
The Terrorist. London: 1926. V. 47
Thy Neighbor's Wife. London: 1923. V. 47; 49; 51; 53
Tidy Tim's Donkey. 1924. V. 47
A Tourist's Guide to Ireland. 1929. V. 52
A Tourist's Guide to Ireland. London: 1929. V. 47; 49; 51; 53; 54
A Tourist's Guide to Ireland. London: 1930. V. 48; 53
Two Lovely Beasts and Other Stories. London: 1948. V. 47
Two Years. London: 1930. V. 49; 51
The White Bitch. with The Jealous hens. 1924. V. 47
The Wild Swan and Other Stories. V. 47
The Wilderness. Dublin: 1978. V. 47

O'FLANAGAN, JOHN
On Fraud (Against Washington Circle Hospital in D.C.). Washington: 1862. V. 50

O'FLARRITY, PADDY, PSEUD.
The Life of Paddy O'Flarrity, Who, from a Shoe Black, Has, By Perserverance and Good Conduct, Arrived to a Member of Congress, Interspersed with Many Curious Anecdotes... 1834. V. 50; 54

OFWOOD, STEPHEN
A Second Part of the Spanish Practices. Or, a Relation of More Paricular Wicked Plots (etc.). London: 1624. V. 50; 53

O'GALLCHOBHAIR, PRIONNSIAS
History of Lanlordism in Donegal. London: 1962. V. 53

OGAWA, K.
Some Japanese Flowers. Yokohama: 1890. V. 48

OGDEN, ADELE
The California Sea Otter Trade, 1784-1848. Berkeley & Los Angeles: 1941. V. 50; 53

OGDEN, CHARLES BURR
The Quaker Ogdens in America. Philadelphia: 1898. V. 51

OGDEN, HUGH W.
Letters from H.W.O. 1917-1918-(1919). 1919. V. 53

OGDEN, JAMES
Ogden on Fly-tying, Etc. Cheltenham: 1879. V. 47
A Poem, on the Museum at Alkrington, Belonging to Ashton Lever, Esq. Manchester: 1800?. V. 48

OGDEN, JOHN C.
An Excursion Into Bethlehem and Nazareth, in Pennsylvania, in the Year 1799. Philadelphia: 1800. V. 53
A View of the New England Illuminati: Who Are Indefatigably Engaged in Destroying the Religion and Government of the United States. Philadelphia: 1799. V. 49; 50

OGDEN, PETER SKENE
Peter Skene Ogden's Snake Country Journals 1824-25 and 1825-1826. London: 1950. V. 48
Traits of American-Indian Life and Character. London: 1853. V. 49

OGDEN Utah. 1910. V. 52

OGHAM.. London: 1979. V. 51

OGIER, CHARLES
Caroli Ogerii Ephemerides, Sive Iter Danicum, Svecicum, Polonicum. Lutetiae Parisiorum: 1656. V. 48

OGILBY, JOHN
Africa: Being an Accurate Description of the Regions of Aegypt, Barbary, Lybia and Billedulgerid, the Land of Negroes, Guinee, Aethiopia and the Abyssines... London: 1670. V. 50
Britannia Depicta or Ogilby Improv'd... London: 1720. V. 48; 51
Britannia; or The Kingdom of England and Dominion of Wales, Actually Survey'd... London: 1698. V. 48
A Description and History of the Island of Jamaica. Kingston: 1851. V. 51

OGILVIE, JAMES
The Ci II History of the Kingdom of Naples... London: 1729-31. V. 49

OGILVIE, JOHN
The Imperial Dictionary. London. V. 48
The Imperial Dictionary. Glasgow: 1851. V. 52
The Imperial Dictionary. London: 1851. V. 52
The Imperial Dictionary. London: 1876. V. 52
Providence, an Allegorical Poem. Boston: 1766. V. 49

OGILVIE, KATHERINE
The Trial of Katherine Nairn and Patrick Ogilvie, for the Crimes of Incest and Murder. Edinburgh: 1765. V. 48

OGILVIE, WILLIAM
Early Days on the Yukon and The Story of Its Gold Finds. London: 1913. V. 49; 50; 53
The Klondike Official Guide. Canada's Great Gold Field, the Yukon District.... Toronto: 1898. V. 53
Lecture on the Klondike Mining District. Victoria: 1897. V. 49

OGILVIE-GRANT, W. R.
Catalogue of the Game Birds (Pterocletes, Gallinae, Opisthocomi, Hemipodii) in the Collection of the British Museum. London: 1893. V. 47
The Gun at Home and Abroad British Game Birds and Wildfowl. London: 1912. V. 47
A Hand-book to the Game-Birds. London: 1895-97. V. 52
A Hand-Book to the Game-Birds. London: 1896-97. V. 51
A Hand-Book to the Game-Birds. London: 1897. V. 51
Reports on the Collections Made by the British Ornithologists' Union Expedition and the Wollaston Expedition in Dutch New Guinea, 1910-13. London: 1916. V. 47; 48; 51

OGILVY, JAMES S.
A Pilgrimage in Surrey. London: 1914. V. 49; 54
Relics and Memorials of London City. London: 1910. V. 54

OGLE, GEORGE
Antiquities Explained, Being a Collection of Figured Gems Illustrated by Similar Descriptions Taken from the Classics. London: 1737. V. 47
Gualtherus and Grielda: or, The Clerk of Oxford's Tale. London: 1739. V. 50

OGLE, GEORGE A., & C0.
Standard Atlas of Buffalo County, Nebraska. Chicago: 1907. V. 48

OGLE, NATHANIEL
Memoirs of Monkeys, &c &c. London: 1825. V. 50

O'GORMAN, EDITH
Convent Life Unveiled. London: 1900. V. 47; 49; 51

O'GRADY, ALICE
The Argyle Cook book. San Antonio: 1941. V. 54

O'GRADY, DESMOND
The Gododdin. Dublin: 1977. V. 48
Stations. Cairo: 1976. V. 52

O'GRADY, STANDISH
Toruigheacht Dhiarmuda Agus Ghrainne; or, The Pursuit after Diarmuid O'Duibhne and Grainne. London: 1857. V. 53

O'GRADY, STANDISH HAYES
Silva Gadelica (I-XXXI): a Collection of Tales in Irish. London: 1892. V. 47

O'GRADY, STANDISH JAMES
Toryism and the Tory Democracy. 1886. V. 49; 50

O'HALLORAN, SYLVESTER
A History of Ireland, an Introduction to the Study of the History and Antiquities of Ireland, and Ierne Defended. Dublin: 1819. V. 53

O'HANLON, JOHN C.
Life and Scenery in Missouri, Reminiscences of a Missouri Priest. Dublin: 1890. V. 53

O'HANLON, REDMOND
In Trouble Again. London: 1988. V. 52; 54
Into the Heart of Borneo: an Account of a Journey Made in 1983 to the Mountains of Batu Tiban with James Fenton. Edinburgh: 1984. V. 54
Joseph Conrad and Charles Darwin. Atlantic Highlands: 1984. V. 52

O'HARA, FRANK
The Collected Poems of Frank O'Hara. New York: 1971. V. 48; 49; 53
Four Poems. Verona: 1983. V. 47
In Memory of My Feelings. New York: 1967. V. 50; 51; 52; 53
Love Poems. New York: 1965. V. 53
Lunch Poems. San Francisco: 1964. V. 53; 54
Meditations in an Emergency. New York: 1957. V. 47; 49; 51; 53
Poems. New York: 1988. V. 49; 51; 53

OHARA, HOUN
Ikebana: the Creative Tradition. Tokyo: 1970. V. 49

O'HARA, JOHN
And Other Stories. New York: 1968. V. 53
Appointment in Samarra. New York: 1934. V. 47; 49; 51; 53; 54
The Farmers Hotel. New York: 1951. V. 51
From the Terrace. 1958. V. 50
Gloria. (Butterfield 8). Paris. V. 51
Here's O'Hara. Three Novels and Twenty Short Stories. New York: 1946. V. 51
Hope of Heaven. New York: 1938. V. 48; 49
The Horse Knows the Way. New York: 1964. V. 53
The Instrument. New York: 1967. V. 48; 49; 51; 53; 54
The Lockwood Concern. 1965. V. 50
The Lockwood Concern. New York: 1965. V. 53; 54
Lovey Childs. New York: 1969. V. 49
Ourselves to Know. New York: 1960. V. 51
Pal Joey. New York: 1940. V. 49; 51
Pal Joey. New York: 1952. V. 51
Pipe Night. New York: 1945. V. 49
A Rage to Live. New York: 1949. V. 47; 48; 51
Sermons and Soda-Water. New York: 1960. V. 48; 49; 50; 51
Sermons and Soda-Water. London: 1961. V. 51
Sweet and Sour: Comments on Books and People. New York: 1954. V. 51
Talalkozas. (Appointment in Samarra). Budapest. V. 51
Waiting For Winter. New York: 1966. V. 49; 53; 54

O'HARA, KANE
Midas: a Burletta... London: 1837. V. 50

O'HARE, KATE RICHARDS
In Prison. New York: 1923. V. 47

OHIO ANTI-SLAVERY SOCIETY
Narrative of the Late Riotous Proceedings Against the Liberty of the Press, in Cincinnati... Cincinnati: 1836. V. 47; 50

OHIO. LAWS, STATUTES, ETC.
Acts of the State of Ohio, Passed and Revised, First Session of the Third General Assembly, Begun and Held at the Town of Chillicothe, December 3, 1804 and in the Third Year of Said State. Chillichote: 1805. V. 49

THE OHIO Railroad Guide, Illustrated. Cincinnati to Erie, Via Columbus and Cleveland. Columbus: 1854. V. 50; 53

OHRNBERGER, D.
The Bamboos of the World, a Preliminary Study of the Names and Distribtuion of the Herbaceous and Woody Bamboos. Dehra Dun: 1990/83-87. V. 48

OHTAISHI, N.
Deer of China - Biology and Management. Amsterdam: 1993. V. 52

OIL PROPERTIES CONSULTANTS, INC.
General Geological Survey of Oil Potentialities in Cuba, February, 1950. Prepared for Cuban-Venezuelan Oil Voting Trust. Pasadena: 1950. V. 49

OIL WELL SUPPLY CO., LTD.
Illustrated Catalogue of Oil and Artesian Well Supplies Manufactured by the Oil Well Supply Co., Ltd., Bradford and Oil City, Pennsylvania. New York: 1884. V. 50

OKADA, TAKAHIKO
Shingu. New York: 1973. V. 51

OKAMURA, K.
Icones of Japanese Algae. Tokyo: 1909-42. V. 48

OKAMURA, O.
Fishes of the Okinawa Trough and the Adjacent Waters. Tokyo: 1984-85. V. 50

O'KEEFE, ADELAIDE
National Characters Exhibited in Forty Geographical Poems. London: 1818. V. 52
Patriarchal Times - or the Land of Canaan. London: 1834. V. 48

O'KEEFE, JOHN
Recollections of the Life of John O'Keefe. London: 1826. V. 50

O'KEEFE, THOMAS M.
The Battle of London Life; or, Box and His Secretary. London: 1849. V. 49

O'KEEFFE, GEORGIA
Georgia O'Keefe. New York: 1976. V. 48; 49; 50; 52; 53
Georgia O'Keeffe. New York: 1978. V. 47

O'KELLY, PATRICK
The Hippocrene: a Collection of Poems. Dublin: 1831. V. 52

O'KELLY, SEUMAS
Ranns and Ballads. Dublin: 1918. V. 48

OKELY, FRANCIS
Memoirs of...Jacob Behman... Northampton: 1780. V. 54

OKES, THOMAS VERNEY
An Account of the Providential Perservation of Eliz. Woodcock, Who Survived a Confinement Under the Snow, of Nearly Eight Days and Nights, in...February 1799. Cambridge: 1799. V. 47

OKLAHOMA. CONSTITUTION
The Constitution of the State of Oklahoma. Guthrie: 1907. V. 49

OKLAND, J.
Lakes and Snails. Environment and Gastropoda in 1500 Norwegian Lakes, Ponds and Rivers. Oegstgeest: 1990. V. 50

OKRI, BEN
The Famished Road. London: 1991. V. 53
Incidents at the Shrine. London: 1986. V. 53

OKUBO, MINE
Citizen 13660. New York: 1946. V. 51

OKUDAIRA, HIEDO
Emaki: Japanese Picture Scrolls. Japan: 1962. V. 52; 54

O'LAVERTY, JAMES
An Historical Account of the Diocese of Down and Connor, Ancient and Modern. Volume II. Dublin: 1880. V. 51
An Historical Account of the Dioceses of Down and Connor: Ancient and Modern. 1878-95. V. 48; 52

OLCOTT, HENRY S.
Old Diary Leaves: the True Story of Theosophical Society. First, Second and Third Series. 1895/1900/1904. V. 47
Sorgho and Imphee, the Chinese and African Sugar Canes. New York: 1857. V. 53

OLCOTT, WILLIAM TYLER
Sun Lore of All Ages, a Collection of Myths and Legends Concerning the Sun and its Worship. New York: 1914. V. 48

OLD Abe's Jokes. New York: 1864. V. 53

OLD and New London. London: 1880. V. 48

OLD Ballads, Historical and Narrative, with Some of Modern Date. London: 1784. V. 54

THE OLD Country Houses of the Old Glasgow Gentry. Glasgow: 1878. V. 51

OLD Customs of Chinese Festivals. V. 50

OLD Dame Trot and Her Comical Cat. London: 1840's. V. 49
OLD Dame Trot and Her Comical Cat. London: 1850. V. 49

OLD England: English Songs of Long Ago. Utrecht: 1917. V. 51

OLD English Drinking Songs. Cincinnati: 1903. V. 51; 53

OLD Fairy Tales. London: 1920's. V. 49

THE OLD Favourite Tales. London: 1865. V. 48

THE OLD Flag. New York: 1864. V. 52

OLD French Nursery Songs. London: 1925. V. 48; 50

OLD Joe Miller: Being a Complete and Correct Copy from the Best Edition of His Celebrated Jests; and Also Including All the Good Things in Above Fifty Jest-Books Published from the Year 1558 to the Present Time. London: 1800. V. 48

OLD King Cole. Scotland: 1985. V. 50

OLD King Cole's Book of Nursery Rhymes. London: 1901. V. 51

OLD Maids: The Varieties, Characters and Conditions. New York: 1835. V. 53

THE OLD Man and the Devils. London: 1890. V. 53

OLD Matthews. (The Dulwich Hermit). London: 1875. V. 47

THE OLD Nursery Rhymes. London: 1933. V. 49

Old Proverbs with new Pictures. London, Paris & New York: 1880. V. 49

OLD Rhymes and New Stories. London: 1930's. V. 51

OLD Rough and Ready Almanac...1849. Philadelphia: 1848. V. 53

THE OLD School: Essays by Divers Hands. London: 1934. V. 50

THE OLD Serpent's Reply (In Verse) to the Electrical Eel. London: 1777. V. 48

OLD Testament Miniatures: a Medieval Picture Book with 283 Paintings from the Creation to the Story of David. New York: 1975. V. 47

OLD Villita. San Antonio: 1939. V. 52

OLD West Antiques and Collectibles. Austin: 1979. V. 50

THE OLD Woman and Her Pig. London: 1845. V. 52

THE OLD Woman Who Lost Her Dumpling. Tokyo: 1902. V. 48

OLD Yorkshire. London: 1881-84. V. 47; 54

OLD-World Love Stories. London: 1913. V. 48

OLDE Tayles Newlye Relayted, Enryched with All Ye Ancyente Embellyshmentes. London: 1883. V. 47

OLDEN, THOMAS
Holy Scriptures in Ireland 1000 Years Ago. 1888. V. 52

OLDENBERG, CLAES
Notes in Hand. 1971. V. 50
Store Days: Documents from the Store (1961) and the Ray Gun Theater (19620). New York: 1967. V. 52; 53

OLDENBERG, HERMANN
Buddha. London: 1904. V. 53

OLDENBURG, HENRY
The Correspondence of Henry Oldenburg. Madison: 1965-73. V. 48
The Correspondence of Henry Oldenburg. Madison & Milwaukee: 1965-75. V. 54

OLDER, FREMONT
The Life of George Hearst, California Pioneer. San Francisco: 1933. V. 50

OLDEROGGE, D.
Negro Art from the Institute of Ethnography, Leningrad. Prague: 1969. V. 54

OLDFIELD, CLAUDE
The Beast. Belfast: 1936. V. 47; 48; 50

OLDFIELD, HENRY AMBROSE
Sketches from Nipal, Historical and Descriptive, with Anecdotes of the Court Life and Wild Sports of the Country in the Time of Majaraja Jang Bahadur... London: 1880. V. 53

OLDFIELD, JOSHUA
An Essay Towards the Improvement of Reason; in the Pursuit of Learning and the Conduct of Life. London: 1707. V. 49

OLDFIELD, OTIS
A Pictorial Journal of a Voyage Aboard the Three Masted Schooner Louise, Last of the Sailing Codfishermen Out of San Francisco... San Francisco: 1969. V. 48; 49; 51

OLDFIELD, THOMAS HINTON BURLEY
An Entire and Complete History, Political and Personal of the Boroughs of Great Britain (Together with the Cinque Ports). London: 1792. V. 47; 53

OLDHAM, J. BASIL
Blind Panels of English Binders. Cambridge: 1958. V. 50; 53
Blind Panels of English Binders. London: 1958. V. 53
English Blind-stamped Bindings. 1952. V. 50; 52
English Blind-Stamped Bindings. Cambridge: 1952. V. 48; 50; 51; 53
English Blind-Stamped Bindings and Blind Panels of English Binders. Cambridge: 1952-58. V. 52
English Blind-Stamped Bindings. (with) Blind Panels of English Binders. 1952/58. V. 48

OLDHAM, J. BASIL continued
Shrewsbury School Library Bindings. Catalogue Raisonne. Oxford: 1943. V. 48; 50; 52; 53

OLDHAM, JOHN
Poems and Translations. London: 1683. V. 47
Satyrs (in Verse) Upon the Jesuits: Written in the Year 1679. (with) Some New Pices Never Before Published. London: 1682/81. V. 47
The Works... Together With His Remains. London: 1686. V. 48; 50
The Works. Together with His Remains. London: 1698. V. 48
The Works...Together with His Remains. London: 1703. V. 48
The Works...Together With His Remains. London: 1730. V. 49

OLDHAM, T.
On the Geological Structure of Part of the Khasi Hills, with Observations on the Meteorology and Ethnology of the District. Calcutta: 1854. V. 52

OLDMIXON, JOHN
The Governour of Cyprus: a Tragedy. London: 1703. V. 47
The History of Addresses. London. V. 54
The History of Addresses By One Very Near a Kin to the Author of the Tale of a Tub. London: 1709. V. 50
The History of England During the Reigns of Henry VIII, Edward VI, Queen Mary, Queen Elizabeth. London: 1739. V. 47
A Letter to the Seven Lords of the Committee, Appointed to Examine Gregg. London: 1711. V. 47; 54
Memoirs of the Life, Writings and Amours of William Congreve, Esq. London: 1730. V. 48

OLDREY, J.
The Devil's Henchmen. London: 1926. V. 48; 52

OLDROYD, I. S.
Marine Shells of the West Coast of North America. 1924-27. V. 48
Marine Shells of the West Coast of North America. Stanford: 1924-27. V. 52; 54
The Marine Shells of the West Coast of North America. Stanford: 1978. V. 48; 50; 51

OLDROYD, OSBORN H.
A Soldier's Story of the Seige of Vicksburg from the Diary of Osborn H. Oldroyd.... Springfield: 1885. V. 47

OLDS, IRVING S.
Bits and Pieces of American History as Told by a Collection of American Naval and Other Historical Prints and paintings, Including Portraits of American Naval Commanders... New York: 1951. V. 49

OLDYS, WILLIAM
A Collection of Epigrams. London: 1735. V. 54

OLEARIUS, ADAM
Voyages Celebres & Remarquables, fAits de Perse aux Indes Orientales par le Sr. Jean Albert Mandelslo... Amsterdam;: 1727. V. 47

O'LEARY, ARTHUR
Miscellaneous Tracts... 1781. V. 47
Miscellaneous Tracts. Dublin: 1781. V. 53
Miscellaneous Tracts on Several Interesting Subjects. 1791. V. 54

O'LEARY, JOHN
Recollections of Fenians and Fenianism. London: 1896. V. 51

O'LEARY, JOSEPH
The Tribute: a Miscellaneous Volume In Prose and Verse... Cork: 1833. V. 47; 49; 53

O'LEARY, PETER
Travels and Experiences in Canada, the Red River Territory and the United States. London. V. 49
Travels and Experiences in Canada, the Red River Territory and the United States. London: 1877. V. 53

OLIM, TRANSINDICUS
The Cabul Question. London: 1869. V. 49

OLIPHANT, CAROLINE
Life and Songs of the Baroness Nairne. Edinburgh: 1896. V. 53; 54

OLIPHANT, GEORGE HENRY HEWITT
The Law of Horses, Including the Law of Innkeepers, Veterinary Surgeons...and of Hunting, Racing, Wagers & Gaming. London: 1865. V. 47

OLIPHANT, LAURENCE
Alitora Peto. Edinburgh: 1883. V. 48; 53
Episodes in a Life of Adventure, or Notes from a Rolling Stone. Edinburgh: 1888. V. 53
Haifa, or Life in Modern Palestine. Edinburgh: 1887. V. 48; 49; 54
Haifa, or Life in Modern Palestine. New York: 1887. V. 53
The Land of Gilead With Excursions in the Lebanon. Edinburgh: 1880. V. 54
The Land of Gilead, with Excursions in the Lebanon. New York: 1881. V. 49; 52
Masollam: a Problem of the Period. Edinburgh: 1886. V. 51; 53
Masollam: a Problem of the Period. London: 1886. V. 54
Minnesota and the Far West. Edinburgh & London: 1855. V. 47; 48; 49; 53; 54
Narrative of the Earl of Elgin's Mission to China and Japan in the Years 1857, 58, '59. Edinburgh: 1859. V. 47; 51; 52
Piccadilly, a Fragment of Contemporary Biography. Edinburgh & London: 1870. V. 50; 53
The Russian Shores of the Black Sea... Edinburgh: 1853. V. 50
The Russian Shores of the Black Sea. London: 1853. V. 49
The Russian Shores of the Black Sea, in the Autumn of 1852, with a Voyage Down the volga... London: 1854. V. 48
Sympneumata or Evolutionary Forces Now Active in Man. Edinburgh: 1885. V. 53
Traits and Travesties Social and Political. Edinburgh: 1882. V. 53

OLIPHANT, MARGARET OLIPHANT WILSON
Annals of a Publishing House. William Blackwood and His Sons, Their Magazine and Friends. Edinburgh: 1897-98. V. 48; 51
The Autobiography and Letters. Edinburgh: 1899. V. 50; 53
Caleb Field. London: 1851. V. 53
Chronicles of Carlingford. Edinburgh: 1864. V. 50
The Chronicles of Carlingford. Edinburgh: 1879. V. 50
Dress. Philadelphia: 1878. V. 51
It Was a Lover and His Lass. London: 1884. V. 50
The Laird of Norlaw. London: 1858. V. 50
The Last of the Mortimers. London: 1862. V. 50
The Literary History of England in the End of the Eighteenth and Beginning of the Nineteenth Century. London: 1882. V. 47; 53
Lucy Crofton. London: 1860. V. 50
Madona Mary. London: 1875. V. 50
Magdalen Hepburn. London: 1854. V. 50
The Makers of Florence... London: 1876. V. 49
The Makers of Florence... London: 1889. V. 50
The Makers of Florence. London: 1901. V. 54
The Makers of Venice, Doges, Conquerors, Painters and Men of Letters. London: 1893. V. 50
Neighbours on the Green. London: 1889. V. 51
Passages in the Life of Mrs. Margaret Maitland, of Sunnyside. London: 1851. V. 50
The Three Brothers. London: 1870. V. 50
Two Stories of the Seen and Unseen. Edinburgh: 1885. V. 48

OLIVEIRA, FRANCISCO XAVIER DE
Memorias das Viagens...Tomo I. Amsterdam: 1741. V. 53

OLIVER, A. W.
Wichita Journal of Commerce, June 1888. Wichita: 1888. V. 49

OLIVER, CHAD
Mists of Dawn. 1952. V. 49
The Winds of Time. 1957. V. 48
The Winds of Time. Garden City: 1957. V. 51
The Winds of Time. New York: 1957. V. 52

OLIVER, D.
Flora of Tropical Africa. Ashford: 1868-1917. V. 52; 53
Illustrations of the Principal Natural Orders of the Vegetable Kingdom. London: 1874. V. 54
Illustrations of the Principal Natural Orders of the Vegetable Kingdom. London: 1893. V. 49

OLIVER, EDITH
Dwarf's Blood. London: 1931. V. 50

OLIVER, EDMUND H.
The Canadian North-West: its Early Development and Legislative Records... Ottawa: 1914/15. V. 48

OLIVER, EDWARD E.
Across the Border or Pathan and Biloch. London: 1890. V. 53

OLIVER, F. S.
The Anvil of War - Letters Between F. S. Oliver and His Brother 1914-1918. London: 1936. V. 47

OLIVER, GEORGE
The History and Antiquities of the Town and Minster of Beverley, in the County of York. Beverley: 1829. V. 47
The History of Exeter. Exeter: 1821. V. 49
The History of the City of Exter. Exeter: 1861. V. 51

OLIVER, J. RUTHERFORD
Upper Teviotdale and the Scotts of Buccleugh. Hawick: 1887. V. 54

OLIVER, J. W.
The Life of William Beckford. London: 1932. V. 53

OLIVER, JEAN
Architecture Of the Kidney in Chronic Bright's Disease. New York: 1939. V. 49; 54

OLIVER, LEON
The Great Sensation. Chicago: 1873. V. 51

OLIVER, MARY
No Voyage and Other Poems. London: 1963. V. 51; 53
No Voyage and Other Poems. Boston: 1965. V. 51
Provincetown. 1987. V. 49; 51
Provincetown. Lewisburg: 1987. V. 52; 53
The River Styx, Ohio and Other Poems. New York: 1976. V. 49
Sleeping in the Forest. Athens: 1977. V. 51

OLIVER, N. W., MRS.
Sephora; a Hebrew Tale, Descriptive of the Country of Palestine and of the Manners and Customs of the Ancient Israelites. London: 1826. V. 50

OLIVER, PETER
A New Chronicle of the Compleat Angler. New York: 1936. V. 47; 51

OLIVER, SAMUEL P.
The True Story of the french Dispute in Madagascar. London: 1885. V. 49

OLIVER, STEPHEN
Scenes and Recollections of Fly Fishing, in Northumberland, Cumberland and Westmorland. London: 1834. V. 47; 50; 52; 53; 54

OLIVER, W. R. B.
The Moas of New Zealand and Australia. Wellington: 1992. V. 53

OLIVER, WILLIAM
A Practical Dissertation on Bath-Waters. 1764. V. 48

OLIVERO, FEDERICO
Edgar Poe. Torino: 1939. V. 48

OLIVERS, THOMAS
Thomas Olivers of Tregynon: the Life of an Early Methodist Preacher Written by Himself. 1979. V. 54

OLIVIA, or the Orphan. London: 1820. V. 50; 54

OLIVIER, ABBE
Memoirs of the Life and Adventures of Signor Rozelli. Giving a Particular Account of His Birth, Education, Slavery... London: 1713. V. 47

OLIVIER, CHARLES P.
Meteors. Baltimore: 1925. V. 53

OLIVIER, EDITH
The Eccentric Life of Alexander Cruden. London: 1934. V. 54

OLIVIER, EUGENE GEORGES HERMAL
Manuel de Reliures Armoriees Francaises. Paris: 1924-38. V. 47

OLIVIER, J.
A Continuation of the Life and Adventures of Signor Rozelli, Late of the Hague. London: 1724. V. 52
Fencing Familiarized: or, a New Treatise on the Art of Sword Play. 1771. V. 51
Fencing Familiarized; or a New Treatise on the Art of Sword Play. London: 1771. V. 53
Fencing Familiarized; or, a New Treatise on the Art of Sword Play. York: 1771. V. 48
Fencing Familiarized: or a New Treatise on the Art of the Small Sword. London: 1780. V. 54

OLLANTA. An Ancient Ynca Drama. London: 1871. V. 48

OLLE'S Ski Trip. New York. V. 52

OLLIER, CHARLES
Ferrers. A Romance of the Reign of George the Second. London: 1842. V. 47

OLLIFF, A. SIDNEY
Australian Butterflies, A Brief Account of the Native Families with a Chapter on Collecting and Preserving Insects. Sydney: 1889. V. 50

OLLIVANT, ALFRED
Bob, Son of Battle. New York: 1898. V. 48; 53
Redcoat Captain. A Story of that country. London: 1907. V. 50

OLLIVANT, J. E.
A Breeze from the Great Salt Lake, or New Zealand to new York by the New Mail Route. London: 1871. V. 50

OLMO, JOSEPH VINCENTE DEL
Nueva Descripcion Del Orbe de la Tierra. En Que Se Trata de Todas Sus Partes Interiores... Valencia: 1681. V. 48

OLMSTEAD, CHARLES H.
Reminiscences of Service with the First Volunteer Regiment of Georgia, Charleston Harbor, in 1863. Savannah: 1879. V. 49

OLMSTED, DENISON
Outlines of Lectures on Meteorology, Delivered at Yale College for the Use of the Students. New Haven: 1837. V. 52

OLMSTED, DUNCAN
40 Years: a Chronology of Announcements & Keepsakes: The Roxburghe Club of San Francisco, 1928-1967. San Francisco: 1968. V. 47
Bartolomeus Zanni, Printer at Venice 1486-1518 and at Portese 1489-90. Berkeley: 1962. V. 52

OLMSTED, FRANCIS ALLYN
Incidents of a Whaling Voyage. New York: 1841. V. 48

OLMSTED, FREDERICK LAW
The Cotton Kingdom: A Travellers Observations on Cotton and Slavery in the American Slave States. New York: 1861. V. 49
Hospital Transports. A Memoir of the Embarkation of the Sick and Wounded From the Peninsula of Virginia in the Summer of 1862. Boston: 1863. V. 49
A Journey in the Back Country. London: 1860. V. 50
A Journey in the Back Country. New York: 1861. V. 49; 53
A Journey in the Seaboard Slave States with remarks on their Economy. New York: 1856. V. 47; 49
Journey through Texas; or, a Saddle Trip on the Southwestern Frontier with a Statistical Appendix. New York: 1857. V. 47; 48; 49; 52; 53
Journey through Texas: or a Saddle-Trip on the Southwestern Frontier. New York: 1859. V. 53
A Journey through Texas, or a Saddle-Trip on the Southwestern Frontier, etc. New York: 1860. V. 49
Walks and Talks of an American Farmer in England. London: 1852. V. 47
Yosemite and the Mariposa Grove: a Preliminary Report, 1865. Berkeley: 1993. V. 52

OLMSTED, T.
The Musical Olio, Containing I. A Concise Introduction to the Art of Singing by Note. II. A Variety of Psalm and Hymn Tunes... New London: 1811. V. 48

OLNEY Hymns, in Three Books. London: 1779. V. 53

OLSCHAUSEN, THEODOR
Geschichte der Mormonen: Oder Jungsten-Tages-Heiligen in Nordamerika. Gottingen: 1856. V. 50

OLSEN, TILLIE
Tell Me A Riddle. Philadelphia: 1961. V. 50

OLSON, CHARLES
Apollonius of Tyana. Black Mountain: 1951. V. 52; 53
Archaeologist of Morning. London: 1970. V. 53
Archeologist of Morning. New York: 1970. V. 51
Call Me Ishmael. New York: 1947. V. 49; 50; 52; 53
Call Me Ishmael. New York: 1958. V. 49
Charles Olson in Connecticut: Last Lectures.... Iowa City: 1974. V. 51; 54
The Complete Correspondence. Santa Barbara: 1980-85. V. 54
In Cold Hell, in Thicket. 1953. V. 54
In Cold Hell, In Thicket. Dorchester: 1953. V. 51; 54
Maximus from Dogwon - 1. San Francisco: 1961. V. 49
The Maximus Poems. New York: 1960. V. 54
The Maximus Poems 1-10. Stuttgart: 1953. V. 48
The Maximus Poems 1-10. (with) The Maximus Poems 11-22. Stuttgart: 1953-56. V. 48; 51; 53; 54
Projective Verse. New York: 1959. V. 51; 52; 53
Proprioception. San Francisco: 1965. V. 48
Some Early Poems. Iowa City: 1978. V. 51; 53; 54
A Some Early Poems. Windhover: 1978. V. 54
The Special View of History. Berkeley: 1970. V. 54
Stocking Cap. 1966. V. 53
West. London: 1966. V. 52; 53

OLSON, EDMUND T.
Utah, a Romance in Pioneer Days. Salt Lake City: 1931. V. 51; 53

OLSON, RUTH
Naum Gabo and Antoine Pevner. New York: 1948. V. 52

OLSON, TOBY
Bird Songs, Eleven New Poems. Mt. Horeb: 1980. V. 47
The Brand. Mt. Horeb: 1969. V. 47; 49; 51; 54
Doctor Miriam. Mt. Horeb: 1977. V. 47; 49; 53; 54
Fishing. A Single Poem with an Original Mixed Media Print by William Eege Da Barba. Driftless: 1973. V. 54
Maps. Mt. Horeb: 1969. V. 51; 54
The Pool, from the Novel Dorit in Lesbos. Mt. Horeb: 1991. V. 51; 54
Three and One. Four Poems. Mt. Horeb: 1976. V. 51; 54
Worms Into Nails. Mt. Horeb: 1969. V. 54

OLSSON, A. A.
Mollusks of the Tropical Eastern Pacific, Panamic-Pacific Pelecypoda. Ithaca: 1961. V. 49; 50; 51; 53

OLVEAGA, LUIS
La Capitana. Told by an eye-witness. London: 1937. V. 49

OLYMPIC Games. B.C. 776-A.D. 1896. Athens & London: 1896. V. 50

OMAGGIO delle Provincie Venete alla Maesta di Carolina Augusta Imperatrice d'Austria. Venice: 1818. V. 47

O'MALLEY, C. D.
Leonardo Da Vinci on the Human Body. The Anatomical Physiological and Embryological Drawings of Leonard Da Vinci. New York: 1952. V. 47; 53

O'MALLEY, JOSEPH
Noah's Ark, Vindicated and Explained, A Reply to Dr. Colenso's Difficulties. Melbourne: 1871. V. 50

OMAN, CHARLES
A History of the Peninsular War. Oxford: 1902-30. V. 51

OMAN, CHARLES C.
Wallpapers: a History and Illustrated Catalogue of the Collection of the Victoria and Albert Museum. London: 1982. V. 50

OMAR KHAYYAM
The Original Rubaiyat of Omar Khayyam. Garden City: 1968. V. 52; 54
The Original Rubaiyat of Omar Khayyam. A New Translation. New York: 1968. V. 50
Penillion Omar Khayyam Wedi eu Cyfieithus o'r Berseg i'r Gymraeg gan John Morris-Jones. Newton: 1928. V. 51; 52; 54
The Quatrains of Omar Khayaam of Nishapour. London: 1898. V. 51
Rose Garden of Omar Khayyam. Worcester: 1910. V. 53
The Rose Garden of Omar Khayyam. Worcester: 1932. V. 47
Ruba'ijat des Omar Chajjam von Neschapur. Leipzig: 1907. V. 51
Rubaiyat. London: 1859. V. 48
Rubaiyat. London: 1872. V. 49; 51
The Rubaiyat. Boston;: 1878. V. 48; 49
Rubaiyat. London: 1879. V. 51; 53
The Rubaiyat. Boston: 1881. V. 49
The Rubaiyat. Boston: 1884. V. 47; 52; 53
Rubaiyat. Boston: 1894. V. 52; 54
Rubaiyat. 1896. V. 51
Rubaiyat. New York: 1897. V. 47
Rubaiyat. Springfield: 1897. V. 47
The Rubaiyat. East Aurora: 1898. V. 51

OMAR KHAYYAM continued
The Rubaiyat. London: 1898. V. 48; 49; 51
Rubaiyat. Portland: 1899. V. 49
Rubaiyat. 1900. V. 49
Rubaiyat... Boston: 1900. V. 48
The Rubaiyat. 1901. V. 49
Rubaiyat. Boston: 1901. V. 53; 54
Rubaiyat. London: 1901. V. 50; 51; 52
Rubaiyat. London: 1903. V. 47; 54
The Rubaiyat. London: 1904. V. 47
The Rubaiyat. 1905. V. 50
Rubaiyat. London: 1909. V. 48; 49; 51; 53
Rubaiyat. New York: 1909. V. 48
The Rubaiyat. London: 1910. V. 47; 50
The Rubaiyat. London: 1913. V. 47; 52
Rubaiyat. London: 1915. V. 52
Rubaiyat. Newark: 1915. V. 51
Rubaiyat. London: 1918. V. 48
Rubaiyat. London & Edinburgh: 1919. V. 47
The Rubaiyat. London: 1920. V. 47; 49; 52
The Rubaiyat. London: 1924. V. 48
The Rubaiyat. London and Glasgow: 1927. V. 49
Rubaiyat. London: 1930. V. 48; 51
Rubaiyat. New York: 1930. V. 48; 54
Rubaiyat. New York: 1935. V. 51
The Rubaiyat. 1942. V. 51
Rubaiyat. Jamaica: 1943. V. 49
The Rubaiyat. Waltham St. Lawrence: 1958. V. 47
Rubaiyat. London: 1980. V. 49

OMAR KHAYYAM CLUB
The Book of the Omar Khayyam Club 1892-1910. London: 1910. V. 48

O'MEARA, BARRY EDWARD
Napoleon at St. Helena. London: 1888. V. 49
Napoleon in Exile...A Voice from St. Helena. London: 1822. V. 49

O'MEARA, JAMES
Broderick and Gwin. The Most Extraordinary Contest for a Seat in the Senate of the United States Ever Known. San Francisco: 1881. V. 52
The Vigilance Committee of 1856. San Francisco: 1887. V. 48

O'MELIA, THOMAS A.
First Year Cantonese... Hong Kong: 1939. V. 50

OMMUNDSEN, H.
Rifles and Ammunition and Rifle Shooting. 1913. V. 54

OMNIA Comesta A Belo or, an Answer Out of the West to a Question Out of the North. London?: 1667. V. 52

OMWAKE, JOHN
The Conestoga Six Horse Bell Teams of Eastern Pennsylvania. Cincinnati: 1930. V. 47; 49; 52; 53; 54
The Conestoga Six-Horse Bell Teams. Cincinnati: 1939. V. 54

ON Gates and Gate-Hanging. Cloghjordan: 1830. V. 47

ON Improvements in Marbling the Edges of Books and Paper, a Nineteenth Century Marbling Account Explained and Illustrated with Fourteen Original Marbled Samples. Newtown: 1983. V. 47

ON Lord Nelson's Victory Over the French Fleet at Abouquir. An Idyl. Pisa: 1798. V. 49

ON Native Grounds: An Interpretation of Modern American prose Literature. New York: 1942. V. 49

ON the Ambitious Projects of Russia in Regard to North West America, with Particular Reference to New Albion & New California. San Francisco: 1955. V. 51; 52

ON the Border of the Ocean. Newport. V. 50

ON the Causes of the Progressive Depreciation of the Price of Grain Prior to the Late Scarcity... Madras: 1834. V. 51

ON the Culture of Potatoes: Extracted From Communications Made to the Board of Agriculture in Great Britain. Boston: 1798. V. 51

ON the Distressed State of the Country. London: 1830. V. 53

ON The Green an Anthology for Golfers. London: 1922. V. 50

O'NAN, STEWART
Snow Angels. New York: 1994. V. 54

ONCE a Mouse... New York: 1961. V. 53

ONDAATJE, MICHAEL
Aardvark. Toronto: 1967. V. 52
Claude Glass. Toronto: 1979. V. 51; 53
The Collected Works of Billy the Kid. New York: 1970. V. 52
The Collected Works of Billy the Kid. Toronto: 1970. V. 51; 52
The Collected Works of Billy the Kid. Toronto: 1974. V. 53
The Collected Works of Billy the Kid. London: 1981. V. 54
Coming Through Slaughter. New York: 1976. V. 48; 52
Coming Through Slaughter. Toronto: 1976. V. 50; 51; 52
Coming through Slaughter. London: 1979. V. 50; 51; 54
The Dainty Monsters. Toronto: 1967. V. 50; 52; 53
Elimination Dance. Ilderton: 1978. V. 51; 53
The English Patient. London: 1992. V. 52; 54
The English Patient. New York: 1992. V. 48; 50; 53
The English Patient. Toronto: 1992. V. 52; 53; 54
In the Skin of a Lion. New York: 1987. V. 51; 54
In the Skin of a Lion. Toronto: 1987. V. 52; 53
Leonard Cohen. Toronto: 1970. V. 53
The Man With Seven Toes. 1969. V. 51
The Man with Seven Toes. Toronto: 1969. V. 52
Running in the Family. Toronto: 1982. V. 53
Secular Love. Toronto: 1984. V. 53

ONDERDONK, JULIAN
The Texas Landscape: Drawings by Julian Onderdonk, 1882-192. Mexico. V. 49

ONE Hundred and Fifty Wood Cuts, Selected From the Penny Magazine... London: 1835. V. 49

ONE Hundred Merrie and Delightsome Stories. Carbonnek: 1924. V. 50
ONE Hundred Merrie and Delightsome Stories. Carbonnek: 1925. V. 52

102. or, The Veteran and His Progeny. Boston: 1828. V. 51

ONE Hundred Years' History of the Chinese in Singapore... 1923. V. 54

ONE Night! Which was Begun "One Day", and is Not Brought to a Conclusion Without Being Finished... London: 1812. V. 51

ONE Thousand Quaint Cuts from Books of Other Days, Including Amusing Illustrations from Children's Books, Fables, Chap-Books. London. V. 48

1007:1: A Portfolio of Photographs Representing the Work of Twelve Significant Photographers in Central Illinois. Urbana: 1972. V. 49

ONE Week at Amer, An American City of the Nineteenth Century. Boston and Cambridge: 1857. V. 48

O'NEAL, HANK
A Vision Shared: a Classic Portrait of America and Its People. 1935-1943. New York: 1976. V. 47

O'NEALL, JOHN BELTON
The Annals of Newberry in Two Parts. Newberry: 1892. V. 48; 52

O'NEIL, ELIZABETH
The War 1914-1916. A History and an Explanation for Boys and Girls. London: 1914-17. V. 47

O'NEIL, HENRY
Lectures on Painting Delivered at the Royal Academy With Additional Notes and Appendix. 1866. V. 49; 50; 54
Lectures on Painting Delivered at the Royal academy with Additional Notes and Appendix. London: 1866. V. 51
Satirical Dialogues. London: 1870. V. 48

O'NEILL, CHARLES
The Textile Colourist: a Monthly Journal of Bleaching, Printing, Dyeing and Finishing Textile Fabrics... Manchester: 1876-77. V. 54

O'NEILL, EUGENE GLADSTONE
Ah, Wilderness. New York: 1933. V. 48; 50; 51; 53
Ah, Wilderness. New York: 1972. V. 48; 51; 52; 54
All God's Chillun Got Wings and Welded. New York: 1924. V. 49; 50; 51; 54
Anna Christie. New York: 1930. V. 50
Before Breakfast: a Play in One Act. New York: 1916. V. 49; 51; 52
Beyond the Horizon. New York: 1920. V. 54
The Complete Works of Eugene O'Neill. New York: 1924. V. 51; 54
Days Without End. New York: 1934. V. 48; 49; 50; 51
Desire Under the Elms. New York: 1925. V. 47; 48; 49; 52
Dynamo. New York: 1929. V. 47; 48; 49; 51; 53; 54
The Emperor Jones. Cincinnati: 1921. V. 49; 53
The Emperor Jones. New York: 1921. V. 47; 48; 49; 53
The Emperor Jones. New York: 1928. V. 47; 49; 54
Gold. New York: 1920. V. 47; 48; 49; 52; 53
The Great God, Brown, The Fountain, The Moon of the Caribbees and Other Plays. New York: 1926. V. 53
The Hairy Ape. New York: 1929. V. 47; 50; 53
The Iceman Cometh. New York. V. 47
The Iceman Cometh. New York: 1946. V. 48
The Iceman Cometh. 1982. V. 48; 50
The Iceman Cometh. New York: 1982. V. 47; 48; 49; 51; 52
Lazaraus Laughed. New York: 1927. V. 48; 49; 50; 51; 52; 53; 54
Long Day's Journey into Night. New Haven: 1956. V. 52
Marco Millions. New York: 1927. V. 50; 53; 54
Mourning Becomes Electra. New York: 1931. V. 47; 48; 49; 50; 51; 52; 53
The Plays. New York: 1934. V. 53
The Plays of Eugene O'Neill. New York: 1934-35. V. 47; 48
Provincetown Plays. The Third Series. New York: 1916. V. 47; 54
Strange Interlude. New York: 1928. V. 47; 52; 53; 54
Thirst. Boston: 1914. V. 47; 48; 49; 50; 52; 53; 54
Thirst and Other One Act Plays. Boston: 1924. V. 51
The Works. New York: 1935. V. 50

O'NEILL, HENRY
The Fine Arts and Civilization of Ancient Ireland. London: 1862. V. 47

O'NEILL, JOHN
Clifford Still. New York: 1979. V. 49

O'NEILL, MR.
Six Etchings by William Crotch, From Sketches by Mr. O'Neill, of the Ruins of the Late Fire at Christ Church, Oxford. Oxford: 1809. V. 48

O'NEILL, ROSE
The Kewpies Their Book. New York: 1913. V. 48

O'NEILL, THOMAS
A Concise and Accurate Account of the Proceedings of the Squadron Under the Command of Rear Admiral Sir Sydney Smith, K.S. &c. in Effecting the Escape of the Royal Family of Portugal to the Brazil, on Nov. 29, 1807... London: 1810. V. 52
A Concise and Accurate Account of the Proceedings of the Squadron Under the Command of Rear Admiral Sir Will. Sidney Smith, K.C. in Effecting the Escape, and Escorting the Royal Family of Portugal and the Brazils on the 29th of November, 1807. London: 1809. V. 48

ONETTI, JUAN CARLOS
The Shipyard. New York: 1968. V. 48

ONGANIA, FERDINAND
Calli E Canali: in Venice and in the islands of the Lagoons. Venice: 1899. V. 51
Early Venetian Printing Illustrated. 1895. V. 53
Early Venetian Printing Illustrated. London: 1895. V. 47; 50

ONION, STEPHEN B.
Narrative of the Mutiny on Board the Schooner Plattsburg, William Hackett, Master. Boston: 1819. V. 47

ONIONS, OLIVER
The Compleat Bachelor. London: 1900. V. 52

ONTARIO. BOARD OF HEALTH
First Annual Report of the Provincial Board of Health of Ontario Being for the Year 1882. Toronto: 1883. V. 47

ONTARIO. BUREAU OF ARCHIVES
Third Report of the Bureau of Archives for the Province of Ontario...1905. Toronto: 1906. V. 51

ONTARIO. LEGISLATIVE ASSEMBLY
Emigration to Canada. Toronto: 1869. V. 50

ONWHYN, THOMAS
Illustrations. London: 1837. V. 49
Nicholas Nickleby. India Proofs printed from the Thirty-Eight Original Steel Plates Engraved by T. Onwhyn. London: 1880. V. 54
Thirty-Two Illustrations to Pickwick, by Onwyhn and Other Eminent Artists. London: 1848. V. 54
Thirty-Two Plates to Illustrate the Cheap Edition of Pickwick, Now Publishing. London: 1847. V. 54
Twelve Illustrations to the Pickwick Club...Drawn and Etched in 1847. London: 1894. V. 54

OOD'OWAH Art. Provo: 1970. V. 51

OORT, E. D. VAN
Ornithologia Neerlandica, De Vogels van Nederland. The Hague: 1918-22-35. V. 51; 52

OOSTEN, HENRY VAN
The Dutch Gardener: or, the Compleat Florist. London: 1711. V. 53

THE OPAL: a Pure Gift for the Holy Days. New York: 1844. V. 48

THE OPAL: a Pure Gift for the Holy Days. MDCCCXLV. New York: 1845. V. 48

THE OPERATIONS of the British and the Allied Arms, During the Campaigns of 1743 and 1744, Historically Deducted. London: 1744. V. 47

OPIE, AMELIA
Adeline Mowbray, or The Mother and Daughter, a Tale. London: 1805. V. 50
Detraction Displayed. London: 1828. V. 49; 50
The Father and Daughter, a Tale in Prose. London: 1804. V. 50
Illustrations of Lying, in All Its Branches. London: 1825. V. 50
Illustrations of Lying, in All Its Branches. Boston: 1841. V. 51
Lays for the Dead. London: 1834. V. 50
Madeline, a Tale. London: 1822. V. 54
Memorials of the Life of Amelia Opie... Norwich: 1854. V. 50
The Negro Boy's Tale. Norwich: 1824. V. 47
New Tales. London: 1818. V. 50
Poems. London: 1802. V. 50
Poems. London: 1804. V. 49; 50
Simple Tales. London: 1806. V. 50; 53
Tales of the Heart. London: 1820. V. 47
Tales of the Pemberton Family for the Use of Children. London: 1825. V. 54
Temper, or Domestic Scenes: a Tale. London: 1812. V. 50
The Warrior's Return, and Other Poems. London: 1808. V. 50

OPIE, EUGENE
Disease of the Pancreas, its Cause and Nature. Philadelphia: 1903. V. 49

OPIE, JOHN
The Catalogue of All the Valuable Collection of Lay Figures, Plaister Casts, French Pencils and Brushes, Easels, Books of Prints & Library of Books...The Whole the Property of John Opie. London: 1807. V. 50; 53
Lectures on Painting, Delivered at the Royal Academy of Arts: With a Letter on the Proposal for a Public Memorial of the Naval Glory of Great Britain... London: 1809. V. 48

OPIE, JOHN N.
A Rebel Cavalryman with Lee Stuart and Jackson. Chicago: 1899. V. 51; 52

OPINIONS of Counsel, on the Rights Vested in the Delaware and Raritan Canal and Camden and Amboy Rail Road and Transportation Companies, by the Acts of the State of New Jersey Passed in Relation to Them. Princeton: 1835. V. 47

OPPE, ADOLF PAUL
English Drawings, Stuart and Georgia Periods, in the Collection of His Majesty the King at Windsor Castle. London: 1950. V. 54
Raphael. London: 1964. V. 54
Raphael. London: 1970. V. 50
Raphael. New York: 1970. V. 51; 53
Thomas Rowlandson: His Drawings and Water-Colours. London: 1923. V. 51
The Watercolours of Turner, Cox and De Wint. London: 1925. V. 50

OPPEN, GEORGE
Alpine. Mt. Horeb: 1969. V. 54
Discrete Series. Cleveland: 1966. V. 53
Primitive. 1978. V. 47; 48; 49
Seascape: Needle's Eye. Fremont: 1972. V. 52
This in Which. New York: 1965. V. 53

OPPENHEIM, HERMANN
Diseases of the Nervous System... Philadelphia/Montreal: 1900. V. 50
Diseases of the Nervous System. Philadelphia/London: 1904. V. 53
Text-Book of Nervous Diseases for Physicians and Students. Edinburgh: 1911. V. 53
Text-Book of Nervous Disorders... Chicago: 1911. V. 54

OPPENHEIM, LEO
Glass and Glassmaking in Ancient Mesopotamia. Corning: 1970. V. 49

OPPENHEIM, M.
A History of the Administration of the Royal Navy and of Merchant Shipping in Relation to the Navy from MDIX to MDCLX. London: 1896. V. 50

OPPENHEIM, MAX VON
Tel Halaf. A New Culture in Oldest Mesopotamia. London: 1931. V. 52

OPPENHEIM, MORITZ
Bilder aus Dem Altjudischen Familien-Leben nach Original-Gemalden...Mit Einfurhung und Erlauterungen von Dr. Leopold Stein. Frankfurt: 1882. V. 47; 53

OPPENHEIMER, JOEL
Acts. Mt. Horeb: 1976. V. 51; 54
Del Quien lo Tomo: a Suite. Mt. Horeb: 1982. V. 47
Del Quien Lo Tomo: a Suite. Mt. Horeb: 1983. V. 54
The Dutiful Son. 1956. V. 52
Generations. Poems. 1986. V. 54
The Great American Desert. New York: 1966. V. 54
New Hampshire Journal. Perry Township: 1994. V. 54
New Hampshire Journal: Poems. Mt. Horeb: 1994. V. 52; 54
Notes Towards the Definition of David. Mt. Horeb: 1984. V. 51; 54
Sirventes on a Sad Occurrence. Mt. Horeb: 1967. V. 51; 54

OPPENHEIMER, LEHMANN J.
The Heart of Lakeland. Manchester: 1908. V. 51; 52

OPPENHEIMER, SEYMOUR
The Surgical Treatment of Chronic Suppration of the Middle Ear and Mastoid. Philadelphia: 1906. V. 47; 51; 54

OPPIANUS
Oppian's Halieuticks; of the Nature of Fishes and Fishing of the Ancients. Oxford: 1722. V. 53

OPPRESSION. A Poem. London: 1765. V. 52

OPUSCULA Romana. Volume IV. Lund: 1962. V. 52

THE ORACULUM; or Book of Fate: Consulted by Napoleon Bonaparte, Who Considered It As His Greatest Treasure, Being in the Habit of Refering to It On All Momentous Occasions, Ever Finding Its Revelations the top edge giltruest in Sight into Futurity. London: 1836-41. V. 47

ORAGE, A. R.
Nietzsche - in Outline and Aphorism. Edinburgh: 1901. V. 51
On Love, Freely Adapted from the Tibetan. London: 1932. V. 50

O'RAHILLY, T. F.
Gadelica: a Journal of Modern-Irish Studies. London: 1912/13. V. 52

ORAM, SAMUEL MARSH
Poems: by the Late Mr. Samuel Marsh Oram... London: 1794. V. 48; 51; 54

ORANGE County and the Santa Ana Valley. Santa Ana: 1900. V. 52

ORATIONS of Arsanes Agaynst Philip the Trecherous Kyng of Macedone: of the Embassadors of Venice Against the Prince that Under Crafty League with Scanderbeg, Layed Snared for Christendome... London: 1560. V. 49

ORATORUM Veterum Orationes... Geneva: 1575. V. 52

ORBELIANI, SULKHAN SABA
The Book of Wisdom and Lies. Hammersmith: 1894. V. 49

ORCHARD, WILLIAM C.
Beads and Beadwork of the American Indian. New York: 1929. V. 48

ORCHARD, WILLIAM C. continued
A Rare Salish Blanket. New York: 1926. V. 50

THE ORCHID Album. London: 1882-83. V. 52

ORCHIDS from the Botanical Register. Basel: 1990. V. 50

ORCHIDS from the Botanical Register, 1815-1847. Boston: 1991. V. 52

ORCHIDS of Australia. Melbourne: 1951. V. 47

ORCUTT, WILLIAM DANA
The Flower of Destiny. London: 1906. V. 48
In Quest of the Pefect Book... Boston: 1926. V. 50
In Quest of the Perfect Book Reminiscences and Reflections of a Bookman. London: 1926. V. 54
The Kingdom of Books. Boston: 1927. V. 50; 51
The Magic of the Book; More Reminiscences and Adventures of a Bookman. Boston: 1930. V. 47; 48; 50
The Princess Kallisto & Other Tales of the Fairies. Boston: 1902. V. 49

ORCZY, BARONESS
Lady Molly of Scotland Yard. London: 1910. V. 53
The League of the Scarlet Pimpernel. New York: 1919. V. 48
The Scarlet Pimpernel. London: 1905. V. 54
The Scarlet Pimpernel. London: 1932. V. 48
Sir Percy Hits Back. New York: 1927. V. 51
The Triumph of the Scarlet Pimpernel. 1922. V. 50
Unto Caesar. London: 1914. V. 54

ORD, W. M.
The Climate and Baths of Great Britain and Ireland. 1895-1902. V. 48

DIE Ordensburg Krossinsee Stammfuhrer U. Fuhreranworter, Wunschen Ihren Reichsorganisationsleiter zu Seinem 49. Krossinsee: 1938. V. 49

ORD-HUME, A. W. J. G.
Clockwork Music. New York & London: 1973. V. 48

ORDINAIRE, CLAUDE NICHOLAS
The Natural History of Volcanoes: Including Submarine Volcanoes, and Other Analogous Phenomena. London: 1801. V. 48; 52; 54

THE ORDINARY of the Mass. With the Masses of All the Saints Days of Obligation ; and of All Those Whih are Celebrated on Sundays throughout the Year, as they Occur. 1738. V. 54

THE ORDNANCE Manual for the Use of the Officers of the United States Army. Richmond: 1861. V. 49

ORDOYNO, THOMAS
Nottinghamiensis, or a Systematic Arrangement of the Plants, Growing Naturally in the County of Nottingham; with Their Linnaen and English Names, Generic and Specific Characters in Latin and English... London: 1807. V. 48

ORDRONAUX, JOHN
The Jurisprudence of Medicine in Its Relation to the Law of Contracts, Torts, and Evidence with a Supplement on the Liabilities of Vendors of Drugs. Philadelphia: 1869. V. 49; 54

ORDWAY, FREDERICK I.
Advances in Space Science and Technology. New York: 1959. V. 49

O'REGAN, WILLIAM
Memoirs of the Legal, Literary and Political Life of the Late the Rt. Hon. John Philpot Curran, Once Master of the Rolls in Ireland... London: 1817. V. 51

OREGON & TRANSCONTINENTAL COMPANY
Second Annual Report of the Board of Directors to the Stockholders, for the Year Ending June 30th, 1883. New York: 1883. V. 47

OREGON. Facts Regarding Its Climate, Soil, Mineral and Agricultural Resources... New York: 1880. V. 48

OREGON. LAWS, STATUTES, ETC.
Statutes of a General Nature Passed by the Legislative Assembly of the Territory of Oregon, at the Second Session, Begun and Held at Oregon City, Dec. 2, 1850. Oregon City: 1851. V. 47; 50

OREGON PIONEER ASSOCIATION
Transactions of the Twenty-First Annual Reunion of the Oregon Pioneer Association for 1893... Portland: 1893. V. 53

OREGON RAILWAY & NAVIGATION CO.
East Washington Territory and Oregon... Portland: 1884. V. 52

OREGON. The Cost, and the Consequences. By a Disciple of the Washington School. Philadelphia: 1846. V. 47

O'REILLY, BERNARD
Greenland and the Adjacent Seas, and the North-West Passage to the Pacific Ocean, Illustrated in a Voyage to Davis's Strait, During the Summer of 1817. London: 1818. V. 47; 50; 52; 53

O'REILLY, EDWARD
An Irish-English Dictionary. V. 51; 52
An Irish-English Dictionary. 1864. V. 49; 50
An Irish-English Dictionary. London: 1864. V. 51

O'REILLY, HARRINGTON
Fifty Years on the Trail, a True Story of Western Life. New York: 1889. V. 49

O'REILLY, HENRY
Origin and Objects of the Slaveholders' Conspiracy Against Democratic Principles, as Well as Against the National Union Illustrated in the Speeches of Andrew Jackson Hamilton. New York: 1862. V. 49

O'REILLY, JOHN
The Anatomy and Physiology of the Placenta. New York: 1860. V. 51

O'REILLY, JOHN BOYLE
Songs, Legends and Ballads. Boston: 1878. V. 51

O'REILLY, MONTAGU
Pianos of Sympathy. Norfolk: 1936. V. 48

O'REILLY, ROBERT, MRS.
Doll World or Play and Earnest. A Study from Real Life. London: 1872. V. 50

OREM, WILLIAM
A Description of the Chanonry in Old Aberdeen, in the Years 1724 and 1725. London: 1782. V. 48

OREY, LEONOR D'
The Silver Service of the Portuguese Crown. Lisbon: 1991. V. 47; 50

ORFILA, M.
Directions for the Treatment of Persons Who Have taken Poison, and Those in a State of Apparent Death... London: 1818. V. 51

ORGANIZATION and Status of Missouri Troops (Union and Confederate) in Service During the War. Washington: 1902. V. 48

ORIBASIUS
Synopseos ad Eustathium Filium Lib. Novem: Quibus Tota Medicina in Compendium Redacta Contrinetur... Paris: 1554. V. 52

ORIENTAL CERAMIC SOCIETY
Transactions. London: 1945-74. V. 49

ORIENTAL Series: China and Japan. Boston and Tokyo: 1901. V. 53

THE ORIENTALIST. London: 1850. V. 53

ORIGEN
Origenis Adamantii Operum Tomi Duo Priores, Cum Tabulis and Indice Generali Proxime Sequentibus. Paris: 1512. V. 50

THE ORIGIN of Printing. London: 1776. V. 48

THE ORIGIN of the Gallic Plant, with Its Baneful Influence in the Garden of Europe. Manchester: 1799. V. 48

ORIGIN of the Town of Hamburg, South Carolina, America, Founded by Henry Shultz, July 2, 1821... Augusta: 1837. V. 48

THE ORIGINAL and Only Punch and Judy. Direct from London. New York: 1890. V. 48

ORIGINAL Compositions in Prose and Verse, Illustrated With Lithographic Drawings; to Which is Added some vocal and Instrumental Music. London: 1833. V. 52

THE ORIGINAL Institution, Power and Jurisdiction of Parliaments. London: 1707. V. 51

AN ORIGINAL Leaf from the First Edition of Alexander Barclay's English Translation of Sebastian Brant's Ship of Fools. San Francisco: 1938. V. 49

AN ORIGINAL Leaf from the Polycronicon Printed by William Caxton at Westminster in the Year 1482. San Francisco: 1938. V. 49

ORIGINAL Letters to an Honest Sailor. London: 1746. V. 47

ORIGINAL Papers Relative to Tanjore; Containing All the Letters Which Passed, and the Conferences Which Passed, and the conferences Which Were Held between His Highness the Nabob of Arcot and Lord Pigiot, on the Subject of the Restoration of Tanjore. London: 1777. V. 48; 52

ORIGINAL Shaker Music Published by the North Family of Mt. Lebanon, Col. Co., New York. New York: 1893. V. 49

THE ORIGINAL Story of Romeo and Juliet from Which Shakespeare Evidently Drew the Subject of His Drama... Cambridge: 1868. V. 51

ORIOLI, GIUSEPPE
Adventures of a Bookseller. Florence. V. 52
Adventures of a Bookseller. Florence: 1932?. V. 50
Adventures of a Bookseller. Florence: 1937. V. 54

O'RIORDAN, MICHAEL
Connolly Column. The Story of the irishmen Who Fought for the Spanish Republic 1936-1939. Dublin: 1979. V. 49

ORLANDI, PELLEGRINO ANTONIO
Repertorium Sculptile-Typicum; or a Complete Collection and Explantion of the Several Marks and Cyphers by Which the Prints of the Best Engravers are Distinguished. London: 1730. V. 49; 51

ORLANDINI, NICOLO
Historiae Societatis Iesv. Antwerp: 1620. V. 51

ORLEANS, CHARLES DE VALOIS, DUC D'
Poems. Paris: 1950. V. 49

ORLEANS, M. LOUISE PHILIP JOSEPH, DUC D'
The Memoire of...accused of High Treason, Before the Tribunal of the Chatelet in Paris; with the Very Interesting Advice of His Counsel as to the Punishment of His Accusers in which is Contained an Authentick Detail of Many Curious Facts... Dublin: 1791. V. 52

ORLEANS, PIERRE JOSEPH D'
The History of the Revolutions in England Under the Family of the Stuarts, From the Year 1603, to 1690. London: 1711. V. 48; 50; 53

ORLEANS, PRINCE HENRI D'
From Tonkin to India by the Sources of the Irawadi 1895-96. London: 1898. V. 49
From Tonkin to India by the Sources of the Irawadi January 95-January 96. New York: 1898. V. 49

ORLEBAR, F. ST. J.
The Adventures of Her Serene Limpness, the Moon-Faced Princess. London: 1888. V. 50

ORLEN, STEVEN
Sleeping on Doors. Lisbon: 1975. V. 54

ORLOFSKY, PATSY
Quilts in America. New York: 1974. V. 53

ORLOV, ALEXANDER
The Secret History of Stalin's Crimes. London: 1954. V. 49

ORLOVSKY, PETER
Lepers Cry. New York: 1972. V. 54

ORME, ROBERT
Historical Fragments of the Mogul Empire. London: 1782. V. 54
A History of the Military Transactions of the British Nation in Indostan, from the Year MDCCXLV. London: 1803-05. V. 54

ORME, WILLIAM
Rudiments of Landscape Drawing and Perspective. London: 1801. V. 48
Rudiments of Landscape Drawing and Perspective. London: 1801-02. V. 50

ORMEROD, GEORGE
History of the County of the Palatine and the City of Chester. London: 1819. V. 47; 50; 53
Parentalia - Genealogical Memoirs. London: 1851. V. 47

ORMEROD, T.
Calderdale, a Descriptive Account of the Streams Forming the Lancashire Calder... Burnley: 1906. V. 48; 53

ORMEROD, W. P.
Clinical Collections and Observations in Surgery, Made During an Attendance on the Surgical Practice of St. Bartholomew's Hospital. London: 1846. V. 50

ORMOND, JOHN
Cathedral Builders and Other Poems. 1991. V. 52

ORMOND, RICHARD
John Sargent Singer. London: 1970. V. 52; 54
John Singer Sargent: Paintings, Drawings, Watercolors. New York: 1970. V. 49; 53

ORMONDE, MARQUIS OF
An Autumn in Sicily. Dublin: 1850. V. 49
The Manuscripts of the Marquis of Ormonde, Preserved at the Castle Kilkenny. (First Series). & (New Series). London: 1895-09/02-08. V. 49

ORMSBY, WATERMAN LILLY
Ormsby's Pentographic Illustrations of the Holy Scriptures; Being Accurate Copies of Sir Edward Thomason's Celebrated Medals with a Condensed History of the Bible. New York: 1835. V. 52

ORNAMENTAL and Early English Alphabets, Initial Letters, &c. For Engravers, Desingers, Marble Masons, Painters, Decorators, Etc. London: 1858. V. 51; 54

ORNAMENTAL PHEASANT SOCIETY OF AMERICA
Yearbook of the Ornamental Pheasant Society of America. Wallingford: 1936. V. 47

ORNAMENTAL Toys and How to Make Them. Boston: 1850. V. 49

ORNDUFF, DONALD R.
Casement of Juniata. As a Man and As a Stockman...One of a Kind. Kansas City: 1975. V. 49

O'RORKE, T.
History, Antiquities and Present State of...Ballysdare & Kilvarnet. London: 1888. V. 47

OROSIUS, PAULUS
Adversus Paganos Historiarum, Libri Spetem. Cologne: 1526. V. 49
Historiae Adversus Paganos. Venice: 1483. V. 53
Historiae Adversus Paganos. Venice: 1499. V. 51; 53

OROZCO
Libro de Las Vidas y Martyrios de los Bienaventurados Sant Juan Baptista, y sant Juan Evangelista. Alcala de Henares: 1581. V. 50

OROZCO, JOSE CLEMENTE
Jose Clemente Orozco. New York: 1932. V. 51

ORPEHUS
The Mystical Initiations; or, Hymns of Orpheus. London: 1787. V. 54

ORPEN, ADELA
The Chronicles of Sid,. London: 1893. V. 52

ORPEN, CHARLES EDWARD HERBERT
Anecdotes and Annals of the Deaf and Dumb. London: 1836. V. 52

ORPEN, GODDARD H.
Ireland Under the Normans. London: 1911/20. V. 53

ORPEN, WILLIAM
An Onlooker in France. 1917-1919. London: 1924. V. 47

THE ORPHAN of the Alps; or, the Victim of Duplicity. Birmingham: 1808. V. 53

ORR, ADRIAN VAN BROCKLIN
Mormonism Dissected, or Knavery "On Two Sticks", Exposed. Lancaster County: 1841. V. 53

ORR, AILEEN
Miss Manners. London: 1909. V. 49

ORR, H. WINNETT
A List of Books and Pamphlets on the History of Surgery and Orthopedic Surgery. The Collection of Dr. H. Winnett Orr. Lincoln: 1943. V. 50

ORR, HECTOR
The Native American: a Gift for the People. Philadelphia: 1845. V. 50

ORR, J. W.
Pictorial Guide to the Falls of Niagara: a Manual for Visiters (sic)... Buffalo: 1842. V. 54

ORR, MONRO S.
The Alphabet Set Forth in Six and Twenty Pictures. London: 1931. V. 49

ORR, THOMAS
Life History of...Pioneer Stories of California and Utah. Placerville: 1930. V. 47

ORRERY, CHARLES BOYLE, 4TH EARL OF
Dr. Bentley's Dissertation on the Epistles of Phalaris and the Fables of Aesop Examin'd. London: 1698. V. 49

ORRERY, ROGER BOYLE, 1ST EARL OF
English Adventures. London: 1676. V. 52
The History of Henry the Fifth and the Tragedy of Mustapha, Son of Solyman the Magnificent. London: 1672. V. 47
A Treatise of the Art of War: Dedicated to the Kings Most Excellent Majesty. London: 1677. V. 53
Two New Tragedies. The Black Prince, and Tryphon. London: 1672. V. 47; 52

ORRIN, H. C.
Facial Grafting in Principle and Practice, an Illustrated Manual of Procedure and Technique. London: 1928. V. 47

ORRINSMITH, LUCY
The Drawing Room, Its Decorations and Furniture. London: 1877. V. 50

ORS, EUGENIO D'
Pablo Picasso. New York: 1930. V. 47; 50; 52

ORSINI, FULVIO
Familiae Romanae Quae Reperiuntur in Antiquis Numismatibus ab Urbe Condita ad Tempora Divi Augusti ex Bibliotheca Fulvii Ursini... Rome: 1577. V. 53

ORSON, B.
Facts and Experiments on the Use of Sugar in Feeding Cattle... London: 1809. V. 50

ORTA, GARCIA DE
Aromatum, et Simplicium Aliquot Medicamentorum Apud Indos Nascentium Historia... Antwerp: 1579. V. 52

ORTEGA, CASIMIRO GOMEZ
Elenchus Plantarum Horti Regii Botanici Matritensis. Madrid: 1796. V. 49

ORTEGA, LUIS B.
California Stock Horse... Sacramento: 1948/49. V. 47
California Stock Horse. Sacramento: 1949. V. 48

ORTELIUS, ABRAHAM
His Epitome of the Theater of the Worlde. London: 1603. V. 47
Thesaurus Geographicus, Recognitus et Auctus... Antwerp: 1596. V. 51

THE ORTHODOX Communicant, by Way of Meditation on the Order for the Administration of the Lords Supper... London: 1721. V. 48; 49

ORTIGUE, PIERRE D'
The Art of Pleasing in Conversation. London: 1708. V. 52

ORTIZ, GEORGE
In Pursuit of the Absolute Art of the Ancient World from the George Oritz Collection. London: 1994. V. 52

ORTIZ, ROXANNE DUNBAR
The Great Sioux Nationa. San Francisco: 1977. V. 50

ORTIZ, SIMON J.
From Sand Creek. Oak Park: 1981. V. 50
Going for the Rain. New York: 1976. V. 50

ORTON, JAMES
The Andes and the Amazons; or, Across the Continent of South America. New York: 1870. V. 51
The Proverbialist and the Poet. Philadelphia: 1852. V. 48
Underground Treasures: How and Where to Find Them. Philadelphia: 1899. V. 47

ORTON, JOE
Entertaining Mr. Sloane. London: 1964. V. 50; 51
Entertaining Mr. Sloane. New York: 1965. V. 54

ORTON, RICHARD H.
Records of California Men in the War of the Rebellion, 1861-1867. Sacramento: 1890. V. 52

ORVIS, CHARLES F.
Fishing with the Fly. Boston: 1892. V. 47

ORWELL, GEORGE
Animal Farm. London: 1945. V. 47; 49; 50
Animal Farm. London: 1946. V. 48
Animal Farm. New York: 1946. V. 47; 48; 50; 51; 52
British Pamphleteers. London: 1948. V. 47; 51
British Pamphleteers from the Sixteenth Century to the Nineteen Thirties. London: 1948-51. V. 48
Burmese Days. New York: 1934. V. 47
Burmese Days. London: 1935. V. 50
The Clergyman's Daughter. New York: 1936. 52; 54
The Collected Essays, Journalism and Letters... London: 1924. V. 51
The Collected Essays, Journalism and Letters... London: 1968. V. 49; 50; 51
The Collected Essays, Journalism and Letters. New York: 1968. V. 49
Coming Up for Air. New York: 1950. V. 47
Critical Essays. London: 1946. V. 47; 50
Dickens, Dali and Others. New York: 1946. V. 50
Down and Out In Paris and London. New York & London: 1933. V. 47; 49; 53
England Your England, and Other Essays. London: 1953. V. 47; 49; 50
The English People. London: 1947. V. 47; 50; 51; 53
Homage to Catalonia. London: 1938. V. 49
Homage to Catalonia. New York: 1952. V. 53
Inside the Whale and Other Essays. London: 1940. V. 50
James Burnham and the Managerial Revolution. London: 1946. V. 48; 49; 52
Keep the Aspidistra Flying. London: 1936. V. 50; 52
Keep the Aspidistra Flying. New York: 1956. V. 48; 51
Kolhosp Tvarin. (Animal Farm). Munich: 1947. V. 51
The Lion and the Unicorn. Socialism and the English Genius. London: 1941. V. 47; 49; 50; 51; 53
Nineteen Eighty-Four. 1948. V. 48; 49; 52; 53; 54
Nineteen Eighty-Four. London: 1949. V. 47; 48; 49; 52; 53
Nineteen Eighty-Four. New York: 1949. V. 47; 48; 50; 51; 53
Nineteen Eighty-Four. London: 1984. V. 53
Politics and the English Language. Evansville: 1947. V. 49
The Road to Wigan Pier. London: 1937. V. 47; 49; 50; 51; 52; 53
The Road to Wigan Pier. New York: 1958. V. 47; 50; 51; 53
Shooting an Elephant and Other Essays. London: 1950. V. 47
Talking to India - a Selection of English Language Broadcasts to India. London: 1943. V. 52
The War Broadcasts and The War Commentaraies. London: 1985. V. 50

OSAWA, S.
Evolution of Life, Fossils and Molecules. Berlin: 1991. V. 48

OSBALDESTON, GEORGE
Squire Osbaldeston: His Autobiography. London: 1926. V. 47

OSBALDISTON, WILLIAM A.
The British Sportsman, or Nobleman, Gentleman and Farmer's Dictionary of Recreation and Amusement. London: 1792. V. 51; 52

OSBECK, PETER
A Voyage to China and the East Indies... London: 1771. V. 48; 53; 54

OSBORN, ALMENA
Biography and Early Life Sketch of the Late Abram Sortore Including His Trip to California and Back. Alexandria: 1909. V. 54

OSBORN, BENJAMIN
Truth Displayed: in a Series of Elementary Principles, Illustrated and Enforced by Practical Observations. Rutland: 1816. V. 51

OSBORN, FRANCIS
The Works...Divine, Moral, Historical, Political. London: 1682. V. 52

OSBORN, H. F.
The Age of Mammals in Europe, Asia and North America. New York: 1910. V. 48
Bibliography of the Published Writings of Henry Fairfield Osborn for the Years 1877-1915. New York: 1916. V. 48
Proboscidea, a Monograph of the Discovery, Evolution, Migration and Extinction... New York: 1936. V. 53
The Titanotheres of Ancient Wyoming, Dakota and Nebraska. Washington: 1929. V. 49

OSBORN, HENRY S.
Plants of the Holy Land with Their Fruits and Flowers. Philadelphia: 1860. V. 53

OSBORN, JOHN JAY
The Paper Chase. Boston: 1971. V. 51

OSBORN, SELLECK
Poems, Moral, Sentimental and Satirical. Boston: 1823. V. 47; 54

OSBORN, SHERARD
A Cruise in Japanese Waters. Edinburgh: 1859. V. 48; 51
The Past and Future of British Relations in China. Edinburgh: 1860. V. 54
Quedah; or, Stray Leaves from a Journal in Malayan Waters. London: 1857. V. 48

OSBORN, WILLIAM COOK
The Plea of "Not Guilty", or the Evils Arising from the Present Mode of Arraigning Prisoners, Considered in a Letter to...Sir G. Grey... London: 1847. V. 48

OSBORNE, CHARLES
Swansong. London: 1968. V. 47

OSBORNE, CHARLES FRANCIS
Historic Houses and Their Gardens. Philadelphia: 1908. V. 51

OSBORNE, DOROTHY
Letters to Sir William Temple 1652-54. New York: 1888. V. 53

OSBORNE, DUFFIELD
Engraved Gems: Signets, Talismans and Ornamental Intaglios, Ancient and Modern. New York: 1912. V. 49

OSBORNE, E. ALLEN
In Letters of Red. London: 1938. V. 50

OSBORNE, E. C.
Osborne's Guide to the Grand Junction, or Birmingham, Liverpool, and Manchester Railway... Birmingham: 1838. V. 54

OSBORNE, FRANCIS
Advice to a Son. The Second Part. London: 1658. V. 50
Political Reflections Upon the Government of the Turks. London: 1656. V. 48
The Works of... London: 1673. V. 53

OSBORNE, JOHN
The Entertainer. London: 1957. V. 50; 53
Epitaph for George Dillon. London: 1958. V. 52
Look Back in Anger. London: 1957. V. 49; 54
Luther. New York: 1962. V. 54
A Place Calling Itself Rome. Helsinki: 1989. V. 48; 53
Tom Jones. London: 1964. V. 53

OSBORNE, L.
Indian Crafts of Guatemala and El Salvador. Norman: 1965. V. 54

OSBORNE, THOMAS
A Catalogue of Some Tracts and Pamphlets Collected by the Late Earl of Oxford... London: 1747. V. 48
A Catalogue of the Libraries of the Honourable Sir. Luke Schaub, Bart. And of Several Noblemen and Gentlemen... London: 1759. V. 54
A Catalogue of the Libraries of the Late Dr. Cromwell Mortimer, Secretary to the Royal Society, Edmund Pargiter, Esq...(together with) The Second Volume... London: 1753-54. V. 54
The First (and Second) Part of T. Osborne's Catalogue of Books, of Several Very Considerable Libraries for the Year 1752. London: 1752. V. 54
Memoirs Relating to the Impeachment of Thomas Earl of Danby...in the Year 1678. London: 1710. V. 50

OSBOURN, JAMES
North Carolina Sonnets, or a Selection of Choice Hymns for the Use of Old School Baptists. Baltimore: 1844. V. 51

OSBOURNE, KATHARINE D.
Robert Louis Stevenson in California. Chicago: 1910. V. 48

OSGOOD, CORNELIUS
The Chinese: a Study of a Hong Kong Community. Tucson: 1975. V. 49; 53

OSGOOD, ERNEST STAPLES
The Day of the Cattleman. Minneapolis: 1929. V. 47; 53; 54
The Field Notes of Captain William Clark, 1803-1805. New Haven and London: 1964. V. 52; 53; 54

OSGOOD, FRANCES S.
The Floral Offering, a Token of Friendship. Philadelphia: 1847. V. 47
The Flower Alphabet in Gold and Colors. Boston: 1845. V. 48
The Poetry of Flowers... New York: 1841. V. 52; 54

OSGOOD, HENRY O.
So This Is Jazz. Boston: 1926. V. 53; 54

OSGOOD, JOSEPH BARLOW FELT
Notes of Travel or Recollections of Majunga, Zanzibar, Muscat, Aden, Mocha and Other Eastern Ports. Salem: 1854. V. 47; 48

OSGOOD, SAMUEL
American Leaves: Familiar Notes of Thought and Life. New York: 1867. V. 48

O'SHAUGHNESSY, ARTHUR
Music and Moonlight: Poems and Songs. London: 1874. V. 51; 53

OSKISON, JOHN M.
Brothers Three. New York: 1935. V. 50
Tecumseh and His Times. New York: 1938. V. 50
A Texas Titan. Garden City: 1929. V. 50
Wild Harvest. New York: 1925. V. 50

OSLER, EDWARD
The Life of Admiral Viscount Exmouth. London: 1835. V. 49; 54

OSLER, F.
Electric Light Fittings. London and Birmingham: 1900. V. 53

OSLER, WILLIAM
Addison's Disease. 1896. V. 49
Aequanimitas and Other Addresses. Philadelphia: 1904. V. 47; 54
Aequanimitas and Other Addresses. Philadelphia: 1905. V. 49; 50; 52; 53
Aequanimitas and Other Addresses. Philadelphia: 1906. V. 49; 50
An Alabama Student. Baltimore: 1896. V. 49
An Alabama Student and Other Biographical Addresses. London: 1909. V. 49; 50; 52
An Alabama Student and Other Biographical Addresses. London: 1926. V. 50
An Alabama Student and Other Biographical Essays. London: 1929. V. 52
An Alabama Student and...Essays. London: 1908. V. 47; 48; 49; 51

OSLER, WILLIAM continued
An Alabama Student and...Essays. New York: 1908. V. 49; 52; 54
Aneurism of the Descending Thoracic Aorta. 1903. V. 49
Aneurysm of the Abdominal Aorta. 1905. V. 49
An Annotated Bibliography with Illustrations. San Francisco: 1988. V. 50; 52
Atrophy of the Stomach, with the Clinical Features of Progressive Pernicious Anaemia. 1886. V. 49; 54
Bibliotheca Osleriana. Oxford: 1929. V. 47; 48; 49; 51; 52; 53; 54; 54
Bibliotheca Osleriana. Montreal: 1969. V. 50
Bibliotheca Osleriana. Montreal: 1987. V. 47; 48; 49; 50; 51
The Bicuspid Condition of the Aortic Valves. 1886. V. 51
The Bicuspid Condition of the Aortic Valves. London: 1886. V. 49
Cancer of the Stomach: a Clinical Study. Philadelphia: 1900. V. 49; 52; 54
Case of Progressive Pernicious Anemia. Montreal: 1877. V. 48; 50
Chronic Infectious Endocarditis. 1909. V. 49; 51
A Clinical Lecture on Erythraemia (Polycythaemia with Cyanosis, Maladie de Vaquez). 1908. V. 49; 54
A Clinical Lecture on the Ball-Valve Gall-Stone in the Common Duct. 1897. V. 49; 54
The Collected Essays of Sir William Osler. Birmingham: 1985. V. 52
The Coming of Age of Internal Medicine in America. 1915. V. 49; 54
A Concise History of Medicine. Baltimore: 1919. V. 50
Doctor and Nurse: Remarks to the First Class of Graduates from the Training School for Nurses of the Johns Hopkins Hospital. Baltimore: 1891. V. 49; 50
Elisha Bartlett, a Rhode Island Philosopher. Providence: 1900. V. 53
The Evolution of Modern Medicine. New Haven: 1921. V. 47; 48; 49; 50; 51
The Evolution of Modern Medicine. New York: 1921. V. 52
The Evolution of Modern Medicine. New Haven: 1922. V. 49; 50
The Evolution of Modern Medicine. New York: 1922. V. 54
Fatal Angina Pectoris, Without Lesions of the Coronary Arteries in a Young Man. 1900. V. 49
Fatal Angina Pectoris Without Lesions of the Coronary Arteries in a Young Man. London: 1900. V. 54
The Growth of Truth as Illustrated in the Discovery of the Circulation of the Blood. London: 1906. V. 52
Incunabula Medica: a Study of the Earliest Printed Medical Books, 1467-1480. Oxford: 1923. V. 52; 54
Internal Medicine as a Vocation. An Address Before the Section on General Medicine at the New York Academy of Medicine, October 19, 1897. V. 47
Internal Secretions, Considered in Their Physiological, Pathological and Clinical Aspects. 1897. V. 47
John Keats. The Apothecary Poet. Baltimore: 1896. V. 47; 49
Lectures on Angina Pectoris and Allied States. New York: 1897. V. 49; 52; 54
Lectures on the Diagnosis of Abdominal Tumors. New York: 1895. V. 52
Lectures on the Diagnosis of Abdominal Tumors... New York: 1898. V. 51; 52
The Life of Sir William Osler. Oxford: 1925. V. 48
The Lumleian Lectures on Angina Pectoris. 1910. V. 49; 54
Man's Redemption of Man. New York: 1913. V. 49; 50
Men and Books. Pasadena: 1959. V. 52; 54
Modern Medicine, Its Theory and Practice. Philadelphia: 1907-10. V. 49; 54
Notes on Aneurism. 1902. V. 49
Notes on Aneurism. London: 1902. V. 54
Observations On the Severe Anaemias of Pregnancy and the Post-Partum State. 1919. V. 49; 54
The Old Humanities and the New Science. 1919. V. 49; 50
The Old Humanities and the New Science. Boston: 1920. V. 47; 49; 50; 52; 54
On a Family form of Recurring Epistaxis, Associated with Multiple Telangiectases of the Skin and Mucus Membranes. 1901. V. 49
On Cholera and Choreiform Affections. Philadelphia: 1894. V. 47; 54
On Six Cases of Addison's Disease, with the Report of a Case Greatly Benefitted by the Use of the Supra-Renal Extract. 1896. V. 49; 54
On Some Points in the Etiology and Pathology of Ulcerative Endocarditis. London: 1881. V. 49; 54
On the Need of a Radical Reform in Our Methods of Teaching Senior Students. 1903. V. 49
The Principles and Practice of Medicine. Edinburgh & London: 1892. V. 52
The Principles and Practice of Medicine. New York: 1892. V. 47; 48; 49; 50; 51; 52; 53; 54
The Principles and Practice of Medicine. New York: 1893. V. 49
The Principles and Practice of Medicine. New York: 1894. V. 54
The Principles and Practice of Medicine. New York: 1896. V. 52; 54
The Principles and Practice of Medicine. New York: 1898. V. 49
The Principles and Practice of Medicine. New York: 1899. V. 50
The Principles and Practice of Medicine. New York: 1900. V. 51
The Principles and Practice of Medicine. London: 1901. V. 47
The Principles and Practice of Medicine. New York and London: 1907. V. 52
The Principles and Practice of Medicine... New York & London: 1909. V. 49; 54
The Principles and Practice of Medicine. Birmingham: 1978. V. 52
Remarks on Arterio-Venous Aneurysm. 1915. V. 54
Remarks on Arterio-Venous Aneurysm. London: 1915. V. 49
Science and Immortality. Boston: 1904. V. 50; 52; 54
Science and Immortality. London: 1904. V. 49
Science and War. Oxford: 1915. V. 49; 54
Studies in Typhoid Fever. Nos. I, II, and III. Baltimore: 1901. V. 49; 50; 52
Teacher and Student. 1893. V. 49
Teacher and Student. London: 1893. V. 50
A Text Book of the Theory and Practice of Medicine. London: 1893-94. V. 50
The Third Corpuscle of the Blood. 1883. V. 54
Thomas Linacre. Cambridge: 1908. V. 49; 52; 54
Unity, Peace and Concord. A Farewell Address to the Medical Profession in the United States. Oxford: 1905. V. 49; 50
A Way of Life... London: 1913. V. 47
A Way of Life. London: 1918. V. 54

OSLO UNIVERSITY. LIBRARY
Bibliotheca Polynesiana. A Catalogue of some of the Books in the Polynesiana Collection Formed by the Late Bjarne Kroepelien and Now in the Oslo University Library. Oslo: 1969. V. 51

OSMASATON, F. P. B.
The Paradise of Tintoretto. Flansham: 1910. V. 54

OSMASTON, F. P. B.
The Paradise of Tintoretto. Bognor, Sussex: 1910. V. 47

OSMOND, R.
John Singer Sargent: Paintings, Drawings, Watercolors. New York: 1970. V. 48; 50; 51

OSMONT, J. B. L.
Dictionnaire Typographique, Historique et Critique des Livres Rares, Singuliers, Estimes et Recherches en tous Genres. Paris: 1768. V. 51

OSORIO, JERONYMO, BP. OF SILVES
De Iustitia Caelesti Libri Decem. Cologne: 1581. V. 48
De Rebus Emmanuelis REgis Lusitaniae Gestis. Cologne: 1574. V. 51
De Regis Institvtione et Disciplina, Libri Octo... Cologne: 1588. V. 51
De Regis Institutione et Disciplina. Lib. VIII. Ad Sereniissiumum et Invictissimum Portugaliae Regem. Sebastianum, E.N.I. Lisbon: 1572. V. 53

OSORIO, MARIANO
Conducta Militar y Politica del General en Gefe del Exercito del Rey en Oposicion con la de los Caudillos que Tiranizaban el Reymo de Chile. Sanliago (sic): 1814. V. 53

OSSIANNILSON, F.
The Psylloidea (Homoptera) of Fennoscandia and Denmark. 1992. V. 50

OSSOLI, SARAH MARGARET FULLER, MARCHESA D'
Conversations with Goethe In the Last Years of His Life. Boston: 1839. V. 50
Life Without and Life Within; or, Reviews, Narratives, Essays and Poems. Boston: 1860. V. 50
The Love Letters of Margaret Fuller 1845-1846. New York: 1903. V. 53
Memoirs of Margaret Fuller Ossoli. Boston: 1852. V. 47; 48; 49; 50; 51; 52
Memoirs of Margaret Fuller Ossoli. London: 1852. V. 49; 52
Memoirs of Margaret Fuller Ossoli. Boston: 1857. V. 47
A Summer on the Lakes in 1843. Boston: 1844. V. 50
Woman in the Nineteenth Century. New York: 1845. V. 53
Woman in the Nineteenth Century and Kindred Papers. Boston: 1855. V. 47; 50; 51; 53
Woman in the Nineteenth Century, And Kindred Papers Relating to Sphere, Condition and Duties of Woman. Boston: 1875. V. 48

OSTRANDER, ALSON B.
An Army Boy of the Sixties: a Story of the Plains. Yonkers: 1924. V. 54

OSTRICH PLUME CO.
The Products of Our Farms... Milwaukee: 1910-20. V. 51

OSTROGORSKI, MOISE
The Rights of Women. London: 1893. V. 50; 51; 53; 54

OSTWALD, WILHELM
Colour Science... London: 1931-33. V. 48

OSTWALD, WOLFGANG
An Introduction to Theoretical and Applied Colloid Chemistry. New York: 1917. V. 50

O'SULLIVAN, DONAL
The Life, Times and Music of an Irish Harper. London: 1958. V. 51

O'SULLIVAN, LAWRENCE
The Miscreant. New York: 1969. V. 54

O'SULLIVAN, M. J.
A Fasciculus of Lyric Verses. Cork: 1846. V. 47; 53

O'SULLIVAN, PHILIP
A Sourcebook on Planning Law in Ireland. 1984. V. 49

O'SULLIVAN, VINCENT
A Book of Bargains. London: 1896. V. 50
The Green Window. London: 1899. V. 50

O'SULLIVAN, WILLIAM
The Economic History of Cork City from the Earliest Times. 1937. V. 48

OSUMI, TAMEZO
Printed Cottons of Asia. Tokyo & Rutland: 1963. V. 51

OSUNA, FRANCISCO DE
Ley de Amor y Quarta Parte del Abecedario Espiritual... Seville: 1542. V. 53

OSWALD, ARTHUR
Country Houses of Dorset. London: 1935. V. 54

OSWALD, FELIX
Index of Figure-Types on Terra Sigillata. 1936-37. V. 52

OSWALD, JOHN
Poems; to Which is Added, the Humours of John Bull, an Operatic Farace, in Two Acts. London: 1789. V. 51

OSWANDEL, J. JACOB
Notes Of the Mexican War, 1846-1847-1848. Philadelphia: 1885. V. 49

OTERO, L. S.
Butterflies: Beauty and Behaviour of Brazilian Species. Rio de Janeiro: 1990. V. 52

OTERO, MIGUEL ANTONIO
My Life on the Frontier 1864-1882. New York: 1935. V. 49
My Nine Years as Governor 1897-1906. Albuquerque: 1940. V. 49; 50
The Real Billy the Kid, With New Light on the Lincoln County War. New York: 1936. V. 49

OTERO, ROBERT
Forever Picasso: an Intimate Look at His Last Years. New York: 1974. V. 50

OTES, TITUS
The Tryals, Convictions and Sentence of Titus Otes, Upon Two Indictments for Willful, Malicious and Corrupt Perjury; at the Kings-Bench-Bar at Westminster, Before the Right Hon. George Lord Jeffreys...Lord Chief Justice of His Majesties Court of Kings... London: 1685. V. 52

OTIS, F. N.
History of the Panama Railroad and of the Pacific Mail Steamship Company. Together with A Traveller's Guide and Buisness Man's Hand-Book for the Panama Railroad. New York: 1867. V. 52
Illustrated History of the Panama Railroad: Together with a Traveller's Guide and Business Man's Handbook... New York: 1861. V. 47

OTIS, GEORGE A.
A Report on Amputations at the Hip-Joint. Washington: 1867. V. 54
A Report on the Excisions of the Head of the Femur for Gunshot Injury. Washington: 1869. V. 52
A Report to the Surgeon General on the Transport of Sick and Wounded by Pack Animals. Washington: 1877. V. 48

OTIS, JAMES
Toby Tyler or Ten Weeks with a Circus. New York: 1881. V. 52

OTLEY, JONATHAN
A Concise Description of the English Lakes, and Adjacent Mountains... Keswick: 1825. V. 52
A Concise Description of the English Lakes and Adjacent Mountains... Keswick: 1834. V. 50; 52
A Concise Description of the English Lakes and Adjacent Mountains... Keswick: 1838. V. 54
A Descriptive Guide to the English Lakes, and Adjacent Mountains... Keswick: 1842. V. 50; 52
A Descriptive Guide to the English Lakes, and Adjacent Mountains. Keswick: 1850. V. 52

OTRANTO, JOSEPH FOUCHE, DUKE OF
Memoirs of Joseph Fouche, Duke of Otranto, Minister of the General Police of France. London: 1825. V. 50

OTT, ISAAC
The Action of Medicines. Philadelphia: 1878. V. 49; 54

OTTAVIANO, E.
Angiosperm Pollen and Ovules. Berlin: 1992. V. 50

OTTER, WILLIAM
The Life and Remains of the Rev. Edward Daniel Clarke. 1824. V. 54

OTTLEY, GEORGE
A Bibliography of British Railway History. (with) Supplement. London: 1983-88. V. 54

OTTLEY, ROI
The Negro in New York: an Informal and Social History. New York: 1967. V. 51

OTTLEY, WILLIAM YOUNG
An Inquiry Concerning the Invention of Printing: In Which the Systems of Meerman, Heinecken, Santander and Koning are Reviewed... London: 1863. V. 48; 51
An Inquiry Into the Origin and Early History of Engraving Upon Copper and In Wood. London: 1816. V. 51; 54

OTTO, ALEXANDER
Mythological Japan or The Symbolisms of Mythology in Relation to Japanese Art. Philadelphia: 1902. V. 48

OTTO, EBERHARD
Ancient Egyptian Art: the Cult of Osiria and Amon. New York: 1967. V. 51

OTTO, WHITNEY
How to Make an American Quilt. New York: 1991. V. 52; 53

OTTOBONI, PIETRO, CARDINAL
Carlo Magno Festa Teatrale in Occasione Della Nascita del Delfino, Offerta Alle Sacre Reali Maesta Cristianissime del Re, e Regina di Francia. Rome: 1729. V. 47

OTTOLENGUI, RODRIGUES
Methods of Filling Teeth. Philadelphia: 1892. V. 51

OTWAY, CAESAR
A Lecture on Miracles!. Dublin: 1823. V. 54
Sketches in Ireland: Descriptive of Interesting and Hitherto Unnoticed Districts in the North and South. Dublin: 1827. V. 50; 53

OTWAY, SILVESTER
Poems; to Which is added, the Humours of John Bull, an Operatical farce, in Two Acts. London: 1789. V. 52

OTWAY, THOMAS
Alcibiades. London: 1687. V. 48
The Atheist; or, the Second Part of the Souldiers Fortune. London: 1684. V. 48; 52
Complete Works. London: 1926. V. 47; 48; 49; 51; 52; 54
Don Carlos of Spain. London: 1686. V. 48
Friendship in Fashion. London: 1678. V. 52
The History and Fall of Caius Marius. London: 1680. V. 47
The Orphan; or, the Unhappy Marriage, a Tragedy. London: 1680. V. 52
Titus and Berenice, a Tragedy. London: 1677. V. 48
Titus and Berenice, a Tragedy. London: 1734. V. 47
Windsor Castle, in Monument to Out Late Sovereign K. Charles II. London: 1685. V. 53
The Works. London: 1768. V. 48

OUDEMANS, ANTHONY CORNELIUS
The Great Sea Serpent. Leiden: 1892. V. 48

OULD, CHARLES
Eve and Lilith. Geneva: 1942. V. 48

OULTON, WALLEY CHAMBERLAIN
Barker's Continuation of Egerton's Theatrical Remembrancer, Barker's Biographia Dramatica. London: 1801. V. 54
The History of the Theatres of London... London: 1796. V. 49
A History of the Theatres of London, Containing an Annual Register of new Pieces, Revivals, Pantomimes &c. London: 1817-18. V. 50

OUR Baby's Record. Norwalk: 1935. V. 53

OUR Exagmination Round His Factification for Incamination of Work in Progress. Paris: 1929. V. 48; 50; 51; 54

OUR Exagmination Round His Factification for Incamination of Work in Progress... 1936. V. 48; 52

OUR Exagmination Round His Factification for Incamination of Work in Progress. London: 1936. V. 54

OUR Friends at the Zoo. London. V. 47

OUR Girls: Poems in Praise of the American Girl. New York: 1907. V. 48

OUR Living Painters: Their Lives and Their Works. London: 1859. V. 47

OUR National Cathedrals...Their History and Architecture From Their Foundation to Modern Times, with Special Accounts of Modern Restorations... London: 1887-88-89. V. 48; 50

OUR Navy. London: 1885. V. 54

OUR Old Nursery Rhymes. London: 1911. V. 49; 52; 53

OUR Western Empire or the New West Beyond the Mississippi. Chicago: 1882. V. 50

OUSPENSKY, P. D.
In Search of the Miraculous, Fragments of an Unknown Teaching. London: 1950. V. 50
The Major Arcana of the Tarot as Described by... Santa Fe: 1975. V. 47
A Record of Some of the Meetings Held by P.D. Ouspensky Between 1930 and 1947 Together with a Further Record Chiefly of Extracts from Meetings Held by P. D. Ouspensky Between 1928 and 1945. Cape Town: 1951/52. V. 54
Strange Life of Ivan Psokin. London: 1947. V. 50

OUSTALET, E.
Mission Scientifique du Cap Horn 1882-83. Zoologie - Oiseaux. Paris: 1891. V. 51

OUT of the West. Northridge: 1979. V. 49; 54

OUT of This World An Anthology of Science Fiction. London: 1960-70. V. 49; 52

OUTCAULT, R. F.
Buster Brown and His Resolutions. New York: 1903. V. 47
Buster Brown's Antics. New York: 1906. V. 47

OUTERBRIDGE, PAUL
Photographing in Color. New York: 1940. V. 47
A Singular Aesthetic: Photos and Drawings 1921-1941. Santa Barbara: 1981. V. 52

OUTHWAITE, GRENBRY
The Little Fairy Sister. London: 1923. V. 49

OUTHWAITE, IDA RENTOUL
Blossom, a Fairy Story. London: 1928. V. 54
Fairyland. Melbourne: 1926. V. 49
The Little Green Road to Fairyland. New York: 1922. V. 49
The Little Green Road to Fairyland. London: 1925. V. 47

OUTLAND, CHARLES
Man-Made Disaster: The Story of St. Francis Dam. Glendale: 1963. V. 50
Stagecoaching on El Camino Real Los Angeles to San Francisco 1861-1901. Glendale: 1973. V. 51

OUTRAM, JAMES
The Conquest of Scinde a Commentary. London: 1846. V. 51

OUTRAM, MARY FRANCIS
Margaret Outram 1778-1863. London: 1932. V. 50

THE OUTSIDER. 1969. V. 51

OUVAROFF, M.
Essay on Mysteries of Elusis. London: 1817. V. 47

OUVRY, HENRY AIME
Stein and His Reforms in Prussia, with Reference to the land Question in England... London: 1873. V. 52

OVALLE, ALONSO DE
An Historical Relation of the Kingdom of Chile, by..., of the Company of Jesus. London: 1703. V. 49

OVENDON, GRAHAM
The Illustrators of Alice in Wonderland and Through the Looking Glass. London: 1972. V. 53

OVER, CHARLES
Ornamental Architecture in the Gothic, Chinese and Modern Taste, Being Above Fifty Intire New Designs of Plans, Sections, Elevations &c. London: 176?. V. 50

OVER the Hills of Hastings to the Haunts of the Gamey Black Bass, the Elusive Speckled Trout and the Fighting Maskinonge... Belleville: 1923. V. 53

OVERBURY, THOMAS
His Observations on His Travailes Upon the State of the XVII Provinces as they Stood Anno Dom. 1609. 1626. V. 47
The Miscellaneous Works in Verse and Prose of Sir Thomas Overbury, Knt. 1753. V. 47

THE OVERLAND Alphabet, from Sketches Taken "En Route" by Isabel D—. London: 1853. V. 52; 54

OVERMAN, FREDERICK
The Manufacture of Iron, In All Its Various Branches. Philadelphia: 1851. V. 49
The Manufacture Of Iron, In All Its Various Branches. Philadelphia: 1854. V. 50
The Moulder's and Founder's Pocket Guide. Philadelphia: 1853. V. 49

OVERMAN WHEEL CO.
The Overman Wheel Co. Manufacturers of Victor Bicycles. Chicopee Falls: 1899. V. 51

OVERS, JOHN
Evenings of a Working Man, Being the Occupation of His Scanty Leisure. London: 1844. V. 47; 54
The True History of the Life and Sudden death of Old John Overs, the Rich Ferry-Man... London: 1744. V. 49

OVERSTONE, SAMUEL JONES LOYD, 1ST BARON
The Evidence Given by Lord Overstone Before the Select Committee of the House of Commons of 1857, on Bank Acts... London: 1858. V. 51
Questions Communicated By Lord Overstone to the Decimal Coinage Commissioners, with Answers. London: 1857. V. 51

OVERTON, CHARLES
The History of Cottingham. Hull: 1861. V. 52

OVERTON, F.
The Health Officer. Philadelphia: 1919. V. 52

OVERTON, RICHARD
Articles of High Treason Exhibited Against Cheap-Side Crosse. London: 1642. V. 50
A New Bull-Bayting; or, a Match Play'd at the Town-Bull of Ely. London: 1649. V. 49; 50

OVERTON, THOMAS COLLINS
The Temple Builder's Most Useful Companion... London: 1774. V. 49

OVID in London: a Ludicrous Poem, in Six Cantos. London: 1814. V. 48

OVIDIUS NASO, PUBLIUS
Amatoria. Additis Guidonis Morilloni in Heroidas & A. Sabini Epistolas, ac in Ibin Argumentis. Basiliae: 1556. V. 47
The Amores... London: 1932. V. 53
The Amores... Waltham St. Lawrence: 1932. V. 47; 49; 50; 51; 52; 53; 54
The Art of Love... London: 1708. V. 48
The Art of Love. New York: 1971. V. 48; 52; 53; 54
Caxton's Translation of Ovid 1480: Hys Booke of Metamorphose: Books 10-15. London: 1924. V. 48
De Rimedi Contra L'Amore Ridotti in Ottava Rima... Avignon: 1576. V. 52
Epistole d'Ovidio di Remigio Fiorentino, Divise in Due Libri... In Vinegia: 1555. V. 50; 53
Fasatorum Lib. VI..., Tristium Lib. V. De Ponto Lib. III. Lyon: 1545. V. 48
Fasti. Venice: 1492. V. 47
The Fifteen Bookes of P. Ovidivs Naso; Entitled Metamorphosis. London: 1612. V. 47
Heroides. Milan: 1953. V. 52; 54
Heroidum Epistolae (etc.). Paris: 1585. V. 51; 54
The Heroycall Epistles of the Learned Poet. London: 1928. V. 47; 52
Hys Booke of Methamorphose. Books X-XV. Stratford-upon-Avon: 1924. V. 52
The Love Books of Ovid. London: 1925. V. 48; 54
Le Metamorfosi... Venice: 1584. V. 54
Metamorphoseon. Venice: 1540. V. 53; 54
Metamorphoseon Libri X. Philadelphia: 1790. V. 52
Metamorphoseon Libri XV. Lugduni: 1554-66-74-74. V. 50
Metamorphoseon. Libri XV. Venice: 1580. V. 49
Les Metamorphoses. Paris. V. 47
The Metamorphoses. Waltham St. Lawrence: 1958. V. 47; 50; 53
The Metamorphoses. London: 1959. V. 48
The Metamorphoses. London: 1968. V. 53
The Metamorphoses of Ovid. New York and Cambridge: 1968. V. 48; 53
Metamorphosis. Oxford: 1632. V. 53
Les Metamorphosis d'Ovide Gravees sur les Desseins des Meilleurs Pientres Francais. Paris: 1767-1770/71. V. 48
Opera Omnia... Amstelodami: 1727. V. 48
Ovid's Art of Love, in 3 Books. Glasgow: 1758. V. 50
Ovid's Art of Love in Three Books, Together with His Remedy of Love. 1764. V. 48
Ovid's Art of Love...with His Remedy of Love. London: 1735. V. 53
Ovid's Elegies. London: 1925. V. 54
Ovid's Epistles. London: 1688. V. 54
Ovid's Epistles: with His Amours. London: 1736. V. 51
Ovid's Heroical Epistles. London: 1639. V. 54
Ovid's Metamorphorsis. London: 1628. V. 48; 50
Ovid's Metamorphoses. London: 1717. V. 47; 48; 53; 54
Ovid's Metamorphoses. Philadelphia: 1790. V. 53
Ovid's Metamorphoses. New York: 1958. V. 47; 52; 54
Ovid's Metamorphoses. Verona: 1958. V. 51; 52; 53; 54
Ovid's Metamorphoses Epitomized in an English Poetical Style, for the Use and Entertainemnt of the Ladies of Great Britain. London: 1760. V. 48
Ovid's Metamorphoses, in Fifteen Books. London: 1733. V. 54
Ovid's Metamorphosis Engished, Mythologiz'd and Represented in Figures. London: 1640. V. 49
Ovid's Metamorphosis Englished... Oxford: 1632. V. 48
P. Ovidii Nasonis Metamorphoseon Libri X. Philadelphia: 1790. V. 47; 52
Preclarum Opus de Novo Impressum. Lugduni: 1511. V. 49
Publii Ovidii Nasonis Heroides, ex Editione Petri Burmanni. London: 1789. V. 47
Publii Ovidii Nasonis. Opera Omnia... Amsterdam: 1727. V. 48; 52
Shakespeare's Ovid: Being Arthur Golding's Translation of the Metamorphoses. London: 1904. V. 51
Le Transforamat-ioni di M. Lodovico Dolce... Venetia: 1555. V. 48
The XV Bookes of P. Ovidius Naso, Entituled Metamorphosis. London: 1593. V. 50
The XV Bookes of P. Ovidius Naso, Entituled, Metamorphosis. London: 1603. V. 52

OVIEDO Y VALDES, GONZALO FERNANDEZ DE
The Conquest and Settlement of the Island of Boriquen or Puerto Rico. Avon: 1975. V. 52; 54

OWEN, A. K.
The Austin-Topolovampo Pacific Railroad Route. Washington: 1875. V. 49
The Austin-Topolovampo Pacific Survey. Philadelphia: 1877. V. 49

OWEN, ANEURIN
Ancient Laws and Institutes of Wales... London: 1841. V. 52

OWEN, CHARLES
An Essay Towards a Natural History of Serpents: In Two Parts. London: 1742. V. 48

OWEN, DAVID DALE
Report of a Geological Exploration of Part of Iowa, Wisconsin, and Illinois... Washington: 1844. V. 47
Report of a Geological Survey of Wisconsin, Iowa and Minnesota. Philadelphia: 1852. V. 49; 52; 53

OWEN, DORA
The Book of Fairy Poetry. London: 1920. V. 51

OWEN, E. A.
Pioneer Sketches of Long Point Settlement or Norfolk's Foundation Builders and their Family Genealogies. Toronto: 1898. V. 53

OWEN, HAROLD
Journey from Obscurity: Wilfred Owen 1893-1918. London: 1963-65. V. 48; 53; 54

OWEN, HUGH
A History of Shrewsbury. London: 1825. V. 52

OWEN, J.
The Ecology of a Garden, the First Fifteen Years. London: 1991. V. 50; 51

OWEN, JOHN
The Fashionable World Displayed. London: 1804. V. 51
The Fashionable World Displayed. London: 1817. V. 48; 50
Travels into Different Parts of Europe, in the Years 1791 and 1792. London: 1796. V. 47

OWEN, MARY ALICIA
Voodoo Tales as Told Among the Negroes of the southwest. New York & London: 1893. V. 50

OWEN, RICHARD
Description of the Fossil Repitlia of South Africa in the Collection of the British Museum. London: 1876. V. 49; 52
Description of the Skeleton of an Extinct Gigantic Sloh, Mylodon Robustus... London: 1842. V. 47; 48; 50
Essays on the Conario-Hypophysial Tract and On the Aspects of the Body in Vertebrate and Invertebrate Animals. London: 1883. V. 52
The Fossil Reptilia of the Cretaceous Formations. London: 1851. V. 47
A History of British Fossil Mammals and Birds. 1846. V. 54
A History of British Fossil Mammals and Birds. London: 1846. V. 48; 50; 51; 53
Key to the Geology of the Globe. Nashville: 1857. V. 47
Lectures on the Comparative Anatomy and Physiology of the Invertebrate (Vertebrate) Animals Delivered at the Royal College of Surgeons in 1843 (1844 and 1846). London: 1843-46. V. 48
Life of Richard Owen. London: 1894. V. 48; 49
Memoir on the Megatherium or Giant Ground-Sloth of America. London: 1860. V. 48
Memoir on the Pearly Nautilus. London: 1832. V. 48
Monograph of the Fossil Reptilia of the Wealden and Purbeck Formations. 1853-89. V. 54
A Monograph on the Fossil Repitilia of the Mesozoic Formations. London: 1874-89. V. 49
A Monograph on the Fossil Reptilia of the Cretaceous Formations. London: 1851-64. V. 49
Odontotgraphy; or a Treatise on the Comparative anatomy of the Teeth. London: 1840-45. V. 48
On the Anatomy of Vertebrates. London: 1866-68. V. 48; 50
On the Classification and Geographical Distribution of the Mammalia... London: 1859. V. 48; 50; 53
On the Fossils Mammals of Australia. Part III (only) Diprotodon Australis. London: 1870. V. 48

OWEN, RICHARD continued
On the Nature of Limbs. London: 1849. V. 50
Palaeontology. Edinburgh: 1860. V. 48; 50
Palaeontology. Edinburgh: 1861. V. 49; 53
Palaeontology or a Systematic Summary of Extinct Animals and Their Geological Relations. London: 1860. V. 51
Palaeontology or a Systematic Summary of Extinct Animals and Their Geological Relations. London: 1861. V. 54

OWEN, ROBERT
Address to All Classes, Sects and Parties, Containing an Official Declaration of Principles, Adapted for Practice by the Congress of the Universal Community Society of Rational Religionists, Held in Leeds, May 1840. London: 1840. V. 53
The Book of the New Moral World. Glasgow: 1837. V. 53
The Book of the New Moral World... London: 1849. V. 49
Congress of the Advanced Minds of the World. London: 1857. V. 53
A Development of the Origin and Effects of Moral Evil and of the Principles and Practices of Moral Good... London: 1838. V. 53
A Dialogue, in Three Parts. Manchester: 1838. V. 53
Essays on the Formation of the Human Character... London: 1840. V. 52
(His) Opening Speech... (and) Memorial to the Republic of Mexico. Cincinnati;: 1829. V. 53
The Life of Robert Owen. 1857-58. V. 47
The Life of Robert Owen. London: 1857-58. V. 54
The Marriage System of the New Moral World with a Faint Outline of the Present Very Irrational System... Leeds: 1838. V. 47
A New View of Society; or, Essays on the Principle of the Formation of the Human Character... (with) Essay Second...Essay Third...Essay Fourth. London: 1813. V. 47
Six Lectures Delivered in Manchester Previously to the Discussion Between Mr. Robert Owen and the Rev. J. H. Roebuck. Manchester: 1837. V. 51

OWEN, ROBERT DALE
Footfalls on the Boundary of Another World. Philadelphia: 1860. V. 52
The Future of the North-West: In Connection With the Scheme of Reconstruction Without New England. Philadelphia: 1863. V. 53
Hints on Public Architecture, containing, Among Other Illustrataions, Views and Plans of the Smithsonian Institution... New York: 1849. V. 47; 48; 50; 52
Labor: Its History and Prospects. New York: 1851. V. 48
Pocahontas: a Historical Drama, in Five Acts. New York: 1837. V. 54
Threading My Way: 27 Years of Autobiography. New York: 1874. V. 49; 52
The Wrong of Slavery. The Right of Emancipation... Philadelphia: 1864. V. 48; 50

OWEN, WILFRED
Collected Letters. London: 1967. V. 47; 50
Collected Poems. 1964. V. 49
The Complete Poems and Fragments. London: 1983. V. 47; 48; 50; 53
Journey from Obscurity: Memoirs of the Owen Family. 1963/65. V. 47
Poems. London: 1920. V. 47; 49; 53
Poems. London: 1921. V. 48
Poems. New York: 1921. V. 50
Poems. London: 1931. V. 47; 51
The Seared Conscience: Nine Poems. London: 1993. V. 52
Selected War Poems. Pasadena: 1983. V. 47
Thirteen Poems. Northampton: 1956. V. 50; 54

OWEN, WILLIAM
Pictorial Sunday Readings; Comprising a series of Scripture Subjects, treated with Special Reference to the Tastes and Requirements of Families... London: 1870. V. 48

OWEN, WILLIAM FITZ WILLIAM
Narrative of Voyages to Explore the Shores of Africa, Arabia, and Madagascar, Performed in H.M. Ships Leven and Barracouta... New York: 1833. V. 54

OWEN CROWTHER, RICHARD
A Letter to the Socialists on the Doctrine of Irresponsiblity &c. Manchester: 1838. V. 53

OWENS, FRANCES E.
Mrs. Owens' Cook Book and Useful Household Hints. 1884. V. 51

OWENS, HARRY
Doctor Faust... Chicago: 1953. V. 47
Doctor Faust. Lexington: 1953. V. 51

OWENS-ADAIR, B. A.
Dr. Owens-Adair. Some of Her Life Experiences. Portland: 1905?. V. 47

OXBERRY, WILLIAM
The Actor's Budget of Wit and Merriment... London: 1820. V. 48; 52
The Actor's Budget of Wit and Merriment, Consisting of Monologues, Prologues, Tales, Comic Songs, Rare and Genuine... London: 1830. V. 48
The Actress of All Work; or, My Country Cousin. London: 1819. V. 52
The Theatrical Banquet; or, the Actor's Budget... London: 1809. V. 47; 48

OXBERRY'S Dramatic Biography and Histronic Anecdotes. 1825-1826. London: 1825. V. 49; 53

OXFORD and Cambridge Miscellany Poems. London: 1708. V. 47; 48

OXFORD, ARNOLD WHITAKER
English Cookery Books to the Year 1850. 1913. V. 47

OXFORD Book of Modern Verse 1892-1935. London: 1936. V. 51; 54

OXFORD, EDWARD HARLEY, 2ND EARL OF
A Catalogue of the Collection of the Right Honourable Edward Earl of Oxford Deceased. London: 1741-42. V. 49; 53
Catalogus Bibliothecae Harleianae. London: 1743-45. V. 49

THE OXFORD English Dictionary. Oxford: 1888-1933. V. 49

OXFORD English Dictionary. Oxford: 1933. V. 50; 51; 52
OXFORD English Dictionary. London: 1961. V. 47
OXFORD English Dictionary. London: 1971-87. V. 50
OXFORD English Dictionary. 1991. V. 48
OXFORD English Dictionary. 1991. V. 51

THE OXFORD History of England. 1985-87. V. 50

OXFORD Latin Dictionary. 1992. V. 48

THE OXFORD List of the Names of the Knights, Citizens, Burgesses and Barons of the Cinque-Ports, That are Returned to Serve in the Parliament Assembled at Oxford the Twenty First of March 1680/81. Oxford: 1681. V. 47

OXFORD Poetry. London: 1928. V. 53

OXFORD Poetry: 1921. New York: 1923. V. 50

OXFORD Prize Poems: Being a Collection of Such English Poems As Have at Various Times Obtained Prizes in the University of Oxford. Oxford: 1816. V. 49

OXFORD Prize Poems: Being a Collection of Such English Poems as Have at Various Times Obtained Prizes in the University of Oxford. Oxford: 1819. V. 50

OXFORD, ROBERT HARLEY, 1ST EARL OF
Articles of Impeachment of High-Treason and Misdeameanors, Against Robert Earl of Oxford and Earl Mortimer. July 9, 1715. London: 1727. V. 48

THE OXFORD Sausage. Cambridge: 1822. V. 47

OXFORD SOCIETY FOR THE STUDY OF GOTHIC ARCHITECTURE
A Guide to the Ar Antiquities in the Neighbourhood of Oxford. Oxford: 1860. V. 47

THE OXFORD University and City Guide... Oxford: 1870. V. 52

OXFORD UNIVERSITY. BODLEIAN LIBRARY
Catalogus Impressorum Librorum Bibliothecae Bodleianae in Academia Oxoniensi... Oxonii: 1738. V. 53
Catalogus Librorum Impressorum Bibliothecase Bodelianae in Academia Oxoniensi. Oxford: 1843. V. 47

THE OXFORD Visitor; or Picturesque Views of all the Colleges and Halls of the University: Public Buildings of the City; and Representations of Curious Works of Art,... London: 1822. V. 52

THE OXFORDSHIRE Contest; or the Whole Controversy Between the Old and New Interest. (with) The New and Old Interest; or a Sequel to the Oxfordshire Contest, Being a Complete Collection... London: 1753. V. 51

OXLEY, JAMES MAC DONALD
Baffling the Blockade. London, Edinburgh & New York: 1896. V. 49
In the Wilds of the West Coast. London: 1895. V. 49

OXLEY, JOHN
Journals of Two Expeditions into the Interior of New South Wales. London: 1820. V. 48; 52; 54

OYE, P. VAN
Biogeography and Ecology in Antarctica. The Hague: 1965. V. 50

OYVED, MOYSHEH
The Book of Affinity. London: 1933. V. 48; 50

OZ, TAHSIN
Turkish Ceramics. Istanbul: 1955. V. 51

OZAKI, YUKIO
Romances of Old Japan. London: 1920. V. 50

OZELL, JOHN
Boileau's Lutrin: a Mock-Eroic Poem. London: 1708. V. 50

OZICK, CYNTHIA
The Pagan Rabbi and Other Stories. New York: 1971. V. 49; 50
Trust. New York: 1966. V. 53

P

PAALZOW, HENRIETTE VON
The Citizen of Prague. London: 1846. V. 53

PAARR, RICHARD
The Life of the Most Reverend Father in God, James Usher, late Lord Arch-Bishop Armagh... London: 1686. V. 51

PAASCH, H.
From Keel to Truck Dictionary of Naval Terms. London: 1937. V. 49

PAASEN, PIERRE VAN
Days of Our Years. New York: 1939. V. 49

PABODIE, WILLIAM J.
Calidore; a Legendary Poem. Boston: 1839. V. 48; 53

PABOR, WILLIAM E.
Colorado as an Agricultural State. New York: 1883. V. 54

PACCAGNINI, G.
Pisanello. London: 1973. V. 50

PACCHONI, ANTIONI
Dissertatones Physico-Anatomicae de Dura meninge Humana Novis Experimentis, & Lucubrationibus Auctae, & Illustratae. Rome: 1721. V. 52

PACE, WILLIAM B.
Rifle and Light Infantry Tactics; for the Exercise and Maneuvers of troops When acting as Light Infantry or Riflemen... Great Salt Lake City: 1865. V. 50

PACEY, H. B.
Considerations Upon the Present State of the Wool Trade, the Laws Made Concerning that Article, and How Far the Same are Consistent with True Policy, and the Real, Interest of the State. London: 1781. V. 50; 54

PACHT, OTTO
Illuminated Manuscripts in the Bodleian Library. Oxford. Oxford: 1966/70/73. V. 50
Illuminated Manuscripts In the Bodleian Library, Oxford. Oxford: 1969-73. V. 48
Illuminated Manuscripts in the Bodleian Library, Oxford. 1970-73. V. 47

PACIFIC & ATLANTIC RAILROAD
Report of the Chief Engineer of the Pacific and Atlantic Rail Road Co. January 1855. San Francisco: 1855. V. 47

PACIFIC RAILROAD COMPANY
People's Pacific Railroad Company. Charter, Organization, Address of the President... Boston: 1860. V. 47

PACIFIC SCIENCE ASSOCIATION
Proceedings of the Ninth Pacific Science Congress. Bangok: 1958-63. V. 48

PACIFIC WHARF COMPANY OF SAN FRANCISCO
By-Laws of the Pacific Wharf Co. of San Francisco, Incorporated June 1st, 1855. San Francisco: 1855. V. 48

PACIOLI, LUCA
Divina Proportione... Venice: 1509. V. 47

PACK, GEORGE
Tumors of the Hands and Feet. St. Louis: 1939. V. 49

PACK, RICHARDSON
A New Collection of Miscellanies in Prose and Verse. London: 1725. V. 50

PACKARD, A. S.
Bombychine Moths of America North of Mexico. Washington?: 1895. V. 51
The Cave Fauna of North America. With Remarks on the Anatomy of the Brain and Origin of the Blind Species. Washington: 1888. V. 53
The Labrador Coast. New York: 1891. V. 54
Monograph of the Bombycine Moths of No. America. London: 1875-1914. V. 52
Monograph of the Bombycine Moths of No. America. Washington: 1895-1914. V. 49; 54

PACKARD, ELIZABETH PARSONS
Modern Persecution, or Insane Asylums Uneviled, as Demonstrated by the Report of the Investigating Committee of the Legislature of Illinois. Hartford: 1873. V. 51
Modern Persecution, or Insane Asylums Unveiled, as Demonstrated by the Report of the Investigating Committee of the Legislature of Illinois. Hartford: 1875/1873. V. 48

PACKARD, FRANCIS R.
The History of Medicine in the United States. Philadelphia: 1901. V. 50; 52
History of Medicine in the United States. New York: 1931. V. 50
History of Medicine in the United States. New York: 1963. V. 53

PACKARD, WELLMAN
Early Emigration to California. Bloomington: 1929. V. 50

PACKE, CHRISTOPHER
Ankographia, sive Convallium Descriptio. Canterbury: 1743. V. 47

PACKE, EDMUND
An Historical Record of the Royal Regiment of Horse Guards, or Oxford Blues. London: 1834. V. 50

PACKER, JAMES E.
The Insulae of Imperial ostia. Rome: 1971. V. 50; 52

PACKER, LONA MOSK
The Rossetti-MacMillan Letters... Berkeley & Los Angeles: 1963. V. 52

PACKMAN, ANA BEGUE
Early California Hospitiality. Glendale: 1938. V. 48

PADDOCK, B. B.
History and Biographical Records of North and West Texas. Chicago: 1906. V. 53
History of Central and Western Texas. Chicago: 1911. V. 48; 53
History of Texas: Fort Worth and the Texas Northwest Edition. Chicago: 1922. V. 53

PADDOCK, JUDAH
A Narrative of the Shipwreck of the Ship Oswego, on the Coast of South Barbary, and of the Sufferings of the Master and the Crew While in Bondage Among the Arabs... New York: 1818. V. 47

PADEN, IRENE
The Big Oak Flat Road: an Account of Freighting from Stockton to Yosemite Valley. San Francisco: 1955. V. 54

PADGETT, ABIGAIL
Child of Science. 1993. V. 54

PADGETT, LEWIS
Tomorrow and Tomorrow and The Fairy Chessmen. New York: 1951. V. 54

PADILLA, VICTORIA
Southorn California Gardens: an Illustrated History. Berkeley & Los Angeles: 1961. V. 52

PADMORE, GEORGE
How Russia Transformed Her Colonial Empire. London: 1946. V. 52

PADWICK, E. W.
A Bibliography of Cricket. London: 1984. V. 49

PAEZ, DON RAMON
Wild Scenes in South America; or Life in the Llanos of Venzuela. New York: 1862. V. 49

A PAGAN Anthology. New York: 1918. V. 47; 50; 53

PAGAN, JAMES
Glasgow Past and Present. Glasgow: 1884. V. 47; 53

PAGAN, WILLIAM
Road Reform: a Plan for Abolishing Turnpike Tolls and Statute Labour Assessments, and for Providing the Funds Necessary for the Public Roads by an Annual Rate on Homes. Edinburgh: 1846. V. 52

PAGE, ANTHEA
Egyptian Sculpture. Warminster: 1976. V. 49

PAGE, DELIA BRYAN
Recollections of Home for My Brothers and Children. Richmond: 1903. V. 50

PAGE, FRANCIS
The Charge of J---- P---- to the Grand Jury of M–x, on Saturday May 22, 1736. London: 1737. V. 52

PAGE, FRANK E.
Homer Watson Artist and Man. Kitchener. V. 53

PAGE, FREDERICK B.
Prairiedom: Rambles and Scrambles in Texas or New Estremadura. New York: 1846. V. 52

PAGE, H. A.
Memoir of Nathaniel Hawthorne... London: 1872. V. 49
Thoreau: His Life and Aims, a Study. London: 1878. V. 49

PAGE, HARRY S.
Between the Flags: The Recollections of a Gentleman Rider. New York: 1929. V. 47

PAGE, I.
Guide for Drawing the Acanthus, and Every Description of Ornamental Foliage. London: 1840. V. 48; 50

PAGE, J. W.
Uncle Robin, In His Cabin in Virginia and Tom Without One in Boston. Richmond: 1853. V. 53

PAGE, JAKE
The Stolen Gods. New York: 1993. V. 54

PAGE, JAMES MADISON
The True Story of Andersonville Prison a Defense of Major Henry Wirz. New York & Washington: 1908. V. 47; 49; 50

PAGE, JAMES R.
A Descriptive Catalogue of the Book of Common Prayer and Related Material in the Collection of James R. Page. Los Angeles: 1955. V. 49; 50

PAGE, JOHN
Receipts for Preparing and Compounding the Principal Medicines Made Use of by the Late Mr. Ward. London: 1763. V. 47; 48; 53

PAGE, JOHN LLOYD WARDEN
The Rivers of Devon from Source to Sea. London: 1893. V. 50

PAGE, LEITCH
Philby: The Spy Who Betrayed and Generation. London: 1968. V. 52

PAGE, P. K.
As Ten As Twenty. Toronto: 1946. V. 47
Magic in Everything. Toronto: 1955. V. 47
Titans. London: 1926. V. 47
The Witches' Brew. London: 1925. V. 47

PAGE, RICHARD
Receipts for Preparing and Compounding the Principal Medicines Made Use Of by the Late Mr. Ward. London: 1763. V. 53

PAGE, THOMAS
Letter to the Right Hon. Lord Ashley, M.P. on the Present Defective State of National Education and the Necesssity of Government Interference. London: 1843. V. 53

PAGE, THOMAS FREDERICK
The Golden Fleece: a Book of Jewish Cabalism. Laconia: 1888. V. 50

PAGE, THOMAS J.
La Plata, the Argentine Confederation and Paraguay. New York: 1859. V. 47

PAGE, THOMAS NELSON
In Ole Virginia or Marse Chan and Other Stories. New York: 1887. V. 50; 54
John Marvel Assistant. New York: 1909. V. 54
Two Little Confederates. New York: 1889. V. 52
The Works of... New York: 1906-12. V. 54

PAGE, W. P.
Page's Prodomus, as a General Nomenclature of All the Plants, Indigenous and Exotic... London: 1818. V. 53

PAGE, WILLIAM
A History of the County of Hertford. London: 1920. V. 51
Victoria County History. Hertfordshire. London: 1902-23. V. 49; 52
The Victoria History of the County of Durham. London: 1905-07. V. 47
York. Volume Three. Victoria History of the Counties of England Series. London: 1913. V. 53

THE PAGEANT. London: 1896-97. V. 48; 52; 54
THE PAGEANT. London: 1897. V. 53

PAGEANT Of Japanese Art. Tokyo: 1952-54. V. 47; 49

PAGEANT of Japanese Art. Volume VI. Architecture and Gardens. Tokyo: 1952. V. 51

PAGES of Glory and History. The 91st Division in Argonne and Flanders. Paris, New York: 1919. V. 52

PAGES, PIERRE MARIE FRANCOIS, VISCOUNT
Travels Round the World, in the Years 1767, 1768, 1769, 1770, 1771... London: 1793. V. 51
Travels Round the World, in the Years 1767, 1768, 1769, 1770, 1771. London: 1793/92. V. 48

PAGET, EDWARD CLARENCE
A Memoir of the Honourable Sir Charles Paget, G. C. H. Toronto: 1911. V. 47; 50

PAGET, FRANCIS EDWARD
Tales of the Village. (Second Series; Series the Third and Last). London: 1840-41. V. 47

PAGET, GUY
The History of the Althorp and Pytchley Hunt, 1634-1920. London: 1937. V. 47
The History of the Althorp and Pytchley Hunt, 1634-1920. London: 1938. V. 47
The Melton Mowbray of John Ferneley. 1782 to 1860. Leicester: 1931. V. 47; 49; 51

PAGET, J. O.
Hunting. London: 1900. V. 48

PAGET, JAMES
Clinical Lectures and Essays. New York: 1875. V. 49; 50; 54

PAGET, JOHN
Hungary and Transylvania; with Remarks on Their Condition, Social, Political and Economical. London: 1855. V. 47; 54

PAGET, THOMAS CATESBY, BARON
Miscellanies in Prose and Verse. London: 1741. V. 51

PAGET, VIOLET
Ariadne in Mantua - A Romance in Five Acts. Oxford and London: 1903. V. 50
Belcaro, Being Essays on Sundry Aesthetical Questions. London: 1883?. V. 49
For Maurice: Five Unlikely Stories. London: 1927. V. 50
Juvenilia: Being a Second Series of Essays on Sundry Aesthetical Questions. London: 1887. V. 53
Miss Brown. Edinburgh: 1884. V. 54
Ottilie: an Eighteenth Century Idyl. London: 1883. V. 50
Pope Jacynth and other Fantastic Tales. London: 1907. V. 50
Proteus - or the Future of Intelligence. London: 1925. V. 52
Renaissance Studies and Fancies: Being a Sequel to Euphorion. London: 1895. V. 54
The Tower of the Mirrors. London: 1914. V. 53
Vernon Lee's Letters. London: 1937. V. 50

PAGLIA, CAMILLE
Sexual Personae. New Haven: 1990. V. 51

PAHER, STANLEY W.
Death Valley Ghost Towns. Las Vegas: 1973. V. 54

PAIGE, CHARLES C.
Story of the Experiences of Lieut. Charles C. Paige in the Civil War of 1861-65. Franklin: 1911. V. 47; 48

PAIJKULL, C. W.
A Summer in Iceland. London: 1868. V. 47

PAILTHORPE, FREDERICK WILLIAM
24 Illustrations to the Pickwick Club. London: 1882. V. 54
Great Expectations. London: 1885. V. 54
Twenty-One Illustrations to Oliver Twist. London: 1886. V. 49

PAIN, B.
The One Before. 1902. V. 47; 51

PAIN, WILLIAM
The Builder's Companion and Workman's General Assistant.... London: 1758. V. 53
Pain's British Palladio; or, the Builder's General Assistant. London: 1786. V. 52
The Practical Builder. London: 1774. V. 53; 54
The Practical Builder. Boston: 1792. V. 53
The Practical Builder. London: 1804. V. 50
The Practical House Carpenter; or Youth's Instructor... Philadelphia: 1797. V. 48
The Practical House Carpenter; or, Youth's Instructor... London: 1805. V. 51

PAINE
Catalogue of Artistic Furniture... Boston: 1880's. V. 52

PAINE, ALBERT BIGELOW
Captain Bill McDonald. New York: 1909. V. 52
Dwellers in Arcady. New York: 1919. V. 52
Mark Twain - a Biography. New York: 1912. V. 47; 48; 49; 52; 53
The Mystery of Evelyn Delorme. Boston: 1894. V. 54
The Tent Dwellers. New York: 1908. V. 52
Thomas Nast His Period and His Pictures. New York: 1904. V. 52; 53

PAINE, BAYARD H.
Pioneers, Indians and Buffaloes. 1935. V. 47

PAINE, D. P.
Aerial Photography and Image Interpretation for Resource Management. New York: 1981. V. 52

PAINE, E. S. M.
The Two James's and the Two Stephensons; or, the Earliest History of Passenger Transit on Railways. London: 1861. V. 49

PAINE, MARTYN
The Institutes of Medicine. New York: 1847. V. 49; 54
Letters on the Cholera Asphyxia, As It Appeared in the City of New York. New York: 1832. V. 50; 51; 52; 54
Materia Medica and Therapeutics. New York: 1848. V. 49

PAINE, THOMAS
The Age of Reason; Being an Investigation of True and Fabulous Theology. London: 1794. V. 53
Agrarian Justice, Opposed to Agrarian Law and to Agrarian Monopoly. Philadelphia: 1797. V. 47; 51; 54
The American Crisis. London: 1817. V. 54
Common Sense: Addressed to the Inhabitants of America. Philadelphia: 1776. V. 50
The Decline and Fall of the English System of Finance. London: 1796. V. 49
The Decline and Fall of the English System of Finance. Paris: 1796. V. 53
The Decline and Fall of the English System of Finance. Philadelphia: 1796. V. 51
Dissertacao Sobre os Principios Fundamentais do Governo, Traduzida da Lingua Ingleza por Zid Es Oan. (Dissertation on First Principles of Government). 1822. V. 48
Dissertation on First Principles of Government. London: 1795. V. 51; 53
Dissertation on First Principles of Government. Paris: 1795. V. 51
Droits de l'Homme. Paris: 1791. V. 47; 54
Examination of the Passages in the New Testament, quoted from the Old and Called Prophecies Concerning Jesus Christ. New York: 1807. V. 51
A Few State Criminals Brought to the Bar Of Public Justice; With Observations on the Last and Advice to the New Parliament, Calling Themselves Representatives of the People. London: 1795. V. 49
The Genuine Trial of Thomas Paine, for a Libel Contained in the Second Part of Rights of Man; at Guildhall, London, December 18, 1792, Before Lord Kenyon and a Special Jury... London: 1792. V. 47
Letter Addressed to the Abbe Raynal on the Affairs of North Ameica. Albany: 1782. V. 51
Letter from Thomas Paine to George Washington, President of the United States of America. London: 1797. V. 47; 48
A Letter to Mr. Secretary Dundas, also Two Letters to Lord Onslow. London: 1792. V. 52
Letters, by the Author of Common Sense. Albany: 1792. V. 51
The Life and Works of Thomas Paine. New Rochelle: 1925. V. 49; 51
Old Truths, Established Facts, Being an Answer to a Very New Pamphlet Indeed!. 1792?. V. 47
The Political and Miscellaneous Works. London: 1819. V. 49
The Political Writings...(with) The Theological Works. (with) Appendix to the Theological Works. (with) Miscellaneous Poems. New York: 1819-35. V. 54
Prospects on the War and Paper Currency. London: 1793. V. 47
Rights of Man. Dublin: 1791. V. 54
Rights of Man. London: 1791. V. 47
Rights of Man. Lunenburg: 1961. V. 48; 51
The Rights of Man. New York: 1961. V. 48; 52
Rights of Man. Part the Second. London: 1792. V. 51
Le Sens-Commun. Ouvrage Adresse Aux Americains. Paris: 1793. V. 47
The Whole Proceedings on the Trial of...Before the Right Honourable Lord Kenyon. London: 1793. V. 49
The Writings. Albany: 1794. V. 52
The Writings... New York: 1894-96. V. 52

PAINTER, C. C.
The Condition of Affairs in Indian Territory and California. Philadelphia: 1888. V. 49

PAINTER, ORRIN CHALFANT
William Painter and His Father, Dr. Edward Painter. Baltimore: 1914. V. 50

PAINTER, WILLIAM
The First (Second) Tome of the Palace of Pleasure, Beautified, Adorned and Well Furnished with Pleasant Histories and Excellent Novels. London: 1813. V. 50
The Palace of Pleasure... London: 1813. V. 50; 53
The Palace of Pleasure. London: 1929. V. 47; 48; 51

THE PAINTER'S and Varnisher's Pocket Manual. London: 1825. V. 47

THE PAINTER'S Object. London: 1937. V. 49

PAINTING, STEPHEN
Four Elegies. I. Morning. II. Noon. III. Evening. IV. Night. London: 1761. V. 54

PAINTINGS from Ajanta Caves. 1954. V. 48

PAIVA D'ANDRADA, DIOGO
Chauleidos Libri Duodecim. Anitur Memoranda Chaulensis Urbis Propugnatio & Celebris Victoria Lustianorum Aduersus Copias Inizae Maluci. Lisbon: 1628. V. 48

PAKENHAM, CAPTAIN
Invention of a Substitute for a Lost Rudder, and to Prevent Its Being Lost Also a Method of Restoring the Masts of Ships, When Wounded, or Otherwise Injured. London: 1793. V. 54

PAKENHAM-WALSH, R. P.
History of the Corps of Royal Engineers. 1958. V. 52

PAKULA, MARVIN J.
Centennial Album of the Civil War. New York: 1960. V. 47

PAL, PARATAPADITYA
Buddhist Book Illuminations. New York: 1988. V. 48

PALACIO FAJARDO, MANUEL
Outline of the Revolution in Spanish America... London: 1817. V. 48

PALARDY, JEAN
The Early Furniture of French Canada. Toronto: 1963. V. 50
The Early Furniture of French Canada. New York: 1965. V. 52

THE PALATINE Note-Book for the Intercommunication of Antiquaries, Bibliophiles and Other Investigators into the History and Literature of the Counties of Lancaster, Chester, etc. Manchester: 1881-84. V. 48; 53

PALATINO, GIOVANNI BATTISTA
Compendio del Gran Volvme Dell'arte del Bene Leggiadramente Scrivere... Venice: 1588. V. 49; 52
Libro di M. Giovam Battista Palatino, Cittadino Romano, Nelqual s'Insegna a Scruer Ogne Sorte Lettera, Antica & Moderna di Qualunque Natione, con le Sue Regole & Misure... Rome: 1561. V. 47; 48; 54

PALAU I FABRE, JOSEP
Picasso: The Early Years 1881-1907. New York: 1981. V. 47; 48; 50; 52; 53

PALERMO, EVANGELIST
A Grammar of the Italian Language. London: 1755. V. 53

PALESTINE EXPLORATION FUND
Annual 1927. No. V. London: 1929. V. 52
Annual I-V. London: 1911-27. V. 52
The Survey of Eastern Palestine. (and) The Survey of Western Palestine. London: 1881-99. V. 52

PALEY, F. A.
Illustrations of Baptismal Fonts. London: 1844. V. 47

PALEY, GRACE
The Collected Stories. New York: 1994. V. 51; 52; 53
Enormous Changes at the Last Minute. New York: 1973. V. 52
Enormous Changes at the Last Minute. New York: 1974. V. 48; 49
Leaning Forward. Penobscot: 1985. V. 47; 51
Leaning Forward. Penobscot: 1986. V. 50
The Little Disturbances of Man. Garden City: 1959. V. 48; 49; 51; 54
The Little Disturbances of Man. London: 1960. V. 54

PALEY, MORTON D.
William Blake. Essays in Honour of Sir Geoffrey Keynes. Oxford: 1973. V. 54

PALEY, WILLIAM
Natural Theology; or Evidences of the Existence and Attributes of the Deity Collected from the Appearances of Nature. London: 1817. V. 47
The Principles of Moral and Political Philosophy. London: 1785. V. 48
The Principles of Moral and Political Philosophy... London: 1786. V. 49
The Principles of Moral and Political Philosophy. Dublin: 1788. V. 49
The Principles of Moral and Political Philosophy. London: 1790. V. 48; 51
A View of the Evidences of Christianity. London: 1794. V. 49
A View of the Evidences of Christianity. London: 1829. V. 52
Works. London: 1803-08. V. 48
The Works... Derby: 1826. V. 52
The Works. London: 1838. V. 47

PALFREY, SARA H.
Herman, or, Young Knighthood. Boston: 1866. V. 48

PALGRAVE, FRANCIS TURNER
The Five Days Entertainemtns at Wentworth Grange. Boston and London: 1868. V. 51
Gems of English Art. London: 1869. V. 52
The Golden Treasury. Cambridge: 1861. V. 51
The Golden Treasury. London: 1900. V. 51
The Golden Treasury. London: 1925. V. 53
The Golden Treasury. New York: 1925. V. 50
A Golden Treasury of Songs and Lyrics. New York: 1921. V. 52
The Golden Treasury of the Best Songs and Lyrical Poems in the English Language. Cambridge: 1861. V. 53; 54
The Golden Treasury Selected from the Best Songs and Lyrical Poems in the English Language... London: 1900. V. 52
Palgrave's Golden Treasury. London: 1907. V. 48

PALGRAVE, ROBERT HARRY INGLIS
Palgrave's Dictionary of Political Economy. London: 1925-26. V. 50

PALGRAVE, WILLIAM GIFFORD
Dutch Guiana. London: 1876. V. 52
Hermann Agha; an Eastern Narrative. London: 1872. V. 47
Narrative of a Year's Journey through Central and Eastern Arabia (1862-63). London: 1865. V. 54

Ulysses or Scenes and Studies in Many Lands. London: 1887. V. 48

PALINGENIUS, MARCELLUS
Stellati Poeta...Zodiacus Vitae. Lyon: 1556. V. 54
The Zodiake of Life... London: 1588. V. 48

PALKE, WILLIAM
The Divinity of Jesus Christ Prov'd from the Words of Thomas, My Lord and My God. A Sermon Preach'd at Exon, Sept. 9, 1719. London: 1719. V. 52

PALLADINO, LAWRENCE B.
Indian and White in the Northwest: a History of Catholicity in Montana, 1831 to 1891. Lancaster: 1922. V. 47; 49

PALLADIO, ANDREA
Andrea Palladio's Architecture, in Four Books. London: 1736. V. 54
Architecture: in four Books. London: 1721. V. 53
The Architecture of A. Palladio, in Four Books. London: 1742. V. 52
The First Book of Architecture... London: 1676. V. 47; 48
The First Book of Architecture... London: 1716. V. 47
I Quattro Libri dell'Architettura. Venice: 1581. V. 52
Traicte des Cinq Ordres d'Architecture...Augmente de...L'Art De Bien Bastir par Le Sr. Le Muet. Paris: 1645. V. 51

PALLADIUS, RUTILIUS TAURUS AEMILIANUS
De Rustica. Libri XIIII. Lyon: 1549. V. 50

PALLAS, PETER SIMON
Flora Rossica Seu Stirpium Imperii Rossici per Europam et Asiam Indigenarum Descriptiones et Icones. St. Petersburg: 1784-88. V. 52; 53
Travels through the Southern Provinces of the Russian Empire in the Years 1793 and 1794. London: 1802-03. V. 47; 50; 54
Travels through the Southern Provinces of the Russian Empire in the Years 1793 and 1794. London: 1812. V. 48; 52

PALLISER, CHARLES
The Quincunx. Edinburgh: 1989. V. 51; 52
The Quincunx. London: 1989. V. 50

PALLISER, FANNY MARRYAT
Historic Devices, Badges and War-Cries. London: 1870. V. 54
History of Lace. London: 1865. V. 48
A History of Lace. London: 1869. V. 51; 52
History of Lace. London: 1902. V. 54
A History of Lace. New York: 1902. V. 47; 48
History of Lace. London: 1910. V. 50

PALLISER, JOHN
Exploration - British North America. London: 1859-65. V. 47
The Papers of the Palliser Expedition 1857-1860. Toronto: 1968. V. 52

PALMA DI CESNOLA, ALEXANDER
Salaminia (Cyprus) The History, Treasures, and Antiquities of Salamis in the Island of Cyprus. London: 1884. V. 51; 54

PALMEDO, ROLAND
Skiing: the International Sport. New York: 1937. V. 47; 48; 50

PALMER, A. B.
A Treatise on Epidemic Cholera and Allied Diseases. Ann Arbor: 1885. V. 51; 54

PALMER, A. H.
The Life of Joseph Wolf Animal Painter. London: 1895. V. 49; 50; 51; 53; 54

PALMER, ARNOLD
Recording Britain. London: 1946-49. V. 47; 52

PALMER, BENJAMIN M.
A Discourse Before the General Assembly of South Carolina, on December 10, 1863, Appointed by the Legislature as a Day of Fasting, Humiliation and Prayer. Columbia: 1864. V. 49

PALMER, BROOKS
The Book of American Clocks. (with) A Treasury of American Clocks. New York: 1950. V. 53

PALMER, CHARLES
A Collection of Select Aphorisms and Maxims... London: 1748. V. 51

PALMER, CHARLOTTE
Letters on Several Subjects, from a Preceptress to Her Pupils who Have Left School. London: 1797. V. 47

PALMER, EDWARD
An Elegy On the Death of Mr. James Bristow, Late Fellow of All Souls. Oxford: 1667. V. 48

PALMER, EDWARD H.
The Desert of the Exodus. Cambridge: 1871. V. 47; 48; 49; 54

PALMER, EDWIN O.
History of Hollywood. Hollywood: 1938. V. 47; 54

PALMER, ELIHU
Principles of Nature; or, a Development of the Moral Causes of Happiness and Misery Among the Human species... London: 1819-24. V. 48
Principles of Nature; or, a Development of the Moral Causes of Happiness and Misery Among the Human Species. London: 1823. V. 51
Principles of Nature; or, a Development of the Moral Causes of Happiness and Misery Among the Human Species. Granville: 1840. V. 48

PALMER, F. P.
The Wanderings of a Pen and Pencil. London: 1846. V. 47; 51

PALMER, FREDERICK
In the Klondyke, Including an Account of a Winter's Journey to Dawson. New York: 1899. V. 54
Report on the Selection of a Terminal Port for the Hudson Bay Railway. London: 1927. V. 54

PALMER, GEORGE
Kidnapping in the South Seas: Being a Narrative of a Three Months' Cruise of H.M. Ship Rosario. Edinburgh: 1871. V. 47; 51; 54

PALMER, HERBERT
In Autumn. London: 1931. V. 48

PALMER, HERBERT EDWARD
The Judgement of Francois Villon. London: 1927. V. 47; 48; 49; 53
Songs of Salvation, Sin and Satire. London: 1925. V. 49

PALMER, HOWARD
Mountaineering and Exploration in the Selkirks. New York: 1914. V. 48; 53

PALMER, J.
The Hesperides. 1936. V. 47; 51
Mushrooms of America. Boston: 1885. V. 54

PALMER, JAMES CROXALL
Thulia: a Tale of the Antarctic. New York: 1843. V. 53

PALMER, JOE H.
Names in Pedigrees. Lexington: 1939. V. 47

PALMER, JOHN
History of the Twenty-Second United States Infantry, 1866-1922. 1922. V. 48; 49
Journal of Travels in the United States of North America and in Lower Canada, Peformed in the Year 1817. London: 1818. V. 53
The New Spouter's Companion; or, a Complete Theatrical Remembrancer and Universal Key to Theatrical Knowledge. London: 1781. V. 53
Papers Relative to the Agreement Made by Government with Mr. Palmer, for the Reform and Improvement of the Posts. London: 1797. V. 52

PALMER, JOHN M.
Personal Recollection of John M. Palmer the Story of an Earnest Life. Cincinnati: 1901. V. 48

PALMER, LUCILE
Heart-Throbs from Reno. Hollywood: 1935. V. 48

PALMER, RALPH S.
Handbook of North American Birds. New Haven: 1962-76. V. 54
Handbook of North American Birds. New Haven: 1962-88. V. 54
Handbook of North American Birds. New Haven: 1976. V. 54

PALMER, RICHMOND
The Bornu Sahara and Sudan. London: 1936. V. 48

PALMER, S.
A General History of Printing; from the First Invention of It In the City of Mentz, to Its Propagation and Progress... London: 1733. V. 50; 52; 53; 54

PALMER, SAMUEL
Moral Essays on Some of the Most Curious and Significant English, Scotch and Foreign Proverbs. London: 1710. V. 48
The Nonconformist's Memorial... London: 1775. V. 47
The Protestant-Dissenter's Catechism. London: 1774. V. 53
St. Pancras; Being Antiquarian, Topographical and Biographical Memoranda, Relating to the Extensive Metropolitan Parish... London: 1870. V. 50; 52

PALMER, SHIRLEY
The Swiss Exile, a Poem. Lichfield: 1804. V. 54

PALMER, SUTTON
Bonnie Scotland. London: 1904. V. 48

PALMER, T. H.
The Historical Register of the United States. Washington City: 1814. V. 51

PALMER, T. S.
Place Names of the Death Valley Region in California and Nevada. 1948. V. 52; 54

PALMER, W. H.
A Review of the Commission of H.M.S. 'Barfleur' on the Mediterranean and China Stations. Nagasaki: 1898. V. 49

PALMER, W. T.
The Complete Hill Walker Rock Climber and Cave Explorer. London: 1934. V. 54
The English Lakes. London: 1905. V. 47; 52
The English Lakes. London: 1908. V. 50; 52

PALMERSTON, HENRY JOHN TEMPLE, 3RD VISCOUNT
The Life of Henry Temple, Viscount Palmerston... London: 1871-74. V. 47
The New Whig Guide. London: 1819. V. 48

PALMERSTON, LORD
Memorandum on the Royal African, Levant and Russia Companies. London: 1851. V. 49

PALMGREN, NILS
Selected Chinese Antiquities from the Collection of Gustav Adolf, Crown Prince of Sweden. Stockholm: 1948. V. 51; 53

PALOU, FRANCISCO
The Expedition Into California of the Venerable Padre Fray Junipero Serra... San Francisco: 1934. V. 47; 48; 52
The Founding of the First California Missions Under the Spiritual Guidance of the Venerable Padre fray Junipero Serra... San Francisco: 1934. V. 51
Historical Memoirs of New California. Berkeley: 1926. V. 48; 52; 54
Life and Apostolic Labors of the Venerable Father Junipero Serra, Founder of the Franciscan Missions of California. Pasadena: 1913. V. 48
Life of Ven. Padre Junipero Serra... San Francisco: 1884. V. 49; 54
Palou's Life of Frey Junipero Serra. Washington: 1955. V. 54

PALTOCK, ROBERT
The Life and Adventures of Peter Wilkins. London: 1751. V. 50; 54
The Life and Adventures of Peter Wilkins. London: 1784. V. 50
The Life and Adventures of Peter Wilkins. London: 1884. V. 48
The Life and Adventures of Peter Wilkins. London: 1928. V. 49
The Life and Adventures of Peter Wilkins. New York: 1928. V. 51; 54

PAMMEL, L. H.
A Manual of Poisonous Plants Chiefly of Eastern North America... Cedar Rapids: 1910-11. V. 48

PAN-AMERICAN MEDICAL CONGRESS
Transactions of the First Pan-American Medical Congress. Washington: 1895. V. 49; 51

THE PANAMA Massacre. Panama: 1856. V. 49

PANAMA-PACIFIC INTERNATIONAL EXPOSITION
Catalogue Deluxe of the Department of Fine Arts, Panama-Pacific International Exposition. San Francisco: 1915. V. 53
Official Catalogue (Illustrated) of the Department of Fine Arts. Panama-Pacific International Exposition (with Awards). San Francisco: 1915. V. 47

PANASSIE, HUGUES
Hot Jazz. New York: 1934. V. 52

PANCAKE, BREECE D'J.
The Stories of Breece D'J Pancake. Boston: 1983. V. 51

PANCEL, L.
Tropical Forestry Handbook. Berlin: 1993. V. 50

PANCHARIS, Queen of Love; or, the Art of Kissing; In All Its Varieties. London: 1722. V. 47

PANCHARIS, Queen of Love; or, Woman Unveil'd. London: 1721. V. 48

PANCHEN, A. L.
The Terrestrial Environment and the Origin of Land Vertebrates. New York: 1980. V. 53

PANCIROLI, GUIDO
Rerum Memorabilium. Commentariis Illustrata et Locis Prope Innumeris Postremum Aucta Ab H. Salmuth. Frankfurt: 1660. V. 47

PANCOAST, CHARLES EDWARD
A Quaker Forty-Niner: the Adventures of...on the American Frontier. Philadelphia: 1930. V. 47

PANCOAST, JOSEPH
A Series of Anatomical Plates... Philadelphia: 1842. V. 54
A Series of Anatomical Plates... Philadelphia: 1843. V. 54
A Treatise on Operative Surgery. Philadelphia: 1844. V. 48; 52; 53; 54

PANCRATIA, or a History of Pugilism. London: 1812. V. 50; 52

PANG Tao (Flat Peaches), Eight Fairies Festival, a Festival Held on the 3rd of the 3rd Lunar Month in Honour of the Goddess Hsi Wang-Mu. 1900. V. 54

PANGBORN, E.
A Mirror for Observors. New York: 1954. V. 49; 54

PANGHORN, J. G.
The New Rocky Mountain Tourist Arkansas Valley and San Juan Guide. The Tour... Chicago: 1878. V. 52; 54

PANKHURST, E. SYLVIA
The Suffragette Movement, an Intimate Account of Persons and Ideals. London: 1931. V. 53; 54
The Suffragette Movement, an Intimate Account of Persons and Ideals. London: 1932. V. 53; 54

PANKHURST, EMMELINE
The Importance of the Vote. London: 1908. V. 50

PANNELL, J. R.
Experiments on Rigid Airship R.29 January 1920. London: 1921. V. 49

PANOFSKY, ERWIN
Albrecht Durer. London: 1945. V. 51
Albrecht Durer. London: 1948. V. 54
Albrecht Durer. Princeton: 1948. V. 47; 50; 51; 53; 54
The Codex Huygens and Leonardo da Vinci's Art Theory. London: 1940. V. 47
Early Netherlandish Painting. Cambridge: 1953. V. 47
Early Netherlandish Painting, its Origins and Character. Cambridge: 1958. V. 49
Early Netherlandish Painting: It's Origins and Character. Cambridge: 1964. V. 54
Early Netherlandish Painting: Its Origins and Character. Cambridge: 1966. V. 54
Problems in Titian. Mostly Iconographic. London: 1969. V. 48
Problems in Titian, Mostly Iconographic. New York: 1969. V. 50; 53; 54
Tomb Sculpture, Its Changing Aspects from Ancient Egypt to Bernini. London: 1964. V. 49; 52

PANSHIN, A.
Rite of Passage. 1969. V. 52

PANTIN, WILLIAM ABEL
Chapters of the English Black Monks. London: 1931-37. V. 54

PANTOMIME Pictures. A Novel Colour Book for Children. London: 1895. V. 48

PANTON, EDWARD
Speculum Juventutis: or, a True Mirror; Where Errors in Breeding Noble and Generous Youth, with the Miseries and Mischiefs that Usually Attend It... London: 1671. V. 47

PANVINIO, ONOFRIO
Antiquitatum Veronensium. Padua: 1648. V. 49
Antiquitatum Veronensium, Libri Octo. Padua: 1647. V. 52
Fasti et Triomphi rom. a Romvlo Rege Vsqve ad Carolum V... Venice: 1557. V. 48; 54

PANZER, G. W. F.
Fauna Insectorum Germanica: Coleoptera... Nuremberg: 1793-1844. V. 54

PAOLO, SERVITA
The Maxims of the Government of Venice. London: 1707. V. 48

PAOLOZZI, EDUARDO
The Metalization of a Dream. London: 1963. V. 48
Underground Design. London: 1986. V. 50

PAPACHRISTOU, T.
Marcel Breuer: New Buildings and Projects. 1970. V. 48; 50

PAPADOPOULO, ALEXANDRE
Islam and Muslim Art. New York: 1978. V. 47
Islam and Muslim Art. New York: 1979. V. 48

PAPADOPOULOS, S. A.
Greek Handicraft. Athens: 1969. V. 49

PAPANICOLAS, G. D.
Usque Adeo? or, What May Be Said for the Ionian People; Being Letters Addressed to Lord John Russell, Earl Grey, Sir John Packington, and Sir Henry Ward, During the Administration of the Latter Gentleman in the Ionian Islands. London: 1853. V. 54

PAPA'S Tour through London with His Son Edward, or a Visit to St. Paul's Westminster Abbey, etc. London: 1830. V. 51

PAPASHVILY, GEORGE
Anything Can Happen. New York: 1945. V. 48
Yes and No Stories: a Book of Georgian Folk Tales. New York: 1946. V. 50

PAPASTRATOS, DORY
Paper Icons. Greek Orthodox Religious Engravings. 1665-1899. Athens: 1990. V. 48

PAPE, AGNES M.
Fair Folk of Many Lands. London: 1920. V. 54

PAPE, FRANK
Composition Strips. No. 1. Picture Stories to Be Fitted With Words. London. V. 53
The Diamond Fairy Book. London: 1912. V. 51

PAPER Dolls and How to Make Them. A Book for Little Girls. New York: 1856. V. 49

PAPERMAKING in Seventeenth Century England. Santa Cruz: 1990. V. 52

PAPERS on Agriculture, Consisting of Communications Made to the Massachusetts Society for Promoting Agriculture. Boston: 1803. V. 51

PAPERS on Agriculture. Consisting of Communications Made to the Massachusetts Society for Promoting Agriculture. Boston: 1804. V. 47

PAPERS Relating to America. Presented to the House of Commons, 1809. London: 1810. V. 47

PAPERS Relating to the Treaty of Washington. Volume I-(V). Washington: 1872. V. 52

PAPERS Relative to the Affairs of British Columbia. London: 1859/59/60/62. V. 47

PAPERS Relative to the Mission of Hon. T. Butler King, to Europe. Milledgeville: 1863. V. 49

PAPIN, DENIS
Nouvelles Experiences du Vvide. Paris: 1674. V. 47

THE PAPISTS Plot of Firing Discovered, in a Perfect Account of the Late Fire in Fetter-Lane, London, the 10th day of April Last... London: 1679. V. 53

PAPON, JEAN
Arresz Notables de Covrts Sovveraines de France. Paris: 1563. V. 51

PAPP, D.
Creation's Doom. 1934. V. 48; 52

PAPWORTH, JOHN BUONAROTTI
Hints on Ornamental Gardening... London: 1823. V. 48; 50; 53
Poetical Sketches of Scarborough. London: 1813. V. 47; 49; 51; 52; 53; 54
Rural Residences, Consisting of a Series of Designs for Cottages, Decorated Cottages, Small Villas and Other Ornamental Buildings... London: 1818. V. 53
Rural Residences, Consisting of a Series of Designs for Cottages, Decorated Cottages, Small Villas and Other Ornamental Buildings. London: 1832. V. 50
Select Views of London with Historical and Descriptive Sketches... London: 1816. V. 48; 50; 51; 52; 54

PAPWORTH, JOHN W.
An Alphabetical Dictionary of Coats of Arms Belonging to Families in Great Britain and Ireland... London: 1874. V. 52

An Alphabetical Dictionary of Coats of Arms Belonging to Families in Great Britain and Ireland, Forming an Extensive Ordinary of British Armorials. Baltimore: 1965. V. 50; 54

THE PARABLES from the Gospels. 1903. V. 49

PARACELSUS
Astronomia Magna: Oder die Gantze Philosophia Sagax der Grossen und der Kleinen Welt... Frankfurt: 1571. V. 47
Avreoli Theophrasti Paracelsi Archidoxorum Seu de Secretis Naturae Mysteriis, Libri Decem. Basileae: 1582. V. 48; 49; 50
De Meteoris Liber Unus De Matrice Liber Alius. De Tribus principiis Liber Tertius. Quibus Astronomica & Astrologia Fragmenta Queda Accesserunt. Basiliae: 1569. V. 49; 50
De Peste. Oppenheim: 1613. V. 47; 50; 53
De Summis Naturae Mysteriis Commentarii Tres a Gerardo Dorn Conversi. Basle: 1584. V. 48
Four Treatises of Theophrastus Von Hohenheim called Paracelsus. Baltimore: 1941. V. 50; 52
The Hermetic and Alchemical Writings.... London: 1894. V. 51
Of the Chymical Transmutation, Genealogy and Generation of Metals & Minerals. London: 1657. V. 52
Of the Supreme Mysteries of Nature; of the Spirits of the Planets... London: 1656. V. 48
Opera Omnia Medico-Chemico-Chirurgica. Geneva: 1658. V. 50
Opus Chyrurgicum. Strassburg: 1564. V. 47; 50; 53
Philosophiae et Medicinae Utriusque Universae. Parisiis: 1567. V. 53
Philosophy Reformed and Improved in Four Profound Tractates. London: 1657. V. 48
Selected Writings. New York: 1941. V. 52
Selected Writings. New York: 1951. V. 50; 52
Wunder Artzney, Vonn Allerley Leibs Gebruchen, unnd zu Fallenden Kranckheiten, ohn Sondere Beschwerung, Unlust unnd Verdrusz... Basel: 1573. V. 53

A PARADOX Against Liberty. London: 1679. V. 48; 54

PARAMORE, EDWARD E.
The Ballad of Yukon Jake. New York: 1928. V. 49

PARBURT, GEORGE R.
Anselmo: a Poem. San Francisco: 1865. V. 52

PARCHER, MARIE LOUISE
Dry Ditches. Bishop: 1934. V. 53

PARDAL, JOSE
Elephant Hunting in Portuguese East Africa. 1990. V. 54
Elephant Hunting in Portuguese East Africa. London: 1990. V. 52

PARDOE, JULIA
The Beauties of Bosphorus. London: 1838. V. 54
The Beauties of Bosphorus... London & Hamburg: 1838-39. V. 48
The Beauties of Bosphorus. London: 1839. V. 48; 52
The Beauties of Bosphorus. London: 1839-40. V. 48
The Beauties of Bosphorus. London: 1855. V. 53; 54
The City of the Sultan: and Domestic Manners of the Turks in 1836. London: 1837. V. 51
The Court and Reign of Francis I King of France. London: 1887. V. 50
The Life of Marie de Medicis, Queen of France. London: 1852. V. 49; 53
Louis the Fourteenth and the Court of France in the Seventeenth Century. London: 1847. V. 52
Louis the Fourteenth and The Court of France in the Seventeenth Century. London: 1886. V. 50
The Romance of the Harem. Philadelphia: 1839. V. 54

PARDON, GEORGE FREDERICK
Beeton's Hand Book of Games. London: 1863?. V. 52
Boldheart the Warrior and His Adventures in the Haunted Wood: A Tale of the Times of Good King Arthur. 1859. V. 52
Parlour Pastimes. London: 1868. V. 47

PARE, AMBROISE
The Apologie and Treatise of Ambroise Pare... London: 1951. V. 52
The Collected Works. New York: 1968. V. 51

PARE, RICHARD
Photography and Architecture, 1839-1939. Montreal: 1982. V. 52

PARENTAL Legacies Consisting of Advice from a Lady of Quality to Her Children. Boston: 1804. V. 54

PARENTINIS, BERNARDUS DE
Expositio Officii Missae. Strassburg: 1487. V. 51

THE PARENT'S Cabinet of Amusement and Instruction. London: 1858-59. V. 51

THE PARENTS' High Commission. London: 1843. V. 52

THE PARENT'S Poetical Anthology: Being a Selection of English Poems, Primarily Designed to Assist in Forming the Taste and the Sentiments of Young Readers. London: 1814. V. 48

PARET, J. PARMLY
Methods and Players of Modern Lawn Tennis. New York: 1915. V. 52
Methods and Players of Modern Lawn Tennis. New York: 1922. V. 54

PARETO, VILFREDO
The Mind and Society. New York: 1935. V. 47

PARETSKY, SARA
Bitter Medicine. New York: 1987. V. 53; 54
Blood Shot. New York: 1988. V. 48; 49; 51
Deadlock. London: 1984. V. 50; 51; 53

PARETSKY, SARA continued
Deadlock. New York: 1984. V. 51; 52; 53; 54
Guardian Angel. 1992. V. 54
Guardian Angel. Bristol: 1992. V. 52
Indemnity Only. London: 1982. V. 54
Indemnity Only. New York: 1982. V. 49
Killing Orders. New York: 1985. V. 51; 52; 54

PARFAICT, FRANCOIS
Histoire du Theatre francois; Depuis Son origine Jusqu'a Present, Avec la Vie des Plus Celebres Poetes Dramatiques, un catalogues Exact de leurs Pieces & des Ntoes Historiques et Critiques. Paris: 1745-49. V. 49

PARINI, JAY LEE
Singing in Time. St. Andrews: 1972. V. 54

PARIS. New York: 1930. V. 49

PARIS Comique: Revue Amusant. Paris: 1844. V. 50

PARIS ET VIANA
The Noble Knight Paris & the Fair Vienne. Kentfield: 1956. V. 50; 53
The Noble Knight Paris & the Fair Vienne. Kentfield: 1961. V. 48

PARIS HILL MANUFACTURING CO.
Annual Illustrated Catalogue and Price List of Children's Carriages, Boys' Carts and Wagons, Sleds &c. Paris: 1876. V. 49

PARIS, JOHN AYRTON
The British Bee Hive. London: 1867. V. 49
The Elements of Medical Chemistry. London: 1825. V. 47; 49
A Guide to the Mount Bay and the Land's End: Comprehending the Topography Botany, Agriculture...of Western Cornwell. London: 1824. V. 47; 48; 53
The Life of Sir Humphry Davy, Bart. LL.D. London: 1831. V. 52
Medical Jurisprudence. London: 1823. V. 48
Miscellanea Practico-Theoretica, or a Miscellany Chiefly concerning Faith and Manners. Cambridge: 1726. V. 49
Pharmacologia... London: 1820. V. 48; 54
Pharmacologia. New York: 1825. V. 51; 52
Pharmacologia. New York: 1828. V. 52
Philosophy in Sport Made Science in Earnest... London: 1827. V. 49; 54
Philosophy in Sport Made Science in Earnest; Being An Attempt to Illustrated the First Principles of Natural Philosophy by the Aid of the Popular Toys and Sports of Youth. Philadelphia: 1847. V. 49
A Treatise on Diet. London: 1826. V. 47; 48; 50

PARIS, LOUIS PHILIPPE ALBERT D'ORLEANS, COMTE DE
Historie de la Guerre Civile en Amerique. Paris: 1874-90. V. 54
History of the Civil War in America. Philadelphia: 1875-88. V. 49; 54

PARIS, MATTHEW
Historia Major. London: 1570. V. 53
Historia Major... Londinii: 1571. V. 51
Historia Major. London: 1640. V. 50

PARIS DE MEYZIEU, J. B.
Bibliotheca Parisiana. London: 1791. V. 52

PARISH, EDMUND
Hallucinations and Illusions. A Study of the Fallacies of Perception. New York: 1897. V. 53

PARISH, ELIJAH
Sacred Geography: or, a Gazetteer of the Bible, Containing, in Alphabetical Order, a Geographical Description of All the Countries, Kingdoms, Nations and Tribes of Men... Boston: 1813. V. 48

THE PARISH Registers of Dalston, Cumberland. Baptisms, 1570-1678; Marriages, 1570-1678; Burials 1570-1678. Dalston: 1893. V. 52

THE PARISH Registers of Dalston, Cumberland. Baptsims, 1679-1812; Marriages 1679-1812, Burials 1678-1812. Dalston: 1895. V. 52

PARISH, ROBERTSON W.
A Vist to Mexico by the West Indian Islands, Yucatan and United States. London: 1853. V. 54

PARISH, W. D.
A Dictionary of the Kentish Dialect and Provincialisms in Use in the County of Kent. Lewes: 1888. V. 53
A Dictionary of the Sussex Dialect and Collection of Provincialisms in Use in the County of Sussex. Lewes: 1875. V. 47; 52

PARISH, WOODBINE
Buenos Ayres and the Provinces of Rio Dela Plata. London: 1839. V. 50; 53

PARISH-WATSON & CO., INC.
Chinese Pottery of the Han, T'Ang and Sung Dynasties; Owned and Exhibited by Parish-Watson & Co., Inc. New York: 1917. V. 47

PARISOT, P. F.
The Reminiscences of a Texas Missionary. San Antonio: 1899. V. 49

PARISOT, PIERRE
Tres-Humbles Representation de Pierre Parisot de Lorraine, a la Nation Angloise au Sujet du Nouvel Etablissement d'Arts & de manufactures; Forme, sous sa Direction, Pars les Ordres a la Generosite de la Famille Royale et des premiers Siegneurs du... London: 1755. V. 49

PARIVAL, J.
The Historie of This Iron Age: Wherein Is Set Down the True State of Europe... London: 1659. V. 47

PARIVAL, JEAN NICHOLAS DE
The History of This Iron Age: Wherein is Set Down the True State of Europe. London: 1656. V. 54

PARK, EDWIN H.
The Park Record... Denver: 1902. V. 47

PARK, GEORGE
Tumors of the Hands and Feet. St. Louis: 1939. V. 54

PARK, JAMES ALAN
Memoirs of William Stevens, Esq. (with) Postscript to Mr. Justice Park's memoirs of the Late William Stevens, Esq. London: 1823. V. 50

PARK, JOHN JAMES
The Topography and Natural History of Hampstead. London: 1814. V. 49; 50; 52
The Topography and Natural History of Hampstead. London: 1818 or later. V. 47; 50; 53

PARK, LAWRENCE
Gilbert Stuart, an Illustrated Descriptive List of His Works. New York: 1926. V. 47; 48; 50

PARK, MAUD WOOD
Front Door Lobby. Boston: 1960. V. 53

PARK, MUNGO
The Journal of a Mission to the Interior of Africa in the Year 1805 together with Other Documents, Official and Private... London: 1815. V. 54
Travels in the Interior Districts of Africa... London: 1799. V. 47; 49; 50; 52
Travels in the Interior Districts of Africa; Performed Under the Direction and Patronage of the African Association in the Years 1795, 1796 and 1797... (with) The Journal of a Mission to the Interior of Africa in the Year 1805... London: 1799/1815. V. 47
Travels in the Interior Districts of Africa, Performed Under the Direction and Patronage of the African Association, in the Years 1795, 1796, and 1797...To Which is added the Life of Mr. Park. London: 1800/1816. V. 52
Travels in the Interior of Africa... London: 1800. V. 47; 51; 52; 54
Travels in the Interior of Africa. London: 1878. V. 54
Travels in the Interior of Africa...Including Both Expeditions... London: 1817. V. 52

PARK, ROBERT EMORY
Sketch of the Twelfth Alabama Infantry. Richmond: 1906. V. 49

PARK, ROSWELL
Selected Papers, Surgical and Scientific. Buffalo: 1914. V. 50; 52

PARK, SAMUEL
Notes of Early History of Union Township, Licking County Ohio. (&) American Antiquities: Read Before a Joint Meeting of the Pioneer Association of the Counties of Franklin, Muskingum and Licing. Terre Haute: 1870. V. 53

PARK, THOMAS
Bibliotheca Anglo-Poetica or a Descriptive Catalogue of a Rare and Rich Collection of Early English Poetry... London: 1815. V. 48
Cupid Turned Volunteer, in a Series of Prints... London: 1804. V. 54
Heliconia. London: 1815. V. 52; 53; 54
Sonnets, and Other Small Poems. London: 1797. V. 48

PARKE, THOMAS HEAZLE
My Personal Experiences in Equatorial Africa As Medical Officer of the Emin Pasha Relief Expedition. London: 1891. V. 54

PARKE, WILLIAM THOMAS
Musical Memoirs; Comprising an Account of the General State of Music in England, from...1784 to the Year 1830... London: 1830. V. 47

PARKER, A. C.
The Code of Handsome Lake, the Seneca Prophet. New York: 1913. V. 54

PARKER, ALFRED BROWNING
You and Architecture; a Practical Guide to the Best Building. New York: 1965. V. 53; 54

PARKER, AMOS A.
Trip to the West and Texas. Concord: 1835. V. 49
Trip to the West and Texas. Concord: 1836. V. 49

PARKER, B.
The Browns: A Book of Bears. London: 1910. V. 47
The History of the Hoppers. Edinburgh. V. 52
The 'Trocious twins at the Sea. London. V. 49

PARKER BROTHERS
The Parker Games 1922. Salem: 1922. V. 54

PARKER, CHARLES ARUNDEL
The Ancient Crosses at Gosforth, Cumberland. London: 1896. V. 52
The Runic Crosses at Gosforth, Cumberland. London: 1882. V. 52

PARKER, CHARLES H.
The Civil Practice Act of the State of California, As Amended... San Francisco: 1863. V. 48; 53

PARKER, DOROTHY
After Such Pleasures. New York: 1933. V. 47; 48; 49; 51; 54
Death and Taxes. New York: 1931. V. 47; 50; 51; 53; 54
Her Lies. The Collected Stories. New York: 1939. V. 47
The Ladies of the Corridor. New York: 1954. V. 47
Laments for the Living. New York: 1930. V. 47; 51
Not so Deep As a Well. New York: 1936. V. 49; 51
The Pleasure of Their Company, an Anthology of Civilized Writing. New York: 1946. V. 49
Sunset Gun. London: 1928. V. 48

PARKER, DOROTHY continued
Sunset Gun. New York: 1928. V. 47; 48; 49
The Viking Portable Library Dorothy Parker. New York: 1944. V. 54

PARKER, EDWARD HARPER
Ancient China Simplified. London: 1908. V. 50

PARKER, F. H. M.
The Pipe Rolls of Cumberland and Westmorland 1222-1260. Kendal: 1905. V. 50; 52

PARKER, G. H.
The Elementary Nervous System. Philadelphia & London: 1919. V. 52

PARKER, GEORGE
Life's Painter of Variegated Characters in Public and Private Life. London: 1789. V. 48
A Survey of the Six Days Works of the Creation: Philosophically Proving the Truth of the Account Thereof... London: 1745. V. 49

PARKER, GEORGE WILLIAMS
A Concise Grammar of the Malagasy Language. London: 1883. V. 50

PARKER, GEORGE WINSHIP
William Caxton. Paper Read at a Meeting of the Club of Odd Volumes in Boston Massachusetts, USA in Jan. 1908. Hammersmith: 1909. V. 51

PARKER, H.
Mail and Passenger Steamships of the Nineteenth Century. Philadelphia: 1928. V. 53

PARKER, HARRY
Naval Battles from the Collection of Prints Formed and Owned by Commander Sir C. L. Cust... London: 1911. V. 54

PARKER, HERBERT
Courts and Lawyers of New England. New York: 1931. V. 49; 50

PARKER, JAMES
Conductor Generalis: or, the Office, Duty and Authority of Justices of the Peace, High Sheriffs... Woodbridge: 1764. V. 47; 50; 51; 53
The Old Army Memories. Philadelphia: 1929. V. 47; 50; 52

PARKER, JOEL
Daniel Webster as a Jurist: An Address to the Students in the Law School of the University of Cambridge. Cambridge: 1853. V. 49

PARKER, JOHN HENRY
The Archaeology of Rome. Oxford and London: 1874. V. 50; 54
A Glossary of Terms Used in Grecian, Roman, Italian and Gothic Architecture. London: 1840. V. 50
A Glossary of Terms Used in Grecian, Roman, Italian and Gothic Architecture. Oxford: 1845. V. 52
A Glossary of Terms Used in Grecian, Roman, Italian and Gothic Architecture. (with) A Companion to the fourth Edition of a Glossary of Terms. Oxford: 1845/46. V. 49
A Hand-Book for Visitors to Oxford. Oxford: 1847. V. 52
A Hand-Book for Visitors to Oxford. Oxford: 1875. V. 50; 53
Some Account of Domestic Architecture in England, from Edward I. to Richard II. Oxford: 1853. V. 53

PARKER, K. LANGLOH
The Eutahlayi Tribe. London: 1905. V. 52

PARKER, LOUIS N.
Pomander Walk. London: 1912. V. 48

PARKER, MISS
A Tour In Scotland in 1863. London: 1984. V. 48

PARKER, NATHAN H.
Iowa As It Is in 1855. Chicago: 1855. V. 47
Iowa As It Is in 1856. Chicago: 1856. V. 53
The Minnesota Handbook, for 1856-57. Boston: 1857. V. 50
The Missouri Hand-Book. St. Louis: 1865. V. 54
Parker's Illustrated Hand Book of the Great West. New York: 1869. V. 48

PARKER, OLIVIA
Under the Looking Glass. Boston: 1983. V. 54
Weighing the Planets. Boston: 1987. V. 54

PARKER, RICHARD A.
The Calendars of Ancient Egypt. Chicago: 1950. V. 51
Demotic Mathematical Papyri. Providence: 1972. V. 49; 51
The Edifice of Taharqa by the Sacred Lake of karnak. Providence: 1979. V. 51

PARKER, RICHARD DUNSCOMBE
Birds of Ireland. 1983. V. 48; 52

PARKER, ROBERT B.
A Catskill Eagle. New York: 1985. V. 48; 52; 54
Ceremony. New York: 1982. V. 50; 52
Double Deuce. New York: 1992. V. 47; 49; 53
Early Autumn. New York: 1981. V. 50
God Save the Child. Boston: 1974. V. 47; 48; 50; 51; 52; 54
God Save the Child. London: 1975. V. 52
The Godwulf Manuscript. Boston: 1973. V. 53
The Godwulf Manuscript. Boston: 1974. V. 50; 51; 52; 54
The Godwulf Manuscript. London: 1974. V. 52
Looking for Rachel Wallace. New York: 1980. V. 49; 52; 53
Mortal Stakes. Boston: 1975. V. 49; 52; 53; 54
Mortal Stakes. London: 1976. V. 48; 52

Pale Kings and Princes. New York: 1987. V. 48
Paper Doll. New York: 1993. V. 49
Parker on Writing. Northridge: 1985. V. 48; 52
Pastime. New York: 1991. V. 48; 49; 52
Playmates. New York: 1989. V. 48; 52
Poodle Springs. London: 1989. V. 48; 52
Promised Land. Boston: 1976. V. 52; 53; 54
Stardust. New York: 1990. V. 48; 52
Surrogate. Northridge: 1982. V. 49; 52
Walking Shadow. New York: 1994. V. 52
The Widening Gyre. New York: 1983. V. 50

PARKER, S. E.
Logic, or the Art of Reasoning Simplified, In This Work Remarks Are Made on Intuitive and Deductive Evidences... Philadelphia: 1837. V. 48

PARKER, SAMUEL
A Discourse of Ecclesiastical Politie: Wherein the Authority of the Civil Magistrate Over the Consciences of Subjects in Matters of External Religion is Asserted. London: 1671. V. 50
Journal of an Exploring Tour Beyond the Rocky Mountains. Ithaca: 1838. V. 53; 54
Journal of an Exploring Tour Beyond the Rocky Mountains. Ithaca: 1840. V. 53
Journal of an Exploring Tour Beyond the Rocky Mountains. Ithaca: 1844. V. 47
Journal of an Exploring Tour Beyond the Rocky Mountains... Auburn: 1846. V. 47; 53
A Journey Beyond the Rocky Mountains in 1835, 1836 and 1837... Edinburgh: 1841. V. 54

PARKER, T. JEFFERSON
Little Saigon. New York: 1988. V. 51

PARKER, THEODORE
John Brown's Expedition Reviewed in a Letter from Rev. Theodore Parker at Rome, to Francis Jackson. Boston: 1860. V. 48
The Present Aspect of Slavery in America and the Immediate Duty of the North: A Speech Delivered in the Hall of the Great State House, Before the Massachusetts Anti-Slavery Convention, on Friday Night, January 29, 1858. Boston: 1858. V. 48

PARKER, THOMAS LISTER
Description of Browsholme Hall. London: 1815. V. 52

PARKER, THOMAS NETHERSON
An Essay, or Practical Inquiry Concerning the Hanging and Fastening of Gates and Wickets. London: 1801. V. 47; 50

PARKER, THOMAS V.
The Cherokee Indians with Special Reference to Their Relations with the Federal Government. New York: 1907. V. 49

PARKER, W. K.
A Monograph On the Structure and Development of the Shoulder Girdle and Sternum in the Vertebrata. London: 1868. V. 49

PARKER, WILLIAM B.
Notes Taken During the Expedition Commanded by Capt. R. B. Marcy, U.S.A. Through Unexplored Texas, in the Summer and Fall of 1854. Philadelphia: 1856. V. 47; 49; 52

PARKER, WILLIAM HARWAR
Recollections of a Naval Officer 1841-1865. New York: 1883. V. 54

PARKER, WILLIAM RILEY
Milton: a Biography. Oxford: 1968. V. 48

PARKES, DOW
Nidus. A Dramatic Poem in Three Voices. Los Angeles: 1950. V. 51

PARKES, EDMUND
The Composition of the Urine in Health and Disease and Under the Action of Remedies. London: 1860. V. 49; 54

PARKES, FANNY
Wanderings of a Pilgrim, In Search of the Picturesque, During Four-and-Twenty Years in the East... London: 1850. V. 51

PARKES, FRANCES BYERLEY
Domestic Duties; or Instructions to Young Married Ladies, on the Management of Their Households and the Regulation of Their Conduct in the Various Relations and Duties of Married Life. London: 1825. V. 53

PARKES, HARRY
The Girl Who Wouldn't Mind Getting Married. 1887. V. 53

PARKES, HENRY
The Beauteous Terrorist. Melborne: 1885. V. 50

PARKES, M. B.
The Medieval Manuscripts of Keble College. London: 1979. V. 48
The Medieval Manuscripts of Kelbe College. 1974. V. 53

PARKES, MARY
Art Monopoly. London: 1850. V. 54

PARKES, OSCAR
British Battleships 1860-1950. London: 1973. V. 50
British Battleships 1860-1950. A History of Design, Construction and Armament. London: 1990. V. 54
British Battleships, 'Warrior' 1860 to 'Vanguard' 1950, a History of Design, Construction and Armament. London: 1956. V. 49

PARKES, SAMUEL
The Rudiment of Chemistry... London: 1810. V. 49

PARKHURST, JOHN L.
Elements of Moral Philosophy. Concord: 1825. V. 47

PARKIN, CHARLES
The History of Great Yarmouth Collected from Antient Records and Other Authentic Materials. Lynn: 1776. V. 50

PARKIN, GEORGE R.
The Great Dominion: Studies of Canada. London: 1895. V. 48

PARKINSON & FRODSHAM
A Brief Account of the Chronometer, with Remarks On Those Furnished by Parkinson and Frodsham to the Expeditions of Captains Ross, Parry, Sabine, King, Lyon, Foster and Other Distinguished Navigators with the Rate of Others Tried at the Royal Ovservatory.. London: 1832. V. 53

PARKINSON, J. C.
The Ocean Telegraph to India, a Narrative and a Diary. Edinburgh and London: 1870. V. 49; 50

PARKINSON, JAMES
The Chemical Pocket-Book... Philadelphia: 1802. V. 50
Organic Remains of a Former World. London: 1804-11. V. 50
Organic Remains of a Former World. London: 1804/08. V. 51
Organic Remains of a Former World. London: 1808-11. V. 48

PARKINSON, JOHN
Outlines of Oryctology. London: 1822. V. 54
Outlines of Oryctology. London: 1831. V. 51
Paradisi in Sole Paradisus Terrestris. London: 1629. V. 52
Paradisi in sole Paradisus Terrestris... London: 1904. V. 47; 49; 53
Theatrum Botanicum... London: 1640. V. 47; 51

PARKINSON, RICHARD
The Experienced Farmer. Philadelphia: 1799. V. 52; 53
Treatise on the Breeding and Management of Live Stock... London: 1810. V. 48

PARKINSON, SYDNEY
A Journal of a Voyage to the South Seas, in His Majesty's Ship, the Endeavour. London: 1773. V. 47; 50; 51; 52
A Journal of a Voyage to the South Seas, In His Majesty's Ship the Endeavour... London: 1784. V. 54
A Journal of a Voyage to the South Seas, in His Majesty's Ship, the Endeavour. Adelaide: 1972. V. 54

PARKINSON, THOMAS
Hart Crane and Yvor Winters - Their Literary Correspondence. Berkeley, Los Angeles: 1978. V. 52
Lays and Leaves of the Forest... London: 1882. V. 53

PARKINSON, WILLIAM
A New Book of Instructions for Beginners on the Piano Forte or Harpsichord. Goulding: 1819. V. 49

PARKMAN, FRANCIS
The California and Oregon Trail. New York: 1849. V. 47; 49
Complete Works. London: 1899-1913. V. 49; 52
Complete Works. Boston: 1907. V. 51
The Discovery of the Great West. Boston: 1869. V. 48
The Frontenac Edition of Francis Parkman's Works. Toronto: 1899. V. 48
History of the Conspiracy of Pontiac, and the War of the North American Tribes. Boston: 1851. V. 50
History of the Conspiracy of Pontiac and the War of the North American Tribes. London: 1851. V. 51
History of the Conspiracy of Pontiac, and the War of the North American Tribes. Boston: 1855. V. 53
The Jesuits in North America in the Seventeenth Century. Boston: 1867. V. 47; 48
The Journals of Francis Parkman. New York: London: 1947. V. 52
The Old Regime in Canada. Boston: 1874. V. 47
The Oregon Trail. Boston: 1892. V. 48; 50; 54
The Oregon Trail. New York: 1943. V. 49; 53
The Oregon Trail. New York: 1945. V. 48
Pioneers of France and England in North America, a Series of Historical Narratives. Boston: 1865. V. 47
Some of the Reasons Against Woman Suffrage. Boston: 1884?. V. 51
Vassall Morton. Boston: 1856. V. 51; 52
Works. Boston: 1899. V. 51
Works. Boston: 1910. V. 52
Works. Boston: 1919. V. 52; 53

PARKS, GORDON
Camera Portraits: The Techniques and Principles of Documentary Portraiture. New York: 1948. V. 47

PARK'S *Infant Tales.* London: 1840. V. 49

PARKS, JOSEPH H.
General Kirby Smith, CSA. Baton Rouge: 1954. V. 47; 52
General Leonidas Polk C.S.A. the Fighting Bishop. Baton Rouge: 1962. V. 52

PARKS, WILLIAM A.
Report on the Building and Ornamental Stones of Canada. Ottawa: 1912-17. V. 52

PARKYNS, GEORGE ISHAM
An Essay on the Different Natural Situations of Gardens. London: 1774. V. 53
Monastic and Baronial Remains, with other Interesting Fragments of Antiquity, in England, Wales and Scotland. London: 1816. V. 48; 49; 51

PARKYNS, J. G.
Monastic and Baronial Remains. London: 1816. V. 53

PARKYNS, MANSFIELD
Life in Abyssinia... London: 1853. V. 54
Life in Abyssinia. New York: 1854. V. 48; 51

PARKYNS, THOMAS
Progymnasmata (Greek Ttile). The Inn-Play: or, Cornish-Hugg Wrestler. London: 1727. V. 50

PARLBY, SAMUEL
Desultory Thoughts on the National Drama Past and Present. London: 1850. V. 52

THE PARLIAMENTARY or *Constitutional History of England: from the Earliest Times to the Restoration of King Charles II...* London: 1762/63. V. 54

THE PARLIAMENTARY *Register, Containing Lists of the Twenty Four Parliaments from 1660 to 1741.* London: 1741. V. 50

THE PARLIAMENTARY *Register; or, History of the Proceedings and Debates of the House of Lords...During the Third Session of the Fourteenth Parliament of Great Britain. Volume VII.* London: 1777. V. 49

PARLOA, M.
The Appledore Cook Book: Containing Practical Receipts for Plain and Rich Cooking. Boston: 1872. V. 49
Camp Cookery. Boston: 1878. V. 48

THE PARLOUR *Spelling-Book.* Philadelphia: 1806. V. 51

PARMALEE, PAUL W.
Decoys and Decoy Carvers of Illinois. DeKalb: 1969. V. 47

PARMELIN, HELENE
Picasso: Intimate Secrets of a Studio at Notre Dame. New York: 1966. V. 47; 48; 50
Picasso: Women. Paris and Amsterdam: 1965. V. 54

PARNASSUS *Biceps, or Several Choice Pieces of Poetry.* London: 1927. V. 47

PARNELL, EDWARD ANDREW
A Practical Treatise on Dyeing and Calico-printing... New York: 1846. V. 53

PARNELL, HENRY
On Financial Reform. London: 1830. V. 49
A Treatise on Roads.... London: 1833. V. 47; 49; 51; 54

PARNELL, R.
The Grasses of Britain. London: 1842-45. V. 50

PARNELL, REGINALD
Baby Jane's Mission. London: 1902. V. 48

PARNELL, THOMAS
Homer's Battle of the Frogs and Mice. London: 1717. V. 51
Poems. Dublin: 1927. V. 48
Poems on Several Occasions. London: 1722. V. 47; 48; 49; 50; 53
Poems on Several Occasions. London: 1722/21. V. 47
Poems on Several Occasions. London: 1737. V. 48; 52
Poems on Several Occasions. Dublin: 1744. V. 48
Poems on Several Occasions. London: 1747. V. 48; 49
Poems on Several Occasions...With the Life of Zoilus and His Remarks on Homer's Battle of the Frogs and Mice... Dublin: 1773. V. 52
The Poetical Works. Edinburgh: 1778. V. 48; 49
The Poetical Works. Glasgow: 1786. V. 47; 48; 49; 51; 53; 54
The Poetical Works of Thomas Parnell. London: 1866. V. 51

PARNELL, WILLIAM
An Enquiry into the Causes of Popular Discontents in Ireland. London: 1805. V. 52
Julietta, or the Triumph of Mental Acquirements Over personal Defects. London: 1802. V. 51
Maurice and Bergheta; or, the Priest of Rahery. Dublin: 1817. V. 51

PARNELL-HAYES, WILLIAM
Maurice and Berghetta; or, the Priest of Rahery. London: 1819. V. 50

PAROCHIAL *Letters from a Beneficed Clergyman to His Curate.* London: 1829. V. 47

PARQUIN, CHARLES
Napoleon's Victories: Authentic memoirs of Captain Charles Parquin of the Imperial Guard. Chicago: 1898. V. 50

PARR, BARTHOLOMEW
The London Medical Dictionary... London: 1809. V. 52

PARR, HARRIET
Mr. Wynyard's Ward. London: 1867. V. 50
Mrs. Denys of Cote. London: 1879. V. 54
Mrs. Denys of Cote. London: 1880. V. 50
This Work-a-Day World. London: 1875. V. 50
The True, Pathetic History of Poor Match. London: 1864. V. 50

PARR, LOUISA
Loyalty George. London: 1888. V. 48
Robin. London: 1882. V. 50

PARR, RICHARD
The Life of James Usher, Late Lord Archbishop of Armagh... 1686. V. 48

PARR, SAMUEL
Bibliotheca Parriana. A Catalogue of the Library. London: 1827. V. 47; 48

PARRA, NICANOR
Emergency Poems. New York: 1972. V. 50

PARRENO, ALBERTO
Spain and Her Colonies in the New World. The Parreno Collection. New York: 1978. V. 47; 50

PARRIS, LESLIE
Constable. London: 1991. V. 49

PARRISH, EDWARD
A Treatise on Pharmacy. Philadelphia: 1867. V. 49

PARRISH, LYDIA
Slave Songs of the Georgia Sea Islands. New York: 1942. V. 50

PARRISH, MORRIS L.
A List of the Writings of Lewis Carroll in the Library at Dormy House, Pine Valley, New Jersey. Collected by M. L. Parrish. (with) A Supplementary List of Writings of Lewis Carroll... Pine Valley: 1928-33. V. 51
A Supplementary List of the Writings of Lewis Carroll (Charles L. Dodgson) in the Library at Dormy House, Pine Valley, New Jersey. 1933. V. 47
Victorian Lady Novelists. V. 54

PARRISH, T. C.
Colorado Springs Its Climate, Scenery and Society. Colorado Springs: 1889. V. 47

PARROT, ANDRE
The Arts of Assyria. New York: 1961. V. 49; 52
Studia mariana. Leiden: 1950. V. 49
Sumer: the Dawn of Art 1. New York: 1960. V. 49; 52

PARROT, FRIEDRICH
Journey to Ararat. London: 1845. V. 51

PARROT, GRAY
Thirty-Four Marbled Papers, Decorated and Arranged By... Hancock: 1993. V. 50; 53

PARROTT, WILLIAM
Paris & the Environs Done on Stone from Nature, with Tinted Grounds. Paris: 1843. V. 49; 52

PARRY, A. N., & CO.
A. N. Parry & Co. Builders of Carriages of the Best Class. Amesbury: 1885-90. V. 52; 53

PARRY, CALEB
Collections from the Unpublished Medical Writings of the Late Caleb Hillier Parry. London: 1825. V. 47

PARRY, D.
The Scarlett Empire. 1906. V. 52

PARRY, E. J.
Parry's Encyclopaedia of Perfumery... London: 1925. V. 49

PARRY, EDWARD
Butter Scotia or a Cheap Trip to Fairy Land. London: 1896. V. 49; 54
The First Book of Krab: Christmas Stories for Young & Old. London: 1897. V. 49

PARRY, HENRY
The Art of Bookbinding. Cambridge: 1818. V. 52
The Art of Bookbinding. London: 1818. V. 54

PARRY, JOHN
A Selection of Welsh Melodies, With Appropriate English Words... London: 1809. V. 49

PARRY, JOHN D.
An Historical and Descriptive Account of the Coast of Sussex. Brighton & London: 1833. V. 47; 50
History and Description of Woburn and Its Abbey... London and Brighton,: 1831. V. 47

PARRY, JUDGE
Don Quixote. London: 1900. V. 51
Don Quixote of the Mancha. New York: 1900. V. 53

PARRY, MRS.
Olive Hastings. London: 1856. V. 54

PARRY, NICHOLAS
In Valleys of Springs of Rivers. Shropshire: 1981. V. 52
A Rook Book. Shropshire: 1988. V. 52

PARRY, OSWALD H.
Six Months in a Syrian Monastery, Being the Record of a Visit to the Head Quarters of the Syrian Church in Mesopotamia... London: 1895. V. 47; 48

PARRY, ROBERT WILLIAMS
Cerdi, Detholaid Gyda Rhagymadrodd gan Thomas Parry. 1980. V. 47

PARRY, THOMAS
On Diet, With its Influence of Man. London: 1844. V. 49

PARRY, WILLIAM EDWARD
Journal of a Second Voyage for the Discovery of a North-West Passage. London: 1824. V. 52; 53; 54
Journal of a Voyage for the Discovery of a North-West Passage. London: 1821. V. 47; 48; 50; 52; 53
Journal of a Voyage for The Discovery of a North-West Passage. Philadelphia: 1821. V. 49; 50
Journal of a Voyage for the Discovery of a North-West Passage from the Atlantic to the Pacific; Performed in the Years 1819-20... New York: 1969. V. 48
Journals of the First, Second and Third Voyages for the Discovery of a Northwest Passage from the Atlantic to the Pacific, in 1819-20-21-22-23-24-25. (with) Narrative of an Attempt to Reach the North Pole in Boats Fitted for the Purpose... London: 1828/29. V. 50
Memoirs of Rear-Admiral Sir W. Edward Parry. London: 1859. V. 48
Narrative of an Attempt to Reach the North Pole, in Boats Fitted for the Purpose and Attached to His Majesty's Ship Hecla, in the Year 1827. London: 1828. V. 54
A Supplement to the Appendix of Captain Parry's Voyage... London: 1824. V. 49

PARSON, ARTHUR JEFFREY
Catalog of the Gardiner Greene Hubbard Collection of Engravings Presented to the Library of Congress by Mrs. Greene. Washington: 1905. V. 53

PARSON, E.C.
Isleta Paintings. Washington: 1962. V. 47

PARSON, EMILY ELIZABETH
Memoir of... Boston: 1880. V. 53

PARSON, WILLIAM
History, Directory and Gazetteer of the Counties of Cumberland and Westmorland... Leeds: 1829. V. 50; 52; 54

THE PARSONIAD; a Satyr. London: 1733. V. 52

PARSONNET, AARON
Applied Electrocaradiography. New York: 1929. V. 54

PARSONS, ALBERT
Life of Albert Parsons with Brief History of the Labor Movement in America. Chicago: 1889. V. 50

PARSONS, CLERE
Poems. London: 1932. V. 52; 54

PARSONS, E. C.
Notes on Zuni. V. 48
A Pueblo Indian Journal 1920-1921: Introduction and Notes. Menasha: 1925. V. 48
The Social Organization of the Tewa of New Mexico. Menash: 1929. V. 54
Taos Pueblo. Menasha. V. 48

PARSONS, EDWARD
The Tourist's Companion; or, the History of the Scenes and Places on the Route by the Railroad and Steam-Packet from Leeds and Selby to Hull. London: 1835. V. 53

PARSONS, GEORGE F.
The Life and Adventures of James W. Marshall... Sacramento: 1870. V. 48
The Life and Adventures of James W. Marshall. San Francisco: 1935. V. 47; 53; 54

PARSONS, HORATIO D.
The Book of Niagara Falls. Buffalo: 1838. V. 54

PARSONS, JAMES
Philosophical Observations on the Analogy Between Propagation of Animals and That of Vegetables... London: 1752. V. 50; 54

PARSONS, JOHN HERBERT
An Introduction to the Theory of Perception. Cambridge: 1927. V. 47

PARSONS, MOSES
A Sermon Preached at Cambridge, Before His Excellency Thomas Hutchinson, Esq., Governor of Massachusetts. Boston: 1772. V. 48

PARSONS, RICHARD C.
Southern Trans-Continental Railway. Supplemental Argument, Showing the Legal Status of the Memphis, El Paso and Pacific Railraod Company in Texas. Washington: 1870. V. 47

PARSONS, ROBERT
Andrea Philopater. Elizabethae Reginae Angliae Edictum...29 Nouemb...MDXCI. Ingolstadt?: 1593. V. 51
A Christian Directory, Guiding Men to Eternal Salvation, Commonly Called the Resolution. 1650. V. 53
Elizabethae Reginae Angliae Edictum...29 Nouemb...MDXCI. Andreae Philopatri ad idem Edictvm Responsio. Ingolstadt?: 1593. V. 54
A Treatise of Three Conversions of England from Paganism to Christian Religion. London: 1688. V. 54

PARSONS' TEXAS CAVALRY BRIGADE ASSOCIATION
Minutes of the Proceedings of Fourth Re-Union of Parsons' Texas Cavalry Brigade Association Held at Alvarado, Johnson Co., Texas, August 1st and 2nd, 1883. Waxahachie: 1883. V. 49

PARSONS, THEOPHILUS
Address Commemorative of Rufus Choate. Boston: 1859. V. 50
Memoirs of Theophilus Parsons, Chief Justice of the Supreme Judicial Court of Massachusetts; With Notices of Some of His Contemporaries. Boston: 1859. V. 49

PARSONS, THOMAS, & SONS, LONDON.
A Few Suggestions for Ornamental Decoration in Painters' and Decorators' Work. London: 1912. V. 54

PARSONS, THOMAS WILLIAM
The First Ten Cantos of the Inferno of Dante Alighieri. Boston: 1843. V. 47
The Shadow of the Obelisk and Other Poems. London: 1872. V. 52

PARSONS, TYLER
Mormon Fanaticism Exposed. Boston: 1841. V. 50
Mormon Fanaticism Exposed. Boston: 1842. V. 53

PARSONS, USHER
Boylston Prize Disserations On 1. Inflammation of the Periostium. 2. Eneuris Irratata. 3. Cutaneous Disases. 4. Cancer of the Breast. Boston: 1839. V. 49; 54

Directions for Making Anatomical Preparations, Formed on the Basis of Pole, Marjolin and Breschet and Including the New Method of Mr. Swan. Philadelphia: 1831. V. 52; 53; 54

PARSONS, WILLIAM
Travelling Recreations. London: 1807. V. 48

PARSONS, WILLIAM BARCLAY
Engineers and Engineering in the Renaissance. Baltimore: 1939. V. 53

PARTINGTON, CHARLES F.
The British Cyclopaedia of Natural History. London: 1834. V. 54

The British Cyclopaedia of the Arts and Sciences... London: 1835. V. 48

The Century of Inventions of the Marquis of Worcester. London: 1825. V. 50

National History and Views of London and Its Environs; Embracing Their Antiquities, Modern Improvements. London: 1834. V. 50; 52

National History and Views of London and its Environs, Embracing Their Antiquities, Modern Improvements etc. London: 1835. V. 50

PARTINGTON, J. R.
A History of Chemistry. London: 1961-64. V. 51

A History of Greek Fire and Gunpowder. Cambridge: 1960. V. 54

PARTINGTON, WILFRED
Thomas J. Wise in the Original Cloth. London: 1946. V. 53; 54

The War Against Malaria and Tropical Diseases. London: 1923. V. 49

PARTON, JAMES
Eminent Women of the Age: Being Narratives of the Lives and Deeds of the Most Prominent Women of the Past Generation. Hartford: 1871. V. 50; 52

Smoking and Drinking. Boston: 1868. V. 47; 49; 54

PARTON, SARA PAYSON
Ruth Hall: a Domestic Tale of the Present Time. New York: 1855. V. 51

PARTRIDGE, EDWARD
A War On Poverty. The One War that Can End War. Winnipeg. V. 54

PARTRIDGE, ERIC
A Dictionary of the Underworld, British and American... London: 1949 i.e. 1950. V. 53

The French Romantic's Knowledge of English Literature (1820-1848) - According to Contemporary French Memoirs, Letters and Periodicals. Paris: 1924. V. 47

Shakespeare's Bawdy - a Literary and Psychological Essay and a Comprehensive Glossary. London: 1947. V. 47

The Spectator - the Story of Addison & Steele's Famous Paper. San Francisco: 1939. V. 52

Three Personal Records of the War. London: 1929. V. 47

PARTRIDGE, FRANCES
Everything to Lose - Diaries 1945-1960. London: 1985. V. 53

A Pacifist's War. London: 1978. V. 53

PARTRIDGE, GEORGE
Report Of the Committee on Improvement of the Mississippi River and Tributaries. St. Louis: 1865. V. 50

PARTRIDGE, HENRY M.
The Most Remarkable Echo in the World. New York: 1933. V. 48

PARTRIDGE, JOHN
Astrological Vade Mecum Briefly Teaching the Whole Art of Astrology... London: 1679. V. 48

Merlinus Liberatus: Being an Almanack for the Year of Our Blessed Saviour's Incarnation, 1698. London: 1698. V. 50

Partridge's Advice to the Protestants of England. 1678. V. 47

PARTRIDGE, WILLIAM
A Practical Treatise on Dying of Woolen, Cotton and Skein Silk... New York: 1823. V. 52

A Practical Treatise on Dying Woollen, Cotton and Silk, Including Recipes for Lac Reds and Scarlets - Chrome Yellows and Oranges-and Prussian Blues-on Silks, cottons and Woolens. New York: 1847. V. 51

PARUTA, PAOLO
Discoris Politici...Divisi in due Libri. (with) Soliloquio. Venetia: 1599. V. 48; 50

Historia Venetiana. Venice: 1605. V. 48; 49

The History of Venice...Likewise, the Wars of Cyprus. London: 1658. V. 53

Perfection de La Vie Politiqve. Paris: 1582. V. 53

PAS, JAN
Mathematische of Wiskundige Behandeling der Schryfl konst, Behelzende een Manier om Alle de Gemeene Letteren...in Alle Haare Gedaantens, Proportien en Evenredigheden Door Passer en Liniaal te Beschryven. Amsterdam: 1737. V. 53

PASADENA ART MUSEUM
Allan Kaprow. September 15 through Octorber 22, 1967. V. 53

PASADENA, California, Illustrated and Described, Showing Its Advantages as a Place for Desirable Homes. Pasadena: 1886. V. 52

PASADENA, San Marino and Vicinity. Pasadena: 1895. V. 54

PASCAL, BLAISE
Monsieur Pascal's Thoughts, Meditations and Prayers, Touching Matters Moral and Divine. London: 1688. V. 50

The Mystery of Jesuitism, Discovered in Certain Letters, Written Upon Occasion of the Present Differences Between the Jansenists and the Molinists, Displaying the Pernicious Maximes of the Late Casuists. London: 1679. V. 47

Les Provinciales; or, the Mysterie of Jesuitisme... London: 1657. V. 52; 53

Les Provinciales, or, the Mystery of Jesuitisme. London: 1658. V. 52; 53

Thoughts on Religion and Other Subjects. London: 1704. V. 48

Traitez de L'Eqvilibre des Liqvevrs. Paris: 1664. V. 48; 52; 54

PASCALIS, FELIX
An Exposition of the Dangers of Interment in Cities: Illustrated by the Account of the Funeral Rites and Customs of Hebrews, Greeks, Romans and Primitive Christians... New York: 1823. V. 53

PASCHAL, GEORGE W.
Concluding Argument of Hon. George W. Paschal, Before the Judiciary Committee of the House of Representatives, on the 25th and 27th April, 1870, in the Case of William McGarrahan. Washington: 1870. V. 49

PASHLEY, ROBERT
Travels in Crete. London: 1837. V. 49

PASKMAN, DAILEY
Gentlemen, Be Seated. Garden City: 1928. V. 48

PASKO, W. W.
American Dictionary of Printing and Bookmaking, Containing a History of These Arts in Europe and America... New York: 1894. V. 48

PASLEY, CHARLES WILLIAM
An Inquiry Into the System of General or Commissariata Contracts, For Supplying His Majesty's Forces in Great Britain with Bread and Meat, As Compared With that of Regimental Purchases... Chatham: 1825. V. 49

EL PASO MUSEUM OF ART
The Samuel H. Kress Collection. El Paso: 1961. V. 53

PASOE, C. F.
Two Hundred Years of the S. P. G.: an Historical Account of the Society for the Progation of the Gospel in Foreign Parts 1701-1900. London: 1901. V. 49

PASOR, GEORG
Grammatica Graeca Sacra Novi Testamenti... 1655. V. 49

PASQUIER, ESTIENNE
Des Recherches de La France, Livres Premier et Second. Paris: 1570. V. 52

PASQUIN, PETER
Flowers from Nature. London: 1824. V. 49

PASSAGES, Incidents and Anecdotes in the Life of Junius Brutus Booth. New York. V. 47

PASSAVANT, G.
Verrocchio Sculpture, Paintings and Drawings. London: 1969. V. 49; 52

PASSAVANTI, JACOBO
Specchio di Vera Penitentia. Florence: 1495/96. V. 48

PASSE, CRISPIJN VAN DE
Hortus Floridus. London: 1928. V. 52

Hortus Floridus. London: 1928/29. V. 52; 54

XII Sibyllarum Icones Elegantissimi... 1601. V. 47; 52; 54

PASSEMANT, CLAUDE SIMEON
Construction d'un Telescope de Reflexion...Avec la Composition de la Matiere des Miroirs... Paris: 1738. V. 49

PASSERANO, ALBERTO RADICATI, CONTE DI
Receuil de Pieces Curieuses sur les Matieres les Plus Interessantes. Rotterdam: 1736. V. 50

PASSERAT, JEAN
Le Premier Livre de Poemes. (with) Kalendae Ianuariae & Varia Quaedam Poemata. Paris: 1602/03. V. 51

Recveil des Oevvres Poetiqves. Paris: 1606. V. 52

PASSERON, R.
Impressionist Prints. New York: 1974. V. 47; 50; 51; 53; 54

THE PASSPORTS Printed by Benjamin Franklin at His Passy Press. Ann Arbor: 1925. V. 52

PASSUTH, KRISZTINA
Laszlo Moholy-Nagy. New York: 1985. V. 49

Moholy-Nagy. London: 1985. V. 53

Moholy-Nagy. A Monograph. New York: 1985. V. 54

PASSY, HIPPOLYTE PHILIBERT
On Large and Small Farms, and Their Influence on the Social Economy. (with) Aristocracy, Considered in its Relations with the Progress of Civilization... London: 1848/48. V. 52

PAST Days in India, or Sporting Reminiscences of the Valley of the Soane and the Basin of Singrowlee. 1874. V. 51

PASTERNAK, BORIS
Bliznets V Tuchakh (Twin in the Clouds). Moscow: 1914. V. 52

Doctor Zhivago. Milan: 1957. V. 47; 50

Doctor Zhivago. London: 1958. V. 47; 50; 51; 52

Doctor Zhivago. New York: 1958. V. 53

PASTEUR, LOUIS
Studies in Fermentation. The Diseases of Beer: Their Causes and the Means of Preventing Them... London: 1879. V. 47; 49; 51; 52; 54

PASTIMES of James Joyce. New York: 1941. V. 47; 49

THE PASTON Letters 1422-1509 A.D. Westminster: 1900-01. V. 51

THE PASTON Letters 1422-1509. A.D. Edinburgh: 1910. V. 49

PASTOR, LUDWIG
The History of the Popes, from the Close of the Middle Ages: Drawn from the Secret Archives of the Vatican and Other Original Sources. St. Louis and London: 1938-53. V. 54

PATCHEN, KENNETH
An Astonished Eye Looks Out of the Air. Waldport: 1944. V. 53
An Astonished Eye Looks Out of the Air. Waldport: 1945. V. 54
Before the Brave. New York: 1936. V. 50; 51; 52
CCCLXXIV Poems. New York: 1948. V. 54
Cloth of the Tempest. New York: 1943. V. 47; 49; 51; 54
Cloth of the Tempest. New York: 1948. V. 53
The Collected Poems. New York: 1968. V. 53
Fables and Other Little Tales. Karlsruhe/Baden: 1953. V. 47; 54
Fables and Other Little Tales. North Carolina: 1953. V. 48
The Famous Boating Party. New York: 1954. V. 54
First Will and Testament. New York: 1939. V. 50
First Will and Testament. Norfolk: 1939. V. 50
First Will and Testament. New York: 1948. V. 54
Hurrah for Anything. Highlands: 1957. V. 54
The Journal of Albion Moonlight. Mount Vernon: 1941. V. 47; 53
Memoirs of a Shy Pornographer. New York: 1945. V. 54
Orchards, Thrones and Caravans. San Francisco: 1952. V. 54
Outlaw of the Lowest Planet. London: 1946. V. 54
Panels for the Walls of Heaven. Berkeley: 1946. V. 54
Pictures of Life and Death. 1946. V. 53
Pictures of Life and Death. New York: 1946. V. 54
A Poem for Christmas. Mountain View: 1976. V. 53
Red Wine and Yellow Hair. New York: 1949. V. 53; 54
See You In the Morning. New York: 1947. V. 54
Selected Poems. New York: 1946. V. 54
Sleepers Awake. New York: 1946. V. 47; 54
To Say If You Love Someone. Prairie City: 1948. V. 54

THE PATENT'S Crime; Or Fatal Curiosity. An Affecting and True History of the Unnatural Murder of James Harden, a Young Sailor, for His Wealth and Who Proved, on the Morning After the Fatal deed, to be the Murderer's Long-Lost and Only Son. London: 1830's. V. 47

PATENTS for Inventions. Abridgements of Specifications Class 144, Wheels of Vehicles, 1897-1908 and 1909-1930. London: 1902-33. V. 49

PATER, WALTER
Appreciations: With an Essay on Style. London and New York: 1901. V. 52
An Imaginary Portrait. The Child in the House. Denys L'Auxerrois. Emerald Uthwart. Portland: 1892, 1900. V. 49
An Imaginary Portrait. The Child in the House. Denys L'Auxerrois. Emerald Uthwart. Portland: 1902/1898/1900. V. 47
Imaginary Portraits. London: 1887. V. 48; 52
Imaginary Portraits and Gaston De La Tour: an Unfinished Romance. London: 1900. V. 52
Marius the Epicurean. His Sensations and Ideas. London: 1885. V. 49; 50
Marius, The Epicurean: His Sensations and Ideas. London: 1892. V. 48; 49
The Renaissance. Verona: 1976. V. 47; 48; 49; 51; 54
Salute the Mountains. London: 1962. V. 54
Sebastian Van Storck. London: 1927. V. 50; 51; 53; 54
Studies in the History of the Renaissance. London: 1873. V. 49; 52; 53

PATERSON, DANIEL
British Itinerary. London: 1800. V. 51
A New and Accurate Description Of All the Direct and Principal Cross Roads in England and Wales. London: 1794. V. 53
New and Accurate Description of all the Direct and Principal Cross Roads in England and Wales & Part of the Roads of Scotland. London: 1808. V. 53
Paterson's British Itinerary. London: 1785. V. 51; 52
Paterson's Roads; Being an Entirely Original and Accurate Description Of All the Direct and Principal Cross Roads in England and Wales... London: 1822. V. 48; 50

PATERSON, JAMES
A Complete Commentary, with Etymological, Explanatory, Critical and Classical Notes on Milton's Paradise Lost. London: 1744. V. 49; 54
The Games Laws of the United Kingdom Comprising the Whole of the Law on the Subject... London: 1861. V. 52
Origin of the Scots and the Scottish Language. Edinburgh: 1855. V. 50
Pietas Londiensis; or, the Present Ecclesiastical State of London... London: 1714. V. 50; 52

PATERSON, SAMUEL
Joineriana, or the Book of Scraps. London: 1772. V. 54

PATERSON, WALTER
The Legend of Iona, with Other Poems. Edinburgh: 1814. V. 48; 54

PATERSON, WILLIAM
An Inquiry Into the Reasonableness and Consequences of an Union with Scotland. London: 1706. V. 50
A Narrative of Four Journeys Into the Country of the Hottentots, and California. London: 1789. V. 47; 52
Twelve Etchings of Views in Edinburgh. Edinburgh: 1816. V. 52

PATIENCE By Perserverance. London: 1860. V. 51

PATMORE, COVENTRY
The Angel in the House. London: 1860-63. V. 48
The Angel in the House. London: 1863. V. 47
The Angel in the House. The Betrothal. London: 1854. V. 50; 52; 54

The Children's Garland from the Best Poets. London: 1862. V. 51
Florilegium Amantis. London: 1879. V. 52
Odes. 1868. V. 49
Poems. London: 1844. V. 50; 51; 54
Principle in Art, Etc. London: 1889. V. 51; 54
Tamerton Church-Tower and Other Poems. London: 1853. V. 50
The Unknown Eros and Other Odes. Odes I-XXXI. London: 1877. V. 51; 54

PATMORE, DEREK
Portrait of My Family. 1783-1896. New York & London: 1935. V. 51; 54

PATMORE, GEORGE
The Life and Struggle of Negro Toilers. London: 1931. V. 50

PATMORE, HENRY
Poems. 1884. V. 54

PATMORE, PETER GEORGE
British Galleries of Art. London: 1824. V. 47

PATMOS, the Treasures of the Monastery. Athens: 1988. V. 48

PATON, ALAN
Cry, the Beloved Country. New York: 1948. V. 47; 48; 51; 52; 53
Debbie Go Home. Helsinki: 1895. V. 48

PATON, ANDREW ARCHIBALD
Highlands and Islands of the Adriatic, Including Dalmatia, Croatia and the Southern Provinces of the Austrian Empire. London: 1885. V. 51

PATON, DAVID
Animals of Ancient Egypt. Princeton: 1925. V. 51
Early Egyptian Record of Travel. Volumes I-IV. Princeton: 1915-22. V. 49; 51

PATON, E. RICHMOND
The Birds of Ayrshire. 1929. V. 54
The Birds of Ayrshire. London: 1929. V. 52

PATON, EVGENY
Reminiscences. Moscow: 1956. V. 49

PATON, JAMES
British History and Papal Claims 1066-1892. 1893. V. 48; 52
Missionary to the New Hebrides. London: 1890. V. 52
Scottish History and Life. Glasgow: 1902. V. 52; 54

PATON, JOSEPH NOEL
Poems by a Painter. Edinburgh: 1861. V. 48

PATON, LUCY ALLEN
American School of Classical Studies at Athens. Cambridge: 1924. V. 50; 53
Selected Bindings from the Gennadius Library. Cambridge: 1924. V. 49; 54

PATON, MAGGIE WHITECROSS
Letters and Sketches from the New Hebrides. London: 1894. V. 48; 50; 51

PATON, NOEL
Poems. London: 1861. V. 49

PATRICK, JAMES
The Posthumous Works of the Late Mr. James Patrick of Houston. Edinburgh: 1836. V. 50

PATRICK, JOHN
A Century of Select Psalms and Portions of the Psalms of David, Especially Those of Praise Turned into Metre... London: 1686. V. 54
The Teahouse of the August Moon. New York: 1952. V. 47; 54

PATRICK, SYMON
The Book of Job Paraphras'd. London: 1697. V. 49
The Book of Psalms Paraphras'd; with Arguments to Each Psalm. London: 1691. V. 49
The Christian Sacrifice. London: 1671. V. 48; 52
The Parable of the Pilgrim... London: 1668. V. 50
A Paraphrase Upon the Books of Ecclesiasates, and the Song of Solomon. London: 1685. V. 49

PATRICK, VINCENT
The Pope of Greenwich Village. New York: 1979. V. 52

THE PATRIOT. Addressed to the People, on the Present State of Affairs in Britain and in France. With Observations on Republican Government and Discussions of the Principles Advanced in the Writings of Thomas Paine. Edinburgh: 1793. V. 53

THE PATRIOT Poet, a Satire. London: 1764. V. 54

PATRIOTIC Competition Against Self-Interested Combination, Recommended; By a Union Between the Nobility, the Landed and Independent Interest, the Clergy and Consumer... London: 1800. V. 49; 52

PATRITII, FABIO
Orationi. Venice: 1587. V. 54

PATRIZI, FRANCESCO
Magia Philosophica... Hamburg: 1593. V. 53; 54
Il Sacro Regno. Venice: 1547. V. 48

PATRONI Eclesiarum: or a List of the Patrons of the Dignities Rectories, Vicarages, Perpetual Curacies Chapelries, Endowed Lectureships, &c. of the United Church of England and Ireland. London: 1831. V. 53

PATTE, PIERRE
Memoires sur les Objets Les Plus Importans de L'Architecture. Paris: 1769. V. 48

PATTEN, C. J.
The Aquatic Birds of Great Britain and Ireland. 1906. V. 49; 50; 54
The Aquatic Birds of Great Britain and Ireland. London: 1906. V. 50; 52; 53

PATTEN, EDMUND
A Glimpse at the United States and the Northern States of America... London: 1853. V. 53

PATTEN, ROBERT
The History of the Late Rebellion. London: 1717. V. 47; 54

PATTEN, WILLIAM
The Book of Sport. New York: 1901. V. 47; 54

PATTERN, BRIAN
The Unreliable Nightingale. London: 1973. V. 47

PATTERSON, ARTHUR J.
The Magyars: Their Country and Institutions. London: 1869. V. 49; 53

PATTERSON, AUGUSTA OWEN
American Homes of To-Day. New York: 1924. V. 47; 51

PATTERSON, BARBE
Chips From Tunis: a Glimpse of Arab Life. 1880. V. 50

PATTERSON, GEORGE
Memoir of the Rev. James MacGregor, D.D. Philadelphia: 1859. V. 53
Sable Island, Its History and Phenomena. Montreal: 1894. V. 53

PATTERSON, IKIE GRAY
Loose Leaves: a History of Delta County. Dallas: 1935. V. 47

PATTERSON, ISAAC FRANKLIN
The Constitutions of Ohio... Cleveland: 1912. V. 47

PATTERSON, J. B.
Autobiography of Ma-Ka-Tai-Me-She-Kia-Kiak or Black Hawk...Together with a History of the Black Hawk War. Oquawka: 1882. V. 52

PATTERSON, JOHN HENRY
In the Grip of the Nyika. New York: 1909. V. 50

PATTERSON, M. L. P.
South Asian Civilizations: a Bibliographic Synthesis. Chicago: 1981. V. 48

PATTERSON, ROBERT
First Steps to Zoology. London & Belfast: 1849. V. 53
Letters on the Natural History of the Insects Mentioned in Shakespeare's Plays. London: 1838. V. 48
The Natural History of the Insects Mentioned in Shakespeare's Plays. London: 1841. V. 52

PATTERSON, SAMUEL
Narrative of the Adventures and Sufferings of Samuel Patterson... Palmer: 1817'. V. 51

PATTERSON, WILLIAM JOHN
I Am Nature. London: 1949. V. 53

PATTILLO, HENRY
Sermons, &c. 1. On the Divisions Among Christians. II. On the Necessity of Regeneration to Future Happiness. III. The Scripture Doctrine of Election. IV. Extract of a letter from Mr. Whitefield to Mr. Wesley. V. An Address to the Deists. Wilmington: 1788. V. 49

PATTISON, JAMES
The Emigrant's Vade-Mecum or Guide to the "Price Grant" in Venezuelan Guayana. London: 1868. V. 53

PATTISON, MARK
Essays (on Historical and Literary Subjects). London: 1889. V. 51
The Estiennes: a Bibliographical Essay by Mark Pattison Illustrated with Original Leaves from Books Printed by the Three Greatest Members of that Distinguished Family. San Francisco: 1949. V. 49; 51
Memoirs. Cambridge: 1885. V. 51

PATTISON, SAMUEL
Original Poems; Moral and Satirical. London: 1792. V. 48

PATTON, JACOB H.
The Triumph of the Presbytery of Hanover. New York: 1887. V. 54

PATTON, WALTER SCOTT
Insects, Ticks, Mites and Venomous Animals of Medical & Veterinary Importance. Croydon: 1929. V. 54
Insects, Ticks, Mites and Venomous Animals of Medical & Veterinary Importance. Croydon: 1929-31. V. 48

PAUKER, JOHN
Excellency. Iowa City: 1967. V. 50

PAUKER, JULIANE
Neuestes Musterbuch Von 102 Ausgezeichnet Strick-Muster Touren. Augsburg: 1837. V. 53

PAUL, ELLIOT
The Life and Death of a Spanish Town. New York: 1937. V. 49
Springtime in Paris. New York: 1950. V. 52; 54
With a Hays Nonny Nonny. New York: 1942. V. 52

PAUL, GEORGE ONESIPHOROUS
An Address Delivered at a General Meeting of the Nobility, Gentry, Clergy and Others, Assessed to the County Rate for the County of Gloucester, Convened by the High Sheriff, for the Purpose of Receiving a Statement of the Proceedings of the Committee... Gloucester: 1792?. V. 53

PAUL, HERMANN
Principles of the History of Language. London: 1891. V. 49

PAUL, HIRAM V.
History of the Town of Durham, North Carolina... Raleigh: 1884. V. 52

THE PAUL Hounds Will Meet. London: 1905. V. 52

PAUL, JAMES BALFOUR
The History of the Royal Company of Archers - The Queen's Body-Guard for Scotland. Edinburgh & London: 1875. V. 51
An Ordinary of Arms Contained in the Public Register of All Arms and Bearings in Scotland. Edinburgh: 1893. V. 52; 54

PAUL, JOHN
Every Landlord or Tenant His Own Lawyer; or, the Whole Law Respecting Landlords, Tenants and Lodgers... London: 1776. V. 52
Every Landlord or Tenant His Own Lawyer; or, the Whole Law Respecting Landlords, Tenants, and Lodgers, Laid Down in a Simple, Easy and Comprehensive Manner, Free from the Technical Terms of the Law... London: 1778. V. 53
The Law of Tythes. London: 1781. V. 52

PAUL, JOHN DEAN
Journal of a Party of Pleasure to Paris, in the Month of August 1802. London: 1802. V. 48; 52
The Man of Ton, a Satire. London: 1828. V. 54

PAUL, JOHN R.
A History of Poliomyelitis. New Haven: 1971. V. 48

PAUL, R. W.
An Account of the Incised and Sepulchral Slabs of North-West Somersetshire... London: 1882. V. 48

PAUL, RODMAN W.
The California Gold Discovery. Georgetown: 1966. V. 52; 54

PAUL, W. J.
Modern Irish Poets. 1894/97. V. 54

PAUL, WILLIAM
Observations on the Cultivation of Roses in Pots... London: 1850. V. 53
The Rose Garden. London: 1848. V. 52
The Rose Garden. London: 1888. V. 54
The Rose Garden. London: 1903. V. 51

PAULDEN, THOMAS
An Account of the Taking and Surrendering of Pontefract Castle, and of the Surprisal of General Rainsborough in His Quarters at Doncaster, anno. 1648. Oxford: 1747. V. 52

PAULDING, HIRAM
Journal of a Cruise of the United States Schooner Dolphin Among the Islands of the Pacific Ocean; and a Visit to the Mulgrave Islands, in Pursuit of the Mutineers of the Whale Ship Globe. New York: 1831. V. 48

PAULDING, JAMES KIRKE
The Backwoodsman. Philadelphia: 1818. V. 49; 52
A Book of Vagaries; Comprising the New Mirror for Travellers and Other Whim-Whams... New York: 1867. V. 50
Chronicles of the City of Gotham, from the Papers of a Retired Common Councilman. New York: 1830. V. 47
Le Coin du Feu d'un Hollandais, ou les Colons de New York Avant l'Independence. Paris: 1832. V. 47
The Dutchman's Fireside. London: 1831. V. 52
The Dutchman's Fireside. New York: 1831. V. 53
John Bull in America; or, the New Munchausen. New York: 1825. V. 47; 53
Koningsmarke, the Long Finne, a Story of the New World. New York: 1823. V. 52
The Lay of the Scottish Fiddle: a Tale of Havre de Grace. New York: 1813. V. 48
The Merry Tales of the Three Wise Men of Gotham. New York: 1826. V. 47; 49; 51
The New Mirror for Travellers; and Guide to the Springs. New York: 1828. V. 49
Salmagundi...First Series, Volumes I and II, Second Series, Volumes I and II. New York: 1835. V. 52
A Sketch of Old England. London: 1822. V. 52; 54
Tales of the Good Woman. New York: 1829. V. 54
Westward Ho. A Tale. New York: 1832. V. 47; 53

PAULHAN, JEAN
De Mauvais Sujets. Paris: 1958. V. 50

PAUL III, POPE
Regula Cancellariae Ap(osto)licae S. D. N. Pauli Papae III. Super Decreto Processum Gratiarum Expectatiuarum... Rome: 1545. V. 51; 54

PAULIN, CHARLES OSCAR
Atlas of the Historical Geography of the United States. Washington/New York: 1932. V. 48; 51

PAULLIN, CHARLES OSCAR
Commodore John Rodgers: Captain, Commodore and Senior Officer of the American Navy, 1773-1838. Cleveland: 1910. V. 51

PAULLINI, CHRISTIAN FRANZ
Cynographica Curisosa Seu Canis Descriptio...et Mantissa Curiosa Eiusdem Argumenti... Nuremberg: 1685. V. 47

PAULSON, RONALD
Hogarth: His Life, Art and Times. New Haven: 1971. V. 48; 50; 54
Hogarth's Graphic Works. New Haven: 1970. V. 48

PAULUS, CAROLUS
The Manor and Parish of Eccleshall. Sheffield: 1927. V. 47; 53

PAULUS AEGINETA
Medicinae Totius Enchiridion. Basileae: 1546. V. 47; 50; 53
Opera a Ioanne Guinterio Andernaco... Strassburg: 1542. V. 52
Praecepta Salubria Guilielmo Copo Basileiensi Interprete. Paris: 1512. V. 54
The Seven Books... London: 1844-4. V. 51
The Seven Books. London: 1844-46-47. V. 53; 54

PAULUS VENETUS
Expositio in Analytica Posteriora Aristotelis. Venice: 1477. V. 54

PAUSANIAS
The Description of Greece. London: 1794. V. 48
The Description of Greece. London: 1824. V. 52
Pausaniae Veteris Graeciae Descriptio. Florence: 1551. V. 49; 54

PAUSE, WALTER
Salute the Mountains. London: 1962. V. 50

PAVEY, L. A.
Moving Pageant. London: 1935. V. 51

PAVIERE, SYDNEY H.
The Devis Family of Painters. Leigh-on-Sea: 1950. V. 47
A Dictionary of British Sporting Painters. Leigh-on-Sea: 1965. V. 47

PAVLOV, IVAN PETROVICH
Die Arbeit der Verdauungsdrusen. Wiesbaden: 1898. V. 47; 48; 50; 52; 53; 54
Conditioned Reflexes: an Investigation of the Physiological Activity of the Cerebral Cortex. London: 1927. V. 52
Conditioned Reflexes: an Investigation of the Physiological Activity Of the Cerebral Cortex. Oxford: 1927. V. 47; 49; 54
Lectures On Conditioned Reflexes. New York: 1928. V. 49; 51
Lectures on Conditioned Reflexes. London: 1928-41. V. 49; 51
Lectures on Conditioned Reflexes. New York: 1928-41. V. 53
Lectures on Conditioned Reflexes. London: 1929. V. 47; 49; 53
Lectures on Conditioned Reflexes. (and) Volume Two: Conditioned Relfexes and Psychiarty. New York: 1941. V. 50; 53
Selected Works. Moscow: 1955. V. 54
The Work of the Digestive Glands. London: 1902. V. 49; 53; 54
The Work of the Digestive Glands. London: 1910. V. 47; 48; 49; 50; 51; 53

PAVRI, M. E.
Parsi Cricket. Bombay: 1901. V. 51

PAVY, FREDERICK W.
The Croonian Lectures on Certain Points Connected with Diabetes. London: 1878. V. 49
A Treatise on Food and Dietetics, Physiologically and Therapeutically Considered. 1875. V. 47
A Treatise on Food and Dietetics, Physiologically and Therapeutically Considered. London: 1875. V. 50

PAXTON, ELISHA FRANKLIN
Memoir and Memorials, Elisha Franklin Paxton, Brigadier General, C.S.A. New York: 1907. V. 49

PAXTON, GEORGE
The Villager, with Other Poems. Edinburgh: 1813. V. 54

PAXTON, JAMES
Illustrations of Paley's Natural Theology. Boston: 1827. V. 52

PAXTON, JOHN D.
Letters on Slavery Addressed to the Cumberland Congregation, Virginia. Lexington: 1833. V. 50

PAXTON, JOSEPH
Paxton's Flower Garden. London: 1882. V. 48
PAXTON'S Flower Garden. London: 1882-84. V. 52
Paxton's Flower Garden. London: 1883-84.. V. 53

PAXTON, PETER
Civil Polity. London: 1703. V. 48
Specimen Physico-Medicum...Or, an Essay Concerning the Knowledge and Cure of Most Diseases... London: 1711. V. 50

PAYER, JULIUS
New Lands Within the Arctic Circle. London: 1876. V. 50; 54
New Lands Within the Arctic Circle. Narrative of the Discoveries of the Austrian Ship 'Tegetthoff in the Years 1872-1874. New York: 1877. V. 50; 52

PAYETTE, B. C.
The Oregon Country Under the Union Jack: a Reference Book of Historical Documents for Scholars and Historians. Montreal: 1962. V. 53

PAYN, JAMES
The Heir of the Ages. London: 1886. V. 51
Leaves from Lakeland. London: 1858. V. 51
The Luck of the Darrells: a Novel. London: 1885. V. 51
Mirk Abbey. London: 1866. V. 51
Murphy's Master, and Other Stories. London: 1873. V. 50; 54
Richard Arbour, or the Family Scapegrace. Edinburgh: 1861. V. 51
Stories and Sketches. London: 1857. V. 50; 51
What He Cost Her. London: 1877. V. 51
The Youth and Middle Age of Charles Dickens... London: 1883. V. 54

PAYNE, A. A.
A Handbook of British and Foreign Orders, War Medals and decorations Awarded to the Army and Navy. Sheffield: 1911. V. 50; 54

PAYNE, BUCKER H.
The Negro: What is His Ethnological Status?. Cincinnati: 1867. V. 53

PAYNE, CHARLES JOHNSON
Four-Legged Friends and Acquaintances. London: 1951. V. 47
More Bandobast. 1936. V. 54
More Bandobast. London: 1936. V. 47; 49
My Sketch Book in the Shiny. London. V. 47; 49
My Sketch Book in the Shiny. 1930. V. 54
'Osses and Obstacles. London: 1935. V. 47

PAYNE, EDWARD F.
The Charity of Charles Dickens... Boston: 1929. V. 49; 54
Dickens Days in Boston. Boston and New York: 1927. V. 54
The Romance of Charles Dickens and Maria Beadnell Winter. Boston: 1929. V. 54

PAYNE, GEORGE PATMORE
Uncle Sam's Peculiarities. London: 184. V. 53

PAYNE, HENRY NEVILLE
The Fatal Jealousie. London: 1673. V. 50

PAYNE, HUMFRY
Archaic Marble Sculpture From the Acropolis. London. V. 50; 54
Archaic Marble Sculpture from the Acropolis. New York: 1950. V. 50; 52
Perachora I: The Sanctuaries of Hera Akraia and Limenia. Oxford: 1940. V. 50

PAYNE, J. B.
Scores and Analyses 1864-1881. Harrogate: 1904. V. 51

PAYNE, JOANNES ARTHINGTON
Disputatio Medica Inauguralis de Neuralgia... Edinburgh: 1813. V. 53

PAYNE, JOHN
The Autobiography of John Payne of Villon Society Fame, Poet and Scholar. Olney, near Bedford: 1926. V. 51
An Epitome of History; or, A Concise View of the Most Important Revolutions and Events in the Principal Empires, Kingdoms, States and Republics. London: 1795. V. 47
An Epitome of History; or, a Concise View of the Most Important Revolutions and Events in the Principal Empires, Kingdoms, States, and Republics. New York: 1795. V. 53
Geographical Extracts, Forming a General View of Earth and Nature, in Four Parts. London: 1796. V. 47
Intaglios Sonnets. London: 1871. V. 49; 50
The Masque of Shadows and Other Poems. London: 1870. V. 49; 50

PAYNE, JOHN HOWARD
Brutus: or, the Fall of Tarquin. New York: 1821. V. 50
Clari; or, the Maid of Milan: an Opera. London: 1823. V. 48
Clari; or, the Maid of Milan, an Opera. New York: 1823. V. 47; 54
Prospectus of a New Periodical. 1833. V. 49
Therese, the Orphan of Geneva, a Drama in Three Acts... New York: 1821. V. 52

PAYNE, ROBERT
Politics and the Military in Modern Spain. Stanford: 1967. V. 49

PAYNE, ROGER
Why Work?. Boston: 1939. V. 51

PAYNE, SOMERSET
East Africa (British), Its History, People, Commerce, Industries and Resources. London: 1908-09. V. 53

PAYNE, WILLIAM
Maxims for Playing the Game of Whilst; With all Necessary Calculations and Laws of the Game. London: 1778. V. 49; 51; 52

PAYNE, WYNDHAM
Town & Country. London: 1926. V. 52

PAYNE-GALLWEY, RALPH
The Book of Duck Decoys: Their Construction, Management and History. London: 1886. V. 49; 53
The Fowler in Ireland. London: 1882. V. 48; 49; 51; 52; 54
High Pheasants in Theory and Practice. London: 1913. V. 49; 51
Letters to Young Shooters. London: 1892-96. V. 54
Letters to Young Shooters. London: 1896-1902. V. 49
Letters to Young Shooters. First Series. Second Series. Third Series. London: 1895/92/96. V. 49
Projectile-Throwing Engines of the Ancients. London: 1907. V. 54

PAYNE'S Orbis Pictus or Book of Beauty for Every Table. Dresden & Leipzig: 1860. V. 50

PAYNE-WESTBROOK, HENRIETTA
The West-Brook Drives. New York: 1902. V. 53

PAYTIAMO, JAMES
Flaming Arrow's People. New York: 1932. V. 49; 53

PAYTON, LEW
Did Adam Sin: Also Stories of Negro Life in Comedy, Drama and Sketches. Los Angeles: 1937. V. 53

PAZ, OCTAVIO
Air Born/Hijos de Aire. Mexico City: 1979. V. 48; 49; 52
Alternating Current. New York: 1973. V. 53
Cuatro Chopos: The Four Poplars. Purchase: 1985. V. 47; 54
Homage and Desecrations. New York: 1987. V. 54
In the Middle of This Phrase. Helsinki: 1987. V. 48
The Labyrinth of Solitude. New York: 1961. V. 49
Return. V. 54
Rufino Tamayo. New York: 1982. V. 47; 50
Selected Poems of Octavio Paz. Bloomington: 1963. V. 53
The Siren and the Seashell: and Other Essays on Poets and Poetry. Austin: 1976. V. 53
Stanzas for an Imaginary Garden. Tuscaloosa: 1990. V. 54
Sun Stone. New York: 1963. V. 54
Three Poems. New York: 1987. V. 49; 50
Tres Poemas/Three Poems. 1987. V. 51; 52; 54

PEABODY, ELIZABETH P.
The Common School Drawing-Master. Boston: 1846. V. 53
Holiness; or the Legend of St. George... Boston: 1836. V. 49; 51
Key to History. Boston: 1833. V. 54
Kindergarten Culture. Washington: 1870. V. 51
Last Evening with Allston and Other Papers. Boston: 1886. V. 50
Record of a School: Exemplifying the General Principles of Spiritual Culture. Boston & New York: 1836. V. 47; 49; 51; 53; 54
Sabbath Lessons, or an Abstract of Sacred History... Salem: 1810. V. 52
To Fathers and Mothers - Letter from Miss Peabody. Boston: 1873. V. 47

PEABODY, JOSEPHINE PRESTON
The Book of the Little Past. Boston: 1908. V. 48
The Book of the Little Past. Boston: 1912. V. 49

PEABODY, MARY TYLER
The Flower People. Hartford: 1842. V. 50

PEACH, B. W.
The Silurian Rocks of Britain. Volume I. Scotland. Glasgow: 1899. V. 54

PEACH, R. E. M.
The Life and Times of Ralph Allen of Prior Park, Bath... London: 1895. V. 49

PEACHAM, HENRY
The Compleat Gentleman. London: 1627. V. 47
The Compleat Gentleman. London: 1634. V. 47; 50; 51; 54
The Compleat Gentleman...To Which is Added the Gentlemans Exercise... London: 1661. V. 47
The Gentlemans Exercise. London. V. 47; 48

PEACHUM, HENRY
The Art of Living in London, or, a Caution How Gentlemen, Countrymen and Stranger, Drawn by Occasion of Business, Should Dispose of Themselves in the Thrifiest Way, Not Onely in the citie, but In All Other Populous Places. London: 1642. V. 49

PEACHY, ARCHIBALD C.
United States District Court, for the Northern District of California. The United States v. Andres Castillero. Mr. Peachy's Agrument, on a Motion for a Commission to Mexico to Take Testimony. 1859. V. 49

PEACOCK, CAESAR
The Spirit of the Times! or, the Contested Election for the City of York, in the Year 1818. York: 1818. V. 51

PEACOCK, EDWARD
The Army Lists of the Roundheads and Cavaliers, Containing the Names of the Officers in the Royal and Parliamentary Armies of 1642. London: 1863. V. 49
English Church Furniture, Ornaments and Decorations, at the Period of the Reformation as Exhibited in a List of the Goods Destroyed in Certain Lincolnshire Churches, A.D. 1566. London: 1866. V. 49

PEACOCK, GEORGE
A Collection of Examples of the Applications of the Differential and Integral Calculus. Cambridge: 1820. V. 49
Life of Thomas Young. London: 1855. V. 50

PEACOCK, JAMES
Oikidia, or Nutshells; Being Ichnographic Distributions for Small Villas... London: 1785. V. 52; 54

PEACOCK, LUCY
The Adventures of the Six Princesses of Babylon, in Their Travels to the Temple of Virtue. London: 1785. V. 48; 51; 53
The Little Emigrant, a Tale: Interspersed with Moral Anecdotes and Instructive Conversations. London: 1802. V. 53
Visit for a Week, or, Hints On the Improvement of Time... Philadelphia: 1796. V. 53

PEACOCK, N.
The Russian Year-Book. London: 1916. V. 47

PEACOCK, ROBERT BACKHOUSE
A Glossary of the Dialect of the Hundred of Lonsdale, North and South of the Sands, in the County of Lancashire. London: 1869. V. 52

PEACOCK, THOMAS LOVE
Collection of Works by... London: 1891-93. V. 47; 49
Crotchet Castle. London: 1831. V. 49; 50; 53
Dramatic Criticisms and Translations and Other Essays. London: 1926. V. 50
The Genius of the Thames: a Lyrical Poem in Two Parts. London: 1810. V. 51; 52; 54
The Genius of the Thames: Palmyra and Other Poems. London: 1812. V. 48; 51
Gryll Grange. London: 1861. V. 49; 51; 54
Gryll Grange. London & New York: 1896. V. 54
Headlong and Nightmare Abbey. London and New York: 1896. V. 54
Headlong Hall. London: 1816. V. 48; 50; 51; 52
Letters to Edward Hookham and Percy B. Shelley. Boston: 1910. V. 51
Maid Marian. London: 1822. V. 52
Maid Marian and Crotchet Castle. London and New York: 1895. V. 54
Melincourt to Sir Oran Haut-Ton... London and New York: 1896. V. 54
The Misfortunes and Rhododaphne. London and New York: 1897. V. 54
The Misfortunes of Elphin. London: 1829. V. 47; 50; 51; 52; 53; 54
The Misfortunes of Elphin. London: 1928. V. 47
The Misfortunes of Elphin. Newtown: 1928. V. 47; 51; 52; 54
Nightmare Abbey: by the Author of Headlong Hall. London: 1818. V. 47
Novels: and Rhododaphne... London: 1895-97. V. 49
Palmyra and Other Poems. London: 1806. V. 51; 53
The Philosophy of Melancholy. London: 1812. V. 51
Rhododaphne: or The Thessalian Spell. London: 1818. V. 47; 51; 54
The Works.. London: 1875. V. 50; 51

PEACOCK, W. F.
The Adventures of St. George After His Famous Encounter with the Dragon. 1858. V. 52

PEAK, JOHN
Memoir of Elder John Peak, Written by Himself. Boston: 1832. V. 53

PEAKE, HOWARD W.
A Ranger of Commerce or 52 Years on the Road. San Antonio: 1929. V. 54

PEAKE, J.
Admonitory Hints on the Use of Sea Bathing. Ramsgate: 1806. V. 47

PEAKE, JAMES
Rudiments of Naval Architecture; or, an Exposition of the Elementary principles of the Science and Practical Application to Naval Construction... London: 1849. V. 50

PEAKE, JOHN
Brown Beer: a Poem. London: 1762. V. 47

PEAKE, MERVYN
Captain Slaughterboard Drops Anchor. London: 1945. V. 48; 50; 54
The Craft of the Lead Pencil. London: 1946. V. 48; 49
Drawings. London: 1949. V. 49; 50; 51
Figures of Speech. London: 1954. V. 51
The Glassblowers. London: 1950. V. 48; 49; 51
Gormenghast. 1950. V. 48; 52; 53
Gormenghast,. London: 1950. V. 48; 49; 51
The Gormenghast Trilogy. Titus Groan. Gormenghast. Titus Alone. London: 1946-59. V. 49
Letters from a Lost Uncle. London: 1948. V. 49; 51; 53
Mr. Pye. London: 1953. V. 52
Mr. Pye. Melbourne: 1953. V. 51; 53
Poems and Drawings. London: 1965. V. 51; 53
A Reverie of Bone. London: 1967. V. 49; 54
Rhymes Without Reason. London: 1944. V. 49; 51
Ride a Cock Horse and Other Nursery Rhymes. London: 1940. V. 50
Shapes and Sounds. London: 1941. V. 48; 51; 52
Titus Alone. London: 1959. V. 50
Titus Groan. Gromenghast. Titus Alone. London: 1946-59. V. 48
Twelve Poems: 1939-1960. Hayes: 1975. V. 49; 51
Twelve Poems 1939-1960. London: 1975. V. 47

PEAKE, ORA BROOKS
The Colorado Range Cattle Industry. Glendale: 1937. V. 50; 52

PEAKE, RICHARD BRINSLEY
The Haunted Inn, a Farce in Two Acts... London: 1832. V. 50

PEAKE, THOMAS
A Compendium of the Law of Evidence. London: 1804. V. 54

PEALE, REMBRANDT
Account of the Skeleton of the Mammoth, a Non Descript Carnivorous Animal of Immense Size Found in America. London: 1802. V. 48; 54

PEARCE, ARTHUR
The History of the Butchers' Company. London: 1929. V. 47

PEARCE, CHARLES E.
The Amazing Duchess, Being the Romantic History of Elizabeth Chudleigh. London: 1920's. V. 48

PEARCE, F. B.
Zanzibar: the Island Metropolis of Eastern Africa. New York: 1920. V. 52

PEARCE, HELEN
The Enchanted Barn. New York: 1929. V. 50

PEARCE, JOSEPH HENRY
Jaco Treloar. A Study of a Woman. London: 1893. V. 54

PEARCE, RICHARD
Marooned in the Arctic - Diary of the MacAlpine Aerial Expedition. 1931. V. 49
The Spleen and Anaemia Experimental and Clinical Studies. Philadelphia: 1918. V. 49

PEARCE, THOMAS
The Justice of the Peace's Pocket-Companion: of the Office and Duty of a Justice Epitomized... London: 1754. V. 48

PEARCE, WALTER J.
Painting and Decorating. London: 1902. V. 48

PEARCE, WILLIAM
Ode to the Memory of the Officers and Men of the Squadron, Under the Command of the Deeply Reverend Lord Nelson... 1805. V. 50; 54

PEARCH, GEORGE
A Collection of Poems in Two Volumes by Several Hands. London: 1768. V. 52

PEARD, W.
A Year of Liberty; or, Salmon Angling in Ireland from February 1 to November 1. London: 1867. V. 49

PEARL of Great Price. Salt Lake City: 1878. V. 52

PEARL, RAYMOND
The Biology of Death. Philadelphia: 1922. V. 52
Studies in Human Biology. Baltimore: 1924. V. 49; 54

PEARS, CHARLES
Observations on the Nature and Treatment of Consumption; Addressed to Patients and Families. London: 1814. V. 51

PEARS, D. F.
The Nature of Metaphysics. London: 1957. V. 54

PEARS, PETER
Moscow Christmas: a Diary. London: 1966. V. 50

PEARS, TIM
In the Place of Fallen Leaves. London: 1993. V. 54

PEARSALL, ROBERT LUCAS DE
A Few Remarks on the Position of the Baronets of Great Britain and Other Branches of the British Gentry, Compared with That of the Continental Lesser Nobility Both at Home and Abroad by a Traveller. Carlsruhe: 1836. V. 47; 48

PEARSE, B. W.
General Report on the Land Round Nanaimo. Victoria: 1860. V. 53

PEARSE, G. E.
Eighteenth Century Architecture in South Africa. London: 1933. V. 49

PEARSE, HENRY H. S.
The History of Lumsden's Horse, a Complete Record of the Corps from Its Formation to Its Disbandment. London: 1903. V. 50

PEARSE, JAMES
A Narrative of the Life of James Pearse, in Two Parts... Rutland: 1825. V. 48

PEARSE, MARY BRIGID
The Home Life of Padraig Pearse as Told by Himself, His Family & Friends. London: 1934. V. 47; 53

PEARSON, ALEXANDER
Annals of Kirkby Lonsdale and Lunesdale in bygone Days. Kendal: 1930. V. 50; 51; 52; 53
The Doings of a Country Solicitor. Kendal: 1947. V. 51; 52

PEARSON, ANTHONY
The Great Case of Tithes Truly Stated, Clearly Open'd and Fully Resolv'd. London: 1754. V. 53
The Great Case of Tithes Truly Stated, Clearly Open'd and Fully Resolv'd... Dublin: 1756. V. 47; 48; 52

PEARSON, CHARLES
What Is to Be Done With Our Criminals? A Letter to the Right Honorable the Lord Mayor...Together with Mr. Pearson's Speech Upon the Same Subject in the House of Commons, May 15, 1849. London: 1857. V. 49

PEARSON, E. S.
Studies in the History of Statistics and Probability. London: 1970. V. 49

PEARSON, EDWIN
Banbury Chap Books and Nursery Toy Book Literature (of the XVIII and early XIX Centuries)... London: 1890. V. 53

PEARSON, G. C.
Overland in 1849: From Missouri to California by the Platt River and Salt Lake Trail. Los Angeles: 1961. V. 54

PEARSON, H. H. W.
The Annals of the Bolus Herbarium. Volume 1-4. Cambridge: 1914-28. V. 48

PEARSON, H. J.
Beyond Petsora Eastward: Two summer Voyages to Novaya Zemlya and the Islands Of the Barents Sea... London: 1899. V. 49
Three Summers Among the Birds of Russian Lapland. London: 1904. V. 49

PEARSON, HESKETH
Modern Men and Mummers. London: 1921. V. 48

PEARSON, HUGH
Memoirs of the Life and Correspondence of the Reverend Christian Frederick Swartz (sic). London: 1834. V. 49

PEARSON, J., & CO.
Very Choice Books Including an Extremely Important Series of Historical Bindings Together with Original and Illuminated Manuscripts Etc. London: 1901. V. 53

PEARSON, J. D.
A Guide to Manuscripts and Documents in the British Isles Relating to Africa. London: 1971. V. 47

PEARSON, J. L.
Copy of Report on Westminster Hall. London: 1884. V. 50

PEARSON, JOHN
Observations on the Effects of Various Articles of the Materia Medica, in the Cure of Lues Venerea... London: 1800. V. 49; 51; 54
Pearson's Political Dictionary; Containing Remarks, Definitions, Explanations, and Customs, Political and Parliamentary... London: 1792. V. 47
A Plain and Rational Account of the Nature and Effects of Animal Magnetism: in a Series of Letters. London: 1790. V. 53
Practical Observations on Cancerous Complaints... 1793. V. 54
Vindiciae Epistolarum S. Ignatii...Accesserunt Isaaci Vossii Epistolae Duae Adversus David Blondellum. Cambridge: 1672. V. 50

PEARSON, JOHN CALDER
The Rowfant Candlesticks. Cleveland: 1959. V. 47

PEARSON, KARL
The Chances of Death and other Studies in Evolution. London: 1897. V. 49; 53
The Grammar of Science. London: 1892. V. 52
Life, Letters and Labours of Francis Galton. Cambridge: 1914-24. V. 47; 54
The Life, Letters and Labours of Francis Galton. Cambridge: 1914-30. V. 49
Two New Pedigrees of Muscular Dystrophy. 1933. V. 53; 54

PEARSON, L.
Diseases and Enemies of Poultry. Harrisburg: 1897. V. 47; 50; 52

PEARSON, T. GILBERT
Birds of America. New York: 1936. V. 53

PEARSON, T. R.
A Short History of a Small Place. New York: 1985. V. 52

PEARSON, W. H.
Hepaticae of the British Isles. London: 1902. V. 49

PEART, EDWARD
On Electric Atmospheres. 1793. V. 48

PEARY, ROBERT E.
Nearest the Pole. London: 1907. V. 49
Nearest the Pole - a Narrative of the Polar Expedition of the Peary Arctic Club in the S.S. Roosevelt, 1905-1906. New York: 1907. V. 49; 50
The North Pole. London: 1910. V. 48; 49
The North Pole. New York: 1910. V. 47; 48; 49; 50; 53
Northward Over the "Great Ice". A Narrative of Life and Work Along the Shores and Upon the Interior Ice-Cap of Northern Greenland in the Years 1886 and 1891-97. London: 1898. V. 49; 51; 52
Northward Over the "Great Ice". A Narrative of Life and Work Along the Shores and Upon the Interior Ice-Cap of Northern Greenland in the Years 1886 and 1891-97. New York: 1898. V. 47; 53

PEASE, ALFRED E.
Biskra and the Oases and Desert of the Zibans, With Information for Travellers. London: 1893. V. 48
The Book of the Lion. 1914. V. 54
The Cleveland Hounds as a Trencher-Fed Pack. London: 1887. V. 47; 48
A Dictionary of the Dialect of the North Riding of Yorkshire with Notes and Comments by Major John Fairfax-Blakeborough, M.C. Whitby: 1928. V. 47

PEASE, E. LLOYD
Scenes from the Saddle, 1921. London: 1921. V. 47

PEASE, EDWARD
The Diaries of Edward Pease. London: 1907. V. 51; 53

PEASE, JOHN C.
A Gazetteer of the States of Connecticut and Rhode-Island. Hartford: 1819. V. 50

PEASE, MARY BALL JOHNSON
Mahlon Johnson Family of Littleton, New Jersey. Morristown: 1931. V. 49; 51

PEASLEE, E. RANDOLPH
Ovarian Tumors: Their Pathology, Diagnosis and Treatment, Especially by Ovariotomy. New York: 1872. V. 49; 54

PEAT, FRANK EDWIN
Christmas Carols. Akron: 1937. V. 53

PEATTIE, D.
Immortal Village. Chicago: 1945. V. 50; 54

PEATTIE, DONALD CULROSS
An Almanac for Moderns. New York: 1938. V. 49
Immortal Village. Chicago: 1945. V. 52
The Road of a Naturalist. Boston: 1941. V. 51

PEATTIE, ELIA W.
Castle, Knight and Troubadour in an Aplogy and Three Tableaux. Chicago: 1903. V. 47; 49

PEBRER, PABLO
Taxation, Revenue, Expenditure, Power, Statistics and Debt of the Whole British Empire. London: 1833. V. 48

PECHEY, JOHN
Promptuarium Praxeos Medicae. London: 1700. V. 52

PECK, FRANCES
Napoleon; or, the Mysteries of the Hundred Days, an Historical Novel. London: 1826. V. 54

PECK, FRANCIS
Desiderata Curiosa; or, a Collection of Divers Scarce and Curious Pieces (Relating Chiefly to Matters of English History). London: 1732/35. V. 51
Desiderata Curiosa: or, A Collection of Divers Scarce and Curious Pieces Relating Chiefly to Matters of English History... London: 1779. V. 49
Memoirs of the Life and Actions of Oliver Cromwell... London: 1740. V. 49; 54
New Memoirs of the Life and Poetical Works of Mr. John Milton. (with) Memoirs of the Life and Actions of Oliver Cromwell. London: 1740. V. 54

PECK, GEORGE W.
Aurifodina; or, Adventures in the Gold Region. New York: 1849. V. 47
Melbourne, and the Chincha Islands; with Sketches of Lima, and a Voyage Round the World. New York: 1854. V. 47; 52

PECK, JOHN
The Political Economy of Democracy. Philadelphia: 1879. V. 51

PECK, JOHN MASON
The Design and Influence of Sunday Schools Promotive of the Best Interests of Our Country. Rock Spring?: 1832. V. 50
A Guide for Emigrants, Containing Sketches of Illinois, Missouri and the Adjacent Parts. Boston: 1831. V. 50
A Guide for Emigrants, Containing Sketches of Illinois, Missouri and the Adjacent Parts. Boston: 1837. V. 53
A New Guide for Emigrants to the West, Containing Sketches of Ohio, Indiana, Illinois, Missouri...Territories of Wisconsin and Arkansas. Boston: 1836. V. 50

PECK, MARY G.
Carrie Chapman Catt, a Biography. New York: 1944. V. 53

PECKHAM, HARRY
A Tour Through Holland, Dutch Brabant, the Austrian Netherlands, and Part of France. London: 1788. V. 53

PECKHAM, JOHN
Perspectivae Communis Libri Tres. Cologne: 1580. V. 51
Registrum Epistoalrum (1279-92). London: 1882-85. V. 49; 52

PECKHAM, P. ANNETTA
Cuttings: Selected from the Writings of Mrs. P. Anneta Peckham. San Francisco: 1877. V. 47

PECKITT, WILLIAM
The Wonderful Love of God to Men, or Heaven Opened in Earth. York: 1794. V. 52

PECOCK, REGINALD
The Repressor of Over Much Blaming of the Clergy. London: 1860. V. 49; 52

THE PECORONE of Ser Giovanni. London: 1897. V. 54

PEDANTIVS. Comoedia, Olim Cantabrig. Acta in Coll. Trin. London: 1631. V. 48; 52

PEDDIE, ALEXANDER
The Manufacturer, Weaver and Warper's Assistant, Containing a new and Correct Set of Tables, Drafts, Cordings, Arithmetical Rules and Examples. Glasgow: 1818. V. 48

PEDDIE, JAMES
Work of a Fiend. Edinburgh: 1892. V. 47

PEDLEY, R. D.
The Diseases of Children's Teeth, Their Prevention and Treatment... London & Philadelphia: 1895. V. 50

PEDRETTI, C.
Leonardo da Vinci on Painting. Berkeley: 1964. V. 50; 51; 53; 54

PEDRICK, GALE
Monastic Seals of the XIIIth Century... London: 1902. V. 49

PEDRO, CAROLINO
The New Guide of the Conversation in Portuguese and English in Two Parts. Boston: 1883. V. 54

PEEK, HEDLEY
The Encyclopaedia of Sport. London: 1897. V. 52

PEEKE, HEWSON
Americana Ebrietatis: The Favorite Tipple of Our Forefathers and the Laws and Customs Relating Thereto. New York: 1917. V. 53

PEEL, CHARLES VINCENT ALEXANDER
Somaliland. London: 1900. V. 50

PEELE, GEORGE
The Works... London: 1888. V. 53

A PEEP At the World. London: 1848. V. 51
A PEEP At the World. London: 1850. V. 52

A PEEP at the World's Fair. London. V. 47
A PEEP at the World's Fair. London: 1884. V. 48

PEEP Bo Pictures. London: 1899. V. 47

A PEEP Into High Life; or, Fashionable Characters Dramatized. London: 1812. V. 49

PEEPS into Wonderland. London: 1880's,. V. 47

THE PEERAGE of Scotland, Including the Dormant, Attained and Extinct Titles, With Their Descent, Marriage, Issue &c. Edinburgh: 1834. V. 54

THE PEERAGE Parallelled: a Poem: In Imitation of the Eighth Satire of Juvenal. London: 1813. V. 48; 51; 54

PEERS, E. ALLISON
Catalonia Infelix. London: 1937. V. 49
Spain in Eclipse 1936-1943. London: 1943. V. 49
The Spanish Tragedy. London: 1936. V. 49

PEET, STEPHEN DENISON
The Cliff Dwellers and Pueblos. Chicago: 1899. V. 52

PEET, T. ERIC
The City of Akhenaten. Parts I-III. London: 1923-51. V. 49

PEETERS, HANS J.
American Hawking. A General Account of Falconry in the New World. Davis: 1970. V. 50

PEGGE, SAMUEL
Curialia Miscellanea, or Anecdotes of Old Times; Regal, Noble, Gentiliatial and Misellaneous. London: 1818. V. 47; 50
The Life of Robert Grosseteste, the Celebrated Bishop of Lincoln... London: 1793. V. 54
The Roman Roads, Ikenild - Street and Bath - Way Discovered and Investigated Through the Country of the Coritani, or the County of Derby. London: 1784. V. 49; 51; 52
Sketch of the History of Bolsover and Peak Castles in the County of Derby. London: 1785. V. 48; 52

PEGUY, CHARLES
Le Mystere de la Charite de Jeanne d'Arc. New York: 1943. V. 48

PEICH, MICHAEL
The Red Ozier: a Literary Fine Press. History and Bibliography 1976-1987. Council Bluffs: 1993. V. 51; 54
The Red Ozier: a Literary Fine Press. History and Bibliography 1976-1987. New York: 1993. V. 49

PEILE, JOHN
New and Complete Tutor for the Violoncello. London: 1820. V. 50

PEILE, W. O.
West of Swardham. London: 1885. V. 54

PEIRAUD Nuevo Libro di Scrittura. Turin: 1722. V. 50; 53

PEIRCE, A. C.
A Man From Corpus Christi or the Adventures of Two Bird Hunters and a Dog in Texan Bogs. New York: 1894. V. 48

PEIRCE, BENJAMIN
A History of Harvard University, from Its Foundation, in...1636 to the Period of the American Revolution. Cambridge: 1833. V. 51
Ideality in the Physical Sciences. Boston: 1881. V. 47
Physical and Celestial Mechanics... Boston: 1855. V. 53

PEIRCE, EBENEEZER W.
Indian History and Genealogy. North Abington: 1878. V. 50

PEIRCE, HENRY AUGUSTUS
Biography of Henry Augustus Peirce. San Francisco: 1880. V. 47

PEIRCE, ISAAC
The Narraganset Chief; or, the Adventures of a Wanderer. New York: 1832. V. 51

PEIRCE, JAMES
The Security of Truth, Without the Assistance of Persecution or Scurrility... London: 1721. V. 52

PEIRCE, KATHLEEN
Divided Touch, Divided Color. XII Poems. Iowa City: 1995. V. 54

PEITHMAN, LEWIS THEOPHILUS
A Refutation of Pierre Franc M'Callum's Remarks On the Royal Military College... London: 1809. V. 50

PEIXOTTO, DANIEL L. M.
Anniversary Discourse, Pronounced before the Society for the Education of Orphan Children and the Relief of Indigent Persons of the Jewish Persuasion. New York: 1830. V. 52

PEIXOTTO, ERNEST C.
Ten Drawings in Chinatown. San Francisco: 1898. V. 48; 53

PELECANOS, GEORGE P.
A Firing Offense. New York: 1992. V. 53

PELEKANIDIS, S. M.
The Treasures of Mount Athos, Illuminated Manuscripts. Athens: 1974. V. 50

PELETIER, JACQUES
De Occulta Parte Numerorum, Quam Algebram Vocant, Libri Duo. Paris: 1560. V. 47

THE PELICAN. From an Ango-Norman Bestiary of 1120. London: 1963. V. 48

PELICAN PRESS
The Types Borders, Ornaments, Initial Letters, Flowers and Decorations of the Pelican Press. London: 1921. V. 52

PELLARIN, C.
The Life of Charles Fourier. New York: 1848. V. 51

PELLEGRINI, CARLOS ENRIQUE
El Descifrador de Marcas. Sistema Indeografico Inventado por...Primera Publicacion. Buenos Aires: 1858. V. 48

PELLETAN, EDOUARD
Revue D'Art. Paris: 1897-98. V. 50

PELLICER SALAS Y TOVAR, JOSE DE
Mission Evangelica al Reyno de Congo por la Serafica Religion de los Capuchinos. Madrid: 1649. V. 50

PELLING, EDWARD
A Practical Discourse Upon Charity In Its Several Branches... London: 1693. V. 53

PELLISON-FONTAINIER, PAUL
The History of the French Academy, Erected at Paris by the Late Famous Cardinal de Richelieu and Consisting of the Most Refined Wits of the Nation. London: 1657. V. 49

PELOUBET, JOSEPH ALEXANDRE DE CHABRIER
Adventures of...at the Time of the French Revolution...His Forebears...Peloubet Family in America. San Francisco: 1953. V. 47

PELTIER, J.
The Late Picture of Paris. London: 1792. V. 47
The Trial of John Peltier, Esq. for a Libel against Napoleon Buonaparte (etc.). London: 1803. V. 52

PELTIER, LESLIE C.
Starlight Nights; the Adventures of a Star-Gazer. London: 1967. V. 53

PELT LECHNER, A. A. VAN
Oologia Neerlandica, Eggs of Birds Breeding in the Netherlands. The Hague: 1910-13. V. 51

PELTON, JOHN C.
Life's Sunbeams and Shadows Poems and Prose with Appendix. San Francisco: 1893. V. 47

PELTZER, LOUIS
The Cattleman's Frontier, A Record of the Trans-Mississippi Cattle Industry from Oxen Trains to Pooling Companies, 1850-1890. Glendale: 1936. V. 49; 50; 53

PELZER, LOUIS
Marches of the Dragoons in the Mississippi Valley. Iowa City: 1917. V. 48; 51

PEMBER, E. H.
Debita Flacco: Echoes of Ode and Epode. London: 1891. V. 48

PEMBERTON, CHRISTOPHER
A Practical Treatise on Various Diseases of the Abdominal Viscera. Worcester: 1815. V. 49; 53; 54

PEMBERTON, EBENEZER
A Funeral Sermon on the Death of that Learned & Excellent Divine the Reverend Mr. Samuel Willard, Pastor of a Church of Christ in Bostom, Willard, Pastor of a Church of Christ in Boston.... Boston: 1707. V. 51; 54

PEMBERTON, ELIZABETH G.
Corinth. Volume XVIII. Part I: The Sanctuary of Demeter and Kore, the Greek Pottery. Princeton: 1989. V. 52

PEMBERTON, H.
The Dispensatory of the Royal College of Physicians, London. London: 1760. V. 47; 51

PEMBERTON, HENRY
Observations on Poetry, Especially the Epic. London: 1738. V. 48
A View of Sir Isaac Newton's Philosophy. Dublin: 1728. V. 49; 51
A View of Sir Isaac Newton's Philosophy. London: 1728. V. 50; 51; 52

PEMBERTON, J. D.
Facts and Figures Relating to Vancouver Island and British Columbia, showing What to expect and How to Get It. London: 1860. V. 49

PEMBERTON, T. J.
Gallipoli Today. London: 1926. V. 47

PEMBERTON, THOMAS
Lord Kingsdown's Recollection of His Life at the Bar and in Parliament. London: 1868. V. 52

PEMBROKE COLLEGE. LIBRARY
A Descriptive Catalogue of the Manuscripts in the Library of Pembroke College, Cambridge. 1905. V. 53

PEMBROKE, GEORGE ROBERT HERBERT, 13TH EARL OF
South-Sea Bubbles. New York: 1872. V. 53

PEMBROKE, HENRY HERBERT, 1ST EARL OF
A Method of Breaking Horses and Teaching Soldiers to Ride, Designed for the Use of the Army. London: 1762. V. 48

PENA, PETRUS
In G. Rondelletii... Methodicam Pharmaceuticam...Dilvcidae Simplicivm Medicamenorvm (sic) Explicationes, & Stirpivm Adversaria... London: 1605. V. 51; 54

PENAFIEL, A.
Monumentos del Arte Mexicano Antiguo... Berlin: 1890. V. 47

THE PENAL Code of California. Sacramento: 1872. V. 48

THE PENAL Enactments of the Slave Registry Bill Examined in a Letter to Charles N. Palmer. London: 1816. V. 47

PENCIL, MARK, PSEUD.
The White Sulphur Papers, or Life at the Springs of Western Virginia. New York: 1839. V. 48

PENDELTON, JOHN
Our Railways: Their Origin, Development, Incident and Romance. London: 1896. V. 50

PENDELTON, NATHANIEL G.
Military Posts-Council Bluffs to the Pacific Ocean... Washington: 1843. V. 47

PENDEREL, RICHARD
Dick Wylder a Romantic Story. London: 1894. V. 47

PENDERGAST, DAVID M.
Excavations at Altun Ha, Belize 1964-1970. Toronto: 1979-82. V. 50; 52

PENDLEBURY, HENRY
A Plain Representation of Transubstantiantion, As it Is Received in the Church of Rome, with the Sandy Foundations It Is Built Upon, and the Arguments that do Clearly Evert and Overturn It. London: 1687. V. 49

PENDLEBURY, J. D. S.
Aegyptiaca: a Catalogue of Egyptian Objects in the Aegean Area. Cambridge: 1930. V. 49

PENDLETON, JOHN
Our Railways, Their Origin, Development, Incident and Romance. London: 1896. V. 48

PENDLETON, LEILA AMOS
A Narrative of the Negro. Washington: 1912. V. 53

PENE DU BOIS, HENRI
Four Private Libraries of New York. New York: 1892. V. 47; 52

PENFIELD, EDWARD
Holland Sketches. New York: 1907. V. 47
Posters in Miniature. New York & London: 1897. V. 54

PENFIELD, WILDER
The Cerebral Cortex of Man: A Clinical Study of Locolization of Function. New York: 1952. V. 47
Epilepsy and Cerebral Localization. Springfield: 1941. V. 47; 54
Epilepsy and the Functional Anatomy of the Human Brain. Boston: 1954. V. 47; 50

PENFOLD, JANE WALLAS
Madeira Flowers, Fruits and Ferns. London: 1845. V. 53

PENGELLY, H.
A Memoir of William Pengelly, of Torquay. London: 1896. V. 51
A Memoir of William Pengelly, of Torquay. London: 1897. V. 52; 53; 54

PENGUIN Modern Poets 24: Kenward Elmslie, Kenneth Koch, James Schuyler. Harmondsworth: 1974. V. 54

THE PENGUIN New Writing. London: 1940-50. V. 48

PENICILLIN: Its Properties, Uses and Preparations. London: 1946. V. 49; 54

PENICILLIN Therapy and Control in Twenty-One Army Groups. London: 1945. V. 54

PENINGTON, ISAAC
Some Few Queries and Considerations Proposed to the Cavaliers. London: 1660. V. 49
The Works... London: 1681. V. 51

THE PENITENT of Egypt. An Heroic Poem. In Eight Books. Dublin: 1781. V. 50

PENKETHAMAN, WILLIAM
Love Without Interest; or, the Man Too Hard for the Master. London: 1699. V. 49

PENKETHMAN, JOHN
A Collection of Several Authentick Accounts of the History and Price of Wheat, Bread, Malt, etc. London: 1748. V. 51

PENLEY, AARON
The English School of Painting In Water-Colours: Its Theory and Practice. London: 1874. V. 50
The English School of Painting in Water-Colours: Its Theory and Practice. London: 1880. V. 47
Sketching from Nature in Water-Colours. London: 1869. V. 49; 50
Sketching from Nature in Water-Colours. London: 1880. V. 50; 54

PENN, GRANVILLE
The Bioscope or Dial of Life, Explained... London: 1814. V. 48
A Comparative Estimate of the Mineral and Mosaical Geologies. 1825. V. 54
Conversations on Geology: Comprising a Familiar Explanation of the Huttonian and Wernerian Systems. London: 1828. V. 54
Memorials of the Professional Life and Times of Sir William Penn, Knt. Admiral and General of the Fleet, During the Interregnum... London: 1833. V. 52
The Policy and Interest of Great Britain, with Respect to Malta, Summarily Considered. London: 1805. V. 48; 50; 52
The Prophecy of Ezekiel, Concerning Gogue...His Discomfiture and Final Fall. London: 1814. V. 54

PENN, I.
The Afro-American Press, and its Editors. Springfield: 1891. V. 48; 53; 54
The United Negro: His Problems and His Progress. Atlanta: 1902. V. 48

PENN, IRVING
Moments Preserved. New York: 1960. V. 47; 50; 51; 52; 54
Worlds in a Small Room. New York: 1974. V. 54

PENN, JAMES
Life of Miss Davis, the Farmer's Daughter of Essex... London: 1810. V. 47
The Life of Miss Davis, the Farmer's Daughter of Essex... London: 1824. V. 47
Under-Grammar Master, Christ's Hospital. London: 1762. V. 53

PENN, WILLIAM
An Address to Protestants of all Perswasions. London: 1692. V. 50
A Brief Answer to a False and Foolish Libell, Called the Quakers opinions, for Their Sakes That Writ It and Read It. 1678. V. 50
A Brief Examination and State of Liberty Spiritual, Both with Respect to Persons in Their Private Capacity and in their Church Society and Communion. London: 1681. V. 50
A Collection of the Works of William Penn....To Which is Prefixed a Journal of His Life. London: 1726. V. 47
Epicedia Academiae Oxoniensis, in Obitum Celesissimi Principis Henrici Ducis Glocestrensis. Oxoniae: 1660. V. 50
Good Advice to the Church of England, Roman Catholick and Protestant Dissenter. London: 1687. V. 53
No Cross, No Crown. London: 1762. V. 50
Some Fruits of Solitude in Reflections and Maxims, Relating to the Conduct of Human Life. London: 1901. V. 48; 53
Some Fruits of Solitude, in Reflections and Maxims...(with) More Fruits of Solitude... London: 1718. V. 48
The Speech of William Penn to His Majesty, Upon His Delivering the Quakers Address. London: 1687. V. 47
To the Churches of Jesus Throughout the World. 1677. V. 50

PENNANT, THOMAS
Arctic Zoology. London: 1784-85. V. 50; 52; 53
Arctic Zoology. London: 1784-87. V. 50
Arctic Zoology. London: 1792. V. 51; 53
British Zoology. Warrington and London: 1776-77. V. 48; 52; 54
British Zoology. London: 1812. V. 47; 48; 50; 54
Genera of Birds. London: 1781. V. 50
The History and Antiquities of London. London: 1813. V. 49
The History and Antiquities of London. London: 1814. V. 50
History of London, Westminster, and Southwark. London: 1814. V. 50; 52
History of Quadrupeds. London: 1793. V. 54
The History of the Parishes of Whiteford and Holywell. London: 1796. V. 48; 51; 52; 54
Indian Zoology. London: 1790. V. 54
The Journey from Chester to London. London: 1782. V. 51
The Journey from Chester to London... London: 1811. V. 52; 54
A Journey from London to the Isle of Wight. London: 1801. V. 50
The Journey to Snowdon. London: 1781. V. 49; 52
The Literary Life of the Late Thomas Pennant. London: 1793. V. 48; 49; 52; 53
Of London. London: 1790. V. 50; 52
Some Account of London. London: 1791. V. 51
Some Account of London. London: 1793. V. 49
Some Account of London. London: 1805. V. 48
Some Account of London, Westminster, and Southark. London: 1814. V. 52
A Tour from Alston-Moor to Harrowgate and Brimham Crags. London: 1804. V. 53
A Tour from Downing to Alston-Moor. London: 1801. V. 48; 50; 52; 53
A Tour from Downing to Alston-Moor. (with) A Tour from Alston Moor to Harrowgate and Brimham Crags, 1773. London: 1801/04. V. 47; 51
A Tour in Scotland, 1769. Chester: 1771. V. 51; 52
A Tour in Scotland, 1769. London: 1772. V. 52; 54
A Tour in Scotland, 1769. Warrington: 1774. V. 49
A Tour in Scotland, 1769 and Voyage to the Hebrides. Warrington: 1776. V. 47
A Tour in Scotland, 1769...and Voyage to the Hebrides, 1772. Warrington: 1774/74. V. 52
A Tour in Scotland, and A Voyage to the Hebrides. London: 1776. V. 48; 49; 51; 54
A Tour in Scotland, and Voyage to the Hebrides, 1772. Chester: 1774. V. 48
A Tour in Wales. London: 1784. V. 47; 48; 49; 51; 53
A Tour in Wales 1773, with Another tour, 1700. London: 1778-83. V. 47
Tours in Wales. London: 1810. V. 54
The View of the Malayan Isles, new Holland and the Spicy Islands. London: 1800. V. 48

PENNECUIK, ALEXANDER
Historical Account of the Blue Blanket; or Craftsmens Banner. Edinburgh: 1780. V. 48

PENNEFATHER, FREDRICK WILLIAM
A Handbook for Travellers in New Zealand. London: 1893. V. 47

PENNEFATHER, JOHN P.
Thirteen Years on the Prairies from Winnipeg to Cold Lake Fifteen Hundred Miles. London: 1892. V. 50

PENNELL, ELIZABETH ROBINS
The Life of James McNeill Whistler. London and Philadelphia: 1908. V. 49
The Life of James McNeill Whistler. Philadelphia: 1911. V. 50
Lithography and Lithographers: Some Chapters in the History of the Art. London: 1915. V. 49
My Cookery Books. Boston and New York: 1903. V. 51; 53
My Cookery Books. Boston: 1930. V. 47
Our Philadelphia. Philadelphia & London: 1914. V. 51

PENNELL, HARRY CHOLMONDELEY
The Family Fairy Tales; or, Glimpses of Elfland at Heatherston Hall. London: 1865. V. 49

PENNELL, JOSEPH
The Adventures of an Illustrator, Mostly In Following His Authors In America and Europe. Boston: 1925. V. 47; 48; 50; 52; 54
Etchers and Etching: Chapters in the History of the Art Together with Technical Explanations of Modern Artistic Methods... New York: 1919. V. 50
Etchers and Etching, Chapters in the History of the Art Together with Technical Explanations of Modern Artistic Methods. New York: 1929. V. 49
The Glory of New York... New York: 1926. V. 48
The Jew at Home. New York: 1892. V. 50
Pen Drawing and Pen Draughtsmen. London: 1897. V. 51
Pen Drawing and Pen Draughtsmen. New York and London: 1920. V. 54
Play in Provence. New York: 1892. V. 49
The Work of Charles Keene... London: 1897. V. 51; 54

PENNELL, T. L.
Among the Wild Tribes of the Afghan Frontier. London: 1909. V. 51; 52

PENNEY, JAMES CASH
Fifty Years with the Golden Rule. New York: 1950. V. 47

PENNEY, NORMAN
The Household Account Book of Sarah Fell of Swarthmore Hall. Cambridge: 1920. V. 52

PENNIE, JOHN FITZGERALD
Corfe Castle; or Keneswitha. London: 1824. V. 54
The Garland of Wild Roses: a Collection of Original Poems, for Youthful Minds. London: 1822. V. 48; 54
The Royal Minstrel; or, the Witcheries of Endor, and Epic Poem in Eleven Books. Dorchester: 1817. V. 48; 54

PENNIMAN, PURCELL
Questions and Expositions of Slavery, Obtained from Those Who Have Experienced It by the Author. Boston: 1856. V. 54

PENNINGTON, GEORGE JAMES
The Currency of the British Colonies. London: 1848. V. 51

PENNINGTON, ISAAC
Light or Darkness, Displaying or Hiding It Self, As It Pleases. London: 1650. V. 52

PENNINGTON, JOHN H.
Aerostation of Steam Aerial Navitation... Baltimore: 1838. V. 50
A System of Aerostation, or Steam Aerial Navigation. Washington City: 1842. V. 50; 53

PENNINGTON, MAY
History of Brenham and Washington County. Houston: 1915. V. 50

PENNINGTON, MONTAGU
Memoirs of the Life of Mrs. Elizabeth Carter. London: 1807. V. 47
Memoirs of the Life of Mrs. Elizabeth Carter. London: 1825. V. 54

PENNINGTON, RICHARD
A Descriptive Catalogue of the Etched Work of Wenceslaus Hollar, 1607-1677. Cambridge: 1982. V. 52
A Descriptive Catalogue of the Etched Work of Wenceslaus Hollar, 1608-1677. 1982. V. 49; 54
Peterley Harvest. London: 1960. V. 50
Peterley Harvest. Toronto: 1963. V. 50

PENNSYLVANIA ACADEMY OF FINE ARTS
Catalogue of the Thirty-Seventh Annual Exhibition, 1860. Philadelphia: 1860. V. 51

PENNSYLVANIA. ADJUTANT GENERAL
Report of the Adjutant General of Pennsylvania, for the Year 1877. Harrisburg: 1878. V. 52

PENNSYLVANIA AGRICULTURAL SOCIETY
Memoirs of the...With Selections from the Most Approved Authors, Adapted to the Use of the Practical Farmers of the United States. 1824. Philadelphia: 1824. V. 47

THE PENNSYLVANIA Hermit. A Narrative of the Extraordinary Life of Amos Wilson, Who Expired in a Cave in the Neighborhood of Harrisburgh (Penn.), After Having Therein Lived in Solitary Retirement for the Space of Nineteen Years... Philadelphia: 1839. V. 47

PENNSYLVANIA IRON MANUFACTURE
Documents Relating to the Manufacture of Iron In Pennsylvania. Philadelphia: 1850. V. 50

PENNSYLVANIA. LEGISLATURE
Acts of the Legislature of Pennsylvania, relating to the Union Canal Company of Pennsylvania. Philadelphia: 1825. V. 51
Report on the Condition of the Insane Within Hospitals of the State of Pennsylvania. 1902. V. 54

THE PENNSYLVANIA State Trials: Containing the Impeachment, Trial and Acquittal of Francis Hopkinson and John Nicholson...the Former Being Judge of the Court of Admiralty and the Latter the Comptroller General of the Commonwealth of Pennsylvania. Philadelphia: 1794. V. 47; 50

PENNY, ANNE
Poems, with a Dramatic Entertainment. London: 1771. V. 47; 48

PENNY, ANNE JUDITH BROWN
The Afternoon of Unmarried Life from the Last London Edition. New York: 1859. V. 54

PENNY, FANNY EMILY FARR
Caste and Creed. London: 1890. V. 54

PENNY, N.
Memoir of the Services of Brigadier N. Penny, C.B. Calcutta: 1851. V. 47

PENROSE, CHARLES BINGHAM
The Rustler Business. Douglas: 1959. V. 51

PENROSE, CHARLES VINICOMBE
Observations on Corporal Punishment, Impressment and Other Matters Relative to the Present State of His Majesty's Royal Navy. Bodmin: 1824. V. 51

PENROSE, ELIZABETH
Tales and Conversations; or, the New Children's Friend. London: 1832. V. 47

PENROSE, MATT R.
Pots O'Gold, Warden Nevada State Prison. Reno: 1935. V. 53

PENROSE, ROLAND
The Road is Wider than Long: an Image Dairy of the Balkans, July August, 1938. London: 1939. V. 49; 51; 53

PENROSE, THOMAS
Poems. London: 1781. V. 54

PENSEYRE, SAMUEL
A New Guide to Astrology; or, Astrology Brought to Light. London: 1726. V. 54

THE PENTAGON Papers. Boston: 1971-72. V. 48

PENTHER, JOHANN FRIEDRICH
Gnomonica Funamentalis & Mechanica. Augsburg: 1752. V. 47

PENTON, STEPHEN
The Guardian's Instruction, or, the Gentleman's Romance... London: 1688. V. 47; 48

PENWARE, JOHN
Contemplation, a Poem: with Tales, and Other Poetical Compositions. London: 1807. V. 48

PENZER, N. M.
Paul Storr, The Last of the Goldsmiths. Boston: 1954. V. 51
Poison-Damsels, and Other Essays in Folklore and Anthropology. London: 1952. V. 54

PEPIN, GUILLAUME
Elucidatio in Confiteor... Venetiis: 1588. V. 53

PEPLER, HILARY DOUGLAS CLARK
Le Boeuf et l'ane, et Deux Autres Pieces Pour marionnettes. Ditchling: 1930. V. 47; 49
Concerning Dragons. Ditchling: 1916. V. 50; 53; 54
The Devil's Devices or Control Versus Service. 1915. V. 49
The Devil's Devices or control Versus Service. Hammersmith: 1915. V. 48; 50; 53
The Hand Press - an Essay Written and Printed by Hand for the Society of Typographic Arts, Chicago... Ditchling: 1934. V. 48; 49; 50; 52; 53
Mimes, Sacred and Profane. Ditchling: 1932. V. 48
Nisi Dominus. Ditchling: 1919. V. 47
Pertinent and Impertinent. 1926. V. 54
The Three Wise Men a Nativity Play. Ditchling: 1929. V. 53

PEPPER, WILLIAM
The Medical Side of Benjamina Franklin. Philadelphia: 1910. V. 50
A System of Practical Medicine by American Authors. Philadelphia: 1885. V. 49; 54
A System of Practical Medicine by American Authors. Philadelphia: 1885-86. V. 54
A Text-Book of the Theory and Practice of Medicine by American Teachers. Philadelphia: 1894. V. 54

PEPYS, CHARLOTTE MARIA, LADY
The Diary and Houres of the Ladye Adolie... London: 1853. V. 50; 51

PEPYS, SAMUEL
The Diary. Boston: 1893. V. 54
The Diary. London: 1904. V. 50; 52
The Diary. London & Cambridge: 1923/24. V. 48
The Diary. London: 1928. V. 47
The Diary... London: 1938. V. 52
The Diary. New York: 1942. V. 51; 53; 54
Diary. London: 1948. V. 47
The Diary. Berkeley: 1971-83. V. 50
The Diary. London: 1971-83. V. 49; 52
The Diary. London: 1978-83. V. 51
The Diary. Berkeley and Los Angeles: 1979. V. 47
The Diary. London: 1983. V. 49; 51
Diary and Correspondence. London: 1875. V. 51
Diary and Correspondence. London: 1875-79. V. 51
Diary and Correspondence. London: 1876-79. V. 48; 50
Diary and Correspondence. New York: 1885. V. 47
Diary and Correspondence... London: 1890. V. 52; 53
Everybody's Pepys, the Diary of Samuel Pepys 1660-1669. London: 1927. V. 48
The Life, Journals and Correspondence of... London: 1841. V. 48; 50; 51
Memoires Relating to the State of the Royal Navy of England, for Ten Years Determin'd December 1688. London: 1690. V. 49; 50; 51; 53
Memoirs: Comprising His Diary from 1659 to 1669... London: 1825. V. 47; 49; 50; 51; 52
Pepys's Memoirs of the Royal Navy 1679-1688. Oxford: 1906. V. 54
The Portugal History; or a Relation of the Troubles that Happened in the Court of Portugal in the Years 1667 and 1668. London: 1677. V. 53
Private and Further Correspondence 1662-1703 of Samuel Pepys. London: 1926-29. V. 51; 54
Ye Minutes of Ye CLXXVIIth Meeting of Ye Sette of Odd Volumes, Extracted from the Diary of Samuel Pepys. Chelsea: 1896. V. 50

PER la Solenne Dedicazione della Statua Equestre Innalzata dal Pubblico di Modena all'Immortale Memoria dell'Altezza Serenissima di Francesco III Gloriosamente Regnante Applausi Poetici... Modena: 1774. V. 47

PERCEVAL, DUDLEY M.
Maynooth and the Jew Bill: Further Illlustrations of the Speech of the Rt. Hon. Spencer Perceval on the Roman Catholic Question, in May 1805.... London and Edinburgh: 1845. V. 54

PERCEVAL, JOHN
An Examination of the Principles... London: 1749. V. 50
A Narrative of the Treatment Experienced by a Gentleman, During a State of Mental Derangement... London: 1838-40. V. 50

PERCIVAL, A. B.
A Game Ranger on Safari. London: 1928. V. 50
A Game Ranger's Note Book. 1927. V. 54
A Game Ranger's Note Book. London: 1927. V. 49
Game Ranger's Note Book. A Game Ranger on Safari. V. 48; 52
A Game Ranger's Notebook. (and) A Game Ranger on Safari. Clinton: 1985/85. V. 49

PERCIVAL, DON
Maynard Dixon Sketchbook. Flagstaff: 1967. V. 52

PERCIVAL, GUY
Paul Reeves: or Life's Mistakes. Columbus: 1879. V. 48

PERCIVAL, JAMES GATES
Poetical Works. Boston: 1863. V. 48

PERCIVAL, JOHN
The Wheat Plant. London: 1921. V. 50; 51

PERCIVAL, ROBERT
An Account of the Island of Ceylon, Containing Its History, Geography, Natural History, with the Manners and Customs Of Its Various Inhabitants... London: 1803. V. 47; 52

PERCIVAL, THOMAS
A Father's Instructions; Consisting of Moral Tales. Warrington: 1784. V. 48
A Father's Instructions: Consisting of Moral Tales. Philadelphia: 1788. V. 53
The Works, Literary, Moral and Philosophical... Bath: 1807. V. 49; 50; 52

PERCIVAL, W. S.
The Land of the Dragon. London: 1889. V. 48

PERCY, JAMES
To the King's Most Excellent Majesty. The Humble Petition of James Percy, Son of Henry Percy...the Heir-Male to Jocelin Percy...Eleventh Earl of Northumberland. 1690?. V. 47

PERCY, JOHN
Metallurgy: the Art of Extracting Metals from Ores and Adapting Them to Various Purposes of Manufacture. London: 1864. V. 50

PERCY, THOMAS, BP. OF DROMORE
Ancient Songs, Chiefly on Morrish Subjects. Oxford: 1932. V. 51
Bishop Percy's Folio Manuscript: Ballads and Romances. London: 1867-68. V. 51
Five Pieces of Runic Poetry. London: 1763. V. 47; 48
The Hermit of Warkworth. London: 1771. V. 47; 53
The Hermit of Warkworth. Alnwick: 1807. V. 48
Miscellaneous Pieces Relating to the Chinese. London: 1762. V. 48
Northern Antiquities, or, a Description of the Manners, Customs, Religion and Laws of the Ancient Danes... London: 1760. V. 50; 54
The Percy Folio of Old English Ballads and Romances. London: 1905-10. V. 49
The Regulations and Establishment of the Household of Henry Algernon Percy, the Fifth Earl of Northumberland, at His Castles of Wrestill and Lekinfield in Yorkshire. London: 1827. V. 47; 54
Reliques of Ancient English Poetry... London: 1765. V. 47; 50; 51; 53
Reliques of Ancient English Poetry... London: 1767. V. 52
Reliques of Ancient English Poetry... London: 1775. V. 48; 51
Reliques of Ancient English Poetry... London: 1794. V. 47; 48; 50
Reliques of Ancient English Poetry... London: 1839. V. 48; 50; 52; 53
Reliques of Ancient English Poetry. Edinburgh: 1858. V. 47
Reliques of Ancient English Poetry. London: 1876. V. 49; 54
Reliques of Ancient English Poetry, Consisting of Old Heroic Ballads, Songs and Other Pieces of Our Earlier Poets. London: 1886. V. 53

PERCY, WALKER
Bourbon. Winston-Salem: 1979. V. 49; 51; 52; 53; 54
Bourbon. Winston-Salem: 1981. V. 48; 49; 51; 52; 53
Diagnosing the Modern Malaise. New Orleans: 1985. V. 54
Lancelot. New York: 1977. V. 49; 52; 54
The Last Gentleman. New York: 1966. V. 47; 50; 51; 53
Lost in the Cosmos. New York: 1983. V. 47; 48; 49; 51; 52; 54
Love in the Ruins. New York: 1971. V. 48; 50; 51; 52; 53; 54
Message in the Bottle: How Queer Man Is, How Queer Language Is, and What One Has To Do with the Other. New York: 1975. V. 47; 54
The Message in the Bottle: How Queer Man Is, How Queer Language Is, and What One Has to Do with the Other. New York: 1976. V. 47
The Movie-Goer. London: 1961. V. 53
The Moviegoer. New York: 1961. V. 49; 50; 51
The Moviegoer. London: 1963. V. 47; 49; 51; 53
The Moviegoer. Franklin Center: 1980. V. 49
Novel Writing in an Apocalyptic Time. New Orleans: 1986. V. 49; 52
Questions They Never Asked Me. 1979. V. 48
Questions They Never Asked Me. Northridge: 1979. V. 47; 52
The Second Coming. New York: 1980. V. 47; 48; 49; 52; 53; 54
The Second Coming. Pennsylvania: 1980. V. 48
The State of the Novel. 1987. V. 50
The State of the Novel. New Orleans: 1987. V. 47; 48; 49; 50; 51; 52; 54
Symbol as Need. New York: 1954. V. 51; 52
Symbols as Hermeneutic in Existentialism. 1956. V. 53
The Thanatos Syndrome. Franklin Center: 1987. V. 49; 52; 53
The Thanatos Syndrome. New York: 1987. V. 48; 51; 52; 53; 54

PERCY, WILLIAM ALEXANDER
The Collected Poems of William Alexander Percy. New York: 1943. V. 52
Lanterns on the Levee. New York: 1941. V. 51

PERCYVALL, RICHARD
A Dictionary in Spanish and English... London: 1623. V. 48; 52

PERDRIEL-VAISSIERES, J.
Rupert Brooke's Death and Burial. New Haven: 1917. V. 50

PEREFIXE, HARDOUIN BEAUMONT DE, ABP.
Histoire du Roy Henry le Grand... Amsterdam: 1661. V. 48
The History of Henry IV. London: 1672. V. 54

PEREGRINUS, PETER
Epistle Of Peter Peregrinus of Maricourt to Sygerus of Foncaucourt, Soldier... London: 1902. V. 48

PEREIRA, BENITO
Adversus Fallaces & Supersitiosas Artes. Id est. De Magia, De Obervatione Somniorum... Lyon: 1592. V. 48
De Magia, De Observatione Somniorvm, et de Divinatione Astrologica. Coloniae Agrippinae: 1598. V. 48; 53

PEREIRA, J.
The Elements of Materia Medica. London: 1839-40. V. 51; 53
The Elements of Materia Medica and Therapeutics. London: 1854. V. 47
The Elements of Materia Medica and Therapeutics. London: 1854-57. V. 50
A Treatise On Food and Diet: With Observations On the Dietetial Regimen Suited for Disordered States of the Digestive Organs... New York: 1843. V. 49; 54
A Treatise on Food and Diet...an Account of the Dietaries of some of the... London: 1843. V. 51; 53

PEREIRA DE BERREDO, BERNARDO
Annaes Historicos do Estado do Maranhao... Lisbon: 1749. V. 48

PERELMAN, S. J.
Acres and Plains. New York: 1972. V. 52
Dawn Ginsbergh's Revenge. 1929. V. 50; 53
Dawn Ginsbergh's Revenge. New York: 1929. V. 54
Eastward Ha!. London: 1977. V. 52
Looke Who's Talking. New York: 1940. V. 51
One Touch of Venus. Boston: 1944. V. 53
Perelman's Home Companion. New York: 1955. V. 54
Strictly From Hunger. New York: 1937. V. 49; 52

THE PERENNIAL; A Collection of Moral and Religious Poetry. London: 1835. V. 54

PERET, BENJAMIN
Air Mexicain. Paris: 1952. V. 47
Remove Your Hat - Twenty Poems. London: 1936. V. 49

PEREZ, GREGORIO
Descripcion Historica del Triunfo Que Erigio a San Rafael, Custodio de Cordoba, el III.... Madrid: 1782. V. 53

PEREZ DE MENDOZA Y QUIJADA, MIGUEL
Principios de Los Cinco Sujetos Principales, de Que se Compone la Philosophia, y Matematica de las Armas, Practica, y Especulativa. Pamplona: 1672. V. 48

PEREZ DE RIBAS, ANDRES
My Life Among the Savage Nations of New Spain...Written in the Year A.D. 1644... Los Angeles: 1968. V. 47

PEREZ DE VILLA-AMIL, GENEARO
Espana y Monumental, Vistas y Descripcion de los Sitios y Monumentos mas Notables de Espana... Paris: 1842-50. V. 47

PEREZ GALDOS, BENITO
Dona Perfecta. New York: 1895. V. 51

PERGOLESI, M. A.
Designs for Various Ornaments. London: 1777-92. V. 50
Eighteenth Century Architecture, Ornamentation, Furniture and Decoration. Boston & New York: 1890. V. 53

PERHAM, JOSIAH
Descriptive and Historical View of the Seven Mile Mirror of the Lakes, Niagara, St. Lawrence and Saguenay Rivers... New York: 1854. V. 52

PERICOT-GARCIA, LUIS
Pre-Historic and Primitive Art. New York: 1968. V. 47
Prehistoric and Primitive Art. London: 1969. V. 50

PERIER, ALESSANDRO
Disinganno de' Peccatori...Utilissimo a Missionarii ed a Tutti i Predicatori, che Solo Deiserano la Salute delle Anime... Rome: 1726. V. 53; 54

PERILS of the Ocean, or Disasters of the Seas. New York: 1830. V. 48

PERING, RICHARD
A Brief Enquiry into the Causes of Premature Decay, in Our Wooden Bulwarks, with an Examination of the Means, Best Calculated to Prolong Their Duration. Plymouth-Dock: 1812. V. 53
On the Preservation of the British Navy, When in a State of Ordinary. Plymouth-Dock: 1813. V. 53
A Reply to Some Strictures in the Quarterly Review, (No. XIX) on Indian-Built Ships. Plymouth-Dock: 1814. V. 53
A Treatise on the Anchor, Shewing How the Component Parts Should Be Combined to Obtain the Greatest Power... Plymouth-Dock: 1819. V. 53

PERIONIUS, JOACHIM
De Optimo Genere Interpretandi Commentarii (Annotationes Ethicorum Librum Decimum). Paris: 1540. V. 49

PERISTIANY, J. G.
The Social Institutions of the Kipsigis (Kenya). London: 1939. V. 49

PERKINS, CHARLES C.
Italian Sculptors: a History of Sculpture in Northern, Southern and Eastern Italy. London: 1868. V. 50; 54
Tuscan Sculptors: Their Lives, Works and Times... London: 1864. V. 49; 50; 52

PERKINS, CHARLES ELIOTT
The Pinto Horse. Santa Barbara: 1937. V. 47; 49

PERKINS, EDNA BRUSH
The White Heat of Mojave. New York: 1922. V. 50

PERKINS, EDWARD T.
Na Motu: or, Reef-Rovings in the South Seas. New York: 1854. V. 47; 52; 54

PERKINS, FRANCIS
A Prognostication for the Year of Our Lord God, 1668... London: 1668. V. 48

PERKINS, FRANCIS BEECHER
Scrope; or, the Lost Library. A Novel of New York and Hartford. Boston: 1874. V. 51

PERKINS, HENRY
The Perkins Library. 1873. V. 53
The Perkins Library. A Catalogue of the Very Valuable and Important Library... Gadsden: 1873. V. 48
Scores of the Cricket Matches Between Oxford and Cambridge From the Commencement Up to Date. London: 1898. V. 51

PERKINS, JACOB B.
J. B.'s Final Bulletin. Cleveland: 1937. V. 47

PERKINS, JAMES
A Tour Round the Globe. Letters to the "City Press". London: 1891. V. 47

PERKINS, JOHN
A Profitable Booke...Treating of the Lawes of England. London: 1581. V. 52
A Profitable Booke...Treating of the Lawes of England. Londoni: 1601. V. 51
A Profitable Booke...Treating of the Lawes of England. London: 1657. V. 51; 52; 53

PERKINS, JOHN C.
Resources of the Philadelphia and Erie Railroad Region, in Letters to the Erie Daily Dispatch, by Its Special Correspondent... Erie: 1868. V. 53

PERKINS, JOSEPH
An Oration Upon Genius, Pronounced at the Anniversary Commencement of Harvard University, in Cambridge, July 19, 1797. Boston: 1797. V. 53

PERKINS, JUSTIN
A Residence of Eight Years in Persia, Among the Nestorian Christians... Andover: 1843. V. 48; 49

PERKINS, LUCY FITCH
The Pickaninny Twins. Boston: 1931. V. 49
Robin Hood. London: 1906. V. 50

PERKINS, SIMEON
The Diary of Simeon Perkins, 1766-1780. Toronto: 1948. V. 52
The Diary of Simeon Perkins, 1780-1812. Toronto: 1958/61/67. V. 48
The Diary of Simeon Perkins 1780-1812. Toronto: 1958/61/67/78. V. 52; 54

PERKINS, WALTER FRANK
Catalogue of the Walter Frank Perkins Agricultural Library. Southampton: 1961. V. 51; 54

PERKINS, WILLARD
The Cactus: 1928. V. 54

PERKINS, WILLIAM
A Discourse of the Damned Art of Witchcraft: so Farr Forth as It Is Reveled in the Scriptures, and Manifest by True Experience. 1609. V. 47
An Exposition of the Symbole or Creede of the Apostles. London: 1631. V. 50
Opera Theologica. Geneva: 1611. V. 52
The Workes of that Famous and Worthy Minister of Christ, in the University of Cambridge, M. William Perkins. London: 1613. V. 52

PERLES, ALFRED
Round Trip. London: 1946. V. 51
Scenes from a Floating Life. London: 1968. V. 54

PERLEY, MOSES HENRY
Reports on the Sea and River Fisheries of New Brunswick. Fredericton: 1852. V. 47; 53

PERLZWEIG, JUDITH
Lamps of the Roman Period, First to Seventh Century after Christ. Princeton: 1961. V. 50; 52

PERNETY, ANTOINE J.
The History of a Voyage to the Malouine (or Falkland) Islands, Made in 1763 and 1764, Under the Command of M. de Bougainville, in Order to Form a Settlement There... London: 1771. V. 47; 52

PERNETY, ROBERT
The History of a Voyage to the Malouine (or Falkland) Islands, Made in 1763 and 1764, Under the Command of M. de Bougainville, in Order to Form a Settlement There... London: 1771. V. 52

PERNKOPF, EDUARD
Atlas of Topographical and Applied Human Anatomy. Philadelphia: 1963-64. V. 54

PERON, FRANCOIS
Voyage de Decouvertes Aux Terres Australes. Paris: 1807-16-24. V. 52
Voyage de Decouvertes Aux Terres Uastrales, Execute par Ordre de sa majeste l'Empereur et Roi, sur Les Corvettes le Geographe, le natraliste, et la Goelette le Casuarina, pendant les Annees, 1800, 1801, 1802, 1803 et 1804. Paris: 1807-16. V. 48

PERON, PIERRE F.
Memoires du Capitaine Peron, sur ses Voyages aux Cotes d'Afrique, en Arabie, a l'ile d'Amsterdam, aux iles d'Anjouan et de Mayotte, Aux Cotes Nord-Ouest de l'Amerique, aux Iles Sandwich, a la Chine,e tc. Paris: 1824. V. 47

PEROTTUS, NICCOLAUS
In Hoc Volumine Habentur Haec - Cornucopiae, Sive Linguae Latinae Com(m)entarii Diligentissime Recogniti... Venice: 1513//17. V. 52

THE PERPETUAL Laws of the Commonwealth of Massachusetts from the Commencement of the Constitution...1780 to...1789. Boston: 1789. V. 53

PERRAIVOS, C.
History of Suli and Parga. Edinburgh: 1823. V. 48

PERRAULT, CHARLES
La Barbe Bleue et La Belle Au Bois Dormant. Asnieres-sur-Seine: 1887. V. 53
Cinderella. New York: 1886?. V. 49
A Fairy Garland. London: 1928. V. 48; 50; 51
Fairy Tales. London: 1922. V. 49
The Fairy Tales. New York: 1922. V. 50
Histoire de Peau d'Ane. Hammersmith: 1902. V. 51; 52
Histoires ou Contes du Tems Passe, Avec des Moralites. A La Haye: 1742. V. 54
Les Hommes Illustres Qui Ont Paru en France Pendant ce Siecle Avec Leurs Portraits au Naturel. Parais: 1696-1700. V. 53; 54
A New History of Blue Beard, Written by Black Beard, for the Amusement of Little Lack Beard and His Pretty sisters. Philadelphia: 1804. V. 52
Old Time Stories. London: 1921. V. 54
Tales of Past Times. London: 1922. V. 48

PERRAULT, CLAUDE
Memoirs for a Natural History of Animals. London: 1688. V. 47; 50
The Natural History of Animals... London: 1702. V. 48; 50; 52
A Treatise of the Five Orders of Columns in Architecture... London: 1708. V. 51

PERRAULT, J.
Lower Canada Agriculturalist: Manufacturing, Commercial, and Colonization Intelligencer. 1861-1862. Montreal: 1863. V. 52

PERRENS, F. T.
The History of Florence Under the Domination of Cosimo, Piero, Lorenzo De' Medicis, 1434-1492. London: 1892. V. 52

PERRIE, GEORGE
Buckskin Mose; or, Life from the Lakes to the Pacific, as Ranger, Gold Digger, Indian Scout, and Guide. New York: 1873. V. 47

PERRIN, JEAN PAUL
Luther's Fore-Runners or a Cloud of Witnesses, Deposing for the Protestant Faith. London: 1624. V. 48

PERRIN, RENE
Album du Nouveau-Bellevue. Paris: 1826. V. 52

PERRINCHIEF, RICHARD
The Royal Martyr: or, the Life and Death of King Charles I... London: 1676. V. 47; 48; 49
The Royal Martyr; or the Life and Death of King Charles I. (with) The Sicilian Tyrant; or, The Life of Agathocles. London: 1684/76. V. 48
The Sicilian Tyrant: or the Life of Agathocles. London: 1676. V. 47; 50; 51; 52

PERRIN DU LAC, FRANCOIS MARIE
Travels through the Two Louisianas, and Among the Savage nations of the Missouri; Also in the United States, along the Ohio and the Adjacent Provinces, in 1801, 1802 and 1803. London: 1807. V. 48; 50

PERRING, F. H.
Atlas of British Flora. London: 1962. V. 51; 52; 54
Atlas of British Flora. (with) Critical Supplement. London: 1962-68. V. 49

PERRINS, C. W. DYSON
Italian Book-Illustrations and Early Printing. 1914. V. 47
Italian Book-Illustrations and Early Printing. Austin: 1994. V. 52

PERRONET, J. R.
Memoire sur la Recherche des Moyens que l'on Pourroit Employer Pour Construire de Grandes Arches de Pierre de Deux Cents, Trois Cents, Quatre Cents & Jusqu'a Cinq Cents Pieds d'Ouverture, Qui Seroient Destinees a Franchir de Prodondes Vallees Bordees ... Paris: 1793. V. 51

PERROT, GEORGES
A History of Art in Ancient Egypt. London: 1883. V. 51
A History of Art in Chaldaea and Assyria. London: 1884. V. 49; 52
History of Art in Persia. London: 1892. V. 47
History of Art in Phoenicia and Its Dependencies. London: 1885. V. 49; 52
History of Art in Phrygia Lydia, Caria and Lycia. London: 1892. V. 52
History of Art in Sardinia, Judaea, Syria and Asia Minor. London: 1890. V. 49; 52

PERROTT, C. L. E.
A Selection of British Birds. 1979. V. 52

PERROUIS, LOUIS
Ancestral Art of Gabon from the Collections of the Barbier-Mueller Museum (Geneva). 1986/87. V. 52

PERRY, B. F.
Biographical Sketches of Eminent American Statesmen with Speeches, Addresses and Letters. Philadelphia: 1887/89. V. 50

PERRY, BLISS
Park-Street Papers. Boston: 1908. V. 54

PERRY, CHARLES
A View of the Levant: Particularly of Constantinople, Syria, Egypt and Greece. London: 1743. V. 54

PERRY, G.
Conchology, or the Natural History of Shells. London: 1811. V. 48; 51; 53
Conchology, or the Natural History of Shells. London: 1825?. V. 47; 48

PERRY, J. EDWARD
Forty Cords of Wood: Memoirs of a Medical Doctor. Jefferson City: 1947. V. 48

PERRY, JAMES
The Electricc Eel; (with) Reply to the Electric Eel. (with) The Old Sperent's Reply to the Electric Eel. (with) The Torpedo... London: 1777/77/77. V. 52
An Epistle from Mademoisell D'Eon to the Right Honorable L---d M------d, C---f J-----e of the C----5 of K--g's B---h on His Determination in Regard to Her Sex. London: 1788. V. 48

PERRY, JOHN
An Account of the Stopping of Daggenham Breach; with the Accidents that Have Attended the Same from the First Undertaking. London: 1721. V. 48
An Account of the Stopping of Daggenham Breach; with the Accidents That Have Attended the Same from the First Undertaking... London: 1721. V. 52
The State of Russia, Under the Present Czar. London: 1716. V. 54

PERRY, JOHN D.
Letter of John D. Perry President of the Union Pacific Railway (Eastern Division) Together with the Reports of the Engineer and the Geologist of the Road. Philadelphia: 1868. V. 47

PERRY, JOHN GARDNER
Letters from a Surgeon of the Civil War. Boston: 1906. V. 51

PERRY, KATE
Reminiscences of a London Drawing Room. Chesham Place, 1849. 1863?. V. 52

PERRY, MATTHEW CALBRAITH
The Japan Expedition (1852-1854). The Personal Journal of Commodore Matthew C. Perry. Washington: 1968. V. 48
Narrative of the Expedition of an American Squadron to the China Seas and Japan... New York: 1856. V. 48
Narrative of the Expedition of an American Squadron to the China Seas and Japan. Washington: 1856. V. 48; 49
Narrative of the Expedition of an American Squadron to the China Seas and Japan Performed in the Years 1852, 1853 and 1854... New York: 1967. V. 49

PERRY, RALPH B.
The Thought and Character of William James... 1935. V. 51

PERRY, RUFUS L.
The Cushite; or, the Children of Ham... New York: 1887. V. 50

PERRY, THOMAS
The Butcher's Boy. New York: 1982. V. 51
Metzger's Dog. New York: 1983. V. 52

PERRY, WILLIAM
The Only Sure Guide to the English Tongue or New Pronouncing Spelling Book... Worcester: 1809. V. 49
The Royal Standard English Dictionary... Brookfield: 1809. V. 53

PERRYWHISTLE, MARMADUKE, PSEUD.
Isn't It Odd?. London: 1822. V. 51

PERSE, G. E.
Eighteenth Century Architecture in South Africa. London: 1933. V. 47

PERSHING, JOHN J.
My Experiences in the World War. New York: 1931. V. 48; 49; 50; 53

THE PERSIAN and Turkish Tales, Compleat. London: 1767. V. 47; 49

PERSIUS, LUDWIG
Architektonische Entwurfe fur den Umbau Vorhandener Gebaude. Potsdam: 1843-49. V. 53

PERSIUS FLACCUS, AULUS
Aulus Flaccus Persius cum Glosis Scipionis Ferrarii Georgii Filii de Monte Ferrato... Venice: 1501. V. 48; 53
The Satires. London: 1799. V. 49
Satyrae cum Commentaris Bartholomaei Fonti. Milan: 1484. V. 53
Satyrs Sex... Nuremberg: 1765. V. 49; 53; 54
The Satyrs of Persius. 1728. V. 47
A Six Satyrs. London: 1719. V. 48

PERSON, CLAUDE
Elements of Anatomy and the Animal Oeconomy. London: 1781. V. 48

PERSON, DAVID
Varities; or, a Surveigh of Rare and Excellent Matters, Necessary and Delectable for all Sorts of Persons. London: 1635. V. 53

PERSOON, C. H.
Mycologia Europaea seu Completa Omnium Fungorum in Variis Europaea Regionibus Detectorum Enumeratio... Erlangen: 1822/25. V. 49; 50

PERSOZ, J.
Traite Theorique et Pratique de l'Impression des Tissus. Paris: 1846. V. 48; 54

PERTELOTE; a Bibliography...October 1936 - April 1943. Waltham St. Lawrence: 1943. V. 52

PERTELOTE, a Sequel to Chanticleer. Being a Bibliography of the Golden Cockerel Press October 1936-1943 April. Waltham St. Lawrence: 1943. V. 49; 51

PERTINENT & Impertinent. An Assortment of Verse. Ditchling: 1926. V. 49

PERUCCI, FRANCESCO
Pompe Funebri di Tutte Le Nationi Del Mondo. Verona: 1639. V. 49; 50; 52; 53

PERUCHIO
La Chiromance, La Physionomie et La Geomance Avec la Signification des Nombres & l'Usage de La Roue de Pytagore. Paris: 1663. V. 52

PERVIGILIUM VENERIS
Pervigilium Veneris. 1910. V. 47
Pervigilium Veneris. Hammersmith: 1911. V. 51
Pervigilium Veneris Incerti Auctoris Carmen de Vere. The Eve of Venus. London: 1924. V. 47
The Vigil of Venus. London. V. 52
The Vigil of Venus. Waltham St. Lawrence: 1939. V. 51
The Vigil of Venus. Cummington: 1943. V. 47; 48; 49; 50; 51; 54
The Vigil of Venus. London: 1952. V. 48

PESHALL, JOHN
The History of the University of Oxford, from the Death of William the Conqueror, to the Demise of Queen Elizabeth. Oxford: 1773. V. 48

PESTALOZZI, JOHANN HEINRICH
Letters On Early Education. London: 1827. V. 49

PETER, JEAN CLOUET
Complete edition of the Drawings, Miniatures and Paintings. London: 1971. V. 49

THE PETER Owen Anthology. London: 1991. V. 49; 51

PETER Pan's ABC. London: 1920. V. 48

PETER Piper's Practical Principles of Plain and Perfect Pronunciation to Which is Added a Collection of Entertaining Conundrums. London: 1870. V. 50; 51

PETER Playfair's Pleasing Book of Boy's Sports. London: 1868. V. 53

PETER, SARAH
Ate Eight. New York: 1994. V. 52
Thirty-Six Drawings. Iceland: 1994. V. 52

PETERKIN, JULIA
Black April. Indianapolis: 1927. V. 48; 49; 50
Bright Skin. Indianapolis: 1932. V. 48; 50; 51
Green Thursday. New York: 1924. V. 49
Roll, Jordan, Roll. New York: 1933. V. 51; 52; 53
Scarlet Sister Mary. Indianapolis: 1928. V. 49; 50
Scarlet Sister Mary. New York: 1928. V. 53

PETER MARTYR ANGELERIUS
De Rebus Oceanicis et Novo Orbe, Decades Tres... Cologne: 1574. V. 52

PETERS, CARL
The Eldorado of the Ancients... London: 1902. V. 47; 51

PETERS, DEWITT C.
Kit Carson's Life and Adventures. Hartford: 1873. V. 51

PETERS, ELIZABETH
Night of Four Hundred Rabbits. New York: 1971. V. 49

PETERS, ELLIS
The Assize of the Dying. New York: 1958. V. 49; 51
Black is the Colour of My True Love's Heart. New York: 1967. V. 52
Death Mask. 1959. V. 53
Death Mask. London: 1959. V. 52
The Devil's Novice. London: 1983. V. 52
An Excellent Mystery. London: 1985. V. 54
Funeral of Figaro. New York: 1964. V. 51
Hortensius: Friend of Nero. New York: 1937. V. 48; 49
The Leper of Saint Giles. London: 1981. V. 54
One Corpse Too Many. London: 1979. V. 49; 50
People of My Own. New York: 1942. V. 50
The Pilgrim of Hate. London: 1984. V. 54
The Potter's Field. London: 1989. V. 54
St. Peter's Fair. New York: 1981. V. 54
The Virgin in the Ice. London: 1982. V. 52
Who Lies Here?. New York: 1965. V. 50
The Will and the Deed. London: 1960. V. 53

PETER'S Enquiries After Knowledge, with the Strange Things He Heard and Saw. London: 1850. V. 52

PETERS, GUSTAV
Die Geschichte Joseph. Harrisburg: 1830's. V. 53

PETERS, HARRY T.
America on Stone: the Other Printmakers to the American People. New York: 1931. V. 47
California on Stone. Garden City: 1935. V. 47; 51; 52; 53
California on Stone. New York: 1935. V. 54
Currier & Ives, Printmakers to the American People. Garden City: 1929. V. 51
Currier & Ives, Printmakers to the American People. New York: 1929-31. V. 50; 52; 53
Currier & Ives, Printmakers to the American People. New York: 1942. V. 50
Currier & Ives, Printmakers to the American People. New York: 1976. V. 47

PETERS, HERMANN
Pictorial History of Ancient Pharmacy: with Sketches of Early Medical Practice. Chicago: 1889. V. 52
Pictorial History of Ancient Pharmacy, with Sketches of Early Medical Practice. Chicago: 1902. V. 52
Pictorial History of Ancient Pharmacy: with Sketches of Early Medical Practice. Chicago: 1906. V. 52

PETERS, J. L.
Check-List of Birds of the World. London: 1931-62. V. 50
Check-List of Birds of the World. Cambridge: 1937-79. V. 54

PETERS, JOHN PUNNETT
Nippur. Or Explorations and Adventures on the Euphrates. London: 1897. V. 49; 51; 54
Painted Tombs in the Necropolis of Marissa (Mareshah). London: 1905. V. 49; 52

PETERS, ROBERT
Ikagnak: The North Wind, with Dr. Kane in the Arctic. Pasadena: 1978. V. 47

PETERS, SAMUEL ANDREW
A General History of Connecticut. London: 1781. V. 47; 49

PETERSEN, K. D.
Plains Indian Art from Marion. Norman: 1971. V. 51

PETERSEN, M. E.
Systematics, Biology and Morphology of World Polychaeta. Copenhagen: 1986. V. 50

PETERSEN, WILLIAM F.
The Patient and the Weather. Ann Arbor: 1936/35/34/34. V. 53

PETERSEN, WILLIAM J.
Steamboating on the Upper Mississippi; The Water Way to Iowa. Iowa City: 1937. V. 49; 50

PETERSHAM, MAUD
An American ABC. New York: 1941. V. 51; 54
Auntie and Celia, Jane and Miki. Garden City: 1932. V. 53
The Christ Child. New York: 1931. V. 51

PETERSON, B. J.
The Battle of Wounded Knee. Gordon: 1941. V. 54

PETERSON, DANIEL H.
The Looking Glass: Being a True Report and Narrative of the Life, Travels and Labors of the Rev. Daniel H. Patterson, a Colored Clergyman... New York: 1854. V. 53

PETERSON, FRANK LORIS
The Hope of the Race. Nashville: 1934. V. 53

PETERSON, HAROLD L.
American Indian Tomahawks. New York: 1965. V. 47; 48

PETERSON, ROBERT W.
Only the Ball Was White. Englewood Cliffs: 1970. V. 50; 54

PETERSON, ROGER TORY
Audubon's Birds of America. New York: 1981. V. 48; 50
The Field Guide Art of Roger Tory Peterson: Western Birds. Norwalk: 1990. V. 54
A Field Guide to the Birds, Giving Field Marks of All Species Found in Eastern North America. Boston and New York: 1934. V. 54

PETERSON, S.
The Living Tradition of Maria Martinez. New York and San Francisco: 1977. V. 51
The Living Tradition of Maria Martinez. Tokyo: 1978. V. 52
Lucy M. Lewis, American Indian Potter. Tokyo: 1984. V. 54

PETERSON, WILLIAM J.
Steamboating on the Upper Missouri. Iowa City: 1937. V. 47

PETERSON, WILLIAM S.
The Kelmscott Press "Golden Legend": a Documentary History of Its Production, Together with a leaf from the Kelmscott Edition. 1990. V. 52

PETHERICK, JOHN
Egypt, the Soudan and Central Africa. Edinburgh and London: 1861. V. 50; 54

PETIS DE LA CROIX, FRANCOIS
The History of Genghizcan the Great, First Emperor of the Ancient Moguls and Tartars... 1722. V. 54
The History of Genghizcan the Great, First Emperor of the Ancient Moguls and Tartars... London: 1722. V. 49
Persian Tales; or the Thousand and One Days... London: 1789. V. 47
The Thousand and One Days: Persian Tales. London: 1738. V. 48

PETIT, A.
Amussat's Lectures on Retention of Urine, Caused by Strictures of the Urethra and on the Diseases of the Prostrate. Philadelphia: 1840. V. 48

PETIT, J. L.
Remarks on Church Architecture. London: 1841. V. 49; 52

PETIT, JEAN
Toros Muertos. New York: 1966. V. 49

PETIT, JEAN LOUIS
A Treatise of the Diseases of the Bones. London: 1726. V. 48; 49

PETIT, PIERRE
Traite Historique Sur Les Amazones... Aleide: 1718. V. 50

LE PETITE *Almanach des Dames, ou Hommage a la Beaute.* Paris: 1816. V. 54

PETITION of Cato West, and Others, in Behalf of Themselves and the Other Inhabitants of the Mississippi Territory. Washington: 1800. V. 47

THE PETITION of Divers Eminent Citizens of London, Presented to the Lord Mayor and Court of Aldermen the 28th of April 1681. London: 1681. V. 52

PETITION of the Inhabitants of Istleworth in the County of Middlesex, Against William Grant, Minister of the Said Parish; Whereunto Is Added One and Twenty Articles Against the Said Minister by His Parishioners, Presented to the Hon. House of Commons. London: 1641. V. 52

PETITION of the Ladies at Court, Intended to be Presented to the House of Lords; Against the Pride and Luxury of the City Dames, &c. London: 1681. V. 47

THE PETITITIONS and Memorials of the Proprietors of East and West Jersey...Etc. (1775-1785). New York: 1785. V. 48

A PETITITON to His Majesty; of the Three Revolting Counties in the West, Wilts, Somerset, and Devon. London: 1645. V. 53

PETKO, EDWARD
At Seventy: Richard J. Hoffman. Los Angeles: 1982. V. 51

PETO, GLADYS
Fireside Stories. London: 1930. V. 48
Gladys Peto's Bedtime Stories. London: 1928. V. 52

PETO, SAMUEL MORTON
Resources and Prospects of America, Ascertained During a Visit to the States in the Autumn of 1865. London & New York: 1866. V. 49; 52; 53

PETRAKIS, HARRY MARK
Chapter Seven from the Hour of the Bell... Mt. Horeb: 1976. V. 51; 54

PETRARCA, FRANCESCO
The Ascent of Mount Ventoux. A Letter from Petrarch. New York: 1989. V. 49; 51; 52
Bucolica, Africa, Epistolae. 1558. V. 47
Il Canzoniere. Venice: 1541. V. 52
De Remediis Utriusque Fortunae. (with) De Rebus Memorandis... Franckfort am Meyn: 1572/66. V. 52
Fifteen Sonnets of Petrarch. New York: 1903. V. 48
Life of Petrarch. London: 1841. V. 53
Il Petrarca. Lyons: 1547. V. 53
Il Petrarcha. Venice: 1514. V. 52
Il Petrarcha. (Sonetti et Cazoni). Venice: 1542. V. 52
Petrarch's View of Human Life. London: 1797. V. 50
Phisicke Against Fortune as Well Prosperous as Adverse. Berkeley: 1993. V. 51
Phyisicke Against Fortune, as Well Prosperous, as Adverse. London: 1579. V. 47
Le Rime del...Brevemente sposte per Lodovico Castelvetro. Basilea: 1582. V. 53
(Rime) Li Sonetti, Canzone e Triumphi del Petrarcha con li Soi Comment Non Senza Grandissima Euigilantia et Summa Diligentia... Venice: 1513. V. 53; 54
Sonetti, Canzoni, et Triomphi... Venetia: 1545. V. 47
The Sonnets. New York: 1965. V. 51
The Sonnets of... Verona: 1965. V. 52; 54
Triomphi Di Meser Francesco Petrarcha Con la Loro Optimas Spositione. (with) Li Sonetti Canzone e Triumphi Del Petrarcha. Venice: 1513/19. V. 53
The Triumphs of Francesco Petrarch. Boston: 1906. V. 48; 54
The Triumphs of Francesco Petrarch. London & Cambridge: 1906. V. 53
Triumphs of Francesco Petrarch. Boston: 1926. V. 53
The Triumphs of Petrarch. San Francisco: 1928. V. 48

PETRA SANCTA, SILVESTRO
De Symbolis Heroicis Libri IX. Antwerp: 1634. V. 50

PETRE, HENRY WILLIAM
An Account of the Settlements of the New Zealand Company from Personal Observation During a Residence There. London: 1841. V. 47; 50

PETRE, JOHN
Trifles. London: 1823. V. 50; 54

PETRIE, ADAM
Rules of Good Deportment, or of Good Breeding. Edinburgh: 1835. V. 52

PETRIE, CONSTANCE C.
Tom Petrie's Reminiscences of Early Queensland Dating from 1837. Brisbane: 1932. V. 48

PETRIE, GEORGE
Christian Inscriptions in the Irish Language. London: 1870/7. V. 47; 53
The Ecclesiastical Architecture of Ireland Anterior to the Anglo-Norman Invasion. 1845. V. 48
The Ecclesiastical Architecture of Ireland Anterior to the Anglo-Norman Invasion... Dublin: 1845. V. 47
The Ecclesiastical Architecture of Ireland Anterior to the Anglo-Norman Invasion. London: 1845. V. 52
Ecclesiastical Architecture of Ireland Anterior to the Anglo-Norman Invasion...an Essay on...the Round Towers of Ireland. London: 1846. V. 47; 53
The Petrie Collection of the Ancient Music of Ireland. Dublin: 1855. V. 48; 49

PETRIE, WILLIAM MATTHEW FLINDERS
Amulets. Warminster: 1972. V. 51
Anthedon. London: 1937. V. 49; 51
Beth-Pelet I (Tell Fara).... London: 1930. V. 51
Ceremonial Slate Palettes. (and) Corpus of Proto-Dynastic Pottery. London: 1953. V. 51
Decorative Patterns of the Ancient World. London: 1930. V. 49; 51; 52
Denderech. London: 1900. V. 51
Ehnasya. (and) Roman Ehnasya. London: 1905. V. 51
The Formation of the Alphabet. London: 1912. V. 49; 50
Gerar. London: 1928. V. 49; 51
Gizeh and Refeh. London: 1907. V. 49; 51
Glass Stamps and Weights With Ancient Weights and Measures. Warminster: 1974. V. 51
Hawara, Biahmu and Arsinoe. London: 1889. V. 49; 51
Heliopolis, Kafr Ammar and Shurafa. London: 1915. V. 49
Historical Scarabs: a Series of Drawings from the Principal Collections. London: 1889. V. 49; 51
A History of Egypt. London: 1899-1924. V. 49; 51
A History of Eygpt. London: 1907, 1894. V. 49
Hyksos & Israelite Cities. London: 1906. V. 49
Inductive Metrology; or, the Recovery of Ancient Measures. London: 1877. V. 49
The Labyrinth, Gerzeh and Maghuneh. London: 1912. V. 49; 51
Memphis I-VI. London: 1909-15. V. 49; 51
Meydum and Memphis (III). London: 1910. V. 49; 51
Naqada and Ballas. London: 1896. V. 49; 51
Naukratis. London: 1886-88. V. 49
Objects of Daily Use Illustrated by the Egyptian Collection in University College, London. Warminster: 1974. V. 51
Prehistoric Egypt. (with) Corpus of Prehistoric Pottery and Palettes Illustrated by the Egyptian Collection in University College, London. Warminster: 1974. V. 51
The Pyramids and Temples of Gizeh. London: 1883. V. 49
Researches in Sinai. London: 1906. V. 49
Researches in Sinai. New York: 1906. V. 51
Roman Portraits and Memphis (IV). London: 1911. V. 49; 50; 51; 52
The Royal Tombs of the First Dynasty, 1900 - Part I. (and) The Royal Tombs of the Earliest Dynasties, 1901 - Part II. London: 1900-01. V. 51
Scarabs and Cylinders with Names Illustrated by the Egyptian. London: 1917. V. 49; 51
Tanis: Part I: 1833-34. Part 2: Nebesheh (Am) and Defenneh (Tahpanhes). London: 1885-88. V. 49; 51
Tarkhan I and Memphis V. London: 1913. V. 49; 51
Tell El Amarna. Warminster: 1974. V. 51
Tools and Weapons Illustrated by the Egyptian Collection in University College, London and 2,000 Outlines from Other Sources. London: 1917. V. 51
Tools and Weapons Illustrated by the Egyptian Collection in University College, London, and 2,000 Outlines from Other Sources. Warminster: 1974. V. 51

PETRONIO, ALESSANDRO TRAJANO
De Victu Romanorum et de Sanitate Tuenda Libri Quinque. Rome: 1581 (1582). V. 52

PETRONIUS ARBITER, TITUS
The Complete Works... London: 1927. V. 50; 51
The Satyrical Works of Titus Petronius Arbiter, in Prose and Verse. London: 1708. V. 48
Le Satyricon. Paris: 1951. V. 51
The Satyricon. New York: 1964. V. 54
The Works... London: 1713. V. 49

PETRUNKEVITCH, A.
A Study of Amber Spiders. 1942. V. 53

PETRUS CHRYSOLOGUS, SAINT
Sermones... Bologna: 1534. V. 52

PETRUS COENOBIUS
Historia Albigensium, et Sacri Belli in Eos Anno MCCIX. Suscepti, Duce & Principe Simone a Monteforti, de in Tolosano Comite... Troyes: 1618. V. 50

PETRUS COMESTER
Historia Scholastica. Strassburg: 1485. V. 47; 49

PETRUS DE BERGAMO
Tabula Operum Thomae Aquinatis. Basel: 1478. V. 51; 53

PETRUS LOMBARDUS, BP. OF PARIS
Liber Sententiarum cum Conclusionibus Henrici Gorichem ac Titulis Quaestionum S. Thomae. Basel: 1488. V. 51
Quadripartitum Opus, Nostri Christianismi Decreta & Orthodoxorum Theologorum Sententias per Varia and Propemodum Infinita Diffusas Abunda Complectens... Paris: 1536. V. 50
Senteniarum Libri IV (with Commentary of St. Bonaventura). Nuremberg: 1491. V. 47

PETRY, ANN
The Common Ground. New York: 1964. V. 54
Country Place. Boston: 1947. V. 54
Harriet Tubman: Conductor on the Underground Railroad. New York: 1955. V. 53
The Narrows. Boston: 1953. V. 51; 53
The Street. Boston: 1946. V. 49; 50; 51; 53

PETTENKOFFER, MAX VON
Outbreak of Cholera Among Convicts an Etiological Study of the Influence of Dwelling, Food, Drinking-Water... London: 1876. V. 48

PETTER, NICOLAS
Der Kunstliche Einger (i.e. Ringer). Amsterdam: 1674. V. 53
Klare Onderrichtinge der Voortreffelijcke Worstel - Konst...met 71 Naeuwkeurige Verbeedlingen... Amsterdam: 1674. V. 49; 53

PETTERSEN, HJALMAR
Dictionary of Anonyms and Pseudonyms in Norwegian Literature. 1924. V. 51; 54

PETTIGREW, J. B.
Design in Nature. London: 1908. V. 52; 54

PETTIGREW, THOMAS
Bibliotheca Sussexiana. A Descriptive Catalogue... London: 1827-39. V. 48; 50; 53
On Superstitions Connected with the History and Practice of Medicine and Surgery. London: 1844. V. 47; 50

PETTIGREW, THOMAS J.
A History of Egyptian Mummies, and an Account of the Worship and Embalming of the Sacred Animals. London: 1834. V. 49

PETTIGREW, THOMAS LETTSOM
Lucien Greville. London: 1833. V. 49

PETTIS, GEORGE H.
Personal Narratives of the Battles of the Rebellion. Santa Fe: 1908. V. 48; 49

PETTIT, EDWARD
The Visions of Government, &c. Wherein the Antimonarachical Principles and Practices of all Phantatical Commonwealths-Men and Jesuitical Politicians are Discovered, Confuted and Exposed... London: 1686. V. 49; 52

PETTUS, JOHN
Fleta Minor. The Laws of Art and Nature in Knowing, Judging, Assaying, Fining, Refining...the Bodies of Confin'd Metals. London: 1683. V. 53
Fleta Minor. The Laws of Art and Nature in Knowing, Judging, Assaying, Fining, Refining...the Bodies of Confin'd Metals. London: 1686/83. V. 54
Fodinae Regales, or the History, Laws and Places of the Chief Mines and Mineral Works... London: 1670. V. 54
Volatiles frm the History of Adam and Eve... London: 1674. V. 48

PETTY, JOHN
The History of the Primitive Methodist Connexion, from Its Origin to the Conference of 1860, the First Jubilee Year of the Connexion. London: 1880. V. 49

PETTY, WILLIAM
The Antient Right of the Commons of England Asserted. London: 1680. V. 50; 51
Five Essays in Political Arithmetick. London: 1687. V. 53
Miscellanea Parliamentaria: Containing Presidents 1. Of Freedom from Arrests. 2. Of Censures. 1. Upon Such as Have Wrote Books to the Dishonour of the Lords of Commons...2. Upon Members for Misdemeanours... London: 1681. V. 50
The Petty-Southwell Correspondence 1676-1687. London: 1928. V. 51
The Political Anatomy of Ireland. London: 1691. V. 51
Political Survey of Ireland...also an Exact List of the Present, Peers, Members of Parliament and Principal Officers of State... London: 1719. V. 49
Tracts; Chiefly Relating to Ireland. Dublin: 1769. V. 48

PEUGNET, EUGENE
The Nature of Gunshot Wounds of the Abdomen, and Their Treatment Based on a Review of the Case of the Late James Fisk, Jr. in Its Medico-Legal Aspects. New York: 1874. V. 49; 54

PEURBACH, GEORG VON
Novae Theoreticae Planetarum...Locis Compluribus Conspurcatae, a Petro Apiano... Venice: 1534. V. 48; 52
Tabulae Eclypsiu(m)... Vienna: 1514. V. 52

PEVSNER, NIKOLAUS
An Enquiry Into Industrial Art in England. Cambridge: 1937. V. 48; 50
High Victorian Design - a Study of the Exhibits of 1851. London: 1951. V. 53
Industrial Art in England. Cambridge: 1937. V. 51
Studies in Art, Architecture and Design. London: 1969. V. 49; 51; 53

PEYRITSCH, J.
Aroideae Maximilianae. Vienna: 1879. V. 49

PEYTON, JOHN LEWIS
Rambling Reminiscences of a Residence Abroad. Staunton: 1888. V. 51

PEYTON, JOHN ROWZEE
3 Letters from St. Louis. Denver: 1958. V. 50

PEZZI, LORENZO
Vinea Domini. Cum Brevi Descriptione Sacramentorum et Paradisi, Limbi Purgatorij, Atque Inferni a Catechismo Catholicisque Patribus Excerpta. Venice: 1588. V. 50; 52

PFANNSTIEL, ARTHUR
Modigliani. Paris: 1929. V. 47; 48; 52

PFEFFER, P. E.
Nuclear Magnetic Resonance in Agriculture. Boca Raton: 1989. V. 50; 52

PFEIFFER, EMILY
Women and Work. London: 1888. V. 50

PFEIFFER, IDA
A Visit to the Holy Land, Egypt and Italy. London: 1852. V. 54

PFEIFFER, ROBERT H.
The Archives of Shilwateshub, Son of the King. Cambridge: 1932. V. 49; 52

PFISTER, R.
The Excavations at Dura-Europos. Final Report IV. Part II: The Textiles. New Haven: 1945. V. 52

PFLUEGER, DONALD H.
Covina: Sunflowers, Citrus Subdivisions. Covina: 1964. V. 48

PFLUG, F. A.
Wagons fur den Eisenbahn-Train der Kaiserl. Russischen Bahn Odessa Kiew. Nach Angaben des Kaiserl. Russisch. Staatsrath Baron von Ungern-Sternberg... Berlin: 1864. V. 51

PFORZHEIMER, WALTER L.
Stocktoniana. Purchase: 1936. V. 51

PHAEDRUS
Ezopische Fabelen Van Fedrus, Gyvryden Slaef des Keizers Augustus. Amsterdam: 1704. V. 51
Fabularum Aesopiarum. Amsterdam: 1701. V. 51
Fabularum Aesopiarum Libri Quinque... Amsterdam: 1667. V. 54
A Poetical Translation of the Fables of Phaedrus. London: 1765. V. 49; 53

PHAIR, CHARLES
Atlantic Salmon Fishing. New York: 1937. V. 47; 54

PHALARIS
The Epistles of Phalaris. London: 1749. V. 47; 48; 54
(Greek title, then) *Phalaridis Agrigentinorum Tyranni. Epistolae.* Oxford: 1718. V. 49

PHANTASIES of a Love Thief. New York: 1994. V. 54

PHANTOM Flowers, a Treatise on the Art of Producing Skeleton Leaves. Boston: 1864. V. 51

PHARMACOPOEA Collegii Medicorum Bergomi, Rationem Componendi Medicamenta Usitatiora Complectens. Bergomi: 1581. V. 47; 50

PHARMACOPOEA Wirtenbergica. Stuttgart: 1750. V. 47

THE PHARMACOPOEIA of the United States of America. Boston: 1820. V. 49; 52; 53; 54
THE PHARMACOPOEIA of the United States of America. Boston: 1828. V. 52; 53
THE PHARMACOPOEIA of the United States of America. New York: 1830. V. 53
THE PHARMACOPOEIA of the United States of America. Philadelphia: 1864. V. 52

PHARR, ROBERT DEANE
The Book of Numbers. Garden City: 1969. V. 50

PHAYRE, ARTHUR PURVES
History of Burma, Including Burma Proper, Pegu, Taungu, Tenasserim and Arakan. London: 1883. V. 54

PHEAR, JOHN BUDD
A Treatise on the Rights of Water, Including Public and Private Rights to Sea and Seashore. London: 1859. V. 53

PHELAN, WILLIAM
A Digest of the Evidence Taken Before the Select Committee of the Two Houses of Parliament, Appointed to Inquire into the State of Ireland; 1824-25. 1826. V. 52
A Digest of the Evidence Taken Before the Select Committee of the Two Houses of Parliament...(with) Notes Historical and Explanatory, and a Copious Index. 1824-25/26. V. 48
The Remains of William Phelan... 1832. V. 48; 52

PHELPS, ALMIRA HART LINCOLN
Lectures to Young Ladies... Boston: 1833. V. 53

PHELPS, CHARLES
Injuries of the Brain and its Membrane from External Violence, With a Special Study of Pistol-Shot Wounds of the Head. New York: 1897. V. 49
Injuries of the Brain and Its Membranes from External Violence, with a Special Study of Pistol-Shot Wounds of the Head in Their Medico-Legal and Surgical Relations. New York: 1900. V. 47
Traumatic Injuries of the Brain and Its Membranes. New York: 1897. V. 47; 53

PHELPS, H. P.
Players of a Century...the Albany Stage. Albany: 1880. V. 47; 49; 52
Players of a Century...the Albany Stage. Albany: 1890. V. 47

PHELPS, J.
The Human Barometer; or, Living Weather Glass. London: 1743. V. 54

PHELPS, JOHN S.
A Letter from Hon. John S. Phelps to Citizens of Arkansas in Relation to a Pacific Railroad. St. Louis: 1858. V. 47

PHELPS, RICHARD H.
Newgate of Connecticut, Its Origin and Early History. Hartford: 1901. V. 51

PHELPS, SYLVANUS DRYDEN
Holy Land, with Glimpses of Europe and Egypt: a Year's Tour. New York: 1864. V. 51

PHELPS, W.
The History and Antiquities of Somersetshire: Being a General and Parochial Survey of that Interesting County. London: 1836. V. 51

PHIBBS, ISABELLE MARY
A Visit to the Russians in Central Asia. London: 1899. V. 50

PHILADELPHIA and the Lakes. Address to the Citizens of Pennsylvania, in Favor of a Railroad to Connect Philadelphia with the Lakes. Philadelphia: 1851. V. 53

THE PHILADELPHIA Book; or Specimens of Metropolitan Literature. Philadelphia: 1836. V. 49

PHILADELPHIA COUNTY PRISON
The First (to the Seventh) Annual Report of the Inspectors of the Philadelphia County Prison, Made to the Legislature. Harrisburg/Philadelphia: 1848-54. V. 49; 51

PHILADELPHIA MUSEUM OF ART
Masters of Seventeenth Century Dutch Genre Painting. Philadelphia: 1984. V. 54

PHILADELPHIA SOCIETY FOR PROMOTING AGRICULTURE
Memoirs of the... Philadelphia: 1808. V. 47

PHILADELPHIA, WILMINGTON & BALTIMORE RAILROAD CO.
Investigation Into the Alleged Official Misconduct of the Late Superintendent of the... Philadelphia: 1854-55. V. 53

PHILANDER, JOAKIM, PSEUD.
Vitulus Aureus; the Golden Calf. London: 1739. V. 47

PHILANDROS, PSEUD.
An Astonishing Affair! The Rev. Samuel Arnold Cast and Tried for His Cruelty, Though His Cause Was Advocated in a Masterly Manner... Concord: 1830. V. 50

PHILBY, H. ST. J. B.
Arabia of the Wahhabis. London: 1928. V. 48
Arabian Days. London: 1948. V. 52
The Heart of Arabia. A Record of Travel and Exploration. London: 1922. V. 48
A Pilgrim in Arabia. 1943. V. 47
A Pilgrim in Arabia. Waltham St. Lawrence: 1943. V. 50
Sheba's Daughters Being a Record of Travel in Southern Arabia. London: 1908. V. 54

PHILBY, KIM
A Handbook of Marxism. London: 1935. V. 52

PHILELFUS, FRANCISCUS
Epistolae. Venice: 1493/94. V. 47; 49
Orationes. Paris: 1515.. V. 48; 52
Satyrarum. 1502. V. 48

PHILIDOR, A. D.
Analyse du Jeu des Echecs. Londres: 1777. V. 53
Analysis of the Game of Chess... To Which Is Added, Several parties Played by the Author Blindfold Against Three Adversaries. London: 1790. V. 49

PHILIP, ALEX J.
The Business of Bookbinding. London: 1912. V. 47; 53

PHILIP, ALEXANDER PHILIP WILSON
An Experimental Inquiry Into the Laws of the Vital Functions, With Some Observations on the Nature and Treatment of Internal Diseasess... Philadelphia: 1818. V. 50; 53
A Treatise on Febrile Diseases, Including Intermitting, Remitting & Continued Fevers... Hartford: 1809. V. 48
A Treatise on Febrile Diseases, Including the Various Species of Fever, and All Diseases Attended with Fever. Hartford: 1816. V. 49; 51; 54
A Treatise on Indigestion and Its Consequences, Called Nervous and Bilious Complaints... London: 1824. V. 47; 49; 51

PHILIP, C. G.
Stratosphere and Rocket Flight (Astronautics). London: 1935. V. 48

PHILIP, DUKE OF EDINBURGH
Wildlife Crisis. London: 1971. V. 49

PHILIP, JOHN
Poems Attempted in the Style of Milton. London: 1762. V. 49

PHILIP, ROBERT KEMP
The Gardener's and Farmer's Reason Why. London: 1860. V. 52

PHILIP, WILLIAM W.
Crathie Churches and Royal Bazaar at Balmoral. Aberdeen: 1896. V. 48

PHILIPON, CHARLES
La Caricature. Paris. V. 47

PHILIPOT, THOMAS
A Brief Historical Discourse of the Original and Grovvth of Heraldry... London: 1672. V. 51

PHILIPOTT, JOHN
Villare Cantianum. London: 1664. V. 47; 50; 53
Villare Cantianum... Lynn: 1776. V. 47

PHILIPPAKI, BARBARA
The Attic Stamnos. Oxford: 1967. V. 50

PHILIPPE, CHARLES LOUIS
Buba de Montparnasse. Paris: 1932. V. 49; 51

PHILIPPS, FABIAN
Plea for the Pardoning Part of the Soveraignty of the Kings of England. London: 1682. V. 48
Tenenda non Tollenda, or the Necessity of Preserving Tenures... London: 1660. V. 53

PHILIPPS, HENRY
The Grandeur of the Law. London: 1684. V. 51; 53

PHILIPPS, JENKIN THOMAS
The History of the Two Illustrious Brothers, Princes of Saxony... London: 1740. V. 47

PHILIPPUS FLORENTINUS, FATHER
Compendino Della Faculta de' Semblici di Tutte Quelle Cose, Che Sono Piu Uso Nell'Arte Della Medicna, con le Ordinationi Nuovamente Fatte da Riformatori, Poste e Proprii Capitoli di Detti Semplici. Fiorenza: 1572. V. 47; 48

PHILIPS, AMBROSE
A Collection of Old Ballads. London: c. 1872. V. 49
The Distrest Mother. London: 1712. V. 47
Pastorals, Epistles, Odes and Other Original Poems... London: 1748. V. 49; 54

PHILIPS, CHARLES
Catalogue of the John Radcliffe Collection, Chetham's Library. Manchester: 1937. V. 48

PHILIPS, ERASMUS
Miscellaneous Works, Consisting of Essays Political and Moral. London: 1752. V. 48

PHILIPS' Family Atlas. London: 1862. V. 53

PHILIPS, JOHN
Blenheim. A Poem. London: 1709. V. 49
Cyder. London: 1708. V. 47; 49; 52; 54
Cyder. London: 1791. V. 49; 54
Cyder. Stafford: 1791. V. 47
Poems. London: 1715. V. 49
Poems on Several Occasions. London: 1728. V. 51
Poems On Several Occasions. (with) Cyder. London: 1728/27. V. 49
Poems On Several Occasions...to Which is Added, His Life by Mr. George Sewell. Dublin: 1730. V. 53
Poems. To Which is Prefix'd His Life. London: 1715. V. 54
Poems. Viz. An Ode to Lord Bolingbroke. the Splendid Shilling. Bleinheim. Cyder. London: 1755. V. 51
A Satyre Against Hypocrites. London: 1689. V. 54
The Splendid Shilling. London: 1705. V. 49; 51; 54
The Whole Works of... Loldon (sic): 1720. V. 47; 49; 50

PHILIPS, KATHERINE
Letters from Orinda to Poliarchus. London: 1705. V. 47
Poems. London: 1664. V. 48; 49
Poems. London: 1667. V. 47
Poems. London: 1669. V. 47
Poems by... London: 1710. V. 53; 54

PHILIPS, N. G.
View of the Old Halls of Lancashire and Cheshire. London: 1893. V. 47
Views in Lancashire and Cheshire of Old Halls and Castles. London: 1821-24. V. 47

PHILLIMORE, FRANCIS
Dickens Memento...Catalogue with Purchasers' Names and Prices Realised of the Pictures, Drawings and Objects of Art of the Late Charles Dickens, Sold by Auction in London...July 9th 1870. London: 1884. V. 51

PHILLIMORE, JOHN GEORGE
Private Law Among the Romans from the Pandects. London: 1863. V. 49

PHILLIMORE, JOSEPH
Substance of the Speech of Joseph Phillimore in the House of Commons...on Moving for Leave to Bring in a Bill to Amend the Marriage Act. London: 1822. V. 50

PHILLIMORE, LUCY
Sir Christopher Wren. London: 1881. V. 50; 53

PHILLIMORE, W. P. W.
Cumberland Parish Registers. Marriages. Volume 1. London: 1910. V. 52

PHILLIP, ARTHUR
The Voyage of Governor Phillip to Botany Bay; with an Account of the Establishment of the Colonies of Port Jackson and Norfolk Island... London: 1789. V. 52

PHILLIP, JAMES
Henry Moore on Sculpture. London: 1966. V. 49

PHILLIP, JOHN
Researches in South Africa... London: 1828. V. 54

PHILLIPPO, JAMES M.
Jamaica: Its Past and Present State. London: 1843. V. 54

PHILLIPPS, E. M.
The Gardens of Italy. London: 1909. V. 52

PHILLIPPS, SAMUEL MARCH
State Trials; or, a Collection of the Most Interesting Trials, Prior to the Revolution of 1688, Reviewed and Illustrated. London: 1826. V. 48

PHILLIPPS, THOMAS
Catalogue of Pictures at Thirlestane House. Cheltenham: 1872. V. 53
Medieval Manuscripts: New Series Parts I-XI. 1965-76. V. 53
Pictures at Middle Hill. 1862. V. 53

PHILLIPPS, WILLIAM
Studii Legalis Ratio: or, Directions for the Study of the Law... London: 1662. V. 54

PHILLIPPS-WOLLEY, CLIVE
Big Game Shooting. London: 1894. V. 47; 49
Big Game Shooting. 1913/01. V. 52; 54
Savage Svanetia. London: 1883. V. 48; 49; 51
A Sportsman's Eden. London: 1888. V. 54
The Trottings of a Tenderfoot: A Visit to the Columbian Fiords and Spitzbergen. London: 1884. V. 48

PHILLIPS, A. V.
Seven Sonnets for Good Friday. V. 49

PHILLIPS, ALFRED, MRS.
Benedicta. London: 1878. V. 49

PHILLIPS, ARTHUR S.
My Wilderness Friends. Fall River: 1910. V. 47

PHILLIPS, C. H.
The History of the Colored Methodist Episcopal Church in America, etc. Jackson: 1925. V. 48

PHILLIPS, C. J.
The New Forest Handbook: Historical and Descriptive. Lyndhurst: 1876. V. 52

PHILLIPS, CARYL
A State of Independence. New York: 1986. V. 53

PHILLIPS, CATHERINE COFFIN
Cornelius Cole, California Pioneer and United States Senator. San Francisco: 1929. V. 51; 54
Coulterville Chronicle. The Annals of a Mother Lode Mining Town. San Francisco: 1942. V. 48
Jessie Benton Fremont - A Woman Who Made History. San Francisco: 1935. V. 48; 49; 50
Portsmouth Plaza. The Cradle of San Francisco. San Francisco: 1932. V. 47; 54

PHILLIPS, CHARLES
Recollections of Curran and some of His Contemporaries. London: 1818. V. 52

PHILLIPS, CHARLES E.
A Brief Historical Account of the Romance of British Columbia. Vancouver: 1934. V. 48

PHILLIPS, CLAUDE
Sir Joshua Reynolds. New York: 1894. V. 51

PHILLIPS, COLES
A Young Man's Fancy. 1912. V. 52

PHILLIPS, D. H.
Diseases of Forest and Ornamental Trees of Europe. London: 1992. V. 49

PHILLIPS, DUNCAN
Arthur B. Davies: Essays On the Man and His Art. Washington: 1924. V. 49; 50

PHILLIPS, E. CAMBRIDGE
The Birds of Breconshire. London: 1899. V. 50

PHILLIPS, E. LORT
On Birds Observed in the Goolis Mountains in Northern Somali-Land. London: 1896. V. 48

PHILLIPS, E. P.
The Genera of South African Flowering Plants. Cape Town: 1926. V. 51

PHILLIPS, EDWARD
The New World of Words. London: 1678. V. 48; 49; 52
The New World of Words; or, Universal English Dictionary. London: 1706. V. 51; 52
The New World of Words; or, Universal English Dictionary... London: 1720. V. 48
Theatrum Poetarum, or a Compleat Collection of the Poets... London: 1675. V. 49; 54

PHILLIPS, G.
Rutland and the Great War. Manchester: 1920. V. 47

PHILLIPS, G. F.
The Art of Drawing and Painting Simplified in a Series of Examples of Parts of the Human Figure... London: 1840. V. 48
A Practical Treatise of Drawing and on Painting with Water Colours. London: 1839. V. 47
Principles of Effect and Colour, as Applicable to Landscape Painting... London: 1833. V. 47; 49
The Theory and Practice of Painting in Water Colours, as Connected with the Study of Landscape. London: 1838. V. 48

PHILLIPS, GEORGE
Rudiments of Curvilinear Design, Illustrated by a Series of Plates in Various Styles of Ancient and Modern Ornament. London: 1839. V. 53

PHILLIPS, GEORGE SEARLE
Transatlantic Tracings, or Sketches of Persons and Scenes in America. London: 1853. V. 53

PHILLIPS, HENRY
Flora Historica: or the Three Seasons of the British Parterre Historically and Botanically Trated. London: 1829. V. 51
Floral Emblems. London: 1825. V. 47; 53
History of Cultivated Vegetables... London: 1822. V. 48; 49; 54
Pomarium Britannicum, an Historical and Botanical Account of Fruits Known in Great Britain. 1821. V. 54
Pomarium Britannicum, an Historical and Botanical Account of Fruits Known in Great Britain. London: 1821. V. 48; 49
Pomarium Britannicum: an Historical and Botanical Account of Fruits Known in Great Britain. London: 1823. V. 49; 51; 52; 53; 54
Sylva Floriefera: the Shrubbery Historically and Botanically Treated. London: 1823. V. 47; 52; 54
The True Enjoyment of Angling. London: 1843. V. 47

PHILLIPS, HOWARD
Further Interiors: Wood-Engravings by Howard Phipps. London: 1992. V. 50

PHILLIPS, J. ARTHUR
The Mining and Metallurgy of Gold and Silver. London: 1847. V. 52

PHILLIPS, JAYNE ANNE
Black Tickets. New York: 1979. V. 50; 52
Counting. New York: 1978. V. 47; 50; 52
Fast Lanes. New York: 1984. V. 47; 48; 51; 52
How Mickey Made It. St. Paul: 1981. V. 47; 48; 50; 51
The Secret Country. Winston Salem: 1982. V. 47; 48
Sweethearts. Carrboro: 1976. V. 47; 52

PHILLIPS, JOHN
A General History of Inland Navigation, Foreign and Domestic... London: 1792. V. 54
Geology of Oxford and the Valley of the Thames. London: 1871. V. 53; 54
The Geology of Oxford and the Valley of the Thames. Oxford: 1871. V. 49; 50; 51; 52
Illustrations of the Geology of Yorkshire. London: 1829. V. 48; 50
Illustrations of the Geology of Yorkshire. York: 1829. V. 54
Illustrations of the Geology of Yorkshire... London: 1829-36. V. 51; 52; 53; 54
Illustrations of the Geology of Yorkshire. London: 1835-36. V. 47; 48
Illustrations of the Geology of Yorkshire. London: 1836-75. V. 52
Illustrations of the Geology of Yorkshire. London: 1875. V. 54
Manual of Geology, Theoretical and Practical. London: 1885. V. 54
Maronides, or Virgil Travestie: Being a New Paraphrase Upon the Fifth book of Virgil's Aeneids in Burlesque Verse. (with) Maronides or Virgil Travesty. London: 1672/78. V. 48
The Rivers, Mountains and Sea-Coast of Yorkshire. London: 1853. V. 49; 52; 53; 54
The Rivers, Mountains and Sea-Coast of Yorkshire. London: 1855. V. 50; 52; 53
The Secret History of the Reigns of K. Charles II and K. James II. London?: 1690. V. 48; 49

PHILLIPS, JOHN CHARLES
American Game Mammals and Birds. Boston: 1930. V. 50
Bibliography of a Natural History of the Ducks. Cambridge: 1926. V. 53
Classics of the American Shooting Field. Boston: 1930. V. 49
A Natural History of the Ducks. Boston & New York: 1922-26. V. 47
A Natural History of the Ducks. London: 1922-26. V. 51
A Sportsman's Scrapbook. 1928. V. 54

PHILLIPS, LANCE
Folks I Knowed and Horses They Rode. Ashland: 1975. V. 53

PHILLIPS, LE ROY
A Bibliography of the Writings of Henry James. 1906. V. 51
A Bibliography of the Writings of Henry James. Boston: 1906. V. 54

PHILLIPS, MARGARET
English Women in Life and Letters. Oxford: 1926. V. 52; 54

PHILLIPS, MARY E.
Edgar Allan Poe the man. Chicago: 1926. V. 48

PHILLIPS, P. LEE
A List of Maps of America in the Library of Congress. Washington: 1901. V. 48

PHILLIPS, PAUL CHARLES
Forty Years on the Frontier as Seen in the Journals and Reminiscences of Granville Stuart, Gold Miner, Trader, Merchant, Rancher and Politician. Glendale: 1967. V. 47
Medicine in the Making of Montana. Missoula: 1962. V. 47

PHILLIPS, PAUL CHRISLER
The Fur Trade. Norman: 1961. V. 47; 49; 50; 52; 54

PHILLIPS, PHILIP
Archaeological Survey in the Lower Mississippi Alluvial Valley 1940-1947. Cambridge: 1951. V. 50; 52
Archaeological Survey in the Lower Yazoo Basin, Mississippi, 1949-1955. Cambridge: 1970. V. 52
The Forth Bridge In Its Various Stages of Construction. Edinburgh: 1890. V. 48
The Forth Bridge In Its Various Stages of Construction. Edinburgh: 1899. V. 51
John Obrisset, Hugenot Carver, Medallist, Horn & Tortoiseshell Worker & snuff Box Maker. London: 1931. V. 47
Paul de Lamerie, Citizen and Goldsmith of London. A Study of His Life and Work 1688-1751. London: 1935. V. 49
Pre-Columbian Shell Engraving from the Craig Mound at Spiro, Oklahoma. Cambridge: 1975. V. 52

PHILLIPS, RICHARD
A Letter to the Schoolmasters and Governesses of England and Wales, on the New Theories of Education, and on the Plans Under Legislative Consideration, for Reforming or Altering the Systems of Public Schools. Sherwood: 1835. V. 52
The Natural and Artificial Wonders of the United Kingdom... London: 1825. V. 54

PHILLIPS, S.
Ulysses - a Drama and a Prologue in Three Acts. London: 1902. V. 47; 51; 53

PHILLIPS, STEPHEN C.
An Address on the Annexation of Texas, and the Aspect of Slavery in the United States... Boston: 1845. V. 50

PHILLIPS, T.
Africa, the Art of a Continent. Munich and New York: 1995. V. 54

PHILLIPS, TERESIA CONSTANTIA
An Apology for the Conduct of Mrs. T. C. Phillips. London: 1750. V. 50

PHILLIPS, THOMAS
The History of the Life of Reginald Pole. London: 1676. V. 54

' PHILLIPS, THOMAS
The History of the Life of Reginald Pole... Oxford and Dublin: 1765/67. V. 49

PHILLIPS, THOMAS
The History of the Life of Reginald Pole... London: 1767. V. 52
A Letter on Books, Printing &c. dedicated to Messrs. Cordeux & Abel. Northampton: 1852. V. 48
A Letter to a Student At a Foreign University on the Study of Divinity. London: 1756. V. 48
The Long Parliament Revived; or, An Act for Continuation, and the Not Dissolving the Long Parliament... London: 1661. V. 47

PHILLIPS, TOM
Dante's Inferno. A Set of Nine Screenprints. London: 1983. V. 49; 53
A Humument - a Treated Victorian Novel. London: 1980. V. 50
The Sketches of Tom Phillips. Kansas City. V. 54

PHILLIPS, VIVIEN
A Trip to Santa Claus Land, or Ruth's Christmas Eve. London: 1905. V. 54

PHILLIPS, W.
Architectural Iron Construction. London: 1870. V. 53

PHILLIPS, W. S.
Indian Tales for Little Folks. 1928. V. 49
Indian Tales for Little Folks. New York: 1928. V. 52

PHILLIPS, WALTER J.
Colour in the Canadian Rockies. Toronto: 1937. V. 54

PHILLIPS, WILLARD
The Inventor's Guide. Boston and New York: 1837. V. 48; 52

PHILLIPS, WILLIAM
The Conquest of Kansas, by Missouri and Her Allies. Boston: 1856. V. 54
A Manual of British Discomycetes. London: 1887. V. 49
Manual of the Mammals of Ceylon. Colombo: 1933. V. 48
Manual of the Mammals of Ceylon. Colombo: 1934. V. 49
Manual of the Mammals of Ceylon. Ceylon & London: 1935. V. 49
Remarks on the Chalk Cliffs Near Dover... London: 1818. V. 52

PHILLPOTTS, EDEN
The Dartmoor Novels. London: 1927-28. V. 51
Delight. London: 1916. V. 53
A Dish of Apples. London and New York: 1921. V. 48; 49; 51; 54
The Red Redmaynes. New York: 1922. V. 49
The Secret Woman. London: 1912. V. 53
The Widecombe Edition of the Dartmoor Novels. London: 1927-28. V. 48

PHILLPS, HOWARD
Further Interiors: Wood Engravings. Lower Marston,: 1992. V. 47

PHILOBIBLION; Volume I-II: 1862-63. New York: 1861-63. V. 51

PHILO JUDAEUS
Scriptoris Eloquentissimi Ac Philosophi Summi. Lyon: 1555. V. 47; 50

PHILOPONUS, JOHANNES
In Primos Quatuor Aristotelis de Naturali Auscultatione Libros Comentaria. Venice: 1535. V. 50; 52; 54

PHILOSOPHICAL Transactions: Giving Some Account of the Present Undertakings, Studies and Labours of the Ingenious in Many Considerable Parts of the World. London: 1665-66. V. 53

PHILOSTRATUS, FLAVIUS
Historiae de Vita Apollonii Tyanel. Lutetiae: 1555. V. 53

PHILP, ROBERT KEMP
The Housewife's Reason Why: Affording to the Manager of Household Affairs Intelligible Reasons for the Various Duties She Has to Perform. London: 1857. V. 54

PHILPOT, CHARLES
An Introduction to the Literary History of the Fourteenth and Fifteenth Centuries.. London: 1798. V. 52

PHILPOTS, J. R.
Oysters and All About Them, a Complete History. London and Leicester: 1890-91. V. 54

PHILPOTT, JOHN
Villare Cantianum: or Kent Surveyed and Illustrated. Lynn: 1776. V. 53

PHILPOTT, WILLIAM BLEDSOE
The Sponsor Souvenir Album and History of the United Confederate Veterans' Reunion, 1895. Houston: 1895. V. 50

PHINNEY, H. F.
The Water Cure in America... New York: 1856. V. 54

PHINNEY, MARY A.
Allen-Isham Genealogy Jirah isham Allen Montana Pioneer, Government Scout, Guide, Interpreter and Famous Hunter... Rutland: 1946. V. 50

PHIPPS, E.
The Fergusons; or, Woman's Love and the World's Favor. London: 1839. V. 54

PHIPPS, HOWARD
Further Interiors... 1992. V. 47; 52
Further Interiors: Wood Engravings. London: 1992. V. 50
Further Interiors: Wood Engravings. Lower Marston: 1992. V. 47
Further Interiors: Wood Engravings. Risbury, Herefordshire: 1992. V. 48

PHIPSON, EMMA
The Animal-Lore of Shakespeare's Time... London: 1883. V. 49

Choir Stalls and Their Carvings. London: 1896. V. 48

PHOTOGRAPHS and Poems by Sioux Children. Rapid City. 1971. V. 50

PHYSIOGLOGUS: The Very Ancient Book of Beasts, Plants and Stones. San Francisco: 1953. V. 49

PHYSIOGNOMICAL Portraits. London: 1824. V. 49

PIACENZA, FRANCESCO
I Campeggiamenti Degli Sacchi...che nel Nuove Arcischacchiere... Turin: 1683. V. 52

PIAF, EDITH
The Wheel of Fortune. Philadelphia: 1965. V. 54

PIAGET, HENRY F.
The Watch: its Construction, Its Merits and Defects. New York: 1860. V. 52

PIAGET, JEAN
The Child's Conception of Number. London: 1952. V. 51
The Child's Conception of Physical Causality. London: 1930. V. 54
The Language and Thought of the Child. New York: 1926. V. 49; 50

PIANKOFF, ALEXANDRE
The Litany of Re. Princeton: 1964. V. 49; 51
Mythological Papyri. New York: 1957. V. 49; 51
The Pyramid of Unas. Princeton: 1968. V. 51
The Shrines of Tut-Ankh-Amon. New York: 1955. V. 49; 51
The Tomb of Ramesses VI. New York: 1954. V. 47; 49; 51
The Wandering of the Soul. Princeton: 1974. V. 51

PIASSETSKY, P.
Russian Travellers in Mongolia and China. London: 1884. V. 49; 52

PIATT, GUY X.
Old Timer's Hand Book. The Story of Butte. Butte: 1897. V. 47

PIAZZA, VINCENZO
Bona Espugnata Poema. Parma: 1694. V. 52

PIC, JEAN
The Dream of Alcibiades. London: 1749. V. 47

PICARD, ADOLPHE
Floral Ornamentation for the Industrial Arts. Boston: 1890. V. 53

PICART, BERNARD
The Ceremonies and Religious Customs of the Various Nations of the Known World.... London: 1733-39. V. 48
A New Drawing Book of Modes. London: 1733. V. 49

PICASSO, PABLO
40 Dessins en Marge du Buffon. Paris: 1957. V. 49
Desire. New York: 1948. V. 54
Graphic Works. 1899-1955; 1955-1965. London: 1966-67. V. 48
Picasso. New York: 1955. V. 47; 50; 52
Picasso 347. New York: 1970. V. 48; 49; 51
Picasso Linoleum Cuts: Bacchanals, Women, Bulls & Bullfighters. New York: 1963. V. 47
Picasso's Variations on Velasquez' Painting "The Maids of Honour" and Other Recent Works. New York: 1959. V. 47; 50
Shakespeare. New York: 1965. V. 47; 48; 50; 52
Trozo de Piel. Cambridge: 1979. V. 47
The Vollard Suite. London: 1956. V. 53

THE PICCADILLY Annual of Entertaining Literature. London: 1870. V. 54

PICCIONE, ANTHONY
Anchor Dragging. New York: 1977. V. 52

PICCOLOMINI, ALESSANDRO
Della Grandezza della Terra et Dell-Acqua. Venice: 1558. V. 52
Della Sfera del Mondo. (with) De le Stelle Fisse... Venice: 1552. V. 48
Della Spera Del Mondo. Venice: 1561. V. 49
La Seconda Parte de la Filosofia Naturale... Venice: 1554. V. 52
La Sfera del Mondo...(and) De le Stelle Fisse... Venice: 1585. V. 54

PICCOLOMINI PETRA, AUGUSTA CATERINA, DUCHESSA
Avvisi di Madama Picolomini Petra,...a Suo Figliuolo, Ovvero, Poema Sulla Condotta Civile della Vita Umana. Londra: 1776. V. 47

PICCOLPASSO, CIPRIANO
The Three Books of the Potter's Art. London: 1934. V. 47
The Three Books of the Potter's Art. London: 1980. V. 52

PICHARDO, JOSE A.
Pichardo's Treaties on the Limits of Louisiana and Texas. Austin: 1931/34/41/46. V. 49; 50

PICHATTY DE CROISSANTE, MONSIEUR
A Brief Journal of What Passed in the City of Marseilles, While It Was Afflicted with Plague, in the Year 1720. 1721. V. 51

PICHON, JEROME
The Life of Charles Henry Count Hoym. New York: 1899. V. 47; 48

PICINELLI, FILIPPO
Mondo Simbolico formato d'Imprese Scelte, Spiegate ed Illustrate con Sentenze ed Eruditioni Sacre, e Profane... Milan: 1669. V. 49

PICK, JOHN F.
Surgery of Repair; Principles, Problems, Procedures. Philadelphia: 1949. V. 54

PICKARD, F. W.
Trout Fishing in New Zealand in War Time. New York: 1940. V. 47

PICKARD, SAMUEL T.
Life and Letters of John Greenleaf Whittier. London: 1895. V. 48

PICKARD-CAMBRIDGE, O.
The Spiders of Dorset. Sherborne: 1879-81. V. 48

PICKELL, JOHN
A New Chapter on the Early Life of Washington in Connection with the Narrative Life of Washington in Connection with the Narrative History of the Potomac Company. New York: 1856. V. 54

PICKEN, ANDREW
The Canadas, as they Presently Commend Themselves to the Enterprize of Emigrants, Colonists and Capitalists... London: 1832. V. 48

PICKEN, EBENEZER
Miscellaneous Poems, Songs &c. Partly in the Scottish Dialect... Edinburgh: 1813. V. 54
Poems and Epistles, Mostly in the Scottish Dialect. Paisley: 1788. V. 54

PICKEN, M. B.
The Secrets of Distinctive Dress. 1918. V. 50

PICKENS, FRANCIS WILKINSON
Message No. 1 of His Excellency F. W. Pickens to the Legislature at the Annual Session of November, 1861. Columbia: 1861. V. 49

PICKENS, WILLIAM
American Aesop: Negro and Other Humor. Boston: 1926. V. 54
Bursting Bonds: Heir of Slaves. Boston: 1929. V. 53

PICKERING, C.
Chronological History of Plants... Dehra Dun: 1986. V. 49; 52

PICKERING, CHARLES
The Gliddon Mummy-Case in the Museum of the Smithsonian Institution. Washington: 1867. V. 51
The Races of Man: and Their Geographical Distribution. London: 1850. V. 47; 51

PICKERING, DANBY
The Statutes at Large from Magna Charta to the End of the Eleventh Parlimanet of Great Britain...1761. Cambridge: 1762-1795. V. 47

PICKERING, EDWARD
An Investigation in Stellar Photography Conducted at the Harvard College Observatory. Cambridge: 1886. V. 47

PICKERING, ELLEN
The Prince and the Pedler; or, the Siege of Bristol... New York: 1839. V. 47; 49
The Secret Foe, an Historical Novel. London: 1841. V. 47; 49; 51

PICKERING, H. G.
Angling of the Test, or True Love Under Stress, Being a Diurnal Postulation of Problems of Connubil Infelicity Which Bring No Comfort to any Married Male Angler. New York: 1936. V. 53

PICKERING, HENRY
The Ruins of Paestum; and Other Compositions in Verse. (with) Athens: and Other Poems. Salem: 1822/24. V. 52

PICKERING, J. E. LATTON
A Dialogue or Confabulation Between Two Travellers Which Treath of Civile and Pollitiking Government in Dyvers Kingdoms and Countries. 1896. V. 53; 54

PICKERING, JOHN
An Essay On a Uniform Orthography for the Indian Languages of North America. Cambridge: 1820. V. 51
A Vocabulary, or Collection of Words and Phrases... Boston: 1816. V. 49; 50; 52; 54

PICKERING, P.
The Pickerings of Barlby, York and Wetherby. London: 1916. V. 49

PICKERING & CHATTO
An Illustrated Catalogue of Old and Rare Books, Illuminated Manuscripts, Specimens of Fine Old and Modern Bindings... London: 1907-09. V. 48

THE PICKERONIAD: or, Exploits of Faction: Celebrated in Mock-Heroic-al, Serio-Comic-al, Hudibrastic-al and Quizzic-al Numbers. Newburyport: 1811. V. 51

PICKETT, A. ST. J.
The Sublime Tragedy of the Lost Cause a Tragic Poem of the War. Columbus: 1884. V. 49

PICKETT, ALBERT JAMES
History of Alabama and Incidentally of Georgia and Mississippi from the Earliest Period. Sheffield: 1896. V. 52

PICKETT, CHARLES EDWARD
Oration Delivered in the Congregational Church, Sacramento, California, July 4, 1857. San Francisco: 1857. V. 48; 49

PICKETT, THOMAS EDWARD
A Soldier of the Civil War, by a Member of the Virginia Historical Society... Cleveland: 1900. V. 49

PICKETT, WILLIAM
Studies for Landscape. London: 1812. V. 50; 52

PICKFORD, MARY
Why Not Try God?. New York: 1934. V. 52

A PICKWICK Portrait Library From the Pens of Divers Admirers of the Illustrious Members of the Pickwick Club, Their Friends and Enemies. London: 1936. V. 50

PICO DELLA MIRANDOLA, GIOVANNI FRANCESCO
De Rervm Praenotione Libri Novem. Strasbourgh: 1507. V. 48; 52

PICOT, EMILE
Catalogue des Livres Composant la Bibliotheque de feu M. le Baron James de Rothschild. New York: 1965. V. 50

PICOT, JEAN
Septem Psalmi Davidici. Paris: 1542. V. 50

PICTET DE ROCHEMONT, CHARLES
Cours d'Agriculture Angloise, Avec Les Developmments Utiles Aux Agriculteurs du Continent. Geneva: 1808-10. V. 50

PICTON, G. W.
The Battle of Waterloo; or, a General History of the Events...from the Period of Bonaparate's Escape from Elba, to His Arrival at St. Helena... London. V. 51

PICTON, J. A.
Memorials Of Liverpool, Historical and Topographical, Including a History of the Dock Estate. London: 1875. V. 49
Memorials of Liverpool, Historical and Topographical Including a History of the Dock Estate. Liverpool: 1907. V. 50

PICTON, THOMAS
Memoirs of Lt.-Gen. Sir Thomas Picton... London: 1835. V. 47

THE PICTON Veil or the Hood of Westminster. London: 1806?. V. 49

PICTORIAL & Genealogical Record of Green County, Missouri. Chicago: 1893. V. 48

THE PICTORIAL Gallery of Arts. London: 1851. V. 50

THE PICTORIAL History of the County of Lancaster. London: 1844. V. 53

A PICTORIAL History of the Negro in the Great World War 1917-18. New York: 1919. V. 54

PICTORIAL Photography in America. Volume 5. New York: 1929. V. 54

PICTORIAL Souvenir of the Police Department and Flint, Michigan. Lansing: 1914. V. 54

THE PICTORIALIST. Los Angeles: 1931. V. 47; 48

A PICTURE Book, for Little Children. Philadelphia: 1812. V. 48; 51

A PICTURE Book of Merry Tales. London: 1860. V. 50

A PICTURE Book of the Life of Saint Anthony the Abbot. London: 1937. V. 53

THE PICTURE of London, for 1806. London: 1806. V. 50

THE PICTURE of London for 1816. London: 1816. V. 52

A PICTURE Story Book with Four Hundred Illustrations. London: 1850. V. 50

PICTURE Story of Preparing Tea. 1900. V. 52

PICTURES and Tales for Little Folk. London: 1880. V. 51

PICTURESQUE America; or, The Land We Live In... New York: 1872-74. V. 47

PICTURESQUE Beauties of Boswell, Twenty Prints Designed and Etched by Two Capital Artists... London: 1786. V. 48; 53

PICTURESQUE Chicago and Guide to the World's Fair. Chicago: 1893. V. 48; 50

PICTURESQUE Description of North Wales: Embellished with Twenty Select Views from Nature. London: 1823. V. 50

PICTURESQUE Europe. London: 1870. V. 49; 52
PICTURESQUE Europe. London: 1876-79. V. 48
PICTURESQUE Europe. London: 1885. V. 53

A PICTURESQUE Guide to Bath, Bristol, Hot-Wells, The River Avon and the Adjacent Country. London: 1793. V. 54

THE PICTURESQUE Land of Gold It's Magnificent Mountain and Water Scenes Its Peaks, Passes and Canyons. White Horse. V. 54

THE PICTURESQUE Mediterranean. London: 1890. V. 52

PICTURESQUE Memorials of Winchester. Winchester: 1830. V. 50

PICTURESQUE Pasadena. Pasadena: 1930?. V. 48

PICTURESQUE Representations of the Dress and Manners of the Russians. London: 1814. V. 54

PICTURESQUE Sketches of Rustic Scenery, Including Cottages and farm Houses. London: 1815. V. 48

PICTURESQUE Views on the River Exe. Tiverton: 1819. V. 48

PICTURESQUE World's Fair. Chicago: 1894. V. 49

PIDDINGTON, HENRY
The Horn-Book of Storms for the Indian and China Seas. London: 1847. V. 49

PIDDINGTON, ROSE
The Last of the Cavaliers. London: 1859. V. 51

PIDGEON, E.
The Fossil Remains of the Animal Kingdom. London: 1840. V. 51; 54

PIDGEON, WILLIAM
Traditions of De-Coo-Dah and Antiquarian Researchers...Mound Builders in America... New York: 1853. V. 54

PIDLSEY, W. E. H.
The Birds of Devonshire. London: 1891. V. 51; 52

PIEDADE E VASCONCELLOS, IGNACIO DA
Historia de Santarem Edificada, Que da Noticia da Sua Fundaca, e das Couzas Mais Notaveis Nella Succedidas... Lisbon: 1740. V. 48

PIER, GARRETT CHATFIELD
Egyptian Antiquities in the Pier Collection. Chicago: 1906. V. 49; 51

PIERCE, BENJAMIN
A History of Harvard University, from Its Foundation in the Year 1636 to the Period of the American Revolution. Cambridge: 1833. V. 54

PIERCE, FRANK CUSHMAN
A Brief History of the Lower Rio Grande Valley. Menasha: 1917. V. 49

PIERCE, GEORGE F.
An Address on Female Education, Delivered in the Chapel of the Georgia Female College... Macon: 1839. V. 48

PIERCE, GERALD S.
Texas Under Arms: The Camps, Posts, Forts and Military Towns of the Republic of Texas, 1836-1846. Austin: 1969. V. 48

PIERCE, GILBERT A.
The Dickens Dictionary. London: 1878. V. 49; 54

PIERCE, HENRY H.
Report of an Expedition from Fort Colville to Puget Sound. Washington: 1883. V. 48; 50

PIERCE, HIRAM DWIGHT
A Forty-Niner Speaks. Oakland: 1930. V. 47; 50

PIERCE, JOHN J.
A Study in Imagination and Evolution. New York: 1987/89. V. 53

PIERCE, LORNE
E. Grace Coombs (Mrs. James Sharp Lawson) A.O.C.A., O.S.A. Toronto: 1949. V. 54

PIERCE, M. B.
Address on the Present Condition and Prospects of the Aboriginal Inhabitants of North America... Philadelphia: 1839. V. 54

PIERCE, RICHARD A.
H. M. S. Sulphur at California, 1837 and 1839. Being the Accounts of Midshipman Francis Guillemard Simpkinson and Captain Edward Belcher. San Francisco: 1969. V. 48; 50

PIERCE, THOMAS
A Collection of Sermons Upon Several Occasions. Oxford: 1671. V. 53

PIERCE, W. E., & CO.
Boise Idaho. Topeka: 1898. V. 52

PIERCE, WALDO
Unser Kent. Cortland: 1930. V. 50

PIERCE, WILLIAM LEIGH
The Year: a Poem in Three Cantos. New York: 1813. V. 54

PIERIS, PAULUS EDWARD
Ceylon and the Hollanders 1658-1796. Tellippalai: 1918. V. 51
Guide to the Collections of the Colombo Museum, Ceylon. Part I. Archaeology and Ethnology. 1912. V. 54

PIERPONT, JOHN
Airs of Palestine, a Poem. Baltimore: 1816. V. 48; 49
The Anti-Slavery Poems. Boston: 1843. V. 52

PIERPONT MORGAN LIBRARY, NEW YORK.
Chinese Calligraphy and Painting in the Collection of John M. Crawford, Jr. London: 1962. V. 54

PIERRE, CHIEF GEORGE
Autumn's Beauty. San Antonio: 1972. V. 50

PIERRE DE SAINTE MARIE MAGDELAINE
Traitte d'Hrlogiographie, Contenant Plvsievrs Manieres de Constrvire svr Tovtes Svrfaces... Paris: 1645. V. 48

PIERREONT, HENRY EVELYN
Historical Sketch of the Fulton Ferry and Its Associated Ferries. Brooklyn: 1879. V. 53

PIERS, F.
Orchids of East Africa. Lehre: 1968. V. 48

PIERS, HARRY
Master Goldsmiths and Silversmiths of Nova Scotia and Their Marks. Halifax: 1948. V. 47

PIERSON, B. T.
Directory of the City of Newark, for 1841-42, with a Historical Sketch. Newark: 1841. V. 51
Directory of the City of Newark for 1844-45. Newark: 1844. V. 51
Directory of the City of Newark for 1849-50. Newark: 1849. V. 51
Directory of the City of Newark, for 1853-54. Newark: 1853. V. 51
Directory of the City of Newark for 1857-58. Newark: 1857. V. 51

PIERSON, CHRISTOFFEL
Explanation of the Famous and Renowned Glas-Work Or Printed Windows, in the Fine and Eminent Church at Gouda. Gouda: 1750?. V. 50

PIERSON, DAVID LAWRENCE
History of the Oranges to 1921. New York: 1922. V. 47; 49; 51

PIERSON, EMILY CATHARINE
Jamic Parker, the Futitive Hartford: 1851. V. 47

PIERSON, JOSIAH
Millennium, a Poem in five Books. Rochester: 1831. V. 47; 52

PIERSON, THOMAS
Roseberry-Toppin; or the Prospect of a Summer's day. Stokesley: 1783. V. 50; 52

PIERS PLOWMAN
The Vision and the Creed of Piers Ploughman. London: 1842. V. 52

PIESSE, G. W. SEPTIMUS
The Art of Perfumery, and the Methods of Obtaining the Odours of Plants... London: 1855. V. 50
Chymical, Natural and Physical Magic... London: 1859. V. 48

A PIETAS Academiae Oxoniensis in Obitum Augustissimae et Desideratissimae Reginae Carolinae. Oxford: 1738. V. 47

PIETAS Oxoniensis. In Memory of Sir Thomas Bodley, Knt. and the Foundation of the Bodleian Library. Oxford: 1902. V. 53

PIETERSE, A. H.
Aquatic Weeds: the Ecology and Management of Nuisance Aquatic Vegetation. London: 1990. V. 52

PIETRASANTA, SILVESTRO
De Symbolis Heroicis Libri IX. Antwerp: 1634. V. 49; 53; 54

PIETSCH, T. W.
Frogfishes of the Great Barrier Reef and Coral Sea. Stanford: 1987. V. 50

PIGAFETTA, ANTONIO
Magellan's Voyage Around the World. Cleveland: 1906. V. 54

PIGAULT-LEBRUN, CHARLES ANTOINE GUILLAUME PIGAULT DE L'EPONY
My Uncle Thomas. A Romance. New York: 1810. V. 52

THE PIGEONS. London: 1817. V. 49

PIGGOTT BROTHERS & CO.
Marquees, Tents and Folding Furniture for Abroad. London: 1910-20. V. 52

PIGGY Wiggy's Picture Book. London: 1890. V. 54

PIGMAN, WALTER
The Journal of Walter Griffith Pigman. Mexico: 1942. V. 47; 50

PIGNA, GIOVANNI BATTISTA
De Principibus Atestinis Historiarum Libri VIII. Ferrara: 1585. V. 47; 50; 53

PIGNA, GIVOANNI BATTISTA
Il Duello...Diviso in Tre Libri, ne Quali dell'Honore, & dell' Ordine Della Cavalleria con Nuovo Modo si Tratta. Venice: 1560. V. 48

PIGNATTI, TERISIO
Giorgione. London: 1971. V. 48; 49; 51; 53
Pietro Longhi Paintings and Drawings. London: 1969. V. 50; 51; 53

PIGNORIA, LORENZO
Patavini de Servis, et Eorum Apud Veteres Ministeriis Commentarius. Augusburg: 1613. V. 51

PIGNOTTI, LORENZO
The History of Tuscany, from the Earliest Era. London: 1826. V. 47
Robert Manners A Poem Translated from the Italian... Florence: 1785. V. 49

PIGOT and Co.'s London and Provincial New Commercial Directory for 1826-27... London: 1826. V. 54

PIGOT, R.
Twenty-Five Years Big Game Hunting. London: 1928. V. 47

PIGOT, RICHARD
The Life of Man, Symbolised by the Months of the Year. London: 1866. V. 52

PIGOTT, CHARLES
The Jockey Club; or a Sketch of the Manners of the Age. New York: 1793. V. 52
*The Jockey Club, or a Sketch of the Manners of the Age, Part Second * The Female Jockey Club.* London: 1792/94. V. 49; 50
A Political Dictionary. London: 1795. V. 48

PIGOTT, HARRIET
The Private Correspondence of a Woman of Fashion. London: 1832. V. 54

PIGOU, A. C.
Industrial Fluctuations. London: 1927. V. 51
A Study in Public Finance. London: 1928. V. 53

PIKE, ALBERT
Nugae. Philadelphia: 1854. V. 49

PIKE, JAMES
The Scout and Ranger. Cincinnati: 1865. V. 49

PIKE, NICHOLAS
A New and Complete System of Arithmetic, Composed for the Use of Citizens of the United States. Newburyport: 1788. V. 47; 48; 50

PIKE, WARBURTON
The Barren Ground of Northern Canada. London: 1892. V. 48; 49; 51; 53; 54
Through the Subarctic Forest. London: 1896. V. 47; 49

PIKE, ZEBULON MONTGOMERY
An Account of a Voyage up the Mississippi River, from St. Louis to Its Source...in the Years 1805 and 1806. Washington?: 1807. V. 47
An Account of Expeditions to the Sources of the Mississippi, and through the Western Parts of Louisiana, to the Sources of the Arkansaw, Kans, La Platte and Pierre Jaun Rivers; Peformed by Order of the Government of the U.S.... Philadelphia: 1810. V. 47; 49; 51; 52
Th Expeditions of Zebulon Montgomery Pike. Minneapolis: 1965. V. 52
The Expeditions of Zebulon Montgomery Pike, to Headwaters of the Mississippi through Louisiana Territory and in New Spain, During the Years 1805-6-7. New York: 1895. V. 51; 53; 54
Exploratory Travels through the Western Territories of North America... London: 1811. V. 49
The Journals of Zebulon Montgomery Pike, With Letters and Related Documents. Norman: 1966. V. 47; 53

PILCHER, LEWIS
A List of Books by Some of the Old Masters of Medicine and Surgery Together with Books on the History of Medicine and on Medical Bibliography in the Possession of Lewis Stephen Pilcher... Brooklyn: 1918. V. 50; 52
The Treatment of Wounds, Its Principles and Practice, General and Special. New York: 1883. V. 51; 54

PILCHER, VELONA
The Searcher - a War Play. London: 1929. V. 48

PILE, GRAFT M.
An Address on Intellectual Development. Delivered...Illinois State University. Springfield: 1856. V. 52

PILES, ROGER DE
The Art of Painting, and the Lives of the Painters... London: 1706. V. 51
The Art of Painting, with Lives and Characters of Above 300 of the Most Eminent Painters... London: 1750?. V. 50; 51; 54

PILGRIM, DAVID
So Great a Man. New York: 1937. V. 50

THE PILGRIM Fathers: a Journal of Their Coming in the Mayflower to New England and Their Life and Adventures There. Waltham St. Lawrence: 1939. V. 47

PILGRIM, THOMAS
Live Boys; or, Charley and Nasho in Texas. Boston & New York: 1878. V. 48; 52

PILKINGTON, H. W.
A Musical Dictionary, comprising the Etymology and Different Meanings of All the Terms That Most Frequently Occur in Modern Composition. Boston: 1812. V. 49

PILKINGTON, JAMES
The Brunynge of Paules Church in London in the Yeare of Our Lord 1561... London: 1563. V. 47

PILKINGTON, JOHN
The History of the Lancashire Family of Pilkington and its Branches from 1066 to 1600. Liverpool: 1894. V. 49

PILKINGTON, JOHN CARTERET
The Real Story of John Carteret Pilkington. London: 1760. V. 48

PILKINGTON, MARY
The Calendar; or, Monthly Recreations... London: 1807. V. 50; 51

PILKINGTON, MATTHEW
A Dictionary of Painters, From the Revival of the Art to the Present Period. London: 1805. V. 49
A Dictionary of Painters From the Revival of the Art to the Present Period... London: 1810. V. 48
A General Dictionary of Painters. London: 1829. V. 49
The Gentleman's and Connoisseur's Dictionary of Painters. London: 1770. V. 48; 54
The Gentleman's and Connoisseur's Dictionary of Painters. London: 1798. V. 49
Poems on Several Occasions. London: 1731. V. 47; 49; 51

PILKINGTON, MRS.
The Force of Example; or, the History of Henry and Caroline... London: 1797. V. 47

PILKINGTON, W.
A Natural and Chymical Treatise of Agriculture, by the Late Count Adolphus Gyllenborg: with Practical Remarks and Additions. Romsey: 1822. V. 53

A PILL to Purge State-Melancholy; or, a Collection of Excellent New Ballads. London: 1715. V. 54

PILLANS, JAMES
Contributions to the Cause of Education. London: 1856. V. 54

PILLAY, DOROTHY
Climbing Days. 1935. V. 53

PILLING, JAMES CONSTANTINE
Bibliography of the Algonquian Languages. Washington: 1891. V. 48
Bibliography of the Iroquoian Languages. Bibliography of the Algonquian Languages. Washington: 1888/91. V. 48; 50
Bibliography of the Siouan (...Eskimor, Iroquoian, Muskhogean, Algonquinian, Athapascan, Salishan, Chinookan, Wakashan) Languages. New York: 1960's. V. 49

PILLSBURY, ARTHUR C.
Picturing Miracles of Plant and Animal Life. Philadelphia: 1937. V. 52

PILLSBURY, PARKER
Acts of the Anti-Slavery Apostles. Concord: 1883. V. 50; 51
The Bible: Its History and Inspiration. Boston: 1848. V. 50

PILON, EDMOND
Scenes Galantes et Libertines des Artistes du XVIII Siecle. Paris: 1909. V. 51

PILON, FREDERICK
Aerostation; Or, the Templar's Stratagem. London: 1784. V. 49

PILSBRY, H. A.
The Aquatic Mollusks of the Belgian Congo. London: 1927. V. 49

PIM, BEDFORD
Dottings on the Roadside, in Panama, Nicaragua and Mosquito. London: 1869. V. 51
The Gate of the Pacific. London: 1863. V. 52; 54

PIM, JONATHAN
The Condition and Prospects of Ireland and the Evils Arising from the Present Distribution of Landed Property... Dublin: 1848. V. 51

PIMENOV, YURI
The Drawings of Eisenstein. Moscow: 1961. V. 50

PINA, DOMINGO DE
Memorial de Suplica, e Informe Que Hazen, Ofrecen, y Ponen a Los Pies de el Illustrissimo Cabildo de la Ciudad de Sevilla...que han Ensenado y Ensenan la Esclarecida y... Seville?: 1675. V. 48

PINCHARD, ELIZABETH
The Blind Child, or Anecdotes of the Wyndham Family. London: 1791. V. 47; 49
The Blind Child; or, Anecdotes of the Wyndham Family. London: 1809. V. 50
Family Affection, a Tale for Youth. Taunton: 1816. V. 53
The Two Cousins. London: 1798. V. 47

PINCKNEY, CHARLES C.
An Address Delivered in Charleston, Before the Agricultural Society of South Carolina... Charleston: 1829. V. 49
Authentic Copies of the Correspondence of Charles Cotesworth Pinckney, John Marshall and Elbridge Gerry, Esqrs. London: 1798. V. 49
Nebuchadnezzar's Fault and Fall: a Sermon Preached at Grace Church, Charleston, S.C. on the 17th of February, 1861. Charleston: 1861. V. 49
Three Letters, Written, And Originally Published, Under the Signature of a South Carolina Planter. Philadelphia: 1799. V. 47

PINCKNEY, DARRYL
High Cotton. New York: 1992. V. 48; 49

PINCKNEY, MARIA HENRIETTA
Essays, Religious, Moral, Dramatic and Poetical, Addressed to Youth... Charleston: 1818. V. 49

PINCKNEY, MARY STEAD
Letter-Book of Mary Stead Pinckney: November 14th 1796 to August 29th 1797. New York: 1946. V. 50

PINCKNEY, PAULINE
Painting in Texas, the Nineteenth Century. Austin: 1967. V. 47; 48; 49; 51

PINCKNEY, STEPHEN R.
National Guard Manual. New York: 1864. V. 54

PINDAR
(Greek Title) Olympia. Glasgow: 1754. V. 52
Izomia (Graece). Glasgua: 1758. V. 53
Nemea (Graece). Glasgua: 1757. V. 53
Odes of Victory: the Olympian and Pythian Odes. London: 1928. V. 51
Olympia, Pythia, Nemea, Isthmia. Geneva: 1599. V. 54
Pindar's Odes of Victory. Stratford-upon-Avon: 1928. V. 51
Pindar's Odes of Victory: The Olympian and Pythian Odes. Stratford-upon-Avon: 1929. V. 52
The Pythian, Nemean and Isthmian odes. London: 1778. V. 48
Pythian Odes. London: 1928. V. 49; 50; 54
Works. Olympia, Pythia, Nemea, Isthmia... Glasguae: 1754/57/58. V. 50

PINDAR, PETER, PSEUD.
The Life of George R----, a Fasionable Swindler, Now Frequenting the Most Polite Circles in London, Bath, Brighton and Other Fashionable Watering Places... London: 1817. V. 50

PINE, GEORGE W.
Beyond the West. Utica: 1870. V. 50; 52
Beyond the West. Utica: 1871. V. 48

PINE, JOHN
The Procession and Ceremonies Observed at the Time of the Installation of the Knights Companions of the Most Honourable Military Order of the Bath, upon Thursday June 17, 1725. London: 1730. V. 50; 53

PINEDA, PEDRO
A New Dictionary Spanish and English and English and Spanish. London: 1740. V. 49
A Short and Compendious Method for Learning to Speak, Read and Write the English and Spanish Languages. London: 1762. V. 49
A Short and Compendious Method for Learning to Speak, Read and Write the Spanish Language... London: 1726. V. 47; 48

PINEL, PHILIPPE
Trate Medico-Philosophique sur l'Alienation Mentale. Paris: 1809. V. 51

PINEL, PHILLIPE
Traite medico-Philosophique sur l'Alienation Mentale. Paris: 1801. V. 52

PINELLI, MAFFEI
A Catalogue of the Magnificent and Celebrated Library of Maffei Pinelli...Sold at Auction. London: 1789. V. 50

PINERO, ARTHUR
The Enchanted Cottage. London: 1922. V. 52

PINERO, ARTHUR W.
The Gay Lord Quex: A Comedy in Four Acts. London: 1900. V. 48

PINGRE, ALEXANDRE GUI
Cometographie ou Traite Historique et Theorique des Cometes... Paris: 1783-84. V. 47

PINGRET, EDOUARD
Costumes des Pyrennees. Paris: 1834. V. 49

PINKERTON, ALLAN
Claude Melmotte As a Detective and Other Stories. Chicago: 1875. V. 48
Claude Melnotte as a Detective, and Other Stories. Toronto: 1875. V. 48
Professional Thieves and the Detective... Toronto: 1880?. V. 48
The Spy of the Rebellion: Being a True History of the Spy System of the United States Army During the Late Rebellion... Boston: 1884. V. 48

PINKERTON, HELEN
Error Pursued. Iowa City: 1959. V. 54

PINKERTON, JAMES N.
Sleep and Its Phenomena. An Essay. London: 1839. V. 53

PINKERTON, JOHN
Ancient Scotish Poems, Never Before in Print. London: 1786. V. 47; 48
An Enquiry into the History of Scotland Preceding the Reign of Malcom III or the Year 1056. London: 1789. V. 48
An Essay on Medals. London: 1789. V. 54
A General Collection of the Best and Most Interesting Voyages and Travels in All Parts of the World. Modern Geography: Empires, Kingdoms, Discoveries. London: 1808-17. V. 47
The History of Scotland From the Accession of the House of Stuart to that of Mary. London: 1797. V. 47; 48; 50; 53; 54
Iconographia Scotia; or Portraits of Illustrious Persons of Scotland Engraved from the Most Authentic Paintings &c. London: 1797. V. 47
The Medallic History of England. London: 1802. V. 52
Modern Geography. London: 1802. V. 53
Recollections of Paris, in the Years 1802-3-4-5. London: 1806. V. 50
Rimes. London: 1782. V. 47; 52
Scotish Poems. London: 1792. V. 50
Select Scottish Ballads. London: 1783. V. 50

PINKERTON, ROBERT
Russia: Observations Past and Present. London: 1833. V. 49; 53

PINKERTON, THOMAS A.
Amy Wynter. London: 1880. V. 49

PINKERTON, WILLIAM
Bank..."Sneak"...Thieves. 1906. V. 50
Train Robberies, Train Robbers and the 'Hold Up' Men. Jamestown: 1907. V. 50

PINKEY, JANE VAUGHAN
The Young Doctor. London: 1851. V. 50

PINKHAM, DANIEL
Symphony No. 1 for Orchestra. New York: 1961. V. 52

PINKNEY, MILES
Sweete Thoughtes of Jesus and Marie or Meditations for All the Feastes of Our B. Saviour and His B. Mother... Paris: 1665. V. 50

PINKS, WILLIAM J.
The History of Clerkenwell. London: 1865. V. 50; 52
The History of Clerkenwell. London: 1880. V. 50

PINNOCK, W.
Iconology: or Emblematic Figures Explained... London: 1830. V. 47

PINO, PEDRO BAUTISTA
Noticias Historicas y Estadisticas de la Antigua Provincia de Nuevo-Mexico... Mexico: 1849. V. 49; 50

PINTER, HAROLD
The Birthday Party. London: 1959. V. 49; 50; 53; 54
The Birthday Party and Other Plays. London: 1960. V. 47; 50
The Collection and the Lover. London: 1963. V. 54
The Dwarfs. London: 1990. V. 54
The French Lieutenant's Woman. Boston: 1981. V. 47; 49; 50; 51; 52
Monologue. London: 1973. V. 48; 49; 51
No Man's Land. London: 1975. V. 47
Old Times. London: 1971. V. 48
Poems. London: 1968. V. 50
Poems. London: 1971. V. 51
The Proust Screenplay. London: 1978. V. 49
The Screenplay of the French Lieutenant's Woman. London: 1981. V. 51
A Slight Ache and Other Plays. London: 1961. V. 54

PINTO DE SOUSA, JOSE CARLOS
Bibliotheca Historica de Portugal, e do Ultramar, na Qual se Contem Varias Historias deste Reino... Lisbon: 1797. V. 48

PIONEERS of Sacramento: A Group of Letters by and About Johann Augustus Sutter, James W. Marshall & John Bidwell. San Francisco: 1953. V. 47

PIOZZI, HESTER LYNCH SALUSBURY THRALE
Anecdotes of the Late Samuel Johnson... London: 1786. V. 47; 48; 50; 51; 52; 53
Anecdotes of the Late Samuel Johnson, LL.D. London: 1826. V. 48
Autobiography, Letters and Literary Remains. London: 1861. V. 48; 50; 51; 51; 54
British Synonymy; or, an Attempt at Regulating the Choice of Words in Familiar Conversation... Dublin: 1794. V. 52
British Synonymy or An Attempt at Regulating the Choice of Words in Familiar Conversation. London: 1794. V. 47; 49; 51; 53
Letters to and From the Late Samuel Johnson, LL.D. London: 1788. V. 51
Observations and Reflections Made in the Course of a Journey through France, Italy and Germany. Dublin: 1789. V. 49; 51; 53
Observations and Reflections Made in the Course of a Journey through France, Italy and Germany. London: 1789. V. 47; 48; 50; 51; 54
The Piozzi Letters, Correspondence of Hester Lynch Piozzi, 1784-1821. Volume I: 1784-1791. 1989. V. 53
The Piozzi Letters, Correspondence of Hester Lynch Piozzi, 1784-1821. Volume II, 1792-1798. 1991. V. 53
The Piozzi Letters, Correspondence of Hester Lynch Piozzi 1784-1821. Volume III: 1799-1804. 1993. V. 53
Piozzi Marginalia... Cambridge: 1925. V. 48
Piozziana or Recollections of the Late Mrs. Piozzi with Remarks by a Friend. London: 1833. V. 48
Retrospection; or a Review of the Most Striking and Important Events, Characters, Situations and their Consequences, Which the Last Eighteen Hundred Years Have Presented to the View of Mankind. London: 1801. V. 48; 51; 52; 54

PIP and Squeak Annual 1923. London: 1923. V. 51

THE PIPE-Rolls, or Sheriff's Annual Accounts of the Revenues of the Crown for the Counties of Cumberland, Westmorland and Durham, During the Reigns of Henry II, Richard I, and John. Newcastle: 1848. V. 53

PIPER, EVELYN
Bunny Lake Is Missing. New York: 1957. V. 52

PIPER, H. B.
Four-Day Planet. 1961. V. 51
Four-Day Planet. New York: 1961. V. 47
Junkyard Planet. 1963. V. 52
Murder in the Gun Room. New York: 1953. V. 54

PIPER, JOHN
Buildings and Prospects. London: 1948. V. 49
John Piper - Paintings, Drawings and Theatre Designs 1932-1954. London: 1955. V. 48; 51
Oxfordshire - a Shell Guide. London: 1953. V. 54
A Painter's Camera, Buildings and Landscapes in Britain 1935-1985. London: 1987. V. 50
Romney Marsh. London: 1950. V. 49

PIPER, MYFANWY
Sea Poems. London: 1944. V. 54

PIPER, W.
The Little Engine That Could. 1930. V. 48; 52

PIPPET, GABRIEL
A Little Rosary. Flansham: 1930. V. 52

PIQUE, EDWARD
A Practical Treatise on the Chemistry of Gold, Silver, Quicksilver and lead, Tracing the Crude Orde from the Mines. San Francisco: 1860. V. 48; 49

THE PIRATE Boy; or, Adventures of Henry Warrington: a Story of the Sea. New York: 1844. V. 54

PIROGOV, NIKOLAI IVANOVICH
Nicol Pirogoff's Chirurgische Anatomie der Arterienstamme und Fascien. Leizpig and Heidelberg,: 1860. V. 52

PIRSIG, ROBERT M.
Zen and the Art of Motorcycle Maintenance. London: 1974. V. 50
Zen and the Art of Motorcycle Maintenance. New York: 1974. V. 47; 49; 51; 52
Zen and the Art of Motorcycle Maintenance. New York: 1994. V. 53

PIRSSON, LOUIS V.
Fly-Fishing Days or the Reminiscences of An Angler. Washington: 1946. V. 47

PIRTLE, ALFRED
The Battle of Tippecanoe. Louisville: 1900. V. 50

PISCATOR, JOHANN
Arithmeticae Compendium, Pro Studiosis Denuo Recognitum & Locupletatum. Wittenberg: 1586. V. 49

PISSARRO, CAMILLE
A Catalogue of the Drawings by Camille Pissarro in the Ashmoleon Museum, Oxford. Oxford: 1980. V. 53

PISSARRO, LUCIEN
The Gentle Art - A Collection of Books and Wood Engravings by Lucien Pissarro. Zurich: 1974. V. 52
The Letters of Lucien to Camille Pissarro 1883-1903. Cambridge: 1993. V. 53
Notes on a Selection of Wood-blocks Held at the Ashmolean Museum, Oxford. Oxford: 1981. V. 48; 50
Notes on the Eragny Press and a Letter to J. B. Manson. 1957. V. 52
Notes on the Eragny Press and a Letter to J. B. Manson. Cambridge: 1957. V. 53
Notes on the Eragny Press and a letter to J. B. Manson. London: 1957. V. 48

PISSARRO, LUCIEN continued
Wood Engravings. Oxford: 1981. V. 51; 53; 54

PISSURLENCAR, PANDURANGA
Portuguese Records on Rustamji Manockji the Parsi Broker of Surat. Nova Goa: 1933. V. 50

PITCAIRN, ARCHIBALD
The Assembly; or, Scotch Reformation; a Comedy. Edinburgh: 1766. V. 53

PITCAIRN, ROBERT
Ancient Criminal Trials in Scotland... Edinburgh: 1829-33. V. 48
Criminal Trials in Scotland... Edinburgh: 1833. V. 50

PITCAIRN, W. D.
Two Years Among the Savages of New Guinea. London: 1891. V. 52

PITCHLYNN, P. O.
To His Excellency the Principal Chief and General Council of the Choctaw Nation. Washington: 1868. V. 48

PITHOU, PIERRE
Extraict d'vn Traicte, De la Grandeur, Droicts, Preeminences & Prerogatiues des Roys & du Royaume de France. 1594. V. 53
Le Premier Livre des Memoires des Comtes Hereditaires de Champagne et de Brie. Paris: 1572. V. 53

PITISCUS, BARTHOLOMAEUS
Canon Manvel des Sinvs, Tovchantaes et Covppantes... Parais: 1619. V. 52

PITISCUS, BARTHOLOMEO
Trigonometry; or, the Doctrine of Triangles. (with) A Canon of Triangles: or the Tables, of Sines, Tangents & Secants, the Radius Assumed to be 100000. London: 1614. V. 47

PITKIN, CALEB
An Address to the Public, the Patrons of Literature and Religion, on the Subject of Establishing a Literary and Theological Institution, in the Connecticut Western Reserve. Pittsburgh: 1822. V. 54

PITKIN, TIMOTHY
A Political and Civil History of the United States... 1828. V. 53
A Political and Civil History of the United States of America, from the Year 1763 to 1797. New Haven: 1828. V. 47; 50
A Statistical View of the Commerce of the United States. Hartford: 1816. V. 52
A Statistical View of the Commerce of the United States. New York: 1817. V. 53

PITMAN, C. M.
The Record of the University Boat Race 1829-1909. London: 1909. V. 47

PITMAN, C. R. S.
A Guide to the Snakes of Uganda. Kampala: 1938. V. 51

PITMAN, JOHN
To The Members of the General Assembly of Rhode-Island. Friends and Fellow-Citizens. Providence?: 1842. V. 51

PITMAN, JOSEPH S.
Report of the Trial of Thomas Wilson Dorr, for Treason Against the State of Rhode Island, Containing the Arguments of Counsel, and the Charge of Chief Justice Durfee. Boston: 1844. V. 53

PITMAN, THOMAS ELDRED
The Bengal Almanack, for the Year 1818... Calcutta: 1817. V. 49

PITROU, ROBERT
Recueil de Differents Projets d'Architecture de Charpente et Autres Concernant la Construction des Ponts. Paris: 1756. V. 53

PITT, CHRISTOPHER
Poems and Translations. London: 1727. V. 50

PITT, J. MARTIN
Twenty-four Nudes. Blackheath: 1985. V. 47

PITT, JOHN
How to Brew Good Beer. London: 1859. V. 50; 51

PITT, WILLIAM
General View of the Agriculture of the County of Stafford... London: 1796. V. 49

PITTAWAY, A. R.
The Hawkmoths of the Western Palearctic. London: 1992. V. 50

PITTENGER, PEGGY
Morgan Horses. S. Brunswick: 1967. V. 52

PITTER, RUTH
First and Second Poems 1912-1925. London: 1927. V. 53
First Poems. London: 1920. V. 51
Persephone in Hades. 1931. V. 49
Poems 1926-1966. London: 1968. V. 52

PITTILOCH, ROBERT
Oppression Under the Colour of the Law, or, My Lord Hercarse His New Praticks As A Way-Marke for Peaceable Subjects to Be Ware of Pleying with a Hot spirited Lord of the Session... Edinburgh: 1827. V. 52; 54

PITTIS, WILLIAM
Dr. Radcliffe's Life and Letters. London: 1736. V. 51
The History and Defence of the Last Parliament. London: 1713. V. 50
Jus Sacrum, or a Discourse Wherein It Is Fully Prov'd and Demonstrated, That No Prince Ought to Be Depriv'd of His Natural Right on Account of Religion &c. London: 1712. V. 53

PITTMAN, PHILIP
The Present State of the European Settlements on the Mississippi. Cleveland: 1906. V. 53

PITT-RIVERS, AUGUSTUS HENRY LANE FOX
Antique Works of Art from Benin, Collected by Lieutenant-General Pitt-Rivers. London: 1900. V. 51
Excavations in Cranborne Chase, Near Rushmore on the Borders of Dorset and Wilts. 1880-88; and in Bokerly and Wansdyke, Dorset and Wilts. 1888-91... London: 1887-1898. V. 51
Excavations in Cranborne Chase, Near Rushmore, on the Borders of Dorset and Wiltshire. London: 1887-1905. V. 50
King John's House, Tollard Royal, Wilts. London: 1890. V. 50

PITTS, J. MARTIN
Gymnopaediae. London: 1989. V. 53

PITTSBURGH PLATE GLASS CO.
Architectural Specifications: Paint-Varnish. 1920. V. 53

LA PITTURA Moderna e l'Arte del Tessuto Stampato (Rapporto di Colori). Milan. V. 48

PITWOOD, JAMES BEATTIE
The Slough of Despond. Los Angeles: 1929. V. 54

PITY'S Gift: a Collection of Interesting Tales to Excite the Compassion of Youth for the Animal Creation. London: 1798. V. 52

PIUS II, POPE
La Discrittione de l'Asia, et Europa... Venice: 1544. V. 47; 48
Epistolae Familiares. Nuremberg: 1486. V. 51; 52; 53
Epistole et Varii Tractatus. Lyons: 1505. V. 51
Le Historie, Costumi et Successi della Nobilissima Provincia deli Boemi... Venice: 1545. V. 50; 53

PIUS XI, POPE
Christian Marriage. New York: 1931. V. 49

PIX, MARY
The Spanish Wives. London: 1696. V. 49; 50; 51; 54

PLACCAET Ende Ordinantie Ons Heeren des Coninks, Daerby Wordt Geboden...Dat Die Placcaten Hiervoormaels Gepubliceert Opt Stuck Vande Calmynen wel...Worden Onderhouden (etc). Brussels: 1590. V. 48; 52

PLACE, FRANCIS
A Letter to a Minister of State, Respecting Taxes on Knowledge. Innes: 1831. V. 51

PLACER County, California. Auburn: 1888. V. 50

PLACER COUNTY IMMIGRATION
Placer County, California. Auburn: 1886. V. 49

PLAIN English: Humbly Offered to the Consideration of His Majesty, and...Parliament. London: 1690. V. 50

THE PLAIN Question Upon the Present Dispute with Our American Colonies. London: 776. V. 47

PLAIN Reading for Plain People! Being an Account of the English Constitution; and the King's Reform Bill. London: 1831. V. 51

PLAIN Reasons Addressed to the People of Great Britain, Against the (Intended) Petittion to Parliament from the Owners and Occupiers of Land in the County of Lincoln, for Leave to Export Wool. Leeds: 1782. V. 49; 51; 52

PLAISTED, BARTHOLOMEW
A Journey from Calcutta in Bengal, by Sea, to Busserah, from Thence Across the Great Desert to Aleppo. London: 1757. V. 47

PLAISTED, H. M.
Report of the Trial of James M. Lowell, for the Murder of...Mary Elizabeth Lowell, etc. Portland: 1875. V. 51

A PLAN for Raising the Supplies During the War, Humbly Submitted to the Two Houses of Parliament, the Landed and Monied Interest, and to All Ranks and Conditions of the People, Capable of Contributing to the Expences of the State. London: 1798. V. 53

PLANCHE, J. R.
A Corner of Kent; or, Some Account of the Parish of Ash-Next Sandwich. London: 1864. V. 47; 53; 54
A Cyclopedia of Costume or Dictionary of Dress... London: 1876-79. V. 54
Extravaganzas. London: 1879. V. 50

PLANCK, MAX
Eight Lectures On Theoretical Physics. New York: 1915. V. 53
Introduction to Theoretical Physics. London: 1933-32. V. 50
Theory of Light. London: 1932. V. 48
Treatise on Thermodynamics. London: 1903. V. 48

PLANKTON-EXPEDITION der Humboldt Stiftung im Atlantischen Ozean, 1889. Lehre: 1971-78. V. 50

PLANS des Hopitaux et Hospices Civils de la Ville de Paris, Leves par Ordre du Conseil General d'Administration de Ces Etablissemens. Paris: 1820. V. 49; 53

PLANS et Dessins des Constructions et Decorations, Ordonnees par la Ville de Paris Pour les Rejouissances Publiques a l'Occasion de al Publication de la Paix le 12 Fevrier 1749. Paris: 1749. V. 53

PLANT, MARJORIE
The English Book Trade - an Economic History of the Making and Sale of Books. London: 1939. V. 54

PLANTA, EDWARD
A New Picture of Paris; or, the Stranger's Guide to the French Metropolis... London: 1837. V. 51

PLANTAGINET-HARRISON, MARSHAL-GENERAL
The History of Yorkshire - Wapentake of Gilling West. London: 1885. V. 47; 53

PLANTE, DAVID
The Ghost of Henry James. Boston: 1970. V. 52
The Ghost of Henry James. London: 1970. V. 48; 50
My Mother's Pearl Necklace. New York: 1987. V. 54
Slides. 1971. V. 49
Slides. London: 1971. V. 48; 53

PLANTER, PSEUD.
Right or Wrong. Grenada: 1882. V. 49

PLASSETSKY, PAVEL IAKOVLEVICH
Russian Travellers in Mongolia and China. London: 1884. V. 54

PLAT, HUGH
A Closet for Ladies and Gentlewomen or, the Art of Preserving, Conserving and Candying. London: 1641. V. 51

THE PLATE
Glass Book...To Which is Added the Compleat Appraiser... London: 1760. V. 51

PLATEA, FRANCISCUS DE
Opus Restitutionum Usuranum et Excommunicationum. Venice: 1474-77. V. 53

PLATH, SYLVIA
Above the Oxbow. Northampton: 1985. V. 48; 53
American Poetry Now. London: 1961. V. 49
Ariel. London: 1965. V. 47; 48; 49; 50; 52; 53
The Bell Jar. London: 1962. V. 51; 54
The Bell Jar. London: 1963. V. 50; 52; 53
The Bell Jar. New York: 1971. V. 47; 49; 54
Collected Poems. London: 1981. V. 54
The Colossus. London: 1960. V. 47; 49; 50
Crossing the Water. London: 1971. V. 52; 54
The Crystal Gazer. London: 1971. V. 47; 48; 49; 53
Dialogue Over a Oiuja Board. London: 1981. V. 48
Fiesta Melons. Exeter: 1971. V. 51; 52
The Green Rock. 1982. V. 49; 51
Lyonesse. London: 1971. V. 48; 49; 51; 53
The Magic Mirror. 1989. V. 48
The Magic Mirror. Rhiwargor, Llandwddyn: 1989. V. 53
Million Dollar Month. Frensham: 1971. V. 47
Million Dollar Month. Surrey: 1971. V. 54
Pursuit. London: 1973. V. 49
The Surgeon at 2 a.m. and Other Poems. Portland: 1971. V. 53
Three Women. London: 1968. V. 47; 48; 49
To Eva Descending the Stair: a Poem. London. V. 49
Two Poems. Knotting: 1980. V. 47
Uncollected Poems. London: 1965. V. 47
Wreath for a Bridal. Frensham: 1970. V. 47

PLATINA, BARTOLOMEO
Delle Vite de Pontifici... Venice: 1590. V. 49
Historia Delle Vite Dei Sommi Pontefici dal Salvator Nostro Sino a Clemente VIII. Venice: 1594. V. 49
The Lives of the Popes. London: 1685. V. 49; 52; 53
The Lives of the Popes. London: 1688. V. 49; 51
Vitae Pontificium. Treviso: 1485. V. 47; 49

PLATO
Crito. Paris: 1926. V. 48; 52; 54
Crito. Paris: 1929. V. 52
Dialogi v. Oxford: 1800. V. 48
The Dialogues. London: 1875. V. 48
The Dialogues... Oxford: 1875. V. 48; 50; 51; 52
The Dialogues... London: 1892. V. 48; 49
The Dialogues... Oxford: 1892. V. 48; 53; 54
Dialogues... New York: 1901. V. 47
The Dialogues of Plato. London: 1924. V. 47
From the Phaedrus. Pownal: 1976. V. 49
(Greek and Latin) Opera Quae Extant Omnia. Geneva: 1578. V. 54
(Greek title) Divini Platonis Opera Omnia Qua Extant. Frankfurt: 1602. V. 52
(Greek title, then) ...Platonis Omnia Opera cum Commentariis Procli in Timaeum & Politica, Thesauro Veteris Philosophiae Maximo... Basileae: 1534. V. 49
Lysis. A Dialogue. London: 1930. V. 51
Lysis, or Friendship. Mt. Vernon: 1968. V. 53
Lysis, or Friendship. New York: 1968. V. 48; 52; 54
Opera... Paris: 1518. V. 52
The Phaedo. Waltham St. Lawrence: 1930. V. 47; 53; 54
Phaedon; or, a Dialogue on the Immortality of the Soul. New York: 1833. V. 52
Phaedrus, a Dialogue. San Francisco: 1976. V. 47
Phaidon. Jena: 1906. V. 54
Plato His Apology of Socrates, and Phaedo or Dialogue Concerning the Immortality of Mans Soul, and Manner of Socrates His Death... London: 1675. V. 48
Platonis et Quae Vel Platonis Esse Feruntur Vel Platonica Solent Comitari Scripta Graece Omnia ad Codices Manuscriptos Recensuit Variasque Inde Lectiones Diligenter Enotavid Immanuel Bekker. London: 1826. V. 48
Plato's Apology of Socrates. Cambridge: 1775. V. 49
Plato's Symposium or Supper. London: 1933. V. 54
The Republic. Glasgow: 1763. V. 48
The Republic. Oxford: 1888. V. 54
The Republic. New York: 1944. V. 53; 54
The Symposium of Socrates. Stuttgart: 1937. V. 54
Three Dialogues of Plato. New York: 1968. V. 49

PLATT, A. E.
The History of the Parish and Grammar School of Sedbergh. London: 1876. V. 47; 52

PLATT, CHARLES A.
Monograph of the Work of Charles A. Platt. New York: 1925. V. 47; 48; 52

PLATT, HUGH
The Jewel House of Art and Nature... London: 1653. V. 52

PLATT, P. L.
Travelers' Guide Across the Plains Upon the Overland Route to California. 1963. V. 48; 52; 54
Travelers' Guide Across the Plains Upon the Overland Route to California. San Francisco: 1963. V. 47; 48; 49; 53

PLATT, T. P.
A Catalogue of the Ethiopic Biblical Manuscripts in the Royal Library of Paris, and in the Library of the British and Foreign Bible Society, Also some Account of Those in the Vatican Library at Rome. London: 1823. V. 52

PLATTES, GABRIEL
A Discovery of Subeterraneal Treasure... London: 1653. V. 49
Practical Husbandry Improved; or, a Discovery of Infinite Treasure, Hidden since the Worlds Beginning. London: 1656. V. 52

PLAUT, JAMES S.
Oskar Kokoschka. London: 1948. V. 49

PLAUTUS, HIERONYMUS
The Happiness of a Religious State. Rouen: 1632. V. 50; 53

PLAUTUS, TITUS MACCIUS
Comedies of Plautus. London: 1769/72-74. V. 50
Comoediae. Antuerpiae: 1566. V. 53
Comoediae. Glasguae: 1763. V. 50; 53
Comoediae Quae Supersunt. Parissis: 1759. V. 53
Comoediae Viginti. Antwerp: 1566. V. 48; 54
Comoediae Viginti... Basileae: 1568. V. 54
M. Plauti Comodiae XX, ex Antiquis, Recentiorbusque Exemplaribus Inucicem Collatis... Paris: 1530. V. 48; 52
(Opera). Lyons: 1577. V. 48

PLAW, JOHN
Fermee Ornee; or Rural Improvements. London: 1803. V. 47
Rural Architecture, or Designs from the Simple Cottage for the Decorated Villa. London: 1794. V. 53
Sketches for Country Houses, Villas and Rural Dwellings...also Some Designs for Cottages. London: 1800. V. 48

PLAY
Hours Story Book. London. V. 52

PLAYBILL
One (-Three). Durband: 1969. V. 54

PLAYER, JOHN
Military Uniforms of the British Empire Overseas. 1938. V. 50
Uniforms of the Territorial Army. 1939. V. 50

PLAYER-FROWD, J. G.
Six Months in California. London: 1872. V. 50

PLAYFAIR, HUGO, R.N., PSEUD.
The Playfair Papers, or Brother Jonathan, the Smartest Nation in All Creation. London: 1841. V. 53

PLAYFAIR, JAMES
A Geographical and Statistical Description of Scotland. Edinburgh: 1819. V. 49

PLAYFAIR, JOHN
Elements of Geometry... Edinburgh: 1814. V. 48
The Works of John Playfair... Edinburgh: 1822. V. 52

PLAYFAIR, R. LAMBERT
A Bibliography of Algeria. London: 1888. V. 47
A Bibliography of Morocco from the Earliest Times to the End of 1891. London: 1893. V. 53
The Scourge of Christendom: Annals of British Relations with Algiers Prior to the French Conquest. London: 1884. V. 54
Travels in the Footsteps of Bruce in Algeria and Tunis. London: 1877. V. 54

PLAYFAIR, WILLIAM
Outlines of a Plan for a New and Sold Balance of Power in Europe. London: 1813. V. 53
Thoughts On the Present State of French Politics and the Necessity and Policy of Diminishing France. London: 1793. V. 49; 52

PLAYFORD, JOHN
An Introduction to the Skill of Musick. London: 1672. V. 48
The Whole Book of Psalms; With the Usual Hymns and Spiritual Songs; Together with All the Ancient and Proper Tunes Sung in churches, With Some of Later Use. London: 1677. V. 48

A PLEA for Moderation. 1642. V. 48

THE PLEADER'S Assistant; Containing a Select Collection of Precedents of Modern Pleadings, in the Courts of King's Bench and Common Pleas. Dublin: 1795. V. 51; 53

PLEASANT Stories for the Little Learner. Philadelphia: 1850's. V. 49

PLEASANTS, J. E., MRS.
History of Orange County, California. Los Angeles: 1931. V. 52

PLEASANTS, J. HALL
Maryland Silversmiths 1715-1830. Baltimore: 1930. V. 48

PLEASONTON, A. J.
The Influence of the Blue Ray of the Sunlight and of the Blue Colour of the Sky, in Developing Animal and Vegetable Life... Philadelphia: 1876. V. 54
The Influence of the Blue Ray of the Sunlight and of the Blue Colour of the Sky, in Developing Animal and Vegetable Life... Philadelphia: 1877. V. 48; 51

THE PLEASURES of Friendship. London: 1823. V. 50

PLEDGER, MAURICE
Game Birds. London: 1981. V. 53

PLEGER, JOHN J.
Bookbinding. Chicago: 1924. V. 50

PLESCH, ARPAD
Botanical Library of Stiftung fur Botanik. London: 1975-76. V. 50
The Magnificent Botanical Library of the Siftung fur Botanik Vaduz Liechtenstein Collected by the Late Arpad Plesch. 1975. V. 47
The Magnificent Botanical Library of the Stiftung Fur Botanik Vaduz Liecchtenstein Collected by the Late Arpad Plesch. London: 1975-76. V. 49; 51; 53

PLESCHEEF, SERGEY
Survey of the Russian Empire. London: 1792. V. 54

PLESKE, T.
Birds of Eurasian Tundra. Boston: 1928. V. 49
Wissenschaftliche Resultate der von N.M. Przewalski nach Central-Asien Unternommen Reisen. St. Petersburg: 1889-1905. V. 51

PLETSCH, OSCAR
Buttercups and Daisies. London: 1871. V. 51
Nursery Carols. London: 1862. V. 51

PLEY, ARTHUR F. E.
St. Paul's Cathedral. London: 1927. V. 52

PLEYNET, MARCELIN
Robert Motherwell. Paris: 1989. V. 48; 51; 52

PLIMPTON, GEORGE A.
The Education of Shakespeare. New York: 1933. V. 49

THE PLIMPTON Press Year Book: an Exhibit of Versatility. Norwood: 1911. V. 52

PLIMSOLL, SAMUEL
Our Seamen. London: 1873. V. 51

PLINIUS CAECILIUS SECUNDUS, C.
An Address of Thanks to a Good Prince, Presented in the Panegyrick of Pliny Upon Trajan, the Best of Roman Emperors. London: 1686. V. 50
C. Plini Secundi Novocomensis Epistolaru(m) Libri Decem... Venetiis: 1508. V. 54
C. Plinii Caecilii Secundi Epistolarum Libri X. London: 1790. V. 47; 48; 50
Epistolae per Philippum Beroaldum Correcte. Bologna: 1498. V. 48; 54
Epistolaru Libri Decem... Venice: 1508. V. 54
Epistolarum Libri X and Panegyricus. Leiden: 1640. V. 52
Epistolarvm Libri X. Eiusdem Panegyricus Traiano. Geneva: 1601. V. 51
The Letters of Pliny the Younger. London: 1751. V. 48; 50
The Letters of Pliny the Younger, with Observations on Each Letter; and an Essay on Pliny's Life Addressed to Charles Lord Boyle by John Earl of Orrery. London: 1752. V. 47
Novocomensis Epistolarum Libri Deceum... Venice: 1508. V. 52

PLINIUS SECUNDUS, C.
Caii Plinii Caecilii Secundi Opera Quae Supersunt Omnia. Glasguae: 1751. V. 54
Histoire de la Pineture Ancienne... London: 1725. V. 48; 52
Historia Mundi Naturalis. Frankfurt am Main: 1582. V. 52
Historia Naturale... Venice: 1580. V. 52
Historiae Naturalis Libri XXXVII ab Alexadro Benedicto Ve. Physico Emendatio res Redditi. 1507. V. 48
The Historie of the World: Commonly called, the Natural Historie of C. Plinius Secundus. London: 1634-35. V. 52; 53; 54
Naturae Historiarum Libri XXXVII. Hagenau: 1518. V. 50
Naturale Historia... Venice: 1481. V. 54
Naturalis Historiae... 1669. V. 47
Natvralis Historiae Prima Pars. Venice: 1540. V. 48

PLOMER, HENRY R.
A Dictionary of the Booksellers and Printers Who Were At Work in England, Scotland and Ireland from 1641 to 1667. 1907. V. 53
A Dictionary of the Booksellers and Printers Who Were at Work in England, Scotland and Ireland from 1641 to 1667. London: 1907. V. 48
A Dictionary of the Printers and Booksellers Who Were At Work in England, Scotland and Ireland from 1726 to 1775. 1932. V. 53
English Printers Ornaments. 1924. V. 53
English Printers' Ornaments. London: 1924. V. 52
Wynkyn de Worde and His Contemporaries from the Death of Caxton to 1935. London: 1925. V. 47

PLOMER, WILLIAM
Address Given at the Memorial Service for Ian Fleming Sept. 15th 1964. V. 53
The Case is Altered. London: 1932. V. 49; 52
Curlew River: A Parable for Church Performance. London: 1964. V. 50
The Family Tree. London: 1929. V. 51
The Fivefold Screen. London: 1932. V. 54
I Speak of Africa. London: 1927. V. 49
Ian Fleming. 28th May 1908-12th Aug. 1964. 1964. V. 54
The Invaders. London: 1934. V. 53
Notes for Poems. London: 1927. V. 51
A Shot in the Park. London: 1955. V. 54
They Never Came Back. New York: 1932. V. 51; 53
Turbott Wolfe. London: 1925. V. 48; 49; 52

PLOMLEY, N. J. B.
Weep In Silence. A History of the Flinders Island Aboriginal Settlement With the Flinders Island Journal of George Augustus Robinson 1835-1839. Hobart: 1987. V. 49

PLON, EUGENE
Thorvaldsen: His Life and Works. London: 1874. V. 50; 51

PLOSS, HERMANN HEINRICH
Woman: an Historical, Gynaecological and Anthropological Compendium. London: 1935. V. 47; 52
Woman: an Historical Gynaecological and Anthropological Compendium. St. Louis: 1938. V. 48

PLOT, ROBERT
The Natural History of Oxford-Shire, Being an Essay Toward the Natural History of England. 1677. V. 52
The Natural History of Oxford-shire, Being an Essay Towards the Natural History of England. Oxford: 1677. V. 47; 51
The Natural History of Oxfordshire... Oxford: 1705. V. 49
Natural History of Stafford-Shire. Oxford: 1686. V. 49; 50

PLOTINUS
The Enneads... London: 1817-30. V. 54
The Ethical Treatises. London: 1917. V. 47

PLOUGHED Under; the Story of an Indian Chief. New York: 1881. V. 50

PLOUGHMAN, WILLIAM
Oeconomy in Brewing. Romsey: 1800. V. 53

PLOWDEN, FRANCIS
An Historical Review of the State of Ireland, from the Invasion of that Country Under Henry II to its Union With Great Britain On the 1st of Jan. 1801. London: 1803. V. 48; 50; 51
A Short History of the British Empire During the last Twenty Months viz. from May 1792 to the Close of the Year 1793. London: 1794. V. 49

PLOWDEN, GENE
The Amazing Ringlings and their Circus. Caldwell: 1967. V. 53

PLOWMAN, GEORGE T.
Etching and Other Graphic Arts. New York: 1922. V. 47; 50; 51; 53; 54

PLOWMAN, MAX
A Subaltern on the Somme In 1916. London: 1927. V. 47

PLUCHE, NOEL ANTOINE
The History of the Heavens, Considered According to the Notions of the Poets and Philosophers, Compared with the Doctrines of Moses. London: 1740. V. 48; 51; 53
Spectacle de la Nature; or Nature Display'd Being Discourses on Such Particulars of Natural History as Were Thought Most Power to Excite the Curiosity and Form the Minds of Youth. London: 1733. V. 47

PLUMB, CHARLES S.
Little Sketches of Famous Beef Cattle. Columbus: 1904. V. 50; 52

PLUMB, R. HUDSON
The Log of Amka. London: 1928. V. 49

PLUMBE, JOHN
Memorial Against Mr. Asa Whitney's Railroad Scheme. Washington: 1850. V. 47

PLUMIER, CHARLES
L'Art de Tourner, ou De faire en Perfection Toutes Sortes d'Ouvrages Au Tour. Lyon: 1701. V. 48
L'Art de Tourner ou De faire en Perfection Toutes Sortes d'Ouvrages au Tour... London: 1706. V. 48

PLUMLEY, MATILDA
Days and Nights in the East. London: 1845. V. 54

PLUMMER, CHARLES
Bethada Naem Nereenn: Lives of irish Saints. London: 1922. V. 52
Betheda Naem Nerenn: Lives of Irish Saints. 1922. V. 49
Vitae Sanctorum Hiberniae Partim Hactenus Ineditae ad Fidem Codicum Manuscriptorum Recognovit Prolegomenis Notis Indicibus Instruxit. Oxonii: 1910. V. 48

PLUMMER, JOHN
The Story of a Blind Inventor. London: 1868. V. 49

PLUMMER, T. ARTHUR
The Ace of Death. London: 1928/30. V. 54
Creaking Gallows!. London: 1934. V. 54
Death Takes a Hand. London: 1934. V. 54

PLUMMER, T. ARTHUR continued
The Devil's Tea-Party. London: 1942. V. 54
The Fool of the Yard. London: 1942. V. 54
Haunting Lights. London: 1932. V. 54
Melody of Death. London: 1940. V. 54
Was the Mayor Murdered?. London: 1936. V. 54

PLUMPTRE, C. E.
Giordano Bruno: a Tale of the Sixteenth Century. London: 1884. V. 52

PLUMPTRE, HELEN
A Word to the Villager, or a Few Hints on the Subject of Clothing Societies &c. &c. Worksop: 1848. V. 51

PLUMPTRE, JAMES
Observations on Hamlet...Being an Attempt to Prove That He Designed It as an Indirect Censure on Mary Queen of Scots. Cambridge: 1796. V. 47

PLUNKET, FREDERIKA
Here and There Among the Alps. London: 1875. V. 50

PLUNKET, WILLIAM CONYNGHAM, 1ST BARON
The Life, Letters and Speeches of Lord Plunket. London: 1867. V. 50; 53

PLUNKETT, ELIZABETH GUNNING
The Packet: a Novel. Dublin: 1794. V. 51

PLUNKETT, GRACE
Doctors Recommend It. London: 1930. V. 53

PLUNKETT, H. M.
Women, Plumbers and Doctors, or Household Sanitation. New York: 1885. V. 54

PLUNKETT, JOSEPH MARY
The Poems of Joseph Mary Plunkett. Dublin: 1916. V. 50

PLUNKETT, LEONARD
Phytographia, Seu Plantae Quam Plurima Novae et Literis Hucusq. London: 1692. V. 48

PLUTARCHUS
Apothegmata. London: 1741. V. 51; 54
Aureus Plutarachi Libellus (Greek Title), Id Est, De Educatione. Frankfurt: 1612. V. 49
Eroticus, Interprete Arnoldo Ferrono Burdigalensi... Leiden: 1557. V. 54
(Greek Title) Moralia Opvscvla, Mvltis Mendarvm Milibvs Expvrgata. Basel: 1542. V. 51; 54
Iside e Osiride..., Tradotto dal Greco con Note Filologiche ed Osservaioni al Testo dal Cav. Sebastiano Ciampi. Florence: 1823. V. 50
Libellus...Quomodo ab Adulatore Discernatur Amicus. Rome: 1514. V. 52
The Lives. London: 1579. V. 52; 54
The Lives. London: 1603. V. 47
The Lives. London: 1631. V. 48; 50
The Lives. London: 1657. V. 52
Lives. London: 1803. V. 52
Lives. London: 1810. V. 52
Lives. London: 1823. V. 50
Lives. London: 1874. V. 51
Lives. London: 1902. V. 50
The Lives. Oxford: 1928. V. 48; 50; 53
The Lives. Stratford-on-Avon: 1928. V. 51
The Lives. Bloomsburgh: 1929. V. 47
The Lives. London: 1929. V. 48; 49
Lives. London: 1929-30. V. 49; 50; 51; 52
The Lives. London: 1930. V. 50
Lives. (with) Life of Plutarch. London: 1770. V. 48
Omnium Quae Exstant Operum. Paris: 1624. V. 48
Opera Moralia. Basileae: 1541. V. 50
The Philosophy, Commonly Called the Morals. London: 1657. V. 53
Plutarchi, Demosthenes et Ciceronis Vitae Parallelae Nunc Primum Separatim Editae. Oxford: 1744. V. 50
Plutarch's Lives. London: 1770. V. 50; 51; 52; 54
Plutarch's Lives. London: 1770-71. V. 48
Plutarch's Lives. London: 1801. V. 49
Plutarch's Lives. London: 1821. V. 50
Plutarch's Lives. Philadelphia: 1822. V. 52
Plutarch's Lives. London: 1893. V. 47
Plutarch's Lives. Boston: 1895. V. 48; 51
Plutarch's Lives and Writings. Boston: 1909. V. 54
Plutarch's Morals. Boston: 1870. V. 47
t'Leven der Doorluchtige Griecken ende Romeynen. (Parallel Lives). Delft: 1644. V. 54
Vitae Illustrium Virorum. Venice: 1496. V. 52

PLYMLEY, JOSEPH
General View of the Agriculture of Shropshire. London: 1803. V. 49

PNEUMANEE; or the Fairy of the Nineteenth Century. London: 1814. V. 51

THE POACHER'S Progress. Edinburgh: 1981. V. 49

POAGE, MICHAEL
Handbook of Ornament. San Francisco: 1979. V. 51

POCAHONTAS.. New York: 1946. V. 53

POCCI, FRANZ
Viola Tricolor. Munchen: 1876. V. 49

POCHIN, W. F.
Angling and Hunting in British Columbia. Vancouver: 1946. V. 48

THE POCKET Companion and History of Free-Masons. London: 1759. V. 47; 49

A POCKET Companion for Oxford. Oxford: 1756. V. 50

A POCKET Companion for Oxford; or Guide through the University. Oxford: 1762. V. 51; 52

POCKLINGTON, JOHN
Altare Christianum; or, the Dead Vicar Plea. London: 1637. V. 52

POCOCK, ISAAC
Rob Roy MacGregor; or, Auld Lang Syne. London: 1820. V. 52

POCOCK, LEWIS
A Chronological List of books and Pamphlets, Relating to the Doctrine of Chances and the Rate of Mortality, Annuities... London: 1842. V. 51

POCOCK, RICHARD
Memorials of the Family of Tufton, Earls of Thanet. Gravesend: 1800. V. 47; 53

POCOCK, W. F.
Designs for Churches and Chapel... London: 1835. V. 52
Modern Finishings for Rooms. London: 1811. V. 50

POCOCK, WILLIAM
Mr. Pocock's Plan, for Establishing the British Nation, in Easy Circumstances, Respecting Her Financial Affairs... London: 1823. V. 51

POCOCKE, RICHARD
A Description of the East, and Some Other Countries. London: 1743-45. V. 48

PODESCHI, JOHN B.
Books on the Horse and Horsemanship. 1981. V. 49
Books on the Horse and Horsemanship. London: 1981. V. 47
Dickens and Dickensiana, a Catalogue of the Richard Gimbel Collection in the Yale University Library. New Haven: 1980. V. 47; 49; 53
Sport in Art and Books. The Paul Mellon Collelction. London: 1982. V. 53

PODMORE, FRANK
Modern Spiritualism, a History and Criticism. London: 1902. V. 48

POE, DAVID
Personal Reminiscences of the Civil War. Charleston: 1908. V. 49

POE, EDGAR ALLAN
Al Aaraaf. New York: 1933. V. 48
Al Aaraaf. Phoenix: 1995. V. 52; 54
Al Aaraaf, Tamerlane and Minor Poems. Baltimore: 1829. V. 48
Anastatic Printing. Northampton: 1975. V. 48; 51
Los Anglo-Americanos en el Polo Sur. Madrid: 1868. V. 47
Arthur Gordon Pym; or, Shipwreck, Mutiny and Famine. London: 1841. V. 48; 53
Arthur Gordon Pym; or, Shipwreck, Mutiny and Famine. London: 1845. V. 53
Les Aventures d'Arthur Gordon Pym De Nantucket. Paris: 1913. V. 48
Les Aventures D'Arthur Gordon Pym De Nantucket. Paris: 1921. V. 48
The Bells and Other Poems. 1912. V. 53
The Bells and Other Poems. London: 1912. V. 47; 48; 49; 50; 51; 52
The Cask of Amontillado. Chicago: 1904. V. 48
Le Chat Noir. Paris: 1927. V. 48
The City in the Sea and Other Poems. London: 1942. V. 50
The Complete Poems and Stories of Edgar Allan Poe. New York: 1946. V. 48; 50
The Complete Poems of Edgar Allan Poe. Boston: 1911. V. 48
The Complete Poetical Works of Edgar Allan Poe. New York: 1889. V. 48
The Complete Poetical Works of Edgar Allan Poe. London: 1909. V. 48
The Complete Works. New York: 1902. V. 48; 51; 52
The Complete Works of Edgar Allan Poe with Biography and Introduction by Nathan Haskell Dole. London & New York: 1908. V. 48
The Conchologist's First Book. Philadelphia: 1839. V. 48; 50; 53
The Conchologist's First Book. Philadelphia: 1840. V. 48
Edgar Allan Poe and the Philadelphia Saturday Courier. Charlottesville: 1933. V. 48
Edgar Allan Poe Letters Till Now Unpublished. Philadelphia & London: 1925. V. 47; 50; 54
English Notes, Intended for Very Extensive Circulation!. Boston: 1842. V. 48
Eureka. New York: 1848. V. 48; 49; 50; 51; 53; 54
Eureka. Paris: 1864. V. 54
Eureka. Paris: 1928. V. 48; 53
Eureka. 1991. V. 52; 54
The Fall of the House of Usher. Paris: 1928. V. 48; 53
The Fall of the House of Usher. Maastricht: 1930. V. 49; 51
The Fall of the House of Usher. New York: 1985. V. 48; 51; 52
The Gold Bug. New York: 1928. V. 48; 51; 54
Histoires Extraordinaires...(with) Nouvelles Histoires Extraordinaires... Paris: 1856-57. V. 52
Hop-Frog Fantastic Tale by Edgar Allan Poe. Braunschweig: 1923. V. 48
Israfel. New York: 1962. V. 51
The Journal of Julius Rodman. San Francisco: 1947. V. 48; 54
The Last Letters of Edgar Allan Poe to Sarah Helen Whitman. New York: 1909. V. 48
Lenore. Boston: 1886. V. 48
Lenore. Troy: 1886. V. 48
The Letters of Edgar Allan Poe. Cambridge: 1948. V. 48
Ligeia. Norfolk: 1991. V. 49; 51
The Literati. New York: 1850. V. 48
The Mask of Red Death. Baltimore: 1969. V. 52; 53

POE, EDGAR ALLAN continued
The Masque. New York: 1995. V. 54
The Masque of the Red Death and Other Tales. Maastricht & London: 1932. V. 53; 54
Mesmerism "In Articulo Mortis". An Astounding and Horrifying Narrative, Shewing the Extraordinary Power of Mesmerism in Arresting the Progress of Death. London: 1846. V. 53; 54
The Murders in the Rue Morgue. Philadelphia: 1895. V. 49
The Murders in the Rue Morgue. New York: 1900. V. 48
The Murders in the Rue Morgue. Chicago: 1933. V. 48
The Murders in the Rue Morgue. Antibes: 1958. V. 47; 49; 52; 53
The Narrative of Arthur Gordon Pym. London: 1838. V. 48; 50
Narrative of Arthur Gordon Pym. New York: 1838. V. 47; 48; 50; 52; 54
The Narrative of Arthur Gordon Pym. New York: 1930. V. 48; 54
Nouvelles Choisies d'Edgar Poe. Le Scarabee d'or. L'Aeronaute Hollandise. Paris: 1853. V. 48
Nouvelles Histoires Extraordinaires... Paris: 1869. V. 53
Phantasy-Pieces. Paris: 1928. V. 48
The Philosophy of Animal Magnetism. Philadelphia: 1837. V. 48
Poemes D'Edgar Poe. Bruxelles: 1888. V. 48
Poems. New York: 1875. V. 48
Poems. London: 1881. V. 48
The Poems. London: 1883. V. 53
Poems. London: 1885. V. 48
The Poems. New York: 1895. V. 48
Poems. London: 1900. V. 52
The Poems. Portland: 1906. V. 48
The Poems. London: 1909. V. 48
Poems. New York: 1936. V. 48
The Poems. New York: 1943. V. 52
Poems. New York: 1950. V. 48
Poe's Contributions to the Columbia Spy. Pottsville: 1929. V. 48; 54
Poe's Raven. A Pennsylvania German Version. Mapleshade: 1891. V. 48
Poe's Tales a Selection. East Aurora: 1922. V. 48
Poe's Tales of Mystery and Imagination. London: 1935. V. 50
The Poetical Works. London: 1853. V. 48
The Poetical Works. New York: 1858. V. 52
The Poetical Works. London: 1866. V. 47
The Poetical Works. Melbourne: 1868. V. 48
The Poetical Works. New York: 1912. V. 47
Politian, an Unfinished Tragedy. Menasha: 1923. V. 48
Politian, an Unfinished Tragedy. Richmond: 1923. V. 48
The Raven. Philadelphia: 1865. V. 48
The Raven. London: 1901. V. 52
The Raven. Easthampton: 1980. V. 48; 53
The Raven. Easthampton: 1985. V. 47; 49; 50
The Raven and Other Poems. New York: 1845. V. 48; 50; 53; 54
The Raven and Other Poems. London: 1846. V. 48
The Raven and other Poems. Detroit: 1936. V. 48
The Raven and other Poems. New York: 1942. V. 48
The Raven and The Pit and the Pendulum. London: 1899. V. 47; 50; 51
The Raven Le Corbeau Poem by Edgar Allan Poe. New York: 1978. V. 48
The Raven...Philosophy of Composition. San Francisco: 1907. V. 47
The Raven...Philosophy of Composition. New York: 1930. V. 51
Le Scarabee d'Or. Paris: 1926. V. 52
Some Edgar Allan Poem Letters. St. Louis: 1905. V. 48
Some Letters of Edgar Allan Poe to E. H. N. Patterson of Oquawka, Illinois... Chicago: 1898. V. 48; 50
Tales. London: 1845. V. 48; 50; 51
Tales. New York: 1845. V. 48; 51
Tales. London: 1846. V. 48
Tales. New York: 1849. V. 48
Tales. Chicago: 1930. V. 47
Tales. New York: 1964. V. 48
The Tales and Poems of... Philadelphia: 1894-95. V. 48
The Tales and Poems of... New York: 1902. V. 52
Tales and Sketches: to Which is Added the Raven: a Poem. London: 1852. V. 49
Tales of Mystery and Imagination. London. V. 53
Tales of Mystery and Imagination. London: 1852. V. 48; 49
Tales of Mystery and Imagination. London: 1919. V. 47; 48; 52
Tales of Mystery and Imagination. New York: 1919. V. 52; 54
Tales of Mystery and Imagination. London & New York: 1920. V. 49
Tales of Mystery and Imagination. 1923. V. 51
Tales of Mystery and Imagination. London: 1923. V. 51
Tales of Mystery and Imagination. New York: 1923. V. 49; 53
Tales of Mystery and Imagination. New York: 1925. V. 47
Tales of Mystery and Imagination. New York: 1933. V. 47
Tales of Mystery and Imagination. London: 1935. V. 47; 48; 49; 51; 53
Tales of Mystery and Imagination. New York: 1936. V. 53
Tales of Mystery and Imagination. New York: 1939. V. 45
Tales of Mystery and Imagination. Baltimore: 1941. V. 48
Tales of the Grotesque and Arabesque. Philadelphia: 1840. V. 48; 50
Tamerlane and other Poems... London: 1884. V. 48; 50; 54
Tamerlane and Other Poems. San Francisco: 1923. V. 48; 50
Tamerlane and Other Poems. London: 1931. V. 48
Two Tales. Beckenham: 1986. V. 47; 50

The Works. New York: 1850. V. 48; 50; 53; 54
The Works. New York: 1850/56. V. 48
The Works. New York: 1853. V. 50
The Works. New York: 1855. V. 48
The Works... London: 1872. V. 49
The Works... Edinburgh: 1874-75. V. 47
The Works. London: 1881?. V. 48
The Works. Edinburgh: 1883. V. 49
The Works. Chicago: 1894. V. 48
The Works. Chicago: 1894-95. V. 47; 54
The Works. London: 1895-98. V. 50
The Works. London: 1896. V. 53; 54

POE, ELISABETH ELLICOTT
Half-Forgotten Romances of American History. Washington: 1922. V. 48

POE, JOHN WILLIAM
The Death of Billy the Kid. Boston and New York: 1933. V. 54

POE, SOPHIE A.
Buckboard Days. Caldwell: 1936. V. 50; 51

A POEM by a Lady on Seeing His Royal Highness the Prince Regent. Edinburgh: 1745. V. 47

POEM for Shakespeare 2. London: 1973. V. 53

POEM OF THE MONTH CLUB
Folios 1-4 (all published). London: 1970-77. V. 50

A POEM Sacred to the Memory of Her Late Majesty, Caroline, Queen Consort of Great Britain. London: 1737. V. 54

POEMS.. London: 1832. V. 54

POEMS By E. Somebody. Dublin: 1806. V. 50

POEMS By Four Authors. Cambridge: 1923. V. 48

POEMS, etc. by Several Hands, Inscribed to the Memory of Abraham Richard Hawksworth, Late Treasurer to the Bristol Infirmary and One of the People Called Quakers. Bristol: 1769. V. 47

POEMS for Alan Hancox. London: 1993. V. 49
POEMS for Alan Hancox. Lower Marston: 1993. V. 53

POEMS for Shakespeare 6. London: 1977. V. 48

POEMS For Spain. London: 1939. V. 50

POEMS from Italy. London: 1945. V. 48; 49; 50

POEMS, Moral, Elegant and Pathetic. London: 1796. V. 52

POEMS of the Great War. London: 1914. V. 54

POEMS on Affairs of State. From the Time of Oliver Cromwell, to the Abdication of K. James the Second. London: 1697. V. 49

POEMS, On Religious, Moral and Descriptive Subjects by an Officer in the Army. London: 1827. V. 54

POESCHE, THEODORE
The New Rome; or, the United States of the World. New York: 1853. V. 48

POESIE per le Gloriose Nozze Dell'...Nobil Uomo Niccolo Foscarini e la Nobil Donna Adriana Barbaro. Venice: 1766. V. 47

THE POET of the Month 1942. New York: 1942. V. 52

POETAE Christiani Veteres. Prvdentii Poetae Opera....Cantica Ioannis Damasceni (etc). Venice: 1501. V. 54

POETAE Graeci Principes Heroici Carminis... Geneva: 1566. V. 50

POETAE Tres Elegantissimi Emendati & Aucti: Michael Marullus. Hieronymus Angerianus. Johannes Secundus. Paris: 1582. V. 51

POETIC Fragments.... 1826. V. 50

A POETICAL Account of the Installation of a Chancellor of the University of Oxford. Oxford: 1810. V. 49

A POETICAL Address to the Ladies of Suffolk. London: 1785. V. 48

A POETICAL Epistle Addressed to Robert Montgomery... Oxford: 1831. V. 50

POETICAL Epistle from Florizel to Perdita: with Perdita's Answer and a Preliminary Discourse Upon the Education of Princes. London: 1781. V. 54

A POETICAL Epistle to the Right Hon. George Canning etc. and Other Poems. Dublin: 1827. V. 54

POETICAL Epistles to the Author of the New Bath Guide, from a Genteel Family in ----shire. London: 1767. V. 51; 54

POETICAL Magazine; Dedicated to the Lovers of the Muse... London: 1809. V. 51

POETICAL Miscellanies, Consisting of Original Poems and Translation. London: 1714. V. 47; 48

POETICAL Miscellanies, Consisting of Original Poems and Translations. London: 1727. V. 53

THE POETICAL Register and Repository of Fugitive Poetry. London: 1802/02. V. 52

POETICAL Sketches of Scarborough. London: 1812. V. 51

A POETRY Folio 1963. San Francisco: 1963. V. 47

POETRY From Oxford in Wartime. London: 1945. V. 48

POETRY London X. London: 1944. V. 47

THE POETRY Of Black America: Anthology of the 20th Century. New York: 1973. V. 53

THE POETRY of Song. Five Tributes to Stephen Sondheim. New York: 1992. V. 49; 51

POETRY of the Anti-Jacobin. London: 1799. V. 47
POETRY of the Anti-Jacobin. London: 1800. V. 49

POETRY Of the Anti-Jacobin: Comprising the Celebrated Political and Satirical Poems, Parodies and Jeux-D'Esprit of the Right Honorable George Canning, the Earl of Carlisle, Marquis Wellesley, the Hon. J. H. Frere, et al. London: 1854. V. 47

THE POETRY of Various Glees, Songs, Etc. as Performed at the Harmonists... London: 1798. V. 50

POETRY Original and Selected. London: 1796-9. V. 49

THE POETRY Quartos. New York: 1929. V. 49

POET'S CLUB
The Second Book of the Poet's Club. London: 1911. V. 52

THE POETS of Great Britain Complete From Chaucer to Churchill. London: 1777-84. V. 50

THE POET'S of Today IV. New York: 1957. V. 52

POGANY, ELAINE
Peterkin. Philadelphia: 1940. V. 53

POGANY, WILLY
Willy Pogany's Mother Goose. London: 1929. V. 54

POGGIO BRACCIOLINI
The Facetiae or Jocose Tales. Paris: 1879. V. 47; 53

POGSON, NORMAN ROBERT
Popular Description of the Total Eclipse of the sun, on August 18th, 1868, Prepared at the Madras Observatory for the Asylum Press Almanac. Madras: 1867 (sic). V. 52

POHL, F.
Gateway. 1977. V. 49
Gateway. New York: 1977. V. 51
Man Plus. New York: 1976. V. 51
Presidential Year. 1953. V. 51
The Reefs of Space. 1965. V. 52
Search the Sky. 1954. V. 52
Search the Sky. New York: 1954. V. 50
The Space Merchants. 1953. V. 47; 51
A Town is Drowning. 1955. V. 48; 52
A Town is Drowning. New York: 1955. V. 51
Wolfbane. London: 1960. V. 48; 52

POINTER, JOHN
An Account of a Roman Pavement, Lately Found at Stunsfield in Oxford-shire, Prov'd to be 1400 Years Old. Oxford: 1713. V. 51; 52
Miscellanea in Usum Juventutis Academicae... London: 1718. V. 54
Miscellanea in Usum Juventutis Academicae... Oxford: 1718. V. 52
A Rational Account of the Weather. London: 1738. V. 51

POINTS of Humour. London: 1823/24. V. 47

POINTZ, ROBERT
Testimonies for the Real Presence of Christes Body and Blood in the Blessed Scarament of the Aultar. Louvain: 1566. V. 52

POISSON, SIMEON DENIS
Recherches sur le Mouvement des Projectiles dans l'air, en Ayant Egard a Leur Figure et Leur Rotation, et l'Influence du Mouvement Diurne de la Terre. Paris: 1839. V. 47

POITEAU, ANTOINE
Pomologie Francaise. Recueil des Plus Beaux Fruits Cultives en France. Paris: 1846. V. 47

POITIER, SIDNEY
This Life. New York: 1980. V. 52

POKAGON, CHIEF SIMON
O-Gi-Maw-Kwe Mit-I-Gwa-Ki (Queen of the Woods). Hartford: 1899. V. 50

POKER As It Is Played in Deadwood in the Fifties. Palo Alto: 1928. V. 54

POLACK, JOEL S.
Manners and Customs of the New Zealanders; with Notes Corroborative of Their Habits, Usages, Etc. and Remarks to Intending Emigrants. London: 1840. V. 47; 52

POLAND: Painting of the Fifteenth Century. New York: 1964. V. 53

POLANUS, AMANDUS
The Substance of Christian Religion... London: 1608. V. 48

POLE, REGINALD
Ad Henricum Octavum Britanniae Regem, Pro Ecclesiasticae Unitatis Defensione, Libri Quatuor. Ingoldstadt: 1587. V. 50; 53

POLE, WILLIAM
A Treatise On the Cornish Pumping Engine... London: 1844-48. V. 54

POLEHAMPTON, EDWARD
The Gallery of Nature and Art. London: 1818. V. 53
The Gallery of Nature and Art. London: 1821. V. 47; 49; 50

POLEMON, JOHN
The Second Part of the Booke of Battailes, Fought in Our Age: Taken Out of the Best Authors and Writers in Sundrie Languages. London: 1587. V. 49; 51

POLENI, GIOVANNI
Epistolarum Mathematicarum Fasciculus. Padua: 1729. V. 54
Memorie Istoriche Della Gran Cupola del Tempio Vaticano e de' Danni di Essa, e De' Ristoramenti Loro, Divise in Libri Cinque. Padua: 1748. V. 53

POLETICA, PIERRE
A Sketch of the Internal Condition of the United States of America and of Their Political Relations with Europe. Baltimore: 1826. V. 50

POLEY, G. HENRY
Domestic Architecture, Furniture and Ornament of England from the 14th to the 18th Century. Boston: 1911. V. 53

POLIDORI, FRANCESCO
Il Losario. Poema Eroico Romanzesco di Ser Francesco Polidori. Firenze: 1851. V. 54

POLIDORI, JOHN WILLIAM
The Vampyre: a Tale. London: 1819. V. 54
The Vampyre, a Tale. Hertfordshire: 1974. V. 48
Vampyren of Lord Byron. Helsingfors: 1824. V. 52

POLISIUS, GOTHOFREDUS SAMUEL
Myrrhologia seu Myrrhae Disquisitio Curiosa ad Normam & Formam Sacri Romani Imperii Academiae Naturae Curiosorum Adornata Variisque Medicamentis Illustrata. Nurnberg: 1688. V. 47

THE POLITE Academy; or, School of Behaviour for Young Gentlemen and Ladies. London: 1786. V. 47

THE POLITE Jester: or, Theatre for Wit... London: 1796. V. 47

POLITI, LEO
Bunker Hill, Los Angeles: Reminiscences of Bygone Days. Palm Desert: 1964. V. 47; 50
Tales of the Los Angeles Parks. Palm Desert: 1966. V. 50

A POLITICAL and Military Survey. London: 1805. V. 50

A POLITICAL and Satirical History of the Years 1756, 1757, 1758 and 1759. London: 1760. V. 48

A POLITICAL and Satirical History of the Years 1756, 1757, 1758, 1759 and 1760... London: 1763?. V. 50

A POLITICAL and Satirical History of the Years 1756 and 1757. London: 1757-60. V. 54

POLITICAL History of England. London: 1906. V. 49

THE POLITICAL History of England. London: 1906-10. V. 52

THE POLITICAL Primer; or, Road to Public Honours. London: 1826. V. 50

POLITTI, LEO
The Song of the Swallows. New York: 1949. V. 51

POLIZIANO, ANGELO
Angeli Politiani, et Aliorum virorum Illustrium, Epistorarum Libri Duodecim. Basel: 1522. V. 53; 54
Illustrium Virorum Epistole ab Angelo Politiano... Paris: 1526. V. 52
Opera Omnia. Rome: 1498. V. 47; 48
Le Stanze...di Nuovo Pubblicate. Parma: 1792. V. 48

POLK, JAMES
The Mexican War. Washington: 1848. V. 49

POLK, JAMES K.
Speech of Mr. James K. Polk, on the Bill to Construct a National Road from Buffalo to New Orleans. Washington: 1830. V. 48

POLK, WILLIS
A Matter of Taste: Willis Polk's Writings on Architecture in the Wave. San Francisco: 1979. V. 53; 54

THE POLL for Knights of the Shire, Begun on Wednesday, May 20th and Finally Closed on Friday June 5th, 1807: Candidates: William Wilberforce, Esquire, the Right Honourable Charles William Wentworth Fitzwilliam...and the Honourable Henry Lascelles. York: 1807. V. 47

THE POLL for Knights of the Shire to Represent the County of Kent... London: 1734. V. 49

THE POLL for Knights of the Shire to Represent the County of Kent; Expressing the Names of the Candidates; and for Which of Them Every Person Voted. London: 1754. V. 53

THE POLL for the Knights of the Shire, to Represent the County of Kent; Taken on Pennenden Heath, on...the 28, 29 and 30th Days of June, 1790. Rochester: 1791. V. 53

THE POLL for Two Knights of the Shire to Represent the Western Division of the County of Stafford...Taken on Tuesday, the Twenty-Fourth of November 1868, Including the whole of the Registered Electors... London: 1868. V. 54

POLLACK, P.
Picture History of Photography, from the Earliest Beginnings to the Present Day. New York: 1969. V. 52

POLLARD, A. F.
Henry VIII. Paris: 1902. V. 54

POLLARD, ALFRED WILLIAM
Anglo-American First Editions 1826-1900 East to West. New York: 1981. V. 54
Bibliographica. London: 1895-97. V. 50
Cobden-Sanderson and the Doves Press. San Francisco: 1929. V. 51; 54
English Embroidered Bookbindings. 1899. V. 53
Fine Books. London: 1912. V. 54
Fine Printing in England and Mr. Bruce Rogers. Newark: 1916. V. 54
Hand-Lists of English Printers 1501-1556. 1895-1913. V. 53
Last Words on the History of the Title Page. 1968. V. 52
Modern Fine Printing in England and Mr. Bruce Rogers. Newark: 1916. V. 49
A Short-title Catalogue of Books Printed in England, Scotland and Ireland. London: 1926. V. 49
A Short-Title Catalogue of Books Printed in England, Scotland and Ireland and of English Books Printed Abroad 1475-1640. London: 1946. V. 49; 54
A Short-Title Catalogue of Books Printed in England, Scotland and Ireland and of English Books Printed Abroad 1475-1640. London: 1986. V. 49
Short-Title Catalogue of Books Printed in England, Scotland and Ireland and of English Books Printed Abroad 1475-1640. London: 1986/76/91. V. 47
Three Hundred Notable Books Added to the Library of the British Museum Under the Keepership of Richard Garnett 1890-1899. London: 1899. V. 54

POLLARD, D. G.
The Times Imperial and Foreign Trade and Engineering Supplement: Canada, Power - Transport - Mining Humber. London: 1929. V. 50

POLLARD, EDWARD ALFRED
Black Diamonds Gathered in the Darkey Homes of the South. New York: 1860. V. 49
The First Year of the War. Richmond: 1862. V. 47; 49; 52
The Lost Cause; a New Southern History of the War of the Confederates. New York: 1866. V. 51
The Second Year of the War. Richmond: 1863. V. 49
Southern History of the Great Civil War in the United States. The First Year of the War. Toronto: 1863. V. 54
Southern History of the War. The Third Year of the War. New York: 1865. V. 54

POLLARD, H. B. C.
British and American Game-Birds. London: 1945. V. 48
Game Birds. Rearing, Preservation and Shooting. London: 1929. V. 49; 52
The Gun Room Guide. London: 1930. V. 49; 51
A History of Firearms. London: 1931. V. 50

POLLARD, JAMES B.
Historical Sketch of the Eastern Regions of New France, from the Various Dates...Prince Edward Island: Military and Civil. Charlottetown: 1898. V. 53

POLLARD, JOSEPHINE
Freaks and Frolics of Little Girls and Boys. New York: 1887. V. 53

POLLARD, PERCIVAL
Posters in Miniature. New York: 1896. V. 52

POLLEN, F. P. L.
Recherches sur la Faune de Madagascar et de Ses Dependances. Leiden: 1868-77. V. 51

POLLEXFEN, HENRY
The Arguments and Reports of Sr. Hen. Pollexfen, Kt. Late Lord Chief Justice of the Court of Common Pleas, in Some Special Cases... London: 1702. V. 47

POLLEY, JOSEPH BENJAMIN
Hood's Texas Brigade: Its Marches, Its Battles, Its Achievements. New York & Washington: 1910. V. 48; 50
A Soldier's Letters to Charming Nellie. New York & Washington: 1908. V. 48; 54

POLLINI, FRANCES
Night. London: 1960. V. 48
Night. Paris: 1960. V. 51

POLLITT, J. MILTON, MRS.
Dorothy Penrose. London & Sydney: 1893. V. 54

POLLNITZ, KARL LUDWIG, FREIHERR VON
Memoirs of Charles-ewis, Baron de Pollnitz. London: 1737-38. V. 48

POLLOCK, FREDERICK
The History of English Law, Before the Time of Edward I. Cambridge: 1911. V. 52
The History of English Law Before the Time of Edward I. 1968. V. 49

POLLOCK, H. E. D.
Round Structures of Aboriginal Middle America. Washington: 1936. V. 52

POLLOCK, JAMES
Railroad to Oregon. Washington: 1848. V. 47

POLLOCK, ROBERT
The Course of Time. New York: 1830. V. 54

POLLOCK, WALTER H.
Fencing...Boxing...Wrestling. London: 1889. V. 51; 54

POLLOK, F.
Incidents of Foreign Sport and Travel. London: 1894. V. 48; 49
Sport in British Burma, Assam, and the Cassyah and Jyntiah Hills. London: 1879. V. 48; 53

POLO and Coaching. London: 1922. V. 54

POLO, MARCO
The Book of Ser Marco Polo, the Venetian Concerning the Kingdoms and Marvels of the east. London: 1875. V. 52; 54
The Book of Ser Marco Polo, The Venetian, Concerning the Kingdoms and Marvels of the East. London: 1926. V. 49
The Travels of Marco Polo 1271-1295. New York: 1936. V. 53

POLONCEAU, A. R.
Notice sur le Nouveau Systeme de Ponts en Fonte Suivi Dans la Construction du pont du Carrousel. Paris: 1839. V. 51

POLSON. CHAMBER OF COMMERCE
Polson Power Lake City and Lower Flathead Valley. Polson: 1915. V. 50

POLSUE, JOSEPH
A Complete Parochial History of the County of Cornwall. Truro: 1866-73. V. 49

POLTINUS
The Enneads. London: 1917-30. V. 48

POLUNIN, O.
Flowers of Europe. London: 1969. V. 54
Flowers of Greece and the Balkans, a Field Guide. London: 1980. V. 47

POLWELL, WILLIAM M.
A History of Minnesota. St. Paul: 1921. V. 54

POLWHELE, RICHARD
Essays by a Society of Gentlemen, at Exeter. Exeter: 1796. V. 48
The Follies of Oxford: or Cursory Sketches on a University Education, from an Undergraduate to His Friend in the Country. London: 1785. V. 54
The History of Cornwall, Civil, Military, Architectural, Agricultural, Commercial... London: 1804-16. V. 51
Reminiscences in Prose and Verse. London: 1836. V. 51
Traditions and Recollections; Domestic, Clerical and Literary. London: 1826. V. 51; 52
Two Letters to the Rev. Robert Hawker, D.D....on His Enthusiasm and fanaticism, Particularly as Exhibited in Cornwall. Helston: 1799. V. 48

POLYAENUS
(Greek) *Polyaeni Stratagematvm Libri Octo.I. Casavbonvs Graece Nunc Primum Edidit*. Lvgdvni: 1598. V. 48

POLYAK, STEPHEN
The Retina: the Anatomy and Histology of the Retina in Man, Ape, and Monkey, Including the Consideration of Visual Functions, The History of Physiological Optics and Histological Laboratory Technique. Chicago: 1941. V. 49
The Vertebrate Visual System. Chicago: 1957. V. 54

THE POLYANTHEA; *of, A Collection of Interesting Fragments in Prose and verse*. London: 1804. V. 49; 51

POLYBIUS
The General History. London: 1761. V. 48
The General History of Polybius in Five Books. London: 1772. V. 47
(Greek) *Historiarum Libri Quinque*. Haganoae: 1530. V. 48
(Greek title) *Polybii Megalopolitani Historiarium Quidquid Superest*. Leipzig: 1689-95. V. 50
Histoire de Polybe, Depuis la Seconde Guerre Punique Jusqu'a Celle de Macedoine. Paris: 1727-30. V. 52
Histoire de Polybe, Nouvellement Traduite du Grec Par Dom Vincent Thuillier, Benedictin de la Congregation de Saint maur... Paris: 1753. V. 52
Historiarum Libri Priores. Basle: 1549. V. 47; 50; 53
Historiarum Libri priores Quinque, Nicolao Perotto Sipontino Interprete. Lugduni: 1554. V. 49; 51; 52
The Hystories of the Most Famous and Worthy Cronographer Polybius: Discoursing of the Warres Betwixt the Romanes & Carthaginenses... London: 1568. V. 47
Opuscula Aliquot Nunc Primum e Graeco in Latinum Conversa, Nempe. Basel: 1544. V. 47; 48; 49; 50
Polybii Lycortae F. Megalopolitani Historiarum Libri qui Supersunt, Interpete Isaaco Casaubono. Amsterdam: 1670. V. 47
Polybii Megalopolitani Historiarum. Lyon: 1554. V. 52
Polybii Megalopolitani Historiarum Quidquid Superest. Leipzig: 1789-95. V. 47
Polybii...Historiarum Libri Qui Supersunt... Paris: 1609. V. 48

POLYBUS
Opuscula Aliquot Nunc Primum e Graeco in Latinum Conversa, Nempe. Basel: 1544. V. 47

POMERANZ, HERMAN
Medicine in the Shakespearean Plays and Dickens's Doctors. New York: 1936. V. 50; 52

POMERIUS, JULIANUS
De Uita Coteplatiua de Uita Actuali. Speyer: 1486. V. 53

POMEROY, JOHN NORTON
An Introduction to Municipal Law. New York: 1864. V. 51; 54
An Introduction to Municipal Law. New York: 1865. V. 52

POMFRET, JOHN
Miscellany Poems on Several Occasions. London: 1702. V. 47
Miscellany Poems on Several Occasions. London: 1707. V. 49

POMPADOUR, JEANNE ANTOINETTE POISSON, MARQUISE DE
Lettres. London: 1776-78. V. 52
Memoirs of the Marchioness of...Written By Herself. London: 1766. V. 50

POMPONATIUS, PETRUS
Opera. De Naturalium Effectuum Admirandorum Causis, Seu de Incantationibus Liber. 1567. V. 47; 51

PONA, FRANCESCO
Cardiomorphoseos sive ex Conde Desumpta Emblemata Sacra. Verona: 1645. V. 49; 53

PONCE, JUAN GARCIA
Leonora Carrington. Mexico City: 1974. V. 53

POND, MIMI
Half Off. Berkeley: 1981. V. 47

POND, S. W.
Two Volunteer Missionaries Among the Dakota. Boston: 1893. V. 50

PONGE, FRANCIS
Braque Lithographs. Monte Carlo: 1963. V. 52
G. Braque. New York: 1971. V. 47; 50; 52

PONICSAN, DARYL
The Last Detail. New York: 1970. V. 51; 52

PONSONBY.. London: 1817. V. 51

PONSONBY: a Tale of Troublous Times. London: 1853. V. 51

PONSONBY, ARTHUR
The Priory and Manor of Lynchmere and Schulbrede. Taunton: 1920. V. 54

PONTANUS, JOANNES JOVIANUS
Iesu Floridor Libri Octo. Augsburg: 1596. V. 50
Opera. Venetijs: 1533. V. 47
Opera in Quatuor Tomos Digesta. Basel: 1556. V. 53
Opera Omnia. Venice: 1519. V. 48
(Poemata) Ioannis Ioviani Pontani Amorum Libri Duo Eiusdem de Amore Coniugali Libri Tres. Strassbourg: 1515. V. 53
Quae in Hoc Enchyridio Contineantur...Urania seu de Stellis Libri Quinque (and other works). Florence: 1514. V. 48; 49; 50

PONTECOULANT
A History of Hailey's Comet. London: 1835. V. 51

PONTEDERA, GUILIO
Anthologia, sive de Floris Natura Libri Tres... Padua: 1720. V. 47

PONTEY, WILLIAM
The Forest Pruner, or Timber Owner's Assistant...With Remarks on the Old and Outlines of a New System for the Management of Oak Wood. London: 1808. V. 50
The Profitable Planter: a Treatise on the Theory and Practice of Planting Forest Trees... London: 1814. V. 47; 49

PONTING, HERBERT G.
The Great White South, or With Scott in the Antarctic... New York: 1923. V. 53
In Lotus-Land Japan. London: 1910. V. 52; 54
In Lotus-Land Japan. London: 1922. V. 54
Japanese Studies. Yokohama: 1906. V. 52

PONTIUS PILATE
Thresor Admirable de la Sentence Prononcee par Ponce Pilate, Contre Notre Sauuer Iesus Christ. Paris: 1581. V. 53

PONTOPPIDAN, ERICH
Den Danske Atlas, Eller Konge-Riget Dannemark, Med dets Naturlige Egenskaber, Elementer, Indbyggere, Vaexter, Dyr Og Andre... Copenhagen: 1763-74. V. 48
The Natural History of Norway... London: 1755. V. 48; 49; 50; 51; 54

POOL, EUGENE
Surgery at the New York Hospital One Hundred Years Ago. New York: 1929. V. 52; 54

POOL, PHOEBE
Poems of Death. London: 1945. V. 51; 53

POOL, ROBERT
Views of the Most Remarkable Public Buildings, Monuments and Other Edifices in the City of Dublin... Dublin: 1780. V. 48

POOLE, BRAITHWAITE
Statistics of British Commerce. London: 1852. V. 49

POOLE, CAROLINE
A Modern Prairie Schooner on the Transcontinental Trail, the Story of a Motor Trip. San Francisco: 1919. V. 47

POOLE, D. C.
Among the Sioux of Dakota: Eighteen Months Experience as an Indian Agent. New York: 1881. V. 47; 49

POOLE, FRANCIS
Queen Charlotte Islands. London: 1872. V. 48; 52

POOLE, GEORGE AYLIFFE
The Churches of Scarborough, Filey and the Neighbourhood. London: 1848. V. 53

POOLE, JACOB
A Glossary, with some Pieces of Verse, of the Old Dialect of the English Colony in the Baronies of Forth and Bargy, County of Wexford, Ireland. London: 1867. V. 48; 50; 52

POOLE, JOHN
Phineas Quiddy, or Sheer Industry. London: 1842. V. 54
Sketches and Recollections. London: 1835. V. 48; 50

POOLE, JOHN H.
American Calvalcade: a Memoir on the Life and Family of Dewitt Clinton Poole. Pasadena: 1939. V. 54

POOLE, JOSHUA
The English Parnassus; or a Help to English Poesie. London: 1657. V. 49
The English Parnassus: or a Help to English Poesie. London: 1677. V. 47; 50

POOLE, SOPHIA
The Englishwoman in Egypt: Letters from Cairo, Written During a Residence There in 1842, 3 & 4. London: 1844. V. 50; 51
The Englishwoman in Egypt: Letters from Cairo, Written During a Residence There in 1842, 3 & 4 with E. W. Lane, Esq. London: 1845-6. V. 47
The Englishwoman in Egypt: Letters from Cairo, Written During a Residence There in 1842, 3 & 4... (with) The Englishwoman in Egypt...Second Series. London: 1846. V. 47

POOLE, W. F.
An Index to Periodical Literature. Boston: 1882 (1883). V. 54

POOLEY, HENRY
John Wyatt, Master Carpenter and Inventor, A.D. 1700-1766. London: 1885. V. 50

POOR Convent Garden! Or, a Scene Rehearsed: an Occasional Prelude, Intended for the Opening of the New Theatre Royal, Covent-Garden, This Season. London: 1792. V. 48

POOR, HENRY V.
Manual of the Railroads of the United States for 1877-78. New York: 1877. V. 53
The Pacific Railroads and the Relations Existing Between Them and the Government of the United States. New York: 1879. V. 47
Poor's Manual of the Railroads. New York: 1886. V. 52

POOR, HENRY WILLIAM
American Bookbindings in the Library of Henry William Poor Described by Henri Pene Du Bois. Jamaica: 1903. V. 48

POOR, M. C.
Denver South Park and Pacific. Denver: 1949. V. 54
Denver South Park and Pacific. Denver: 1976. V. 54
Pictorial Supplement to Denver South Park and Pacific. Denver: 1959. V. 54

THE POOR Unhappy Transported Felon's Sorrowful Account of His Fourteen Years Transportation, at Virginia, in America. York: 1830. V. 50

POORE, BENJAMIN PERLEY
The Life and Public Serivices of Ambrose E. Burnside, Soldier-Citizen Statesman. Providence: 1882. V. 49

POP Goes the Weasel Songster. Philadelphia, New York: 1855. V. 51

POPA, VASKO
Give Me Back My Rags. Portland: 1985. V. 47
The Little Box. Washington: 1970. V. 47

POPE, A.
Reproductions of Some of the Important Paintings and Of Their Details Illustrating the Technique of the Artists. Boston: 1936. V. 50

POPE, A. WINTHROP
Remarks on Some Masonic Book Plates in America and their Owners. Boston: 1908/11. V. 50

POPE, ALEXANDER
Celeberrimi Popii Tentamen de Modis Criticis Scripta Dijudicandi. London: 1745. V. 47
The Corresondence of Alexander Pope. Oxford: 1910. V. 52
The Dunciad. London: 1729. V. 47; 48; 50; 53; 54
The Dunciad. London: 1735. V. 48; 49
The Dunciad, in Four Books. London: 1743. V. 47; 48; 50; 54
An Epistle from Mr. Pope to Dr. Arbuthnot. London: 1734. V. 47; 48; 49; 51; 52; 54
An Epistle from Mr. Pope, to Dr. Arbuthnot. London: 1734-35. V. 49
An Epistle from Mr. Pope, to Dr. Arbuthnot. London: 1735. V. 54
An Epistle to the Right Honourable Richard Earl of Burlington. London: 1731. V. 48
An Epistle to the Right Honourable Richard Lord Visc. Cobham. London: 1733. V. 47; 48; 49; 51; 54
Epistola de Heloyza a Abaylard, Compsota no Idioma Inglez... London: 1801. V. 50
Essai sur l'Homme. 1736. V. 52
Essai sur l'Homme... Strasbourg: 1772. V. 47; 50
Essai sur l'Homme...avec l'original Anglois; Ornee de Figures en Taille-Douce. Lausanne: 1745. V. 49
An Essay on Criticism. San Francisco: 1920's. V. 48
An Essay on Criticism. San Francisco: 1928. V. 48; 49; 50; 53
An Essay on Criticism. (with) An Essay on Man. London: 1743. V. 48
An Essay on Man. London: 1734. V. 47
Essay on Man. London: 1745. V. 52
An Essay on Man. Dublin: 1771. V. 48
An Essay on Man. London: 1773-74. V. 48
An Essay on Man. London: 1777. V. 48
An Essay on Man. London: 1786. V. 48
An Essay on Man. London: 1819. V. 50; 54
An Essay on Man. Oxford: 1962. V. 47; 48; 50; 54
The First Epistle of the First Book of Horace Imitated. London: 1737. V. 47
The First Satire of the Second Book of Horace, Imitated in a Dialogue Between Alexander Pope of Twickenham in Com. Midd. Esq. on the One Part, and His Learned Counil on the Other. London: 1733. V. 47; 54
Inart: I Principi della Morale, o Sia Saggio Sopra l'Uomo, Poema Ingl. Venice: 1758. V. 51
Inart: I Principj Della Morale o Sia Saggio Sopra l'Uomo, Poema Ingles. Venice: 1784. V. 47
Inart: Il Riccio Rapito e le Lodi di Neuton Poemi Inglesi Tradotti in oscani dal Sig. Andrea Bonducci Accademia Fiorentino con Altri Nuovi Componimenti. In Napoli: 1760. V. 47
A Key to the Lock. London: 1715. V. 52; 54
Letters of Mr. Alexander Pope and Several of His Friends. London: 1737. V. 52

POPE, ALEXANDER continued

Letters of Mr. Pope, and Several Eminent Persons, From the Year 1705 to 1735. London: 1735. V. 47; 48; 49; 54
Miscellaneous Poems and Translations. London: 1712. V. 48
The New Dunciad: as It Was Found in the Year 1741... London: 1742. V. 47; 54
Ode for Musick on St. Cecilia's Day. London: 1719. V. 47
Oeuvres Diverses de M. Pope. Amsterdam and Leipzig: 1753. V. 48; 49
Of the Characters of Women; an Epistle to a Lady... London: 1735. V. 47; 48; 49; 52
Of the Knowledge and Characters of Men. An Epistle to the Right Honourable Richard Lord Visct. Cobham. London: 1733. V. 47; 50
Of the Use of Riches, an Epistle to Lord Bathurst. London: 1732. V. 47; 48; 49; 54
Of the Use of Riches, an Epistle to the Right Honourable Allen Lord Bathurst. London: 1733. V. 54
One Thousand Seven Hundred and Thirty Eight. Dialogue II. London: 1738. V. 47; 48; 49
Les Pensees de Pope, avec un Abrege de sa vie, Extraits de l'edition Angloise, de M. Warburthon, par M.***. Geneva and Paris: 1766. V. 47
Poetical Miscellanies. The Sixth Part. London: 1709. V. 48
The Poetical Works. Glasgow: 1773. V. 50
The Poetical Works. Glasgow: 1785. V. 47; 49; 53; 54
The Poetical Works. London: 1821. V. 47; 51
The Poetical Works. London: 1831. V. 48; 52
The Poetical Works. London: 1835. V. 52
The Poetical Works. London: 1875. V. 49
The Poetical Works. London: 1891. V. 48
Pope's Own Miscellany... London: 1935. V. 47; 50; 54
Pope's Poetical Works. Princeton: 1828. V. 52
Prose Works. Oxford: 1936-86. V. 53
The Rape of the Lock. London: 1714. V. 47; 48; 49; 52; 53
The Rape of the Lock. London: 1714/15. V. 49
The Rape of the Lock. Preston: 1790. V. 48
The Rape of the Lock. London: 1798. V. 49; 51; 53
The Rape of the Lock. London: 1896. V. 47; 50
The Rape of the Lock. London: 1897. V. 47
The Rape of the Lock. New Rochelle: 1902. V. 53
The Rape of the Lock. London: 1925. V. 51
Several Copies of Verses on Occasion of Mr. Gulliver's Travels. London: 1727. V. 47
The Sixth Epistle of the First Book of Horace Imitated. London: 1737. V. 54
Sober Advice from Horace, to the Young Gentlemen About Town. London: 1734. V. 48
Sober Advice from Horace, to the Young Gentlemen About Town. London: 1735. V. 53
The Temple of Fame: a Vision. London: 1715. V. 47
The Works. London. V. 51
The Works. London: 1717. V. 49; 52
The Works. London: 1717-35. V. 47
The Works... London: 1717/35/37/41. V. 47
The Works. London: 1735. V. 49
The Works. London: 1737/41. V. 51
The Works. London: 1739. V. 48
The Works. London: 1751. V. 49; 52; 53; 54
The Works. London: 1764. V. 53; 54
The Works... London: 1766. V. 50; 51; 52
The Works. Edinburgh: 1767. V. 52
The Works. Edinburgh: 1776. V. 50
The Works... London: 1778. V. 53
The Works. London: 1822. V. 47; 51
The Works. London: 1824. V. 47; 51
Works. London: 1835. V. 48; 51
The Works. London: 1847. V. 49; 50; 51; 54
Works. London: 1871-86. V. 49

POPE, ARTHUR

Reproductions of Some of the Most Important Paintings and of Their Details Illustrating the Technique of the Artists. Boston: 1936. V. 54

POPE, C. H.

The Reptiles of China. New York: 1935. V. 51

POPE, CLARENCE

An Oil Scout in the Permian Basin. 1924-1960. El Paso: 1972. V. 48

POPE, FRANKLIN LEONARD

Evolution of the Electric Incandescent Lamp. Elizabeth: 1889. V. 49
Evolution of the Electric Incandescent Lamp. Elizabeth: 1894. V. 49; 53

POPE, HILL

The Sherlock Holmes Hoax. Athens: 1952. V. 50

POPE, JESSIE

Babes and Beasts. London: 1912. V. 48
The Cat Scouts. London: 1912. V. 48
The Terrible Land of "Don't". London. V. 51
War Poems. London: 1915. V. 48

POPE, JOHN

Brief Statement of the Case of Fitz John Porter. 1864. V. 51
Report of the Secretary of War, Communicating the Report of an Exploration of the Territory of Minnesota, by Brevet Captain Pope. Washington: 1850. V. 48
Roster of Troops Serving in the Department of the Missouri...Headquarters - Fort Leavenworth, Kansas. Fort Leavenworth: 1875. V. 50

POPE, JOHN ALEXANDER

Chinese Porcelains from the Ardebil Shrine. Washington: 1956. V. 48; 52
The Freer Chinese Bronzes. Washington: 1967-69. V. 49

POPE, SIMEON

Interesting Suggestions to Proprietors and Trustees of Estates, Respecting the Land-Tax Sale and Redemption Act. London: 1798. V. 48

POPE, THOMAS

A Treatise on Bridge Architecture; in Which the Superior Advantages of the Flying pedent Lever Bridge are Fully Proved. New York: 1811. V. 47; 48; 50; 51; 53; 54

POPE, WALTER

Canticum Catholicum, Sive Invitatio ad Religionem Romanum. London: 1675. V. 47
The Catholick Ballad: or an Invitation to Popery... London: 1678. V. 47
The Wish. London: 1710. V. 51; 54

POPE-HENNESSY, JOHN

Catalogue of Italian Sculpture in the Victoria and Albert Museum. London: 1964. V. 50; 52; 54
Catalogue of Renaissance Bronzes from the Samuel H. Kress Collection. London: 1965. V. 54
Cellini. New York: 1985. V. 53
The Complete Work of Paolo Uccello... London: 1950. V. 50
Drawings of Domenichino. London: 1948. V. 52; 54
Fra Angelico. Ithica: 1974. V. 51
Italian High Renaissance and Baroque Sculpture. London: 1963. V. 47; 49; 51; 53; 54
Italian Renaissance Sculpture. London: 1958. V. 50
Paolo Uccello. London: 1969. V. 50
Renaissance Bronzes from the Samuel H. Kress Collection. London: 1965. V. 49

POPE-HENNESSY, UNA

Charles Dickens 1812-1870. London: 1945. V. 54
Early Chinese Jades. London: 1923. V. 49; 51; 52

POPHAM, A. E.

Correggio's Drawings. London: 1957. V. 50; 54
Italian Drawings in the Department of Prints and Drawings in the British Museum. London: 1950. V. 53; 54
Italian Drawings in the Department of Prints and Drawings in the British Museum. London: 1967. V. 53
Italian Drawings on the XV and XVI Centuries. London: 1949. V. 52; 54

POPHAM, HOME

Telegraphic Signals; or Marine Vocabulary: with Observations on Signal Flags and the Best Mode of Employing Them. London: 1812. V. 49

POPHAM, M. R.

Lefkandi I: The Iron Age. The Settlement the Dememteries. London: 1980-79. V. 52

POPP, J.

Bruno Paul. Munchen: 1920's. V. 51; 53

POPPER, HANS

Liver: Structure and Function. New York: 1957. V. 54

POPPER, R.

Agam. New York: 1983. V. 51

POPPING, J. F.

Orbis Illustratus seu Nova Historico-Politico-Geographica, Imperiorum Rerumque Publicarum per Totum Terrarum Orbem, Descriptio. Razeburg: 1668. V. 54

POPPLE, WILLIAM

A Rational Catechism. London: 1687. V. 47
A Rational Catechism... London: 1712. V. 52

POPULAR Encyclopaedia, or Conversations Lexicon. A General Dictionary of Arts, Sciences, Literature, Biography, History and Politics. London: 1890-93. V. 52

POPULAR History of the United States from the First Discovery of the Western Hemisphere by the Northmen, to the End of the Civil War... New York: 1881. V. 47

POPULAR Pastimes. London: 1816. V. 51

A POPULAR View of the Effects of the Venereal Disease Upon the Constitution Collected from the Best Writers. Edinburgh: 1794. V. 49; 50; 51; 54

POR, F. D.

The Legacy of Tethys. Dordrecht: 1989. V. 50

PORADA, EDITH

Corpus of Ancient Near Eastern Seals in North American Collections: the Collection of the Pierpont Morgan Library. Washington: 1948. V. 49

PORCACCHI, TOMMASO

Funerali Antichi di Diversi Popoli, et Nationi... Venice: 1591. V. 49; 51

PORCHER, JEAN

French Miniatures From Illuminated Manuscripts. London: 1960. V. 48
Medieval French Miniatures. New York: 1959. V. 47

PORCIA, ANTONIO

Voices. Consigny: 1978. V. 50

PORDAGE, SAMUEL

The Siege of Babylon. London: 1678. V. 53

PORDEN, WILLIAM
The Exhibition, or a Second Anticipation... London: 1779. V. 50

PORGES, I.
Edgar Rice Burroughs - the Man Who Created Tarzan. 1975. V. 51

PORNY, MARK ANTHONY
The Elements of Heraldry... London: 1765. V. 48; 53
The Elements of Heraldry... London: 1771. V. 47

PORPHYRY
Porphyrii de Non Necandis ad Epulandium Animantibus Libri IV. Florence: 1548. V. 48

PORRENO, BALTHASAR
Oraculos de Los Doce Sibilas. Cuenca: 1621. V. 50

PORSON, RICHARD
Adversaria. Notae et Emendationes in Poetas Graecos. Cambridge: 1812. V. 48
The Correspondence. 1867. V. 48
The Devil's Walk; a Poem. London: 1830. V. 48
Eloisa en Dishabille... London: 1801. V. 48; 54
Eloisa en Dishabille. London: 1822. V. 48
Letters to Mr. Archdeacon Travis, in answer to His Defence of the Three Heavenly Witnesses. London: 1790. V. 48; 52
Tracts and Miscellaneous Criticisms. London: 1815. V. 48

PORT TOWNSEND. CHAMBER OF COMMERCE
Reports On the Naval Station Site, Relations with Canada, and the North Pacific Fisheries. Port Townsend: 1889. V. 50; 52

PORTA, GIOVANNI BATTISTA DELLA
De Furtivis Literarum Notis... Naples: 1591. V. 54
De i Miracoli et Maravigliosi Effeti Dalla Natvra Prodotti. Venice: 1588. V. 50
De I Miracoli et Maravigliosi Effeti Da La Natura Prodotti: Libri Quattro. Venice: 1628. V. 50
De Occultis Literarum Notis, Seu Artis Animi Sensa Occulte Aliis Significandi... Strasbourg: 1606. V. 48
Fisionomia Naturale di Gio. Battista dall Porta... Philadelphia: 1626/27. V. 54
Historiae Brytannicae Defensio. London: 1573. V. 53
Magiae Naturalis, Sive de Miraculis Rervm Natvralivm. Antwerp: 1564. V. 47
Magiae Naturalis, Sive Libri IV. Antwerp: 1560. V. 47
Natural Magic... London: 1658. V. 48
La Physionomie Humaine... Rouen: 1655. V. 52

PORTAL, ABRAHAM
Nuptial Elegies. London: 1774. V. 48; 51
Poems. London: 1781. V. 47; 48

PORTAL, ROBERT
Letters from the Crimea 1854-55. Winchester: 1900. V. 51

PORTALIS, ROGER, BARON
Les Dessinatures d'Illustrations au dix-Huitieme Siecle. Paris: 1877. V. 47

PORTENKO, L. A.
Birds of the Chukchi Peninsula and Wrangel Island. New Delhi: 1981. V. 50

PORTEOUS, BEILBY
Death: a Poetical Essay. Cambridge: 1759. V. 49

PORTEOUS, CRICHTON
Pioneers of Fertility. London. V. 50; 54

PORTEOUS, JOHN
The Trial of Capt. John Porteous, Before the High Criminal Court, or Lords of Justiciary, in Scotland. London: 1736. V. 51

PORTER, ANNA MARIA
The Barony. London: 1830. V. 47; 49
Don Sebastian; or, the House of Braganza. London: 1809. V. 47; 52
The Knight of St. John, a Romance. London: 1818. V. 50
The Recluse of Norway. London: 1814. V. 50

PORTER, ANNE AGNES
The Triumphs of Reason: Exemplified in Seven Tales. London: 1791. V. 54

PORTER, ARTHUR KINGSLEY
Medieval Architecture its Origins and Development. London: 1919. V. 49

PORTER, BERTHA
Topographical Bibliography of Ancient Egyptian Hieroglyphic Texts, Reliefs and Paintings VI: Upper Egypt-Chief Temples... Oxford: 1970. V. 51

PORTER, BRUCE
Art in California. San Francisco: 1916. V. 50; 53
Art in California. Irvine: 1988. V. 48

PORTER, BURTON B.
One of the People. His Own Story. 1907. V. 48

PORTER, COLE
103 Lyrics of Cole Porter. V. 54
Red Hot and Blue. New York: 1936. V. 54

PORTER, DAVID
Constantinople and its Environs. New York: 1835. V. 48; 49
Journal of a Cruise Made to the Pacific Ocean...in the United States Frigate Essex, in the Years 1812, 1813, and 1814. Philadelphia: 1815. V. 53; 54
A Voyage in the South Seas, in the years 1812, 1813 and 1814. London: 1823. V. 47; 50

PORTER, DAVID D.
The Naval History of the Civil War. New York: 1886. V. 52

PORTER, EDNA
Double Blossoms: Helen Keller Anthology. New York: 1931. V. 49

PORTER, EDWIN H.
The Fall River Tragedy - a History of the Borden Murders. Fall River: 1893. V. 47; 52; 54

PORTER, ELEANOR H.
Pollyana. Boston: 1913. V. 53

PORTER, ELIOT
All Under Heaven: The Chinese World. New York: 1983. V. 49
Antarctica. New York: 1978. V. 48; 49
Appalachian Wilderness: The Great Smoky Mountains. New York: 1970. V. 47
Forever Wild: The Adirondacks. Blue Mountain Lake: 1966. V. 50
Galapagos: the Flow of Wildness. San Francisco: 1967/68. V. 52
Galapagos, the Flow of Wildness. 1968. V. 54
Galapagos, the Flow of Wildness. San Francisco: 1968. V. 47; 51; 54
In Wildness is the Preservation of the World. San Francisco: 1962. V. 54
Intimate Landscapes. New York: 1979. V. 52
The Place No One Knew. Glen Canyon on the Colorado. San Francisco: 1963. V. 48; 51
The Place No One Knew: Glen Canyon On the Colorado. Sierra Club: 1963. V. 53

PORTER, F. SCARLETT
A Family Chronicle. London: 1875. V. 51; 54

PORTER, G. R.
The Progress of the Nation, In Its Various Social and Economical Relations, from the Beginning of the Nineteenth Century. London: 1851. V. 51
The Tropical Agriculturist... London: 1833. V. 54

PORTER, GENE STRATTON
Birds of the Bible. Cincinnati: 1909. V. 52
The Fire Bird. 1922. V. 50
Freckles. New York: 1904. V. 49; 51
The Harvester. Garden City: 1912. V. 53
Homing with the Birds. Garden City: 1919. V. 54
Laddie: a True Blue Story. Garden City: 1913. V. 48; 49; 51
Michael O'Halloran. Garden City: 1915. V. 54
The Song of the Cardinal. Indianapolis: 1903. V. 51
The White Flag. Garden City: 1923. V. 52

PORTER, HENRY M.
Pencilings of an Early Western Pioneer. Denver: 1929. V. 49; 50

PORTER, HORACE
Campaigning with Grant. New York: 1897. V. 50

PORTER, J.
The Two Princes of Persia. London: 1801. V. 48

PORTER, JANE
The Pastor's Fire-Side, a Novel. London: 1817. V. 49; 50
The Scottish Chiefs. London: 1810. V. 50
The Scottish Chiefs. London: 1816. V. 47
The Scottish Chiefs. London: 1841?. V. 50
The Scottish Chiefs. London: 1921. V. 48
The Scottish Chiefs. New York: 1921. V. 49
The Scottish Chiefs. New York: 1923. V. 48
Sir Edward Seaward's Narrative of His Shipwreck, and Consequent Discovery of Certain Islands in the Caribbean Sea... London: 1831. V. 52
Sir Edward Seaward's Narrative of His Shipwreck, and Consequent Discovery of Certain Islands in the Caribbean Sea... London: 1832. V. 47; 50; 54

PORTER, JOHN
The Case Between Mr. Cant and Mr. Porter, Truly and Impartially Stated (etc.). London: 1742. V. 47
History of the Fylde of Lancashire. London: 1876. V. 48; 53

PORTER, JOHN GREY V.
Some Agricultural and Political Irish Questions Calmly Discussed. London: 1843. V. 52

PORTER, JOHN W. H.
Record of Events in Norfolk County, Virginia, from April 19th 1861 to May 10th 1862. Portsmouth: 1892. V. 49

PORTER, JONATHAN
All Under Heaven. The Chinese World. New York: 1983. V. 51

PORTER, KATHERINE ANNE
A Christmas Story. New York: 1967. V. 50; 52; 53; 54
The Collected Essays and Occasional Writings of... New York: 1970. V. 50; 53; 54
The Days Before. New York: 1952. V. 53
A Defense of Circe. New York: 1954. V. 49
Flowering Judas. New York: 1930. V. 47; 48; 49
Flowering Judas. New York: 1935. V. 47; 48; 49; 53
French Song Book. Paris: 1933. V. 48; 49; 50; 51; 52; 54
Hacienda. New York: 1934. V. 47; 48; 49; 50; 51; 53; 54
Hacienda. Paris: 1934. V. 48; 49; 50
The Leaning Tower and Other Stories. New York: 1944. V. 51; 53; 54
My Chinese Marriage. 1921. V. 50
My Chinese Marriage. New York: 1921. V. 47; 49; 51; 54
My Chinese Marriage. New York: 1922. V. 51; 54

PORTER, KATHERINE ANNE continued
Noon Wine. Detroit: 1937. V. 47; 48; 51
Pale Horse, Pale Rider. New York: 1939. V. 48; 49; 51; 53
Ship of Fools. Boston: 1962. V. 47; 49; 52; 53

PORTER, KENNETH WIGGINS
The Jacksons and the Lees: Two Generations of Massachusetts Merchants 1765-184. Cambridge: 1937. V. 48
The Jacksons and the Lees; Two Generations of Massachusetts Merchants 1765-1844. New Haven: 1937. V. 47

PORTER, LAVINIA HONEYMAN
By Ox Team to California. A Narrative Crossing the Plains in 1860. Oakland: 1910. V. 52

PORTER, MILLIE JONES
Memory Cups of Panhandle Pioneers. 1945. V. 48

PORTER, NOAH
The Human Intellect: with an Introduction Upon Psychology and the Soul. New York: 1868. V. 48

PORTER, PETER
Jonah. London: 1973. V. 51
The Lady and the Unicorn. London: 1975. V. 51

PORTER, ROBERT KER
A Narrative of the Campaign in Russia, During the Year 1812. London: 1813. V. 49; 52
A Series of Engravings, After Drawings...from the Celebrated Odes of Anacreon. London: 1805. V. 52
Travelling Sketches in Russia and Sweden, During the years 1805, 1806, 1807, 1808. London: 1809. V. 50
Travelling Sketches in Russia and Sweden During the Years 1805, 1806, 1807, 1808. London: 1813. V. 47; 48
Travels in Georgia, Persia, Armenia, Ancient Babylonia...During the Years 1817, 1818, 1819 and 1820. London: 1821. V. 54

PORTER, ROBERT P.
Report of Indians Taxed and Not Taxed in the United States... Washington: 1894. V. 54
Report of Indians Taxed and Not Taxed in the United States. Washington: 1984. V. 53

PORTER, RUFUS
Aerial Navitation: the Practicability of Traveling Pleasantly and Safely from New York to California in Three Days. San Francisco: 1935. V. 47; 50
A Choice Selection of Valuable and Curious Arts and Interesting Experiments... Concord: 1832. V. 52
A New Collection of Genuine Receipts, for the Preparation and Execution of Curious Arts and Interesting Experiments... Concord: 1831. V. 52; 53
A Select Collection of Valuable and Curious Arts and Interesting Experiments. Concord: 1826. V. 51; 52; 53

PORTER, THOMAS
The Villain, a Tragedy. London: 1670. V. 48; 53

PORTER, WILLIAM D.
State Sovereignty and the Doctrine of Coercion...Together with a Letter from Hon. J(ames) K(irke) Paulding, Former Sec. of Navy. Charleston: 1860. V. 49

PORTER, WILLIAM OGILVIE
Sir Edward Seaward's Narrative of His Shipwreck, and Conquest Discovery of Certain Islands in the Caribbean Sea... London: 1831. V. 47; 49

PORTER, WILLIAM SYDNEY
Cabbages and Kings. New York: 1904. V. 47; 48; 51; 54
The Complete Writings of O. Henry. Garden City: 1917. V. 53
The Gift of the Magi. London: 1939. V. 47
The Heart of the West. New York: 1907. V. 53
The Hiding of Black Bill. New York: 1913. V. 53; 54
Let Me Feel Your Pulse. New York: 1910. V. 54
Sixes and Sevens. Garden City: 1915. V. 49
The Stories of O. Henry. New York: 1965. V. 54
Strictly Business. New York: 1910. V. 48; 50
The Voice of the City. New York: 1908. V. 50; 51
The Voice of the City. New York: 1935. V. 48; 50; 51; 52; 53; 54
Waifs and Strays. Garden City: 1917. V. 47; 48; 51

PORTER, WILLIAM WARREN
Engravings from Drawings of the Late Rev. William Warren Porter, fellow of St. John's College, Oxford. London: 1806. V. 52; 53

PORTEUS, STANLEY
The Psychology of a Primitive People. London: 1931. V. 52

THE PORTFOLIO Artistic Monographs: Containing Richmond on the Thames; Royal English Bookbindings; Greek Bronzes. London: 1896-98. V. 54

A PORTFOLIO Honoring Harold Hugo for His Contribution to Scholarly Printing. 1978. V. 50

A PORTFOLIO of Estates: Sunset Islands, Miami Beach. Miami Beach. V. 53

THE PORTFOLIO of Fine Comic Art. 1978. V. 47; 50; 51

A PORTFOLIO of Proof Impressions selected from Scribner's Monthly and St. Nicholas. New York: 1879. V. 50

PORTFOLIO: The Annual of the Graphic Arts. 1950-51. V. 50

PORTHER, LUTHER H.
Wheels and Wheeling. Boston: 1892. V. 47

PORTINARO, PIERLUIGI
The Cartography of North America, 1500-1800. New York: 1987. V. 54

PORTIS, CHARLES
Norwood. New York: 1966. V. 49; 52
True Grit, a Novel. 1968. V. 50

THE PORTLAND Directory... Portland: 1834. V. 50

PORTLAND, DUKE OF
The Red Deer of Langwell and Braemore. 1935. V. 54

PORTLOCK, J. E.
Report on the Geology of the County of Londonderry and of Parts of Tyrone and Fermanagh. Dublin: 1843. V. 47; 48; 50; 53; 54

PORTLOCK, NATHANIEL
An Abridgement of Portlock and Dixon's Voyage Round the World. London: 1789. V. 47
A Voyage Round the World, but More Particularly to the North-West Coast of America, Performed in 1785, 1786, 1787, 1788 in the King George and Queen Charlotte, Captains Portlock and Dixon. London: 1789. V. 47; 49; 50; 51; 52
A Voyage Round the World; but More Particularly to the North-West Coast of America; Performed in 1785, 1786, 1787 and 1788 in King George and Queen Charlotte, Captains Portlock and Dixon. Amsterdam: 1968. V. 48; 50; 54

PORTOGHESI, PAOLO
The Rome of Borromini: Architecture as Language. New York: 1968. V. 47

PORTRAIT and Biographical Record of Denver and Vicinity Colorado. Chicago: 1898. V. 49

PORTRAIT and Biographical Record of Hunterdon and Warren Counties, New Jersey. New York: 1898. V. 49

PORTRAIT and Biographical Record of the State of Colorado. Chicago: 1899. V. 49

PORTRAIT of a Publisher, 1915-1965. New York: 1965. V. 48

A PORTRAIT OF Masonry and Antimasonry, as Drawn by Richard Rush, John Quincy Adams, Wiliam Wirt, &c. Providence: 1832. V. 50

PORTRAITS and Characters of the Kings of England from William the Conqueror to George the Third. Part 2. London: 1830. V. 49

PORTRAITS Illustrative of the Novels, Tales and Romances of the Author of "Waverley". London. V. 54

PORTRAITS of Curious Characters in London, With Descriptive and Entertaining Anecdotes. London: 1809. V. 51

PORTRAITS of Eminent Conservatives and Statesmen With Genealogical and Historical Memoirs. First (and Second) Series. London: 1836-46. V. 49

PORTRAITS of William Harvey. London, New York, Toronto: 1913. V. 49; 52

PORTRAITS to Illustrate the Novels, Tales and Romances of the Author of Waverley. London: 1824. V. 53

PORTRAITURE of K. Charles I. Illuminated, With Several of His Memorable Actions Very Proper to Be Read on the 30th of January, Before Sermon. London: 1700. V. 53

PORTSMOUTH RELIEF ASSOCIATION
Report of the Portsmouth Relief Association to the Contributors of the Fund for the Relief of Portsmouth, Virginia, During the Prevalence of the Yellow Fever in that Town in 1855... Richmond: 1856. V. 48

PORTUGAL: Being Some Account of Lisbon and its Environs, and Of a Tour in the Alemtejo, from a Journal Kept by a Lady During Three Years' Actual Residence. London: 1830. V. 50

PORTUGAL. TREATIES, ETC.
Tratado de Commercio, e Navegacado Entre...O Principe Regente de Portugal, e El Rey do Reino Unido da Grande Bretanha e Irlanda, Assinado no Rio de Janeiro...19 de Feveiro de 1810. Bahia: 1811. V. 48

PORTUS, AEMYLIUS
Dictionarium Doricum Graecolatinum, Quod Totius Theocriti, Moschi Syracusani, Bionis, Smyrnaie & Simmiae Rhodii... Frankfurt: 1603. V. 52

PORZIO, SIOME
Se l'Huomo Diventa Buono o Cattivo Volontariamente... 1551. V. 47

POSADA, JOSE GUADALUPE
100 Original Woodcuts by Posada. Mexico/Colorado Springs: 1947. V. 50
Monografia: Las Obras... Mexico City: 1930. V. 53; 54

POSEY, ALEXANDER
Alex Posey, the Creek Indian Poet, the Poems of Alexander Lawrence Posey. Topeka: 1910. V. 49
The Poems of Alexander Lawrence Posey. Topeka: 1910. V. 50

POSEY, WILLIAM
The Wills Hospital of Philadelphia. Philadelphia: 1931. V. 50; 52

POSITIVE Medical Agents: Being a Treatise on the New Alkaloid, Resinoid and Concentrated Preparations of Indigenous and Foreign Medical Plants. New York: 1855. V. 49; 54

POSNER, DAVID
A Rake's Progress; a Poem in Five Sections. 1967. V. 52
A Rake's Progress, a Poem in Five Sections. London: 1967. V. 50

POSNER, DONALD
Annibale Carracci: a Study in the Reform of Italian Painting Around 1590. New York: 1971. V. 49

POSSELIUS, JOHANNES
Familiarium Colloquiorum Libellus Graece & Latine, Auctus & Recognitum. Londini: 1642. V. 50

POSSEVINO, ANTONIO
Moscovia, et, Alia Opera, De Statv Hvivs Secvli, Aduersus Catholicae Ecclesiae Hostes. Cologne: 1587. V. 48

POSSINO, GASPARE
I Celebri Freschi di Gaspare Possino Nell Chiesa Du S. Martino A'Mont in Roma. Roma: 1810. V. 50

POST, AUSTIN
Glacier Ice. Toronto: 1971. V. 52

THE POST Chaise Companion: or Traveller's Directory through Ireland... Dublin: 1810?. V. 51

POST, CHANDLER RATHFON
A History of Spanish Painting. Cambridge: 1930-38. V. 54

POST, CHARLES C.
Ten Years a Cowboy. Chicago: 1889. V. 51

POST, ISAAC
Voices from the Spirit World, Being Communications from Many Spirits. Rochester: 1852. V. 50

THE POST OFFICE Directory for 1814. London: 1814. V. 50

POST Office Directory for 1829. London: 1829. V. 52

THE POST Office London Directory for 1823. London: 1823. V. 52

POST, PIERRE
Les Ouvrages d'Architecture. Leide: 1715. V. 48; 49

POSTAN, ALEXANDER
The Complete Graphic Work of Paul Nash. London: 1973. V. 48

POSTANS, MARIANNE
Cutch; or, Random Sketches, Taken During a Residence in One of the Northern Provinces of Western Indian. London: 1839. V. 50

POSTE, BEALE
The History of the College of All Stains, Maidstone. Maidstone: 1847. V. 53

POSTELLO, GULIELMO
Cosmographicae... Basel: 1561. V. 52
De Magistratibus Atheniensium Liber, ad Intelligendam Non Solum Graecorum. Basileae: 1551. V. 53
De Orbis Terrae Concordia Libri Quatuor. Basle: 1544. V. 49

POSTERITAS, PSEUD.
The Siege of London. London: 1885. V. 47

POSTL, KARL
Life in the New World; or Sketches of American Society. New York: 1844. V. 47; 51

POSTLEHWAYT, JAMES
The History of the Public Revenue, from the Revolution in 1688 to Christmas 1758. London: 1759. V. 52

POSTLETHWAITE, JOHN
The Geology of the English Lake District... Keswick: 1897. V. 50; 52
The Geology of the English Lake District with Notes on Minerals. Carlisle: 1906. V. 54
Mines and Mining in the English Lake District. Leeds: 1889. V. 54
Mines and Mining in the (English) Lake District. Whitehaven: 1913. V. 54

POSTLETHWAYT, MALACHY
Britain's Commercial Interest Explained and Improved. London: 1757. V. 47; 49; 51

POSTON, CHARLES D.
Apache Land. San Francisco: 1878. V. 49
The Parsees. V. 48; 50; 52
Speech of Hon. Charles D. Poston, of Arizona on Indian Affairs. New York: 1864. V. 49
Speech of Hon. Charles D. Poston, of Arizona, on Indian Affairs. New York: 1865. V. 47; 52

POSTSCRIPTS On Dwiggins. New York: 1960. V. 47; 50

POTAMIAN, BROTHER
Makers of Electricity. New York: 1909. V. 50

POTE, JOSEPH
The History and Antiquities of Windsor Casatle, and the Royal College and Chapel of St. George... 1749. V. 51
The History and Antiquities of Windsor Castle, and the Royal College and Chapel of St. George... Eton: 1749. V. 53

POTE, WILLIAM
The Journal of Captain William Pote, Jr., During His Captivity in the French and Indian War from May 1745-Aug. 1757. New York: 1896. V. 53

POTOCKI, COUNT
Dogs' Eggs: a Study In Powsology. France: 1968-75. V. 53

POTOCKI, JAN
The Saragossa Manuscript. London: 1962. V. 53

POTOCKI, JOSEPH
Sport in Somoliland. 1988. V. 54

POTOK, CHAIM
Tho Chosen. New York: 1967. V. 51
The Chosen. New York: 1992. V. 52

POTT, PERCIVALL
An Account of a Particular Kind of Rupture, Frequently Attendant Upon New Born Children, and Sometimes in Adults. London: 1765. V. 47
The Chirurgical Works. London: 1775. V. 51; 52
Further Remarks on the Useless State of the Lower Limbs in Consequence of a Curvature of the Spine... London: 1782. V. 53
Observations on that Disorder of the Corner of the Eye, Commonly Called Fistual Lachrymalis. London: 1769. V. 47; 48; 49; 50; 51
Observations on the Nature and Consequences of Those Injuries to Which the Head is Liable from the External Violence. London: 1771. V. 51; 54
Remarks on the Disease, Commonly Called a Fistula in Ano. London: 1767. V. 47
Some Few General Remarks on Fractures and Disclocations. London: 1769. V. 51; 52; 53; 54
A Treatise on Ruptures. London: 1763. V. 47

POTTER, AMBROSE GEORGE
A Bibliography of the Rubaiyat of Omar Khayyam. London: 1929. V. 47; 48; 52

POTTER, BEATRIX
Appley Dapply's Nursery Rhymes. London: 1917. V. 47; 49; 51; 54
Cecily Parlsey's Nursery Rhymes.. London: 1922. V. 48; 54
The Fairy Caravan. Philadelphia: 1929. V. 49
The Fairy Caravan. London: 1952. V. 47
Ginger and Pickles. London: 1909. V. 51
Peter Rabbit's Almanac for 1929. New York: 1928. V. 49
The Pie and the Patty-Pan. London. V. 48
The Roly-Poly Pudding. London: 1908. V. 47
The Roly-Poly Pudding. London: 1926. V. 50
The Songs of Peter Rabbit. London: 1951. V. 47
The Story of Miss Moppet. New York: 1906. V. 52
The Story of Miss Moppet. London: 1916. V. 49
The Tailor of Gloucester. London: 1803. V. 52
The Tailor of Gloucester. London: 1902. V. 50; 51; 54
The Tailor of Gloucester. London: 1903. V. 47; 48; 49; 50; 51
The Tailor of Gloucester. London & New York: 1933. V. 53
The Tale of Benjamin Bunny. London: 1904. V. 48; 49; 52
The Tale of Jemima Puddle-Duck. London: 1908. V. 47; 48; 49; 51; 52
The Tale of Jemima Puddle-Duck. London: 1920's. V. 49
The Tale of Johnny Town-Mouse. London: 1918. V. 51; 53
The Tale of Johnny Town-Mouse. London: 1919. V. 48; 52
The Tale of Little Pig Robinson. London: 1930. V. 51; 52; 54
The Tale of Mr. Jeremy Fisher. London: 1906. V. 48; 51; 52; 53
The Tale of Mr. Tod. London: 1912. V. 47; 48; 49; 51; 52; 53; 54
The Tale of Mrs. Tiggy-Winkle. London: 1905. V. 48; 51; 52
The Tale of Mrs. Tittlemouse. London: 1910. V. 47; 48; 50; 51; 52; 53
The Tale of Mrs. Tittlemouse. New York: 1910. V. 48
The Tale of Mrs. Tittlemouse. 1979. V. 49
The Tale of Peter Rabbit. London: 1901. V. 47
The Tale of Peter Rabbit. London: 1902. V. 48; 49; 54
The Tale of Peter Rabbit. Philadelphia: 1904. V. 52
Tho Tale of Peter Rabbit. New York: 1916. V. 48
The Tale of Peter Rabbit. Cleveland: 1931. V. 50
The Tale of Peter Rabbit. London: 1993. V. 48; 50
The Tale of Peter Rabbit. Kingston: 1995. V. 54
The Tale of Pigling Bland. London: 1913. V. 48; 49; 49; 50; 51; 52; 53; 54
The Tale of Samuel Whiskers. London: 1962. V. 54
The Tale of Squirrel Nutkin. London: 1903. V. 47; 48
The Tale of the Faithful Dove. New York: 1956. V. 53
The Tale of the Flopsy Bunnies. London: 1909. V. 52; 53
The Tale of the Flopsy Bunnies. New York: 1909. V. 48
The Tale of Timmy Tiptoes. London: 1911. V. 47; 48; 49; 50; 52; 53
The Tale of Timmy Tiptoes. New York: 1911. V. 48
The Tale of Tom Kitten. London: 1907. V. 48; 51; 53
The Tale of Two Bad Mice. London: 1904. V. 48; 50; 52; 53
Wag-by-Wall. London: 1944. V. 48

THE POTTER Country Club: a Feature of the Potter Hotel. Santa Barbara: 1901-20. V. 54

POTTER, ELIZA
A Hairdresser's Experience in High Life. Cincinnati: 1859. V. 48

POTTER, FRANCIS
An Interpretation of the Number 666. Oxford: 1642. V. 52; 54

POTTER, G. W. J.
A History of the Whitby and Pickering Railway. London: 1906. V. 51

POTTER, ISRAEL R.
Life and Remarkable Adventures of Israel R. Potter. Providence: 1824. V. 52

POTTER, JACK
Cattle Trails of the Old West. 1939. V. 54

POTTER, JACK M.
Land Steer and other Tales. Clayton: 1939. V. 48

POTTER, JOHN
Archaeologia Graeca; or, The Antiquities of Greece. London: 1722. V. 47
Archaeologia Graeca; or the Antiquities of Greece. London: 1728. V. 54
Archaeologia Graeca; or the Antiquities of Greece. London: 1740. V. 49
Archaeologia Graeca, or the Antiquities of Greece. Edinburgh: 1820. V. 54

POTTER, MARY
Poetry of Nature, Comprising, a Selection of the Most Sublime and Beautiful Apostrophes, Histories, Songs, Elegies, &c... Londini: 1789. V. 48

POTTER, NATHANIEL
A Memoir on Contagion, More Especially As It Respects the Yellow Fever. Baltimore: 1818. V. 51

POTTER, O. M.
The Colour of Rome: Historic, Personal and Local. London: 1914. V. 49

POTTER, ROBERT
Observations on the Poor Laws, on the Present State of the Poor and on Houses of Industry. London: 1775. V. 48

POTTER, SIDNEY PELL
A History of Wymeswold (Leicestershire). London: 1915. V. 52

POTTER, STEPHEN
The Glittering Coffin. London: 1960. V. 48
Pedigree: Words From Nature, Essays on the Etymology of Words From Nature. London: 1973. V. 48; 49

POTTER, T. R.
The History and Antiquities of Charnwood Forest. London: 1842. V. 47
The History and Antiquities of Charnwood Forest. Nottingham: 1842. V. 50

POTTER, THEODORE E.
The Autobiography of... Concord: 1913. V. 47; 49

POTTER, THOMAS
Concrete: Its Use in Building and the Construction of Concrete Walls, Floors, etc. London: 1894. V. 53

POTTER, THOMAS J.
Legends, Lyrics and Hymns. Dublin: 1862. V. 53

POTTER, W. R., MRS.
History of Montague County. Austin: 1912. V. 53

POTTER, WOODBURNE
The War in Florida: Being an Exposition of Its Causes, and an Accurate History of the Campaigns of Generals Clinch, Gaines and Scott... Baltimore: 1836. V. 48

POTTERY
Making at Poole. East Quay, Poole, Dorset: 1925. V. 49

POTTINGER, DAVID T.
The French Book Trade in the Ancient Regime 1500-1791. Cambridge: 1958. V. 52

POTTLE, FREDERICK A.
Boswell and the Girl from Botany Bay. New York: 1937. V. 54
Shelley and Browning - A Myth and Some Facts. Chicago: 1923. V. 53
Stretchers - the Story of a Hospital Unit on the Western Front. New Haven: 1929. V. 49

POTTS, NATHAN R.
Catalogue of the Valuable Law Library of the Late Nathan R. Potts, Esq. to be sold by order of executrix on Tuesday Afternoon April 8, 1862 at the Auction Rooms 139 and 141 S. Fourth St. Upstairs... Philadelphia: 1862. V. 51

POTTS, T.
The British Farmer's Cyclopaedia... London: 1809. V. 54

POTTS, T. H.
Out in the Open: a Budget of Scraps of Natural History Gathered in New Zealand. Christchurch: 1882. V. 49

POTTS, THOMAS
Potts's Discovery of Witches in the County of Lancester. Manchester: 1845. V. 47

POUCHER, W. A.
A Camera in the Cairngorms. London: 1947. V. 52
The Magic of Skye. London: 1949. V. 52; 54
Perfumes, Cosmetics and Soaps. New York: 1936-36-36. V. 47; 48; 51

POUCHET, F. A.
The Universe, or the Infinitely Great and Infinitely Little. Shanghai: 1904. V. 51; 54

POUCHOT, M. PIERRE
Memoir Upon the Late War in North America Between the French and English 1755-60. Roxburgy: 1866. V. 48

POUHAULT, PIERRE SIMON
Traite des Pleyes de Tete. Turin: 1720. V. 53

POULET, W.
The Arts and Spectacles Over Five Centuries. London: 1980. V. 49

POULSEN, FREDERIK
Delphi. London: 1920. V. 50
Greek and Roman Portraits in English Country Houses. Oxford: 1923. V. 50; 52

POULSON, GEORGE
The History and Antiquities of the Seignory of Holderness, in the East-Riding of the County of York, Including the Abbeys of meaux and Swine, with Priories of Nunkeeling and Burstall... Hull: 1840. V. 47; 49

POULTNEY, EVAN
An Appeal to the Creditors of the Bank of Maryland and the Public Generally. Baltimore: 1835. V. 47

POUNCY, JOHN
Dorsetshire Photographically Illustrated. London: 1857. V. 51

POUND, EZRA LOOMIS
ABC of Economics. London: 1933. V. 53
ABC of Reading. London: 1934. V. 48; 49; 52; 53
ABC of Reading. New Haven: 1934. V. 48
Active Anthology. 1933. V. 49
Alfred Venison's Poems. London: 1935. V. 50
Antheil & the Treatise on Harmony with Supplement Notes by Ezra Pound. Chicago: 1927. V. 49
An Autobiographical Outline Written for Louis Untermeyer. New York: 1980. V. 47
Canto CX. Cambridge: 1965. V. 49
Canto CX. Paris: 1967. V. 48; 51
The Cantos. New York: 1948. V. 54
The Cantos. London: 1954. V. 52
The Cantos. London: 1968. V. 54
Cantos 110-16. New York: 1967. V. 47; 48
Cantos LII-LXXI. London: 1940. V. 48; 53
Canzoni of Ezra Pound. London: 1911. V. 48; 53
Cathay. 1915. V. 49
Cathay. London: 1915. V. 48; 54
Cathay. Poems After Lio Po. New York: 1992. V. 49
Cavalacanti Poems. London: 1966. V. 47; 50
Confucian Analects. New York: 1951. V. 51
Confucio Studio Integrale. 1942. V. 47
Diptych Rome-London Homage to Sextus Propertius & Hugh Selwyn Mauberley Contacts and Life. London: 1957. V. 50; 51
A Draft of XXX Cantos. Paris: 1930. V. 49; 53
A Draft of XXX Cantos. 1933. V. 49
A Draft of XXX Cantos. New York: 1933. V. 51
A Draft of XXX Cantos. London: 1993. V. 49
Drafts and Fragments of Cantos CX-CXVII. 1968. V. 47
Drafts and Fragments of Cantos CX-CXVII. New York & Iowa City: 1968. V. 48; 49; 50; 53; 54
Drafts and Fragments of Cantos CX-CXVII. London: 1969. V. 48; 53
Eleven New Cantos XXXI to XLI. New York: 1934. V. 51; 54
Etre Ditoyan Romain Etait un Privilege Etre Citoyen Moderne est une Calamite. Liege: 1965. V. 47
The Exile. Dijon & Chicago: 1927-28. V. 52
Exultations. London: 1909. V. 48
The Fifth Decade of Cantos. London: 1937. V. 47; 48; 51
Forked Branches. Iowa City: 1985. V. 48; 50; 52; 54
Gaudier-Brzeska. London & New York: 1916. V. 47; 53; 54
Homage to Sextus Propertius. London: 1934. V. 47; 48; 49; 54
How to Read. London: 1931. V. 53
Hugh Selwyn Mauberley. London: 1920. V. 47; 49
Hugh Selwyn Mauberly by E.P. London: 1969. V. 53
Imaginary Letters. Paris: 1930. V. 52; 53
An Immortality. 1980. V. 47
Indiscretions; or, Une Revue De Deux Mondes. Paris: 1923. V. 47; 48; 49
Jefferson and/Or Mussolini. New York: 1936. V. 47
The Letters of Ezra Pound 1907-1941. London: 1941. V. 52
The Letters of Ezra Pound 1907-1941. New York: 1950. V. 53
Literary Essays. London: 1954. V. 51; 52
The Literary Essays. Norfolk: 1954. V. 48
Lumina. London: 1970. V. 47
Lustra. London: 1916. V. 48; 51
Lustra. New York: 1917. V. 51; 52; 54
Make It New. London: 1934. V. 53
Passages from the Letters of John Butler Yeats. Churchtown, Dundrum: 1917. V. 52
Pavannes and Divisions. New York: 1918. V. 54
Personae. 1909. V. 49
Personae. London: 1909. V. 54
Personae. New York: 1926. V. 47; 48; 49; 52; 53
The Pisan Cantos. New York: 1948. V. 48
The Pisan Cantos. London: 1949. V. 51
Poems 1918-1921. New York: 1921. V. 52; 53; 54
Provenca. Boston: 1910. V. 50; 51; 52; 53; 54
Quia Pauper Amavi. London: 1919. V. 47; 48; 50; 53
Redondillas, or Something of that Sort. San Francisco: 1967. V. 51
Rene Crevel. Paris: 1992. V. 51
Rene Crevel. Paris: 1992/93. V. 48
Ripostes. London: 1912. V. 48
Ripostes, Whereto are Appended the Complete Poetical Works of T.E. Hulme. London: 1915. V. 47; 53; 54
Section: Rock-Drill 85-95 de los Cantares. 1956. V. 49; 54
Selected Poems. London: 1928. V. 47
Social Credit. London: 1935. V. 50; 53

POUND, EZRA LOOMIS continued
Sonnets and Ballate of Guido Cavalcante. London: 1912. V. 53
Sophokles Women of Trachis. London: 1956. V. 48
The Spirit of Romance. London: 1910. V. 47; 50; 54
The Spirit of Romance. Norfolk: 1952. V. 48; 51
The Spirit of Romance. New York: 1953. V. 51
The Spirit of Romance. Norfolk: 1953. V. 48
Ta Hio. The Great Learning. Seattle: 1928. V. 49
Ta Hio: The Great Learning. London: 1936. V. 48; 50
Thirty-Three Sonnets of Guido Cavalcanti. San Francisco: 1991. V. 47
Thrones - 96 109 de Los Cantares. London: 1960. V. 54
Translations by Ezra Pound. London: 1915. V. 52
The Translations of Ezra Pound. London: 1953. V. 49
Umbra - The Early Poems of Ezra Pound... London: 1920. V. 50; 53

POUND, OMAR
Arabic and Persian Poems. London: 1970. V. 54

POUND, ROSCOE
An Introduction to the Philosophy of Law. New Haven: 1922. V. 52

POUQUEVILLE, F. C. H. L.
Travels through the Morea, Albania and Several Other Parts of the Ottoman Empire, to Constantinople. During the Years 1798, 1799, 1800 and 1801. London: 1806. V. 48; 50

POWEL, ROBERT HARE
Mr. Powel's Remarks on the Termination of the Pennsylvania Rail-Way. Philadelphia?: 1829. V. 53

POWELL, AARON MACY
Personal Reminiscences of the Anti-Slavery and other Reforms and Reformers. New York: 1899. V. 50
State Regulation of Vice. New York: 1878. V. 50

POWELL, ACE
Tales of Glacier Park. Kalispell: 1967. V. 54

POWELL, ANTHONY DYMOKE
The Acceptance World - a Novel. London: 1955. V. 49; 51
Afternoon Men. London: 1931. V. 50
Afternoon Men. New York: 1932. V. 54
Agents and Patients. London: 1936. V. 49
At Lady Molly's. London: 1937. V. 49
At Lady Molly's. Boston: 1957. V. 49; 53
At Lady Molly's. London: 1957. V. 48; 51; 53
Autobiography. London: 1976-82. V. 47
Books Do Furnish a Room. London: 1971. V. 49; 51
A Buyer's Market. London: 1952. V. 48
A Buyer's Market. New York: 1953. V. 49; 53
Casanova's Chinese Reataurant. London: 1960. V. 47; 48; 49; 49; 50; 53
A Dance to the Music of Time. London: 1951-75. V. 47; 49; 52
The Fisher King. London: 1986. V. 53; 54
Hearing Secret Harmonies. London: 1975. V. 48; 53; 54
John Aubrey and His Friends. London: 1948. V. 50; 52
The Kindly Ones. London: 1962. V. 48; 49; 50; 51; 54
The Military Philosophers. London: 1968. V. 51; 54
Mr. Zouch: Superman: From a View to a Death. New York: 1934. V. 50; 51; 53
O, How the Wheel Becomes It!. London: 1983. V. 53; 54
A Question of Upbringing. New York: 1951. V. 52; 53; 54
A Reference for Mellors. London: 1966. V. 51
A Reference for Mellors. London: 1994. V. 52; 53; 54
The Soldier's Art. London: 1966. V. 49; 51
To Keep the Ball Rolling. Memoirs. London: 1976-82. V. 48; 49; 50; 51; 54
The Valley of Bones. London: 1964. V. 50; 51; 53

POWELL, CHARLES
Bound Feet. Boston: 1938. V. 52

POWELL, CUTHBERT
Twenty Years of Kansas City's Live Stock Trade and Traders. Kansas City: 1893. V. 47

POWELL, E. ALEXANDER
Slanting Lines of Steel. New York: 1933. V. 49

POWELL, FRED WILBUR
Hall Jackson Kelley, Prophet of Oregon. Portland: 1917. V. 53

POWELL, GEORGE
Alphonso King of Naples, a Tragedy. London: 1691. V. 48; 53

POWELL, H. M. T.
The Santa Fe Trail to California, 1849-1852. San Francisco: 1931. V. 47; 48; 49
The Santa Fe Trail to California 1849-1852. New York: 1981. V. 47; 48; 50

POWELL, J. W. DAMER
Bristol Privateers and Ships of War. Bristol: 1930. V. 48; 49

POWELL, JOHN J.
The Golden State and Its Resources. San Francisco: 1874. V. 54
Nevada: The Land of Silver. San Francisco: 1876. V. 52

POWELL, JOHN WESLEY
Down the Colorado. New York: 1969. V. 48; 53
The Exploration of the Colorado River and the High Plateaus of Utah in 1871-72. Salt Lake City: 1948-49. V. 48
Exploration of the Colorado River of the West and its Tributaries Explored in 1869, 1870, 1871 and 1872 Under the Direction of the Secretary of the Smithsonian Institution. Washington: 1872. V. 51
Exploration of the Colorado River of the West and Its Tributaries. Explored in 1869, 1870, 1871 and 1872, Under the Directions of the Secretary of the Smithsonian Institution. Washington: 1875. V. 47; 48
Introduction to the Study of Indian Languages. Washington: 1800. V. 48
Introduction to the Study of Indian Languages. Washington: 1880. V. 52
Report of the Lands of the Arid Regions of the United States, with a More Detailed Account of the Lands of Utah. Washington: 1879. V. 47; 51

POWELL, LAWRENCE CLARK
Book Shops by L.C.P. Los Angeles: 1965. V. 51
California Classics, The Creative Literature of the Golden State. Los Angeles: 1971. V. 53
Eucalyptus Fair: a Memoir in the Form of a Novel. 1992. V. 50; 51
From the Heartland: Profiles of People and Places of the Southwest and Beyond. Flagstaff: 1976. V. 47
Heart of the Southwest: a Selective Bibliography of Novels, Stories and Tales Laid in Arizona and New Mexico and Adjacent Lands. Los Angeles: 1955. V. 50; 54
Land of Fact, a Companion to Land of Fiction.. Los Angeles: 1992. V. 50; 54
Madeleine. Pasadena: 1990. V. 47; 51
Musical Blood Brothers: Wolfgang Amadeus Mozart, Franz Josef, Haydn. Malibu: 1966. V. 52
Mysterious Transformation; or When Does History Become Literature and Other Uncollected Essays and Addresses on Landscape, Literature, History and Morality. 1993. V. 50; 51
A Passion For Books. 1958. V. 48
Robinson Jeffers; The Man and His Work. Los Angeles: 1934. V. 48; 49; 51; 54
Robinson Jeffers: the Man and His Work. Pasadena: 1940. V. 54
Southwestern Book Trails, a Reader's Guide to the Heartland of New Mexico and Arizona. Albuquerque: 1963. V. 48; 53
W. W. Robinson, 1891-1972: Eulogy, spoken By... Los Angeles: 1974. V. 47

POWELL, PETER J.
People of the Sacred Mountain. San Francisco: 1979. V. 51
People of the Sacred Mountain. San Francisco: 1981. V. 50
Sweet Medicine. Norman: 1969. V. 50; 54

POWELL, RICHARD
Proceedings of a General Court Martial Held at the Horse-Guards, on the 24th and 27th of March, 1792, for the Trial of Capt. Richard Powell, Lieutenant Christopher Seton and Lieutenant John Hall, on Several Charges Preferred Against Them... London: 1809. V. 48

POWELL, ROBERT HUTCHINSON
A Medical Topography of Tunbridge Wells; Illustrating the Beneficial Influence of Its Mineral Waters, Climate, Soil, etc.. London: 1846. V. 52
A Medical Topography of Tunbridge Wells, Illustrating the Beneficial Influence of Its Mineral Waters, Climate, Soil, etc. In Restoring and Preserving Health. Tunbridge Wells: 1846. V. 53

POWELL, THOMAS
The Attornies Almanacke. London: 1627. V. 51; 54
The Blind Wife; or, the Student of Bonn. London: 1843. V. 51; 54
The Living Authors of America. New York: 1850. V. 48; 54

POWELL, WALTER
A Catalogue of the Birmingham Collection Including Printed Books and Pamphlets, Manuscripts, Maps, Views, Portraits, etc. 1918. V. 47
A Catalogue of the Birmingham Collection...(with) Supplement. London: 1918. V. 51
A Catalogue of the Birmingham Collection...(with) Supplement. London: 1918-31. V. 54

POWELL, WILFRED
Wanderings in a Wild Country; or, Three Years Amongst the Cannibals of New Britain. London: 1884. V. 52

POWELL, WILLIAM H.
A History of the Organzation and Movements of the Fourth Regiment of Infantry, United States Army, From May 30, 1796, to December 31, 1870; Together with a Record of the Military Services of All Officers. Washington City: 1871. V. 50

POWELL, WILLIS J.
Tachyhippodamia, or Art of Quieting Wild Horses in a Few Hours as Discovered by the Author, in the Year 1814. New Orleans: 1838. V. 47

POWELL-COTTON, P. H. G.
A Sporting Trip through Abyssinia. 1902. V. 48

POWER, BERTHA KNIGHT
William Henry Knight California Pioneer. 1932. V. 47

POWER, D'ARCY
Portraits of Dr. William Harvey. Oxford: 1913. V. 47; 50; 51; 53
A System of Syphilis. London: 1908. V. 54

POWER, E. B.
The Smaller American House... Boston: 1927. V. 50; 51

POWER, EILEEN
Medieval English Nunneries c. 1275-1535. London: 1922. V. 49

POWER, JOHN CARROLL
History of Springfield, Illinois, Its Attractions as a Home and Advantages for Business, Manufacturing, Etc. Springfield: 1871. V. 50

POWER, KEVIN
Heidegger My Way and Scarcely: a Long Poem. Amsterdam: 1982. V. 54

POWER, P.
Sambo's Legacy. Philadelphia. V. 53

POWER, TYRONE
Impressions of America, During the Years 1833, 1834 and 1835. London: 1836. V. 48; 49; 50; 52; 53; 54
Sketches in New Zealand, with Pen and Pencil. London: 1849. V. 47; 52

A POWERFULL, Pitifull, Citi-full Cry, of Plentiful Children and Their Admirable, Lamentable Compliant. London: 1643. V. 49

POWERS, ALAN
The Marches: a Picturesque Tour. 1989. V. 52

POWERS, ALFRED
History of Oregon Literature. 1935. V. 50

THE POWERS and Duties of the Town Officer, as Contained in the Statutes of Maine. Hallowell: 1824. V. 52

POWERS, CALEB
Great Speech of Caleb Powers Before the Jury That Sentenced Him to Death Upon the Charge of Being an Accessory Before the Fact to the Murder of William Goebel. Georgetown: 1903. V. 48; 53

POWERS, J. F.
The Old Bird: a Love Story. Minneapolis: 1991. V. 48
The Presence of Grace. Garden City: 1956. V. 49
Prince of Darkness and Other Stories. Garden City: 1947. V. 54

POWERS, PERRY F.
A History of Northern Michigan and its People. Chicago: 1912. V. 49

POWERS, RICHARD
The Gold Bug Variations. New York: 1991. V. 50; 51; 52; 53; 54
Operation Wandering Soul. New York: 1994. V. 51
Prisoner's Dilemma. New York: 1988. V. 51
Three Farmers on Their Way to a Dance. New York: 1985. V. 48; 49; 50; 51; 52; 53; 54
Three Farmers On Their Way to a Dance. New York: 1988. V. 51

POWERS, STEPHEN
Afoot and Alone, a Walk from Sea to Sea. Hartford: 1872. V. 47; 48; 50; 51; 54

POWERS, TIM
The Anubis Gates. London: 1985. V. 52
Dinner at Deviant's Palace. London: 1986. V. 51
On Stranger Tides. 1987. V. 48; 52
The Stress of Her Regard. Lynbrook: 1989. V. 50; 52

POWERSCOURT, VISCOUNT
A Description and History of Powerscourt. London: 1903. V. 50

POWICKE, F. M.
King Henry III and the Lord Edward: the Community of the Realm in the Thirteenth Century. London: 1947. V. 52

POWLETT, CHARLES
A Father's Reasons for Being a Christian. London: 1812. V. 49

POWNALL, HENRY
Some Particulars Relating to the History of Epsom... Epsom: 1825. V. 49; 51

POWNALL, THOMAS
Notices and Descriptions of antiquities of the Provincia Romana of Gaul... London: 1788. V. 48; 53

POWNEY, RICHARD
The Stag in Windsor Forest. London: 1739. V. 53

POWYS, JOHN COWPER
Confessions of Two Brothers. Rochester: 1916. V. 48; 53
Debate! Is Modern Marriage a Failure?. New York: 1930. V. 53
Dorothy M. Richardson. London: 1931. V. 51; 53
Ducdame. London: 1925. V. 48; 53
Ducdame. New York: 1925. V. 54
Enjoyment of Literature. New York: 1938. V. 53
A Glastonbury Romance. New York: 1932. V. 53
A Glastonbury Romance. London: 1933. V. 51
Homer and the Aether. London: 1959. V. 49; 51; 53
In Defence of Sensuality. London: 1930. V. 47; 51
In Defence of Sensuality. New York: 1930. V. 48
Jobber Skald. London: 1935. V. 50; 51; 53
Lucifer... 1956. V. 53
Lucifer. London: 1956. V. 48; 51
Maiden Castle. New York: 1936. V. 53
Maiden Castle. London: 1937. V. 50
Mandragora. New York: 1917. V. 50
The Meaning of Culture. New York: 1929. V. 53
Morwyn or, the Vengenace of God... London: 1937. V. 53
Odes and Other Poems. London: 1896. V. 53
One Hundred Best Books. New York: 1922. V. 53
Owen Glendower. New York: 1940. V. 51; 53
A Philosophy of Solitude. New York: 1933. V. 53
Poems. London: 1896. V. 53
Poems. London: 1899. V. 53
Psychoanalysis and Morality. San Francisco: 1923. V. 50
Samphire: Poems. New York: 1922. V. 53
The Secret of Self Development. Girard: 1926. V. 53
Visions and Revisions: a Book of Literary Devotions. New York: 1915. V. 53; 54
The War and Culture. New York: 1914. V. 50
Weymouth Sands. New York: 1934. V. 50; 54
Wolf Solent. London: 1929. V. 48; 51
Wolf Solent. New York: 1929. V. 51
Wolfe's Bane. Rhymes. New York: 1915. V. 48
Wolf's Bane. Rhymes. New York: 1916. V. 49; 50; 54
Wood and Stone. New York: 1915. V. 53

POWYS, LLEWELYN
A Baker's Dozen. Herrin: 1939. V. 53; 54
Black Laughter. London: 1925. V. 48
The Book of Days. Waltham St. Lawrence: 1937. V. 47
Confessions of Two Brothers. Rochester: 1916. V. 54
Ebony and Ivory. New York: 1923. V. 53
Now That the Gods Are Dead. An Essay. New York: 1932. V. 49; 51
Old English Yuletide. Herrin: 1940. V. 54
The Twelve Months. London: 1936. V. 48; 51

POWYS, THEODORE FRANCIS
Black Bryony. London: 1923. V. 50; 51; 53
Christ in the Cupboard. London: 1930. V. 53
The Dewpond. London: 1928. V. 47; 49; 54
Fables. London: 1929. V. 51; 53
God's Eyes a-Twinkle. London: 1947. V. 54
An Interpretation of Genesis. London: 1929. V. 53
An Interpretation of Genesis. New York: 1929. V. 47; 50
Kindness in a Corner. London: 1930. V. 50; 51; 53
The Left Leg: Containing The Left Leg, Hester Dominy, Abraham Men. London: 1923. V. 51
Mark Only. London: 1924. V. 51
Mr. Tasker's Gods. London: 1925. V. 51; 53
Mr. Weston's Good Wine. London: 1927. V. 47; 50; 53
Mockery Gap. London: 1925. V. 51
The Only Penitent. London: 1931. V. 47; 48; 51; 53
The Soliloquy of a Hermit. London: 1916. V. 48
The Soliloquy of a Hermit. New York: 1916. V. 53
The Soliloquy of a Hermit. London: 1918. V. 47; 48; 49; 51; 53
Unclay. London: 1931. V. 48; 49; 51
Uncle Dottery. Bristol: 1930/31. V. 48; 53
When Thou Was Naked. Waltham St. Lawrence: 1931. V. 50; 54
The White Paternoster and Other Stories. London: 1930. V. 50; 51; 52; 53

POYAS, CATHARINE GENDRON
Year of Grief, and Other Poems. Charleston: 1869. V. 54

POYET, BERNARD
Nouveau Systeme de Pont en Bois et en Fer Forge... Paris: 1820/21. V. 53

POYNDER, JOHN
A History of the Jesuits; to which is Prefixed a Reply to Mr. Dallas's Defence of that Order. London: 1816. V. 49; 54

POYNTER, EDWARD J.
The National Gallery. London: 1899. V. 49
The National Gallery. London: 1899/1900. V. 48

POYNTER, ELEANOR FRANCES
My Little Lady. London: 1871. V. 54

POYNTER, F. N. L.
A Bibliography of Gervase Markham 1568?-1637. London: 1962. V. 47; 51; 54
A Catalogue of Incunabula in the Wellcome Historical Library. London: 1954. V. 47; 48; 51; 52
The History and Philosophy of Knowledge of the Brain and Its Functions. Springfield: 1958. V. 47

POYNTING, F.
Eggs of British Birds with an Acount of Their Breeding Habits: Limicolae. London: 1895-96. V. 52

POYNTING, JOHN HENRY
Collected Scientific Papers. Cambridge: 1920. V. 50

POYNTON, F. J.
Researches on Rheumatism. New York: 1914. V. 49; 51; 54

POZZI, S.
Treatise on Gynaecology, Medical and Surgical. New York: 1891-92. V. 54

POZZO, ANDREA
Perspectivae Pictorum Atque Architectorum. Augsburg: 1719. V. 49; 50
Prospettive De Pittori et Architetti... Rome: 1702/1700. V. 51
Rules and Examples of Perspective Proper for Painters and Architects... London: 1707. V. 47; 49; 52
Rules and Examples of Perspective Proper for Painters and Architects, Etc. London: 1725. V. 53

POZZO, BARTOLOMEO, CONTE DAL
Le Vite de'Pittori de gli Scultori et Architetti Veronesi... Verona: 1718. V. 53

PRACH, IVAN
(Title in Cyrillic) Russian Popular folks Songs. St. Petersburg: 1815. V. 49

PRACTICAL Guide and Receipt Book for the Liquor Merchant, Being a Clear and Comprehensive Treatise on the Manufacture and Imitation of Brandy, Rum, Gin and Whisky. New York: 1868. V. 48

A **PRACTICAL** Guide to the English Kinder-Garten (Children's Garden) for the Use of Mothers, Nursery Governesses and Infant Teachers. London: 1863. V. 50

PRACTICAL Manual of Health and Temperance Embracing the Treatment of Common Diseases, Accidents and Emergencies, the Alcohol and Tobacco Habits... Battle Creek: 1886. V. 50

PRADE, JEAN LE ROYER
The History of Gustavus Adolphus Surnamed the Great, King of Sueden. London: 1689. V. 54

PRADHAN, U. C.
Sikkim-Himalayan Rhododendrons. Kalimpong: 1990. V. 50

PRAED, CYRIL WINTHROP MACKWORTH
Birds of the Southern Third of Africa. London: 1962. V. 53

PRAED, ROSA CAROLINE MURRAY-PRIOR
An Australian Heroine. London: 1890. V. 53
Fugitive Anne: a Romance of the Unexplored Bush. London: 1902. V. 50
Mrs. Tregaskiss: a Novel of Anglo-Australian Life. New York: 1895. V. 47; 49; 50; 51
Policy and Passion. London: 1881. V. 54

PRAED, WINTHROP MACKWORTH
Australasia. A Poem Which Obtained the Chancellor's Medal at the Cambridge Commencement. July 1823. Cambridge: 1823. V. 54
The Etonian. Windsor: 1821. V. 48
Lillian: a Fairy Tale. London: 1823. V. 54
The Poems. London: 1864. V. 47; 48; 51; 52

PRAEGER, R. L.
Irish Topographical Botany. Dublin: 1901. V. 54
Natural History of Ireland, A Sketch of Its Flora and Fauna. London: 1950. V. 54
A Populous Solitude. Dublin: 1941. V. 54
Some Irish Naturalists. Dundalk: 1949. V. 54
The Way That I Went, an Irishman in Ireland. London: 1937. V. 50; 52; 53; 54

PRAEGER, S. ROSAMUND
Further Adventures of the Three Bold Babes. London: 1898. V. 50

PRAGETER, EDITH
The Assize of the Dying. London: 1958. V. 54

PRAGNELL, F.
The Green Man of Kilsona. 1936. V. 47

PRAMBHOFER, JOHANNES
Wunderseltsame, Wahrhaffte, Beynabens Lacherliche Traum-Gesichter... Augsburg: 1712. V. 52

PRANCERIANA. A Select Collection of Fugitive Pieces, Published Since the Appointment of the Present Provost of the University of Dublin. Dublin: 1775. V. 51

PRANDO, PETER PAUL
History of the Old Testament. Montana: 1890's. V. 48

PRANG, LOUIS
Prang's Standard Alphabets. Boston: 1886. V. 47; 49; 50

PRATCHETT, TERRY
Strata. Gerrards Cross: 1981. V. 52

PRATO, DANIELLO DA
Trattato Della Preservantia Intitolato Corona di Serui D'Iddio... Venice: 1544. V. 52

PRATT, A. E.
To the Snows of Tibet through China. London: 1892. V. 49; 52
Two Years Among New Guinea Cannibals... London: 1906. V. 52

PRATT, ANNE
Chapters on the Common Things of the Sea-Coast. London: 1853. V. 54
The Flowering Plants, Grasses, Sedges and Ferns of Great Britain... London: 1874. V. 47; 52
The Flowering Plants, Grasses, Sedges and Ferns of Great Britain. London: 1875. V. 54
The Flowering Plants, Grasses, Sedges and Ferns, of Great Britain... London: 1889. V. 51
The Flowering Plants, Grasses, Sedges and Ferns of Great Britain... London: 1899-1900. V. 53; 54
The Flowering Plants of Great Britain. Volume IV. Grasses, Sedges and Ferns. London: 1865. V. 54
Flowers and Their Associations. London: 1840. V. 54
Poisonous, Noxious and Suspected Plants of Our Fields and Woods. London: 1865. V. 54
Things of the Sea Coast. London: 1853. V. 52
Wild Flowers. London: 1857. V. 54
Wild Flowers. London: 1860. V. 53; 54
Wild Flowers. London: 1880. V. 48

PRATT, CHARLES STUART
Baby Land. Boston: 1899. V. 51
Bye O Baby Ballads. Boston: 1886. V. 49; 51

PRATT, CHARLES T.
A History of Cawthorne. Manchester: 1882. V. 50

PRATT, DANIEL
Autobiography of Daniel Pratt, Jr., A.A.S. of Boston, formerly of Prattville, Chelsea, Mass. Boston: 1855. V. 52

PRATT, E. J.
The Fables of the Goats and Other Poems. Toronto: 1937. V. 49; 50
The Iron Door. Toronto: 1927. V. 47
Titans. London: 1926. V. 48; 54

PRATT, ELLIS
The Art of Dressing the Hair. Bath: 1770. V. 48; 54

PRATT, ENOCH
A Comprehensive History, Ecclesiastical and Civil of Eastham, Welfleet and Orleans, County of Barnstable, Mass. from 1644 to 1844. Yarmouth: 1844. V. 54

PRATT, FLETCHER
Land of Unreason. New York: 1942. V. 52

PRATT, H. B.
Commercial Airships. London: 1920. V. 49

PRATT, IDA A.
Ancient Egypt: Sources of Information in the New York Public Library. (with) Ancient Egypt 1925-1941: a Supplement. New York: 1925/42. V. 49; 51

PRATT, JULIUS HOWARD
Reminiscences Personal and Otherwise. 1910. V. 47

PRATT, PARLEY PARKER
The Autobiography of Parley Parker Pratt, One of the Twelve Apostles of the Church of Jesus Christ of Latter-Day Saints, Embracing His Life, Ministry and Travels... Chicago: 1888. V. 47
History of the Late Persecution Inflicted by the State of Missouri Upon the Mormons, in Which Ten Thousand American Citizens Were Robbed, Plundered and Driven from the State and Many Others Imprisoned, Martyred, &c. Detroit: 1839. V. 47
Key to the Science of Theology. Liverpool: 1855. V. 50
The Millennium, a Poem. Boston: 1835. V. 54
A Voice of Warning and Instruction to All People... New York: 1837. V. 52
A Voice of Warning and Instruction To All People. Liverpool: 1854. V. 51
A Voice of Warning and Instruction to All People. Plano: 1863. V. 49

PRATT, SAMUEL JACKSON
Emma Corbett. London: 1789. V. 47
Family Secrets, Literary and Domestic. Cork: 1800. V. 48
Pity's Gift: a Collection of Interesting Tales to Excite the Compassion of Youth for the Animal Creation. London: 1798. V. 49

PRAVAL, CHARLES
The Idioms of the French Language, Compared with Those of English, In a Series of Polite and Instructive Conversations. Dublin: 1794. V. 52

PRAZ, MARIO
An Illustrated History of Interior Decoration from Pompeii to Art Nouveau. London: 1964. V. 47; 53
On Neoclassicism. London: 1969. V. 54
Studies in Seventeenth Century Imagery. Michigan: 1976. V. 54

PREBLE, GEORGE H.
Notes for a History of Steam Navigation. Philadelphia: 1881. V. 53

PRECHAC, JEAN DE
Le Seraskier Bacha. Novvelle de Temps. Paris: 1685. V. 54

PREISTLEY & WEALE
Useful and Necessary Works of Architecture. London: 1824. V. 53

PRELLEUR, PETER
A Brief History of Musick; Wherein is Related the Several Changes, Additions and Improvements, From Its Origin to This Present Time. London: 1730?. V. 47

PREMIUMS Offered by the Dublin Society, for Agriculture, Planting and Fine Arts. 1800. Dublin: 1800. V. 49

PRENDERGAST, J. P.
The Tory War of Ulster... 1868. V. 54

PRENDERGAST, MAURICE
A Sketchbook of Maurice Prendergast. Erie: 1974. V. 52

PRENDERGRAST, MAURICE
Water-Color Sketchbook 1899. Boston & Cambridge. V. 48

PRENSHAW, PEGGY WHITMAN
Eudora Welty: Critial Essays. Jackson: 1979. V. 48

PRENTICE, E. PARMALEE
The Influence of Hunger On Human History. Williamstown: 1938. V. 49; 52; 54

PRENTICE, H.
Captured by Apes; or, How Philip Garland Became King of Apeland. 1888. V. 48; 52

PRENTICE, H. W.
The Beagle in American and England (and) Chronological Table of Winners at Beagle Field Trials 1890-1919. London: 1920. V. 47

PRENTICE, WORTHY A.
Polk County Wisconsin as Seen by Worthy A. Prentice. 1921?. V. 54

PRENTIS, NOBLE L.
Kansas Miscellanies. Topeka: 1889. V. 52

PRENTISS, CHARLES
A Collection of Fugitive Essays in Prose and Verse. Leonminster: 1797. V. 54
The Life of the Late Gen. William Eaton...Principally Collected From His Correspondence and Other Manuscripts. Brookfield: 1813. V. 47; 52

PRENTISS, GEORGE L.
A Memoir of S. S. Prentiss. New York: 1855. V. 47

PREOBRAZHENSKY, B. V.
Contemporary Reefs. Rotterdam: 1993. V. 50

PRESBYTERIAN CHURCH
The Westminster Shorter Catechism Ratified by the General Assembly of the Presbyterian Church in the United States at Augusta, GA, Dec. 4th, 1861. Richmond & Texarkana: 1861. V. 51

PRESBYTERIAN CHURCH OF CANADA
A Historical and Statistical Report of the Presbyterian Church of Canada, in Connection with the Church of Scotland, for the Year 1866. Montreal: 1867. V. 54

PRESBYTERIAN CHURCH OF NOVA SCOTIA, SYNOD.
The Report of a Commitee, Appointed by the Synod of the Presbyterian Church of Nova Scotia to Prepare a Statement of Means for Promoting Religion in the Church... Halifax: 1818. V. 53

PRESCOT, KENRICK
Poems. 1772. V. 49

PRESCOTT, G. W.
Bibliographia Desmidiacearum Universalis. Koenigstein: 1984. V. 53

PRESCOTT, GEORGE B.
The Electric Telephone. New York: 1890. V. 53
History, Theory and Practice of the Electric Telegraph. Boston: 1860. V. 50; 52; 54
The Speaking Telephone, Electric Light, and Other Recent Inventions. London: 1879. V. 48

PRESCOTT, HENRY P.
Tobacco and Its Adulterations. London: 1858. V. 50

PRESCOTT, J. E.
The Register of the Priory of Wetheral. London: 1897. V. 50; 52
The Statutes of the Cathedral Church of Carlisle. London: 1903. V. 52

PRESCOTT, KENNETH W.
The Complete Graphic Works of Ben Shahn. New York: 1973. V. 48; 53; 54

PRESCOTT, WILLIAM HICKLING
The Complete Works. London. V. 50; 53
Complete Works. London: 1896. V. 51
Complete Works. London: 1900. V. 52
The History of Ferdinand and Isabella. Boston: 1839. V. 48
History of the Conquest of Mexico. London: 1843. V. 52
History of the Conquest of Mexico. New York: 1843. V. 51; 52; 53; 54
History of the Conquest of Mexico, with a Preliminary View of the Ancient Mexican Civilisation, and Life of the Conqueror Hernando Cortes. London: 1844. V. 54
History of the Conquest of Mexico. (with) History of the Conquest of Peru. London: 1899/1903. V. 47; 51
History of the Conquest of Peru. London: 1847. V. 51; 54
The History of the Conquest of Peru. New York: 1847. V. 48; 50; 53
History of the Conquest of Peru... Paris: 1847. V. 48
History of the Conquest of Peru, 1524-1550. Mexico City: 1957. V. 52
History of the Reign of Ferdinand and Isabella. London: 1838. V. 51
History of the Reign of Ferdinand and Isabella. London: 1855/59. V. 54
History of the Reign of Ferdinand and Isabella. London: 1858. V. 51
History of the Reign of Ferdinand and Isabella. New York: 1967. V. 49; 53
History of the Reign of Philipp the Second, King of Spain. London: 1855-59. V. 54
Memoir of the Honorable Abbott Lawrence. 1856. V. 48
Memoir of the Honorable Abbott Lawrence. London: 1856. V. 47
William H. Prescott's Works. Philadelphia and London: 1904. V. 48; 49; 50; 51; 52; 54
Works. New York: 1847-52. V. 50
Works. Philadelphia: 1871. V. 50
The Works. London: 1875. V. 51
The Works. Philadelphia: 1895. V. 51

PRESCOTT, WINWARD
A List of Canadian Bookplates, with a Review of the History of Ex-Libris in the Cominion. Boston & Toronto: 1919. V. 47

PRESCOTT-WESTCAR, V.
Big Game, Boers and Boches. London: 1937. V. 47

THE PRESENT Case Stated: or, the Oaths of Allegiance and Supremacy No Badges of Slavery. London: 1689. V. 53

THE PRESENT Judiciary System of South Carolina; Its Defects Reviewed and Modes Suggested for Its Improvement. Charleston: 1850. V. 52

THE PRESENT State of Germany. London: 1738. V. 47

THE PRESENT State of Ireland: Together with Some Remarques Upon the Antient State Thereof. Likewise a Description of the Chief Towns. London: 1673. V. 54

THE PRESENT State of the Game Law, and the Question of Property, Considered. Edinburgh: 1772. V. 52

THE PRESENT State of the Stage in Great-Britain and Ireland. And the Theatrical Characters of the Principal Performers...Impartially Considered. London: 1753. V. 49

THE PRESENT State of the West-Indies: Containing an Accurate Description of What Parts are Possessed by the Several Powers in Europe... London: 1778. V. 54

A PRESENT to Children. New York and Baltimore: 1820. V. 50

PRESENTATION of a Timepiece to Alexander Hamilton and W. A. Blackwell by Ten Fellow Sportsmen and True Friends on the Occasion of the 1947 Quail Hunt on the Delightful Ranch of Alexander Hamilton. Cuero: 1947. V. 52

THE PRESENTMENT of the Grand Jury for the City of London, at the Sessions of Peace and Gaol Delivery at Justice-Hall in the Old Baily, on thursday 19th April 1683. London: 1683. V. 52

PRESS, C. A. M.
Westmorland Lives Social and Political. London: 1900. V. 52

PRESS-O-Grams. Arkansas: 1939. V. 49

PRESSLAND, DAVID
The Art of the Tin Toy. New York: 1976. V. 54

PREST, THOMAS PECKETT
Nickelas Nickelbery. 1840. V. 54
Pickwick in America. 1838-39. V. 49
Pickwick in America. Bloomsbury: 1838-39. V. 54
The Pickwick Songster. London: 1837. V. 49
The Sketch Book by "Bos".... London: 1837?. V. 54

PRESTET, JEAN
Nouveaux Elemens des Mathematiques ou Principes Generaux de Toutes les Sciences qui ont les Grandeurs Pour Objet. Paris: 1695. V. 48

PRESTON, ANNIE
Dame Durden's Copper Kettle. London: 1890. V. 49

PRESTON, CHLOE
The Chunkies. London: 1916. V. 51
Peek-A-Boo Peter. Springfield: 1927. V. 53
The Peek-A-Boos-In-Town. London. V. 50
Somebody's Darlings. London: 1936. V. 49

PRESTON, ISAAC
Mr. Preston's Reply to a Libel, Intitl'd a Narrative of the Disputes Between Isaac Preston, Esq... Norwich: 1758. V. 48

PRESTON, JOHN
Every Man His Own Teacher; or, Lancaster's Theory of Education, Practically Displayed... New York: 1817. V. 54

PRESTON, LYMAN
Preston's Tables of Interest Showing the Interest on any Sum from One Dollar to Five Hundred Dollars Inclusive. Utica: 1828. V. 50

PRESTON, MARGARET J.
A Handful of Monographs: Continental and English. New York: 1886. V. 47

PRESTON, PAUL, PSEUD.
The Fireside Magician; or, The Art of Natural Magic Made Easy. New York: 1870. V. 50

PRESTON, THOMAS
The Life and Opinions of Thomas Preston, Patriot and Shoemaker... London: 1817. V. 52
The Theory of Heat. London and New York: 1894. V. 50

PRESTON, WILLIAM
Illustrations of Masonry... London: 1812. V. 47
The Poetical Works. Dublin: 1793. V. 49; 50
Seventeen Hundred and Seventy-Seven; or, a Picture of the Manners and Character of the Age. Dublin: 1777. V. 48

PRESTWICH, EDMUND
The Hectors; or the False Challenge. London: 1656. V. 52

PRESTWICH, J.
A Geological Enquiry Respecting the Water Bearing Strata of the Country Around London, with Reference Especially to the Water Supply of the Metropolis. London: 1851. V. 48; 50; 53
Geology Chemical, Physical and Stratigraphical. Oxford: 1886. V. 52
Geology: Chemical, Physical and Stratigraphical. London: 1886-88. V. 54

PRESTWICH, JOHN
Republica; or a Display of the Honours, Ceremonies and Ensigns of the Commonwealth Under the Protectorship of Oliver Cromwell. London: 1787. V. 51

THE PRETTY and Entertaining History of Tom Thumb With His Wonderful Escape from the Cow's Belly. Otley: 1820. V. 49

PRETTY Peggy and other Ballads. London: 1890. V. 52

PRETTY Pictures for Little Eyes. London: 1885. V. 48

PRETTY Polly. London: 1899. V. 52

PRETTY Tales for the Nursery. London: 1863. V. 50

PRETTYMAN, W. S.
Indian Territory. A Frontier Photographic Record... Norman: 1957. V. 49

PREVERT, JACQUES
Adonides. Paris: 1975. V. 51

PREVOST, ANTOINE FRANCOIS, CALLED PREVOST D'EXILES
Histoire du Chevalier des Grieux et du Manon Lescaut. Stamford: 1958. V. 47

PREVOST, ANTOINE FRANCOIS, CALLED PREVOST D'EXILES continued
The Life and Entertaining Adventures of Mr. Cleveland, Natural Son of Oliver Cromwell. London: 1734/35. V. 48; 53
Manon Lescaut. London: 1841. V. 53
Manon Lescaut. London: 1928. V. 49; 51; 52; 53; 54
Manon Lescaut. New York: 1928. V. 48

PREVOST, LOUIS
California Silk Grower's Manual. San Francisco: 1867. V. 50

PREWETT, FRANK
Poems. Richmond: 1921. V. 53

PRICE, A. GRENFELL
The Explorations of Capt. James Cook in the Pacific as Told by Selections of His Own Journals 1768-1779. New York: 1957. V. 47

PRICE, ANTHONY
The Alamut Ambush. London: 1971. V. 51
Colonel Butler's Wolf. London: 1972. V. 49; 51
Other Paths to Glory. London: 1974. V. 51
Our Man in Camelot. London: 1975. V. 47
War Game. London: 1976. V. 47

PRICE, CON
Trails I Rode. Pasadena: 1947. V. 50; 53

PRICE, D. J.
The Texarkana Gateway to Texas and the Southwest. St. Louis: 1896. V. 54

PRICE, EDMUND E.
The Science of Self-Defence. New York: 1867. V. 47

PRICE, EDWARD
Norway and Its Scenery. London: 1853. V. 51; 52
Twelve Views in Dovedale and Ilam, from Drawings by Mr. Edward Price. Ashbourne: 1845. V. 54

PRICE, ELEANOR C.
The Adventures of King Arthur. London: 1931. V. 51

PRICE, F. G. HILTON
A Catalogue of the Egyptian Antiquities in the Possession of F. G. Hilton Price. London: 1897. V. 49; 51
A Handbook of London Bankers: with Some Account of Their Predecessors, the Goldsmiths. London: 1876. V. 51

PRICE, FLORENCE ALICE
The White Witch. London: 1884. V. 47

PRICE, FRANCIS
The British Carpenter; or, a Treatise on Carpentry. London: 1759. V. 48
The British Carpenter...(and) A Supplement to the British Carpenter... London: 1735. V. 53
A Series of Particular and Useful Observations, Made With Great Diligence and Care, Upon the Admirable Structure, the Cathedral-Church of Salisbury. London: 1753. V. 48
A Treatise on Carpentry. London: 1733-35. V. 48

PRICE, FREDERIC NEWLIN
The Etchings and Lithographs of Arthur B. Davies. New York/London: 1929. V. 48; 49; 50; 52; 53
Horatio Walker. New York: 1928. V. 50

PRICE, FREDERICK GEORGE HILTON
The Signs of Old Lombard Street. London: 1887. V. 53

PRICE, GEORGE F.
Across the Continent With the Fifth Cavalry. New York: 1883. V. 47; 51; 53
Across the Continent with the Fifth Cavalry. New York: 1961. V. 48

PRICE, H.
A Letter to the Kidderminster Carpet Manufacturers, by Their Native Townsman... 1830. V. 50

PRICE, HARRY
An Account of Some Further Experiments with Rudi Schneider, a Minute-by-Minute Record of 27 Seances. London: 1933. V. 48
Confessions of a Ghost-Hunter. London: 1936. V. 48
Search for Truth. London: 1942. V. 48
Short-Title Catalogue of Works on Psychical Research, Spiritualism, Magic, Psychology, Legerdemain and Other Methods of Deception...(with) Supplement. London: 1929-35. V. 51; 53

PRICE, J.
The Buyers' Manual and Business Guide... San Francisco: 1872. V. 49; 52; 53; 54

PRICE, J. H.
The Shore Environment. Volume 2: Ecosystems. London: 1980. V. 53

PRICE, JACOB M.
France and the Chesapeake. 1973. V. 49

PRICE, JOHN
Historiae Brytannicae Defensio. London: 1573. V. 50
An Historical Account of the City of Hereford. Hereford: 1796. V. 54
A Moderate Reply to the Citie-Remonstrance...Containing Several Reasons Why Many Well Affected Citizens Cannot Assent Thereunto. London: 1646. V. 53
Some Considerations Humbly Offered to the Honourable Members of the House of Commons, for Building a Stone Bridge over the River Thames, from Westminster to Lambeth. London: 1735. V. 51
Walwins Wiles; or the Manifestors Manifested. London: 1649. V. 50; 53

PRICE, JOHN EDWARD
A Descriptive Account of the Guildhall of the City of London: Its History and Associations. London: 1886. V. 49

PRICE, JOHN FREDERICK
Ootacamund. A History. Madras: 1908. V. 52

PRICE, JOSEPH
An Historical Account of Bilston, from Alfred the Great to 1831, Particularly of the Ancient Chapel, the Dissolution Thereof and Its Re-establishment Contests for the Incumbency. (with) A Narrative of the Proceedings Relative to the Internal Election... Bilston: 1835/36. V. 50
A Second Letter to the Right Honourable Edmund Burke, Esq; on the Subject of the Evidence Refered to in the Second Report of the Select Committee of the House of Commons... London: 1782. V. 47
A Series of Facts, Shewing the Present Political State of India, as Far As Concerns the Powers at War; and the Probable Consequences of a General Pacification in Europe, Before We Shall Have Decided Our Contests in the Carnatic. London: 1783. V. 47

PRICE, JULIUS M.
From the Arctic Ocean to the Yellow Sea. London: 1892. V. 54
From the Arctic Ocean to the Yellow Sea. New York: 1892. V. 47; 48; 52

PRICE, LAMBART
The Two Americas: an Account of Sport and Travel. London: 1877. V. 47

PRICE, LANGFORD LOVELL
Economic Science and Practice. London: 1896. V. 52

PRICE, LAWRENCE
Flora's Farewel; or, the Shepherds Love Passion Song. London: 1693?. V. 47

PRICE, LUCY
The Sydney-smith & Clagett-Price Genealogy. Strasburg: 1927. V. 54

PRICE, M.
The Work of Dwight James Baum, Arachitect. New York: 1927. V. 51

PRICE, MARY
A Treasury of Great Recipes: Famous Specialties of the World's Foremost Restaurants... 1965. V. 48

PRICE, R. K.
Astbury, Wheldon and Ralph Wood Figures and Toby Jugs Collected by.... London: 1922. V. 51

PRICE, R. N.
Holston Methodism. Nashville: 1904-14. V. 52

PRICE, REYNOLDS
The Annual Heron. New York: 1980. V. 53
Back Before Day. Rocky Mount: 1989. V. 53
Blue Calhoun. New York: 1992. V. 54
The Collected Stories. New York: 1993. V. 50
Country Mouse, City Mouse. 1981. V. 53
A Final Letter: Robinson Mayfield in Essex, North Carolina to Huchins Mayfield in Oxford, England, June 15 to November 27, 1955. Los Angeles: 1980. V. 51; 52
A Generous Man. New York: 1966. V. 48; 49; 51
The Honest Account of a Memorable Life: an Apocryphal Gospel. Rocky Mount: 1994. V. 52; 53
Late Warning. New York: 1968. V. 48; 51
A Long and Happy Life. New York: 1962. V. 47; 48; 49; 50; 51; 52; 53
A Long and Happy Life. New York: 1963. V. 52
Love and Work. New York: 1968. V. 48
The Names and Faces of Heroes. New York: 1963. V. 47; 50
Oracles: Six Versions from the Bible. Durham: 1977. V. 47; 50
Private Contentment. New York: 1984. V. 50
Question and Answer. The Second Archibald Yell Smith IV Lecture. Chattanooga: 1979. V. 51
Real Copies. Will Price, Crichton Davis, Phyllis Peacock and More. Rocky Mount: 1988. V. 49
A Start (Early Work). 1981. V. 47
The Thing Itself. Durham: 1966. V. 53
Things Themselves. New York: 1972. V. 52
The Tongues of Angels. New York: 1950. V. 54
The Tongues of Angels. New York: 1990. V. 47
Vital Provisions. New York: 1982. V. 49

PRICE, RICHARD
The Breaks. New York: 1983. V. 51
Clockers. Boston: 1992. V. 53
Discourse on the Love of Our Country, Delivered on Nov. 4, 1789, 15 the Meeting-House in Old Jewry, to the Society for Commemorating the Revolution in Great Britain, with an Appendix... London: 1790. V. 48
Ladies' Man. Boston: 1978. V. 52
Observations on Reversionary Payments; on Schemes for Providing Annuities for Widows, and for Persons in Old Age... London: 1772. V. 47; 49
Observations on Reversionary Payments; on Schemes for Providing Annuities for Widows, and for Persons in Old Age.... London: 1792. V. 48; 52
Observations on the Importance of the American Revolution, and the means of making It a Benefit to the World. London: 1785. V. 48
Observations on the Importance of the American Revolution, and the Means of Making It a Benefit to the World. Philadelphia: 1785. V. 48
Observations on the Nature of Civil Liberty, the Principles of Government, and the Justice and Policy of the War with America... London: 1776. V. 47

PRICE, RICHARD continued
Observations on the Nature of Civil Liberty, the Principles of Government and the Justice and Policy of the War With America.... (with) Additional Observations on the Nature and Value of Civil Liberty, and the War with America... London: 1776/77. V. 52

A Review of the Principal Questions and Difficulties in Morals... London: 1769. V. 51

The Wanderers. Boston: 1974. V. 51; 53

The Wanderers. Boston: 1976. V. 48

PRICE, ROBERT
Holland. The Horrors of Invasion, a Poem. Wrexham: 1804. V. 54

PRICE, ROSE LAMBART
A Summer on the Rockies. London: 1898. V. 47; 53

The Two Americas: an Account of Sport and Travel. London: 1877. V. 52

PRICE, SARAH
Illustrations of the Fungi of Our Fields and Woods Drawn From natural Specimens. London: 1864-65. V. 48; 49; 51; 52

PRICE, UVEDALE
An Essay on the Picturesque, as Compared with the Sublime and the Beautiful; and on the Use of Studying Pictures for the Purpose of Improving Real Landscape. London: 1794. V. 49; 54

Essays on the Picturesque, as Compared with the Sublime and the Beautiful; and, on the Use of Sudying Pictures for the Purpose of Improving Real Landscape. London: 1810. V. 52

Thoughts on the Defence of Property. Addressed to the County of Hereford. Hereford: 1797. V. 52

PRICE, VINCENT
The Vincent Price Treasury of American Art. Waukesha: 1972. V. 52

PRICE, W.
The Whole Art of Bookbinding. (with) The Whole Process of Marbling Paper. Austin: 1987. V. 47

PRICE, WILLIAM
Clement Falconer; or, the Memoirs of a Young Whig. Baltimore: 1838. V. 52; 54

PRICHARD, A.
A History of Infusoria, Living and Fossil. London: 1849. V. 54

PRICHARD, H. HESKETH
Hunting Camps in Wood and Wilderness. London: 1910. V. 48; 54

Through Trackless Labrador. London: 1911. V. 49; 54

PRICHARD, ILTUDUS
The Chronicles of Budgepore; or, Sketches of Life in Upper India. London: 1870. V. 54

PRICHARD, JAMES COWLES
An Analysis of the Egyptian Mythology... London: 1819. V. 51

The Natural History of Man. London: 1855. V. 52

On the Different Forms of Insanity, in Relation to Jurisprudence, Designed for the Use of Persons Concerned in Legal Questions Regarding Unsoundness of Mind. 1842. V. 54

A Treatise on Insanity and Other Disorders Affecting the Mind. London: 1835. V. 52

A Treatise on Insanity and Other Disorders Affecting the Mind. Philadelphia: 1837. V. 47

PRICHARD, JAMES G.
The Eastern Origin of the Celtic Nations Proved by a Comparison Between Their Dialects with Sanskrit, Greek... 1857. V. 49

PRICHARD, REES
Canwyll Y Cymru, sef Gwaith Mr. Rees Prichard... The Divine Poems of Mr. Rees Prichard. 1766. V. 48

The Welshman's Candle; or the Divine Poems... Carmarthen: 1771. V. 47

The Welshman's Candle; or the Divine Poems of Mr. Rees Prichard, Sometime Vicar of Landovery... Carmarthen: 1781. V. 50; 54

PRIDDEN, W.
Australia, Its History and Present Condition. London: 1843. V. 50

PRIDEAUX, HUMPHREY
The Old and New Testament Connected in the History of the Jews and Neighbouring Nations, from the Declension of the Kingdoms of Israel and Judah to the Time of Christ. London: 1720-18. V. 50

The True Nature of Imposture Fully Display'd in the Life of Mahomet. London: 1698. V. 53

The True Nature of Imposture Fully Display'd in the Life of Mahomet with a Discourse Annex'd for the Vindicating of Christianity from This Charge: Offered to the Consideration of the Deists of the Present Age. London: 1708. V. 47

The True Nature of Imposture Fully Display'd In the Life of Mahomet with a Discourse Annex'd for the Vindication of Christianity from This Charge. London: 1723. V. 50; 53

PRIDEAUX, MATHIAS
An Easy and Compendious Introduction for Reading All Sorts of Histories... Oxford: 1650. V. 49

An Easy and Compendious Introduction for Reading All Sorts of Histories... Oxford: 1664. V. 48

An Easy and Compendious Introduction for Reading All Sorts of Histories... Oxford: 1682. V. 47

PRIDEAUX, S. T.
Aquatint Engraving. A Chapter in the History of Book Illustration. London: 1909. V. 47

Bookbinders and Their Craft. New York: 1903. V. 47; 49; 52; 54

A Catalogue of Books Bound by S. T. Prideaux Between MDCCCXC and MDCCCC with Twenty-Six Illustrations. London: 1900. V. 47; 50

An Historical Sketch of Bookbinding. London: 1893. V. 47; 48; 51; 53; 54

Modern Bookbindings: their Design and Decoration. London: 1906. V. 48; 51; 54

PRIDEAUX, W. F.
Notes for a Bibliography of Edward Fitzgerald. London: 1901. V. 50

PRIDHAM, CHARLES
An Historical, Political and Statistical Account of Ceylon and its Dependencies. London: 1849. V. 54

PRIEST, C. D.
The Birds of Southern Rhodesia. London: 1933-36. V. 48; 50; 51

PRIEST, JOSEPH
American Antiquities and Discoveries in the West. Albany: 1833. V. 47; 52; 54

PRIEST, JOSIAH
Slavery, As it Relates to the Negro, or African Race, Examined in the Light of Circumstances, History and the Holy Scriptures... Albany: 1843. V. 50

Stories of the Revolution. Albany: 1838. V. 48

The Wonders of Nature and Providence, Displayed. Albany: 1825. V. 53

PRIEST, WILLIAM
Travels in the United States of America; Commencing in the Year 1793 and Ending in 1797. London: 1802. V. 53

PRIESTLEY, ANN FREEBORN
How to Know Japanese Colour Prints. New York: 1927. V. 49

PRIESTLEY, ERIC J.
Flame and Smoke!. Los Angeles: 1974. V. 52

PRIESTLEY, HERBERT INGRAM
Franciscan Explorations in California. Glendale: 1946. V. 51

PRIESTLEY, JOHN BOYNTON
Angel Pavement. London: 1930. V. 47; 51; 52

Black-Out in Gretley. London: 1942. V. 51

Brief Diversions. Cambridge: 1922. V. 48

Britain at War. New York: 1942. V. 51

Britain Speaks. New York: 1940. V. 51

Daylight in Saturday. London: 1943. V. 51

Delight. London: 1949. V. 51

Delight. 1978. V. 47

Figures in Modern Literature. London: 1924. V. 54

Four-in-Hand. London: 1934. V. 51

The Good Companions. London: 1934. V. 51

Johnson Over Jordan. the Play. New York: 1939. V. 51

Midnight on the Desert. London: 1937. V. 51

Out of the People. London: 1941. V. 51

Postscripts. London: 1980. V. 51

Rain Upon Godshill. London: 1939. V. 51

They Walk in the City: the Lovers in the Stone Forest. Leipzig: 1937. V. 51

Three Men in New Suits. London: 1945. V. 51

Three Plays... London: 1935. V. 51

Three Plays. London: 1943. V. 51

The Town Major of Miracourt. London: 1930. V. 48; 53

Two Time Plays. Time and Conways. I Have Been Here Before. London: 1938. V. 48; 50; 51

PRIESTLEY, JOSEPH
An Answer to Mr. Paine's Age of Reason. London: 1795. V. 48

An Appeal to the Public, On the Subject of the Riots in Birmingham. Birmingham: 1791. V. 52

An Appeal to the Public, on the Subject of the Riots in Birmingham. Birmingham: 1792. V. 52

The Conduct to be Observed by Dissenters in Order to Procure the Repel of the Corporation and Test Acts Recommended in a Sermon, Preached Before the Congregations of the Old and New Meetings, at Birmingham, Nov. 5, 1789. Birmingham: 1789. V. 50; 54

A Descriptive System of Biography, with a Catalogue of All the Names Inserted In it and the Dates Annexed to Them. Philadelphia: 1803. V. 51

Directions for Impregnating Water with Fixed Air, In Order to Communicate to it the Peculiar spirit of Pyrmont Water, and Other Mineral Waters of a Similar Nature. London: 1772. V. 51

Dr. Priestley's Letter to the Inhabitants of Birmingham... London: 1791. V. 52

An Essay on the First Principles of Government and On the Nature of Political, Civil and Religious Liberty... London: 1771. V. 48; 51; 53

Experiments and Observations on Different Kinds of Air. London: 1774. V. 52

Experiments and Observations on Different Kinds of Air, and Other Branches of Natural Philsopy Connected with the Subject. Birmingham: 1790. V. 54

A Familiar Introduction to the Theory and Practice of Perspective. London: 1780. V. 50

A Harmony of the Evangelists in English... London: 1780. V. 49

Historical Account of the Navigable Rivers, Canals, and Railways of Great Britain. London: 1831. V. 54

The History and Present State of Discoveries Relating to Vision, Light and Colours. London: 1772. V. 54

The History and Present State of Electricity, with Original Experiments... London: 1767. V. 50; 53; 54

The History and Present State of Electricity, with Original Experiments. London: 1775. V. 53

An History of Early Opinions Concerning Jesus Christ. London: 1786. V. 47

An Interesting Appendix to Sir William Blackstone's Commentaries on the Laws of England. Philadelphia: 1772. V. 48

Lectures On History, and General Policy... Birmingham: 1788. V. 52

Lectures on History and General Policy... Dublin: 1791. V. 50

Lectures on History, and General Policy... London: 1791. V. 54

A Letter to the Right Honourable William Pitt...On the Subject of Toleration and Church Establishments; Occasioned by His Speech Against the Repeal of the Test and Corporation Acts, on Wednesday the 28th of March, 1787. London: 1787. V. 48

Letters to a Philosophical Unbeliever. Part I (with) Part II. Birmingham: 1787/87. V. 49; 52

Letters to the Jews... (with) Letters to the Jews. Part II. Birmingham: 1786/87. V. 49

PRIESTLEY, JOSEPH continued
Letters to the Right Honourable Edmund Burke Occasioned by His Reflections on the Revolution in France &c. Birmingham: 1791. V. 48; 52
Letters to the Right Honourable Edmund Burke, Occasioned by His Reflections on the Revolution in France &c. London: 1791. V. 52
A Twig of Birch for a Butting Calf; or Strictures Upon Remarks on the Emigration of Doctor Joseph Priestley, &c... New York: 1795. V. 48

PRIESTLEY, MARY
A Book of Birds. London: 1937. V. 48

PRIME Evil. West Kingston: 1988. V. 48; 49; 51; 52

PRIME, NATHANIEL S.
A History of Long Island, From Its First Settlement by Europeans to the Year 1845. New York: 1845. V. 54

PRIME, SAMUEL I.
Travels in Europe and the East: a Year in England, Scotland, Ireland, Wales, Belgium, Holland, Germany, Austria, Greece, Turkey, Syria, Palestine and Egypt. New York: 1855. V. 48
Travels in Europe and the East: a Year in England, Scotland, Ireland, Wales...Greece, Turkey, syria, Palestine and Egypt. New York: 1864. V. 49

PRIME, WILLIAM C.
Pottery and Porcelain of All Times and Nations... New York: 1878. V. 49
Pottery and Porcelain of All Times and Nations. New York: 1879. V. 47

THE PRIMER, Or Office of the Blessed Virgin Marie, in Latin and English. Antwerp: 1650. V. 49

PRIMERA, y Breve Relacion de las Favorables Noticias Que Con Fechas de Seis, y Veinte y Ocho de Enero de este ano de 1703 se han Tenido por Cartas de Don Luis (i.e. Juan) de Zuniga, Governador de la Florida, y D. Luis Chacon, Governador de la Havana. Madrid: 1703. V. 48

PRIMITIVE Christian Discipline, Not to Be Slighted; or Man, Look Home and Know Thy Self. London?: 1658. V. 48; 49

PRIMOGENITA, PSEUD.
Recollections of Childhood; or, Sally, the Faithful Nurse. London: 1840. V. 54

PRIMROSE, JAMES
De Vulgi in Medicina Erroribus.... London: 1640. V. 51; 54
Popular Errours. Or the Errours of People of Physick, First Written in Latine... London: 1651. V. 47; 49

PRIN, ALICE
Kiki's Memoirs. Paris: 1930. V. 48; 50; 53

PRINCE Albert's Golden Precepts; or, the Opinions and Maxims of His Royal Highness the Prince Consort. London: 1862. V. 53

PRINCE, F. T.
Memoirs in Oxford. London: 1970. V. 54
Soldiers Bathing. London: 1954. V. 47

PRINCE, JOHN
Danmonii Orientales Illustres; or, the Worthies of Devon... Exeter: 1701. V. 51
Danmonii Orientales Illustres; or the Worthies of Devon... London: 1810. V. 54
Danmonii Orientales Illustres; or, the Worthies of Devon. Plymouth: 1810. V. 50; 54
A Wreath of St. Crispin: Being Sketches of Eminent Shoemakers. Boston: 1848. V. 54

PRINCE, JOHN DYNELEY
Materials for a Sumerian Lexicon With a Grammatical Introduction. Leipzig: 1908. V. 49; 52

PRINCE, L. BRADFORD
Historical Sketches of New Mexico from the Earliest Records to the Occupation. New York: 1883. V. 49
New Mexico A Defence of the People and Country... Santa Fe: 1882. V. 52
New Mexico's Struggle for Statehood: Sixty Years of Effort to Obtain Self Government. Santa Fe: 1910. V. 53
The Present and Future of New Mexico A Land of Prosperity and Happiness. Santa Fe: 1891. V. 52
Spanish Mission Churches of New Mexico. Cedpar Rapids: 1915. V. 51

PRINCE, MORTON
Clinical and Experimental Studies in Personality. Cambridge: 1929. V. 54

PRINCE, NANCY
A Narrative of the Life and Travels of Mrs. Nancy Prince Written by Herself. Boston: 1853. V. 54

THE PRINCE Of Peace. Christmas Canticles. Flemington: 1965. V. 52

PRINCE, THOMAS
Extraordinary Events the Doings of God, and Maravellous in Pious Eyes. Boston: 1746. V. 52
The Vade Mecum for America; or, a Companion for Traders and Travellers... Boston: 1732. V. 47; 51; 52

PRINCE, WILLIAM
Catalogue of Fruit and Ornamental Trees, Flowering Shrubs and Plants, Green House Shrubs and Plants...Cultivated and for Sale at the Linnaean Botanic Garden, Flushing, Long Island, Near New York. 1826. V. 47

PRINCE, WILLIAM ROBERT
The Pomological Manual; or, a Treatise on Fruits... New York: 1831. V. 50; 51; 53; 54
A Treatise on the Vine... New York: 1830. V. 50; 51

PRINCE DE BEAUMONT, MARIE
The Young Misses Magazine... New York: 1807. V. 54

THE PRINCE'S Cabala; or Mysteries of State. London: 1715. V. 53

THE PRINCES Fire-Flash and Fire-Fade. London: 1888. V. 53
THE PRINCES Fire-Flash and Fire-Fade. Tokyo: 1888. V. 50

THE PRINCESS Elizabeth Gift Book. 1933. V. 48; 52

PRINCESS Mary's Gift Book. 1914. V. 49

PRINCETON UNIVERSITY
Laws of the College of New Jersey, Reviewed, Amended and Finally Adopted...in September 1802... Philadelphia: 1802. V. 49

THE PRINCIPAL Events in the History of Ireland, in the Form of Stories. London: 1829. V. 52

PRINCIPLES of Design in Architecture Traced in Observations on Buildings, in a Series of Letters to a Friend. London: 1809. V. 49

PRING, JOSEPH
Particulars of the Grand Suspension Bridge, Erected Over the Straits of menai, by Order of Government... Bangor: 1826. V. 51

PRINGLE, EDWARD J.
Slavery in the Southern States. Cambridge: 1852. V. 48; 49

PRINGLE, J. F.
Lunenburgh or the Old Eastern District Its Settlement and Early Progress... Cornwall: 1890. V. 54

PRINGLE, J. J.
Twenty Years' Snipe-Shooting. New York: 1899. V. 47

PRINGLE, JOHN
A Discourse on the Theory of Gunnery. London: 1778. V. 50; 54
Observations on the Diseases of the Army. London: 1753. V. 51; 52
Observations On the Diseases of the Army. London: 1764. V. 53
Observations on the Diseases of the Army, with Notes. Philadelphia: 1810. V. 48
Observations on the Nature and Cure of Hospital and Jayl-Fevers. London: 1750. V. 52
Six Discourses, Delivered by John Pringle, Bart. When President of the Royal Society. London: 1783. V. 47; 48

PRINGLE, M. A.
Towards the Mountains of the Moon. Edinburgh: 1884. V. 51

PRINGLE, ROGER
A Garland for the Laureate - Poems - Poems Presented to Sir John Betjeman on His 75 th Birthday. Stratford-upon-Avon: 1981. V. 54
Poems for Shakespeare. London: 1977. V. 54

PRINGLE, THOMAS
African Sketches. London: 1834. V. 54

PRINGY, MME. DE MARENVILLE DE
Les Differens Caracteres des Femmes du Siecle, Avec la Description de l'Amour Propre... Paris: 1694. V. 50; 53; 54

THE PRINTER. The Guide to Trade. London: 1845. V. 52

A PRINTER'S Dozen: Eleven Spreads from Unrealised Books... 1993. V. 52; 54

PRINTING in the Twentieth Century: a Survey. London: 1930. V. 51

PRINTING with the Handpress. Kentfield: 1969. V. 49; 50

PRINTZ, H.
The Vegetation of the Siberian-Mongolian Frontiers (the Sayansk Region). Trondhjem: 1921. V. 51

PRINZING, FRIEDRICH
Epidemics Resulting from Wars. Oxford: 1916. V. 50; 51; 52; 54

PRINZMETAL, M.
The Auricular Arrhythmias. Springfield: 1952. V. 49; 54

PRIOR, JAMES
The Life of Oliver Goldsmith. Philadelphia: 1837. V. 48
Memoir of the Life and Character of the Right Hon. Edmund Burke... London: 1824. V. 51
Memoir of the Life and Character of the Right Hon. Edmund Burke, with Specimens of His Poetry and Letters... London: 1839. V. 54
Narrative of a Voyage in the Indian Seas, in the Nisus Frigate, to the Cape of Good Hope, Isle of Bourbon, France and Seychelles... London: 1820. V. 49; 50

PRIOR, M.
Voyage and the Eastern Coast of Africa, to Mosambique, Johanna and Quiloa... London: 1819. V. 47

PRIOR, MATTHEW
An English Ballad. London: 1695. V. 53
The Hind and the Panther Transvers'd to the Story of the City Mouse and the Country Mouse. London: 1687. V. 47; 49; 52
The History of His Own Time. London: 1740. V. 48
Miscellaneous Works Consisting of Poems on Several Occasions. London: 1740. V. 50; 53
An Ode, Humbly Inscrib'd to the Queen. London: 1706. V. 48; 53; 54
Poems on Several Occasions. London: 1709. V. 47; 48; 49; 52; 54
Poems on Several Occasions. London: 1718. V. 47; 49; 50; 51; 52; 53; 54
Poems on Several Occasions. London: 1721. V. 51
Poems on Several Occasions. London: 1741. V. 53
Poems on Several Occasions. London: 1766/67. V. 49
Poems on Several Occasions. Dublin: 1768. V. 48; 49
Poems On Several Occasions. Glasgow: 1771. V. 49
The Poetical Works... London: 1779. V. 47; 50; 54

PRIOR, MATTHEW continued
The Poetical Works. London: 1866. V. 51

PRIOR, R.
Lusus Westmonasaterienses, sive Epigrammatum et Poematum Minorum Delectus... Londini: 1740. V. 53

PRIOR, R. C. A.
Ancient Danish Ballads. London & Edinburgh: 1860. V. 49
On the Popular Names of British Plants, an Explanation of the Origin and meaning of the Names of the Indigenous and Most Commonly Cultivated Species. London: 1879. V. 52

PRIOR, THOMAS
A List of the Absentees of Ireland, and the Yearly Value of Their Estates and Incomes Spent Abroad. 1729. V. 47
A List of the Absentees of Ireland, and the Yearly Value of Their Estates and Incomes Spent Abroad. Dublin: 1745. V. 48
Observations on Coin in General. Dublin: 1729. V. 51

PRIOR, WILLIAM MATTHEW
The King's Vesture: Evidence from Scripture and History. Boston: 1862. V. 54

PRISCIANUS CAESARIENSIS
Prisciani Grammatici Caesariensis Libri Omnes... Venice: 1527. V. 48; 50; 52

PRISK, W. F.
Nevada County Mining Review. Grass Valley: 1895. V. 50

PRISON Etiquette: The Convict's Compendium of Useful Information by the Inmates. Bearsville: 1950. V. 51

PRITCHARD, ANDREW
A History of Infusoria Animalcules, Living and Fossil. London: 1852. V. 52
A History of Infusoria, Including the Desmidiaceae and Diatomaceae, British and Foreign. London: 1861. V. 51; 52
A History of Infusoria, Living and Fossil. London: 1841. V. 47
A History of Infusoria, Living and Fossil... London: 1842. V. 52
The Microscopic Cabinet of Select animated Objects. London: 1832. V. 49

PRITCHARD, ERIC, MRS.
The Cult of Chiffon. London: 1902. V. 52

PRITCHARD, H. BADEN
The Studios of Europe. New York: 1882. V. 51

PRITCHARD, JAMES A.
The Overland Diary of James A. Pritchard from Kentucky to California in 1849. Denver: 1959. V. 48; 50; 53; 54

PRITCHARD, JAMES B.
The Ancient Near East in Pictures Relating to the Old Testament. (and) Ancient Near Eastern Texts Relating to the Old Testament. Princeton: 1969/74. V. 52

PRITCHETT, R. T.
Pen and Pencil Skethces of Shipping and Craft all Round the World. London: 1899. V. 51

PRITCHETT, V. S.
Marching Spain. London: 1928. V. 53
When My Girl Comes Home. New York: 1961. V. 52

PRITT, T. E.
An Anglers Basket, Filled in Sunshine and Shade through the Space of Forty Years... London: 1896. V. 53

PRITTS, JOSEPH
Incidents of Border Life, Illustrative of the Times and Condition of the First Settlements in Parts of the Middle and Western States. Chambersburg: 1839. V. 48

PRITZEL, G. A.
Thesaurus Botanicae. Mansfield: 1995. V. 53

PRIVATE Anecdotes of Foreign Courts...With Anecdotes of the French Court by the Perfect of the Imperial Palace. London: 1827. V. 54

PRIVATE Letter from an American in England to His Friends in America. London: 1769. V. 52

PRIVATE Letters from Phyllis to Marie or the Art of Child-Love. Or the Adventures and Experiences of a Little Girl. London and Paris: 1898. V. 50

THE PRIVATE Life of the Late Benjamin Franklin, LL.D. London: 1793. V. 48

THE PRIVATE Stable Its Establishment, Management and Appointments. Boston: 1899. V. 54

PRIVATE Worth the Basis of Public Decency. An Address to People of Rank and Fortune. Dublin: 1789. V. 48

THE PRIVILEDGES Of the Citizens of London: Contained in the Charters, Granted to Them by Several Kings Of This Realm... London: 1682. V. 52

THE PRIVILEGES and Practice of Parliaments in England: Collected out of the Common Laws of This Land. London: 1680. V. 48; 52

PRIVILEGGI e Statuti Della Venerabile Archiconfraternita dell'Anime Piu' Bisognose del Purgatorio eretta in Roma Sotto il Patrocino di Gesu Maria, e S. Giuseppe dal Venerabile Servo di Dio Papa Innocenzo XI. Rome: 1734. V. 52; 54

PRIZE Stories 1964. The O. Henry Awards. Garden City: 1964. V. 51

PROBY, DOUGLAS JAMES
A Catalogue of the Pictures at Elton Hall in Huntingdonshire in the Possession of Col. Douglas James Proby. London: 1924. V. 47

PROBYN, JOHN WEBB
Essays on Italy and Ireland and the United States of America. London: 1868. V. 47

PROBYN, MAY
Poems. London: 1881. V. 48

THE PROCEEDINGS at the Assizes Holden at York, the 24th day of July 1680...Against Several Prisoners Then Indicted for the Horrid Popish Plot...With an Account at Large of the Arraignment of Sir Miles Stapleton...and of the Tryal...of Mr. Thomas Thwing. London: 1681. V. 53

THE PROCEEDINGS At the Guild-Hall in London on Thursday, July 29th, 1680. London: 1680. V. 52; 53

PROCEEDINGS at the Laying of the Corner Stone of the New Capitol Building, at Des Moines, Iowa, November 23, 1871. Des Moines: 1871. V. 53

PROCEEDINGS at the Reception and Dinner, in Honor of George Peabody, Esq. of London, by the Citizens of the Old Town of Danvers, October 9, 1856. Boston: 1856. V. 47; 50

PROCEEDINGS in Behalf of the Morton Testimonial. Boston: 1861. V. 50

THE PROCEEDINGS in The Cause of the King Against the Dean of St. Asaph, on the Prosecution of William Jones, Gent, for a Libel; at the Great Session Held at Wrexham... Chester: 1783. V. 47

PROCEEDINGS of a General Court Martial held at the Horse-Guards, on the 24th and 27th of March, 1792, for the Trial of Capt. Richard Powell, Lieut. Christopher Seton, and Lieut. John Hall of the 54th Regiment of Foot; on Several Charges... London: 1809. V. 49

PROCEEDINGS of an Indian Council Held at the Buffalo Creek Reservation, State of New York, Fourth Month, 1842. Baltimore: 1842. V. 48

THE PROCEEDINGS of Corpus Christi College, Oxon, in the Case of Mr. Ayscough, Vindicated. London: 1730. V. 53

PROCEEDINGS of Public Meetings Held at Various Times in Charleston, Calling Upon the City Council to Make Subscriptions to Rail Roads... Charleston: 1854. V. 48

PROCEEDINGS of the Citizens of Philadelphia Relative to the Rail Road to Erie, and of the Convention at Williamsport, Lycoming County, Pa. Philadelphia: 1836. V. 53

PROCEEDINGS Of the Convention to Consider the Opening of the Indian Territory. Kansas City: 1888. V. 49

THE PROCEEDINGS of the Executive of the United States, Respecting the Insurgents, 1794. Philadelphia: 1795. V. 51

THE PROCEEDINGS of the Grand-Jury of Middlesex, in Easter Term. 1681. London: 1681. V. 52

THE PROCEEDINGS of the Present Parliament Justified by the Opinion of the Most Judicious and Learned Hugo Grotius; with Considerations Thereupon. London: 1689. V. 52

PROCEEDINGS of the Public Meeting Held at Freemason's Hall, on the 18th June, 1824, for Erecting a Monument to the Late James Watt. London: 1824. V. 50

PROCEEDINGS of the Tribunal of Arbitration, Convened at Paris...for the Determination of Questions...in the Waters of the Bering Sea. Washington: 1895. V. 52

THE PROCEEDINGS of the United States Anti-Masonic Convention, Held at Philadelphia, September 11, 1830. Philadelphia: 1830. V. 48

PROCEEDINGS of the Vice-Chancellor and the University of Cambridge Against Dr. Bentley, Stated and Vindicated. London: 1719. V. 53

PROCHASKA, GEORGE
A Dissertation on the Functions of the Nervous System. London: 1851. V. 47; 54

PROCLUS
The Fragments That Remain of the Lost Writings of Proclus, Surnamed the Platonic Sucessor. London: 1825. V. 48
Sphaera. Astronomiam Discere Incipientibus Utilissima. Vienna: 1511. V. 47

PROCOPIUS
Arcana Historia...Ex Bibliotheca Vaticana Nicolaus Alemannus Protilit Latine Reddidit. Lyons: 1623. V. 50
The History of the Warres of the Emperour Justinian in Eight Books. London: 1653. V. 47; 50

PROCTER, ADELAIDE ANNE
A Chaplet of Verses. London: 1862. V. 50; 53
Legends and Lyrics. London: 1866. V. 47; 48; 49; 50; 54
Legends and Lyrics. London: 1871. V. 51

PROCTER BROS.
The Fishermens' Own Book Comprising the List of men and Vessels Lost from the Port of Gloucester, Mass., from 1874 to April 1, 1882, and a Table of Losses from 1830. Together with Valuable Statistics of the Fisheries. Gloucester: 1882. V. 49

PROCTER, BRYAN WALLER
An Autobiographical Fragment and Biographical Notes, with Personal Sketches of Contemporaries, Unpublished Lyrics and Letters. London: 1877. V. 51
Dramatic Scenes. London: 1857. V. 49
English Songs and Other Small Poems. London: 1832. V. 54
Marcian Colonna, an Italian Tale. London: 1820. V. 48; 54
The Poetical Works of Barry Cornwall. London: 1822. V. 48
A Sicilian Story, With Diego De Montilla and Other Poems. London: 1820. V. 48; 54

PROCTER, ELLEN A.
A Brief Memoir of Christina G. Rossetti. London: 1895. V. 49; 50; 52

PROCTOR, A. PHIMISTER
An Ascent of Half Dome in 1884. San Francisco: 1945. V. 50

PROCTOR, FRANK
Under Six Sovereigns: Fox Hunting In Canada. Toronto: 1955. V. 47

PROCTOR, FREDERICK TOWNE
The Frederick Towne Proctor Collection of Antique Watches and Table Clocks. Utica: 1913. V. 53

PROCTOR, GEORGE
The Lucubrations of Humphrey Ravelin (Pseud), Late Major in the **Regiment of Infantry. London: 1823. V. 47

PROCTOR, HENRY HUGH
Between Black and White: Autobiographical Sketches. Boston: 1925. V. 53

PROCTOR, L. B.
The Bench and Bar of New York:. New York: 1870. V. 48; 54
Lives of Eminent Lawyers and Statesmen of the State of New York, and Notes of Cases Tried by Them... New York: 1892. V. 52

PROCTOR, R.
The Printing of Greek in Fifteenth Century. Oxford: 1900. V. 47

PROCTOR, RICHARD A.
Watched by the Dead, a Loving Study of Charles Dickens' Half Told Tale. London: 1887. V. 47

PROCTOR, ROBERT
Bibliographical Essays. London: 1905. V. 51; 54
Jan Van Doesborgh, Printer at Antwerp. London: 1894. V. 48; 50

PRODDOW, PENNY
American Jewelry: Glamour and Tradition. New York: 1987. V. 49

PROEMS. London: 1938. V. 49

PROFESSIONAL Anecdotes, or Ana of Medical Literature... London: 1825. V. 48

PROGRESS. 1893. Commerce. The Century's Progress. Yorkshire: 1893. V. 50

PROGRESS. 1893. Commerce. The Ports of the Bristol Channel. 1893. V. 50

PROGRESS. 1894. Commerce. Rivers of the North. Their Cities and Their Commerce. 1894. V. 50

THE PROGRESS of a Female Mind, in Some Interesting Enquiries. London: 1764. V. 48

PROGRESS of Saskatchewan (Year Book). Saskatoon: 1932. V. 53

THE PROGRESS of the Wheaten Loaf. Baltimore: 1810. V. 50

THE PROGRESSES of H.M. Queen Victoria & H.R.H. Prince Albert in France, Belgium and England. London: 1844. V. 48

PROGRESSIVE Drawing Book; Containing a Series of Easy and Comprehensive Lessons for Drawing Landscape, Architecture, the Human Figure, Shipping, Animals &c... London: 1853. V. 48; 50

PROGRESSIVE Men of the State of Montana. Chicago: 1902. V. 49

PROKOSCH, FREDERIC
The Asiatics. New York: 1935. V. 48; 53
The Assassins. New York: 1936. V. 54
The Carnival. New York, London: 1938. V. 49; 53; 54
Chosen Poems. Garden City: 1947. V. 51; 54
The Conspirators. New York: 1943. V. 54
Death at Sea. New York & London: 1940. V. 53; 54
Night of the Poor. New York: 1939. V. 54
Nine Days to Mukalla. New York: 1953. V. 51
The Red Sea. 1935. V. 52
The Skies of Europe. New York & London: 1941. V. 54
Storm and Echo. New York: 1948. V. 47
The Stranger. New Haven: 1931. V. 52
A Tale of Midnight. Boston: 1955. V. 54

THE PROMISED Visit: Including an Account of the Various Methods of Manufacturing Paper in different Countries. London: 1818. V. 49

PRONY, GASPARD FRANCOIS CLAIR MARIE RICHE DE
Nouvelle Architecture Hydraulique, Contenant l'art d'Elever l'eau au Moyen de Differentes machines, de Construire dans ce Fluide, de la Diriger, et Generalement de l'Appliquer... Paris: 1790/96. V. 51

PRONY, MARC ANTOINE, PSEUD.
Models of Letters in French and English... London: 1797. V. 52

PRONZINI, BILL
Cat's Paw. Richmond: 1983. V. 52
A Killing in Xanadu. Richmond: 1980. V. 52

PROPERT, J. L.
A History of Miniature Art. London: 1887. V. 53; 54

PROPERT, W. A.
The Russian Ballet, 1921-29. London: 1931. V. 50
The Russian Ballet in Western Europe 1909-1920. New York & London: 1921. V. 52; 54

PROPERTY Re-Asserted, in Answer to the Arguments & Exceptions in a Late Paper Intituled Property Vindicated. Dublin: 1640. V. 47

A PROPHESIE. Which Hath Been in Manuscript, in the Lord Powis's Family Sixty Years. 1679. V. 47

A PROPOSAL for Humbling Spain. London: 1730. V. 47

PROPOSALS for Opening a Scotch Eating House or, North Country Ordinary, and Scotch Chocolate House, in the Neighbourhood of St. James's... London: 1799. V. 47

PROPOSALS for Raising a Million of Money Out of the Forfeited Estates in Ireland: Together, With the Answer of the Irish to the Same, and a Reply Thereto. London: 1694. V. 50

PROPOSED State of Sequoyah Mr. Foraker Presented the Following Memorial From Citizens of Indian Territory, Praying for Admission Into the Union Upon and Equal Footing with the Original States...To Be Known as the State of Sequoyah. Washington: 1906. V. 48

PROPRIETES et Les Fonctions du Systeme Nerveus dan Les Animaux Vertebre. Paris: 1824. V. 47

PROSCH, CHARLES
Reminiscences of Washington Territory, Scenes, Incidents and Reflections of the Pioneer period on Puget Sound. Seattle: 1904. V. 48; 52

PROSCH, T. W.
David S. Maynard and Catherine T. Maynard: Biographies of two of the Oregon Immigrants of 1850. Seattle: 1906. V. 51
McCarver and Tacoma. Seattle: 1906. V. 47; 48

PROSE, e Versi per Onorare la Memoria di Livia Doria Caraffa...di Alcuni Rinomati Autori. Parma: 1784. V. 50; 51; 52; 53; 54

PROSE E Versi Per Onorare La Memoria Di Livia Doria Caraffa. Parma: 1793. V. 48

PROSE Masterpieces from Modern Essayists. London: 1896. V. 51; 54

PROSKOURIAKOFF, TATIANA
An Album of Maya Architecture. Washington: 1946. V. 52
Jades from the Cenote of Sacrifice Chichen Itza, Yucatan. Cambridge: 1974. V. 52
A Study of Classic Maya Sculpture. Washington: 1950. V. 50

PROSPECCTUS of Mr. Sheldrake's Undertaking to Cure Distortion of the Spine and Distortions of the Legs and Feet of Children, at His Residence No. 10, Adams Street, Adelphia, London at Richmond and at Bath. London: 1816. V. 52

THE PROTESTANT Antidote. 1680. V. 52

PROTESTANT EPISCOPAL CHURCH
Constitution of the Protestant Episcopal Church in the Confederate States of America and Digest of the Canons Adopted in General Council, in Augusta, Georgia, November, 1862. Augusta: 1863. V. 49

PROTESTANT MISSIONARIES OF CHINA
Records of the General conference of the...Held at Shanghai, May 1-24, 1877. Shanghai: 1878. V. 49

THE PROTESTANT Petition and Address. London April 30, 1681. Upon Thursday Last There Was Presented to the Lord Mayor and Court of Aldermen... London: 1681. V. 52

PROTHERO, D. R.
Eocene-Oligocene Climatic and Biotic Evolution. Princeton: 1992. V. 52
The Evolution of Perissodactyls. Oxford: 1989. V. 50

PROUD, ROBERT
The History of Pennsylvania, in North America, from the Original Institution and Settlement of that Province, Under the First Proprietor and Governor William Penn in 1681, Till After the Year 1742... Philadelphia: 1797-98. V. 47; 54

PROUDFIT, ALEXANDER
A Sermon Preached in the First Presbyterian Church in Newburyport, Oct. 4th, 1827. Newburyport: 1828. V. 53

PROUDHON, PIERRE JOSEPH
Advertissement aux Proprietaires... Paris: 1841. V. 52

PROULX, E. ANNIE
The Complete Dairy Foods Cookbook. Emmaus: 1982. V. 53
The Fine Art of Salad Gardening. Emmaus: 1985. V. 52; 54
The Gourmet Gardener. New York: 1987. V. 54
Heart Songs. New York: 1988. V. 50; 51; 52; 53
Postcards. New York: 1992. V. 50; 51; 52; 53; 54
Postcards. London: 1993. V. 54
The Shipping News. New York: 1993. V. 51; 52; 53; 54

PROUST, MARCEL
The Captive. New York: 1929. V. 50; 53
Cities of the Plain. 1927. V. 50
Du Cote de Chez Swann. Paris: 1914. V. 51
Jean Santeuil. Paris: 1952. V. 47
Letters of Marcel Proust. New York: 1949. V. 54
Les Plaisirs et les Jours. Paris: 1896. V. 49
A La Recherche du Temps Perdu. Paris: 1914-13/1918-27. V. 53
A La Recherche du Temps Perdu. Paris: 1919. V. 53
Remembrance of Things Past. London: 1943. V. 47
Remembrance of Things Past. London: 1964. V. 51
Remembrance of Things Past. London: 1967-71. V. 47

PROUST, MARCEL continued
Time Regained. London: 1931. V. 50
A Vision of Paris. New York: 1963. V. 50; 51; 52; 53

PROUT, SAMUEL
Hints on Light and Shadow, Composition, etc., as Applicable to Landscape Painting... London: 1838. V. 47; 53
Hints on Light and Shadow, Composition, Etc. as Applicable to Landscape Painting. London: 1848. V. 50; 53
A New Drawing Book, in the Manner of Chalk... London: 1819. V. 48
A New Drawing Book in the Manner of Chalk, Containing Twelve Views in the West of England. London: 1821. V. 47
Picturesque Studies of Cottages, Old Houses, Castles, Bridges, Ruins, Etc. in the Manner of Chalk. London: 1840. V. 48
Progressive Fragments... London: 1817. V. 53
Progressive Fragments, Drawn and Etched in a Broad and Simple Manner... London: 1818. V. 48
Prout's Microcosm. The Artist's Sketch-Book of Groups of Figures, Shipping and Other Picturesque Objects. London: 1841. V. 48
Prout's Microcosm. The Artist's Sketchbook of Groups of Figures, Shipping, and Other Picturesque Objects. London: 1881. V. 47
Rudiments of Landscape... London: 1813. V. 49
Rudiments of Landscape: in Progressive Studies, in Imitation of Chalk, Indian Ink and Colours. London: 1814. V. 48
A Series of Easy Lessons in Landscape Drawing, Contained in Forty Plates... London: 1820. V. 48
Studies of Boats and Coast Scenery for Landscape and Marine Painters, Drawn and etched in Imitation of Chalk. London: 1816. V. 47

PROUT, WILLIAM
Chemistry, Meteorology and the Function of Digestion Considered with Reference to Natural Theology. Philadelphia: 1834. V. 48
An Inquiry Into the Nature and Treatment of Gravel, Calculus, and Other Diseases Connected with a Deranged Operation of the Urinary Organs. London: 1821. V. 49; 51
On the Nature and Treatment of Stomach and Renal Diseases... London: 1848. V. 52
On the Nature and Treatment of Stomach and Urinary Diseases: Being an Inquiry into the Connexion of Diabetes, Calculus and Other Affections of the Kidney and Bladder with Indigestion. London: 1840. V. 54

PROUTY, OLIVE HIGGINS
Now, Voyager. Boston: 1941. V. 47; 48; 49

PROVERBS Exemplified, and Illustrated by Pictures from Real Life.
London: 1790. V. 52

PROVINCE of Ontario Gazetteer and Directory 1907-08.
Ingersoll: 1907. V. 53

PROVINCIARUM Europae Geographica Descriptio: Europa, Mit Angrentzenden Welt-Theilen Denen Staats-Kriegs und Gelehrten Personen...
Augsburg: 1679. V. 47

PROVOST, ANDREW J.
Biographical and Genealogical Notes of the Provost Family from 1545 to 1895. New York: 1895. V. 49; 51

PROWELL, GEORGE R.
The History of Camden County, New Jersey. Philadelphia: 1886. V. 49; 51

PROWELL, SANDRA WEST
By Evil Means. 1993. V. 54
By Evil Means. New York: 1993. V. 51

PROWN, JULES DAVID
American Painting: From Its Beginnings to the Armory Show: The 20th Century. Geneva: 1969. V. 49
John Singleton Copley. Cambridge: 1966. V. 49; 50; 52; 53

PROWSE, D. W.
A History of Newfoundland from the English, Colonial and Foreign Records. London: 1896. V. 53
The Newfoundland Guide Book 1905 Including Labrador and St. Pierre. London: 1905. V. 47; 52

PRUDDEN, NEHEMIAH
To Marry a Wife's Sister, Not Inconsistent with the Divine Law. To Which is Added Some Remarks on Dr. Trumbull's Late Appeal to the Public. Hartford: 1811. V. 50

PRUDEN, DUNSTAN
Silversmithing. Its Principles and Practice in Small Workshops. Ditchling: 1933. V. 47; 49

PRUDENTIUS, AURELIUS CLEMENS
Opera. Amsterdam: 1631. V. 52
Opera. Paris: 1687. V. 49
Opera Ex Fide Decem Liborum Manuscriptorum Emendatus, Et in Eum, Ejusdem Victoris Giselini Commentarius. (and) Symmachi, et Ambrosii de Roterodami in Duos Hymnos Aur. Prudentii Commentarius. Antwerp: 1564. V. 47; 53

PRUIETT, MOMAN
Moman Pruiett, Criminal Lawyer. 1945. V. 47

PRUIETT, MONAN
Moman Pruiett, Criminal Lawyer. Oklahoma City: 1945. V. 53

PRUNETTI, MICHELANGELO
Regras de Arte da Pintura, com Breves Reflexoes Criticas Sobre os Caracteres Distinctivos de Suas Escolas, Vidas, e Quadros de Seus Mais Celebres professores. Lisbon: 1815. V. 47

PRUYN, ANNA PARKER
Catalogue of Books Relating to the Literature of the Law Collected by the Late John v. L. Pruyn of Albany, New York. Albany: 1901. V. 48

PRY, PAUL, PSEUD.
Oddities of London Life. London: 1838. V. 52

PRYCE, F. N.
Catalogue of Sculpture in the Department of Greek and Roman Antiquities of the British Museum. London: 1928. V. 50; 52

PRYCE, GEORGE
Memorials of the Canynges' Family and Their Times. Bristol: 1854. V. 49; 53

PRYCE, WILLIAM
Archaeologia Cornu-Britannica; or, an Essay to Preserve the Ancient Cornish Language. Sherborne: 1790. V. 48; 51; 53
Mineralogia Cornubiensis: a Treatise on Minerals, Mines and Mining... London: 1778. V. 47; 48; 49; 53; 54

PRYCE-JONES, ALAN
Little Innocents. London: 1932. V. 51

PRYER, ADA
A Decade in Borneo. London: 1893. V. 54

PRYME, GEORGE
Ode to Trinity College, Cambridge. London: 1812. V. 52

PRYNNE, WILLIAM
Antiquae Constitutiones regni Angliae, Sub Regibus Joanne, Henrico Tertio, et Edoardo Primo, Circa Jurisdictionem et Potestatem Ecclesiasticam. London: 1672. V. 47
A Brief Survey and Censure of Mr. Cozens His Couzening Devotions. London: 1628. V. 53
The Doome of Cowardisze and Treachery, or, a Looking Glasse for Cowardly or Corrupt Govenours, and Souldiers, Who through Pusillanimity or Bribery, Betray Their Trusts... London: 1643. V. 48
The Falsities and Forgeries of the Anonymous author of a Late Pamphlet (Supposed to be Printed at Oxford but in Truth at London) 1644, Intituled The Fallacies of Mr. William Prynne, Discovered and Confuted, in a Short View of His Books. London: 1644. V. 48
The First and Second Part of the Signal Loyalty and Devotion of Gods True Saints and Pious Christians...Towards Their Kings. London: 1660. V. 50
Mr. William Prynn His Defence of Stage-Plays, or A Retraction of a Former Book of His Called Historio-Mastix. London: 1822. V. 53
A Moderate Apology Against a Pretended Calumny. London: 1644. V. 48
A New Discovery of the Prelates Tyranny, in Their Late Prosecutions of Mr. William Pryne, Dr. John Bastwick and Mr. Henry Burton. London: 1641. V. 47
Romes Master-Peece. Or the Grand Conspiracy of the Pope and His Jesuited Instruments... London: 1643. V. 47
The Second Tome of an Exact Chronological Vindication and Historical Demonstration of Our British, Roman, Saxon, Danish, Norman, English Kings Supream Ecclesiastical Jurisdiction. London: 1665. V. 47; 50; 53
The Soveraigne Power of Parliaments and Kingdomes: Divided Into Foure Parts. London: 1643. V. 48
The Treachery and Disloyalty of Papists to Their Soveraignes...Together with The First (through Fourth) part(s) of the Soveraigne Power of Parliaments and Kingdomes. London: 1643. V. 47
The Unlovelinesse, of Love-Lockes. London: 1628. V. 53

PRYOR, A. R.
The Flora of Hertfordshire. London: 1887. V. 50; 51

PRYSE, G. SPENCER
Four Days - an Account of a Journey in France Made Between August 28th and 31st, 1914. London: 1932. V. 49

PRYSE, JOHN
Pryse's Handbook to the Radnorshire and Breconshire Mineral Springs... Llanidloes: 1880. V. 54

PSALIGRAPHY..
Boston: 1868. V. 51

PSALMANAZAR, GEORGE
An Historical and Geographical Description of Formosa... London: 1704. V. 47
Historical and Geographical Description of Formosa. London: 1705. V. 47; 49; 51; 54
An Historical and Geographical Description of Formosa, An Island Subject to the Emperor of Japan. London: 1926. V. 50; 52; 53; 54
Memoirs of... London: 1764. V. 48

PSALMS, Hymns and Anthems: Sung in the Chapel of the Hospital, for the Maintenance and Education of Exposed and Deserted Young Children.
London: 1795. V. 54

PSELLUS, MICHAEL
De Victus Ratione. Basileae: 1529. V. 47; 50; 53

PTLOMAEUS, CLAUDIUS
Geographia Universalis, vetus et Nova. Basil: 1545. V. 52

PTOLEMAEUS, CLAUDIUS
Geographiae Universae tum Veteris tum Novae Absolutissimum Opus Duobus Voluminibus Distinctum... Colonia: 1597. V. 48; 49
De Praedictionibus Astronomicus Cui Titulum Fecerunt Qudripartitum, Libri Quatuor. Perugia: 1664. V. 47

THE PUBLIC Buildings of Westminster Described.
London: 1831. V. 47

THE PUBLIC Edifices of the British Metropolis; with Historical and Descriptive Accounts of the Different Buildings...
London: 1825. V. 50; 53

PUBLIC School Verse, an Anthology. Volume IV. 1923-24.
London: 1924. V. 50

PUBLIC School Verse: an Anthology: Volume V, 1924-25.
London: 1925. V. 49

PUBLICOLA, PSEUD.
The New Vade Mecum; or a Pocket Companion for Lawyers... Concord: 1819. V. 50

PUCKETT, J. L.
History of Oklahoma and Indian Territory and Homeseeker's Guide. Vinita: 1906. V. 53

PUCKETT, NEWBELL NILES
Folk Beliefs of the Southern Negro. Chapel Hill: 1926. V. 48; 50

PUCKLE, BERTRAM S.
Funeral Customs, Their Origin and Development. London: 1926. V. 50

PUCKLE, JAMES
The Club...Dialogue Between Father and Son. London: 1713. V. 54
The Club...Dialogue Between Father and Son. London: 1817. V. 52; 54
England's Path to Wealth and Honour. London: 1718. V. 48; 54
England's Path to Wealth and Honour... London: 1750. V. 48; 52

PUCKLER-MUSKAU, PRINZ VON
Hints on Landscape Gardening. Boston and New York: 1917. V. 52; 53
Tour in England, Ireland and France in the Years 1828 and 1829... London: 1832. V. 47; 49

PUDNEY, JOHN
Atlantic Bridge - the Offical Account of R.A.F. Transport Command's Ocean Ferry. London: 1945. V. 47
Dispersal Point and Other Air Poems. London: 1942. V. 47
Ten Summers - Poems (1933-1945). London: 1944. V. 47

PUEBLO Indian Painting. Santa Fe: 1979. V. 54

PUFFENDORF, SAMUEL, FREIHERR VON
De Officio Hominis et Civis Juxta Legem Naturalem Libri Duo. London: 1715. V. 52
The Divine Feudal Law. London: 1703. V. 53
An Introduction to the History of the Principal Kingdoms and State of Europe. London: 1719. V. 47
Of the Law of Nature and Nations. Oxford: 1703. V. 48
The Present State of Germany. London: 1690. V. 53
Thaten Carl Gustavs Konigs in Schweden. Nuremberg: 1697. V. 49
The Whole Duty of Man According to the Law of Nature. London: 1716. V. 47

PUFFING Billy and Its Creator. Wylam: 1964. V. 51; 53

THE PUGET Sound Iron Co. San Francisco: 1882. V. 50

PUGET DE LA SERRE, JEAN
The Mirrour Which Flatters Not... London: 1639. V. 47; 48; 53

PUGH, DAVID
London: Being an Accurate History and Description of the British Metropolis and Its Neighbourhood, to Thirty Miles Extent, from an Actual Perambulation. London: 1805-09. V. 52

PUGH, EDWARD
Cambria Depicta; a Tour through North Wales, Illustrated with Picturesque Views. London: 1816. V. 49; 52

PUGH, ELLIS
A Salutation to the Britains, To Call Them From the Many Things, to the One Thing Needful, for the Saving of Their Souls. Philadelphia: 1727. V. 48

PUGH, JOHN
Remarkable Occurrences in the Life of Jonas Hanway, Esq... London: 1787. V. 50
Remarkable Occurrences in the Life of Jonas Hanway, Esq. London: 1798. V. 50
A Treatise on the Science of Muscular Action. London: 1794. V. 52

PUGIN, AUGUSTUS CHARLES
Examples of Gothic Architecture... Edinburgh: 1895. V. 48
Illustrations of the Public Buildings of London. London: 1825-28. V. 50
Paris and Its Environs. London: 1829. V. 52
Paris and Its Environs. London: 1830-1831. V. 47
Paris and Its Environs. London: 1831. V. 47; 51; 52
Paris and Its Environs. London: 1833. V. 52
Pugin's Gothic Ornaments. London: 1831. V. 50
Specimens of Gothic Architecture. London: 1825. V. 49
Specimens of the Architecture of Normandy. London: 1874. V. 49

PUGIN, AUGUSTUS WELBY NORTHMORE
An Apology for the Revival of the Christian Architecture in England. London: 1843. V. 53
Contrasts: or, a Parallel Between the Noble Edifices of the Middle Ages, and Corresponding Buildings of the Present Day... London: 1841. V. 50
Designs for Iron and Brass Work in the Style of the XV and XVI Centuries. London: 1836/. V. 53
Details of Antient Timber Houses of the 15th and 16th Centuries. London: 1836. V. 52
Floriated Ornament: a Series of Thirty-One Designs. London: 1849. V. 50
Glossary of Ecclesiastical Ornament and Costume. London: 1846. V. 49; 52; 54
Gothic Furniture: Consisting of Twenty-Seven Coloured Engravings from Designs By A. Pugin. London: 1828. V. 52
The Present State of Ecclesiastical Architecture in England. London: 1843. V. 47
Pugin's Gothic Furniture. London: 1835. V. 49
Select Views of Islington, Pentonville, Highbury, Canonbury, etc. London: 1819. V. 47; 49
A Treatise on Chancel Screens and Rood Lofts. London: 1851. V. 52
The True Principles of Pointed or Christian Architecture. London: 1841. V. 47; 52
The True Principles of Pointed or Christian Architecture...(with) An Apology for the Revivial of Christian Architecture in England. London: 1853/43. V. 49

PUGSLEY, ALFRED
The Works of Isambard Kingdom Brunel. An Engineering Appreciation. London: 1976. V. 52

PUGSLEY, H. W.
A Prodromus of the British Hieracia. London: 1948. V. 50

PUIG, MANUEL
Betrayed by Rita Hayworth. New York: 1971. V. 53; 54
Kiss of the Spider Woman. New York: 1979. V. 49

PULCI, LUIGI
Il Morgante Maggiore. Florence: 1732. V. 48

PULGAR, HERNANDO DEL
Cronica de Los Senores Reyes Cataolicos Don Fernando y Dona Isabel de Castilla y de Aragon... Valencia: 1780. V. 52

PULIGA, COMTESSE DE
Madame Sevigne De, Her Correspondents and Contemporaries. London: 1873. V. 52

PULL My Daisy. New York: 1961. V. 54

PULLAN, MATILDA MARTIAN CHESNEY
The Lady's Manual of Fancy-Work... New York: 1859. V. 47

PULLE, A.
An Enumeration of the Vascular Plants Known from Surinam... Leiden: 1906. V. 52

PULLEN & POPPLEWELL
Experimental Engineering. Manchester: 1900/01. V. 53

PULLEN-BURRY, BESSIE
In a German Colony or Four Weeks in New Britain. London: 1909. V. 52
Nobly Won: a Novel. London: 1888. V. 54

PULLER, TIMOTHY
The Moderation of the Church of England, Considered as Useful for Allaying the Present Distempers Which the Indisposition of the Time has Contracted. London: 1679. V. 49; 52

PULLIN, A. W.
History of Yorkshire County Cricket 1902-1923. Leeds: 1924. V. 47; 48

PULMAN, GEORGE P. R.
The Book of the Axe... London: 1875. V. 49
The Vade-Mecum of Fly-Fishing for Trout. London: 1846. V. 49
The Vade-Mecum of Fly-Fishing for Trout. London: 1851. V. 49; 53

PULSIFER, WILLIAM H.
Notes for a History of Lead and an Inquiry into the Development of the Manufacture of White Lead and Lead Oxides. New York: 1888. V. 49; 50

PULSZKY, FRANCIS
The Tricolor On the Atlas. London: 1854. V. 51

PULTENEY, RICHARD
Historical and Biographical Sketches of the Progress of Botany in England From Its Origin to the Introduction of the Linnaean System. London: 1790. V. 47; 48; 49

PULTENEY, WILLIAM
The Case of the Revival of the Salt Duty, Fully Stated and Considered; With Some Remarks on the Present State of Affairs. London: 1732. V. 47
The Case of the Sinking Fund, and the Right of Publick Creditors to It Considered at Large; with Some Farther Observations on the National Debts, the Civil List, the Bank Contract... London: 1735. V. 47
An Enquiry into the Conduct of Our Affairs, from the Year 1721, to the Present Time... London: 1734. V. 47
A Letter from a Member of Parliament to a Friend in the Country, Concerning the Sum of 115, 0001. Granted for the Service of the Civil List. London: 1729. V. 47
The Politicks on Both Sides, with Regard to Foreign Affairs, Stated from their own Writings, and Examined by the Course of Events. London: 1734. V. 50
Some Considerations on the National Debts, the Sinking Fund, and the State of Publick Credit: In a Letter to a Friend in the Country. London: 1729. V. 47
Thoughts on the Present State of Affairs with America, and the means of Conciliation. London: 1778. V. 47
Thoughts on the Present State of Affairs with America, and the Means of Conciliation... London: 1788. V. 47

PULTON, FARDINANDO
An Abstract of all the Penal Statutes Which Be General, in Force and Use. London: 1586. V. 52
An Abstract Of All the Penal Statutes Which be General, in Force and Use. London: 1600. V. 51
A Collection of Sundry Statutes, Frequent in Use: with Notes in the Margent and References to the Book Cases and Books of Entries and Registers, Where They be Treated of... London: 1640. V. 52
De Pace Regis et Regni, viz. A Treatise Delcaring Which be the Great and Generall Offences of the Realme... London: 1615. V. 51

PUMA, RICHARD DANIEL
Etruscan Tomb-Groups: Ancient Pottery and Bronzes in Chicago's Field Museum of Natural History. Mainz am Rhein: 1986. V. 52

PUMPELLY, RAPHAEL
Across America and Asia. New York: 1870. V. 47; 52
Geological Research in China, Mongolia and Japan during the Years 1862 to 1865. 1866. V. 53
Geological Researches in China, Mongolia and Japan During the Years 1862 to 1865. Washington: 1867. V. 54

PUMPHREY, STANLEY
Indian Civilization: a Lecture. Philadelphia: 1877. V. 52; 53

PUNCH and Judy. London: 1828. V. 54
PUNCH and Judy. London: 1881. V. 50

PUNIN, NATAN
N. Pamiatnik III Internatsionaia. Petrograd: 1920. V. 52

PUNKIN, JONATHAN, PSEUD.
Downfall of Freemasonry, Being an Authentic History of the Rise, Progress and Triumph of Anti-Masonry... Harrisonburg: 1838. V. 48; 52; 54

THE PUPPET-Showman's Album. London: 1848. V. 47

PURCELL, E.
Sporting Sketches. London: 1823. V. 47

PURCELL, EDWARD J.
Report on a Visit to Atomic Energy Commission Nevada Test Site to Witness Operation Cue, April 21, 1955-May 7, 1955. Worcester: 1955. V. 54

PURCELL, HENRY
Orpheus Britannicus... London: 1698. V. 48
Orpheus Britannicus. London: 1706/02. V. 48
Orpheus Britannicus. London: 1706/12. V. 53

PURCELL, LESLIE HARPER
Miracle in Mississippi, Laurence C. Jones of Piney Woods. New York: 1956. V. 47; 48

PURCELL, MAE FISHER
History of Contra Costa County. Berkeley: 1940. V. 54

PURCELL, MRS.
The Orientalist, or Electioneering in Ireland. London: 1820. V. 51

PURCHAS, JOHN
The Miser's Daughter, or the Lover's Curse, a Comedy: and Miscellaneous Poems. London: 1839. V. 53

PURCHAS, SAMUEL
Hakluytus Posthumous, or Purhcas His Pilgrimes. Glasgow/New York: 1905. V. 47; 53
Purchas His Pilgrimage. London: 1613. V. 50
Purchas, His Pilgrimage, or Relations of the World and the Religions Observed in all Ages and Places. London: 1617. V. 47; 48
Purchas His Pilgrimes. (with) Purchas His Pilgrimage. London: 1625/26. V. 47; 48; 50; 52
A Theatre of Politicall Flying Insects. London: 1657. V. 48

PURCHON, R. D.
The Biology of the Mollusca. Oxford: 1977. V. 49; 52

PURDY, AL
The Blur in Between. 1960-61. Toronto: 1962. V. 47; 52
The Crafte So Longe to Lerne. Toronto: 1959. V. 47
Emu, Remember!. Fredericton: 1956. V. 47
Morning and it's Summer: a Memoir. Dunvegan: 1983. V. 52
No Second Spring. Coatsworth: 1977. V. 52
On the Bearpaw Sea. Burnaby: 1973. V. 52
Pressed on Sand. Toronto: 1955. V. 47; 52
Two Poems. 1990. V. 54

PURDY, JAMES
63: Dream Palace. New York: 1956. V. 47
63: Dream Place. Helsinki: 1991. V. 48
Are You In the Wintertree. 1987. V. 52
The Candles of Your Eyes. New York: 1985. V. 51
Color or Darkness. New York: 1957. V. 50
A Day After the Fair. New York: 1977. V. 48; 51
Don't Call Me by My Right Name and Other Stories. New York: 1956. V. 47; 48; 51; 52
Eustace Chisholm and His Works. New York: 1967. V. 54
Lessons and Complaints. New York: 1978. V. 48; 51; 54
Malcolm. New York: 1959. V. 48
Mr. Evening. 1968. V. 47; 48; 49
Mr. Evening. Los Angeles: 1968. V. 54
An Oyster is a Wealthy Beast. 1967. V. 47; 48; 49
Pioneers of the Valley of the Maumee Rapids and their Improvements. Mansfield: 1882. V. 51
Proud Flesh: Four Short Plays. Northridge: 1980. V. 48; 52
Scrap of Paper and the Berry-Picker. Los Angeles: 1981. V. 51
Two Plays. Dallas: 1979. V. 47

PURDY, RICHARD LITTLE
Thomas Hardy: a Bibliographical Study. London: 1968. V. 53

PURDY, THOMAS
Resolutions and Articles of the Union for Parliamentary Reform, According to the Constitution, Established in Leeds... Leeds: 1817?. V. 49

PUREY-CUT, A. P.
The Heraldry of York Minster. Leeds: 1890-96. V. 53; 54
Walks Round York Minster. Leeds: 1907. V. 53

PURMANN, MATTHAUS GOTTFIRED
Chirurgia Curiosa: or, The Newest and Most Curious Observations and Operations in the Whole Art of Chirurgery... London: 1706. V. 48; 49

PURPLE, EDWIN R.
In Memoriam. New York: 1881. V. 47

PURRINGTON, JAMES
Horrid Massacre!! Sketches of the Life of Captain James Purrington, Who On the Night of the Eighth of July 1806, Murdered His Wife, Six Children and Himself... Augusta: 1806. V. 50

PURRY, JEAN PIERRE
Memorial Presented to His Grace My Lord the Duke of Newcastle, Chamberlain of His Majesty King George, &c. and Secretary of State... Augusta: 1880. V. 50

PURSER, WILLIAM E.
Palmerin of England. Some Remarks On This Romance and On the Controversy Concerning Its Authorship. Dublin: 1904. V. 53

PURSH, FREDERICK
Flora Americae Septentrionalis, or Systematic Arrangement and Description of the Plants of North America. London: 1816. V. 54

PURVES, DAVID LAING
The English Circumnaviagtors: the Most Remarkable Voyages Round the World by English Sailors. London: 1876. V. 54

PURVIS, J. B.
Through Uganda to Mount Elgon. London: 1909. V. 48; 54

PURVIS, ROBERT
Sir William Arrol. A Memoir. Edinburgh: 1913. V. 49
A Tribute to the Memory of Thomas Shipley, the Pilanthropist. Philadelphia: 1836. V. 52

PUSEY, E. B.
A Letter on...the Laws Prohibiting Marriage Between Those Near of Kin. (with) Evidence Given Before the Commission Appointed to Inquire into...the Law of Marriage...(with) God's Prohibition of the Marriage with a Deceased Wife's Sister. London: 1842. V. 51

PUSEY, W.
The History and Epidemiology of Syphilis. Springfield: 1933. V. 50
The Practical Application of the Roentgen Rays in Therapeutics and Diagnosis. Philadelphia: 1904. V. 49; 54

PUSHKIN, ALEKSANDR SERGEEVICH
Boris Godounov. Paris: 1927. V. 53
Il Cavaliere di Bronzo. 1968. V. 52; 54
Eugene Onegin. New York: 1943. V. 47; 48; 52; 54
Eugene Onegin. New York: 1964. V. 47; 49; 52; 54
Four Stories. The Squire's Daughter. The Queen of Spades. The Blizzard. The Shot. Greenbrae: 1987. V. 48; 54
Gabriel, a Poem in One Song. New York: 1929. V. 47; 53
The Golden Cockerel. New York: 1938. V. 48; 53
The Golden Cockerel. New York: 1950. V. 48; 52; 54
The Queen of Spades. London: 1928. V. 48; 53; 54
The Tale of the Golden Cockerel. St. Petersburg: 1910. V. 53
The Tale of the Golden Cockerel. 1936. V. 47
The Tale of the Golden Cockerel. Waltham St. Lawrence: 1936. V. 50
The Talisman. St. Petersburg: 1835. V. 50; 52
Zolotoi Petushak. (The Golden Cockerel). Moscow: 1909. V. 47

PUSS in Boots. London: 1880. V. 49
PUSS in Boots. New York: 1934. V. 47; 53; 54
PUSS in Boots. U.S.A: 1935. V. 50
PUSS in Boots. New York: 1944. V. 48; 49
PUSS in Boots. London: 1951. V. 47

PUSSIES at Mischief. London: 1870. V. 49

PUSSYCAT'S Rag Book. London: 1910. V. 54

PUTER, STEPHEN A. DOUGLAS
Looters of the Public Domain... Portland: 1908. V. 49; 50

PUTERSCHEIN, HERMANN
Paraphs. New York: 1928. V. 50

PUTNAM, ALLEN
Witchcraft of New England Explained by Modern Spiritualism. Boston: 1888. V. 52

PUTNAM, G. P.
The Book Buyer's Manual: a Catalogue of Foreign and American Books in Every Department of Literature. New York: 1852. V. 51; 53
The Home Book of the Picturesque; or American Scenery, Art and Literature... New York: 1852. V. 47; 50

PUTNAM, GEORGE GRANVILLE
Salem Vessels and Their Voyages, Series I, II & III. Salem: 1924-25. V. 53

PUTNAM, J. PICKERING
The Open Fire-Place In All Ages. Boston: 1881. V. 53
The Open Fireplace In All Ages. Boston: 1882. V. 49

PUTNAM, JAMES JACKSON
Addresses on Psycho-Analysis. London: 1921. V. 51
Studies in Neurological Diagnosis. Boston: 1902. V. 53

PUTNAM, NINA WILCOX
Sunny Bunny. Chicago: 1918. V. 54

PUTNAM, R.
William the Silent, Prince of Orange, the Moderate man of the Sixteenth Century. New York and London: 1895. V. 49

PUTNAM, SALLIE B.
Richmond During the War; Four Years of Personal Observation. New York: 1867. V. 49

PUTNAM, SAMUEL
The World of Jean de Bosschere. London: 1932. V. 51

PUTNAM'S Library of Choice Stories. Sea Stories. Now First Collected and Forming, the Fifth Volume... New York: 1858. V. 52

PUTRON, P. DE
Nooks and Corners of Old Sussex. Choice Examples in Sussex Archaeology. Lewis: 1875. V. 48

PUXLEY, F. L.
In African Game Tracks. 1929. V. 54
In African Game Tracks. London: 1929. V. 48; 52

PUYDT, EMILE DE
Les Orchidees. Paris: 1880. V. 54

PUYSEUR, MARECHAL DE
Art de la Guerre, par Principes et par Regles. Paris: 1749. V. 53

PUZO, MARIO
The Dark Arena. New York: 1955. V. 54
The Godfather. London: 1969. V. 51
The Godfather. New York: 1969. V. 54

PYCROFT, JAMES
The Collegian's Guide; or, Recollections of College Days, Setting Fourth the Advantages and Temptations of a University of Education. London: 1845. V. 48
The Cricket-Field. London: 1873. V. 51
Cricketana. London: 1864. V. 49
Cricketana. London: 1865. V. 51
Twenty Years in the Church. An Autobiography. London: 1861. V. 50; 54

PYE, CHARLES
Provincial Copper Coins or Tokens, Issued Between the Years 1787 and 1796... London: 1795. V. 51
The Stranger's Guide to Modern Birmingham, With an Account of Its Public Buildings and Institutions, Its Show Rooms and Manufactories. Birmingham: 1825. V. 52; 54

PYE, D.
George Leigh Mallory. A Memoir. 1927. V. 53

PYE, HENRY JAMES
Alfred: an Epic Poem, in Six Books. London: 1801. V. 50
Amusement. A Poetical Essay. London: 1790. V. 50; 54
The Aristocrat, a Novel. London: 1799. V. 48
Beauty, a Poetical Essay. London: 1766. V. 47
The Democrat; or Intrigues and Adventures of Jean Le Noir, From His Inlistment as a Drummer in General Rochembeau's Army and Arrival at Boston to His Being Driven from England. New York: 1795. V. 47
Faringdon Hill. Oxford: 1774. V. 48
Naucratia; or Naval Dominion. London: 1798. V. 54
Summary of the Duties of a Justice of the Peace. London: 1808. V. 48

PYE, JAEL HENRIETTA MENDEZ
Poems by a Lady. (with, as issued) A Short View of the Principal Seats and Gardens in and About Twickenham. London: 1767. V. 48

PYE, JOHN
Patronage of British Art. London: 1845. V. 47; 48; 49

PYE, THOMAS
Canadian Scenery, District of Gaspe. Montreal: 1866. V. 53

PYLE, HOWARD
Howard Pyle's Book of Pirates. New York: 1921. V. 48; 54
Howard Pyle's Book of the American Spirit. New York & London: 1923. V. 47; 49; 51; 52; 53
A Modern Aladdin, or the Wonderful Adventures of Oliver Munier. New York: 1892. V. 53
Pepper and Salt, or Seasoning for Young Folk. New York: 1886. V. 48; 52; 53
The Ruby of Kishmoor. New York: 1908. V. 48; 49; 51; 52; 53
The Story of King Arthur and His Knights. New York: 1903. V. 50
The Story of the Champions of the Round Table. New York: 1905. V. 50
The Story of the Grail and the Passing of Arthur. New York: 1910. V. 49

PYM, BARBARA
Excellent Women. London: 1952. V. 47
Jane and Prudence. London: 1953. V. 48; 50; 52; 53
Less Than Angels. New York. V. 48; 51
Less Than Angels. London: 1955. V. 48; 50; 51; 52; 53; 54
Less than Angels. New York: 1957. V. 50; 53; 54

PYM, JOHN
The Churche's Lamentation for the Good man His Loose. London: 1644. V. 47; 48
The Heads of a Conference Delivered by Mr. Pym At a Committee of Both Houses, Juni 24 1641. London: 1641. V. 53
March 17. Master Pym's Speech in Parliament. Wherein is Expressed His Zeal and Reall Affection to the Publick Good. London: 1641. V. 47
Mr. Pym His Speech in Parliament, the XXV of January MDCXLI. Against the Bishops Charge, Hastening Their Triall. London: 1641. V. 48
A Speech Delivered By Mr. Pym, at a Conference of Both Houses...June 15, 1642. London: 1642. V. 49; 51

PYM, T.
Skipping Time. London: 1890. V. 48

PYMELL, CHARLES
Forever Wider. NJ/London: 1985. V. 48; 51

PYNCHON, J. C.
Record of the Pynchon Family in England and America. Springfield: 1885. V. 49

PYNCHON, THOMAS
El Arco Iris de Gravedad (Gravity's Rainbow). Bar: 1978. V. 52
The Crying of Lot 49. Philadelphia: 1965. V. 49
The Crying of Lot 49. Philadelphia: 1966. V. 47; 48; 49; 50; 51; 52; 53
The Crying of Lot 49. London: 1967. V. 49; 51; 52
The Crying of Lot 49. Philadelphia & New York: 1967. V. 47
Gravity's Rainbow. London: 1973. V. 47; 50; 53
Gravity's Rainbow. New York: 1973. V. 47; 49; 50; 51; 52; 53; 54
Slow Learner. Boston: 1984. V. 47; 49; 50; 52; 53
Slow Learner. London: 1984. V. 52
The Tale of the Body Thief. New York: 1992. V. 49
V. London: 1963. V. 47; 49; 50; 53; 54
V. Philadelphia: 1963. V. 47; 49; 51; 52; 53; 54
Vineland. Boston: 1990. V. 47; 49; 53; 54

PYNE, HENRY R.
The History of the First New Jersey Cavalry. (Sixteenth Regiment New Jersey Volunteers). Trenton: 1871. V. 47; 49; 51

PYNE, JAMES BAKER
The First Series of the Mountain, River, Lake and Landscape Scenery of Great Britain... Leeds: 1877-79. V. 52
Lake Scenery of England. London: 1859. V. 48; 52

PYNE, W. B.
Lancashire Illustrated in a Series of Views, Towns, Public Buildings, Streets, Docks, Churches, Antiquities, Abbeys, Castles, Seats of Nobility... London: 1831. V. 48; 53

PYNE, WILLIAM HENRY
The Costumes of Great Britain. London: 1808. V. 50
Etchings of Rustic Figures, for the Embellishment of Landscape. London: 1815. V. 49
The History of the Royal Residences. London: 1819. V. 52
On Rustic Figures, in Imitation of Chalk. London: 1813. V. 50
On Rustic Figures in Imitation of Chalk. London: 1817. V. 50
Wine and Walnuts; or, After Dinner Chit Chat. London: 1823. V. 47
The World in Miniature: England, Scotland, and Ireland. London: 1827. V. 48

PYTHAGORAS
Aurea Pythagoreorum Carmina. Paris: 1585. V. 47

Q

QUACKENBOS, JOHN D.
Geological Ancestors of the Brook Trout, and Recent Saibling Forms from Which It Evolved. New York: 1916. V. 49; 50; 53
Illustrated History of Ancient Literature, Oriental and Classical. New York: 1882. V. 51

QUADRILLES, or Fashionable French Dances. London: 1816. V. 51

QUAIFE, JAMES
The Hackney Coach Directory. London: 1821. V. 50

QUAIFE, MILO MILTON
Yellowstone Kelly, the Memoirs of Luther S. Kelly. New Haven: 1926. V. 53; 54

QUAIN, JONES
A Series of Anatomical Drawings. London: 1842. V. 48
The Viscera of the Human Body. London: 1840. V. 53

QUAIN, RICHARD
A Dictionary of Medicine Including General Pathology, General Therapeutics, Hygiene and the Diseases Peculiar to Women and Children, by Various Authors. New York: 1884. V. 47
A Dictionary of Medicine Including General Pathology, General Therapeutics, Hygiene and the Diseases Peculiar to Women and Children, by Various Writers. London: 1886. V. 54
The Diseases of the Rectum. London: 1854. V. 54

THE QUAKERS Elegy On the Death of Charles Late King of England. 1685. V. 50

QUAMMEN, DAVID
To Walk the Line. New York: 1970. V. 52

QUARITCH, BERNARD
A Catalogue of Books and Mansucripts Issued to Commemorate the One Hundredth Anniversary of the Firm of Bernard Quaritch 1847-1947. London: 1947. V. 54
A Catalogue of Books In English History and Literature from the Earliest Times to the End of the Seventeenth Century. London: 1930. V. 50
A Catalogue of English and Foreign Bookbindings Offered for Sale by Bernard Quaritch Ltd. London: 1921. V. 48; 50; 51; 54
A Catalogue of Illuminated and Other Manuscripts Together with Some Works on Palaeography. London: 1931. V. 52
Contributions Towards a Dictionary of English-Collectors, as Also of Some Foreign Collectors Whose Libraries Were Incorporated in English Collections or Whose Books Are Chiefly Met With in England. London: 1892-Dec. 1896. V. 47
A General Catalogue of Books. London: 1868. V. 49
A General Catalogue of Books. London: 1874. V. 49; 54
A General Catalogue of Books Offered for Sale to the Public at the Affixed Prices by Bernard Quaritch. The Supplement 1875-77. London: 1877. V. 49; 54

QUARITCH, BERNARD continued
A General Catalogue of Books Offered to the Public at the Affixed Prices. London: 1880. V. 49
A General Catalogue of Books Offered to the Public at the Affixed Prices Supplement 1875-77. London: 1874/77. V. 50
Monumenta Typographica. London. V. 48

QUARLES, BENJAMIN
Frederick Douglass. Washington: 1948. V. 52
The Negro in the Civil War. Boston: 1953. V. 48

QUARLES, FRANCIS
Boanerges and Barnabas; Judgment and Mercy, or, Wine and Oil for Wounded and Afflicted Souls. London: 1664. V. 52
Divine Fancies: Digested into Epigrammes, Meditations and Observations. London: 1638. V. 51
Divine Poems. London: 1633. V. 47; 49
Divine Poems. London: 1638. V. 48; 50; 53
Divine Poems, Containing the History of Jonah, Ester, Job, Sampson. Together with Sions Sonnets, Elegies. London: 1674. V. 52
Emblems, Divine and Moral. London: 1839. V. 52
Emblems, Divine and Moral; Together with Hieroglyphics of the Life of Man... London: 1723. V. 54
Emblems, Divine and Moral: Together with Hieroglyphics of the Life of Man. London: 1736. V. 48
Emblems, Divine and Moral: Together with Hieroglyphics of the Life of Man. London: 1778. V. 48; 49
Quarles' Emblems. London: 1861. V. 52

QUARLES, JOHN
Divine Meditations Upon Several Subjects. London: 1679. V. 49

QUARTO-MILLENARY: The First 250 Publications and the First 25 Years, 1929-1954, of the Limited Editions Club: a Critique, A Conspectus, a Bibliography, Indexes. 1959. V. 54

QUASIMODO, SALVATORE
The Tall Schooner. New York: 1980. V. 52

QUATUOR Sermones. 1883. V. 54
QUATUOR Sermones. London: 1883. V. 48

THE QUEBEC Bridge Carrying the Transcontinental Line of the Canadian Government Railways Over the St. Lawrence River Near the City of Quebec, Canada. Quebec: 1918. V. 49

QUEBEC CENTRAL RAILWAY
Sights and Scenes for the Tourist, Pen and Pencil Sketches of Quebec City, The Chaudiere and St. Francis Valleys and Lower St. Lawrence River. Sherbrooke: 1893. V. 49; 50

QUECKETT MICROSCOPICAL CLUB
Journal. London: 1907-15. V. 54

QUEEN, ELLERY
101 Years' Entertainment. Boston: 1941. V. 54
The Adventures of Ellery Queen. New York: 1934. V. 47; 52
The American Gun Mystery. 1933. V. 53
The Brown Fox Mystery. Boston: 1948. V. 52
Calamity Town. Boston: 1942. V. 47; 49
The Detective Short Story, a Bibliography. Boston: 1942. V. 47
The Devil to Pay. New York: 1938. V. 50
The Dragon's Teeth. New York: 1939. V. 52
The Egyptian Cross Mystery. London: 1933. V. 53
Ellery Queen, Master Detective. New York: 1941. V. 47; 48
The Misadventures of Sherlock Holmes. Boston: 1944. V. 47
The Murder is a Fox. Boston: 1945. V. 49; 53
Queen's Quorum. A History of the Detective-Crime Short Story as Revealed by the 106 Most Important Books Published in This field Since 1845. New York: 1951. V. 47
The Roman Hat Mystery. New York: 1929. V. 51
The Roman Hat Mystery. New York: 1979. V. 48

QUEEN Victoria's Dolls. London: 1894. V. 47

QUEEN Victoria's Jubilee, The Great Procession of June 22, 1897 in the Queen's Honor, Reported Both in the Light of History and as a Spectacle. V. 52

THE QUEEN'S Book of the Red Cross. London: 1939. V. 48

QUEENS of the Circulating Library. Selections from Victorian Lady Novelists, 1850-1900. London: 1950. V. 54

QUEENSBERRY, CATHERINE DOUGLAS, DUCHESS OF
A Proper Reply to a Late Very Extraordinary Letter from the Hon. T(homa)s H(erve)y, Esq. to Sir Thomas Hanmer, Bart. London: 1742. V. 48

QUEENY, EDGAR M.
Cheechako, The Story of an Alaskan Bear Hunt. New York: 1941. V. 47; 53
Prairie Wings. New York: 1946. V. 47; 48; 52; 53
Prairie Wings. Philadelphia: 1946. V. 54
Prairie Wings. Philadelphia & New York: 1947. V. 47; 52; 53

QUEER Stories About Queer Animals, Told in Rhymes and Jingles. Philadelphia: 1905. V. 52

QUEKETT, J.
Lectures on Histology Delivered at the Royal College of Surgeons of England 185-51, 1851-52. London: 1852-54. V. 49; 52
A Practical Treatise on the Use of the Microscope... London: 1852. V. 52

QUENNELL, NANCY
Epicure's Anthology. London: 1936. V. 48
The Epicure's Anthology. Waltham St. Lawrence: 1936. V. 48
A Lovers Progress: Seventeenth Century Lyrics. Waltham St. Lawrence: 1938. V. 54

QUENNELL, PETER
Masques and Poems. Berkshire: 1922. V. 50; 54
Masques and Poems. Waltham St. Lawrence: 1922. V. 51; 54
Poems. London: 1926. V. 48

QUERIES Containing the Truth of the New Forest Case. London?: 1720-40. V. 47

QUERRY, RON
The Death of Bernadette Lefthand. Santa Fe: 1993. V. 50; 51; 54

QUESNEL, PASQUIER
The History of the Wonderful Don Ignatius Loyola de Guipuscoa... London: 1754. V. 50

QUESTIER, MATHURIN
Predictions Vniverselles Povr les Annees 1648. 1649. 1650. 1651. & 1652. Paris: 1648. V. 54

QUEVEDO, DON FRANCISCO DE
The Dog and the Fever. Hamden: 1954. V. 49

QUEVEDO Y VILLEGAS, FRANCISCO GOMEZ DE
The Life and Adventures of Buscon, the Witty Spaniard. London: 1670. V. 47
El Parnaaso Espanol, y Musas Castellanas...Corregidas, i Enmendadas de Nuevo en Esta Impression, por el Doctor Amuso Cultifragio... Madrid: 1668. V. 53
The Visions. 1673. V. 47
The Visions. London: 1678/67. V. 48
Visions. London: 1766. V. 48; 52
The Works... Edinburgh: 1798. V. 50; 51

QUIA Amore Langueo. 1902. V. 48

QUIBELL, J. E.
Catalogue General des Antiquites Egyptiennes du Musee du Caire, Nos. 51001-51191: Tomb of Yuaa and Thuiu. Le Caire: 1908. V. 51
The Monastery of Apa Jeremias. Le Caire: 1912. V. 51
The Ramesseum. London: 1898. V. 49
Teti Pyramid, North Side (Excavations at Saqqara). Le Caire: 1927. V. 49; 51

QUICK, ARMAND
The Hemorrhagic Diseases and the Physiology of Hemostasis. Springfield: 1942. V. 54

QUICK, JOHN
A Serious Inquiry into the Weighty Case of Conscience, Whether a Man May Lawfully Marry His Deceased Wife's Sister. London: 1703. V. 51

QUICK, ROBERT
A Portfolio of Birds. San Francisco: 1958. V. 53

QUICK, WILLIAM HARVEY
Negro Stars in All Ages of the World. Richmond: 1898. V. 53

QUICKSILVER MINING CO.
Charter and By-Laws, Proceedings of the Annual Meeting of the Stockholders Held at Philadelphia, February 22, 1865. New York: 1865. V. 48; 49

QUIGGIN, E. C.
A Dialect of Donegal Being the Speech of Meenawanna. Cambridge: 1906. V. 50

QUILLER-COUCH, ARTHUR THOMAS
Dead Man's Rock: a Romance. London: 1887. V. 48
In Powder and Crinoline. London: 1912. V. 49
In Powder and Crinoline. London: 1913. V. 48; 53
The Oxford Book of English Verse: 1250-1918. Oxford: 1039. V. 48
The Sleeping Beauty and Other Fairy Tales. London: 1910. V. 49; 50; 51; 53
The Twelve Dancing Princesses and Other Fairy Tales.. New York: 1920. V. 50

QUILLER-COUCH, MABEL
A Book of Children's Verse. London: 1911. V. 48; 51

QUILLET, CLAUDE
Callipaedia; or, the Art of Getting Pretty children. London: 1729. V. 48
Callipaediae; or, an Art to Have Handsome Children. London: 1710. V. 54

QUILLINAN, DORA WORDSWORTH
Journal of a Few Month's Residence in Portugal, Glimpses of the South of Spain. London: 1858. V. 47

QUILLINAN, EDWARD
Ball Room Votaries; or, Canterbury and Its Vicinity. London: 1810. V. 54
Elegiac Verses, Addressed to a lady. Kent: 1817. V. 48
New Canterbury Tales; or, The Glories of the Garrison. London: 1811. V. 47
Woodcuts and Verses. Kent: 1820. V. 49

QUIN, CLARA
So Young, My Lord, and True. London: 1878. V. 49

QUIN, MICHAEL JOSEPH
A Visit to Spain: Detailing the Transactions Which Occurred During a Residence in that Country. London: 1823. V. 54

QUINBY, JANE
Beatrix Potter. New York: 1954. V. 53

QUINCY, ELIZA SUSAN MORTON
Memoir of the Life of Eliza S. M. Quincy. Boston: 1861. V. 47; 50

QUINCY, JOHN
...A Compleat English Dispensatory... London: 1720. V. 49
The American Medical Lexicon, on the Plan of Quincy's lexicon Physico-Medicum... New York: 1811. V. 50
Lexicon Physico-Medicum; or, A New Medicinal Dictionary... London: 1736. V. 48
Medicina Stataica: Being the Aphorisms of Sanctorius... London: 1728. V. 49; 54
Medicina Stratica... London: 1718. V. 49
Pharmacopoeia Officinalis & Extemporanea, or, a Compleat English Dispensatory, in Four Parts. London: 1742. V. 49
Pharmacopoeia Officinalis & Extemporanea; or, a Compleat English Dispensatory, in Two Parts, Theoretic and Practical. London: 1749. V. 52

QUINCY, JOSIAH
The History of Harvard University. Cambridge: 1840. V. 47
The History of Harvard University. Boston: 1860. V. 51
Observations on the Act of Parliament Commonly Called the Boston Port-Bill; with Thoughts on Civil Society and Standing Armies. Philadelphia: 1774. V. 47
Remarks on Some of the Provisions of the Laws of Massachusetts, Affecting Poverty, Vice and Crime. Cambridge: 1822. V. 52
Speech of the Hon. Josiah Quincy...In Relation to Maritime Protection. Alexandria: 1812. V. 49
Speech of...on the Passage of the Bill to Enable the People of the Territory of Orleans, to Form a Constitution and State Government. Baltimore: 1811. V. 48

QUIN DASKEIN, TARELLA
Chimney Town. London: 1934. V. 49

QUINN, ARTHUR HOBSON
Edgar Allan Poe a Critical Biography. New York: 1941. V. 48
Edgar Allan Poe Letters and Documents in the Enoch Pratt Free Library. New York: 1941. V. 48

QUINN, D. B.
The Roanoke Voyages 1584-1590. London: 1955. V. 54

QUINN, EDWARD
Max Ernst. Paris: 1976. V. 52
Max Ernst. London: 1978. V. 49; 51; 53

QUINN, JOHN
The Library. New York: 1923. V. 51
The Library. New York: 1923-24. V. 54

QUINN, SEABURY
Roads. Sauk City: 1948. V. 48

QUINNEY, THOMAS
Sketches of a Soldier's Life in India. Glasgow: 1853. V. 48

QUINQUABOREUS, JOHANN
De Re Grammatica Hebraeorum. Paris: 1556. V. 50

QUINTANILLA, LUIS
Franco's Black Spain. New York: 1946. V. 47

THE QUINTESSENCE of English Poetry; or, a Collection of all the Beautiful Passages in Our Poems and Plays... London: 1740. V. 50

QUINTIANUS STOA, JOHANNES F.
De Syllabarum Quantitate Epographiae Sex... Venice: 1519. V. 52

QUINTILIAN, MARCUS FABIUS
Institutionum Oratoriarum, Libri XII. Parisiis: 1542. V. 47

QUINTILIANUS, MARCUS FABIUS
Declamationes Vndeviginti. Lugduni: 1549. V. 53

QUINTILLIANUS, MARCUS FABIUS
De Institutione Oratoria Libri Duodecim. Oxford: 1693. V. 48
Institutionum Oratoriarum, Libri XII... Venice: 1522. V. 48

QUIRKE, W. M.
Recollections of a Violinist. London: 1914. V. 54

QUIROS, JOSE MARIA
Memoria de Instituto en que se Manifesta Que el Comercio ha llamado Siempre la Atencion de Todas las Naciones... Havana: 1814. V. 53

THE QUIVER of Love. A Collection of Valentines Ancient and Modern. London: 1876. V. 50

R

R & C Golden Jubilee, 1931-1981. Los Angeles: 1981. V. 51

R., L. F.
The Harpstring, a Collection of Original Poems. Nazareth: 1838. V. 49

RABADAN, MAHOMET
Mahometism Fully Explained. London: 1723. V. 53

RABAN, WILLIAM
Origin of the Pindaraies; Preceded by Historical Notices on the Rise of the Different Mahratta States. London: 1818. V. 48; 49

RABAN, ZE'EV
Palestine. Jerusalem: 1931. V. 47
The Story of Ruth. New York: 1930. V. 48

RABAUT DE SAINT-ETIENNE, JEAN PAUL
An Impartial History of the Late Revolution in France. Philadelphia: 1794. V. 53

RABB, KATE MILNER
Indiana Coverlets and Coverlet Weavers. Indianapolis: 1928. V. 47

RABELAIS, FRANCOIS
All the Extant Works. New York: 1929. V. 50; 51
Catalogue of the Choice Books Found by Pantagruel in the Abbey of Saint Victor. Burlingame: 1952. V. 47
The Complete Works. London: 1927. V. 48; 54
The Complete Works. London: 1933. V. 48
Five Books of the Lives, Heroic Deeds and Sayings of Gargantua and His Son Pantagruel. London: 1892. V. 50
Five Books of the Lives, Heroic Deeds and Sayings of Gargantua and His Son Pantagruel. London: 1904. V. 49
Five Books of the Lives, Heroic Deeds and Sayings of Gargantua and His Son Pantagruel. London: 1970. V. 49
Gargantua and Pantagruel. London: 1904. V. 54
Master Francis Rabelais: Five Books of the Lives, Heroic Deeds and Sayings of Gargantua and His Son Pantagruel. London: 1892. V. 53
Les Oevvres. Antwerp: 1605-8. V. 52
Pantagruel. Dijon: 1946. V. 52
Pantagruel. Dijon: 1946. V. 54
Songes Drolatiques de Pantagruel. Paris: 1797. V. 49
The Works... London: 1737. V. 51
The Works... London: 1784. V. 49
The Works. London: 1807. V. 51
The Works. London: 1849. V. 51
The Works. London: 1901. V. 52
The Works. London: 1904. V. 51
The Works... London: 1921. V. 48

RABLEY, CHARLES A.
Devonshire Trout Fishing. London: 1912. V. 52

RACHFORD, BENJAMIN KNOX
Neurotic Disorders of Childhood Including a study of Auto and Intestinal Intoxications, Chronic Anaemia, Fever, Eclampsia, Epilepsy, Migraine, Chorea, Hysteria, Asthma, etc. New York: 1905. V. 52

RACINE, JEAN
Andromache. Lexington: 1986. V. 54
Oeuvres de Jean Racine. Paris: 1783. V. 48
Phaedra. San Francisco: 1968. V. 49
Phaedra Britannica. London: 1975. V. 52
Theatre. Paris: 1928. V. 49

RACINET, ALBERT CHARLES AUGUST
L'Ornement Polychrome. Paris: 1875. V. 50; 52

RACKHAM, ARTHUR
The Allies Fairy Book. London: 1916. V. 48
The Allies' Fairy Book. Philadelphia: 1916. V. 54
The Arthur Rackham Fairy Book. London: 1933. V. 53
The Arthur Rackham Fairy Book. London: 1933. V. 47; 50
Arthur Rackham's Book of Pictures. London: 1913. V. 47; 51; 53; 54
Arthur Rackham's Book of Pictures. New York: 1913. V. 52
Arthur Rackham's Book of Pictures. London: 1920. V. 51
The Land of Enchantment. London: 1907. V. 52
Once Upon a Time. London: 1972. V. 47
Some British Ballads. New York. V. 52

RACKHAM, BERNARD
The Ancient Glass of Canterbury Cathedral. London: 1949. V. 47; 52
Catalogue of the Glaisher Collection of Pottery & Porcelain in the Fitzwilliam Museum. Cambridge: 1935. V. 48
English Pottery. New York: 1924. V. 47; 51

RADAU, HUGO
Early Babylonian History Down to the End of the Fourth Dynasty of Ur, to Which is Appended an Account of the E. A. Hoffman Collection of Babylonian Tablets in the General Theological Seminary, New York, U.S.A. New York: 1900. V. 52
Letters to Cassite Kings from the Temple Arachives of Nippur. Philadelphia: 1908. V. 49; 52
Sumerian Hymns and Prayers to God Ninib from the Temple Library of Nippur. Philadelphia: 1911. V. 49

RADBIL, SAMUEL X.
Bibliography of Medical Ex-Libris Literature. Los Angeles: 1951. V. 49

RADCLIFF, THOMAS
A Report on the Agriculture of Eastern and Western Flanders... London: 1819. V. 47; 49

RADCLIFFE, ALEXANDER
The Ramble: an Anti Heroick Poem. London: 1682. V. 47

RADCLIFFE, ANN WARD
The Castles of Athlin and Dunbayne. London: 1793. V. 47

RADCLIFFE, ANN WARD continued
The Castles of Athlin and Dunbayne. Dublin: 1794. V. 54
The Complete Novels. London: 1987. V. 48
Gaston de Blondeville, or the Court of Henry III. St. Alban's Abbey. London: 1826. V. 50
The Italian, or the Confessional of the Black Penitents. London: 1797. V. 47; 48; 49
A Journey Made in 1794 to Holland and the Western Frontier of Germany, with a Return Down the Rhine... Dublin: 1795. V. 48; 49; 51
The Mysteries of Udolpho. London: 1794. V. 47; 48; 49; 51; 52
The Mysteries of Udolpho, a Romance. London: 1810. V. 47
The Romance of the Forest. London: 1791. V. 48
The Romance of the Forest. London: 1792. V. 48
The Romance of the Forest. London: 1796. V. 50
The Romance of the Forest. Dublin: 1801-1800. V. 49
The Romance of the Forest; Interspersed With some Pieces of Poetry. London: 1816. V. 47
A Sicilian Romance. London: 1792. V. 51
A Sicilian Romance. London: 1818. V. 47; 49

RADCLIFFE, CHARLES BLAND
On Diseases of the Spine and of the Nerves. Philadelphia: 1871. V. 53

RADCLIFFE, FREDERICK PETER DELME
The Noble Science. London: 1839. V. 47; 48; 49; 52
The Noble Science. London: 1875. V. 49
The Noble Science. London: 1911. V. 47; 49

RADCLIFFE, JOHN
Dr. Radcliffe's Life and Letters, with a True Copy of His Last Will and Testament... London: 1716. V. 47
Pharmacopoeia Radcliffeana; or, Dr. Radcliffe's Prescriptions... London: 1716. V. 49; 53

RADCLYFFE, C. E.
Big Game Shooting in Alaska. London: 1904. V. 54

RADCLYFFE, CHARLES W.
Memorials of Westminster School, Drawn and Lithographed. London: 1860. V. 50
The Palace of Blenheim. Oxford: 1842. V. 52

RADDATZ, FRITZ J.
Lithographies 1959-1973. Paris: 1974. V. 52

RADEN, WOLDEMAR
Switzerland: Its Mountains and Valleys. London: 1878. V. 49; 54

RADER, JESSE L.
South of Forty, From the Mississippi to the Rio Grande: a Bibliography. Norman: 1947. V. 48

RADFORD, DOLLIE
Songs for Somebody. London: 1893. V. 50

RADFORD, ERNEST
Dante Gabriel Rossetti: a Biographical Study. London: 1905. V. 48

RADFORD, GEORGE
Yorkshire by the Sea. Leeds: 1891. V. 47; 53

RADFORD, MAITLAND
Poems. London: 1945. V. 47

RADFORD, W.
On the Construction of the Ark, as Adapted to the Naval Architecture of the Present Day on the Equipment of Vessels and on Steam Navigation to India. London: 1840. V. 54

RADI, BERNARDINO
Variae Inventione per Depositi. Rome: 1625. V. 51

THE RADICAL Programme. London: 1885. V. 47; 49; 52

RADICAL Reform: or a Better Cure for Poverty and Distress, Than Burning Corn Stacks and Destroying Thrashing Machines. Doncaster: 1831. V. 51

RADICAL Rule: Military Outrage in Georgia. Arrest of Columbus Prisoners: with Facts Connected With Their Imprisonment and Release. Louisville: 1868. V. 50

RADIGUET, RAYMOND
Devil in the Flesh. Washington: 1948. V. 49

RADIN, PAUL
African Folktales and Sculpture. New York: 1952. V. 52
African Folktales and Sculpture. New York: 1964. V. 50
African Folktales and Sculpture. New York: 1966. V. 54
Crashing Thunder: the Autobiography of an American Indian. New York: 1926. V. 50
The Italians of San Francisco, Their Adjustment and Acculteration (sic). 1935. V. 51

RADIO CORPORATION OF AMERICA
Exhibition Catalog for Radio Corportation of America, April 25, 1927. New York: 1927. V. 52

RADLOV, NICHOLAS
The Cautious Carp and Other Fables in Pictures. New York: 1938. V. 52; 54

RADO, A.
Guide-Book to the Soviet Union. New York: 1928. V. 51

RADSTOCK, WILLIAM WALDEGRAVE
The British Flag Triumphant!. London: 1806. V. 49

RADZINOWICZ, LEON
A History of English Criminal Law and Its Administration from 1750. London: 1948-56. V. 52

RAE, EDWARD
The White Sea Peninsula, a Journey in Russian Lapland and Karelia. London: 1881. V. 54

RAE, JOHN
Granny Goose!. Joliet: 1926. V. 54
John Rae's Correspondence with the Hudson's Bay Company on Arctic Exploration, 1844-1855. London: 1953. V. 47; 49
Life of Adam Smith. London: 1895. V. 49; 53
Narrative of an Expedition to the Shores of the Arctic Sea in 1846 and 1847. London: 1850. V. 49
Rae's Arctic Correspondence 1844-55. London: 1953. V. 49
Stanley Gordon. London: 1889. V. 51

RAE, PETER
The History of the Late Rebellion; Rais'd Against His Majesty King George, by the Friends of the Popish Pretender. Dumfries: 1718. V. 50; 53

RAE, THOMAS
Adventures of John M'Alpine. London: 1985. V. 50

RAEBURN, BEN
Treasury for the Free World. New York: 1946. V. 48

RAFFALD, ELIZABETH
The Experienced English Housekeeper. London: 1771. V. 48
The Experienced English Housekeeper. Manchester: 1799. V. 49
The Experienced English Housekeeper. London: 1803?. V. 47; 49
The Experienced English Housekeeper. London: 1808. V. 47
The Experienced Housekeeper. London: 1801. V. 48
The Experienced Housekeeper. London: 1814. V. 53

RAFFALOVICH, ANDRE
Roses of Shadow. 1895. V. 48

RAFFE, W. G.
Graphic Design. London: 1927. V. 50

RAFFLES, SOPHIA
Memoir of the Life and Public Services of Sir Thomas Stamford Raffles. London: 1830. V. 48; 52

RAFFLES, THOMAS
Letters, During a Tour Through Some Parts of France, Savoy, Switzerland, Germany and the Netherlands in the Summer of 1817. Liverpool: 1818. V. 51
Letters, During a Tour through Some Parts of France, Savoy, Switzerland, Germany, and the Netherlands in the Summer of 1817. Liverpool: 1819. V. 51

RAFFLES, THOMAS STAMFORD
The History of Java. London: 1817. V. 50
Memoirs of the Life and Ministry of the Rev. Thomas Raffles, D.D., LL.D. London: 1864. V. 51

RAFINESQUE, C. S.
Ancient History, or Annals of Kentucky; with a Survey of the Ancient Monuments of North America, and a Tabular View of the Principal Languages and Primitive Nations of the Whole Earth. Frankfort: 1824. V. 47
The Complete Writings... New York, London, Paris: 1864. V. 48; 54
Ichthyologia Ohiensius, or Natural History of the Fishes Inhabiting the River Ohio and Its Tributary Streams, Preceded by a Physical Description of the Ohio and Its Branches. Lexington: 1820. V. 48
A Life of Travels and Researches in North America and South Europe, of Outlines of the Life, Travels and Researches of... Philadelphia: 1836. V. 51; 53
Medical Flora; or, Manual of the Medical Botany of the United States of North America. Philadelphia: 1828-30. V. 50
A Monograph On the Fluviatile Bivalve Shells of the River Ohio, Containing Twelve Genera & Sixty-Eight Species. Philadelphia: 1832. V. 51

RAFN, C. C.
Antiquitates Americanae Sive Scriptores Septentrionales Reerum Ante-Columbianarum in America. Hafnie: 1837. V. 48

RAGGETT, JOHN JAMES
A Series of Plans for Single-Fronted Residences with Quantities for Estimating Their Approximate Cost. Birmingham: 1900. V. 47

RAGGUAGLIO Delle Nozze della Maesta di Filippo Quinto e di Elisabette Farnese...Celebrate in Parma l'Anno 1714. Parma: 1717. V. 53

RAGLAND, J. FARLEY
Rhymes of the Times. New York: 1946. V. 53

RAGOZIN, ZENAIDE A.
Media, Babylon and Persia, Including a Study of the Zend-Avesta or Religion of Zend-Avesta or Religion of Zoroaster. London: 1900. V. 54

RAGUET, CONDY
A Treatise on Currency and Banking. Philadelphia: 1839. V. 54

RAHEB, BARBARA
A Dark, Dark Tale. Agoura Hills: 1995. V. 52

RAHMAS, S.
A Day in Fairyland. 1940. V. 54

RAHT, CARLYSLE GRAHAM
The Romance of Davis Mountains and Big Bend Country. El Paso: 1919. V. 47; 48; 51

RAIKER, ALICE M.
The Story of Dulicbella and Fairies. London. V. 49

RAIKES, G. A.
History of the Honourable Artillery Company. London: 1878. V. 50

RAIKES, RICHARD
Considerations on the Alliance Between Christianity and Commerce, Applied to the Present State of this Country. London: 1806. V. 52

RAIKES, THOMAS
A Visit to St. Petersburg, in the Winter of 1829-30. London: 1838. V. 47; 53

RAIL, DE WAYNE
Going Home Again. Mt. Horeb: 1971. V. 49; 51; 54

THE RAILROAD Jubilee. An Account of the Celebration Commemorative of the Opening of Railroad Communication... Boston: 1852. V. 53

RAILTON, J.
The Army's Regulator, or the British Monitor. London: 1738. V. 50

RAILWAY ABC. Read's Railway Alaphabet. London: 1861. V. 51

RAILWAY Directors and Investments. Manchester: 1846. V. 54

RAILWAY Engineering and Maintenance Cyclopedia. New York: 1926. V. 53

RAIMBACH, ABRAHAM
Memoirs and Recollections of the Late Abraham Raimbach, Esq... London: 1843. V. 50

RAINE, CRAIG
A Free Translation. Edinburgh: 1981. V. 52

RAINE, JAMES
Catterick Church, in the County of York. London: 1834. V. 47; 53
Historians of the Church of York and Its Archbishops. London: 1879-94. V. 49
Saint Cuthbert: With an Account of the State In Which His Remains Were Found Upon the Opening of His Tomb in Durham Cathedral in the Year MDCCCXXVII. Durham: 1828. V. 49; 53; 54

RAINE, KATHLEEN
Blake and Tradition. New York: 1968. V. 53
Blake and Tradition. Princeton: 1968. V. 53
Faces of Day and Night. London: 1972. V. 47
The Hollow Hill. London: 1965. V. 53
The Lost Country. Dublin: 1971. V. 48
The Written Word. A Speech Delivered at the Annual Luncheon of the Poetry Society 1963. London: 1967. V. 49; 52

RAINE, WILLIAM MAC LEOD
A Daughter of Raasay. New York: 1902. V. 51

RAINES, C. W.
Bibliography of Texas 1536 to 1896. Austin: 1934. V. 50

RAINEY, GEORGE
The Cherokee Strip. 1925. V. 54
The Cherokee Strip. Enid: 1933. V. 53
The Cherokee Strip. Guthrie: 1933. V. 47
No Man's Land, the Historic Story of a Landed Orphan. Enid: 1937. V. 51; 54

RAINOLDS, JOHN
The Overthrow of Stage-Playes, by the Way of Controversie Betwixt D. Gager and D. Rainoldes... Oxford: 1629. V. 52
The Svmme of the Conference Betweene Iohn Rainoldes and Iohn Hart. London: 1584. V. 48; 50
Th'overthrow of Stage-Players, by the Way of Controversie Betwixt D. Gager and D. Rainoldes, Wherein All the Reasons That Can Be Made for Them are Notably Refuted... Middleburg: 1599. V. 50

RAINOLDS, WILLIAM
De Ivsta Reipvb. Christianae In Reges Impios et Haereticos Avthoritate... Antwerp: 1592. V. 48; 50

RAINS, GEORGE WASHINGTON
Notes on Making Saltpetre from the Earth of the Caves. New Orleans: 1861. V. 49

RAINY, ALEXANDER
On the Transfer of Property By Public Auction and private Contract; The Reciprocity of Allowance System, etc. London: 1845. V. 49

RAISTRICK, ARTHUR
The Lead Industry of Wensleydale and Swaledale. Buxton: 1975. V. 47; 53
Lead Mining in the Mid-Pennines. Truro: 1973. V. 54
Quakers in Science and Industry. London: 1950. V. 47

RAITHBORNE, AARON
The Surveyor: in Foure Bookes. London: 1616. V. 54

RAITHBY, JOHN
The Study and Practice of the Law, Considered in Their Various Relations to Society, etc. Portland: 1806. V. 47; 52

THE RAKE'S Progress; or, the Humours of Drury Lane. London: 1880. V. 47

RALEIGH & GASTON RAILROAD
Proceedings of the Fourteenth Annual Meeting of the Stockholders of the Raleigh & Gaston Rail Road Company... Raleigh: 1864. V. 49

RALEIGH, WALTER
Aphorisms of State. London: 1661. V. 49
The Arraignment and Conviction of Sr. Walter Rawleigh, at the Kings Bench-Barre at Winchester...17 of November 1603... London: 1648. V. 53
The Arts of Empire and Mysteries of State Discabineted. London: 1692. V. 53
The Cabinet-Council: Containing the Chief Art of Empire... London: 1658. V. 51
The Discoverie of the Large, Rich and Bewtiful Empyre of Guiana, with a Relation of the Great and Golden Citie of Manoa (Which the Spanyards call El Dorado) and of the Provinces of Emeria, Arromaia, Amapaia, and Other Countries. London: 1595. V. 52; 53; 54
The Discovery of the Large, Rich and Beautiful Empire of Guiana, with a Relation of the Great and Golden City of Manoa... London: 1848. V. 52
The Historie of the World. London: 1671. V. 49
The History of the World. London: 1614. V. 48; 51
The History of the World. 1621. V. 47
The History of the World... London: 1652. V. 49
The History of the World. London: 1687. V. 51
The History of the World in Five Bookes... London: 1687. V. 48
The History of the World in Five Bookes. London: 1677. V. 48; 51
The History of the World, in Five Books. London: 1736. V. 48; 52
An Introduction to a Breviart of the History of England, with the Reign of King William the I. London: 1693. V. 52
Judicious and Select Essayes and Observations. London: 1650. V. 47; 48; 51; 52; 53
The Life and Death of Mahomet... London: 1637. V. 51
The Marrow of Historie, or an Epitome of All Historical Passages from the Creation to the End of the Last Macedonian War. London: 1650. V. 50
The Marrow of History or, an Epitome of All Historical Passages. London: 1662. V. 50; 52
The Poems of Sir Walter Raleigh, Now First Collected. 1814. V. 52
The Prerogative of Parliaments in England... 1628. V. 48
The Prerogative of Parliaments in England... London: 1628. V. 47; 49; 52
The Prerogative of Parliaments in England. London: 1640. V. 50
The Prerogative of Parliaments in England: Proued in a Dialogue...Betweene a Councellour of State and a Justice of Peace. Middleburg: 1628. V. 53; 54
A Report of the Truth Concerning the Last Sea-Fight of the Revenge. V. 50
A Report on the Truth Concerning the Last Sea-Fight of the Revenge. Boston: 1902. V. 54
Three Discourses...1. Of a War with Spain...II. Of the Original, and Fundamental Cause of Natural, Arbitrary and Civil War. III. Of Ecclesiastical Power. London: 1702. V. 54

RALFE, JAMES
The Naval Chronology of Great Britain... London: 1820. V. 49

RALFE, P. G.
The Birds of the Isle of Man. Edinburgh: 1924. V. 48

RALFS, JOHN
The British Desmidieae. London: 1848. V. 48

RALPH, BENJAMIN
The Ax Laid to the Root of Christian Priestcraft. (with) The Axe (Once More) Laid to the Root of the Tree. London: 1742/43. V. 48
The School of Raphael; or, the Student's Guide to Expression in Historical Painting. London: 1825. V. 50

RALPH DE DICETO
Opera Historica. London: 1876. V. 49

RALPH, J.
Our Great West. A Study of Present Conditions and Future Possibilities of the New Commonwealths and Capitals of the United States. New York: 1893. V. 54

RALPH, JAMES
A Critical Review of the Public Buildings, Statues, and Ornaments in and About London and Westminster... London: 1783. V. 50
The Fashionable Lady; or, Harlequin's Opera. London: 1730. V. 52
Night: a Poem. In Four Books. London: 1729. V. 48
Of the Use and Abuse of Parliaments; in Two Historical Discourses... London: 1744. V. 50; 51
The Other Side of the Question; or, an Attempt to Rescue the Characters of the Two Royal Sisters Q. Mary and Q. Anne... London: 1742. V. 47; 49; 50; 53
The Taste of the Town; or, a Guide to All Publick Diversions. London: 1731. V. 47; 48; 49; 53

RALPH, JULIAN
On Canada's Frontier: Sketches of History, Sport and Adventure and of the Indians, Missionaries, Fur-Traders and Newer Settlers. London: 1892. V. 49
On Canada's Frontier. Sketches of History, Sport and Adventure and of the Indians, Missionaries Fur-Traders and Newer Settlers. New York: 1892. V. 53

RALPH Walker-Architect of Voorhees, Gmelin & Walker Vorrhees Walker Foley & Smith Voorhees Walker Smith & Smith. New York: 1957. V. 47; 48

RALSTON, J. K.
Rhymes of a Cowboy. Billings: 1969. V. 48

RALSTON. Memorial of William C. Ralston... San Francisco: 1875. V. 51

RAM, JAMES
A Treatise on Facts as Subjects of Inquiry by a Jury. New York: 1873. V. 53

RAMAMOORTHY, T. P.
Biological Diversity of Mexico. London: 1993. V. 50

RAMASWAMY, C. V., & SON
No. I. A Digest of the Different Castes of the Southern Division of Southern India, with Descriptions of Their Habits, Customs, Etc. Bombay: 1847. V. 49

RAMBAUD, ALFRED
History of Russia from the Earliest Times. Boston: 1879. V. 49

RAMBLE, REUBEN
The Child's Treasury of Knowledge and Amusement; or Reuben Ramble's Picture Lessons. London: 1840. V. 54

RAMBLE, ROBERT
The Book of Fishes. Philadelphia: 1845. V. 50

THE RAMBLES and Surprising Adventures of Captain Bolio. London: 1839. V. 52

RAMBOVA, N.
The Shrines of Tut-ankh-amon. New York: 1955. V. 48

RAMEAU, JEAN PHILIPPE
A Treatise of Music, Containing the Principles of Composition. London: 1775. V. 47

RAMEL, JEAN PIERRE
Narrative of the Deportation to Cayenne, of Barthelemey, Pichegru, Willot, Marbois, La Rue, Ramel, etc., etc. in Consequence of the Revolution of the 18th Fructidor (September 4, 1797)... London: 1799. V. 54

RAMELLI, AGOSTINO
Schatzkammer, Mechanischer Kuenste. Leipzig: 1620. V. 53

RAMHOFFSKY, JOHANN HEINRICH
Drey Beschreibungen, Erstens: Des Koniglichen Einzugs, Welchen Ihre Konigliche Majestat...Maria Theresia, zu Hungarn und boheim Konigin... Prague: 1743. V. 52

RAMIE, GEORGES
Picasso's Ceramics. New York. V. 47; 48; 50; 52

RAMIREZ, JOSE F.
A Memorial Setting forth the Rights and Reasons Which the Government of the United States of Mexico Has, for Not Recognizing the Validity of the Privilege Granted to D. Jose Garay,... New York: 1852. V. 47

RAMMOHUN ROY, RAJAH
The Last Days in England of the Rajah Rammohun Roy. London: 1866. V. 53

RAMON Y CAJAL, S.
Degeneration and Regeneration of the Nervous System. New York: 1959. V. 49; 52
Degeneration and Regneration of the Nervous System. Birmingham: 1984. V. 47
Histology. Baltimore: 1933. V. 48; 49; 53; 54
Precepts and Councils on Scientific Investigation: Stimulants of the Spirit. Mountain View: 1951. V. 50; 52
Recollections of My Life. Philadelphia: 1937. V. 52
Studies on the Cerebral Cortex. Springfield: 1955. V. 47

RAMOS DE ARIZPE, MIGUEL
Memoria que el Doctor Ramos de Arispe...Presenta a el Augusto Congreso, Sobre el Estado... Cadiz: 1812. V. 50

RAMPANT LIONS PRESS
The First 10. Some Ground Covered at the Rampant Lions Press by Will Carter 1949-58. Cambridge: 1958. V. 50
THE Rampant Lions Press, A Printing Workshop Through Five Decades: Catalogue of an Exhibition at the Fitzwilliam Museum, Cambridge. 1982. V. 54

RAMPART Mining Company, Rampart, Alaska. Worcester: 1901. V. 52

RAMPP, LARRY C.
The Civil War in the Indian Territory. Austin: 1975. V. 49; 54

RAMSAY, A. MAITLAND
Atlas of External Diseases of the Eye. Glasgow: 1898. V. 49; 51; 54

RAMSAY, ALLAN
The Ever Green, Being a Collection of Scots Poems, Wrote by the Ingenious Before 1600. Edinburgh: 1724. V. 50
The Ever Green, Being a Collection of Scots Poems, Wrote by the Ingenious Before 1600. Edinburgh: 1761. V. 47
The Gentle Shepherd. Glasgow: 1788. V. 48
The Gentle Shepherd. Glasgow: 1796. V. 48; 51
The Gentle Shepherd. Edinburgh: 1808. V. 48; 51; 52; 54
The Gentle Shepherd. New York: 1852. V. 49
The Morning-Interview. Edinburgh: 1719. V. 53
Poems. Edinburgh: 1721. V. 53
Poems. London: 1731. V. 51
The Poems. London: 1800. V. 50
Poems on Several Occasions. Berwick: 1793. V. 50
The Poetical Works... London & New York: 1866-68. V. 48
The Tea-Table Miscellany: a Collection of Choice Songs Scots and English. Glasgow: 1871. V. 53
The Tea-Table Miscellany; or, Allan Ramsay's Collection of Scots Sangs. London: 1730. V. 50

RAMSAY, ANDREW JOHN
Win-on-ah: or the Forrest Light and Other Poets. Toronto: 1869. V. 49

RAMSAY, ANDREW MICHAEL
An Essay Upon Civil Government: Wherein Is Set Forth, the Necessity, Origine, Rights, Boundaries and Different Forms of Sovereignty. London: 1722. V. 48; 52
The Life of Francis de Salignac de la Motte Fenelon, Arch-bishop and Duke of Cambray. London: 1723. V. 52
The Travels of Cyrus. London: 1730. V. 51
The Travels of Cyrus. London: 1739. V. 48
The Travels of Cyrus... London: 1752. V. 48
The Travels of Cyrus. Boston: 1795. V. 47; 48

RAMSAY, DAVID
The History of South Carolina, From Its First Settlement in 1670, to the Year 1808. Charleston: 1809. V. 47
History of South Carolina, From Its First Settlement in 1670 to the Year 1808. Newberry: 1858. V. 48
The History of the American Revolution. Trenton: 1811. V. 47
The History of the Revolution in South Carolina, From a British Province to An Independent State. Trenton: 1785. V. 48
History of the United States, from Their First Settlement as English Colonies in 1607, to the Year 1808, or the Thirty-Third of Their Sovereignty and Independence. Philadelphia: 1816. V. 47
The Life of George Washington, Commander in Chief of the Armies of the United States in the War Which Established Their Independence; and First President of the United States. London: 1807. V. 47
The Life of George Washington, Commander in Chief...and First President of the United States. New York: 1807. V. 48; 50
Military Memoirs of Great Britain; or, a History of the War 1755-1763. Edinburgh: 1779. V. 50; 51; 53

RAMSAY, DEAN
Reminiscences of Scottish Life and Character. Edinburgh and London. V. 49; 54

RAMSAY, EDWARD BANNERMAN
Two Lectures on Some Changes in Social Life and Habits. Edinburgh: 1857. V. 49; 52

RAMSAY, GEORGE
A New Dictionary of Anecdotes, Illustrative of Character and Events: From Genuine Sources. London: 1822. V. 50
A New Encyclopaedia of Anecdotes. London: 1830. V. 51

RAMSAY, JAMES
Examination of the Rev. Mr. Harris's Scriptual Researches on the Licitness of the Slave Trade. London: 1788. V. 51; 52
Objections to the Abolition of the Slave Trade, with Answers. London: 1788. V. 51; 52

RAMSAY, JOHN
Scotland and Scotsmen in the Eighteenth Century. London: 1888. V. 49

RAMSAY, W. M.
Studies in the History and Art of the Eastern Provinces in the Roman Empire. Aberdeen: 1906. V. 49; 52; 54
The Thousand and One Churches. London: 1909. V. 49

RAMSBOTHAM, FRANCIS H.
The Principles and Practice of Obstetric Medicine and Surgery,... London: 1845. V. 50; 54

RAMSDELL, CHARLES EUGUENE BARKER
The South in the Building of the Nation. Richmond: 1909. V. 48

RAMSDEN, CHARLES
Bookbinders of the United Kingdom (Outside London) 1780-1840. London: 1954. V. 48; 49; 50; 54
French Bookbinders 1789-1848. London: 1950. V. 49; 50; 54
London Bookbinders 1780-1840. London: 1956. V. 49; 50; 54

RAMSEY, C. G.
Architectural Graphic Standards. New York: 1966. V. 48

RAMSEY, J. G. M.
The Annals of Tennessee to the End of the Eighteenth Century: Comprising Its Settlement. Philadelphia: 1860. V. 47

RAMSEY, PAUL
Eve, Singing. Easthampton: 1976. V. 48

RAMSEY, STANLEY C.
Small Houses of the Late Georgian Period 1750-1820. 1919-23. V. 47
Small Houses of the Late Georgian Period, 1750-1820. London: 1919-23. V. 50; 53; 54
Small Houses of the Late Georgian Period, 1750-1820. New York: 1923 and 1924. V. 51
Small Houses of the Late Georgian Period 1750-1820. London: 1923/24. V. 50

RAMSEYER, U.
The Art and Culture of Bali. Oxford: 1977. V. 51

RAN Away to Sea. By Hard Clam. New York: 1873. V. 54

RANBY, JOHN
The Method of Treating Gun-Shot Wounds. London: 1760. V. 48
A Narrative of the Last Illness of the Right Honourable the Earl of Orford (Robert Walpole)... London: 1745. V. 49; 54

RANCHERE, GABRIEL
Narrative of a Voyage to the Northwest Coast of America in the Years 1811, 1812, 1813 and 1814. New York: 1854. V. 54

RAND, A. L.
Handbook of New Guinea Birds. 1967. V. 54
Handbook of New Guinea Birds. London: 1967. V. 49; 52; 53
Handbook of New Guinea Birds. Garden City: 1968. V. 54

RAND, AYN
Atlas Shrugged. 1957. V. 47
Atlas Shrugged. New York: 1957. V. 47; 48; 49; 52; 53
Capitalism: the Unknown Ideal. 1966. V. 50
Capitalism: the Unknown Ideal. New York: 1966. V. 48; 53
For the New Intellectual: the Philosophy of Ayn Rand. New York: 1961. V. 52
The Fountainhead. Indianapolis: 1943. V. 49; 50; 53
The Fountainhead. London: 1947. V. 48; 51
We the Living. 1936. V. 50
We the Living. London: 1936. V. 47
We the Living. New York: 1959. V. 54
What is Capitalism?. New York: 1965. V. 47

RAND, PAUL
Thoughts on Design. New York: 1947. V. 51
The Trademarks. Wittenborn: 1960. V. 47

RANDALL, DAVID
Thirteen Author Collections of the Nineteenth Century and Five Centuries of Familiar Quotations. New York: 1950. V. 50; 52

RANDALL, ISABELLA
A Lady's Ranche Life in Montana. London: 1887. V. 47

RANDALL, J. E.
Fishes of the Great Barrier Reef and Coral Sea. Honolulu: 1990. V. 50; 51

RANDALL, JAN
When Toys Could Talk. Akron: 1939. V. 50

RANDALL, JOHN
Our Coal and Iron Industries and the Men Who Have Wrought in Connection with Them - the Wilkinsons... Barrow-in-Furness: 1917. V. 50; 52; 54

RANDALL, JOSEPH
An Introduction to So Much of the Arts and Sciences, More Immediately Concerned in an Excellent Education for Trade In Its Lower Scenes and More Genteel Professions... London: 1765. V. 50; 54
The Semi-Virgilian Husbandry, Deduced From Various Experiments... London: 1764. V. 47

RANDALL, LORA VROOMAN
Josiah B. Vrooman: His Ancestors and Descendants. El Paso: 1946. V. 49

RANDALL, THOMAS E.
History of the Chippewa Valley, a Faithful Record of All Important Events, Incidents and Circumstances that Have Transpired in the Valley of the Chippewa from Its Earliest Settlement by White People, Indian Treaties... Eau Claire: 1875. V. 52

RANDALL-MACIVER, DAVID
Buhen. Philadelphia: 1911. V. 51
The Iron Age in Italy: a Study of those Aspects of the Early Civilization Which Are Neither Villanovan nor Etruscan. Oxford: 1927. V. 50; 52

RANDIS, ROBERT J.
An Eye for Justice: the Third Private Eye Writers of America Anthology. New York: 1988. V. 51; 54

RANDISI, ROBERT J.
The Eyes Have It. New York: 1984. V. 51; 54
Justice for Hire: the Fourth Private Eye Writers of America Anthology. New York: 1990. V. 51
Mean Streets. New York: 1986. V. 48; 49; 51; 52; 54

RANDOLPH, EDMUND
A Vindication of Mr. Randolph's Resignation. Philadelphia: 1795. V. 47

RANDOLPH, EDWARD
Edward Randolph; Including His Letters and Official Papers from the New England, Middle & Southern Colonies in America, with Other Documents Relating Chiefly to the Vacating of the Royal Charter of the Colony of Massachusetts Bay, 1676-1703. Boston: 1898. V. 47

RANDOLPH, FRANCIS
Observations on the Present State of Denmark, Russia and Switzerland, in a Series of Letters. London: 1784. V. 49

RANDOLPH, JOHN
Letters of John Randolph, to a Young Relative. Philadlephia: 1834. V. 51
To the Freeholders of Charlotte, Buckingham, Prince Edward and Cumberland. 1812. V. 52

RANDOLPH, MARY
The Virginia Housewife.... Baltimore: 1831. V. 50
The Virginia Housewife; or, Methodical Cook. Baltimore: 1836. V. 52; 53

RANDOLPH, THOMAS
Cornelianum Dolium. London: 1638. V. 49
Poems. London: 1652. V. 47; 49; 50
Poems, With the Muses Looking-Glasse, and Amyntas. Oxford: 1640. V. 49

RANDOLPH, VANCE
The Ozarks: an American Survival of Primitve Society. New York: 1931. V. 53

RANDOLPH, WILLIAM FITZHUGH
With Stonewall Jackson, at Chancellorsville. N.P: 1905. V. 49; 50

RANDS, W. B.
Lilliput Revels and Innocents' Island. London. V. 47

RANHOFER, CHARLES
The Epicurean. New York: 1912. V. 47
The Epicurean. Chicago: 1920. V. 53
The Epicurean. Evanston: 1920. V. 48

RANK, OTTO
Art and Artist. New York: 1932. V. 48

RANKE, LEOPOLD VON
The Ecclesiastical and Political History of the Popes of Rome. London: 1840. V. 49
The History of Servia, and the Servian Revolution. London: 1853. V. 48
A History of Servia, and the Servian Revolution, from Original Mss. and Documents. London: 1847. V. 50
The History of the Popes, Their Church and State, and Especially of Their Conflicts with Protestantism in the Sixteenth and Seventeenth Centuries. London: 1847-48. V. 48
The Ottoman and the Spanish Empires, in the Sixteenth and Seventeenth Centuries. Philadelphia: 1845. V. 52
Universal History. The Oldest Historical Group of Nations and the Greeks. London: 1884. V. 48

RANKIN, ADAM
Dialogues, Pleasant and Interesting, Upon the All-Important Question in Church Government, What Are the Legitimate terms of Admission to Visible Church Communion?. Lexington: 1819. V. 48

RANKIN, DANIEL J.
The Zambesi Basin and Nyassaland. Edinburgh: 1893. V. 54

RANKIN, DANIEL S.
Kate Chopin and Her Creole Stories. Philadelphia: 1932. V. 49

RANKIN, F. HARRISON
The White Man's Grave; a Visit to Sierra Leone in 1834. London: 1836. V. 47; 49

RANKIN, JAMES L.
Walther Pistols. Coral Gables: 1980/nd/1981. V. 51

RANKIN, M. WILSON
Reminiscences of Frontier Days. Denver: 1935. V. 47; 48; 50

RANKIN, MELINDA
Twenty Years Among the Mexicans. Cinncinatti: 1875. V. 47

RANKIN, REGINALD
The Inner History of the Balkan War. London: 1914. V. 48

RANKINE, JOHN
A Treatise on the Law of Leases in Scotland. Edinburgh: 1887. V. 51

RANKINE, W. J. M.
A Manual of Applied Mechanics. London: 1870. V. 50
Miscellaneous Scientific Papers... London: 1881. V. 53

RANKING, JOHN
Historical Researches on the Conquest of Peru, Mexico, Bogota, Natchez and Talomeco, in the Thirteenth Century. London: 1827. V. 54
Historical Researches on the Wars and Sports of the Mongols and Romans. London: 1826. V. 54

RANLETT, WILLIAM H.
The Architect... New York: 1849. V. 48

RANSOM, J. H.
Who's Who (and Where) in Horsedom. V. 53

RANSOM, JOHN CROWE
Armageddon. Charleston: 1923. V. 54
Chills and Fever. New York: 1924. V. 47; 48; 53; 54
Grace After Meat. London: 1924. V. 49; 53
Poems About God. New York: 1919. V. 51; 53; 54
Selected Poems. New York: 1945. V. 47; 48; 50; 53
Selected Poems. New York: 1952. V. 52
Selected Poems. New York: 1964. V. 53
Two Gentlemen in Bonds. New York: 1927. V. 47; 51; 53
The World's Body. New York: 1938. V. 53

RANSOM, WILL
Kelmscott, Doves and Ashendene - the Private Press Credos. New York: 1952. V. 52
Little Dutchy Nursery Songs from Holland. London: 1925. V. 50; 54
Private Presses and Their Books. New York: 1929. V. 48; 50; 51; 53; 54
Private Presses and Their Books. New York: 1992. V. 49

RANSOME, ARTHUR
Aladdin and His Wonderful Lamp. New York: 1919. V. 49
Aladdin and His Wonderful Lamp in Rhyme. London: 1919. V. 51
The Big Six. London: 1940. V. 54
Missee Lee. London: 1941. V. 54
The Soldier and Death. A Russian Folk Tale. London: 1920. V. 47

RANSON, R.
The Assembled Alphabet: or, Acceptance of A's Invitation... London: 1809. V. 53

RANTOUL, ROBERT
Letter to Robert Schuyler, Esq., President of the Illinois Central Railroad, on the Value of the Public Lands of Illinois. Boston: 1851. V. 53

RAPELJE, GEORGE
Narrative of Excursions, Voyages and Travels... New York: 1834. V. 52

RAPER, ELIZABETH
The Receipt Book. Soho: 1924. V. 47

RAPHAEL
The Complete Works of Raphael. New York: 1969. V. 47
The Familiar Astrologer: an Easy Guide to Fate, Destiny and Foreknowledge, As Well as to the Secret and Wonderful Properties of Nature. London: 1831. V. 47
The Seven Cartoons of Raphael Urbin... London: 1721. V. 50

RAPHAEL, FREDERIC
Obbligato. London: 1956. V. 54

RAPHAEL, HERBERT H.
A Descriptive Catalogue of the Artistic and Literary Illustrations Collected by the Author of the Extension of the Original Edition of Walpole's letters... Bristol: 1909. V. 51

RAPHAEL, MAX
Prehistoric Pottery and Civilization in Egypt. Washington: 1947. V. 49; 51

RAPHALL, M. J.
Bible View of Slavery. New York: 1861. V. 53

RAPHALL, M. J. continued
The Constancy of Israel Delivered Before the Congregation Shearit Israel, Charleston, South Carolina on Shabat Parah, Adar 18, 5610. Charleston: 1850. V. 50

RAPIN, RENE
Hortorvm Libri IV. Parisiis: 1665. V. 48; 54
Rapin of Gardens. London: 1718. V. 48; 54
Two Odes from the Latin of the Celebrated Rapin.... London: 1710. V. 50

RAPIN-THOYRAS, PAUL DE
The History of England. London: 1732-33. V. 50
The History of England... London: 1732-47. V. 50
The History of England. London: 1757-59. V. 54
History of England. 1760. V. 53

RAPOU, A.
Typhoid Fever and its Homoeopathic Treatment. Cincinnati: 1853. V. 48

RAPP, GEORGE
Excavations at Nichoria in Southwest Greece. Minneapolis: 1978-92. V. 50; 52

RAPPOPORT, S.
History of Eygpt, from 330 B.C. to the Present Time. London: 1904. V. 48

RAPPORT, LEONARD
Rendezvous With Destiny, a History of the 101st Airborne Division. Washington: 1948. V. 47

RARE Books and Collections of the Reynolds Historical Library. A Bibliography. Birmingham: 1968. V. 53

RASHDALL, HASTINGS
The Universities of Europe in the Middle Ages. London: 1936. V. 52
The Universities of Europe in the Middle Ages. London: 1937. V. 49
The Universities of Europe in the Middle Ages. 1942. V. 50
The Universities of Europe in the Middle Ages. Oxford: 1969. V. 47; 49

RASHLEIGH, PHILIP
Specimens of British Minerals Selected from the Cabinet of Philip Rashleigh. London: 1797-1802. V. 47

RASK, ERASMUS
A Grammar of the Danish Language. Copenhagen: 1830. V. 50

RASK, RASMUS KRISTIAN
Vejledning til det Islandske eller Gamle Nordiske Sprog. Copenhagen: 1811. V. 54

RASLES, SEBASTIAN
A Dictionary of the Abnaki Language in North America...Volume 1. Cambridge: 1833. V. 53

RASMUSSEN, E. MICHAEL
The First Night. New York: 1947. V. 48

RASMUSSEN, KNUD
Greenland By the Polar Sea. London: 1921. V. 49; 50
The People of the Polar North: a Record. London: 1908. V. 53

RASMUSSEN, W. D.
Agriculture in the United States, a Documentary History. New York: 1975. V. 50; 52

RASPE, RUDOLF ERICH
The Adventures of Baron Munchausen. London: 1866. V. 48
Surprising Adventures of Baron Munchausen. London: 1895. V. 48
The Travels and Surprising Adventures of Baron Munchausen. London: 1868. V. 50

RASPE, RUDOLPH ERICH
The Travels and Surprising Adventures of Baron Munchausen. London: 1869. V. 54

RASTELL, JOHN
The Pastime of People, or the Chronicles of Divers Realms and Most Especially of the Realm of England. London: 1811. V. 47; 51; 54
Les Termes de la Ley; or, Certain Difficult and Obscure Words and Terms of the Common and Statute Laws of This Realm, Now in Use, Expounded and Explained. London. V. 52
Les Termes de la Ley; or, Certain Difficult and Obscure Works and Terms of the Common and Statute Laws... London: 1721. V. 47

RASTELL, WILLIAM
A Collection in English, o the Statutes Now In Force, Continued from the Beginning of Magna Charta, Made in the 9 Yeare of the Reigne of King H. 3 Until the End of the Parliament Holden the 7. Yeeare of the Reign of Our Sovereign Lord King James... London: 1611. V. 53

RASWAN, CARL
The Arab and His Horse. Des Moines: 1955. V. 53
The Raswan Index and Handbook for Arabian Breeders. Ames: 1969. V. 49

RATCH, JERRY
Chaucer Marginalia. Berkeley: 1979. V. 52; 54

RATCHFORD, FANNY
The Brontes Web of Childhood. New York: 1941. V. 52; 54
The Brontes Web of Childhood. New York: 1949. V. 54
Letters of Thomas J. Wise to John Henry Wrenn. A Further Inquiry Into the Guilt of Certain 19th Century Forgers. New York: 1944. V. 51; 54

RATCLIFF, CARTER
Andy Warhol. New York: 1983. V. 49
Carter & George. Complete Pictures 1971-1985. New York: 1986. V. 53
John Singer Sargent. Oxford: 1983. V. 49
Jorge Castillo. Drawing, Painting, Sculpture. New York: 1986. V. 50
Red Grooms. New York: 1984. V. 51

RATCLIFFE, DOROTHY UNA
Nightlights. London: 1929. V. 48; 50

RATHBONE, BASIL
In and Out of Character. Garden City: 1962. V. 54

RATHBONE, FREDERICK
Wedgwood. Merion: 1968. V. 50

RATHBONE, HANNAH MARY
The Poetry of Birds, Selected from Various Authors... Liverpool: 1833. V. 52
So Much of the Diary of Lady Willoughby as Relates to Her Domestic History, & to the Eventful period fo the Reign of Charles the First... London: 1846. V. 49

RATHBONE, PERRY T.
Westward the Way. The Character and Development of the Louisiana Territory as Seen by Artists and Writers of the Nineteenth Century. St. Louis: 1954. V. 52

THE RATIONAL Humourist: Consisting of a Selection of Anecdotes, Bon Motes &c... London: 1799. V. 48; 51

RATTENBURY, HAROLD B.
Face to Face with China. London: 1945. V. 53

RATTENBURY, JOHN
Memoirs of a Smuggler... London: 1837. V. 51

RATTIGAN, TERENCE
The Collected Plays. London: 1953. V. 52; 53
Ross - a Dramatic Portrait. London: 1960. V. 47
Ross: a Dramatic Portrait. New York: 1962. V. 54
The Winslow Boy. London: 1946. V. 50

RATTRAY, ALEXANDER
Vancouver Island and British Columbia. London: 1862. V. 48; 54

RATTRAY, DAVID
A Red-Framed Print of the Summer Palace. New York: 1983. V. 49; 50; 52
To the Blue Wall. New York: 1993. V. 51

RATTRAY, R. S.
Ashanti. London: 1923. V. 51
The Tribes of the Ashanti Hinterland. Oxford: 1932-69. V. 54

RATTRAY, W. J.
The Scot in British North America. Toronto: 1880. V. 53

RATZES, FRIEDRICH
The History of Mankind. London: 1896. V. 47

RAUCH, FREDERICK AUGUSTUS
Psychology, or a View of the Human Soul, including Anthropology. New York: 1840. V. 47; 54
Psychology, or a View of the Human Soul, Including Anthropology. 1841. V. 47
Psychology, or a View of the Human Soul, Including Anthropology. New York: 1841. V. 49; 54

RAUCH, JOHN
Public Parks: Their Effects Upon the Moral, Physical and Sanitary Condition of the Inhabitants of Large Cities: With Special Reference to the City of Chicago. Chicago: 1869. V. 50

RAUCOURT DE CHARLEVILLE, A.
A Manual of Lithography... London: 1821. V. 47
A Manual of Lithography: Clearly Explaining the Whole Art, and the Accidents That May Happen in Printing... London: 1832. V. 49; 52

RAULSTON, MARION C.
Memories of Owen Humphrey Churchill and His Family. 1950. V. 47

RAUMER, FREDERICK VON
America and the American People. New York: 1846. V. 52
The Corn Laws of England. London: 1841. V. 49
England in 1835. London: 1836. V. 50
Italy and the Italians. London: 1840. V. 49

RAUNICK, SELMA M.
Kothmanns of Texas 1845-1930. Austin: 1931. V. 51; 52

RAUSCHENBERG, ROBERT
Robert Rauschenberg: Photographs. New York: 1981. V. 49; 51

RAUSCHER, FRANK
Music on the March 1862-65. Philadelphia: 1892. V. 47

RAUTHMEL, RICHARD
Antiqitates Bremertonacenses; or the Roman Antiquities of Overborough. Kirkby Lonsdale: 1824. V. 48
The Roman Antiquities of Overborough. London: 1746. V. 50; 52; 53
The Roman Antiquities of Overborough. Kirkby Lonsdale: 1823. V. 47
The Roman Antiquities of Overborough. Kirkby Lonsdale: 1824. V. 50; 52; 53

RAUWOLF, LEONHART
Aigentliche Beschreibung der Raiss, So er Vor Diser Zeit Gegen Auffgang Inn Die Morgenlander... Lauingen: 1582. V. 47

RAVEL, JEROME
Raoul, or the Magic Star, A Fairy Pantomine in One Act and Ten Tableaux. New York: 1849. V. 54

RAVEL, OSCAR E.
Descriptive Catalogue of the Collection of Tarentine Coins Formed by M. P. Vlasto. London: 1947. V. 48

RAVEN, C. E.
English Naturalists from Neckam to Ray... Cambridge: 1947. V. 48
John Ray, Naturalist: His Life and Works. Cambridge: 1942. V. 50
John Ray, Naturalist: His Life and Works. Cambridge: 1950. V. 53

RAVEN, HENRY CUSHIER
Anatomy of the Gorilla. New York: 1950. V. 49; 52
The Henry Cushier Raven Memorial Volume. The anatomy of the Gorilla. New York: 1950. V. 49

RAVEN, JOHN JAMES
The Church Bells of Suffolk... London: 1890. V. 53

RAVEN, SIMON
Brother Cain. London: 1959. V. 51; 52; 53
Doctors Wear Scarlet. London: 1960. V. 49
The Feathers of Death. London: 1959. V. 49
Places Where they Sing. London: 1970. V. 49
The Rich Pay Late. London: 1964. V. 47

RAVENEAU DE LUSSAN, SIEUR
Raveneau de Lussan, Buccaneer of the Spanish Main and Early French Filibuster of the Pacific. Cleveland: 1930. V. 50

RAVENHILL, ALICE
The Native Tribes of British Columbia. Victoria: 1938. V. 49

RAVENSTEIN, E. G.
Martin Behaim, His Life and His Globe. London: 1908. V. 50

RAVERAT, GWEN
Period Piece. A Cambridge Childhood. London: 1952. V. 49; 51

RAVIGLIO ROSSO, GIULIO
Historia d'Inghilterra, Dopo la Morte di Odoarado Sesto. Ferrara: 1591. V. 47; 53
I Successi d'Inghilterra Dopo a Morte di Odoardo Sesto. Ferrara: 1560. V. 53

RAVILIOUS, ERIC
The Complete Wedgwood Designs of Eric Ravilious. London: 1986. V. 53
For Shop Use Only: Curwen & Dent Stock Blocks and Devices. 1993. V. 54
The Wood Engravings of Eric Ravilious. London: 1972. V. 47; 48; 53

RAVISIUS TEXTOR, JEAN
Epithetorvm Epitome. Lyon: 1548. V. 53
Officinae Historicis Poeticis Referrae Disciplinis (etc.). (with) Cornucopia (etc.). Venice: 1541. V. 52

RAVITCH, MARK M.
A Century of Surgery 1880-1980. Philadelphia: 1981. V. 52

RAWLET, JOHN
A Dialouge Betwixt Two Protestants.... London: 1685. V. 49
Poetick Miscellanies of Mr. John Rawalet, B.D. and Late Lecturer of S. Nicholas Church in the Town and County of New-castle Upon Tine. London: 1687. V. 49; 50

RAWLING, C. G.
The Land of the New Guinea Pygimes. London: 1913. V. 52

RAWLINGS, MARJORIE KINNAN
Cross Creek Cookery. New York: 1942. V. 47; 48; 49; 50; 51; 53
Golden Apples. New York: 1935. V. 51; 53
The Secret River. New York: 1955. V. 48; 52; 53
The Sojourner. New York: 1953. V. 50; 54
South Moon Under. New York: 1933. V. 47; 50; 51
When the Whippoorwill. New York: 1940. V. 48; 51; 52; 53; 54
The Yearling. New York: 1938. V. 47; 53; 54
The Yearling. New York: 1939. V. 51; 53

RAWLINGS, THOMAS
The Confederation of the British North American Provinces... London: 1865. V. 48

RAWLINSON, GEORGE
The Five Great Monarchies of the Ancient Eastern World... London: 1871. V. 48
The Five Great Monarchies of the Ancient Eastern World. London: 1862-67. V. 50
Five Great Monarchies of the Ancient Eastern World... New York: 1881. V. 54
History of Ancient Egypt. New York: 1882. V. 50
The Works of George Rawlinson. New York: 1900. V. 48

RAWLINSON, HENRY
The Russians in Central Asia. London. V. 49

RAWLINSON, RICHARD
The English Topographer. London: 1720. V. 52

RAWLINSON, ROBERT
Designs for Factory, Furnace and Other Tall Chimney Shafts. London: 1858. V. 49; 52

RAWLINSON, WILLIAM GEORGE
Turner's Liber Studiorum, a Description and a Catalogue. London: 1878. V. 51
The Water-Colours of J. M. W. Turner. London. V. 48

RAWLS, WALTON
The Great Book of Currier & Ives' America. New York: 1979. V. 53

RAWNSLEY, HARDWICKE DRUMMOND
A Book of Bristol Sonnets. London: 1877. V. 54
The Book of the Coronation Bonfires. Carlisle: 1911. V. 51
Chapters at the English Lakes. Glasgow: 1913. V. 54
The Darkened West. Keswick: 1896. V. 54
Edward Thring. Teacher and Poet. London: 1889. V. 54
Five Addresses of the Lives and Work of St. Kentigern and St. Herbert, Delivered in St. Kentigern's Church, Crosthwaite. Carlisle: 1888. V. 52
Five Addresses on the Lives and Work of St. Kentigern and St. Herbert. Carlisle: 1889. V. 48; 50; 52; 54
Flower-Time in the Oberland. Glasgow: 1904. V. 54
Henry Whitehead 1825-1896. Glasgow: 1898. V. 52; 54
Literary Associations of the English Lakes. Glasgow: 1894. V. 54
Past and Present at the English Lakes. Glasgow: 1916. V. 54
Poems, Ballads and Bucolics. London: 1890. V. 54
The Resurrection of Oldest Egypt. Laleham: 1904. V. 54
The Resurrection of Oldest Egypt. Staines: 1904. V. 52; 54
Sonnets Round the Coast. London: 1887. V. 54
The Undoing of Harcla: a Ballad of Cumberland. London: 1892. V. 54

RAWNSLEY, R. DRUMMOND B.
Christian Exhortation. Sermons Preached in Country Churches. Third Series. London: 1871. V. 54

RAWORTH, TOM
The Big Green Day. London: 1968. V. 47
Muted Hawks. Berkeley: 1995. V. 51

RAWSON, GEOFFREY
Bligh of the "Bounty". London: 1930. V. 54
Nelson's Letters from the Leeward Islands and Other Original Documents in the Public Record Office and the British Museum. Waltham St. Lawrence: 1953. V. 50

RAWSON, MRS.
Notes of Eastern Travel: Being Selections from the Diary of a Lady. Manchester: 1864. V. 52

RAWSTORNE, LAWRENCE
Gamonia: or, the Art of Preserving Game... London: 1837. V. 50; 51; 52; 53; 54
Gamonia; or, the Art of Preserving Game. London: 1929. V. 52

RAY, C.
The Underwater Guide to Marine Life. New York: 1956. V. 53

RAY, CYRIL
The Complete Imbiber: an Entertainment. London: 1956-71. V. 48

RAY, D. M.
Roster of the 16th Texas Cavalry (Dismounted). 1907. V. 49

RAY, DEE
The Bunkhouse Boys from the Lazy Daisy Ranch. Flagstaff: 1974. V. 54

RAY, EMMA J. SMITH
Twice Sold and Twice Ransomed, The Autobiography of Mr. & Mrs. L. P. Ray. Chicago: 1926. V. 53

RAY, GORDON N.
Books as a Way of Life. New York: 1988. V. 52
The Illustrator and the Book in England from 1790 to 1914. 1976. V. 50
The Illustrator and the Book in England from 1790 to 1914. New York: 1976. V. 47; 54

RAY, ISAAC
Contributions to Mental Pathology. Boston: 1873. V. 48; 52
Conversations on the Animal Economy; Designed for the Instruction of Youth, and the Perusal of General Readers. Portland: 1829. V. 48; 54
Mental Hygiene. Boston: 1863. V. 47
A Treatise on the Medical Jurisprudence of Insanity. Boston: 1853. V. 48; 52

RAY, JAMES
A Compleat History of the Rebellion, From Its First Rise in 1745 to Its Total Suppression at the Glorious Battle of Culloden, in April 1746. London: 1758. V. 54

RAY, JOHN
Catalogus Plantarum Angliae, et Insularum Adjacentium... Londini: 1670. V. 49; 50; 51; 52; 54
A Collection of Curious Travels and Voyages. London: 1693. V. 51; 52
A Collection of English Proverbs Digested Into a Convenient Method for the Speedy Finding Any One Upon Occasion... Cambridge: 1670. V. 51; 53
A Collection of English Proverbs Digested Into a Convenient method for the Speedy Finding Any One Upon Occasion... Cambridge: 1678. V. 48; 49
A Collection of English Words Not Generally Used, with Their Significations and Original... London: 1691. V. 49; 51; 53
A Compleat Collection of English Proverbs... London: 1737. V. 48
A Compleat Collection of English Proverbs... London: 1768. V. 51
A Compleat Collection of English Proverbs... London: 1818. V. 53
Correspondence (Further Correspondence). London: 1848-1928. V. 53
Further Correspondence. London: 1928. V. 54
Historia Plantarum Species Hactenus Editas Aliasque Insuper Multas Noviter Inventas & Descriptas. London: 1686-88. V. 48
Joannis Raii Synopsis Methodica Avium & Piscium; Opus Postumum... London: 1713. V. 51; 52
Methodus Plantarum Emendata et Aucta. Londini: 1703. V. 51
Methodus Plantarum Nova. Londini: 1682. V. 48; 49
Miscellaneous Discourses Concerning the Dissolution and Changes of the World... London: 1692. V. 48; 51; 53

RAY, JOHN continued
Nomenclator Classicus, Sive Dictionarum Trilingue... London: 1706. V. 51
A Persuasive to a Holy Life. London: 1719. V. 53
Philosophical Letters Between the Late Learned Mr. Ray and Several of His Ingenious Correspondents, Native and Foreigners. London: 1718. V. 48
Philosophical Letters Between the Late Learned Mr. Ray and Several of His Ingenious Correspondents, Natives and Foreigners. London: 1718. V. 47; 49; 51
Select Remains of the Learned John Ray, with His Life... London: 1760. V. 51
Synopsis Methodica Animalium Quadrupedum et Serpentini Genris. London: 1693. V. 49
Synopsis Methodica Avium & Piscium: Opus Posthumum Quod Vivus Recensuit & Perfecit Ipse Insignissimus Author. London: 1713. V. 51; 53
Synopsis Methodica Stirpium Britannicaru, Tum Indigenis, tum in Agris Cultis... Londini: 1696. V. 51
Synopsis Methodica Stirpium Britannicarum: Tum Indigenis, Tum in Agris Cultis Locis Suis... Londini: 1724. V. 49; 50; 51; 52
Three Physico-Theological Discourses, Concerning I. The Primitive Chaos and Creation of the World. II. The General Deluge, Its Causes and Effects. III. The Disscolution of the World and Future Conflagration. London: 1693. V. 51
Travels through the Low-Countries, Germany, Italy and France... London: 1738. V. 51; 52
The Wisdom of God Manifested in the Works of the Creation. London: 1709. V. 54
The Wisdom of God Manifested in the Works of the Creation. London: 1722. V. 51
The Wisdom of God Manifested in the Works of the Creation. London: 1727. V. 49
The Wisdom of God Manifested in the Works of the Creation. London: 1743. V. 51

RAY, MAN
Alphabet Pour Adultes. Paris: 19070. V. 54
Photographs by Man Ray 1920 Paris 1934. Hartford: 1934. V. 52; 53
Revolving Doors. Turin: 1972. V. 50
Self Portrait. Boston: 1963. V. 52
Self Portrait. London: 1963. V. 50

RAY, MILTON S.
The Farallones, the Painted World and Other Poems of California. San Francisco: 1934. V. 51; 52

RAY, OPHELIA
Daughter of the Tejas. Greenwich: 1965. V. 49; 51; 53; 54

RAY, PATRICK HENRY
Report of the International Polar Expedition to Point Barrow, Alaska, In Response to the Resolution of the House of Representatives of December 11, 1884. Washington: 1885. V. 50; 54

RAY, PERLEY ORMAN
The Repeal of the Missouri Compromise: Its origin and Authorship. Cleveland: 1909. V. 48

RAYE, CHARLES
A Picturesque Tour through the Isle of Wight. London: 1825. V. 49; 51

RAYER, P. F.
A Theoretical and Practical Treatise on the Diseases of the Skin. Philadelphia: 1845. V. 54

RAYLEIGH, JOHN WILLIAM STRUTT, BARON
Argon, a New Constituent of the Atmosphere. Washington: 1896. V. 50; 52; 53; 54
The Theory of Sound. 1894-96. V. 54

RAYLEIGHT, JOHN WILLIAM STRUTT, BARON
The Theory of Sound. London: 1926. V. 52

RAYMOND, A.
Flash Gordon in the Caverns of Mongo. 1936. V. 48

RAYMOND, ANTONIN
Antonin Raymond, Architectural Details. New York: 1947. V. 48; 50; 53; 54

RAYMOND, DORA N.
Captain Lee Hall of Texas. Norman: 1940. V. 49

RAYMOND, ELEANOR
Early Domestic Architecture of Pennsylvania. New York: 1931. V. 54

RAYMOND, FREEMAN, & CO.
Texas Real Estate Brokerage, Collecting and Land Agency...Sir: We Hereby Propose a Business Correspondence With You. Austin: 1850. V. 48

RAYMOND, GEORGE
Memoirs of Robert William Elliston, Comedian. London: 1846. V. 48
Memoirs of Robert William Elliston Comedian. London: 1884-85. V. 49; 53

RAYMOND, GEORGE B.
Catalogue of Books on Angling, Shooting, Field Sports, natural History, The Dog, Gun, Horse, Racing and Kindred Subject. New York: 1904. V. 47

RAYMOND, J.
Oscar Wilde Recollections. Bloomsbury: 1932. V. 51

RAYMOND, JAMES G.
The Life of Thomas Dermody... 1806. V. 47
The Life of Thomas Dermody. London: 1806. V. 49

RAYMOND, JEAN PAUL
Oscar Wilde, Recollections. Bloomsbury: 1932. V. 54
Recollections of Oscar Wilde. Bloomsbury: 1932. V. 47; 50

RAYMOND, JOHN
An Itinerary Contayning a Voyage Made through Italy, in the Yeare 1646 and 1647. London: 1648. V. 48

RAYMOND, ROSSITER W.
Camp and Cabin. Sketches of Life and Travel in the West. New York: 1880. V. 54
Mineral Resources of the States and Territories West of the Rocky Mountains. Washington: 1869. V. 48
Statistics of Mines and Mining in the States and Territories West of the Rocky Mountains. Washington: 1870-72. V. 48

RAYNAL, GUILLAUME THOMAS FRANCOIS
Histoire Philosophique et Politique des Etablishsemens et du Commerce des Europeens Dans les Deux Indes. Geneve: 1781. V. 49; 53
Revolution de l'Amerique... Londres i.e. Paris?: 1781. V. 47
The Revolution of America. London: 1781. V. 47
The Revolution of America... New York: 1792. V. 50

RAYNAL, MAURICE
Picasso. Munchen: 1921. V. 49; 52

RAYNBIRD, WILLIAM
An Old Man's Legacy; or, the Labour of Many Years Devoted to Biblical, Artistic and Historical Literature, to Works of Fiction and to the Collection of Aphorisms. London: 1867. V. 47

RAYNE, H.
The Ivory Raiders. London: 1923. V. 52

RAYNER, ARTHUR E.
Accuracy in the X-Ray Diagnosis of Urinary Stone. Preston: 1909. V. 52

RAYNER, B. L.
Sketches of the Life, Writings and Opinions of Thomas Jefferson. New York: 1832. V. 50

RAYNER, D. H.
The Geology and Mineral Resources of Yorkshire. 1974. V. 53

RAYNER, J. L.
The Complete Newate Calendar. London: 1926. V. 48

RAYNER, JOHN
A Digest of the Law Concerning Libels: Containing All the Resolutions in the Books on the Subject, and Many Manuscript Cases. London: 1765. V. 47; 50

RAYNER, SIMEON
The History and Antiquities of Haddon Hall. Derby: 1836. V. 48
The History and Antiquities of Haddon Hall. Derby: 1836-37. V. 53

RAYNER, WILLIAM
Miscellanies in Prose and Verse, Original and Translated. Ipswich: 1767. V. 50

RAYNOLDS, W. F.
Report...on the Explorations of the Yellowstone and the Country Drained by that River. Washington: 1868. V. 47

RAZINOWICZ, LEON
A History of English Criminal Law and Its Administration from 1750. London: 1948-56. V. 54

RAZZI, GIROLAMO
La Balia. Comedia. Nuouamente Ristampata. Florence: 1564. V. 51; 54
Vite di Qvattro Huomini Illustri. Florence: 1580. V. 52

RAZZI, SILVANO
La Vita, Overo Azzioni Della Contessa Matelda... Firenza: 1587. V. 54

RE-UNION of Col. Dan McCooks's Third Brigade Second Division Fourteenth A.C. "Army of the Cumberland". Assault of Col. Dan McCook's Brigade on Kenesaw Mountain, Ga., June 27, 1864. Chicago: 1900. V. 49

REA, ALICE
Dalefolk. London: 1895. V. 47

REA, JOHN
Flora: seu de Florum Cultura. London: 1665. V. 52; 53; 54
Flora: Seu, De Florum Cultura. Or, A Complete Florilege, Furnished with all Requisites Belonging to a Florist. London: 1676. V. 47; 48

REACH, ANGUS B.
Clement Lorimer; or, the Book with the Iron Clasps. London: 1849. V. 48; 49; 51; 52; 53
Clement Lorimer; or, The Book with the Iron Clasps. London: 1855. V. 49

READ and Circulate. John Charles Fremont. A California Statement of His Connection with Palmer, Cook & Co. Together with a Brief Review of His Military and Financial Career, from the Record. 1856. V. 48

READ, CHARLES A.
The Cabinet of Irish Literature... London: 1879-80. V. 53
The Cabinet of Irish Literature: Selections from the Works of the Chief Poets, Orators and Prose Writers of Ireland. London: 188-?. V. 48

READ, CHARLES HERCULES
Antiquities from the City of Benin and From Other Parts of West Africa in the British Museum. London: 1899. V. 47; 48; 49
The Waddesdon Bequest. Catalogue of the Works of Art Bequeathed to the British Museum by Baron Ferdinand Rothschild, M.P., 1898. London: 1902. V. 54

READ, CHARLES R.
Squash Rackets. New York: 1937. V. 47

READ, HERBERT
Art Now: An Introduction to the Theory of Modern Painting and Sculpture. London: 1933. V. 51
Barbara Hepworth Carvings and Drawings. London: 1952. V. 54
Collected Poems 1913-1925. London: 1926. V. 47
English Stained Glass. London: 1926. V. 48

READ, HERBERT continued
Lord Byron at the Opera - a Play for Broadcasting. North Harrow: 1963. V. 52
Marino Marini: The Complete Works. New York: 1970. V. 47; 48; 50; 52; 53
Mutations of the Phoenix. Richmond: 1923. V. 53
Naked Warriors: Poems. London: 1919. V. 47; 53
The Parliament of Women. 1960. V. 52; 54
The Parliament of Women. London: 1960. V. 50; 54
The Practice of Design. London: 1946. V. 47
Surrealism. London: 1936. V. 51; 53; 54
Unit 1: The Modern Movement in English Architecture, Painting and Sculpture. London: 1934. V. 49; 51

READ, J. A.
Journey to the Gold Diggins (sic) by Jeremiah Saddlebags. Burlingame: 1950. V. 48

READ, JOHN E.
Nansen in the Frozen World... Philadelphia: 1897. V. 48

READ, JOHN MEREDITH
A Historical Inquiry Concerning Henry Hudson, His Friends, Relatives and Early Life, His Connection with the Muscovy Company and Discovery of Delaware Bay. Albany: 1866. V. 47

READ, OPIE
Bolanyo: a Novel. Chicago: 1897. V. 48

READ, PIERS PAUL
The Train Robbers. London: 1978. V. 47

READ, W. W.
Annals of Cricket, a Record of the Game... London: 1896. V. 48

READE, ALEYN LYELL
Johnsonian Gleanings. New York: 1968. V. 48; 50; 52
The Mellards, and Their Descendants, Including the Bibbys of Liverpool. London: 1915. V. 49; 52

READE, BRIAN
Ballet Designs and Illustrations 1581-1940. A Catalogue Raisonne. London: 1967. V. 54
Beardsley. London: 1967. V. 54

READE, CHARLES
The Cloister and the Hearth. London: 1861. V. 51; 54
The Cloister and the Hearth. New York: 1861. V. 47; 51
Come Over and Stay Till Domesday. 1937. V. 48
The Course of True Love Never Did Run Smooth. London: 1857. V. 47; 50; 54
Cream. London: 1858. V. 48
Griffith Gaunt; or, Jealousy. London: 1867. V. 48
A Hero and a Martyr: a True Narrative. New York: 1875. V. 50; 54
It Is Never to Late to Mend. Boston: 1856. V. 50; 53
It Is Never Too Late to Mend. London: 1856. V. 54
Peg Woffington. New York: 1887. V. 48
Peg Woffington. London: 1899. V. 47
Put Yourself In His Place. London: 1870. V. 48
A Simpleton. Boston: 1873. V. 53
A Simpleton. London: 1873. V. 48
A Terrible Temptation. London: 1871. V. 47; 50
White Lies. London: 1857. V. 47; 52
A Woman-Hater. Edinburgh and London: 1877. V. 48; 54
The Works. London: 1910. V. 52

READE, COMPTON
The Smith Family: Being a Popular Account of Most Branches of Name, However Spelt, from the 14th Century Downwards. 1902. V. 49; 54
The Smith Family: Being a Popular Account of Most Branches of the Name, However Spelt, from the 14th Century Downwards. London: 1902. V. 51
The Smith Family: Being a Popular Account of Most Branches of the Name, However Spelt, from the 14th Century Downwards. 1942. V. 50

READE, JOHN EDMUND
Prose from the South. London: 1847. V. 49
Prose from the South... London: 1849. V. 49

READE, WINWOOD
The African Sketch-Book. London: 1873. V. 50
The Outcast. London: 1875. V. 48
Savage Africa: Being the Narrative of a Tour in Equatorial South Western and North Western Africa... London: 1864. V. 54

READER, E. E.
Priestess and Queen. London: 1899. V. 52

READING, JOSEPH H.
The Ogowe Band: a Narrative of African Travel. Philadelphia: 1901. V. 47

READING, PETER
Shitheads. London: 1989. V. 51
Water and Waste. Walthom on Thames, Surrey: 1970. V. 47

READING Races; or, The Berkshire Beauties. 1777. V. 51

READING Races; or, the Berkshire Beauties. London: 1777. V. 48

READINGS and Musick, at Free-Masons Hall, This Evening (Wednesday) February 28 at Seven O'Clcock. Titchfield-street: 1787?. V. 47

READY, OLIVER
Life and Sport in China. 1904. V. 52; 54

REAGAN, RONALD
An American Life. New York: 1990. V. 49
House of the Oireachtas Joint Sitting. Dublin: 1984. V. 48, 51

THE REAL Home Keeper. Vancouver: 1913. V. 54

REAL Life in Dolly Land. Chicago: 1913. V. 52

REAL Life in Ireland; or, the Day and Night Scenes, Rovings, Rambles and Sprees, Bulls, Blunders, ...of Brian Boru, Esq. and His Elegant Friend Sir Shawn O'Dogherty. London: 1830?. V. 51

REAL Life in London. 1824. V. 50; 54

REAL Life. Pages from the Portfolio fo a Chronicler. Edinburgh: 1832. V. 52

REANEY, JAMES
The Dance of Death at London, Ontario. London: 1963. V. 47
The Red Heart. Toronto: 1949. V. 47
Twelve Letters to a Small Town. Toronto: 1962. V. 47

REANEY, PERCY H.
Records of Queen Elizabeth Grammar School, Penrith. Kendal: 1915. V. 50; 52

REAR-Admiral Denman, Mr. Layard (Late Her Majesty's Under Secretary of State for Foreign Affairs), and the British Community of Valparaiso. Liverpool: 1866. V. 53

REARDEN, TIMOTHY H.
Petrarch and Other Essays. San Francisco: 1897. V. 47

REARICK, JANET C.
The Drawings of Pontormo. 1964. V. 50

REASONS Against a Registry for Lands, Etc. Shewing Briefly the Great Disadvantages, Charges and Inconveniences that May Accrue to the Whole Nation in General Thereby, Much Overbalancing the Particular Advantages That are Imagined... London: 1678. V. 52

REASONS for a Registry: Shewing briefly the Great Benefits and Advantages that May Accrue to this Nation Thereby. London: 1678. V. 52

REASONS for Giving Up Gibraltar.... London: 1749. V. 47

REASONS for the Inexpediency of Chartering a National Bank. New York: 1841. V. 53

REASONS Humbly Offer'd for the Making a Law to Prohibit the Exportation of All silver and to Prevent the Clipping of Our Money. London: 1694/95. V. 49

REASONS Humbly Offer'd to the Honourable House of Commons, Against Dividing the Ancient Parish of St. James Clerkenwell. 1723. V. 52

REASONS Humbly Offered for Preventing the Melting Down the Coin, and for Circulating of Money, and Encouraging a Coinage, and to Preserve the Manufacture of Wrought Plate. 1718?. V. 53

REASONS of Dissent from the Sentence and Resolution of the Commission of the General Assembly Met at Edinburgh, March 11, 1752, Concerning the Conduct of the Presbytery of Dunfermilne... Edinburgh: 1752. V. 54

REASONS Why the Present System of Auctions Ought to Be Abolished. New York: 1828. V. 51

REAUGH, FRANK
Paintings of the Southwest. Dallas: 1930. V. 49
Prose Sketches to Accompany the Series of Paintings by Frank Reaugh Entitled Twenty Four Hours with the Herd. Dallas: 1934. V. 49

REAUMUR, RENE ANTOINE FERCHAULT DE
L'Art de Convertir Le Fer Forge Acier... Paris: 1722. V. 51
The Art of Hatching and Bringing Up Domestic Fowls of All Kinds. London: 1750. V. 48; 51; 53; 54
Memoires Pour Servir a l'Historie des Insects. Paris: 1734-42. V. 50; 51; 53
The Natural History of Bees. London: 1744. V. 53

REAVEY, GEORGE
The Colours of Memory. New York: 1955. V. 51; 53

REAVIS, JAMES ADDISON
In the United States Court of Private Land Claims Santa Fe District...Peralta Grant, Amended Answer and Cross-Petition of the United States; Translations, Documentary Evidence and Exhibits of the Government... Santa Fe: 1895. V. 54

REAVIS, LOGAN URIAH
The Empire of the Mississippi Valley. St. Louis: 1877. V. 53
The Life and Military Services of Gen. Selby Harney. St. Louis: 1878. V. 47

REBAY, HILLA
In Memory of Wassily Kandinsky. 1945. V. 50
In Memory of Wassily Kandinsky - The Solomon R. Guggenheim Foundation Presents a Survey of the Artist's Painting and Writings. New York: 1945. V. 54

RECANANTI, MENACHEM
Piskei Halachoth. Bologna: 1538. V. 53

RECAPITULATION of All Masonry; or a Description...of the Universal Heiroglyph... Dublin: 1883. V. 52

RECENT Expeditions to Eastern Polar Seas. London: 1882. V. 54

RECENT Scenes and Occurences in Ireland; or Amiadversions on a Pamphlet Entitled "One Year of the Administration of the Marquess of Wellesley". 1823. V. 54

RECHY, JOHN
City of Night. New York: 1963. V. 54
Numbers. New York: 1967. V. 54

RECKITT, W.
Some Account of the Life and Labours of... Philadelpha: 1783. V. 53

RECLUS, ELISEE
The Earth: A Descriptive History of the Phenomena of the Life of the Globe. London: 1876. V. 49
The Earth and Its Inhabitants. New York: 1886-95. V. 52
The Earth and Its Inhabitants: Oceanica. New York: 1890. V. 52
The Ocean, Atmosphere and Life. London: 1873. V. 49
The Ocean Atmosphere and Life. London: 1888. V. 50

RECOLLECTIONS Of Childhood; or, Sally the Faithful Nurse. Canterbury: 1840. V. 47

RECOLLECTIONS of Sheridan County Nebraska. Rushville: 1976. V. 50

RECORD of Service of the Forty-Fourth Massachusetts Volunteer Militia in North Carolina, August 1862 to May 1863. Boston: 1887. V. 54

RECORD of the Celebration of...the Introduction of the Art of Printing Into Aberdeen by Edward Raban. Aberdeen: 1922. V. 54

A RECORD of the Commemoration, November Fifth to the Eighth 1886, On the Two Hundred and Fiftieth Anniversary to the Founding of Harvard College. Cambridge: 1887. V. 53

RECORD of the Federal Dead Buried from Libby, Belle Isle, Danville & Camp Lawton Prisons, and at City Point, and in the Field Before Petersburg and Richmond. Philadelphia: 1865. V. 49

RECORD of the Service of the Forty-Fourth Massachusetts Volunteer Militia in North Carolina August 1862 to May 1863. Boston: 1887. V. 47

RECORD, ROBERT
The Urinal of Physick Whereunto Is Added an Ingenious Treatise, Concerning Physicians, and Chyrugians, Set Forth by a Doctor in Queen Elizabeth's Days. (with) Faults in Unskilful Physitians, Ignorant and Careless Apothecaries... London: 1665/1662. V. 47

RECORDE, ROBERT
The Ground of Arts, Teaching the Perfect Worke and Practise of Arithmeticke... London: 1623. V. 49

RECORDS of Officers and Men of New Jersey in Wars, 1791-1815. Trenton: 1909. V. 47; 49

RECORDS of the Lives of Ellen Free Pickton and Featherstone Lake Osler. Oxford: 1915. V. 52

RECORDS of the Royal Military Academy. Woolwich: 1851. V. 52

RECORDS of the Royal Military Academy, 1741-1892. Woolwich;: 1892. V. 50

RECREATIONS In Natural History, or Popular Sketches of British Quadrupeds: Describing Their Natures, Habits and Dispositions... 1815. V. 54

RECREATIONS In Natural History, or Popular Sketches of British Quadrupeds... London: 1815. V. 49; 50; 52; 53

RECREATIONS in Shooting. London: 1846. V. 52

RECREATIONS of the Rabelais Club. London. V. 54

RECREATIVE Science: a Record and Remembrancer of Intellectual Observation. London: 1860-62. V. 50

RECTOR, HENRY M.
Inaugural Address of Henry M. Rector, Delivered Before the General Assembly of Arkansas, 15th November, 1860. V. 52

RECUEIL des Loix Constitutives des Colonies Angloises, Confederees sous la Denomination d'Etats-Unis de l'Amerique Septentrionale. Philadelphia: 1778. V. 47

RECUEIL d'Estampes Representant les Differents Evenements de la Guerre qui a Procure l'Independence aux Etats Uns de l'Amerique. Paris: 1784?. V. 52; 53; 54

THE RED Brothers. Philadelphia: 1846. V. 50

RED, GEORGE PLUNKETT
The Medicine Man in Texas. Houston: 1930. V. 49

RED Riding Hood. New York: 1891. V. 52
RED Riding Hood. London: 1895. V. 49
RED Riding Hood. New York: 1915. V. 54
RED Riding Hood. London: 1950. V. 54

RED River Insurrection. Hon. Wm. McDougall's Condut Reviewed. Montreal: 1870. V. 52

RED, White and Blue Socks. New York: 1864. V. 52

REDDIE, JAMES CAMPBELL
Laura Middleton Her Brother and Her Lover. Brussels: 1890. V. 50

REDDING, CYRUS
A History and Description of Modern Wines. London: 1833. V. 48
A History and Description of Modern Wines. London: 1851. V. 52
Memoirs of Remarkable Misers. London: 1863. V. 54

REDDING, J. SAUNDERS
To Make a Poet Black. Chapel Hill: 1939. V. 50; 52

REDE, LEMAN THOMAS
Anecdotes & Biography, Including Many Modern Characters in the Circles of Fashionable and Official Life... London: 1799. V. 48

REDE, WILLIAM LEMAN
Peregrinations of Pickwick. New York and Philadelphia: 1837. V. 54

REDEL, CARL ADOLPH
Das Sehenswurdige Prag Worinnen alle Sehensmerck- und Wunderwurdige Begebenheiten, Denckmahle und Antiquitaten... Nuremberg & Prag: 1710. V. 53

REDESDALE, LORD
The Garter Mission to Japan. London: 1906. V. 53
Memories. London: 1915. V. 54
A Treatise on the Pleadings in Suits in the Court of Chancery by English Bill. London: 1814. V. 49

REDFEATHER
The Faithful Indians of Ignatius. 1907. V. 50

REDFIELD, AMASA A.
A Hand-book of the U.S. Tax Law, (Approved July 1, 1862), with All the Amendments, to March 4, 1863: Comprising the Decisions of the Commissioner of Internal Revenue... New York: 1863. V. 52

REDFIELD, H. V.
Homicide, North and South, Being a Comparative View of Crime Against the Person in Several Parts of the United States. Philadelphia: 1880. V. 52

REDFIELD, W. C.
Letter to the Secretary of the Treasury, on the History and Causes of Steamboat Explosions, and the Means of Prevention. New York: 1839. V. 54
Sketch of the Geographical Rout (sic) of a Great Railway, by Which It is Proposed to Connect the Cannals and Navigable Waters, of New-York, Pennsylvania, Ohio, Indiana, Illinois, Michigan, Missouri and the Adjacent States and Territories... New York: 1830. V. 47

REDGRAVE, MICHAEL
In My Mind's I. New York: 1983. V. 53
The Mountebank's Tale. London: 1959. V. 52

REDGROVE, PETER
An Explanation of the Two Visions. Leamington Spa: 1985. V. 51
Work in Progress. London: 1968. V. 48

REDI, FRANCESCO
Experimenta Circa Generationem Insectorum. Amsterdam: 1671. V. 48
Osservazioni...Intorno Agli Animali Viventi che si Trovano Negli Animali Viventi. Florence: 1684. V. 47; 49; 51

REDLICH, JOSEF
The Procedure of the House of Commons. London: 1903. V. 51

REDMAYNE, J. S.
Fruit Farming On the "Dry Belt" of British Columbia; The Why and Wherefore. London: 1910. V. 47; 52

REDON, ODILON
L'Oeuvre Graphique de Odilon Redon. The Hague: 1913. V. 51

REDOUTE, PIERRE JOSEPH
Beautiful Flowers and Fruits. New York: 1985. V. 50; 51; 52; 54
A Catalogue of Redouteana. Exhibited at the Botanical Library, 21 April to 1 August, 1963. Pittsburgh: 1963. V. 49
Choix des Plus Belles Fleurs Prises dans Differentes Families du Regne Vegetal et de Quelques Branches des Plus Beaux Fruits. Paris: 1829. V. 53
Choix des Plus Belles Fleurs Prises dans Differentes Familles du Regne Vegetal et de Quelques Branches des plus Beaux Fruits. Paris: 1827-33. V. 47
Facsimile Prints Made from Mostly Unpublished Original Paintings from the Collection of the Hunt Institute for Botanical Documentataion. Regensburg & Pittsburg: 1972. V. 53
A Redoute Treasury. New York: 1986. V. 51
Roses. New York and London: 1954-56. V. 50; 51
Les Roses. (with) A Volume of Commentaries. Antwerp: 1974-76. V. 50

REDPATH, JAMES
Echoes of Harper's Ferry. Boston: 1860. V. 53
The Public Life of Capt. John Brown. Boston: 1860. V. 48; 49

REDSHAW, THOMAS DILLON
Hill Field. Poems and Memoirs for John Montague on His Sixtieth Birthday, 28 Feb. 1989. Minneapolis: 1989. V. 48; 50

REECE, BYRON HERBERT
The Season of Flesh. New York: 1955. V. 51

REED, ANDREW
A Narrative of the Visit to the American Churches, by the Deputation from the Congregational Union of England and Wales. London: 1835. V. 53

REED, EDWARD J.
Japan: Its History, Traditions and Religions. London: 1880. V. 54
Shipbuilding in Iron and Steel. London: 1869. V. 54
A Treatise on the Stability of Ships. London: 1885. V. 53

REED, EPHRAIM
Musical Monitor; or New-York Collection of Devotional Church Music... Utica: 1817. V. 50

REED, F. W.
A Bibliography of Alexander Dumas, Pere. London: 1933. V. 54

REED, HELEN LEAH
Brenda's Summer at Rockley. Boston: 1901. V. 47

REED, HENRY
Lessons of the War. New York: 1970. V. 48; 53

REED, ISAAC
Bibliotheca Reediana. London: 1807. V. 52
Diaries 1762-1804. 1946. V. 54
The Repository: a Select Collection of Furitive Pieces of Wit and Humour... London: 1790. V. 52

REED, ISHMAEL
Cab Calloway Stands In for the Moon. Flint: 1986. V. 50
The Free-Lance Pallbearers. Garden City: 1967. V. 48; 50; 51; 53
The Last Days of Louisiana Red. New York: 1974. V. 53
Mumbo Jumbo. Garden City: 1972. V. 53
Reckless Eyeballing. New York: 1986. V. 53
Yellow Back Radio Broke-Down. Garden City: 1969. V. 51; 53

REED, J. T. A.
Cow Pox Inoculation... Respecting the Efficacy and Success of Vaccine Inoculation... Buckingham: 1810. V. 47; 48; 49; 50

REED, JOHN
The Day in Bohemia, or, Life Among the Artists... New York: 1913. V. 47; 50
Sangar to Lincoln Steffens. Riverside: 1913. V. 47
Ten Days That Shook the World. New York: 1919. V. 49; 52; 53

REED, JOHN A.
History of the 101 Regiment Pennsylvania Volunteers Infantry. Chicago: 1910. V. 49

REED, JOSEPH
Tom Jones, a Comic Opera: as it is Performed at the Theatre Royal in Covent Garden. London: 1769. V. 52; 53

REED, KIT
Lighthouse. Middletown: 1966. V. 50

REED, LAURA COATES
In Memoriam: Sarah Walter Chandler Coates. Kansas City: 1898-99. V. 54

REED, LEAR B.
Human Wolves: Seventeen Years of War on Crime. Kansas City: 1941. V. 47

REED, MYRTLE
Flower of the Dusk. New York: 1908. V. 50
The Master Violin. New York: 1904. V. 52

REED, REBECCA T.
Six Months In a Convent, or, the Narrative of Rebecca Teresa Reed who was Under the Influence of the Roman Catholics About Two Years, and an Inmate of the Ursuline Convent on Mount Benedict, Charlestown, Mass... Boston: 1835. V. 52

REED, RONALD
The Nature and Making of Parchment. 1975. V. 54
The Nature and Making of Parchment. Leeds: 1975. V. 49; 51

REED, S. G.
A History of the Texas Railroads and of Transportation Conditions Under Spain and mexico... Houston: 1941. V. 48

REED, TALBOT BAINES
A History of the Old English Letter Foundries... London: 1887. V. 47; 51
A History of the Old English Letter Foundries. London: 1952. V. 51

REED, THOMAS ALLEN
The Reporter's Guide. London: 1869. V. 53

REED, WALT
Harold Von Schmidt Draws and Paints the Old West. Flagstaff: 1972. V. 48; 50; 51
John Clymer an Artist Rendezvous with the Frontier West. Flagstaff: 1976. V. 47; 50; 52; 53; 54

REED, WALTER
The Propagation of Yellow Fever Based on Recent Researches. Baltimore: 1901. V. 52; 54
Yellow Fever. A Compilation of Various Publications. Results of the Work of Maj. Walter Reed, Medical Corps, United States Army, and the Yellow Fever Commission. Washington: 1911. V. 52

REED, WILLIAM
De Grazia, the Irreverent Angel. 1971. V. 54
De Grazia, the Irreverent Angel. San Diego: 1971. V. 48; 51
Olaf Wieghorst. Flagstaff: 1969. V. 47; 53

REED, WILLIAM B.
Haud Immemor. a Few Personal Recollections of Mr. Thackeray in Philadelphia. Philadelphia: 1864. V. 47; 54
A Letter on American History. Philadelphia: 1847. V. 54
Oration Delivered at Philadelphia By...February 22, 1849. Philadelphia: 1849. V. 49

REEDER, ELLEN D.
Hellenistic Art in the Walters Art Gallery. Baltimore: 1988. V. 50; 52

REEDER, RED
Omar Nelson Bradley, The Soldiers' General. Champaign: 1969. V. 50

REEMELIN, CHARLES
The Vine-Dresser's Manual, an Illustrated Treatise on Vineyards and Wine-Making. New York: 1856. V. 51; 54
The Vine-Dressers Manual, an Illustrated Treatise on Vineyards and Wine-Making. New York: 1858. V. 52

REES, A. R.
The Growth of Bulbs, Applied Aspects of the Physiology of Ornamental Bulbous Crop Plants. New York: 1972. V. 48

REES, ABRAHAM
The Cyclopaedia; or, Universal Dictionary of Arts, Sciences and Literature. London: 1819-20. V. 47; 51; 53
Ree's Manufacturing Industry (1819-20). 1972. V. 52
Rees's Manufacturing Industry, A Selection from the Cyclopedia; or Universal Dictionary of Arts, Sciences and Literature. London: 1972. V. 49

REES, ENNIS
More of Brer Rabbit's Tricks. New York: 1968. V. 51; 52

REES, IOAN BOWEN
The Mountains of Wales: an Anthology. Newtown: 1987. V. 47

REES, J. D.
H.R.H. the Duke of Clarence and Avondale in Southern India with a Narrative of Elephant Catching in Mysore.... London: 1891. V. 53

REES, THOMAS
A New System of Stenography, or Short Hand. Philadelphia: 1800. V. 51

REESE, A. M.
The Alligator and Its Allies. New York: 1915. V. 51

REESE, DAVID MEREDITH
Humbugs of New York: Being a Remonstrance Against Popular Delusion...Etc. New York: 1838. V. 48

REESE, HARRY
The Sandragraph: Between Printing and Painting. Los Angeles: 1987. V. 51

REESE, LIZETTE WOODWORTH
A Branch of May. Poems. Baltimore: 1887. V. 54

REEVE, CLARA
Edwin, King of Northumberland. London: 1802. V. 47
The Exiles. London: 1788. V. 48
The Old English Baron: A Gothic Story. London: 1780. V. 53
The Old English Baron: a Gothic Story. London: 1789. V. 49
The Old English Baron: a Gothic Story. London: 1794. V. 50; 52; 53; 54

REEVE, H.
The Greville Memoirs; a Journal of...Regins of King(s) George IV, William IV and Queen Victoria. 1888. V. 48

REEVE, J. ARTHUR
Monograph of Fountains Abbey, Yorkshire. London: 1892. V. 51

REEVE, J. STANLEY
A Foxhunter's Journal. Philadelphia: 1952. V. 54
Foxhunting Formalities. New York: 1930. V. 51
Foxhunting Recollections a Journal of the Radnor Hounds and Other Packs. Philadelphia: 1928. V. 47

REEVE, JOHN
A Transcendent Spiritual Treatise Upon Several Heavenly Doctrines, from the Holy Spirit of the Man Jesus... London. V. 49; 52

REEVE, L.
Elements of Conchology... London: 1860. V. 53

REEVE, R. D.
Nightways. Colorado Springs: 1987. V. 50

REEVE, TAPPING
The Law of Baron and Femme; of Parent and Child; of Guardian and Ward; of Master and Servant; and of the Powers of Courts of Chancery. With an Essay on the Terms, Heir, Heirs and Heirs of the Body. New Haven: 1816. V. 49

REEVES, ARTHUR MIDDLETON
The Finding of Wineland the Good: The History of the Icelandic Discovery of America... London: 1895. V. 54

REEVES, C. N.
Valley of the Kings: the Decline of a Royal Necropolis. London & New York: 1990. V. 49

REEVES, DIANNE L.
From Fiber to Paper. Houston. V. 51; 52

REEVES, GEORGE
The Lady's Practical Guide to the Science of Horsemanship. Bath: 1838. V. 47

REEVES, JAMES
Arcadian Ballads. 1977. V. 47
The Closed Door. 1977. V. 52
Collected Poems 1929-1974. London: 1974. V. 54
Subsong. London: 1969. V. 54

REEVES, JAMES J.
History of the Twenty-fourth Regiment New Jersey Volunteers. Camden: 1889. V. 48; 49; 51; 54

REEVES, RICHARD STONE
Classic Lines. Birmingham: 1975. V. 50; 52
Decade of Champions. New York: 1980. V. 52
Legends. The Art of Richard Stone Reeves. Birmingham: 1989. V. 52
Thoroughbreds I Have Known. S. Brunswick: 1973. V. 53

REEVES, ROLEYNE
Colburn's Kalendar of Amusements in Town and Country, for 1840. London: 1840. V. 51

REEVES, WILLIAM
The Life of St. Columba. 1857. V. 50; 54
The Life of St. Columba. London: 1857. V. 51

REEVES, WILLIAM PEMBER
New Zealand. London: 1908. V. 48

REFLECTIONS on Our Common Failings. London: 1701. V. 52

REFLECTIONS On the Causes and Probable Consequences of the Late Revolution in France... Edinburgh: 1790. V. 50

REFLECTIONS on the Importation of Bar-Iron, from Our Own Colonies of North-Ameirca. London: 1757. V. 47; 49

REFLECTIONS on the Petition and Apology for the Six Deprived Bishops. London: 1690. V. 53

REFLECTIONS On the Powers of the General Government and the Inherent Rights of American Citizens: Suggested by a Perusal of the Constitution and Congressional Debates in Relation to Territorial Governments. Kalamazoo: 1857. V. 48

REFLECTIONS Upon the Late Horrid Conspiracy Contrived by Some of the French Court to Murther His Majesty in Flanders: and for Which Monsieur Grandvall, One of the Assassinates Was Executed. London: 1692. V. 53

REFLEXIONS on Courtship and Marriage in Two Letters to a Friend. London: 1759. V. 50; 51

THE REFORM Medical Practice: With a History of Medicine, from the Earliest Period, Until the Present Time, and a Synopsis of Principles On which the Reform Practice is Founded. Macon: 1857. V. 54

THE REFUGE. London: 1801. V. 47

REGAE, PAULINE, PSEUD.
Story of O. New York: 1965. V. 53

REGAN, C. TATE
Biologia Centrali-Americana: Pisces. London: 1906-08. V. 51

REGEMORTER, BERTHE
Some Oriental Bindings in the Chester Beatty Library. Dublin: 145. V. 47

REGIMEN SANITATIS SALERNITANUM
De Conservanda Bona Valetudine. Francoforti: 1557. V. 53
De Conservanda Bona Valetudine. Venetiis: 1587. V. 47; 50; 53
Regimen Sanitatais Salerni... London: 1541. V. 48
Regimen Sanitatis Salerni; or the Schoole of Salernes Regiment of Health. London: 1634. V. 47; 50
Regimen Sanitatis Salerni; or, the Schoole of Salernes Regiment of Health. London: 1649. V. 52
Regimen Sanitatis Salernitanum. Paris: 1490. V. 48
The School of Salernum: Regimen Sanitatis Salerni. Salerno: 1966. V. 54

REGIMENTAL Orders of the Second Ohio Heavy Artillery, From Its First Organization, September 23, 1863. N.P: 1864. V. 49

REGIMENTAL Standing Orders: issued by the Colonel; to Be Observed by the 17th or Royal Meath Regiment of Militia. Cork: 1796. V. 51

REGINA Tornado June 30 1912 Regina Saskatchewan Canada. 1912. V. 48

REGINALD, R.
Science Fiction and Fantasy Literature. A Checklist 1700-1974. (with) *Contemporary Science Fiction Authors II.* Detroit: 1979. V. 52

A REGISTER of Officers and Agents, Civil, Military and Naval. Washington: 1828. V. 48

REGISTER of the Commissioned Officers and Privates of the New Jersey Volunteers, in the Service of the United States. Jersey City: 1863. V. 47; 51

THE REGISTERS of Middleton-in-Lonsdale, Westmorland. 1670-1812. Penrith: 1925. V. 52

THE REGISTERS Of Millom, Cumberland, 1591-1812. Kendal: 1925. V. 52

THE REGISTERS of St. Michael's, Pennington in Furness 1612-1702; The Registers of Urswick in Furness 1608-1695. Cambridge: 1907. V. 52

THE REGISTERS of the Parish Church of Torver 1599-1792; the Registers of the Parish Chruch of Kirkby Ireleth 1681-1812. Rochdale: 1911. V. 52

THE REGISTERS of Warcop Westmorland 1597-1744. Kendal: 1914. V. 52

REGISTRUM Malmesburiense. London: 1879-80. V. 52

REGLAMENTO Para la Milicia Civica Del Estado de Coahuila Y Texas. Monclova: 1834. V. 49

REGLER, GUSTAV
The Owl of Minerva. Autobiography. London: 1959. V. 49

REGNAULT, ELIAS
The Criminal History of the English Government; From the First Massacre of the Irish to the Poisoning of the Chinese. New York: 1843. V. 53

REGNAULT, THEODORE
Tableaux Analytiques De L'Esprit Des Lois, De Montesquieu Suivis De la Comparison de Plusieurs Principes et Passages de Montesquieu et de Blackstone. Paris: 1824. V. 53

REGNERY, DOROTHY F.
The Battle of Santa Clara, Jan. 2, 1847. San Jose: 1978. V. 54

REGRA & Statutos da Hordem Adujs. Colophon: 1516. V. 48

REGULATIONS and Instructions for the Cavalry Sword Exercise. London: 1819. V. 52

REGULATIONS and Orders Observed In His Majesty's 12th, or Prince of Wale's Regiment of Light Dragoons. London: 1813. V. 49

REGULATIONS for Governing the Province of the Californias...1781. San Francisco: 1929. V. 47; 52

REHBERG, FREDERICK
Drawings Faithfully Copied From Nature at Naples and with Permission Dedicated to the Right Honourable Sir William Hamilton. Rome: 1794. V. 48

REHDER, A.
Bibliography of Cultivated trees and Shrubs Hardy in the Cooler Temperate Regions of the Northern Hemisphere. Jamaica Plain: 1949. V. 47; 48; 52; 53; 54
The Bradley Bibliography, a Guide to the Literature of the Woody Plants of the World Published Before the Beginning of the Twentieth Century. Cambridge: 1911-18. V. 47

REIBEHAND, CHRISTOPH
Filium Araiadnes, das ist.. Leipzig & Gotha: 1690. V. 53

REIBISCH, F. M.
Eine Auswahl Merkwurdiger Gegenstande aus der Konigl. Sachsischen Rustkammer. (and) Perspecktivischer Plan Von Alt-Dresden. Dresden: 1825-27. V. 47

REICH, SHELDON
John Marin: a Stylistic Analysis and Catalogue Raisonne. Tucson: 1970. V. 47; 48; 49; 50; 52; 53; 54

REICH, WILHELM
The Function of the Orgasm: Sex-Economic Problems of Biological Energy. New York: 1942. V. 52
Listen Little Man: a Document from the Archives of the Orgone Institute. New York: 1948. V. 51
People in Trouble. 1953. V. 51
Psychischer Kontakt und Vegetative Stromung. Copenhagen: 1935. V. 52
The Sexual Revolution: Toward a Self-Governing Character Structure. New York: 1945. V. 52

REICHARD, GLADYS
Navaho Religion. A Study in Symbolism. New York: 1950. V. 51

REICHARD, GLADYS A.
Dezba, Woman of the Desert. New York: 1939. V. 54
Navaho Religion. A Study of Symbolism. New York: 1950. V. 49
Navajo Medicine Man, Sandpaintings and Legends of Miguelito. New York: 1939. V. 48; 52; 53; 54

REICHELT, JULIUS
Exercitatio, de Amuletis, Aeneis Figuris Illustrata. Strassburg: 1676. V. 48

REICHENBACH, H. G. L.
Illustratio Generis Aconiti Atque Delphinii...Neue Bearbeitung der Gattungen Aconitum und Delphinum. Leipzig: 1823-25. V. 48
Monographia Generis Aconiti. Volume 1. Leipzig: 1820-21. V. 48; 49; 50

REICHENOW, A.
Vogelbilder aus Fernen Zonen. Abbildungen und Beschreibungen der Papageien. London: 1878-83. V. 48

REICHERT, IRVING FREDERICK
Judaism and the American Jew. San Francisco: 1953. V. 53

REICHERT, MADELEINE NEUMANN
Wonderful World. San Francisco: 1961. V. 52

REID, ALEXANDER
The Resources and Manufacturing Capacity of the Lower Fox River Valley, Appleton Wisconsin. Appleton: 1874. V. 49

REID, ARNOT
From Peking to Petersburg. London: 1899. V. 50

REID, ARTHUR
Reminiscences of the Revolution; or, Le Loup's Bloody Trail from Salem to Fort Edward. Utica: 1859. V. 47

REID, B. L.
The Man from New York - John Quinn and His Friends. New York: 1968. V. 53

REID, DAVID BOSWELL
Ventilation in American Dwellings; with a Series of Diagrams, Presenting Examples in Different Classes of Habitation. New York: 1864. V. 50; 53

REID, E. P.
Historical and Literary Botany...To Which is Added Flowers... Windsor: 1826. V. 50

REID, FORREST
The Garden God: a Tale of Two Boys. London: 1905. V. 53
Illustrators of the Sixties. London: 1928. V. 54

REID, FORREST continued
Notes and Impressions. 1942. V. 53
Pender Among the Residents. London: 1922. V. 51
Peter Waring. London: 1937. V. 53
Retrospective Adventures. London: 1941. V. 48
Uncle Stephen. London: 1931. V. 53
W. B. Yeats - a Critical Study. London: 1915. V. 54
Walter de la Mare - a Critical Study. London: 1929. V. 53

REID, HENRY
The Science and Art of the manufacture of Portland Cement. London: 1877. V. 50

REID, HIRAM A.
History of Pasadena: Comprising an Account of the Native Indian, the early Spanish, the Mexican, the American, the Colony and the Incorporated City. Pasadena: 1895. V. 52

REID, HUGO
The Indians of Los Angeles County. Los Angeles: 1926. V. 52

REID, J.
Feather Masterpieces of the Ancient and Andean World. London: 1990. V. 51

REID, JAMES
The Life of Christ. New York: 1930. V. 54

REID, JAMES SEATON
The History of the Presbyterian Church in Ireland... Edinburgh: 1834. V. 52

REID, JESSE WALTON
History of the Fourth Regiment of S.C. Volunteers, from the Commencement of the War Until Lee's Surrender. Greenville: 1892. V. 49

REID, JOHN
Bibliotheca Scoto-Celtica; or an Account of all the Books Which Have Been Printed in the Gaelic Language, with Bibliographical and Biographical Notices. Glasgow: 1832. V. 54
Essays on Hypochondriacal and Other Nervous Affections. Philadelphia: 1817. V. 54
Essays on Hypochondriasis, and Other Nervous Affections. London: 1816. V. 52
Physiological, Anatomical and Pathological Researches. Edinburgh: 1848. V. 47; 50
Physiological, Anatomical and Pathological Researches. Edinburgh: 1858. V. 49
Turkey and the Turks: The Present Stat of the Ottoman Empire. London: 1840. V. 48; 49; 53
The Young Surveyor's Preceptor and Architect's and Builder's Guide... London: 1859. V. 53

REID, K. E. J.
The Book of Wedding Days, Quotations for Every Day in the Year. London: 1889. V. 47

REID, MAYNE
The Bandalero. London: 1866. V. 51
The Child Wife: A Tale of the Two Worlds. London: 1868. V. 47; 54
The Child Wife: a Tale of the Two Worlds. New York: 1869. V. 51
Croquet. London: 1865. V. 51
The Desert Home: or, The Adventures of a Lost Family in the Wilderness. London: 1852. V. 47
The English Family Robinson. The Desert Home of The Adventures of a Lost Family in the Wilderness. London: 1854. V. 54
The Flag of Distress: a Story of the South Sea. London: 1876. V. 54
The Free Lances. London: 1881. V. 48
The Giraffe Hunters. London: 1867. V. 54
Gwen Wynn: a Romance of the Wye. London: 1877. V. 51
The Headless Horseman: a Strange Tale of Texas. London: 1866. V. 47
The Maroon. London: 1862. V. 48
No Quarter!. London: 1888. V. 51; 54
The Plant Hunters; or, Adventures Among the Himalaya Mountains. Boston: 1858. V. 47
The Quadroon; or, a Lover's Adventures in Louisiana. London: 1856. V. 47; 52; 54
The Rifle Rangers; or, Adventures of an Officer in Southern Mexico. London: 1850. V. 51
The Young Voyagers, or the Boy Hunters in the North. London/New York: 1862. V. 53

REID, ROBIE L.
The Assay Office and the Proposed Mint at New Westminster: a Chapter in the History of the Fraser River Mines. Victoria: 1926. V. 51; 54

REID, SAMUEL C.
The Scouting Expeditions of McCulloch's Texas Rangers; or, the Summer and Fall Campaign of the Army of the United States in Mexico - 1846... Philadelphia: 1859. V. 47

REID, STUART J.
Life and Letters of the First Earl of Durham, 1792-1840. London: 1906-07. V. 48

REID, THOMAS
An Essay on the Nature and Cure of the Phthisis Pulmonalis. London: 1782. V. 49; 51; 54
An Essay on the Nature and Cure of the Phthisis Pulmonalis; or, Consumption of the Lungs... Philadelphia: 1785. V. 48
Essays on the Active Powers of Man. Edinburgh: 1788. V. 49; 52
Essays on the Intellectual Powers of Man. Edinburgh: 1785. V. 49
Essays on the Powers of the Human Mind... London: 1822. V. 54
An Inquiry Into the Human Mind on the Principles of Common Sense. Edinburgh: 1765. V. 49
An Inquiry Into the Human Mind, On the Principles of Common Sense... London: 1769. V. 48; 52
An Inquiry Into the Human Mind on the Principles of Common Sense. Glasgow: 1817. V. 47
An Inquiry Into the Human Mind on the Principles of Common Sense... Edinburgh: 1818. V. 47

REID, WILLIAM
An Attempt to Develop the Law of Storms by Means of Facts, Arranged According to Place and Time, and Hence to Point Out a Cause for the Variable Winds, with the View to Practical Use in Navigation. London: 1850. V. 47
The Progress of the Development of the Law of Storms and of the Variable Winds. London: 1849. V. 54

REID, WILLIAM JAMESON
Through Unexplored Asia. Boston: 1899. V. 53

REIFENBERG, ADOLF
Ancient Jewish Coins. Jerusalem: 1947. V. 47

REIGART, J. FRANKLIN
The Life of Robert Fulton... Philadelphia: 1856. V. 47; 52; 54

REIGN of Fear. Fiction and Film of Stephen King. Los Angeles: 1988. V. 49; 51

THE REIGN of George VI. London: 1763. V. 49

REILLY, CATHERINE W.
Lake Victorian Peotry 1880-1899. London: 1994. V. 52

REILY, HUGH
Ireland's Case Briefly Stated: or, A Summary Account of the Most Remarkable Transactions in that Kingdom Since the Reformation. 1720. V. 48

REINACH, THEODORE
Jewish Coins. London: 1903. V. 47

REINECK, REINERUS
Chronicon Hierosolymitanvm, Id est, De Bello Sacro Historia. Helmstadt: 1584-85. V. 52

REINHARDT, AD
Art as Art. The Selected Writings of Ad Reinhardt. New York: 1975. V. 53

REINKE DE VOS
Speculum Vitae Aulicae. De Admirabili Fallacia et Astutia Vulpeculae Reinikes Libri Quatuor... Frankfurt: 1584. V. 54

REINZ, GERHARD F.
Bernard Buffet. Gravures/Engravings/Radierungen 1948-1967. New York: 1968. V. 50

REISER, RUTH
Lawton Kennedy, Printer. San Francisco: 1988. V. 50

REISNER, GEORGE ANDREW
The Cemeteries of Naga-ed-Der. Leipzig and Berkeley: 1908-65. V. 51
The Development of the Egyptian Tomb Down to the Accession of Cheops. Cambridge: 1936. V. 51
Harvard Excavations at Samaria 1908-1910. Cambridge: 1924. V. 52
Mycerinus: The Temples of the Third Pyramid at Giza. Cambridge: 1931. V. 51

REISS, WINOLD
American Indian Portraits on Exhibit at the Buffalo Museum of Science April 1929. Buffalo: 1929. V. 54

REITLINGER, GERALD
A Tower of Skulls, a Journey through Persian and Turkish Armenia. London: 1932. V. 50

REITLINGER, HENRY SCIPIO
Old Master Drawings. London: 1922. V. 50; 54

RELACAM da Mais Extraordinaria Admiravel, e Lastimosa Tormenta de Vento, Que Entre as Memoraueis do Mundo Socedeo na India Oriental, na Cidale de Bacaim & seu Destricto, na Era de 1618. aos 17 do Mes de Mayo. Lisbon: 1619. V. 54

RELACION de las Exequias que a la Magestad del Rey Catolico D. Ferdinand VI. Rome: 1760. V. 47

RELAND, ADRIAAN
Palaestina ex Monumentis Veteribus Illustrata. Utrecht: 1714. V. 51; 52; 54

A RELATION Of the Engagement of His Majesty's Fleet with the Enemies, on the 11th August, 1673. London: 1673. V. 53

RELATION Veridique Qui a l'air d'un songe. A La Haye: 1782. V. 54

RELATIONE del Successo nell'Isola della Terzera. Naples: 1583. V. 51; 54

RELAZIONE de 'Funerali a Benedetto XIV Pontefice...Celebrati in Bologna il di 10. Giugno 1758 nella Chiesa di San Bartolommeo... Bologna: 1758. V. 47

RELF, SAMUEL
Infidelity, or the Victims of Sentiment. Philadelphia: 1797. V. 47

RELFORD, THOMAS
Report and Estimates Relative to a Proposed Road in Scotland from Kyle-Rhea in Inverness-shire to Killin in Perthshire, by Rannoch-Moor. Investigated by Order of the Commissioners for Highland Roads and Bridges... London: 1810. V. 51

RELHAN, R.
Flora Cantabrigiensis. London: 1785. V. 49; 54
Flora Cantabrigiensis. London: 1802. V. 54

RELIGION As Now Practised Opposed to the Laws of God, or Remarks On the Necessity of Immediately Reviving Primitive Christianity and Community of Goods. Manchester: 1838. V. 53

A RELIQUE of the Princess Charlotte Augusta, or a Selection of Psalms and Hymns with the Appropriate Tunes, Being an Exact Copy of the Genuine Hymn Book, Used Jointly by the Late Princess Charlotte and Prince Leopold of Saxe Cobourg... London: 1818. V. 49

RELIQUES of Ancient English Poetry. London: 1794. V. 52

RELIQUES of Ancient English Poetry: Consisting of Old Heroic Ballads, Songs and Other Pieces of Our Earlier Poets; Together with Some Few of Later Date. London: 1823. V. 54

RELPH, JOSIAH
A Miscellany of Poems, Consisting of Original Poems, Translations, Pastorals in the Cumberland Dialect, Familiar Epistles, Fables, Songs and Epigrams. Glasgow: 1747. V. 48
Poems by Josiah Relf of Sebergham. London: 1798. V. 53
Poems...With the Life of the Author. Carlisle: 1798. V. 47; 48; 50

RELY, JEHAN DE
L'Order Tenu et Garde en l'Assemblee des Trois Estats, Representans tout le Royaume de France... Paris: 1558. V. 48; 52; 53; 54

REMAINS of St. Mary's Abbey, Dublin. Their Explorations and Researches, A.D. 1886. Dublin: 1887. V. 48; 50; 53

REMARKABLE Shipwrecks, or a Collection of Interesting Accounts of Naval Disasters, with Many Particulars of the Extraordinary Adventures and Sufferings of the Crews... Hartford: 1813. V. 47

REMARKABLE Visions. Comprising Highly Important Revelations Concerning the Life After Death. Boston: 1844. V. 50

REMARKS by a Junior to His Senior, On an Article in the Edinburgh Review of January, 1844 on the State of Ireland, and the Measures for Its Improvement. London: 1844. V. 49; 52

REMARKS On a General Improvement of the River Nene. April 24th, 1849. Northampton: 1849. V. 49

REMARKS On a Pamphlet, Intitled, a Inquiry In to the Revenue, Credit and Commerce of France, Exposing the False Quotations and False Reasoning of the Author, and Evil Tendency of His Pamphlet. London: 1742. V. 48

REMARKS On a Report from a Select Committee of the Late House of Commons, on the Publication of Printed Ppaers. London: 1837. V. 51

REMARKS on African Colonization and the Abolition of Slavery. Winsro: 1833. V. 48

REMARKS on Dr. Price's Observations on the Nature of Civil Liberty, &c. London: 1776. V. 47

REMARKS on the Calumnies Published in the Quarterly Review, on the English Ship-builders. London: 1814. V. 50

REMARKS on the Miscellaneous Observations Upon authors Antient and Modern. London: 1731. V. 49

REMARKS on the Morality of Dramatic Compositions with Particular Reference to "La Traviata", etc. London: 1856. V. 52

REMARKS on the Novel of Reginald Dalton (by John Gibson Lockhart) with Extracts from that Work, Illustrative of Life in Oxford. Oxford: 1824. V. 47

REMARKS on the Present State of the Coal Trade with a Retrospective Glance At Its History; addressed to the Marquis of Londonderry. London: 1843. V. 53

REMARKS On the Rights of Inventors and the Influence of Their Studies in Promoting the Enjoyments of Life and Public Prosperity. Boston: 1807. V. 52

REMARKS on the Tragedy of the Lady Jane Grey; in a Letter to Mr. Rowe. London: 1715. V. 49

REMARKS on Upper Canada Surveys, and Extracts from the Surveyor's Reports, Contain a Description of the Soil and Timber of the Townships in the Ottawa River and Georgian Bay Section... Ottawa: 1867. V. 50; 53

REMARKS Relating to a Canal, Intended to be Made from the City of Chester, to Join the Navigation from the Trent to the Mersey, at or Near Middlewich. Chester: 1770. V. 54

REMARKS Upon the Emigration of Hill Coolies. London: 1840. V. 54

REMARQUE, ERICH MARIA
All Quiet on the Western Front. Boston: 1929. V. 48; 53; 54
All Quiet on the Western Front. London: 1929. V. 47; 53
Im Western Nichts Neues. Berlin: 1929. V. 47
The Road Back. Boston: 1931. V. 47; 52
Three Comrades. London: 1937. V. 47

REMBERT, W. R.
The Georgia Bequest. Augusta: 1854. V. 47
The Georgia Bequest. Manolia; or the Vale of Tallulah. Augusta: 1856. V. 54

REMBRANDT
The Complete Work. Paris: 1897-1906. V. 50
The Drawings. London: 1973. V. 50

A REMEDY for Sedition. 1933. V. 53

REMEY, CHARLES MASON
Architectural Compositions in the Indian Style. N.P: 1923. V. 49

REMINGTON ARMS CO.
Revised Price List October, 1897. New York: 1897. V. 50

REMINGTON, FREDERIC
Crooked Trails. New York & London: 1898. V. 47
Done in the Open. New York: 1902. V. 47; 48; 49; 50; 51
Done in the Open. New York: 1903. V. 47
Drawings. New York: 1897. V. 47; 48
The Frederic Remington Book - A Pictorial History of the West. New York: 1966. V. 53
Frontier Sketches. Chicago: 1898. V. 47; 50; 52; 53
Men With the Bark On. New York/London: 1900. V. 49; 50; 51; 53
Men With the Bark On. New York: 1901. V. 53
Paintings and Drawings from the Old West. Alhambra: 1963. V. 53
Pony Tracks. New York: 1895. V. 47; 51
Sundown Leflare. New York & London: 1899. V. 48; 51

REMINISCENCES of Michael Kelly of the King's Theatre, and Theatre Royal Drury Lane, Includes a Period of Half a Century. London: 1826. V. 47

REMINISCENCES Of the Boston Female Asylum. Boston: 1844. V. 50

REMISE, JAC
The Golden Age of Toys. 1967. V. 52; 53
The Golden Age of Toys. Greenwich: 1967. V. 50

A REMONSTRANCE of the Declaration...In Answer to a Declaration...Concerning the Businesse of Hull. London: 1642. V. 50; 53

REMONSTRANCE of the General Assembly of the Kirk In Scotland to His Majestie, Sent from the Committee of Both Kingdoms the 12 of June Last to Sir Thomas Fairfax to Be By Him Sent with a Trumpeter to His Majesties Quarters... London: 1645. V. 48; 51

REMONSTRANCE of William Smith, Et Al, of Covington, Kentucky Against the Admission of Deseret Into the Union. Washington: 1850. V. 51

REMUSAT, MME. DE
Letters of Mme. de Remusat, to Her Husband and Son, 1804-1813. London: 1881. V. 50
Memoirs of Mme. de Remusat, 1802-1808. London: 1880. V. 50

REMY, JULES
A Journey to Great Salt-Lake City...with a Sketch of the History, Religion and Customs of the Mormons... London: 1861. V. 47; 51; 53
Voyage au Pays des Mormons: Relation, Geographie, Histoire Naturelle, Histoire, Theologie, Moeurs et Costumes. Paris: 1860. V. 49

REMY, NICHOLAS
Demonolatry. London: 1930. V. 47; 50; 52

RENAN, ERNEST
The Life of Jesus. London: 1864. V. 51

RENAUD, E. B.
Archaeological Survey Series. Petroglyphs of North Central New Mexico. Denver: 1938. V. 48

RENAUDOT, EUSEBIUS
Ancient Accounts of India and China. London: 1773. V. 47

RENAULT, MARY
The Charioteer. New York: 1959. V. 54
Kind Are the Answers. New York: 1940. V. 50
The Middle Mist. New York: 1945. V. 52

RENDALL, VERNON
The London Nights of Belsize. London: 1917. V. 50

RENDEL, J. M.
Report of the Drainage of the Nene Valley. Northampton: 1849. V. 49

RENDELL, RUTH
The Best Man to Die. Garden City: 1970. V. 49
The Crocodile Bird. London: 1993. V. 52
A Demon In My View. London: 1976. V. 52
The Face of Trespass. London: 1974. V. 52
The Fallen Curtain and Other Stories. London: 1976. V. 48; 52
A Judgement in Stone. London: 1977. V. 52
The Lake of Darkness. Garden City: 1980. V. 52
Master of the Moor. London: 1982. V. 52; 53
Matters of Suspense. Helsinki: 1986. V. 48; 53
Put Out by Cunning. London: 1981. V. 52
Shake Hands Forever. London: 1975. V. 47; 52
Some Lie and Some Die. London: 1973. V. 52
The Speaker of Mandarin. London: 1983. V. 53
Three Cases for Chief Inspector Wexford. Helsinki: 1990. V. 47
Three Cases for Chief Inspector Wexford. Helsinki: 1991. V. 48
Three Stories. Helsinki: 1987. V. 48
The Tree of Hands. London: 1984. V. 52
Wolf to the Slaughter. Garden City: 1968. V. 52

RENDLE, B. J.
World Timbers. London: 1969-69-70. V. 52

RENDLE, WILLIAM
Old Southwark and its People. London: 1878. V. 50

RENDU, M. LE CHANOINE LOUIS
Theory of the Glaciers of Savoy. London: 1874. V. 48

RENFREW, COLIN
The Emergence of Civilization: The Cyclades and the Aegean in the Third Millennium B.C. London: 1972. V. 50

RENGA.. New York: 1971. V. 53

RENICK, WILLIAM
Memoirs, Correspondence and Reminiscences. Circleville: 1880. V. 50

RENIER, G. J.
Oscar Wilde. London: 1933. V. 53

RENINGER, GEBBERT & SCHALL, CHICAGO
Electro-Medical Instruments and Their Management, and Illustrated Price List of Electro-Medical Apparatus, By Reninger, Gebbert and Schall, Chicago. Bristol: 1893. V. 50

RENN, LUDWIG
War. London: 1928. V. 47
War. (and) After War. London: 1929/31. V. 53

RENNE, J.
The Architecture (Domestic Habits, Faculties) of Birds. London: 1831-35. V. 54

RENNELL, JAMES
A Bengal Atlas. London: 1781. V. 48; 49
Illustrations (Chiefly Geographical) of the History of the Expedition of Cyrus, From Sardis to Babylonia... London: 1816. V. 48

RENNER, FREDERIC G.
Charles M. Russell: Paintings, Drawings and Sculpture in the Amon Carter Museum. New York: 1974. V. 51; 54

RENNERT, JACK
Alphonse Mucha: The Complete Posters and Panels. Boston: 1984. V. 52

RENNIE, D. F.
Peking and the Pekingese During the First Year of the British Embassy at Peking. London: 1865. V. 51

RENNIE, GEORGE
General View of the Agriculture of the West Riding of Yorkshire, Surveyed by Messrs. Rennie, Brown and Shirreff. London: 1793. V. 50

RENNIE, HILL
The Theory, Formation and Construction of British and Foreign Harbours. London: 1854. V. 52

RENNIE, JAMES
Alphabet of Scientific Angling for the Use of Beginners. London: 1833. V. 47

RENNIE, JOHN
Autobiography of Sir John Rennie, F.R.S. London: 1875. V. 49
Insect Architecture (Transformations, Miscellanies). London: 1830-31. V. 51; 54
Report and Estimate on the Improvement of the Drainage and Navigation of the South and Middle Levels of the Great Level of the Fens. London: 1810. V. 47; 49; 51; 53; 54
The Theory, Formation and Construction of British and Foreign Harbours. London: 1854. V. 49

RENNIE, R.
Essays on the Natural History and Origin of Peat Moss... Edinburgh: 1807. V. 48; 52; 54

RENOIR, JEAN
My Life and My Films. New York: 1974. V. 50; 53

RENOUARD, P. V.
History of Medicine, From its Origin to the 19th Century. Cincinnati: 1856. V. 50

RENOUARD DE BUSSIERRE, M. T., BARON
Lettres Sur L'Orient. Paris and Strasbourg: 1829. V. 53

RENSHAW, RICHARD
Voyage to the Cape of Good Hope, the Indian Ocean and Up the Red Sea, with Travels Into Egypt... Manchester: 1821. V. 51

RENTON, GEORGE
The Grazier's Ready Reckoner; or, a Useful Guide for the Buying and Selling Cattle. Berwick: 1798. V. 50

RENTOUL, ANNIE R.
Fairyland. New York: 1901. V. 54
Fairyland. New York: 1929. V. 53
The Little Green Road to Fairyland. London: 1947. V. 48

RENVERSEMENT de la Morale Chretienne par les Desordres du Monachisme. 169?. V. 47

RENVERSEMENT de la Morale Chretienne Par les Desordres du Monachisme. Amsterdam?: 1700. V. 49

A **REPLY** to a Pamphlet, Entitled the Case of the Duke of Portland, Respecting Two Leases Granted by the Lords of the Treasury to Sir James Lowther, Bart. London: 1768. V. 52

A **REPLY** to the Letter of the Hon. Marcus Morton, Late Governor of Massachusetts, on the Rhode Island Question. Providence: 1842. V. 51

REPORT Of the Committee On the Conduct of the War on the Attack of Petersburg on the 30th day of July, 1864. Washington: 1865. V. 50

REPORT of the Cruise of the U.S. Revenue Cutter Bear and the Overland Expedition for the Relief of the Whalers in the Arctic Ocean, from November 27, 1897 to September 13, 1898. Washington: 1899. V. 52

REPORT of the Great Conspiracy Case, the People of the State of Michigan Versus Abel F. Fitch. Detroit: 1851. V. 54

A **REPORT** of the Judgment Delivered...by Right Honourable Sir William Scott (Lord Stowell)...in the Case of Dalrymple the Wife Against Dalrymple the Husband. London: 1811. V. 51

A **REPORT** of the Proceedings of the Artizans of Birmingham, at Their meeting, Held at the Shakespeare Tavern, on Wednesday, the 17th of June 1812 and of Other Circumstances Connected Therewith. Birmingham: 1812. V. 50

REPORT of the State Trials, Before a General Court Martial Held at Montreal in 1838-9; Exhibiting a Complete History of the Late Rebellion in Lower Canada. Montreal: 1839. V. 52

REPORT of the Trial of Peter Heaman and Francois Gautiez or Gautier, for the Crimes of Piracy and Murder, Before the High Court of Admiralty, Held at Edinburgh. Edinburgh: 1821. V. 51

REPORT of the Trial of the Students on the Charge of Mobbing, Rioting and Assault, at the College (i.e. University of Edinburgh) on Jan. 11 & 12, 1838. Edinburgh: 1838. V. 48; 52

REPORT On the Petition of William Forsyth, of the Niagara Falls Pavilion, Complaining of Military Outrage. Toronto: 1835. V. 51

REPORT on the Zoological Collections Made in the Indo-Pacific Ocean, During the Voyage of H.M.S. Alert 1881-2. London: 1884. V. 53

REPORT to the Secretary of State for the Home Department from the Poor Law Commissioners on the Training of Pauper Children. London: 1841. V. 49

REPORT to the Trustees of the Dick Bequest for the Benefit of the Parochial Schoolmasters and Schools in the Counties of Aberdeen, Banff and Moray. Edinburgh: 1844. V. 54

THE **REPORTS** of the Commissioners Appointed to Examine, Take, and State the Public Accounts of the Kingdom... London: 1783. V. 53

REPORTS of the Operations of the Army of Northern Virginia from June 1862 to and Including the Battle of Fredericksburg, Dec. 13, 1862. Richmond: 1864. V. 51

REPORTS Of the Selectmen, and Other Officers of the Town of Concord. Concord: 1861. V. 54

REPORTS of the Swedish Deep-Sea Expedition 1947-1948 on the Motor Schooner "Albatross". Gothenburg & Stockholm: 1951-66. V. 47

REPORTS of the United States Commissioners to the Paris Universal Exposition, 1878. Washington: 1880. V. 52

REPORTS on Plague Investigations in India. Cambridge: 1911. V. 49; 51

REPORTS Regarding Sir William Thomson's Compass and Sounding Machine. Glasgow: 1877. V. 50

REPP, ED EARL
Hell in the Saddle. New York: 1936. V. 48

A **REPRESENTATION** Made by the Lower House of Convocation to the ArchBishops (sic) and Bishops: The Greater Part of Whom, Are of the Diligence of the Lower, and the Remissness of the Upper-House in Suppressing Books Published Against the Truth of... London: 1705. V. 48; 53

A **REPRESENTATION** of the Impiety and Immorality of the English Stage, with Reasons for Putting a Stop Thereto: and Some Questions Addrest to Those Who Frequent the Play-Houses. London: 1704. V. 51

REPRESENTATIONS of the Embossed, Chased and Engraved Subjects and Descriptions Which Decorate the Tobacco Box and Cases, Belonging to the Past Overseers Society of the Parishes of St. Margaret and St. John the Evangelist in the City of Westminster. London: 1824. V. 50; 53

REPS, JOHN W.
Cities of the American West, a History of Frontier Urban Planning. Princeton: 1979. V. 48
Views and Viewmakers of Urban America. Columbia: 1984. V. 50

REPTON, HUMPHRY
Designs for the Pavilion at Brighton. London: 1822. V. 54
Fragments On the Theory and Practice of Landscape Gardening. London: 1816. V. 53
The Landscape Gardening and Landscape Architecture. London: 1840. V. 51; 54
Observations on the Theory and Practice of Landscape Gardening. London: 1803. V. 48
Observations On The Theory and Practice of Landscape Gardening... London: 1805. V. 47; 48; 54
Observations on the Theory and Practice of Landscape Gardening... London: 1980. V. 47
Odd Whims; and Miscellanies. London: 1804. V. 48; 51
The Red Books of Humphry Repton, Including Red Books Prepared for Anthony House, Cornwall... London: 1976. V. 47; 49; 51
Variety; or a Collection of Essays Written in the Year 1787. London: 1788. V. 47; 52

REPTON, J. A.
A Trewe & Feythfull Hystorie of the Redoubtable Prynce Radapanthus. London: 1820. V. 50

REPUBLICAN Campaign Edition for the Million. Containing the Republican Platform, the Lives of Fremont and Dayton, with Beautiful Steel Portraits of Each... Boston: 1856. V. 51

REPUBLICAN NATIONAL PARTY
The Virginia Address... Richmond: 1828?. V. 47

REQUA, R. S.
Architectural Details; Spain and the Mediterranean... Los Angeles: 1926. V. 48
Architectural Details, Spain and the Mediterranean. Cleveland: 1927. V. 52
Old World Inspiration for American Architecture. 1929. V. 51
Old World Inspiration for American Architecture. Los Angeles: 1929. V. 48; 50

THE **REQUEST**, a Poem. London: 1762. V. 53

RERESBY, JOHN
The Memoirs of... London: 1734. V. 53
The Travels and memoirs of Sir John Reresby Bart. London: 1813. V. 49

RERESBY, TAMWORTH
A Miscellany of Ingenious Thoughts and Reflections in Verse and Prose. London: 1721. V. 48; 49

RESENIUS, JOHANN PAUL
Scholia Succincta et Facilia, in Arithmeticam Gemmae Frisii. Wittenberg: 1611. V. 49

RESEWITZ, FRIEDRICH
Die Erziehung des Burgers zum Gebrauch des Gesunden Verstandes... Copenhagen: 1773. V. 52

RESOLUTIONS of the Assoiated Architects; with the Report of a Committee by Them Appointed to Consider the Causes of Frequent Fires and the Best means of Preventing the Like in Future. 1793. V. 47

RESOLUTIONS of the State of Texas, Concerning Peace, Reconstruction and Independence. Richmond: 1865. V. 49

RESOLVE for Districting the Commonwealth, for the Purpose of Choosing Federal Representatives. Boston: 1792. V. 51

RESOURCES of Dakota 1887. Sioux Falls: 1887. V. 54

THE RESOURCES of New Mexico. Prepared Under the Auspices of the Bureau of Immigration fro the Territorial fair to Be Held at Albuquerque, N.M., October 3rd to 8th, 1881. Santa Fe: 1881. V. 49

RESOURCES of the Salt River Valley: Maricopa County Arizona. Phoenix: 1891. V. 54

RESTA, SEBASTIANO
The True Effigies of the Most Eminent Painters, and Other Famous Artists That Have Flourished in Europe Curiously Engraved Upon Copper-Plates. London: 1694. V. 49; 54

RESTANY, PIERRE
Botero. New York: 1984. V. 50
Yves Klein. New York: 1982. V. 50

RESTATEMENT of the Law, Second, Torts 2d. St. Paul: 1965. V. 52

RESTIF DE LA BRETONNE, NICOLAS EDME
Monsieur Nicolas of the Human Hear Unveiled Intimate Memoirs. London: 1930. V. 50
L'Oeuvre... Paris: 1930-32. V. 48
Le Paysan Perverti, La Paysane Pervertie, and Les Figures. Paris: 1782-84. V. 50

RESULTS of the First United States Manned Orbital Space Flight, Feb. 20, 1962. Washington: 1962. V. 54

A RETROSPECT of Andrew Jackson's Administration. 1832. V. 51

THE RETROSPECT of Practical Medicine and Surgery. New York: 1840-73. V. 51

RETURNS from the Several Chartered Banks, Stating the Name and Place of Residence of Each Stockholder, with the Number and Nominal Value of the Shares Held by Them. Quebec: 1860. V. 52

RETZ, JEAN FRANCOIS PAUL DE GONDI, CARDINAL
Memoirs of the Cardinal de Retz... London: 1723. V. 54

REUBEN, DAVID
Everything You Always Wanted to Know About Sex But Were Afraid to Ask. New York: 1969. V. 54

REUCHLIN, JOHANN
Vocabularius Breviloquus. Strassburg: 1501. V. 50
Vocabularius Breviloquus. Strassburg: 1501. V. 47

REUNION of the Dickinson Family, at Amherst, Mass., August 8th and 9th, 1883. Binghamton: 1884. V. 51

REUSNER, NICOLAUS
Icones Imagines Virovm Literis Illvstrivm (etc.). Strasbourg: 1587. V. 53

THE REV. John Smith Died--and Went to Jupiter Via Hell. New York: 1933. V. 49

REVERDY, PIERRE
Selected Poems. New York: 1969/55. V. 50

REVERE, JOSEPH WARREN
Keel and Saddle: A Retrospect of Forty Years of Military and Naval Service. Boston: 1872. V. 48
A Tour of Duty in California... New York: 1849. V. 50; 52

REVEREND, DOMINIQUE
Letters to Monsieur H**** Concerning the Most Antient Gods or Kings of Egypt, and the Antiquity of the First Monarchs of Babylon and China. London: 1734. V. 48

REVESI BRUTI, OTTAVIO
Archisesto per Formar Con Facilita li Cinque Ordini d'Architettura. Vicenza: 1627. V. 53

REVIEW of an Address of the Minority in Congress of Their Constituents, on the Subject of the War with Great Britain. Trenton: 1812. V. 51

A REVIEW of Some of the Arguments Which are Commonly Advanced Against Parliamentary Interference on behalf of the Negro Salves. Manchester: 1824. V. 51

A REVIEW of the Characters of the Principal Nations in Europe. London: 1770. V. 49

A REVIEW Of the Principles of Radical Reformers and the Measures Which They Have Proposed fro a Reform in Parliament. Edinburgh: 1820. V. 53

A REVIEW of the Prosecution Against Abner Kneeland, for Blasphemy. Boston: 1835. V. 50

A REVIEW of the State of John Bull's Family, Ever Since the Probate of His Last Will and Testament. London: 1713. V. 49

REVILLE, ALBERT
Lectures on the Origin and Growth of Religion as Illustrated by the Native Religions of Mexico and Peru. London: 1884. V. 51

REVILLE, F. DOUGLAS
History of the County of Brant. Brantford: 1920. V. 48

REVILLON FRERES, PARIS
Revillon Freres Trade Catalogue of Women's Fur Coats and Wraps. Paris: 1928-29. V. 53
Revillon Freres Trade Catalogue of Women's Furs. Paris: 1929-30. V. 53

THE REVIVAL of Printing: a Bibliographical Catalogue of Works Issued by the Chief Modern English Presses. London: 1912. V. 47; 51

REVOLUTION Politicks; Being a Compleat Collection Of All the Reports, Lyes, and Stories, Which are the Fore-Runners of the Great Revolution in 1688; Commencing from the Death of King Charles II. And From Thence Regularly Continued... London: 1733. V. 48; 50

REWALD, JOHN
Degas Sculpture. The Complete Works. London: 1957. V. 49; 50
Paul Cezanne: The Watercolours. A Catalogue Raisonne. London: 1984. V. 49; 51; 53
Renoir Drawings. New York: 1946. V. 49

THE REWARD: or, The History of the Goldfinch and the Lark. 1820. V. 47

REXROTH, KENNETH
The Art of Worldly Wisdom. Santa Barbara: 1980. V. 50
Between Two Wars. Selected Poems... Athens & San Francisco: 1982. V. 54
The Elastic Retort. New York: 1973. V. 52
In What Hour. 1940. V. 53
In What Hour. New York: 1940. V. 49; 51
Lovers Who Feed Goldfish In the Fontaine De Medicis Will Always Be True to One Another. Cambridge: 1972. V. 48
The New British Poets. Verona: 1948. V. 53
The Phoenix and the Tortoise. 1944. V. 47; 48

REY, EMMANUEL GUILLAUME, BARON
Voyage dans le Haouran, et aux Bords de la mer Morte, Execute Pendant les Annees 1857 et 1858. Paris: 1861. V. 49

REY, G.
The Matterhorn. 1907. V. 53
The Matterhorn. London: 1907. V. 52
Peaks and Precipices: Scrambles in the Dalomites and Savoy. London: 1914. V. 48; 52

REY, H. A.
Anybody at Home?. Boston: 1942. V. 51
Anybody At Home?. London: 1950. V. 54
Curious George Learns the Alphabet. Boston: 1963. V. 51
Curious George Rides a Bike. Boston: 1952. V. 51
Elizabite Adventures of a Carnivorous Plant. New York: 1950. V. 52
Raffy and the 9 Monkeys. London: 1939. V. 50
See the Circus. London: 1945. V. 54
We Three Kings and Other Christmas Carols. New York: 1944. V. 51
Where's My Baby?. Boston: 1943. V. 51
Where's My Baby?. London: 1945. V. 54

REYMOND, E. A. E.
Catalogue of Demotic Papyri in the Ashmolean Museum. Volume I: Embalmers' Archives from Hawara, Including Greek Documents and Subscriptions. Oxford: 1973. V. 49; 51

REYNAL, EUGENE S.
Thoughts Upon Hunting Kit in a Series of Nine Letters to a Friend. Millbrook: 1934. V. 47

REYNARD, FRANK H.
The Ninth Royal Lancers (Queen's Royal) Lancers, 1715-1903. London: 1904. V. 50

REYNARDSON, C. T. S. BIRCH
Down the Road; or, Reminiscences of a Gentleman Coachman. London: 1875. V. 47
Down the Road or the Reminiscenses of a Gentleman Coachman. London: 1887. V. 47; 48

REYNARD THE FOX
Reynard the Fox. London: 1852. V. 47
Reynard the Fox. London: 1885. V. 51
Reynard the Fox. An Old Story retold. London: 1886. V. 48
Reynard the Fox In South Africa, or Hottentot Fables and Tales. London: 1864. V. 53
Reynard the Foxe. 1892. V. 54

REYNAUD, LEONCE
Memoir Upon the Illumination and Beaconage of the Coasts of France. Washington: 1876. V. 48; 50
Memoirs Upon the Lighting, Beaconage and Buoyage of the Coasts of France. Washington: 1871. V. 54

REYNIER, MARGUERITE
Wild Animals at Home. New York: 1935. V. 49

REYNOLDS, DANIEL C.
Romance in Smoke. Providence: 1876. V. 48

REYNOLDS, FRANK
Mr. Pickwick Illustrated in Colour. London: 1910. V. 54

REYNOLDS, FREDERICK
The Blind Bargain, or, Hear It Out. London: 1805. V. 49
The Life and Times of Frederick Reynolds. London: 1826. V. 47; 51; 53
The Rage: a Comedy. Dublin: 1795. V. 47

REYNOLDS, G. W.
The Aloes of South Africa. Johannesburg: 1950. V. 48
The Aloes of South Africa. Rotterdam: 1982. V. 49; 50; 51

REYNOLDS, GEORGE
The Mormon Metropolis. An Illustrated Guide to Salt Lake and Its Environs. Salt Lake City: 1883. V. 52

REYNOLDS, GEORGE W. M.
The Anatomy of Intemperance; or a Key to Teetolalism. London: 1840. V. 53
Ellen Percy; or, the Memoirs of an Actress. London: 1860. V. 48
Grace Darling; or, the Heroine of the Fern Islands. London: 1839. V. 54
Master Timothy's Book-Case; or the Magic-Lanthorn of the World. London: 1843. V. 54
Pickwick Abroad. London: 1839. V. 49; 54
Pickwick Abroad. London: 1847. V. 54
Pickwick Abroad... London: 1864. V. 54

REYNOLDS, HELEN WILKINSON
Dutchess County Doorways and Other Examples of Period-Work in Wood 1730-1830. New York: 1931. V. 50

REYNOLDS, HENRY REVELL
An Address to the Ladies, from a Young Man. London: 1796. V. 47; 48; 51

REYNOLDS, HORACE
A Providence Episode in the Irish Literary Renaissance. Providence: 1929. V. 47

REYNOLDS, J. H.
The Fancy. 1905. V. 54

REYNOLDS, J. RUSSELL
Lectures on the Clinical Uses of Electrcity. Philadelphia: 1872. V. 54
A System of Medicine. Philadelphia: 1880. V. 47; 49

REYNOLDS, JAN
William Callow R.W.S. London: 1980. V. 54

REYNOLDS, JEREMIAH N.
Voyage of the United States Frigate "Potomac"...During the Circumnavigation of the Globe, in the Years 1831, 1832, 1833 and 1834. New York: 1835. V. 48; 51

REYNOLDS, JOHN
A Discourse Upon a Prodigious Abstience... London: 1669. V. 48
Friendship's Offering: a Sketch of the Life of Dr. John Mason Peck. Belleville: 1858. V. 52
My Own Times, Embracing Also. The History of My Life. Belleville: 1855. V. 47
The Pioneer History of Illinois, Containing the Discovery, in 1673, and the History of the Country to the Year Eighteen Hundred and Eighteen, When the State Government was Organized. Belleville: 1852. V. 47
Sketches of the Country, on the Northern Route from Belleville, Illinois, to the City of New York and Back by the Ohio Valley; Together with a Glance at the Crystal Palace. Belleville: 1854. V. 47

REYNOLDS, JOHN HAMILTON
The Fancy: a Selection From the Poetical Remains of the Late Peter Corcoran, of Gray's Inn, Student at Law. London: 1820. V. 50
One, Two, Three, Four, Five: by Advertisement; a Musical Entertainment, in One Act... London: 1819. V. 48

REYNOLDS, JOSHUA
A Collection of Six Discourses Delivered to Students at the Royal Academy in the Years 1769, 1770, 1774, 1776, 1782 and 1790 (Comprising the 1st, 3rd, 5th, 7th, 11th and 15th Discourses). London: 1769-90. V. 54
A Discourse Delivered to His Students of the Royal Academy on the Distribution of the Prizes, December 10, 1782, by the President. London: 1783. V. 48
A Discourse Delivered to the Students of the Royal Academy. London: 1769. V. 48
Johnson and Garrick. London: 1816. V. 48; 49; 51; 52; 54
Seven Discourses Delivered at the Royal Academy by the President. London: 1778. V. 48; 49; 53
Unique Collection of Drawings and Prints. A Catalogue of All the Great and Valuable Collection of Ancient Drawings, Scarce Prints and Books of Prints, Which Belonged to Sir Joshua Reynolds, Deceased... London: 1798. V. 48
The Works... London: 1798. V. 48; 51
The Works... London: 1801. V. 49
The Works. London: 1809. V. 48; 53

REYNOLDS, RICHARD
Letters of Richard Reynolds. London: 1852. V. 54

REYNOLDS, ROBERT
Rio Grande. Portland: 1975. V. 54

REYNOLDS, STEPHEN
The Voyage of the New Hazard to the Northwest Coast, Hawaii and China, 1810-1813. Salem: 1938. V. 48; 50; 53

REYNOLDS, THOMAS
The Life of Thomas Reynolds, Esq. Formerly of Kilkea Casatle, in the County of Kildare. 1839. V. 54

REYNOLDS, WILLIAM
The Theory of the Law of Evidence as Established in the United States and of the Conduct of the Examination of Witnesses. Chicago: 1883. V. 48

REYNOLDSON, JOHN
Practical and Philosophical Principles of Making Malt... Newark: 1809. V. 50
Practical and Philsosophical Principles of Making Malt, in Which the Efficacy of the Sprinkling System is Contrasted with the Hertfordshire Methods... Newark: 1808. V. 53

REY ROSA, RODRIGO
The Path Doubles Back. New York: 1982. V. 52; 53; 54

REZAC, J.
96 Photographs. 1964. V. 52

REZANOV, NIKOLAI PETROVICH, COUNT
Rezanov Reconnoiters California, 1806. San Francisco: 1972. V. 53
The Rezanov Voyage to Nueva California in 1806... San Francisco: 1926. V. 47; 48

REZEK, ANTOINE IVAN
History of the Diocese of Sault Ste. Marie and Marquette... Houghton: 1906. V. 49

REZNIKOFF, CHARLES
By the Well of Living and Seeing. New and Selected Poems. 1918-1973. Los Angeles: 1974. V. 50; 51
Early History of a Sewing Machine Operataor. New York: 1936. V. 54
Five Groups of Verse. New York: 1927. V. 53; 54
Going to and Fro and Walking Up and Down. New York: 1941. V. 54
Nine Plays. New York: 1927. V. 47; 54
Poems 1918-1936, 1937-1975. Santa Barbara: 1976/77. V. 50
Separate Way. New York: 1936. V. 53; 54
Testimony. New York: 1934. V. 53
Testimony: The United States (1885-1915) Recitative. Santa Barbara: 1978. V. 50

RHAZES
A Treatise On the Small-Pox and Measles. London: 1848. V. 51

RHEAD, G. WOOLLISCOFT
History of the Fan. London: 1910. V. 47; 52

RHEAD, G. WOOLLISCROFT
Staffordshire Pots and Potters. London: 1906. V. 51

RHEAD, LOUIS
American Trout-Stream Insects. New York: 1916. V. 47
A Collection of Book Plate Designs. Boston: 1907. V. 49
The Speckled Brook Trout... New York: 1902. V. 47

RHEEDE TOT DRAAKESTEIN, ADRIAAN VAN
Hortus Indicus Malabaricus, Continens Regni Malabarici Apud Indos Celeberrimis Generis Plantae Rariori, Latinis, Malabaricis... 1979-83. V. 47; 48; 49

RHEES, WILLIAM JONES
The Smithsonian Institution. Washington: 1901. V. 50; 52

RHEIMS, MAURICE
The Age of Art Nouveau. London: 1966. V. 50
Bernard Buffet: Graveur, 1948-1980. Nice. V. 52
The Flowering of Art Nouveau. New York: 1966. V. 48; 49; 50; 52
Hector Guimard. New York: 1988. V. 54

RHENANUS, BEATUS
Autores Historiae Ecclesiasticae. Eusebii Pamphili Caesariensis...Ruffino Libri Duo...Theodorito Episcopo Cyrensi, Sozomeno, et Socrate Constantinapolitano...Epiphanio Scholastico...Nicephori...Victoris Episcopi...Theodoriti Libri V. Graece. Basel: 1535. V. 54

RHIND, ALEXANDER HENRY
Facsimiles of Two Papyri Found in a Tomb at Thebes. London: 1863. V. 49

RHIND, W.
A History of the Vegetable Kingdom. London. V. 48
A History of the Vegetable Kingdom. London: 1855. V. 51
A History of the Vegetable Kingdom. London: 1868. V. 52; 53; 54
A History of the Vegetable Kingdom. London: 1877. V. 53

RHOADS, FRED
Rhoads' West. Flagstaff: 1972. V. 49

RHODA.. London: 1816. V. 49

RHODE, CHRISTIAN DETLEV
Cimbrisch-Hollsteinische Antiquitaten-Remarques... Hamburg: 1720. V. 52

RHODE ISLAND. (COLONY). LAWS, STATUTES, ETC.
Acts and Laws of His Majesty's Colony of Rhode Island and Providence Plantations in New England, in america. Newport: 1752. V. 52

RHODE ISLAND. GENERAL ASSEMBLY
Report of the Important Hearing on the Memorial of the New England Mining Company for Encouragement from the State...Before the Select Special Committee of the General Assembly of Rhode Island. 1838. V. 52

RHODE ISLAND. LAWS, STATUTES, ETC.
Election Law. State of Rhode Island and Providence Plantations in General Assembly, January Session, A.D. 1844. An Act to Regualte the Election of Civil Officers. Providence: 1844. V. 54

RHODE ISLAND SOLDIERS' & SAILORS' HISTORICAL SOCIETY
Personal Narratives of Events in the War of the Rebellion, Being Papers Read Before the Rhode Island Soldiers' and Sailors Historical Society. Sixth Series. Nos. 1-10. Providence: 1903-05. V. 52
Personal Narratives of the Battles of the Rebellion. Providence: 1878-79. V. 50

RHODE, JOHN
The Last Suspect. New York: 1952. V. 50; 52
Murder of a Chemist. London: 1936. V. 51

RHODES, ALEXANDRE DE
Divers Voyages de la Chine, et Autres Royaumes de l'Orient. Paris: 1681. V. 47

RHODES, CECIL JOHN
A Chronicle of the Funeral Ceremonies from Muizenberg to the Matoppos March April 1902. 1972. V. 53

RHODES, CHARLES D.
History of the Cavalry of the Army of the Potomac... Kansas City: 1900. V. 49

RHODES, DENNIS E.
Bookbindings and Other Bibliophily. Essays in Honour of Anthony Hobson. Verona: 1994. V. 53
Essays in Honour of Victor Scholderer. Mainz: 1970. V. 47; 54

RHODES, E.
Yorkshire Scenery: or Excursions in Yorkshire with Delineations of Some of the Most Interesting Objects. London: 1826. V. 47

RHODES, EUGENE MANLOVE
Beyond the Desert. Boston: 1934. V. 51; 53
Bransford in Arcadia or the Little Eohippus. New York: 1914. V. 51; 53; 54
Good Men and True. New York: 1910. V. 51; 53
The Little World Waddies. 1946. V. 48; 49
The Little World Waddies. Chicago: 1946. V. 48; 51
The Little World Waddies. Chico: 1946. V. 51; 53
Penalosa. 1934. V. 47; 48
Penalosa. Santa Fe: 1934. V. 49; 51; 53; 54
Penalosa. Santa Fe: 1943. V. 51
Say Now Shibboleth. 1921. V. 48; 49
Say Now Shibboleth. Chicago: 1921. V. 52

RHODES, GODFREY
Tents and Tent-Life, from the Earliest Ages to the Present Time. London: 1859. V. 52

RHODES, JAMES FORD
History of the United States From the Compromise of 1850 to the Restoration of Home Rule at the South in 1877. New York: 1904-07. V. 48

RHODES, JOHN W.
Melini, or the Victim of Guilt. Boston: 1844. V. 51

RHODES, RICHARD S.
The Audiphone, and How to Use It In Hearing through the Teeth. Chicago: 1895. V. 54

RHODES, W. H.
Caxton's Book. 1876. V. 52

RHODES, WILLIAM BARNES
Bibliotheca Dramatica. A Catalogue of the Entire...Dramatic Library of William Barnes Rhodes. London: 1825. V. 50; 53

RHODIUS, HANS
Schonheit und Reichtum des Lebens. Walter Spies (Maler and Musiker auf Bali 1895-1942). Den Haag: 60's. V. 48

RHUEMANN, HELMUT
The Cleaning of Paintings, Problems and Potentialities... London: 1968. V. 49

RHYMERS' CLUB, LONDON.
The Book of the Rhymers' Club. 1892. V. 50
The Second Book of the Rhymers' Club. London: 1894. V. 47; 49; 50

RHYMES and Roundelayes in Praise of a Country Life. London: 1875. V. 51

RHYOLITE: Metropolis of Southern Nevada. 1907. V. 50; 53

RHYS, CHARLES HORTON
A Theatrical Trip for a Wager!. London: 1861. V. 53
A Theatrical Trip for a Wager!. Vancouver: 1966. V. 53

RHYS, ENREST
A London Rose and Other Rhymes. London: 1894. V. 48

RHYS, JEAN
After Leaving Mr. Mackenzie. London: 1930. V. 48
Good Morning Midnight. London: 1939. V. 53
The Left Bank. London: 1927. V. 50; 53
Voyage in the Dark. London: 1934. V. 53
Voyage in The Dark. London: 1967. V. 52; 53
Wide Sargasso Sea. 1966. V. 54
Wide Sargasso Sea. London: 1966. V. 49; 51; 52

RHYS, JOHN
Celtic Folklore: Welsh and Manx. Oxford: 1901. V. 48

RIBADENEIRA, PEDRO
The Lives of the Saints, with Other Feasts of the Year, According to the Roman Calendar. London: 1730. V. 52
The Lives of the Saints, with Other Feasts of the Year, According to the Roman Calendar... Dublin: 1763. V. 48
Princeps Christianvs Adversvs Nicolavm Machiavellvm. Cologne: 1604. V. 51
Vita Ignatii Loiolae. Lyons: 1595. V. 50

RIBALOW, HAROLD U.
Arnold Wesker. New York: 1965. V. 54

RIBBLESDALE, THOMAS, 4TH BARON
The Queen's Hounds and Stag-Hunting Recollections. London: 1897. V. 47

RIBEIRO DE MACEDO, DUARTE
Iuizo Historico, Iuridico, Politico Sobre a Paz Celebrada Entre as Coroas de Franca & Castella no anno de 1660. Lisbon: 1666. V. 53

RIBEIRO ROCHA, MANOEL
Ethiope Resgatado, Empenhado, Sustentado, Corregido, Instruido, e Libertado. Lisbon: 1758. V. 48

RIBERA, JUAN DE
Lettera Annua della Vice-Provincia delle Filippine. Venice: 1605. V. 51; 54

RIBERA, MANUEL MARIANO
Real Capilla de Barcelona, Illustrada y Defendida. Barcelona: 1698. V. 47

RIBOT, THEODULE A.
Diseases of Memory: an Essay in the Positive Psychology... New York: 1882. V. 48; 50; 52
Diseases of Memory, Diseases of the Will and Diseases of Personality. New York: 1885. V. 47

RIBTON-TURNER, C. J.
A History of Vagrants and Vagrancy, and Beggars and Begging. London: 1887. V. 49

RICARDO, DAVID
On the Principles of Political Economy and Taxation. London: 1817. V. 50; 52; 53
On the Principles of Political Economy and Taxation. London: 1819. V. 50; 51
Principes de l'Economie Politique, et de l'Impot. Paris: 1819. V. 48; 54

RICCHIERI, LODOVICO, KNOWN AS LODOVICUS CAELIUS RHODOGINUS
Lectionum Antiquarum. Lyon: 1562. V. 47

RICCI, BARTOLOMEO
Apparatvs Latinae Locvtionis. Argentoarati: 1535. V. 53
Apparatvs Latinae Locvtionis. Argentorati: 1535. V. 49; 50

RICCI, CORADO
Baroque Architecture and Sculpture in Italy. Stuttgart: 1926. V. 54
Pintoricchio. His Life, Work and Time. London: 1902. V. 54

RICCI, ELISA
Old Italian Lace. London: 1913. V. 52

RICCI, JAMES
The Development of Gynaecological Surgery and Instruments... Philadelphia: 1949. V. 50; 52
The Development of Gynaecological Surgery and Instruments. San Francisco: 1990. V. 48
The Geneaology of Gynaecology, History of the Development of Gynaecology throughout the Ages 2000 BC-1800 AD.... Philadelphia: 1950. V. 52
One Hundred Years of Gynaecology, 1800-1900. Philadelphia: 1945. V. 50

RICCI, MATTEO
De Christiana Expeditione apud Sinas Suscepta ab Societata Iesu. Cologne: 1617. V. 53
Historia von Einfuehrung der Christlichen Religion in Dass Grosse Konigreich China Durch die Societet Jesu. Augusburg: 1617. V. 53

RICCI, SEYMOUR DE
Catalogue of a Collection of Mounted Porcelain Belonging to E. M. Hodgkins. Paris: 1911. V. 48
A Catalogue of Early English Books in the Library of John L. Clawson. Philadelphia: 1924. V. 50
A Census of Caxtons. London: 1909. V. 48
A Census of Caxtons. Oxford: 1909. V. 47; 52
English Collectors of Books and Manuscripts (1530-1930) and Their Marks of Ownership. London: 1930. V. 53
English Collectors of Books and Manuscripts (1530-1930) and Their Marks of Ownership. New York: 1930. V. 52
French Signed Bindings in the Mortimer L. Schiff Collection. New York: 1935. V. 47
A Hand List of a Collection of Books and Manuscripts Belonging to the Rt. Hon. Lord Amherst of Hackney at Didlington Hall, Norfolk. Cambridge: 1906. V. 52

RICCIUS, BARTHOLOMAEUS
De Imitatione Libri Tres Ad Al Fonsum Atestium principem... Venetiis: 1545. V. 48

RICCIUTI, I. W.
New Orleans and Its Environs: the Domestic Architecture 1727-1870. New York: 1938. V. 51; 53; 54

RICCOBINI, MARIE JEANNE
Letters of Adelaide de Sancerre, to Count De Nance. Newbern: 1801. V. 53

RICCOBONI, LEWIS
A General History of the Stage, from Its Origin. London: 1754. V. 52
An Historical and Critical Account of the Theatres in Europe... London: 1741. V. 49; 54

RICCOBONI, MARIE JEANNE
Letters From Sophia de Valiere to her friend Louisa Hortensia de Canteleu... London: 1772. V. 48; 50; 52

RICE, ALICE HEGAN
The Honorable Percival. New York: 1914. V. 51
Mr. Opp. New York: 1909. V. 51

RICE, ANNE
Beauty's Punishment. New York: 1984. V. 47; 48; 51; 53; 54
Beauty's Punishment. London: 1987. V. 51
Beauty's Release. New York: 1985. V. 47; 49; 51; 52; 53; 54
Belinda. New York: 1986. V. 51; 52; 53
The Claiming of Sleeping Beauty. New York: 1976. V. 47
The Claiming of Sleeping Beauty. New York: 1983. V. 48; 53
The Claiming of Sleeping Beauty. London: 1987. V. 51
Cry to Heaven. New York: 1982. V. 49; 50; 52; 53
Exit to Eden. New York: 1985. V. 51; 52; 53

RICE, ANNE continued
The Feast of All Saints. New York: 1971. V. 47
The Feast of All Saints. New York: 1979. V. 51; 52; 53; 54
Interview with the Vampire. London: 1976. V. 47; 50
Interview with the Vampire. New York: 1976. V. 47; 48; 49; 50; 51; 52; 53; 54
Interview with the Vampire. New York: 1986. V. 52
Lasher. New York: 1993. V. 51; 52
The Mummy. New York: 1989. V. 51; 53; 54
The Queen of the Damned. 1988. V. 48; 52
The Queen of the Damned. New York: 1988. V. 49; 50; 51; 52
The Tale of the Body Thief. New York: 1992. V. 47; 48; 49; 50; 51; 53; 54
Taltos. New York: 1994. V. 51; 54
The Vampire Chronicles. New York: 1990. V. 51
The Vampire Lestat. New York: 1976. V. 53
The Vampire Lestat. London: 1985. V. 49
The Vampire Lestat. New York: 1985. V. 47; 48; 49; 50; 51; 52; 53; 54
The Witching Hour. New York: 1990. V. 47; 49; 52

RICE, CRAIG
Eight Faces At Three. New York: 1939. V. 51
Having Wonderful Crime. New York: 1943. V. 49

RICE, DAVID
Slavery Inconsistent with Justice and Good Policy. New York: 1804. V. 54
Slavery Inconstitent with Justice and Good Policy... London: 1793. V. 47

RICE, DAVID TALBOT
The Church of Haghia Sophia at Trebizond. Edinburgh: 1968. V. 48; 49; 50; 52; 54

RICE, E. G.
Wild Flowers of the Cape of Good Hope. Kirstenbosch: 1951. V. 50

RICE, ELMER
Cue for Passion. New York: 1959. V. 54
The Grand Tour. New York: 1952. V. 54
The Show Must Go On. New York: 1949. V. 54

RICE, GRANTLAND
Songs of the Open. New York: 1924. V. 50
Songs of the Stalwart. New York: 1917. V. 50
Sportlights of 1923. New York: 1924. V. 51

RICE, HOWARD
The American Campaigns of Rochambeau's Army 1780, 1781, 1782, 1783. The Journals of Clermont-Crevecoeur, Verger & Berthier. 1972. V. 49

RICE, HOWARD C.
The American Campaigns of Rochambeau's Army 1780, 1781, 1782, 1783. Princeton and Providence: 1972. V. 47; 50; 54

RICE, JAMES
History of the British Turf, From the Earliest Times to the Present Day. London: 1879. V. 48

RICE, JOHN A.
Catalogue of Mr. John A. Rice's Library to Be sold at Auction On...March 21st 1870 and Five Following Days by Bangs, Merwin & Co. New York: 1870. V. 51

RICE, NATHAN P.
Trials of a Public Benefactor, as Illustrated in the Discovery of Etherization. New York: 1858. V. 53
Trials of a Public Benefactor as Ilustrated in the Discovery of Etherization. New York: 1859. V. 48; 50

RICE, SARA SIGOURNEY
Edgar Allan Poe. A Memorial Volume. Baltimore: 1877. V. 48; 49

RICE, T. TALBOT
Icons. London: 1958. V. 50

RICE, WILLIAM
Tiger-Shooting in India: Being an Account of Hunting Experiences on Foot in Raipootana, During the Hot Seasons from 1850 to 1854. London: 1857. V. 54

RICE-PEREIRA, IRENE
The Lapis. New York: 1957. V. 50

RICETTARIO Fiorentino. Fiorenza: 1574. V. 47; 50

RICH, ADRIENNE
A Chance of World. New Haven: 1951. V. 50; 51; 52; 53
Leaflets: Poems 1965-1968. New York: 1969. V. 52
Not I, But Death: a Play in One Act. Baltimore: 1941. V. 51

RICH, ANTHONY
A Dictionary of Roman and Greek Antiquities. London: 1874. V. 50

RICH, ARNOLD
The Pathogenesis of Tuberculosis. Springfield: 1944. V. 49; 51

RICH, BEN C.
Mr. Durant of Salt Lake City. Salt Lake City: 1893. V. 47

RICH, CHARLES H.
Specimens of the Art of Ornamental Turning, In Eccentric and Concentric Patterns... Southampton: 1825. V. 52

RICH, CLAUDIUS JAMES
Memoirs on the Ruins of Bablyon. (with) Second Memoir on Babylon... London: 1815.18. V. 50
Narrative of a Residence in Koordistan and on the Site of Ancient Nineveh. London: 1836. V. 47

RICH, DANIEL CATTON
Edgar Hilaire Germain Degas. New York: 1951. V. 51

RICH, EDWIN ERNEST
Cumberland House Journals and Inland Journal 1775-82; First Series 1775-79. London: 1952. V. 48; 49
The History of the Hudson's Bay Company 1670-1870. London: 1958-59. V. 49; 52
Hudson's Bay Copy Booke of Letters Commissions Instructions Outward 1688-1696. London: 1957. V. 48
John Rae's Corrspondence with the Hudson's Bay Company on Arctic Exploration, 1844-1855. London: 1953. V. 48
London Correspondence Inward From Eden Colvile 1849-1852. London: 1956. V. 48
Peter Skene Ogden's Snake Country Journals 1824-25 and 1825-26. London: 1950. V. 48

RICH, O.
Bibliotheca Americana Nova: A Catalogue of Books in Various Languages Relating to America... New York: 1968?. V. 50

RICH, ROBERT
A Letter...to the Right Honourable Lord Viscount Barrington, His Majesty's Secretary at War... London: 1775. V. 47

RICH, WINIFRED
Tony's White Room and How the White Rose of Love Bloomed and Flourished There. San Francisco: 1911. V. 48

RICHARD and Alice, a Tale, Founded on Facts; Which Occurred in Portsmouth in the Regin of Queen Elizabeth. Portsmouth: 1840. V. 47

RICHARD, HENRY
Letters On the Social and Political Condition of the Principality of Wales. London: 1866?. V. 52

RICHARD, JOHN
A Tour From London to Petersburgh, and from Thence to Moscow. Dublin: 1781. V. 50

RICHARD, JULES
Types et Uniformes -L'Armee Francaise. Paris: 1885-89. V. 49; 50

RICHARD, OF CIRENCESTER
Speculum Historiale de Gestis Regum Angliae. London: 1863-69. V. 49; 52

RICHARDS, A. M., MRS.
Memoires of a Grandmother. Boston: 1854. V. 50

RICHARDS, ALFRED B.
Croesus, King of Lydia. London: 1845. V. 50
Medea: a Poem. London: 1869. V. 49
A Sketch of the Career of Richard F. Burton. London: 1886. V. 51

RICHARDS, ANTHONY
From a Satyric Country. London: 1971. V. 52

RICHARDS, DAVID
Ioseph, Llywodraethwr yr Aipht; Awen-Gerdd, yn Saith rain...Gan Ddafydd Ionawr. Dolgelleu: 1809. V. 50

RICHARDS, DAVID ADAM
Small Heroics. Fredericton: 1972. V. 47; 51

RICHARDS, EDWARD A.
Shadows-Selected Poems. Saint Thomas: 1933. V. 52

RICHARDS, EUGENE
Few Comforts or Surprises: the Arkanasa Delta. Cambridge and London: 1973. V. 52

RICHARDS, FRANCES
The Acts of the Apostles. Engravings. London: 1980. V. 51

RICHARDS, FRANK
Billy Bunter and the Blue Mauritius. London: 1952. V. 51
Old-Soldier Sahib. London: 1936. V. 52

RICHARDS, GEORGE
Modern France: a Poem. Oxford: 1793. V. 54
Monody on Admiral Lord Viscount Nelson, Who After a Series of Transcendent and Heroic Services, Fell Gloriously Oct. 21, 1805, in the Battle of Trafalgar... Oxford: 1805. V. 54

RICHARDS, GORDON
My Story. London: 1955. V. 50

RICHARDS, I. A.
Practical Criticism - a Study of Literary Judgment. London: 1929. V. 48

RICHARDS, J. M.
High Street. London: 1938. V. 50; 51; 52

RICHARDS, JOHN
The Gentleman's Steward and Tenants of Manors Instructed. London: 1730. V. 50

RICHARDS, LAURA E.
Captain January. Boston: 1898. V. 47; 51
Julia Ward Howe 1819-1910. Boston & New York: 1915. V. 50; 51; 54
More Five Minute Stories. Boston: 1903. V. 48

RICHARDS, MARIA T.
Life in Israel; or, Portraitures of Hebrew Character. New York and Chicago: 1857. V. 51; 52

RICHARDS, NAT
Otis Dunn, Manhunter. Port Washington: 1974. V. 54

RICHARDS, P. F.
Old Soldier. London: 1936. V. 52

RICHARDS, R. N.
Report on the Maritime Canal Connected the Mediterranean at Port Said, with the Red Sea At Suez. London: 1870. V. 47

RICHARDS, RAYMOND
Old Cheshire Churches. London: 1948. V. 47
Old Cheshire Churches. Manchester: 1973. V. 49

RICHARDS, T. ADDISON
American Scenery Illustrated. New York: 1854. V. 50; 53; 54

RICHARDS. T. ADDISON
Tallulah and Jocassee; or, Romances of Southern Landscape and Other Tales. Charleston: 1852. V. 54

RICHARDS, THOMAS
Cambriae Suspiria in Obitum Desideratissimae Reginae Carliane. Salopiae: 1738. V. 48; 49

RICHARDS, VYVYAN
T. E. Lawrence Book Designer, His Friendship with Vyvyan Richards. Wakefield: 1985. V. 53; 54

RICHARDS, WALTER
Her Majesty's Army. London: 1889?. V. 54
Her Majesty's Army. A Descriptive Account of the Various Regiments Now Comprising the Queen's Forces... London: 1841. V. 52
Her Majesty's Army, Indian and Colonial Forces. London: 1900. V. 50
His Majesty's Territorial Army... London: 1905. V. 50

RICHARDS-WILCOX MANUFACTURING CO.
Door Hangers and Hardware Specialities. Aurora: 1910. V. 54

RICHARDS, WILLIAM
Heimburg, a Tale; and Other Poems. London: 1853. V. 53

RICHARDSON & CO.
Texas Almanac for 1870 and Emigrants Guide to Texas. Galveston. V. 48
The Texas Almanac for 1870 and Emigrant's Guide to Texas. Galveston: 1869. V. 50
Texas Almanac for 1872 and Emigrant's Guide to Texas. Galveston: 1871. V. 48

RICHARDSON, ALBERT D.
Beyond the Mississippi. Hartford: 1867. V. 47

RICHARDSON, ALBERT E.
The Art of Architecture. London: 1938. V. 53
The English Inn Past and Present. London: 1925. V. 47; 53
Monumental Classic Architecture in Great Britain and Ireland During the Eighteenth and Nineteenth Centuries. London: 1914. V. 53
Regional Architecture of the West of England. London: 1924. V. 50; 53; 54
The Smaller English House of the Later Renaissance 1660-1830. London: 1933. V. 53; 54

RICHARDSON, ALEX
The Evolution of the Parsons Steam Turbine. 1911. V. 54
The Evolution of the Parsons Steam Turbine. London: 1911. V. 49; 53
Vickers Sons and Maxim, Limited: their Works and Manufactures. London: 1902. V. 53

RICHARDSON, BENJAMIN
The Cause of the Coagulation of the Blood, Being the Astley Cooper Prize Essay for 1856. London: 1858. V. 49

RICHARDSON, C. S.
Report of...On the Oil, Coal, Salt & Iron Lands, 62,860 Acres, of the 'Little Kanawha and Elk River Petroleum and Mining Co.', West Virginia. New York: 1865. V. 50

RICHARDSON, CHARLES
Cassell's New Book of the Horse. London: 1911. V. 54
A New Dictionary of the English Language. London: 1836-37. V. 52
A New Dictionary of the English Language. London: 1839. V. 48
A New Dictionary of the English Language. Philadelphia: 1847. V. 53
A New Dictionary of the English Language, Combining Explanation with Etymology... London: 1855. V. 48
Racing at Home & Abroad. London: 1923-31. V. 47

RICHARDSON, CHARLES JAMES
The Englishman's House from a Cottage to a Mansion. London: 1870. V. 49; 54

RICHARDSON, CHARLES L.
Selected Shore Plants of Southern California. Pasadena: 1992. V. 49

RICHARDSON, DOROTHY
The Long Day. The Story of a New York Working Girl, as Told by Herself. New York: 1905. V. 50

RICHARDSON, DOROTHY M.
Clear Horizon. London: 1935. V. 47; 53
John Austen and the Inseparables. London: 1930. V. 49; 50; 51; 53; 54
Pilgrimage. London: 1938. V. 47; 53
The Trap. London: 1925. V. 51; 53

RICHARDSON, EDWARD
Anglo-Belgica. The English Netherdutch Academy. Amsterdam: 1677. V. 47

RICHARDSON, GEORGE
A Collection of Ornaments in the Antique Style Comprised in XXXVII Plates... London: 1816. V. 51
New Designs of Vases and Tripods, Decorated in the Antique Taste. (with) Capitals of Columns and Friezes, Measured from the Antique. London: 1793/93. V. 53
Supplement to the Vitruvius Britannicus; or the British Architect. London: 1800. V. 50

RICHARDSON, GEORGE W.
Speech of George W. Richardson, of Hanover, in Committee of the Whole, On the Report of the Committee on Federal Relations, in the Convention of Virginia, April 4, 1861. Richmond: 1862. V. 49; 50

RICHARDSON, HAROLD
The Poet and Other Animals. London: 1909. V. 52

RICHARDSON, HENRY
The Loss of the Tigris. A Poem. London: 1840. V. 51

RICHARDSON, HENRY HANDEL, PSEUD.
The Fortunes of Richard Mahony. (with) The Way Home: Being the Second Part of the Chronicle of the Fortunes of Richard Mahony. (with) Ultima Thule: Being the Third Part of... London: 1917/25/29. V. 54
Ultima Thule Being the Third Part of the Chronicles of the Fortunes of Richard Mahony. London: 1929. V. 47

RICHARDSON, HENRY S.
Greenwich; Its History, Antiquities, Improvements and Public Buildings. Greenwich: 1934. V. 50

RICHARDSON, HESTER DORSEY
Side-Lights on Maryland History, with Sketches of Early Maryland Families. Baltimore: 1913. V. 49

RICHARDSON, J.
The Museum of Natural History... London: 1859-62. V. 53

RICHARDSON, JAMES
Narrative of a Mission to Central Africa Performed in the years 1850-51... London: 1853. V. 47; 52
Report on Geological Exploration in British Columbia. Montreal: 1874. V. 49
Report on the Coal Fields of Vancouver Island, with Map of Their Distribtuion. Ottawa: 1872. V. 52
Travels in the Great Desert of Sahara, in the years 1845 and 1846. London: 1848. V. 52

RICHARDSON, JAMES D.
A Compilation of the Messages and Papers of the Confederacy, Including the Diplomatic Correspondence 1861-1865. Nashville: 1906. V. 49

RICHARDSON, JOHN
The Canadian Brothers; or, the prophecy Fulfilled. Montreal: 1840. V. 48
Ecarte; or, the Salons of Paris. London: 1829. V. 51
Erebus and terror, Zoology of the Voyage: Fishes. London: 1844-48. V. 49
Fauna Boreali-Americana; or the Zoology of the Northern Parts of British America. Part First Quadrupeds. London: 1829. V. 52
A Grammar of the Arabic Language. London: 1776. V. 49
A Grammar of the Arabic Language. London: 1801. V. 49; 51
The Museum of Natural History. London: 1868. V. 51
The Museum of Natural History. London: 1870. V. 52
The Philosophical Principles of the Science of Brewing... York;: 1788. V. 54
Recollections, Political, Literary, Dramatic and Miscellaneous, of the Last Half Century. London: 1855. V. 51
Recollections, Political, Literary, Dramatic and Miscellaneous, of the Last Half Century. London: 1856. V. 48
Remarks on a Pamphlet Entitled Hydrometrical Observations and Experiments in the Brewery... London: 1785. V. 54
Richardson's War of 1812 with Notes and a Life of the Author by Alexander Clark Casselman. Toronto: 1902. V. 47
Statical Estimates of the Materials of Brewing... London: 1784. V. 54
The War of 1812. Toronto: 1902. V. 52

RICHARDSON, JOHN F.
The Director's Collection - The Kill. 1989. V. 54
The Director's Collection - The Kill. Gaborone: 1989. V. 53

RICHARDSON, JONATHAN
An Account of Some of the Statues, Bas Reliefs, Drawings and Pictures in Italy, &c. London: 1722. V. 47
Explantory Notes and Remarks on Milton's Paradise Lost. London: 1734. V. 54
Two Discourses. 1. An Essay on the Whole Art of Criticism as It Relates to Painting...1. Of the Goodness of a Picture. II. Of the Hand of the Master. III. Whether 'tis an Original or a Copy. II. An Argument in Behalf of the Science... London: 1725. V. 54
The Works... London: 1773. V. 47; 49; 54
The Works. London: 1792. V. 48; 49; 52; 54

RICHARDSON, JOSEPH
The Album of Streatham; or, Ministerial Amusements... London: 1788. V. 48
Jekyll: a Political Eclogue. London: 1788. V. 52
A Practical Treatise on Mechanical Dentistry. Philadelphia: 1869. V. 50

RICHARDSON, LEANDER
The Dark City, or Cutoms of the Cockneys. Boston: 1886. V. 52

RICHARDSON, M. A.
The Local Historian's Table Book of Remarkable Occurences, Historical Facts, Legendary and Descirptive Ballads, Etc. Newcastle upon Tyne: 1841-46. V. 54
The Local Historian's Table Book of Remarkable Occurrences, Historical Facts, Traditions, Legendary and Descriptive Ballads Etc... London: 1841-46. V. 50

RICHARDSON, M. T.
Practical Blacksmithing... New York: 1889-95. V. 53

RICHARDSON, OWEN WILLANS
The Electron Theory of Matter. Cambridge: 1914. V. 48; 54

RICHARDSON, ROBERT
The Law of Testaments and Last Wills. In the Savoy: 1744. V. 48

RICHARDSON, RUPERT
The Comanche Barrier to South Plains Settlement. Glendale: 1933. V. 51; 54
The Comanche Barrier to South Plains Settlement. Abilene: 1991. V. 48; 49; 52
The Frontier of Northwest Texas, 1846-1876: Advance and Defense by Pioneer Settlers of the Cross Timbers and Prairies. Glendale: 1963. V. 48; 51
The Greater Southwest. Glendale: 1935. V. 51; 53

RICHARDSON, S. T.
The Friends in Council. Darlington: 1875. V. 47; 49; 53

RICHARDSON, SAMUEL
An Answer to the London Ministers Letter, from Them to His Excellency and His Counsel of War. London: 1649. V. 50; 53
Clarissa. London: 1748. V. 48; 54
Clarissa. London: 1751/50/51. V. 48
Clarissa. London: 1759. V. 52
Clarissa. London: 1768. V. 49
Clarissa. London: 1774. V. 53
Clarissa. Oxford: 1930. V. 51; 54
Clarisse Harlowe. Paris: 1802. V. 51
The Correspondence of Samuel Richardson... London: 1804. V. 49; 51
Crime and Criminal Offenders, in Connexion with Popular Education and Morals: an Essay. London and Norwich: 1855. V. 53
The History of Sir Charles Grandison. London: 1754. V. 47; 49; 53
The History of Sir Charles Grandison. London: 1762. V. 48; 50
The History of Sir Charles Grandison. London: 1765. V. 48
The History of Sir Charles Grandison, Abridged from the Works... Wilmington: 1812. V. 50
The History of Sir Charles Grandison. (bound with, probably as issued) Clarissa. New Haven: 1810/10. V. 49
The History of Sir Charles Grandison. In A Series of Letters Published from the Originals. London: 1754. V. 52
The History of Sir Charles Grandison. (with) Clarissa. Suffield: 1798. V. 52
Letters and Passages Restored from the Original Manuscripts of the History of Clarissa... London: 1751. V. 48
Letters from Sir Charles Grandison. London: 1896. V. 52
Lettres Angloises ou Histoire de Miss Clarisse Harlove. Dresden: 1751-52. V. 48
The Novels. New York: 1901. V. 50; 52; 54
The Novels of Mr. Samuel Richardson. London: 1902. V. 47
The Novels of Samuel Richardson. London: 1824. V. 52
Pamela. London: 1741/1762. V. 53
Pamela: a Comedy. 1742. V. 47
Pamela: or, Virtue Reward. London: 1741-42. V. 49; 51
Pamela, or Virtue Rewarded. London: 1785. V. 49; 50; 52
Pamela; or Virtue Rewarded. London: 1801. V. 48
Pamela, ou la Vertue Recompensee. Londres: 1742. V. 52
Tenants Law: or, the Laws Concerning Landlords, Tenants and Farmers. London: 1760. V. 48
The Works. London: 1792/81. V. 48
The Works. Edinburgh and London: 1883. V. 52

RICHARDSON, SARAH WATTS
Ethelred, a Legendary Tragic Drama... London: 1809?. V. 49

RICHARDSON, STANLEY
Air-Raid over Barcelona. A Poem. 1938. V. 49

RICHARDSON, T. C.
East Texas, its History and Its Makers. New York: 1940. V. 48; 52

RICHARDSON, T. D.
Modern Figure Skating. London: 1938. V. 48

RICHARDSON, T. M.
Memorials of Old Newcastle Upon Tyne. Edinburgh: 1880. V. 47; 49

RICHARDSON, THOMAS
Richardson's New London Fashionable Gentleman's Valentine Writer, or The Lover's Own Book for This Year... Derby: 1825. V. 48

RICHARDSON, W.
The Chemical Principles of the Metallic Arts...Principal Diseases Incident to the Different Artificers: the Means of Prevention and Cure... Birmingham: 1790. V. 49; 54
Dr. Zell and the Princess Charlotte. 1892. V. 48; 52

RICHARDSON, W. A.
Reprints of Rare Tracts and Imprints of Antient Manuscripts., &c. Newcastle-upon-Tyne: 1847-49. V. 53; 54

RICHARDSON, WIGHAM
Visit of the British Association to Newcastle-upon-Tyne 1889. Newcastle-upon-Tyne: 1889. V. 50

RICHARDSON, WILLIAM
Anecdotes of the Russian Empire. London: 1784. V. 47; 52; 53
Curious Traveller, Who Shall Visit the Giant's Causeway. Coleraine: 1811. V. 47
Cursory Remarks on Tragedy, on Shakespeare and on Certain French and Italian Poets. London: 1774. V. 47
Essays on Shakespeare's Dramatic Characters of Macbeth, Hamlet, Jacques and Imogen, (with) Essays on...Richard the Third, King Lear, and Timon of Athens... (with) An Essay on the Faults of Shakespeare... 1785. V. 47
Essays on Shakespeare's Dramatic Characters of Macbeth, Hamlet, Jaques and Imogen.,(with) an Introduction... (with) Essays on...Richard the Third, King Lear and Timon of Anthens. London: 1785. V. 50
Essays on Shakespeare's Dramatic Characters of Richard the Third, King Lear, and Timon of Athens. London: 1784. V. 50
The Maid of Lochlin: a Lyrical Drama with Legendary Odes and Other Poems. London: 1801. V. 54
The Monastic Ruins of Yorkshire. York: 1843. V. 48; 50; 53
A Philosophical Analysis and Illustration of some of Shakespeare's Remarkable Characters. Edinburgh: 1774. V. 53

RICHARDSON, WILLIAM H.
Journal of William H. Richardson, a Private Soldier in Col. Doniphan's Command. Baltimore: 1847. V. 47; 49
Journal of William H. Richardson a Private Soldier in the Campaign of New and Old Mexico. Baltimore: 1848. V. 50
A Manual of Infantry and Rifle Tactics, with Honors Paid by the Troops, Inspections-- Reviews, &c. Richmond: 1861. V. 49

RICHARDSON'S Virginia & North Carolina Almanac, for the Year of Our Lord 1863.. Richmond: 1862. V. 49

RICHELIEU & ONTARIO NAVIGATION CO.
From Niagara to the Sea: the Finest Inland Water Trip in the World. Office Guide, 1902. Montreal;: 1902. V. 52

RICHERS, THOMAS
The History of the Royal Genealogy of Spain. London: 1724. V. 47

RICHET, CHARLES
Physiology and Histology of the Cerebral Convolutions. New York: 1879. V. 47

RICHEY, MATTHEW
The Necessity and Efficiency of the Gospel: a Sermon Preached Before the Branch Methodist Missionary Society of Halifax. Halifax: 1827. V. 53
Sermons Delivered On Various Occasions. Toronto: 1840. V. 47

RICHIE, DONALD
Design and Craftsmanship of Japan. New York: 1964. V. 53
The Erotic Gods. Tokyo: 1967. V. 50
The Masters' Book of Ikebana: Background and Principles of Japanese Flower Arrangement, with Lesons by the Masters of Japan's Three Foremost Schools. Tokyo: 1966. V. 47; 49; 50

RICHIE, WARD
John Gutenberg - A Fanciful Story of the Fifteenth Century. Los Angeles: 1940. V. 52

RICHLER, MORDECAI
The Acrobats. New York: 1954. V. 49
The Apprenticeship of Duddy Kravitz. Boston: 1959. V. 50

RICHMAN, IRVING BERDINE
California Under Spain and Mexico, 1535-1847. New York: 1911. V. 51; 53; 54

RICHMOND. BOARD OF HEALTH
Official List from the Office of the Board of Health of All Colored Males Over the Age of 19 Who Have Died in the City of Richmond Between the Dates October 1st, 1889 and November 1st 1890. Richmond: 1890. V. 50
Official List from the Office of the Board of Health of all Colored males Over the Age of 21 Who Have Died in the City of Richmond, between the Dates September 1886 and October, 1889. Richmond: 1889. V. 50

RICHMOND, C. W.
A History of the County of Du Page, Illinois... Chicago: 1857. V. 50

RICHMOND, IAN A.
The City Wall of Imperial Rome: an Account of its Architectural Development from Aurelian to Narses. Oxford: 1930. V. 50; 52

RICHMOND, JAMES C.
A Midsummer's Day-Dream: Libellous; or, a Little Book of the Vision of Shawmut. Boston: 1847. V. 51; 52

RICHMOND, LEGH
A Statement of Facts Relative to the Supposed Abstience of Ann Moore of Tutbury, Staffordshire... Burton-on-Trent: 1813. V. 50

RICHON, C.
Atlas des Champignons Comestibles et Veneneux de la France et des Pays Circonvoisins. London: 1888. V. 49

RICHTER, CHRISTIAN
Saxoniae Electoralis Miraculosa Terra, Oder des Weltberuhmten Chur-Sashsen-Landes Bewunders-Wurdige Erde... Schneeberg: 1732. V. 47

RICHTER, CONRAD
Brothers of No Kin. New York: 1924. V. 47; 48
The Free Man. New York: 1943. V. 49
The Grandfathers. New York: 1964. V. 54
A Simple Honorable Man. New York: 1962. V. 51; 53
The Town. New York: 1950. V. 52
The Trees. New York: 1940. V. 47; 48; 49
The Trees/ The Fields/ The Town. New York: 1940/46/50. V. 48

RICHTER, F. C.
The Reach Official American League Baseball Guide for 1908. 1908. V. 50

RICHTER, GEORGE MARTIN
Giorgio Da Casatelo-Franco, Called Giorgione. Chicago: 1937. V. 51

RICHTER, GISELA M. A.
Animals and Greek Sculpture. New York: 1930. V. 48
The Archaic Gravestones of Attica. London: 1961. V. 49; 52; 54
Archaic Greek Art Against Its Historical Background. New York: 1949. V. 50
Catalogue of Engraved Gems: Greek, Etruscan and Roman. Roma: 1956. V. 50; 52
Catalogue of Greek Sculptures. Cambridge: 1954. V. 50; 52
Engraved Gems of the Greeks, Etruscans and Romans. London: 1968-71. V. 50; 52
The Furniture of the Greeks, Etruscans and Romans. London: 1966. V. 49
Kouroi: a Study of the Development of the Greek Kouros from the Late Seventh to the Early Fifth Century B.C. New York: 1942. V. 48; 49
Kouroi, Archaic Greek Youths, A Study of the Development of the Kouros Type in Greek Sculpture. London: 1970. V. 50; 52
The Portraits of the Greeks. London: 1965. V. 49; 50; 52
The Portraits of the Greeks. London: 1965-72. V. 52
Red-Figured Athenian Vases in the Metropolitan Museum of Art. New Haven: 1936. V. 50; 52
The Sculpture and Sculptors of the Greeks. New Haven: 1967. V. 50; 52
Three Critical Periods in Greek Sculpture. Oxford: 1951. V. 50

RICHTER, H. D.
Floral Art, Decoration and Design. London: 1932. V. 54

RICHTER, HANS
Hans Richter. Neuchatel: 1965. V. 51
Hans Richter. London: 1971. V. 48; 50; 53; 54

RICHTER, HENRY
Day-Light; A Recent Discovery in the Art of Painting; With Things on the Philosophy of the Fine Arts, and On that of the Human Mind, as First Dissected by Emanuel Kant. London: 1817. V. 48

RICHTER, J.
Flower, Fruit and Thorn Pieces. Leipzig: 1871. V. 52

RICHTER, JEAN PAUL
The Golden Age of Classic Christian Art. London: 1904. V. 49; 52; 54

RICHTOFEN, WALTER, BARON VON
Cattle-Raising on the Plains of North America. New York: 1885. V. 47

RICKARD, T.
Across the San Juan Mountains. New York: 1903. V. 49
Journeys of Observation. San Francisco: 1907. V. 54

RICKARDS, CONSTANTINE GEORGE
The Ruins of Mexico. London: 1910. V. 50; 52

RICKARDS, E. A.
The Art of E. A. Rickards... London: 1920. V. 48
The Art of E. A. Rickards. New York: 1920. V. 53

RICKE, HERBERT
The Beit el-Wali Temple of Ramesses II. Chicago: 1967. V. 51

RICKERT, MARGARET
The Reconstructed Carmelite Missal. London: 1952. V. 50

RICKETS, BENJAMIN
The Surgery of the Heart and Lungs: a History and Resume of Surgical Conditions Found Therein... New York: 1904. V. 50

RICKETS, HOWARD TAYLOR
Contributions to Medical Science by Howard Taylor Rickets 1870-1910. Chicago: 1911. V. 50

RICKETSON, ANNA
Daniel Ricketson and His Friends. Boston & New York: 1902. V. 54

RICKETSON, OLIVER G.
Uaxactun, Guatemala. Washington: 1937. V. 50; 52

RICKETSON, SHADRACH
Means of Preserving Health, and Preventing Diseases... New York: 1806. V. 48; 50; 51; 52

RICKETT, H. W.
Wild Flowers of the United States. New York: 1966. V. 48; 49; 50; 52; 53
Wild Flowers of the United States. New York: 1966-71. V. 47
Wild Flowers of the United States. New York: 1966-73. V. 53
Wild Flowers of the United States. New York: 1967. V. 49; 50
Wild Flowers of the United States. New York: 1971. V. 50
Wild Flowers of the United States. New York: 1973. V. 50
Wild Flowers of the United States: Volume Four - the Southwestern States. New York: 1970. V. 52

RICKETTS, CHARLES
Beyond the Threshold. 1927. V. 47
De La Typographie et de L'Harmonie de la Page Imprimee. 1898. V. 49
A Defence of the Revival of Printing. 1899. V. 51; 52; 54
A Defence of the Revival of Printing. London: 1899. V. 47; 48; 49; 50; 54
Dell' Arate della Stampa. 1926. V. 54
Dell'Arte della Stampa. Verona: 1926. V. 52
Oscar Wilde: Recollections by Jean Paul Raymond and Charles Ricketts. London: 1932. V. 48; 50; 51; 52; 53; 54
Pages from a Diary in Greece. Edinburgh: 1978. V. 51; 52

Pages on Art. London: 1913. V. 48
Self Portrait - Letters and Journals of Charles Ricketts. London: 1939. V. 49
Sixty Five Illustrations by Charles Ricketts. London: 1933. V. 50; 54
Unrecorded Histories. London: 1933. V. 48; 51; 52; 54

RICKETTS, HOWARD TAYLOR
Contributions to Medical Science by Howard Taylor Ricketts 1870-1910. Chicago: 1911. V. 51

RICKETTS, R.
First Class Polo Tactics and Match Play. Aldershot: 1928. V. 51

RICKETTS, W. P.
50 Years in the Saddle. Sheridan: 1942. V. 47; 54

RICKEY, DON
Forty Miles on Beans and Hay. Norman: 1963. V. 53

RICKLARD, T. A.
Journeys of Observation. San Francisco: 1907. V. 51

RICKMAN, P.
A Bird-Painter's Sketch Book. London and New York: 1931. V. 47; 53; 54

RICKMAN, PHILIP
Bird Sketches and some Field Observations. London: 1938. V. 48; 50; 52; 53
A Bird-Painter's Sketch Book. London: 1931. V. 47
A Selection of Bird Paintings and Sketches. 1979. V. 48; 52
A Selection of Bird Paintings and Sketches. London: 1979. V. 50; 52; 53

RICKMAN, THOMAS
An Attempt to Discriminate the Styles of Architecture in England, from the Conquest. Oxford: 1881. V. 54
An Attempt to discriminate the Styles of Architecture in England from the Conquest to the Reformation. London: 1848. V. 47; 48

RICKMAN, THOMAS CLIO
Corruption, a Satire. London: 1806. V. 47; 49

RICKMERS, W. RICKMER
The Duab of Turkestan. Cambridge: 1913. V. 50

RICORD, FREDERICK W.
History of Union County, New Jersey. Newark: 1897. V. 47; 49; 51

RICORD, PHILIPPE
Illustrations of Syphilitic Disease... Philadelphia: 1825. V. 49
Illustrations of Syphilitic Disease. Philadelphia: 1852. V. 49
A Practical Treatise on Venereal Diseases; or, Critical and Experimental Researches on Inoculation, Applied to the Study of These Affections. New York: 1842. V. 51; 52; 54
A Practical Treatise on Venereal Diseases; or, Critical and Experimental Researches on Inoculation, Applied to the Study of These Affections. New York: 1849. V. 51
Traite complet des Maldies Veneriennes. Clinique Iconographique de l'Hopital des Veneriens. London: 1851. V. 52

RIDDELL, J. H.
Methodism in the Middle West. Toronto: 1946. V. 49; 54

RIDDELL, J. H., MRS.
Austin Friars. London: 1870. V. 51

RIDDELL, JOHN
The John Riddell Murder Case. New York: 1930. V. 53

RIDDELL, MARIA
The Metrical Miscellany. London: 1802. V. 50
The Metrical Miscellany... London: 1803. V. 47

RIDDELL, R.
A Manual of Gardening for Western India. Madras: 1845. V. 51

RIDDELL, ROBERT
The Carpenter and Joiner, Stair Builder and Hand-Railer. London: 1860. V. 51

RIDDLE, ALBERT GALLATIN
Ansel's Cave: a Story of Early Life in the Western Reserve. Cleveland: 1893. V. 50; 54

RIDDLE, DANIEL S.
The Law and Practice in Proceedings Supplementary to Execution, Under the New York code, and Adpated to All the Other States Having Similar Practice. New York: 1886. V. 50

RIDDLE, KENYON
Records and Maps of the Old Santa Fe Trail. West Palm Beach: 1963. V. 53

RIDE a Cock Horse to Banbury Cross. London: 1895. V. 48

THE RIDE on the Sled; or the Punishment of Disobedience. Boston: 1839. V. 48

RIDEING, WILLIAM H.
A Saddle in the Wild West. New York: 1879. V. 47

RIDER, CARDANUS
Rider's British Merlin: for the Year of Our Lord God 1780. London: 1780. V. 48

RIDER, FREMONT
Rider's California, A Guide-Book for Travelers with 28 maps and plans... New York: 1925. V. 48

RIDERS (1699) British Merlin: Bedecke with many Delightful Varieties and useful Verities, Fitting the Longitude and Latitude of all Capacities Within the Islands of Great Britain's Monarchy... London: 1699. V. 47

RIDER'S British Merlin for the Year of Our Lord 1814. London: 1814. V. 48

RIDGAWAY, HENRY BASCOM
The Lord's Land: a Narrative of Travels in Sinai, Arabia Petraea and Palestine, from the Red Sea to the Entering in of Hamath. New York: 1876. V. 48

RIDGE, C. H.
Records of the Worshipful Company of Shipwrights 1428 to 1858. London: 1939/46. V. 47

RIDGE, JOHN R.
Joaquin Murieta The Brigand Chief of California. San Francisco: 1932. V. 54
Ridge's Poems. San Francisco: 1868. V. 47; 50

RIDGE, LOLA
Firehead. New York: 1929. V. 49
The Ghetto and Other Poems. New York: 1918. V. 48; 51

RIDGELY, DAVID
Annals of Annapolis, Comprising Sundry Notices of that Old City from the Period of the First Settlements In its Vicinity in the Year 1640, Until the War of 1812... Baltimore: 1841. V. 50

RIDGEWAY, WILLIAM
The Early Age of Greece. Cambridge: 1931. V. 52
The Origin and Influence of the Thoroughbred Horse. Cambridge: 1905. V. 51; 53

RIDGWAY, BRUNILDE SISMONDO
The Severe Style in Greek Sculpture. Princeton: 1970. V. 50; 52

RIDGWAY, R.
The Birds of North and Middle America... Washington: 1901-50. V. 54
Color Standards and Color Nomenclature. Washington: 1912. V. 50
A Manual of North American Birds. New York: 1887. V. 54
A Manual of North American Birds. Philadelphia: 1896. V. 54
A Nomenclature of Colors for Naturalists. Boston: 1886. V. 51

RIDING, LAURA
Americans. Los Angeles: 1934. V. 54
The Close Chaplet. London: 1926. V. 49
The Close Chaplet. New York: 1926. V. 47
Collected Poems. London: 1938. V. 52
The Collected Poems of... New York: 1938. V. 47
Contemporaries and Snobs. Garden City: 1928. V. 48; 51
Description of Life. New York: 1980. V. 50; 51; 53; 54
Everybody's Letters. London: 1933. V. 50
Four Unposted Letters to Catherine. Paris: 1930. V. 53
Laura and Francesca. Deya, Majorca: 1931. V. 48; 51; 53
The Life of the Dead. London: 1933. V. 47; 49; 54
Lives of Wives. London: 1939. V. 48
Love as Love, Death as Death. London: 1928. V. 48
Poet: a Lying Word. London: 1933. V. 48; 49; 50
Progress of Stories. London: 1935. V. 50; 51
Some Communications of Broad Reference. Northridge: 1983. V. 48
The Telling. London: 1972. V. 51
A Trojan Ending. Deya: 1937. V. 53
Twenty Poems Less. Paris: 1930. V. 47; 51; 54

RIDINGER, JOHANN ELIAS
Enswurf Einiger Thiere... Augsburg: 1738-55. V. 47

RIDINGS, SAM P.
The Chisholm Trail. Guthrie: 1936. V. 47; 48; 49; 51; 53; 54

RIDLER, A. W.
Holidays in Animal Land. London: 1919. V. 49

RIDLER, ANNE
Dies Natalis. Poems of Birth and Infancy. Oxford: 1980. V. 52
A Dream Observed and Other Poems. London: 1941. V. 49
The Jesse Tree. 1972. V. 54
The Jesse Tree. London: 1972. V. 48
Poems. London: 1939. V. 49
Ten Poems. Leamington Spa: 1984. V. 51

RIDLEY, BROMFIELD L.
Battles and Sketches of the Army of Tennessee. Mexico: 1906. V. 47

RIDLEY, GLOCESTER
The Life of Dr. Nicholas Ridley, Sometime Bishop of London; Shewing the Plan and Progress of the Reformation. London: 1763. V. 47; 49

RIDLEY, H. N.
Report on the Botany of the Wollaston Expedition to Dutch New Guinea, 1912-13. London: 1916. V. 51

RIDLEY, HUMPHREY
Observationes Quadedam Medico-Practicae & Physiologicae, Inter Quas Aliquanto Surius Agitur. London: 1703. V. 47; 48; 50

RIDLEY, JAMES
The Tales of the Genii... London: 1765. V. 54
The Tales of the Genii. London: 1781. V. 49
The Tales of the Genii. London: 1786. V. 48
The Tales of the Genii. London: 1805. V. 51
The Tales of the Genii. London: 1820. V. 51

RIDLEY, MARK
A Short Treatise of Magneticall Bodies and Motions. London: 1613. V. 52

RIDLEY, NICHOLAS
De Coena Dominica Assertio. Geneva: 1556. V. 51; 54

RIDLEY, THOMAS
A View of the Civile and Ecclesiasticall Law... Oxford: 1676. V. 51

RIDLEY, WILLIAM
Snapshots from the North Pacific Letters Written by the Right Rev. Bishop ridley (late of Caledonia). London: 1904. V. 48

RIDOLFI, CARLO
Le Meraviglie dell'Arte, Overo le Vite de gl'illustri Pittori Veneti, e delo Stato. Venice: 1648. V. 53

RIDPATH, GEORGE
The Border History of England and Scotland, Deduced from the Earliest Times to the Union of the Two Crowns. London: 1776. V. 47; 53
The Stage Condemned, and the Encouragement Given to the Immoralities and Profaneness of the Theatre... London: 1698. V. 51

RIDPATH, JOHN CLARK
Ridpath's History of the World. New York: 1886. V. 53

RIEDER, HERMANN
Atlas of Urinary Sediments: with Special Reference to their Clinical Significance. London: 1899. V. 49; 54

RIEDESEL, FRIEDRICH ADOLPH VON
Memoirs, and Letters and Journals, of Major General Riedesel During His Residence in America. Albanay: 1868. V. 47

RIEFENSTAHL, LENI
Coral Gardens. London: 1978. V. 52
The Last of the Nuba. New York: 1974. V. 51
The People of Kau. New York/Hagerstown: 1976. V. 53
Vanishing Africa. New York: 1982. V. 52; 53

RIEFSTAHL, ELIZABETH
Ancient Egyptian Glass and Glazes in the Brooklyn Museum. Brooklyn: 1968. V. 51

RIEFSTAHL, R. MEYER
The Parish-Watson Collection of Mohammadan Potteries. New York: 1922. V. 47; 48; 49

THE RIEL Rebellion 1885. Montreal: 1885. V. 50

RIENAECKER, VICTOR
John Sell Cotman 1782-1842. Leigh-on-Sea: 1953. V. 53

RIESBECK, KASPAR, BARON
Travels through Germany, in a Series of Letters. Dublin: 1787. V. 47

RIFLE and Infantry Tactics. Mobile: 1861. V. 54

RIGAUD, JACQUES
Livre de Paysages et Marines, Ou Sont Representez les Avantures des Voyageurs. Paris: 1730. V. 49; 53

RIGBY, ELIZABETH
A Residence on the Shores of the Baltic. London: 1841. V. 52

RIGBY, R. G. K.
Time Honoured Lancaster. Lancaster: 1891. V. 48; 51; 53

RIGG, ARTHUR
A Practical Treatise on the Steam Engine. London: 1878. V. 50; 53

RIGGE, AMBROSE
A Brief and Serious Warning to Such as Are Concerned in Commerce and Trading, Who Go Under the Profession of Truth, to Keep Within the Bounds Thereof, in Righteousness, Justice and Honesty Towards All Men... London: 1771. V. 48; 49

RIGGIN, AILEEN
Modern Swimming and Diving. New York: 1931. V. 47

RIGGS, ALFRED L.
Wicoie Wowapi Kin. New York: 1887. V. 54

RIGGS, ELIAS
A Manual of the Chaldee Language... boston: 1832. V. 50

RIGGS, LYNN
Green Grow the Lilacs. New York: 1954. V. 52
Listen, Mind. Los Angeles: 1933. V. 54

RIGGS, STEPHEN R.
Dakota Grammar, Texts and Ethnography. Washington: 1893. V. 51
A Dakota-English Dictionary. Washington: 1890. V. 52
Grammar and Dictionary of the Dakota Language. Washington: 1851. V. 48
Mary and I. Chicago: 1880. V. 50
Model First Reader Wayawa Tokeheya, Prepared in English-Dakota. Chicago: 1873. V. 52
Wayawa Tokaheya, Model First Reader. Chicago: 1873. V. 50

RIGGS, T. C.
Home Seekers Should Purchase Homes in the Northern Portion of San Joaquin County, California. Stockton: 1887. V. 52

THE RIGHT Of Electing Sheriffs of London and Middlesex, Briefly Stated and Declared. London: 1682. V. 52

RIGHTON, HENRY
Lord Leclerg, and Other Poems. London: 1865. V. 48; 50; 52

RIGHTS and Privileges of the Freemen of Exeter; Being an Account of All Legacies Left to the Poor of the Said City...First Printed in the Year 1736 by Samuel Izacke... Exeter: 1785. V. 49

RIGHTS, EDITH ANDERSON
The Bookplates of Arthur Nelson MacDonald. Montclair: 1986. V. 49

RIGOLEY DE JUVIGNY, JEAN ANTOINE
Les Bibliotheques Francoises De La Croix Du Maine et De Du Verdier Sieur de Vauprivas. Paris: 1772-73. V. 48; 50

RIIS, JACOB A.
The Battle with the Slum. New York: 1902. V. 54
How the Other Half Lives. New York: 1890. V. 47; 49
How the Other Half Lives. London: 1891. V. 54
How the Other Half Lives. New York: 1891. V. 52
Theodore Roosevelt the Citizen. New York: 1904. V. 54

RIJNHART, SUSIE CARSON
With the Tibetans in Tent and Temple. Chicago: 1901. V. 53
With the Tibetans in Tent and Temple. Edinburgh: 1901. V. 48
With the Tibetans in Tent and Temple. London: 1901. V. 50

RIKHOFF, JIM
Hunting the Big Cats. Clinton: 1981. V. 53

RILEY & SARGENT
Price Ten Cents. Multum In Paro, or, the Travelers' Companion, Containing Distance Tables To All Parts of the United States. Philadelphia: 1869-70. V. 52

RILEY, ATHELSTAN
Athos, or the Mountain of the Monks. London: 1887. V. 48; 49

RILEY, BENNETT
Message from the President...Relating to the Protection of the Trade Between Missouri and Mexico. Washington: 1830. V. 50

RILEY, C. V.
Insect Life, Devoted to the Economy and Life-Habits of Insects... Washington: 1888-95. V. 50

RILEY, E. BAXTER
Among Pauan Headhunters. Philadelphia: 1925. V. 52

RILEY, ELIHU SAMUEL
Stonewall Jackson a Thesaurus of Anecdotes and Incidents in the Life Of Lieut. General Thomas Jonathan Jackson, C.S.A. Annapolis: 1920. V. 52

RILEY, FREDERIC
Guide to Settle and District. Settle. V. 47
The Ribble From Its Source to the Sea. Settle: 1914. V. 54
The Settle District and North-West Yorkshire Dales. Settle: 1923. V. 53

RILEY, HENRY ALSOP
An Atlas of the Basal Ganglia, Brain Stem and Spinal Cord. Baltimore: 1943. V. 49
An Atlas of the Basal Ganglia, Brain Stem and Spinal Cord. New York: 1960. V. 54

RILEY, JAMES
An Authentic Narrative of the Loss of the American Brig Commerce, Wrecked on the Western Coast of Africa... Lexington: 1823. V. 50

RILEY, JAMES WHITCOMB
Armazindy. Indianapolis: 1894. V. 49; 50
The Boy Lives on Our Farm. Indianapolis: 1908. V. 49
A Child-World. Indianapolis & Kansas City: 1897. V. 49; 53; 54
The Complete Works of... Indianapolis: 1913. V. 47
The Complete Works of... New York: 1916. V. 47
Defective Santa Claus. Indianapolis: 1904. V. 49
The Flying Islands of the Night. Indianapolis: 1892. V. 51
The Flying Islands of the Night. Indianapolis: 1900. V. 49
The Flying Islands of the Night. Indianapolis: 1913. V. 50; 51
The Girl I Loved. Indianpolis: 1910. V. 48
Green Fields and Running Brooks. Indianapolis: 1893. V. 49; 54
Home Again with Me. Indianapolis: 1908. V. 48
A Hoosier Romance. Indianapolis: 1912. V. 48
An Old Sweetheart of Mine. Indianapolis: 1902. V. 48
An Old Sweetheart of Mine. Indianapolis: 1903. V. 49; 52
The Old Swimmin'-Hole and 'Leven More Poems. Indianapolis: 1883. V. 51; 53
Old-Fashioned Roses. London: 1888. V. 49; 52
Old-Fashioned Roses. London: 1896. V. 52
The Raggedy Man. Indianapolis: 1907. V. 50
The Riley Baby Book. Indianapolis: 1913. V. 51
Riley's Roses. Indianapolis: 1909. V. 47; 48; 49
The Runaway Boy. Indianapolis: 1906. V. 49
While the Heart Beats Young. Indianpaolis: 1906. V. 49
Works. New York: 1910. V. 49

RILING, RAY
Guns and Shooting, a Bibliography. Greenberg: 1951. V. 51
The Powder Flask Book. New York: 1953. V. 48; 51; 52

RILKE, RAINER MARIA
Duineser Elegien. Leipzig: 1923. V. 47; 51; 52
Duineser Elegien. 1931. V. 52
Duineser Elegien. London: 1931. V. 53; 54
Duino Elegies - The German Text, with English Translation... London: 1939. V. 50

Illustrationen zu Rainer Maria Rilke "Die Aufzeichnungen des Malte Laurids Brigge". Zurich: 1986. V. 47
The Lay of Love and Death of Cornet Christopher Rilke. London: 1948. V. 54
The Lay of the Love and Death of Cornet Christoph Rilke. San Francisco: 1963. V. 53
The Lay of the Love and Death of Cornet Christoph Rilke. San Francisco: 1983. V. 52
The Lay of the Love and Death of Cornet Christoph Rilke. San Francisco: 1983. V. 47; 48; 50
Primal Sound and Other Prose Pieces. Cummington: 1943. V. 47; 49; 50; 53
Les Roses. Bussum: 1927. V. 53
Selected Poems. New York: 1981. V. 47
Die Sonette an Orpheus. Leipzig: 1923. V. 49
Wartime Letters - 1914-1921. New York: 1940. V. 47
Die Weise Von Lieb und Tod Des Cornets Christoph Rilke. San Francisco: 1983. V. 51

RIMBAUD, ARTHUR
Le Bateau Ivre: Drunken Boat. Reading: 1976. V. 47
Drunken Boat. Reading: 1976. V. 52
A Season in Hell. Norfolk: 1939. V. 51
A Season in Hell. London: 1986. V. 47
A Season in Hell. New York: 1986. V. 47; 48; 49; 51; 52; 53
Ten Poems. New York: 1982. V. 50; 54

RIME di Diversi Antichi Avtori Toscani in Dieci Libri Raccolte. Venice: 1532. V. 51

RIMMEL, EUGENE
The Book of Perfumes. London: 1865. V. 49
The Book of Perfumes. London: 1871. V. 50

RIMMER, ALFRED
About England with Dickens. London: 1883. V. 53; 54
Ancient Stone Crosses of England. London: 1875. V. 52

RIMMER, ROBERT H.
The Harrad Experiment. Los Angeles: 1966. V. 52

RIMMER, W.
Elements of Design. Book First. Boston: 1864. V. 52

RINDER, FRANK
Old World Japan. Legends of the Land of the Gods. London: 1895. V. 47; 49; 54

RINEHART, F. A.
Rinehart's Indians. Omaha: 1899. V. 53

RINEHART, MARY ROBERTS
The Bat. New York: 1926. V. 52
The Circular Staircase. Indianapolis: 1908. V. 48; 51; 54
The Red Lamp. New York: 1925. V. 48
Through Glacier Park: the Log of a trip with Howard Eaton. Boston: 1916. V. 50

RING, JOHN
The Commemoration of Handel. London: 1786. V. 50
The Commemoration of Handel. London: 1819. V. 47

RING O'Roses. A Nursery Rhyme Picture Book. London: 1921. V. 52

RINGEL, FRED J.
America as Americans See It. New York: 1932. V. 47

RINGHIERI, INNOCENTIO
Cento Givochi Liberali, et D'Ingegno. Bologna: 1551. V. 47

RINHART, FLOYD
American Daguerreian Art. New York: 1967. V. 52
American Miniature Case Art. South Brunswick & New York: 1969. V. 52

RINK, EVALD
Technical Americana. Millwood: 1981. V. 48

RINK, HENRY
Danish Greenland. Its People and Its Products. London: 1877. V. 51
Tales and Traditions of the Eskimo With a Sketch of Their Habits, Religion, Language and Other Peculiarities. Edinburgh & London: 1875. V. 54

RIO, ANTONIO DEL
Description of the Ruins of an Ancient City, Discovered Near Palenque, in the Kingdom of Guatemala, in Spanish America. London: 1822. V. 47

RIO VERDE CANAL CO.
Alfalfa in the Salt River Valley, Arizona. Minneapolis: 1896. V. 49

RIOLAN, JOHANNES
Opera Omnia. Paris: 1610. V. 47

RIORDAN, JOSEPH W.
The First Half Century of St. Ignatius Church and College. San Francisco: 1905. V. 51

RIOS, JULIAN
Kitaj. Pictures and Conversations. London: 1994. V. 51

RIPA, CAESAR
Iconologia; or, Moral Emblems. London: 1709. V. 54

RIPLEY, ALEXANDRA
Scarlet: the Sequel to Gone with the Wind. New York: 1992. V. 54

RIPLEY, DOROTHY
The Extraordinary Conversion, and Religious Experience of Dorothy Ripley, With Her First Voyage and Travels in America. New York: 1810. V. 50

RIPLEY, ELIZA
The Obligations of Parents to Give Their Children a Virtuous Education and to Provide Schools for this Purpose with Advice to Scholars...a Sermon, Delivered Sept. 7, 1820... Cambridge: 1820. V. 53

RIPLEY, GEORGE
A Farewell Discourse, Delivered to the Congregational Church in Purchase Street, March 20, 1841. Boston: 1841. V. 48; 50
A Letter Addressed to the Congregational Church in Purchase Street (Boston). Boston: 1840. V. 50

RIPLEY, HENRY
Hand-Clasp of the East and West. Denver: 1914. V. 48; 50

RIPLEY, JAMES
Original Letters on Various Subjects by James Ripley, Now, and for Thirty Years Past, Ostler at the Red Lion, Barnet. London: 1781. V. 51
Select Original Letters on Various Subjects. London: 1781. V. 48; 50; 53; 54

RIPLEY, MARY CHURCHILL
The Oriental Rug Book. New York: 1904. V. 52

RIPLEY, ROBERT L.
Believe it or Not!. 1928. V. 48; 52
Believe It or Not!. New York: 1929. V. 51; 53

RIPLEY, ROSWELL S.
The War with Mexico. New York: 1849. V. 47

RIPLEY, S. D.
Ornithological Books in the Yale University Library. New Haven: 1961. V. 51
Rails of the World. Boston: 1977. V. 49
Rails of the World. London: 1977. V. 48; 51; 53
Rails of the World. Toronto: 1977. V. 54
Rails of the World. U.S.A: 1977. V. 50; 52

RIPLEY, WARREN
Artillery and Ammunition of the Civil War. New York: 1970. V. 53

RIPON Millenary. A Record of the Festival. Also a History of the City Arranged Under Its Wakemen and Mayors from the Year 1400. Ripon: 1892. V. 51; 54

RIPPERDA, JOAN WILLEM VAN, DUQUE
Memoirs of the Duke de Ripperda: first Ambassador from the States-General to His Most Catholick Majesty, Then Duke and Grandee of Spain... London: 1740. V. 47; 49; 51

RIPPEY, SARA CORY
The Sunny-Sulky Book. London. V. 50

RIPPON, JOHN
A Selection of Hymns from the Best Authors, Including a Great Number of Originals... London: 1800. V. 53

RIPPON, SARAH
The True State of the Case of Sarah Rippon, Widow. London: 1756?. V. 47

RISBECK, JOHANN KASPAR
Travels through Germany. Dublin: 1787. V. 50

RISHEL, C. D.
The Life and Adventures of David Lewis, the Robber and Counterfeiter, the Terror of the Cumberland Valley. Newville: 1890. V. 47

RISK, ALLAH HABEEB
The Thistle and The Cedar of Lebanon. London: 1853. V. 48

RISK, R. T.
Erhard Ratdolt, Masater Printer. Francestown: 1982. V. 51; 52

RISTER, CARL COKE
Border Captives, The Traffic in Prisoners by Southern Plains Indians 1835-1875. Norman: 1940. V. 48; 50; 52
Comanche Bondage. Glendale: 1955. V. 48; 49; 51; 53
The Southwestern Frontier 1865-1881. Cleveland: 1928. V. 50; 52

RITCH, WILLIAM G.
Aztian. The History, Resources and Attractions of New Mexico. Boston: 1885. V. 49
Illustrated New Mexico. Santa Fe: 1883. V. 52
Inaugural Address of...Historical Society of New Mexico Delivered Before the Society Feb. 21, 1881 at the Palace, Santa Fe, N.M. Santa Fe: 1881. V. 54

RITCHIE, ANNE ISABELLA THACKERAY, LADY
A Book of Sibyls. Mrs. Barbauld, Miss Edgeworth, Mrs. Opie, Miss Austen. London: 1883. V. 48
Records of Tennyson, Ruskin and Browning. London: 1892. V. 54
The Story of Elizabeth. London: 1863. V. 47; 49
Toilers and Spinsters and other Essays. London: 1874. V. 50
The Village On the Cliff. London: 1867. V. 50; 50

RITCHIE, JAMES
The Influence of Man on Animal Life in Scotland. Cambridge: 1920. V. 48; 52; 54

RITCHIE, JAMES S.
Wisconsin and Its Resources. Philadelphia: 1857. V. 47

RITCHIE, LEITCH
Ireland Picturesque and Romantic. London: 1837. V. 50
A Journey to St. Petersburg and Moscow. London: 1836. V. 54
Schinderhannes, the Robber of the Rhine. Philadelphia: 1833. V. 50
Scott and Scotland. London: 1835. V. 52; 54

Travelling Sketches in the North of Italy, the Tyrol, and On the Rhine. London: 1832. V. 48
Travelling Sketches on the Rhine, and in Belgium and Holland. London: 1833. V. 49
Travelling Sketches on the Sea Coasts of France. London: 1834. V. 48; 50; 53
Wanderings by the Loire. London: 1833. V. 48
Wanderings by the Seine. London: 1834. V. 50
Wanderings by the Seine. London: 1835. V. 54
Wearyfoot Common. New York: 1854. V. 53

RITCHIE, THOMAS EDWARD
An Account of the Life and Writings of David Hume, Esq. London: 1807. V. 52

RITCHIE, WARD
Adventures With Authors. Laguna Beach: 1978. V. 51; 54
Art Deco, the Books of Francois-Louis Schmied, Artist-Engraver-Printer with Recollections and Descriptive Commentaries on the Books. San Francisco: 1987. V. 49
Art Deco: The Books of Francois-Louis Schmied, Artist/Engraver/Printer, with Recollections and Descriptive Commentaries on the Books. 1987. V. 54
Jane Grabhorn: The Roguish Printer of the Jumbo Press. Laguna Beach: 1985. V. 49
Job Printing in California. Los Angeles: 1955. V. 54
MacIntyre. Laguna Beach: 1975. V. 54
Merle Armitage: His Loves and His Many Lives. Laguna Beach: 1982. V. 51; 54
Quince, etc. Exposing the Several Disguises of Ward Ritchie, Poet... Laguna Beach: 1976. V. 54
Some Books with Illustrations by Paul Landacre. Northrdige: 1978. V. 54

RITIUS, MICHAEL
De Re di Francia Libri III. Dr Re D'Ispagna. Libri III, etc. Venice: 1543. V. 48

RITNER, WILLIAM D.
Juan, the White Slave; and the Rebel Planter's Daughter. Philadelphia: 1865. V. 52

RITSON, ANNE
Exercises for the Memory... London: 1814. V. 50

RITSON, JOSEPH
Ancient English Metrical Romances. London: 1802. V. 48; 50
Ancient Popular Poetry from Authentic Manuscripts and Old Printed Copies. Edinburgh: 1884. V. 47; 52
Ancient Songs and Ballads, from the Reign of King Henry the Second to the Revolution. London: 1829. V. 50
Ancient Songs, From the Time of King Henry the Third, to the Revolution. London: 1790. V. 50
Annals of the Caledonians, Picts. and Scots... Edinburgh: 1828. V. 53; 54
The English Anthology. London: 1793-94. V. 49
Fairy Tales Now First Collected... London: 1831. V. 49
Gammer Gurton's Garland, or, the Nursery Parnassus. Edinburgh: 1866. V. 52
Memoirs of the Celts or Gauls. London: 1827. V. 54
Northern Garlands, a Collection of Songs... Edinburgh: 1887. V. 50
Northern Garlands. The Bishopric Garland; The Yorkshire Garland; The Northumnberland Garland; The North Country Chorister. London: 1810. V. 50
The Office of Bailiff of a Liberty. London: 1811. V. 52
Pieces of Ancient Popular Poetry. London: 1791. V. 52
Pieces of Ancient Popular Poetry; From Authentic Manuscripts and Old Printed Copies. London: 1833. V. 47
Pieces of Ancient Popular Poetry...Adorned with Cuts. London: 1791. V. 53
Robin Hood, a Collection of Poems, Songs and Ballads Relative to that Celebrated English Outlaw. London: 1884. V. 54
Scottish Songs. Glasgow: 1869. V. 50
A Select Collection of English Songs, With Their Original Airs... London: 1813. V. 47; 50
The Spartan Manual, or Tablet of Morality... London: 1785. V. 54

RITSOS, YANNIS
Return and Other Poems. 1983. V. 54
Return and other Poems. Birmingham: 1983. V. 49; 52

RITTENHOUSE, JACK D.
American Horse-Drawn Vehicles. Los Angeles: 1948. V. 48; 53; 54
Carriage Hundred: a Bibliography on Horse-Drawn Transportation. Houston: 1961. V. 48; 54
New Mexico Civil War Bibliography. Houston: 1961. V. 54
The Santa Fe Trail - a Historical Bibliography. Albuquerque: 1971. V. 47; 48; 52

RITTER, KARL
Atlas zu Reise nach Hayti. Stuttgart: 1836. V. 51

RITTER, MARY BENNETT
More Than Gold in California 1849-1933. Berkeley: 1933. V. 50

RITTS, HERB
Duo: Herb Ritts Photographs Bob Paris and Rod Jackson. 1991. V. 48
Pictures. Altadena: 1988. V. 54

RITUAL of the Methodist Episcopal Church, South. Richmond: 1851. V. 48

RITZ, CHARLES
A Fly Fisher's Life. 1959. V. 54
A Fly Fisher's Life. New York: 1959. V. 53
A Fly Fisher's Life. New York: 1960. V. 53

RIVA AGUERO, JOSE DE LA
Exposicion de Don Jose de la Riva Aguero Acerca de Su Conducta Politica en el Tiempo Que Ejercio la Presidencia de la Republica del Peru. London: 1824. V. 48

THE RIVAL Roses; or Wars of York and Lancaster. London: 1813. V. 49

RIVE, RICHARD
Emergency. London: 1964. V. 48; 53

RIVERA, DIEGO
Mexican History: Diego Rivera's Frescoes in the National Palace of Mexico City. Mexico City: 1952. V. 49

RIVERA CAMBAS, I. M.
Los Gobernantes de Mexico... Mexico: 1872-73. V. 47

RIVERO, MARIANO
Antiquidades Peruanas. Vienna: 1851. V. 47
Peruvian Antiquities. New York: 1854. V. 48
Peruvian Antiquities. New York: 1855. V. 50

RIVERS, EDITH
The Reformed Woman; or, Passages from the Life of Mrs. Anna Cooley. Boston: 1859. V. 50

RIVERS, GEORGE
Captain Shays. A Populist of 1786. Boston: 1897. V. 50

RIVERS, GEORGE PITT, 1ST BARON
Letters to a Young Nobelman, Upon Various Subjects, Particularly on Government and Civil Liberty. London: 1784. V. 52

RIVERS, HENRY
Accidents: Popular Directions for Their Intermmediate Treatment with Observations on Poisons and Their Antidotes. Boston: 1845. V. 49; 54

RIVERS, HENRY J.
The Tale of Two Cities, a Drama in Three Acts, and a prologue... London: 1862?. V. 54

RIVERS, LARRY
What Did I Do?. New York: 1992. V. 48; 49; 51; 54

RIVERS of Great Britain, Rivers of the East Coast, Descriptive, Historical, Pictorial. London: 1892. V. 53

RIVERS, W. H. R.
The History of the Melanesian Society. Cambridge: 1914/14. V. 48; 54
Psychology and Ethnology, International Library of Psychology, Philosophy and Scientific Method. London: 1926. V. 49; 51

RIVERS, WILLIAM JAMES
Rivers' Account of the Raising Of Troops in South Carolina for State and Confederate Service, 1861-65. Columbia: 1899. V. 49
A Sketch of the History of South Carolina to the Close of the Proprietary Government by the Revolution of 1719. Charleston: 1856. V. 50

RIVERSIDE and Vicinity. (cover title): Souvenir of Riverside and Vicinty Cal. Home of the Orange. Columbus: 1887. V. 47

RIVES, GEORGE LOCKHART
The United States and Mexico, 1821-1848: a History of the Relations Between the Two Countries from the Independence of Mexico to the Close of the War with the United States. New York: 1913. V. 49

RIVES, JUDITH PAGE WALKER
Tales and Souvenirs of a Residence in Europe. Philadelphia: 1842. V. 52

RIVES, REGINALD
The Coaching Club Its History, Records and Activities. New York: 1935. V. 50; 54

RIVES, WILLIAM C.
Letter From the Hon. William C. Rives to a Friend. Richmond: 1860. V. 50

RIVIERE, LAZARE
Observationes Medicae, et Curationes Insignes. Geneva: 1656. V. 48
Opera Medica Universa. Francofurti: 1674. V. 48; 49
The Practice of Physic in Seventeen Several Books. London: 1672. V. 48
The Practice of Physick. London: 1678. V. 48; 52
The Secrets of the Famous Lazarus Riverius, Counsellor and Physician to the French King... London: 1685. V. 53

RIVIERE, R.
Examples of Modern Bookbinding. London: 1919. V. 47; 53

RIVIERE, R. B.
A History of the Birds of Norfolk. London: 1930-32. V. 52

RIVINGTON, WALTER
The Medical Profession: Being the Essay...Awarded First Carmichael Prize...Royal College of Surgeons, Ireland, 1879. 1879. V. 54

RIVIUS, GREGORIUS
Puritani Monatica Historia Occidentis Scabra et Salebrosa Floribus Constrata... Leipsiz: 1737. V. 49

RIVOIRA, G. T.
Lombardic Architecture, its Origin, Development and Derivatives. London: 1910. V. 47; 48; 52; 53
Moslem Architecture. Its Origin and Development. London: 1918. V. 48
Roman Architecture and Its Principles of Construction Under the Empire. Oxford: 1925. V. 50; 52

RIX, HERBERT
Prince Pimpernel, or Kittys Adventures in Fairyland and the Regions Adjoining. London: 1909. V. 51

RIX, M.
The Art of the Plant World, the Great Botanical Illustrators and Their Work. Woodstock: 1981. V. 47; 48; 51

ROACH, ALVA C.
The Prisoner of War, and How Treated. Indianapolis: 1865. V. 52; 54

ROADKILLS: a Collection of Prose and Poetry... 1981. V. 48; 51

THE ROADS and Railroads, Vehicles and Modes of Travelling of Ancient and Modern Countries... London: 1839. V. 49

ROBACK, C. W.
The Mysteries of Astrology, and the Wonders of Magic. Boston: 1854. V. 47; 52

ROBB, JAMES
A Southern Confederacy. Chicago: 1863. V. 49

ROBB, JOHN S.
Streaks of Squatter Life, and Far-West Scenes. Philadelphia: 1847. V. 47; 48; 52; 54

THE ROBBER Kitten. Philadelphia: 1904. V. 49

ROBBINS, ARCHIBALD
A Journal, Comprising an Account of the Loss of the Brig Commerce, of Hartford,... Hartford: 1817. V. 50

ROBBINS, ELIZA
The New Year Improved... Philadelphia: 1821. V. 47

ROBBINS, GUY
The Breast. Austin: 1984. V. 52

ROBBINS, TOM
Another Roadside Attraction. Garden City: 1971. V. 47; 49; 50; 51; 52; 53
Another Roadside Attraction. London & New York: 1973. V. 47; 51
Candy from a Stranger: a Tom Robbins Reader. New York: 1994. V. 53
Even Cowgirls Get the Blues. Boston: 1976. V. 47; 48; 50; 51; 53; 54
Guy Anderson. Seattle: 1965. V. 53
Jitterbug Perfume. New York: 1984. V. 49
Skagit Valley Artists. Seattle: 1974. V. 51
Skinny Legs and All. New York: 1990. V. 52
Still Life with Woodpecker. New York: 1980. V. 47; 49; 51; 52; 53

ROBBINS, W.
African Art in American Collections. New York: 1966. V. 51

ROBBINS-LANDON, H. C.
Beethoven: a Documentary Study. New York: 1970. V. 49

ROBERT Granjon: Sixteenth Century Type Founder and Printer. Brooklyn: 1931. V. 49; 54

ROBERT, OF GLOUCESTER
Chronicle. Oxford: 1810. V. 54
Metrical Chronicle of Robert of Gloucester. London: 1887. V. 49; 52
Robert of Gloucester's Chronicle. Oxford: 1724. V. 49; 52
Robert of Gloucester's Chronicle. London: 1810. V. 47; 53
Robert of Gloucester's Chronicle. Oxford: 1810. V. 50

ROBERT SIMPSON COMPANY LIMITED
Avon House. Galleries of Fine Furniture, Fourth and Fifth Floors. Toronto: 193-?. V. 54

ROBERT, THE HERMIT
Life and Adventures of Robert; the Hermit of Massachusetts, Who Has Lived Fourteen Years in a Cave... Providence: 1829. V. 52

ROBERT-HOUDIN, JEAN EUGENE
Card-Sharping Exposed. London: 1882. V. 48
Memoirs of Robert-Houdin Ambassador, Author and Conjuror. London: 1859. V. 49

ROBERTI, ANTONIUS
Clavis Homerica, sive Lexicon Vocabulorum Omnium, Quae Continentur in Homeri Iliade et Potissima Parate Odyssaea. London: 1741. V. 47; 49

ROBERT LE DIABLE
Robert the Devil. Iowa City: 1981. V. 52; 54
Roberte the Deuyll. London: 1798. V. 49; 53

ROBERTON, JOHN
A Practical Treatise on the Power of Cantharides When Used Internally... Edinburgh: 1806. V. 49; 51; 54

ROBERTS, AUSTIN
The Mammals of South Africa. South Africa. V. 51
The Mammals of South Africa. 1951. V. 54
The Mammals of South Africa. London: 1951. V. 52
The Mammals of South Africa. Cape Town: 1954. V. 54

ROBERTS, B.
A Bibliography of D. H. Lawrence. London: 1963. V. 49

ROBERTS, B. H.
Defense of the Faith and the Saints. Salt Lake City: 1907. V. 51
The Missouri Persecutions. Salt Lake city: 1900. V. 52
The Rise and Fall of Nauvoo. Salt Lake City: 1900. V. 52
The Seventy's Course in Theology. Salt Lake City: 1907. V. 53

ROBERTS, BARRE CHARLES
Letters and Miscellaneous Papers... London: 1814. V. 50

ROBERTS, CECIL
Autobiography. London: 1967-74. V. 47

ROBERTS, CHARLES
The Private Library of the Late Charles Roberts of Philadelphia, Comprising an Extensive Collection of Quakeriana. New York: 1918. V. 51

ROBERTS, CHARLES G. D.
The Iceberg and Other Poems. Toronto: 1934. V. 48; 50
The Land of Evangeline and the Gateways Thither, with Many Illustrations and Appendices for Sportsman and Tourist. Kentville: 1895. V. 54
The Sweet o' the Year and Other Poems. Toronto: 1925. V. 54

ROBERTS, DAN W.
Rangers and Sovereignty. San Antonio: 1914. V. 47; 54

ROBERTS, DANIEL
Some Memoirs of the Life of John Roberts. York: 1750?. V. 47; 51

ROBERTS, DAVID
The Holy Land. London, Paris, New York: 1879-84. V. 49; 52
The Holy Land, Syria, Idumea, Arabia, Egypt and Nubia. London: 1855-56. V. 50
The Military Adventures of John Newcome, with An Account of His Campaigns on the Peninsula and in Pall Mall... London: 1815. V. 47; 53
Sketches in Egypt and Nubia, with Historical Descriptions... Den Haag: 1992. V. 51
La Terre Sainte. (The Holy Land). Brussels: 1843. V. 54

ROBERTS, E.
Colorado Springs and Manitou. Chicago: 1883. V. 54
Forty-One Years in India from Subaltern to Commander-in-Chief. London: 1911. V. 51
Gogebic, Eagle River, Ashland and Other Resorts in Northern Michigan and Wisconsin... Chicago: 1886. V. 54

ROBERTS, E. ELLIS
Samuel Rogers and His Circle. New York: 1910. V. 49

ROBERTS, EDWARD
Santa Barbara and Around There. Boston: 1888. V. 47
With the Invader: Glimpses of the Southwest. San Francisco: 1885. V. 49

ROBERTS, ELIZABETH MADOX
A Buried Treasure. New York: 1931. V. 51; 53
The Great Meadow. New York: 1930. V. 51; 53
The Time of Man. New York: 1945. V. 54

ROBERTS, EMMA
Hindostan Its Landscapes, Palaces, Temples, Tombs, The Shores of the Red Sea and the Sublime and Romantic Scenery of the Himalaya Mountains Illustrated in a Series of Views Drawn by Turner, Stanfield, Prout, Cattermole, Roberts, Allom, etc... London: 1840's. V. 52
Memoirs of the Rival Houses of York and Lancaster Historical and Biographical... London: 1827. V. 48
Oriental Scenes, Dramatic Sketches and Tales. Calcutta: 1830. V. 53; 54
Scenes and Characteristics of Hindostan, with Sketches of Anglo-Indian Society. London: 1835. V. 49
Views in India, China and On the Shores of the Red Sea... 1835. V. 54
Views in India, China and On the Shores of the Red Sea; Drawn by Prout, Stanfield, Cattermole, Purser, Cox, Austen &c... London: 1835. V. 50; 51

ROBERTS, FRANCIS
Clavis Bibliorum. The Key of the Bible, Unlocking the Richest Treasury of the Holy Scriptures... London: 1648. V. 48

ROBERTS, G. E.
Rocks of Worcestershire. London: 1860. V. 53

ROBERTS, GEORGE
The Life, Progresses and Rebellion of James Duke of Monmouth...Capture and Execution...Bloody Assize. London: 1844. V. 54

ROBERTS, HENRY
The Dwellings of the Labouring Classes. London: 1850. V. 48
The Green Book of Golf. San Francisco: 1926. V. 51

ROBERTS, HENRY D.
A History of the Royal Pavilion, Brighton. London: 1939. V. 54

ROBERTS, JACK
The Wonderful Adventures of Ludo the Little Green Duck. Paris: 1924. V. 48

ROBERTS, JAMES
History of Wetton, Thor's Cave and Ecton Mines in the Neighbourhood of Dovedale, Manifold Valley and Beresford Dale. Ashbourne: 1900. V. 54
Introductory Lessons, with Familiar Examples in Landscape, for the Use of Those Who Are Desirous of Gaining Some Knowledge of the Pleasing Art of Painting in Water-Colours. London: 1800. V. 48; 50
Introductory Lessons, with Familiar Examples in Landscape...Painting in Water Colours...Instructions for Executing Transparencies. London: 1808. V. 47
Narrative of James Roberts Soldier in the Revolutionary War and at the Battle of New Orleans. Hattiesburg: 1945. V. 54

ROBERTS, JOHN
Roberts on Billiards. London: 1869. V. 49

ROBERTS, JOHN BINGHAM
Surgery of Deformities of the Face Including Cleft Palate. New York: 1912. V. 54

ROBERTS, JOSEPH
The Hand-Book of Artillery. Richmond: 1861. V. 49
The Hand-Book of Artillery for the Service of the United States (Army and Militia). Richmond: 1862. V. 49

ROBERTS, KATE
Two Old Men and Other Stories. 1981. V. 51; 54
Two Old Men and Other Stories. Newtown: 1981. V. 47; 48; 52

ROBERTS, KEITH
The Boat of Fate. London: 1971. V. 50
The Chalk Giants. London: 1974. V. 51
The Furies. 1966. V. 51
Machines and Men. 1973. V. 49; 51; 54

ROBERTS, KENNETH
Antiquamania. Garden City: 1928. V. 49
Black Magic. Indianapolis: 1924. V. 50
Boon Island. Garden City: 1956. V. 49; 51; 52; 54
The Collector's What Not. 1923. V. 53
Cowpens: The Great Morale Builder. Kalamazoo: 1957. V. 49
Cowpens: the Great Morale-Builder. Westholm: 1957. V. 53
Europes Morning After. New York: 1921. V. 49
Florida. New York: 1926. V. 50
For Authors Only and Other Gloomy Essays. Garden City: 1935. V. 49
For Authors Only and Other Gloomy Essays. New York: 1935. V. 51
The Furies. 1966. V. 47
Henry Gross and His Dowsing Rod. 1951. V. 52
Henry Gross and His Dowsing Rod. (with) The Seventh Sense. Garden City: 1951/53. V. 50
It Must Be Your Tonsils. Garden City: 1936. V. 49
The Lively Lady: a Chronicle of Arundel. Garden City: 1933. V. 49
Lydia Bailey. Garden City: 1947. V. 47; 48; 49; 51; 53; 54
March to Quebec. 1938. V. 53
March to Quebec: Journals of the Members of Arnold's Expedition. Garden City: 1938. V. 52
Northwest Passage. Garden City: 1937. V. 50; 51; 52; 53
Northwest Passage. New York: 1937. V. 51; 52
Oliver Wiswell. New York: 1940. V. 53
Rabble in Arms. 1934. V. 53
Rabble in Arms. London: 1939. V. 50
Sun Hunting. Indianapolis: 1922. V. 51; 53
Trending Into Maine. 1938. V. 50
Trending Into Maine. Boston: 1938. V. 49; 51; 53
Why Europe Leaves Home. Indianapolis: 1922. V. 48; 50
Why Europe Leaves Home. New York: 1922. V. 48; 49

ROBERTS, LORD
Forty-One Years in India. From Subaltern to Commander-in-Chief. London: 1897. V. 50; 52

ROBERTS, M.
Ruins and Old Trees, Associated with Memorable Events in English History. London: 1850. V. 53

ROBERTS, M. J.
The Spiders of Great Britain and Ireland. Colchester: 1984-87. V. 48
The Spiders of Great Britain and Ireland. Volume 2: Linyphiidae and Check List. London: 1987. V. 49

ROBERTS, M. N.
Memory. Luba Art and the Making of History. New York: 1996. V. 54

ROBERTS, MARGARET
The Atelier du Lys or an Art Student in the Reign of Terror. London: 1876. V. 54
Denise. New York: 1864. V. 48
Rose and Emily; or, Sketches of Youth. New York: 1813. V. 49

ROBERTS, MARY
Voices from the Woodlands, Descriptive of Forest Trees, Ferns, Mosses and Lichens. London: 1850. V. 47

ROBERTS, MICHAEL
New Country - Prose and Poetry by the authors of "New Signatures". London: 1933. V. 47; 52; 53
New Signatures: Poems by Several Hands. London: 1932. V. 49

ROBERTS, MORLEY
W. H. Hudson - a Portrait. London: 1924. V. 53
The Western Avernus or, Toil and Travel in Further North America. London: 1887. V. 47

ROBERTS, O. M.
A Description of Texas, Its Advantages and Resources, with Some Account of Their Development, Past, Present and Future. St. Louis: 1881. V. 47
Texas, Confederate Military History. V. 49

ROBERTS, OLIVER
The Great Understander; True Story of the Last of the Wells Fargo Express Messengers. Aurora: 1931. V. 53

ROBERTS, OWEN J.
The Court and the Constitution. Cambridge: 1951. V. 53

ROBERTS, PETER
The Cambrian Popular Antiquities; or An Account of Some Traditions, Customs and Superstitions of Wales with Observations as to Their Origin, &c. London: 1815. V. 50
Sketch of the Early History of the Cymry, or Ancient Britons, from the Year 700 Before Christ to A.D. 500. London: 1803. V. 49; 53; 54

ROBERTS, RICHARD
Hanes Taith Drwy Unol Daleithiau Yn Nghyd A America, Yn Y Blynyddoedd 1841, 1842; Yn Cynwys Desrifiad O'r Unol Faleithiau, Yn Nghyd A Hyfforddiant I'r Ymfudwr. Caernarfon: 1842. V. 47

ROBERTS, RICHARD SAMUEL
A True Likeness. The Black South of Richard Samuel Roberts 1920-1936. Chapel Hill: 1920-36. V. 51
A True Likeness. The Black South of Richard Samuel Roberts 1920-1936. Chapel Hill: 1986. V. 51

ROBERTS, ROBERT
The House Servant's Directory, or, a Monitor for Private Families. Boston: 1827. V. 50
The House Servant's Directory, or a Monitor for Private Families. New York: 1827. V. 52
The House Servant's Directory, or a Monitor for Private Families... Boston: 1843. V. 54

ROBERTS, S. C.
Doctor Watson: Prolegomena to the Study of a Biographical Problem, with a Bibliography of Sherlock Holmes. London: 1931. V. 53
The Evolution of Cambridge Publishing. Cambridge: 1956. V. 52

ROBERTS, SAMUEL
The Blind Man and His Son. London: 1816. V. 51; 54
The State Lottery, a Dream. London: 1817. V. 51

ROBERTS, T.
The Birds of Pakistan. London: 1991-92. V. 51

ROBERTS, T. T.
An Indian Glossary; Consisting of Some Thousand Words and Terms Commonly Used in the East Indies. London: 1800. V. 53

ROBERTS, THOMAS
The English Bowman, or Tracts on Archery; To Which is added the Second part of the Bowman's Glory. London: 1801. V. 48

ROBERTS, THOMAS S.
The Birds of Minnesota. Minneapolis/London: 1932. V. 54

ROBERTS, VERNE L.
Bibliotheca Mechanica. New York: 1991. V. 47; 48; 49; 50

ROBERTS, W.
The Book-Hunter in London. Historical and Other Studies of Collectors and Collecting. Chicago: 1895. V. 49
Catalogue of the Collection of Pictures Formed by John H. McFadden, Esq. of Philadelphia, Pa. London: 1917. V. 52; 54
Letter-Writing from the Earliet Period to the Fifth Century. 1842. V. 48
Memoirs of Christie's. A Record of Art Sales from 1766 to 1896. London: 1897. V. 49

ROBERTS, W. ADOLPHE
The Haunting Hand. New York: 1926. V. 53

ROBERTS, W. F.
Wheatley, R.A. His Life and Works. London: 1910. V. 53

ROBERTS, W. L.
Encyclopaedia of Minerals. London: 1990. V. 48; 50

ROBERTS, WARREN
A Bibliography of D. H. Lawrence. London: 1963. V. 47; 50; 53

ROBERTS, WILLIAM
4.5 Howitzer Gunner R.F.A. - 1916-1918. London. V. 47
An Account of the First Discovery, and Natural History of Florida. London: 1763. V. 47
Memoirs of the Life and Correspondence of Mrs. Hannah More. London: 1834. V. 50
Memoirs of the Life and Correspondence of Mrs. Hannah More. London: 1835. V. 52
Memoirs of the Life and Correspondence of Mrs. Hannah More. New York: 1835. V. 53
A Treatise on the Construction of the Statutes...Relating to Voluntary and Fraudulent Conveyances, etc. Hartford: 1825. V. 53

ROBERTS, WILLIAM HAYWARD
Poems. London: 1774. V. 48
A Poetical Essay, on the Existence of God. London: 1771. V. 48

ROBERTSON, AGNES J.
The Laws of the Kings of England from Edmund to Henry I. 1925. V. 49

ROBERTSON, ALEC
In the Little Things: an Act of Worship for Radio. Worcester: 1969. V. 49

ROBERTSON, ALEXANDER
The Philosophy of the Unconditioned. London: 1866. V. 54
Poems on Various Subjects and Occasions... Edinburgh: 1751?. V. 54

ROBERTSON, BEN
Travelers' Rest. Clemson: 1938. V. 53

ROBERTSON, BRUCE
Sopwith - The Man and His Aircraft. Letchworth: 1970. V. 50

ROBERTSON, BRYAN
Elisabeth Frink Sculpture. 1984. V. 54
Jackson Pollock. New York: 1960. V. 47; 48; 50; 51; 52
Jackson Pollock: Works on Paper. New York: 1969. V. 49

ROBERTSON, COLIN
Colin Robertson's Correspondence Book, September 1817 to September 1822. London: 1939. V. 47; 48
Colin Robertson's Correspondence Book, September 1817 to September 1822. Toronto: 1939. V. 51; 53

ROBERTSON, D. GULIELMI
Disseratio Medica in Auguralis, De Colica. Edinburgh: 1777. V. 48

ROBERTSON, DAVID
Poems. Edinburgh: 1784. V. 54
Reports of the Trials of Colonel Aaron Burr (Late Vice-President of the United States) for Treason and for Misdemeanor... Philadelphia: 1808. V. 47
A Tour through the Isle of Man: To Which is Subjoined a Review of the Manks History. London: 1794. V. 48

ROBERTSON, E. GRAEME
Early Buildings of Southern Tasmania. Melbourne: 1970. V. 48

ROBERTSON, ETIENNE GASPARD
La Minerve, Vaisseau Aerien Destine Aux Decouvertes... Paris: 1820. V. 48

ROBERTSON, G. S.
Chitral. The Story of a Minor Siege. London: 1898. V. 47
Kafiristan and Its People. London: 1895. V. 47

ROBERTSON, GEORGE
An Outline of the Life of George Robertson... Lexington: 1876. V. 50

ROBERTSON, GILES
Giovanni Bellini. Oxford: 1968. V. 49

ROBERTSON, H. R.
Life on the Upper Thames. London: 1875. V. 50

ROBERTSON, HANNAH
The Life of Mrs. Robertson. Grand-Daughter of Charles II. Edinburgh: 1792. V. 49
The Life, Written by Herself. Edinburgh: 1792. V. 51

ROBERTSON, HENRY
A General View of the Natural History of the Atmosphere an Of Its Connection with the Sciences of Medicine and Agriculture. Edinburgh: 1808. V. 52

ROBERTSON, J. B.
Reminiscences of a Campaign in Mexico. Nashville: 1849. V. 47

ROBERTSON, J. C.
Materials for the History of Thomas Becket. London: 1876-85. V. 49; 52

ROBERTSON, J. P.
Letters on Paraguay:. London: 1839. V. 48; 49

ROBERTSON, JAMES
A Concise Historical Proofs Respecting the Gael of Alban... Edinburgh: 1865. V. 54
A Gaelic Topography of Scotland. Edinburgh: 1869. V. 53; 54
General View of the Agriculture in the County of Perth; with Observations on the Means of Its Improvement. Perth: 1799. V. 51; 52
History of the Mission of the Secession Church to Nova Scotia and Prince Edward Island from Its Commencement in 1765. Edinburgh: 1847. V. 53
The Journal of James Robertson. Scarsdale: 1911. V. 48

ROBERTSON, JOHN
Angling Streams and Angling Quarters in the Scottish Lowlands. Edinburgh: 1859. V. 47
Michigan In the Civil War. Lansing: 1882. V. 49
Michigan in the War. (1861-1865). Lansing: 1880. V. 49

ROBERTSON, JOHN DRUMMOND
The Evolution of Clockwork with a Special Selection on the Clocks of Japan... London: 1931. V. 53

ROBERTSON, JOHN ROSS
The History of Freemasonry in Canada, From Its Introduction in 1749. Toronto: 1899. V. 53
Robertson's Landmarks of Toronto: a Collection of Historical Sketches of the Old Town of York from 1792 Until 1833 and of Toronto from 1834 to 1893-(1914). Toronto: 1894-1914. V. 50; 53

ROBERTSON, JOHN W.
Bibliography of the Writings of Edgar A. Poe. (and) Commentary on the Bibliography of Edgar A. Poe. San Francisco: 1934. V. 48
Edgar A. Poe. A Psychopathic Study. New York: 1923. V. 48
Edgar A. Poe. A Study. San Francisco: 1921. V. 48
Francis Drake and Other Early Explorers Along the Pacific Coast. San Francisco: 1927. V. 48; 52

ROBERTSON, JOSEPH
Catalogue of the Jewels, Dresses, Furniture, Books and Paintings of Mary Queen of Scots 1556-1569. Edinburgh: 1863. V. 48
An Essay on Punctuation. London: 1786. V. 52
The Parian Chronicle, or the Chronicle of the Arundelian Marbles: with a Dissertation Concerning Its Authenticity. London: 1788. V. 48

ROBERTSON, MANNING
Dun Laoghaire: the History, Scenery and Developemtn of the District. 1936. V. 52

ROBERTSON, MARTIN
A History of Greek Art. London: 1975. V. 48

ROBERTSON, MERLE GREENE
The Sculpture of Palenque. Princeton: 1983-91. V. 50; 52

ROBERTSON, ROBERT
An Essay on Fevers; Wherein Their Theoretic Genera, Species and Various Denominations, are, From Observation and Experience for Thirty Years... London: 1790. V. 49; 51; 54

ROBERTSON, THORBURN BRAILSFORD
The Chemical Basis of Growth Senescence. Philadelphia: 1923. V. 47

ROBERTSON, W. GRAHAM
The Blake Collection of W. Graham Robertson. London: 1952. V. 48

ROBERTSON, W. GRAHAM continued
Gold, Frankincense and Myrrh and Other Pageants for a Baby Girl. London: 1908. V. 48; 51; 52
Letters From... London: 1953. V. 49

ROBERTSON, W. S.
Mvskoke Nakcokv Eskereetv Esvhokkolat. Creek Second Reader. New York: 1860?. V. 54

ROBERTSON, WILLIAM
A Collection of Various Forms of Stoves, Used for Forcing Pine Plants, Fruit Trees and Preserving Tender Exotics. London: 1798. V. 47
From Private to Field-Marshall. London: 1921. V. 49
A Gate or Door to the Holy Tongue, Opened in English. London: 1653. V. 48; 50; 52
(Hebrew Title) The First Gate, or the Outward Door to the Holy Tongue Opened in English. (with) The Second Gate, or the Inner Door to the Holy Tongue. London: 1654. V. 47
L'Histoire de l'Amerique. Paris: 1780. V. 49
An Historical Disquisition Concerning Knowledge Which the Ancients Had of Indian and the Progress of Trade with That Country Prior to the Discovery of the Passage To It... London: 1817. V. 49
Historical Disquisition Concerning the Knowledge Which the Ancients Had of India. Basil: 1792. V. 49; 54
An Historical Disquisition Concerning the Knowledge Which the Ancients Had of India... Philadelphia: 1792. V. 47; 52
The History of America. London: 1777. V. 53
The History of America. London: 1788. V. 53
The History of America... London: 1803. V. 47
The History of America, Books IX and X. Philadelphia: 1799. V. 47
The History of America: Containing the History of Virginia to the Year 1688 and of New England to the Year 1652. London: 1822. V. 48
The History of Scotland During the Reigns of Queen Mary and of King James IV Till His Accession to the Crown of England with a Review of Scottish History.. Basil: 1791. V. 54
The History of the Emperor Charles V with a View of the progress of Society in Europe from the Subversion of the Roman Empire to the Beginning of the Sixteenth Century. London: 1806. V. 48
History of the Reign of Charles the Fifth. London: 1857. V. 54
The History of the Reign of the Emperor Charles V. London: 1769. V. 48
The History of the Reign of the Emperor Charles V. London: 1806. V. 47; 51
Phraseologia Generalis... Cambridge: 1681. V. 50
Thesaurus Graecae Linguae, Inepitomen, Sive Compendium, Redactus... Cantabrigiae: 1676. V. 50
Works. London: 1799-1803. V. 49
The Works. Edinburgh: 1818. V. 53
The Works... Chiswick: 1824. V. 52
The Works. London: 1840. V. 48; 49

ROBERTSON, WILLIAM H. P.
The History of Throughbred Racing in America. Englewood Cliffs: 1964. V. 47

ROBESON, DAVE
Al G. Barnes, Master Showman. Caldwell: 1935. V. 53

ROBESON, ESLAND GOODE
Paul Robeson, Negro. London: 1930. V. 48

ROBESON, KENNETH
The Man of Bronze. New York: 1933. V. 47; 49
Quest of the Spider. New York: 1933. V. 47; 49

ROBESON, PAUL
Here I Stand. London: 1958. V. 48; 50
Here I Stand. New York: 1958. V. 48; 49; 51
Notes and Queries on Anthropology. London: 1929. V. 49

ROBICSEK, FRANCIS
The Maya Book of the Dead: the Ceramic Codex. The Corpus of Codex Style Ceramics of the Late Classic Period. Norman: 1981. V. 50; 52
The Smoking Gods: Tobacco in Maya Art, History and Religion. Norman: 1978. V. 50; 52; 54

ROBIDA, A.
Le Coeur de Paris, Splendeurs et Souvenirs. Paris: 1895. V. 47

ROBIDA, ALBERT
Les Villes Martyres. Paris: 1914. V. 51

ROBIDOUX, ORRALL M.
Memorial to the Robidoux Brothers Who Blazed the Western Trails for Civilization. Kansas City: 1924. V. 51

ROBIN, ABBE
New Travels through North America: In a Series of Letters, Exhibiting the History of the Victorious Campaign of the Allied Armies...in the Year 1781. Boston: 1784. V. 47; 50

ROBIN the Conjuror and Other Tales in Verse. London: 1880. V. 53

ROBIN HOOD
The Ballads of Robin Hood. 1977. V. 51
Five Ballads about Robin Hood. Birmingham: 1899. V. 52
A Lytell Geste of Robyn Hode and His Meiny. San Francisco: 1932. V. 48; 51
A Lyttel Geste of Robin Hode with Other Ancient and Modern Ballads and Songs Relating to this Celebrated Yeoman. London: 1847. V. 47
Robin Hood. New York: 1917. V. 49
Robin Hood: a Collection of All the ancient Poems, Songs and Ballads, Now Extant, Relative to that Celebrated Outlaw. London: 1795. V. 49; 52
Robin Hood's Garland: Being a Complete History of All the Notable and Merry Exploits Performed by Him and His Men on Many Occasions. Kidderminster: 17--?. V. 52

Robin Hood's Garland, Being a Complete History of all the Notable Exploits Performed by Him and His Merry Men. York: 1800?. V. 47

ROBINS, BENJAMIN
A Discourse Concerning the Nature and Certainty of Sir Isaac Newton's Methods of Fluxions and of Prime and Ultimate Ratios. London: 1735. V. 51

ROBINS, EDWARD COOKWORTHY
Technical School and College Building. London: 1887. V. 54

ROBINS, ELIZABETH
Portrait of a Lady. London: 1941. V. 53

THE ROBIN'S Jubilee: Being a Collection of Poetry Relative to the Robin Red-Breast. London: 1826. V. 47; 51

ROBINSON & STEINMAN
Bridges Lasting and Beautiful. New York: 1935. V. 53

ROBINSON, A. H. W.
Marine Cartography in Britain. 1962. V. 51

ROBINSON, ALAN JAMES
The Banging Rocks, a Dissertation On the Origins of a Species of Rock Descended With Modification from the Ancient Piroboli... Easthampton: 1990. V. 48
Cetecea, the Great Whales. Easthampton. V. 47
Cheloniidae Sea Turtles. Easthampton: 1987. V. 52
A Fowl Alphabet. Easthampton: 1986. V. 47; 49; 50; 51
Game Animals: Ten Etchings Hand-Watercolored by Alan James Robinson. Easthampton: 1981. V. 47
Game Fishes. Easthampton: 1981. V. 47
HPM. A Celebration of Fifty Years of Printing. Easthampton: 1991. V. 50
An Odd Bestiary. Easthampton: 1982. V. 52
Roadkills. Easthampton: 1981. V. 52

ROBINSON, ALFRED
Life in California Before the Conquest. San Francisco: 1925. V. 47; 48
Life in California: During a Residence of Several Years in that Territory... New York: 1846. V. 47

ROBINSON, ARMIN L.
The Ten Commandments: Ten Short Novels of Hitler's War Against the Moral Code. New York: 1943. V. 54

ROBINSON, B.
The Basket Weavers of Arizona. Albuquerque: 1954. V. 51

ROBINSON, B. W.
A Descriptive Catalogue of the Persian Paintings in the Bodleian Library. 1958. V. 50
A Descriptive Catalogue of the Persian Paintings in the Bodleian Library. London: 1958. V. 54

ROBINSON, BERT
The Basket Weavers of Arizona. Albuquerque: 1954. V. 52

ROBINSON, BRAD
Suddens. Toronto: 1965. V. 47

ROBINSON, CHANDLER
J. Evetts Haley, Cowman, Historian. El Paso: 1967. V. 48; 49; 50

ROBINSON, CHARLES
Annual Message of Gov. Charles Robinson, Kansas. Lawrence: 1862. V. 50
Babes and Blossoms. London: 1908. V. 49
Black Bunnies. London: 1907. V. 54
A Bookful of Fun. Jingle Rhymes for Merry Times. London: 1905. V. 49
The Kansas Conflict. New York: 1892. V. 50; 53
Thanksgiving Proclamation. The Second Year of Our Existence As a State Is Drawing to a Close. Topeka: 1862. V. 48

ROBINSON, CHARLES HENRY
Hausland, or Fifteen Hundred Miles through the Central Soudan. London: 1896. V. 50

ROBINSON, CHARLES N.
The British Tar in Fact and Fiction. New York: 1909. V. 54
Celebrities of the Army. London: 1900. V. 54
Old Naval Prints, Their Artists and Engravers. London: 1924. V. 47; 48; 49; 52; 54

THE ROBINSON Crusoe Picture Book. London: 1880. V. 51

ROBINSON, DANIEL
Practical Suggestions for the Reclamation of Waste lands and Improvement in the Condition of the Agricultural Population of Ireland. London: 1846. V. 51; 52; 53
Practical Suggestions for the Reclamation of Waste Lands and Improvements in the Condition of the Agricultural Population of Ireland. London: 1845. V. 49

ROBINSON, DAVID M.
A Catalogue of the Greek Vases in the Royal Ontario Museum of Archaeology, Toronto. Toronto: 1930. V. 50
Excavations at Olynthus. Part IV: The Terracottas of Olynthus Found in 1928. Baltimore: 1936. V. 50; 52
Excavations at Olynthus. Part VIII: The Hellenic House. Baltimore: 1938. V. 50; 52
Excavations at Olynthus, Part X: Metal and Minor Miscellaneous Finds... Baltimore: 1941. V. 52

ROBINSON, DOANE
Encyclopedia of South Dakota. Pierre: 1925. V. 53
History of South Dakota. Chicago: 1930. V. 47
South Dakota Stressing the Unique and Dramatic in South Dakota History. Chicago: 1930. V. 52

ROBINSON, DR.
Magistrate's Pocket-Book; or an Epitome of the Duties and Practice of a Justice of the Peace, Out of Sessions. London: 1837. V. 52

ROBINSON, E.
Biblical Researches in Palestine, Mount Sinai and Arabia Petraea. London: 1841. V. 48

ROBINSON, E. A.
The Mite. Grimsby: 1891. V. 49

ROBINSON, E. S. G.
Catalogue of Greek Coins Collected by Godfrey Locker Lampson. London: 1923. V. 48
Catalogue of the Greek Coins of Cyrenaica. London: 1927. V. 48

ROBINSON, EDWARD
Calmet's Dictionary of the Holy Bible... Boston/New York: 1832. V. 54

ROBINSON, EDWIN ARLINGTON
Amaranth. New York: 1934. V. 54
Cavender's House. New York: 1929. V. 53; 54
Cavender's House. London: 1930. V. 51
The Children of the Night. Boston: 1897. V. 47; 48
Collected Poems. New York: 1921. V. 51
Collected Poems. Cambridge: 1927. V. 51
Collected Poems. New York: 1927. V. 49
Dionysus in Doubt. New York: 1925. V. 52
Fortvnatvs. Reno: 1928. V. 49
The Glory of the Nightingales. New York: 1930. V. 54
The Man Who Died Twice. New York: 1924. V. 54
Matthias at the Door. New York: 1931. V. 51
Merlin. New York: 1917. V. 48; 52
Modred. A Fragment. New York: 1929. V. 51
Roman Bartholomew. New York: 1923. V. 49; 51; 53; 54
Talifer. New York: 1933. V. 54
Thoreau's Last Letter, With a Note on His Correspondent, Myron B. Benton. Amenia: 1925. V. 48
The Torrent and the Night Before. Cambridge: 1896. V. 48; 54
The Torrent and the Night Before. Princeton: 1928. V. 54
Tristram. New York: 1927. V. 54

ROBINSON, ELISHA
Atlas of the City of Brooklyn, New York, Embracing All Territory Within Its Corporate Limits. New York: 1886. V. 49

ROBINSON, EMMA
Caesar Borgia; an Historical Romance. London: 1846. V. 47

ROBINSON, F.
The War of the Worlds. 1914. V. 48; 52

ROBINSON, F. J. G.
Eighteenth Century British Books: an Author Union Catalogue... London. V. 49
Eighteenth Century British Books, An Author Union Catalogue Extracted from the British Museum General Catalogue of Printed Books, the Catalogues of the Bodleian Library and of the University Library, Cambridge. Folkestone: 1981. V. 48; 49

ROBINSON, FAYETTE
An Account of the Organization of the Army of the United States... Philadelphia: 1848. V. 48; 53
Mexico and Her Military Chieftains... Philadelphia: 1847. V. 48

ROBINSON, FRANCIS KILDALE
A Glossary of Yorkshire Words and Phrases, Collected in Whitby and the Neighbourhood. London: 1855. V. 52

ROBINSON, FREDERICK WILLIAM
For Her Sake. London: 1869. V. 50
No Church. London: 1861. V. 50
Prison Characters Drawn from Life. London: 1866. V. 49
Wildflower. London: 1857. V. 50

ROBINSON, GEORGE
Travels in Palestine and Syria. Volume II (Syria). London: 1837. V. 48

ROBINSON, H. B.
Memoirs of Lt.-Gen. Sir Thomas Picton, Including His Correspondence. London: 1815. V. 50

ROBINSON, H. C.
The Birds of the Malay Peninsula. London: 1927-76. V. 47; 49

ROBINSON, H. CRABB
Diary, Reminiscences and Correspondence... London: 1869. V. 50; 51; 52; 54
Diary, Reminiscences and Correspondence. London: 1888. V. 51

ROBINSON, H. M.
The Great Fur Land or Sketches of Life in Hudson's Bay Territory. New York: 1879. V. 54
The Great Fur Land or Sketches of Life in the Hudson's Bay Territory. New York: 1882. V. 54

ROBINSON, H. P.
Pictorial Effect in Photography, Being Hints on Composition and Chiaroscuro for Photographers. Philadelphia: 1881. V. 47

ROBINSON, J. C.
Catalogue of the Works of Art Forming the Collection of Robert Napier of West Shandon, Dumbartonshire. London: 1865. V. 47
The Treasury of Ornamental Art... London: 1857. V. 51

ROBINSON, J. W.
Railroad and Steamboat Sketches, Between New York and Kansas. Philadelphia: 1857. V. 47

ROBINSON, JACOB
Wrestling and Wrestlers: Biographical Sketches and Celebrated Athletes of the Northern Ring... London: 1893. V. 50; 52

ROBINSON Jeffers: Ave Vale. San Francisco;: 1962. V. 52; 54

ROBINSON, JOHN
An Account of Sueden: Together with an Extract of the History of that Kingdom. London: 1711. V. 50; 52
An Account of Sweden. London: 1694. V. 50
Elements of Mechanical Philosophy, Being the Substance of a Course of Lectures on that Science. Edinburgh: 1804. V. 52
A Guide to the Lakes, in Cumberland, Westmorland and Lancashire... London: 1819. V. 50; 52; 54
Letter to Sir John Sinclair, Bart...5th April, 1794. London: 1794. V. 53
Whitney's Railroad to the Pacific. Washington: 1850. V. 47

ROBINSON, JOHN R.
The Life of Robert Coates, Better Known as 'Rome' and 'Diamond' Coates the Celebrated 'Amateur of Fashion'. London: 1891. V. 51
Old Q a Memoir of William Douglas, Fourth Duke of Queensberry, Kt. London: 1895. V. 54

ROBINSON, K. S.
Green Mars. London: 1993. V. 51
Green Mars. 1994. V. 54

ROBINSON, LEIGH
The South Before and At the Battle of the Wilderness. Richmond: 1878. V. 50

ROBINSON, LENNOX
The Cross Roads: a Play in a Prologue and Two Acts. 1911. V. 54
The Cross Roads: a Play in a Prologue and Two Acts. London: 1911. V. 51
The Irish Theatre. London: 1939. V. 53

ROBINSON, M. S.
A Pageant of the Sea, The MacPherson Collection of Maritime Prints and Drawings in the National Museum Greenwich. London: 1950. V. 50; 53; 54

ROBINSON, MARY
Lyrical Tales. London: 1800. V. 48; 49
Memoirs of... London: 1801. V. 53
Memoirs of... Philadelphia: 1802. V. 50
Memoirs of ... London: 1894. V. 53
Memoirs of... London: 1895. V. 48; 50
Poems. London: 1791. V. 53
Vancenza, or the Danger of Credulity. London: 1792. V. 54

ROBINSON, MATTHEW
Considerations on the Measures Carrying on with Respect to the British Colonies in North America. London: 1774. V. 47

ROBINSON, MERLE GREENE
The Sculpture of Palenque. Princeton: 1983-85. V. 47

ROBINSON, MORGAN P.
Virginia Counties: those Resulting from Virginia Legislation. Richmond: 1916. V. 54

ROBINSON, N.
Verses Upon Fourteen Different Occasions: Composed in Albany Gaol, in the Year 1768. Boston: 1773. V. 54

ROBINSON, P. F.
Designs for Farm Buildings. London: 1830. V. 51
Designs for Farm Buildings. London: 1837. V. 48
Designs for Gate Cottages, Lodges and Park Entrances, in Various Styles, from the Humblest to the Castellated. London: 1837. V. 48
Designs for Ornamental Villas. London: 1836. V. 52
Rural Architecture, or a Series of Designs for Ornamental Cottages. London: 1823. V. 53
Rural Architecture; or a Series of Designs for Ornamental Cottages. London: 1836. V. 49
Vitruvius Britannicus. History of Hardwicke Hall. London: 1835. V. 49
Vitruvius Britannicus. History of Hatfield House. London: 1833. V. 49
Vitruvius Britannicus. History of Woburn Abbey. (and) Hatfield House. London: 1827/33. V. 47

ROBINSON, PATRICK
Classic Lines. Birmingham: 1975. V. 47
Decade of Champions: the Greatest Years in the History of Thoroughbred Racing, 1970-1980. New York: 1980. V. 47

ROBINSON, PERCY J.
Toronto During the French Regime: the History of Toronto Region from Brule to Simcoe, 1615-1793. Toronto: 1933. V. 52

ROBINSON, PETER
Gallows View. Markham: 1987. V. 49
With Equal Eye. Toronto: 1979. V. 51

ROBINSON, R. W.
The Dog. Bedford: 1850. V. 51

ROBINSON, ROBERT
Bremers and Their Kin in Germany and Texas. Wichita Falls: 1977. V. 51; 52
Thomas Bewick His Life and Times. Newcastle-upon-Tyne: 1887. V. 48; 50; 51; 52

ROBINSON, ROWLAND EVANS
Forest and Stream Fables. New York: 1886. V. 48

ROBINSON, S.
Copyright Violation. 1990. V. 47
Facts for Farmers... New York: 1864/63. V. 50
Facts for Farmers; Also for the Family Circle. New York: 1864. V. 48; 52

ROBINSON, S. F. H.
Celtic Illuminative Art in the Gospel Books of Durrow, Lindisfarne & Kells. Dublin: 1908. V. 48

ROBINSON, S. G.
Tineid Genera of Australia. East Melbourne: 1993. V. 50

ROBINSON, SAMUEL
A Course of Fifteen Lectures, on Medical Botany... Columbus: 1829. V. 48

ROBINSON, SARA T. L.
Kansas: Its Interior and Exterior Life. Boston: 1856. V. 47

ROBINSON, SELMA
City Child. New York: 1931. V. 47; 54

ROBINSON: Some Account of the Family of Robinson of the White House, Appleby, Westmoreland. London: 1874. V. 52

ROBINSON, SUE ANN
Quercus Psalter. Washington: 1993. V. 53

ROBINSON, THOMAS
The Common Law of Kent; or the Customs of Gavelkind. London: 1741. V. 47
An Essay Towards a Natural History of Westmorland and Cumberland. London: 1707. V. 53
An Essay Towards a Natural History of Westmorland and Cumberland. London: 1709. V. 50; 52

ROBINSON, THOMAS ROMNEY
Juvenile Poems... Belfast: 1806. V. 48
Juvenile Poems...To Which is Prefixed, a Short Account of the Author... Belfast: 1807. V. 49

ROBINSON, TOM
The Longcase Clock. Suffolk: 1981. V. 53

ROBINSON, VICTOR
Encyclopaedia Sexualis: A Comprehensive Encyclopedia-Dictionary of the Sexual Sciences. New York: 1936. V. 50; 52
Pathfinders in Medicine. New York: 1929. V. 51; 53

ROBINSON, W.
Flora and Sylvia. London: 1903-04. V. 48
A Flying Trip to the Tropics. Cambridge: 1895. V. 51
The Parks and Gardens of Paris. London: 1878. V. 48

ROBINSON, W. HEATH
Absurdities A Book of Collected Drawings. London: 1934. V. 48
The Adventures of Uncle Lubin. London: 1902. V. 47
The Adventures of Uncle Lubin. London: 1934. V. 50
Bill the Minder. London: 1912. V. 48; 49; 54
Book of Goblins. London. V. 48
Hunlikely. London: 1916. V. 47; 49
Railway Ribaldry. London: 1935. V. 49; 51
Some "Frightful" War Pictures. London: 1915. V. 48; 50
Then and Now. Manchester: 1921. V. 49

ROBINSON, W. R.
Guide to Richmond: Comprising Historical and Descriptive Notices of the Castle, Monastic Remains, Walks, View, &c. Richmond: 1833. V. 47; 53

ROBINSON, W. W.
The Indians of Los Angeles: Story of the Liquidation of a People. Los Angeles: 1952. V. 50
Land in California. Berkeley & Los Angeles: 1948. V. 48; 53
The Malibu. Los Angeles: 1958. V. 53; 54
Ranchos Become Cities. Pasadena: 1939. V. 51; 52
Tarnished Angels: Paradisical Turpitude in Los Angeles. Los Angeles: 1964. V. 51

ROBINSON, WILLIAM
The English Flower Garden. London: 1883. V. 54
Friends of Half a Century: Fifty Memorials with Portraits of Members of the Society of friends, 1840-1890. London: 1891. V. 49
Gleanings from French Gardens. London: 1869. V. 54
The Histories and Antiquities the Parish of Tottenham. London: 1840. V. 47; 51; 53
The Parks and Gardens of Paris. London: 1878. V. 52
The Parks Promenades and Gardens of Paris... London: 1869. V. 49

ROBINSON, WILLIAM DAVIS
Memoirs of the Mexican Revolution... Philadelphia: 1820. V. 47; 50

ROBINSON, WILLIAM HENRY
The Story of Arizona. Story. Phoenix: 1919. V. 47

ROBINSON, WILLIAM MORRISON
The Confederate Privateers. New Haven: 1928. V. 47

ROBINSON, WILLIAM WILCOX
Maps of Los Angeles: From Ord's Survey of 1849 to the End of the Boom of the Eighties. Los Angeles: 1966. V. 47

ROBINSON'S Atlas of Essex County, New Jersey. New York: 1890. V. 47

ROBISON, JOHN
Proofs of a Conspiracy Against All the Religions and Governments of Europe, Carried On In the Secret Meetings of Free Masons, Illuminati and Reading Socieities. Edinburgh: 1797. V. 50
A System of Mechanical Philosophy. Edinburgh: 1822. V. 48

ROBLES, ANTONIO DE
Resguardo Contra el Olvido, en el Breve Compendio de la Vida Admirable, y Virtudes Heroycas del Illmo. Mexico: 1757. V. 48

ROBLES DOMINGUEZ DE MAZARIEGOS, MARIANO
Memoria Historica de la Provincia de Chiapa, Una de las de Guatemala, Presentada al Augusto Congeso. Cadiz: 1813. V. 48

ROBSJOHN-GIBBINGS, T. H.
Furniture of Classical Greece. New York: 1963. V. 52

ROBSON, A. W. MAYO
Cancer of the Stomach. New York: 1907. V. 49; 54

ROBSON, ALBERT H.
Canadian Landscape Painters. London: 1932. V. 50
Canadian Landscape Painters. Toronto: 1932. V. 53; 54

ROBSON, ARTHUR H.
A. Y. Jackson. Toronto: 1938. V. 47
Tom Thompson. Toronto: 1937. V. 47

ROBSON, EDWARD ROBERT
School Architecture. London: 1874. V. 48

ROBSON, G. C.
Monograph of Recent Cephalopoda, Based on Collections in the British Museum. London: 1929-32. V. 49

ROBSON, GEORGE FENNELL
Scenery of the Grampian Mountains. London: 1814. V. 52; 54

ROBSON, ISABEL S.
Two Lady Missionaries in Tibet. London: 1909. V. 54

ROBSON, JAMES, & CO.
A Catalogue, &c. London: 1775-76. V. 49

ROBSON, JOHN S.
How a One-Legged Rebel Lives. Charlottesville: 1888. V. 49
How a One-Legged Rebel Lives. Charlottesville: 1891. V. 49

ROBSON, JOSEPH
An Account of Six Years Residence in Hudson's Bay, from 1733-1736 and 1744-47. London: 1752. V. 51

ROBSON, STEPHEN
The British Flora. York: 1777. V. 54
The British Flora. York: 1778. V. 49

ROBSON, THOMAS
The British Herald, or Cabinet of Armorial Bearings of the Nobility and Gentry of Great Britain and Ireland, from the Earliest to the Present Time... Sunderland: 1830. V. 50

ROBSON, WILLIAM
Grammigraphia; or the Grammar of Drawing. London: 1799. V. 53

ROBY, JOHN
Jokeby, a Burlesque on Rokeby, a Poem. London: 1813. V. 53
Popular Traditions of Lancashire. London: 1843. V. 48

ROCHAS, HENRICUS DE
Traicte des Observations Nouvelles et Vraye Cognoissance des Eaux Minerales & de Leurs Qualitez & Vertus... Paris: 1634. V. 54

ROCHDALE EQUITABLE PIONEERS SOCIETY
Catalogue of the Library. Rochdale,: 1868. V. 54

ROCHE, HARRIET A.
On Trek, in the Transvaal; or, Over Berg and Veldt in South Africa. London: 1878. V. 53; 54

ROCHE, JAMES JEFFREY
John Boyle O'Reilly. His Life and Poems and Speeches... New York: 1891. V. 53
Life of John Boyle O'Reilly. Philadelphia: 1891. V. 51
Story of the Filibusters. London/New York: 1891. V. 48; 50

ROCHE, REGINA MARIA
Bridal of Dunamore; and Lost and Won. London: 1823. V. 50
The Children of the Abbey. London: 1798. V. 48
The Children of the Abbey. Paris: 1807. V. 47
The Children of the Abbey. London: 1835. V. 50
Contrast. London: 1828. V. 47
The Discarded Son; or, Haunt of the Banditti: a Tale. London: 1825. V. 50

ROCHEFORT, CHARLES CESAR DE
The History of the Barbados St. Christophers, Mevis, St. Vincents, Antego, Martinico, Monserrat and the Rest of the Carribby-Islands. London: 1666. V. 47

ROCHESTER, JOHN WILMOT, 2ND EARL OF
Collected Works. London: 1926. V. 48; 50
The Works. London: 1714. V. 48

ROCHFORT, EDITH
The Lloyds of Ballymore. A Story of Irish Life. London: 1890. V. 50

ROCHON, ALEXIS MARIE DE
A Voyage to Madagascar, and the East Indies... London: 1792. V. 54

ROCK, JAMES L.
Southern and Western Texas Guide for 1878. St. Louis: 1878. V. 47; 54

ROCK-A-Bye Baby. New York: 1916. V. 54

ROCKEFELLER, MICHAEL CLARK
The Journal of Michael Clark Rockefeller. 1966. V. 51

ROCKER, RUDOLF
The Tragedy of Spain. New York: 1937. V. 49

ROCKER SILVER MINING CO.
Prospectus of the Rocker Silver Mining Company, Jefferson Co., Montana... New York: 1879. V. 50

ROCKET PRESS
Rocket Ephemera. Steventon: 1996. V. 54

ROCKFELLOW, JOHN ALEXANDER
Log of an Arizona Trail Blazer. Tucson: 1933. V. 51; 53

ROCKHILL, WILLIAM WOODVILLE
The Land of the Lamas. Notes of a Journey through Cina, Mongolia and Tibet. New York: 1891. V. 48

ROCKWELL, A.
Lectures on Electricity (Dynamic and Franklinic) in Its Relations to Medicine and Surgery. New York: 1881. V. 54

ROCKWELL, CHARLES
Sketches of Foreign Travel and Life at Sea... Boston: 1842. V. 49

ROCKWELL, JOHN A.
Canal Or Railroad Between the Atlantic and Pacific Oceans. Washington: 1849. V. 47
A Compilation of Spanish and Mexican Law, in Relation to Mines, and Titles to Real Estate, in Force in California, Texas and New Mexico. New York: 1851. V. 47; 52; 53
States vs. Territories. A True Solution of the Territorial Question by an Old Line Whig. Washington: 1860. V. 49

ROCKWELL, MOLLY
Willie Was Different: the Tale of an Ugy Thrushling. New York: 1969. V. 52

ROCKWELL, NORMAN
My Adventures as An Illustrator. Garden City: 1960. V. 47; 48; 49; 50
Willie Was Different. New York: 1969. V. 52; 53

ROCKWELL, THOMAS
Norman Rockwell's Hometown. New York: 1970. V. 49

THE ROCKY Mountain Directory and Colorado Gazetteer, for 1871. Denver: 1870. V. 48; 49; 54

ROCKY Mountain Scenery...Along the Line of the Denver and Rio Grande Railroad. New York: 1888. V. 52

ROCKY Mountain Views on Canadian Pacific Railway. West Selkirk. V. 48

ROCOLES, JEAN BAPTISTE DE
Les Imposteurs Insignes. Amsterdam: 1683. V. 48; 49

ROCQUE, JOHN
A New and Accurate Survey of the Cities of London and Westmisnter, the Borough of Southwark, with the Country About It. London: 1748. V. 47
A Plan of the Cities of London and Westminster and Borough of Southwark with the Continuous Buildings, from an Actual Survey Taken by John Rocque... V. 52
A Plan of the Cities of London and Westminster and Borough of Southwark...(with) An Alphabetical Index of the Streets, Squares, Lanes, Alleys... London: 1746-47. V. 47; 49
A Topographical Survey of the County of Berks(hire) in Eighteen Sheets. London: 1761. V. 54

A ROD For Rome, or, a Description of the Popish Clergy: Their Popes, Cardinals, Monks, Fryers, &c. In Their Proper Colours. London: 1679. V. 47

A ROD for Tunbridge Beaus, Bundl'd Up at the Request of the Tunbridge Ladies. London: 1701. V. 48

RODAKOWSKI, ERNEST DE
The Channel Ferry. Advantages and Feasibility of a Train-Ferry Between England and France. London: 1905. V. 48; 51

RODD, RENNELL
Bulletin of the Keats-Shelley memorial Rome. 1910-13. V. 49
The Princes of Achaia and the Chronicles of Morea. London: 1907. V. 49
Rose Leaf and Apple Leaf. Philadelphia: 1882. V. 52

RODDENBERRY, GENE
Star Trek. 1979. V. 52; 53

RODDIS, LOUIS
A Short History of Nautical Medicine. New York: 1941. V. 52

RODEN, CLAUDIA
A Book of Middle Eastern Food. London: 1968. V. 49

RODGERS, H. J.
Twenty-Three Years Under a Sky-Light, or Life and Experiences of a Photographer. Hartford: 1872. V. 48; 54
Twenty-Three Years Under a Sky-Light or Life and Experiences of a Photographer. Hartford: 1873. V. 51

RODGERS, RICHARD
Me and Juliet. New York: 1953. V. 54
Six Plays by Rodgers and Hammerstein. New York: 1955. V. 54

RODIN, AUGUSTE
Cathedrals of France and Later Drawings. Boston: 1965. V. 48

RODITI, EDOUARD
New Old and New Testaments. New York: 1983. V. 54
Orphic Love. New York: 1986. V. 52; 53; 54
Poems 1928-1948. Norfolk: 1949. V. 49
Poems for M. Paris: 1935. V. 48; 50
Thrice Chosen. Santa Barbara: 1981. V. 48

RODKER, JOHN
Adolphe 1920. 1929. V. 51
Dartmoor. Paris: 1926. V. 53
Hymns. London: 1920. V. 47
Memoirs of Other Fronts. London: 1932. V. 47

RODMAN, SELDEN
Horace Pippin: a Negro Painter in America. New York: 1947. V. 52
The Poetry of Flight: an Anthology. New York: 1941. V. 52

RODMAN, WILLIAM
Diseases of the Breast with Special Reference to Cancer. Philadelphia: 1908. V. 54

RODNEY, GEORGE BRYDGES
As a Cavalryman Remembers. Caldwell: 1944. V. 54

RODNEY, JANET
The Forest. Mt. Horeb: 1978. V. 49

RODOCANACHI, C. P.
Forever Ulysses. New York: 1938. V. 50; 51; 53

RODOREDA, MERCE
Two Tales. New York: 1983. V. 54

RODRIGO, LUIS CARLOS
Picasso in His Posters. Madrid: 1992. V. 50

RODRIGUES, J. C.
Bibliotheca Brasiliense. Catalogo Annotado dos Livros Sobre o Brasil e de Alguns Autographos e Manuscriptos Pertencentes a... New York: 1966. V. 47

RODRIGUES DE MATTOS, ANDRE
Dialogo Funebre Entre o Reyno de Portugal, e o Rio Tejo, Glosando o Famoso Soneto, Fermoso Tejo Meu, Quam Differente... Lisbon: 1690. V. 53

RODRIGUEZ, ANTONIO
A History of Mexican Mural Painting. London: 1969. V. 49

RODRIGUEZ, CHRISTOVAL
Bibliotheca Universal de la Polygraphia Espanola... Madrid: 1738. V. 53

RODRIGUEZ DE CASTRO, JOSE
Biblioteca Espanola. Madrid: 1781. V. 47

RODRIGUEZ DE ROBLES, ANTONIO
Senor. Antonio rodriguez de Robles Dize, Que aun Que en el Real consejo de las Indias se ha Tratado Sobre Auer de ser Renunciables los Officios de Pluma de la Nueua Espana... 1606?. V. 48

RODRIGUEZ DE SAN MIGUEL, JUAN
Documentos Relativos al Piadoso Fondo de Missiones para Conversion y Civilizacion de las Numerosas Tribus Barbaras de la Antigua y Nueva California. Mexico: 1845. V. 48; 49

RODWAY, L.
The Tasmanian Flora. Hobart: 1903. V. 53

RODWELL, ANNE
The Juvenile Pianist, or a Mirror of Music for Infant Minds. London: 1836. V. 49

RODWELL, G. F.
South by East: Notes of Travel in Southern Europe. London: 1877. V. 47; 51

RODWELL, GEORGE HERBERT
The Memoirs of an Umbrella. London: 1845. V. 52
Old London Bridge, a Romance of the Sixteenth Century. London: 1860. V. 50; 52

RODWELL, HERBERT
The First Rudiments of Harmony. London: 1830. V. 49

RODWELL, J. S.
British Plant Communities. Volume I: Woodlands and Scrub. London: 1991. V. 48

RODWELL, JAMES
Queen Cora; or, Slavery and Its Downfall. London: 1856. V. 49

ROE, F. GORDON
Cox The Master, The Life and Art of David Cox: (1783-1859). Leigh-on-Sea: 1946. V. 50
The North American Buffalo. Toronto: 1951. V. 52
The North American Buffalo: a Critical Study of the Species in Its Wild State. Toronto: 1972. V. 53
Sea Painters of Britain. Leigh-on-Sea: 1947-48. V. 50; 54
Sporting Prints of the Eighteenth and Early Nineteenth Centuries. New York: 1927. V. 53

ROE, FRANCIS M.
Army Letters from a Officer's Wife, 1871-1888. New York: 1909. V. 47; 50; 52; 54

ROE, P. F.
Poems: Characteristic, Itinerary and Miscellaneous. London: 1868. V. 49

ROE, THOMAS
Sir Thomas Rowe His Speech at the Councell-Table Touching Brasse-Money, or Against Brasse Money... London: 1641. V. 52

ROEBLING, W. A.
Pneumatic Tower Foundations of the East River Suspension Bridge. New York: 1872. V. 51

ROEBUCK, CARL
Ionian Trade and Colonization. New York: 1959. V. 50; 52

ROEBUCK, JOHN ARTHUR
The Colonies of England: a Plan for the Government of Some Portion of Our Colonial Possessions. London: 1849. V. 50
History of the Whig Ministry of 1830, to the Passing of the Reform Bill. London: 1852. V. 51

ROEDER, GUNTHER
Agyptische Bronzewerke. Gluckstadt: 1937. V. 49

ROEMER, F.
Fauna Arctica. Jena: 1900-32. V. 48

ROEMER, FERDINAND
Texas. San Antonio: 1935. V. 50
Texas. Mit Besonderer Rucksicht auf Deutsche Auswanderung... Bonn: 1849. V. 49

ROEMER, J. J.
Genera Insectorum Linnaei et Fabricii Iconibus Illustrata. Wintherur: 1789. V. 53; 54

ROENTGEN, WILHELM
Eine Neue Art Von Strahlen. Wurzburg: 1896. V. 47; 48; 50

ROERICH, GEORGE N.
Trails to Inmost Asia, Five Years of Exploration with the Roerich Central Asian Expedition. New Haven: 1931. V. 49

ROESEL VON ROSENHOF, A. S.
Historia Naturalis Ranarum Nostratium... Nuremberg: 1758. V. 49

ROESLER, HUGO
Atlas of Cardio-Roentgenology. Springfield: 1940. V. 54

ROESLIN, EUCHARIUS
The Birth of Mankinde, Othervvise Named the Womans Booke. London: 1634. V. 49
The Birth of Mankinde, Otherwyse Named the VVoman's Booke. London: 1598. V. 49; 50
De Partu Hominis, et Qua Circa Ipsum Accidunt. Venice: 1536. V. 51; 53

ROESSLE, THEOPHILUS
Roessle's Gardener's Hand-Books. No. 1. How to Cultivate and Preserve Celery. Albany: 1860. V. 52

ROETHEL, H. K.
Kandinsky: Catalogue Raisonne of the Oil Paintings. London: 1982. V. 51; 53; 54

ROETHER, SUSAN
Reflections on Color. San Francisco: 1982. V. 49

ROETHKE, THEODORE
I Am! Says the Lamb. Garden City: 1961. V. 49; 53
The Lost Son and Other Poems. Garden City: 1948. V. 48; 53
The Lost Son and Other Poems. London: 1949. V. 48
Open House. New York: 1941. V. 47; 48; 49; 51; 52; 53
The Poetry of Louise Bogan. 1961. V. 54
Praise to the End!. New York: 1951. V. 50; 51; 52
Sequence Sometimes Metaphysical Poems. Iowa City: 1963. V. 51; 53; 54
The Waking. Garden City: 1953. V. 54
The Waking. New York: 1953. V. 52
Words for the Wind. London: 1957. V. 47; 51
Words for the Wind. Garden City: 1958. V. 54
Words For the Wind. New York: 1958. V. 47; 48

ROETHLISBERGER, BIANCO
Cavalier Pietro Tempesta and His Time. 1970. V. 52
Claude Lorrain, the Drawings. Berkeley: 1968. V. 47; 50; 51; 53; 54

ROFF, JOE T.
A Brief History of Early Days in Northern Texas and the Indian Territory. 1930. V. 54

ROGER, OF HOVEDEN
Chronica. London: 1868-71. V. 49; 52

ROGER, OF WENDOVER
The Flowers of History from 1154; Flores Histoiarum (1154-1235). London: 1886-89. V. 49; 52

ROGER-MARX, CLAUDE
Variations. Drawings, Water-Colors, Etchings and Lithographs. Greenwich: 1961. V. 52

ROGERS, AMMI
Memoirs of the Rev. Ammi Rogers, A.M., a Clergyman of the Episcopal Church, Educated at Yale College in Connecticut, Ordained in Trinity Church in the City of New York. Schenectady: 1826. V. 51

ROGERS, ARTEMAS
Trial of Daniel Davis Farmer, for the Murder of the widow Anna Ayer, at Toffstown, on the 4th of April, 1821. Concord: 1821. V. 51

ROGERS, BRUCE
An Account of the Making of the Oxford Lectern Bible. London: 1936. V. 53
Books. What They Represent to Some of Those Who Have Written, Read and Loved Them. 1945. V. 54
Golden Years. A Sonnet Sequence. Mount Vernon: 1924. V. 51
The Last Letter, A Story of the Museum Press. Locust Valley: 1975. V. 47
Paragraphs on Printing Elicited from Bruce Rogers in Talks with James Hendrickson on the Functions of the Book Designer. New York: 1943. V. 47; 51
Report on the Typography of the Cambridge University Press, Prepared in 1917 at the Request of the Syndics by Bruce Rogers and Now Printed in Honour of His Eightieth brithday. Cambridge: 1950. V. 47
Typographical Partnership: Ten Letters Between Bruce Rogers and Emery Walker 1907-31. Cambridge: 1971. V. 54

ROGERS, CHARLES
Boswelliana. The Commonplace Book of James Boswell. London: 1874. V. 53

ROGERS, DANIEL
Naaman the Syrian His Disease and Cure. London: 1642. V. 48

ROGERS, EBENEZER PLATT
Daniel Webster. A Discourse Pronounced in the First Presbyterian Church in Augusta, Sunday Evening November 28th, 1852. Augusta: 1853. V. 49

ROGERS, FAIRMAN
A Manual of Coaching. London: 1900. V. 47
A Manual of Coaching. Philadelphia: 1900. V. 50; 54
A Manual of Coaching. New York & London: 1901. V. 47

ROGERS, FRANCIS
The Law and Practice of Elections with Analytical Tables... London: 1820. V. 52
List of the Editions of the Libro del Infante Dom Pedro de Portugal. Lisbon: 1959. V. 47

ROGERS, FRED BLACKBURN
Soldiers of the Overland. San Francisco: 1938. V. 47; 51
William Brown Ide, Bear Flagger. San Francisco. V. 48

ROGERS, G. ALBERT, MRS.
A Winter in Algeria 1863-64. London: 1865. V. 49

ROGERS, GEORGE
My Adopted Country: a Poem... New York: 1851. V. 49

ROGERS, HENRY
Essays, Selected From Contributions to the Edinburgh Review. London: 1850. V. 54

ROGERS, HENRY J.
Rogers and Black's American Semaphoric Signal Book for the Use of Vessels Employed in the United States Naval, Revenue and Merchant Service. Baltimore: 1847. V. 51

ROGERS, HOWELL
Voyager's Medical Companion. Norwich: 1847. V. 50

ROGERS, J. B.
War Pictures. Experiences and Observataions of a Chaplain in the U.S. Army in the War of the Southern Rebellion. Chicago: 1863. V. 52

ROGERS, J. SMYTH
Catalogue of a Cabinet of Materia Medica. New York: 1826. V. 48

ROGERS, JAMES EDWIN THOROLD
Cobden and Modern Political Opinion. Essays on Certain Political Topics. London: 1873. V. 49; 52
Six Centuries of Work and Wages. London: 1884. V. 52

ROGERS, JASPER W.
Letter to the Landlords and Ratepayers of Ireland, Detailing means for the Permanent and Profitble Employment of the Peasantry, Without Ultimate Cost to the Land or the Nation... London: 1846. V. 52

ROGERS, JOHN GODFREY
Sport in Vancouver and Newfoundland. Toronto: 1912. V. 52

ROGERS, JOHN R.
The Inalienable Rights of Man. Olympia: 1900. V. 48

ROGERS, JOHN WILLIAM
Finding Literature on the Texas Plains. Dallas: 1931. V. 47; 48; 52; 54

ROGERS, JUSTUS H.
Colusa County: Its History Traced from a State of Nature Through the Early Period of Settlement and Development, to the Present Day with a Description of its Resources... Orland: 1891. V. 49; 50

ROGERS, MARY ELIZA
Domestic Life in Palestine. London: 1862. V. 54

ROGERS, MEYRIC R.
Carl Milles: an Interpretation of His Work. New Haven: 1940. V. 47; 48; 49; 50; 52
Carl Milles: an Interpretation of His Work. New Haven: 1948. V. 51

ROGERS, R. A.
The Lonely Island. London: 1926. V. 48

ROGERS, RICHARD
Carousel. New York: 1946. V. 51

ROGERS, ROBERT
A Concise Account of North America: Containing a Description of Several British Colonies on that Continent...the Interior or Westerly Parts of that Country, Upon the Rivers St. Laurence, the Mississippi, Christino, and the Great Lakes. London: 1765. V. 47; 48; 54
Journals of Major Robert Rogers: Containing an Account of the Several Excursions He Made Under the Generals Who Commanded Upon the Continent of North America, During the Late War. London: 1765. V. 52; 53

ROGERS, SAMUEL
Human Life, a Poem. London: 1819. V. 47; 49; 50; 51
Italy, a Poem. London: 1823. V. 51
Italy, a Poem. London: 1830. V. 48
Italy, a Poem. London: 1830/34. V. 48; 53
Italy, a Poem. London: 1838. V. 49
Italy, a Poem. London: 1844. V. 52
The Pleasures of Memory. London: 1793. V. 48
The Pleasures of Memory. London: 1795. V. 53
The Pleasures of Memory. London: 1875. V. 47; 48
Poems. London: 1812. V. 53
Poems. London: 1822. V. 51
Poems. London: 1834. V. 48; 49; 50; 53; 54
Poems. London: 1838. V. 51
Poems. (with) Italy, a Poem. London: 1839/40. V. 52
Recollections of (His) Table-Talk. New Southgate: 1887. V. 53
The Voyage of Columbus. London: 1810?. V. 49

ROGERS, THOMAS
The Faith, Doctrine and Religion, Professed and protected in the Realme of England and Dominions of Same, Expressed in Thirty Nine Articles. London: 1625. V. 50

ROGERS, W. H.
Records of the Cheriton Otter Hounds. Taunton; Somerset: 1925. V. 47

ROGERS, W. H. HAMILTON
The Antient Sepulchral Efigies and Monumental and memorial Sculpture of Devon. Exeter: 1877. V. 48

ROGERS, WILL
Ether and Me. New York: 1929. V. 53
How We Elect Our Presidents. Boston: 1952. V. 53
Letters of a Self-Made Diplomat to His President. New York: 1926. V. 53

ROGERS, WOODES
A Cruising voyage Round the World; First to the South-Seas, Thence to the East-Indies, and Homewards by the Cape of Good Hope. London: 1712. V. 48; 50; 52

ROGERSON, IAN
Agnes Miller Parker: Wood Engraver and Book Illustrator 1895-1980. Wakefield: 1990. V. 47; 48; 49; 50; 52; 54
Agnes Miller Parker: Wood Engravings from the Fables of Esope; the Story of a Remarkable Book. 1996. V. 54

ROGERSON, JOHN BOLTON
A Voice from the Town and Other Poems. London: 1842. V. 51; 54

ROGERSON, SIDNEY
Both Sides of the Road. London: 1949. V. 54
Our Bird Book. London: 1947. V. 51

ROGER WILLIAMS BANK, PROVIDENCE
The Charter of the Roger Williams Bank, in Providence. Providence: 1803. V. 54

ROGET, PETER MARK
Animal and Vegetable Physiology Considered with Reference to Natural Theology. London: 1834. V. 49; 51
Thesaurus of English Words, So Classified and Arranged As to Facilitate the Expression of Ideas and Assist in Literary Ideas. Boston: 1854. V. 54

ROGOZHIN, V. N.
V. S. Sopikov. An Essay in Russian Bibliography, or a Complete Dictionary of Works Printed in the Church Slavonic & Russian Language from the Introduction of Printing to the Year 1813. London: 1962. V. 48

ROH, F.
Foto Auge/Oeil Et Photo/Photo Eye. Stuttgart: 1929. V. 52

ROH, FRANZ
German Art in the 20th Century. 1968. V. 48; 50; 51; 53; 54

ROHDE, ELEANOUR SINCLAIR
Herbs and Herb Gardening. London: 1936. V. 54
The Old English Gardening Books... London: 1924. V. 49; 52; 54
The Old English Herbals. London: 1922. V. 50; 52; 53; 54
Oxford's College Gardens. London: 1932. V. 54

ROHE, GEORGE
A Text-Book of Hygiene. Baltimore: 1885. V. 49; 51; 54

ROHEIM, GEZA
Animism, Magic and the Divine King. New York: 1930. V. 52
Australian Totemism. London: 1925. V. 52
The Eternal Ones of the Dream. New York: 1945. V. 48; 52

ROHLEDER, H.
Test Tube Babies. 1934. V. 48; 52

ROHLFS, ANNA KATHARINE GREEN
Marked "Personal". New York: 1893. V. 52

ROHLFS, GERHARD
Adventures in Morocco and Journeys through the Oases of Draa and Tafilet... London: 1874. V. 51; 54

ROHMER, SAX
The Bat Flies Low. Garaden City: 1935. V. 48
Bim-Bashi Baruk of Egypt. New York: 1944. V. 47; 48; 49; 53; 54
Daughter of Fu Manchu. Garden City: 1931. V. 47
The Day the World Ended. New York: 1945. V. 53
Dope. 1919. V. 48
The Drums of Fu Manchu. Garden City: 1939. V. 50; 53
Fu Manchu's Bride. 1933. V. 54
The Insidious Dr. Fu-Manchu. New York: 1913. V. 47
The Island of Fu Manchu. Garden City: 1941. V. 53
The Mask of Fu Manchu. 1932,. V. 49
President Fu Manchu. Garden City: 1936. V. 50; 53; 54
The Return of Dr. Fu-Manchu. New York: 1916. V. 51; 52; 53
She Who Sleeps. Garden City: 1928. V. 47
The Trail of Fu Manchu. Garden City: 1934. V. 53

ROHR, JULIUS BERNHARD
...Neuer Moralischer Tractat Von der Liebe Gegen die Personen Andern Geschlechts, Darinnent so Wohl Uberhaupt Die Regeln der Klugheit so Bey Liebes-Affairen Vorzukommen Pflegen, Vorgestellet Werden... Leipzig: 1717. V. 52

ROJANKOVSKY, FEODOR
Daniel Boone Historic Adventures of an American Hunter Among the Indians. Paris: 1931. V. 47

ROKITANSKY, CARL
A Manual of Pathological Anatomy. London: 1854. V. 54
A Manual of Pathology Anatomy. London: 1849-54. V. 47

ROLAND, CHARLES P.
Albert Sidney Johnston: Soldier of Three Republics. Austin: 1964. V. 47

ROLAND, GEORGE
An Introductory Course of Fencing. Edinburgh: 1837. V. 51; 54
A Treatise on the Theory and Practice of the Art of Fencing. London: 1824. V. 51

ROLAND, JEANNE MARIE PHILIPON
Works. London: 1796-1800. V. 48

ROLAND, JEREMY
Gathering the Decade. San Francisco: 1972. V. 51

ROLEWINCK, WERNER
Fasciculus Temporum. Strassburg: 1490. V. 52

ROLFE, FREDERICK WILLIAM
The Armed Hands and Other Stories and Pieces. London: 1974. V. 54
The Cardinal Perfect of Propaganda and Other Stories. London: 1957. V. 53
Chronicles of the House of Borgia. 1901. V. 54
Chronicles of the House of Borgia. London: 1901. V. 52
Chronicles of the House of Borgia. New York: 1901. V. 48
Collected Poems. London: 1974. V. 49
The Desire and Pursuit of the Whole. London: 1934. V. 47; 48; 50; 51; 54
Don Renato: an Ideal Content. London: 1963. V. 48; 52
Hubert's Arthur. London: 1935. V. 47; 54
In His Own Image. London & New York: 1901. V. 47; 51; 54
In His Own Image. London: 1902. V. 48
In His Own Image. New York: 1925. V. 49
Letters to C. H. C. Pirie Gordon,...to Leonard Moore, ... to R. M. Dawkins. London: 1959-62. V. 50
Letters to C. H. C. Pirie Gordon...to Leonard Moore...to R.M. Dawkins. 1959-62. V. 52
Letters to C. H. C. Pirie-Gordon. London: 1959. V. 54
Letters to Grant Richards. Berkshire: 1952. V. 48
Letters to Harry Bainbridge. London: 1977. V. 53
Letters to James Walsh. London: 1972. V. 53
Nicholas Crabbe or the One and the Many. London: 1960. V. 47; 48; 54
Stories Toto Told Me. London: 1898. V. 51
Tarcissus; the Boy Martyr of Rome, in the Diocletian Persecution. Saffron Walden: 1880. V. 47
Three Tales of Venice. London: 1950. V. 49
The Weird of the Wanderer. London: 1912. V. 51
Without Prejudice. London: 1963. V. 48; 51; 53

ROLFE, JOHN
A True Relation of the State of Virginia Left by Sir Thomas Dale Knight in May Last 1616. London: 1951. V. 47
A True Relation of the State of Virginia lefte by Sir Thomas Dale Knight in May Last 1616. New Haven: 1951. V. 48

ROLLAND, R.
The Revolt of the Machines or Invention Run Wild. 1932. V. 48; 52

ROLLAND, SANDY
Raffles His Sons and Daughters. Burlington: 1974. V. 54

ROLLE, HENRY
Un Abridgment des Plusieurs Cases et Resolutions del Common Ley... London: 1668. V. 47

ROLLESTON, C. W.
Parsifal, or the Legend of the Holy Grail. New York: 1912. V. 54

ROLLESTON, H. D.
Diseases of the Liver, Gall-Bladder and Bile Ducts. Philadelphia: 1905. V. 50

ROLLESTON, HUMPHRY
Cardio-Vascular Diseases Since Harvey's Discovery. Cambridge: 1928. V. 50; 52
The Endocrine Organs in Health and Disease with an Historical Review. London: 1936. V. 50

ROLLESTON, HUMPHRY continued
Some Medical Aspects of Old Age. London: 1922. V. 50; 52; 54

ROLLESTON, J. D.
The History of the Acute Exanthemata. London: 1937. V. 51

ROLLESTON, SAMUEL
Oinos Krithinos. Oxford: 1750. V. 53

ROLLESTON, THOMAS WILLIAM HAZEN
Lohengrin. London: 1913. V. 48
Parsifal, or the Legend of the Holy Grail. London: 1912. V. 48; 53

ROLLEY, CLAUDE
Greek Bronzes. London: 1986. V. 52

ROLLIN, CHARLES
The Ancient History of the Egyptians, Carthaginians, Assyrians, Babylonians, Medes & Persians, Grecians & Macedonians. London: 1800. V. 48
The Ancient History, The Roman History and Belles Lettres. London: 1768-69. V. 48; 51; 53
The Method of Teaching and Studying the Belles Letters, or an Introduction to Languages, Poetry, Rhetoric, History, Moral Philosophy, Physicks, &c. London: 1749. V. 50
The Method of Teaching and Studying the Belles Lettres; or, an Introduction to Languages, Poetry, Rheotric, History, Moral, Philosophy, Physics... Dublin: 1778. V. 52
New Thoughts Concerning Education. Done From the French, with Notes. London: 1735. V. 53

ROLLIN, M.
The Ancient History of the Egyptians, Assyrians, Babylonians, Medes and Persians, Grecians, and Macedonians. London: 1851. V. 51

ROLLINS, CHARLEMAE
Christmas Gif'. Chicago: 1963. V. 51

ROLLINS, HYDER E.
Cavalier and Puritan Ballads and Broadsides Illustrating the Period of the Great Rebellion 1640-1660. New York: 1923. V. 49
Tottel's Miscellany 1557-1587. 1928-29. V. 50

ROLLINS, PHILIP A.
The Discovery of the Oregon Trail, Robert Stuarts Narratives. New York: 1935. V. 51
Robert Stuart's Narrative. The Discovery of the Oregon Trail. New York: 1935. V. 47

ROLLO, W. K.
Fly Fishing in Northern Streams. London: 1924. V. 53

ROLLOCK, ROBERT
Lectures Upon the Epistle of Paul to the Colossians. London: 1603. V. 48; 52

ROLPH, J. ALEXANDER
Dylan Thomas: a Bibliography. London: 1956. V. 53

ROLPH, THOMAS
A Brief Account, Together with Observations, Made During a Visit in the West Indies, and a Tour through the United States of America, In Parts of the Years 1832-33. Dundas: 1836. V. 54

ROLT, L. T. C.
High Horse Riderless. London: 1947. V. 50
Mariners' Market. Liverpool: 1961. V. 50

ROLT, RICHARD
A New and Accurate History of South-America, Containing a Particular Account of Some Accidents leading to the Discovery of the New World. London: 1756. V. 48
A New History of France, by Question and Answer. London: 1754. V. 54

ROMAINS, JULES
Stefan Zweig - Great European. New York: 1941. V. 54

ROMAN, ALFRED
The Military Operations of General Beauregard in the War Between the States 1861 to 1865. New York: 1844. V. 49
The Military Operations of General Beauregard in the War Between the States 1861 to 1865 Including a Brief Personal Sketch and a Narrative of His Services in the War with Mexico, 1846-48. New York: 1884. V. 47; 50

ROMAN, C. V.
American Civilization and the Negro, the Afro-american in Relation to national progress. Philadelphia: 1916. V. 50
American Civilization and the Negro: The Afro-American in Relation to National Progress. Philadelphia: 1921. V. 54

A ROMAN Story. London: 1711. V. 53

THE ROMANCE of El Camino Real. With Authentic Kaloprints Attesting to the Period of Construction (1769-1830), the Period of Depeltion (1835-) and Partial Preservation of the Historic California Missions. Los Angeles: 1937. V. 48

THE ROMANCE of the Appenines. London: 1808. V. 54

ROMAN DE LA ROSE
Cy Est le Rommant de la Roze... 1531. V. 53
The Romaunt of the Rose. London: 1908. V. 53

ROMANE Historiae Anthologia Recognita et Aucta. London: 1658. V. 48

ROMANES, G. J.
Darwin and After Darwin: an Exposition of the Darwinian theory and a Discussion of Post Darwinian Questions. Chicago: 1892/95. V. 49
Darwin and After Darwin, an Exposition of the Darwinian Theory and a Discussion of Post Darwinian Questions. Chicago: 1901-06-06. V. 53
Jelly-Fish, Star-Fish and Sea-Urchins Being a Research on Primitive Nervous Systems. London: 1885. V. 49
Mental Evolution in Ainmals... London: 1883. V. 48; 54

ROMANIS, J. MANNERS
The Great Western Mystery: or, From the Caucasus to the "Caucus". London: 1886. V. 54

ROMANS, BERNARD
Annals of the Troubles in the Netherlands. Hartford: 1778/82. V. 49

ROMAYNE, NICOLAUS
Dissertatio Inauguralis de Puris Generatione. Edinburgh: 1780. V. 49; 53

ROMBAUER, IRMA S.
The Joy of Cooking. Indianapolis: 1936. V. 48

ROMER, F.
Makers of History. Hartford: 1926. V. 53

ROMER, ISABELLA FRANCES
A Pilgrimage to the Temples and Tombs of Egypt, Nubia and Palestine in 1845-46. London: 1846. V. 52

ROMERO, CARLOS OROZCO
13 Mexican Painters. Mexico: 1929. V. 48

ROMILLY, ESMOND
Boadilla. London: 1937. V. 49

ROMILLY, GILES
Out of Bounds. The Education of Giles Romilly and Esmond Romilly. London: 1935. V. 49
The Privileged Nightmare. London: 1954. V. 53

ROMILLY, HUGH
From My Verandah in New Guinea. London: 1889. V. 52
The Western Pacific and New Guinea. London: 1886. V. 48; 52

ROMILLY, SAMUEL
Memoirs of the Life of Sir Samuel Romilly. London: 1840. V. 54
Memoirs of the Life of Sir Samuel Romilly. London: 1841. V. 48
Observations on a Late Publication, Intituled, Thoughts on Executive Justice... London: 1786. V. 52

ROMINE, WILLIAM BETHEL
A Story of the Original Ku Klux Klan. Pulaski: 1934. V. 52

ROMNEY, HENRY SIDNEY, EARL OF
Diary of the Times of Charles II. London: 1843. V. 47

ROMOLI, DOMENICO
La Singolar Dottrina...Di Nuouo Con somma Diligenza Ricorretta, and Ristampata... Venice: 1598. V. 51

RONALDS, ALFRED
The Fly-Fisher's Entomology. London: 1836. V. 54
The Fly-Fisher's Entomology. London: 1862. V. 48; 51
The Fly-Fisher's Entomology. London: 1868. V. 52
The Fly-Fisher's Entomology. London: 1877. V. 52
The Fly-Fisher's Entomology... London: 1883. V. 47; 48
The Fly-Fisher's Entomology... Liverpool: 1913. V. 47; 50; 51; 53
The Fly-Fisher's Entomology. London: 1913. V. 52

RONALDS, FRANCIS
Catalogue of Books and Papers Relating to Electricity, Magnetism, the Electric Telegraphy &c. London and New York: 1880. V. 54

RONAN, PETER
Historical Sketch of the Flathead Indian Nation from the Year 1813 to 1890. Helena: 1890. V. 48; 50; 53

RONAYNE, PHILIP
A Treatise of Algebra in Two Books, the first Treating of the Arithmetical and the Second of the Geometrical Part. London: 1717. V. 48

RONDELET, GUILLAUME
Methodus Curandorum Omnium Morborum Corporis Humani. Lyons: 1586. V. 47; 50

RONDELET, J.
Memoire Historique sur le Dome du Pantheon Francais. Paris: 1797. V. 53
Traite Theorique et Pratique de l'art de Batir. Paris: 1802-17. V. 53

RONGE, J.
A Practical Guide to the English Kinder-Garten... London: 1863. V. 48

RONSARD, PIERRE DE
Abrege de l'Art Poetique Francois. 1903. V. 49
Choix de Sonnets. London: 1902. V. 49
Florilege des Amours de Ronsard. Paris: 1948. V. 50
Songs and Sonnets of Pierre de Ronsard, Gentleman of Vendomois. Boston: 1903. V. 48
Sonnets for Helen. South Pasadena: 1932. V. 54

ROOD, STANDISH
The Silver Districts of Nevada, and Prospectus of the Pan-ranagat Valley Silver Mining Co. New York: 1866. V. 52

ROOKE, HAYMAN
A Description of the Great Oak in Salcey Forest, in the County of Northampton. Nottingham: 1797. V. 50
Descriptions and Sketches of Some Remarkable Oaks, in the Park at Welbeck, in the county of Nottingham, a Sea of His Grace the Duke of Portland. London: 1790. V. 53

ROOKE, HAYMAN continued
A Narrative of What Passed at the Resolution House at Whittington, County of Derby, in...1688. Nottingham: 1788. V. 53

ROOKMAAKER, L. C.
The Zoological Exploration of Southern Africa. Rotterdam: 1989. V. 52

ROOME, THOMAS
The Self Instructed Philosopher, or Memoirs of the Late Joseph Whitehead, of Sutton in Ashfield, Notts. Mansfield: 1817. V. 52

ROOP, G.
Villas and Palaces...1508-1580. Milan: 1968. V. 48; 50; 51

ROORDA, T.
Grammatica Arabica, Breviter in Usum Scholarum Academicarum Conscripta... Leovardiae: 1858. V. 51

ROOS, EVA
Lullabies and Baby Songs. London: 1900. V. 50

ROOS, HENRI
Etudes d'Animaux. Vienna: 1799. V. 47

ROOSEVELT, ANNA ELEANOR
It's Up to Women. New York: 1933. V. 54

ROOSEVELT, B. BARNWELL
Fish Hatching, and Fish Catching. Rochester: 1879. V. 47

ROOSEVELT, ELEANOR
India and the Awakening East. New York: 1953. V. 47
On My Own. New York: 1958. V. 50
This I Remember. New York: 1949. V. 49; 50

ROOSEVELT, FRANKLIN DELANO
On Our Way. New York: 1934. V. 48; 53
The Public Papers and Addresses of Franklin D. Roosevelt. New York: 1938. V. 47

ROOSEVELT, THEODORE
African Game Trails. London: 1910. V. 49
African Game Trails. New York: 1910. V. 48; 50; 53
African Game Trails. London: 1926. V. 47
American Big-Game Hunting. Edinburgh: 1893. V. 48; 49
American Big-Game Hunting. New York: 1893. V. 47
Big Game Hunting in the Rockies and on the Great Plains. New York: 1899. V. 47; 49; 50; 54
Fear God and Take Your Own Part. New York: 1916. V. 47; 48
Historic Towns - New York. London: 1891. V. 51
Hunting in Many Lands; The Book of the Boone and Crockett Club. New York: 1895. V. 47; 48
Hunting Trips of a Ranchman: Sketches of Sport on the Northern Cattle Plains. New York & London: 1885. V. 47; 54
Hunting Trips of a Ranchman. Sketches of Sport on the Northern Cattle Plains. New York: 1886. V. 47; 49
If You Ask Me. New York: 1946. V. 47
Inaugural Addresses of Franklin D. Roosevelt: President of the United States. Worcester: 1945. V. 52
New York. New York: 1891. V. 47; 48
Outdoor Pastimes of an American Hunter. 1905. V. 52
Outdoor Pastimes of an American Hunter. London: 1905. V. 48
Outdoor Pastimes of an American Hunter. New York: 1905. V. 47; 51
Ranch Life and the Hunting Trail. New York: 1888. V. 47; 52; 53
Ranch Life and the Hunting Trail. New York: 1899. V. 47; 53
Rank and File: True Stories of the Great War. New York: 1928. V. 48
The Rough Riders. New York: 1899. V. 53; 54
Strenuous Epigrams. New York Boston: 1904. V. 51
The Summer Birds of the Adirondacks in Franklin County, New York. (with) Notes on some of the Birds of Oyster Bay, Long Island. New York: 1925. V. 47
Through the Brazilian Wilderness. London: 1914. V. 47
Through the Brazilian Wilderness. New York: 1914. V. 50
Trail and Camp Fire; the Book of the Boone and Crockett Club. New York: 1897. V. 48
Trailing the Giant Panda. New York: 1929. V. 54
The Winning of the West. New York: 1900. V. 52
The Works of... New York: 1923-26. V. 48; 50; 54
The Works of... New York: 1926. V. 54

ROOT, EDWARD W.
Philip Hooker: a Contribution to the Study of the Renaissance in America. New York: 1929. V. 53

ROOT, FRANK A.
The Overland Stage to California. Topeka: 1901. V. 47; 48; 50; 51; 52; 54
The Overland Stage to California. Topeka: 1911. V. 47

ROOT, HENRY
Henry Root, Surveyor, Engineer and Inventor. Personal History and Reminiscences. San Francisco: 1921. V. 47; 49
Personal History and Reminiscences with Personal Opinions on Contemporary Events 1845-1921. San Francisco: 1921. V. 47

ROOT, M. A.
The Camera and the Pencil; or the Heliographic Art. Philadelphia: 1864. V. 47

ROOT, SIDNEY
Primary Bible Questions for Young Children. Atlanta: 1864. V. 47

ROOTS, GEORGE
The Charters of the Town of Kingston Upon Thames. London: 1797. V. 50; 53

ROPER, WILLIAM
The Mirrour of Vertue in Worldly Greatness or the Life of Sir Thomas More, Knight. London: 1902. V. 53
A Relation of the Defeating Card. London: 1666. V. 49

ROPES, HANNAH
Six Months in Kansas. Boston: 1856. V. 47

ROPES, JOHN C.
Story of the Civil War... Boston: 1894. V. 48
The Story of the Civil War: a Concise Account of the War in the United States of America Between 1861 and 1865. New York: 1894-1913. V. 47
The Story of the Civil War; a Concise Account of the War in the United States of America Between 1861 and 1865. New York: 1933. V. 50

ROQUEFORT, JEAN BAPTISTE BONAR DE
Vues Pittoresques et Perspectives des Dalles du Musee des Monuments Francais... Paris: 1816. V. 48

ROQUES, JOSEPH
Phytographie Medicale, Histoire des Substances Herioques Dea Poison Tires du Regne Vegetal. Paris & Lyon: 1835. V. 52
Plantes Usuelles, Indigenes et Exotiques. Paris: 1809. V. 53; 54

ROQUET, ANTOINE ERNEST
Le Relieurs Francais (1500-1800). Paris: 1893. V. 47

ROREM, NED
Paul's Blues. New York: 1984. V. 53; 54

RORSCHACK, HERMANN
Psychodiagnostics: a Diagnostic Test Based on Perception. New York: 1942. V. 52

RORTY, JAMES
What Michael Said to the Census Taker. San Francisco: 1922. V. 47

ROS, AMANDA MC KITTRICK
Bayonets of Bastard Sheen. London: 1949. V. 47
Fumes of Formation (Poems). Belfast: 1933. V. 51
Irene Iddesleigh. Belfast: 1897. V. 47; 48; 49; 50; 53
Irene Iddesleigh. Bloomsbury: 1926. V. 50

ROSA in London and Other Tales; by the Author of the Young Mother, or Albinia. London: 1809. V. 47

ROSA, JOSEPH G.
Alias Jack McCall A Pardon or Death?. Kansas City: 1967. V. 49

ROSA, THOMAS
Idaea, Sive de Iacobi Magnae Britanniae, Galliae et Hybernaie... Londini: 1608. V. 49

ROSALES, VINCENTE PEREZ
California Adventure. San Francisco: 1947. V. 48

ROSALIE: or, the Castle of Montalbretti. Richmond: 1811. V. 54

ROSCOE and Hayden's Book of Magic and Mystery. 1870. V. 47

ROSCOE, E.
Floral Illustrations of the Seasons... London: 1829. V. 48; 50; 51

ROSCOE, HENRY
A Digest of the Law of Evidence in Criminal Cases. Philadelphia: 1840. V. 52
Lives of Eminent British Lawyers. London: 1830. V. 50

ROSCOE, HENRY E.
Spectrum Analysis. London: 1869. V. 52
Spectrum Analysis. New York: 1869. V. 49
Spectrum Analysis. London: 1870. V. 54

ROSCOE, JOHN
The Baganda, an Account of Their Native Customs and Beliefs. London: 1911. V. 52
The Soul of Central Africa, A General Account of the Mackie Ethnological Expedition. London: 1922. V. 50; 54

ROSCOE, MARGARET LACE
Floral Illustrations of the Seaons, Consisting of Representations Drawn From Nature of Some of the Most Beautiful, Hardy and Rare Herbaceous Plants Cultivated in the Flower Garden... London: 1831. V. 47; 48; 50

ROSCOE, S.
John Newbery and His Successors 1740-1814. Hertfordshire: 1973. V. 47
John Newbery and His Successors 1740-1840. A Bibliography. London: 1973. V. 53

ROSCOE, THOMAS
Chevy Chase, a Poem Founded on the Ancient Ballad. London: 1813. V. 54
The German Novelists... London: 1826. V. 49
The Pleasant History of Reynard the Fox. London: 1873. V. 51
The Tourist in France. London: 1834. V. 48; 50
The Tourist in Italy. London: 1831. V. 48
The Tourist in Italy. 1832. V. 47
The Tourist in Spain. London: 1830. V. 48
The Tourist in Spain and Morocco. London: 1838. V. 48
The Tourist in Spain, Granada... London: 1835. V. 51
The Tourist in Switzerland and Italy. London: 1830. V. 48
Wanderings and Excursions in North (and South) Wales. London: 1840. V. 47; 50; 53

ROSCOE, THOMAS continued
Wanderings and Excursions in North Wales. (with) *Wanderings and Escursions in South Wales.* London: 1836/c.1837. V. 51
Wanderings and Excursions in North Wales. (with) *Wanderings and Escursions in South Wales, with the Scenery of the River Wye.* London: 1853. V. 52
Wanderings and Excursions in South Wales; Including the Scenery of the River Wye. London: 1837. V. 51

ROSCOE, WILLIAM
The Butterfly's Ball and the Grasshopper's Feast. Boston: 1977. V. 50
Catalogue of the Very Select and Valuable Library of William Roscoe, Esq. Liverpool: 1816. V. 50; 53
Catalogue of the Very Select and Valuable Library of William Roscoe, Esq. Which Will Be Sold by Auction... London: 1816. V. 48; 51; 52
Illustrations Historical and Critical of the Life of Lorenezo Medici, Called the Magnificent. London: 1822. V. 48
The Life and Pontificate of Leo the Tenth. Liverpool: 1805. V. 47; 50; 51
The Life of Lorenzo De Medici, Called the Magnificent. London: 1796. V. 50
The Life of Lorenzo de Medici, Called the Magnificent. 1797. V. 47
The Life of Lorenzo De Medici, Called the Magnificent. London: 1797. V. 50; 53
The Life of Lorenzo De Medici, Called the Magnificent. Philadelphia: 1803. V. 52
Memoir of Richard Roberts Jones, of Aberdaron, in the County of Carnarvon, in North Wales; Exhibiting a Remarkable Instance of a Partial Power and Cultivation of Intellect. London: 1822. V. 49
Mount Pleasant; a Descriptive Poem, To Which is added an Ode. Warrington: 1777. V. 48
Occasional Tracts Relative to the War Between Great Britain and France... London: 1810. V. 52

ROSCOMMON, WENTWORTH DILLON, EARL OF
An Essay on Translated Verse. London: 1684. V. 49
An Essay on Translated Verse. London: 1685. V. 49
An Essay On Translated Verse. London: 1709. V. 48; 52
Poems by the Earl of Roscommon. London: 1717. V. 47; 48; 50

ROSE, A.
Napoleon's Campaign in Russia Anno 1812, Medico-Historical. New York: 1913. V. 52

ROSE, ALFRED
Register of Erotic Books. New York: 1965. V. 53

ROSE, BARBARA
Claes Oldenburg. New York: 1969. V. 51
Claes Oldenburg. New York: 1970. V. 50
Frankenthaler. New York. V. 47; 48; 49; 50; 52

THE ROSE: Being a Detection of the Pernicious Tendency of Two Libels Lately Published, viz. in the Old English Journal, and a Pamphlet Entitled, The Thistle. London: 1747. V. 48

ROSE, BERNICE
Jackson Pollock, Works on Paper. New York: 1969. V. 50

ROSE, COWPER
Four Years in Southern Africa. London: 1829. V. 49; 52

ROSE, D. MURRAY
Historical Notes and Essays on the '15 and '45. Edinburgh: 1897. V. 52; 54

ROSE, DAN
The Abyss. Madison: 1969. V. 54

ROSE, FREDRICK G. G.
The Wind of Change in Central Australia: the Aborigines of Angas Downs, 1962. Berlin: 1965. V. 52

ROSE, G. MAC LEAN
A Cyclopaedia of Canadian Biography, Being Chiefly Men of the Time. Toronto: 1888. V. 53

ROSE, GEORGE
Observations on the Historical Work of the Late Right Honorable Charles James Fox. London: 1809. V. 48; 53; 54
Observations Respecting the Public Expenditure, and the Influence of the Crown. London: 1810. V. 50

ROSE, GUSTAV
Elemente der Krystallographie, Nebst Einer Tabellarischen Uebersicht der Mineralien nach den Krystallformen... Berlin: 1833. V. 47

ROSE, H.
The Elements of Botany... London: 1775. V. 52; 53

ROSE, HENRY
A Manual of Analytical Chemistry. London: 1831. V. 50

ROSE, HENRY JOHN
Fifty Cottage Prints from Sacred Subjects...Intended Chiefly for Distribution Amongst the Poor, and Rewards to Sunday-School Children. London: 1851. V. 47

ROSE, HUGH JAMES
A New General Biographical Dictionary... 1853. V. 52

ROSE, JOSHUA
Modern Machine-Shop Practice. London: 1886-7. V. 51; 52

ROSE, STEWART
St. Ignatius Loyola and the Early Jesuits. New York: 1891. V. 53

ROSE, STUART
An Essex Dozen. Colchester: 1953. V. 48

ROSE, THOMAS
Westmorland, Cumberland, Durham and Northumberland. London: 1832. V. 47; 48
Westmorland, Cumberland, Durham and Northumberland, Illustrated. London: 1832-35. V. 48; 49; 50; 53

ROSE, VICTOR M.
The Life and Services of Gen. Ben McCulloch... Philadelphia: 1888. V. 50
Ross' Texas Brigade. Being a Narrative of Events Connected With Its Service in the Late War Between the States. Louisville: 1881. V. 51; 54

ROSE, W.
Lost Copper. Banning: 1980. V. 53

ROSE, WILLIAM
The Surgical Treatment of Neuralagia of the Fifth Nerve. London: 1892. V. 47; 48; 49; 50

ROSEN, ERIC VON
Popular Account of Archaeological Research During the Swedish Chaco-Cordillera-Expedition 1901-02. Stockholm: 1924. V. 50; 52

ROSEN, GEORGE
The History of Miners' Diseases. A Medical and Social Interpretation. New York: 1943. V. 53

ROSEN, KENNETH
The Man to send Rain Clouds. New York: 1974. V. 50
Voices of the Rainbow. Contemporary Poetry by American Indians. New York: 1975. V. 50

ROSEN, PETER
Pa-Ha-Sa-Pah, or the Black Hills of South Dakota. St. Louis: 1895. V. 53; 54

ROSEN, R. D.
Strike Three You're Dead. New York: 194. V. 47

ROSENAU, H.
Boullee & Visionary Architecture. London: 1976. V. 54

ROSENAU, MILTON
Preventive Medicine and Hygiene. New York: 1913. V. 51; 54

ROSENBACH, ABRAHAM SIMON WOLF
Book Hunter's Holiday: Adventures with Books and Manuscripts. Boston & New York: 1936. V. 49; 52; 53
Books and Bidders. The Adventures of a Bibliophile. Boston: 1927. V. 49; 50; 51; 52
The Collected Catalogues of Dr. A. S. W. Rosenbach, 1904-1951. New York: 1967. V. 53
The Earliest Christmas Books. Philadelphia: 1927. V. 52
Early American Children's Books. Portland: 1933. V. 47; 48; 49; 51
Early American Children's Books. 1966. V. 53
An Introduction to Herman Melville's Moby Dick. New York: 1924. V. 54
The Libraries of the Presidents of the United States. Worcester: 1935. V. 52
The Unpublishable Memoirs. New York: 1917. V. 49; 54

ROSENBACH CO., PHILADELPHIA
1776 Americana: a Catalogue of Autograph Letters and Documents Realting to the Declaration of Independence and the Revolutionary War. Philadelphia: 1926. V. 50

ROSENBAUM, ELISABETH
A Catalogue of Cyrenaican Portrait Scultpure. London: 1960. V. 52

ROSENBAUM, J.
The Plague of Lust, Being a History of Veneral Disease in Classical Antiquity... Paris: 1901. V. 47; 49

ROSENBERG, B.
Olana's Guide to American Artists: a Contribution Toward a Bibliography. New York: 1978/80. V. 51

ROSENBERG, C. B. H. VON
Der Malayische Archipel. London: 1878. V. 48

ROSENBERG, D.
Explication of an Engraving Called the Origin of the Rites and Worship of the Hebrews... New York: 1859. V. 54

ROSENBERG, HAROLD
De Kooning. New York: 1973. V. 48
De Kooning. New York: 1978. V. 48; 49; 50
Portraits. New York: 1976. V. 47

ROSENBERG, ISAAC
The Collected Works of Isaac Rosenberg - Poetry - Prose - Letters - and Some Drawings. London: 1937. V. 47; 52
Poems. London: 1922. V. 52

ROSENBERG, LOUIS
Canada's Jews: a Social & Economic Study of the Jews in Canada. Montreal: 1939. V. 51

ROSENBERG, LOUIS CONRAD
Cottages, Farmhouses and Other Minor Buildings in England of the 16th, 17th and 18th Centuries. New York: 1923. V. 51; 54
The Davanzati Palace, Florence Italy. New York: 1922. V. 50

ROSENBERG, M.
The Art of Advertising. New York: 1930. V. 53

ROSENBERG, MARY ELIZABETH
The Museum of Flowers. London: 1845. V. 48

ROSENBERG, PETER CARL JOHANN VON
Von Rosenberg Family of Texas. Boerne: 1949. V. 48

ROSENBLATT, JOE
Dream Craters. Erin: 1974. V. 52

ROSENFIELD, JOHN
Texas History Movies. Dallas: 1943. V. 48

ROSENGARTEN, MORTON
The Lines of the Poet. Toronto: 1981. V. 47

ROSENSTEIN, I. G.
Theory and Practice of Homoeopathy. First Part. Louisville: 1840. V. 52

ROSENTHAL, DORIS
Prim-Art Series Volume 1: Animal Motifs. New York: 1926. V. 48

ROSENTHAL, JACQUES
Incunabula Typographica... Munich: 1900-06. V. 48

ROSENTHAL, LEONARD
The Kingdom of the Pearl. New York. V. 48
The Kingdom of the Pearl. New York: 1920. V. 47

ROSENTHAL, NAN
George Rickey. New York: 1977. V. 51

ROSENWALD, LESSING J.
Vision of a Collector, the Lessing J. Rosenwald Collection in the Library of Congress. Washington: 1991. V. 48

ROSENWEIG, FRANZ
Der Stern der Erlosung. Frankfurt: 1921. V. 48

ROSETT, JOSHUA
Intercortical Systems of the Human Cerebrum. New York: 1933. V. 48

ROSETTA STONE INSCRIPTION
Report Of the Committee Appointed by the Philomathean Society of the University of Pennsylvania to Translate the Inscription on the Rosetta Stone. Philadelphia: 1858. V. 51
Report of the Committee Appointed by the Philomathean Society of the University of Pennsylvania to Translate the Inscription on the Rosetta Stone. Philadelphia: 1859. V. 47

ROSETTI, GIOANVENTURA
The Plictho...Instructions in the Art of the Dyers Which Teaches the Dyeing of Woolen Cloths, Linens, Cottons and Sild by the Great Art as Well as the Common. Cambridge: 1969. V. 52; 54

ROSHER, HAROLD
In the Royal Naval Air Service. Being the Letters of the Late Harold Rosher to His Family. London: 1916. V. 47

ROSICKY, MARY
Bohemian-American Cook Book. Omaha: 1915. V. 54

ROSIS, ANGELO
A New Book of Ornaments, Consisting of Compartment Decorations of Theatres, Ceilings, Chimney Pieces, Doors, Windows and Other Beautyful Forms Usefull to Painters, Carvers, Engravers, &c. London: 1753. V. 52

ROSKILL, S. W.
War at Sea. London: 1954. V. 48; 49; 51; 53
The War at Sea 1939-1945. London: 1954-61. V. 49
The War at Sea 1939-1945. London: 1954/56. V. 51

ROSMAN, CHARLES
Enchanted Rock Views of a Texas Batholith. Austin: 1985. V. 51

ROSS, ALAN
Jolakottur, Yuillis Yald and Similar Expressions. London: 1937. V. 53
Time Was Away. A Notebook of Corsica. London: 1948. V. 54

ROSS, ALEXANDER
Adventures of the First Settlers on the Oregon or Columbia River... London: 1849. V. 53
Adventures of the First Settlers on the Oregon or Columbia River 1810-1813. Cleveland: 1904. V. 48; 53
The Fortunate Shepherdress, a Pastoral Tale, in Three Cantos... Aberdeen: 1768. V. 49
Fur Hunters of the Far West. London: 1855. V. 47; 54
Mel Heliconium: or, Poeticall Honey, Gathered Out of the Weeds of Parnassus. London: 1642. V. 50
Pansebeia (in Greek letter): or, a View of All Religions in the world. London: 1675. V. 49; 51; 52
Pansebeia; or, a View of all Religions in the World, from the Creation. to These Times. London: 1653. V. 49
Pansebeia; or a View of all Religions in the World, with the Several Church Governments...also a Discovery of all Known Heresies in All Ages and Places. London: 1655. V. 51
Panzebeia (Graece): or a View of All Religions in the World. London: 1696. V. 53
The Red River Settlement: its Rise, Progress and Present State. London: 1856. V. 47; 50; 52; 54
View of All Religions in the World... London: 1655. V. 48; 52
View of All Religions in the World... London: 1675. V. 47
Virgilii Evangelisantis Christiados Libri XIII. Londini: 1638. V. 49; 54

ROSS, CHARLES H.
The Book of Cats. London: 1868. V. 52
A London Romance. London: 1869. V. 47
Merry Conceits and Whimsical Rhymes. London: 1883. V. 51
The Story of a Honeymoon. London: 1869. V. 49

ROSS, DANIEL H.
Protest by the Lawful Delegates of the Civilized Nations of Indians of the Indian territory (Herein Named) On Their Behalf and on Behalf of the Indian Race, Against the Passage of a Law by Congress Transferring them and Their Property to Military Control. Washington: 1876. V. 48
To the Congress of the United States. Washington: 1875. V. 48

ROSS, DAVID
The Land of the Five Rivers and Sindh. London: 1883. V. 51

ROSS, E. DENISON
Persian Art. London: 1930. V. 50

ROSS, EDMUND
History of the Impeachment of Andrew Johnson, President of the United States by the House of Representatives and His Trial by the Senate for High Crimes and Misdeameanors in Office. Santa Fe: 1896. V. 49; 52

ROSS, FITZGERALD
A Visit to the Cities and Camps of the Confederate States. Edinburgh & London: 1865. V. 49

ROSS, FREDERICK
The Ruined Abbeys of Britain. London: 1880. V. 54
The Ruined Abbeys of Britain. London: 1882. V. 50; 51; 53; 54
The Ruined Abbeys of Great Britain. London. V. 50

ROSS, HUGH
Induced Cell-Reproduction and Cancer. Philadelphia: 1911. V. 49; 51; 54

ROSS, JAMES
From Wisconsin to California, and Return, as Reported for the "Wisconsin State Journal"... Madison: 1869. V. 47
Handbook of the Diseases of the Nervous System. Philadelphia: 1885. V. 53

ROSS, JAMES CLARK
A Voyage of Discovery and Research in the Southern and Antarctic Regions During the Years 1839-43. London: 1847. V. 48

ROSS, JOHN
The Book of the Red Deer and Empire Big Game. London: 1925. V. 47; 52
Joanni Rossi Antiquarii Warwicensis Historia Regum Angliae. E Codice in Bibliotheca Bodlejana... Oxonii: 1716. V. 52
The Last Voyage of Capt. Sir John Ross, R.N. Knt. to the Arctic Regions, for the Discovery of a North West Passage, Performed in the Years 1829, 30-31-32 and 33... London: 1836. V. 47; 50
Letter from John Ross, the Principal Chief of the Cherokee Nation to a Gentleman at Philadelphia. Philadelphia: 1837. V. 52
Narrative of a Second Voyage in Search of a North-West Passage and of a Residence in the Arctic Regions During 1829, 1830, 1831, 1832, 1833. London: 1835. V. 47; 49; 50; 51; 52; 54
Narrative of a Second Voyage in Search of a North-West Passage, and of a Residence in the Arctic Regions, During the Years 1829, 1830, 1831, 1832, 1833. Philadelphia: 1835. V. 50
Narrative of a Second Voyage in Search of a North-West Passage and of a Residence in the Arctic Regions During the years 1829, 1830, 1831, 1832, 1833. New York: 1969. V. 50
Narrative of a Second Voyage in Search of a Northwest Passage and of a Residence in the Arctic Regions...1829-1833. Paris: 1835. V. 53
A Treatise on Navigation by Steam; Comprising a History of the Steam Engine... London: 1828. V. 54
A Voyage of Discovery, Made Under the Orders of the Admiralty in His Majesty's Ships Isabella and Alexander... London: 1819. V. 47; 53

ROSS, JOHN D.
Scottish Poets in America with Biographical and Critical Notices. New York: 1889. V. 54

ROSS, JOHNNY
The Biggin Hill Frescoes. 1975. V. 52; 54

ROSS, MALCOLM
Machine Age in the Hills. New York: 1933. V. 53

ROSS, MARGERY
Robert Ross - Friend of Friends. London: 1952. V. 52

ROSS, MARVIN C.
The Art of Karl Faberge and His Contemporaries; Russian Imperial Portraits and Mementos... Norman: 1965. V. 49; 51
Russian Porcelains...the Collections of Marjorie Merriweather Post, Hillwood, Washington, D.C. Norman: 1968. V. 52

ROSS, MRS.
The Bachelor and the Married Man, or the Equilibrium of the "Balance of Comfort". London: 1817. V. 50
The Balance of Comfort; or the Old Maid and Married Woman. London: 1817. V. 50; 54
The Balance of Comfort; or the Old Maid and Married Woman. London: 1818. V. 50

ROSS, PETER V.
California Unreported Cases, being Those Decisions ...Not Officially Reported... San Francisco: 1913. V. 51

ROSS, ROBERT
The American Latin Grammar... Newburyport: 1780?. V. 47
The American Latin Grammar; or, a Complete Introduction to the Latin Tongue. Newburyport: 1794?. V. 50
Aubrey Beardsley. London: 1909. V. 54
Friend of Friends. London: 1952. V. 54

ROSS, RONALD
Memoirs with a Full Account of the Great Malaria problem and its Solution. London: 1923. V. 51

ROSS, RONALD continued
Studies on Malaria. London: 1928. V. 49; 51

ROSS, SINCLAIR
As for Me and My House. New York: 1941. V. 51

ROSS, WALTER
The Immortal. New York: 1958. V. 54

ROSS, WILLIAM
The French Scholar's Guide; or a New and Compendious Grammar of the French Tongue. Glasgow: 1772. V. 47

ROSS, WILLIAM P.
Indian Territory. Remarks In Opposition to the Bill to Organize the Territory of Oklahoma. Washington: 1874. V. 48

ROSS, WILLIAM P., MRS.
The Life and Times of Hon. Wm. P. Ross of the Cherokee Nation. Ft. Smith: 1893. V. 49

ROSS COCKERILL, W.
The Husbandry and Health of the Domestic Buffalo. Rome: 1974. V. 54

ROSS-CRAIG, STELLA
Drawings of British Plants. London: 1948-56. V. 51
Drawings of British Plants. London: 1948-73. V. 48
Drawings of British Plants. London: 1948-74. V. 50

ROSSE, WILLIAM PARSONS, 3RD EARL OF
The Scientific Papers, Collected and Republished by the Hon. Sir Charles Parsons. London: 1926. V. 53

ROSSEL, LOUISE
Sea Sprites or, What Happened in Fishland. London. V. 54

ROSSET, FRANCOIS DE
Novveav Recveil des Plvs Beavx Vers de ce Temps. Paris: 1609. V. 51; 54

ROSSET, PIERRE FULCARAND DE
L'Agriculture. Paris: 1774/82. V. 49

ROSSETTI, CHRISTINA
Annus Domini. Oxford and London: 1874. V. 51
Called to Be Saints. London: 1881. V. 51
Commonplace and Other Short Stories. London: 1870. V. 47; 51
The Face of the Deep, a Devotional Commentary on the Apocalypse. London: 1892. V. 51
The Family Letters. London: 1908. V. 48
The Family Letters, with Some Supplementary Letters and Appendices. New York: 1908. V. 54
Goblin Market. London: 1862. V. 51
Goblin Market. London: 1879. V. 51
Goblin Market. London: 1893. V. 47; 48; 49; 50; 51
Goblin Market. Chicago: 1905. V. 47
Goblin Market. London: 1933. V. 49; 51; 52; 54
Letter and Spirit. Notes on the Commandments. London: 1883. V. 48; 51
Maude. Chicago: 1897. V. 51
Maude. London: 1897. V. 51
New Poems.... London: 1896. V. 49; 50; 51; 52; 53; 54
A Pageant and Other Poems. Boston: 1881. V. 47; 49
A Pageant and Other Poems. London: 1881. V. 48; 49; 50; 51; 52; 53; 54
Poems. Boston: 1866. V. 50; 54
Poems. Boston: 1888. V. 52
Poems. London: 1890. V. 51
Poems. London: 1891. V. 51; 52
Poems. London: 1892. V. 54
Poems. London: 1910. V. 47; 48; 51
Poems. London: 1913. V. 48
Poems Chosen By Walter De La Mare. Newtown: 1930. V. 47; 49; 51; 52
Poems. (with) New Poems by Christina Rossetti Hitherto Unpublished or Uncollected. London: 1895/96. V. 48
The Poetical Works of... Boston: 1899. V. 54
The Poetical Works of... London: 1904. V. 51
The Poetical Works of... London: 1908. V. 48
The Prince's Progress and Other Poems. London: 1866. V. 51; 53
Seek and Find. London: 1879. V. 51
Sing Song. Boston: 1872. V. 48; 52
Sing Song. London: 1893. V. 51
Sing-Song. London: 1872. V. 47; 49; 51; 52; 53
Speaking Likenesses. London: 1874. V. 47; 48; 49; 50; 51; 53; 54
Time Flies, a Reading Diary. London: 1885. V. 51
Verses. London: 1893. V. 51

ROSSETTI, DANTE GABRIEL
The Ballad of Jan Hunks. London: 1929. V. 47; 49
Ballads & Sonnets. London: 1881. V. 49
Ballads and Narrative Poems. London: 1893. V. 49; 52; 54
Ballads and Sonnets. Boston: 1881. V. 54
Ballads and Sonnets. London: 1881. V. 51; 53; 54
Ballads and Sonnets. Boston: 1882. V. 48
Ballads and Sonnets. London: 1903. V. 49
Ballads and Sonnets. Portland: 1903. V. 50; 52
The Blessed Damozel. New York: 1886. V. 53
The Blessed Damozel. 1898. V. 52
The Blessed Damozel. London: 1898. V. 49; 51
The Blessed Damozel. Portland: 1901. V. 48
The Collected Works. London: 1886. V. 47; 49
The Collected Works. London: 1888. V. 54
Collected Works. London: 1890. V. 48; 49; 51
The Collected Works. London: 1897. V. 47; 48
Dante and His Circle: With the Italian Poets Preceding Him... London: 1874. V. 50; 51
Dante and His Circle with the Italian Poets Preceding Him (100-1200-1300). London: 1892. V. 49
Dante Gabriel Rossetti His Family Letters with a Memoir. Boston: 1895. V. 47
Dante Gabriel Rossetti to William Allingham 1854-1870. New York: 1898. V. 49
The Early Italian Poets 1100-1200-1300. London: 1861. V. 50; 51; 54
Hand and Soul. London: 1850. V. 47
Hand and Soul. London: 1869. V. 48; 52
Hand and Soul. Hammersmith: 1895. V. 50; 52; 54
Hand and Soul. London: 1895. V. 47
Hand and Soul. 1899. V. 48; 49
Hand and Soul. London: 1944. V. 49
Henry the Leper. Boston: 1905. V. 49
The House of Life. Boston: 1894. V. 47; 49
The House of Life. Edinburgh: 1904. V. 47
Letters to William Allingham, 1854-1870. London: 1897. V. 54
Letters to William Allingham 1854-1870. New York: 1897. V. 50
The New Life of Dante Alighieri. New York: 1901. V. 49
Poems. Boston: 1870. V. 49; 50; 51
Poems. London: 1870. V. 47; 49; 51; 54
Poems. Leipzig: 1873. V. 47; 51
Poems. London: 1881. V. 51; 53
The Poems. Troy: 1903. V. 50
The Poems. London: 1904. V. 49; 51
Poems and Ballads. London: 1898/1903. V. 49
Poems. (with) Ballads and Sonnets. London: 1870/81. V. 47
Poems. (with) Ballads and Sonnets. Portland: 1902/03. V. 54
The Poetical Works. London: 1897. V. 48
The Poetical Works. London: 1900. V. 49
Sister Helen. New Haven: 1939. V. 49
Sonnets and Lyrical Poems. 1894. V. 49
Sonnets and Lyrical Poems. Hammersmith: 1894. V. 52
The White Ship, a Little Book of Poems. Boston: 1896. V. 47

ROSSETTI, DOMENICO
Il Sepolcro di Winckelmann in Trieste. Venezia: 1823. V. 52

ROSSETTI, DONATO
Composizione e Passioni de' Vetri, Overo Dimostrazioni Fisico-Matematiche delle Gocciole, e de' Fili del Vetro, che Rotto in Qualsisia Parte Tutto Quanto si Stritola. Livorno: 1671. V. 49

ROSSETTI, GABRIELE
Disquisitions on the Antipapal Spirit Which Produced the Reformation: Its Secret Influence of the Literature of Europe in General and of Italy in Particular. London: 1834. V. 49
Iddio e L'Uomo - Salterio. Londra: 1833. V. 51
Versi. Losanna: 1847. V. 51

ROSSETTI, MARIA FRANCESCA
A Shadow of Dante. London: 1871. V. 51
A Shadow of Dante. London, Oxford: 1872. V. 51; 53; 54
A Shadow of Dante Being an Essay Towards studying Himself, His World and His Pilgrimage. Boston: 1897. V. 49

ROSSETTI, WILLIAM MICHAEL
Bibliography of the Works of Dante Gabriel Rossetti. London: 1905. V. 49; 54
The Germ: Thoughts Towards Nature in Poetry, Literature and Art. London: 1850. V. 47
Letters Concerning Whitman, Blake & Shelley to Anne Gilchrist and Her Son Herbert Gilchrist. 1934. V. 49
Memoir of Shelley. London: 1886. V. 47; 49; 54
The P.R.B. Journal - William Michael Rossetti's Diary of the Pre-Raphaelite Brotherhood 1849-1853, Together with Other Pre-Raphaelite Documents. London: 1975. V. 53
Rossetti Papers 1862-1870. London: 1903. V. 51
Ruskin: Rossetti: Pre-Raphaelitism. Papers 1854 to 1862. London: 1899. V. 47; 51
Swinburne's Poems and Ballads. London: 1866. V. 47; 48; 49; 50; 51; 54

ROSSI, FILIPPO
Italian Jeweled Arts. New York: 1954. V. 47; 50
Italian Jeweled Arts. London: 1957. V. 50; 52; 53

ROSSI, G. B. DE
La Roma Sotterranea Christiana. Roma: 1864-77. V. 50

ROSSI, GIROLAMO
De Distillatione Liber: in Quo Stillatitiorum Liquorum, Qui ad Medicinam Faciunt, Methodus ac Vires Explicantur... Basle: 1585. V. 47

ROSSI, J. V.
Snakes of the United States and Canada Keeping Them Health in Captivity. Volume I. Eastern Area. Melbourne: 1992. V. 50

ROSSI, MARIO M.
Pilgrimage in the West. 1933. V. 49
Pilgrimage in the West. Dublin: 1933. V. 53

ROSSIG, CARL G.
Die Nelken nach Ihren Arten, Besonders Nach der J. C. Etlers in Schneeberg und Andem Beruhmten Sammlungen, in Blattern Nach der natur Gezeichnet und Ausgemahlt... Leipzig: 1800-08. V. 52

ROSSIGNOL, L.
L'Art d'Ecrire Contenant Une Collection des Meilleurs Examples... Paris: 1756. V. 53

ROSSITER, HENRY P.
M. & M. Karolik Collection of American Water Colors and Drawings, 1800-1875. Boston: 1962. V. 51; 53

ROSSITER, W. RAYMOND
Mineral Resources of the States and Territories West of the Rocky Mountains. Washington: 1869. V. 50

ROSSKAM, EDWIN
Washington: Nerve Center. New York: 1939. V. 47

ROSSLIN, EUCHARIUS
The Byrth of Mankynde, Otherwyse Named the Womens Boke. 1552. V. 47
Der Swangern Frauwen und Hebammen Rosegarten. Strassburg: 1513. V. 47

ROSSMAN, CHARLES
Enchanted Rock, Views of a Texas Batholith. Austin: 1985. V. 53

ROSSO, G.
Relatione Astrologica Della Cometa Novamente Apparsa a 20 Di Decembre 1680. Palermo: 1681. V. 50

ROSS-OF-BLADENSBURG, JOHN
The Coldstream Guards 1914-1918. 1928. V. 49

ROST, J. L.
Die Wohlangerichtete Neuerfundene Tugendschule in Welcher Vier und Zwantzig Anmuthige Historien zu Erlaubter Gemuths-Ergotzung der Jugend. Frankfurt & Leipzig: 1743?. V. 52

ROSTAND, EDMOND
Cyrano de Bergerac. New York: 1898. V. 48

ROSTELLINI, HIPPOLYTUS
Elementa Linguae Aegyptiacae Vulgo Copticae... Rome: 1837. V. 54

ROSTEN, LEO
People I Have Loved, Known or Admired. New York: 1970. V. 52

ROSTEN, NORMAN
Return Again, Traveler. New Haven: 1940. V. 51

ROSTLUND, ERHARD
Freshwater Fish and Fishing in Native North America. Berkeley and Los Angeles: 1952. V. 53; 54

ROSTOVTZEFF, M.
Iranians and Greeks in South Russia. Oxford: 1922. V. 52
The Social and Economic History of the Hellenistic World. Oxford: 1953. V. 50

ROT, DIETER
246 Little Clouds. New York: 1968. V. 52
Scheisse. Providence: 1966. V. 51

ROTARI, GIUSEPPE
Geanaforo Economico Per Transportar Terra Per Aria a Qualunque Altezza. Verona: 1822. V. 53

ROTCH, THOMAS
Pediatrics: The Hygiene and Medical Treatment of Children. Philadelphia: 1896. V. 49

ROTCH, WILLIAM
Memorandum Written by...in the Eightieeth Year of His Age. Boston & New York: 1916. V. 54

ROTH, A.
Zwei Wohnhauser. Stuttgart: 1927. V. 51

ROTH, ALBRECHT WILHELM
Novae Plantarum species Praesertim Indiae Orientalis. Halberstadt: 1821. V. 49

ROTH, EDWARD
Christmas Judex, Legend of the White Mountains. Boston: 1892. V. 48

ROTH, H. LING
The Aborigines of Tasmania. Hobart. V. 52
The Natives of Sarawak and British North Boreno. London: 1896. V. 52
Notes On Continental Irrigation. London: 1882. V. 50; 54

ROTH, HENRY
Call It Sleep. New York: 1934. V. 49
Call It Sleep. New York: 1935. V. 48
Call It Sleep. London: 1963. V. 53
Mercy of a Rude Stream. New York: 1994. V. 51
Nature's First Green. New York: 1979. V. 48; 51; 52; 54

ROTH, IRVING
Cardiac Arrythmias, Clinical Features and Mechanism of the Irregular Heart. New York: 1928. V. 54

ROTH, PHILIP
The Anatomy Lesson. New York. V. 52; 54
The Anatomy Lesson. Franklin Center: 1983. V. 52
The Anatomy Lesson. New York: 1983. V. 49; 53; 54
Elfenbeinzahne. Ivory Tusks. Gedichte eines Afroamerikaners. Heidelberg: 1956. V. 47
The Facts. A Novelist's Autobiography. New York: 1988. V. 54
Goodbye, Columbus. Boston: 1959. V. 48; 49; 51; 52; 54
Goodbye, Columbus. London: 1959. V. 53
Goodbye, Columbus. New York: 1959. V. 48
Goodbye, Columbus. 1978. V. 49
Goodbye, Columbus and Other Stories. Franklin Center: 1978. V. 54
His Mistress's Voice. Lewisburg: 1995. V. 52
Novotny's Pain. Los Angeles: 1980. V. 51
On the Air. A Long Story. New York: 1970. V. 48; 52
A Philip Roth Reader. New York: 1980. V. 49; 50
Portnoy's Complaint. New York: 1969. V. 48; 51; 52; 53; 54
The Professor of Desire. New York: 1977. V. 50
Zuckerman Bound: The Ghost Writer: Zuckerman Unbound: The Anatomy Lesson, Epilogue: the Prague Orgy. New York: 1985. V. 49
Zuckerman Unbound. New York: 1981. V. 52; 53; 54

ROTH, SAMUEL
The Beau Book. New York: 1926-27. V. 48
Stone Walls Do Not. The Chronicle of a Captivity. New York: 1930. V. 51

ROTH, WALTER E.
Ethnological Studies Among the North-West Central Queensland Aborigines. Brisbane: 1897. V. 52

ROTHCHILD, HERBERT L.
A Survey of Modern Bookmaking. San Francisco: 1931. V. 50

ROTHE, DAVID
The Analecta of... Dublin: 1884. V. 53

ROTHENBERG, JEROME
A Big Jewish Book. New York: 1978. V. 48
The History of Dada. 1982. V. 49; 53
Improvisations. New York: 1991. V. 51; 53
A Merz Sonata. 1985. V. 51
A Poem to Celebrate the Spring and Diane Rothenberg's Birthday. Mt. Horeb: 1975. V. 51
Poland/ 1931. 1970. V. 47
Senecca Journal I, a Poem of Beavers. Mt. Horeb: 1973. V. 54
Shaking the Pumpkin. Traditional Poetry of the Indian North Americas. New York: 1972. V. 50
Sightings I-IX and Red Easy a Color. London: 1968. V. 47

ROTHENSTEIN, JOHN
The Artists of the 1890's. London: 1928. V. 47
Autobiography. London: 1965-70. V. 50
Francis Bacon. Milano;: 1966. V. 54
Paul Nash (1889-1946). London: 1961. V. 51
Turner. London: 1965. V. 50; 53

ROTHENSTEIN, WILLIAM
Men and Memories. London: 1931/32/39. V. 49
Men and Memories: Recollections...1872-1900; Men and Memories: Recollections...1900-1922. Since Fifty Men and Memories 1922-1938. London: 1931-38. V. 49
Twelve Portraits. London: 1929. V. 54

ROTHERAM, JOHN
An Essay on Human Liberty. Newcastle upon Tyne: 1782. V. 47; 51; 52
A Philosophical Inquiry Into the Nature and Properties of Water. Newcastle-upon-Tyne: 1770. V. 48

ROTHERT, OTTO A.
A History of Muhlenberg County...With More than Two Hundred Illustrations and a Complete Index. Louisville: 1913. V. 47
The Outlaws of Cave-in-Rock, Historical Accounts of the Famous Highwayman and River Pirates in Pioneer Days Upon the Ohio and Mississippi Rivers and Over the Old Natchez Trace. Cleveland: 1927. V. 53
The Outlaws of Cave-in-Rock, Historical Accounts of the Famous Highwaymen and River Pirates Who Operated in Pioneer Days Upon the Ohio and Mississippi Rivers and Over the Old Natchez Trace. Cleveland: 1924. V. 47

ROTHERY, CHARLES WILSON
Notes on a Yacht Voyage to Hardanger Fjord, and the Adjacent Estauries. London: 1855. V. 50

ROTHERY, G. A.
A Diary of the Wreck of His Majesty's Ship Challenger, On the Western Coast of South America, in May 1835. London: 1836. V. 54

ROTHERY, MARY C. HUME
The Bridesmaid, Count Stephen and Other Poems. London: 1853. V. 48; 50; 52

ROTHSCHILD Collection at Waddesdon Manor. Gold Boxes. Serge Grandjean, Kirsten Aschengreen, Piacenti, Charles Truman and Anthony Blunt. 1975. V. 49

ROTHSCHILD, FERDINAND DE, BARON
Livre d'Or. Cambridge: 1957. V. 48

ROTHSCHILD, JAMES A. DE
Gold Boxes and Miniatures of the Eighteenth Century. Fribourg: 1975. V. 47

ROTHSCHILD, LORD
The Genus Dedrolagus (Tree Kangaroos). London: 1936. V. 48; 49; 54

ROTHSCHILD, MIRIAM
Dear Lord Rothschild. Birds, Butterflies and History. London: 1983. V. 52
Fleas, Flukes and Cuckoos. London: 1952. V. 48

THE ROTHSCHILD Miscellany. Jerusalem: 1989. V. 51; 52

ROTHSCHILD, NATHAN JAMES EDOUARD, BARON DE
Catalogue des Livres. New York: 1965. V. 48

ROTHSCHILD, NATHANIEL M. V.
Two Bindings by Robert Payne in the Library of Lord Rothschild. Cambridge: 1947. V. 48
Two Bindings by Roger Payne in the Library of Lord Rothschild. London: 1947. V. 49

ROTHSCHILD, VICTOR
The History of Tom Jones, a Changeling - Caveat Emptor. Cambridge: 1951. V. 53

ROTHSCHILD, W.
The Avifauna of Laysan and the Neighbouring Islands... London: 1893-1900. V. 51
Extinct Birds. London: 1907. V. 51
Revision of the Lepidopterous Family Sphingidae. London: 1903. V. 49

ROTHWELL, C. F. SEYMOUR
The Printing of Textile Fabrics, a Practical manual on the Printing of Cotton, Wool, Silk and Half Silk Fabrics... London: 1897. V. 47

ROTTIERS, BERNARD EUGENE ANTOINE
Monuments de Rhodes. Brussels: 1828. V. 54

ROTZ, JEAN
The Maps and Text of the Boke of Idrography Presented by Jean Rotz to Henry VIII Now in the British Library. London: 1981. V. 50
The Maps and Text of the Boke of Idrography Presented by...to Henry VIII Now in the British Library. Oxford: 1981. V. 54

ROUART, DENIS
Degas Monotypes. Paris: 1948. V. 53

ROUAULT, GEORGES
Miserere. London: 1950. V. 48

ROUCHER, JEAN ANTOINE
Collection Universelle des Memoires Particuliers Rleatifs a l'Histoire de France. Londres et se Trouve: 1785-91. V. 53

ROUCK, THOMAS DE
Adelyk Toneel of Historische Beschrijvinge Van Allerley Trappen Van Adeldom. Amsterdam: 1673. V. 53; 54

ROUFF, MAGGY
La Philosophie de l'Elegance. Paris: 1945. V. 51

ROUGHEAD, WILLIAM
Trial of Mrs. M'Lachlan. Glasgow: 1911. V. 50
Trial of Oscar Slater. Edinburgh & Glasgow: 1910. V. 49

ROUGHEY, T. C.
Fishes of Australia and Their Technology. Sydney: 1916. V. 48; 50; 51; 54

ROUILLE, GUILLAUME
La Premiere - Seconde Partie du Promptuaire des Medalles. Lyon: 1553. V. 54
Promptuarii Iconum Insigniorum a seculo Hominum... Lyon: 1553. V. 48

ROUNDELAY Or the New Syren. A Collection of Choice Songs Including the Modern. London: 1785. V. 48

ROUNDELL, C., MRS.
Cowdray; the History of a Great English House. London: 1884. V. 47
Ham House, Its History and Art Treasures. London: 1904. V. 51

ROUNTREE, HARRY
Dicky Duck and Wonderful Walter. London. V. 54
Rountree's Ridiculous Rabbits. No. 1 The Furlimbunnmie Family. London: 1930. V. 51

ROUPEL, A. E.
Specimens of the Flora of South Africa. London: 1849. V. 54

ROUQUET, ANDRE
L'Art Nouveau de la Peinture en Fromage ou en Ramequin Inventree Pour Suivre Le Louable Projet de Trouver Graduellement des Facons de Peindre Inferieures a Celles Qui Existent. A Marolles (i.e. Paris): 1755. V. 52

ROUQUETTE, ADRIEN
Critical Dialgoue Between Aboo and Caboo on a New Book on a Grandissime Acension. Mingo City: 1880. V. 48

ROUQUETTE, L. F.
Le Grand Silence Blanc (Roman Vecu d'Alaska). Paris: 1928. V. 53

ROURKE, C.
Charles Sheeler: Artist in the American Tradition. New York: 1938. V. 50; 51; 53; 54

ROURKE, J.
The Proteas of Southern Africa. Cape Town: 1980. V. 49

ROUS AND MANN
Toronto: The Capital of Ontario. Eleven Reproductions of Etchings Made in the Art Department of Rous and Mann. Toronto: 1921. V. 52

ROUS, FRANCIS
Archaeologiae Atticae Libri Septem. Oxford: 1649. V. 48
Archaeologiae Atticae Libri Septem. Oxfordd: 1658. V. 48
Archaeologiae Atticae Libri Septem. Oxford: 1667. V. 49

ROUS, GEORGE
A Letter to the Right Honurable Edmund Burke... London: 1791. V. 51
Thoughts on Government: Occasioned by Mr. Burke's Reflections, &c. London: 1790. V. 51

ROUS, HENRY JOHN
On the Laws and Practice of Horse Racing, etc., etc. London: 1866. V. 47

ROUSE, WILLIAM
The Doctrine of Chances, or, The Theory of Gaming Made Easy to Every Person... London: 1814. V. 47; 52

ROUSSEAU, JEAN JACQUES
Aphorisms on Education... London: 1800. V. 48
The Confessions. London: 1783. V. 50
The Confessions. Philadelphia: 1902. V. 51
The Confessions. London: 1904. V. 51
Confessions. London: 1938. V. 53
The Confessions. New York: 1955. V. 49
Le Devin du Village. Paris: 1753. V. 49
Eloisa; a Series of Original Letters. London: 1810. V. 47
Eloisa; or, a Series of Original Letters. London: 1761. V. 47
Emile, ou de l'Education. Francfort: 1762. V. 47
Emilius; or, an Essay on Education. London: 1763. V. 47; 48; 49; 53; 54
An Inquiry into the Nature of the Social Contract; or Principles of Political Right. London: 1791. V. 48; 49
Julia; or, the New Eloisa. Edinburgh: 1794. V. 47
Letters of an Italian Nun and an English Gentleman. Worcester: 1796. V. 51
Letters on the Elements of Botany. London: 1791. V. 51; 52; 53
The Miscellaneous Works. London: 1767. V. 54
Original Letters, to M. de Malesherbes, M. D'Alembert, Madame la M. de Luxembourg, &c. London: 1799. V. 48
A Treatise on the Social Compact. London: 1764. V. 54
A Treatise on the Social Compact. London: 1795. V. 47

ROUSSEAU, SAMUEL
A Dictionary of Mohammedan Law, Bengal Revenue Terms, Shanscrit, Hindoo, and Other Words Used in the East Indies... London: 1802. V. 47
Punctuation; or, an Attempt to Facilitate the Art of Painting, on the Principles of Grammar and Reason. London: 1813. V. 52

ROUSSEAU, V.
The Messiah of the Cylinder. 1917. V. 48; 52

ROUSSEAU DE LA VALETTE, MICHEL
The Life of Count Ulfeld, Great Master of Denmark and of the Countess of Eleonora His Wife. London: 1695. V. 52

ROUSSELET, LOUIS
India and Its Native Princes... 1876. V. 54

ROUSSET DE MISSY, J.
Histoire du Cardina Alberoni, et de Son Ministere. La Haye: 1720. V. 49
The History of Cardinal Alberoni...to the Year 1719. (with) Considerations Upon the Present State of the Spanish Monarchy. London: 1719. V. 47; 53

ROUSSIN, ANDRE
The Little Hut. New York: 1953. V. 54

ROUT, E. A.
Maori Symbolism, Being an Account of the Origin, Migration and Culture of the New Zealand Maori... London: 1926. V. 51

ROUTH, MARTIN J.
Reliquiae Sacrae: sive, Auctorum Fere Jam Perditorum Secundi Tertiique Saeculi Post Christum Natum Quae Supersunt. Oxford: 1846. V. 50

ROUTLEDGE, EDMUND
Every Boy's Book. London: 1884. V. 51

ROUTLEDGE, JAMES
Chapters in the History of Popular Progress, Chiefly in Relation to the Freedom of the Press and Trial by Jury. 1660-1820. London: 1876. V. 51

ROUTLEDGE, SCORESBY
The Mystery of Easter Island, the Story of an Expedition. 1919. V. 49

ROUTLEDGE, WILLIAM
The Children's Musical Cinderella. London: 1879. V. 49

ROUTLEDGE'S Coloured Scrap Book. London: 1870. V. 47

ROUTLEDGE'S Nursery Book. London: 1866. V. 48

ROUX, HUGHES
Acrobats and Mountebanks. London: 1890. V. 49

ROUX, J.
Ornithologie Provencale. Marseille & Paris: 1825-30. V. 47

ROUX, JOSEPH
Carte de la mer Mediterranee en Douze Feuilles. Marseilles: 1764. V. 49

ROVILLE, GUILLAUME
Pomptvarii Iconvm Insigniorvm A Secvlo Hominum. Lyon: 1553. V. 47; 49; 53

ROWAN, ALFRED
The Military Operations of General eaureard in the War Between the States 1861 to 1865... New York: 1884. V. 47

ROWAN, ARCHIBALD HAMILTON
Report Of the Trial...On an Information, Filed, Ex Officio, by the Attorney General, for the Distribution of a Libel... New York: 1794. V. 51; 52

ROWAN, JOHN J.
The Emigrant and Sportsman in Canada. London: 1876. V. 52

ROWAN, PETER
History of the Flathead Indian. Helena: 1890. V. 49

ROWE, ALAN
A Catalogue of Egyptian Scarabs, Scaraboids, Seals and Amulets in the Palestine Archaeological Museum. Le Caire: 1936. V. 49

ROWE, ELEANOR
Studies from the Museums. Wood Carvings from the South Kensington Museum. London: 1889. V. 49

ROWE, ELIZABETH
Friendship in Death: In Twenty Letters from the Dead to the Living. New York: 1795. V. 53
Friendship in Death; in Twenty Letters...to which are added, Letters Moral and Entertaining... London: 1745. V. 50

ROWE, G.
Forty-Eight Views of Cottages and Scenery at Sidmouth, Devon, Drawn from Nature and on Stone. Sidmouth: 1826. V. 47

ROWE, GEORGE STRINGER
The Life of John Hunt, Missionary to the Cannibals. London: 1860. V. 48

ROWE, HENRY
Fables in Verse. London: 1810. V. 47
Poems. London: 1796. V. 50

ROWE, NICHOLAS
The Ambitious Step-Mother. London: 1702. V. 49
Ode for the New Year MDCCXVI. London: 1716. V. 50
The Royal Convert. London: 1702. V. 48
The Royal Convert. London: 1708. V. 47; 48
Tamerlane. London: 1703. V. 48
The Tragedy of Jane Shore. London: 1710. V. 48
The Tragedy of Jane Shore. London: 1714. V. 48; 51
The Tragedy of Lady Jane Gray. London: 1715. V. 48
Ulysses. London: 1706. V. 47
The Works. London: 1766. V. 48; 53

ROWE, R. P. P.
Rowing. London: 1898. V. 54

ROWELL, MARGIT
Jean Dubuffet: a Retrospective. New York: 1973. V. 48
Miro. New York: 1970. V. 47; 48; 50; 52

ROWLAND, ERON OPHA MOORE
Varina Howell Wife of Jefferson Davis. New York: 1927-31. V. 50

ROWLAND, WILLIAM
Judiciall Astrologie Judicially Condemned Upon a Survey and Examination of Sr. Christopher Heydons Apology for It in Answer to Mr. Chambers. London: 1652. V. 50

ROWLANDS, HENRY
Mona Antigua Restaurata. London: 1766. V. 49; 51; 53

ROWLANDS, JOHN
Historical Notes of the Counties of Glamorgan, Carmarthen & Cardigan and List of the Members of Parliament for South Wales from Henry VIII to Charles II. Cardiff: 1866. V. 52

ROWLANDS, SAMUEL
Tis Merry When Gossips Meet. London: 1818. V. 53

ROWLANDS, WALTER
Curious Old Gravestones in and About Boston. Boston: 1924. V. 50; 53

ROWLANDSON, THOMAS
The Adventures of Doctor Comicus or the Frolicks of Fortune. London: 1815. V. 50
The Adventures of Doctor Comicus or the Frolicks of Fortune. London: 1915. V. 47
Chesterfield Travestie, or School for Modern Manners. London: 1809. V. 47; 49
Country Characters. London: 1800. V. 48
Doctor Syntax in Paris, or a Tour in Search of the Grotesque. London: 1820. V. 51
The English Dance of Death... London: 1815-16. V. 49
The Grand Master, or Adventures of Qui Hi?. London: 1816. V. 51
The History of Johnny Quae Genus, the Little Foundling of the Late Dr. Syntax. London: 1822. V. 51
Hugarian and Highland Broad Sword. 1799. V. 51
Loyal Volunteers of London and Environs. London: 1798-99. V. 49; 50; 53; 54
Medical Caricatures. V. 51
Medical Caricatures. New York: 1971. V. 47; 48; 50; 53; 54
The Military Adventures of Johnny Newcome with an Account of His Campaign on the Peninsula and In Pall Mall. London: 1816. V. 50
Miseries of Human Life. London: 1808. (1823-25). V. 54
Naples and the Campagna Felice in a Series of Letters, Addressed to a friend in England in 1802. London: 1815. V. 48; 51
Pretty Little Games. 1930's. V. 48
Rowlandson's Characteristic Sketches of the Lower Orders... London: 1820. V. 53
The Tour of Doctor Syntax through London, or the Pleasures and Miseries of the Metropolis. London: 1820. V. 53
The World in Miniature. London: 1817. V. 52

ROWLATT, RICHARD
Entranced with a Dream. London: 1883. V. 54
Fishing in Deep Waters. London: 1879. V. 54

ROWLES, THOMAS
Report on the Survey of the Proposed Elysville and Canton RailRoad. Baltimore: 1853. V. 53

ROWLES, WALTER
A General History of Maidstone... London: 1809. V. 47

ROWLEY, G. D.
Ornithological Miscellany. London: 1876-78. V. 51; 52; 53

ROWLEY, HUGH
Gamosagammon; or, Hints on Hymen. London: 1870. V. 49
Puniana; or, Thoughts Wise and Other-Wise. London: 1867. V. 49

ROWLEY, WILLIAM
Schola Medicinae, or, the New Universal History and School of Medicine. London: 1803. V. 51; 52; 53

ROWNING, J.
A Compenious System of Natural Philosophy. Cambridge: 1735-36. V. 53

ROWNTREE, ARTHUR
The History of Scarborough: Yorkshire. London: 1931. V. 51; 54

ROWSE, A. L.
A Cornishman Abroad. London: 1976. V. 50

ROWSON, CHARLOTTE
Charlotte. A Tale of Truth. Philadelphia: 1794. V. 51; 52

ROWSON, SUSANNA HASWELL
An Abridgment of Universal Geography, Together with Sketches of History, Designed for the Use of Schools and Academics in the United States. Boston;: 1806. V. 54
Biblical Dialogues Between a Father and His Family... Boston: 1822. V. 54
Charlotte Temple, a tale of Truth. Cincinnati: 1828. V. 50
Miscellaneous Poems. Boston: 1804. V. 48; 49
A Spelling Dictionary, Divided into Short Lessons for the Easier Committing to Memory of Children and Young Persons... Boston: 1807. V. 52

ROXBURGHE CLUB
Chronological List of Members: Catalogue of Books; Rules and Regulations. London: 1850. V. 48
List of Members 1812-1991. List of Books 1814-1990. 1991. V. 54

ROXBURGHE CLUB OF SAN FRANCISCO
Chronology of 25 Years, 1928-1953. San Francisco: 1954. V. 53

ROY, ANDREW
A History of the Coal Miners of the United States - from the Development of the Mines to the Close of the Anthracite Strike of 1902... Columbus: 1904. V. 52

ROY, C. S.
Heart-Beat and Pulse-Wave. 1890. V. 49

ROY, CAMPBELL
The Collected Poems of Roy Campbell. London: 1949. V. 47

ROY, CLAUDE
Hans Erni. Geneva: 1955. V. 51

ROY, JAMES A.
The Heart is Highland. Toronto: 1947. V. 53

ROY, JOHN
Helen Treveryan, or the Ruling Race. London: 1892. V. 54

ROY, JUST JEAN ETIENNE
The Adventures of a French Captain, at Present a Planter in Texas... New York: 1878. V. 47

ROY, WILLIAM
The Military Antiquities of the Roman in Britain. London: 1793. V. 54

ROYAL ACADEMY
Abstract of the Constitution. London: 1815. V. 50; 53

ROYAL ACADEMY OF ARTS
The Chinese Exhibition. A Commemorative Catalogue of the International Exhibition of Chinese Art. Royal Academy of Arts. November 1935-March 1936. London: 1936. V. 49

ROYAL AGRICULTURAL SOCIETY OF ENGLAND
The Journal of the Royal Agricultural Society of England. London: 1840-1941. V. 49

ROYAL CANADIAN ACADEMY OF ARTS
Records of the Founding of the Royal Canadian Academy by His Excellency the Marquis of Lorne and Her Royal Highness the Princess Louise 1879-80. Toronto: 1883. V. 50

THE ROYAL Canadian Air Force Overseas: The Sixth year. Toronto: 1949. V. 52

ROYAL COLLEGE OF PHYSICIANS
The Dispensatory. London: 1746. V. 53

ROYAL COMMISSION ON HISTORICAL MONUMENTS
Herefordshire. London: 1931-34. V. 47
An Inventory of the Historical Monuments in London. East London: 1924-30. V. 48

ROYAL GEOGRAPHIC SOCIETY OF LONDON
Proceedings of the Royal Geographic Society of London. Volume II Session 1857-58. Numbers I to VI. London: 1858. V. 47
Proceedings of the Royal Geographic Society of London. Volume VI. Session 1861-62. Numbers I to V. London: 1862. V. 47; 51
Proceedings of the....Volume II Session 1857-58. Nos. I to VI. London: V. 51

ROYAL GEOLOGICAL SOCIETY OF CORNWALL
Transactions. Volume the First. London: 1818. V. 54
Transactions. Volume the Fourth. Penzance: 1832. V. 54
Transactions. Volume the Second. Penzance: 1822. V. 54
Transactions. Volume the Third. Penzance: 1827. V. 54

ROYAL HISTORICAL SOCIETY
Transactions. London: 1927-88. V. 49

ROYAL HORTICULTURAL SOCIETY
Dictionary of Gardening. London: 1951. V. 47; 48; 50
Dictionary of Gardening. Oxford: 1951. V. 49
Dictionary of Gardening. London: 1956. V. 48; 50
Dictionary of Gardening. Oxford: 1956/65-69. V. 48
Dictionary of Gardening. Oxford: 1965-69. V. 50; 51
Dictionary of Gardening, A Practical and Scientific Encyclopaedia of Horticulture. Oxford: 1974. V. 48
The Fruit Yearbook. London: 1947-58. V. 52; 53
The Lindley Library. Catalogue of Books, Pamphlets, Manuscripts and Drawings. London: 1927. V. 49
The New Dictionary of Gardening. London: 1992. V. 48; 50; 51

ROYAL HOSPITAL CHELSEA
Papers Illustrative of the Original and Early History... London: 1872. V. 50

ROYAL HUMANE SOCIETY
Fifty-Fourth Annual Report of the Royal Humane Society, Instituted 1774, to Collected and Circulate the Most Approved and Effectual Methods for Recovering Persons Apparently Drowned or Dead... London: 1828. V. 49

ROYAL INSTITUTE OF BRITISH ARCHITECTS
Catalogue of the Royal Institute of British Architects Library. Folkstone: 1972. V. 49

ROYAL INSTITUTE OF BRITISH ARCHTIECTS
Papers Read at the Royal Institute of British Architects. London: 1859-65. V. 52

ROYAL INSTITUTION
Notices of the Proceedings at their Meetings of the Members of the Royal Institution, With Abstracts of the Discourse Delivered at the Evening Meetings. London: 1854-1918. V. 52

ROYAL INSTITUTION OF BRITISH ARCHITECTS
Industrial Housing in Wartime. London: 1940. V. 53
Report On Brickwork Tests Conducted by a Sub-Committee of the Science Standing Committee of the Royal Institute of British Architects. London: 1905. V. 53

ROYAL INSTITUTION OF CORNWALL
Twenty-Seventh-Thirty Fourth Annual Report. Truro: 1846-53. V. 52

ROYAL INSTITUTION OF GREAT BRITAIN
The Archives in Facsimile: Minutes of Managers' Meetings 1799-1903. London: 1971-76. V. 49

ROYAL INSTITUTION OF GREAT BRITAIN. LONDON. LIBRARY
A Catalogue of the Library of the Royal Institution of Great Britain... London: 1821. V. 47; 53

ROYAL *Investigation; or Authentic Documents, Containing the Acquittal of H.R.H. the P(rince)ss of W(ale)s (etc.).* London: 1807. V. 48

ROYAL IRISH ACADEMY
Transactions. Volume I/II. 1787/88. V. 52

THE ROYAL *Navy List or Who's Who in the Navy.* London: 1916. V. 54

THE ROYAL *Punch and Judy.* London: 1870. V. 52

ROYAL SCOTTISH GEOGRAPHICAL SOCIETY
Atlas of Scotland. Edinburgh: 1895. V. 50

ROYAL SOCIETY
Biographical Memoirs of Fellows of the Royal Society. London: 1972-83. V. 47
The Philosophical Transactions 1700-1720. London: 1721. V. 50

THE ROYAL *Society of British Artists 1824-1893 and The New English Art Club 1888-1917.* 1987. V. 54

ROYAL SOCIETY OF LONDON
Biographical Memoirs of Fellows. London: 1955-80. V. 49; 51
Catalogue of a Collection of Early Printed Books in the Library of the Royal Society. London: 1910. V. 54
Catalogue of Scientific Books in the Library... London: 1839. V. 54
Philosophical Transactions, From Their Commencement in 1665 to the Year 1800... London: 1809. V. 48; 49
The Record of the Royal Society of London for the Promotion of Natural Knowledge. London: 1940. V. 54
The Royal Society. Some Account of the "Letters and Papers" of the Period 1741-1806 in the Archives with an Index of Authors. Oxford: 1908. V. 54

THE ROYAL *Sovereign - A New Year's Gift.* London: 1825. V. 54

ROYAL COLLEGE OF SURGEONS, LONDON
A Descriptive and Illustrated Catalogue of the Calculi & Other Animal Concretions Contained in the Museum. London: 1842. V. 48

ROYALL, ANNE NEWPORT
Sketches of History, Life and Manners in the United States. New Haven: 1826. V. 48
The Tennessean: a Novel Founded on Facts. New Haven: 1827. V. 47; 52; 53

THE ROYALL *Martyr, or Charles the First No Man of Blood but a Martyr for His People.* London: 1660. V. 49; 53

ROYALL, WILLIAM L.
Some Reminiscences. New York: 1909. V. 49

ROYAL OBSERVATORY, GREENWICH
Astronomical and Meteorological Observations Made at the Royal Observatory, Greenlwch. Edinburgh. 1902-1932. V. 47
Astronomical and Meteorological Observations made at the Royal Observatory, Greenwich Under the Direction of W. H. M. Christie, 100-1931. Edinburgh: 1901-31. V. 50

ROYCE, ANNE OGDEN
Records of a Quaker Family: The Richardsons of Cleveland. London: 1889. V. 49

ROYCE, C. C.
John Bidwell, Pioneer, Statesman, Philanthropist. A biographical Sketch. (with) Addresses, Reminiscences, etc. Chico: 1906-07. V. 50

ROYCE, GEORGE MONROE
Two Englishmen. London: 1885. V. 53

ROYCE, JOSIAH
The Basic Writings of...(with) The Letters of Josiah Royce. Chicago: 1969-70. V. 51
California from the Conquest in 1846 to the Second Vigilance Committee in San Francisco... Boston/New York: 1886. V. 47; 53

ROYCE, SARAH
A Frontier Lady: Recollections of the Gold Rush and Early California. New Haven: 1932. V. 50

ROYDE-SMITH, NAOMI
Children in the Wood. London: 1928. V. 51
The Housemaid. New York: 1926. V. 51
The Lover. London: 1928. V. 51

ROYEN, ADRIAN VAN
Florae Leydensis Prodromus, Exhibens Plantas Quae in Horto Academico Lugduno-Batavo Aluntur. Leiden: 1740. V. 49

ROYLE, J. F.
An Essay on the Antiquity of Hindoo Medicine, Including an Introductory Lecture to the Course of Materia Medica and Therapeutics, Delivered at King's College. London: 1837. V. 52
The Fibrous Plants of India Fitted for Cordage, Clothing and Paper. London: 1855. V. 49
Illustrations of the Botany and Other Branches of the Natural History of the Himalayan Mountains and of the Flora of Cashmere. London: 1839. V. 48; 50; 51
On the Culture and Commerce of Cotton in India and Elsewhere... London: 1851. V. 52

ROYS, RALPH L.
The Book of Chilam Balam of Chumayel. Washington: 1933. V. 50; 52

ROYSTON, VISCOUNT
Cassandra. Cambridge: 1806. V. 48

ROZSA, MIKLOS
Double Life: the Autobiography of... Turnbridge Wells: 1982. V. 51

ROZWADOWSKI, ZDISLAW
50 Years of Breeding Pure Blood Arabians in Poland in Their Genealogical Charts 1918-1968. Warsaw: 1972. V. 53

RUARK, ROBERT
Grenadine's Spawn. Garden City: 1952. V. 50; 53
Grenadine's Spawn. New York: 1982. V. 50
I Didn't Know It Was Loaded. Garden City: 1948. V. 53
The Old Man and the Boy. New York: 1957. V. 50
The Old Man's Boy Grows Older. New York: 1961. V. 53
Poor No More. New York: 1959. V. 53
Uhuru; a Novel of Africa Today. New York: 1962. V. 51

RUBENS, ALFRED
A History of Jewish Costume. New York: 1973. V. 53

RUBEUS, THEODOSIUS
Discursus Circa Literas Apostolicas in Forma Brevis S.D.M. Urvani Papae VIII. Rome: 1639. V. 52

RUBIN, LAWRENCE
Frank Stella Paintings 1958-1965. London: 1986. V. 49; 54

RUBIN, R.
Rubin: My Life, My Art: an Autobiography and Selected Paintings. New York: 1970. V. 52

RUBIN, WILLIAM S.
Dada and Surrealist Art. New York. V. 49; 52
Dada and Surrealist Art. New York: 1968. V. 48; 54
Dada and Surrealist Art. London: 1969. V. 47

RUBINSTEIN, ARTHUR
My Young Years. New York: 1973. V. 49

RUBIONE, GUGLIELMUS
Disputatorum In Quatuor Libros Magisri Sententiarum. Paris. V. 52

RUBLOWSKY, J.
Pop Art. New York: 1965. V. 53; 54

RUCKER, MAUDE
The Oregon Trail and Some Of its Makers. New York: 1930. V. 48; 52

RUCKER, WILBUR
A History of the Opthalmoscope. Rochester: 1971. V. 52

RUDD, DAN A.
From Slavery to Wealth: The Life of Scott Bond, The Rewards of Honesty, Industry, Economy and Perserverance. Madison: 1917. V. 53

RUDD, SAYER
The Certain Method to Know the Disease. London: 1742. V. 51

RUDDER, SAMUEL
The History and Antiquites of Gloucester: Including the Civil and Military Affairs of that Ancient City... Cirencester: 1781. V. 49
A New History of Gloucestershire. Cirencester: 1779. V. 47; 48; 50

RUDDIMAN, THOMAS
Grammatical Exercises, On the Moods, Tenses and Syntax of the Latin Language... Charleston: 1823. V. 48

RUDENSTINE, ANGELICA ZANDER
Russian Avant-Garde Art. The George Costakis Collection. London: 1981. V. 49; 51

RUDGE, THOMAS
The History of the County of Gloucester, Compressed and Brought Down to the Year 1802. London: 1803. V. 48
The History of the County of Gloucester: Compressed, and Brought Down to the Year 1803. Gloucester: 1803. V. 51; 52

RUDIMENTS of Ancient Architecture, Containing an Historical Account of the Five Orders, With Their Proportions and Examples of Each From Antiques. London: 1794. V. 48

RUDING, WALT
An Evil Motherhood: an Impressionist Novel. V. 50
An Evil Motherood: an Impressionist Novel. London: 1896. V. 49

RUDISILL, RICHARD
Mirror Image: The Influence of the Daguerreotype on American Society. Albuquerque: 1971. V. 47; 54

RUDKIN, DAVID
Will's Way. Halford: 1993. V. 52
Will's Way. Shipston-on-Stour: 1993. V. 54

RUDNAI, JUDITH A.
The Social Life of the Lion. Kenya: 1973. V. 54

RUDOLF, CROWN PRINCE OF AUSTRIA
Notes on Sport and Ornithology. London: 1889. V. 50; 51; 52; 53
Tafeln Aus dem Werke Eine Orientreise. Vienna: 1884. V. 54
Travels in the East Including a Visit to Egypt and the Holy Land. London: 1884. V. 48

RUEFF, JACOB
De Conceptu et Generatione Hominis... Zurich: 1554. V. 48
Hebammen Buch, Daraus Man Alle Heimligkeit Desz Weiblichen Geschlechts Erlehmen, Welcherley Gestadt der Mensch in Mutter Leib Empfangen, Zunimpt und Geboren Wirdt. Franckfort am May: 1588. V. 49; 50

RUESS, EVERETT
On Desert Trails with Everett Ruess. El Centro: 1940. V. 50
On Desert Trails With Everett Ruess. Palm Desert: 1950. V. 51

RUFF, SIEGFRIED
Compendium of Aviation Medicine. Washington: 1942. V. 49

RUFFHEAD, OWEN
The Life of Alexander Pope, Esq. London: 1769. V. 52; 53

RUFFIN, EDMUND
Agricultural, Geological and Descriptive Sketches of Lower North Carolina and the Similar Adjacent Lands. Raleigh: 1861. V. 49; 51
Anticipiations of the Future, to Serve as Lessons for the Present Time. Richmond: 1860. V. 52
An Essay on Calcareous Manures. Petersburg: 1832. V. 47

RUFFIN, FRANK GILDARAT
The Negro as a Political and Social Factor. Richmond: 1888. V. 53

RUFFNER, E. H.
Explorations and Surveys in the Department of the Missouri. Washington: 1878. V. 54
Lines of Communication Between Colorado and New Mexico. Washington: 1878. V. 49; 52

RUFFNER, HENRY
Address to the People of West Virginia; Shewing and Slavery is Injurious to the Public Welfare. Louisville: 1847. V. 50

RUFFNER, W. H.
A Report on Washington Territory. New York: 1889. V. 52

RUFUS FESTUS, SEXTUS
Le Dignita de Consoli, e de gl'Imperadori, e i Fatti de' Romani.... Venice: 1561. V. 52

RUGE, A.
Logic. Encyclopeida of the Philosophical Sciences. London: 1913. V. 49

RUGELEY, ROWLAND
Miscellaneous Poems, and Translations from La Fontaine and Others. Cambridge: 1763. V. 47; 54

RUGGIERI, CLAUDE
Precis Historique sur les Fetes, les Spectacles et les Rejouissances Publiques. Paris: 1830. V. 52

RUGGLE, GEORGE
Ignoramus. Comoedia Coram Regia Maiestate Jacobi Regis Angliae. Londini: 1630. V. 48; 50

RUHEMANN, HELMUT
The Cleaning of Paintings, Problems and Potentialities. London: 1968. V. 52

RUHL, LUDWIG SIGISMUND
Capricci. London: 1827. V. 53

RUHMER, EBERHARD
Cosimo Tura Paintings and Drawings. London: 1958. V. 50
Tura. Paintings and Drawings. London: 1958. V. 54

RUHRAH, JOHN
Pediatrics of the Past. New York: 1925. V. 52; 53

RUIZ DE MORO, PEDRO
Decisiones de Rebus in Sacro Auditorio Lituanico... Cracow: 1563. V. 50

RUIZ-VILAPLANA, A.
Burgos Justice: a Year's Experience of Nationalist Spain. London: 1938. V. 49

RUKEYSER, MURIEL
Elegies. Germany: 1949. V. 48
The Green Wave (Poems). New York: 1948. V. 54
Theory of Flight. New Haven: 1935. V. 47; 48; 49; 53

RULAND, MARTIN
De Lingua Graeca, Eiusque Dialectis Omnibus Libri V. Tiguri (Zurich): 1556. V. 47; 50
Synonyma. Copia Graecorum Verborum Omnium Absolutissima... Augustburg: 1563. V. 51

RULE, BOB
Champions Golf Club 1957-1976. Houston: 1976. V. 52

THE RULE of Life. London: 1776. V. 53

RULE, ROGER C.
The Rifleman's Rifle. Northridge: 1982. V. 53

RULE, WILLIAM HARRIS
History of the Inquisition from Its Establishment in the Twelfth Century to Its Extinction in the Nineteenth. London: 1874. V. 47

RULES and Articles for the Better Government of the Troops Raised, or to Be Raised and Kept in Pay by and at the Expense of the United States of America. Philadelphia: 1776. V. 49

THE RULES and Constitutions for Governing and Managing the Maiden-Hospital, Founded by the Company of Merchants, and Mary Erskine, in Anno 1695. Edinburgh: 1731. V. 51

RULES and Regulations for the Field Exercise and Manoeuvres of Infantry, Compiled and Adpated to the Organization of the Army of the United States, Agreeably to a Resolve of Congress, Dated December 1814. New York: 1815. V. 48

RULES and Regulations for the Field Exercise and Manoeuvres of Infantry, Compiled and Adapted to the Organization of the Army of the United States, Agreeably to a resolve of Congress, Dated December 1814. Concord: 1817. V. 48

RULES for the Management and Cleaning of the Rifle Musket, Model 1863 for the Use of Soldiers, Springfield Armory, April 28th, 1863. Washington: 1863. V. 48

RULES of Practice for the Courts of Equity of the United States, Promulgated by the Supreme Court of the United States, Jan. Term, 1842. Indianapolis: 1842. V. 50; 53

RULES, Orders and Regulations, to Be Observed and Enforced fro the Government of the House in Correction, at Wakefield, in the West-Riding of the County of York. Wakefield: 1801. V. 50; 54

RULES Under the Surpeme Court of Judicataure. (Ireland) Act, 1877. Dublin: 1891. V. 49

RULFO, JUAN
El Llano en Llamas. Mexico City: 1953. V. 48
Pedro Paramo. Mexico City: 1955. V. 53
Perdo Paramo. New York: 1959. V. 53

RULHIERE, CLAUDE
A History, or Anecdotes of the Revolution in Russia, in the Year 1762. Boston: 1798. V. 53

RUMFORD, BENJAMIN THOMPSON, COUNT
The Complete Works. Boston: 1870. V. 47
The Complete Works. London: 1875-76. V. 53

RUMI, JALALUDDIN MOHAMMAD
Letters. New York: 1987. V. 50; 54
On the Art of Painting. New York: 1989. V. 50
The Parrot and the Merchant. New York: 1981. V. 49; 50
The Reed. New York: 1989. V. 50

RUMILLA, JOSEPH
El Orinoco Illustrado, y Defendido, Historia Natural, Civil y Geographica de este Gran Rio, y de sus Caudalosas Vertientes... Madrid: 1745. V. 53

RUMPF, GEORG EVERHARD
D'Amboinsche Rariteitkamer, Behelzende Eene Beschryvinge van Allerhande Zoo Weeke als Harade Schaalvisschen... Amsterdam: 1741. V. 49

RUMPLE, JETHRO
A History of Rowan County, North Carolina... Raleigh: 1929. V. 47; 50

RUMSEY, JAMES
A Short Treatise on the Application of Steam, Whereby is Clearly Shewn from Actual Experiments.... Philadelphia: 1788. V. 48; 51

RUNDALL, L. B.
The Ibex of Sha-Ping and Other Himalayan Studies. 1915. V. 52; 54
The Ibex of Sha-Ping and Other Himalayan Studies. London: 1915. V. 48; 49

RUNDALL, MARY ANN
Symbolic Illustrations of the History of England from the Roman Invasion to the Present Time. London: 1815. V. 50

RUNDELL, MARIA ELIZA
A New System of Domestic Cookery. Exeter: 1808. V. 48; 50
A New System of Domestic Cookery... 1810. V. 53
A New System of Domestic Cookery. London: 1815. V. 50
A New System of Domestic Cookery... London: 1819. V. 49

RUNDLE, MARIA ELIZA
A New System of Domestic Cookery. London: 1813. V. 52

RUNDLE, T.
A Sermon Preached at St. George's Church, Hanover Square, On Sunday Feb. 17, 1733-34. To Recommend the Charity for Establishing the New Colony of Georgia. London: 1734. V. 52

RUNDT, CARL
A Walk Round Oxford. Berlin: 1851. V. 49; 50

RUNNING a Time Table. A Brakeman's Story. Burlington: 1873. V. 54

RUNNING, JOHN
Honor Dance. Native American Photographs. Reno: 1985. V. 50

RUNNINGTON, CHARLES
A Treatise on the Action of Ejectment. Dublin: 1792. V. 52

RUNSTALL, WILLIAM
St. Cyprian's Discourse to Donatus. London: 1717. V. 48

RUNYON, DAMON
The Best of Runyon. 1938. V. 50
In Our Town: Twenty Seven Slices of Life. New York: 1946. V. 48; 49
Runyon A La Carte. Philadelphia: 1944. V. 52
The Tents of Trouble. New York: 1911. V. 51

THE RUPERT Book. 1948. V. 52

RUPERT Edward Inglis. Chaplain to the Forces, Rector of Frittenden. Born 17 May, 1863, Killed in Action Near Ginch in the Battle of the Somme, 18 Sept. London: 1918. V. 47

RUPERT, PRINCE, COUNT PALATINE
Historical Memoirs of the Life and Death of...Prince Palatine of the Rhine, Duke of Cumberland, &c... London: 1683. V. 53

RUPIN, ERNEST
L'Oeuvre de Limoges. Paris: 1890-91. V. 51

RUPP, I. DANIEL
Early History of Western Pennsylvania, and of the West...1754-1833. Pittsburgh: 1846. V. 53
He Pasa Ekklesia. An Original History of the Religious Denominations at Present Exhisting in the United States. Philadelphia/Harrisburg: 1844. V. 47; 54
The History and Topography of Dauphin, Cumberland, Franklin, Bedford, Adams, and perry Counties... Lancaster City: 1846. V. 50
History of All the Religious Denominations in the United States... Harrisburg: 1852. V. 53
History of the Counties of Berks and Lebanon. Lancaster: 1844. V. 54

RUPPELL, E.
Neue Wirbelthiere zu der Fauna von Abyssinien Gehorig. London: 1835-40. V. 51

RUPPERT, KARL
Archaeological Reconnaissance in Campeche, Quintana Roos and Peten. Washington: 1943. V. 50
The Caracol at Chichen Itza, Yucatan, Mexico. Washington: 1935. V. 52
The Mercado, Chichen Itza, Yucatan. Washington: 1943. V. 52

THE RURAL Songster: a Collection of National and Sentimental Songs, for Rural Life. Dayton: 1850. V. 51

RUSBY, HENRY HURD
Morphology and Histology of Plants Designed Especially as a Guide to Plant-Analysis and Classification... New York: 1899. V. 52

RUSCELLI, GIROLAMO
De Secretis Libri, Mira Quadam Rerum Varietate Utilitateq Referti, Longe Castigatiores & Ampliores Quam Priore Editione. Basel: 1560. V. 49; 50; 52
Epistres des Princes, Lesqvelles, ov sont Addresses Avx Princes, ov Traittent les Affaires des Princes... Paris: 1572. V. 48; 52
Le Imprese Illvstri. Venice: 1584/83. V. 50; 53
Le Imprese Illustri... Con la Giunta di Altre Imprese Tutto Riordinato e Corretto da Fran. Venice: 1572. V. 50
Lettere di Principi, le Quali o'si Scrivono da Principi, o'a' Principi, o' Ragionan di Principi. Libro Primo. In Questa Seconda Editione Tutto Riordinato & Migliorato. (Libro Secondo). 1564-75. V. 47
Lettvra Sopra vn Sonetto dell'....Signor della Terza alla...Signora Marchesa del Vasto... Venice: 1552. V. 48
The Secretes of the Reuerende Maister Alexis of Piemount. London: 1568/68?/66/69. V. 50
The Secretes of the Reverende Maister Alexis of Piemount... London: 1566. V. 47
Tre Disccorsi a M. Lodovico Dolce. Venice: 1553. V. 48; 50; 53

RUSCHA, EDWARD
Crackers. Hollywood: 1969. V. 51
Every Building on the Sunset Strip. Los Angeles: 1966. V. 47
A Few Palm Trees. Hollywood: 1971. V. 51

RUSCHENBERGER, WILLIAM S. W.
Three Years in the Pacific; Containing Notices of Brazil, Chile, Bolivia, Peru, &c. in 1831, 1832, 1833, 1834. London: 1835. V. 47; 52; 53
A Voyage Round the World, Including an Embassy to Muscat and Siam in 1835, 1836 and 1837. Philadelphia: 1838. V. 50

RUSH, BENJAMIN
Essays, Literary, Moral and Philosophical. Philadelphia: 1798. V. 52
An Eulogium, Intended to Perpetuate the Memory of David Rittenhouse, Late President of the American Philosophical Society, Delivered Before the Society in the First Presbyterian Church in High Street, Philadelphia on the 17th Dec. 1796. Philadelphia: 1796. V. 47; 48; 52; 54
Letters of Benjamin Rush, 1761-1813. Princeton: 1951. V. 50; 52
Medical Inquiries and Observations. Philadelphia: 1793. V. 51
Medical Inquiries and Observations. Philadelphia: 1794-98. V. 54
Medical Inquiries and Observations. Philadelphia: 1805. V. 49
Medical Inquiries and Observations. Philadlephia: 1809. V. 48
Medical Inquiries and Observations Upon the Diseases of the Mind. Philadelphia: 1812. V. 52
Medical Inquiries and Observations Upon the Diseases of the Mind. Philadelphia: 1818. V. 50; 52
Medical Inquiries and Observations Upon the Diseases of the Mind. Philadelphia: 1827. V. 49; 54
Medical Inquiries and Observations Upon the Diseases of the Mind. Philadelphia: 1830. V. 52
Medical Inquiries and Observations Upon the Diseases of the Mind. Philadelphia: 1835. V. 47; 52

RUSH, JACOB
Charges and Extracts of Chargers, on Moral and Religious Subjects...to Which is Annexed the Act of the Legislature of the State of Pennsylvania, Respecting Vice and Immorality. Philadelphia: 1804. V. 54

RUSH, JAMES
The Philosophy of the Human voice... Philadelphia: 1833. V. 49
The Philosophy of the Human Voice. Philadelphia: 1855. V. 52; 53
The Philosophy of the Human Voice. Philadelphia: 1859. V. 54

RUSH, NORMAN
Whites. New York: 1986. V. 47; 49; 52

RUSH, RICHARD
Memoranda of a Residence at the Court of London. Philadelphia: 1833. V. 53
Memoranda of a Residence at the Court of London. Philadelphia: 1845. V. 47; 52
A Residence at the Court of London. London: 1833. V. 50; 52; 54

RUSHBY, G. G.
No More the Tusker. London: 1965. V. 52

RUSHDIE, SALMAN
East, West. London: 1994. V. 53
Grimus. London: 1975. V. 47; 51; 52; 53
Grimus. Woodstock: 1979. V. 54
Haroun and the Sea of Stories. London: 1990. V. 48; 49; 51; 52; 53
Haroun and the Sea of Stories. New York: 1991. V. 47; 53
Imaginary Homelands. London: 1991. V. 53
Imaginary Homelands. New York: 1991. V. 47
The Jaguar Smile. New York: 1987. V. 50
Midnight's Children. New York: 1980. V. 48; 52; 54
Midnight's Children. London: 1981. V. 49; 51; 52
Midnight's Children. New York: 1981. V. 49; 51; 52; 54
Midnight's Children. London: 1988. V. 51
The Moor's Last Sigh. V. 53; 54
The Moor's Last Sigh. London: 1995. V. 54
The Satanic Verses. London: 1988. V. 48; 49; 50; 51; 52; 53
The Satanic Verses. New York: 1988. V. 48; 54
The Satanic Verses. New York: 1989. V. 51
The Satanic Verses. Dover: 1992. V. 53
Shame. London: 1983. V. 50; 51
Two Stories. London: 1989. V. 47; 49; 53

RUSHER, J. G.
Anecdotes for Good Children, Being Select Pieces... Banbury: 1820. V. 51
The Children in the Wood, Restored. Banbury: 1820. V. 49
Galloping Guide to the ABC, or the Child's Agreeable Introduction to a Knowledge of the Gentleman of the Alphabet. Banbury: 1830's. V. 51
The Interesting Story of the Children in the Wood. Banbury: 1830's. V. 51
Trial of an Ox, for Killing a Man; with the Examination of the Witnesses, Before Judge Lion, at Quadruped Court, Near Brest Park. Banbury: 1830's. V. 51

RUSHFORTH, G. MC. N.
Medieval Christian Imagery as Illustrated by the Painted Windows of Great Malvern Priory Church. Oxford: 1936. V. 49

RUSHMORE, HELEN
The Dancing Horses of Acoma. Cleveland: 1963. V. 51

RUSHTON, EDWARD
Poems. London: 1806. V. 54

RUSHTON, ELMER THEODORE
Engraved Style Book of Monograms, Lettering, Inscriptions for Jewelers, Engravers and Artists. Portland: 1914. V. 50

RUSHWORTH, JOHN
Historical Collections of Private Passages of State. London: 1659-80. V. 48; 49
Mr. Rushworth's Historical Collections Abridg'd and Improv'd. London: 1703-08. V. 49; 53

RUSKIN, ARTHUR
Classics in Arterial Hypertension. Springfield: 1956. V. 50; 52

RUSKIN, JOHN
Aratra Pentelici. London: 1890. V. 54
Arrows of Chase. Orpington: 1880. V. 47; 50
Arrows of the Chace, Being a Collection of Scattered Letters Published Chiefly in the Daily Newspapers, 1840-80. Sunnyside: 1880. V. 47
The Art of England. Orpington: 1884. V. 50; 51; 54
Catalogue of the Educational Series 1-18. London: 1871. V. 53
Complete Works of... London: 1903-12. V. 52
The Crown of Wild Olive. London: 1866. V. 50; 51
Dame Wiggins of Lee and Her Seven Wonderful Cats. London: 1885. V. 50; 51
The Eagle's Nest. London: 1899. V. 54
The Elements of Drawing. London: 1857. V. 49; 50; 51
The Elements of Drawing. London: 1900. V. 54
The Ethics of the Dust. London: 1866. V. 50
Ethics of the Dust. London: 1883. V. 47
The Ethics of the Dust. London: 1900. V. 54
Fors Clavigera. London: 1899-96. V. 54
Fors Clavigera. Letters to the Workmen and Labourers of Great Britain. Orpington, Kent: 1871-87. V. 50
The Harbours of England. London and Sunnyside: 1895. V. 54
Hortus Inclusus, Messages from the Wood to the Garden. Sunnyside, Orpington, Kent: 1887. V. 50; 54
A Joy For Ever. London: 1900. V. 54
The King of the Golden River. London: 1907. V. 54
The King of the Golden River. New York: 1930. V. 53
The King of the Golden River. London: 1932. V. 51
The King of the Golden River. London: 1932. V. 47; 48; 49; 51
Lectures on Architecture and Painting Delivered at Edinburgh in November 1853. London: 1854. V. 47; 50
Lectures On Art. New York: 1870. V. 50; 52
Lectures on Landscape Delivered at Oxford In Lent Term, 1871. London: 1897. V. 49
Lectures on Landscape Delivered at Oxford in Lent Term 1871. Orpington: 1897. V. 50
Letters Addressed by Professor Ruskin, D.C.L. tot he Clergy on the Lord's Prayer and the Church. 1879. V. 47
Letters from John Ruskin to William Ward. London: 1893. V. 50
Letters on Art and Literature. London: 1894. V. 52; 54
Modern Painters. London: 1843. V. 50; 54
Modern Painters. London: 1844. V. 49
Modern Painters. London: 1846-60. V. 47; 49
Modern Painters. London: 1848-60. V. 51
Modern Painters. London: 1867/56/60. V. 49
Modern Painters. London: 1888. V. 47; 54
Modern Painters. London: 1897. V. 54
Modern Painters. New York: 1950. V. 48
Modern Painters. (and) The Stones of Venice. New York: 1880. V. 52
Mornings in Florence: Being Simple Studies of Christian Art, For English Travellers. Orpington: 1875-77. V. 49
Munera Pulveris. London: 1899. V. 54
The Nature of Gothic: a Chapter of the Stones of Venice. Hammersmith: 1892. V. 54
The Nature of Gothic, a Chapter of the Stones of Venice. London: 1892. V. 54
Notes by Mr. Ruskin on Samuel Prout and William Hunt... London: 1880. V. 52
Notes on the Turner Gallery. (with) Notes on Some of the Principal Pictures in the Rooms of the Royal Academy. Number III(-V). London: 1856-9. V. 51
Of Queen's Gardens. Edinburgh;: 1902. V. 48
On the Old Road. Orpington: 1885. V. 47
Our Fathers Have Told Us Sketches of the History of Christendom for Boys and Girls Who Have been Held at Its Fonts... Sunnyside, Orpington, Kent: 1883/1881-85. V. 47
The Pleasures of England. London: 1884. V. 51
The Poems. London: 1891. V. 50; 51
The Poems. Sunnyside, Orpington: 1891. V. 48; 49
The Poems. London: 1900. V. 54
The Poetry of Architecture: or the Architecture of the Nations of Europe... London: 1893. V. 49; 54
The Poetry of Architecture; or, The Architecture of the Nations of Europe Considered In Its Association with Natural scenery and National Character. Orpington, Kent: 1893. V. 48
The Political Economy of Art. London: 1857. V. 50; 51
The Political Economy of Art. New York: 1858. V. 50
Praeterita. London: 1899. V. 54
Praeterita. Outlines of Scenes and Thoughts Perhaps Worthy of Memory in My Past Life. London: 1886-87-1900. V. 51
Praeterita. Outlines of Scenes and Thoughts Perhaps Worthy of Memory in My Past Life. Sunnyside, Orpington, Kent: 1886-89. V. 52
Praeterita. Outlines of Scenes and Thoughts Perhaps Worthy of Memory in My Past Life. London: 1949. V. 54
Pre-Raphaelitism. London: 1851. V. 54
Properina. Studies of Wayside Flowers. (with) Deucalion. Collected STudies of the Lapse of Waves and Life of Stones. 1879-80-83. V. 47
The Queen of the Air: Being a Study of the Greek Myths of Cloud ad Storm. London: 1900. V. 54
Salsette and Elephanta. Oxford: 1839. V. 53; 54
Selections From the Writings of... Edinburgh: 1907. V. 48
Sesame and Lilies. London: 1884. V. 47
Sesame and Lilies. London: 1900. V. 54
The Seven Lamps of Architecture. London: 1849. V. 48; 51; 52
The Seven Lamps of Architecture. London: 1855. V. 50; 54
The Seven Lamps of Architecture. New York: 1871. V. 48
The Seven Lamps of Architecture. London: 1880. V. 50
The Seven Lamps of Architecture. Orpington, Kent: 1883. V. 48
The Seven Lamps of Architecture. Orpington, Kent: 1889. V. 47; 52
The Seven Lamps of Architecture. London: 1898. V. 49
The Stones of Venice. London: 1873-4-4. V. 47; 50; 52
The Stones of Venice. London: 1886. V. 50
The Stones of Venice. London: 1898. V. 54
The Storm Cloud of the Nineteenth Century. Sunnyside, Orpington: 1884. V. 48; 49
Studies in Both Arts... London: 1895. V. 54
Time and Tide by Weare and Tyne Twenty Five Letters to a Working Man of Sunderland on the Laws of Work. London: 1900. V. 54
The Two Paths: Being Lectures on Art, and Its Appliation to Decoration and Manufacture Delivered in 1858-59. London: 1859. V. 47
The Two Paths: Being Lectures On Art and Its Application to Decoration and Manufacture, Delivered in 1858-59. London: 1900. V. 54
Unto This Last. 1902. V. 54
Unto This Last. 1907. V. 49; 51
Unto This Last. Hammersmith: 1907. V. 49
Unto This Last. London: 1907. V. 50
Verona and Other Lectures. London: 1894. V. 48
Works. Boston: 1900. V. 49; 50; 52
The Works. London: 1903-12. V. 48; 49; 50
Works. Boston: 1910. V. 48

RUSS, CAROLYN HALE
The Log of a Forty-Niner. Boston: 1923. V. 49; 54

RUSS, KARL
The Speaking Parrots: a Scientific Manual. London: 1884. V. 50

RUSSEL, ALEXANDER
The Salmon. Edinburgh: 1864. V. 47

RUSSEL, E. F.
Sinister Barrier. 1948. V. 49

RUSSEL, J.
Max Ernst: Life and Work. London: 1967. V. 54

RUSSEL, JAMES
Letters from a Young Painter Abroad to His Friends in England. London: 1748. V. 47; 52
Letters from a Young Painter Abroad to His Friends in England. London: 1750. V. 52

RUSSEL, M.
Polynesia: or, an Historical Account of the Principal Islands in the South Sea, Including New Zealand... Edinburgh: 1865. V. 52

RUSSEL, RICHARD
A Dissertation on the Use of Sea-Water in the Diseases of the Glands. London: 1752. V. 48

RUSSEL, ROBERT ROYAL
Economic Aspects of Southern Sectionalism, 1840-1861. Urbana: 1924. V. 48

RUSSELL, A. J.
On Champlain's Astrolabe, Lost on the 7th June, 1613, and Found in August 1867... Montreal: 1879. V. 48
Union Pacific R.R. Views Across the Continent, West from Omaha. 1869-70. V. 47

RUSSELL, ADDISON PEALE
Sub-Coelum: a Sky-Built Human World. Boston & New York: 1893. V. 54

RUSSELL, BENJAMIN
An Address Delivered Before the Massachusetts Charitable Mechanics Assocaition, December 21, 1809... Boston: 1810. V. 52

RUSSELL, BERTRAND
The Amberley Papers: The Letters and Diaries of Bertrand Russell's Parents. New York: 1937. V. 47; 48
The Analysis of Matter. London: 1927. V. 50
The Archives of Bertrand Russell Continuum 1. London: 1967. V. 53
A Critical Exposition of the Philosophy of Leibniz, with an Appendix. 1900. V. 52
Free Though and Other Official Propaganda. New York: 1922. V. 48
History of the World in Epitome. London: 1962. V. 47
Human Knowledge Its Scopes and Limits. London: 1948. V. 49
Marriage and Morals. New York: 1929. V. 48
Mysticism and Logic. New York: 1929. V. 50
Political Ideals. London: 1916. V. 48; 51
The Principles of Mathematics. Cambridge: 1903. V. 48; 52; 54
Satan in the Suburbs and Other Stories. London: 1953. V. 50

RUSSELL, C. E. M.
Bullet and Shot in Indian Forest, Plain and Hill. 1900. V. 52
Bullet and Shot in Indian Plain and Hill. London: 1900. V. 53

RUSSELL, CHARLES E.
English Mezzotint Portraits and Their States. London: 1926. V. 50

RUSSELL, CHARLES MARION
Back Trailing on the Old Frontiers. Great Falls: 1922. V. 47
Forty Pen and Ink Drawings. Pasadena: 1947. V. 54
Good Medicine. Garden City: 1929. V. 50
Good Medicine. New York: 1929. V. 48; 51
Good Medicine. Garden City: 1930. V. 47
Good Medicine. New York: 1930. V. 50
How the Buffalo Lost His Crown. 1894. V. 50
More Rawhides. Great Falls: 1925. V. 50; 52; 54
Paper Talk: 12 Full Color Reproductions of Illustrated Letters. Ft. Worth: 1962. V. 49
Pen Sketches. Great Falls: 1898-99. V. 48
Pen Sketches. Great Falls: 1899. V. 47
Pen Sketches. Alhambra: 1964. V. 48; 54
Rawhide Rawlins Stories. Great Falls: 1921. V. 47; 49; 52
Studies of Western Life. New York: 1890. V. 50
Trails Plowed Under. Garden City: 1927. V. 47; 52; 53
Trails Plowed Under. New York: 1927. V. 53

RUSSELL, CHARLES WILLIAM
The Life of Cardinal Mezzofanti; with an Introductory Memoir of Eminent Linguists, Ancient and Modern. London: 1863. V. 47

RUSSELL, DON
One Hundred and Three Fights and Scrimmages. The Story of General Reuben F. Bernard. Washington: 1936. V. 47

RUSSELL, E. F.
Dark Tides. 1962. V. 52
Sinister Barrier. 1948. V. 47; 48; 49; 51; 54

RUSSELL, E. L.
The Russell Reader. 1956. V. 49

RUSSELL, F.
The Medusae of the British Isles. Volume 2. Pelagic Scyphozoa... Cambridge: 1970. V. 49

RUSSELL, F. M. M.
A Social Failure. Liverpool: 1895. V. 53

RUSSELL, FRANCIS
A Short History of the East India Company... London: 1793. V. 48

RUSSELL, FRANK
Art Nouveau Architecture. New York: 1979. V. 48; 50; 51; 53; 54
Explorations in the Far North. Iowa City: 1898. V. 51

RUSSELL, FREDERIC WILLIAM
Kett's Rebellion in Norfolk; Being a History of the Great Civil Commotion that Occurred at the Time of the Reformation, in the Right of Edward VI. London: 1859. V. 52

RUSSELL, GEORGE
A Tour Through Sicily in the Year 1815. London: 1819. V. 49

RUSSELL, GEORGE WILLIAM
By Still Waters, Lyrical Poems Old and New. Dundrum: 1906. V. 51; 52; 54
The Candle of Vision. London: 1928. V. 49
Co-Operation and Nationality. Dublin: 1912. V. 49; 50
Dark Weeping. London: 1929. V. 54
The Divine Vision and Other Poems. New York: 1904. V. 49; 50
The Earth Breath and Other Poems. New York: 1897. V. 51
Enchantment and Other Poems. New York. V. 49; 50
Enchantment and Other Poems. New York: 1930. V. 51; 54
Homeward Songs by the Way. Dublin: 1894. V. 49
The Inner and Outer Ireland. Dublin: 1921. V. 48
Midsummer Eve. New York: 1928. V. 47
Some Passages from the Letters of A.E. to W. B. Yeats. Dublin: 1936. V. 48; 52; 54
Thoughts for a Convention...Memorandum on the State of Ireland. Dublin and London: 1917. V. 52

RUSSELL, HENRY PATRICK
Biarritz and the Basque Countries. London: 1873. V. 52

RUSSELL, JOHN
A Complete and Useful Book of Cyphers. London. V. 48
An Essay on the History of the English Government and Constitution, from the Reign of Henry VII to the Present Time. London: 1821. V. 53
Francis Bacon. Greenwich: 1971. V. 47; 50
The History of the War, Between the United States and Great Britain, Which Commenced in June, 1812, and Closed in Feb. 1815... Hartford: 1815. V. 47; 53
Instructions for the Drill and the Method of Performing the Eighteen Manoeuvres. Philadelphia: 1814. V. 51; 52
Letters from a Young Painter Abroad to His Friends in England. London: 1750. V. 53
The Life and Times of Charles James Fox. London: 1859-66. V. 47
The Life of William Lord Russell; with Some Account of the Times in Which He Lived. London: 1819. V. 50; 51
Max Ernst: Life and Work. New York. V. 48
Max Ernst: Life and Work. London: 1967. V. 47; 49; 50; 51; 53
Max Ernst: Life and Work. New York: 1967. V. 53
The Nun of Arrouca. London: 1822. V. 51
The Speech...In the House of Commons, Feb. 8, 1850, on Colonial Policy; with a View to Promote the General Wealth and Population of the Colonies... London: 1850. V. 49
A Tour in Germany and Some of the Southern Provinces of the Austrian Empire in 1820, 1821 and 1822. Edinburgh: 1828. V. 49

RUSSELL, JOHN A.
Remains of the Late Rev. Charles Wolfe, A.B. Dublin: 18252. V. 51

RUSSELL, JOHN SCOTT
The Modern System of Naval Architecture. London: 1864-65. V. 51

RUSSELL, LORIS S.
A Heritage of Light: lamps and Lighting in the Early Canadian Home. Toronto: 1968. V. 50

RUSSELL, M.
Polynesia: A History of the South Sea Islands Including New Zealand, With a Narrative of the Introduction of Christianity... London: 1842. V. 48

RUSSELL, M. C.
Uncle Dudleys' Odd Hours. Western Sketches, Indian Trail Echoes, Straws of Humor. Lake City: 1904. V. 54

RUSSELL, MARY ANNETTE BEAUCHAMP RUSSELL, COUNTESS
The April Baby's Book of Tunes. London: 1900. V. 47; 51; 53
Elizabeth and Her German Garden. London: 1899. V. 47; 48
The Solitary Summer. New York & London: 1899. V. 47; 48

RUSSELL, MICHAEL
Palestine, or The Holy Land. New York: 1832. V. 53

RUSSELL, OSBORNE
Journal of a Trapper. Boise: 1921. V. 47; 52; 53
Journal of a Trapper. Portland: 1955. V. 48; 50

RUSSELL, P.
An Account of Indian Serpents, Collected on the Coast of Coromandel...(with) A Continuation of an Account of Indian Serpents. Parts I and II only. London: 1796-1801. V. 54

RUSSELL, PATRICK
A Treatise on the Plague: Containing an Historical Journal and Medical Account of the Plague, at Aleppo in the Years 1760, 1761 and 1762. London: 1791. V. 53

RUSSELL, RACHEL WRIOTHESLEY VAUGHAN
Letters. London: 1773. V. 47; 50; 54
Letters. London: 1801. V. 47; 52
Letters. London: 1852. V. 54
Letters. London: 1853. V. 52

RUSSELL, RICHARD
A Dissertation on the Use of Sea-Water in Diseases of the Glands. London: 1752. V. 51
A Dissertation on the Use of Sea-Water in the Diseases of the Glands. London: 1755. V. 48
The Oeconomy of Nature in Acute and Chronical Diseases of the Glands. London: 1755. V. 47
The Oeconomy of Nature in Acute and Chronical Diseases of the Glands. London: 1765. V. 49; 54

RUSSELL, ROSS
Bird Lives! The High Life and Hard Times of Charlie (Yardbird) Parker. New York: 1973. V. 50; 52

RUSSELL, THOMAS
Sonnets and Miscellaneous Poems by the Late Thomas Russell, Fellow of New College. Oxford: 1789. V. 48; 54

RUSSELL, THOMAS H.
Pictures from the Wonderful Wizard of Oz. Chicago: 1903-04. V. 49

RUSSELL, W. CLARK
My Shipmate Louise. The Romance of a Wreck. London: 1890. V. 50
The Tale of the Ten. London: 1896. V. 48

RUSSELL, W. H.
The British Expedition to the Crimea. London: 1958. V. 54

RUSSELL, WALTER
The Universal One: an Exact Science of the One Visible and Invisible Universe of Mind and the Registration of All Idea of Thinking Mind in Light, Which is Matter and Also Energy. Waynesboro: 1974. V. 53

RUSSELL, WILLIAM
The History of Modern Europe. Philadelphia: 1802. V. 47; 51
Life, With some Account of the Times in Which He Lived. London: 1820. V. 51
Recollections of a Detective Police-Officer. London: 1856. V. 53
A Treatise on the Reform Act. London: 1832. V. 51; 53

RUSSELL, WILLIAM CLARK
Fra Angelo: a Tragedy. London: 1865. V. 52
The Lady Maud: Schooner Yacht. London: 1882. V. 53
Memoirs of Mrs. Laetitia Boothby. London: 1872. V. 51; 54
The Phantom Death and Other Stories. London: 1895. V. 53
Rose Island. Chicago: 1899. V. 54
A Sea Queen. London: 1883. V. 51
The Yarn of Old Harbour Town. London: 1905. V. 53

RUSSELL, WILLIAM HOWARD
The Adventures of Doctor Brady. London: 1868. V. 47
Canada: Its Defences, Condition and Resources. London: 1865. V. 47
A Memorial fo the Marriage of H.R.H, the Prince of Wales, and H.R.H. Alexandra, Princess of Denmark. London: 1864. V. 48
My Diary In India, in the year 1858-59. London: 1860. V. 50; 51

RUSSELL, WILLIAM HOWARD continued
My Diary North and South. Boston: 1863. V. 49
My Diary North and South. London: 1863. V. 47; 49; 52; 53
My Diary North and South. (with) Canada: its Defences, Condition and Resources. London: 1863/65. V. 53
The War: from the Landing at Gallipoli to the Death of Lord Raglan. London: 1855. V. 50

RUSSETTI, WILLIAM MICHAEL
Ruskin: Rossetti: Pre-Raphealitism: Papers 1854-62. London: 1899. V. 48

RUSSO, RICHARD
Mohawk. New York: 1986. V. 51

RUSSOLI, FRANCO
Modigliani. London: 1959. V. 50

RUSSOM, J.
A Word to the Working Classes on Their Improvement and Elevation (with Other Pieces). London: 1850. V. 52

RUST, BRIAN
The American Dance Band Discography 1917-1942. New Rochelle: 1975. V. 47
Jazz Records. 1897-1942. London: 1970. V. 47; 52
Jazz Records, 1897-1942. New Rochelle: 1978. V. 54

RUST, GEORGE
A Letter of Resolution concerning Origen and the Chief of His Opinions. London: 1661. V. 49; 51

RUST, S. F.
Railway, Commercial and Tourist's Guide to Colorado with Correct State and Sectional Maps Giving a General Description of the Cities and towns, Pleasure Resorts, etc. Denver: 1883. V. 48

RUST, WILLIAM
Britons in Spain. A History of the British Battalion of the XVth International Brigade. London: 1939. V. 49

RUSTICUS, MERCURIUS
Bibliophobia. Remarks On the Present Languid and Depressed State of Literature and the Book Trade. London: 1832. V. 50

RUSTLING, JAMES F.
Across America or the Great West and the Pacific Coast. New York: 1874. V. 53

RUSTON, ARTHUR G.
Hooton Pagnell. London: 1934. V. 47; 53

RUTGERS, A.
Birds of Europe. Birds of Australia. Birds of Asia. Birds of New Guinea. Birds of South America. London: 1966-72. V. 52
Encyclopaedia of Aviculture. London: 1970-77. V. 49; 52

RUTHERFORD, ERNEST
The Collected Papers of Lord Rutherford Nelson. London: 1962-65. V. 50
Radio-Activity. Cambridge: 1904. V. 50; 54
Radio-activity. Cambridge: 1905. V. 48; 50; 54
Radioactive Substances and Their Radiations. Cambridge: 1913. V. 50; 54
Radioactive Transformations. London: 1906. V. 50; 53; 54

RUTHERFORD, JAMES H.
The History of the Linlithgow and Stirlingshire Hunt 1775-1910. Edinburgh & London: 1911. V. 48

RUTHERFORD, LIVINGSTON
Family Records and Events. New York: 1894. V. 47

RUTHERFORD, SAMUEL
Joshua Redivivus, or Mr. Rutherfoord's Letters, Divided In Two Parts... Edinburgh?: 1671. V. 48
Joshua Redivivus: Or, Three Hundred and Fifty-Two Letters. Glasgow: 1765. V. 52
A Survey of the Survey of that Summe of Church Discipline Penned by Mr. Thomas Hooker, Late Pastor of the Church at Hartford Upon Connecticut in New England... London: 1658. V. 48

RUTHERSTON, ALBERT
Sixteen Designs for the Theatre. London: 1928. V. 54

RUTILIUS LUPUS, PUBLIUS
De Figuris Sententiarum Ac Verborum... Lyon: 1542. V. 52

RUTKOW, I. M.
The History of Surgery in the United States 1775-1900. San Francisco: 1988. V. 47; 48; 49; 50; 51; 52; 53; 54
The History of Surgery in the United States 1775-1900. San Francisco: 1988-92. V. 49; 50; 54
The History of Surgery in the United States 1775-1900. Volume 2. San Francisco: 1992. V. 48; 49; 50; 51; 53; 54

RUTLAND, HENRY MANNERS, 8TH DUKE OF
The Haddon Hall Library. London: 1899-1903. V. 54

RUTLAND, JOHN HENRY MANNERS, 5TH DUKE OF
Journal of a Tour Round the Southern Coasts of England. (with) Journal of a Tour to the Northern Parts of Great Britain. London: 1805/13. V. 50
Journal of a Trip to Paris...July MDCCXIV. (with) Journal of a Short Trip to Paris During the Summer of MDCCXV. London: 1814/15. V. 54
A Tour Through Part of Belgium and the Rhenish Provinces. London: 1822. V. 47; 52
Travels in Great Britain. London: 1805. V. 48

RUTLEDGE, ARCHIBALD
The Banners of the Coast. Columbia: 1908. V. 53
South of Richmond. Chambersburg: 1923. V. 53

RUTLEDGE, DICK
Brief Sketches in the Life of Col. Dick Rutledge, the Last Living Indian Scout. V. 53

RUTLEDGE, HUGH
Everest: the Unfinished Adventure. London: 1937. V. 54

RUTLEDGE, LEO
That Some May Follow. 1989. V. 53

RUTLEDGE, SARAH
House and Home: Or, The Carolina Housewife. Charleston: 1855. V. 48; 52

RUTSALA, VERN
Small Songs. 1969. V. 53
Small Songs. Iowa City: 1969. V. 54

RUTT, JOHN TOWILL
Diary of Thomas Burton, Esq. Member in the Parliaments of Oliver and Richard Cromwell from 1656 to 1659... London: 1828. V. 52

RUTTAN, HENRY
Ventilation and Warming of Buildings. New York: 1862. V. 53

RUTTER, FRANK
The British Empire Panels Designed for the House of Lords, by Frank Brangwyn. Essex: 1933. V. 50

RUTTER, JOAN
Here's Flowers: an Anthology of Flower Poems. 1937. V. 47
Here's Flowers, An Anthology of Flower Poems. Waltham St. Lawrence: 1937. V. 49; 54

RUTTER, JOHN
The Banwell and Cheddar Guide; Including a Descriptive Account of the antediluvian Bone Caverns on Banwell and Hutton Hills; of Cheddar Cliffs and of Druidical Temple at Stanton Drew, in somersetshire. London: 1829. V. 51
Delineations of the North West Division of Somerset and of Its Antediluvian Bone Caverns... London: 1829. V. 48
Delineations of the North-West Division of Somerset. Shaftesbury: 1829. V. 47

RUTTER, OWEN
The Court-Martial of the "Bounty" Mutineers. London: 1931. V. 54
The Pagans of North Borneo. London: 1929. V. 53

RUTTLEDGE, H.
Attack on Everest. 1935. V. 52
Everest 1933. 1934. V. 53
Everest 1933. London: 1934. V. 52
Everest: The Unfinished Adventure. 1937. V. 53
Everest Unfinished Adventure. London: 1937. V. 52; 54

RUTTY, JOHN
A History of the Rise and Progress of the People Called Quakers, in Ireland from the Year 1653 to 1700. London: 1811. V. 49
Observations on the London and Edinburgh Dispensatories: with an Account of the Virtues of Various Subjects of the Materia Medica, Not Contained in Either of Those Works. London: 1776. V. 47
A Spiritual Diary and Soliloquies. London: 1776. V. 48
A Spiritual Diary and Soliloquies... London: 1796. V. 53

RUXNER, GEORG
Thurnierbuch. Frankfort: 1578. V. 53

RUXTON, GEORGE FREDERIC
Adventures in Mexico and the Rocky Mountains. London: 1847. V. 47; 49
Adventures in Mexico and the Rocky Mountains. New York: 1848. V. 53
Life in the Far West. Edinburgh: 1849. V. 47
Life in the Far West. New York: 1849. V. 47; 48
Life in the Far West. (with) Adventures in Mexico and the Rocky Mountains. New York: 1849/48. V. 47

RUYI, YAN
Out of the Mountains. Honolulu: 1991. V. 49

RUYL, BEATRICE BAXTER
Little Indian Maidens at Work and Play. London & New York: 1907. V. 51

RUYSCH, FREDERIC
The Celebrated Dr. Frederic Ruysch's Practical Observations in Surgery and Midwifery. London: 1751. V. 48; 50
Opera Omnia Anatomica-Medico-Chirurgica... Amstelodami: 1737-43. V. 48

RUZICKA, RUDOLPH
Speaking Reminiscently... New York: 1986. V. 52
Studies in Type Design. Hanover: 1968. V. 49; 51

RYALL, E. CANNY
Operative Cystoscopy. London: 1925. V. 47
Operative Cystoscopy. St. Louis: 1925. V. 47

RYAN, ABRAM JOSEPH
Father Ryan's Poems. Mobile: 1879. V. 49; 52

RYAN, CHARLES S.
Under the Red Crescent: Adventures of an English Surgeon with the Turkish Army at Plevna and Erzeroum, 1877-1878. London: 1897. V. 48

RYAN, DANIEL JOSEPH
Ohio in Four Wars: a Military History. Columbus: 1917. V. 54

RYAN, J. G.
Life and Adventures of Gen. W. A. C. Ryan, the Cuban Martyr... New York and Chicago: 1876. V. 52

RYAN, JAMES
A Letter from Mr. James Ryan...on His Method of Ventilating Coal Mines.... London: 1816. V. 50

RYAN, JOHN
Captain Pugwash - a Private Story. London: 1957. V. 50
The Life of William the Third. Dublin: 1836. V. 49; 50; 51; 54
Popery Unmasked. London: 1845. V. 53

RYAN, KATHRYN WHITE
Golden Pheasant - Poems. New York & London: 1925. V. 52

RYAN, MICHAEL
A Manual of Medical Jurisprudence. Philadelphia: 1832. V. 48

RYAN, PETER
Encyclopedia of Papua New Guinea. Melbourne: 1972. V. 52

RYAN, WILLIAM REDMOND
Personal Adventures in Upper and Lower California in 1848-49: With the Author's Experience at the Mines... London: 1851. V. 47

RYBERG, INEZ SCOTT
Panel Reliefs of Marcus Aurelius. New York: 1967. V. 52

RYCAUT, PAUL
The History of the Turkish Empire from the Year 1623 to the Year 1677. London: 1680-79. V. 48; 49; 53
The Lives of the Popes... London: 1688. V. 49

RYCK, JOHN
The Rector of Amesty. London: 1891. V. 51

RYDELL, ROBERT W.
The Books of the Fairs: Materials About World's Fairs 1834-1916 in the Smithsonian Institution Libraries. Chicago and London: 1992. V. 49

RYDEN, STIG
Archaeological Researches in the Department of La Candelaria. Goteborg: 1936. V. 52

RYDER, ARTHUR W.
The Panchatantra. New York: 1972. V. 47

RYDER, JOHN
Four Years' Service in India. Leicester: 1853. V. 47
Intimate Leaves from a Designer's Notebook. Newtown: 1993. V. 49; 50; 53
Intimate Leaves from a Designer's Notebook: Essays. 1993. V. 52; 54

RYE, E. C.
British Beetles: an Introduction to Our Indigenous Coleoptera. London: 1866. V. 47; 48; 50

RYE, EDGAR
The Quirt and the Spur. Chicago: 1909. V. 47; 49; 51; 53

RYE, GEORGE
A Treatise Against the Nonconforming Nonjurors. London: 1719. V. 49; 54

RYE, WALTER
A Catalogue of Fifty of the Norfolk Manuscripts in the Library of Mr. Walter Rye at Winchester House, Putney. Norwich: 1889. V. 49

RYERSON, EGERTON
The Journal of Education for Upper Canada. Volume II - For the Year 1849; Volume III for the Year 1850. Toronto: 1849-50. V. 47
The Loyalists of America and Their Times: from 1620 to 1816. Toronto: 1880. V. 50

RYERSON, LOUIS JOHNES
The Genealogy of the Ryerson Family in America, 1646-1902. New York: 1902. V. 49

RYFF, WALTER HERMANN
Die Kleyner Chirurgi.... (bound with) Recht Grundliche Bewerte Cur des Steins, Sandt und Lenden, unnd alle Schwere Zufell... Strassburg: 1542/43. V. 49
Schwangerer Frawen Rosengarten. Frankfurt am Mayn: 1561. V. 47

RYLAND, JOHN
An Easy Introduction to Mechanics, Geometry, Plane Trigonometry, Measuring...Optics, Astronomy. London: 1768. V. 53
Serious Essays On the Truths of the Glorious Gospel, and the Various Branches of Vital Experience. London: 1771. V. 49

RYLAND, R. H.
The History of Topography and Antiquities of Waterford. London: 1982. V. 49; 50; 51
The History, Topography and Antiquities of the County and City of Waterford... 1824. V. 47

RYLANDS, GEORGE
A Distraction of Wits Nutured in Elizabethan Cambridge; an Anthology. Cambridge: 1958. V. 53
Poems. London: 1931. V. 49; 50; 51; 52; 53
Russet and Taffeta. London: 1925. V. 49; 51; 53

RYLANDS, JOHN
The English Bible in the John Rylands Library 1525 to 1640. London: 1899. V. 48

RYLANDS, THOMAS GLAZEBROOK
The Geography of Ptolemy Elucidated. Dublin: 1893. V. 49

RYLANDS, W. HARRY
The Ars Moriendi. London: 1881. V. 48

RYLE, GILBERT
The Concept of Mind. London: 1949. V. 54
Plato's Progress. Cambridge: 1966. V. 48

RYLEY, A. BERESFORD
Old Paste. London: 1913. V. 51; 53

RYLEY, SAMUEL WILLIAM
Roderick Random, a Comic Opera... Huddersfield: 1800. V. 47

RYLEY, WILLIAM
The Visitation of Middlesex, Began in the Year 1663. Salisbury: 1820. V. 47; 53

RYMER, THOMAS
Foedera, Conventiones, Literae, et Cujuscunque Generis Acta Publica... London: 1704-1735. V. 47
Foedera, Conventiones, Literae, et Cujuscunque Generis Acta Publica, Inter Reges Angliae et Alios Quosvis Imperatores... The Hague: 1739-45. V. 50; 53
A General Draught and Prospect of Government in Europe and Civil Policy. London: 1681. V. 51
A Short View of Tragedy: Its Original, Excellency and Corruption... London: 1693. V. 47; 48; 49; 51; 52; 54
The Tragedies of the Last Age Consider'd and Examin'd by the Practice of the Ancients, and by the Common Sense of All Ages. London: 1678. V. 50; 54

RYMNIKSKI, ALEXANDER SUVOROV, COUNT
History of the Campaigns of Prince Alexander Suworow, in the Service of the Emperor of all the Russias. London: 1799. V. 50

RYMSDYK, JOHN
Museum Britannicum: or, a Display in Thirty-Two Plates, of Antiquities and Natural Curiosities in that Noble and Magnificent Cabient, the British Museum. London: 1791. V. 47; 54

RYNNING, THOMAS
Gun Notches. New York: 1931. V. 53

RYRIE BROS.
Diamond Hall Catalogue. Toronto: 1900. V. 50

RYTHER, JOHN
A Plat for Mariners; or, the Seaman's Preacher. (with) The Day of God's Patience to Seamen Improved. London: 1675. V. 50

RYVES, LAVINIA J. H. DE SERRES
An Appeal for Royalty: a Letter to Her Most Gracious Majesty Queen Victoria from Lavinia Princess of Cumberland. London: 1858. V. 47

RYVES, THOMAS
Historia Navalis Antiqva...Historia Navalis Mediae. London: 1633/40. V. 51; 54

S

S., C. H.
Essay on the Military System of Bonaparte, with a Brief Account of the French Revolution and the Coronation of His Corsican Majesty. London: 1811. V. 50

S., E.
The Bogey Book. London: 1905. V. 50
The Godmother's Tales. London: 1808. V. 48
The Godmother's Tales. London: 1813. V. 52

S., H.
The History of the Davenport Family. London: 1798. V. 49

S., J.
Syllogologia (Graece); or, an Historical Discourse of Parliaments in Their Originall Before the Conquest, and Continuance Since... London: 1656. V. 50

S., L.
A Letter to a Noble Peer of the Realm, About His Late Speech and Petition to His Majesty. London: 1681. V. 47

S. MITCHELL Weir: *Memorial Addresses and Resolutions.* Philadelphia: 1914. V. 47

SA, LUIZ
Gigi and Gogo. New York: 1943. V. 51

SAA, P. ANTONIO DE
Sermao da Conceicam da Virgem Maria Nossa Senhora, que Pregou...na Igreia Matriz do Recife de Pernambuco anno de 1658. Coimbra: 1675. V. 48; 50

SAAD, ZAKI YOUSSEF
Ceiling Stelae in Second Dynasty Tombs from the Excavations at Helwan. Le Caire: 1957. V. 51
Royal Excavations at Helwan (1945-1947). Le Caire: 1951. V. 49; 51

SAADI, MUSLE-HUDDEEN
Gulistan or Rose Garden. Boston: 1865. V. 51

SAAR, JOHANN JACOB
Ost-Indianische Funfzehen-Jahrige Kriegs Dienste und Wahrhafftige Beschreibung...von 1644 bis 1659... Nuremberg: 1672. V. 47

SAARINEN, EERO
Eero Saarinen on His Work. New Haven & London: 1962. V. 48; 51

SAAVEDRA FAJARDO, DIEGO DE
Idea Principis Christiano-Politici. Amstelodami: 1651. V. 53
Idea Principis Christiano-Politici. Parisiis: 1660. V. 48

SABARTES, JAIME
Picasso Toreros. New York, Monte Carlo: 1961. V. 49; 52; 53

SABATIER, WILLIAM
Letter to Robert Peel, Esq. London?: 1796. V. 49

SABATINI, RAFAEL
Bellarion. London: 1926. V. 50
The Carolinian. Boston: 1925. V. 53
Fortune's Fool. Boston: 1923. V. 48
Fortune's Fool. London: 1923. V. 50
Heroic Lives. Boston: 1934. V. 49
The Historical Nights Entertainment: Third Series. Boston: 1938. V. 49
The Hounds of God. London: 1928. V. 50; 51
The Nuptials of Corbal. Boston: 1927. V. 52
The Writings of... Boston: 1924-30. V. 52

SABBATH Bells Chimed by the Poets. London. V. 48

SABERNA. A Saxon Eclogue. London: 1778. V. 54

SABIN, ARTHUR K.
Medea and Circe and Other Poems. East Sheen: 1911. V. 51

SABIN, EDWIN LEGRAND
Building the Pacific Railway. Philadelphia: 1919. V. 47; 48
Kit Carson Days. Adventures in the Path of Empire. New York: 1935. V. 49

SABIN, JOSEPH
A Bibliographical Catalogue of the Waltonian Library...of Robert W. Coleman. New York: 1866. V. 47
A Dictionary of Books Relating to America, from Its Discovery to the Present Time. New York: 1868-1936. V. 47
A Dictionary of Books Relating to America, From its Discovery to the Present Time. New York: 1967. V. 48; 49; 52

SABINE, EDWARD
The North George Gazette, and Winter Chronicle. London: 1821. V. 47

SABINE, LORENZO
Notes on Duels and Duelling, Alphabetically Arranged... Boston: 1855. V. 47; 49; 52
Report on the Principal Fisheries of the American Seas. Washington: 1853. V. 47

SABINE, W. H. W.
Historical Memoris from 16 March 1763 to 9 July 1776; 12 July, 1776 to 25 July, 1778, of William Smith, Historian of the Province of New York... New York: 1956. V. 52

SACHEM TEZUCO
The Rescue of Tula. New York: 1859. V. 50

SACHER-MASOCH, LEOPOLD VON
Venus in Furs. New York: 1928. V. 51

SACHEVERELL, WILLIAM
An Account of the Isle of Man, Its Inhabitants, Language, Soil, Remarkable Curiosities, the Succession of Its Kings and Bishops, Down to the Present Time. London: 1702. V. 54

SACHS, A. J.
Late Babylonian Astronomical and Related Texts. Providence: 1955. V. 49

SACHS, BERNARD
A Treatise On the Nervous Diseases of Children for Physicians and Students. New York: 1905. V. 53

SACHS, ERNEST
The Diagnosis and Treatment of Brain Tumors. St. Louis: 1931. V. 49; 54

SACHS, J. VON
History of Botany (1530-1860). Oxford: 1890. V. 48

SACK, ISRAEL
American Antiques from Israel Sack Collection. 1974-81. V. 51

SACKETT, FRANCIS ROBERTSON
Dick Dowling. Houston: 1937. V. 48

SACKETT, S. P.
Mother, Nurse and Infant: A Manual Especially Adapted for the Guidance of Mothers and Monthly Nurses... New York: 1889. V. 48

SACKHEIM, ERIC
The Blues Line. A Collection of Blues Lyrics. Tokyo & New York: 1969. V. 48; 49

SACKS, OLIVER W.
Awakenings. Garden City: 1974. V. 51
Awakenings. New York: 1987. V. 48

SACKVILLE, CHARLES
A Treatise Concerning the Militia, in Four Sections. London: 1752. V. 47

SACKVILLE, GEORGE
The Proceedings of a General Court-Martial Held at the Horse-Guards on Friday the 7th, the Continued by Several Adjournments...& of a General Court-Martial Held at the Horse-Guards on Tuesday the 25th of March,...Upon the Trial of Lord George Sackville. London: 1760. V. 50; 54

SACKVILLE, MARGARET
The Travelling Companions: and Other Stories for Children. London: 1915. V. 50

SACKVILLE-WEST, EDWARD
The Apology of Arthur Rimbaud. London: 1927. V. 51
The Rescue. London: 1945. V. 47; 48
Simpson, a Life. London: 1931. V. 48

SACKVILLE-WEST, VICTORIA MARY
All Passion Spent. London: 1931. V. 49; 52; 53; 54
Andrew Marvelll. London: 1929. V. 51
Aphra Behn. London: 1927. V. 51; 52
Challenge. New York: 1923. V. 48; 50
Collected Poems - Volume One. London: 1933. V. 51
Constantinople: Eight Poems. London: 1915. V. 48; 52; 53
The Dark Island. London: 1934. V. 47; 48; 49; 50; 52
Devil at Westease - The Story as Related by Roger Liddiard. New York: 1947. V. 52
The Eagle and the Dove - a Study in Contrasts - St. Teresa of Avila - St. Therese of Lisieux. London: 1943. V. 52
The Eagle and the Dove - a Study in Contrasts - St. Theresa of Avila - St. Therese of Lisieux. London: 1953. V. 50
The Easter Party. London: 1953. V. 49
The Easter Party. New York: 1953. V. 54
The Edwardians. London: 1930. V. 51; 52; 53
The Garden. London: 1946. V. 49; 52; 54
The Heir... London: 1922. V. 48
The Heir. New York: 1922. V. 51
Heritage. New York: 1919. V. 48; 51
Joan of Arac. London: 1937. V. 53
Knole and the Sackvilles. London: 1922. V. 48; 53
The Land. London: 1926. V. 47; 49; 54
More for Your Garden. London: 1955. V. 50
Nursery Rhymes. London: 1947. V. 48
Orchard and Vineyard. London: 1921. V. 47; 48; 49; 52; 53
Pepita. London: 1937. V. 47; 49; 50; 54
Poems of West and East. London: 1917. V. 52
Saint Joan of Arc. London: 1936. V. 47; 49
Seducers in Ecuador. London: 1924. V. 47; 51; 54
Seducers in Equador. New York: 1925. V. 51
Selected Poems. London: 1935. V. 54
Selected Poems. London: 1941. V. 51
Sissinghurst. London: 1931. V. 49
Twelve Days. London: 1928. V. 48; 54
The Women's Land Army. London: 1944. V. 53; 54

SACRE, PSEUD.
Sidelights. Being an Official Series of Caricature Portraits. Military. First Series. London: 1918. V. 47

THE SACRED Books of China, The Texts of Taosim. Oxford: 1891. V. 48

SACRED To the Memory of Our Late Revered Sovereign, George IV; Under Whose Reign...Great Britain has Attained a Dignity and Splendour...and a Perfection in the Arts and Sciences...Far Above Other Nations... London: 1830. V. 47

SACROBOSCO, JOHANNES DE
Algorismus. colophon: 1523. V. 47
De Anni Ratione, seu...Computus Ecclesiastaicus. Paris: 1551. V. 51
Opusculu Johannis de Sacrobusto Spericum cu Figuris Optimis et Novis Textu in se Sine Ambiguitate declarantibus. Leipzig: 1494. V. 52
La Sfera. Florence: 1579. V. 54
Sphaera Mundi... Venice: 1499. V. 53
Sphaera Mundi. Venice: 1519. V. 47
Sphaera...D.D. Ordinum Hollandiae & West-Frisiae... Leyden: 1656. V. 49

SACRORUM Rituum Congreagtione...Beatificationis et Canonizationis...Roberti Bellarmini Societatis Iesu. Rome: 1712. V. 52; 54

SACY, LOUIS DE
A Discourse on Friendship. London: 1707. V. 53

SADDLEBAGS, JEREMIAH
Journey to the Gold Diggins. 1950. V. 54

SADE, DONATIEN ALPHONSE FRANCOIS, COMTE, CALLED MARQUIS DE
Histoire de Justine ou Les Malheurs de la Vertu... (with) Histoire de Juliette ou les Prosperites du Vice... En Hollande: 1797. V. 52
The Story of Juliette. Paris: 1958-65. V. 51

SADE, JACQUES FRANCOIS PAUL ALDONCE DE
The Life of Petrarach. Dublin: 1777. V. 49

SADELER, AEGIDIUS
Vestigi delle Antichita di Roma, Tivoli, Pozzuolo ed Altri Luoghi. Prague: 1606 but later. V. 47; 53

SA' DI
The Gulistan... Hertford: 1850. V. 53

SA' DI continued
The Gulistan. London: 1880. V. 48; 54

SADLEIR, MICHAEL
The Anchor - a Love Story. London: 1918. V. 50; 53
Authors and Publishers. London: 1932. V. 50
Daumier, The Man and the Artist. London: 1924. V. 48
Desolate Splendour. London: 1923. V. 50; 53
Desolate Splendour. New York: 1923. V. 50
Desolate Splendour. Toronto: 1923. V. 50
Desolate Splendour. London: 1948. V. 50
The Evolution of Publisher's Binding Styles, 1770-1900. London: 1930. V. 54
Excursions in Victorian Bibliography. London: 1922. V. 49; 50; 51; 54
Fanny by Gaslight. London: 1940. V. 54
Forlorn Sunset. New York: 1946. V. 50
Forlorn Sunset. London: 1947. V. 50; 53
Michael Ernest Sadleir (Sir Michael Sadleir K.C.S.I.) - Memoir by His Son. London: 1949. V. 50
Minerva Press Publicity. London: 1940. V. 47
Mr. Michael Sadleir's Collection of XIXth Century Fiction. London: 1945. V. 50
More Wrangham - a Supplement to the Paper: "Archdeacon Francis Wrangham 1769-1842". 1939. V. 50
More Wrangham - a Supplement to the Paper: 'Archdeacon Francis Wrangham 1769-1842'... London: 1939. V. 53
The Noblest Family. London: 1925. V. 50
The Northanger Novels - A Footnote to Jane Austen. London: 1927. V. 50
The Politcal Career of Richard Brinsley Sheridan. London: 1912. V. 50
The Political Career of Richard Brinsley Sheridan. Oxford: 1912. V. 53
Privilege - a Novel of the Transition. London: 1921. V. 50
Privilege - a Novel of the Transition. New York: 1921. V. 50
The Sadleir Library. London: 1955. V. 50; 53
Servants of Books - a Lecture Delivered to the London Branch of the Associated Booksellers at Stationers' Hall, 24th September 1924. London: 1925. V. 50
Thackeray's Letters: a Review. London: 1947. V. 50
These Foolish Things. London: 1937. V. 50; 53
These Foolish Things. New York: 1937. V. 50
These Foolish Things... Leipzig: 1937?. V. 50
These Foolish Things. London: 1944. V. 50
These Special Things. New York: 1937. V. 50
Trollope: a Bibliography. London: 1977. V. 53
Trollope. A Commentary. London: 1927. V. 51
XIX Century Fiction. 1951. V. 51
XIX Century Fiction... Cambridge: 1951. V. 47
XIX Century Fiction. London: 1951. V. 47
XIX Century Fiction. New York: 1969. V. 49; 51
XIX Century Fiction. 1992. V. 52
XIX Century Fiction. Cambridge: 1992. V. 47; 51

SADLEIR, RICHARD
The Aborigines of Australia. Sydney: 1883. V. 52

SADLEIR, THOMAS U.
A Brief Memoir of the Rt. Hon. Sir Ralph Sadleir. Hereford: 1907. V. 54

SADLER, HENRY
Masonic Facts and Fictions. London: 1887. V. 52
Masonic Reprints and Historical Revelations. London: 1898. V. 53

SADLER, JOHN
Rights of the Kingdom; or, Customs of Our Ancestors. London: 1682. V. 48

SADLER, MICHAEL
Modern Art and Revolution. London: 1932. V. 51

SADLER, MICHAEL T.
Ireland: its Evils and Their Remedies: Being a Refutation of the Errors of the Emigration Committee and Others, Touching that Country. London: 1829. V. 50

SADLER, RALPH
Letters and Negotiations of Sir Ralph Sadler, Ambassador of King Henry VIII of England... Edinburgh: 1720. V. 54
The State Papers and Letters. Edinburgh: 1809. V. 50; 54

SADOLETO, JACOPO, CARDINAL
De Liberis Recte Insituendis, Liber. Paris: 1534. V. 52
Epistolarum Libri Sexdecim. Cologne: 1580. V. 50

SAENGER, PAUL
A Catalogue of the Pre-1500 Western Manuscript Books at the Newberry Library. Chicago: 1989. V. 47; 50

A SAFE and Easy Way to Obtain Free and Peaceable Elections, without Imposition, Noise or Charge; Proposed...Now the Regulation of Elections is Under Debate... London: 1679. V. 47

SAFFORD, JAMES M.
Geology of Tennessee. Nashville: 1869. V. 47

SAFFORD, WILLIAM H.
The Life of Harman Blennerhassett. Chillicothe: 1850. V. 53
The Life of Harman Blennerhassett... Cincinnati: 1853. V. 49

SAFRONI-MIDDLETON, A.
Gabrielle of the Lagoon - a Romance of the South Seas. London: 1919. V. 52

THE SAGA of Frankie & Johnny. New York: 1930. V. 48

THE SAGA of King Olaf Tryggwason Who Reigned Over Norway A.D. 995 to A.D. 1000. London: 1895. V. 53

SAGAN, FRANCOISE
Aimez-vous Brahms. Paris: 1959. V. 51
Un Certain Sourire. (A Certain Smile). Paris: 1956. V. 51

SAGATOO, MARY A.
Wah Sash Kah Moqua; or, Thirty-Three Years Among the Indians. Boston: 1897. V. 50

SAGE, JOHN
The Principles of the Cyprianic Age... London: 1695. V. 47; 49

SAGE, KAY
Mordicus. Paris: 1962. V. 52

SAGE, RUFUS
Rufus B. Sage, His Letters and Papers, 1836-1847. Glendale: 1956. V. 48; 51; 52; 53

SAGE, SIDNEY
Stand-Ups: The Tale of Peter Rabbit. Akron: 1934. V. 49

SAGE, WALTER N.
Sir James Douglas and British Columbia. Toronto: 1930. V. 47

SAGGIO de Caratteri Della Fonderia Reale di Torino. Turin: 1830. V. 50; 54

SAGRA, RAMON DE LA
Cinco Meses en Los Estados-Unidos de la America del Norte Desde el 20 de Abril a 23 de Septiembre de 1835. Paris: 1836. V. 53
Histoire Physique Politique et Naturelle de l'Ile de Cuba. Paris: 1839. V. 53; 54

SAGREDO, GIOVANNI
Memorie Istoriche De' Monarchi Ottomani. Venice: 1679. V. 48

SAHAGUN, FRAY BERNADINO DE
Historia General de las Cosas de Nueva Espana. Mexico: 1982. V. 52

SAHAK, JUDY HARVEY
Dorothy Drake and the Scripps College Pess. Claremont: 1992. V. 49

SAIA, NONIUS MARCELLUS
Tractatus in Quo Adversus Antiquorum... Paris: 1575. V. 53

SAIGON: Sketches and Words from the Artist's Journal. New York: 1971. V. 51

SAINSBURY, W. NOEL
Original Unpublished Papers Illustrative of the Life of Sir Peter Paul Rubens as Artist and Diplomatist, Preserved in HM State Paper Office. London: 1859. V. 50

SAINT Cecelia; or, the British Songster. Edinburgh: 1782. V. 48

THE SAINT Helena Almanac and Annual Register, for...1857...Containing a Detailed account of the Public Departments and Local Institutions... St. Helena: 1856. V. 49

SAINT Hilda. Durham: 1830. V. 50

SAINT LOUIS & SAN FRANCISCO RAILROAD
Tenth Annual Report of the St. Louis & San Francisco Railway Company. For the Year Ending December 31, 1886. St. Louis: 1887. V. 47
There Is Something to See Along the Frisco Line. St. Louis: 1900. V. 53

SAINT LOUIS IRON MOUNTAIN AND SOUTHERN RAILWAY
The Hot Springs of Arkansas. America's Baden-Baden. St. Louis: 1877. V. 51

SAINT, W.
Memoirs of the Life, Character, Opinions and Writings, of that Learned and Eccentric man, the Late John Fransham, of Norwich. Norwich: 1811. V. 47

SAINT AUBIN DE TERAN, LISA
Keepers of the House. London: 1982. V. 54

SAINT CLAIR, ARTHUR
A Narrative of the Manner in Which the Campaign Against the Indians...Was Conducted, Under the Command of Major General St. clair... Philadelphia: 1812. V. 47; 48
The St. Clair Papers. Cincinnati: 1882. V. 47; 51

SAINT CLAIR, GEORGE
Creation Records Discovered In Egypt. London: 1898. V. 51

SAINT CLEMENT, J.
A Paper-Basket, into Which Have Been Thrown Some Pieces of Prose and Rhyme. Bombay: 1856. V. 47

SAINT-CRICQ, LAURENT
Travels in South America from the Pacific Ocean to the Atlantic ocean. London: 1875. V. 51

SAINT DENIS, RUTH
Ruth St. Denis, an Unfinished Life. New York: 1939. V. 50

SAINTE BEUVE, L. A.
Causeries de Lundi. Nouveau Lundis. Premiers Lundis. Paris: 1880. V. 50

SAINTE-CROIX, GUILLAUME EMMANUEL JOSEPH
History of the Rise and Progress of the Naval Power of England, Interspersed with Various Important Notices, Relative to the French Marine... London: 1802. V. 52

SAINT ETIENNE, CLAUDE
Nouvelle Instruction Pour Connoistre les Bons Fruits, Selon les Mois de l'Annee. Paris: 1670. V. 49

SAINT ETIENNE, M. RABAUT DE
The History of the Revolution of France. Dublin: 1792. V. 49; 54

SAINT EVREMOND, CHARLES DE MARGUETEL ST. DENIS, SEIGNEUR DE
The Works. London: 1728. V. 53

SAINT EXUPERY, ANTOINE DE
Flight to Arras. New York: 1942. V. 50; 53
The Little Prince. New York: 1943. V. 48; 49; 50; 51; 53
The Little Prince. London: 1944. V. 48
The Little Prince. New York: 1944. V. 53
Night-Flight. London: 1932. V. 51
Night-Flight. New York: 1932. V. 51
Night-Flight. Paris: 1932. V. 50
Wind, Sand and Stars. London: 1939. V. 49
Wind, Sand and Stars. New York: 1939. V. 48

SAINT GERMAIN, CHRISTOPHER
The Dialogues in English, Betweene a Doctor of Divinity and a Student in the Lawes of England. 1580. V. 47
The Dialogues in English, Betweene a Doctor of Divinity and a Student in the Lawes of England. Londini: 1580. V. 48; 50
The Dialogues in English, Betweene a Doctor of Divinity and a Student in the Lawes of England. London: 1623. V. 49
The Dialogues in English, Betweene a Doctor of Divinity and a Student in the Lawes of England. London: 1638. V. 47; 53
The Exact Abridgement of that Excellent Treatise Called Doctor and Student. London: 1630. V. 52
Two Dialogues in English, Between a Doctor of Divinity... London: 1673. V. 47; 50
Two Dialogues in English, Between a Doctor of Divinity... London: 1709. V. 48

SAINTHILL, RICHARD
The Old Countess of Desmond: an Inquiry. London: 1861/63. V. 47
The Old Countess of Desmond: an Inquiry. London: 1863-63. V. 53

SAINT JOHN, BAYLE
The Subalpine Kingdom; or, Experiences and Studies in Savoy, Piedmont, and Genoa. London: 1856. V. 52; 54
Village Life in Egypt: With Sketches of the Said. Boston: 1853. V. 49

SAINT JOHN, CHARLES
Natural History and Sport in Moray. 1863. V. 52
Natural History and Sport in Moray. Edinburgh: 1863. V. 54
Natural History and Sport in Moray. London: 1863. V. 52
Natural History and Sport in Moray. London: 1882. V. 48
Short Sketches on the Wild Sports and Natural History of the Highlands... London: 1893. V. 47
Sketches of the Wild Sports and Natural History of the Highlands. London: 1878. V. 52; 54
A Tour in Sutherlandshire. London: 1849. V. 51; 53
A Tour in Sutherlandshire. 1884. V. 54
Wild Sports and Natural History of the Highlands. London: 1919. V. 54

SAINT JOHN, DAVID
For Lerida. Lisbon: 1973. V. 51; 54

SAINT JOHN, FERDINAND
Rambles in Germany, France, Italy and Russia in Search of Sport. London: 1853. V. 50

SAINT JOHN, HENRY
Letters On the Spirit of Patriotism: On the Idea of a Patriot King: and On the State of Parties. London: 1749. V. 49

SAINT JOHN, HENRY CRAVEN
Notes and Sketches from the Wild Coasts of Nipon... Edinburgh: 1880. V. 54

SAINT JOHN, JAMES AUGUSTUS
Egypt and Mohammed Ali; or, Travels in the Valley of the Nile. London: 1834. V. 53
Egypt and Nubia, Their Scenery and Their People, Being Incidents of History and Travel, from the Best and Most Recent Authorities, Including J. L. Burckhardt and Lord Lindsay. London: 1840. V. 48
The History of the Manners and Customs of Ancient Greece. London: 1842. V. 50
Oriental Album. Characters, Costumes and Modes of Life in the Valley of the Nile. London: 1848. V. 48

SAINT JOHN, JUDITH
The Osborne Collection of Early Children's Books, 1566-1910. Toronto: 1966. V. 50; 53

SAINT JOHN, MOLYNEUX
The Province of British Columbia, Canada. Its Resources, Commercial Position and Climate and Description of the New Field Opened Up by the Canadian Pacific Railway... Montreal?: 1886. V. 47
The Sea of Mountains. An Account of Lord Dufferin's Tour through British Columbia in 1876. London: 1877. V. 47; 50

SAINT JOHN, OLIVER
The Speech and Declaration of... Delivered at a Conference of Both Houses of Parliament Held 16 Caroli, 1640. London: 1641. V. 50

SAINT JOHN, PERCY BOLINGBROKE
A Hunter's Experiences in the Southern States...Being an Account of the Various Quadrupeds and Birds Which are the Objects of Chase. London: 1866. V. 48; 49
The Texan Ranger, or Real Life in the Blackwoods by Captain Flack. London: 1866. V. 47

SAINT JOHN, SPENSER
Life in the Forests of the Far East. London: 1862. V. 49
Life in the Forests of the Far East... London: 1863. V. 47

SAINT JOHN, WILLIAM CHARLES
Catechism of the History of Newfoundland... Boston: 1855. V. 47

SAINT LEGER, FRANCIS BARRY BOYLE
Mr. Blount's MSS. Being Selections from the Papers of a Man of the World. London: 1826. V. 47; 49; 54

SAINT LO, GEORGE
England's Safety; or, a Bridle to the French King. London: 1693. V. 54

SAINT MARTHE, SCEVOLE DE
Paedotrophia; or, the Art of Rearing Children. London: 1797. V. 52

SAINT MAURE, CHARLES DE
A New Journey through Greece, Aegypt, Palestine... London: 1725. V. 48

SAINT PALAYE, JEAN BAPTISTE DE LA CURNE DE
Literary History of the Troubadors. London: 1807. V. 52; 54
Memoirs of the Life of Froissart. London: 1801. V. 49

SAINT PAUL, HENRY
Our Home and Foreign Policy. Mobile: 1863. V. 49

SAINT PHALE, MME. DE
The History of Mademoiselle De St. Phale. London: 1787. V. 50; 51; 53

SAINT PIERRE, JACQUES HENRI BERNARDIN DE
Amasis. London: 1799. V. 48
Beauties of the Studies of Nature: Selected from the Works of Saint Pierre. New York: 1799. V. 54
Botanical Harmony Delineated. Worcester: 1797. V. 49
Harmonies of Nature. London: 1815. V. 48
The Indian Cottage. Philadelphia: 1794. V. 50
Paul and Mary, an Indian Story. London: 1789. V. 48
Paul and Virginia. London: 1789. V. 52
Paul and Virginia. London: 1799. V. 48
Paul and Virginia. Philadelphia: 1808. V. 48
Paul and Virginia. London: 1819. V. 49
Paul and Virginia. London: 1839. V. 53
Paul and Virginia. London: 1888. V. 53
Paul et Virginie. Paris: 1838. V. 49
Studies of Nature... London: 1796. V. 52
Studies of Nature... London: 1796-99. V. 52
Studies of Nature. Dublin: 1798. V. 53
A Vindication of Divine Providence. Worcester: 1797. V. 49
A Voyage to the Island of Mauritius, (Or, Isle of France), The Isle of Bourbon, The Cape of Good Hope, &c. London: 1775. V. 48; 53

SAINT PIERRE, PAUL DE
Sufferings and Death of Henry Roberts, Esq. Dublin: 1748. V. 48

SAINT PRIEST, FRANCOIS EMMANUEL GUIGNARD, COMTE DE
Malte, Par Un Voyageur Francois. Valetta: 1791. V. 52

SAINT QUENTIN, DOMINIQUE DE
A Poetical Chronology of the Kings of England, from William the Conqueror to George the Third Inclusive... Reading: 1792. V. 54

SAINT REAL, CAESAR VISCHARD DE
Conspiracy of the Spaniards Against Venice and of John Lewis Fiesco Against Genoa. Boston: 1828. V. 54
The Memoires of the Dutchess Mazarine... London: 1676. V. 47; 52; 53

SAINTSBURY, GEORGE
Minor Poets of the Caroline Period... Oxford: 1905-06-21. V. 47
Minor Poets of the Caroline Period. London: 1968. V. 51
A Scrap Book in Three Volumes. London: 1922. V. 49
Specimens of English Prose Style. London: 1885. V. 54

SAINT SIMON, MARQUIS DE
Histoire de la Guerre des Bataves et des Romains... Amsterdam: 1770. V. 47

SAINT VINCENT, J. B. G. M. BORY DE
Voyage to, and Travels through the Four Principal Islands of the Africa Seas, Performed in Order of the French Government, During the Years 1801 and 1802... London: 1805. V. 54

SAINT VINCENT, OF LERINS
Pro Catholicae Fidei Antiqvitate & Veritate, Aduersus Prophanas Omnium Haerese Nouationes... London: 1591. V. 48

SAJOUS, CHARLES
The Internal Secretions and the Principles of Medicine. Philadelphia: 1903-07. V. 51

SAKAGAMI, S. F.
Natural History of Social Wasps and Bees in Equatorial Sumatra. 1990. V. 50

SAKEL, MANFRED JOSHUA
The Pharmacological Shock Treatment of Schizophrenia. New York/Washington: 1938. V. 52

SALA, ANGELO
Descriptio Brevis Antidoti Pretiosi. Marburg: 1620. V. 48

SALA, GEORGE AUGUSTUS
America Reivisted: from the Bay of New York to the Gulf of Mexico. London: 1885. V. 54
The Great Exhibition "Wot is to Be". London: 1850. V. 47
The Hats of Humanity, Historically, Humorously and Aesthetically Considered, A Homily. Manchester: 1870's. V. 53

SALA, GEORGE AUGUSTUS continued
A Journey Due North: Being Notes of a Residence in Russia, In the Summer of 1856. London: 1858. V. 49
The Life and Adventures of George Augustus Sala. London Paris & Melbourne: 1895. V. 53; 54
My Diary in America in the Midst of War. London: 1865. V. 53
The Seven Sons of Mammon: a Story. London: 1862. V. 52
A Trip to Barbary by a Roundabout Route. London: 1866. V. 53
Under the Sun. London: 1886. V. 51
William Hogarth: Painter, Engraver and Philosopher. London: 1866. V. 48; 54

SALAMAN, MALCOLM C.
British Book Illustration, Yesterday and Today. London: 1923. V. 50; 53
The Etchings of James McBey. London: 1929. V. 49; 52; 54
The Etchings of Sir Francis Seymour Haden. London: 1923. V. 47; 49; 51; 52; 53
Fine Prints of the Year. London: 1925. V. 47
French Colour-Prints of the XVIII Century. London: 1913. V. 52
French Colour-Prints of the XVIII Century. Philadelphia: 1913. V. 47
Old English Colour-Prints. London: 1909. V. 53
Old English Mezzotints. London: 1910. V. 53

SALAMAN, REDCLIFFE N.
The History and Social Influence of the Potato... Cambridge: 1949. V. 51

SALARAR YLARREGUI, JOSE
Datos de Los Trabajos Astronomicos Y Topograficos, Dispuestos en Forma de Diario. Mexico: 1850. V. 47; 52

SALCEDO CORONEL, JOSE GARCIA DE
Ariadna... Madrid: 1624. V. 48

SALE, FLORENTIA
A Journal of the Disasters in Afghanistan, 1841-42. London: 1843. V. 51

SALE, P. F.
The Ecology of Fishes on Coral Reefs. London: 1991. V. 50; 51

THE SALEM Collection of Classical Sacred Musick; in Three and Four Parts: Consisting of Psalm Tunes and Occasional Pieces... Boston: 1806. V. 48

SALES, EDITH TUNIS
Interiors of Virginia Houses of Colonial Times: From the Beginnings of Virginia to the Revolution. Richmond: 1927. V. 50; 52

SALINGER, JEROME DAVID
The Catcher in the Rye. Boston: 1951. V. 47; 49; 51; 52
The Catcher in the Rye. London: 1951. V. 50; 51; 52
The Complete Uncollected Short Stories. 1974. V. 47; 52
Franny and Zooey. Boston & Toronto: 1961. V. 49; 50; 51; 52
Nine Stories. Boston: 1953. V. 47; 48; 49; 51; 52
Raise High the Roof Beam, Carpenter. Boston: 1959. V. 48; 49
Raise High the Roof Beam, Carpenter. Boston: 1963. V. 47
With Love and Squalor and Other Stories. London: 1953. V. 51

SALINGER, PIERRE
A Tribute to John F. Kennedy. Chicago: 1964. V. 50

SALIS, BAPTISTA DE
Summa Casuum Conscientiae... Nuremberg: 1488. V. 50
Summa Casuum Conscientiae. Venice: 1499. V. 48; 49

SALISBURY, FRANK O.
The Art of Frank O. Salisbury. Leigh-On-Sea, Essex: 1936. V. 47

SALISBURY, JAMES
Malaria. New York: 1885. V. 49

SALISBURY, JESSE
A Glossary of Words Used in S.E. Worcestershire, Together with Sayings, Customs, Etc. London: 1893. V. 54

SALISBURY, MARQUIS OF
Calendar Manuscripts of the Marquis of Salisbury, Etc., Preserved at Hatfield House, Hertfordshire. London: 1883-1906. V. 49

SALISBURY, STEPHEN
Troy and Homer. Remarks on the Discovers of Dr. Heinrich Schliemann in the Troad. Worcester: 1875. V. 52

SALIVET, LOUIS GEORGES ISAAC
Manuel Du Tourneur, Ouvrage Dans Lequel on Enseigne aux Amateurs la Maniere Dexecuter sur la Tour a Pointes, a Lunette, en l'Air, Excentrique, Ovale, a Guillocher, Quatre, a Portraits & Autres... Paris: 1792-96. V. 51

SALK, JONAS
Man Unfolding. New York: 1972. V. 52
The Survival fo the Wisest. New York: 1973. V. 51
Vaccination Against Paralytic Poliomyelitis Performance and Prospects. 1955. V. 49

SALKELD, WILLIAM
Reports of Cases Adjudged in the Court of King's Bench; Together with Several Special Cases. London: 1724. V. 52

SALKEY, ANDREW
The Adventures of Catullus Kelly. London: 1969. V. 53
The Late Emancipation of Jerry Stower. London: 1968. V. 53

SALLANDER, HANS
Bibliotheca Walleriana... New York. V. 49
Bibliotheca Walleriana. Stockholm: 1955. V. 50
Bibliotheca Walleriana... New York: 1990. V. 49
Bibliotheca Walleriana. New York: 1991. V. 48

SALLER, SYLVESTER J.
Excavations at Bethany (1949-1953). Jerusalem: 1957. V. 49; 52
The Excavations at Dominus Flevit (Mount Olivet, Jerusalem). Part II: The Jebusite Burial Place. Jerusalem: 1964. V. 49; 52
Memorial of Moses on Mount Nebo. Jerusalem: 1941-50. V. 49

SALLEY, H. E.
History of California Post Offices, 1849-1976. La Mesa: 1977. V. 47
Rhododendron Hybrids. London: 1992. V. 49

SALLIS, JAMES
A Few Last Words. New York: 1970. V. 51

SALLUSTIUS CRISPUS, C.
C. Crispi Sallustii Belli Catilinarii et Jugurthini Historiae. Edinburgh: 1739. V. 52
C. Crispi Sallustii Opera Omnia Quae Extant... Amstelodami: 1690. V. 53
La Conjuracion de Catalina y la Guerra de Jugurta por Cayo Salustio Cispo. Madrid: 1772. V. 48; 51
De Conivratione Catilinae. Venice: 1521. V. 52
The Historian Made English. London: 1719. V. 48
Opera Omnia. London: 1789. V. 48
Opera Quae Supersunt, Omnia. Glasgow: 1777. V. 47; 48; 49
The Two Most Worthy and Notable Histories... London: 1608-09. V. 52

SALLY Miller. 1840. V. 52
SALLY Miller. New Orleans?: 1845?. V. 54

SALMI, MARIO
Italian Miniatures. London: 1957. V. 54

SALMON, JOSEPH WHITTINGHAM
Moral Reflections in Verse, Begun in Hawkstone Park, May 20th and 21st 1794... 1796. V. 54

SALMON, NATHANIEL
The History of Hertfordshire... London: 1728. V. 47

SALMON, THOMAS
The Chronological Historian. London: 1747. V. 47; 53
A Critical Essay Concerning Marriage. London: 1724. V. 48; 50; 51
Hedendaagsche Historie: Tegenwoordige Staat van Africa. Amsterdam: 1763. V. 47
The Modern Gazetteer; or, a Short View of the Several Nations of the World... London: 1747. V. 52
Modern History; or, the Present State of All Nations... London: 1726. V. 54
A New Abridgement and Critical Review of the State Trials (etc.). Dublin: 1741. V. 48
A New Geographical and Historical Grammar... London: 1758. V. 51; 52
A New Geographical and Historical Grammar. London: 1759. V. 50
New Geographical and Historical Grammar. London: 1772. V. 54
A New Historical Account of St. George for England and the Original of the most Noble Order of the Garter. London: 1704. V. 50; 52
South Shields: Its Past, Present and Future Being a Decennial Supplement to the Town Clerk's Published Lecture. South Shields: 1866. V. 50

SALMON, WILLIAM
Botanologia. The English Herbal; or, History of Plants. London: 1710. V. 53
Dictionnaire Hermetique, Contenant l'Explication des Termes, Fables, Enigmes, Emblemes & Manieres de Parler des Vrais Philosophes. Paris: 1695. V. 48
Horae Mathematicae Seu Urania, The Soul of Astrology... London: 1679. V. 48
Iatrica: seu Praxis Medendi. The Practice of Curing: Being a medicinall History of Many Famous Observations. London: 1684. V. 52
The London and Country Builder's Vade Mecum, or, the Compleat and Universal Archtiect's Assistant. London: 1755. V. 50
Medicina Practica: or, Practical Physick... London: 1692. V. 48
Palladio Londinensis; or, the London Art of Building. London: 1738. V. 48
Pharmacopoeia Londinensis; or, the New London Dispensatory. London: 1707. V. 48
Polygraphice; or the Arts of Drawing, Engraving, Etching, Limning, Painting... London: 1673. V. 52
Polygraphice: or the Arts of Drawing, Engraving, Etching Limning, Painting... London: 1681. V. 51
Polygraphice; or the Arts of Drawing, Engraving, Etching, Limning, Painting... London: 1685. V. 47
Polygraphice; or the Arts of Drawing, Engraving, Etching, Limning, Painting... London: 1701. V. 48
Praxis Medica. The Practice of Physick... London: 1707. V. 48
Synopsis Medicinae; or, a Compendium of the Theory and Practce of Physick... London: 1695. V. 51

SALMONIUS, JOANNES
Lyricorvm Libri Dvo, ad Franciscvm Valesivm...Epithalamiorvm Liber Vnvs. Paris: 1531. V. 48

SALMONS, C. H.
The Burlington Strike: its Motives and Methods, Including the Causes of the Strike...Action Taken by Order Brotherhood R.R. Brakemen, Order Railway Conductors and Knights of Labor... Aurora: 1889. V. 51

SALM-REIFFERSCHEID-DYCK, JOSEPH, FURST VON
Cacteae in Horto Dyckensi Cultae. Dusseldorf: 1842. V. 49
Cacteae in Horto Dyckensi Cultae... Paris: 1845. V. 49

SALNOVE, ROBERT DE
La Venerie Royale, Divisee en IV Parties... Paris: 1665. V. 47

SALOMONS, DAVID L.
Breguet. (1747-1823). London: 1921. V. 53
Breguet. (1747-1823). London: 1923. V. 53

SALOMONSEN, C. J.
Bacteriological Technology for Physicians. New York: 1890. V. 54

SALOMONSEN, FINN
The Birds of Greenland. Kobenhavn: 1950. V. 53
The Birds of Greenland. Copenhagen: 1950-51. V. 50; 51; 52; 53; 54

EL SALON de la Moda. Ano V-VI. Barcelona: 1888-89. V. 54

SALPETER, HOWARD
Dr. Johnson and Mr. Boswell. New York: 1929. V. 52

SALPOINTE, J. B.
Soldiers of the Cross. Banning: 1898. V. 51; 54

SALT, HENRY
A Plea for Vegetarianism and Other Essays. Manchester: 1886. V. 54
A Voyage to Abyssinia, and Travels Into the Interior of that Country, Executed Under the Orders of the British Government, in the Years 1809 and 1810... London: 1814. V. 50; 51; 52

SALT, HENRY S.
The Life of Henry David Thoreau. London: 1890. V. 49
Percy Bysshe Shelley. Poet and Pioneer, a Biographical Study. London & New York: 1896. V. 51

SALT Lake City Illustrated. Salt Lake City: 1887. V. 51

SALT Lake City with a Sketch of the Route of the Central Pacific Railroad from Omaha to Salt Lake City and Thence to San Francisco. London/Edinburgh/: 1870's. V. 51

SALT, T. J.
Trentham Hymnal. Newcastle-under-Lyme: 1894. V. 52; 54

SALTEN, FELIX
Bambi. New York: 1928. V. 52; 54
Walt Disney's Bambi. Boston: 1944. V. 53

SALTER, EDWIN
History of Monmouth and Ocean Counties, Embracing a Genealogical Record of Earliest Settlers in Monmouth and Ocean Counties and Their Descendants... Bayonne: 1890. V. 47; 49; 51
Old Times in Old Monmouth. Freehold: 1887. V. 47; 49

SALTER, ELIZABETH
Will to Survive. London: 1958. V. 53

SALTER, H. E.
A Cartulary of the Hospital of St. John the Baptist. London: 1914-17. V. 49; 52

SALTER, HENRY
On Asthma: its Pathology and Treatment. New York: 1882. V. 49

SALTER, J.
A Treatise Upon Bulbous Roots, Greenhouse Plants, Flower Gardens, Fruit Trees, the Cultivation of Sea Cale, Destruction of Insects &c. Bath: 1816. V. 47

SALTER, J. W.
A Catalogue of the Collection of Camarian and Silurian Fossils Contained in the Geological Museum of the University of Cambridge. London: 1873. V. 54

SALTER, JAMES
The Arm of Flesh. New York: 1961. V. 50; 52
Dusk and Other Stories. San Francisco: 1988. V. 51
The Hunters. New York: 1956. V. 51; 52
Light Years. New York: 1974. V. 48; 52
Light Years. New York: 1975. V. 52; 53
Solo Faces. Boston: 1979. V. 48; 50; 51; 52
Solo Faces. New York: 1994. V. 53
A Sport and a Pastime. Garden City: 1967. V. 50; 51; 52
A Sport and a Pastime. New York: 1967. V. 54
A Sport and a Pastime. London: 1987. V. 52

SALTER, ROBERT
The Modern Angler, In a Series of Letters. Oswestry: 1811. V. 47

SALTER, T. F.
The Angler's Guide, Being a Complete Practical Treatise on Angling... London: 1815. V. 48
The Angler's Guide, Being a Plain and Complete Practical Treatise on the Art of Angling for Sea River and Pond Fish. 1841. V. 54
The Troller's Guide, a New and Complete Practical Treatise on the Art of Trolling or Fishing for Jack and Pike... London: 1820. V. 47
The Troller's Guide: Being a Complete Practical Treatise on the Art of Trolling... London: 1841. V. 47

SALTONSTALL, WILLIAM GORDON
Reminiscences of the Civil War and Autobiography. N.P: 1913. V. 49

SALTUS, EDGAR EVERTSON
The Philosophy of Detachment. Boston: 1885. V. 48

SALUS Populi Supreme Lex. Or; the Free Thoughts of a Well Wisher, for a Good Settlement. In a Letter to a Friend. Edinburgh: 1689. V. 53

SALVADORI, T.
Catalogue fo the Columbae, or Pigeons, in the Collection of the British Museum. London: 1893. V. 47

SALVAGE, JEAN GALBERT
Anatomie Du Gladiateur Combatant, Applicable Aux Beaux Arts ou Traite des Os des Muscles, Du Mecanisme des Mouvemens des Proprtions et des Cracateres du Corps Human. Paris: 1812. V. 53

SALVATOR, LUDWIG, ARCHDUKE OF AUSTRIA
The Caravan Route Between Egypt and Syria. London: 1881. V. 48

SALVATOR, LUDWIG LOUIS
Los Angeles in the Sunny Seventies: a Flower from the Golden Land. Los Angeles: 1929. V. 51; 54

SALVERTE, EUSEBE
The Occult Sciences. London: 1846. V. 48

SALVIATI, LEONARDO
Lo' nfarinato Secondo Ovvero dello' nfarinato Accademico della Crusca, Risposta al Libro Intitolato Replica di Camillo Pellegrino ec. Florence: 1588. V. 52
Il Primo Libro delle Orazioni. Firenze: 1575. V. 47

SALVIN, F. H.
Falconry in the British Isles. London: 1855. V. 47

SALVIN, O.
Biologia Centrali-Americana: Aves. London: 1879-1904. V. 51; 52; 54
Catalogue of the Picariae in the Collection of the british Museum. Upupae and Trochili...Coraciae. London: 1892. V. 47
On the Avifauna of the Galpagos Arachipelago. London: 1876. V. 51

SALVO, CARLO, MARQUIS DE
Travels in the Year 1806, from Italy to England, through the Tyrol, Styria, Bohemia, Gallicia (sic) Poland and Livonia... Troy: 1808. V. 49; 51

SALVO BARCELLONA, GEMMA
The Sculptors of the Cassaro. Palermo: 1971. V. 50

SALWAY, CHARLOTTE M.
Fans of Japan. London: 1894. V. 48

SALZMAN, L. F.
Building in England. Oxford: 1967. V. 50

SALZMAN, MARK
Iron and Silk. New York: 1986. V. 52

SALZMANN, CHRISTIAN GOTTHILF
Elements of Morality, for the Use of Children... London: 1792-91-92. V. 49
Gymnastics for Youth... London: 1800. V. 51
Gymnastics for Youth... Philadelphia: 1802. V. 49

SAMAAN HANNA, A.
Moods That Endure. Worcester: 1978. V. 54

SAMARAS, LUCAS
Samaras Album: Autointerview. Autobiography. Autopolaroid. New York: 1971. V. 53

SA MATTOS, MANOEL DE
Bibliotheca Elementar Chirurgico-Anatomica, ou Compendio Historico-Critico, e Chronolgico Sobre a Cirurgia e Anatomia em Geral, Que Contem os Seus Principios, Incrementos e Ultimo Estado, Assim em Portugal, Como Nas Mais Partes Cultas do Mundo... Porto: 1788. V. 53

SAMBUCUS, JOHANNES
Emblemata. Antverpiae: 1584. V. 49; 50

SAMMES, AYLETT
Britannia Antiqua Illustrata: or, the Antiquities of Ancient Britain. London: 1676. V. 47; 48; 50

SAMOUELLE, GEORGE
The Entomological Cabinet. London: 1834. V. 47
The Entomologist's Useful Compendium; or an Introduction to the Knowledge of British Insects. London: 1819. V. 48; 53

SAMPSON Against the Philistines, or the Reformation of Lawsuits... Philadelphia: 1805. V. 54

SAMPSON, HENRY
A History of Advertising From the Earliest Times. London: 1875. V. 48

SAMPSON, JOHN
XXI Welsh Gypsy Folk-Tales. Newtown: 1933. V. 47; 52; 54

SAMPSON, MARMADUKE B.
Raionale of Crime. New York: 1846. V. 48

SAMPSON, WILLIAM
Memoirs of William Sampson... New York: 1807. V. 51
Memoirs of William Sampson... Leesburg: 1817. V. 51

SAMS, CONWAY WHITTLE
The Conquest of Virginia, the Forest Primeval. New York: 1916. V. 53

SAMS, S.
A Complete and Universal System of Stenography, or Short-Hand, Rendered Easy and Familiar... London: 1812. V. 48; 52

SAMS, WILLIAM
A Tour Through Paris Illustrated with Twenty-One Coloured Plates Accompanied by Descriptive Letter-Press. London: 1822-24. V. 50

SAMUEL, ARTHUR MICHAEL
The Herring. London: 1918. V. 49

SAMUEL Beckett: an Exhibition Held at Reading University Library May - July, 1971. London: 1971. V. 50

SAMUEL Sowerby; Or, Doings at Ravensdale Priory. London: 1839. V. 48; 54

SAMUELS, EDWARD A.
Ornithology and Oology of New England... Boston: 1867. V. 50
Our Northern and Eastern Birds... New York: 1883. V. 48

SAMUELS, MAURICE VICTOR
The Florentines: a Play. New York: 1904. V. 48

SAMUELS, SAMUEL
From the Forecastle to the Cabin. New York: 1887. V. 47

SAMUELSON, JAMES
The Earthworm and the Common Housefly. London: 1858. V. 53

SAMWELL, DAVID
Captain Cook and Hawaii. San Francisco/London: 1957. V. 49

SAMY, RENE GABRIEL
Le Home Moderne. Paris: 1926. V. 54

SAN DIEGO. CHAMBER OF COMMERCE
San Diego "Our Italy". San Diego: 1895. V. 47; 49; 50
Sunny San Diego: an Illustrated Souvenir. San Diego: 1896. V. 52

SAN FRANCISCO
San Francisco Municipal Reports for the Fiscal Year 1871-2, ending June 30, 1872. San Francisco: 1872. V. 51
San Francisco Municipal Reports for the Fiscal year 1874-5 Ending June 30, 1875. San Francisco: 1875. V. 51
San Francisco Municipal Reports for the Fiscal Year 1875-6, Ending June 30, 1876. San Francisco: 1876. V. 53; 54
San Francisco Municipal Reports for the Fiscal Year 1892-3, Ending June 30, 1893. San Francisco;: 1893. V. 53
San Francisco Municipal Reports of the Fiscal Year 1886-7, Ending June 30, 1887. San Francisco: 1887. V. 51

THE SAN Francisco Directory for the Year Commencing December, 1869. San Francisco: 1869. V. 52

THE SAN Francisco Directory for the Year Commencing October, 1868. San Francisco: 1868. V. 52

SAN FRANCISCO MECHANIC'S INSTITUTE
Report of the First Industrial Exhibition of the Mechanics' Institute of the City of San Francisco... San Francisco: 1858. V. 48

SAN Francisco Offical Guide and Indexed Map, Showing Topography of the City. San Francisco: 1904. V. 53

SAN Joaquin County California. San Francisco: 1915. V. 47

SANBORN, ALVAN FRANCIS
Paris and the Social Revolution. Boston: 1905. V. 47

SANBORN, FRANK
Recollections of Seventy Years. Boston: 1909. V. 53

SANBORN, FRANKLIN B.
A. Bronson Alcott His Life and Philosophy. Boston: 1893. V. 54
Thoreau the Poet Naturalist. Boston: 1902. V. 54

SANBORN, JOHN WENTWORTH
Hymnal in the Seneca Language Also Ten Psalms of David. Clear Sky: 1892. V. 48

SANBORN, P. E.
The Sick Man's Friend: Being a Plain, Practical Medical Work on Vegetable or Botanical Principles. Boston: 1844. V. 48

SANBORN, RALPH
A Bibliography of the Works of Eugene O'Neill. New York: 1931. V. 49

SANCHEZ, GASPAR
Conciones, in Dominicis, et Feriis Qvadragesimae... Brescia: 1599. V. 48; 52

SANCHEZ, SONIA
Love Poems. New York: 1973. V. 51

SANCHEZ, THOMAS
Four Visions of America. Santa Barbara: 1977. V. 50

SANCHEZ CANTON, FRANCISCO J.
Goya. New York: 1964. V. 48

SANCHEZ SALAVAR, LEANDRO A.
Murder in Mexico; The Assassination of Leon Trotsky. London: 1950. V. 49

SANCHO, IGNATIUS
Letters of the Late Ignatius Sancho, an African. London: 1782. V. 53

SANCROFT, WILLIAM
The Proceedings and Tryal in the Case of...William (Sancroft), Lord Archbishop of Canterbury...Anno Dom. 1688. London: 1716. V. 53

SANCTA ELLA, RODERICUS DE
Oratio in Die Parasceve Anno Domini MCCCCLXXVII. Rome: 1481-87. V. 53

SANCTI Benedicti Regula. Codex Sangallensis R914. Woodmere: 1992. V. 54

SANCTO VENANTIO, ROMANUSA
Syllabus Praesulum Jaurinensium... Iaurini: 1794. V. 51

SAND, GEORGE, PSEUD. OF MME. DUDEVANT
La Comtesse de Rudolstadt. Paris: 1845. V. 48
Correspondence 1812-1876. Paris: 1882-83. V. 53
The Devil's Pool. New York: 1894. V. 48; 52; 53
Francis the Waif. London: 1889. V. 48; 50; 52; 53
Germain's Marriage. New York: 1892. V. 52; 53
Handsome Lawrence. Boston: 1871. V. 53
Historic and Romantic Novels. Philadelphia: 1900. V. 49
Indiana. Paris: 1847. V. 53
Indiana. Paris: 1856. V. 53
Jean De La Roche. Paris: 1860. V. 50
Letters. London: 1886. V. 48; 51
The Master Mosaic-Workers. Boston: 1895. V. 48
The Masterpieces of George Sand. Philadelphia: 1900-02. V. 53
Pauline. Paris: 1841. V. 50
La Petite Fadette. Paris. V. 50
Winter in Majorca. London: 1956. V. 51

SAND, MAURICE
The History of the Harlequinade. London: 1911. V. 49

SANDBACH, MARGARET
Poems. London: 1840. V. 50

SANDBURG, CARL
Abraham Lincoln, 1809-1959. The Address by... Worcester: 1959. V. 50
Abraham Lincoln, the Prairie Years. New York: 1926. V. 53
Abraham Lincoln, the Prairie Years... New York: 1926/39. V. 51; 53
Abraham Lincoln: The Prairie Years... New York: 1937. V. 49
Abraham Lincoln the War Years. New York: 1939. V. 48; 51; 53; 54
Address of Carl Sandburg Before a Joint Session of Congress, Feb. 12, 1959. New York: 1959. V. 52; 53
Always the Young Strangers. New York: 1952. V. 47
Always the Young Strangers. New York: 1953. V. 49; 51
The American Songbag. New York: 1927. V. 47; 52
Bronze Wood. San Francisco: 1941. V. 48; 51
Chicago Poems. New York: 1916. V. 48; 49; 51; 54
Early Moon. New York: 1930. V. 47; 48
Good Morning America. New York: 1928. V. 53
Home Front Memo. New York: 1943. V. 48
Lincoln Collector. New York: 1949. V. 47; 49; 53; 54
Lincoln Collector.... New York: 1950. V. 49
The People, Yes. New York: 1936. V. 47; 53
Remembrance Rock. New York: 1948. V. 47; 48; 50; 51; 52; 53; 54
Seven Poems. New York: 1970. V. 52; 53
Slabs of the Sunburnt West. New York: 1922. V. 48; 50; 52
Smoke and Steel. New York: 1920. V. 54
Steichen the Photographer. New York: 1929. V. 48; 50; 54
Storm Over the Land. New York: 1942. V. 51; 53
Wind Song. New York: 1960. V. 50

SANDBY, PAUL
A Collection of Landscapes, Drawn by P. Sandby, Esq. R.A... London: 1777. V. 51

SANDBY, WILLIAM
The History of the Royal Academy of Arts from Its Foundation in 1768 to the Present Time. London: 1862. V. 54

SANDEMAN, CHRISTOPHER
Thyme and Bergamot. London: 1947. V. 51

SANDEMAN, ROBERT
Letters on Theron and Aspasio, Addressed to the Author (James Hervey). Edinburgh: 1803. V. 47

SANDER, AUGUST
Antlitz Der Zeit. Muchen: 1929. V. 47
Men without Masks. Greenwich: 1971. V. 54
Men Without Masks. Faces of Germany 1910-1938. Greenwich: 1973. V. 47

SANDER, GUNTHER
August Sander: Photographer Extraordinary. London: 1973. V. 48; 54

SANDER, NICHOLAS
Historia Ecclesiastaica del Scisma del Reyno de Ingalaterra. Emberes: 1594. V. 48

SANDERS, ALVIN HOWARD
At the Sign of the Stock Yard Inn. Chicago: 1915. V. 47
A History of Aberdeen-Angus Cattle with Particular Reference to their Introduction, Distribution and Rise to Popularity in the Field of Fine Beef Production in North America. Chicago: 1928. V. 54
A History of the Percheron Horse. Chicago: 1917. V. 47
Red White & Roan. Chicago: 1936. V. 49
The Story of the Herefords. Chicago: 1914. V. 52

SANDERS, CONES AND CO.
The Rail and Its Localities; or, a Guide to Places Along the Railway Line from Howrah to Raneegunj, Containing Brief Notices of Howrah, Bali, Serampore (etc.)... Calcutta: 1855. V. 47

SANDERS, DANIEL CLARKE
A History of the Indian Wars... Montpelier: 1812. V. 47
A History of the Indian Wars... Rochester: 1828. V. 53
A History of the Indian Wars... Rochester: 1893. V. 49
Tales of the Revolution and Thrilling Stories, Founded on Facts. Methuen: 1837. V. 52

SANDERS, DORI
Clover. Chapel Hill: 1990. V. 51

SANDERS, EDWARD
The Hymenoptera Aculeata of the British Islands... London: 1896. V. 50

SANDERS, ELIZABETH ELKINS
Reviews of a Part of Pescott's History of Ferdinand and Isabella and of Campbell's Lectures on Poetry. Boston: 1841. V. 47

SANDERS, FRANCIS
An Abridgement of the Life of James II, King of Great Britian, &c... London: 1704. V. 50

SANDERS, G. D.
Elizabeth Cleghorn, with a Bibliography by Clark S. Northup. New Haven: 1929. V. 52

SANDERS, HENRY A.
The Minor Prophets in the Freer Collection and the Berlin Fragment of Genesis. New York: 1927. V. 52; 54

SANDERS, JOHN
Memoirs On the Military Resources of the Valley of the Ohio, As Applicable to Operations on the Gulf of Mexico; and on a System for the Common Defence of the United States. Pittsburgh: 1845. V. 50

SANDERS, LESLIE YORATH
A Soldier of England. Memorials of Leslie Yorath Sanders. Born July 5th 1893, Killed in Action March 10th, 1917. Dumfries: 1920. V. 47

SANDERS, NICHOLAS
De Origine ac Progressu Schismatis Anglicani, Libri Tres... Ingoldstadt: 1587. V. 49
Doctissimi Viri Nicolai Sanderi De Origine ac Progressu Schismatis Anglicani Liber. Coloniae Agrippinae,: 1585. V. 50

SANDERS, WILLIAM BLISS
Examples of Carved Oak Woodwork... London: 1883. V. 50

SANDERS E. W. C.
The Indian Sappers and Miners. Chatham: 1948. V. 51

SANDERSON, ALFRED
Historical Sketch of the Union Fire Company, No. 1, of the City of Lancaster, Pennsylvania. Lancaster: 1879. V. 52

SANDERSON, E.
Africa in the Nineteenth Century. London: 1898. V. 49

SANDERSON, GEORGE
A Brief History of the Early Settlement of Fairfield County. Lancaster: 1851. V. 47

SANDERSON, GEORGE P.
Thirteen Years Among the Wild Beasts of India... London: 1878. V. 48
Thirteen Years Among the Wild Beasts of India... London: 1879. V. 47; 52
Thirteen Years Among the Wild Beasts of India. London: 1882. V. 48

SANDERSON, IVAN T.
John and Juan in the Jungle. New York: 1953. V. 49

SANDERSON, J.
An Ocean Cruise and Deep Water Regatta of the Pacific Yacht Club, July 1884. San Francisco: 1884. V. 54

SANDERSON, JAMES
Rural Architecture... London: 1860. V. 53

SANDERSON, PATRICK
The Antiquities of the Abbey or Cathedral Church of Durham. Newcastle-upon-Tyne: 1767. V. 49; 50

SANDERSON, ROBERT
Nine Cases of Conscience: Occasionally Determined... (with) Episcopacy (As Established by Law in England) Not Prejudicial to Regal Power. London: 1685/83. V. 52
Twenty Sermons Formerly Preached. XVI and Aulam III... London: 1656. V. 54
XXXIV Sermons. London: 1674. V. 54

SANDERSON, THOMAS
Original Poems. Carlisle: 1800. V. 54

SANDERSON, WILLIAM
A Compleat History of the Life and Raigne of King Charles from His Cradle to His Grave. London: 1658. V. 47
Graphice, or, the Use of the Pen and Pensill. London: 1658. V. 51

SANDERUS, ANTONIUS
Chorographia Sacra Brabantiae, Sive Celebrium Aliquot in ea Provincia Abbatianum, Coenobiorum... The Hague: 1727. V. 47

SANDFORD, CHRISTOPHER
Primeval Gods. Manaton, Devon: 1934. V. 50

SANDFORD, ELIZABETH POOLE
Female Improvement. London: 1836. V. 52
Woman, in Her Social and Domestic Character. Boston: 1833. V. 50; 51

SANDFORD, FRANCIS
A Genealogical History of the Kings and Queens of England. London: 1707. V. 52; 54
A Genealogical History of the Kings of England and Monarachs of Great Britain &c... London: 1677. V. 47; 50
The History of the Coronation of the Most High, Most Mighty and Most Excellent Monarch, James II... In the Savoy: 1687. V. 50

SANDFORD, K. S.
Paleolithic Man and the Nile Valley in Nubia and Upper Egypt. Chicago: 1933. V. 49; 51; 52

SANDFORD, LETTICE
Wood-Engravings. Pinner. V. 47

SANDHAM, ALFRED
Coins, Tokens and Medals of the Dominion of Canada. Montreal: 1869. V. 52; 54

SANDHAM, ELIZABETH
The Adventures of Poor Puss. London: 1809. V. 54
The History of Elizabeth Woodville; or the Wars of the House of York and Lancaster. London: 1822. V. 51
More Trifles!. London: 1804. V. 52
The Twin Sisters; or the Advantages of Religion. London: 1805. V. 51

SANDHURST, PHILLIP T.
The Great Centennial Exhibition. Philadelphia: 1876. V. 50

SANDLER, I.
Alex Katz. New York: 1979. V. 53; 54

SANDOZ, MARI
The Battle of Little Bighorn. New York: 1966. V. 51; 53
The Beaver Men: Spearheads of Empire. New York: 1964. V. 53
The Buffalo Hunters: the Story of the Hide Men. 1954. V. 48
The Cattlemen From the Rio Grande Across the Far Marias. New York: 1958. V. 47; 50
Cheyenne Autumn. New York: 1953. V. 47
Crazy Horse. New York: 1942. V. 50; 54
Love Song to the Plains. New York: 1961. V. 47; 53; 54
Miss Morissa: Doctor of the Gold Trail. New York: 1955. V. 54
Son of the Gamblin' Man. New York: 1960. V. 53; 54

SANDOZ, MAURICE
The Maze. Garden City: 1945. V. 47; 49; 50; 53; 54

SANDS, B. F.
Reports on the Total Solar Eclipse of August 7, 1869. Washington: 1870. V. 53

SANDS, BENJAMIN
Metamorphosis; or, a Transformation of Pictures, with Poetical Explanations, for the Amusement of Young Persons. Philadelphia: 1810. V. 50
Metamorphosis; or, a Transformation of Pictures, with Poetical Explanations, for the Amusement of Young Persons. New York: 1815. V. 48

SANDS, J.
Out of the World; or, Life in St. Kilda. Edinburgh: 1878. V. 53

SANDS, ROBERT CHARLES
The Bridal of Vaumond; a Metrical Romance. New York: 1817. V. 52
The Executioner; Being a True, Impartial and Most Extraordinary Account of What Happened to the Man Who Burnt the Rev. John Rogers as Related by His Son James Rogers. Philadelphia: 183-?. V. 50

SANDWEISS, MARTHA
Laura Gilpin an Enduring Grace. Ft. Worth: 1986. V. 53

SANDWELL, B. K.
The Molson Family. Montreal: 1933. V. 47

SANDWICH, JOHN, EARL OF
The Sandwich Papers. The Private Papers of John, Earl of Sandwich, First Lord of the Admiralty 1771-7182. London: 1932-38. V. 54

SANDWITH, HUMPHRY
The Hekim Bashi; or the Adventures of Giuseppe Antonelli, a Doctor in the Turkish Service.. London: 1864. V. 48

SANDYS, CHARLES
Consuetudines Kanciae. London: 1851. V. 47; 49; 53

SANDYS, EDWIN
Europae Speculum; or a Survey of the State of Religion in the Western Parts of the World. London: 1687. V. 53

SANDYS, FREDERICK
Reproductions of Woodcuts. 1860-1866. 1910. V. 49

SANDYS, GEORGE
Anglorum Speculum, or the Worthies of England in Church and State. London: 1684. V. 47
A Paraphrase Upon the Divine Poems. London: 1676. V. 53
A Relation of a Journey Begun An. Dom. 1610. London: 1632. V. 49

SANDYS, JOHN E.
A History of Classical Scholarship. New York: 1967. V. 53

SANDYS, RUTH
Numerous Names Nimbly Narrated. London: 1930. V. 53

SANDYS, WILLIAM
Christmas Carols, Ancient and Modern. London: 1833. V. 49; 52

SANDYS, WILLIAM continued
Christmastide: its History, Festivities and Carols. London: 1852. V. 52
Specimens of Macaronic Poetry. London: 1831. V. 54

SANDZEN, BIRGER
The Mountains. McPherson: 1925. V. 51

SANFORD, JOHN
A Man Without Shoes. Santa Barbara: 1982. V. 48; 54

SANGER, C. P.
The Structure of Wuthering Heights. London: 1926. V. 54

SANGER, DONALD BRIDGMAN
James Longstreet. I. Soldier. II. Politican, Officeholder and Writer. Baton Rouge: 1952. V. 49

SANGER, GEORGE
Seventy Years a Showman. London: 1908. V. 47

SANGER, MARGARET
An Autobiography. New York: 1938. V. 50; 51
Woman and the New Race. New York: 1920. V. 47; 53

SANGER, WILLIAM
The History of Prostitution: Its Extent, Causes and Effects Throughout the World. New York: 1858. V. 52

SANGSTER, AMOS W.
Niagara River from Lake to Lake. Buffalo: 1886. V. 53
Niagara River...from Lake to Lake. Buffalo: 1886-89. V. 51

SANGSTER, CHARLES
Hesperus, and Other Poems. Montreal and Kingston: 1860. V. 48; 51; 54

SANGSTER, MARGARET E.
Lyrics of Love. New York: 1901. V. 54

SANGUINETI, A.
La Serrurerie Au XIX Siecle. Paris: 1875?. V. 48

THE SANITARY Commission of the United States Army: a Succinct Narrative Of Its Works and Purposes. New York: 1864. V. 52

SANITARY Economy: Its Principles and Practice; and Its Moral Influence On the Progress of Civilization. Edinburgh: 1850. V. 49; 52; 54

SAN MARTIN, GREGORIO DE
Sucessos Felices Intinulados, Finezas de Amor... Lisbon: 1642. V. 48

SANN, ALEXANDER
Deposition Strategy, Law and Forms. New York: 1985. V. 49

SANNAZARO, JACOBO
Arcadia Del Sannazaro. (wtih) Sonetti, E Canzoni del Sannazaro. Venice: 1534. V. 52
Opera Omnia. Lyon: 1540. V. 53; 54

SANSAY, LEONORA HASSALL
Secret History; or, the Horrors of St. Domingo, in a Series of Letters... Philadelphia: 1808. V. 50; 54

SANSOM, JOSEPH
Letters from Europe, During a Tour through Switzerland and Italy. Philadelphia: 1805. V. 51
Travels in Lower Canada, with Author's Recollections of the Soil and Aspect; the Morals, Habits and Religious Institutions of that Country. London: 1820. V. 51

SANSOM, WILLIAM
Christmas. London: 1968. V. 48
The Equilibriad. London: 1948. V. 49; 52; 53
Fireman Flower, and Other Stories. London: 1944. V. 49; 51

SANSON, HENRY
Memoirs of the Sansons (1688-1847) from the Private Notes and Documents. London: 1876. V. 53

SANSOVINO, FRANCESCO
Concetti Politici. Venice: 1578. V. 51; 53
Le Osservationi Della Lingua Volgare. Venice: 1565. V. 48
The Quintessence of Wit. London: 1590. V. 50

SANTA Catalina Island... Los Angeles: 1900?. V. 52

SANTA Catalina Island. Los Angeles: 1910. V. 54

SANTA Cruz County: a Faithful Reproduction in Print and Photography of its Climate, Capabilities and Beauties. 1896. V. 52

SANTA ANNA, JOAQUIM JOSE DE
Elementos de Cirurgia Ocular Offerecidos a Sua Alteza Real o Senhor D. Joao Principe do Brazil. Lisboa: 1793. V. 48

SANTA FE, LIBERAL & ENGLEWOOD RAILROAD
Scenes Along the Line of the Santa Fe, Liberal & Englewood Railroad and Canadian Railroad. New York: 1906. V. 49

SANTA MARIA, VICENTE DE
The First Entry Into San Francisco Bay, 1775. San Francisco: 1971. V. 48; 50; 51

SANTAREM, PEDRO DE
Tracatus de Assecurationibus, et Sponsionibus Mercatorum... Coloniae: 1599. V. 50

SANTA RITA DURAO, JOSE DE
Caramaru. Poema Epico do Descubrimento da Bahia. Lisbon: 1781. V. 53

SANTAYANA, GEORGE
Lucifer, or the Heavenly Truce; a Theological Tragedy. Cambridge: 1924. V. 47
Poems. London: 1922. V. 49; 51; 54
The Realm of Matter: Book Second of Realms of Being. London: 1930. V. 47
The Sense of Beauty: Being the Outlines of Aesthetic Cthory. London: 1896. V. 48
Sonnets and Other Verses. Cambridge: 1894. V. 52
Sonnets and Other Verses. New York: 1896. V. 47
The Works of... New York: 1936-37. V. 51; 54
The Works of... New York: 1936-50. V. 52

SANTEE, ROSS
The Bubbling Spring. New York: 1949. V. 48; 54
Cowboy. 1928. V. 48
Cowboy. New York: 1928. V. 48
Men and Horses. New York: 1926. V. 50; 51; 52; 54
Spike. The Story of a Cowpuncher's Dog. New York: 1931. V. 51

SANTERRE, GEORGE H.
White Cliffs of Dallas, the Story of La Reunion: the Old French colony. Dallas: 1955. V. 47

SANTI, DOMENICO
Varii Modioni. Bologna: 1683. V. 51

SANTIAGO, DANNY
Famous All Over Town. New York: 1983. V. 49

SANTILLAN, D. A. DE
After the Revolution Economic Reconstruction in Spain Today. New York: 1937. V. 49

SANTORIO, SANTORIO
Medicina Statica: Being the Aphorisms... London: 1712. V. 50; 54
Medicina Statica: Being the Aphorisms... London: 1723. V. 47; 53
(Opera Omnia)...Commentaria in Prima Fen Primi Libri Canonis Avicennae.../...Methodi Vitandorum.../...Commentaria in Artem Medicinalem Galeni... Venice: 1660. V. 52

SANTOS, FRANCISCO DE LOS
A Description of the Royal Palace, and Monastery of St. Laurence, Called The Escurial... London: 1760. V. 48

SANTOS-DUMONT, ALBERTO
My Airships; the Story of My Life. London: 1904. V. 48; 49

SANTOS E SILVA, THOMAZ ANTONIO DOS
Braziliada, ou Portugal Immune, e Salvo: Poema Epico em Doze Cantos... Lisbon: 1815. V. 48

SANTUCCI, BERNARDO
Anatomia do Corpo Humano, Recopilada com Doutrinas Medicas, Chimicas, Filosoficas, Mathematicas, com Indices, e Estampas, Representantes Todas as Partes do Corp Humano... Lisboa: 1739. V. 53

SANTUCCI, LUIGI
La Donna Con La Bocca Aperta. (The Woman With Her Mouth Open). 1980. V. 52

SANYER, EUGENE T.
The Life and Career of Tiburcio Vasquez the California Brandit and Murderer... San Jose: 1875. V. 54

SAPATQAYN. Twentieth Century Nez Perce Artists. Seattle/Lewiston: 1991. V. 50

SAPHIRE, LAWRENCE
Fernand Leger: The Complete Graphic Work. New York: 1978. V. 50; 52

SAPPHO
Fragments. Paris: 1933. V. 48
Fragments... 1973. V. 52
(Greek Title) Songs of Sappho. 1922. V. 51; 52; 54
Poems and Fragments. Ann Arbor: 1965. V. 53
Sappho. London: 1885. V. 48
Sappho. London: 1887. V. 48
Sappho. London: 1982. V. 51; 52

SAPPINGTON, JOHN
The Theory and Treatment of Fevers. Arrow Rock: 1844. V. 48; 49; 50; 51; 54

SARAGENT, EPES
Velasco: a Tragedy. New York: 1839. V. 54

THE SARAH-AD: or, a Flight for Fame. London: 1742. V. 49; 51; 54

SARASIN, PAUL
Reisen in Celebes Ausgefuhrt in den Jahren 1839-1896 und 1902-1903. Wiesbaden: 1905. V. 48

SARAYNA, TORELLUS
Le Histoire E Fatti de Veronesi Nelli Tempi d'il Popolo et Signori Scaligeri. Verona: 1542. V. 52

SARBER, MARY
Photographs from the Border. El Paso: 1977. V. 51

SARDA, DANIEL
Conte de Maitre Espapidour. New York: 1927. V. 52; 54

SARDI, PIETRO
Corona Imperiale dell'Archiettura Militare Divisa in due Trattati. Venice: 1618. V. 52; 54

SARDOU, VICTORIEN
Rabagas, Comedie en Cinq Actes, en Prose. Paris: 1872. V. 51

SARG, TONY
Tony Sarg's Book for Children from Six to Sixty. New York. V. 51
Tony Sarg's Surprise Book. New York: 1941. V. 54

SARGANT, ALICE
Crystal Ball: A Child's Book of Fairy Ballads. London: 1894. V. 48

SARGANT, JANE ALICE
Two Letters to the Queen, and an Address to the Females of Britain. Maidenhead: 1820. V. 52

SARGANT, WILLIAM LUCAS
Recent Political Economy. London: 1867. V. 52
Robert Owen and His Social Philosophy. London: 1860. V. 52
The Science of Social Opulence. London: 1856. V. 51

SARGEANT, I.
Views in Kensington Gardens from Drawings by Mr. I. Sargeant. London: 1831. V. 50; 53

SARGENT & CO.
Locks and Hardware. New Haven: 1922. V. 50

SARGENT & ROHRABACHER
Fortunes of a Decade: a Graphic Recital of the Struggles of the Early Days of Cripple Creek, the Greatest Gold Camp on Earth, With Stories of Its Mines... Colorado Springs: 1900. V. 54

SARGENT, C. P.
Plantae Wilsonianae, an Enumeration of the Woody Plants Collected in Western China for the Arnold Arboretum of Harvard University During the Years 1907, 1908, 1910. Portland: 1988. V. 47

SARGENT, CHARLES SPRAGUE
Report on the Forests of North America (Exclusive of Mexico). Washington: 1884. V. 49; 50
The Silva of North America... New York: 1894-98. V. 50
Silva of North America. New York: 1947. V. 49

SARGENT, DANIEL
My Account of the Flood by Noah's Brother-in-Law. Ditchling: 1930. V. 53

SARGENT, EPES
Songs of the Sea, With Other Poems. Boston: 1847. V. 47

SARGENT, HENRY WINTHROP
A Treatise on the Theory and Practice of Landscape Gardening, Adapted to North America... New York: 1859. V. 47

SARGENT, JAMES
James Sargent's Descriptive Catalogue of Patent Magnetic Bank and Safe Locks, Manufacatured at 62 Buffalo St., Rochester, New York. Rochester: 1867. V. 51

SARGENT, JOHN
The Mine: a Dramatic Poem. London: 1785. V. 47; 53

SARGENT, LUCIUS MANILUS
Dealings with the Dead. Boston: 1856. V. 54

SARGENT, MARTIN P.
Pioneer Sketches: Scenes and Incidents of Former Days. Erie: 1891. V. 47

SARGENT, WINTHROP
The Life and Career of Major John Andre, Adjutant-General of the British Army in America. Boston: 1861. V. 47
The Loyalist Poetry of the Revolution. Philadelphia: 1857. V. 53
Papers in Relation to the Official Conduct of Winthrop Sargent, 2nd January 1801, Referred to the Committee Appointed on the 22nd Ultimo, to Enquire Into the Offical Conduct of Winthrop Sargent, Governor of the Mississippi Territory. Washington: 1801. V. 47

SARIANIDI, VIKTOR IVANOVITCH
The Golden Board of Bactria from the Tillya-tepe Excavations in Northern Afghanistan. New York: 1985. V. 50

SARNELLI, POMPEO
Antica Basilicografia. Naples: 1686. V. 49

SAROYAN, WILLIAM
An Act or Two of Foolish Kindness. Lincoln: 1977. V. 47; 48; 50; 53
The Adventures of Wesley Jackson. New York: 1946. V. 48; 54
The Assyrian and Other Stories. New York: 1950. V. 49; 51
The Beautiful People, Sweeney in the Trees and Across the Board on Tomorrow Morning. New York: 1941. V. 53
A Christmas Psalm. San Francisco: 1935. V. 47; 51
The Daring Young Man on the Flying Trapeze. New York: 1934. V. 51; 53; 54
The Daring Young Man on the Flying Trapeze... 1984. V. 52; 54
The Daring Young Man on the Flying Trapeze... California: 1984. V. 48
The Daring Young Man on the Flying Trapeze... Covela: 1984. V. 49
Don't Go Away Mad and Two Other Plays. New York: 1949. V. 49
The Fiscal Hoboes. New York: 1949. V. 48; 49; 54
Fragment. San Francisco: 1938. V. 48; 53
Harlem as Seen by Hirschfeld. New York: 1941. V. 53
The Human Comedy. New York: 1943. V. 49
Inhale and Exhale. London: 1936. V. 49
Inhale and Exhale. New York: 1936. V. 49; 50; 51; 53
Little Children. New York: 1937. V. 48; 49; 51
Look at Us,...etc. New York: 1967. V. 54
Morris Hirshfield. Milan: 1976. V. 53
Morris Hirshfield. Parma: 1976. V. 51
My Heart's in the Highlands. New York: 1939. V. 49
My Name is Aram. New York: 1940. V. 47; 51; 54
A Native American. San Francisco: 1938. V. 51; 54
Peace, It's Wonderful. New York: 1939. V. 51; 53; 54
Places Where I've Done Time. New York: 1972. V. 51
Razzle Dazzle. New York: 1942. V. 49; 54
Rock Wagram. London: 1952. V. 53; 54
Sam, the Highest Jumper of Them All, or the London Comedy. London: 1961. V. 53
The Saroyan Special. New York: 1948. V. 53
Saroyan's Fables. New York: 1941. V. 47; 49; 53
The Special Announcement. New York: 1940. V. 47; 48
Those Who Write Them and Those Who Collect Them. Chicago: 1936. V. 51; 53
Three Plays: My Heart's in the Highlands. The Time of Your Life. Love's Old Sweet song. New York: 1940. V. 48
Three Times Three. Los Angeles: 1936. V. 49; 51; 53; 54
The Time of Your Life. New York: 1939. V. 51
The Trouble with Tigers. 1938. V. 49
The Trouble with Tigers. New York: 1938. V. 51; 53
The Trouble with Tigers. London: 1939. V. 53

SARPI, PAOLO
The Historie of the Councel of Trent. London: 1620. V. 47; 53
The Historie of the Councel of Trent. London: 1629. V. 53
The History of the Council of Trent... London: 1676. V. 50; 51
The History of the Inquisition... London: 1655. V. 50; 54
The Letters of the Renowned Father Paul, Counsellor of State. London: 1693. V. 52
The Rights of Sovereigns and Subjects... London: 1722. V. 48; 51; 52

SARRATT, J. H.
A Treatise on the Game of Chess. London: 1808. V. 50

SARRAUTE, NATHALIE
The Age of Suspicion. New York: 1963. V. 50
Do You Hear Them?. New York: 1973. V. 50
Fools Say. New York: 1977. V. 50
Tropisms. New York: 1967. V. 50

SARRIS, ANDREW
The Films of Josef von Sternberg. New York: 1966. V. 54

SARTAIN, JOHN
The Reminiscences of a Very Old Man. New York: 1899. V. 50

SARTIN, STEPHEN
Thomas Sidney Cooper, C.V.O., R.A. 1803-1902. Leigh-on-Sea: 1976. V. 53

SARTON, GEORGE
A History of Science. Cambridge: 1952-59. V. 49; 51
Introduction to the History of Science. Washington: 1927-47. V. 51
Introduction to the History of Science. Baltimore: 1927-48. V. 49
Introduction to the History of Science. Washington: 1927-48. V. 50
Introduction to the History of Science. Baltimore: 1927-48/50. V. 54
Introduction to the History of Science. Baltimore: 1931. V. 52
Introduction to the History of Science... Baltimore: 1968. V. 47
Introduction to the History of Science. Volume II. from Rabi Ben Ezra to Roger Bacon. Baltimore: 1931. V. 53; 54

SARTON, MAY
Coming Into Eighty. Concord: 1992. V. 47; 49; 51; 52
A Durable Fire: Poems. New York: 1972. V. 54
Encounter In April. Boston: 1937. V. 49; 54
Forward Into the Past. Concord: 1992. V. 49
Honey in the Hive. Boston: 1988. V. 54
The House by the Sea. London: 1977. V. 54
The Land of Silence and Other Poems. New York: 1953. V. 51
The Leaves of the Tree. Mt. Vernon: 1950. V. 47; 49; 54
Punch's Secret. New York: 1974. V. 51
The Single Hound. Boston: 1938. V. 47

SARTORIUS, CARL CHRISTIAN
Mexico. Landscapes and Popular Sketches. London: 1858. V. 54

SARTRE, JEAN PAUL
Being and Nothingness. New York: 1956. V. 51
Les Chemins de la Liberte. Paris: 1945-49. V. 49
Five Plays. 1978. V. 48
Five Plays. Franklin Center: 1978. V. 50; 53
Les Mains Sales. Paris: 1948. V. 52
The Wall and Other Stories. 1948. V. 48
The Wall and Other Stories. 1949. V. 52

SARYCHEV, GAVRIL A.
Account of a Voyage of Discvoery to the North-East of Siberia, the Forzen Ocean and the North-East Sea. London: 1806-07. V. 50

SASOWSKY, N.
The Prints of Reginald Marsh. New York: 1976. V. 53

SASS, HENRY
A Journey to Rome and Naples, Performed in 1817; Giving an Account of the Present State of Society in Italy; and Containing Observations on the Fine Arts... London: 1818. V. 53

SASSI, GIUSEPPE ANTONIO
Specimen Virtutis Avitae...Expressum in Funebri Apparatu Solemnium Exequiarum. Milan: 1743. V. 53

SASSOON, SIEGFRIED LORRAINE
Counter-Attack and Other Poems. New York: 1908. V. 50
Counter-Attack and Other Poems. London: 1918. V. 47; 52; 53
Counter-Attack and Other Poems. New York: 1918. V. 47; 48; 50
The Daffodil Murderer. London: 1913. V. 49; 52
Four Poems. Cambridge: 1918. V. 49; 53
The Heart's Journey. New York & London: 1927. V. 47; 49; 50; 52; 53; 54
The Heart's Journey.... New York: 1929. V. 49
In Sicily. London: 1930. V. 47; 48; 51; 54
Memoirs of a Fox-Hunting Man. London: 1920. V. 52
Memoirs of a Fox-Hunting Man. London: 1928. V. 52; 53
Memoirs of a Fox-Hunting Man... London: 1928/30/36. V. 50
Memoirs of a Fox-Hunting Man. London: 1929. V. 50; 51; 54
Memoirs of a Fox-Hunting Man. New York: 1929. V. 51; 54
Memoirs of a Fox-Hunting Man. 1977. V. 47
Memoirs of a Fox-Hunting Man. Great Britain: 1977. V. 53
Memoirs of an Infantry Officer. London: 1930. V. 47; 49; 50; 51; 52; 53; 54
Memoirs of an Infantry Officer. London: 1931. V. 47; 48; 49; 50; 53
Memoirs of an Infantry Officer. New York: 1981. V. 47; 51; 54
Nativity. New York: 1927. V. 48; 49; 53
An Octave. 1966. V. 49; 51
An Octave. London: 1966. V. 47; 49; 50; 53
The Old Century and Seven More Years. London: 1938. V. 50; 51; 53
The Old Huntsman and Other Poems. London: 1917. V. 47; 48; 49; 51
The Old Huntsman and Other Poems. New York: 1918. V. 50
The Old Huntsman and Other Poems. New York: 1918/17. V. 48
The Path to Peace. Worcester: 1960. V. 47; 52; 54
Picture Show. Cambridge: 1919. V. 47
Poems. London: 1931. V. 48
Poems. London: 1958. V. 53
Poems by Pinchbeck Lyre. London: 1931. V. 51
Poems From Italy. London: 1945. V. 50; 51
Rhymed Ruminations: Poems. London: 1940. V. 49; 53
The Road to Ruin. London: 1933. V. 48; 51; 53
Satirical Poems. London: 1926. V. 50
Sherston's Progress. London: 1936. V. 48; 49; 50; 51; 52; 53
Something About Myself. Worcester: 1966. V. 48; 49
To My Mother. London: 1928. V. 48; 50; 51
Vigils. Bristol: 1934. V. 47; 49
The War Poems. London: 1919. V. 47; 49; 50; 51

SASTRES, FRANCESCO
An Introduction to Italian Grammar... London: 1777. V. 50

SATGE ST. JEAN, CAROLINE, VICOMTESSE DE
The Cave of the Huguenots: a Tale of the XVIIth Century, and Other Poems. Bath: 1848. V. 53

SATIE, ERIK
Sports & divertissements. Paris: 1919. V. 47

A SATIRE Upon Physicians, or an English Paraphrase, with Notes and References, of Dr. King's Most Memorable Oration, Delivered at the Dedication of the Faclivian Library in Oxford. London: 1755. V. 54

SATTERLEE, MARION P.
The Massacre at the Redwood Indian Agenccy, on Monday, August 18, 1862. Minneapolis: 1916. V. 52

SATTERTHWAIT, WALTER
Wall of Glass. New York: 1987. V. 53

SATURINO DA COSTA PEREIRA, JOSE
Observations on the Analysis Made by Sr. Souza Martins of Doctor Saturnino's Finance Project, by the Author of that Project. Rio de Janeiro: 1844. V. 48

A SATYR Against Dancing. London: 1702. V. 49

A SATYR Against the French. London: 1691. V. 47; 48

SATYRE Menippee De La Vertv Dv Catholicon D'Espagne, Et De La Tenve Des Estats de Paris. 1595. V. 48

SAUDEK, JAN
The World of Jan Saudek. 1983. V. 52

SAUER, GORDON C.
John Gould, The Bird Man. Melbourne: 1982. V. 53

SAUER, MARTIN
An Account of a Geographical and Astronomical Expedition to the Northern Parts of Russia, for Ascertaining the Degree of Latitude and Longitude of the Mouth of the River Kovima... London: 1802. V. 47; 48

SAUERLANDER, WILLIBALD
Gothic Sculpture in France, 1140-1270. New York: 1973. V. 50; 54

SAUGRAIN, CLAUDE MARIN
Code de la Librairie et Imprimerie de Paris. Paris: 1744. V. 52

SAULCY, F. DE
Narrative of a Journey Round the Dead Sea and In the Bible Lands in 1850 and 1851. London: 1853. V. 48; 51

SAUMAISE, CLAUDE DE
Ad Johannem Miltonum Hesponsio Opus Posthumum. Londini: 1660. V. 54

SAUNDBY, ROBERT
Lectures on Bright's Disease. London: 1889. V. 54

SAUNDERS, ANN
Narrative of the Shipwreck and Sufferings of Miss Ann Saunders, Who Was a Passenger on Board the Ship Francis (!) Mary, Which foundered at Sea on the 5th Feb. 1826 On Her Passage from New Brunswick to Liverpool. Providence: 1827. V. 51

SAUNDERS, D.
Australian Ecosystems: 200 Years of Utilization, Degradation and Reconstruction. Chipping Norton: 1990. V. 52

SAUNDERS, EDWARD
The Hemiptera of the British Islands. London: 1892. V. 53
The Hymenoptera Aculeata of the British Islands, a Descriptive Account of the Families, Genera and Species Indigenous to Great Britain and Ireland. London: 1896. V. 47; 53

SAUNDERS, F.
Memories of the Great Metropolis; or, London, from the Tower to the Crystal Palace. New York: 1852. V. 54

SAUNDERS, FREDERIC
The Author's Printing and Publishing Assistant. London: 1839. V. 50; 52; 54

SAUNDERS, GEORGE W.
The Trail Drivers of Texas. 1924. V. 50

SAUNDERS, HENRY S.
100 Whitman Photographs. Toronto: 1939. V. 50

SAUNDERS, J. B. DE C. M.
Andreas Vesalius Bruxelensis: The Bloodletting Letter of 1539. London: 1948. V. 48
The Illustrations from the Works of Andreas Vesalius of Brussels, with Annotations and Translations... Cleveland: 1950. V. 47; 50; 52

SAUNDERS, JAMES
The Compleat Fisherman. London: 1724. V. 49
Next Time I'll Sing to You - a Play in Two Acts. London: 1963. V. 50

SAUNDERS, JAMES EDMOND
Early Settlers of Alabama... New Orleans: 1899. V. 47; 52; 53

SAUNDERS, JAMES M.
A Collection of Miscellaneous Pieces, in Prose and Verse. Philadelphia: 1834. V. 51

SAUNDERS, JOHN
Israel Mort, Overman. London: 1873. V. 54

SAUNDERS, JOHN CUNNINGHAM
A Treatise on Some Practical Points Relating to the Diseases of the Eye... London: 1811. V. 48
A Treatise on Some Practical Points Relating to the Diseases of the Eye. Philadelphia: 1821. V. 48

SAUNDERS, LOUISE
The Knave of Hearts. New York: 1925. V. 48; 51; 53
The Knave of Hearts. Racine: 1925. V. 47; 49; 53; 54

SAUNDERS, MARSHALL
Beautiful Joe: An Autobiography. Philadelphia: 1894. V. 51
Beautiful Joe: an Autobiography. Toronto: 1894. V. 53
Daisy. Philadelphia: 189-?. V. 50

SAUNDERS, O. ELFRIDA
English Illumination. Florence & New York: 1928. V. 48; 49; 51

SAUNDERS, RICHARD
Angelographia Sive Pneumata Leiturgia Pneumatalogia, or, a Discourse of Angels... London: 1701. V. 49
Physiognomie, and Chiromancie, Metoposcopie, the Symmetrical Proportions and Signal Moles of the Body. London: 1653. V. 50
Poor Richard: the Almanacks for the Years 1733-1758. Philadelphia: 1964. V. 52; 54

SAUNDERS, T. W.
A Practical Treatise on the Law of Assault and Battery; Including the Remedies by Action, Indictment, Summary Proceedings Before Magistrates and Sureties to Keep the Peace. London: 1842. V. 47

SAUNDERS, W. B.
Nautilus, the Biology and Paleobiology of a Living Fossil. New York: 1987. V. 50

SAUNDERS, W. W.
Refugium Botanicum... London: 1869-82. V. 50

SAUNDERS, WILLIAM
Through the Light Continent. London Paris & New York: 1879. V. 54
A Treatise on the Chemical History and Medicinal Powers of Some of the Most Celebrated Mineral Waters... London: 1800. V. 48
A Treatise on the Chemical History and Medicinal Powers of Some of the Most Celebrated Mineral Waters... London: 1805. V. 48
A Treatise On the Structure, Economy and Diseases Of the Liver... London: 1793. V. 49; 50; 54
A Treatise on the Structure, Economy and Diseases of the Liver... London: 1795. V. 51
Treatise on the Structure, Economy and Diseases of the Liver... Walpold: 1810. V. 48

SAUNDERSON, FRANCIS
The Case Stated of Education As It Was and Ought to Be Restored; and As It Now and Ought to be Discontinued. Dublin: 1862. V. 52

SAUNDERSON, NICHOLAS
The Method of Fluxions Applied to a select Number of Useful Problems... London: 1756. V. 51

SAUNDERSON, ROBERT
Twelve Sermons, Preached. London: 1637. V. 49

SAUNDES, WAYNFLETE HENRY PATTEN
Black and Gold; or "The Don! The Don!". London: 1864. V. 47

SAUNIER, CLAUDIUS
A Treatise of Modern Horlogy of Theory and Practice. London: 1887. V. 47

SAUVAGE, SILVAIN
Cinquante Eaux-Fortes de Sylvain Sauvage Pour Illustrer les Memoirs de Jacques Casanova de Seingalt Venitien. 1930?. V. 48

SAUVAGES, FRANCOIS BOISSIER DE
Nosologia Methodica Sistens Morborum Classes, Juxta syndehami mentem & Botanicorum Ordinem... London: 1768. V. 53

SAUVAN, JEAN BAPTISTE BALTHAZAR
Picturesque Tour of the Seine from Paris to the Sea. London: 1821. V. 49

SAVAGE, C. R.
The Reflex or Salt Lake City and Vicinity. Salt Lake City: 1890. V. 52

THE SAVAGE Club Papers. London: 1897. V. 48

SAVAGE, EDWARD H.
Boston Events. A Brief Mention and the Date of More than 5,000 Events that Transpired in Boston from 1630 to 1880. Boston: 1884. V. 51

SAVAGE, GEORGE
The American Birds of Dorthy Doughty. Worcester: 1962. V. 49
English Ceramics. New York: 1981. V. 47

SAVAGE, HENRY
A Long Spoon and the Devil. A Parody of the Spoon River Anthology. London: 1922. V. 49

SAVAGE, JOHN
The Art of Prudence: or, a Companion for a Man of Sense... London: 1702. V. 49
Horace to Scaeva. London: 1730. V. 47; 48

SAVAGE, MARMION W.
The Bachelor of the Albany. London: 1848,. V. 51
The Falcon Family; or, Young Ireland. London: 1845. V. 51

SAVAGE MINING CO.
Annual Report of the Savage Mining Company, for the Fiscal year Ending July 11th, 1873. San Francisco: 1873. V. 49

SAVAGE, RICHARD
The Wanderer: a Poem. London: 1729. V. 51
The Works of Richard Savage... 1775. V. 47
The Works of Richard Savage... London: 1775. V. 48; 50
The Works of Richard Savage. London: 1777. V. 48; 50; 52; 53

SAVAGE, W. SHERMAN
The History of Lincoln University. Jefferson City: 1939. V. 48; 53

SAVAGE, WILLIAM
A Dictionary of the Art of Printing. London: 1841. V. 50
Practical Hints on Decorative Printing, with Illustrations Engraved on Wood... London: 1822. V. 48

SAVANNAH & MEMPHIS RAILROAD
Its Local Advantages and Importance as the Central Link in the Combined Line from St. Louis to Savannah, with the St. Louis & Iron Mountain Railroad, Mobile & Ohio Railroad, Central R. R. & Banking Co. of Georgia, Bankers and Financial Agents... New York: 1873. V. 47

SAVARY, A. W.
A Genealogical and Biographical Record of the Savery Families (Savory and Savary) and of the Severy Family (Severit...). Boston: 1893. V. 53

SAVARY, CLAUDE E.
Letters on Egypt. Dublin: 1787. V. 53
Letters on Egypt... London: 1787. V. 51

SAVELLE, MAX
The Diplomatic History of the Canadian Boundary, 1749-1763. New Haven/Toronto: 1940. V. 51

SAVE-SODERBERGH, TORGNY
The Navy of the Eighteenth Egyptian Dynasty. Uppsala & Leipzig: 1946. V. 51
Private Tombs at Thebes. Oxford: 1957-63. V. 49; 51

SAVIGNY, J. B. HENRY
Narrative of a Voyage to Senegal in 1816... Comprising the Shipwreck of the Medusa...etc. London: 1818. V. 50

SAVIGNY, JOHN HENRY
A Catalogue of Chirurgical Instruments, Made and Sold...No. 28, King-Street, Covent-Garden. London: 1804. V. 51
Treatise on the Management and Use of a Razor, With Practical Directions Relative to Its Appendages... London: 1786. V. 48

SAVILE, A. R.
Cyprus. London: 1878. V. 49

SAVILE, ALBANY
Thirty Six Hints to Sportsman. Okehampton: 1825. V. 47; 52

SAVILE, F.
Beyond the Great South Wall: the Secret of the Antarctic. 1901. V. 48
Beyond the Great South Wall: The Secret of the Antarctic. New Amsterdam: 1901. V. 52
The River of the Giraffe, a Chronicle of Desert, Stream and Forest Shotting in the Southern Sudan. London: 1925. V. 48

SAVILE, GEORGE
A Character of King Charles the Second. London: 1750. V. 48; 50; 53

SAVILE, HENRY
Advice to a Painter. London: 1679. V. 54
Rervm Anglicaravm Scriptores Post Bedam Praecipvi, ex Vetvstissimis Codicibvs Manvscriptis Nvnc Primvm in Ivcem Editi (etc.). Frankfurt: 1601. V. 51; 54

SAVILL, THOMAS
Clinical Lectures of Neurastahenia. London: 1899. V. 51; 54

SAVILLE, FRANK
The High Grass Trail. London: 1924. V. 48

SAVILLE, HENRY M.
Rhymes and Reminiscences (Humorous and Serious). Boston: 1929. V. 49

SAVILLE, M. H.
The Antiquities of Manabi Ecuador. New York: 1907/10. V. 51

SAVINO, ALBERT
The Departure of the Argonaut. New York: 1986. V. 48

SAVO BARCELLONA, GEMMA
The Sculptors of the Cassaro. Palermo: 1971. V. 53

SAVONAROLA, GIROLAMO
Compendio di Revelatione. Florence: 1495. V. 47; 49
Devotissimi Patris Fratris Hieronymi Sauonarole Ferrariensis, Praedicatorum Ordinis Opuscula, de Simplicitate Vitae Christianae. Alcala: 1530. V. 48
Expositione de Reuerendissimo in Christo Padre Frate Hieronymo...Sopra la Oratione della Vergine Gloriosa. Florence: 1495. V. 47; 49
Sermone del Oratione a M.A.d.S. Composto da Frate Hieronymo da Ferrara Dellordine de Frati Predicatori. Florence: 1500. V. 47
Tractato di Frate Hieronymo De Ferraria Delordine De Fr. Pred. in Defensione et Commedatione Della Oratione Mentale. Florence: 1494. V. 47; 49
Trattato Della Reuelatione della Reformatione della Chiesa Diuninitus. Venice: 1536. V. 52

SAVORY, H. S.
Geometric Turning: Comprising a Description of the New Geometric Chuck Constructed by Mr. Plant of Birmingham. London: 1873. V. 52

SAVORY, ISABEL
A Sportswoman In India. London: 1900. V. 50; 51

THE SAVOY. London: 1896. V. 47; 52

SAVOY, WILLARD
Alien Land. New York: 1949. V. 54

SAVVA, MONK
The Book of Wisdom and Lies. Hammersmith: 1894. V. 50; 52; 54

SAWARD, BLANCHE C.
Decorataive Painting. London: 1883. V. 52

SAWERS, WILLIAM
Essays, on Subjects Moral and Divine, In Prose and Verse... Berwick: 1796. V. 48

SAWITZKY, WILLIAM
Matthew Pratt, 1734-1805. New York: 1942. V. 53

SAWKINS, JAMES GAY
A Pictorial Tour of Hawaii 1850-1852. San Francisco: 1991. V. 51
Reports on the Geology of Jamaica... 1869. V. 53

SAWYER, ALVAH LITTLEFIELD
A History of the Northern Peninsula of Michigan and Its People. Chicago: 1911. V. 50

SAWYER, CHARLES J.
English Books 1475-1900. London: 1927. V. 47; 48; 49
English Books 1475-1900... Westminster: 1927. V. 47; 49; 54

SAWYER, EDMUND
Sir Ralph Winwood: Memorials of the Affairs of State, in the Reigns of Elizabeth and James I... London: 1725. V. 53

SAWYER, ELBERT HENRY
The National Military Park, Established by the Government to Commemorate the Gallant Deeds of the Federal and Confederate Armies in the Four Major Battles, Fredericksburg, Chancellorsville, Wilderness & Spotsylvania, Va. 1932. V. 52

SAWYER, EUGENE T.
The Life and Career of Tiburcio Vasquez, the California State Robber. Oakland: 1944. V. 48

SAWYER, JOSEPH
System of Book-Keeping, Drawn Up for and Expressly Adapted to the Tanning Trade...in two parts. London: 1862. V. 49

SAWYER, LORENZO
Way Sketches. New York: 1926. V. 47; 50; 53

SAWYER, RUTH
The Long Christmas. New York: 1941. V. 48
Maggie Rose: Her Birthday Christmas. New York: 1952. V. 48

SAXBY, HENRY
The British Customs: Containing an Historical and Practical Account of Each Branch of that Revenue... London: 1757. V. 49

SAXBY, HENRY L.
The Birds of Shetland with Observations on Their Habits, Migration and Occasional Appearance. Edinburgh: 1874. V. 52; 54

SAXBY, JESSIE M. E.
Joseph Bell. An Appreciation by an Old Friend. Edinburgh and London: 1914. V. 49

SAXE, JOHN G.
Progress: a Satire. New York: 1847. V. 47; 54

SAXE, MAURICE
Reveries, or Memoirs Upon the Art of War...Together with His Reflections Upon the Propagation of the Human Species. London: 1757. V. 51

THE SAXON Chronicle. London: 1823. V. 47

SAY, BENJAMIN
A Short Compilation of the Extraordinary Life and Writings of Thomas Say. New York: 1805. V. 53

SAY, JEAN BAPTISTE
Letters to Mr. Malthus, on Several Subjects of Political Economy, and on the Cause of Stagnation of Commerce. London: 1821. V. 51
A Treatise on Political Economy... London: 1821. V. 50; 54

SAY, THOMAS
American Conchology, or Descriptions of the Shells of North America. New Harmony: 1830. V. 52
American Conchology, or Descriptions of the Shells of North America,... New Harmony: 1830-38?. V. 48
American Entomology, or Descriptions of the Insects of North America. Philadelphia: 1824-25-28. V. 48; 50; 52; 53; 54
Complete Writings of Thomas Say on the Entomology of North America. New York: 1859. V. 54
The Complete Writings of Thomas Say on the Entomology of North America. Philadelphia: 1891. V. 53

SAYCE, A. H.
The Astronomy and Astrology of the Babylonians, with the Translations fo the Tablets Relating to These Subjects. London: 1874. V. 48

SAYE, JAMES HODGE
Memoirs of Major Joseph McJunkin. Greenwood: 1925. V. 48

SAYER, CAPTAIN
The History of Gibraltar and of Its Political Relation to Events in Europe... London: 1862. V. 51

SAYER, EDWARD
Observations On the Police and Civil Government of Westminster, with a Proposal for a Reform. London: 1784. V. 50

SAYER, FREDERIC
The History of Gibraltar and of its Political Relation to Events in Europe. London: 1865. V. 48

SAYER, OLIVER M.
Max Reinhardt and His Theatre. New York: 1924. V. 54

SAYER, ROBERT J.
The Artist's Vade Mecum; Being the Whole Art of Drawing, Taught in a New Work... London: 1766. V. 54
Dramatic Characters or Different Portraits of the English Stage. London: 1771-72. V. 49
Dramatic Characters, or Different Portraits of the English Stage. London: 1773. V. 49

SAYER, WILLIAM FREDERICK
Spare Moments. Hackney: 1853. V. 50; 51
The Warehouse Boy, in Six Discourses... London: 1849. V. 47

SAYERS, DOROTHY L.
Aeneas at the Court of Dido. London: 1945. V. 49
Busman's Holiday - a Love Story with Detective Interruptions. London: 1937. V. 47
Busman's Honeymoon. London: 1937. V. 49; 51; 52
Busman's Honeymoon. New York: 1937. V. 50; 52
The Documents in the Case. New York: 1930. V. 47
The Emperor Constantine. London: 1951. V. 49
Gaudy Night. London: 1935. V. 47; 49; 50; 51; 53
Gaudy Night. New York: 1936. V. 48
Great Short Stories of Detection, Mystery and Horror. London: 1928. V. 53
In the Teeth of the Evidence and Other Stories. London: 1939. V. 47; 49; 51; 53
In the Teeth of the Evidence and Other Stories. 1940. V. 53
Lord Peter Views the Body. London: 1928. V. 51
The Mysterious English. London: 1941. V. 53
The Nine Tailors. London: 1934. V. 48
The Nine Tailors. New York: 1934. V. 52
The Story of Adam and Christ. Greenwich: 1955. V. 51
The Story of Easter. Greenwich: 1955. V. 51
Strong Poison. London: 1930. V. 48
Strong Poison. New York: 1930. V. 48; 52
The Unpleasantness at the Bellona Club. London: 1928. V. 48
Whose Body?. New York: 1923. V. 50

SAYERS, FRANCES CLARKE
Bluebonnets for Lucinda. New York: 1934. V. 53

SAYERS, R. S.
The Bank of England 1891-1944. Cambridge: 1976. V. 51

SAYERS, TOM
By Order of the Executors of Tom Sayers, Late "Champion of England". A Catalogue of the Whole of the Valuable Trophies, Won By and Presented to the Late Tom Sayers... Colophon London: 1865. V. 49

SAYLE, C. E.
A Catalogue of the Bradshaw Collection of Irish Books in the University Library, Cambridge. Cambridge: 1916. V. 49
Early English Printed Books in the University Library, Cambridge (1475-1640). 1900-07. V. 47; 49
Early English Printed Books in the University Library, Cambridge (1475-1640). Cambridge: 1900-07. V. 51; 54

SAYLER, OLIVER M.
Inside the Moscow Art Theatre. New York: 1925. V. 47; 54
Max Reinhardt and His Theatre. New York: 1926. V. 50

SAYLES, JOHN
Annotated Statutes of the State of Texas. St. Louis: 1898. V. 52
Early Laws of Texas. St. Louis: 1888. V. 50
Pride of the Bimbos. Boston: 1975. V. 48; 50; 52; 53
Union Dues. Boston: 1977. V. 50

SAYLOR, HENRY H.
Bungalows: Their Design, Construction and Furnishing. New York: 1926. V. 48

SAYRE, LEWIS ALBERT
Partial Paralysis from Reflex Irritation, Caused By Congenital Phimosis and Adherent Prepuce. Philadelphia: 1870. V. 52
Spinal Disease and Spinal Curvature, Their Treatment, Suspension and the Use of the Plaster of Paris Bandage. London: 1878. V. 47; 49

SAYRE, STEPHEN
The Trial of the Cause on An Action Brought by Stephen Sayre, Esq. Against the Right Honourable Henry Earl of Rochford, for False Imprisonment...in the Court of Common Pleas in Westminster-Hall on Thursday the 27th of June, 1776. London: 1776. V. 53

SAYWELL, J. L.
The History and Annals of Northallerton, Yorkshire... Northallerton: 1885. V. 50; 53

SCACCHI, FRANCESCO
De Salvbri Potv Dissertatio. Rome: 1622. V. 53

SCADDING, HENRY
Early Notices of Toronto. Toronto: 1865. V. 53
Toronto of Old: Collections and Recollections... Toronto: 1873. V. 52; 53
Toronto of Old: Collections and Recollections. Toronto: 1878. V. 52
Toronto: Past and Present: Historical and Descriptive. Toronto: 1884. V. 52; 54

SCALES, ALFRED M.
The Battle of Fredericksburg. Washington: 1884. V. 49

SCALIGER, JOSEPH JUSTUS
Cyclometrica Elementa Duo. (with) Mesolabium. Leiden: 1594. V. 47
Notitia Galliae. Amsterdam: 1697. V. 52

SCAMMON, CHARLES M.
The Marine Mammals of the North Western Coast of North America, Described and Illustrated. San Francisco: 1874. V. 53

SCAMMON, L. N.
Spanish Missions California. San Francisco: 1926. V. 48; 51

SCAMOZZI, VINCENZO
Discorsi Sopra L'Antichita di Roma. Venice: 1583. V. 54
The Mirror of Architecture; or the Ground-Rules of the Art of Building... London: 1721. V. 52

SCAMUZZI, ERNESTO
Egyptian Art in the Egyptian Museum of Turin. New York: 1965. V. 50; 51; 52; 53

SCANNELL, VERNON
Of Love and Music. Canterbury: 1980. V. 50

SCAPULA, JOHANN
Lexicon Graecolatinum Novum. 1580. V. 50

SCARBOROUGH, DOROTHY
On the Trail of Negro Folk-Songs. Cambridge: 1925. V. 48; 49

SCARFE, FRANCIS
Inscapes - Poems. London: 1940. V. 52

SCARGILL, WILLIAM PITT
Blue-Stocking Hall. London: 1827. V. 53
The Puritan's Grave. London: 1833. V. 54

SCARLET and Gold. Vancouver: 1919. V. 50

SCARPA, ANTOINE
Practical Observations on the Principal Diseases of the Eyes. London: 1806. V. 53

SCARPA, ANTOINE continued
Traite Pratique des Hernies, ou Memoires Anatomiques et Chirirgicaux sur ces Maladies. Paris: 1823. V. 52

SCARRON, PAUL
The Comical Romance and Other Tales. London: 1892. V. 49
Scarron's Comical Romance: or, a Facetious History of a Company of Strowling Stage-Players. London: 1676. V. 48; 50
The Whole Comical Works of Scarron, Containing His Comical Romance of a Company of Stage Players... London: 1703. V. 47; 48

SCATTERGOOD, THOMAS
Memoirs of Thomas Scattergood, Late of Philadelphia, a Minister of the Gospel of Christ. London: 1845. V. 49; 54

SCENERY of the East India Islands, Etc. London: 1811-13. V. 52

SCENES from the Land of the Midnight Sun, Yukon and Alaska. Dawson: 1908. V. 50

SCENES in China, Exhibiting the Manners, Customs, Diversions, and Singular Peculiarities of the Chinese, together With the Mode of Travelling, Navigation, &c... London: 1820?. V. 48

SCHAACK, MICHAEL J.
Anarchy and Anarchists a History of the Red Terror... Chicago: 1889. V. 47
Anarchy and Anarchists, a History of the Red Terror... New York: 1980. V. 51

SCHAAFSMA, POLLY
Indian Rock Art of the Southwest. Albuquerque: 1980. V. 54

SCHAARSCHMIDT-RICHTER, I.
Japanese Gardens. New York: 1979. V. 50; 51

SCHADE, WERNER
Cranach: a Family of Master Painters. New York: 1980. V. 51

SCHADOW, JOHANN GOTTFRIED
Wittenbergs Denkmaler. Wittenberg: 1825. V. 53

SCHAEFER, E. A.
Quain's Anatomy: Splanchnology. London: 1896. V. 48

SCHAEFER, JACK
The Great Endurance Horse Race... 1963. V. 51; 54
The Great Endurance Horse Race. Santa Fe: 1963. V. 54
Monte Walsh. Boston: 1963. V. 54
Shane. Boston: 1949. V. 54
Shane. Boston: 1954. V. 51

SCHAEFFER, CASPER
Memoirs and Reminiscences Together with Sketches of the early History of Sussex County, New Jersey. Hackensack: 1907. V. 47; 49; 51

SCHAEFFER, JACOB CHRISTIAN
Fungorum Qui in Baaria et Palatinatu Circa Ratisbonam Nascuntur... Erlangae: 1800. V. 49; 52

SCHAEFFER, LUTHER MELANCTHON
Sketches of Travels in South America, Mexico and California. New York: 1860. V. 47; 48; 49; 54

SCHAEFFER, SAMUEL BERNARD
Morning Noon Night. New York: 1937. V. 52
Pose Please. New York: 1936. V. 51

SCHAFER, JURGEN
Early Modern English Lexicography. London: 1989. V. 51

SCHAFF, PHILIP
A Religious Encyclopedia; or Dictionary of Biblical, Historical, Doctrinal and Practical Theology. New York: 1889. V. 47

SCHAFFER, JACOB CHRISTIAN
Vorlaufige Beogachtungen der Schwamme um Regensburg. Regensburg: 1759. V. 49; 52

SCHALDACH, WILLIAM J.
Carl Rungius, Big Game Painter. West Hartford: 1945. V. 47; 53
Coverts and Casts. Field Sports and Angling in Words and Pictures. New York: 1943. V. 47; 52
Fish by Schaldach. London: 1937. V. 50; 52
Fish by Schaldach... Philadelphia: 1937. V. 48
Upland Gunning. New York: 1946. V. 52
Upland Gunning... West Hartford: 1946. V. 53
The Wind On Your Cheek. New York: 1972. V. 50

SCHAPERA, I.
The Bantu-Speaking Tribes of South Africa. London: 1937. V. 51

SCHARF, GEORGE
A Descriptive and Historical Catalogue of the Collection of Pictures at Woburn Abbey. London: 1890. V. 49

SCHARF, JOHN THOMAS
History of Westchester County... Philadelphia: 1886. V. 49
History of Westchester County. 1992. V. 49

SCHARFT, GEORGE
A Descriptive and Historical Catalogue of the Collection of Pictures at Woburn Abbey. 1890. V. 52

SCHARL, JOSEF
Josef Scharl. New York: 1945. V. 47; 51

SCHARLING, CARL HENRIK
Noddebo Parsonage. London: 1867. V. 48

SCHARMANN, HERMANN B.
Scharmann's Overland Journey to California. New York: 1918. V. 47

SCHARY, DORE
The Devil's Advocate. New York: 1961. V. 54

SCHATZ, BORIS
Boris Schatz. His Life and Work. Jerusalem: 1925. V. 48

SCHATZ, OLGA
Juval Sings Into the Spirit of Art. Berkeley: 1949. V. 53

SCHAU, MICHAEL
J. C. Leydendecker. New York: 1974. V. 48; 50; 52

SCHECKLEY, R.
Watchbird. 1990. V. 47

SCHEDEL, HARTMANN
Liber Chronicarum. Nuremberg: 1493. V. 48; 50; 54
The Nuremberg Chronicle. New York: 1979. V. 50; 53

A SCHEDULE of the Ancient Colored Inhabitants of Charlestown, Massachusetts, on Record Prior to 1800. 1870. V. 51

SCHEEL, J. J.
Atlas of Killifishes of the Old World. Portsmouth: 1990. V. 50

SCHEELE, CARL WILHELM
The Chemical Essays... London: 1786. V. 48; 54
Chemical Observations and Experiments on Air and Fire. London: 1780. V. 48
Memoires de Chymie Tires des Memoires de l'Academie Royale des Sciences de Stockholm... Paris: 1785. V. 50
Opuscula Chemica et Physica. Leipzig: 1788-89. V. 48
Supplement au Traite Chimique de l'Air et Du Feu... Paris: 1785. V. 48; 53
Traite Chimique de l'Air et du Feu... Paris: 1781. V. 48; 53

SCHEER, FREDERICK
Kew and Its Gardens. London: 1840. V. 49

SCHEFFER, JOHN
The History of Lapland. 1674. V. 50
The History of Lapland... Oxford: 1674. V. 52

SCHEIDIG, WALTHER
Crafts of the Weimar Bauhaus 1919-1924. London: 1967. V. 49; 51; 53

SCHEITHAUER, W.
Hummingbirds. London: 1967. V. 54

SCHELL, JAMES P.
In the Ojibway Country - A Story of Early Missions on the Minnesota Frontier. Walhalla: 1911. V. 54

SCHELLEN, H.
Spectrum Analysis, In its Application to Terrestrial Substances and the Physical Constitution of the Heavnely Bodies. New York: 1872. V. 50

SCHENCK, J. H.
The Wild Ranger of Santa Fe. 1886. V. 48; 50

SCHENCK, P. L.
Historical Sketch of the Zabriskie Homestead (Removed 1877), Flatbush, L.I.... Brooklyn: 1881. V. 53

SCHENK, PETER
Het-Loo and Rosendael. 1700. V. 48

SCHERPF, G. A.
Entstehungsgeschichte und Gegenwartiger Zustand des Neuen, Unabhangigen, Amerikanischen Staates Texas. Augsburg: 1841. V. 49

SCHERZER, KARL
Narrative of the Circumnavigation of the Globe by the Austrian Frigate Novara... London: 1861-63. V. 50

THE SCHERZER Rolling Lift Bridge Company. Chicago: 1904. V. 49

SCHETKY, JOHN CHRISTIAN
Sketches and Notes of a Cruise in Scottish Waters on Board His Grace the Duke of Rutland's Yacht Resolution, in the Summer of 1848. London: 1850. V. 48

SCHEUCHZER, JOHANN JAKOB
Physica Sacra. 1731-35. V. 53
Specimen Lthographiae Helveticae Curiosa, quo Lapides ex Figuratis Helveticis Selectissimi Aeri Incisi Sistuntur & Describuntur... Zurich: 1702. V. 49

SCHEURL, CHRISTOPH
Libellus: de Sacerdotum...Prestantia... Nuremberg: 1513. V. 52

SCHEVILL, JAMES
Ghost Names...Ghost Numbers. Providence: 1985. V. 51
Quixote Visions. Providence: 1991. V. 51

SCHIAPARELLI, GIOVANNI V.
Astronomy in the Old Testament. Oxford: 1905. V. 50

SCHIDLOFF, B.
Venus Oceanica, Anthropological Studies in the Sex Life of the South Sea Natives. New York: 1935. V. 51

SCHIEFER, JOHN FREDERIC
An Explanation of the Practice of Law... Dublin. V. 51

SCHIFF, MORTIMER L.
Catalogue of the Famous Library, Principally of Fine Bindings, Rare Engravings, Illustrated Books and French Literature Formed by... London: 1938. V. 48; 51; 54
French Signed Bindings in the Mortimer L. Schiff Collection. New York: 1935. V. 47
French Signed Bindings in the Mortimer L. Schiff Collection... Paris: 1935. V. 51

SCHIFF, S.
Whispers. 1973-87. V. 52

SCHILLER, A. ARTHUR
Ten Coptic Legal Texts. New York: 1932. V. 49; 51

SCHILLER, GERTRUD
Iconography of Christian Art. Greenwich: 1971. V. 54

SCHILLER, JOHANN CHRISTOPH FRIEDRICH VON
Aesthetical and Philosophical Essays. Boston: 1902. V. 53
The Bride of Messina. London: 1837. V. 54
Complete Works. Philadelphia: 1861. V. 49
Demetrius. Munchen: 1922. V. 51
The Dragon of the Isle of Rhodes. London: 1829. V. 53; 54
History of the Rise and Progress of the Belgian Republic, Until the Revoltuion Under Philip II. London: 1807. V. 52
Maria Stuart ein Trauerspiel. Tubingen: 1801. V. 47
The Piccolomini, or, The First Part of Wallenstein, a Drama. London: 1800. V. 47; 49; 52
The Robbers. London: 1792. V. 53
The Robbers. London: 1799. V. 52
Sammtliche Werke. Stuttgart: 1869. V. 47
The Song of the Bell. London: 1841. V. 54
The Those-Seer; or, Apparitionist. London: 1795. V. 47

SCHILLER, JUSTIN G.
The Distinguished Collection of L. Frank Baum and Related Oziana Including W. W. Denslow Formed by Justin G. Schiller. Sale 11/2/78. New York: 1978. V. 47

SCHILLING, ARTHUR
The Ojibway Dream. Montreal: 1986. V. 50

SCHILLINGER, FRANCES
Joseph Schillinger: a Memoir by His Wife. New York: 1949. V. 54

SCHILLINGS, CARL GEORG
In Wildest Africa. London: 1907. V. 53
With Flashlight and Rifle. London: 1906. V. 48; 50

SCHIMANSKI, STEFAN
Knight and Devil. Billericay: 1942. V. 54

SCHIMELLPENNINCK, MARY ANNE
Select Memoirs of Port Royal. (with) A Tour to Alet. London: 1835. V. 49

SCHIMMELPENNINCK, MARY ANNE
Life of Mary Anne Schimmelpenninck, Author of "Select Memoirs of Port Royal". Philadelphia: 1859. V. 53
Narrative of the Demolition of the Monastery of Port Royal des Champs, Including Biogrpaphical Memoirs of Its Latter Inhabitants... London: 1816. V. 50

SCHIMPER, A. F. W.
Plant Geography Upon a Physiological Basis. Oxford: 1903. V. 49
Plant Geography Upon a Physiological Basis. London: 1977. V. 50; 51

SCHINDLER, RUDOLF
Gastroscopy, the Endoscopic Study of Gastric Pathology. Chicago: 1937. V. 49; 54

SCHINDLER, VALENTIN
Lexicon Pentaglottum. London: 1635. V. 54

SCHINKEL, KARL FRIEDRICH
Collection of Architectural Designs... Chicago: 1981. V. 47; 48; 49; 50
Sammlung Architektonischer Entwurfe... Berlin: 1858. V. 48

SCHIOLER, E. L. T. L.
Danmarks Fugle, Med Henblick Paa de in Gronland... Copenhagen: 1925-31. V. 49; 51; 53

SCHIOTZ, A.
The Treefrogs (Rhacophoridae) of West Africa. Copenhagen: 1967. V. 54

SCHIWETZ, E. M.
Houston Past and Present... Houston. V. 49
Houston Past and Present. Houston: 1927-28. V. 50
The Schiwetz Legacy. An Artist's Tribute to Texas, 1910-1971. Austin: 1972. V. 49

SCHLECHTENDAL, D. F. L.
Flora von Deutschland. Gera: 1880-89. V. 51

SCHLECHTER, R.
The Orchidaceae of German New Guinea. Leiden: 1982. V. 48
The Orchidaceae of German New Guinea. Melbourne: 1982. V. 52; 53

SCHLEGAL, AUGUSTUS WILLIAM
A Course of Lectures on Dramatic Art and Literature. London: 1815. V. 50; 54

SCHLEGEL, FRIEDRICH VON
Collected Works in English. London: 1846-59. V. 51

SCHLEGEL, H.
De Vogels van Nederlandsch Indie/Les Oiseaux Indies Neerlandaises. Haarlem: 1863-66. V. 54
Fauna van Nederland: De Vogels Van nederland. Leiden: 1854-58. V. 51
Traite de Fauconnerie. New York: 1980. V. 52

SCHLEGEL, JOHAN FRIEDRICH WILHELM
Neutral Rights; or, an Impartial Examination of the Right of Search of Neutral Vessels Under Convoy... Philadelphia: 1801. V. 48; 50

SCHLEICHER, GUSTAV
Memorial Addresses Life and Character of... Washington: 1879. V. 51; 52

SCHLEIDEN, J. M.
Principles of Scientific Botany; or, Botany as an Inductive Science. London: 1849. V. 50

SCHLEIERMACHER, FRIEDRICH
Brief Outline of the Study of Theology. Edinburgh: 1850. V. 49

SCHLESINGER, ARTHUR M.
Oretes A. Brownson: A Pilgrim's Progress. Boston: 1939. V. 48

SCHLEY, FRANK
Frank Schley's American Partridge and Pheasant Shooting. Frederick: 1877. V. 47

SCHLEY, WINFIELD SCOTT
Report of Winfield S. Schley, Commander U.S. Navy, Commanding Greeley Relief Expedition of 1884. Washington: 1887. V. 51; 54
The Rescue of Greely. London: 1885. V. 49

SCHLICH, W.
Manual of Forestry. London: 1889-1904. V. 49; 51

SCHLIEMANN, HENRY
Ilios: The City and Country of the Trojans. London: 1880. V. 48; 52
Ilios: The City and Country of the Trojans. New York: 1881. V. 47
Mycenae: a Narrative of Researaches and Discoveries at Mycenae and Tiryns. New York: 1878. V. 52
Mycenae: a Narrative of Researches and Discoveries at Mycenae and Tiryns. New York: 1880. V. 48; 52
Mycenes. Paris: 1879. V. 48
Tiryns... New York: 1880. V. 49
Tiryns... New York: 1885. V. 48
Tiryns. London: 1886. V. 50; 52; 54
Troja. Results of the Latest Researches & Discoveries on the Site of Homer's Troy. New York: 1884. V. 48
Trojanischer Alterthumer. Bericht uber Die Ausgrabungen in Troja. Leipzig: 1874. V. 52
Troy and Homer. Remarks on the Discoveries of...in the Troad. Worcester: 1875. V. 48
Troy and Its Remains a Narrative of Researches and Discoveries Made on the site of Ilium and in the Trojan Plain. London: 1875. V. 54

SCHLOSS, DAVID FREDERICK
Methods of Industrial Remuneration. London: 1892. V. 52

SCHLOSSER, FRIEDRICH C.
History of the Eighteenth Century and of the Nineteenth Till the Overthrow of the French Empire, with Particular Reference to Mental Cultivation and Progress. London: 1843-52. V. 49; 53

SCHLOSSER, LEONARD B.
A Pair on Paper. North Hills: 1976. V. 48; 50

SCHLOSS'S English Bijou Almanac for 1840. London: 1840. V. 54

SCHLOSS'S English Bijou Almanac for 1842. London: 1842. V. 54

SCHLOTEL, A. E.
Still a Wife's Sister: a Novel. London: 1886. V. 54

SCHMALENBACH, WERNER
Kurt Schwitters. New York: 1967. V. 51; 53; 54
Kurt Schwitters. London: 1970. V. 47
Kurt Schwitters. New York: 1970. V. 52

SCHMID, HERMAN
The Bavarian Highlands and The Salzkammergut. London: 1874. V. 49

SCHMID, L. J.
Description Historique et technique du Grandpont Suspendu en fil der fer, a fribourg en Suisse. Fribourg: 1839. V. 51

SCHMID, R.
Dictionary of Biotechnology in English-Japanese-German. Berlin: 1986. V. 50; 53

SCHMIDT, DOREY
Larry McMurtry: Unredeemed Dreams: a Collection of Bibliography, Essays and Interview. Edinburgh: 1978. V. 52

SCHMIDT, ERICH F.
The Alishar Huyuk Seasons of 1928 and 1929. Part II (only). London: 1933. V. 49
The Alishar Huyuk Seasons of 1928 and 1929. Parts I & II. Chicago: 1932-33. V. 49
Excavations at Tepe Hissar Damghan with an Additional Chapter on the Sasanian Building at Tepe Hissar by Fiske Kimball. Philadelphia: 1937. V. 49; 52

SCHMIDT, GEORG
Ten Reproductions in Facsimile of Paintings by Paul Klee. New York: 1946. V. 47; 48; 50; 52

SCHMIDT, K. P.
Contributions to the Herpetology of the Belgian Congo. 1919-24. V. 51

SCHMIDT, OTTO IULEVICH
The Conquest of the Arctic. Moscow: 1939. V. 50

SCHMIED, FRANCOIS LOUIS
Art-Deco: The Books of Francois-Louis Schmied, Artist/Engraver/Printer, with Recollections and Descriptive Commentaries on the Books by Ward Ritchie. San Francisco: 1987. V. 53
Ruth et Booz. Paris: 1930. V. 51

SCHMITZ, CARL
Oceanic Sculpture. 1962. V. 52

SCHMITZ, J.
A Nice Day for Screaming and Other Tales of the Hub. 1965. V. 48

SCHMITZ, JAMES H.
The Witches of Karres. Philadelphia: 1966. V. 52

SCHMOBERG, R. C. F.
Unknown Karakoram. London: 1936. V. 48

SCHMOLDER, BRUNO
Neuer Praktischer Wegweiser Furauswanderer Nach Nord-Amerika in Drei Abtheilungen... Mainz: 1849. V. 47

SCHMOLLER, HANS
Chinese Decorated Papers: Chinoiserie for Three. Newtown: 1987. V. 48; 53
Mr. Gladstone's Washi. Newtown: 1984. V. 47; 48; 49; 51; 52; 53; 54
Mr. Gladstone's Washi... North Hills: 1984. V. 49

SCHMOLLER, T.
Remondini and Rizzi. New Castle: 1990. V. 47

SCHMORANZ, GUSTAV
Old Oriental Gilt and Enamelled Glass Vessels Extant in Public Museums and Private Collections Reproduced in Their Original Colouring... London: 1899. V. 48

SCHMUTZLER, ROBERT
Art Nouveau. New York: 1962. V. 47

SCHNAPPER, E. B.
The British Union Catalogue of Early Music Printed Before the Year 1801. London: 1957. V. 54

SCHNEEBERGER, PIERRE F.
The Baur Collection, Geneva. Chinese Jades and Other Hardstone. Geneva: 1976. V. 51; 53

SCHNEIDER, G.
The Book of Choice Ferns for the Garden, Conservatory and Stove. London: 1892-94. V. 52; 53

SCHNEIDER, ISADORE
Doctor Transit. 1925. V. 49; 54
The Temptation of Anthony and Other Poems. New York: 1928. V. 48

SCHNEIDER, PIERRE
Matisse. London: 1984. V. 52; 54

SCHNEIDER, REINHOLD
Imperial Mission. New York: 1948. V. 53

SCHNEIR, JACQUES
Sculpture in Modern America. 1948. V. 53

SCHNIER, JACQUES
Sculpture in Modern America. Berkeley: 1948. V. 50

SCHNIEWIND, CARL O.
A Sketch Book by Toulouse-Lautrec Owned by the Art Institute of Chicago. New York: 1952. V. 51

SCHNITZLER, ARTHUR
Casanova's Homecoming. New York: 1947. V. 49
Rhapsody. London: 1928. V. 49

SCHOALES, JOHN
Reports of Cases Argued and Determined in the High Court of Chancery in Ireland (1802-1807). London & Dublin: 1806/21. V. 48

SCHOBERL, FREDERIC
Excursions in Normandy, Illustrated of the Character, Manners, Customs and Traditions of the People; or the State of Society in General... London: 1841. V. 52
The World in Miniature: Africa, Containing a Description of the Manners and Customs, With Some Historical Particulars of the Moors of the Zahara and of the Negro Nations Between the Rivers Senegal... London: 1821. V. 50

SCHOENBAUM, S.
William Shakespeare: a Documentary Life. London: 1975. V. 51

SCHOENBERG, ARNOLD
Style and idea. New York: 1950. V. 49

SCHOENER, ALLON
Harlem on My Mind. Cultural Capital of Black America 1900-1968. New York: 1968. V. 48

SCHOENFELD, SEYMOUR
The Negro in the Armed Forces: His Value and Status-Past, Present and Potential. Washington: 1945. V. 53

SCHOENHOF, JACOB
The Economy of High Wages. New York: 1892. V. 52

SCHOENRICH, OTTO
The Legacy of Christopher Columbus. Glendale: 1949. V. 49; 54
The Legacy of Christopher Columbus. Glendale: 1949-50. V. 51; 52

SCHOFIELD, F. H.
The Story of Manitoba. Winnipeg/Vancouver/Montreal: 1913. V. 47

SCHOFIELD, JAMES
An Historical and Descriptive Guide to Scarbrough and Its Environs. London: 1787. V. 53

SCHOFIELD, JOHN M.
Forty-Six Years in the Army, by Lieutenant-General John M. Schofield. New York: 1897. V. 48

SCHOFIELD, LILY
Billy Ruddylox, an Ancient British Boy. London: 1904. V. 52
Tom Catapus and Potiphar. London: 1903. V. 54

SCHOLASTIC Dialogue. Northampton: 1968. V. 47

SCHOLDERER, VICTOR
Fifty Essays in Fifteenth and Sixteenth Century Bibliography. Amsterdam: 1966. V. 47; 50; 54
Greek Printing Types, 1465-1927. 1927. V. 47
Greek Printing Types, 1465-1927. London: 1927. V. 49
Women of Troy: Poems. 1965. V. 54

SCHOLES, JAMES C.
Documentary Notes Relating to the District of Turton. Bolton: 1882. V. 53

SCHOLES, PERCY A.
The Great Dr. Burney. His Life, His Travels, His Works, His Family and His Friends. London: 1948. V. 51
The Life and Activities of Sir John Hawkins, Musician, Magistrate and Friend of Johnson. Oxford: 1953. V. 48

SCHOLTZ, C. H.
Insects of Southern Africa. Durban: 1989. V. 53

SCHOLTZ, CHRISTIAN
Christiani Scholtz, ... Grammatica Aegyptiaca Utriusque Dialecti... Oxonii: 1778. V. 50

SCHOMBURGK, ROBERT H.
A Description of British Guiana, Geographical and Statistical... London: 1840. V. 50

SCHONBORN, GRAFINN VON
Costumes des Trauerspiels von Schiller: Maria Stuart. Vorgestellt auf dem Gesellschafts - Theater des Herrn Grafen Clam Gallas. Vienna: 1816. V. 49

SCHONFIELD, H. J.
The New Hebrew Typography. London: 1932. V. 52

SCHOOCK, MARTINUS
Admiranda Methodvs Novae Philosophiae Renati Des Cartes. Maastricht: 1643. V. 47

THE SCHOOL for Satire: or, A Collection of Modern Satirical Poems Written During the Present Regin. V. 51; 54

THE SCHOOL for Satire: or, a Collection of Modern Satirical Poems Written During the Present Reign. London: 1801. V. 48

THE SCHOOL for Satire: or, a Collection of Modern Satirical Poems Written During the Present Reign. London: 1802. V. 50

THE SCHOOL of Arts Improved... Gainsborough: 1776. V. 51

THE SCHOOL of Arts; or, New Book of Useful Knowledge. London: 1790. V. 51

THE SCHOOL of Good Manners. Boston: 1808. V. 48

A SCHOOL of Purposes. A Selection of Fougasse Posters, 1939-1945. London: 1946. V. 54

SCHOOLCRAFT, HENRY ROWE
The American Indians, Their History, Condition and Prospects from Original Notes and Manuscripts. Buffalo: 1851. V. 51
Historical and Statistical Information...Indian Tribes of the United States... Philadelphia: 1851. V. 54
Historical and Statistical Information...Indian Tribes of the United States... Philadelphia: 1851-55. V. 49
Historical and Statistical Information...Indian Tribes of the United States. 1970's. V. 53
Information, Respecting the History, Condition and Prospects of the Indian Tribes of the United States... Philadelphia: 1853. V. 47
Inquiries, Respecting the History, Present Condition and Future Prospects of the Indian Tribes of the United States. Washington: 1847. V. 47
Journal of a Tour in the Interior of Missouri and Arkansas. London: 1821. V. 47; 48; 52
Letter from Secretary of War, Transmitting Report of Schoolcraft's Expedition Among the Northwestern Indians. Washington: 1833. V. 47
The Myth of Hiawatha, and Other Oral Legends, Mythologic and Allegoric of the North American Indians. Philadelphia: 1856. V. 47
Narrative Journal of Travels through the Northwestern Regions of the United States. Albany: 1821. V. 47; 52
Narrative of an Expedition through the Upper Mississippi to Itasca Lake, the Acutal Source of This River... New York: 1834. V. 47; 52
Notes on the Iroquois... New York: 1846. V. 51
Notes on the Iroquois... Albany: 1847. V. 47; 52
Oneota, or the Red Face of America: Their History, Traditions, Customs, Poetry, Picture-Writing, &c. New York: 1844-45. V. 47

SCHOOLCRAFT, HENRY ROWE continued
Personal Memoirs of a Residence of Thirty Years With the Indian Tribes on the American Frontier... Philadelphia: 1851. V. 47
Personal Memoirs of a Residence of Thirty Years with the Indian Tribes on the American Frontiers... Norman: 1972. V. 54
Report of the Sec. of Interior Communicating a Report by H. R. Schoolcraft on the State of Indian Statistics. Washington: 1854. V. 52
Summary Narrative of an Exploratory Expedition to the Sources of the Mississippi River, in 1820... Philadelphia: 1855. V. 47
A View of the Lead Mines of Missouri... New York: 1819. V. 47; 50

SCHOOLING, WILLIAM
The Hudson Bay Company, 1670-1920. The Governor and Company of Adventurers of England Trading into Hudson's Bay During two Hundred and Fifty Years. London: 1920. V. 51

SCHOOL OF ST. AFRA, MEISSEN, GERMANY
Statuta et Leges... Meissen: 1764. V. 52

SCHOONENBEEK, ADRIEN
Courte Description des Ordres des Femmes et Filles Religieuses. Amsterdam: 1691. V. 49; 53

SCHOPENHAUER, ARTHUR
Uber die Freiheit des Willens. Trondheim: 1840. V. 50

SCHOPF, J. W.
Earth's Earliest Biosphere, Its Origin and Evolution. Princeton: 1983. V. 53

SCHORER, MARK
Sinclair Lewis - an American Life. New York: 1961. V. 52

SCHOTT, GASPAR
Anatomia Physico-Hydrostatica Fontium ac Fluminum Libri VI. Wurzburg: 1663. V. 48
Mechanica Hydraulico-Pneumatica... Wurzburg: 1657. V. 52; 54
Pantometrum Kircherianum, Hoc Est Instrumentum Geometricum Novum a Celeberrimo Viro P. Athanasio Krichero Ante Hac Inventum... Frankfurt: 1660. V. 50
Thaumaturgus Physicus Sive Magiae Unversalis Naturae: et Artis Pars IV et Ultima. Wurzburg: 1659. V. 47

SCHOTT, SIEGFRIED
Wall Scenes from the Mortuary Chapel of the Mayor Paser at Medinet Habu. Chicago: 1957. V. 49; 51

SCHOTTUS, FRANCISCUS
Itinerariae Italiae Rerumque Romanorum. Antwerp: 1600. V. 53

SCHOUVALOFF, ALEXANDER
Set and Costume Designs for Ballet and Theater. The Thyssen-Bornemisza Collection. New York: 1987. V. 54

SCHRAM, F. R.
Crustacea. London: 1986. V. 49

SCHRAMM, JACK E.
Detroit's Street Railways. Chicago: 1978/80. V. 51

SCHRANTZ, WARD L.
Jasper County, Missouri, in the Civil War. Carthage: 1923. V. 49

SCHREIBER, CHARLOTTE
Journals, Confidences of a Collector of Ceramics and Antiques Throughout Britain, France, Holland, Belgium, Spain, Portugal, Turkey, Austria and Germany from 1869-1885. London: 1911. V. 47

SCHREIBER, FRED
The Estiennes. An Annotated Catalogue of 300 Highlights of Their Various Presses. New York: 1982. V. 47

SCHREIBER, GEORGES
Portraits and Self-Portraits. Boston: 1936. V. 51

SCHREIBER, MARTIN H.
Last of a Breed. 1982. V. 49

SCHREINER, OLIVE
Dream Life and Real Life: a Little African Story. London: 1893. V. 51
Dreams. 1891. V. 49
Dreams. 1901. V. 49
So Here Then Are Dreams. East Aurora: 1901. V. 48
The Story of an African Farm. Westerham, Kent. V. 49
The Story of an African Farm. Westerham, Kent: 1961. V. 49
Trooper Peter Halket of Mashonaland. Boston: 1897. V. 52; 53; 54
Woman and Labour. London: 1911. V. 50
Woman and Labour. Toronto: 1911. V. 48

SCHREINER, WILLIAM H.
Schreiner's Sporting Manual. Philadelphia: 1841. V. 47

SCHRENCK, P. L. VON
Vogel des Amur-Landes. St. Petersberg: 1860. V. 52

SCHRETLEN, M. J.
Dutch and Flemish Woodcuts of the Fifteenth Century. Boston and New York: 1925. V. 50; 54
Dutch and Flemish Woodcuts of the Fifteenth Century. London: 1925. V. 51

SCHREYVOGEL, CHARLES
My Bunkie and Others. New York: 1909. V. 47; 48

SCHROCK, RAYMOND L.
Broken Hearts of Hollywood: a Story of a Mother's Love, Fame and Triumph. New York: 1926. V. 51

SCHRODER, JOHN
Catalogue of Books and Manuscripts by Hupert Brooke, Edward Marsh and Christopher Hassall. Cambridge: 1970. V. 54
The Compleat Chymical Dispensatory in Five Books. London: 1669. V. 48

SCHRODER, TIMOTHY B.
The Gilbert Collection of Gold and Silver. London: 1988. V. 49
The Gilbert Collection of Gold and Silver. Los Angeles: 1988. V. 54

SCHROECK, LUCAS
Historia Moschi... Augsburg: 1682. V. 53

SCHROEDER, ERIC
Persian Miniatures in the Fogg Museum of Art. Cambridge: 1942. V. 48

SCHROEDER, HENRY
The Annals of Yorkshire. Leeds: 1851/52. V. 51; 52; 54

SCHROEDER, THEODORE
Obscene Literature and Constitutional Law, A Forensic Defense of Freedom of the Press. New York: 1911. V. 53

SCHROEDER VAN DER KOLK, JACOB L. C.
On the Minute Structure and Functions of the Spinal Cord and Medulla Oblongata... London: 1859. V. 50; 52; 53

SCHROER, H. M. D.
From the Pigeons to the Piutes. 1926. V. 47

SCHROETER, JOHANN FRIEDRICH
Allgemeine Geschichte der Lander und Volker von America. Halle: 1752-53. V. 53

SCHROETER, JOHANN HIERONYMUS
Selenotopographische Fragmente zur Gernauern Kenntniss der Mondflache, ihrer Erlittenen Veranderungen und Atmosphare... Lilienthal: 1791. V. 50; 52; 54

SCHUBERT, G. H. VON
Atlas of the Natural History of the Animal Kingdom. (with) Explanatory Text to S.R. Urbino's Charts... Boston: 1869. V. 51

SCHUBERT, H. R.
History of the British Iron and Steel Industry from 450 B.C. to A.D. 1775. London: 1957. V. 50

SCHUBLER, JOHANN JACOB
Nutzliche Anweisung zur Unentbehrlichen zu Zimmermanns-Kunst. Nuremberg: 1749. V. 53

SCHUCK, H.
Alfred Nobel. London: 1929. V. 47

SCHUFELDT, ROBERT W.
Reports of Explorations and Surveys, to Ascertain the Practicability of a Ship-Canal Between the Atlantic and Pacific Oceans by the Way of the Isthmus of Tehuantepec. Washington: 1872. V. 51; 54

SCHUG, ALBERT
Art of the Twentieth Century. New York: 1969. V. 50

SCHULBERG, BUDD
A Face in the Crowd. New York: 1957. V. 54
The Harder They Fall. New York: 1947. V. 53; 54
Waterfront. New York: 1955. V. 54
What Makes Sammy Run?. 1941. V. 50
What Makes Sammy Run?. New York: 1941. V. 48

SCHULBERT, BUDD
Swan Watch. New York: 1975. V. 54

SCHULLIAN, DOROTHY M.
A Catalogue of Incunabula and Manuscripts in the Army Medical Library. New York: 1950. V. 50

SCHULTES, R. E.
Native Orchids of Trinidad and Tobago. London: 1960. V. 54

SCHULTZ, CHRISTIAN
Travels on an Inland Voyage through the States of New York, Pennsylvania, Virginia, Ohio, Kentucky and Tennessee... New York: 1810. V. 47
Travels on an Inland Voyage through the States of New York, Pennsylvania, Virginia, Ohio, Kentucky and Tennessee. New York: 1812. V. 47

SCHULTZ, CHRISTOPH
Kurze Fragen Ueber die Christiche Glaubens-Lehre...Den Christlichen Glaubens-Schulern... Philadelphia: 1784. V. 48

SCHULTZ, J. W.
My Life as an Indian the Story of a Red Woman and a White Man in the Lodges of the Blackfeet. New York: 1907. V. 47

SCHULZ, ALBERT
An Essay on the Influence of Welsh Tradition Upon the Literature of Germany, France, and Scandinavia. Llandovery: 1841. V. 54

SCHULZ, CHARLES
Christmas is Together - Time. San Francisco: 1964. V. 53

SCHULZ, H. C.
A French Miniature Book of Hours Leaf, with an Essay Entitled "French Illuminated Manuscripts". 1958. V. 52; 54
A French Miniature Book of Hours Leaf, with an Essay Entitled "French Illuminiated Manuscripts". San Francisco: 1958. V. 48; 51
The Gothic Script of the Middle Ages. San Francisco: 1939. V. 50
A Leaf from a Fifteenth Century Flemish Book of Hours... 1938. V. 51
A Leaf from a Fifteenth Century Flemish Book of Hours... San Francisco: 1938. V. 48
A Monograph on the Italian Choir Book. San Francisco: 1941. V. 52

SCHUMACHER, GOTTLIEB
Across the Jordan... London: 1886. V. 51

SCHUMANN Album of Children's Pieces for Piano;. London: 1915. V. 52

SCHUMANN, ELKA
The Dream of the Dirty Woman: a Play in One Act Based On a Dream of Elka Schumann. Newark: 1980. V. 50

SCHUMPETER, JOSEPH A.
Business Cycles. New York & London: 1939. V. 51

SCHURER, EMIL
A History of the Jewish People in the Time of Jesus. Edinburgh and New York: 1908. V. 49; 52

SCHURIG, MARTIN
Spermatologia Historico-Medica. h. e. Seminis Humani Consideratio Physico-Medico-Legalis... Frankfurt: 1720. V. 52

SCHUSTER, R. M.
Hepaticae & Anthocerotae of North America. New York: 1969. V. 50
Hepaticae & Anthocerotae of North America. New York: 1969-80. V. 49

SCHUSTER, THOMAS E.
Printed Kate Greenaway: a Catalogue Raisonne. London: 1986. V. 50
Printed Kate Greenaway: a Catalogue Raisonne. London: 1987. V. 52

SCHUTZ, ALEXANDER
Die Renaissance in Italien. Hamburg: 1893-1907. V. 50

SCHUTZ, ANTON
New York Its Etchings. New York: 1939. V. 47

SCHUTZE, ALBERT
Travis County Directory, 1894-95. Austin: 1895. V. 54

SCHUYLER, EUGENE
Turkistan. Notes of a Journey in Russian Turkestan, Khokand, Bukhara and Kuldja. London: 1876. V. 48; 50
Turkistan, Notes of a Journey in Russian Turkistan, Khokand, Bukhara and Kuldja. New York: 1876. V. 52
Turkistan. Notes of A Journey in Russian Turkistan, Khokand, Bukhara and Kuldja. New York: 1877. V. 47; 49; 50; 53

SCHUYLER, H.
The Roeblings, a Century of Engineers, Bridge-Builders and Industrialists. Princeton: 1931. V. 49

SCHUYLER, JAMES
The Home Book. Prose and Poems, 1951-1970. Calais: 1977. V. 50

SCHUYLER, MONTGOMERY
The Woolworth Building. New York: 1913. V. 53

SCHUYT, M.
Fantastic Architecture: Personal and Eccentric Visions. New York: 1980. V. 51; 53

SCHWAB, G.
Tribes of the Liberian Hinterland. 1947. V. 54

SCHWABACHER, E. K.
Arshille Gorky. 1957. V. 51
Arshille Gorky. New York: 1957. V. 53; 54

SCHWABE, WILLMAR
Pharmacopoea Homoeopathica Polyglotta. New York: 1880. V. 50

SCHWANDNER, JOHANN GEORG
Dissertatio Episolaris de Calligraphiae Comenclatione, Cultu, Praestantia, Utilitate. Vienna: 1756. V. 53

SCHWANN, THEODOR
Microscopical Researches Into the Accorance in the Structure and Growth of Animals and Plants. London: 1847. V. 49; 50; 54
Mikroskopische Untersuchungen Uber die Uebereinstimmung in der Struktur und dem Wachthum der Thiere und Pflanzen. Berlin: 1839. V. 49; 54

SCHWANTES, G.
Flowering Stones and Mid-Day Flowers... London: 1957. V. 54

SCHWARAZ, KARL
Das Graphische Werk von Lovis Corinth. Berlin: 1917. V. 48

SCHWARTZ, A.
Amphibians and Reptiles of the West Indies. Gainesville: 1991. V. 48; 50; 51

SCHWARTZ, DELMORE
In Dreams Begin Responsibilities. New York: 1938. V. 53
In Dreams Begin Responsibilities. Norfolk: 1938. V. 48; 49; 52; 53
Shenandoah. Norfolk: 1941. V. 47; 48; 49
Successful Love and Other Stories. New York: 1961. V. 52; 54
Summer Knowledge. Garden City: 1959. V. 47; 48; 51
Vaudeville for a Princess. New York: 1950. V. 53
The World is a Wedding. Norfolk: 1948. V. 52; 53; 54
The World is a Wedding... London: 1949. V. 48; 53
The World is a Wedding. Norfolk: 1949. V. 48

SCHWARTZ, J. H.
The One-Humped Camel in Eastern Africa... Weikersheim: 1992. V. 49
Orang-Utan Biology. Oxford: 1988. V. 50

SCHWARTZ, J. VAN DER POOTEN
God's Fool: a Koopstad Story. London: 1892. V. 53

SCHWARTZ, JOZUA MARIUS WILLEM
God's Fool: a Koopstad Story. London: 1892. V. 52

SCHWARTZ, LYNNE SHARON
The Accounting. Great Barrington: 1983. V. 51

SCHWARZ, ARTURO
The Complete Works of Marcel Duchamp. New York: 1969. V. 53
The Complete Works of Marcel Duchamp. New York: 1970. V. 47; 48; 50
The Complete Works of Marcel Duchamp. New York: 1996. V. 53
Marcel Duchamp: Notes and Projects for the Large Glass. New York. V. 50; 52

SCHWARZ, GEORGE
Almost Forgotten Germany. London: 1936. V. 53

SCHWARZ, H.
David Octavius Hill, Master of Photographer. New York: 1931. V. 52

SCHWARZ, TED
Arnold Friberg, the Passion of a Modern Master. Flagstaff: 1985. V. 52

SCHWATKA, FREDERICK
Along Alaska's great River. New York: 1885. V. 47
The Children of the Cold. New York: 1886. V. 49
Report of a Military Reconnaissance in Alaska, Made in 1883. Washington: 1885. V. 50
A Summer in Alaska. St. Louis: 1894. V. 48

SCHWEIDLER, MARY
The Amber Witch. London: 1846. V. 48
The Amber Witch. London: 1903. V. 49; 51

SCHWEINFURTH, C.
Orchids of Peru. Chicago: 1958-61. V. 52

SCHWEINFURTH, GEORG
The Heart of Africa. London: 1873. V. 50; 54
The Heart of Africa. London: 1874. V. 48
The Heart of Africa... New York: 1874. V. 52

SCHWEINGRUBER, F. H.
Trees and Wood in Dendrochronology. Berlin: 1993. V. 50

SCHWEITZER, ALBERT
J. S. Bach. London: 1911. V. 47
Out of My Life and Thought, an Autobiography. New York: 1949. V. 54

SCHWEITZER, BERNHARD
Greek Geoemtric Art. London: 1971. V. 50

SCHWERDT, C. F. G. R.
The Hampshire Hunt. London: 1929. V. 54
Hunting, Hawking & Shooting. London: 1928-37. V. 47; 49; 52
Hunting, Hawking & Shooting. London: 1985. V. 47; 48

SCHWERNER, ARMAND
Redspel/Eleven American Indian Adaptations. Mt. Horeb: 1974. V. 51; 53; 54
Sounds of the River Naranjana & The Tablets I-XXIV. Barrytown: 1983. V. 49
The Tablets I - VIII. West Branch: 1968. V. 47
Triumph of the Will. Mt. Horeb: 1976. V. 54

SCHWETTMANN, CARL
Santa Rita: The University of Texas Oil Discovery. Austin: 1943. V. 48

SCHWIEBERT, ERNEST
Trout. 1979. V. 54
Trout. London: 1979. V. 49

SCHWIMMER, NY ROSIKA
Tisza Tales. Garden City: 1928. V. 50

SCHWIND, MORITZ VON
Bilder fur die Jugend, Volkstrachten. Vienna: 1825. V. 53

SCHWOB, MARCEL
Mimes with a Prologue. Portland: 1901. V. 49

SCIDMORE, ELIZA RUHAMAH
Appletons' Guide Book to Alaska and the Northwest Coast. New York: 1895. V. 51; 53

LA SCIENCE Curieuse, ou Traite de La Chyromance; Recueilly des Plus Graves Autheurs qui Ont Traite de Cette Matiere... Paris: 1665. V. 53

A SCIENCE Fiction and Fantasy Songbook Being Mostly Words Without Music. 1960. V. 51

THE SCIENCE-Fictional Sherlock Holmes. Denver: 1960. V. 53

SCIENTIFIC American. New York: 1885-Dec. 1887. V. 51

SCLATER, PHILIP LUTLEY
Argentine Ornithology. London: 1888-89. V. 48
The Book of the Antelopes. London: 1894-1900. V. 50; 51; 52; 53
Catalogue of the Passeriformes or Perching Birds in the Collection of the British Museum. Tracheophonae, or the Families Dendrocoplapt Idae, Formicariidae, Conopophagidae and Pteroptochidae. London: 1890. V. 47
Catalogue of the Picariae in the Collection of the British Museum. London: 1891. V. 47
A Monograph of the Birds Forming the Tanagrine Genus Calliste. London: 1857-58. V. 48
A Monograph of the Jacamars and Puff-Birds, or Families Galbulidae and Bucconidae. London: 1879-82. V. 48; 52; 53; 54
On Certain Species of Deer Now or Lately Living in the Society's Menagerie. London: 1817. V. 54
On Certain Species of Deer Now or Lately Living in the Society's Menagerie. London: 1871. V. 51

SCLATER, WILLIAM
An Exposition with Notes Upon the First and Second Epistles to the Thessalonians. London: 1630. V. 52

SCLATER, WILLIAM L.
The Mammals of South Africa. London: 1900-01. V. 53
Systema Avium Ethiopicarum... London: 1924-30. V. 52

SCOBELL, HENRY
A Collection of Acts and ordinances of General Use, Made in the Parliament Begun...November, Anno 1640...unto...1656... London: 1658. V. 50

SCOBIE & Balfour's Canadian Almanac, and Repository of Useful Knowledge for the Year 1848 (1849). Toronto: 1847/48. V. 54

SCOBIE, I. H. MAC KAY
An Old Highland Fencible Corps; the History of the Reay Fencible Highland Regiment of Foot, or Mackay's Highlanders 1794-1802. Edinburgh/London: 1914. V. 50

SCOFFERN, JOHN
Chemistry No Mystery; or, A Lecturer's Bequest. London: 1839. V. 49
The Manufacture of Sugar, in the Colonies and at Home, Chemically Considered. London: 1849. V. 47

SCOFIELD, SAMUEL
A Practical Treatise on Vaccinia or Cowpock. New York: 1810. V. 51; 54

SCOLES, IGNATIUS
Sketches of African and Indian Life in British Guiana. Demerara: 1885. V. 52

SCOPOLI, J. A.
Deliciae Florae et Faunae Insubricae, Seu Novae. Pavia: 1786-88. V. 49

SCORESBY, WILLIAM
An Account of the Arctic Regions. London: 1969. V. 47
Journal of a Voyage to Australia and Round the World, for Magnetical Research. London: 1859. V. 47; 49; 52
Journal of a Voyage to the Northern Whale-Fishery... Edinburgh: 1823. V. 52; 53

SCORUP, STENA
J. A. Scorup, A Utah Cattleman. Provo: 1945. V. 48

SCOT, REGINALD
The Discoverie of Witchcraft... London: 1584. V. 52
Discoverie of Witchcraft... London: 1665. V. 48
The Discoverie of Witchcraft. 1930. V. 48; 50; 52
The Discoverie of Witchcraft. Bungay: 1930. V. 48
The Discoverie of Witchcraft... London: 1930. V. 49

SCOT, REYNOLDE REGINALD
A Perfite Platform of a Hop Garden. London: 1574. V. 52

SCOT, WALTER
A True History of Several Honourable Families of the...Name of Scot, in...Roxburgh and Selkirk and Others Adjacent. (with) Satchels's Post'ral. Edinburgh: 1776. V. 49

THE SCOTCH Hut, a Poem, Addressed to Euphorbus; or, the Earl of the Grove. London: 1779. V. 48; 51; 54

THE SCOTCH Portmanteau Opened at York. London: 1761. V. 50; 54

SCOTCHER, GEORGE
The Fly Fisher's Legacy. 1974. V. 47; 53
The Fly Fisher's Legacy. London: 1974. V. 47

SCOTIA Rediviva: a Collection of Tracts Illustrative of the History and Antiquities of Scotland. Edinburgh: 1826. V. 54

SCOTLAND For Ever: a Gift Book of the Scottish Regiments. London: 1910. V. 50

SCOTLAND: Her Sons and Scenery, as Sung by Her Bards, and Seen in the Camera. London: 1868. V. 52

SCOTLAND. LAWS, STATUTES, ETC. - 1650
An Act to Prohibit all Commerce and Traffique Between England and Scotland and Enjoyning the Departure of Scots Out of This Commonwealth. London: 1650. V. 47

SCOTLAND. LAWS, STATUTES, ETC. - 1681
The Laws and Acts of Parliament Made by King James the First (to) ...King Charles the Second Who Now Presently Reigns, Kings and Queens of Scotland. Edinburgh: 1681. V. 50; 53

SCOTLAND. LAWS, STATUTES, ETC. - 1703
The Laws and Acts of Parliament, Of Our Most High and Dread Sovereign, Anne, Holden and Begun at Edinburgh the Sixth Day of May 1703... Edinburgh: 1703. V. 48; 53

SCOTLAND. LAWS, STATUTES, ETC. - 1706
Anno Regni Annae Reginae...Quinto...An Act for the Union of the Two Kingdoms of England and Scotland (and) Anno Sextae Annae Reginae. An Act for Rendering the Union...More Intire and Complete... London: 1706. V. 47

THE SCOTS Farmer, or Select Essays on Agriculture Adapted to the Soil and Climate of Scotland. Edinburgh: 1773-74. V. 54

SCOTT & DAY
Carriage Materials of Every Description. Philadelphia: 1876. V. 51

SCOTT, BENJAMIN
A State Iniquity: its Rise; Extension and Overthrow. London: 1890. V. 50

SCOTT, C. H. H.
Hymns to Robert E. Lee. Lynchburg: 1915. V. 49

SCOTT, CAROLINE LUCY
A Marriage in High Life. London: 1828. V. 50

SCOTT, CHARLES A.
My Unknown Friend. London: 1883. V. 54

SCOTT, COLONEL
A Journal of a Residence in the Esmailla of Abd-El-Kader: and of Travels in Morocco and Algiers. London: 1842. V. 54

SCOTT, DANIEL
The Stricklands of Sizergh Castle. Kendal: 1908. V. 50; 52; 54

SCOTT, DAVID
The Engineer and Machinist's Assistant; Being a Series of Plans, Sections and Elevations of Steam Engines, spinning Machines, Mills for Grinding, Tools, etc. Glasgow & London: 1847. V. 49
The History of Scotland. Westminster: 1728. V. 54

SCOTT, DUNCAN CAMPBELL
To the Canadian Mothers and Three Other Poems. 1917. V. 49

SCOTT, EDWARD B.
Squaw Valley... Crystal Bay, Lake Tahoe: 1960. V. 53

SCOTT, EMMETT J.
Scott's Official History of the American Negro in the World War. N.P: 1819. V. 48

SCOTT, EVELYN
Background in Tennessee. New York: 1937. V. 51
A Calendar of Sin: American Melodramas. New York: 1931. V. 54
On William Faulkner's The Sound and the Fury. New York: 1929. V. 53
The Wave. New York: 1929. V. 51; 52

SCOTT, F. R.
Events and Signals. Toronto: 1954. V. 47

SCOTT, FLORENCE
Historical Heritage of the Lower Rio Grande. San Antonio: 1937. V. 50

SCOTT, FRANK J.
The Art of Beautifying Suburban Home Grounds of Small Extent... New York: 1886. V. 51

SCOTT, G. FIRTH
From Franklin to Nansen: Tales of Arctic Adventure. London: 1899. V. 53

SCOTT, GEOFFREY
A Box of Paints: Poems. London: 1923. V. 49; 53

SCOTT, GEORGE
The Labrador Dog. Its Home and History. Leeds: 1990. V. 49

SCOTT, GEORGE GILBERT
An Essay on the History of English Church Architecture Prior to the Separation of England from the Roman Obedience. London: 1881. V. 48; 49; 53
Gleanings from Westmisnter Abbey. London: 1861. V. 52
On the Conservation of Ancient Architectural Monuments and Remains. Oxford & London: 1864. V. 49
Personal and Professional Recollections by the Late Sir Gilbert Scott. London: 1879. V. 48

SCOTT, GEORGE RYLEY
The History of Cockfighting. London. V. 47; 49
The History of Cockfighting. 1957. V. 49

SCOTT, GEORGE W.
The Black Hills Story. Ft. Collins: 1953. V. 51

SCOTT, H. L.
Headquarters of the Army, National Palace of Mexico, Sept. 17, 1847. Mexico City: 1847. V. 49

SCOTT, HUGH STOWELL
From One Generation to Another. London: 1892. V. 54
Prisoners and Captives. London: 1891. V. 54
The Slave of the Lamp. London: 1892. V. 51; 54
With Edged Tools. London: 1894. V. 54
The Works of... London: 1909. V. 48
Young Mistley. London: 1888. V. 53

SCOTT, J.
Combination Atlas Map of Bucks County. Philadelphia: 1876. V. 53

SCOTT, J. E.
A Bibliography of the Works of Sir Henry Rider Haggard 1856-1925. 1947. V. 51
A Bibliography of the Works of Sir Henry Rider Haggard 1856-1925. London: 1947. V. 54
A Bibliography of the Works of Sir Henry Rider Haggard 1856-1925. Takeley: 1947. V. 54
A Bibliography of the Works of Sir Henry Rider Haggard 1856-1925. 1974. V. 49

SCOTT, J. S.
An Introduction to the Sea Fishes of Malaya. Kuala Lumpur: 1959. V. 51

SCOTT, JAMES
The Perils of Poetry: and Epistle to a Friend. 1776. V. 54

SCOTT, JAMES BROWN
The Status of the International Court of Justice. New York: 1916. V. 54

SCOTT, JAMES GEORGE
Burma: a Handbook of Practical Information. London: 1906. V. 54
The Burman: His Life and Notions. London: 1896. V. 54

SCOTT, JAMES L.
A Journal of a Missionary Tour through Pennsylvania, Ohio, Indiana, Illinois, Iowa, Wiskonson and Michigan. Providence: 1843. V. 47

SCOTT, JESUP WAKEMAN
A Presentation of Causes Tending to Fix the Position of the Future Great City of the World in the Central Plain of North America... Toledo: 1876. V. 50

SCOTT, JOB
Journal of the Life...Job Scott. New York: 1797. V. 47; 50; 52; 53
Journal of the Life...Job Scott. Dublin: 1798. V. 49; 54
Journal of the Life...Job Scott. London: 1815. V. 54

SCOTT, JOCK
Fine and Far Off, Salmon Fishing Methods in Practice. London: 1952. V. 53
Greased Line Fishing for Salmon. London: 1935. V. 53

SCOTT, JOHN
The Indiana Gazetteer, or Topographical Dictionary... Indianapolis: 1833. V. 47
The Indiana Gazetteer, or Topographical Dictionary... Indianapolis: 1849. V. 47
Paris Revisited, in 1815. London: 1816. V. 48
Partisan Life with Col. John S. Mosby. New York: 1867. V. 48; 49
The Poetical Works. London: 1782. V. 50; 52
The Sportsman's Repository... London: 1820. V. 49
A Visit to Paris in 1814: Being a Review of the Moral, Political, Intellectual and Social Condition of the French Capital. London: 1816. V. 49

SCOTT, JOHN F.
The Danzantes of Monte Alban. Washington: 1978. V. 50; 52

SCOTT, JOHN ROBERT
A Dissertation On the Progress of the Fine Arts. London: 1800. V. 48; 54

SCOTT, JONATHAN
Tales, Anecdotes and Letters. Translated from the Arabic and Persian. Shrewsbury: 1800. V. 47

SCOTT, JOSEPH
A Geographical Dictionary... Philadelphia: 1805. V. 47
The United States Gazetteer... Philadelphia: 1795. V. 50

SCOTT, JULIA H. KINNEY
Prize Tale. The Sacrifice: a Clergyman's Story. New York: 1837. V. 47

SCOTT, KENNET
Homage - a Book of Sculptures. London: 1938. V. 52

SCOTT, LYDIA
Trevelyan. London: 1833. V. 49; 54

SCOTT, M. H. BAILLIE
Houses and Gardens. London: 1933. V. 50

SCOTT, MARY W.
Houses of Old Richmond. Richmond: 1941. V. 51
Old Richmond Neighborhoods. Richmond: 1950. V. 51

SCOTT, MICHAEL
Tom Cringle's Log. Edinburgh: 1833. V. 47; 48; 49; 50; 51; 52

SCOTT, PAUL
After the Funeral. Andoversford & London: 1979. V. 52; 53
The Alien Sky. London: 1953. V. 47; 50
The Birds of Paradise. London: 1962. V. 49
The Corrida at San Feliu. London: 1964. V. 49; 52
The Day of the Scorpion. London: 1968. V. 49; 51; 52
The Day of the Scorpion. New York: 1968. V. 49
The Day of the Scorpion. London: 1969. V. 53
A Division of the Spoils. London: 1975. V. 49; 50
I Gerontius - a Trilogy: The Creation - The Dream - The Cross: a Poem. London: 1941. V. 47
The Jewel in the Crown. London: 1966. V. 51
The Jewel in the Crown. New York: 1966. V. 49
Johnnie Sahib. London: 1952. V. 49
A Male Child. London: 1956. V. 52
The Mark of the Warrior. London: 1958. V. 52
Paul's Letters to His Kinsfolk. Edinburgh: 1816. V. 53
Six Days in Marapore. Garden City: 1953. V. 54
Staying On. London: 1977. V. 53

SCOTT, PETER
Morning Flight. London: 1935. V. 47; 49; 52
Morning Flight and Wild Chorus. London: 1935 and 1938. V. 53
Wild Chorus. London: 1938. V. 47; 48; 49; 52; 53

SCOTT, REGINALD
Scots Discovery of Witchcraft... London: 1651. V. 47

SCOTT, ROBERT
Elegies. London: 1764. V. 54
A Regular Series of Chronology, from the Creation of the World, to the Year 5813... Poughkeepsie: 1810. V. 47

SCOTT, ROBERT FALCON
Captain Scott's Message to England. London: 1913. V. 51; 54
Scott's Last Expedition. London: 1913. V. 49; 53
Scott's Last Expedition. New York: 1913. V. 49
Scott's Last Expedition. London: 1914. V. 47; 50
The Voyage of the "Discovery". London: 1905. V. 49; 51

SCOTT, ROBERT N.
The War of the Rebellion: a Compilation of the Union and Confederate Armies. Series I - Volumes I & II. Washington: 1880. V. 52

SCOTT, S. H.
A Westmorland Village. London: 1904. V. 50; 52

SCOTT, SARAH
A Dscription of Millenium Hall, and the Country Adjacent: Together With the Characters of the Inhabitants, and Such Historical Anecdotes and Reflections... London: 1762. V. 51

SCOTT, SUTTON SELWYN
Southbooke. Columbus: 1880. V. 54

SCOTT, TEMPLE
Oliver Goldsmith Bibliographically and Biographically Considered. New York: 1928. V. 48; 53
The Silver Age and Other Dramatic Memories. New York: 1919. V. 51; 52; 54

SCOTT, THOMAS
Robert Earle of Essex His Ghost, Sent from Elizian, to the Nobility, Gentry and Communaltie of England. London: 1624. V. 47
Vox Populi, or Newes from Spayne. 1620. V. 49; 50; 51; 53; 54

SCOTT, W.
A New Spelling, Pronouncing and Explanatory Dictionary of the English Language. Edinburgh: 1786. V. 53

SCOTT, W. A.
The Giant Judge: or the Story of Samson the Hebrew Hercules. San Francisco: 1858. V. 53
Wedge of Gold or Achan in El Dorado. Philadelphia: 1855. V. 53

SCOTT, W. B.
A History of Land Mammals in the Western Hemisphere. New York: 1913. V. 51
Ornithology of the Princeton University Expeditions to Patagonia. Princeton: 1904-28. V. 51
Reports of the Princeton University Expedition to Patagonia, 1896-99. Princeton: 1903-14. V. 51
Reports of the Princeton University Expediton to Patagonia 1896-99. Volume III. Zoology. Parts 1-7. Princeton: 1905-11. V. 51

SCOTT, W. L. L., MRS.
Views in the Himalayas, Drawn on the Spot By... London: 1852. V. 53

SCOTT, W. W.
A History of Orange County, Virginia. Richmond: 1907. V. 50

SCOTT, WALTER
The Abbot. Edinburgh: 1820. V. 48; 49; 50; 54
The Abbot. Philadelphia: 1821. V. 47
The Ancient British Drama. (with) The Modern British Drama. London: 1810. V. 52
Anne of Geierstein; or, the Maiden of the Mist. Edinburgh: 1829. V. 47; 49
Auld Robin Gray: a Ballad. Edinburgh: 1825. V. 53
Les Aventures de Nigel. Paris: 1822. V. 47
The Border Antiquities of England and Scotland. London: 1814. V. 53
The Border Antiquities of England and Scotland. London: 1814-17. V. 49
The Border Antiquities of England and Scotland... London: 1823-26. V. 54
Catalogue fo the Library at Abbotsford. Edinburgh: 1838. V. 49
Chronicles of the Canongate... Edinburgh: 1827/28. V. 50
Chronicles of the Canongate... Edinburgh: 1828. V. 47
The Collected Works of Walter Scott. 1894. V. 49
Demonology and Witchcraft. London: 1868. V. 48
The Doom of Devorgoil, a Melo-Drama. Edinburgh: 1830. V. 51
Familiar Letters of Sir Walter Scott. Edinburgh: 1894. V. 54
A Few Hours With Scott: Being Sketches in the Way of Supplement to the Two Poems of "The Lord of the Isles" and of "Rokeby". Edinburgh: 1856. V. 48
The Field of Waterloo: A Poem. Edinburgh: 1815. V. 48
The Fortunes of Nigel. Edinburgh & London: 1822. V. 47; 48; 49; 50; 51; 54
The Fortunes of Nigel. Philadelphia: 1822. V. 50
Guy Mannering; or, the Astrologer. Edinburgh: 1815. V. 48
Guy Mannering; or the Astrologer. 1817. V. 47
Halidon Hill. Edinburgh: 1822. V. 52; 53
Halidon-Hill... Paris: 1822. V. 47
Ivanhoe... Edinburgh: 1820. V. 47
Ivanhoe. New York: 1940. V. 52; 53; 54
Ivanhoe. New York: 1951. V. 52; 54

SCOTT, WALTER continued
The Journal of Sir Walter Scott from the Original manuscript at Abbotsford. Edinburgh: 1890. V. 47; 49
The Journal of Sir Walter Scott from the Original Manuscript at Abbotsford. Edinburgh: 1891. V. 54
Kenilworth... Edinburgh: 1821. V. 47; 48; 51; 53; 54
Kenilworth. 1966. V. 51
Kenilworth. Burlington: 1966. V. 53
The Lady of the Lake. Edinburgh: 1810. V. 47; 49; 51; 52; 53; 54
The Lady of the Lake. London: 1811. V. 51
The Lady of the Lake... Edinburgh: 1814. V. 52
The Lady of the Lake. Boston: 1853. V. 54
The Lady of the Lake. Edinburgh: 1857. V. 54
The Lady of the Lake. Edinburgh: 1869. V. 47; 51; 53
The Lady of the Lake. 1910. V. 48; 52
The Lay of the Last Minstrel... London: 1805. V. 53
The Lay of the Last Minstrel. London: 1807. V. 52
The Lay of the Last Minstrel. London: 1809. V. 50
The Lay of the Last Minstrel. Edinburgh: 1854. V. 51; 52; 54
The Letters, 1787-1832. London: 1932. V. 51
Letters on Demonology & Witchcraft, Addressed to J. G. Lockhart... London: 1830. V. 47; 48; 52
Letters on Demonology & Witchcraft, Addressed to J. G. Lockhart. London: 1831. V. 52; 53; 54
The Life of Napoleon Buonaparte, Emperor of the French... Edinburgh & London: 1827. V. 52; 53; 54
The Life of Napoleon Buonaparte, Emperor of the French... Philadelphia: 1827. V. 47; 50
Lives of the Novelists. Paris: 1825. V. 48; 54
London: on Demonology and Witchcraft. London: 1831. V. 47
The Lord of the Isles, a Poem. Edinburgh: 1815. V. 50
The Lord of the Isles, a Poem. Philadelphia: 1815. V. 50
Marmion, a Tale of Flodden Field. Edinburgh: 1808. V. 51
Marmion: a Tale of Flodden Field. London: 1866. V. 47
Minstrelsy of the Scottish Border. Kelso: 1802. V. 52
Minstrelsy of the Scottish Border... Edinburgh: 1803. V. 50; 52; 53; 54
O Misantropo, Ou o Anao das Pedras Negras...Vertido em Portuguezpelo Dr. Caetano Lopes de Moura, Natural de Bahia... (The Black Dwarf). Paris: 1838. V. 50
Miscellaneous Poems. Edinburgh: 1820. V. 47
The Monastery. 1820. V. 48; 52
The Monastery. Edinburgh: 1820. V. 49
Novels and Tales. London: 1822-33. V. 48
Novels and Tales... Edinburgh: 1822/22/24. V. 49
Peveril of the Peak. Edinburgh: 1822. V. 47; 49; 54
The Pirate. Edinburgh: 1822. V. 49; 51; 53; 54
The Pirate. London: 1822. V. 50
The Poetical Works. Edinburgh & London: 1820. V. 48
The Poetical Works. Edinburgh: 1830. V. 54
The Poetical Works. Edinburgh: 1850. V. 47
Poetical Works... Edinburgh: 1856. V. 47
The Poetical Works. Boston: 1866. V. 53
Poetical Works. Edinburgh: 1881. V. 54
The Poetical Works. London: 1886. V. 47
The Poetical Works... London: 1893. V. 52
The Poetical Works. London: 1900. V. 54
Provincial Antiquities and Picturesque Scenery of Scotland with Descriptive Illustrations by... London: 1826. V. 54
Quentin Durward. Edinburgh: 1823. V. 49
Redgauntlet. Edinburgh: 1824. V. 47; 49
Redgauntlet... Paris: 1824. V. 47
Redgauntlet. Philadelphia: 1824. V. 49
Religious Discourses. New York: 1828. V. 50; 53
Rob Roy. Edinburgh: 1818. V. 47; 51
Rokeby... Edinburgh: 1813. V. 49; 50; 51; 52; 54
Rokeby. Edinburgh: 1869. V. 52
St. Ronan's Well. Edinbrugh: 1824. V. 47; 49; 50; 54
A Second Letter to the Editor of the Edinburgh Weekly Journal, from Malachi Malagrowther, esq. on the Proposed Change of Currency and Other Late Alterations, as They Affect, or are Intended to Affect, the Kingdom of Scotland. Edinburgh: 1826. V. 48
The Select Poetical Works. Lay of the Last Minstrel, Marmion, Lady of the Lake and Rokeby. London: 1846. V. 47
Some Unpublished Letters of Walter Scott, from the Collection in the Brotherton Library. Oxford: 1932. V. 54
Tales of a Grandfather. Edinburgh: 1828-30. V. 54
Tales of a Grandfather. Edinburgh: 1829. V. 47; 48
Tales of My Landlord, Fourth and Last Series... Edinburgh: 1832. V. 47; 48; 50; 54
Tales of My Landlord. Second Series. Edinburgh: 1818. V. 47
Tales of My Landlord. Third Series. Edinburgh: 1819. V. 47
Tales of the Crusaders. Edinburgh: 1825. V. 47; 48; 51; 53
The Vision of Don Roderick. Edinburgh: 1811. V. 47; 48; 49; 50; 51
The Visionary: Nos. I, II, III. Edinburgh: 1819. V. 48
Waverley... Edinburgh: 1814. V. 48; 54
Waverley. Boston: 1815. V. 50
Waverley Novels. Edinburgh: 1829-34. V. 48
Waverley Novels... Edinburgh: 1830-55. V. 50
The Waverley Novels. Edinburgh: 1842. V. 50; 52; 53
Waverley Novels. Edinburgh: 1842-47. V. 47; 49; 51; 53
Waverley Novels. Edinburgh: 1852-53. V. 49; 51; 52
The Waverley Novels. Philadelphia: 1857. V. 53
The Waverley Novels. Edinburgh: 1865-68. V. 47; 51
Waverley Novels. Edinburgh: 1877. V. 52
Waverley Novels. Philadelphia: 1879. V. 48
The Waverley Novels. Edinburgh: 1886. V. 53
Waverley Novels. London and Edinburgh: 1892. V. 49
Waverley Novels. London: 1892-94. V. 47; 50; 51
The Waverley Novels. 1904. V. 49
The Waverley Novels. Oxford: 1909-12. V. 47
Waverley; or, 'Tis Sixty Years Since. Edinburgh: 1817. V. 47
Woodstock; or, the Cavalier. Edinburgh: 1826. V. 49; 53

SCOTT, WALTER SIDNEY
The Athenians. London: 1943. V. 50
Harriet & Mary Being the Relations Between Percy Bysshe Shelley, Harriet Shelley, Mary Shelley and Thomas Jefferson Hogg... Waltham St. Lawrence: 1944. V. 49

SCOTT, WILLIAM
Picturesque Scenery in the County of Sussex, sketched from Nature, Drawn on Stone... London: 1821. V. 52

SCOTT, WILLIAM BELL
Albert Durer: His Life and Works... London: 1869. V. 49
Antiquarian Gleanings in the North of England... London: 1850. V. 50; 52; 53
Antiquarian Gleanings in the North of England. London: 1851. V. 47; 48
The Ornamentist, or Artisan's Manual in the Various Branches of Ornamental Art... London: 1853. V. 52
William Blake. London: 1878. V. 47; 49
The Year of the World: a Philosophical Poem on "Redemption from the Fall". Edinburgh: 1846. V. 51; 54

SCOTT, WILLIAM HENRY
British Field Sports. Sherwood: 1818. V. 48
The Sportsman's Calendar; or, Monthly Remembrancer of Field Diversions. London: 1818. V. 48

SCOTT, WILLIAM W.
History of Passaic and Its Environs. Historical-Biographical. New York: 1922. V. 47; 49; 51

SCOTT, WINFIELD
Memoirs of Lieut. General Scott, LL.D. Written by Himself. New York: 1864. V. 48; 49
Official List of Officers Who Marched with the Army Under the Command of Major General Winfield Scott. Mexico: 1848. V. 47

SCOTT-ELLIOT, W.
The Story of Atlantis. London: 1896. V. 48

SCOTT-HERON, GIL
The Nigger Factory. New York: 1972. V. 47
The Vulture. New York: 1970. V. 49

THE SCOTTISH Students' Song Book. Glasgaow: 1897. V. 49

SCOTT-JAMES, ANNE
The Pleasure-Garden - an Illustrated History of British Gardening. London: 1977. V. 47

SCOTT MONCRIEFF, CHARLES KENNETH
Evensong and Morwe Song. London: 1923. V. 50; 53

SCOTTON, S.
Del Norte County California and Its Industries, Resources and Capabilities. Lumbering, Dairying, Fishing and Mining. Crescent City: 1909. V. 47

SCOTTOWE, JOHN
John Scottowe's Alphabet Books. 1974. V. 47

SCOTT'S Texas Pacific Bill. Ought It to Be Passed!. Washington: 1875. V. 49

SCOTT-STEVENSON, MRS.
Our Ride through Asia Minor. London: 1881. V. 50

SCOTT-WARING, JOHN
An Epistle from Oberea, Queen of Otaheite to Jospeh Banks, Esq. London: 1774. V. 50

SCOTT-WATSON, KEITH
Single to Spain. London: 1937. V. 49

SCOTUS, ROMOALDUS
Svmmarivm Rationvm, Qvibvs Cancellarivs Angliae et rolocvtor Pvckeringius Elizabethae Anglaie Reginae Persuaserunt Occidendam Esse. Cologne: 1627. V. 53

THE SCOUNDREL'S Dictionary, or an Explantion of the Cant Words Used by the Thieves, Horse-Breeders, Street-Robbers and Pick-Pockets About Town. London: 1754. V. 52

SCRANTON, ROBERT LORENTZ
Corinth. Volume I. Part III: Monuments in the Lower Agora and North of the Archaid Temple. Princeton: 1951. V. 52
Corinth. Volume XVI: Mediaeval Architecture in the Central Area of Corinth. Princeton: 1957. V. 52
Greek Walls. Cambridge: 1941. V. 52

SCRATCHLEY, J.
The London Dissector; or System of Dissection Practised in the Hospitals and Lecture Rooms of the Metropolis. London: 1816. V. 52

SCREIBER, MARTIN H.
Last of a Breed. Texas: 1982. V. 49

SCRIPPS, JOHN L.
The Undeveloped Northern Portion of the American Continent. Chicago: 1856. V. 48

SCRIPTORES REI RUSTICAE
Libri de re Rustica. 1528. V. 47
Libri de re rustica. Zurich: 1528. V. 50

SCRIPTURAL History Versified, from the Creation to the Food. Columbia: 1863. V. 49

SCRIPTURE Illustrations. London: 1834. V. 54

SCRIVERIUS, PETRUS
Het Oude Goutsche Chronycxken. Het. Amsterdam: 1663. V. 47; 51

SCROGGS, WILLIAM
The Practice of Courts-Leet, and Courts-Baron...Likewise, Several Curious Matters and Notes in Law, Relating to Presentments, Distress... London: 1714. V. 47

SCROPE, GEORGE JULIUS POULETT
The Geology and Extinct Volcanos of Central France. London: 1858. V. 47; 49; 51; 52; 53; 54
How Its Ireland to Be Governed? A Question Addressed to the New Administration of Lord Melbourne in 1834, with a Postscript, In Which the Same Question is Addressed to the Administration of Sir Robert Peel in 1846. London: 1846. V. 49
Memoir of the Life of Lord Sydenham. London: 1843. V. 47; 49; 53
Volcanos. London: 1862. V. 47; 48; 51

SCROPE, GEORGE POULETT
Volcanos... London: 1872. V. 50

SCROPE, RICHARD
A Letter to — —, Esq. Occasioned by a Late Misrepresentation of the Circumstances of a Prosecution Commenced A.D. 1763. Salisbury: 1773. V. 48; 53

SCROPE, WILLIAM
Days and Nights in the Tweed...Natural History and Habits of the Salmon... London: 1843. V. 49; 53; 54
Days and Nights in Tweed...Natural History and Habits of the Salmon. London: 1854. V. 53

SCRUTON, WILLIAM
Thornton and the Brontes. 1898. V. 52
Thornton and the Brontes. Bradford: 1898. V. 51; 54

SCUDAMORE, CHARLES
A Treatise on the Nature and Cure of Gout... London: 1816. V. 47; 49
A Treatise on the Nature and Cure of Gout... Philadelphia: 1819. V. 48

SCUDAMORE, JAMES
Homer a la Mode. Oxford: 1664. V. 48

SCUDDER, I. W.
Memorial of Colonel Abram Zabriskie, by the Bar of Hudson County, New Jersey. Jersey City: 1864. V. 48

SCUDDER, S. H.
Butterflies of Eastern United States and Canada with Special Reference to New England. Cambridge: 1889. V. 54

SCUDERY, GEORGE DE
Curia Politae; or, the Apologies of Several Princes... London: 1654. V. 47; 48; 49; 51

SCUDERY, MADELEINE DE
Almahide; or, the Captive Queen. London: 1677. V. 49; 53

SCULL, E. MARSHALL
Hunting in the Arctic and Alaska. London: 1914. V. 53

SCULLY, DENIS
A Statement of Penal Laws, Which Aggrieve the Catholics of Ireland... 1812. V. 47

SCULPTURA Historico-Technica; or, the History and Art of Engraving. London: 1770. V. 54

SCULTETUS, JOANNES
Armamentarium Chirurgicum Bipartitum... Francofurti: 1666. V. 54
Cheiroplotheke (in Greek) seu...Armamentarium Chirurgicum... Venice: 1665. V. 54
The Chyrurgeons Store-House: Furnished with Forty-Three Tables Cut in Brass... London: 1674. V. 47

SCUPHAM, PETER
The Gift - Love Poems. London: 1973. V. 48

SCUPOLI, LORENZO
The Spiritual Conflict... Paris: 1652-51. V. 48

SCURFIELD, GEORGE
A Stickful of Nonpareil. Cambridge: 1956. V. 53

THE SEA Book: a Nautical Repository of Perils and Pleasures, Adventures, Joys and Sufferings on the Briny Deep... London. V. 47

THE SEA, The Ship and the Sailor. Tales of Adventure from Log Books and Original Narratives. Salem: 1925. V. 51; 52

SEA-GREEN & Blue, See Which Speaks True. London: 1649. V. 50

SEABORN, EDWIN
The March of Medicine in Western Ontario. Toronto: 1944. V. 50

SEABORNE Trade. The Period of Unrestricted Submarine Warfare with a Map and Statistical Diagrams. London: 1924. V. 49

SEABROOK, WHITEMARSH B.
An Appeal to the People of the Northern and Eastern States, on the Subject of Negro Slavery in South Carolina. New York: 1834. V. 50

SEABROOK, WILLIAM BUEHLER
Diary of Section VIII American Ambulance Field Service. Boston: 1917. V. 48; 52

SEABURY, SAMUEL
American Slavery Distinguished from the Slavery of English Theorists and Justified by the Law of Nature. New York: 1861. V. 50

SEACOMBE, JOHN
Memoirs, Containing a Genealogical and Historical Account of the Antient and Honourable House of Stanley... Manchester: 1767. V. 47

THE SEAFARER. Bangor: 1991. V. 50; 52

SEAGAL, RALPH H.
Bodyscope,. New York: 1935. V. 48

SEAGER, JOHN
A Supplement to Dr. Johnson's Dictionary of the English Language... London: 1819. V. 52; 53

SEALLY, JOHN
The Loves of Calisto and Emira... London: 1776. V. 54

SEALSFIELD, CHARLES
Austria As It is; or, Sketches of Continental Courts. London: 1828. V. 48
The Cabin Book; or, National Characteristics. London: 1852. V. 47; 48; 49; 52
Das Cajutenbuch Oder Nationale Charaktertistiken. Zurick: 1841. V. 49
Lebensbilder aus Beiden Hemispharen... Zurich: 1835-37. V. 47; 49

SEALY, HENRY NICHOLAS
A Treatise on Coins, Currency and Banking, with Observations on the Bank Act of 1844 and on the Reports of the Committees of the House of Lords and of the House of Commons on the Bank Acts. London: 1858-67. V. 52

SEALY, THOMAS HENRY
The Little Old Man of the Wood; or the Tale of a Comical Stick. London: 1845?. V. 49

SEAMAN, M.
Popular Pslamody, Being a Selection of Congregational Psalm and Hymn Tunes... London: 1836. V. 53

SEAMAN, OWEN
The Battle of the Bays. London: 1896. V. 49

SEAMAN, ROBERT
An Exposition of the Vice Slander; its Causes and Effects; with Some Cursory Observataions Upon Education and Religion. London: 1795. V. 48

THE SEAMAN'S Protestation. Concerning their Ebbing and Flowing to and from the Parliament House at Westminster, upon Tuesday the 11 day of Ianuary. 1642. London: 1642. V. 53

SEARIGHT, FRANK THOMPSON
The Doomed City. Chicago: 1906. V. 52; 53

SEARIGHT, THOMAS B.
The Old Pike. A History of the National Road, With Incidents, Accidents and Anecdotes Thereon. Uniontown: 1894. V. 47

SEARLE, MARK
Turn-Pikes and Toll-Bars. London: 1930. V. 50; 53; 54

SEARLE, RONALD
Forty Drawings. 1946. V. 53
Forty Drawings. Cambridge: 1946. V. 48
Merry England, etc. New York: 1957. V. 53
Ronald Searle in Perspective. London: 1983. V. 53
Slightly Foxed - But Still Desirable. London: 1989. V. 48
Which Way Did He Go?. London: 1961. V. 53

SEARLES, MICHAEL
The Land Steward's and Farmer's Assistant... London: 1779. V. 52

SEARLS, NILES
The Diary of a Pioneer and Other Papers. San Francisco: 1940. V. 54

SEARS, GEORGE W.
Woodcraft: by "Nessmuk". New York: 1884. V. 47

SEARS, LOUIS MARTIN
John Slidell. Durham: 1925. V. 48

SEARS, ROEBUCK & CO.
Catalogue of Books and Stationery. Chicago: 1897. V. 53

A SEASONABLE Address to the Right Honurable the Lord Mayor, Court of Aldermen and Commoners of the City of London, Upon Their Present Electing of Sherifs. London?: 1680. V. 52

A SEASONABLE Letter to the King. London: 1779?. V. 48

SEATON, J.
The Ball-Room Manual and Etiquette of Dancing. Halifax: 1853. V. 51

SEATON, R. C.
Six Letters from the Colonies. Hull: 1886. V. 50

SEATTLE.. Seattle: 1892. V. 50

SEATTLE & WALLA WALLA RAILROAD
Report of the Chief Engineer of the Seattle and Walla Walla Railroad Company... Seattle: 1874. V. 47

SEAVER, GEORGE
Albert Schweitzer - the Man and His Mind. London: 1955. V. 50
The History of the Seaver Family...of Heath Hall, Co. Armagh and Their Connection. 1950. V. 50; 54
The History of the Seaver Family...of Heath Hall, Co. Armagh and Their Connections. London: 1950. V. 49; 51

SEAVER, JAMES E.
Deh-He-Wa-Mis: or a Narrative of the Life of Mary Jemison... Batavia: 1842. V. 47
Deh-He-Wa-Mis: or a Narrative of the Life of Mary Jemison... Batavia: 1844. V. 53
Deh-He-Wa-Mis: or a Narrative of the Life of Mary Jemison... Shebbear: 1847. V. 47
A Narrative of the Life of Mrs. Mary Jemison... Canadaigua: 1824. V. 47; 54
A Narrative of the Life of Mrs. Mary Jemison... Howden: 1826. V. 47
A Narrative of the Life of Mrs. Mary Jemison... Otley: 1842. V. 47

SEAWARD, EDWARD
Narrative of His Shipwreck, and Consequent Discovery of Certain Islands in the Caribbean Sea...1733 to 1749. London: 1832. V. 51

SEAWARD, JOHN
Observations on the Re-Building of London Bridge... London: 1824. V. 51

SEAWELL, MARY WRIGHT
Our Father's Care. A Ballad. Richmond: 1864. V. 49

SEBA, A.
Locupletissimi Rerum naturalium Thesauri Accurata Descriptis et Iconibus Artificiocissimis Expressio... Amsterdam: 1734-65. V. 51

SEBASTIANI, F. GIUSEPPE DE S. MARIA
Viaggio e Navigatione di...prima Vescovo di Hierapoli... Roma: 1687. V. 49

SEBASTIAO, KING OF PORTUGAL
Ordenacam da Nova Ordem do Juyzo, Sobre o Abreviar das Demandas & Execucoes dellas. Lisbon: 1578. V. 48

SEBOTH, JOSEPH
Alpenpflanzen Nach der Natur Gemalt. Prague: 1879-84. V. 47; 49

SEBRIGHT, GEORGIANA MARY MUIR MAC KENZIE, LADY
Travels in the Slavonic Provinces of Turkey in Europe. London & New York: 1866. V. 51

SECCHI, GIAMPIETRO
Monumenti Inediti d'un Antico Sepolcro Greco Scoperto in Roma. Rome: 1843. V. 53

SECCOMBE, JOSEPH
Some Occasional Thoughts on the Influence of the Spirit. Boston: 1742. V. 52

SECCOMBE, THOMAS S.
The Good Old Story of Cinderella, Re-Told in Rhyme. New York: 1882. V. 50

SECHENOV, IVAN
Selected Works. Moscow: 1935. V. 47; 49; 50; 54

SECKLE, DIETRICH
Emakimono. New York: 1959. V. 50

THE SECOND American Caravan. New York: 1928. V. 48; 51

A SECOND Letter to the Right Honourable the Earl of B***. London: 1761. V. 47

A SECOND Modest Enquiry Into the Causes of the Present Disasters in England, and Who They Are that Brought the French Fleet into the English Channel... London: 1690. V. 54

THE SECOND Part of Whipping-Tom; or, a Rod for a Proud Lady. Bundled Up In Five Feeling Discourses, Both Serious and Merry. London: 1722. V. 48

THE SECONDE Tome of Homelyes of Such Matters As Were Promised and Intituled in the former Part of Homelyes, Set Out by the Aucthoritie of the Quenes Maiestie... London: 1563. V. 49

SECRET Anecdotes of the Revolution of the 18th Fructidor: (September 4th, 1797); and New Memoirs of the Persons Deported to Guiana, Written by Themselves... London: 1799. V. 49; 52

THE SECRET History of Persia. London: 1745. V. 47; 53

THE SECRET History of the Court and Cabinet of St. Cloud, in a Series of Letters from a Gentleman in Paris to a Nobleman in London, Written During the Months of August, September and October, 1805. London: 1806. V. 47; 50; 53

THE SECRET History of the Court and Cabinet of St. Cloud, in a Series of letters from a Gentleman in Paris to a Nobleman in London, Written during the Months of August, September and October, 1805. London: 1895. V. 50

THE SECRET History of the Dutchess of Portsmouth. London: 1690. V. 50

SECRET History of the Most Renown'd Q. Elizabeth and Earl of Essex. Cologne: 1761. V. 50

THE SECRET History of the Most Renown'd Q. Elizabeth and the Earl of Essex. Cologne: 1680. V. 53

THE SECRET History of the Reigns of K. Charles II and K. James II. London: 1690. V. 54

SECRET Memoirs of (French Courts). London: 1909. V. 48

SECRET Memoirs of the Life of Dr. Henry Sachevell... London: 1710. V. 53

SECRET Transactions During the Hundred Days Mr. William Gregg Lay in Newgate Under Sentence of Death for High-Treason, from the Day of His Sentence, to the day of His Execution. London: 1711. V. 49

SECRETA Monita Societatis Jesu. The Secret Instructions of the Jesuits. London: 1723. V. 47

SECRETAN, LOUIS
Mycographie Suisse, ou Description des Champignons qui Croissent en Suisse... Geneve: 1833. V. 49; 52

THE SECRETARY of the Scots Army, His Relation to the Commissioners Concerning the King, How His Majesty Came Within Two Miles of London: the Garrisons He Marched Through, and His Coming to the Scots. London: 1646. V. 52

SECUNDUS, JOANNES NICOLAI
Kisses... London: 1768. V. 48
Kisses. London: 1775. V. 52
Kisses. London: 1927. V. 51
Opera, Emendata & Aucta: Quorum Catalogum Proxima Facies Enumerabit. Paris: 1582. V. 48
Opera, Nunc Secundam in Lucem Edita... Paris: 1561. V. 51

SEDDON, JOHN
The Pen-Mans Paradis Both Pleasant and Profitable. London: 1695. V. 50; 53

SEDDON, JOHN P.
King Rene's Honeymoon Cabinet. London: 1898. V. 49

SEDDON, THOMAS
Memoir and Letters of the Late Thomas Seddon, Artist. London: 1858. V. 49

SEDDON, WILLIAM
Coal Mining Made Easy, Safe and Healthy. Manchester: 1887. V. 49

SEDGEWICK, HENRY DWIGHT
Refutation of the Reasons Assigned by the Arbitrators, for Their Award in the Case of the Two Greek Frigates. New York: 1826. V. 48

SEDGWICK, ADAM
A Discourse on the Studies of the University of Cambridge. London: 1860. V. 48; 50
A Memorial by the Trustees of Cowgill Chapel... Cambridge: 1868. V. 47

SEDGWICK, CATHERINE MARIA
Letters from Abroad to Kindred at Home. New York: 1841. V. 47; 49; 50; 51; 53
The Linwoods; or "Sixty Years Since" in America. New York: 1835. V. 54
A Love Token for Children, Designed For Sunday-School Libraries... New York: 1838. V. 48
Married or Single?. New York: 1857. V. 54
Means and Ends, or Self-Training by the Author of... Boston: 1839. V. 54
A New-England Tale. London: 1822. V. 47
Tales and Sketches by... Philadelphia: 1835. V. 54
Tales of City Life. Philadelphia: 1850. V. 49

SEDGWICK, JAMES
Remarks Critical and Miscellaneous, on the Commentaries of Sir William Blackstone. London: 1800. V. 49

SEDGWICK, THEODORE
A Memoir of the Life of William Livingston, Member of Congress in 1774, 1775 and 1776... New York: 1833. V. 47
Thoughts on the Proposed Annexation of Texas to the United States. New York: 1844. V. 52

SEDGWICK, WILLIAM
Principles of Sanitary Science and the Public Health with Special Reference to the Causation and Prevention of Infectious Diseases. New York: 1902. V. 54

SEDLEY, CHARLES
As Modeus; or, The Devil in London: a Sketch. London: 1808. V. 51
Bellamira, or the Mistress, a Comedy... London: 1687. V. 48; 51; 54
The Miscellaneous Works of the Honourable Charles Sedley. London: 1702. V. 47; 48; 52
The Poetical Works...and His Speeches in Parliament... London: 1707. V. 47; 50; 51; 53

SEDULIUS, C.
The Four Evangelists... Lexington: 1955. V. 51

SEEBOHM, BENJAMIN
Memoirs of the Life and Gospel Labours of Stephen Grellet. London: 1860. V. 53

SEEBOHM, HENRY
The Birds of Siberia. London: 1901. V. 52; 53; 54
The Birds of the Japanese Empire. London: 1890. V. 48
Coloured Figures of the Eggs of British Birds. London: 1896. V. 49; 52; 53
The Geographical Distribution of the Family Charadriidae, or the Plovers, Sand-pipers, Snipes and Their Allies. London: 1888. V. 51
A History of British Birds. London: 1883-85. V. 48; 49; 51; 52; 54
A History of British Birds... London: 1885. V. 52; 53
A Monograph of the Turdidae, or Family of Thrushes. London: 1902. V. 48; 51
Siberia in Asia: a Visit to the Valley of the Yenesay in East Siberia... London: 1882. V. 50
Siberia in Europe: a Visit to the Valley of the Petchora in North-East Russia... London: 1880. V. 54

SEECOMBE, JOSEPH
Some Occasional Thoughts on the Influene of the Spirit. Boston: 1742. V. 54

SEEGER, ALAN
Alan Seeger Le Poete de la Legion Etrangere. Paris: 1918. V. 50
Poems. New York: 1916. V. 50; 53
Poems. London: 1917. V. 47

SEEGER, PETE
The Bells of Rhymney. New York: 1964. V. 49

SEELE, KEITH C.
The Tomb of Tjanefer at Thebes. Chicago: 1959. V. 49; 51

SEELEY, B.
Stowe: a Description of the Magnificent House and Gardens...with Descriptions of the Inside of the House. London: 1766. V. 47

SEELEY, H. G.
Researches on the Structure, Organisation and Classification of the Fossil Repitilia. London: 1887-95. V. 49

SEELEY, JOHN
Ecce Homo; a Survey of the Life and Work of Jesus Christ. London: 1866. V. 50

SEELEY, JOHN BENJAMIN
The Wonders of Elora; or the Narrative of a Journey to the Temples and Dwellings Excavated Out of a Mountain of Granite and Extending Upwards of a Mile and a Quarter... London: 1824. V. 48; 53

SEELEY, JOHN ROBERT
The Expansion of England: Two Courses of Lectures. London: 1906. V. 54
Life and Times of Stein, or Germany and Prussia in the Napoleonic Age. 1878. V. 53
Life and Times of Stein, or Germany and Prussia in the Napoleonic Age. Cambridge: 1878. V. 50
A Short History of Napoleon the First. Boston: 1886. V. 50

SEELEY, ROBERT BENTON
Remedies Suggested for Some of the Evils Which Constitute "The Perils of the Nation". London: 1844. V. 52

SEELIGER, U.
Coastal Plant Comunities of Latin America. London: 1992. V. 50

SEELY, HOWARD
Lone Star Bo-Peep and other Tales of Texas Ranch Life. New York: 1885. V. 50

SEELY, JOHN
A Voice from India, in Answer to the Reformers of England. London: 1824. V. 52

SEEMANN, BERTHOLD
Narrative of the Voyage of H.M.S. Herald During the Years 1845-51, Under the Command of Captain Henry Kellett. London: 1853. V. 50
Viti: An Account of a Government Mission to the Vitian of Fijian Islands... Cambridge: 1862. V. 47; 52
Viti: an Account of a Government Mission to the Vitian or Fijian Ilands. London: 1862. V. 47; 49

THE SEERLESS of Prevorst. (Justinus Kerner, Chief Physician at Weinsberg). London: 1845. V. 52

SEGALE, BLANDINA
At the End of the Santa Fe Trail. Columbus: 1932. V. 49

SEGAR, E. C.
Popeye Cartoon Book. Akron: 1934. V. 49
Popeye with the Hag of the Seven Seas. Chicago: 1935. V. 49

SEGAR, WILLIAM
Honor, Military and Civill Cotnained in Four Books viz. 1. Justice and Jurisdiction Military. 2. Knighthood in General... 3. Combats... 4. Precedencie of Great Estates... London: 1602. V. 47

SEGARD, W.
Picturesque Views of Public Edifices in Paris. London: 1814. V. 49; 53

SEGER, HERMANN AUGUST
The Collected Writings, Prepared from the Records of the Royal Porcelain Factory at Berlin... Easton: 1902. V. 54

SEGER, JOHN H.
Early Days Among the Cheyenne and Arapaho Indians. Norman: 1924. V. 52

THE SEGREGATION Decisions. Papers Read at a Session of the Twenty-first Annual Meeting of the Southern Historical Association, Memphis, Tennessee, November 10, 1955. Atlanta: 1956. V. 50

SEGUIN, E. C.
Medical Thermometry and Human Temperature. New York: 1876. V. 49; 54

SEGUIN, EDWARD
Idiocy: and Its Treatment by the Physiological Method. New York: 1866. V. 47

SEGUR, COMTESSE DE
Old French Fairy Tales. 1920. V. 47
Old French Fairy Tales. Philadelphia: 1920. V. 51

SEGUY, E. A.
Bouquets et Frondaisons. 60 Motifs en Couleur. Paris: 1928. V. 48

SEIDENFADEN, G.
The Orchids of Peninsular Malaysia and Singapore. Fredensborg: 1993. V. 50
The Orchids of Thailand, a Prelimary List. Bangkok: 1959-65. V. 51; 52

SEIDLITZ, W. VON
A History of Japanese Colour-Prints. London: 1910. V. 49
A History of Japanese Colour-Prints. Philadelphia: 1920. V. 51

SEIGNEBOSC, FRANCOISE
The Big Rain. New York: 1961. V. 51
Biquette the White Goat. New York: 1953. V. 49
Chouchou. New York: 1958. V. 49; 54
Franchette and Jeannot. New York: 1937. V. 49; 53
Jeanne Marie Counts Her Sheep. New York: 1951. V. 51
Jeanne Marie in Gay Paris. New York: 1956. V. 49
The Things I Like. New York: 1960. V. 49

SEILLIERE, BARON
Catlaogue of an Important Portion of the Very Choice Library of the Late Baron Seilliere. 1887. V. 47

SEITZ, A.
The Macrolepidoptera of the World. Stuttgart: 1929. V. 54
Macrolepidoptera of the World: Palaearctic Fauna. Stuttgart: 1906-12-16. V. 54
Macrolepidoptera of the World. Volume 13. African Butterflies. Stuttgart: 1925. V. 53
Macrolepidoptera of the World. Volume 2. Palaearctic Bombycides and Sphingides. Stuttgart: 1913. V. 53
Les Macrolepidopteres du Globe. Vols. 1-4, Les Macrolepidopteres de la Region Patearctique. Stuttgart: 1906-21. V. 49; 52

SEITZ, RON
Monk's Pond. Old Hermit. Monterey: 1988. V. 47; 48

SEITZ, WILLIAM C.
Abstract Expressionist Painting in Ameirca. Cambridge: 1983. V. 47

SEIXAS, JAMES
Manual Hebrew Grammar for the Use of Beginners. Andover: 1833. V. 49; 53

SEIXAS BRANDAO, JOAQUI IGNACIO DE
Memorias dos Annos de 1775 a 1780 Para Servirem de Historia a Analysi (sic) e Virtudes das Agoas Thermaes da villa das Caldas da Rinha... Lisbon: 1781. V. 48

SEIXAS DE LOVERA, FRANCISCO
Theatre Naval Hydrographique, des Fluxet Reflux, des Courans des Mers, Detroits, Archipels & Passages... Paris: 1704. V. 53

SEIZ, JOHANN CHRISTIAAN
Het Derde Jubeljaar der Uitgevondene Boekdrunkkonst, Behelzende Een Beknopt Historis Verhaal van de Uitvinding der Edele Boekdrukkonst... Haerlem: 1740. V. 48

SEKLER, EDUARD
Josef Hoffmann: Architectural Work. Princeton: 1985. V. 48

SELBY, CHARLES
Barnaby Rudge. A Domestic Drama in Three Acts. London: 1841. V. 54
Maximums and Specimens of William Muggins, Natural Philosopher and Citizen of the World. London: 1841. V. 50

SELBY, HUBERT
Last Exit of Brooklyn. New York: 1964. V. 51; 52; 53

SELBY, PRIDEAUX JOHN
A History of British Forest Trees Indigenous and Introduced. London: 1842. V. 49; 50; 51; 52; 53
Illustrations of British Ornithology. Edinburgh: 1833. V. 52
The Natural History of Pigeons. Edinburgh: 1835. V. 50
The Natural History of Pigeons. London: 1835. V. 48
Ornithology: Pigeons. London: 1885. V. 47

SELDEN, AMBROSE
Love and Folly. London: 1749. V. 48

SELDEN, CATHARINE
Villasantelle; or the Curious Impertinent. London: 1817. V. 50

SELDEN, JOHN
A Brief Discourse Touching the Office of Lord Chancellor of England. London: 1677. V. 48; 49
A Briefe Discourse Concerning the Power of the Peeres and Commons of Parliament, in Point of Judicature. London: 1640. V. 54
De Dis Syris Syntagmata II. Adversaria Nempe de Numinibus Commentitiis... London: 1617. V. 51; 52; 54
De Dis Syris Syntagmata II. Adversaria Nempe de Numinibus Commentitiis... Lipsiae: 1672. V. 51; 52; 54
De Iure Naturali & Gentium Iuxta Disciplinam Ebraeorum, Libri Septem. London: 1640. V. 50
An Historical and Political Discourse of the Laws and Government of England, From the First Times to the End of the Reign of Queen Elizabeth. London: 1689. V. 48; 50
The Historie of Tithes. London: 1618. V. 51
Mare Clausem seu de Domino Maris Libri Duo. Londini: 1635. V. 47
Mare Clausum: the Right and Dominion of the Sea. London: 1663. V. 54
Of the Dominion, or, Ownership of the Sea. (bound with) Dominium Maris... London: 1652. V. 49
The Priviledges of the Baronage of England, When They Sit in Parliament. London: 1642. V. 48
Seldeniana; or, the Table Talk of John Selden, Esq... London: 1789. V. 49
Table-Talk... London: 1696. V. 53
Table-Talk... London: 1716. V. 47
The Table-Talk. London: 1847. V. 49
The Table-Talk. London: 1856. V. 48; 52
Titles of Honour. London: 1631. V. 54
Titles of Honour... London: 1672. V. 47; 53
Tituli Honorum... Francofurti: 1696. V. 54
Uxor Ebraica, seu de Nuptiis et Divortiis ex Jure Civili, id est, Divino & Talmudico (together with) De Successionibus ad Leges Ebraeorum (etc.). Frankfurt: 1673. V. 47

SELECT and Approved Forms of Judicial Writs, and Other Process: With Their... and Entries in the Court of Common Pleas at Westminster. As Also Special Pleadings to Writs of Scire Facias (etc.). London: 1679. V. 53

A **SELECT** Collection of Fugitive Political Pieces, Published During the Administration of Lord Townshend in Ireland. Dublin: 1777. V. 48

A **SELECT** Collection of Hymns Universally Sung in all the Countess of Huntingdon's Chapels. London: 1802. V. 54

SELECT Comic Tales, from the Best Authors. Edinburgh: 1813. V. 48

SELECT Emblems, and Other Short Poems: Religious and Moral. Banbury: 1820. V. 52; 54

SELECT Portions of Psalms and Hymns Taken from Various Collections and Adapted to Public Worship... 1827. V. 51

SELECT Portions of the Psalms of David, According to the Version of Dr. Brady and Mr. Tate...Hymns for..Church Holy-Days and Festivals. Sydney: 1828. V. 52

SELECT Psalms and Hymns for the Use of the Parish Church of Cardington, in the County of Bedford. London: 1786. V. 52

SELECT Psalms and Hymns, For the Use of the Parish Church of Dardington, in the County of Bedford. Bedford: 1787. V. 48

SELECT Specimens Etched from the Old Masters: Stoop - Dietrich- Adrian Vandervelde - Betghem - Paul Potter - and Karl du Jardin. London: 1822. V. 54

SELECTED Poems. By John Hall, Keith Douglas and Norman Nicholson. London: 1943. V. 49

A **SELECTION** from the Harleian Miscellany of Tracts, Which Principally Regard the English History... London: 1793. V. 47; 54

A **SELECTION** from the Harleian Miscellany of Tracts, Which Principally Regard the English History... London: 1794. V. 52

A **SELECTION** of Sacred Harmony: Containing Lessons Explaining the Gamut, Keys and Characters Used in Vocal Music... Philadelphia: 1797. V. 52

SELECTION of Tables for the Instruction of Youth. New York: 1811. V. 50

SELECTIONS from the Spectator, Tatler, Guardian and Freeholder... London: 1804. V. 51

SELETZ, EMIL
Surgery of Peripheral Nerves. Springfield: 1951. V. 47

SELF, WILL
The Quantity Theory of Insanity. London: 1991. V. 51; 52; 54

THE SELF-Instructor, or, Young Man's Best Companion... Liverpool: 1814. V. 47

SELFRIDGE, THOMAS OLIVER
Reports of Explorations and Surveys to Ascertain the Practicability of a ship Canal Between the Atlantic and Pacific oceans by Way of the Isthmus of Darien. Washington: 1874. V. 50; 52; 53
Trial of Thomas O. Selfridge, Attorny at Law, Before the Hon. Isaac Parker, Esquire, for Killing Charles Austin, on the Public Exchange in Boston, August 4th 1806. Boston: 1806. V. 52

SELIGMAN, C.
Pagan Tribes of the Nilotic Sudan. London: 1932. V. 48

SELIGMAN, GERMAIN
The Drawings of Georges Seurat. New York: 1947. V. 49; 50; 52; 54
Roger De La Fresnaye. Catalogue Raisonne. Greenwich: 1969. V. 50

SELKIRK, THOMAS DOUGLAS, 5TH EARL OF
A Narrative of Occurences in the Indian Countries of North America, Since the Connexion of the Right Hon. The Earl of Selkirk with the Hudson's Bay Company... London: 1817. V. 49
Observations on the Present State of the Highlands of Scotland. London: 1805. V. 50; 52
On the Necessity of a More Effectual System of National Defence, and the Means of Establishing the Permanent Security of the Kingdom. London: 1808. V. 48
A Sketch of the British Fur Trade in North America; with Observations Relative to the North-West Company of Montreal... London: 1816. V. 52

SELLARS, JOHN CARRINGTON
Chemistianity, a Poem... Birkenhead: 1873. V. 51

SELLECK, HENRY B.
Occupational Health in America. Detroit: 1962. V. 53

SELLER, A.
The Antiquities of Palmyra. London: 1696. V. 53

SELLERS, CHARLES COLEMAN
Benjamin Franklin in Portraiture. New Haven: 1962. V. 50; 54

SELLERS, WILLIAM, & CO.
A Treatise on Machine-Tools... Philadelphia: 1877. V. 52

SELLINK, J. L.
Dutch Antique Domestic Clocks, ca. 1670-1870 and Some Related Examples. Leiden: 1973. V. 53

SELOUS, EDMUND
The Bird Watcher in the Shetlands. London: 1905. V. 54
Bird Watching. London: 1901. V. 49

SELOUS, FREDERICK COURTENEY
African Nature Notes and Reminiscences. 1908. V. 54
African Nature Notes and Reminiscences. London: 1908. V. 47; 52

Big Game Hunting and Angling. London: 1914. V. 48
The Gun at Home and Abroad: The Big Game of Africa & Europe. London: 1914. V. 52; 53
A Hunter's Wanderings in Africa. London: 1893. V. 52; 53
A Hunter's Wanderings in Africa... London: 1919. V. 47; 52
Recent Hunting Trips in British North America. 1907. V. 52; 54
Recent Hunting Trips in British North America. London: 1907. V. 47; 52
Sport and Travel, East and West. London: 1900. V. 47; 48
Sport and Travel, East and West. London: 1901. V. 48
Sunshine and Storm in Rhodesia. London: 1896. V. 47; 48; 52; 54
Travel and Adventure in South East Africa. London: 1893. V. 47; 48
Travel and Big Game. London: 1897. V. 54
Travel and Big Game. New York: 1897. V. 47

SELOUS, H. C.
Illustrations... of "Hereward the Wake" by Charles Kingsley. London: 1870. V. 53

SELTMAN, C. T.
Athens: Its History and Coinage Before the Persian Invasion. Cambridge: 1924. V. 48

SELTSAM, W. H.
Metropolitan Opera Annals: a Chronicle of Artists and Performances. New York: 1947. V. 49

SELWAY, N. C.
James Pollard, 1792-1867. Leigh-on-Sea: 1965. V. 47
The Regency Road. The Coaching prints of James Pollard. London: 1957. V. 49

SELWYN, ALFRED R. C.
Journal and Report of Preliminary Explorations in British Columbia... Montreal: 1872. V. 50

SELWYN, WILLIAM
An Abridgment of the Law of Nisi Prius. New Haven: 1831. V. 54

SEMI-Tropical Livermore, Alameda County, California... Livermore: 1887. V. 47

SEMMELWEIS, IGNAZ PHILLIP
Die Aetiologie, der Bergriff und die Prophylaxis des Kindbettfiebers. Pest, Vienna & Leipzig: 1861. V. 47
Offener Brief an Sammtliche Professoren der Geburtshilfe. Often: 1862. V. 49

SEMMES, RAPHAEL
The Campaign of General Scott in the Valley of Mexico. Cincinnati: 1852. V. 47
The Cruise of the Alabama and the Sumter. New York: 1864. V. 47; 50
Memoirs of Service Afloat, During the War Between the States. Baltimore: 1869. V. 49
Service Afloat; or, The Remarkable Career of the Confederate Cruisers Sumter and Alabama During the War Between the States. Baltimore: 1877. V. 49

SEMON, RICHARD
In the Australian Bush and on the Coast of the Coreal Sea. London: 1899. V. 50; 52; 54

SEMONIDES OF ARMORGOS
Women. Brisbane: 1983. V. 47

SEMPER, C. G.
Reisen im Archipel der Philippinen...Wissenschaftliche Resultate. Leipzig & Wiesbaden: 1868-1914. V. 49

SEMPLE, EUGENE
Report of the Governor of Washington Territory to the Secretary of the Interior. Olympia: 1888. V. 52

SEMPLE, ROBERT
Memoirs on Diphteria. London: 1859. V. 50; 51; 54
Sketch of the Present State of Caracas; including a Journey from Caracas through La Victoria and Valencia to Puerto Cabello. London: 1812. V. 50

SEMPLE, ROBERT B.
History of the Rise and Progress of the Baptists in Virginia. Richmond: 1810. V. 54

SEMS, JOHAN
Practica des Landmessens: Darinnen Gelehrt Wirdt, Wie Man Alle Recht Und Krumseitige Land... Amsterdam: 1616. V. 47; 48; 49

SENAC, JEAN
Treatise on the Hidden Nature and Treatment of Intermitting & Remitting Fevers. Philadelphia: 1805. V. 48; 52

SENALUT, J. F.
The Use of Passions. London: 1671. V. 53

SENATOR, H.
Health and Disease in Relation to Marriage and the Married State. New York: 1904. V. 54

SENAULT, LOUIS
Heures Nouvelles Tirees De La Sainte Ecriture. Paris: 1690. V. 49
Hevres Nouvelles Dediees A Madame La Davphine. Paris: 1680. V. 48; 49; 52

SENCOURT, ROBERT
Spain's Ordeal. A Documentary Survey of Recent Events. London: 1938. V. 49

SENDAK, JACK
The Happy Rain. New York: 1956. V. 49

SENDAK, MAURICE
Higglety Pigglety Pop!. New York: 1967. V. 49
The Juniper Tree and Other Tales From Grimm. New York: 1973. V. 53
The Love for Three Oranges. New York: 1984. V. 48; 51
The Nutshell Library: Chicken Soup with Rice - A Book of Months, One Was Johnny - A Counting Book, Pierre - a Cautionary Tale. Alligators All Around - an alphabet. London: 1964. V. 49
Outside Over There. New York: 1981. V. 51

SENDAK, MAURICE continued
Pictures by Maurice Sendak. New York: 1971. V. 47
Posters by Maurice Sendak. New York: 1986. V. 51
The Sign on Rosie's Door. New York: 1960. V. 49
Very Far Away. New York: 1957. V. 49; 52
Where the Wild Things Are. New York: 1988. V. 54

SENDAK, PHILIP
In Grandpa's House. New York: 1985. V. 53

SENDER, RAMON J.
Seven Red Sundays. London: 1936. V. 47; 49
The War in Spain. London: 1937. V. 49; 53

SENDIVOGIUS, MICHAEL
A New Light of Alchymy: Taken Out of the Fountain of Nature and manual Experience... London: 1674. V. 50
Philsophical Account of Nature in General and the Generation of the Three Principles of Nature, Viz. Mercury, Sulphur, Salt, Out of the Four Elements. London: 1722. V. 52

SENECA, LUCIUS ANNAEUS
Cinco Libros de Seneca. Seville: 1491. V. 51; 52
The Epistles of Lucius Annaeus Seneca... London: 1786. V. 50
His Tenne Tragedies. London: 1927. V. 53
L. Annaei Seneca Philosophi: et M. Annaei Senecae Rhetoris Quae Extant Opera... Paris: 1613. V. 47
Morals by Way of Abstract. London: 1722. V. 49
A New Translation of the Morals of Seneca, in Five Parts. London: 1745. V. 50; 54
Opera Philosophica. Epistolae, etc. Venice: 1490. V. 51
Opera Quae Exstant Omnia: a Iusto Lipsio Emendata et Scholiis Illustrata. Antwerp: 1652. V. 50
Philosophi Opera... Antwerp: 1605. V. 47
Philosophi Opera... Antwerp: 1632. V. 47
Seneca's Morals, the Third and Last Part. London: 1678. V. 50
Tragedie cum Duobus Commentariis. Venice: 1510. V. 54
Tragoediae... London: 1624. V. 50
Tragoediae. Amsterdam: 1678. V. 48
Workes Both Morrall and Natural... London: 1614. V. 47; 48
The Works of Lucius Annaeus Seneca... London: 1620. V. 47; 52

SENEFELDER, ALOIS
A Complete Course of Lithography. London: 1819. V. 48; 52
The Invention of Lithography. New York: 1911. V. 51

SENEX, JOHN
The Roads through England Delineated or Ogilby's Survey... London: 1759. V. 54

SENHOUSE, PETER
The Right Use and Improvement of Sensitive Pleasures and More Particularly of Musick. London. V. 47

SENIOR, NASSAU WILLIAM
Four Introductory Lectures on Political Economy, Delivered Before the University of Oxford. London: 1852. V. 53
A Journal Kept in Turkey and Greece in the Autumn of 1857 and the Beginnng of 1858. London: 1859. V. 51
Journals, Conversations and Essays Relating to Ireland. London: 1868. V. 47; 51
Statement of the Provision for the Poor and of the Condition of the Labouring Classes, in a Considerable Portion of America and Europe... London: 1835. V. 53

SENIOR, WILLIAM
The Thames from Oxford to the Tower. London: 1891. V. 51
Travel and Trout in the Antipodes; An Angler's Sketches in Tasmania and New Zealand. London: 1880. V. 47

SENN, NICHOLAS
Intestinal Surgery. Chicago: 1889. V. 53; 54
The Pathology and Surgical Treatment of Tumors. Philadelphia: 1895. V. 54
Surgical Bacteriology. Philadelphia: 1889. V. 51; 54
Tuberculosis of Bones and Joints. Philadelphia: 1892. V. 47

SENNERT, DANIEL
Epitome Naturalis Scientiae. Oxford: 1664. V. 52
Institutionum Medicinae Libri V. Wittemberg: 1667. V. 47; 53

SENNETT, A. R.
Garden Cities in Theory and Practice. London: 1905. V. 48

SENTENTIAE et proverbia ex Poetis Latinis. His Adiecimus. Leosthenis Colvandri Sententias Prophanas... Venice: 1550. V. 52

THE SENTIMENTS. A Poem to the Earl of Danby in the Tower. By a Person of Quality. London: 1679. V. 53

SEPP, J. C.
Beschouwing der Wonderen Gods in de Minstgeachtte Schepzelen. Of Nederlandsche Insecten. Amsterdam: 1762-1821. V. 49

A SEQUEL to the Endless Amusement, Containing Nearly 400 Interesting Experiments in Various Branches of Science... London: 1826. V. 52

THE SERAPHICAL Young Shepherd. London: 1762. V. 52

SERDONATI, M. FRANCESCO
De Fatti D'Arme de'Romani, Libri Tre. Venetia: 1572. V. 53

SERGE, VICTOR
From Lenin to Stalin. London: 1937. V. 49

SERGEANT, ADELINE
The Mistress of Quest. London: 1895. V. 48

SERGEANT, ELIZABETH SHEPLEY
Robert Frost: The Trial By Existence. New York: 1960. V. 49

SERGEANT, JANE
Souvenirs of a Tour on the Continent. London: 1827. V. 49

SERGENT, ANTOINE FRANCOIS
Portraits des Grands Hommes, Femmes Illustres, et Sujets memorables de France, Graves et Imprimes en Couleurs... Paris: 1789-92. V. 50

SERJEANTSON, R. M.
The Serjeantsons of Hanlith. V. 48
The Serjeantsons of Hanlith. London. V. 47

SERLE, AMBROSE
The American Journal of Ambrose Serle: Secretary to Lord Howe, 1776-1778. San Marino: 1940. V. 51

SERLE, GEORGE
Dialling Universal. London: 1664. V. 49

SERLE, JOHN
A Plan of Mr. Pope's Garden, As it Was Left at His Death... London: 1745. V. 51

SERLING, ROD
The Season to Be Wary. Boston: 1967. V. 54

SERMAISE, ROBERT
The Fleshly Prelude. Paris: 1938. V. 51

A SERMON Preached to the Society in Brattle Street, Boston, October 20, 1793, and Occasioned by the Death of His Excellency John Hancock, Governor of Massachusetts. Boston: 1783. V. 48

SERMONS by Artists. Waltham St. Lawrence: 1934. V. 51; 54

SERNA-SANTANDER, CARLOS ANTONIO DE LA
An Historical Essay on the Origin of Printing. Newcastle: 1819. V. 48

SEROTTA, EDWARD
Out of the Shadows: a Photographic Portrait of Jewish Life in Central Europe Since the Holocaust. 1991. V. 48

SERRA, JUNIPERO
An Allegorical ABC Book Where-in the ABCs Tell Stories of Junipero Serra. Richmond: 1977. V. 49

SERRES, DOMINICK
Liber Nauticus and Instructor in the Art of Marine Drawing. London: 1805-06. V. 51

SERRES, J. T.
The Little Sea Torch, or True Guide for Coasting Pilots... London: 1801. V. 50

SERRES, JEAN DE
A Generall Historie of France. London: 1624. V. 47
La Vie de Messire Gaspar de Colligny, Seigneur de Chastillon, Admiral de France. Leiden: 1643. V. 51; 52

SERRES, OLIVIER DE
The Perfect Vse of Silkwormes and Their Benefit. London: 1607. V. 53

SERT, JOSE LUIS
Can Our Cities Survive?. Cambridge: 1942. V. 47; 50

SERVEN, JAMES E.
Colt Firearms 1836-1954. Santa Ana: 1954. V. 51

SERVICE Afloat Comprising the Personal Narrative of a Naval Officer Employed During the Late War and the Journal of an Officer Engaged in the Late Surveying Expedition Under the Command of Captain Owen on the Western Coast of Africa. London: 1933. V. 50; 52

SERVICE, JAMES
Metrical Legends of Northumberland. Alnwick: 1834. V. 53

SERVICE, ROBERT WILLIAM
Ballads of a Bohemian. New York: 1921. V. 49
Ballads of a Cheechako. Toronto: 1909. V. 47; 54
The Poisoned Paradise. London: 1922. V. 54
Rhymes for My Rags. London: 1956. V. 53
Rhymes of a Red Cross Man. New York: 1916. V. 53
Rhymes of a Red Cross Man. Toronto: 1916. V. 52; 53
Rhymes of a Red Cross Man... London: 1920. V. 49
The Trial of Ninety-Eight. New York: 1911. V. 47
Why Not Grow Young?. New York & Newark: 1928. V. 53

SERVIES, JAMES A.
A Bibliography of Florida. Volume I. Pensacola: 1993. V. 50

SERVISS, G.
The Moon Metal. New York: 1900. V. 47; 51

SERVIUS MAURUS, HONORATUS
Commentarii in Vergilii Opera. Rome: 1470. V. 47

SESSIONS, ROGER
Quintet (for 2 Violins, 2 Violas and Cello). New York: 1959. V. 52

SESTI, GIOVANNI BATTISTA
Piante Delle Citta, Piazze, E Castelli Fortificati in Questo Stato di Milano. Milan: 1707. V. 49

IL SESTO Libro Delle Rime Di Diversi Eccellenti Avtori, Nvovamente Raccolte... Venice: 1553. V. 53

SETCHELL, W. A.
The Marine Algae of the Pacific Coast of North America. Berkeley: 1919-25. V. 50

SETEN, J. M.
Indian Costume Book. Santa Fe: 1938. V. 51

SETH, VIKRAM
From Heaven Lake. Travels through Sinkiang and Tibet. London: 1983. V. 51
The Golden Gate. New York: 1986. V. 48; 51; 53
Mappings. 1980. V. 53
A Suitable Boy. 1993. V. 51
A Suitable Boy. London: 1993. V. 53

SETH-SMITH, D.
Parrakeets: a Handbook... London: 1902-03. V. 50
Parrakeets, a Handbook... London: 1903. V. 49

SETON, ERNEST THOMPSON
The Arctic Prairies... New York: 1911. V. 48
The Biography of a Grizzly. New York: 1900. V. 51
The Forester's Manual. Garden City: 1912. V. 52; 54
Life Histories of Northern Animals. London: 1910. V. 48; 50; 51
Lives of Game Animals. Garden City: 1925-28. V. 50
Lives of the Hunted: Containing a True Account of the Doings of Five Quadrupeds and Three Birds. London: 1901. V. 50
The Trail of the Sandhill Stag. New York: 1899. V. 47; 48; 51
Two Little Savages. New York: 1903. V. 53
Wild Animals I Have Known. New York: 1898. V. 47; 48; 49
Wild Animals I Have Known. New York: 1900. V. 48
Woodmyth and Fable. New York: 1905. V. 53

SETON, WILLIAM
The Interest of Scotland in Three Essays. 1700. V. 48

SETON-KARR, H. W.
Bear-Hunting in the White Mountains or Alaska and British Columbia Revisited. London: 1891. V. 48
My Sporting Holidays. London: 1904. V. 48; 49

SETON WATSON, ROBERT W.
The Southern Slav Question, and the Habsburg Monarchy. London: 1911. V. 49

SETOUN, GABRIEL
The Child World. London: 1896. V. 48; 49; 50

SETTLE, ELKANAH
Absalom Senior; or, Achitophel Transpos'd. A Poem. London: 1682. V. 53
Cambyses King of Perisa. London: 1671. V. 49
The Heir of Morocco, with the Death of Gayland. London: 1682. V. 48
Ibrahim the Illustrious Bassa. London: 1677. V. 47; 50
A Narrative... London: 1683. V. 48; 49; 50
A Pindarick Poem, To His Grace Christopher Duke of Albemarle &c., Lately Elected Chancellour of the University of Cambridge. London: 1682. V. 49
The Virgin Prophetess; or, The Fate of Troy. London: 1701. V. 47

SETTLE, MARY LEE
Blood Tie. Boston: 1977. V. 53
The Killing Ground. New York: 1982. V. 54
The Kiss of Kin. New York: 1955. V. 51; 52
Know Nothing. New York: 1960. V. 53
The Love Eaters. London: 1954. V. 48
The Love Eaters. New York: 1954. V. 48; 49; 51; 52; 54
Prisons. New York: 1973. V. 53

SETTLE, RAYMOND W.
The March of the Mounted Riflemen. Glendale: 1940. V. 47; 48; 50; 51; 54

SEUELL, MALCHUS M.
The Mad Pagan and Verse. Downey: 1959. V. 54

SEUPHOR, MICHEL
Piet Mondrian: Life and Work. New York: 1956. V. 47; 48; 50; 52; 54

SEUTONIUS TRANQUILLUS, CAIUS
Vitae XII Caesarum. Venice: 1500. V. 48

THE SEVEN Champions of Christendom. London: 1801. V. 49

SEVEN Happy Days. London: 1914. V. 49

SEVEN SAGES
Dicta Septem Sapientium, et Eorum Qui Cum Iis Numerantur. Paris: 1569-70. V. 50; 53
The Sayings of the Seven Sages of Greece. 1976. V. 52
The Sayings of the Seven Sages of Greece. Verona: 1976. V. 47

SEVEN WISE MASTERS
The History of the Seven Wise Masters of Rome. London: 1697. V. 48

SEVENTH Day Baptists in Europe and America. A Series of Historic Papers...100th Anniversary. Plainfield: 1910. V. 53

SEVENTY Negro Spirituals for Low Voice. Philadelphia: 1926. V. 50

SEVERANCE, CAROLINE M. SEYMOUR
The Mother of Clubs. Los Angeles: 1906. V. 50

SEVERINO, MARCO AURELIO
Il Filocofia Overo il Perche Degli Scacchi (with) Dell'Antica Pettia Overo che Palamede non e Stato L'Inventor Degli Scacchi... Napoli: 1690. V. 52; 53; 54

SEVERINUS, PETRUS
Idea medicinae Philosphicae, Fundamenta continens Totius Doctrinae Paracelsicae, Hippocrates & Galenicae... Basel: 1571. V. 47; 48; 49

SEVERN, EMMA
Anne Hathaway: Or, Shakespeare in Love. London: 1845. V. 48

SEVERN, WALTER
The Golden Calendar. London: 1865. V. 52
Pen and Ink Sketches. 1853. V. 49

SEVERUS, SULPICIUS
Opera Omnia Quae Extant. Lvgd. Batavorum: 1643. V. 53

SEVIGNE, MARIE DE RABUTIN-CHANTAL, MARQUISE DE
Letters... London: 1764. V. 47; 50
Letters... London: 1811. V. 53
The Letters. Philadlephia: 1927. V. 52
Lettres de Madame de Sevigne, de sa Famille et de Ses Amis. Paris: 1818. V. 48; 54
Recueil des Lettres de Madame de Sevigne. Paris: 1801. V. 47

SEVILLE, WILLIAM P.
History of the First Regiment, Delaware Volunteers...to the Final Muster-Out at the Close of the Rebellion. Wilmington: 1884. V. 48

SEWALL, R. K.
Sketches of St. Augustine, with a View of Its History and Advantages as a Resort for Invalids. New York: 1848. V. 47

SEWALL, RICHARD B.
The Life of Emily Dickinson. New York: 1974. V. 51

SEWALL, SAMUEL
Phaenomena Quaedam Apocalyptica ad Aspectum Novi Orbis Configurata... Boston: 1727. V. 47
The Selling of Joseph: a Memorial. Northampton: 1968. V. 51

SEWALL, SAMUEL E.
How to Settle the Texas Question. Boston: 1845. V. 49

SEWALL, STEPHEN
An Hebrew Grammar... Boston: 1763. V. 49; 53

SEWALL, THOMAS
A Lecture Delivered at the Opening of the medical Department of the Columbian College in the District of Columbia... Washington City: 1826. V. 50

SEWARD, ALBERT C.
Catalogue of the Mesozoic Plants. London: 1894-1915. V. 49; 52
Darwin and Modern Science... Cambridge: 1909. V. 50; 52; 53
Darwin and Modern Science. Cambridge: 1910. V. 53

SEWARD, ANNA
Elegy on Captain Cook. London: 1780. V. 54
Letters...Written Between the Years 1784 and 1807. Edinburgh: 1811. V. 47; 50; 51; 52
Memoirs of the Life of Dr. Darwin... London: 1804. V. 50; 51
Memoirs of the Life Of Dr. Darwin... Philadelphia: 1804. V. 47
Monody on Major Andre... Lichfield: 1781. V. 48; 54

SEWARD, JOHN
The Spirit of Anecdote and Wit. London: 1823. V. 51

SEWARD, WILLIAM
Anecdotes...Distinguished Persons... London: 1795-96. V. 48; 51
Anecdotes...Distinguished Persons... London: 1798. V. 51
Anecdotes...Distinguished Persons... London: 1804. V. 48
Biographiana. London: 1799. V. 48

SEWARD, WILLIAM H.
The Elements of Empire in America. New York: 1844. V. 50
Our North Pacific States. Speeches of...in Alaska, Vancouver's and Oregon. August 1869. Washington: 1869. V. 49

SEWARD, WILLIAM W.
Collectanea Politica; or the Political Transactions of Ireland. London: 1801-04. V. 47
The Rights of the People Asserted, and the Necessity of a More equal Representation in Parliament States and Proved. Dublin: 1783. V. 48

SEWEL, WILLIAM
A Compendious Guide to the Low-Dutch Language... Amsterdam: 1760. V. 48
The History of the Rise, Increase and Progress of the Christian People Called Quakers... London: 1722. V. 53
The History of the Rise, Increase and Progress of the Christian People Called Quakers... London: 1725. V. 49
A Large Dictionary English and Dutch, in Two Parts... Amsterdam: 1735. V. 52

SEWELL, ANNA
Black Beauty... London: 1878. V. 50
Black Beauty. London: 1880. V. 50
Black Beauty. Boston: 1890. V. 47; 47; 50; 51; 54
Black Beauty. London: 1915. V. 50
Black Beauty. New York: 1952. V. 49; 52; 54

SEWELL, B.
Three Private Presses: Saint Dominic's Press: The Press of Edward Walters: Saint Albert's Press. Wellinborough: 1979. V. 47

SEWELL, BROCARD
Joseph Delteil: a Symposium. Aylesford: 1962. V. 48

SEWELL, ELIZABETH MISSING
Principles of Education, Drawn From Nature and Revelation and Applied to Female Education in the Upper Classes. New York: 1866. V. 48; 50; 51
Ursula. A Tale of Country Life. New York: 1858. V. 50

SEWELL, GEORGE
A New Collection of Original Poems, Never Printed in Any Miscellany. London: 1720. V. 47

SEWELL, HELEN
The Three Tall Tales. New York: 1947. V. 49

SEWELL, MAY WRIGHT
The World's Congress of Representative Women. Chicago: 1894. V. 50

SEWELL, WILLIAM G.
The Ordeal of Free Labor in the British West Indies. New York: 1861. V. 54
The Ordeal of Free Labor in the British West Indies. New York: 1862. V. 49

THE SEXAGENARIAN; or the Recollections of a Literary Life. London: 1818. V. 49

SEXBY, EDWARD
Killing no Murder... London: 1689. V. 54
Killing no Murder. Edinburgh: 1749. V. 51; 52
Killing No Murder... London: 1792. V. 51; 52
Traicte Politique...(Killing No Murder). Paris: 1793. V. 52

SEXE, MARCEL
Two Centuries of Fur-Trading 1723-1923, Romance of the Revillion Family. 1924. V. 54

SEXTON, ANNE
All My Pretty Ones. Boston: 1962. V. 47; 49
The Book of Folly. Boston: 1972. V. 48; 49; 51
The Death Notebooks. Boston: 1974. V. 49; 52
To Bedlam and Part Way Back. Boston: 1960. V. 47; 49; 52; 53; 54
Transformations. Boston: 1971. V. 50; 51

SEXTON, ERIC H. L.
A Descriptive and Bibliographical List of Irish Figure Sculptures of the Early Christian Period. Portland: 1946. V. 52

SEXTON, R. W.
The Logic of Modern Architecture: Exteriors and Interiors of Modern American Buildings. New York: 1929. V. 50
The Rationalists: Theory and Design in the Modern Movement. London: 1978. V. 48
Spanish Influence on American Architecture and Decoration. New York: 1927. V. 48; 50

SEXTON, SAMUEL
The Ear and its Diseases. Ear. New York: 1888. V. 47

SEYBERT, ADAM
Statistical Annals: Embracing Views of the Population, Commerce, Navigation... Philadelphia: 1818. V. 47; 50

SEYBOLT, PAUL S.
A Catalogue of the First Editions of First Books in the Collection of Paul S. Seybolt. Boston: 1946. V. 54

SEYER, SAMUEL
Memoirs Historical and Topographical of Brisol and it's Neighbourhood. Bristol: 1821-23. V. 53
Memoirs Historical and Topographical of Bristol and its Neighbourhood. London: 1821-23. V. 49

SEYFFERT, O.
Spielzeug. Berlin: 1920. V. 51

SEYMER, JOHN GUNNING
The Romance of Ancient Egypt: Second Series of the Romance of Ancient History. London: 1835. V. 51

SEYMOUR, CHARLES
The Intimate Papers of Colonel House. Boston: 1926. V. 48
The Intimate Papers of Colonel House. Boston: 1926-28. V. 48

SEYMOUR, E. H.
Remarks, Critical, Conjectural and Explanatory Upon the Plays of Shakespeare... London: 1805. V. 50

SEYMOUR, E. S.
Sketches of Minnesota, the New England of the West, With Incidents of Travel in that Territory During the Summer of 1849. New York: 1850. V. 53

SEYMOUR, H. D.
Russia on the Black Sea and Sea of Azof. London: 1855. V. 47; 49

SEYMOUR, HAMILTON
The Golden Pin or a Week of Madness. London: 1884. V. 47

SEYMOUR, HENRY
The Reproduction of Sound, Being a Description of the Mechanical Appliances and Technical Processes Employed in the Art. London: 1918. V. 48

SEYMOUR, MARJORIE F.
The Doings of Dinky Dandy. London: 1917. V. 51

SEYMOUR, RICHARD
The Compleat Gamester. London: 1739. V. 53

SEYMOUR, ROBERT
Comic Readings of Byron and Shakespeare. London: 1830's. V. 52
Humorous Sketches. London: 1878. V. 51; 52
Maxims and Hints for an Angler and Miseries of Fishing. London: 1833. V. 49
Seymour's Humorous Sketches. London: 1841. V. 49
Seymour's Humorous Sketches. London: 1846. V. 54
Sketches by Seymour. London: 1835-36. V. 53
Sketches by Seymour. London: 1840. V. 49; 54

SEYMOUR, SILAS
Incidents of a Trip through the Great Platte Valley, to the Rocky Mountains and Laramie Plains... New York: 1867. V. 47

SEYMOUR, W. D.
Journal of a Voyage Round the World. Cork: 1877. V. 47

SEYMOUR, WILLIAM N.
1855. Wm. N. Seymour's Madison Directory and Business Advertiser. Madison: 1855. V. 47

SEZAWA, KATSUTADA
Elastic Waves Formed by Local Stress Changes of Different Rapidities. Tokyo: 1936. V. 53

SGANZIN, M. L.
An Elementary Course of Civil Engineering. Boston: 1827. V. 49

SHAARA, MICHAEL
The Killer Angels. New York: 1974. V. 48; 50; 51; 54

SHABERMAN, RAPHAEL B.
George MacDonald, a Bibliographical Study. London: 1990. V. 51

SHABISTARI, MAHMUD IBN ABD AL-KARIM
Mahmud Schebisteri's Rosenflor des Geheimnisses. Persich und Deutsch Herausgegeben von Hammer-Purstall. Pesth and Leipzig: 1838. V. 48

SHACKLEFORD, OTIS M.
Lillian Simmons. Kansas City: 1915. V. 54
Seeking the Best. Kansas City: 1911. V. 53

SHACKLETON, EDWARD
Arctic Journeys. London: 1936. V. 54

SHACKLETON, ERNEST HENRY
Aurora Australis. Auckland: 1988. V. 48; 49
The Heart of the Antarctic. London: 1909. V. 48; 49; 50; 52
The Heart of the Antarctic... Philadelphia: 1909. V. 50
South - the Story of Shackleton's Last Expedition 1914-17. New York: 1920. V. 49

SHACOCHIS, BOB
Easy in the Islands. New York: 1985. V. 50

SHADBOLT, JACK
In Search of Form. Toronto: 1968. V. 52

SHADBOLT, SYDNEY H.
The Afghan Campaigns of 1878-1880. London: 1882. V. 51
The Afghan Campaigns of 1878-1880. London: 1982. V. 51

SHADWELL, CHARLES
Five New Plays. Viz. The Hasty Wedding. The Sham Prince. Rotheric O'Connor, King of Connaught. The Plotting Lovers. Irish Hospitality. London: 1720. V. 49

SHADWELL, THOMAS
The Address of John Dryden, Laureat to His Highness the Prince of Orange. London: 1689. V. 47
Bury-Fair. London: 1689. V. 47; 52
The Complete Works. London: 1927. V. 47; 48; 49; 50; 52; 54
The Libertine: a Tragedy. London: 1676. V. 49; 50
The Scowrers. London: 1691. V. 47
The Sullen Lovers; or, the Impertinents. London: 1670. V. 53
The Virtuoso. London: 1676. V. 53
The Virtuoso. London: 1704. V. 48
The Volunteers; or, The Stock Jobbers. London: 1693. V. 47; 53

SHAFFER, ANTHONY
Withered Murder. London: 1955. V. 50; 53

SHAFFER, ELLEN
A Check-List of the Mark Twain Collection Assembled by the Late Willard S. Morse. Los Angeles: 1942. V. 53
The Garden of Health: an Account of two Herbals... 1957. V. 52
The Garden of Health. An Account of Two Herbals... San Francisco: 1957. V. 49

SHAFFER, NEWTON MELMAN
Selected Essays on Orthopaedic Surgery. New York: 1923. V. 47; 50

SHAFFER, PETER
Black Comedy and White Lies. New York: 1967. V. 50
The Collected Plays of Peter Shaffer. New York: 1982. V. 50
Equus. London: 1973. V. 50; 51
Five Finger Exercise... London: 1958. V. 50; 51; 52
Five Finger Exercise... New York: 1959. V. 48
The Private Ear and the Public Eye. London: 1962. V. 50
The Woman in the Wardrobe. London: 1951. V. 47

SHAFFNER, TALIAFERRO P.
The War in America: Being an Historical and Political Account of the Southern and Northern States. London: 1862. V. 49

SHAFTESBURY, ANTHONY ASHLEY COOPER, 3RD EARL OF
Characteristicks of Men, Manners, Opinions... London: 1714. V. 47
Characteristicks of Men, Manners, Opinions... London: 1732. V. 47
Characteristicks of Men, Manners, Opinions... London: 1737-38. V. 47
Characteristicks of Men, Manners, Opinions... Birmingham: 1773. V. 48; 49; 50; 51; 53; 54
Characteristicks of Men, Manners, Opinions... Birmingham: 1783. V. 52
Letters of Earl of Shaftesbury, Author of the Characteristicks. 1746. V. 48

SHAH, IDRIES
Tale of the Sands. Del Mar: 1980. V. 52

SHAHN, BEN
The Alphabet of Creation. An Ancient Legend from the Zohar. New York: 1954. V. 52; 53
The Complete Graphic Works. New York: 1973. V. 47; 50; 52
Love and Joy About Letters. New York: 1963. V. 50; 52; 53; 54
Love and Joy About Letters. London: 1964. V. 53
Sweet Was the Song. New York: 1965. V. 52

SHAHN, BERNARDA BRYSON
Ben Shahn. New York. V. 47; 48; 49; 50; 52
Ben Shahn. New York: 1972. V. 48; 50; 51; 52; 53

SHAIRP, JOHN CAMPBELL
Life and Letters of James David Forbes, F.R.S. London: 1873. V. 51

SHAKESPEAR, H.
The Wild Sports of India... London: 1860. V. 48
The Wild Sports of India... London: 1862. V. 48

SHAKESPEARE. A Review and A Preview. New York: 1939. V. 49

SHAKESPEARE, EDWARD O.
Report of Cholera in Europe and India. Washington: 1890. V. 53

SHAKESPEARE, WILLIAM
All the Love Poems of Shakespare. New York: 1947. V. 51
Anthony and Cleopatra. Paris. V. 52
Antony & Cleopatra. 1979. V. 47; 54
As You Like It. Hammersmith: 1799. V. 52
As You Like It. London: 1799. V. 49
As You Like It. London: 1900. V. 47
As You Like It. East Aurora: 1903. V. 51; 53
As You Like It. London: 1909. V. 54
As You Like It. London: 1910. V. 47; 50
As You Like It. London: 1930. V. 49; 51
Bell's Edition of Shakespeare's Plays, As They Are Now Performed at the Theatres Royal in London. (with) *Poems Written by Shakespeare.* London: 1773-74/74. V. 49
A Book of Shakespeare's Songs. New York: 1903. V. 51
Cassell's Illustrated Shakespare. London. V. 48
A Collection of Poems. London: 1709. V. 48
The Comedies... New York: 1896. V. 47
The Comedies. New York: 1899. V. 52
Comedies... London: 1915. V. 48
Comedies, Histories, and Tragedies... London: 1632. V. 49; 52; 54
Comedies, Histories and Tragedies. London: 1685. V. 48; 49; 50; 52
Comedies, Histories and Tragedies... London: 1909. V. 49; 51
The Comedies, Histories and Tragedies. New York: 1939-40. V. 52; 54
The Comedies, Histories and Tragedies... New York: 1939-40/41. V. 50; 52; 54
The Comedies, Histories, Tragedies, and Poems. London: 1851. V. 50
The Comedies, Histories, Tragedies and Poems. London: 1851-52. V. 48
Comedies, Histories, Tragedies and Poems. London: 1858. V. 50
Comedies, Histories, Tragedies and Poems. Cambridge: 1901. V. 53
The Comedy of Errors. London: 1909. V. 52
The Complete Oxford Shakespeare Histories, Tragedies & Comedies. London: 1994. V. 53
The Complete Works... London: 1850. V. 49
Complete Works. New York: 1856. V. 53
The Complete Works... Halifax: 1864. V. 49
The Complete Works... New York: 1874. V. 53
Complete Works... Philadelphia: 1896. V. 52
The Complete Works. Boston: 1900. V. 49
The Complete Works. Oxford: 1901. V. 48
The Complete Works. London: 1904-07. V. 53
Complete Works. New York: 1904-44. V. 50
Complete Works. New York: 1907. V. 47
The Complete Works... New York: 1907-09. V. 53
The Complete Works... Edinbrugh: 1910. V. 49
The Complete Works. London and Glasgow: 1919. V. 49
The Complete Works. Garden City: 1936. V. 47; 50; 51
The Complete Works. New York: 1940-44. V. 52
The Complete Works. London: 1953. V. 47; 48; 49; 52; 53
Coriolanus... London: 1734-35. V. 51
Coriolanus. Hammersmith: 1941. V. 54
Dramatic Works. Oxford: 1786. V. 48
The Dramatic Works... London: 1802. V. 47; 49
The Dramatic Works. London: 1812-15. V. 47
The Dramatic Works. London: 1823. V. 54

Dramatic Works. Boston: 1850-51. V. 52
Dramatic Works. London: 1857. V. 51
Dramatic Works. Edinburgh: 1883. V. 50
Dramatic Works. London: 1885. V. 49; 52
Everybody's Shakespeare. Woodstock: 1934. V. 51
Excerpts from The Sonnets. Amsterdam and Paris: 1993. V. 52
The Family Shakespeare. London: 1825. V. 48; 52
The First Collected Edition of the Dramatic Works of William Shakespeare. London: 1866. V. 48
The First Folio of Shakespeare. London: 1968. V. 50; 53
The First Folio of Shakespeare. New York: 1968. V. 48
Four Sonnets. Providence: 1994. V. 53
Fourteen Shakespeare Sonnets, XIV Original Woodcuts. Providence: 1987. V. 51
Hamlet... Leipzig: 1907. V. 52
Hamlet. Philadelphia: 1918. V. 48
Hamlet... London: 1922. V. 51; 53
Hamlet. Santa Fe: 1949. V. 51
Hamlet. Alpignano: 1978. V. 50
The Handy Volume Shakespeare. London: 1865. V. 49
The Handy Volume Shakespeare. London: 1875. V. 48
The Handy Volume Shakespeare. London: 1900. V. 52
The Handy-Volume Shakespeare. (Works). London: 1890. V. 47
Henry the Eighth. New York: 1939. V. 51
Henry the Fourth. Part I. New York: 1939. V. 49; 51
Henry the Fourth. Part II. New York: 1939. V. 51
The Historie of Henry the Fourth... London: 1639. V. 48; 49
Julius Caesar. Dublin: 1726. V. 52
Julius Caesar. New York: 1939. V. 51
King Henry the Eighth. London: 1762. V. 49; 54
King Henry the Eighth. London: 1903. V. 49; 50
King Henry the Sixth: Part One. New York: 1940. V. 51
King Lear. San Francisco: 1930. V. 50
King Lear. West Burke: 1987. V. 51
The Kingsway Shakespeare. London: 1932. V. 54
The Life and Death of King Richard the Second. London: 1623. V. 54
The Life of King Henry V. New York: 1951. V. 52
The Life of Timon of Athens. London: 1900. V. 48
Love's Labour's Lost. London: 1924. V. 52
Lucrece. Hammersmith: 1915. V. 48; 51
Macbeth. New York: 1939. V. 51
Macbeth. New York: 1946. V. 49; 53
Macbeth. 1970. V. 47
Macbeth. Guildford: 1970. V. 53
Macbeth. London: 1970. V. 52
The Merchant of Venice. London: 1920. V. 48
The Merry Wives of Windsor. London: 1910. V. 48; 50
A Midsummer Night's Dream. New York. V. 54
A Midsummer Night's Dream. London: 1895. V. 53; 54
A Midsummer Night's Dream. London: 1908. V. 47; 48; 50; 54
A Midsummer Night's Dream. New York: 1912. V. 51
A Midsummer Night's Dream. London: 1914. V. 47; 52
A Midsummer Night's Dream. New York: 1914. V. 48
A Midsummer Night's Dream. London: 1920. V. 49
A Midsummer Night's Dream. London: 1924. V. 52
A Midsummer Night's Dream. Hellerau: 1926. V. 50
A Midsummer Night's Dream. London: 1929. V. 51
Mr. William Shakespeare, His Comedies, Histories and Tragedies. London. V. 53
The Old Spelling Shakespare: Being the Works of Shakespeare in the Spelling of the Best Quarto and Folio Texts. New York & London: 1907-19. V. 54
Othello... London: 1695. V. 52; 53
Othello. New York: 1939. V. 51
Othello. Northampton: 1973. V. 49; 51
The Passionate Pilgrim. 1896. V. 47; 52; 54
The Passionate Pilgrim... London: 1896. V. 52
The Phoenix and the Turtle. 1937. V. 51
The Plays... London: 1765. V. 49
The Plays. London: 1773. V. 48; 49; 51
The Plays... London: 1774. V. 49
The Plays. London: 1785. V. 52; 54
The Plays... London: 1793. V. 47
The Plays. London: 1798-1800. V. 48
The Plays... London: 1806. V. 47
Plays... London: 1813. V. 50
The Plays. London: 1825. V. 48; 51; 54
Plays. London: 1845. V. 48; 53
The Plays... London: 1847. V. 48; 51
The Plays... London: 1849. V. 53
The Plays. London: 1853. V. 51
The Plays. London: 1900. V. 50
Plays. New York: 1904. V. 48
The Plays. New York: 1958. V. 49
The Plays and Poems... Dublin: 1794. V. 49
The Plays and Poems... Philadelphia: 1795-96. V. 47
The Plays and Poems... London: 1821. V. 47; 50; 53

SHAKESPEARE, WILLIAM continued
The Poems... Boston: 1807. V. 48; 54
The Poems... 1893. V. 54
The Poems... Hammersmith: 1893. V. 48; 49
Poems... London: 1899. V. 47; 48; 50
The Poems. London: 1941. V. 49
Poems. 1967. V. 51
Poems. London: 1967. V. 49
Poems and Sonnets. Waltham St. Lawrence: 1960. V. 47
The Rape of Lucrece. Hammersmith: 1915. V. 47; 49
Richard the Second. New York: 1940. V. 51
Romeo and Juliet. Philadelphia: 1833. V. 53
Romeo and Juliet. Philadelphia: 1913. V. 48
Romeo et Juliette. Paris. V. 48
The Royal Shakespeare (sic) The Poet's Works, in Chronological Order... London: 1883. V. 48
The Royal Shakespeare: The Poet's Works in Chronological Order. London: 1905/03. V. 48
Shakespeare's Comedies, Histories and Tragedies. Oxford: 1902. V. 47
Shakespeare's Comedy of Twelfth Night or What You Will. London. V. 48
Shakespeare's Plays: With His Life. New York: 1847. V. 48
Shakespeare's Quarto's in Facsimile. Venus and Adonis - Lucrece - the Passionate Pilgrim - Pericles - The Sonnets. Oxford: 1905. V. 49
Shakespeare's Sonnets. London: 1899. V. 50
Shakespeare's Sonnets. London: 1925. V. 54
Shakespeare's Sonnets. 1982. V. 47; 53
Shakespeare's The Tragedie of Macbeth. London: 1923. V. 51
Shakespeare's Venus and Adonis. Oxford: 1905. V. 51
Shakespeare's Works. London: 1882-83. V. 54
Shakespearian Tales in Verse. London: 1880. V. 49
The Songs and Sonnets... London. V. 47
The Songs and Sonnets. London: 1915. V. 48; 50; 51; 54
The Songs and Sonnets... Philadelphia: 1915. V. 49
Songs from Shakespeare's Plays. 1974. V. 49
Songs from Shakespeare's Plays. Verona: 1974. V. 48; 54
The Songs of Shakespeare. London: 1872. V. 54
Sonnet XXIX. 1919. V. 48
The Sonnets... Mount Vernon. V. 48
The Sonnets... London: 1895. V. 50
The Sonnets... New Rochelle: 1901. V. 48
The Sonnets... New York: 1901. V. 47; 48
Sonnets. Hammersmith: 1909. V. 51; 54
Sonnets. Oxford: 1947. V. 48; 53
Sonnets... Toronto: 1970's?. V. 53
The Sonnets... Los Angeles: 1974. V. 48
Sonnets. Wantage: 1974. V. 48
Sonnets. London: 1979. V. 49
Sonnets. London: 1982. V. 48
Tales from Shakespeare. London: 1909. V. 52
The Taming of the Shrew... London: 1623. V. 50
The Taming of the Shrew. London: 1909. V. 52
The Taming of the Shrew. Palo Alto: 1967. V. 48
The Tempest. New York. V. 48; 50
The Tempest. London: 1898. V. 49; 53
The Tempest. London: 1901. V. 54
The Tempest. London: 1908. V. 48; 49; 50; 52; 53; 54
The Tempest. London: 1911. V. 54
The Tempest. New York: 1920. V. 51
The Tempest. London: 1926. V. 47; 50; 51; 53
The Tempest. Paris: 1975. V. 47
The Tempest. Lexington: 1993. V. 49
Titus Andronicus... London: 1687. V. 52; 53
Titus Andronicus. Northampton: 1973. V. 47; 48; 49; 51; 54
The Tragedie of Anthony and Cleopatra. Hammersmith: 1912. V. 49; 50; 51
The Tragedie of Anthony and Cleopatra. London: 1912. V. 52
The Tragedie of Cymbeline. London: 1923. V. 48; 51; 52
The Tragedie of Julius Caesar. 1913. V. 47
The Tragedie of Julius Caesar. Hammersmith: 1913. V. 51
The Tragedie of Julius Caesar. San Francisco: 1954. V. 48; 54
The Tragedie of King Lear. East Aurora: 1904. V. 49
The Tragedie of King Lear. 1927. V. 52
The Tragedie of King Lear. London: 1927. V. 48
The Tragedie of King Lear. Bangor: 1986. V. 52; 54
The Tragedies of Shakespeare. London: 1903. V. 54
The Tragedy of Coriolanus. 1623. V. 53
The Tragedy of Coriolanus. 1914. V. 49
The Tragedy of Coriolanus. Hammersmith: 1914. V. 47; 48; 51; 54
The Tragedy of Hamlet. High Wycombe: 1933. V. 51
The Tragedy of Hamlet.... London: 1933. V. 47
The Tragedy of Hamlet... New York: 1933. V. 48; 53
The Tragedy of Julius Caesar. London: 1900. V. 52
The Tragedy of Richard the Third. 1953. V. 52
The Tragical Historie of Hamlet. Hammersmith: 1909. V. 48; 51; 52; 54
Twelfth Night... London: 1920. V. 48; 50
Twelfth Night. Waltham St. Lawrence: 1932. V. 51; 53; 54
Twenty of the Plays of Shakespeare. London: 1766. V. 53
Venus and Adonis. Tempe: 1894. V. 51
Venus and Adonis. Stratford-on-Avon: 1905. V. 48
Venus and Adonis. Hammersmith: 1912. V. 47; 49; 51
Venus and Adonis. London: 1912. V. 51
Venus and Adonis. Paris: 1930. V. 47; 48; 49; 50
Venus and Adonis. Rochester: 1931. V. 47; 48; 49; 53
Venus and Adonis. New York: 1934. V. 48
Venus and Adonis. San Francisco: 1975. V. 48
Venus and Adonis. Tempe: 1984. V. 48
The Whole Historical Dramas. London: 1811. V. 50
With Fairest Flowers While Summer Lasts. Poems from Shakespeare. Garden City: 1971. V. 52; 53
The Works. London. V. 50; 54
The Works. London: 1709/10. V. 51; 52
The Works. London: 1723-25. V. 48
The Works... London: 1733. V. 50; 54
The Works. London: 1740. V. 48
The Works... Edinburgh: 1753. V. 48
The Works. London: 1762. V. 53
The Works... Oxford: 1771-70. V. 48
The Works. London: 1773. V. 52
Works. London: 1785-87. V. 51
Works. London: 1840. V. 48; 50
Works. London: 1843. V. 48; 51
Works. London: 1844. V. 48
Works. London: 1845. V. 50
The Works. London: 1860. V. 48
The Works. London: 1864. V. 51
The Works... Cambridge: 1866. V. 47
Works. London: 1866. V. 49; 52
The Works... London: 1870. V. 49; 53
The Works. London: 1873. V. 51
The Works... London: 1875. V. 49
The Works. London: 1875-76. V. 52
The Works... London: 1880. V. 50
The Works... Boston: 1881. V. 50
The Works. London: 1886. V. 51
The Works. London: 1888-90. V. 48
Works. London: 1890. V. 50
Works. London: 1895. V. 47
Works. London: 1901-04. V. 50
The Works. London: 1902. V. 50
Works. New York: 1902. V. 47; 52
The Works. Glasgow: 1904. V. 48
The Works. London: 1904. V. 48; 54
The Works. Stratford-on-Avon: 1904. V. 48; 54
The Works. Stratford-on-Avon: 1904-07. V. 47; 49; 51
The Works... London: 1929-33. V. 48; 49; 50; 51; 53; 54
The Works... New York: 1929-33. V. 48; 50; 51; 52
Works. London: 1930. V. 48
The Works... Oxford: 1934. V. 48
The Works. New York: 1939-41. V. 49; 51

A SHAKESPEAREAN Memento 1964. Worcester: 1964. V. 48

SHAKESPEARE'S England. An Account of the Life and Manners of His Age.. London: 1917. V. 49

SHAKESPEARE'S England. An Account of the Life and Manners of His Age, All by Brilliant Authors. Oxford: 1966. V. 49

SHAKESPEARE'S Heroes and Heroines. After Sir A. Callcott, R.A., C.R., Leslie, R.A., D. Maclise... 1891. V. 47

SHAKESPEARE'S Household Words. London: 1859. V. 53

SHALER, N. S.
American Highways. New York: 1896. V. 52
A Comparison of the Features of the Earth and the Moon. Washington: 1903. V. 50

SHALL GIRLS Propose? And Other Papers on Love and Marriage... New York: 1891. V. 48

SHAMBAUGH, BERTHA
The Community of True Inspiration. Iowa City: 1908. V. 48

SHAND, ALEXANDER INNES
General John Jacob, Commandant of the Sind Irregular Horse and Founder of Jacobabad. London: 1900. V. 48
Shooting... London: 1872. V. 48; 49; 54
Shooting. London: 1902. V. 49

SHAND, P. MORTON
Modern Theatres and Cinemas. London: 1930. V. 51

SHANDHAM, ELIZABETH
Lucilla; or, the Reconditiation. London: 1819. V. 50

SHANGE, NTOZAKE
A Daughter's Geography. New York: 1983. V. 51
For Colored Girls Who Have Considered Suicide... San Lorenzo: 1975. V. 51; 53; 54

SHANGE, NTOZAKE continued
For Colored Girls Who Have Considered Suicide... New York: 1977. V. 53
From Okra to Greens. St. Paul: 1984. V. 53

SHANHAGAN, ROGER
The Exhibition, or a Second Anticipation... London: 1779?. V. 48; 53

SHANKS, EDWARD
The Dogs of War. London: 1948. V. 54

SHANKS & CO., GLASGOW
Sanitary Appliances. Baths & Bath Fittings, Lavatories & Lavatory Fittings, Water Closets and Urinals, Fireclay Sinks, Slate Sinks, Sanitary Earthenware & Water Fittings of Every Description. Glasgow: 1886. V. 54

SHANNON, A. H.
The Negro in Washington. New York: 1930. V. 53

SHANNON, C. HAZELWOOD
The Pageant. London: 1896-97. V. 53; 54
The Pageant. London: 1897. V. 52

SHANNON, C. HAZLEWOOD
The Pageant. London: 1897/98. V. 52

SHANNON, FRANCIS BOYLE, VISCOUNT
Discourses Useful for the Vain Modish Ladies and Their Gallants. London: 1696. V. 47

SHANNON, FRED ALBERT
The Organization and Administration of the Union Army 1861-1865. Cleveland: 1928. V. 48

SHAPED Poetry: a Suite of 30 Typographic Prints Chronicling This Literary From from 300 B.C. to the Present. San Francisco: 1981. V. 49; 54

SHAPIRO, DAVID
Jasper Johns Drawings 1954-1984. New York: 1984. V. 53
Jim Dine: Painting What One Is. New York: 1981. V. 47; 50

SHAPIRO, KARL JAY
Auden (1907-1973). 1974. V. 52
Auden (1907-1973). A Poem. Davis: 1974. V. 48
Edsel. 1971. V. 51
Edsel. New York: 1971. V. 54
Five Young American Poets. Second Series 1941. Norfolk: 1941. V. 50
Poems. Baltimore: 1935. V. 48; 50; 51; 52; 53; 54

SHAPLEIGH, JOHN
Highways: a Treatise, Shewing the Hardships and Inconveniences of Presenting, or Indicting Parishes, Towns &c. for Not Repairing the Highways. London: 1750. V. 52; 54

SHAPLEY, FERN RUSK
Paintings from the Samuel H. Kress Collection Italian Schools XVI-XVIII Century. London: 1973. V. 52; 54

SHAPLEY, RUFUS E.
Solid for Mulhooly... Philadelphia: 1889. V. 50

SHAPTER, THOMAS
The Climate of the South of Devon and Its Influence Upon Health... London: 1842. V. 54

SHARP, A. MARY
Point and Pillow Lace. New York: 1899. V. 50

SHARP, CECIL JAMES
The Dance. An Historical Survey of Dancing in Europe. London: 1924. V. 50

SHARP, CUTHBERT
A Brief Summary of the Contents of a Manuscript, Formerly elonging to the Lord William Howard of Naworth. Durham: 1819. V. 50
Catalogue of Rare and Curious Books, Copperplates and Wood Cuts and Valuable Literary Copyrights. Newcastle upon Tyne: 1849. V. 48
The Duke of Wellington's Visit to Sunderland, 1827. Durham: 1827. V. 50
Seaham Harbour. Durham: 1828. V. 50

SHARP, D.
The Rationalists: Theory and Design in the Modern Movement. London: 1978. V. 50; 51; 53; 54

SHARP, EVELYN
The Child's Christmas. London: 1906. V. 49
The Story of the Weathercock. London: 1907. V. 48; 53; 54

SHARP, GRANVILLE
An Account of the Ancient Division of the English Nation Into Hundreds and Thirthings. London: 1784. V. 47
A Declaration of the People's Natural Right to a Share in the Legislature... London: 1774. V. 48
The Gilbart Prize Essay on the Adaptation of Recent Discoveries and Inventions in Science and Art to the Purposes of Practical Banking. London: 1854. V. 51
The Law of Retribution; or a Serious Warning to Great Britain and Her Colonies... London: 1776. V. 52; 53
Remarks Concerning the Encroachments ont he River Thames near Durham-Yard... London: 1771. V. 48; 54
A Short Treatise on the English Tongue. London: 1767. V. 52
A Tract on the Law of Nature, and Principles of Action in Man. London: 1777. V. 48

SHARP, GUSTAVUS
The Confessions of an Attorney. New York: 1853. V. 48

SHARP, HENRY
Modern Sporting Gunnery. A Manual of Practical Information for Shooters of To-Day. London: 1906. V. 48
Practical Wildfowling. London: 1895. V. 49

SHARP, JAMES
Rolling Carts and Waggons (a Descriptive Advertisement, in Three Letterpress Columns Beneath Woodcut of Large Wagon Drawn by an Eight-Horse Team). London: 1770. V. 47

SHARP, MARY A.
The History of Ufton Court, of the Parish of Ufton in the county of Berks, and of the Perkins Family... London: 1892. V. 53

SHARP, RICHARD
Episles in Verse. London: 1828. V. 50; 54

SHARP, SAMUEL
A Critical Enquiry into the Present State of Surgery. London: 1750. V. 47
A Critical Enquiry into the Present State of Surgery. London: 1761. V. 51; 53
Letters From Italy, Describing the Customs and Manners of that Country... London: 1766. V. 49
Letters from Italy, Describing the Customs and Manners of that Country. Dublin: 1767. V. 51
Letters from Italy, Describing the Customs and manners of that Country... London: 1767. V. 50; 54
A Treatise on the Operations of Surgery. London: 1740. V. 48
A Treatise on the Operations of Surgery... London: 1761. V. 47
A View of the Customs, Manners, Drama &c. of Italy, As They Are Described in the Frustra Letteraria; and in the Account of Italy in English, Written by Mr. Baretti... London: 1768. V. 53

SHARP, THOMAS
A Charity-Sermon, for the Relief of Poor Widows, and Children of Clergymen, Within the Diocese of Durham... York: 1721. V. 50
A Dissertation on the Pageants or Dramatic Mysteries Anciently Performed at Coventry... Coventry: 1825. V. 50
Kenilworth Illustrated, or, the History of the Caste, Priory and Church of Kenilworth. Chiswick: 1821. V. 47; 53

SHARP, WILLIAM
An Account of a New Method of Treating Fractured Legs... London: 1767. V. 48
Dante Gabriel Rossetti: a Record and a Study. London: 1882. V. 51
The Last Supper. 1952. V. 48
The Mountain Lovers. Boston: 1895. V. 47
Vistas. Derby: 1894. V. 52

SHARPE, CHARLES KIRKPATRICK
A Ballad Book, or Popular and Romantic Ballads and songs Current in Annandale and Other Parts of Scotland. Edinburgh: 1883. V. 52
Metrical Legends, and Other Poems. Oxford: 1807. V. 47; 54

SHARPE, D.
Fossil Remains of Mollusca Found in the Chalk. (with) A Survey of the Fossil Cephalapoda of the Chalk of Great Britain... London: 1853-57/1951. V. 50

SHARPE, EDMUND
A Visit to the Domed Churches of Charente, France, by the Architectural Association of London, in the Year 1875. London: 1884. V. 53

SHARPE, GREGORY
A Short Dissertation Upon that Species of Misgovernment, Called an Oligarchy. London: 1748. V. 52

SHARPE, JOHN
Fifteen Sermons Preached on Several Occasions. London: 1701. V. 49
A Sermon Preached at Trinity-Church in New York, in America, August 13, 1706. London: 1706?. V. 47; 51

SHARPE, LEWIS
The Noble Stranger. London: 1640. V. 50

SHARPE, REGINALD R.
Calendar of Letter-Books Preserved Among the Archives of the City of London at the Guildhall. From A.D. 1275-(Henry VI). London: 1899-1911. V. 52
London and the Kingdom. London: 1894-95. V. 48

SHARPE, RICHARD BOWDLER
Catalogue of the Fulicariae (Ralidae and Heliornithidae) and Alectorides (Aramidae, Eurypygidae, Meditidae, Rhinocheretidae, Gruidae Psophiidae and Otididae) in the Collection of the British Museum. London: 1894. V. 47
A Hand-List of the Genera and Species of Birds. London: 1899-1909. V. 53
A Handbook to the Birds of Great Britain. London: 1896-97. V. 52
Lloyd's Natural History. London: 1896-97. V. 53
Matabele Land and the Victoria Falls, from the Letters and Journals of the Late Frank Oates, F.R.G.S. London: 1882. V. 52
A Monograph of the Alcedinidae; or, Family of Kingfishers. London: 1868-71. V. 48; 51
A Monograph of the Hirundinidae, or Family of the Swallows. London: 1885-94. V. 52; 53; 54
Monograph of the Paradiseidae, or Birds of Paradise and Ptilonorhynchidae, or Bower Birds. London: 1891-98. V. 49; 51; 52
On a Collection of Birds Made by Dr. A. Donaldson Smith During His Recent Expedition in Western Somali-Land. London: 1895. V. 52
On the Birds Collected by Professor J. B. Steere in the Philippine Archipelago. London: 1877. V. 51; 52
On the Birds of Zululand... London: 1897. V. 52
Scientific Results Of the Second Yarkand Mission... London: 1891. V. 51

SHARPE, RICHARD SCRAFTON
Theodore; or, the Gamester's Progress. London: 1824. V. 54

SHARPE, SAMUEL
Egyptian Hieroglyphics; Being an Attempt to Explain Their Nature, Origin and Meaning. London: 1861. V. 51
The History of Eygpt, from the Earliest Times Till the Conquest of the Arabs, A.D. 640. London: 1859. V. 50
A Treatise On the Operations of Surgery, with a description and Representation of the Instruments Used in Performing Them... London: 1761. V. 51

SHARPE, THOMASIN E.
A Royal Descent; with Other Pedigrees and Memorials. London: 1875. V. 53

SHARPE, TOM
Blott on the Landscape. London: 1975. V. 50
Indecent Exposure. London: 1973. V. 48; 54
Riotous Assembly. London: 1971. V. 50; 54
The Wilt Alternative. London: 1979. V. 50

SHARROCK, ROBERT
An Improvement to the Art of Gardening... London: 1694. V. 52

SHATNER, W.
The Tekwar. 1989. V. 48

SHATTUCK, GEORGE BURBANK
The Bahama Islands. New York & London: 1905. V. 50

SHATTUCK, GEORGE CHEYNE
Three Dissertations on Boylston Prize Questions for the Years 1806 and 1807. Boston: 1808. V. 48; 54

SHATTUCK, LEMUEL
Report to the Committee of the City Council Appointed to Obtain the Census of Boston for the Year 1845, Embracing Collateral Facts and Statistical Researches Illustrating the History and Condition of the Population and Their Means of Progress... Boston: 1846. V. 47; 51

SHAVER, RUTH M.
Kabuki Costume. Rutland & Tokyo: 1966. V. 48

SHAW, ALEXANDER
Narrative of the Discoveries of Sir Charles Bell in the Nervous System. London: 1839. V. 47; 48

SHAW, B.
The Palace of Eternity. London: 1970. V. 52

SHAW, BARNABAS
Memorials of Southern Africa. London: 1841. V. 50

SHAW, BYAM
Life's Ironies. London: 1912. V. 47

SHAW, CHARLES
A Topographical and Historical Description of Boston, from the First Settlement of the Town to the Present Period; with Some Account of Its Environs. Boston: 1817. V. 54

SHAW, DAVID A.
Eldorado or California as Seen by a Pioneer. Los Angeles: 1900. V. 47

SHAW, DUNCAN
The History and Philosophy of Judaism... Edinburgh: 1787. V. 49

SHAW, EDWARD
Civil Architecture: Or, a Complete Theoretical and Practical System of Building. Boston: 1832. V. 53
Civil Architecture; or a Complete Theoretical and Practical System of Building. Boston: 1834. V. 52

SHAW, FLORA L.
A Tropical Dependency. London: 1905. V. 50

SHAW, FREDERICK
Oil Lamps and Iron Ponies. San Francisco: 1949. V. 54

SHAW, G.
Museum Leveriarnum containing Select Specimens from the Museum of the Late Sir Ashton Lever Kt... London: 1791/92/93. V. 53

SHAW, GEORGE
General Zoology... London: 1800-01. V. 54
A Select Cabinet of Natural History... London: 1820. V. 54
Zoological Lectures Delivered at the Royal Institution in 1806 and 1807. London: 1809. V. 54

SHAW, GEORGE A.
Madagascar and France. London: 1885. V. 47; 48

SHAW, GEORGE BERNARD
The Apple Cart: a Political Extravaganza. London: 1930. V. 48; 49; 50; 51; 52; 53
The Apple Cart: a Political Extravaganza. New York: 1931. V. 48
Back to Methuselah. London: 1921. V. 53
Buoyant Billions. London: 1949. V. 49; 53
Cashel Byron's Profession. London: 1886. V. 48; 53; 54
Cashel Byron's Profession. Chicago: 1901. V. 49
Collected Plays with Their Prefaces. London: 1979-71-74. V. 51
The Collected Works. V. 47
The Collected Works. New York: 1930. V. 49; 54
The Collected Works. New York: 1930-32. V. 54
The Complete Plays... London: 1931. V. 49
The Complete Plays... London: 1931-34. V. 49
Complete Works. London: 1931-50. V. 51
Cymbeline Refinished: a Variation by Bernard Shaw. Edinburgh: 1937. V. 53
The Doctor's Dilemma: Getting Married, the Shewing-Up of Blanco Posnet. London: 1911. V. 52
Dramatic Opinions and Essays with an Apology. London: 1907. V. 54
Fabian Essays in Socialism. London: 1889. V. 47; 50; 54
Fabian Essays in Socialism. New York: 1891. V. 52
The Fabian Essays in Socialism. Boston: 1911. V. 48
Farfetched Fables: by a Fellow of the Royal Society of Literature. London: 1949. V. 53
Flyleaves. Austin: 1977. V. 52
Geneva: a Fancied Page of History in Three Acts. London: 1939. V. 52
How to Settle the Irish Question. London and Dublin: 1917. V. 51
The Intelligent Woman's Guide to Socialism and Capitalism. London: 1928. V. 48; 50; 53
The Irrational Knot. London: 1905. V. 54
Is Free Trade Alive or Dead?. London: 1906. V. 53
London Music in 1888-1889 as Heard by Corno di Bassetto (Later Known as Bernard Shaw) with Some Further Autobiographical Particulars. New York: 1937. V. 50
Love Among the Artists. Chicago: 1900. V. 49; 53
Love Among the Haystacks. Chicago: 1900. V. 54
Man and Superman... Westminster: 1903. V. 48
Man and Superman. New York: 1962. V. 48; 50; 51
Misalliance, Dark Lady of Sonnets. London: 1914. V. 47; 49; 50; 51; 52; 53
Misalliance, the Dark Lady of the Sonnets... New York: 1914. V. 49
Mrs. Warren's Profession: a Play in Four Acts. London: 1902. V. 51
On Going to Church. East Aurora: 1896. V. 53; 54
On the Rocks: Political Fantasy.... London: 1933. V. 53
Passion Play. Iowa City: 1971. V. 51; 53
Passion Play... London: 1971. V. 48; 52; 54
Plays: Pleasant and Unpleasant. Chicago & New York: 1898. V. 49
Plays: Pleasant and Unpleasant. London: 1898. V. 51
Prefaces. London: 1934. V. 54
Pygmalion and Candida. Avon: 1974. V. 47; 50
The Quintessence of Ibsenism. London: 1891. V. 51; 54
Saint Joan. London: 1904. V. 54
Saint Joan. London: 1924. V. 47; 49; 50; 51
Saint Joan... New York: 1924. V. 47; 48
The Sanity of Art... London: 1908. V. 50; 54
The Sanity of Art. New York: 1908. V. 52
Selected Passages from the Works of Bernard Shaw. London: 1912. V. 53; 54
Shakes versus Shav: a Puppet Play... London: 1949. V. 53
Shaw Gives Himself Away. Newtown: 1939. V. 47; 50; 51; 54
Shaw's Music: the Complete Musical Criticism. London: 1981. V. 51
The Shewing-Up of Blanco Posnet. London: 1923. V. 48
Statement of the Evidence in Chief by (G.B.S.) Before the Joint Committee on Stage Plays. 1909. V. 50
Three Plays for Puritans: The Devil's Disciple, Caesar and Cleopatra and Captain Brassbound's Conversion. London: 1901. V. 54
Too True to Be Good, Village Wooing and On th Rocks. London: 1934. V. 53
Widower's Houses. London: 1893. V. 49
The Works... London: 1930-38. V. 48
The Works of... London: 1930. V. 53

SHAW, GEORGE C.
The Chinook Jargon and How to Use It. Seattle: 1909. V. 48

SHAW, HENRY
Alphabets Numerals and Devices of the Middle Ages. London: 1845. V. 51
A Booke of Sundry Draughtes. London: 1848. V. 51; 54
The Decorative Arts, Ecclesiasatical and Civil of the Middle Ages. London: 1851. V. 49; 50; 52
Details of Elizabethan Architecture. London: 1834. V. 50; 51
Details of Elizabethan Architecture. London: 1839. V. 48
Dresses and Decorations of the Middle Ages. London: 1843. V. 48; 50; 51; 53
Dresses and Decorations of the Middle Ages... London: 1858. V. 52
The Encyclopaedia of Ornament. London: 1842. V. 49; 52
The Handbook of Medieaval Alphabets & Devices. London: 1853. V. 49; 53
A Handbook of the Art of Illumination as Practised during the Middle Ages. London: 1866. V. 47; 50; 52
Illuminated Ornaments Selected from Manuscripts and Early Printed Books from the Sixth to the Seventeenth Centuries. London: 1833. V. 50
Specimens of Ancient Furniture. London: 1836. V. 48; 52

SHAW, HENRY WHEELER
Josh Billings, His Book of Sayings. London: 1866. V. 49

SHAW, IRWIN
Bread Upon Waters. New York: 1941. V. 51
The Gentle People. New York: 1939. V. 51
Mixed Company. New York: 1950. V. 49
Report on Israel. New York: 1950. V. 48; 51
Two Weeks In Another Town. New York: 1960. V. 54
Voices of a Summer Day. New York: 1965. V. 54
The Young Lions. New York: 1948. V. 54

SHAW, JAMES
Early Reminiscences of Pioneer Life in Kansas. Atchison: 1886. V. 51
Sketches of the History of the Austrian Netherlands With Remarks On the Constitution, Commerce, Arts and General State of These Provinces. London: 1786. V. 53

SHAW, JAMES BYAM
Drawings by Old Masters at Christ Church, Oxford. 1976. V. 51
Drawings by Old Masters at Christ Church, Oxford. London: 1976. V. 49
Drawings by Old Masters at Christ Church, Oxford. Oxford: 1976. V. 53
Paintings by Old Masters at Christchurch, Oxford. London: 1967. V. 50

SHAW, JOHN
The Divine Art of Memory; or the Sum of the Holy Scriptures Delivered in Acrostick Verses... London: 1683. V. 47
Woolton Green: a Domestic Tale... Liverpool: 1825. V. 48; 53

SHAW, JOSEPH
The Practical Justice of Peace... London: 1736. V. 49
The Practical Justice of Peace... London: 1751. V. 47

SHAW, JOSEPH T.
Danger Ahead. New York: 1932. V. 52
The Hard-Boiled Omnibus. Early Stories From Black Mask. New York: 1946. V. 48

SHAW, L. O.
The Duel, the Battle of Waterloo, and other Poems. 1836?. V. 50

SHAW, LUELLA
True History of Some of the Pioneers of Colorado. Hotchkiss: 1909. V. 47; 54

SHAW, NAPIER
The Air and Its Ways: the Rede Lecture (1921) in the University of Cambridge, With Other Contributions to Meteorology for Schools and Colleges. Cambridge: 1923. V. 54
Manual of Meteorology. Cambridge: 1932/36/42/19. V. 53

SHAW, P. J.
An Old York Church, All Hallows in North Street. York: 1908. V. 54

SHAW, PETER
Pharmacopoeia Edinburgensis or, the Dispensatory of the Royal College of Physicians in Edinburgh. London: 1740. V. 53
The Reflector: Representing Human Affairs, As They are, and May be Improved. London: 1750. V. 49

SHAW, PRINGLE
Ramblings in California... Toronto: 1860?. V. 51

SHAW, R. C.
Across the Plains in Forty-Nine. Farmland: 1896. V. 47

SHAW, R. CUNLIFFE
Kirkham in Amounderness. Preston: 1949. V. 48; 53

SHAW, RALPH R.
American Bibliography, a Preliminary Checklist 1801 (to 1834). New York: 1958-65. V. 51

SHAW, RICHARD NORMAN
Architectural Sketches from the Continent. London: 1858. V. 47; 51; 52
Architectural Sketches from the Continent. London: 1872. V. 52
Sketches for Cottages and Other Buildings Designed to Be Constructed in the Patent Cement Slab System of W. H. Lascelles. London: 1878. V. 49

SHAW, ROBERT
A Card from Morocco. New York: 1969. V. 54

SHAW, ROBERT BARKLEY
Visits to High Tartary, Yarkand, and Kashgar... London: 1871. V. 48; 51

SHAW, S.
A Tour to the West of England in 1788... London: 1789. V. 52

SHAW, SIMEON
An Atlas of Nature... London: 1823. V. 54

SHAW, T. E.
More Letters from T. E. Shaw to Bruce Rogers. 1936. V. 52

SHAW, THOMAS
The History of Wharfdale. Otley: 1830. V. 53
Travels, Or Observations Relating to Several Parts of Barbary and the Levant. Oxford: 1738. V. 49; 53; 54
Travels, or Observations Relating to Several Parts of Barbary and the Levant. London: 1757. V. 51; 52; 54

SHAW, VERO
The Illustrated Book of the Dog... London: 1883-86. V. 51; 53

SHAW, WILLIAM
An Analysis of the Galic Language. Edinburgh: 1778. V. 48; 53
Golden Dreams and Walking Realities. London: 1851. V. 47; 53
The Land of Promise; or, My Impressions of Australia. London: 1854. V. 51
Memoirs of the Life and Writings of the Late Dr. Samuel Johnson.... London: 1785. V. 48

SHAW, WILLIAM ARTHUR
Manchester Old and New. London: 1894. V. 48; 53

SHAW, WILLIAM FRANCIS
Liber Estriae; or Memorials of the Royal Ville and Parish of Eastry, Kent. London: 1870. V. 53

SHAW, WILLIAM H.
History of Essex and Hudson Counties, New Jersey. Philadelphia: 1884. V. 47; 51

SHAWN, TED
Gods Who Dance. New York: 1929. V. 47; 52

SHAWN, WALLACE
Our Late Night. New York: 1984. V. 54

SHAY, JOHN C.
Twenty Years in the Backwoods of California. Boston: 1923. V. 54

SHAZKI: Tales and Legends of Old Russia. New York: 1926. V. 47

SHEA, JOHN
Catholic Church in Colonial Days... New York: 1886. V. 53

SHEA, JOHN GILMARY
Discovery and Exploration of the Mississippi Valley with the Original Narratives of Marquette, Allouez, Membre, Hennepin and Anastase Dovay. Albany: 1903. V. 49
Early Voyages Up and Down the Mississippi, by Cavelier St. Cosme, Le Sueur, Gravier and Guignas... Albany: 1861. V. 47
The Fallen Brave: a Biographicl Memorial of the American Officers Who Have Given Their Lives for the Preservation of the Union. New York: 1861. V. 47
Perils of the Ocean and Wilderness... Boston: 1856. V. 47

SHEA, MICHAEL
Nifft the Lean. Woodinville: 1994. V. 52

SHEARD, CHARLIE KILNER
Descriptive Paper of Railway Practice and Mountain Railways of a Similar Description to the Tasmanian Railways Now Under Construction. Hobart: 1886. V. 49

SHEARER, FREDERICK E.
The Pacific Tourist. J. R. Bowman's Illustrated Trans-Continental Guide of Travel from the Atlantic to the Pacific Ocean... New York: 1882-83. V. 47

SHEARER, W. H.
Atlases of the Goldfield, Tonopah and Bullfrog Mining Districts of Nevada. Chicago: 1905. V. 49

SHEARS, EDWARD HORNBY
Active-Service Diary - 21 January 1917 - 1 July 1917. London: 1919. V. 47

SHEBBEARE, JOHN
A Fourth Letter to the People of England, On the Conduct of M----rs in Alliances, Fleets and Armies, Since the First Differences on the Ohio, to the Taking of Minorca, by the French. London: 1756. V. 47
A Letter to the People of England, Upon the Militia, Continental Connections, Neutralities, and Secret Expeditions. London: 1757. V. 50
Letters on the English Nation. London: 1755. V. 48; 52
Letters to the People of England: I-V. London: 1756/57/57. V. 52

SHECKLEY, ROBERT
Citizen in Space. 1955. V. 48; 52
Journey Beyond Tomorrow. London: 1964. V. 48; 52
Specialist. New York: 1993. V. 51
Untouched by Human Hands. London: 1955. V. 50; 54

SHECUT, JOHN L. E. W.
Flora Carolinaeensis; or a Historical, Medical and Economical Display of the Vegetable Kingdom. Charleston: 1806. V. 53; 54

SHEE, MARTIN ARACHER
Elements of Art, a Poem, in Six Cantos... London: 1809. V. 49; 53

SHEEHAN, JOSEPH EASTMAN
General and Plastic Surgery, with Emphasis on War Injuries. New York and London: 1945. V. 54
Plastic Surgery of the Orbit. New York: 1927. V. 54

SHEELER, CHARLES
The University Museum: Section of Oriental Art. Philadelphia: 1917. V. 54

SHEEN, JACK H.
Aesthetic Rhinoplaty. Medical Illustrator, Hermene Kavanau. St. Louis: 1978. V. 54

SHEERES, HENRY
An Essay on the Certainty and Causes of the Earth's Motion on Its Axis, &c. London: 1698. V. 47

THE SHEFFIELD Assay Office Register. A Copy of the Register of the Persons Concerned in the Manufacture of Silver Wares, and of the Marks Entered by Them from 1773 to 1907. Sheffield: 1911. V. 53

SHEFFIELD, JOHN BAKER HOLYROYD, 1ST EARL OF
Observations on the Commerce of the American States. London: 1784. V. 47
Observations on the Manufactures, Trade and Present State of Ireland. London: 1785. V. 49
Strictures on the Necessity of Inviolably Maintaining the Navigation and Colonial System of Great Britain. London: 1804. V. 52

SHEFFY, L. F.
Colonization of West Texas: The Life and Times of Timothy Dwight Hobart, 1855-1935. Canyon: 1950. V. 48

SHEIL, RICHARD LALOR
Sketches of the Irish Bar. New York: 1854. V. 48

SHEILDS, G. O.
Cruisings in the Cascades. Chicago: 1889. V. 54

SHELDON, CHARLES
The Wilderness of Denali. New York: 1930. V. 47; 52; 53
The Wilderness of the North Pacific Coast Islands... London: 1912. V. 53
The Wilderness of the North Pacific Coast Islands. New York: 1912. V. 47; 50; 52
The Wilderness of the Upper Yukon... London: 1911. V. 48

SHELDON, CHARLES continued
The Wilderness of the Upper Yukon. New York: 1911. V. 47; 49; 53
The Wilderness of the Upper Yukon... Toronto: 1911. V. 53
The Wilderness of the Upper Yukon. New York: 1919. V. 50
The Wilderness of the Upper Yukon... 1983. V. 48; 52; 54

SHELDON, FRANKLIN J.
Nonsense, Common Sense, Incense. Enfield: 1925/26/27. V. 47
A Sketch of Enfield Rapids of Connecticut River, Past Present Future. Enfield: 1915. V. 47

SHELDON, FREDERICK
The Minstrelsy of the English Border. London: 1847. V. 52

SHELDON, G. W.
American Painters. New York: 1879. V. 47; 50; 51; 53

SHELDON, GEORGE
A History of Deerfield, Massachusetts... Deerfield: 1895. V. 51

SHELDON, H. HORTON
Television. Present Methods of Picture Transmission. New York: 1930. V. 52; 54

SHELDON, HAROLD P.
Tranquility... New York: 1936. V. 47; 48
Tranquility... New York: 1940. V. 47
Tranquility... 1945. V. 50; 54
Tranquility... West Hartford: 1945. V. 47; 53

SHELDON, LIONEL A.
General Orders No. 1. Territory of New Mexico: 1881. V. 49

SHELDON, WILLIAM
History of the Heathen Gods, and Heroes of Antiquity. Boston: 1816. V. 47

SHELDON, WILLIAM G.
Exploring for Wild Sheep in British Columbia in 1931 and 1932. Clinton: 1981. V. 53

SHELDON, WILLIAM HERBERT
Atlas of Men: a Guide for Somatotyping the Adult Male at All Ages. New York: 1954. V. 48; 52

SHELDON-WILLIAMS, RALF
The Canadian Front in France and Flanders. London: 1920. V. 47

SHELFORD, LEONARD
The Act for the Commutation of Tithes in England and Wales... London: 1837. V. 53

SHELFORD, ROBERT WALTER CAMPBELL
A Naturalist in Boreno. London: 1916. V. 51

SHELLABARGER, SAMUEL
Union Pacific Railroad. Argument of Samuel Shellabarger, before the Committee on the Pacific Railroad in House of Representatives Delivered March 13th and 14th, 1878, in Regard to the Power of Congress to Order and Seizure and Possession of the... Washington City: 1878. V. 47

SHELLEY, E.
Hunting Big Game with Dogs in Africa. Columbus: 1924. V. 49

SHELLEY, GEORGE
The Second Part of Natural Writing...Making a Compleat Body of Penmanship. London: 1714. V. 50

SHELLEY, GEORGE ERNEST
A Handbook to the Birds of Egypt. London: 1872. V. 48; 51; 53
A Monograph of the Nectariniidae or Family of Sun Birds. London: 1876-80. V. 48; 51; 52

SHELLEY, HARRIET
Letters from Harriet Shelley to Catherine Nugent. London: 1889. V. 47; 48

SHELLEY, MARY WOLLSTONECRAFT GODWIN
The Choice. A Poem on Shelley's Death. London: 1876. V. 48
Frankenstein. New York. V. 51
Frankenstein... London: 1818. V. 47; 49; 51; 54
Frankenstein... London: 1831. V. 54
Frankenstein... Philadelphia: 1833. V. 48; 51
Frankenstein... Boston and Cambridge: 1869. V. 52; 54
Frankenstein... New York: 1930. V. 53
Frankenstein... London: 1930's. V. 50
Frankenstein. New York: 1934. V. 49; 52; 53; 54
Frankenstein. 1983. V. 52; 53
Frankenstein. New York: 1983. V. 51; 53
Frankenstein. West Hatfield: 1983. V. 50; 51
Frankenstein... West Hatfield: 1984. V. 48; 52; 54
History of a Six Weeks' Tour through a Part of France, Switzerland, Germany and Holland... London: 1817. V. 54
The Last Man. London: 1826. V. 47; 50; 51
Letters Of... Boston: 1918. V. 50; 54
Lives of the Most Eminent French Writers. Philadelphia: 1840. V. 48
Original Compositions in Prose and Verse. London: 1833. V. 48
Rambles in Germany and Italy 1840-43. London: 1844. V. 53; 54
Tales and Stories by Mary Wollstonecraft Shelley. London: 1891. V. 49
Valperga; Or, The Life and Adventures of Casataruccio, Prince of Lucca. London: 1823. V. 49; 52

SHELLEY, PERCY BYSSHE
Adonais. London: 1886. V. 54
Adonais. London: 1900. V. 52
Adonais... San Francisco: 1922. V. 48
Alastor, or the Spirit of Solitude and Other Poems. London: 1886. V. 53
The Banquet of Plato. Chicago: 1895. V. 51
The Cenci. Italy: 1819. V. 47; 48
The Cenci... London: 1821. V. 50; 51
Complete Poetical Works. Cambridge: 1892. V. 49; 50
The Complete Poetical Works. Oxford: 1904. V. 50
The Complete Works. London & Boston: 1904. V. 54
The Complete Works... London: 1927. V. 48
The Complete Works... 1927-30. V. 47; 51
The Complete Works... London: 1927-30. V. 53
Complete Works. New York & London: 1965. V. 49
The Daemon of the World...The First Part as Published in 1816 with Alastor... London: 1876. V. 48
Epipsychidion... London: 1821. V. 47; 49
Epipsychidion. London: 1921. V. 50
Epipsychidion. 1923. V. 54
Essays, Letters from Abroad. London: 1840. V. 48; 50; 51; 52
Harriet & Mary... Waltham St. Lawrence: 1944. V. 52
Laon and Cynthia. London: 1818. V. 50
Laon and Cynthia... London: 1829. V. 52; 54
Letters from Percy Bysshe Shelley to J. H. Leigh Hunt. London: 1894. V. 47; 50
Lives of the Most Eminent French Writers. Philadelphia: 1840. V. 48
The Lyrical Poems and Translations of Percy Bysshe Shelley. New York: 1924. V. 48
The Masque of Anarchy. London: 1832. V. 47; 49; 51; 52; 54
A Philosophical View of Reform. London: 1920. V. 52
Poems. London: 1880. V. 50
Poems. London: 1889. V. 47
The Poems... London/New York: 1901-02. V. 53
Poems. London: 1902. V. 48; 50; 51; 54
The Poems... London: 1910. V. 50
Poems. Hammersmith: 1914. V. 47; 50; 51
Poems. London: 1914. V. 50; 52
Poems... London: 1922. V. 47
The Poems... Cambridge: 1971. V. 52
Poetical Works. London: 1837. V. 49; 51
The Poetical Works... London: 1839. V. 47; 49; 50; 51; 52; 53; 54
The Poetical Works. London: 1844. V. 48
The Poetical Works... New York: 1845. V. 50
The Poetical Works... London: 1853. V. 48; 51; 54
The Poetical Works... London: 1870. V. 48
The Poetical Works... London: 1872/73/75/75. V. 49
The Poetical Works... London: 1876-80. V. 53
The Poetical Works... London: 1880. V. 49
The Poetical Works... London: 1892. V. 47; 48
The Poetical Works... Hammersmith: 1894-95. V. 47
The Poetical Works. London: 1894-95. V. 47
The Poetical Works. Hammersmith: 1895. V. 48; 52
Posthumous Poems. London: 1824. V. 50; 54
Prometheus Unbound. London: 1820. V. 47; 48; 51; 52; 54
Prometheus Unbound. The Hague: 1917. V. 51; 52; 54
Queen Mab... London: 1813. V. 47
Queen Mab. London: 1821. V. 47; 48; 52
Queen Mab. London: 1829. V. 49
Relics of Shelley. London: 1862. V. 52
The Revolt of Islam: a Poem. London: 1818. V. 49; 52
Rosalind and Helen... London: 1819. V. 47; 48; 50; 52; 53; 54
St. Irvyne; or, the Rosicrucian; a Romance. London: 1811. V. 53; 54
Select Letters of Percy Bysshe Shelley. London: 1882. V. 53
The Sensitive Plant. London: 1899. V. 51
The Sensitive Plant. London: 1911. V. 48; 53
Shelley Memorials: from Authentic Sources. London: 1859. V. 48; 52
Shelley Memorials from Authentic Sources. London: 1875. V. 52
The Shelley Papers. 1833. V. 47
The Shelley Papers. London: 1833. V. 48; 50
Verse and Prose from the Manuscripts of Percy Bysshe Shelley. London: 1934. V. 52
We Pity the Plumage, but Forget the Dying Bird. London: 1835. V. 54
The Works. London: 1834. V. 53
The Works. London: 1836. V. 52
Works... London: 1876. V. 52
The Works... London: 1880. V. 54
The Works. London: 1934. V. 54
Zastrozzi... London: 1810. V. 47
Zastrozzi. London: 1955. V. 51
Zastrozzi. Waltham St. Lawrence: 1955. V. 52

SHELTON, CAROLINE
King William Street, San Antonio, Texas. 1977. V. 50; 51; 52

SHELTON, FREDERICK W.
The Trollopiad; or, Traveling Gentlemen in America. Providence: 1837. V. 52; 53

SHELTON, WILLIAM HENRY
The Jumal Mansion: Being a Full History of the House on Harlem Heights Built by Roger Morris Before the Revolution. Boston: 1916. V. 47; 50

SHELTON, WILLIAM HENRY *continued*
The Salmagundi Club. Boston & New York: 1918. V. 48; 51

SHELVOCKE, GEORGE
Memoirs of the Life of M. du Gue-Trouin, Chief of a Squadron In the Royal Navy of France. London: 1743. V. 48
A Voyage Round the World by the Way of the Great South Sea... London: 1726. V. 50
A Voyage Round the World by the Way of the Great South Sea... London: 1757. V. 48; 50

SHENANDOAH VALLEY RAILWAY CO.
Shenandoah Valley Railway Company Corporate History. Philadelphia: 1891. V. 50

SHENNAN, ROBERT
Tales, Songs and Miscellaneous Poems, Descriptive of Rural Scenes and Manners... Dumfries: 1831. V. 48; 50; 51; 54

SHENSTONE, WILLIAM
The Judgement of Hercules, a Poem. London: 1741. V. 48; 54
The Poetical Works... London: 1798. V. 50
The Poetical Works. Edinburgh: 1854. V. 51
The Works in Verse and Prose... London: 1764. V. 47
The Works in Verse and Prose. London: 1764-69. V. 47; 54
The Works in Verse and Prose. Edinburgh: 1765. V. 50
The Works in Verse and Prose. Edinburgh: 1768. V. 49
The Works in Verse and Prose... London: 1768. V. 51
The Works in Verse and Prose... London: 1773. V. 50
Works in Verse and Prose. London: 1777. V. 50; 52

SHEPARD, ANNA O.
Plumbate... 1948. V. 54
Plumbate... Washington: 1948. V. 50

SHEPARD, ERNEST
Fun and Fantasy. London: 1927. V. 47; 50

SHEPARD, GERALD F.
The Shepard Families of New England. 1971-73. V. 52

SHEPARD, L.
Life During Wartime. 1987. V. 48

SHEPARD, LORENZO B.
The Dignity of Mechanical Labor. New York: 1852. V. 54

SHEPARD, LUCIUS
The Jaguar Hunter. Sauk City: 1987. V. 51
The Jaguar Hunter. U.K: 1988. V. 52
Nantucket Slayrides. Nantucket: 1989. V. 52

SHEPARD, ODELL
Pedlar's Progress; the Life of Bronson Alcott. Boston: 1937. V. 47; 48; 50

SHEPARD, RUPERT
Passing Scene: Eighteen Images of Southern Africa. London: 1966. V. 52

SHEPARD, SAM
Five Plays. Chicago/Icarus's Mother/Red Cross/Fourteen Hundred Thousand/Melodrama. Indianapolis: 1967. V. 51
Fool for Love and other Plays: Angel City: Melodrama Play: Cowboy Mouth: Action: Suicide in B-Flat: Seduced: Geography of a Horse Dreamer. 1984. V. 49
Hawk Moon. Los Angeles: 1973. V. 50; 52
Operation Sidewinder. Indianapolis: 1970. V. 53

SHEPARD, THOMAS
The Parable of the Ten Virgins, Opened and Applied. London: 1660. V. 48
The Parable of the Ten Virgins Opened and Applied. Cambridge: 1695. V. 53

SHEPARD, WILLIAM
Touchstone of Common Assurances; or a Plain and Familiar Treatise, Opening the Learning of the Common Assurances, or Conveyances of the Kingdom. London: 1820. V. 53

THE SHEPHERD Boy; or, Rural Scenes. London: 1840. V. 50

SHEPHERD, C. W.
The North-West Peninsula of Iceland, Being the Journal of a Tour in...1862. London: 1867. V. 48

SHEPHERD, DAVID
An Artist in Africa. 1969. V. 54

SHEPHERD, HENRY ELLIOT
Life of Robert Edward Lee. New York: 1906. V. 49

SHEPHERD, J. C.
Italian Gardens of the Renaissance. London: 1925. V. 51

SHEPHERD, RICHARD
An Essay on Education in a Letter to Sir William Jones, Esq. London: 1782. V. 53

SHEPHERD, RICHARD HERNE
The Bibliography of Carlyle. London: 1881. V. 51
The Bibliography of Dickens. London: 1880. V. 51
The Bibliography of Thackeray. London: 1880. V. 54
The Bibliography of Thackeray. London: 1881. V. 50
Tennysoniana. Notes Biographical and Critical on Early Poems of Alfred and C. Tennyson. London: 1866. V. 51
Waltoniana. London: 1878. V. 50

SHEPHERD, THOMAS H.
London and Its Environs in the Nineteenth Century. London: 1829. V. 54
Metropolitan Improvements... London: 1827-28. V. 50; 53
Metropolitan Improvements... London: 1830. V. 49; 52
Modern Athens, Displayed in a Series of Views... London: 1829. V. 47; 48
Modern Athens, Displayed in a Series of Views... London: 1833. V. 49; 53

SHEPHERD, W.
Systematic Education; or Elementary Instruction in the Various Departments of Literature and Science... London: 1815. V. 52
Systematic Education; or Elementary Instruction in Various Departments of Literature and Science... London: 1817. V. 52

SHEPHERD, WILLIAM
The Life of Poggio Bracciolini. Liverpool: 1802. V. 47
Prairie Experiences in Handling Cattle and Sheep. 1885. V. 47
Prairie Experiences in Handling Cattle and Sheep. New York: 1885. V. 48; 54

SHEPHERD, WILLIAM ASHTON
Life in Bombay and the Neighbourhood of the Persian Gulf. London: 1857. V. 47

THE SHEPHERDESS of the Alps. Newcastle-upon-Tyne: 1820. V. 50

SHEPPARD, EDGAR
Lectures on Madness in Its Medical, Legal and Social Aspects. London: 1873. V. 47

SHEPPARD, ELIZABETH SARA
Charles Auchester: a Memorial. London: 1853. V. 54

SHEPPARD, ERIC WILLIAM
Bedford Forrest, the Confederacy's Greatest Cavalryman. New York: 1930. V. 48; 49; 52

SHEPPARD, J. P.
Literae Cantuarienses, the Letter Books of the Monastery of Christ Church, Canterbury. London: 1887-89. V. 49

SHEPPARD, JAMES
Hints to the Landlord and Tenant: Being a Review of the Present Averages and Showing Their Fallacy, with a Plan for Alteration in Taking the Graduated Scale of Duties, and Remarks Upon Lord Milton's Letter. Doncaster: 1833. V. 49

SHEPPARD, MURIEL EARLEY
Cabins in the Laurel Land. Chapel Hill: 1935. V. 48

SHEPPARD, T.
Bibliography of Yorkshire Geology. 1915. V. 54
Bibliography of Yorkshire Geology. Hull: 1915. V. 53
Handbook to Hull and the East Riding of Yorkshire. London: 1922. V. 47

SHEPPARD, WILLIAM
The Practical Counsellor in the Law. London: 1671. V. 47
The Touch-Stone of Common Assurances... London: 1648. V. 53
The Touch-Stone of Common Assurances... London: 1780. V. 52
The Touch-Stone of Common Assurances. London: 1784. V. 50; 52
Touch-Stone of Common Assurances... London: 1820. V. 48; 50

SHEPPERSON, WILLIAM G.
War Songs of the South. Richmond: 1862. V. 49

SHERARD, ROBERT HARBOROUGH
Emile Zola: a Biographical and Critical Study. London: 1893. V. 53

SHERARD, WILLIAM
Schola Botanica Sive Catalogus Plantarum, Quas ab Aliquot Annis in Horto Regio Parisiensi Studiosis... Amsterdam: 1689. V. 47

SHERATON, THOMAS
The Cabinet Makers Dictionary. London: 1803. V. 52

SHERBORN, CHARLES DAVIES
Index Animalium, sive Index Nominum Quae ab A.D. MDCCLVIII Generibus et Speciebus Animalium Imposita Sunt. Cantabrigiae & London: 1902-32. V. 49
A Sketch of the Life and Work of Charles William Sherborn, Painter-Etcher, with a Catalogue of His Bookplates... London: 1912. V. 50; 53

SHERBURN, GEORGE
The Early Career of Alexander Pope. London: 1934. V. 54

SHERBURNE, HENRY
The Oriental Philanthropist, or True Republican. Portsmouth: 1800. V. 52

SHERBURNE, JOHN HENRY
The Life and Character of John Paul Jones... New York: 1851. V. 47

SHERE, JOHN
The Life and Adventures of a Gold-Digger. London: 1853. V. 50

SHERER, J. W.
Daily Life During the Indian Mutiny. London: 1898. V. 53

SHERER, MOYLE
Military Memoirs of Field Marshal the Duke of Wellington. London: 1830-32. V. 54
Notes and Reflections During a Ramble in Germany. London: 1826. V. 48; 49
Sketches of India... London: 1824. V. 48
Tales of the Wars of Our Time. London: 1829. V. 51

SHERIDAN, FRANCES
The History of Nourjahad. London: 1767. V. 54
Memoirs de Miss Sidney Bidulph. Amsterdam: 1762. V. 54
Memoirs of Miss Sidney Bidulph. London: 1761. V. 47

SHERIDAN, JOHN
A Complete Treatise on the Art of Distillation... London: 1830. V. 47

SHERIDAN, PHILIP HENRY
Outline Descriptions of the Posts in the Military Division of the Missouri. Chicago: 1872. V. 47; 49

Outline Descriptions of the Posts in the Military Division of the Missouri... Chicago: 1876. V. 49

Personal Memoirs of P. H. Sheridan General United States Army. New York: 1888. V. 48; 50; 51

Personal Memoirs of P. H. Sheridan, General United States Army. New York: 1891. V. 53; 54

Records of Engagements with Hostile Indians With the Military Division of the Missouri From 1868-1882. Chicago: 1882. V. 49

Report of Lieut. General P. H. Sheridan Dated September 20, 1881 of His Expedition through the Big Horn Mountains, Yellowstone National Park, Etc. Washington: 1882. V. 50

Reports of Inspection Made in the Summer of 1877...of Country North of the Union Pacific Railroad. Washington: 1878. V. 54

SHERIDAN, RICHARD BRINSLEY BUTLER
The Critic. London: 1781. V. 48; 50; 52
The Critic... London: 1797. V. 47
The Duenna... London: 1775. V. 48
The Duenna... Dublin: 1786. V. 54
The Duenna. Dublin: 1794. V. 51
The Governess, a Comic Opera: As it Is Performed at the Theatre-Royal in Crow-Street. Dublin: 1777. V. 49
The Letters... Oxford: 1966. V. 52
The Love Epistles of Aristaenetus. London: 1771. V. 50
Pizarro: a Tragedy. London: 1799. V. 51
The Plays and Poems of Richard Brinsley Sheridan. Oxford: 1928. V. 51
The Rivals: a Comedy. London: 1775. V. 48
The Rivals: a Comedy. London: 1953. V. 53
The School for Scandal. Dublin: 1781. V. 51; 52
The School for Scandal. London: 1797?. V. 47
The School for Scandal. New York & London: 1910. V. 49
The School for Scandal. London: 1911. V. 48; 51; 54
The School for Scandal... Oxford: 1934. V. 52
The School for Scandal. London: 1949. V. 49
The Speeches. London: 1842. V. 47; 51
Verses to the Memory of David Garrick. London: 1779. V. 47; 49; 53; 54
The Works. London: 1821. V. 48; 49; 51; 52
The Works. London: 1873. V. 50

SHERIDAN, THOMAS
British Education: or, the Source of the Disorders of Great Britain. London: 1756. V. 52
British Education; or, the Source of the Disorders of Great Britain. London: 1769. V. 47
A Complete Dictionary of the English Language Both with Regard to Sound and Meaning... London: 1789. V. 52
A Course of Lectures on Elocution; Together with Two Dissertations on Language... London: 1762. V. 48; 52
A Course of Lectures on Elocution: Together with Two Dissertations on Language... Dublin: 1764. V. 49
A Course of Lectures on Elocution; Together with Two Dissertations on Language... London: 1781. V. 52
A Discourse of the Rise and Power of Parliaments. London: 1677. V. 50; 51
A Full Vindication of the Conduct of the Manager of the Theatre Royal. Dublin: 1747. V. 53
A General Dictionary of the English Language. London: 1780. V. 48; 50
The Life of Dr. Jonathan Swift, Dean of St. Patarick's Dublin. London: 1787. V. 48; 52
A Rhetorical Grammar of the English Language Calculated Solely for the Purpose of Teaching Pronunciation and Justness of Delivery, in That Tongue, by the Organs of Speech. Philadelphia: 1783. V. 49

SHERIDANIANA; or Anecdotes of the Life of Richard Brinsley Sheridan: His Table-talk and Bon Mots. London: 1826. V. 50

SHERIDAN'S and Henderson's Practical Method of Reading and Reciting English Poetry. London: 1796. V. 52

SHERINGHAM, H. T.
A Library in Miniature. London: 1948. V. 51

SHERINGHAM, HUGH
The Book of the Fly-Rod. Boston and New York: 1931. V. 53
The Book of the Fly-Rod. London: 1931. V. 48; 51; 53

SHERK, MICHAEL GONDER
Pen Pictures of Early Pioneer Life in Upper Canada. Toronto: 1905. V. 50

SHERLOCK, HERBERT A.
Black Powder Snapshots. Huntington: 1946. V. 51
Black Powder Snapshots. Huntington: 1948. V. 53

SHERLOCK, MARTIN
Letters from an English Traveller. (with) *New Letters from an English Traveller.* London: 1780/81. V. 48; 51
Lettres d'un Voyageur Anglois. Londres: 1779-80. V. 51

SHERLOCK, THOMAS
A Letter from the Lord Bishop of London, to the Clergy and People of London and Westminster, On Occasion of the Late Earthquakes. London: 1750. V. 53

SHERLOCK, W. P.
Drawing Book of Landscapes, Shipping and Animals, from Designs by Westall, Girtin, Smith, Marlow, Wheatly, Ibbotson, Hill, Anderson. London: 1819. V. 52

SHERLOCK, WILLIAM
The Notes of the Church, As Laid Down by Cardinal Bellarmin; Examined and Confuted. London: 1688. V. 52
A Practical Discourse Concerning Death. London: 1751. V. 49

SHERMAN, ELEAZER
The Narrative of Eleazer Sherman, Giving an Account of His Life, Experience, Call to the Ministry of the Gospel and Travels as Such to the Present Time. Providence: 1828. V. 54

SHERMAN, FRANK DEMPSTER
Little-Folk Lyrics. Boston and New York: 1892. V. 54

SHERMAN, JOHN
A Description of Trenton Falls, Oneida County, New York. Utica: 1828. V. 48

SHERMAN, LYDIA
The Poison Fiend! Life, Crimes and Conviction of Lydia Sherman. Philadelphia: 1873. V. 54

SHERMAN, WILLIAM TECUMSEH
General Orders No. 24. Headquarters, Southern Division of Louisiana. New Orleans: 1865. V. 48
Memoirs of Gen. William T. Sherman, Written by Himself... New York: 1891. V. 52

SHERRIFF, R. C.
Journey's End. A Novel. London: 1930. V. 47; 51; 53

SHERRILL, HUNTING
An Essay on Epidemics as They Appeared in Dutchess County, from 1809 to 1825... New York: 1832. V. 54

SHERRIN, G. C.
The Montagu Motor Book. London: 1912?. V. 47

SHERRIN, R. A. A.
Brett's Historical Series. Auckland: 1890. V. 49

SHERRING, CHARLES A.
Western Tibet and the British Borderland, the Sacred Country of Hindus and Buddhists... 1906. V. 54

SHERRING, M. A.
The Sacred City of the Hindus: an Account of Benares in Ancient and Modern Times. London: 1868. V. 50

SHERRINGTON, CHARLES S.
Inhibition as a Coordinative Factor. Stockholm: 1933. V. 47; 50; 51; 53
The Integrative Action of the Nervous System. London: 1906. V. 50
The Integrative Action of the Nervous System. London: 1911. V. 47; 49; 50; 51; 54
The Integrative Action of the Nervous System. New Haven: 1911. V. 53
The Integrative Action of the Nervous System. Cambridge: 1947. V. 54
Man On His Nature. New York: 1941. V. 50; 52
Note on the Knee-Jerk and the Correlation of action of antagonistic Muscles. V. 50; 53
Selected Writings. New York: 1940. V. 47; 50; 52; 53

SHERWELL, JOHN W.
A Descriptive and Historical Account of the Guild of Saddlers of the City of London. London: 1889. V. 47; 52

SHERWELL, SAMUEL
Old Recollections of an Old Boy. New York: 1923. V. 47

SHERWIN, HENRY
Mathematical Tables. London: 1726. V. 48; 49

SHERWIN-WILLIAMS
The Home Decorator. 1936. V. 51

SHERWOOD, ADIEL
Conversation in a Tent. Macon: 186?. V. 49

SHERWOOD, LORENZO
An Act to Authorise and Provide for the Construction of a Military and Postal Road from Galveston, in the State of Texas, to Fort Gibson in the Indian Territory, with a Branch to Little Rock, in Arkansas. Washington: 1867. V. 47

SHERWOOD, MARGARET
Undercurrents of Influence in English Romantic Poetry. Cambridge: 1934. V. 52

SHERWOOD, MARY MARTHA BUTT
The History of Henry Milner, a Little Boy, Who Was Not Brought Up According to the Fashions of This World. (with) *Second part.* (with) *Third Part.* (with) *Fourth Part.* London: 1822/26/31/37. V. 48
The History of John Marten, a Sequel to the Life of Henry Milner. London: 1844. V. 47
The Lady of the Manor. London: 1825. V. 52
The Lady of the Manor. London: 1841. V. 47; 49; 50; 51; 53
The Lady of the Manor. London: 1860. V. 47
The Life of Mrs. Sherwood, Chiefly Autobiographical. London: 1857. V. 52
My Three Uncles, and the Swiss Cottage. London: 1837-45. V. 47
Roxobel. London: 1831. V. 47; 50; 54

SHERWOOD, MIDGE
Days of Vintage, Years of Vision. San Marino: 1982. V. 53

SHERWOOD, ROBERT
Abe Lincoln in Illinois. New York: 1939. V. 50

SHERWOOD, ROBERT EMMET
Idiot's Delight. New York: 1927. V. 50
Idiot's Delight. New York: 1936. V. 49; 53
The Petrified Forest. New York: 1935. V. 49; 50; 52; 53; 54

SHERWOOD, ROBERT EMMET continued
The Road to Rome. New York: 1927. V. 50; 54
There Shall Be No Night. New York: 1940. V. 50

SHERZER, W. H.
Geologic Atlas of the United States. Washington: 1916. V. 54

SHEW, JOEL
Children Their Hydropathic Management in Health and Disease... New York: 1852. V. 50
Facts in Hydropathy, or Walter Cure. New York: 1847. V. 51
The Hydropathic Family Physician. New York: 1854. V. 51
Hydropathy; or, the Water-Cure: its Principle Modes of Treatment, &c. New York: 1844. V. 48
Hydropathy; or, the Water-Cure; Its Principles, Modes of Treatment &c. New York: 1845. V. 52

SHEW, M. L., MRS.
Water-Cure for Ladies: a Popular Work on the Health, Diet and Regimen of Females and Children, and the Prevention and Cure of Diseases... New York: 1844. V. 52

SHIEL, M. P.
Cold Steel. London: 1929. V. 53
Dr. Krasinski's Secret. New York: 1929. V. 48
How the Old Woman Got Home. London: 1927. V. 47
How the Old Woman Got Home. New York: 1928. V. 53
The Isle of Lies. London. V. 47
The Isle of Lies. London: 1908. V. 54
The Last Miracle. London: 1906. V. 53
The Lord of the Sea. 1901. V. 47
The Lord of the Sea. London: 1901. V. 53
The Pale Ape and Other Pulses. London. V. 47
The Purple Cloud. London: 1901. V. 47
This Knot of Life. London: 1909. V. 49
The Weird O' It. 1902. V. 49

SHIELD, ARNOLD
Billy Boy, the Ferry Boat. London: 1948. V. 50

SHIELD, WILLIAM
Principles and Practice of Harbour Construction. London: 1895. V. 53

SHIELDS, CAROL
Intersect. Ottawa: 1974. V. 54
Others. Ottawa: 1972. V. 53
The Republic of Love. Toronto: 1992. V. 54
Small Ceremonies. Toronto: 1976. V. 53
The Stone Diaries. Toronto: 1993. V. 54

SHIELDS, F. W.
The Strains on Structures of Ironwork; With Practical Remarks on Iron Construction. London: 1861. V. 49

SHIELDS, GEORGE OLIVER
The American Book of the Dog. Chicago: 1891. V. 49
The Big Game of North America. 1890. V. 54
The Big Game of North America... Chicago & New York: 1890. V. 47; 53
The Big Game of North America. London: 1890. V. 52

SHIELLS, WILLIAM
An Account of the Atholl System of Planting and Rearing Larch, as Practised by the Late Duke of Atholl, at Dunkeld. Edinburgh: 1831. V. 53

SHIELS, ARCHIE
San Juan Islands, the Cronstadt of the Pacific. Juneau: 1938. V. 54

SHIERA, EDWARD
Sumerian Texts of Varied Contents. Chicago: 1934. V. 51

SHIFREEN, LAWRENCE J.
A Bibliography of Primary Sources 1919-1992. London: 1993. V. 53
Henry Miller... Ann Arbor: 1993. V. 51
Henry Miller... Paris: 1993. V. 49; 50; 51

SHIGEMORI, K.
The Artistic Garden of Japan. Tokyo: 1957. V. 51

SHILAND, ANDREW
From Ocean to Ocean with Notes and Observations on the Way. New York: 1892. V. 47

SHILLABER, BENJAMIN PENHALLOW
Knitting Work: a Web of Many Textures, Wrought by Ruth Partington. Boston: 1859. V. 51; 52
Life and Sayings of Mrs. Partington. New York & Boston: 1854. V. 52; 54
A Midnight Race. Boston: 1888. V. 54
Mrs. Partington's Tea Party... 1855. V. 47
Mrs. Partington's Tea Pary... London: 1855. V. 50
Partingtonian Patchwork. Boston: 1873. V. 52

SHILLIBEER, JOHN
A Narrative of the Briton's Voyage to Pitcairn's Island. Taunton: 1817. V. 50; 52; 53

SHILLINGFORD, M. A.
Helena the Recluse of the Lake. London: 1840. V. 47

SHILLITO, CHARLES
The Country Book-Club... London: 1788. V. 50; 52
The Country Book-Club... 1964. V. 49

The Country Book-Club. London: 1964. V. 51

SHILLITOE, THOMAS
Journal of the Life, Labours and Travels of Thomas Shillitoe, in the Service of the Gospel of Jesus Christ. London: 1839. V. 54

SHILOH BATTEFIELD COMMISSION
Illinois at Shiloh. Chicago: 1905?. V. 52; 54

SHILTON, RICHARD PHILLIPS
The History of the Town of Newark Upon Trent, In the County of Nottingham, Comprising an Account of Its Antiquities... Newark: 1820. V. 47

SHIMEALL, R. C.
Propsectus for the Publication of the Following Work. New York: 1844. V. 49

SHIMMIN, HUGH
Liverpool Sketches... London: 1862. V. 47

SHINE, THOMAS
The Australian Portrait Gallery and Memoirs of Representative Colonial Men. Sydney: 1885. V. 51

SHINN, CHARLES HOWARD
Graphic Description of Pacific Coast Outlaws: Thrilling Exploits of their Arch-Enemy, Sheriff Harry N. Morse... San Francisco: 1887. V. 47
Mining Camps: a Study in American Frontier Government. New York: 1885. V. 49

SHINN, G. HAZEN
Shoshean Days, Recollections of a Residence of Five Years Among the Indians of Southern California 1885-1889. Glendale: 1941. V. 47

SHINN, JOHN L.
Discussion Between Rev. John L. Shinn, of the Universalist Church and Elder mark H. Forscutt, of the Reorganized Church of Jesus Christ of Later Day Saints, Held at Rock Creek, Ills., August 10th-13th 1875. Plano: 1875. V. 47; 49; 50

SHINWELL, EMANUEL
Conflict Without Malice. London: 1955. V. 52
I've Lived Through It All. London: 1973. V. 54
Lead with the Left. London: 1981. V. 52
Shinwell Talking - a Conversational Biography to Celebrate His Hundredth Birthday. London: 1984. V. 52

SHIP and Short: or Leaves from the Journal of a Cruise to the Levant. New York: 1835. V. 49

A SHIP Called the Bon Jesus of One Thousand Tuns, Sometime Since Loaded on Board at Portobello in the West Indies... 1710?. V. 48

SHIPLEY, MALCOLM A.
Artiticial Flies and How to Make Them. Philadelphia: 1888. V. 47

SHIPLEY, WILLIAM
A True Treatise on the Art of Fly-Fishing. London: 1838. V. 47; 49; 51

SHIPLEY, WILLIAM DAVIES
The Rights of Juries Vindicated. London: 1785. V. 48

SHIPMAN, O. L., MRS.
The Big Bend of Texas. New York: 1928. V. 50

SHIPP, JOHN
Memoirs of the Extraordinary Military Career of John Shipp. London: 1832. V. 47; 50
the Military Bijou; or the Contents of a Soldier's Knapsack; Being the Gleanings of Thirty-Three Years' Active Service. London: 1831. V. 52

SHIPPEN, WILLIAM
Moderation Display'd: a Poem. London: 1704. V. 54

THE SHIP'S Bell. Baltimore: 1927. V. 52; 54

SHIPTON, CLIFFORD K.
National Index of American Imprints through 1800: The Short-Title Evans. Worcester: 1969. V. 48

SHIPTON, E. E.
Nanda Devi. 1936. V. 53
Nanda Devi. London: 1936. V. 54

SHIPWAY, WILLIAM
The Campanalogia; or, Universal Instructor in the Art of Ringing... London: 1813/16. V. 48

SHIRAI, S.
Squalean Phylogeny, a New Framework of 'Squaloid' Sharks... Tokyo: 1992. V. 50; 51

SHIRAKAWA, YOSHIKAZU
Himalayas. New York: 1971. V. 48
Himalayas. 1986. V. 53

SHIRAZI, J. K. M.
Life of Omar Al-Khayyami. V. 50
Life of Omar Al-Khayyami. Edinburgh & London: 1905. V. 54

SHIRIS, GEORGE
Hunting Wild Life with Camera and Flashlight... Washington: 1935. V. 50
Hunting Wild Life with Camera and Flashlight. U.S.A: 1936. V. 52

SHIRK, DAVID
The Cattle Drives of David Shirk, from Texas to the Idaho Mines, 1871 and 1873... Portland: 1956. V. 47; 53

SHIRLEY, ANDREW
Bonington (1801-1828). London: 1940. V. 50

SHIRLEY, DAME
California in 1851, the Letters of Dame Shirley. San Francisco: 1933. V. 53

SHIRLEY, E. P.
Some Account of English Deer Parks with Notes on the Management of Deer. London: 1867. V. 54

SHIRLEY, F.
Rodeo Town (Canadian Texas). Denver: 1953. V. 53

SHIRLEY, JAMES
The Court Secret. London: 1653. V. 48; 49
The Imposture. London: 1652. V. 49
Six New Plays, viz. The Brothers; The Sisters; The Doubtful Heir; The Imposture; The Cardinal; The Court Secret. London: 1652-53. V. 52
The Tragedie of Chabot, Admirall of France... London: 1639. V. 47

SHIRLEY, JOHN
The Life of the Valiant and Learned Sir Walter Raleigh, Knight. London: 1677. V. 48

SHIRLEY, RODNEY W.
The Mapping of the World. London: 1984. V. 48; 49; 53

SHIRLEY, THOMAS
An Address...Grand (Masonic) Lodge of Illinois at Springfield. Alton: 1854. V. 53

SHIRLEY, W. W.
Royal and Historical Letters Illustrative of the Reign of Henry III 1216-1272. London: 1862-66. V. 49; 52

SHIRLEY, WILLIAM
A Letter...to His Grace the Duke of Newcastle with a Journal of the Siege of Louisbourg, and Other Operations of the Forces. London: 1748. V. 54

SHIROKOGOROFF, S. M.
Psychomental Complex of the Tungus. London: 1935. V. 52

SHIRREFS, ANDREW
Poems, Chiefly in the Scottish Dialect. Edinburgh. V. 49
Poems, Chiefly in the Scottish Dialect. Edinburgh: 1790. V. 47; 48; 51

SHOBERL, FREDERIC
Austria; Containing a Description of the Manners, Customs, Character and Costumes. Philadelphia: 1828. V. 48
A Historical Account Interspersed with Biographical Anecdotes of the House of Saxony.... London: 1816. V. 50
Persia, Containing a Brief Description of the Country... London: 1822. V. 53
Persia: Containing a Description of the Country, With an Account Of Its Government, Laws and Religion and of the Chracter, Manners and Customs, Arts, Amusements, Etc. Philadelphia: 1828. V. 48
Picturesque Tour from Geneva to Milan by Way of the Simplon... London: 1820. V. 47; 50; 53
Tales of Woman. London: 1828. V. 50
The World in Miniature... London: 1821. V. 48
The World in Miniature. London: 1822. V. 52
The World in Miniature. London: 1825. V. 47
The World in Miniature: Austria. London: 1823. V. 52
The World in Miniature: Illryia and Dalmatia. London: 1821. V. 52

SHOCK, NATHAN
A Classified Bibliography of Gerontology and Geriatrics. Stanford: 1951. V. 50; 52; 54

SHOEMAKER, R. M.
Reports of Preliminary Surveys for the Union Pacific Railway, Eastern Division, from Fort Riley to Denver City. Cincinnati: 1866. V. 47

SHOENBERG, WILFRED P.
Jesuit Mission Presses in the Pacific Northwest: a History and Bibliography of Imprints 1876-1899. Portland: 1957. V. 54

SHOLOKHOV, MIKHAIL
And Quiet Flows the Don. London: 1934. V. 47; 50
The Don Flows Home to the Sea. London: 1940. V. 47

SHONE, RICHARD
Bloomsbury Portraits. London: 1976. V. 50; 52

SHONTS, EVA MARSHALL
Bells. Chicago: 1926. V. 53

SHOOK, EDWIN M.
Mound E-III-3, Kaminaljuyu, Guatemala. Washington: 1952. V. 52
Tikal Reports Numbers 1-11 in 3 Parts. Philadelphia: 1958-61. V. 52

SHOOTING in the Southwest, Illustrated: Respectfully Dedicated to Ye Lovers of Dog, Gun and Rod. St. Louis: 1880. V. 47

SHOOTING Notes and Comments: a Book Containing Matters of Interest to Sportsmen. Birmingham: 1910. V. 47

SHORE, FREDERICK JOHN
Notes on Indian Affairs. London: 1837. V. 50

SHORE, JOHN
A Charge Deliver'd At The General Quarter Sessions of the Peace, for the County of Sussex, Held at Chichester, on Monday the Fifth Day of April, 1714. London: 1714. V. 53

SHORE, JOHN, BARON TEIGNMOUTH
Memoirs of the Life, Writings and Correspondence... London: 1804. V. 48

SHORE, W. T.
Kent. London: 1907. V. 50

A **SHORT** Account of Algiers...With a Concise View of the Origin of the Rupture Between Algiers and the United States. Philadelphia: 1794. V. 51

A **SHORT** Account of the Late Application to Parliament Made by the Merchants of London Upon the Neglect of Their Trade... London: 1742. V. 47

A **SHORT** Account of the Life and Work of Wynkyn De Worde with a leaf from the Golden Legend Printed by Him at the Sign of the Sun in Fleet Street London, the Year 1527. San Francisco: 1949. V. 48; 49

A **SHORT** Address to the People of Scotland, on the Subject of the Slave Trade. Edinburgh: 1792. V. 47

SHORT, C.
Dramas for the Use of Young Ladies. Birmingham: 1792. V. 47

SHORT, C. W.
Public Buildings: a Survey of Architecture of Projects Constructed by Federal and Other Governmental Bodies Between the Years 1933 and 1939... Washington: 1939. V. 48; 53

A **SHORT** Examination of the Spirit of Quakerism. V. 47

A **SHORT** Explication of Such Foreign Words, as Are Made Use of In Musick Books. London: 1724. V. 47

SHORT, FRANK
Modern Masters of Etching. Sir Frank Short, R. A., P.R.E. London: 1925. V. 50

SHORT, FRANK HAMILTON
Selected Papers: Being Addresses, Civic Studies and Public Letters. San Francisco: 1923. V. 47

SHORT, L.
Woodpeckers of the World. Delaware: 1982. V. 49; 52

A **SHORT** Review of the Recent Affair of Honor Between His Royal Highness the Duke of York, and Lieutenant Colonel Lenox. London: 1789. V. 50

SHORT, THOMAS
Discourses on Tea, Sugar, Milk, Made-Wines, Spirits, Punch, Toobacco &c. with Plain and Useful Rules for Gouty People. London: 1750. V. 47; 49; 54
Medicina Britannica; or, a Treatise on Such Phsycial Plants as Are Generally to be Found in the Fields or Gardens in Great Britain... London: 1746. V. 11
The Natural, Experimental and Medicinal History of the Mineral Waters of Derbyshire, Lincolnshire and Yorkshire... (with) An Essay Towards a Natural, Experimental and Medicinal History of the Principle Mineral Waters of Cumberland, Northumberland... London: 1734/40. V. 52
The Natural, Experimental and Medicinal History of the Mineral Waters of Derbyshire, Lincolnshire and Yorkshire... (with) An Essay Towards a Natural, Experimental and Medicinal History of the Principle Mineral Waters of Cumberland, Northumberland... Sheffield: 1740. V. 50

A **SHORT** Treatise on that Useful Invention called the Sportsman's Friend; or, the Farmer's Footman. Newcastle: 1801. V. 47

A **SHORT** Trip To, At and From Paris. Addressed Not Only to Such as Propose Being Present at the Ceremony of the Marriage of Comte d'Artois, Grandson to the French King... London: 1773. V. 48; 54

A **SHORT** View of the Dispute Between the Merchants of London, Bristol and Liverpool, and the Advocates of a New Joint-Stock Company Concerning the Regulation of the African Trade. London: 1750. V. 54

A **SHORT** View of the Life and Reign of King Charles (The Second Monarch of Great Britain) from His Birth to His Burial. London: 1658. V. 47

A **SHORT** Way to Know the World; or the Rudiments of Geography: Being a New Familiar Method of Teaching Youth the Knowlede of the Globe, and the Four Quarters of the World. London: 1712. V. 53

A **SHORT-HAND** Dictionary, To Which is Prefixed All the Rules or Principles of that Useful and Pleasing Art... London: 1777?. V. 52

SHORT-Title Catalog of Books Printed in Italy and of Books in Italian Printed Abroad 1501-1600 Held in Selected North American Libraries. Boston: 1970. V. 49

SHORT-Title Catalogue of Books Printed in England, Scotland and Ireland and of English Books printed Abroad 1475-1640. London: 1986-76/91. V. 48

SHORTEN, MONICA
Squirrels. London: 1954. V. 48; 52; 53

SHORTER, ALFRED H.
Paper Mills and Paper Makers in England 1495-1800. Hilversum: 1957. V. 48

SHORTER, CLEMENT K.
The Brontes... London: 1908. V. 50
The Brontes. New York: 1908. V. 50
The Brontes... New York: 1909. V. 51
Charlotte Bronte and Her Circle. London: 1896. V. 53

SHORTHOUSE, J. D.
Biology of Insect-Induced Galls. London: 1992. V. 50

SHORTHOUSE, JOSEPH HENRY
Blanche, Lady Falaise: a Tale. London: 1891. V. 53
John Inglesant. A Romance. Birmingham: 1880. V. 47
John Inglesant: a Romance. London: 1881. V. 51
Sir Percival. London: 1886. V. 48; 54

SHORTLAND, E.
Traditions and Superstitions of the New Zealanders. London: 1856. V. 51

SHORTRIDGE, G. C.
The Mammals of South West Africa. London: 1934. V. 47; 48; 49; 51; 52

SHORTT, ADAM
Canada and Its Provinces, a History of the Canadian People and Their Institutions. Toronto: 1914. V. 47

SHORTT, W. T. P.
Collectanea Curiosa Antiqua Dunmonia; or, an Essay on Some Druidical Remains in Devon, and Also On Its Noble Ancietn Camps and Circumvallations... Exter: 1840's. V. 47

SHOSOIN OFFICE
Treasures of the Shosoin. Tokyo: 1965. V. 49

SHOTWELL, AMBROSE M.
Annals of Our Colonial Ancestors and Their Descendants; or, Our Quaker Forefathers and their Posterity... Concord: 1897?. V. 47

SHOUP, PAUL
Side Tracks from the Main Line: Being Occasional Excursions Away from the Business World to the Pleasant Places of Literary Recreation. San Francisco: 1924. V. 51

SHOURDS, THOMAS
History and Genealogy of Fenwick's Colony. Bridgeton: 1876. V. 47; 49; 51

SHOVE'S Business Advertiser and Detroit Directory for 1852-53, Containing a Correct Census of the City for 1852. Detroit: 1852. V. 48

SHOW Window Backgrounds. London: 1934. V. 52

SHOWER, JOHN
Practical Reflections on the Late Earthquakes in Jamaica, England, Sicily, Malta &c. Anno 1692. London: 1693. V. 52; 53

SHRADY, JOHN
The College of Physicians and Surgeons...Founders, Officers, Instructors, Benefactors, and Alumni, a History. New York: 1903. V. 53

SHREVE, F.
Vegetation and Flora of the Sonoran Desert. Stanford: 1964. V. 47

SHREWSBURY, EARL OF
Minutes of Evidence Taken Before the Committee of Privileges to Whom Were Referred the Petition of the Right Honorable Henry John Chetwynd, Earl Talbot to Her Majesty, Praying Her Majesty that the Title Dignity and Peerage or Honors... London: 1857. V. 51

SHUBRICK, W. B.
Robert Frost. A Bibliography. Amherst: 1937. V. 49

SHUCK, OSCAR TULLY
Bench and Bar in California, History, Anecdotes, Reminiscences. San Francisco: 1889. V. 50
California Scrap Book. New York: 1869. V. 48; 50
Historical Abstract of San Fransico. San Francisco: 1897. V. 51
Representative & Leading men of the Pacific... San Francisco: 1870. V. 48
Sketches of Leading and Representative Men of San Francisco. London: 1875. V. 49

SHUCKFORD, SAMUEL
The Sacred and Profane History of the World... London: 1731-37. V. 49
The Sacred and Profane History of the World... Oxford: 1848. V. 48

SHUDAKOY, GRIGORY
Pioneers of Soviet Photography. New York: 1983. V. 49

SHUFELDT, ROBERT W.
Reports of Explorations and Surveys, to Ascertain the Practicability of a Ship Canal Between the Atlantic and Pacific Oceans, by Way of the Isthumus of Tehuantepec. Washington: 1872. V. 47; 50
Reports of Explorations and Surveys to Ascertain the Practicability of a Ship-Canal Between the Atlantic and Pacific Oceans, by the Way of the Isthmus of Tehuantepec. Washington: 1982. V. 53

SHUFFREY, WILLIAM ARTHUR
The Churches of the Deanery of North Craven. Leeds: 1914. V. 53

SHULMAN, DAVID
An Annotated Bibliography of Cryptography. London: 1976. V. 49

SHULMAN, NEIL
Finally I'm a Doctor. New York: 1976. V. 51; 52; 53; 54
What? Dead...Again?. Baton Rouge: 1979. V. 51; 52; 53; 54

SHUMAY, HARRY IRVING
War in the Desert. 1938. V. 54

SHUMWAY, A. L.
Oberliniana: a Jubilee Volume of Semi-Historical Anecdotes Connected with the Past and Present of Oberlin College. Cleveland: 1883. V. 50

SHUMWAY, GEORGE
Conestoga Wagon 1750-1850. 1964. V. 51
Conestoga Wagon 1750-1850, Freight Carrier for 100 Years of America's Western Expansion. York: 1964. V. 47; 50; 53

SHURE, DAVID S.
Hester Bateman. Queen of English Silversmiths.. Garden City: 1959. V. 48
Hester Bateman, Queen of English Silversmiths. London: 1959. V. 54
Hester Bateman. Queen of English Silversmiths. New York: 1959. V. 54

SHURLOCK, MAINWARING
Tiles from Chersey Abbey, Surrey... London: 1855. V. 47

SHUTE, NEVIL
The Chequer Board. London: 1947. V. 49
In The Wet. Melbourne: 1953. V. 51
Most Secret. London: 1945. V. 52
No Highway. London: 1948. V. 53
An Old Captivity. London: 1940. V. 53
On the Beach. London: 1957. V. 48; 49
On the Beach. Melbourne: 1957. V. 50; 53
On the Beach. New York: 1957. V. 47
Pied Piper. New York: 1942. V. 48
A Town Like Alice. London: 1950. V. 53

SHUTTLE, PENELOPE
Delicious Babies. London: 1996. V. 54

SHUTTLEWORTH, ROBERT
A Manual for the Assistance of Magistrates... London: 1815. V. 51

SHWACHMAN, IRENE
We Grew Up in Manhattan: Notes for an Autobiography. Boston: 1984. V. 54

SHWARTZMAN, GREGORY
Phenomenon of Local Tissue Reactivity and Its Immunological, Pathological and Clinical Significance. New York: 1937. V. 49; 51

SIBERELL, LLOYD EMERSON
A Bibliography of the First Editions of John Cowper Powys. Cincinnati: 1934. V. 54

SIBLEY, C. G.
Distribution and Taxonomy of Birds of the World. London: 1991. V. 49
Distribution and Taxonomy of Birds of the World. London: 1991-93. V. 52
Phylogeny and Classification of Birds, a study in Molecular Evolution. London: 1991. V. 49

SIBLEY, CELESTINE
The Magical Realm of Sallie Middleton. Birmingham: 1980. V. 48

SIBLEY, H. H.
Minnesota Territory: Its Present Condition and Prospects. Washington: 1852. V. 48

SIBLEY, JOHN LANGDON
History of the Town of Union, in the County of Lincoln, Maine, to the Middle of the Nineteenth Century. Boston: 1851. V. 50

SIBLY, EBENEZER
The Celestial Science of Astrology: Or, the Art of Foretelling Future Events and Contingencies by the Aspects, Positions and Influences of the Heavenly Bodies. London: 1784-88. V. 50
A Key to Physic and the Occult Sciences. London: 1794. V. 50
A Key to Physic and the Occult Sciences. 1800. V. 54
The Medical Mirror. 1795. V. 54
The Medical Mirror. London: 1795. V. 50

SIBORNE Battle of Waterloo. London: 1830. V. 50

SIBREE, JAMES
Fifty Years' Recollections of Hull; or Half-a-Century of Public Life and Ministry. Hull: 1884. V. 50
A Naturalist in Madagascar, a Record of Observation...During a Period of Over Fifty Years. London: 1915. V. 48

SIBSON, FRANCIS
Medical Anatomy. London: 1869. V. 52

SIBSON, T.
Sketches of Expeditions from the Pickwick Club. London: 1885. V. 54

SIBYLLINE Leaves; or Anonymous Papers: Containing a Letter to the Lord Mayor of London. London: 1755. V. 53

SICHEL, EDITH
The Story of Two Salons. London: 1895. V. 50

SICHEL, JULES
Spectacles: Their Uses and Abuses in Long and Short Sightedness; and the Pathological Conditions Resulting from their Irrational Employment. Boston: 1850. V. 52

SICK, H.
Birds in Brazil, a Natural History. Princeton: 1993. V. 50; 52

SICKLER, JOSEPH
The History of Salem County, New Jersey. Salem: 1937. V. 47; 49; 51

SIDDONS, ANNE RIVERS
The House Next Door. Atlanta: 1993. V. 51
John Chancellor Makes Me Cry. Garden City: 1975. V. 53; 54

SIDDONS, G. A.
The Cabinet-Maker's Guide; or, Rules and Instructions in the Art of Varnishing, Dying, Staining, Japanning, Polishing, Lackering and Beautifying Wood, Ivory, Tortoise-shell & Metal... London: 1830. V. 47; 53

SIDDONS, HENRY
Practical Illustrations of Rhetorical Gesture and Action, Adapted to the English Drama. London: 1807. V. 54

SIDDONS, SARAH KEMBLE
The Story of Our First Parents, Selected from Milton's Paradise Lost... London: 1822. V. 49; 54

SIDGWICK, FRANK
Frank Sidgwick's Diary - and other Material Relating to A. H. Bullen and the Shakespeare Head Press. Oxford: 1975. V. 54
Legendary Ballads. London: 1908. V. 49; 51

SIDGWICK, HENRY
The Elements of Politics. London: 1891. V. 52
The Principles of Political Economy. London: 1883. V. 53

SIDIS, BORIS
Psychopathological Researches: Studies in Mental Dissociation. New York: 1902. V. 52

SIDNEY, ALGERNON
The Arraignment, Tryal and Condemnation of Algernon Sidney, Esq. for High Treason. For Conspiring the Death of the King, and Intending to Raise a Rebellion in This Kingdom. London: 1684. V. 48
Discourses Concerning Government. London: 1698. V. 54
Discourses Concerning Government. London: 1704. V. 48; 52; 53
Discourses Concerning Government. Edinburgh: 1750. V. 47; 50
Discourses Concerning Government. London: 1751. V. 48; 53
Discourses Concerning Government... London: 1763. V. 54
Letters of the Honourable Alglernon Sydney, to the Honourable Henry Savile, Ambassador to France. London: 1742. V. 54
The Works. London: 1772. V. 53

SIDNEY, JOHN APSLEY
A Scheme For Improving Small Sums of Money... Rochester: 1801. V. 49; 52

SIDNEY, MARGARET
The Five Little Peppers and How They Grew. Boston: 1909. V. 50

SIDNEY, PHILIP
Arcadia, Modernised by Mrs. Stanley. London: 1725. V. 47
Astrophel and Stella. London: 1931. V. 47; 48; 50
The Complete Poems. London: 1877. V. 51; 53
The Countess of Pembroke's Arcadia... London: 1598. V. 48
The Countess of Pembroke's Arcadia... London: 1627. V. 50
The Countess of Pembroke's Arcadia. London: 1627-28. V. 51
The Countess of Pembroke's Arcadia... Dublin: 1638. V. 48
The Countess of Pembrokes Arcadia. London: 1638. V. 47; 48; 51
The Countess of Pembroke's Arcadia... London: 1655. V. 47; 50
The Countess of Pembroke's Arcadia. London: 1662. V. 53
The Countess of Pembroke's Arcadia. London: 1674. V. 50; 52; 53
The Countess of Pembroke's Arcadia. London: 1891. V. 54
The Defence of Poesie. London: 1810. V. 48
The Defence of Poesie... Chiswick: 1906. V. 54
The Defence of Poesie... London: 1906. V. 47; 49
The Defence of Poesie... Boston: 1908. V. 47
The Lad Philisides: Being a Selection of Songs, Pastoral Eclogues & Elegies from the Countess of Pembroke's Arcadia. Llandogo: 1988. V. 52
The Miscellaneous Works. Boston: 1860. V. 47; 50
The Prose Works of Sir Philip Sidney. London: 1962. V. 48
Sir Philip Sidney's Astrophel and Stella Wherein the Excellence of Sweet Poesy is Concluded. London: 1888. V. 53
The Works in Prose and Verse. London: 1725. V. 54

SIDNEY, RICHARD CHASE
A Brief Memoir of the Life of...Algernon Sidney, with a short Account of His Trial etc. London: 1835. V. 52

SIDNEY, SAMUEL
The Book of the Horse. London: 1893. V. 48; 51
The Three Colonies of Australia: New South Wales, Victoria, South Australia: Their Pastures, Copper Mines and Gold Fields. London: 1852. V. 48

SIDONIUS, CAIUS SOLLIUS APOLLINARIS
Opera ex Veteribus Libris Aucta & Emendata: Notisque petri Colvi. Lyon: 1598. V. 48
Poema Aureum Eiusdemque Epistole. Milan: 1498. V. 51; 53

SIEBECK, RUDOLPH
Guide Pratique du Jardinier Paysagiste... Paris: 1863. V. 48

SIEBERT, WILBUR H.
The Underground Railroad from Slavery to Freedom. New York: 1899. V. 48

SIEBOLD, P. F. VON
Annales d'Horticulture et de Botanique Pour Flore des Jardins du Royaume des Pays-Bas, et Histoire des Plantes Cultivees... Leiden: 1858-62. V. 47
Siebold's Florilegium of Japanese Plants: Florilegium Plantarum Japonicarum Sieboldii... Tokyo: 1993. V. 50; 51

SIEGEL, C.
Structure and Form in Modern Architecture. 1962. V. 48; 50
Structure and Form in Modern Architecture. New York: 1962. V. 51; 54

SIEGEL, HENRY A.
The Derrydale Press, A Bibliography. Goshen: 1981. V. 47

SIEGL, HELEN
A Felicity of Carols. Barre: 1970. V. 54
A Little Bestiary. A Portfolio of Eight Wood Blocks Cut by Helen Siegl. Philadelphia: 1961. V. 52

SIEGRIST, WALTER W.
The First Seventeen Years and the Dallas Story. Dallas: 1971. V. 47

SIEMENS, C. WILLIAM
On the Conversation of Solar Energy. London: 1883. V. 51; 53
The Scientific Works. London: 1889. V. 48

SIEMENS, GEORGE
The History of the House of Siemens. Freiburg: 1957. V. 50

SIEMENS, WERNER VON
Inventor and Entrepreneur. Recollections of Werner von Siemens. London: 1966. V. 50
Personal Recollections of Werner von Siemens. London: 1893. V. 50

SIEMIENOWICZ, CASIMIR
Artis Magnae Artilleriae. Amsterdam: 1650. V. 52

SIENKIEWICZ, HENRYK
In Vain. Boston: 1899. V. 50
Quo Vadis?. Verona: 1959. V. 48; 53; 54

SIEVEKING, LANCELOT DE GIBERNE
Bats in the Belfry: The Collected Nonsense Poems. London: 1926. V. 48
Smite and Sapre Not. London: 1933. V. 47

SIEVWRIGHT, WILLIAM
Historical Sketch of the Perth Cricket Club (The Premier Club of Scotland) from Its Origin in 1826-27 till 1879. London: 1880. V. 52

SIFFERATH, N. L.
A Short Compendium of the Catechism for the Indians with the Approbation of the Rt. Rev. Frederic Barga, Bishop of Sau Sainte Marie, 1864. Buffalo: 1869. V. 50

SIGAL, CLANCY
Zone of the Interior. New York: 1976. V. 54

SIGERIST, HENRY E.
American Medicine. New York: 1934. V. 50
The Great Doctors. New York: 1933. V. 50; 52
A History of Medicine. New York: 1951-61. V. 53

SIGERSON, GEORGE
History of the Land Tenures and Land Classes of Ireland, with an Account of the Various Secret Agrarian Confederacies. London: 1871. V. 51

SIGNATURES.. 1991. V. 50

SIGONIO, CARLO
Caroli Sigonii de Antiquo Iure Civium Romanorum Libri Duo. (with) Orationes Caroli Sigonii. Paris: 1573/73. V. 52
De Republica Hebraeorum Libri VII. Bologna: 1582. V. 47
De Republica Hebraeorum Libri VII. Frankfurt: 1585. V. 49

SIGOURNEY, LYDIA MARIA HUNTLEY
Illustrated Poems. Philadelphia: 1849. V. 53
Letters to Young Ladies. Hartford: 1833. V. 49; 50; 51; 53
Letters to Young Ladies. New York: 1840. V. 51
Moral Pieces in Prose and Verse. Hartford: 1815. V. 48
Past Meridian. New York: 1864. V. 53
Pocahontas and Other Poems. London: 1841. V. 53
Pocahontas and Other Poems. New York: 1841. V. 53; 54
Sketches. Philadelphia: 1834. V. 54

SIGSBEE, CHARLES D.
Deep-Sea Sounding and Dredging. Washington: 1880. V. 50

SIGSBY, WILLIAM
Life and Adventures of Timothy Murphy... Schoharie: 1839. V. 47; 52
Life and Adventures of Timothy Murphy. Schoharie: 1863. V. 47

SIGUENZA Y GONGORA, DON CARLOS DE
The Mercurio Volante of Don Carlos de Siguenza Y Gongora. Los Angeles: 1932. V. 50

SIGURJONSSON, JOHANN
Loftur, a Play. 1939. V. 51; 54

SIKORSKY, IGOR
Story of the Winged-S. New York: 1948. V. 54

SILBER, EVELYN
The Sculpture of Epstein. London: 1986. V. 48
The Sculpture of Epstein. Oxford: 1986. V. 49

SILBERER, HERBERT
Problems of Mysticism and Its Symbolism. New York: 1917. V. 51

SILCOX, DAVID P.
Christopher Pratt. Toronto: 1981. V. 47
Christopher Pratt. Toronto: 1982. V. 54

SILFORD, WILLIAM
The Court Register and Statesman's Remembrancer... London: 1782. V. 52

SILICATE PAINT CO.
A Handbook on Paint. London: 1939. V. 52

SILIUS ITALICUS, GAIUS
De Bello Punico Libri... Paris: 1531. V. 52; 54
De Bello Punico, Libri... Antwerp: 1567. V. 48
De Bello Punico Libri... Antwerp: 1601. V. 54
De Bello Punico Secundo XVII Libri Nuper Diligentissime Castigati. Venice: 1523. V. 49; 52
Poetae de Belo Punico Libri Septemdecim. Paris: 1533. V. 48

SILIUS ITALICUS, GAIUS continued
Punica. Venice: 1483. V. 48; 54
Punica. Venice: 1493. V. 54
(Punica)...Cum Commentariis Petri Marsi. Venice: 1492. V. 47

SILKO, LESLIE MARMON
Almanac of the Dead. New York. V. 50
Almanac of the Dead. New York: 1977. V. 52
Almanac of the Dead. New York: 1991. V. 53; 54
Ceremony. New York: 1977. V. 47; 50; 51
Laguna Woman. Greenfield Center: 1974. V. 52
Storyteller. New York: 1980. V. 54
Storyteller. New York: 1981. V. 50; 52; 54

SILL, EDWARD ROWLAND
Field Notes. Berkeley: 1882. V. 49
The Prose of Edward Rowland Sill. Boston and New York: 1900. V. 54

SILLAR, DAVID
Poems... Kilmarnock: 1789. V. 48; 51; 52; 53; 54

SILLAR, FREDERICK CAMERON
The Symbolic Pig. Edinburgh & London: 1961. V. 54

SILLIMAN, BENJAMIN
Elements of Chemistry, in the Order of the Lectures Given in Yale College. New Haven: 1830-31. V. 54
A Journal of Travels in England, Holland and Ireland...in the Years 1805 and 1806. New York: 1810. V. 54
Remarks Made On a Short Tour Between Hartford and Quebec, in the Autumn of 1819. New Haven: 1824. V. 48; 52
Review of the Nature, Resources and Plan of Development (Now in Progress) Of the Northern Division of the mariposa Estate. New York: 1873. V. 49
A Tour to Quebec, in the Autumn of 1819. London: 1822. V. 47
A Visit to Europe in 1851. New York: 1856. V. 51

SILLITOE, ALAN
The Death of William Posters. London: 1965. V. 48; 51
The Loneliness of the Long-Distance Runner. London: 1959. V. 51; 54
The Ragman's Daughter. London. V. 54
The Ragman's Daughter. London: 1963. V. 49; 51
The Rats and other Poems. London: 1960. V. 48; 51
Saturday Night and Sunday Morning. London: 1958. V. 51; 54
Saturday Night and Sunday Morning. New York: 1959. V. 49

THE SILLY Jelly Fish. London: 1890. V. 53

SILONE, IGNAZIO
Bread and Wine. New York: 1937. V. 49

SILTZER, FRANK
The Story of British Sporting Prints. 1925. V. 51
The Story of British Sporting Prints. London: 1925. V. 47; 49
The Story of British Sporting Prints. New York: 1925. V. 49; 53; 54
The Story of British Sporting Prints. London: 1929. V. 51

SILVA, ERCOLE
Dell'Arte Dei Giardini Inglesi. Milan: 1801. V. 52

SILVA, OWEN
Mission Music of California: a Collection of Old California Mission Hymns and Masses. Los Angeles: 1941. V. 48

SILVA, T.
A Monograph of Macaws and Conures. North Pickering: 1993. V. 51

SILVANELLA, or the Gypsey: a Novel. Glocester: 1812. V. 54

SILVATICUS, MATTHAEUS
Liber Pedectarum Medicinae. Vicenza: 1480. V. 49

SILVAY, CHALLISS
Pagan Fires. Philadelphia: 1929. V. 51

SILVER, ARTHUR P.
Farm-Cottage, Camp and Canoe In Maritime Canada or the Call of Nova Scotia to the Emigrant and Sportsman. London: 1910. V. 51

SILVER CITY MINING AND MILLING CO.
Silver City Mining and Milling Company. Organized January 25th, 1882. New York: 1882. V. 52

SILVER, DR.
A Poetical Account of the Installation of a Chancellor of the University of Oxford. Oxford: 1810. V. 47

SILVER, GEORGE
A Practical Treatise on the Prevention and Cure of Smoky Chimneys. Glasgow: 1836. V. 52

SILVER, JACOB MORTIMER WIER
Sketches of Japanese Manners and Customs With Original Colored Pictures by Native Artists Reproduced in Facsimile by Means of Chromolithography. London: 1869. V. 51

THE SILVER Mines of Nevada. New York: 1864. V. 49

SILVER Voice: a Fairy Tale Being the Adventures of Harry's Mother, Harry's Sweetheart and Harry Himself. London: 1887. V. 54

SILVERBERG, R.
Lion Time in Timbuctoo. 1990. V. 52
Lord Valentine's Castle. 1980. V. 49; 54
A Time for Changes. London: 1973. V. 49

SILVERBERG, ROBERT
Hawksbill Station. Garden City: 1968. V. 52; 53
Revolt on Alpha C. New York: 1955. V. 52

SILVERSMITH, JULIUS
The Miner's Companion and Guide... San Francisco: 1861. V. 52

THE SILVERTIP Gold Mining and Milling Company... Florence: 1898. V. 50

SILVESTRE, J. B.
Alphabet-Album (or) Collection de 60 Feuilles d'Alphabets... Paris: 1843-44. V. 53

SILVESTRE, M. J. B.
Universal Palaeography; or, Facsimiles of Writings of all Nations and Periods, Copied from the Most Celebrated and Authentic Manuscripts in the Libraries and Archives of France, Italy, Germany and England. London: 1850. V. 47

SIM, T. R.
The Ferns of South Africa... Cambridge: 1915. V. 51
The Forests and Forest Flora of the Colony of the Cape of Good Hope. Aberdeen: 1907. V. 49
Handbook of the Ferns of Kaffraria. Aberdeen: 1891. V. 49

SIMAK, CLIFFORD D.
All Flesh is Grass. New York: 1965. V. 47
City. 1952. V. 47; 49; 52; 54
City. 1954. V. 48; 51
City. London: 1954. V. 47
Destiny Doll. 1971. V. 48; 52
They Walked Like Men. 1960. V. 48
They Walked Like Men. New York: 1962. V. 47; 52
Way Station. Garden City: 1963. V. 54
Way Station. New York: 1963. V. 54
Why Call Them Back from Heaven?. Garden City: 1967. V. 52
The Worlds of Clifford Simak. 1960. V. 48; 52

SIMCOE and Norfolk County: in Commemoration of the Simcoe Reunion of Norfolk Cty. Old Boys Aug. 2nd-7th 1924. Simcoe: 1924. V. 48

SIMCOE, ELIZABETH
The Diary of Mrs. John Graves Simcoe... Toronto: 1911. V. 54

SIMCOE, JOHN GRAVES
The Correspondence of Lieut. Governor John Graves Simcoe, with Allied Documents Relating to His Administration of the Government of Upper Canada. Toronto: 1923-31. V. 50
Simcoe's Military Journal. New York: 1844. V. 48

SIMCOX, G. A.
Recollections of a Rambler. London: 1874. V. 51

SIME, DAVID
The Edinburgh Musical Miscellany: A Collection of the Most Approved Scotch, English and Irish Songs... Edinburgh: 1792. V. 49
In Manbury City. London: 1876. V. 54

SIME, WILLIAM
King Capital: a Tale of Provincial Ambition. London: 1883. V. 54

SIMENON, GEORGES
The First-Born. New York: 1947. V. 54
The Glass Cage. New York: 1973. V. 49
Maigret Afraid. New York: 1983. V. 49
Maigret Chez Le Ministre. Lakeville: 1954. V. 47
Maigret Sits It Out. New York: 1941. V. 50
November. New York: 1970. V. 50
The Patience of Maigret. New York: 1940. V. 48
The Rich Man. New York: 1971. V. 50
The Shadow Falls. New York: 1945. V. 53
The Snow Was Black. New York: 1950. V. 53

SIMEON, JOHN
Sixty Sermons Preach'd on Several Occasions. Oxford: 1724. V. 50

SIMEON, OF DURHAM
Opera Omnia. London: 1882-85. V. 49

SIMEONI, GABRIELE
Epitome de l'Origine et Svccession de la Dvche De Ferrare. Paris: 1553. V. 48; 52
Les Illustres Observations Antiques... Lyons: 1558. V. 47; 49; 50

SIMES COMPANY, INC.
The Simes Company, Inc. Lighting Consultants. A Valuable Reference of Lighting In All Its Branches, Covering the Application of Traditional Styles and Contemporary Trends. New York: 1939. V. 47

SIMIC, CHARLES
Biography and a Lament Poems 1961-1967. Hartford: 1976. V. 48; 52
The Chicken Without a Head: a New Version. Portland: 1983. V. 47
Displaced Person. New York: 1995. V. 54
Interlude. Salem: 1981. V. 48
Sharing at Night. Poems. San Francisco: 1982. V. 47; 54
Somewhere Among Us a Stone is Thinking Notes. San Francisco: 1969. V. 47
They Forage at Night. New York: 1980. V. 47; 50; 54

SIMIC, CHARLES continued
White. London: 1972. V. 52
White. New York: 1972. V. 48

SIMIENOWIC, CASIMIR
The Great Art of Artillery... London: 1729. V. 50; 54

SIMINGTON, ROBERT C.
The Civil Survey, AD 1654-56, County of Tipperary. 1931/34. V. 52

SIMKIN, RICHARD
British Yeomanry Uniforms. 1971. V. 50

SIMMA, BRUNO
The Charter of the United Nations, A Commentary. New York: 1994. V. 53

SIMMONDS, PETER LUND
The Curiosities of Food. London: 1859. V. 54
Sir John Franklin and the Arctic Regions: Showing the Progress of British Enterprise for the Discovery of the North-West Passage During the Nineteenth Century. London: 1851. V. 48
Tropical Agriculture, a Treatise on the Culture, Preparation, Commerce and Consumption of the Principal Products of the Vegetable Kingdom. London: 1877. V. 48

SIMMONDS, RALPH
All About Airships. London: 1911. V. 47

SIMMONS, A. D.
Wing Shots. A Series of Camera Studies of American Game Birds and Other Birds of Field and Stream on the Wing. New York: 1936. V. 49

SIMMONS, AMELIA
American Cookery; Or the Art of Dressing Viands, Fish, Poultry and Vegetables. Walpole: 1812. V. 50
American Cookery, or the Art of Dressing Viands, Fish, Poultry and Vegetables... Brattleborough: 1814. V. 49

SIMMONS, C. F.
Home, Sweet Home. A Home In Sunny South Texas for a Song. San Antonio: 1906. V. 49; 52

SIMMONS, DAN
Carrion Comfort. 1989. V. 54
Carrion Comfort. Arlington Heights: 1989. V. 52
Carrion Comfort. 1990. V. 54
Children of the Night. 1992. V. 47
Children of the Night. Northridge: 1992. V. 48; 49; 51; 52; 53; 54
Entrophy's Bed at Midnight. 1990. V. 51
Entrophy's Bed at Midnight. Northampton: 1990. V. 49
Entropy's Bed at Midnight. Northridge: 1990. V. 49; 54
The Fall of Hyperion. New York: 1990. V. 54
The Hollow Man. 1992. V. 47; 49; 51; 52; 54
The Hollow Man. Northridge: 1992. V. 48; 49; 51; 54
Hyperion. 1989. V. 48
Hyperion. New York: 1989. V. 49; 52; 54
Phases of Gravity. London: 1989. V. 49
Phases of Gravity. 1990. V. 54
Phases of Gravity. London: 1990. V. 52
Prayers to Broken Stones. Arlington Heights: 1990. V. 52
Song of Kali. New York: 1985. V. 51; 52
Song of Kali. 1987. V. 54
Summer Sketches. 1992. V. 47; 49; 51; 54
Summer Sketches. Northridge: 1992. V. 48; 49; 50; 51; 54

SIMMONS, ENOCH SPENCER
A Solution of the Race Problem of the South. Raleigh: 1898. V. 49

SIMMONS, J. C.
The History of Southern Methodism on the Pacific Coast. Nashville: 1886. V. 51

SIMMONS, JAMES
The Diaries of James Simmons: Paper Maker of Haslemere, 1831-1868. 1990. V. 47
The Diaries of James Simmons: Paper Maker of Haslemere, 1831-1868. London: 1990. V. 50
Out On the Edge. Leeds: 1958. V. 51

SIMMONS, JOHN
An Account of a Simple, Easy and Effectual Method for Preserving His Majesty's Navy, From Its Present Great Decays. London: 1774. V. 52

SIMMONS, MARC
Along the Santa Fe Trail. Albuquerque: 1986. V. 54

SIMMONS, NOAH
Heroes and Heroines of the Fort Dearborn Massacre. Lawrence: 1896. V. 52

SIMMONS, OWEN
The Book of Bread. London: 1903. V. 48; 50; 51

SIMMONS, P. L.
The Arctic Regions and Polar Discoveries During the Nineteenth Century. London New York: 1878. V. 50

SIMMONS, RALPH B.
Boulder Dam and the Great Southwest. Los Angeles: 1936. V. 53

SIMMONS, SAMUEL
Elements of Anatomy and the Animal Economy. London: 1775. V. 52

SIMMS, D.
The Text-Book; or Easy Instructions in the Elements of the Art of Printing... Belfast: 1826. V. 48

SIMMS, FREDERICK WALTER
Practical Tunnelling... London: 1860. V. 49
Practical Tunnelling. London: 1896. V. 53
Public Works of Great Britain Consisting of Railways...Cast Iron Bridges, Iron and Gas Works. London: 1838. V. 50
A Treatise on the Principal Mathematical Instruments Employed in Surveying, Levelling and Astronomy. London: 1836. V. 48

SIMMS, HARRY
Martin Chuzzlewit. A Drama in Four Acts. London: 1886. V. 49
Nicholas Nickleby. London: 1883?. V. 49

SIMMS, JEPTHA R.
Trappers of New York: or, a Biography of Nicholas Stoner and Nathaniel Foster... Albany: 1851. V. 48

SIMMS, WILLIAM GILMORE
Atalantis. New York: 1832. V. 53
Beauchampe, or the Kentucky Tragedy. Philadelphia: 1842. V. 53; 54
The Charleston Book. Charleston: 1845. V. 54
Count Julian; or the Last Days of the Goth. London: 1846. V. 54
The Damsel of Darien. Philadelphia: 1839. V. 48; 53; 54
Donna Florida. Charleston: 1843. V. 49
Guy Rivers. New York: 1834. V. 54
The Life of Captain John Smith, the Founder of Virginia. New York: 1846. V. 47
The Life of Nathanael Greene, Major General in the Army of the Revolution. New York: 1849. V. 47; 52; 53
The Life of the Chevalier Bayard; "The Good Knight". New York: 1847. V. 47; 51
The Lily and the Totem, or, the Huguenots in Florida. New York: 1850. V. 53; 54
Marie de Berniere. Philadelphia: 1853. V. 53; 54
Martin Faber, the Story of a Criminal. New York: 1837. V. 53; 54
Pelayo. New York: 1828. V. 53
Pelayo. New York: 1838. V. 54
Poems, Descriptive, Dramatic, Legendary and Contemplative. New York: 1853. V. 53; 54
Richard Hurdis; or, the Avenger of Blood. Philadelphia: 1838. V. 48
Southern Passages and Pictures. New York: 1839. V. 50; 53; 54
Southward Ho! A Spell of Sunshine. New York: 1854. V. 47
Transatlantic Tales, Sketches and Legends. London: 1842. V. 53; 54
War Poetry of the South. New York: 1867. V. 51
The Wigwam and the Cabin. First (and Second) Series. New York: 1845. V. 52

SIMOENS, GUILLAUME
The Gold and the Tin in the South East of Ireland. Dublin: 1921. V. 53

SIMON, ANDRE
Bibliotheca Vinaria. London: 1979. V. 51
The Star Chamber Dinner Accounts, Being Some Hitherto Unpublished Accounts of Dinners Provided for the Lords of the Privy Council in the Star Chamber, Westminster... London: 1959. V. 48

SIMON, CHARLES
An Introduction to the Study of Infection and Immunity Including Chapters on Serum Therapy, Vaccine Therapy, Chemotherapy and Serum Diagnosis. Philadelphia: 1912. V. 51

SIMON, JOHN
English Sanitary Institutions, Reviewed in Their Course of Development, and In some of Their Political and Social Relations. London: 1890. V. 50; 51
English Sanitary Institutions, Reviewed In Their Course of Development and In Some of Their Political and Social Relations. London: 1897. V. 50; 52
General Pathology, As Conducive to the Establishment Of Rational Principles for the Diagnosis and Treatment of Disease. Philadelphia: 1852. V. 49; 52; 54

SIMON, NEIL
Barefoot in the Park. New York: 1964. V. 51
The Gingerbread Lady. New York: 1971. V. 50
The Odd Couple. New York: 1966. V. 52
Promises, Promises. New York: 1969. V. 50

SIMON, OLIVER
A Conversation Piece. London: 1933. V. 49
The Curwen Press Miscellany. 1931. V. 53
The Curwen Press Miscellany. Plaistow: 1931. V. 47
The Double Crown Club. V. 54
Printing of To-Day: an Illustrated Survey. London & New York: 1928. V. 48; 50; 52

SIMON, OSWALD JOHN
The World and the Cloister, a Novel. London: 1890. V. 49

SIMON, RICHARD
The Critical History of the Religions and Customs of the Eastern Nations. London: 1685. V. 49
The History of the Original and Progress of Ecceiasatical Revenues... London: 1685. V. 54

SIMON, THOMAS
Medals, Coins, Great Seals and Other Works. London: 1780. V. 47

SIMOND, LOUIS
Journal of a Tour and Residence in Great Britain, During the Years 1810 and 1811... Edinburgh: 1815. V. 52
Journal of a Tour and Residence in Great Britain, During the years 1810 and 1811. Edinburgh: 1817. V. 50; 52

SIMONDE DE SISMONDI, JEAN CHARLES LEONARD
Historical View of the Literature of the South of Europe... London: 1823. V. 47; 52
Historical View of the Literature of the South of Europe. New York: 1827. V. 47
Political Economy and the Philosophy of Government. London: 1847. V. 47; 52

SIMONIN, L.
Underground Life. London: 1869. V. 54

SIMONS, ALBERT
Charleston, South Carolina. New York: 1927. V. 51

SIMON'S Essay on Irish Coins and the Currency of Foreign Monies in Ireland...with Mr. Snelling's Supplement and an Additional Plate. Dublin: 1810. V. 47

SIMONS, J.
Handbook for the Study of Egyptian Topographical Lists Relating to Western Asia. Leiden: 1937. V. 49
Jerusalem in the Old Testament; Researches and Theories. Leiden: 1952. V. 52

SIMONS, JOHN HUME
The Planter's Guide and Family Book of Medicine. Charleston: 1849. V. 48

SIMONSEN, R.
Atlas and Catalogue of the Diatom Types of Friedrich Hustedt. Berlin: 1987. V. 50

SIMONSON, GEORGE A.
Francesco Guardi, 1712-1793. London: 1904. V. 51; 53

SIMOPOULOS, KYRIAKOS
How Foreigners Saw the Greece of 1821. Athens: 1981-87. V. 48

SIMPLE Studies of Natural History: Birds. London: 1835. V. 47; 50

SIMPSON, ALEXANDER
The Sandwich Islands: Progress of Events Since Their Discovery by Captain Cook. London: 1843. V. 50

SIMPSON, ANNA PRATT
Problems Women Solved. San Francisco: 1915. V. 50; 53

SIMPSON, ARTHUR J.
Southwest Texans. San Antonio: 1953. V. 53

SIMPSON, C. T.
A Descriptive Catalogue of the Naiades or Pearly Freshwater Mussels. Detroit: 1914. V. 54

SIMPSON, CHARLES
The Harboro' Country. London: 1927. V. 47
El Rodeo. London: 1925. V. 48
Trencher & Kennel. Some famous Yorkshire Packs. London: 1927. V. 47

SIMPSON, DAVID
A Discourse On Dreams and Night-Visions With Numerous Examples Ancient and Modern. Macclesfield: 1791. V. 50
A Plea for Religion and the Sacred Writings; Addressed to the Disciples of Thomas Paine, and Wavering Christians of Every Persuasion... (with) A Remarkable Narrative of the Murder of a French Lady. Manchester: 1823/24. V. 47

SIMPSON, EDWARD
A Treatise on Ordnance and Naval Gunnery, Compiled and Arranged as a Text Book for the U.S. Naval Academy. New York: 1862. V. 48

SIMPSON, ELIZABETH
Earthlight, Wordfire. The Work of Ivan Doig. Moscow: 1992. V. 50

SIMPSON, EVELYN
A Study of the Prose Works of John Donne. 1924. V. 54

SIMPSON, F. A.
Journal of M. M. Marmaduke Of a trip from Flin, Missouri to Santa Fe, New Mexico in 1824. Columbia: 1911. V. 51

SIMPSON, F. GERALD
Watermills and Military Works on Hadiran's Wall. London: 1891. V. 48
Watermills and Military Works on Hadrian's Wall. Kendal: 1976. V. 47

SIMPSON, FRANK
The Chester Volunteers with Special Reference to "A" Company, 3rd Volunteer Battalion The Cheshire Regiment (1914-1920). Chester: 1922. V. 48; 53
A History of the Church of St. Peter in Chester. Chester: 1909. V. 50; 53

SIMPSON, GEORGE
Journal of Occurrences in the Athabasca Department... 1820 and 1821... London: 1938. V. 47; 48
Journal of Occurrences in the Athabasca Department...1820 and 1821... Toronto: 1938. V. 51
Narrative of a Journey Round the World During the Years 1841 and 1842. London: 1847. V. 47; 48; 49; 50; 51; 52
Narrative of a Voyage to California Ports in 1841-42. Together with Voyages to Sitka, the Sandwich Islands & Okhotsk... San Francisco: 1930. V. 47; 48; 53; 54
An Overland Journey Round the World, During the Years 1841 and 1842. Philadelphia: 1847. V. 47; 53
Part of Dispatch from George Simpson, Esq., Governor of Ruperts Land, to the Governor and Committee of the Hudson's Bay Company, London, March 1, 1829. London: 1947. V. 47; 49; 53; 54
Part of Dispatch from George Simpson Esqr. Governor of Ruperts Land to the Governor and Committee of the Hudson's Bay Company London, March 1, 1829, Continued and Completed March 24 and June 5, 1829. Toronto: 1947. V. 51

SIMPSON, HAROLD B.
Hood's Texas Brigade in Poetry and Song. Hillsboro: 1968. V. 54

SIMPSON, HENRY
The Lives of Eminent Philadelphians, Now Deceased. Philadelphia: 1859. V. 50

SIMPSON, HENRY I.
The Emigrant's Guide to the Gold Mines. Haverford: 1978. V. 47; 48; 51; 54

SIMPSON, HENRY TRAIL
Archaeologia Adelensis, or a History of the Parish of Adel, in the West Riding of Yorkshire, Being an Attempt to Delineate Its Past and Present Associations... London: 1879. V. 54

SIMPSON, JAMES H.
Report from the Secretary of War Communicating...the Report and Map of the Route From Fort Smith Arknasas, to Santa Fe, New Mexico. Washington: 1850. V. 47
Report of Explorations Across the Great Basin of the Territory of Utah... Washington: 1876. V. 47
Report of the Secretary of War, Communicating...Captain Simpson's Report and Map of Wagon Road Routes in Utah Territory. Washington: 1859. V. 47
Report of...On the Union Pacific Railroad and Branches, Central Pacific Railroad of California, Northern Pacific Railroad, Wagon Roads in the Territories of Idaho, Montana, Dakota and Nebraska, and the Washington Aqueduct... Washington: 1866. V. 47
Route from Fort Smith to Santa Fe. Letter from the Secretary of War, Transmitting...a Report and Map of Lieutenant Simpson, of the Route from Fort Smith to Santa Fe... Washington: 1850. V. 47
The Shortest Route to California. Philadelphia: 1869. V. 47

SIMPSON, JAMES YOUNG
Acupressure, a New Method of Arresting Surgical Haemorrahge and of Accelerating the Healing of Wounds. Edinburgh: 1864. V. 52
Antiquarian Notices of Leprosy and Leper Hospitals in Scotland and England. Edinburgh: 1841. V. 48
Archaic Sculpturings of Cups, Circles, &c. Upon Stones and Rocks in Scotland, England and Other Countries. Edinburgh: 1867. V. 47; 51
The Cat-Stane, Edinburghshire... Edinburgh: 1862. V. 51
Clinical Lectures on Diseases of Women. Philadelphia: 1863. V. 50; 52
The Obstetric Memoirs and Contributions. Philadelphia: 1855. V. 50
Selected Obsterical and Gynaecological Works... New York: 1871. V. 48; 49; 50

SIMPSON, JOHN
A Complete System of Cookery, on a Plan Entirely New. London: 1815?. V. 48

SIMPSON, KEITH
Forensic Medicine. London: 1947. V. 54

SIMPSON, LESLEY BYRD
The Encomienda in New Spain: Forced Native Labour in the Spanish Colonies, 1492-1550. Berkeley: 1929. V. 52
The San Saba Papers. San Francisco: 1959. V. 54

SIMPSON, LOUIS
Armidale. Brockport: 1979. V. 52
The Arrivistes. New York: 1949. V. 48; 49
The Invasion of Italy. Easthampton: 1976. V. 48
The Invasion of Italy. Northampton: 1976. V. 47
Poets of Today II. New York: 1955. V. 49

SIMPSON, MONA
The Lost Father. New York: 1992. V. 52

SIMPSON, N. DOUGLAS
A Bibliographical Index of British Flora... Bournemouth: 1960. V. 52; 53

SIMPSON, PERCY
Proof-Reading in the Sixteenth, Seventeenth and Eighteenth Centuries. London: 1935. V. 47

SIMPSON, RICHARD, CO., LTD.
Largest Dealers in Baby Carriages, Baby Vehicles and Reed Furniture in Canada. Toronto: 1902. V. 52

SIMPSON, ROBERT
The History and Antiquities of the Town of Lancaster. Lancaster: 1852. V. 48; 53

SIMPSON, STEPHEN
The Lives of George Washington and Thomas Jefferson. Philadelphia: 1833. V. 53

SIMPSON, T.
Observations on Asiatic Cholera: and facts Regarding the Mode of Its Diffusion. London: 1849. V. 48
A Specimen of Sketching Landscapes, in a Free and Masterly Manner... London: 1781. V. 50

SIMPSON, THOMAS
The Doctrine and Application of Fluxions. London: 1806. V. 49; 51
Essays on Several Curious and Useful Subjects, in Speculative and Mix'd Mathematics. London: 1740. V. 49
Mathematical Dissertations on a Variety of Physical and Analytical Subjects. London: 1743. V. 49
The Nature and Laws of Chance. London: 1792. V. 49
Select Exercises for Young Proficients in the Mathematicks. London: 1752. V. 51; 52
A Treatise of Algebra: Wherein the Fundamental Principles are Fully and Clearly Demonstrated and Applied to the Solutions of a Great Variety of Problems. London: 1745. V. 48

SIMPSON, W. J.
A Treatise on Plague Dealing with the Historical Epidemiological, Clinical, Therapeutic and Preventive Aspects of the Disease. Cambridge: 1905. V. 50; 51

SIMPSON, WALTER
A History of the Gipsies with Specimens of the Gipsy Language. London: 1865. V. 50

SIMPSON, WILLIAM
Hydrologia Chymica; or, the Chymical Anatomy of the Scarbrough (sic) and Other Spaws in Yorkshire. London: 1669. V. 48; 50; 54
Meeting the Sun: a Journey All Round the World, Through Egypt, China, Japan and California... London: 1874. V. 50
Picturesque People. London: 1876. V. 52
A Private Journal Kept During the Niger Expedition, from the Commencement in May 1841, Until the Recall of the Expedition in June 1842. London: 1843. V. 54
The Seat of the War in the East. London: 1855. V. 51
The Seat of the War in the East. First and Second Series. London: 1855-56. V. 47

SIMPSON, WILLIAM KELLY
Papyrus Reisner. Boston: 1963. V. 51

SIMS, AGNES C.
San Cristobal Petroglyphs. Santa Fe: 1950. V. 49

SIMS, GEORGE
An Illustrated design Book of Cabinet Furniture, Manufactured of the Best Seasoned Materials and the Most Approved Styles. London: 1868. V. 52
The Sand Dollar. London: 1969. V. 49
Sleep No More. London: 1966. V. 52

SIMS, GEORGE R.
Living London, Its Works and the Plays. London: 1902. V. 50

SIMS, JOHN
Dissertatio Medica Inauguralis, Quaedam de Cerebri Concussione Malisque Inde Oriundis... Edinburgh: 1818. V. 53

SIMS, JOSEPH PATTERSON
Old Philadelphia Colonial Details. New York: 1914. V. 51

SIMS, ORLAND
Gun-Toters I Have Known. Austin: 1967. V. 49

SIMS, R. G.
Sayings and Doings. London: 1994. V. 50; 53

SIMS, RICHARD
A Manual for the Genealogist, Topographer, Antiquary, and Legal Professor... London: 1856. V. 50; 54

SIMSON, JOHN
The Case of Mr. John Simson Professor of Divinity in the University of Glasgow. Edinburgh: 1727. V. 48

SIMSON, ROBERT
Opera Quaeda Reliqua... Glasgow: 1776. V. 48
Sectionum Conicarum Libri Quinque. London: 1750. V. 50
Sectionum Conicarum Libri Quinque. London: 1750. V. 54
A Treatise Concerning Porisms. Canterbury: 1777. V. 49

SINCE Man Began to Eat Himself. Mt. Horeb: 1986. V. 49; 54

SINCLAIR, A. G.
The Critic Philosopher; or Truth Discovered... London: 1789. V. 48

SINCLAIR, ARTHUR
Two Years in Alabama. Boston: 1895. V. 49
Two Years On the Alabama. London: 1896. V. 49

SINCLAIR, CATHERINE
Hill and Valley, or Hours in England and Wales. Edinburgh: 1838. V. 50; 54
Lord and Lady Harcourt; or, Country Hospitalities. London: 1850. V. 50
Modern Accomplishments, or The March of Intellect. Edinburgh: 1836. V. 53
Modern Accomplishments, or the March of Intellect. Edinburgh: 1838. V. 49; 50; 51
Modern Flirtations: or, a Month at Harrowgate. London: 1843. V. 47
Modern Society; or, the March of Intellect. Edinburgh: 1847. V. 53

SINCLAIR, GEORGE
Hortus Gramineus Woburnensis... London: 1825. V. 52; 54
Hortus Gramineus Woburnensis... London: 1826. V. 54
Useful and Ornamental Planting. London: 1832. V. 54

SINCLAIR, IAIN
Downriver. London: 1991. V. 54
White Chappell... London: 1987. V. 51
White Chappell. Uppingham: 1987. V. 53; 54

SINCLAIR, J. A.
Airships in Peace and War. London: 1934. V. 49

SINCLAIR, JOHN
An Account of the Systems of Husbandry Adopted in the More Improved Districts of Scotland. Edinburgh: 1812. V. 52; 54
An Account of the Systems of Husbandry Adopted in the More Improved Districts of Scotland. London: 1812. V. 49
Address to the Society for the Improvement of British Wool, Constituted at Edinburgh on Monday Jan. 31, 1791. London: 1791. V. 52; 53
The Code of Agriculture. London: 1819. V. 53
The Code of Agriculture... London: 1832. V. 47
The Correspondence of the Right Honourable Sir John Sinclair, Bart. London: 1831. V. 51
The History of the Public Revenue of the British Empire. London: 1785. V. 48
The Night the Bear Came Off the Mountain. Santa Fe: 1991. V. 52
Observations of the Scottish Dialect. London: 1782. V. 48
The Propriety of Retaining Gibraltar Impartially Considered. London: 1783. V. 47
Radon Daughters. London: 1994. V. 54

SINCLAIR, MAY
Feminism. London. V. 52
The Rector of Wyck. London: 1925. V. 51

SINCLAIR, TOLLEMACHE
A Defence of Russia and the Christians of Turkey... London: 1877. V. 48

SINCLAIR, UPTON
Between Two Worlds. New York: 1941. V. 52
The Book of Life Mind and Body. Pasadena: 1921. V. 52
Cliff Farady in Command or the Fight of His Life... New York: 1899. V. 51; 52
Co-op: A Novel of Living Together. Pasadena: 1936. V. 48
Dragon's Teeth. New York & Pasadena: 1942. V. 48
The Goose-Step: a Study of American Education. Pasadena: 1923. V. 50
The Jungle. New York: 1906. V. 47; 48; 50; 51; 53
The Jungle. Ann Arbor: 1945. V. 53; 54
The Jungle. Baltimore: 1965. V. 53; 54
The Millennium. 1929. V. 52
No Pasaran! (They Shall Not Pass). 1937. V. 49
No Pasaran! (They Shall Not Pass). Girard: 1937. V. 49
O Shepherd, Speak!. Monrovia: 1949. V. 54
One Clear Call. New York: 1948. V. 52
One Hundred Percent. The Story of a Patriot. Pasadena: 1920. V. 52
Our Lady. New York: 1938. V. 54
The Overman. New York: 1907. V. 48
Presidential Agent. New York and Monrovia: 1944. V. 50; 52
Roman Holiday. Pasadena: 1931. V. 54
Springtime and Harvest. New York: 1901. V. 48
Theirs Be the Guilt. New York: 1959. V. 50
World to Win. Monrovia: 1946. V. 53
World's End. New York: 1940. V. 54

SINDERMANN, C. J.
Principal Diseases of Marine Fish and Shellfish. New York: 1990. V. 49; 52

SINECURE, SHANDY, PSEUD.
Fiar Play, or, Who Are the Adulterers, Slandereres and Demoralizers. London: 1820. V. 47

SINEL, JOSEPH
A Book of American Trade-Marks & Devices. New York: 1924. V. 47; 50; 52

SINGER, CHARLES
The Evolution of Anatomy: a Short History of Anatomical and Physiological Discovery to Harvey. New York: 1925. V. 50; 52
From Magic to Science: Essays on the Scientific Twilight. London: 1928. V. 50; 52; 54
A History of Technology. Oxford: 1954-58. V. 53
A History of Technology. New York and London: 1954-58/57-59. V. 50
A History of Technology. Oxford and New York: 1954-84. V. 49
A History of Technology. Oxford: 1956-58. V. 49
A History of Technology. Oxford: 1967-84. V. 47
A Prelude to Modern Science... Cambridge: 1946. V. 49; 50
A Prelude to Modern Science. London: 1946. V. 51; 52; 53
Science, Medicine and History. London New York: 1953. V. 54
A Short History of Medicine. Oxford: 1928. V. 52
Studies in the History and Method of Science. Oxford: 1917-21. V. 47; 48; 49; 50; 51; 52; 53
Studies in the History and Method of Science. Oxford: 1917-21/56. V. 54
Studies in the History and Method of Science. Oxford: 1921. V. 47; 48; 50; 51
Studies in the History and Method of Science. 1975. V. 47
Vesalius on the Human Brain. London: 1952. V. 53

SINGER, D. W.
Catalogue of Latin and Vernacular Plague Texts in Great Britian and Eire in Manuscripts Written Before the Sixteenth Century. Paris and London: 1950. V. 49

SINGER, H. W.
Complete Etchings of Rembrandt. New York: 1921. V. 51

SINGER, I. J.
The Brothers Ashkenzai. 1936. V. 53
East of Eden. London: 1939. V. 49
The Sinner. New York: 1933. V. 48

SINGER, ISAAC BASHEVIS
The Collected Stories. New York: 1982. V. 47; 48; 50; 51
A Crown of Feathers. New York: 1973. V. 51
A Day of Pleasure: Stories of a Boy Growing Up in Warsaw. New York: 1969. V. 54
The Death of Methuselah. Franklin Center: 1988. V. 48
Death of Methuselah. New York: 1988. V. 47; 54
Elijah the Slave. New York: 1970. V. 53
Enemies, a Love Story. New York: 1972. V. 53
The Estate. New York: 1969. V. 53
The Family Moskat. New York: 1950. V. 47; 48; 49; 51; 53; 54
The Fearsome Inn. New York: 1967. V. 52
The Fools of Chelm and Their History. New York: 1973. V. 54
The Gentleman from Cracow. New York: 1979. V. 47; 48; 49; 50; 51; 53
Gentleman from Cracow... Northampton: 1979. V. 49; 54
The Golem. New York. V. 52
The Golem. New York: 1982. V. 54

SINGER, ISAAC BASHEVIS continued
The Image and Other Stories. New York: 1985. V. 51; 54
Joseph and Koza or the Sacrifice to the Vistula. New York: 1970. V. 53
The King of the Fields. New York: 1988. V. 54
A Little Boy in Search of God: Mysticism in a Personal Light. Garden City: 1976. V. 53
Lost in America. Garden City: 1981. V. 49; 54
Lost in America. New York: 1981. V. 47
Love and Exile. Garden City: 1984. V. 49
The Manor. New York: 1967. V. 54
National Book Award Acceptance Speech, April 18, 1974. New York: 1974. V. 52
Nobel Lecture. New York: 1979. V. 54
Old Love. New York: 1979. V. 53; 54
One Day of Happiness. New York: 1982. V. 47; 48; 52; 53; 54
The Penitent. 1983. V. 51
The Penitent. Franklin Center: 1983. V. 52
Reaches of Heaven. New York: 1980. V. 48; 49
Satan in Goray. New York: 1955. V. 47; 49; 50; 52
Satan in Goray. New York: 1981. V. 51
Short Friday and Other Stories. New York: 1964. V. 54
Shosha. New York: 1978. V. 54
The Slave. New York: 1962. V. 54
The Spinoza of Market Street. New York: 1961. V. 54
Stories for Children. New York: 1984. V. 54
A Tale of Three Wishes. New York: 1976. V. 52; 53
The Topsy-Turvy Emperor of China. New York: 1971. V. 53
Yentil the Yeshiva Boy. New York: 1983. V. 50
Yentl, the Yeshiva Boy. New York: 1985. V. 51
A Young Man in Search of Love. Garden City: 1978. V. 48; 50; 52; 53; 54
Zlateh the Goat and Other Stories. New York: 1966. V. 52; 53

SINGER, ISIDORE
The Jewish Encyclopedia... New York: 1901-06. V. 51

SINGER, KURT
Diseases of the Musical Profession: a Systematic Presentation of Their Causes, Symptoms and methods of Treatment. New York: 1932. V. 47; 49; 50; 52

SINGER, SAMUEL WELLER
Researches into the History of Playing Cards with Illustrations of the Origin of Printing and Engraving on Wood. London: 1816. V. 47

SINGH, CHANDRAMANI
Textile and Costumes from the Maharaja Sawai Man Singh II Museum. Jaipur: 1979. V. 52

SINGH, MADANJEET
Himalayan Art: Wall-Painting and Sculpture in Ladakh... Greenwich: 1968. V. 50; 54

SINGLETON, E.
The Orchestra and its Instruments. New York: 1917. V. 49

SINGLETON, ESTHER
The Furniture of Our Fore-Fathers. New York: 1901. V. 47

SINGLETON-GATES, P.
The Black Diaries: an Account of Roger Casement's Life and Times... London: 1959. V. 47; 53

SINIGAGLIA, LEONE
Climbing Reminiscences of the Dolomites. 1896. V. 53
Climbing Reminiscences of the Dolomites... London: 1896. V. 51

SINISTRARI D'AMENO, LOUIS MARIE
Demoniality, Or Incubi and Succubi: a Treatise Wherein Is Shown That There are in Existence on Earth Rational Creatures Besides Man. Paris: 1879. V. 50

SINKANKAS, JOHN
Gemology: an Annotated Bibliography. Methuchen: 1993. V. 49; 50

SINKER, ROBERT
Catalogue of the Fifteenth-Century Printed Books in the Library of Trinity College, Cambridge. Cambridge: 1876. V. 47
The Library of Trinity College, Cambridge. Cambridge: 1891. V. 47

SINKIEWICZ, HENRYK
Quo Vadis?. Verona: 1959. V. 52

SINKS of London Laid Open. London: 1848?. V. 53

SINNETT, C.
The Emigrant Solders' Gazette and Cape Horn Chronicle. Victoria: 1907. V. 48; 53

SINNOTT, JOHN
A Military Catechism, Designed for the Use of the Non-Commissioned Officers and Others of the Infantry. Portsmouth: 1844. V. 53

SIODMAK, CURT
Donovan's Brain. New York: 1943. V. 47

SIPE, C. HALE
The Indian Wars of Pennsylvania. Harrisburg: 1929. V. 50

SIPES, WILLIAM B.
The Pennsylvania Railroad: Its Origin, Construction, Condition and Connections. Philadelphia: 1875. V. 47

SIPLEY, LOUIS WALTON
Frederick E. Ives: Photo-Graphic Inventor. Philadelphia: 1956. V. 51; 54

SIR Frantic, the Reformer; or, the Humours of the Crown and Anchor: a Poem in Two Cantos. London: 1809. V. 47; 54

SIR Harry Herald's Graphical Representation of the Dignitaries of England... London: 1820. V. 52

SIR Roger De Coverley. London: 1850. V. 49

SIR Winston S. Churchill Honorary Citizen of the United States of America...April 9, 1963. Worcester: 1964. V. 49

SIRAT BANI HILAL
The Celebrated Romance of the Stealing of the Mare. London: 1892. V. 50; 51
The Celebrated Romance of the Stealing of the Mare. Newtown: 1930. V. 47; 50; 51

SIREN, OSVALD
China and Gardens of Europe of the Eighteenth Century. New York: 1950. V. 47; 50; 54
Chinese Paintings in American Collections. Paris and Brussels: 1927-28. V. 53
Early Chinese Paintings: A. W. Bahr Collection. London: 1938. V. 51; 52; 54
Gardens of China. New York: 1949. V. 48; 54
A History of Early Chinese Painting. London: 1933. V. 50; 54
The Walls and Gates of Peking. London: 1924. V. 52

SIRINGO, CHARLES ANGELO
A Cowboy Detective. Chicago: 1912. V. 47; 48
History of 'Billy the Kid'. Santa Fe: 1920. V. 50
A Lone Star Cowboy. Santa Fe: 1919. V. 49; 52; 54
Riata and Spurs. Boston: 1927. V. 47; 49; 51
A Texas Cowboy... Chicago: 1885. V. 47
A Texas Cowboy... New York: 1886. V. 47
A Texas Cowboy... New York: 1950. V. 53

SIRR, HENRY CHARLES
Ceylon and the Cingalese: Their History, Government and Religion. London: 1850. V. 54
China and the Chinese: Their Religion, Character, Customs and Manufactures... London: 1859. V. 54

SISKIND, AARON
Photographs. New York: 1959. V. 47
Places. New York: 1976. V. 47
The Siskind Variations: a Quartet of Photographs and Contemplations. Toronto: 1990. V. 47; 50

SISMONDE DE SISMONDI, JEAN CHARLES LEONARD
Historical View of the Literature of the South of Europe. London: 1823. V. 53
Historie des Republiques Italiennes du Moyen Age... Paris: 1818. V. 50
Political Economy, and the Philosophy of Government. London: 1847. V. 48

THE SISTERS of Sefton Hall; or the Athenian Vase. Glasgow: 1824. V. 47

SITGREAVES, LORENZO
Northern and Western Boundary Line of the Creek Country. Washinton: 1858. V. 47
Report of an Expedition Down the Zuni and Colorado Rivers. Washington: 1853. V. 47; 48; 49

SITJAR, BONAVENTURE
Vocabulary of the Language of San Antonio Mission, California. New York: 1861. V. 48

SITWELL, EDITH
Alexander Pope. London: 1930. V. 51; 52; 53; 54
A Book of the Winter. New York: 1951. V. 53; 54
Buccolic Comedies. London: 1923. V. 47
Clown's Houses. Oxford: 1918. V. 48
The Collected Poems of Edith Sitwell. London: 1930. V. 52
The Collected Poems of Edith Sitwell. New York: 1954. V. 47; 54
The Death of Venus. New York: 1983. V. 49; 50; 52
Elegy on Dead Fashion. London: 1926. V. 47
England Reclaimed. London: 1927. V. 48
The English Eccentrics. London: 1933. V. 52; 54
Epithalamium. London: 1931. V. 49
Facade. Kensington: 1922. V. 47
Facade. London: 1954. V. 47
Five Poems. London: 1928. V. 54
Five Variations on a Theme. London: 1933. V. 50; 53; 54
Gardeners and Astronomers. New York: 1953. V. 54
Gold Coast Customs. London: 1929. V. 50; 54
In Spring. A Poem. London: 1931. V. 54
Music and Ceremonies. New York: 1963. V. 54
The Outcasts. London: 1962. V. 50
A Poet's Notebook. Boston: 1950. V. 54
Poor Young People. London: 1925. V. 47
Popular Song. London: 1928. V. 53; 54
Rustic Elegies. London: 1927. V. 47
Shadow of Cain. London: 1947. V. 48; 50
The Song of the Cold. London: 1945. V. 49; 50
The Song of the Cold. New York: 1948. V. 54
Victoria of England. London: 1936. V. 54
Wheels... Oxford: 1916. V. 53
Wheels. Oxford: 1916-21. V. 49
Wheels... Oxford: 1917. V. 52
Wheels... Oxford: 1919. V. 47

SITWELL, GEORGE
On the Making of Gardens. London: 1909. V. 50; 53
On the Making of Gardens. London: 1949. V. 50

SITWELL, H. D. W.
The Crown Jewels. London: 1953. V. 47; 48; 52

SITWELL, OSBERT
Argonaut and Juggernaut. London: 1919. V. 50
At the House of Mrs. Kinfoot - Consisting of Four Satires. London: 1921. V. 47
Brighton. London: 1935. V. 49
The Collected Satires and Poems. London: 1931. V. 49
England Reclaimed. London: 1927. V. 47; 48; 49; 54
Four Songs of the Italian Earth. Vermont: 1948. V. 47; 53
Great Morning. London: 1948. V. 53
Left Hand Right Hand!. London: 1945/46/48/50. V. 54
Left Hand Right Hand!. London: 1945/6/8/9/50. V. 50
Left Hand Right Hand!. London: 1948-50. V. 48; 51
The Man Who Lost Himself. London: 1929. V. 53
Miracle on Sinai. London: 1933. V. 54
Miss Mew. 1929. V. 51
Noble Essences. Boston: 1950. V. 54
Out of the Flame: Poems. London: 1923. V. 49
Penny Foolish. London: 1935. V. 53
The People's Album of London Statues. London: 1928. V. 49; 53
Three-Quarter Length Portrait of Michael Arlen. London: 1931. V. 47
Triple Fugue. London: 1924. V. 49
The True Story of Dick Whittington: a Christmas Story for Cat-Lovers. London: 1945. V. 49
Who Killed Cock-Robin?. London: 1921. V. 52
The Winstonburg Line - 3 Satires. London: 1919. V. 50
The Winstonburg Line: Three Satires. 1919. V. 53
Winters of Content and Other Discursions on Mediterranean Art and Travel. London: 1950. V. 54
Wrack At Tidesend: a Book of Balnearaics. London: 1952. V. 54

SITWELL, SACHEVERELL
A Book of Towers and Other Buildings of Southern Europe. London: 1928. V. 51
British Architects and Craftsmen: a Survey of Taste, Design and Style During three Centuries, 1600 to 1830. London: 1947/45. V. 48
Conversation Pieces - A Survey of English Domestic Portraits and Their Painters. London: 1936. V. 54
The Cyder Feast. London: 1927. V. 49; 53
Doctor Donne & Gargantua... London: 1921. V. 47
Doctor Donne & Gargantua. London: 1930. V. 48; 51; 53
Exalt the Eglantine and other Poems. London: 1926. V. 48
Far From My Home: Stories, Long and Short. London: 1931. V. 51
Fine Bird Books. London and New York: 1953. V. 48; 49; 50; 51; 52; 53; 54
Fine Bird Books... London: 1990. V. 52
Great Bird Books. 1700-1900. London and New York: 1953. V. 51
Great Flower Books 1700-1900. London: 1956. V. 47; 48; 50; 51; 52; 53
Narrative Pictures. London: 1937. V. 49
Old Garden Roses. London: 1955-57. V. 47; 53
The People's Palace. Oxford: 1918. V. 47
The Romantic Ballet in Lithographs of the Time. London: 1938. V. 47
Spanish Baroque Art. London: 1931. V. 49
The Thirteenth Caesar and Other Poems. London: 1924. V. 49
To E. S. (with) A Notebook On My New Poems. London: 1968/73. V. 50
Two Poems, Ten Songs. London: 1929. V. 48; 54

SIVARAMAMURTI, C.
Nataraja in Art, Thought and Literature. New Delhi: 1974. V. 48; 52

SIVIERO, RODOLFO
Jewelry and Amber of Italy: a Collection in the National Museum of Naples. New York: 1959. V. 51; 53; 54

SIVLESTRE, J. B.
Alphabet-album (or) Collection de 60 Feuilles dAlphabets... Paris: 1843-44. V. 49

SIVRIGHT, THOMAS
(Sale) Catalogue of the Extensive and Valuable Collection of Books, Pictures, Drawings, Prints and Painters' Etchings, Ancient Bronzes and Terracttas, Gems and Precious Stones... Edinburgh: 1836. V. 53

SIX Hundred Dollars a Year. A Wife's Effort at Low Living, Under High Prices. Boston: 1867. V. 50

SIX Poems of Mutabilitie by Divers Writers. Shaker Heights: 1992. V. 52

SIX Progressive Lessons for Flower Painting... London: 1810. V. 50; 51

SIX Views of the Scenery at Nesscliff. London: 1824. V. 52

SIXTEEN Contemporary Wood Engravers. Newcastle: 1982. V. 52

SIXTEEN Views of the Lakes in Cumberland and Westmorland. London: 1795. V. 49

SIZZI, FRANCESCO
Dianoia Astronomica, Optica, Physica, qua Syderei Nuncii Rumor de Quatuor Planetis a Galileo Galileo Mathematico.. Venice: 1611. V. 47

SJOSTEDT, YNGVE
Wissenschaftliche Ergebnisse der Schwedischen Zoologischen Expedition Nach dem Kilimandjaro, Dem Meru... Stockholm: 1910. V. 48

SKAGGS, WILLIAM
Central Texas Business and Professional Directory. Austin. V. 53

SKAGUAY The Gateway to the Klondike. Skaguay: 1898. V. 49

SKAIFE, THOMAS
A Key to Civil Architecture; or the Universal British Builder. London: 1774. V. 49
A Key to Civil Architecture, or The Universal British Builder. London: 1776. V. 53

SKARSTEN, M. O.
George Drouillard, Hunter and Interpreter for Lewis and Carl and Fur Trader, 1807-10. Glendale: 1964. V. 47; 50; 51; 53

SKEAD, C. J.
The Canaries, Seedeaters and Buntings of Southern Africa. Cape Town: 1960. V. 52
The Sunbirds of Southern Africa... Cape Town: 1967. V. 48; 52

SKEAT, WALTER WILLIAM
An Etymological Dictionary of the English Language. Oxford: 1882. V. 51
An Etymological Dictionary of the English Language. Oxford: 1888. V. 52
An Etymological Dictionary of the English Language. Oxford: 1910. V. 47
Malay Magic. London: 1900. V. 48
Pagan Races of the Malay Peninsula. London: 1906. V. 48; 54

SKEET, FRANCIS JOHN ANGUS
The Life and Letters of H. R. H. Charlotte Stuart, Duchess of Albany, only Child of Charles III, King of Great Britain, Scotland, France and Ireland. London: 1932. V. 49
The Life of the Right Hourable James Radcliffe, Third Earl of Derwentwater... London: 1929. V. 51; 52
Stuart Papers, Pictures, Relics, Medals and Books. Leeds: 1930. V. 52; 54

SKEETERS, PAUL
Sidney H. Sime - Master of Fantasy. 1978. V. 47

SKELDING, SUSIE BARSTOW
Flowers from Dell and Bower Poems Illustrated. New York: 1886. V. 54

SKELTON, CHRISTOPHER
The Engravings of Eric Gil. Wellingborough: 1983. V. 51

SKELTON, JOHN
Charles I. London, Paris: 1898. V. 52; 54
Mary Stuart. Paris & London: 1893. V. 49
Pithy Pleasant and Profitable Workes. London: 1736. V. 50
A Sculptor's Work 1950-1975. Wellingborough: 1977. V. 52

SKELTON, JOSEPH
Engraved Illustrations of the Principal Antiquities of Oxfordshire... Oxford: 1823-27. V. 52
Pietas Oxoniensis, or, Records of Oxford Founders. Oxford: 1828. V. 49
Skelton's Engraved Illustrations of the Principal Antiquities of Oxfordshire. Oxford: 1823. V. 48; 49

SKELTON, PHILIP
Truth in a Mask. Dublin: 1744. V. 47

SKELTON, R. A.
County Atlases of the British Isles 1519-1850. A Bibliography. 1579-1703. London: 1970. V. 51
Decorative Printed Maps of the 15th to 18t Centuries. London: 1952. V. 50; 54
A Description of Maps and Architectural Drawings in the Collection Made by William Cecil, First Baron Burghley, Now at Hatfield House. Oxford: 1971. V. 47
Explorers' Maps. London: 1958. V. 54
The Vinland Map and the Tartar Relation. New Haven & London: 1965. V. 54

SKELTON, W. C.
Reminiscences of Joe Bowman and the Ullswater Foxhounds. Kendal: 1923. V. 54

SKEMPTON, MARY
The Wood Engravings of Mary Skempton. Marlborough: 1989. V. 47

SKENE, FELICIA MARY FRANCES
Hidden Depths. Edinburgh: 1866. V. 50
Use and Abuse, a Tale. London: 1849. V. 47

SKENE, J. W.
Th Danubian Principalities, the Frontier Lands of the Christian and the Turk. London: 1854. V. 48

SKENE, JOHN
De Verborum Significatione. The Exposition of the Termes and Difficil Wordes Conteined in the Foure Buikes of Regiam Majestatem. Edinburgh: 1820. V. 54
De Verorum Significatione. The Exposition of the termes and Difficill Wordes Conteined in the Four Buikes of Regiam Majestatem... London: 1820. V. 49
Regiam Maiestatem. The Auld Lawes and Constitutions of Scotland Faithfullie Collected Furth of the Register, and Other Auld Authentick Bukes, Fray the Dayes of King Malcolme, the Second... Edinburgh: 1609. V. 48
Regiam Majestatem. The Auld Lawes and Constitutions of Scotland, Faithfullie Collected Furth of the Register and Other Auld Authentick Bukes etc. (with) An Examination of Some of the Arguments for the High Antiquity of Regiam Majestatem (etc.). Edinburgh: 1609/1769. V. 51

SKENE, PETER
Peter Skene Ogden's Snake Country Journal, 1826-27. London: 1961. V. 51

SKENE, WILLIAM F.
Celtic Scotland; a History of Ancient Alban. Edinburgh: 1876-80. V. 53

SKERMAN, P. J.
Tropical Grasses. Rome: 1990. V. 47; 48

SKERTCHLY, SYDNEY BARBER JOSIAH
Our Island. Hong Kong: 1893. V. 54

SKETCH of St. Anthony and Minneapolis, Minnesota Territory. St. Anthony: 1857. V. 48; 51; 53

A SKETCH of the Life and Character of Gen. Taylor the American hero and People's Man: Together with a concise History of the Mexican War. Boston: 1847. V. 49

A SKETCH of the Life and Public Services of General Zachary Taylor, the People's Candidate for the Presidency. Washington: 1848. V. 47

SKETCH of the Life, Personal Appearance, Character and Manners of Charles S. Stratton, the Man in Miniature, Known as General Tom Thumb, Twenty-two Years Old, Thirty-Two Inches High and Weighing only Thirty-Two Pounds... New York: 1860. V. 47

A SKETCH of the Present State of France. London: 1805. V. 54

SKETCH of the Public Services of Rear Admiral S. F. Du Pont, United States Navy. Wilmington: 1865. V. 54

SKETCH, WALTER
The Down-Trodden; or, Black Blood and White. New York: 1853. V. 52

SKETCHES and Eccentricities of Col. David Crockett of West Tennessee. London: 1834. V. 50

SKETCHES from "Nine Sharp". London: 1938. V. 52

SKETCHES from Nature, Intended for the Use of Young Persons. London: 1801. V. 48; 54

SKETCHES in Natural History. History of the Mammalia. London: 1849. V. 54

SKETCHES of a Tour in Egypt and Palestine, During the Spring of 1856. London: 1857. V. 54

SKETCHES of Character, or Specimens of Real Life. London: 1813. V. 51

SKETCHES Of Character, or Specimens of Real Life. London: 1815. V. 51

SKETCHES of Imposture, Description and Credulity... London: 1837. V. 47

SKETCHES of Portuguese Life, Manners, Costume and Character. London: 1826. V. 53

SKETCHES of Universal History. New Haven: 1811. V. 54

SKETCHLEY, ARTHUR
Mrs. Brown On the Alabama Claims. London: 1872. V. 52

SKETCHLEY, W.
The Cocker: Containing Every Information to the Breeders and Amateurs of that Noble Bird, The Game Cock. London: 1814. V. 49

SKETCHWELL, BARNABY, PSEUD.
London Characters; or, Anecdotes, Fashions, and Customs of the Present Century. London: 1809. V. 50; 51

SKEY, FREDERIC
A Practical Treatise on the Venereal Disease. London: 1840. V. 51; 54

SKEY, WILLIAM
The Heraldic Calendar: a List of the Nobility & Gentry. London: 1846. V. 47

SKIDMORE, CHARLES
A Catalogue of the Library of Wakefield Books in the Possession of Charles Skidmore... 1897. V. 49

SKIDMORE, LEWIS
A Choice Selection of the Latest Social and Camp Meeting Hymns and Spiritual Songs... Baltimore: 1825. V. 50

SKIDMORE, THOMAS
The Rights of Man to Property!. New York: 1829. V. 50

THE SKILFUL Housewife's Guide; a Book of Domestic Cookery, Compiled from the Best Authors. Montreal: 1848. V. 48

SKILLING, THOMAS
The Science and Practice of Agriculture. Dublin: 1846. V. 54

SKINNER, ADA M.
A Child's Book of Country Stories. New York: 1925. V. 47
A Child's Book of Modern Stories. New York: 1920. V. 47; 49
The Turquoise Story Book. New York: 1918. V. 48

SKINNER, ALANSON
Material Culture of the Menomini. New York: 1921. V. 48

SKINNER, BELLE
The Belle Skinner Collection of Old Musical Instruments. Holyoke: 1933. V. 49

SKINNER, BURRHUS FREDERICK
The Behavior of Organisms: an Experimental Analysis. New York: 1938. V. 54
Walden Two. New York: 1948. V. 51

SKINNER, CHARLES M.
Do Nothing Days. Philadelphia: 1899. V. 47; 49
With Fleet to the Earth. Philadelphia: 1899. V. 47

SKINNER, HENRY
The Origin of Medical Terms. Baltimore: 1949. V. 50; 52

SKINNER, ISRAEL
A History of the Revolutionary War Between Great Britain and the United States in Verse. Binghampton: 1829. V. 49

SKINNER, J. D.
The Mammals of the Southern African Subregion. Pretoria: 1990. V. 48; 60

SKINNER, J. RALSTON
A Key to the Hebrew-Egyptian Mystery in the Source of Measures Originating the British Inch and the Ancient Cubit. Cincinnati: 1875. V. 48

SKINNER, JOHN
Amusements of Leisure Hours; or Poetical Pieces, Chiefly in the Scottish dialect... Edinburgh: 1809. V. 47; 49

SKINNER, JOHN EDWIN HILARY
After the Storm; or, Jonathan and His Neighbours in 1865-66. London: 1866. V. 49

SKINNER, JOHN R.
History of the Fourth Illinois Volunteers in Their Relation to the Spanish American War... Logansport: 1899. V. 49

SKINNER, JOSEPH
The Present State of Peru... London: 1805. V. 47; 52

SKINNER, OTIS A.
The Theory of William Miller, Concerning the End of the World in 1843... Boston: 1840. V. 54

SKINNER, STEPHEN
Etymologicon Linguae Anglicanae, Seu Explicato vocum Anglicarum Etymologia ex Propriis Fontibus... London: 1671. V. 50

SKINNER, THOMAS
The Life of General Monk, Late Duke of Albemarle... London: 1723. V. 47

SKIPP, JOHN
Book of the Dead. Shingletown: 1989. V. 52

SKIPTON, E.
Blank On the Map. 1938. V. 53

SKIPWITH, P.
The Great Bird Illustrators and Their Art 1730-1930. London: 1979. V. 52

SKODA, JOSEPH
Auscultation and Percussion. Philadelphia: 1854. V. 49; 54

SKOLSKY, SIDNEY
Don't Get me Wrong - I Love Hollywood. New York: 1975. V. 52; 54

SKORKOWSKI, EDWARD
The Arab Horse in Poland. Warsaw: 1930. V. 48

SKORY, EDMUND
An Extract Out of the Historie of the Last French King Henry the Fourth. London: 1610. V. 50; 54

SKOTTOWE, AUGUSTINE
The Life of Shakespeare... London: 1824. V. 47; 51

SKREBNESKI, VICTOR
Skrebneski Portraits: a Matter of Record. New York: 1978. V. 47

SKRINE, HENRY
A General Account of All the Rivers of Note in Great Britain... London: 1801. V. 49

SKUE, G. E. M.
Side-Lines, Lights and Reflections. London: 1932. V. 53

SKUES, G. E. M.
Nymph Fishing for Chalk Stream Trout. London: 1939. V. 47; 53
Silk, Fur and Feather. 1950. V. 53
The Way of a Man With a Trout. London: 1977. V. 53
The Way of a Trout with a Fly. London: 1935. V. 53
The Way of a Trout with a Fly, with Some Further Studies in Minor Tactics. London: 1921. V. 49

SKURRAY, FRANCIS
Bidcombe Hill... London: 1808. V. 48; 51
Bidcombe Hill... London: 1824. V. 50

SKUSE'S Complete Confectioner. London: 1890. V. 47

SKUTCH, ALEXANDER F.
Life Histories of Central American Birds. Berkeley: 1954-60-69. V. 54
The Life of the Woodpecker. London: 1985. V. 50
Life of the Woodpecker. Santa Monica: 1985. V. 50; 51; 52

SKVORECKY, JOSEF
The Engineer of Human Souls. Toronto: 1984. V. 51

THE SKYLARK. (The Thrush). (The Nightingale): A Choice Selection of the Most Admired Popular Songs. London: 1825. V. 48; 49; 54

SKYRME, F. H. E.
The Yanktsze-Kiang. Shanghai: 1937. V. 49

SLADE, ADOLPHUS
Records of Travels in Turkey, Greece, &c. and A Cruise of the Black Sea with the Captain Pasha in the Years 1829, 1830 and 1831. London: 1833. V. 53
Travels in Germany and Russia: Including a Steam Voyage by the Danube and the Euxine from Vienna to Constantinople in 1838-39. London: 1840. V. 52

SLADEN, DOUGLAS
In Sicily. 1896-1898-1900. London: 1901. V. 50
More Queer Things About Japan. 1905. V. 54
On the Cars and Off. Being the Journal of a Pilgrimage Along the Queen's Highway... London: 1895. V. 47
On the Cars and Off, Being the Journal of a Pilgrimage Along the Queen's Highway... London: 1898. V. 48; 49

SLADEN, F. L. W.
The Humble Bee, Its Life History and How to Domesticate It... London: 1912. V. 49; 52; 53

SLADEN, W. P.
Report on the Asteroidea Collected by H.M.S. Challenger During the Years 1873-76. London: 1889. V. 49

SLAFTER, EDMUND F.
Sir William Alexander & American Colonization, Including Three Royal Charters... Boston: 1873. V. 50

SLANGE, NIELS
Den Stormaegtigste Konges Christian Den Fierdes, Konges Til Danmark og Norge... Kjobenhavn: 1749. V. 49; 53

SLATER, HENRY H.
Manual of the Birds of Iceland. London: 1901. V. 50

SLATER, HUMPHREY
The Heretics. London: 1946. V. 49

SLATER, ISAAC
Slater's Royal National and Commercial Directory of Gloucestershire, Monmouthshire and North and South Wales... Manchester: 1858-59. V. 47
Slater's Royal National Commercial Directory of Cumberland and Westmorland... Manchester: 1869. V. 50
Slater's Royal National Commercial Directory of the Counties of Cumberland, Durham, Northumberland and Westmorland with the Cleveland District. Manchester: 1884. V. 51

SLATER, J. H.
Early Editions. A Bibliographical Survey of the Works of Some Popular Modern Authors. London: 1894. V. 51; 53

SLATER, JOHN M.
El Morro: Inscription Rock, New Mexico. Los Angeles: 1961. V. 53

SLATER, P. L.
Argentine Ornithology. A Descriptive Catalogue of the Birds of the Argentine Republic. London: 1888-89. V. 51
The Book of Antelopes. London: 1894-1900. V. 48; 49
A Monograph of the Jacamars and Puff-Birds, or Families Galbulidae and Bucconidae. London: 1879-82. V. 51
On the Curassows Now or Lately Living in the Society's Gardens. (with) Supplementary Notes. London: 1875/75-79. V. 49

SLATER, PHILEMON
History of the Ancient Parish of Guiseley. Leeds: 1880. V. 51

SLATER, THOMAS FREDERICK
The Troller's Guide, A New and Complete Treatise on the Art of Trolling or Fishing for Jack and Pike... London: 1820. V. 51

SLATIN, RUDOLPH CARL, FREIHERR VON
Fire and Sword in the Sudan. London, New York: 1896. V. 47; 48; 49; 50; 52

SLATTER, HENRY
The Oxford University and City Guide, on a New Plan... Oxford: 1825. V. 54
Views of All the Colleges, Halls and Public Buildings In the University and City of Oxford... Oxford: 1802. V. 50
Views of All the Colleges, Halls and Public Buildings in the University and City of Oxford... Oxford: 1830. V. 49

SLATYER, WILLIAM
The History of Great Britanie, from the First Peopling of this Island to This Present Raigne of ...K. Iames... Colophon: 1621. V. 47

SLAUGHTER, MIHILL
Railway Intelligence, Jan. 1859. London: 1859. V. 49

SLAUGHTER, PHILIP
A History of St. Mark's Parish, Culpeper County, Virginia... Richmond: 1877. V. 48

SLAVE Songs of the United States. New York: 1867. V. 54

SLAVERY. A Treatise, Showing that Slavery is Neither a Moral, Political, nor Social Evil. Penfield: 1844. V. 49

SLEDD, JAMES H.
Dr. Johnson's Dictionary, Essays in the Biography of a Book. Chicago: 1955. V. 52

SLEEMAN, J. L.
Tales of a Shikari. Big Game Shooting in India. 1919. V. 52

SLEEMAN, W. H.
A Journey through the Kingdom of Oude in 1849-1850. London: 1858. V. 49
Rambles and Recollections of an Indian Official. 1844. V. 54
Rambles and Recollections of an Indian Official. London: 1844. V. 48; 50; 51

THE SLEEPING Beauty... Newcastle-upon-Tyne: 1810. V. 50

THE SLEEPING Beauty. London: 1920. V. 51

SLEEPING Beauty. New York: 1933. V. 47
SLEEPING Beauty. London: 1961. V. 49

SLEIDAN, JOHANNES PHILIPPSON
Dos Informaciones Mvy Vtiles, la Vna Dirigida a...Carlo Quinto...la Otra, a Los Estados del Imperio... 1559. V. 49
De Quatuor Monarchiss Libri Tres. Cambridge: 1686. V. 53

SLEIGH, W. CAMPBELL
A Handy Book of Criminal Law, Applicable Chiefly to Commercial Transactions. London: 1858. V. 52

SLICER, THOMAS R.
From Poet to Premier. The Centennial Cycle 1809-1910. London & New York: 1909. V. 48

SLIGHT, BENJAMIN
Indian Researches; or, Facts Concerning the North American Indians. Montreal: 1844. V. 47
Intellectual Greatness. Montreal: 1847. V. 51

SLINGSBY, W. C.
Norway - the Northern Playground. Oxford: 1941. V. 51

SLIVE, SEYMOUR
Frans Hals. 1970. V. 49
Frans Hals. London: 1970. V. 50
Frans Hals. London: 1970-74. V. 51

SLOAN, ERIC
Camouflage Simplified. New York: 1942. V. 51
Clouds, Air and Wind. New York: 1941. V. 51

SLOAN, JAMES
An Oration, Delivered at a Meeting of the Democratic Association of the County of Gloucester, Held in the Court House at Woodbury, on the Fourth Day of March 1802. Trenton: 1802. V. 49; 51

SLOAN, JOHN
Gist of Art. New York: 1939. V. 54

SLOAN, JOHN ALEXANDER
North Carolina in the War Between the States. Washington: 1883. V. 49

SLOAN, MARGY
Infiltration: Poems. Mexico: 1989. V. 54

SLOAN, PAT
John Cornford: a Memoir. London: 1938. V. 49

SLOAN, ROBERT W.
Utah Gazetteer and Directory of Logan, Ogden, Provo and Salt Lake Cities for 1884. Salt Lake City: 1884. V. 49

SLOAN, SAMUEL
City and Suburban Architecture.. Philadelphia: 1859. V. 47; 48
Sloan's Constructive Architecture: a Guide to the Practical Builder and Mechanic. Philadelphia: 1859. V. 48
Sloan's Constructive Architecture; a Guide to the Practical Builder and Mechanic... Philadelphia: 1866. V. 48
Sloan's Homestead Architecture, Containing Forty Designs for Villas, Cottages and Farm Houses.... Philadelphia: 1861. V. 51; 54

SLOAN, W. B.
The Complete Farrier or Horse Doctor. Chicago: 1849. V. 47

SLOANE, ERIC
ABC Book of Early Americana. Garden City: 1963. V. 53
Legacy. New York: 1979. V. 51
The Spirits of '76. New York: 1973. V. 53

SLOANE, H.
An Account of a Most Efficacious Medicine for Soreness, Weakness and Several Other Distempers of the Eyes. London: 1745. V. 52

SLOANE, HANS
A Voyage to the Islands of Madera, Barbados, P. Nevis, S. Christopher and Jamaica, with the Natural History of the Herbs and Trees, Four-footed Beastes, Fishes, Birds, Insects, Reptiles, &c. London: 1707-25. V. 47; 48; 49

SLOANE, T. O'CONOR
Electric Toy Making for Amateurs. New York: 1899. V. 53

SLOANE, WILLIAM MILLIGAN
Life of Napoleon Bonaparte. New York: 1896. V. 48

SLOCOMB, WILLIAM
The Federal Calculator, or, a Concise System of Practical Aritmetick... Wheeling: 1828. V. 49

SLOCUM, CHARLES EILHU
The Life and Services of Major General Henry Warner Slocum. Toledo: 1913. V. 53

SLOCUM, JOHN J.
A Bibliography of James Joyce (1882-1941). New Haven: 1953. V. 47
The Youth of Hamlet: an Interpretation. South Pasadena: 1932. V. 49; 54

SLOCUM, ROBERT
Grail Field Notes. Easthampton: 1995. V. 53

SLOW, EDWARD
Wiltshire Rhymes. London: 1881. V. 54

SLOW Horses Made Fast and Fast Horses Made Faster. New York: 1871. V. 49

SMAIL, DAVID CAMERON
Prestwick Golf Club. Prestwick: 1989. V. 50; 52; 54

SMALL, ANDREW
Interesting Roman Antiquities Recently Discovered in Fife... Edinburgh: 1823. V. 52

A SMALL Collection of Moral Precepts from the Best Persian Authors with a Translation in Hindostani Verse for the Use of Schools. Lucknow: 1835. V. 47

A SMALL Garden of Flora. Oxford: 1990. V. 52

SMALL, GEORGE G.
Fred Douglass and His Mule: a Story of the War. New York: 1886. V. 49; 52
H--L. New York: 1878. V. 47

SMALL, GEORGE RAPHAEL
Ramos Martinez. His Life and Art. Westlake Village: 1975. V. 51

SMALL, HAROLD A.
Adventures of Joseph Alexandre de Chabrier de Peloubet at the Time of the French Revolution. San Francisco: 1953. V. 52; 54

SMALL, HENRY BEAUMONT
Canadian Forests - Forest Trees, Timber and Forest Products. Montreal: 1884. V. 47
Canadian Handbook and Tourist's Guide. Montreal: 1866. V. 47
The Canadian Handbook and Tourist's Guide... Montreal: 1867. V. 49

SMALL, J. K.
Iris Species Described in Addisonia. Addisonia: 1930. V. 49

SMALL, JOHN WILLIAM
Scottish Woodwork of the Sixteenth and Seventeenth Centuries. New York: 1877. V. 49
Scottish Woodwork of the Sixteenth and Seventeenth Centuries. Stirling: 1878. V. 51

SMALL Rain Upon the Tender Herb. London: 1830. V. 48

SMALL, TUNSTALL
Mouldings of the Wren and Georgian Periods. London. V. 51

SMALL World Alphabet. Seattle: 1992. V. 52; 54

SMALLEY, DAN S.
The American Phonetic Dictionary of the English Language. Cincinnati: 1855. V. 47

SMALLEY, EUGENE V.
History of the Northern Pacific Railroad. New York: 1883. V. 47

SMART, ADAM
Prehistoric Beasts Discovered for His Grandchildren. San Francisco;: 1937. V. 54

SMART, BILL
From Mexico to Montreal on a Cow Pony. Ft. Worth: 1928. V. 50

SMART, CHRISTOPHER
The Midwife, or Old Woman's Magazine. London: 1751. V. 47
The Poems of the Late Christopher Smart. Reading: 1791. V. 52
Poems on Several Occasions. London: 1752. V. 49; 52
The Student, or, The Oxford and Cambridge Monthly Miscellany. Oxford: 1750. V. 49
The Student's Companion: Being a Collection of Historical Quotations from the best Ancient and Modern Authors... London: 1748. V. 48

SMART, ELIZABETH
By Grand Central Station I Sat Down and Wept. London: 1945. V. 49; 50; 54

SMART, JAMES FRANCIS
The Steam Packet. Bristol: 1823. V. 54

SMART, JOHN
Tables of Interest, Discount, Annuities, etc. London: 1726. V. 47; 53
Tables of Time. London: 1710. V. 52

SMART, T. H.
Pre-Columbian Historical Treasures. The Flatey Book and Recently Discovered Vatican Manuscripts Concerning Americ as Early as the Tenth Century. London: 1906. V. 49

SMART, WILLIAM
The National Income and its Distribution. London: 1899. V. 49

SMEAD, ISAAC D.
Ventilation and Warming of Buildings, Upon the principles as Designed and Patented by Isaac D. Smead. Toledo: 1889. V. 50

SMEATON, JOHN
Experimental Enquiry Concerning the Natural Power of Wind and Water to Turn Mills and Other Machines Depending On a Circular Motion. London: 1796. V. 53
An Historical Report on Ramsgate Harbour: Written by Order Of and Addressed to the Trustees. London: 1791. V. 51
John Smeaton's Diary of His Journey to the Low Countries 1755 From the Original MS in the Library of Trinity House. Leamington Spa: 1938. V. 50; 52; 54
The Report...Concerning the Drainage of the North Level of the Fens, and the Outfall of the Wisbeach River. Austhorpe: 1768. V. 52
The Report...concerning the Drainage of the North level of the Fens, and the Outfall of the Wisbeach River. London: 1768. V. 54
Reports of the Late John Smeaton, F.R.S. Made on Various Occasions, in the Course of His Employment as a Civil Engineer, (with Life). (with) The Miscellaneous Papers of John Smeaton, Comprising His Communications to the Royal Society... London: 1812-14. V. 47

SMEDLEY, EDWARD
Erin. A Geographical and Descriptive Poem. London: 1810. V. 48; 51; 54
The Parson's Choice of Town or Country... London: 1821. V. 54
Sketches from Venetian History. London: 1831. V. 48

SMEDLEY, FRANK E.
Harry Coverdale's Courtship and All that Came of It. London: 1852. V. 47
Harry Coverdale's Courtship and All That Came Of It. London: 1855. V. 54
Lewis Arundel; or, the Railroad of Life. London: 1852. V. 50; 54

SMEDLEY, HAROLD HINSDILL
Fly Patterns and their origins. Muskegon: 19743. V. 51

SMEDLEY, JONATHAN
Gulliveriana; or a Fourth Volume of Miscellanies. London: 1728. V. 47
A Hue and Cry After the Examiner Dr. S—t. Occasiond by a True and Exact Copy of Part of His own Diary, Found in His Pocket-Book, Wherein He Has Set Down a Faithful Account of Himself... London: 1714. V. 48

SMEDLEY, R. C.
History of the Underground Railroad in Chester and the Neighboring Counties of Pennsylvania. Lancaster: 1883. V. 48

SMEDLEY, WILLIAM
Across the Plains in '62. Denver: 1916. V. 47

SMEE, ALFRED
Instinct and Reason: Deduced from Electro-Biology. London: 1850. V. 47; 49; 54
My Garden: its Plan and Culture. London: 1872. V. 52; 53

SMELLIE, WILLIAM
Anatomical Tables, with Explanations and an Abridgement of the Practice of Midwifery.. Edinburgh: 1787. V. 48; 53
The Philosophy of Natural History. Edinburgh: 1790. V. 49; 53; 54
The Philosophy of Natural History. Edinburgh: 1790-99. V. 48; 52; 53; 54

SMET, HEINRICH
Prosodia...Quae Syllabarum Positione & Dipthongis Carentium. Cantabrigiae: 1654. V. 48; 53

SMET, PIERRE JEAN DE
Letters and Sketches; with a Narrative of a Year's Residence Among the Indian Tribes of the Rocky Mountains. Philadelphia: 1843. V. 53
New Indian Sketches. New York: 1863. V. 47; 50
Oregon Missions and Travels Over the Rocky Mountains in 1845-46. New York: 1847. V. 47

SMETHAN, HENRY
Rambles Round Churches (in the Vicinity of Maidstone, Rochester and Chatham). Chatham: 1925-28. V. 52

SMIALOWSKI, ARTHUR
Photography in Medicine. Springfield: 1960. V. 49

SMIDS, LUDOLPH
Pictura Loquens, sive Heroicarum Tabularum Hadirani Schoonebeeck Enarratio et Explicatio. Amsterdam: 1695. V. 47; 54

SMILES, SAMUEL
A Boy's Voyage Round the World, Including a Residence in Victoria, and a Journey by Rail Across North America. New York: 1872. V. 53
Duty: with Illustrations of Courage, Patience and Endurance. London: 1880. V. 52
George Moore, Merchant and Philanthropist. London: 1878. V. 52
History of Ireland and the Irish People, Under the Government of England. London: 1844. V. 53
Huguenots. Their Settlements, Churches and Industries in England and Irleand. London: 1868. V. 54
Life and Labour. London: 1887. V. 49
Life of a Scotch Naturalist: Thomas Edward Associate of the Linnean Society. London: 1876. V. 50
The Life of George Stephenson... London: 1857. V. 49
The Life of George Stephenson. London: 1858. V. 49
Lives of Boulton and Watt. London: 1865. V. 48; 50; 54
Lives of the Engineers... London: 1861-62. V. 48; 50; 53
Lives of the Engineers... London: 1861-65. V. 48
Lives of the Engineers. London: 1862-65. V. 54
Lives of the Engineers. London: 1862-68. V. 54
Lives of the Engineers. London: 1874-91. V. 51
Lives of the Engineers. 1968. V. 54
Men of Invention and Industry. London: 1884. V. 54
Robert Dick, Baker of Thurso, Geologist and Botanist. London: 1878. V. 49
Thrift. London: 1875. V. 52

SMILEY, JANE
The Age of Grief. New York: 1987. V. 50; 52; 54
At Paradise Gate. New York: 1981. V. 48; 49; 51; 52; 53
Barn Blind. New York: 1980. V. 51; 52; 53; 54
Duplicate Keys. London: 1984. V. 53
Duplicate Keys. New York: 1984. V. 49; 51; 52; 53; 54
The Greenlanders. New York: 1988. V. 50; 51
The Life of the Body. Minneapolis: 1990. V. 50; 51
Moo. New York: 1995. V. 51
A Thousand Acres. New York: 1991. V. 50; 51; 52; 53; 54

SMILEY'S Atlas for the Use of Schools and Families. Philadelphia: 1839. V. 49

SMIRDIN, A.
(Russian title) Rospis' Rossijskim Knigam... St. Petersburg: 1828-29-32. V. 54

SMIRKE, EDWARD
The Case of Vice Against Thomas, Determined on Appeal Before the Lord Warden of the Stannaries of Cornwall... London: 1843. V. 48

SMIT, PIETER
History of the Life Sciences. An Annotated Bibliography. Amsterdam: 1974. V. 47

SMITH, A.
Empire State, a History. New York: 1931. V. 54
The Wassail - Bowl. London: 1843. V. 53

SMITH, A. C.
Guide to British and Roman Antiquities of the North Wiltshire Downs in a Hundred Square Miles Round Abury. 1885. V. 52

SMITH, A. DUNCAN
Trial of Maedleine Smith. London: 1905. V. 52

SMITH, A. H.
A Catalogue of Engraved Gems in the British Museum. London: 1888. V. 50; 52
Marbles and Bronzes: Fifty Plates from Selected Subjects in the Department of Greek and Roman Antiquities. London: 1914. V. 50; 52
The Place Names of the West Riding of Yorkshire. 1961-63. V. 47

SMITH, A. J. M.
News of the Phoenix. Toronto/New York: 1943. V. 47; 48; 51
A Sort of Ecstacy. East Lansing: 1954. V. 47

SMITH, A. LEDYARD
Archaeological Reconnaissance in Central Guatemala. Washington: 1955. V. 50
Excavations at Nebaj, Guatemala. Washington: 1951. V. 50
Explorations in the Motagua Valley, Guatemala. Washington: 1943. V. 52
Uaxactun, Guatemala: Excavations of 1931-1937. Washington: 1950. V. 52

SMITH, A. MURRAY, MRS.
The Roll-Call of Westminster Abbey. London: 1912. V. 51
Westminster Abbey. London: 1904. V. 52

SMITH, AARON
The Atrocities of the Pirates... New York: 1824. V. 48; 49; 50
The Atrocities of the Pirates. Waltham St. Lawrence: 1919. V. 53
The Atrocities of the Pirates... Waltham St. Lawrence: 1929. V. 51

SMITH, ADAM
A Catalogue of the Library of Adam Smith, author of the "Moral Sentiments" and "The Wealth of Nations". London: 1894. V. 47; 50; 53
Essays on Philosophical Subjects. London: 1795. V. 50; 52
An Inquiry Into the Nature and Causes of the Wealth of Nations. London. V. 47
An Inquiry into the Nature and Causes of the Wealth of Nations... Dublin: 1776. V. 51; 53
An Inquiry into the Nature and Causes of the Wealth of Nations... London: 1776. V. 48; 54
An Inquiry Into the Nature and Causes of the Wealth of Nations... London: 1778. V. 50; 53
An Inquiry into the Nature and Causes of the Wealth of Nations... London: 1784. V. 51
An Inquiry into the Nature and Causes of the Wealth of Nations. Philadelphia: 1789-96-89. V. 52
An Inquiry Into the Nature and Causes of the Wealth of Nations. London: 1793. V. 48; 51; 54
An Inquiry Into the Nature and Causes of the Wealth of Nations. Dublin: 1793-1801. V. 49
An Inquiry into the Nature and Causes of the Wealth of Nations. London: 1796. V. 48; 50
An Inquiry into the Nature and Causes of the Wealth of Nations. London: 1796/93. V. 49
An Inquiry Into the Nature and Causes of the Wealth of Nations. Dublin: 1801. V. 54
An Inquiry Into the Nature and Causes of the Wealth of Nations. Hartford: 1804. V. 54
An Inquiry Into the Nature and Causes of the Wealth of Nations. London: 1805. V. 52; 53
An Inquiry Into the Nature and Causes of the Wealth of Nations. London: 1812. V. 49; 51
An Inquiry into the Nature and Causes of the Wealth of Nations. Edinburgh and London: 1817. V. 52
An Inquiry into the Nature and Causes of the Wealth of Nations. London: 1819. V. 47
An Inquiry Into the Nature and Causes of the Wealth of Nations. Edinburgh: 1828. V. 47; 51
An Inquiry into the Nature and Causes of the Wealth of Nations. Edinburgh: 1846. V. 49
An Inquiry Into the Nature and Causes of the Wealth of Nations. Oxford: 1869. V. 52
An Inquiry Into the Nature and Causes of the Wealth of Nations... London: 1930. V. 48
The Theory of Moral Sentiments. London: 1761. V. 48; 53
The Theory of Moral Sentiments... London: 1781. V. 48; 49; 50
The Theory of Moral Sentiments... London: 1804. V. 47
The Theory of Moral Sentiments... Edinburgh: 1813. V. 47
The Theory of Moral Sentiments... Philadelphia: 1817. V. 49

SMITH, AGNES
Glimpses of Greek Life and Scenery. London: 1884. V. 48; 49

SMITH, ALAN G. R.
The Last Years of Mary Queen of Scots. 1990. V. 54

SMITH, ALBERT RICHARD
The Drama Founded on the New Christmas Annual of Charles Dickens, Esq. Called the Battle of Life. London: 1846. V. 54
The Entirely New and Original Drama in Three Parts. London: 1845. V. 54
Hop-O-My-Thumb, or, The Seven League Boots. London: 1846. V. 47; 51
A Month at Constantinople. London: 1850. V. 48
The Natural History of "Stuck-Up" People. London: 1847. V. 54
The Natural History of a Gent. London: 1847. V. 47
The Pottleton Legacy, a Story. London: 1849. V. 54
Sketches of London Life and Character. London: 1870. V. 52
The Story of Mont Blanc. London: 1853. V. 48
The Struggles and Adventures of Christopher Tadpole... London: 1848. V. 48; 51
The Struggles and Adventures of Christopher Tadpole. London: 1850. V. 51
Stuck-Up People. London: 1840. V. 51
To China and Back: Being a Diary Kept, Out and HOme. London: 1859. V. 47

SMITH, ALEXANDER
Dreamthorp. London: 1863. V. 47; 48; 50; 52
A Summer in Skye. London: 1865. V. 49

SMITH, ALFRED E.
Progressive Democracy, Addresses and State Papers of Alfred E. Smith. New York: 1928. V. 52

SMITH, ALFRED RUSSELL
A Catalogue of Ten Thousand Tracts and Pamphlets, and Fifty Thousand Prints and Drawings, Illustrating the Topography and Antiquities of England, Wales, Scotland and Ireland. London: 1878. V. 53

SMITH, ALICE R. HUGER
The Dwelling Houses of Charleston, South Carolina. London: 1917. V. 47

SMITH, AMANDA
An Autobiography, the Story of the Lord's Dealings with Mrs. Amanda Smith, the Colored Evangelist... Chicago: 1893. V. 47; 48; 52

SMITH, ANDREW
Essays in Philosophical Criticism. London: 1883. V. 49
Illustrations of the Zoology of South Africa. London: 1849. V. 53

SMITH, ANN ELIZA BRAINARD
Atla: a Story of the Lost Island. New York: 1886. V. 50

SMITH, ANNE
Anthology of Love. London: 1985. V. 52

SMITH, ARTHUR DONALDSON
Through Unknown African Countries. London: 1897. V. 51

SMITH, ASHBEL
A Brief Description of the Climate, Soil and Productions of Texas. Philadelphia: 1841. V. 48; 50; 52
Reminiscences of the Texas Republic. Galveston: 1876. V. 49

SMITH, B.
The Art of the First Fleet and Other Early Australian Drawings. London: 1988. V. 50

SMITH, BAKER PETER
A Journal of an Excursion Round the South-Eastern Coast of England. London: 1834. V. 50

SMITH, BERNARD E.
Designs and Sketches for Furniture in the Neo-Jacobean & Other Styles. London: 1876. V. 48

SMITH, BETTY
A Tree Grows in Brooklyn. New York: 1943. V. 49; 51

SMITH, BRADLEY
20th Century Masters of Erotic Art. New York: 1980. V. 53

SMITH, BRYDON
Donald Judd. A Catalogue of the Exhibition at the National Gallery of Canada, Ottawa 24 May - 6 July 1975. (with) Complete Writings 1959-1975... Ottawa/Halifax: 1975/75. V. 50

SMITH, BUCKINGHAM
Rudo Ensayo, Tenative de Una Prevencional Description Geographica de la Provincia de Sonora... St. Augustine: 1863. V. 47

SMITH, C. C.
The Life and Work of Jacob Kenoly. Cincinnati: 1912. V. 48; 53

SMITH, C. H. J.
Landscape Gardening; or, Parks and Pleasure Grounds. New York: 1853. V. 51

SMITH, CECIL
The Birds of Somersetshire. London: 1869. V. 52

SMITH, CECIL H.
Collection of J. Pierpont Morgan. Bronzes, Antique Greek, Roman, etc... Paris: 1913. V. 52

SMITH, CHARD POWERS
Prelude to Man. Mt. Vernon: 1936. V. 48

SMITH, CHARLES
The American War, from 1775 to 1783, with Plans. New York: 1797. V. 47
The Ancient and Present State of the County and City of Cork. Cork: 1815. V. 51
The Ancient and Present State of the County and City of Waterford. Dublin: 1774. V. 47
Elegiac Sonnets. London: 1792. V. 52
The Monthly Repository, Respectfully Inscribed to the Military of the United States of America. New York: 1796-97. V. 47

SMITH, CHARLES A.
A Comprehensive History of Minnehaha County, South Dakota. Mitchell: 1949. V. 52

SMITH, CHARLES HAMILTON
Costume Of the Army of the British Empire According to the Last Regulations, 1814. London: 1812-15. V. 49
Horses. The Equidae or Genus Equus. Edinburgh: 1841. V. 50; 53
The Natural History of Horses. Edinburgh: 1841. V. 47
The Natural History of the Human Species... London. V. 47
The Natural History of the Human Species. Edinburgh: 1848. V. 53
The Natural History of the Human Species... London: 1852. V. 53

SMITH, CHARLES JOHN
Historical and Literary Curiosities. London: 1840. V. 48; 51; 52; 53
Historical and Literary Curiosities... London: 1847. V. 48
Historical and Literary Curiosities... London: 1875. V. 49; 53

SMITH, CHARLES ROACH
The Antiquities of Richborough, Reculver and Lymne, in Kent. London: 1850. V. 53
Catalogue of the Museum of London Antiquities. London: 1854. V. 50; 53

SMITH, CHARLES W.
Check-List of Books and Pamphlets Relating to the History of the Pacific Northwest. Olympia: 1909. V. 53
Journal of a Trip to California, Across the Continent from Weston, Mo. to Weber Creek, Cal. in the Summer of 1850. New York: 1920. V. 54
Old Virginia in Block Prints. Richmond: 1929. V. 50

SMITH, CHARLIE
Canaan. New York: 1984. V. 50; 51

SMITH, CHARLOTTE
Celestina. A Novel. London: 1791. V. 47
Desmond. London: 1792. V. 48
Elegiac Sonnets. London: 1786. V. 48
Elegiac Sonnets. London: 1795. V. 49
Elegiac Sonnets. London: 1795-97. V. 54
The Emigrants, a Poem. London: 1793. V. 49
Emmeline, the Orphan of the Castle. London: 1789. V. 48
Ethelinde; or the Recluse of the Lake. London: 1820. V. 53
Minor Morals, Interspersed with Sketches of Natural History, Historical Anecdotes and Original Stories. London: 1806. V. 49
Montalbert, a Novel. London: 1795. V. 54
A Narrative of the Loss of the Catherine, Venus and Piedmont Transports and the Thomas, Golden Grove and Aeolus Merchant Ships Near Weymouth on Wednesday the 18th of November Last. London: 1796. V. 48
Rambles Farther: a Continuation of Rural Walks... Dublin: 1796. V. 48

SMITH, CHETWOOD
Rogers Groups: Thought & Wrought by John Rogers. Boston: 1934. V. 48

SMITH, CLARE SYDNEY
The Golden Reign - The Story of My Friendship with Lawrence of Arabia. London: 1940. V. 53

SMITH, CLARK ASHTON
The Abominations of Yondo. Sauk City: 1960. V. 48; 52
The Dark Chateau. Sauk City: 1951. V. 52
The Double Shadow and Other Fantasies. 1933. V. 52
The Double Shadow and Other Fantasies. Auburn: 1933. V. 49
Genius Loci. Sauk City: 1948. V. 47; 51; 52
The Immortals of Mercury. 1932. V. 47; 51
Lost Worlds. Sauk City: 1944. V. 48; 52; 54
Nero and other Poems. Lakeport: 1937. V. 48; 54
Poems in Prose. Sauk City: 1965. V. 51
Poems in Prose. Sauk City: 1965/64. V. 48
Sandalwood. 1925. V. 51; 53
Spells and Philtres. Sauk City: 1958. V. 50
The Star-Treader and other Poems. 1912. V. 48; 52
The Star-Treader and Other Poems. San Francisco: 1912. V. 50
Tales of Science and Sorcery. Sauk City: 1964. V. 50; 51

SMITH, DAVE
Gray Soldiers. 1983. V. 48; 53; 54
Gray Soldiers. Winston-Salem: 1983. V. 49; 51

SMITH, DAVID EUGENE
History of Mathematics. Boston: 1923-25. V. 54
Rare Arithmetica: a Catalogue of the Arithmetics Written Before the Year MDCI with a Description of Those in the Library of George Arthur Plimpton. Boston & London: 1908. V. 48; 50; 52; 54

SMITH, DAVID SETH
Jolly Families. Surrey: 1950. V. 53

SMITH, DAVID WILLIAM
Gazetteer of the Province of Upper Canada: to Which is Added, An Appendix... New York: 1813. V. 53

SMITH, DIANE SOLETHER
The Armstrong Chronicle, a Ranching History. Corona: 1986. V. 53

SMITH, E. BALDWIN
The Dome. A Study in the History of Ideas. Princeton: 1950. V. 50
Egyptian Architecture as Cultural Expression. New York: 1938. V. 48; 51

SMITH, E. BOYD
My Village. New York: 1896. V. 47; 50

SMITH, E. W.
The Ila Speaking People of Northern Rhodesia. London: 1920. V. 51

SMITH, EDGAR C.
A Short History of Naval and Marine Engineering. Cambridge: 1937. V. 50

SMITH, EDGAR W.
Baker Street Inventory. Summit: 1945. V. 47
Letters from Baker Street. New York: 1942. V. 49; 51
Profile by Gaslight. New York: 1944. V. 47

SMITH, EDMUND
Phaedra and Hippolitus. London: 1707. V. 48

SMITH, EDMUND W.
A Tomato Can Chronicle and Other Stories of Fishing & Shooting. New York: 1937. V. 47

SMITH, EDMUND WARE
The One-Eyed Poacher of Privilege. New York: 1941. V. 48; 52
Tall Tales and Short. New York: 1938. V. 52; 53

SMITH, EDWARD
Dietaries for the Immates of Workhouses. London: 1866. V. 51
The Life of Joseph Banks, President of the Royal Society, with some Notices of His Friends and Contemporaries. London/New York: 1911. V. 53
Smith's Trial. A Full an Authentic Report of the Trial of Ensign Edward Smith, for a Rape Alledged to Have Been Committed on the Body of Miss Sarah Rawson..County of Dublin, on Tuesduay, the 7th Day of October, 1800. Dublin: 1800. V. 53

SMITH, EDWARD C.
A History of Lewis County, West Virginia. Weston: 1920. V. 52

SMITH, EDWARD E.
First Lensman. London: 1955. V. 51
Galactic Patrol. 1950. V. 54
Second Stage Lensmen. 1953. V. 52
Second Stage Lensmen. Reading: 1953. V. 50
The Skylark of Space. 1946. V. 47; 51; 52
The Skylark of Space. Providence: 1946. V. 52
The Skylark of Space. 1947. V. 48; 52
The Skylark of Valeron. 1949. V. 48; 51; 52
Skylark Three. 1948. V. 48
Spacehounds of IPC. 1947. V. 48; 52
Triplanetary. 1948. V. 47; 48; 51; 52
Triplanetary... Reading: 1948. V. 48
Triplanetary... London: 1954. V. 51
The Vortex Blasater. 1960. V. 52

SMITH, EDWIN
Cuts. 1992. V. 52

SMITH, EGERTON
The Melange, a Variety of Original Pieces in Prose and Verse... Liverpool: 1834. V. 49

SMITH, ELBERT H.
Ma-Ka-Tai-Me-She-Kia-Kiak: or Black Hawk and Scenes in the West. New York: 1848. V. 47; 49; 50

SMITH, ELI
Researches of the Rev. E. Smith and Rev. H. G. O. Dwight in Armenia... Boston: 1833. V. 47

SMITH, ELIAS
The American Physician and Family Assistant in Five Parts. Boston: 1837. V. 51; 54
A Discourse on Government and Religion; Delivered at Gray, (Maine), July Fourth, 1810, at the Celebration of American Independence. Portland: 1810. V. 54
An Essay on the Fall of Angels & Men... Boston: 1812. V. 49
The Peoples' Book. Boston: 1836. V. 48

SMITH, ELIZA
The Compleat Housewife... London: 1737. V. 50

SMITH, ELIZABETH
Fragments...Prose and Verse... Bath: 1811. V. 53
Fragments...Prose and Verse. Burlington: 1811. V. 54

SMITH, ELIZABETH OAKES
The Newsboy. Amsterdam: 1856. V. 52

SMITH, ELLA
Starring Miss Barbara Stanwyck. New York: 1974. V. 51

SMITH, ERNEST BRAMAH
English Farming and Why I Turned It Up. London: 1894. V. 48; 50; 51
The Eyes of Max Carrados. London: 1923. V. 48
A Guide to the Varieties and Rarity of English Regal Copper Coins. 1671-1860. London: 1929. V. 48
The Kai Lung Omnibus. London: 1936. V. 47
Kai Lung Unrolls His Mat. 1928. V. 48; 50
Kai Lung Unrolls His Mat. London: 1928. V. 50
Kai Lung Unrolls the Mat. New York: 1928. V. 47; 49
Kai Lung's Golden Hours. London. V. 52
Kai Lung's Golden Hours. London: 1922. V. 51
Kai Lung's Golden Hours. London: 1924. V. 48; 51; 53
Kai Lung's Golden Hours. London: 1929. V. 51; 53
A Little Flutter. London: 1930. V. 53
Max Carrados Mysteries. 1927. V. 53
The Mirror of Kong Ho. London: 1905. V. 52
The Return of Kai Lung. New York: 1937. V. 51
The Transmutation of Ling. London: 1911. V. 48
The Transmutation of Ling. New York: 1911. V. 49
The Wallet of Kai Lung. 1900. V. 51; 53
The Wallet of Kai Lung. London: 1900. V. 47; 48
The Wallet of Kai Lung. London: 1923. V. 48; 50; 52; 53

SMITH, ETHAN
Key to the Revelation. In Thirty-Six Lectures, Taking the Whole Book in Course. New York: 1833. V. 50

SMITH, EUSTACE
Clinical Studies of Diseases in Children. Diseases of the Lungs, Acute Tuberculosis. London: 1876. V. 54

SMITH, FAY JACKSON
Father Kind in Arizona. 1966. V. 49

SMITH, FERRIS
Plastic and Reconstructive Surgery: a Manual of Management. Philaldephia: 1950. V. 54

SMITH, FLORENCE M.
Mary Astell. New York: 1916. V. 54

SMITH, FRANCIS
Report Of a Committee Appointed by the Sanitary Commission to Prepare a Paper on the Value of Vaccination in Armies. Philadelphia: 1861. V. 50
Some Observations Upon the Late Tryals of Sir George Wakeman, Corker and Marshall &c. London: 1679. V. 53

SMITH, FRANCIS HOPKINSON
Outdoor Sketching. New York: 1915. V. 48
A White Umbrella in Mexico. London: 1889. V. 48

SMITH, FRANK MERIWEATHER
San Francisco Vigilance Committee of '56, With Some Interesting Sketches of Events Succeeding 1846. San Francisco: 1883. V. 48

SMITH, FREDERICK
The Early History of Veterinary Literature and Its British Development. London: 1976. V. 50; 52
A Manual of Veterinary Hygiene. London: 1887. V. 49

SMITH, G.
The Highflyers Guide, or How to Breed and Train Tipplers, Tumblers, Rollers, Cumulets and Cross-Breds. Nottingham: 1890. V. 52

SMITH, G. E. KIDDER
A Pictorial History of Architecture in America. New York: 1976. V. 49; 50

SMITH, G. ELLIOT
A Catalogue of Rare or Remarkable Phaenogamous Plants Collected in South Kent. London: 1829. V. 51
Egyptian Mummies. London: 1924. V. 49
Egyptian Mummies. New York: 1924. V. 53
Egyptian Mummies. New York: 1925. V. 48
Elephants and Ethnologists. London, New York: 1924. V. 49; 50; 51

SMITH, G. MUNRO
A History of the Bristol Royal Infirmary. Bristol: 1917. V. 54

SMITH, GARDEN G.
The World of Golf. London: 1898. V. 53

SMITH, GEOFFREY
A Naturalist in Tasmania. Oxford: 1909. V. 52

SMITH, GEORGE
Assyrian Discoveries. London: 1875. V. 47; 49; 51; 52
Assyrian Discoveries... New York: 1875. V. 47; 48
The Cassiterides: an Inquiry into the Commercial Operations of the Phoenicians in Western Europe... London: 1863. V. 49; 54
A Compleat Body of Distilling, Explaining the Mysteries of that Science... London: 1725. V. 48
A Compleat Body of Distilling, Explaining the Mysteries of that Science. London: 1731. V. 48
A Compleat Body of Distilling, Explaining the Mysteries of that Science... London: 1738. V. 48
Essay on the Construction of Cottages, Suited for the Dwellings of the Labouring Classes, for which the Premium was Voted by the Highland Society of Scotland. Glasgow: 1834. V. 47
History of Assurbanipal, Translated from the Cuneiform Inscriptions. London: 1871. V. 47
History of Delaware County, Pennsylvania, from the Discovery of the Territory Included Within Its Limits to the Present Time... Philadelphia: 1862. V. 47
History of Sennacherib. London: 1878. V. 47
The Oldest London Bookshop. A History of Two Hundred Years... London: 1928. V. 53

SMITH, GEORGE ALBERT
Correspondence of Palestine Tourists; Comprising a Series of Letters. Salt Lake City: 1875. V. 52
The Rise, Progress and Travels of the Church of Jesus Christ of Latter Day Saints... Salt Lake City: 1872. V. 47; 53
The Rise, Progress and Travels of the Church of Jesus Christ of Latter Day Saints. Liverpool & London: 1873. V. 47

SMITH, GEORGE, ARCHITECT
Essay On the Construction of Cottages... Glasgow: 1834. V. 50; 53

SMITH, GEORGE BARNETT
Shelley. A Critical Biography. Edinburgh: 1877. V. 52

SMITH, GOLDWIN
A Letter to a Whig Member of the Southern Independence Association. London: 1864. V. 54
The United Kingdom: a Political History. London: 1899. V. 52

SMITH, GUSSE THOMAS
Birds of the Arizona Desert. Phoenix: 1941. V. 47

SMITH, GUSTAVUS WOODSON
The Battle of Seven Pines. New York: 1891. V. 49
Confederate War Papers. Fairfax Court House, New Orleans, Seven Pines, Richmond and North Carolina. New York: 1884. V. 49

SMITH, GYLES, PSEUD.
Serious Reflections on the Dangerous Tendency of the Common Practices of Card-Playing... London: 1754. V. 48

SMITH, H. ALLEN
Lo, the Former Egyptian!. Garden City: 1947. V. 51; 53
Lost in the Horse Latitudes. Garden City: 1944. V. 51

SMITH, H. M.
The Fresh-Water Fishes of Siam, or Thailand. 1945. V. 51
Synopsis of the Herpetofauna of Mexico. Augusta & No. Bennington: 1971-80. V. 53

SMITH, H. S.
Saqqara Demotic Papyri I. London: 1983. V. 49; 51

SMITH, HAMMOND
Albert Goodwin, R.W.S., 1845-1932. Essex: 1977. V. 54
Albert Goodwin R.W.S., 1845-1932. Leigh on Sea: 1977. V. 49
Peter de Wint 1784-1849. London: 1982. V. 50

SMITH, HARRY B.
Robin Hood: a Comic Opera. New York: 1896. V. 48

SMITH, HARRY WORCESTER
Life and Sport in Aiken and Those Who Made It. New York: 1935. V. 47; 50
A Sporting Family of the Old South. Albany: 1936. V. 49
A Sporting Tour Through Ireland, England, Wales and France. Columbia: 1925. V. 47

SMITH, HENRY
Observations on the Prevailing Practice of Supplying Medical Assistance to the Poor, Commonly Called the Farming of Parishes... London: 1819. V. 50; 52; 54
The Sermons...Together With Other His Learned Treatises...also the Life of the Reverend and Learned Author. London: 1675. V. 53

SMITH, HENRY ECROYD
The History of Conisborough Castle with Glimpses of Ivanhoe-Land. Worksop: 1887. V. 53
Reliquiae Isurianae: the Remains of the Roman Isurium... London: 1852. V. 48

SMITH, HENRY HOLMES
Henry Holmes Smith. Portfolio Two. Louisville: 1973. V. 54

SMITH, HERBERT H.
Brazil. The Amazons and the Coast. New York: 1879. V. 51

SMITH, HORACE
Amarynthus, the Hympholept. London: 1821. V. 52
Arthur Arundel, a Tale of the English Revolution. London: 1844. V. 50
Brambletye House; or, Cavaliers and Roundheads. London: 1826. V. 49; 51
Brambletye House; or, Cavaliers and Roundheads. Paris: 1826. V. 50
Horace in London: Consisting of Imitations of the First Two Bookes of the odes of Horace. London: 1813. V. 51
The Moneyed Man, or the Lesson of Life. London: 1841. V. 50
The New Forest. London: 1829. V. 50
Oliver Cromwell, an Historical Romance. London: 1840. V. 53
Quadrilling; a Favourite Song, by the Author of Rejected Addresses. Birmingham: 1822. V. 51
Tales of the Early Ages. London: 1832. V. 53
The Tin Trumpet... London: 1836. V. 48
The Tin Trumpet. Philadelphia: 1836. V. 53
The Tor Hill. London: 1826. V. 47; 49; 51
Walter Colyton: a Tale of 1688. London: 1830. V. 51

SMITH, HORACE W.
Nuts for Future Historians to Crack... Philadelphia: 1856. V. 47

SMITH, HUGH
Formulae Medicamentorum; or, a Compendium of the Modern Practice of Physic. London: 1772. V. 48
Letters to Married Ladies, to Which is Added A Letter on Corsets... New York: 1827. V. 53
Letters to Married Women, on Nursing and Management of Children. Philadelphia: 1792. V. 48
Medicanmentorum Formulae: ad Varias Medendi Intentiones Concinnatae. London: 1760. V. 48

SMITH, I. B.
The Speculative Dictionary... New York: 1835. V. 49

SMITH, IRWIN
The Theatrical Journey-Work and Anecdotal Recollections of Sol Smith. Philadelphia: 1854. V. 47

SMITH, J.
Sixteen Views of the Lakes in Cumberland and Westmorland. London. V. 48

SMITH, J. BUCKNALL
A Treatise Upon Cable or Rope Traction, as Applied to Working of Street and Other Railways. London: 1887. V. 47; 50; 54

SMITH, J. C.
Tempest an Opera. 1756. V. 52

SMITH, J. CALVIN
The Illustrated Hand-Book, A New Guide for Travelers through the United States of America... New York: 1848. V. 47

SMITH, J. F.
John Cassell's Illustrated History of England. London: 1857-64. V. 53

SMITH, J. GRAY
A Brief Historical, Statistical and Descriptive Review of East Tennessee, United States of America, Developing Its Immense Agricultural, Mining and Manufacturing Advantages, with Remarks to Emigrants... London: 1842. V. 47

SMITH, J. GREIG
Abdominal Surgery. Philadelphia: 1887. V. 54

SMITH, J. L. B.
The Fishes of the Seychelles. Grahmastown: 1963. V. 49
The Sea Fishes of Southern Africa. Cape Town: 1961. V. 51

SMITH, J. S.
Anthems Composed for the Choir Service of the Church of England. London: 1793. V. 52

SMITH, J. THORNE
Biltmore Oswald, The Diary of a Hapless Recruit. New York: 1918. V. 48
Haunts and By-Paths, and Other Poems. New York: 1919. V. 48

SMITH, JAMES
An Account of the Remarkable Occurrences in the Life... Philadelphia: 1831. V. 51
An Account of the Remarkable Occurrences in the Life... Philadelphia: 1834. V. 53
The Mechanic, or Compendium of Practical Inventions... Liverpool: 1818. V. 50
The Panorama of Science and Art. Liverpool: 1815. V. 50; 54
Rejected Addresses. London: 1812. V. 51
Remarks on thorough Draining and Deep Ploughing. Stirling: 1837. V. 53
Remarks on Thorough Draining and Deep Ploughing. Stirling: 1844. V. 49
The Winter of 1840 in St. Croix, with an Excursion to Tortola and St. Thomas. New York: 1840. V. 49

SMITH, JAMES EDWARD
English Botany. London: 1863-72. V. 51
The English Flora. London: 1828-29. V. 49
Exotic Botany... London: 1804-05. V. 49; 52
Fifteen Views Illustrative of a Tour to Hafod, In Cardiganshire, The Seat of Thomas Johnes, Esq. M.P. London: 1810. V. 48
Filamentous Fungi. New York: 1975-78. V. 49
Flora Britannica, Auctore Jacobo Edvardo Smith. London: 1800-04. V. 49
A Grammar of Botany, Illustrative of Artificial, as Well as Natural Classification... London: 1821. V. 53
A Grammar of Botany, Illustrative of Artificial, as Well as Natural Classification... New York: 1822. V. 51; 53
Icones Pictae Plantarum Rariorum... London: 1790-93. V. 48
Icones Pictae Plantarum Rariorum... London: 1792. V. 54
An Introduction to Physiological and Systematical Botany. Boston: 1814. V. 54
An Introduction to Physiological and Systematical Botany. Philadelphia: 1814. V. 49
An Introduction to Physiological and Systematical Botany. London: 1819. V. 48
An Introduction to Physiological and Systematical Botany. London: 1826. V. 52; 53
A Sketch of a Tour on the Continent. London: 1793. V. 48; 53
Sketch of a Tour on the Continent... London: 1807. V. 54

SMITH, JAMES L.
Autobiography of James L. Smith... Norwich: 1881. V. 48; 53

SMITH, JAMES, MRS.
The Booandik Tribe of South Austrlian Aborigines. Adelaide: 1880. V. 52

SMITH, JAMES POWER
General Lee at Gettysburg. Richmond: 1905. V. 49
Stonewall Jackson and Chancellorsville. Richmond: 1904. V. 49

SMITH, JEDEDIAH STRONG
The Southwest Expedition of Jedediah S. Smith. His Personal Account of the Journey to California 1826-1827. Glendale: 1977. V. 48; 51; 53

SMITH, JEROME VAN CROWNINSHIELD
Natural History of the Fishes of Massachusetts, Embracing a Practical Essay on Angling. Boston: 1833. V. 48; 50; 54
Trout and Angling. New York: 1929. V. 47; 48; 50; 51

SMITH, JESSIE WILCOX
A Child's Stamp Book of Old Verses. New York: 1915. V. 48

SMITH, JOHN
Advertisements fro the Unexperienced Planters of New England or Anywhere; or, the Pathway to Erect a Planatation. Boston: 1865. V. 47
Chronicon Rusticum - Commerciale; or, Memoirs of Wool, &c. London: 1747. V. 51; 52
Curiosities of Common Water; or, the Advantages Thereof in Preventing and Curing Many Diseases... London: 1851. V. 54
A Description of New England... Boston: 1865. V. 51
Fruits and Farinacea, the Proper Food of Man... London: 1845. V. 48
Galice Antiquities: Consisting of a History of the Druids, Particularly Those of Caledonia... Edinburgh: 1780. V. 47
The Generall Historie of Virginia, New England and the Summer Isles. Glasgow: 1907. V. 53
The Generall Historie of Virginia, New England and the Summer Isles... Cleveland: 1966. V. 48
The Pourtract of Old Age. London: 1666. V. 52
The Pourtract of Old Age. London: 1676. V. 47
The Printer's Grammar... London: 1755. V. 48
The Printer's Grammar... London: 1787. V. 51
Select Discourses Treating, 1. Of the True Way of Method of Attaining to Divine Knowledge. 2. Of Superstition. 3. Of Atheism. 4. Of the Immortality of the Soul. 5. Of the Existence and Nature of God. 6. of Prophecy. London: 1660. V. 50
Travels and Works of Captain John Smith, President of Virginia and Admiral of New England. London: 1910. V. 52
The True Art of Angling; Being a Clear and Speedy Way of Taking All Sorts of fresh-Water Fish, with the Worn, Fly, Paste and Other Baits in Their Proper Seasons. London: 1770. V. 50
A True Relation of Virginia. Boston: 1866/65. V. 51
The True Travels, Adventures and Observations of Captaine John Smith. New York: 1930. V. 54
The True Travels and Adventures and Observations of Captaine John Smith. Richmond: 1819. V. 47
Works. 1608-1631. Birmingham: 1884. V. 52

SMITH, JOHN, DEALER IN PICTURES
A Catalogue Raisonne of the Works of the Most Eminent Dutch, Flemish and French Painters. London: 1908. V. 54

SMITH, JOHN FREDERICK
Stanfield Hall: an Historical Romance. London: 1888-9. V. 53

SMITH, JOHN JAY
American Historical and Literary Curiosities... Philadelphia: 1847. V. 48
American Historical and Literary Curiosities... New York: 1860. V. 54
Recollections of John Jay Smith. Philadelphia: 1892. V. 51

SMITH, JOHN, OF THE INNER TEMPLE
Iconographica Scotica; or, Portraits of Illustrious Persons of Sccotland... London: 1798. V. 50

SMITH, JOHN RUSSELL
Bibliotheca Cantiana: a Bibliographica Account of What Has Been Published on the History, Topography...of the County of Kent. London: 1837. V. 47; 48; 49; 50; 53; 54
(Sale) Catalogue of Unique Collection of Ancient English Broadside Ballads. London: 1856. V. 50

SMITH, JOHN SIDNEY
A Treatise on the Practice of the Court of Chancery... Philadelphia: 1839. V. 50

SMITH, JOHN STORES
Mirabeau: a Life History. London: 1848. V. 49

SMITH, JOHN TALBOT
A Woman of Culture. New York: 1883. V. 47; 52

SMITH, JOHN THOMAS
Ancient Topography of London... London: 1815. V. 47; 50; 52
An Antiquarian Ramble in the Streets of London, with Anecdotes of Their More Celebrated Residents. London: 1846. V. 50
Antiquites of London and Its Environs. London: 1791-1800. V. 48; 49
Antiquities of Westminster. London: 1807. V. 47; 50; 51
Antiquities of Westminster. London: 1807-09. V. 48; 52; 54
Nollekens and His Times... London: 1828. V. 51; 54
Nollekens and His Times... London: 1829. V. 48; 50; 54
Remarks on Rural Scenery. London: 1797. V. 49; 50; 52
Vagabondiana, or, Anecdotes of Mendicant Wanderers through the Streets of London.. London: 1815-17. V. 53
Vagabondiana; or, Anecdotes of Mendicant Wanderers through the Streets of London... London: 1817. V. 50

SMITH, JOSEPH
Bibliotheca Smithiana, Sue Catalogues Librorum D. Josephi Smithii Angli per Cognomina Authorum dispositus. Venice: 1755. V. 48; 51
The Book of Doctrine and Covenants, of the Church of Jesus Christ of Latter-Day Saints... Liverpool: 1854. V. 51
A Catalogue of Books Adverse to the Society of Friends... London: 1873. V. 51
Old Redstone; or, Histoical Sketches of Western Presbyterianism, Its Early Ministers, Its Perilous Times and Its First Records. Philadelphia: 1854. V. 47; 50
The Pearl of Great Price. Salt Lake City: 1888. V. 51

SMITH, JOSEPH R.
Observations on Texas Cattle. Concord: 1884. V. 49

SMITH, JOSHUA HETT
An Authentic Narrative of the Causes Which Led to the Death of Major Andre. London: 1808. V. 47; 50; 51
An Authentic Narrative of the Causes Which led to the Death of Major Andre... New York: 1809. V. 51

SMITH, JOSHUA TOULMIN
The Discovery of America by the Northmen in the Tenth Century. London: 1839. V. 47
Journal in America, 1837-1838. 1925. V. 53

SMITH, JUDITH
The Mary Calendar. Ditchling: 1930. V. 47

SMITH, JULIA
Letters of the Swedish Court, Written Chiefly in the Early Part of the Reign of Gustavus III, to Which is added an Appendix Containing an Account of the Assassination of that Monarch... London: 1809. V. 54

SMITH, JULIE
Death Turns a Trick. New York: 1982. V. 54
The Sourdough Wars. New York: 1984. V. 54

SMITH, JUSTIN HARVEY
Annexation of Texas. New York: 1941. V. 52
Our Struggle for the Fourteenth Colony Canada and the American Revolution. New York: 1907. V. 47
The War With Mexico, 1846-1848. New York: 1919. V. 54

SMITH, KAY
Footnote to the Lord's Prayer and Other Poems. Montreal: 1951. V. 47

SMITH, KENNETH M.
Mumps Measles and Mosaics. London: 1954. V. 48

SMITH, L. P.
Trivia. 1917. V. 50

SMITH, LEE
Black Mountain Breakdown. New York: 1980. V. 53; 54
Bob, a Dog. Chapel Hill: 1988. V. 53
Cakewalk. New York: 1981. V. 49
Fancy Strut. New York: 1973. V. 47; 53
The Last Day the Dogbushes Bloomed. New York: 1968. V. 49; 50; 51
Oral History. New York: 1983. V. 50; 51
Something in the Wind. New York & Evanston: 1971. V. 49; 50; 51; 52; 53

SMITH, LILLIAN
The Journey. Cleveland: 1954. V. 48
Killers of the Dream. London: 1950. V. 48

SMITH, LOGAN PEARSALL
A Portrait of Logan Pearsall Smith - Drawn from His Letters and Diaries... 1950. V. 53
The Prospects of Literature. London: 1927. V. 53
Robert Bridges. Oxford: 1931. V. 50
Songs and Sonnets. London: 1909. V. 54
Stories from the Old Testament. London: 1920. V. 51
The Youth of Parnassus and Other Stories. London: 1895. V. 49; 53

SMITH, LUCY MACK
Biographical Sketches of Joseph Smith, the Prophet, and His Progenitors for Many Generations. Liverpool & London: 1853. V. 47; 52

SMITH, M. A.
Fauna of British India, Reptilia and Amphibia. Volume 3. Serpentes. London: 1943. V. 51

SMITH, MADELEINE
Full Report, of the Extraordinary and Interesting Trial of Miss Madeleine Smith. London: 1857. V. 52
The Story of Minie l'Angelier or Madeleine Hamilton Smith. Edinburgh: 1857. V. 52

SMITH, MARGARET
Leaves from Margaret Smith's Journal in the Province of Massachusetts Bay 1678-79. Boston: 1849. V. 47

SMITH, MARGARET BAYARD
A Winter in Washington Or, Memoirs of the Seymour Family. New York: 1824. V. 49

SMITH, MARK
The Death of the Detective. New York: 1974. V. 53

SMITH, MARTIN CRUZ
Canto for a Gypsy. New York: 1972. V. 50
Gypsy in Amber. New York: 1971. V. 50
Nightwing. New York: 1977. V. 50

SMITH, MARTIN F.
A Book of Canadian and American Poems. Hamilton: 1863. V. 49

SMITH, MARTIN L.
Report of the Secretary of War....A map of the Valley of Mexico From Surveys By... Washington: 1849. V. 49

SMITH, MARY
An Affecting Narrative of the Captivity and Sufferings of Mrs. Mary Smith, Who With Her Husband and Three Daughters Was taken Prisoner by the Indians, in August 1814... 1818. V. 48; 51; 52
Young Puritan's in Captivity. Boston: 1907. V. 49

SMITH, MARY ANNE PELLEW
Six Years' Travels in Russia. London: 1859. V. 50

SMITH, MARY STUART
Virginia Cookery-Book. New York: 1885. V. 47

SMITH, MATTHEW
Memoirs of Secret Service. London: 1699. V. 53

SMITH, MAURICE L.
Who Cares. New York: 1968. V. 54

SMITH, MEREDITH J.
Marsupials of Australia. Melbourne: 1980. V. 53

SMITH, MICHAEL
A Geographical View of the British Possessions in North America. Baltimore: 1814. V. 53
Geographical View of the Province of Upper Canada... New York: 1813. V. 47; 53
A Geographical View of the Province of Upper Canada... Philadelphia: 1813. V. 47
A Geographical View of the Province of Upper Canada. Trenton: 1813. V. 47; 50; 53

SMITH, MISS
Studies of Flowers from Nature... 1820. V. 47; 51; 52; 53

SMITH, MOSES
History of the Adventures and Sufferings of Moses Smith, During Five Years of His Life... Brooklyn: 1812. V. 53
History of the Adventures and Sufferings of Moses Smith, During Five Years of His Life. Albany: 1814. V. 48; 51

SMITH, MR.
A Short and Direct Method of Painting in Water Colour. London: 1730. V. 48

SMITH, NATHAN
Medical and Surgical Memoirs. Baltimore: 1831. V. 47; 48; 49; 50; 51; 53; 54
A Practical Essay on Typhous Fever. New York: 1824. V. 48; 50; 51; 52

SMITH, NORA ARCHIBALD
Boys and Girls of Bookland. New York: 1923. V. 47; 49; 50

SMITH, NORTON B.
Practical Treatise on the Breaking and Training of Wild and Vicious Horses, With over Forty Illustrations. London: 1892. V. 48

SMITH, O. H.
Early Indiana Trials and Sketches. Cincinatti: 1858. V. 47; 52

SMITH, OLIVER P.
The Domestic Architect... Buffalo: 1854. V. 47; 49

SMITH, P. E.
Experimental Evidence...Role of the Anterior Pituitary in the Development and Regulation of the Genital System. Philadelphia: 1927. V. 48

SMITH, PAUL JORDAN
A Key to the Ulysses of James Joyce. Chicago: 1927. V. 49

SMITH, PERCIVAL GORDON
Hints and Suggestions as to the Planning of Poor Law Buildings... London: 1901. V. 49

SMITH, PHILIP
New Directions in Bookbinding. 1974. V. 51
New Directions in Bookbinding. London: 1974. V. 48; 54
New Directions in Bookbinding. New York: 1974. V. 49

SMITH, R. A.
A History of Dickinson County Iowa, Together with an Account of the Spirit Lake Massacre and the Indian Troubles on the Northeastern Frontier. Des Moines: 1902. V. 50

SMITH, R. BOSWORTH
Life of Lord Lawrence. London: 1885. V. 54

SMITH, R. D.
Citadel. Cairo: 1942. V. 52

SMITH, R. G.
The Familiar Astrologer: an East Guide to Fate, Destiny & Foreknowledge. London: 1832/31. V. 49

SMITH, R. MORRIS
The Burlington Smiths: a Family History. Philadelphia: 1877. V. 47

SMITH, R. MURDOCH
A History of the Recent Discoveries at Cyrene. London: 1864. V. 53

SMITH, R. R. R.
Hellenistic Royal Portraits. Oxford: 1988. V. 50; 52

SMITH, RALPH CLIFTON
Life and Work of Henry Wolf. Champlain: 1927. V. 49

SMITH, RAY THOMAS
The Wonders of Nature and Art. London: 1803. V. 54

SMITH, RICHARD
Notes Made During a Tour in Denmark, Holstein, Mecklenburg-Schwerin, Pomerania, the Isle of Rugen, Prussia, Poland, Saxony, Brunswick, Hannover, The Hanseataic Territories... London: 1827. V. 47; 49

SMITH, RICHARD PENN
Col. Crockett's Exploits and Adventures in Texas...a Full Account of His Journey from Tennessee to the Red River and Natchitoches... New York: 1848. V. 49
The Miscellaneous Works of the Late Richard Penn Smith. Philadelphia: 1856. V. 48; 54

SMITH, RICHARD SHIRLEY
Richard Shirley Smith: Wood Engravings, a Selection, 1960-77. Pinner: 1983. V. 49
The Wood Engravings of Richard Shirley Smith. Cambridge: 1994. V. 52; 54
Wood Engravings...1960-1977. Ravelston: 1983. V. 53
Wood-Engravings...1960-1977. 1983. V. 47

SMITH, ROBERT
A Compleat System of Opticks... Cambridge: 1738. V. 48; 50; 52; 54
Harmonics, or the Philosophy of Musical Sounds... Cambridge: 1749. V. 53
Harmonics, or the Philosophy of Musical Sounds... 1759-62. V. 47
Harmonics, or the Philosophy of Musical Sounds... London: 1824. V. 50
Railroad to the Pacific Ocean. Washington: 1846. V. 47

SMITH, ROBERT ANGUS
Loch Etive and the Songs of Uisnach. London: 1879. V. 50; 52

SMITH, ROBERT C.
A Manual of Astrology, or the Book of the Stars, Being the Art of Foretelling Future Events by the Influences of the Heavenly Bodies. London: 1828. V. 48
Raphael's Witch!!! Or the Oracle of the Future. London: 1839. V. 48

SMITH, ROBERT E.
Ceramic Sequence at Uaxactun, Guatemala. New Orleans: 1955. V. 50

SMITH, ROBERT H.
Native Trout of North America. Portland: 1984. V. 53

SMITH, ROBERT HOUSTON
Pella of the Decapolis... Wooster: 1973. V. 50; 52
Pella of the Decapolis. Wooster: 1973-89. V. 50; 52

SMITH, ROBERT, RAT CATCHER
The Universal Directory for Taking Alive and Destroying Rats, and All Other Kinds of Four Footed and Winged Vermin. London: 1841. V. 54

SMITH, ROSS
Reminiscences of an Old Timer. 1930. V. 49

SMITH, S. COMPTON
Chile Con Carne or the Camp and the Field. New York: 1887. V. 52

SMITH, S. SKILBECK
A Subaltern in Mesopotamia and Judaea, 1916-17. London: 1930. V. 49

SMITH, SAMUEL
The History of the Colony of Nova Caesaria, or New Jersey... Burlington: 1765. V. 48; 50

SMITH, SAMUEL B.
The Wonderful Adventures of a Lady of French Nobility, and the Intrigues of a Popish Priest, Her Confessor, to Seduce and Murder Her. New York: 1836. V. 52

SMITH, SAMUEL STANHOPE
An Essay on the Causes of the Variety of Complexion and Figure in the Human Species. Philadelphia: 1787. V. 48
An Essay on the Causes of the Variety of Complexion and Figure in the Human Species... Edinburgh: 1788. V. 48
An Essay on the Causes of the Variety of Complexion and Figure in the Human Species... New Brunswick: 1810. V. 47; 49; 54
An Oration, Upon the Death of General George Washington, Delivered in the State-House at Trenton, on the 14th of January, 1800... Trenton: 1800. V. 51

SMITH, SEBA
John Smith's Letters, with "Pictiers" to Match. New York: 1839. V. 48; 52

SMITH, SIDNEY LAWTON
Sidney Lawton Smith, Designer, Etcher, Engraver. Boston: 1931. V. 49

SMITH, SOL
The Theatrical Apprenticeship and Anecdotal Recollections. Philadelphia: 1846. V. 54
Theatrical Management in the West and South for Thirty Years. New York: 1868. V. 47; 49; 52; 54

SMITH, STEPHEN
The City That Was. New York: 1911. V. 50

SMITH, STEVIE
A Good Time Was Had by All. London: 1937. V. 52
Harold's Leap. London: 1950. V. 47; 48; 49; 51; 53
The Holiday. London: 1949. V. 53
Mother, What Is Man? Poems. London: 1942. V. 48
Novel on Yellow Paper... London: 1936. V. 51; 52; 54
Novel on Yellow Paper. New York: 1937. V. 48; 51
Over the Frontier. London: 1918. V. 53
Over the Frontier. London: 1938. V. 50; 51
Selected Poems. London: 1965. V. 47

SMITH, SYDNEY
Bon-Mots. London: 1893. V. 54
Elementary Sketches of Moral Philosophy, Delivered at the Royal Institution, in the Years 1804, 1805 and 1806. London: 1849. V. 48
The Works. London: 1839-40. V. 54
The Works. London: 1848. V. 47

SMITH, SYDNEY K.
Life, Army Record and Public Services of D. Howard Smith. Louisville: 1890. V. 49

SMITH, T.
The Naturalist's Cabinet. London: 1806-07. V. 54

SMITH, T. MARSHALL
Legends of the War of Independence, and of The Earlier Settlements in the West. Louisville: 1855. V. 47

SMITH, T. R.
Poetica Erotica. New York: 1921-22. V. 47; 49

SMITH, T. ROGER
Acoustics in Relation to Architecture and Building: the Laws of Sound as Applied to the Arrangement of Buildings. London: 1870's. V. 50

SMITH, T. WATSON
History of the Methodist Church Within the Territories...of Eastern British America.... Halifax: 1877. V. 48

SMITH, THADDEUS L.
The Twenty-Fourth Iowa Volunteers. Des Moines: 1893-95. V. 48

SMITH, THOMAS
An Account of the Greek Church, As To its Doctrine and Rites of Worship... London: 1680. V. 48; 51
The Commonwealth of England... London: 1609. V. 47; 50
The Commonwealth of England. London: 1635. V. 47
De Repubica et Administratione Anglorum Libri Tres. Londini: 1610. V. 54
De Republica Anglorum Libri Tres. Lug. Batavorum: 1630. V. 52
De Republica Anglorum Libri Tres... Leyden: 1630-27. V. 50
De Republica Anglorum Libri Tres. Lug. Batavor: 1641. V. 48
Epistolae Duae, Quarum Altera de Moribus ac... London: 1672. V. 49
Epistolae Duae, Quarum Altera de Moribus ac... Oxonii: 1672. V. 48
Extracts from the Diary of a Huntsman. London: 1838. V. 52; 53
Journals of the Rev. Thomas Smith and the Rev. Samuel Deane, Pastors of the First Church in Portland... Portland: 1849. V. 47; 50
The Life of a Fox, Written by Himself. London: 1843. V. 54
The Miner's Guide, Being a Description and Illustration of a Chart of Sections of the Principal Mines of Coal and Ironstone in the Counties of Stafford, Salop, Warwick and Durham. London: 1836. V. 53
Remarks Upon the Manners, Religion and Government of the Turks. London: 1678. V. 48
A Topographical and Historical Account of the Parish of St. Mary-Le-Bone. London: 1833. V. 54
Vitae Quorundam Eruditissimorum et Illustrium Virorum. London: 1707. V. 47
The Young Artist's Assistant in the Art of Drawing in Water colours, Exemplified in a Course of Twenty-Nine Progressive Lessons, on Animals, Fruit, Flowers, Still Life, Portrait, Miniature, Landscape, Perspective, Architecture and Sculpture... London: 1835. V. 48

SMITH, THOMAS ASSHETON
Reminiscences of the Late Thomas Assheton Smith, Esq... London: 1860. V. 47

SMITH, THOMAS L.
Elements of the Laws; or, Outlines of the System of Civil and Criminal Laws in Force in the United States, and in the Several States of the Union. Philadelphia: 1878. V. 50

SMITH, THOMAS LACEY
Chronicles of Turkeytown; or, The Works of Jeremy Peters. Philadelphia: 1829. V. 47

SMITH, THOMAS SHARPE
On the Economy of Nations. London: 1842. V. 52

SMITH, THOMAS SOUTHWOOD
Statement of the Preliminary Inquiry by T. Southwood Smith, Esq., M.D. and John Sutherland, Esq., M.D. on Epidemic at Croydon... London: 1853. V. 51

SMITH, THORNE
The Glorious Pool. New York: 1934. V. 49
The Night Life of the Gods. New York: 1931. V. 49
Out of Luck. New York: 1919. V. 49
Rain in the Doorway. New York: 1933. V. 49
Topper. New York: 1926. V. 49; 51; 53

SMITH, TOM
Sporting Incidents in the Life of Another Tom Smith. London: 1867. V. 47; 50

SMITH, TOM C.
History of the Parish Church of Preston in Amounderness. Preston: 1892. V. 48

SMITH, TRUMAN
An Examination of the Question of Anaesthesia, on the Memorial of Charles Thomas Wells, Referred to a Select Committee of the Senate of the United States... Washington: 1853?. V. 50
Speech of Mr. Truman Smith, of Connecticut, of the Physical Character of the Northern States of Mexico... Washington: 1848. V. 47; 49

SMITH, VERN E.
The Jones Men. Chicago: 1974. V. 53

SMITH, VINCENT A.
A History of Fine Art in India and Ceylon. Bombay: 1960. V. 50

SMITH, W.
A Synopsis of the British Diatomaceae. London: 1853. V. 52
Synopsis of the British Diatomaceae... London: 1853-56. V. 52
Synopsis of the British Diatomaceae... London: 1856. V. 49

SMITH, W. A.
The Anson Guards: Company C, Fourteenth Regiment, North Carolina Volunteers, 1861-1865. Charlotte: 1914. V. 49

SMITH, W. C. S.
A Journey to California in 1849. 1925. V. 49; 50

SMITH, W. H.
Smith's Family Physician... Montreal: 1873. V. 54

SMITH, W. H., MRS.
The Children's Japan. Tokyo: 1890. V. 51

SMITH, W. P.
The Book of the Great Railway Celebrations of 1857. New York: 1858. V. 53

SMITH, W. RAMSAY
Myths and Legends of the Australian Aboriginals. London: 1930. V. 52
Myths and Legends of the Australian Aboriginals. New York: 1930. V. 52

SMITH, W. W.
The Genus Primula. Edinburgh: 1941-50. V. 53
The Genus Primula. London: 1977. V. 50

SMITH, WALLACE D.
Prodigal Sons, the Adventures of Christopher Evans and John Sontag. Boston: 1951. V. 53; 54

SMITH, WALTER
Art Education, Scholastic and Industrial. Boston: 1872. V. 52

SMITH, WALTER E.
The Bronte Sisters, A Bibliographical Catalogue. Los Angeles: 1991. V. 47; 49; 53; 54
Charles Dickens in the Original Cloth... Los Angeles: 1982-83. V. 49; 50; 51; 52; 54

SMITH, WALTER H. B.
Pistols and Revolvers. Washington: 1946. V. 48

SMITH, WALTER PARRY HASKETT
Climbing in the British Isles. London: 1894-95. V. 54

SMITH, WATSON
Kiva Mural Decorations at Awatovi and Kaw-aika- With a Survey of Other Wall Paintings in the Pueblo Southwest. Cambridge: 1952. V. 48; 51

SMITH, WILBUR
Cry Wolf. London: 1976. V. 51

SMITH, WILLIAM
An Account of the Proceedings of the Illinois (sic) and Oubache Land Companies, in Pursuance of Their Purchases Made of the Independent Natives, July 5th, 1773 and 18th October 1775. Philadelphia: 1796. V. 48
An Answer to Mr. Franklin's Remarks, on a Late Protest. Philadelphia: 1764. V. 47
A Brief State of the Province of Pennsylvania...and the True Cause of the Continual Encroachments of the French Displayed... London: 1755. V. 50
A Brief State of the Province of Pennsylvania...and the True Cause of the Continual Encroachments of the French Displayed. London: 1756. V. 47
A Dictionary of Christian Antiquites. (with) A Dictionary of Christian biography, Literature. Sects and Doctrines. London: 1875-80/75-87. V. 52
A Dictionary of Christian Biography, Literature, Sects and Doctrines. London: 1877-87. V. 47
A Dictionary of Greek and Roman Geography. London: 1878-73. V. 54
A Dictionary of the Bible. London: 1863. V. 48
Discourses on Public Occasions in America. London: 1762. V. 47; 49
An Examination of the Connecticut Claim to Lands in Pennsylvania. Philadelphia: 1774. V. 47
Gravenhurst or Thoughts on Good and Evil. Edinburgh & London: 1875. V. 49
The History and Antiquities of Morley, in the West Riding of the County of York. London: 1876. V. 53
History of Canada, from Its First Discovery to the Peace of 1763... Quebec: 1815. V. 49; 52
History of New-York. Albany: 1814. V. 47; 51
The History of the Post Office in British North America, 1639-1870. Cambridge: 1920. V. 50; 52; 54
The History of the Province of New York, from the First Discovery... London: 1757. V. 47; 50
The History of the Province of New York, from the First Discovery... London: 1776. V. 47
The History of the Province of New York, from the First Discovery... Philadelphia: 1792. V. 48
Journal of a Voyage in the Missionary Ship Duff, to the Pacific Ocean in the Years 1796, 7, 8, 9, 1800, 1, 2 &c. New York: 1813. V. 48
Memoirs of William Smith. London: 1844. V. 52
Morley, Ancient and Modern. London: 1886. V. 51
Old Yorkshire. London: 1881-84. V. 50
Old Yorkshire. Volume 2. London: 1881. V. 53
Old Yorkshire. Volume 3. London: 1882. V. 53
An Oration in Memory of General Montgomery, and of the Officers and Soldiers, Who Fell With Him, December 31, 1775, Before Quebec; Drawn Up (and Delivered February 19th, 1776) at the Desire of the Honorable Continental Congress. Philadelphia: 1776. V. 47
Peace and Unity Defended... Glasgow: 1766. V. 50
The Poetic Works... Chester: 1782. V. 54
The Progress of Civil and Mechanical Engineeering and Shipbuilding (Illustrated). 1877. V. 47
The Progress of Civil and Mechanical Engineering and Shipbuilding (Illustrated)... London: 1877. V. 54
Relation Historique de l'Expedition Contre les Indiens de l'Ohio en MDCCLXIV. Amsterdam: 1769. V. 48
Speech of Mr. Smith, of South Carolina, on the Admission of Missouri. Washington: 1820. V. 49
Trial of William Smith for Piracy, as One of the Crew of the Confederate Privateer. Philadelphia: 1861. V. 53
A Yorkshireman's Trip to the United States and Canada. London: 1892. V. 47

SMITH, WILLIAM A.
Lectures on the Philosophy and Practice of Slavery...in the United States: With the Duties of Masters to Slaves. Nashville: 1856. V. 49

SMITH, WILLIAM ANDERSON
Temperate Chile: a Progressive Spain. London: 1899. V. 51

SMITH, WILLIAM B.
Incidents of a Journey from Pennsylvania to Wisconsin Territory in 1837, Being the Journal of... Chicago: 1927. V. 50; 52
On Wheels and How I Came There... New York: 1892. V. 54
On Wheels and How I Came There. New York: 1893. V. 52

SMITH, WILLIAM C.
Indiana Miscellany: Consisting of Sketches of Indian Life, the Early Settlement, Customs and Hardships of the People... Cincinnati: 1867. V. 51
The Tracts Upon the Union. 1831. V. 49

SMITH, WILLIAM CUSACK
An Authentic Report of the Address of Baron William Sir William Smith, to Chief Constable Blake, and Others of the Constabulary, on Their Acquittal at the Last Assizes at Mullingar. Mullingar: 1831. V. 48
The Maze a Poem... London: 1815. V. 50
Miracles, a Rhapsody. London: 1823. V. 54

SMITH, WILLIAM H.
The St. Clair Papers. The Life and Public Services of Arthur St. Clair Soldier of the Revolutionary War... Cincinnati: 1882. V. 47

SMITH, WILLIAM HAWKES
Kenilworth Castle in the 16th, 18th and 19th Centuries, Displayed in Thirteen Lithographic Plates. Birmingham: 1821. V. 47

SMITH, WILLIAM HENRY
The Mediterranean, a Memoir: Physical, Historical and Nautical. London: 1854. V. 47
A Political History of Slavery... New York: 1903. V. 54
The Sea-Wall Question Analysed and Practically Resolved: by a Principle Applicable to all Marine Structures. London: 1849. V. 51

SMITH, WILLIAM L.
The Speeches of Mr. Smith, Of South Carolina, Delivered in the House of Representatives of the United States in January 1794, on the Subject of Certain Commercial Regulations, Proposed by Mr. Madison, in the Committee of the Whole, on the Report... London: 1794. V. 49

SMITH, WILLIAM, OF BESTHORP
The True Light Shining in England. London: 1660. V. 49

SMITH, WILLIAM R.
The History of Wisconsin. Madison: 1854. V. 47
Observations On the Wisconsin Territory. Philadelphia: 1838. V. 48; 53

SMITH, WILLIAM S.
The Trials of Williams S. Smith and Samuel G. Ogden, for Misdemeanours, Had in the Circuit Court of the United States for the New York District in July 1806. New York: 1807. V. 50

SMITH, WILLIAM STEVENSON
A History of Egyptian Sculpture and Painting in the Old Kingdom. London: 1946. V. 47
A History of Egyptian Sculpture and Painting in the Old Kingdom. London: 1949. V. 51
Interconnections in the Ancient Near East: a Study of the Relationships Between the Arts of Egypt, the Aegean and Western Asia. New Haven: 1965. V. 50

SMITH, WILLOUGHBY
The Rise and Extension of Submarine Telegraphy. London: 1891. V. 50

SMITHERS, HENRY
Observations Made During a Residence in Brussels and Several Tours through the Netherlands... Brussels: 1822. V. 53
Observations Made During a Tour in 1818 and 1817, Through that Part of the Netherlands, which Comprises Ostend, Bruges, Ghent, Brussels, malines & anatwerp with Remarks on the Works of Art, in Carving, Painting and Scupture and Enquiries... Brussels: 1818?. V. 48

SMITH'S *Classical Atlas, Containing Distinct Maps of the Countries Described in Ancient History, Both Sacred and Profane.* London: 1817. V. 48

SMITHS' CASH STORE, SAN FRANCISCO
On the Klondike How to Go When to Go Where to Go What to Take Where To Get It. San Francisco: 1897. V. 52

SMITHSONIAN INSTITUTION
Annual Report of the Board of Regents of the Smithsonian Institution, Showing the Operations, Expenditures and Condition of the Institution for the Year 1880. Washington: 1881. V. 48

SMITHURST, BENJAMIN
Britain's Glory and England's Bravery. London: 1689. V. 54

SMITHWICK, NOAH
Evolution of a State. Austin: 1900. V. 53
Revolution of a State: Recollections of Old Texas Days. Austin. V. 49

SMOLLETT, TOBIAS GEORGE
The Adventures of Ferdinand Count Fathom. London: 1753. V. 47; 50; 51; 53
The Adventures of Ferdinand Count Fathom. London: 1771. V. 48
The Adventures of Gil Blas. London: 1819. V. 51
The Adventures of Peregrine Pickle. London: 1751. V. 47; 48; 49; 51; 52; 53; 54
The Adventures of Peregrine Pickle. London: 1765. V. 50
The Adventures of Peregrine Pickle. London: 1769. V. 48; 50
The Adventures of Peregrine Pickle. London: 1776. V. 53
The Adventures of Peregrine Pickle. London: 1784. V. 49; 52
The Adventures of Peregrine Pickle. Edinburgh: 1793. V. 50; 54
The Adventures of Peregrine Pickle. Harrisburgh: 1807. V. 47
The Adventures of Peregrine Pickle. London: 1831. V. 49
The Adventures of Peregrine Pickle. London: 1904. V. 48
The Adventures of Roderick Random. London: 1748. V. 49; 54
The Adventures of Sir Launcelot Greaves... London: 1774. V. 50; 51
Aventures de Sir Williams Pickle... Paris: 1799. V. 48
A Complete History of England... London: 1757/60/60/61. V. 52
A Complete History of England... London: 1758-59/60-61. V. 53
A Complete History of England... London: 1758-60. V. 54
The Expedition of Humphry Clinker. London: 1671 (1771). V. 47
The Expedition of Humphry Clinker. London: 1671/71/71. V. 54
The Expedition of Humphry Clinker. London: 1683. V. 47
The Expedition of Humphry Clinker. Dublin: 1771. V. 48
The Expedition of Humphry Clinker. London: 1771. V. 47; 48; 49; 51; 52; 53; 54
The Expedition of Humphry Clinker. London: 1772. V. 47; 50
The Expedition of Humphry Clinker. Dublin: 1790. V. 48
The Expedition of Humphry Clinker. London: 1793. V. 52
The Expedition of Humphry Clinker. London: 1795. V. 48
The Expedition of Humphry Clinker. London: 1831. V. 49
The History and Adventures of an Atom. London: 1769. V. 48; 53
The History and Adventures of an Atom. London: 1786. V. 48

SMOLLETT, TOBIAS GEORGE continued
The History of England, from the Revolution to the Death of George the Second. London: 1794. V. 51
The History of England, from the Revolution to the Death of George the Second. London: 1796. V. 52
The Miscellaneous Works... Edinburgh: 1806. V. 51; 54
The Miscellaneous Works... Edinburgh: 1817. V. 51
The Miscellaneous Works. London: 1850. V. 54
The Miscellaneous Works... London: 1858. V. 50; 54
A North Briton Extraordinary. London: 1765. V. 48
The Novels. London: 1925-26. V. 51
The Novels. Boston & New York: 1926. V. 49; 52
Plays and Poems....With memoirs of the Life and Writings of the Author. London: 1777. V. 51
The Regicide: or, James the First of Scotland. London: 1749. V. 48
The Reprisal; or, the Tears of Old England. London: 1757. V. 50
Select Essays on Commerce Agriculture, Mines, Fisheries and Other Subjects. London: 1754. V. 48; 51; 52; 53; 54
The Tears of Scotland. 1746?. V. 50
Travels through France and Italy... London: 1766. V. 50; 53
Travels through France and Italy. London: 1778. V. 48
The Works. London: 1797. V. 48
The Works... Westminster: 1899-1900. V. 54
The Works. London: 1910. V. 48; 52
Works. London: 1925. V. 47
Works. London: 1930. V. 49

SMOLNIKAR, ANDREW B.
Secret Enemies of True Republicanism, Most Important Developments Regarding the Inner Life of Man and the spirit World... Springhill: 1859. V. 49

SMYTH, AMELIA GILLESPIE
Probation and Other Tales. Edinburgh: 1832. V. 50

SMYTH, CHARLES PIAZZI
Life and Works at the Great Pyramids During the Months of January, February, march & April, 1865. Edinburgh: 1867. V. 50
Our Inheritance in the Great Pyramid. London: 1864. V. 47
Teneriffe, an Astronomer's Experiment. London: 1858. V. 47; 48

SMYTH, COKE
Sketches in the Canadas. Toronto: 1968. V. 47; 50

SMYTH, ELAINE
Plain Wrapper Press 1966-1988. Austin: 1993. V. 53; 54

SMYTH, ETHEL
Inordinate (?) Affection. London: 1936. V. 47; 49

SMYTH, H. WARINGTON
Mast and Sail in Europe and Asia. London: 1906. V. 52

SMYTH, HENRY DE WOLF
Atomic Energy for Military Purposes. Princeton: 1945. V. 48; 52; 54
A General Account of the Development of Methods of Using Atomic Energy for Military Purposes. 1945. V. 52
A General Account of the Development of Methods of Using Atomic Energy for Military Purposes... London: 1945. V. 48
A General Account of the Development of Methods of Using Atomic Energy for Military Purposes... Oak Ridge: 1945. V. 49
A General Account of the Development of Methods of Using Atomic Energy for Military Purposes... Washington: 1945. V. 48; 50; 54

SMYTH, JAMES CARMICHAEL
A Description of the Jail Distemper, As It Appeared Amongst the Spanish Prisoner, at Winchester, in the Year 1780. London: 1795. V. 47; 49
The Effect of the Nitrous Vapour in Preventing and Destroying Contagion... Philadelphia: 1799. V. 47; 48; 49; 50; 51; 53

SMYTH, JOHN
A Paterne of True Prayer. London: 1624. V. 50

SMYTH, PAUL
The Cardinal Sins: a Bestairy Seven Ottava Rimas... Northampton: 1980. V. 48
Thistles and Thorns: Abraham and Sarah at Bethel. Omaha: 1977. V. 48; 50

SMYTH, PHILIP
Rhyme and Reason: Short and Original Poems... London: 1803. V. 50

SMYTH, R. BROUGH
The Aborigines of Victoria: with Notes Relating to the Habits of the Natives of Other Parts of Australia and Tasmania. London: 1878. V. 52

SMYTH, W. H.
The Cycle of Celestial Objects Continued at the Hartwell Observatory to 1859. London: 1860. V. 52

SMYTH, WILLIAM
English Lyricks. Liverpool: 1797. V. 52
Erin's Fairy Spell; or, the Palace of Industry and Pleasure; a Vision. 1865. V. 47
Erin's Fairy Spell; or, the Palace of Industry and Pleasure: a Vision. Dublin: 1865. V. 54

SMYTH, WILLIAM HENRY
Descriptive Catalogue of a Cabinet of Roman Family Coins Belonging to His Grace the Duke of Northumberland, K.g. London: 1856. V. 48
Descriptive Catalogue of a Cabinet of Roman Imperial Large Brass Medals. Bedford: 1834. V. 48

SMYTHE, CHARLES W.
Our Own Primary Grammar for the Use of Beginners. Greensborough: 1861. V. 49

SMYTHE, F.
An Alpine Journey. 1934. V. 53
Camp Six. London: 1937. V. 52
Edward Whymper. 1940. V. 52; 53
Kamet Conquered. 1932. V. 52; 53
Kamet Conquered. London: 1932. V. 52
The Valley of Flowers. 1938. V. 53

SMYTHE, H.
Historical Sketch of Parker County and Weatherford, Texas. St. Louis: 1877. V. 48; 52

SMYTHE, ROBERT
Historical Account of Charter House. London: 1808. V. 47; 52

SMYTHE, SARAH MARIA BLAND
Ten Months in the Fiji Islands. Oxford & London: 1864. V. 47; 50; 52

SMYTHE, THOMAS
The Sin and the Curse: or, the Union, the True Source of Disunion, and Our Duty in the Present Crisis. Charleston: 1860. V. 47

SMYTHE, W. DUMVILLE
An Historical Account of the Worship Company of Girdlers, London. London: 1905. V. 47

SMYTHE, WILLIAM
Narrative of a Journey from Lima to Para, Across the Andes and Down the Amazon. London: 1836. V. 52

SMYTHE, WILLIAM ELLSWORTH
The Conquest of Arid America. New York: 1907. V. 53
History of San Diego 1542-1908. San Diego: 1908. V. 50

SMYTHIES, BERTRAM EVELYN
The Birds of Borneo. Edinburgh: 1960. V. 49; 53
The Birds of Borneo. London: 1960. V. 49
The Birds of Borneo. Edinburgh: 1968. V. 54
The Birds of Borneo. London: 1968. V. 51; 54
Birds of Burma. Rangoon: 1940. V. 49; 50; 51; 53
The Birds of Burma. Edinburgh: 1953. V. 48
The Birds of Burma. London: 1953. V. 49; 50; 52; 53; 54

SMYTHIES, MISS
The Stage-Coach: Containing the Character of Mr. Manly, and the History of His Fellow-Travellers. London: 1753. V. 50

SNAGG, ROBERT
The Antiquity & Original of the Court of Chancery, and Authority of the Lord Chancellor of England. London: 1654. V. 47

SNAPE, ANDREW
The Anatomy of an Horse. London: 1683. V. 47
The Anatomy of an Horse. London: 1686. V. 47

SNART, JOHN
Thesaurus of Horror... London: 1817. V. 51

SNEDECOR, V. GAYLE
A Directory of Greene County for 1855-56. Mobile: 1856. V. 53

SNELGRAVE, WILLIAM
A New Account of Some Parts of Guinea, and the Slave Trade. London: 1734. V. 49

SNELL, CHARLES
The Art of Writing. In its Theory and Practice By... London: 1712. V. 52

SNELL, JAMES P.
History of Sussex and Warren Counties, New Jersey... Philadelphia: 1881. V. 47; 49; 51

SNELL, S.
A Story of Railway Pioneers Being an Account of the Inventions and Works of Isaac Dodds and His Son Thomas Weatherburn Dodds. London: 1921. V. 49

SNELL, WILLEBRORD
Tiphys Batavus, Sive Histiodromice, De Navium Cursibus, et re Navali. Leiden: 1624. V. 47

SNELLING, HENRY H.
The History and Practice of the Art of Photography... London: 1853. V. 47

SNELLING, THOMAS
Miscellaneous Views of The Coins Struck by English Princes in France, Counterfeit Sterlings, Coins Struck by the East India Company, etc. (with) A View of the Origin, Nature and Use of Jettons or Counters. (with) A View of the Silver Coin & Coinage... London: 1769/69/94. V. 53
Snellings Seventy-One Plates of Gold and Silver Coin, with Their Weight, Fineness and Value. London: 1788-92. V. 57
A View of the Gold Coinage of England, from Henry the Third to the Present Time. London: 1763. V. 53
A View of the Silver Coin and Coinage of England. (with) A View of the Gold Coin and Coinage of England. (with) A View of the Copper Coin and Coinage of England. London: 1762-63/66. V. 53

SNELLING, WILLIAM J.
Tales of the Northwest; or, Sketches of Indian Life and Character. Boston: 1830. V. 48; 54
Tales of Travels West of the Mississippi. Boston: 1830. V. 50

SNEYD, WALTER
Portraits of the Spruggins Family. 1829. V. 49; 54

SNIDER, BENJAMIN
A New Year's Address...Concerning the Origin, Titles and Attributes of Speculative Free-Masonry.... Geneseo: 1828. V. 48

SNIDER, C. H. J.
Annals of the Royal Canadian Yacht Club 1852-1937 with a Record of the Club's Trophies and the Contests for Them. Toronto: 1937. V. 53

SNIDER, DENTON J.
A Walk in Hellas, or the Old in the New. St. Louis: 1881. V. 52

SNIPP, Snapp, Snurr and the Gingerbread. Chicago: 1936. V. 53

SNODGRASS, A. M.
The Dark Age of Greece: an Archaeological Survey of the Eleventh to the Eighth Centuries B.C. Edinburgh: 1971. V. 50

SNODGRASS, JOHN JAMES
Narrative of the Burmese War... London: 1827. V. 49; 51; 52

SNODGRASS, W. D.
The Boy Made of Meat. Concord. 1983. V. 48; 51
Heart's Needle. New York: 1959. V. 48; 50; 51; 53; 54
Heart's Needle... Hessle: 1960. V. 50; 53
If Birds Build With Your Hair. New York: 1979. V. 49; 50; 54
The Kinder Capers. New York: 1986. V. 50; 54
To Shape a Song. New York: 1988. V. 54
Traditional Hungarian Songs. Baltimore: 1978. V. 52

SNORRI STURLASON
The Heimskringla... London: 1889. V. 49
Heimskringla... 1932. V. 47

SNORRI STURULSON
The Heimskringla... London: 1844. V. 54

SNOW, C. P.
Death Under Sail. Garden City: 1932. V. 51
Dickens and the Public Service. London: 1970. V. 54
The Light and the Dark. London: 1947. V. 50
The Search. London: 1934. V. 49
The Search. Indianapolis: 1935. V. 48

SNOW, CHARLES WILIBERT
Songs in the Neukluk. Council, Alaska: 1912. V. 49

SNOW, D. W.
An Atlas of Speciation in African Non-Passerine Birds. London: 1978. V. 49

SNOW, E. E.
A History of Leicestershire Cricket. Leicester: 1949. V. 48

SNOW, EDGAR
Journey to the Beginning: a Personal View of Contemporary History. New York: 1958. V. 50

SNOW, EDWARD ROWE
Great Gales and Dire Disasters. New York: 1952. V. 50

SNOW, JACK
The Magical Mimics in Oz. Chicago: 1946. V. 53
The Shaggy Man of Oz. Chicago: 1949. V. 49; 52
Who's Who In Oz. Chicago: 1954. V. 47; 49; 54

SNOW, PHILIP
The People from the Horizon. Oxford: 1979. V. 52

SNOW, W. PARKER
A Two Years' Cruise off Tierra del Fuego, the Falkland Islands, Patagonia, and in the River Plate... London: 1857. V. 48

SNOW White and the Seven Dwarfs. New York: 1972. V. 48; 51

SNOWDEN, JAMES R.
The Cornplanter Memorial. An Historical Sketch of Gy-Ant-Wa-Chia - the Cornplanter. Harrisburg: 1867. V. 47

SNOWDEN, RICHARD
The American Revolution. Clinton: 1815. V. 47; 48; 50; 54

SNOWDON, ANTONY CHARLES ROBERT ARMSTRONG-JONES, EARL OF
Snowdown: a Photo-graphic Autobiography. New York: 1979. V. 51

SNOWMAN, KENNETH
Eighteenth Century Gold Boxes of Europe. Boston: 1966. V. 48

SNYDER, F.
Rhymes for Kindly Children. 1916. V. 47

SNYDER, FRANK M.
Building Details. New York: 1906-09. V. 53

SNYDER, GARY
All in the Family. Davis: 1975. V. 53
The Back Country. London: 1967. V. 47; 48; 49; 50; 53; 54
The Blue Sky. New York: 1969. V. 53; 54
Earth House Hold: Technical Notes and Queries to Fellow Dharma Revolutionaries. New York: 1969. V. 47
Myths and Texts. New York: 1960. V. 47
Myths and Texts. New York: 1978. V. 48
North Pacific Lands and Waters. A Further Six Sections. Waldron Island: 1993. V. 52
A Range of Poems. London: 1966. V. 47; 50; 54
Regarding Wave. Iowa City: 1969. V. 54
Riprap. Ashland: 1959. V. 47; 49; 50; 53
Six Sections from Mountains and Rivers Without End. London: 1967. V. 47; 53; 54
Smokey the Bear Sutra. Oakland: 1993. V. 53
Tree Song. San Francisco: 1986. V. 48
True Night. North San Juan: 1980. V. 48
Turtle Island. New York: 1974. V. 49; 53

SNYDER, MARTIN
City of Independence: Views of Philadelphia Before 1800. New York: 1975. V. 53

SOANE, ELY BANISTER
To Mesopotamia and Kurdistan in Disguise. Boston: 1912. V. 49
To Mesopotamia and Kurdistan in Disguise. London: 1912. V. 53

SOANE, GEORGE
The Dwarf of Naples. London: 1819. V. 51

SOANE, JOHN
Description of the House and Museum on the North Side of Lincoln's Inn Fields, the residence of Sir John Soane. London: 1835. V. 48; 50
Designs in Architecture, Consisting of Plans, Elevations... London: 1789. V. 49
Lectures on Architecture. London: 1929. V. 49
Plans, Elevations and Sections of Buildings... London: 1788. V. 48; 50
The Portrait of Sir John Soane, R. A. (1753-1837). London: 1927. V. 48
Sketches in Architecture Containing Plans and Elevations of Cottages, Villas and other Useful Buildings with Characteristic Scenery. London: 1793. V. 48

SOAVE, FRANCESCO
Novelle Morali...Colla Spiegazione Inglese di Vari Idiomi e Frasi che in Esse s'Incontrano. Chelsea: 1799. V. 47

SOBEL, BERNARD
Burleycue: an Underground History of Burlesque Days. New York: 1931. V. 50

A SOBERT, Yet Jocular Answer to Heraclitus Ridens. London: 1682?. V. 47

SOBIESKI, JOHN
Lays of the Deer Forest. London: 1985. V. 48; 49; 50
The Life Story and Personal Reminiscences of... Shelbyville: 1900. V. 47
The Life Story and Personal Reminiscences of... Los Angeles: 1907. V. 54

SOBIN, GUSTAF
Ten Sham Haikus for my Friend, Brad Morrow. New York: 1983. V. 54

SOBOTTA, JOHANNES
Atlas of Human Anatomy. New York: 1927. V. 54
Atlas Of Human Anatomy. New York: 1936. V. 49

SOBY, JAMES THRALL
Ben Shahn-Paintings. New York: 1963. V. 51
The Early Chirico. New York: 1941. V. 47
The Prints of Paul Klee. New York: 1945. V. 50
Tchelitchew - Paintings - Drawings. New York: 1942. V. 52

SOCIALISTIC LABOR PARTY
Platform of the Socialistic Labor Party. 1877. V. 53

SOCIETE DES ANTIQUAIRES DE PICARDIE
La Picardie, Historique et Monumentale Suite. Amiens and Paris: 1893-1940. V. 50

SOCIETY FOR PURE ENGLISH
Tracts I-XL. Oxford: 1919-34. V. 52

SOCIETY FOR THE DIFFUSION OF USEFUL KNOWLEDGE
British Husbandry. London: 1834-37. V. 53

SOCIETY FOR THE IMPROVEMENT OF NAVAL ARCHITECTURE
An Address to the Public, from the Society for the Improvement of Naval Architecture. 1791. V. 52

SOCIETY FOR THE PROMOTION OF AGRICULTURE
Transactions of...Volume I. Albany: 1801. V. 47

SOCIETY FOR THE REFORM OF COLONIAL GOVERNMENT
Second Annual Address of the Society... London: 1851. V. 54

SOCIETY FOR THE SUPPRESSION OF BEGGARS
The Eighth Report of the Society, Instituted in Edinburgh on 2th Jan. 1813, for the Suppression of Beggars, for the Relief of Occasional Distress, and for the Encouragement of Industry Among the Poor. Edinburgh: 1820. V. 53

SOCIETY OF ANTIQUARIES OF LONDON
The Antiquaries Journal Being the Journal of... 1973-89. V. 52

SOCIETY OF ARTISTS OF GREAT BRITAIN
A Catalogue of the Pictures, Sculptures, Models, Drawings, Prints, &c. Exhibited by the Society of Artists of Great Britain, at the Great Room in Spring-Garden, Charing-Cross, May the 9th, 1761. London: 1761. V. 48; 52

SOCIETY OF ARTISTS OF THE UNITED STATES
First Annual Exhibiton of the Society of Artists of the United States. Philadelphia: 1811. V. 47

SOCIETY OF BEAUX-ARTS ARCHITECTS
Winning Designs 1904-1927 Paris Prize in Architecture. New York: 1928. V. 47; 48

SOCIETY OF CALIFORNIA PIONEERS
Constitution and By-Laws of the Society of California Pioneers. San Francisco: 1850. V. 53; 54

SOCIETY OF DILETTANTI
Report of the Committee of the Society of Dilettanti, Appointed by the Society to Superintend the Expedition Lately sent by Them to Greece and Ionia... London: 1814. V. 49
Unedited Antiquities of Attica. London: 1817. V. 49

SOCIETY OF FRIENDS
An Epistle from Our General Spring Meeting of Ministers. 1755. V. 52

SOCIETY OF ICONOPHILES
Catalogue of the Engravings Issued by the Society of Iconophiles, 1908. New York: 1908. V. 51

SOCIETY OF THE FRIENDS OF THE PEOPLE
The State of the Representation of England and Wales, Delivered to the Society, the Friends of the People, Associated for the Purpose of Obtaining a Parliamentary Reform on Saturday the 9th of Feburary 1793. London: 1793. V. 51

SODDY, F.
The Interpretation of Radium. London: 1909. V. 53

SODERHOLTZ, E. E.
Colonial Architecture and Furniture. Boston: 1895. V. 53

SOHO Centenary, a Gift from Artists, Writers and Musicians to the Soho Hospital for Women. London: 1944. V. 54

SOLA, A. E.
Klondyke: Truth and Facts of the New El Dorado. London: 1897. V. 54

SOLANO, SOLITA
Statue in a Field. 1934. V. 53
Statue in a Field. 1935. V. 54

SOLANO DE LUQUE, FRANCISCO
New and Extraordinary Observations Concerning the Prediction of Various Crises by the Pulse, Independent of the Critical Signs Delivered by the Ancients... London: 1741. V. 47

A SOLDIER'S Album. London: 1826. V. 51; 54

THE SOLDIER'S Hymn Book. Chicago: 1863. V. 52

SOLDINI, FRANCESCO MARIA
De Anima Brutorum Commentaria. Florence: 1776. V. 48; 50

SOLE, W.
Menthae Britannicae. Bath: 1798. V. 47; 52

SOLERI, PAOLO
Arcology: The City in the Image of Man. Cambridge: 1969. V. 47

SOLEY, JAMES RUSSELL
Historical Sketch of the United States Naval Academy. Washington: 1876. V. 47

SOLINUS, CAIUS JULIUS
De Mirabilibus Mundi. Venice: 1498. V. 51
Joannis Camertis Minoritani. Artium, et Sacrae Theologiae Doctoris, in C. Julii Solini... Vienna: 1520. V. 47

SOLIS Y RIBADENEYRA, ANTONIO DE
Historia de la Conquista de Mexico, Poblacion, y Progresos de la America Septentrional, Conocida por el Nuenra Espana. Barcelona: 1691. V. 52
The History of the Conquest of Mexico by the Spaniards. London: 1724. V. 50; 52; 54
Varias Poesias, Sagradas y Profanas, Que Dexo Escritas... Madrid: 1692. V. 53

SOLL, IVAN
C: O: L: O: N. Madison: 1995. V. 54
Tryangulations. Madison: 1991. V. 47; 48; 50; 51; 52; 54

SOLLEYSEL, JACQUES DE
The Compleat Horseman... London: 1696. V. 47
The Compleat Horseman... London: 1729. V. 47

SOLLY, HENRY
James Woodford, Carpenter and Chartist. London: 1881. V. 54

SOLLY, N. NEAL
Memoir of the Life of David Cox with Selections from His Correspondence... London: 1873. V. 54
Memoir of the Life of William James Miller. London: 1875. V. 54

SOLLY, S. EDWIN
A Handbook of Medical Climatology Embodying its Principles and Therapeutic Application with Scientific Data of the Chief Health Resorts of the World. Philadelphia: 1897. V. 54

SOLLY, SAMUEL
The Human Brain... London: 1836. V. 48
The Human Brain... London: 1847. V. 48
The Human Brain... Philadelphia: 1848. V. 53
Surgical Experiences: The Substance of Clinical Lectures. London: 1865. V. 47

SOLMS-BRAUNFELS, CARL, PRINCE OF
Texas 1844-1845. 1936. V. 54

SOLMS-GRAUNFELS, CARL, PRINCE OF
Texas 1844-1845. Houston: 1936. V. 51

SOLODKOFF, ALEXANDER VON
Russian Gold and Silver. London: 1981. V. 54

THE SOLOMON Guggenheim Museum. New York: 1960. V. 47

SOLON, L. M.
The Art of the Old English Potter. London: 1885. V. 52

SOLT, MARY ELLEN
Flowers in Concrete. Bloomington: 1966. V. 52
Flowers in Concrete. Bloomington: 1969. V. 47; 52
Marriage. Champaign: 1975. V. 54

SOLTAU, HENRY WILLIAM
The Holy Vessels and Furniture of the Tabernacle of Israel. London: 1860. V. 54

SOLVYNS, BALT
The Costume of Hindoostan...with Descriptions in English and French Taken in the Years 1798 and 1799. London: 1804. V. 48

SOLZHENITSYN, ALEXANDER
August 1914. New York: 1987. V. 48
August 1914. New York: 1989. V. 48; 53
The Gulag Archipelago 1918-1956. Paris: 1973-75. V. 50
The Gulag Archipelago 1918-1956. London: 1974. V. 48
(in Russian) The Gulag Archipelago: 1918-1956. Paris: 1973. V. 47
The Oak and the Calf. Paris: 1975. V. 50
The Oak and the Calf. New York: 1980. V. 53
One Day in the Life of Ivan Denisovich. London: 1963. V. 52
Stories and Prose Poems. New York: 1971. V. 47; 52
We Never Make Mistakes. Columbia: 1963. V. 52
A World Split Apart. New York: 1978. V. 50

SOMADEVA BHATTA
The Ocean of Story. London: 1924-28. V. 47

SOMARE, G.
The Nagas. Disciplined Forms of Beauty. 1992. V. 54

SOMBRE, DYCE
Mr. Dyce Sombre's Refutation of the Charge of Lunacy Brought Against Him in the Court of Chancery. Paris: 1849. V. 50

SOME Account of Suffragan Bishops in England. London: 1785. V. 48

SOME Account of that Ancient and Honourable Society, Vulgarly Denominated the Henpecked Club. Workington: 1810. V. 47

SOME Account of the Ancient Monuments in the Priory Church, Abergavenny. Newport: 1872. V. 47

SOME Account of the Conduct of the Religious Society of Friends Towards the Indian Tribes in the Settlement of the Colonies of East and West Jersey and Pennsylvnaia... London: 1844. V. 48; 51

SOME Account of the English Stage, from the Restoration in 1660 to 1830. Bath: 1832. V. 52

SOME Account of the Family of Robinson Of the White House, Appleby, Westmoreland. London: 1874. V. 50

SOME Account of the Family of the Butlers, But More Particularly of the Late Duke of Ormond, the Earl of Offory His father, and James Duke of Ormond His Grandfather. London: 1716. V. 54

SOME Account of the Public Life of the Late Lieutenant-General Sir George Prevost, Bart, Particularly of His Services in the Canadas. London: 1823. V. 48

SOME British Ballads. London: 1919. V. 48; 51; 52
SOME British Ballads. New York: 1919. V. 47

SOME Early American Hunters, Being Stories from the Cabinet of Natural History and American Rural Sports... New York: 1928. V. 53

SOME Examples of the Work of American Designers. Philadelphia: 1918. V. 54

SOME Fragments for C.R.H. Lexington: 1967. V. 52; 54

SOME Imagist Poets. Boston & New York: 1917. V. 53

SOME Minor Arts as Practised in England. London: 1894. V. 53

SOME Observataions Concerning Jealousies Betweene King and Parliament, With Their Causes and Cures. London: 1642. V. 51

SOME Papers of the Commissioners of Scotland, Given in Lately to the Houses of Parliament Concerning the Propositions of Peace. London: 1646. V. 51

SOME Remarkable Passages in the Life and death of Mr. John Mason, Late Minister of Water-Stratford, in the County of Bucks... London: 1694. V. 48

SOME Remarks on a Late Pamphlet (by Josiah Tucker) intituled, Reflections on the Expediency of Opening the Trade to Turky (sic). London: 1753. V. 49; 52; 53

SOME Seasonable Thoughts Relating to Our Civil and Ecclesiastical Constitution: Wherein is Occasionally Consider'd The Case of Professors of Popery. 1751. V. 49

SOME Southwestern Trails. El Paso: 1948. V. 52

SOME Thoughts on the Present State Of Our Trade to India. London: 1754. V. 49

SOME Thoughts Upon a Bill for General Naturalization: Addressed to those of All Denominations Who Act Upon Whig-Principles. London: 1751. V. 50

SOME Transactions Between the Indians and Friends in Pennsylvania in 1791 and 1792. London: 1792. V. 49

SOME Trout. North Humberside: 1989. V. 51; 52

SOME Vorticist Poetry and a Piece of Prose. London: 1985. V. 50

SOMEREN, V. G. L.
The Birds of East Africa. Volume 1 Ploceidae. London: 1973. V. 49

SOMERS, JOHN, LORD
Anguis in Herba; or the Fatal Consequences of a Treaty with France. London: 1702. V. 47
A Collection of Scarce and Valuable Tracts...Chiefly Such as Relate to the History and Constitution of These Kingdoms. London: 1809-15. V. 50; 53
Iura Populi Anglicani; or, the Subject's Right of Petitioning Set Forth... London: 1772. V. 52
The Judgement of Whole Kingdoms and Nations, Concerning the Rights, Power and Prerogative of Kings, and the Rights, Priveledges and Properties of the People. London: 1710. V. 54
A Letter, Ballancing the Necessity of Keeping a Land-Force, in Times of Peace; with the Dangers That May Follow On It. London: 1697. V. 53

SOMERS, ROBERT
Letters from the Highlands; or, the Famine of 1847. London: 1848. V. 53

SOMERSET and Dorset, Particulars, Plans, Illustrations of the West of England Freehold Estates of General Viscount Bridport...an Important Mansion Known as Cricket House... London: 1895. V. 53

SOMERTON, ALICE
Ida; or, the Last Struggles of the Welsh for Independence. London: 1858. V. 54

SOMERTON, WILLIAM HENRY
A Narrative of the Bristol Riots, on the 29th, 30th and 31st of October, 1831, Consequent on the Arrival of the Recorder, Sir C(harles) Wetherell to Open the Commission of Assize... Bristol;: 1831. V. 53

SOMERVELL, JOHN
Some Westmorland Wills 1686-1738. Kendal: 1928. V. 50; 52
Water-Power Mills of South Westmorland, on the Kent, Bela and Gilpin and Their Tributaries. Kendal: 1930. V. 52

SOMERVILLE, ALEXANDER
The Autobiography of a Working Man. London: 1848. V. 52
Canada, a Battle Ground; About a Kingdom in America. Hamilton: 1862. V. 48
Conservative Science of Nations. Montreal: 1860. V. 51
Narrative of the Fenian Invasion of Canada... Hamilton: 1866. V. 53

SOMERVILLE, EDITH OE.
Dan Russell the Fox, an Episode in the Life of Miss Rowan. London: 1911. V. 50
Dan Russell the Fox. An Episode in the Life of Miss Rowan. Toronto: 1911. V. 47
Further Experiences of an Irish R.M. London: 1908. V. 48; 49; 50
In Mr. Knox's Country. London: 1915. V. 50; 53; 54
In the Vine Country. London: 1893. V. 50
An Incorruptible Irishman: Being an Account of Chief Justice Charles Kendal Bushe... 1932. V. 52
An Incorruptible Irishman: Being an Account of Chief Justice Charles Kendal Bushe... London: 1932. V. 48
Mount Music. London: 1919. V. 53
A Patrick Day's Hunt. Westminster: 1902. V. 47
Slipper's ABC of Fox Hunting by... London: 1903. V. 51; 54
Some Experiences of an Irish R.M. London: 1899. V. 50
Some Irish Yesterdays. London: 1906. V. 50
The Sporting Works: Som Experiences of an Irish R.M.; Further Experiences of an IRish R.M.; In Mr. Knox's Country; Dan Russel the Fox; All on the Irish Shore; Wheel Tracks; IRish Memories. New York: 1927. V. 47
The States through Irish Eyes. Boston and N: 1930. V. 52; 54
Stray-Aways. London: 1920. V. 53

SOMERVILLE, ELIZABETH
The Village Maid; or, Dame Burton's Moral Stories for the Instruction and Amusement of Youth. London: 1801. V. 51

SOMERVILLE, H. G.
Curiosities of Impecuniosity. London: 1896. V. 49

SOMERVILLE, JAMES
The Baronial House of Somerville. Glasgow: 1920. V. 54

SOMERVILLE, JOHN
The System Followed During the Last Two Years by the Board of Agriculture Further Illustrated with Dissertations on the Produce and Growth of Sheep and Wool... London: 1800. V. 54

SOMERVILLE, MARTHA
Personal Recollections, from Early Life to Old Age, of Mary Somerville; with Selections from Her Correspondence... London: 1874. V. 53

SOMERVILLE, MARY
The Connexion of the Physical Sciences. London: 1834. V. 54

SOMERVILLE, THOMAS
The History of Political Transactions and of Parties, from the Restoration of King Charles the Second, to The Death of King William. London: 1792. V. 47
The History of Political Transactions and of Parties, from the Restoration of King Charles the Second to the Death of King William. (with) The History of Great Britain During the Reign of Queen Anne. London: 1792-98. V. 50

SOMERVILLE, WILLIAM
The Chace. London: 1735. V. 47; 48; 51
The Chace... London: 1757. V. 49
The Chace. Birmingham: 1767. V. 47; 51; 52; 53; 54
The Chace... London: 1796. V. 48; 54
The Chace... Dublin: 1799. V. 49
The Chace. London: 1802. V. 47; 49; 53
The Chace... London: 1804. V. 48
The Chace... Edinburgh: 1812. V. 47
The Chace... London: 1812. V. 49
The Chace. London: 1896. V. 51
The Chace. Garden City: 1929. V. 51; 52
Field Sports. A Poem. London: 1742. V. 54
Occasional Poems, Translations, Fables, Tales &c. London: 1727. V. 47; 48

SOMETHING on Ruskinism: With a 'Vestibule' in Rhyme. London: 1851. V. 50

SOMETIME, Never. London: 1956. V. 47

SOMMER, FREDERICK
The Constellations That Surround Us. Toronto: 1992. V. 47; 48

SOMMERFELDT, HAKON A.
Elementary and Practical Principles of the Construction of Ships for Ocean and River Service. London: 1860-61. V. 50

SOMMERFIELD, JOHN
The Imprinted - Recollections of Then, Now and Later On. London: 1977. V. 50
Volunteer in Spain. London: 1937. V. 49

SOMNER, WILLIAM
The Antiquities of Canterbury. London: 1703. V. 47; 49; 52; 53
Dictionarium Saxonico-Latino-Anglicum... Oxonii: 1659. V. 48
Julii Caesaris Portus Iccius Illustratus... Oxonii: 1694. V. 50
A Treatise of the Roman Ports and Forts in Kent. Oxford: 1693. V. 47; 50; 53
Vocabularium Anglo-Saxonicum... Oxoniae: 1701. V. 48

SONDHEIM, STEPHEN
Gypsy. New York: 1960. V. 53
A Little Night Music. New York: 1973. V. 54
Sunday in the Park. New York: 1986. V. 49; 50; 51; 52; 54
Sweeney Todd: the Demon Barber of Fleet Street. New York: 1979. V. 52

SONDLEY, F. A.
A History of Buncombe County, North Carolina. Asheville: 1930. V. 52

A SONG in Favour of Bundling. Leicester: 1961. V. 48

A SONG in Favour of Bundling. Leicester: 1963. V. 52

SONGS and Poems of the Class of 1829. Boston: 1859. V. 54

SONGS and Spirituals of Negro Composition; Also Patriotic Songs, Songs of Colleges and College Fraternities and Sororities. Chicago: 1928. V. 49

SONGS for the Philogists. London: 1936. V. 51

SONGS from Many Lands: Being a Popular Collection of English, Scotch, Irish, Love, Negro, Comic, Naval, Military and Other Songs. Glasgow: 1880?. V. 47

SONGS from Shakespeare's Plays. Verona: 1974. V. 51

SONGS of Adieu: a Little Book of Finale and Farewell. Portland: 1893. V. 51

SONGS of Our Grandfathers. London: 1935. V. 48

SONGS of Our Grandfathers Re-Set in Guinness Time. Dublin: 1936. V. 51

SONGS, Recitatives, &c. In the Entertainment of Pandora's Box; or, the Plagues of Mankind, as Performed at Sadler's Wells. London: 1793. V. 50

THE SONGSTER'S Jewel. Durham: 1838. V. 50

SONMEZ, NEDIM
Ebru. Turkish Marbled Paper. Tubingen: 1987. V. 47

SONN, ALBERT H.
Early American Wrought Iron. New York: 1928. V. 49; 54

SONN, HAROLD A.
A History of Colonel Joseph Beavers (2nd Regt. N. J. Militia) (1728-1816) of Hunterdon County, New Jersey. Short Hills: 1948. V. 47; 49; 51

SONNECK, O. G.
Beethoven Letters in America. New York: 1927. V. 49

SONNERAT, PIERRE
Voyage aux Indes Orientales et a la Chine. Paris: 1782. V. 48; 49

SONNET, THOMAS
Satyre Contre les Charlatanes, et Pseudomedecins Empyriques. Paris: 1610. V. 48; 49

SONNICHSEN, C. L.
El Paso Salt War of 1877. El Paso: 1961. V. 51
Pass of the North... El Paso: 1968. V. 51; 52
Pass of the North. El Paso: 1968/80. V. 53

SONNINI, C. S.
Travels in Upper and Lower Egypt. London: 1800. V. 49; 52

SONTAG, SUSAN
The Benefactor. New York: 1963. V. 48; 54
Brother Carl. New York: 1974. V. 54
Death Kit. New York: 1967. V. 51
Duet for Cannibals. New York: 1970. V. 54

SOPER, ALEXANDER COBURN
The Evolution of Buddhist Architecture in Japan. Princeton: 1942. V. 49

SOPHOCLES
Antigone. New York: 1930. V. 53
The Antigone... New York: 1939. V. 54
Antigone. Haarlem: 1074. V. 48
Antigone. Haarlem: 1975. V. 53; 54
Antigone. Greenbrae: 1978. V. 47
(Greek title) Sophoclis Tragoediae VII. 1579-80. V. 52
(Greek Title) Sophoclis Tragoediae VII. Leyden: 1593. V. 48
Oedipus at Colonus. New York: 1941. V. 54
Oedipus Rex. New York: 1949. V. 54
Oedipus the King. New York: 1955. V. 48; 49
Sophoclis Tragoediae VII... Antwerp: 1579/80. V. 48
Sophoclis Tragoediae Septem; cum Versione Latina et Notis. Oxford: 1814. V. 47
Trag Diae Quotquot Extant Carmine Latino Reddite. Antwerp: 1584. V. 50
A Tragedy by Sophocles. 1978. V. 51
Tragoediae Septem. (With Greek Title). Paris: 1528. V. 53
Tragoediae Septem...cum Latinis Ioach. Cameraii... 1568. V. 47

SOPPE, JOAN M.
Living Room. 1994. V. 52
Trespasses. An Artist's Book. Cedar Rapids: 1993. V. 52

SOPWITH, THOMAS
An Account of the Mining Districts of Alston Moor, Weardale and Teesdale, in Cumberland and Durham. Alnwick: 1833. V. 54

SORCAR, P. C.
Sorcar on Magic. 1960. V. 51

SOREDD, CURTIUS
One Hundred and Thirty Quatrains by Curtius Soredd. Pasadena: 1928. V. 52

SOREL, CHARLES
The Comical History of Francion, Wherein the Variety of Vices that Abuse the Ages are Satyrically Limn'd In Their Native Colours... London: 1655. V. 47; 50

SORENSEN, ALFRED
The Story of Omaha From the Pioneer Days to the Present Time. Omaha: 1923. V. 48

SORENSEN, JON
Fridtjof Nansen's Saga. Oslo: 1940. V. 50

SORENSON, THEODORE C.
Kennedy. New York: 1965. V. 48

SORIA, MARTIN S.
The Paintings of Zurbaran. London: 1953. V. 49; 50; 52
The Paintings of Zurbaran. London: 1955. V. 51

SORLEY, CHARLES HAMILTON
Marlborough and Other Poems. Cambridge: 1916. V. 47; 52

SORLIER, CHARLES
Chagall's Posters: a Catalogue Raisonne. New York: 1975. V. 48; 50; 51; 52; 53; 54
The Lithographs of Marc Chagall. Volume IV: 1969-1973. New York: 1974. V. 50
The Lithographs of Marc Chagall. Volume V: 1974-1979. New York: 1984. V. 50
The Lithographs of Marc Chagall. Volume VI. New York: 1978. V. 50

SOROCOLD, THOMAS
Supplications of Saints, a Book of Prayers and Praises. London: 1693. V. 51; 54

SORREL, GILBERT MOXLEY
Recollections of a Confederate Staff Officer. New York: 1905. V. 53

SORRENTINO, GILBERT
A Beehive Arranged on Humane Principles. 1986. V. 52
A Beehive Arranged On Humane Principles. New York: 1986. V. 54
Black and White. New York: 1964. V. 53
The Darkness Surrounds Us. Highlands: 1960. V. 47
Darkness Surrounds Us. Penlands: 1960. V. 53
Flawless Play Restored. Los Angeles: 1974. V. 50
Mulligan Stew. New York: 1979. V. 53
Mulligan Stew. London: 1980. V. 53
The Perfect Fiction. New York: 1968. V. 53
Sculpicia Elegidia/Elegiacs of Sulpicia. Mt. Horeb: 1977. V. 47; 51; 53; 54
The Sky Changes. New York: 1966. V. 53

SOSEKI, MUSO
Sun at Midnight... 1985. V. 52
The Sun at Midnight. New York: 1985. V. 53; 54

SOTBENE, OSWOLD
The Shrine of Aesculapius. Cleveland: 1905. V. 50

SOTEROPOULOS, S.
The Brigands of the Morea. London: 1868. V. 52

SOTHARD, CHARLES ALFRED
The Monumental Effigies of Great Britain... London: 1817-32. V. 49

SOTHEBY, SAMUEL LEIGH
Principia Typographica. London. V. 48
Ramblings in the Elucidation of the Autograph of Milton. London: 1861. V. 49; 51; 54
Specimen of Mr. S. Leigh Sotheby's Principia Typographica... London: 1858. V. 48

SOTHEBY, WILLIAM
Constance De Castile. London: 1810. V. 50; 52
Oberon, a Poem. London: 1826. V. 48
Poems. London: 1825. V. 48; 50
Saul: a Poem, In Two Parts. Boston: 1808. V. 49
A Tour through Parts of Wales, Sonnets, Odes and Other Poems. London: 1794. V. 48; 49; 51; 54

SOTHERAN, HENRY, & CO.
Bibliotheca Chemico-Mathematica: Catalogue of Works in Many tongues on Exact and Applied Science. London: 1921. V. 51

SOTHERAN, HENRY, LTD.
Annotated Catalogue(s) of Works On Chemistry, Pure and Applied. London: 1934-54. V. 49

SOTHEY & CO.
Catalogues of Valuable Printed Books, Illuminated Manuscripts, Autograph Letters and Historical Documents... London: 1938-75. V. 50

SOTO, HERNANDO DE
The Discovery of Florida... 1946. V. 50
The Discovery of Florida. San Francisco: 1946. V. 52

SOUCHAL, FRANCOIS
French Sculptors of the 17th and 18th Centuries, The Reign of Louis XIV. London: 1977/81/87/93. V. 50

SOUDER, CASPER
The Mysteries and Miseries of Philadelphia, as Exhibited and Illustrated by a late Presentment of the Grand Jury and by a Sketch of the Condition of the Most Degraded Classes of the City. Philadelphia: 1853. V. 52

SOULBY, W. H.
The Surprise Art Album a new Book Containing Over One Hundred Amusing and Interesting Picture Puns. London: 1885. V. 47

THE SOULDIERS
Language; Or a Discourse Between Two Souldiers, the One Coming from York, the Other from Bristol, Shewing How the Warres Go On and How the Souldiers Carrie and Demean Themselves. London: 1644. V. 50

SOULE, D. F.
Marine Organisms as Indicators. Berlin: 1988. V. 50

SOULE, FRANK
The Annals of San Francisco.. New York San Francisco: 1855. V. 48; 52
Annals of San Francisco. Palto Alto: 1968. V. 48; 53

SOULE, WINSOR
Spanish Farm Houses and Minor Public Buildings. New York: 1924. V. 48

SOULES, FRANCOIS
Histoire des Troubles de l'Amerique Anglaise, Ecrite sur les Memoires les Plus Authentiques... Paris: 1787. V. 47

SOULSBY, B.
A Catalogue of the Works of Linnaeus.... London: 1933. V. 48

SOUPAULT, PHILIPPE
Souvenirs de James Joyce. Alger: 1943. V. 47

SOUSA, ANTONIO CAETANO DE
Historia Genealogica da Casa Real Portugueza Desde a Sua Origem ate o Presente... Coimbra: 1946-54. V. 47

SOUSA, JOHN PHILIP
The Fifth String. Indianapolis: 1902. V. 51

SOUSA COUTINHO, LOPO DE
Copey Eines Sendbriefs der...dem...Kunig zu Portugal auss India...Zugeschichkt...auss Portugallesischer in Italianische vnd auss Derselben in Teutsche Sprach Transferiert...Worden. Dillingen: 1572. V. 51

SOUSTER, RAYMOND
As Is. Toronto: 1967. V. 47; 52
City Hall Street. Toronto: 1951. V. 52
The Colour of the Times. Toronto: 1964. V. 47; 52
Crepe-Hanger's Carnival: Selected Poems 1955-58. Toronto: 1958. V. 47
For What Time Slays: Poems. Toronto: 1955. V. 48; 49
Go To Sleep, World. Toronto: 1947. V. 47; 52
A Local Pride. Toronto: 1962. V. 47; 52; 54
On Target. Toronto: 1972. V. 50
Place of Meeting: Poems 1958-1960. Toronto: 1961. V. 54
Place of Meeting: Poems 1958-1960. Toronto: 1962. V. 47; 51
Shake Hands with the Hangman: Poems 1940-1952. Toronto: 1953. V. 52
When We Are Young. Montreal: 1946. V. 47; 51; 52

SOUTEHRNE, THOMAS
The Spartan Dame. London: 1719. V. 47

SOUTH CAROLINA
The Correspondence Between the Commissioners of the State of South Carolina to the Government at Washington and the President of the United States... Charleston: 1861. V. 54

SOUTH CAROLINA COLLEGE
Catalogue of the Library of the South Carolina College. Columbia: 1848. V. 47

SOUTH CAROLINA. CONVENTION
Journal of a Convention of the People of South Carolina: Assembled at Columbia on the 19th November, 1832... Columbia: 1833. V. 47

SOUTH CAROLINA. CONVENTION continued
Journal of the Convention of the People of South Carolina, Held in 1860-'61. Together with Reports, Resolutions &c. Charleston: 1861. V. 49
Report on the Address of the Portion of the Members of the General Assembly of Georgia. Charleston: 1860. V. 49; 54

SOUTH Carolina Deed Abstracts 1791-1772. Easley: 1983. V. 52

SOUTH CAROLINA. GOVERNOR
Correspondence Relating to the Post Office. Charleston: 1861. V. 54

SOUTH CAROLINA. LAWS, STATUTES, ETC.
Memorial of the Legislature of the State of South Carolina, Remonstrating Against the Passing of Laws by Congress, Increasing the Duties Upon Importations, for the Encouragement of Domestic Manufactures (etc.). Washington: 1828. V. 51

SOUTH CAROLINA. SECRETARY OF STATE
Correspondence with the Collector (of the Port of Charleston) 29th January, 1861. Charleston: 1861. V. 54

A SOUTH Dakota Guide. Pierre: 1938. V. 51; 53

SOUTH Dakota Historical Collections. Volume XI. 1922. V. 54

SOUTH Louisiana and the Beautiful Gulf Coast, Featuring Oil, Sulphur, Gas, Rice, Sugar, Salt, Cotton, Lumber... New Orleans: 1937. V. 49

SOUTH, ROBERT
Posthumous Works... London: 1717. V. 48

SOUTH Wales Association for the Improvement of Roads, Instituted in the Year 1789. London: 1792. V. 51

SOUTHAM, A. D.
From Manuscript to Bookstall. London. V. 54

SOUTHARD, ELMER ERNEST
Neurosyphilis: Modern Systematic Diagnosis and Treatment Presented in One Hundred and Thirty-Seven Case Histories. Boston: 1917. V. 52; 53
Shell-Shock and Other Neuropsychiatric Problems Presented in 589 Histories From the War Literature 1914-1918. Boston: 1919. V. 52; 53

SOUTHCOTT, JOANNA
Letters and Communications of...the Prophetess of Exeter... Stourbridge: 1804. V. 47; 48; 50; 51
Prophecies Announcing the Birth of the Prince of Peace... London: 1814. V. 48
The Trial of Joanna Southcott, During Seven Days Which Commenced on the Fifth and Ended on the Eleventh of December, 1804, at the Neckinger House, Bermondsey... London: 1804. V. 53
Wisdom Excelleth the Weapons of War, and Herein Is Shewn What Judgments are the Strange Works of the Lord, But Mery His Darling Attribute. (with) Communication Sent in a Letter to the Rev. Mr. P. in 1797, with an Explanation Thereon Now Given. London: 1814. V. 53

SOUTHERN & Western Guide. 1877. V. 53

SOUTHERN BAPTIST THEOLOGICAL SEMINARY
Second Annual Catalogue of the Southern Baptist Theological Seminary, Greenville, South Carolina. Charleston: 1861. V. 50

SOUTHERN California: Pomona Illustrated and Described. Pomona: 1888. V. 54

SOUTHERN Coast, a Hand-Book of Travel, a Picturesque, Antiquarian and Topographical Description of the Scenery, Towns and Ancient Remains. London: 1849. V. 51

THE SOUTHERN Coast of England. London: 1849 or later. V. 49

A SOUTHERN HARVEST: Short Stories by Southern Writers. Boston: 1937. V. 52; 53

SOUTHERN Historical Society Papers. Millwood: 1977. V. 50

SOUTHERN IMMIGRATION CO.
Texas, Her Resources and Capabilities... New York: 1881. V. 52

SOUTHERN RIGHTS ASSOCIATION
Address of the Southern Rights Association of Yazoo County. Jackson: 1850. V. 50

SOUTHERN States Embracing a Series of Papers Condensed from the Earlier Volumes of De Bow's Review Upon Slavery and the Slave Institutions of the South... Washington: 1856. V. 53

SOUTHERN, TERRY
Blue Movie. New York: 1970. V. 54
Flash and Filigree. London: 1958. V. 48
Flash and Filigree. New York: 1958. V. 53
The Magic Christian. London: 1959. V. 54
Red Dirt Marijuana and Other Tastes. New York: 1967. V. 54

THE SOUTHERN Warbler. Charleston: 1845. V. 49

SOUTHERNE, THOMAS
The Fate of Capua. London: 1700. V. 52
The Maids Last Prayer: or, Any, Rather Than Fail. London: 1693. V. 47; 52
The Spartan Dame. London: 1719. V. 48
The Works of Mr. Thomas Southerne. London: 1721. V. 47; 48

SOUTHESK, JAMES CARNEGIE, 9TH EARL OF
Saskatchewan and the Rocky Mountains. Edinburgh: 1875. V. 54

SOUTHEY, CAROLINE BOWLES
The Cat's Tail: Being the History of Childe Merlin. Edinburgh: 1831. V. 49

SOUTHEY, ROBERT
The Annual Anthology. Bristol: 1799-1800. V. 48
The Book of the Church. London: 1824. V. 51
Carmen Triumphale, for the Commencement of the Year 1814. London: 1814. V. 54
Common-Place Book. London: 1849-51. V. 51
The Doctor, &c. London: 1834-47. V. 48; 52; 54
The Expedition of Orsua; and the Crimes of Aguirre. London: 1821. V. 47
History of Brazil. London: 1810-19. V. 47
History of the Peninsular War. London: 1823-32. V. 54
History Of the Peninsular War... London: 1828-37. V. 50; 51
Joan of Arc... Boston: 1798. V. 53
Joan of Arc. Bristol: 1798. V. 48
The Lay of the Laureate. Carmen Nuptiale. London: 1816. V. 48
A Letter to William Smith, Esq. from Robert Southey, Esq. London: 1817. V. 54
Letters Written...Portugal. Bristol: 1797. V. 54
Letters Written...Portugal. London: 1808. V. 48
The Life of Nelson. London: 1813. V. 52
The Life of Nelson. London: 1895. V. 50
The Life of Nelson. London: 1895. V. 54
The Life of the Rev. Andrew Bell. London: 1844. V. 52
Lives of Uneducated Poets, to Which are added Attempts in Verse, by John Jones, an Old Servant. London: 1836. V. 50
Odes to His Royal Highness the Prince Regent, His Imperial Majesty the Emperor of Russia and His Majesty the King of Prussia. London: 1814. V. 54
Omniana, or Horae Otiosiores. London: 1812. V. 48; 49; 50
Poems... Bath: 1795. V. 48
Poems. Bristol: 1797. V. 51
The Poetical Works. London: 1837/38. V. 49
The Remains of Henry Kirke White, of Nottingham, Late of St. John's College, Cambridge, with an Account of His Life. London: 1823. V. 50
Roderick, the Last of the Goths. London: 1815. V. 49
Roderick, the Last of the Goths. London: 1818. V. 50
Sir Thomas More... London: 1831. V. 52
Specimens of the Later English Poets, with Preliminary Notices. London: 1807. V. 47
Thalaba the Destroyer. London: 1801. V. 50
A Vision of Judgement and the Vision of Judgement by Lord Byron. 1932. V. 53

SOUTHEY, THOMAS
Chronological History of the West Indies. London: 1827. V. 47

SOUTHGATE, FRANK
Wildfowl and Waders. London: 1928. V. 49; 52; 53

SOUTHGATE, HORATIO
Narrative of a Tour through Armenia, Kurdistan, Persia and Mesopotamia... New York: 1840. V. 48

SOUTHGATE, RICHARD
Sermons Preached to Parochial Congregations with a Bibliographical Preface by George Gaskin. London: 1799. V. 49

SOUTH KENSINGTON MUSEUM, LONDON
Universal Catalogue of Books on Art. New York: 1968. V. 47; 54

SOUTHWARD, JOHN
Modern Printing. Raithby: 1900. V. 50; 54
Modern Printing... London: 1921-2. V. 51

THE SOUTHWARK Address. London: 1681. V. 52

SOUTHWART, ELIZABETH
Bronte Moors and Villages. London: 1923. V. 48; 54

SOUTHWELL, CHARLES
Socialism Made Easy; or, a Plain Exposition of Mr. Owen's Views. London: 1840. V. 51

SOUTHWELL, ROBERT
St. Peter's Complaint and Other Poems... London: 1817. V. 53

SOUTHWELL, THOMAS
The Seals and Whales of the British Seas. London: 1881. V. 48

THE SOUTHWEST: Six Billion Doctor Market, Twelve Million People... Dallas: 1927. V. 47

SOUTHWICK, SOLOMON
Five Lessons for Young Men. Albany: 1837. V. 47
A Layman's Aplogy... Albany: 1834. V. 48; 50; 51; 53

SOUTHWOOD, T. R. E.
Land and Water Bugs of the British Isles. 1959. V. 54

SOUTHWORTH, SYLVESTER S.
Trial, Life and Confession of Amos Miner, Who Was Executed on Friday, dec. 27, 1833, for the Murder of John Smith, Late Town-Sergeant of Foster. With His Speech Under the Gallows; Also the Trial and Sentence of Charles Brown, for Highway Robbery... Providence: 1834. V. 47

SOUVENIR Album of the Great West. Columbus: 1890. V. 47

SOUVENIR de la Procession et des Solennites qui Ont eu Lieu a Gand en 1867 a l'Occasion du Jubile Huit Fois Seculaire de Saint Macaire. Ghent: 1869. V. 47; 53

SOUVENIR Diamond Jubilee Guide. Rat Portage and the Lake-of-the-Woods. 1897. V. 54

SOUVENIR of Colorado. Denver: 1885. V. 47

SOUVENIR of Edinburgh. London: 1892. V. 50

SOUVENIR of Jerusalem. Jerusalem: 1880. V. 53

SOUVENIR of Los Angeles and Vicinity. Columbus: 1887. V. 47

SOUVENIR Of Monterey, California. San Francisco: 1883. V. 53

SOUVENIR of San Diego. Columbus: 1886. V. 47

SOUVENIR of Santa Barbara, California. San Francisco: 1888. V. 47

SOUVENIR of Scotland, Its Cities, Lakes and Mountains. London: 1890. V. 50; 52

SOUVENIR of Scotland, Its Cities, Lakes and Mountains. London: 1897. V. 54

SOUVENIR of Silver Islet Port Arthur and Fort William's Healthful Summer Resort 1913. Port Arthur: 1913. V. 50

SOUVENIR of the Dominion Exhibition Winnipeg 1904. Winnipeg: 1904. V. 50

SOUVENIR of the Island of Jersey: Its Towns, Antiquities and Objects of Interest. London: 1892. V. 47

SOUVENIR of the Klondyke. Dawson: 1901. V. 52

SOUVENIR of the West Highlands and the Caledonian Canal. London: 1892. V. 52; 54

SOUVENIR Of....Toronto...Photo-Gravures. Brooklyn: 1899. V. 50

SOUVESTRE, EMILE
Translations from the French of Emile Souvestre. 1856. V. 52

SOUVIELLE, E. M.
The Ulyssiad. Jacksonville: 1896. V. 54

THE SOVEREIGN: or a Political Discourse Upon the Office and Obligations of the Supreme Magistrate. London: 1680. V. 49

THE SOVEREIGNS Prerogative and the Subjects Priviledge: Discussed Betwixt Courtiers and Patriots in Parliament, the Third and Fourth Yeares of the Reign of King Charles... London: 1657. V. 54

SOWDONE OF BABYLONE
The Romaunce of the Sowdone of Babyloyne and of Ferumbras His Sone Who Conquered Rome. London: 1854. V. 48

SOWELL, A. J.
Early Settlers and Indian Fighters of Southwest Texas. Austin: 1900. V. 50; 53
Life of Big-Foot Wallace. Bandera: 1934. V. 54
Rangers and Pioneers of Texas. New York: 1964. V. 51

SOWERBY, ARTHUR DE CARLE
The Naturalist in Manchuria. Tientsin: 1922-23. V. 48; 51
A Naturalist's Holiday by the Sea. London: 1923. V. 54
A Naturalist's Note-Book in China. Shanghai: 1925. V. 48
Nature in Chinese Art. New York: 1940. V. 49
Sport and Science on the Sino-Mongolian. London: 1918. V. 49
A Sportsman's Miscellany (In China). London: 1917. V. 48

SOWERBY, G. B.
A Catalogue of the Shells Contained in the Collection of the Late Earl of Tankerville... London: 1825. V. 53
A Conchological Manual. London: 1839. V. 53
A Conchological Manual... London: 1846. V. 47
A Conchological Manual. London: 1852. V. 49
The Genera of Recent and Fossil Shells. London: 1820-34. V. 53
Illustrated Index of British Shells. London: 1859. V. 51; 54
Miscellanies. London: 1859. V. 51
Popular British Conchology. London: 1854. V. 50; 53
Popular History of the Aquarium of Marine and Fresh-Water Animals and Plants. London: 1857. V. 54
Prose Idylls, New and Old. London: 1873. V. 51
A Selection of 150 Plates from Sowerby's Thesaurus Conchyliarum or Genera of Shells. London: 1847-87. V. 52
Sermons on National Subjects, Preached in a Village Church. London: 1852. V. 51
Thesaurus Conchyliorum or, Monographs of Genera of Shells. London: 1847. V. 53

SOWERBY, GITHA
The Bright Book. London: 1920. V. 49
The Bumbletoes. London: 1907. V. 49; 50
Cinderella. V. 54
The Dainty Book. London: 1915. V. 49
The Gay Book. London: 1915. V. 49
The Pretty Book. London: 1920. V. 49

SOWERBY, J. G.
Afternoon Tea. London: 1880. V. 48

SOWERBY, JAMES
British Mineralogy... London: 1802-07-17. V. 47
British Mineralogy... London: 1804-17. V. 47; 49
The British Miscellany: or Coloured Figures of New, Rare of Little Known Animal Subjects. London: 1804-06-75. V. 51
The British Miscellany; or Coloured Figures of New, Rare of Little Known Animal Subjects... London: 1805-06-75. V. 49
Coloured Figures of English Fungi or Mushrooms. London: 1797-103-15. V. 52
An Easy Introduction to Drawing Flowers According to Nature... London: 1788. V. 51
English Botany. London: 1790-1814. V. 48; 51; 54
English Botany... London: 1790-1849. V. 49; 50
English Botany... London: 1832-46. V. 49
English Botany. London: 1846. V. 49
English Botany... London: 1847-49-54. V. 49
English Botany. London: 1863-67. V. 49
English Botany. London: 1902. V. 52; 53
An Introduction to Drawing Flowers According to Nature...originally Designed for the Use of His Pupils. London: 1788. V. 48
A New Elucidation of Colours, Original Prismatic and Material... London: 1809. V. 52; 54
Tortoises, Terrapins and Turtles Drawn From Life. London: 1872. V. 49; 53

SOWERBY, JOHN EDWARD
British Wild Flowers. London: 1863. V. 52
British Wild Flowers. London: 1876. V. 48; 49; 50
British Wild Flowers. London: 1914. V. 50
The Grasses of Great Britain. London: 1858-61. V. 49
Wild Flowers. London: 1882. V. 54

SOWERBY, MILLICENT
Cinderella. London: 1918. V. 47

SOWERBY, R. R.
Historical Kirkby Stephen and North Westmorland. Kendal: 1950. V. 52

SOYER, ALEXIS
The Modern Housewife or Menagere. London: 1849. V. 49
The Modern Housewife or Menagere. London: 1861. V. 47

SOYER, RAPHAEL
Self-Revealment: a Memoir. New York: 1969. V. 49; 52; 54
Sixteen Etchings. New York: 1964. V. 51

SOYINKA, WOLE
Ake. New York: 1981. V. 53
Death and the King's Horseman. New York: 1987. V. 53
Idanre and Other Poems. New York: 1967. V. 53
Madmen and Specialists. London: 1971. V. 54
The Man Died. New York: 1972. V. 51; 53
Mandela's Earth and Other Poems. New York: 1988. V. 53
Season of Anomy. New York: 1974. V. 53
A Shuttle in the Crypt. New York: 1972. V. 53

SOZINSKEY, THOMAS
Medical Symbolism in Connection with Historical Studies in the Arts of Healing and Hygiene. Philadelphia: 1891. V. 50; 52

SPACH, E.
Histoire Naturelle des Vegetaux. Phanerogames. 1834-48. V. 47

SPACKMAN, W. M.
Heyday. New York: 1953. V. 53

SPACKMAN, WILLIAM FREDERICK
An Analysis of the Railway Interest of the United Kingdom... London: 1845. V. 48

SPAENDONCK, GERRIT VAN
Souvenirs de Van-Spaendonck, ou Recueil de Fleurs, Lithographiees d'Apres les Dessins de ce Celebre Professeur... Paris: 1826. V. 48

SPAETH, SIGMUND
Barber Shop Ballads: A Book of Close Harmony. New York: 1925. V. 48

SPAFFORD, HORATIO GATES
A Gazetteer of the State of New York... Albany: 1813. V. 53

SPAGNUOLI, BAPTISTA MANTUANUS
The Bucolicks of Baptist Mantuan in Ten Eclogues. London: 1656. V. 47

SPAIGHT, ASHLEY W.
The Resources, Soil and Climate of Texas. Galveston: 1882. V. 49; 53

SPAIN. CONSTITUTION
Constitucion Politica de la Monarquia Espanola. Promulgada en Cadiz 19 de Marzo de 1812. Cadiz: 1812. V. 53
Constitucion Politica de la Monarquia Espanola. Promulgada en Cadiz 19 de marzo de 1812. Mexico: 1812. V. 53

SPAIN, October 1934. Paris: 1934. V. 49

SPAIN. TREATIES, ETC.
Articles of Peace, Entercovrse and Commerce, Concluded in the Names of...Charles...and Philip the Fourth King of Spaine, &c. in a Treaty at Madrit (sic)...MDCXXX. London: 1630. V. 54
Convencion Para Explicar, Ampliar, y Hacer Efectivo lo Estipulado en al Articulo Sexto del Tratado Definitivo de Paz del Ano de 1783; concluida Entre el rey Nuestro Seno y el Rey de la Gran Bretana, Firmada en londres a 14 de Julio de 1786. Madrid: 1786. V. 48

SPALDING, CHARLES C.
Annals of the City of Kansas: Embracing Full Details of the Trade and Commerce of the Great Plains, Together with Statistics of the Agricultural, Mineral and Commercial Resources of the Country West, South and Southwest... Kansas City: 1858. V. 49; 50

SPALDING, J. A.
From New England to the Pacific. Notes of a Vacation Trip Across the Continent in April, May and June, 1884. Hartford: 1884. V. 47

SPALDING, LYMAN
An Inaugural Dissertation on the Production of Animal Heat: Read and Defended at a Public Examination... Walpole: 1797. V. 52; 53

SPALDING, PHEBE ESTELLE
Patron Saints of California. San Diego Santiago: 1934-35. V. 54

SPALDING, RUFUS P.
Oration of...Battle of Lake Erie...Corner-Stone of the Monument... Sandusky: 1859. V. 51

SPALDING, WILLIAM
Italy and the Italian Islands from the Earliest Ages to the Present Time. Edinburgh: 1841. V. 48
Italy and the Italian Islands, from the Earliest Ages to the Present Time. Edinburgh: 1845. V. 47; 52

SPALLANZANI, LAZZARO
De Fenomeni Della Circolazione Osservata Nel Giro Universae de Vasi... Modena: 1773. V. 48; 49; 54
Experiments Upon the Circulation of the Blood Throughout the Vascular System. London: 1801. V. 54
Travels in the Two Sicilies, and Some Parts of the Apennines. London: 1798. V. 47

SPALTEHOLZ, WERNER
Hand Atlas of Human Anatomy. Philadelphia: 1930. V. 49; 54
Handatlas der Anatomie des menschen. Mit Unterstutzung von Wilhelm His...Mit 1011 Abbildungen. Leipzig: 1919-20. V. 48

SPANDUGINO, THEODORO
I Commentari di Theodoro Spandugino Cantacuscino Gentilhumomo Costantinopolitano, Dell'Origine de Principi Turchi... Florence: 1551. V. 51; 52

SPANG, WILLIAM
Rerum Nuper in Regno Scotiae Gestarum Historia, Seu Verius Commentarius... Dantisci: 1641. V. 47

A SPANISH Voyage to Vancouver and the North-West Coast of America; Being the Narrative of the Voyage Made in the Year 1792 by the Schooners Sutil and Mexicana to explore the Strait of Juan De Fuca. London: 1930. V. 48; 50

SPANNER, E. F.
This Airship Business. London: 1927. V. 49

SPARCK, R.
The Zoology of the Faroes. Copenhagen: 1928-71. V. 47

SPARGO, JOHN
The Potters and Potteries of Bennington. Boston: 1926. V. 51

SPARK, MURIEL
The Abbess of Crewe. London: 1974. V. 48
The Bachelors. London: 1960. V. 48
The Ballad of Peckham Rye. London: 1960. V. 49
Child of Light; a Reassessment of Mary Wollstonecraft Shelley. Essex: 1951. V. 47; 51
The Comforters. London: 1957. V. 47; 48; 50
The Driver's Seat. New York: 1970. V. 47
Emily Bronte. London: 1953. V. 53
The Fanfarlo and other Verse. Kent: 1952. V. 49
A Far Cry from Kensington. London: 1988. V. 49
Memento Mori. London: 1959. V. 49
Not to Distrub. London: 1971. V. 54
The Portobello Road. Helsinki: 1991. V. 48
The Prime of Miss Jane Brodie. London: 1961. V. 49; 51; 53
Robinson. 1958. V. 51

SPARKE, MICHAEL
Truth Brought to Light; or, the History of the First 14 Years of King James I. London: 1692. V. 52

SPARKMAN, ROBERT
Day in the Life of Lon Tinkle. Dallas: 1981. V. 51; 52
The Texas Surgical Society: The First Fifty Years. Dallas: 1965. V. 49

SPARKS, A. W.
The War Between the States As I Saw It, Reminiscent, Historical and Personal. Tyler: 1901. V. 49

SPARKS, EDWIN ERLE
The English Settlement in Illinois. London: 1907. V. 48; 53

SPARKS, JARED
Correspondence of the American Revolution: Being Letters of Eminent Men to George Washington, From the Time of His Taking Command of the Army to the End of His Presidency. Boston: 1853. V. 47
The Library of American Biography. Boston: 1834-38. V. 53
The Library of American Biography. Boston: 1844. V. 52
The Life of George Washington. Boston: 1839. V. 50; 53
The Life of Gouverneur Morris, with Selections from His Correspondence and Papers... Boston: 1832. V. 50; 52
The Life of John Ledyard, the American Traveller... Cambridge: 1828. V. 47; 48
Memoirs of the Life and Travels of John Ledyard, from His Journals and Correspondence. London: 1828. V. 47
Travels and Adventures of John Ledyard... London: 1834. V. 47

SPARLING, HENRY HALLIDAY
The Kelmscott Press and William Morris Master Craftsman. London: 1924. V. 50; 51; 52; 54

SPARRMAN, ANDERS
A Voyage Round the World with Captain James Cook in H.M.S. Resolution... London: 1944. V. 51; 52
A Voyage Round the world with Captain James Cook in H.M.S. Resolution. Waltham St. Lawrence: 1944. V. 51; 53
A Voyage to the Cape of Good Hope, Towards the Antarctic Polar Circle, and Round the World... London: 1785. V. 50

SPARROW 25-36. Los Angeles: 1975. V. 50; 53
SPARROW 25-36. Santa Barbara: 1977. V. 47

SPARROW 37-48. Santa Barbara: 1975-76. V. 53

SPARROW 49-60. Los Angeles: 1976. V. 53
SPARROW 49-60. Santa Barbara: 1977. V. 47; 50

SPARROW 61-72. Los Angeles: 1977. V. 53
SPARROW 61-72. Santa Barbara: 1978. V. 47; 50

SPARROW, ANTHONY
A Collection of Articles, Injunctions, Canons, Orders, Ordinances and Constitutions Ecclesiastical... London: 1671. V. 52

SPARROW, GEOFFREY
The Crawley and Horsham Hunt. London: 1930. V. 49

SPARROW, JOHN
Lapidaria Quinta. 1965. V. 54
Line Upon Line: an Epigraphical Anthology. Cambridge: 1967. V. 47; 51; 53

SPARROW, WALTER SHAW
A Book of British Etching from Francis Barlow to Francis Seymour Haden. London: 1926. V. 50; 54
A Book of Sporting Painters. London: 1931. V. 47; 49; 53
British Sporting Artists. London: 1922. V. 47; 50
Frank Brangwyn and His Work. London: 1910. V. 50; 54
George Stubbs and Ben Marshall. London: 1929. V. 47
Henry Alken. London & New York: 1927. V. 47; 48; 49; 50; 54
John Lavery and His Work. London. V. 54
Prints and Drawings by Frank Brangwyn, With Some Other Phases of His Art. London: 1914. V. 50; 54

SPATE, VIRGINIA
Orphism. The Evolution of Non-Figurative Painting in Paris 1910-1914. 1979. V. 49; 52; 54

SPAULDING, LYMAN
An Inaugural Dissertation on the Production of Animal Heat... Walpole: 1797. V. 54

SPEAKING Picture Book... New York: 1875-92. V. 49

THE SPEAKING Picture Book... 1885. V. 49
THE SPEAKING Picture Book... Germany: 1885. V. 47

THE SPEAKING Picture Book. Germany: 1893. V. 49

SPEAR, ELSA
Bozeman Trail Scrapbook. Sheridan: 1967. V. 52
Fort Phil Kearny, Dakota Territory 1866-1868. Sheridan: 1939. V. 47

SPEARMAN, FRANK H.
Whispering Smith. New York: 1906. V. 51
Whispering Smith. Toronto: 1906. V. 53

SPEARS, HEATHER
Asylum Poems and Others. Toronto: 1958. V. 47

SPEARS, JOHN R.
A History of the Mississippi Valley from its Discovery to the End of Foreign Domination. New York: 1903. V. 50
Illustrated Sketches of Death Valley, and Other Borax Deserts of the Pacific Coast. Chicago: 1892. V. 48; 49; 53
Illustrated Sketches of Death Valley, and Other Borax Deserts of the Pacific Coast. New York: 1892. V. 51

SPECHT, RICHARD
Mozart. Vienna: 1915. V. 51

A SPECIMEN of Southern Devotion; or, the Prayer of a Rebel Saint. Philadelphia?: 1862. V. 54

SPECIMENS of Books printed at Oxford, With the Types Given to the University by John Fell... Oxford: 1925. V. 48

SPECIMENS of the American Poets; with Critical Notices and a Preface. London: 1822. V. 49

SPECK, FRANK G.
Midwinter Rites of the Cayuga Long House. Philadelphia: 1949. V. 54
Naskapi: the Savage Hunters of the Labrador Peninsula. Norman: 1935. V. 48

SPECK, WILLIAM A.
The William A. Speck Collection of Goetheana. New Haven: 1940. V. 54

SPECK-STERNBURG, MAX, BARON VON
Verzeichniss der von Speckschen Gemalde-Sammlung... Leipzig: 1827. V. 47

SPECKTER, OTTO
Puss in Boots. London: 1860. V. 48

THE SPECTATOR. London: 1765. V. 48
THE SPECTATOR. London: 1767. V. 50
THE SPECTATOR. London: 1788. V. 50
THE SPECTATOR. Edinburgh: 1800?. V. 49
THE SPECTATOR. London: 1817. V. 49

THE SPECTATOR... Edinburgh: 1819. V. 51

THE SPECTATOR. London: 1970. V. 53
THE SPECTATOR. Oxford: 1987. V. 52

SPECTORSKY, A. C.
The Book of the Sea. New York. 1954. V. 47; 51; 52

SPECULUM Crape-Gownorum: or, a Lesson of Instruction to Those Pragmatical Pr—sts, Who Turn the Pulpit into a Prattling Box... London: 1739. V. 48; 49

SPECULUM Exemplorum. Strassburg: 1495. V. 53

SPEECE, CONRAD
The Mountaineer. Staunton: 1823. V. 54

A SPEECH Made by a True Protestant English Gentleman, to Incourage the City of London to Petition for the Sitting of the Parliament. 1679. V. 52

SPEECHLY, WILLIAM
A Treatise on the Culture of the Vine... (with) A Treatise on the Culture of the Pine Apple... London: 1821. V. 52; 54

SPEED, ADOLPHUS
Adam Out of Eden, or, An Abstract of Divers Excellent Experiments Touching the Advancement of Husbandry. London: 1659. V. 48

SPEED, JAMES
Opinion on the Constitutional Power of the Military to Try and Execute the Assassins of the President. Washington: 1865. V. 47

SPEED, JOHN
England. London: 1953-54. V. 49
The History of Great Britaine Under the Conquests of the Romans, Saxons, Danes and Normans. London: 1623. V. 50
The Theatre of the Empire of Great Britain, with the Prospect of the Most Famous Parts of the World. London: 1991. V. 49

SPEED, LANCELOT
A Sojourn in the Highlands, 1885 Achanalt, Ross Shire. London: 1885. V. 48

SPEED, ROBERT
The Counter-Scuffle. London: 1680. V. 47; 50

SPEEDY, THOM
Craigmillar and Its Environs. Selkirk: 1892. V. 52; 54

SPEEDY, TOM
The Natural History of Sport in Scotland with Rod and Gun. London: 1920. V. 52; 54

SPEER, EMORY
Lincoln, Lee, Grant and Other Biographical Addresses. New York and Washington: 1909. V. 50

SPEER, OCIE
Texas Jurist... 1936. V. 53
Texas Jurist. Austin; 1936. V. 48

SPEER, WILLIAM
Encyclopedia of the New West...Texas, Arkansas, Colorado, New Mexico and Indian Territory. Marshall: 1881. V. 53

SPEERT, HAROLD
Iconographia Gyniatrica: a Pictorial History of Gynecology and Obstetrics. Philadelphia: 1973. V. 50
Obstetric and Gynecologic Milestones: Essays and Eponymy. New York: 1958. V. 50; 53

SPEIGHT, HARRY
Chronicles and Stories of Old Bingley. London: 1898. V. 47; 53
The Craven and North-West Yorkshire Highlands. London: 1892. V. 47; 50; 53
Lower Wharfedale. London: 1902. V. 47; 53
Nidderdale and the Garden of the Nidd: a Yorkshire Rhineland. London: 1894. V. 47; 53; 54
Nidderdale, from Nun Monkton to Whernside. London: 1906. V. 47; 53
Romantic Richmondshire. London: 1897. V. 47; 53
Upper Nidderdale, with the Forest of Knaresborough. London: 1906. V. 47
Upper Wharfedale. London: 1900. V. 47; 53; 54

SPEISER, E. A.
Excavations at Tepe Gawra. Philadelphia: 1935. V. 52
Excavations at Tepe Gawra, Levels I-XX. Philadelphia: 1935-50. V. 52

SPEKE, HUGH
The Prince of Orange His Third Declaration. 1688. V. 53
The Prince of Orange's Third Declaration. London: 1688?. V. 49

SPEKE, JOHN HANNING
Journal of the Discovery of the Source of the Nile. Edinburgh & London: 1863. V. 48; 51; 52; 54
Journal of the Discovery of the Source of the Nile. London: 1864. V. 50; 52

SPELLMAN, A. B.
The Beautiful Days. New York: 1965. V. 52

SPELMAN, HENRY
De Non Temerandis Eccelefis, Churches Not to Be Violated. Oxford: 1668. V. 47
The English Works of Sir Henry Spelman Kt. London: 1727. V. 47
Glossarium Archaiologicum... London: 1664. V. 50; 51; 52
Glossarium Archaiologicum. London: 1687. V. 49; 50
Glossarium Archaiologicum: Continens Latino-Barbara...Scholiis and Commentariis Illustrata. London: 1664. V. 52
The History of Fate of Sacrilege, Discover'd by Examples of Scripture, of Heathens and of Christians. London: 1698. V. 50

The Larger Treatise concering Tithes...Together with Some Other Tracts of the Same Author... London: 1647. V. 48
The Larger Treatise Concerning Tithes...Together with Some Other Tracts of the Same Author... London: 1647/46. V. 50
Villare Anglicum; or a View of All the Cities, Towns and Villages in England... London: 1678. V. 47; 49

SPELMAN, W. W. R.
Lowestoft China. Norwich: 1905. V. 47

SPELMAN, WILLIAM
A Dialoge or Confabulation Between Two Travellers Which Treateth of Civile and Pollitike Gouvernment in Dyvers Kingdoms and Contries. London: 1896. V. 51; 54

SPELTZ, ALEXANDER
The Colored Ornament of All Historical Styles. Leipzig: 1914-15. V. 47

SPENCE, ELEANOR P.
The Sobieski Hours. London: 1977. V. 50

SPENCE, ELIZABETH ISABELLA
Dame Rebecca Berry, or, Court Scenes in the Reign of Charles the Second. London: 1827. V. 54

SPENCE, JAMES
The American Union; its Effect on National Character and Policy, with an Inquiry into Secession as a Consitutional Right and the Causes of the Disruption. London: 1861. V. 47; 49
The American Union: Its Effect on National Character and Policy, with an Inquiry into Succession as a Constitutional Right and the Causes of the Disruption. London: 1862. V. 47

SPENCE, JOSEPH
Anecdotes, Observations and Character of Books and Men. London & Edinburgh: 1820. V. 47; 50; 51
Crito: or a Dialogue of Beauty. Edinburgh: 1885. V. 53
An Essay on Mr. Pope's Odyssey. London: 1737. V. 48
Moralities; or, Essays, Letters, Fables... London: 1753. V. 53
A Parallel: in the Manner of Plutarch... Strawberry Hill: 1758. V. 48; 49; 50; 52; 53
A Parallel: in the Manner of Plutarch:. Twickenham: 1758. V. 53
Polymetis; or, an Enquiry Concerning the Agreement Between the Works of the Roman Poets... London: 1747. V. 48; 50
Polymetis; or, an Enquiry Concerning the Agreement Between the Works of the Roman Poets... London: 1755. V. 47
Polymetis; or, an Enquiry Concerning the Agreement Between the Works of the Roman Poets... London: 1774. V. 52

SPENCE, ROBERT TRAILL
Minstrelsey of Edmund the Wanderer. New York: 1810. V. 49; 52

SPENCE, RUTH ELIZABETH
Prohibition in Canada: a Memorial to Francis Stephens Spence. Toronto: 1919. V. 50; 52

SPENCE, S. A.
Antarctica Its Books and Papers from the Earliest to the Present Time. London: 1966. V. 52

SPENCE, THOMAS
Manitoba, and the North-West of the Dominion, Its Resources and Advantages to the Emigrant and Captialist. Quebec: 1876. V. 52
The Prairie Lands of Canada; ...New and Inviting Field...for the Capitalist and New... Montreal: 1879. V. 48; 49; 50

SPENCER, A. J.
Catalogue of Egyptian Antiquites in the British Museum. V: Early Dynastic Objects. London: 1980. V. 49

SPENCER, BALDWIN
Across Australia. London: 1912. V. 48; 52
The Arunta. A Study of a Stone Age People. London: 1927. V. 52
The Horn Expedition. II: Zoology. London: 1896. V. 52
The Native Tribes of Central Australia. London: 1899. V. 48; 52
The Native Tribes of Central Australia. London: 1899/1938. V. 54
The Native Tribes of Central Australia. London: 1938. V. 52
Native Tribes of the Northern Territory of Australia. London: 1914. V. 52
The Northern Tribes of Central Australia. London: 1904. V. 48; 52
Notes on Certain of the Initiation Ceremonies of the Arunta Tribe, Central Australia. Melbourne: 1898. V. 52
Wanderings in Wild Australia. London: 1928. V. 49; 51

SPENCER, BENJAMIN
Chrysomeson, A Golden Meane; or, a Middle Way for Christians to Walk by; Wherein All Seekers of Truth and Shakers in the Faith, May Find the True Religion Independing Upon Mans Inventions... London: 1659. V. 49

SPENCER, BERNARD
Agean Islands and Other Poems. London: 1946. V. 52

SPENCER, BRIAN A.
Prairie School Tradition; the Prairie Archives of the Milwaukee Art Center. New York: 1979. V. 48; 54

SPENCER, E.
The Sobieski Hours. A Manuscript in the Royal Library at Windsor Castle. 1977. V. 47

SPENCER, EDMUND
A Tour of Inquiry through France and Italy, Illustrating Their Present Social, Political and Religious Condition;. London: 1853. V. 49
Travels in European Turkey, in 1850. London: 1851. V. 47

SPENCER, EDWARD
The King's Racehorses. London: 1902. V. 47

SPENCER, ELIZABETH
Fire in the Morning. New York: 1948. V. 49
Marilee. Three Stories. 1981. V. 51
On the Gulf. Jackson: 1991. V. 47; 48; 49
Ship Island and Other Stories. New York: 1968. V. 48; 50
The Stories of Elizabeth Spencer. Garden City: 1980. V. 48
This Crooked Way. New York: 1952. V. 48; 51; 52
The Voice at the Back Door. New York: 1956. V. 50

SPENCER, FREDERIC CHARLES
The Vale of Bolton: a Poetical Sketch and Other Poems. London: 1840. V. 50; 53

SPENCER, GEORGE
Private Papers. London: 1913-24. V. 52

SPENCER, GILBERT
Memoirs of a Painter. London: 1974. V. 49

SPENCER, HAZELTON
Elizabethan Plays... London: 1934. V. 54

SPENCER, HERBERT
First Principles. London: 1867. V. 51
The Principles of Psychology. London: 1855. V. 54
The Principles of Psychology. London: 1870-72. V. 49
Railway Morals and Railway Policy. London: 1855. V. 49
Works. New York: 1897. V. 53

SPENCER, ISOBEL
Walter Crane. New York: 1975. V. 53

SPENCER, JESSE AMES
The East: Sketches of Travel in Egypt and the Holy Land. New York: 1850. V. 48; 51; 52
History of the United States from the Earliest Period to the Administration of James Buchanan. New York: 1858. V. 52

SPENCER, JOHN
A Discourse Concerning Prodigies... London: 1665. V. 48; 50; 53
Things New and Old (Kaina Kaipalaia (Greek type)). London: 1658. V. 53

SPENCER, SPENCE
The Scenery of Ithaca and the Head Waters of the Cayuga Lake... Ithaca: 1866. V. 52

SPENCER, STANLEY
Scrapbook Drawings of Stanley Spencer. London: 1964. V. 50; 53

SPENCER, THEODORE
An Acre in the Seed. Cambridge: 1949. V. 50
A Garland for John Donne - 1631-1931. Cambridge: 1931. V. 52

SPENCER, THOMAS
Instructions for the Multiplication of Works of Art in Metal by Voltaic Electricity. Glasgow: 1840. V. 50; 53

SPENCER, WILLIAM ROBERT
Poems. London: 1811. V. 54
The Year of Sorrow. London: 1804. V. 49

SPENCER, WILLIAM V.
Lincolniana. Boston: 1865. V. 49

SPENCER-CHURCHILL, E. G.
Catalogue of Antiquites from the Northwick Park Collection, the Property of the Late Captain E. G. Spencer-Churchill, M.D....June 21, 1965 and the Two Following Days... London: 1965. V. 52

SPENCE-WATSON, ROBERT
A Visit to Wazan, the Sacred City of Morocco. London: 1880. V. 54

SPENDER, HAROLD
Through the Pyrenees... London: 1898. V. 48; 52

SPENDER, JOHN
Therapeutic Means for the Relief of Pain. London: 1874. V. 54

SPENDER, STEPHEN
China Diary. London: 1982. V. 52; 53
Collected Poems - 1928-1953. London: 1955. V. 50
Forward from Liberalism. London: 1937. V. 54
Generous Days. Boston: 1969. V. 48; 52; 53; 54
Henry Moore O. M. - A Memorial Address. London: 1986. V. 50
Henry Moore, O.M.: a Memorial Address. London: 1987. V. 53
I Sit At the Window: a Poem. 1939-40. V. 47
Journals 1939-1983. Franklin Center: 1984. V. 49
Letters to Christopher. Santa Barbara: 1980. V. 48; 49
Poems. London: 1933. V. 47; 49; 50; 51; 53; 54
Poems. London: 1934. V. 47; 52; 53
Poems. New York: 1934. V. 51
Poems for Spain. London: 1939. V. 48; 49
Poems of Dedication. London: 1947. V. 50
Recent Poems. London: 1978. V. 52
Returning to Vienna. 1947. V. 47; 48; 52; 53; 54
The Still Centre. London: 1939. V. 49
Three Poems. Verona: 1971. V. 47
Three Versions from the German. London: 1955. V. 48; 54
Trial of a Judge: a Tragedy. London: 1938. V. 51; 53
Twenty Poems. Oxford: 1930. V. 49
Twenty-Two Poems. Helsinki: 1988. V. 48
Vienna. London: 1934. V. 49
The Year of the Young Rebels Revisited. USA: 1984. V. 53

SPENDLOVE, F. ST. GEORGE
The Face of Early Canada: Pictures of Canada Which Have Helped to Make History. Toronto: 1958. V. 52

SPENSER, EDMUND
Calendarium Pastorale, sive Aeglogae Duodecim... London: 1653. V. 50
Colin Clouts Come Home Againe. London: 1595. V. 48; 53; 54
Complete Works in Verse and Prose. London: 1882-84. V. 50; 53
The Epithalamion. Campden, Gloucestershire: 1901. V. 51
Epithalamion. London: 1901. V. 49; 52
Epithalamion. London: 1901. V. 52
Epithalamion. New Rochelle: 1902. V. 48
Epithalamion. London: 1938. V. 51
The Faerie Queene... 1611. V. 52
The Faerie Queene... London: 1611. V. 47; 48
The Faerie Queene... London: 1611-09-12. V. 52
The Faerie Queene... London: 1615. V. 52
The Faerie Queene... London: 1617. V. 47; 53
The Faerie Queene... London: 1758. V. 48; 50
The Faerie Queene. Oxford: 1883-90. V. 51
The Faerie Queene. London: 1897. V. 47; 48; 49
The Faerie Queene. Cambridge: 1909. V. 49; 50
The Faerie Queene. Chelsea: 1923. V. 47
The Faerie Queene. New York: 1953. V. 50
The Faerie Queene. Oxford: 1953. V. 52; 53; 54
The Fairie Queen. 1953. V. 51
Poems of Spenser. Edinburgh: 1906. V. 48; 54
The Poetical Works. London: 1802. V. 51
The Poetical Works... Boston: 1839. V. 53
The Poetical Works. London: 1839. V. 54
Poetical Works. Boston: 1855. V. 47; 48
The Poetical Works... Edinburgh: 1859. V. 54
The Poetical Works... London: 1866. V. 51
Poetical Works. London: 1909-10. V. 51
Prothalamion: Epithalamion. Boston & New York: 1902. V. 49; 50; 51
The Shepheard's Calendar. 1898. V. 49
The Shepheard's Calendar. London & New York: 1898. V. 47; 48; 51; 52; 53; 54
The Shepheard's Calendar... London: 1930. V. 48; 53
Sonnets. London: 1948. V. 51
Spencer's Faerie Queene. London: 1894-97. V. 48; 49; 52
Spenser's Faerie Queen. London: 1896-97. V. 53
Spenser's Faerie Queene. London: 1895-97. V. 51
Spenser's Minor Poems... 1925. V. 51; 52; 54
Spenser's Minor Poems. London: 1925. V. 47
Thalamos or the Brydall Boure Being the Epithalamion and Prothalamion... 1932. V. 52
The Wedding Songs. Waltham St. Lawrence: 1923. V. 48
The Works... London: 1679. V. 48; 49; 50
The Works... London: 1805. V. 50
The Works. London: 1862. V. 49; 51
The Works. London: 1865. V. 54
The Works... London: 1873. V. 53
The Works... Oxford: 1930. V. 53
Works. Oxford: 1930-32. V. 48

SPERONI, SPERONE
Canace, Tragedia. Venice: 1597. V. 51; 54
Dialoghi... Venice: 1550. V. 52; 53

SPETH, B.
Die Kunst in Italien. Munich: 1819-23. V. 53

SPEWACK, SAMUEL
Kiss Me Kate. New York: 1953. V. 52

SPEYER, LEONORA
American Poets. Munich: 1923. V. 49; 51
American Poets... Munich: 1925. V. 47
Oberammergau. 1922. V. 49

SPICE, ROBERT P.
The Wanderings of the Hermit of Westminster Between New York & San Francisco... London: 1882. V. 47

SPICER, JACK
A Lost Poem. Verona: 1974. V. 51; 52; 54

SPICER, JOHN L.
Correlation Methods of Comparing Idiolects in a Transition Area. 1952. V. 52; 53

SPICER, MURIEL HANDLEY
Toy Dogs. How to Bread and Rear Them, Being the Life of a Griffon Bruxellois. London: 1902. V. 48

SPICER, WILLIAM HENRY
The Last Evening of Cataline; with Other Poems. London: 1834. V. 48

SPIECER, PETER, & SONS
Stalking Records. Leamington & Inverness,: 1913. V. 48

SPIEGELBERG, WILHELM
Catalogue General des Antiquites Egyptiennes du Musee du Caire. Leipzig Strassburg &: 1904-32. V. 49
Hieratic Ostraka and Papyri Found by J. E. Quibell in the Ramesseum 1895-96. London: 1898. V. 51

SPIEGELMAN, ART
4 Mice: Mause + Mouse. Cat + Maus. Mickey, Maus + Mouse. Nadja, Mickey + Mause. New York: 1992. V. 53
Maus. New York: 1986. V. 51; 53
Maus... New York: 1991. V. 51; 53

SPIELBERG, STEVEN
Close Encounters of the Third Kind. New York: 1977. V. 51

SPIELMANN, JACOB REINBOLD
Pharmacopoea Generalis... Venice: 1785-86. V. 47

SPIELMANN, M. H.
Hugh Thomson, His Art, His Letters, His Humour and His Charm. London: 1931. V. 48; 49
Kate Greenaway. London: 1905. V. 47; 48; 49; 50; 51; 53; 54
Kate Greenaway. New York: 1905. V. 51; 53
Littledom Castle and Other Tales. London: 1903. V. 54
The Rainbow Book. London: 1909. V. 51

SPIELMANN, PERCY EDWIN
Catalogue of the Library of Miniature Books Collected by Percy Edwin Spielmann. Together with Some Descriptive Summaries. London: 1961. V. 50

SPIES, AUGUST
Auto-Biography. Chicago: 1887. V. 52

SPIES, WERNER
The Return of La Belle Jardiniere. Max Ernst 1950-1970. New York: 1971. V. 47; 50
Sculpture by Picasso with a Catalogue of His Works. New York: 1971. V. 50; 52
Victor Vasarely. New York: 1971. V. 47; 50; 52

SPIKES, NELLIE W.
Through the Years: a History of Crosby County Texas. San Antonio: 1952. V. 52

SPILLANE, JOHN D.
The Doctrine of the Nerves. Chapters in the History of Neurology. London: 1981. V. 54

SPILLANE, MICKEY
The Body Lovers. New York: 1967. V. 51
I, the Jury. New York: 1947. V. 49; 51; 52
Kiss Me, Deadly. 1953. V. 53
Tomorrow I Die. New York: 1984. V. 53
Vengenace is Mine!. New York: 1950. V. 47

SPILLER, BURTON L.
Firelight. New York: 1937. V. 47
Hunt. New York: 1935. V. 48
More Grouse Feathers. New York: 1938. V. 47; 49
Thoroughbred. New York: 1936. V. 47; 52

SPILLER, JURG
Paul Klee Notebooks. London: 1973/78. V. 50; 54

SPILLER, ROBERT E.
A James Fenimore Cooper: Descriptive Bibliography of (His) Writings. New York: 1934. V. 49
The Philobiblon Club of Philadelphia, 1893-1973. North Hills: 1973. V. 50
The Philobiblon Club of Philadelphia,...1893-1973. Philadelphia: 1973. V. 49

SPILMAN, THOMAS E.
Semi-Centenarians of Butler Grove Township Montgomery Co., III. 1878. V. 50

SPILSBURY, FRANCIS B.
Account of a Voyage to the Western Coast of Africa; Performed in His Majesty's Sloop Favourite, in the Year 1805... London: 1807. V. 50
Picturesque Scenery in the Holy Land and Syria, Delineated During the Campaigns of 1799 and 1800. London: 1819. V. 50

SPILSBURY, WILLIAM HOLDEN
Lincoln's Inn Its Ancient and Modern Buildings With an Account of the Library. London: 1850. V. 50

SPIN Top Spin and Rosemarie and Thyme. New York: 1929. V. 53

SPINACH from Many Gardens, Gathered by the Typophiles and Fed to Frederic W. Goudy on His Seventieth Anniversary, 1935. New York: 1935. V. 48; 49; 51

SPINDEN, HERBERT JOSEPH
Maya Art and Civilization. Indian Hills: 1957. V. 54
Songs of the Tewa. New York: 1933. V. 50
A Study of Maya Art; Its Subject Matter and Historical Development. Cambridge: 1913. V. 50; 52

SPINDLER, CARL
The Natural Son. London: 1835. V. 51; 54

SPINDLER, WILL
Rim of the Sandhills. Mitchell: 1941. V. 52

SPINETO, MARQUIS
The Elements of Hieroglyphics and Egyptian Antiquities. London: 1576. V. 51
The Elements of Hieroglyphics and Egyptian Antiquities. London: 1845. V. 49

THE SPINNER'S Book of Fiction. San Francisco: 1907. V. 47; 50; 54

SPINNIKER, ADRIAAN
Leerzaame Zinnebeelden. Haarlem: 1714. V. 52
Vervolg der Lerrzaame Zinnebeelden... Haarlem: 1758. V. 50

SPINOZA, BARUCH DE
Renati Descartes Principiorum Philosophiae... Cogitata Metaphysica. Amsterdam: 1663. V. 51
Renati Descartes Principiorum Philosophiae Parts I & II, More Geometrico Demonstratae... (with) Opera Posthuma, Quorum Series Post Praefationem Exhibetur. Amsterdam: 1663/77. V. 47

SPINOZA, BENEDICTUS DE
B. D. S. Opera Posthuma, Quorum Series Post Praefationem Exhibitur. Amsterdam: 1677. V. 48
Tractatus Theologico-Politicus Continens Dissertationes Aliquot... Hamburg: 1670. V. 52
Tractatus Theologico-Politicus, Cui Adjunctus est Philosphia S. Scripturae Interpres. 1674. V. 48; 53
A Treatise Partly Theological, and Partly Political. London: 1689. V. 48

THE SPIRIT of Canada: Dominion and Provinces 1939 - a Souvenir of Wlecome to H. M. King George VI and H.M. Queen Elizabeth. 1939. V. 47; 50

THE SPIRIT of Election Wit, at the City of Exeter, and County of Devon: Together with the Burlesque at Ide, in the Year 1812... Exeter: 1812. V. 49

SPIRIT of English Wit; or, Post-Chaise Companion... London: 1812. V. 51

THE SPIRIT of the Fair. New York: 1864. V. 47

THE SPIRIT of the Public Journals for the Year M.DCCC.XXII: Being an Impartial Selection of the Most Exquisite Essays... London: 1824. V. 47

SPIRITUALISTS' and Liberalists' Camp-Meeting. Lake Pleasant. Montague, Mass. August 4th to August 30th, 1875. Springfield: 1875. V. 48

SPIRONCINI, GINIFACCIO, PSEUD.
Il Corriero Svaligiato Publicato da Ginifaccio Spironcini...(with) Continuszione del Corriero Svaligiato... Villafranca (Geneva?): 1644/60. V. 51; 53

SPITERIS, TONY
The Art of Cyprus. New York: 1970. V. 54

SPITTA, PHILIPP
John Sebastian Bach. His Work and Influence on the Music of Germany, 1685-1750. London: 1884-85. V. 52

SPITTAL, JOHN KER
Contemorary Criticisms of Dr. Samuel Johnson - His Works and His Biographers. London: 1923. V. 49

SPIVAK, JOHN LOUIS
Georgia Nigger. London: 1933. V. 50

SPIVEY, RICHARD L.
Maria. Flagstaff: 1979. V. 52; 54

SPIZELIUS, THEOPHILUS
Vetus Academia Jesu Christi in Qua XXII. Augustae Vindelic: 1671. V. 53

SPLAN, JOHN
Life with the Trotters. Chicago: 1889. V. 47

SPLATT, CYNTHIA
Isadora Duncan & Gordon Craig. The Prose and Poetry of Action. 1988. V. 48; 54

SPLAWN, A. J.
Ka-Mi-Akin The Last Hero of the Yakimas. Portland: 1917. V. 47

SPOCK, BENJAMIN
The Psychological Aspects of Pediatric Practice. 1938. V. 50

SPOERKE, D. G.
Toxicity of Houseplants. London: 1990. V. 51

SPOERRI, JAMES FULLER
Finnegans Wake a Check List - Including Publications of Portions Under the Title Work in Progress. Evanston: 1953. V. 52

SPOFFORD, HARRIET ELIZABETH PRESCOTT
Art Decoration Applied to Furniture. New York: 1878. V. 52
The Maid He Married. Chicago: 1899. V. 49

SPOFFORD, HARRY
The Mysteries of Worcester; or, Charley Temple and His First Glass of Liquor. Worcester: 1846. V. 54

SPON, ERNEST
Workshop Receipts for the Use of Manufacturers, Mechanics and Scientific Amateurs (First-Fifth Series);. London: 1889-92. V. 49

SPON, ISAAC
The History of the City and State of Geneva, From Its First Foundation to This Present Time. London: 1687. V. 52

SPON, JACOB
Histoire de Geneve. Geneva: 1730. V. 47

SPOONER, LYSANDER
A Letter to Thomas F. Bayard: Challenging His Right-and that of All the Other So-Called Senators and Representatives in Congress-to Exercise any Legislative Power Whatever Over the People of the United States. Boston: 1882. V. 54
The Unconstitutionality of Slavery. Boston: 1845. V. 51

SPOONER, ZILPHA H.
Poems of the Pilgrims Selected by... Boston: 1886. V. 47

SPORTING Anecdotes; Original and Select; Including Characteristic Sketches of Eminent Persons Who Have Appeared on the Turf, etc... London: 1808. V. 47

THE SPORTING Repository, Containing Horse Racing, Hunting, Coursing, Shooting, Archery, Trotting and Tandem Matches, Cocking, Pedestrianism, Pugilism, Anecdotes on Sporting Subjects, Interspersed with Essays... London: 1822. V. 47

SPORTING Sketches: Home and Abroad. London: 1866. V. 52

THE SPORTSMAN in Ireland. London: 1897. V. 49

THE SPORTSMAN'S Cabinet or a Correct Delineation of the Various Dogs Used in the Sports of the Field, Etc. London: 1803/04. V. 51

THE SPORTSMAN'S Dictionary: Containing Instructions for Various Methods to be Observed in Riding, Hunting, Fowling, Setting, Fishing, Racing, Farriery, Hawking, Breeding and Feeding Horses for the Road and Turf... London: 1807. V. 47

SPORTSMAN'S Dictionary, or the Gentleman's Companion for Town and Country. London: 1792. V. 47; 50; 52

THE SPORTSMAN'S Portfolio of American Field Sports. Boston: 1855. V. 47
THE SPORTSMAN'S Portfolio of American Field Sports. New York: 1929. V. 47

THE SPORTSMAN'S Vocal Library... London: 1812. V. 49

SPOTISWOODE, ROBERT
Practicks of the Laws of Scotland... Edinburgh: 1706. V. 50

SPOTORNO, GIOVANNI BATISTA
Memorials of Columbus... London: 1823. V. 53

SPOTTE, S.
Captive Seawater Fishes: Science and Technology. London: 1992. V. 50

SPOTTISWOOD, JOHN
The History of the Church of Scotland. Edinburgh: 1850. V. 53
The History of the Church of Scotland, Being the Year of Our Lord 203 and Continued to the Reign of king James the VI of Ever Blessed Memory. London: 1666. V. 49
Refutatio Libelli de Regimine Ecclesiae Scoticanae. London: 1620. V. 50

SPOTTS, DAVID L.
Campaigning with Custer and the Nineteenth Kansas Volunteer Cavalry on the Washita Campaign 1868-69. Los Angeles;: 1928. V. 49; 54

SPRACKLAND, R. G.
Giant Lizards. London: 1992. V. 51

SPRADBERY, J. PHILIP
Wasps, an Account of the Biology and Natural History of Solitary and Social Wasps With Particular Reference to Those of the British Isles. 1973. V. 54

SPRAGUE, ISAAC
Beautiful Wild Flowers of America. Troy: 1892. V. 50
Flowers of Field and Forest. Boston: 1882. V. 54
Life of Isaac W. Sprague, the Living Skeleton. New York: 1882. V. 54

SPRAGUE, P. E.
The Drawings of Louis Henry Sullivan: a Catalogue of the Frank Lloyd Wright Collection at the Avery Arch. Library. Princeton: 1979. V. 50; 51; 54

SPRANGE, JASPER
The Tunbridge Wells Guide: or an Account of the Ancient and Present State of That Place... London: 1801. V. 54
The Tunbridge Wells Guide: or An Account of the Ancient and Present State of that Place... Tunbridge Wells: 1801. V. 50

SPRAT, THOMAS
The History of the Royal Society of London. London: 1667. V. 47; 48; 51; 54
The History of the Royal Society of London. London: 1702. V. 48; 50; 52; 54
The History of the Royal Society of London... London: 1722. V. 47; 49; 51; 52
The History of the Royal Society of London... London: 1734. V. 53
The History of the Royal Society of London... London: 1848. V. 49
A Relation of the Late Wicked Contrivance of Stephen Blackhead and Robert Young... London: 1693. V. 53
Sermons Preached on Several Occasions. London: 1722. V. 49
A True Account and Declaration of the Horrid Conspiracy Against the Late King, His Present Majesty and the Government... London: 1686. V. 48; 49

SPRATLIN, V. B.
Juan Latino: Slave and Humanist. New York: 1938. V. 54

SPRATLING, WILLIAM
Little Mexico. New York: 1932. V. 50

SPRATT, G., MRS.
Flora and Thalia; or, Gems of Flowers and Poetry... London: 1835. V. 54
The Language of Birds...Poetic and Prose Illustrations of the Most Favourite Cage Birds... London: 1837. V. 54

SPRATT, GEORGE
Obstetric Tables: Comprising Graphic Illustrations with Descriptions and Practical Remarks... Philadelphia: 1848. V. 49
Obstetric Tables: Comprising Graphic Illustrations with Descriptions and Practical Remarks... Philadelphia: 1850. V. 53

SPRATT, T. A. B.
Travels and Researches in Crete. London: 1865. V. 49

SPREAT, W.
Picturesque Sketches of the Churches of Devon. Exeter: 1842. V. 51

SPRENGEL, K.
An Introduction of Cryptogamous Plants in Letters. London: 1807. V. 49; 50; 52

SPRENGELL, CONRAD
The Aphorisms of Hippocrates, and the Sentences of Celsus... London: 1735. V. 51; 52; 53

SPRENGER, MAJA
The Etruscans: Their History, Art and Architecture. New York: 1983. V. 53

SPRENGLING, MARTIN
Barhebraeus' Scholia on the Old Testament. Chicago: 1931. V. 52

SPREUL, JOHN
Some Remarkable Passages of the Lord's Providence. Edinburgh: 1832. V. 54

SPRIGG, CHRISTOPHER
The Airship. Its Design, History, Operation and Future. London: 1931. V. 49

SPRIGGE, ELIZABETH
Jean Cocteau: The Man and the Mirror. London: 1968l. V. 53

SPRIGGE, JOSHUA
Angliae Rediviva; England's Recovery... London: 1647. V. 47

SPRIGGE, S. SQUIRE
The Methods of Publishing. London: 1890. V. 51

SPRIGGS,, A. O.
Champion Anatomy for Embalmers. Springfield and Toronto: 1934. V. 52

SPRIGGS, A. O.
Champion Restorative Art. Springfield & Toronto: 1934. V. 52
Textbook on Embalming. Springfield and Toronto: 1933. V. 52

SPRING, AGNES WRIGHT
The Cheyenne and Black Hills Stage and Express Routes. Glendale: 1949. V. 50; 51
Seventy Years. A Panoramic History of the Wyoming Stock Growers Association. 1942. V. 54
William Chapman Deming of Wyoming: Pioneer Publisher and State and Federal Official. Glendale: 1944. V. 53

SPRING, GARDINER
Memoirs of the Rev. Samuel J. Mills, Late Missionary to the South Western Section of the United States... New York: 1820. V. 47; 48

SPRING, SAMUEL
Giafar Al Barmeki, a Tale of the Court of Haroun al Raschid. New York: 1836. V. 54

SPRINGER, ANTON
Albrecht Durer. Mit Tafeln und Illustrationem im Text. Berlin: 1892. V. 47

SPRINGER, JOHN S.
Forest Life and Forest Trees: Comprising Winter Camp Life Among the Loggers and Wild Wood Adventure. New York: 1851. V. 47

SPRINGETT, EVELYN CARTIER
For My Children's Children. Montreal: 1937. V. 48

SPRINGS, Water-Falls, Sea-Bathing Resorts and Mountain Scenery of the United States adn Canada... New York: 1855. V. 47

SPROAT, GILBERT MALCOLM
Scenes and Studies of Savage Life. London: 1868. V. 47; 48; 51

SPROD, DAN
Proud Intrepid Heart. Leichhardt's First Attempt to the Swan River. 1846-1847. Hobart: 1989. V. 49

SPROTT, THOMAS
Thomae Sprotti Chronica. E Codice Antiquo... Oxonii: 1719. V. 52

SPROULE, JOHN
The Resources and Manufacturing Industry of Ireland as Illustrated by the Exhibition of 1853. 1853. V. 49

SPRUCE, RICHARD
Notes of a Botanist on the Amazon and Andes. London: 1908. V. 48

SPRUNGER, S.
Orchids from Curtis's Botanical Magazine. London: 1987. V. 47; 48; 50
Orchids from the Botanical Register, 1815-1847. Boston: 1991. V. 51

SPRUNT, A.
South Carolina Bird Life. Columbia: 1949. V. 49

SPRUNT, JAMES
Chronicles of the Cape Fear River... Raleigh: 1914. V. 48
Chronicles of the Cape Fear River, 1600-1916. Raleigh: 1916. V. 53
Derelicts. Wilmington: 1920. V. 49

SPRY, IRENE M.
The Papers of the Palliser Expedition, 1857-1860. Toronto: 1968. V. 48; 49; 53

SPRY, W.
The British Coleoptera Delineated... London: 1861. V. 52

SPRY, WILLIAM JAMES JOSEPH
The Cruise of Her Majesty's Ship "Challenger". Voyages Over Many Seas, Scenes in Many Lands. New York: 1877. V. 47; 50
The Cruise of Her Majesty's Ship "Challenger". Voyages over Many Seas, Scenes in Many Lands. Toronto: 1877. V. 52

SPURGEON, CHARLES HADDON
C. H. Spurgeon's Autobiography. London: 1897. V. 51
The Rev. C. H. Spurgeon's Anecdotes and Stories,.... London: 1866. V. 51

SPURR, GEORGE G.
A Fight with a Grizzly Bear. A Story of Thrilling Interest. Boston: 1886. V. 52

SPURR, HARRY A.
A Cockney in Arcadia. London: 1899. V. 54
The Dumas Fairy Tale Book. London: 1924. V. 49

SPURR, JOSIAH EDWARD
Geology of the Aspen Mining District, Colorado with Atlas. Washington: 1898. V. 48
Through the Ukon Gold Diggings. Boston: 1900. V. 47

SPURSTOW, WILLIAM
The Spiritual Chymist, or Six Decades of Divine Meditations on Several Subjects. London: 1666. V. 53

SPURZHEIM, JOHANN GASPAR
The Anatomy of the Brain with a General View of the Nervous System. Boston: 1836. V. 53
Observations on the Deranged Manifestations of the Mind, or, Insanity. Boston: 1833. V. 50; 52; 53
Observations On the Deranged Manifestations of the Mind; or, Insanity. Boston: 1836. V. 47; 51
Phrenology... London: 1825. V. 51
Phrenology... Boston: 1832. V. 50; 54
The Physiognomical System of Drs. Gall and Spurzheim... London: 1815. V. 50; 53
A Sketch of the Natural Laws of Man. London: 1828. V. 48; 49
A View of the Elementary Principles of Education, Founded on the Study of the Nature of man. Edinburgh: 1821. V. 48
A View of the Elementary principles of Education, Founded on the Study of the Nature of Man. Boston: 1832. V. 47
View of the Elementary Principles of Education, Founded on the Study of the Nature of Man. Boston: 1833. V. 48

SPYRI, JOHANNA
Heidi. Boston: 1899. V. 54

SQUIER, EPHRAIM GEORGE
Nicaragua; its People, Scenery, Monuments and the Proposed Interoceanic Canal. New York: 1852. V. 47; 51
Notes on Central America... New York: 1855. V. 47; 51; 52
Peru. Incidents of Travel and Exploration in the Land of the Incas. London: 1877. V. 48
Peru. Incidents of Travel and Exploration in the Land of the Incas. New York: 1877. V. 47; 49; 52
Tropical Fibres; Their Production and Economic Extraction. London and New York: 1863. V. 51
Waikna; or, Adventures on the Mosquito Shore. New York: 1855. V. 51
Waikna; or Adventures On the Mosquitore Shore. London: 1855. V. 51

SQUIRE, J. C.
If It Happened Otherwise. 1931. V. 51
Speech at the Opening Ceremony of the Lewis Carroll Centenary Exhibition, 28th June 1932. London: 1932. V. 47

SQUIRE, JOHN
Cheddar Gorge: a Book of English Cheeses. London: 1937. V. 49

SQUIRE, SAMUEL
An Enquiry into the Foundation of the English Constitution... London: 1745. V. 47
An Enquiry Into the Foundation of the English Constitution... London: 1753. V. 48

SQUIRE, WATSON C.
Resources and Development of the Territory of Washington. Seattle: 1886. V. 50

SQUIRES, FREDERICK
Architec-tonics, the Tales of Tom Thumtack, Architect. New York: 1914. V. 54

SQVITINIO *Della Liberta Veneta.* Mirandola: 1612. V. 48

SREEVE, JOHN
The Divine Musick Scholar's Guide, Being a Choice Collection of Psalm-Tunes, Hymns and Anthems. London: 1740. V. 48

SRONKOVA, OLGA
Gothic Fashions in Women's Dress. Prague: 1954. V. 54

ST. *James's: a Satirical Poem, in Six Epistles to Mr. Crockford.* London: 1827. V. 48; 50; 51

ST. LOUIS. POLICE DEPARTMENT
Manual of the Metropolitan Police Department of the City of St. Louis. St. Louis: 1902. V. 49

STABLES, W. GORDON
A Boy's Book of Battleships. London: 1909. V. 47; 49
The Cruise of the Land Yacht 'Wanderer'; or, Thirteen Hundred Miles in May Caravan. London: 1886. V. 53
Turkish and Other Baths. A Guide to Good Health and Longevity. London: 1883. V. 51

STACEY, C. P.
The Canadian Army 1939-1945 - an Official Historical Summary. Ottawa: 1948. V. 52
Official History of the Canadian Army in the Second World War. Ottawa: 1957-60. V. 54

STACEY, J.
A Topographical and Historical Account of the City of Norwich... Norwich: 1819. V. 47

STACKHOUSE, J.
Nereis Britannica: Containing all the Species of Fuci, Natives of the British Coasts. Bath: 1795-1801. V. 49; 52
Nereis Britannica: Containing All the Species of Fuci, Natives of the British Coasts. Bath: 1795/1801. V. 53

STACKHOUSE, THOMAS
A Fair State of the Controversy Between Mr. Woolston and His Adversaries:... London: 1730. V. 50
A New History of the Holy Bible. London: 1742. V. 50

STACPOOLE, H. DE VERE
The Garden of God. 1923. V. 48
Pierrette. London: 1900. V. 49

STACY, EDMUND
The Black-Bird's Tale. London: 1710. V. 54

STACY-JUDD, ROBERT B.
Atlantis - Mother of Empires. Los Angeles: 1939. V. 48; 50

STADE, HANS
The Captivity of Hans Stade of Hesse, in A.D. 1547-1555, Among the Wild Tribes of Eastern Brazil. London: 1874. V. 53

STAEHLIN VON STORCKSBURG, JAKOB
An Account of the New North Archipelago, Lately Discovered by the Russians in the Seas of Kamtschatka and Anadir. London: 1774. V. 50

STAEL, GEORGII ERNESTI
Theoria Medicavera. Physiologiam & Pathologiam, Tanquam Doctrinae Medicae partes Vere Contemplativas, E. Nature & Artis Veris Fundamentis, Intaminata Ratione & Inconcussa Experientia Sistens. Halae: 1708. V. 51

STAEL-HOLSTEIN, ANNE LOUISE GERMAINE NECKER, BARONNE DE
An Appeal to the Nations of Europe Against the Continental System. London: 1813. V. 54
Considerations Sur Les Principaux Evenements De La Revolution Francoise. Londres: 1819. V. 50
Corinna; or, Italy... London: 1807. V. 48
Corinna, or Italy. London: 1894. V. 52; 53
Corinne ou l'Italie. Paris: 1807. V. 48; 50
De L'Allemagne. Paris: 1813. V. 50
Germany. London: 1813. V. 47; 50
Germany. London: 1814. V. 49
Letters and Reflections of the Austrian Field-Marshall Prince De Ligne... Philadelphia: 1809. V. 49; 50; 53
A Treatise on Ancient and Modern Literature. London: 1803. V. 54

STAEL-HOLSTEIN, AUGUSTE LOUIS, BARON DE
Letters on England. London: 1825. V. 51

STAFFORD, JEAN
Boston Adventure. New York: 1944. V. 47
The Collected Stories of Jean Stafford. New York: 1969. V. 52; 53
A Mother in History. New York: 1966. V. 52

STAFFORD, MALLIE
The March of Empire Through Three Decades Embracing Sketches of California History...Crossing the Plains with Ox Teams... San Francisco: 1884. V. 47

STAFFORD, MARQUIS OF
Catalogue Raisonne of the Pictures...in the Gallery of Cleveland House, Comprising a List of the Pictures, with Illustrative Anecdotes and Descriptive Accounts of the Execution, Composition and Characteristic Merits of the Principal Paintings. London: 1808. V. 47

STAFFORD, MARSHALL
The Life of James Fisk, Jr., Being a Full and Accurate Narrative of All the Enterprises in Which He Has Been Engaged. New York: 1872. V. 51

STAFFORD, THOMAS
Pacata Hibernia. Ireland Appeased and Reduced, or, an Historie of the Late Warraes of Ireland... London: 1633. V. 50
Pacata Hibernia; or, a History of the Wars in Ireland. Dublin: 1810. V. 47; 53
Pacata Hibernia, or a History of the Wars in Ireland... London: 1896. V. 51

STAFFORD, WILLIAM
All About Light. Athens: 1978. V. 51
Braided Apart. Lewiston: 1976. V. 51
The Design on the Oriole. 1977. V. 51
Eleven Untitled Poems. Mt. Horeb: 1968. V. 51; 52; 54
Going Places. Poems. Reno: 1974. V. 51
In the Clock of Reason. Victoria: 1973. V. 51
Listening Deep. Great Barrington: 1984. V. 49; 50
The Rescued Year. New York: 1966. V. 50
Segues a Correspondence in Poetry. Boston: 1983. V. 47
Sleeping At a Friend's House. 1981. V. 51
Smoke's Way. Port Townsend: 1978. V. 51
Sometimes Like a Legend. Puget Sound County. 1981. V. 54
Stories and Storms and Strangers. Rexburg: 1984. V. 50

STAFFORD, WILLIAM continued
Temporary Facts. Athens: 1970. V. 51
That Other Alone. Mt. Horeb: 1973. V. 51; 53; 54
Traveling through the Dark. New York: 1962. V. 48; 50; 51
Tuft by Puff. Mt. Horeb: 1978. V. 54
Weather. Mt. Horeb: 1969. V. 49
Wyoming Circuit. 1980. V. 51; 52; 53

STAFLEU, F. A.
Taxonomic Literature. The Hague: 1976-88. V. 54
Taxonomic Literature. The Hague: 1983. V. 50
Taxonomic Literature, Supplement. 1993. V. 50

THE STAGE in 1816. A Satirical Poem. In Three Parts. London: 1816. V. 54

STAGG, JOHN
The Cumbrian Minstrel... Manchester: 1821. V. 50; 52; 54
Miscellaneous Poems. Carlisle: 1790. V. 54
Miscellaneous Poems. Carlisle: 1804. V. 49

STAHL, GEORG ERNST
Anweisung zur Metallurgie. Leipzig: 1720. V. 47
Collegium Casuale, Sic Dictum Minus, in Quo Complectuntur Casus Centum & Duo Diversi Argumenti, Numerum Plerorumque Morborum Absolventes, cum Epicrisibus & Resolutionibus Theoretico Practicis... Suidnitii & Hirschbergae: 1734. V. 48
Opusculum Chymico-Physico-Medicum, Seu Schediasma Tum a Pluribus Annis Variis Occasionibus in Publicum Emissorum Nunc Quadantenus Etiam Auctorum et Deficientibus Passim Exemplaribus in Unum Volumen Iam Collectorum... Halle: 1715. V. 47

STAHLSCHMIDT, J. C. L.
The Church Bells of Kent; Their Inscriptions, Founders, Uses and Traditions. London: 1887. V. 53

STAIG, R. A.
The Fabrician types of Insects in the Hunterian Collection at Glasgow University. Coleoptera. Parts 1 and 2. Cambridge: 1931-40. V. 50

STAINER, C. L.
King Blacksack and His Sword. London: 1909. V. 53

STAINTON, H. T.
British Butterflies and Moths: an Introduction to the Study of Our Native Lepidoptera. London: 1867. V. 50
The Entomologist's Annual for 1855 (to 1874). London: 1855-74. V. 48
The Natural History of the Tineina. London: 1855-73. V. 50

STALEY, ALLEN
The Pre-Raphaelite Landscape. 1973. V. 49

STALEY, WILLIAM
The Tryal of William Staley, Goldsmith, for Speaking Treasonable Words Against His Most Sacred Majesty... London: 1678. V. 53

STALIN, JOSEF
Works. London: 1953-55. V. 49

STALIN-Wells Talk. London: 1934. V. 53

STALLWORTHY, JON
Wilfred Owen - as Biography. London: 1975. V. 47

STAMBAUGH, J. LEE
A History of Collin County, Texas. Austin: 1958. V. 47

STAMBAUGH, SAMUEL C.
A Faithful History of the Cherokee Tribe of Indians, from the Period of Our First Intercourse with Them... Washington: 1846. V. 47; 52

STAMMA, PHILLIP
The Noble Game of Chess; or, a New and Easy Method to Learn to Play Well in a Short Time. London: 1745. V. 54

STAMPFLE, FELICE
Rubens and Rembrandt in Their Century, Flemish and Dutch Drawings of the 17th Century from the Pierpont Morgan Library. New York: 1979. V. 50

THE STANBROOK Abbey Press 1956-1990. 1992. V. 47

STANBROOK Abbey Press. Ninety Two Years of Its History, Written and Illustrated by the Benedictines of Stanbrook. Worcester: 1970. V. 51

STANDARD Atlas of Hamilton County, Nebraska Including a Plat Book... Chicago: 1923. V. 50

STANDARD Atlas of Lapeer County Michigan Including a Plat Book of Villages, cities and Townships of the County. Chicago: 1906. V. 49

STANDARD Blue Book of U.S.A. South Texas Edition Deluxe. 1926. V. 49
STANDARD Blue Book of U.S.A. South Texas Edition Deluxe. 1929-30. V. 49

THE STANDARD Blue Book, Texas 1920. San Antonio: 1920. V. 47

STANDARD Rules for Married Ladies: Containing Instructions to Make Good and Honest Female Servants; with Hints for Their Own Happiness. Manchester: 1831. V. 48

STANDARD Uniforms and Patterns of the Army, Navy, Militia, Volunteers, Civil Service, Court Dress, Etc. London: 1880. V. 50

STANDING BEAR, CHIEF LUTHER
Land of the Spotted Eagle. Boston: 1933. V. 50
My People and the Sioux. Boston: 1928. V. 50

STANDLEY, P. C.
Studies of American Plants, I-XI. Chicago: 1929-40. V. 48; 51
Trees and Shrubs of Mexico. Washington: 1920-26. V. 52
Trees and Shrubs of Mexico. Washington: 1967. V. 50

STANESBY, SAMUEL
The Bridal Souvenir. London: 1857. V. 50
The Floral Gift, an Illuminated Souvenir. London: 1863. V. 49
The Wisdom of Solomon. London: 1861. V. 52

STANFIELD, CLARKSON
Stanfield's Coast Scenery. London: 1836. V. 51; 52
Stanfield's Coast Scenery. London: 1847. V. 53

STANFORD, DON
New England Earth and Other Poems. San Francisco: 1941. V. 53

STANFORD, EDWARD
The University Atlas of Classical and Modern Geography Including All the Recent Geographical Discoveries. London: 1874. V. 50

STANFORD, JANE KINDERLY
A Lady's Gift, or Woman as She Ought to Be. Philadelphia: 1836. V. 54

STANFORD, JOHN
The Winters of that Country. 1984. V. 47; 48

STANFORD Short Stories 1964. Stanford: 1964. V. 50

STANFORD, WILLIAM
An Exposition of the Kinges Prerogative, Collected Out of the Great Abridgement of Iustice Fitzherbert, and Other Olde Writers of the Lawes of England...1577. 1577. V. 47

STANGE, STANISLAUS
The Singing Girl. New York: 1895. V. 49

STANGER, FRANK M.
Peninsula Community Book. San Mateo: 1946. V. 51

STANHOPE, CHARLES STANHOPE, 3RD EARL OF
Considerations on the Means of Preventing Fraudulent Practices on the Gold Coin. London: 1775. V. 53
Principles of the Science of Tuning Instruments with Fixed Tones. London: 1806. V. 47

STANHOPE, EUGENIA
The Deportment of a Married Life. London: 1798. V. 48; 49; 50

STANHOPE, HESTER
Memoirs as Related by Herself in Conversations With Her Physician... London: 1845. V. 50; 54
Memoirs of the Lady Hester Stanhope, as Related by Herself... London: 1846. V. 51

STANHOPE, LEICESTER
Greece in 1823 and 1824: Being a Series of Letters and Other Documents on the Greek Revolution. London: 1824. V. 49

STANHOPE, LOUISA SIDNEY
The Crusaders. London: 1820. V. 50

STANHOPE, PHILIP HENRY STANHOPE, 5TH EARL OF
History of England from the Peace of Utrecht to the Peace of Versailles, 1713-1783. London: 1853. V. 52; 54

STANIHURST, RICHARD
De Rebus in Hibernia Gestis. Leyden: 1584. V. 47
Hebdomada Mariana, Ex Orthodoxis Catholice Romane Ecclesiae Patribus Collecta (etc.). Antwerp: 1609. V. 53

STANLEY, ARTHUR PENRHYN
Historical Memorials of Westmisnter Abbey. London: 1886. V. 49
The Life and Correspondence of Thomas Arnold, D.D. London: 1868, V. 54
Sermon Preached by Arthur Penrhyn Stanley, Dean of Westminster... London: 1870. V. 49; 54
Sinai and Palestine in Connection With Their History. London: 1856. V. 48
Sinai and Palestine in Connection with Their History. London: 1858. V. 50; 52

STANLEY, AUTUMN
Mothers and Daughters of Invention, Notes for a Revised History of Technology. Metuchen: 1993. V. 48

STANLEY BELCHER & MASON
General Laboratory Apparatus Etc. Birmingham: 1939. V. 54

STANLEY, CHARLES HENRY
The Chess Player's Instructor; or, Guide to Beginners... New York: 1859. V. 52
Paul Morphy's Match Games. New York: 1859. V. 52

STANLEY, DAVID SLOANE
War Department. Report on the Yellowstone Expedition of 1873. Washington: 1874. V. 50

STANLEY, E.
A Familiar History of Birds, Their Nature, Habits and Instincts. London: 1835. V. 53

STANLEY, EDWARD
Before and After Waterloo: Letters from Edward Stanley, 1802, 1814 and 1816. New York: 1908. V. 50
Elmira, a Dramatick Poem: With Thoughts on Tragedy. Norwich: 1790. V. 47; 49

STANLEY, EDWIN J.
Life of Rev. L. B. Stateler: or, Sixty-Five Years on the Frontier Containing Incidents, Anecdotes and Sketches of Methodist History in the West and Northwest. Nashville: 1907. V. 47; 50; 52
Rambles in Wonderland. New York: 1878. V. 52

STANLEY, F.
The Apache of New Mexico, 1540-1940. Pampa: 1962. V. 52
Ciudad Santa Fe. 1958-65. V. 54
The Civil War in New Mexico. Denver: 1960. V. 48
Clay Allison. Denver: 1956. V. 49; 50
Desperadoes of New Mexico. Denver: 1953. V. 51; 53
Ike Stockton. Denver: 1959. V. 53
Longhair Jim Courtright. Denver: 1957. V. 49
Socorro, the Oasis. Denver: 1950. V. 50
Story of the Texas Panhandle Railroads. Borger: 1976. V. 48
The Las Vegas Story (Mexico). Denver: 1951. V. 49

STANLEY, HENRY MORTON
The Autobiography of Sir Henry Morton Stanley... London: 1909. V. 49
The Congo and the Founding of its Free State... London: 1885. V. 48
The Congo and the Founding of Its Free State. New York: 1885. V. 47; 52; 53; 54
The Congo and the Founding of Its Free State... London: 1886. V. 47
Coomassie and Magdala: the Story of Two British Campaigns in Africa. London: 1874. V. 54
Coomassie and Magdala: The Story of Two British Campaigns in Africa. New York: 1874. V. 47
How I Found Livingstone... London: 1872. V. 47; 53
How I Found Livingstone... Montreal: 1872. V. 52
In Darkest Africa. London: 1890. V. 48; 51; 52; 53
In Darkest Africa. New York: 1890. V. 47; 48; 49; 50; 52; 53
In Darkest Africa... London: 1891. V. 54
My Dark Companion and Their Strange Stories. London: 1893. V. 54
My Early Travels and Adventures in America and Asia. London: 1895. V. 51; 53; 54
Slavery and the Slave Trade in Africa. New York: 1893. V. 49
Through the Dark Continent or the Sources of the Nile Around the Great Lakes of Equatorial Africa and down the Livingstone River to the Atlantic Ocean. New York: 1878. V. 49
Through the Dark Continent or the Sources of the Nile Around the Great Lakes of Equatorial Africa and Down the Livingstone River to the Atlantic Ocean. London: 1899. V. 49; 54

STANLEY, J. L.
The Arts of Africa. An Annotated Bibliography. 1988/89. V. 51

STANLEY, JOHN A.
In the County Court of the County Court of the City and County of San Francisco. September Term, 1870. In the Matter of Application for the Confirmation of the Report of the Second Street Commissioners. Opinion of John A. Stanley, County Judge. San Francisco: 1870. V. 49

STANLEY, JOHN THOMAS
An Account of the Hot Springs in Iceland... Edinburgh?: 1794. V. 50

STANLEY, LEE WRIGHT
Knapsack Stories. New York: 1917. V. 48

STANLEY, RICHARD
The London Bookshop. (with) The London Bookshop. Being Part Two... Pinner, Middlesex: 1971/77. V. 50

STANLEY, ROBERT
Angling Anecdotes. London: 1900. V. 53

STANLEY, T. D.
Flora of South Eastern Queensland. Brisbane: 1983-89. V. 48; 50; 51

STANLEY, THOMAS
Historia Philosophiae Orientalis. Amsterdam: 1690. V. 50
History of Philosophy... London: 1656. V. 47
The History of Philosophy... London: 1687. V. 48; 52
The History of Philosophy... London: 1701. V. 48
The History of Philosophy... London: 1743. V. 47; 52; 54

STANLEY, WILLIAM
The Case of the Fox...A Political Utopia. London: 1903. V. 47

STANLEY, WILLIAM OWEN
Memoirs on Remains of Ancient Dwellings in Holyhead Island, Called Cyttiau'r Gwyddelod, Explored in 1862, 1868, 1876. London: 1871. V. 50

STANLEY-STONE, A. C.
The Worshipful Company of Turners of London. London: 1925. V. 47

STANNARD, HENRIETTA ELIZA VAUGHAN
Cavalry Life or, Sketches and Stories in Barracks and Out. London: 1881. V. 54

STANSBURY, CAROLINE M. KIRKLAND
Montacute: or, a New Home - Who'll Follow. 1840. V. 47

STANSBURY, ELIJAH
Life and Times of Hon. Elijah Stansbury... Balitmore: 1874. V. 50

STANSBURY, HOWARD
Exploration and Survey of the Valley of the Great Salt Lake of Utah. Philadelphia: 1852. V. 47; 49; 50; 52; 53
Exploration and Survey of the Valley of the Great Salt Lake of Utah.... Washington: 1853. V. 47; 53

STANSFIELD, ABRAHAM
Flora of Todmorden... Todmorden: 1911. V. 54

STANTON, BERIT
Eleonora: a Fairy Tale. New York: 1993. V. 50

STANTON, ELIZABETH CADY
Address in Favor of Universal Suffrage, for the Election of Delegates to the Constitutional Convention. Albany: 1867. V. 53
Address in Favor of Universal Suffrage, for the Election of Delegates to the Constitutional Convention. New York: 1867. V. 50
Eighty Years and More (1815-1897) Reminiscences of Elizabeth Cady Stanton. New York: 1898. V. 53

STANTON, G. SMITH
When the Wildwood Was in Flower. New York: 1909. V. 47

STANTON, HENRY B.
Debate at the Lane Seminary, Cincinnati: Speech of James A. Thome, of Kentucky...Letter of the Rev. Dr. Samuel H. Cox, Against the American Colonization Society. Boston: 1834. V. 47

STANTON, IRVING
Sixty Years in Colorado Reminiscences and Reflections of a Pioneer of 1860. Denver: 1922. V. 48; 54

STANTON, SAMUEL WARD
American Steam Vessels. New York: 1895. V. 53

STANTON, STEPHEN B.
The Bering Sea Controversy. New York: 1892. V. 47

STANWOOD, AVIS A.
Fostina Woodman, the Wonderful Adventurer. Boston: 1850. V. 49

STANYAN, ABRAHAM
An Account of Switzerland. London: 1714. V. 47; 50

STANYAN, TEMPLE
The Grecian History. London: 1781. V. 47

STAPF, O.
Iconu Botanicarum Index Londinensis. Oxford: 1929-31. V. 47

STAPHYLUS, FRIEDRICH
The Apologie of Fridericus Staphylus, Counseller to the Late Emperour Ferdinandus &c. Antwerp: 1565. V. 54

STAPLEDON, WILLIAM OLAF
Darkness and the Light. London: 1942. V. 53
Last and First Men. London: 1930. V. 48; 54
Last and First Men. 1931. V. 52
Last and First Men. London: 1931. V. 49
Last and First Men... New York: 1931. V. 50
Last and First Men. London: 1934. V. 51
Last Men in London. London: 1932. V. 48; 49
Odd John. London: 1935. V. 54

STAPLES, WILLIAM R.
The Documentary History of the Destruction of the Gaspee. Providence: 1845. V. 54

STAPLETON, MILES
The Tryal of Sr. Miles Stapleton Bart, for High Trason in Conspring the Death of the King &c. at York Assizes on the 18th Day of July 1681. London: 1681. V. 48

STAPLETON, THOMAS
An Politici Horum Temporum in Numero Christianorum Sint Habendi oratio Academica. Germany: 1602. V. 50

STAPP, WILLIAM P.
The Prisoners of Perote: Containing a Journal kept by the Author, Who Was Captured by the Mexicans, at Mier... Philadelphia: 1845. V. 49

STAR Science Fiction Stories. 1954. V. 48; 52

STAR Short Novels. 1954. V. 48; 52

STARBACK, EDITH
Crossing the Plains. Nashville: 1922. V. 52

STARBUCK, ALEXANDER
History of the American Whale Fishery From Its Earliest Inception to the Year 1876. Waltham: 1878. V. 52
History of the American Whale Fishery From Its Earliest Inception to the Year 1876. Washington: 1878. V. 53

STARBUCK, W. G.
Latimer's Luck: by the author... London: 1865. V. 49

STARFORTH, JOHN
The Architecture of the Farm. Edinburgh & London: 1853. V. 47

STARK, A. W.
Instruction for Field Artillery... Richmond: 1864. V. 49

STARK, ADAM
The History and Antiquities of Gainsbrugh, (Com. Linc.) Together with a Topographical and Descriptive Account of Stow, Principally in Illustration of Its Claim to be Considered as the Roman Sidnacester. London: 1817. V. 47

STARK, ARTHUR
The Fauna of South Africa. London: 1900-01. V. 50; 52

STARK BROS.
Centennial Fruits, the Products of a Hundred Years Successful Tree Growing 1816-1916. Louisiana: 1916. V. 50; 51; 52; 54

STARK, CORDELIA
A Female Wanderer; or the Remarkable Disclosures of Cordelia and Edwin. Boston: 1857. V. 48
The Remarkable Narrative of Cordelia Krasts; or the Female Wanderer. Boston: 1846. V. 47

STARK, FREYA
Baghdad Sketches. Baghdad: 1932. V. 49; 52
Letters. 1914-80. Salisbury: 1974-82. V. 52
The Lyrican Shore. London: 1956. V. 54
Rome on the Euphrates - the Story of a Frontier. London: 1966. V. 49
Seen in the Hadhramaut. London: 1938. V. 48; 49
Space, Time and Movement in Landscape. London: 1969. V. 48; 49; 51
Space, Time and Movement in Landscape. London: 1980?. V. 54
Traveller's Prelude (Autobiography to 1928). - Beyond Euphrates, Autobiography 1928-1933. - The Coast of Incense, Autobiography 1933-1939. London: 1950-53. V. 50

STARK, GLADYS
The Old Ship Meeting House of Hingham, Massachusetts. Boston: 1951. V. 48

STARK, JAMES
Scenery of the Rivers of Norfolk, Comprising the Yare, the Waveney and the Bure. Norwich & London: 1834. V. 51; 52; 53; 54

STARK, JAMES HENRY
Stark's History and Guide to the Bahama Islands. Boston: 1891. V. 53

STARKE, JAMES
Picturesque Views on and Near Eastern Coast of England... London: 1834. V. 47; 50

STARKE, MARIANA
Information and Directions for Travellers on the Continent. London: 1824. V. 50

STARKE, RICHARD
The Office ad Authority of a Justice of Peace Explained and Digested Under Proper Titles. Williamsburg: 1774. V. 50

STARKEY, JAMES
At Christmas: Verses. Dublin: 1934. V. 54
An Epilogue to the Praise of Angus. Dublin: 1914. V. 50
Facetiae et Curiosa. 1937. V. 54
The Lamplighter and Other Poems. London. V. 53
Personal Talk, a Book of Verses. 1936. V. 54
Poems, 1930-1938. 1938. V. 54
This Is the House and Other Verses. 1942. V. 54
Twenty-Five Lyrics. 1933. V. 48

STARKEY, WILLIAM
Poems and Translations. Dublin: 1875. V. 53

STARKMAN, S. B.
The Contemplative Man's Recreation. Vancouver: 1970. V. 48; 53

STARKWEATHER, GEORGE B.
The Law of Sex: Being an Exposition of the Natural Law by Which the Sex of Offspring is Controlled in Man and the Lower Animals. London: 1883. V. 49

STARLING, ERNEST
The Fluids of the Body. Chicago: 1909. V. 49; 54
Recent Advances in the Physiology of Digestion. Chicago: 1906. V. 54

STARNES, EBENEZER
The Slaveholder Abroad... Philadelphia: 1860. V. 49

STARPAROLA, GIOVANNI FRANCESCO
Facetious Nights. London: 1898. V. 50

STARR, F. RATCHFORD
Farm Echoes. New York: 1901. V. 52

STARR, FREDERICK
Ancient Pictures for Little Moderns; or, Things Once Seen by Jewish Children. New Haven: 1889. V. 50
Catalogue of a Collection of Objects Illustrating the Folklore of Mexico. London: 1899. V. 47; 51
Indians of Southern Mexico, an Ethnographic Album. Chicago: 1899. V. 51
Notes Upon the Ethnography of Southern Mexico. Davenport: 1902. V. 54

STARR, H., & CO.
Great Ocean Mail Line Via the Isthmus of Panama to California and British Columbia. London: 1866. V. 53

STARR, JIMMY
365 Nights in Hollywood. Hollywood: 1926. V. 50
Three Short Biers. Hollywood: 1945. V. 50

STARR, MOSES ALLEN
Atlas of Nerve Cells. Columbia: 1896. V. 48
Atlas of Nerve Cells. New York: 1896. V. 49; 50; 54
Brain Surgery. New York: 1893. V. 49
Familiar Forms of Nervous Diseases. New York: 1890. V. 47
Organic Nervous Diseases. Philadelphia: 1903. V. 47

STARRETT, VINCENT
221B. Studies in Sherlock Holmes by Various Hands. New York: 1940. V. 49
Ambrose Bierce - a Bibliography. Philadelphia: 1929. V. 51
Bibliography of Stephen Crane. Glendale: 1949. V. 53
Bookman's Holiday. The Private Satisfactions of an Uncurable Collector. New York: 1942. V. 49
Books and Bipeds. New York: 1947. V. 49
The Case-Book of Jimmy Lavender. New York: 1944. V. 54
Coffins for Two. Chicago: 1924. V. 50
Et Cetera, a Collector's Scrap-Book. Chicago: 1924. V. 53; 54
Flame and Dust. Chicago: 1924. V. 47
Monologue in Baker Street. New York: 1960. V. 54
Oriental Encounters. Two Essays in Bad Taste. Chicago: 1938. V. 50
Penny Wise and Book Foolish. New York: 1929. V. 49; 52
Persons from Porlock & Other Interruptions. Chicago: 1938. V. 47; 49; 51; 54
The Private Life of Sherlock Holmes. New York: 1933. V. 53
The Quick and the Dead. Sauk City: 1965. V. 54
Stephen Crane - a Bibliography. Philadelphia: 1923. V. 48; 49; 50

STATE Atlas of New Jersey... New York: 1872. V. 47; 49; 51

THE STATE Farce: A Lyrick. Written at Clermont and Inscribed to His Grace the Duke of Newcastle. London: 1756. V. 49

STATE of Facts. Shewing the Right of Certain Companies to the Lands Lately Purchased by Them from the State of Georgia. Philadelphia: 1795. V. 48

THE STATE of Innocence, and the Fall of Man. Trenton: 1813. V. 49; 54

THE STATE of Nebraska and Its Resources. Lincoln: 1879. V. 48

STATE of Oregon Recorded Marks and Brands 1918. V. 50

THE STATE of Representation of England and Wales, Delivered to the Society, the Friends of the People, Associated for the Purpose of Obtaining a Parliamentary Reform, on Saturday the 9th of Feb. 1793. London: 1793. V. 53

STATE of the British and French Colonies in North America, with Respect to Number of People, Forces, Forts, Indians, Trade and other Advantages... London: 1755. V. 50

STATE of the East India Company's Affairs, With a View to the Intended Bill for Regulating the Dividend, December 1767. London: 1768. V. 47

THE STATE of the Nation. Cincinnati: 1940. V. 47; 51

THE STATE of the Nation, with a General Balance of the Publick Accounts. Together with: a Suplemtn (sic) to the State of the Nation... London: 1748. V. 47

THE STATE of the Trade and Manufactory of Iron in Great Britain Considered. London: 1750. V. 51

STATE Papers and Publick Documents of the United States from the Accession of George Washington to the Presidency, Exhibiting a Complete View Of Our Foreign Relations Since that Time... Boston: 1817. V. 47

STATE Papers on Nullification Including...the Proclamation of the President of the United States, and the Proceedings of the Several State Legislatures. Boston: 1834. V. 49; 53

STATE Tracts: Being a Collection of Several Treatises Relating to the Government. (with) State Tracts: Being a Farther Collection of Several Choice Treatises Relating to the Government From the Year 1660 to 1689. London: 1689. V. 51

STATE Tracts: Being a Collection of Several Treatises Relating to the Government. (with) State Tracts: Being a Farther Collection... London: 1692. V. 47

STATEMENT of Certain Immoral Practices Prevailing in His Majesty's Navy; Addressed to the Lords Commissioners of the Admiralty. London: 1822. V. 51

STATEMENT of the Oregon and Washington Delegation, In Regard to the War Claims of Oregon and Washington. Washington: 1860. V. 48

A STATEMENT of the Quantity of Mackerel Packed from Hingham Vessels, from 1815 to 1828. Hingham: 1829. V. 54

A STATISTICAL Account of the Schuylkill Permanent Bridge, Commenced September 5th, 1801. Opened January 1st 1805. Philadelphia. V. 49

STATISTICAL Account of the Shetland Isles by the Ministers of the Respective Parishes. London: 1841. V. 52; 54

STATISTICAL History of John Ridgway's Vertical Revolving Battery. Boston: 1865. V. 49

STATIUS, PUBLIUS PAPINIUS
Opera (with commentaries). Venice: 1499. V. 47
Statii Sylvarum Libri V./ Achilleidos Libri XII./ Thebaidos Libri II./ Orthographia et Flexus Dictionum Graecarum Omnium... Venice: 1502. V. 52
Statii Sylvarum Libri V./ Achilleidos Libri XII./ Thebaidos Libri II./ Orthographia et Flexus Dictionum Graecarum Omnium... Venice: 1519. V. 52
The Thebaid. Oxford: 1767. V. 48

STATON, FRANCES M.
A Bibliography of Canadiana... Toronto: 1934/59. V. 53
A Bibliography of Canadiana: Being Items in the Public Library of Toronto, Canada, Relating to the Early History and Development of Canada. Toronto: 1934. V. 47; 50; 51
A Bibliography of Canadiana; First and Second Supplements. Toronto: 1934-85. V. 51; 52
A Bibliography of Canadiana...early History and Development of Canada. Toronto: 1934-59. V. 50

THE STATUTES at Large Made for the Preservation of the Game. London: 1734. V. 48; 52

STAUFFACHER, JACK
Porter Garrett: Philosophical Writings on the Ideal Book. 1994. V. 54
Porter Garrett: Philosophical Writings on the Ideal Book. San Francisco: 1994. V. 52

STAUFFER, DAVID M.
American Engravers Upon Copper and Steel. 1960. V. 52; 53

STAUNFORD, WILLIAM
An Exposition of the Kinges Prerogative Collected Out of the Great Abridgement of Justice Fitzherbert... London: 1573. V. 52
An Exposition of the Kinges Prerogative Collected Out of the Great Abridgement of Justice Fitzherbert... London: 1590. V. 50
Les Plees del Coron, Diuisees in Plusors Titles & Comon Lieux. London: 1583. V. 47

STAUNTON, GEORGE LEONARD, BART
An Authentic Account of an Embassy from the King of Great Britain to the Emperor of China. London: 1797. V. 50
An Authentic Account of an Embassy from the King of Great Britain to the Emperor of China. London: 1798. V. 47; 49; 52
An Authentic Account of an Embassy from the King of Great Britain to the Emperor of China. Philadelphia: 1799. V. 47

STAUNTON, GEORGE THOMAS
Memoirs of the Chief Incidents of the Public Life of Sir George Thomas Staunton, Bart... London: 1856. V. 51
Miscellaneous Notices Relating to China, and Our Commercial Intercourse With That Country. London: 1822. V. 51

STAUNTON, HOWARD
The Chess-Player's Text Book: a Concise and Easy Introduction to the Game. London: 1849. V. 52

STAVELEY, THOMAS
The Romish Horseleech: or, an Impartial Account of the Intolerable Charge of Popery to This Nation... London: 1674. V. 48; 49

STAVENOW-HIDEMARK, ELISABET
18th Century Textiles: the Anders Berch Collection at the Nordiska Museet. Stockholm: 1990. V. 48; 53

STAVERT, W. J.
The Church Warden's Accounts of the Parish of Burnsall-in-Craven, 1704-1769. Skipton: 1899. V. 47; 53

STAWELL, MAUD MARGARET KEY
My Days with Fairies. New York: 1913. V. 52

STAWELL, RODOLOPH
My Days with the Fairies. London: 1913. V. 49

STEAD, CHRISTINA
The Salzburg Tales. New York: 1934. V. 47; 49
The Salzburg Tales. New York: 1943. V. 53

STEAD, WILLIAM T.
If Christ Came to Chicago!. Chicago: 1894. V. 49

STEADMAN, RALPH
Sigmund Freud. New York: 1979. V. 51
Still Life with Raspberry or the Bumper Book of Steadman. London: 1969. V. 50

STEALINGWORTH, SLIM
Tom Wesselmann. New York: 1980. V. 52; 53

STEAMERS v. Stages; or, Andrew and His Spouse. London: 1830. V. 50

STEARN, WILLIAM T.
The Australian Flower Paintings of Ferdinand Bauer. 1976. V. 52
The Australian Flower Paintings of Ferdinand Bauer. London: 1976. V. 48

STEARNS, CHARLES
The Ladies' Philosophy of Love. Leonminster: 1797. V. 48

STEARNS, E.
Notes on Uncle Tom's Cabin... Philadelphia: 1853. V. 52

STEARNS, HAROLD
Confessions of a Harvard Man. Canada and Santa Barbara: 1984. V. 54
The Confessions of a Harvard Man. Sutton West: 1984. V. 48

STEARNS, JOSIAH
A Sermon Preached at Epping, in New Hampshire on Lord's Day, September 19, 1779. Exeter: 1780. V. 52
A Sermon Preached at the Ordination of the Rev. Mr. Nicolas Dudley. Newbury-port: 1778. V. 52

STEARNS, SAMUEL
The American Oracle. London: 1791. V. 53

STEARNS, WILLIAM AUGUSTUS
Adjutant Stearns. Boston: 1862. V. 49

STEARNS, WINFRID ALDEN
Labrador; a Sketch of Its Peoples, Its Industries and Its Natural History. Boston: 1884. V. 54

STEBBING, HENRY
The Christian in Palestine, or, Scenes of Sacred History... London: 1847. V. 53

STEBBING, WILLIAM
Analysis of Mr. Mill's Sytem of Logic. London: 1864. V. 51

STECHOW, WOLFGANG
Dutch Landscape Painting of the Seventeenth Century. London: 1966. V. 49

STECKBECK, JOHN S.
Fabulous Redman: The Carlisle Indians and Their Famous Football Teams. Harrisburg: 1951. V. 54

STEDMAN, CHARLES
The History of the Origin, Progress and Terimination of the American War... London: 1794. V. 47; 53; 54

STEDMAN, EDMUND C.
Alice of Monmouth. An Idyl of the Great War, with Other Poems. New York: 1864. V. 51
An American Anthology 1787-1900. Cambridge: 1900. V. 47; 51
Edgar Allan Poem. Boston: 1881. V. 48
Poets of America, Victorian Poets, a Victorian Anthology. (and) An American Anthology. Cambridge: 1885-1900. V. 50

STEDMAN, JOHN
Laelius and Hortensia; or, Thoughts on the Nature and Objects of Taste and Genius, in a Series of Letters to Two Friends. Edinburgh: 1782. V. 52

STEDMAN, JOHN GABRIEL
Narrative of a Five Years' Expedition against the Revolted Negroes of Surinam... London: 1796. V. 48
Narrative of a Five Years' Expedition Against the Revolted Negroes of Surinam... London: 1803. V. 47
Narrative of a Five Years' Expedition Against the Revolted Negroes of Surinam... London: 1806-13. V. 52
Narrative of a Five Years' Expedition Against the Revolted Negroes of Surinam... London: 1813. V. 52
Narrative of a Five Years' Expedition Against the Revolted Negroes of Surinam... Barre: 1971. V. 48; 50; 51; 52; 54

STEEDMAN, A.
Wanderings and Adventures in the Interior of Southern Africa. London: 1835. V. 49
Wanderings and Adventures in the Interior of Southern Africa. Cape Town: 1966. V. 48; 52

STEEDMAN, AMY
Legends and Stories of Italy. London: 1909. V. 53

STEEHOLM, CLARA
The House at Hyde Park. New York: 1950. V. 54

STEEL, A. G.
Cricket. London: 1888. V. 51

STEEL, DAVID
The Art of Sail-Making as Practised in the Royal Navy, and According to the Most Approved Methods...etc... London: 1843. V. 53
Seamanship, Both in Theory and Practice. London: 1795. V. 52
The Ship-Masters Assistant and Owners manual... London: 1795. V. 49
Steel's Elements of Mastmaking, Sailmaking and rigging. London: 1932. V. 52

STEEL, FLORA ANNIE WEBSTER
English Fairy Tales... London: 1918. V. 54
English Fairy Tales. New York: 1919. V. 51

STEEL, JOHN H.
An Analysis of the Mineral Waters of Saratoga and Ballston, with Practical Remarks on their Use in Various Diseases. Saratoga Springs: 1825. V. 48

STEEL, SAMUEL AUGUSTUS
The Sunny Road: Home Life in Dixie During the War. Mephis: 1925. V. 49

STEELE, ANNE
Poems On Subjects Chiefly Devotional. London: 1760. V. 50

STEELE, FRANCESCA M.
The Great Auk's Eggs. London: 1886. V. 54
Naomi's Transgression. London: 1907. V. 54

STEELE, FREDERICK
General Orders, No. 39. Headquarters Department of Arkansas. Little Rock: 1864. V. 48

STEELE, JAMES W.
Frontier Army Sketches. Chicago: 1883. V. 48
A Golden Era. The New Gold Fields of the United States. Chicago: 1897. V. 52
Guide to the Pacific Coast, Santa Fe Route. Chicago: 1893. V. 48; 50; 52
Rand, McNally & Co.'s New Guide to the Pacific Coast. Santa Fe Route. Chicago: 1890. V. 47
The Sons of the Border. Sketches of the Life and People of the Far Frontier. Topeka: 1873. V. 48; 49

STEELE, JOHN
Across the Plains in 1850. Chicago: 1930. V. 47
In Camp and Cabin. Mining Life and Adventure, in California During 1850 and Later... Lodi: 1901. V. 47

STEELE, JOSHUA
An Essay Towards Establishing the Melody and Measure of Speech to be Expressed and Perpetuated by Peculiar symbols. London: 1775. V. 51; 53

STEELE, MATTHEW FORNEY
American Campaigns. Washington: 1909. V. 49
American Campaigns. Washington: 1922. V. 50

STEELE, OLIVER G.
Steele's Book of Niagara Falls. Buffalo: 1840. V. 50

STEELE, RICHARD
The Christian Hero: an Argument Proving that No Principles but Those of Religion are Sufficient to Make a Great Man. London: 1701. V. 47
The Conscious Lovers. Londra: 1724. V. 47
The Crisis; or a Discourse Representing the Most Authentic Record, the Just Causes of the Late Happy Revolution... London: 1714. V. 54
Dramatic Works. London: 1760-68. V. 47
The Englishman: Being the Sequel of the Guardian. London: 1714. V. 48
An Essay Upon Gardening, Containing a Catalogue of Exotic Plants for the Stoves and Green-Houses of the British Gardens... York: 1793. V. 52
Essays. London: 1914. V. 52
The Guardian. London: 1797. V. 48
The Ladies Library. London: 1714. V. 47
The Ladies Library. London: 1722. V. 48
A Letter to the Earl of O----d, Concerning the Bill of Peerage. London: 1719. V. 50; 54
The Lover and the Reader. London: 1718. V. 47
The Plebians. London: 1719. V. 47
Poetical Miscellanies, Consisting of Original Poems and Translations. London: 1714. V. 47; 48
The State of the Case Between the Lord Chamberlain of His Majesty's Household and the Governor of the Royal Company of Comedians. London: 1720. V. 54
The Theatre...To Which are Added, The Anti-Theatre; the Character of Sir John Edgar, Steele's Case with the Lord Chamberlain; the Crisis of Property, with the Sequel, Two Pasquins, &c, &c. London: 1791. V. 52; 53

STEELE, ROBERT
The Earliest English Music Printing. London: 1903. V. 48
The Earliest Music Printing. London: 1903. V. 49
The Revival of Printing: a Bibliographical Catalogue of Works Issued by the Chief Modern English Presses. London: 1912. V. 50; 51
Some Old French and English Ballads. Hammersmith: 1905. V. 47

STEELE, THOMAS SEDGWICK
Canoe and Camera: a Two Hundred Mile Tour through the Maine Forests. New York: 1880. V. 50
Canoe and Camera: a Two Hundred Mile Tour through the Maine Forests. Boston: 1882. V. 49
Canoe and Camera: a Two Hundred Mile Tour Through the Maine Forests. New York: 1882. V. 47

STEELE, WILLIAM
Beauties of Gilsland. London: 1836. V. 52; 53

STEELE'S Book of Niagara Falls. Buffalo: 1840. V. 52

STEEL'S Original and Correct List of the Royal Navy, Hired Armed-Vessels, Gunboats, Revenue and Excise Cutters, Packets and India Ships, With Their Commanders and Stations... London: 1797. V. 50

STEEN, MARGUERITE
Oakfield Plays Including the Inglemere Christmas Play. London: 1932. V. 50; 52
William Nicholson. London: 1943. V. 49

STEENTOFT, M.
Flowering Plants in West Africa. London: 1988. V. 49; 50; 52

STEER, G. L.
The Tree of Gernika. A Field Study of Modern War. London: 1938. V. 49

STEERE, C. A.
When Things Were Doing. Chicago: 1908. V. 54

STEFANSKI, ELIZABETH
Coptic Ostraca from Medinet Habu. Chicago: 1952. V. 49; 51

STEFANSSON, VILHJALMUR
The Adventure of Wrangel Island. New York: 1925. V. 49; 51
Arctic Manual. New York: 1950. V. 53
The Friendly Arctic. London: 1921. V. 48
The Friendly Arctic. New York: 1921. V. 50; 52; 53
Hunters of the Great North. New York: 1922. V. 52
Hunters of the Great North. London: 1923. V. 54
My Life with the Eskimo. New York: 1951. V. 50

STEFFEN, RANDY
The Horse Soldier 1776-1943. Norman: 1977. V. 50

STEFFENS, LINCOLN
The Shame of the Cities. New York: 1904. V. 51

STEGER, HARRY PEYTON
Letters of 1899-1912. Austin: 1915. V. 50

STEGGALL, JOHN
An Essay on Mineral, Vegetable, Animal and Aerial Poisons. London: 1833. V. 47

STEGGERDA, M.
Maya Indians of Yucatan. 1941. V. 54

STEGMAIER, MARK J.
James F. Milligan: His Journal of Fremont's Fifth Expedition, 1853-1854... Glendale: 1988. V. 50; 54

STEGMANN, C. VON
Architecture of the Renaissance in Tuscany. New York: 1924. V. 48

STEGNER, WALLACE
All the Little Live Things. New York: 1967. V. 49
Angle of Repose. Garden City: 1971. V. 48; 50; 52
Angle of Repose. New York: 1971. V. 49; 53
Beyond the Hundredth Meridian. Boston: 1954. V. 47; 50; 52
The Big Rock Candy Mountain. New York: 1943. V. 50; 52
The Big Rock Candy Mountain. Franklin Center: 1978. V. 52
The City of the Living. 1956. V. 51
The City of the Living. London: 1957. V. 53
The Collected Stories of Wallace Stegner. New York: 1990. V. 52
Conversations with Wallace Stegner on Western History & Literature. 1983. V. 49; 50; 51; 54
Crossing to Safety. 1987. V. 48
Crossing to Safety. Franklin Center: 1987. V. 52
Crossing to Safety. New York: 1987. V. 49
Fire and Ice. New York: 1941. V. 52
Mormon Country. New York: 1942. V. 48
On a Darkling Plain. New York: 1940. V. 48; 51; 54
On the Teaching of Creative Writing... 1988. V. 49; 50
On the Teaching of Creative Writing. Hanover: 1988. V. 53
Remembering Laughter. Boston: 1937. V. 48; 50
Second Growth. Boston: 1947. V. 49
A Shooting Star. New York: 1961. V. 47; 48; 50
The Sound of Mountain Water. Garden City: 1969. V. 50
The Spectator Bird. Franklin Center: 1976. V. 51
The Uneasy Chair: a Biography of Bernard De Voto. Garden City: 1974. V. 47
Where the Bluebird Sings to the Lemonade Springs: Living and Writing in the West. New York: 1992. V. 49; 51
The Women on the Wall. Boston: 1950. V. 51

STEICHEN, EDWARD
The Blue Ghost. New York: 1947. V. 47
The Family of Man. New York: 1955. V. 50
The First Picture Book. Everyday Things for Babies. New York: 1991. V. 51; 53
A Life in Photography. Garden City: 1963. V. 52
A Life in Photography. New York: 1963. V. 48
Sandburg. New York: 1966. V. 51
The Second Picture Book. New York: 1931. V. 47

STEILACOOM LIBRARY ASSOCIATION
Constitution, By-Laws, and Rules and Orders of the Steilacoom Library Association, Washington Territory. Organized in March 1858. Steilacoom: 1860. V. 50

STEIN, AUREL
The Indo-Iranian Borderlands: Their Prehistory in the Light of Geography and of Recent Explorations. V. 50
Marco Polo's Account of a Mongol Inroad Into Kashmir. V. 50
Old Routes of Western Iran. London: 1940. V. 51
On Alexander's Track to the Indus. London: 1929. V. 48; 50; 51; 54
On Ancient Central-Asia Tracks. London: 1933. V. 49; 51
Ruins of Desert Cathay, Personal Narrative of Explorations in Central Asia and Westernmost China. London: 1912. V. 53
Wall Paintings from Ancient Shrines in Central Asia. London: 1948. V. 48; 52

STEIN, ELIZABETH P.
David Garrick, Dramatist. New York: 1938. V. 52

STEIN, F.
Der Organismus der Infusionsthiere Nach Eigenen Forschungen in systematischer Reihenfolge Bearbeitet. Leipzig: 1859-83. V. 48

STEIN, GERTRUDE
An Acquaintance with Description. London: 1929. V. 47; 51; 54
Alice B. Toklas Cook Book. New York: 1954. V. 53
Alphabets and Birthdays. New Haven: 1957. V. 51
The Autobiography of Alice B. Toklas. London: 1933. V. 48; 50
The Autobiography of Alice B. Toklas. New York: 1933. V. 47; 51; 52
Blood on the Dining-Room Floor. 1948. V. 51; 52; 53
Blood on the Dining-Room Floor. New York: 1948. V. 50
Composition as Explanation. London: 1926. V. 51; 53
Dix Portraits. Paris: 1930. V. 49; 51; 53
An Elucidation. Paris: 1927. V. 47; 48; 50
Everybody's Autobiography. New York: 1937. V. 48; 49; 51; 53
Everybody's Autobiography. London: 1938. V. 49
Four in America. New Haven: 1947. V. 51
Four Saints in Three Acts. New York: 1934. V. 49; 53
From To Do, A Book of Alphabets and Birthdays for All Children Everywhere. Tujunga: 1947. V. 48
The Geographical History of America or the Relation of Human Nature to the Human Mind. New York: 1936. V. 47
Geography and Plays. Boston: 1922. V. 47; 50; 51; 52; 53; 54
The Gertrude Stein First Reader & Three Plays. Dublin & London;: 1946. V. 49; 51; 53
Gertrude Stein's America. Washington: 1965. V. 54
How to Write. Paris: 1931. V. 49; 53
How Writing is Written: Volume II of the Previously Uncollected Writings. Los Angeles: 1974. V. 50
Ida: a Novel. New York: 1941. V. 50
In Savoy, or Yes Is for a Very Young Man. London: 1946. V. 51; 54
In Savoy or Yes Is for a Very Young Man. London: 1947. V. 53
Lectures in America. New York: 1935. V. 48; 49; 50; 51; 53; 54
Lily. Venice: 1969. V. 53
Lucretia Borgia. New York: 1968. V. 51; 52

STEIN, GERTRUDE continued
Lucy Church Amiably. Paris: 1930. V. 47; 53
The Making of Americans. Paris: 1925. V. 47; 48; 49
The Making of Americans. New York: 1926. V. 48
The Making of Americans. New York: 1966. V. 54
Matisse, Picasso and Gertrude Stein. Paris: 1933. V. 47
Money. Los Angeles: 1973. V. 50; 51
Narration. Chicago: 1935. V. 48; 49; 51; 53
A Novel of Thank You. New Haven: 1958. V. 51
Opera and Plays. Paris: 1932. V. 53; 54
Paris, France. London: 1940. V. 51
Paris France. New York: 1940. V. 53; 54
Picasso. London: 1938. V. 50
Picasso. Paris: 1938. V. 49
Picasso. London: 1939. V. 47; 49; 51; 52; 54
Picasso. New York: 1992. V. 49
Portrait of Mabel Dodge at the Villa Curonia. Florence: 1912. V. 48
Portraits and Prayers. New York: 1934. V. 48; 49; 50; 51; 52; 53; 54
A Primer for the Gradual Understanding of Gertrude Stein. Los Angeles: 1971. V. 54
Reflection on the Atomic Bomb. Volume I of the Previously Uncollected Writings. Los Angeles: 1973. V. 50
Selected Writings of Gertrude Stein. New York: 1946. V. 51
Things as They Are. Pawlet: 1950. V. 48; 50; 51
Three Lives. New York: 1909. V. 47; 52
Three Lives. London: 1920. V. 47
Three Lives. New York: 1933. V. 51
Useful Knowledge. London. V. 51
Useful Knowledge. London: 1928. V. 52; 53
Wars I Have Seen. London: 1945. V. 52
Wars I Have Seen. New York: 1945. V. 53
What Are Masterpieces. Los Angeles: 1940. V. 50; 52; 54
The World Is Round. New York: 1939. V. 48; 49; 51; 52; 53

STEIN, HEINRICH F. KARL, BARON
Life and Times of Stein, or Germany and Prussia in the Napoleonic Age. London: 1878. V. 52

STEIN, JOSEPH
Fiddler on the Roof. New York: 1965. V. 52
Zorba: a Musical. New York: 1969. V. 50

STEINBECK, JOHN ERNST
Acceptance Speech. 1962. V. 51
Bombs Away. New York: 1942. V. 48; 49; 51; 52; 54
Burning Bright. New York: 1950. V. 49; 50; 51; 52; 53; 54
Cannery Row. New York: 1945. V. 47; 48; 49; 50; 51; 53
Chapter Thirty-Four from the Novel East of Eden. Bronxville: 1952. V. 53
The Collected Poems of Amnesia Glasscock. San Francisco: 1976. V. 48
Cup of Gold. New York: 1929. V. 47; 49; 51; 53
Cup of Gold. New York: 1936. V. 48; 51; 54
East of Eden. New York: 1952. V. 47; 48; 49; 50; 51; 52; 53; 54
Flight. 1984. V. 52; 54
The Forgotten Village. New York: 1941. V. 48; 49; 50; 51; 53; 54
The Grapes of Wrath. New York: 1938. V. 50
The Grapes of Wrath. London: 1939. V. 50; 51; 54
The Grapes of Wrath. New York: 1939. V. 47; 48; 49; 50; 51; 52; 53; 54
The Grapes of Wrath. New York: 1940. V. 49; 50; 53; 54
The Grapes of Wrath. New York: 1941. V. 53
His Language. Aptos: 1970. V. 53
How Edith McGillcuddy Met R.L.S. Cleveland: 1943. V. 47; 53
In Dubious Battle. 1936. V. 50
In Dubious Battle. New York: 1936. V. 53; 54
John Emery. New York: 1964. V. 52; 53
Journal of a Novel: The East of Eden Letters. New York: 1969. V. 48; 51; 52
A Letter from John Steinbeck. Aptos: 1964. V. 53
A Letter from John Steinbeck. San Francisco: 1964. V. 48
Letter Written in Reply to a Request for a Statement About His Ancestry. Stamford: 1940. V. 51
Letters to Elizabeth. San Francisco: 1978. V. 47; 51; 53; 54
The Log from the Sea of Cortez. New York: 1951. V. 50; 52
The Log from the Sea of Cortez. London: 1958. V. 47; 50
The Long Valley. New York: 1938. V. 49; 50; 51; 52; 53
The Long Valley. London: 1939. V. 53
The Moon is Down. London: 1942. V. 48; 51
The Moon is Down. New York: 1942. V. 47; 48; 49; 50; 51; 53
Neznamemu Bohu. (To a God Unknown). Praha: 1970. V. 49
Nothing So Monstrous. New York: 1936. V. 47; 51; 54
Nothing so Monstrous... New York: 1938. V. 51
Of Mice and Men. London: 1937. V. 52
Of Mice and Men. New York: 1937. V. 47; 48; 49; 50; 51; 52; 53; 54
Of Mice and Men. New York: 1970. V. 52; 53; 54
On a California Ranch. Munich: 1950. V. 51
Once There Was a War. New York: 1958. V. 48; 50
Once There Was a War. London: 1959. V. 48
The Pastures of Heaven. New York: 1932. V. 53
The Pastures of Heaven. New York: 1937. V. 50
The Pearl. New York: 1947. V. 49; 52
The Red Pony. New York: 1937. V. 52; 53
A Russian Journal. New York: 1948. V. 51; 54
St. Katy the Virgin. New York: 1936. V. 53
Sea of Cortez. New York: 1941. V. 48; 52; 53
The Short Novels of John Steinbeck. New York: 1953. V. 51; 52
The Short Reign of Pippin IV. A Fabrication. New York: 1957. V. 48; 49; 53
Slunce A Vino Chudych. (Tortilla Flat). Praha: 1947. V. 49
Speech Accepting the Nobel Prize for Literature. New York: 1962. V. 53
Steinbeck: A Life in Letters. New York: 1975. V. 48
Sweet Thursday. New York: 1954. V. 48; 49
To a God Unknown. New York: 1933. V. 47; 50; 53
Tortilla Flat. New York: 1935. V. 49; 50; 52; 53; 54
Tortilla Flat. New York: 1947. V. 49; 51
Toulavy Autobus. (The Wayward Bus). Praha: 1948. V. 49
Travels With Charley. New York: 1962. V. 49; 51; 53; 54
Vanderbilt Clinic. New York: 1947. V. 48
Viva Zapata!. 1975. V. 52
The Wayward Bus. New York: 1947. V. 48; 49; 51
The Winter of Our Discontent. New York: 1961. V. 51

STEINBERG, SAUL
All in Line. New York: 1945. V. 53

STEINBOCK, R. TED
Paleopathological Daignosis and interpretation: Bone Diseases in Ancient Human Populations. Springfield: 1976. V. 52

STEINDLER, ARTHUR
Mechanics of Normal and Pathological Locomotion in Man. Springfield: 1935. V. 47
Orthopedic Operations: Indications, Technique and End Results. Springfield: 1940. V. 47

STEINER, A. RALPH
Dartmouth. Brooklyn: 1922. V. 47; 48; 51; 54

STEINER, GEORGE
Anno Domini. London: 1964. V. 50
The Death of Tragedy. London: 1961. V. 50

STEINER, JESSE F.
The North Carolina Chain Gang. Chapel Hill: 1927. V. 50

STEINER-PRAG, HUGO
Der Golem/Prager Phantasien. Leipzig: 1916. V. 47

STEINFELD, CECILIA
Early Texas Furniture and Decorative Arts. San Antonio: 1973. V. 49; 50; 54

STEINGRUBER, JOHANN DAVID
Architectural Alphabet, 1773. London: 1972. V. 48

STEINHOUSE, T. B. H.
The Rocky Mountain Saints: a Full and Complete History of the Mormons, from the First Vision of Joseph Smith to the Last Courtship of Brigham Young. New York: 1873. V. 50

STEINMETZ, ANDREW
The Gaming Table: its Votaries and Victims. London: 1870. V. 47; 53

STEINMETZ, CHARLES PROTEUS
Four Lectures on Relativity and Space. New York: 1923. V. 50

STEINMETZ, MORITZ
Arithmeticae Praecepta, in Quaestiones Redacta cum Exemplis Utilibus. Leizpig: 1575. V. 49

STEJNEGER, L.
Georg Wilhelm Steller. The Pioneer of Alaskan Natural History. Cambridge: 1936. V. 54
Herpetology of Japan and Adjacent Territory. Washington: 1907. V. 49; 52
Results of Ornithological Explorations in the Commander Islands and Kamtschatka. Washington: 1885. V. 48

STEKEL, WILHELM
Sadism and Masochism, the Psychology of Hatred and Cruelty. London: 1935. V. 50

STELL, CHARLES
Aleck Hormby. New York: 1898. V. 50

STELL, JAMES
The Hasting's Guide... London: 1794. V. 49
The Hasting's Guide. London: 1815. V. 52

STELLA, ANTONIUS
Antonii Stellae Clerici Veneti, Elogia Venetorum Navali Pugna Illustrium, Ad. Sereniss. Reip. Venetae Principem, Laurentium Priolum, Cum Privilegio Liber Primus. Venice: 1558. V. 49

STELLA, BENEDETTO
Il Tabacco. Opera...Nella Quale si Tratta dell'Origine, Historia, Coltura... Rome: 1669. V. 50; 51; 52

STELLA, CLAUDINE BAUZONNET
Pastorales. Paris: 1667. V. 53

STELLE, F.
Headquarters, Army of the Rio Grande. General Orders No. 4. Brownsville: 1865. V. 48

STELLUTI, FRANCESCO
Trattato del Legno Fossile Minerale Nuovamente Scoperto nel Quale Brevemente si Accenna la Varia... Rome: 1637. V. 49

STENELAUS and Amylda; a Christmas Legend. London: 1858. V. 49

STENGEL, CASEY
Casey at the Bat. The Story of My Life in Baseball. New York: 1962. V. 51

STENGER, ERICH
The March of Photography. London: 1958. V. 49

STENHOUSE, T. B. H.
The Rocky Mountain Saints: a Full and Complete History of the Mormons... New York: 1873. V. 53; 54

STENNETT, SAMUEL
Discourses on Domestick Duties. London: 1783. V. 48

STEPHANINI, J.
The Narrative of J. Stephanini, a Native of Arts, in Greece. Charleston: 1829. V. 48
The Personal Narrataive of the Sufferings of J. Stephanini... New York: 1839. V. 49

STEPHANUS, HENRY
Auli Gellii Noctes Atticae, sev Vigili ae Atticae... Parisiis: 1585. V. 48

STEPHEN, ALEXANDER
Hopi Journal of Alexander M. Stephen. New York: 1969. V. 51

STEPHEN, GEORGE
The Adventures of a Gentleman in Search of a Horse. London: 1836. V. 51
The Adventures of a Gentleman in Search of a Horse. Philadelphia: 1857. V. 52
Adventures of an Attorney in Search of Practice. London: 1839. V. 50

STEPHEN, J. K.
Lapsus Calami. Cambridge: 1891. V. 47

STEPHEN, JAMES
Questions for Law Students on the Sixth Edition of Mr. Serjeant Stephen's New Commentaries on the Laws of England. London: 1869. V. 48; 49
War in Disguise; or, The Frauds of the Netral Flags. New York: 1806. V. 48

STEPHEN, JAMES FITZJAMES
A Digest of the Law of Evidence. St. Louis: 1879. V. 52
Essays by a Barrister. London: 1862. V. 47
A History of the Criminal Law of England. London: 1883. V. 53
Liberty, Equality, Fraternity. London: 1873. V. 49
The Story of Nuncomar and the Impeachment of Sir Elijah Impey. London: 1885. V. 52

STEPHEN, LESLIE
The English Utilitarians. New York: 1900. V. 47
Essays on Freethinking and Plainspeaking. London: 1873. V. 51
George Eliot. London: 1902. V. 47
Hours in a Library... London: 1874-79. V. 52
Hours in a Library. London: 1892. V. 47; 48
Hours in a Library. New York & London: 1894. V. 49; 52
Hours in a Library. London: 1899. V. 49
Hours in a Library. London: 1909. V. 54
Life of Henry Fawcett. London: 1885. V. 54
The Playground of Europe. London: 1894. V. 50; 51
Samuel Johnson. London: 1880. V. 54
The Science of Ethics. London: 1882. V. 52; 53
Sketches from Cambridge. London: 1865. V. 52
Studies of a Biographer. London: 1899. V. 50

STEPHEN, RICHARD H.
The Bibliography of Thackeray. London: 1880. V. 47

STEPHENS, ALEXANDER
Memoirs of John Horne Tooke. London: 1813. V. 49

STEPHENS, ALEXANDER H.
Extract from a Speech by Alexander H. Stephens, Vice President of the Confederate States, delivered in the Secession Convention of Georgia, January 1861. Boston: 1861. V. 50

STEPHENS, ANN S.
The Ladies' Complete Guide to Crochet, Fancy Knitting, and Needlework. New York: 1854. V. 47
Malaeska; The Indian Wife of the White Hunter. New York: 1860. V. 49; 52; 53
The Portland Sketch Book. Portland: 1836. V. 52

STEPHENS, EDWARD
Reflections Upon the Occurrences of the Last Year. From 5 Nov. 1688 to 5 Nov. 1689. London: 1689. V. 52

STEPHENS, FERRIS J.
Voitive and Historical Texts from Babylonia and Assyria. New Haven: 1937. V. 50; 52

STEPHENS, FREDERIC GEORGE
English Children as Painted by Sir Joshua Reynolds. London: 1867. V. 54
Flemish Relics; Architectural, Legendary and Pictorial, as Connected with Public Buildings in Belgium. London: 1866. V. 52
A History of Gibraltar and Its Sieges. London: 1870. V. 50; 54
Memoirs of Sir Edwin Landseer. London: 1874. V. 54
Notes on a Collection of Drawings and Woodcuts by Thomas Bewick, Exhibited at the Fine Art Society's Rooms. London: 1881. V. 47

STEPHENS, GEORGE
Gertrude and Beatrice: or the Queen of Hungary. London: 1839. V. 53
Incidents of Travel in Egypt, Arabia, Praetaea and the Holy Land. London: 1838. V. 52
Old Norse Fairy Tales, Gathered from the Swedish Folk. London: 1860. V. 54
The Practical Irrigator. Edinburgh: 1829. V. 53
The Practical Irrigator and Drainer. London: 1834. V. 48
Prof. S. Bugge's Studies on Northern Mythology Shortly Examined. London: 1993. V. 51

STEPHENS, H. MORSE
The Pacific Ocean in History. New York: 1917. V. 48

STEPHENS, HENRY
The Book of the Farm, Detailing the Labours of the Farmer... Edinburgh & London: 1842. V. 49
The Book of the Farm, Detailing the Labours of the Farmer... London: 1844. V. 51; 52
Journeys and Experiences in Argentina, Paraguay and Chile Including a Side Trip to the Source of the Paraguay River in the State of Matto Grosso, Brazil... New York: 1920. V. 54
A Manual of Practical Draining. London: 1846. V. 49

STEPHENS, J. F.
Illustrations of British Entomology. London: 1828-35-46. V. 54
Illustrations of British Entomology, Haustellata Only. London: 1828-34. V. 50; 51
Illustrations of British Entomology: Mandibulata. Haustellata. London: 1828-35. V. 54

STEPHENS, JAMES
The Adventures of Seumas Beg. London: 1915. V. 48
Collected Poems. London: 1926. V. 47; 49; 53
The Crock of Gold. London: 1912. V. 47; 50; 51; 52
The Crock of Gold. London: 1926. V. 47; 52; 53
The Crock of Gold. New York: 1931. V. 53
Etched in Moonlight. New York: 1928. V. 53
Green Branches. 1916. V. 48
Here Are Ladies. London: 1913. V. 48; 49
Hunger. Dublin: 1918. V. 48; 49; 50; 52
In the Land of Youth. London: 1924. V. 49; 51
The Insurrection in Dublin. Dublin and London: 1916. V. 52
Insurrections. Dublin: 1909. V. 52
Irish Fairy Tales. London: 1912. V. 49
Irish Fairy Tales. London: 1920. V. 47; 49; 51; 54
Irish Fairy Tales. New York: 1920. V. 47
Julia Elizabeth. New York: 1929. V. 47; 50; 51; 52; 53
Kings and the Moon. London: 1938. V. 48
Little Things. 1924. V. 48
On Prose and Verse. New York: 1928. V. 47; 50
Optimist. Gaylordsville: 1929. V. 48; 50
Stars Do Not Make a Noise. Los Angeles: 1931. V. 54
Theme and Variations. New York: 1930. V. 50; 52

STEPHENS, JAMES WILSON
An Historical and Geographical Account of Algiers; Containing a Circumstantial and Interesting Detail of Events Relative to the American Captives, Taken From Their Own Testimony. Brooklyn: 1800. V. 52

STEPHENS, JOHN LLOYD
Incidents of Travel in Central America, Chiapas & Yucatan. London: 1841. V. 49
Incidents of Travel in Central America, Chiapas & Yucatan. New York: 1841. V. 47; 48; 51; 52; 53
Incidents of Travel in Central America, Chiapas & Yucatan. London: 1846. V. 52
Incidents of Travel in Central America, Chiapas & Yucatan... London: 1854. V. 52; 54
Incidents of Travel in Egypt, Arabia Petraea, and the Holy Land. New York: 1845. V. 48
Incidents of Travel in Egypt, Arabia, Petraea and the Holy Land. New York: 1853. V. 49
Incidents of Travel in Greece, Turkey, Russia and Poland. New York: 1838. V. 52
Incidents of Travel in Greece, Turkey, Russia and Poland. New York: 1839. V. 49
Incidents of Travel in Yucatan. London: 1843. V. 49; 51; 52
Incidents of Travel in Yucatan. New York: 1843. V. 52

STEPHENS, L. DOW
Life Sketches of a Jayhawker of '49. 1916. V. 53; 54

STEPHENS, STEPHEN DE WITT
The Mavericks. New Brunswick: 1950. V. 47; 49; 51

STEPHENS, THOMAS
A Brief Account of the Causes That Have Retarded the Progress of the Colony of Georgia in America. London: 1743. V. 47; 50
A New System of Broad and Small Sword Exercise Comprising the Broad Sword Exercise for Cavalry and Artillery, and the Small Sword Cut and Thrust Practice for Infantry and Navy. Milwaukee: 1861. V. 48
Stephens's Philadelphia Directory for 1796; or, Alphabetical Arrangement... Philadelphia: 1795. V. 48; 50

STEPHENS, W. R. W.
Memorials of the South Saxon See and Cathedral Church of Chichester. London: 1876. V. 53

STEPHENS, WALTER
Notes on the Mineralogy of Part of the Vicinity of Dublin... 1812. V. 48; 52; 54
Notes on the Mineralogy of the Part of the Vicinity of Dublin, Taken Principally from Papers of the Late... London: 1812. V. 52

STEPHENS, WILLIAM
An Account of the Growth of Deism in England. London: 1709. V. 48
A State of the Province of Georgia, Attested Upon Oath in the Court of Savannah, November 10, 1740. London: 1742. V. 47

STEPHENSEN, P. R.
The Well of Sleevelessness - a Tale fo the Least of this Little Ones. London: 1929. V. 49

STEPHENSON, ALAN M. G.
The Victorian Archbishops of Canterbury. 1991. V. 52; 54
The Victorian Archbishops of Canterbury. Blewbury: 1991. V. 53

STEPHENSON, BLAKE & CO.
Lining Type Borders, Brass Rule, &c. Material and Machinery. London: 1915/19. V. 52
Specimen of Printing Types, Borders, Ornaments, Plain and Fancy... 1895. V. 47
Specimens of Printing Types, Borders, Ornaments, Plain and Fancy... Sheffield: 1895. V. 52

STEPHENSON, ELIZA TABOR
Nature's Nobleman. London: 1869. V. 47

STEPHENSON, JOHN
Medical Botany; or, Illustrations and Descriptions of the Medical Plants of the London, Edinburgh and Dublin Pharmacopoeias...Indigenous to Great Britain. London: 1831. V. 54
Medical Zoology, and Mineralogy; or Illustrations and Descriptions of the Animals and Minerals Employed in Medicine and of the Preparations Derived from Them... London: 1838. V. 48

STEPHENSON, MARMADUKE
A Call From Death to Life, and Out of the Dark Wayes and Worships of the World Where the Seed Is held in Bondage Under the Merchants of Babylon.. London: 1660. V. 48

STEPHENSON, P. R.
The Legend of Aleister Crowley. London: 1930. V. 47

STEPHENSON, ROBERT
Report on the Atmospheric Railway System. London: 1844. V. 51

STEPHENSON, SIMON
Representations of the Embossed, Chased and Engraved Subjects and Inscriptions Which Decorate the Tobacco Box and Cases Belonging to the Past Overseers Society, Of the Parishes of St. Margaret and St. John the Evangelist in the City of Westminster. London: 1824. V. 49

STEPHENSON, T. A.
The British Sea Anemones. London: 1928-35. V. 50; 51; 52

STEPHENSON, TERRY ELMO
Caminos Viejos: Tales Found in the History of California of Especial Interest to Those Who Love the Valelys and Hills and the Canyons of Orange County, Its Traditions and Its Landmarks. Santa Ana: 1930. V. 54
Don Bernadino Yorba. Los Angeles: 1941. V. 47

STEPNEY & HACKNEY
Customs and Privileges of the Manors of Stepney and Hackney. London: 1736. V. 53

STEPNEY, CATHERINE
The Courtier's Daughter. London: 1841. V. 47
The New Road to Ruin. London: 1833. V. 50

STEPNEY, GEORGE
An Epistle (in verse) To Charles Montague, Esq; on His Majesty's Voyage to Holland. London: 1691. V. 48
A Poem Dedicated to the Blessed memory of Her Late Gracious Majesty Queen Mary. London: 1695. V. 48; 50; 53

STEPTOE, JOHN
Uptown. New York: 1970. V. 53

STERBEECK, FRANCISCUS VAN
Theatrum Fungorum oft Het Tooneel der Campernoelien Waer.... Antwerpen: 1712. V. 49

STERLAND, W. J.
The Birds of Sherwood Forest. London: 1869. V. 54

STERLING, CHARLES
Still Life Painting. Paris: 1959. V. 49

STERLING, GEORGE
Continent's End: an Anthology of California Poets. San Francisco: 1925. V. 54
The House of Orchids and Other Poems. San Francisco: 1911. V. 50; 53; 54
Ode on the Opening of the Panama-Pacific International Exposition. San Francisco: 1915. V. 51
Robinson Jeffers, the Man and the Artist. New York: 1926. V. 54
Rosamund: a Dramatic Poem. San Francisco: 1920. V. 50
The Testimony of the Suns. San Francisco: 1907. V. 52
Truth. Chicago: 1923. V. 54

STERLING, JOSEPH
Poems. London: 1789. V. 54

STERLING, Kansas. The Actual Advantages and Resources of a Grand Young Town Carefully and Candidly Discussed. Sterling: 1887. V. 52

STERLING, LOUIS
The Sterling Library. A Catalogue of Printed Books and Literary Manuscripts Collected by...and Presented by Him to the University of London. 1954. V. 48; 50; 52

STERLING, RICHARD
Our Own Second Reader: for the Use of Schools and Families. Greensboro: 1862. V. 49; 50

STERLING, WILLIAM
Annals of the Artists of Spain. London: 1848. V. 52; 54

STERN, BERT
The Last Sitting. New York: 1982. V. 50

STERN, DANIEL
The Suicide Academy. New York: 1968. V. 50

STERN, F. C.
Snowdrops and Snowflakes, a Study of the Genera Galanthus and Leucojum. 1956. V. 54
A Study of the Genus Paeonia. London: 1946. V. 47; 48; 51; 52

STERN, GERALD
The Naming of Beasts and Other Poems. Omaha: 1973. V. 54

STERN, HENRY A.
Wanderings Among the Falashas in Abyssinia: Together with a Description of the Country and Its Various Inhabitants... London: 1862. V. 51

STERN, JAMES
The Heartless Land. New York: 1932. V. 49
The Man Who Was Loved. New York: 1951. V. 50
The Man Who Was Loved. London: 1952. V. 48

STERN, MADELEINE B.
A Phrenological Dictionary of Nineteenth Century Americans. Westport: 1982. V. 49

STERN, RENE B.
Book Trails. Chicago: 1946. V. 49

STERNBERG, GEORGE M.
Disinfection and Disinfectants: Their Application and Use in the Prevention and Treatment of Disease and in Public and Private Sanitation. Concord: 1888. V. 51; 54
Immunity, Protective Inoculations In Infectious Diseases and Serum-Therapy. New York: 1895. V. 51; 54
Photomicrographs and How to Make Them. Boston: 1884. V. 54
Report on the Etiology and Prevention of Yellow Fever. Washington: 1890. V. 51; 54
A Text-Book of Bacteriology. New York: 1896. V. 51

STERNBERG, HARRY
Silk Screen Color Printing. New York: 1942. V. 50

STERNBERG, MAXIMILIAN
Acromegaly. London: 1899. V. 47; 49; 50; 54

STERNBERG, THOMAS
The Dialect and Folk-lore of Northamptonshire. London: 1851. V. 52

STERNDALE, ROBERT ARMITAGE
The Afghan Knife. London: 1879. V. 54
Seonee; or, Camp Life on the Satpura Range. Calcutta: 1887. V. 49

STERNE, HENRY
A Statement of Facts, Submitted to the Right Hon. Lord Gleneig, His Majesty's Principal Secretary of State for the Colonies, Prepatory to an Appeal About to Be made by the author... London: 1837. V. 52

STERNE, LAURENCE
The Beauties of Sterne... London: 1782. V. 48; 52; 54
The Beauties of Sterne... London: 1809. V. 49; 50
A Facsimile Reproduction of a Unique Catalogue of Laurence Sterne's Library. London: 1930. V. 50
Gleanings From the Works. London: 1796. V. 48
Das Leben und die Meynungen des Hern Tristram Shandy. Berlin and Stralsund: 1769-72. V. 54
Letters from Yorick to Eliza. Dublin: 1775. V. 49
Letters from Yorick to Eliza. London: 1775. V. 48; 51
Letters of the Late Rev. Mr. Laurence Sterne. London: 1775. V. 47; 48; 49; 51; 53
Letters of the Late Rev. Mr. Laurence Sterne, to His Most Intimate Friends. London: 1776. V. 47
Lettres d'Yorick a Eliza, et d'Eliza a Yorick. Lausanne: 1786. V. 47
The Life and Letters of Laurence Sterne. London. V. 52
The Life and Opinions of Tristram Shandy... London: 1760. V. 48
The Life and Opinions of Tristram Shandy. London: 1760-67. V. 48; 50; 51
The Life and Opinions of Tristram Shandy... York & London: 1760-69. V. 50; 51; 52; 54
The Life and Opinions of Tristram Shandy... York & London: 1760/59-67. V. 49
The Life and Opinions of Tristram Shandy. London: 1770. V. 47
The Life and Opinions of Tristram Shandy... London: 1772-73. V. 54
The Life and Opinions of Tristram Shandy... London: 1786. V. 47
The Life and Opinions of Tristram Shandy... London: 1794. V. 51
The Life and Opinions of Tristram Shandy... London: 1832. V. 53
The Life and Opinions of Tristram Shandy... London: 1883. V. 52
The Life and Opinions of Tristram Shandy. London: 1886. V. 50
The Life and Opinions of Tristram Shandy. London: 1911. V. 48
Life and Opinions of Tristram Shandy... London: 1926. V. 54
The Life and Opinions of Tristram Shandy. Waltham St. Lawrence: 1929/30. V. 47; 51; 54
The Life and Opinions of Tristram Shandy. New York: 1935. V. 50
The Life and Opinions of Tristram Shandy... San Francisco: 1988. V. 48; 53
Original Letters of the Late Reverend Mr. Laurence Sterne. London: 1788. V. 47
A Sentimental Journey through France and Italy. London: 1768. V. 47; 48; 50; 51; 52; 54
A Sentimental Journey through France and Italy... York: 1774. V. 49
A Sentimental Journey through France and Italy. London: 1778. V. 54
A Sentimental Journey through France and Italy. London: 1790. V. 48
A Sentimental Journey through France and Italy. London: 1794. V. 51
A Sentimental Journey Through France and Italy. London: 1809. V. 50; 53
A Sentimental Journey Through France and Italy. New York: 1884. V. 49
A Sentimental Journey through France and Italy. New York: 1885. V. 52
A Sentimental Journey through France and Italy. Boston: 1905. V. 47
A Sentimental Journey through France and Italy. London: 1928. V. 48
A Sentimental Journey through France and Italy. Waltham St. Lawrence: 1928. V. 47; 49; 51; 52; 54

STERNE, LAURENCE continued
A Sentimental Journey through France and Italy. Paris: 1929. V. 49
A Sentimental Journey through France and Italy. High Wycombe: 1936. V. 48; 52; 54
A Sentimental Journey Through France and italy. New York: 1936. V. 50
The Sermons... London: 1711/70/69. V. 51
The Sermons... London: 1760/66. V. 48
The Sermons... London: 1764-66. V. 47
The Sermons. London: 1765-69. V. 54
The Sermons... London: 1771/70/69. V. 48
The Sermons... London: 1773-70-69. V. 49; 51
The Sermons... London: 1773/73/69. V. 48; 53
La Vie et les Opinions de Tristram Shandy. Neuchatel: 1777-77/85-85. V. 51
Works. London: 1760. V. 49
The Works. London: 1788. V. 53
The Works... London: 1793. V. 51; 53
The Works... London: 1795. V. 54
The Works... London: 1808. V. 48
The Works. London: 1815. V. 48; 49; 51
The Works. London: 1819. V. 47; 50; 52
The Works. London: 1823. V. 47; 48; 49; 51; 53; 54
The Works... London: 1873. V. 50
The Works... London: 1885. V. 48
The Works... New York: 1904. V. 49; 51
The Works. Oxford: 1927. V. 54
Yoricks Kanslosamma Resa Igenom Frankrike Och Italien. (Sentimental Journey). Stockholm: 1790-91. V. 54

STERNE, LOUIS
Seventy Years of an Active Life. London: 1912. V. 47; 50

STERNE, MAURICE
Murals in the Department of Justice Building in Washington, D.C. V. 47

STETSON, LYDIA BACON
Biography of Mrs. Lydia B. Bacon. Boston: 1856. V. 50

STETZ, MARGARET D.
England in the 1880's Old Guard and Avant-Garde. Charlottesville: 1989. V. 50

STEUART, HENRY
The Planter's Guide; or a Practical Essay on the Best Method of Giving Immediate Effect to Wood. Edinburgh & London: 1828. V. 48; 49; 52
The Planters Guide; or a Practical Essay on the Best Method of Giving Immediate Effect to Wood... New York: 1832. V. 47

STEUART, JOHN ALEXANDER
In the Day of Battle. A Romance. London: 1894. V. 54

STEUART, R. H. J.
March, Kind Comrad. London: 1931. V. 49

STEUBEN, FRIEDRICH W. A. H. F., BARON VON
Regulations for the Order and Discipline of the Troops of the United States. Halifax: 1794. V. 48
Regulations for the Order and Discipline of the Troops of the United States... New York: 1794. V. 48
Regulations for the Order and Discipline of the Troops of the United States... Albany: 1803. V. 48
Regulations for the Order and Discipline of the Troops of the United States. Philadelphia: 1809. V. 47; 50
The Soldier's Monitor: Being a Systlem of Discipline for the Use of the Infantry of the United States.... Rutland: 1814. V. 50

STEVENS, ABEL
The Women of Methodism; Its Three Foundresses, Susanna Wesley, the Countess of Huntingdon and Barbara Heck... New York: 1866. V. 47

STEVENS, AGNES
How Men Propose. Chicago: 1888. V. 48

STEVENS, ALEXANDER
Public Characters of 1799-1800. London: 1799. V. 51

STEVENS, AUGUSTA DE GRASSE
The Lost Dauphin; Louis XVII. Or Onwarenhiiaki, the Indian Iroquois Chief. Sunnyside: 1887. V. 48

STEVENS, CHARLES W.
Fly-Fishing in Maine Lakes; or, Camp-Life in the Wilderness. Boston: 1881. V. 50

STEVENS, E. T.
Guide to the Blackmore Museum, Salisbury. (with) Account of the Museum. London: 1870. V. 47

STEVENS, F. L.
Through Merrie England. London: 1928. V. 54

STEVENS, FRANCIS
Domestic Architecture. London: 1815. V. 48

STEVENS, FRANK E.
The Black Hawk War Including a Review of Black Hawk's Life. Chicago: 1903. V. 48

STEVENS, FREDERICK P.
Denver: The Coming City. Denver: 1902. V. 48

STEVENS, G. R.
Canadian National Railways... Toronto: 1960-62. V. 48
Canadian National Railways. Toronto: 1962. V. 53

STEVENS, GEORGE ALEXANDER
George Stevens's Celebrated Lecture on Heads, Which Has Been Exhibited Upwards of Two Hundred and Fifty Successive Nights, to Crowded Audiences and Met with the Most Universal Applause. London: 1766. V. 47
A Lecture on Heads... With Additions by Mr. Pilon; as Delivered by Mr. Charles Lee Lewis. London: 1799. V. 49
Songs Comic and Satyrical. London: 1772. V. 53

STEVENS, GEORGE THOMAS
Three Years in the Sixth Corps. Albany: 1866. V. 47
Three Years in the Sixth Corps. New York: 1867. V. 52

STEVENS, HAZARD
The Life of Isaac Ingalls Stevens. Boston and New York: 1901. V. 51; 53

STEVENS, HENRY
An Account of the Proceedings at the Dinner Given by Mr. George Peabody to the Americans Connected with the Great Exhibition. London: 1851. V. 50; 52
American Books With Tails to 'Em. London: 1873. V. 48
Catalogue of My English Library. London: 1853. V. 47; 48; 51; 54
Historical Nuggets Bibliotheca Americana... London: 1862. V. 52
Rare Americana: a Catalogue of Historical and Geographical Books, Pamphlets and Manuscripts Relating to America. London: 1926. V. 52
Recollections of Mr. James Lenox of New York and the Formation of His Library. London: 1886. V. 53; 54

STEVENS, HENRY N.
Ptolemy's Geography. A Brief Account of All the Printed Editions Down to 1730. London: 1908. V. 49

STEVENS, ISAAC I.
Address on the Northwest Before the American Geographical and Statistical Society. Washington: 1858. V. 47; 50
Campaigns of the Rio Grande and of Mexico. New York: 1851. V. 47; 52

STEVENS, J. LEE
Wood Paving in London; a Practical Treatise. London: 1842. V. 54

STEVENS, JAMES
An Historical and Geographical Account of Algiers...Relative to the American Captives. Philadelphia: 1797. V. 54

STEVENS, JOHN
Examen du Gouvernement D'Angleterre, Compare aux Constitutions des Etats-Unis. Paris: 1789. V. 47; 48
The Royal Treasury of England; or, an Historical Account of all Taxes, Under What Denomination Soever, fromthe Conquest to This Present Year... London: 1725. V. 52

STEVENS, JOHN W.
Reminiscences of the Civil War. Hillsboro: 1902. V. 47; 49

STEVENS, LEWIS TOWNSEND
The History of Cape May County, New Jersey... Cape May City: 1897. V. 47; 49; 51

STEVENS, LINWOOD L.
Virgin Hannah. Philadelphia: 1977. V. 53

STEVENS-NELSON PAPER CORPORATION
Specimens: a Paper Catalogue of Hand Made and Mould Made Paper. New York: 1953. V. 53; 54

STEVENS, SAMUEL
A Wilding Posy. London: 1925. V. 52

STEVENS, WALLACE
The Auroras of Autumn. New York: 1950. V. 48; 52; 53
The Blue Guitar. 1977. V. 51
The Collected Poems. New York: 1954. V. 52
Collected Poems. London: 1955. V. 49; 54
Estheique du Mal. Cummington: 1945. V. 48; 51; 52; 53; 54
Harmonium. New York: 1923. V. 47; 49; 50; 51; 53
Harmonium. New York: 1931. V. 52; 53
Ideas of Order. New York: 1936. V. 48; 51; 53
Letters of Wallace Stevens. New York: 1966. V. 52; 53
the Man with the Blue Guitar... New York: 1937. V. 48; 51; 53
The Man with the Blue Guitar... New York: 1952. V. 49; 53
The Necessary Angel. New York: 1951. V. 47; 48; 49; 50; 51; 53; 54
The Necessary Angel. London: 1960. V. 54
Notes Toward a Supreme Fiction. Cummington: 1942. V. 50; 52; 53; 54
Notes Toward a Supreme Fiction. Cummington: 1943. V. 53
Opus Posthumous. New York: 1957. V. 47; 50; 52; 53
Part of a World. New York: 1942. V. 47; 48
A Primitive Like an Orb. New York: 1948. V. 49; 52; 53
The Relations Between Poetry and Painting. New York: 1951. V. 51; 53
Selected Poems. London: 1952. V. 49; 53; 54
Selected Poems. London: 1953. V. 51; 53
Three Academic Pieces. The Realm of a Resemblance, Someone Puts a Pineapple Together and Of Ideal Time and Choice. Cummington: 1947. V. 53
Transport to Summer. New York: 1947. V. 48; 49; 50; 51; 52; 53

STEVENS, WALTER B.
St. Louis, the Fourth City, 1764-1909. St. Louis: 1909. V. 54

STEVENS, WILLIAM
A Discourse on the English Constitution; Extracted From a Late Eminent Writer, and Applicable to the Present Times. London: 1776. V. 48
Observations on the Healthy and Diseased Properties of the Blood. London: 1832. V. 48
A System for the Discipline of the Artillery of the United States of America, or, the Young Artillerist's Pocket Companion... New York: 1797. V. 48

STEVENS, WILLIAM BAGSHAW
Poems. London: 1782. V. 47; 51; 52; 54

STEVENSON, ADLAI E.
Call to Greatness. New York: 1954. V. 50; 54

STEVENSON, ALAN
Biographical Sketch of the Late Robert Stevenson. Edinburgh: 1861. V. 50

STEVENSON, D. ALAN
The World's Lighthouses Before 1820. London: 1959. V. 50

STEVENSON, DAVID
Life of Robert Stevenson, Civil Engineer. Edinburgh: 1878. V. 50
The Principles and Practice of Canal and River Engineering. Edinburgh: 1886. V. 48
Sketch of the Civil Engineering of North America. London: 1838. V. 49; 53

STEVENSON, EDWARD LUTHER
Terrestrial and Celestial Globes. New Haven: 1921. V. 54

STEVENSON, J.
British Fungi. Hymenomycetes. London: 1886. V. 54
Two Centuries of Life in County Down, 1600-1800. Belfast: 1920. V. 52

STEVENSON, J. B.
The Species of Rhododendron. London: 1930. V. 53

STEVENSON, JOHN
On the Morbid Sensibility of the Eye, Commonly called Weakness of Sight. Hartford: 1815. V. 47; 49; 51; 53; 54

STEVENSON, JOHN HALL
Crazy Tales. London: 1769. V. 49; 51; 54
Makarony Fables... London: 1768. V. 53
Makarony Fables. London: 1897. V. 54

STEVENSON, MATILDA COXE
Ethnobotany of the Zuni Indians. Washington: 1915. V. 52

STEVENSON, MATTHEW
Poems. London: 1665. V. 53

STEVENSON, MERRITT R.
Marine Atlas of the Pacific Coastal Waters of south America. Berkeley/Los Angeles: 1970. V. 52

STEVENSON, R. RANDOLPH
The Southern Side; or, Andersonville Prison. Baltimore: 1876. V. 49

STEVENSON, ROBERT
Report Relative to Granton Harbour. Edinburgh: 1834. V. 51

STEVENSON, ROBERT LOUIS BALFOUR
Across the Plains With Other Memories and Essays. London: 1892. V. 53
The Adventures of David Balfour. London. V. 54
Aes Triplex. 1898. V. 49; 52
The Amateur Emigrant. Chicago: 1895. V. 49; 54
Ballads. London: 1890. V. 47; 49; 53; 54
Being Memoirs of the Adventures of David Balfour in the Year 1751. London: 1886. V. 49
The Best Thing in Edinburgh: an Address. San Francisco: 1923. V. 50; 52; 54
The Black Arrow. London: 1888. V. 47; 53
The Castaways of Soledad. Buffalo: 1928. V. 48; 49
Catriona; a Sequel to "Kidnapped". London: 1893. V. 49; 53
A Child's Garden of Verses. London. V. 47; 49; 52
Child's Garden of Verses. London: 1885. V. 48; 49; 51
A Child's Garden of Verses. New York: 1885. V. 47
A Child's Garden of Verses. London: 1896. V. 51; 52; 54
A Child's Garden of Verses. New York: 1902. V. 49
A Child's Garden of Verses. New York: 1905. V. 47
A Child's Garden of Verses. London: 1907. V. 47
A Child's Garden of Verses. London: 1908. V. 47; 48; 49
A Child's Garden of Verses. London: 1909. V. 48
A Child's Garden of Verses. Philadelphia: 1926. V. 47
A Child's Garden of Verses. London: 1931. V. 48; 54
A Child's Garden of Verses. New York: 1944. V. 52
A Child's Garden of Verses. New York: 1947. V. 48
A Child's Garden of Verses. San Francisco: 1978. V. 52
Collected Works. London: 1906-07. V. 50; 51
David Balfour. New York: 1893. V. 53
David Balfour. New York: 1924. V. 49; 50
Diogenes at the Savile Club. Chicago: 1921. V. 48; 52
Diogenes in London. San Francisco: 1920. V. 47
The Dynamiter. London: 1885. V. 49
The Ebb-Tide. Chicago and Cambridge: 1894. V. 54
The Ebb-Tide. London: 1894. V. 49; 51; 53
Edinburgh: Picturesque Notes. London: 1879. V. 49
Essays in the Art of Writing. London: 1905. V. 51
Fables. London: 1914. V. 54
Fables. New York: 1914. V. 52
Father Damien. London: 1890. V. 53; 54
Father Damien. San Francisco: 1930. V. 47; 48
A Footnote to History. London: 1892. V. 52
The Graver and the Pen: or Scenes from Nature with Appropriate Verses. Edinburgh: 1882. V. 50
The Image of the White Man as Projected in the Published plays of Black Americans, 1847-1973. Bloomington: 1976. V. 54
In the South Seas. London: 1900. V. 48; 51
An Inland Voyage. London: 1878. V. 49; 51; 52; 53
An Inland Voyage. Boston: 1883. V. 54
An Inland Voyage. Stamford: 1938. V. 48
Island Night's Entertainments. London, Paris, Melbourne: 1893. V. 47; 48; 49; 50; 51; 52; 53; 54
The Jolly Jump-Ups Child's Garden of Verses. Springfield: 1946. V. 52
Kidnapped. London: 1886. V. 50; 52; 53; 54
Kidnapped. New York: 1886. V. 47; 49; 50; 54
Kidnapped... London: 1886/93. V. 48; 52
Kidnapped. London: 1913. V. 49
Kidnapped. New York: 1913. V. 48
Kidnapped. 1930. V. 51
Kidnapped. London: 1930. V. 49
Kidnapped. London: 1938. V. 48
Kidnapped. New York: 1938. V. 52; 54
The Letters of Robert Louis Stevenson. London: 1901. V. 49
The Letters to His Family and Friends. London: 1900. V. 52; 54
A Lodging for the Night. East Aurora: 1902. V. 48; 49
A Lodging for the Night. New York: 1923. V. 51
The Master of Ballantrae. London: 1889. V. 47; 48; 49
The Master of Ballantrae. New York: 1965. V. 53
Memories and Portraits. London: 1887. V. 47; 53
The Merry Men. London: 1887. V. 47; 52; 53; 54
The Merry Men. New York: 1887. V. 51; 54
More New Abrabian Nights: the Dynamiter. London: 1885. V. 47; 52; 53
A Mountain Town in France. London: 1896. V. 53
New Arabian Nights. London: 1882. V. 49
New Arabian Nights. Avon: 1976. V. 53
The Novels and Tales of Robert Louis Stevenson. New York: 1895-1902. V. 53
On the Thermal Influence of Forests. Edinburgh: 1878. V. 47
Poems. Boston: 1917. V. 48
Poems. Boston: 1921. V. 49
La Porte de Maletroit. 1952. V. 54
La Porte de Maletroit. Cagnes-sur-Mer: 1952. V. 48
Prayers Written at Valima. London: 1910. V. 50; 52
Prince Otto. Boston: 1886. V. 54
Prose Writings. Boston: 1921. V. 51
R.L.S. to J.M. Barrie: a Valima Portrait. San Francisco: 1962. V. 47
Robert Louis Stevenson to His Good Friend M. Donat. San Francisco: 1925. V. 48; 49; 53
St. Ives... New York: 1897. V. 48
St. Ives... Toronto: 1897. V. 53
St. Ives. London: 1898. V. 47; 49; 53; 54
The Silverado Squatters. London: 1883. V. 51; 53
The Silverado Squatters. Boston: 1884. V. 54
Some College Memories. New York: 1899. V. 49
Some Letters By Robert Louis Stevenson. New York: 1902. V. 47
Songs of Travel and Other Verses. London: 1896. V. 53
Songs of Travel and Other Verses. London: 1908. V. 50
A Stevenson Medley. London: 1899. V. 47; 48; 50; 52; 53
Stevenson's Workshop: with Twenty-Nine Ms. Facsimiles. Boston: 1921. V. 47
Strange Case of Dr. Jekyll and Mr. Hyde. London: 1886. V. 47; 49; 50; 51; 52; 54
Strange Case of Dr. Jekyll and Mr. Hyde. New York: 1886. V. 49; 50; 51; 54
Strange Case of Dr. Jekyll and Mr. Hyde. London: 1930. V. 53
The Strange Case of Dr. Jekyll and Mr. Hyde. New York: 1930. V. 51
Three Letters (to Mrs. Sitwell). 1902. V. 47
Three Plays. Deacon Brodie. Beau Austin. Admiral Guinea. London: 1892. V. 48
Three Short Poems. Chicago: 1902. V. 53; 54
Ticonderoga. Edinburgh: 1887. V. 48; 53; 54
Travels with a Donkey. New York: 1957. V. 52; 54
Treasure Island. New York. V. 48
Treasure Island. London: 1883. V. 49; 50; 51; 52
Treasure Island. Boston: 1884. V. 53; 54
Treasure Island. London: 1884. V. 50; 51
Treasure Island. Chicago & New York: 1895. V. 51
Treasure Island. New York: 1911. V. 48
Treasure Island. 1920. V. 52
Treasure Island. New York: 1927. V. 54
Treasure Island. London: 1929. V. 50
Treasure Island. New York: 1929. V. 53
Treasure Island. London: 1934. V. 52
Treasure Island. London: 1947. V. 51; 52
Treasure Island. London: 1973. V. 51
Treasure Island. London: 1985. V. 49; 51
Two Mediaeval Tales. London: 1929. V. 49
Two Mediaeval Tales. New York: 1930. V. 53

STEVENSON, ROBERT LOUIS BALFOUR continued
Underwoods. London: 1887. V. 49; 53
Vailima Letters: Being Correspondence Add-ressed by Robert Louis Stevenson to Sidney Colvin: November, 1890- October 1894. Chicago: 1895. V. 48
Virginibus Puerisque. London: 1881. V. 47; 50; 53
The Waif Woman. London: 1916. V. 51; 52
Weir of Hermiston. London: 1896. V. 47; 53; 54
When the Devil Was Well. Boston: 1921. V. 47; 51
Will O' the Mill. East Aurora: 1901. V. 54
Works. London: 1896-1901. V. 53; 54
The Works... New York: 1905/12. V. 50; 53
Works. London: 1906. V. 47; 49
Works. 1909-14. V. 48
The Works. London: 1911-12. V. 50; 51
The Works. 1921-23. V. 49
Works. New York: 1921-23. V. 48
Works. London: 1922. V. 48; 50
Works. London: 1922-23. V. 51
The Works... London: 1922-33. V. 49
The Works. London: 1924-26. V. 49
The Wrecker. London: 1892. V. 53
The Wrecker. New York: 1892. V. 53
The Wrong Box. London: 1889. V. 51

STEVENSON, ROGER
Military Instructions for Officers Detached in the Field: Containing a Scheme for Forming a Corps of a Partisan. Philadelphia: 1775. V. 47; 48; 52

STEVENSON, THOMAS
The Design and Construction of Harbours. Edinburgh: 1864. V. 50
The Design and Construction of Harbours. Edinburgh: 1874. V. 50

STEVENSON, W. F.
Wounds in War: The Mechanism of Their Production and Their Treatment. New York: 1898. V. 47

STEVENSON, WILLIAM B.
A Historical and Descritpive Narrative of Twenty Years' Residence in South America, Containing Travels in Arauco, Chile, Peru and Colombia... London: 1825. V. 47

STEVIN, SIMON
De Beghinselen der Weeghconst...(with) De Weeghdaet Praxis artis Ponderaria...(with) De Beghinselen des Waterwichts... Leiden: 1586. V. 47
Les Oeuvres Mathematiques, ou Sont Inseres les Memoires Mathematiques Esquelles s'est Exerce le... Leyden: 1634. V. 50

STEWARD, AUSTIN
Twenty-Two Years a Slave, and Forty Years a Free Man, Embracing a Correspondence of Several Years, While President of Wilberforce Colony, London, Canada West. Canadaigua: 1867. V. 53

STEWARD, JULIAN H.
Notes on Hillers' Photographs of the Paiute and Ute Indians Taken on the Powell Expedition of 1873. Washington: 1939. V. 47

STEWARD, RICHARD
An Answer to a Letter Written at Oxford, and Superscribed to Dr. Samuel Turner, Concerning the Church and the Revenues Thereof. 1647. V. 52
Catholique Divinity; or, the Most Solid and Sententious Expressions of the Primitive Doctors of the Church. London: 1657. V. 52

STEWARD, WILLIAM
The First Edition of Steward's Healing Art, Corrected and Improved by the Original Hand. Saco: 1827. V. 52
Gouldtown, a Very Remarkable Settlement of Ancient Date: Studies of Some Sturdy Examples of the Simple Life... Philadelphia: 1913. V. 51; 53; 54

STEWART, A. F.
Paintings, Drawings and Prints in the Collection of...Catalogued by R. G. Watkin. 1920. V. 47

STEWART, BASIL
Japanese Colour-Prints and the Subjects They Illustrate. New York: 1920. V. 48
Subjects Portrayed in Japanese Colour-Prints. London: 1922. V. 52

STEWART, C. P.
Lind's Treatise on Scurvy: a Bicentenary Volume... Edinburgh: 1953. V. 50

STEWART, CAROL
Poems of Sleep and Dream. London: 1947. V. 54

STEWART, CATHERINE
New Homes in the West. Nashville. V. 48

STEWART, CECIL
Topiary. Waltham St. Lawrence: 1954. V. 47; 54

STEWART, CHARLES
The Killin Collection of Gaelic songs with Music and Translations. Edinburgh: 1884. V. 49

STEWART, CHARLES JAMES
Catalogue of the Works of Writers of the Seventeenth and Later Centuries, Interspersed with Additions to that of the Sixteenth... London: 1860. V. 50
Two Sermons on Family Prayer, with Extracts from Various Authors; and a Collection of Prayers, Selected and Compiled by the Hon. and Rev. Charles Stewart, A. M. Minister of St. Armand, Lower Canada and Chaplain to the Lord Bishop of Quebec. Montreal: 1814. V. 52

STEWART, CHARLES S.
Journal of a Residence in the Sandwich Islands, During the Years 1823, 1824 and 1825. London: 1828. V. 47; 52
A Visit to the South Seas, in the U.S. Ship Vincennes... London: 1832. V. 50
A Visit to the South Seas, in U.S. Ship Vincennes... New York: 1833. V. 52

STEWART, CHRISTINA DUFF
The Taylors of Ongar: an Analytical Bio-Bibliography. New York: 1975. V. 51

STEWART, DAVID
Sketches of the Character, Manners and Present State of the Highlanders of Scotland. Edinbrugh: 1822. V. 50
Sketches of the Character, Manners and Present State of the Highlanders of Scotland... Edinburgh: 1825. V. 50

STEWART, DONALD OGDEN
Writers Take Sides on the Question: Are Your for, Or Are You Against Franco Fascism?. New York: 1938. V. 49

STEWART, DOROTHY N.
Handbook of Indian Dances. Santa Fe: 1950. V. 50

STEWART, DUGALD
Elements of the Philosophy of the Human Mind. London: 1792/1814/27. V. 49
Elements of the Philosophy of the Human Mind. Philadelphia: 1793. V. 49
Elements of the Philosophy of the Human Mind... Edinburgh: 1814. V. 48
Elements of the Philosophy of the Human Mind. Edinburgh: 1814-16. V. 49; 51; 52
Elements of the Philosophy of the Human Mind. Edinburgh: 1814-16. V. 53
Outlines of Moral Philosophy. Edinburgh: 1793. V. 48
Philosophical Essays. Edinburgh: 1810. V. 49; 50
A Short Statement of Some Important Facts, Relative to the Late Election of a Mathematical Professor (i.e. John Leslie) in the University of Edinburgh... Edinburgh: 1805. V. 50

STEWART, EDGAR I.
Custer's Luck. Norman: 1955. V. 52

STEWART, FRANK A.
Cross Country with Hounds. London: 1936. V. 49
Hark to Hounds. London: 1937. V. 47
Hunting Countries. London: 1935. V. 47; 49

STEWART, FRANK H.
Notes on Old Gloucester County, New Jersey. Woodbury: 1917-64. V. 47; 49; 51

STEWART, FRIDA
Songs of the Basque Children. London: 1939. V. 49

STEWART, GEORGE
The Story of the Great Fire in St. John, N.B. June 20th, 1877. Toronto: 1877. V. 53

STEWART, GEORGE R.
Earth Abides. New York: 1949. V. 49; 52
Take Your Bible In One Hand: the Life of William Henry Thomas... San Francisco: 1939. V. 53

STEWART, H. M.
Egyptian Stelae, Reliefs and Paintings from the Petrie Collection. Warminster: 1976-83. V. 51

STEWART, J.
A View of the Past and Present State of the Island of Jamaica... Edinburgh: 1823. V. 51

STEWART, J. I. M.
The Man Who Wrote Detective Stories and Other Stories. London: 1959. V. 51

STEWART, J. MRS.
The Missing Law; or, Woman's Birthright. London: 1869. V. 50

STEWART, JAMES
The Index of Abridgement, Of the Acts of Parliament and Convention, from the First Parliament of King James I. Holden the 26 Maii, anno 1424 to the Fourth Session of the First Parliament of Her Majesty Queen Anne, Concluded 25 March 1707... Edinburgh: 1707. V. 47
James Stewart's Answer to Mijn Heer Fagel Pensioner to the States of Holland and West-Frisland, Concerning the Repeal of the Penal Laws and Tests. London: 1688. V. 50
Jimmy Stewart and His Poems. New York: 1989. V. 52
Plocacosmos; or the Whole Art of Hair Dressing. London: 1782. V. 50
Rudyard Kipling, a Bibliographical Catalogue. Toronto: 1959. V. 53; 54

STEWART, JOHN
An Account of Jamaica, and Its Inhabitants. London: 1808. V. 52
An Account of Prince Edward Island, in the Gulph of St. Lawrence, North America. London: 1806. V. 49
Genevieve; or, the Spirit of the Brave. London: 1810. V. 54
An Important and Invaluable Secret Discovered and Developed in the Laws of Human Nature, to Render the Valour of British Soldiers and the Freedom of British Citizens Invincible. London: 1807. V. 50
The Pleasures of Love. A Poem. London: 1806. V. 47
Ten Photographs of Venice. Geneva: 1983. V. 54
A View of the Past and Present State of the Island of Jamaica... Edinburgh: 1823. V. 52

STEWART, JOHN ROBERT
A Description of Some Ancient Monuments, with Inscriptions, Still Existing in Lydia and Phyrgia, Several of Which Are Supposed to Be Tombs of the Ancient Kings. London: 1842. V. 51

STEWART, P. M.
Travel and Sport in Many Lands. New York: 1929. V. 54

STEWART, PHILEMON
A Holy, Sacred and Divine Roll and Book; from the Lord God of heaven, to the Inhabitants of Earth; Revealed in the United Society at New Lebanon... Canterbury: 1843. V. 47

STEWART, ROBERT
The American Farmer's Horse Book... Cincinnati: 1867. V. 52

STEWART, S. A.
A Flora of the North-East of Ireland. Cambridge: 1888/95. V. 53
A Flora of the North-East of Ireland. Belfast: 1938. V. 50; 51

STEWART, THOMAS GRAINGER
An Introduction to the Study of the Diseases of the Nervous System: Being Lectures Delivered in the University of Edinburgh During the Tercentenary Year. Philadelphia: 1885. V. 53
A Practical Treatise on Bright's Diseases of the Kidneys. New York: 1871. V. 54

STEWART, VIRGINIA
45 Contemporary Mexican Artists. Stanford: 1951. V. 48

STEWART, W. C.
The Practical Angler. 1857. V. 53
The Practical Angler... Edinburgh: 1857. V. 47

STEWART, W. FRANK
Pleasant Hours in an eventful Life. San Francisco: 1869. V. 49

STEWART, WILLIAM GRANT
The Popular Supersititons and Festive Amusements of the Highlanders of Scotland. London: 1851. V. 53

STEWART, WILLIAM M.
The Mineral Resources of the Pacific States and Territories. New York: 1865. V. 52
Reminiscences of Senator William M. Stewart of Nevada. New York and Washington: 1908. V. 47; 52; 54
Report on Government Aid to Pacific Railroads. Washington: 1869. V. 47

STEWART-MURPHY, CHARLOTTE A.
A History of British Circulating Libraries. Newtown: 1992. V. 50; 51

STEYERMARK, J. A.
Contributions to the Flora of Venezuela. Chicago: 1951-57. V. 48

STICHANER, JOSEPH VON
Sammlung Romischer denkmaler in Baiern...Mit Lithographischen Abdruken. Munchen: 1808. V. 50

STICKLEY, GUSTAV
Craftsman Homes. New York: 1909. V. 50; 52
More Craftsman Homes. New York: 1912. V. 54

STIEGLITZ, ALFRED
America and Alfred Stieglitz: a Collective Portrait. Garden City: 1934. V. 49; 51
Camera Work. Issue Number 1. New York: 1903. V. 47
Camera Work. Issue Number II. New York: 1903. V. 47
Camera Work. Issue Number VIII. New York: 1904. V. 47
Georgia O'Keeffe: a Portrait. New York: 1978. V. 48; 54
Stieglitz Memorial Portfolio, 1864-1946. New York: 1947. V. 48

STIEGLITZ, C. L.
Zeichnungen Aus der Schonen Baukunst Oder Darstellung Idealischer und Ausgefuhrter Gebaude... Leipzig: 1805. V. 48

STIEHL, HENRY
Autobiography of...The Life of a Frontier Builder. Salt Lake City: 1941. V. 47

STIELER, KARL
The Rhine: from Its Source to the Sea. Philadelphia: 1898. V. 53

STIERIUS, JOANNIUS
Praecepta Doctrinae Logicae, Ethicae, Physicae, Metaphysicae, Sphericae... London: 1652. V. 49

STIERLIN, HENRI
Art of the Incas and its origins. New York: 1984. V. 54

STIFF, EDWARD
The Texan Emigrant... Cincinnati: 1840. V. 47; 52

STIGAND, CHAUNCEY H.
Central Afrcan Game and Its Spoor. London: 1906. V. 53
The Game of British East Africa. London: 1913. V. 54
Hunting the Elephant in Africa and Other Recollections of Thirteen Years' Wanderings. New York: 1913. V. 47; 52
The Land of Zinj. London: 1913. V. 48; 54

STILES, EZRA
A Family Tablet: Containing a Selection of Original Poetry. Boston: 1796. V. 48
A History of Three of the Judges of King Charles I: Major-General Whaley, Major-General Goffe, and Colonel Dixwell, Who, at the Restoration in 1660, Fled to America... Hartford: 1794. V. 47; 50

STILES, HENRY REED
Bundling: Its Origin, Progress and Decline In America. Albany: 1871. V. 52

STILES, JOSEPH CLAY
Modern Reform Examined; or, the Union of North and South On the Question of Slavery. Philadelphia: 1858. V. 50
National Rectitude, the Only True Basis fo National Prospertiy: An Appeal to the Confederate States. Petersburg: 1863. V. 49

STILL, ANDREW T.
Autobiography... Kirksville: 1897. V. 49; 51
Autobiography. Kirksville: 1908. V. 54

STILL, GEORGE F.
Common Disorders and Diseases of Childhood. London: 1909. V. 47

STILL, I.
The Hastings Guide; Containing a Description of that Ancient Town and Port... Hastings: 1804. V. 49

STILL, JAMES
On Troublesome Creek. New York: 1941. V. 49; 51
River of Earth. New York: 1940. V. 53

STILL, WILLIAM
The Underground Rail Road. Philadelphia: 1872. V. 52
The Underground Rail Road... Philadelphia: 1878. V. 48

STILLE, ALFRED
Epidemic Meningitis, or Cerebro-Spinal Meningitis. Philadelphia: 1867. V. 53

STILLE, CHARLES J.
Major General Anthony Wayne and the Pennsylvania Line in the Continental Army. Philadelphia: 1893. V. 47; 50

STILLINGFLEET, BENJAMIN
An Essay on Conversation. London: 1737. V. 54
Miscellaneous Tracts Relating to Natural History, Husbandry and Physick. London: 1762. V. 48
Miscellaneous Tracts Relating to Natural History, Husbandry and Physick. London: 1775. V. 54
Principles and Power of Harmony. London: 1771. V. 48
Some Thoughts Occasioned by the Late Earthquake. London: 1750. V. 53; 54

STILLINGFLEET, EDWARD
The Bishop of Worcester's Answer to Mr. Locke's Second Letter... London: 1698. V. 53
Fifty Sermons Preached Upon Several Occasions... London: 1707. V. 51
The Grand Question, Concerning the Bishops Right to Vote in Parliament In Cases Capital, Stated and Argued, From the Parliament Rolls and the History of Former Times. London: 1680. V. 47
Origines Britannicae, or, the Antiquities of the British Churches. London: 1685. V. 47; 50
The Unreasonableness of Separation: or, an Impartial Account of the History, Nature and Pleas of the Present Separation from the Communion of the Church of England... London: 1681. V. 53
Works. Together with His Life and Character. London: 1710. V. 50

STILLMAN, CHAUNCEY
Charles Stillman, 1810-1875. New York: 1956. V. 49

STILLMAN, DAMIE
English Neo-Classical Architecture. London: 1988. V. 54

STILLMAN, JACOB DAVIS BABCOCK
The Horse in Motion as Shown by Instantaneous Photography... Boston: 1882. V. 53
The Horse in Motion as Shown by Instantaneous Photography. London: 1882. V. 47
Seeking the Golden Fleece; a Record of Pioneer Life in California... San Francisco: 1877. V. 51
Wanderings in the Southwest, 1855. Spokane: 1990. V. 48

STILLMAN, SAMUEL
Death, the Last Enemy, Destroyed by Christ. Philadelphia: 1776. V. 47

STILLMAN, W. J.
Poetic Localities of Cambridge. Boston: 1876. V. 50; 54

STILLWELL, HART
Old Soggy, No. 1, the Uninhibited Story of Slate Rodgers. New York: 1954. V. 48; 53

STILLWELL, JOHN E.
The History of the Burr Portraits... 1928. V. 47
The History of the Burr Portraits. New York: 1928. V. 50; 54

STILLWELL, MARGARET BINGHAM
The Awakening Interest in Science During the First Century of Printing 1450-1550. New York: 1970. V. 47; 50
Gutenberg and the Catholicon of 1460: A Biblio-graphical Essay. New York: 1936. V. 48
Incunabula and Americana, 1450-1800. New York: 1931. V. 53; 54
Noah's Ark in Early Woodcuts and Modern Rhymes. New York: 1942. V. 51
The Pageant of Benefit Street Down through the Years. Providence: 1945. V. 51
While Benefit Street Was Still Young. Providence: 1933. V. 48

STILLWELL, R.
Princeton Encyclopedia of Classical Sites. Princeton: 1979. V. 54
The Theatre. Princeton: 1952. V. 52

STIMSON, ALEXANDER L.
History of the Express Business: Including the Origin of the Railway system in America, and the Relation of Both to the Increase of New Settlements and the Prosperity of Cities in the United States. New York: 1881. V. 51; 53
History of the Express Companies: and the Origin of American Railroads.... New York: 1858. V. 50

STIMSON, MARY
Marijuana Mystery. Philadelphia: 1940. V. 47

STIRLING, A. M. W.
The Hothams. London: 1918. V. 47; 53

STIRLING, A. M. W. continued
The Richmond Papers from the Correspondence and Manuscripts of George Richmond, R.A. and His Son William Richmond... London: 1926. V. 49

STIRLING, D. M.
The Beauties of the Shore: or a Guide to the Watering Places on the South-East Coast of Devon. Exeter: 1838. V. 54

STIRLING, EDWARD
The Battle of Life, a drama in Three Acts. London: 1847. V. 54
The Cricket on the Hearth... London: 1846. V. 54
Martin Chuzzlewit!. London: 1844. V. 54
Martin Chuzzlewit!... London: 1850. V. 49
Martin Chuzzlewit!... London: 1850/46. V. 54
Mrs. Harris! A farce In One Act. London: 1846. V. 49; 54
Nicholas Nickleby. London: 1838?. V. 49; 54
Old Drury Lane. Fifty Years' Recollections of Author, Actor and Manager. London: 1881. V. 47
The Pickwick Club; or, The Age We Live In. London: 1837?. V. 49; 54

STIRLING, H. S.
Two Simple Tales for Simple Folks. Chicago. V. 48

STIRLING, JAMES
Letters from a Slave State. London: 1857. V. 49; 53

STIRLING, JAMES HUTCHISON
Sir William Hamilton: Being the Philosophy of Perception. London: 1865. V. 53

STIRLING, JOHN
A System of Rhetorick, in a Method Entirely new. Dublin: 1786. V. 52

STIRLING, MAXWELL
The Canon. An Exposition of the Pagan Mystery Perpetuated in the Cabala as the Rule of All the Arts. London: 1897. V. 51

STIRLING, PATRICK JAMES
The Australian and Californian Gold Discoveries and Their Probable Consequences. Edinburgh: 1853. V. 49; 50; 54
The Philosophy of Trade; or, Outlines of a Theory of Profits and Prices... Edinburgh: 1846. V. 52; 54

STIRLING, WILLIAM
Some Apostles of Physiology. London: 1902. V. 48; 49; 54

STIRLING, WILLIAM ALEXANDER, 1ST EARL OF
Recreation with the Muses. London: 1637. V. 48; 50; 52

STIRLING-MAXWELL, CAROLINE ELIZABETH SARAH SHERIDAN NORTON
Lost and Saved. London: 1863. V. 54

STIRLING-MAXWELL, SIR WILLIAM, BART
Antwerp Delivered in 1577... Edinburgh: 1878. V. 47
Sopra l'Effigie di Cesare, fatta per M. Enea Vico da Parma. London: 1868. V. 47

STIRN & LYON, NEW YORK
Catalogue and Price List of Patent Electro-Radiant Magica Lanterns and Views. New York: 1887. V. 53

STISTED, GEORGIANA M.
The True Life of Capt. Sir Richard F. Burton... London: 1896. V. 48; 50

STITH, WILLIAM
The History of the First Discovery and Settlement of Virginia... Williamsburg: 1747. V. 48

STOAT, JOHN
A Description of the System of Inquiry; or Examination by the Scholars Themselves, by Means of Circulating Classes, etc... London: 1826. V. 49

STOBAEUS, JOHANNES
Eclogarvm Libri Dvo. Antverpiae: 1575. V. 48

STOBART, J. C.
The Glory that was Greece. (and) The Grandeur that was Rome. London: 1936/34. V. 51

STOBO, ROBERT
Memoirs of Major Robert Stobo, of the Virginia Regiment. Pittsburgh: 1854. V. 47; 50; 52

STOCK, DENNIS
Jazz Street. Garden City: 1960. V. 47

STOCK, EUGENE
The History of the Church Missionary Society. London: 1899. V. 53

STOCK, JOHN
An Inaugural Essay on the Effects of Cold Upon the Human Body. Philadelphia: 1797. V. 54

STOCKBAUER, J.
Ausgewahlte Kunstwerke Aux Dem Schatze der Reichen Capelle in der Koniglichen Residenz Zu Munchen. Munich: 1876. V. 50

STOCKDALE, FREDERICK WILLIAM LITCHFIELD
A Concise Historical and Topographical Sketch of Hastings, Winchelsea & Rye. London: 1817. V. 47
Etchings...of Antiquities... London: 1810-11. V. 47
Etchings...of Antiquities in the County of Kent. London: 1910. V. 52

STOCKDALE, J. J.
Sketches Civil and Military of the island of java and its Immediate Dependencies... London: 1811. V. 48

STOCKDALE, JAMES
Annales Caermoelenses; or, Annals of Cartmel. Ulverston: 1872. V. 50; 52
Annals of Cartmel. Whitehaven: 1978. V. 50

STOCKDALE, MARY R.
The Panorama of Youth. Edinburgh: 1811. V. 50

STOCKER, K. F.
Medical Use of Snake Venom Proteins. London: 1990. V. 50

STOCKHAM, ALICE B.
Karezza. Ethics of Marriage. Chicago: 1897. V. 52; 53
Koradine Letters. (cover title) Koradine, a Propehtic Story. Chicago: 1894. V. 51; 53

STOCKLEIN, JOSEPH
Allerhand So Lehr-Als Geistreiche Brief Scrifften und Reis-Beschreibungen. Augsburg & Gratz: 1726-30. V. 47

STOCKLEY, C. H.
Shikar. London: 1928. V. 48
Stalking in the Himalayas and Northern India. 1936. V. 52; 54

STOCKLEY, CHARLES V. M.
Big Game Shooting in India, Burma and Somaliland. 1913. V. 54

STOCKTON, FRANK RICHARD
Afield and Afloat. London: 1901. V. 54
Ardis Claverden. London: 1890. V. 47
The Casting Away of Mrs. Lecks and Mrs. Aleshine. (with) The Dusantes. New York: 1886/88. V. 53; 54
The Floating Prince and Other Fairy Tales. New York: 1881. V. 53; 54
The Great Stone of Sardis. London and New York: 1898. V. 52
The Lady, or the Tiger? and Other Stories. New York: 1884. V. 53
The Squirrel Inn. New York: 1891. V. 51
Ting-a-Ling. London: 1870. V. 47
Ting-A-Ling. New York: 1870. V. 48; 51
What Might Have Been Expected. London: 1875. V. 54

STOCKTON, T. H.
Poems: with Autobiographic and Other Notes. Philadelphia: 1862. V. 54

STOCKTON, THOMAS COATES
The Stockton Family of New Jersey and Other Stocktons. Washington: 1911. V. 49

STODART, M. A.
Every-Day Duties; in Letters to a Young Lady. London: 1841. V. 52
Female Wirters: Thoughts on Their Proper Sphere and On Their Powers of Usefulness. London: 1842. V. 54

STODART, ROBERT R.
Memorials of the Browns of Fordell, Finmount and Vicarsgrange. Edinburgh: 1887. V. 53
Scottish Arms Being a Collection of Armorial Bearings A.D. 1370-1678. Edinburgh: 1881. V. 52

STODDARD, AMOS
Sketches, Historical and Descriptive of Louisiana... Philadelphia: 1812. V. 47; 52

STODDARD, HERBERT L.
The Bobwhite Quail... New York: 1931. V. 49; 53
The Bobwhite Quail. New York: 1950. V. 52

STODDARD, JAMES
Torula Infection in Man. A Group of Cases, Characterized by Chronic Lesions of the Central Nervous System... New York: 1916. V. 47

STODDARD, JOHN L.
John L. Stoddard's Lectures. Boston: 1904. V. 50

STODDARD, RICHARD HENRY
The Story of Little Red Riding Hood. New York: 1864. V. 47

STODDARD, SENECA RAY
In Mediterranean Lands The Cruise of the Friesland 1895. Glen Falls: 1896. V. 48

STODDARD, T. LOTHROP
The French Revolution in San Domingo. Boston: 1914. V. 51

STODDARD, W. O.
The Great Union Pacific Railroad Excursion... Chicago: 1867. V. 47; 52
The Great Union Pacific Railroad Excursion... New York: 1867. V. 47

STODDART, ANNA M.
The Life of Isabella Bird. London: 1906. V. 54

STODDART, ISABELLA
Arthur Montieth: a Moral Tale, Founded on an Historical fact... London: 1822. V. 48

STODDART, JOHN
A Journal of the Life, Travels, Sufferings and Labour of Love...of William Edmundson, Who Departed This Life, the 31st of the 6th Month 1712. London: 1774. V. 49
Remarks on Local Scenery & Manners in Scotand During the Years 1799 and 1800. London: 1801. V. 48; 50; 51; 53

STODDART, THOMAS TOD
Abel Massinger; or the Aeronaut. Edinburgh: 1846. V. 48
The Angler's Companion to the Rivers and Lochs of Scotland. Edinburgh: 1847. V. 47
An Angler's Companion to the Rivers and Lochs of Scotland. London: 1847. V. 50; 51; 53
Angling Songs. London: 1889. V. 54
The Art of Angling, as Practised in Scotland. Edinburgh: 1835. V. 47; 52

STOEVER, DIETRICH HEINRICH
The Life of Sir Charles Linnaeus... London: 1794. V. 47; 49; 51; 52

STOEVESANDT, J. C.
Deutsche Anweisung zur Feuerwerkerey, Worinnen alle Gebrauchliche Arten der Lust und Ernstfeuer Nebst Derselben Verfertigung und Denen Dazu Notigen Werkzeugen Ordentlich und Genau Beschreiben und Mit Kupfern Erlautert Werden. Leipzig: 1757. V. 49

STOKER, BRAM
Dracula. New York. V. 51
Dracula. Westminster: 1897. V. 48; 49; 50; 51; 53
Dracula. New York: 1965. V. 48; 53
Famous Imposters. New York: 1910. V. 50; 53; 54
The Jewel of Seven Stars. London: 1904. V. 53
The Jewel of Seven Stars. New York: 1904. V. 50; 52
The Lair of the White Worm. 1911. V. 48
Miss Betty. London: 1898. V. 49; 51
The Mystery of the Sea. New York: 1902. V. 49; 54
Personal Reminiscences of Henry Irving. London: 1906. V. 49; 50; 51
Personal Reminiscences of Henry Irving. New York: 1906. V. 53
The Snake's Pass. London: 1891. V. 51
The Snake's Pass... London: 1891/90. V. 48
Under the Sunset. London: 1882. V. 47; 48; 49; 51
The Watter's Mou'. London: 1895. V. 53
The Watter's Mou'. New York: 1895. V. 48
The Watter's Mou. Westminster: 1895. V. 51

STOKES, ANSON PHELPS
Church and State in the United States. New York: 1950. V. 52
Stokes Records: Notes Regarding the Ancestry and Lives of Anson Phelps Stokes and Helen Louisa (Phelps) Stokes. New York: 1910. V. 52
Stokes Records: Notes Regarding the Ancestry and Lives of Anson Phelps Stokes and Helen Louisa Phelps Stokes. New York: 1910-15. V. 50

STOKES, GEORGE
A List of Books, Connected with the English Reformation, and Chiefly in the English Language, in the Possession of George Stokes of Cheltenham. 1844. V. 52

STOKES, GEORGE T.
Pococke's Tour in Ireland in 1752. London: 1891. V. 51

STOKES, I. N. PHELPS
American Historical Prints, Early Views of American Cities, Etc. New York: 1932. V. 48
American Historical Prints, Early Views of American Cities, etc. New York: 1933. V. 47; 50; 51; 52

STOKES, J.
The Complete Cabinet Maker and Upholsterers' Guide... London: 1829. V. 53

STOKES, J. LORT
Discoveries in Australia: During the Voyage of HMS Beagle in the Years 1837-43. Adelaide: 1969. V. 52
Discoveries in Australia...During the Voyage of HMS Beagle in the Years 1837-43. London: 1846. V. 48; 54

STOKES, JOHN
Modern Clinical Syphilology. Springfield: 1927. V. 51

STOKES, MAIVE
Indian Fairy Tales Collected and Translated. Calcutta: 1879. V. 52

STOKES, MARGARET
Early Christian Architecture in Ireland. London: 1878. V. 53

STOKES, RALPH
A Text-Book of Rand Metallurgical Practice... London: 1913-12. V. 48
A Text-Book of Rand Metallurgical Practice... London: 1926-19. V. 48

STOKES, SEWELL B.
The China Cow and Other Stories. London: 1929. V. 53

STOKES, WHITLEY
Gwreans an Bys. The Creation of the World, a Cornish Mystery. 1864. V. 52
Saltair Na Rann. 1883. V. 49
Thesaurus Palaeohibernicus: A Collection of Old-Irish Glosses, Scholia Prose and Verse. 1901-03. V. 49; 51
The Tripartite Life of St. Patrick, with Other Documents Relating to the Saint. 1887. V. 48; 52
Tripartite Life of St. Patrick, with Other Documents Relating to the Saint. London: 1888. V. 49

STOKES, WILLIAM
The Diseases of the Heart and Aorta. Dublin: 1854. V. 49
The Diseases of the Heart and Aorta. Philadelphia: 1855. V. 49; 54
Lectures on the Theory and Practice of Physic. Philadelphia: 1837. V. 47; 54
The Life and Labours in Art and Archaeology of George Petrie. 1868. V. 52
Medicine in Modern Times or Discourses Delivered at a Meeting of the British medical Association at Oxford. London: 1869. V. 50
A Treatise On the Diagnosis and Treatment of Diseases of the Chest. Philadelphia: 1837. V. 49; 54
A Treatise on the Diagnosis and Treatment of Diseases of the Chest. Philadelphia & New Orleans: 1839. V. 48
Treatise on the Diagnosis and Treatment of Diseases of the Chest... London: 1882. V. 52; 54

STOKES, WINSTON
The Story of Hiawatha. New York: 1910. V. 47

STOLBERG, FREDERIC LEOPOLD, GRAF VON
Travels through Germany, Switzerland, Italy and Sicily. London: 1797. V. 47

STOLL, CASPAR
Representation Exactement Coloriee d'Apres Nature des Cigales... Amsterdam: 1788. V. 52

STOLL, WILLIAM T.
Silver Strike. The True Story of Silver Mining in the Coeur d'Alenes. Boston: 1932. V. 48

STONE, ALBERT H.
Historic Lushan. Hankow: 1921. V. 51

STONE, ARTHUR L.
Following Old Trails. Missoula: 1913. V. 47; 48

STONE, CAMERON
A Glossary of the Construction, Decoration and Use of Arms and Armor in all Countries and In all Times... 1961. V. 54

STONE, EDWARD MARTIN
The Invasion of Canada in 1775... Providence: 1867. V. 47

STONE, EDWIN M.
Our French Allies...in the Great War of the American Revolution from 1778 to 1782... Providence: 1884. V. 50

STONE, ELIZABETH ARNOLD
Uinta County: its Place in History. Laramie: 1924. V. 51; 53; 54

STONE, HENRY LANE
Morgan's Men a Narrative of Personal Experiences. Louisville: 1919. V. 47

STONE, HERBERT L.
Millions for Defense. New York: 1934. V. 54

STONE, HERBERT STUART
First Editions of American Authors. Cambridge: 1893. V. 48; 50; 52; 54

STONE, I. F.
The Hidden History of the Korean War. New York: 1952. V. 54

STONE, IRVING
False Witness. New York: 1940. V. 53; 54
Men to Match My Mountains. New York: 1956. V. 53; 54
Sailor On Horseback. Boston: 1938. V. 47; 50
Those Who Love. New York: 1965. V. 48

STONE, JOHN BENJAMIN
Children in Norway, or a Holiday on the Ekeberg. London: 1884. V. 47

STONE, LIVINGSTON
The Cold Spring Trout Ponds, Charleston, N.H. 1870?. V. 47

STONE, MARY AMELIA BOOMER
A Summer in Scandinavia. New York: 1885. V. 54

STONE, MELVILLE E.
A Book of American Prose Humor. (and) A Book of American Humorous Verse. Chicago: 1904. V. 54

STONE, OLIVER
Evita. Hollywood: 1989. V. 53

STONE, REYNOLDS
Boxwood: Sixteen Engravings. London: 1957. V. 51
Engraved Lettering in Wood. Wakefield: 1992. V. 47; 48
Engravings. Brattleboro: 1977. V. 48
Engravings. London: 1977. V. 47; 50; 52; 53; 54
Reynolds Stone Engravings. London: 1978. V. 53
The Turn of the Years. London: 1982. V. 47
The Turn of the Years. Salisbury: 1982. V. 49; 54
The Wood Engravings of Thomas Bewick. London: 1953. V. 50

STONE, ROBERT
Children of Light. London: 1986. V. 51; 53
Dog Soldiers. Boston: 1974. V. 47; 48; 49; 50; 51; 52; 53
A Flag for Sunrise. New York: 1981. V. 47; 51
A Hall of Mirrors. Boston: 1966. V. 52; 53; 54
A Hall of Mirrors. Boston: 1967. V. 47; 48; 49; 50; 51; 52; 54
A Hall of Mirrors. London: 1968. V. 47; 48
Helping. New York: 1987. V. 51; 52
Helping. 1993. V. 52
Helping. New York: 1993. V. 51; 53
Outerbridge Reach. Boston: 1991. V. 47
Outerbridge Reach. Franklin Center: 1992. V. 51; 53
Outerbridge Reach. New York: 1992. V. 48; 49; 50; 51; 52; 53; 54

STONE, STUART
The Kingdom of Why. Indianapolis: 1913. V. 52

STONE, W.
Bird Studies at Old Cape May. Philadelphia: 1937. V. 50

THE STONE Wall Book of Short Fictions. Iowa City: 1973. V. 54

STONE, WILBUR FISK
History of Colorado. Chicago: 1918. V. 51

STONE, WILBUR MACEY
A Snuff-Boxfull of Bibles. Newark: 1926. V. 50
The Triptych's Penny Toys. V. 47

STONE, WILLIAM
A Practical Treatise on Benefit Building Societies, Embracing Their Origin, Constitution and Change of Character... London: 1851. V. 52

STONE, WILLIAM G. M.
The Colorado Hand-book: Denver and Its Outings. A Guide for Tourists and Book of General Information with Some Bits of Early History. Denver: 1892. V. 48

STONE, WILLIAM L.
The Campaign of Lieut. Gen. John Burgoyne and the Expedition of Lieut. Col. Barry St. Leger. Albany: 1877. V. 47
Life of Joseph Brant... New York: 1838. V. 47; 52; 53
Life of Joseph Brant... New York: 1865. V. 50
The Life...of Sir William Johnson, Bart. Albany: 1865. V. 53
Ups and Downs in the Life of a Distressed Gentleman. New York: 1836. V. 47

STONE, WITMER
Bird Studies at Old Cape May: An Ornithology of Coastal New Jersey. Philadelphia: 1937. V. 47; 49; 51

STONEBACK, H. R.
Cartographers of the Deus Loci: The Mill House. Newtown: 1982. V. 48; 51
Cartographers of the Deus Loci: The Mill House. North Hills: 1982. V. 47; 48; 54

STONEBRAKER, JOSEPH R.
A Rebel of '61. New York: 1899. V. 49

STONEHAM, CHARLES
The Birds of the British Islands. London: 1906-11. V. 50
Wanderings in Wild Africa. London: 1932. V. 50

STONER, F.
Chelsea Bow and Derby Porcelain Figures, Their distinguishing Characteristics. Newport: 1955. V. 48

STONES, M.
The Endemic Flora of Tasmania. London: 1967-79-71. V. 48

STONEY, SAMUEL GAILLARD
Plantations of the Carolina Low Country. Charleston: 1939. V. 51

STOOKEY, BYRON
Surgical and Mechanical Treatment of Peripheral Nerves. Philadelphia: 1922. V. 47; 52; 53; 54

STOOTER, JOAO
Arte de Brilhantes Vernizes, & das Tinturas, Fazelas, & o Como Obrar com Ellas. E dos Ingredientes de Que o Dito se Deve Compor... Antwerp: 1729. V. 48

STOPES, CHARLOTTE CARMICHAEL
British Freewomen Their Historical Privilege. London: 1894. V. 50

STOPES, H.
Malt and Malting, an Historical, Scientific and Practical Treatise... London: 1885. V. 49

STOPES, MARIE
Contraception (Birth Control). Its Theory, History and Practice. London: 1924. V. 50; 52
Married Love, a New Contribution to the Solution of Sex Difficulties. London: 1918. V. 49

STOPFORD, FRANCIS
The Romance of the Jewel. London: 1920. V. 49; 53

STOPPARD, TOM
After Magritte. London: 1971. V. 54
Albert's Bridge and If You're Glad I'll be Frank: Two Plays for Radio. London: 1969. V. 54
Artist Descending a Staircase and Where Are They Now? Two Plays for Radio. London: 1973. V. 54
Dalliance and Undiscovered Country. London and Boston: 1986. V. 49
Dirty Linen and New-Found-Land. London: 1976. V. 54
Dogg's Hamlet and Cahoot's Macbeth. London: 1979. V. 54
Enter a Free Man. London: 1968. V. 54
Four Plays for Radio. London: 1984. V. 51
Jumpers. London: 1972. V. 53
Lord Malquist and Mr. Moon. London: 1966. V. 47; 49; 50; 51; 53
Rosencrantz and Guildenstern are Dead. London: 1967. V. 49; 53; 54
Rosencrantz and Guildenstern are Dead. New York: 1967. V. 54
Travesties. London: 1975. V. 54
Travesties. New York: 1975. V. 48; 51

STORCH, HENRY
The Picture of Petersburg. London: 1801. V. 48

STORCK, ANTON
An Essay on the Medicinal Nature of Hemlock... Edinburgh: 1762. V. 49

STORCK, KARL
Musik und Musiker in Karikatur. Oldenburg: 1910. V. 52

STORER, D. H.
A Synopsis of the Fishes of North America. Cambridge: 1846. V. 48; 53

STORER, EDWARD
I've Quite Forgotten Lucy - Poems. Printed in Rome: 1932. V. 54

STORER, HENRY
Mesmerism in Disease. Bath: 1845. V. 48

STORER, HORATIO
The Causation, Course and Treatment of Reflex Insanity in Women. Boston: 1871. V. 47

STORER, J.
Ancient Reliques; or, Delineations of Monastic, Castellated, & Domestic Architecture and Other Interesting Subjects... London: 1812-13. V. 54
Antiquarian and Topographical Cabinet. London: 1807-11. V. 48; 52; 54
The Antiquarian Itinerary. London: 1815-18. V. 52
The Antiquarian Itinerary, Comprising Specimens of Architecture, Monastic, Castelalted and Domestic... London: 1816. V. 53
Cowper, Illustrated by a Series of Views in or Near the Park of Weston-Underwood, Bucks. London. V. 52
Delineations, Graphical and Descriptive of Fountains' Abbey, in the West Riding of the County of York. London: 1830. V. 50
Delineations Graphical and Descriptive of Fountains' Abbey, in the West Riding of the County of York. Ripon: 1840. V. 52
Graphic and Historic Description of the Cathedrals of Great Britain. London: 1814-19 plates. V. 53
History and Description of the Parish of Clerkenwell. London: 1828. V. 50; 52
The Wild White Cattle of Great Britain, an Account of Their Origin, History and Present State. London: 1880. V. 53

STORER, MARIA LONGWORTH NICHOLS
In Memoriam Bellamy Storer, with Personal Remembrances of President McKinley, President Roosevelt. London: 1923. V. 54

STOREY, DAVID
The Changing Room. New York: 1972. V. 54
Flight Into Camden. London: 1960. V. 49; 50; 51; 53
This Sporting Life. London: 1959. V. 54
This Sporting Life. London: 1960. V. 54

STOREY, GLADYS
Dickens and Daughter. London: 1939. V. 49

STOREY, HARRY
A Ceylon Sportsman's Diary. 1921. V. 54
Hunting and Shooting in Ceylon. London: 1907. V. 53; 54

STOREY, THOMAS
A Journal of the Life of Thomas Storey... Newcastle-upon-Tyne: 1747. V. 54
Report on the Great North of England Railway, Connecting Leeds and York, with Newcastle-upon-Tyne. Darlington: 1836. V. 51

STORIES About Birds. London: 1856. V. 51

STORIES by American Authors. New York: 1884-85. V. 54

STORIES, by Jean Stafford, John Cheever, Daniel Fuchs, William Maxwell. New York: 1956. V. 48

THE STORIES of the Jubilee Singers with Their Songs. London: 1877. V. 53

STORIES Selected from the History of Scotland, for Children, Intended as a Companion to the Stories Selected fromt he History of England. London: 1820. V. 49

STORK, WILLIAM
An Account of East-Florida, with a Journal, Kept by John Bartram of Philadelphia, Botanist to His Majesty for the Floridas... London: 1766. V. 47; 48; 53

STORM, COLTON
A Catalog of the Everett D. Graff Collection of Western American. Chicago: 1968. V. 52

STORM, HYEMEYOHSTS
Seven Arrows. New York: 1972. V. 50; 54

STORRER, WILLIAM ALLIN
The Architecture of Frank Lloyd Wright. Cambridge: 1979. V. 50

STORRS, AUGUSTUS
Answers of Augustus Storrs, of Missouri, to Certain Queries Upon the Origin, Present State and Future Prospect of Trade and Intercourse Between Missouri and the Internal Provinces of Mexico. Washington: 1825. V. 47

STORY, JOSEPH
Charge of Mr. Justice Story, on the Law of Treason, Delivered to the Grand Jury of the Circuit Court of the United States, Holden at Newport, for the Rhode Island District, June 15, 1842. Providence: 1842. V. 54
Commenataries on Equity Jurisprudence, as Administered in England and America. Boston: 1886. V. 50
Commentaries on the Conflict of Laws, Foreign and Domestc, in Regard to Contracts, Rights and Remedies and Especially in Reagrad to Marriages, Divorces, Wills, Successions and Judgments. Boston: 1872. V. 48; 54
Commentaries on the Constitution of the United States... Boston: 1833. V. 52
Commentaries on the Law of Bills of Exchange, Foreign and Inland as Administered in England and America. London: 1843. V. 53
Commentaries on the Law of Partnership, as a Branch of Commercial and Maritime Jurisprudence, with Occasional Illustrations from the Civil and Foreign Law. London: 1841. V. 52
Life and Letters of Joseph Story. Boston: 1851. V. 51
The Power of Solitude. A Poem. Salem: 1804. V. 50
A Practical Treatise on Bills of Exchange, Checks on Bankers, Promissory Notes, Bankers' Cash Notes and Bank Notes. Boston: 1809. V. 50

THE STORY of a Little Red Indian. V. 51

THE STORY of Beauty and the Beast. London: 1908. V. 48

THE STORY of Bunty. Racine: 1935. V. 51

THE STORY of Calgary and Tuxedo Park. Calgary and Toronto: 1911. V. 53

THE STORY of Horrockses. 1950. V. 54

THE STORY of How Amnon Ravished His Sister Thamar. Pigotts: 1930. V. 51

THE STORY OF Jack and the Giants. London: 1851. V. 49; 53

THE STORY of Jesus. London: 1940. V. 49

STORY of King David. London. V. 51

STORY of the American Fireman. New York: 1908. V. 48; 54

THE STORY Of the Bristol Training Ship, H.M.S. "Formidable". 1884. V. 54

THE STORY of the Fifty-Fifth Regiment Illinois Volunteer Infantry in the Civil War. Clinton: 1887. V. 52; 54

THE STORY of the Jubilee Singers With Their Songs. London: 1876. V. 47

THE STORY of the Typewriter 1873-1923, Published in Comemeoration of the Fiftieth Anniversary of the Invention of the Writing Machine. Herkimer: 1923. V. 54

STORY, ROBERT
Craven Blossoms; or, Poems Chiefly Connected with the District of Craven, by Robert Storey... Skipton: 1826. V. 54
Love and Literature; Being the Reminiscences, Literary Opinions, and Fugitive Pieces of a Poet in Humble Life. London: 1842. V. 51

STORY, T. W.
Notes on the Old Haworth Registers. Haworth: 1909. V. 54

STORY, THOMAS
Journal of the Life of Thomas Story. Newcastle Upon Tyne: 1747. V. 47; 49; 50; 51; 54

STORY, WILLIAM WETMORE
Roba di Roma. London: 1864. V. 47

STORY Worth Telling: Or Mental Food for Young Minds. Boston: 1830. V. 48

STOTHARD, C. A.
The Monumental Effigies of Great Britain... London: 1817-32. V. 48

STOTHARD, CHARLES
Letters Written During a Tour through... France in 1818, by Mrs. Charles Stothard. London: 1820. V. 50

STOTZ, CHARLES MORSE
The Early Architecture of Western Pennsylvania, a Record of Building Before 1860. New York: 1936. V. 48

STOUFFER, SAMUEL A.
Studies in Social Psychology. Princeton: 1949-50. V. 48

STOUT, GARDNER D.
The Shorebirds of North America. New York: 1967. V. 50; 52; 53; 54
The Shorebirds of North America. New York: 1968. V. 49

STOUT, HOSEA
On the Mormon Frontier - The Diary of Hosea Stout 1844-1861. 1964. V. 54

STOUT, L. H.
Reminiscences of General Braxton Bragg. Hattiesburg: 1942. V. 49

STOUT, PETER F.
Nicaragua: Past, Present and Future... Philadelphia: 1859. V. 52

STOUT, REX
And Be a Villain. New York: 1948. V. 50; 52
The Broken Vase. New York: 1941. V. 49
The Doorbell Rang. New York: 1965. V. 53
Double for Death. New York: 1939. V. 54
Fer-de-Lance. London: 1935. V. 53
The Final Deduction. London: 1962. V. 53
The Golden Spiders. New York: 1953. V. 53
How Like a God. New York: 1929. V. 48
If Death Ever Slept. New York: 1957. V. 52
The Illustrious Dunderheads. New York: 1942. V. 48; 49; 50
Not Quite Dead Enough. New York: 1944. V. 50
Prisoner's Base. New York: 1952. V. 53
The Second Confession. New York: 1949. V. 49; 53
The Silent Speaker. New York: 1946. V. 48; 49; 50
The Silent Speaker. London: 1947. V. 53
Too Many Cooks. 1938. V. 52; 53
Too Many Cooks. New York: 1938. V. 49
Where There's A Will. New York: 1940. V. 49

STOUT, SAMUEL H.
An Address on Education, Delivered in Pulaski, Tennessee at the Close of the Examination of the Students of Wurtemburg Academy... Pulaski: 1851. V. 48

STOUT, TOM
Montana It's Story and Biography. Chicago: 1921. V. 50

STOVALL, ALLAN
Nueces Headwater Country. San Antonio: 1959. V. 49; 52; 54

STOVER, DONALD L.
Tischlermeister Jahn. San Antonio: 1978. V. 48

STOVER, ELIZABETH M.
Son-Of-a Gun Stew. Dallas: 1945. V. 50

STOW, J.
Certaine Worthye Manuscript Poems of Great Antiquitie Reserved Long in the Studie of a Northfolke Gentleman. Colophon Edinburgh: 1812. V. 50

STOW, JOHN
Annales, or, a Generall Chronicle of England. (with) An Appendix of Corollary of the Foundations and Descriptions of the Three Most Famous Universities of England... (with) The Third Universities of England... London: 1631/32/31. V. 52
A Summarie of the Chronicles of England. London: 1598. V. 53
A Survay (sic) of London. London: 1599. V. 52
A Survay (sic) of London. London: 1603. V. 50
The Survey of London. London: 1633. V. 51

STOW, MARIETTA LOIS
Probate Chaff; or, Beautiful Probate; or, Three Years Probating in San Francisco. 1879. V. 53
Probate Confiscation. Unjust Laws Which Govern Woman. 1877. V. 48

STOW, WILLIAM
Remarks on London: Being an Exact Survey of the Cities of London and Westminster, Borough of Southwark and the Suburbs and Liberties Contiguous to Them. London: 1722. V. 50

STOWE, DAVID
The Training System, Religious, Intellectual and Moral, a Manual for Schools... Glasgow: 1846. V. 53

STOWE, HARRIET ELIZABETH BEECHER
The American Woman's Home; or Principles of Domestic Science. New York: 1869. V. 47; 48; 50
Dred. Boston: 1856. V. 47; 48; 49; 50; 51; 52; 53; 54
Dred... London: 1856. V. 51
Earthly Care, a Heavenly Discipline. Boston: 1854. V. 47
Herinneringen uit Vreemde Landen. (Sunny Memories in Foreign Lands). Amsterdam: 1859. V. 47
A Key to Uncle Tom's Cabin. Boston: 1853. V. 52; 53
The Key to Uncle Tom's Cabin. London: 1853. V. 47; 48; 49; 53
Light and Darkness. Religious Poems. London: 1867. V. 47
Little Pussy Willow. Boston: 1881. V. 51; 52; 53
The Mayflower; or, Sketches of Scenes and Characters Among the Descendants of the Pilgrims. New York: 1844. V. 53
Men of Our Times. 1868. V. 53
Men of Our Times. Hartford: 1868. V. 52; 53
The Minister's Wooing. London: 1859. V. 51
The Minister's Wooing. New York: 1859. V. 53
Oheim Tom's Hutte... Boston: 1853. V. 52
Old Town Folks. Boston: 1865. V. 53
Oldtown og dets Beboere. Et Tidsbillede af Livet i Amerika i Gamle Dage. Copenhagen: 1876. V. 47
Onkel Tom's Hutte, Oder: leben Unter den Verstossnen. Philadelphia: 1853. V. 51
Our Charley. Boston: 1858. V. 51; 54
Palmetto Leaves. Boston: 1873. V. 51; 52
Pictures and Stories from Uncle Tom's Cabin. Boston: 1853. V. 47; 54
Pink and White Tyranny. Boston: 1871. V. 52; 54
Queer Little People. Boston: 1867. V. 52
Religious Poems. Boston: 1867. V. 48; 51
Sunny Memories of Foreign Lands. Boston: 1854. V. 47; 50; 52; 54
Sunny Memories of Foreign Lands. London: 1854. V. 53
Uncle Tom's Cabin. Boston: 1852. V. 48; 49; 51; 52; 53; 54
Uncle Tom's Cabin. Leipzig: 1852. V. 49
Uncle Tom's Cabin... London: 1852. V. 47; 48; 49; 50; 51; 52; 53; 54
Uncle Tom's Cabin. London: 1853. V. 53
Uncle Tom's Cabin. London: 1880. V. 49
Uncle Tom's Cabin... Cambridge: 1892. V. 47
Uncle Tom's Cabin. 1938. V. 53
Uncle Tom's Cabin. New York: 1938. V. 52; 53
We and Our Neighbors. New York: 1875. V. 53
Woman in Sacred History. New York: 1873. V. 49
Woman in Sacred History. New York: 1874. V. 49; 51
The Writings of Harriet Beecher Stowe... Boston: 1896. V. 48; 50; 52

STOWELL, JOHN
Don Coronado Through Kansas 1541 Then Known as Quivira. Seneca: 1908. V. 49

STOWELL, MYRON
Fort Frick or the Siege of Homestead. Pittsburg: 1893. V. 47; 52

STOWER, CALEB
The Printer's Grammar; or, Introduction to the Art of Printing... London: 1808. V. 48; 54

STOWITS, GEORGE H.
History of the One Hundredth Regiment of New York State Volunteers. Buffalo: 1870. V. 47

STRABO
En Tibi Lector Studiose Strabonis Geographicorum Co(m)me(n)tarios, Olim a Guarino Versonese & Gregorio Trifernate Latinitate Donatus... Basel: 1523. V. 54
Geographia. Venice: 1494. V. 53
(Greek title) Strabonis De Situ Orbis Librix XVII. Basel: 1549. V. 52
Rervm Geographicarvm. Basel: 1571. V. 53

STRACHEY, LYTTON
Books and Characters. London: 1922. V. 49; 54
Elizabeth and Essex. New York and London: 1928. V. 50; 51; 53; 54
Eminent Victorians. London: 1918. V. 53
Ermyntrude and Esmeralda. London: 1969. V. 50; 53
Portraits in Miniature. London: 1931. V. 51
Queen Victoria. London: 1921. V. 49; 50; 53

STRACHEY, MARJORIE
Mazzini, Garibaldi and Cavour. London: 1937. V. 49

STRACHEY, RACHEL
The Cause. London: 1928. V. 48; 50; 51; 53

STRACHEY, RICHARD
Catalogue of the Plants of Kumaon and of the Adjacent Portions of Garhwal and Tibet, Based on the Collections Made by Strachey and Winterbottom During the Years 1846 to 1849... London: 1906. V. 47

STRACHEY, ROY
Marching On. New York: 1923. V. 50; 52

STRACK, HENRY
Brick and Terra-Cotta Work During the Middle Ages and the Renaissance in Italy. New York: 1914?. V. 50

STRADA, FAMIANO
De Bello Belgico. The History of the Low-Countrey Warres. London: 1650. V. 50; 51; 52; 53

STRADA, JACOB DE
Epitome Thesauri Antiquitatum, Hoc Est, Impp. rom. Orientalium et Occidentalium Iconum, Ex Antiquis Numismatibus Quam Fidelisme Deliniatarum. Tiguri: 1557. V. 48

STRAFFORD, THOMAS WENTWORTH, 1ST EARL OF
The Earl of Strafforde's Letters and Despatches, with an Essay Towards His Life by Sir George Radcliffe... London: 1739. V. 51
La Harangve dv Vice-Roy d'Irlande...Decapite a Londres...le 12 May 1641. Paris: 1641. V. 52
Letters and Dispatches. Dublin: 1740. V. 47
The Tryal of Thomas Earl of Strafford...Upon an Impeachment of High Treason By the Commons Then Assembled in Parliament... London: 1680. V. 48

STRAHAN, A.
The Geology of the Isle of Purbeck and Weymouth. London: 1898. V. 51; 52; 53; 54

STRAHAN, S. A. K.
Marriage and Disease. A Study of Heredity and the More Important Family Degenerations. New York: 1892. V. 54

STRAHORN, CARRIE ADDELL
Fifteen Thousand Miles by Stage. New York: 1911. V. 48
Fifteen Thousand Miles by Stage. New York: 1915. V. 53

STRAHORN, ROBERT EDMUND
Gunnison and San Juan. A Late and Reliable description of the Wonderful Gold and Silver Belts and Iron and Coal of that Newest and Best Land for Prospector and Capitalist, South Western Colorado. Omaha: 1881. V. 48; 52
The Hand-Book of Wyoming and Guide to the Black Hills and Big Horn Regions for Citizen, Emigrant and Tourist... Cheyenne: 1877. V. 52

STRAHORN, ROBERT G.
Idaho, The Gem of the Mountain, The Resources and Attractions of Idaho Territory, Facts Regarding Climate, Soil, Minerals, Agricultural and Grazing Lands, Forests, Scenery, etc. Boise City: 1881. V. 47; 50; 52

STRAIN, ISAAC G.
Sketches of a Journey in Chili, and the Argentine Provinces in 1849. New York: 1853. V. 47

STRAKER, D. AUGUSTUS
The New South Investigated. Detroit: 1888. V. 53
A Trip to the Windward Islands. Detroit: 1896. V. 54

STRAKER, E.
Wealden Iron. London: 1969. V. 49

STRALEY, W.
Pioneer Sketches of Nebraska and Texas. Hico: 1915. V. 48

STRAND; *A Profile.* Iowa City: 1979. V. 47

STRAND, MARK
Art of the Real. New York: 1983. V. 51; 53
The Continuous Life. Iowa City: 1990. V. 47; 49; 53; 54
Elegy for My Father. Robert Strand. Iowa City: 1973. V. 51; 53; 54
The Late Hour. New York: 1978. V. 53
Prose: Four Poems. 1987. V. 52
Prose: Four Poems. Portland: 1987. V. 47; 49; 50
Reasons for Moving. New York: 1968. V. 53
The Sargeantville Notebook. Providence: 1973. V. 47; 53
Strand: a Profile. Iowa City: 1979. V. 53
A Suite of Appearances: a Poem. 1993. V. 52; 53
A Suite of Appearances: a Poem. Oregon: 1993. V. 49; 54

STRAND, PAUL
Ghana: an African Portrait. 1976. V. 52
Living Egypt. Dresden: 1969. V. 54
Living Egypt. New York: 1969. V. 49
The Mexican Portfolio. New York: 1967. V. 54
Paul Strand: a Retrospective Monograph, the Years 1915-1968. Millerton: 1971. V. 47
A Retrospective Monograph. The Years 1915-1968. Millerton: 1971/72. V. 54
Time in New England. New York: 1950. V. 47; 52
Tir A'Mhurain: Outer Hebrides. London: 1962. V. 48

STRANG, HERBERT, MRS.
The Rose Fairy Book. London: 1912. V. 51

STRANG, JAMES J.
Ancient and Modern Michilimackinac, Including an Account of the Controversy Between Mackinac and the Mormons. Burlington: 1894?. V. 47
The Book of the Law of the Lord, Consisting of All Inspired Translation of Some of the Most Important Parts of the Laws Given to Moses. Beaver Island: 1856. V. 47

STRANG, JOHN
The Cruise, with Other Poems. London: 1812. V. 54

STRANG, PETER
History of Missions in Southern Saskatachewan. Regina: 1929. V. 51

STRANG, WILLIAM
The Doings of Death. London: 1901. V. 52; 54

STRANGE, EDWARD F.
The Colour-Prints of Hiroshige. London: 1925. V. 47; 48

STRANGE, J. D.
The Price of Victory. London: 1930. V. 47

STRANGE, ROBERT
A Descriptive Catalogue of a Collection of Pictures... London: 1769. V. 47; 49

STRANGE, T. A.
French Interiors, Furniture, Decoration, Woodwork and Allied Arts. London: 1907. V. 50; 51

STRANGE *Visitors. A Series of Papers.* New York: 1869. V. 48

STRANGFORD, PERCY CLINTON SYDNEY SMYTHE, VISCOUNT
Poems. Dublin: 1796. V. 47

STRANSBURY, HOWARD
Exploration and Survey of the Valley of the Great Salt Lake of Utah... Washington: 1853. V. 51

STRAPAROLA, GIOVANNI FRANCESCO
The Most Delectable Nights of Straparola of Caravaggio. Paris: 1906. V. 48
The Nights of Straparola. London: 1894. V. 51; 52; 53; 54

STRASSER, ALEX
Victorian Photography. London and New York: 1942. V. 48

STRATAGEMS *Of Chess, or a Collection of Critical and Remarkable Situations, Selected from the Works of Eminent Masters...* London: 1817. V. 49

STRATHMORE, MARY ELEANOR BOWES, COUNTESS OF
The Confessions of the Countess of Strathmore: Written by Herself. London: 1793. V. 52

THE STRATHMORE *Quality Deckle-Edge Bookpapers: Strathmore Japan, Old Choice, Strathmore, Old Stratford, Alexandra. Manufactured by Mittineague Paper Company.* Mittineague: 1906. V. 48

STRATTON, ARTHUR
The English Interior. London: 1920. V. 48
The Orders of Architecture: Greek, Roman and Renaissance with Selected Examples of Their Application. London: 1931. V. 47

STRATTON, CHARLES
An Account of the Life, Personal Appearance, Character and Manners of Charles S. Stratton, the American Man in Miniature... London: 1844. V. 51
The American General Tom Thumb. New York: 1850. V. 49
Grandmamma Easy's General Tom Thumb. Boston: 1850. V. 52
The Life of General Tom Thumb. Troy: 1856. V. 47

STRATTON, FLORENCE
The White Plume, or O. Henry's Own Short Story. Beaumont: 1931. V. 53

STRATTON, GEORGE
Defences of George Stratton, Esq. London: 1778. V. 48; 52

STRATTON, HELEN
The Lily of Life. London: 1910. V. 50

STRATTON, MARY CHENOWETH
Shaw on Women. Lewisburg: 1992. V. 49

STRATTON, ROBERT BURCHER
The Heroes in Gray. Lynchburg: 1894. V. 49

STRATTON, ROYAL B.
Captivity of the Oatman Girls... Chicago: 1857. V. 47
Captivity of the Oatman Girls... New York: 1859. V. 53
Life Among the Indians or the Captivity of the Oatman Girls Among the Apache and Mohave Indians. San Francisco: 1935. V. 51; 53

STRATTON-PORTER, GENE
Laddie. A True Blue Story. New York: 1913. V. 47

STRAUB, PETER
Ghost Story. London: 1979. V. 47; 52
Ghost Story. New York: 1984. V. 51
If You Could See Me Now. 1977. V. 47; 51
If You Could See Me Now. New York: 1977. V. 51

STRAUB, PETER continued
Ishmael. 1972. V. 49; 54
Julia. 1975. V. 54
Julia. New York: 1975. V. 51; 53
Julia. 1976. V. 51
Julia. London: 1976. V. 47
Marriages. London: 1973. V. 53
Marriages. New York: 1973. V. 53

STRAUS, RALPH
John Baskerville a Memoir. Cambridge: 1907. V. 54
The Unspeakable Curll... London: 1927. V. 52
The Unspeakable Curll. New York: 1928. V. 52

STRAUSBURGER, RALPH BEAVER
Pennsylvania German Pioneers... Norristown: 1934. V. 54

STRAUSS, DAVID FRIEDRICH
The Life of Jesus... London: 1846. V. 50; 53

STRAUSS, LEO
The Political Philosophy of Hobbes: its Basis and Its Genesis. Oxford: 1936. V. 47

STRAUSS, WALTER
The Complete Drawings of Albrecht Durer. New York: 1974. V. 53

STRAVINSKY, IGOR
An Autobiography. New York: 1936. V. 49
Selected Correspondence. London: 1982-85. V. 50

STREAMER, D.
Ruthless Rhymes for Heartless Homes. London: 1899. V. 52

STREATFEILD, R. A.
Samuel Butler: Records and Memorials. Cambridge: 1903. V. 52

STREATFEILD, THOMAS
Lympsfield and Its Environs... Westerham: 1838. V. 47; 52; 53

STRECKFUSS, ADOLF
Der Ausgewiesene. Leipzig: 1848. V. 48

STREET, ALFRED B.
A Digest of Taxation in the States, Under Three Heads. 1. Mode or Machinery of Taxation. 2. Standard of Valuation. 3. Property Liable to and Exempt from Taxation. Albany: 1863. V. 52
The Indian Pass. New York: 1869. V. 54
Woods and Waters; or, the Saranacs and Racket. New York: 1860. V. 50

STREET, B.
Historical Notes on Grantham and Grantham Church. Grantham: 1857. V. 51

STREET, GEORGE
Che! Wah! or, the Modern Montezumas in Mexico. Rochester: 1883. V. 47; 49
Some Account of Gothic Architecture in Spain. London: 1869. V. 53

STREET, HENRY
A Plea for the Removal of Jewish Disabilities. London: 1849. V. 54

STREET, PARK
Courts of the Order of the Alamo: 1940-1949. V. 49

STREET Sketches of London Life. London: 1890. V. 52

STREET, THOMAS ATKINS
The Foundations of Legal Liability, a Presentation of the Theory and Development of the Common Law. New York: 1906. V. 50

STREETER, EDWARD
Same Old Bill, en Mable!. New York: 1919. V. 54

STREETER, EDWIN W.
The Great Diamonds of the World. London: 1882. V. 48
Precious Stones and Gems, their History and Distinguishing Characteristics. London: 1879. V. 50
Precious Stones and Gems, Their History and Distinguishing Characteristics. London: 1882. V. 47
Precious Stones and Gems, Their History and Distinguishing Characteristics. London: 1884. V. 50

STREETER, FLOYD B.
Prairie Trails and Cow Towns. Boston: 1936. V. 47; 49

STREETER, THOMAS WINTHROP
Bibliography of Texas, 1795-1845... Cambridge: 1960. V. 48
Bibliography of Texas, 1795-1845. Woodbridge: 1983. V. 48
Bibliography of Texas, 1795-1845. 1996. V. 54
The Celebrated Collection of Americana... New York: 1966-69. V. 47; 48; 52
The Celebrated Collection of Americana... New York: 1966-70. V. 48; 49; 53
The Celebrated Collection of Americana... New York: 1968. V. 53
The Celebrated Collection of Americana... New York: 1970. V. 54
Sale of the Celebrated Collection of Americana. Index. New York: 1970. V. 48

STREETT, WILLIAM B.
Gentlemen Up. New York: 1930. V. 47; 48; 50

STREHLNEEK, E. A.
Chinese Pictorial Art. Shanghai: 1914. V. 47; 50; 54

STRESSEMANN, E.
Ornithology from Aristotle to the Present. London: 1975. V. 51

STRETCH, LYSCOMBE MALTBEE
The Beauties of History; or, Pictures of Virtue and Vice, Drawn from Real Life... Dublin: 1788. V. 53

STRETCH, R. H.
Reports on the Spring Valley Hydraulic Gold Company, comprising, the Cherokee Flat Blue Gravel and Spring Valley Mining and Irrigating Company's Property. New York: 1879. V. 47

STRETE, CRAIG KEE
Burn Down the Night. 1982. V. 50
Paint Your face on a Drowning in the River. New York: 1978. V. 50

STRETSER, THOMAS
A New Description of Merryland: Containing, a Topographical, Geographical and Natural History of that Country. London: 1742. V. 48

STRETTON, CHARLES
Memoirs of A Chequered Life. London: 1862. V. 49
Sport and Sportsmen, A Book of Recollections. London: 1866. V. 47; 50

STRETTON, HESBA
The Clives of Burcot. London: 1867. V. 50

STRETZER, THOMAS
Merryland Displayed: or, Plagiarism, Ignorance and Impudence detected. Bath: 1741. V. 49

STREVELL, CHARLES NETTELTON
As I Recall Them. V. 54
As I Recall Them. 1943. V. 53

STRIBLING, ROBERT MACKEY
Gettysburg Campaign and Campaigns of 1864 and 1865 in Virginia. Petersburg: 1905. V. 47; 49; 50; 54

STRIBLING, T. S.
Clues of the Caribees. Garden City: 1929. V. 54
The Cruise of the Dry Dock. Chicago: 1917. V. 54

STRICKER, SALAMON
Manual of Human and Comparative Histology. London: 1870. V. 49

STRICKER, THOMAS PERRY
Marginalia to Life: Being Notes from the Private Papers of Anthony Hillyer. Los Angeles: 1931. V. 54

STRICKLAND, AGNES
Floral Sketches, Fables and Other Poems. London: 1861. V. 54
The Little Tradesman; or, a Peep Into English Industry by the author of "The Moss House"... London: 1825. V. 49
Lives of the Queens of England... London: 1851. V. 49
Lives of the Queens of England... London: 1857. V. 48
Lives of the Queens of England... London: 1864. V. 48
Lives of the Queens of England... London: 1882. V. 51
Lives of the Queens of England... London: 1885. V. 47; 51
Lives of the Queens of England. Philadelphia: 1902. V. 47; 51; 52; 54
The Pilgrims of Walsingham; or Tale of the Middle Ages. London: 1835. V. 53
Queen Victoria from Her Birth to Her Bridal. London: 1840. V. 49
Rosetta's Birthday; for the Entertainment and Instruction of Little Girls. London: 1824. V. 47; 50

STRICKLAND, F.
A Manual of Petrol Motors and Motor Cars. London: 1907. V. 47

STRICKLAND, JANE
The Orphan Captive or Christian Endurance. London: 1845. V. 47; 49

STRICKLAND, MARY
A Memoir of the Life, Writings and Mechanical Inventions of Edmund Cartwright, D.D. F.R.S., Inventor of the Power Loom... London: 1843. V. 54

STRICKLAND, REX W.
El Paso in 1854. El Paso: 1969. V. 48; 52

STRICKLAND, SAMUEL
Twenty-Seven Years in Canada West; or, The Experience of an Early Settler. London: 1853. V. 48

STRICKLAND, WILLIAM
Address Upon a Proposed Rail Road from Wilmington to the Susquehanna. Philadelphia: 1835. V. 53

STRICTURES On Female Education; Chiefly As it Relates to the Culture of the Heart. Norwich: 1792. V. 50

STRID, A.
Mountain Flora of Greece. London: 1986-91. V. 49; 50; 52
Mountain Flora of Greece. Volume 2. Edinburgh: 1991. V. 49

STRILING, EDWARD
The Fortunes of Smike. London: 1840?. V. 54

STRINDBERG, AUGUST
Gespenstersouper. 1987. V. 51
Plays. First, Second and Third Series. London: 1912-13. V. 48
Plays. (with) Plays Second Series. (and) Plays Third Series. London: 1912-23. V. 50

STRINGER, GEORGE ALFRED
Leisure Moments in Gough Square, or the Beauties and Quaint Conceits of Johnson's Dictionary. Buffalo: 1886. V. 47; 50; 54

STRINGFELLOW, THORNTON
Slavery: Its Origin, Nature and History Considered in the Light of Bible Teachings, Moral Justice and Political Wisdom. New York: 1861. V. 47

STROBRIDGE, IDAH MEACHAM
The Land of Purple Shadows. Los Angeles: 1909. V. 53
The Loom of the Desert. Los Angeles: 1907. V. 53

STRODE, HUDSON
Jefferson Davis. New York: 1955-66. V. 49

STRODE, MURIEL
My Little Book of Prayer. Chicago: 1906. V. 47

STRODE, WILLIAM
The Floating Island. London: 1655. V. 52

STROMMENGER, EVA
5000 Years of the Art of Mesopotamia. New York: 1964. V. 50; 52

STRONG, A. B.
The American Flora, or, History of Plants and Wild Flowers... New York: 1846. V. 51

STRONG, CHARLES
Specimens of Sonnets from Most Celebrated Italian Poets: with Translations. London: 1827. V. 48; 54

STRONG, D. E.
Catalogue of the Carved Amber in the Department of Greek and Roman Antiquities. London: 1966. V. 50

STRONG, EUGENIE
Catalogue of the Greek and Roman Antiques in the Possession of the Right Honourable Lord Melchett. Oxford: 1928. V. 50

STRONG, JAMES CLARK
Biographical Sketch of... Los Gatos: 1910. V. 47; 49; 52

STRONG, LEONARD ALFRED
Don Juan and The Wheelbarrow. London: 1932. V. 47
The Hansom Cab and Pigeons. Waltham St. Lawrence: 1935. V. 50; 52

STRONG, NATHANIEL T.
Appeal to the Christian Community on the Condition and Prospects of the New York Indians, In Answer to a Book, Entitled The Case of the New York Indians, and Other Publications of the Society of Friends. New York: 1841. V. 48

STRONG, PHIL
State Fair. New York: 1932. V. 50

STRONG, R. M.
A Bibliography of Birds... Chicago: 1939. V. 50
Bibliography of Birds. Chicago: 1939-59. V. 49; 53

STRONG, R. P.
The African Republic of Liberia and the belgian Congo.... Cambridge: 1930. V. 49; 51; 53

STRONG, ROY
The English Icon - Elizabethan & Jacobean Portraiture. London: 1969. V. 50; 52; 54
Splendour at Court - Renaissance Spectacle and Illusion. London: 1973. V. 53
Tudor & Jacobean Portraits, National Portrait Gallery, London. London: 1969. V. 50

STRONG, WILLIAM
Strawberry Hill. A Catalogue of Singularly Choice Collection of Rare and Valuable Books...Principally from the Collection of Horace Walpole. Bristol: 1843. V. 53

STRONG, WILLIAM DUNCAN
Archaeological Studies in Peru 1941-1942. New York: 1943. V. 50

STROTHER, DAVID HUNTER
The Capital of West Virginia and the Great Kanawha Valley; Advantages, Resources and Prospects. Charleston: 1872. V. 51
Virginia Illustrated... New York: 1857. V. 53; 54

STROTHER, EDWARD
Criticon Febrium; or, a Critical Essay on Fevers with the Diagnosticks and methods of Cure. London: 1716. V. 49
Dissertations Upon the Ingraftment of the Small-Pox, According to the Method of Turkey... London: 1722. V. 48; 51
Dr. Radcliffe's Practical Dispensatory. London: 1721. V. 49
The Family Companion for Health, or the Housekeeper's Physician... London: 1750. V. 52

STROUD, DOROTHY
The Architecture of Sir John Soane. London: 1961. V. 49; 53
Capability Brown. London: 1950. V. 48
Capability Brown. London: 1957. V. 53

STROUD, T. B.
The Elements of Botany, Physiological and Systematical to Which is Added a Comprehensive Dictionary of All Terms... Greenwich: 1821. V. 50

STROUD, VIRGIL C.
In Quest of Freedom. Dallas: 1963. V. 54

STROUSE, NORMAN H.
C-S the Master Craftsman. Harper Woods: 1969. V. 50
The Passionate Pirate. North Hills: 1964. V. 49; 51

The Silverado Episode. 1966. V. 48

STROYER, JACOB
My Life in the South. Salem: 1898. V. 48; 50; 51; 53

STROZZI, TITO VESPASIANO
Strozii Poetae Pater et Filius. Venice: 1513. V. 48
Strozii Poetae Pater et Filius. Venice: 1513/14. V. 52

STRUBBERG, FRIEDRICH ARMAND
Amerikanisches Jagd-Und Reiseabenteuer aus Meinem leben in den Westlichen Indianergebieten. Stuttgart und Augsburg: 1858. V. 49

STRUCTIONS *for Surgeons Under the Commissioners for Conducting His Majesty's Transport Service, for Taking Care of Sick and Wounded Seamen, and for the Care and Custody of Prisoners of War.* London: 1809. V. 54

STRUENSEE, JOHANN F., COUNT VON
Authentic Elucidation of the History of Counts Struensee and Brandt, and of the Revolution in Denmark in the Year 1772. London: 1789. V. 47

STRUTHER, JAN
Mrs. Miniver. New York: 1940. V. 49
The Modern Strewwelpeter. London: 1936. V. 48

STRUTHERS, JOHN
Anatomical and Physiological Observations. Part I. Edinburgh: 1854. V. 49

STRUTT, ELIZABETH
Domestic Residence in Switzerland. London: 1842. V. 47

STRUTT, JACOB GEORGE
Sylva Britanica, or, Portraits of Forest Trees... London: 1830. V. 47; 49; 51; 52; 53; 54
Sylva Britannica; or, Portraits of Forest Trees. London: 1822-26. V. 53
Sylva Britannica, or Portraits of Forest Trees. London: 1830-36. V. 47; 48; 50

STRUTT, JOHN WILLIAM
Argon, a New Constituent of the Atmosphere. Washington: 1896. V. 48

STRUTT, JOSEPH
The Bumpkins' Disasater, or the Journey to London... London: 1808. V. 50
A Complete View of the Dress and Habits of the People of England. London: 1796. V. 47
A Complete View of the Dress and Habits of the People of England... 1799. V. 54
A Complete View of the Dress and Habits of the People of England... London: 1842. V. 48; 52
(Glig Gamena Angel-Deod.)... London: 1801. V. 51
(Glig Gamena Angel-Deod.)... London: 1810. V. 51; 52
Horda Angel-Cynnan: or a Compleat View of the Manners, Customs, Arms, Habits, &c. of the Inhabitants of England, from the Arrival of the Saxons, Till the Reign of Henry the Eighth. London: 1775-76. V. 54
Queen-Hoo Hall, A Romance: and Ancient Times. Edinburgh: 1808. V. 47; 52
The Regal and Ecclesiastical Antiquities of England. London: 1777. V. 47; 51; 54
The Regal and Ecclesiastical Antiquities of England... London: 1842. V. 47; 52
The Sports and Pastimes of the People of England. London: 1801. V. 47
The Sports and Pastimes of the People of England. London: 1830. V. 51; 52
The Sports and Pastimes of the People of England. London: 1833. V. 48
The Sports and Pastimes of the People of England... London: 1849. V. 50
The Sports and Pastimes of the People of England... London: 1876. V. 51
The Test of Guilt; or Traits of Ancient Superstition. London: 1808. V. 47; 49; 50; 54

STRUVE, CHRISTIAN AUGUST
Asthenology; or, the Art of Preserving Feeble Life; and of Supporting the Constitution... London: 1801. V. 52
A Practical Essay on the Art of Recovering Suspended Animation... Albany: 1803. V. 48; 50; 51; 53

STRUVE, FRIEDRICH GEORG WILHELM
Stellarum Duplicium et Multiplicum Mensurae Micrometriciae per Magnum Frauhoferi Tubum Annis a 1824 ad 1837 in Specula Dorpatensi Intitutae... St. Petersburg: 1837. V. 47

STRUVE, J. C. VON
Travels in the Crimea. A History of the Embassy from Petersburg to Constantinople in 1793. London: 1802. V. 49

STRUYS, JAN
The Voiages and Travels of John Struys through Italy, Greece, Muscovy, Tartary, Media, Persia, East-India, Japan and Other Countries in Europe... London: 1684. V. 51

STRYKER, ROY
In This Proud Land: America 1935-1943 As Seen in the FSA Photographs. Greenwich: 1973. V. 54

STRYKER, WILLIAM S.
The Battles of Trenton and Princeton. Boston: 1898. V. 49; 51
Official Register of the Officers and Men of New Jersey in the Revolutionary War. Trenton: 1872. V. 51
Record of Officers and Men of New Jersey in the Civil War 1861-1865. Trenton: 1876. V. 47; 51

STRYPE, JOHN
Ecclesiastical Memorials; Relating Chiefly to Religion and the Reformation of It, and the Emergencies of the Church of England Under King Henry VIII, King Edward VI and Queen Mary the First. London: 1721. V. 53
The History of the Life and Acts of...Edmund Grindal. London: 1710. V. 47
The Life and Acts of John Whitgift. Oxford: 1822. V. 47
The Life and Acts of Matthew Parker. Oxford: 1821. V. 47
The Life and Acts of the Most Reverend Father in God, John Witgift, D. D. London: 1718. V. 48

STRYPE, JOHN continued
The Life of the Learned Sir Thomas Smith Kt. Doctor of the Civil Law... London: 1698. V. 48
Memorials of the Most Reverend Father in God, Thomas Cranmer... London: 1694. V. 47; 50; 53
Works. Oxford: 1824-28. V. 48

STRZELECKI, P. E. DE
Physical Description of New South Wales and Van Diemen's Land. London: 1845. V. 52

STUART, A. H., MRS.
Washington Territory. Information Concerning Its Resources, Population and General Statistics... Olympia: 1880. V. 48

STUART, ANDREW
Considerations on the Present State of East-India Affairs and Examination of Mr. Fox's Bill; Suggesting Certain Material Alterations for Averting Dangers and Preserving the Benefits of that Bill. London: 1784. V. 52
Genealogical History of the Stewarts, from the Earliest Period to the Present...Particular Account of the...Stuarts of Darnley, Lennox and Aubigny... London: 1798. V. 50
A Letter to the Right Honourable Lord Amherst, from Andrew Stuart, Esq. London: 1781. V. 52
Letters to the Right Honourable Lord Mansfield... London: 1773. V. 50; 52
Letters to the Right Honourable Lord Mansfield. Dublin: 1775. V. 51; 54

STUART, CHARLES
A Letter to General Richard Smith, in Reply to the Charges Introduced into the Ninth Report of the Select Committee, Affecting the Character of Mr. Stuart. London: 1783. V. 47

STUART, CHARLES B.
Lives and Works of Civil and Military Engineers of America. New York: 1871. V. 49; 50

STUART, CONSTANCE M. VILLIERS
Gardens of the Great Mughals. London: 1913. V. 49; 53

STUART, DUDLEY COUTTS
Address of the Literary Association of the Friends of Poland, to the People of Great Britain and Ireland. London: 1846. V. 49

STUART, E. J.
Land of Opportunities, Being an Account of the Author's Recent Expedition to Explore the Northern Territories of Australia. London: 1923. V. 52

STUART, FRANCIS
The Coloured Dome. 1932. V. 54
The Coloured Dome. London: 1932. V. 48; 50; 51
Glory. London: 1933. V. 48; 51
A Hole in the Head. 1977. V. 47
Pigeon Irish. London: 1932. V. 48
Try the Sky. London: 1933. V. 48; 50
Victors and Vanquished. Ohio: 1959. V. 47
We Have Kept the Faith... Dublin: 1923. V. 48
We Have Kept the Faith. London: 1923. V. 48
The White Hare. London: 1936. V. 48
Women and God - a Novel. London: 1931. V. 48

STUART, GILBERT
An Historical Dissertation Concerning the Antiquity of the English Constitution. Edinburgh: 1768. V. 48
A View of Society in Europe, In Its Progress from Rudeness to Refinement. Edinburgh: 1778. V. 48; 51
A View of Society in Europe, in Its Progress from Rudeness to Refinement... London: 1782. V. 52
A View of Society in Europe, In Its Progress from Rudeness to Refinement... London: 1783. V. 47; 49
A View of Society in Europe, its Progress from Rudeness to Refinement... Edinburgh: 1792. V. 51

STUART, GLORIA
Boating with Bogart. Los Angeles: 1993. V. 50

STUART, GRANVILLE
Forty Years...Gold Miner, Trader, Merchant, Rancher and Politician. Cleveland: 1925. V. 48; 50; 52; 54
Forty Years...Gold Miner, Trader, Merchant, Rancher and Politician. Glendale: 1957. V. 53

STUART, H. A.
A Pilgrimage in the South Seas. San Francisco: 1871. V. 47

STUART, HENRY
The Planter's Guide; or, a Practical Essay on the Best Method to Giving Immediate Effect to Wood... Edinburgh & London: 1828. V. 52

STUART, JAMES
Critical Observations on the Buildings and Improvements of London. London: 1771. V. 48
Poems on Various Subjects. Belfast: 1811. V. 54
Three Years in North America. Edinburgh: 1832. V. 50
Three Years in North America. Edinburgh: 1833. V. 47; 52; 54
Three Years in North America. London: 1833. V. 53

STUART, JAMES F.
Open Letter to the President of the United States, the Secretary of the Interior, the Members of Congress, and the Judges of the Supreme Court of the United States. Washington: 1878. V. 49
Senate Bill 238. For the Relief of the Heirs and Legal Representatives of Juan Miranda, Deceased. Washington: 1865. V. 49

STUART, JESSE
Beyond Dark Hills. New York: 1938. V. 51; 53; 54
Head O' W-Hollow. New York: 1936. V. 53
Honest Confessions of a Literary Sin. Detroit: 1977. V. 53
Kentucky Was My Land. New York: 1951. V. 47
Man With a Bull-Tongue Plow. New York: 1934. V. 48; 53
Man With a Bull-Tongue Plow. New York: 1936. V. 49; 54
Men of the Mountains. New York: 1941. V. 54
Taps for Private Tussie. New York: 1943. V. 48; 50; 51; 53; 54
Tree of Heaven. New York: 1940. V. 47; 48; 51; 54

STUART, JOHN
Records of the Priory of the Isle of May. Edinburgh: 1868. V. 53; 54

STUART, JOHN SOBIESKI
Lays of the Deer Forest. Edinburgh & London: 1848. V. 54

STUART, JOSEPH A.
My Roving Life, a Diary of Travels and Adventures by Sea and Land, During Peace and War... Auburn: 1895. V. 47

STUART, LOUISA
Notes on George Selwyn and His Contemporaries. New York and London: 1928. V. 49; 52

STUART, MOSES
A Grammar of the Hebrew Language. Andover: 1828. V. 50
A Hebrew Grammar Without the Points... Andover: 1813. V. 53

STUART, REGINALD R.
Calvin B. West of the Umpqua. An Obscure Chapter in the History of Southern Oregon. Stockton: 1961. V. 49

STUART, ROBERT L.
Catalogue of the Library of Robert L. Stuart. New York: 1884. V. 50; 52

STUART, RUTH MC ENERY
The River's Children. New York: 1904. V. 48
The Story of Babette, a Little Creole Girl. New York & London: 1898. V. 48; 50; 52

STUART, VILLIERS
Adventures Amidst the Equatorial Forests and Rivers of South America... London: 1891. V. 51
Nile Gleanings Concerning the Ethnlogy, History and Art of Ancient Egypt as Revealed by Egyptian Paintings and Bas-Reliefs. London: 1879. V. 48

STUART, W. J.
Forbidden Planet. 1956. V. 48; 52

STUART, WILLIAM
Sketches of the Life of William Stuart, the First and Most Celebrated Coutnerfeiter of Connecticut. Bridgeport: 1854. V. 53

STUART-GLENNIE, JOHN STUART
Greek Folk-songs from the Ottoman Provinces of Northern Hellas. London: 1888. V. 49

STUART-WORTLEY, EMMELINE CHARLOTTE ELIZABETH MANNERS, LADY
Travels in the United States, etc. During 1849 and 1850. London: 1851. V. 48; 53
Travels in the United States, etc., During 1849 and 1850. New York: 1851. V. 51; 53

STUART-YOUNG, J. M.
Osrac, the Self Sufficient and Other Poems. London: 1905. V. 48; 50; 53

STUBBES, GEORGE
A Dialogue on Beauty. London: 1731. V. 49; 53
A New Adventure of Telemachus. London: 1731. V. 47; 49; 53

STUBBES, HENRY
A Justification of the Present War Against the United Netherlands. London: 1672. V. 49

STUBBINGS, FRANK H.
Mycenaean Pottery from the Levant. Cambridge: 1951. V. 50

STUBBLEBINE, JAMES H.
Duccio di Buoninsegna and His School. Princeton: 1979. V. 48

STUBBS, AMELIA
Family Tales for Children. London: 1824. V. 50

STUBBS, CHARLES WILLIAM
The Land and the Labourers. London: 1884. V. 52

STUBBS, GEORGE
The Anatomy of the Horse. London: 1938. V. 47
An Illustrated Lecture on Sketching from Nature in Pencil and Water Colour. London: 1850. V. 53

STUBBS, LAURA
Stevenson's Shrine. London: 1903. V. 54

STUBBS, LUCAS PETER
A Guide to Pawnbroking Being the Statutes Regulating Pawns and Pawnbrokers. London: 1866. V. 51; 52

STUBBS, STEPHEN
Agnes; or the Power of Love. Boston: 1845. V. 51

STUBBS, W.
The Crown Circuit Companion... Dublin: 1766. V. 50

STUBBS, WILLIAM
Chronicles and Memorials of the Reign of Richard I. London: 1864-65. V. 49; 52
Chronicles of the Reigns of Edward I and Edward II. London: 1882-83. V. 49; 52
The Constitutional History of England In its Origin and Development. London: 1880. V. 52

STUBBS, WILLIAM continued
The Crown Circuit Companion. London: 1738. V. 48

STUCK, HUDSON
Voyages on the Yukon and Its Tributaries: a Narrative of Summer Travel on the Interior of Alaska. New York: 1917. V. 49

STUCKEY, RONALD
The Lithographs...1931-72. Boston: 1974. V. 48; 50; 53; 54

STUCKLE, HENRY
Interoceanic Canals. An Essay on the Question of Location for a Ship Canal Across the American Continent. New York: 1870. V. 51

THE STUDENT, or, *The Oxford and Cambridge Monthly Miscellany.* Oxford: 1750-51. V. 51

STUDER, JACOB H.
The Birds of North America... Columbus: 1878. V. 54
The Birds of North America. Montreal: 1881. V. 54
The Birds of North America. New York and Columbus: 1881. V. 54
The Birds of North America. New York: 1888. V. 50
The Birds of North America. Barre: 1977. V. 54
Studer's Popular Ornithology: The Birds of North America. New York and Columbus: 1881. V. 50

STUDIES in History and Philosophy of Science. London: 1970-81. V. 49

STUDIES in the Age of Chaucer. University of Tennessee: 1980-91. V. 49

STUDIES in the Book Trade: In Honor of Graham Pollard. Oxford: 1975. V. 48

STUDIES Presented to F.L.I. Griffith. London: 1932. V. 49

THE STUDIO. Modern Book-Bindings and Their Designers. London: 1899-1900. V. 50; 52

THE STUDIO. Modern Book-Bindings and Their Designers... London: 1900. V. 52

STUDLEY, J. T.
The Journal of a Sporting Nomad. London: 1892. V. 48

STUDLEY, VANCE
Specimens of Handmade Botanical Papers. Los Angeles: 1979. V. 52

STUMPF, FRANZ, MRS.
San Antonio's Menger. 1953. V. 48

STURDIVANT, JONATHAN
A Collection of Hymns for the Use of Christians. Poughkeepsie: 1806. V. 54

STURGE, JOSEPH
Reconciliation Between the Middle and Labouring Classes. Edinburgh: 1842. V. 53
A Visit to the United States in 1841. Boston: 1842. V. 49
A Visit to the United States in 1841. London: 1842. V. 50; 51
The West Indies in 1837; Being a Visit to Antigua, Montserrat, Dominica, St. Lucia, Barbadoes and Jamaica... 1838. V. 50
The West Indies in 1837; Being the Journal of a Visit to Antigua, Monteserrat, Dominica, St. Lucia, Barbados and Jamaica... London: 1838. V. 47

STURGEON, THEODORE
Caviar. 1955. V. 52
The Dreaming Jewels. New York: 1950. V. 48; 50; 51; 52
E Pluribus Unicorn. New York: 1953. V. 48; 50
The Joyous Invasions. London: 1965. V. 47; 51
The Joyous Invasions. 1966. V. 48; 52
More than Human. 1953. V. 48; 52
More Than Human. New York: 1953. V. 48; 50
More Than Human. London: 1954. V. 49; 54
A Touch of Strange. Garden City: 1958. V. 52
A Way Home. 1955. V. 47; 51
A Way Home. New York: 1955. V. 52
Without Sorcery. 1948. V. 49; 54

STURGES, JOCK
The Last Days of Summer. New York: 1991. V. 53

STURGES, LEE
Salmon Fishing on Cain River, New Brunswick. Chicago: 1919. V. 47

STURGIS, WILLIAM
The Oregon Question. Boston: 1845. V. 48

STURGIS, WILLIAM BAYARD
New Lines for Flyfishers. New York: 1936. V. 47; 49

STURLA THORDARSON
Anecdotes of Olave the Black, King of Man, and the Hebridian Princes of the Somerled Family, To Which are Added XVIII, Eulogies on Haco King of Norway... Copenhagen: 1780. V. 47

STURLESON, S.
The Heimskringla; or Chronicle of the Kings of Norway. London: 1844. V. 53

STURM, ALEXANDER
From Ambush to Zig-Zag. New York: 1942. V. 50

STURM, C. C.
Reflections On the Works of God...Throughout All Nature. London: 1823. V. 51

STURM, JACOB
Deutschlands Fauna in Abbildungen Nach der natur Mit Beschreibungen... 1829-34. V. 51

STURM, JOHANN CHRISTOPH
Mathesis Enucleata; or, the Elements of Mathematicks. London: 1724. V. 49

STURMER, FREDERICK JOHN
The Plagues of Egypt, a Poem and Other Pieces. Gainsborough: 1851. V. 51

STURMY, JOHN
Love and Duty; or, The Distress'd Bride. London: 1722. V. 49

STURT, CHARLES
Narrative of an Expedition Into Central Australia...During 1844, 5 and 6. London: 1849. V. 52
Two Expeditions into the Interior of Southern Australia during the Years 1828, 1829, 1830 and 1831. London: 1833. V. 52

STURT, GEORGE
The Journals, 1890-1927. Cambridge: 1967. V. 50

STUTFIELD, H.
Climbs and Exploration in the Canadian Rockies. London: 1903. V. 53

STYFFE, KNUT
The Elasticity, Extensibility and Tensile Strenth of Iron and Steel. London: 1869. V. 49

STYLE, WILLIAM
Regestum Practicale: or the Practical Register, Consisting of Rules, Orders and Observations Concerning the Common-Laws, and the Practice Thereof...Particularly Applicable to the Proceedings in the Upper Bench. London: 1657. V. 48

STYLIANOU, ANDREAS
The History of Cartography of Cyprus. Nicosia: 1980. V. 48

STYRON, WILLIAM
Admiral Robert Penn Warren. 1981. V. 47
Admiral Robert Penn Warren and the Snows of Winter. North Carolina: 1978. V. 51; 52
Admiral Robert Penn Warren and the Snows of Winter. Winston Salem: 1981. V. 47
Against Fear. 1981. V. 47; 49; 54
As He Lay Dead, a Bitter Grief. New York: 1981. V. 47; 51
Blankenship. 1988. V. 48; 51
Christchurch. Davidson: 1977. V. 48; 51
Confessions of Nat Turner. New York: 1967. V. 48; 49; 50; 51; 53
The Confessions of Nat Turner. London: 1968. V. 49; 51
Darkness Visible: a Memoir of Madness. New York: 1990. V. 50
Inheritance of Night. Durham & London: 1993. V. 49; 50; 51; 53
Lie Down in Darkness. Indianapolis & New York: 1951. V. 48; 49; 50; 51; 52; 53
The Long March. New York: 1952. V. 49; 51
The Message of Auschwitz. Blacksburg: 1979. V. 48
Set This House on Fire. New York: 1960. V. 48; 52
Shadrach. Los Angeles: 1979. V. 47; 48; 51
Sophie's Choice. Franklin Center: 1979. V. 52; 53; 54
Sophie's Choice. New York: 1979. V. 47; 48; 49; 51; 52
This Quiet Dust. 1967. V. 51
This Quiet Dust. New York: 1967. V. 53
This Quiet Dust. New York: 1982. V. 47; 48; 49; 51; 52; 53
A Tidewater Morning. New York: 1993. V. 51; 54

THE SUBJECT Of Supremacie. The Right of Caesar. Resolution of Conscience. London: 1643. V. 53

THE SUBSTANCE of a Charge Delivered to the Grand Jury of Wiltshire,, at the Summer Assizes 1827, by the Lord Chief Justice Best. London: 1827. V. 52

THE SUBSTANCE of the Evidence Delivered to a Committee of the Honourable House of Commons by the Merchants and Traders of London, Concerned in the Trade to Germany and Holland, and of the Dealers in Foreign Linens, as Summed Up by Mr. Glover. London: 1774. V. 47

SUBSTANCE of the Speech of Joseph Phillimore in the House of Commons On Moving for Leave to Bring in a Bill to Amend the Marriage Act. London: 1822. V. 52

SUCH, ROD
George Jackson: Death of a Black Revolutionary. 1971. V. 48

SUCKLING, ALFRED
The History and Antiquities of the County of Suffolk... London: 1848/. V. 53

SUCKLING, JOHN
A Ballad Upon a Wedding. 1927. V. 47
A Ballad Upon a Wedding. Berkshire: 1927. V. 48
A Ballad Upon a Wedding. Waltham Saint Lawrence: 1927. V. 48; 52; 53
Fragmenta Aurea. London: 1646. V. 47; 48
Fragmenta Aurea. London: 1648. V. 47
Fragmenta Aurea... London: 1658. V. 52
The Poems... London: 1896. V. 47; 49
Poems. Halifax: 1933. V. 47
The Poems, Plays and Other Remains. London: 1874. V. 50
The Works. Dublin: 1766. V. 48; 49; 52; 54

SUCKOV, LORENZ JOHANN DANIEL
Erste Grunde der Burgerlichen Baukunst in Einem Zusammenhange Entworfen... Jena: 1781. V. 47

SUDDEN Fiction. American Short Stories. Layton: 1986. V. 52

SUDEK, JOSEF
Fotografie. Prague: 1956. V. 49
Magic In Stone. London: 1947. V. 47; 50

SUDERMANN, HERMANN
The Joy of Living. New York: 1902. V. 53

SUDHOFF, KARL
Essays in the History of Medicine. New York: 1926. V. 50; 54

SUE, EUGENE
The Mysteries of Paris. London: 1844. V. 54
Paula Monti: or the Hotel Lambert. London: 1845. V. 48
The Rival Races; or, the Sons of Joel. London: 1863. V. 51
The Wandering Jew. 1844. V. 54
The Wandering Jew. London: 1844. V. 52
The Wandering Jew. London: 1844-45. V. 51; 53
The Wandering Jew. London & New York: 1889. V. 49
Works. London & Boston. V. 49; 50
Works. Boston: 1900. V. 50

SUE, JEAN JOSEPH
A Series of Engravings, Representing Bones of the Human Skelton: With the Skeltons of Some of the Lower Animals. London: 1819-20. V. 47

SUESS, EDUARD
The Face of the Earth. 1904. V. 49
The Face of the Earth. 1904-09. V. 54
The Face of the Earth. Oxford: 1904-09. V. 49

SUETONIUS TRANQUILLUS, GAIUS
The Historie of Twelve Caesars, Emperors of Rome... London: 1931. V. 47; 51
Lives of the Twelve Caesars. 1930. V. 48; 51; 54
The Lives of the Twelve Caesars. Verona: 1963. V. 47
Suetonii Tranquillus XII Caesares, Cum Libera Versione, in Qua Idiomatis Anglici Ratio... London (in fact York): 1732. V. 50
Twelve Caesars. Antwerp: 1591. V. 50
The Twelve Caesars. Baltimore: 1957. V. 50
The Twelve Caesars. London: 1962. V. 51
Vitae XII Caesares. Milan: 1480. V. 48; 54
Vitae XII, Caesarum. Bologna: 1493. V. 49
Works. Leyden: 1751. V. 51; 54

THE SUFFOLK Garland. Ipswich: 1818. V. 54

SUFFOLK, HENRY CHARLES HOWARD, 18TH EARL OF
Racing and Steeple-Chasing. London: 1886. V. 54

THE SUFFOLK Tourist, or Excursions Through Suffolk. London: 1818. V. 47

SUFFOLK TRUST & INVESTMENT CO.
Suffolk Trust and Invetment Co....Incorporated by Special Character Massachusetts Legislature, 1887. Boston: 1887. V. 49

SUGDEN, ALAN VICTOR
A History of English Wallpaper 1509-1914. London: 1925. V. 52
Potters of Darwen. 1839-1939. Manchester: 1939. V. 53

SUGDEN, EDWARD BURTENSHAW, BARON ST. LEONARD'S
A Practical Treatise of the Law of Vendors and Purchasers of Estates. Philadelphia: 1807. V. 48
A Series of Letters to a Man of Property, on the Sale, Purchase... Philadelphia: 1811. V. 51
A Series of Letters to a Man of Property, on the Sale, Purchase... London: 1815. V. 50; 52

SUGERMAN, DANNY
The Doors: The Illustrated History. New York: 1983. V. 50

SUGG, REDDING S.
The Horn Logs of Walter Inglis Anderson. Memphis: 1973. V. 49

SUGUENZA Y GONGORA, DON CARLOS
The Mecurio Volante of...An Account of the First Expedition of Don Diego de Vargas into New Mexico in 1692. Los Angeles: 1932. V. 49

SUHAILI, ANVAR I.
The Lights of Canopus. London. V. 54

SUKARNO
Paintings and Statues From the Collection of President Sukarno of the Republic of Indonesia. Jakarta: 1964. V. 47; 49

SUKENIK, E. L.
The Dead Sea Scrolls of the Hebrew University. Jerusalem: 1955. V. 48
The Third Wall of Jerusalem: an Account of Excavations. Jerusalem: 1930. V. 52

SULIVAN, GEORGE LYDIARD
Dhow Chasing in Zanzibar Waters and on the Eastern Coast of Africa. London: 1873. V. 54

SULIVAN, LAURENCE
Queen Square, 3d April 1773. N.P: 1773. V. 47

SULLIVAN, A. M.
A Visit to the Valley of Wyoming. Dublin: 1865. V. 53

SULLIVAN, ARABELLA JANE
Recollections of a Chaperon. London: 1833. V. 50
Recollections of a Chaperon. London: 1849. V. 53; 54
Tales of the Peerage and the Peasantry. London: 1835. V. 47; 49; 50; 51; 52

SULLIVAN, CHARLES T.
Snitching Niggers. New York: 1974. V. 54

SULLIVAN, CONSTANCE
Nude Photographs 1850-1980. New York: 1980. V. 53

SULLIVAN, DENNIS
A Picturesque Tour through Ireland. London: 1824. V. 48

SULLIVAN, EDWARD
Rambles and Scrambles in North and South America. London: 1852. V. 47
Yachting. London: 1894. V. 54

SULLIVAN, ELEANOR
Whodunit: a Biblio-Bio Anecdotal memoir of Frederic Dannay. New York: 1984. V. 48; 51; 52; 54

SULLIVAN, FRANCIS STOUGHTON
An Historical Treatise on the Feudal Law, and the Constitution and Laws of England... London: 1772. V. 54
Lectures on the Constitution and Laws of England. London: 1776. V. 47; 52; 54

SULLIVAN, J. F.
The British Working Man By One Who Does Not Believe in Him, and Other Sketches. London: 1878. V. 48

SULLIVAN, JAMES
The History of the District of Maine. Boston: 1795. V. 47

SULLIVAN, JOHN
Letters and Papers of... Concord: 1930-39. V. 50
Tracts Upon India: Written in the Years 1779, 1780, and 1788. London: 1795. V. 48

SULLIVAN, JOHN LANGDON
Prospective Economy, in the Future Public Works of the State of New York... Albany: 1827. V. 53

SULLIVAN, JOHN T.
Report of Historical and Technical Information Relating to the Problem of Interoceanic Communication by Way of the American Isthmus. Washington: 1883. V. 52

SULLIVAN, LOUIS H.
The Autobiography of an Idea. New York: 1924. V. 47
Kindergarten Chats... 1934. V. 47; 48
Kindergarten Chats. New York: 1947. V. 50
A System of Architectural Ornament... New York: 1924. V. 48; 54
A System of Architectural Ornament. New York: 1990. V. 50

SULLIVAN, MARK
Our Times. New York: 1927-35. V. 51
Our Times 1900-1925. New York: 1935. V. 53

SULLIVAN, MAURICE S.
Jedediah Smith, Trader and Trail Breaker. New York: 1936. V. 47; 48; 53
The Travels of Jedediah Smith... Santa Ana: 1934. V. 47; 51; 52

SULLIVAN, MAY KELLOGG
A Woman Who Went to Alaska. Boston: 1902. V. 53

SULLIVAN, NANCY
The Treasury of American Short Stories. New York: 1981. V. 51

SULLIVAN, RICHARD JOSEPH
A View of Nature, in Letters to a Traveller from the alps. London: 1794. V. 49

SULLIVAN, T. D.
Poems. Dublin: 1880. V. 48; 50

SULLIVAN, THOMAS
Born Burning. New York: 1989. V. 51

SULLIVANT, WILLIAM S.
Icones Muscorum, or Figures and Descriptions of Most of Those Mosses Peculiar to Eastern North America. Cambridge and London: 1864/74. V. 47; 48; 49; 52; 53
The Musci and Hepataicae of the United States East of the Mississippi River. New York: 1856. V. 52

SULLY, JAMES
The Human Mind: a Text-Book of Psychology. London: 1892. V. 54
Pessimisim; a History and a Criticism. London: 1877. V. 48; 50

SULLY, MAXIMILLIAN DE BETHUNE, DUC DE
Memoires... Amstelredam: 1638. V. 48
Memoires. Londres: 1745. V. 54
Memoirs... London: 1761. V. 47; 53
Memoirs... Edinburgh: 1770. V. 51

SULLY, MAXIMILLIAN DE BETHUNE, DUC OF
Memoirs... London: 1778. V. 52

SULZBERGER, CYRUS
The Resistentialists. New York: 1962. V. 48; 51

SULZER, FRIEDRICH GABRIEL
Versuch Einer Naturgeschichte des Hamsters. Gottingen & Gotha: 1774. V. 49

SULZER, JOHANN HEINRICH
Die Kennzeichen der Insekten nach Anleitung...Karl Linnaeus. Zurich: 1761. V. 51; 54

A SUMMARY and Philosophic View of the Genius, Character, Manners, Government and Politics of the Dutch. London: 1788. V. 48

SUMMARY View of the Millennial Church, Or United Society of Believers (Commonly Called Shakers)... Albany: 1823. V. 48

A SUMMER Month; or, Recollections of a Visit to the Falls of Niagara, and the Lakes. Philadelphia: 1823. V. 53

SUMMER Rambles, or Conversations, Instructive and Entertaining for the Use of Children. London: 1801. V. 49

SUMMERHAYES, MARTHA
Vanished Arizona, Recollections Of My Army Life. Philadelhia: 1908. V. 50; 53
Vanished Arizona: Recollections of My Army Life. Salem: 1911. V. 48; 53

SUMMERING in Colorado. Denver: 1874. V. 47; 52

SUMMERS, JAMES
Rudiments of the Chinese Language, with Dialogues, Exercises and a Vocabulary. London: 1864. V. 50

SUMMERS, MONTAGUE
Antinous and Other Poems. London: 1907. V. 50; 53
The Gothic Quest. London. V. 52
The Grimoire and other Supernatural Stories. London: 1936. V. 49
Malleus Maleficarum. Bungay: 1928. V. 50
Malleus Maleficarum. London: 1928. V. 49
The Marquis de Sade. A Study in Algolagnia. London: 1920. V. 50
The Playhouse of Pepys. London: 1935. V. 54
A Popular History of Witchcraft. London: 1937. V. 52
The Restoration Theatre - an Account of the Technique of the Playwrights of Charles II and the Practical Staging of Plays in the Restoration Theatre. London: 1934. V. 49
Victorian Ghost Stories. London: 1933. V. 49
Witchcraft and Black Magic. London: 1946. V. 52

SUMMERSELL, CHARLES GRAYSON
The Cruise of the C. S. S. Sumter. Tuscaloosa: 1965. V. 49

SUMMERSETT, HENRY
Probable Incidents; or, Scenes in Life, a Novel. London: 1797. V. 48

SUMMERSON, JOHN
Georgian London. London: 1945. V. 52
Georgian London. London: 1948. V. 49

SUMNER, CHARLES
Argument of Charles Sumner, Esq. Against the Constitutionality of Separate Colored Schools, in the Case of Sarah C. Roberts vs. the City of Boston. Before the Supreme Court of Mass. Dec. 4, 1849. Boston: 1849. V. 52; 53
The Barbarism of Slavery. Washington: 1860. V. 50
Freedom National; Slavery Sectional. Washington: 1852. V. 50
The Landmark of Freedom. Speech of the Hon. Charles Sumner Agaisnt the Repeal of the Missiouri Prohibition of Slavery North of 36 Degrees, 30 Minutes... Boston: 1854. V. 47
Orations and Speeches. Boston: 1850. V. 53
The Speech of Hon. Charles Sumner, of Massachusetts, on the Cession of Russian America to the United States. Washington: 1867. V. 47; 53

SUMNER, CHARLES PINCKNEY
The Compass. Boston: 1795. V. 54

SUMNER, HEYWOOD
Sintram and His Companions. London: 1883. V. 49

SUMNER, JAMES
The Mysterious Marbler. North Hills: 1976. V. 53

SUMNER, JAMES B.
The Enzymes: Chemistry and Mechanism in Action. New York: 1950. V. 48

SUMNER, L.
Birds and Mammals of the Sierra with Records from Sequoia and Kings Canyon National Parks. Berkeley: 1953. V. 54

SUMPTER, JESSE
Paso Del Aguila, a Chronicle of Frontier Days on the Texas Border as Recorded in the Memoirs of Jesse Sumpter. Encino: 1969. V. 53

THE SUN Calendar 1920. London: 1920. V. 51

THE SUN Princess Fairy Stories. London: 1930. V. 49

SUN BEAR
At Home in the Wilderness. Sparks: 1968. V. 50

SUNDAY Alphabet by C.S.C. London: 1861. V. 49

SUNDAY Water-Party. A Poem Published for the Benefit of the Benevolent Society, for the Relief of the Sick and Aged Poor, at Cambridge. Cambridge: 1804. V. 54

SUNDAY, WILLIAM
Gah Dah Gwa Stee. Pryor: 1953. V. 52

SUNDBERG, JOHN
Health Hints for Travelers. Philadelphia: 1884. V. 54

SUNDEVALL, C.
Svenska Foglarna. Stockholm: 1856-86. V. 47

SUNDRY Items. Grimsby: 1887. V. 49

SUNSET COPPER MINING CO.
Prospectus of the Sunset Copper Mining Company of Everett, Washington. New York: 1900. V. 52

SUNSHINE in the Country. A Book of Rural Poetry. London: 1861. V. 54

SUNU, CHOI
5000 Years of Korean Art. Seoul: 1979. V. 47

A SUPPLEMENT to the Court of Adultery. Addressed to the Maid of Honour. London: 1778. V. 48

SUPPRESSION of the Taiping Rebellion in the Departments Around Shanghai. Shanghai: 1871. V. 52

SUPRON, L. F.
Medical and Civil Defense in Total War. Jerusalem: 1961. V. 52

SURBY, RICHARD W.
Grierson's Raids and Hatch's Sixty-Four Days March, with Biographical Sketches, and the Life and Adventures of Chickasaw, the Scout. Chicago: 1865. V. 48; 54

SURDAM, CHARLES E.
Beautiful Homes of Morris County and Northern New Jersey. Morristown: 1915?. V. 49

A SURE Guide to Merchants, Custom-House Officers, &c. or the Modern Practice of the Court of Exchequer, in Prosecutions Relating to His Majesty's Revenue of the Customs. London: 1730. V. 54

THE SURF Riders of Hawaii. Honolulu: 1920. V. 47

SURIREY DE SAINT-REMY, PIERRE
Memoires d'Artillerie. Amsterdam: 1702. V. 53

SURIUS, LAURENTIUS
Commentarivs Brevis Rervm in Orbe Gestaravm, ab Anno Salvtis M.D. Vsqve in Annvm MDLXXIIII. Coloniae: 1574. V. 53

LES SURPRISES. Livre D'Images. Paris: 1870. V. 48

SURR, THOMAS SKINNER
Richmond; or, Scenes in the Life of a Bow Street Officer, Drawn Up From His Private Memoranda. London: 1827. V. 51
A Winter in London; or, Sketches of Fashion; a Novel. London: 1806. V. 50; 51

SURREY Archaeological Collections. Guildford, Surrey: 1901-89. V. 50

SURREY, HENRY HOWARD, EARL OF
Poems... London: 1717. V. 50; 51
The Poems of Henry Howard Earl of Surrey. London: 1866. V. 51
The Works of. London: 1815. V. 48

SURTEES, ROBERT SMITH
Analysis of the Hunting Field... London: 1846. V. 47
Ask Mamma. London: 1857-58. V. 52; 54
Ask Mamma. London: 1858. V. 47; 48; 50; 51
Handley Cross... London. V. 49; 51; 54
Handley Cross... London: 1843. V. 49
Handley Cross... London: 1853-54. V. 54
Handley Cross... London: 1854. V. 48; 49; 53
Handley Cross... London: 1854/65. V. 48; 50
Handley Cross... London: 1920. V. 49; 50
Hawbuck Grange; or, The Sporting Adventures of Thomas Scott, Esq. London: 1847. V. 47
Hillingdon Hall; or, the Cockney Squire, A Tale of Country Life. London: 1845. V. 47
The Horseman's Manual. London: 1831. V. 47; 48; 52
The Horseman's Manual... New York: 1832. V. 47
Hunts with Jorrocks. London. V. 51
Jorrocks' Jaunts and Jollities. London. V. 54
Jorrocks' Jaunts and Jollities... Philadelphia: 1838. V. 47
Jorrocks' Jaunts and Jollities... London: 1843. V. 53
Jorrocks' Jaunts and Jollities. London: 1869. V. 47; 49
Mr. Facey Romford's Hounds. London: 1864-65. V. 54
Mr. Facey Romford's Hounds. London: 1865. V. 50
Mr. Facey Romford's Hounds. London: 1865. V. 47; 48; 49; 50; 51
Mr. Sponge's Sporting Tour. London. V. 50
Mr. Sponge's Sporting Tour. London: 1852. V. 48
Mr. Sponge's Sporting Tour. London: 1852-53. V. 47
Mr. Sponge's Sporting Tour. London: 1853. V. 48; 51
Mr. Sponge's Sporting Tour. New York: 1856. V. 48
Mr. Sponge's Sporting Tour. London: 1860. V. 52; 53
Mr. Sponge's Sporting Tour. London: 1875. V. 48; 51
Mr. Sponge's Sporting Tour. London: 1888. V. 51
Mr. Sponge's Sporting Tour. London: 1890. V. 51
Novels... London: 1847-65. V. 47
The Novels... London: 1853/54/58/60/. V. 48
The Novels... London: 1880. V. 48
Novels... London: 1880s. V. 47
Novels. London: 1888. V. 51
Novels. London: 1929-30. V. 47; 50
Plain or Ringlets?. London: 1859-60. V. 48
Plain or Ringlets?. London: 1860. V. 48; 49; 50; 52; 53
Scenes and Characters. London: 1948. V. 47
Selected Works, Including: Ask Mamma; Plain or Ringlets; Hawbuck Grange; Mr. Sponge's Sporting Tour; Mr. Romford's Hounds; and Handley Cross. London. V. 52
Sporting Novels. London: 1880. V. 47; 50
Sporting Novels. London: 1890. V. 47
Sporting Novels. London: 1890's. V. 52
The Sporting Novels. London: 1899. V. 49

SURTEES, ROBERT SMITH continued
Thoughts on Hunting and Other Matters. Edinburgh: 1925. V. 47
Works: Handley Cross; Plain or Ringlets; Hawbuck Grange' Mr. Sponge's Sporting Tour; Mr. Facey Romford's Hounds; Ask Mamma; Hillingdon Hall; Young Tom Hall; Mr. Jorrocks's Jaunts and Jollitites. 1981-88. V. 47
Young Tom Hall; His Heart-Aches and Horses. Edinburgh: 1926. V. 51

SURTEES, VIRGINIA
Dante Gabriel Rossetti. 1828-1882. A Catalogue Raisonne... London: 1971. V. 49
Dante Gabriel Rossetti 1828-1882. The Paintings and Drawings. A Catalogue Raisonne. Oxford: 1971. V. 49; 52; 54

SURTEES, WILLIAM
Twenty-Five Years in the Rifle Brigade. Edinburgh: 1833. V. 51

SURVIVAL This Way: Interviews with American Indian Poets. Tucson: 1987. V. 51

SUSANNE
Famous Saddle Horses. Louisville: 1942/42/47. V. 53
Famous Saddle Horses. Louisville: 1947. V. 49; 51

SUSSEX ARCHAELOGICAL SOCIETY
Sussex Archaeological Collections. London: 1848-1980. V. 49; 52

SUSSEX ARCHAEOLOGICAL SOCIETY
Sussex Archaeological Collections. London: 1954-92. V. 52

SUTCLIFF, ROBERT
Travels in Some Parts of North America, in the Years 1804, 1805 & 1806. New York: 1804-06. V. 47
Travels in Some Parts of North America, in the Years 1804, 1805 & 1806. York: 1811. V. 49; 50; 52; 53
Travels in Some Parts of North America, in the Years 1804, 1805 & 1806. Philadelphia: 1812. V. 47; 53
Travels in Some Parts of North America, in the Years 1804, 1805 & 1806. York: 1815. V. 54

SUTCLIFFE, G. LISTER
The Modern Carpenter, Jointer and Cabinet-Maker. London: 1902-04. V. 51

SUTCLIFFE, HALLIWELL
The Striding Dales. London: 1929. V. 53

SUTCLIFFE, JOHN
Drawing Book of Horses, in Progressive Lessons. London: 1855. V. 50
Drawing Book of Horses, in Progressive Lessons. London: 1860. V. 48

SUTCLIFFE, JOHN H.
British Optical Association Library and Museum Catalogue. London: 1932. V. 49

SUTCLIFFE, R. J.
Richard Sutcliffe. The Pioneer of Underground Belt Conveying. Edinburgh: 1955. V. 50

SUTER, H.
Manual of the New Zealand Mollusca. London: 1913-15. V. 54

SUTHERLAND, A.
A Summer in Prairie-Land: Notes of a Tour Through the North-West Territory. Toronto: 1882. V. 47

SUTHERLAND, ALEXANDER
St. Kathleen; or, the Rock of Dunnismoyle. London: 1820. V. 50; 54

SUTHERLAND, C. H. V.
Roman Coins. New York: 1974. V. 48

SUTHERLAND, DAVID
A Tour Up the Straits, From Gibraltar to Constantinople... London: 1790. V. 47; 51

SUTHERLAND, DUCHESS OF
Wayfarer's Love Contributions from Living Poets. Westminster: 1904. V. 48

SUTHERLAND, G. A.
The Heart in Early Life. London: 1914. V. 49
A System of Diet and Dietetics. London: 1908. V. 49

SUTHERLAND, GEORGE
A Manual of the Geography and Natural and Civil History of Prince Edward Island. Charlottesville: 1861. V. 48; 51
The South Australian Company, a Study in Colonisation. London: 1898. V. 50

SUTHERLAND, GRAHAM
Complete Graphic Work. London: 1978. V. 54

SUTHERLAND, J.
The Adventures of an Elephant Hunter. London: 1912. V. 49

SUTHERLAND, JAMES
Essays on the Eighteenth Century, Presented to David Nichol Smith in Honour of His Seventieth Birthday. Oxford: 1945. V. 53

SUTHERLAND, JOHN
Other Canadians. Montreal: 1946. V. 52

SUTHERLAND, LIEUT.
Accurate Account of the Loss of His Majesty's Ship Litchfield...On the Coast of Barbary. London: 1809. V. 53

SUTHERLAND, REDDING, MRS.
Five Years Within the Golden Gate. London: 1868. V. 50

SUTHERLAND, ROBERT
Zambesi Camp Fires. London: 1935. V. 49

SUTHERLAND, ROBERT Q.
The Book of Colt Firearms. Kansas City: 1971. V. 52

SUTHERLAND, W.
The Sign Writer and Glass Embosser. Manchester: 1898. V. 53

SUTHERLAND HARRIS, ANN
Andrea Sacchi. London: 1977. V. 49; 52; 54

SUTPHEN, W. G. VAN T.
The Golfer's Alphabet. New York: 1898. V. 54

SUTRO
Catalogue of Mexican Pamphlets in the Sutro Collection 1623-1888. With Supplements 1605-1887. New York: 1971. V. 48; 51

SUTRO, ADOLPH
Closing Argument of Adolph Sutro on the Bill Before Congress to Aid the Sutro Tunnel... Washington: 1872. V. 48; 52
The Mineral Resources of the United States and the Importance and the Necessity of Inaugurating a Rational System of Mining... Baltimore: 1868. V. 47
The Sutro Tunnel to the Comstock Lode in the State of Nevada. New York: 1866. V. 52
The Sutro Tunnel...to the Comstock Lode in the State of Nevada. London: 1873. V. 51

SUTRO, ALFRED
The Batheaston Parnassus Fairs: a Manuscript Identified. San Francisco: 1936. V. 47
Words at Play by Adam Smart. San Francisco: 1939. V. 47

SUTRO, OSCAR
Some Remarks On Shakespeare. Before the Roxburghe Club of San Francisco on the Evening of September 18, 1933. San Francisco: 1933. V. 48

SUTRO, THEODORE
The Sutro Tunnel Company and the Sutro Tunnel... New York: 1887. V. 47

SUTTER, BARTON
Cedarhome. Bockport: 1977. V. 52

SUTTER, JOHANN AUGUST
The Diary of Johann August Sutter. San Francisco: 1932. V. 47

SUTTER, JOHN
New Helvetia Diary. A Record of Events kept by John A. Sutter and His Clerks at New Helvetia, California, from September 9, 1845 to May 25 1848. San Francisco: 1939. V. 48; 54

SUTTON & SONS
Sutton's Spring Catalogue for 1875. Reading: 1875. V. 49

SUTTON, EDWARD
Anthropophagus: the Man Eater. London: 1624. V. 47

SUTTON, G.
The Life and Writings of Menlove Edwards. London: 1961. V. 52; 53

SUTTON, G. M.
Exploration of Southampton Island, Hudson Bay. 1929-30. Pittsburgh: 1932-36. V. 53

SUTTON, RICHARD L.
An African Holiday. 1924. V. 48; 54
An African Holiday. St. Louis: 1924. V. 52; 54
Tiger Trails in Southern Asia. 1926. V. 48

SUZOR, RENAUD
Hydrophobia. London: 1887. V. 50; 51; 54

SUZUKI, D. T.
Essays in Zen Buddhism. First Series. London: 1927. V. 51
Essays in Zen Buddhism. Second Series. London: 1933. V. 51

SUZUKI, M.
Wooden Houses. New York: 1979. V. 50; 51; 53

SVEVO, ITALO
Confessions of Zeno. London & New York: 1930. V. 48; 52

SVININ, PAUL
Picturesque United States of America 1811, 1812, 1813... New York: 1930. V. 53

SVOBODA, A.
The Seven Churches of Asia. London: 1869. V. 48; 49

SVOBODA, ANTONIN
Computing Mechanisms and Linkages. New York: 1948. V. 48; 50; 52; 54

SWAAN, W.
The Gothic Cathedral. London: 1969. V. 54

SWAIM, WILLIAM
A Treatise on Swaim's Panacea: Being a Recent Discovery, for the Cure of Scrofula or King's Evil, Mercurial Disease, Deep-Seated Syphilis... Philadelphia: 1822. V. 50

SWAIN, DAVID L.
Early Times in Raleigh: Addresses. Raleigh;: 1867. V. 48

SWAIN, JOHN
The Historical Volume and Reference Works covering Bassett, City of Industry, La Habra, La Mirada, La Puente, Pico Rivera, Santa Fe Springs, Walnut, Whittier. Whittier: 1963. V. 50

SWAINSON, WILLIAM
On the History and Natural Arrangement of Insects. London: 1840. V. 54
On the Natural History and Classification of Birds. London: 1836-37. V. 49
A Selection of the Birds of Brazil and Mexico. London: 1841. V. 48
Taxidermy, Bibliography and Biography. London: 1840. V. 54
A Treatise on the Geography and Classification of Animals. London: 1835. V. 54
Zoological Illustrations, or Original Figures and Descriptions of New, Rare, or Interesting Animals... London: 1820-33. V. 48; 49; 50; 54

SWALES, FRANK
Driving As I Found It. What to Drive. How to Drive. London: 1891. V. 47

SWALLOW, GEORGE CLINTON
Geological Report of the Country Along the Line of the South Western Branch of the Pacific Railroad, State of Missouri... St. Louis: 1859. V. 47; 48

SWAMMERDAM, J.
Biblia Naturae; Sive, Historia Insectorum. Leiden: 1737-38. V. 47

SWAN, ABRAHAM
The British Architect, or the Builder's Treasury of Stair-Cases... London: 1765?. V. 53
A Collection of Designs in Architecture. London: 1770. V. 50

SWAN, ANNIE S.
The Woman at Home. London: 1898-1904. V. 50

SWAN, JAMES G.
The Haidah Indians of Queen Charlotte's Islands, British Columbia. (with) The Indians of Cape Flattery, at the Entrance to the Strait of Fuca, Washington Territory. Washington: 1874/70. V. 53
The Northwest Coast; or, Three Years' Residence in Washington Territory. New York: 1857. V. 51

SWAN, JOHN
Explanation of an Improved Mode of Tanning; Laid Down from Practical Results... London: 1821. V. 52
Speculum Mundi... London: 1635. V. 54
Speculum Mundi. Cambridge: 1643. V. 53

SWAN, JOHN A.
A Trio to the Gold Miner of California in 1882. San Francisco: 1960. V. 52

SWAN, JOSEPH
The Brain in Relation to the Mind. London: 1854. V. 47
Delineations of the Brain in Relation to Voluntary Motion. London: 1864. V. 51; 53; 54
A Demonstration of the Nerves of the Human Body. London: 1834. V. 47
Illustrations of the Comparative Anatomy of the Nervous System. London: 1864. V. 53; 54

SWAN, JOSEPH R.
A Treatise on the Law Relating to the Powers and Duties of Justices of the Peace and Constables in the State of Ohio, with Practical Forms. Columbus: 1837. V. 53

SWANK, JAMES B.
Statistics of the Iron and Steel Production of the United States. Washington: 1881. V. 54

SWANN, HOWARD KIRKE
A Monograph of the Birds of Prey... London: 1930-45. V. 49; 50
A Monograph of the Birds of Prey; Accipitres. London: 1924-45. V. 48; 52; 53; 54
Nature in Acadie. London: 1895. V. 47
A Synopsis of Accipitres (Diurnal Birds of Prey)... London: 1922. V. 50; 51; 53; 54

SWANN, THOMAS BURNETT
Alas, in Lilliput. Worcester: 1964. V. 52

SWAN'S Views of the Lakes of Scotland: a Series of Views...with Historical and Descriptive Illustrations... Glasgow: 1836. V. 51

SWANSEA, HENRY HUSSEY VIVIAN, 1ST BARON
Notes of a Tour in America. From August 7th to November 17th, 1877. London: 1878. V. 53

SWANSON, VERN G.
The Biography and Catalogue Raisonne of the Paintings of Sir Lawrence Alma-Tadema. London: 1990. V. 52; 53

SWANTON, JOHN R.
Social Condition, Beliefs, Linguistic Relationship of Tinglit Indians. Washington: 1908. V. 50

SWANWICK, MICHAEL
Stations of the Tide. New York: 1981. V. 51
Stations of the Tide. 1991. V. 49
Stations of the Tide. New York: 1991. V. 51; 52

SWARBRECK, S. D.
Sketches in Scotland Drawn from Nature and On Stone. London: 1845. V. 48; 52

SWARBRICK, JOHN
Robert Adam and His Brothers: Their Lives, Work and Influence on English Architecture, Decoration and Furniture. London: 1915. V. 52

SWART, P.
Afbeelding Van de Zaal En't Praalbed Waar Op...Willem Karel Hendrik Friso, Prinse Van Oranje...(with) Lyk-Staetsie Van Zyne Door-Luchtigste...Willem Carel Hendrik Friso... Amsterdam: 1752. V. 48

SWASEY, WILLIAM F.
The Early Days and Men of California... Oakland: 1891. V. 50

SWAUGER, J. L.
Rock Art of the Upper Ohio Valley. Graz: 1974. V. 51

SWAYNE, GEORGE C.
Lake Victoria. Edinburgh: 1868. V. 49

SWAYNE, H. G. C.
Seventeen Trips through Somaliland. London: 1895. V. 48
Through the Highlands of Siberia. 1904. V. 52

SWAYSLAND, WALTER
Familiar Wild Birds... London: 1883. V. 50
Familiar Wild Birds. London: 1894-99. V. 50; 54
Familiar Wild Birds. London: 1901-03. V. 49

SWAYZE, NATHAN L.
Engraved Powder Horns of the French and Indian War and Revolutionary War Era. Yazoo City: 1978. V. 51

SWEDBURG, JOHAN
Dissertatio Gradualis de Svionum in America Colonia... Uppsala: 1709. V. 47

SWEDEN. TREATIES, ETC.
Wanskaps och Handels Tractat Emellan...Swerige och the Forrente Staterne i Norra America...Traite d'Amitie et de Commerce entre...Suede et les etats Unis de l'Amerique Septentrionale... Stockholm: 1785. V. 48

SWEDENBORG, EMANUEL
Arcana Coelestia: Heavenly Arcana... London: 1926-09. V. 51
Swedenborg's Works. London: 1930. V. 52
A Treatise on the Nature of Influx, or, of the Intercourse Between the Soul and Body, Which is Supposed to be Either by Physical Influx, or by spiritual Influx or by Pre-Established Harmony. Boston: 1794. V. 52

SWEDENBORG, EMMANUEL
The True Christian Religion... Boston: 1833. V, 47

SWEDIAUR, FRANCOIS XAVIER
A Complete Treatise on the Symptoms, Effects, Nature and Treatment of Syphilis. Philadelphia: 1815. V. 50
Practical Observations on the More Obstinate and Inveterate Venereal Complaints. London: 1784. V. 47
Practical Observations on Venereal Complaints. New York: 1788. V. 52

SWEENEY, JAMES JOHNSON
Antoni Gaudi. London: 1960. V. 50
Marc Chagall. 1946. V. 50
Marc Chagall. New York: 1946. V. 47
Three Young Rats and Other Rhymes. New York: 1944. V. 48; 49; 53

SWEENEY, THOMAS W.
Military Occupation of California 1849-1853. Washington: 1907. V. 52

SWEENEY, W. ALLISON
History of the American Negro in the Great World War: His Splendid Record in the Battle Zones of Europe. 1919. V. 53

SWEET, ALEXANDER E.
On a Mexican Mustang, Through Texas, from the Gulf to the Rio Grande. Hartford: 1883. V. 48; 53; 54
On a Mexican Mustang, Through Texas, from the Gulf to the Rio Grande. London: 1883. V. 54
On a Mexican Mustang through Texas, From the Gulf to the Rio Grande. London: 1884. V. 48
Sketches from Texas Siftings. New York: 1882. V. 49
Three Dozen Good Stories from Texas Siftings...With Nearly 100 Illustrataions by Thomas Worth and Other Artists. New York & Chicago: 1887. V. 48

SWEET, ROBERT
The Botanical Cultivator; or Instructions for the Management and Propagation of the Plants Cultivated in...Great Britain. London: 1821. V. 48
The British Flower Garden. London: 1823-38. V. 50
Cistinae. The Natural Order of Cistus, or Rock Rose. London: 1825-30. V. 47; 48; 51
Flora Australasica; or, a Slection of Handsome, or Curious Plants, Nataives of New Holland and the south Sea Islands... London: 1827-28. V. 53
Hortus Suburbanus Londinensis; or, a Catalogue of Plants Cultivated in the Neighbourhood of London... London: 1818. V. 49

SWEETS for Leisure Hours. London: 1820. V. 47
SWEETS for Leisure Hours. London: 1825. V. 50

SWEETSER, M. F.
Chisholm's Mount-Desert Guide-Book. Portland: 1888. V. 54

SWEETSER, WILLIAM
A Treatise on Consumption... Boston: 1836. V. 54

SWEM, EARL GREGG
A Bibliography of Virginia. Richmond: 1915-17. V. 51
A Bibliography of Virginia, Part I. Richmond: 1916. V. 54
Brothers of the Spade. Worcester: 1949. V. 47
The Jamestown 350th Anniversary Historical Booklets. Richmond: 1957. V. 51

SWETE, E. H.
Flora Birstoliensis. London & Bristol;: 1854. V. 54

SWETT, SAMUEL
History of Bunker Hill Battle. (with) Notes to His Sketch of Bunker-Hill Battle. Boston: 1825. V. 47

SWIETEN, GERARD VAN
The Commentaries Upon the Aphorisms of Dr. Herman Boerhaave, the Late Learned Professor of Physick in the University of Leyden. London: 1744-73. V. 53

SWIFT, GRAHAM
Ever After. London: 1992. V. 47
Learning to Swim and Other Stories. London: 1982. V. 47; 49
Shuttlecock. London: 1981. V. 47; 49; 50; 53
The Sweet Shop Owner. London: 1980. V. 48; 50
Waterland. London: 1983. V. 49; 51; 52; 54

SWIFT, JONATHAN
The Adventures of Captain Gulliver, in a Voyage to Lilliput. Glasgow: 1815. V. 49
Baucis and Philemon: a Poem...Together with Mrs. Harris's Earnest Petition....As Also An Ode Upon Solitude. London: 1709. V. 54
The Beauties of Swift; or, the Favorite Offspring of Wit & Genius. London: 1782. V. 47
The Benefit of Farting Explain'd; or the Fundament-All Cause of the Distempers Incidental to the Fair Sex... Longford: 1722. V. 53
Cadenus and Vanessa. London: 1726. V. 48
Capitain Lemuel Gullivers Resor, til Atskillige... Wasteras: 1772. V. 48; 50; 52
A Complete Collection of Genteel and Ingenious Conversation, According to the Most Polite Mode and Method Now Used at Court... London: 1738. V. 47; 49; 51; 53
The Complete Works of Jonathan Swift. London: 1869. V. 47
The Conduct of the Allies, and of the Late Ministry, In Beginning and Carrying On the Present War. London: 1711. V. 48; 52; 54
The Conduct of the Allies and the Late Ministry in Beginning and Carrying Out the Present War. London: 1712. V. 48
A Discourse Of the Contests and Dissensions Between the Nobles and the Commons in Athens and Rome, With the Consequences They Had Upon Both Those States. London: 1701. V. 50
Gulliver's Travels. London: 1803. V. 52
Gulliver's Travels. London: 1875. V. 51
Gulliver's Travels. Philadelphia: 1900. V. 49
Gulliver's Travels. London: 1909. V. 48; 49; 50; 51; 52; 54
Gulliver's Travels. London: 1910. V. 49
Gulliver's Travels. Chicago: 1912. V. 49
Gulliver's Travels. London: 1912. V. 53
Gulliver's Travels. Philadelphia: 1918. V. 49
Gulliver's Travels... London: 1920. V. 51
Gulliver's Travels. 1930. V. 51
Gulliver's Travels. London: 1930. V. 50; 53; 54
Gulliver's Travels... London: 1937. V. 47
Gulliver's Travels. London: 1939. V. 48
Her Majesties Most Gracious Speech to Both Houses of Parliament, On Thursday the Ninth Day of April, 1713. (and) The Humble Address Of the...Lords Spiritual and Temporal...Presented to her Majesty on Saturday the Eleventh Day of April, 1713. London: 1713. V. 49
The Hibernian Patriot. London: 1730. V. 52; 54
The Hibernian Patriot. London: 1750. V. 53
The History of the Four Last Years of the Queen. London: 1758. V. 47; 48; 49; 50; 51; 54
The Intelligencer. Dublin: 1729. V. 47; 48
The Intelligencer. London: 1729. V. 48
The Intelligencer. London: 1730. V. 48
Journal to Stella. Oxford: 1948. V. 49
The Lady's Dressing Room. London: 1732. V. 52
Letters Written by the Late Jonathan Swift... London: 1766. V. 47; 48
Letters Written by the Late Jonathan Swift... London: 1766-68. V. 47; 54
The Life and Genuine Character of Doctor Swift. London: 1733. V. 48; 51; 52; 54
Miscellaneous Poems. Waltham St. Lawrence: 1928. V. 48; 50; 52
Miscellaneous Works, Comical and Diverting. London i.e. The Hague: 1720. V. 48
Miscellanies in Prose and Verse. London: 1711. V. 47; 49; 54
Miscellanies in Prose and Verse. London: 1713. V. 47; 50; 51; 54
Miscellanies in Prose and Verse. London: 1713(1714). V. 50
Miscellanies: the Last Volume. 1728. V. 50
A New Journey to Paris: Together with Secret Transactions Between the F(renc)h K(in)g and an Eng-(lish) Gentleman. London: 1711. V. 54
On Poetry: a Rapsody. Dublin: 1733. V. 48; 52
On Poetry: a Rapsody. London: 1733. V. 49; 50
Poems of Dr. Jonathan Swift. Glasgow: 1774. V. 49
The Poetical Works. London: 1833-34. V. 48
The Poetical Works. London: 1853. V. 52
The Poetical Works... London: 1866. V. 51
Political Tracts. London: 1738. V. 48; 49; 53
A Proposal for Correcting, Improving and Ascertaining the English Tongue... London: 1712. V. 47
A Proposal Humbly Offered to the P------t, for the Most Effectual Preventing the Further Growth of Popery. Dublin: 1731. V. 52
Prose Works. Oxford: 1939-68. V. 52
The Publick Spirit of the Whigs... London: 1714. V. 48; 49; 50; 53
The Right of Precedence Between Physicians and Civilians Enquir'd Into. Dublin: 1720. V. 47
The Right of Precedence Between Physicians and Civilians Enquir'd Into. London: 1720. V. 48; 53
A Satire on Dr. D---ny. By Dr. Sw--t. London: 1730. V. 47
Selected Essays. London: 1925. V. 48
Selected Essays... Waltham St. Lawrence: 1925. V. 47; 48
Some Remarks On the Barrier Treaty. London: 1712. V. 49
The Swearer's-Bank; or, Parliamentary Security for Establishing a New Bank in Ireland. Dublin: 1721. V. 50
A Tale of a Tub. London: 1704. V. 47; 48; 54
A Tale of A Tub. London: 1710. V. 47; 49; 51; 53; 54
A Tale of a Tub. 1711. V. 52
A Tale of a Tub... London: 1711/14. V. 47
A Tale Of a Tub. London: 1724. V. 48
A Tale of a Tub. London: 1739. V. 48
A Tale of a Tub. Paris: 1781. V. 48
Tale of a Tub. Philadelphia: 1846. V. 54
A Tale of a Tub... 1970. V. 51
Travells Into Several Remote Nations of the World. London: 1726. V. 47; 48; 49; 51; 52; 53; 54
Travels Into Several Remote Nations of the World. London: 1727. V. 51; 52
Travels Into Several Remote Nations of the World. London: 1742. V. 48; 49; 51
Travels Into Several Remote Nations of the World... London: 1840. V. 53
Travels Into Several Remote Nations of the World... London: 1860. V. 51
Travels Into Several Remote Nations of the World. Waltham St. Lawrence: 1925. V. 49; 50; 51; 52; 53; 54
The Travels of Lemuel Gulliver. Baltimore: 1929. V. 48
Unpublished Letters of Dean Swift. London: 1899. V. 50
Verses on the Death of Doctor Swift... London: 1739. V. 52
Verses on the Death of Dr. Swift. 1992. V. 48
Verses on the Death of Dr. Swift... Market Drayton: 1992. V. 50
A Voyage to Lilliput and a Voyage to Brobdingnag Made by Lemuel Gulliver. New York: 1950. V. 49; 52; 54
Voyages du Capitaine Lemuel Gulliver, en Divers Pays Eloignez. The Hague: 1727. V. 54
The Wonderful Wonder of Wonders. London: 1722. V. 53
The Works... London: 1754-75. V. 53
The Works... London: 1755-64. V. 53
The Works... London: 1760-67. V. 51
The Works. London: 1768. V. 53
The Works. Dublin: 1768-72. V. 48
The Works... London: 1768-79/87. V. 52
The Works... London: 1768/75/69/68. V. 51
The Works. Edinburgh: 1778. V. 47
Works. London: 1801. V. 48; 54
Works. London: 1803. V. 52
Works. Edinburgh: 1814. V. 50; 53
The Works. Edinburgh: 1824. V. 49; 50; 51
The Works... London: 1850. V. 48; 54

SWIFT, THEOPHILUS
Letter to the King; In Which the Conduct of Mr. Lenox, and the Minister, in the Affair of the Duke of York, Is Fully Considered. London: 1789. V. 48

SWIFT, ZEPHANIAH
An Address to the Rev. Moses C. Welch, Containing an Answer to His Reply to the Corespondent, with Some Observations Respecting Certain Late Extraordianry Transactions at Woodstock. Windham: 1794. V. 51

SWIGGETT, HOWARD
War Out of Niagara: Walter Butler and the Tory Rangers. New York: 1933. V. 54

SWIGGETT, S. A.
The Bright Side of Prison Life. Experiences in Prison and Out.. Baltimore: 1897. V. 48; 49

SWINBURNE, ALGERNON CHARLES
The Age of Shakespeare. London: 1908. V. 51
Astrophel and Other Poems. London: 1894. V. 51
Atalanta in Calydon. London: 1865. V. 47; 51; 53; 54
Atalanta in Calydon. Boston: 1866. V. 51
Atalanta in Calydon. Boston: 1886. V. 47
Atalanta in Calydon... Hammersmith: 1894. V. 49
The Ballad of Bulgarie. London: 1893. V. 48
The Ballad of Dead Men's Bay. London: 1889. V. 47
Bothwell: a Tragedy. London: 1874. V. 48
A Channel Passage and Other Poems. London: 1904. V. 53
Charles Dickens. London: 1913. V. 47
Chastelard... London: 1865. V. 47; 50; 51; 52; 54
Chastelard. London: 1866. V. 47; 49; 51
Chastelard... New York: 1866. V. 51
The Devil's Due. London: 1897. V. 49
Essays and Studies. London: 1875. V. 51
Grace Darling. London: 1893. V. 47
The Heptalogia... London: 1880. V. 51
The Heptalogia. Portland: 1898. V. 49
Hide-and-Seek. London: 1975. V. 52
Hymn to Prosperpine. Waltham St. Lawrence: 1944. V. 52
In the Album of Adah Menken. London: 1883. V. 47
Laus Veneris... New York: 1866. V. 47; 53
Laus Veneris. London: 1948. V. 47
Laus Veneris. Waltham St. Lawrence: 1948. V. 49; 50; 51; 52
Letters from (the author) to A. H. Bullen. London: 1910. V. 49; 50
The Letters of Algernon Charles Swinburne. New York: 1919. V. 52
Letters to Edward Dowden and Other Correspondents. London: 1914. V. 49
Locrine a Tragedy. London: 1887. V. 47; 52
Love's Cross Currents, a Year's Letters. London: 1905. V. 51
Lucretia Borgia. The Chronicle of Tebaldeo Tebaldei. Renaissance Period. London: 1942. V. 48; 54
Marino Faliero. London: 1885. V. 54
Mary Stuart. London: 1881. V. 47; 51; 54
Miscellanies. London: 1886. V. 52; 54
Note of an English Republican on the Muscovite Crusade. London: 1876. V. 47; 49; 51; 54

SWINBURNE, ALGERNON CHARLES continued
A Note on Charlotte Bronte. London: 1877. V. 51; 52; 54
Notes on Poems and Reviews. London: 1866. V. 49; 51; 54
Notes on the Royal Academy Exhibition 1868. London: 1868. V. 51
Ode on the Proclamation of the French Republic. London: 1870. V. 51
Ode to Mazzini. The Saviour of Society. Liberty and Loyalty. Boston: 1913. V. 49
Pasiphae. Waltham St. Lawrence: 1950. V. 49; 52
The Poems. London: 1904. V. 49; 51; 53
The Poems... London: 1909. V. 50
The Poems... New York: 1928. V. 51
Poems and Ballads. London: 1866. V. 49; 51; 54
Poems and Ballads. London: 1908. V. 52
Poems and Ballads, Second Series. London: 1878. V. 47; 48
Posthumous Poems. London: 1917. V. 49; 54
Private and Confidential. 1892. V. 48
The Queen Mother. (and) Rosamund. London: 1860. V. 48; 49; 50; 51; 52
The Queen-Mother and Rosamond. London: 1868. V. 49
Rondeaux Parisiens. London: 1917. V. 49
Rosamund, Queen of the Lombards... London: 1899. V. 47; 49
Rosamund, Queen of the Lombards. London: 1900. V. 53
Selected Poems... London: 1928. V. 47; 48
Selected Poems. New York: 1928. V. 51
Siena. London: 1868. V. 47; 48; 50
Some Unpublished Verses to a Mistress. New York: 1903. V. 50
A Song Of Italy. London: 1867. V. 48; 49; 51; 54
Songs Before Sunrise. Boston: 1871. V. 48
Songs Before Sunrise. London: 1871. V. 47; 49; 51
Songs Before Sunrise. London: 1909. V. 47; 48; 49; 50; 52; 53; 54
Songs of Two Nations. London: 1875. V. 50
The Springtide of Life. London: 1918. V. 48; 50; 51; 52
The Springtide of Life. Garden City: 1926. V. 52
Studies in Prose and Poetry. London: 1894. V. 47; 51
A Study of Ben Johnson. London: 1889. V. 47; 51
The Swinburne Letters. New Haven: 1959-62. V. 49
The Tragedies... London: 1905. V. 53
The Tragedies. London: 1905-06. V. 51; 52; 53; 54
Under the Miscroscope. London: 1872. V. 51; 54
William Blake. London: 1868. V. 48; 49; 51
A Word for the Navy. London: 1887. V. 51; 54
A Year's Letters. Portland: 1901. V. 51

SWINBURNE, HENRY
The Courts of Europe, at the Close of the Last Century. London: 1841. V. 49
A Treatise of Testaments and Last Wills, Fit to Be Understood By All men, That They May Know, Whether, Whereof, and How to Make Them (etc.). London: 1677. V. 48

SWINDLER, MARY HAMILTON
Ancient Painting. New Haven: 1929. V. 49; 52

SWING, GILBERT S.
...Events in the Life and History of the Swing Family. Camden: 1889. V. 47; 49; 51

SWINHOE, ROBERT
Narrative of the North China Campaign of 1860. London: 1861. V. 51
On Some Birds from Hakidadi in Northern Japan. London: 1874-76. V. 48

SWINNTERTON, EMILY
George Eliot, Her Early Home. London: 1880. V. 51

SWINTON, ALAN A. CAMPBELL
The Principles and Practice of Electric Lighting. London: 1884. V. 53

SWINTON, ANDREW
Travels Into Norway, Denmark and Russia. In the Years 1788, 1789, 1790 and 1791. Dublin: 1792. V. 51

SWINTON, ARCHIBALD
Report of the Trial of Alexander Humphrys or Alexander Claiming the Title of Earl of Stirling, Before the High Court of Justiciary at Edinburgh, for the Crime of Forgery. Edinburgh: 1839. V. 48

SWINTON, JOHN
Considerations Concerning a Proposal for Dividing the Court of Session into Classes or Chambers; and for Limiting Litigation in Small Causes; and for the Revival of Jury-Trial in Certain Civil Actions. Edinburgh: 1789. V. 53

SWINTON, WILLIAM
The Twelve Decisive Battles of the War: a History of the Eastern and Western Campaigns in Relation to the Actions that Decided Their Issue. New York: 1867. V. 47

SWIRE, HERBERT
The Voyage of the Challenger. Waltham St. Lawrence: 1938. V. 47; 50

SWISHER, JAMES
How I Know, or Sixteen Years Eventful Experience... Cincinnati: 1881. V. 47; 52

SWISS Everest Expeditions. Everest. 1954. V. 53

SWISS Pictures. London. V. 54

SWITZER, STEPHEN
Ichnographia Rustica; or, the Nobleman, Gentleman and Gardener's Recreation. London: 1742. V. 49
The Practical Fruit Gardener. London: 1724. V. 48; 49

SWOPE, JOHN
Camera Over Hollywood. New York: 1939. V. 47

THE SWORN Book of Honorius the Magician.. Heptangle: 1977. V. 52

SWYNNERTON, C. F. M.
The Tsetse Flies of East Africa. 1936. V. 54
The Tsetse Flies of East Africa. London: 1936. V. 52

SYBEL, HEINRICH C. L. VON
History of the French Revolution. London: 1867-69. V. 49; 53

SYDENHAM, EDWARD A.
Aes Grave, a Study of the Cast Coinages of Rome and Central Italy. London: 1926. V. 48
The Coinage of Caesaria in Cappadocia. London: 1933. V. 48
The Roman Republican Coinage. London: 1952. V. 48

SYDENHAM, THOMAS
The Entire Works of Dr. Thomas Sydenham, newly Made English From the Originals... London: 1742. V. 48
Opera Medica; in Hae Novissima Editione Variis Variorum Praestantissimorum Medicorum Observation-ibus... Venice: 1762. V. 52
Opera Universa. London: 1685. V. 51
Opera Universa. Lugduni Batavorum: 1726. V. 49; 50
Processus Integri In Morbis Fere Omnibus Curandis... London: 1726. V. 48; 49; 50
The Works... London: 1788. V. 48
The Works... Philadelphia: 1809. V. 52
Works... London: 1848-50. V. 49; 50; 52; 54

SYDNEY, ALGERNON
Discourse Concerning Government. London: 1763. V. 51; 52
The Works of Algernon Sydney. London: 1772. V. 54

SYDNEY Harbour Bridge. London: 1932. V. 49

SYDNEY, PHILIP
Sir Philip Sydney's Defence of Poetry, and Observations on Poetry and Eloquence from the Discoveries of Ben Jonson. London: 1787. V. 52

SYDNEY'S Letter to the King; and Other Correspondence, Connected with the Reported Exclusion of Lord Byron's Monument from Westminster Abbey. London: 1828. V. 54

SYKES, ARTHUR ASHLEY
An Essay on the Nature, Design and Origin of Sacrifices. London: 1748. V. 47
A Paraphrase and Notes Upon the Epistle to the Hebrews. London: 19755. V. 52

SYKES, C. A.
Service and Sport on the Tropical Nile. London: 1903. V. 47

SYKES, CHRISTOPHER
Wassmuss, "The German Lawrence". London: 1936. V. 50

SYKES, D. F. E.
Dorothy's Choice. Huddersfield: 1910. V. 48
Miriam: A Tale of Pole Moor and the Greenfield Hills. Huddersfield: 1912. V. 48

SYKES, EDWARD TURNER
Walthall's Brigade. 1916. V. 49; 53

SYKES, ELLA
Through Deserts and Oases of Central Asia. London: 1920. V. 48; 50; 51

SYKES, GEORGE
The Life and Death of Sir Henry Vane, Kt. Or a Short Narrative of the Main Passages of His Early Pilgrimage... London: 1662. V. 48; 50

SYKES, JOHN
Local Records...Register of Remarkable Events...Northumberland... Newcastle-upon-Tyne: 1824. V. 50
Local Records...Register of Remarkable Events...Northumberland... Newcastle: 1866-67. V. 47

SYKES, MARK MASTERMAN
A Catalogue of the Highly Valuable Collection of prints, the property of the Late Sir Mark Masterman Sykes...of Sledmere House. London: 1824. V. 48; 50
Catalogue of the Splendid, Curious and Extensive Library... London: 1824. V. 50

SYKES, PERCY
A History of Persia. London: 1920. V. 50

SYKES, PERCY MOLESWORTH
Ten Thousand Miles in Persia or Eight Years in Iran. London: 1902. V. 54

SYLVAN
Formula of Prescriptions, and Various Instructions for the Service and Guidance of Those Who Have Applied, Are Applying, or Shall Apply, to the Enemy of Human Diseases... Providence: 1812. V. 49; 54

SYLVAN'S Pictorial Handbook to the English Lakes. London: 1847. V. 52

SYLVANUS, GEORGIUS
Scholia in Librum Plutarchi (Greek title) seu De Liberorum Educatione. Londini: 1684. V. 50

SYLVEIRA, MANOEL DA
Sermao na Profissam das Madres Soror Clara Maria de Jesus, Soror Anna da Santissima Trindade, Soror Ignez de Santa Tereza, Soror Joanna da Natividade... Lisbon: 1747. V. 48

SYLVESTER, CHARLES
The Philosophy of Domestic Economy... Nottingham: 1819. V. 53

SYLVESTER, HERBERT MILTON
Indian Wars of New England. Boston: 1910. V. 50

SYLVESTER, J. J.
The Collected Mathematical Papers. Cambridge: 1904-12. V. 50

SYLVESTER, NATHANIEL BARTLETT
Historical Sketches of Northern New York and the Adirondack Wilderness... Troy: 1877. V. 54

SYLVIUS, FRANCISCUS DE LA BOE
Opera Medica. Amsterdam: 1679. V. 47
Opera Medica. Amsterdam: 1680. V. 53

SYME, JAMES
The Principles of Surgery. Edinburgh: 1837. V. 48; 49; 50; 51; 53

SYME, P.
A Treatise on British Song Birds. Edinburgh: 1823. V. 49

SYME, PATRICK
Werner's Nomenclature of Colours, with Additions... Edinburgh: 1814. V. 54

SYMEONOGLOU, SARANTIS
The Topography of Thebes from the Bronze Age to Modern Times. Princeton: 1985. V. 50

SYMES, MICHAEL
An Account of an Embassy to the Kingdom of Ava, Sent by Governor-General of India in the Year 1795. London: 1800. V. 54

SYMES PRIDEAUX, T.
On Economy of Fuel, Particularly with Reference to Reverberatory Furnaces for the Manufacture of Iron and to Steam Boilers. London: 1853. V. 50

SYMINGTON, JOHN ALEXANDER
The Brotherton Library. Leeds: 1931. V. 53
Some Unpublished Letters of Walter Scott from the Collection in the Brotherton Library. Oxford: 1932. V. 52; 54

SYMINGTON, N.
The Night Climbers of Cambridge. 1937. V. 53

SYMINTON, ANDREW JAMES
Samuel Lover: a Biographical Sketch. London: 1880. V. 51

SYMMACHUS, QUINTUS AURELIUS
Epistolarvm...Libri Decem. Paris: 1580. V. 48

SYMMES, FRANK R.
History of the Old Tennent Church. Cranbury: 1904. V. 47; 49; 51

SYMMONS, CHARLES
The Life of John Milton. London: 1810. V. 49; 54
Some Account of the Life and Writings of John Milton. London: 1826. V. 54

SYMMONS, JOHN
Thoughts On the Present Prices of Provisions, Their Causes and Remedies; Addressed to All Ranks of People. London: 1800. V. 52

SYMOND, ARTHUR
An Introduction to the Study of Browning. London: 1886. V. 48

SYMONDS, ARTHUR
Silhouettes. London: 1892. V. 47

SYMONDS, B.
A Treatise on Field Diversions. Yarmouth: 1823. V. 47
A Treatise on Field Diversions. 1825. V. 52
A Treatise on Field Diversions. Yarmouth: 1825. V. 51

SYMONDS, EMILY MORSE
At John Murray's 1843-1892. Records of a Literary Circle. L: 1932. V. 51
B. R. Haydon and His Friends. London: 1905. V. 52
Social Caricature in the Eighteenth Century. London: 1905. V. 50

SYMONDS, JOHN ADDINGTON
Anima Figura. London: 1882. V. 47; 48; 52
Blank Verse. London: 1895. V. 48
The Escorial - a Prize Poems, Recited in the Theatre, Oxford. London: 1860. V. 47; 48; 53
Essays Speculative and Suggestive. London: 1890. V. 47
Fragilia Labilia. Portland: 1902. V. 47
In the Key of Blue and Other Prose Essays. London and New York: 1893. V. 48; 50
The Letters 1844-1893. 1967-69. V. 52
The Life of Michelangelo Buonarroti: Based on Studies in the Archives of the Buonarroti Family at Florence. London: 1893. V. 50; 52
Many Moods. London: 1878. V. 48
Medieval Latin Student Songs. San Francisco: 1928. V. 47
Our Life in the Swiss Highlands. London: 1892. V. 52; 54
A Problem in Greek Ethics... London: 1901. V. 49; 53
A Problem in Modern Ethics, Being an Inquiry Into the Phenomenon of Sexual Inversion... London: 1896. V. 49
Renaissance in Italy. New York. V. 49
Renaissance In Italy... London: 1875. V. 53
Renaissance in Italy. London: 1875-86. V. 49; 52
Renaissance in Italy. London: 1877-86. V. 48
The Renaissance in Italy. London: 1880-86. V. 49; 52
Renaissance in Italy... London: 1886. V. 48
Shakespeare's Predecessors in the English Drama. London: 1884. V. 51
Shakespere's Predecessors in the English Drama. London: 1900. V. 51
Sleep and Dreams: Two Lectures Delivered at the Bristol Literary and Philosophical Institution. London & Bristol: 1851. V. 48
Vagabunduli Libellus. London: 1884. V. 48
Walt Whitman: a Study. London: 1893. V. 54
Wine, Women and Song... London: 1907. V. 48
Wine, Women and Song. Portland: 1918. V. 53

SYMONDS, MARY
Needlework Through the Ages. London: 1928. V. 53

SYMONDS, ROBERT WEMYSS
English Furniture from Charles II to George II. London: 1929. V. 48; 49; 50
Furniture Making in Seventeenth and Eighteenth Century England. London: 1955. V. 49
Masterpieces of English Furniture and Clocks. London: 1940. V. 53
Thomas Tompion: His Life and Work. London: 1941. V. 53
Thomas Tompion. His Life and Work. London: 1951. V. 54
Thomas Tompion: His Life and Work. London: 1969. V. 53

SYMONDS, WILLIAM
Pisgah Evangelica. London: 1606. V. 49

SYMONS, ALPHONSE JAMES ALBERT
Anthology of 'Nineties' Verse. 1928. V. 54
An Anthology of 'Nineties' Verse. London: 1928. V. 49
Emin. London: 1928. V. 52
An Episode in the Life of the Queen of Sheba. London: 1929. V. 50; 52
H. M. Stanley. London: 1933. V. 49
The Nonesuch Century. London: 1936. V. 48; 51; 53
The Quest for Corvo. London: 1934. V. 47

SYMONS, ARTHUR
Aubrey Beardsley. London: 1905. V. 51
The Cafe Royal and Other Essays. London: 1923. V. 51; 53; 54
Charles Baudelaire - a Study. London: 1920. V. 52
The Collected Works of Arthur Symons. London: 1924. V. 54
Confessions: a Study in Pathology. New York: 1930. V. 53; 54
Days and Nights. London: 1889. V. 48
Figures of Several Centuries. London: 1916. V. 53
From Catullus: Chiefly Concerning Lesbia. London: 1924. V. 54
Images of Good and Evil. London: 1899. V. 49; 53
An Introduction to the Study of Browning. London: 1886. V. 49; 53
Love's Cruelty. London: 1923. V. 54
Plays, Acting and Music - A Book of Theory. London: 1909. V. 54
Silhouettes. London: 1892. V. 47
Studies in Prose and Verse. London: 1904. V. 53
Studies in Strange Souls. London: 1929. V. 52; 53
Studies on Modern Painters. New York: 1925. V. 54
A Study of Walter Pater. London: 1932. V. 52
The Symbolist Movement in Literature. London: 1899. V. 53
Thomas Hardy. London: 1927. V. 52
Tragedies. London: 1916. V. 50
William Blake. London: 1907. V. 47
William Blake. London: 1970. V. 53

SYMONS, G. J.
The Eruption of Krakatoa and Subsequent Phenomena. London: 1888. V. 49
The Floating Island in Derwent Water, Its History and Mystery, With Notes of Other Dissimilar Islands. London: 1888. V. 50; 54

SYMONS, J.
Synopsis Plantarum Insulis Britannicis Indigenarum. London: 1798. V. 53

SYMONS, JULIAN
Confusions About X. London: 1939. V. 49
The Immaterial Murder Case. London: 1945. V. 50
The Modern Crime Story. Helsinki: 1986. V. 48
The Second Man - Poems. London: 1943. V. 49; 52
Somebody Else. Helsinki: 1990. V. 48

SYMONS, THOMAS W.
Report of an Examination of the Upper Columbia River and the Territory In Its Vicinity in September and October, 1881 to Determine Its Navigability and Adaptability to Steamboat Transportation. Washington: 1882. V. 48

SYMPSON, SAMUEL
A New Book of Cyphers, More Compleat and Regular Than Any Ever Publish'd. London: 1750?. V. 50; 52; 54
A New Book of Cyphers, More Compleat and Regular Than Ever Publish'd... London: 1736. V. 48; 49

SYMSON, PATRICK
The Historie of the Chvrch Since the Dayes of Our Saviour. London: 1624. V. 53

SYNGE, GEORGINA M.
A Ride through the Wonderland. London: 1892. V. 49

SYNGE, JOHN MILLINGTON
The Aran Islands. London: 1906. V. 48
The Aran Islands. Dublin/London: 1907. V. 48; 53
The Complete Works of... 1910. V. 49
The Complete Works of... Boston: 1912. V. 48
Deirdre of the Sorrows. Churchtown: 1910. V. 53

SYNGE, JOHN MILLINGTON continued
Deirdre of the Sorrows. New York: 1910. V. 51; 52
Playboy of the Western World. Dublin: 1907. V. 47; 54
The Playboy of the Western World. Dublin: 1912. V. 50
The Playboy of the Western World. Barre: 1970. V. 51
The Playboy of the Western World. Dublin: 1970. V. 49
Poems and Translations. Churchtown, Dundrum: 1909. V. 47
Poems and Translations. New York: 1909. V. 51
The Shadow of the Glen and Riders to the Sea. London: 1905. V. 47
The Works... Dublin: 1910. V. 53; 54
The Works. London: 1910. V. 50; 52; 53
The Works. London: 1911. V. 53
The Works... Boston: 1912. V. 49; 50

SYR Perceyvelle of Gales. Hammersmith: 1895. V. 54

SYRACUSE ORNAMENTAL CO., SYRACUSE, NEW YORK
Period Carvings. 1923. V. 50; 52

SYRETT, NETTA
The Old Miracle Plays of England. London: 1911. V. 47

SYRIACAE Linguae Pria Elementa. Antwerp: 1572. V. 48; 52

A SYSTEM of Civil and Criminal Law for the District of Columbia and for the Organization of the Courts Therein. Washington: 1833. V. 52

A SYSTEM of Exercise and Instruction of Field Artillery Including Manoeuvres for Light or Horse-Artillery. Boston: 1829. V. 49

SZABAD, EMERIC
Hungary Past and Present: Embracing its History from Magyar Conqest to the Present Time. Edinburgh: 1854. V. 49; 54

SZARKOWSKI, JOHN
Callahan. New York: 1976. V. 50
The Idea of Louis Sullivan. Minneapolis: 1956. V. 50; 51; 53
Irving Penn... Boston: 1984. V. 54
Irving Penn. New York: 1984. V. 50
William Eggleston's Guide. New York: 1976. V. 48
The Work of Atget. New York: 1981/82. V. 49
The Work of Atget. New York: 1981/82/83/85. V. 54

SZE, MAI MAI
The Tao of Painting... New York: 1956. V. 49; 53
The Tao of Painting. Princeton: 1963. V. 50

SZECHENYI, ZSIGMOND
Land of Elephants. 1935. V. 54
Land of Elephants. London: 1935. V. 47

SZEKELEY, EDMOND BORDEAUX
The World Picture of Zarathustra. Tecate: 1953. V. 48

SZIGETI, JOSEPH
With Strings Attached. New York: 1947. V. 49

SZUKALSKI, STANISLAW
Projects in Design, Sculpture and Architecture. Chicago: 1929. V. 51; 53
The Works of... Chicago: 1923. V. 51

SZYK, ARTHUR
Ink and Blood, a Book of Drawings. New York: 1946. V. 51
The New Order. New York: 1941. V. 48; 50; 51; 53

T

T., A.
Rich Storehouse or Treaxurie for the Diseased. London: 1631. V. 50

T., D.
Hieraginisticon: or, Corah's Doom, Being an Answer to Two Letters of Enquiry into the Grounds and Occasions of the Contempt of the Clergy and Religion. London: 1672. V. 47

T., E. S.
Another Nile Journal, and Notes from Egypt and Egypt and Elsewhere. Bayswater: 1881. V. 51

T., F.
The Wonders of a Week at Bath; in a Doggrel Address to the Hon. T. S-, from F. T-, Esq. of that City. London: 1811. V. 51

T., M. I. S.
Annine. A Novel. London: 1871. V. 54

T., O.
Tell-Tale Cupids Lately Discover'd in the Eyes of a Certain Court Lady, Now Displac'd. London: 1735. V. 48

T., R.
The Mother the Best Governess. London: 1839. V. 52

Tenants Law: a Treatise of Great Use, for Tenants and Farmers of All Kinds, and All Other Persons Whatsoever. London: 1674. V. 52
Ye Ancient Ballad of Chevy Chase. 1890. V. 54

T., T.
A Short Way to Know the World; Or the Rudiments of Geography. London: 1712. V. 47

TAAFE, DENNIS
An Impartial History of Ireland, from the Period of the English Invasion to the Present Time. Dublin: 1809-10-10-11. V. 53

TABB, JOHN BANISTER
Later Lyrics. London and New York: 1902. V. 50; 54
Poems by John B. Tabb. Boston: 1894. V. 48; 51

LE TABLEAU De La Croix Represente dans les Ceremonies de la Ste. Messe. Paris: 1653 at end. V. 49

TABOR, ELIZA STEPHENSON
Diary of a Novelist. London: 1871. V. 50
Hester's Sacrifice. London: 1866. V. 50

TABOR, J. A.
On the Improvement of the Colne Navigation: more especially from Colchester to Wivenhoe, in the County of Essex. Colchester: 1840. V. 51

TACHARD, GUY
Voyage de Siam. Paris: 1686. V. 49

TACITUS, CORNELIUS
The Annales of Cornelius Tacitus. (with) The End of Nero. London: 1640. V. 47; 49
The Annales. (with) The End of Nero and Beginning of Galba. The Life of Agricola. London: 1612. V. 48
The Annals and History of Cornelius Tacitus: His Account of the Ancient Germans and the Life of Agricola. London: 1716. V. 48
C. Cornelii Taciti Opera Quae Exstant, a Iusto Lipsio Postremum Recensita, Eiusque Auctis Emendatisque Commentariis Illustrata... Antwerp: 1648. V. 47
De Moribus Germanorum, et de Vita Agricolae; ex Editione Gabrielis Brotier. Londini: 1788. V. 48; 52
De Vita et Moribus Julii Agricolae Liber. Hammersmith: 1900. V. 48; 51; 52; 54
Exacta Cura Recognitus, et Emandatus. Venice: 1534. V. 50
Gli Annali di Cornelio Tacito Cavalier Romano de Fatti, e Guerre de Romani... Venetia: 1582. V. 50
Historiae Augustae. Venice: 1497. V. 48; 54
Opera Omnia. London: 1790-94. V. 48
Opera Quae Supersunt. Glasguae: 1753. V. 53
The Works. London: 1805. V. 47; 50; 52

TACOMA. CHAMBER OF COMMERCE
Second Annual Report of the Chamber of Commerce, of Tacoma, Washington Territory, with an Appendix. Tacoma: 1886. V. 47
Tacoma Illustrated. Chicago: 1889. V. 52

TACQUET, ANDREAS
Arithmeticae Theory et Praxis. Antwerp: 1682. V. 52

TADEMA, LAWRENCE ALMA
The Courting of Mary Smith. London: 1886. V. 50
The Keeper of the Keys. London: 1890. V. 50

TAFF, JOSEPH ALEXANDER
Maps of Segregated Coal Lands in the...Indian Territory. Washington: 1904. V. 49

TAFT, ROBERT
Photography and the American Scene. A Social History, 1839-1889. New York: 1938. V. 47

TAFT, WILLIAM H.
Address of William H. Taft In Response To Notification Speech at Cincinnati, Ohio, July 28, 1908. New York: 1908. V. 48

TAGAULT, JEAN
De Chirurgica Institutione Libri Quinque. Lyons: 1560. V. 48

TAGE LA COUR
The Murder of Santa Claus. Lars Bo: 1954. V. 51

TAGER, ALEXANDER B.
The Decay of Czarism, the Beiliss Trial, a Contribution to the History of the Political Reaction During the Last Years of Russian Czarism. Philadelphia: 1935. V. 51

TAGGARD, GENEVIEVE
For Eager Lovers. New York: 1922. V. 48

TAGLIENTI, GIOVANNI ANTONIO
Componimento Di Parlamenti, Nuovamente Stampato. In Vineggia: 1537. V. 47
Lo Presente Libro Insegna la Vera Arte delo Exclele(n)te Scrivere de Diverse Varie Sorti de Litere. Venice: 1550. V. 47

TAGORE, RABINDRANATH
Chitra. London: 1913. V. 49
Chitra... New York: 1914. V. 47; 48; 50
Gitanjal (Song Offerings). London: 1912. V. 49; 50
The King of the Dark Chamber. New York: 1914. V. 48; 50
The Post Office: a Play. 1914. V. 53
The Wreck. London: 1921. V. 53

TAGORE, SOURINDRO MOHUN
Victoria Samrajyan, or Sanskrit Stanzas (with a translation) on the Various Dependencies of the British Crown, Each Composed and Set to the Respective National Music, in Commemoration of the Assumption by Her Most Gracious Majesty the Queen Victoria... Calcutta: 1876. V. 52

TAHSIN AL-DIN
The Loves of Camarupa and Camalta, an Ancient Indian Tale. London: 1793. V. 52

TAILLANDIER, YVON
Indelible Miro. New York: 1972. V. 47; 50; 51; 52; 53

THE TAIN. Dublin: 1969. V. 50

TAINE, HIPPOLYTE ADOLPH
A History. London: 1886. V. 51
On Intelligence. New York: 1872. V. 49; 50
A Tour through the Pyrenees. New York: 1874. V. 49
A Tour through the Pyrenees. New York: 1875. V. 51

TAINE, JOHN
Before the Dawn. 1934. V. 52
The Crystal Horde. Reading: 1952. V. 50
The Forbidden Garden. 1947. V. 54
The Forbidden Garden. Reading: 1947. V. 52
G.O.G. 666. Reading: 1954. V. 50; 52
Quayle's Invention. New York: 1927. V. 52
Seeds of Life. 1951. V. 47; 51
Seeds of Life. Reading: 1951. V. 52
The Time Stream. 1946. V. 52

TAIT, HUGH
The Art of the Jeweller: a Catalogue of the Hull Grundy Gift to the British Museum: Jewellery, Engraved Gems and Goldsmiths' Work. London: 1984. V. 53

TAIT, JOHN
The Cave of Morar, the Man of Sorrows. London: 1774. V. 48
The Cave of Morar, the Man of Sorrows. London: 1775. V. 49

TAIT, R. LAWSON
The Pathology and Treatment of Diseases of the Ovaries... Birmingham: 1883. V. 51

TAIT, THOMAS
Bamburgh Castle; a Poem in Two Parts. Edinburgh: 1818. V. 54

TAIT, WILLIAM
Cruise of H.M.S. Cleopatra, 1892-1895. Plymouth: 1896. V. 51

TAKAHASHI, M.
Catalogue of Special Books on Christian Missions. Tenri: 1932/55/73. V. 47

TAKANO, S.
Birds of Japan in Photographs. Tokyo: 1981. V. 49

TAKASHIMA, S.
Illustrations of Japanese Life. Tokyo: 1896. V. 48

TAKA-TSUKASA, PRINCE
The Birds of Nippon. Tokyo: 1932-39. V. 48
The Birds of Nippon. Tokyo & London: 1932-43. V. 47

TAKESHI, KUNO
A Guide to Japanese Sculpture. Tokyo: 1963. V. 50

TAKHTAJAN, A.
Floristic Regions of the World. London: 1986. V. 48; 52

TAKING Possession of Monterey. Washington: 1843. V. 53

TAKINGS: or the Life of a Collegian. London: 1821. V. 54

TALAMANTEZ, INES
Tse-Gihi. Del mar: 1975. V. 49

TALBOT, CATHERINE
Essays on Various Subjects. London: 1772. V. 48

TALBOT, CLARE RYAN
Historic California in Bookplates. Los Angeles: 1936. V. 47; 49; 51; 54
In Quest of the Perfect Bookplate. Claremont: 1933. V. 47; 49; 54

TALBOT, D. AMAURY
Woman's Mysteries of Primitive People. London: 1915. V. 54

TALBOT, EDITH ARMSTRONG
Samuel Chapman Armstrong: a Biographical Study. New York: 1904. V. 52

TALBOT, EDWARD ALLEN
Five Years' Residence in the Canadas: Including a Tour through Part of the United States of America in the Year 1823. London: 1824. V. 53

TALBOT, ELEANOR W.
My Lady's Casket of Jewels and Flowers for Her Adorning. Boston: 1885. V. 47

TALBOT, EUGENE
Interstitial Gingivitis or so-Called Pyorrhoea Alveolaris. Philadelphia: 1899. V. 51; 54

TALBOT, FREDERICK A.
Making Good in Canada. London: 1912. V. 48; 50; 52
Motor-Cars and Their Story. London: 1912. V. 51

TALBOT, P. A.
Life in Southern Nigeria; the Magic, Beliefs and Customs of the Ibibio Tribe. London: 1923. V. 54

TALBOT, ROBERT
Letters on the French Nation, Considered in Its Different Departments... London: 1771. V. 54

TALBOT, S.
The Marvelous Book. Shanghai: 1930. V. 47

TALBOT, THEODORE
The Journals of Theodore Talbot. Portland: 1931. V. 50

TALBOT, WILLIAM
The Rev. Mr. Talbot's Narrataive of the Whole of His Proceedings Relative to Jonathan Britain. Bristol: 1772. V. 48; 53

TALBOT-KELLY, R. B.
The Way of Birds. London: 1937. V. 50

TALBOTT, JAMES
The Christian School-Master; or, the Duty of Those Who Are Employed in the Public Instruction of Children... London: 1811. V. 52

THE TALE of Mr. Tootleo and Tootleo Two. London: 1925/27. V. 49

THE TALE of the Weapon-Firthers Englished Out of the Icelandic. Edinburgh: 1902. V. 50

A TALE of the West, or, Life with a Sister. Providence: 1846. V. 51

A TALE of the Winds and the Waves: a Mournful Chant of Merrie Christmas. London: 1849. V. 53

TALES and Stories for Black Folks. Garden City: 1971. V. 54

TALES for Domestic Instruction: Containing the Histories of Ben Hallyard; Hannah Jenkins; John Aplin; Edward Fletcher, or the Necessity of Curbing Our Passions... London: 1806. V. 50

TALES of the Academy. London: 1820/21. V. 51

TALES of the Classics: a New Delineation of the Most Popular Fables, Legends and Allegories Commemorated in the Works of Poets, Painters and Sculptors. London: 1830. V. 52

THE TALES of the Genii. London: 1820. V. 50

TALES Original and Translated from the Spanish. By a Lady. London: 1810. V. 54

TALESE, GAY
New York: a Serendipiter's Journey. New York: 1961. V. 52

TALFOURD, THOMAS NOON
Final Memorials of Charles Lamb... London: 1848. V. 47; 50
Ion, A Tragedy. London: 1835. V. 47; 48
Ion: a Tragedy. London: 1836. V. 48

TALIAFERRO, HARDEN E.
Fisher's River (North Carolina): Scenes and Characters. New York: 1859. V. 47; 54

TALIESIN
The Poems of Taliesin. 1989. V. 52

TALLACK, WILLIAM
The California Overland Express. Los Angeles: 1935. V. 54
Friendly Sketches in America. London: 1861. V. 53

TALLENT, ANNIE D.
The Black Hills of the Last Hunting Ground of the Dakotahs. St. Louis: 1899. V. 47; 49

TALLENTYRE, S. G.
The Friends of Voltaire. London: 1906. V. 47
The Life of Voltaire. London: 1903. V. 50

TALLEY, THOMAS W.
Negro Folk Rhymes, Wise and Otherwise. New York: 1922. V. 53; 54

TALLEYRAND-PERIGORD, CHARLES MAURICE, PRINCE DE BENEVENT
Bibliotheca Splendidissima. A Catalogue of a Superlatively Splendid and Extensive Library Consigned from the Continent. London: 1816. V. 48
Memoirs. London: 1891-92. V. 47

TALLIS, ROBERT
Lancashire Illustrated, From Original Drawings... London: 1831. V. 48

TALLIS'S History and Description of the Crystal Palace and the Exhibition of the World's Industry in 1851. London: 1851. V. 48

TALLIS'S London Street Views, Exhibiting Upwards of One Hundred Buildings in Each Number, Elegantly Engraved on Steel... London: 1847. V. 50; 52

TALLONE, ENRICO
Le Carte e La Filigrana. Belgioioso: 1991. V. 50

TALMA, J.
A Chronological Account and Brief History of the Events of the French Revolution, from the taking of the Bastile, in 1789, to the Conquest of Holland, in 1795... London: 1795. V. 49

TALMUD
The Living Talmud. New York: 1960. V. 49; 52

TALON, NICOLAS
The Holy History. London: 1653. V. 47; 54

TALTAVALL, JOHN
Telegraphers of To-Day. Descriptive, Historical, Biographical. New York: 1893. V. 50

TALWAR, KAY
Indian Pigment Paintings on Cloth. Ahmedabad: 1979. V. 48; 54

TALWAR, P. K.
Inland Fishes of India and Adjacent Countries. Rotterdam: 1991. V. 50

TAMERLANE and Other Poems. Baltimore: 1939. V. 50

TAN, AMY
The Hundred Secret Senses. New York: 1995. V. 54
The Joy Luck Club. London: 1989. V. 51
The Joy Luck Club. New York: 1989. V. 47; 48; 49; 50; 51; 52; 53; 54
The Kitchen God's Wife. Franklin Center: 1991. V. 53
The Kitchen God's Wife. New York: 1991. V. 51; 52; 53; 54
Moon Lady. New York: 1992. V. 49; 51; 53

TANAKA, ICHIMATSU
The Art of Korin. Tokyo: 1959. V. 49

TANAKA, YOSHINO SUKE
Textile Designs. Art Sea. Kyoto: 1929. V. 48

TANG, W. C.
Chinese Drugs of Plant Origin. Berlin: 1992. V. 48; 52

TANGYE, H. LINCOLN
In New South Africa: Travels in the Transvaal and Rhodesia. London: 1896. V. 47

TANGYE, NIGEL
Red, White and Spain. London: 1937. V. 49

TANIZAKI, JUNICHERO
The Key. New York: 1961. V. 54

TANNEHILL, WILKINS
Sketches of the History of Literature, from the Earliest Period to the Revival of Letters in the Fifteenth Century. Nashville: 1827. V. 48; 53

TANNER, ADAM
Universa Theologia Scholastica, Speculativa, Practica, ad methodum S. Thomae. Ingolstadt: 1626. V. 50

TANNER, CLARA LEE
Southwest Indian Craft Arts. Tucson: 1968. V. 51
Southwest Indian Printing, a Changing. Tucson: 1973. V. 50

TANNER, HEATHER
A Country Book of Days. London: 1986. V. 48
Wiltshire Village. London: 1939. V. 47; 52
Woodland Plants. London: 1981. V. 54

TANNER, HENRY SCHENK
The American Traveller.... Philadelphia: 1836. V. 47
The American Traveller. Philadelphia: 1840. V. 47
The American Traveller... New York: 1844. V. 47; 48
The Central Traveller, or Tourist's Guide through the States of Pennsylvania, New Jersey, Delaware, Maryland, Virginia, the District of Columbia and Parts of New York and Other Adjoining States. New York: 1844. V. 47
A Description of the Canals and Rail-roads of the United States. New York: 1840. V. 47
A New Universal Atlas Containing Maps of the Various Empires. Philadelphia: 1844. V. 53; 54
A New Universal Atlas Containing Maps of the Various Empires. Philadelphia: 1845. V. 50

TANNER, J. M.
A Biographical Sketch of James Jensen... Salt Lake City: 1911. V. 47

TANNER, JOHN
Angelus Britannicus... London: 1687. V. 50
The Hidden Treasures of the Art of Physick. London: 1659. V. 53; 54
The Hidden Treasures of the Art of Physick... London: 1672. V. 47; 50
An Indian Captivity (1789-1822). John Tanner's Narrative of His Captivity Among the Ottawa and Ojibwa Indians. San Francisco: 1940. V. 53

TANNER, MATTHAIS
Societas Jesu Apostolorum Imitrix Sive Gesta Praeclara et Virtutes Eorum. Prague: 1694. V. 52

TANNER, ROBIN
A Country Book of Days. London: 1986. V. 49

TANNER, THOMAS
Notitia Monastica or a Short History of the Religious Houses in England and Wales. Oxford: 1695. V. 51
Notitia Monastica; or, an Account of all the Abbies, Priories and Houses of Friers Formerly in England and Wales... Cambridge: 1787. V. 47

TANNER, V.
Outlines of the Geography, Life, and Customs of Newfoundland-Labrador. Cambridge: 1947. V. 54

TANQUEREL DES PLANCHES, LOUIS
Lead Diseases: A Treatise with Notes and Additions on the Use of Lead Pipe and... Lowell: 1848. V. 47; 54
Traite des Maladies de Plomb. Paris: 1838. V. 47; 48; 50; 52; 53

TANSELLE, G. THOMAS
Guide to the Study of United States Imprints. Cambridge: 1971. V. 47

TANSILLO, LUIGI
The Nurse. Liverpool: 1798. V. 49; 53

TANSLEY, A. G.
The British Islands and Their Vegetation. Cambridge: 1939. V. 53
The British Islands and Their Vegetation. London: 1949. V. 48
The British Isles and Their Vegetation. London: 1953. V. 51

TANTIVY
Scottish Hunts. Glasgow: 1902. V. 47

TANTY, FRANCOIS
La Cuisine Francaise: French Cooking for Every Home. Los Angeles: 1894. V. 54

TAORMINA: Wilhelm von Gloeden. Pasadena: 1986. V. 52

TAPERELL, JOHN
A New Miscellany. London: 1763. V. 47

TAPLEY, HARRIET SILVESTER
Salem Imprints, 1768-1825: a History of the First Fifty Years of Printing in Salem, Massachusetts... Salem: 1927. V. 48

TAPLIN, GEORGE
Narrinyeri: an Account of the Tribes of South Australian Aborigines Inhabiting the Country Around the Lakes Alexandria, Albert and Coorong and the Lower Part of the River Murray, Their Manner and Customs. Adelaide: 1878. V. 52

TAPLIN, WILLIAM
The Gentleman's Stable Directory; or, Modern System of Farriery. London: 1788. V. 49
The Gentleman's Stable Directory; or, Modern System of Farriery. London: 1788/91. V. 47
The Gentleman's Stable Directory; or, Modern System of Farriery. London: 1793. V. 50
The Sporting Dictionary and Rural Repository of General Information Upon Every Subject Appertaining to Sports of the Field. London: 1803. V. 49; 52; 54
The Sportsman's Cabinet; or, a Correct Delineation of the Various Dogs Used in the Sports of the Field... London: 1803-04. V. 47; 52; 53

TAPPAN, H.
Paleobiology of Plant Protists. San Francisco: 1980. V. 50

TAPPAN, LEWIS
Narrative of the Lake Riotous Proceedings Against the Liberty of the Press, in Cincinnati. Cincinnati: 1836. V. 53

TAPPING, THOMAS
A Treatise On the Derbyshire Mining Customs and Mineral Court Act 1852. London: 1854. V. 54

TAPPLY, WILLIAM G.
Death at Charity's Point. New York: 1984. V. 50; 52; 53
The Dutch Blue Error. New York: 1984. V. 47; 52

TARASCON, LEWIS
Petition of Lewis A. Tarascon (and Others) Praying the Opening of a Wagon Road from the River Missouri to the River Columbia. Washington: 1824. V. 47; 50

TARAVAL, SIGISMUNDO, FATHER
The Indian Uprising in Lower California 1734-1737. Los Angeles: 1931. V. 48; 49

TARBELL, HARLAN
The Tarbell Course in Magic, Volume I. New York: 1946. V. 47

TARBELL, IDA M.
Florida Architecture of Addison Mizner. New York: 1928. V. 51
The History of the Standard Oil Company. New York: 1904. V. 48

TARBUCK, EDWARD LANCE
The Builder's Practical Director... Leipzig & Dresden: 1855-58. V. 53
The Builder's Practical Director. Leipzig and Dresden: 1860. V. 47
The Encyclopaedia of Practical Carpentry and Joinery...The Choice, Preservation and Strength of Materials. Leipzig & Dresden: 1857-59. V. 47

TARDY, MARY T.
The Living Female Writers of the South. Philadelphia: 1872. V. 54
Southland Writers. Philadelphia: 1870. V. 54

TARG, WILLIAM
Abacus Now: Footnotes to Indecent Pleasures and Observations on Fine Book Printing, Book Collecting and Matters Personal... New York: 1984. V. 48; 51; 52; 54
Bibliophile in the Nursery. Cleveland: 1957. V. 48; 51
The Making of the Bruce Rogers World Bible. Cleveland and New York: 1949. V. 48; 49

TARKINGTON, BOOTH
Beasley's Christmas Party. New York & London: 1909. V. 47
Cherry. New York: 1903. V. 54
Christmas This Year. Los Angeles: 1945. V. 54
Claire Ambler. New York: 1928. V. 51; 53
The Conquest of Canann. New York: 1905. V. 53
The Fascinating Stranger: and Other Stories. Garden City: 1923. V. 48
The Fascinating Stranger and Other Stories. New York: 1923. V. 51
The Gentleman from Indiana. New York: 1899. V. 48; 52; 53; 54
Harlequin and Columbine. Garden City: 1921. V. 49
In the Arena. New York: 1905. V. 54
Lady Hamilton and Her Nelson. New York: 1945. V. 47; 50
Little Orvie. Garden City: 1934. V. 54
Mary's Neck. Garden City: 1932. V. 53
Monsieur Beaucaire. New York: 1961. V. 52
Penrod. Garden City: 1914. V. 51

TARKINGTON, BOOTH continued
Penrod. New York: 1914. V. 53
Penrod Jashber. Garden City: 1929. V. 48; 51
Penrod Jashber. New York; 1929. V. 54
Some Old Portraits. New York: 1939. V. 49
The Two Vanrevels. New York: 1902. V. 54

TARLETON, BANASTRE
History of the Campaigns of 1780 and 1781 in the Southern Provinces of North America. Dublin: 1787. V. 47; 48; 54
A History of the Campaigns of 1780 and 1781 in the Southern Provinces of North America. London: 1787. V. 48; 49; 50

TARN, NATASHA
Multitude of One. New York: 1994. V. 54

TARN, NATHANIEL
The Forest, in Part, from a Much Larger Work. Mt. Horeb: 1978. V. 51; 54

TARR, RALPH STOCKMAN
Alaskan Glacier Studies of the National Geographic Society in the Yakutat Bay, Prince William sound and Lower Copper River Regions. Washington: 1914. V. 52

TARRANT, MARGARET W.
Rhymes of Old Times. London: 1925. V. 49

TARRIN, W. A.
The Italian Confectioner. London: 1861. V. 52

TARTAGLIA, NICCOLO
Nova Scientia Inventa... (bound with) Quesiti, et Inventioni Diverse... 1537/46. V. 49

TARTT, DONNA
The Secret History. New York: 1992. V. 48; 52

TASHJIAN, VIRGINIA A.
Once There Was and Was Not - Armenian Tales Retold. Boston and Toronto: 1966. V. 52

TASMAN, ABEL JANSZOON
Abel Janzoon Tasman's Journal of His Discovery of Van Diemen's Land and New Zealand in 1642, with Documents Relating to His Exploration of Australia in 1644. London: 1965. V. 47
Abel Janzoon Tasman's Journal of His Discovery of Van Diemen's Land and New Zealand in 1642, with Documents Relating to His Exploration of Australia in 1644. Los Angeles: 1965. V. 49; 52

TASSI, ROBERTO
Graham Sutherland: Complete Graphic Work. London: 1978. V. 49; 52; 54
Graham Sutherland: Complete Graphic Work. New York: 1978. V. 53

TASSIE, JAMES
A Descriptive Catalogue of a General Collection of Ancient and Modern Engraved Gems, Cameos, as Well as Intaglios, Taken from the Most Celebrated Cabinets in Europe... London: 1791. V. 50

TASSO, BERNARDO
Li Tre Libri Delle Lettere...Alli Quali Nuovamente s'Aggiunto il Quarto Libro. Venice: 1559. V. 52

TASSO, TORQUATO
Aminta... In Leida: 1656. V. 53
Aminta. Amsterdam: 1678. V. 47
Amyntas, a Tale of the Woods... London: 1820. V. 49
La Gerusalemme Liberata. Genova: 1590. V. 50
La Gerusalemme Liberata.... Genua: 1617. V. 52
La Gerusalemme Liberata. Parigi: 1771. V. 53
La Gerusalemme Liberata... London: 1778. V. 54
Il Godfredo... Venetia: 1583. V. 48; 50
Godfrey of Bulloigne... London: 1687. V. 48; 51; 54
Godfrey of Bulloigne... 1726. V. 47
Godfrey of Bulloigne... London: 1817. V. 52
Il Goffredo... Venice: 1588. V. 50
Jerusalem Delivered... London: 1764. V. 51
Jerusalem Delivered... Paris: 1794. V. 54
Jerusalem Delivered... London: 1803. V. 51
Jerusalem Delivered... Newburyport: 1810. V. 47
Jerusalem Delivered. Huntington: 1828. V. 47
O Godfredo... Lisbon: 1682. V. 48
Ventiquattro Sonetti. Vienna: 1939. V. 52

TATAM, GEORGE HARDY
The Buggy; or, Mr. Turnbull's Adventures in the New World. London: 1860. V. 49; 53

TATE, ALLEN
Christ and the Unicorn. West Branch: 1966. V. 47; 52; 54
Collected Poems 1919-1976. New York: 1977. V. 51
The Fathers. New York: 1938. V. 49
Fragment of a Meditation/MCMXXVIII. Cummington: 1947. V. 52
The Golden Mean and Other Poems. Nashville: 1923. V. 48; 52; 53
Jefferson Davis: His Rise and Fall. New York: 1929. V. 52
The Mediterranean and Other Poems. 1936. V. 47
The Mediterranean and Other Poems. New York: 1936. V. 52; 53
Mr. Pope and Other Poems. New York: 1928. V. 47; 50; 51; 52; 53; 54
On the Limits of Poetry. Selected Essays: 1928-1948. New York: 1948. V. 53
Poems. Chicago: 1961. V. 50
Poems: 1928-1931. New York: 1932. V. 52
Reactionary Essays on Poetry and Ideas. New York: 1936. V. 52
Reason in Madness. Critical Essays. New York: 1941. V. 52; 53
Requiescat in Pace. Iowa City: 1957/20/56. V. 54
Selected Poems. New York: 1937. V. 52; 54
Sonnets at Christmas. Cummington. 1941. V. 52
Stonewall Jackson: The Good Soldier. New York: 1928. V. 49; 52
Three Poems: Ode to the Confederate Dead. London: 1930. V. 53
(Three Poems). Ode to the Confederate Dead. New York: 1930. V. 53
Two Conceits for the Eye to Sing, if Possible. Cummington: 1950. V. 48; 52; 53
Who Owns America?. Boston: 1936. V. 49; 52
The Winter Sea, A Book of Poems. Cummington: 1944. V. 52; 54

TATE, CHARLES MONTGOMERY
Chinook as Spoken by the Indians of Washington Territory, British Columbia and Alaska... Victoria: 1889. V. 49

TATE, CHARLES S.
Pickway, a True Narrative. Chicago: 1905. V. 47

TATE, JAMES
Bewitched... 1989. V. 52
Bewitched. Llannynog: 1989. V. 53
Hottentot Ossuary. Cambridge: 1973. V. 53
Just Shades. 1985. V. 49
Land of Little Sticks. Worcester: 1981. V. 48; 54
The Lost Pilot. New Haven: 1967. V. 48
Notes of Woe. Iowa City: 1968. V. 48; 53; 54

TATE, JAMES RODDAM
Maderia; or, the Spirit of Anti-Christ in 1846, as Exhibited in a Series of Outrages Perpetrated in August last on British Subjects and Portuguese Protestant Christians. London: 1847. V. 47

TATE, NAHUM
Characters of Vertue and Vice. London: 1691. V. 52
Dido and Aeneas. Bangor/Newark: 1989. V. 52
A Duke and No Duke. London: 1685. V. 52
An Elegy on the Most Reverend Father in God, His Grace, John, Late Lord Archbishop of Canterbury. London: 1695. V. 53
An Essay of a Character of the Late Right Honourable Sir George Treby Kt. Lord Chief Justice of His Majesty's Cout of Common-Pleas. London: 1700. V. 48
The Kentish Worthies... 1701. V. 48
The Kentish Worthies. London: 1701. V. 49
On the Sacred memory of Our Late Sovereign (In Verse)... London: 1685. V. 48
A Poem Upon Tea; with a Discourse on Its Sov'rain Virtues; and Directions in the Use of It for Health. London: 1702. V. 47

TATE, WILLIAM
The Modern Cambist; Forming a Manual of Foreign Exchanges, in the Direct, Indirect and Cross Operations of Bills of Exchange and Bullion... Paris: 1834. V. 52

TATE ALLEN
The Hovering Fly and Other Essays. Cummington: 1949. V. 51

TATHAM, JOHN
The Dramatic Works. London: 1879. V. 49

TATHAM, JOSEPH
Rules and Instructions for the Regular Management of the Seminary, Kept by Joseph Tatham, Leeds. Leeds: 1817. V. 52

TATIANUS
Oratio Ad Graecos. Hermiae Irrisio Gentilim Philosophorum... Oxoniae: 1700. V. 48

THE TATLER... London: 1710-11. V. 48
THE TATLER... London: 1764. V. 51; 53
THE TATLER. London: 1806. V. 48; 49

TATLOW, JOSEPH
Fifty Years of Railway Life. London: 1948. V. 49

TATTAM, HENRY
Lexicon Aegyptiaco-Latinum ex Veteribus Linguae Aegyptiacae Monumentis... Oxonii: 1835. V. 54

TATTERSALL, C. E. C.
A Thousand End-Games. Leeds: 1910-11. V. 50

TATTERSALL, GEORGE
Sporting Architecture. London: 1841. V. 47
Tablets of an Itinerant. London: 1836. V. 50; 52

TATUM, LAWRIE
Our Red Brothers and the Peace Policy of President Ulysses S. Grant. Philadelphia: 1899. V. 48

TAUBERT, SIGRED
Bibliopola. Hamburg & London: 1966. V. 50; 52; 54

TAUNT, HENRY W.
A New Map of the River Thames from Oxford to London, from Entirely New Surveys, Taken During the Summer of 1871... Oxford: 1872. V. 47
A New Map of the River Thames, from Thames Head to London... Oxford: 1886. V. 47; 48

TAUSSIG, HELEN
Congenital Malformations of the Heart. London: 1947. V. 54

TAUT, BRUNO
Houses and People of Japan. Tokyo: 1937. V. 52
Houses and People of Japan. London: 1938. V. 48
Modern Architecture. London. V. 52

TAUTPHOEUS, JEMIMA MONTGOMERY, FREIFRAU VON
At Odds. London: 1863. V. 48
The Initials. London: 1850. V. 48
Quits: a Novel. London: 1857. V. 48
Quits: a Novel. Leipzig: 1858. V. 47; 48

TAVENOR PERRY, J.
Dinanderie: A History and Description of Mediaeval Art Work in Copper, Brass and Bronze. London: 1910. V. 50

TAVERNER, ERIC
The Angler's Week-End Book. London: 1935. V. 47
The Fly Fishers' Club Library Catalogue. London: 1935. V. 47
The Making of a Trout Stream. London: 1953. V. 51; 52
Salmon Fishing. London: 1931. V. 53
Trout Fishing From All Angles. London: 1929. V. 52; 53

TAVERNER, JAMES
An Essay Upon the Witham Spa. London: 1737. V. 49

TAVERNER, JOHN
Certaine Experiments Concerning Fishe and Fruite. New York, London: 1928. V. 47

TAVERNIER, J. B.
Collections of Travels through Turkey to Persia and the East Indies... London: 1684. V. 51

TAXATIO
Ecclesiastica Angliae et Walliae Auctoritate P. Nicholai IV. Circa A.D. 1291. London: 1802. V. 49

TAYLER, CHARLES BENJAMIN
A Fireside Book, or the Account of Christmas Spent at Old Court... London: 1828. V. 51; 54
A Fireside Book, or the Account of Christmas Spent at Old Court. London: 1829. V. 49
Legends and Records, Chiefly Historical. London: 1836. V. 54
May You Like It... London: 1823. V. 51

TAYLOR & TAYLOR
Types, Borders and Miscellany of Taylor and Taylor. San Francisco: 1939. V. 49

TAYLOR, ALFRED
Birds of a County Palatine. London: 1913. V. 50; 52; 53

TAYLOR, ALFRED SWAINE
A Manual of Medical Jurisprudence. London: 1846. V. 50
On Poisons in Relation to Medical Jurisprudence and Medicine. Philadelphia: 1859. V. 54
On Poisons in Relation to Medical Jurisprudence and Medicine. Philadelphia: 1875. V. 52
The Principles and Practice of Medical Jurisprudence. London: 1865. V. 51
The Principles and Practice of Medical Jurisprudence... London: 1873. V. 51

TAYLOR, ALRUTHEUS AMBUSH
The Negro in Reconstruction of Virginia. Washington: 1926. V. 52

TAYLOR, ANDREW T.
The Towers and Steeples Designed by Sir Christopher Wren. London: 1881. V. 48

TAYLOR, ANN
City Scenes or a Peep into London for Children. London: 1818. V. 47; 49
Little Ann and Other Poems. London: 1883. V. 47
My Mother, a Poem Embellished with Designs by a Lady... London: 1807. V. 48

TAYLOR, ARNOLD
Four Great Castles: Caernarfon, Conway, Harlech, Beaumaris. Newtown: 1983. V. 47; 50

TAYLOR, ARTHUR
The Glory of Regality: an Historical Treatise of the Anointing and Crowning of the Kings and Queens of England. London: 1820. V. 52; 54
The Glory of Regality: an Historical Treatise of the Anointing and Crowning of the Kings and Queens of England. (with) *The Queen's claim to Coronation Examined.* London: 1820/21. V. 50

TAYLOR, BAYARD
A Book of Romances, Lyrics and Songs. Boston: 1852. V. 52
Eldorado, or Adventures in the Path of Empire. London: 1850. V. 47; 50
Eldorado, or Adventures in the Path of Empire. New York: 1850. V. 47; 50; 52
India, China and Japan. New York: 1855. V. 53

TAYLOR, BENJAMIN F.
January and June. Chicago: 1860. V. 49

TAYLOR, CHARLES
A Familiar Treatise on Drawing, for Youth. Sherwood: 1827. V. 47
A Familiar Treatise on Perspective, in Four Essays. London: 1816. V. 47; 49; 53
Surveys of Nature... London: 1787. V. 53
Surveys of Nature. London: 1787-89. V. 54

TAYLOR, CHARLES FAYETTE
On the Mechanical Treatment of Disease of the Hip Joint. New York: 1873. V. 50

TAYLOR, CHARLES S.
The Old Commonwealth of Virginia: Its Social Life and Civilization. Alexandria: 1885. V. 50

TAYLOR, CONYNGHAM CRAWFORD
Toronto "Called Back", from 1892 to 1847. Toronto: 1892, 1890. V. 53
Toronto "Called Back", from 1894 to 1847. Toronto: 1894. V. 54

TAYLOR, DEEMS
Walt Disney's Fantasia. New York: 1940. V. 47; 48; 49; 53

TAYLOR, DREW KIRKSEY
Taylor's Thrilling Tales of Texas. 1926. V. 54

TAYLOR, EDGAR
Lays of the Minnesingers or German Troubadours of the Twelfth and Thirteenth Centuries... London: 1825. V. 54

TAYLOR, EDWARD
Cursory Remarks on Tragedy, on Shakespear, and On Certain French and Italian Poets... London: 1774. V. 50; 54

TAYLOR, EDWARD SAMUEL
The History of Playing Cards, with Anecdotes of their Use in Conjuring, Fortune-Telling and Card-Sharping. London: 1865. V. 51; 52; 54

TAYLOR, ELIZABETH
Angel. London: 1957. V. 50
At Mrs. Lippincote's. London: 1945. V. 51
A Dedicated Man - and Other Stories. London: 1965. V. 52
The Devastating Boys and Other Stories. London: 1972. V. 52
Hester Lilly and Other Stories. London: 1954. V. 51
Mossy Trotter. London: 1967. V. 52
Nibbles and Me. New York: 1946. V. 48
The Sleeping Beauty. London: 1953. V. 51; 52
The Wedding Group. London: 1968. V. 52

TAYLOR, FENNINGS
The Hon. Thos. D'Aracy McGee: a Sketch of His Life and Death. Montreal: 1868. V. 53

TAYLOR, FRANK
The Wars of Marlborough 1702-1709. Oxford: 1921. V. 49

TAYLOR, FREDERICK WINSLOW
The Principles of Scientific Management. New York & London: 1911. V. 48; 49; 54

TAYLOR, G.
An Account of the Genus Meconopsis. London: 1934. V. 52

TAYLOR, G. L.
The Architectural Antiquities of Rome. London: 1821-22. V. 52

TAYLOR, GEORGE
An Exposition of the Swedish Movement-Cure, Embracing the History of Philosophy of This System of Medical Treatment, With Examples of Single Movements... New York: 1860. V. 49
A History of the Rise, Progress, Cruelties and Suppression of the Rebellion in the County of Wexford in the Year 1798. Belleville: 1864. V. 48; 54
Taylor & Skinner's Survey of the Roads of Scotland on an Improved Plan to Which Is(n't) Prefixed an Accurate Map of Scotland. Edinburgh. V. 48
Taylor and Skinner's Maps of the Roads of Ireland, Surveyed 1777. London: 1778. V. 48

TAYLOR, GEORGE WATSON
The Profligate, a Comedy. London: 1820. V. 47

TAYLOR, GLADYS
When the Stars Sang. San Francisco: 1950's. V. 51

TAYLOR, GRIFFITH
With Scott: The Silver Lining. London: 1916. V. 48
With Scott: the Silver Lining. New York: 1916. V. 49

TAYLOR, H. M.
Anglo-Saxon Architecture. 1965-78. V. 50; 54
Anglo-Saxon Architecture. Cambridge: 1965/65/78. V. 50

TAYLOR, HARRIET OSGOOD
Japanese Gardens. London: 1880. V. 54
Japanese Gardens. London: 1912. V. 51
Japanese Gardens. London: 1928. V. 47

TAYLOR, HENRIETTA
The History of the Rebellion in the Years 1745 and 1746. Oxford: 1944. V. 48; 50

TAYLOR, HENRY
The Apology of Benjamin Ben Mordecai to His Friends, for Embracing Christianity. London: 1771. V. 47
Autobiography. London: 1885. V. 53
Old Halls in Lancashire and Cheshire. Manchester: 1884. V. 48; 53
Philip Van Artevelde; a Dramatic Romance. London: 1834. V. 52
The Statesman. London: 1836. V. 52

TAYLOR, HENRY OSBORN
The Mediaeval Mind: a History of the Development of Thought and Emotion in the Middle Ages. London: 1911. V. 49

TAYLOR, HOWARD, MRS.
The Call of China's Great North-West or Kansu and Beyond. 1925. V. 50; 51

TAYLOR, ISAAC
Beginnings of Biography, Being the Lives of One Hundred Persons Eminent in British History. London: 1824. V. 47
Beginnings of European Biography. London: 1828?. V. 49
Fanaticism. London: 1833. V. 52; 52; 53
Home Education. London: 1838. V. 49
Physical Theory of Another Life. London: 1836. V. 51
Scenes in Africa. London: 1824. V. 48

TAYLOR, ISAAC *continued*
Scenes in America, for the Amusement and Instruction of Little Tarry-at-Home Travellers. London: 1821. V. 50; 52
Scenes in Asia, for the Amusement and Instruction of Little Tarry-at-Home Travellers. London: 1819. V. 50
Scenes in England. London: 1826. V. 50
Scenes in Europe for the Amusement and Instruction of Litte Tarry-at-Home Travellers. London: 1823. V. 48; 51
Scenes in Europe for the Amusement and Instruction of Little Tarry-at-Home Travellers.... London: 1825. V. 49
Scenes of Commerce, By Land and Sea... London: 1830. V. 49; 52
Self Cultivation Recommended; or, Hints to a Youth Leaving School... London: 1817. V. 48
The Ship. London: 1833. V. 48; 49
Specimens of Gothic Ornaments Selected from the Parish Church of Lavenham in Sufolk. London: 1796. V. 52
Spiritual Despotism. London: 1835. V. 52

TAYLOR, J. J.
The Physician as a Business Man; or, How to Obtain the Best Financial Results in the Practice of Medicine. Philadelphia: 1892. V. 52

TAYLOR, J. W.
A Monograph of the Land and Freshwater Molluscs of the British Isles. Leeds: 1894-1914. V. 47

TAYLOR, JAMES
Paralysis and Other Diseases of the Nervous System in Childhood and Early Life. Philadelphia: 1905. V. 53

TAYLOR, JAMES BAYARD
Views A-Foot: or Europe Seen with Knapsack and Staff. New York: 1846. V. 54
Ximena; or, the Battle of the Sierra Morena, and Other Poems. Philadelphia: 1844. V. 47; 54

TAYLOR, JAMES MONROE
Vassar. New York: 1915. V. 50

TAYLOR, JAMES WICKES
Legislature of Minnesota. Northwest British America, and Its Relations to the State of Minnesota. St. Paul: 1860. V. 47; 50
The Railroad System of the State of Minnesota With Its Railroad, Telegraphic and Postal Connections. Saint Paul: 1859. V. 50
Relations Between the United States and Northwest British America. Washington: 1862. V. 47

TAYLOR, JANE
The Associate Minstrels. London: 1810. V. 48
City Scenes or a Peep into London. London: 1818. V. 50
City Scenes or a Peep Into London... London: 1823. V. 52
City Scenes or a Peep Into London. London: 1828. V. 47
The Contributions of Q.Q.... London: 1824. V. 49
The Contributions of Q.Q. London: 1838. V. 49
Essays in Rhyme on Morals and Manners. London: 1816. V. 48; 50
Little Ann and Other Poems. London: 1882. V. 48; 51
Little Ann and Other Poems. London: 1883. V. 48; 49; 50
Memoirs and Poetical Remains. London: 1826. V. 50
Rhymes for the Nursery. London: 1811. V. 48; 49
Rural Scenes or a Peep Into the Country for Children. London: 1826. V. 48
Signor Topsy-Turvy's Wonderful Magic Lantern: or, the World Turned Upside Down. London: 1810. V. 48

TAYLOR, JEFFERYS
The Forest; or Rambles in the Woodland. London: 1832. V. 49
A Month in London... London. V. 48
A Month in London. London: 1832. V. 52
Old English Sayings: Newly Expounded in Prose and Verse. London: 1827. V. 47; 48

TAYLOR, JEREMY
Antiquitates Christianae; or, The History of the Life and Death of the Holy Jesus... London: 1675. V. 49; 54
Antiquitates Christianae: or the History of the Life and Death of the Holy Jesus. London: 1694. V. 47
A Course of Sermons for All the Sundaies of the Year. (with) Sermons Preached At Golden Grove. (with) Discourse Of the Divine Institution. London: 1653/51/. V. 53
Ductor Dubitantium; or, the Rule of Conscience In All Her General Measures... London: 1696. V. 51
The Great Exemplar of Sanctity and Holy Life... London: 1649. V. 48; 50
The Great Exemplar of Sanctity and Holy Life... London: 1653. V. 48
The Great Exemplar of Sanctity and Holy Life. London: 1667. V. 47
Holy Living and Holy Dying. London: 1852. V. 51
The Rule and Exercises of Holy Dying. London: 1655. V. 48; 49
The Rule and Exercises of Holy Dying. London: 1845. V. 53
The Rule and Exercises of Holy Living... London: 1693/93. V. 50
The Rule and Exercises of Holy Living. Philadelphia: 1810. V. 53
The Rule and Exercises of Holy Living. London: 1847. V. 49
A Selection from His Works. Waltham St. Lawrence: 1923. V. 51
A Selection of His Works. Berkshire: 1923. V. 50
Taylor's Opuscula. The Measures of Friendship. London: 1684. V. 50
Unum Necessarium. Or, The Doctrine and Practice of Repentance. London: 1655. V. 48
The Whole Works... London: 1822. V. 49
The Whole Works... London: 1839. V. 49
The Worthy Communicant: or, a Discourse of the...Lords Supper. London: 1678. V. 52

TAYLOR, JOHN
African Rifles & Cartridges. 1948. V. 48; 52
African Rigles & Cartridges. Georgetown: 1948. V. 48; 49
All the Workes. London: 1630. V. 48; 49; 53
Big Game and Big Game Rifles. London: 1953. V. 49
A Dog of War. London: 1927. V. 52
Geological Essays and Sketch of the Geology of Manchester and the Neighbourhood. London: 1864. V. 53
A History of the Ten Baptist Churches, Of Which the Author Has Been Alternately a Member... Frankfort: 1823. V. 48
An Inquiry Into the Principles and Policy of the Government of the United States. Fredericksburg: 1814. V. 47; 50
Monsieur Tonson. London: 1830. V. 50
The Music Speech at the Public Commencement in Cambridge July 6, 1730. London: 1730. V. 47; 49
Poems and Translations; Including the First Four Books of Ovid's Fasti.... Liverpool: 1839. V. 54
Pondoro, Last of the Ivory Hunters. 1955. V. 54
Saint Hillaries Teares. London: 1642. V. 47
Tyranny Unmasked. Washington City: 1822. V. 47; 48; 49

TAYLOR, JOHN, & CO.
Tables Showing the Value of Silver and Gold, per Ounce Troy, at Different Degrees of Fineness, for John Taylor & Co., Importer of Assayers' Materials... San Francisco: 1860. V. 48

TAYLOR, JOHN HENRY
Taylor On Golf. London: 1902. V. 53

TAYLOR, JOSEPH
Arbores Mirabiles; or, a Description of the Most Remarkable Trees, Plants and Shrubs, in all Parts of the World. London: 1812. V. 48
The General Character of the Dog... London: 1804. V. 48

TAYLOR, JOSEPH HENRY
Beavers Their Ways and Other Sketches. Washburn: 1906. V. 53
Frontier & Indian Life and Kaleidoscopic Lives. Valley City: 1932. V. 54
Kaleidoscopic Lives. Washburgn: 1902. V. 52
Sketches of Frontier and Indian Life on the Upper Missouri and Great Plains Embracing the Author's Personal Recollections... Pottstown: 1889. V. 47

TAYLOR, JOSHUA C.
William Page, the American Titian. Chicago: 1957. V. 49; 53

TAYLOR, L. J. ORR
Life History of Thomas Orr, Jr. Pioneer of California and Utah. 1930. V. 47; 49

TAYLOR, LANDON
The Battle Field Reviewed. Chicago: 1881. V. 47; 48; 50

TAYLOR, LIEUT. COLONEL
Letters on India, Political, Commercial and Military, Relative to Subjects Importance to the British Interests in the East. London: 1800. V. 48

TAYLOR, MARLY L.
The Tiger's Claw. 1956. V. 52

TAYLOR, MARSHALL W.
Collection of Revival Hymns and Plantation Melodies. Cincinnati: 1883. V. 47
The Fastest Bicycle Rider in the World. Worcester: 1928. V. 48

TAYLOR, MAURICE
Bulletin in Bold Characters. A Bibliography of the Seton Village Press. Santa Fe: 1990. V. 50

TAYLOR, MEADOWS
Confessions of a Thug. London: 1839. V. 47
Tara. Edinburgh and London: 1863. V. 50

TAYLOR, MICHAEL
A Bibliography of St. Dominic's Press 1916-1937. London: 1995. V. 52
St. Dominic's Press: a Bibliography. Herefordshire: 1994. V. 52; 53
Saint Dominic's Press: a Bibliography 1916-1937. 1995. V. 47
Tables of Logarithms of All Numbers, from 1 to 101000; and of the Sines and Tangents to Every Second of the Quadrant... London: 1792. V. 49; 54

TAYLOR, MICHAEL WAISTELL
The Old Manorial Halls of Westmorland and Cumberland. Kendal: 1892. V. 50; 52; 54

TAYLOR, MR.
The History of Little Bob; with Memoirs of the Camelford Family. Uxbridge: 1820. V. 53

TAYLOR, N. G.
Relief for East Tennessee. Meeting at Cooper Institute, Thursday Evening, March 10, 1864. Address of Hon. N. G. Taylor. New York: 1864. V. 49

TAYLOR, NATHANIEL
The Coming Empire or Two Thousand Miles in Texas on Horseback. New York: 1877. V. 49

TAYLOR, NEVILLE
Ibex Shooting on the Himalayas. 1903. V. 52; 54
Ibex Shooting on the Himalayas. London: 1903. V. 49

TAYLOR, PAUL S.
An American-Mexican Frontier. Chapel Hill: 1934. V. 50

TAYLOR, PETER
The Collected Stories... 1969. V. 51
The Collected Stories. New York: 1969. V. 52
The Early Guest. 1982. V. 47; 54
Happy Families Are All Alike... London: 1959. V. 51

TAYLOR, PETER continued
Happy Families Are All Alike. New York: 1959. V. 48; 49; 51; 52; 54
Happy Families Are All Alike... London: 1960. V. 50
In the Miro District. London: 1977. V. 53
A Long Fourth and Other Stories. New York: 1947. V. 52
A Long Fourth and Other Stories. New York: 1948. V. 49; 52; 54
Miss Leonora When Last Seen. New York: 1963. V. 48; 49; 50; 52; 53; 54
The Old Forest. Garden City: 1985. V. 52
The Old Forest. London: 1985. V. 52
The Oracle at Stoneleigh Court. New York: 1993. V. 49
A Stand in the Mountains. New York: 1986. V. 52
A Summons to Memphis. New York: 1986. V. 47; 48
Tennessee Day in St. Louis. New York: 1957. V. 49; 54
The Widow of Thornton. New York: 1954. V. 48; 52; 53; 54
A Woman of Means. New York: 1950. V. 48; 52

TAYLOR, PETER ALFRED
Some Account of the Taylor Family (Originally Taylard). London: 1875. V. 54

TAYLOR, PHILIP MEADOWS
Confessions of a Thug. London: 1873. V. 52
Tara: a Mahratta Tale. London: 1863. V. 54

TAYLOR, PHOEBE ATWOOD
The Cape Cod Mystery. Indianapolis: 1931. V. 48
The Criminal C. O. D. New York: 1940. V. 47
Dead Ernest. New York: 1944. V. 51
Diplomatic Corpse. Boston: 1951. V. 50

TAYLOR, R.
A Key to the Knowledge of Nature... London: 1825. V. 50

TAYLOR, R. V.
The Biographia Leodiensis; or, Biographical Sketches of the Worthies of Leeds and Neighbourhood, from the Norman Conquest to the Present Time. London: 1865. V. 53; 54

TAYLOR, RICHARD
Destruction and Reconstruction: Personal Experiences of the Late War. New York: 1879. V. 48; 49; 50
The Past and Present of New Zealand. 1868. V. 54

TAYLOR, ROBERT H.
Authors at Work: an Address Delivered by Robert H. Taylor at the Opening of an Exhibition of Literary Manuscripts at the Grolier Club Together with a Catalogue of the Exhibition by Herman W. Liebert and Facsimiles of Many of the Exhibits. New York: 1957. V. 52

TAYLOR, ROBERT LEWIS
Adrift in a Boneyard. Garden City: 1947. V. 50

TAYLOR, ROBERT W.
A Clinical Atlas of Venereal and Skin Diseases Including Diagnosis, Prognosis and Treatment. Philadelphia: 1889. V. 48; 49; 51; 52; 53; 54
A Practical Treatise on Sexual Disorders of the Male and Female. Philadelphia: 1897. V. 51; 54

TAYLOR, SAMUEL
Sabrina Fair. New York: 1954. V. 50

TAYLOR, SAMUEL T.
Angling In All Its Branches, Reduced to a Complete Science. London: 1800. V. 48; 50
Dress Cutting Simplified and Reduced to Science. Baltimore: 1850. V. 52

TAYLOR, SARAH
Glenalpin, or the Bandit's Cave. London: 1828. V. 50

TAYLOR, T. U.
The Chisholm Trail and Other Routes. San Antonio: 1936. V. 51
Jesse Chisolm. Bandera: 1939. V. 47

TAYLOR, THEODORE
Thackeray, the Humourist and the Man of Letters. London: 1864. V. 50
Thackeray the Humourist and the Man of Letters. New York: 1864. V. 49; 51

TAYLOR, THOMAS
The Eleusinian and Bacchic Mysteries. New York: 1875. V. 48
The Parable of the Sower and of the Seed... London: 1634. V. 53
Two Orations of the Emperor Julian, One to the Sun and the Other to the Mother of the Gods. London: 1793. V. 50

TAYLOR, THOMAS E.
Running the Blockade: a Personal Narrative of Adventures, Risks and Escapes During the American Civil War. London: 1896. V. 49

TAYLOR, TOM
Leicester Square: Its Association and Its Worthies. London: 1874. V. 54
Life of Benjamin Robert Haydon, Historical Painter, from His Autobiography and Journals. 1853. V. 47
The Railway Station Painted by W. P. Frith, Esq., R.A. Described. London: 1862. V. 54
A Tale of Two Cities. London: 1860. V. 49; 54

TAYLOR, UNA
Early Italian Love Stories. London: 1899. V. 48

TAYLOR, W.
Historic Survey of German Poetry, Interspersed with Various Translations. London: 1828-30. V. 54

TAYLOR, W. A.
Intermere. 1901. V. 52

TAYLOR, W. THOMAS
Texfake. Austin: 1991. V. 51
Twenty-One Years of Bird & Bull. 1980. V. 47; 48; 49; 50; 51; 52; 53; 54
Twenty-One Years of Bird & Bull. North Hills: 1980. V. 48; 49; 50

TAYLOR, WALTER HERRON
Four Years With General Lee. New York: 1878. V. 49

TAYLOR, WILLIAM
California Life Illustrated. New York: 1858. V. 54
Christian Adventures in South Africa. New York: 1879. V. 52
A Concise Statement of Transactions and Circumstances Respecting the King's Theatre, in the Haymarket. London: 1791. V. 47
Observations on the Street Paving of the Metropolis; with an Account of a Peculiar System Adopted at the London and North Western Railway Station, Euston Square. London: 1850. V. 54
On a New and Successful Treatment for Febrile and Other Diseaes through the Medium of the Cutaneous Surface. London: 1850. V. 51; 54
Scenes and Adventures in Affghansitan... London: 1842. V. 48; 51
Scots Poems. Edinburgh: 1787. V. 52
Seven Years Street Preaching in San Francisco, California, Embracing Incidents, Triumphant Death Scenes. New York: 1857. V. 51; 53

TAYLOR, WILLIAM COOKE
Ancient and Modern India. London: 1851. V. 49
The Natural History of Society in the Barbarous and Civilized State... London: 1840. V. 52

TAYLOR, ZACHARY
A Sketch of the Life and Character of Gen. Taylor, the American Hero and People's Man... New York: 1847. V. 52

TAYLOUR, WILLIAM
Mycenean Pottery in Italy and Adjacent Areas. Cambridge: 1958. V. 50

TCHELITCHEW, PAVEL
Drawings. New York: 1947. V. 52

TCHEREPNIN, ALEXANDER
American Civil-War Battle Pieces, for Piano. London: 1951. V. 51

TCHERIKOVER, AVIGDOR
Corpus Papyrorum Judicarum. Cambridge: 1960. V. 47

THE TEA Cyclopaedia. Calcutta: 1881. V. 52

THE TEA Planter's Vade Mecum... Calcutta: 1885. V. 52

TEALE, THOMAS PRIDGIN
Dangers to Health: a Pictorial Guide to Domestic Sanitary Defects. London: 1881. V. 51; 53; 54
A Treatise on Neuralgic Diseases, Dependent Upon Irritation of the Spinal Marrow and Ganglia of the Sympathetic Nerve. Philadelphia: 1830. V. 53

TEALL, J. J. HARRIS
British Petrography... London: 1888. V. 50; 54

TEASDALE, SARA
Dark of the Moon. New York: 1926. V. 49; 51

TEASDALE-BUCKELL, G. T.
Experts On Guns and Shooting. London: 1900. V. 49; 51

TEBB, W. SCOTT
A Century of Vaccination and What it Teaches. London: 1899. V. 52

TEBBS, LOUISA A.
The Art of Bobbin Lace. London: 1908. V. 50

TECHENER, J.
Histoire de la Bibliophile. Reliures. Recherches sur les Bibliotheques des Plus Celebres Amateurs. Paris: 1861-64. V. 53

TEDDY Tail Waddle Book. London: 1934. V. 49

TEDLOCK, E. W.
Touch & Go. London: 1920. V. 49

TEEFY, J. R.
The Archdiocese of Toronto and Archbiship Walsh. Toronto: 1892. V. 48

TEERINK, H.
A Bibliography of the Writings of Jonathan Swift. Philadelphia: 1962. V. 53
A Bibliography of the Writings of Jonathan Swift. Philadelphia: 1963. V. 47

TEGETMEIER, DENIS
The Seven Deadly Virtues. London. V. 51
The Seven Deadly Virtues. London: 1934. V. 49
The Seven Deadly Virtues. London: 1938. V. 51

TEGETMEIER, WILHELM BERNHARD
Pallas's Sand Grouse: It's Natural History. London: 1888. V. 50
Pheasants for Coverts and Aviaries. London: 1873. V. 50; 51; 52; 53
Pheasants Their Natural History and Practical Management. London: 1897. V. 48
Pigeons, Their Structure... London. V. 47
Pigeons: Their Structure, Varities, Habits and Management. London: 1868. V. 47; 49
The Poultry Book. London: 1867. V. 49; 50; 53

TEGGART, FREDERICK J.
Catalogue of the Hopkins Railway Library. Palo Alto: 1895. V. 49

TEGNER, ESAIAS
Axel and Svea. London: 1840. V. 47; 48; 51; 54
Frithiof's Saga... London: 1833. V. 51
Frithiof's Saga. London: 1835. V. 54
Frithiof's Saga. London: 1839. V. 54
Frithiof's Saga... Stockholm: 1839. V. 53

TEHAUNTEPEC RAILWAY CO.
The Tehauntepec Railway. Its Location, Features and Advantages Under the La Sere Grant of 1869. New York: 1869. V. 47

TEICHMANN, EMIL
A Journey to Alaska in the Year 1868. Kensington: 1925. V. 47; 48
A Journey to Alaska in the Year 1868... New York: 1963. V. 49; 50; 53

TEICHMANN, HOWARD
The Solid Gold Cadillac. New York: 1954. V. 54

TEIGNMOUTH, JOHN SHORE, LORD
Memoirs of the Life, Writings and Correspondence of Sir William Jones. London: 1804. V. 48

TEISER, RUTH
Lawton Kennedy, Printer. San Francisco: 1988. V. 49; 52
Valenti Angelo: Art and Books: A Glorious Variety. Berkeley: 1980. V. 48

TEIT, J. A.
Traditions of the Thompson River Indians of British Columbia. Boston: 1898. V. 47; 48

TEIXEIRA, JOSE
Rervm ab Henrici Boronii Franciae Protoprincipis Majoribus Gestarum, Epitome... Paris: 1598. V. 52

TELENY or the Reverse of the Medal. London: 1893. V. 48

TELESIO, BERNARDINO
Varii de Naturalibus Rebus Libelli ab Antonio Persio Editi. Venice: 1590. V. 47

TELEVISION Today, Practice and Principles Clearly Explained. London: 1935. V. 53

TELFORD, JOHN
Sayings and Portraits of John Wesley. London: 1924. V. 49
Sayings and Portraits of John Wesley. London: 1927. V. 49

TELFORD, THOMAS
English and Bristol Channels Ship Canal. Prospectus and Mr. Telfords Preliminary Report, Dated 2d August, 1824. London: 1824. V. 51
London and Liverpool Roads. Mr. Telford's Reports, Estimates and Plans for Improving the Road from London to Liverpool. London: 1829. V. 51; 54
Report and Estimates Relative to a Proposed Road in Scotland from Kyle-Rhea in Inverness-Shire to Killin in Perthshire... London: 1810. V. 54
Report from the Committee Appointed to Examine Into Mr. Telford's Report and Survey, Relative to the Communication Between England and Ireland...(and) The Charts and Plans Referred to in Mr. Telford's Report and Survey on the Communication Between ... London: 1809. V. 51; 54
Report from the Committee Upon the Roads Between Carlisle and Port Patrick. London: 1811. V. 54
Report of Thomas Telford, Civil Engineer, February 1834, on the means of Supplying the Metropolis with Pure Water. London: 1834. V. 51
Ship Canal, for the Junction of the English and Bristol Channels, Reports of Mr. Telford and Captain Nicholls... London: 1824. V. 51; 54

THE TELL-Tale; or, Anecdotes Expressive of Characters of Persons Eminent for Rank, Learning, Wit or Humour. London: 1756. V. 48

TELLER, H. M.
Letter from the Secretary of the Interior...Lands in the Indian Territory... Washington: 1884. V. 52
Letter From the Secretary of the Interior...Lands in the Indian Territory. Washington: 1885. V. 52

TELLIER, JULES
Abd-er-Rhaman in Paradise. Waltham St. Lawrence: 1928. V. 48; 50; 51; 52; 53

TEMANZA, TOMMASO
Vite dei Piu Celebri Architetti e Scultori Venziani che Fioriono nel Secodo Decimosesto. Venice: 1778. V. 53

TEMMINCK, COENRAAD J.
Les Oiseaux d'Europe. Paris: 1848. V. 47

TEMPERANCE Cook Book: Being a Collection of Receipts for Cooking from Which All Intoxicating Liquids are Excluded. Philadelphia: 1841. V. 47; 51

TEMPERLEY, H. W. V.
A History of the Peace Conference of Paris. London: 1920-24. V. 48

TEMPLE, A. G.
Wantage Collection. A Catalogue of Pictures Forming the Collection of Lord and Lady Wantage. London: 1905. V. 52

TEMPLE, EDMOND
The Life of Pill Garlick; Rather a Whimsical Sort of Fellow. London: 1813. V. 48

THE TEMPLE of Compassion; a Poem, Addressed to a Lady. London: 1771. V. 48

THE TEMPLE of Death, a Poem. London: 1695. V. 48; 54

TEMPLE, RICHARD
Journals Kept in Hyderbad, Kashmir, Sikkim and Nepal. London: 1887. V. 54
Palestine Illustrated. London: 1888. V. 52

TEMPLE, ROBERT C.
The Itinerary of Ludovico di Varthema of Bologna, from 1502 to 1508... London: 1928. V. 51

TEMPLE, SARAH B. G.
The First Hundred Years. Atlanta: 1935. V. 50

TEMPLE, WILLIAM
Further Proposals for Amending and Settling the Coyn. London: 1696. V. 50
An Introduction to the History of England. London: 1695. V. 49; 50
Letters Written by... and Other Ministers of State... London: 1700/03. V. 48
Letters Written by...and Other Ministers of State... London: 1700. V. 53
Memoirs of the Life, Works and Correspondence. London: 1836. V. 50
Memoirs of What Past in Christendom from the War Begun 1672 to the Peace Concluded 1679. London: 1692. V. 50; 51
Memoirs of What Past in Christendom from the War Begun 1672 to the Peace Concluded 1679. London: 1700. V. 53
Miscellanea. London: 1690. V. 48
Miscellanea: Parts I and II & Part III. 1705/01. V. 49; 50
Miscellanea, the Third Part. Dublin: 1701. V. 53
Observations Upon the United Provinces of the Netherlands... London: 1690/81. V. 49
Observations Upon the United Provinces of The Netherlands. London: 1693. V. 49
The Works... London: 1720. V. 48
The Works. London: 1731. V. 47

TEMPLEMAN, JAMES
Gilbert; or, the Young Carrier. London: 1808. V. 50; 54

TEMPLES of the Fairies. London: 1804. V. 47

TEMPLETON, WILLIAM
The Locomotive Engine Popularly Explained and Illustrated by Lithographic Designs. London: 1841. V. 53
The Operative Mechanic's Workshop Companion. London: 1845. V. 48

TEMPLI Carmina. Songs of the Temple, or Bridgewater Collecton of Sacred Music. Boston: 1819. V. 50

TEMPLIN, HUGH
Fergus: the Story of a Little Town. Fergus: 1933. V. 53

TEMPORA Mutantur. A Memorial of the Fordington Times Society. London: 1859. V. 48

TEN Little Coloured Boys. New York: 1942. V. 49

TEN Little Negro Boys. New York: 1880. V. 52

TEN Little Nigger Boys and Ten Little Dollies. London: 1920. V. 47

THE TEN Little Niggers. London: 1870. V. 47; 51

TEN Months in the Field with the Boers. London: 1901. V. 50

TEN Ring Circus Books. New York: 1949. V. 50

TEN Singers - An Anthology. London: 1925. V. 54

TEN Tales. Huntington Beach: 1994. V. 51; 52

TEN Thousand Hackney Coach Fares... London: 1800. V. 50

TENANTS Law; or, the Laws Concerning Landlords, Tenants and Farmers... London: 1737. V. 48

TEN CATE, P. H. J. HOUWINK
The Luwian Population Groups of Lycia and Cilicia Aspera During the Hellenistic Period. Leiden: 1961. V. 50

TENCIN, CLAUDINE ALEXANDRINE GUERIN DE
The Siege of Calais, an Historical Novel. London: 1751. V. 50; 52

TENESLES, NICOLAS
The Indian of New-England, and the North Eastern Provinces... Middletown: 1851. V. 53

TENISON, LOUISA
Castille and Andalucia. London: 1853. V. 53

TENN, W.
Of All Possible World. 1955. V. 52

TENNANT, CHARLES
The Bank of England; and the Organisation of Credit in England. London: 1865. V. 51
A Tour through Parts of the Netherlands, Holland, Germany, Switzerland, Savoy and France in the year 1821-22. London: 1824. V. 49

TENNANT, EMMA
Alice Fell. London: 1980. V. 53
The Time of the Crack. London: 1973. V. 48

TENNANT, JAMES EMERSON
Ceylon: an Account of the Island, Physical, Historical and Topographical with Notices of Its Natural History, Antiquities and Productions. London: 1860. V. 54

TENNANT, STEPHEN
My Brother Aquarius - Poems. London: 1961. V. 47

TENNANT, W.
Indian Recreations. London: 1804. V. 54

TENNANT, WILLIAM
Anster Fair. Baltimore: 1815. V. 54

TENNENT, GILBERT
The Necessity of Holding Fast the Truth Represented in Three Sermons on Rev. III. 3. Preached at New York. April 1742. Boston: 1743. V. 47; 51
Two Sermons Preached at New-Brunswick in the Year 1741. On the Priestly Office of Christ. And the Virtue of Charity. Boston: 1742. V. 47; 51

TENNENT, JAMES EMERSON
Ceylon. An Account of the Island, Physical, Historical and Topographical. London: 1860. V. 48

TENNESSEE
Tennessee Reports, or Cases Ruled and Adjudged in the Superior Courts of Law and Equity and Federal Courts for the State of Tennessee. Knoxville: 1813. V. 50; 53

TENNESSEE. LAWS, STATUTES, ETC.
Public Acts of the State of Tennessee, Passed at the Extra Session of the Thirty-Third General Assembly, April, 1861. Nashville: 1861. V. 49

TENNESSEE. LEGISLATURE. HOUSE OF REPRESENTATIVES
Journal of the House of Representatives of the State of Tennessee. Begun and Held at Knoxville, on Saturday the Thirtieth Day of July, One Thousand Seven Hundred and Ninety Six. Knoxville/Nashville: 1796/1852. V. 47

TENNESSEE. MILITIA
Regulations Adopted for the Provisional Force of the Tennessee Volunteers, Together with the Act of Tennessee Legislature of 1861 Organizing Such Provisonal Force. Nashville: 1861. V. 49

TENNESSEE. TREASURY
Report of James Y. Dunlap, Comptroller of the Treasury to the General Assembly of Tennessee, October 1861. Nashville: 1861. V. 52

TENNEY, E.
Colorado and Homes in the New West. Boston/New York: 1880. V. 47

TENNEY, HORACE KENT
Vert and Venison. 1924. V. 54

TENNIEL, JOHN
Illustrations to Lewis Carroll's Alice's Adventures in Wonderland and Through the Looking Glass. London: 1988. V. 50

TENNYSON, ALFRED TENNYSON, 1ST BARON
12 Verses from "The Day Dream". London: 1995. V. 52; 54
A Collection of Poetical Works by... (with) Maud and Other Poems: The Princess: a Medley: In Memoriam: and Enoch Arden, etc. London: 1866-67. V. 47
The Death of Oenone, Akbar's Dream, and Other Poems. London: 1892. V. 51; 54
Demeter and Other Poems. Edinburgh: 1889. V. 51
Demeter and Other Poems. London: 1889. V. 53
The Devil and the Lady. London: 1930. V. 50; 51
A Dream of Fair Women and Other Poems. London: 1900. V. 49
Elaine. London: 1867. V. 51
Elaine. London: 1868. V. 48
Enid. London: 1868. V. 48
Enoch Arden. London: 1864. V. 47; 48; 54
Enoch Arden. Boston: 1865. V. 51
Fairy Lilian. Boston: 1888. V. 50
Gems from Tennyson. Boston: 1866. V. 47
Guinevere. New York: 1868. V. 48
Guinevere & Other Poems. London: 1912. V. 48; 49; 50
Idylls of the King. London: 1859. V. 51; 53; 54
Idylls of the King. London: 1864. V. 51
Idylls of the King. London: 1867. V. 52
The Idylls of the King. London: 1868. V. 48
The Idylls of the King. London: 1911. V. 50; 54
Idylls of the King. New York: 1952. V. 48
In Memoriam. Boston: 1850. V. 47; 50; 51; 52
In Memoriam. London: 1850. V. 50; 51; 52; 53
In Memoriam. Boston: 1855. V. 49
In Memoriam. London: 1885. V. 47; 50
In Memoriam. London and New York: 1894. V. 51
In Memoriam. London: 1896. V. 52; 54
In Memoriam. London: 1900. V. 51
In Memoriam. London: 1933. V. 47; 50; 52; 54
The Lady of Shalott. New York: 1881. V. 47; 49
The Lover's Tale... London: 1875. V. 54
The Lover's Tale. London: 1879. V. 48
Lyrical Poems. London: 1885. V. 50
Lyrical Poems. London & New York: 1906. V. 49
Maud. London: 1855. V. 47; 50; 51; 52; 53; 54
Maud... London: 1861-63. V. 50; 51
Maud. 1893. V. 51; 52
Maud... Hammersmith: 1893. V. 54
Maud. London: 1893. V. 47; 49; 50; 51
Maud. London: 1922. V. 54
The May Queen. London: 1860. V. 47
The May Queen. London: 1861. V. 51
The May Queen. London: 1870. V. 49
Ode on the Death of the Duke of Wellington. London: 1852. V. 50; 51; 53; 54
Ode on the Death of Wellington. London: 1853. V. 54
Ode to Virgil. Bangor: 1890. V. 54
The Passing of Arthur. London: 1884. V. 54
Poems. London: 1842. V. 47; 49; 50; 52
Poems. London: 1843. V. 54
Poems. London: 1846. V. 51; 54
Poems. London: 1857. V. 51
Poems. London: 1859. V. 49
Poems. London: 1866. V. 48
Poems ... Boston: 1872. V. 51
Poems. London: 1872. V. 47
The Poems. London: 1888/89. V. 53
Poems... London: 1889. V. 48
Poems. London: 1893. V. 52; 53
Poems. 1900. V. 49
Poems. London: 1900. V. 54
Poems. London: 1905. V. 52; 54
Poems... London: 1907. V. 50
Poems. London: 1917. V. 47
Poems. 1974. V. 47; 51
Poems. London: 1974. V. 49
Poems. New York: 1974. V. 48; 54
Poems, by Two Brothers. London: 1827. V. 47; 48
Poems, Chiefly Lyrical. London: 1830. V. 47; 48; 50; 51; 53; 54
Poems MDCCCXXX - MDCCCXXXIII. London: 1862. V. 48
Poems. MDCCCXXX. MDCCCXXXIII. 1862. V. 48; 54
The Poetic and Dramatic Works. Boston: 1929. V. 48
The Poetical Works. Boston: 1856. V. 54
The Poetical Works... London: 1878. V. 51; 52
Poetical Works. London: 1899. V. 50
The Princess. London: 1847. V. 50; 51; 54
The Princess... London: 1853. V. 48
The Princess. London: 1867. V. 50; 51
The Princess... London: 1880. V. 48; 49
The Princess. London & New York: 1899. V. 49
Queen Mary. London: 1875. V. 47
A Selection from the Works of Alfred Tennyson. London: 1876. V. 47; 51
Seven Poems and Two Translations. Hammersmith: 1902. V. 47; 48; 49; 51; 54
Seven Poems and Two Translations. London: 1902. V. 51; 52
Timbuctoo. Cambridge: 1829. V. 53; 54
Tiresias and Other Poems. London: 1885. V. 47; 51
A Welcome. London: 1863. V. 53
The Window; or, the Loves of the Wrens. V. 54
The Works... London: 1872-73. V. 53
The Works... London: 1880. V. 53
The Works... London: 1881. V. 48
The Works. London: 1884. V. 51
The Works... London: 1894. V. 51
Works. Boston: 1895. V. 49; 52
Works. New York: 1895. V. 52
Works.... London: 1902. V. 53
Works. London: 1906-11. V. 53

TENNYSON, CHARLES
Sonnets and Fugitive Pieces. Cambridge: 1830. V. 47; 53

TENNYSON, FREDERICK
Days and Hours. V. 47; 49
Days and Hours. London: 1854. V. 48
Poems of the Day and Year. London: 1895. V. 53; 54

TENNYSON, HALLAM LORD
Alfred Lord Tennyson. London: 1897. V. 54

TENNYSON D'EYNCOURT, CHARLES
Eustace an Elegy. London: 1851. V. 52

TEONGE, HENRY
The Diary of Henry Teonge, Chaplain on Board His Majesty's Ships Assistance, Bristol & Royal Oak, Ano 1675 to 1679... London: 1825. V. 47; 51; 52

TERENTIUS AFER, PUBLIUS
The Brothers. Kentfield: 1968. V. 53
Comediae... Amsterdam: 1650. V. 52
Comedies. London: 1749. V. 52
The Comedies... London: 1765. V. 47
A Comedy... Verona: 1971. V. 49; 54
Comoediae... Parisiis: 1541. V. 48; 54
Comoediae... Venetiis: 1543. V. 54
Comoediae. Paris: 1551, 1550. V. 53
Comoediae. Venice: 1569. V. 48
Comoediae. Venice: 1586. V. 52
Comoediae. Cambridge: 1701. V. 48
Comoediae... Hague: 1732. V. 47
Comoediae. Dublin: 1745. V. 49
Comoediae. Edinburgh: 1758. V. 48
Comoediae. Birminghamiae: 1772. V. 47; 50; 51; 51; 52; 53
Comoediae... London: 1820. V. 51
Comoediae. Londini: 1854. V. 48

TERENTIUS AFER, PUBLIUS continued
Comoedias... Leipzig: 1577. V. 48; 52
Four Comedies. Dublin: 1824. V. 51
P. Terentius Afer A. M. Antonio Mureto Emendatus Venice: 1560. V. 52
P. Terentius Afer A. M. Antonio Mureto Emendatvs Eiusdem. Mureti Argumenta et Scholia. Venice: 1575. V. 52
Poetae Lepidissimi Comoediae Omnes. Venetiis: 1567. V. 54
Publii Terentii Afri Comoediae, Phaedri Fabulae Aesopiae, Publii Syri et Aliorum Veterum Sententiae. Cambridge: 1726. V. 48
Terence in English. London: 1641. V. 49
Terentius A. M. Antonio Mureto, Locis. (with) Annotationes. Antwerp: 1565. V. 52
Terentius, in Quem Triplex Edita est P. Antesignani. Lyons: 1560. V. 52

TERENZIO, S.
The Prints of Robert Motherwell: a Catalogue Raisonne 1943-84. New York: 1984. V. 47; 50; 51; 53

TERESA, SAINT
The Life...Holy Mother Teresa... London: 1671. V. 49
The Life...Holy Mother Teresa... London: 1671/69. V. 47
The Works... London: 1675. V. 50
The Works... London: 1679. V. 49

TERHUNE, ALFRED MCKINLEY
The Life of Edward Fitzgerald. London: 1947. V. 50

TERHUNE, MARY VIRGINIA HAWES
Miriam. New York: 1862. V. 48
Moss-Side. New York: 1857. V. 48
Nemesis. New York: 1861. V. 48
Sunnybank. New York: 1866. V. 48

TERKEL, STUDS
Giants of Jazz. New York: 1957. V. 48; 50; 52

TERMAN, LEWIS M.
Genetic Studies of Genius. Stanford: 1925/26. V. 50

TERNISIEN-D'HAUDRICOURT
Fastes de la Nation Francaise... Paris: 1807/16. V. 48

TERRACE, EDWARD L. B.
Egyptian Paintings of the Middle Kingdom. London: 1968. V. 50; 54

TERRAY, L.
Conquistadors of the Useless. 1963. V. 53

TERREL, WILLIAM
Under Heaven. Madison: 1968. V. 54

TERRELL, J. C.
Reminiscences of Early Days of Fort Worth. Forth Worth: 1906. V. 47

TERRELL, JOHN UPTON
Estevanico the Black. Los Angeles: 1968. V. 54

THE TERRIBLE Tragedy at Washington, Assassination of President Lincoln. Philadelphia: 1865. V. 52

TERRINGTON, WILLIAM
Cooling Cups and Dainty Drinks. London: 1869. V. 53

TERRY, ALFRED
The Field Diary of Alfred II Terry, Texas Yellowstone Expedition 1876. Bellevue: 1969. V. 49

TERRY, CHARLES SANFORD
The Life and Campaigns of Alexander Leslie, First Earl of Leven. London New York & Bombay: 1899. V. 54

TERRY, DANIEL
The Antiquary; a Musical Play. London: 1820. V. 52

TERRY, ELLEN
The Story of My Life. London: 1908. V. 48; 54

TERRY, G. E.
Unknown North Queensland. Victoria: 1937. V. 52

TERRY, G. W.
The Alphabet Annotated for Youth and Adults, in Doggerel Vese by and Old Etonian. London: 1853. V. 53

TERRY, MICHAEL
Across Unknown Australia. London: 1925. V. 52
Across Unknown Australia. London: 1926. V. 52
Hidden Wealth and Hiding People. New York: 1931. V. 48
Sand and Sun: with Camels in the Dry Lands of Central Australia. London: 1937. V. 52

TERRY, T. PHILIP
Terry's Japanese Empire. Boston: 1914. V. 47

TERSANSKY, JOSEPH EUGENE
The History of Hungary. Budapest: 1920. V. 50

TERTRE, R. P. JEAN BAPTISTE DU
Histoire Generale des Isles des Christophe, de la Guadeloupe, de la Martinique, et Autres dans l'Amerique. Paris: 1654. V. 48

TERTULLIAN
Q. Septimii Florentis Tertulliani (Opera). Basel: 1562. V. 52

TERUJI, YOSHIDA
The Life and Works of Toshusai Sharaku. Tokyo: 1957. V. 53

TESLA, NIKOLA
Experiments with Alternate Currents of High Potential and High Frequency. New York: 1896. V. 52

TESSIER, THOMAS
How We Died. Dublin: 1970. V. 54
In Sight of Chaos. 1971. V. 49; 54
In Sight of Chaos. London: 1971. V. 52
The Night Walker. New York: 1980. V. 51; 52
Phantom. New York: 1982. V. 51; 52

TESSIN, CARL GUSTAF
Letters from an Old Man to a Young Prince, with the Answers. London: 1756. V. 47
Letters From an Old Man to a Young Prince with the Answers. London: 1759. V. 48; 50

A TEST for the Times: or, the Treachery and Inconsistency of Democratic Politics Manifested, in the Case Especially of Somers Versus Somers. Dublin: 1795. V. 48

THE TESTAMENT of Charlotte B. 1988. V. 52

TESTE, A.
The Homoeopathic Materia Medica. Philadelphia: 1854. V. 50; 52

TESTIMONY in Relation To the Ute Indian Outbreak. Washington: 1880. V. 50

TESTOLINI, GAETANO
Elements of Drawing. London: 1795. V. 50
A Suite of Four Fine Aquatint Plates of Surrey Views. London: 1810. V. 54

TESUKIWASHI Taikan. Tokyo: 1974. V. 47; 48

TETIUS, HIERONYMUS
Aedes Barberinae. Rome: 1647. V. 54

TETTI, CARLO
Discorso delle Fortificationi. Venice: 1575. V. 53

TEVIS, A. H.
Beyond the Sierras: or, Observations on the Pacific Coast. 1877. V. 48

TEVIS, WALTER S.
The Hustler. New York: 1959. V. 51
The Hustler. London: 1960. V. 49

TEW, DAVID
The Oakham Canal. Wymondham: 1968. V. 51; 52

TEXAS
General Regulations for the Government of the Army of the Republic of Texas. Houston: 1839. V. 52
Senate and House Journals of the Tenth Legislature...State of Texas. Austin: 1965. V. 52

TEXAS & PACIFIC & NEW ORLEANS RAILROAD
To All Stock and Security Holders of the Texas and Pacific and New Orleans Railway Company. Philadelphia: 1886. V. 49

TEXAS & PACIFIC RAILROAD
The Texas and Pacific Railway. Memoranda of Surveys Showing the General Features of the Line, and Character and Resources of the Country Along Its Route, Together with Reasons for Its Prompt Completion. Philadelphia: 1876. V. 47

TEXAS & PACIFIC RAILWAY COMPANY
Argument of John C. Brown, Vice President Texas and Pacific Railway Company, Before House Committee on Pacific Railroads, January 25, 1878, in Behalf of the Texas and Pacific Railway Company. Washington City: 1878. V. 47

TEXAS Almanac for 1857 with Statistics, Historical and Biographical Sketches &c. Relating to Texas. Galveston: 1856. V. 53

TEXAS Almanac for 1859. Galveston: 1858. V. 53

TEXAS Almanac for 1861. Galveston: 1860. V. 53

TEXAS Almanac for 1867. Galveston: 1866. V. 53

TEXAS Almanac for 1868. Galveston: 1867. V. 53

TEXAS Almanac for 1869... Galveston: 1868. V. 53

TEXAS Almanac for 1870... 1869. V. 49
TEXAS Almanac for 1870... Galveston: 1869. V. 53

TEXAS Almanac for 1872... 1871. V. 49

TEXAS Almanac for 1873... Galveston: 1872. V. 53

TEXAS. CONSTITUTION
The Constitution... Washington: 1845. V. 49
The Constitution... Austin: 1861. V. 49
The Constitution... Austin: 1866. V. 49

THE TEXAS Cook Book... Houston: 1883. V. 47

TEXAS COPPER MINING AND MANUFACTURING CO.
Charter and By-Laws of the Texas Cooper Mining and Manufacturing Company. Dallas: 1883. V. 54

TEXAS FOLKLORE SOCIETY
Publications of...2. Austin: 1923. V. 50

TEXAS. LAWS, STATUTES, ETC.
General Laws of the Extra session of the Ninth Legislature of the State of Texas. Austin: 1863. V. 49

TEXAS. LAWS, STATUTES ETC.
General Laws of the Ninth Legislature of the State of Texas. Houston: 1862. V. 49

TEXAS. LAWS, STATUTES, ETC.
General Laws of the Seventh Legislature of the State of Texas. Austin: 1858. V. 48
Laws Passed by the First Legislature of the State of Texas. Austin: 1846. V. 49
Special Laws of the Sixth Legislature of the State of Texas. Austin: 1856. V. 49

TEXAS.
The Vast Importance of Correct Views, as to the Various Questions of Policy...in the Proposed Annexation of Texas... 1844. V. 49

TEXAS, TOPOLOBAMPO & PACIFIC RAILROAD & TELEGRAPH CO.
Reports of Geo. W. Simmons, Jr., Dr. B. R. Carman and John E. Price, Esq. Upon the Route of a Railroad from Topolobampo Bay on the Gulf of California to Piedras Negras on the Rio Grande. Boston: 1881. V. 49

TEXIER, CHARLES
The Principal Ruins of Asia Minor, Illustrated and Described. London: 1865. V. 49

TEXTBOOK of Small Arms. London: 1929. V. 49

TEXTOR, BENEDICTUS
Stirpium Differentiae... Paris: 1534. V. 52

TEY, J.
The Daughter of Time. London: 1951. V. 51

THACHER, JAMES
American Medical Biography: or Memoirs of Eminent Physicians Who Have Flourished in America. Boston: 1828. V. 48; 50
American Medical Practice: or, a Simple Method of Prevention and Cure of Diseases. Boston: 1817. V. 53; 54
A Military Journal During the American Revolutionary War... Boston: 1823. V. 48
A Military Journal During the American Revolutionary War... Boston: 1827. V. 48; 51; 53; 54
Military Journal of the American Revolution, from the Commencement to the Disbanding of the American Army... Hartford: 1862. V. 49
The New American Dispensatory. Boston: 1810. V. 49; 54
Observations on Hydrophobia, Produced by the Bite of a Mad Dog, or Other Rabid Animal. Boston: 1812. V. 54

THACHER, PETER
Historical Sketch of the Insitution, Design &c. of the Society for Propagating the Gospel Among the Indians and Others in North America. 1798. V. 49
A Sermon Preached to the Society in Brattle Street, Boston, October 20, 1793. Boston: 1793. V. 47

THACKER, THOMAS
The Courser's Annual Remembrancer and Stud Book... London: 1842-58. V. 48
The Courser's Companion. Derby: 1834/35. V. 47

THACKERAY, WILLIAM MAKEPEACE
The Adventures of Philip... London: 1862. V. 48; 49; 50; 51; 52; 53; 54
The Adventures of Philip. New York: 1862. V. 54
The Awful History of Bluebeard. New York: 1924. V. 50
Ballads. (with) Barry Lyndon. London: 1855/56. V. 52
The Complete Works. Boston: 1889. V. 47; 48
Contributions to "Punch". London: 1885-86. V. 49
Denis Duval. New York: 1864. V. 48; 54
Denis Duval. London: 1867. V. 49
Doctor Birch and His Young Friends. London: 1849. V. 48; 53; 54
English Humourists. New York: 1853. V. 53
An Essay on the Genius of George Cruikshank. London: 1840. V. 51
Etchings by the late William Makepeace Thackeray. London: 1878. V. 54
La Foire Aux Vanites. Paris: 1855. V. 50
The Four Georges. London: 1861. V. 51; 54
The Great Hoggarty Diamond. New York: 1848. V. 48
The History of Henry Esmond... London: 1842. V. 51
The History of Henry Esmond. London: 1852. V. 48; 50; 51
The History of Henry Esmond. New York: 1852. V. 51
The History of Henry Esmond... London: 1956. V. 49
History of Henry Esmond. New York: 1956. V. 50; 52; 54
The History of Pendennis. London: 1848-50. V. 47; 48
The History of Pendennis. London: 1849. V. 51; 54
The History of Pendennis. London: 1849-50. V. 47; 48; 49; 50
The History of Pendennis. New York: 1850. V. 47
The History of Samuel Titmarsh and the Great Hogarty Diamond. London: 1849. V. 47; 49; 50; 51; 52; 54
The Irish Sketch-Book. London: 1843. V. 52
The Kickleburys on the Rhine. 1850. V. 53
The Kickleburys on the Rhine. London: 1850. V. 48; 52
The Kickleburys on the Rhine... London: 1866. V. 51
A Little Dinner at Timmins's: & the Bedford-Row Conspiracy. London: 1856. V. 51
Lovel the Widower. London: 1861. V. 53
The Loving Ballad of Lord Bateman. London: 1839. V. 48
The Loving Ballad of Lord Bateman. London: 1871. V. 52
Men's Wives. New York: 1852. V. 47; 53
Miscellanies: Prose and Verse. London: 1855-57. V. 54
Mrs. Perkins's Ball. London: 1847. V. 50; 52; 53; 54
The Newcomes. London: 1835-55. V. 51
The Newcomes. London: 1853-55. V. 47; 48; 50; 52; 53; 54
The Newcomes. London: 1854. V. 49; 50; 54
The Newcomes. London: 1854-55. V. 47; 48; 50; 51; 53; 54
The Newcomes. London: 1855. V. 47; 52
The Newcomes. Cambridge: 1954. V. 49
The Newcomes. New York: 1955. V. 52; 54
Notes of a Journey from Cornhill to Grand Cairo. London: 1846. V. 47; 53; 54
The Orphan of Pimlico, and Other Sketches, Fragments and Drawings. London: 1876. V. 48
Our Street. London: 1848. V. 54
The Paris Sketch Book. London: 1840. V. 47
Punch's Prize Novelists, the Fat contributor, and Travels in London. New York: 1853. V. 53
Reading a Poem. London: 1891. V. 50
Reading a Poem. New York: 1911. V. 51
Rebecca and Rowena. London: 1850. V. 49; 52; 53; 54
The Rose and the Ring. London: 1855. V. 54
The Rose and the Ring. New York: 1855. V. 54
The Rose and the Ring. New York: 1942. V. 48; 52; 54
Roundabout Papers. London: 1863. V. 47; 54
Roundabout Papers. New York: 1863. V. 47
A Shabby Genteel Story. New York: 1852. V. 50
Sketches and Travels in London. London: 1856. V. 53
Sultan Stork and Other Stories and Sketches Now First Collected. London: 1887. V. 47; 49
Thackerayana Notes - Anecdotes. London: 1875. V. 51
Vanity Fair. London: 1847-48. V. 53
Vanity Fair. London: 1848. V. 47; 48; 49; 50; 51; 52; 53; 54
Vanity Fair. New York: 1848. V. 48
Vanity Fair. London: 1849. V. 47; 48
Vanity Fair. 1931. V. 53
Vanity Fair. New York: 1931. V. 49
Vanity Fair. Oxford: 1931. V. 52; 53; 54
The Virginians. London: 185/59. V. 49
The Virginians. London: 1857-59. V. 47; 48; 49; 53; 54
The Virginians. London: 1858. V. 50; 51
The Virginians. London: 1858-59. V. 47; 48; 49; 51; 53; 54
Works. Oxford. V. 48
The Works. London: 1858-69. V. 51
The Works. London: 1867-69. V. 51
Works. London: 1869. V. 51
The Works. London: 1869-86. V. 53
The Works. London: 1874-76. V. 48; 51
Works. London & New York: 1878. V. 48; 51
The Works... London: 1878-79/86. V. 50; 52
The Works... London: 1883-86. V. 50
Works. London: 1899-1906. V. 48
The Works... New York: 1903-04. V. 51
Works. London: 1904. V. 50
The Works. New York & London: 1910. V. 50; 54
The Works... London: 1911. V. 51

THACKRAH, CHARLES TURNER
The Effects of Arts, Trades and Professions, and of Civic States and Habits of Living... London: 1832. V. 48

THACKWELL, PAUL
A Collection of Miscellaneous and Religious Poems. Ross: 1820. V. 50

THAKUR, R. S.
Major Medicinal Plants of India. Lucknow: 1989. V. 52; 54

THALATTA: A Book for the Sea-Side. Boston: 1853. V. 50

THE THAMES. "Waterway of the World". London: 1893. V. 50

THE THAMES From Its Source to the Sea. London: 1892. V. 52

THANE, J.
British Autography. A Collection of Fac-Similes of the Hand Writing of Royal and Illustrious Personages, with Their Authentic Portraits. London. V. 52
British Autography. A Collection of Fac-Similes of the Hand-writing of Royal and Illustrious Personages, with Their Authentic Portraits. London: 1790. V. 52

THATCHER, BENJAMIN BUSSEY
Indian Biography: or, An Historical Account of Those Individuals Who Have Been Distinguished Among the North American Natives as Orators. New York: 1832. V. 47

THATCHER, MARGARET
The Downing Street Years. New York: 1993. V. 51

THATCHER, MARSHALL P.
A Hundred Battles in the West. Detroit: 1884. V. 47

THATCHER, RICHMOND
Life and Times of Jem Punch, Being an Account of the Life of a Worthy, Brave Hearted Citizen... Sydney: 1885. V. 50

THAXTER, CELIA
Among the Isles of Shoals. Boston: 1873. V. 52
The Cruise of the Mystery and Other Poems. Boston and New York: 1886. V. 51
Drift Weed. Boston: 1879. V. 52
An Island Garden. Boston: 1894. V. 48; 49; 50
An Island Garden. Boston & New York: 1895. V. 47; 48; 54
Poems. New York: 1872. V. 48

THAXTER, CELIA continued
Poems. New York: 1875. V. 48

THAYER, A. W.
The Life of Ludwig Van Beethoven. London: 1960. V. 49

THAYER, CAROLINE MATILDA WARREN
The Gamesters; or, Ruins of Innocence. Boston: 1805. V. 48; 54

THAYER, ELISHA
Family Memorial. 1835. V. 52

THAYER, EMMA HOMAN
Wild Flowers of Colorado. New York: 1885. V. 48; 50; 51; 52
Wild Flowers of the Rocky Mountains. New York: 1887. V. 47
Wild Flowers of the Rocky Mountains. New York: 1889. V. 49; 50; 51
Wild Flowers of the Rocky Mountains. New York: 1989. V. 48

THAYER, GERALD H.
Concealing colouration in the Animal Kingdom. New York: 1909. V. 47; 50; 51; 53
Concealing Colouration in the Animal Kingdom. New York: 1918. V. 52

THAYER, JAMES BRADLEY
Legal Essays. Cambridge: 1927. V. 50
A Western Journey with Mr. Emerson. Boston: 1884. V. 51

THAYER, JOHN
An Account of the Conversion of the Reverend Mr. John Thayer, Lately a Protestant Minister at Boston in North America... Baltimore: 1788. V. 52

THAYER, JOHN ELIOT
Catalogue of a Collection of Books on Ornithology in the Library of John E. Thayer. Boston: 1913. V. 51
Ornithological Collection of John Eliot Thayer. Lancaster: 1910?. V. 51

THAYER, PHINEAS
Casey at the Bat. Chicago: 1912. V. 50

THEAKSTON, MICHAEL
British Angling Flies. London: 1862. V. 47
British Angling Flies. Ripon: 1883. V. 47

THEAKSTON, S. W.
Theakston's Guide to Scarborough... Scarborough: 1862. V. 54

THEARLE, SAMUEL J. P.
The Modern Practice of Shipbuilding in Iron and Steel. London: 1891. V. 49

THE THEATRE, Tragic and Comic. Edinburgh: 1776. V. 49

THE THEATRE-Royal Turn'd Into a Mountebank's Stage. London: 1718. V. 51

THE THEATRIC Count, a Tragic Comedy, in Five Acts. London: 1809. V. 51

THEATRICAL Monopoly; Being an Address to the Public on the Present Alarming Coalition of the Managers of the Winter Theatres. London: 1779. V. 47

THEATRICAL Records; or, an Account of English Dramatic Authors, and Their Works. London: 1756. V. 48

THEATRUM Europaeum. Frankfurt: 1662-1738. V. 53

THELLER, EDWARD A.
Canada in 1837-38, Showing, by Historical Facts, the Causes of the Late Attempted Revolution and Of its Failure... Philadelphia: 1841. V. 50

THEMISTIUS, EUPHRADA
Omnia Themistii Opera, Hoc est Paraphrases, et Orationes. Venice: 1534. V. 48; 50

THEOBALD, F. V.
A Monograph of the Culicidae or Mosquitoes. London: 1901-10. V. 50; 51
Physiologue Theobaldi Episcopi De Naturis Duodecim Animalium. Bloomington: 1964. V. 52; 54
The Plant Lice or Aphididae of Great Britain. London: 1926-29. V. 49; 52

THEOBALD, JOHN
Miscellaneous Poems and Translations. London: 1724. V. 49
An Oxford Odyssey. 1955. V. 54

THEOBALD, LEWIS
Double Falshood; or, the Distrest Lovers. London: 1728. V. 47
The History of the Loves of Antiochus and Stratonice; In which are Interspers'd Some Accounts Relating to Greece and Syria. London: 1717. V. 52
Shakespeare Restored: or, a Specimen of the Many Errors, as well Committed, as Unamended by Mr. Pope in His Late edition of this Poet. London: 1726. V. 52; 54

THEOCRITUS
Commentari Vetera in Theocriti Eglogas...(Scholia to Theocritis). Venice: 1539. V. 52
The Complete Poems. London: 1929. V. 51; 54
Idyllia, Eiusdem Epigrammata. Geneva: 1579. V. 48
Idyls. London: 1910/11. V. 53
Idyls, Rendered Into English Prose. London: 1922. V. 48
Sixe Idyllia. London: 1971. V. 47
Sixe Idyllia. New York: 1971. V. 50; 52; 54
Theocriti Syracusii Quae Supersunt. Oxford: 1770/72. V. 48
Theocritus, Bion & Moschus. London: 1922. V. 49; 50; 52

THEODORE Low DeVinne. Printer. New York: 1915. V. 53

THE THEOPHILANTHROPIST. New York: 1810. V. 47

THEOPHRASTUS
The Characters: Illustrated by Physionomical Sketches. Boston: 1831. V. 53; 54
Characters of Theophrastus. London: 1824. V. 54
Libellus de Odoribus... Paris: 1556. V. 49
The Moral Characters of Theophrastus. London: 1714. V. 52
Notationes Morum. Lyons: 1599. V. 54

THEORETICAL, Practical and Analytical as Applied to the Arts and Manufactures. London: 1882. V. 48

THE THEORY of the Whizgig Considred; Inasmuch as it Mechanically Exemplifies the Three Working Properties of Nature... London: 1822. V. 47

THEORY of Theatrical Dancing. London: 1888. V. 47; 52

THEOSEBIA.. London: 1749. V. 53

THEROUX, ALEXANDER
An Adultery. New York: 1987. V. 48; 52; 53
Darconville's Cat. Garden City: 1981. V. 48; 52; 53
The Great Wheadle Tragedy. Boston: 1975. V. 51; 52; 53
History is Made at Night. West Chester: 1992. V. 51; 52; 53; 54
The Lollipop Trollops and Other Poems. Naperville: 1992. V. 52; 53
The Lollipop Trollops and Other Poems. Normal: 1992. V. 52; 53
The Primary Colors. New York: 1994. V. 52
The Schinocephalic Waif. Boston: 1975. V. 51; 52
Theroux Metaphrastes. Boston: 1975. V. 48; 52; 53
Three Wogs. Boston: 1972. V. 50; 51; 52
Watergraphs. Boston: 1994. V. 51; 52; 53

THEROUX, PAUL
The Black House. Boston: 1974. V. 53; 54
A Christmas Card. Boston: 1978. V. 51
The Consul's File. Boston: 1977. V. 47
The Family Arsenal. London: 1976. V. 50
Fong and the Indians. Boston: 1968. V. 48; 49; 54
Fong and the Indians. Boston: 1969. V. 47
Fong and the Indians. London: 1976. V. 49; 51; 52; 53; 54
Girls at Play. Boston: 1969. V. 49; 51; 52; 53; 54
The Great Railway Bazaar. Boston: 1975. V. 51; 53; 54
Half Moon Street. Boston: 1984. V. 51; 54
Jungle Lovers. Boston: 1971. V. 48; 51; 54
Jungle Lovers. London: 1971. V. 54
The Kingdom By the Sea. Boston: 1983. V. 47; 51; 54
The London Embassy. Boston: 1983. V. 53
London Snow... London: 1973. V. 52
London Snow. London: 1979. V. 51; 53; 54
London Snow. Salisbury: 1979. V. 47; 48; 49; 50; 51; 53; 54
London Snow. Wiltshire: 1979. V. 54
The Mosquito Coast. Boston: 1882. V. 54
The Mosquito Coast. London: 1981. V. 51
The Mosquito Coast. Boston: 1982. V. 49; 51; 52; 53; 54
My Secret History. London: 1989. V. 48; 49; 51; 52
The Old Patagonian Express. Boston: 1979. V. 52; 53
Picture Palace. Boston: 1978. V. 47; 50
Sailing through China. Salisbury: 1983. V. 47; 48; 51
Sailing through China. Boston: 1984. V. 53
Saint Jack. Boston: 1973. V. 47; 50; 54
Saint Jack. London: 1973. V. 54
Sinning with Annie. Boston: 1972. V. 49; 52; 54
Sunrise with Seamonsters. Boston: 1985. V. 53
V. S. Naipaul: an Introduction to His Work. London: 1972. V. 52; 54
Waldo. Boston: 1967. V. 47; 48; 49; 51; 52; 53; 54
Waldo. London: 1967. V. 48
World's End and Other Stories. Boston: 1980. V. 53; 54

THESAURUS Dramaticus. London: 1924. V. 52

THESIGER, WILFRED
Arabian Sands. London: 1959. V. 49; 53; 54
Desert Marsh and Mountain. The World of a Nomad. London: 1979. V. 49
Visions of a Nomad. London: 1987. V. 49

THE THESPIAN Dictionary. London: 1802. V. 50; 54

THESPIAN Dictionary, or Dramatic Biography of the Present Age, Containing Sketches of the Lives...Of All the Principal Dramatists, Composers, Commentators, Managers, Actors and Actresses of the United Kingdom. London: 1805. V. 52

THE THESPIAN Preceptor; or, a Full Display of the Scenic Art... Boston: 1810. V. 52; 53; 54

THEVENOT, JEAN DE
The Travels of Monsieur de Thevenot into the Levant. London: 1687. V. 51

THEVENOT, MELHISEDEC
Relations de Divers Voyages qui n'ont Point Este Publiees, et quW. B. O'Neill NS18-on a Traduit ou Tire des Originaux des Voyageurs Francois, Espagnols, Allemands, Portugais, Anglois, Hollandois, Persans, Arabes & Autres Orientaux... Paris: 1697. V. 48

THEY Still Draw Pictures: a Collection of 60 drawings Made by Spanish Children During the War. New York: 1938. V. 49

THEY Still Draw Pictures!. New York: 1938. V. 48; 53

THIBAUDEAU, COLLEEN
Lozenges: Poems in the Shapes of Things. London: 1965. V. 47

THICKNESSE, ANN
Sketches of the Lives and Writings of the Ladies of France. London: 1780-81. V. 54

THICKNESSE, PHILIP
Memoirs and Anecdotes of Philip Thicknesse... London: 1788. V. 52
Memoirs and Anecdotes of Philip Thicknesse... Dublin: 1790. V. 47
A Year's Journey through France and Part of Spain. Bath: 1777. V. 47; 50
A Year's Journey Through France and Part of Spain. London: 1778. V. 50

THIELEN, BETH
Why the Revolving Door: the Neighborhood, the Prisons. 1993. V. 52

THIERS, LOUIS ADOLPHE
The History of the French Revolution. London: 1881. V. 52

THIERS, M. A.
The History of the French Revolution. London: 1838. V. 47; 51

THIMM, CARL A.
A Complete Bibliography of Fencing and Duelling... London: 1896. V. 50

THINGS By Their Right Names; a Novel. Boston: 1812. V. 47; 52

THIRA; or, the Cairn Branch. London: 1879. V. 47

THIRD Appendix to the Abridgement of the Statutes of Ireland. V. 49

THIRTY Favorite Paintings by Leading American Artists. New York: 1908. V. 49

THIRTY Old-Time Nursery Songs. London: 1915. V. 51

THIRTY Plates Illustrative of natural Phenomena, Etc. With a Short Description Annexed to Each Plate. London: 1849. V. 48

THIRTY Views of Ramsgate. 1870. V. 50

THIRTY Years Among the Zunis, Oct. 11, 1897 to Oct. 11, 1927. Muskegon: 1927. V. 54

THIRTY-SECOND Infantry Division WWII. Blakely: 1955. V. 52

THIRTY-THREE Triads. Dublin: 1955. V. 49

THISSELL, G. W.
Crossing the Plains in '49. Oakland: 1903. V. 47; 48; 51; 53

THISTED, VALDEMAR ADOLPH
Letters from Hell. London and Copenhagen: 1866. V. 54

THISTLEWAITE, BERNARD
The Bax Family. London: 1936. V. 49

THISTLEWOOD, ARTHUR
The Trial of Arthur Thistlewood, on a Charge of High Treason. Tried At Old Bailey, April 17th, 1820, Before the Lord Chief Justice Abbott. London: 1820. V. 53

THOBURN, J.
A History of Oklahoma. San Francisco: 1908. V. 54

THOINAN, ERNEST
Le Reliures Francais. Paris: 1893. V. 53; 54

THOM, ADAM
The Claims of the Oregon Territory Considered. London: 1844. V. 47; 48; 49; 54

THOM, ROBERT
A Brief Account of the Shaws Water Scheme, and Present State of the Works: with...Drawings and Descriptions of the Various Hydraulic Contrivances Employed in Collected, Economizing and Bringing Home the Water to the Mills... Greenock: 1825. V. 51

THOM, WILLIAM
Rhymes and Recollections of a Hand-Loom Weaver. London and elsewhere: 1844. V. 54
The Trial of a Student at the College of Clutha in the Kingdom of Oceana. Glasgow: 1768. V. 53

THOMA, KURT H.
Oral Roentgenology: a Roentgen Study of the Anatomy and Pathology of the Oral Cavity. Boston: 1922. V. 52

THOMAS, A. S.
Laboratories of the Spirit. 1976. V. 49

THOMAS, ABEL C.
A Brief Memoir Concerning Abel Thomas, a Minister of the Gospel of Christ in the Society of Friends... Philadelphia: 1824. V. 49
Complete Refutation of Miller's Theory of the End of the World in 1843. Philadelphia: 1843. V. 51

THOMAS, ALAN G.
Great Books and Great Book Collectors. London: 1975. V. 47

THOMAS, ANTOINE LEONARD
Essay on the Character, Manners and Genius of Women in Different Ages. Philadelphia: 1774. V. 48; 50; 51

THOMAS, BENJAMIN P.
Abraham Lincoln: a biography. New York: 1952. V. 50

THOMAS, BERTRAM
Alarms and Excursions in Arabia. London: 1931. V. 51
Arabia Felix: Across the "Empty Quarter" of Arabia. New York: 1932. V. 48

THOMAS, C.
Lists of Elevations and Distances in That Portion of the United States West of the Mississippi River. Washington: 1872. V. 47

THOMAS, CAITLIN
Not Quite Posthumous Letter to My Daughter. Boston: 1963. V. 53

THOMAS, CASSIUS M.
Centennial Congress 1876. Washington: 1876. V. 52

THOMAS, CLARENCE
General Turner Ashby the Centaur of the South A Military Sketch. Winchester: 1907. V. 49

THOMAS, CORBINIANUS
Manductio ad Astronomiam, Juxta Modum Bayerii... Leipzig & Nurnberg: 1730. V. 47

THOMAS, D. M.
Birthstone. London: 1980. V. 52; 53
D. M. Thomas. Berkhamsted, Herts: 1974. V. 54
Logan Stone. London: 1971. V. 48
Personal and Possessive. London: 1964. V. 52
Selected Poems. New York: 1983. V. 54
Two Voices. London: 1968. V. 48; 54
The White Hotel. London: 1981. V. 48; 54
The White Hotel. Toronto: 1981. V. 48

THOMAS, DAVID
Travels through the Western Country in the Summer of 1816... Auburn: 1819. V. 47; 54

THOMAS, DAVIS
People of the First Man - Life Among the Plains Indians in Their Final Days of Glory... New York: 1976. V. 47
People of the First Man: Life Among the Plains Indians in Their Final Days of Glory... New York: 1982. V. 54

THOMAS, DWIGHT
The Poe Log. A Documentary Life. Boston: 1987. V. 48

THOMAS, DYLAN MARLAIS
18 Poems. London. V. 51
18 Poems. London: 1932. V. 51
18 Poems. London: 1934. V. 48; 49; 50; 52; 53; 54
Adventures in the Skin Trade. London: 1955. V. 47; 48; 50; 53
Adventures in the Skin Trade... New York: 1955. V. 53
Adventures in the Skin Trade... Norfolk: 1955. V. 48; 52
Botteghe Obscure No. 9. London: 1952. V. 49
A Child's Christmas in Wales. Norfolk: 1954. V. 48; 53
A Child's Christmas in Wales. Norfolk: 1955. V. 53
Collected Poems. London: 1952. V. 47; 52; 53; 54
Collected Poems. New York: 1953. V. 51
Conversation About Christmas. New York: 1954. V. 48; 51; 54
Deaths and Entrances. London: 1946. V. 47; 48; 49; 50; 53
The Doctor and the Devils. New York: 1953. V. 47; 54
The Doctor and the Devils... New York: 1966. V. 49
In Country Sleep. 1952. V. 50
In Country Sleep. New York: 1952. V. 47; 48; 49; 51; 53
Letter to Loren. London: 1993. V. 49
Letter to Loren. Swansea: 1993. V. 54
The Map of Love. London: 1939. V. 47; 49; 51; 52; 53; 54
The Mouse and the Woman. San Diego: 1988. V. 47; 53
New Poems. Norfolk: 1943. V. 47; 48; 49; 50
Poems. 1980. V. 48
The Poetry of Dylan Thomas. Chicago: 1954. V. 48; 50
Portrait of the Artist as a Young Dog. London: 1940. V. 50
Portrait of the Artist as a Young Dog. Norfolk: 1940. V. 48; 54
Portrait of the Artist As A Young Dog. Norfolk: 1944. V. 48
A Prospect of the Sea: and Other Stories and Prose Writings. London: 1955. V. 54
Quite Early One Morning. London: 1954. V. 48; 50
Twelve More Letters. London: 1969. V. 49
Twelve More Letters. Stoke Ferry: 1969. V. 48; 51
Twenty-Five Poems. London: 1936. V. 48; 49; 50; 53; 54
Twenty-Six Poems. London: 1949. V. 49
Under Milk Wood. 1954. V. 51
Under Milk Wood. London: 1954. V. 47; 48; 49; 51; 52; 54
Under Milk Wood. New York: 1954. V. 48; 50; 52; 53
The World I Breathe. 1939. V. 47; 48
The World I Breathe. Connecticut: 1939. V. 48
The World I Breathe. Norfolk: 1939. V. 49; 51; 54

THOMAS, EBENEZER SMITH
Reminiscences of the Last Sixty-Five Years, Commencing With the Battle of Lexington. Hartford: 1840. V. 48

THOMAS, EDITH M.
Babes of the Nations. New York: 1889. V. 49

THOMAS, EDWARD
Algernon Charles Swinburne. London: 1912. V. 48; 49
Beautiful Wales. London: 1905. V. 51
Chosen Essays. Newtown: 1926. V. 50
Cloud Castle an Other Papers. London: 1922. V. 52; 53

THOMAS, EDWARD continued
Collected Poems. London: 1920. V. 47; 52
The Diary of Edward Thomas, 1 January to 16 April, 1917. Gloucestershire: 1977. V. 48
The Diary of Edward Thomas: 1 January to 8 April 1917. London: 1977. V. 48
Feminine Influence On the Poets. London: 1910. V. 50; 51
George Borrow. The Man and His Books. London: 1912. V. 49
The Heart of England. London: 1906. V. 47; 48; 50
Horae Solitariae. London: 1902. V. 47; 48; 52; 54
In Pursuit of Spring. London: 1914. V. 50
Last Poems. London: 1918. V. 47; 49; 50
The Last Sheaf. Essays. London: 1928. V. 48
Light and Twilight. London: 1911. V. 54
A Literary Pilgrim in England. New York: 1917. V. 50
Maurice Maeterlinck. New York: 1911. V. 49
Oxford. London: 1903. V. 49; 50; 54
Poems. London: 1917. V. 51; 53
Rest and Unrest. London: 1910. V. 54
Richard Jefferies: His Life and Work. London: 1909. V. 49; 54
Selected Poems. Newtown: 1927. V. 47; 48; 51; 52; 54
Six Poems... Flansham: 1916. V. 51
Six Poems... 1921. V. 52
Twelve Poets. A Miscellany in New Verse. London: 1918. V. 50
Two Poems. London: 1927. V. 47; 48; 52
The Woodland Life. Edinburgh & London: 1897. V. 47; 49; 50; 51

THOMAS, ELIZABETH PATTERSON
Old Kentucky Homes and Gardens. Louisville: 1939. V. 51

THOMAS, F. W.
Low and I. A Cooked Tour in London. London: 1923. V. 51

THOMAS, FRANK J.
Mark Twain Roughed It Here. Los Angeles: 1964. V. 47
The Myths of California Isle. Los Angeles: 1966. V. 51

THOMAS, FREDERICK
The Trial of Lieut. Col. Thomas of the First Regiment of Foot-Guards on a Charge Exhibited by Lieut. Col. Cosmo Gordon... London: 1781. V. 47

THOMAS, FREDERICK WILLIAM
East and West. Philadelphia: 1836. V. 48
The Emigrant, or Reflections While Descending the Ohio. Cincinnati: 1833. V. 49; 52

THOMAS, H. B.
Uganda. London: 1935. V. 54

THOMAS, H. S.
The Rod in India...with Remarks on the Natural History of Fish. London: 1881. V. 49

THOMAS, HENRY
Andres Brun. Calligrapher of Saragossa. Some Account of His Life and Work. Paris and New York: 1928. V. 49
Andres Brun, Calligrapher of Saragossa, Some Account of His Life and Work... Paris: 1929. V. 50
Early Spanish Bookbindings XI-XV Centuries. London: 1939. V. 48; 50; 51

THOMAS, HENRY F.
A Twentieth Century History of Allegany County, Michigan. Chicago: 1907. V. 49

THOMAS, HENRY SULLIVAN
The Rod in India: Being Hints How to Obtain Sport, with Remarks on the Natural History of Fish, Their Culture and Value.... 1881. V. 53

THOMAS, HENRY WALTER
History of the Doles-Cook Brigade Army of Northern Virginia, C.S.A. Containing Muster Rolls of Each Company of the Fourth, Twelfth, Twenty First and Forty-Fourth Georgia Regiments. Atlanta: 1903. V. 54

THOMAS, ISAIAH
The History of Printing in America. Worcester: 1810. V. 47; 48; 50
The History of Printing in America... Albany: 1874. V. 50
The History of Printing in America. Albany: 1876. V. 53
The History of Printing in America. Barre: 1970. V. 49; 51; 54

THOMAS, J. A. W.
A History of Marlboro County... Atlanta: 1897. V. 47; 50

THOMAS, J. B.
Observations on Borzoi, Called in America Russian Wolfhounds. Boston: 1912. V. 49

THOMAS, J. J.
Rural Affairs: A Practical and Copiously Illustrated Register of Rural Economy and Rural Taste... Albany: 1868. V. 48

THOMAS, JAMES A.
A Pioneer Tobacco Merchant in the Orient. Durham: 1928. V. 48

THOMAS Jefferson - Architect and Builder. Richmond: 1931. V. 47; 48

THOMAS, JERRY
How to Mix Drinks, or the Bon-vivant's Companion... New York: 1862. V. 48; 54

THOMAS, JOHN
Practical Observations on Chronic Affections of the Digestive Organs, and on Bilious and Nervous Disorders... Cheltenham: 1821. V. 47; 49

THOMAS, JOHN J.
The American Fruit Culturist, Containing Practical Directions for the Propagation and Culture of All Fruits Adapted to the United States. New York: 1875. V. 49

THOMAS, JOHN PEYRE
Career and Character of General Micah Jenkins, C.S.A. Columbia: 1903. V. 47; 49; 50

THOMAS, JOSEPH
A Comprehensive Medical Dictionary... Philadelphia: 1865. V. 49

THOMAS, JOSEPH B.
Hounds and Hunting through the Ages... New York: 1928. V. 47
Hounds and Hunting Through the Ages... New York: 1929. V. 47

THOMAS, JOYCE CAROL
Bitter Sweet. San Jose: 1973. V. 53

THOMAS, LAURIE
Arthur Boyd Drawings 1934-1970. 1973. V. 51
Arthur Boyd Drawings 1934-1970. London: 1973. V. 53

THOMAS, LEWIS
Quartet. Berkeley: 1986. V. 51

THOMAS, LYNALL
Rifled Ordnance. A Practical Treatise on the Application of the Principle of the Rifle to Guns and Mortars of Every Calibre, by Dunamikos. London: 1857. V. 48
A Theory for Obtaining the Maximum Range of Shot from Cannon, with the Employment of the Least Possible Quantity of Material Necessary for Durability... London: 1855. V. 54
The True Basis for Construction of Heavy Artillery. London: 1869. V. 54

THOMAS, MANUEL
Insulana. Antwerp: 1635. V. 48

THOMAS, MARGARET
Cambridge Women's Verse. An Anthology. London: 1931. V. 51

THOMAS, MATT
Hopping on the Border: the Life Story of a Bellboy. San Antonio: 1951. V. 53

THOMAS, N. W.
Anthropological Report on the Edo-Speaking Peoples of Nigeria. London: 1910. V. 54
Kinship Organisations and Group Marriage in Australia. Cambridge: 1906. V. 52
Natives of Australia. London: 1906. V. 52

THOMAS, OF MONMOUTH
The Life and Miracles of St. William of Norwich. 1896. V. 50

THOMAS, OLDFIELD
The Duke of Bedford's Zoological Exploration in Eastern Asia. London: 1906-07. V. 51

THOMAS, OWEN
Agricultural and Pastoral Prospects of South Africa. London: 1904. V. 50

THOMAS, P. P.
A Dissertation On the Ancient Chinese Vases Of the Shang Dynasty, from 1743-1496, BC. London: 1851. V. 50

THOMAS, PASCOE
A True and Impartial Journal of a Voyage to the South Seas, and Round the Globe, In His Majesty's Ship the Centurion Under the Command of Commodore George Anson. London: 1745. V. 50

THOMAS, PETER
Bikupan, the Story of a Trip to Visit a Hand Paper Mill in Sweden, with a Bit of History Added in for Good Measure. Santa Cruz: 1992. V. 49
A Collection of Paper Samples from Hand Papermills in the United States of America. Santa Cruz: 1993. V. 51

THOMAS, R. S.
An Acre of Land. Newtown: 1952. V. 49
The Bright Field. Babel: 1986. V. 53
Collected Poems 1945-1990. 1993. V. 51
Collected Poems 1945-1990. London: 1993. V. 49; 50
Destinations. 1985. V. 49
Destinations. Warwickshire: 1985. V. 54
Frieze Babel. Babel: 1992. V. 51
Laboratories of the Spirit. Newtown: 1976. V. 47
The Minister. Newtown: 1953. V. 47
The Mountains. New York: 1968. V. 47; 48; 52
Pieta. London: 1966. V. 49
Poet's Meeting. Stratford-upon-Avon: 1983. V. 53; 54
Selected Poems 1946-1968. London: 1974. V. 51
Song at the Year's Turning. London: 1955. V. 50; 53; 54
The Stones of the Field. 1946. V. 49
The Stones of the Field. Carmarthen: 1946. V. 47; 49
Words and the Poet - The W. D. Thomas Memorial Lecture Delivered at the University College of Swansea on November 19, 1963. Cardiff: 1964. V. 51

THOMAS, RALPH
Serjeant Thomas and Sir J. E. Millais Bart. London: 1901. V. 51; 54

THOMAS, ROBERT
The Modern Practice of Physic... New York: 1811. V. 49; 51
The Modern Practice of Physic. New York: 1813. V. 50; 51; 54
The Modern Practice of Physic. New York: 1824. V. 54
The Modern Practice of Physic... New York: 1825. V. 51

THOMAS, ROSE HAIG
Stone Gardens. London: 1905. V. 47

THOMAS, ROSS
The Backup Men. New York: 1971. V. 50; 52; 53
The Brass Go-Between. New York: 1969. V. 52; 53
Briarpatch. New York: 1984. V. 48; 52
Cast a Yellow Shadow. New York: 1967. V. 47; 48; 49; 50; 52; 53
Cast A Yellow Shadow. London: 1968. V. 49
The Cold War Swap. New York: 1966. V. 49; 50; 52; 53
The Fools in Town Are On Our Side. London: 1970. V. 53
The Fools in Town Are On Our Side. New York: 1971. V. 48; 49; 50
The Highbinders. New York: 1973. V. 48
The Highbinders. New York: 1974. V. 50; 52; 53; 54
If You Can't Be Good. New York: 1973. V. 48; 51; 52; 53
The Money Harvest. New York: 1975. V. 52; 53
No Questions Asked. New York: 1976. V. 53
Out on the Rim. New York: 1987. V. 48; 52
The Porkchoppers. New York: 1972. V. 49; 52; 53
The Porkchoppers. New York: 1975. V. 53
The Procane Chronicle. New York: 1972. V. 51; 53; 54
Protocol for a Kidnapping. New York: 1971. V. 52; 53
The Seersucker Whipsaw. New York: 1967. V. 52; 53
The Singapore Wink. New York: 1969. V. 52; 53
Spies, Thumbsuckers, Etc. Northridge. V. 48
Spies, Thumbsuckers, etc. Northridge: 1989. V. 53
Spy in the Vodka. 1967. V. 53
Yellow-Dog Contract. New York: 1977. V. 52; 53

THOMAS, W. BEACH
With the British on the Somme. London: 1917. V. 47

THOMAS, WILLIAM
A Collection of Early Prose Romances. London: 1827/28. V. 52
Hints, for Establishing an Office in Newcastle... Newcastle: 1815. V. 51
The Historye of Italye. London: 1561. V. 51
A Survey of the Cathedral Church of Worcester... London: 1737. V. 51

THOMAS, WILLIAM H.
On Land and Sea, or, California in the Years 1843, '44, '45. Boston: 1884. V. 47

THOMAS, WILLIAM RUSSELL
Sunlight Views of Fort Collins and Surroundings. Fort Collins: 1907. V. 52

THOMAS, WILLIAM S.
Hunting Big Game with Gun and Kodak. New York: 1906. V. 47; 48; 52; 54
Hunting Big Game with Gun and Kodak. New York: 1966. V. 54

THOMAS A KEMPIS
The Following of Christ... London: 1686. V. 52; 54

THOMAS AQUINAS, PSEUD.
De Arte et Vero Modo Predicandi. Memingen: 1483. V. 50

THOMAS AQUINAS, SAINT
Aquinas Ethicus: or, the Moral Teaching of St. Thomas. London: 1892. V. 51
Catena Aurea Super Omnia Evangelia Dominicalia et Ferialia. Venice: 1494. V. 51; 52
Cathena Aurea in Q(ua)ttuor Eva(n)ngelia. Lyon: 1520. V. 48; 50
Diuus Thomas in Octo Politicorum Aristotelis Libros Cum Textu Eiusdem Leonardo Aretino Interprete Nouissime Recognitus. Venice: 1514. V. 53
Divi Thomae Aquinitatis, In Beati Ioannis Apocalypism Expositio.... Florence: 1549. V. 50
In Evangelium Beati Joannis Evageliste Aurea Expositio... Paris: 1520. V. 52
In Mattheum Evangelistam, Esayamq. et Hieremiam Prophetas, Necno Eiusde Hieremie Trenos Commentaria. 1531. V. 50
Opus Aureum Sancti Thome de Aquino Super Quatuor Evangelia. Venice: 1493. V. 52
Saint Thomas Aquinas. Selections from His Works Made by George N. Shuster. Chatham: 1969. V. 51
Selections from His Works. 1969. V. 52
Selections from His Works. New York: 1969. V. 50
Summa Totius Theologiae... (with) Prima Secundae Partis Summae Theologicae... Antwerp: 1569. V. 50
Super Tertio Libro Sententiarum. Venice: 1490. V. 47; 49; 50; 53
Theologorum Principis. 1520. V. 50

THOMAS ATTRABATENSIS
Quaestiones super Quattuor Libris Sententiarum. Lyons: 1491. V. 54

THOMAS HERBERT
Chapters in American Obstetrics. Springfield: 1933. V. 52

THOMAS ISAIAH
The History of Printing in America. Barre: 1970. V. 48

THOMASIUS, THOMAS
Thomae Thomasii Dictionarium... Cantabrigiae: 1606. V. 47; 50; 51

THOMAS JEANETTE BELL
Devil's Ditties: Being Stories of the Kentucky Mountain People. Chicago: 1931. V. 47

THOMASON, CAROLINE
Youth of Color. New York: 1951. V. 54

THOMASON, GEORGE
Catalogue of the Pamphlets, Books Newspapers, and Manuscripts Relating to the Civil War, the Commonwealth and Restoration, Collected by George Thomason 1640-1661. London: 1908. V. 52; 53

THOMAS-STANFORD, CHARLES
Early Editions of Euclid's Elements. London: 1926. V. 49; 51; 54
Sussex in the Great Civil War and the Interregnum 1642-1660. London: 1910. V. 50

THOMLINSON, M. H.
The Garrison of Fort Bliss, 1849-1916. El Paso: 1945. V. 47

THOMOND, DOWAGER MARCHIONESS OF
Catalogue of the Very Valuable and Highly Important Collection of Ancient and Modern Pictures... (with) Catalogue of Drawings by Old Masters Chiefly of the Italian school... London: 1821. V. 47

THOMPSON & WEST
Official Historical Atlas Map of Alameda County, California. Fresno: 1976. V. 54

THOMPSON, A. HAMILTON
The History of the Hospital and the New College of the Annunciation of St. May in the Newarke, Leicester. Leicester: 1937. V. 49

THOMPSON, A. M.
The Galley Slave and His Daughter. Dublin: 1858. V. 50

THOMPSON, A. R.
Gold-Seeking on the Dalton Trail. Boston: 1900. V. 47

THOMPSON, ALBERT
They Were Open Range Days, Annals of a Western Frontier. Denver: 1946. V. 52

THOMPSON, ALICE
A Bibliography of Nursing Literature, 1859-1960, with An Historical Introduction. London: 1968. V. 52

THOMPSON, ANTHONY
PFE, Pacific Fruit Express. Wilton: 1992. V. 53

THOMPSON, ARTHUR
The Ancient Races of the Thebaid, Being an Anthropometrical study of the Inhabitants of Upper Egypt from the Earliest Prehistoric Times to the Mohammedan Conquest Based Upon the Examination of Over 1500 Crania. Oxford: 1905. V. 49

THOMPSON, BENJAMIN
Inventions, Improvements and Practice of Benjamin Thompson... Newcastle: 1847. V. 50

THOMPSON, BENJAMIN F.
The History of Long Island; From Its Discovery and Settlement to the Present Time. New York: 1843. V. 53

THOMPSON, C. HALFORD
The Pyrenees Described in Verse and Illustrated with a Camera. 1898. V. 54

THOMPSON, C. J. S.
The Mystery and Lore of Monsters with Account of Some Giants, Dwarfs and Prodigies. New York: 1931. V. 52; 54
The Quacks of Old London. London: 1923. V. 49

THOMPSON, C. PATRICK
Adventures in Investing. London: 1936. V. 53

THOMPSON, CHARLES
Rules for Bad Horsemen. London: 1763. V. 50

THOMPSON, CHARLES W.
Life if a Jest. The Testimony of a Wanderer. London: 1924. V. 48

THOMPSON, DANIEL PIERCE
The Adventures of Timothy Peacock, Esq. Middlebury: 1835. V. 49; 54
The Green Mountain Boys: a Historical Tale of the Early Settlement of Vermont. Montpelier: 1839. V. 48
Locke Amsden, or the Schoolmaster: a Tale. Boston: 1847. V. 48
May Martin: or the Money Diggers. Montpelier: 1835. V. 54

THOMPSON, D'ARCY W.
On Growth and Form. Cambridge: 1942. V. 52

THOMPSON, DAVID
David Thompson's Narrative... -1812. Toronto: 1916. V. 47; 50
David Thompson's Narrative, 1784-1812. Toronto: 1962. V. 53
History of the Late War Between Great Britain and the United States of America... Niagara: 1832. V. 47; 53

THOMPSON, DEBORAH
Coptic Textiles in the Brooklyn Museum. Brooklyn: 1971. V. 49
Stucco from Chal Tarkhan-Eshgabad near Rayy. Warminster: 1976. V. 50; 52

THOMPSON, DON W.
Men and Meridians: the History of Surveying and Mapping in Canada. Ottawa: 1975/72/69. V. 50

THOMPSON, DOROTHY
I Saw Hitler. 1932. V. 53
I Saw Hitler. New York: 1932. V. 49

THOMPSON, DUNSTAN
The Third Murderer. London: 1944. V. 47

THOMPSON, E. P.
William Morris - Romantic to Revolutionary. London: 1955. V. 53

THOMPSON, EDWARD
The Demi-Rep. London: 1766. V. 54
The Meretrciad. London: 1765. V. 54
Roentgen Rays and Phenomena of the Anode and Cathode. New York: 1896. V. 54

THOMPSON, EDWARD H.
The Chultunes of Labna, Yucatan. Cambridge: 1897. V. 50; 52

THOMPSON, EDWARD MAUNDE
An Introduction to Greek and Latin Paleography. Oxford: 1912. V. 48

THOMPSON, ELIZABETH
Kindergarten Homes. New York: 1882. V. 47

THOMPSON, ERA BELL
American Daughter. Chicago: 1947. V. 53

THOMPSON, FLORA
Bog-Myrtle and Peat. London: 1922. V. 49

THOMPSON, FRANCIS
Collected Poetry. London: 1913. V. 50; 54
Literary Criticisms by Francis Thompson.... 1948. V. 51
The Mistress of Vision. Ditchling: 1918. V. 51
New Poems. Boston: 1897. V. 53
Shelley. London: 1909. V. 54
Sister Songs. London: 1895. V. 47; 49; 50; 53
Works. London: 1913. V. 47; 49; 50

THOMPSON, FRANCIS BENJAMIN
The Universal Decorator. London: 1860. V. 52

THOMPSON, GEORGE
Catharine and Clara; or the Double Suicide. Boston: 1854. V. 52
Lectures On British India... Pawtucket: 1840. V. 54
Letters and Addresses by George Thompson, During His Mission in the United States, from Oct. 1st, 1834 to Nov. 27, 1835. Boston: 1837. V. 54
The Prison Bard; or Poems on Various Subjects. Hartford: 1848. V. 52
Prison Life and Reflections. Hartford: 1849. V. 52
Prison Life and Reflections; or, a Narrative of the Arrest, Trial, Conviction, Imprisonment, Observations, Reflections and Deliverance of Work, Burr and Thompson, Who Suffered an Unjust and Cruel Imprisonment in Missouri Penitentiary... Hartford: 1850. V. 50
The Substance of a Speech Delivered in the Wesleyan Methodist Chapel, Irwell St., Salford, Manchester, on Monday, Aug. 13th, 1832... London: 1832. V. 48; 53
Thompson in Africa, or an Account of the Missionary Labors, Sufferings, Trials, Observations &c. of George Thompson in Western Africa, or the Mendi Mission. Cleveland: 1852. V. 53
Travels and Adventures in Southern Africa. London: 1827. V. 47; 50; 51; 52; 54

THOMPSON, HARRY STEPHEN
Ireland in 1839 and 1869. London: 1870. V. 52

THOMPSON, HARRY V.
The Rabbit. London: 1956. V. 48; 53

THOMPSON, HENRY
The Diseases of the Postrate, Their Pathology and Treatment. London: 1868. V. 49; 54
The Motor Car, It's Nature, Use and Management. London: 1902. V. 52; 54
Sketches of Characters: Moral & Political Condition of the Republic; the Judiciary &c. Philadelphia: 1839. V. 48; 49

THOMPSON, HENRY, BART
Modern Cremation: Its History and Practice, with Information Relating to the Recently Improved Arrangements Made by the Cremation Society of England. London: 1889. V. 51

THOMPSON, HERBERT
A Family Archive from Siut from Papyri in the British Museum Including an Account of a Trial Before the Laocritae in the Year B.C. 170. Oxford: 1934. V. 49

THOMPSON, HUNTER S.
Fear and Loathing on the Campaign Trail '72. San Francisco: 1973. V. 48; 51; 52; 53
The Great Shark Hunt. New York: 1979. V. 50
Hell's Angels. New York: 1967. V. 48; 49; 51

THOMPSON, ISAAC
Poetic Essays, on Nature, Men and Morals. Newcastle upon Tyne: 1750. V. 47

THOMPSON, J. ERIC S.
An Archaeological Reconnaissance in the Cotzumalhuapa Region, Escuintla, Guatemala. Washington: 1948. V. 52
A Commentary on the Dresden Codex. Philadelphia: 1972. V. 47; 50; 53
Excavations at San Jose, British Honduras. Washington: 1939. V. 50; 52
Maya Hieroglyphic Writing. 1950. V. 51
Maya Hieroglyphic Writing... Washington: 1950. V. 50
Maya Hieroglyphic Writing. Norman: 1960. V. 51

THOMPSON, J. V.
A Catalogue of Plants Growing in the Vicinity of Berwick upon Tweed. London: 1807. V. 50; 52; 53

THOMPSON, J. W.
Sketches, Historical and Descriptive of Noted Maine Horses. Portland: 1874/87. V. 52

THOMPSON, JAMES
Poems in the Scottish Dialect. Edinburgh: 1801. V. 54

THOMPSON, JAMES MAURICE
My First Voyage and Other Stories by Noted Authors. Boston: 1890. V. 50
The Witchery of Archery: a Complete Manual of Archery. New York: 1878. V. 52

THOMPSON, JAMES WESTFALL
The Frankfort Book Fair, the Francofordiense Emporium of Henri Estienne. Chicago: 1911. V. 49; 50

THOMPSON, JERRY
Sabers on the Rio Grande. Austin: 1974. V. 52

THOMPSON, JIM
Bad Boy. New York: 1953. V. 49
The Criminal. New York: 1953. V. 52
The Getaway. New York: 1959. V. 51; 53
The Grifters. Evanston: 1963. V. 53
Ironside. New York: 1967. V. 52
The Kill-Off. New York: 1957. V. 52
The Nothing Man. New York: 1954. V. 52
Nothing More than Murder. New York: 1949. V. 50; 51
Now and On Earth. New York: 1942. V. 53
Pop. 1280. Greenwich: 1964. V. 48
Pop. 1280. New York: 1964. V. 49
The Undefeated. New York: 1969. V. 52

THOMPSON, JOHN
The Life of John Thompson, a Fugitive Slave... Worcester: 1856. V. 47; 54

THOMPSON, JOHN R.
The Genius and Character of Edgar Allan Poe. 1929. V. 48; 49
Oration and Poem. Richmond: 1856. V. 52

THOMPSON, JOHN S. D.
The Execution of Louis Riel. speech of the Hon. John S. D. Thompson, Minister of Justice. Delivered March 22, 1886. V. 53

THOMPSON, JOHN W.
The Adventures of General Marbot. New York: 1935. V. 50

THOMPSON, JOSEPH A.
El Gran Capitan. Jose De la Guerra. A Historical Biographical Study. Los Angeles: 1961. V. 50

THOMPSON, KAY
Eloise. New York: 1955. V. 47
Eloise at Christmastime. New York: 1958. V. 49; 53
Eloise in Moscow. London: 1959. V. 51
Eloise in Moscow. New York: 1959. V. 47; 48; 49; 51; 54
Eloise in Moscow. New York: 1960. V. 49
Eloise in Paris. New York: 1957. V. 47
Eloise in Paris. London: 1958. V. 52
Miss Pooky Peckinpaugh. New York: 1970. V. 50

THOMPSON, LAWRENCE
Moby Dick: the Passion of Ahab. 1968. V. 54
Moby Dick; the Passion of Ahab. Barre: 1968. V. 52

THOMPSON, MARGARET
The New Style Silver Coinage of Athens. New York: 1961. V. 50

THOMPSON, MAURICE
The Boy's Book of Sports and Outdoor Life. New York: 1886. V. 51

THOMPSON, NATHANIEL
The Tryal of Nathaniel Thompson, William Pain and John Farwell...for Writing, Printing and Publishing Libels. London: 1682. V. 52

THOMPSON, OTIS
A Poem Delivered in the Chapel of Rhode Island College...December 27, 1797. Providence: 1798. V. 50

THOMPSON, P.
Healthy Moral Homes for Agricultural Labourers. London: 1863. V. 48

THOMPSON, P. A.
Siam an Account of the Country and the People. Boston and Tokyo: 1910. V. 54

THOMPSON, PISHEY
The History and Antiquities of Boston, and the Villages of Skirbeck, Fishtoft, Freiston, Butterwick, Benington, Leverton, Leake and Wrangle... Boston: 1856. V. 50

THOMPSON, R. A.
Conquest of California Capture of Sonoma by Bear Flag Men June 14, 1846... Santa Rosa: 1896. V. 47

THOMPSON, R. CAMPBELL
A Dictionary of Assyrian Botany. London: 1949. V. 50; 54
Late Babylonian Letters, Transliterations and Translations Of a Series of Letters Written in Babylonian Cuneiform... London: 1906. V. 50; 52

THOMPSON, R. R.
The Fifty-Second (Lowland) Division 1914-1918. Glasgow: 1923. V. 54

THOMPSON, RALPH
An Artist's Safari. London: 1970. V. 50; 52; 53

THOMPSON, ROBERT
The Gardener's Assistant: Practical and Scientific. London: 1859. V. 47; 48; 49; 51
The Gardener's Assistant: Practical and Scientific. London: 1870. V. 54
The Gardener's Assistant: Practical and Scientific... London: 1884. V. 50
The Gardener's Assistant: Practical and Scientific... London: 1923. V. 54

THOMPSON, ROBERT B.
President Heber C. Kimball's Journal, Seventh Book of the Faith-Promoting Series. Salt Lake City: 1882. V. 47

THOMPSON, ROBERT FARRIS
African Art in Motion. Icon and Act in the Collection of Katherine Coryton White. Washington: 1974. V. 52
Black Gods and Kings. Yoruba Art at UCLA. 1971. V. 51; 52

THOMPSON, RUTH PLUMLY
The Cowardly Lion of Oz. 1923. V. 47
The Cowardly Lion of Oz. Chicago: 1923. V. 49
The Giant Horse of Oz. Chicago: 1928. V. 47; 49; 50
The Gnome King of Oz. Chicago: 1927. V. 47; 49
The Gnome King of Oz. Chicago: 1935. V. 51
The Hungry Tiger of Oz. 1926. V. 47; 54
The Hungry Tiger of Oz. Toronto: 1926. V. 48; 54
Jack Pumpkinhead of Oz. Chicago: 1929. V. 47
The Land of Nod, and Rocking Horse Hill. New York: 1920. V. 49
The Lost King of Oz. 1925. V. 47
The Lost King of Oz. Chicago: 1925. V. 49; 53
Ojo in Oz. Chicago: 1933. V. 47
Old Doc Turtle and Lucky Peter. New York: 1920. V. 49
Ozoplaning with the Wizard of Oz. Chicago: 1939. V. 54
The Silver Princess in Oz. Chicago: 1938. V. 47; 49
Tommy in Topsy Turvey Land. New York: 1920. V. 49
The Wishing Horse of Oz. Chicago: 1935. V. 49

THOMPSON, SILVANUS P.
The Life of William Thomson, Baron Kelvin of Largs. London: 1910. V. 48; 50; 52; 54
Memorials of John Ford. London: 1877. V. 49; 54

THOMPSON, SYLVIA
The Battle of the Horizons. Boston: 1928. V. 49

THOMPSON, T. D.
Facts for the People, Relating to the Teeth... Boston: 1854. V. 52

THOMPSON, THEOPHILUS
Annals of Influenza or Epidemic Catarrhal Fever in Great Britain from 1510 to 1837. London: 1852. V. 49; 50; 51; 52; 54

THOMPSON, THOMAS
An Account of Two Missionary Voyages by the Appointment of the Society for the Propagation of the Gospel in Foreign Parts. London: 1758. V. 47
A History of the Scottish People from the Earliest Times. London: 1895. V. 54
Ocellum Promontorium; or, Short Observations on the Ancient State of Holderness. (and) Historic Facts Relative to Ravenspurne in Holderness. Hull: 1821-22. V. 54

THOMPSON, THOMAS H.
Official Historical Atlas Map of Fresno County. V. 52
Official Historical Atlas Map of Fresno County. Tulare: 1891. V. 52

THOMPSON, WADDY
Recollections of Mexico. New York: 1846. V. 47; 48; 52

THOMPSON, WILLIAM
Appeal to One Half of the Human Race, Women Against the Pretentions Of the Other Half, Men... London: 1825. V. 50
An Hymn to May. London: 1746. V. 47; 48
An Illustrated Guide to Sedbergh Garsdale and Dent... Leeds: 1894. V. 51
Reminiscences of a Pioneer. San Francisco: 1912. V. 47; 48
Sedbergh Garsdale and Dent. Leeds: 1892. V. 48; 50; 52; 53
Sedbergh Garsdale and Dent. Leeds: 1910. V. 48; 50; 52; 53
Sickness. London: 1745-45-46. V. 49

THOMPSON, WILLIAM TAPPAN
John's Alive; or, the Bride of a Ghost and Other Sketches. Philadelphia: 1883. V. 54

THOMPSON, ZADOCK
History of Vermont, Natural, Civil and Statistical... Burlington: 1853. V. 49
Natural History of Vermont. An Address Delivered...Before the Boston Society of Natural History, June 1850. Burlington: 1850. V. 50

THOMS, HERBERT
Chapters in American Obstetrics. Springfield: 1933. V. 50
Classical Contributions to Obstetrics and Gynecology. Springfield: 1935. V. 50

THOMS, P. P.
A Dissertation on the Ancient Chinese Vases of the Shang Dynasty, from 1743-1496. London: 1851. V. 47

THOMS, W. J.
Early English Prose Romances. London: 1904. V. 54

THOMSON, ADAM
Time and Timekeepers. London: 1842. V. 50

THOMSON, ALEXANDER
The Paradise of Taste. London: 1796. V. 48; 49; 51
Sonnets, Odes and Elegies. Edinburgh: 1801. V. 54

THOMSON, ALEXIS
On Neuroma and Neuro-Fibromatosis. Edinburgh: 1900. V. 47

THOMSON, ALLEN
History of the Walker Horse. The Morrills... 1893. V. 52
History of the Walker Horse. The Morrills... Woodstock: 1893. V. 54

THOMSON, ANDREW
The Hendersonian Testimony... Edinburgh, London: 1849. V. 52

THOMSON, ANTHONY TODD
The London Dispensatory... London: 1831. V. 50

THOMSON, CHARLES WYVILLE
The Atlantic. New York: 1878. V. 47
The Depths of the Sea. London: 1873. V. 54
The Depths of the Sea... London: 1873 or 1874. V. 49
The Depths of the Sea. London: 1874. V. 49; 51
Report on the Scientific Results of the Voyage of H.M.S. Challenger During the Years 1873-76 Under the Command of Capt. George S. Nares, R.N., F.R.S. and Captain Frank Tourle Thomson. London: 1882. V. 52
The Voyage of the "Challenger". London: 1877. V. 48; 50; 51; 52; 53; 54
The Voyage of the "Challenger"... New York: 1878. V. 50

THOMSON, CLARA J.
Samuel Richardson - a Biographical and Critical Study. London: 1900. V. 52

THOMSON, CYRUS
Facts Respecting the Tomsonian Plan of Medicine... Syracuse: 1853. V. 51

THOMSON, DAVID CROAL
Life and Labours of Hablot Knight Browne... V. 52
Life and Labours of Hablot Knight Browne. London: 1884. V. 49; 53
The Water-Colour Drawings of Thomas Bewick. 1930. V. 48
The Water-Colour Drawings of Thomas Bewick. Chipping-Campden: 1930. V. 48

THOMSON, DONALD
Economic Structure and the Ceremonial Exchange Cycle in Arnhem Land. Melbourne: 1949. V. 52

THOMSON, EDWARD
The Adventures of a Carpet Bag; Respectfully Addressed to Travellers in General. London: 1853. V. 50

THOMSON, GLADYS SCOTT
The Russells in Bloomsbury. London: 1940. V. 52

THOMSON, H. BYERLEY
The Laws of War, Affecting Commerce and Shipping. London: 1854. V. 51

THOMSON, J.
Alfred: a Masque. London: 1740. V. 48

THOMSON, J. C.
Bibliography of the Writings. Wimbledon: 1905. V. 51

THOMSON, J. J.
Conduction of Electricity through Gases. Cambridge: 1903. V. 54
The Corpuscular Theory of Matter. London: 1907. V. 53
Electricity and Matter. New York: 1904. V. 50

THOMSON, JAMES
Biographical and Critical Studies. London: 1896. V. 53
Britannia. A Poem. London: 1729. V. 54
The Castle of Indolence: an Allegorical Poem. London: 1748. V. 48; 54
The City of Dreadful Night and Other Poems. London: 1880. V. 47; 48; 53
Coriolanus. London: 1749. V. 48
Edward and Eleonora. London: 1739. V. 47
A Great Free City. The Book of Silchester. The Dramatic Complemental History of the Remarkable Atebatian Stronghold... London: 1924. V. 51
Illustrations of Shakespeare. London: 1830. V. 47
Liberty. A Poem. London: 1735. V. 48
On the Mummy Cloth of Egypt... London: 1834. V. 50
A Poem Sacred to the Memory of Sir Isaac Newton. London: 1727. V. 54
Poems, Essays and Fragments. London: 1892. V. 48
The Poetical Works. Glasgow: 1784. V. 48; 54
Poetical Works. London: 1862. V. 48; 51
The Poetical Works. Edinburgh: 1863. V. 48
Retreats: a Series of Designs, Consisting of Plans and Elevations for Cottages, Villas and Ornamental Buildings. London: 1833. V. 51
The Seasons. London: 1728. V. 47
The Seasons... London: 1730. V. 47; 48; 52; 53
The Seasons. London: 1758. V. 53
The Seasons. Edinburgh: 1768. V. 50
The Seasons. London: 1793. V. 48
The Seasons. Perth: 1793. V. 49; 50
The Seasons. London: 1797. V. 50
The Seasons... London: 1802. V. 49; 51; 53
The Seasons. London: 1805. V. 48; 50; 51
The Seasons. London: 1823. V. 48
The Seasons... London: 1841. V. 54
The Seasons. London: 1842. V. 51; 54
The Seasons. London: 1852. V. 50; 52; 53
The Seasons. London: 1927. V. 48; 49; 50; 51; 52; 53
The Seasons. London: 1981. V. 54
Spring. A Poem. London: 1728. V. 47
Vane's Story, Weddah and Om-El-Bonain and Other Poems. London: 1881. V. 48
A Voice from the Nile and Other Poems. London: 1884. V. 48
The Works. London: 1750. V. 54

THOMSON, JAMES continued
The Works... London: 1762. V. 48; 51; 54
The Works. London: 1766. V. 47; 49
The Works. London: 1773. V. 48; 49
Works... London: 1788. V. 50

THOMSON, JAMES, WEAVER IN KENLEITH
Poems, in the Scottish Dialect. Edinburgh: 1801. V. 52

THOMSON, JOHN
An Account of the Varioloid Epidemic Which Has Lately Prevailed in Edinburgh and Other Parts of Scotland... London: 1820. V. 47; 52
A Descriptive Catalogue of the Books Forming the Library of Clarence H. Clark, Chestnut-World. Philadelphia: 1888. V. 50
Etymons of English Worlds. Edinburgh: 1826. V. 52
Illustrations of China and Its People. London: 1873. V. 51
The Letters of Curtius... Richmond: 1804. V. 47; 51
Report of Observations Made in the British Military Hospitals in Belgium after the Battle of Waterloo. Edinburgh: 1816. V. 47
Tables of Interest, at 3, 4, 4 1/2 and 5 per cent. London: 1837. V. 50

THOMSON, JOSEPH
To the Central African Lakes and Back: The Narrative of the Royal Geographical Society's East Central African Expedition 1878-80. London: 1881. V. 51

THOMSON, KATHARINE
Memoirs of the Life of Sir Walter Ralegh. London: 1830. V. 47; 48

THOMSON, MATT
Early History of Wabaunsee County, Kansas with Stories of Pioneer Days. Alma: 1901. V. 48

THOMSON, PETER G.
A Bibliography of the State of Ohio, Being A Catalogue of the Books and Pamphlets Relating to the History of the State. Cincinnati: 1880. V. 49

THOMSON, RICHARD
Chronicles of London Bridge. London: 1827. V. 52; 53
Chronicles of London Bridge. London: 1839. V. 49
Historical Notes and Other Literary Materials Now First Collected Towards the Formation of a Systematic Bibliographical Description of Medieval Illuminated Manuscripts... London: 1858. V. 54

THOMSON, ROBERT
A Cruise in the Western Hebrides, or a Week on Board the S.S. "Hebridean". Glasgow: 1891. V. 54
Duty and Office of a Messenger at Arms, with a Copious Introduction... Edinburgh: 1790. V. 53

THOMSON, S. HARRISON
Latin Bookhands of the Later Middle-Ages 1100-1500. Cambridge: 1969. V. 47

THOMSON, S. J.
The Real Indian People. London: 1914. V. 53

THOMSON, SAMUEL
An Earnest Appeal to the Public, Showing the Misery Caused by the Fashionable Mode of Practice of the Doctors of the present Day... Boston: 1824. V. 48
The Law of Libel. Report of the Trial of Dr. Samuel Thomson, the Founder of the Thomsonian Practice, for an Alleged Libel in Warning the Public Against the Impositions of Paine D. Badger, as a Thomsonian Physician Sailing Under False Colors, Before... Boston: 1839. V. 48
Learned Quackery Exposed; or Theory According to Art. Boston: 1824. V. 52
A Narrative of the Life and Medical Discoveries of Samuel Thomson... Columbus: 1833. V. 53
New Guide to Health; or Botanic Family Physician. Boston: 1822. V. 50
New Guide to Health: or Botanic Family Physician. Hallowell: 1833. V. 48
New Guide to Health; or Botanic Family Physician. Boston: 1835. V. 52; 54

THOMSON, THOMAS
Elements of Chemistry. Philadelphia: 1810. V. 50
The History of Chemistry. London: 1830-31. V. 49; 54
The History of Chemistry. London: 1835. V. 49
History of the Royal Society from its Institution to the End of the Eighteenth Century. London: 1812. V. 48; 49; 51; 53
An Outline of the Sciences of Heat and Electricity. Edinburgh: 1830. V. 50

THOMSON, VIRGIL
Eighteen Portraits. New York: 1985. V. 50
Missa pro Defunctis. New York: 1960. V. 48
Portraits for Piano Solo - Album 2. New York: 1949. V. 49
Selected Letters of Virgil Thomson. New York: 1988. V. 49

THOMSON, W. G.
A History of Tapestry. London: 1930. V. 47

THOMSON, WILLIAM
The Chartist Circular. Glasgow: 1841. V. 50
Graves' Disease with and Without Exophthalmic Goitre. New York: 1904. V. 49
Letters from Scandinavia on the Past and Present State of the Northern Nations of Europe. London: 1796. V. 53
A Practical Treatise on the Cultivation of the Grape Vine. Edinburgh: 1865. V. 50
A Tour in England and Scotland in 1785. London: 1788. V. 48; 51
A Tradesman's Travels in the United States and Canada, in the Years 1840, 41 & 42. Edinburgh: 1842. V. 49

THOMSON, WILLIAM M.
The Land and the Book; or, Biblical Illustrations Drawn from the Manners and Customs and Scenes and Scenery of the Holy Land. London: 1886. V. 54
Lebanon, Damascus and Beyond Jordan. New York: 1886. V. 47

THOMSONBY
Cricketers in Council. London: 1871. V. 53

THOMSON-GREGG, W.
A Desperate Character: a Tale of the Gold Fever. London: 1873. V. 54

THONNER, F.
The Flowering Plants of Africa, an Analytical Key to the Genera of African Phanerogams. 1962. V. 48

THORBURN, ARCHIBALD
Birds of Prey. 1985. V. 54
British Birds. London: 1916. V. 52
British Birds. London: 1917-18. V. 48
British Birds... London: 1918. V. 47; 51; 53
British Birds. London: 1925-26. V. 49; 51
British Birds. London: 1931-35. V. 50; 51; 52; 53; 54
British Mammals. London: 1920. V. 51
British Mammals. London: 1920-21. V. 48; 51; 52; 53
Game Birds and Wild Fowl. London: 1923. V. 47; 49; 50; 52; 53
A Naturalist's Sketch Book. London: 1919. V. 47; 48; 49; 50; 51; 52; 53
Thorburn's Birds of Prey. London: 1985. V. 54

THORBURN, S. S.
The Punjab in Peace and War. Edinburgh: 1904. V. 50

THORBURN, W. STEWART
A Guide to the Coins of Great Britain and Ireland, in Gold, Silver and Copper... London: 1888. V. 51

THOREAU, HENRY DAVID
Autumn. Boston & New York: 1892. V. 47; 52; 53
Autumn... Cambridge: 1894. V. 54
Cape Cod. Boston: 1865. V. 47; 48; 51; 52; 53; 54
Cape Cod. Cambridge: 1894. V. 49; 54
Cape Cod. Boston and New York: 1896. V. 54
Cape Cod. Portland: 1968. V. 49; 53
Civil Disobedience. Boston: 1969. V. 50
Collected Poems of... Chicago: 1943. V. 54
The Correspondence of Henry David Thoreau. Washington Square: 1958. V. 51
Early Spring in Massachusetts. Boston: 1881. V. 51; 52
Early Spring in Massachusetts... Boston: 1881-92. V. 50
Excursions. Boston: 1863. V. 47; 48; 51; 52; 53
Excursions. Cambridge: 1894. V. 54
Familiar Letters of Henry David Thoreau. Boston and New York: 1894. V. 54
The First and Last Journeys of Thoreau. Boston: 1905. V. 53; 54
The Heart of Thoreau's Journals. Boston & New York: 1927. V. 54
Henry David Thoreau Quotations from His Writings Selected by Amy W. Smith. Worcester: 1948. V. 48; 53
Letters... Boston: 1865. V. 47; 48; 49; 52; 53
Life Without Principle, Three Essays. Stanford: 1946. V. 48
Little Book of Nature Themes. Portland: 1912. V. 53
The Maine Woods. Boston: 1864. V. 47; 48; 50; 52; 53
Men of Concord. Boston: 1936. V. 52
Miscellanies...with a Biographical Sketch by Ralph Waldo Emerson. Cambridge: 1894. V. 54
The Moon. Boston: 1927. V. 51; 54
Poems of Nature. Boston & New York: 1895. V. 50
The Service. Boston: 1902. V. 47
Sir Walter Raleigh. Boston: 1905. V. 47; 51; 52; 54
Solitude, an Essay from Walden by Henry David Thoreau. Baltimore: 1971. V. 47
Summer... Boston: 1884. V. 51
Summer... London: 1884. V. 54
Summer... Boston and New York: 1894. V. 52; 53; 54
Summer... Cambridge: 1894. V. 54
Thoreau: Two Fragments from the Journals. Iowa City: 1968. V. 53; 54
Thoreau's Thoughts, Selections from the Writings of Thoreau. Boston & New York: 1890. V. 51
Thoreau's Turtle Nest from the Journal Notes of Henry David Thoreau. Worcester: 1967. V. 48
Transmigration of the Seven Brahmans. New York: 1931. V. 47
Transmigration of the Seven Brahmans. New York: 1932. V. 51; 52
Two Early Poems. Skidmore College: 1974. V. 50
Unpublished Poems by Bryant and Thoreau. Boston: 1907. V. 52
Walden. Boston: 1854. V. 47; 48; 52; 53; 54
Walden. Boston: 1864. V. 49
Walden. Boston: 1869. V. 52; 54
Walden. London: 1886. V. 47; 50; 51; 54
Walden. Boston and New York: 1897. V. 49; 54
Walden... Boston: 1909. V. 50; 54
Walden... London: 1927. V. 51; 53
Walden... Chicago: 1930. V. 47; 48; 49
Walden. Boston: 1936. V. 48; 50; 52; 53; 54
Walden... New York: 1939. V. 48
Walking. Santa Barbara: 1988. V. 49

THOREAU, HENRY DAVID continued
Walking. Sherman Oaks: 1988. V. 49
A Week on the Concord and Merrimack Rivers. Boston and Cambridge: 1849. V. 47; 49; 53; 54
A Week on the Concord and Merrimack Rivers. Boston: 1862. V. 52; 53; 54
A Week on the Concord and Merrimack Rivers. Boston: 1868. V. 47; 54
A Week on the Concord and Merrimack Rivers. London: 1895. V. 54
A Week on the Concord and Merrimack Rivers. 1975. V. 52; 54
A Week on the Concord and Merrimack Rivers. Lunenburg: 1975. V. 54
Where I Lived and What I Lived For. Waltham St. Lawrence: 1924. V. 50; 54
Wild Apples. Worcester: 1956. V. 47
Winter: from the Journal of Henry D. Thoreau. Boston and New York: 1888. V. 47; 48; 52; 54
Winter from the Journal of Henry David Thoreau. Cambridge: 1894. V. 54
A Winter Walk. Bangor: 1991. V. 52
Works. London: 1910. V. 48
Works. London: 1912. V. 51
The Writings of Henry David Thoreau. Cambridge: 1894. V. 54
The Writings of Henry David Thoreau. Boston and New York: 1906. V. 53; 54
A Yankee in Canada. Boston: 1866. V. 50; 52; 53; 54
A Yankee in Canada, with Anti-Slavery and Reform Papers. Boston: 1872. V. 54

THOREK, MAX
The Human Testis: Its Gross Anatomy, Histology, Physiology, Pathology, With Particular Reference to Its Endocrinology... Philadelphia: 1924. V. 49; 54

THORELL, T.
Descriptive Catalogue of the Spiders of Burma Based Upon the Collection Made by E. W. Oates. London: 1895. V. 49

THORER, ALBAN
De Re Medica. Basel: 1528. V. 52

THORESBY, RALPH
Ducatus Leodiensis; or the Topography of Ancient and Populous Town and Parish of Leedes... London: 1715. V. 48; 53
Ducatus Leodiensis; or, the Topography of the Ancient and Populous Town and Parish of Leedes... London: 1816. V. 52

THORIUS, RAPHAEL
Hymnus Tabaci; a Poem in Honour of Tabaco. London: 1651. V. 47; 52
Tabacu Poema. Libris Duobus. London: 1716. V. 50

THORLEY, JOHN
(Melisselogia) or, the Female Monarchy. London: 1744. V. 49

THORN & ARROWSMITH BROS.
Illustrated Catalogue of Coffins and Caskets. New York. V. 49

THORN, ISMAY
In and Out. London: 1885. V. 54
In and Out. London: 1890. V. 49

THORNBER, WILLIAM
Penny Stone; or, a Tradition of the Spanish Armada. Preston: 1886. V. 53

THORNBOROUGH, JOHN
A Discourse Shewing the Great Happinesse That Hath, and May Still Accrue to His majesties Kingdomes of England and Scotland... London: 1641. V. 49

THORNBURN, J. M.
India and Malayasia. Cincinnati: 1892. V. 54

THORNBURY, GEORGE WALTER
Art and Nature: at Home and Abroad. London: 1856. V. 54
Every Man His Own Trumpeter. London: 1858. V. 54
The Monarachs of the Main; or, Adventures of the Buccaneers... London: 1855. V. 49

THORNBURY, WALTER
The Life of J. M. W. Turner, R.A. London: 1862. V. 47; 48; 50; 54
Old and New London... London Paris & New York: 1881. V. 50
Old and New London. London: 1892-93. V. 50; 53
Turkish Life and Character. London: 1860. V. 49

THORNDIKE, EDWARD L.
Educational Psychology. New York: 1903. V. 50

THORNDIKE, LYNN
A Catalogue of Incipits of Medieval Scientific Writings in Latin. Cambridge: 1963. V. 47
A History of Magic and Experimental Science... New York: 1934-58. V. 49
A History of Magic and Experimental Science... New York: 1940. V. 47
A History of Magic and Experimental Science... New York: 1943-58. V. 54
A History of Magic and Experimental Science. New York: 1958. V. 48
A History of Magic and Experimental Science. New York & London: 1964-66. V. 52

THORNDYKE, RUSSELL
Sybil Thorndyke. London: 1929. V. 48
The Tragedy of Mr. Punch. London: 1923. V. 49

THORNE, EBENEZER
The Queen of the Colonies; or Queensland as I Knew it by an Eight Years' Resident. London: 1876. V. 50

THORNE, JAMES
Handbook to the Environs of London. London: 1876. V. 50

THORNE, JOHN JULIUS
Humble Hours of Solitude. Wilson: 1904. V. 54

THORNE, ROSS
Theatre Buildings in Australia to 1905. Sydney: 1971. V. 54

THORNE, SABINA
Of Gravity and Grace. Newark: 1982. V. 54

THORNELEY, JAMES L.
The Monumental Brasses of Lancashire and Cheshire. Hull: 1893. V. 53

THORNHILL, J. B.
Adventures in Africa Under the British, Belgian and Portuguese Flags. London: 1915. V. 48

THORNLEY, BERRY
Canadian Pacific Rockies. 1920's. V. 47

THORNLEY, JOHN J.
The Ancient Church Registers of the Parish of Kirkoswald, Cumberland, Baptisms, Marriages, Burials, 1577-1812. Workington: 1901. V. 52

THORNTON, ABEL
The Life of Elder Abel Thornton, Late of Johnston, R.I. Providence: 1828. V. 49

THORNTON, ALFRED
The Adventures of a Post Captain. London: 1817. V. 48; 50; 51; 52
Adventures of a Post Captain. London: 1822. V. 47
Don Juan. London: 1821-22. V. 51; 53
The Post Captain: Or, Adventures of a True British Tar by a Naval Officer. London: 1817-18. V. 49

THORNTON, CATHERINE
The Fothergills of Ravenstonedale. London: 1905. V. 50; 54

THORNTON, EDWARD
The History of the British Empire in India. London: 1841-45. V. 47; 49; 54
Illustrations of the History and Practices of the Thugs. London: 1837. V. 49
India, Its State and Prospects. London: 1835. V. 47; 52

THORNTON, ERNEST
Leaves from an Afghan Scrapbook. London: 1910. V. 50; 51

THORNTON, JAMES HOWARD
Memories of Seven Campaigns. London: 1895. V. 53

THORNTON, JESSY QUINN
Memorial of J. Quinn Thornton, Praying the Establishment of a Territorial Government in Oregon... Washington: 1848. V. 47
Oregon and California in 1848... New York: 1855. V. 47

THORNTON, ROBERT JOHN
Botanical Extracts; or Philosophy of Botany. (with) Elementary Botanical Plates... London: 1810/10. V. 53
The British Flora; or, Genera and Species of British Plants... London: 1812. V. 52
Elements of Botany. London: 1812. V. 47; 48; 50; 53
A Family Herbal. London: 1814. V. 49; 53
A Grammar of Botany... London: 1811. V. 49
A Grammar of Botany... London: 1814. V. 54
Illustrations of the School-Virgil, in copper-Plates and Wood-Cuts... London: 1814. V. 50
Medical Extracts. On the Nature of Health and the Laws of the Nervous and Fibrous Systems. London: 1798. V. 49
A New Family Herbal... London: 1810. V. 47; 49
New Illustration of the Sexual System of Linnaeus. London: 1799-1805?. V. 47
New Illustration of the Sexual System of... Linnaeus... London: 1799-1807. V. 49
The Philosophy of Medicine; or, Medical Extracts on Nature of Health and Disease... London: 1799-1800. V. 49
Temple of Flora... London: 1812. V. 48; 51
Temple of Flora. London: 1951. V. 49; 52; 53

THORNTON, THOMAS
King's Bench, June 27, 1801. London: 1801. V. 49
A Sporting Tour through the Northern Parts of England and Great Part of the Highlands of Scotland. London: 1804. V. 49; 50; 51
A Sporting Tour through the Northern Parts of England and Great Part of the Highlands of Scotland. London: 1896. V. 48
A Sporting Tour Through Various Parts of France, in the Year 1802. London: 1806. V. 50

THORNTON, WILLIAM
Political Economy: Founded in Justice and Humanity, in a Letter to a Friend. Washington City: 1804. V. 53

THORNTON, WILLIAM THOMAS
Over-Population and Its Remedy; or, an Inquiry Into the Extent and Causes of the Distress Prevailing Among the Labouring Classes of the British Islands, and Into the Means of Remedying It. London: 1846. V. 49
A Plea for Peasant Proprietors; with the Outlines of a Plan for Their Establishment in Ireland. London: 1848. V. 51

THORNWELL, JAMES HENLEY
The Rights and Duties of Masters. A Sermon Preached at the Dedication of a Church Erected in Charleston, S.C. for the Benefit and Instruction of the Coloured Population. Charleston: 1850. V. 49
The State of the Country... Columbia: 1861. V. 49

THOROLD, JOHN
The Wreath of Heraldry. Bath. V. 49

THOROTON, ROBERT
The Antiquities of Nottinghamshire... London: 1677. V. 53

THORP, JOSEPH
Early Days in the West Along the Missouri One Hundred Years Ago. Liberty: 1924. V. 53
Eric Gill. London: 1929. V. 53

THORP, RAYMOND W.
Bowie Knife. Albuquerque: 1948. V. 53

THORP, WILLIAM H.
An Architect's Sketchbook at Home and Abroad. Leeds: 1884. V. 54

THORPE, ADAM
Ulverton. London: 1992. V. 51; 53

THORPE, BENJAMIN
Ancient Laws and Institutes of England: Comprising Laws Enacted Under the Anglo-Saxon Kings from Aethelbirht to Cnut... London: 1840. V. 48
Diplomatarium Anglicum Aevi Saxonici: a Collection of English Charters, from the Regin of King Aethelberht A.D. to William the Conqueror. London: 1865. V. 49

THORPE, FRANCIS
Benjamin Franklin and the University of Pennsylvania. Washington: 1893. V. 50

THORPE, JAMES
English Illustration: the Nineties. London: 1935. V. 53

THORPE, T. BANGS
The Hive of the "Bee-Hunter", a Repository of Sketches Including Peculiar American Character, Scenery and Rural Sports. New York: 1854. V. 47; 50

THORPE, T. E.
Reports...On the Use of Phosphorus in the Manufacture of Lucifer Matches 1899. London: 1899. V. 50

THORPE, THOMAS BANGS
Our Army at Monterey. Philadelphia: 1847. V. 47
Our Army on the Rio Grande... Philadelphia: 1846. V. 47
Thorpe's Scenes in Arkansaw. Philadelphia: 1868. V. 54

THORPE, THOMS BANGS
The Mysteries of the Backwoods; or Sketches of the Southwest. Philadelphia: 1846. V. 48; 53; 54

THORSON, G.
Reproduction and Larval Development of Danish Marine Bottom Invertebrates... Copenhagen: 1946. V. 48

THOU, JACQUES AGUSTE DE
Histoire Universelle, Depuis 1543 Jusqu'en 1607. Londres: 1734. V. 50
Monseiur de Thou's History of His Own Time. London: 1729. V. 47

THOUGHTS on Education in Ireland, and on National Education and Improvements Generally in the Present Times. London: 1832. V. 52

THOUGHTS On Libels; and an Impartial Inquiry Into the Present State of the British Army... London: 1809. V. 48

THOUGHTS on Population and the Means of Comfortable Subsitence; With Suggestions Regarding an Increased Supply and Lessened Cost of Food for Childhood and the Industrial Classes. London: 1863. V. 51

THOUGHTS on the Canada Bill, Now Depending in Parliament. London: 1791. V. 50

THOUGHTS on the Conduct Both of the Ministers and Opposition, Submitted, by A True-Born Englishman... London: 1797. V. 50

THOUGHTS on the Destiny of man, Particularly with Reference to the Present Times. New Harmony: 1824. V. 48

THOUGHTS on the Importance of the Manners of the Great to General Society. Philadelphia: 1788. V. 49; 50; 51; 54

THOUIN, GABRIEL
Plans Raisonnes de Toutes les Especes de Jardins. Paris: 1838. V. 47

THRALL, HOMER
Pictorial History of Texas. St. Louis: 1879. V. 53

THRALL, MIRIAM M. H.
Rebellious Fraser's. New York: 1934. V. 54

THRAPP, DAN L.
Encyclopedia of Frontier Biography. Glendale: 1988. V. 48; 51
Encyclopedia of Frontier Biography. Glendale & Spokane: 1988/94. V. 54
Encyclopedia of Frontier Biography. 1990. V. 48
Encyclopedia of Frontier Biography. Glendale: 1990. V. 48; 50; 54

THRASHER, MAX BENNET
Tuskegee. Boston: 1900. V. 52

THRASHER, WILLIAM
The Marrow of Chymical Physick; or, The Practice of making Chymical medicines. London: 1669. V. 50

THE THREE Bears. Portland: 1983. V. 52

THREE Birthday Tributes. New York: 1954/55/57. V. 47

THE THREE Chances. London: 1858. V. 54

THREE Characters. London: 1995. V. 54

THREE Choruses from Opera Libretti, by Lou Harrison to Robert Duncan. Highlands: 1960. V. 52

THREE Early French Essays on Paper Marbling, 1642-1765. 1987. V. 52

THREE Early French Essays on Paper Marbling, 1642-1765. Newtown: 1987. V. 49

THREE Erfurt Tales, 1497-1498. 1962. V. 51

THREE Erfurt Tales, 1497-1498. North Hills: 1962. V. 48; 53

THREE Famous New Songs Called Effects of Whiskey. The Valley Below. Larry O'Gaff. Paisley: 1820. V. 51; 52; 53

THREE Frontiers, Memories and a Portrait of Henry Littleton Pitzer. Muscantine: 1938. V. 47

THE THREE Kittens. London. V. 53

THREE Letters Addressed to a Friend in India, by a Proprietor. London: 1793. V. 54

THREE Lions and the Cross of Lorraine: Bartholomaeus Anglicus, John of Trevisa, John Tate, Wynkyn de Worde, and De Propietatibus Rerum. Newtown: 1992. V. 50

THE THREE Little Kittens. London: 1870. V. 52

THE THREE Little Pigs. London: 1930. V. 47

THREE Months in York: Containing Among Other Matter, Remarks and Strictures on the Construction and Peculiar Mode of Making a Weekly Newspaper... 1821. V. 51

THREE Nights' Public Discussion Between the Revds. C. W. Cleeve, James Robertson and Philip Cater, and Elder John Taylor, of the Church of Jesus Christ of Latter-day Saints, at Boulognersur-mer, France. Liverpool: 1850. V. 48; 49

THREE Notable Stories. London: 1890. V. 51

THE THREE Prize Essays On Agriculture and the Corn Law. Manchester: 1842. V. 50

THREE Speeches Spoken at Common-Hall, Thursday the 3 of July, 1645. By Mr. Lisle, Mr. Tate, Mr. Brown, Members of the House of Commons... London: 1645. V. 52

THE THREE Tiny Pigs. London: 1880's. V. 48

THREE Winter Poems (by) Michael Hays, William Keens, G. A. O'Connell. Lisbon: 1973. V. 54

THRELKELD, C.
Synopsis Stirpium Hibernicarum Alphabetice Dispositarum... Dublin: 1727. V. 52

THRELKELD, LANCELOT EDWARD
An Australian Grammar, Comprehending the Principles and Natural Rules of the Language, as Spoken by the Abrorigines, in the Vicinity of Hunter's River, Lake Macquarie &c. Sydney: 1834. V. 49

THRENODIA: or, an Elegy On the Unexpected and Unlamented Death of the M- of B-;... Oxford: 1753. V. 50; 54

THRING, EDWARD
Borth Lyrics. Uppingham: 1881. V. 50

THRING, THEODORE
Criminal Law of the Navy... London: 1877. V. 51

THROSBY, JOHN
Thoroton's History of Nottinghamshire: Republished with Large Additions, and Embellished with Picturesque and Select Views of Seats of the Nobility and Gentry, Towns, Village Churches and Ruins. London: 1797. V. 54

THROUGH Shot and Flame; the Adventures and Experiences of J.D. Kestell, Chaplain to President Steyn and General Christian De Wet. London: 1903. V. 50

THROWER, NORMAN J. W.
A Leaf from the Mercataor-Hondius World Atlas. Fullerton: 1985. V. 48

THRUM, THOMAS G.
Hawaiian Folk Tales. Chicago: 1907. V. 51

THRUPP, G. A.
The History of Coaches. London: 1877. V. 47

THRUSTON, GATES P.
The Antiquities of Tennessee and the Adjacent States and the State of Aboriginal Society in the Scale of Civilization Represented by Them a Series of Historical and Ethnological Studies. Cincinnati: 1897. V. 47

THUBRON, COLIN
The God in the Mountain. London: 1977. V. 51; 54
The Hills of Adonis - a Quest of Lebanon. London: 1968. V. 53; 54
Jerusalem. London: 1969. V. 51
Mirror for Damascus. London: 1967. V. 50; 53

THUCYDIDES
De Bello Peloponnesiaco Libri Octo, Cum Adnotationibus Integris H. Stephani... Amsterdam: 1731. V. 48
The Eight Bookes of the Peloponnesian Warre. London: 1634. V. 53
The Funeral Oration of Pericles. 1929. V. 47
The History of the Grecian War. London: 1676. V. 48; 52
The History of the Grecian War. London: 1723. V. 52
History of the Peloponnesian War. V. 48
The History of the Peloponnesian War. London: 1876. V. 48

THUCYDIDES continued
History of the Peloponnesian War. 1930. V. 52; 54
History of the Peloponnesian War. Chelsea: 1930. V. 47; 48; 50; 52; 54
History of the Peloponnesian War. London: 1930. V. 54
The History of the Peloponnesian War. Connecticut: 1974. V. 47
The History of Thucydides. London: 1829. V. 47; 51
(Opera) Graece & Latine. Edinburgh: 1804. V. 48
Otto Libri Delle Guerre. Venice: 1550. V. 50
Thucydides Translated into English. Oxford: 1881. V. 54
Thucydides Translated into English... Chelsea: 1930. V. 47
Thucydidis de Bello Peloponnesiaco Libri Octo, Cum Adnotationibus Integris H. Stephani, & J. Hudsoni. Amsterdam: 1731. V. 49; 51

THUDICHUM, J. L. W.
The Spirit of Cookery. London and New York: 1895. V. 52
A Treatise on the Pathology of the Urine, Including a Complete Guide to Its Analysis. London: 1858. V. 49; 54

THULDEN, THEODORE VAN
Les Travaux d'Ulysse. Paris: 1639. V. 53

THE THUMB Ready Reckoner: Containing Calculations from One-Sixteenth of a Penny to Nineteen Shillings and Ninepence... London: 1895. V. 50

THUNBERG, C. P.
C. P. Thunberg Collection of Drawings of Japanese Plants: Icones Plantarum Japonicarum Thunbergii, Held in the Library of the Komarov Botanicl Institute. Tokyo: 1993. V. 50

THURAH, LAURIDS DE
Hafina Hodierna...Description Circonstantiee de la Residence Roiale et Capitale de Copenhague. Copenhagen: 1748. V. 49

THURBER, JAMES GROVER
The 13 Clocks. New York: 1950. V. 53
Alarms and Diversions. New York: 1957. V. 50
The Beast in Me: and other Animals. New York: 1948. V. 52
Fables for Our Time. New York: 1940. V. 49; 51; 53
Further Fables for Our Time. New York: 1956. V. 50
The Great Quillow. New York: 1944. V. 51
Is Sex Necessary?. New York: 1929. V. 49
The Last Flower - a Parable in Pictures. London: 1939. V. 50
The Last Flower: a Parable in Pictures. New York: 1939. V. 47; 48; 49
Many Moons. New York: 1943. V. 48
The Middle-Aged Man on the Flying Trapeze. 1935. V. 50
The Middle-Aged Man on the Flying Trapeze. London: 1935. V. 51
The Middle-Aged Man on the Flying Trapeze. New York: 1935. V. 48; 49
The Seal in the Bedroom and Other Predicaments. New York: 1932. V. 50
The Thurber Album. New York: 1952. V. 49
The Thurber Carnival. London: 1945. V. 51
The Thurber Carnival. New York: 1945. V. 49; 53
Thurber Country, A New Collection of Pieces About Males and Females Mainly Of Our Own Species. New York: 1953. V. 48
Thurber's Dogs. 1955. V. 50
Thurber's Dogs. New York: 1955. V. 51
Thurber's Men, Women and Dogs. New York: 1943. V. 53
The White Deer. New York: 1945. V. 49; 53
The Wonderful O. New York: 1957. V. 49

THURET, GUSTAVE
Etudes Phycologiques: Analyses d'Algues Marines... Paris: 1878. V. 48; 52

THURLOE, JOHN
A Collection of the State Papers of John Thurloe, Esq. London: 1742. V. 48; 51

THURLOW, EDWARD HOVEL
Arcita and Palamon: after the Excellent Poet Geoffrey Chaucer. London: 1822. V. 54

THURMAN, HOWARD
Deep River: an Interpretation of Negro Spirituals. Mills College: 1945. V. 53

THURMAN, W. C.
Non-Restance, or the Spirit of Christinaity Restored. Charlottsville (sic): 1862. V. 50

THURMAN, WALLACE
The Interne. New York: 1932. V. 54
Negro Life in New York's Harlem. Girard. V. 47; 48

THURNEISSER ZUM THURN, LEONHARD
Prokatalepsis Oder Praeoccupatio, Durch Zwoelff Verscheidenlicher Tracaten. Frankfurt an der Oder: 1571. V. 47

THURSTON, A. B.
African Incidents: Personal Experiences in Egypt and Unyoro. London: 1900. V. 54

THURSTON, ADA
Check List of Fifteenth Century printing in the Pierpont Morgan Library. New York: 1939. V. 47; 48

THURSTON, CLARA BELL
The Jingle of a Jap. Boston: 1906. V. 53
The Jingle of a Jap. Boston: 1908. V. 53

THURSTON, E. TEMPLE
The Open Window. London: 1913. V. 51

THURSTON, GATES P.
The Antiquities of Tennessee and the Adjacent States and the State of Aboriginal Society in the Scale of Civilization Represented by Them. Cincinnati: 1890. V. 47

THURSTON, GEORGE H.
Pittsburgh As It Is. Pittsburgh: 1857. V. 47

THURSTON, JOSEPH
The Toilette. London: 1730. V. 47; 48; 49; 52; 54

THURSTON, LORRIN A.
Thurston's Hawaiian Guide Book: and Auto Road Guide to the Island of Oahu. Honolulu: 1927. V. 47

THURTLE, FRANCES
Ashford Rectory; or, the Spoiled Child Reformed. London: 1818. V. 51

THWAITE, LEO
Alberta: an Account of its Wealth and Progress. Chicago/New York: 1912. V. 50; 52

THWAITES, REUBEN GOLD
Frontier Defense on the Upper Ohio 1777-1778. Madison: 1912. V. 54

THYNNE, H. & G., LTD., HEREFORD.
Fireplaces Made by H. & G. Thynne Ltd. 1930's. V. 50

TIBETAN Medical Thangka of the Four Medical Tantras. 1988. V. 49

TIBULLUS
Elegies de Tibulle. Paris: 1798. V. 52

TICE, GEORGE A.
Paterson. 1972. V. 52

TICE, JOHN H.
Over the Plain, on the Mountains; or Kansas, Colorado and the Rocky Mountains; Agriculturally, Mineralogically and Aesthetically Described. St. Louis: 1872. V. 47; 52

TICEHURST, CLAUD B.
A History of the Birds of Suffolk. London: 1932. V. 50; 52; 53

THE TICHBORNE Romance: Its Matter-of-Fact and Moral. London: 1872. V. 47

TICKELL, RICHARD
Anticipation: Containing the Substance of His M-----y's Most Gracious Speech to Both H-----s of P---l---t, on the Opening of the Approaching Session... London: 1778. V. 47
Epistle from the Honourable Charles Fox, Partridge Shooting, to the Honourable John Townshend, Cruising. London: 1779. V. 48; 51; 54
Probationary Odes for the Laureatship... London: 1785. V. 50
The Project. London: 1778. V. 48; 51; 54
The Wreath of Fashion,, or, the Art of Sentimental Poetry. London: 1778. V. 48

TICKELL, THOMAS
Kensington Garden. London: 1722. V. 47
Oxford. A Poem. London: 1707. V. 48
Oxford. A Poem. London: 1707/06. V. 48; 53

TICKNOR, GEORGE
History of Spanish Literature. London: 1849. V. 49; 51
Life of William Hickling Prescott. Boston: 1864. V. 49; 50; 54

TIDCOMBE, MARIANNE
The Bookbindings of T. J. Cobden-Sanderson. 1984. V. 47
The Bookbindings of T. J. Cobden-Sanderson. London: 1984. V. 48; 50; 52; 53
The Bookbindings of T. J. Cobden-Sanderson... London and New Castle: 1984/91. V. 48
The Doves Bindery. 1991. V. 47
The Doves Bindery. London & New Castle: 1991. V. 47; 50; 53

TIDY Twinkle "I Squeak". London: 1940. V. 50

TIDYMAN, ERNEST
Shaft. New York: 1970. V. 53

TIECK, L.
Tales from the "Phantasus", Etc. 1845. V. 48

TIEDEMANN, F.
Plates of the Arteries of the Human Body... Edinburgh: 1831. V. 51

TIEMANN, GEORGE, & CO.
American Armamentarium Chirurgicum. San Francisco: 1989. V. 50; 52

TIERNEY, GEORGE
The Real Situation of the East-India Company Considered, With Respect to Their Rights and Privileges, Under the Operation of the Late Acts of Parliament... London: 1787. V. 51; 52

TIERNEY, M. A.
The History and Antiquities of the Castle and Town of Arundel... London: 1834. V. 52

TIETJENS, EUNICE
Body and Raiment. New York: 1919. V. 51; 54

TIETZE, HANS
The Drawings of the Venetian Painters in the 15th and 16th Centuries. New York: 1944. V. 50; 54

THE TIFFANY Studios Collection of Antique Chinese Rugs. New York: 1908. V. 51

THE TIFFANY Studios Collection of Notable Antique Oriental Rugs. New York: 1906. V. 51

TIGHE, MARY BLANCHFORD
Psyche, with Other Poems. London: 1811. V. 53

TIGHT Lines and a Happy Landing. Anticost: 1937. V. 47

TIJOU, JOHN
A New Booke of Drawings Invented and Designed by John Tijou. London: 1723. V. 51

TILDEN, SAMUEL JAMES
The New York City "Ring": Its Origin, Maturity and Fall, Discussed in a Reply to the New York Times. New York: 1873. V. 48

TILFORD, OLIVE DARGAN
The Welsh Pony. Boston: 1913. V. 47

TILGHMAN, CHRISTOPHER
On the Rivershore. New York: 1990. V. 53

TILGHMAN, OSWALD
History of Talbot County, Maryland, 1661-1861... Baltimore: 1915. V. 47

TILGHMAN, ZOE A.
Marshal of the Last Frontier: Life and Services of...Tilghman... Glendale: 1940. V. 51
Marshal of the Last Frontier: Life and Services of...Tilghman. Glendale: 1949. V. 47
Quanah, The Eagle of the Comanches. Oklahoma City: 1938. V. 48; 53

TILING, MORITZ
German Element in Texas from 1820-1850 With Historical Sketches of Texas... Houston: 1913. V. 53

TILKE, MAX
Oriental Costumes. London: 1923. V. 48

TILLEY, FRANK
Teapots and Tea. London: 1957. V. 51

TILLEY, HENRY A.
Eastern Europe and Western Asia. Political and Social Sketches on Russia, Greece and Syria in 1861-2-3. London: 1871. V. 48

TILLI, MICHEL ANGELO
Catalogus Plantarum Horti Pisani. Florence: 1723. V. 48; 52

TILLIE, A.
Yule and Christmas. Their Place in the Germanic Year. London: 1899. V. 51

TILLOTSON, JOHN
The Golden Americas. London: 1869. V. 50
The New Waverly Album. London: 1859. V. 53
The Rule of Faith: or an Answer to the Treatise of Mr. I. S. Entituled, Sure-Footing, &c. (with) A Reply to Mr. I.S. His (Third) Appendix... London: 1666. V. 51
The Works. London: 1735. V. 51
The Works. London: 1752. V. 50

TILLOTT, P. M.
A History of Yorkshire - the City of York. Oxford: 1961. V. 48

TILLYARD, R. J.
The Insects of Australia and New Zealand. Sydney: 1926. V. 52; 53

TILMAN, H. W.
The Ascent of the Nanda Devi. Cambridge: 1937. V. 51
The Ascent of the Nanda Devi. London: 1937. V. 52
Snow On the Equator. London: 1937. V. 50
Two Mountains and a River. 1949. V. 52

TILNEY, EDMUND
A Brief and Pleasant Discourse of Duties in Mariage, etc. London: 1568. V. 48; 52

TILNEY, F. C.
The Pictorial Annual of the Royal Photographic Society of Great Britain, 1926. London: 1926. V. 47
The Pictorial Annual of the Royal Photographic Society of Great Britain, 1927. London: 1927. V. 47
The Pictorial Annual of the Royal Photographic Society of Great Britain, 1928. London: 1928. V. 47

TILNEY, FREDERICK
The Brain from Ape to Man. New York: 1928. V. 49

TILNEY, ROBERT
My Life in the Army. Three Years and a Half with the Fifth Army Corps, Army of the Potomac 1862-1865. Philadelphia: 1912. V. 52

TILSON, JAKE
Excavator Barcelona Excavador. London: 1986. V. 52; 54

TILSON, R. L.
Tigers of the World, the Biology, Biopolitics, Management and Conservation of an Endangered Species. New Jersey: 1987. V. 49

TILTON, E. STEVENS, MRS.
Home Dissertations. An Offering to the Household for Economical and practical Skill in Cookery, Orderly Domestic Management... Los Angeles: 1891. V. 48

TILTON, THEODORE
Golden-Haired Gertrude: a Story for Children. New York: 1865. V. 50
The Two Hungry Kittens. New York: 1866. V. 52

TIMBERLAKE, HENRY
The Memoirs of Lieut. Henry Timberlake. London: 1765. V. 47

TIMBS, JOHN
Abbeys, Castles and Ancient Halls of England and Wales: their Legendary Lore and Popular History. London. V. 54
Anecdote Lives of Hogarth, Reynolds, Gainsborough, Fuseli, Lawrence and Turner. London: 1865. V. 47
Clubs and Club Life in London. London: 1872. V. 47; 49; 51
Curiosities of London. London: 1855. V. 50
Curiosities of London. London: 1867. V. 47; 54
The Harlequin, a Journal of Drama. London: 1829. V. 51
Mountain Adventures in the Various Countries of the World. London: 1869. V. 54

THE TIME-LIFE Encyclopedia of Gardening. Alexandria & New York: 1971-79. V. 47; 51

TIMERMAN, JACOBO
Prisoner Without a Name, Cell Without a Number. New York: 1981. V. 48

TIMIRYAZEV, KLIMENT ARKADIEVICH
Solntse, Zhizn, Klorofill. Moscow & St. Petersburg: 1923. V. 47

TIMLIN, WILLIAM
The Ship that Sailed to Mars. London. V. 51
The Ship that Sailed to Mars. London: 1920. V. 53
The Ship That Sailed to Mars. London: 1923. V. 47; 48; 49; 51; 54

TIMM, WERNER
The Graphic Art of Edvard Munch. Greenwich: 1969. V. 48; 50; 52

TIMMINS, THOMAS
Examples of Iron Roofs. London: 1882. V. 49; 53

TIMMONS, WILBERT H.
Morelos of Mexico; Priest, Soldier, Statesman. El Paso: 1963. V. 48

TIMOSHENKO, STEPHEN P.
Collected Papers of...Timoshenko. New York: 1953. V. 50
History of Strength of Materials. New York: 1953. V. 53
Theory of Elastic Stability. New York and London: 1936. V. 54

TIMPERLAKE, JAMES
Illustrated Toronto: Past and Present, Being an Historical and Descriptive Guide-Book... Toronto: 1877. V. 52; 53

TIMPERLEY, CHARLES HENRY
A Dictionary of Printers and Printing, with the Progress of Literature, Ancient and Modern... London: 1838-39. V. 48
A Dictionary of Printers and Printing, with the progress of Literature, Ancient and Modern... London: 1839. V. 50; 53
A Dictionary of Printers and Printing, with the Progress of Literature, Ancient and Modern. London: 1939. V. 52
Encyclopaedia of Literary and Typographical Anecdote... London: 1842. V. 48; 52
The Printer's Manual, Containing Instructions to Learners. London: 1838. V. 51
Songs of the Press and Other Poems... Nottingham: 1833. V. 49
Songs of the Press and other Poems... London: 1845. V. 50; 53

TIMPERLEY, H. W.
A Cotswod Book. London: 1931. V. 48

TIMPSON, LILIAN
The Fairy Prince Next Door. London: 1915. V. 49

TIMROD, HENRY
The Poems of Henry Timrod. New York: 1873. V. 54

TINCKER, MARY AGNES
By the Tiber. London: 1881. V. 50

TINDAL, MATTHEW
Four Discourses on the Following Subjects: viz. I. Of Obedience to the Supreme Powers, and the Duty of Subjects in All Revolutions. II. Of the Law of Nations... III. Of the Power of the Magistrate... IV. Of the Liberty of the Press. London: 1709. V. 48

TINDAL, WILLIAM
The History and Antiquities of the Abbey and Borough of Evesham. Evesham: 1794. V. 52
Remarks on Dr. Johnson's Life, and Critical Observations on the Works of Mr. Gray. London: 1782. V. 48

TINDALE, NORMAN B.
Aboriginal Tribes of Australia... Berkeley: 1974. V. 51; 52

TINDALE, THOMAS KEITH
The Handmade Papers of Japan. Vermont & Tokyo: 1952. V. 52

TINDALL, GEORGE B.
South Carolina Negroes 1877-1900. Greenville: 1952. V. 54

TINDALL, JOHN
Yorkshire Fishing and Shooting (with Frank). London. V. 48

THE TINDER Box. New York: 1945. V. 49

TINEL, JULES
Nerve Wounds: Symptomatology of Peripheral Nerve Lesions Caused by War Wounds. New York: 1917. V. 53

TING, WALASSE
Hot and Sour Soup. 1969. V. 50
One Cent Life. Bern: 1964. V. 51; 52

TINGLEY, ELBERT R.
Poco Loco; Sketches of New Mexico Life. Blair: 1900. V. 52

TINKER, CHAUNCEY BREWSTER
Addresses Commemorating the Hundredth Anniversary of the Birth of William Morris - Delivered Before the Yale Library Associates in the Sterling Memorial Library, XXIX October MCMXXXIV. 1935. V. 52
A New Portrait of James Boswell. Cambridge: 1927. V. 50
Painter and Poet. Cambridge: 1938. V. 54
The Tinker Library. A Bibliographical Catalogue of Books and Manuscripts. Storrs. V. 54

TINKER, F. G.
Some Still Live. Experiences of a Fighting-Plane Pilot in the Spanish War. London: 1938. V. 49

TINKHAM, GEORGE H.
Californian Men and Events, Time, 1769-1890. Stockton: 1915. V. 49

TINKLE, LON
J. Frank Dobie, the Makings of An Ample Mind. Austin: 1968. V. 47

TINLEY, G. F.
Colour Planning of the Garden. London: 1924. V. 47; 48

TINNEY, J.
Compendious Treatise of Anatomy. London: 1808. V. 47; 48; 49; 50; 51; 53

TIPHAIGNE DE LA ROCHE, CHARLES FRANCOIS
Giphantia; or a View of What Has Passed, What is Now Passing and During the Present Century, What Will Pass, in the World... London: 1760. V. 47
Giphantia; or a View of What Has Passed, What is Now Passing and During the Present Century, What Will Pass, in the World. London: 1761. V. 47; 48

TIPPING, HENRY AVRAY
English Gardens. London: 1925. V. 49; 51; 52; 53; 54
English Homes - Period IV - Volume I. Late Stuart, 1649-1714. London: 1929. V. 47; 54
English Homes. Period III. volume I. Late Tudor and Early Stuart 1558-1649. London: 1922-29. V. 49
English Homes. Periods 1-6. London: 1921-26. V. 52
Gardens Old and New. London: 1915. V. 51; 54
Gibbons and the Woodwork of His Age (1648-1720). London: 1914. V. 52
Grinling Gibbons and the Wood-Work of His Age (1648-1720). London: 1914. V. 47; 51

TIPTREE, J.
Ten Thousand Light-Years from Home. London: 1975. V. 52

TIR A'Mhurain: *Outer Hebrides.* London: 1962. V. 47

TIRAQUEAU, ANDRE
Tractatus, Cessante Causa Effectus. Paris: 1551. V. 50

TIRPITZ, VON
My Memoirs. London: 1919. V. 52

TISCHBEIN, HEINRICH WILHELM
Figures d'Homere Dessinees d'Apres l'Antique... (with) Tome Second, Odyssee. Metz: 1801-02. V. 53

TISCHNER, HERBERT
Oceanic Art. New York: 1954. V. 52

TISSANDIER, GASTON
A History and Handbook of Photography. London: 1876. V. 49; 50
Popular Scientific Recreations in Natural Philosophy, Astronomy, Geology, Chemistry, etc... London: 1880's. V. 50
Popular Scientific Recreations in Natural Philosophy, Astronomy, Geology, Chemistry, Etc. Chicago: 1885. V. 50

TISSOT, J. JAMES
The Life of Our Saviour Jesus Christ. London: 1897. V. 48; 54
The Life of Our Saviour Jesus Christ. New York: 1899. V. 48

TISSOT, SAMUEL AUGUSTE ANDRE DAVID
Advice to the People in General, with Regard to Their Health. London: 1768. V. 52
Traite des Nerfs et de Leurs Maladies. Lausanne: 1784. V. 49

TISSOT, SIMON ANDRE
Onanism: or a Treatise Upon the Disorders Produced by Masturbation. London: 1767. V. 54

TISSOT, VICTOR
Unknown Switzerland. New York: 1890. V. 49

TITCHENER, EDWARD B.
Experimental Psychology. New York: 1905. V. 51

TITI, PLACIDO
De Diebus Decretoriis et Aegrorum Decubitu. (with) De Diebus Decretoriis et Morborum Causa Caelesti. Ticini Regii: 1660/65. V. 50
Primum Mobile... London: 1820. V. 48
Tabulae Primi Mobilis cum Thesibus ad Theoricen & Canonibus ad Praxim, Additis in Rerum Demonstrationem & Supputationum Exemplum Triginta Clarissimorum Natalium Thematibus. Padua: 1657. V. 50

TITSINGH, M. ISAAC
Illusrations of Japan; Consisting of Private Memoirs and Anecdotes of the Djogouns, or, Sovereigns of Japan. London: 1822. V. 51; 52

TITTERTON, W. R.
Me As a Model. London: 1914. V. 50

TITUS and Vespasian or the Destruction of Jerusalem. London: 1905. V. 48; 51; 52

TIXIER, VICTOR
Tixier's Travels on the Osage Prairies. Norman: 1940. V. 47

TJADER, RICHARD
The Big Game of Africa. New York: 1910. V. 47

TO Brokers, Attornies & Landlords. Oppression, Robbery and Neglect, Exemplified in the Distressing Case of Henry Smith vs. Charles Hall and the Conduct of J. Searle, Attorney at Law, Fetter Lane. London: 1815. V. 52

TO Col. Aaron Ogden, Sir, As You Refused to Receive a Letter That I Sent You by General Dayton Yesterday, I Will Give It Publicity Through Another Channel.... Elizabethtown: 1816. V. 47

TO Harvey Cushing Master Surgeon and Teacher These Medical Essays and Papers are Affectionately Dedicated by His Pupils on the Occasion of His Sixtieth Birthday. April 8, 1929. V. 54

TO the High and Honourable Court of Parliament. The Nobility, Knights, Gentry, Ministers, Freeholders and Inhabitants of the County of Surrey... London?: 1642. V. 49

TO the Marine Society, in Praise of the Great and Good Work They Have Done by Clothing and Fitting Out for the Sea-Service 2682 men and 1868 Boys, in the Space of Fifteen Months, to the 6th of October Last... London: 1758?. V. 48; 51

TO the Members of the Pharmaceutical Association, and to Apothecaries in General throughout England and Wales. London: 1805. V. 49

TO The Millers of the United States. Take Notice -- That Congress Did on the 21st of Jan. 1808, Pass the Following Act: An Act for the Relief of Oliver Evans. Philadelphia?: 1809. V. 52

TO The People of Great Britain. 1788. V. 50

TO the Right Honourable the Lord Mayor, Alderman and Common Council of the City of London. 1768?. V. 49

TOASTS and Maxims. London: 1910. V. 49

TOBACK, C. W.
The Mysteries of Astrology, and the Wonders of Magic. Boston: 1854. V. 49

TOBIN, AGNES
Letters, Translations, Poems. San Francisco: 1958. V. 47; 48

TOBIN, J.
Journal of a Tour Made in the Years 1828-1829, Through Syria, Carniola and Itlay, Whilst Accompanying the Last Sir Humphry Davy. London: 1832. V. 52

TOCQUE, PHILIP
Kaleidoscope Echoes Being Historical, Philosophical, Scientific and Theological Sketches. Toronto: 1895. V. 47
Newfoundland: As It Was, And As It Is In 1877. London: 1878. V. 49
Newfoundland: As It Was and As It is in 1877. Toronto: 1878. V. 47

TOCQUEVILLE, ALEXIS CHARLES HENRI MAURICE CLEREL DE
Correspondence and Conversations of Alexis de Tocqueville with Nassau William Senior from 1834 to 1859. London: 1872. V. 49
De La Democratie en Amerique. Bruxelles: 1835. V. 49
Democracy in America. London: 1836. V. 49
Democracy in America. New York: 1840/41. V. 50
Democracy in America. New York: 1841. V. 47
Democracy in America. London: 1862. V. 48

TODD, CHARLES W.
Woodville; or, the Anchoret Reclaimed. Knoxville: 1832. V. 49; 52

TODD, DOROTHY
The New Interior Decoration. An Introduction to Its Principles and International Survey of Its Methods. New York: 1929. V. 54

TODD, F. S.
Waterfowl, Ducks, Geese and Swans of the World. New York: 1979. V. 50; 54

TODD, FRANK MORTON
Eradicating Plague from San Francisco. San Francisco: 1909. V. 50; 52
The Story of the Exposition. New York: 1921. V. 50

TODD, GEORGE W.
Castellum Huttonicum. York: 1824. V. 50; 54

TODD, GLENN
Shaped Poetry... San Francisco: 1981. V. 47; 48

TODD, HENRY JOHN
Illustrations of the Lives and Writings of the Lives and Writings of Gower and Chaucer. London: 1810. V. 54
A Letter to His Grace the Archbishop of Canterbury, Concerning the Authorship of Eikon Basilike. London: 1825. V. 49
Memoirs of the Life and Writings Of the Right Rev. Brian Walton, D.D. London: 1821. V. 49; 54
Some Account of the Life and Writings of John Milton. London: 1809. V. 53
Some Account of the Life and Writings of John Milton. London: 1826. V. 49

TODD, JOHN
California and Its Wonders. London: 1884. V. 51
A Catalogue of Books, Ancient and Modern, Now Selling at the prices Affixed to Each Article. York: 1821. V. 51

TODD, JOHN R.
Prince William's Parish and Plantations. Richmond: 1935. V. 49

TODD, ROBERT BENTLEY
Clinical Lectures on Paralysis, Disease of the Brain and Other Affections of the Nervous System. Philadelphia: 1855. V. 47; 48; 49; 50
Descriptive and Physiological Anatomy of the Brain, Spinal Cord and Ganglions and of Their Coverings. London: 1845. V. 53

TODD, RUTHVEN
The Acerage of the Heart. Glasgow: 1944. V. 49
Loser's Choice. London: 1953. V. 51
Ten Poems. Edinburgh: 1940. V. 49; 53
Until Now. Poems. London: 1942. V. 51

TODD, W. B.
Tauchnitz International Editions in English 1841-1955. A Bibliographical History. New York: 1988. V. 52

TODD, W. E. C.
Birds of the Labrador Peninsula and Adjacent Areas... Pittsburgh: 1963. V. 54
Birds of the Labrador Peninsula and Adjacent Areas. Toronto: 1963. V. 53
The Birds of the Santa Marta Region of Colombia, a Study in Altitudinal Distribution. 1922. V. 49; 52

TODHUNTER, ISAAC
A History of the Mathematical Theories of Attraction and the Figure of the Earth from the Time of Newton to that of Laplace. London: 1873. V. 49
A History of the Mathematical Theories of Attraction and the Figure of the Earth from the Time of Newton to that of Laplace. New York: 1962. V. 49
A History of the Progress of the Calculus of Variations During the Nineteenth Century. London: 1861. V. 49
A History of the Theory of Elasticity and Of the Strength of Materials from Galilei to the Present Time... London: 1886-93. V. 49
Researches in the Calculus of Variations Principally on the Theory of Discontinuous Solutions. London: 1871. V. 52
A Treatise on Analytical Statics with Numerous Examples. Cambridge: 1853. V. 48

TODHUNTER, JOHN
An Essay in Search of a Subject. 1904. V. 54
An Essay in Search of a Subject. London: 1904. V. 51
Forest Songs - and Other Poems. London: 1881. V. 50
How Dreams Come True. London: 1890. V. 49
Ye Minutes of Ye CLXXVIIth Meeting of Ye Sette of Odd Volumes... 1896. V. 48
Ye Minutes of Ye CLXXVIIth Meeting of Ye Sette of Odd Volumes. Hertford: 1896. V. 48
Ye Minutes of ye CLXXVIIth Meeting of Ye Sette of Odd Volumes... London: 1896. V. 50; 53

TOESCA, PIETRO
Florentine Painting of the Trecento. Florence: 1929. V. 52
The Mosaics in the Church of St. Mark in Vence. London: 1958. V. 52; 54

TOFFTEEN, OLAF A.
Researches in Biblical Archaeology. Chicago: 1907-09. V. 50; 52

THE TOKEN. Boston: 1830. V. 50
THE TOKEN. Boston: 1831. V. 53; 54
THE TOKEN. Boston: 1833. V. 52; 53
THE TOKEN. Boston: 1837. V. 47; 54
THE TOKEN. Boston: 1838. V. 50; 51; 52

THE TOKEN and Atlantic Souvenir. Boston: 1837. V. 52
THE TOKEN and Atlantic Souvenir. Boston: 1838. V. 52
THE TOKEN and Atlantic Souvenir. Boston: 1840. V. 47; 53

TOKLAS, ALICE B.
The Alice B. Toklas Cook Book. London: 1954. V. 50
What Is Remembered. London: 1963. V. 54
What Is Remembered. New York: 1963. V. 54

TOLAND, JOHN
An Account of the Courts of Prussia and Hanover: Sent to a Minister of State in Holland. London: 1714. V. 48
The Art of Governing by Partys... London: 1701. V. 48; 51
The Life of John Milton... London: 1699. V. 51; 53
The Life of John Milton... London: 1761. V. 48; 49; 54
Nazarenus; or, Jewish, Gentile and Mahometan Christianity. London: 1718. V. 51
Tetradymus. London: 1720. V. 51

TOLAR, A. H. H.
Central Texas Review: Devoted to the Interest of Agriculture, Live Stock, Commerce, and the Development of Central Texas Generally... Abilene: 1887. V. 49

TOLDERVY, W.
Select Epitaphs. London: 1755. V. 53

TOLEDO, Ypsilanti and Saginaw Air Line Railroad. Detroit: 1870. V. 48

TOLENTINO, RAUL
De Luxe Catalogue of the Rare Artistic Properties Collected by Signor Raoul Tolentino. New York: 1920. V. 52

TOLFREY, FREDERIC
The Sportsman in Canada. London: 1845. V. 52

TOLKIEN, JOHN RONALD REUEL
The Adventures of Tom Bombadil. London: 1962. V. 47; 49; 50
The Adventures of Tom Bombadil. Boston: 1963. V. 53
Farmer Giles of Ham. 1949. V. 47; 51
Farmer Giles of Ham. London: 1949. V. 47; 49; 52; 53
Farmer Giles of Ham. 1950. V. 49; 54
Farmer Giles of Ham. Boston: 1950. V. 49; 51; 53
The Fellowship of the Ring. 1954. V. 48; 52
The Fellowship of the Ring... London: 1954-55. V. 48
The Fellowship of the Ring... London: 1990. V. 47
The History of Middle-Earth. 1984-92. V. 51
The Hobbit. 1937. V. 47; 48; 50; 54
The Hobbit. London: 1937. V. 51
The Hobbit. 1938. V. 52; 54
The Hobbit. Boston: 1966. V. 52
The Hobbit. London: 1976. V. 50
The Letters of J. R. R. Tolkien. 1981. V. 54
The Lord of the Rings. London: 1954-55. V. 49; 52
The Lord of the Rings... London: 1954-56. V. 49
The Lord of the Rings. 1954-56/56. V. 52; 53
The Lord of the Rings... 1954/54/55. V. 48
The Lord of the Rings. London: 1955. V. 54
The Lord of the Rings... 1961. V. 47
The Lord of the Rings. London: 1962. V. 48
The Lord of the Rings. London: 1966. V. 50
The Lord of the Rings. 1967. V. 48; 52
The Lord of the Rings. 1969. V. 49
The Lord of the Rings. London: 1969. V. 47; 50
The Lord of the Rings. London: 1993. V. 51
Middle English "Losenger"; Sketch of an Etymological and Semantic Enquiry. Paris: 1953. V. 53
The Return of the King. 1955. V. 49; 52; 53
The Return of the King. 1956. V. 48; 54
The Silmarillion. 1977. V. 49
The Silmarillion. Boston: 1977. V. 48
The Silmarillion. London: 1977. V. 48; 49; 51
Smith of Wootton Major. Boston: 1967. V. 50
Smith of Wootton Major. London: 1967. V. 50; 51
Smith of Wootton Major. London: 1971. V. 50
Tree and Leaf. 1964. V. 49; 54
Tree and Leaf. Boston: 1965. V. 49

TOLLER, ERNEST
Hinkerman. Potsdam: 1925. V. 52

TOLLER, ERNST
Brokenbrow. London. V. 47
Brokenbrow. London: 1926. V. 52; 54
Masses and Man. London: 1923. V. 48; 51
Pastor Hall: a Play. London: 1939. V. 49; 53

TOLLER, R. NORTHCOTE
An Anglo-Saxon Dictionary... London: 1964-66. V. 51

TOLLET, ELIZABETH
Poems on Several Occasions. London: 1775. V. 50

TOLLOT, JEAN BAPTISTE
Nouveau Voyage Fait au Levant es Annees 1731 & 1732. Paris: 1742. V. 53; 54

TOLMER, A.
Mise en Page. The Theory and Practice of Lay-Out. London: 1931. V. 48

TOLMIE, W. F.
Comparative Vocabularies of the Indian Tribes of British Columbia. Montreal: 1884. V. 48

TOLNAY, CHARLES DE
Hieronymus Bosch. 1966. V. 49; 51
Hieronymus Bosch. New York: 1966. V. 51
Hieronymus Bosch. U.S.A: 1966. V. 53

TOLOMEI, CLAUDIO
De Le lettere...Lib. Sette. Venice: 1547. V. 48

TOLSON, FRANCIS
The Battle of Dettingen. Northampton: 1743. V. 47
Hermathenae, or Moral Emblems and Ethnick Tales, with Explanatory Notes. London: 1740. V. 48; 51

TOLSON, M. B.
Libretto for the Republic of Liberia. New York: 1953. V. 48

TOLSTOI, LEV NIKOLAEVICH
Anna Karenina. Moskva: 1878. V. 47; 51
Anna Karenina. New York: 1886. V. 51; 53; 54
Anna Karenina. Moscow: 1933. V. 53
Anna Karenina. Cambridge: 1951. V. 48; 52; 53; 54
Anna Karenina. New York: 1951. V. 53; 54
Childhood, Boyhood, Youth. New York: 1886. V. 52
Childhood, Boyhood, Youth. New York: 1972. V. 52; 54
Christ's Christianity. London: 1885. V. 54
Katia. New York: 1888. V. 50; 51
The Kingdom of God is Within You' Christianity Not as a Mystic Religion But As a New Theory of Life. London: 1894. V. 51
The Kreutzer Sonata. Boston: 1890. V. 52
Master and Man. London: 1895. V. 54
My Religion. New York: 1855. V. 49
Novels and Other Works. New York: 1899-1900. V. 51

TOLSTOI, LEV NIKOLAEVICH continued
Preliminary Sketch of the "Kreutzer Sonata". Berkeley Heights: 1965. V. 51
Resurrection. New York: 1900. V. 48
Resurrection. New York: 1963. V. 52; 54
A Russian Proprietor. New York: 1887. V. 53
A Russian Proprietor... London: 1888. V. 48
Sebastopol. New York: 1887. V. 48; 51
Stories and Legends. New York. V. 50
Vojnaimir (War and Peace.). Moscow: 1868-69. V. 48
War and Peace. New York: 1886. V. 49
War and Peace. New York: 1886-87. V. 47
War and Peace. London: 1887. V. 53
War and Peace. 1889. V. 50
War and Peace. Glasgow: 1938. V. 51; 52; 53; 54
War and Peace. New York: 1938. V. 54
What Is Religion? And Other New Articles and letters. New York: 1902. V. 49
What Men Live By. Flemington: 1970. V. 48
The Works. New York: 1925. V. 47

TOM Marchmont. London: 1867. V. 49

TOM of Bedlam's Song. San Francisco: 1931. V. 48

TOM Thumb. London: 1880. V. 53

TOM Thumb's Play-Book to Teach Children Their letters As Soon as They Can Speak... Newcastle: 1824. V. 49; 52

TOMAS, BENITO LUCIANO
Gems of Modern Poetry. New York: 1939. V. 47

TOMASINI, JACOPO FILIPPO
Illustrium Virorum Elogia Iconibus Exornata. Patavii: 1630. V. 50

THE TOMBES, Monuments, and Sepulchral Inscriptions, Lately Visible in St. Paul's Cathedral and St. Faith's Under It, Completely Rendered in Latin and English. London: 1684. V. 47

TOMBLESON, WILLIAM
Eighty Picturesque Views on the Thames and Medway. London: 1834, but later. V. 52
Views of the Rhine. London: 1832. V. 49

TOME, PHILIP
Pioneer Life; or Thirty Years a Hunter. Buffalo: 1854. V. 47

TOMES, ROBERT
Japan and the Japanese: a Narrative of the U. S. Government Expedition to Japan. London: 1859. V. 54
Panama in 1855, an Account of the Panama Rail-Road of the Cities of Panama and Aspinwall with Sketches of Life and Character on the Isthumus. New York: 1855. V. 48

TOMKINS, CHARLES
Six Views in the West of England. London: 1802. V. 48

TOMKINS, PELTRO WILLIAM
To the Queen This Book of Etchings, from Papers Cut by the Right Honourable Lady Templeton, in the Collection of Her Majesty... London: 1790. V. 50

TOMKINS, T.
A Tale of Midas the King. London: 1714. V. 49

TOMKINS, THOMAS
The Beauties of Writing, Exemplified in a Variety of Plain and Ornamental Penmanship. London: 1777. V. 51
Poems on Various Subjects; Selected to Enforce the Practice of Virtue. London: 1780. V. 49; 50; 54

TOMKINSON, G. S.
A Select Bibliography of the principal Modern Presses Public and Private in Great Britain and Ireland. London: 1928. V. 48; 50; 51; 52; 54

TOMLINE, GEORGE
Memoirs of the Life of the Rt. Hon. William Pitt. London: 1821. V. 47; 49

TOMLINE, WILLIAM EDWARD PRETYMAN
A Speech on the Character of the Right Hon. William Pitt, Delivered at Trinity College Chapel Cambridge, Dec. 17, 1806. Cambridge: 1806. V. 52

TOMLINS, WILLIAM L.
The Child's Garden of Song. Chicago: 1895. V. 48

TOMLINSON, CHARLES
Cyclopaedia of Useful Arts, Mechanical and Chemical, Manufactures, Mining and Engineering. London & New York: 1851?. V. 51
Cyclopaedia of Useful Arts, Mechanical and Chemical, Manufactures, Mining and Engineering. London: 1854. V. 52; 53
Pneumatics; for the Use of Beginners. London: 1848. V. 50
Relations and Contraries. Aldington: 1951. V. 49; 54
A Rudimentary Treatise on Warming and Ventilation... London: 1850. V. 50

TOMLINSON, DAVID
African Wildlife in Art. 1991. V. 52; 54
African Wildlife in Art. London: 1991. V. 52; 53

TOMLINSON, HENRY MAJOR
All Our Yesterdays. London: 1930. V. 47
All Our Yesterdays. New York: 1930. V. 53
A Brown Owl. Garden City: 1928. V. 48; 52
London River. London: 1921. V. 48
The Sea and the Jungle. London: 1912. V. 47; 48; 53
The Sea and the Jungle. London: 1930. V. 48; 50; 51; 52
The Sea and the Jungle. New York: 1930. V. 52; 53
Thomas Hardy. New York: 1929. V. 51; 52; 54
Tide Marks Some Record of a Journey to the Beaches of the Moluccas and the Forest of Malaya in 1923. New York: 1924. V. 48
Under the Red Ensign. London: 1926. V. 48
War Books. Cleveland: 1930. V. 51

TOMLINSON, JOHN
Doncaster from the Roman Occupation to the Present Time. Doncaster: 1887. V. 53

TOMLINSON, ORA F.
The John Brown Raid. Charles Town: 1918. V. 50; 51

TOMLINSON, RALPH
A Slang Pastoral Being a Parody of a Celebrated Poem of Dr. Byron's. (sic). London: 1780. V. 50

TOMLINSON, WILLIAM
A Epistle to the Flock, Professing the True Light Which Lighteth Every One that Cometh Into the World... London: 1674. V. 51

TOMLINSON, WILLIAM WEAVER
Denton Hall and Its Associations. London: 1894. V. 47

TOMPKINS, CHARLES
Views of Reading Abbey... London: 1805. V. 53

TOMPKINS, FRANK H.
Chasing Villa, the Story Behind the Story of Pershings Expedition into Mexico. Harrisburg: 1934. V. 53
Riparian Lands of the Mississippi River. New Orleans: 1901. V. 47

TOMPKINS, P. W.
To Her Royal Highness the Princess Amelia, This Book Representing the Birth-Day Gift or the Joy of a New Doll... London: 1796. V. 52

TOMPSON, BENJAMIN
New-England's Crisis. Boston: 1894. V. 48

THE TON: Anecdotes, Chit-Chat, Hints and On Dits... London: 1819. V. 51

TONER, J. M.
The Medical Men of the Revolution, with a Brief History of the Medical Department of the Continental Army... Philadelphia: 1876. V. 52; 53

TONEY, MARCUS BRECKENRIDGE
The Privations of a Private. Nashville: 1905. V. 49
The Privations of a Private. Nashville and Dallas: 1907. V. 50

TONEYAMA, KOJIN
Relief Sculptures of Ancient Mexico: Rubbings of Objects from the Mayan and Aztec World. Boston: 1971. V. 47; 50

TONGE, THOMAS
Denver by Pen and Picture. Denver: 1900. V. 52

TONGUE, CORNELIUS
The Kennel Stud Book. London: 1866. V. 47

TONGUE Cut Sparrow. London & Sydney: 1888. V. 50

TONGUE, MARGARET
A Book of Kinds. Iowa City: 1958. V. 47; 54

TONNA, CHARLOTTE ELIZABETH
Derry, a Tale of the Revolution. London: 1833. V. 50; 52; 53; 54
Mesmerisim. London: 1844. V. 50
Osrie, a Missionary Tale: With the Garden and Other Poems. London: 1826. V. 49
The Rockite. London: 1830. V. 49

TONSBERG, C.
Norge Fremstillet i Tegninger Med Onlysende Text. Christiania: 1855. V. 47

TONTINE COFFEE-HOUSE
The Constitution and Nominations of the Subscribers to the Tontine Coffee-House. New York: 1796. V. 48

TONY Sarg's Surprise Book. New York: 1941. V. 48

TOOGOOD, C. G.
Index to James' Naval History (Edition 1886). London: 1895. V. 53

TOOHEY, JOHN L.
A History of the Pulitzer Prize Plays. New York: 1967. V. 53

TOOKE, ANDREW
The Pantheon, Representing the Fabulous Histories of the Heathen Gods, and Most Illustrious Heroes... London: 1774. V. 47; 54

TOOKE, JOHN HORNE
The Diversion of Purley. London: 1798-1815. V. 49; 53
Eiiea litepoenta. Or, The Diversions of Purley. London: 1798/1815. V. 48
Epea Pteroenta. London: 1798. V. 49
Epea Pteroenta. London: 1798-1805. V. 52
Epea Pteroenta... London: 1829. V. 52

TOOKE, THOMAS
Considerations on the State of the Currency. London: 1826. V. 51; 53
A History of Prices, and of the State of the Circulation from 1793 to 1837...(with) A History of Prices, and of the State of the Circulation in 1838 and 1839... London: 1838/40. V. 52

TOOKE, WILLIAM
History of Russia: from the Foundation of the Monarchy by Rurik, to the Accession of Catharine the Second. London: 1800. V. 49; 51
The Life of Catherine II, Empress of All the Russias... Philadelphia: 1802. V. 50; 51; 53
A New and General Biographical Dictionary... London: 1798. V. 47; 51

TOOKER, RICHARD
The Dawn Boy. Philadelphia: 1932. V. 52

TOOLE, JOHN KENNEDY
A Confederacy of Dunces. Baton Rouge & London: 1980. V. 47; 48; 51; 53
A Confederacy of Dunces. London: 1981. V. 51
A Confederacy of Dunces. Baton Rouge: 1983. V. 50

TOOLE, JOHN LAWRENCE
Reminiscences of J. L. Toole Related by Himself, and Chronicled by Joseph Hatton. London: 1889. V. 47

TOOLE-STOTT, RAYMOND
A Bibliography of English Conjuring 1581-1876. Derby: 1976-78. V. 51
Circus and the Allied Arts. Derby: 1958-71. V. 51; 52

TOOLE STOTT, RAYMOND
Circus and the Allied Arts... Derby: 1958-71/92. V. 54

TOOLEY, RONALD VERE
Collectors' Guide to Maps of the African Continent and Southern Africa. London: 1969. V. 50
English Books with Coloured Plates... Boston: 1954. V. 51
English Books with Coloured Plates 1790-1860. Folkstone: 1973. V. 48
A History of Cartography: 2500 Years of Maps and Mapmakers. London: 1969. V. 53
Landmarks of Mapmaking. New York: 1976. V. 49; 50; 53
The Mapping of America. London: 1980. V. 54
Some English Books with Coloured Plates. London: 1935. V. 48
Tooley's Dictionary of Mapmakers. Tring: 1979. V. 48

TOOMER, JEAN
Essentials. Chicago: 1931. V. 47; 48; 49; 52; 53
The Flavor of Man. London: 1949. V. 50
The Flavor of Man. Philadelphia: 1949. V. 51

TOON, CHAN, MRS.
For Love of the King. London: 1922. V. 53

TOONDER, MARTEN
Tom Puss Tales. London. V. 48

TOONDER, MARTIN
Tom Puss Tales. London: 1930. V. 50

TOONE, WILLIAM
A Chronological Record of the Remarkable Public Events, Political, Historical, Biographical, Literary, Domestic and Miscellaneous. London: 1834. V. 53
A Glossary and Etymological Dictionary of Obsolete and Uncommon Words, Antiquated Phrases, Proverbial Expressions, Obscure Allusions, and Of Words which Have Changed Their Significations. London: 1832. V. 48

TOOVEY, JAMES
Catalogue of an Extensive and Extraordinary Assemblage of the Productions of the Aldine Press, From Its First Establishment at Venice in 1494, Together with Lyonese and Venetian Counterfeits, the Giunta and Other Works Illustrative of the Series. London: 1880. V. 47

TOPENCE, ALEXANDER
The Reminiscences of Alexander Topence, Pioneer. 1923. V. 49

TOPHAM, E.
The British Album. Dublin: 1790. V. 50; 54

TOPHAM, EDWARD
The Poetry of "The World". London: 1788. V. 52

TOPHAM, W. F.
The Lakes of England. London: 1869. V. 50; 52; 54

TOPLADY, AUGUSTUS
The Scheme of Christian and Philosophical Necessity Asserted. London: 1775. V. 52

TOPLIS, GRACE
Jefferies' Land - a History of Swindon and Its Environs. London: 1896. V. 49

TOPONCE, ALEXANDER
Reminiscences of Alexander Toponce, Pioneer 1839-1923. Ogden: 1923. V. 47; 52

TOPP, C. BERESFORD
The 42nd Battalion C.E.F. Royal Highlanders of Canada in the Great War. Montreal: 1931. V. 48; 50

TOPP, CHESTER W.
Victorian Yellowbacks and Paperbacks 1849-1905, Volume One, George Routledge. Denver: 1993. V. 52; 54
Victorian Yellowbacks and Paperbacks 1849-1905. Volume Two, Ward & Lock. Denver: 1995. V. 52; 54

TOPSELL, EDWARD
The Fowles of Heaven or History of Birds. Austin: 1972. V. 54
The Historie of Four Footed Beasts... New York: 1967. V. 50
The Historie of Four Footed Beasts... London: 1973. V. 51
The Historie of Serpents, or The Second Book of Living Creatures... London: 1973. V. 51

TORBETT, D.
On Trial: The Story of A Woman At Bay... New York: 1928. V. 48

TORBUCK, JOHN
A Collection of Welsh Travels and Memoirs of Wales. London: 1749. V. 47

TORCHIANA, HENRY ALBERT VAN COENEN
Story of Mission Santa Cruz. San Francisco: 1933. V. 47; 54

TORCZYMER, HARRY
Magritte. Ideas and Images. New York: 1977. V. 47; 48; 50; 52

TORDAY, E.
On the Trail of the Bushongo. London: 1925. V. 54

TORELLI, LELIO
Raguaglio della Marciata, e Comparsa a' Uso di Guerra con L'Artiglieria... Urbino: 1640. V. 52

TORMES, LAZARILLO DE
The Pleasant History of Lazarillo de Tormes. 1991. V. 52

TORNE, L'ABBE
Sermons Preches Devant Le Roi, Pendant Le Careme de 1764. Paris: 1765. V. 52

TORNEL, JOSE MARIA
Tejas Y Los Estados-Unidos de America, en Sus Relaciones con la Republica Mexicana. Mexico: 1837. V. 47

TORNIELLO DA NOVARA, FRANCESCO
The Alphabet. 1971. V. 52
The Alphabet...Followed by a Comparison With the Alphabet of Fra Luca Padioli. Verona: 1971. V. 53

TORONTO.. Toronto: 188-. V. 52

TORONTO - Street Directory. Toronto: 1895. V. 54

TORONTO ARCHITECTURAL EIGHTEEN CLUB
Catalogue of the Fourth Exhibition. Toronto: 1905. V. 51

THE TORONTO City Directory for 1890. Toronto: 1890. V. 54

TORONTO of To-Day. To Commemorate the Twelfth International Geological Congress, Toronto. Toronto: 1913. V. 52; 54

TORONTO PUBLIC LIBRARY
The Osborne Collection of Early Children's Books 1566-1910. A Catalogue. Toronto: 1975. V. 47; 49; 53

TORONTONENSIS, 1900: A Yearly Record and Memorial of Student Life in the University of Toronto. Toronto: 1900. V. 52

TORQUEMADA, ANTONIO DE
The Spanish Mandevile of Miracles, or the Garden of Curious Flowers. London: 1600. V. 48

TORQUEMADA, JUAN DE, CARDINAL
Expositio Super Psalterio. Augsburg: 1471. V. 51; 53

TORR, JAMES
The Antiquities of York City. York: 1719. V. 47; 49; 50; 51

TORRANCE, JARED SIDNEY
The Descendants of Lewis Hart and Anne Elliott. Los Angeles: 1923. V. 47

TORRE, CARLO
Il Ritratto di Milano, Divisio in Tre Libri... Milan: 1674. V. 53

TORRE, NICHOLAS LEE
Translations of the Oxford and Cambridge Latin Prize Poems. Second Series. London: 1831. V. 52
Translations of the Oxford Latin Prize Poems. First Series. London: 1831. V. 52

TORRE FARFAN, FERNANDO DE LA
Fiestas de la S. Iglesia Metropolitana, y Patriarcal de Sevilla, al Nuevo Culto del Senor Rey S. Fernando el Tercero de Castilla y de Leon... Seville: 1671. V. 48

TORRENCE, RIDGELY
Granny Maumee: the Rider of Dreams: Simon the Cyrenian. New York: 1917. V. 48; 52
Poems. New York: 1941. V. 54

TORRENS, HENRY D'OYLEY
Travels in Ladak Tartary, and Kashmir. London: 1862. V. 48; 51

TORREY, JESSE
The Moral Instructor, and Guide to Virtue and Happiness. Ballston Spa: 1819. V. 47
A Portraiture of Domestic Slavery, in the United States... Philadelphia: 1817. V. 47

TORREY, JOHN
A Compendium of the Flora of the Northern and Middle States... New York: 1826. V. 47; 48
Explorations and Surveys for a Railroad Route from the Mississippi River... Washington: 1856. V. 52
A Flora of North America. New York: 1838-40. V. 47; 48
A Flora of the State of New York... Albany: 1843. V. 47; 54
Flora of the State of New York... Albany: 1943. V. 51
Plantae Fremontianae, or Descriptions of Plants Collected by Col. J. C. Fremont in California. Washington: 1850. V. 47

TORREY BOTANICAL CLUB, NEW YORK.
Index to American Botanical Literature 1886-1966. Boston: 1969. V. 53

TORRIANO, G.
Rome Exactly Described, As to the Present State of it Under Pope Alexander the Seventh. London: 1664. V. 48

TORRINGTON, JOHN BYNG, 5TH VISCOUNT
The Torrington Diaries: Containing the Tours through England and Wales of the Hon. John Byng. London: 1934-38. V. 50

TORROJA, EUDARDO
The Structures...; an Autobiography of Engineering Accomplishment. New York: 1958. V. 54

TORSELLINO, ORAZIO
the History of Our B. Lady of Loreto. 1608. V. 52
The History of Our B. Lady of Loreto. St. Omer: 1608. V. 48

TORY, GEOFFROY
Champ Fleury. New York: 1927. V. 47; 48; 49; 51; 52; 53; 54

THE TOTNESS Address Transversed. London: 1727. V. 53

TOTT, FRANCOIS DE, BARON
Memoirs...On the Turks and the Tartars. Dublin: 1785. V. 53
Memoirs...on the Turks and the Tartars. London: 1785. V. 52

TOTTEN, GEORGE OAKLEY
Maya Architecture. Washington: 1926. V. 48; 51

TOTTEN, JOSEPH
Report in Relation to the Military and Naval Defences of the Country. Washington: 1850. V. 48

TOTTENHAM, GEORGE L.
The Peasant Proprietors of Norway. 1889. V. 52
Terence McGowan, the Irish Tenant. London: 1870. V. 47

TOUCH and Go: A Book of Changing Pictures. London: 1895. V. 49

THE TOUCHSTONE of Precedents Relating to Judicial Proceedings at Common Law. London: 1682. V. 52

THE TOUCHSTONE: or Paradoxes Brough to the Test of a Rigorous and Fair Examination for the Settling of Dubious Points to the Satisfaction of the Curious and Conscientious... 1732. V. 54

TOUCHSTONE, S. F.
History of Celebrated English and French Thorough-Bred Stallions and French Mares Which Appeared on the Turf from 1764 to 1887. London: 1890. V. 47

TOULMIN, H. A.
With Pershing in Mexico. Harrisburg: 1935. V. 53

TOULOUSE-LAUTREC, HENRI DE
The Posters. Boston: 1966. V. 51

A TOUR in Germany in the Years 1820, 1821, 1822. Edinburgh: 1824. V. 53

THE TOUR of Doctor Syntax through London, Or the Pleasures and Miseries of the Metropolis. London: 1820. V. 51; 52; 54

TOUR to the Loire and La Vendee in 1835. London: 1836. V. 52

TOURE, ASKIA MUHAMMAD
Songhai!. New York: 1972. V. 54

TOURGEE, ALBION WINEGAR
The Story of a Thousand, Being a History fo the Service of the 105th Ohio Volunteer Infantry, in the War for the Union from August 21, 1862 to June 6, 1865. Buffalo: 1896. V. 48; 54
With Gauge & Swallow, Attorneys. Philadelphia: 1889. V. 52

THE TOURIST or Pocket Manual for Travellers on the Hudson River, the Western Canal; and Stage Road to Niagara Falls Down Lake Ontario and the St. Lawrence to Montereal and Quebec... New York: 1834. V. 49

A TOURIST'S Companion to Ripon, Studley Park, Fountains Abbey, Hackfall... Ripon: 1822. V. 47

TOURIST'S Guide to the English Lakes. London: 1870. V. 50; 52

THE TOURIST'S Illustrated Hand-Book for Ireland. 1861. London: 1861. V. 53

TOURNEFORT, JOSEPH PITTON DE
Institutiones Rei Hebariae. Lugduni juxta Exemplar: 1719. V. 47; 53
Relation d'un Voyage au Levant. Amsterdam: 1718. V. 48
A Voyage Into the Levant... London: 1718. V. 50
A Voyage Into the Levant... London: 1741. V. 48

TOURNEUR, CYRIL
The Plays and Poems of Cyril Tourneur. London: 1878. V. 54
The Works... London: 1930. V. 49

TOURNIER, MICHEL
Gilles and Jeanne. Helsinki: 1990. V. 48
Le Jardin D'Hammamet. Northridge: 1986... V. 48

TOURTEL, MARY
A Horse Book. London: 1901. V. 50

TOUSARD, ANNE LOUIS DE
American Artillerist's Companion, or Elements of Artillery. Philadelphia: 1809. V. 54

TOUSSAINT, FRANCOIS V.
Manners. London: 1749. V. 52

TOUSSAINT, MANUEL
Colonial Art in Mexico. 1967. V. 48

TOUT, T. F.
Chapters in the Adminstrative History of Medieaval England: The Wardrobe, The Chamber and the Small Seals. Manchester: 1967. V. 49

TOWARDS a New American Poetics: Essays and Interviews. Santa Barbara: 1978. V. 50; 52

THE TOWER of Babel... 1975. V. 52

THE TOWER of Babel. West Burke: 1975. V. 54

TOWER, PHILO
Slavery Unmasked: Being a Truthful Narrative of a Three Years' Residence and Journeying in Eleven Southern States... Rochester: 1856. V. 51; 53

TOWERS, JOSEPH
Memoirs of the Life and Reign of Frederick the Third, King of Prussia. Dublin: 1789. V. 47; 53

TOWERSON, GABRIEL
An Explication of the Cathechism of the Church of England. London: 1658/81/80/86/. V. 51

TOWLE, ELEANOR A.
My Sister Rosalind. London: 1876. V. 50

TOWLE, NANCY
Vicissitudes Illustrated, in the Experience of Nancy Towle, in Europe and America. Charleston: 1832. V. 53
Vicissitudes Illustrated, in the Experience of Nancy Towle, in Europe and America. Portsmouth: 1833. V. 50

TOWLER, JOHN
The Silver Sunbeam... New York: 1879. V. 54

THE TOWN and Country Mouse and Other Fables. London: 1870. V. 54

THE TOWN and Country Toy Book. London: 1880. V. 47; 49

TOWN, HAROLD
Enigmas, Enigmas. Montreal: 1964. V. 47
Tom Thompson: the Silence and the Storm. Toronto: 1977. V. 47; 53; 54

TOWN, ITHIEL
Atlantic Steam-Ships. Some Ideas and Statements, the Result of Considerable Reflection on the Subject of Navigating the Atlantic Ocean with Steam Ships of Large Tonnage... New York: 1838. V. 49

TOWNE, RICHARD
A Treatise of the Diseases Most Frequent in the West-Indies and Herein More Particularly of Those Which Occur in Barbadoes. London: 1726. V. 49; 53

TOWNE, ROBERT
Chinatown: A Screenplay. Santa Barbara: 1983. V. 50

TOWNE, ROSA M.
Plant Lore of Shakespeare. Louisville: 1974. V. 52

TOWNLEY, JAMES
High Life Below Stairs. London: 1759. V. 48; 49
Tally Ho-To Hark Forward. 1803. V. 47

TOWNS.. 1985. V. 49
TOWNS. London: 1985. V. 53

TOWNSEND, C. H.
Condition of Seal Life on the Rookeries of the Pribilof Islands and Pelagic Sealing in Bering Sea and North Pacific Ocean, 1893-95. Washington: 1896. V. 51; 54
Illustrations Showing Condition of Fur-Seal Rookeries in 1895 and Method of Killing Seals... Washington: 1896. V. 54

TOWNSEND, CHARLES
Rio Grande: an Original Drama in 3 Acts. Boston: 1891. V. 50; 51

TOWNSEND, F.
Flora of Hampshire... London: 1904. V. 54

TOWNSEND, F. TRENCH
Ten Thousand Miles of Travel, Sport and Adventure. London: 1869. V. 51

TOWNSEND, GEORGE A.
Campaigns of a Non-Combatant and His Roamings Abroad During the War. New York: 1866. V. 48; 50; 52

TOWNSEND, JOHN K.
Excursion to the Oregon. 1846. V. 47
Narrative of a Journey Across the Rocky Mountains. Philadelphia: 1839. V. 47; 48; 52

TOWNSEND, JOHN SEALY EDWARD
Electricity in Gases. Oxford: 1915. V. 50

TOWNSEND, JOSEPH
The Character of Moses Established for Veracity as an Historian, Recording Events from the Creation to the Deluge. Bath: 1813. V. 47
Elements of Therapeutics; or, A Guide to Health: Being Cautions and Directions in the Treatment of Diseases. Boston: 1802. V. 49
Etymological Researches... Bath: 1824. V. 48
Free Thoughts on Despotic and Free Governments, as Connected with the Happiness of the Governor and the Governed. London: 1781. V. 47
A Guide to Health: Being Cautions and Directions in the Treatment of Diseases. London: 1795-96. V. 49

TOWNSEND, LUTHER TRACY
History of the 16th Regiment, New Hampshire Volunteers. 1897. V. 48; 52
History of the 16th Regiment, New Hampshire Volunteers. Washington: 1897. V. 50; 54

TOWNSEND, RICHARD EDWARD AUSTIN
Visions of the Western Railways. London: 1838. V. 48

TOWNSEND, RICHARD H.
Original Poems. Baltimore: 1809. V. 53
Scenes at Washington; a Story of the Last Generation. New York: 1848. V. 47; 52

TOWNSEND, W. G. PAULSON
Measured Drawings of French Furniture from the Collection in South Kensington Museum. London: 1900. V. 51
Modern Decorative Art in England. London: 1922. V. 51

TOWNSEND, W. H.
A System of Foliage, with Hints on the Acquirement of a Touch... London: 1844. V. 47; 49

TOWNSEND, WILLIAM C.
The Lives of Twelve Eminent Judges of the Last and of the Present Century. London: 1846. V. 51

TOWNSEND, WILLIAM THOMPSON
The Cricket on the Hearth. London: 1860. V. 54
The Cricket on the Hearth. London: 1873. V. 54

TOWNSHEND, CHARLES
A Defence of the Minority in the House of Commons on the Question Relating to General Warrants. London: 1764. V. 54

TOWNSHEND, CHAUNCY HARE
Facts in Mesmerism, or Animal Magnetism... London: 1840. V. 53
Facts in Mesmerism, or Animal Magnetism... Boston: 1841. V. 48
Facts in Mesmerism, With Reasons for a Dispassioante Inquiry Into It. London: 1844. V. 49; 50
Religious Opinions of the Late Reverend Chauncy Hare Townshend. London: 1869. V. 54

TOWNSHEND, FREDERICK TRENCH
Ten Thousand Miles of Travel, Sport and Adventure. London: 1869. V. 47; 48; 52; 53
Wild Life in Florida. London: 1875. V. 50

TOWNSHEND, GEORGE TOWNSHEND, 1ST MARQUIS
A Brief Narrative of the Late Campaigns in Germany and Flanders. London: 1751. V. 47
A Political and Satyrical History of the Years 1756, 1757, 1758 and 1759. London: 1760. V. 50; 52

TOWNSHEND, SAMUEL NUGENT
Our Indian Summer in the Far West. London: 1880. V. 47; 54

TOWNSHEND, THOMAS
Poems. London: 1796. V. 48

TOYNBEE, ARNOLD
Survey of International Affairs 1939-46: The World in March 1939. Oxford: 1952. V. 49

TOYNBEE, ARNOLD J.
Armenian Atrocities - the Murder of a Nation. London: 1915. V. 47
Greek Policy Since 1882. London: 1914. V. 48; 51
A Study of History. London: 1956. V. 50

TOYNBEE, JOSEPH
The Diseases of the Ear: Their Nature, Diagnosis and Treatment. Philadelphia: 1860. V. 47

TOZER, HENRY FANSHAW
Lectures on the Geography of Greece. London: 1873. V. 52
Researches in the Highlands of Turkey... London: 1869. V. 51

TOZZER, ALFRED M.
Chichen Itza and its Cenote of Sacrifice: a Comparative Study of Contemporaneous Maya and Toltec. Cambridge: 1957. V. 52
A Preliminary Study of the Prehistoric Ruins of Nakum Guatemala. Cambridge: 1913. V. 50; 52

TRABER, ZACHARIAS
Nervus Opticus Sive Tractatus Theoricus, in Tres Libros Opticam, Catoptricam, Dioptricam Distributus. Vienna: 1675. V. 47

THE TRACKLESS Trolley as an Investment. Los Angeles: 1912. V. 53

THE TRACT Primer. New York: 1840's. V. 51

TRACY, W. BURNETT
Lancashire at the Opening of the Twentieth Century - Contemporary Biographies. Brighton: 1903. V. 53; 54

TRADE Index and Guide Book of New York City. 1877. V. 53

TRADES HOUSE, GLASGOW.
The Records of the Trades House of Glasgow, 1605-1678. Glasgow: 1910. V. 49

THE TRAGEDY of Nero. London: 1633. V. 50

THE TRAGIC-Comic History of the Burial of Cock Robin; With the Lamentation of Jenny Wren... Philadelphia: 1821. V. 48

THE TRAGICAL History of the Children in the Wood. Wilmington: 1809. V. 54

TRAGICUM Theatrum Actorum, & Casuum Tragicorum Londini Publice Celebratorum. Amsterdam: 1649. V. 48; 49; 50; 52; 54

TRAICE, W. H. J.
Hand-Book of Mechanics' Institutions, with Priced Catalogue of Books Suitable for Libraries and Periodicals for Reading Rooms. London: 1863. V. 52

TRAIL, WILLIAM
Account of the Life and Writings of Robert Simson. London: 1812. V. 52
Elements of Algebra. London: 1789. V. 49

TRAILL, CATHERINE PARR STRICKLAND
Afar in the Forest; or, Pictures of Life and Scenery in the Wilds of Canada. London: 1869. V. 53
The Backwoods of Canada... London: 1835-46. V. 50
The Backwoods of Canada... London: 1836. V. 48; 50; 52; 54
The Backwoods of Canada... London: 1838. V. 50
The Backwoods of Canada. London: 1846. V. 53
Canada and the Oregon. The Backwoods of Canada. London: 1846. V. 48; 52
The Canadian Settler's Guide. Toronto: 1857. V. 53
Canadian Wild Flowers. Montreal: 1869. V. 51; 52; 53
Pearls and Pebbles; or, Notes of an Old Naturalist. Toronto: 1894. V. 53
Stories of the Canadian Forest; or, Little Mary and Her Nurse. New York: 1857. V. 48
Stories of the Canadian Forest; or, Little Mary and Her Nurse. Boston: 1862. V. 53
Studies of Plant Life in Canada; or Gleanings from Forest, Lake and Plain. Ottawa: 1885. V. 52; 54

TRAILL, H. D.
The Building of Britain and the Empire. London: 1914. V. 49; 52
Social England: a Record of the Progress of the People. New York & London: 1901-04. V. 53

TRAILL, THOMAS W.
Chain Cables and Chains. London: 1885. V. 50

TRAIN, JOSEPH
Strains of the Mountain Muse. Edinburgh: 1814. V. 51; 54

TRAIN, PERCY
Medicinal Uses of Plants by Indian Tribes of Nevada. Washington: 1941. V. 47

TRAITTEUR, G. DE
Plans, Profils, Vues Perspectives et Details des Ponts en Chaines Executes a Saint Petersburg. St. Petersburg: 1824. V. 49; 53

TRAKI, GEORG
Gedichte.l. Leipzig: 1913. V. 49

TRALBAUT, MARC EDO
Vincent Van Gogh. London: 1969. V. 50

TRALL, R. T.
The New Hydropathic Cook-Book. New York: 1873. V. 53
Water-Cure for the Million, the Processes of Water-Cure Explained. New York: 1860. V. 51

TRALLES, BALTHASAR LUDOVICUS
Usus Opii. Breslau: 1757-62. V. 47; 53

TRAMEZZANI, DIOMIRO
Three Italian Arietts. London: 1793. V. 54

TRANSATLANTIC Sketches; or, Sixty Days in America. London: 1865. V. 53

THE TRANSFORMATION of a Beech Tree; or, the History of a Black Chair. London: 1828. V. 48

TRANSITION. No. 25. London: 1936. V. 52

TRANSITION. No. 26. London: 1937. V. 50

TRANSITION Stories. New York: 1929. V. 50

A TRANSLATION of the Charter of King Edward the Sixth, Whereby a Free Grammar School Was Founded for the Benefit of the Town of Louth, in the County of Lincoln. Louth: 1813. V. 51

THE TRANSMIGRATION of the Seven Brahmans. New York: 1931. V. 54

TRANT, THOMAS ABERCROMBIE
Two Years in Ava. From May 1824 to May 1826. London: 1827. V. 54

TRAPMANN, A. H.
The Greeks Triumphant. London: 1915. V. 48

TRAPP, JOHN
A Clavis to the Bible. 1650. V. 47

TRAPP, JOSEPH
Abra-Mule; or, Love and Empire. London: 1704. V. 51

TRAQUAIR, RAMSAY
The Old Architecture of Quebec: a Study of the Buildings Erected in New France from the Earliest Explorers to the Middle of the Nineteenth Century. Toronto: 1947. V. 47; 52

TRASK, JOHN B.
Report on the Geology of the Coast Mountains, and Part of the Sierra Nevada: Embracing their Industrial Resources in Agriculture and Mining. Sacramento: 1854. V. 49
Report on the Geology of the Coast Mountains; Embracing Their Agricultural Resources and Mineral Productions Also, Portions of the Middle and Northern Mining Districts. Sacramento: 1855. V. 49

TRATTINNICK, LEOPOLD
Die Essbaren Schwamme des Oesterreichischen Kaiserstaates. Wien and Triest: 1809. V. 49; 52

TRAUBEL, HORACE L.
Camden's Compliment to Walt Whitman. May 31, 1889. Philadelphia: 1889. V. 48; 49
In Re Walt Whitman. Philadelphia: 1893. V. 51
With Walt Whitman in Camden. Boston: 1906. V. 51

TRAUTMANN, W.
Riot. Chicago: 1922?. V. 54

TRAUX, CHARLES
The Mechanics of Surgery (1899). San Francisco: 1988. V. 47; 48; 49; 50

TRAVELERS Rest Arabian Horses. Franklin: 1943. V. 53

THE TRAVELLER; or, an Entertaining Journey Round the Habitable Globe... London: 1820. V. 54

THE TRAVELLER'S Guide through the Kingdom of the Netherlands. Ostend: 1828. V. 47; 50

THE TRAVELLER'S Pocket Directory and Stranger's Guide... Schenectady: 1831. V. 47

TRAVELS Into Several Remote Nations of the World. London: 1727. V. 51

THE TRAVELS of Captains. Lewis & Clarke, From St. Louis, By Way of the Missouri and Columbia Rivers, to the Pacific Ocean. London: 1809. V. 47

THE TRAVELS of Several learned Missioners of the Society of Jesus, into Divers Parts of the Archipelago, India, China and America. London: 1714. V. 51

TRAVELS Through Flanders, Holland, Germany, Sweden and Denmark. London: 1693. V. 50

TRAVEN, B.
The Bridge in the Jungle. New York: 1938. V. 47
The Cotton Pickers. London: 1956. V. 52
The Death Ship. London: 1934. V. 49
The Death Ship. New York: 1934. V. 47; 49; 53
The Rebellion of the Hanged. London: 1952. V. 51
The Rebellion of the Hanged. New York: 1952. V. 49; 51; 52
The Treasure of the Sierra Madre. New York: 1935. V. 49; 50; 51; 53
The White Rose. London: 1965. V. 49

TRAVER, ROBERT
Danny and the Boys. Cleveland: 1951. V. 51
Trouble Shooter. New York: 1943. V. 48; 53

TRAVERS, BENJAMIN
An Inquiry Concerning that Disturbed State of the Vital Functions Usually denominated Constitutional Irritation. New York: 1826. V. 49
A Synopsis of the Diseases of the Eye, and Their Treatment, to Which a prefixed, a Short Anatomical Description and Sketch of the Physiology of that Organ. London: 1820. V. 53

TRAVERS, HENRY
Miscellaneous Poems and Translations. London: 1731. V. 47; 48; 51; 54

TRAVERS, MORRIS W.
The Discovery of the Rare Gases. London: 1928. V. 49

TRAVERS, PAMELA LYNDON
Aunt Sass. New York: 1941. V. 54
Mary Poppins. 1934. V. 54
Mary Poppins. London: 1934. V. 50
Mary Poppins. New York: 1934. V. 47; 51
Mary Poppins. New York: 1935. V. 49
Mary Poppins in the Park. New York: 1952. V. 49
Mary Poppins Opens the Door. New York: 1943. V. 48
Mary Poppins Opens the Door. New York: 1944. V. 52; 53

TRAVIS-COOK, J.
Notes Relative to the Manor of Myton. Hull: 1890. V. 53

TRAVLOS, JOHN
Pictorial Dictionary of Ancient Athens. London: 1971. V. 52

TREADWELL, EDWARD F.
The Cattle King. New York: 1931. V. 50; 54
The Cattle King. Boston: 1950. V. 54

TREASURE Land. Tucson: 1897. V. 47

TREASURES of a London Temple. London: 1951. V. 48; 53

TREASURES of Japanese Architecture. Castles. Tokyo: 1962. V. 48

TREASURES of the Shosoin. Tokyo: 1965. V. 53

TREATIES, Conventions, International acts, Protocols and Agreements Between the United States of America and Other Powers 1776-1909. New York: 1968. V. 50

A TREATISE of Distresses, Replevins and Avowries...Containing the Common and Statute Law for Securing the Payment of Rents...Also Divers Statutes Touching the Office of Sheriffs... London: 1761. V. 51

A TREATISE of Feme Coverts; or, the Lady's Law. London: 1732. V. 48; 54

TREATISE on Ammunition. London: 1881. V. 47

A TREATISE on Greyhounds with Observations on the Treatment & Disorders of Them. By a Sportsman. London: 1819. V. 47; 48

TREATISE on Military Finance; Containing the Pay of the Forces on the British and Irish Establishment, With the Allowances in Camp, Garrison and Quarters. London: 1804. V. 48

TREATISE on the Custom of Counting Noses. London: 1779. V. 48; 50

TREATISES On Architecture, Building, Masonry, Joinery and Carpentry. Edinburgh: 1846. V. 50

TREATT, STELLA COURT
Cape to Cairo. London: 1927. V. 54

THE TREBLE Almanack for the Year 1823. Dublin: 1822. V. 50

TREDGOLD, THOMAS
Elementary Principles of Carpentry... London: 1820. V. 53
Elementary Principles of Carpentry... London: 1853. V. 49
Elementary Principles of Carpentry... London: 1870. V. 53
Elementary Principles of Carpentry... London: 1886. V. 49
Practical Essay on the Strength of Cast Iron and other Metals... London: 1842/47. V. 49
The Principles of Warming and Ventilating Public Buildings, Dwelling-Houses, manufactories, Hospitals, Hot-Houses, Conservatories &c... London: 1836. V. 50; 53; 54
The Steam Engine, Its Invention and an Investigation of Its Principles, for Navigation, Manufactures and Railways. London: 1838. V. 53
Tracts on Hydraulics... London: 1836. V. 48
Tredgold on the Steam Engine Marine Engines and Boilers... London: 1850. V. 48

TREE, HERBERT BEERBOHM
Souvenir of the Charing Cross Hospital Bazaar. London: 1899. V. 51

TREE, IRIS
Poems. Nassau: 1917. V. 49

TREECE, HENRY
Dylan Thomas. London: 1949. V. 48
Herbert Read - an Introduction to His Work by Various Hands. London: 1944. V. 54
Towards a Personal Armageddon. Prairie City: 1941. V. 49

TREES, ARTHUR
Open Space in the Inner City. New York: 1971. V. 47

TREFUSIS, VIOLET
Don't Look Round. London: 1952. V. 50

TREGEAR, E.
The Maori Race. Wangantui: 1904. V. 54

TREGELLAS, JOHN TABOIS
The Amusing Adventures of Josee Cock, the Perran Cock-Fighter, the Author's Address to Captain Peard, Bozzy Paul, Zacky Martin and others... London: 1857. V. 49
The St. Agnes Bear Hunt and the Perran Cherrybeam. Truro: 1851. V. 54

TREGENNA, CHARLES
Lascare. A Tale. London: 1876. V. 50

TREGONING, JOSEPH
Laws of the Stanneries of Cornwall with Marginal Notes and References to Authorities. Truro: 1808. V. 51

TREHERNE, J.
Key Environments: Galapagos, Sahara Desert, Madagascar, Amazonia, Antarctica, Red Sea, Western Mediterranean, Malaysia. London: 1984-86. V. 48

TRELAWNY, EDWARD JOHN
Recollections of the Last Days of Shelley and Byron. Boston: 1858. V. 54
Recollections of the Last Days of Shelley and Byron. London: 1858. V. 54

TRELEASE, W.
Agave in the West Indies. Washington: 1913. V. 54

TREMAIN, HENRY EDWIN
The Closing Days About Richmond; or, the Last Days of Sheridan's Cavalry. New York: 1873. V. 49
The Closing Days About Richmond, or, the Last Days of Sheridan's Cavalry. Edinburgh: 1884. V. 49
Last Hours of Sheridan's Cavalry. New York: 1904. V. 52; 54

TREMAINE, MARIE
A Bibliography of Canadian Imprints 1751-1800. Toronto: 1952. V. 52

TREMEARNE, A. J. N.
The Ban of the Bori. Demons and Demon-Dancing in West and North Africa. London: 1925. V. 53
The Tailed Headhunters of Nigeria... London: 1912. V. 54

TREMENHEERE, HUGH SEYMOUR
Notes on Public Subjects, Made During a Tour in the United States and Canada. London: 1852. V. 47; 50; 53

TRENCH, CHARLOTTE V.
The Wrays of Donegal, Londonderry & Antrim. 1945. V. 50; 54
The Wrays of Donegal, Londonderry & Antrim. London: 1945. V. 49; 51

TRENCH, FREDERICK WILLIAM
A Collection of Papers Relating to the Thames Quay; With Hints for Some Further Improvements in the Metropolis. London: 1827. V. 51; 53
A Collection of Papers Relating to the Thames Quay with Hints for Some Further Improvements in the Metropolis. (with) A Group of Later Material and Printed Correspondence Relating to the Architecture and Planning of London. London: 1852. V. 53

TRENCH, RICHARD CHENEVIX
Poems. London: 1865. V. 54

TRENCH, W. S.
Ireland's Struggle for Life in the 19th Century. Leipzig: 1930. V. 54

TRENCHANT, JAN
L'Arithmeticque...Departie en trois Liures. Rouen: 1632. V. 47

TRENCHARD, JOHN
An Argument, Shewing that a Standing Army is Inconsistent with a Free Government and Absolutely Destructive to the Constitution of the English Monarchy. London: 1697. V. 53
An Argument Showing, that a Standing Army is Inconsistent with a Free Government, and Absolutely Destructive to the Constitution of the English Monarchy... London: 1698. V. 47
A Letter from the Author of the Argument Against a Standing Army, to the Author (Somers) of the Ballancing Letter. London: 1697. V. 53
A Short History of Standing Armies in England. London: 1698. V. 53

TRENDALL, A. D.
Early South Italian Vase Painting. Mainz: 1974. V. 50; 52
The Red-Figured Vases of Apulia. Volume I: Early and Middle Apulian. Oxford: 1978. V. 50; 52
The Red-Figured Vases of Lucania, Campania and Sicily. Oxford & London: 1967-83. V. 50; 52
The Red-Figured Vases of Paestum. London: 1987. V. 52

TRENHOLM, VIRGINIA C.
Footprints on the Frontier, Saga of the Laramie Region of Wyoming. Douglas: 1945. V. 51

TRENT, COUNCIL OF, 1545-1563.
Sacrosancti et Oecumenici Concilii Tridentini Pauli III. Iulio III. et Pio IV. Pont. Max. Celebrati Canones & Decreta... Cologne: 1647. V. 48
Vera, et Catholica Doctrina, Qvod in Missa Vervm Sacrificivm, et Propitiatorivm Offeratvr... Brescia: 1563. V. 48; 52

TRENT, WILLIAM P.
Edgar Allan Poe. A Centenary Tribute. Baltimore: 1910. V. 48

THE TRENTON City Directory, for 1869. Trenton: 1869. V. 51

TRESCOT, WILLIAM HENRY
The Diplomatic History of the Administration of Washington and Adams, 1789-1801. Boston: 1857. V. 51
Memorial of the Life of J. Johnston Pettigrew, Brig. Gen. of the Confederate States Army. Charleston: 1870. V. 49

TRESHAM, HENRY
Le Avventure Di Saffo. Roma: 1784. V. 51

TREVATHAM, CHARLES E.
The American Thoroughbred. V. 47

TREVELYAN, G. M., MRS.
The Life of Mrs. Humphrey Ward. London: 1923. V. 53

TREVELYAN, GEORGE OTTO
The American Revolution. London: 1899-1907. V. 49
The American Revolution. London: 1899-1914. V. 51
The Life and Letters of Lord Macaulay. London: 1876. V. 51; 54

TREVELYAN, R. C.
Beelzebub and Other Poems. London: 1935. V. 51
The Deluge and Other Poems. London: 1926. V. 48
Meleager. London: 1927. V. 49
Poems and Fables. London: 1925. V. 51

TREVERS, JOSEPH
An Essay to the Restoring of Our Decayed Trade. London: 1675. V. 52

TREVITHICK, FRANCIS
Life of Richard Trevithick, with an Account of His Inventions. London and New York: 1872. V. 51; 54

TREVOR, ELLESTON
The Striker Portfolio. London: 1969. V. 48

TREVOR, WILLIAM
Beyond the Pale and Other Stories. New York. V. 47
The Boarding House. London: 1965. V. 49; 50; 51; 54
The Collected Stories. London: 1993. V. 51; 53
Collected Stories. New York: 1993. V. 50
The Day We Got Drunk on Cake. London: 1967. V. 50
Dreaming. London: 1973. V. 53
Excursions in the Real World. London: 1993. V. 50; 51; 53; 54
Fools of Fortune. New York: 1983. V. 47
The Last Lunch of the Season. London: 1973. V. 49
The Love Department. London: 1966. V. 51
Lovers of Their Time. 1978. V. 49
Lovers of Their Time. London: 1978. V. 47; 48; 53
Marrying Damian: a Story. 1995. V. 54
Miss Gomez and the Brethren. London: 1971. V. 47; 48; 50; 51; 53
Mrs. Eckdorf in O'Neill's Hotel. London: 1969. V. 50; 51; 53
The News from Ireland and Other Stories. London: 1985. V. 47
The Old Boys. London: 1964. V. 49
The Old Boys. New York: 1964. V. 47; 48; 51
Other People's Worlds. London: 1980. V. 48
The Silence in the Garden. London: 1988. V. 48; 49; 51; 53; 54
A Standard Behaviour. London: 1958. V. 49; 53

TREVOR-BATTYE, AUBYN
Ice-Bound on Kolguev. London: 1895. V. 47; 48
Ice-Bound on Kolguev. Westminster: 1895. V. 51

TREW, CHRISTOPH JAKOB
De Vasis Linguae Salivalibus Atque Sanguiferis Epistola. Nurnberg: 1734. V. 47

THE TRI-QUARTERLY Anthology of Contemporary Latin American Literature. New York: 1969. V. 50

TRIA, GIOVANNI ANDREA
Prima Dioecesana Synodus Larinensis. Rome: 1728. V. 54

THE TRIAL at Bar Between Campbell Craig, Lessee of James Annesley, Esq; Plantiff, and the Right Honourable Richard Earl of Anglesey, Defendant... London: 1744. V. 53

THE TRIAL, Before the Lord President of the Court of Session, Lord MacKenzie and a Special Jury, ... of the issues in the Action of Damages at the Instance of Lady Ramsay Widow of the Late Colonel Sir Thomas Ramsay. Edinburgh: 1833. V. 52

TRIAL for Murder. The People vs. James K. Polk. Counsel for the People, J. Q. Adams...for the Prisoner, John Tyler. Boston: 1847. V. 52

THE TRIAL of Antichrist, Otherwise the Man of Sin, for High Treason against the Son of God... Dublin: 1806. V. 51; 54

THE TRIAL of Edward Gibbon Wakefield, William Wakefield and Frances Wakefield, Indicted with One Edward Thevenot, a Servant for a Conspiracy and for the Abduction of Miss Ellen Turner, the only Child and Heiress of William Turner. London: 1827. V. 54

TRIAL Of Eugene Aram. London: 1820. V. 50

THE TRIAL of James Lackey, Isaac Evertson (et al)...for Kidnapping Capt. William Morgan; at the Ontario General Sessions, Held at Canandaigua, Ontario County, Aug. 22, 1827. New York: 1827. V. 48

TRIAL of John Jasper for the Murder of Edwin Drood. Philadelphia: 1914. V. 48

THE TRIAL of Lord Grey of Werk, Robert Charnock, Anne Charnock, David Jones, Frances Jones, and Rebecca Jones...for Unlawful Tempting and Inticing, the Lady Henrietta Berkeley (etc). London: 1716. V. 50

TRIAL of Marshal Ney, Preceded by a Memoir of His Life... Glasgow: 1829. V. 52

TRIAL of the Officers and Crew of the Privateer Savannah on the Charge of Piracy, in the United States Circuit Court for the Southern District of New York, Hon. Judges Nelson and Shipman Presiding. New York: 1862. V. 50

THE TRIAL of Thomas Hunter, Peter Hacket, Richard M'Neil, James Gibb and William M'Lean, the Glasgow Cottonspinners, Before the Hight court of Justiciary, at Edinburgh, on Charges of Murder... Edinburgh: 1838. V. 53

A TRIALL of the English Lyturgie. London: 1643. V. 48; 49

TRIALS for Adultery: or, the History of Divorces. Together with the Letters, &c., That Have Been Intercepted Between the Amorous Parties. London: 1779. V. 47

THE TRIALS of Arthur Thistlewood, James Ings, John Thomas Brunt, Richard Tidd, William Davidson and Others for High Treason. At the Sessions House in the Old Bailey...April 1820. London: 1820. V. 53

THE TRIALS of James, Duncan and Robert McGregor, Three Sons of the Celebrated Rob Roy, Before the High Court of Justiciary (etc). Edinburgh: 1818. V. 51

THE TRIALS of Jeremiah Brandreth, William Turner, Isaac Ludlam, George Weightman and Others for High Treason, Under a Special Commission at Derby...October 1817. London: 1817. V. 53

THE TRIALS of Thomas Hardy, John Horne Tooke and John Thelwell, for High Treason. London: 1794. V. 53

TRIANA, JOSE MARIA MARTIN
Suite Lirica: en Homenaje a Wallace Stevens. 1982. V. 52; 54

A TRIBUTE to Carl Hertzog. Keepsake No. Two. El Paso: 1983. V. 48

A TRIBUTE to Huddie Ledbetter. London: 1946. V. 52

A TRIBUTE to Jim Lowell. Cleveland: 1967. V. 48; 52

TRIBUTES to Brooke Crutchley on His Retirement as University Printer. Cambridge: 1975. V. 47

TRIBUTES to Edward Johnston, Calligrapher. 1948. V. 47

TRICASSO, PATRICIO
Chyromantia...Nuouamente Reuista & Con Somma Diligentia Corretta & Ristampata. Venice: 1543. V. 53

TRICHTERN, VALENTIN
Pferd-Buch... Pferd-Anatomie. Nuremberg: 1716-17. V. 52

THE TRICKS OF London Laid Open: Being a True Caution to Both Sexes in Town and Country. London: 1780. V. 52

THE TRICKS of London Laid Open; Being a True Caution to Both Sexes in Town and Country. London: 1785. V. 54

THE TRICKS of the Town Laid Open; or, a Compassion for Country Gentlemen. London: 1772. V. 49

TRICKY Dick and His Pals. New York: 1974. V. 54

TRIER, EDUARD
Jean Arp, Sculpture... London: 1968. V. 50; 54
Jean Arp, Sculpture... New York: 1968. V. 48
The Sculpture of Marino Marini. New York: 1961. V. 47; 48; 50; 52; 53

TRIER, JESPER
Ancient Paper of Nepal. Copenhagen: 1972. V. 51; 52

TRIER, WALTER
Quite Crazy - 8192 More Crazy People. London: 1949. V. 53

TRIEWALD, MARTEN
Short Description of the Atmospheric Engine Published at Stockholm, 1734. London: 1928. V. 50; 52; 54

TRIGGS, HARRY INIGO
Formal Gardens in England and Scotland. London: 1902. V. 47; 48; 50
Garden Craft in Europe. New York: 1913. V. 51; 54

TRIGGS, J. H.
History and Directory of Laramie City, Wyoming, Territory... (with) History of Cheyenne and Northern Wyoming... Laramie City/Omaha: 1875/76. V. 51

TRILLING, LIONEL
Matthew Arnold. London: 1939. V. 49; 53

TRIMBLE, ISAAC P.
A Treatise on the Insect Enemies of Fruit and Fruit Trees... New York: 1865. V. 52; 53

TRIMBLE, WILLIAM J.
The Mining Advance Into the Inland Empire... Madison: 1914. V. 47; 53

TRIMBLE, WILLIAM TENNANT
The Trimbles & Cowens of Dalston, Cumberland. 1935. V. 50
The Trimbles & Cowens of Dalston, Cumberland. Carlisle: 1935. V. 48; 52; 54

TRIMEN, R.
South-African Butterflies: a Monograph of the Extra-Tropical Species. London: 1887-89. V. 54

TRIMMER, K.
Flora of Norfolk. London: 1866. V. 50

TRIMMER, SARAH
Comment on Dr. Watt's Divine Songs for Children, With Questions... London: 1789. V. 47
A Description of a Set of Prints of Ancient History; Contained in a set of Easy Lessons. London: 1787. V. 47
Fabulous Histories. London: 1793. V. 48
Fabulous Histories... London: 1811. V. 52
Some Account of the Life and Writings of Mrs. Trimmer.... London: 1814. V. 51
The Teacher's Assistant; Consisting of Lectures in the Catechetical Form; Being Part of a Plan of Appropriate Instruction for the Children of the Poor. London: 1820. V. 52

TRINITY College Apocalypse. London: 1967. V. 50

TRINITY COLLEGE. LIBRARY
Descriptive Catalogue of the Medieval and Renaissance Latin Manuscripts. 1991. V. 47

TRINITY HISTORICAL SOCIETY
Laws and Regulations of the College Historical Society. Dublin: 1836. V. 50

TRINKLER, EMIL
The Stormswept Roof of Asia. London: 1931. V. 51; 53
Wissenschaftliche Ergebnisse der Dr. Trinkler'schen Zentralasien Expedition. Berlin: 1932. V. 54

TRIO. First Poems by Gael Turnbull, Phyllis Webb, E. W. Mandel. 1954. V. 52

TRION, ISAAK
Nieuwe en Beknopte Hand Atlas. Amsterdam: 1769. V. 53

TRIP, TOM
Tom Trip's Museum; or, a Peep at the Feathered Creation. London: 1832. V. 54

TRIPLE Cross. New York: 1972. V. 49

TRIPLER, CHARLES S.
Hand-Book for the Military Surgeon. Cincinnati: 1861. V. 52
Hand-Book for the Military Surgeon. Cincinnati: 1862. V. 49

TRIPLETT, FRANK
The Life, Times and Treacherous Death of Jesse James. Chicago: 1882. V. 53; 54
The Life, Times and Treacherous Death of Jesse James. St. Louis: 1882. V. 54

THE TRIPOD of Helen: a Grecian Tale. Witney, Oxon: 1822. V. 50

TRIPP, C. E.
Ace High, the "Frisco Detective" Or, the Girl Sport's Double Game: a Story of the Sierra & the Golden Gate City. San Francisco: 1948. V. 47

TRIPP, F. E.
British Mosses, Their Homes, Aspects, Structure & Uses. London: 1874. V. 49; 51; 52; 53; 54
British Mosses: Their Homes, Aspects, Structure & Uses. London: 1888. V. 48

TRISMOSIN, SALOMON
Aureum Vellus Oder Guldin Schatz und Kunst-Kammer, Darinnen der...Bewehrtesten Auctorum, Schriften und Bucher aus dem gar Uralten Schatz der Uberlibnen... Hamburg: 1708. V. 48

TRISSEL, JAMES
Daedalus. 1993. V. 54
Daedalus. Colorado Springs: 1993. V. 54
Silence. Colorado Springs: 1995. V. 54

TRISSINO, GIOVANNI GIORGIO
La Italia Liberata da Gotthi. Rome: 1547. V. 53

TRISTAN
Le Roman de Tristan et Iseut. Paris: 1914. V. 48
The Romance of Tristan & Iseult. London: 1913. V. 47
The Romance of Tristram & Iseault. London and Philadelphia: 1910. V. 48; 49; 54

TRISTRAM, ERNEST W.
English Medieval Wall Painting. 1944. V. 47

TRISTRAM, HENRY BAKER
The Great Sahara: Wanderings South of the Atlas Mountains. London: 1860. V. 51
The Land of Israel: a Journal of Travels in Palestine. London: 1865. V. 50; 52
The Land of Israel; a Journal of Travels in Palestine... London: 1866. V. 48; 51
The Land of Moab. Travels & Discoveries of the East Side of the Dead Sea & Jordan. New York: 1873. V. 48
Rambles in Japan, the Land of the Rising Sun. London: 1895. V. 48
Scenes in the East, Consisting of Twelve Coloured Photographic Views of Places Mentioned in the Bible... London: 1880. V. 48; 50; 52

TRISTRAM, WILLIAM OUTRAM
Coaching Days and Coaching Ways. London & New York: 1888. V. 47; 49
Coaching Days and Coaching Ways. London: 1901. V. 53
Coaching Days and Coaching Ways. London: 1914. V. 48

TRITHEMIUS, JOHANN
Steganographia: Hoc Est: Ars per Occultam Scripturam Animi Sui Volunatem Absentibus Aperiendi Certa. (with) Clavis Generalis Triplex in Libros Steganographicos. Darmbstadii: 1621. V. 49; 50

TROELSCH, HENRY W.
The Kill van Kull Bridge Between Bayonne, New Jersey and Port Richmond, New York Built by the Port of New York Authority. New York?: 1931. V. 49

TROGUS POMPEIUS
Historiae in Compedivm ab Ivstino Redactae. Venice: 1522. V. 48; 54
Historiarvm Philippicarvm Epitoma... Paris: 1581. V. 48; 54
The History of Justin, Taken Out of the Four and Forty Books of Trogus Pompeius. London: 1664. V. 54
Justinus de Historiis Philippicis... London: 1798. V. 52

TROIL, UNO VON, ABP. OF UPSALA
Letters On iceland...Made During a Voyage Undertaken in the Year 1772.... Dublin: 1780. V. 49; 50
Letters on Iceland...Made During a Voyage Undertaken in the Year 1772... London: 1780. V. 50; 54

TROILI, GIULIO
Paradossi Per Pratticare La Propsettiva... Bologna: 1683. V. 48; 51; 52

TROLLOPE, ANTHONY
The American Senator. London: 1877. V. 47; 50; 52; 54
The American Senator. Toronto: 1877. V. 47
The American Senator. Toronto: 1878. V. 48
Australia and New Zealand. London: 1873. V. 47
An Autobiography. Edinburgh and London: 1883. V. 47; 50; 51
An Autobiography. New York: 1883. V. 51
Ayala's Angel... London: 1881. V. 47; 49; 52
The Barchester Novels. Boston: 1926. V. 47
Barchester Towers... London: 1857. V. 47; 52
Barchester Towers. New York: 1945. V. 51
Barchester Towers. Mt. Vernon: 1958. V. 53
The Barsetshire Novels. (with) An Autobiography. Oxford: 1929. V. 47; 48
The Belton Estate. London: 1865. V. 47
The Belton Estate... London: 1866. V. 48; 50; 51; 53; 54
The Belton Estate. Philadelphia: 1866. V. 49; 52
The Belton Estate. London: 1870. V. 47; 50
The Bertrams. London: 1859. V. 47; 48; 52
British Sports and Pastimes. London: 1868. V. 47; 54
Can You Forgive Her?. London: 1864. V. 47; 50; 52
Can You Forgive Her?. London: 1864-65. V. 47; 48; 49
Castle Richmond. Leipzig: 1860. V. 47
Castle Richmond. London: 1860. V. 52
Castle Richmond. 1862. V. 54
The Chronicles of Barsetshire. London: 1879. V. 48
The Chronicles of Barsetshire. London: 1879-87. V. 49
The Chronicles of Barsetshire... New York: 1893. V. 51
The Claverings. New York: 1866/67?. V. 47; 50; 51; 52
The Claverings. London: 1867. V. 47; 48; 51
The Claverings. New York: 1867. V. 47
Clergymen of the Church of England. London: 1866. V. 47; 48
The Commentaries of Caesar. Edinburgh and London: 1870. V. 47
Cousin Henry. London: 1879. V. 47; 48; 53
Cousin Henry. London: 1881. V. 52
Cousin Henry. London: 1883. V. 51
Doctor Thorne. New York: 1858. V. 47; 48; 51; 52; 54
Dr. Wortle's School. London: 1881. V. 47
The Duke's Children. London: 1880. V. 47; 51; 54

TROLLOPE, ANTHONY continued
An Editor's Tales. London: 1870. V. 47; 51; 52; 54
An Editor's Tales. London: 1876. V. 50
The Eustace Diamonds. New York: 1872. V. 48; 50; 51; 52; 53
The Eustace Diamonds... London: 1873. V. 48; 50
The Fixed Period. Edinburgh: 1882. V. 48
The Fixed Period... Leipzig: 1882. V. 51
Framley Parsonage. London: 1861. V. 47; 48; 51; 52; 54
Framley Parsonage. New York: 1861. V. 48
The Golden Lion of Granpere. London: 1872. V. 47; 48; 50; 51; 53
The Golden Lion of Granpere. New York: 1872. V. 51
The Golden Lion of Granpere. London: 1873. V. 48
Harry Heatchcote of Gangoil. London: 1890?. V. 51
He Knew He Was Right. London: 1868-22May 1869. V. 47; 51
He Knew He Was Right. London: 1869. V. 47; 48; 49; 50; 51; 52; 54
He Knew He was Right. New York: 1869. V. 47
He Knew He Was Right. New York: 1869/70. V. 51
How the "Mastiffs" Went to Iceland. London: 1878. V. 47
Hunting Sketches. London: 1865. V. 47; 52
Is He Popenjoy?. London: 1878. V. 47; 49
John Caldigate. London: 1879. V. 47; 51; 53
The Kellys and the O'Kellys. London. V. 47; 53
The Kellys and the O'Kellys... London: 1848. V. 47; 48
The Kellys and the O'Kellys. London: 1859. V. 47; 50
The Kellys and the O'Kellys. London: 1861. V. 50
The Kellys and the O'Kellys. London: 1867. V. 47
Kept in the Dark. London: 1882. V. 47; 51
Kept in the Dark. London: 1883. V. 47
Lady Anna. London: 1874. V. 47; 51; 52
Lady Anna... Toronto: 1874. V. 47
The Landleaguers. London: 1883. V. 47; 51; 52; 54
The Last Chronicle of Barset. 1867. V. 47
The Last Chronicle of Barset. London: 1867. V. 47; 48; 49; 50; 51; 52; 53; 54
The Last Chronicle of Barset. New York: 1867. V. 48; 51; 53; 54
The Last Chronicle of Barset. London: 1872. V. 51
The Life of Cicero. London: 1880. V. 47; 54
The Life of Cicero. New York: 1881. V. 47
Lord Palmerston. London: 1882. V. 48
Lotta Schmidt and Other Stories. London: 1867. V. 47; 48; 51; 54
Lotta Schmidt and Other Stories. London: 1870. V. 47
The MacDermots of Ballycloran. London. V. 47
The Macdermots of Ballycloran. London: 1847. V. 51; 52; 54
The Macdermots of Ballycloran. London: 1871. V. 51
Marion Fay. London: 1882. V. 47; 51; 52; 54
Miss Mackenzie. London: 1865. V. 51
Miss Mackenzie. London: 1885. V. 51
Mr. Scarborough's Family. London: 1883. V. 47; 48; 51; 52; 54
New Zealand. London: 1875. V. 52
North America. London: 1862. V. 47; 51; 53
North America. New York: 1862. V. 47; 51; 52; 54
North America. Philadelphia: 1862. V. 53
An Old Man's Love. Edinburgh & London: 1884. V. 47; 48; 51; 54
Orley Farm. London: 1861-Oct. 1862. V. 48
Orley Farm. London: 1862. V. 47; 48; 49; 50; 51; 53; 54
Orley Farm. New York: 1862. V. 51
Orley Farm. London: 1866. V. 48; 52
Orley Farm. New York: 1871. V. 51
Orley Farm. New York: 1873. V. 51
Phineas Finn, the Irish Member. New York: 1868. V. 47; 51
Phineas Finn, the Irish Member. London: 1869. V. 47; 48; 50; 51
Phineas Redux. London: 1873. V. 47
Phineas Redux. London: 1874. V. 47; 48; 50; 51
The Prime Minister. London: 1876. V. 48; 50; 51; 52; 54
The Prime Minister. Toronto: 1876. V. 48; 53
Rachel Ray. London: 1868. V. 50; 52
Ralph the Heir. London: 1871. V. 47; 48; 51; 53
Ralph the Heir. New York: 1871. V. 48; 51
(Selected) Works. Philadelphia: 1900. V. 47
Sir Harry Hotspur of Humblethwaite. London: 1871. V. 47; 54
The Small House at Allington. London: 1864. V. 47; 48; 50; 51; 52; 53; 54
The Small House at Allington. New York: 1864. V. 47
The Small House at Allington. London: 1869. V. 51
The Struggles of Brown, Jones and Robinson. London: 1870. V. 47; 49
Tales of all Countries. London: 1861. V. 47
Tales of All Countries... London: 1864. V. 47
The Three Clerks. London: 1858. V. 47; 48; 51
The Three Clerks. London: 1859. V. 47
The Three Clerks. New York: 1860. V. 47
The Three Clerks. London: 1861. V. 47
Travelling Sketches. London: 1866. V. 47; 49; 52
Tremordyn Cliff. Brussels: 1835. V. 47
La Vendee. London: 1850. V. 47; 48; 52
The Vicar of Bullhampton. London: 1870. V. 47; 48; 49; 50; 51; 54
The Warden. London. V. 48
The Warden. London: 1855. V. 47; 48; 50
The Warden. London: 1870. V. 47
The Warden. London: 1926. V. 48
The Warden. New York: 1955. V. 51
The Way We Live Now. London: 1875. V. 47; 48; 51; 52; 54
The Way We Live Now. New York: 1875. V. 50; 51; 52; 53; 54
The West Indies and the Spanish Main. London: 1859. V. 52
The West Indies and the Spanish Main. London: 1860. V. 51
The West Indies and the Spanish Main. New York: 1860. V. 50
Works. New York: 1911-14. V. 47
Works. Oxford: 1948. V. 48

TROLLOPE, FRANCES ELEANOR TERNAN
Like Ships Upon the Sea. London: 1883. V. 53
Mabel's Progress. London: 1867. V. 48

TROLLOPE, FRANCES MILTON
The Abbess, a Romance. London: 1833. V. 50
The Barnabys in America; or, Adventures of the Widow Wedded. London: 1843. V. 53
Belgium and Western Germany in 1833... Brussels: 1834. V. 50; 54
Belgium and Western Germany in 1833.... London: 1834. V. 54
Domestic Manners of the Americans. London: 1832. V. 47; 48
Domestic Manners of the Americans. New York: 1832. V. 53
Father Eustace: a Tale of the Jesuits. London: 1847. V. 51
The Homes and Haunts of the Italian Poets. London: 1881. V. 48
Jessie Phillips. A Tale of the Present Day. London: 1843. V. 54
Jessie Phillips, a Tale of the Present Day. London: 1844. V. 50; 52; 53
The Life and Adventures of a Clever Woman. London: 1854. V. 54
The Life and Adventures of a Clever Woman. London: 1864. V. 50
The Life and Adventures of Jonathan Jefferson Whitlaw: or Scenes on the Mississippi. London: 1836. V. 50
The Life and Adventures of Michael Armstrong. London: 1840. V. 50
The Lottery of Marriage. London: 1849. V. 50
The Mother's Manual. London: 1833. V. 47; 48; 50; 52
One Fault. London: 1840. V. 50
Paris and Parisians in 1835. London: 1836. V. 47
Paris and Parisians in 1835. New York: 1836. V. 47
Paris and Parisians in 1835. Paris: 1836. V. 51
Tremordyn Cliff. Brussels: 1835. V. 49
Tremordyn Cliff. London: 1835. V. 50; 51
The Vicar of Wrexhill. London: 1837. V. 50; 51
Vienna and the Austrians: with Some Account of a Journey through Swabia, Bavaria, the Tyrol and the Salzbourg. London: 1838. V. 49
A Visit to Italy. London: 1842. V. 54
The Widow Barnaby. London: 1839. V. 51; 53
The Widow Barnaby. London: 1840. V. 50; 51
The Widow Barnaby. Paris: 1840. V. 52; 53
The Widow Married. London: 1840. V. 51
The Widow Wedded; or, Adventures of the Barnabys in America. London: 1858. V. 50
The Young Heiress. London: 1867. V. 50

TROLLOPE, THOMAS ADOLPHUS
Artingale Castle. London: 1867. V. 48
A Decade of Italian Women. London: 1859. V. 47; 48; 50; 52
Filippo Strozzi. London: 1860. V. 49
The Garstangs and Garstang Grange. London: 1869. V. 50
Giulio Malatesta: a Novel. London: 1863. V. 51; 54
A History of the Commonwealth of Florence, From the Earliest Independence of the Commune to the Fall of the Republic in 1531. London: 1865. V. 47
Marietta. London: 1862. V. 51
Sketches from French History. London: 1878. V. 50
A Summer in Brittany. London: 1840. V. 47; 48
A Summer in Western France. London: 1841. V. 48
What I Remember. London: 1877. V. 47
What I Remember. London: 1887. V. 47

TROLLOPE, WILLIAM
A History of the Royal Foundation of Christ's Hospital... London: 1834. V. 53

THE TROLLOPIAN. A Journal of Victorian Fiction. London: 1945/49. V. 52

TROMHOLT, SOPHUS
Under the Rays of the Aurora Borealis; in the Land of the Lapps and Kvaens. Boston: 1885. V. 48

TROMMSDORFF, T. W. VON
Pharmacy Guide or the Fundamentals of Healing Art. Moscow: 1811. V. 53

TRONCON, JEAN
L'Entree Triomphante de Leurs Maiestez Louis XIV, Roy de France et de Navarre, et Marie Threse d'Austriche, son Espouse, dans la Ville de Paris... Paris: 1662. V. 47

TROPPAU UND JAEGERNDORFF, ELEONORA MARIA ROSALIA, DUCHESS OF
Freywillig- Auffgesprungener Granat-Apffell dess Christlichen Samaritans. Vienna: 1695. V. 47

TROTMAN, MISS
Catalogue of the Useful Household Furniture...and a Small Library of Books...Removed from Wanstrow Rectory and Castle House, Frome... Frome: 1868. V. 54

TROTSKII, LEV
The Case of Leon Trotsky. London: 1937. V. 51
The Revolution in Spain. New York: 1931. V. 49
The Spanish Revolution in Danger!. New York: 1931. V. 49
Whither Russia? Toward Capitalism or Socialism. New York: 1926. V. 49

TROTTER, J. K.
The Niger Sources and the Borders of the New Sierra Leone Protectorate. London: 1898. V. 54

TROTTER, JAMES M.
Music and Some Highly Musical People... Boston & New York: 1882. V. 48

TROTTER, JOHN B.
Walks through Ireland, in the Years 1812, 1814 and 1817...in a Series of letters to an English Gentleman. London: 1819. V. 49

TROTTER, THOMAS
A Proposal for Destroying the Fire and Choak-Damp of Coal-Mines... Newcastle: 1805. V. 50
A View of the Nervous Temperament: Being a Practical Enquiry into the Increasing Prevalence, Prevention and Treatment of Those Diseases Commonly Called Nervous, Billious, Stomach and Liver Complaints... Newcastle: 1807. V. 49
A View of the Nervous Temperament: Being a Practical Inquiry into the Increasing Prevalence, Prevention and Treatment of Those Diseases Commonly Called Nervous, Billious, Stomach and Liver Complaints... New York: 1808. V. 52

TROTTER, WILLIAM EDWARD
Select Illustrated Topography of Thirty Miles Round London. London: 1839. V. 51

TROTULA OF SALERNO
The Diseases of Women... Los Angeles: 1940. V. 49

TROUBETZKOY, PAUL
Exodus A.D. - A Warming to Civilians. London: 1934. V. 52

THE TROUBLES of a Good Husband. Northampton: 1818. V. 51

THE TROUBLES Of Life; or, The Guinea and the Shilling. 1810. V. 50

TROUGHTON, R. ZOUCH
Nina Sforza. London: 1855. V. 54

TROUP, GEORGE M.
Georgia and the General Government. Milledgeville: 1826. V. 48

TROUP, J. ROSE
With Stanley's Rear Column. London: 1890. V. 54

TROUP, R. S.
The Silviculture of Indian Trees. Dehra Dun: 1986. V. 50

TROUPE, QUINCY
Embryo. New York: 1972. V. 47

TROUSSEAU, ARMAND
Lectures on Clinical Medicine Delieevered at the Hotel-Dieu, Paris. London: 1869-82. V. 50
Treatise on Therapeutics. New York: 1880. V. 52

TROUT, PETER LAIRD
Prospectors' Manual Being a Full and Complete History and Description of the Newly Discovered Gold Mines on Granite Creek, the Canyon of the Tulameen River, and Other New Mineral Discoveries in the Similkameen Country... Victoria: 1886. V. 52

TROVHERTIGHE Vermaninghe Aende Verheerde Nederlantsche Provintien. 1586. V. 52

TROVILLART, PIERRE
Memoires des Comtes de Maine. Le Mans: 1643. V. 51

TROVILLION, VIOLET
The Sundial in Our Garden. Herrin: 1935. V. 53

TROWARD, RICHARD
A Collection of the Statutes Now in Force Relative to Elections. London: 1790. V. 47

TROWBRIDGE, BERTHA CHADWICK
Old Houses of Connecticut, from Material Collected by the Committee on Old Houses of the Connecticut Society of the Colonial Dames of America. New Haven: 1923. V. 47

TROWBRIDGE, JOHN TOWNSEND
Cudjo's Cave. (and) The Three Scouts. London: 1867. V. 51; 53
The Old Battle-Ground. New York: 1860. V. 54

TROWBRIDGE, MARY E.
Pioneer days. The Life Story of Gershom and Elizabeth Day. Philadelphia: 1895. V. 49

TROWBRIDGE, THOMAS R.
Grandfather's Voyage Around the World in the Ship "Betsey" 1799-1801. New Haven: 1895. V. 47

TROWBRIDGE, W. R. H.
Cagliostro the Splendour and Misery of a Master of Magic. London: 1910. V. 47

TROWELL, M.
African Arts and Crafts, Their Development in the School. London: 1937. V. 54

TROWELL, S.
A New Treatise of Husbandry, Gardening and Other Matters Relating to Rural Affairs... London: 1739. V. 51; 52; 52; 54

TRUAX, CHARLES
The Mechanics of Surgery. Chicago: 1899. V. 50; 51; 52
The Mechanics of Surgery. San Francisco: 1988. V. 51

TRUBLET, NICHOLAS CHARLES
Essais sur Divers Sujts de Litterature et de Morale. Paris: 1749-60. V. 49

TRUCCHI, LORENZA
Francis Bacon. New York: 1975. V. 48; 50; 52

TRUCHSES-WALDBURG, FRIEDRICH LUDWIG, COUNT
A Narrative of Napoleon Buonaparte's Journey from Fontainebleau to Frejus in April 1814. London: 1815. V. 54

A **TRUE** Account of What Past at the Old-Bailey, May the 18th, 1711. Relating to the Tryal of Richard Thornhill, Esq.; Indicted for the Murder of Sir Cholmley Dering, Bar. London: 1711. V. 48

A **TRUE** Account of What Was Transacted in the Assembly of the United Ministers of Devon and Cornwal... Exon: 1719. V. 52

A **TRUE** and Authentick Narrative of the Action Between the Northumberland and Three French Men of War. London: 1745. V. 48

THE **TRUE** and Eccentric Life of Betty Bolaine, (Late of Canterbury) a Well-Known Character for Avarice, Meanness, and Vice, Who Died June 6, 1805, Aged Eighty Two, Whilst Eating a Brown Crust, Although Worth Twenty-Thousand Pounds!. London: 1805. V. 51

A **TRUE** and Exact Relation of the Death of Two Catholics Who Suffered for Their Religion at the Summer Assizes, Held at Lancaster in the Year 1628... London: 1737. V. 53

A **TRUE** and Faithful Account of the Island of Veritas; Together with the Forms of Their Liturgy... London: 1790?. V. 52

A **TRUE** and Faithful Account of...the Late Dreadful burning of the City of London. London: 1667. V. 47; 50

THE **TRUE** and Real Interest of Great Britain, Impartialy Considered: with Regard to The Rupture, Among the Northern Powers.... London: 1749. V. 48

A **TRUE** Copie of the Master-Piece of All Those Petitions Which Have Formerly Beene Presented by the Major (sic), Aldermen and the Rest of the Common Counsell of the Citie of London. London: 1641/42. V. 53

A **TRUE** Copy of the Indictment Which is Preferred Against Archibald Earl of Argile, for High Treason...to be Tryed on Monday the 12th day of this Instant December 1681... Edenbrough: 1681. V. 47

A **TRUE** Copy of the Journal-Book of the Last Parliament, Begun 1678/9... London: 1680. V. 50

A **TRUE** Description of the Bull-Feast. London: 1683. V. 47

A **TRUE** Dialogue Between Thomas Jones, a Trooper, Lately Return'd from Germany and John Smith, a Serjeant in the First Regiment of Foot-Guards. London: 1743. V. 53

TRUE, F. W.
Whalebone Whales of the Western North Atlantic. Washington: 1904. V. 51

A **TRUE** Narrative of the Examination, Tryall and Sufferings of James Nayler with Copies of Sundry Petitions. London: 1657. V. 54

A **TRUE** Narrative of the Proceedings at Guild-Hall, London, The Fourth of this Instant February, in Their Unanimous Election of Their Four Members to Serve in Parliament. London: 1681. V. 52; 53

TRUE News From Oxford Being a Relation of the Magnificent Valour of the Scholars in Number 500, Completely Armed... London: 1642. V. 48

THE **TRUE** Protestant Lettany. 1680. V. 47

A **TRUE** Relation of the Manner of Deposing of King Edward II. Together with the Articles Which Were Exhibited Against Him in Parliament. London: 1689. V. 48

A **TRUE** Relation of the Manner of the Deposing of King Edward III...As Also, an Exact Account of the Proceedings...Against King Richard II. London: 1689. V. 50

TRUE Stories from the History of Scotland; Intended As a Companion to "True Stories from English History". London: 1829. V. 50

TRUE Stories of an Old Woman. London: 1853. V. 50

TRUEHART, JAMES L.
The Perote Prisoners. San Antonio: 1934. V. 48

TRUELOVE, EDWARD
The Queen v. Edward Truelove, for Publishing Robert Dale Owen's Moral Physiology and "Individual, Family and National Poverty". London: 1878. V. 47

TRUEMAN, A.
British Carboniferous Non-Marine Lamelhbranchia. London: 1946-68. V. 50; 51; 52; 53

TRUEMAN, R. H.
Views of Glacier House District Selkirk Mountains. Vancouver: 1895. V. 52

TRUEMAN, T., PSEUD.
The Unrivalled Adventures of that Great Aeronaut and Glum, Peter Wilkins... London: 1802. V. 50

TRUMAN, BENJAMIN C.
Occidental Sketchs... San Francisco: 1881. V. 49
Tourists' Illustrated Guide to the Celebrated Summer and Winter Resorts of California Adjacent to and Upon the Lines of the Central and Southern Pacific Railroads. San Francisco: 1883. V. 52

TRUMAN, C. M.
The Ypres Alphabet. London: 1915. V. 47

TRUMAN, HARRY S.
Memoirs. Garden City: 1955. V. 47; 51; 53
Memoirs. New York: 1955. V. 47
Memoirs. Garden City: 1955-56. V. 50; 52
Mr. Citizen. New York: 1960. V. 47; 48; 51; 53
Mr. President. New York: 1952. V. 48
The Truman Program. Washington: 1949. V. 48; 50; 51
Truman Speaks. New York: 1960. V. 47

TRUMBO, DALTON
Eclipse. London: 1935. V. 47; 48
Johnny Got His Gun. New York: 1939. V. 51
The Remarkable Andrew. Philadelphia: 1941. V. 48
Washington Jitters. London: 1936. V. 53
Washington Jitters. New York: 1936. V. 52

TRUMBULL, BENJAMIN
A Plea in Vindication of the Connecticut Title to the Contested Lands, Lying West of the Province of New York, Addressed to the Public. New Haven: 1774. V. 47

TRUMBULL, HENRY
Life and Adventures of Robert, the Hermit of Massachusetts, Who Has Lived 14 Years in a Cave, Secluded from Human Society... Providence: 1829. V. 47; 51
Life and Remarkable Adventures of Israel R. Potter... Providence: 1824. V. 47; 48

TRUMBULL, JAMES HAMMOND
Natick Dictionary. Washington: 1903. V. 47

TRUMBULL, JOHN
Autobiography, Reminiscences and Letters of John Trumbull from 1756 to 1841. New York: 1841. V. 52
Catalogue of Paintings by Colonel Trumbull: Including 8 subjects of the American Revolution, with near 250 portraits... New Haven: 1835. V. 52
An Elegy On the Times... New Haven: 1774. V. 49
An Elegy on the Times. New Haven: 1775. V. 48
The Poetical Works. Hartford: 1820. V. 50

TRUMBULL, L. R.
A History of Industrial Paterson; Being a Compendium of the Establishment, Growth and Present Status in Paterson, N.J. of the Silk, Cotton, Flax, Locomotive, Iron and Miscellaneous Industries... Paterson: 1882. V. 47

TRUSLER, JAMES
The London Adviser and Guide... London: 1790. V. 50

TRUSLER, JOHN
The Art of Carving. Cambridge: 1931. V. 50; 54
The Differences Between Words, Esteemed Synonymous, in the English Language; and the Proper Choice of Them Determined... London: 1766. V. 52
The Honours of the Table, or, Rules for Behaviour During Meals. Dublin: 1791. V. 48
The London Advertiser and Guide: Containing Every Instruction and Information Useful and Necessary to Persons Living in London and Coming to Reside There... London: 1790. V. 47
Memoirs of the Life of the Rev. Dr. Trusler, with His Opinions On a Variety of Interesting Subjects, and His Remarks... (with) A Prospectus of a Work Which the Author Proposes to Publish, Under the Title of Sententiae Variorum, and the Conditions. Bath: 1806/c. 1800. V. 52
Modern Times, or, the Adventures of Gabriel Outcast. London: 1785. V. 47
Proverbs Exemplified, and Illustrated by Pictures From Real Life... London: 1790. V. 48
Proverbs in Verse, or Moral Instructions Conveyed in in Pictures, for the Use of Schools... London: 1820. V. 51
The Works of William Hogarth. London: 1821. V. 51

TRUTH, SOJOURNER
Narrative of Sojourner Truth... Boston: 1850. V. 54
Narrative of Sojourner Truth... Boston: 1875. V. 54
Narrative of Sojourner Truth... Battle Creek: 1881. V. 54

TRUTH Will Out! The Foul Charges of the Tories Against the Editor of the Aurora Repelled by Positive Proof and Plain Truth. Philadelphia: 1798. V. 47; 54

THE TRYAL and Condemnation of Several Notorious Malefactors, at a Sessions of Oyer and Terminer...Beginning July 6, 1681...at Sessions House in the Old Bayly. Together with an Account of the Proceedings Against the Earl of Shaftesbury, & Lord Howard Baron... 1681. V. 53

THE TRYAL Between Sir W----m M--rr--s, Baronet, Plaintiff, and Lord A---gst---s F--tz-r--y, Defendant, for Criminal Conversation with the Plaintiff's Wife, at the Kings-Bench Bar, Westminster. London: 1742. V. 47; 50; 51

THE TRYALS and Condemnation of Thomas White, Alias Whitebread (and others), all Jesuits and Priests; for High Treason in Conspiring the Death of the King, the Subversion of Government and Protestant Religion. London: 1679. V. 50

THE TRYALS Of Haagen Swendsen, Sarah Baynton, John Hartwell and John Spurr. For Feloniously Stealing Mrs. Pleasant Rawlins, a Virgin and Heiress of a Considerable Fortune; with an Intent to Cause and Procure the Said Pleasant Rawlins Against Her Will... London: 1703. V. 47

THE TRYALS of Henry Cornish, Esq; for Conspiring the Death of the King, and Raising a Rebellion in This Kingdom; and John Fernley, William King and Elizabeth Gaunt, for Harbouring and Maintaining Rebels...Oct. 19, 1685. London: 1685. V. 52; 54

THE TRYALS of Robert Green, Henry Berry & Lawrence Hill, for the Murder of Sr. Edmond-Bury Godfrey Knt..., Before the Right Honourable Sir William Scroggs...10th of February 1678/79. London: 1679. V. 52

TRYE, JOHN
Jus Filizarii; or, the Filacer's Office in the Court of King's-Bench (etc.). London: 1684. V. 52

TRYON, G. W.
Structural and Systematic Conchology. Philadelphia: 1882-84. V. 48

TRYON, THOMAS
A New Art of Brewing Beer, Ale and Other Sorth of Liquors. London: 1691. V. 47
The Other. New York: 1971. V. 51
The Way to Health, Long Life and Happiness... London: 1691. V. 54

TRYPANIS, C. A.
The Elegies of a Glass Adonis. New York: 1967. V. 48; 49; 52; 54

TSA TOKE, MONORE
The Peyote Ritual: Visions and Descriptions. San Francisco: 1957. V. 51; 53

TSCHERNING, M.
Physiologic Optics. Dioptrics of the Eye, Functions of the Retina Ocular Movements & Binocular Vision. Philadelphia: 1900. V. 47

TSCHICHOLD, JAN
Asymmetric Typography. New York: 1967. V. 51
Designing Books. New York: 1950. V. 51
Treasury of Alphabets and Lettering: a Source Book. 1966. V. 53; 54

TSCHINK, CAJETAN
The Victim of Magical Delusion; or the Mystery of the Revolution of P-1. Dublin: 1795. V. 47

TSCHUDI, CLARA
Napoleon's Son. London: 1912. V. 50

TSENG, HSIEN-CHI
The Charles B. Hoyt Collection in the Museum of Fine Art, Boston. Boston: 1964. V. 53
The Charles B. Hoyt Collection in the Museum of Fine Art, Boston. Boston: 1964/72. V. 49

TSUBOI, ISUKE
Illustrations of the Japanese Species of Bamboo. Gifu: 1916. V. 54

TSUN-SHEN YING, YU-LONG ZHANG
The Endemic Genera of Seed Plants of China. Beijing: 1993. V. 50

TUBBY, A. H.
Deformities: a Treatise on Orthopaedic Surgery, Its Pathology, Symptoms and Treatment. Edinburgh: 1895. V. 51
Modern Methods in the Surgery of Paralyses with Special Reference to Muscle-Grafting, Tendon Transplantation and Arthrodesis. London: 1903. V. 47

TUBERVILLE, A. S.
Johnson's England, an Account of the Life and Manners of His Age. Oxford: 1933. V. 48

TUCCI, GIUSEPPE
Rati-Lila: an Interpretation of the Tantric Imagery of the Temples of Nepal. Geneva: 1969. V. 50

TUCHMAN, BARBARA
The Lost British Policy. London: 1938. V. 47; 50

TUCHMAN, MAURICE
David Hockney: a Retrospective. New York: 1988. V. 53

TUCK, EDWARD
Some Works of Art Belonging to Edward Tuck in Paris. London: 1910. V. 54

TUCK, JOHN
Thoughts and Stories on Tobacco for American Lads, or Uncle Toby's Anti-Tobacco Advice to His Nephew Billy Bruce. Boston: 1852. V. 50

TUCKER, ABRAHAM
An Abridgment of the Light of Nature Purused, by Abraham Tucker, Esq. London: 1807. V. 48

TUCKER, ALAN
In Line - Poems to Eight Collages by Morris Cox. Stroud, Gloucestershire: 1988. V. 54
In Line, the Poems, and In Line, the Collages. Stroud: 1988. V. 50

TUCKER, BENJAMIN
Observations on a Pamphlet Which Has Been Privately Circulated, Said to be "A Concise Statement of Facts, and the Treatment Experienced by Sir Home Opham, Since His Return from the Red Sea". London: 1804. V. 53

TUCKER, BENJAMIN R.
Instead of a Book By a Man Too Busy to Write One. New York: 1897. V. 48

TUCKER, C.
Abbeokuta; or, Sunrise Within the Tropics... London: 1853. V. 47

TUCKER, ELIZABETH S.
The Lawrence Memorial Album... Lawrence: 1895. V. 52
Old Youngsters. New York: 1897. V. 49; 54

TUCKER, GEORGE
The Life of Thomas Jefferson, Third President of the United States, with Parts of His Correspondence Never Before Published... London: 1837. V. 47

TUCKER, GILBERT NORMAN
The Naval Service of Canada: Its Official History. Ottawa: 1952. V. 53

TUCKER, HENRY ST. GEORGE
Commentaries on the Laws of Virginia... Delivered to the Winchester Law School. Winchester: 1831. V. 54

TUCKER, HENRY ST. GEORGE continued
Commentaries on the Laws of Virginia...Delivered to the Winchester Law School. Winchester: 1836-37. V. 51

TUCKER, J. C.
To the Golden Goal and Other Sketches. San Francisco: 1895. V. 47

TUCKER, JOSIAH
A Brief Essay on the Advantages and Disadvantages Which Respectively Attend France and Great Britain, with Regard to Trade. London: 1787. V. 51
Four Letters on Important National Subjects, Addressed to the Right Honourable the Earl of Shelburne, His Majesty's First Lord Commissioner of the Treasury. Glocester: 1783. V. 52
A Letter to Edmund Burke...in Answer to His Printed Speech, Said to be Spoken in the House of Commons on the Twenty Second of March, 1775. Glocester: 1775. V. 47
A Series of Answers to Certain Popular Objections, Against Separating from the Rebellious Colonies and Discarding Them Entirely... Glocester: 1776. V. 47; 51

TUCKER, MISS
Abbeokuta: or, Sunrise Within the Tropics; an Outline of the Origin and Progress of the Yoruba Mission. London: 1853. V. 50

TUCKER, NATHANIEL BEVERLY
George Balcome. New York: 1836. V. 48; 54
A Key to the Disunion Conspiracy. The Partisan Leader. New York: 1861. V. 47
The Partisan Leader: a Tale of the Future. Washington: 1836. V. 50; 54

TUCKER, PATRICK T.
Riding the High country. Caldwell: 1933. V. 47; 50; 52; 54

TUCKER, PETER
Haslewood Books: the Books of Frederick Etchells & Hugh Macdonald. 1990. V. 52; 54
Haslewood Books. The Books of Frederick Etchells & Hugh Macdonald. Hanborough Parrot, Church: 1990. V. 52
The Interpretation of a Classic, the Illustrated Editions of Candide. Oxon: 1993. V. 52

TUCKER, SARAH
The Rainbow in the North: a Short Account of the First Establishment of Christianity in Rupert's land by the Church Missionary Society. New York: 1854. V. 50

TUCKER, ST. GEORGE
A Dissertation on Slavery: With a Proposal for the Gradual Abolition of It, in the State of Virginia. Philadelphia: 1796. V. 48; 53

TUCKER, W.
Prison Planet. 1947. V. 48; 52
The Year of the Quiet Sun. 1971. V. 47; 51

TUCKER, WILLIAM
The Family Dyer and Scourer; Being a Complete Treatise on the Arts of Dyeing and Cleaning Every Article of Dress, Bed and Window Furniture, Silks, Bonnets, Feathers, &c... Hartford: 1831?. V. 48

TUCKER MACHETTA, BLANCHE ROOSEVELT
The Home Life of Henry W. Longfellow. New York: 1882. V. 54

TUCKERMAN, ARTHUR LYMAN
A Short History of Architecture. New York: 1887. V. 52

TUCKERMAN, EDWARD
Collected Lichenological Papers of Edward Tuckerman. Wineheim: 1964. V. 51

TUCKERMAN, FREDERICK GODDARD
The Complete Poems. New York: 1965. V. 50; 52; 53
The Cricket. Cummington: 1950. V. 51; 52; 54

TUCKERMAN, HENRY T.
Artist-Life: or, Sketches of American Painters. New York: 1847. V. 47; 51; 53
Characteristics of Literature Illustrated by the Genius of Distinguished Men. Philadelphia: 1849. V. 49
The Collector. London: 1868. V. 49

TUCKETT, F.
A Pioneer in the High Alps. London: 1920. V. 52

TUCKETT, HARVEY
The Indian Revenue System as It Is. A Letter Addressed to the President, Vice-President and Members of the Manchester Chamber of Commerce and Manufactures.....for the East India Company. London: 1840. V. 53

TUCKEY, JAMES KINGSTON
Narrative of an Expedition to Explore the River Zaire, Usually Called the Congo, in South Africa in 1816. London: 1818. V. 47; 54
Narrative of an Expedition to Explore the River Zaire, Usually Called the Congo, in South Africa in 1816. New York: 1818. V. 54

TUCKNEY, ANTHONY
The Balme of Gilead, for the Wounds of England. London: 1643. V. 49

TUDOR *Church Music.* London: 1923. V. 54

TUDOR, TASHA
Alexander the Gander. New York: 1939. V. 54
Around the Year. New York: 1957. V. 51
A Is For Annabelle. New York: 1954. V. 51
Pumpkin Moonshine. New York: 1938. V. 54
Tasha Tudor's Favorite Stories. Philadelphia: 1965. V. 48
A Time to Keep, the Tasha Tudor Book of Holidays. Chicago: 1977. V. 51

TUDOR-CRAIG, ALGERNON
Catalogue of the Contents of the Museum at Freemason's Hall in the Possession of the United Grand Lodge of England. (with) Catalogue of the Portraits and Prints and Catalogue of the Manuscripts and Library. London: 1938. V. 47

TUER, ANDREW WHITE
1,000 Quaint Cuts from Books of Other Days... London. V. 47; 50
1,000 Quaint Cuts From Books of Other Days... London: 1875. V. 49
Bartolozzi and His Works. London: 1881. V. 53
The Book of Delightful and Strange Designs. London: 1893. V. 48; 50
The Follies and Fashions of Our Grandfathers. London: 1886/87. V. 48
History of the Horn Book. London: 1896. V. 48
History of the Horn-Book. London: 1897. V. 47; 50; 54
Luxurious Bathing... London. V. 47
Luxurious Bathing. London: 1880. V. 49
Old London Street Cries. London: 1885. V. 49
Pages and Pictures from Forgotten Children's Books. London: 1898-99. V. 47; 49
Quads, for Authors, Editors & Devils. London: 1884. V. 48; 49
Quads within Quads. London: 1884. V. 48; 52

TUESDAY NIGHT CLUB OF NEWBURYPORT
The Records of the Tuesday Night Club of Newburyport, Comprising an Account of Its Sixth Century of Meetings. 1946-69. V. 48

TUFTS, JAMES
A Tract Descriptive of Montana Territory; With a Sketch of Its Mineral and Agricultural Resources. New York: 1865. V. 47; 50

TUFTS, MARSHALL
A Tour Through College: Containing Some Remarks From Experience on the Nature of the Learning There Acquired... Lexington: 1833. V. 48

TUIT, J. E.
The Tower Bridge. 1894. V. 51; 54
The Tower Bridge... London: 1894. V. 47

TUKE, DANIEL HACK
Illustrations of the Influence of the Mind Upon the Body in Health and Disease. London: 1872. V. 47
Illustrations of the Influence of the Mind Upon the Body in Health and Disease... Philadelphia: 1873. V. 49; 52
Illustrations of the Influence of the Mind Upon the Body in Health and Disease... Philadelphia: 1884. V. 52
Rules and List of the Present Members of the Society for Improving the Condition of the Insane; and the Prize Essay Entitled The Progressive Changes Which Have Taken Place Since the Time of Pinel in the Moral Management of the Insane and the Various... London: 1854. V. 52
Sleep-Walking and Hypnotism. London: 1884. V. 47

TUKE, HENRY
Memoirs of George Whitehead; A Minister of the Gospel in the Society of Friends... York: 1830. V. 49; 54
Memoirs of the Life Of Stephen Crisp, With Selections from His Works. York: 1824. V. 49; 54

TUKE, JOHN BATTY
The Insanity of Over-Exertion of the Brain. Edinburgh: 1894. V. 53

TUKE, SAMUEL
The Adventures of Five Hours. London: 1663. V. 48; 50; 54
Description of the Retreat, an Institution Near York, for Insane Persons of the Society of Friends. York: 1813. V. 49

TULARD, JEAN
Napoleon, the Myth of the Saviour. London: 1984. V. 50

TULASNE, LUDOVICUS RENATUS
Fungi Hypogaei, Histoire et Monographie des Champignons Hypoges. Paris: 1841. V. 52
Fungi Hypogaei, Histoire et Monographie des Champignons Hypoges. Paris: 1851. V. 49
Selecta Fungorum Carpologia... Paris: 1861-65. V. 49
Selecta Fungorum Carpologia. London: 1931. V. 47; 48; 50
Selecta Fungorum Carpologia. Oxford: 1931. V. 49

TULL, JETHRO
The Horse-Hoeing Husbandry... London: 1733. V. 54
Horse-Hoeing Husbandry... London: 1751. V. 49; 54
The Horse-Hoeing Husbandry... London: 1822. V. 50
The Horse-Hoeing Husbandry... London: 1829. V. 47; 49; 51; 52; 53; 54
Horse-Hoeing Husbandry... London: 1851. V. 50

TULLIBARDINE, MARCHIONESS
A Military History of Perthshire 1899-1902. Perth: 1908. V. 54

TULLIDGE, EDWARD W.
History of Salt Lake City. Salt Lake City: 1886. V. 47; 50
Tullidge's Histories. (Volume II). Containing the History of All the Northern Eastern and Western Counties of Utah; also the Counties of Southern Idaho. Salt Lake City: 1889. V. 47

TULLIE, ISAAC
A Narrative of the Siege of Carlisle, in 1644 and 1645. Carlisle: 1840. V. 50

TULLOCH, JOHN
Rational Theology and Christian Philosophy in England in the Seventeenth Century. Edinburgh & London: 1874. V. 48; 49

TULLY, J. D.
The History of Plague, As it Has Lately Appeared in the Islands of Malta, Gozo, Corfu, Cephaolonia &c. London: 1821. V. 49

TULLY, JIM
Beggars of Life. New York: 1924. V. 49

TULLY, MISS
Narrative of a Ten Years' Residence at Tripoli in Africa... London: 1817. V. 54

TULLY, RICHARD
Letters Written During a Ten Years' Residence at the Court of Tripoli. London: 1819. V. 51; 53

TULLY, SAMUEL
The Life of Samuel Tully, who Was Executed at South Boston, Dec. 10, 1812 for Piracy. Boston: 1812. V. 49

TUMBLE, THOMAS
The Life of General Monck, with Remarks Upon His Actions. London: 1671. V. 47

TUMBLETY, FRANCIS
A Few Passages in the Life of Dr. Francis Tumblety, the Indian Herb Doctor... Cincinnati: 1866. V. 47

THE TUNBRIDGE Wells Guide: or, an Account of the Ancient and Present State of that Place, To Which is Added a Particular Description of the Towns and Village, Gentlemans Seats, Remains of Antiquity, Founderies, &c . London: 1786. V. 50

THE TUNBRIDGE Wells Guide; or, an Account of the Ancient and Present State of that Place to Which is Added a Particular Description of the Towns and Village, Gentlemans Seats, Remains of Antiquity, Founderies &c... Tunbridge Wells: 1786. V. 54

TUNNARD, C.
Gardens in the Modern Landscape. London: 1950. V. 51; 54

TUNNEY, GENE
A Man Must Fight. Boston: 1932. V. 53

TUNNICLIFF, WILLIAM
A Topographical Survey of the Counties of Stafford, Chester and Lancaster... Nantwich: 1787. V. 53

TUNNICLIFFE, C. F.
Both Sides of the Road. London: 1949. V. 53; 54
Mereside Chronicle. London: 1948. V. 51; 52

TUNNICLIFFE, CHARLES
Shorelands Summer Diary. London: 1952. V. 48; 51; 52; 53; 54

TUPPER, FERDINAND BROCK
The Life and Correspondence of Major-General Sir Isaac Brock, K.B. Interspersed with Notices of the Celebrated Indian Chief, Tecumseh. London: 1845. V. 47

TUPPER, J. H. E.
Stone Carving and Inlaying in the Bombay Presidency. Bombay: 1906. V. 48

TUPPER, MARTIN FARQUHAR
Proverbial Philosophy: a Book of Thoughts and Arguments. London: 1838. V. 49
Proverbial Philosophy: A Book of Thoughts and Arguments. Boston: 1851. V. 48
Proverbial Philosophy: a Book of Thoughts and Arguments. London: 1854. V. 51
Rides and Reveries of the Late Mr. Aesop Smith. London: 1858. V. 54

TURBERVILLE, A. S.
Johnson's England: an Account of His Life and Manners of His Age. Oxford: 1933. V. 54
Johnson's England. An Account of the Life and Manners of His Age. Oxford: 1965. V. 48

TURBERVILLE, GEORGE
The Booke of Falconrie or Havvking...(with) The Noble Art of Venerie or Hvnting (etc.). London: 1611. V. 51; 54

TURBERVILLE, HENRY
Manual of Controversies Clearly Demonstrating the Truth of the Catholic Religion. Douai: 1654. V. 48; 50; 53

TURBEVILLE, DEBORAH
Unseen Versailles. Garden City: 1981. V. 54
Wallflower. New York: 1978. V. 54

TURBLET, NICHOLAS CHARLES JOSEPH
Essais Sur Divers Sujets de Litterature et de Morale. Paris: 1749-60. V. 48

THE TURF. London: 1831. V. 51

THE TURF Seat; or, More Village Stories. Salisbury: 1807. V. 48

TURGENEV, IVAN SERGEEVICH
Fathers and Sons. New York: 1867. V. 48; 50
Fathers and Sons. New York: 1872. V. 54
Fathers and Sons. New York: 1951. V. 52; 53; 54
The Novels and Stories. New York: 1903-04. V. 47; 49; 51
The Novels and Stories. London: 1905. V. 51; 53
Virgin Soil. London: 1878. V. 49

TURGOT, ANNE R. J.
The Life and Writings of Turgot, Comptroller General of France, 1774-76. London: 1895. V. 49

TURLEY, EDWARD
First Lines of Education: A Course of Four Lectures, Delivered to the Literary and Scientific Institution, Worcester, In the Spring Session of 1839. Worcester: 1839. V. 53

TURNBULL, GAEL
As from Fleece; a Long Poem. 1990. V. 52
Circus: Poems. Cradley, Malvern: 1984. V. 54
Land That I Knew. Toronto: 1962. V. 47; 52
A Trampoline, Poems 1952-64. London: 1968. V. 50

TURNBULL, GEORGE
A Curious Collection of Ancient Paintings, Accurately Engraved from Excellent Drawings, lately Done After the Originals... London: 1744. V. 48
Observations Upon Liberal Education, In All Its Branches...Designed for the Assistance of Younge Gentlemen... London: 1742. V. 48

TURNBULL, LAURENCE
The Advantages and Accidents of Artificial Anaesthesia... Philadelphia: 1878. V. 47

TURNBULL, ROBERT
The Theatre in its Influence Upon Literature, Morals, and Religion. Boston: 1839. V. 52

TURNBULL, ROBERT J.
A Visit to the Philadelphia Prison; Being an Accurate and Particular Account of the Wise and Humane Administration Adopted in Every Part of that Building. London: 1797. V. 48; 52
Visite a la Prison de Philadelphie, ou Enonce Exact de la Sage Administration qui a Lieu Dans les Divers Departemens de Cette Maison... Paris: 1809. V. 47

TURNBULL, ROBERT JAMES
Address to the People of South Carolina, by Their Delegates in Convention. Columbia: 1832. V. 53
The Crisis: or, Essays on the Usurpation of the Federal Government. Charleston: 1827. V. 49

TURNBULL, W. B. D. D.
Catalogue of the Extensive and Valuable Library of... London: 1851. V. 48

TURNBULL, W. P.
The Birds of East Lothian and a Portion of the Adjoining Counties. Glasgow: 1867. V. 47

TURNER, A. J.
The Time Museum. Volume I: The Measuring Instruments. Part I: Astrolabes, Astrolabe Related Instruments. Rockford: 1985. V. 53
The Time Museum. Volume I: The Measuring Instruments. Part III. Water-clocks, Sand-clocks, Fire-clocks. Rockford: 1984. V. 53

TURNER, AVERY, MRS.
Into the West. Amarillo: 1938. V. 53

TURNER, BENJAMIN
St. George's Church and Schools, Barnsley. Retrospect: 1821-1912. Barnsley: 1904. V. 53

TURNER, CHARLES QUINCY
Yosemite Valley through the Stereoscope. New York: 1902. V. 51

TURNER, DANIEL
A Discourse Concerning Fevers. London: 1727. V. 51
Siphylis. A Practical Dissertation on the Venereal Disease in Two Parts. London: 1732. V. 47; 49

TURNER, DAWSON
Architectural Antiquities of Normandy. 1822. V. 47
The Botanist's Guide through England and Wales. London: 1805. V. 51; 54
Descriptive Index of the Contents of Five Manuscript Volumes, Illustrative of the History of Great Britain, in the Library of Dawson Turner, Esq. Great Yarmouth: 1851. V. 50; 52
Fuci sive Plantarum Fucorum Generi... London: 1809. V. 50; 54
Muscologiae Hibernicae Spicilegium. Yarmouth and London: 1804. V. 48; 52
Proof Impressions of Engravings Designed to Illustrate Mr. Roscoe's Catalogue of the Manuscript Library at Holkham. London: 1835. V. 50
Sketch of the History of Caister Castle. London: 1842. V. 52

TURNER, DECHERD
The Rhemes New Testament. Being a Full and Particular Account of the Origins, Printing and Subsequent Influences of the First Roman Catholic New Testament in English, with the Divers Controversies Occasioned by Its Publication Diligently Expounded... San Francisco: 1990. V. 48

TURNER, EDWIN B.
Reminiscences of Morris, and History of the Congregational Church. Chicago: 1865. V. 49; 50

TURNER, ERNEST
Hints to Househunters and Householders. London: 1883. V. 52

TURNER, FREDERICK JACKSON
The Character and Influence of the Indian Trade in Wisconsin. Baltimore: 1891. V. 50
The Frontier in American History. New York: 1920. V. 50
The Frontier in American History. New York: 1921. V. 48
The Significance of the Frontier in American History. Ithaca: 1956. V. 48; 51

TURNER, GEORGE
Nineteen Years In Polynesia, Missionary Life, Travels and Researches in the Islands of the Pacific. London: 1861. V. 47; 50

TURNER, HENRY GLYES
A History of the Colony of Victoria from Its Discovery to Its Absorption into the Commonwealth of Australia. London: 1904. V. 52

TURNER, HENRY WARD
The Pleistocene Geology of the South Central Sierra Nevada... San Francisco: 1900. V. 54

TURNER, J. B.
Mormonism in All Ages; or the Rise, Progress and Causes of Mormonism, with the Biography of Its Author and Founder, Joseph Smith, Junior. New York: 1842. V. 53

TURNER, J. HORSFALL
Ancient Bingley: or, Bingley, Its History and Scenery. Bingley: 1897. V. 48; 53
Haworth Past and Present, a History of Haworth, Stanbury & Oxenhope. 1879. V. 52; 53; 54
History of Brighouse, Raistrick and Hipperholme... 1893. V. 48; 53
Yorkshire Anthology: Ballads and Songs - Ancient and Modern... Bingley: 1901. V. 53
Yorkshire Genealogist. 1888. V. 53; 54

TURNER, JAMES
Memoirs of His Own Life and Times 1632-1670. Edinburgh: 1829. V. 49
A Treatise on the Foot of the Horse, and a New System of Shoeing... London: 1832. V. 47

TURNER, JAMES A.
Remarks on the Linnaean Order of Insects Forming a Short and Familiar Introduction to the Study of Entomology... London: 1828. V. 54

TURNER, JESSE
A Page from the English State Trials. 1907. V. 51

TURNER, JOHN
A Letter of Resolution to a Friend, Concerning the Marriage of Cousin Germans... London: 1682. V. 53
A Resolution of Three Matrimonial Cases... London: 1684. V. 54

TURNER, JOHN PETER
The North-West Mounted Police 1873-1893. Ottawa: 1950. V. 50; 52; 54

TURNER, JOSEPH MALLORD WILLIAM
Architectural Remains Removed to Farnley, by Walter Hawkes, Esq. from Different Ancient Hall Houses in His Possession. London: 1821. V. 47
Liber Fluviorum; or, River Scenery of France. London: 1853. V. 54
The Liber Studiorum. London: 1899. V. 51
Liber Studiorum. London: 1920. V. 54
Picturesque Views on the Southern Coast of England... London: 1826. V. 47
The Rivers of France. London: 1837. V. 51
Turner's Annual Tour, 1833. Wanderings by the Loire. London: 1833. V. 53
Views in Richmondshire. 1823. V. 48
Wanderings by the Loire. London: 1833. V. 49

TURNER, LUCIEN MC SHAW
Contributions to the Natural History of Alaska. Washington: 1886. V. 49; 52

TURNER, M. J.
The Bank Tree. London: 1937. V. 49

TURNER, MATTHEW
An Account of the Extraordinary Medicinal Fluid, Called Aether. Liverpool: 1761. V. 48

TURNER, MORRIE
Black and White Coloring Book. San Francisco: 1969. V. 48

TURNER, NICHOLAS
An Essay on Draining and Improving Peat Bogs... Chichester: 1784. V. 53

TURNER, NOEL D.
American Silver Flatware 1837-1910. South Brunswick: 1973. V. 47

TURNER, RICHARD
An Easy Introduction to the Arts and Sciences... London: 1791. V. 53; 54
A New and Easy Introduction to Universal Geography; in A Series of Letters to a Youth at School. London: 1800. V. 48

TURNER, ROBERT
Maria Stuarta, Regina Scotiae, Doctaria Franciae, Haeres Angliae et Hyberniae, Martyr Ecclesiae Innocens a Caede Darleana... Ingolstadt: 1588. V. 51
Oratoris et Philosophi...Orationes XIV. Antwerp: 1597. V. 53

TURNER, SAMUEL
My Climbing Adventures in Four Continents. 1911. V. 53
My Climbing Adventures in Four Continents. London: 1911. V. 49
Siberia. A Record of Travel, Climbing and Exploration. London: 1905. V. 48

TURNER, SAMUEL BLOIS
Turner Genealogy. London: 1884. V. 47; 53

TURNER, SILVIE
Handmade Paper Today, a Worldwide Survey of Mills, Papers, Techniques and Uses. London: 1983. V. 48

TURNER, T.
The Three Gilt Balls; or, My Uncle, His Stock-in-Trade and Customers. London: 1864. V. 48

TURNER, T. HUDSON
Some Account of Domestic Architecture in England. Oxford: 1851/53. V. 51
Some Account of Domestic Architecture in England...from the Conquest through the XVth Century. London: 1859. V. 53

TURNER, THOMAS
Narrative of a Journey, Associated with a Fly, from Gloucester to Aberystwith and from Aberystwith through North Wales. July 31st to September 8th 1837. London: 1840. V. 54

TURNER, TIMOTHY GILMAN
Gazetteer of the St. Joseph Valley, Michigan and Indiana, with a View of Its Hydraulic and Business Capacities. Chicago: 1867. V. 50
Turner's Guide from the Lakes to the Rocky Mountains. Chicago: 1868. V. 47

TURNER, TOMKYNS HILGROVE
Thoughts and Anecdotes Military and Historical. London: 1811. V. 47

TURNER, W. J.
Seven Sciagraphical Poems. London: 1929. V. 47

TURNER, WHITELY
A Spring-Time Saunter Round and About Bronte-Land. 1913. V. 54

TURNER, WILLIAM
Sound Anatomiz'd, in a Philosophical Essay on Musick. London: 1724. V. 48
William Adams an Old English Potter. London: 1904. V. 54

TURNER, WILLIAM A.
Even More Confederate Faces. Orange: 1983. V. 48

TURNER, WILLIAM H.
Selections from the Records of the City of Oxford, with Extracts from other Documents Illustrating the Municipal History... Oxford and London: 1880. V. 50

THE TURNER'S Companion. Philadelphia: 1867. V. 53

TURNER-TURNER, J.
Life in the Blackwoods. London: 1890. V. 48
Three Years Hunting and Trapping in America and the Great North West. 1888. V. 52; 54
Three Years Hunting and Trapping in America and the Great North West. London: 1888. V. 48

TURNILL, REGINALD
Jane's Spaceflight Directory 1986. London: 1985. V. 49
Jane's Spaceflight Directory 1987. London: 1986. V. 49
Jane's Spaceflight Directory, 1988-89. Coulsdon, Surrey: 1988. V. 53

TURNLEY, JOSEPH
The Language of the Eye: as Indicative of Female Beauty, Mainly Genius and General Character with Many Illustrations. London: 1856. V. 47

TURNLEY, PARMENAS TAYLOR
Reminiscences of Parmenas Taylor Turnley from the Cradle to Three-Score and Ten. Chicago: 1892. V. 47; 48; 50

TURNOR, EDMUND
Collections for the History of the Town and Soke of Grantham. London: 1806. V. 51

TUROW, SCOTT
One L. New York: 1977. V. 50; 51; 52; 53
Presumed Innocent. New York: 1987. V. 50; 52

TURPIN, RICHARD
The Trial of the Notorious Highwayman Richard Turpin, at York Assizes, on the 22d Day of March 1739. York: 1739. V. 49; 52

TURPIN, WATERS EDWARD
These Low Grounds. New York: 1937. V. 53

TURPIN DE CRISSE, LANCELOT, COUNT
An Essay on the Art of War. London: 1761. V. 52

THE TURQUOISE Trail. Boston: 1928. V. 53

TURRILL, CHARLES B.
California Notes: First Volume. San Francisco: 1876. V. 47

TURRILL, W. B.
Royal Botanic Gardens, Kew, Past and Present. London: 1959. V. 54

THE TURTLE Dove's Wedding. London: 1820. V. 49

TURTON, JOHN
The Angler's Manual; or, Fly-Fisher's Oracle. London: 1836. V. 47

TURTON, THOMAS
A Vindication of the Literary Character of the Late Professor Porson, from the Animadversions of the Right Reverend Thomas Burgess. Cambridge: 1827. V. 48

TURTON, W.
British Fauna. Swansea: 1807. V. 52
Conchylia Insularum Britannicarum: The Shells of the British Islands, Systematically Arranged. Exeter: 1822. V. 51
A Manual of the Land and Fresh-Water Shells of the British Islands. London: 1840. V. 51; 52; 53

TURTON, ZOUCH H.
To the Desert and Back: or, Travels in Spain, the Barbary States, Italy, Etc., in 1875-76. London: 1876. V. 49

TUSCARORA & COLD RUN TUNNEL & RAILROAD CO.
An Act to Incorporate the Tuscarora and Cold Run Tunnel and Rail Road Company. Pottsville: 1830. V. 53

TUSON, EDWARD WILLIAM
Myology Illustrated: a supplement to Myology. London: 1825-28. V. 52
Spinal Debility: Its Prevention, Pathology and Cure, in Relation to Curvatures, Paralysis, Epilepsy and Various Deformities. London: 1861. V. 47
A Supplement to Myology. London: 1828. V. 53

TUSSER, THOMAS
...Five Hundred Pointes of Good Husbandrie...Mixed in Everie Month with Huswiferie. London: 1590. V. 52
Five Hundred Points of Good Husbandry.... London: 1672. V. 48
Five Hundred Points of Good Husbandry... London: 1744. V. 49
Five Hundred Points of Good Husbandry. London: 1812. V. 47; 48; 49; 53
Five Hundred Points of Good Husbandry. 1931. V. 51; 52

TUTEN, FREDERIC
The Adventures of Mao. New York: 1971. V. 54
Tintin in the New World. New York: 1993. V. 51

TUTHILL, FRANKLIN
The History of California. San Francisco: 1866. V. 49

TUTHILL, LOUISA CAROLINE
The Young Lady at Home and In Society. New York: 1869. V. 50

TUTIN, T. G.
Flora Europaea. London: 1964-80. V. 49

TUTT, J. W.
A Natural History of the British Lepidoptera. London: 1899-1909. V. 53

TUTTIETT, MARY GLEED
The Last Sentence: a Novel. London: 1893. V. 48; 51
The Reproach of Annesley. London: 1889. V. 48

TUTTLE, CHARLES R.
Annual New England Official Directory and General Hand-Book for 1878-79. Boston: 1878. V. 49
A New Centennial History of the State of Kansas. Madison: 1876. V. 51
Our North Land: Being a Full Account of the Canadian North-West and Hudson's Bay Route... Toronto: 1885. V. 47

TUTTLE, FRANCIS
Report of the Cruise of the U.S. Revenue Cutter Bear and the Overland Expedition for the Relief of the Whalers in the Arctic Ocean from Nov. 27, 1897 to Sept. 13, 1898. Washington: 1899. V. 52

TUTTLE, GEORGE
Stories About Whale-Catching. New Haven: 1845. V. 49

TWEDDELL, ROBERT
Remains of the Late John Tweddell...a Selecton of His letters... London: 1815. V. 50

TWEED, JOHN
The Invasion or, England's Glory. Bocking: 1798?. V. 49

TWEEDDALE, ARTHUR HAY, MARQUIS OF
Contributions to the Ornithology of the Philippines. London: 1877-79. V. 49
The Ornithological Works of Arthur, 9th Marquis of Tweeddale. London: 1881. V. 48; 54

TWEEDIE, ALEXANDER
Clinical Illustrations of Fever. Comprising a Report of the Cases Treated at the London Fever Hospital 1828-1829. Philadelphia: 1831. V. 47

TWEEDIE, R. A.
Arts in New Brunswick. Fredericton: 1967. V. 47

TWEEDIE, W.
The Arabian Horse: His Country and People. Edinburgh & London: 1894. V. 48
The Arabian Horse: His Country and People... Beirut: 1960. V. 48

TWEEDIE, W. K.
Jerusalem and its Environs; or, the Holy City As It Was and Is. London: 1860. V. 52
The Rivers and Lakes of Scripture. London: 1857. V. 49

TWELVE American Writers. Easthampton: 1974. V. 50

THE TWELVE Months of the year: With a Picture for Each Month. Concord: 1846. V. 48

TWELVE PHOTOGRAPHERS of the American Social Landscape. New York: 1967. V. 48

TWELVE Poets of the Pacific. Norfolk: 1937. V. 53

TWELVE Southerners. I'll Take My Stand. New York: 1930. V. 53

TWELVE Steps and Twelve Traditions. 1953. V. 51

TWEMLOW, GEORGE
Facts and Fossils Adduced to Prove the Deluge of Noah and Modify the Transmutation System of Darwin. London & Guildford: 1868. V. 49

TWENEY, GEORGE H.
The Washington 89. Seattle: 1989. V. 48

TWENTEITH Century History of Southwest Texas, Illustrated. Chicago: 1907. V. 53

TWENTY-FIVE Years of the Weather Bird Press. Pasadena: 1993. V. 51

THE TWENTY-THIRD Canadian Field Regiment (S.P.), Royal Canadian Artillery. Lochem: 1945. V. 50

TWENTY-TWENTY Vision: In Celebration of the Peninsula Hills. Palo Alto: 1982. V. 51

TWICI, WILLIAM
Le Art de Venerie. En France: 1883. V. 47
The Art of Hunting, by...Huntsman to King Edward the Second. Daventry: 1843. V. 47

TWICKEL, IOANNES WILELMUS DE
Paraphrasis Canonica Libri V. Strasbourg: 1701. V. 54

TWIGDEN, B. L.
The Fifty Rarest Birds of the World. Auckland: 1991. V. 49
Pisces Tropicani. Melbourne: 1978. V. 52

TWINE, LAURENCE
The Patterne of Painefull Adventures Gathered Into English. New Rochelle: 1903. V. 47; 49

TWINING, E. W.
The Art & Craft of Stained Glass. London: 1928. V. 49; 53

TWINING, HENRY
On the Philosophy of Painting: a Theoretical and practical Treatise. London: 1849. V. 50; 52

TWINING, LOUIS
Workhouses and Pauperism and Women's Work in the Administration of the Poor Laws. London: 1898. V. 49

TWINING, RICHARD
An Answer to the Second Report of the East India Directors, Respecting the Sale and Prices of Tea. London: 1785. V. 52

THE TWINS. London: 1927. V. 49

TWISS, HENRY F. BERRY
A History of the Royal Dublin Society. London: 1915. V. 54

TWISS, HORACE
An Enquiry Into the Means of Consolidating and Digesting the Laws of England. London: 1826. V. 52
The Public and Private Life of Lord Chancellor Eldon, with Selections from His Corresopndence. London: 1844. V. 47; 54
The Public and Private Life of Lord Chancellor Eldon, with Selections from His Correspondence. Philadelphia: 1844. V. 52

TWISS, RICHARD
An Heroick Answer (in Verse)... Dublin: 1776. V. 48
A Trip to Paris, in July and August, 1792. Dublin: 1793. V. 50
A Trip to Paris, in July and August, 1792. London: 1793. V. 52

TWISS, TRAVERS
Considerations of a Plan for Combining the Professional System with the System of Public Examinations in Oxford. Oxford: 1839. V. 47
Monumenta Juridica. The Black Book of the Admiralty... London: 1871-76. V. 49
On Certain Tests of a Thriving Population. London: 1845. V. 52
On the Relations of the Duchies of Schleswig and Holstein to the Crown of Denmark and the Germanic Confederation, and on the Treaty-Engagements of the Great European Powers in Reference Thereto. London: 1848. V. 48; 50; 53
The Oregon Question, in Respect to Facts and the Law of Nations. London: 1846. V. 47; 48

TWITCHELL, RALPH EMERSON
History of the Military Occupation of the Territory of New Mexico from 1846-1851. Denver: 1909. V. 48
The Leading Facts of New Mexican History. Cedar Rapids: 1911-17. V. 49; 53
The Leading Facts of New Mexican History. Albuquerque: 1963. V. 48; 49; 54
The Military Occupation of New Mexico. Denver: 1909. V. 49
The Spanish Archives of New Mexico. Cedar Rapids: 1914. V. 47

TWO Eleven. Being the History of 211 Siege Battery R.G.A. on the Western Front. Portsmouth: 1925. V. 47

TWO Epistles on Happiness: to a Young Lady. Salisbury: 1754. V. 54

TWO Humble Petitions of the Apprentices of London & Parts Adjacent, for Lawful Recreations: the First Presented to the Rt. Hon. the Lords & Commons Assembled in Parliament on Tuesday, Feb. 9, 1646...The Other Presented to Rt. Hon. Lord Mayor Alderman... London: 1647. V. 47; 52

THE TWO Hundred and Fiftieth Anniversary of the Settlement of the Jews in the United States. Addressed Delivered at Carnegie Hall, New York on Thanksgiving Day MCMV. Together With Other Selected Addresses and Proceedings. New York: 1906. V. 51

TWO Petitions of the County of Yorke...3d of June, 1642. London: 1642. V. 50; 53

TWO Right Profitable and Fruitfull Concordances... London: 1619. V. 51

TWOHY LAND CO.
Twohy Land Company's Review of the Famous Yakima Valley. North Yakima: 1909. V. 52

TWYMAN, F.
Prism and Lens Making: a Text Book for Optical Glassworkers. London: 1944. V. 53

TWYMAN, MICHAEL
Printing 1770-1970. London: 1970. V. 50; 51; 52

TWYN, JOHN
An Exact Narrative of the Tryal and Condemnation of John Twyn, for Printing and Dispersing of a Treasonable Book, with the Tryals of Thomas Brewster, Bookseller, Simon Dover, Printer, Nathan Brooks, Bookbinder, for Printing, Publishing & Uttering of... London: 1664. V. 48

TWYNE, BRIAN
Antiquitatis Academiae Oxonienes Apologia... Oxford: 1608. V. 48

TWYSDEN, ROGER
Historiae Anglicanae Sciptores X, Simeon Monachus Dumelmensis... London: 1652. V. 53
An Historical Vindication of the Church of England In Point of Schism... London: 1675. V. 51

TYACKE, RICHARD H.
The Sportsman's Manual in Quest of Game in Kulu, Lahoul and Ladak to the Tso Morari Lake. 1907. V. 47

TYAS, ROBERT
Beautfiul Birds Described. London: 1868. V. 54
Favourite Field Flowers; or Wild Flowers of England Popularly Described. London: 1850. V. 54

TYERS, THOMAS
An Historical Essay on Mr. Addison. London: 1783. V. 54

TYLER, ANNE
The Accidental Tourist. New York: 1978. V. 54
The Accidental Tourist. New York: 1985. V. 47; 50; 51; 53; 54
Breathing Lessons. 1988. V. 48
Breathing Lessons. Franklin Center: 1988. V. 50; 51; 53
Breathing Lessons. New York: 1988. V. 49; 51
Celestial Navigation. New York: 1974. V. 48; 49; 50; 51; 52
The Clock Winder. New York: 1972. V. 52; 53
Dinner at the Homesick Restaurant. New York: 1982. V. 48; 51; 53; 54
Earthly Possessions. New York: 1990. V. 51
If Morning Ever Comes. New York: 1964. V. 49; 50; 51; 52; 53
If Morning Ever Comes. London: 1965. V. 48; 52
Ladder of Years. Franklin Center: 1995. V. 54
Ladder of Years. New York: 1995. V. 51; 54
Morgan's Passing. London: 1980. V. 53
Morgan's Passing. New York: 1980. V. 47; 50; 52; 53
Saint Maybe. Franklin Center: 1991. V. 53
Saint Maybe. New York: 1991. V. 47; 49; 50; 51; 54
Saint Maybe. New York: 1993. V. 49
Searching for Caleb. New York: 1976. V. 48; 51; 52
A Slipping Down Life. New York: 1970. V. 47; 48; 50; 51; 52; 53
A Slipping Down Life. London: 1983. V. 50
The Tin Can Tree. New York: 1965. V. 50; 53; 54
The Tin Can Tree. London: 1966. V. 49; 51
Tumble Tower. New York. V. 54
A Visit with Eudora Welty. Chicago: 1980. V. 47; 50; 51; 52
Your Place is Empty. Concord: 1992. V. 48; 49; 53; 54

TYLER, DANIEL
A Concise History of the Mormon Battalion in the Mexican War 1846-1847. N.P: 1881. V. 51
A Concise History of the Mormon Battalion in the Mexican War 1846-47. 1881. V. 47; 51
A Concise History of the Mormon Battalion in the Mexican War 1846-47. Washington: 1881. V. 53

TYLER, GEORGE W.
For a Railway Commission. Speech of Hon. Geo. W. Tyler Senator, from Bell, in the Senate of Texas. Austin: 1889. V. 49
History of Bell County. San Antonio: 1936. V. 48; 49; 50; 52

TYLER, GILLIAN
The Good Wine. Thetford: 1965. V. 52
Perhaps a Poem. Thetford: 1967. V. 54

TYLER, J. O.
Shooting in Monmouthshire 1789-1923. Pontypool: 1923. V. 48

TYLER, JOHN
Message from...Correspondence with the Government of Mexico. Washington: 1842. V. 47

TYLER, LYON G.
The Letters and Times of the Tylers. Richmond: 1884-85. V. 52
The Letters and Times of the Tylers. Williamsburg: 1885/96. V. 47
The Letters and Times of the Tylers. New York: 1971. V. 52
Men of Mark in Virginia. Washington: 1906. V. 52

TYLER, MOSES COIT
The Literary History of the American Revolution 1763-1783. New York & London: 1897. V. 52

TYLER, RON
Audubon's Great National Work. Austin: 1993. V. 50

TYLER, ROYAL
The Yankey in London... New York: 1809. V. 48; 54

TYLER, WILLIAM N.
The Dispatch Carrier...Adventures...in the Late War; The Capture, Imprisonment, Escape and Recapture of a Union Solider. Port Byron: 1892. V. 48

TYLOR, EDWARD BURNET
Anahuac; or Mexico and the Mexicans, Ancient and Modern. London: 1861. V. 52
Researches Into the Early History of Mankind and the Development of Civilization. London: 1865. V. 49

TYLOR, J. J.
The Tomb of Paheri. London: 1895. V. 49; 51

TYMER, THOMAS
The Tragedies of the Last Age Consider'd and Examin'd by the Practice of the Ancients, and by the Common Sense of All Ages. London: 1678. V. 47

TYMMS, W. R.
The Art of Illuminating, as Practiced in Europe from the Earliest Times... London: 1865. V. 54
The Art of Illuminating as Practised in Europe from the Earliest Times. London: 1870's. V. 53

TYNAN, KATHARINE
Twenty-One Poems. Dundrum: 1907. V. 54
The Wild Harp. London: 1913. V. 48

TYNAN, KENNETH
Bull Fever. London: 1955. V. 52

TYNDALE, JOHN
The Study of Physics, from a Lecture Delivered by Professor Tyndale in the Royal Institution of Great Britain in the Spring of 1854. V. 53

TYNDALE, WALTER
An Artist in Egypt. London: 1912. V. 50
An Artist in Italy. London: 1913. V. 48
Below the Cataracts. London: 1907. V. 49

TYNDALE, WILLIAM
The Whole Works. London: 1572. V. 50

TYNDALL, JOHN
Essays on the Floating-Matter of the Air in Relation to Putrefaction and Infection. London: 1881. V. 48
Essays on the Floating-Matter of the Air in Relation to Putrefaction and Infection. New York: 1882. V. 47; 52; 53; 54
Essays on the Use and Limit of the Imagination of Science. London: 1870. V. 50
Faraday As a Discoverer. London: 1868. V. 48; 53
The Glaciers of the Alps. London: 1860. V. 48
Heat Considered as a Mode of Motion: Being a Course of Twelve Lectures. London: 1863. V. 53; 54
Mountaineering in 1861. a Vacation Tour. 1862. V. 53
Mountaineering in 1861. A Vacation Tour. London: 1862. V. 54

TYNER, J. W.
Our People and Where They Rest. Norman: 1969-78. V. 52

TYNESIDE NATURALISTS' FIELD CLUB
Transactions of the Tyneside Naturalists' Field Club 1846-1850. Newcastle-upon-Tyne: 1850-64. V. 47

TYPE and Alphabet. Lafayette: 1973. V. 50

TYPIS Sacrae Congregationis De Propoganda Fide, The Vatican. Regi Gustavo...Adfuerit Iterumque Ad Officinae Librariae Cognitionem...Litterarium formarum Omnigenearum Specimen Laeti Libentes Dedicant... Rome, the Vatican: 1784. V. 52

TYPOGRAPHIA, or the Printer's Instructor. London: 1824. V. 53

TYPOGRAPHIA...Ode On Printing... Roanoke: 1926. V. 48

TYPOGRAPHIA...Ode on Printing. Williamsburg: 1926. V. 54

A TYPOGRAPHICAL Commonplace-Book. 1932. V. 52
A TYPOGRAPHICAL Commonplace-Book. Paris: 1932. V. 48

TYPOGRAPHYCS. New York: 1994. V. 51

TYRELL, JAMES
Bibliotheca Politica: or an Enquiry into the Ancient Constitution of the English Government. London: 1693-94. V. 54

TYRRELL, FREDERICK
A Practical Work on the Diseases of the Eye, and Their Treatment Medically, Topically and by Operation. London: 1840. V. 47; 49; 53

TYRRELL, HENRY
England's Battles by Sea and Land from the Commencement of the Great French Revolution to the Present Time... 1858. V. 50
The History of the War with Russia... London: 1854-56. V. 50
The History of the War With Russia. London: 1855-58. V. 50
The History of the War With Russia... London and New York: 1860. V. 52

TYRRELL, JAMES
Bibliotheca Politica; or, an Enquiry Into the Ancient Constitution of the English Government... London: 1727. V. 48
Patriarcha non Monarcha. The Patriarch Unmonarch'd... London: 1681. V. 47

TYRRELL, JAMES W.
Across the Sub-Arctics of Canada: a Journey of 3200 Miles by Canoe... London: 1898. V. 49
Across the Sub-Arctics of Canada: a Journey of 3200 Miles by Canoe... Toronto: 1908. V. 50; 52
Coast and Harbour Surveys in Hudson Bay and Strait. Toronto: 1890. V. 48

TYRWHITT, J.
The Heart of the City: Towards the Humanization of Urban Life. New York: 1952. V. 50

TYRWHITT, R. ST. JOHN
A Hand Book of Pictorial Art... Oxford: 1868. V. 51

TYSON, EDWARD
Orang-Outang, Sive Homo Sylvestris; or, The Anatomy of a Pygmie Compared With That of a Monkey, An Ape and a Man. London: 1699. V. 50

TYSON, JAMES
The Cell Doctrine: Its History and Present State. Philadelphia: 1878. V. 49

TYSON, JAMES L.
Diary of a Physician in California... New York: 1850. V. 47; 50; 52

TYSON, PHILIP T.
Geology and Industrial Resources of California. Baltimore: 1851. V. 47; 48

TYSSOT DE PATOT, SIMON
The Travels and Adventures of James Massey. London: 1743. V. 48; 51

TYTLER, ALEXANDER FRASER
Elements of General History. Edinburgh: 1801. V. 54
Essay on the Principles of Translation. London: 1791. V. 50; 54

TYTLER, ALEXANDER FRASER continued
Memoirs of the Life and Writings of the Honourable Henry Home of Kames. Edinburgh: 1814. V. 54
Plan and Outlines of a Course of Lectures on Universal History, Ancient and Modern, Delivered in the University of Edinburgh. Edinburgh: 1782. V. 49; 50
Universal History from the Creation of the World to the Beginning of the Eighteenth Century. London: 1835. V. 54

TYTLER, JAMES
A Treatise on the Plague and Yellow Fever... Salem: 1799. V. 48; 50

TYTLER, PATRICK FRASER
England Under the Reigns of Edward VI and Mary. London: 1839. V. 49; 53
Historical View of the Progress of Discovery on the More Northern Coasts of America... 1832. V. 54
History of Scotland 1249-1603. Edinburgh: 1828-43. V. 53
History of Scotland 1249-1603. Edinburgh: 1841-43. V. 52
The History of Scotland from the Accession of Alexander III to the Union. Edinburgh: 1864. V. 54
Lives of Scottish Worthies. London: 1831. V. 54
Progress of Discovery on the More Northern Coasts of America. New York: 1833. V. 54

TYTLER, SARAH
Jane Austen and Her Works. London: 1880. V. 52
The Life of Her Most Gracious Majesty the Queen. London: 1885. V. 48

TYTLER, WILLIAM
An Historical And Clinical Enquiry Into the Evidence Produced by the Earls of Murray and Morton, Against Mary Queen of Scots. Edinburgh: 1760. V. 49; 53
An Inquiry, Historical and Critical, Into the Evidence of the Histories of Dr. Robertson and Mr. Hume, with Respect to that Evidence. London: 1790. V. 51

TZARA, TRISTAN
Le Signe de Vie. Paris: 1946. V. 47

U

UBALDI, GUIDO
Le Mechaniche. Venice: 1615. V. 54

UBALDINI, JOANNES PAULUS
Carmina Poetarvm Nobilivm. Milan: 1563. V. 48

UBALDIS, BALDUS DE
Lectura Super Prima et Secunda Parte Infortiati. (and) Lectura Super Digesto Novo. Lyons: 1498. V. 47; 49; 50; 53

UCHARD, MARIO
My Uncle Barbassou. London: 1888. V. 49

UCHIDA, D.
Photographs of Bird-Life in Japan. Tokyo & Osaka: 1930-31. V. 48

UCHIDA, S.
Birds of East Asia,. Tokyo: 1943-44. V. 48
Study of Birds from Foot of Fujiyama. Tokyo: 1927. V. 48

UDALL, WILLIAM
The Historie of the Life and Death of Mary Stuart, Queen of Scotland. London: 1636. V. 47; 48; 50

UDELL, JOHN
Incidents of Travel to California, Across the Great Plains; Together with the Return Trip through Central America and Jamaica. Jefferson: 1856. V. 47

UDRY, JANICE MAY
Let's Be Enemies. New York: 1961. V. 49

UEBELACKER, FRANZ
System des Karlsbader Sinters, Unter Vorstellung Schoner und Seltener Stucke Samt Einem Versuche Einer Mineralischen Geschichte Desselben. Erlangen: 1781. V. 47; 48

UGONIUS, FLAVIUS LEXIUS
Dialogo Della Vigilia, et del Sonno. Venice: 1562. V. 53; 54

UHLEMANN, MAXIMILIAN ADOLPH
Three Days in Memphis: or Sketches of the Public and Private Life of the Old Egyptians. Philadelphia: 1858. V. 49

UHLMAN, FRED
Reunion. London: 1971. V. 54

UKERS, WILLIAM H.
All About Coffee. New York: 1922. V. 52; 53
All About Coffee. New York: 1935. V. 48
All About Tea. New York: 1935. V. 50

UKIYO-E. "The Floating World". San Francisco: 1962. V. 47; 48; 54

ULANOV, BARRY
The Incredible Crosby. New York: 1948. V. 54

ULE, LOUIS
A Concordance to the Shakespeare Apocrypha. London: 1987. V. 51

ULLAO, ANTONIO
A Voyage to South America. London: 1772. V. 50

ULLMAN, JAMES RAMSEY
The Day on Fire. Cleveland: 1958. V. 54

ULLMAN, JOE
What's the Odds? Funny, True and Clean Stories of the Turf. New York: 1903. V. 47

ULLMANN, DANIEL
Address by Daniel Ullmann, LL.D., Before the Soldier's and Sailor's Union of the State of New York, on the Organization of Colored Troops and the Regeneration of the Office. Washington: 1868. V. 50

ULLOA, DON ANTONIO DE
A Voyage to South America... London: 1805. V. 48; 50

ULMANN, DORIS
The Appalachian Photographs of Doris Ulmann. Penland: 1971. V. 50; 51; 53
A Book of Portraits of the Faculty of the Medical Department of the Johns Hopkins University Baltimore. Baltimore: 1922. V. 50; 52
A Portrait Gallery of American Editors Being a group of XLIII Likenesses by Doris Ulmann. New York: 1925. V. 49

ULMO, GIOVANNI FRANCESCO
Francisci Ulmi...De Liene Libellus. Paris: 1578. V. 52

ULRICH, CAROLYN F.
Books and Printing. A Selected List of Periodicals 1800-1942. New York: 1943. V. 48

ULRICI, HERMANN
Shakespeare's Dramatic Art and His Relation to Calderon and Goethe. London: 1846. V. 51

ULRICK, ANTHONY
Fifty Reasons or Motives Why the Roman Catholick Apostolick Religion Out to be Preferr'd to All the Sects This Day in Christendom, and Which Induced His Most Serene Highness Anthony Ulrick, Duke of Brunswick and Lunenburg... Antwerp: 1715. V. 49

ULSTAD, PHILIPP
Coelum Philosophorum, Seu Liber de Secretis Naturae...ex Variis Autoribus Accurate Selectus, Varrisque Figuris Illustratus. Lyon: 1553. V. 47

UMFREVILLE, EDWARD
The Present State of Hudson's Bay. London: 1790. V. 47; 54

UMLAUFT, F.
The Alps. London: 1889. V. 48

UNCLE Buncle's Account of Tea in China. London: 1865. V. 50

UNCLE Tom in England. London: 1852. V. 49

THE UNCLE'S Present, a New Battledoor. Philadelphia: 1810. V. 50; 51

THE UNDEAD. Orange: 1984. V. 49

THE UNDER-Sheriff: Containing the Office and Duty of High-Sheriffs, Under-Sheriffs and Bailiffs... London: 1766. V. 51; 52

UNDERHILL, EDWARD BEAN
Alfred Saker: Missionary to Africa. London: 1884. V. 54

UNDERHILL, FRANCIS T.
Driving for Pleasure, or, the Harness Stable and Its Appointments. New York: 1896. V. 47
Driving for Pleasure, or, the Harness Stable and its Appointments. New York: 1897. V. 47; 51; 52

UNDERHILL, HAROLD A.
Plan-on-Frame Models and Scale Masting and Rigging. Glasgow: 1958. V. 52

UNDERRETNING Om det Tit Gamle soldaters...Fadaer-og Moderalose Soldater Borns. Copenhagen: 1773. V. 53

UNDERWOOD, CLARENCE F.
Love Songs Old and New. Indianapolis: 1907. V. 54

UNDERWOOD, E. ASHWORTH
Science Medicine and History. Essays on the Evolution of Scientific Thought and Medical Practice. London: 1953. V. 47; 50

UNDERWOOD, GEORGE C.
History of the Twenty-Sixth Regiment of North Carolina Troops in the Great War, 1861-65. Goldsboro: 1901. V. 47; 49

UNDERWOOD, J. C.
Gilbert; or, Then and Now. Philadelphia: 1902. V. 53

UNDERWOOD, LAMAR
Hunting the North Country. Clinton: 1982. V. 49

UNDERWOOD, LEON
Animalia. New York: 1926. V. 53
Leon Underwood His Wood Engravings. 1986. V. 51
Leon Underwood: His Wood Engravings. London: 1986. V. 53
The Siamese Cat. New York: 1928. V. 50

UNDERWOOD, PAUL A.
The Kariye Djami. New York: 1966. V. 50

THE UNEMBARRASSED Countenance, a New Ballad. London: 1746. V. 48

THE UNFORTUNATE Englishmen; or, a Faithful Narrative of the Distresses and Adventures of John Cockburn, and Five Other English Mariners... London: 1773. V. 47

THE UNFORTUNATE Lovers; the History of Argalus and Parthenia. London: 1760?. V. 48

UNGAR, GLADYS
The Divine Woman. New York: 1928. V. 51

UNGARELLI, LUIGI MARIA
Interpretatio Obeliscorum Urbis ad Gregorium XVI Pontificem Maximum Digesta per Aloisium Mariam Unarellium Sodallem Barnabitam. Romae: 1842. V. 49; 51

UNGER, DOUGLAS
Leaving the Land. New York: 1984. V. 50

UNGERER, TOMI
Fornicon. New York: 1969. V. 53
Horrible. 1960. V. 50

THE UNHAPPY Lovers; or, the History of James Welston, Gent. Together with His Voyages and Travels. London: 1732. V. 48

UNION CENTRAL CONSTRUCTION CO., DALLAS
Nuggets from an East Texas Gold Mine. 1905. V. 54

UNION COLONY OF COLORADO
First Annual Report of the Union Colony of Colorado, Including a History of the Town of Greeley... New York: 1871. V. 49

UNION Jack. Volume II. 1880-81. V. 53

THE UNION of the Roses, a Tale of the Fifteenth Century in Six Cantos, with Notes. London: 1821. V. 54

UNION PACIFIC RAILROAD
Annual Report. 1905-16. V. 54
Don't Go West in Search of a Home, Until You Have Obtained Full Particulars Regarding the Rich Farming Lands for Sale very Cheap by the Union Pacific Railway Co.... 2,000,000 Acres in Eastern Nebraska, in the Great Platte Valley, the Garden of the West. Cleveland: 1880's. V. 47
Guide to the Union Pacific Railroad Lands. 12,000,000 Acres... Omaha: 1870. V. 52
Guide to the Union Pacific Railroad Lands. 12,000,000 Acres... Omaha: 1873. V. 50
Hand-Buch Zu Den Union-Pacific Eisenbahn-Landereien 12,000,000...in Dem Staate Nebraska Und Den Territorien Colorado, Wyoming Und Utah... Omaha: 1871. V. 52
Reply of J. I. Blair, President of the Sioux City Branch Union Pacific Railroad Company. Yankton: 1868. V. 47
Report. 1891-97. V. 54
Report to the Stockholders of the Union Pacific Railway Company for the Year 1879. New York: 1880. V. 47
Report to the Stockholders of the Union Pacific Railway Company for the year 1883. New York: 1884. V. 47
The Resources and Attractions of Colorado. Council Bluffs: 1888. V. 52
The Resources and Attractions of Colorado. Chicago: 1889. V. 52
The Union Pacific R. R. Cheap Homes! Farms Nebraska, 3,000,000 Acres! Land Guide, 1880. Omaha: 1880. V. 52
The Union Pacific Railroad: A Trip Across the North American Continent from Omaha to Ogden. New York: 1871. V. 47; 51
The Union Pacific Railroad from Omaha, Nebraska, Across the Continent, Making With Its Connections, an Unbroken Line from the Atlantic to the Pacific Ocean... New York: 1867. V. 47
Union Pacific Railroad: The Great National Highway Between the Missouri River and California. The Direct Route to Colorado, Idaho, Utah, Montana, Nevada and California. Chicago: 1868. V. 47
The Union Pacific Railroad...Progress of Their Road, West from Omaha, Nebraska...540 Miles, Completed December, 1867. New York: 1868. V. 47

THE UNIQUE; a Series of Lives and Portraits. London: 1823. V. 47

UNITED BROTHERHOOD OF CARPENTERS & JOINERS OF AMERICA
By-laws of Butte Union No. 112 of the United Brotherhood of Carpenters and Joiners of America Organized Feb. 22, 1890. Butte: 1891. V. 52

UNITED DAUGHTERS OF THE CONFEDERACY
Confederate Women of Arkansas in the Civil War, 1861-'65. Little Rock: 1907. V. 47

UNITED NATIONS
Charter of the United Nations. New York: 1720. V. 51

UNITED STATES. ARCHITECT OF THE CAPITOL - 1899
Annual Report of the Architect of the United States... Washington: 1899. V. 52

UNITED STATES. ARMY - 1813
Military Laws and Rules and Regulations for the Armies of the United States. Washington: 1813. V. 52

UNITED STATES. ARMY - 1840
Official Army Register, 1840-1855. Washington: 1840-55. V. 49

UNITED STATES. ARMY - 1851
Annual Report of the Quartermaster General, of the Operations of the Quartermaster's Department, for the Fiscal Year Ending on the 30th June, 1850. Washington: 1851. V. 52

UNITED STATES. ARMY - 1866
Official Army Register for 1866 and 1867. Washington: 1866/67. V. 52

UNITED STATES. ARMY - 1886
Annual Report of Brigadier General Nelson A. Miles, U.S. Army, Commanding Department of Arizona, 1886. Albuquerque: 1886. V. 52

THE UNITED States Army and Navy 1776-1899. Akron: 1899. V. 50

UNITED STATES. ARMY CORPS OF ENGINEERS - 1872
Preliminary Report Concerning Explorations and Surveys Principally in Nevada and Arizona. Washington: 1872. V. 49

UNITED STATES. ARMY CORPS OF TOPOGRAPHICAL ENGINEERS
An Examination By the Direction of the Hon. Jefferson Davis, Secretary of War, of the Reports of Explorations for Railroad Routes from the Mississippi to the Pacific... Washington: 1855. V. 47

UNITED STATES. ARMY MEDICAL MUSEUM - 1866
Catalogue (sic) Prepared Under the Direction of the Surgeon General. Washington: 1866-67. V. 49

UNITED STATES. BOARD ON CONSTRUCTION OF PACIFIC RAILROAD
Report of Board Convened to Determine a Standard for Construction of the Pacific Railroad, Made to Honorable James Harlan, Secretary of the Interior, Feb. 24, 1866, with Accompanying Documents. Washington: 1866. V. 47

UNITED STATES. BUREAU OF AMERICAN ETHNOLOGY - 1883
Second Annual Report of the Bureau of Ethnology to the Secretary of the Smithsonian Institution 1880-81. Washington: 1883. V. 50

UNITED STATES. BUREAU OF AMERICAN ETHNOLOGY - 1888
Sixth Annual Report of the Bureau of American Ethnology to the Secretary of the Smithsonian Inst. 1884-25. Washington: 1888. V. 52

UNITED STATES. BUREAU OF AMERICAN ETHNOLOGY - 1891
Eight Annual Report. 1886-87. Washington: 1891. V. 54
Seventh Annual Report...1885-86. Washington: 1891. V. 52

UNITED STATES. BUREAU OF AMERICAN ETHNOLOGY - 1892
Fourteenth Annual Report of the Bureau... Washington: 1896. V. 54

UNITED STATES. BUREAU OF AMERICAN ETHNOLOGY - 1893
Tenth Annual Report of the Bureau of Ethnology to the Secretary of the Smithsonian Inst. 1888-89. Washington: 1893. V. 52

UNITED STATES. BUREAU OF AMERICAN ETHNOLOGY - 1894
Eleventh Annual Report of the...1889-'90. Washington: 1894. V. 48; 52
Twelfth Annual Report of the Bureau of American Ethnology.... Washington: 1894. V. 52

UNITED STATES. BUREAU OF AMERICAN ETHNOLOGY - 1896
Fourteenth Annual Report of the Bureau of Ethnology to the Secretary of the Smithsonian Inst. 1892-93. Washington: 1896. V. 48; 52

UNITED STATES. BUREAU OF AMERICAN ETHNOLOGY - 1899
Eighteenth Annual Report of the Bureau of American Ethnology to the Secretary of the Smithsonian Institution 1896-97. Washington: 1899. V. 47; 53

UNITED STATES. BUREAU OF AMERICAN ETHNOLOGY - 1904
Twenty-Second Annual Report of the Bureau of American Ethnology to the Secretary of the Smithsonian Institution 1900-1901. Part I (only). Washington: 1904. V. 52

UNITED STATES. BUREAU OF AMERICAN ETHNOLOGY - 1912
Twenty-Eighth Annual Report of the Bureau of American Ethnology to the Secretary of the Smithsonian Institution 1906-1907. Washington: 1912. V. 52

UNITED STATES. BUREAU OF AMERICAN ETHNOLOGY - 1915
Thirteenth Annual Report. Washington: 1915. V. 54

UNITED STATES. BUREAU OF AMERICAN ETHNOLOGY - 1916
Thirty First Annual Report 1909-10. Washington: 1916. V. 54

UNITED STATES. BUREAU OF AMERICAN ETHNOLOGY - 1922
Thirty-Fourth Annual Report of the.... Washington: 1922. V. 52

UNITED STATES. BUREAU OF AMERICAN ETHNOLOGY - 1928
Forty-First Annual Report of the Bureuan of American Ethnology to the Secretary of the Smithsonian Inst. 1919-1924. Washington: 1928. V. 52

UNITED STATES. BUREAU OF INDIAN AFFAIRS - 1866
Report of the Commissioner of Indian Affairs for the Year 1866. Washington: 1866. V. 53

UNITED STATES. CENSUS OFFICE - 1791
Return of the Whole Number of Persons Within the Several Districts of the United States. Philadelphia: 1791. V. 47

UNITED STATES. CENSUS OFFICE - 1872
Ninth Census. Washington: 1872. V. 47

UNITED STATES. CENSUS OFFICE - 1880
Report of the Manufactures of the United States at the Tenth Census (June 1, 1880). Washington: 1883. V. 47

UNITED STATES. CENSUS OFFICE - 1883
Statistics of the Population of the United States at the Tenth Census (June 1, 1880). Washington: 1883. V. 47

UNITED STATES. CENSUS OFFICE - 1885
Reports of the Water-Power of the United States (Vol. XVI, Part I-II in 2 volumes). Washington: 1885. V. 47

UNITED STATES. CENSUS OFFICE - 1886
Report of the Mortality and Vital Statistics of the United States as Returned at the Tenth Census (June 1, 1880). Part II. Washington: 1886. V. 53

UNITED STATES. CENSUS OFFICE - 1894
Report on Indians Taxed and Indians Not Taxed in the United States (Except Alaska) at the Eleventh Census, 1890. Washington: 1894. V. 54

UNITED STATES. CENSUS OFFICE - 1896
Report on vital and Social Statistics in the United States at the Eleventh Census: 1890. Part I, Analysis and Rare Tables. Washington: 1896. V. 47

UNITED STATES. CIRCUIT COURT - 1872
Proceedings in the Ku Klux Trials, at Columbia, S.C. Columbia: 1872. V. 50

UNITED STATES. COAST SURVEY - 1850
Report of Prof. Alexander D. Bache, Superintendent of the Coast Survey Showing the Progress of that Work for the Year Ending October 1850. Washington: 1850. V. 47

UNITED STATES. CONGRESS - 1782
Journals of Congress, Containing the Proceedings from January 1, 1779 to January 1, 1780. Volume V. Philadelphia: 1782. V. 47

UNITED STATES. CONGRESS - 1783
Addresses and Recommendations to the States. By the United States in Congress Assembled. Philadelphia: 1783. V. 47

UNITED STATES. CONGRESS - 1787
Journals of Congress and of the United States in Congress Assembled, for the Year 1781. Volume VII. New York: 1787. V. 47

UNITED STATES. CONGRESS - 1791
Laws of the United States of America. New York: 1791. V. 50

UNITED STATES. CONGRESS - 1792
A Bill for Registering Ships or Vessels, for Regulating Those Employed in the Coasting, Trade and Fisheries, and for Other Purposes. Philadelphia: 1792. V. 50

UNITED STATES. CONGRESS - 1800
Journals of Congress: Containing Their Proceedings from September 5, 1774 to January 1, 1776 (-November 5, 1787 to November 3, 1788). Chiefly Philadelphia: 1800-1801. V. 47; 50

UNITED STATES. CONGRESS - 1823
Journals of the American Congress: from 1774 to 1788. Washington: 1823. V. 50

UNITED STATES. CONGRESS - 1824
Congressional Directory of the Second Session of the Eighteenth Congress. Washington: 1824. V. 48

UNITED STATES. CONGRESS - 1848
Acts and Resolutions Passed at the First Session of the Thirtieth Congress of the United States. Washington: 1848. V. 50

UNITED STATES. CONGRESS - 1850
Pacific Rail-Road. A Review of the Reports of the Committees of the Senate and House of Representatives of the Last Session. New Orleans: 1850. V. 47

UNITED STATES. CONGRESS - 1860
Difficulties on Southwestern Frontier. 3th Cong. 1st. Sess. Ex. Doc. 52. Washington: 1860. V. 47

UNITED STATES. CONGRESS - 1875
The Pacific Railroad. Congressional Proceedings in the Thirty-seventh, Thirty-eighth and Forty-first Congresses. West Chester: 1875. V. 47

UNITED STATES. CONGRESS - 1911
Investigation of the Department of the Interior and the Bureau of Forestry. Washington: 1911. V. 51

UNITED STATES. CONGRESS. HOUSE OF REPRESENTATIVES - 1812
Report, or Manifesto on the Causes and Reasons of War with Great Britain. Presented to the House of Representatives by the Committee of Foreign Relations, June 3, 1812. Washington: 1812. V. 52

UNITED STATES. CONGRESS. HOUSE OF REPRESENTATIVES - 1829
Exposition and Protest, Reported by the Special Committee of the House of Representatives, on the Tariff, Read and Ordered to Be Printed Dec. 19th, 1828. Columbia: 1829. V. 49

UNITED STATES. CONGRESS. HOUSE OF REPRESENTATIVES - 1838
Bridge at Wheeling, Virginia: Report No. 993. Washington: 1838. V. 51

UNITED STATES. CONGRESS. HOUSE OF REPRESENTATIVES - 1839
From Document No. 229 of the House of Representatives, 3d Session 25th Congress of the U.S. Containing Allegations of Fraud 'In Relation to the Settlement of the Claims of the Half-Breed Relatives of the Winnebagoe Indians', In Which Case the... Harrisburg: 1839. V. 50

UNITED STATES. CONGRESS. HOUSE OF REPRESENTATIVES - 1845
...Joint Resolution Declaring the Terms on Which Congress Will Admit Texas Into the Union as a State. Washington: 1845. V. 47

UNITED STATES. CONGRESS. HOUSE OF REPRESENTATIVES - 1848
A Bill to Set Apart and Sell to Asa Whitney, of New York, a Portion of the Public Lands, to Enable Him to Construct a Railroad from Lake Michigan to the Pacific Ocean. Washington: 1848. V. 47

Thirtieth Congress - First Session. Report no. 230 (to Accompany Bill H.R. No. 224). (House of Representatives). Alabama, Florida and Georgia Railroad. Washington: 1848. V. 47

UNITED STATES. CONGRESS. HOUSE OF REPRESENTATIVES - 1852
A Bill to Set Apart and Sell to Asa Whitney, of New York, a Portion of the Public Lands, to Enable Him to Construct a Railroad from Lake Michigan or the Mississippi River to the Pacific Ocean. Washington: 1852. V. 47

UNITED STATES. CONGRESS. HOUSE OF REPRESENTATIVES - 1854
An Amendment to Provide for the Establishment of Railroad and Telegraphic Communication Between the Atlantic States and the Pacific Ocean, and for Other Purposes. Washington: 1854. V. 47

UNITED STATES. CONGRESS. HOUSE OF REPRESENTATIVES - 1860
Reports of the Majority and Minority of the Select Committee on the Pacific Railroad. Washington: 1860. V. 47

UNITED STATES. CONGRESS. HOUSE OF REPRESENTATIVES - 1861
Reports of the Select Committee of Thirty-Three on the Disturbed Condition of the Country. Washington: 1861. V. 53

UNITED STATES. CONGRESS. HOUSE OF REPRESENTATIVES - 1872
Report of the Commissioners and Evidence Taken by the Committee on Mines and Mining of the House of Representatives of the United States, In Regard to the Sutro Tunnel... Washington: 1872. V. 52

UNITED STATES. CONGRESS. HOUSE OF REPRESENTATIVES - 1873
Report of the Select Committee to Investigate the Alledged Credit Mobilier Bribery, Made to the House of Representatives, February 18, 1873. Washington: 1873. V. 47

UNITED STATES. CONGRESS. HOUSE OF REPRESENTATIVES - 1875
43rd Congress, 2d Session. H. Res. 142. Printer's No. 4454. Washington: 1875. V. 49

UNITED STATES. CONGRESS. HOUSE OF REPRESENTATIVES - 1876
Texas Frontier Troubles. Washington: 1876. V. 49

UNITED STATES. CONGRESS. HOUSE OF REPRESENTATIVES - 1878
Committee on Military Affairs. Testimony Taken by the Committee...in Relation to the Texas Border Troubles. Washington: 1878. V. 49

House Committee on Pacific Railroad, Discussion of the Pro-Rata Bill. Argument of...in Behalf of the Lines Connecting with the Union Pacific Railroad, at Council Bluffs. Tuesday, March 5, 1878. Washington City: 1878. V. 47

UNITED STATES. CONGRESS. HOUSE OF REPRESENTATIVES - 1889
Investigation of the Fur-Seal and Other Fisheries of Alaska. Report from the Committee on Merchant Marine and Fisheries of the House of Representatives. Washington: 1889. V. 50

UNITED STATES. CONGRESS. HOUSE OF REPRESENTATIVES - 1890
The Executive Documents of the House of Representatives for the First Session of the Fifty-First Congress, 1889-90. Washington: 1890. V. 47

UNITED STATES. CONGRESS. HOUSE OF REPRESENTATIVES - 1893
The Executive Documents of the House of Representatives fro the First Session of the Fifty-Third Congress. 1893. Washington: 1893. V. 47

UNITED STATES. CONGRESS. HOUSE OF REPRESENTATIVES - 1903
Appendix II. Foreign Relations of the United States, 1902. United States vs. Mexico. Washington: 1903. V. 47

UNITED STATES. CONGRESS. HOUSE OF REPRESENTATIVES - 1909
Atlas Illustrating Report of March 20, 1909, of Board of Examination and Survey of Mississippi River Creased by Act of Congress Approved March 2, 1907. Washington: 1909. V. 47

UNITED STATES. CONGRESS. SENATE - 1845
A Bill to Provide for the Annexation of Texas to the United States and to Restore the Ancient Limits of the Republic. Washington: 1845. V. 47

UNITED STATES. CONGRESS. SENATE - 1846
A Bill to Set Apart a Portion of the Public Lands with Which to Construct a Railroad from Lake Michigan to the Pacific Ocean. New York: 1846. V. 47

UNITED STATES. CONGRESS. SENATE - 1848
In the Senate of the United States July 13, 1848...Mr. Borland, Made the Following Report (to Accompany Bill S. No. 253), the Committee on Public Lands, to whom was referred... Washington: 1848. V. 47

UNITED STATES. CONGRESS. SENATE - 1851
Report of the Secretary of War, Communicating a Copy of W. H. Sidell's Survey of a Route for a Railroad from the Great Bend, on Red River, to Providence on the Mississippi River. Feb. 28, 1851. Washington: 1851. V. 47

UNITED STATES. CONGRESS. SENATE - 1852
Executive Documents Printed by Order of the Senate of the United States During the First Session of the Thirty-Second Congress, 1851-52. Washington: 1852. V. 47

UNITED STATES. CONGRESS. SENATE - 1853
A Bill to Provide for the Construction of a Military and Postal Railroad through the Territories of the United States Lying Between the Atlantic States and the State of California. Washington: 1853. V. 47

UNITED STATES. CONGRESS. SENATE - 1854
Report of the Select Committee of the Senate of the United States on the Sickness and Mortality on Board Emigrant Ships. Washington: 1854. V. 50; 51; 52; 54

UNITED STATES. CONGRESS. SENATE - 1856
Reports of Explorations and Surveys to Ascertain the Most Practicable and Economical Route for a Railroad from the Mississippi River to the Pacific Ocean...in 1853-54. Volume 4. Washington: 1856. V. 50

UNITED STATES. CONGRESS. SENATE - 1867
A Bill to Aid in the Construction of the San Francisco Central Pacific Railroad. Washington: 1867. V. 47

UNITED STATES. CONGRESS. SENATE - 1869
In Compliance with a Resolution of the Senate of Dec. 14, 1868 Information in Relation to the Late Indian Battle on the Washita River. Washington: 1869. V. 54

UNITED STATES. CONGRESS. SENATE - 1870
Senate Bill No. 469. Will Congress Preserve Good Faith with Central Branch Union Pacific R.R. Company?. Washington: 1870. V. 47

UNITED STATES. CONGRESS. SENATE - 1880
Removal of the Ponca Indians...(with) Removal of the Northern Cheyennes. Washington: 1880. V. 50

UNITED STATES. CONGRESS. SENATE - 1889
California, Oregon and Nevada State War Claims. Washington: 1889-94. V. 53

UNITED STATES. CONGRESS. SENATE - 1900
Compilation of Narratives of Exploration in Alaska. Washington: 1900. V. 50

UNITED STATES. CONGRESS. SENATE - 1904
Conditions in Alaska. Report of the Subcommittee of Committee on Territories Appoiinted to Investigate Conditions in Alaska. Washington: 1904. V. 53

UNITED STATES. CONGRESS. SENATE - 1906
Proceedings Before the Committe on Privileges and Elections of the United States Senate in the Matter of the Protests Against the Right of Hon. Reed Smoot, a Senator from the State of Utah, to Hold His Seat. Washington: 1906. V. 52

UNITED STATES. CONSTITUTION - 1783
Constitutions des Treize Etats-Unis de l'Amerique. Philadelphia & Paris: 1783. V. 48; 50

UNITED STATES. CONSTITUTION - 1800
The Constitutions of the United States, According to the Latest Amendments: to Which are Prefixed the Declaration of Independence, and the Federal Constitution, with the Amendments. Philadelphia: 1800. V. 53

UNITED STATES. CONSTITUTION - 1804
The Constitutions of the United States, According to the Latest Amendments. Philadelphia: 1804. V. 51

UNITED STATES. CONSTITUTION - 1811
The Constitutions of the United States, According to the Latest Amendments: To Which are Prefixed, the Declaration of Independence... Gettysburg: 1811. V. 47

UNITED STATES. CONSTITUTION - 1828
The Constitution of the United States of America: the Rules of the Senate and of the House of Representatives: with (Thomas) Jefferson's Manual. Washington: 1828. V. 48

UNITED STATES. CONSTITUTION - 1925
The Constitution of the United States and Related Articles. 1925. V. 53
The Constitution of the United States and Related Articles. London: 1925. V. 54

UNITED STATES. CONSTITUTION - 1987
Constitution of the United States of America. 1987. V. 52
The Constitution of the United States of America. San Francisco: 1987. V. 47; 48; 49; 53

UNITED STATES. CONSTITUTIONAL CONVENTION - 1788
Debates, Resolutions and Other Proceedings, of the Convention of the Commonwealth of Massachusetts Convened at Boston, on the 9th of Jan., 1788...for the Purpose of Assenting to and Ratifying the Constitution Recommended by the Grand Federal... Boston: 1788. V. 53

UNITED STATES. CONSTITUTIONAL CONVENTION - 1805
Debates and Other Proceedings of the Convention of Virginia, Convened at Richmond, on Monday the Second Day of June, 1788, for the Purpose of Deliberating on the Constitution Recommended by the Grand Federal Convention. Richmond: 1805. V. 53

UNITED STATES. CONTINENTAL CONGRESS - 1774
Extracts from the Votes and Proceedings of the American Continental Congress, Held at Philadelphia, on the Fifth of September, 1744. Philadelphia: 1774. V. 47

UNITED STATES. CORPS OF TOPOGRAHICAL ENGINEERS - 1848
Report of the Secretary of War Communicating...A Report and Map of the Examination of New Mexico, Made by Lieutenant J. W. Abert... Washington: 1848. V. 47

UNITED STATES. COURT OF CLAIMS - 1863
In the Court of Claims. No. 1882. William S. Grant vs. the United States. Washington: 1863-64. V. 52

UNITED STATES. DECLARATION OF INDEPENDENCE - 1970
The Declaration of Independence. Worcester: 1970. V. 47

UNITED STATES. DEPARTMENT OF AGRICULTURE - 1893
A Report on Irrigation and Cultivation of the Soil Thereby. Washington: 1893. V. 47

UNITED STATES. DEPARTMENT OF AGRICULTURE - 1900
Report on the Big Trees of California. Washington: 1900. V. 54

UNITED STATES. DEPARTMENT OF AGRICULTURE - 1902
A Report of the Secretary of Agriculture in Relation to the Forests, Rivers and Mountains of the Southern Appalachian Region. Washington: 1902. V. 47; 52

UNITED STATES. DEPARTMENT OF AGRICULTURE - 1932
Forest Service. Southern Forest Experiment Station. Occasional Papers 27-28. New Orleans: 1932-38. V. 50

UNITED STATES. DEPARTMENT OF AGRICULTURE - 1933
Descriptions of Types of Principal American Varities of Cabbage, Carrots, Garden Peas, Onions, Spinach, Tomatoes. Washington: 1933-41. V. 54

UNITED STATES. DEPARTMENT OF INTERIOR - 1850
Report of the Secretary of the Interior. Information in Relation to the Operations of the Commission Appointed to Run and Mark the Boundary Between the United States and Mexico... Washington: 1850. V. 47; 49

UNITED STATES. DEPARTMENT OF INTERIOR - 1851
Report of the Secretary of the Interior Communicating a Copy of the Report of William Carey Jones, Special Agent to Examine the Subject of land Titles in California. Washington: 1851. V. 50

UNITED STATES. DEPARTMENT OF INTERIOR - 1852
Report of the Secretary of the Interior...Information in Relation to the Commission Appointed to Run and Mark the Boundaries Between the United States and Mexico. Washington: 1852. V. 47

UNITED STATES. DEPARTMENT OF INTERIOR - 1855
Report of the Interior...January 22, 1855. Communicates a Report and Map of A.B. Gray, Relative to the Mexican Boundary... Washington: 1855. V. 47

UNITED STATES. DEPARTMENT OF INTERIOR - 1859
Pacific Wagon Roads. Letter from the Secretary of the Interior Transmitting a Report Upon the Several Wagon Roads Constructed Under the Direction of the Interior Department. Washington: 1859. V. 47

UNITED STATES. DEPARTMENT OF INTERIOR - 1867
Report of the Secretary of the Interior, Communicating...Reports of the Government Directors of the Union Pacific Railroad Company. Washington: 1867. V. 47

UNITED STATES. DEPARTMENT OF INTERIOR - 1876
Department of the Interior Land Office. In the Matter of the Applications for Patents for Mining Claims Situated in Townships 16 and 17 North, Range 21, East, Mount Diablo Meridian... New York: 1876. V. 49

UNITED STATES. DEPARTMENT OF INTERIOR - 1879
Atlantic Local Coast Pilot. Sub-Division 6. Cape Ann to Cohasset. Washington: 1879. V. 47

UNITED STATES. DEPARTMENT OF INTERIOR - 1882
Letter from the Secretary of the Interior...Concerning a Tract of Land in Colorado Patented to Charles Beaubien. Washington: 1882. V. 52

UNITED STATES. DEPARTMENT OF INTERIOR - 1883
Letter of the Secretary of Interior...in Relation to the Leavenworth, Pawnee, and Western Railroad. Washington: 1883. V. 47

UNITED STATES. DEPARTMENT OF INTERIOR - 1903
Annual Reports of the Department of the Interior for the Fiscal Year Ending June 30, 1902. Indian Affairs. Part II. Commission to the Five Civilized Tribes. Indian Inspector for Indian Territory. Indian Contracts. Washington: 1903. V. 47

UNITED STATES. DEPARTMENT OF INTERIOR - 1909
Survey of Mississippi Atlas. Volume 2. Washington: 1909. V. 47

UNITED STATES. DEPARTMENT OF INTERIOR - 1917
Negro Education. A Study of the Private and High Schools for Coloured People in the United States. Washington: 1917. V. 50

UNITED STATES. DEPARTMENT OF THE GULF - 1864
Memorandum. Headquarters, Department of the Gulf, New Orleans, February 15th 1864. 1. Heads of Staff Departments, with Their Assistants...2. Aides-de-Camp to the Major General Commanding... New Orleans?: 1864?. V. 47

UNITED STATES. DISTRICT COURT - 1858
District Court of the United States. Northern District of California. Opinion, Delivered by His Honor, Ogden Hoffman, U.S. District Judge. The United States vs. Jose Y. Limantour. San Francisco: 1858. V. 49

UNITED STATES. DISTRICT COURT - 1913
In the District Court of the United States, Western District of New York. The United States of America v. Eastman Kodak Company of New York, Eastman Kodak Company of New Jersey and Others. New York: 1913. V. 50

UNITED STATES. GENERAL LAND OFFICE - 1849
Report of the...Commissioner of the General Land Office. December 14, 1848. Washington: 1849. V. 47

UNITED STATES. GENERAL LAND OFFICE - 1869
Circular (No. 26) from the General Land Office, Showing the Manner of Proceeding to Obtain Title to Public Lands...Issued March 10, 1869. Washington: 1869. V. 52

UNITED STATES. GENERAL LAND OFFICE - 1871
Abstract of Patented lands...Arranged by County...From January 1, 1867 to August 31, 1871, Divided into Yearly Parts. Austin: 1871. V. 53

UNITED STATES. GENERAL LAND OFFICE - 1878
Abstract of Land Titles Comprising the Titles, Patented and Located Lands in the State; Volume I. Galveston: 1878. V. 53

UNITED STATES. GENERAL LAND OFFICE - 1882
Letter from the Secretary of the Interior, Transmitting...the Report of the Commissioner of the General Land Office Upon the Survey of the United States and Texas Boundary Commission. Washington: 1882. V. 52

UNITED STATES. GEOGRAPHICAL SURVEY - 1878
Annual Report Upon the Geographical Surveys...In the States and Territories of California, Colorado, Kansas, Nebraska, Nevada, Orgeon, Texas, Arizona, Idaho, Montana, New Mexico, Utah, Washington and Wyoming. Washington: 1878. V. 47

UNITED STATES. GEOGRAPHICAL SURVEY - 1879
Report Upon the U.S. Geographical Surveys West of the One Hundredth Meridian, Etc. Volume VII. Washington: 1879. V. 54

UNITED STATES. GEOLOGICAL & GEOGRAPHICAL SURVEY - 1878
Maps and Panoramas. Twelfth Annual Report of the United States Geological and Geographical Survey of the Territories. Washington: 1878. V. 47
Tenth Annual Report of the United States Geological and Geographical Survey of the Territories, Embracing Colorado and Parts of Adjacent Territories. Washington: 1878. V. 47

UNITED STATES. GEOLOGICAL & GEOGRAPHICAL SURVEY - 1879
Eleventh Annual Report of the United States Geological and Geographical Survey of the Territories, Embracing Idaho and Wyoming, Being a Report of Progress of the Exploration for the Year 1877. Washington: 1879. V. 47

UNITED STATES. GEOLOGICAL SURVEY - 1852
Report of a Geological Survey of Wisconsin, Iowa and Minnesota; and Incidentally of a Portion of Nebraska Territory. Philadelphia: 1852. V. 47

UNITED STATES. GEOLOGICAL SURVEY - 1855
The First and Second Annual Reports of the Geological Survey of Missouri. Jefferson City: 1855. V. 47

UNITED STATES. GEOLOGICAL SURVEY - 1872
Preliminary Report of the United States Geological Survey of Montana and Portions of Adjacent Territories... Washington: 1872. V. 47

UNITED STATES. GEOLOGICAL SURVEY - 1873
Sixth Annual Report of the U.S.G.S. of the Territories. Washington: 1873. V. 53

UNITED STATES. GEOLOGICAL SURVEY - 1876
(Eighth) Annual Report of the United States Geological and Geographical Survey of the Territories, Embracing Colorado and Parts of Adjacent Territories. Washington: 1876. V. 47

UNITED STATES. GEOLOGICAL SURVEY - 1877
Ninth Annual Report of the United States Geological and Geographical Survey of the Territories, Embracing Colorado and Parts of Adjacent Territories for the Year 1875. Washington: 1877. V. 47

UNITED STATES. GEOLOGICAL SURVEY - 1880
First Annual Report of the United States Geological Survey to the Hon. Carl Schurz, Secretary of the Interior. Washington: 1880. V. 47

Second Annual Report of the United States Geological Survey to the Secretary of the Interior, 1800-1801. Washington: 1882. V. 51; 53

UNITED STATES. GEOLOGICAL SURVEY - 1884
Fifth Annual Report of the United States Geological Survey. Washington: 1884. V. 48

UNITED STATES. LAWS, STATUTES, ETC. - 1791
Acts Passed at the First (Second, Third) Session of the Congress of the United States. Philadelphia: 1791. V. 54

UNITED STATES. LAWS, STATUTES, ETC. - 1794
Act Making Appropriations for the Support of the Military Establishment of the United States for the Year One Thousand Seven Hundred Ninety-Four. Philadelphia: 1794. V. 52

UNITED STATES. LAWS, STATUTES, ETC. - 1796
The Laws of the United States of America. Philadelphia: 1796. V. 47

UNITED STATES. LAWS, STATUTES, ETC. - 1797
Acts Passed at the First Session of the Fifth Congress of the United States of America: Begun and Held at the City of Philadelphia, the in the State of Pennsylvania, on Monday the Fifteenth of May, 1797 and of the Independence of the United States... Philadelphia: 1797. V. 47

UNITED STATES. LAWS, STATUTES, ETC. - 1798
The Laws of the United States of America. (with) Act Passed at the First, Second and Third Sessions of Congress. Philadelphia: 1796/98?. V. 53

UNITED STATES. LAWS, STATUTES, ETC. - 1799
Acts Passed at the Third Session of the Fifth Congress of the U.S. and the Constitution of the U.S. of America: as Prosposed by the Convention, Held at Philadelphia, Sept. 17, 1787... Philadelphia: 1799. V. 51

UNITED STATES. LAWS, STATUTES, ETC. - 1803
Acts Passed At the First Session of the Eighth Congress of the United States of America, Begun and Held at the City of Washington, in the District of Columbia, on Monday the Seventeenth of October, in the Year 1803... Washington: 1803. V. 49

UNITED STATES. LAWS, STATUTES, ETC. - 1810
Acts Passed at the First Session of the Eleventh Congress of the United States. (with) Acts Passed at the Second Session. 1810. V. 53

UNITED STATES. LAWS, STATUTES, ETC. - 1812
An Act, Establishing Rules and Articles for the Government of the Armies of the United States; with the Regulations of the War Department. Albany: 1812-13. V. 47; 50

UNITED STATES. LAWS, STATUTES, ETC. - 1816
Acts of the Fourteenth Congress of the United States, Passed at the First Session...James Madison, President. Washington: 1816. V. 51

UNITED STATES. LAWS, STATUTES, ETC. - 1818
Acts Passed at the First Session of the Fifteenth Congress of the United States. Washington: 1818. V. 51

UNITED STATES. LAWS, STATUTES, ETC. - 1821
Acts Passed at the Second Session of the Sixteenth Congress of the United States. Washington: 1821. V. 49

UNITED STATES. LAWS, STATUTES, ETC. - 1832
An Act to Provide for Liquidating and Paying Certain Claims of the State of Virginia. Washington: 1832. V. 52

UNITED STATES. LAWS, STATUTES, ETC. - 1850
Acts and Resolutions Passed at the First Session of the Thirty-First Congress of the United States;... Washington: 1850. V. 49

UNITED STATES. LAWS, STATUTES, ETC. - 1862
An Act to Aid in the Construction of a Railroad and Telegraph Line from the Missouri River to the Pacific Ocean. Washington: 1862. V. 47

Laws Relating to the Direct and Excise Taxes, Passed During the First and Second Sessions of the Thirty-Seventh Congress. Washington: 1862. V. 49

UNITED STATES. LAWS, STATUTES, ETC. - 1863
An Act to Grant the Proceeds of the Sales of Certain Public Lands to Aid in the Construction of a Northern Pacific Railroad. Washington. V. 47

UNITED STATES. LAWS, STATUTES, ETC. - 1867
An Act to Aid in the Construction of a Railroad & Telegraph Line from the Missouri River to the Pacific Ocean. Approved July 1, 1862. New York: 1867. V. 47

UNITED STATES. LAWS, STATUTES, ETC. - 1877
Acts of Congress Relating to the Union Pacific Railroad and Branches. Compiled December 1877. Washington: 1877. V. 47

UNITED STATES. LIBRARY OF CONGRESS - 1802
Catalogue of Books, Maps and Charts Belonging to the Library of the Two Houses of Congress. Washington City: 1802. V. 48

UNITED STATES. LIBRARY OF CONGRESS - 1901
A List of Maps of America in the Library of Congress. Washington: 1901. V. 52

UNITED STATES. LIBRARY OF CONGRESS - 1909
List of Geographical Atlases in the Library of Congress with Bibliographical Notes. Washington: 1909. V. 47

A List of Geographical Atlases in the Library of Congress with Bibliographical Notes. Washington: 1909-20. V. 53

UNITED STATES. LIBRARY OF CONGRESS - 1912
The Lowery Collection. A Descriptive List of maps of the Spanish Possessions Within the Present Limits of the United States 1502-1820. Washington: 1912. V. 51

UNITED STATES. LIBRARY OF CONGRESS - 1914
List of Geographical Atlases in the Library of Congress with Bibliographical Notes - Volume 3 and 4. Washington: 1914/20. V. 52

UNITED STATES. LIBRARY OF CONGRESS - 1975
Children's Books in the Rare Book Division of the Library of Congress. Totowa: 1975. V. 52

UNITED STATES. LIBRARY OF CONGRESS - 1995
A List of Geographical Atlases in the Library of Congress... 1995. V. 54

A List of Geographical Atlases in the Library of Congress. Mansfield: 1995. V. 54

UNITED STATES NATIONAL CENTER FOR HEALTH STATISTICS
The International Classification of Diseases 9th Revision Clinical Modification Icd.9.Cm. Volume 1: Diseases: Tabular List. 2: Diseases: Alphabetic List. 3: Procedures: Tabular List and Alphabetic Index. Ann Arbor: 1978. V. 52

UNITED STATES. NATIONAL LIBRARY OF MEDICINE - 1967
A Catalogue of Sixteenth Century Printed Books in the National Library of Medicine. Bethesda: 1967. V. 51

UNITED STATES. NATIONAL LIBRARY OF MEDICINE - 1979
A Short Title Catalogue of Eighteenth Century Printed Books in the National Library of Medicine. Bethesda: 1979. V. 51

UNITED STATES NAVAL ASTRONOMICAL EXPEDITION, 1849-1852.
The U.S. Naval Astronomical Expedition to the Southern Hemisphere, During the Years 1849-52. Washington: 1855. V. 47; 52; 53

UNITED STATES NAVAL ASTRONOMICAL EXPEDITION, 1849-1852
The U.S. Naval Astronomical Expedition to the Southern Hemisphere, during the Years 1849-52. Volume II: The Andes and the Pampas. Washington: 1855. V. 50

UNITED STATES. NAVY DEPARTMENT
Letter from the Secretary of the Navy...Report Lt. G. B. Harber, USN Concerning the Search for the Missing Persons of the Jeanette Expedition and the Transportation of the Remains of Lt. Commander Delong and Companions to the U.S. 48th Cong... Washington. V. 50

UNITED STATES. NAVY DEPARTMENT - 1811
Letter From the Secretary of the Navy, Transmitting Sundry Documents Exhibiting Certain Preliminary Experiments Which Have Been Made in the City and Harbor of New York, in Conformity With the Act of Congress, Entitled "Act Making an Appropriation...". Washington: 1811. V. 50

UNITED STATES. NAVY DEPARTMENT - 1844
Report of the Navy Department of the United States, on American Coals Applicable to Steam Navigation and to Other Purposes. Washington: 1844. V. 53

UNITED STATES. NAVY DEPARTMENT - 1865
Letter of the Secretary of the Navy, Communicating the Report of the Commission Appointed Under the Joint Resolution of Congress, Approved June 30, 1864, "To Select the Most Approved Site for a Naval Yard or Naval Station on the Mississippi River...". 1865. V. 47

UNITED STATES. NAVY DEPARTMENT - 1869
Uniform for the United States Navy, Prepared Under Direction of the Secretary of the Navy. Washington: 1869. V. 50

UNITED STATES. NAVY DEPARTMENT - 1880
Ordnance Instructions. Washington: 1880. V. 50

UNITED STATES. NAVY DEPARTMENT - 1886
Regulations Governing the Uniform of Commissioned Officers, Warrant Officers, and Enlisted Men of the Navy of the United States. Washington: 1886. V. 53

UNITED STATES. NAVY DEPARTMENT - 1899
Flags of Maritime Nations. Washington: 1899. V. 47

UNITED STATES. NAVY DEPARTMENT - 1948
Proceedings of a Symposium on Large-Scale Digital Calculating Machinery. Cambridge: 1948. V. 54

UNITED STATES. PARLIAMENT. HOUSE OF LORDS - 1835
First (and second) Report from the Select Committee of the House of Lords Appointed to Inquire Into the Present State of the Several Gaols and Houses of Correction in England and Wales. London: 1835. V. 49

UNITED STATES. PRESIDENT - 1795
A Message of the President of the United States, to Congress, Relative to France and Great Britain: Delivered December 5, 1793, with the Papers Therein Referred to. Philadelphia: 1795. V. 50

The Proceedings of the Executive of the United States, Respecting the Insurgents. 1794. Philadelphia: 1795. V. 47

UNITED STATES. PRESIDENT - 1796
A Collection of the Speeches of the President of the United States to Both Houses of Congress, at the Opening of Every Session with Their Answers. Boston: 1796. V. 47

UNITED STATES. PRESIDENT - 1803
An Account of Louisiana, Being an Abstract of Documents... Philadelphia: 1803. V. 47

UNITED STATES. PRESIDENT - 1806
Message from the President...Communicating Discoveries Made in Exploring the Missouri, Red River and Washita... New York: 1806. V. 47

UNITED STATES. PRESIDENT - 1807
Message from the President of the United States... Touching an Illegal Combination of Private Individuals Against the Peace and Safety of the Union, and a Military Expedition Planned By Them Against the Territories of a Power in Amity... Washington: 1807. V. 51

Travels in the Interior Parts of America.... London: 1807. V. 50

UNITED STATES. PRESIDENT - 1809
Message from the President of the United States Transmitting Extracts from the Correspondence of Mr. Pinkney. Washington: 1809. V. 52

UNITED STATES. PRESIDENT - 1817
Message from the President of the United States (Dec. 15, 1817). Communicates Information of the Proceedings of Certain Persons Who Took Possession of Amelia Island and of Galvezton (sic) During the Summer of the Present Year,... Washington: 1817. V. 47; 49

UNITED STATES. PRESIDENT - 1818
Message from the President of the United States Transmitting Information Relative to the Arrest and Imprisonment of Certain American Citizens at Santa Fe, by Authority of the Government of Spain, April 1818. Washington: 1818. V. 47

UNITED STATES. PRESIDENT - 1819
Message from the President of the United States...Information Relative to the Arrest and Imprisonment of Certain American Citizens at Santa Fe, by Authority of the government of Spain, April 15, 1818. Boston: 1819. V. 49

Message of the President...Transmitting a Report to the Secretary of War, in Compliance With a Resolution of the Senate of the 25th of January Last Requesting Him "To Cause to Be Laid Before It, a Copy of the Rules and Regulations Adopted for...". Washington: 1819. V. 52

UNITED STATES. PRESIDENT - 1822
Message from the President of the United States...Relative to the Introduction of Slaves Into the United States. Washington: 1822. V. 49

Message...Transmitting...Communications From the Agents of the United States With the Governments South of the U. States Which Have Declared Independence... Washington: 1822. V. 48; 49

UNITED STATES. PRESIDENT - 1823
Message from the President...to Both Houses of Congress, at the Commencement of the First Session of the Eighteenth Congress Dec. 2, 1823. Washington: 1823. V. 53; 54

Message from...Communicating the Letter of Mr. Prevost, and other Documents Relating to an Establishment Made at the Mouth of Columbia River. Washington: 1823. V. 47; 50

UNITED STATES. PRESIDENT - 1824
Message From the President of the United State, Transmitting a Report of the Secretary of State, Upon the Subject of the Present Condition and Future Prospects of the Greeks. Washington: 1824. V. 48; 49; 50

UNITED STATES. PRESIDENT - 1825
Message From the President of the United States, Transmitting Information Relative to Piratical Depredations &c. Washington: 1825. V. 48

Message from...Transmitting an Abstract of Licenses Granted to Persons to Trade in the Indian Country.... Washington: 1825. V. 50

UNITED STATES. PRESIDENT - 1828
Navigation of the Saint Lawrence: Message from the President of the United States, Transmitting a Report from the Secretary of State, and the Correspondence with the Government of Great Britain, Relative to the Free Navigation of the River St. Lawrence. Washington: 1828. V. 48

UNITED STATES. PRESIDENT - 1831
Message from...Relative to the British Establishments on the Columbia, and the State of the Fur Trade... Washington: 1831. V. 54

UNITED STATES. PRESIDENT - 1832
Message from the President of the United States...Concerning the Fur Trade and Inland Trade to Mexico. Washington: 1832. V. 47; 50

UNITED STATES. PRESIDENT - 1835
Message from the President of the United States. Washington: 1835. V. 53

UNITED STATES. PRESIDENT - 1836
Condition of Texas. Message from the President of the U.S., Upon the Subject of the Political, Military, and Civil Condition of Texas. Washington: 1836. V. 52

UNITED STATES. PRESIDENT - 1842
Message from the President...Proceedings of the Commissioner Appointed to Run the Boundary Line Between the U.S. and the Republic of Texas. Washington: 1842. V. 50

UNITED STATES. PRESIDENT - 1845
Message from the President of the United States. Washington: 1845. V. 47

UNITED STATES. PRESIDENT - 1847
Message from the President of the United States, To the Two Houses of Congress, at the Commencmenet of the First Session of the Thirtieth Congress, December 7, 1847. Washington: 1847. V. 47; 54

UNITED STATES. PRESIDENT - 1848
Message from the President of the United States to the Two Houses of Congress. Washington: 1848. V. 47; 53

Message of the President of the United States, Communicating the Proceedings of the Court Martial In the Trial of Lieutenant-Colonel Fremont. Washington: 1848. V. 48; 52

UNITED STATES. PRESIDENT - 1849
Message from the President of the United States to the Two Houses of Congress, at the Commencement of the First Session of the Thirty-First Congress, December 24, 1849...Part II. Washington: 1849. V. 47; 52; 53

UNITED STATES. PRESIDENT - 1850
California and New Mexico. Message from the President... Washington: 1850. V. 47; 53

UNITED STATES. PRESIDENT - 1851
Message From the President of the United States to the Two Houses of Congress... Washington: 1851. V. 48; 54

UNITED STATES. PRESIDENT - 1853
Message from the President of the U. S...at the Commencement of the First Session of the 33rd Congress. Washington: 1853. V. 52

UNITED STATES. PRESIDENT - 1854
Message from the President of the U.S...at the Commencement of the Second Session of the 33d Congress. Dec. 4, 1854. Washington: 1854. V. 52

UNITED STATES. PRESIDENT - 1856
Message of the President...Calling for Information Relating to the Boundary Line and the Payment of the $3,000,000 Under the Treaty with Mexico of June 30, 1853. Washington: 1856. V. 49

UNITED STATES. PRESIDENT - 1858
A Proclamation...Concerning the Utah War and Its Necessity. Washington: 1858. V. 52

UNITED STATES. PRESIDENT - 1860
Message of the President of the United States Communicating...Information Relative to the Massacre at Mountain Meadows and Other Massacres in Utah Territory. Washington: 1860. V. 47; 49; 54

Message of the President...Concerning the Alledged Hostilities Existing on the Rio Grande... Washington: 1860. V. 49

UNITED STATES. PRESIDENT - 1863
Message of the President...Transmitting...the Report of Hon. Reverdy Johnson, as Commissioner of the United States in New Orleans. Washington: 1863. V. 49

UNITED STATES. PRESIDENT - 1864
For Five Hundred Thousand Volunteers. By the President of the United States of America. A Proclamation. Washington: 1864. V. 54

UNITED STATES. PRESIDENT - 1876
Message from the President...Communicating, In Answer to a Senate Resolution of July 20, 1876, Information in Relation to the Slaughter of American Citizens at Hambrugh (sic) S.C. Washington: 1876. V. 49

UNITED STATES. PRESIDENT - 1877
Mexican Border Troubles. Message from the President... Washington: 1877. V. 49

UNITED STATES. PRESIDENT - 1879
Message From the President of the United States...Information in Relation to an Alleged Occupation of a Portion of the Indian Territory by White Settlers. Washington: 1879. V. 52

UNITED STATES. PRESIDENT - 1882
Message from the President of the United States...with a Draft of a Bill to Accept and Ratify an Agreement with the Crow Indians for the Sale of a Portion of Their Reservation in the Territory of Montana Required for the Northern Pacific Railroad... Washington: 1882. V. 47

UNITED STATES. PRESIDENT - 1886
Message from...Transmitting a Report from the Secretary of State Relative to the Frontier Line Between Alaska and British Columbia. Washington: 1886. V. 52

UNITED STATES. PRESIDENT - 1889
Message from the President of the United States Transmitting, in Response to Senate Resolution of February 11, 1889. A Report Upon the Case of Louis Riel. Washington: 1889. V. 47

UNITED STATES. PRESIDENT - 1897
A Compilation of the Messages and Papers of the Presidents. Prepared Under the Dir. of the Joint Committee on Printing, House and Senate. Washington: 1897-1922. V. 53

UNITED STATES. PRESIDENT - 1902
Message from the President of the United States. Transmitting a Report of the Secretary of Agriculture in Relation to the Forests, Rivers and Mountains of the southern Appalachian Region. Washington: 1902. V. 47; 53

UNITED STATES. PRESIDENT - 1917
Address of the President of the United States, Delivered at a Joint Session of the Two Houses of Congress April 2, 1917. Garden City: 1917. V. 50

UNITED STATES. PRESIDENT - 1967
No Retreat from Tomorrow. 1967. V. 50

UNITED STATES. PUBLIC LANDS COMMISSION - 1880
Report of the Public Lands Commission...Relating to Public Lands in the Western Portion of the United States and to the Operation of Existing Land Laws. Washington: 1880. V. 47

UNITED STATES. QUARTERMASTER GENERAL - 1850
Annual Report of the Quartermaster General, of the Operations of the Quartermaster's Department for the Fiscal Year Ending on the 30th June, 1850. Washington: 1850. V. 47

UNITED STATES. QUARTERMASTER GENERAL - 1851
Annual Report of the Quartermaster General of the Operations of the Quartermaster's Department for the Fiscal Year Ending on the 30th June, 1850. Washington: 1851. V. 47

THE UNITED States Sanitary Commission. A Sketch of its Purposes and its Work. Boston: 1863. V. 52

UNITED STATES. STATE DEPARTMENT - 1808
Letters from the Secretary of State to Mr. Monroe, on the Subject of Impressments, &c. Washington: 1808. V. 50

THE UNITED States Strategic Bombing Survey - the Effects of Atomic Bombs on Hiroshima and Nagasaki. 1946. V. 49

THE UNITED States Strategic Bombing Survey - The Effects of Atomic Bombs on Hiroshima and Nagasaki. Washington: 1946. V. 50; 54

UNITED STATES. SUPREME COURT - 1793
A Case Decided in the Supreme Court of the United States, February, 1793..."Whether a State Be Liable to Be Sued by a Private Citizen of Another State?". Boston: 1793. V. 48; 49

A Case Decided in the Supreme Court of the United States, February, 1793..."Whether a State be liable to be sued by a private person of another state?". Philadelphia: 1793. V. 49

UNITED STATES. SUPREME COURT - 1829
Opinion of the Supreme Court of the United States, Delivered by Mr. Chief Justice Marshall, March 9, 1829...in the Case of Foster & Elam, Plaintiffs in Error vs. Neilson, Defendant in Error. Messrs. Webster and R. S. Coxe for Plaintiffs & Mr. W. Jones... 1829. V. 50

UNITED STATES. SUPREME COURT - 1841
Argument...Before the Supreme Court of the United States, in the Case of the United States, Appelants vs. Cinque and Others, Africans, Captured in the Schooner Amistad by Lieut. Gedney, Delivered on the 24th of Feb. and 1st of March 1841... New York: 1841. V. 51

UNITED STATES. SUPREME COURT - 1856
Supreme Court of the United States, December Term, 1855. Field v. Seabury et al, No. 113, Same v. Same No. 114. Washington: 1856. V. 49

UNITED STATES. SUPREME COURT - 1859
Supreme Court of the United States. No. 242 - December Term, 1858. The United States, Appellants vs. Charles Fossatt. 1859. V. 49

UNITED STATES. TREASURY DEPARTMENT - 1828
Letter from the Secretary of the Treasury, Transmitting the Information Required by a Resolution of the House of Presentations...in Relation to the Growth and Manufacture of Silk. Washington: 1828. V. 52

UNITED STATES. TREASURY DEPARTMENT - 1845
Report of the Secretary of the Treasury...In Relation to the Claim to Land in the State of Louisiana, Called the "Houmas Claim". Washington: 1845. V. 48

UNITED STATES. TREASURY DEPARTMENT - 1884
Report on the Internal Commerce of the United States. Washington: 1884. V. 47

UNITED STATES. TREASURY DEPARTMENT - 1886
Annual Report of the Supervising Architect...1886. Washington: 1886. V. 48

UNITED STATES. TREASURY DEPARTMENT - 1896
Letter from the Secretary of the Treasury Transmitting, in Response to the House Resolution of the 22d Instant, a Copy of the Report of Henry W. Elliott on the condition of the Fur-Seal Fisheries of Alaska. Washington: 1896. V. 47; 49

Reports of Agents, Officers and Persons, Acting Under the Authority of the Secretary of the Treasury, in Relation to the Condition of Seal Life on the Rookeries of the Pribilof Islands and to Pelagic Sealing in Bering Sea and the North Pacific Ocean... Washington: 1896. V. 49; 51

UNITED STATES. TREASURY DEPARTMENT - 1898
Seal and Salmon Fisheries and General Resources of Alaska. Washington: 1898. V. 51

UNITED STATES. TREASURY DEPARTMENT - 1901
A History of Public Buildings Under the Control of the Treasury Department. Washington: 1901. V. 53

UNITED STATES. TREATIES, ETC. - 1795
Treaty of Amity, Commerce and Navigation, Between His Britannic Majesty and the United States of America, Conditionally Ratified by the Senate of the United States... Philadelphia: 1795. V. 47

UNITED STATES. TREATIES, ETC. - 1834
Treaty Between the United States and the Cherokee Nation of Indians, West of the Mississippi. Washington: 1834. V. 50

Treaty Between the United States of America and the Seminole Nation of Indians. Concluded at Fort Gibson, March 28, 1833. Washington: 1834. V. 50

UNITED STATES. TREATIES, ETC. - 1848
The Treaty Between the U.S. and Mexico and the Proceedings of the Senate Thereon...From Which the Injunction of Secrecy Has Been Removed. Washington: 1848. V. 52

Treaty of Guadalupe Hidalgo. Washington: 1848. V. 49

UNITED STATES. TREATIES, ETC. - 1856
United States Micha Chahta Micha Chickasha Aiena Traty Anampa ai Itim Apesa Tok. Proclaimed March 4, 1856. Washington: 1856. V. 50

UNITED STATES. TREATIES, ETC. - 1866
A Treaty Between the United States and the Choctaws and Chickasaws. Washington: 1866. V. 50

Treaty (of the Little Arkansas River) Between the United States and the Comanche and Kiowa Tribes of Indians, Concluded October 18, 1865. Ratification Advised May 22, 1866. Proclaimed May 26, 1866. Washington: 1866. V. 49

UNITED STATES. TREATIES, ETC. - 1868
Treaty With Russia. Washington: 1868. V. 52

UNITED STATES. TREATIES, ETC. - 1949
Treaty of Guadalupe Hidalgo. Berkeley: 1949. V. 49

UNITED STATES. WAR DEPARTMENT - 1816
Letter from the Secretary of War, Transmitting Documents Exhibiting the General Expenses of the Indian Department, Embracing Annuities and Presents and the General and Particular Views of the Indian Trade, in Obedience to a Resolution... Washington: 1816. V. 51

UNITED STATES. WAR DEPARTMENT - 1820
Report of the Secretary of War, or the Terms on Which Contracts Have Been Made for the Transportation of Troops Ordered on the Expedition. Washington: 1820. V. 47

UNITED STATES. WAR DEPARTMENT - 1823
Letter from the Secretary of War, Transmitting...Reports of the Newspapers, Journals, and Other Periodical Publications, Charts and Instruments, Maps and prints, Taken at the Public Expense... Washington: 1823. V. 51

UNITED STATES. WAR DEPARTMENT - 1826
Indian Treaties, and Laws and Regulations. Relates to Indian Affairs: to Which is Added an Appendix, Containing the Proceedings of the Old Congress, and Other Important State Papers, in Relation to Indian Affairs. Washington City: 1826. V. 47

UNITED STATES. WAR DEPARTMENT - 1834
Letter from the Secretary of War, Transmitting a Map and Report of Lieut. Allen and H. B. Schoolcraft's Visit to the Northwest Indians in 1832. Washington: 1834. V. 52

UNITED STATES. WAR DEPARTMENT - 1835
Little Rock and Memphis Road. Letter from the Secretary of War, Transmitting a Report from the Topographical Bureau, in Relation to the Survey of So Much of the Little Rock and Memphis Road as Lies Between the St. Francis and Mississippi Rivers... Washington: 1835. V. 47

Report from the Secretary of War, with an Abstract of Licenses to Trade with the Indians... Washington: 1835. V. 50

Survey of Cumberland River. Letter from the Secretary of War Transmitting a Report of the Survey of the Cumberland River, Feb. 24, 1835. Washington: 1835. V. 47

UNITED STATES. WAR DEPARTMENT - 1837
Letter from the Secretary of War Transmitting Various Reports in Relation to the Protection of the Western Frontier. Washington: 1837. V. 52

UNITED STATES. WAR DEPARTMENT - 1838
Report from the Secretary of War... in Relation to the Protection of the Western Frontier of the United States. Washington: 1838. V. 47

UNITED STATES. WAR DEPARTMENT - 1840
Report from the Secretary of War, Transmitting...Copies of Reports, Plans, and Estimates for the Improvement of the Neenah, Wiskonsin and Rock Rivers; the Improvement of the Haven of Rock River; and the Construction of a Pier at the Northern Extremity... Washington: 1840. V. 52

UNITED STATES. WAR DEPARTMENT - 1850
California and New Mexico. Message from the President. Washington: 1850. V. 49

Pembina Settlement... Washington: 1850. V. 47

Report of the Secretary of War, Communicating Information in Relation to the Geology and Topography of California. April 3, 1850. Washington: 1850. V. 47

Report of the Secretary of War...The Report of an Exploration of the Territory of Minnesota, by Brevet Captain Pope. Washington: 1850. V. 47

UNITED STATES. WAR DEPARTMENT - 1853
Reports of Explorations and Surveys.... Volume V. Washington: 1853. V. 47

UNITED STATES. WAR DEPARTMENT - 1855
Report of the Secretary of War Communicating the Several Pacific Railroad Explorations. Volume 2. Washington: 1855. V. 48

Report of the Secretary of War on...Pacific Railroad Exploration. Washington: 1855. V. 47; 48; 50

Reports of Explorations and Surveys, to Ascertain the Most Practicable & Economical Route for a Railroad from the Mississippi River to the Pacific Ocean... Washington: 1855. V. 47

Reports of Explorations and Surveys to Ascertain the Most Practicable & Economical Route for a Railroad from the Mississippi River to the Pacific Ocean... Washington: 1855-60. V. 50; 51

Reports of Explorations and Surveys, to Ascertain the Most Practicable & Economical Route for a Railroad from the Mississippi River to the Pacific Ocean... Washington: 1855-61. V. 47; 48

UNITED STATES. WAR DEPARTMENT - 1856
Reports of Explorations and Surveys, to Ascertain the Most Practicable & Economical Route for a Railroad from the Mississippi River to the Pacific Ocean. Volume III. Washington: 1856. V. 47; 53

UNITED STATES. WAR DEPARTMENT - 1857
Reports and Explorations and Surveys, to Ascertain the Most Practicable & Economical Route for a Railroad from the Mississippi River to the Pacific Ocean. Volume VII. Washington: 1857. V. 47; 53

Reports of Explorations and Surveys. Volume VI. Washington: 1857. V. 47

UNITED STATES. WAR DEPARTMENT - 1859
Report of the Secretary of War...Colonel Wright's Late Campaign Against the Indians in Oregon & Washington Territories. Washington: 1859. V. 53

Reports of Explorations and Surveys, to Ascertain the Most Practicable & Economical Route for a Railroad from the Mississippi River to the Pacific Ocean...Vol. 10. Washington: 1859. V. 53

UNITED STATES. WAR DEPARTMENT - 1860
Reports of Explorations and Surveys, to Ascertain the Most Practicable & Economical Route for a Railroad from the Mississippi River to the Pacifc Ocean... Washington: 1860. V. 47

UNITED STATES. WAR DEPARTMENT - 1861
The Medical and Surgical History of the War of the Rebellion, 1861-1865. Washington: 1870-88. V. 47

Reports of Explorations and Surveys, to Ascertain the Most Practicable & Economical Route for a Railroad from the Mississippi River to the Pacifc Ocean... Washington: 1861. V. 47

UNITED STATES. WAR DEPARTMENT - 1863
Letter of the Secretary of War. Communicates The Report of Major D. Fergusson on the Country, Its Resources and the Route Between Tucson and Lobos Bay, March 14, 1863. Washington: 1863. V. 47

UNITED STATES. WAR DEPARTMENT - 1865
Letter of the Secretary of War, Communicating...Military Commissions by Which Were Tried and Convicted E. W. Andrews, of South Carolina; J. M. Brown and C. C. Reese of Georgia; J. L. McMillan and Neill McGill of North Carolina. 1865. V. 50

UNITED STATES. WAR DEPARTMENT - 1872
Letter from the Secretary of War. Communicating, in Compliance with a Resolution of the Senate of March 7, 1872, a Preliminary Report of Lieutenant George M. Wheeler, Corps of Engineers, of the Progress of the Engineer Exploration of the Public... Washington: 1872. V. 47

UNITED STATES. WAR DEPARTMENT - 1875
Letters from the Secretary of War, Relative to the Improvement of the Navigation of the Holston and Tennessee Rivers, February 3, 1875. Washington: 1875. V. 47

UNITED STATES. WAR DEPARTMENT - 1879
Report of the Secretary of War... Washington: 1879. V. 53

UNITED STATES. WAR DEPARTMENT - 1882
Posts of the Rio Grande Frontier. Letter from Secretary of War... Washington: 1882. V. 49

UNITED STATES. WAR DEPARTMENT - 1887
Letter from the Secretary of War...Correspondence with General Miles Relative to the Surrender of Geronimo. Washington: 1887. V. 49

UNITED STATES. WAR DEPARTMENT - 1891
Atlas to Accompany the Official Records of the Union and Confederate Armies. Washington: 1891-95. V. 47

UNITED STATES. WAR DEPARTMENT - 1893
Opening of the Cherokee Strip. Washington: 1893. V. 49

UNITED STATES. WAR DEPARTMENT - 1899
The War of the Rebellion. Official Records of the Union and Confederate Armies, Series I. Index to Battles, Campaigns, Etc. Washington: 1899. V. 47

UNITED STATES. WAR DEPARTMENT - 1919
Manual of Neuro-Surgery Authorized by the Secretary of War. Washington: 1919. V. 52; 53; 54

UNITED STATES. WAR DEPARTMENT - 1972
The War of the Rebellion: a Compilation of the Official Records of the Union and Confederate Armies. Gettysburg: 1972. V. 48

THE UNIVERISTY of Virginia. Thirty-Two Woodcuts by Charles W. Smith. V. 48

UNIVERSAL Catalogue of Books on Art. New York: 1978. V. 54

UNIVERSAL History, from the Earliest Account of Time... London: 1747-48. V. 47

AN UNIVERSAL History, from the Earliest Account of Time. London: 1747-54. V. 47

THE UNIVERSAL Songster; or, Museum of Mirth... London: 1832. V. 49
THE UNIVERSAL Songster; or, Museum of Mirth... London: 1834. V. 49

UNIVERSITY OF ARIZONA MUSEUM OF ART
Navajo Blankets. From the Collection of Anthony Berlant. 1974. V. 54

UNIVERSITY OF NORTH CAROLINA
Catalogue of the Faculty and Students of the University of North Carolina. September 1, 1823. Raleigh: 1824. V. 47
Catalogue of the Faculty and Students of the University of North Carolina. September 1, 1824. Raleigh: 1824. V. 47

THE UNIVERSITY Printing Houses at Cambridge from the 16th to the 20th Century. Cambridge: 1962. V. 51

UNIVERSITY OF KING'S COLLEGE, TORONTO
Proceedings at the Ceremony of Laying the Foundation Stone, April 23, 1842; and at the Opening of the University, June 8, 1843. Toronto: 1843. V. 54

UNNA, WARREN
The Coppa Murals. A Pageant of Bohemian Life in San Francisco at the Turn of the Century. San Francisco: 1952. V. 53

UNSWORTH, BARRY
The Greeks Have a Word For It. London: 1967. V. 50
Mooncranker's Gift. London: 1973. V. 54
The Partnership. London: 1966. V. 49; 50; 52; 54
Sacred Hunger. London: 1992. V. 51; 53

UNTERMEYER, JEAN STARR
Private Collection. New York: 1965. V. 47; 48

UNTERMEYER, LOUIS
Doorways to Poetry. New York: 1938. V. 49
James Branch Cabell... Virginia: 1970. V. 47; 48; 49
Moses. New York: 1938. V. 48

UNTERMYER, IRWIN
Bronzes, Other Metalwork and Sculpture in the Irwin Untermyer Collection. New York: 1962. V. 50; 53; 54
Chelsea and Other English Porcelain Pottery and Enamel in the Irwin Untermyer Collection. Cambridge: 1957. V. 52
The Irwin Untermyer Collection. London: 1956-63. V. 50

UNTOPICAL Songs. London: 1959. V. 54

UNTRACHT, OPPI
Jewelry Concepts and Technology. New York: 1982. V. 51
Jewelry Concepts and Technology. New York: 1985. V. 47

UNVARNISHED Facts About the Carlsbad Project Carlsbad. Carlsbad: 1908. V. 50

UNWIN, A. HAROLD
West African Forests and Forestry. New York: 1920. V. 49; 52

UNWIN, GEORGE
Letters, Remarks &c. London: 1790. V. 47

UNWIN, STANLEY
The Truth About Publishing. London: 1926. V. 47

UNZER, JOHN AUGUSTUS
The Principles of Physiology. London: 1851. V. 50; 53

UP DE GRAFF, F. W.
Head-Hunters of the Amazon. London: 1923. V. 52

UPCOTT, WILLIAM
A Bibliographical Account of Principal Works Relating to English Topography. London: 1818. V. 52
A Bibliographical Account of the Principal Works Relating to English Topography. New York: 1968. V. 52; 53

UPDIKE, DANIEL BERKELEY
Printing Types: Their History, Forms and Use. Cambridge: 1922. V. 49
Printing Types, Their History, Forms and Use. Cambridge: 1927. V. 47; 53
Printing Types Their History, Forms and Use. Cambridge: 1937. V. 47; 51; 54
Printing Types, Their History, Forms and Use. London: 1937. V. 50
Some Aspects of Printing Old and New. New Haven: 1941. V. 51; 54

UPDIKE, JOHN
The Afterlife... Leamington: 1987. V. 52; 54
The Afterlife. Warwickshire: 1987. V. 51
The Afterlife... New York: 1994. V. 51; 52; 53
The Angels. Pensacola: 1968. V. 51; 53
Assorted Prose. New York: 1965. V. 47; 49; 50; 53
Baby's First Steps. Huntington Beach: 1993. V. 51
Bath After Sailing. Stevenson: 1968. V. 51
Bech: a Book. New York: 1970. V. 47; 48; 49; 51
Bech is Back. New York: 1982. V. 47; 48; 49; 50; 51; 53; 54
The Beloved. Northridge: 1982. V. 48; 51
Bottom's Dream. New York: 1969. V. 47; 49; 54
Brazil. New York: 1994. V. 51; 54
Brother Grasshopper. Worcester: 1990. V. 47; 49; 50; 51; 53
Buchanan Dying. New York: 1974. V. 48; 49; 54
The Carpentered Hen... New York: 1956. V. 52
The Carpentered Hen. New York: 1958. V. 47; 49; 50; 53
The Centaur. New York: 1963. V. 47; 51; 52; 53
The Centaur. New York: 1964. V. 49
The Chaste Planet. Worcester: 1980. V. 54
A Child's Calendar. New York: 1965. V. 47; 49; 51; 52
Collected Poems 1953-1993. New York: 1993. V. 50; 51
Concert at Castle Hill. Northridge: 1993. V. 48
The Coup. New York: 1978. V. 47; 48; 49; 51; 54
Couples. New York: 1968. V. 49; 51; 52
Cunts. New York: 1974. V. 47; 49; 51
Ego and Art in Walt Whitman. New York: 1980. V. 48; 49; 51; 52
From the Journal of a Leper. Northridge: 1978. V. 47
Getting Older. Helsinki: 1986. V. 48; 49
Getting the Words Out. Northridge: 1988. V. 48; 51; 53
Going Abroad. Helsinki: 1988. V. 48; 49; 52
A Good Place. 1973. V. 51
Hawthorne's Creed. New York: 1981. V. 52
Heroes and Anti Heroes. New York: 1991. V. 49
Hoping for a Hoopoe. London: 1959. V. 49; 50; 51; 52; 54
Hub Fans Bid Kid Adieu. Northridge: 1977. V. 49; 50; 51; 54
Impressions. Los Angeles: 1986. V. 51
In Memoriam Felis Felis. Warwickshire: 1989. V. 47
In Memoriam Felis Felis. Leamington Spa: 1990. V. 53
In the Cemetery High Above Shillington. Concord: 1995. V. 54
Invasion of the Book Envelopes. Concord: 1981. V. 51
Iowa. Portland: 1980. V. 54
Jester's Dozen. Northridge: 1984. V. 47; 49; 54
Just Looking. V. 51
Just Looking. New York: 1989. V. 47; 48; 51; 53
The Magic Flute. New York: 1962. V. 50; 52
Marry Me. Franklin Center: 1976. V. 54
Marry Me. New York: 1976. V. 48; 49; 53
Memoirs of the Ford Administration. New York: 1992. V. 47; 48; 49; 51
Midpoint and other Poems. New York: 1969. V. 48; 49; 51; 52; 53
A Month of Sundays. New York: 1975. V. 47; 48; 49; 50; 51; 52; 53
Museums and Women and Other Stories. New York: 1972. V. 51; 52; 53
The Music School. New York: 1966. V. 47; 48; 49; 51; 52; 54
Odd Jobs. Essays and Criticism. New York: 1991. V. 48; 51
Of the Farm. New York: 1965. V. 48; 49; 51; 52; 54
On Meeting Authors. Newburyport: 1968. V. 50
On the Move. Cleveland: 1988. V. 49
A Pear Like a Potato. Northridge: 1986. V. 48
People One Knows. Northridge: 1980. V. 48; 51
Picked-Up Pieces. New York: 1975. V. 48; 49; 52
Pigeon Feathers and Other Stories. New York: 1962. V. 47; 48; 49; 50; 52; 53
The Poorhouse Fair. London: 1959. V. 50; 53
The Poorhouse Fair. New York: 1959. V. 47; 49; 52; 53
Problems. New York: 1975. V. 47
Problems. New York: 1979. V. 47; 49; 51; 53
Query. New York: 1974. V. 48; 51
Rabbit at Rest. New York: 1960. V. 50
Rabbit at Rest. 1990. V. 50
Rabbit at Rest. New York: 1990. V. 47; 48; 49; 51; 52; 53
Rabbit Is Rich. New York: 1981. V. 47; 48; 51; 53; 54
Rabbit Redux. New York: 1971. V. 48; 49; 51; 52; 53
Rabbit, Run. New York: 1960. V. 47; 48; 49; 50; 52; 54
Rabbit Run. Franklin Center: 1977. V. 50; 54

UPDIKE, JOHN continued
Recent Poems. Helsinki: 1990. V. 49
Recent Poems. Helsinki: 1991. V. 48
The Ring. New York: 1964. V. 49; 51
Roger's Version. New York: 1986. V. 48; 51; 53; 54
S. London: 1988. V. 48; 53
S. New York: 1988. V. 47; 49; 51; 53
S. London: 1989. V. 47
The Same Door. New York: 1959. V. 47; 48; 49; 51; 52; 53
The Same Door. London: 1962. V. 53
Self Consciousness. New York: 1989. V. 47; 48; 49; 51; 52; 53
Six Poems. 1973. V. 51
Small-City People. Northridge: 1982. V. 48
A Soft Spring Night in Shillington. Northridge: 1986. V. 48; 51; 54
Spring Trio. 1982. V. 47; 50; 53
Talk from the Fifties. Northridge: 1979. V. 49; 51; 52; 54
Telephone Poles. New York: 1963. V. 49
Three Illuminations in the Life of an American Author. New York: 1979. V. 47; 48; 51; 54
Trust Me. New York: 1987. V. 48; 49; 51
The Twelve Terrors of Christmas. New York: 1993. V. 53
The Twelve Terrors of Christmas. New York: 1994. V. 53
Warm Wine. New York: 1973. V. 47; 51; 54
The Witches of Eastwick. Franklin Center: 1984. V. 52
The Witches of Eastwick. London: 1984. V. 48
The Witches of Eastwick. New York: 1984. V. 47; 48; 49; 51; 52; 53
The Young King. New York: 1962. V. 52

UPDIKE, WILKINS
A History of the Episcopal Church in Narragansett Rhode Island. Boston: 1907. V. 50; 51
Memoirs of the Rhode-Island Bar. Boston: 1842. V. 50

UPFIELD, ARTHUR W.
Bony and the Mouse. London: 1959. V. 47
Bushranger of the Skies. London: 1963. V. 49
The Mystery of Swordfish Reef. New York: 1943. V. 53
The Mystery of Swordfish Reef. London: 1960. V. 49
Winds of Evil. London: 1938. V. 48

UPHAM, CHARLES WENTWORTH
Lectures on Witchcraft: Comprising a History of the Delusion in Salem in 1692. Boston: 1831. V. 47
Speech of Charles W. Upham, of Salem, in the House of Representatives of Massachusetts, on the Compromises of the Constitution... Salem: 1849. V. 47

UPHAM, SAMUEL C.
Notes of a Voyage to California Via Cape Horn Together with Scenes in El Dorado, in the Years 1849-50. Philadelphia: 1878. V. 47; 53

UPHAM, THOMAS C.
Elements of Intellectual Philosophy: Designed as a Text-Book. Portland: 1827. V. 47; 49; 54
Elements of Mental Philosophy. Portland: 1828. V. 47; 49; 54
Elements of Mental Philosophy. Portland: 1831. V. 54
A Philosophical and Practical Treatise on the Will. Portland: 1834. V. 47; 54

UPPER MISSOURI MINING & PROSPECTING CO.
Prospectus of the Upper Missouri Mining and Prospecting Co. New York: 1865. V. 50

UPS and Downs in Picture Town. London: 1890. V. 54

UPSHUR, ABEL PARKER
A Brief Enquiry into the True Nature and Character of the Federal Government... Petersburg: 1840. V. 48

UPTON, BERTHA
The Adventures of Two Dutch Dolls. London: 1895. V. 47; 48; 49
The Golliwogg at the Sea-Side. London: 1898. V. 49
The Golliwogg in Holland. London: 1904. V. 48; 51
The Golliwogg's Air-ship. London: 1902. V. 49; 50; 52
The Golliwogg's Auto-Go Cart. London: 1901. V. 50; 51
The Golliwogg's Auto-Go-Cart. New York: 1901. V. 54
The Golliwogg's Bicycle Club. London: 1896. V. 51
The Golliwogg's Bicycle Club. London: 1898. V. 49
The Golliwogg's Christmas. London: 1907. V. 54
The Golliwogg's Fox-Hunt. London: 1905. V. 51
The Vege-men's Revenge. London: 1897. V. 48

UPTON, CHARLES E.
Pioneers of El Dorado. Placerville: 1906. V. 49; 54

UPTON, JOHN
Critical Observations on Shakespeare. London: 1748. V. 53

UPTON, ROBERT
Gleanings from the Desert of Arabia. London: 1881. V. 47

UPWARD, EDWARD
In the Thirties. London: 1962. V. 53
Journey to the Border. London: 1938. V. 49

URBAN, MARTIN
Emil Nolde - Landscapes. New York: 1970. V. 50
Emil Nolde: Catalogue Raisonne of the Oil Paintings. Volume I. 1895-1914. London: 1987. V. 47
Emil Nolde: Flowers and Animals, Watercolors and Drawings. London: 1966. V. 47; 48; 50; 52

URBINO, L. B.
Art Recreations. Boston: 1860. V. 50

URE, ANDREW
A Dictionary of Arts, Manufactures and Mines... London: 1853. V. 50
Dictionary of Arts, Manufactures and Mines... London: 1863. V. 54
A Dictionary of Arts, Manufactures and Mines... New York: 1873. V. 47
A Dictionary of Chemistry, on The Basis of Mr. Nicholson's... London: 1821. V. 49
Ure's Dictionary of Arts, Manufactures and Mines. London: 1878-81. V. 49

URE, DAVID
The History of Rutherglen and East-Kilbride. Glasgow: 1793. V. 48; 52; 54

URE, GEORGE P.
The Hand-Book of Toronto; Containing Its Climate, Geology, Natural History, Educational Institutions, Courts of Law, Municipal Arrangements. Toronto: 1858. V. 54

URE, JOHN
A Tour Round the World. Glasgow: 1885. V. 47

URE-SMITH, SYDNEY
Adrian Feint: Flower Paintings. Sydney: 1948. V. 52

URIEL a Poetical Address to the Right Honourable Lord Byron, Written on the Continent... London: 1822. V. 53; 54

URIS, LEON
The Angry Hills. New York: 1955. V. 48; 49; 52; 53
Battle Cry. 1953. V. 50
Battle Cry. New York: 1953. V. 49; 53
Exodus. Garden City: 1958. V. 53
Exodus. Franklin Center: 1977. V. 51

URQHUART, THOMAS
(Ekskubalauron): or, the Discovery of a Most Exquisite Jewel, More Precious then (sic) Diamonds Inchased in Gold, the like Whereof was Never Seen In Any Age... London: 1652. V. 51

URQUHART, BERYL LESLIE
The Camellia. Sharpthorne, Sussex: 1956-60. V. 47
The Rhododendron. 1958-62. V. 52
The Rhododendron. Sharpthorne: 1958-62. V. 47; 48
The Rhododendron. London: 1962. V. 49

URQUHART, DAVID
The Pillars of Hercules; or, a Narrative of Travels in Spain and Morocco. London: 1850. V. 54

URQUHART, H. M.
The History of the 16th Battalion (The Canadian Scottish), Candian Expeditionary Force, in the Great War, 1914-1919. Toronto: 1932. V. 48

URQUHART, JANE
I Am Walking in the Garden of His Imaginary Palace. Toronto: 1932. V. 47

URQUHART, THOMAS
The Works of. Edinburgh: 1834. V. 54

URQUHART, WILLIAM POLLARD
Essays on Subjects in Political Economy. Aberdeen: 1850. V. 53

URWICK, W.
Indian Pictures Drawn with Pen and Pencil. London. V. 54

USSHER, JAMES
Annales Veteris Testamenti (et Novi Testamenti), a Prima Mundi Origine Deducti... 1650/54. V. 47
A Body of Divinity, or The Summe and Substance of Christian Religion. London: 1648. V. 53
Clio: or, a Discourse on Taste. 1770. V. 47
Clio, or a Discourse on Taste. London: 1803. V. 51
A Discourse of the Religion Anciently Professed by the Irish and British. 1631. V. 48
A Discourse on the Religion Anciently Professed by the Irish and British. Dublin: 1815. V. 51
The Iudgement of Doctor Rainoldes Touching the Original of Episcopacy... London: 1641. V. 49; 54

USTERI, JOHN MARTIN
The Lord's Prayer of an Unterwaldener. London: 1805. V. 51

USTINOV, PETER
The Love of Four Colonels. New York: 1953. V. 54
Romanoff and Juliet. New York: 1958. V. 54

USUARD
Martyrologium, Quo Romana Ecclesia, ac Permultae Aliae Utuntur... Louvain: 1573. V. 50

UTAH. CONSTITUTION
Constitution of the State of Utah. Adopted by the convention april 27, 1882. Ratified by the People, May 22, 1882. Salt Lake City: 1881. V. 49

UTAH Scenes. New York: 1889. V. 51

UTAH, the Inland Empire Illustrated. Salt Lake City: 1902. V. 53

UTAH. UNIVERSITY
The Deseret First Book. By the Regents of the Deseret University. Salt Lake City: 1868. V. 48

UTAMARO, KITAGAWA
Twelve Woodblock prints of Kitagawa Utamaro... San Francisco: 1965. V. 47; 48; 52

UTTERSON, A. T.
Letters of an Antiquary. London: 1938. V. 51

UTTERSON, EDWARD VERNON
Letters of a Literary Antiquary. London: 1938. V. 50
Select Pieces of Early Popular Poetry: Re-Published Principally from Early Printed Copies in Black Leather. London: 1817. V. 47

UTTLEY, ALISON
The Adventures of Peter and Judy in Bunnyland. London: 1935. V. 49
The Button-Box and Other Essays. London: 1968. V. 54
Little Grey Rabbit's Party. London: 1936. V. 52

UZANNE, OCTAVE
The Fan. London: 1884. V. 47; 49
La Femme a Paris. Paris: 1894. V. 54
The French Bookbinders of the Eighteenth Century. Chicago: 1904. V. 47; 48; 51; 52
The Frenchwoman of the Century. London: 1886. V. 53; 54
Le Memoir du Monde: Notes et Sensations de la Vie Pittoresque. Paris: 1888. V. 54
Son Altesse La Femme. Paris: 1885. V. 54
The Sunshade - The Glove - The Muff. London: 1883. V. 54

UZZIAH and Jotham. A Poem. London: 1690. V. 54

V

VACARESCO, HELENE
The Bard of the Dimbovitza. London: 1892-97. V. 49; 52
The Bard of the Dimbovitza... London: 1892/94. V. 47; 50; 51

VACHSS, ANDREW
Flood. New York: 1985. V. 49

VAENIUS, ERNESTUS
Tractatus Physiologicus de Pulchritudine. Brussels: 1662. V. 49

VAGO, A. L.
Orthodox Phrenology... London: 1871. V. 50

VAHLE, JOSEPH
The Irish Prince and Hebrew Prophet a Masonic Tale of the Captive Jews and the Ark of the Covenant. New York: 1896. V. 49

VAIL, ALFRED
The American Electro Magnetic Telegraph... Philadelphia: 1845. V. 47
Description of the American Electro Magnetic Telegraph... Washington: 1845. V. 47

VAIL, ISRAEL E.
Three Years on the Blockade. New York: 1902. V. 49

VAILL, THEODORE FRELINGHUYSEN
History of the Second Connecticut Volunteer Heavy Artillery, Originally the Nineteenth Connecticut Volunteers. Winstead: 1868. V. 47

VAILLANT, ANNETTE
Bonnard. Greenwich: 1965. V. 47; 48; 50; 51; 52

VAILLANT, CLEMENT
De La Commodite de L'Appange. Paris: 1585. V. 48

VAILLANT, PAUL
Catalogus Librorum apud Paulum Vaillant, Bibliopolam, Londini Venales Prostantium: or, a Catalogue of Books in Most Languages and Faculties, Sold by Paul Vaillant, Bookseller, in the Strand. London: 1745. V. 50

VAILLANT, SEBASTIEN
Botanicon Parisiense ou Denombrement par Ordre Alphabetique des Plantes... Leiden & Amsterdam: 1727. V. 48; 49

VAIRASSE, DENIS
A Short and Methodical Introduction to the French Tongue. Paris: 1683. V. 50

VAJDA, MIKLOS
Winged By Their Own Need: Poems by the Winners and the Jurors of the Robert Graves Prize for Best Hungarian Poem of the Year 1970-1986. Deia, Mallorca: 1988. V. 49

VAKHRAMEEV, V. A.
Jurassic and Cretaceous Floras and Climates of the Earth. London: 1991. V. 52

VALA Moro/Tanz. Vienna: 1924. V. 51

VALDES, GONZALO FERNANDEZ DE OVIEDO Y
The Conquest and Settlement of the Island of Boriquen or Puerto Rico. Connecticut: 1975. V. 47

VALDEZ, GIOVANNI MELENDEZ
Meriggio, Ode...Tradotto dal Dottore Giuseppe Adorni. Parma: 1800. V. 49

VALDEZ, R.
Wild Sheep and Wild Sheep Hunters of the Old World. 1983. V. 52

VALDOR, JEAN
Les Triomphes de Louis le Juste XIII. Du Nom, Roy de France et de Navarre... Paris: 1649. V. 51

VALE, JOSEPH G.
Minty and the Cavalry. A History of Cavalry Campaigns in the Western Armies. Harrisburg: 1886. V. 48

VALENTI Angelo, Author, Illustrator, Printer. San Francisco: 1976. V. 48; 51

VALENTINE and Orson. London: 1919. V. 49

VALENTINE, DAVID
Valentine's Manuals. New York: 1916-28. V. 48

VALENTINE, DAVID T.
History of the City of New York. New York: 1853. V. 47

VALENTINE, L.
Heroes of the United Service. London: 1900. V. 50

VALENTINER, W. R.
The Bamberg Rider, Studies of Medieval German Sculpture. Los Angeles: 1956. V. 50
Jacques Louis David and the French Revolution. New York: 1929. V. 51
Studies of Italian Renaissance Sculpture. London: 1950. V. 49; 50; 52; 54

VALENTINI, CHRISTOPH BERNHARD
Tournefortius Contractus, Sub Forma Tabularum Sistens Instiutiones Rei Herbariae Juxta Methodum Modernorum, Cum Laboratorio Parisiensi Ejusdem Autoris. Frankfurt: 1715. V. 47; 53

VALENTINI, MICHAEL
Novellae Medico-Legales Seu Responsa medico-Forensia. Frankfurt: 1711. V. 50; 52

VALERIANO BOLZANO, GIOVANNI PIETRO
Hieroglyphica, Seu de Sacris Aegyptiorum... Venice: 1604. V. 54
Hieroglyphica Sive de Sacris Aegyptiorum, Aliarumque Gentium Literis Commentarii Ioannis Pierii Valeriani Bolzanii Bellunensis... Basle: 1575. V. 50

VALERIUS, MAXIMUS
Facta et Dicta Memorabilia.... Venice: 1493. V. 54

VALERIUS FLACCUS, CAIUS
Argomavticon. Antverpiae: 1566. V. 53; 54
Argonautica. Venice: 1523. V. 52
Argonauticon. Antwerp: 1565. V. 48
Argonauticon Libri Octo. Paris: 1532. V. 47; 49; 50

VALERIUS MAXIMUS
Dictorum ac Factorum Memorabilium tam Romanorum, Quam Extremorum Collectanea... Paris: 1535. V. 47; 50
Facta et Dicta Memorabilia... Venice: 1493. V. 48
(Facta et Dicta Memorabilia). Paris: 1531. V. 47
Valerio Massimo Volgare Novamente Coretto (sic). Venice: 1526. V. 52
Valerius Maximus Nuper Editus Index Copiosissimus Rerum Omnium, et Personarum, de Quibus in His Libris Agitur. Venice: 1534. V. 52

VALERY, PAUL
Charmes ou Poemes. Paris: 1922. V. 49
Le Cimetiere Marin. Paris: 1920. V. 50; 52
Le Cimetiere Marin. (The Graveyard by the Sea.). Verona: 1946. V. 51
Degas. Danse. Dessin. Paris: 1936. V. 54
An Evening with Mr. Teste. Paris: 1925. V. 54
The Graveyard by the Sea. London: 1945. V. 52
The Graveyard by the Sea. London: 1946. V. 48; 51; 52
Introduction to the Method of Leonardo da Vinci. London: 1929. V. 49; 50
Parallelement. Paris: 1889. V. 50

VALIN, JONATHAN
Final Notice. New York: 1980. V. 51

VALLA, LAURENTIUS
Elegantiarum Adeps, ex Eius de Lingua Latina Libris per Bonum Accursum Pisanum... Paris: 1548. V. 51; 54

VALLADARES DE SOTOMAYOR, ANTONIO
Historia Geografica, Civil Y Politica de la Isla De S. Juan Bautista de Puerto Rico. Madrid: 1789. V. 47

VALLANCE, AYMER
William Morris, His Art, His Writings and His Public Life. London: 1897. V. 47; 49; 51

VALLANCEY, CHARLES
The Art of Tanning and Currying Leather... London: 1774. V. 48
The Art of Tanning and Currying Leather... London: 1780. V. 50
A Grammar of the Iberno-Celtic or Irish Language. Dublin: 1782. V. 54

VALLANS, W.
A Tale of Two Swannes... London: 1953. V. 52

VALLAVINE, PETER
Observations on the Present Condition of the Current Coin of This Kingdom. London: 1742. V. 48; 51

VALLE, PIETRO DELLA
Les Frameux Voyages...dans la Turquie, l'Egypte la Palestine, la Perse & les Indes Orientales. Paris: 1662-65. V. 48
The Travels of...Into East-India and Arabia Deserta. London: 1665. V. 49; 53

VALLEE, RUDY
Vagabond Dreams Come True. New York: 1930. V. 53

VALLEJO, BORIS
The Boy Who Saved the Stars. 1978. V. 47; 51
The Fantastic Art of Boris Vallejo. 1978. V. 47

VALLEMONT, PIERRE LE LORRAIN DE
Curiosities of Nature and Art in Husbandry and Gardening. London: 1707. V. 54
La Physique Occulte, ou Traite de la Baguette Divinatoire... Paris: 1696. V. 49

VALLE PONTES, SEBASTIAO
Oracao Funebre nas Exequias do Illustrissimo, e Reverendissimo Senhor D. Rodrigo de Moura Telles, Arcebispo, e Senhor de Braga...Celebradas na Cathedral da Bahia a 28 de Marco de 1729...Peo Arcebispo da Bahia... Lisboa Occidental: 1730. V. 48

VALLES, FRANCISCO DE
De Iis Quae Scripta Sunt Physice in Libris Sacris, sive de Sacra Philosophia, Liber Singularis... Leiden: 1588. V. 48

VALLETTE, ELIE
The Deputy Commissary's Guide Within the Province of Maryland, Together with Plain and Sufficient Directions for Testators... Annapolis: 1774. V. 50

THE VALLEY Road. A History of the Traffic Association of California, the League of Progress, the North American Navigation Co., the Merchant's Shipping Association and the San Francisco and San Joaquin Valley Railway... San Francisco: 1896. V. 53

VALLIER, DORA
Henri Rousseau. New York: 1962. V. 47; 49; 51; 53
Henri Rousseau. London: 1979. V. 50

VALLS I SUBIRA, ORIOL
A Lively Look at Papermaking. North Hills: 1980. V. 53; 54

VALMIER, GEORGES
Collection Decors et Couleurs. Paris: 1930. V. 52

VALMIN, M. N.
The Swedish Messenia Expedition. Lund: 1938. V. 50; 52

VALPY, RICHARD
Poetical Chronology of Ancient and English Poetry with Historical and Explanatory Notes. London: 1795. V. 54

VALTRINUS, IOANNES
De Re Militari Veterum Romanorum Libri Septem. Cologne: 1597. V. 48

VALUABLE Secrets Concerning Arts and Trades...from the Best Artists... London: 1775. V. 47; 48; 51; 52
VALUABLE Secrets Concerning Arts and Trades...from the Best Artists... Dublin: 1778. V. 47; 48; 50; 51

VALUABLE Secrets Concerning Arts and Trades...from the Best Artists. Norwich: 1795. V. 48

VALUABLE Secrets Concerning Arts and Trades...from the Best Artists... Boston: 1798. V. 52

VALUABLE Secrets in Arts and Trades; or, Approved Directions from the Best Artists. London: 1791?. V. 52

VALUABLE Secrets in Arts, Trades, &c. Selected from the Best Authors and Adapted to the Situation of the United States. New York: 1809. V. 47; 49; 52

VALVASONE, ERASMO DI
La Caccia. Beramo: 1593. V. 53

VALVERDE DE HAMUSCO, JUAN
Anatome Corporis Humani... Venice: 1589. V. 48
Anatome Corporis Humani.... Venetiis: 1607. V. 48

VALZANIA, FRANCISCO ANTONIO
Instituciones de Arquitectura... Madrid: 1792. V. 53

VAMBERY, ARMINIUS
History of Bokhara from the Earliest Period Down to the Present. London: 1873. V. 50
Sketches of Central Asia. London: 1868. V. 51
Travels in Central Asia... 1864. V. 54
Travels in Central Asia. London: 1864. V. 50
Travels in Central Asia... New York: 1865. V. 48

VAMBERY, HERMANN
The Toorkmans and their Position Towards Russia. Calcutta: 1874. V. 49

VAN DER BURG,
School of Painting for the Imitation of Woods and Marbles. London: 1899. V. 48

VAN DER ELSKEN, ED
Sweet Life. New York. V. 48; 51

VAN DER HAEGHEN, FERDINAND
Bibliotheca Belgica... 1979. V. 48
Bibliotheca Belgica. Brussels: 1979. V. 50

VAN DER HORST, K.
Illuminated and Decorated Medieval Manuscripts in the University Library, Utrecht. Cambridge: 1989. V. 47

VAN DER KELLEN, D.
Illustrated International Architecture. The Hague: 1966. V. 50

VAN DER OSTEN, H. H.
Explorations in Central Anatolia: Season of 1926. Chicago: 1929. V. 50

VAN DER POST, LAURENS
The Dark Eye in Africa. London: 1955. V. 40
The Heart of the Hunter. London: 1961. V. 52
In a Province. London: 1934. V. 50; 53
The Lost World of the Kalahari. London: 1958. V. 53

VAN DER WOUDE, S.
Studia Bibliographica in Honorem Herman De La Fontaine Verwey. A Collection of Essays and Studies in Bibliography and Allied Subjects. Amsterdam: 1966. V. 50

VAN DER ZEE, JAMES
James Van Der Zee. Dobbs Ferry: 1973. V. 54

VAN DE VELDE, CAREL WILLEM MEREDITH
Le Pays D'Israel: Collection de Cent Vues Prises d'Apres Nature Dans la Syrie et la Palestine par C.W.M. van de Velde Pendant son Voyage d'Exploration Geographique en 1854 et en 1852. Paris: 1856. V. 53

VAN DE VELDE, M. S.
Cosmopolitan Recollections. London: 1889. V. 47

VAN DE WATER, FREDERIC F.
Glory-Hunter a Life of General Custer. New York: 1934. V. 50

VAN ALEN, W. K.
The Sutro Tunnel In Congress. Explanatory Remarks. 1870. V. 52

VAN ALSTYNE, LAWRENCE
Diary of an Enlisted Man. New Haven: 1910. V. 51; 53

VAN ANTWERP, WILLIAM C.
A Collector's Comment on His First Editions of the Works of Sir Walter Scott. San Francisco: 1932. V. 51; 53

VAN ASSEN, BENEDICTUS ANTONIO
The British Dance of Death, Exemplified by a Series of Engravings, from Drawings by Van Assen... London: 1828. V. 47

VAN BAAL, J.
Dema. Description and Analysis of Marind-Anim Culture (South New Guinea). The Hague: 1966. V. 52

VAN BOEKEL, GEORGETTE MARIA EUGENIE CORNELIA
Roman Terracotta Figurines and Masks from the Netherlands. Groningen: 1987. V. 52

VANBRUGH, JOHN
The Complete Works. Bloomsbury: 1924. V. 50; 54
The Complete Works... Bloomsbury: 1927. V. 47; 52
Complete Works. London: 1927. V. 50; 52; 53
The Complete Works. London: 1927-28. V. 47; 48; 49; 52; 53
The Mistake. London: 1706. V. 48
The Provok'd Husband; or, a Journey to London. London: 1728. V. 50
The Provok'd Husband; or, a Journey to London. 1737. V. 51
The Provok'd Wife: a Comedy. London: 1709. V. 52
A Short Vindication of the Relapse and the Provok'd Wife, from Immorality and Prophaneness. London: 1698. V. 47

VAN BUREN, A. DE PUY
Jottings of a Year's Sojourn in the South; or First Impressions of the Country and Its People... Battle Creek: 1859. V. 47

VAN BUREN, E. DOUGLAS
Archaic Fictile Revetments in Sicily and Magna Graecia. London: 1923. V. 49
Clay Figurines of Babylonia and Assyria. New Haven: 1930. V. 52
Figurative Terra-Cotta Revetments in Etruria and Latium in the VI and V Centuries B.C. London: 1921. V. 49
Greek Fictile Revetments in the Archaic Period. London: 1926. V. 52

VAN BUREN, MARTIN
Considerations in Favour of the Appointment of Rufus King, to the Senate of the United States. Submitted to the Republican Members of the Legislature of...New York. New York: 1819. V. 52

VAN BUREN, W. H.
Lectures Upon Diseases of the Rectum and the Surgery of the Lower Bowel. New York: 1881. V. 54
A Practical Treatise on the Surgical Diseases of the Genito-Urinary Organs Including Syphilis. New York: 1874. V. 51; 54

VAN BUTCHELL, MARTIN
Causes of Crim. Con. also Barrenness - and the King's Evil: Advice-New-Guinea... London: 1795. V. 48

VAN CAPELLEVEEN, PAUL
Prototype. 1991. V. 52

VANCE, ANDREW
The Green Book; or, Reading Made Easy of the Irish Statutes, Containing an Account of the Principal Reported Decisions at Law and in Equity, on the Irish Statues, Rules and Orders of Court, From Magna Charta to the Present Time. Dublin: 1862. V. 52

VANCE, JACK
Big Planet. 1957. V. 54
Big Planet. 1978. V. 52
Cadwal II: Ecce and Old Earth. Novato: 1991. V. 52
Cadwal III: Throy. Novato: 1992. V. 52
The Dying Earth. 1976. V. 54

VANCE, JACK continued
Eight Fantasms and Magics. 1969. V. 47
The Faceless Man. The Brave Free Men. The Asutra. San Francisco: 1983. V. 52
The Five Gold Bands. Novato: 1993. V. 52
The Fox Valley Murders. 1966. V. 54
Light from a Lone Star. 1985. V. 49; 54
The Seventeen Virgins & The Bagful of Dreams. 1979. V. 49; 54
Take My Face. 1957. V. 54
To Live Forever. 1956. V. 49; 54
To Live Forever. New York: 1956. V. 51
Vandals of the Void. 1953. V. 48; 52
When the Five Moons Rise. San Francisco: 1992. V. 52

VAN CLEVE, CHARLOTTE OUISCONSIN
Three Score Years and Ten, Life Long Memories of Fort Snelling, Minnesota and Other Parts of the West. Minneapolis: 1888. V. 47; 49
Three Score Years and Ten, Life Long Memories of Fort Snelling, Minnesota and Other Parts of the West. Minneapolis: 1895. V. 49; 51; 53

VAN COURT, DEWITT
The Making of Champions in California. Los Angeles: 1926. V. 52; 54

VANCOUVER, CHARLES
General View of the Agriculture in the County of Essex; with Observations on the means Of its Improvement. London: 1795. V. 50
General View of the Agriculture of the County of Devon... London: 1808. V. 51

VANCOUVER. FIRE DEPARTMENT
Rules and Regulations of the Fire Department, Vancouver, B.C. Vancouver: 1908. V. 53

VANCOUVER, GEORGE
Vancouver in California, 1792-1794. Los Angeles: 1953. V. 51
Vancouver in California, 1792-1794. Los Angeles: 1953/54. V. 54
Vancouver in California, 1792-1794. Los Angeles: 1954. V. 54
Voyage de Decouvertes, a L'Ocean Pacifique du Nord, et Autour du Monde... Paris: 1797. V. 51
A Voyage of Discovery to the North Pacific Ocean and Round the World... London: 1798. V. 47; 51
A Voyage of Discovery to the North Pacific Ocean, and Round the World... London: 1801. V. 51
A Voyage of Discovery to the North Pacific Ocean, and Round the World... Amsterdam, New York: 1967. V. 48; 49; 50; 52

VANDELEUR, CECIL FOSTER SEYMOUR
Campaigning on the Upper Nile and Niger. London: 1898. V. 48

VANDEN BERGH, L. J.
On the Trail of the Pigmies, an Anthropological Exploration Under the Cooperation of the American Museum of Natural History and American Universities. New York: 1921. V. 51

VAN DENBURGH, J.
The Reptiles of Western North America. 1922. V. 51

VANDENDAEL, A.
Fruits, Their Character and Qualities... Brussels: 1954. V. 54

VANDENHOFF, G.
A Plain System of Elocution... New York: 1845. V. 48

VANDERBILT, HAROLD S.
The Story of the Defense of the America's Cup in 1930. New York: 1931. V. 47

VANDER BURG, JESSIE M.
A History of the Union Steamship company of British Columbia 1889-1943. 1943. V. 53

VANDER ELST, JOANNES FRANCISCUS
Prael-Treyn Verrykt Door Ry-Benden, Prael-Wagens Zinne-Beelden en Andere Opronkingen Toegeschikt Aen Het Duyzend-Jaerig Jubile... Mechelen: 1775. V. 52

VANDERMONDE, ALEXIS T.
Procedes de la Fabrication des Armes Blanches, Publies Par Ordre du Comite de Salut Public. Paris: 1793. V. 53

VAN DERSAL, SAMUEL
Van Dersal's Stock Growers Directory of Marks and Brands for the State of North Dakota, 1902... Saint Paul: 1902. V. 54

VANDERVELL, H. E.
A System of Figure-Skating, Being the Theory and Practice of the Art as Developed in England, with a Glance At Its Origin and History. London: 1869. V. 50

VAN DEUSEN, JOHN G.
The Black Man in White America. Washington: 1938. V. 54

VANDEWATER, ROBERT J.
The Tourist, of Pocket Manual for Travellers on the Hudson River, the Western and Northern Canals and Railroads. New York: 1838. V. 47; 49

VANDIVER, CLARENCE
The Fur Trade and Early Western Exploration. Cleveland: 1929. V. 49

VANDOR, PAUL E.
History of Fresno County California with Biographical Sketches. Los Angeles: 1919. V. 47

VAN DOREN, CARL
Benjamin Franklin. New York: 1938. V. 47; 52
Letters From Carl. 1951. V. 48; 50

VAN DOREN, MARK
An Anthology of World Poetry. New York: 1936. V. 51
Henry David Thoreau. Boston & New York: 1916. V. 49; 54
The Life of Thomas Love Peacock. London: 1911. V. 49

VAN DRUTEN, JOHN
I Remember Mama. New York: 1945. V. 47
The Return of the Soldier. London: 1928. V. 54

VAN DUSEN, CONRAD
The Indian Chief an Account of the Labours, Losses, Sufferings and Oppression of Ke-zig-ko-e-ne-ne (David Sawyer)... London: 1867. V. 54

VAN DUYN, MONA
Valentines to the World. 1958. V. 54

VAN DYK, HENRY
The Gondola. London: 1827. V. 47

VAN DYKE, HARRY
The Physiology and Pharmacology of the Pituitary Body. Chicago: 1936-39. V. 47; 49

VAN DYKE, HENRY
The National Sin of Literary Piracy. New York: 1888. V. 50
The Travel Diary of an Angler. New York: 1929. V. 48; 53

VAN DYKE, THEODORE STRONG
The City and the County of San Diego. San Diego: 1888. V. 47; 54
Southern California: Its Valley, Hills, and Streams: Its Animals, Birds and Fishes... New York: 1886. V. 47

VANE, CHARLES
Memoirs and Correspondence of Viscount Castlereagh, Second Marquess of Londonderry. London: 1848. V. 54

VANE, HENRY
The Tryal of Sir Henry Vane...Together with What He Intended to Have Spoken the day of His Sentence... London: 1662. V. 48

VANEGAS, MIGUEL
A Natural and Civil History of California. London: 1759. V. 47

VAN EVERY, EDWARD
Sins of New York as "Exposed" by the Police Gazette. New York: 1930. V. 51

VAN EVRIE, J. H.
Negroes and Negro 'Slavery' the First, an Inferior Race - the Latter, Its Normal Condition. Baltimore: 1854. V. 50

VAN GIESON, JUDITH
Mercury Retrograde. Huntington Beach: 1994. V. 52; 53
North of the Border. 1988. V. 54
North of the Border. New York: 1988. V. 47
Raptor. New York: 1990. V. 53; 54

VAN GULIK, ROBERT
The Chinese Bell Murders. London: 1958. V. 47; 50; 51
The Chinese Bell Murders... London: 1963. V. 52
The Chinese Lake Murders. London: 1960. V. 53
The Chinese Maze Murders. Hague and Bandung: 1956. V. 52; 53
The Chinese Maze Murders. 1957. V. 53
The Chinese Nail Murders. London: 1961. V. 51; 53
Dee Gong An, Three Murder Cases Solved by Judge Dee. 1949. V. 53
The Emperor's Pearl. London: 1963. V. 52
The Given Day - an Amsterdam Mystery. Kuala Lumpur: 1964. V. 50; 51
The Haunted Monastery... Kuala Lumpur: 1961. V. 50
The Haunted Monastery. London: 1963. V. 51
The Haunted Monastery. New York: 1969. V. 52
Poets and Murder. London: 1968. V. 49; 50
Sexual Life in Ancient China - a Preliminary Survey of Chinese Sex and Society from ca. 1500 B.C. till 1644 A.d. Leiden: 1961. V. 47

VAN HEURCK, HENRI
The Microscope: Its Construction and Management. London: 1893. V. 50

VAN HORNE, THOMAS BUDD
History of the Army of the Cumberland. Cincinnati: 1875. V. 51

VANINI, GUILIO CESARE
Amphitheatrum Aeternae Providentiae Divino-Magicum. Lyon: 1615. V. 48

VAN KAMPEN, N.
The Dutch Florist: or, True Method of Managing All Sorts of Flowers with Bulbous Roots... London: 1764. V. 47

VAN KAMPEN, N. G.
The History and Topography of Holland and Belgium. London: 1837. V. 52

VAN LAREN, A. J.
Cactus. Los Angeles: 1935. V. 49; 53
Succulents Other Than Cacti. Los Angeles: 1934. V. 53

VAN LEAR, A. H. F.
Documents Relating to New Netherland 1624-1626. San Marino: 1924. V. 49

VAN LENNEP, HENRY JOHN
Bible Lands: Their Modern Customs and Manners Illustrative of Scripture. New York: 1875. V. 48; 51

VAN LIER, HELPERUS RITZEMA
The Power of Grace Illustrated. London: 1792. V. 51

VAN LOO, CARLO
Recueil de Differentes Charges Dessignee a Rome. Paris: 1729-38. V. 53

VAN LOON, HENDRIK WILLEM
America. New York: 1927. V. 50; 53
Ancient Man, the Beginning of Civilization. London: 1923. V. 51

VAN LUSTABADER, ERIC
The Sunset Warrior. Garden City: 1977. V. 51

VAN MILLINGEN, ALEXANDER
Byzantine Constantinople. The Walls of the City and Adjoining Historical Sites. London: 1899. V. 48; 49
Constantinople. London: 1906. V. 51

VAN NESS, WILLIAM PETER
An Examination of the Various Charges Exhibited Against Aaron Burr, Esq... New York: 1803. V. 47
Examination of the Various Charges Exhibited Against Aaron Burr, Esq... Philadelphia: 1803. V. 47
The Speeches at Full length of Mr. Van Ness, Mr. Caines, the Attorney-General, Mr. Harrison and General Hamilton in the Great Cause of the people Against Harry Croswell on an Indictment for a Libel on Thomas Jefferson. New York: 1804. V. 50; 51

VAN NORDEN, WARNER
Who's Who of the Chinese in New York. New York: 1918. V. 47

VAN NOSTRAND, JEANNE
A Pictorial and Narrative History of Monterey, Adobe Capital of California 1770-1847. San Francisco: 1968. V. 53; 54
San Francisco, 1806-1906, in Contemporary Paintings, Drawings and Watercolors. San Francisco: 1975. V. 47; 48; 53; 54

VAN OSDEL, A. L.
Historic Landmarks in the Great American Northwest, Being a History of Early Explorers and Fur Traders with a Narrative of Their Adventures in the Winds of the Great Northwest Territory. 1915. V. 53

VAN PATTEN, NORMAN
There Are Some Who Mourn. Salem: 1948. V. 47; 48; 49

VAN PEEBLES, MELVIN
The Big Heart. San Francisco: 1957. V. 52

VAN PELT, GARRETT
Old Architecture of Southern Mexico. Cleveland: 1926. V. 52

VAN REGEMORTER, BERTHE
Some Oriental Bindings in the Chester Beatty Library. Dublin: 1961. V. 49

VAN RENSSELAER, FLORENCE
The Livingston Family in America and Its Scottish Origins. New York: 1949. V. 49; 51

VAN RENSSELAER, MARIANA GRISWOLD
History of the City of New York in the 18th Century. New York: 1909. V. 52

VAN RENSSELAER, MAY KING
Newport Social Capital. Philadelphia & London: 1905. V. 50

VAN RENSSELAER, SOLOMON
A Narrative of the Affair of Queenstown in the War of 1812. New York: 1836. V. 47; 52

VAN ROYEN, P.
The Orchids of the High Mountains of New Guinea. London: 1980. V. 52
The Orchids of the High Mountains of New Guinea. Vaduz: 1980. V. 52

VAN SICHEM, CHRISTOFFEL
Bibels Tresor, Ofte dere Ziellen Lusthof, Vytgebeelt in Figueren, Door Verschyeden Meesters. Amsterdam: 1646. V. 52

VAN SINDEREN, ADRIAN
Canter Please! Random Memories of Glenholme Farm and of Our Playmates and Playgrounds. New York: 1935. V. 47

VANSITTART, HENRY
A Letter to the Proprietors of East-India Stock - Occasioned by a Late Anonymous Pamphlet and by the East India Observer. London: 1767. V. 48; 53

VANSITTART, NICHOLAS
An Inquiry into the State of the Finances of Great Britain: in Answer to Mr. Morgan's Facts. London: 1796. V. 53

VANSITTART, ROBERT
Certain Ancient Tracts Concerning the Management of Landed Property Reprinted. London: 1767. V. 49
The Singing Caravan. Newtown: 1932. V. 47; 51; 54

VAN SOMEREN, G. R. C.
Van Somerens' Birds. Volume 2. London: 1994. V. 52

VAN SOMEREN, V. G. L.
The Birds of East Africa. Sarasota: 1973. V. 50
The Birds of East Africa. Volume I. Ploceidae. London: 1973. V. 52

VANSTON, GEORGE T. B.
The Law Relating to Local government in Ireland. Dublin: 1915-05-19. V. 48

VAN TRAMP, JOHN C.
Prairie and Rocky Mountain Adventures... Columbus: 1858. V. 47; 49

VAN URK, J. BLAN
The Horse The Valley and the Chagrin Valley Hunt. New York: 1947. V. 47
The Story of American Foxhunting. New York: 1940/41. V. 52

The Story of Rolling Rock. New York: 1947. V. 47
The Story of Rolling Rock. New York: 1950. V. 47; 52; 53

VAN VECHTEN, CARL
Sacred and Profane Memories. New York: 1932. V. 49; 61
Spider Boy: a Scenario for a Moving Picture. New York: 1928. V. 51; 52
The Tattooed Countess: a Romantic Novel with a Happy Ending. New York: 1924. V. 50

VANVITELLI, LUIGI
Dichiarazione Dei Disegni del Reale Palazzo di Caserta... Naples: 1756. V. 47; 53

VAN VOGT, A. E.
Masters of Time. 1950. V. 48; 49; 52
Slan. Sauk City: 1946. V. 47; 51
Slan. 1953. V. 54
The Voyage of the Space Beagle. 1950. V. 52
The Weapon Makers. 1947. V. 48; 52
The Weapon Makers. Providence: 1947. V. 52

VAN WALLEGHEN, MICHAEL
The Wichita Poems. Iowa City: 1973. V. 54

VAN WART, IRVING
A Recollection of Wonderous Wanderings. Fontainebleau: 1864. V. 49; 53

VAN WATERS, GEORGE
The Poetical Geography, Being a Classification of the Principal Rivers, Towns, Islands, Mountains and Lakes of the World, Woven Into Verse: the Object of Which is to Aid the Memory. Ogdensburgh: 1841. V. 54

VAN WINKLE, DANIEL
History of the Municipalities of Hudson County, New Jersey, 1630-1923. New York: 1924. V. 49; 51

VAN WINKLE, W. M.
Henry William Herbert (Frank Forester). A Bibliography of His Writings 1832-1858. Portland: 1936. V. 47; 49

VAN WYCK, WILLIAM
Robinson Jeffers. Los Angeles: 1938. V. 51; 53; 54

VAN ZANDT, NICHOLAS B.
A Full Description of the Soil, Water, Timber and Prairies of Each Lost, or Quarter Section of the Military Lands Between the Mississippi and Illinois Rivers. Washington: 1818. V. 47

VAN ZANTEN, D. T.
Walter Bruley Griffin: Selected Designs. Palos Park: 1970. V. 51

VAN ZILE, E. S.
That Marvel - the Movie - A Glimpse At ts Reckless Pasts, Its Promising Present and Its Significant Future. New York: 1923. V. 53

VAN ZYL, JOHANNES
Theatrum Machinarum Universale; of Groot Algemeen Moolen-Boek. Amsterdam: 1761. V. 53

VARAGNAC, ANDRE
French Costumes. London: 1939. V. 48

VARCHI, BENEDETTO
De Sonetti...Parte Prima (and) Parte Secunda. Florence: 1555-57. V. 52

VARDY, JOHN
Some Designs of Mr. Inigo Jones and Mr. William Kent. London: 1744. V. 52

VAREKAMP, MARJOLEIN
Francesco. Groningen: 1987. V. 52; 54

VARGA, JUDY
Gemlins on the Job. London, Canada: 1943. V. 50

VARGA: The Esquire Years. A Catalogue Raisonne. New York: 1987. V. 49; 53

VARGAS LLOSA, MARIO
Captain Pantoja and the Special Service. New York: 1978. V. 47
Conversation in the Cathedral. New York: 1975. V. 47; 49; 53
The Cubs. Helsinki: 1990. V. 48
The Green House. New York: 1968. V. 49
The Real Life of Alejandro Mayta. New York: 1986. V. 52; 53
The War of the End of the World. New York: 1984. V. 53

LES VARIETES Amusantes. Paris: 1782. V. 53

VARIETIES in Woman. London: 1819. V. 50; 54

VARIETIES of Life; or Conduct and Consequences. London: 1815. V. 51

VARILLAS, ANTOINE DE
Anekdota Eterouiaka (graece) or, The Secret History of the House of Medicis. London: 1686. V. 50; 52

VARIOUS Methods to Prevent Fires in Houses and Shipping and for Preserving...Lives...an Account of Remarkable Accidents by Fire... London: 1775. V. 52

VARLEY, JOHN
Blue Champagne. Niles: 1986. V. 52
The Gaean Trilogy, Being Titan, Wizard and demon. 1979/80/84. V. 48; 52
A Practical Treatise on Perspective... London: 1815-20. V. 47

VARLO, CHARLES
The Essence of Agriculture...With the Author's Twelve Months Tour thro' America... London: 1786. V. 48
Nature Display'd a New Work. London: 1793. V. 52
A New System of Husbandry.... Philadelphia: 1785. V. 48; 51; 54

VARNEY, ALMON C.
Our Homes and Their Adornments; or How to Build, Finish, Furnish and Adorn a Home. Detroit: 1884. V. 50

VARNUM, JAMES M.
The Case, Trevett Against Weeden: On Information and Complaint, for Refusing Paper Bills in Payment...at Par with Specie... Providence: 1787. V. 48; 51

VARRO, MARCUS TERENTIUS
Opera Quae Supersunt... Geneva: 15181. V. 52
Opera Quae Supersunt. Basle: 1581. V. 48

VASARI, GIORGIO
Lives of Seventy of the Most Eminent Painters, Sculptors and Architects. London: 1897. V. 51
Lives of the Most Eminent Painters... London: 1850-52. V. 48
Lives of the Most Eminent Painters. 1966. V. 52; 54
The Lives of the Most Eminent Painters. Verona: 1966. V. 48; 49; 52
Opere de... Firenze: 1822-23. V. 50

VASCONCELLOS, SIMAO DE
Vida do Veneravel Padre Joseph de Anchieta da Companhia de Iesu, Taumaturgo do Nouo Mundo, na Provincia do Brasil... Lisbon: 1672. V. 48

VASCONCELOS, EDMUNDO
Modern Methods of Amputation. 1945. V. 54

VAS DIAS, ROBERT
The Life of Parts, or Thanking You for the Book on Birdfeeders. Mt. Horeb: 1972. V. 51; 54

VASEY, G.
Grasses of the Pacific Slope... Washington: 1890-91. V. 52

VASON, GEORGE
An Authentic Narrative of Four Years' Residence at Tongataboo, One of the Friendly Islands, in the South Sea. London: 1810. V. 51

VASSALL, SPENCER THOMAS
Memoir of the Life of Lieutenant-Colonel Vassall. Bristol: 1812. V. 49

VASSAR, J. J.
Copies From a Correspondence and Substance of Communications, with Mr. Huskisson, Mr. Perceval, &c. &c... London: 1810. V. 50

VASSE, A.
Souvenir de Beloeil, Dedie a Son Altesse Serenissime La Princesse de Ligne, nee Princesse Lubomirska. Brussels: 1853. V. 52

VASSE, LOYS
In Anatomen Corporis Humani Tabulae Quatuor... Venice: 1549. V. 53; 54

VASSOS, JOHN
Phobia. New York: 1931. V. 50

VASSOS, JOHN & RUTH
Contempo. New York: 1929. V. 50; 51; 53; 54
Ultimo: an Imaginative Narration Of Life Under the Earth with Projections... New York: 1930. V. 48; 50; 51; 53

VASSOS, RUTH
Humanities. New York: 1935. V. 52

THE VAST Importance of Correct Views, As to the Various Questions of Policy...In the Proposed Annexation of Texas... 1844. V. 48

VASTEY, POMPEE-VALENTIN, BARON DE
Reflexions Politiques sur Quelques ouvrages et Journax Francais, Concernant Hayti. Sans Souci: 1817. V. 49

VATABLUS, FRANCISCUS
In Hoc Opere Continentvr Totivs Philosophiae Naturalis Paraphrases. Paris: 1533. V. 52

VATTEL, EMMERICH DE
The Law of Nations; or Principles of the Law of Nature... Dublin: 1787. V. 48
The Law of Nations; or Principles of the Law of Nature... New York: 1796. V. 50
The Law of Nations; Or Principles of the Law of Nature. Northampton: 1805. V. 50

VAUGHAN, BENJAMIN
Letters on the Subject of the Concert of Princes, and the Dismemberment of Poland and France. London: 1793. V. 52

VAUGHAN, HAROLD STEARNS
Congenital Cleft Lip, Cleft Palate and Associated Nasal Deformities. Philadelphia: 1940. V. 54

VAUGHAN, HENRY
The Poems. London & New York: 1896. V. 47
Poems. 1924. V. 49
Poems. Newtown: 1924. V. 49
Sacred Poems. London: 1897. V. 51
Secular Poems of...Including a Few Pieces by His Twin-Brother Thomas. Hull: 1893. V. 48
Silex Scintillans... London: 1847. V. 54
Silex Scintillans... London: 1858. V. 47; 52
The Works... Oxford: 1914. V. 48

VAUGHAN, HENRY HALFORD
New Readings and New Renderings of Shakespeare's Tragedies. London: 1886. V. 53

VAUGHAN, J. D.
The Manners and Customs, of the Chinese of the Straits Settlements. Singapore: 1879. V. 48; 51

VAUGHAN, JOHN
The Reports and Arguments... London: 1677. V. 47; 50; 52

VAUGHAN, KEITH
Journal and Drawings 1939-1965. London: 1966. V. 48

VAUGHAN, MALCOLM
Chandor's Portraits. New York: 1942. V. 47

VAUGHAN, RICE
A Treatise on Money or a Discourse of Coin and Coinage... London: 1675. V. 47

VAUGHAN, ROBERT
The History of England Under the House of Stuart, Including the Commonwealth A.D. 1603-1688. London: 1840. V. 49
The Life and Opinions of John de Wycliffe... London: 1828. V. 47
Memorials of the Stuart Dynasty from the Decease of Elizabeth to the Abdication of James II. London: 131. V. 49

VAUGHAN, SALLIE WERNER
Illusion of Two. Houston: 1981. V. 52
Seeds of Snow. Houston: 1981. V. 52

VAUGHAN, T. W.
Recent Madreporaria of the Hawaiian Islands and Laysan. Washington: 1907. V. 53

VAUGHAN, THOMAS
Isabel de Bohun, or the Siege of Hereford: and Other Poems. Hereford: 1858. V. 54
The Works of Thomas Vaughan. London: 1919. V. 48

VAUGHAN, W.
Advice to Young Gentleman, Concerning the Conduct of Life. London: 1710. V. 47

VAUGHAN, W. E.
Autobiographica with a Gossip on the Art of printing in Colours. 1900. V. 51

VAUGHAN, WALTER
The Life and Work of Sir Willian Van Horne. New York: 1920. V. 53

VAUGHAN, WILLIAM
The Church Militant (in Verse), Historically Continued From the Yeare of Our Saviours Incarnation 33. Until This Present, 1640. London: 1640. V. 48
Memoir of William Vaugham... London: 1839. V. 50

VAURIE, C.
The Birds of the Palaearctic Fauna. London: 1959-65. V. 52; 54
The Birds of the Palearctic Fauna. Volume 2. Non-Passeriformes. London: 1965. V. 48; 50; 51
Tibet and its Birds. London: 1972. V. 49; 50; 51; 52; 53; 54

VAUX, CALVERT
Villas and Cottages. New York: 1857. V. 47; 52
Villas and Cottages... 1864. V. 51
Villas and Cottages. New York: 1864. V. 47; 50; 53; 54
Villas and Cottages. New York: 1867. V. 47; 48
Villas and Cottages. 1869. V. 51
Villas and Cottages... New York: 1869. V. 48; 50; 53

VAUX, FRANCES BOWYER
Henry: a Story, Intended for Little Boys and Girls From Five to Seven Years Old. London: 1825. V. 48

VAUX, ROBERTS
Memoirs of the Life of Anthony Benezet... Philadelphia: 1817. V. 52

VAVILOV, N. I.
Origin and Geography of Cultivated Plants. London: 1992. V. 49; 52

VAVRA, JAROSLAV R.
5000 Years of Glass-Making. The History of Glass. Prague: 1954. V. 48

VAZ DE ALMADA, FRANCISCO
Tratado do Successo Que Teve a Nao Sam Joam Baptista, e Iornada, Que fez a gente, Que della Escapou Desde Trinta, & Tres Graos no Cabo da Boa Esperanca, Onde Fez Naufragio, Ate Zofala, Indo Sempre Marchando por Terra. Lisbon: 1625. V. 48

VEAL, GEORGE
Joel Collier Redivivus, an enitrely New Edition, of That Celebrated Author's "Musical Travels"... London: 1818. V. 47
Musical Travels through England. London: 1785. V. 47

VEBLEN, THORSTEIN
The Theory of the Leisure Class. An Economic Study in the Evolution of Institutions. New York: 1899. V. 47

VEDDER, DAVID
The Story of Reynard the Fox. London. V. 49
The Story of Reynard the Fox... London: 1830. V. 49

VEDDER, ELIHU
The Digressions of Elihu Vedder. Boston: 1910. V. 47; 49; 51
Doubt and Other Things. Boston: 1922. V. 54

VEECH, JAMES
The Monoghaela of Old; or, Historical Sketches of South-Western Pennsylvania to the Year 1800. Pittsburgh: 1858-92. V. 47; 50

VEEN, JAN VAN DER
Zinne-Beelden, oft Adams Appel...Mitsgagders Signe en Nieuwe Ongemeene Bruylofs Zege-Zangen, Raetselen... Amsterdam: 1659. V. 47; 48; 50; 52

VEEN, OCTAVIO VAN, KNOWN AS OTTO VAENIUS
Amoris Divina Emblemata, Studio et Aere Othonis Vaeni Concinnata. Antwerp: 1660. V. 53
Emblemata Horatiana, Imaginibus in Aes Incisis Atque Latino, Germanico, Gallico et Belgico Carmine Illustrata. Amsterdam: 1684. V. 47; 48
Vita D. Thomae Aquinatis. Brussels: 1778. V. 47
Zinnebeelden Getrokken uit Horatius Flaccus, Naer de Geestrijke Vinding van den Geleerden Otto van Veen. Amsterdam: 1683. V. 47

VEENHOVEN, WILLEM A.
Case Studies on Human Rights and Fundamental Freedoms. The Hague: 1975/76. V. 49

VEER, GERRIT DE
The Three Voyages of William Barents to the Arctic Regions (1594, 1595 and 1596). London: 1876. V. 47; 49

VEGA CARPIO, LOPE FELIX DE
The Star of Seville. Newtown: 1935. V. 51; 53; 54

LAS Vegas Hot Springs, Las Vegas, New Mexico on the Line of the Atchison, Topeka and Santa Fe. Chicago: 1882. V. 49

LAS Vegas Hot Springs, New Mexico. Prepared for the Information of Tourists, Tired People, Invalids of All Classes and Those Who Seek a Summer or Winter Resort, with the Benefit to be Derived from Medicinal Baths and Mineral Waters. Chicago: 1887. V. 49

VEGETIUS
Military Institutions of Vegetius, in Five Books. London: 1767. V. 48

VEHLING, JOSEPH DOMMERS
Platina and the Rebirth of Man. Chicago: 1941. V. 51

VEITCH, JAMES, & SONS
A Manual of Orchidaceous Plants Cultivated Under Glass in Great Britain. London: 1887-94. V. 48
A Manual of the Coniferae... London: 1881. V. 47; 48
Manual of the Coniferiae. London: 1900. V. 47; 48

VEITCH, JAMES H.
Hortus Veitchi. A History of the Rise and Progress of the Nurseries of Messrs. James Veitch & Sons... London: 1906. V. 51; 52; 53
A Traveller's Notes...India, Malaysia, Japan, Corea, the Australian Colonies and New Zealand. London: 1896. V. 51

VEITCH, JOHN
The Feeling for Nature in Scottish Poetry. London: 1887. V. 52; 54
Institutes of Logic. Edinburgh: 1885. V. 50; 51

VEITCH, JOHN, & SONS
A Manual of Orchidaceous Plants. London: 1887. V. 50
Manual of the Coniferiae. London: 1900. V. 50; 54

VEITH, ILZA
Huang Ti Nei Ching Su Wen. The Yellow Emperor's Classic of Internal Medicine. Baltimore: 1949. V. 54

VELARDE, PABILTA
Old Father: the Story Teller. Globe: 1960. V. 48

VELASCO, FRANCISCO
Sonora: its Extent, Population, Natural Productions, Indian Tribes, Mines, Mineral Lands, Etc., Etc. San Francisco: 1861. V. 48

VELASCO DE GOUVEIA, FRANCISCO
Perfidia de Alemania y de Castilla, en la Prision, Entrega, Accusacion, y Processo del Serenissimo Infante de Portugal D. Duarte. Lisbon: 1652. V. 53

VELASQUEZ, PEDRO
Memoir of an Eventful Expedition in Central America... New York: 1850. V. 47

VELDE, KARL FRANZ VAN DER
Tales from the German. Boston: 1837. V. 50

VELEZ DE JAEN, FERNANDO
Discurso Historico de los Servicios Que Juanetin Mortara Patricio Genoves Hizo a Su Magestad del Rey don Felipe III. Madrid: 1612. V. 48

VELIKOVSKY, IMMANUEL
Earth in Upheaval. London: 1956. V. 51
Worlds in Collision. 1950. V. 54
Worlds in Collision. New York: 1950. V. 49

VELLEIUS PATERCULUS, MARCUS
The Roman History. London: 1721. V. 54
The Roman History... Edinburgh: 1722. V. 49

VELOSO, JOSE MARIA DA CONCEICAO
Naturalista Instruido nos Diversos methodos Antigos, e Modernos de Ajuntar, Preparar, e Conservar as Producoes dos tres Reinos de Natureza Colligido das Differentes Authores, Dividio em Varios Livros. Lisbon: 1800. V. 48

VELPEAU, A.
A Treatise on the Diseases of the Breast and Mammary Region. London: 1856. V. 54

VELSERUS, MARCUS
Antiqua Monumenta Das Ist Alte Bilder, Gemahlde und Schrifften zu Augspurg Gefunden. Frankfurt: 1595. V. 53

VENABLES, R. LISTER
Domestic Scenes in Russia... London: 1839. V. 50

VENABLES, ROBERT
The Experienced Angler. London: 1827. V. 47; 51; 52; 54

VENCENTI, LAELIUS
Absolvtissima Qvaestio De Animae Immortalitate... Venice: 1588. V. 48

VENEDEY, JACOB
Ireland and the Irish During the Repeal Year, 1843... Dublin: 1844. V. 53

VENEGAS, MIGUEL
Juan Maria de Salvatierra of the Company of Jesus; Missionary in the Province of New Spain and Apostolic Conquerer of the California. Cleveland: 1929. V. 50; 51
A Natural and Civil History of California... London: 1759. V. 47; 53; 54

VENERONI, GIOVANNI
The Complete Italian Master... London: 1763. V. 47
The Italian Master; or, The Easiest and Best method for Attaining that Language. London: 1729. V. 52

VENESS, W. T.
El Dorado, or, British Guiana as a Field for Colonisation. London: 1867. V. 49; 52

VENIERO, MAFFIO
Hidalba: Tragedia. Venice: 1596. V. 51; 54

VENN, JOHN
Catalogue of a Collection of Books on Logic Presented to the Library by John Venn. Cambridge: 1889. V. 49
The Logic of Chance. An Essay on the Foundations and Province of the Theory of Probability... London: 1888. V. 49
The Principals of Empirical or Inductive Logic. London: 1889. V. 51

VENNER, T.
Via Recta ad Vitam Longam. Or, a Treatise Wherein the Right Way and Best manner of Living for Attaining to a Long and Healthful Life is Clearly Demonstrated. London: 1650. V. 53

VENNING, MARY ANNE
A Geographical Present: Being Descriptions of the principal Countries of the World. London: 1817. V. 47; 49
A Geographical Present: Being Descriptions of the Principal Countries of the World. London: 1818. V. 48; 50
A Geographical Present: Being Descriptions of the Principal Countries of the World. New York: 1829. V. 48; 53

VENNOR, HENRY G.
Our Birds of Prey, or the Eagles, Hawks and Owls of Canada. Montreal: 1876. V. 48

VENTENAT, ETIENNE PIERRE
Description des Plantes Nouvelles et Peu Connues, Cultivees dans le Jardin de J. M. Cels. Paris: 1800-03. V. 51

VENTOUILLAC, L. T.
The French Librarian, or Literary Guide, Pointing Out the Best Works of the Principal Writers of France, in Every Branch of Literature. London: 1829. V. 47

VENTURA, COMINO
Tresor Politiqve Diuise en Trois Liures. Paris: 1608. V. 51; 53

VENTURI, LIONELLO
Marc Chagall. New York: 1945. V. 50

VENTURI, ROBERT
Complexity and Contradiction in Architecture. New York: 1966. V. 49
Learning from Las Vegas. Cambridge: 1972. V. 50; 51; 53

VENUS Attiring the Graces. London: 1777. V. 48; 54

VENUS Oceanica. New York: 1935. V. 48; 52

VENUTI, FILIPPO
Dittionario Volgare, & Latino... (with) Dictionarium Latinvm (etc.). Venice: 1596. V. 51; 54

VENUTI, NICCOLO MARCELLO DI, MARQUIS
A Description of the First Discoveries of the Antient City of Herculaneum. London: 1750?. V. 48

VERARD, ANTOINE
Antoine Verard. London: 1900. V. 48; 50

VER BECK, FRANK
Little Black Sambo and the Tiger Kitten. New York: 1935. V. 54

VERBEEK, R. D. M.
Krakatau. Brussels: 1886. V. 49

VERDICT of 13 a Detection Club Anthology. London: 1979. V. 52

VERE, FRANCIS
The Commentaries of Sr Francis Vere. Cambridge: 1657. V. 51

VEREY, ROSEMARY
A Country-woman's Notes. 1989. V. 47
A Countrywoman's Notes. Barnsley: 1989. V. 47

VERGA, GIOVANNI
The House by the Medlar Tree. New York: 1890. V. 51
Little Novels of Sicily. New York: 1925. V. 47

VERGANI, ANGELO
The Beauties of English Poetry, or a Collection of Poems Extracted from the Best Authors. Paris: 1803. V. 47; 52

VERGILIUS, POLYDORUS
An Abridgement of the Notable Worke of Polidore Virgile. London: 1560. V. 50
Anglicae Historiae Libri Uigintisex... Basel: 1546. V. 50; 53
Anglicae Historiae Libri Vigintiseptem. Basle: 1555. V. 47; 50; 53
Anglicae Historiae Libri XXVI. Basileae: 1534. V. 49
De Inventoribus Rerum Libri VIII. Et de Prodigiis Libri III. Amstelodami: 1671. V. 48
De Rerum Inventoribus Libri Octo. Romae: 1585. V. 51
Les Memoires et Histoire de l'Origine, Invention & Autheurs des Choses. Paris: 1582. V. 52
A Pleasant and Compendious History of the First Inventers and Institutors of the Most Famous Arts, Mistries, Laws, Customs and Manners in the Whole World. London: 1686. V. 48
Proverbium Libellus. Venice: 1500. V. 51; 54

VERGILIUS MARO, PUBLIUS
The Aeneid... Boston: 1872. V. 54
The Aeneid... Boston & New York: 1906. V. 52
The Aeneid. New York: 1944. V. 48; 50; 52; 54
The Aeneid. London: 1952. V. 48; 53
The Aeneids of Virgil; Done into English Verse by William Morris. London: 1902. V. 48; 51
Aeneis. Edinburgh: 1710. V. 49; 50; 51; 53; 54
Bucolica... Edinburgh: 1743. V. 52
Bucolica... 1750. V. 47
Bucolica... London: 1750. V. 48; 49; 50
Bucolica... Birmingham: 1757. V. 47; 51; 52
Bucolica... Birmingham: 1766. V. 52
Bucolica... London: 1774. V. 48; 52; 53; 54
Bucolica... Glasgow: 1778. V. 48; 52; 53
Bucolica... Paris: 1798. V. 52
Bucolica... London: 1800. V. 52
Bucolica. London: 1810. V. 50
Bucolica... London: 1821. V. 52
Les Bucoliques. Paris: 1955. V. 48
Eclogae and Georgica Latine et Germanice. 1926. V. 54
The Eclogues. London: 1813. V. 50
Les Eclogues. 1926. V. 52
Les Eclogues... Weimar: 1926. V. 47; 52
The Eclogues. New York: 1960. V. 50; 52; 53
L'Eneide. Venice: 1576. V. 48
L'Eneide Fidelement... Paris: 1658. V. 49; 51; 52; 54
An English Version of the Eclogues of Virgil. London: 1883. V. 52; 54
Georgica, et Aeneis. Glasguae: 1778. V. 50
Georgica/Les Georgiques. Paris: 1937-43-50. V. 52; 54
The Georgics... London: 1741. V. 49
The Georgics... London: 1810. V. 49
The Georgics. New York: 1952. V. 48; 49; 54
The Georgics. Verona: 1952. V. 49; 52; 54
Opera... Lyon: 1527/1528. V. 49
Opera. Amsterdam: 1746. V. 52
Opera. London: 1753. V. 54
Opera. Londini: 1775. V. 53
Opera. Londini: 1781. V. 48
Opera. London: 1793. V. 48; 51
Opera. Parma: 1793. V. 52
Opera ex Antiquis Monimentis Illustrata, Cura, Studio & Sumtibus Henrici Justice, Armigeri, Rufforthii Toparchae. The Hague: 1757-65. V. 49
Opera Omnia... London: 1819. V. 52
Opera Omnia. 1912. V. 54
Opera Omnia. London: 1912. V. 50
L'Opere...Nvovamente...Tradotte... Florence: 1556. V. 51
Paesaggi Virgiliani. Milan: 1981. V. 48
Philippi Melanchthonis Adnotatiunculis, ut Brevissimis, Ita Doctissimis Illustatus. Parisiis: 1535. V. 48
Publii Virgilii Maronis Georgicorum...The Georgicks...with and English Translation and Notes (and) The Bucolicks... London: 1746/49. V. 54
Virgil's Husbandry, or an Essay on the Georgics... London: 1724. V. 48
The Whole XII Bookes of the Aenedios of Virgil. London: 1573. V. 47
The Works... London: 1654. V. 47; 53; 54
The Works... London: 1697. V. 50; 54
The Works... London: 1709. V. 48
The Works... London: 1731. V. 52
The Works... London: 1731-35. V. 47
The Works... London: 1735. V. 52
The Works... London: 1753. V. 48
Works. Brussels: 1765. V. 47
The Works... Birmingham: 1766. V. 54
The Works... Glasgow: 1775. V. 48
The Works. London: 1792. V. 48
Works. London: 1821. V. 50
The Works... New York: 1823. V. 52

VERHAEREN, EMILE
Five Tales. New York: 1924. V. 49; 51
Les Petits Vieux. London: 1901. V. 49

VERHEIDEN, JACOB
Af-Beeldingen Van Sommighe in Godts-Woort Ervarene Mannen, Die Bestreden Hebben Den Roomschen Antichrist. The Hague: 1603. V. 50

VERHOEFF, MARY
The Kentucky River Navigation. Louisville: 1917. V. 50

VERHOEVEN, J. T. A.
Fens and Bogs in the Netherlands: Vegetation History, Nutrient Dynamics and Conservation. Dordrecht: 1992. V. 50

VERHULST, GABRIEL FRANCOIS JOSEPH
Catalogue d'une Riche et Precieuse Collection de Tableaux. Brussels: 1779. V. 47

VERICH, THOMAS
English Magnolias: an Exhibition of Mississippi Fiction Printed in England. Jackson: 1992. V. 54

VERINI, GIOVAM BAPTISTA
Luminario; or, the Third Book of the Liber Elementorum Litterarum on the Construction of Roman Capitals. Cambridge and Chicago: 1947. V. 48; 51; 53

VERINO, UGOLINO
Vita di Santa Chiara Vergine. 1921. V. 52; 54
Vita di Santa Chiara Vergine Composta per Ugolino Verino Cittadino Fiorentino. Chelsea: 1921. V. 47
Vita di Santa Chiara Vergine Composta per Vgolino Verino Cittadino Florentino. London: 1921. V. 54

VERITY, FRANK T.
Flats, Urban Houses and Cottage Homes. London: 1906. V. 51; 52

VERLAINE, PAUL MARIE
Epigrammes. Paris: 1894. V. 47; 51
Fetes Galantes. Paris: 1928. V. 54

VERLARDE, PABLITA
Old Father. The Story Teller. 1960. V. 52

VERLET, PIERRE
The James A. de Rothschild Collection at Waddesdon Manor: the Savonnerie, its History - The Waddlesdon Collection. Fribourg: 1982. V. 52

VERLIUS MAXIMUS
Valerio Massimo Volgare Novamente Coretto (sic). Venice: 1526. V. 48

VERMEULE, CORNELIUS C.
Roman Imperial Art in Greece and Asia Minor. Cambridge: 1968. V. 52

VERMEULE, EMILY D. T.
Toumba tou Skourou: a Bronze Age Potters' Quarter on Morphou Bay in Cyprus. Cambridge: 1990. V. 52

VERMIGLIOVI, G. B.
Saggio di Bonzi Etruschi Trovatai Nell'Agro Perugino L'Aprile del 1812. Perugia: 1813. V. 50

VERMILLE, THOMAS E.
Funeral Discourse Occasioned by the Death of the Hon. Stephen Van Rensselaer. Albany: 1839. V. 47
Funeral Discourse Occasioned by the Death of the Hon. Stephen Van Rensselaer. New York: 1839. V. 48

THE VERMIN Killer. Being a Compleat and Necessary Family-Book. London. V. 49

VERNE, JULES
Abandoned. London: 1875. V. 54
Adventures in the Land of the Behemoth. Boston: 1874. V. 49
Around the World in Eighty Days. Los Angeles: 1962. V. 51
Doctor Ox, and Other Stories. Boston: 1874. V. 49
The Exploration of the World-Famous Travels and Travelers. New York: 1879. V. 47; 49; 51
Facing the Flag. 1897. V. 49; 51; 54
Five Weeks in a Balloon. New York: 1869. V. 47; 54
Foundling Mick. 1895. V. 50
From the Clouds to the Mountains: Comprising Narratives of Strange Adventures by Air, Land and Water. Boston: 1874. V. 48; 49
From the Earth to the Moon and Around the Moon. New York: 1970. V. 48; 51; 52; 54
Godfrey Morgan - a Californian Mystery. New York: 1883. V. 47
The Great Navigators of the Eighteenth Century. London: 1880. V. 51
Great Navigators of the Eighteenth Century, Great Explorers of the XIX Century, Famous Travels and Travellers. New York: 1887. V. 48
A Journey to the Center of the Earth. New York: 1874. V. 47; 54
A Journey to the Center of the Earth. New York: 1966. V. 53
A Journey to the North Pole. London: 1875. V. 51
Meridiana. New York: 1874. V. 49; 51
Michael Strogoff... New York: 1877. V. 47; 54
Michael Strogoff. Paris: 1880's. V. 47
Michael Strogoff... New York: 1927. V. 50
Mistress Branican. London: 1891. V. 47
The Mysterious Island. Baltimore: 1959. V. 48; 51; 53
Mysterious Island. New York: 1959. V. 52; 53
Robur-Le-Conquerant. Paris: 1886. V. 47

VERNE, JULES continued
La Tour du Monde en Quatre-Vignets Jours. Paris: 1872. V. 47; 48
The Tour of the World in 80 Days. Boston: 1873. V. 47; 48
Twenty-Thousand Leagues Under the Sea. V. 47
Twenty-Thousand Leagues Under the Sea. Los Angeles: 1956. V. 54
A Voyage Around the World - South America. 1876. V. 48
A Voyage Around the World - South America. London: 1876. V. 52
The Will of an Eccentric. London: 1900. V. 54
The Works of Jules Verne. New York. V. 51
Works of Jules Verne. New York, London: 1911. V. 50
The Works of Jules Verne. New York: 192-?. V. 53
The Wreck of the Chancellor. Boston: 1875. V. 49
The Wreck of the Chancellor. Toronto: 1875. V. 53

VERNER, COOLIE
The Northpart of America. Toronto: 1979. V. 47; 49; 50

VERNER, WILLOUGHBY
My Life Among the Wild Birds in Spain. London: 1909. V. 51
Sketches in the Soudan. London: 1886. V. 49

VERNEUIL, A.
Kaleidoscope, Ornements Abstraits. Paris: 1929. V. 48; 50

VERNEUIL, M. P.
L'Animal dans la Decoration. Paris: 1898. V. 47
Etude de la Plante. Son Application aux Industries d'Art. Paris: 1900. V. 47

VERNEY, FRANCES PARTHENHOPE
Memoirs of the Verney Family. London: 1892/94/99. V. 51
Memoirs of the Verney Family. London: 1970. V. 48

VERNEY, G. L.
The History of the 7th Armoured Division, 1938-1945. London: 1954. V. 50

VERNIER, CHARLES
Les Bals de Paris & Souvenirs de Caranval. Paris: 1859-60. V. 48

VERNON, EDWARD
A Specimen of Naked Truth, from a British Sailor. London: 1746. V. 52

VERNON, EDWARD JOHNSTON
A Guide to the Anglo-Saxon Tongue: a Grammar... London: 1846. V. 52

VERNON, FRANCIS
Oxonium Poema. Oxon: 1667. V. 48

VERNON-HARCOURT, LEVESON FRANCIS
Rivers and Canals. The Flow, Control and Improvement of Rivers and the Design, Construction and Development of Canals Both for Navigation and Irrigation. Oxford: 1896. V. 47; 50; 52

VERNOR, HENRY G.
Our Birds of Prey or the Eagles, Hawks and Owls of Canada. Montreal: 1876. V. 47

VERO *Raggvaglio dell'alto Ricevimento, Che la Citta di Burgos Fece Alla Serenissima Regina Donna Anna (etc.).* Rome: 1571. V. 53

VEROLA, PAUL
Rama. Poeme Dramatique En Trois Actes, Illustrations de Alphonse Mucha. Paris: 1898. V. 51

VERPLANCK, GULIAN C.
Discourses and Addresses on Subjects to American History, Arts and Literature. New York: 1833. V. 49
The Influence of Moral Causes Upon Opinion, Science and Literature. (with) The Right Moral Influence and Use of Liberal Studies. (with) Discources and Addresses. New York: 1834/33/33. V. 48; 52

VERRAL, CHARLES
Poems: Including Servius Tullius, a Tragedy and Saladin, a Dramatic Romance. Upper Mary-le-Bone St: 1815?. V. 48

VERRALL, G. H.
British Flies. Volume 8: Platypezidae, Pipunculidae and Syrphidae. London: 1901. V. 52

VERRENT, ANN
The Three Little Black Boys. London: 1950. V. 53

VERRILL, A. E.
Monograph of the Shallow-Water Starfishes of the North Pacific Coast from the Arctic Ocean to California. London: 1914. V. 49

VERSAILLES Illustrated, or Divers Views of the Several Parts of the Royal Palace... London: 1740. V. 52

VERSES from Alice. London: 1944. V. 49

VERSES in Memory of a Lady. London: 1768. V. 54

VERSES Inscribed to Captain James Duncan of the Rose Bud Privateer. England: 1822. V. 47

VERSES Made on the Sudden Death of Six Young Women and One Boy, Who Were Drowned at Jamestown, Rhode-Island, July 13, 1782. Newport: 1798?. V. 47

VERSES to the Memory of the Late Right Hon. Charles Earl Camden, to Which are added, Two Poetical Essays, viz. The Ruin of Athens and the Shepherds of Lebanon, With Alcander and Evanthe, a Tale. Dublin: 1795. V. 50

VERSTEGEN, RICHARD
A Restitution of Decayed Intelligence... Antwerp: 1604. V. 53
A Restitution of Decayed Intelligence... Antwerp: 1605. V. 49; 50
A Restitution of Decayed Intelligence... London: 1628. V. 49; 50
A Restitution of Decayed Intelligence... London: 1634. V. 47; 53
A Restitution of Decayed Intelligence... London: 1673. V. 47; 50

VERTES, MARCEL
The Stronger Sex, as Seen by Vertes. New York: 1941. V. 48

VERTKOV, K.
Atlas of Musical Instruments of the Peoples Inhabiting the USSR. Moscow: 1975. V. 49

VERTOT, RENE AUBERT DE, ABBE
Histoire des Chevaliers Hospitaliers de S. Jean de Jerusalem... Paris: 1726. V. 54
The History of the Revolution in Portugal in the Year 1640, or, an Account of Their Revolt from Spain, and Setting the Crown on the Head of Don Juan of Braganza. London: 1700. V. 47
The History of the Revolutions in Sweden... London: 1696. V. 47; 50; 53
The History of the Revolutions in Sweden. London: 1723. V. 47
The History of the Revolutions That Happened in the Government of the Roman Republic... London: 1720. V. 48
An History of the Revolutions that Happened in the Government of the Roman Republic. London: 1770. V. 50

VERVE: an Artistic and Literary Quarterly. Paris: 1937. V. 52

VERVILLE, BEROALDE DE
Fantastic Tales; or, The Way to Attain. Carabonnek: 1890. V. 53

VERVLIET, HENDRIK D. L.
The Book Through Five Thousand Years. London: 1972. V. 49

VERVOORT, FRANS
Hortulus Anime. Antwerp: 1562. V. 54

VERY, JONES
Essays and Poems. Boston: 1839. V. 49; 51; 52; 53; 54
Poems. Boston: 1883. V. 54

VERY, LYDIA L. A.
Poems. Andover: 1856. V. 52; 54
Red Riding Hood. Boston: 1863. V. 50
A Strange Disclosure. Boston: 1898. V. 51

THE VERY Remarkable Trial of John Holloway, and Owen Haggerty...Guilty...of the Wilful Murder of Mr. J. C. Steele...to Which is added the Trial of Elizabeth Godfrey for the Murder of Richard Prince etc. London: 1807?. V. 52

VESALIUS, ANDREAS
Chirurgia Magna in Septem Libros Digesta. Venice: 1569. V. 47
De Humani Corpori Fabrica. Basel: 1555. V. 53
De Humani Corporis Fabrica Libri Septem. Basel: 1543. V. 47
De Humani Corporis Fabrica Libri Septem. Venice: 1568. V. 53
Icones Anatomicae. New York and Munich: 1934. V. 54
Opera Omnia Antomica and Chirurgica... Leiden: 1725. V. 52; 54

VESLING, JOHANN
Syntagma Anatomicum. Padua: 1647. V. 47; 49

VESPUCCI, AMERIGO
The Letter of Amerigo Vespucci Describing His Four Voyages to the World 1497-1504. San Francisco: 1926. V. 47

VESPUCCIUS, ALBERICUS
The Voyage from Lisbon to India, 1505-06, Being an Account and Journal By... London: 1894. V. 53

VEST, GEORGE GRAHAM
Man's Best Friend: a Plea to a Jury by... New York: 1920. V. 47

VESTAL, STANLEY
Big Foot Wallace. A Biography. Boston: 1942. V. 51
Fandango, Ballads of the Old West. Boston & New York: 1927. V. 47; 48; 49; 50; 53
Joe Meek. The Merry Moutain Men. A Biography. Caldwell: 1952. V. 53
New Sources of Indian History. Norman: 1934. V. 49; 54
Queen of Cowtowns, Dodge City. "The Wickedest Little City in America" 1872-1886. New York: 1952. V. 53
Sitting Bull Champion of the Sioux a Biography. Boston & New York: 1932. V. 47
Warpath. The True Story of the Fighting Sioux Told in a Biography of Chief White Bull. Boston & New York: 1934. V. 51; 52

VESTIGIA Veritatis: or, the Controversy Relating to the Act of the Thirty fifth of Elizabeth... London: 1681. V. 49; 51

VETALAPANCAVIMASTI
Vikram and the Vampire... 1870. V. 48; 50; 52
Vikram and the Vampire... London: 1870. V. 50; 52
Vikram and the Vampire. London: 1893. V. 51

VETH, CORNELIS
Comic Art in England. Amsterdam: 1930. V. 52

VETROMILE, EUGENE
The Abnakis and Their History of Historical Notices on the Aborigines of Acadia. New York: 1866. V. 47; 53

VETSCH, EARNEST
A New Story of Little Black Sambo. Racine: 1926. V. 49

VETTORI, PIETRO
Epistolarum Libri X. Orationes XIIII. Et Liber De Lavdibvs Ioannae Avstriacae. Florence: 1586. V. 48
Liber de Laudibus Ioannae Austriacae, Natae Reginae Vngarie, et Boemiae. Florence: 1566. V. 50
Oratio Fvnebris De Lavdibvs Ioannis Medicis. Florence: 1562. V. 48; 53

VEVER, HENRY
Catalogue of Highly Important Japanese Prints, Illustrated Books and Drawings from the Henri Vever Collection. London: 1974/75/77. V. 50

VIAN, BORIS
L'Automne a Pekin. Paris: 1956. V. 52

VIANA, FRANCISCO JAVIER DE
Dairio Del Viage Explorador de Las Corbetas Espanolas "Descubierta" y "Atrevida" en Los Anos de 1789 a 1794, Llevado Por el Teniente de Anvio D. Francisco Janvier de viana, Y Ofrecido Para Su Publicacion, en Su Original Inedito... Cirrito de la Victoria: 1849. V. 52

VICAIRE, GEORGES
Bibliographie Gastronomique. London: 1954. V. 48
Manuel de l'Amateur de Livres du XIXe Siecle... 1974-75. V. 49

THE VICAR of Bray: a Tale. London: 1771. V. 50

VICARY, THOMAS
The English-Mans Treasure. London: 1633. V. 48

VICEDOM, GEORG F.
Die Mbowamb. Hamburg: 1943-48. V. 52

VICERY, ELIZA
Emily Hamilton, a Novel. Worcester: 1803. V. 52

VICKERS, ALFRED GEORGE
Russia &c. London: 1840. V. 54

VICKERS, BRIAN
Shakespeare; The Critical Heritage. London: 1974-81. V. 51

VICKERS, C. L.
History of Arkansas Valley, Colorado. Chicago: 1881. V. 52

VICKERS, HENRY
(Sale) Catalogue of Furniture...Library of Books...Oil Paintings and Engravings. Bridgnorth: 1865. V. 53

VICKERS, LEONARD B.
The Loud Voice: Rev. X. 3, and Everlasting Gospel; Rev. XIV 6. New York: 1865. V. 52

VICKERS, ROY HENRY
Solstice. The Art of Henry Vickers. Tofino: 1988. V. 53
Some Like the Dead. London: 1960. V. 52

VICKERY, SUKEY
Emily Hamilton. Worcester: 1803. V. 50; 51; 53

VICKRIS, RICHARD
Truth and Innocency Defended. London: 1692/93. V. 51

VICK'S Flower and Vegetable Garden. Rochester: 1900. V. 52

VICO, ENEA
Sic Romae Antiqui Sculptores ex Acre et Marmore Faciebant. Rome: 1543 and 1552. V. 53

VICQ D'AZYR, FELIX
Oeuvres. Recueillies et Publiees avec des Notes et un Discours sur sa Vie et ses Ouvrages... Paris: 1805. V. 51
Traite d'Anatomie et de Physiologie... Paris: 1786. V. 51; 53

VICTOR, BENJAMIN
Memoirs of the Life of Barton Booth, Esq... London: 1733. V. 51
The Widow of the Wood. London: 1755. V. 47; 49; 51

VICTOR, FRANCES AURETTA FULLER
All Over Oregon and Washington. San Francisco: 1872. V. 47
The Early Indian Wars of Oregon. Salem: 1894. V. 48; 53
Eleven Years in the Rocky Mountains and Life on the Frontier... Hartford: 1877. V. 51
The New Penelope and Other Stories and Poems. San Francisco: 1877. V. 54
The River of the West: Life and Adventure in the Rocky Mountains and Oregon, Embracing Events in the Life-Time of a Mountain-Man and Pioneer, with the Early History of the North-Western Slope. Hartford: 1870. V. 50

VICTOR Hammer: an Artist's Testament. Lexington: 1988. V. 51

VICTOR, METTA VICTORIA FULLER
Fresh Leaves from Western Woods. Buffalo: 1852. V. 54
Maum Guinea, and Her Plantation "Children" or, Holiday-Week on a Louisiana Estate. A slave Romance. New York: 1861. V. 52
The Senator's Son; or, The Maine Law; a Last Refuge; A Story Dedicated to the Law-Makers. Cleveland: 1853. V. 50

VICTOR, ORVILLE JAMES
The Private and Public Life of Abraham Lincoln. New York: 1865. V. 48

VICTOR Robinson Memorial Volume. Essays on History of Medicine in Honor of Victor Robinson on His Sixteith Birthday, August 16, 1946. New York: 1948. V. 53

VICTORIA & ALBERT MUSEUM
Catalogue of English Porcelain Earthenware Enamels and Glass Collected by Charles Screiber and the Lady Charlotte Elizabeth Schreiber and Presented to the Museum in 1884. London: 1924-30. V. 51
Catalogue of Watercolor Paintings by British Artists and Foreigners Working in Great Britain. London: 1927. V. 49; 52

VICTORIA County History of Bedfordshire. London: 1904-1972. V. 47

VICTORIA County History. Sussex. Volume I. London: 1905. V. 52

VICTORIA County History. Sussex. Volume II. London: 1907. V. 52

VICTORIA History of the County of... London: 1905. V. 47

VICTORIA, QUEEN OF GREAT BRITAIN
The Girlhood of Queen Victoria: a Selection from Her Majesty's Diaries Between the Years 1832 and 1840. London: 1912. V. 49
Leaves from the Journal Of Our Life in the Highlands from 1848 to 1861. London: 1868. V. 47; 48; 49; 50; 52
Leaves from the Journal of Our Life in the Highlands from 1848 to 1861...(with) More Leaves from the Journal of a Life in the Highlands from 1862 to 1882. London: 1868-84. V. 48; 49
The Letters of Queen Victoria. London: 1907-32. V. 47; 49; 52

VICTORIA, R. I., A Collection of Books, Manuscripts, Autograph Letters, Original Drawings, etc. San Francisco: 1969. V. 49; 54

VICTORIA, R. I. A Collection of Books, Manuscripts, Autograph letters, Original Drawings, Etc. London: 1969-70. V. 51

VICTORIA, R. I. A Collection of Books, Manuscripts, Autograph Letters, Original Drawings, Etc... San Francisco: 1969-70. V. 47; 48

VICTORIA, The Good Queen and Empress. London: 1897. V. 47; 51

VICTORIA UNIVERSITY OF MANCHESTER. LIBRARY
Catalogue of Medical Books in Manchester University Library 1480-1700. Manchester: 1972. V. 49; 51; 52

A VICTORIAN Anthology 1837-1895. Boston: 1906. V. 54

THE VICTORIANS. London: 1949. V. 53

VICTORIANS Abroad: Observations of Five Travellers. London: 1995. V. 54

VICTORIUS, PETRUS
Petri Victorii Variarum lectionum... Lyon: 1554. V. 52
Variarum Lectionum Libri XXV. Lyons: 1554. V. 48

VIDA, MARCO GIROLAMO, BP. OF ALBA
Christiados Libri Sex. Cremonae: 1535. V. 53
Dialogi De Rei Pbvlicae Dignitate. Cremona: 1556. V. 53
The Game of Chess. London: 1921. V. 48; 53
The Game of Chess. London: 1926. V. 50
Opera. Antwerp: 1567. V. 50
Poemata Omnia... Creomona: 1550. V. 52
The Poetics of... Sunderland: 1793. V. 47; 52
Sacchia Ludus: or, the Game of Chess. London: 1736. V. 51
The Silkworn: a Poem. (with) Scacchia, Ludus: a Poem on the Game of Chess. Dublin: 1750/50. V. 50
Vida's Art of Poetry. 1725. V. 53
Vida's Art of Poetry. London: 1725. V. 47; 48; 49; 50; 54
Vida's Art of Poetry. London: 1742. V. 48

VIDAL, EMERIC ESSEX
Picturesque Illustrations of Buenos Ayres and Monte Video... London: 1820. V. 49

VIDAL, GORE
1876. 1976. V. 50
1876. New York: 1976. V. 48; 49
The City and the Pillar. London: 1949. V. 47
Creation. New York: 1981. V. 49; 51
Dark Green, Bright Red. New York: 1950. V. 48; 49; 51
Death Before Bedtime. New York: 1953. V. 48; 49; 52
Death in the Fifth Position. New York: 1952. V. 48; 49; 52
Death Likes It Hot. New York: 1954. V. 48
Empire. New York: 1987. V. 48; 51
In a Yellow Wood. New York: 1947. V. 51
The Judgement of Paris. New York: 1952. V. 47; 48; 49; 50; 52
Julian. Boston: 1964. V. 54
The Ladies in the Library. Helsinki: 1985. V. 48
Lincoln. 1984. V. 53
Lincoln. Franklin Center: 1984. V. 52
Lincoln. New York: 1984. V. 49; 51; 53
Myra Breckinridge. Boston: 1968. V. 50; 51
Reflections Upon a Sinking Ship. Boston: 1968. V. 54
Rocking the Boat. Boston: 1962. V. 54
Romulus. New York: 1966. V. 54
A Search for the King. New York: 1950. V. 53; 54
Sex Is Politics. Los Angeles: 1979. V. 51
Two Sisters. Boston: 1970. V. 54
Visit to a Small Planet and Other Television Plays. Boston: 1956. V. 54
Williwaw. New York: 1946. V. 47; 49; 51

VIDOCQ, FRANCOIS EUGENE
Memoires de Vidocq... Paris: 1828-29. V. 50
Memoirs of Vidocq. London: 1829. V. 48
Memoirs of Vidocq... London: 1829-30. V. 47

VIDYASAGAR, ESHWAR CHANDRA
Marriage of Hindu Widows. Calcutta: 1856. V. 49

LE VIE et les Actions Memorable du Sr. Michel de Ruyter, Duc. Chevalier, & Lt. Amiral General des Provinces Unies. Amsterdam: 1677. V. 48

VIEILLOT, LOUIS J. P.
La Galerie des Oiseaux. 1834. V. 47
Songbirds of the Torrid Zone. 1979. V. 52; 54
Songbirds of the Torrid Zone. London: 1979. V. 50; 53

VIELE, EGBERT L., MRS. (TERESA GRIFFIN)
Following the Drum: A Glimpse of Frontier Life. New York: 1858. V. 47; 48; 52

VIETZEN, R. C.
The Ancient Ohioans and their Neighbors. Ohio: 1946. V. 51

VIEUSSEUX, ANDRE
Anselmo: a Tale of Italy. London: 1825. V. 50
Italy and the Italians in the Nineteenth Century... London: 1824. V. 47

LA VIEUX Natura Breuium, Dernierment Corrigee et Amend... Londini: 1580. V. 51

VIEW Book of Hamilton, Ontario. Hamilton: 1900. V. 53

A VIEW of London and Westminster: or, the Town Spy. London: 1725. V. 53

A VIEW of Paris, and Places Adjoining. London: 1701. V. 47

A VIEW of the Relative State of Great Britain and France, at the Commencement of...1796. London: 1796. V. 50; 53

A VIEW of the Several Changes, Made in the Administration of Government, Since the Accession of His Present Majesty. London: 1767. V. 48

VIEWS in Cheltenham. Cheltenham: 1830. V. 52

VIEWS In Edinburgh and its Vicinity. Edinburgh: 1820. V. 51

VIEWS in London, Consisting of the Most Remarkable Buildings, With an Historical Description of Each. London: 1825. V. 50

VIEWS in Oxford. 1850. V. 47

VIEWS of British Columbia and Alaska. Victoria: 1888?. V. 47

VIEWS of Denver Colorado 1889. Denver: 1889. V. 52

VIEWS of Los Angeles & Vicinity, California. 1888. V. 47

VIEWS of Lyford Texas and Vicinity in the Heart of the Magic Valley Formerly Known as the Lower Rio Grande Valley. Lyford: 1915. V. 53

VIEWS Of Niagara Falls, New York. Columbus: 1890. V. 54

VIEWS of Pompeii. London: 1828. V. 52

VIEWS of the English Lakes, Drawn and Engraved by W. Banks, Edinburgh. Windermere: 1860. V. 54

VIEWS of the Parish Churchs in York: With a Short Account of Each. York: 1831. V. 51

VIEYRA, ANTONIO
A Dictionary of the Portuguese and English Languages, in Two Parts... London: 1840. V. 50
A New Pocket Dictionary of the English and Portuguese Languages. Lisbon: 1841-45. V. 51; 54

VIGEE-LEBRUN, MARIE LOUISE ELISABETH
Souvenirs of Madame Vigee le Brun. London: 1879. V. 52

VIGFUSSON, GUDBRANDUR
Corpus Poeticum Boreale. The Poetry of the Old Northern Tongue, From the Earliest Times to the Thirteenth Century. Oxford: 1883. V. 48

VIGNAUD, HENRY
Toscanelli and Columbus. The Letter and Chart of Toscanelli on the Route to the Indies by Way of the West, Sent in 1474 to the Portuguese Fernam Martins and Later On to Christopher Columbus. London: 1902. V. 50

VIGNE, GODFREY T.
Six Months in America. London: 1832. V. 47; 53

VIGNIER, NICOLAS
Theatre de l'Antechrist. La Rochelle: 1610. V. 49

VIGNOLA, GIACOMO BAROZZIO, CALLED
Le Due Regole Della Propsettiva Prattica Di M. Jacomo Barozzi de Vignola... In Bologna: 1782. V. 47
Reigle des Cinq Ordres d'Architecture. Paris. V. 53
Il Vignola Illustrato Proposto da Giambattista Spampani, e Carlo Antonini... Rome: 1770. V. 50

VIGNOLES, CHARLES
Observations Upon the Floridas. New York: 1823. V. 47
Statements Respecting the Method and Cost of Producing Coke from Turf. London: 1850. V. 52

VIGNY, ALFRED DE
Poemes. Paris: 1822. V. 48

VIGO, GIOVANNI DE
Prattica Vtilissima et Necessaria Di Cirvgia dello Eccell M. Giovanni Di Vico, con Novove Figvre Adornata. Venetia: 1558. V. 48

VIGORS, NICHOLAS AYLWARD
An Inquiry Into the Nature and Extent of Poetick Licence. London: 1810. V. 54

VIGOUREUX, JEAN
Paris: Twenty-Eight Drawings by... Los Angeles: 1942. V. 50

VILLA and Cottage Architecture: Select Examples of Country and Suburban Residences Recently Erected. London: 1869. V. 51; 52

VILLA, JOSE GARCIA
A Celebration for Edith Sitwell on the Occasion of Her Visit to the United States. Norfolk: 1948. V. 47

VILLAGE Annals, Containing Austerus and Humanus. Philadelphia: 1814. V. 49; 51

THE VILLAGE Harmony; or, Youth's Assistant to Sacred Musick... Newburyport: 1813. V. 50

THE VILLAGE Orphan: a Tale for Youth. To Which is Added, The Basket-Maker, an Original Fragment. Philadelphia: 1800. V. 53

VILLAGE Tales, or Juvenile Amusements. New York: 1803. V. 49

VILLAGOMEZ Y LORENZANA, GREGORIO ALFONSO
Prima Oratio Habita in Regio ac Pontificio Angelopolitano Seminario Sanct. Apost. Petri & Joann. in Laudem Angelici Doctoris D. Thomae Aquinatis... Puebla de Los Angeles: 1770. V. 53

VILLAULT, SIEUR DE BELLEFOND
Relation of the Coasts of Africk called Guinee: with a Description of the Countreys, Manners...Being Collected in a Voyage...in the Years 1666 and 1667. London: 1670. V. 48

VILLEGAGNON, NICHOLAS DURAND DE
Caroli V Imperatoris Expeditio in Africam. Paris: 1542. V. 51

VILLEHARDOUIN, GEOFFRY DE
The Chronicle of Geoffry de Villehardouin... Leicester: 1829. V. 51
Histoire de l'Empire de Constantinople Sous les Empereurs Francois. Paris: 1657. V. 54

VILLIERS, ALAN J.
An Account of Sailing with the Arabs in their Dhows, in the Red Sea, round the Coasts of Arabia, and to Zanzibar and Tanganyika... London: 1940. V. 50
The Sea in Ships: The Story of a Sailing Ship's Voyage Round Cape Horn. New York: 1932. V. 51
Whalers of the Midnight Sun. New York/London: 1934. V. 53

VILLIERS, DAVID
A Winter Fireworks. Waltham St. Lawrence: 1937. V. 51; 54

VILLIERS, FREDERIC
Days of Glory - The Sketch Book of a Veteran Correspondent at the Front. New York: 1920. V. 47

VILLIERS DE L'ISLE-ADAM, JEAN MARIE MATHIAS PHILIPPE
Olympe & Henriette. Sherman Oaks: 1992. V. 49; 51
Queen Ysabeau. Chicago: 1925. V. 53

VILLON, FRANCOIS
Autres Poesies. London: 1901. V. 48
Ballads Done Into English from the French. Portland: 1904. V. 50
The Ballads of Francois Villon. San Francisco: 1927. V. 48; 51; 54
Le Lais, Le Testament et Sea Balaldes. The Hague: 1926. V. 52
The Lyrical Poems Of... New York: 1979. V. 48; 52; 54
The Lyrics of Francois Villon... Croton Falls: 1933. V. 47
The Lyrics of Francois Villon. New York: 1933. V. 48; 52; 53
Oeuvres Completes. Paris: 1892. V. 50
The Poems of Francois Villon. London: 1946. V. 49

VILLON, JACQUES
Cent Croquis 1894-1904. Paris: 1959. V. 52

VILNAY, ZEV
The Holy Land in Old Prints and Maps. Jerusalem: 1965. V. 48

VILVAIN, ROBERT
Enchiridion Epigrammatum Latino-Anglicum. London: 1654. V. 48; 51; 54

VIMERCATI, FRANCESCO
In...Libros Aristotelis Meteorologicorum Commentarij (etc). Venice: 1565. V. 52

VINCARD, B.
L'Art du Typographe. Ouvrage Utile a MM. les Hommes de Lettres, Bibliographes, et Typographes. Paris: 1806. V. 48

VINCARTIUS, JOANNES
Sacrarum Heroidum Epistolae. Tornaci: 1640. V. 53; 54

VINCE, SAMUEL
The Principles of Fluxions: Designed for the Use of Students in the University. Philadelphia: 1812. V. 47; 49; 50

VINCENT, C. W.
Chemistry, Theoretical, Practical and Analytical as Applied to the Arts and Manufactures. London: 1882. V. 52; 54

VINCENT DE BEAUVAIS
Speculum Naturale. Strassburg?: 1481. V. 47; 50; 53
Speculum Naturalis. 1486. V. 48

VINCENT, FRANK
Actual Africa; or, the Coming Continent. New York: 1895. V. 54

VINCENT, JOHN
Fowling. A Poem. London: 1808. V. 50; 51; 52; 54
Fowling, a Poem. London: 1812. V. 51; 52

VINCENT, LEON
Dewitt Miller, a Biographical Sketch. Cambridge: 1912. V. 47

VINCENT, LEVINUS
Wondertooneel der Nature, Geopent in Een Korte Beschryvinge der Hoofddeelen van de Byzondere Zeldsaamheden daar in Begrepen... Amsterdam: 1706-15. V. 49

VINCENT, STEPHEN
Passages. San Francisco: 1983. V. 54

VINCENT, THOMAS
Christ's Sudden and Certain Appearance to Judgment. Wheeling: 1823. V. 48
Gods Terrible Voice in the City. London: 1667. V. 50

VINCENT, WILLIAM
The Voyage of Nearchus from the Indus to the Euphrates. London: 1797. V. 50

VINCENT OF LERINS, SAINT
Pro Catholicae Fidei Antiquitate...Adversus Prophanas...Haeresen Nouationes, Liber. Paris: 1561. V. 48

A **VINDICATION** of Oliver Cromwell, and the Whiggs of Forty One, to Our Modern Low Churchmen. London: 1712. V. 53

A **VINDICATION** of Sir Thomas Player and Those Loyal Citizens Concerned with Him... 1679. V. 47

A **VINDICATION** of the Celts, From Ancient Authorities. London: 1803. V. 47

A **VINDICATION** of the Conduct and Principles of the Catholics of Ireland, from the Charges Made Against Them by Certain Late Grand Juries and Other Interested Bodies in that Country... London: 1793. V. 51

A **VINDICATION** of the Honourable the Sheriffs and Recorder of London, from Those Impudent Reflections Cast Upon Them in Fitzharris's Libel, Entituled His Confession. London: 1681. V. 52; 53

A **VINDICATION** of the Lord Russel's Speech and Paper, &c. from the Foul Imputations of Falsehood. London: 1683. V. 47

A **VINDICATION** of the Present M(inistr)y from the Clamours Rais'd Against Them Upon Occasion of the New Preliminaries. London: 1711. V. 49

A **VINDICATION** of the Proceedings in the Case of Mr. Ayscough of Corpus-Christi-College, Oxon. London: 1731. V. 53

VINDING, ERASMUS PAUL
Regia Academia Hauniensis in Regibus... Copenhagen: 1665. V. 48

VINE, BARBARA
Asta's Book. 1993. V. 54
Asta's Book. Bristol: 1993. V. 52

VINE, FRED K. T.
Practical Bread-Making: a Useful Guide for All in the Trade. London: 1897. V. 50

VINES, RICHARD
The Hearse of the Renowned, the Right Honourable Robert Earle of Essex... London: 1646. V. 52

VINETTE, A.
Buena Vista and Tributary Mining Camps: A Sketch of the Mines of Cottonwood and La Plata Districts, Chaffee County, Colorado. Buena Vista: 1882. V. 52

VINGE, J.
The Snow Queen. 1980. V. 51
The Snow Queen. New York: 1980. V. 47

VINGE, VERNOR
A Fire Upon the Deep. New York: 1992. V. 52
A Fire Upon the Deep. Toronto: 1992. V. 51

VINOGRADOV, A. P.
The Elementary Chemical Composition of Marine Organisms. New Haven: 1953. V. 53

VINTON, FRANCIS
Louis XVII and Eleazar Williams Were They the Same Person?. New York: 1868. V. 53

VINTON, STALLO
John Colter, Discoverer of Yellowstone Park. New York: 1926. V. 47; 52

VINYCOMB, JOHN
On the Processes for the Production of Ex-Libris (Book-plates). London: 1894. V. 49

VIOLA, JEROME
The Painting and Teaching of Philip Pearlstein. New York: 1982. V. 51; 53

VIOLLET-LE-DUC, EUGENE EMMANUEL
Dictionnaire Raisonne de l'Architecture Francaise du XI au XVIe Siecle. Paris: 1868-74. V. 50
Discourses on Architecture. New York: 1959. V. 48; 51; 53
Lectures on Architecture. London: 1877-81. V. 53
On Restoration and a Notice of His Works in Connection with the Historic Monuments of France. London: 1875. V. 51

VIRCHOW, RUDOLF
Cellular Pathology as Based Upon Physiological and Pathological Histology. New York: 1860. V. 49
Die Cellularpathologie in Ihrer Begrundung auf Physiologische und Pathologische Gewebelehre. Berlin: 1858. V. 47; 48; 53
Die Krankhaften Geschulste. Berlin: 1863-67. V. 47; 48; 50

VIRGINIA
The Code of Virginia...and Constitution of Virginia. Richmond: 1849. V. 53

VIRGINIA CENTRAL RAILROAD
Address of the President of the Virginia Central Railroad Co., to the Stockholders, on the Subject of Withdrawal of the Mails by the Postmaster General. Richmond: 1864. V. 49

VIRGINIA COMPANY OF LONDON
The Records of the Virginia Company of London: The Court Book: 1619-22. II: 1622-24. Washington: 1906. V. 51

VIRGINIA. CONSTITUTION
Constitution of the State of Virginia, and the Ordinances Adopted by the Convention Which Assembled at Alexandria On the 13th Day of February, 1864. Alexandria: 1864. V. 49

VIRGINIA. CONVENTION
Debates and other Proceedings of the convention of Virginia... Richmond: 1805. V. 49

VIRGINIA, CONVENTION
Journal, Acts of Proceedings of a General Convention of the State of Virginia, Assembled at Richmond, On Monday, The Fourteenth Day of October, 1850. Richmond: 1850. V. 48

VIRGINIA. CONVENTION
Virginia Bill of Rights, Passed June 12, 1776; Adopted Without Alteration by the Convention of 1829-30, and Re-Adopted, with Amendments, by the Convention of 1850-51, and Now Re-Adopted as Passed June 12, 1776. Richmond: 1861. V. 52; 54

VIRGINIA. GENERAL ASSEMBLY
Acts of the General Assembly of the State of Virginia, passed in 1861-62. Richmond: 1862. V. 47

VIRGINIA. GOVERNOR
Message of the Governor of Virginia, and Accompanying Documents. Richmond: 1863. V. 53; 54

VIRGINIA. LAWS, STATUTES, ETC.
Acts of the General Assembly of the State of Virginia... 1861-62. (with) Acts of the General Assembly...Passed at Extra Session, 1862. (with) Ordinances Adopted by the Convention of Virginia...1861. Richmond: 1862. V. 50
Acts of the General Assembly of the State of Virginia...1863...(with) Acts of the General Assembly...1863-64. Richmond: 1863-64. V. 50
A Collection of All Such Acts of the General Assembly of Virginia. Richmond: 1794. V. 48
Virginia General Assembly and Revised Code of the Laws of Virginia (to 1819). (together with) Supplement. Richmond: 1819. V. 54

THE **VIRGINIA** Primer. Richmond: 1864. V. 50

VIRTUE, an Ethic Epistle. London: 1759. V. 48

VIRTUE In a Cottage; or, a Mirror for Children in Humble Life. London: 1790?. V. 53

VISCHER, EDWARD
Edward Vischer & His "Pictorial of California". San Francisco: 1932. V. 53; 54
Edward Vischer's Drawings of the California Missions, 1861-1878. San Francisco: 1982. V. 51

VISCHER, WILLIAM LIGHTFOOT
Black Mammy: Song of the Sunny-South. Cheyenne: 1885. V. 48
Black Mammy: Song of the Sunny-South... Cheyenne: 1886. V. 47; 50
Poems of the South; and Other Verse. Chicago: 1911. V. 50
Vissch. St. Joseph: 1873. V. 48

VISCOSE. The Chlorantine Fast Colours of the Society of Chemical Industry in Basle. Basel. V. 48

VISCOUNT ST. ALBANS
Opuscula Varia Posthuma, Philosophica, Civila, et Theolgoica... Amstelodami: 1663. V. 48

VISHNIAC, ROMAN
Polish Jews: a Pictorial Record. New York: 1947. V. 49; 52
A Vanished World. New York: 1983. V. 53

THE **VISION** of Hades, or the Region Inhabited by the Departed Spirits of the Blessed... London: 1825. V. 51; 54

A **VISIT** to Aunt Agnes. London: 1864. V. 49

VISITATION of Suffolke, Made by William Hervey, Clarenceau King of Arms, 1561. Lowestoft: 1866. V. 51

THE **VISITATION** of the County Palatine of Duresme... Sunderland: 1820. V. 53; 54

VISITING Dieppe and a Weekend in Dieppe. London: 1981. V. 53

VISITORS Guide to the Centennial Exhibiton and Philadelphia. May 10th to November 10th 1876. V. 49

VISSER, H. F. E.
Asiatic Art. Amsterdam: 1960. V. 53

VITA De'Beati Gaspar e Niccolo... Turin: 1788. V. 52; 54

VITRUVIUS POLLIO, MARCUS
Architecture General Reduite et Abrege par M. Perrault. Amsterdam: 1681. V. 47
The Civil Architecture of Vitruvius. London: 1812. V. 52
Della Architettvra Di Gio. Antonio Rvsconi, Con Centoses-Santa Figure Dissegnate Dal Medessimo, Secondo... In Ventia: 1590. V. 53
Los Diez Libros de Architectura. Madrid: 1787. V. 47
Les Dix Livres d'Architecture. 1684. V. 47
Les Dix Livres d'Architecture... Paris: 1684. V. 48

VITRUVIUS POLLIO, MARCUS continued
I Dieci Libri Della'Architettura. Venice: 1567. V. 48
M. L. Vitrvuio Pollione di Architettura dal Vero Esemplare Latino Nella Volgar Lingua... Venice: 1535. V. 50
M. Vitruvius Per Iocundum Sollto Castigatior Factus Cum Figuris et Tabula ut Iam Legi et Intelligi Possit. Venice: 1511. V. 49

VITRY, PAUL
French Sculpture During the Reign of Saint Louis, 1226-1270. Florence: 1938. V. 47; 49; 51
Hotels & Maisons de La Renaissance Francaise... Paris: 1909-14. V. 49

VITTORI, ANGELO
De Palpitatione Cordis, Fractura Costarum Aliisque Affectionibus B. Philippi Nerii... Rome: 1613. V. 47

VITZETELLY, HENRY
The Wines of the World Characterized and Classed. London: 1875. V. 53

VIVALDI, ANTONIO
The Four Seasons. New York: 1984. V. 48; 51; 54

VIVANCO, AURELIO DE
Baja California al Dia, Lower California Up To Date. Los Angeles: 1924. V. 50

VIVIAN, A. PENDARVES
Wanderings in the Western Land. London: 1879. V. 51
Wanderings in the Western Land. London: 1880. V. 54

VIVIAN, H. HUSSEY
Notes of a Tour in America. From August 7th to November 17th, 1877. London: 1878. V. 49; 52
Notes on a Tour in America. From August 7th to November 17th, 1877. London: 1877. V. 47

VIVIANI, DOMENICO
Florae Libycae Specimen sive Plantarum Enumeratio Cyrenaicam, Pentapolim, Magnae Syrteos Desertum et Regionem Tripolitanam... Genoa: 1824. V. 49

VIVIENNE, MAY
Travels in Western Asutralia. London: 1902. V. 47

VIVISECTION. The Royal Society for the Prevention of Cruelty to Animals and the Royal Commission. London: 1876. V. 50; 52

VIZENOR, GERALD ROBERT
The Everlasting Sky. New York: 1972. V. 50
Two wings the Butterfly. St. Cloud: 1962. V. 50
Wordarrows. Indians and Whites in the New Fur Trade. Minneapolis: 1978. V. 50

VIZETELLY, HENRY
Berlin Under the New Empire. London: 1879. V. 54
Christmas with the Poets... London: 1862. V. 54
Facts About Champagne and Other Sparkling Wines. London: 1879. V. 47
Four Months Among the Gold-finders in Alta California; Being the Diary of an Expedition from San Francisco to the Gold Districts. London: 1849. V. 53
A History of Champagne with Notes on the Other Sparkling Wines of France. London: 1882. V. 52
Paris in Peril. London: 1882. V. 47

VLADIMIR Nabokov: In Memoraim 1899-1977. New York: 1977. V. 47

VLIET, R. G.
Events & Celebrations, Poems. New York: 1966. V. 47
Sand is the Tool. New York: 1953. V. 52
Solitude. New York: 1977. V. 49; 52

VOCABULA Amatoria: a French-English Glossary of Words, Phrases and Allusions Occurring in the Works of Rabelais, Voltaire, Moliere, Rousseau, Beranger, Zola and others with English Equivalents and Synonyms. London: 1896. V. 49; 52

THE VOCAL Companion: Consisting of Songs, Duets, Glees, Catches, Canons and Canzonets... Boston: 1815-12. V. 48

THE VOCAL Enchantress Containing an Elegant Selection of all the Newest Songs Lately Sung at the Theatres Royal Drury Lane, Covent Garden, Haymarket, Royalty Theatre, Vaux Hall, &c, &c. London: 1788. V. 47

THE VOCAL Enchantress Presenting an Elegant Selection of the Most Favourite Hunting Sea, Love and Miscellaneous Songs... London: 1783. V. 54

VOCAL Music: or, the Songster's Companion. London: 1775. V. 49; 54

VOET, LEON
The Plantin Press at Antwerp 1555-1589, A Bibliography of the Works Printed and Published by Christopher Plantin at Antwerp and Leiden. Amsterdam: 1980-82. V. 48

VOGE, CECIL
The Chemistry and Physics of Contraceptives. London: 1933. V. 54

VOGEL, GERTRUIDA
Spring Flowers. London: 1916. V. 52

VOGEL, JULIUS
Anno Domini 2000; or Woman's Destiny. London: 1889. V. 48; 50; 54
Anno Domini 2000; or Woman's Destiny. 1890. V. 47

VOGEL, S. M.
African Aesthetics, the Carlo Monzino Collection. 1986. V. 51

VOGT, A. E.
The Voyage of the Space Beagle. 1950. V. 48

VOGT, C.
The Natural History of Animals (Class Mammalia). London: 1887. V. 50; 51

VOGTS, M. M.
Proteas, Know Them and Grow Them: on Cultivation of the South African Proteaceae. Johannesburg: 1959. V. 47

A VOICE from Greece in Appeal to the Sympathies and Charities of America. V. 47

THE VOICE of the Prophets. Mesianic Prophecies. Flemington: 1970. V. 51

A VOICE to America; or, the Model Republic, Its Glory, Or its Fall, with a Review of the Causes of the Decline and Failure of the Republics of South America, Mexico and of the Old World... New York: 1855. V. 50

VOIGT, J. O.
Hortus Suburbanus Calcuttensis... Dehra Dun: 1984. V. 50

VOINOVICH, VLADIMIR
The Ivankiad. New York: 1977. V. 54

VOLAVKOVA, HANA
A Story of the Jewish Musuem in Prague. Prague: 1968. V. 53

VOLBACH, WOLFGANG FRITZ
Early Christian Art. London: 1961. V. 52; 54
Early Christian Art. New York: 1961. V. 54

VOLGA. St. Petersburg: 1904. V. 53

VOLGER, G.
Indonesian Textiles. Symposium 1985. 1991. V. 54

VOLK, ERNEST
The Archaeology of the Delaware Valley. Cambridge: 1911. V. 50; 52

VOLLMANN, WILLIAM T.
An Afghanistan Picture Show. New York: 1992. V. 51; 52
Butterfly Stories. 1993. V. 52
Butterfly Stories. London: 1993. V. 51; 53; 54
Butterfly Stories. New York: 1993. V. 53
Butterfly Stories. 1994. V. 52
The Convict Bird. 1987. V. 51; 52
The Convict Bird. San Francisco: 1987. V. 48; 54
Fathers and Crows. London: 1992. V. 51
Fathers and Crows. New York: 1992. V. 51
The Grave of Lost Stories. Los Angeles: 1993. V. 51
The Grave of Lost Stories. Sacramento: 1993. V. 52
The Happy Girls. New York: 1990. V. 53
The Ice Shirt. London: 1990. V. 51; 52; 53
The Ice Shirt. New York: 1990. V. 49; 52
Rainbow Stories. New York: 1988. V. 49
The Rainbow Stories. 1989. V. 50; 51; 54
The Rainbow Stories. London: 1989. V. 50; 51; 53; 54
The Rainbow Stories. New York: 1989. V. 52; 54
The Rifles. New York: 1993. V. 50
Thirteen Stories and Thirteen Epitaphs. London: 1991. V. 50; 51; 52; 53
Thirteen Stories and Thirteen Epitaphs. New York: 1991. V. 52; 54
Whores for Gloria. London: 1991. V. 51
Whores for Gloria. New York: 1991. V. 51; 52; 53
Whores for Gloria. New York: 1992. V. 52
You Bright and Risen Angels. 1987. V. 50; 51; 52
You Bright and Risen Angels. London: 1987. V. 50; 51; 52
You Bright and Risen Angels. New York: 1987. V. 50; 51; 52; 54

VOLNEY, CONSTANTIN FRANCOIS, COMTE DE
The Law of Nature, or Principles of Morality, Deduced from the Physical Constitution of Mankind and the Universe. London: 1796. V. 52
A New Translation of Volney's Ruins; Or Meditations on the Revolution of Empires. Paris: 1802. V. 48
The Ruins: or a Survey of the Revolutions of Empires... London: 1795. V. 48
Tableau du Climat et du Sol des Etats-Unis D'Amerique. Paris: 1803. V. 52
Travels through Egypt and Syria, in the years 1783, 1784 and 1785. New York: 1798. V. 50
Travels through Syria, and Egypt in the Years 1783, 1784 and 1785. Dublin: 1788. V. 48
Travels through Syria and Egypt. In the Years 1783, 1784 and 1785. London: 1788. V. 52
View of the Climate and Soil of the United States of America... London: 1804. V. 48
A View of the Soil and Climate of the United States of America... Philadelphia: 1804. V. 47; 50

VOLSUNGA SAGA
The Story of the Volsungs and Niblungs With Certain Songs from...Edda. London: 1870. V. 53
Story of the Volsungs and Niblungs with Certain Songs from...Edda. London: 1901. V. 49; 51
A Tale of the House of the Volsungs and All the Kindreds of the Mark... London: 1901. V. 51

VOLTA, ALLESSANDRO
Vola Le Opere. Milan: 1918-29. V. 48

VOLTAIRE, FRANCOIS MARIE AROUET DE
The Age of Louis XIV. London: 1779-81. V. 53
Le Brutus... Paris: 1731. V. 48
Candide... London: 1759. V. 50
Candide... Paris?: 1759. V. 47; 48

VOLTAIRE, FRANCOIS MARIE AROUET DE continued
Candide... Paris: 1759/61. V. 47
Candide. Paris: 1922. V. 54
Candide... New York: 1927. V. 51
Candide. 1928. V. 50
Candide. New York: 1928. V. 49; 51; 52; 53; 54
Candide... Paris: 1930. V. 47
Candide... New York: 1973. V. 47; 52; 54
Collected Works. New York: 1901. V. 48
Collection Complete des Oeuvres de Mr. De Voltaire. Geneva: 1768-77. V. 52
Critical Essays on Dramatic Poetry. London: 1761. V. 53
A Defence of My Uncle. London: 1768. V. 48
Elemens de la Philosophie de Neuton... Amsterdam: 1738. V. 49; 54
The Elements of Sir Isaac Newton's Philosophy. London: 1738. V. 50
Essay on Milton. 1954. V. 52
L'Examen Important de Milord Bolinbroke. Ecrit sur la fin de 1736. Londres: 1776. V. 54
The General History and State of Europe, from the Time of Charlemain to Charles V. London: 1754-57. V. 50
La Henriade. Londres: 1728. V. 52
The Henriade. London: 1797. V. 48; 49; 50; 51; 53; 54
The Henriade... Mobile: 1834. V. 53
Histoire de l'Empire de Russie sous Pierre le grand. 1765. V. 51
The History of Charles XII King of Sweden. London: 1732. V. 48
The History of the Misfortunes of John Calas, a Victim of Fanaticism. Edinburgh: 1776. V. 53
The History of the War of Seventeen Hundred and Forty One. London: 1756. V. 48
The History of Zadig; or, Destiny. New York: 1952. V. 48
The History of Zadig; or, Destiny. Paris: 1952. V. 48; 52; 53; 54
The Ignorant Philosopher. London: 1779. V. 54
L'Ingenu; or, the Sincere Huron. Glasgow: 1768. V. 49
Irene. Paris: 1779. V. 47; 50; 52
Letters Concerning the English Nation. London: 1733. V. 48; 49; 52
Letters from M. de Voltaire, to Several of His Friends. London: 1770. V. 52
Memoirs of the Life of Voltaire. Dublin: 1784. V. 53
Memoirs of the Life of Voltaire. London: 1784. V. 48; 50; 52
Le Micromegas... Londres: 1752. V. 48
Micromegas... London: 1753. V. 47
Oeuvres. Neufchatel: 1773. V. 48
Oeuvres Completes. Paris: 1785-89. V. 49
Oeuvres Completes. Paris: 1835-38. V. 47
The Philosophical Dictionary... Catskill: 1796. V. 51; 53
The Philosophical Dictionary... London: 1819. V. 51
La Philosophie de l'Histoire. Amsterdam: 1765. V. 48
Poem Upon the Lisbon Disaster. 1977. V. 49
Poem Upon the Lisbon Disaster. Lincoln: 1977. V. 48; 49; 51; 54
The Prince of Babylon... London: 1927. V. 50; 52; 53
La Pucelle... 1789. V. 49
La Pucelle... Paris: 1795. V. 49
La Pucelle... London: 1899. V. 53
The Pupil of Nature; a True History, Found Amongst the Papers of Father Quesnel. London: 1771. V. 47; 53
Romances, Novels and Tales. London: 1806. V. 53
Select Pieces. Viz. Zadig; or Destiny. An Eastern History. Memnon. A Letter from a Turk... London: 1754. V. 48
Therese, a Fragment. Cambridge: 1981. V. 48; 50; 54
A Treatise on Toleration; the Ignorant Philosopher... London: 1779. V. 52
Voltaire's Essay on Milton. Cambridge: 1954. V. 47; 51; 53
The Works. London: 1761-69. V. 50
The Works... London: 1761-74. V. 51
The Works... Paris, London, New York: 1901. V. 50
Zadig... London: 1748. V. 48
Zadig... 1749. V. 48
Zadig... London: 1774. V. 48
La Zayre... Paris: 1733. V. 48

A VOLUME of Memoirs and Genealogy of Representative Citizens of Northern California, Including Biographies of Many of Those Who Have Passed Away. Chicago: 1901. V. 49; 50

VOLUSPA: The song of the Sybil. Iowa City: 1968. V. 53; 54

VOLWILER, ALBERT T.
George Croghan and the Westward Movement 1741-1782. Cleveland: 1926. V. 47; 49

VON DER OSTER, GERD
Art of the Sixties. Koln: 1971. V. 50

VON BOTHMER, DIETRICH
The Amasis Painter and His World: Vase-Painting in Sixth Century B.C. Athens. New York: 1985. V. 50; 52

VON BRAUN, WERNHER
Moon - Man's Greatest Adventure. New York: 1970. V. 48

VON BUCH, LEOPOLD
Travels through Norway and Lapland During the Years 1806, 1807, and 1808. London: 1813. V. 54

VONDEL, JOOST VAN DEN
Vorstelijcke Warande der Dieren: Waer in De Zeden-Rijcke Philosophie, Poetisch, Morael, en Historiael... Amsterdam: 1682. V. 50

VON EGLOFFSTEIN, F. W.
Contributions to the Geology and Physical Geography of Mexico, Including a Geological and Topographical Map... New York: 1864. V. 50

VON ERDBERG, E.
Chinese Influence on European Garden Structures. Cambridge: 1936. V. 54

VON FALKE, JACOB
Art in the House. Historical, Critical and Aesthetical Studies on the Decoration and Furnishing of the Dwelling. Boston: 1879. V. 52

VON GEBLER, KARL
Galileo Galilei and the Roman Curia. London: 1879. V. 54

VON GIMMELSHAUSEN, JOHANN JAKOB C.
The Adventures of Simplicissimus. New York: 1981. V. 51

VON HADELN, DETLEV, BARON
Titian's Drawings. London: 1927. V. 50

VON HAGEN, VICTOR WOLFGANG
The Aztec and Maya Papermakers. New York: 1944. V. 48
Jungle in the Clouds. New York: 1940. V. 52
Maya Explorer: John Lloyd Stephens and the Lost Cities of Central America and Yucatan. Norman: 1947. V. 50

VON HOLST, H. V.
Modern American Homes. Chicago: 1916. V. 53

VON HORN, W. O.
Der Rhein. Wiesbaden: 1881. V. 49

VON KARMAN, THEODORE
Collected Works of Theodore Von Karman, 1902-1913 & 1914-1932. London: 1956. V. 50

VON KOTTZEBUE, AUGUSTUS
Sketch of the Life and Literary Career of Augustus Von Kotzebue. New York: 1801. V. 49

VON LOHER, FRANZ
Cyprus: Historical and Descriptive, from the Earliest times to the Present Day. New York: 1878. V. 48; 49

VON LUSCHAN, F.
Die Altertumer Von Benin. Berlin & Leipzig: 1919. V. 54

VONNEGUT, KURT
Between Time and Timbuktu or Prometheus 5. 1972. V. 49; 54
Between time and Timbuktu, or Prometheus 5. New York: 1972. V. 49; 51
Bluebeard. New York: 1987. V. 51; 53
Breakfast of Champions. New York: 1973. V. 49; 51; 53
Canary in a Cat House. Greenwich: 1961. V. 47; 49; 51
Cat's Cradle. New York: 1963. V. 49
Conversations with Kurt Vonnegut. Jackson: 1988. V. 50
Deadeye Dick. New York: 1982. V. 49; 51; 52; 53; 54
Fates Worse Than Death. New York: 1991. V. 49; 51
Galapagos. New York: 1985. V. 48; 50; 51; 52; 53
God Bless You, Mr. Rosewater... 1965. V. 48; 52
God Bless You, Mr. Rosewater... London: 1965. V. 54
God Bless You, Mr. Rosewater. New York: 1965. V. 49; 51; 53
Happy Birthday, Wanda June. New York: 1971. V. 51; 52
Happy Birthday Wanda June. London: 1973. V. 49; 53; 54
Hocus Pocus. New York: 1990. V. 47; 48
Jailbird. 1979. V. 54
Jailbird. London: 1979. V. 49; 51
Jailbird. New York: 1979. V. 49; 50; 51; 52; 53
Mother Night. Greenwich: 1962. V. 47; 49
Mother Night. 1966. V. 49; 54
Mother Night. London: 1966. V. 49
Mother Night. New York: 1966. V. 48; 49; 51; 52; 53
Mother Night. London: 1968. V. 48; 49; 50; 51
Nothing Is Lost Save Honor. Jackson: 1984. V. 51; 52; 53
One Great Novelist of the 70's Writes About Another. 1974. V. 49; 51
Palm Sunday. New York: 1981. V. 48; 49; 51; 53
Player Piano. New York: 1952. V. 47; 48; 49; 51; 52; 53; 54
Player Piano. London: 1953. V. 51; 52
The Sirens of Titan. Boston: 1959. V. 53
Sirens of Titan. New York: 1959. V. 51; 52; 53
The Sirens of Titan. Boston: 1961. V. 49
Slapstick. Franklin Center: 1976. V. 52
Slapstick. London: 1976. V. 49; 51
Slapstick... New York: 1976. V. 48; 49; 51; 53
Slaughterhouse Five... 1969. V. 48; 49; 53; 54
Slaughterhouse Five... New York: 1969. V. 48; 49; 51; 54
Slaughterhouse Five... Franklin Center: 1978. V. 49; 50; 51
Sun Moon Star. New York: 1980. V. 49; 51
Wampeters, Foma and Granfalloons Opinions. New York: 1974. V. 49; 51; 53; 54
Welcome to the Monkey House. London: 1968. V. 49; 51
Welcome to the Monkey House. New York: 1968. V. 49; 52; 54
Welcome to the Monkey House. 1969. V. 49
Welcome to the Monkey House. London: 1969. V. 54

VON NEUMANN, JOHN
Theory of Games and Economic Behavior. Princeton: 1944. V. 54

VON RAUMER, FREDERICK
England in 1835: Being a Series of Letters. London: 1836. V. 52; 54

VON REICHENBACH, CHARLES, BARON
The Old Force: Letters on a Newly Discovered Power in Nature, and Its Relation to Magnetism, Electricity, Heat and Light. Boston: 1854. V. 53
Physico-Physiological Researches in the Dynamics of Magnetism, Electricity, Heat, Light, Crystallization and Chemism, in Their Relations to "Vital Force". New York: 1850. V. 47

VON REZZORI, GREGOR
Memoirs of an Anti-Semite. New York: 1981. V. 51

VON ROSENBERG-TOMLINSON, ALMA
Von Rosenberg Family of Texas: a Record with Historical Facts and Legends. (with) The Von Rosenberg Family Record Book II. Boerne/Waco: 1949/1974. V. 52
Von Rosenberg Family of Texas: a Record with Historical Facts and Legends. (with) The Von Rosenberg Family Record Book II. Boerne: 1974. V. 51

VON STADEN, HEINRICH
Herophilus: the Art of Medicine in Early Alexandria. 1989. V. 49

VON STEUBEN, FREDERICK WILLIAM
Regulations for the Order and Discipline of the Troops of the United States. Hartford: 1782. V. 47

VON SYDOW, E.
Afrikanische Plastaik. New York and Berlin: 1954. V. 54

VON TEMPSKY, G. F.
Mitla. A Narrative of Incidents and Personal Adventures on a Journey in Mexico, Guatemala and Salvador, in the Years 1853 to 1855. London: 1858. V. 51

VON THIELMANN, MAX, BARON
Journey In the Caucasus, Persia and Turkey in Asia. London: 1875. V. 49

VON WARTENBURG, YOREK, COUNT
Atlas to Accompany Napoleon as a General. West Point: 1942. V. 54

VON WELLING, GEORGII
Opus Mago-Cabbalisticum et Theosophicum... Frankfurt: 1760. V. 47

VON WINNING, HASSO
Pre-Columbian Art of Mexico and Central America. New York: 1968. V. 47; 50; 52
The Shaft Tomb Figures of West Mexico. Highland Park: 1974. V. 50

VOORHEES, J. M.
The Game of Ring Hockey. New York: 1903. V. 50

VOORHEES, LUKE
Personal Recollections of Pioneer Life on the Mountains and Plains of the Great West. Cheyenne: 1920. V. 47

VOORN, HENK
Old Ream Wrappers. North Hills: 1969. V. 48; 51; 53

VORONOFF, SERGE
Rejuvenation by Grafting. New York: 1925. V. 54

VOSBURG, KEITH
Azusa Old and New. Azusa: 1921. V. 53

VOSBURGH, W. S.
Cherished Portraits of Thoroughbred Horses, from the Collection of William Woodward. New York: 1929. V. 47
Racing in America 1866-1921, Racing in America 1922-1936 & Racing in America 1665-1865. New York: 1922-37. V. 54
Thoroughbred Types 1900-1925. New York: 1926. V. 47; 48; 49

VOSE, GEORGE L.
Bridge Disasters of America. Boston: 1887. V. 49

VOSE, JOHN
A System of Astronomy, on the Copernicus. Concord: 1827. V. 50

VOSS, GERARD JOHANN
Rhetorices Contractae, sive Partitionum Oratoriarum. Libri. Oxford: 1651. V. 51

VOSTELL, WOLF
Fantastic Architecture. n.d. V. 48

VOTH, H. R.
Brief Hopi Miscellaneous Hopi Papers - The Stanley McCormick Hopi Expedition. Chicago: 1912. V. 53
The Oraibi Marau Ceremony. 1912. V. 54

VOX *Patriae: or the Resentments & Indignation of the Free-Born Subjects of England Popery, Arbitrary Government, the Duke of York, or Any Popish Succesor...* London: 1681. V. 49

VOX *Populi: or, England's General Lamentation for the Dissolution of the parliament.* London: 1681. V. 47

THE VOYAGE of Sebastian Vizcaino to the Coast of California, Together with a Map and Sebastian Vizcaino's Letter Written at Monterey, December 28, 1602. San Francisco: 1933. V. 47; 54

A VOYAGE Round the World, in His Majesty's Ship the Colophin, Commanded by...Commodore Byron... London: 1776. V. 47

A VOYAGE through the Islands of the Pacific Ocean. Dublin: 1824. V. 50

VREAM, WILLIAM
A Description of the Air-Pump, According to the Late Mr. Hawksbee's Best and Last Improvements... London: 1717. V. 47

VREDENBURG, EDRIC
In Nurseryland with Louis Wain. London: 1916. V. 51

VREELAND, NICHOLAS GARRETSON
History and Genealogy of the Vreeland Family. Jersey City: 1909. V. 49

VRIES, HUGO DE
Intracellular Pangenesis Including a Paper on Fertilization and Hybridization. Chicago: 1910. V. 48; 50; 52; 54
The Mutation Theory. Chicago: 1909-10. V. 48
Species and Varieties, Their Origin by Mutation. Chicago: 1905. V. 50; 53
Species and Varieties: Their Origin by Mutation. London: 1905. V. 54
Species and Varieties, Their Origin by Mutation... Chicago: 1906. V. 52; 53

VRIES, JAN
Architectura. Die Kostliche Unnd WeitberumbteKhunst, Welche Besteht in Fufferly Art Der Edifitien... The Hague: 1606. V. 51

VRIESEN, GUSTAV
Robert Delaunay: Light and Color. New York: 1967. V. 51

VUILLIAMY, C. E.
Byron. London: 1948. V. 50

VUILLIER, GASTON
A History of Dancing From the Earliest Ages to Our Own Times. London: 1898. V. 48; 51; 54

THE VULGARITIES of Speech Corrected: with Elegant Expressions for Provincial and Vulgar Scots and Irish... London: 1829. V. 52

VULPIUS, CHRISTIAN AUGUST
The Life Surprising Adventures, and Most Remarkable Escapes of Rinaldo Rinaldini, Captain of a Banditti of Robbers. London: 1801. V. 54

VYNER, ROBERT THOMAS
Notitia Venatica... London: 1841. V. 47
Notitia Venatica... London: 1842. V. 47
Notitia Venatica... London: 1847. V. 47
Notitia Venatica... London: 1871. V. 47
Notitia Venatica. London: 1890. V. 49
Notitia Venatica... London: 1892. V. 47; 48
Notitia Venatica... London: 1910. V. 49

VYSE, CHARLES
The Tutor's Guide. London: 1779. V. 51

W

W. C. BROWNELL: Tributes and Appreciations. New York: 1929. V. 50

W., R.
An Essay on Grief; with Causes and Remedies Of it. Oxford: 1695. V. 50

W., S.
A Visit to London, Containing a Description of the Principal Curiosities in the British Metropolis. London: 1805. V. 47; 48; 51
A Visit to London Containing a Description of the Principal Curiosities in the British Metropolis. London: 1820. V. 52
The Warren Family, or Scenes at Home. London: 1820. V. 48
The Warren Family, or Scenes at Home. London: 1825. V. 49

W., T.
The Natural Interest of Great Britain, In Its Present Circumstances, Demonstrated in a Discourse. London: 1748. V. 47

W., W.
Animadversions on the Late Vindication of Slingsby Bethel, Esq.; Wherein the Ancient and Laudable Customs of the City of London are Asserted... Hamborough: 1681. V. 52

WAAC - The Woman's Story of the War. London: 1930. V. 49

WAAGEN, G. F.
Treasures of Art in Great Britain... (with) Calleries and Cabinets of Art in Great Britain... London: 1854/57. V. 47
Works of Art and Artists in England. London: 1838. V. 47
Works of Art. Treasures of Art in Great Britain. Galleries and Cabinets of Art in Great Britain. 1970. V. 49

WABASH RAILROAD
The Wabash Line, the Banner Route, Official Time Tables, Corrected to April 1st, 1897. V. 54

WABNER, ROBERT
Ventilation in Mines. London: 1903. V. 49; 53

WACE, ALAN
The Marlborough Tapestries at Blenheim Palace and Their Relation to Other Military Tapestries of the War of the Spanish Succession. London: 1968. V. 54

WACK, H. W.
The Story of the Congo Free State, Social, Political and Economic Aspects of the Belgian System of Government in Central Africa. New York and London: 1905. V. 54

WADD, WILLIAM
Nugae Chirurgicae; or, a Biographical Miscellany. London: 1824. V. 47; 48; 49; 50

WADDELL, ALFRED MOORE
A Colonial Officer and His Times. 1754-1773. Raleigh: 1890. V. 47
A History of New Hanover County and the Lower Cape Fear Region, 1723-1800. Volume I. Wilmington: 1909. V. 48

WADDELL, J. A. L.
Bridge Engineering. New York: 1916. V. 51

WADDELL, JAMES D.
Biographical Sketch of Linton Stephens... Atlanta: 1877. V. 49

WADDELL, JOHN ADDISON
Annals of Augusta County, virginia. N.P: 1885. V. 49

WADDELL, L. A.
Among the Himalayas. London: 1899. V. 48

WADDINGHAM, WILSON
The Celebrated Ada Elmore Gold and Silver Mine of South Boise, Idaho Territory. 1866. V. 50

WADDINGTON, ALFRED
The Fraser Mines Findicated; or, the History of Four Months. Vancouver: 1949. V. 49
Overland Route Through British North America; or, The Shortest and Speediest Road to the East. London: 1868. V. 47

WADDINGTON, GEORGE
Columbus. Cambridge: 1813. V. 48; 54

WADDINGTON, MIRIAM
Green World. Montreal: 1945. V. 47
The Season's Lovers. Toronto: 1958. V. 47

WADDLETON, NORMAN
Waddleton Chronology of Books with Colour Printed Illustrations of Decorations: 15th to 20th Century. 1993. V. 49
Waddleton Chronology of Books with Colour Printed Illustrations of Decorations: 15th to 20th Century. York: 1993. V. 50

WADE, ALLEN
A Bibliography of the Writings of W. B. Yeats. London: 1951. V. 47
A Bibliography of the Writings of W. B. Yeats. London: 1958. V. 49
A Bibliography of the Writings of W. B. Yeats. London: 1968. V. 53

WADE, DAVID
Pattern in Islamic Art. London: 1976. V. 49; 52; 54

WADE, EDWARD
A Proposal for Improving and Adorning the Island of Great Britain... London: 1755. V. 48

WADE, JOHN
The Black Book; or, Corruption Unmasked. London: 1820. V. 48; 49; 50
The Black Book; or, Corruption Unmasked... London: 1820/23. V. 53

WADE, MARK SWEETEN
Mackenzie of Canada. Edinburgh: 1927. V. 49
The Overlanders of '62. Victoria: 1931. V. 47; 48; 54
The Thompson Country. Kamloops: 1907. V. 48

WADE, W. M.
Walks in Oxford. Oxford: 1818. V. 50

WADE, WALTER
Plantae Rariores in Hibernia Inventae... Dublin: 1804. V. 47; 53

WADMORE, J. F.
Some Account of the Worshipful Company of Skinners of London, Being the Guild or Fraternity of Corpus Christi. London: 1902. V. 47

WADSTROM, CARL BERNHARD
An Essay on Colonization, Particularly Applied to the Western Coast of Africa... London: 1794-95. V. 49

WADSWORTH, CHARLES
Sailing-Ships and Barges of the Western Mediterranean and Adriatic Seas. London: 1926. V. 47

WADSWORTH, JAMES
The Copies of Certain Letters Which Have Passed Between Sapian and England in Matter of Religion. London: 1685. V. 50

WADSWORTH, R. D.
The Temperance Manual; or Teetotaler's Pocket Companion. Montreal: 1847. V. 54

WAFER, LIONEL
A New Voyage and Description of the Isthumus of America... London: 1699. V. 50

WAGENAAR, JAN
'T Verheugd Amsterdam ter Gelegenheid van het Plegtig Bezock...Willem Prinse van Oranje... Amsterdam: 1768. V. 47; 53; 54

WAGHORN, HENRY THOMAS
Cricket Scores, Notes, Etc. from 1730-1773. London: 1899. V. 51

WAGHORN, THOMAS
A Vade-Mecum from India to Europe, by Way of Egypt. London: 1827. V. 49

WAGNER, ARTHUR L.
The United States Army and Navy... Akron: 1899. V. 53

WAGNER, GLENDOLIN DAMON
Blankets and Moccassins. Caldwell: 1933. V. 47
Old Neutriment. Boston: 1934. V. 49; 53

WAGNER, HENRY RAUP
California Imprints. Berkeley: 1922. V. 54
California Voyages 1539-1541. San Francisco: 1925. V. 48; 49; 50
The Cartography of the Northwest Coast of America to the Year 1800. Berkeley: 1937. V. 48; 53
The Cartography of the Northwest Coast of America to the Year 1800. Amsterdam: 1968. V. 48; 51
The Grabhorn Press: a Catalogue of Imprints in the Collection of Henry R. Wagner. Los Angeles: 1938. V. 54
Juan Rodriguez Cabrillo, Discoverer of the Coast of California. San Francisco: 1941. V. 50; 53; 54
The Library of Fernando Colon. Santa Ana: 1934. V. 54
Peter Pond, Fur Trader and Explorer. New Haven: 1955. V. 47
The Plains and the Rockies... San Francisco: 1937. V. 47; 48; 50; 53
The Plains and the Rockies... Columbus: 1953. V. 51; 53
The Plains and the Rockies. 1972. V. 47
The Plains and the Rockies... London: 1982. V. 49
The Plains and the Rockies. San Francisco: 1982. V. 47; 49; 50; 51; 52; 53; 54
The Rise of Fernando Cortes. Berkeley: 1944. V. 47
Sir Francis Drake's Voyage Around the World. San Francisco: 1926. V. 47; 48; 52; 53; 54
Sir Francis Drake's Voyage Around the World... Amsterdam: 1969. V. 48
Sixty Years of Book Collecting. Los Angeles: 1952. V. 54
Spanish Explorations in the Strait of Juan de Fuca. Santa Ana: 1933. V. 49; 53; 54
The Spanish Southwest 1542-1794. Albuquerque: 1937. V. 48; 49
Spanish Voyages to the Northwest Coast of America in the Sixteenth Century. San Francisco: 1929. V. 52; 53; 54
Spanish Voyages to the Northwest Coast of America in the Sixteenth Century. Amsterdam: 1966. V. 48; 50; 52

WAGNER, HERMANN
The Instructive Picture-Book. London: 1877. V. 50

WAGNER, KARL EDWARD
Horrorstory: Volume III. Novato: 1991/92. V. 52
Horrorstory: Volume IV. Novato: 1990. V. 52
Horrorstory: Volume V. Novato;: 1989. V. 52

WAGNER, RICHARD
Beethoven. Indianapolis: 1873. V. 49
The Nietzsche-Wagner Correspondence. New York: 1921. V. 50
Parsifal... London: 1912. V. 47
Parsifal. Wien: 1915. V. 49
The Rhinegold & the Valkyrie. London: 1910. V. 47; 49; 50; 51; 52
The Rhinegold & the Valkyrie. New York: 1910. V. 51; 53
The Rhinegold & the Valkyrie... London: 1910/11. V. 48
The Rhinegold & the Valkyrie. London: 1918. V. 49
The Rhinegold & the Valkyrie. London: 1920. V. 47
Richard to Minna Wagner. London: 1909. V. 54
The Ring of the Nibelung. London: 1939. V. 52
The Ring of the Nibelung. London: 1980. V. 47; 51
Siegfried & the Twilight of the Gods. London: 1911. V. 47; 51; 54
Siegfried & the Twilight of the Gods. New York: 1911. V. 49; 54
Siegfried & The Twilight of the Gods. London: 1924. V. 47
Siegfried and the Twilgiht of the Gods. London: 1930. V. 51
The Tale of Lohengrin Kight of the Sun. London. V. 48
Tannhauser. London: 1911. V. 48
Tannhauser. New York: 1920. V. 53
Uber Schauspieler und Sanger. Leipzig: 1872. V. 49

WAGNER, W. F.
Adventures of Zenas Leonard, Cleveland Fur Trader and Trapper, 1831-1836. Cleveland: 1904. V. 49
Leonard's Narrative Adventures of Zenas Leonard Fur Trader and Trapper 1831-1836... Cleveland: 1904. V. 47

WAGSTAFF, ALEXANDER E.
Life of David S. Terry: Presenting an Authentic, Impartial and Vivid History of His Eventful Life and Tragic Death. San Francisco: 1892. V. 51; 54

WAGSTAFFE, THOMAS
A Letter Out of Lancashire to a Friend in London, Giving some Account of the Late Trials There, Together with Some Seasonable and Proper Remarks Upon It. London: 1694. V. 47
A Vindication of K. Charles the Martyr...(with) A Defence of the Vindication of K. Charles the Martyr... London: 1711/1699. V. 49

WAGSTAFFE, WILLIAM
The Character of Richard St—le, Esq. London: 1713. V. 47; 53
A Comment Upon the History of Tom Thumb. London: 1711. V. 51; 54
Miscellaneous Works... London: 1725. V. 47
Miscellaneous Works of Dr. William Wagstaffe, Physician to St. Bartholomew's Hospital. London: 1726/25. V. 54
The Story of the St. Albans Ghost, or the Apparition of Mother Haggy. London: 1712. V. 50

WAH, FRED
Mountain. Buffalo: 1967. V. 47

WAHBI, MAGDI
Johnsonian Studies, Including a Bibliography of Johnsonian Studies 1950-1960. Cairo: 1962. V. 53

WAHLENBERG, ANNA
Old Swedish Fairy Tales. New York: 1925. V. 52
Old Swedish Fairy Tales. Philadelphia: 1925. V. 49

WAHLSTROM, CARL E.
Abraham Lincoln: Servant of the People. Worcester: 1942. V. 49

WAILES, B. L. C.
Report on the Agriculture and Geology of Mississippi... 1854. V. 48; 52

WAIN, JOHN
Letters to Five Artists. London: 1969. V. 49
Mid-Week...Return: Home Thoughts. Stratford: 1982. V. 53
Poems for the Zodiac. 1980. V. 54
Thinking About Mr. Person. Beckenham: 1980. V. 47

WAIN, LOUIS
Cats at Play. London: 1917. V. 54
Days in Catland. London: 1912. V. 49
The Happy Family. London: 1910. V. 47
In Animal Land with Louis Wain. London. V. 49
The Kittens Seaside Holiday. 1897/98. V. 48
Louis Wain's Annual 1921. London: 1921. V. 51
Our Darlings. London. V. 48
Pa Cats Ma Cats and Their Kittens. London: 1901. V. 49
Pussies and Puppies. London. V. 51
The Story of Tabbykin Town in School and at Play. London: 1920. V. 48

WAINEWRIGHT, JEREMIAH
A Mechanical Account of the Non-Naturals.... London: 1718. V. 51

WAINEWRIGHT, LATHAM
The Literary and Scientific Pursuits Which Are Encouraged and Enforced in the University of Cambridge... London: 1815. V. 52

WAINEWRIGHT, THOMAS GRIFFITHS
Essays and Criticisms, Now First Collected With Some Account of the Author... London: 1880. V. 54

WAINWRIGHT, ALFRED
A Bowland Sketchbook. Kendal: 1981. V. 53
The Central Highlands. Kendal: 1977. V. 54
A Coast to Coast Walk. Kendal: 1973. V. 54
The Eastern Highlands. Kendal: 1978. V. 54
The Far Eastern Fells. Kentmere: 1957. V. 52; 54
Fellwanderer. The Story Behind the Guidebooks. Kendal: 1966. V. 52
A Fifth Lakeland Sketchbook. Kendal. V. 52
A Furness Sketchbook. Kendal: 1979. V. 52
Kendal in the Nineteenth Century. Kendal: 1977. V. 52; 54
Lakeland Mountain Drawings. Volume Five. Kendal: 1984. V. 54
A Lune Sketchbook. Kendal: 1980. V. 54
The North-Western Highlands. Kendal: 1976. V. 54
The Northern Fells. Kentmere: 1962. V. 54
The Northern Highlands. Kendal: 1974. V. 54
A Second Lakeland Sketchbook. Kendal: 1970. V. 50; 52
The Southern Fells. Kendal: 1960. V. 54
A Third Lakeland Sketchbook. Kendal: 1977. V. 52
Three Westmorland Rivers. Kendal: 1979. V. 54
Wainwright in Lakeland. Kendal: 1983. V. 50; 52; 54
Westmorland Heritage. Kendal: 1975. V. 51; 52

WAINWRIGHT, J. M.
The Land of Bondage; its Ancient Monuments and Present Condition; Being the Jouranl of a Tour in Egypt. New York: 1852. V. 48

WAINWRIGHT, JOHN
The Medical and Surgical Knowledge of William Shakespeare With Explanatory Notes. New York: 1907. V. 50; 52
The Medical Knowledge of William Shakespeare with Explanatory Notes. New York: 1915. V. 52
Yorkshire. An Historical and Topographical Introduction to a Knowledge of the Ancient State of the Wapentake of Strafford and Tickhill. Sheffield: 1829. V. 48; 53

WAINWRIGHT, JONATHAN M.
A Set of Chants Adapted to the Hymns in the Morning and Evening Prayer and to the Communion Service of the Protestant Episcopal Church in the United States of America. Boston: 1819. V. 51

WAINWRIGHT, NICHOLAS B.
Philadelphia in the Romantic Age of Lithography. Philadelphia: 1958. V. 50; 54

WAIT, A. E.
The Real History of the Rosicrucians. London: 1887. V. 52

WAIT, BENJAMIN
Letters from Van Dieman's Land, Written During Four Years Imprisonment for Political Offences Committed in Upper Canada... Buffalo: 1843. V. 47; 53

WAIT, FRONA EUNICE
Yermah the Dorado. San Francisco: 1897. V. 51

WAITE, ARTHUR EDWARD
Azoth: or the Star in the East: Embracing the First Matter of the magnum Opus, the Evolution of Aphrodite-Urania, The Supernatural Genration of the Son of the Sun, and the Alchemical Transfiguration of Humanity. London: 1893. V. 47
The Book of Ceremonial Magic: Including the Rites and Mysteries of Goetic Theurgy, Sorcery and Infernal Necromancy. London: 1911. V. 52
A Book of Mystery and Vision. London: 1902. V. 48
The Brotherhood of the Rosy Cross. London: 1924. V. 47; 48
The Hermetic Museum: Restored and Enlarged... London: 1953. V. 47
The Holy Kabbalah. London: 1929. V. 50
Lives of Alchemystical Philosophers: Based on Materials Collected in 1815. London: 1888. V. 47
The Mysteries of Magic: a Digest of the Writings of Eliphas Levi... London: 1886. V. 47
The Mysteries of Magic: a Digest of the Writings of Eliphas Levi... London: 1897. V. 47

WAITE, D. B.
Artefacts from the Solomon Islands, in the Julius L. Brenchley Collection. London: 1987. V. 54

WAITE, OTIS F. R.
New Hampshire in the Great Rebellion. Claremont: 1870. V. 48; 50; 52

WAITZ, JULIA ELLEN LE GRAND
The Journal of Julia Le Grand, New Orleans, 1862-1863. Richmond: 1911. V. 49; 53

WAKE, C. STANILAND
The Development of Marriage and Kinship. London: 1889. V. 52

WAKE, WILLIAM
The Excellency and Benefits of a Religious Education: A Sermon Preach'd in the parish-Church of St. Sepulchre, June...1715...with The Methods Used for Erecting Charity-Schools... London: 1715. V. 50

WAKEFIELD, D. R.
Some Trout. Poetry on Trout and Angling by Various Authors. North Humberside: 1989. V. 53
The Sporting Fishes of the British Isles. 1985. V. 52
The Sporting Fishes of the British Isles. London: 1985. V. 47

WAKEFIELD, EDWARD GIBBON
An Account of Ireland, Statistical and Political. London: 1812. V. 49
The British Colonization of New Zealand... London: 1837. V. 47
England and America. A Comparison of the Social and Political State of Both Nations. London: 1833. V. 48
New Zealand After Fifty Years. London: 1889. V. 47
The Trial in Full of Edw. Gibbon Wakefield and Others, for the Abduction of Miss Turner (etc). London: 1827. V. 52
A View of the Art of Colonization in Letters Between Statesman and a Colonist. 1914. V. 50
A View of the Art of Colonization with Present Reference to the British Empire... London: 1849. V. 49; 52

WAKEFIELD, GILBERT
Observations on Pope. London: 1796. V. 48
Poetical Translations from the Ancients. London: 1795. V. 48; 53; 54

WAKEFIELD, JOHN A.
History of the War Between the United States and the Sac and Fox Nations of Indians... Jacksonville: 1834. V. 48

WAKEFIELD, JOSEPHUS
History of Waupaca County, Wisconsin. Waupaca: 1890. V. 52

WAKEFIELD, PAUL L.
Campaigning Texas. Houston: 1932. V. 48

WAKEFIELD, PRISCILLA
Excursions in North America, Described in Letters from A Gentleman and His Young Companion, to Their Friends in England. London: 1806. V. 47
Excursions in North America, Described in Letters from a Gentleman and His Young Companion to Their Friends in England. London: 1819. V. 47
An Introduction to Botany. Dublin: 1796. V. 49; 54
An Introduction to Botany... London: 1798. V. 48
An Introduction to the Natural History and Classification of Insects. London: 1816. V. 54
Juvenile Anecdotes, Founded on Facts. Philadelphia: 1809. V. 47
Mental Improvements: or, the Beauties and Wonders of Nature and Art. Dublin: 1800. V. 54
Perambulations in London and its Environs. London: 1809. V. 48; 49

THE WAKEFIELD Second Nativity Play. London: 1917. V. 48; 53
THE WAKEFIELD Second Nativity Play. Weybridge: 1917. V. 47

WAKEFIELD, W.
The Happy Valley: Sketches of Kashmir and the Kashmiris. London: 1879. V. 50; 54

WAKELY, ANDREW
The Mariner's Compass Rectified. London: 1775. V. 49

WAKEMAN, EDGAR
The Log of an Ancient Mariner. San Francisco: 1878. V. 47; 48; 50; 51; 54

WAKEMAN, GEOFFREY
Aspects of Victorian Lithography; Anastatic Printing and Photozincography. Wymondham: 1970. V. 51
Bradbury & Evans: Colour Printers. Oxford: 1984. V. 53
English Marbled Papers, a Documentary History. Loughborough: 1978. V. 47; 48
Functional Developments in Bookbinding. New Castle: 1993. V. 52
The Literature of Letterpress Printing 1849-1900. Kidlington: 1986. V. 49
Nineteenth Century Trade Binding. 1983. V. 53

WAKEMAN, GEOFFREY continued
Nineteenth Century Trade Binding. Kidlington: 1983. V. 48
Twentieth Century English Vat Paper Mills. Loughborough: 1980. V. 48

WAKEMAN, STEPHEN H.
The Stephen H. Wakeman Collection of Books. New York: 1924. V. 52
The Stephen H. Wakeman Collection of Nineteenth Century American Writers. New York: 1922. V. 48

WAKINSHAW, JOSEPH W.
The Parliamentary Career of Sir W. R. Plummer, M.P. Newcastle-upon-Tyne: 1904. V. 50

WAKLEY, B. J.
Bradman the Great. London: 1959. V. 51

WAKOSKI, DIANE
Coins and Coffins. New York: 1962. V. 48
The Collected Greed, Parts 1-13. Santa Barbara: 1984. V. 54
Dancing on the Grave of a Son of a Bitch. Los Angeles: 1973. V. 51
The Diamond Merchant. Cambridge: 1968. V. 50
Discrepancies and Apparitions. Garden City: 1966. V. 49
The George Washington Poems. New York: 1967. V. 50
George Washington's Camp Cups. Madison: 1976. V. 52; 54
Greed. Parts 1-2. Los Angeles: 1968. V. 48; 51
Greed. Parts 3-4. 1969. V. 51
Greed. Parts 5-7. Los Angeles: 1971. V. 48; 51
Greed. Parts 8, 9, 11. Los Angeles: 1973. V. 48; 51; 52
The Ice Queen. Alabama: 1994. V. 52; 53; 54
The Laguna Contract. Wisconsin: 1976. V. 51
The Lament of the Lady Bank Dick. Cambridge: 1969. V. 48; 49; 54
The Magician's Feastletters. Santa Barbara: 1982. V. 49
Making a Sacher Torte. Mt. Horeb: 1981. V. 47; 51; 53; 54
The Managed World. New York: 1980. V. 52; 54
Overnight Projects with Wood. A Poem. Madison: 1977. V. 52
The Pumpkin Pie. 1972. V. 48
Thanking My Mother for Piano Lessons. Mount Horeb: 1969. V. 51; 52; 53; 54
Trophies. Santa Barbara: 1979. V. 47; 49
The Wandering Tattler. 1974. V. 48
The Wandering Tattler. Mt. Horeb: 1974. V. 51; 53
The Wandering Tattler. Wisconsin: 1974. V. 54

WAKOWSKI, DIANE
The Purple Finch Song. Mt. Horeb: 1972. V. 47

WALBERG, GISELA
Provincial Middle Minoan Pottery. Mainz am Rhein: 1983. V. 50; 52

WALBRAN, JOHN T.
British Columbia Caosat Names 1592-1906. Ottawa: 1909. V. 48; 49; 53; 54

WALCH, JAN
De Vreeselijke Avonturen van Scholastica. Bussum: 1933. V. 47

WALCOT, W.
Architectural Water-colours and Etchings of W. Walcot. London: 1919. V. 50

WALCOTT, C. D.
Cambrian Brachiopoda. Washington: 1912. V. 49; 52

WALCOTT, DEREK
Another Life. New York: 1973. V. 53
The Arkansas Testament. New York: 1987. V. 50; 51
Caribbean Poetry. New York: 1983. V. 48; 49; 53
The Castaway and Other Poems. London: 1965. V. 49; 53
The Castaway and Other Poems. New York: 1965. V. 53
Collected Poems 1948-1984. New York: 1986. V. 53
Dream on Monkey Mountain. New York: 1970. V. 54
The Gulf. London: 1969. V. 53
The Gulf. New York: 1970. V. 50
In a Green Night. London: 1962. V. 48; 49; 51
The Joker of Seville and O Babylon!. New York: 1978. V. 48; 50; 53
Malcauchon. Trinidad: 1966. V. 54
Omeros. New York: 1990. V. 49
Omeros. New York: 1993. V. 52
Poems of the Caribbean. New York: 1983. V. 48
Sea Grapes. New York: 1976. V. 53; 54
Selected Poems. New York: 1964. V. 47; 51; 52; 53; 54
The Star-Apple Kingdom. New York: 1979. V. 49; 53

WALCOTT, GEORGE
The George Walcott Collection of Used Civil War Patriotic Covers. New York: 1934. V. 52

WALCOTT, M. V.
North American Wild Flowers. Washington: 1925. V. 54

WALCOTT, MAC KENZIE E. C.
Scot-Monasticon. The Ancient Church of Scotland. London: 1874. V. 52; 54

WALCOTT, MARY VAUX
Illustrations of North American Pitcherplants. Washington: 1935. V. 48

WALCOTT, PAUL
Chats About Miniature Books. Boston: 1932. V. 49; 50

WALCOTT, THOMAS
A True Copy of a Paper Written by Capt. Tho. Walcott in Newgate, After His Condemnation and Delivered to His Son, Immediately Before His Execution. Colophon: 1683. V. 47; 54

WALDBERG, PATRICK
Marino Marini. Complete Works. New York: 1970. V. 50
Max Ernst. Paris: 1958. V. 50
Rene Magritte. Brussels: 1965. V. 47; 50

WALDEGRAVE, JAMES, EARL OF
Memoirs from 1754 to 1758. London: 1821. V. 50

WALDHORN & CO.
Antiques, a Rare Collection from Old Creole Families. New Orleans: 1905-11. V. 51

WALDMAN, DIANE
Roy Lichtenstein... New York: 1969. V. 50
Roy Lichtenstein. New York: 1971. V. 48; 49; 50; 52; 54

WALDMANN, EMIL
Albrecht Altdorfer. London: 1923. V. 51

WALDMEIER, THEOPHILUS
The Autobiography of T. Waldmeier, Missionary... London: 1886. V. 53

WALDO, SAMUEL PUTNAM
Biographical Sketches of Distinguished American Naval Heroes in the War of the Revolution. Hartford: 1823. V. 52
Memoirs of Andrew Jackson, Major-General in the Army of the United States... Hartford: 1819. V. 48
The Tour of James Monroe, President of the U.S. through the Northern and Eastern States in 1817. Hartford: 1819. V. 53
The Tour of James Monroe, President of the U.S...Through the States of Maryland, Pennsylvania, New Jersey, New York, Connecticut, Rhode Island, Massachusetts, New Hampshire, Vermont and Ohio... Hartford: 1818. V. 47

WALDRON, FRANCIS GODOLPHIN
Free Recollections on Miscellaneous Papers and Legal Instruments, Under the Hand and Seal of William Shakespeare... London: 1796. V. 51

WALDROP, KEITH
Songs from the Decline of the West. Mt. Horeb: 1970. V. 51

WALDROP, ROSEMARIE
Sping is an Season and Nothing. Mt. Horeb: 1970. V. 51

WALDSCHMIDT, JOHANN J.
Opera Medico-Practica... Frankfurt: 1695. V. 49

WALDSEEMULLER, MARTIN
The Cosmographiae Introductio (In Facimile) Followed by the Four Voyages of Amerigo Vespucci... New York: 1907. V. 48

WALE, JOHN
Divers Works of Early Masters in Christian Decoration... London: 1846. V. 47

WALE, W. J. JAMES
Hubert and John Van Eyck, Their Life and Work. London: 1908. V. 50

WALES, GEORGE C.
Etchings and Lithographs of American Ships. Boston: 1927. V. 53

WALES, PHILIP
Report On Yellow Fever in the U.S.S. Plymouth in 1878-79. Washington: 1880. V. 50

WALES, PRINCE OF
Sport and Travel in East Africa. 1934. V. 54

WALEY, ARTHUR
The Poet Li Po A.D. 701-762. (A Paper Read before the China Society at the School of Oriental Studies on November 21, 1918). 1919. V. 47
The Year Book of Oriental Art and Culture, 1924-1925. London: 1925. V. 47
Zen Buddhism and Its Relation to Art. Luzac: 1922. V. 47

WALEY, HUBERT
The Revival of Aesthetics. London: 1926. V. 48; 49

WALFORD, CORNELIUS
Fairs, Past and Present: a Chapter in the History of Commerce. London: 1883. V. 50

WALFORD, EDWARD
Londiniana. London: 1879. V. 54

WALFORD, JAMES F.
A Book of Orchid Paintings. London: 1971. V. 51

WALFORD, LIONEL A.
Marine Game Fishes of the Pacific Coast from Alaska to the Equator. Berkeley: 1937. V. 50

WALFORD, LUCY BERTHA
A Little Legacy and Other Stories. Chicago: 1899. V. 49
Twelve English Authoresses. London: 1892. V. 48; 50

WALFORD, WILLIAM
A True Account From On Board the Good Ship Caesar, in Her Voyage to the East Indies. London: 1687. V. 47

WALGAMOTT, CHARLES S.
Reminiscences of Early Days. Twin Falls: 1926-27. V. 50

WALKE, HENRY
Naval Scenes and Reminiscences of the Civil War in the United States, on the southern and Western Waters During the Years 1861, 1862 and 1863. New York: 1877. V. 53

WALKEM, W. WYMOND
Stories of Early British Columbia. Vancouver: 1914. V. 52

WALKER, A.
A Philosophical Estimate of the Causes, Effects and Cure of Unwholsome Air in Large Cities. London: 1777. V. 54

WALKER, A. EARL
A History of Neurological Surgery. Baltimore: 1951. V. 48; 52; 52
The Late Effects of Head Injury. Springfield: 1969. V. 47
Penicillin in Neurology. Springfield: 1946. V. 47
Posttraumatic Epilepsy. Springfield: 1949. V. 47

WALKER, ADAM
Ideas Suggested on the Spot in a Late Excursion through Flanders, Germany, France and Italy. London: 1790. V. 54
Remarks Made in a Tour from London to the Lakes of Westmoreland and Cumberland, in the Summer of MDCCXCI. London: 1792. V. 52

WALKER, ALEXANDER
Beauty: Illustrated Chiefly by an Analysis and Classification of Beauty in Woman. London: 1836. V. 54
Intermarriage; or the Mode in Which and the Causes Why, Beauty, Health and Intellect, Result... London: 1838. V. 50

WALKER, ALEXANDER, MRS.
Female Beauty, as Preserved and Improved By Regimen, Cleanliness and Dress... London: 1837. V. 53

WALKER, ALICE
The Color Purple. New York: 1970. V. 52
The Color Purple. New York: 1982. V. 47; 48; 51; 52; 53
Good Night, Willie Lee, I'll See You in the Morning. 1979. V. 50
Good Night, Willie Lee, I'll See You in the Morning. New York: 1979. V. 47; 51; 52; 53; 54
Good Night Willie Lee, I'll See You in the Morning. London: 1984. V. 51
Her Blue Body Everything We Know. San Diego, New York,: 1991. V. 48; 49; 52; 54
Horses Make a Landscape Look More Beautiful. New York: 1984. V. 52
Horses Make a Landscape Look More Beautiful. San Diego: 1984. V. 51
In Love and In Trouble. Stories of Black Women. New York: 1973. V. 48
In Search of Our Mothers' Gardens. San Diego, New York: 1983. V. 50; 51; 52; 53; 54
Langston Hughes, American Poet. New York: 1974. V. 51; 53
Living by the Word. San Diego: 1988. V. 51
Meridian. London: 1976. V. 50; 51; 52; 53
Meridian. New York: 1976. V. 47; 48; 52
On Sight. 1983. V. 47
Once. New York: 1968. V. 47
Possessing the Secret of Joy. New York: 1992. V. 47; 48; 49; 51; 52
Possessing the Secret of Joy. San Diego: 1992. V. 47; 51
Revolutionary Petunias. New York: 1973. V. 47
The Temple of My Familiar. San Diego/New York: 1989. V. 48; 53
The Third Life of Grange Copeland. New York: 1970. V. 47; 48; 52; 53
To Hell With Dying. 1988. V. 47
To Hell With Dying. New York: 1988. V. 52
You Can't Keep a Good Woman Down. New York: 1981. V. 53; 54

WALKER, ANNA LOUISA
Lady's Holm. London: 1878. V. 49

WALKER, ANNE
Rose Rose. Paris: 1993. V. 52

WALKER, ARTHUR N.
The Holcombe Hunt. Manchester: 1937. V. 47

WALKER, BERTRAM
Tales of the Bark Lodges. Oklahoma City: 1919. V. 54

WALKER, C. B.
The Mississippi Valley and Prehistoric Events... Burlington: 1879. V. 48

WALKER, CHARLES M.
History of Athens County, Ohio... Cincinnati: 1869. V. 48

WALKER, CHARLES THOMAS
Reply to William Hannibal Thomas the 20th Century Slanderer of the Negro Race. New York: 1901?. V. 51

WALKER, CLEMENT
Relations and Observations, Historical and Politick, Upon the Parliament, begun Anno Dom. 1640. London: 1648. V. 49
Relations and Observations, Historical and Politick, Upon the Parliament Begun Anno Dom. 1640. London: 1648-51. V. 53
Relations and Observations, Historicall and Politick, Upon the Parliament Begun Anno Dom. 1640. London: 1660. V. 54

WALKER, CORNELIUS IRVINE
The Life of Lieutenant General Richard Heron Anderson, of the Confederate states Army. Charleston: 1917. V. 48; 49

WALKER, D. E.
A Resume of the Story of 1st Battalion, the Saskatoon Light Infantry (MG) Canadian Army, Overseas. Saskatoon: 1946. V. 52

WALKER, DALE L.
Death Was the Black Horse: The Story of Rough Rider Buckey O'Neill. Austin: 1975. V. 48
Jack London, Sherlock Holmes and Sir Arthur Conan Doyle. Amsterdam: 1974. V. 53

WALKER, DONALD
Defensive Exercises... London: 1840. V. 51

WALKER, E. P.
Mammals of the World. New York: 1991. V. 48

WALKER, EDWARD
Historical Collections of Several Important Transactions Relating to the Late Rebellion and Civil Wars of England... London: 1707. V. 53
Historical Discourses Upon Several Occasions: Together with Perfect Copies of All the Votes, Letters, Proposals, Answers Relating Unto and that Passed in, the Treaty Held at Newport, in the Isle of Wight... London: 1705. V. 47

WALKER, ELDRED G. F.
Canadian Trails Re-Visited. London: 1925?. V. 47

WALKER, EWING A.
Old Cocking Poems and Prints. 1927. V. 47

WALKER, F.
List of the Specimens of Dipterous Insects in the Collection of the British Museum. London: 1848-55. V. 50

WALKER, F. A., & CO.
Illustrated Catalogue of Useful and Ornamental Goods Suitable for the Parlor, Dining Room, Kitchen and Laundry. Boston: 1871. V. 53
Illustrated Supplement to Our Catalogue of 1871...Choice House and Kitchen Furnishing Goods... Boston: 1872. V. 53

WALKER, F. W.
The History of the Old 2/4th (City of London) Battalion the London Regiment Royal Fusiliers. London: 1919. V. 47

WALKER, FRANCIS A.
General Hancock. New York: 1897. V. 47

WALKER, FRANKLIN
The Seacoast of Bohemia. San Francisco: 1966. V. 47
The Wickedest Man in San Francisco. San Francisco: 1941. V. 49

WALKER, FREDERICK
English Rustic Pictures. London: 1882. V. 49
English Rustic Pictures. Routledge: 1882/82. V. 54

WALKER, G. GOOLD
The Honourable Artillery Company, 1537-1926. London: 1926. V. 50

WALKER, GEORGE
The Battle of Waterloo. London: 1815. V. 54
Chess Made Easy... Baltimore: 1837. V. 49
The Costume of Yorkshire. London: 1814. V. 49; 52; 54
Descriptive Catalogue of a Choice Assemblage of Original Pictures... Edinburgh: 1807. V. 47
The House of Tynian. London: 1795. V. 48
A New Treatise on Chess... London: 1832. V. 52
On the Doctrine of the Sphere. London: 1777 (altered). V. 53
Scottish Scenery. London: 1807. V. 53
Sermons on Various Subjects. London: 1790. V. 47
The Three Spaniards, a Romance. Dublin: 1800. V. 54
A True Account of the Siege of London-Derry. London: 1689. V. 53; 54

WALKER, GERALD
Cruising. New York: 1970. V. 54

WALKER, H. W.
Wanderings Among South Sea Savages and in Borneo and the Philippines. London: 1910. V. 50

WALKER, HOVENDEN
Journal, or Full Account of the Late Expedition to Canada. London: 1720. V. 47; 51

WALKER, ISAAC
Dress: as It Has Been, Is and Will Be. New York: 1885. V. 54

WALKER, J.
The History of Penrith, from the Earliest Period to the Present Time. Hodgson: 1857. V. 52
The History of Penrith, from the Earliest Period to the Present Time. Penrith: 1865. V. 50; 52

WALKER, J. CRAMPTON
Irish Life and Landscape. 1926. V. 49; 50
Irish Life and Landscape. London: 1926. V. 51

WALKER, J. RUSSELL
Pre-Reformation Churches in Fifeshire. Edinburgh: 1895. V. 50

WALKER, J. W.
Wakefield: Its History and People. Wakefield: 1934. V. 47

WALKER, JAMES
Report to the Directors of the Liverpool and Manchester Railway, on the Comparative Merits of Locomotive and Fixed Engines... Philadelphia: 1831. V. 47
A Sermon, Preached in Brooklyn, Connecticut, at the Installation of Rev. Samuel Joseph May, November 5, 1823. Boston: 1824. V. 48

WALKER, JAMES R.
Be Firm My Hope. New York: 1955. V. 53

WALKER, JAMES S.
The Theory of the Common Law. Boston: 1852. V. 51

WALKER, JAMES SCOTT
Accurate Description of the Liverpool and Manchester Railway... Liverpool: 1832. V. 54

WALKER, JOHN
The Academic Speaker; or, a Selection of Parliamentary Debates, Orations, odes, Scenes and Speeches. London: 1803. V. 52
An Attempt Towards Recovering an Account of the Numbers and Sufferings of the Clergy of the Church of England... London: 1714. V. 47; 51; 53
A Critical Pronouncing Dictionary...of the English Language. London: 1797. V. 52
A Critical Pronouncing Dictionary...of the English Language... London: 1806. V. 52
A Critical Pronouncing Dictionary...of the English Language. London: 1854. V. 53
A Dictionary of the English Language, Answering at Once the Purposes of Rhyming, Spelling and Pronouncing. London: 1775. V. 52
Elements of Elocution. London: 1781. V. 52
Elements of Elocution... Boston: 1810. V. 49
Hand-Book of Ireland. An Illustrated Guide. London. V. 53
Oxoniana. Oxford: 1809. V. 47
A Rhyming Dictionary; Answering, at the Same Time, the Purposes of Spelling and Pronouncing the English Language... London: 1806. V. 52

WALKER, JOSEPH COOPER
Historical Memoir On Italian Tragedy from the Earliest Period to the Present Time... London: 1799. V. 47; 49; 53; 54
Memoirs of A. Tassoni.... London: 1815. V. 49

WALKER, JOSIAH
The Defence of Order, a Poem. Edinburgh: 1803. V. 49

WALKER, JUDSON ELLIOTT
Campaigns of General Custer in the North-West and the Final Surrender of Sitting Bull. New York: 1881. V. 47; 50

WALKER, MARGARET
For My People. New Haven: 1942. V. 48; 51; 53
Jubilee. Boston: 1965. V. 49
Jubilee. Boston: 1966. V. 49; 53

WALKER, MARY
Reminiscences of the Life of the World Renowned Charlotte Cushman. Boston: 1876. V. 50

WALKER, MARY ADELAIDE
Through Macedonia to the Albanian Lakes. London: 1864. V. 52; 54

WALKER, MARY E.
Hit. New York: 1871. V. 48; 53; 54

WALKER, MARY WILLIS
The Red Scream. New York: 1994. V. 53; 54
Under the Bettle's Cellar. New York: 1995. V. 54

WALKER, OBADIAH
Of Education Especially of Young Gentlemen. Oxford: 1673. V. 47; 53; 54

WALKER, PERCY
Lost in the Cosmos. New York: 1983. V. 51

WALKER, R.
The Flora of Oxfordshire, and its Contiguous Counties... Oxford: 1833. V. 52

WALKER, R. J.
Letter of Mr. Walker of Mississippi, Relative to the Reannexation of Texas; in Replying to the Call of the People of Carroll County, Kentucky, to Communicate His Views on that Subject. Washington: 1844.. V. 47

WALKER, RALPH
Ralph Walker, Architect. New York: 1957. V. 47

WALKER, RICHARD
Memoirs of Medicine... London: 1799. V. 49; 51; 53
Regency Portraits. London: 1985. V. 50

WALKER, ROBERT
An Inquiry into the Small-Pox, Medical and Political. London: 1790. V. 47; 51

WALKER, ROBERT JOHN
Letter of...Relative to the Reannexation of Texas. Washington: 1844,. V. 49

WALKER, S.
The Road: Leaves From the Sketch-book of a Commercial Traveller. London: 1872. V. 49

WALKER, SAMUEL
Reformation of Manners Promoted by Argument, in Several Essays, Viz. of Reproof...Drunkeness...Lust of Impurity...Swearing...the Lord's Day. London: 1711. V. 54
Reformation of Manners Promoted by Argument, in Several Essays, Viz. Of Reproof...Drunkenness... Lust or Impurity... Swearing... The Lord's Day. 1711. V. 49

WALKER, T.
Mountain Days in the Highlands and Alps. London: 1937. V. 53

WALKER, TACETTA B.
Stories of Early Days in Wyoming, Big Horn Basin. Casper: 1936. V. 49; 53

WALKER, THOMAS
Journal of an Exploration in the Spring of the Year 1750. Boston: 1888. V. 47
The Quaker's Opera. London: 1728. V. 48
A Review of Some of the Political Events Which Have Occccurred in Manchester, During the Last Five Years. London: 1794. V. 51

WALKER, THOMAS A.
The Severn Tunnel: Its Construction and Difficulties. 1872-1887. London: 1888. V. 51
The Severn Tunnel: Its Construction and Difficulties. 1872-1887. London: 1890. V. 54
The Severn Tunnel: Its Construction and Difficulties 1872-1887... London: 1891. V. 48; 49

WALKER, THOMAS DIXON
An Analysis of the Waters of Dinsdale & Croft, with Practical Observations on Their Medicinal Powers... Durham: 1828. V. 51
Dinsdale and Croft. Part I and II only. Darlington: 1856. V. 50; 54
Facts Relative to the Medicinal Properties of the Dinsdale and Croft Sulpher Springs. Darlington: 1835. V. 50

WALKER, W. S.
Between the Tides Comprising, Sketches, Tales and Poems, Including H-U-N-G-R-Y L-A-N-D. Los Gatoes: 1885. V. 47

WALKER, WILLIAM
Idiomatologia Anglo-Latina, Sive Dictionarium Idiomaticum AngloR.F.G. Hollett & Son SU96-Latinum... London: 1685. V. 54
Jottings of an Invalid in Search of Health, Comprising a Run through British India and a Visit to Singapore and Java. Bombay: 1865. V. 49
The Missionary Pioneer, or a Brief Memoir of the Life, Labours and Death of John Stewart... New York: 1827. V. 50
Some Improvements to the Art of Teaching, Especially in the First Grounding of a Young Scholar in Grammar Learning. London: 1693. V. 48; 49
A Treatise of English Particles; Shewing Much of the Variety of Their Significations and Uses in English... London: 1663. V. 51
The War in Nicaragua. Mobile: 1860. V. 52

WALKER, WILLIAM SIDNEY
The Appeal of Poland. Cambridge: 1816. V. 48; 54
Gustavus Vasa and Other Poems. London: 1813. V. 47; 52
Poems from the Danish. London: 1815. V. 47

WALKINGAME, FRANCIS
The Tutor's Assistant... London: 1793. V. 47
The Tutor's Assistant... Toronto: 1847. V. 50

WALKLEY, THOMAS
A New Catalogue of the Dukes, Marquesses, Earles, Viscounts, Barons, That Sit in This Present Parliament. London: 1644. V. 53

WALKOWITZ, ABRAHAM
100 Paintings and Drawings from the Objective to the Abstract. New York: 1925. V. 53
From Life to Life. Girard: 1951. V. 53

WALKS *About Richmond A Story for Boys, and a Guide to Persons Visiting the City, Desiring to See the Principal Points of Interest...* Richmond: 1870. V. 49

WALL, ALFRED H.
A Manual of Artistic Colouring, as Applied to Photographs. London: 1861. V. 50; 52; 54

WALL, BERNARD
Headlong Into Change. An Autobiography and a Memoir of Ideas Since the Thirties. London: 1969. V. 49

WALL, BERNHARDT
Following General Sam Houston: 1793-1863. Lime Rock: 1935. V. 47; 53
The Russian Players in America: The Moscow Art Theatre, Balieff's chauve-souris. New York: 1923. V. 48

WALL, DOROTHY
Blinky Bill Grows Up. Sydney: 1934. V. 49

WALL, E. J.
The History of Three Colour Photography. Boston: 1925. V. 49

WALL, GARRET D.
An Address to the Legislature of New Jersey, on the Subject of Internal Improvements. 1835. V. 51

WALL, JOHN P.
The Chronicles of New Brunswick, New Jersey 1667-1931. New Brunswick: 1931. V. 47; 51
History of Middlesex County, New Jersey, 1664-1920. New York: 1921. V. 47; 51
History of Middlesex County, New Jersey 1667-1931. New Brunswick: 1931. V. 49

WALL, MARTIN
Clinical Observations on the Use of Opium in Low Fevers, and in the Synochus... Oxford: 1786. V. 48; 53

WALL *Paintings in the Kondo Horyuji Monastery.* Kyoto: 1951. V. 48

WALL, THOMAS
The Voyage of Sir Nicholas Carewe to the Emperor Charles V in the Year 1529. Cambridge: 1959. V. 48; 51

WALL, WALTER
Spider Poems. Madison: 1967. V. 52

WALLACE & WARNER
The Work of Wallace & Warner architects. Philadelphia: 1930. V. 48

WALLACE, ALFRED RUSSEL
Australasia. London: 1884. V. 53; 54
Contributions to the Theory of Natural Selection. London: 1875. V. 54
Darwinism... London: 1889. V. 48; 49; 50; 53; 54
Darwinism. London: 1890. V. 49
Darwinism an Exposition of the Theory of Natural Selection. London: 1889. V. 48; 49; 50
The Geographical Distribution of Animals. London: 1876. V. 47; 48; 50; 54
The Geographical Distribution of Animals. New York: 1876. V. 47; 48; 54

WALLACE, ALFRED RUSSEL continued
Is Mars Habitable?. London: 1907. V. 48
Island Life. London: 1880. V. 48; 49; 50; 51; 54
Island Life... New York: 1881. V. 54
Island Life. London: 1892. V. 48; 54
Island Life... London: 1895. V. 54
Island Life. London: 1902. V. 54
The Malay Archipelago. London: 1869. V. 47; 49; 51; 52; 54
The Malay Archipelago. New York: 1869. V. 51; 52; 54
Der Malayische Archipel. Braunschweig: 1869. V. 51
Man's Place in the Universe. New York: 1903. V. 49
My Life: a Record of Events and Opinions. London: 1905. V. 49
A Narrative of Travels on the Amazon and Rio Negro... London: 1853. V. 52
A Narrative of Travels on the Amazon and Rio Negro... London: 1889. V. 54
Palm Trees of the Amazon and Their Uses. London: 1853. V. 52; 53
Studies Scientific & Social. London: 1900. V. 48; 51
Tropical Nature and Other Essays. London: 1878. V. 48; 50; 51; 52; 53
The Wonderful Century. London: 1898. V. 51; 52; 53; 54

WALLACE, ANDREW
Gen. August V. Kautz and the Southwestern Frontier. Tucson: 1967. V. 49

WALLACE, ARTHUR
The Trial of Arthur Wallace, Assistant Deputy Post-Master of Carlow, for Stealing Notes Out of the Post Bag and for Forgery. Dublin: 1800. V. 50

WALLACE, C. LEIGH HUNT, MRS.
Physianthropy; or, the Home Cure and Eradication of Disease. London. V. 50

WALLACE, DAVID FOSTER
The Broom of the System. New York: 1987. V. 47; 51; 52; 53; 54
The Girl With the Curious Hair. New York: 1989. V. 53

WALLACE, DONALD MAC KENZIE
Russia. London: 1877. V. 48; 52
Russia. London: 1905. V. 51
Russia... Boston and Tokyo: 1910. V. 54

WALLACE, E.
The Mission That Failed. 1898. V. 53
Unofficial Dispatches. London: 1900. V. 53

WALLACE, EDGAR
The Four Just Men. London: 1905. V. 51
The Tomb of Ts'in. London: 1916. V. 48
Writ in Barracks. 1900. V. 53
Writ in Barracks. London: 1900. V. 51

WALLACE, EDWARD J.
The Oregon Question. London: 1846. V. 50

WALLACE, ELIZABETH
Mark Twain and the Happy Island. Chicago: 1913. V. 47; 48

WALLACE, ELLERSLIE
The Amateur Photographer. A Manual of Photographic Manipulation. Philadelphia: 1884. V. 47

WALLACE, F. W.
Roving Fisherman. An Autobiography. Gardenvale: 1955. V. 52

WALLACE, FREDERICK WILLIAM
Record of Canadian Shipping. Toronto: 1929. V. 50

WALLACE, HAROLD FRANK
The Big Game of Central and Western China. London: 1913. V. 48; 49
British Deer Heads. 1913. V. 52; 54

WALLACE, HENRY
Uncle Henry's Own Story of His Life: Personal Reminicences. Des moines: 1917-18-19. V. 50

WALLACE, ISABEL
Life and Letters of General W. H. L. Wallace. Chicago: 1909. V. 48; 50

WALLACE, J. H.
Wallace's American Trotting Register. New York: 1871. V. 49

WALLACE, JAMES
Every Man His Own Letter Writer; or, the New and Complete Art of Letter-Writing. London: 1782?. V. 52

WALLACE, JOHN
The Horse in America. New York: 1897. V. 50

WALLACE, JOHN WILLIAM
An Old Philadelphia, Colonel William Bradford, the Patriot Printer of 1776. Sketches of Life. Philadelphia: 1884. V. 48

WALLACE, LEW
An Autobiography. New York: 1906. V. 48; 53
Ben Hur. New York: 1880. V. 48; 53
Ben Hur... New York: 1892. V. 52
Ben Hur... London: 1902. V. 51
Ben Hur. London: 1926. V. 53
Life of General Ben Harrison. Philadelphia, Chicago: 1888. V. 47; 48

WALLACE NUTTING INC.
Wallace Nutting Windsors. Correct Windsor Furniture. 1918. V. 52

WALLACE, PATRICK MAXWELL STEWART
The Trials of Patrick Maxwell Stewart Wallace and Michael Shaw Stewart Wallace, for Wilfully Destroying the Big Dryad, Off Cuba, with Intent to Defraud the Marine Assurance Companies. London: 1841. V. 52; 54

WALLACE, PHILIP B.
Colonial Ironwork in Old Philadelphia. The Craftmanship of the Early Days of the Republic. New York: 1930. V. 54

WALLACE, R. I.
British Cage Birds. London: 1880. V. 50

WALLACE, ROBERT
Characteristics of the Present Political State of Great Britain. London: 1758. V. 50; 53
A Dissertation on the Numbers of Mankind in Antient and Modern Times... Edinburgh: 1753. V. 48
A Dissertation on the Verb of the English Language, Its Moods, Tenses and Inflections, Delivered Before the Members of the Literary and Philosophical Society of Chesterfield, Dec. 7, 1832. Chesterfield: 1832. V. 52
Essai sur la Difference du Nombre des Hommes Dans les Tems Anciens et Modernes, Dans Lequel on Tablet Qu'il Etoit Plus Considerable Dans l'Antiquite. Londres: 1754. V. 54
Various Prospects of Mankind, Nature and Providence. London: 1761. V. 48
A View of Internal Policy of Great Britain. London: 1764. V. 48

WALLACE, SUSAN
The Land of the Pueblos. New York: 1888. V. 53

WALLACE, W.
A Treatise on the Venereal Disease. London: 1833. V. 51

WALLACE, W. STEWART
Documents Relating to the North West Company. Toronto: 1934. V. 48

WALLACE, WILLIAM SWILLING
Antoine Robidoux 1794-1860. Los Angeles: 1953. V. 50; 54

WALLACE-CRABBE, CHRIS
Apprehensions. Melbourne: 1994. V. 54
Drawing. Melbourne: 1994. V. 54
Phantoms in the Park. Melbourne: 1995. V. 54

WALLACE-DUNLOP, MADELINE
The Timely Retreat; or a Year in Bengal Before the Mutinies. London: 1858. V. 50; 51

WALLACE-DUNLOP, MARION
Fairies, Elves and Flower-Babies. London: 1899. V. 47

WALLACE'S American Trotting Register. New York: 1874. V. 52

WALLASCHEK, RICHARD
Primitive Music. London: 1893. V. 49

WALLEN, HENRY DAVIES
Report of the Secretary of War Communicating...the Report of Captain H.D. Wallen of His Expedition, in 1859, From Dalles City to Great Salt Lake and Back. Washington: 1860. V. 47

WALLER, AUGUSTUS D.
Eight Lectures on the Signs of the Life. London: 1903. V. 54
An Introduction to Human Physiology. London: 1891. V. 49
An Introduction to Human Physiology. London: 1893. V. 54
Lectures on Physiology. First Series: on Animal Electricity. London: 1897. V. 47; 49; 54

WALLER, EDMUND
Poems... London: 1668. V. 48
Poems... London: 1682. V. 53
Poems... London: 1705. V. 51
Poems... London: 1712. V. 50
The Poems. London: 1893. V. 51; 53
Songs and Verse Selected From the Works of Edmund Waller. South Harting: 1902. V. 49
Songs and Verses. New York: 1911. V. 54
The Works of Edmund Waller, Esq. London: 1729. V. 47; 48; 50
The Works of Edmund Waller, Esq. London: 1730. V. 48; 52; 53; 54
The Works...in Verse and Prose. London: 1753. V. 52

WALLER, EFFIE
Songs of the Months. New York: 1904. V. 54

WALLER, ERIK
Bibliotheca Walleriana... New York. V. 47
Bibliotheca Walleriana. Stockholm: 1955. V. 47; 50; 54
Bibliotheca Walleriana. New York: 1990. V. 47; 50; 52
Bibliotheca Walleriana. Stockholm: 1991. V. 54

WALLER, J.
The Everlasting Hills. London: 1939. V. 53

WALLER, JOHN AUGUSTINE
A Voyage in the West Indies. London: 1820. V. 50

WALLER, JOHN FRANCIS
Pictures from English Literature. London. V. 52

WALLER, ROBERT JAMES
The Bridges of Madison County. New York: 1992. V. 49; 50; 51; 52; 53; 54

WALLER, ROBERT JAMES continued
The Bridges of Madison County. London: 1993. V. 50
The Bridges of Madison County. New York: 1993. V. 53
Iowa. 1991. V. 51
Iowa: Perspectives on Today and Tomorrow. Ames: 1991. V. 50
Love in Black and White. 1992. V. 51; 54
One Good Road is Enough. 1990. V. 51

WALLER, WILLIAM
Divine Meditations Upon Several Occasions... London: 1680. V. 53
An Essay on the Value of the Mines, Late of Sir Carbery Price. London: 1698. V. 47; 51
The Tragical History of Jetzer: or, a Faithful Narrative of the Feigned Visions, Counterfeit Revelations and False Miracles of the Dominican Fathers of the Covent of Berne in Switzerland... London: 1679. V. 52
Vindication of the Character and Conduct of Sir William Waller, Knight... London: 1793. V. 47; 48

WALLHAUSEN, JOHANN JACOBI VON
Art De Cheualerie. Frankfort: 1616. V. 49

WALLICH, G. C.
Eminent Men of the Day...Scientific Series. London: 1870. V. 48
The North-Atlantic Sea-Bed: Comprising a Diary of the Voyage on Board H.M.S. Bulldog in 1860...Part I. 1862. V. 47

WALLICH, J. U.
Religio Turcica, Mahomtis Vita, et Occidentali Antichristo Comparatio. Stade: 1659. V. 49

WALLING, GEORGE W.
Recollections of a New York Chief of Police... New York: 1887. V. 54
Recollections of a New York Chief of Police. New York: 1888. V. 54

WALLING, H. F.
New Topographical Atlas of the State of Ohio. Cincinnati: 1872. V. 47
Tackabury's Atlas of the Dominion of Canada and General Description. Montreal: 1876. V. 54

WALLIS, ALFRED
Examples of the Book-Binders' Art of the XVI and XVII Centuries. Exeter: 1890. V. 48; 51; 54

WALLIS, FRANK E.
Old Colonial Architecture and Furniture. Boston: 1887. V. 53

WALLIS, G. HARRY
Illustrated Catalogue of Classical Antiquities from the Site of the Temple of Diana, Nemi, Italy. Nottingham: 1893. V. 50; 52; 53

WALLIS, GEORGE
The Art of Preventing Diseases and Restoring Health. London: 1793. V. 48; 50
The Art of Preventing Diseases and Restoring Health... London: 1796. V. 48

WALLIS, HELEN
Carteret's Voyage Round the World 1766-1769. Cambridge: 1965. V. 52; 54
My Hand is a Map. Essays and Memoirs in Honour of R. V. Tooley. London: 1973. V. 51

WALLIS, HENRY
The Cloud Kingdom. London: 1905. V. 49

WALLIS, JAMES
An Historical Account of the Colony of New South Wales and Its Dependent Settlements... London: 1821. V. 54
Wallis's New Pocket Edition of the English Counties... London: 1810?. V. 51
Wallis's New Pocket Edition of the English Counties. London: 1814. V. 53

WALLIS, JOHN
The Cornwall Register... Bodmin: 1847. V. 50
A Defence of the Royal Society, and the Philosophical Transactions, Particulary Those of July, 1670... London: 1678. V. 48
Grammatica Linguae Anglicanae... Londini: 1765. V. 48; 52; 53
Grammatica Linguae Anglicanae. London: 1765/64. V. 50
The Natural History and Antiquities of Northumberland... London: 1769. V. 49; 54

WALLIS, JONNIE L.
Sixty Years on the Brazos - the Life and Letters of Dr. John Washington Lockhart 1824-1900. Los Angeles: 1930. V. 54

WALLIS, PETER
Newton and Newtoniana 1672-1975. Kent: 1977. V. 50; 54

WALLIS, R. V.
Bio-bibliography of British Mathematics and Its Applications. Part II: 1701-1760. Newcastle-upon-Tyne: 1986. V. 49

WALLIS, THOMAS
The Farrier's and Horseman's Complete Dictionary... London: 1764. V. 49

WALLIS, THOMAS WILKINSON
Autobiography of...Sculptor in Wood and Extracts from His Sixty Years' Journal... Louth: 1899. V. 52

WALLIS, WILSON D.
The Canadian Dakota. New York: 1947. V. 48

WALLIS TAYLER, A. J.
Motor Cars Power-Carriages for Common Roads. London: 1897. V. 49

WALLRICH, J. U.
Religio Turica, Mahometis Vita, et Orientalis cum Occidentali Antichristo Comparatio. Stade: 1659. V. 48

WALLS, WILLIAM J.
The African Methodist Episcopal Zion Church: Reality of the Black Church. Charlotte: 1974. V. 53

WALMSLEY, EDWARD
Physiognomical Portraits. London: 1822-24. V. 48

WALMSLEY, HUGH MULLENUEX
The Chasseur d'Afrique and Other Tales. London: 1865. V. 54

WALN, ROBERT
Life of the Marquis of LaFayette: Major-General in the Service of the United States of America, in the War of the Revolution. Philadelphia: 1825. V. 47

WALPOLE, FREDERICK
The Ansayrii, and the Assassins, with Travels in the Further East in 1850-51. London: 1851. V. 48; 51
Four Years in the Pacific. London: 1849. V. 50

WALPOLE, GEORGE AUGUSTUS
The New British Traveller: or, a Complete Modern Universal Display of Great Britain and Ireland... London: 1784. V. 54

WALPOLE, HORACE
Aedes Walponianae... London: 1767. V. 53
Anecdotes of Painting in England... London: 1762-71. V. 48; 50; 51
Anecdotes of Painting in England... London: 1782. V. 52
Anecdotes of Painting in England... London: 1828. V. 47; 51
Anecdotes of Painting in England... London: 1849. V. 50
Anecdotes of Painting with Some Account of the Principal Artists...Etc. London: 1826. V. 49
Il Castello di Otranto. Londra: 1795. V. 48
The Castle of Otranto. London: 1765. V. 48
The Castle of Otranto... London: 1765/64. V. 47; 49; 50; 51; 52
The Castle of Otranto. London: 1769. V. 48
The Castle of Otranto. London: 1782. V. 48
Castle of Otranto. London: 1796. V. 54
The Castle of Otranto... London: 1800. V. 53
The Castle of Otranto. London: 1825. V. 52
Castle of Otranto... London: 1924. V. 49
The Castle of Otranto. Westerham: 1975. V. 47; 52; 54
A Catalogue of Horace Walpole's Library. (with) Horace Walpole's Library. London: 1969. V. 52
A Catalogue of the Royal and Noble Authors of England... Dublin. V. 48
A Catalogue of the Royal and Noble Authors of England... 1758. V. 51
A Catalogue of the Royal and Noble Authors of England. Strawberry Hill: 1758. V. 54
A Catalogue of the Royal and Noble Authors of England... London: 1759. V. 47
A Catalogue of the Royal and Noble Authors of England... London: 1806/07. V. 48
A Catalogue of the Royal and Noble Authors of England, Scotland And Ireland... London: 1806. V. 47; 48; 49; 50; 51; 52
The Correspondence of Walpole and the Rev. William Mason. London: 1851. V. 53
Correspondence...with George Montagu, Esq., H.S. Conway... London: 1837. V. 48; 50; 51; 53
Essay on Modern Gardening... 1785. V. 47
Essay on Modern Gardening. Strawberry Hill: 1785. V. 52
Farthing Hall. London: 1929. V. 47
Fugitive Pieces in Verse and Prose. Strawberry Hill: 1758. V. 50
Hieroglyphic Tales. London: 1926. V. 54
Historic Doubts on the Life and Reign of King Richard the Third. London: 1768. V. 47; 48; 49; 50; 51; 52; 53; 54
Journal of the Printing Office at Strawberry Hill. 1923. V. 51; 53
Journal of the Printing Office at Strawberry Hill. London: 1923. V. 49
Journal of the Reign of King George the Third, from the Year 1771 to 1783. London: 1859. V. 51
A Letter to the Editor of the Miscellanies of Thomas Chatterton. Strawberry Hill: 1779. V. 47; 49; 54
The Letters... London: 1843-44. V. 49
The Letters... London: 1846. V. 53
The Letters... London: 1857-59. V. 53
The Letters. London: 1861. V. 53
The Letters. London: 1877. V. 48
The Letters... London: 1880. V. 50
Letters... London: 1890. V. 48
Letters. London: 1891. V. 48
The Letters... Edinburgh: 1906. V. 51
Letters to William Cole and Others from the Year 1745 to the Year 1782. London: 1818. V. 50; 54
Letters...Countess of Ossory... London: 1848. V. 48
Letters...Countess of Ossory. London: 1903. V. 53; 53
Letters...George Montagu, from the Year 1736-1770. London: 1818. V. 50; 52; 54
Letters...Sir Horace Mann... London: 1833. V. 51
Letters...Sir Horace Mann... London: 1843. V. 51
The Letters...Sir Horace Mann, His Britannic Majesty's Resident at the Court of Florence, from 1760-1785. London: 1840/43-44. V. 47
Lord Orford's Reminiscences. London: 1818. V. 50
Memoirs of the Last Ten Years of the Reign of George the Second. London: 1822. V. 48
Memoirs of the Reign of King George the Second. London: 1847. V. 48; 50
Memoirs of the Reign of King George the Third. London: 1845. V. 52

WALPOLE, HORACE continued
Miscellaneous Antiquities; or, a Collection of Curious Papers... Strawberrry Hill: 1772. V. 47; 48
The Mysterious Mother. London: 1781. V. 48
The Mysterious Mother. Dublin: 1791. V. 48; 50; 52
A Notebook of Horace Walpole. New York: 1927. V. 48
Private Correspondence of Horace Walpole, Earl of Orford. London: 1820. V. 49; 53
Works. London: 1798. V. 49; 50

WALPOLE, HORATIO WALPOLE, BARON
The Complaints of the Manufacturers, Relating to the Abuses in Marking the Sheep, and Winding the Wool, Fairly Stated, and Impartially Considered, in a Letter to the Marquis of Rockingham. London: 1742. V. 52
The Complaints of the Manufacturers, Relating to the Abuses in Marking the Sheep, and Winding the Wool, Fairly Stated, and Impartially Considered, in a Letter to the Marquis of Rockingham. London: 1752. V. 50; 54
The Convention Vindicated from the Misrepresentation of the Enemies of Our Peace. London: 1739. V. 51; 53
The Grand Question, Whether War, or No War, with Spain, Impartially Considered... London: 1739. V. 53

WALPOLE, HUGH
All Souls Night. London: 1933. V. 49
Anthony Trollope. London: 1928. V. 51
The Apple Trees. Waltham St. Lawrence: 1932. V. 51; 54
Captain Nicholas. London: 1934. V. 54
The Cathedral. London: 1922. V. 54
The Fortress. London: 1931. V. 51; 52
Harmer John. London: 1926. V. 51
The Herries Chronicles. London: 1930-33. V. 50
The Inquisitor. London: 1935. V. 54
Jeremy. London: 1919. V. 47
The Joyful Delaneys. London: 1938. V. 54
Judith Paris. London: 1931. V. 51; 53
The Old Ladies. London: 1924. V. 54
A Prayer for My Son. London: 1936. V. 54
Rogue Herries. (with) Judith Paris. (with) The Fortress. (with) Vanessa. (with) The Bright Pavillions. London: 1930-1-2-3-40. V. 50
Seven Pillars of Wisdom: T. E. Lawrence in Life and Death. London: 1985. V. 53
Vanessa. London: 1933. V. 51; 52
Wintersmoon. London: 1928. V. 51
The Wooden Horse. London: 1909. V. 51
The Young Enchanted. London: 1921. V. 51

WALPOLE, ROBERT
Ades Walpolianae; or, a Description of the Collection of Pictures at Houghton-Hall in Norfolk. London: 1752. V. 48
Memoirs Relating European and Asiatic Turkey and Other Countries of the East. London: 1818. V. 51
Some Considerations Concerning the Publick Funds, The Publick Revenues, and the Annual Supplies, Granted by Parliament. London: 1735. V. 47

WALPOLE SOCIETY
The Walpole Society Notebooks, 1951-1961. Portland: 1951-61. V. 48

WALPOLE-BOND, JOHN
A History of Sussex Birds. London: 1938. V. 49; 52

WALSDORF, JOHN J.
Men of Printing, Anglo-American Profiles. Easthampton: 1976. V. 48; 53

WALSER, RICHARD
The Black Poet: Being the Remarkable Story (Partly Told by Himself) of George Moses Horton, a North Carolina Slave. New York: 1966. V. 54

WALSH, CHRISTY
intercollegiate Football. New York: 1934. V. 50

WALSH, E.
A Narrative of the Expedition to Holland, in the Autumn of the Year 1799. London: 1800. V. 50; 54

WALSH, JOHN HENRY
British Rural Sports: Comprising Shooting, Hunting, Coursing, Fishing, Hawking, Racing, Boating, Harvey, Hind, etc. London: 1872. V. 51
The Dogs of the British Islands. London: 1867. V. 47; 52
The Dogs of the British Islands... London: 1972. V. 49
Every Horse Owner's Cyclopedia... Philadelphia: 1871. V. 48
The Greyhound: a Treatise on the Art of Breeding, Rearing, Training Greyhounds for Public Running... London: 1869. V. 47
Hints to Sportsmen on Guns and Shooting... 1880. V. 54
The Horse, in the Stable and the Field. London: 1862. V. 47
Manual of British Rural Sports... London: 1859. V. 49
The Modern Sportsman's Gun and Rifle. London: 1988. V. 51; 52
On the Management of Dogs, in Point of Food and Lodging, with Remarks on the Treatment of Distemper, Mange, Worms, Ticks, etc. London: 1872. V. 49

WALSH, LANGTON PRENDERGAST
Under the Flag and Somali Coast Stories. London: 1912. V. 47

WALSH, MICHAEL
A New System of Mercantile Arithmetic... Newburyport: 1804. V. 50

WALSH, PAUL
Irish Chiefs and Leaders. 1960. V. 49

Irish Chiefs and Leaders. London: 1960. V. 51

WALSH, ROBERT
The American Review of History and Politics and General Repository of Literature and States Papers. Philadelphia: 1811-12. V. 47
An Appeal from the Judgments of Great Britain Respecting the United States of America. Philadelphia: 1819. V. 47; 48
Constantinople and the Scenery of the Seven Churches of Asia Minor Illustrated... London: 1840. V. 50
A Letter On the Genius and Dispositions of the French Government... Baltimore: 1810. V. 49; 52
A Letter on the Genius and Dispositions of the French Government... Boston: 1810. V. 50
Narrative of a Journey from Constantinople to England. Philadelphia: 1828. V. 48
Notices of Brazil in 1828 and 1829. London: 1830. V. 53; 54
Notices of Brazil in 1828 and 1829. Boston: 1831. V. 53

WALSH, T. J.
A Tribute to Wilfred Owen. Birkenhead: 1964. V. 47

WALSH, THOMAS
Journal of the Late Campaign in Egypt... London: 1803. V. 47; 52

WALSH, WILLIAM
A Dialogue Concerning Women, Being a Defence of the Sex. London: 1691. V. 47
A Funeral Elegy Upon the Death of the Queen. London: 1695. V. 48

WALSHE, WALTER
On the Nature and Treatment of Cancer. London: 1846. V. 49
A Practical Treatise on the Diseases of the Heart and Great Vessels, Including the Principles of Physical Diagnosis. Philadelphia: 1862. V. 49; 54

WALSINGHAM, FRANCIS
A Search Made Into Matters of Religion. St. Omer: 1609. V. 51; 52

WALSINGHAM, THOMAS DE GREY, 6TH BARON
Shooting. London: 1886. V. 52; 54
Shooting: Field and Covert. (and) Shooting: Moor and Marsh. London: 1895/93. V. 52

WALTER Browning; or, the Slave's Protector. Cincinnati: 1856. V. 47; 48

WALTER, H.
Studies of Cattle from Nature. London: 1821. V. 52

THE WALTER Hagen Story. New York: 1956. V. 48

WALTER, HENRY
A History of England. London: 1840. V. 51; 52

WALTER, JAMES
Shakespeare's True Life. London: 1890. V. 50

WALTER, JOHN
First Impressions of America. London: 1867. V. 53

WALTER, OF COVENTRY
The Historical Collections. London: 1872-73. V. 52

WALTER, RICHARD
Anson's Voyage Round the World. London & Boston: 1928. V. 49; 52; 53
A Voyage Round the World... London: 1748. V. 47; 48; 49; 50; 51; 52; 52; 53; 54
A Voyage Round the World... London: 1749. V. 51; 52; 53
A Voyage Round the World... London: 1756. V. 52
A Voyage Round the World... Edinburgh: 1796. V. 51

WALTER, RYE
The Norfolk Antiquarian Miscellany. Second Series. Parts 1, 2 and 3. Norwich: 1906/07/08. V. 52

WALTER, WEEVER
Letters from the Continent: Containing Sketches of Foreign Scenery and Manners; with Hints as to the Different Modes of Travelling, Expense of Living, etc. London: 1828. V. 51

WALTER, WILLIAM W.
The Great Understander: True Life Story of the Last of the Wells Fargo Shotgun Express Messengers. Aurora: 1931. V. 47; 48

WALTERS, E.
The Serpent's Presence. London: 1954. V. 54

WALTERS, E. W.
Heroines of the World Ward. London: 1916. V. 47

WALTERS, H. B.
Marbles and Bronzes: Fifty-Two Plates from Selected Subjects in the Department of Greek and Roman Antiquities. London: 1928. V. 50; 52
Select Bronzes, Greek, Roman and Etruscan in the Department of Antiquities. London: 1915. V. 50; 52

WALTERS, HENRY
Incunabula Typographica. Baltimore: 1906. V. 49; 50; 51; 52; 53

WALTERS, HENRY LITTLEJOHN MASTER
Arab Life. London and Liverpool: 1861. V. 54

WALTERS, JOHN
A Dissertation on the Welsh Language, Pointing Out It's Antiquity, Copiousness, Grammatical Perception, with Remarks On it's Poetry... Cowbridge: 1771. V. 52
Poems. With Notes. Oxford: 1780. V. 48
Poems With Notes. (with) Translated Specimens of Welsh Poetry in English Verse. Oxford: 1780/82. V. 50

WALTERS, L. O'D.
The Year's at the Spring. London: 1920. V. 47; 50; 51; 53; 54

WALTERS, LORENZO D.
Tombstone's Yesterday. Tucson: 1928. V. 48; 53

WALTERS, MINETTE
The Scold's Bridle. Bristol: 1994. V. 52
The Sculptress. London: 1993. V. 52; 54

WALTERS, S. M.
The European Flora. London: 1986-89. V. 50
The European Garden Flora. Cambridge: 1986-89. V. 50; 51

WALTERS, SAMUEL
His Memoirs. London: 1949. V. 53

WALTERS ART GALLERY, BALTIMORE
The History of Bookbinding 525-1950 A.D. An Exhibition Held at the Baltimore Museum of Art. Baltimore: 1957. V. 47

WALTHER, RUDOLPH
Argumenta Omnium Tam Veteris Quam Novi Testamenti, Capitum... 1554. V. 47

WALTON, AUGUSTUS Q.
A History of the Detection, Conviction, Life and Designs of John A. Murel (sic), the Great Western Land Pirate; Together with His System of Villiany, and Plan of Exciting a Negro Rebellion... Cincinnati: 1835. V. 47

WALTON, DANIEL
The Book Needed for the Times, Containing the Latest Well-Authenticated Facts from the Gold Regions. Boston: 1849. V. 48

WALTON, E.
The Virign and the Swine. 1936. V. 47; 51

WALTON, ELIJAH
The Coast of Norway from Christiania to Hammerfest. London: 1871. V. 50

WALTON, IZAAK
The Compleat Angler. London. V. 47; 53
The Compleat Angler... London: 1661. V. 47
The Compleat Angler... London: 1750. V. 47; 49; 52
The Compleat Angler... London: 1759. V. 47
The Compleat Angler. London: 1760. V. 47; 53
The Compleat Angler. London: 1766. V. 47
The Compleat Angler... London: 1775. V. 47; 48
The Compleat Angler. London: 1784. V. 47
The Compleat Angler. London: 1808. V. 47; 48; 51; 52; 54
The Compleat Angler. London: 1810. V. 50
The Compleat Angler. London: 1815. V. 47; 48; 49; 51; 52
The Compleat Angler... London: 1822. V. 47
The Compleat Angler. London: 1823. V. 47; 48; 49; 51
The Compleat Angler. London: 1824. V. 47; 48; 49; 54
The Compleat Angler. London: 1825. V. 48; 50
The Compleat Angler. Chiswick: 1826. V. 47
The Compleat Angler. London: 1826. V. 50; 52; 53
The Compleat Angler. London: 1827. V. 53
The Compleat Angler. London: 1835. V. 47; 48; 50; 52; 54; 54
The Compleat Angler. London: 1836. V. 50; 53
The Compleat Angler. London: 1842. V. 47
The Compleat Angler. London: 1844. V. 47
The Compleat Angler. New York, London: 1847. V. 48; 49; 50; 51
The Compleat Angler... New York: 1848. V. 51
The Compleat Angler. New York: 1852. V. 47
The Compleat Angler... Boston: 1867. V. 51
The Compleat Angler... Boston: 1870. V. 51
The Compleat Angler. London: 1876. V. 47
The Compleat Angler. London: 1880. V. 53
The Compleat Angler. London: 1885. V. 48
The Compleat Angler. London: 1888. V. 47
The Compleat Angler. Boston: 1889. V. 47
The Compleat Angler... New York: 1889. V. 48
The Compleat Angler. London: 1893. V. 54
The Compleat Angler. London: 1896. V. 47
The Compleat Angler. London: 1897. V. 49
The Compleat Angler... London: 1900. V. 51
The Compleat Angler. London: 1903, or later. V. 53
The Compleat Angler. Boston & New York: 1909. V. 49
The Compleat Angler... Cambridge: 1909. V. 49
The Compleat Angler. New York: 1911. V. 54
The Compleat Angler. London: 1927. V. 48
The Compleat Angler. New York: 1927. V. 47
The Compleat Angler... Boston: 1928. V. 50
The Compleat Angler... London: 1929. V. 47; 50; 51; 52; 54
The Compleat Angler. London: 1930. V. 51; 53
The Compleat Angler. London: 1931. V. 47; 48; 49; 50; 51; 52; 53; 54
The Compleat Angler. Philadelphia: 1931. V. 49
Izaak Walton: His Wallet Book. London: 1885. V. 48
The Life of Dr. Sanderson, Late Bishop of Lincoln. London: 1678. V. 48; 52; 54
The Life of Mr. George Herbert... London: 1670. V. 52
The Life of Mr. Rich. Hooker. London: 1665. V. 48
The Lives. London: 1825. V. 48; 49; 51; 52; 54
The Lives of Dr. John Donne; Sir Henry Wotton; Mr. Richard Hooker; Mr. George Herbert; and Dr. Robert Sanderson. V. 53
The Lives of Mr. Richard Hooker, Mr. George Herbert and Dr. Robert Sanderson. London: 1847. V. 54
The Universal Angler. London: 1676. V. 47
The Works of that Learned and Judicious Divine, Mr. Richard Hooker. Oxford: 1850. V. 52

WALTON, JOHN
The Oxford Companion to Medicine. New York: 1986. V. 52

WALTON, JOSEPH
China and the Present Crisis. London: 1900. V. 50

WALTON, MURRAY
Scrambles in Japan and Formosa. London: 1934. V. 53

WALTON, PAUL H.
The Drawings of John Ruskin. London: 1972. V. 50; 54

WALTON, WILLIAM
Concerto for Viola and Orchestra. London: 1929. V. 54
Facade. London: 1972. V. 47
An Historical and Descriptive Account of the Four Species of Peruvian Sheep, Called Carneros de la Tierra... London: 1811. V. 50
A Narrative of the Captivity and Sufferings of Benjamin Gilbert and His Family... London: 1790. V. 49; 54
Portsmouth Point...an Overture. London: 1925. V. 54

WALTZBURG; a Tale of the Sixteenth Century. London: 1833. V. 48

WALWYN, JAMES
The Voluntary Exile, a Poetical Essay. London: 1784. V. 54

WALZ, ANTHONY
President's Boyhood Home... 1965. V. 49

WALZ, ARTHUR
Presidents Boyhood Home. Austin: 1965. V. 51; 52

THE WANDERER, or Horatio and Laetitia: a Poem. New York: 1811. V. 54

WANDERING Cries. London: 1860. V. 48; 51

WANDERINGS in the Land of Ham. London: 1858. V. 51

WANDERINGS over Bible Lands and Seas. London: 1866. V. 49

WANDREI, DONALD
Dark Odyssey. St. Paul: 1931. V. 47; 48; 49
Ecstasy. Athol: 1928. V. 47; 54
The Eye and the Finger. Sauk City: 1944. V. 48; 51; 52
Poems for Midnight. Sauk City: 1964. V. 54
The Web of Easter Island. Sauk City: 1948. V. 47; 52

WANG, C. C.
C. C. Wang. Landscape Paintings. Seattle: 1986. V. 53

WANG, TSENG-TSU
Bamboo. Its Cult and Culture. Berkeley: 1986. V. 53

WANGERMEE, R.
Flemish Music and Society in the 15th and 16th Centuries. New York: 1968. V. 49

WANLEY, HUMFREY
The Letters. London: 1989. V. 49

WANLEY, NATHANIEL
The History of Man: or the Wonders of Human Nature, in Relation to the Virtues, Vices and Defects of Both Sexes. Dublin: 1791. V. 49
The Wonders of the Little World: or, a General History of man. London: 1678. V. 48; 50
The Wonders of the Little World; or, a General History of Man... London: 1809. V. 50
The Wonders of the World... London: 1768. V. 51

WANOSTROCHT, NICHOLAS
Felix On the Bat; Being a Scientific Enquiry Into the Use of the Cricket Bat... London: 1845. V. 49

WANSEY, HENRY
An Excursion to the United States of North America in the Summer of 1794. Salisbury: 1798. V. 47
The Journal of an Excursion to the United States of North America, in the Summer of 1794. Salisbury: 1796. V. 53

WANSKAPS och Handels Tractat Emellan...Swerige och the Forenie Staterne i Norra America...Traite d'Amitie et de Commerce Entre...Suede et les Etats Unis de l'Amerique Septentrionale... Stockholm: 1785. V. 47

THE WAR and Its Heroes Illustrated. Richmond: 1864. V. 47

THE WAR Correspondence of the "Daily News" 1877: Forming a Continuous History of the War Between Russia and Turkey. (with) The War Correspondence of the "Daily News": Continued from the Fall of Kars to the Preliminaries of Peace. London: 1878/78. V. 53

THE WAR In Italy. I. On the High Mountains. II. The Carso. III. The Battle Between the Brenta and the Adige. Milan: 1916. V. 47

THE WAR of the Rebellion: a Compilation of the Official Records of the Union and Confederate Armies. Washington: 1880-1901. V. 54

WAR Pictures by British Artists. First and Second Series. 1942/43. V. 49

WARBASSE, JAMES
Medical Sociology: a Series of Observations Touching Upon the Sociology of Health and the Relations of Medicine to Society. London: 1878. V. 52
Medical Sociology: a Series of Observations Touching Upon the Sociology of Health and the Relations of Medicine to Society. New York: 1909. V. 54

WARBURTON, ELIOT
The Crescent of the Cross; or, Romance and Realities of Eastern Travel. London: 1890. V. 54
Darien; or, the Merchant Prince. London: 1852. V. 53
Hochelaga; or, England in the New World. London: 1846. V. 48
Hochelaga: or, England in the New World. London: 1847. V. 53
Memoirs of Prince Rupert and the Cavaliers. London: 1849. V. 47; 49; 53

WARBURTON, GEORGE DROUGHT
The Conquest of Canada. London: 1849. V. 53
A Memoir of Charles Mordaunt Earl of Peterborough and Monmouth. London: 1853. V. 54

WARBURTON, JOHN
History of the City of Dublin, from the Earliest Accounts to the Present Time. London: 1818. V. 51

WARBURTON, PETER EGERTON
Journey Across the Western Interior of Australia. London: 1875. V. 52

WARBURTON, R. E. E.
Hunting Songs, Ballads... Chester: 1834. V. 54
Hunting Songs, Ballads. London: 1846. V. 47

WARBURTON, WILLIAM
Letters from a Late Eminent Prelate to One of His Friends (Hurd). Kidderminster: 1808. V. 47; 50

WARD, A. E.
The Sportsman's Guide to Kashmir & Ladak, &c. Calcutta: 1883. V. 48

WARD, ADOLPHUS WILLIAM
The Cambridge History of English Literature. Cambridge: 1908-16. V. 48
Cambridge History of English Literature. Cambridge: 1949-53. V. 51
Dickens. London: 1882. V. 47; 53; 54
A History of English Dramatic Literature to the Death of Queen Anne. London: 1875. V. 49; 52
A History of English Dramatic Literature to the Death of Queen Anne. London: 1899. V. 51

WARD, ARTEMAS
The Grocer's Encycopedia. New York: 1911. V. 52
The Grocers' Handbook and Directory for 1883. Philadelphia: 1882. V. 50; 51
The Grocers' Handbook and Directory for 1883. Philadelphia: 1883. V. 49
The Grocer's Handbook and Directory for 1886. Philadelphia: 1886. V. 49

WARD, ARTEMUS
Artemus Ward's Panorama. New York: 1869. V. 54
Encyclopedia of Food... New York: 1923. V. 53

WARD, BERNARD
The Eve of Catholic Emancipation. London: 1911-12. V. 49

WARD, C. S.
Hints on Driving. London: 1870. V. 47

WARD, CATHERINE GEORGE
The Cottage on the Cliff, a Sea Side Story. London: 1823. V. 54
The Mysteries of St. Clair; or, Mariette Mouline. London: 1824. V. 50
The Rose of Claremont, or Daughter, Wife and Mother. London: 1821. V. 47

WARD, EDWARD
Hudibras Redivivus; or, a Burlesque Poem on the Times. London: 1705-07. V. 47
The Insinuating Bawd, and the Repenting Harlot. London?: 1758. V. 52
The Republican Procession; or, the Tumultuous Cavalcade. 1714. V. 48
A Trip to Jamaica: with a True Character of the People and Island. Londod (sic): 1700. V. 49
A Vade Mecum for Malt-Worms; or, a Guide to Good Fellows, Being a Description of the Manners and Customs of the Most Eminent Publick Houses... London: 1840. V. 54
The Whigs Unmask'd... London: 1721. V. 48
The Whole Pleasures of Matrimony: or Scenes in Life... London: 1820. V. 50

WARD, ELIZABETH STUART PHELPS
Burglars in Paradise. Boston & New York: 1886. V. 50
Chapters from a Life. Boston and New York: 1897. V. 52
The Gates Between. Boston & New York: 1887. V. 53
The Silent Partner. Boston: 1899. V. 53

WARD, EVELYN D.
The Children of Bladensfield. New York: 1978. V. 50

WARD, FRANCIS
An Account of Three Camp-Meetings, Held by the Methodists, at Sharon in Litchfield County, Connecticut. Brooklyn: 1806. V. 49

WARD, FRANCIS KINGDON
Burma's Icy Mountains. London: 1949. V. 51
Field Notes of Rhododendrons... London: 1927. V. 47
Field Notes of Rhododendrons... London: 1929. V. 47

WARD, FREDERICK WILLIAM
Pessimus: a Rhapsody, and a Paradox... London: 1865. V. 47; 49

WARD, GEORGE B.
National Collection of Head and Horns. Cody: 1993. V. 53

WARD, H. C.
Wild Flowers of Switzerland, or a Year Amongst the Flowers of the Alps... London: 1883. V. 53

WARD, HARRY PARKER
Some American College Bookplates. Columbus: 1915. V. 47; 49

WARD, HENRY
The Vintner...the White Fox Chased. 1766. V. 47
The Vintner...the White Fox Chased. Belfast: 1766. V. 50

WARD, HERBERT
Mr. Poilu. Notes and Sketches with the Fighting French. London: 1916. V. 47

WARD, HUMPHREY
A Biographical and Critical Essay with a Catalogue Raisonne of His Works. London: 1904. V. 49; 52; 54

WARD, JAMES
Colour Harmony and Contrast. London: 1903. V. 48
Colour Harmony and Contrast. London: 1912. V. 50
A Series of Lithographic Drawings of Celebrated Horses. London: 1823-24. V. 49; 53
Threatened Social Disorganisation of France. London: 1848. V. 53

WARD, JANE GRAY
From This Hill. Cummington: 1941. V. 49

WARD, JOHN
Greek Coins and Their Parent Cities. Accompanied By a Catalogue of the Author's Collection by g. f. Hill. London: 1902. V. 48
The Lives of the Professors of Gresham College... London: 1740. V. 47; 48; 49; 51
The Sacred Beetle: a Popular Treatise on Egyptian Scarbs in Art and History. London: 1902. V. 49; 54
The Young Mathematician's Guide. London: 1707. V. 49
The Young Mathematician's Guide... London: 1728. V. 49
The Young Mathematician's Guide... London: 1758. V. 50; 54

WARD, JONATHAN
American Slavery, and the Means of Its Abolition. Boston: 1840. V. 54

WARD, L. F.
Status of the Mesozoic Floras of the United States. Washington: 1905. V. 48

WARD, LYND
God's Man... London: 1929. V. 51
God's Man. New York: 1929. V. 51
God's Man. London: 1930. V. 50
Gods' Man... New York: 1930/29. V. 48; 51
Madman's Drum. London and Toronto: 1930. V. 48; 51; 52; 53
Madman's Drum... New York: 1930. V. 52; 54
Song Without Words. New York: 1936. V. 54
Storyteller Without Words. New York: 1974. V. 48; 51
Wild Pilgrimage. New York: 1932. V. 53; 54

WARD, MARCUS
A Practical Treatise on the Art of Illuminating with Examples.... London: 1870. V. 51
The Royal Illuminated Book of Legends. London: 1872. V. 48

WARD, MARIA E.
Bicycling for Ladies, With Hints As to the Art of Wheeling... New York: 1896. V. 51
The Common Sense of Bicycling: Bicycling for Ladies, with Hints as to the Art of Wheeling - Advice to Beginners - Dress - Care of the Bicycle - Mechanics - Training - Exercise, Etc., Etc. New York: 1896. V. 48

WARD, MARY AUGUSTA ARNOLD
The Coryston Family. New York: 1913. V. 53
England's Effort - Six Letters to an American Friend. London: 1916. V. 47
Fenwick's Career. London: 1906. V. 48; 54
Fenwick's Career. New York: 1906. V. 53
Helbeck of Bannisdale. London: 1898. V. 50; 51
The History of David Grieve. London: 1892. V. 47; 50; 51; 54
Marcella. New York: 1894. V. 48
The Marriage of William Ashe. New York: 1905. V. 53
Robert Elsemere. London: 1888. V. 50; 52; 53
Sir George Tressady. London: 1896. V. 48
William Thomas Arnold - Journalist and Historian. Manchester: 1907. V. 51; 54
The Writings of... Boston and New York: 1909-12. V. 47; 48; 54

WARD, MATTHEW FLOURNEY
Letters from Three Continents. New York: 1851. V. 50

WARD, MRS.
Entomology in Sport and Entomology in Earnest. London: 1859. V. 54
Waves on the Ocean of Life: a Dalriadian Tale. London: 1869. V. 48; 50
A World of Wonders Revealed by the Microscope. London: 1859. V. 48

WARD, N. L.
Oriental Missions in British Columbia. London: 1925. V. 48

WARD, NATHANIEL
A Word to Mr. Peters, and Two Words for the Parliament and Kingdom. London: 1647. V. 48

WARD, NATHANIEL BAGSHAW
On the Growth of Plants in Closely Glazed Cases. London: 1842. V. 47; 49; 51; 53

WARD, NED
The London Spy, by the Author of the Trip to Jamaica. London: 1699-1701. V. 48

WARD, PATIENCE
The Speech of the Right Honourable Sir Patience Warade, Lord Mayor Elect, at Guild-Hall, London, September 29, 1680... London: 1680. V. 52

WARD, R. GERALD
American Activities in the Central Pacific 1790-1870... Ridgewood: 1966. V. 48; 49; 51

WARD, ROBERT PLUMER
De Clifford; or, the Constant Man. London: 1841. V. 47; 48; 53
De Vere: or, the Man of Independence. London: 1827. V. 51
An Enuiry Into the Manner In Which Different Wars in Rueope Have Commenced During the Last Two Centuries... London: 1805. V. 50
Fielding; Or, Society. Atticus; or, The Retired Statesman and St. Lawrence. Philadelphia: 1837. V. 48
An Historical Essay on the Real Character and Amount of the Precedent of the Revolution of 1688... London: 1838. V. 47
Illustrations of Human Life. London: 1837. V. 52
Pictures of the World at Home and Abroad. London: 1839. V. 52
Tremaine. London: 1825. V. 47; 48; 53
Tremaine... London: 1827. V. 47
Tremaine. London: 1833. V. 47

WARD, ROWLAND
The English Angler in Florida. London: 1898. V. 49
Horn Measurements and Weights of the Great Game of the World, Being a Record for the Use of Sportsmen and Naturalists. London: 1892. V. 48
Records of Big Game. London: 1896. V. 49
Records of Big Game. 1899. V. 52; 54
Records of Big Game. London: 1899. V. 48; 49
Records of Big Game. London: 1903. V. 49
Records of Big Game. 1907. V. 52
Records of Big Game. London: 1907. V. 48; 49
Records of Big Game. 1910. V. 52
Records of Big Game. London: 1910. V. 48; 49
Records of Big Game... London: 1914. V. 47
Records of Big Game. 1922. V. 52
Records of Big Game. London: 1922. V. 48; 49
Records of Big Game. 1928. V. 52; 54
Records of Big Game. London: 1928. V. 48; 53
Records of Big Game... London: 1935. V. 48
Records of Big Game. 1975. V. 48
Records of Big Game. London: 1975. V. 49
Records of Big Game (Africa). 1962/64/66. V. 52
The Sportsman's Handbook to Practical Collecting and Preserving Trophies. 1888. V. 54
The Sportsman's Handbook to Practical Collecting and Preserving Trophies. 1891. V. 52
The Sportsman's Handbook to...Preserving and Setting-Up Trophies and Specimens. London: 1894. V. 50

WARD, SAMUEL
A Modern System of Natural History. London: 1775-76. V. 54

WARD, SETH
Vindiciae Academiarum... Oxford: 1654. V. 51; 53

WARD, T.
Rambles of an Australian Naturalist. London: 1907. V. 53

WARD, THOMAS
The Bird Fancier's Recreation: Being Curious Remarks on the Nature of Song-Birds... London: 1770. V. 52
England's Reformation... Hambourgh: 1710. V. 50; 51
England's Reformation... London: 1715. V. 50
England's Reformation... London: 1716. V. 52
England's Reformation. London: 1747. V. 47; 49

WARD, WILLIAM
Farewell Letters to a Few Friends in Britain and America, on Returning to Bengal in 1821. New York: 1821. V. 47

WARD, WILLIAM A.
The Role of the Phoenicians in the Interaction of Mediterranean Civilizations. Beirut: 1968. V. 50; 52

WARDE, BEATRICE
Words in Their Hands. Cambridge: 1964. V. 51

WARDE, FREDERIC
Bruce Rogers Designer of Books. Cambridge: 1925. V. 53
Printers Ornaments Applied to the Composition of Decorative Borders, Panels and Patterns. London: 1928. V. 50; 52; 53

WARDELL, JAMES
An Historical, Antiquarian and Picturesque Account of Kirkstall Abbey and Embellished with Engravings from Original Drawings... Leeds: 1827. V. 50

WARDELL, JOHN WILFORD
A History of Yarm. London: 1957. V. 51; 53

WARDEN, A. J.
The Linen Trade, Ancient and Modern. London: 1867. V. 49

WARDEN, C. F.
The Battle of Waterloo. London: 1817. V. 52

WARDEN, DAVID B.
A Statistical, Political and Historical Account of the United States of North America. Edinburgh: 1819. V. 47; 50

WARDEN, WILLIAM
Letters Written on Board His Majesty's Ship the Northumberland, and at Saint Helena... London: 1816. V. 48

WARDENBURG, FRED A.
Operation Safari. (with) Safari Encore. 1948. V. 52

WARDER, WILLIAM
Minutes of the Eleventh Bethel Baptist Association, Held at Union M.H., Logan County, Ky. on the 26th, 27th and 28th of Sept. 1835. Hopkinsville: 1835. V. 50

WARD-JACKSON, PETER
English Furniture Designs of the Eighteenth Century. London: 1958. V. 49; 54

WARDLAW, JOSEPH G.
Genealogy of the Wardlaw Family. 1929. V. 50

WARDLE, M. K.
An Alphabet From the Trenches - by Two Infantry Officers. London: 1916. V. 47

WARD-PERKINS, JOHN B.
Roman Architecture. New York: 1977. V. 50

WARDROP, A. E.
Days and Nights with Indian Big Game, with Chapters by C. W. G. Morris. London: 1923. V. 47
Modern Pig Sticking. 1914. V. 54

WARDROP, ANDREW
An Address to the Members of the Royal College of Surgeons, on the Regulation of the Surgical Department of the Royal Infirmary. Edinburgh: 1800. V. 49

WARDROP, JAMES
The Morbid Anatomy of the Human Eye. London: 1834. V. 48; 52
On the Nature and Treament of the Diseases of the Heart; With Some New Views on the Physiology of the Circulation. Part 1. London: 1837. V. 47

WARE, EUGENE F.
The Indian War of 1864, Being a Fragment of the Early History of Kansas, Nebraska, Colorado and Wyoming. Topeka: 1911. V. 49

WARE, FABIAN
The Immortal Heritage. An Account of the Work and Policy of the Imperial War Graves Commission During Twenty Years. 1917-1937. Cambridge: 1937. V. 47
The Immortal Heritage. An Account of the Work and Policy of the Imperial War Graves Commission During Twenty Years. 1917-1937. London: 1937. V. 47

WARE, FRANCIS
Driving. New York: 1903. V. 54

WARE, HENRY
Papers on the Diaries of William Nicolson, Sometime Bishop of Carlisle. Kendal: 1905. V. 52
A Sermon Delivered at the Ordination of Rev. Chandler Robbins, Over the Second Congregational Church in Boston, December 4, 1833. Boston: 1833. V. 52

WARE, HIBBERT
History of the Foundations in Manchester of Christ's College, Chetham's Hospital and the Free Grammar School. London: 1828-33. V. 49

WARE, I. D.
The Coach-Makers' Illustrated Hand-Book. Philadelphia: 1875. V. 54

WARE, ISAAC
The Plans, Elevations and Sections; Chimney Pieces and Ceilings of Houghton in Norfolk; the Seat of the Rt. Honourable Sir Robert Walpole. London: 1735. V. 49

WARE, JAMES
The Antiquities and History of Ireland... Dublin: 1704-05. V. 50
The History and Antiquities of Ireland ... The Writers of Ireland. Dublin: 1764. V. 53
Remarks on Opthalmology, Psorophthalmy and Purulent Eye. London: 1787. V. 53
The Works of Sir James Ware. Volume II: The History and Antiquities of Ireland..The Writers of Ireland. Dublin: 1764. V. 47

WARE, JONATHAN
Apology for New Principles in Education. Boston: 1818. V. 54

WARE, ROBERT
The Hunting of the Romish Fox, and the Quenching of Sectarian Fire Brands... Dublin: 1683. V. 48

WARE, SAMUEL
Remarks on Theatres; and on the Propriety of Vaulting Them With Brick and Stone; with Observations on the Construction of Domes, and the Vaults of the Free and Accepted Masons. London: 1809. V. 53
A Treatise on the Properties of Arches. London: 1809. V. 53

WARE, WILLIAM ROTCH
The Georgian Period. New York: 1901-08. V. 52
The Georgian Period. New York: 1923. V. 51

WARFIELD, CATHERINE ANNE WARE
The Household of Bouverie; or, the Elixir of Gold. New York: 1860. V. 47; 49

WARFIELD, EDGAR
A Confederate Soldier's Memoirs by Edgar Warfield Member and Co-Organizer of the "Old Dominion Rifles" of Alexandria, Later Company H, Seventeenth Virginia Infantry, Confederate States Army. Richmond: 1936. V. 47

WARGENTIN, I. E.
Gruppen des Lebens mit Arabesken von E. Lamoral. Stuttgart & Tubingen: 1825. V. 49

WARHOL, ANDY
A. New York: 1968. V. 48; 49, 54
Andy Warhol. Stockholm: 1968. V. 53
Andy Warhol. London: 1970. V. 48
Andy Warhol's Children's Book. Zurich: 1983. V. 53; 54
Andy Warhol's Exposures. London: 1979. V. 47
Andy Warhol's Exposures. New York: 1979. V. 48; 49; 50; 52; 53
Andy Warhol's Index Book. New York: 1967. V. 47; 48; 49; 50; 51; 53
From A to B & Back Again: the Philosophy of Andy Warhol. London: 1975. V. 53
Holy Cats. 1954. V. 47; 51
The Philosophy of... New York and London: 1975. V. 47; 48; 49; 50; 51; 52; 53; 54
Portraits of the 70s. New York: 1979. V. 47; 52

WARING, C.
The Minstrelsy of the Woods. London: 1832. V. 48; 51; 53

WARING, EDWARD
Bibliotheca Therapeutica or Bibliography of Therapeutics. London: 1878. V. 54
Pharmacopoeia of India. London: 1868. V. 49; 50

WARING, GEORGE E.
Earth-Closets and Earth Sewage. New York: 1870. V. 53

WARING, JANET
Early American Stencils on Walls and Furniture. New York: 1937. V. 48; 51; 53

WARING, JOHN BURLEY
Art Treasures of the United Kingdom. London: 1858. V. 52; 54
Examples of Pottery and Porcelain. London: 1858. V. 49
Illustrations of Architecture and Ornament. London: 1865. V. 52

WARING, ROBERT
The Picture of Love Unveil'd. London: 1722. V. 48

WARING, ROBERT LEWIS
As We See It. Washington: 1918. V. 52

WARING, THOMAS
A Treatise on Archery, or the Art of Shooting with the English Bow... London: 1847. V. 50; 52
A Treatise on Archery, or the Art of Shooting, With the Long Bow. London: 1814. V. 50

WARING, WILLIAM R.
Report to the City Council of Savannah on the Epidemic Disease of 1820. Savannah: 1821. V. 48

WARING & GILLOW, LTD., LONDON
Carpets of Quality by Waring & Gillow, Ltd., Furnishers and Decorators to H.M. the King. 1900-10. V. 51

WARINGTON, J.
The Nurse's Guide. Philadelphia: 1839. V. 47

WARKENTIN, JOHN
Historical Atlas of Manitoba: A Selection of Facsimile Maps, Plans and Sketches, from 1612 to 1969. Winnipeg: 1970. V. 53

WARKWORTH, LORD
Notes from a Diary in Asiatic Turkey. London: 1898. V. 49

WARMAN, CY
The Story of the Railroad. New York: 1900. V. 51; 53

WARNER, C. A.
Texas Oil and Gas Since 1543. Houston: 1939. V. 48; 54

WARNER, CHARLES DUDLEY
The Complete Writings of... Hartford: 1904. V. 52

WARNER, ELISHA
The History of Spanish Fork. Spanish Fork: 1930. V. 49

WARNER, FERDINANDO
A Full and Plain Account of Gout... London: 1768. V. 53
A Full and Plain Account of Gout... London: 1772. V. 48; 51

WARNER, FRANK
The Silk Industry of the United Kingdom, Its Origin and Development. London: 1921. V. 49

WARNER, G. F.
Illuminated Manuscripts in the British Museum. London: 1899-1903. V. 52
Illuminated Manuscripts in the British Museum. London: 1903-04. V. 47

WARNER, H. T.
Texans and Their State: a Newspaper Reference Work. Houston;: 1920's. V. 53

WARNER, H. W.
Report of the Trial of Charles N. Baldwin, for a Libel, in Publishing, in the Republican Chronicle, Certain Charges of Fraud and Swindling, in the Management of Lotteries in the State of New York. New York: 1818. V. 51

WARNER, JUAN J.
An Historical Sketch of Los Angeles County. Los Angeles: 1876. V. 48; 49; 50
An Historical Sketch of Los Angeles County... Los Angeles: 1936. V. 54

WARNER, LANGDON
The Craft of the Japanese Sculptor. New York: 1936. V. 50
Japanese Sculpture of the Tempyo Period. Cambridge: 1959. V. 48

WARNER, OPIE L.
A Pardoned Lifer, Life of George Sontag Former Member Evans-Sontag Gang of Train Robbers. San Bernadino: 1909. V. 49; 51

WARNER, P. F.
Imperial Cricket... London: 1912. V. 49; 52

WARNER, R.
Select Orchidaceous Plants. London: 1874. V. 52
Select Orchidaceous Plants. Jacksonville: 1975. V. 52

WARNER, RALPH
Dutch and Flemish Flower and Fruit Painters of the XVIIth and XVIIIth Centuries. London: 1928. V. 50

WARNER, REBECCA
Original Letters from Richard Baxter, Matthew Prior, Lord Bolingbroke, Alexander Pope, Dr. Cheyne, Dr. Hartley, Dr. Samuel Johnson, Mrs. Montague, Rev. William Gilpin, Rev. John Newton, George Lord Lyttleton, Rev. Dr. Claudius Buchanan, &c, &c. Bath: 1817. V. 47

WARNER, REX
The Kite. Oxford: 1936. V. 49
The Professor. 1938. V. 53
The Professor. London: 1938. V. 51
The Wild Goose Chase. 1937. V. 53
The Wild Goose Chase. London: 1937. V. 48; 51

WARNER, RICHARD
Antiquitates Culinariae; or, Curious Tracts relating to the Culinary Affairs of the Old English. London: 1791. V. 47
Bath Characters: or Sketches from the Life. London: 1808. V. 50
Excursions from Bath. Bath: 1801. V. 51
Hampshire Extracted From Domes-Day Book... London: 1789. V. 48
A History of the Abbey of Galston, and of the Town of Glastonbury. Bath: 1826. V. 47; 50; 51
A Letter to David Garrick, Esq. London: 1768. V. 47; 49; 54
Rebellion in Bath: or, the Battle of the Upper-Rooms: an Heroico-odico-tragico-comico poem, in Two Cantos. London: 1808. V. 49
A Second Walk through Wales...In August and September 1798. Bath: 1799. V. 50
A Tour through the Northern Counties of England and the Borders of Scotland. Bath: 1802. V. 52; 53; 54
A Walk through Some of the Western Counties of England. Bath: 1800. V. 51
A Walk through Wales in August 1797... Bath: 1798. V. 52; 54

WARNER, S. A.
Fair Play's a Jewel: a Narrative of Circumstances Connected With My Mode of National Defence Against the Whole World. London: 1849. V. 53

WARNER, SUSAN BOGART
The Old Helmet. London: 1864. V. 52; 53
Queechy. New York: 1852. V. 53

WARNER, SUSAN BOGERT
Queechy. London: 1853. V. 48; 54

WARNER, SYLVIA TOWNSEND
After the Death of Don Juan. London: 1938. V. 48; 52
Boxwood. London: 1958. V. 47
Elinor Barley. London: 1930. V. 48; 49; 50
A Garland of Straw and Other Stories. London: 1943. V. 47
Mr. Fortune's Maggot. New York: 1927. V. 49
Opus 7. London: 1931. V. 53
Sixteen Engravings by Reynolds Stone. London: 1957. V. 49
Summer Will Show. London: 1916. V. 53
Whether a Dove or a Seagull - Poems. New York: 1933. V. 54

WARNER, WORCESTER REED
Selections from Oriental Objects of Art Collected by Warner and Presented to the Cleveland Museum of Art. Tarrytown: 1921. V. 54

WARNERY, CHARLES D.
Remarks on Cavalry; by the Prussian Major General of Hussars, Warnery. London: 1798. V. 48

WARNES, JOHN
On the Cultivation of Flax; the Fattening of Cattle with Native Produce... London: 1846. V. 50

WARNE'S *Mounted Toy Picture Book.* London: 1875. V. 47

WARRACK, GUY
Sherlock Holmes and Music. London: 1947. V. 50

WARREN, ARTHUR
The Charles Whittinghams Printers. New York: 1896. V. 48; 50; 51

WARREN, ASA
Views of the Summer-Land or the Poems of Rev. Asa Warren. Hannibal: 1887. V. 51

WARREN, B. H.
Report on the Birds of Pennsylvania. Harrisburg: 1888. V. 48; 49
Report on the Birds of Pennsylvania. Harrisburg: 1890. V. 49; 50; 53; 54

WARREN, CHARLES
The Supreme Court in United States History. Boston: 1922. V. 47; 48

WARREN, EDWARD
The Life of John Collins Warren, M.D. Boston: 1860. V. 49; 50; 51; 54
The Life of John Warren, M.D. Boston: 1874. V. 52; 53; 54

WARREN, EDWARD H.
The Rights of Margin Customers Against Wrongdoing Stockbrokers and Some Other Problems in the Modern Law of Pledge. Norwood: 1941. V. 52
Spartan Education. Boston: 1942. V. 52

WARREN, ELIZA SPALDING
Memoirs of the West. Portland: 1916. V. 47; 51; 53
Memoirs of the West. Portland: 1917. V. 52

WARREN, ELIZABETH
Spiritual Thrift... (with) The Good Old Way Vindicated... London: 1647/46. V. 49

WARREN, FRANCIS E.
The Proposed State of Wyoming. Proclamation, bill for Admission, Reports and Other Papers Relating to Statehood. Cheyenne: 1889. V. 48

WARREN, GOUVERNEUR K.
Explorations in the Dacota Country, in the Year 1855. Washington: 1856. V. 47
Geographical Surveys in the United States. Remarks Upon Professor J. D. Whitney's Article in the North American Review, July 1875, Concluding with an Account of the Origination of the Pacific Railroad. Washington: 1877. V. 47

WARREN, HENRY M.
To and Fro. Philadelphia: 1908. V. 48

WARREN, J. MASON
Surgical Observations, with Cases and Operations. New York: 1867. V. 49; 54

WARREN, JOHN C.
Remarks on Some Fossil Impression in the Sandstone Rocks of Connecticut River. Boston: 1854. V. 52

WARREN, JOHN COLLINS
A Comparative View of the Sensoral and Nervous System of Man and Animal. Boston: 1822. V. 54
Description of an Egyptian Mummy Presented to the Massachusetts General Hospital; With an Account of the Operation of Embalming, in Ancient and Modern Times. 1821. V. 52
The Healing of Arteries After Ligatures in Man and Animal. New York: 1886. V. 47; 48; 49
The Introductory Discourse and Lectures Delivered in Boston, Before the Convention of Teachers, and Other Friends of Education, Assembled to From the American Insitute of Instruction. August 1830. Boston: 1831. V. 50
The Life of John Collins Warren, M.D. Boston: 1860. V. 47; 48
The Mastodon Giganteus of North America. Boston: 1855. V. 48
Physical Education and the Preservation of Health. Boston: 1846. V. 49; 50; 52; 54
Surgical Observations on Tumours, with Cases and Operations. London: 1839. V. 49
A View of the Mercurial Practice in Febrile Diseases. Boston: 1813. V. 49; 51; 54

WARREN, JOSEPH H.
Hernia, Strangulated and Reducible. Boston: 1881. V. 54

WARREN, MERCY
History of the Rise, Progress and Termiantion of the American Revolution. Boston: 1805. V. 50
Poems, Dramatic and Miscellaneous. Boston: 1790. V. 47; 53; 54

WARREN, ROBERT PENN
All the King's Men. New York: 1946. V. 47; 50; 51
All the King's Men. 1948. V. 50
All the King's Men. London: 1948. V. 49; 52
All the King's Men. 1977. V. 49
All The King's Men. Franklin Center: 1977. V. 48; 49
All The King's Men. New York: 1981. V. 47
All the King's Men. New York: 1990. V. 51
At Heaven's Gate. New York: 1943. V. 47; 49; 53
Audubon: a Vision. New York: 1969. V. 47
Ballad of a Sweet Dream of Peace: a Charade for Easter. Dallas. V. 47
Ballad of a Sweet Dream of Peace: a Charade for Easter. Dallas: 1980. V. 50
Band of Angels. New York: 1955. V. 47; 51; 54
Being Here. New York: 1980. V. 47; 48; 49; 51
Blackberry Winter. 1946. V. 47
Blackberry Winter. Cummington: 1946. V. 47; 48; 53
Brother to Dragons. New York: 1979. V. 49; 51
The Cave. New York: 1959. V. 54
Chief Joseph of the Nez Perce. New York. V. 54
Chief Joseph of the Nez Perce. New York: 1983. V. 49; 50
The Circus in the Attic. New York: 1947. V. 47; 48; 51; 52; 54
The Circus in the Attic and Other Stories. London: 1952. V. 51
Democracy and Poetry. Cambridge: 1975. V. 51
Dream of a Dream. New York: 1976. V. 51
Eleven Poems on the Same Theme. Norfolk: 1942. V. 47; 48; 51
The Gods of Mount Olympus. New York: 1959. V. 48; 51; 53
Homage to Theodore Dreiser. New York: 1971. V. 50; 51
How Texas Won Her Freedom: The Story of Sam Houston and the Battle of San Jacinto. San Jacinto Monument Texas: 1959. V. 52
Jefferson Davis Gets His Citizenship Back. Lexington: 1980. V. 51
John Brown. New York: 1929. V. 47; 48; 49; 51; 52; 53
John Greenleaf Whittier's Poetry. Minneapolis: 1971. V. 54
The Legacy of the Civil War. New York: 1961. V. 54
Love: Four Versions. 1981. V. 47; 48
Meet Me In the Glen. Flagstaff: 1965. V. 48
Meet Me in the Green Glen. New York: 1971. V. 47; 48; 51; 53; 54
New and Selected Poems... Franklin Center: 1985. V. 49
New and Selected Poems... New York: 1985. V. 48; 51
New and Selected Poems. Helsinki: 1986. V. 53
Night Rider. Boston: 1939. V. 47; 48; 49
Now and Then. New York: 1978. V. 54
Old Flame. 1978. V. 47
Or Else, Poem/Poems 1968-1974. New York: 1974. V. 51
A Place to Come To. New York: 1977. V. 50; 51; 52
A Place to Come To. New York: 1981. V. 53
A Plea in Mitigation. Macon: 1966. V. 48
Rebuke of the Rock. V. 47
Remember the Alamo!. New York: 1958. V. 48; 49; 51; 54
Rumor Verified. New York: 1981. V. 49; 51
Segregation. New York: 1956. V. 47
Selected Poems. New York: 1976. V. 53
Selected Poems 1923-1943. London. V. 48; 49
Selected Poems 1923-1966... New York: 1966. V. 48; 49; 53; 54
Selected Poems 1923-1975. V. 51
Selected Poems of Herman Melville. New York: 1970. V. 51
Snowfall. 1984. V. 48
A Southern Harvest. Boston: 1937. V. 53
Two Poems. 1979. V. 47
Two Poems. Winston Salem: 1979. V. 48
Wilderness. A Tale of the Civil War. New York: 1961. V. 49; 51
William Faulkner and His South. 1951. V. 48; 50
William Faulkner and His South. Charlottesville: 1951. V. 47; 54
World Ehough and Time. New York: 1950. V. 48

WARREN, SAMUEL
Collected Works. London: 1854-55. V. 50; 51
Now and Then. Edinburgh: 1854. V. 48
Passages from the Diary of a Late Physician. Edinburgh: 1838. V. 49
Ten Thousand a year. Philadelphia: 1840-41. V. 48; 49; 52
Ten Thousand a Year. Edinburgh & London: 1841. V. 47; 50; 51; 54
Ten Thousand a Year. Paris: 1841. V. 48
Ten Thousand a Year. Edinburgh: 1853. V. 50
Works. Edinburgh: 1867/54-55. V. 49

WARREN, T. HERBERT
By Severn Sea: and Other Poems. London: 1898. V. 50

WARREN, T. ROBINSON
Dust and Foam; or, Three Oceans and Two Continents... New York: 1859. V. 47

WARREN, WILLIAM F.
Paradise Found. The Cradle of the Humane Race at the North Pole. A Study of the Preshistoric World. Boston: 1885. V. 53

WARREN, WILLIAM THORN
Winchester Illustrated. London: 1905. V. 54

WARRINER, FRANCES
Cruise of the United States Frigate Potomac Round the World, During the Years 1831-34. New York: 1835. V. 52

WARRINGTON, WILLIAM
The History of Wales, in Nine Books... London: 1788. V. 49; 51

WARTHIN, ALDRED SCOTT
The Physician of the Dance of Death: a Historical Study of the Evolution of the Dance of Death Myths in Art. New York: 1931. V. 48

WARTON, JOSEPH
An Essay on the Writing and Genius of Pope. London: 1756. V. 47
An Essay on the Writing and Genius of Pope. London: 1762/82. V. 47
Odes on Various Subjects. London: 1747. V. 54

WARTON, THOMAS
The History of English Poetry, from the Close of the Eleventh Cenmtury to the Commencement of the Eighteenth Century. London: 1774-81. V. 50
The History of English Poetry, from the Close of the Eleventh Century to the Commencement of the Eighteenth Century. London: 1774-78-81/1806. V. 52
The History of English Poetry, from the Close of the Eleventh Century to the Commencement of the Eighteenth Century. London: 1840. V. 51
History of English Poetry from the Twelfth to the Close of the Sixteenth Century. London: 1871. V. 48; 51
The Life of Sir Thomas Pope, Founder of Trinity College, Oxford, Chiefly Compiled from Original Evidences. London: 1780. V. 50; 54
The Lives of those Eminent Antiquaries John Iceland, Thomas Hearne and Anthony a Wood... Oxford: 1772. V. 49; 52
Observations on the Fairy Queen of Spenser. London: 1754. V. 49; 50
Observations on the Fairy Queen of Spenser... London: 1762. V. 47; 48; 53
Observations on the Fairy Queen of Spenser. Oxford: 1762. V. 48
The Oxford Sausage. London: 1777. V. 54
The Oxford Sausage... Oxford: 1777. V. 48
The Pleasures of Melancholy. London: 1747. V. 48; 49; 54
Poems... London: 1748. V. 51
Poems. London: 1777. V. 48; 53
The Poems... London: 1791. V. 53
Poetical Works. Oxford: 1802. V. 50
Specimen of a History of Oxfordshire... 1783. V. 54
Specimen of a History of Oxfordshire. London: 1783. V. 49; 50; 51
The Triumph of Isis, a Poem. London: 1750. V. 51; 54

WARVILLE, J. P. BRISSOT DE
New Travels in the United States of America. Performed in 1788. Dublin: 1792. V. 52

WARWICK, EARL OF
The Earl of Warwick Letter to the...Committee of Lords and Commons at Derby-House, Containing a Narrative of His Proceedings in Pursuit of the Revolted Ships, and Their Declining the Engagement... London. V. 48

WARWICK, JOHN
Market Charters, Charities and Benevolent Institutions Belonging to the Town and Parish of Workington. Workington: 1914. V. 50

WARWICK, PHILIP
Memoires of the Reigne of King Charles I. London: 1701. V. 48; 50

WASCHER-JAMES, SANDE
How Long?... 1993. V. 52
How Long?. Renton: 1993. V. 52

WASE, CHRISTOPHER
Considerations Concerning Free-Schools, as Settled in England. 1678. V. 54
Considerations Concerning Free-Schools, as Settled in England. Oxford: 1678. V. 49

WASEURTZ AF SANDELS, G. M.
A Sojourn in California by the King's Orphan: The Travels and Sketches of a Swedish Gentleman Who Visited California in 1842-1843. San Francisco: 1945. V. 47

WASHBURN, CEPHAS
Reminiscences of the Indians. Richmond: 1869. V. 54

WASHBURN, EMORY
A Manual of Criminal Law, Including the Mode of Procedure by Which It is Enforced. Chicago: 1878. V. 52
A Treatise on the American Law of Real Property. Boston: 1876. V. 51

WASHBURN, STANLEY
Trails, Trappers and Tender-Feet in the New Empire of Western Canada. London: 1913. V. 54

WASHBURNE, ELIHU BENJAMIN
Sketch of Edward Coles, Second Governor of Illinois and of the Slavery Struggle of 1823-1824. Chicago: 1882. V. 50; 52; 53

WASHINGTON, BOOKER T.
Character Building, Being Addresses Delivered On Sunday Evenings to the Students of Tuskegee Inst. New York: 1902. V. 53
The Man Farthest Down. Garden City: 1912. V. 52; 53; 54
The Man Farthest Down. New York: 1913. V. 54
The Negro in the South. Philadelphia: 1907. V. 48
A Protest Against the Burning and Lynching of Negroes. Tuskegee: 1904. V. 53
Putting the Most Into Life. New York: 1906. V. 48; 52
Sowing and Reaping. New York: 1900. V. 49
The Story of My Life and Work. Naperville: 1900. V. 48
The Story of Slavery. Dansville: 1913. V. 51
Tuskegee and its People. New York: 1905. V. 48
Up From Slavery. New York: 1901. V. 49; 50; 51; 52; 53
Up from Slavery. New York: 1970. V. 53
Working with the Hands. New York: 1904. V. 48; 50; 53

WASHINGTON County, Oklahoma. Industrial-Labor Review. Kansas City: 1914. V. 48; 52

WASHINGTON, GEORGE
The Diary of George Washington from 1789 to 1791... Richmond: 1861. V. 47
Epistles Domestic, Confidential and Official from General Washington, Written About the Commencement of the American Contest, When He Entered on the Command of the Army of the United States. New York: 1796. V. 47
Journal of Colonel George Washington, Commanding a Detachment of Virginia Troops... Albany: 1893. V. 47
The Journal of Major George Washington... London: 1754. V. 47; 50
Letters from His Excellency George Washington to Arthur Young, Esq. F.R.S. and Sir John Sinclair... Alexandria: 1803. V. 47; 50
Official Letters to the Honourable American Congress, Written During the War Between the United Colonies and Great Britain... London: 1795. V. 47
Washington...Farewell Address. Kingsport: 1932. V. 50
Washington's Farewell Address to the People of the United States the XIX Day of September MDCCXCVI. San Francisco: 1922. V. 52
Washington's Political Legacies. Boston: 1800. V. 47
Washington's Rules of Civility and Decent Behavior in Company and Conversation. Washington: 1888. V. 50
Washington's...Farewell Address... Philadelphia: 1858. V. 51
The Will of Gen. George Washington. New York: 1800. V. 47
The Writings. Boston: 1834-37. V. 47; 50; 52

WASHINGTON, JOSEPH
An Exact Abridgment of All the Statutes of King William and Queen Mary, and of King William III and Queen Anne, in Force and in Use. London: 1704. V. 51
An Exact Abridgment of all the Statutes of King William and Queen Mary, and of King William III and Queen Anne, in Force and in Use. London: 1708. V. 47

WASHINGTON, M. BUNCH
The Art of Romare Bearden: the Prevalence of Ritual. New York: 1972. V. 52

WASHINGTON. (TERRITORY). LAWS, STATUTES, ETC.
Statutes of the Territory of Washington, Made and Passed...at the City of Olympia...1865. Olympia: 1865. V. 54
Statutes of the Territory of Washington, Made and Passed...at the City of Olympia...1866. Olympia: 1866. V. 54
Statutes of the Territory of Washington, Made and Passed...at the City of Olympia...1867. Olympia: 1867. V. 54

WASHINGTON UNIVERSITY. LIBRARY
Dictionary Catalog of the Pacific Northwest Collection of the University of Washington Libraries, Seattle. Boston: 1972. V. 53

WASHINGTON INSURANCE CO., PROVIDENCE
Charter of the Washington Insurance Co. in Providence. Providence: 1800. V. 54

WASHINGTON'S MANUAL LABOUR SCHOOL AND MALE ORPHAN ASYLUM
Monuments of Washington's Patriotism. Washington: 1841. V. 47

WASIELEWSKI, W. J. D.
The Violoncello and Its History, Rendered Into English. London: 1894. V. 49

WASSERMANN, AUGUST
Immune Sera: Haemolysins, Cytotoxins and preceipitins. New York: 1904. V. 51

WASSING, RENE S.
African Art. Its Background and Traditions. New York: 1968. V. 52

WASSING-VISSER, R.
Royal Gifts from Indonesia. Historical Bonds with the House of Orange-Nassau (1600-1938). Zwolle: 1995. V. 54

WASSON, JOHN MACAMY
Annals of Pioneer Settlers On the Whitewater and Its Tributaries, in the Vicinity of Richmond, Ind. from 1804 to 1830. Richmond: 1875. V. 49; 50

WASSON, JOSEPH
Bodie and Esmeralda...Account of the Revival of Affairs in two Singularly Interesting and Important Mining Districts... San Francisco: 1878. V. 47; 53

WASSON, ROBERT GORDON
The Hall Carbine Affair... New York: 1941. V. 50
The Hall Carbine Affair. Danbury: 1971. V. 47; 48
Maria Sabina and Her Mazatec Mushroom Velada. New York & London: 1974. V. 48; 49; 52
Soma, Devine Mushroom of Immortality. New York: 1968. V. 48; 49; 52
Soma: Divine Mushroom of Immortality. New York: 1971. V. 52
The Wondrous Mushroom: Mycolatry in Mesoamerica. New York: 1980. V. 49; 51

WASSON, VALENTINA PAVLOVNA
Mushrooms, Russia and History. New York: 1957. V. 47; 48; 49; 52

THE WATER Cure Illustrated. London: 1870. V. 50

WATER Poetry. London: 1771. V. 49

WATERER, JOHN W.
Leather in Life, Art and Industry: Being an Outline of its Preparation and Uses in Britain Yesterday and Today Together with Some Reflections of its Place in the World of Synthetics Tomorrow. London: 1946. V. 49

WATERFIELD, MARGARET
Flower Grouping in English, Scotch & Irish Gardens. 1907. V. 54
Flower Grouping in English, Scotch & Irish Gardens. London: 1907. V. 48

WATERHOUSE, BENJAMIN
The Botanist. Boston: 1811. V. 48; 52; 54
An Essay on Junius and His Letters... Boston: 1831. V. 52
A Journal of a Young Man of Massachusetts, Late a Surgeon on Board and American Privateer, Who Was Captures at Sea by the British. Boston: 1816. V. 47
The Rise, Progress and Present State of Medicine. Boston: 1792. V. 52
A Synopsis of a Course of Lectures, on the Theory and Practiceof Medicine. Boston: 1786. V. 50; 53

WATERHOUSE, E. G.
Camellia Trail. Sydney: 1952. V. 52

WATERHOUSE, EDWARD
The Gentlemans Monitor; or, a Sober Inspection Into the Vertues, Vices, and Ordinary Means, of the Rise and Decay of men and Families. London: 1665. V. 48
An Humble Apologie for Learning and Learned Men. London: 1653. V. 53
A Short Narrative of the Late Dreadful Fire in London. London: 1667. V. 50; 52

WATERHOUSE, ELIZABETH
A Little Book of Life and Death. London: 1909. V. 51

WATERHOUSE, ELLIS
Gainsborough. London: 1958. V. 54
Gainsborough. London: 1966. V. 54
Reynolds. London: 1941. V. 50

WATERHOUSE, KEITH
Billy Liar. London: 1959. V. 47; 54

WATERLAND, DANIEL
Advice to a Young Student. London: 1730. V. 53

WATERMAN, CATHERINE H.
Flora's Lexicon: An Interpretation of the Language and Sentiment of Flowers...Etc. Philadelphia: 1839. V. 50

WATERMAN, LEROY
Royal Correspondence of the Assyriad Empire. Ann Arbor: 1930-36. V. 50; 52

WATERMAN, THOMAS TILESTON
Domestic Colonial Architecture of Tidewater Virginia. New York: 1932. V. 51
Domestic Colonial Architecture of Tidewater Virginia. Chapel Hill: 1947. V. 47

WATERMAN, THOMAS TILESTON continued
The Early Architecture of North Carolina. Chapel Hill: 1941. V. 48
The Early Architecture of North Carolina. Chapel Hill: 1947. V. 53
The Early Architecture of North Carolina. Chapel Hill: 1965. V. 48; 52

WATERS, ALAN
A Lotos Eater in Capri. London: 1893. V. 52

WATERS, D. W.
The Art of Navigation in England in Elizabethan and Early Stuart Times. New Haven: 1958. V. 53
The Ruttes of the Sea. The Sailing Directions of Pierre Garcie. New Haven & London: 1967. V. 47

WATERS, E. G. R.
The Anglo Norman Voyage of St. Brendan. London: 1928. V. 47

WATERS, EATON W.
The Waters or Walter Family of Cork. London: 1939. V. 47; 53

WATERS, FRANK
Below Grass Roots. New York: 1937. V. 48
Book of the Hopi. New York: 1963. V. 48; 50; 53
The Colorado. New York: 1946. V. 47
The Earp Brothers of Tombstone: The Story of Mrs. Virgil Earp. New York: 1960. V. 50
The Flight from Fiesta. Santa Fe: 1986. V. 51
Leon Gaspard. Santa Fe: 1981. V. 50
The Man Who Killed the Deer. New York: 1942. V. 47; 53
The Man Who Killed the Deer. Flagstaff: 1965. V. 48; 51; 52; 54
The Man Who Killed the Deer. Northland: 1965. V. 48; 49
Masked Gods. 1950. V. 49
Masked Gods... Albuquerque: 1950. V. 51; 52
Masked Gods. Albuquerque: 1950. (1964). V. 54
Pike's Peak: a Family Saga. Chicago: 1971. V. 50
The Yogi of Cockroach Court. New York: 1947. V. 48; 49; 50; 52; 54

WATERS, GEORGE
Indian Gleanings and Thoughts of the Past. Chatham: 1864. V. 48

WATERS, GEORGE VAN
The Poetical Geography... Louisville: 1858. V. 53

WATERS, JOHN
Shock Value. New York: 1981. V. 51

WATERS, WILLIAM E.
Life Among the Mormons, and a March to Their Zion. New York: 1868. V. 47

WATERSTON, JOHN JAMES
The Collected Scientific Papers. Edinburgh & London: 1928. V. 52

WATERTON, CHARLES
Wanderings in South America... London: 1825. V. 48; 50; 52
Wanderings in South America. London: 1828. V. 50; 54
Wanderings in South America. London: 1879. V. 54
Wanderings in South America. London Edinburgh: 1891. V. 49

WATESON, GEORGE
A Rich Store-House; or, Treasury for the Diseased. London: 1650. V. 54

WATHEN, JONATHAN
The Conductor and Containing Splints; or, a Description of two Instruments, for the Safer Conveyance and More Perfect Cure of Fractured Legs. London: 1781. V. 52

WATHERSTON, JAMES H.
The Gold Valuer; Being a Table for Ascer-taining the Value of Gold, as Naturally Produced or Artificially Amal-gamated... London: 1852. V. 54

WATKIN, EDWARD W.
Catalogue of the Library of Sir Edward W. Watkin, M.P. Rose Hill, Northenden. Manchester: 1875. V. 51; 54

WATKIN, W.
Roman Cheshire; or, a Description of Roman Remains in the County of Cheshire. Liverpool: 1886. V. 53
Roman Lancashire; or, a Description of Roman Remains in the County Palatine of Lancaster. Liverpool: 1883. V. 53

WATKINS, ALFRED
The Old Straight Track. London: 1925. V. 50

WATKINS, CHARLES
A Treatise on Copyholds. London: 1821. V. 54

WATKINS, CHARLES FREDERICK
The Human Hand and Other Poems. London: 1852. V. 50

WATKINS, E. A.
A Dictionary of the Cree Language, as Spoken by the Indians of the Hudson's Bay Company's Territories. London: 1865. V. 50; 54

WATKINS, EDWARD W.
Canada and the States: Recollections 1851 to 1886. London/New York: 1887. V. 48; 54

WATKINS, JOHN
A Biographical Dictionary of Living Authors of Great Britain and Ireland. London: 1816. V. 49; 52
An Essay Towards a History of Bideford, in the County of Devon. Exeter: 1792. V. 50

Memoirs of the Public and Private Life of Richard Brinsley Sheridan.. London: 1817. V. 47; 51
Scarborough Tales. London: 1830. V. 47
An Universal Biographical and Historical Dictionary...of All Ages and All Countries. London: 1800. V. 50; 53

WATKINS, PAUL
Night Over Day Over Night. London: 1988. V. 51
Night Over Day Over Night. New York: 1988. V. 47

WATKINS, ROBERT
Digest of the Laws of the State of Georgia...to 1798. Philadelphia: 1800. V. 50

WATMOUGH, EDMUND C.
Scrbblings and Sketches, Diplomatic, Piscatorial and Oceanic. Philadelphia: 1844. V. 47; 53

WATNEY, VERNON JAMES
Catalogue of the Library of V. J. Watney at Cornbury. 1917. V. 47; 49
Cornbury and the Forest of Wychwood. London: 1910. V. 48; 54

WATON, AUGUSTUS Q.
A History of the Detection, Conviction, Life and designs of John A. Murel. New York: 1839. V. 48

WATROUS, ANGEL
History of Larimer County Colorado. Ft. Collins: 1911. V. 47

WATROUS, GEORGE R.
The History of Winchester Firearms 1866-1975. New York: 1975. V. 53

WATSON, A. E. T.
King Edward VII as a Sportsman. London: 1911. V. 49

WATSON, ANDREW G.
Catalogue of Dated and Datable Manuscripts c. 435-1600 in Oxford Libraries. Oxford: 1984. V. 47; 48

WATSON, B. A.
The Sportsman's Paradise; or the Lake Lands of Canada. Philadelphia: 1888. V. 50; 54

WATSON, DAVID K.
History of American Coinage. New York: 1899. V. 51

WATSON, DOUGLAS SLOANE
California in the Fifties... San Francisco: 1936. V. 47
Joaquin Murieta, the Brigand Chief of California. San Francisco: 1932. V. 51; 53
The Spanish Occupation of California... San Francisco: 1934. V. 47; 48; 50; 53

WATSON, ELIZABETH SOPHIA
A High Little World and What Happened There. London: 1892. V. 50

WATSON, ELKANNAH
Men and Times of the Revolution; or, Memoirs of...Including Journals of Travel in Europe and America, from 1777 to 1842. New York: 1856. V. 47

WATSON, FREDERICK
Hunting Pie: The Whole Art and Craft of Foxhunting. New York: 1931. V. 47

WATSON, G.
Three Rolling Stones in Japan. London: 1904. V. 48

WATSON, GEORGE
Bygone Penrith. Penrith: 1893. V. 52
The New Cambridge Bibliography of English Literature. 1969-77. V. 47; 50
A Rich Store-House; or, Treasury for the Diseased. London: 1650. V. 53

WATSON, GOW & CO.
Open and Close Fire Ranges, Grilling Stoves, Hot Plates & Section V.M. Glasgow: 1880. V. 54

WATSON, H.
The Decline and Fall of the British Empire; or, the Witch's Cavern. 1890. V. 54

WATSON, H. R. C.
Catalogue of Morgan Horses at Edge View Farm Brandon Vermont, Property of H. R. C. Watson. 1915. V. 49

WATSON, HENRY
Narrative of Henry Watson, a Fugitive Slave. Boston: 1848. V. 52
Narrative of Henry Watson, a Fugitive Slave. Boston: 1849. V. 51

WATSON, HEWETT COTTRELL
Remarks on the Geographical Distribution of British Plants Chiefly in Connection with Latitude, Elevation and Climate. London: 1835. V. 54

WATSON, I.
The Embedding. 1973. V. 48

WATSON, IAN
Conversations with Ayckbourn. London: 1988. V. 54

WATSON, J.
The Confessions of a Poacher. London: 1890. V. 51

WATSON, J. W.
A Short Account of Wigton School and the Neighbourhood, with Lists of Teachers and Scholars. Wigton: 1892. V. 51

WATSON, J. Y.
A Compendium of British Mining, With Statistical Notices of the Principle Mine in Cornwall. London: 1843. V. 53; 54

WATSON, JAMES
The Spirit of the Doctor... Manchester: 1820. V. 50; 54
The Trial of James Watson, for High Treason, at the Bar of the Court of King's Bench...June 1817. London: 1817. V. 53

WATSON, JAMES D.
The Double Helix. 1968. V. 47
The Double Helix. London: 1968. V. 53
The Double Helix. New York: 1968. V. 48; 50; 51

WATSON, JAMES, MRS.
Lower Rio Grande Valley of Texas and Its Builders. Mission: 1927. V. 49

WATSON, JOHN
The Adventure of the Peerless Peer. Boulder: 1974. V. 51
The History and Antiquities of the Parish of Halifax, in Yorkshire. London: 1765. V. 50
The History and Antiquities of the Parish of Halifax, in Yorkshire. London: 1775. V. 48
Kant and His English Critics: a Comparison of Critical and Empirical Philosophy. Glasgow: 1881. V. 47
The Medical Profession in Ancient Times. An Anniversary Discourse Delivered Before the New York Academy of Medicine, November 7, 1855. New York: 1856. V. 52
Memoirs of the Ancient Earls of Warren and Surrey. London: 1785. V. 48
Psychology: from the Standpoint of a Behaviorist. Philadelphia: 1919. V. 52

WATSON, JOHN BROADUS
Behaviorism. New York: 1924. V. 54

WATSON, JOHN F.
Annals of Philadelphia and Pennsylvania in the Olden Time. Philadelphia: 1927. V. 50; 52; 53

WATSON, L.
The Grass Genera of the World. Wallingford: 1992. V. 49; 51

WATSON, LARRY
Montana 1948. Minneapolis: 1993. V. 50; 52; 54

WATSON, M. L.
Designs Illustrative of Samuel Rogers Poem "Human Life". London: 1851. V. 48

WATSON, PETER D.
The History of Greensboro: The First 200 Years. Greensboro: 1990. V. 49

WATSON, PETER WILLIAM
Dendrologia Britannia, or Trees and Shrubs That Will Live in the Open Air of Britain throughout the Year. London: 1825. V. 52; 53

WATSON, RALPH
A Brief Explanatory Statement of the Principle and Application of a Plan for Preventing Ships Foundering at Sea... London: 1829. V. 50

WATSON, RICHARD, BP. OF LLANDAFF
Anecdotes of the Life of Richard Watson, Bishop of Landaff, Written by Himself... London: 1817. V. 51
An Apology for Christianity. (with) An Apology for the Bible...Addressed to Thomas Paine. New Brunswick: 1796. V. 53
An Apology for the Bible, Addressed to Thomas Paine... Bhowanipore: 1855. V. 48
Chemical Essays. London: 1782-87. V. 54
Chemical Essays. 1793-96. V. 54
Chemical Essays. Dublin: 1793-96. V. 50
Chemical Essays. London: 1800. V. 47; 49
A Collection of Theological Tracts. Cambridge: 1785. V. 51

WATSON, RICHARD, BP OF LLANDAFF
Historicall Collections of Ecclesiastaick Affairs in Scotland and Politick Related to Them... London: 1657. V. 50; 52

WATSON, RICHARD, BP. OF LLANDAFF
A Letter to His Grace the Archbishop of Canterbury. London: 1783. V. 49

WATSON, ROBERT
The History of the Reign of Philip the Second, King of Spain... London: 1803-08. V. 47; 50
The History of the Reign of Philip the Second, King of Spain. London: 1812. V. 53

WATSON, ROBERT GRANT
Spanish and Portuguese South America During the Colonial Period. London: 1884. V. 52

WATSON, ROBERT PATRICK
Memoirs of Robert Patrick Watson: a Journalist's Experience of Mixed Society. London: 1899. V. 54

WATSON, S. H.
A Folio of Old Songs. Waxahachie: 1912. V. 52

WATSON, SERENO
Report of the Geological Exploration of the Fortieth Parallel. Volume V. Botany. Washington: 1871. V. 52

WATSON, W. H. L.
A Company of Tanks. London: 1920. V. 47

WATSON, W. P.
Japan Aspects and Destinies. London: 1904. V. 48
The Mattioli Woodblocks. London & Amsterdam: 1989. V. 47

WATSON, WILBUR J.
Bridge Architecture... New York: 1927. V. 48; 50; 51; 53

WATSON, WILLIAM
The Adventures of a Blockade Runner; or, Trade in Time of War. London: 1892. V. 54
The Clergy-Man's Law; or, the Complete Incumbent... London: 1701. V. 51
The Clergy-Man's Law; or, the Complete Incumbent... London: 1725. V. 47
The Collected Poems of... New York & London: 1899. V. 47
The Eloping Angels. London: 1893. V. 49; 51
Experiments and Observations Tending to Illustrate the Nature and Properties of Electricity. (with) A Sequel to the Experiments and Observations... London: 1746. V. 47
The Hope of the World and Other Poems. London: 1898. V. 53
Life in the Confederate Army, Being the Observations and Experiences of an Alien in the South During the American Civil War. New York: 1888. V. 49
Orchids: Their Culture and Management... London: 1890. V. 54
Orchids: Their Culture and Management... London: 1903. V. 48
The Poems of William Watson. London & New York: 1905. V. 54

WATSON, WILLIAM HENRY
A Practical Treatise on the Office of Sheriff: Comprising the Whole of the Duties, Renumeration, and Liabilities of Sheriffs, in the execution and Return of Writs (etc.). London: 1848. V. 48

WATSON, WINSLOW C.
The Military and Civil History of the County of Essex, New York. Albany: 1869. V. 54

WATT, ALEXANDER
The Art of Paper-Making... London: 1890. V. 49
The Art of Paper-Making. New York: 1907. V. 51

WATT, GEORGE
Indian Art at Delhi 1903. London: 1904. V. 49; 54

WATT, ISAAC
The Knowledge of the Heavens and Earth Made Easy... London: 1726. V. 54

WATT, J. A.
Mediaeval Studies Presented to Aubrey Gwynn, S.J. 1961. V. 48
Mediaeval Studies Presented to Aubrey Gwynn, S.J. Dublin: 1961. V. 51

WATT, JAMES
Correspondence of the Late James Watt on His Discovery of the Theory of the Composition of Water... London: 1846. V. 51

WATT, ROBERT
Bibliotheca Britannica or a General Index to British and Foreign Literature. New York. V. 47
Bibliotheca Britannica; or a General Index to British and Foreign Literature. Edinburgh: 1824. V. 49

WATT, STUART, MRS.
In the Heart of Savagedom. London: 1912. V. 50

WATT, WILLIAM
Remarks on Shooting; to Which is Added, a Part of the Game-Laws; Both Written in Familar Verse. London: 1835. V. 47

WATTER, EMILE
Le Progres de Seduction. Paris: 1833. V. 54

WATTERS, THOMAS
A Guide to the Tablets in a Temple of Confucius. Shanghai: 1879. V. 49

WATTERS, WILLIAM
A Short Account of the Christian Experience, and Ministereal Labours. Alexandria: 1806. V. 49

WATTERSON, GEORGE
The L... Family at Washington; or, a Winter in the Metropolis. Washington: 1822. V. 52

WATTERSTON, GEORGE
The Lawyer, or Man As He Ought Not to Be. Pittsburg: 1808. V. 53

WATTEVILLE, V. DE
Out in the Blue (Big Game Hunting in Kenya, Uganda and the Congo). London: 1927. V. 49
Speak to the Earth, Wanderings and Reflections Among Elephants and Mountains... London: 1935. V. 49

WATTLES, GURDON WALLACE
Autobiography of...Genealogy. Los Angeles: 1922. V. 47
Autobiography of...Genealogy. New York: 1922. V. 48

WATTS, ALAN W.
Beat Zen Square Zen and Zen. San Francisco: 1959. V. 52
Beyond Theology: the Art of Godmanship. New York: 1964. V. 49
Buddhism in the Modern World. Cecil Court: 1930's. V. 52
Nature, Man and Woman. New York: 1958. V. 52
An Outline of Zen Buddhism. London: 1932. V. 52
This Is It and Other Essays on Zen and Spiritual Experience. New York: 1960. V. 52
The Wisdom of Insecurity. New York: 1951. V. 49; 51; 52
Zen Buddhism. London: 1947. V. 52; 53

WATTS, DR.
The Union Collection of Hymns and Sacred odes... London: 1827. V. 48

WATTS, GEORGE FREDERICK
Pictures By... New York: 1904. V. 49

WATTS, HENRY
A Dictionary of Chemistry and the Allied Branches of Other Sciences. London: 1883-81. V. 53

WATTS, ISAAC
Divine and Moral Songs... London: 1803. V. 52
Divine Songs...for the Use of Children. London: 1777. V. 52

WATTS, ISAAC continued
Divine Songs...for the Use of Children. London: 1780. V. 52
Divine Songs...for the Use of Children. London: 1804. V. 52
Divine Songs...for the Use of Children. Glasgow: 1814. V. 51
Divine Songs...for the Use of Children. Derby: 1840. V. 52
Dr. Watts's Divine Songs for Children... Banbury: 1810. V. 49
The First Principles of Astronomy and Geography Explained by the Use of Globes and Maps. London: 1765. V. 49
Humility Represented in the Character of St. Paul, The Chief Springs Of it Opened. London: 1737. V. 51
Hymns and Spiritual Songs. London: 1767. V. 51
The Improvement of the Mind or a Supplement to the Art of Logic. London: 1784. V. 49
The Improvement of the Mind or a Supplement to the Art of Logic... Berwick: 1801. V. 52
The Knowledge of the Heavens and the Earth Made Easy; or, the First Principles of Astronomy and Geography Explain'd by the Use of Globes and Maps. London: 1760. V. 52
Logick; or, the Right Use of Reason in the Enquiry after Truth... London: 1726. V. 53
Logick; or, the Right Use of Reason in the Enquiry After Truth. London: 1736. V. 50
Logick; or, The Right Use of Reason in the Enquiry After Truth. London: 1782. V. 48; 49
Logick; or, the Right Use of Reason in the Enquiry After Truth... London: 1822. V. 52
Philosophical Essays on Various Subjects, Viz. Space, Substance, Body, Spirit, the Operations of the Soul in Union with the Body... London: 1733. V. 47
The Psalms of David Imitated in the Language of the New Testament and Apply'd to The Christian State and Worship. London: 1719. V. 47
The Psalms of David, Imitated in the Language of the New-Testament and Applied to the Christian State and Worship; and Hymns and Spiritual Songs. In Three Books. With a Valuable Collection of Sacred Musick, Adapted to the Various Metres in Watts. Exeter: 1818. V. 47
Reliquiae Juveniles: Miscellaneous Thoughs in Prose and Verse, on Natural, Moral and Divine Subjects. London: 1734. V. 48; 54
Reliquiae Juveniles: Miscellaneous Thoughts in Prose and Verse, on Natural, Moral and Divine Subjects... London: 1752. V. 52
Reliquiae Juveniles. Miscellaneous Thoughts, in Prose and Verse, on Natural, Moral and Divine Subjects... Portsmouth: 1796. V. 50
Songs, Divine and Moral. London: 1826. V. 48; 50
The Works... London: 1753. V. 51
The Works... Leeds: 1800. V. 49

WATTS, JOHN
A True Relation of the Inhumane and Unparallel'd Actions, and Barbarous Murders of Negroes or Moors... London: 1672. V. 50

WATTS, JOHN S.
Armendaris Grant, Fort Craig, New Mexico. Argument by John S. Watts, Attorney. Santa Fe: 1870. V. 49

WATTS, M. S.
George Frederic Watts. New York. V. 51
George Frederick Watts... London: 1912. V. 49

WATTS, STUART, MRS.
In the Heart of Savagedom. London: 1912. V. 51

WATTS, WILLIAM
The Seats of Nobility and Gentry, in a Collection of the Most Interesting and Picturesque Views... London: 1779. V. 48; 50; 53; 54
The Seats of Nobility and Gentry, in a Collection of the Most Interesting and Picturesque Views. Chelsea: 1779-86. V. 47; 50
The Seats of the Nobility and Gentry, in a Collection of the Most Interesting and Picturesque Views. London: 1779-86. V. 53
The Yahoo: a Satirical Rhapsody. (with) The Mohawks: a Satirical Poem with Notes. New York: 1830/22. V. 50

WATTS, WILLIAM W.
Old English Silver. London: 1924. V. 49
Old English Silver. New York: 1924. V. 50
Works of Art in Silver and Other Metals Belonging to Viscount and Viscountess Lee of Fareham. London: 1936. V. 47

WATTS-DUNTON, THEODORE
Aylwin. London: 1899. V. 51; 54

WAUGH, ALEC
The Fatal Gift. London: 1973. V. 50
Georgian Stories. London: 1926. V. 51
The Prisoners of Mainz. London: 1919. V. 47
Resentment - Poems. London: 1918. V. 47
The Year-Boke of the Sette of Odd Volumes. London: 1935. V. 52

WAUGH, ARTHUR
The Square Book of Animals. London: 1899. V. 47

WAUGH, EDWIN
Home-Life of the Lancashire Factory Folk During the Cotton Famine. London: 1867. V. 47

WAUGH, EVELYN
Basil Seal Rides Again. Boston: 1963. V. 47; 48; 50; 51; 52; 53; 54
Basil Seal Rides Again. London: 1963. V. 47; 49; 51; 54
Black Mischief. London: 1932. V. 47; 48; 49; 50; 51; 52; 53
Brideshead Revisited. London: 1944. V. 53
Brideshead Revisited. Boston: 1945. V. 47; 48; 51; 53
Brideshead Revisited. London: 1945. V. 47; 49; 51; 53
Brideshead Revisited. New York: 1945. V. 53
Brideshead Revisited... Boston: 1946. V. 49
Decline and Fall. London: 1928. V. 53
Decline and Fall. 1929. V. 50
Decline and Fall. Garden City: 1929. V. 51
Edmund Campion. London: 1935. V. 49; 50
Edmund Campion. Boston: 1946. V. 53
A Handful of Dust. London: 1928. V. 53
A Handful of Dust. London: 1934. V. 49; 50; 51; 53
A Handful of Dust. New York: 1934. V. 49
Helena. London: 1950. V. 50; 51; 52
The Holy Places. New York: 1953. V. 50
Labels. London: 1930. V. 49; 50; 51; 52; 53; 54
The Life of the Rt. Rev. Ronald Knox. London: 1959. V. 48; 50; 53
Love Among the Ruins. London: 1953. V. 49; 50; 51; 52
The Loved One. Boston: 1948. V. 49; 52
The Loved One. London: 1948. V. 47; 48; 51; 52; 53
Men At Arms. London: 1952. V. 50
Men at Arms... London: 1952/55/61. V. 49
Mexico: an Object Lesson. Boston: 1939. V. 47; 53
Mr. Loveday's Little Outing. Boston: 1936. V. 48
Mr. Loveday's Little Outing. London: 1936. V. 47; 48; 49; 51
Ninety-Two Days. London: 1934. V. 50; 52; 54
Ninety-Two Days. USA: 1934. V. 53
Officers and Gentlemen. Boston: 1955. V. 50
Officers and Gentlemen. London: 1955. V. 54
The Ordeal of Gilbert Pinfold. London: 1957. V. 48; 50; 53; 54
PRB: An Essay on the Pre-Raphaelite Brotherhood 1847-54. London: 1926. V. 50
PRB: an Essay on the Pre-Raphaelite Brotherhood 1847-54. 1982. V. 54
Put Out More Flags. Boston: 1942. V. 48
Put Out More Flags. London: 1942. V. 47; 50; 51; 53
Remote People. London: 1931. V. 49; 51; 54
Robbery Under Law: The Mexican Object Lesson. London: 1939. V. 53
Robbery Under Law: the Mexican Object Lesson. London: 1940. V. 50
Rossetti. New York: 1928. V. 54
Scoop. London: 1933. V. 48; 50
Scoop. 1938. V. 50
Scoop. London: 1938. V. 47; 50; 51; 53
Sword of Honour. London: 1952/55/61. V. 54
Sword of Honour. London: 1961. V. 51
Sword of Honour. London: 1965. V. 49; 51; 54
Sword of Honour... London: 1990. V. 53
Tactical Exercise. Boston: 1954. V. 50
They Were Still Dancing. New York: 1931. V. 54
They Were Still Dancing. New York: 1932. V. 47; 50; 54
They Were Still Dancing. USA: 1932. V. 53
Unconditional Surrender. London: 1961. V. 49; 53
Vile Bodies. London: 1930. V. 53; 54
Vile Bodies. New York: 1930. V. 48
Waugh in Abyssinia. London: 1936. V. 48; 49; 50; 51; 52; 53
When the Going Was Good. London: 1946. V. 51
When the Going Was Good. Boston: 1947. V. 50
Wine in Peace and War. London: 1947. V. 48; 49; 50; 51; 53
Wine in Peace and War. London: 1949. V. 47; 52
Work Suspended. London: 1942. V. 53

WAUGH, FRANCIS G.
The Athenaeum Club and Its Associations. London: 1900. V. 54

WAUGH, IDA
Holly Berries... London: 1880. V. 50
Holly Berries. New York: 1881. V. 47
When Mother Was a Little Girl. London: 1915. V. 47

WAUGH, JULIA NOTT
Castroville and Henry Castro, Empresario. San Antonio: 1934. V. 51; 52

WAUGH, LORENZO
The Autobiography of Lorenzo Waugh. Oakland: 1883. V. 47

WAUGH, NORAH
Corsets and Crinolines. London: 1954. V. 47; 52

WAUGHBURTON, RICHARD, PSEUD.
Innocence and Design. London: 1935. V. 48

WAURIN, JEHAN DE
A Collection of Chronicles and Ancient Histories of Great Britain. London: 1864-91. V. 49

WAUTERS, A. J.
Stanley's Emin Pasha Expedition. London: 1890. V. 54

WAVELL, ARCHIBALD
Generals and Generalship. London: 1941. V. 48

WAVELL, ARCHIBALD PERCIVAL WAVELL, 1ST EARL OF
Other Men's Flowers: an Anthology of Poetry. London: 1944. V. 49

WAX Flowers, How to Make Them. Boston: 1864. V. 51

WAY, GEORGE P.
Story of Earthquake. Detroit: 1906. V. 51; 53

WAY, THOMAS ROBERT
Ancient Royal Palaces In and Near London. London and New York: 1902. V. 53

WAY, THOMAS ROBERT continued
Memories of James McNeill Whistler. London: 1912. V. 48; 52
Reliques of Old London Suburb North of Thames. London: 1898. V. 50

WAY, VIRGIL GILMAN
History of the Thirty-Third Regiment Illinois Veteran Volunteer Infantry in the Civil War 22nd August, 1861 to 7th December 1865... Gibson City: 1902. V. 50

WAY, W. IRVING
Migratory Books: Their Haunts and Habits. Los Angeles: 1924. V. 51

WAYLAND, FRANCIS
The Elements of Moral Science. New York: 1835. V. 53
The Elements of Political Economy. New York: 1837. V. 49
A Memoir of the Life and Labors of the Rev. Adoniram Judson, D.D. Boston: 1853. V. 47; 52

WAYLAND, JOHN WALTER
Battle of New Market Memorial Address Sixty-Second Anniversary of the Battle of New Market, Virginia, May 15, 1926 wit Maps. New Market: 1926. V. 49; 54
The German Element of the Shenandoah Valley of Virginia. Charlottesville: 1907. V. 47
A History of Rockingham County, Virginia. Dayton: 1912. V. 47
Stonewall Jackson's Way. Staunton: 1940. V. 49

WAYNE, JOHN
America, Why I Love Her. New York: 1977. V. 53

WAYSS, G. A.
Das System Monier. (Eisengerippe mit Cementumhullung) in Seiner Anwendung auf das Gesammte Bauwesen. Berlin: 1887. V. 52

WAYTE, GEORGE HODGSON
Prospecting: or Eighteen Months in Australia and New Zealand. Colophon: 1879. V. 48

WAYTE, SAMUEL C.
The Equestrian's Manual; or, the Science of Equitation, with Advice to Purchasers of Horses, Saddlery. London: 1850. V. 47

WAYTH, C.
Trout Fishing: or, the River Darent. London: 1845. V. 47

WAYZGOOSE One: the Australian Journal of Book Arts. Number One. Sydney: 1985. V. 54

WE Japanese: being Descriptions of Many of the Customs, Manners, Ceremonies, Festivals, Arts and Crafts of the Japanese. Hakone, Japan: 1964. V. 49

THE WEAL-Reaf, a Record of the Essex Institute Fair. Salem: 1860. V. 47; 53

WEALE, GEORGE
An Interesting Memoir of George Weale...From the Time of His Leaving His Father at the Age of Fourteen... Leamingon: 1838. V. 52

WEALE, JOHN
Divers Works of Early Masters in Christian Decoration... London: 1846. V. 51
Ensamples of Railway Making... London: 1843. V. 49
Monograms, Old Architectural Ornaments, Sacred Illustrations, Borders and Alphabets Collected on the Continent and In England... London: 1845. V. 48
Monograms, Old Architectural Ornaments, Sacred Illustrations, Borders and Alphabets Collected on the Continent and in England. London: 1885. V. 48; 51
The Theory, Practice and Architecture of Bridges. London: 1843. V. 49; 54

WEALE, W. H. JAMES
Bookbindings and Rubbings of Bindings in the Victoria and Albert Museum. London: 1962. V. 49

WEALTH and Biography of the Wealthy Citizens of Philadelphia. Philadelphia: 1845. V. 47

THE WEALTH Of Great Britain in the Ocean... London: 1749. V. 48; 52

WEARE, W. K.
Songs of the Western Shore. San Francisco: 1879. V. 51; 52

WEATHERHEAD, D. HUME
Madagascar, Past and Present. London: 1847. V. 54

WEATHERLEY, FREDERIC E.
Lays for Little Ones. London: 1898. V. 53

WEATHERLY, FREDERIC E.
Out of Town. London: 1880. V. 48
Punch and Judy. London: 1885. V. 47; 48; 52
Rainbow Stories and Verses. London: 1890. V. 54
Through the Meadows. London: 1885. V. 48

WEATHERS, J.
Commercial Gardening, a Practical and Scientific Treatise for Maraket Gardeners, Marker Growers, Fruit, Flower and Vegetable Growers, Nurserymen, Etc. London: 1913. V. 47; 50; 51; 52

WEAVER, C. S.
Living Volutes, a Monograph of the Recent Volutidae of the World. Greenville: 1970. V. 50; 51; 53

WEAVER, JOHN
Anatomical and Mechanical Lectures Upon Dancing. London: 1721. V. 47
An Essay Towards an History of Dancing, In Which the Whole Art and Its Various Excellencies are in Some Measure Explain'd. London: 1712. V. 47

WEAVER, LAWRENCE
English Leadwork Its Art and History. London: 1909. V. 51

The House and Its Equipment. London: 1912. V. 50
The House and its Equipment. London: 1920. V. 49
Houses and Gardens by E. L. Lutyens. London: 1913. V. 50; 51; 54
Houses and Gardens by E. L. Lutyens. London: 1914. V. 47; 48
Houses and Gardens by E. L. Lutyens... London: 1925. V. 51; 53; 54
Memorials and Monuments Old and New: Two Hundred Subjects Chosen from Seven Centuries. London: 1905. V. 50
Small Country Houses of Today. London: 1922/22. V. 54
Small Country Houses: Their Repair and Enlargement. London: 1914. V. 51

WEAVER, R.
Monumenta Antiquae; or the Stone Monuments of Antiquity Yet Remaining in the British Isles, Particularly as Illustrated by Scripture. London: 1840. V. 48

WEAVER, RAYMOND
Herman Melville: Mariner and Mystic. New York: 1921. V. 52

WEAVER, T.
Memoir on the Geological Relations to the East of Ireland. 1819. V. 53

WEAVER, WILEY M., MRS.
Imperial Valley: 1901-1915. 1916. V. 48

WEAVER, WILLIAM AUGUSTUS
Examination and Review of a Pamphlet Printed and Secretly Circulated by M. E. Gorostiza...Respecting the Passage of the Sabine by the Troops Under the Command of General Gaines. Washington: 1837. V. 49

WEAVER, WILLIAM D.
Catalogue of the Wheeler Gift of Books, Pamphlets and Periodicals in the Library of the American Institute of Electrical Engineers. New York: 1909. V. 52; 54

WEBB, A. P.
A Bibliography of the Works of Thomas Hardy 1865-1915. London: 1916. V. 49

WEBB, BENJAMIN
Sketches of Continental Ecclesiology, or Church Notes in Belgium, Germany and Italy. London: 1848. V. 49

WEBB, CHARLES HENRY
Liffith Lank, or Lunacy. New York: 1866. V. 54

WEBB, CLIFFORD
The North Pole Before Lunch. London: 1936. V. 53
The Story of Noah. New York: 1949. V. 54

WEBB, CORNELIUS
The Posthumous Papers, Facetious and Fanciful, of a Person Lately About Town. London: 1828. V. 48

WEBB, DANIEL
An Inquiry Into the Beauties of Painting... London: 1761. V. 49
An Inquiry into the Beauties of Painting... Dublin: 1764. V. 47
An Inquiry Into the Beauties of Painting... London: 1769. V. 52
Observations on the Correspondence Between Poetry and Music. (with) Remarks on the Beauties of Poetry. London: 1769/62. V. 52
Remarks on the Beauties of Poetry... Dublin: 1754/54. V. 49
Remarks on the Beauties of Poetry. London: 1762. V. 47; 48; 49; 52; 54
Remarks on the Beauties of Poetry... London: 1762/69/69. V. 49
Remarks on the Beauties of Poetry... Dublin: 1764. V. 48; 49

WEBB, DAVE
Old Paper Specimens of Three Centuries. Chillicothe: 1946. V. 54

WEBB, E. A.
The Records of St. Bartholomew's Priory and of the Church and Parish of St. Bartholomew in Great West Smithfield. Oxford: 1921. V. 54

WEBB, E. B.
On Iron Breakwaters and Piers. London: 1862. V. 51

WEBB, EDITH BUCKLAND
Indian Life at the Old Missions. Los Angeles: 1952. V. 50; 51; 54

WEBB, EDWARD A.
The Historical Directory of Sussex County, N.J. 1872. V. 47; 49; 51

WEBB, FRANCIS
Friendship: a Poem Inscribed to a Friend; To Which is Added, an Ode. London: 1779. V. 48; 52
Panharmonicon, Designed as an Illustration of an Engraved Plate... London: 1815. V. 50
Somerset a Poem. London: 1811. V. 48; 54

WEBB, FRANK J.
The Garies and Their Friends. London and New York: 1857. V. 47

WEBB, GEORGE
The Practice of Quietness, Directing a Christian How to Live Quietly in this Troublesome World. 1705. V. 52

WEBB, GEORGE W.
Chronological Lists of Engagements Between the Regular Army of the United States and Various Tribes of Hostile Indians Which Occurred During the Years 1790-1898, Inclusive. St. Joseph: 1939. V. 48; 50

WEBB, J. B., MRS.
The Life and Adventures of Charles Durand; Shewing the Manners and Customs of Eastern Nations. London: 1850. V. 54

WEBB, JAMES JOSIAH
Adventures in the Santa F. Trade, 1844-1847. Glendale: 1931. V. 48; 51; 52; 54

WEBB, MARIA
The Fells of Warthmoor Hall, and Their Friends... London: 1865. V. 49; 50; 52; 54
The Penns and Peningtons of the Seventeenth Century. London: 1867. V. 50; 52; 54

WEBB, MARION ST. JOHN
The Flower Fairies. London: 1925. V. 49
The Forest Fairies. London: 1932. V. 54
The Heath Fairies. London: 1925. V. 49
The Orchard Fairies. London: 1925. V. 49; 54
The Pond Fairies. London: 1925. V. 49
The Sea-shore Fairies. London. V. 49
The Seed Fairies. London. V. 50
The Seed Fairies. 1920. V. 54
The Seed Fairies. London: 1925. V. 49
The Twilight Fairies. London: 1925. V. 49
Twilight Fairies. London: 1928. V. 54
The Weather Fairies. London: 1925. V. 49
The Wild-Fruit Fairies. London: 1932. V. 49

WEBB, MARY
The Chinese Lion. London: 1937. V. 48; 49; 50
The Gold Arrow. London: 1916. V. 48; 50
Gone to Earth. London: 1917. V. 49; 50
Memoir of Mrs. Chloe Spear, a Native of Africa, Who Was Enslaved in Childhood, and Died in Boston January 3, 1815...Aged 65 Years. Boston: 1832. V. 50
Precious Bane. London: 1924. V. 53
The Works. London: 1939-43. V. 48

WEBB, MAURICE E.
Raffles Division. A Record of His Life and Work from 1870 to 1926. London: 1927. V. 53

WEBB, PHILIP CARTERET
A Short Account of Danegeld; with Some Further Particulars Relating to Will. The Conqueror's Survey. London: 1756. V. 53
A State of Facts in Defence of His Majesty's Right to Certain Fee-Farm Rents in the County of Norfolk. London: 1758. V. 53

WEBB, PHYLLIS
Even Your Right Eye. Toronto: 1956. V. 47
The Sea Is Also a Garden. Toronto: 1962. V. 47

WEBB, RICHARD D.
The Life and Letters of Captain John Brown, Who Was Executed at Charlestown (!), Virginia, Dec. 2, 1859, for an Armed Attach Upon American Slavery... London: 1861. V. 47; 54

WEBB, SAMUEL B.
Records of North American Big Game. 1952. V. 52; 54

WEBB, SIDNEY
The Eight Hours Day. London: 1891. V. 51
The History of Trade Unionism. London: 1896. V. 54
Soviet Communism: a New Civilisation?. London. V. 49

WEBB, T.
A New Select Collection of Epitaphs, Panegyrical and Moral, Humorous, Whimsical, Satyrical and Inscriptive. London: 1775. V. 52

WEBB, THOMAS H.
Information for Kansas Immigrants. Boston: 1855. V. 50
Information for Kansas Immigrants. Boston: 1859/60. V. 52

WEBB, THOMAS S.
The Freemason's Monitor; or, Illustrations of Masonry... New York: 1802. V. 54

WEBB, TODD
Georgia O'Keeffe. The Artist's Landscape. Pasadena: 1984. V. 54

WEBB, W.
Dwellers at the Source. Southwestern Indian Photographs of A. C. Vroman, 1895-1904. New York: 1973. V. 51

WEBB, W. L.
Battles and Biographies of Missourians, or the Civil War Period Of Our State. Kansas City: 1900. V. 49

WEBB, WALTER PRESCOTT
Flat Top: a Story of Modern Ranching. El Paso;: 1960. V. 48; 51; 52
The Great Plains. Boston: 1931. V. 50; 53
The Texas Rangers. Boston: 1935. V. 47; 52; 53; 54
The Texas Rangers... New York: 1935. V. 52
Toward the Morning Sun: a Tribute to Walter Prescott Webb. Austin: 1967. V. 49

WEBB, WILLIAM
Dwellers at the Source: Southwestern Indian Photographs of A. C. Vroman, 1895-1904. New York: 1973. V. 47

WEBB, WILLIAM SEWARD
California and Alaska and Over the Canadian Pacific Railway. New York/London: 1891. V. 48; 49
Shelburne Farms Stud (Shelburne, Chittenden County, Vermont) of English Hackneys, Harness and Saddle Horses, Ponies and Trotters. New York: 1893. V. 47

WEBBER, ALEXANDER
Shooting: a Poem Comprising a General Description of Field Sports... London: 1841. V. 50; 52

WEBBER, BYRON
James Orrock, R.I. Painter, Connoisseur, Collector. London: 1903. V. 54

WEBBER, CHARLES WILKINS
The Hunter-Naturalist. Romance of Sporting; or, Wild Scenes and Wild Hunters. Philadelphia: 1852. V. 49
Jack Long; or, Shot in the Eye. New York: 1846. V. 52
Old Hicks the Guide: or, Adventures in the Camanche Country in Search of a Gold Mine. New York: 1848. V. 47
Wild Scenes and Song Birds. New York: 1854. V. 54
Wild Scenes and Song-Birds. New York: 1858. V. 54
Wild Scenes and Wild Hunters of the World. Philadelphia: 1854. V. 47

WEBBER, H. J.
The Citrus Industry. Berkeley: 1948. V. 47

WEBBER, JOHN
Views in the South Seas, from Drawings by the Late James (sic) Webber, Draftsman on Board the Resolution, Captain James Cooke (sic)... London: 1808. V. 50

WEBBER, SAMUEL
War, a Poem. Cambridge: 1823. V. 51; 52

WEBER, BRUCE
Bear Pond. 1990. V. 54
Bruce Weber. Los Angeles: 1983. V. 48; 51
Bruce Weber. New York: 1989. V. 47
Sam Shepard. New York: 1990. V. 48

WEBER, C.
A Thousand and One Fore-Edge Paintings. Waterville: 1949. V. 50

WEBER, CARL J.
Fore-edge Painting. A Historical Survey of a Curious Art in Book Decoration. Irvington-on-Hudson: 1966. V. 48; 49; 53
Fore-Edge Painting. A Historical Survey of a Curious Art in Book Decoration. London: 1966. V. 52
Thomas Hardy in Maine. Portland: 1942. V. 54
A Thousand and One Fore-Edge Paintings. Maine: 1949. V. 51
A Thousand and One Fore-Edge Paintings. Waterville: 1949. V. 48; 52

WEBER, GEORGE W.
The Ornaments of Late Chou Bronzes. New Brunswick: 1973. V. 54

WEBER, JOSEPH
Memoires Concernant Marie Antoinette, Archiduchesse d'Autriche, Reine de France... Londres: 1804-06-09. V. 51

WEBER, MAX
Cubist Poems. London: 1914. V. 49; 50; 51
Essays on Art. New York: 1916. V. 48

WEBER, SARAH STILWELL
The Musical Tree. Songs and Pictures. Philadelphia: 1925. V. 50

WEBER, WILHELM
A History of Lithography. New York: 1966. V. 53

WEBSTER, BENJAMIN
Holly Tree Inn. London: 1907?. V. 49; 54
Mrs. Sarah Gamp's Tea and Turn Out; a Bozzian Sketch, in One Act. London: 1846. V. 54

WEBSTER, C. K.
The Foreign Policy of Castereagh 1812-1822. London: 1931/34. V. 48

WEBSTER, CHARLES A.
The Diocese of Ross; Its Bishops, Clergy &c. 1936. V. 48

WEBSTER, DANIEL
Daniel Webster, On the Powers of Government Assigned to It by the Constitution. Worcester: 1952. V. 47
Discourse, Delivered at Plymouth, December 22, 1820, in Commemoration of the First Settlement of New England by... Boston: 1826. V. 49
A Discourse in Commemoration of the Lives and Services of John Adams and Thomas Jefferson, Delivered in Fanueil Hall, Boston, August 2, 1826. Boston: 1826. V. 49; 53
Mr. Webster's Address at Andover, November 9, 1843. Boston: 1843. V. 48
Mr. Webster's Address at the Laying of the Corner Stone of the Addition to the Capitol: July 4, 1851. Washington: 1851. V. 52
Mr. Webster's Speech on the Greek Revolution. Washington City: 1824. V. 52
The Private Correspondence of Daniel Webster. Boston: 1857. V. 47
The Rhode Island Question. Washington: 1848. V. 54
Speech at the National Republican Convention in Worcester, October 12, 1832. Boston: 1832. V. 50
Speech Delivered by Daniel Webster at Niblo's Saloon in New York, on the 15th of March, 1837. New York: 1837. V. 48
Speech of Daniel Webster in Reply to Mr. Hayne, of South Carolina: The Resolution of Mr. Foot, of Connecticut, Relative to the Public Lands, Under Consideration, Delivered in the Senate, January 26, 1830. Washington: 1830. V. 47
Speech of Hon. Daniel Webster, on Mr. Clay's Resolutions in the Senate of the United States, March 7, 1850. Washington: 1850. V. 48; 49
Speech of the Hon. Daniel Webster to the Young Men of Albany Wednesday, May 28, 1851. Washington: 1851. V. 52
Speech...On the Subject of Slavery...Marh 7, 1850. Boston: 1850. V. 50; 53
The Works of Daniel Webster. Boston: 1851. V. 50; 53
The Works of Daniel Webster. Boston: 1890. V. 52

WEBSTER, DAVID
The Angler and the Loop Rod. Edinburgh: 1885. V. 47

WEBSTER, EDWARD A.
An Interpretation of the Twelve Steps on the Alcoholics Anonymous Program. Minneapolis: 1946. V. 51

WEBSTER, GEORGE C.
Around the Horn in '49. Wethersfield: 1898. V. 52; 53

WEBSTER, GEORGE P.
Santa Claus and His Works. New York: 1880. V. 50

WEBSTER, GRACE
Ingliston. Edinburgh;: 1840. V. 50

WEBSTER, J. D.
Message From the President...Communicating the Report of Lieutenant Webster of a Survey of the Gulf Coast at the Mouth of the Rio Grande. Washington: 1850. V. 49

WEBSTER, J. PALMER
A Treatise on Phrenology, Embracing a Chart. Washington: 1843. V. 49

WEBSTER, JOHN
The Complete Works. London: 1927. V. 53
The Displaying of Supposed Witchcraft Wherein is Affirmed that There are Many Sorts of Deceivers and Imposters and Divers persons Under a Passive Delusion of Melancholy and Fancy. London: 1677. V. 54
The Duchess of Malfi. London: 1896. V. 47
The Duchess of Malfi. 1945. V. 53
The Duchess of Malfi. London: 1945. V. 50; 51
Elements of Mechanical and Chemical Philosophy. Taunton: 1816. V. 47
Elements of Natural Philosophy. London: 1804. V. 53
Love's Graduate. 1885. V. 52; 54
Love's Graduate. Oxford: 1885. V. 52
Metallographia: or, an History of Metals. London: 1671. V. 52; 53
The Works. London: 1830. V. 52; 54

WEBSTER, JOHN WHITE
A Description of the Island of St. Michael... Boston: 1821. V. 52; 53

WEBSTER, KIMBALL
The Gold Seekers of '49. Manchester: 1917. V. 47; 49; 52; 54

WEBSTER, LYDIA GERTRUDE HAMILTON
When Dreams Come True. 1925. V. 52

WEBSTER, NOAH
An Address to the Freemen of Connecticut. Hartford: 1803. V. 49
An American Dictionary of the English Language. New York: 1828. V. 47; 48; 49; 50; 51; 52; 54
An American Dictionary of the English Language... Springfield: 1857. V. 48; 53
The American Spelling Book. Philadelphia: 1805. V. 53
The American Spelling Book... Montreal: 1836. V. 47
A Collection of Essays and Figitive Writings. Boston: 1790. V. 47
A Compendious Dictionary of the English Language. Hartford: 1806. V. 47
A Dictionary of the English Language... London: 1831-32. V. 47
Dissertations on the English Language... Boston: 1789. V. 47; 49; 53
The Elementary Spelling Book... New Brunswick: 1840. V. 52
Elements of Useful Knowledge. Hartford: 1802. V. 52
A Grammatical Institute, of the English Language. Hartford: 1784. V. 49
A Letter to Dr. David Ramsay, of Charleston (S.C.) Respecting the Errors in Johnson's Dictionary and Other Lexicons. New Haven: 1807. V. 52
Webster's International Dictionary of the English Language. Springfield: 1903. V. 52

WEBSTER, REDFORD
Miscellaneous Remarks on the Police of Boston, as Respects Paupers; alms and Work House; Clases of Poor and Beggars... Boston: 1814. V. 52

WEBSTER, ROBERT
Gems. Their Sources, Descriptions and Identification. London: 1962. V. 49

WEBSTER, THOMAS
The American Family Encyclopedia of Useful Knowledge or Book of 4223 Receipts and Facts. New York: 1856. V. 50
An Encyclopaedia of Domestic Economy... London: 1844. V. 47
Encyclopaedia of Domestic Economy. New York: 1845. V. 47; 50
An Encyclopaedia of Domestic Economy... London: 1847. V. 49

WEBSTER, WILLIAM
Narrative of a Voyage to the Southern Atlantic Ocean, in the Years 1828, 29, 30, Performed in H. M. Sloop Chanticleer, Under the Command of the Late Capt. Henry Foster. London: 1834. V. 47; 50; 52

WEBSTER'S Third New International Dictionary of the English Language Unabridged. With Seven Language Dictionary. London: 1966. V. 51

WECHSELMANN, WILHELM
The Treatment of Syphilis with Salvarsan. New York: 1911. V. 51; 54

WEDDELL, ALEXANDER WILBOURNE
A Description of Virginia House, in Henrico County, Near Richmond, Virginia...Together with an Account of Some of the Furniture, Pictures, Curiosities... Richmond: 1947. V. 47
A Memorial Volume of Virginia Historical Portraiture, 1585-1830. Richmond: 1930. V. 54

WEDDLE, ROBERT S.
Plow-Horse Cavalry, the Canery Creek Boys of Thirty-Fourth Texas. Austin: 1974. V. 49; 54

WEDEL, GEORG WOLFGANG
Compendium Praxeos Clinicae Exemplaris Secundum Orinem Casuum Timaei a Guldenklee. Jena: 1706. V. 52

WEDELL, MRS.
The City Farce: Designed for the Theatre-Royal in Drury Lane. London: 1737. V. 47

WEDGWOOD, ALEXANDRA
A. W. N. Pugin and the Pugin Family. London: 1985. V. 50

WEDGWOOD, ETHEL KATE
Wind Along the Waste. 1902. V. 52
Wind Along the Waste. Oxford: 1902. V. 47; 53

WEDGWOOD, JOSIAH C.
The Life of Josiah Wedgwood, from His Private Correspondence and Family Papers... London: 1865. V. 50
The Life of Josiah Wedgwood from His Private Correspondence and Family Papers... London: 1865/66. V. 48
Staffordshire Pottery and its History. London: 1913. V. 49
Wedgwood's Catalogue of Cameos, Intaglios, Medals, Bas-Reliefs, Busts and Small Statues... London: 1873. V. 49

WEDGWOOD, WILLIAM B.
The Reconstruction of the Government of the United States of America... New York: 1861. V. 51; 53

WEDMORE, FREDERICK
Etchings by Frederick Wedmore. New York: 1911. V. 47
Whistler's Etchings: a Study and a Catalogue. London: 1886. V. 47

WEED, FRANK
Military Hospitals in the United States. Washington: 1923. V. 50; 52

WEED, LEWIS H.
A Reconstruction of the Nuclear Masses in the Lower Portion of the Human Brain Stem. Washington: 1914. V. 47

WEED, THOMAS A.
A Souvenir of the Trans-Continental Excursion of Railroad Agents, 1870. Albany: 1871. V. 47

WEED, WALTER HARVEY
Geology and Ore Deposits of the Butte District, Montana. Washington: 1912. V. 53

WEED, WILLIAM H.
To Texas and Back. New York: 1877. V. 52

WEEDEN, HOWARD
Bandanna Ballads Including "Shadows on the Wall". New York: 1899. V. 54
Shadows On the Wall. Huntsville: 1899. V. 49; 50
Sons of the Old South. New York: 1901. V. 48

WEEDON, GEORGE
Valley Forge Orderly Book of General George Weedon of the Continental Army Under Command of Genl. George Washington in the Campaign of 1777-78. New York: 1902. V. 47

WEEDON, L. L.
The Land of Long Ago, a Visit to Fairyland with Humpty Dumpty. London. V. 47
The Land of Long Ago: A Visit to Fairyland with Humpty Dumpty. London: 1890's. V. 54

WEEGEE
Naked City. New York: 1945. V. 49

A WEEK Away From Time. Boston: 1887. V. 48

WEEKES, HENRY
Lectures on Art, Delivered at the Royal Academy, London. London: 1880. V. 54

WEEKES, MARY
Trader King, as Told to Mary Weekes, the Thrilling Story of Forty Years' Service in the North-West Territories... Regina/Toronto: 1949. V. 50

WEEKS, A. G.
Illustrations of Diurnal Lepidoptera, with Descriptions. Boston: 1905. V. 49
Illustrations of Diurnal Lepidoptera, with Descriptions. Boston: 1905-11. V. 52
Massasoit of the Wampanoags. Fall River: 1920. V. 54

WEEKS, DONALD
T. E. Lawrence - an Hitherto Unknown Biographical bibliographical Note. Edinburgh: 1983. V. 53
T. E. Lawrence: an Hitherto Unknown Biographical/Bibliographical Note. London: 1983. V. 53

WEEKS, EDWARD P.
A Treatise on the Law of Depositions (etc.). San Francisco: 1880. V. 51

WEEKS, STEPHEN B.
Southern Quakers and Slavery: a Study in Institutional History. Baltimore: 1896. V. 52
The University of North Carolina in the Civil War. Richmond: 1896. V. 49

WEEMS, MASON LOCKE
The Bad Wife's Looking Glass or God's Revenge Against Cruelty to Husbands. Charleston: 1823. V. 50
The Drunkard's Looking Glass... Philadelphia: 1818. V. 50
God's Revenge Against Adultery, Awfully Exemplified in the Following Cases of American Crim. Con. 1. The Accomplished Dr. Theodore Wilson (Delaware)...2. The Elegant James O'Neale, Esq.... Philadelphia: 1816. V. 50
God's Revenge Against Duelling, or the Duelist's Looking Glass... Philadelphia: 1821. V. 50
God's Revenge Against Gambling. Philadelphia: 1822. V. 48; 50
God's Revenge Against Murder... Philadelphia: 1808. V. 53
God's Revenge Against Murder... Philadelphia: 1823. V. 50

WEEMS, MASON LOCKE continued
Hymen's Recruiting-Sergeant; or the New Matrimonial Tat-Too, for Old Bachelors. Hartford: 1823. V. 47
Das Leben des Georg Waschington. Lebanon: 1810. V. 53; 54
The Life of George Washington. Knoxville: 1842. V. 47
The Philanthropist; or, a Good Twenty-Five Cents Worth of Political Love Powder, for Honest Adamites and Jeffersonians. Dumfries: 1799. V. 53

WEETHE, J. P.
The Battle of Armageddon; or, the World of God Against the World. Boston: 1849. V. 47

WEEVER, JOHN
Ancient Funeral Monuments...Great Britain, Ireland and the Islands Adjacent... London: 1631. V. 49; 51; 52; 53; 54
Ancient Funeral Monuments...Great Britian, Ireland and the Islands Adjacent. London: 1767. V. 53

WEGELIN, OSCAR
Early American Poetry. New York: 1930. V. 50

WEGENER, ELSE
Greenland Journey, the Story of Wegener's German Expedition to Greenland in 1930-31... London & Glasgow: 1939. V. 50

WEGERT, FRIEDRICH
Die Farbe Als Stimmungselement. Munich: 1929. V. 47

WEGLIN, OSCAR
Micah Hawkins and the Saw-Mill. New York: 1917. V. 49

WEGMAN, WILLIAM
ABC. New York: 1964. V. 52
The Making of Little Red. N.P: 1993. V. 49

WEGMANN, EDWARD
The Design and Construction of Dams, Including Masonry, Earth, Rock-Fill & Timber Structures... 1904. V. 51

WEHMAN Bros.: How to Box and Gymnastics Without a Teacher. New York: 1890. V. 47

WEHMAN'S New Book of Tricks & Ventriloquist's Guide. New York: 1889. V. 47

WEIBERT, DON
Custer, Cases and Cartridges. The Weibert Collection Analyzed. Billings: 1989. V. 51

WEICHARDT, K.
Die Vereinigten Staaten von Nord-Amerika... Captain J. C. Fremont's Reisen nach dem Felsengebirge, Oregon und Nord-Californien in den Jahren 1842-1844. Leipzig: 1848. V. 47; 50

WEIDENMANN, J.
Beautifying Country Homes. New York: 1870. V. 50; 51

WEIDLER, JOHANN FREIDRICH
Historia Astronomiae Sive de Ortu et Progressu Astronomiae. Wittenberg: 1741. V. 47

WEIDMAN, JEROME
I Can Get It For You Wholesale. New York: 1927. V. 49
I Can Get It for You Wholesale. New York: 1937. V. 47; 48; 50

WEID-NEUWIED, ALEXANDER PHILIPP MAXIMILIAN, PRINZ VON
Travels in Brazil in 1815, 1816, 1817. London: 1820. V. 53

WEIERMAIR, PETER
The Hidden Image. Photographs of the Male Nude in the Nineteenth and Twentieth Centuries. Cambridge/London: 1988. V. 54

WEIGALL, ARTHUR
Ancient Egyptian Works of Art. London: 1924. V. 53

WEIGEL, CHRISTOPH
Celebriores Veteris Testamenti Iconibus Repraesentatae et Selectis Epigrammatibus Exornatae in Lucem Olim Datae (and) Historiae Celebriores Novi Testamenti. Noribergae: 1712. V. 48

WEIGELIUS, VALENTINE
Astrology Theologized: Wherein is Set Forth What Astrologie, and the Light of Nature Is. London: 1797. V. 47

WEIGHT, CAREL
The Curious Captain, War Artist 1939-1945: Letters to Helen Roeder. 1989. V. 52

WEIGHTMAN, R. H.
To the Congress of the United States...Requesting the Passage of a Bill Declaring New Mexico One of the United States of America on Certain Conditions. Washington: 1851. V. 52

WEIGL, BRUCE
The Giver of Morning: On the Poetry of Dave Smith. Birmingham: 1982. V. 51

WEIHE, A.
Die Deutschten Brombeerstrauche (Rubi Germanici). Elberfeld: 1822-27. V. 48; 49; 50

WEIK, JOHANN
Californien Wie Es Ist oder Handbuch von Californien, mit Besonderer Berssucksichtigung fur Auswanderer. Philadelphia und Leipzig: 1849. V. 47; 48; 49

WEIL, ERNST
Albert Einstein 14th March 1879 (Ulm)-18th April, 1955. (Princeton, N.J.) A Bibliography of His Scientific Papers. 1901-1954. London: 1960. V. 51
The Collected Catalogues... Mansfield: 1995. V. 54

WEIL, SIMONE
The Iliad or the Poem of Force. Iowa City: 1973. V. 54

WEILER, MILTON C.
Classic Shorebird Decoys. New York: 1971. V. 47; 50; 51

WEIMANN, CHRISTOPHER
Marbled Papers. Los Angeles: 1978. V. 51

WEIMANN, INGRID
Christopher Weinmann (1946-1988): a Tribute. Tubingen: 1991. V. 47

WEINBAUM, STANLEY
Dawn of Flame and Other Stories. 1936. V. 49
A Martian Odyssey and Others. Reading: 1949. V. 49
The New Adam. 1939. V. 49
The Red Peri. 1952. V. 49; 54

WEINBERG, MARTIN
Homosexuality: an Annotated Bibliography. New York: 1972. V. 50

WEINBERG, SAUL S.
Corinth. Volume I. Part V: The Southeast Building and Twin Basilicas, the Mosaic House. Princeton: 1960. V. 52

WEINBERGER, BERNHARD W.
Orthodontics an Historical Review of Its Origin and Evolution Including an Extensive Bibliography of Orthodontic Literature... St. Louis: 1926. V. 54
Pierre Fauchard, Surgeon-Dentist... Minneapolis: 1941. V. 50

WEINBERGER, MARTIN
Michelangelo the Sculptor. London & New York: 1967. V. 47; 48; 53

WEINTHAL, LEO
The Story of the Cape to Cairo Railway and River Route from 1887 to 1922. London: 1923-24. V. 54

WEIR, HARRISON
The Camel. London: 1850. V. 47
The Cow. London: 1850. V. 47
The Horse. London: 1850. V. 47
The Sheep. London: 1850. V. 47

WEIR, L. H.
Parks, a Manual of Municipal and County Parks Compiled as a Result of a Nation-Wide Study of Municipal and County Parks Conducted by the Playground and Recreation Association of America. New York: 1928. V. 47

WEIR, R. W.
The History of the 3rd Batt. King's Own Scottish Borderers, 1798-1907. Dumffies: 1907. V. 48

WEIR, ROBERT
Uncle Samuel's Whistle; and What It Costs. A Tale. New York: 1864. V. 51

WEIRD Science. 1979. V. 47

WEIRD Tales, English (Scottish: Irish; American, German). London & Edinburgh: 1890. V. 48

WEIRD Tales for Spring. 1988. V. 49

WEISBORD, ALBERT
The Conquest of Power. New York: 1937. V. 51

WEISMANN, AUGUST
Essays Upon Heredity and Kindred Biological problems. Oxford: 1889. V. 52; 53
Essays Upon Heredity and Kindred Biological Problems. Oxford: 1891. V. 54
Essays Upon Heredity and Kindred Biological Problems. London: 1891-92. V. 49; 54
The Evolution Theory. London: 1904. V. 49
The Germ-Plasm: a Theory of Heredity. London: 1893. V. 49
The Germ-Plasm. A Theory of Heredity. New York: 1893. V. 49
Studies in the Theory of Descent. London: 1882. V. 48

WEISS, DIANNE
A Carrousel. Mill Valley. V. 51

WEISS, H. B.
Thomas Say, Early American Naturalist. Springfield: 1931. V. 53

WEISS, JOSEPH
The Hand Book of Hydropathy; for Professional and Domestic Use... London: 1844. V. 47

WEISS, PETER
Bodies and Shadows. New York: 1969. V. 54
The Persecution and Assassination of Jean Paul Marat as Peformed by the Inmates of the Asylum of Charenton Under the Direction of the Marquis de Sade. New York: 1965. V. 54

WEISS, SAMUEL
Diseases of the Liver, Gall Bladder, Ducts and Pancreas. New York: 1935. V. 54

WEISS, SUSAN ARCHER
Home Life of Poe. New York: 1907. V. 48

WEISSE, FRANZ
The Art of Marbling. North Hills: 1980. V. 48; 54

WEISSENBORN, HELLMUTH
A B C of Names: From Antiquity to the Present. London: 1980. V. 48
Hellmuth Weissenborn, Engraver. Andoversford: 1983. V. 49; 51
Hellmuth Weissenborn, Engraver. London: 1983. V. 48; 50; 53

WEISSENBORN, HELLMUTH continued
Painter and Graphic Artist. Andoversford: 1976. V. 51

WEIST, JACOB R.
The Medical Department in the War. Cincinnati: 1886. V. 51

WEITENKAMPF, FRANK
The Illustrated Book. Cambridge: 1938. V. 49; 53
The Illustrated Book. Chicago: 1938. V. 50

WEITZMANN, KURT
Age of Spirituality: Late Antique and Early Christina Art, Third to Seventh Century. New York: 1979. V. 52

WELBORN, MARY ETHEL
History - Zonta Club of Dallas 1924-1961. Dallas: 1961. V. 47

WELBY, HORACE
Signs Before Death and Authenticated Apparitions... London: 1825. V. 51

WELBY, J. E.
Memoirs of the Belvoir Hounds. Grantham, Lincs: 1867. V. 47

WELBY, T. EARLE
The Victorian Romantics, 1850-70. London: 1929. V. 49; 50; 54

WELCH, ANDREW
A Narrative of the Early Days and Remembrances of Oceola Nikkanochee, Prince of Econchatti, a Young Seminole Indian... London: 1841. V. 47

WELCH, CHARLES
History of the Cutlers' Company of London and of the Minor Cutlery Crafts. London: 1916/23. V. 47
History of the Tower Bridge and of Other Bridges Over the Thames Built by the Corporation of London. London: 1894. V. 51
History of the Worshipful Company of Paviors of the City of London. London: 1909. V. 47; 49

WELCH, CHARLES A.
History of the Big Basin. Deseret: 1940. V. 51

WELCH, DENTON
Brave and Cruel. London: 1948. V. 47; 48; 53
I Left My Grandfather's House. 1958. V. 49; 52
I Left My Grandfather's House. London: 1958. V. 48; 50; 51; 52; 53
In Youth is Pleasure. London: 1944. V. 47; 50; 53; 54
A Last Sheaf. London: 1951. V. 53; 54
The Loved One. London: 1948. V. 53
A Lunch Appointment. 1993. V. 52; 53
A Lunch Appointment. North Pomfret: 1993. V. 51; 52
A Lunch Appointment. Vermont: 1993. V. 49
A Lunch Appointment. North Pomfret: 1994. V. 51
Maiden Voyage. 1943. V. 49
Maiden Voyage. London: 1943. V. 47; 53
A Voice through a Cloud. London: 1950. V. 48; 53

WELCH, JAMES
Fools Crow. New York: 1986. V. 51; 52; 53
Riding the Earthboy 40... 1971. V. 48; 49
Riding the Earthboy 40. New York and Cleveland: 1971. V. 50; 51; 52; 53; 54
Riding the Earthboy 40. New York: 1976. V. 51
Winter in the Blood. New York: 1974. V. 50; 52; 53
Winter in the Blood. New York: 1975. V. 51; 52; 54

WELCH, JOSEPH
A List of Scholars at St. Peter's College, Westminster, As They Were Selected to Christ Church College, Oxford, and Trinity College, Cambridge... London: 1788. V. 47; 49; 50; 52; 53

WELCH, ORRIN
Knights Templars' Tactics and Drill for the Use of Commanderies, and the Burial, Service of the Orders of Masonic Knighthood. New York: 1872. V. 52

WELCH, S. L.
Southern California Illustrated, Containing an Epitome of the Growth and Industry of the Three Southern Counties. Los Angeles: 1886-87. V. 52

WELCH, SPENCER GLASGOW
A Confederate Surgeon's Letters to His Wife. New York & Washington: 1911. V. 49

WELCH, WILLIAM HENRY
Contributions to the Science of Medicine Dedicated by His Pupils on the Twenty-Fifth Anniversary of His Doctorate. Baltimore: 1900. V. 54
Papers and Addresses. Baltimore: 1920. V. 48; 50; 51; 52; 54

WELCOME to Charles Dickens. The Boz Ball. To Be Given Under the Direction of a Committee of Citizens of New York, at the Park Theatre, on the Evening of the Fourteenth of February Next. New York: 1842. V. 50

WELD, CHARLES RICHARD
A History of the Royal Society, with Memoirs of the Presidents. London: 1848. V. 47; 49; 51; 52

WELD, EDWARD F.
The Ransomed Bride: a Tale of the Inquisition. New York: 1846. V. 49; 52

WELD, ISAAC
Illustrations of the Scenery of Killarney and the Surrounding Country. London: 1807. V. 48; 50; 51
Travels through the States of North America and the Provinces of... London: 1799. V. 47; 48; 49; 50; 54
Travels through the States of North America, and the Provinces of... London: 1800. V. 54
Travels through the States of North America and the Provinces of... London: 1807. V. 47; 53; 54

WELDON, ANTHONY
A Brief History of the Kings of England, Particularly Those of the Royal House of Stuart, of Blessed Memory. London: 1755. V. 53
History of the Court and Character of King James I, and of the Intrigues & Tragical Events of His Reign. London: 1817. V. 48
A Perfect Description of the People and Country of Scotland. London: 1649. V. 49

WELFORD, RICHARD
History of Newcastle and Gateshead. London: 1884-87. V. 48; 53

WELFORD, RICHARD GRIFFITHS
The Influences of the Game Laws... London: 1846. V. 51; 52; 54

WELL Dressed Lines. Stripped from the Reels of Five New Englanders. New York: 1962. V. 47; 52

WELLBELOVED, C.
Account of St. Mary's Abbey, York. London: 1829. V. 48; 53

WELLBELOVED, ROBERT
A Treatise On the Law Relating to Highways... London: 1829. V. 51

WELLBY, M. S.
Twixt Sirdar & Menelik. London: 1901. V. 54

WELLCOME HISTORICAL MEDICAL LIBRARY
A Catalogue of Arabic Manuscripts on Medicine and Science in the Wellcome Historical Medical Library. London: 1967. V. 50
A Catalogue of Printed Books in the Wellcome Historical Medical Library. London: 1962-66. V. 50
A Catalogue of Printed Books in the Wellcome Historical Medical Library. 1962-76. V. 50; 51; 52; 54
Catalogue of Western Manuscripts on Medicine and Science in the Wellcome Historical Medical Library. London: 1962-73. V. 50

WELLEK, RENE
Concepts of Criticism. New Haven and London: 1963. V. 52
The Criticism of T. S. Eliot. 1956. V. 54
A History of Modern Criticism. London: 1955-66. V. 51

WELLENS, H. J. J.
Electrical Stimulation in the Heart in the Study and Treatment of Tachycardias. Baltimore: 1971. V. 54

WELLER, S. ALLEN
Art USA Now. Switzerland & New York: 1962. V. 47

WELLER, SAMUEL
The Trial of Mr. Whitefield's Spirit. London: 1741. V. 51

WELLES, C. M.
Three Years' Wanderings of a Connecticut Yankee in South-America, Africa, Australia and California. New York: 1859. V. 49; 51; 53

WELLESLEY, DOROTHY
Desert Wells. London: 1946. V. 53
Early Poems. London: 1913. V. 48
Jupiter and the Nun. London: 1932. V. 48; 53
Lost Planet and Other Poems. London: 1942. V. 53
The Poets and Other Poems. 1943. V. 53
Rhymes for Middle Years. London: 1954. V. 53
Selections from the Poems. London: 1936. V. 49; 53

WELLESLEY, RICHARD COLLEY, MARQUIS
Memoirs and Correspondence of Richard Marquess Wellesley. London: 1846. V. 47
Primitiae et Reliquiae. London: 1840. V. 48

WELLESLEY, WILLIAM LONG
A View of the Court of Chancery. London: 1830. V. 51

WELLINGTON, ARTHUR WELLESLEY, 1ST DUKE OF
Primitiae et Reliquiae. London: 1841. V. 49; 54
A Selection from the Private Correspondence of the First Duke of Wellington. London: 1952. V. 48
The Speeches of the Duke of Wellington in Parliament. London: 1854. V. 54

WELLMAN, JOHN
Opera Brevis, a Play. Boston: 1977. V. 52; 54

WELLMAN, M.
Who Fears the Devil. Sauk City: 1963. V. 47; 51

WELLMAN, MANLY WADE
Lonely Vigils. Chapel Hill: 1981. V. 52
Worse Things Waiting. Chapel Hill: 1973. V. 52

WELLMAN, PAUL ISELIN
Death in the Desert: the Fifty Years' War for the Great Southwest. New York: 1935. V. 47

WELLS, CAROLYN
The Merry-Go-Round. New York: 1901. V. 49

WELLS, CATHERINE
The Book of Catherine Wells. London: 1928. V. 48

WELLS, CATHERINE continued
The Book of Catherine Wells. New York: 1928. V. 49

WELLS, CHARLES JEREMIAH
Stories From Nature. London: 1822. V. 47

WELLS, CHARLES KNOX POLK
Life and Adventures of Polk Wells, the Notorious Outlaw. Halls: 1907. V. 49

WELLS, DAVID A.
How Much Carriage Building Is Helped by the Present Tariff. Wilmington: 1884. V. 47

WELLS, EDWARD
The Young Gentleman's Astronomy, Chronology and Dialling. London: 1712. V. 51

WELLS, EDWARD LAIGHT
Hampton and His Cavalry in '64. Richmond: 1899. V. 53
A Sketch of the Charleston Light Dragoons from the Earliest Information of the Corps. Charleston: 1888. V. 49

WELLS, F. E.
The Marine Flora and Fauna of Albany, Western Australia. Leiden: 1990-91. V. 50

WELLS, GABRIEL
Edgar Allan Poe as a Mystic. Metuchen: 1934. V. 52

WELLS, H. GIDEON
The Chemical Aspects of Immunity. New York: 1925. V. 51; 54

WELLS, HENRY P.
Fly-rods and Fly-Tackle Suggestions as to Their Manufacture and Use. New York: 1885. V. 51

WELLS, HERBERT GEORGE
The Adventures of Tommy. London: 1929. V. 48; 52
All Aboard for Ararat. London: 1940. V. 53
Ann Veronica. London: 1909. V. 51; 53
Ann Veronica. New York: 1909. V. 50
Anticipations of the Reaction of Mechanical and Scientific Progress Upon Human Life and Thought. London: 1902. V. 48; 49; 52; 53
Apropos of Dolores. London: 1938. V. 53; 54
The Autocracy of Mr. Parkham. London: 1930. V. 48; 51; 53
Boon, the Mind of the Race, the Wild Asses of the Devil, and the Last Trump. New York: 1915. V. 53; 54
The Brothers. London: 1938. V. 54
Brothers. New York: 1938. V. 53
Certain Personal Matters. London: 1898. V. 47
The Country of the Blind... 1911. V. 52; 53
The Country of the Blind. London: 1939. V. 50; 53
The Country of the Blind. Waltham St. Lawrence: 1939. V. 47; 50
The Desert Daisy. USA: 1957. V. 53
The Door in the Wall. New York & London: 1911. V. 48; 50
The Door in the Wall. London: 1915. V. 54
The Dream. New York: 1924. V. 49
An Englishman Looks at the World, being a Series of Unrestrained Remarks Upon contemporary Matters. London: 1914. V. 49
Experiment in Autobiography. 1934. V. 49
Experiment in Autobiography. New York: 1934. V. 54
The First Men in the Moon. London: 1901. V. 47; 48; 49; 51; 54
Floor Games. London: 1911. V. 48
The Food of the Gods. New York: 1904. V. 48
The History of Mr. Polly. London: 1910. V. 49; 50; 51
In the Days of the Comet. New York: 1906. V. 48; 50; 51
The Invisible Man. 1897. V. 47
The Invisible Man. London: 1897. V. 50; 51; 52; 53; 54
The Invisible Man. New York: 1897. V. 54
The Invisible Man. New York: 1967. V. 48; 50; 51; 52; 54
The Island of Dr. Moreau. 1896. V. 48
The Island of Dr. Moreau. Chicago: 1896. V. 52
The Island of Dr. Moreau. London: 1896. V. 47; 48; 50; 51; 52
The Island of Doctor Moreau... New York: 1896. V. 53
The King Who Was a King. London: 1929. V. 48; 49; 51
Mankind in the Making. London: 1903. V. 48
Meanwhile - the Picture of a Lady. London: 1927. V. 48
Meanwhile (The Picture of a Lady). New York: 1927. V. 50
Men Like Gods. 1923. V. 47
Men Like Gods. London: 1923. V. 48; 50; 51; 53
Mr. Blettsworthy on Rampole Island. London: 1928. V. 48; 49; 50; 51; 54
New America: the New World. London: 1935. V. 53
The Outline of History. London: 1919-20. V. 48; 51; 53
The Outlook for Homo Sapiens... London: 1942. V. 52; 53
The Passionate Friends, a Novel. London: 1913. V. 48
Phoenix - a Summary of the Inescapable Conditions of World Reorganisation. London: 1942. V. 52
The Plattner Story and Others. London: 1897. V. 48
Russia in the Shadows. London: 1920. V. 47
Russia in the Shadows. New York: 1921. V. 48
The Science of Life. 1931. V. 48
The Science of Life. Garden City: 1931. V. 50; 52
The Science of Life. New York: 1931. V. 47; 51; 52
The Sea Lady. New York: 1902. V. 52
The Secret Places of the Heart. London: 1922. V. 48; 50; 51
Select Conversations with an Uncle. 1895. V. 47; 51
Select Conversations with an Uncle. London: 1895. V. 49; 53; 54
Select Conversations With an Uncle. New York: 1895. V. 48
Select Conversations with an Uncle. 1900. V. 49; 54
The Shape of Things to come - The Ultimate Revolution. London: 1933. V. 47
The Soul of A Bishop. London: 1917. V. 54
The Soul of a Bishop. New York: 1917. V. 54
The Stolen Bacillus. London: 1895. V. 48; 52; 53
Stories of Men and Women in Love... London: 1933. V. 54
Tales of Life and Adventure. 1923. V. 53
Tales of Life and Adventure. London: 1923. V. 52
Tales of Space and Time. New York: 1899. V. 52
Tales of Space and Time. 1900. V. 48; 52
Tales of Space and Time. London: 1900. V. 48; 53
The Time Machine. London: 1895. V. 47; 48; 49; 50; 52; 53
The Time Machine... New York: 1931. V. 52
The Time Machine... New York: 1964. V. 53
Tono-Bungay. London: 1909. V. 50
Twelve Stories and a Dream. 1903. V. 52
Twelve Stories and a Dream. London: 1903. V. 53
The Undying Fire. London: 1919. V. 49; 51
The Undying Fire. New York: 1919. V. 48; 51; 54
University of London Election (an Electoral Address). London: 1922. V. 50
War and the Future - Italy, France and Britain at War. London: 1917. V. 48
The War in the Air... London: 1908. V. 48; 50; 53
The War in the Air. New York: 1908. V. 53; 54
The War of the Worlds. London: 1898. V. 48; 49; 51; 52; 53; 54
The War of the Worlds... New York: 1964. V. 48; 51; 53
The Wheels of Chance. 1896. V. 53
The Wheels of Chance. London: 1896. V. 49
The Wheels of Chance. New York: 1896. V. 54
When the Sleeper Wakes. New York & London: 1899. V. 48; 50; 51; 52; 53; 54
When the Sleeper Wakes. 1900. V. 48
The Wonderful Visit. London: 1895. V. 47; 49; 51; 52; 53; 54
The Work, Wealth and Happiness of Mankind. New York: 1931. V. 51
Works. London: 1924. V. 49
The Works. London: 1924-27. V. 49; 52
The World of William Clissold. London: 1926. V. 51; 53
The World Set Free. 1914. V. 49; 51; 52; 53; 54
The World Set Free. New York: 1914. V. 47

WELLS, J. E.
Life and Labors of Robert Alex. Fyfe, D.D., Founder and for Many Years Principal of the Canadian Literary Institute. Toronto: 1885. V. 47

WELLS, JAMES W.
Exploring and Travelling Three Thousand Miles through Brazil from Rio de Janeiro to Maranhao... London: 1886. V. 49
Exploring and Travelling Three Thousand Miles Through Brazil, from Rio de Janeiro to Maranhao. London: 1887. V. 49
With Touch of Elbow or Death Before Dishonor. Philadelphia: 1909. V. 47; 49

WELLS, JOHN G.
Wells' Pocket Hand-Book of Iowa; Past, Present and Prospective. New York: 1857. V. 50; 52

WELLS, JOHN SOELBERG
A Treatise on the Diseases of the Eye... Philadelphia: 1873. V. 47
A Treatise on the Diseases of the Eye. Philadelphia: 1880. V. 47
A Treatise on the Diseases of the Eye. Philadelphia: 1883. V. 47

WELLS, NATHANIEL ARMSTRONG
The Picturesque Antiquities of Spain... London: 1846. V. 48; 53

WELLS, OLIVER
An Anthology of the Younger Poets. Philadelphia: 1932. V. 47; 49; 53

WELLS, POLK
Life and Adventures of Polk Wells... 1907. V. 48; 52

WELLS, ROBERT
A Correspondence Between the Rev. Robert Wells, M.A. Chaplain to the Earl of Dunmore, and a Gentleman Under the Signature of Publicola Relative to the Riots at Birmingham... London: 1791. V. 47
The Pastry Cook and Confectioner's Guide for Hotels, Restaurants, and the Trade in General, Adapted Also for Family Use Including a Large Variety of Modern Recipes. London: 1889. V. 50

WELLS, ROLLA
Episodes of My Life. St. Louis: 1933. V. 48

WELLS, S. Y.
Testimonies Concerning the Character and Ministry of Mother Ann Lee and the First Witnesses of the Gospel of Christ's Second Appearing; give by some of the Aged Brethern and Sisters of the United Society. Albany: 1827. V. 52

WELLS, THOMAS SPENCER
Surgery Past, Present and Future and Excessive Mortality After Surgical Operations. London: 1877. V. 48

WELLS, WILLIAM CHARLES
An Essay on Dew, and Several Appearances Connected With It. London: 1814. V. 47; 48; 49; 50; 51; 54

WELLS, WILLIAM CHARLES continued
An Essay on Dew, and Several Appearances Connected With It. Philadelphia: 1838. V. 48; 50
Two Essays: One Upon single Vision with two Eyes; the Other on Dew. Edinburgh: 1818. V. 51; 52

WELLS, WILLIAM V.
Explorations and Adventures in Honduras, Comprising Sketches of Travel in the Gold Regions of Olancho and a Review of the History and General Resources of Central America... New York: 1857. V. 49

WELLS-BARNETT, IDA B.
Lynch Law in Georgia. Chicago: 1899. V. 48; 49

WELSER, MARCUS
Antiqua Monumenta: Das ist alte Bilder Gemahlde unnd Schriften... Frankfurt am Main: 1595. V. 49

WELSH, JAMES
Military Reminiscences... London: 1830. V. 50

WELSH, WILLIAM
Taopi and His Friends, or the Indians Wrongs and Rights. Philadelphia: 1869. V. 48

WELSTED, LEONARD
Epistles, Odes &c. London: 1724. V. 49; 52; 54

WELTY, EUDORA
Acrobats in a Park. 1977. V. 52; 53
Acrobats in a Park. Northridge: 1980. V. 48; 50; 51; 53
The Bride of Innisfallen. 1955. V. 50; 53
The Bride of Innisfallen... London: 1955. V. 54
The Bride of Innisfallen. New York: 1955. V. 47; 48; 49; 50; 51; 52; 53; 54
Bye-Bye Brevoort. Jackson: 1980. V. 47; 48; 49; 51; 53
The Collected Stories... New York, London: 1980. V. 47; 48; 50; 51; 52
A Curtain of Green. Garden City: 1941. V. 53; 54
A Curtain of Green. New York: 1941. V. 51
Delta Wedding. New York: 1946. V. 47; 48; 50; 51; 52; 53; 54
Eudora Welty Photographs. Jackson: 1989. V. 47
The Eye of the Story. New York: 1977. V. 47; 51; 53
The Eye of the Story. New York: 1978. V. 53
Fairy Tale of the Natchez Trace. Jackson: 1975. V. 48; 49
A Flock of Guinea Hens Seen From a Car. New York: 1970. V. 51
Four Photographs. Northridge: 1984. V. 47
The Golden Apples. New York: 1949. V. 47; 48; 49; 51; 53; 54
Henry Green: a Novelist of the Imagination. 1961. V. 52
Henry Green: a Novelist of the Imagination. Austin: 1961. V. 53
Ida M'Toy. Urbana: 1979. V. 48; 51
In Black and White. Northridge: 1985. V. 49; 50; 53
The Key. Garden City: 1941. V. 53
The Little Store. Newton: 1985. V. 49; 52
Losing Battles. New York: 1970. V. 47; 48; 49; 50; 52; 53
Morgana. Jackson and London: 1988. V. 47; 48; 53; 54
Music from Spain. Greenville: 1948. V. 48; 49; 53
On Short Stories. New York: 1949. V. 47; 50; 53
One Time, One Place. New York: 1971. V. 49; 50; 52; 53
One Time, One Place... Jackson: 1996. V. 54
One Writer's Beginning. V. 53
One Writer's Beginning. Cambridge: 1984. V. 47; 48; 49; 50; 51; 52; 54
One Writer's Beginning. Cambridge: 1989. V. 53
The Optimist's Daughter. New York: 1972. V. 47; 49; 50; 53
The Optimist's Daughter. 1980. V. 47; 49; 50
The Optimist's Daughter. Franklin Center: 1980. V. 49
A Pageant of Birds. New York: 1974. V. 47; 48; 50; 52; 53; 54
Photographs. London & Jackson: 1989. V. 47; 48; 49; 50; 51; 52; 53
Place in Fiction. New York: 1957. V. 49; 51; 52; 53; 54
The Ponder Heart. New York: 1954. V. 48; 49; 50; 51; 52; 53
The Ponder Heart. New York: 1956. V. 48
Primo Amore. Milano: 1947. V. 52
Retreat. 1981. V. 47; 49; 51; 52; 53
Retreat. Winston Salem: 1981. V. 48; 53
The Robber Bridegroom. Garden City: 1942. V. 47; 50; 51; 52; 53; 54
The Robber Bridegroom. New York: 1942. V. 51
The Robber Bridegroom. 1987. V. 52; 54
The Robber Bridegroom. West Hatfield: 1987. V. 48
Selected Stories. New York: 1954. V. 50
The Shoe Bird. New York: 1964. V. 47; 48; 50; 52; 53; 54
Short Stories. New York: 1949. V. 51; 53
Short Stories. New York: 1950. V. 51
Some Notes on Time in Fiction. Jackson: 1973. V. 52; 53
Three Papers on Fiction. Northampton: 1962. V. 47; 52; 53
White Fruitcake. New York: 1980. V. 52
The Wide Net. New York: 1943. V. 47; 48; 49; 50; 51; 53; 54
The Wide Net... London: 1945. V. 53
Women! Make Turban in Own Home. 1979. V. 51
Women! Make Turban in Own Home. Winston Salem: 1979. V. 48

WELWITSCH, F.
Catalogue of the African Plants Collected in 1853-61. London: 1896-1901. V. 54

WELWOOD, JAMES
Memoirs of the Most Material Transactions in England, for the Last Hundred Years, Preceding the Revolution in 1688. Glasgow: 1749. V. 50
Memoirs of the Most Material Transactions in England, for the Last Hundred Years, Preceding the Revolution in 1688. London: 1700. V. 47; 50; 53

WEMBER, PAUL
Miro - the Graphic Work. 1957. V. 54
Miro - The Graphic Work. Krefeld: 1957. V. 50

WEMYSS, FRANCIS COURTNEY
Theatrical Biography, or the Life of an Actor and Manager. Glasgow: 1848. V. 53

WENIG, BERNHARD
Ex Libris. Berlin: 1902. V. 54

WENTWORTH, D'ARCY
Nursery Nonsense or Rhymes Without Reason. London: 1865. V. 48

WENTWORTH, FRANK L.
Aspen on the Roaring Fork. Lakewood: 1950. V. 50
A Silver Baron. Boston: 1896. V. 54

WENTWORTH, JUDITH ANNE DOROTHEA WENTWORTH BLUNT-LYTTON
The Authentic Arabian Horse... London: 1945. V. 47; 53
The Authentic Arabian Horse. London: 1962. V. 51
The Authentic Arabian Horse. New York: 1963. V. 49
Drift of the Storm. Oxford: 1951. V. 51
Thoroughbred Racing Stock and Its Ancestors. New York: 1938. V. 48
Thoroughbred Racing Stock and Its Ancestors. London: 1960. V. 54
Thoroughbred Racing Stock and its Ancestors. New York: 1962. V. 47; 49

WENTZ, ROBY
The Grabhorn Press. San Francisco: 1981. V. 47; 51; 53

WEPFER, JOHANNES
Observationes Medico-Practicae, De Affectibvs Capitis Internis & Externis. 1727. V. 53
Observationes Medico-Practicae, De Affectibvs Capitis Internis & Externis. Ziegleri: 1727. V. 47; 48

WERDMUELLER, OTTO
A Spiritual and Most Precious Perle, Teachynge All Men to Love and Imbrace Ye Crosse... London: 1555?. V. 50

WERENFELS, SAMUEL
A Dissertation Upon Superstition in Natural Things, Which are Added, Occasional Thoughts on the Power of Curing the King's-Evil... London: 1748. V. 48

WERFEL, FRANZ
The Forty Days of Musa Dagh. New York: 1934. V. 52
Hearken Unto the Voice. New York: 1938. V. 52
The Pascarella Family. New York: 1935. V. 52
Poems. Princeton: 1945. V. 52
The Song of Bernadette. New York: 1942. V. 52; 53
The Twilight of a World. New York: 1937. V. 52
Verdi. New York: 1926. V. 52

WERNE, FERDINAND
Expedition to Discover the Sources of the White Nile, in the Years 1840, 1841... London: 1849. V. 54

WERNER, A.
The Natives of British Central Africa. London: 1906. V. 47

WERNER, ALFRED
New Ideas on Inorganic Chemistry. New York, Bombay: 1911. V. 50

WERNER, ALLEN S.
Art USA Now. Lucerne: 1962. V. 53

WERNER, ARNO
One Man's Work: a Lecture. Easthampton. V. 52
One Man's Work: a Lecture. Easthampton: 1982. V. 53; 54

WERNER, CARL
Nile Sketches, Painted from Nature During His Travels Through Egypt. Wandsbec: 1871-75. V. 47
Nile Sketches, Painted from Nature During Travels through Egypt. London: 1871-75. V. 52

WERNER, CHARLES J.
Eric Mullica and His Descendants. New Gretna: 1930. V. 49; 51

WERNER, HELMUT
From the Aratus Globe to the Zeiss Planetarium. Stuttgart: 1957/53. V. 48

WERNER, J. R.
A Visit to Stanley's Rear-Guard at Major Barttelot's Camp on the Aruhwimi... 1889. V. 47
A Visit to Stanley's Rear-Guard at Major Barttelot's Camp on the Aruhwimi... Edinburgh: 1889. V. 47
A Visit to Stanley's Rear-Guard at Major Barttelot's Camp on the Aruhwimi. London: 1889. V. 48

WERTENBAKER, THOMAS JEFFERSON
The Planters of Colonial Virginia. Princeton: 1922. V. 47

WERTHAM, FREDRIC
Seduction of the Innocent. New York: 1954. V. 49

WERTHEIM, BARBARA
The Lost British Policy. Britain and Spain Since 1700. London: 1938. V. 49

WERTHEIM, CHEVALIER FRANCOIS DE
Manuel de l'Outillage des Arts et Metiers... Vienna: 1869. V. 49; 53

WERTHEIMER, JOHN
The Law Relating to Clubs. London: 1885. V. 48

WESCHER, HERTA
Collage. New York: 1968. V. 48; 50; 51; 53; 54
Collage. New York: 1979. V. 52

WESCHER, P.
Jean Fouquet and His Time. Basle: 1947. V. 50

WESCOTT, GLENWAY
The Babe's Bed. Paris: 1930. V. 49; 51; 52; 54
A Calendar of Saints for Unbelievers. Paris: 1932. V. 47
Good-Bye Wisconsin. New York & London: 1928. V. 48; 52
Images of Truth: Remembrances and Criticism. New York: 1962. V. 54

WESKER, ARNOLD
Six Sundays in January. Helsinki: 1990. V. 48

WESLEY, CHARLES
Gloria Patri, &c. or Hymns to the Trinty. Bristol: 1764. V. 53
Hymns for Those That Seek and Those That Have Redemption in the Blood of Jesus Christ. Wilmington: 1770. V. 49
A Sermon Preached at the Opening of the New Meeting-House at Wakefield. Leeds: 1774. V. 51
Wesley His Own Biographer. London: 1891. V. 54

WESLEY, CHARLES H.
The History of Alpha Phi Alpha: a Development in Negro College Life. Washington: 1929. V. 52
Negro Labor in the United States 1850-1925: A Study in American Economic History. New York: 1927. V. 52; 53

WESLEY, JOHN
A Collection of Hymns for the Use of the People Called Methodists. Derby: 1817. V. 48; 49
A Collection of Psalms and Hymns. Bristol: 1771. V. 53
A Companion for the Altar. London: 1744. V. 50
A Compendium of Natural Philosophy Being a Survey of the Wisdom of God in the Creation. London: 1840. V. 54
An Extract from Mr. Law's Serious Call to a Holy Life. Philadelphia: 1793. V. 47
An Extract of the Life and Death of Mr. John Janeway. London: 1753. V. 53
An Extract of the Life of Monsieur De Renty. Bristol: 1760. V. 53
An Extract of the Rev. Mr. John Wesley's Journal from His Embarking for Georgia. To His Return to London. Bristol: 1843. V. 47
Funeral Hymns. Bristol: 1770. V. 53
Hymns and Spiritual Songs, Intended for the Use of Real Christians, of all Denominations. Bristol: 1773. V. 53
Hymns for New-Year's Day. Bristol: 1758. V. 53
Hymns for Our Lord's Resurrection. Dublin: 1751. V. 53
Hymns for the Nativity of Our Lord. Bristol: 1764. V. 53
Hymns for the Watch-Night. 1770?. V. 53
Hymns for the Year 1756. Bristol: 1756. V. 53
Hymns of Intercession for all Mankind. Dublin: 1759. V. 53
Hymns of Petition and Thanksgiving for the Promise of the Father. Bristol: 1760. V. 53
Hymns on God's Everlasting Love. London: 1756. V. 53
The Journal of the Rev. John Wesley, A.M. London: 1909-16. V. 48
A Short Account of the Life and Death of Nathanael Othen, Who Was Shot in Dover Castle, Oct. 26, 1757. Bristol: 1758. V. 53
Wesley His Own Biographer. London: 1891. V. 51

WESLEY, MARY
The Sixth Seal. London: 1969. V. 51

WESLEY, SAMUEL
A Letter From a Country Divine to His Friend in London. London: 1703. V. 49
Maggots; or, Poems on Several Subjects, Never Before Handled. London: 1685. V. 52
The Pious Communicant Rightly Prepar'd; or, a Discourse Concerning the Blessed Sacrament... London: 1700. V. 53
Poems on Several Occasions... London: 1736. V. 48; 51; 52
Poems on Several Occasions. Cambridge: 1743. V. 50
Poems on Several Occasions. London: 1743. V. 54

WEST, BENJAMIN
Catalogue of Pictures, Representing Christ Rejected, Christ Healing in the Temple and a Design of Our Saviour's Crucifixion. London: 1815. V. 50
Catalogue of the First Part of the Superb Collection of Prints and Drawings... London: 1820. V. 47
Description of the Picture of Christ Healing the Sick in the Temple... London: 1811. V. 50; 53
A Description of...the Picture of Christ Healing the Sick in the Temple. Philadelphia: 1818. V. 47
A Discourse Delivered to the Students of the Royal Academy, on the Distribution of the Prizes, December 10, 1792, by the President. London: 1793. V. 51
Miscellaneous Poems, Translations and Imitations. Northampton: 1780. V. 54
The Paintings of Benjamin West. New Haven: 1986. V. 48

WEST By One and By One. San Francisco: 1965. V. 49; 54

WEST, CHARLES
An Inquiry into the Pathological Importance of Ulceration of the Os Uteri. Philadelphia: 1854. V. 49; 54
Lectures on Diseases of Infancy and Childhood. London: 1854. V. 49
Lectures on Diseases of Infancy and Childhood. London: 1859. V. 52
On Some Disorders of the Nervous System in Childhood... Philadelphia: 1871. V. 47; 48; 49; 50; 51; 53; 54

WEST, CLARENCE J.
Bibliography of Bibliographies on Chemistry and Chemical Technology 1900-1924 and First Supplement 1924-1928. Washington: 1925-29. V. 49

WEST, D. PORTER
Early History of Pope County. Ressellville: 1906. V. 47

WEST, DOROTHY
The Living is Easy. Boston: 1948. V. 54

WEST, EDWARD
Homesteading: Two Prairie Seasons. London: 1918. V. 48

WEST, EDWARD W.
The Diary Of the Late Rajah of Kolhapoor, During His Visit to Europe in 1870. London: 1872. V. 53

WEST India Agricultural Distress and a Remark on Mr. Wilberforce's Appeal. London: 1823. V. 48; 52

THE WEST Indian; or, the Happy Effects of Diligence and Self-Control; Exemplified in the History of Philip Montague. Wellington: 1827. V. 52; 53

WEST, JAMES
A Tale of the Times. Alexandria: 1801. V. 54

WEST, JANE
Alicia de Lacy: an Historical Romance. London: 1814. V. 47; 50
A Gossip's Story, and a Legendary Tale. London: 1798. V. 48; 49
The Infidel Father. London: 1802. V. 50
Letters Addressed to a Young Man, On His First Entrance Into Life and Adapted to the Peculiar Circumstances of the Present Times. London: 1802. V. 50
The Loyalists: an Historical Novel. London: 1812. V. 49; 50
The Refusal. London: 1810. V. 47; 50
The Refusal. London: 1819. V. 50
Sidney, Comte D'Avondel: par Mistriss West. Paris: 1813. V. 54
A Tale of the Times. London: 1799. V. 50

WEST JERSEY SURVEYORS' ASSOCIATION
Proceedings, Constitution, By-Laws, List of Members, &c. of the Surveyors' Association of West New Jersey. Camden: 1880. V. 47

WEST, JESSAMYN
The Friendly Persuasion. New York: 1945. V. 48

WEST, JOHN
Mathematical Treatises... Edinburgh: 1838. V. 50

WEST, LEONARD
The Natural Trout Fly and Its Imitation. Ravenhead, St. Helens: 1912. V. 47; 50
The Natural Trout Fly and It's Imitation. London: 1921. V. 51; 52
The Natural Trout Fly and Its Imitations. St. Helens: 1921. V. 53

WEST, MARY
Allegra. London: 1887. V. 48

WEST, MICHAEL
Clair de Lune and Other Troubadour Romances. London. V. 54
Clair de Lune and Other Troubadour Romances. New York. V. 54
Clair de Lune and Other Troubadour Romances. Saynt Albans: 1915. V. 48

WEST, NANCY GLASS
Jose Vives-Atsara: His Life and His Art. Austin: 1976. V. 51; 52

WEST, NATHANAEL
The Ancestry, Life and Times of Hon. Henry Hastings Sibley. St. Paul: 1889. V. 47
A Cool Million. New York: 1934. V. 52; 53; 54
The Day of the Locust. 1951. V. 54
The Dream Life of Balso Snell. Paris: 1931. V. 50
Miss Lonelyhearts. New York: 1933. V. 50; 51
Miss Lonelyhearts. London: 1949. V. 50

WEST NEW JERSEY BAPTIST ASSOCIATION
Minutes of the....(9th- 12th, 14th, 15th, 17th-49th anniversary), 1820-(1860). 1820-60. V. 47

WEST, PAUL
Bela Lugosi's White Christmas. New York: 1972. V. 50
Enigmas of Imagination: Woolf's Orlando through the Looking Glass. 1957. V. 54
The Fossils of Piety. New York: 1959. V. 49
The Growth of the Novel. Toronto: 1959. V. 52
The Spellbound Horses. Toronto: 1960. V. 52

WEST Point Tic Tacs. New York: 1878. V. 51

WEST, REBECCA
Black Lamb and Grey Falcon - the Record of a Journey through Yugoslavia in 1937. London: 1941. V. 51
Harriet Hume. London: 1929. V. 54
Henry James. London: 1916. V. 50
The Modern "Rake's Progress". London: 1934. V. 54
The Return of the Soldier. London: 1918. V. 54
The Return of the Soldier. New York: 1918. V. 48; 52; 54
The Thinking Reed - a Novel. London: 1936. V. 47

WEST SALTON FRIENDLY SOCIETY
Articles of Constitution, of West-Salton Friendly Society, 1804. Haddington: 1804. V. 49

WEST TEXAS
Constitution of the State of West Texas. Austin: 1868. V. 49

WEST, THOMAS
The Antiquities of Furness... London: 1774. V. 50, 52
The Antiquities of Furness... London: 1784. V. 50
The Antiquities of Furness... Ulverston: 1805. V. 50; 52
The Antiquities of Furness. Ulverston: 1822. V. 52
The Antiquities of Furness. Beckermet: 1977. V. 54
A Guide to the Lakes, in Cumberland, Westmorland and Lancashire. London: 1780. V. 50
A Guide to the Lakes in Cumberland, Westmorland, and Lancashire. London: 1784. V. 52; 54
A Guide to the Lakes in Cumberland, Westmorland and Lancashire... London: 1793. V. 52
A Guide to the Lakes, in Cumberland, Westmorland and Lancashire. London: 1799. V. 50
A Guide to the Lakes, in Cumberland, Westmorland and Lancashire. Kendal: 1812. V. 50; 52
A Guide to the Lakes, in Cumberland, Westmorland and Lancashire. Kendal: 1821. V. 50; 52

WEST to the Water. Six Poets: a Santa Cruz Portfolio. Santa Cruz: 1972. V. 51

WEST, W.
A Monograph of the British Desmidiaceae. London: 1904-12. V. 49
A Monograph of the British Desmidiaceae. London: 1904-23. V. 52; 53

WEST, WILLIAM
Cornered. New York: 1964. V. 53
Fifty Years Recollections of an Old Bookseller. London: 1837. V. 48
Fifty Years' Recollections of an Old Bookseller... London: 1837/35. V. 48
The First ...& the Second Part of Symboleography... London: 1632/27. V. 51
The First...& the Second Part of Simboleography.... London: 1622/27. V. 48
The First...& The Second Part of Symboleography. London: 1610/01. V. 48; 52
Tavern Anecdotes and Reminiscences of the Origin of Signs, Clubs, Coffee-Houses, Streets, City Companies, Wards &c. London: 1825. V. 53

WESTAL, STANLEY
Joe Meek. The Merry Mountain Man. A Biography. Caldwell: 1952. V. 53

WESTALL, WILLIAM
The Mansions of England. London: 1828-43. V. 49
Picturesque Tour of the River Thames. London: 1828. V. 50
Rob of Roy's Court. London: 1892. V. 54
Thirty-Five Views on the Thames at Richmond, Eton, Windsor and Oxford. London: 1824. V. 50
Views of Ragland Castle. London: 1843. V. 52

WESTBY-GIBSON, JOHN
The Bibliography of Shorthand. London: 1887. V. 52

WESTCOTT, EDWARD NOYES
David Harun. New York: 1900. V. 54

WESTCOTT, THOMPSON
Centennial Portfolio: a Souvenir of the International Exhibition. Philadelphia: 1876. V. 50; 52

WESTELL, W. PERCIVAL
The Book of the Animal Kingdom - Mammals. London: 1910. V. 47

WESTERMARCK, EDWARD
The History of Human Marriage. London: 1894. V. 47; 50; 52
The History of Human Marriage. London: 1921. V. 48; 53
The Origin and Development of the Moral Ideas. London: 1924-26. V. 49
Ritual and Belief in Morocco. 1926. V. 47
Ritual and Belief in Morocco. London: 1926. V. 50

WESTERN Canada: Manitoba, Alberta, Saskatchewan and New Ontario. Montreal: 1906. V. 51

THE WESTERN Primer, Ornamented with Engravings. Columbus: 1847. V. 47

WESTERN RAILROAD CORP.
Reports of the Engineers of the Western Rail Road Corporation, Made to the Directors in 1836-7. Springfield: 1838. V. 52

THE WESTERN Sanitary Commission: a Sketch of Its Origin, History, Labors for the Sick and Wounded of the Western Armies, and Aid Given to Freedmen and Union Refugees... St. Louis: 1864. V. 50; 52

WESTERN SOUTH DAKOTA STOCK GROWERS ASSOCIATION
Brand Book of the Western South Dakota Stock Growers Association. Omaha: 1901. V. 54

WESTERNERS. CHICAGO CORRAL
The Westerners Brand Book, 1944. Chicago: 1946. V. 53

WESTERNERS. DENVER POSSE
1952 Brand Book. Sixteen Original Studies in Western History. Colorado: 1953. V. 53
Denver Westerners Brand Book - Brand Book 1945. Denver: 1946. V. 48
Denver Westerners Brand Book - Brand Book 1946. Denver: 1947. V. 48; 53
The Westerners. (Denver Posse) 1948 Brand Book. Denver: 1949. V. 53

WESTERNERS. LOS ANGELES CORRAL
The Westerners Brand Book, I. Los Angeles: 1947. V. 48; 53
Westerners Brand Book, III. Los Angeles: 1949. V. 53; 54
Westerners Brand Book, IV. Los Angeles: 1949. V. 47; 54
Westerners Brand Book, VII. Los Angeles: 1957. V. 54
The Westerners Brand Book, VIII. Los Angeles: 1959. V. 54

WESTERNERS. SAN DIEGO CORRAL
Brand Books Numbers 1-8 together with Troopers West (1970). San Diego: 1968-87. V. 48

WESTERVELT, FRANCES A.
History of Bergen County, New Jersey, 1630-1923. New York: 1923. V. 49; 51

WESTERVELT, W. D.
Hawaiian Legends of Gods and Ghosts. Boston/London: 1915. V. 52

WESTGARTH, WILLIAM
Half a Century of Australasian Progress, a Personal Retrospect. London: 1889. V. 50; 53; 54
Victoria and the Australian Gold Mines in 1857. London: 1857. V. 47; 52; 54
Victoria; Late Australia Felix, or Port Philip District of New South Wales; Being an Historical and Descriptive Account of the Colony and Its Gold Mines. Edinburgh: 1853. V. 53; 54

WESTHEIMER, DAVID
Von Ryan's Express. Garden City: 1964. V. 53

WESTHOFEN, W.
The Forth Bridge. London: 1890. V. 49; 53

WESTINGHOUSE BRAKE CO. LTD.
The Westinghouse Air Brake Co. Pittsburgh: 1882. V. 51

WESTLAKE, DONALD E.
God Save the Mark. New York: 1967. V. 52
Horse Laugh. Helsinki: 1991. V. 48

WESTLAKE, HERBERT F.
Westminster Abbey; the Church, Convent, Cathedral and College of St. Peter, Westminster. London: 1923. V. 52

WESTLAKE, N. H. J.
History of Design in Painted Glass. London: 1881-94. V. 48

WESTMACOTT, CHARLES MOLLOY
The English Spy. London: 1825. V. 49
The English Spy. London: 1825-26. V. 48; 51; 53
Fitzalleyne of Berkeley. London: 1825. V. 52
Points of Misery, or Fables for Mankind: Prose and Verse, Chiefly Original. London: 1823. V. 50
The Punster's Pocket-Book, or,t he Art of Punning Enlarged. London: 1826. V. 50

WESTMAN, ERIK G.
The Swedish Element in America: a Comprehensive History of Swedish-American Achievements from 1638 to the Present Day. Chicago: 1931. V. 52

WESTMINSTER Kennel Club. New York: 1929. V. 47

WESTMORELAND, Cumberland, Durham and Northumberland. London: 1832. V. 51

THE WESTMORLAND Note-Book. Volume I 1888-1889. London: 1890. V. 52

WESTON, EDWARD
California and the West. New York: 1940. V. 51
The Daybooks of Edward Weston. Rochester: 1961/1966. V. 47
Edward Weston Nudes. Millerton: 1977. V. 49
Fifty Photographs. New York: 1947. V. 47; 50
My Camera on Point Lobos. 1950. V. 52
My Camera on Point Lobos. Boston: 1950. V. 47; 50; 54
Seeing California with Edward Weston. 1939. V. 47

WESTON, H. W.
Chancery Infamy; or, a Plea for an Anti-Chancery League. London: 1849. V. 54

WESTON, JESSIE L.
From Ritual to Romance. Cambridge: 1920. V. 50; 53
Legend of Sir Lancelot du Lac - Studies Upon Its Origin, Development and Position in the Arthurian Romantic Cycle. London: 1901. V. 49
Romance, Vision and Satire: English Alliterative Poems of the 14th Century. London: 1912. V. 53
The Rose-Tree of Hildesheim and Other Poems. London: 1896. V. 53

WESTON, R.
The English Flora. (with) The Supplement to the English Flora. London: 1775-80.. V. 53
The Gardener's and Planter's Calendar. London: 1773. V. 51
Tracts on Practical Agriculture and Gardening. London: 1769. V. 53
Tracts on Practical Agriculture and Gardening. London: 1773. V. 49; 53

WESTON, STEPHEN
Letters from Paris, During the Summer of 1791. London: 1792. V. 47
Two Sketches of France, Belgium and Spa in Two Tours During the Summers of 1771 and 1816. London: 1817. V. 48; 50
Viaggiana; or, Detached Remarks on the Buildings, Pictures, Statues, Inscriptions &c. of Ancient and Modern Rome. London: 1776. V. 47

WESTON, THOMAS
Memoirs of that Celebrated Comedian and Very Singular Genius Thomas Weston. London: 1776. V. 51

WESTON, WALTER
Mountaineering and Exploration in the Japanese Alps. London: 1896. V. 50
The Playground of the Far East. London: 1918. V. 50

WESTON, WILLIAM
The Art and Process of Carbon Printing. New York: 1896. V. 54
New Dialogues of the Dead. London: 1762. V. 49

WESTON, WILLIAM continued
Report of William Weston, Esquire, on the Practicability of Introducing the Water of the River Bonx into the City of New York:. New York: 1799. V. 52

WESTROPP, J. E., MRS.
Summer Experiences of Rome, Perugia, and Siena, in 1854; and Sketches of the Islands in the Bay of Naples. London: 1856. V. 48

WESTROPP, M. S. DUDLEY
Irish Glass. An Account of Glass-Making in Ireland from the XVIth Century to the Present Day. London: 1920. V. 47; 54

WESTRUP, EMILY
Doggy Doggerel. London. V. 51

WESTWOOD, JOHN OBADIAH
Arcana Entomologica... London: 1841-54. V. 48
British Butterflies and Their Transformations. London: 1849. V. 48
The Butterflies of Great Britain. London: 1854. V. 48
The Butterflies of Great Britain. London: 1887. V. 49
The Entomologist's Text Book... London: 1838. V. 48
Illuminated Illustrations of the Bible... 1846. V. 52
Illuminated Illustrations of the Bible. London: 1846. V. 48; 53
An Introduction to the Modern Classification of Insects. London: 1839-40. V. 51
Palaeographia Sacra Pictoria. London: 1843-45. V. 48; 49; 50; 54
Palaeographia Sacra Pictoria... London: 1845. V. 47; 54
Palaeographia sacra Pictoria... London: 1849. V. 50

WESTWOOD, THOMAS
Bibliography Piscatoria. London: 1966. V. 47
Bibliotheca Piscatoria... London: 1883. V. 47; 49
The Chronicle of The "Compleat Angler" of Izaak Walton and Charles Cotton. London: 1864. V. 47
A New Bibliotheca Piscatoria; or, General Catalogue of Angling and Fishing Literature. London: 1861. V. 47

WETENHALL, EDWARD
A View of Our Lord's Passion: With Meditations on the Most Important Passages Thereof. London: 1710. V. 48

WETHERELL, ELIZABETH, PSEUD.
The Old Helmet. London: 1864. V. 50
The Wide, Wide World; or, the Early History of Ellen Montgomery. London: 1852. V. 50

WETHERELL, JOHN
The Adventures of John Wetherell. London: 1954. V. 48

WETMORE, ALPHONSO
Gazetteer of the State of Missouri... St. Louis: 1837. V. 47

WETMORE, HELEN CODY
Last of the Great Scouts: the Life Story of Col. William F. Cody. Duluth: 1899. V. 47; 48; 50

WETMORE, PROSPER
Lexington, with Other Fugitive Poems. New York: 1830. V. 52

WETTE, ADELHEID
Hansel and Gretel. A Fairy Opera... London: 1894. V. 49

WETZEL, CHARLES M.
American Fishing Books. Newark: 1950. V. 47; 48; 54

WETZEL, G.
Howard Phillips Loveraft Memoirs, Critiques and Bibliographies. 1955. V. 52; 53

WEXLEY, JOHN
The Judgement of Julius and Ethel Roesenberg. New York: 1955. V. 53
They Shall Not Die. New York: 1934. V. 48

WEYGAND, JAMES LAMAR
A Collection of Pressmarks Gathered from America's Private Presses and from Others Not so Private. Nappanee: 1956. V. 47
The Devout Tightwad and the Isfahan Columbian. Nappanee: 1975. V. 50
The Tightwads Guide to Gold Stamping. Nappanee: 1972. V. 49
The Weygand Tightwad Beater... Nappanee: 1970. V. 48

WEYMAN, STANLEY JOHN
A Gentleman of France: Being the Memoirs of Gaston de Bonne Sieur de Marsac. London: 1893. V. 51; 52; 54
The New Rector. London: 1891. V. 54
Under the Red Robe. London: 1894. V. 51

WEYMOUTH, ANTHONY
Through the Leper-Squint: a Study of Leprosy From Pre-Christian Times to the Present Day. London: 1938. V. 48

THE WHALE *and the Dangers of the Whale-Fishery.* New Haven. V. 51; 52

WHALEY, GOULD
William Wittliff and the Encino Press: a Bibliography. Dallas: 1989. V. 51

WHALEY, JOHN
A Collection of Original Poems and Translations. London: 1745. V. 48; 49
A Collection of Poems. London: 1732. V. 48

WHALEY, JOYCE IRENE
The Art of Calligraphy, Western Europe and America. London: 1980. V. 49

WHALL, W. B.
Sea Songs and Shanties. Glasgow: 1927. V. 52

WHALLEY, R.
Revolution of Philosophy, Containing a Concise Analysis and Synthesis of the Universe. Manchester: 1835. V. 48

WHALLEY, THOMAS SEDGWICK
Edwy and Edilda: a Tale. London: 1779. V. 48
Edwy and Edilda, a Tale... London: 1794. V. 48; 53

WHANSLAW, H. W.
Everybody's Marionette Book. (with) Animal Puppetry. London: 1935/35. V. 51

WHARBURTON, CHARLES
A Memoir of Charles Mordaunt Earl of Peterborough and Monmouth... London: 1853. V. 52; 54

WHARFDALE; *or, a Description of the Several Delightful Features of that Extensive, Splendid and Fascinating Valley, Interspersed with other Topographical Illustrations of Its Towns and Villages.* Otley: 1813. V. 50; 53

WHARTON, ANNE HOLLINGSWORTH
Through Colonial Doorways. Philadelphia: 1893. V. 51

WHARTON, CLARENCE R.
History of Fort Bend County. San Antonio: 1939. V. 49
Satanta, the Great Chief of the Kiowas and His People. Dallas: 1935. V. 48; 50
Texas. Chicago: 1930. V. 53

WHARTON, EDITH
The Age of Innocence. 1973. V. 48; 51
The Age of Innocence. New York: 1973. V. 52; 54
Artemis to Actaeon. London: 1909. V. 51; 52
Artemis to Actaeon... New York: 1909. V. 52
Au Temps de L'Innocence. Paris: 1921. V. 48
A Backward Glance. New York: 1934. V. 52
The Book of the Homeless. New York: 1916. V. 48; 49; 50; 52; 53
The Buccaneers. 1938. V. 50
The Buccaneers. New York: 1938. V. 47; 51; 52
Certain People. New York: 1930. V. 48; 50
The Children. New York: 1928. V. 50; 51
Crucial Instances. New York: 1901. V. 47; 49; 52; 54
The Custom of the Country. London: 1913. V. 52
The Custom of the Country. New York: 1913. V. 47; 48; 49; 51; 52
The Decoration of Houses. New York: 1897. V. 49; 50; 53; 54
The Decoration of Houses. New York: 1902. V. 50
The Descent of Man and Other Stories. New York: 1904. V. 47; 52
Ethan Frome. London: 1911. V. 49; 50
Ethan Frome. New York: 1911. V. 48; 49; 51; 53; 54
Ethan Frome. New York: 1922. V. 47; 48; 50; 51
Ethan Frome. New York: 1939. V. 50; 51
Ethan Frome. Portland: 1939. V. 50
Fighting France from Dunkerque to Belfort. New York: 1925. V. 48; 49
The Fruit of the Tree. New York: 1907. V. 49; 50; 52; 54
A Gift from the Grave. London: 1900. V. 52; 54
Glimpses of the Moon. New York: 1922. V. 47; 48; 49
Gods Arrive. New York: 1927. V. 51; 53
The Gods Arrive. New York & London: 1932. V. 48; 51; 52; 53; 54
The Greater Inclination. London: 1899. V. 49; 50
The Greater Inclination. New York: 1899. V. 50; 52
Here and Beyond. New York: 1926. V. 49
The Hermit and the Wild Woman. New York: 1908. V. 51
The House of Mirth. New York: 1905. V. 49; 50; 51; 53; 54
The House of Mirth. Leipzig: 1906. V. 54
The House of Mirth. New York: 1975. V. 50
Hudson River Bracketed. New York: 1929. V. 48; 51; 52
Human Nature. New York: 1933. V. 47; 53
In Morocco. New York: 1920. V. 49; 50; 52
Italian Backgrounds. New York: 1905. V. 54
Italian Villas and Their Gardens. London: 1904. V. 50
Italian Villas and Their Gardens. New York: 1904. V. 53
Madame de Treymes. New York: 1907. V. 48; 50; 51; 52; 53
The Marne. London: 1918. V. 52
The Marne. New York: 1918. V. 48; 49; 50; 52
The Mother's Recompense. New York & London: 1925. V. 49; 50; 51; 52; 53
A Motor-Flight through France. New York: 1908. V. 48; 50; 54
A Motor-Flight through France. West Hatfield: 1987. V. 48
The Old Maid. New York: 1939. V. 54
Old New York. New York: 1924. V. 51; 54
Old New York. New York: 1927. V. 50
The Reef, a Novel. New York: 1912. V. 51; 54
Sanctuary. New York: 1903. V. 54
A Son at the Front. New York: 1923. V. 48; 49; 50; 52; 54
Summer. New York: 1917. V. 50; 54
Tales of Men and Ghosts. New York: 1910. V. 49; 50; 51
The Touchstone. New York: 1900. V. 52; 53
Twilight Sleep. New York: 1927. V. 51
The Valley of Decision. New York: 1902. V. 49; 50; 51; 52; 54

WHARTON, EDITH continued
The World Over. New York: 1936. V. 49; 52
The Writing of Fiction. London: 1925. V. 52
Xingu. New York: 1916. V. 47

WHARTON, EDWARD ROSS
The Whartons of Wharton Hall, with a Memorial of the Author. Oxford: 1898. V. 48; 51; 54

WHARTON, FRANCIS
Wharton and Stille's Medical Jurisprudence. Philadelphia: 1882/84/84. V. 48

WHARTON, GEORGE
Bellum Hybernicale: or, Ireland's Warre Astrologically Demonstrated. 1647. V. 49; 50; 54
Bellum Hybernicale: or, Ireland's Warre Astrologically Demonstrated. London: 1647. V. 51
Calendarium Ecclesiasticum: or A New Almanack After the Old Fashion. London: 1658. V. 49

WHARTON, GRACE
The Wits and Beaux of Society. London: 1890. V. 52; 54

WHARTON, HENRY
A Defence of Pluralities, or, Holding Two Benefices with Cure of Souls, as Now Practised in the Church of England. London: 1692. V. 50

WHARTON, HENRY E.
The Practice of Surgery... Philadelphia: 1899. V. 47; 48; 49; 50; 51; 54

WHARTON, JAMES B.
Squad. London: 1929. V. 54

WHARTON, JAMES GEORGE
Arizona: the Wonderland. Boston: 1917. V. 48

WHARTON, THOMAS
The Union; or Scots and English Poems. Dublin: 1761. V. 52

WHARTON, THOMAS, MARQUIS OF
Memoirs of the Life of...His Speeches in Parliament...His Lordship's Character, by Sir Richard Steele... London: 1715. V. 47

WHARTON, WILLIAM
Birdy. New York: 1979. V. 54
Franky Furbo. 1989. V. 48; 52
A Midnight Clear. New York: 1982. V. 52; 54

WHARTON, WILLIAM H.
Texas Address...Delivered in New York, on Tuesday, April 26, 1836... New York: 1836. V. 50

WHAT Farmers Say of Their Personal Experience in the Canadian North-West. Ottawa: 1884. V. 47

WHAT Happened to Tommy?. Rochester: 1921. V. 53

WHAT is to Be Done? Or Past, Present and Future. London: 1844. V. 49; 52

WHAT The Salt River Valley Offers to the Immigrant, Capitalist and Invalid... Chicago: 1887. V. 50

WHAT to Observe at the Bed-Side After Death in Medical Cases. Philadelphia: 1855. V. 49

WHAT Will They Think of Next?. London: 1960. V. 54

WHATELY, RICHARD
Considerations on the Law of Libel, as Relating to Publications on the Subject of Religion. London: 1833. V. 54
Elements of Logic. New York: 1832. V. 49
Elements of Rhetoric... Oxford: 1828. V. 50
Introductory Lectures on Political Economy, Delivered at Easter Term, MDCCCXXXI. London: 1832. V. 51; 52
Miscellaneous Lectures and Reviews. London: 1861. V. 52

WHATELY, T.
Observations on Modern Gardening. London: 1777. V. 49

WHATELY, THOMAS
Practical Observations on the Cure of Wounds and Ulcers of the Legs, Without Rest... London: 1799. V. 48

WHATLEY, STEPHEN
A Criticism Upon Mr. Ramsay's Travels of Cyrus... London: 1729. V. 47

WHATMAN, SUSANNA
Her Housekeeping Book. Cambridge: 1952. V. 47

WHEARE, DEGORY
Degorei Wheari Prael. Hist. Camdeniani. Oxford: 1628. V. 50
The Method and Order of Reading Both Civil and Ecclesiastical Histories... London: 1685. V. 47; 49; 54
Relectiones de Ratione & Methodo Legendi Utrasque Historias, Civiles & Ecclesiasticas... Cambridge: 1684. V. 54

WHEAT, CARL IRVING
Books of the California Gold Rush. San Francisco: 1949. V. 47; 53
Mapping the Transmississippi West, 1540-1861. San Francisco: 1957-61. V. 49
Mapping the Transmississippi West, 1540-1861. San Francisco: 1957-63. V. 47; 48; 50; 51; 54
Mapping the Transmississippi West, 1540-1861. Storrs-Mansfield: 1995. V. 53
The Maps of the California Gold Region, 1848-1857. San Francisco: 1942. V. 48; 51; 53; 54
The Maps of the California Gold Region, 1848-1857. 1995. V. 54

The Maps of the California Gold Region, 1848-1857. Storrs-Mansfield: 1995. V. 52; 54
The Pioneer Press of California. Oakland: 1948. V. 47; 50; 52

WHEAT, JAMES CLEMENT
Maps and Charts Published in America Before 1800. London: 1978. V. 47

WHEAT, MARVIN T.
Progress and Intelligence of Americans, Whether in the Northern, Central or Southern Portion of the Continent, Founded Upon the Normal and Absolute Servitude of Inferior... N.P: 1865. V. 53

WHEATER, W.
The History of the Parishes of Sherburn and Cawood with Notices of Wistow and Saxton, Towton, etc. London: 1882. V. 48; 52

WHEATLEY, DENNIS
Black August - a Novel. London: 1934. V. 49
Come Into My Parlour. London: 1946. V. 49
The Devil Rides Out - a Novel. London: 1935. V. 49
The Forbidden Territory. London: 1933. V. 49
Herewith the Clues. London: 1939. V. 48
The Malinsay Massacre. London: 1938. V. 48
Murder Off Miami. London: 1936. V. 48
Old Masters, Old brandies and a Few Great Wines. London: 1930. V. 49
Old Rowley - a Private Life of Charles II. London: 1933. V. 49
Saturdays with Bricks (and other Days Under Shell-Fire). London: 1961. V. 49
The Scarlet Impostor - a Novel. London: 1940. V. 49
The Secret War - a Novel. London: 1937. V. 49
Sixty Days to Live - a Novel. London: 1939. V. 49
They Found Atlantis. London: 1936. V. 49
Who Killed Robert Prentice?. London: 1937. V. 48

WHEATLEY, GEORGE
An Address on the Principles and Formation of Political Societies, Delivered on the Occasion of Establishing the Whitehaven Patriotic Association, the 7th August, 1832. Whitehaen: 1832. V. 49

WHEATLEY, HENRY B.
London Past and Present. Its History, Associations and Traditions. London: 1891. V. 47; 48
Round About Piccadilly and Pall Mall... London: 1870. V. 50; 54

WHEATLEY, HEWITT
The Rod and Line, or Practical Hints and Dainty Devices. London: 1849. V. 48; 53

WHEATLEY, PHILLIS
Poems on Various Subjects, Religious and Moral. London: 1773. V. 48

WHEATLEY, RICHARD
Cathedrals and Abbeys in Great Britain and Ireland. New York: 1890. V. 51

WHEELER, ALFRED
Land Titles in San Francisco, and the Laws Affecting the Same, with a Synopsis of All Grants and Sales of Land Within the Limits Claimed by the City. San Francisco: 1852. V. 47

WHEELER, ANDREW C.
The Chronicles of Milwaukee. Milwaukee: 1861. V. 47
The Iron Trail. A Sketch. New York: 1876. V. 47

WHEELER, ANNE
The Westmorland Dialect... Kendal: 1821. V. 50; 52
The Westmorland Dialect... London: 1851. V. 52

WHEELER, ARTHUR OLIVER
Eye-Witness; or, Life Scenes in the Old North State, Depicting the Trials and Sufferings of the Unionists During the Rebellion. Boston: 1865. V. 49
The Selkirk Range. Ottawa: 1905. V. 48; 52; 53

WHEELER, BENJAMIN
Ode at the Encaenia, Held at Oxford, July 1773; for the Reception of the Right Honourable Frederic Lord North, Chancellor of the University. Oxford: 1773. V. 53

WHEELER, C. A.
Sportascrapiana...by Celebrated Sportsmen, with Unpublished Anecdotes of the 19th Century. London: 1867. V. 50

WHEELER, C. H.
Ten Years on the Euphrates; or, Primitive Missionary Policy Illustrated. Boston: 1868. V. 49

WHEELER, CANDACE
The Development of Embroidery in America. New York & London: 1921. V. 47; 48

WHEELER, DANIEL
Extracts from the Letters and Journal of Daniel Wheeler, Now Engaged in a Religious Visit to the Inhabitants of the Islands of the Pacific Ocean, Van Dieman's land, and New South Wales, Accompanied by His Son, Charles Wheeler. London: 1839. V. 52
Memoirs of the Life and Gosepl Labours of the Late Daniel Wheeler.... London: 1842. V. 49; 50; 54

WHEELER, ETHEL ROLT
Famous Blue-Stockings. London: 1910. V. 48

WHEELER, GEORGE AUGUSTUS
Castine, Past and Present: the Ancient Settlement of Pentagoet and the Modern Town. Boston: 1896. V. 50

WHEELER, GEORGE MONTAGUE
Preliminary Report Concerning Explorations and Surveys Principally in Nevada and Arizona. Washington: 1872. V. 47; 53

WHEELER, GEORGE MONTAGUE continued
Progress Report Upon Geographical and Geological Explorations and Surveys West of the One Hundredth Meridian in 1872. Washington: 1874. V. 47
Report Upon Geographical...Surveys West of the One Hundredth Meridian. Washington: 1875. V. 47
Report Upon Geographical...Surveys West of the One Hundredth Meridian... Washington: 1881. V. 47
Report Upon Geographical...Surveys West of the One Hundreth Meridian. Washington: 1879-89. V. 52; 53

WHEELER, GERVASE
The Choice of a Dwelling. London: 1872. V. 50

WHEELER, HOMER W.
The Frontier Trail - a Personal Narrative... Los Angeles: 1923. V. 54

WHEELER, JAMES
Manchester: Its Political, Social and Commercial History, Ancient and Modern. London: 1836. V. 48; 53

WHEELER, JAMES TALBOYS
Adventures of a Tourist from Calcutta to Delhi. Calcutta: 1868. V. 49
Early Records of British India: a History of the English Settlements in India, as Told in the Government Records, the Works of Old Travellers and Other Contemporary Documents. London: 1878. V. 48

WHEELER, JOHN H.
Historical Sketches of North Carolina, From 1584 to 1851. Philadelphia: 1851. V. 47

WHEELER, JOSEPH
The Santiago Campaign 1898. Boston, New York, London: 1898. V. 47

WHEELER, JOSEPH TOWNE
The Maryland Press 1777-1790. Baltimore: 1938. V. 47

WHEELER, MONROE
A Typographical Commonplace Book. Paris: 1932. V. 51

WHEELER, OF GLOUCESTER
The Royal Grammar Reformed into A More Easie Method for the Better Understanding of the English; and More Speedy Attainment of the Latin Tongue. London: 1695. V. 47

WHEELER, OLIN D.
The Trail of Lewis and Clark, 1804-1904. New York: 1904. V. 51

WHEELER, ROBERT
At a Meeting of the Manufacturers of Guns, Fowling Pieces and Pistols, and the Component Parts Thereof, in the Town of Birmingham... Birmingham: 1813. V. 48

WHEELER, W. H.
A History of the Fens of South Lincolnshire, Being a Description of the Rivers Witham and Welland and Their Estuary, and an Account of the Reclamation, Drainage and Enclosure of the Fens Adjacent Thereto. Boston. V. 53
Tidal Rivers. London: 1893. V. 50

WHEELER, WILLIAM OGDEN
Inscriptions on Tombstones and Monuments in the Burying Grounds of the First Presbyterian church and St. Johns Church at Elizabeth, New Jersey. 1664-1892. 1892. V. 49; 51
The Ogden Family in America, Elizabethtown Branch and Their English Ancestry. Philadelphia: 1907. V. 49; 51

WHEELING CORRUGATING CO.
Wheeling Metal Ceilings. Catalog No. 316. 1910's. V. 54

WHEELOCK, ELEZAR
A Sermon Preached Before the Second Society in Lebanon, June 30, 1763, at the ordination of the Rev. Mr. Charles Jeffry Smith, with A view to His Going as a Missionary to the Remote Tribes of the Indians in this Land... London: 1767. V. 49

WHEELOCK, JOHN HALL
The Bright Doom. New York: 1927. V. 54
Poems 1911-1936. New York: 1936. V. 48
Poems Old and New. New York: 1956. V. 47
Poets of Today VII. James Dickey. Paris Leary. Jon Swan. New York: 1960. V. 51

WHEELOCK, JULIA
The Boys in White: the Experience of a Hospital Agent in and Around Washington. New York: 1870. V. 50; 52

WHEELOCK, THOMPSON B.
Journal of Colonel Dodge's Expedition from Fort Gibson to the Pawnee Pict Village. Washington: 1834. V. 47

WHEELWLRIGHT, CHARLES APTHORP
Poems Original and Translated. London: 1811. V. 54

WHEELWRIGHT, HORACE WILLIAM
Natural History Sketches... London: 187-. V. 52
Natural History Sketches. 1880. V. 54
A Spring and Summer In Lapland by an Old Bushman. London: 1871. V. 53
Ten Years in Sweden. London: 1865. V. 50

WHEELWRIGHT, JOHN
Mirrors of Venus. Boston: 1938. V. 48; 51
Rock and Shell. Poems 1923-1933. Boston: 1933. V. 50

WHEELWRIGHT, MARY C.
Emergence Myth According to the Hanethnayhe or Upward Reaching Rite. Santa Fe: 1949. V. 49
The Myth and Prayers of the Great Star Chant and The Myth of the Coyote Chant. Santa Fe: 1956. V. 52

WHELAN, EDWARD
The Union of the British Provinces. Charlottetown: 1865. V. 54

WHELAN, M.
Wonderworks. 1979. V. 54

WHELDON, J. A.
The Flora of West Lancashire. Eastbourne: 1907. V. 50; 54

WHELER, GORGE
A Journey into Greece in Company of Dr. Spon of Lyons. London: 1682. V. 48

WHELER, R. B.
History and Antiquites of Stratford-upon-Avon... Stratford-upon-Avon: 1806. V. 47; 49; 51; 52

WHELLAN, FRANCIS
History, Topography and Directory of Northamptonshire... London: 1874. V. 53

WHELLAN, T., & CO.
History and Topography of the City of York: The Ainsty Wapentake; and the East Riding of Yorkshire. London: 1855. V. 48

WHELLAN, WILLIAM
The History and Topography of the Counties of Cumberland and Westmorland. Pontefract: 1860. V. 50; 52

WHELPLEY, SAMUEL
A Compend of History from the Earliest Times... Boston: 1820. V. 47

WHEN We Talk About Raymond Carver. Layton: 1991. V. 53

WHERE the Two Came to Their Father: a Navaho War Ceremonial... Princeton: 1969. V. 52

WHERRY, GEORGE
Alpine Notes and the Climbing Foot. Cambridge: 1896. V. 50

WHEWELL, WILLIAM
Astronomy and General Physics, Considered with Reference to Natural Theology. London. V. 52
English Hexameter Translations from Schiller, Goethe, Homer, Callinus and Meleager. London: 1847. V. 52
History of the Inductive Sciences... London: 1837. V. 52; 54
History of the Inductive Sciences... London: 1847. V. 49; 52
History of the Inductive Sciences... London: 1857. V. 49
The Mechanics of Engineering. Cambridge: 1841. V. 50
On the Principles of English University Education. London: 1838. V. 49
The Philosophy of the Inductive Sciences, Founded Upon Their History. London: 1840. V. 47
The Philosophy of the Inductive Sciences, Founded Upon Their History. London: 1847. V. 48; 50; 52; 54

WHICH: Lord Byron or Lord Byron: a Bet. San Francisco: 1932. V. 48; 50

WHICHCOTE, BENJAMIN
Moral and Religious Aphorisms, Collected From Ms. Papers and Pub. in 1703. London: 1753. V. 47

WHICHER, GEORGE F.
Alas All's Vanity or a leaf from the First American Edition of Several Poems by Anne Bradstreet Printed at Boston anno 1678. New York: 1942. V. 52

WHIG PARTY, VIRGINIA
Address of the Whig Convention for the Nomination of Electors, to the People of Virginia. Richmond: 1840?. V. 50

WHINCOP, THOMAS
Scanderbeg; or, Love and Liberty. London: 1717. V. 50
Scanderbeg; or, Love and Liberty. London: 1747. V. 47; 53

WHIPPELL, J., & CO.
Abridged and Condensed Catalogue of Church Furniture, Carved Wood and Stone Work, Mission Church & School Furniture... Exeter: 1894. V. 51

WHIPPING-Tom: or, a Rod for a Proud Lady, Bundled Up in Four Feeling Discourses, Both Serious and Merry. In Order to Touch the Fair Sex to the Quick. London: 1722. V. 48

WHIPPLE, A. W.
Report...Lieutenant Whipple's Expedition from San Diego to the Colorado. Washington: 1851. V. 47; 49

WHIPPLE, EDWIN PERCY
Charles Dickens: the Man and His Work. Boston: 1912. V. 49; 54

WHIPPLE, FRED L.
The Collected Contributions of Fred L. Whipple. Cambridge: 1972. V. 51

WHIPPLE, GEORGE
Typhoid Fever: Its Causation, Transmission and Prevention. New York: 1908. V. 54

WHISHAW, FRANCIS
Analysis of Railways: Consisting of a Series of Reports on the Railways Projects in England and Wales, in the Year 1837. London: 1838. V. 51

WHISHAW, FRED J.
Out of Doors in Tsarland. A Record of Seeings and Doings of a Wanderer in Russia. London: 1893. V. 49

WHISTLER, JAMES ABBOTT MC NEILL
Eden Versus Whistler. The Baronet and the Butterfly. A Valentine with a Verdict. New York: 1899. V. 48

WHISTLER, JAMES ABBOTT MC NEILL continued
Eden Versus Whistler: the Baronet and the Butterfly: a Valentine with a Verdict. Paris: 1899. V. 50
The Gentle Art of Making Enemies. London: 1890. V. 47; 48; 50; 54
The Gentle Art of Making Enemies. New York: 1890. V. 49; 50; 51
The Lithographs of Whistler. New York: 1914. V. 54
Mr. Whistler's Ten O'Clock. London: 1888. V. 50
Mr. Whistler's Ten O'Clock. San Francisco: 1940. V. 52
The Red Rag. Easthampton: 1970. V. 47
The Red Rag. Easthampton: 1980. V. 48
Ten O'Clock, a Lecture. Portland: 1920. V. 54

WHISTLER, LAURENCE
The Burning-Glass. London: 1941. V. 53
Children of Hertha and Other Poems. Oxford: 1929. V. 50
The Emperor Heart. London: 1936. V. 48; 53
The English Festivals. London: 1947. V. 52
The Imagination of Vanbrugh and His Fellow Artists. London: 1954. V. 53; 54
In Time of Suspense. London: 1940. V. 53
Oho?. London: 1946. V. 49
Sir John Vanbrugh... London: 1938. V. 52
Sir John Vanbrugh... New York: 1939. V. 49
Who Live in Unity. London: 1944. V. 53
The Work of Rex Whistler. London: 1960. V. 49; 51; 53; 54

WHISTLER, REX
The Konigsmark Drawings. London: 1952. V. 50; 52; 53
The New Forget-Me-Not: a Calendar. London: 1929. V. 52

WHISTON, WILLIAM
Astronomical Principles of Religion, Natural and Reveal'd. London: 1725. V. 47
Memoirs of the Life and Writings of (and) of Several of His Friends Also. London: 1749. V. 51; 52; 53
A New Theory of the Earth... London: 1696. V. 51; 52; 53
A New Theory of the Earth... London: 1722. V. 53
A New Theory of the Earth... London: 1737. V. 51
Sir Isaac Newton's Mathematick Philosophy More Easily Demonstrated... London: 1716. V. 51; 52
Whiston's Account of the Exact Time when Miraculous Gifts Ceas'd in the Church. London: 1749. V. 51; 52

WHITAKER, ARTHUR P.
The Spanish-American Frontier: 1783-1795. Boston & New York: 1927. V. 50

WHITAKER, CHARLES HARRIS
Bertram Grosvenor Goodhue - Architect and Master of Many Arts. New York: 1925. V. 47; 48; 49; 50; 53

WHITAKER, E. A.
Rectified Lunar Atlas, Supplement Number to the Photographic Lunar Atlas. 1963. V. 49

WHITAKER, EDWARD
The Death, Burial and Resurrection of the Act of the 35th of Eliza...Being an Answer to a late Lying Pamphlet Entituled, The Life and Death of the 35th of Eliz. Colophon: 1681. V. 49; 51
A Short History of the Life and Death of the Act Made the 35th of Elizabeth... London: 1681. V. 49; 51

WHITAKER, J.
The Birds of Tunisia. London: 1905. V. 47; 49; 50; 51
British Duck Decoys of Today, 1918. London: 1918. V. 49

WHITAKER, JOHN
The History of Manchester. London: 1773. V. 52
The Seraph, A Collection of Sacred Music, Suitable to Public or Private Devotion. London: 1825-28. V. 48; 49

WHITAKER, MILO LEE
Pathfinders and Pioneers of the Pueblo Region Comprising a History of Pueblo from the Earliest Times. Pueblo: 1917. V. 49; 54
Pathfinders and Pioneers of the Pueblo Region Comprising a History of Pueblo from the earliest Times. Pueblo: 1917. V. 49

WHITAKER, THOMAS DUNHAM
The History and Antiquities of the Deanery of Craven, in the County of York. London: 1805. V. 48; 53
The History and Antiquities of the Deanery of Craven, in the County of York. Halifax: 1812. V. 48
The History and Antiquities of the Deanery of Craven, In the County of York. London: 1812. V. 48
The History and Antiquities of the Deanery of Craven, in the County of York. Leeds: 1878. V. 47; 48
The History and Antiquities of the Deanery of Craven, in the County of York. London: 1878. V. 48; 52; 53; 54
A History of Richmondshire, in the North Riding of the County of York. London: 1823. V. 53
A History of the Original Parish of Whalley and Honor of Clitheroe in the Counties of Lancaster and York. Blackburn: 1801. V. 53
An History of the Original Parish of Whalley and Honor of Clitheroe in the Counties of Lancaster and York. London: 1818. V. 47; 48
An History of the Original Parish of Whalley and Honor of Clitheroe, To Which is Subjoined An Account of the Parish of Caratmel. London: 1872. V. 48
Loidis and Elmete: or, an Attempt to Illustrate the Districts Described in Those Words by Bede. Leeds: 1816. V. 53

WHITAKER, W.
The Geological Record. London: 1875-89. V. 53; 54
Geology of London and Of Part of the Thames Valley. London: 1889. V. 52

WHITAKER, WILLIAM
Adversus Thomae Stapletoni... Cambridge: 1594. V. 47
Disputatio de Sacra Scriptura Contra Hujus Temporis Papistas Imprimis Robertum Bellarminum... Cantabrigiae: 1588. V. 53
Dispvtatio de Sacra Scriptvra; Contra Hvivs Temporis Papistas (etc.). Herborn: 1590. V. 54

WHITBOURNE, RICHARD
Westward Hoe for Avalon in the New-found-land as Described by... London: 1870. V. 47

WHITBY, DANIEL
Ethices Compendium, in Usum Academicae Juventutis. Oxford: 1684. V. 47

WHITCOMBE, CHARLES EDWARD
The Canadian Farmer's Manual of Agricutlure... Toronto: 1879. V. 48

WHITE, A.
A Popular History of Birds. London: 1855. V. 54
A Popular History of British Crustacea. London: 1857. V. 54
A Popular History of Mammalia... London: 1850. V. 54

WHITE, ALAIN
A Sketchbook of American Chess Problematists. Stamford: 1942. V. 47
The Stapeliae... Pasadena: 1933. V. 49; 50; 52
The Stapeliae. Pasadena: 1937. V. 54
The Succulent Euphorbieae (Southern Africa). Pasadena: 1941. V. 54

THE WHITE Alphabet. V. 51

WHITE, ANTONIA
Frost in May. London: 1933. V. 49; 52

WHITE, ARTHUR SILVA
From Sphinx to Oracle. London: 1899. V. 51; 53

WHITE, C. R.
By the Sea. Portland: 1889. V. 47

WHITE, CARLOS
Ecce Femina: an Attempt to Solve the Woman Question. Hanover: 1870. V. 50

WHITE, CHARLES
An Account of the Regular Gradation in Man... London: 1799. V. 48; 51
An Account of the Topical Applicaton of the Spunge, in Stopping of Haemorrhages... London: 1762. V. 51
The Adventures of a King's Page. London: 1829. V. 51
Almack's Revisited. London: 1828. V. 51
Almack's Revisited... New York: 1828. V. 47
Cases in Surgery with Remarks. London: 1770. V. 47; 49; 52
Herbert Milton. London: 1828. V. 47
Sporting Scenes. London: 1840. V. 47
A Treatise on the Management of Pregnant and Lying in Women, and the Means of Curing, but More Especially of Preventing the Principal Disorders to Which they are Liable. Worcester: 1793. V. 53

WHITE, CHRISTOPHER
The Flower Drawings of Jan Van Huysum 1682-1749. Leigh-on-Sea: 1964. V. 49; 52; 54
Rembrandt as an Etcher. London: 1969. V. 49; 52

WHITE, CLAYTON
Physics and Medicine of the Upper Atmosphere. Albuquerque: 1952. V. 49; 54

WHITE, D.
Fossil Flora of the Lower Coal Measures of Missouri. Washington: 1899. V. 53

WHITE, DABNEY
East Texas: Its History and Its makers. New York: 1940. V. 48

WHITE, DIANA
The Descent of Ishtar. 1903. V. 49; 52; 53; 54
The Descent of Ishtar. Hammersmith: 1903. V. 50; 54
The Descent of Ishtar. London: 1903. V. 47; 50
Preface to an Album of Poems from the Livre de Jade. 1948. V. 53

WHITE, E. W.
Cameos from the Silver Land; or the Experiences of a Young Naturalist in the Argentine Republic. London: 1881-82. V. 53

WHITE, EDGAR
Sati the Rastifarian. New York: 1973. V. 53

WHITE, EDMUND
Forgetting Elena. New York: 1973. V. 50
Genet: a Biography. New York: 1992. V. 54
Nocturnes for the King of Naples. New York: 1978. V. 48; 50; 51; 52
States of Desire: Travels in Gay America. London: 1980. V. 53
States of Desire: Travels in Gay America. New York: 1980. V. 54

WHITE, EDWARD
Evansville and Its Men of Mark. Evansville: 1873. V. 52

WHITE, EDWARD LUCAS
Lukundoo & Other Stories. New York: 1927. V. 47

WHITE, EDWARD SKEATE
The Maltster's Guide... London: 1860. V. 49

WHITE, ELIJAH
Testimonials and Records. Together with Arguments in Favor of Special Action for Our Indian Tribes. Washington: 1861. V. 47

WHITE, ELIZA
Gertrude... London: 1823. V. 52

WHITE, ELLSBERRY VALENTINE
The First Iron Clad Naval Engagement in the World. New York: 1906. V. 49

WHITE, ELWYN BROOKS
Alice through the Cellophane. New York: 1933. V. 53
Charlotte's Web. New York: 1952. V. 47; 48; 49; 53
The Fox of Peapack. New York: 1938. V. 52; 53
Ho Hum: Newsbreaks from The New Yorker. New York: 1931. V. 47; 48
The Lady is Cold. New York: 1929. V. 47; 48
One Man's Meat. New York: 1942. V. 48; 50; 51
Stuart Little. New York & London: 1945. V. 47; 48; 49; 53
Stuart Little in the Schoolroom. 1960. V. 48; 52

WHITE, ERIC WALTER
Stravinsky's Sacrifice. London: 1930. V. 51

WHITE, EUGENE E.
Service on the Indian Reservations. Little Rock: 1893. V. 52

WHITE, F.
Forest Flora of Northern Rhodesia. London: 1962. V. 54

WHITE, FRANCIS
A Replie to Jesuit Fishers Answere to Certain Questions Propounded by His Most Gratious Ma'tie King James... London: 1624. V. 48; 53
A Treatise of the Sabbath Day...Against Sabbatarian Novelty. London: 1635. V. 48; 54

WHITE, G.
English Illustration "The Sixties" 1855-70. Westminter: 1897. V. 50
English Illustration "The Sixties" 1855-70. London: 1903. V. 47

WHITE, GEORGE
Combination and Arbitration Laws, Artisans and Machinery, Abstracts of the Acts Repealing the Laws of Combinations of Workmen and Emigration of Artisans... London: 1824. V. 47

WHITE, GEORGE FRANCIS
Views in India, Chiefly Among the Himalaya Mountains... London and Paris: 1836. V. 53
Views in India, Chiefly Among the Himalaya Mountains... London: 1838. V. 49; 52

WHITE, GEORGE S.
Memoir of Samuel Slater, the Father of American Manufactures. Philadelphia: 1836. V. 47; 50

WHITE, GERALD T.
Baptism in Oil: Stephen F. Peckham in Southern California, 1865-66. San Francisco: 1984. V. 47

WHITE, GILBERT
The Journals. 1754-1793. London: 1986-89. V. 51
The Natural History and Antiquities of Selborne. London: 1789. V. 47; 50; 51; 52; 53; 54
The Natural History and Antiquities of Selborne... London: 1813. V. 49; 50; 51; 52; 53; 54
The Natural History and Antiquities of Selborne... London: 1836. V. 47; 48
The Natural History and Antiquities of Selborne... London: 1874. V. 47
Natural History and Antiquities of Selborne. London: 1875. V. 47; 50
The Natural History and Antiquities of Selborne... London: 1877. V. 49; 54
The Natural History and Antiquities of Selborne. London: 1880. V. 51
The Natural History and Antiquities of Selborne. London: 1884. V. 49
The Natural History and Antiquities of Selborne. London: 1890. V. 54
The Natural History and Antiquities of Selborne. London & Philadelphia: 1900. V. 50; 51; 52; 53; 54
The Natural History of Selborne. London: 1825. V. 49; 51; 52; 53; 54
The Natural History of Selborne. 1837. V. 54
The Natural History of Selborne. London: 1854. V. 53
The Natural History of Selborne... London: 1861. V. 48
The Natural History of Selborne... London: 1870. V. 49
The Natural History of Selborne. London: 1900. V. 49
The Natural History of Selborne. London: 1902. V. 52
The Natural History of Selborne. 1972. V. 48; 51; 54
The Natural History of Selborne. Ipswich: 1972. V. 47; 52; 53
The Natural History of Selborne. London: 1972. V. 49
The Natural History of Selborne. New York: 1972. V. 48
A Naturalist's Calendar. London: 1795. V. 47; 50; 51; 52; 53
A Naturalist's Calendar, with Observations in Various Branches of History. London: 1795. V. 48
Works in Natural History. London: 1802. V. 47; 51
The Writings of Gilbert White of Selborne... London: 1928. V. 48
The Writings of Gilbert White of Selborne. London: 1938. V. 47; 48; 50; 53; 54

WHITE, GLEESON
Book-Song, an Anthology of Poems of Books and Bookmen from Modern Authors. London: 1893. V. 47; 49
Children's Books and Their Illustrators. London: 1897. V. 52
Children's Books and Their Illustrators. London: 1897/98. V. 54
Christmas Cards and Their Chief Designers. London: 1895. V. 51

WHITE, HENRY
Geology, Oil Fields and Minerals, of Canada West... Toronto: 1865. V. 48; 51; 52; 54
Gold Regions of Canada. Gold: How and Where to Find It!. Toronto: 1867. V. 54

WHITE, HENRY ALEXANDER
Robert E. Lee and the Southern Confederacy 1807-1870. New York & London: 1910. V. 50

WHITE, HENRY KIRKE
Clifton Grove, A Sketch in Verse. London: 1803. V. 50
The Poetical Works. London: 1853. V. 47
The Poetical Works... London: 1867. V. 51
The Remains...With an Account of His Life by Robert Southey. London: 1819/22. V. 49

WHITE, HERBERT M.
Old Ingleborough. London: 1904. V. 53

WHITE, J.
An Essay on the Indigenous Grasses of Ireland. Dublin: 1808. V. 52

WHITE, J. CLAUDE
Sikhim & Bhutan, Twenty-One Years on the North-East Frontier 1887-1908. 1909. V. 54

WHITE, J. T.
The History of Torquay. Torquay: 1878. V. 50

WHITE, JAMES
The Adventures of John of Gaunt, Duke of Lancaster. London: 1790. V. 50; 54
The Adventures of Sir Frizzle Pumpkin. Edinburgh: 1836. V. 49
The Adventures of Sir Frizzle Pumpkin... London: 1836. V. 51
A Compendium of the Veterinary Art... Canterbury: 1802. V. 47
Earl Strongbow; or, the History of Richard de Clare and the Beautiful Geralda. London: 1789. V. 50; 54
English Country Life. London: 1843. V. 52
A New Century of Inventions, Being Designs and Descriptions of One Hundred Machines, Relating to Arts, Manufactures, & Domestic Life. Manchester: 1822. V. 51

WHITE, JAMES E.
A Genealogical History of the Descendants of Peter White, of New Jersey, from 1670 and of William White and Deborah Tilton his Wife Loyalists. St. John: 1906. V. 49; 51

WHITE, JOHN
Art's Treasury of Rarities; and Curious Inventions. Glasgow: 1773. V. 54
The Birth and Rebirth of Pictorial Space. London: 1967. V. 52; 54
An Essay on the Formation of Harbours of Refuge, and the Improvement of the Navigation of Rivers and Sea Ports, by the Adoption of Moored Floating Constructions as Breakwaters of the Force of the Sea Tides and Currents of Sea Coasts... London: 1840. V. 51
The First Century of Scandalous, Malignant Priests, Made and Admitted Into Benefices of the Prelates, in Whose Hands the Ordination of Ministers and Government of the Church Hath Been. London: 1643. V. 50
Journal of a Voyage to New South Wales with Sixty-Five Plates of Non-Descript Animals, Birds, Lizards, Serpents, Curious Cones of Trees and Other Natural Productions. London: 1790. V. 51; 54
Sketches from America. London: 1870. V. 47
Some Account of the Proposed Improvements of the Western Part of London, by the Formation of the Regent's Park, the New Street,, the New Sewer &c. (with) Brief Remarks on the Proposed Regent's Canal. London: 1815/12. V. 53
Three Letters to a Gentleman Dissenting From the Church of England. London: 1748. V. 49

WHITE, JOHN, ARCHITECT
Rural Architecture: Illustrated in a New Series of Designs for ornamental Cottages and Villas. Glasgow: 1852. V. 49

WHITE, JOHN, U. S. N.
A Voyage to Chochin China. London: 1824. V. 48

WHITE, JOSEPH BLANCO
Vargas: a Tale of Spain... London: 1822. V. 50

WHITE, KENNETH
Itineraire. Paris: 1986. V. 51
A Walk Along the Shore. Guildford: 1977. V. 47

WHITE, LESLIE A.
Pioneers in American Anthropology: the Bandelier-Morgan Letters, 1873-1883. Albuquerque: 1940. V. 47; 53

WHITE, LUKE
The Complete Dublin Catalogue of Books In All Arts and Sciences. (Printed in Ireland) from the Beginning of this Century, to the Present Time. Dublin: 1786. V. 52

WHITE, MARGARET E.
A Sketch of Chester Harding, Artist: Drawn by His Own Hand. Boston: 1929. V. 53

WHITE, MINOR
Mirror, Messsages, Manifestations. New York: 1969. V. 47; 51

WHITE, NEWMAN IVEY
American Negro Folk-songs. Cambridge: 1928. V. 50
An Anthology of Verse by American Negroes. Durham: 1924. V. 47

WHITE, OWEN P.
The Autobiography of a Durable Sinner. New York: 1942. V. 48; 50
A Frontier Mother. New York: 1929. V. 48; 50; 53
Out of the Desert. The Historical Romance of El Paso. El Paso: 1923. V. 50; 54

WHITE, PALMER
Poiret. London: 1974. V. 50

WHITE, PATRICK
The Aunt's Story. London: 1948. V. 48; 51; 52
The Burnt Ones. London: 1964. V. 52
The Cockatoos - Shorter Novels and Stories. London: 1974. V. 51

WHITE, PATRICK continued
The Eye of the Storm. London: 1973. V. 51
Flaws in the Glass. London: 1981. V. 51
Four Plays. London: 1965. V. 49; 51; 52
Happy Valley. New York: 1940. V. 48; 50
The Living and the Dead. New York: 1941. V. 49
Riders in the Chariot. London: 1961. V. 52
The Tree of Man. New York: 1955. V. 47; 48; 49; 50; 53
The Tree of Man. 1956. V. 50
The Tree of Man. London: 1956. V. 51; 52
The Twyborn Affair - a Novel. London: 1979. V. 51
Voss. London: 1957. V. 52

WHITE, PERCY
Mr. Bailey-Martin. London: 1894. V. 53

WHITE, PHILO
Philo White's Narrative of a Cruise in the Pacific to South America and California on the U.S. Sloop-of-War "Dale" 1841-1843. Denver: 1965. V. 53; 54

WHITE, PRISCILLA
Diabetes in Childhood and Adolesence. Philadelphia: 1932. V. 54

WHITE, RANDY WAYNE
Batfishing in the Rainforest. New York: 1991. V. 53

WHITE, RICHARD GRANT
Memoirs of the Life of William Shakespeare. Boston: 1866. V. 53
Poetry, Lyrical, Narrative and Satirical of the Civil War. New York: 1866. V. 52
Revelations: a Companion to the "New Gospel of Peace". New York: 1863. V. 48

WHITE, RICHARDSON D.
Aesop's Fables in Rhyme for Children. Akron: 1903. V. 51

WHITE, SALLIE ELIZABETH JOY
Business Openings for Girls. Boston: 1891. V. 47

WHITE, SAMUEL S.
Catalogue of Dental Materials, Furniture, Instruments, Etc...January 1, 1867. Philadelphia: 1866. V. 51

WHITE, STANFORD
Sketches and Designs by...with an Outline of His Career by His Son.... New York: 1920. V. 47; 48

WHITE, STEWART EDWARD
The Claim Jumpers. New York: 1901. V. 51
Gold. Garden City: 1913. V. 54
Gold... New York: 1913. V. 48

WHITE, TERENCE HANBURY
The Book of Beasts. London: 1954. V. 48
Burke's Steerage. London: 1938. V. 50
Darkness at Pemberley. London: 1932. V. 48
Earth Stopped or Mr. Marx's Sporting Tour. London: 1934. V. 48
The Elephant and the Kangaroo. London: 1947. V. 48
The Elephant and the Kangaroo. New York: 1947. V. 54
The Elephant and the Kangaroo. London: 1948. V. 48; 51
England Have My Bones. London: 1936. V. 48; 50
Farewell Victoria. London: 1933. V. 48
First Lesson. London: 1932. V. 48; 49; 53; 54
First Lesson. New York: 1933. V. 51
Gone to Ground. London: 1935. V. 48; 52
The Green Bay Tree, or the Wicked Man Touches Wood. 1929. V. 48
The Ill Made Knight. London: 1942. V. 51
Loved Helen and Other Poems. London: 1929. V. 48; 49; 52; 53
The Master. London: 1957. V. 51
The Once and Future King. London: 1958. V. 48; 49; 52
The Sword in the Stone. London: 1938. V. 48; 50; 51; 52; 53
The Sword in the Stone. New York: 1939. V. 48; 51; 53
They Winter Abroad. London: 1932. V. 48; 53; 54
They Winter Abroad. New York: 1932. V. 48
The Witch in the Wood. London: 1940. V. 48; 49

WHITE, THOMAS
The Beauties of Occult Science Investigated; or, the Celestial Intelligencer... London: 1810. V. 48
Institututionum Peripateticarum ad mentem Summi Viri, Clarissimique Philosophi Kenelmi Equitis... London: 1647. V. 48
Naval Researches; or A Candid Inquiry into the conduct of Admirals Byron, Graves, Hood and Rodney, in the Actions Off Grenanda, Chesapeak, St. Christopher's and of the Ninth and Twelfth of April, 1782... London: 1830. V. 47

WHITE, THOMAS P.
Archaeological Sketches in Scotland: District of Kintyre. Edinburgh & London: 1873. V. 49

WHITE, W.
Observations on Strictures of the Rectum and Other Afffections Which Diminish the Capacity of that Intestine... Bath: 1820. V. 54
A Sailor-Boy's Log-Book from Portsmouth to the Peiho. London: 1862. V. 47

WHITE, W. C.
An Album of Chinese Bamboos. Toronto: 1939. V. 50
Tomb Tile Pictures of Ancient China. Toronto: 1939. V. 50

WHITE, WALTER
Eastern England from the Thames to the Humber. London: 1865. V. 49; 50
A Londoner's Walk to the Land's End, and a Trip to the Scilly Isles. London: 1855. V. 50
A Month in Yorkshire. London: 1861. V. 53
Northumberland, and the Border. London: 1859. V. 53
On Foot through Tyrol in the Summer of 1855. London: 1856. V. 48; 53
A Rising Wind. Garden City: 1945. V. 53
Rope & Faggot: a Biography of Judge Lynch. New York: 1929. V. 53

WHITE, WILLIAM
The Evils of Quarantine Laws, and Non-Existence of Pestilential Contagion... London: 1837. V. 50
History, Gazetteer, and Direcctory of the West-Riding of Yorkshire, with the City of York and Port of Hull... Sheffield: 1837-38. V. 48
History, Gazetteer and Directory of Devonshire and the City and County of the City of Exeter... London: 1850. V. 50
History, Gazetteer and Directory of Norfolk and the City and County of Norwich. Sheffield & London: 1864. V. 53

WHITE, WILLIAM ALLEN
In Our Town. New York: 1906. V. 54

WHITE, WILLIAM F.
A Picture of Pioneer Times in California, Illustrated with Anecdotes and Stories Taken from Real Life. San Francisco: 1881. V. 53

WHITE, WILLIAM S.
The Professional Lyndon B. Johnson. Boston: 1964. V. 48

WHITEBROOK, ROBERT B.
Coastal Exploration of Washington. Palo Alto: 1959. V. 47

WHITECHAPEL GALLERY, LONDON
David Hockney. Paintings, Prints & Drawings 1960-70. London April-May, 1970. 1970. V. 53

WHITEFIELD, GEORGE
A Journal of A Voyage from Gibralter to Georgia... London: 1738. V. 48
A Letter to the Rev. the President and Professors, Tutors and Hebrew Instructor, of Harvard College in Cambridge, in Answer to a Testimony Publish'd by them Against the Reverend Mr. George Whitefield, and His Conduct. Boston: 1745. V. 54
The True Nature of Beholding the Lamb of God, and Peter's Denial of His Lord, Opened and Explained in Two Sermons. London: 1753. V. 53

WHITEHALL in Cumberland. London: 1865. V. 50; 52

WHITEHEAD, ALFRED NORTH
The Axioms of Projective Geometry. Cambridge: 1906. V. 47
Principia Mathematica. Cambridge: 1910/12/27. V. 47
Principia Mathematica. Cambridge and New York: 1927-50. V. 54
Principia Mathematica. Cambridge: 1950. V. 48
The Principle of Relativity with Applications to Physical Science. Cambridge: 1922. V. 50
Religion in the Making. New York: 1926. V. 48
Symbolism its Meaning and Effect. Cambridge: 1928. V. 52
A Treatise on Universal Algebra with Applications.... Cambridge: 1898. V. 48

WHITEHEAD, CHARLES
The Autobiography of Jack Ketch. London: 1835. V. 48
Lives and Exploits of English Highwaymen, Pirates and Robbers. London: 1834. V. 47

WHITEHEAD, CHARLES E.
The Camp-Fires of the Everglades or Wild Spots in the South. Edinburgh: 1891. V. 47; 51; 52
Wild Sports in the South; or, the Camp-Fires of the Everglades. New York: 1860. V. 47

WHITEHEAD, G. KENNETH
The Ancient White Cattle of Britain and Their Descendants. London: 1953. V. 50
Deer and Their Management. 1950. V. 48
Deer and Their Management... London: 1950. V. 54
The Deer of Great Britain and Ireland. London: 1964. V. 48; 50; 52
Deer of the World. 1972. V. 52
Deer of the World. London: 1972. V. 48; 49
The Deer Stalking... 1960. V. 54
The Deer Stalking. London: 1960. V. 49
Encyclopaedia of Deer. London: 1992. V. 53
The Whitehead Encyclopaedia of Deer. Shrewsbury: 1992. V. 48
The Whitehead Encyclopedia of Deer. London: 1993. V. 49; 52

WHITEHEAD, GEORGE
A Sober Expostulation with Some of the Clergy Against Their Pretended Convert Fracnis Bugg, His Repeated Gross Abuse of the People Called Quakers in His Books and Pamphlets. London: 1697. V. 47
The Way of Life and Perfection Living Demonstrated in some Serious Animadversions...Upon the Book Entituled The Middle Way of Perfection... London: 1676. V. 51

WHITEHEAD, H.
Jumbee and Other Uncanny Tales. Sauk City: 1944. V. 47; 49; 51; 54

WHITEHEAD, HENRY S.
West India Lights. Sauk City: 1946. V. 51

WHITEHEAD, JOHN
The Judicial and Civil History of New Jersey. Boston?: 1897. V. 47; 51
The Passaic Valley, New Jersey, in Three Centuries. New York: 1901. V. 49; 51

WHITEHEAD, P. J. P.
Chinese Natural History Drawings. London: 1974. V. 48; 50; 53
Clupeoid Fishes of the World. Rome: 1985-88. V. 52
Forty Drawings of Fishes Made by the Artists Who Accompanied Captain James Cook... London: 1968. V. 54

WHITEHEAD, PAUL
The Case of the Hon. Alex. Murray, Esq. In an Appeal to the People of Great Britain; More Particularly, the Inhabitants Of... Wesminster: 1851/. V. 53
The Gymnasiad, or Boxing Match. London: 1744. V. 50
Honour. London: 1747. V. 48
Manners. London: 1739. V. 48; 51; 54
The Poems and Miscellaneous Compositions with Explanatory Notes and His Life... London: 1777. V. 49
The Poems and Miscellaneous Compositions...with Explanatory Notes and His Life... London: 1787. V. 54
The State Dunces. London: 1733. V. 54

WHITEHEAD, SARAH R.
The Two Families: an Episode in the History of Chapelton. London: 1852. V. 50; 54

WHITEHEAD, THOMAS
History of the Dales Congregational Churches. Bradford: 1930. V. 53
Illustrated Guide to Nidderdale and a History of Its Congregational Churches. Bradford: 1932. V. 51; 53

WHITEHEAD, WILLIAM
A Charge to the Poets. London: 1762. V. 54
The Goat's Bread. London: 1777. V. 48
An Hymn to the Nymph of Bristol Spring. London: 1751. V. 51
Plays and Poems. London: 1774. V. 48
Plays and Poems. (with) Memoirs of His Life and Writings. London: 1774/88. V. 50
Variety. London: 1776. V. 49; 54
Verses to the People of England. 1758. London: 1758. V. 48

WHITEHEAD, WILLIAM A.
Contributions to the Early History of Perth Amboy and Adjoining Country, with Sketches of Men and Events in New Jersey During the Provincial Era... New York: 1856. V. 49; 51
East Jersey Under the Proprietary Governments: a Narrative of Events Connected With the Settlement and Progress of the Province, Until the Surrender of the Government to the Crown in 1703... Newark: 1875. V. 47; 49; 51

WHITEHOUSE, JOHN
Odes Moral and Descriptive by the Rev. John Whitehouse, of St. John's College, Cambridge. London: 1794. V. 54

WHITEHOUSE, MARY
Whatever Happened to Sex?. London: 1977. V. 48

WHITEHURST, JOHN
An Inquiry Into the Original State and Formation of the Earth... London: 1778. V. 49; 50
An Inquiry Into the Original State and Formation of the Earth... London: 1786. V. 48; 49
The Works, with Memoirs of His Life and Writings. 1792. V. 54

WHITELAW, ALEX
The Casquet of Literary Gems. Glasgow: 1850. V. 50
The Republic of Letters, a Selection, in Poetry and Prose, From the Works of the Most Eminent Writers with Many Original Pieces. Glasgow: 1835. V. 48

WHITELAW, GEORGE
A View of Old London as It Appeared in 1660. London: 1851. V. 54

WHITELAW, JAMES
An Essay on the Population of Dublin. 1805. V. 47

WHITELOCKE, BULSTRODE
The Diary. London: 1989. V. 52
A Journal of the Swedish Embassy, in the Years 1653 and 1654. London: 1772. V. 53
Memorials of the English Affairs... London: 1682. V. 52; 54
Memorials of the English Affairs... London: 1709. V. 47; 48
Memorials of the English Affairs... London: 1732. V. 48
Memorials of the English Affairs... London: 1853. V. 47
Notes Upon the Kings Writt...Being Disquisitions on the Government of England by King, Lord and Commons... London: 1766. V. 53
Whitelock's Notes Upon the Kings Writt for Choosing Members of Parlement XIII Car. II. London: 1766. V. 48

WHITELOCKE, JAMES
A Learned and Necessary Argument to Prove that Each Subject Hath a Prioriety in His Goods. London: 1641. V. 49

WHITELOCKE, JOHN
The Whole Proceedings of the Court Martial Held on General Whitelocke for Misconduct... London: 1808. V. 51

WHITELY, IKE
Rural Life in Texas. Atlanta: 1891. V. 47; 51

WHITER, WALTER
A Specimen of a Commentary on Shakespeare. London: 1794. V. 48; 49

WHITESIDE, J.
Sharpe in Bygone Days. Kendal: 1904. V. 50; 52

WHITESIDE, JAMES
Italy in the Nineteenth Century... London: 1848. V. 49
Italy in the Nineteenth Century. London: 1849. V. 53

WHITFIELD, A. STANTON
Mrs. Gaskell. Her Life and Work. London: 1929. V. 51

WHITFIELD, CHRISTOPHER
Lady from Yesterday. Waltham St. Lawrence: 1939. V. 47; 50
Mr. Chambers and Persephone. Waltham St. Lawrence: 1937. V. 51; 52
Together and Alone. London: 1945.. V. 52
Together and Alone. Waltham St. Lawrence: 1945. V. 47; 52

WHITFORD, NOBLE E.
History of the Barge Canal of New York State. Albany: 1922. V. 50; 54

WHITFORD, WILLIAM C.
Colorado Volunteers in the Civil War, the New Mexico Campaign of 1862. Denver: 1906. V. 49

WHITING, D. P.
Army Portfolio. New York: 1848. V. 47

WHITING, F. B.
Grit, Grief and Gold: a True Narrative of an Alaska Pathfinder. Seattle: 1933. V. 48

WHITING, GERTRUDE
A Lace Guide for Makers and Collectors. New York: 1920. V. 54
Tools and Toys of Stitchery. New York: 1928. V. 47; 48; 50

WHITING, HENRY
Ontwa, the Son of the Forest. New York: 1822. V. 48

WHITING, JOHN
Persecution Exposed, in Some Memoirs Relating to the Sufferings of John Whiting, and Many Others of the People Called Quakers, for Conscience Sake in the West of England... London: 1791. V. 49; 54

WHITING, LILIAN
The World Beautiful. Boston: 1895. V. 48

WHITING, SAMUEL
The Connecticut Town-Officer...Containing...the Powers and Duties of Towns...Town Officers (and) Religious and School Societies. Danbury: 1814. V. 52

WHITING, WILLIAM
The War Powers of the President and the Legislative Powers of Congress in Relation to Rebellion, Treason and Slavery. Boston: 1862. V. 51

WHITLAW, CHARLES
A Treatise on the Causes and Effects of Inflammation, Fever, Cancer, Scrofula, and Nervous Affections... London: 1831. V. 48; 49; 50; 51; 52; 54

WHITLEY, EDNA TALBOTT
Kentucky Ante-Bellum Portraiture. Paris: 1956. V. 48

WHITLEY, T. W.
The Parliamentary Representation of the City of Coventry from the Earliest Times to the Present Date. Coventry: 1894. V. 53

WHITLEY, WILLIAM T.
Artists and their Friends in England, 1700-1799. New York: 1968. V. 50

WHITLING, H. J.
Pictures of Nuremberg and Rambles in the Hills and Valleys of Franconia. London: 1850. V. 54

WHITLOCK, RICHARD
Zootomia, or, Observations on the Present Manners of the English... London: 1654. V. 51; 53

WHITMAN, ALBERT
An Idyl of the South. New York: 1901. V. 54

WHITMAN, ALFRED
Charles Turner. London: 1907. V. 47
Samuel Cousins. London: 1904. V. 54

WHITMAN, MALCOLM D.
Tennis: Origins and Mysteries. New York: 1932. V. 50

WHITMAN, RUTH
Tall Grasses. Boston: 1965. V. 48

WHITMAN, SARAH HELEN
Edgar Poe and His Critics. New York: 1860. V. 48; 49; 50; 52; 53
Hours of Life, and Other Poems. Providence: 1853. V. 48; 52
Poems. Boston: 1879. V. 48

WHITMAN, WALT
After All, Not to Create Only. Boston: 1871. V. 51
American Bard. Satna Cruz: 1981. V. 53
Autobiographia. New York: 1892. V. 54
Calamus: A Series of Letters Written by Walt Whitman. Boston: 1897. V. 47; 48; 52
Complete Poems and Prose of Walt Whitman. 1888. V. 50
The Complete Poetry and Selected Prose and Letters. London: 1938. V. 54
Complete Prose... Philadelphia: 1892. V. 48
Complete Prose. New York: 1914. V. 48
The Complete Writings. New York: 1902. V. 50; 52
Criticism: an Essay. Newark;: 1913. V. 52
Democratic Vistas, and Other Papers. London: 1888. V. 52
Drum-Taps. (with) Sequel to Drum-Taps. New York: 1865. V. 51
Franklin Evans; or the Inebriate. New York: 1842. V. 49; 54
Gems from Walt Whitman. Philadelphia: 1889. V. 51

WHITMAN, WALT continued
Good-Bye My Fancy. Philadelphia: 1891. V. 47; 48; 50; 51; 52
The Half-Breed and other Stories. New York: 1927. V. 47; 49; 51; 52
Have We a National Literature?. 1891. V. 49
Hymn on the Death of President Lincoln. London: 1900. V. 52
Leaves of Grass. Brooklyn: 1855. V. 48; 54
Leaves of Grass. Brooklyn: 1856. V. 50; 52
Leaves of Grass. Boston: 1860. V. 47; 48; 51; 54
Leaves of Grass. Boston: 1860-65. V. 52
Leaves of Grass. Boston: 1881-82. V. 49
Leaves of Grass. Philadelphia: 1882. V. 52
Leaves of Grass. Philadelphia: 1884. V. 49
Leaves of Grass. Philadelphia: 1891-92. V. 47; 49; 50; 52
Leaves of Grass. London: 1907. V. 53
Leaves of Grass. Portland: 1919. V. 47
Leaves of Grass. Garden City: 1928. V. 49
Leaves of Grass. 1930. V. 52; 54
Leaves of Grass. New York: 1930. V. 47; 48; 52
Leaves of Grass. New York: 1936. V. 49
Leaves of Grass. New York: 1937. V. 52
Leaves of Grass. New York: 1940. V. 51
Leaves of Grass. New York: 1942. V. 47; 48; 51; 53
Leaves of Grass. Tokyo: 1966. V. 51
Memoranda During the War. Camden: 1875-76. V. 51
Memories of President Lincoln. When Lilacs Last in the Dooryard Bloom'd. O Captain! My Captain... Portland: 1912. V. 49
New York Dissected - a Sheaf of Recently Discovered Newspaper Articles by the Author of Leaves of Grass. London: 1936. V. 52
Notebook Used Along the New Jersey Coast September & October 1883. Montclair: 1992. V. 49; 50; 51; 52
November Boughs. Philadelphia: 1888. V. 47; 48; 49; 50; 51; 52; 54
November Boughs. London: 1889. V. 52
November Boughs. 1891. V. 52
On the Beach at Night. 1992. V. 54
On the Beach at Night. Maine: 1992. V. 53
Out of the Cradle Endlessly Rocking. Santa Cruz & Torrance: 1976-78. V. 47
Out of the Cradle Endlessly Rocking. Torrance: 1978. V. 51; 53
Overhead the Sun. Lines from Walt Whitman. New York: 1969. V. 53
Poems. London: 1868. V. 48; 49; 52
President Lincoln's Funeral Hymn. London: 1900. V. 52; 54
Rivulets of Prose: Critical Essays. New York: 1928. V. 50
Selected Poems. New York: 1892. V. 48; 50; 51; 52; 53
Selected Poems. 1979. V. 52
Selected Poems. Sussex: 1979. V. 54
Song of the Open Road. 1990. V. 54
Song of the Open Road. New York: 1990. V. 51
Songs At Parting... San Francisco: 1930. V. 52
Specimen Days and Collect. 1882-83. V. 49
Specimen Days and Collect. Philadelphia: 1882-83. V. 47; 51; 52; 54
Specimen Days and Collect. Glasgow: 1883. V. 48; 51
Specimen Days and Collect. London: 1883. V. 54
Specimen Days in America. London: 1887. V. 51
There Was a Child Went Forth. Northampton: 1969. V. 50
Two Rivulets. Camden: 1876. V. 47; 54
Walt Whitman in Camden: a Selection of Prose from Specimen Days. Camden: 1938. V. 47
Walt Whitman's Blue Book. New York: 1968. V. 49
Walt Whitman's Diary in Canada with Extracts from Other of His Diaries and Literary Notebooks. Boston: 1904. V. 53
Walt Whitman's Workshop. Cambridge: 1928. V. 51; 53
The Wound Dresser: a Series of Letters Written from the Hospitals in Washington During the War of Rebellion. Boston: 1898. V. 49
Wrenching Times; Poems from Drum Taps. 1991. V. 52; 54
Wrenching Times: Poems from Drum Taps. Newtown: 1991. V. 47; 48

WHITMORE, ROSA TULLOCH
Memoir of a Lady, Daughter of Major Francis Tulloch, and Sister to the Marchioness of Stacpoole... Paris: 1827. V. 48

WHITMORE, TERRY
Memphis-Nam-Sweden: the Autobiography of a Black American Exile. Garden City: 1971. V. 54

WHITNEY, ADELINE DUTTON TRAIN
Faith Gartney's Girlhood. Boston: 1863. V. 53
The Gayworthys: a Story of Threads and Thrums. London: 1865. V. 47
Sights and Insights: Patience Strong's Story of Over the Way. Boston: 1877. V. 49

WHITNEY, ASA
Address of Mr. A. Whitney, Before the Legislature of Pennsylvania, on His Project for a Railroad from Lake Michigan to the Pacific. Harrisburg: 1848. V. 47
Memorial of A. Whitney, Praying, a Grant of Land to Enable Him to Construct a Railroad from Lake Michigan to the Pacific Ocean. Washington: 1848. V. 47
Memorial of A. Whitney, Praying, A Grant of Public Land to Enable Him to Construct a Railroad from Lake Michigan to the Pacific Ocean. Washington: 1846. V. 47
A Project for a Railroad to the Pacific. New York: 1849. V. 47
Report on Memorial of Thomas Allen and Others...in Favour of the Plan of Mr. Asa Whitney. Washington: 1850. V. 47

WHITNEY, C.
Musk-Ox, Bison, Sheep and Goat. London: 1904. V. 48

WHITNEY, CARRIE WESTLAKE
Kansas City, Missouri: Its History and Its People, 1808-1908. Chicago: 1908. V. 49

WHITNEY, CASPAR
Charles Adelbert Canfield. New York: 1930. V. 47; 49
Jungle Trails and Jungle People. New York: 1905. V. 52
Of Snow-Shoes to the Barren Ground. 1896. V. 52
On Snow-Shoes to the Barren Ground. New York: 1896. V. 47

WHITNEY, CHARLES S.
Bridges. A Study in their Art, Science and Evolution. New York: 1929. V. 49; 50; 53

WHITNEY, COURTNEY
MacArthur His Rendezvous with History. New York: 1956. V. 49

WHITNEY, D.
Andy Warhol Portraits of the '70's. New York: 1979. V. 54
Andy Warhol: Portraits of the '70's. New York: 1979/80. V. 51; 53

WHITNEY, DANIE H.
The Family Physician, and Guide to Health, in Three Parts. New York: 1833. V. 50

WHITNEY, GEOFFREY
Whitney's "Choice of Emblems". London: 1866. V. 48

WHITNEY, HARRY
Hunting with the Eskimos. London: 1910. V. 48; 50
Hunting with the Eskimos. New York: 1910. V. 53

WHITNEY, HELEN HAY
The Bed-Time Book. New York: 1907. V. 49

WHITNEY, J. P.
Le Colorado Aux Etats-Unis d'Amerique... Paris: 1867. V. 47

WHITNEY, J. PARKER
Reminiscences of a Sportsman. New York: 1906. V. 50

WHITNEY, JOHN
The Gentell Recreation; or, the Pleasure of Angling, a Poem. London: 1820. V. 47

WHITNEY, JOSIAH DWIGHT
The Yosemite Guide-Book: a Description of the Yosemite Valley and the Adjacent Region of the Sierra Nevada, and of the Big Tress of California. Sacramento: 1870. V. 54

WHITNEY, LEVI H.
To the Hon. Committee on Public Lands, House of Representatives of the United States. Washington: 1866. V. 49

WHITNEY, ORSON FERGUSON
Elias, an Epic of the Ages. New York: 1904. V. 48
History of Utah. Salt Lake City: 1892-1904. V. 53

WHITNEY, SALEM TUTT
Mellow Mussings. Boston: 1926. V. 48

WHITNEY, SUMNER
A Catalogue of Law Books.... San Francisco: 1869. V. 50

WHITNEY, W. D.
The Hayden Expedition. New Route to Yellowstone. New York: 1873. V. 54

WHITNEY, WILLIAM DWIGHT
Century Dictionary and Cyclopedia. New York: 1900. V. 47

WHITNEY, WILLIAM H.
Union and Confederate Campaigns in the Lower Shenandoah Valley. Boston: 1884. V. 54

WHITSELL, LEON O.
One Hundred Years of Freemasonry in California. San Francisco: 1950. V. 48

WHITTAKER, EDMUND T.
A History of Theories of Aether and Electricity. Dublin: 1910. V. 48; 50
A History of Theories of Aether and Electricity. London: 1951-53. V. 49

WHITTAKER, FREDERICK
Popular Life of Gen. George A. Custer. New York: 1876. V. 54

WHITTAKER, JOSEPH
The Deer Parks and Paddocks of England. 1892. V. 54

WHITTAKER, WALTER C.
Richard Hooker Wilmer Second Bishop of Alabama. Philadelphia: 1907. V. 50

WHITTARD, W. F.
The Ordovician Trilobites of the Shelve Inlier, West Shropshire. London: 1955-67. V. 49

WHITTED, J. A.
History of the Negro Baptists of North Carolina. Raleigh: 1908. V. 53

WHITTEL, JOHN
Constantinus Redivivus; or a Full Account of the Wonderful Providences and Unparallell'd Successes That Have All Along Attended the Glorious Enterprises of the Heroical Prince, William the 3d, now King of Great Britain... London: 1693. V. 50; 53

WHITTELL, H. M.
The Literature of Australian Birds... Mansfield: 1994. V. 53

WHITTEMORE, EDWARD
Quin's Shanghai Circus. New York: 1974. V. 51

WHITTICK, ARNOLD
Eric Mendelsohn. London: 1940. V. 49

WHITTIER, JOHN GREENLEAF
At Sundown. Cambridge: 1890. V. 51; 54
At Sundown. Boston & New York: 1892. V. 50
At Sundown. Cambridge: 1892. V. 52
The Complete Poetical Works of John Greenleaf Whittier. Boston: 1875. V. 49
History of Pennsylvania Hall, Which Was Destroyed by a Mob on the 17th of May 1838. Philadelphia: 1838. V. 53
Home Ballads. Boston: 1860. V. 50
The King's Missive and Other Poems. Boston: 1881. V. 54
Lays of My Home and Other Poems. Boston: 1843. V. 54
Legends and Lyrics. Boston & New York: 1890. V. 47
Legends of New England. Hartford: 1831. V. 48; 49; 50
The Life and Letters of John Greenleaf Whittier. Boston: 1894. V. 52
The Literary Remains of John G. C. Brainard, with a Sketch of His Life. Hartford: 1832. V. 52
Miriam. Boston: 1871. V. 52
Moggmegone. A Poem. Boston: 1836. V. 53
Moll Pitcher, a Poem. Boston: 1832. V. 52
Narrative of James Williams, an American Slave, Who Was for Several Years a Driver on a Cotton Plantation in Alabama. New York: 1838. V. 52
National Lyrics. Boston: 1866. V. 50
Our Countrymen in Chains!. New York: 1835-36. V. 47
The Panorama and Other Poems. Boston: 1856. V. 52
Poems. Boston: 1849. V. 53; 54
Poetical Works. Boston: 1864. V. 48
The Poetical Works. Boston: 1868. V. 47
The Poetical Works... London: 1900. V. 54
Prose Works. Boston: 1866. V. 51
Prose Works. Boston: 1872. V. 50
The Red River Voyageur. Winnipeg: 1892. V. 48
A Sabbath Scene. Boston: 1854. V. 50
Saint Gregory's Guest and Recent Poems. Cambridge: 1886. V. 52
Snow-Bound. Boston: 1866. V. 47; 48; 50; 51
Snow-Bound... Boston & New York: 1892. V. 52
Snow-Bound. New York: 1930. V. 54
Songs of the Free. Boston: 1836. V. 47
Songs of Three Centuries. Boston: 1876. V. 52
The Supernaturalism of New England. London: 1847. V. 47; 54
The Supernaturalism of New England. New York: 1847. V. 51; 53
The Writings. Cambridge: 1888. V. 50

WHITTINGTON PRESS
A Miscellany of Type. Andoversford: 1990. V. 47; 48
Nine Artists and a Press. An Exhibition of the Work of Nine Artists Working for the Whittington Press, Held at the Fiery Beacon Gallery, 2-17, December '89. Andoversford: 1989. V. 51
Type Specimen. Andoversford: 1990. V. 48

WHITTINGTON, ROBERT
Roberti Whitintoni Lichfeldiensis Lucubrationes. De Synonimis. London: 1522. V. 47

WHITTLE, PETER ARMSTRONG
The History of the Borough of Preston, in the County Palatine of Lancaster. Preston: 1821-37. V. 48

WHITTLE, WILLIAM C.
Cruises of the Confederate States Steamers 'Shenandoah' and 'Nashville'. N.P: 1910. V. 49

WHITTLESEY, CHARLES
Early History of Cleveland, Ohio, Including Original Papers and Other Matter Relating to the Adjacent Country... Cleveland: 1867. V. 51
War Memoranda. Cheat River to the Tennessee, 1861-62. Cleveland: 1884. V. 49

WHITTLESEY, J. H.
Report On National Military Education, with the Plan of a System for the United States, Based on Existing Educational Agencies. Washington: 1867. V. 50

WHITTOCK, ARNOLD
Eric Mendelsohn. London: 1940. V. 51

WHITTOCK, N.
A Picturesque Guide through Dublin. 1846. V. 54

WHITTOCK, NATHANIEL
The Art of Drawing and Colouring, from Nature, Birds, Beasts, Fishes and Insects. London: 1830. V. 50
The Costumes of the Members of the University of Oxford... London: 1830. V. 47
The Decorative Painters' and Glaziers' Guide... London: 1827. V. 48; 54
The Decorative Painter's and Glaziers' Guide. London: 1828. V. 49; 54
The Microcosm of Oxford... Oxford: 1830. V. 50
The Oxford Drawing Book, or the Art of Drawing... London: 1825. V. 49; 53
The Oxford Drawing Book, or the Art of Drawing... London: 1830. V. 48; 50
Roman Antiquities, from Trajans Column and Other Authorities. Oxford: 1830?. V. 49
The Youth's New London Self-Instructing Drawing Book... London: 1834. V. 48; 50

WHITWORTH, CHARLES
An Account of Russia as It Was in the Year 1710. Strawberry Hill: 1758. V. 48; 49; 50; 52; 54

WHITWORTH, JOSEPH
Miscellaneous Papers on Mechanical Subjects. London: 1858. V. 53

WHITWORTH, ROBERT
A Report and Survey of the Canal Proposed to Be Made on One Level, from Waltham-Abbey to Moorfields. London: 1773. V. 54
A Report and Survey of the Canal, Proposed to Be Made On One Level, from Waltham-Abbey to Moorfields. London: 1774. V. 51

WHO Burnt Columbia?. Charleston: 1873. V. 49

WHO Stole My Nest?. New York: 1870-80. V. 52

WHOLE Art of Bookbinding, Containing Valuable Recipes For Sprinkling, Marbling (sic), Colouring &c. Oswestry: 1811. V. 48

THE WHOLE Art of Bookbinding. The Whole Process of Marbling Paper. Austin: 1987. V. 48

WHOLE Art of Conjuring, or, Hocus Pocus. Philadelphia New York: 1850. V. 51

THE WHOLE Art of Dress! Or, The Road to Elegance and Fashion... London: 1830. V. 48; 50

THE WHOLE Art of Fishing. London: 1714. V. 47

THE WHOLE Art of Gymnastics and Muscular Development. London: 1870?. V. 47

THE WHOLE Family. New York: 1908. V. 52; 53

THE WHOLE Proceedings on the Special Commissions of Oyer and Terminer and Goal Delivery, for the County of Sussex, Held at Chichester, the 16th, 17th and 18th Days of January Last; Before the Hon. Mr. Justice Foster, Mr. Baron Clive, and Mr. Justice Birch... London: 1749. V. 47

THE WHORE of Babylon's Pockety Priest; or, a True Narrative of the Apprehensions of William Geldon Alias Bacon, a Secular Priest of the Church of Rome Now Prisoner in Newgate. London: 1679/80. V. 48

WHO'S Who in China. Shanghai: 1920. V. 54

WHO'S Who in Cumberland and Westmorland. London: 1937. V. 50; 52

WHO'S Who in Nazi Germany. London: 1943. V. 47

WHO'S Who in Professional Portraiture in America. Cleveland: 1927. V. 47

WHY Abstract?. New York: 1945. V. 50

WHY the Sea Is Salt - and Other Fairy Stories. London: 1946. V. 52

WHYMPER, CHARLES
Egyptian Birds for the Most Part Seen in the Nile Valley. London: 1909. V. 47; 49; 54

WHYMPER, EDWARD
The Ascent of the Matterhorn. London: 1880. V. 51; 52
Chamonix and the Range of Mont Blanc. London: 1896. V. 48
How to Use the Aneroid Barometer. 1891. V. 53
How to Use the Aneroid Barometer. London: 1891. V. 52
Letter Addressed to Members of the Alpine Club (On the Controversy over a Leap by Christian Almer). 1900. V. 53
Scrambles Amongst the Alps in the Years 1860-69. London: 1871. V. 51; 52
The Scrambles Amongst the Alps in the Years 1860-69. London: 1893. V. 51; 53
Scrambles Amongst the Alps in the Years 1860-69. London: 1900. V. 50; 52
Travels Amongst the Great Andes of the Equator... London: 1891-92. V. 52
Travels Amongst the Great Andes of the Equator. London: 1892. V. 48; 50; 52; 53; 54
Travels Amongst the Great Andes of the Equator. New York: 1892. V. 47; 49; 51; 54

WHYMPER, FREDERICK
Travel and Adventure in the Territory of Alaska, Formerly Russian America... London: 1868. V. 48; 53; 54
Travel and Adventure in the Territory of Alaska, Formerly Russian America... New York: 1869. V. 52

WHYTE, FREDERIC
The Life of W. T. Stead. New York: 1925. V. 52

WHYTE, JOHN
Carl Rungius, Painter of the Western Wilderness. Vancouver: 1985. V. 53

WHYTE, LAURENCE
Original Poems on Various Subjects, Serious, Moral and Diverting. (with) Part the Second. 1742. V. 47
Original Poems on Various Subjects, Serious, Moral and Diverting...To This Edition, are Added the Following Poems Never Before Published viz... Dublin: 1742. V. 50

WHYTE, SAMUEL
A Collection of Poems, the Productions of the Kingdom of Ireland. London: 1773. V. 51
Miscellanea Nova... Dublin: 1801. V. 47
The Shamrock; or, Hibernian Cresses. Dublin: 1772. V. 47

WHYTE, W. E.
O'Er the Atlantic, or a Journal of a Voyage to and From Europe... New York: 1870. V. 47

WHYTE-MELVILLE, GEORGE JOHN
The Arab's Ride to Cairo: a Legend of the Desert. Edinburgh: 1857. V. 53
The Brookes of Bridlemere. London: 1864. V. 51
Cerise: a Tale of the Last Century. London: 1866. V. 51
General Bounce or the Lady and the Locusts. London: 1855. V. 48
The Gladiators. London: 1863. V. 51
Good for Nothing; or, All Down Hill. London: 1861. V. 51
Kate Coventry; an Autobiography. London: 1856. V. 51

WHYTE-MELVILLE, GEORGE JOHN continued
Novels. London: 1890. V. 52
The Queen's Maries. London: 1862. V. 51
Roy's Wife. London: 1878. V. 54
Tilbury Nogo; or, Passages in the Life of an Unsuccessful Man. London: 1854. V. 51
The Works... 1890. V. 50
Works. London: 1890's. V. 48
The Works... London: 1899-1902. V. 50

WHYTT, ROBERT
An Essay on the Virtues of Lime-Water in the Cure of the Stone. Edinburgh: 1755. V. 50; 53
An Essay on the Vital and Involuntary Motions of Animals. Edinburgh: 1763. V. 53
Observations on the Nature, Causes and Cure of the Diseases Which Have Been Commonly Called Nervous Hypochondriac, or Hysteric. Edinburgh: 1765. V. 53
Observations on the Nature, Causes and Cure of Those Diseases Which Have Been Commonly Called Nervous Hypochondriac, or Hysteric... Edinburgh: 1764-65. V. 52
The Works. Edinburgh: 1768. V. 47

WICHELMAN'S Ocean, River and Land Distance Tables, Compiled for the Traveling Public of the United States. Chicago: 1869. V. 50

WICHMANN, SIEGFRIED
Japonisme. New York: 1981. V. 48

WICK, P. A.
The Book Beautiful and the Binding as Art. New York and Boston: 1983/85. V. 50

WICKENDEN, WILLIAM
Adventures Before Sebastopol. London: 1855. V. 51

WICKERSHAM, JAMES
A Bibliography of Alaskan Literature 1724-1924. Cordova: 1927. V. 51; 54
Old Yukon. Tales - Trails and Trials. Washington: 1938. V. 48

WICKES, CHARLES
Illustrations of the Spires and Towers of the Mediaeval Churches of England. Boston: 1889. V. 50

WICKES, GEORGE
Lawrence Durrell and Henry Miller A Private Correspondence. New York: 1963. V. 54

WICKES, STEPHEN
History of Medicine in New Jersey and of Its Medical Men, from the Settlement fo the Province to A.D. 1800. Newark: 1879. V. 47; 49; 51

WICKHAM, J. D. C.
Records by Spade and Terrier. Bath: 1910. V. 54

WICKHOFF, FRANZ
Roman Art: Some of its Principles and Their Application to Early Christian painting. London: 1900. V. 50; 52

WICKSTED, CHARLES
The Cheshire Hunt: a Song. Chester: 1837. V. 47

WICKSTEED, JOSEPH H.
Blake's Innocence and Experience. A Study of the Songs and Manuscripts. London: 1928. V. 48; 49
Blake's Vision of the Book of Job With Reproductions of the Illustrations. London: 1910. V. 51

WICQUEFORT, ABRAHAM DE
L'Ambassadeur et Ses Fonctions. The Hague: 1680-81. V. 53

WIDDICOMBE Fair. London and New York: 1899. V. 50

WIDE, THOMAS JAMES
A Complete Bibliography of the Writings of John Ruskin, LL.D. London: 1893. V. 48

WIDEMAN, JOHN EDGAR
Brothers and Keepers. New York: 1984. V. 51
Damballah. London: 1984. V. 52
Fever. New York: 1989. V. 53
A Glance Away. New York: 1967. V. 47; 48; 49; 52; 53
Hiding Place. London: 1984. V. 52
The Homewood Trilogy. London: 1984. V. 51
Hurry Home. New York: 1970. V. 52
The Lynchers. New York: 1973. V. 51; 52
Philadelphia Fire. New York: 1990. V. 52; 53
Reuben. New York: 1987. V. 53
Sent for You Yesterday. London: 1984. V. 53
The Stories of John Edgar Wideman. New York: 1992. V. 52; 53

WIDENER, P. A. B.
Pictures in the Collection of P. A. B. Widener at Lynnewood Hall, Pennysylvania. Philadelphia: 1913/15/16. V. 50

WIEBEKING, CARL FRIEDRICH VON
Memoire sur des Ponts Supsendus en Chaines de Fer, Relatif aux Ponts Construits dans le Dernier Temps en Angleterre et en Russie, et Lequel Servira de Complement a l'Ouvrage sur l'Architecture-Civile. Munich: 1832. V. 53

WIEDEMANN, ALFRED
Religion of the Ancient Egyptians. London: 1897. V. 48; 51

WIED-NEUWIED, MAXIMILIAN, PRINZ VON
Abbildungen zur Naturgeschichte Brasiliens. Weimar: 1822-31. V. 47

WIEGLEB, JOHANN CHRISTIAN
A General System of Chemistry. London: 1789. V. 53

WIELAND, CHRISTOPH MARTIN
Oberon, a Poem, from the German of Wieland. London: 1708. V. 50

WIELAND, TERRY
Spiral-Horn Dreams. 1955. V. 54

WIENER, LEO
Mayan and Mexican Originals. Cambridge: 1926. V. 48; 54

WIENER, NORBERT
Collected Works. Cambridge: 1976-85. V. 47
Cybernetics or Control and Communication in the Animal and the Machine. New York: 1948. V. 47; 48; 49; 54
Cybernetics or Control and Communication in the Animal and the Machine. New York: 1949. V. 47; 49; 50
Cybernetics, or Control and Communication in the Animal and the Machine. Cambridge: 1961. V. 54
Cybernetics, or Control and Communication in the Animal and the Machine. Cambridge: 1962. V. 54
Ex-Prodigy, My Childhood and Youth. New York: 1953. V. 51
The Human Use of Human Beings. Boston: 1950. V. 47; 49; 50

WIENERS, JOHN
Ace of Pentacles. New York: 1964. V. 47; 53
Chinoiserie. San Francisco: 1965. V. 47
The Hotel Wentley Poems. San Francisco: 1958. V. 51
Unhired. Mt. Horeb: 1968. V. 52

WIERZBICKI, F. P.
California As It Is and As It May Be. San Francisco: 1933. V. 47; 54

WIESEL, ELIE
The Golem. New York: 1983. V. 52
Night. London: 1960. V. 48
Night. New York: 1960. V. 54
Twilight. New York: 1988. V. 49; 51

WIESER, FRIEDRICH VON
Natural Value... London: 1893. V. 51

THE WIFE; or, Women as They Are. London: 1835. V. 51

WIFFEN, JEREMIAH HOLMES
Historical Memoirs of the House of Russell, from the Time of the Norman Conquest. London: 1833. V. 50; 53
Verses Written in the Portico of the Temple of Liberty at Woburn Abbey, on Placking Before It the Statues of Locke and Erskine in the Summer of 1835. London: 1836. V. 50

WIGFALL, LOUIS T.
Speech of Hon. L. T. Wigfall of Texas, on Relation of States. Delivered in the Senate of the United States May 22 & 23, 1860. Washington: 1860. V. 49

WIGG, JOHN GODDARD
Family Records. A Brief Memoir of the Rev. John Carter, of Mattishall, Norfolk. Carlton, Melbourne: 1880. V. 51

WIGGERS, CARL
Modern Aspects of the Circulation in Health and Disease. Philadelphia: 1915. V. 49; 54

WIGGIN, KATE DOUGLAS
Bluebeard: a Musical Fantasy. New York and London: 1914. V. 47; 48; 51
A Child's Journey with Dickens. Boston: 1912. V. 52
A Child's Journey with Dickens. Boston: 1915. V. 47
A Child's Journey with Dickens. Boston: 1922. V. 52
Penelope's Irish Adventures. Boston and New York: 1901. V. 53
Rebecca of Sunnybrook Farm. Boston: 1903. V. 50; 53
Rebecca of Sunnybrook Farm. Boston: 1904. V. 54
The Romance of a Christmas Card. 1916. V. 50; 53
The Story of Patsy. San Francisco: 1883. V. 53
Susanna and Sue. Boston: 1909. V. 50
The Village Watch Tower. Boston: 1895. V. 51

WIGGINS, EZEKIEL S.
The Architecture of the Heavens... Montreal: 1864. V. 47

WIGGINS, LIDA KECK
The Life and Works of Paul Laurence Dunbar. Naperville & Memphis: 1907. V. 49; 51; 54

WIGGINS, MARIANNE
Went South. New York: 1980. V. 50; 54

WIGGINS, WALT
Kid Russell, a Rare Collection of Early Cowboy Art Montana Territory in the 1880's. Rudioso: 1989. V. 50

WIGHAM, ELIZA
The Anti-Slavery Cause in America and Its Martyrs. London: 1863. V. 52

WIGHT, ALEXANDER
An Inquiry Into the Rise and Progress of Parliament, Chiefly in Scotland... Edinburgh: 1784. V. 48
An Inquiry Into the Rise and Progress of Parliament, Chiefly in Scotland... (with) Election Cases, Decided in the Court of Session, House of Peers and High Court of Justiciary, Chiefly from 1784 to 1796... Edinburgh: 1784/96. V. 51
A Treatise on the Laws Concerning the Election of the Different Representatives Sent from Scotland to The Parliament of Great Britain. Edinburgh: 1773. V. 48

WIGHT, ANDREW
A Catalogue of the Entire Library of Andrew Wight of Philadelphia. New York: 1864. V. 48

WIGHT, AUSTIN TAPPAN
Islandia. New York: 1942. V. 49

WIGHT, J.
Sunday in London. London: 1833. V. 48

WIGHT, R.
Illustrations of Indian Botany... Madras: 1840-50. V. 47

WIGHT, THOMAS
A History of the...People Called Quakers in Ireland from... Dublin: 1751. V. 48; 49; 50; 51; 52; 54
A History of the...People Called Quakers in Ireland from... 1800. V. 49; 50; 54
A History of the...People Called Quakers in Ireland from... London: 1800. V. 47; 51; 53

WIGHT, WILLIAM
Cottage Poems. Edinburgh: 1820. V. 54

WIGHT, WILLIAM WARD
Eleazer Williams - His Forerunners, Himself. Milwaukee: 1896. V. 48

WIGHTMAN, ROBERT
Information for Robert Wightman and Others Against the Earl of Hopeton. Edinburgh: 1730. V. 53

WIGHTMAN, W. P. D.
Science and the Renaissance: an Introduction to the Study of the Emergence of the Sciences in the Sixteenth Century. Edinburgh & London: 1962. V. 54

WIGHTWICK, GEORGE
Hints to Young Architects... London: 1846. V. 48; 50; 53
The Palace of Architecture. London: 1840. V. 47; 50

WIGMORE, JOHN HENRY
A Treatise on the Anglo-American System of Evidence in Trials at Common Law. Boston: 1923. V. 51

WIGRAM, W. A.
The Cradle of Mankind Life in Eastern Kurdistan. London: 1914. V. 54

WIGSTEAD, HENRY
Remarks on a Tour to North and South Wales. London: 1800. V. 47; 51

WIJDEVELD, H. T.
The Life Work of the American Architect Frank Lloyd Wright. Santpoort: 1925. V. 49; 52

WIJDEVELD, T.
Wendingen. Amsterdam: 1921. V. 51

WIJNBLAD, CARL
Afhandling om Mur-och Tak-Tegelbruks. Stockholm: 1761. V. 47

WILBARGER, J. W.
Indian Depredations in Texas. Austin: 1935. V. 54

WILBER, C. D.
The Great Valleys and Prairies of Nebraska and the Northwest. Omaha: 1881. V. 47

WILBER, MARGUERITE EYER
Vancouver in California, 1792-1794: the Original Account of George Vancouver. Los Angeles: 1953. V. 50

WILBERFORCE, R. I.
The Life of William Wilberforce. London: 1838. V. 54

WILBERFORCE, REGINALD G.
An Unrecorded Chapter of the Indian Mutiny. London: 1894. V. 53

WILBERFORCE, WILLIAM
An Appeal to the Religion, Justice and Humanity of the Inhabitants of the British Empire, In Behalf of the Negro Slaves in the West Indies. London: 1823. V. 50
A Letter on the Abolition of the Slave-Trade; addressed to the Freeholders and Other Inhabitants of Yorkshire. London: 1807. V. 52

WILBRAHAM, RICHARD
Travels in the Trans-Caucasian Provinces of Russia, And Along the Southern Shore of the Lakes of Van and Urumiah, in the Autumn and Winter of 1837. London: 1839. V. 48; 54

WILBUR, HOMER
The Biglow Papers. Cambridge: 1848. V. 49

WILBUR, K. M.
Physiology of Mollusca. London: 1964-66. V. 49; 52; 53

WILBUR, MARGUERITE E.
The Indian Uprising in Lower California, 1734-1737... Los Angeles: 1931. V. 53

WILBUR, RICHARD
The Beautiful Changes. New York: 1947. V. 47; 49; 51; 52; 53
A Bestiary. New York: 1955. V. 48; 50; 53
Ceremony. New York: 1950. V. 49
Complaint. New York: 1968. V. 54
Pedestrian Flight. 1981. V. 48; 51
Poems 1943-1956. London: 1957. V. 48
Things of This World. New York: 1956. V. 51

WILCOCK, JOHN
The Autobiography and Sex-Life of Andy Warhol. New York: 1971. V. 50

WILCOCK, PETER
The Lives of the Abbots of Wearmouth. Sunderland: 1818. V. 53

WILCOCKE, SAMUEL HULL
A Narrative of Occurrences in the Indian Countries of North America, Since the Connexion of the Right Hon. the Earl of Selkirk with the Hudson's Bay Company and His Attempt to Establish a Colony on the Red River. London: 1817. V. 52
Report of the Proceedings Connected with the Disputes Between the Earl of Selkirk and the North-West Company, at the Assizes, Held at York, in Upper Canada, October 1818. London: 1819. V. 52

WILCOCKS, JOSEPH
Roman Conversations; or, a Short Description of the Antiquities of Rome, and the Characters of Many Eminent Romans. London: 1792. V. 50; 53

WILCOX, B.
The Atlas of Dog Breeds of the World. London: 1991. V. 50

WILCOX, CADMUS M.
History of the Mexican War. Washington: 1892. V. 47

WILCOX, DANIEL
The Noble Stand: or a Just Vindication of Those Brave Spirits Who in the Late Memorable Actions at Salters-Hall Distinguished Themselves. London: 1719. V. 53

WILCOX, ELLA WHEELER
The Love Sonnets of Abelard and Heloise. Hammond: 1907. V. 53
Poems of Passion and Pleasure. London: 1912. V. 51
Poems of Pleasure. London: 1910?. V. 53
Shells. Milwaukee: 1873. V. 48

WILCOX, MICHAEL
Twelve Bindings. Austin: 1985. V. 47; 48

WILCOX, THOMAS
A Right Godly and Learned Exposition, Upon the Whole Booke of Psalmes... London: 1586. V. 52

WILCOX, WALTER DWIGHT
The Rockies of Canada. New York: 1900. V. 47

WILCOXSIN, W.
History of Stratford, CT. 1639-1939. Stratford: 1939. V. 53

WILD, CHARLES
An Illustration of the Architecture and Sculpture of the Cathedral Church of Lincoln. London: 1819. V. 47; 49; 50; 54
An Illustration of the Architecture of the Cathedral Church of Lichfield. (with) An Illustration of the Architecture of the Cathedral Church of Chester. London: 1813. V. 49; 50
Select Examples of Architectural Grandeur in Belgium, Germany and France. London: 1843. V. 47
Twelve Perspective Views of the Exterior and Interior Parts of the Metropolitical Church of York... London: 1809. V. 50

WILD Flowers and Their Teachings. Bath & London: 1845. V. 48

WILD Flowers of America. New York: 1894. V. 51

WILD Flowers of Canada. Montreal. V. 48; 54
WILD Flowers of Canada. Montreal: 1895. V. 49

WILD, FRANK
Shackleton's Last Voyage. New York. V. 50
Shackleton's Last Voyage. London: 1923. V. 50

WILD, J. C.
The Valley of the Mississippi. St. Louis: 1948. V. 49

WILD, JOSEPH
The Lost Ten Tribes: and 1882. New York: 1879. V. 47

WILD, ROBERT
Iter Boreale. London: 1660. V. 49
Iter Boreale... London: 1670. V. 47
Iter Boreale. London: 1671. V. 50

WILDE, JANE FRANCESCA ELGEE, LADY
Ancient Cures, Charms and Usages of Ireland. 1890. V. 49; 50
Ancient Cures, Charms and Usages of Ireland. London: 1890. V. 53
Poems by Speranza. Glasgow: 1870. V. 53

WILDE, JOHN
44 Wilde 1944: Being a Selection of 44 Images from a Sketchbook... Mt. Horeb: 1984. V. 51; 52; 54
An Address to the Lately Formed Society of the Friends of the People. Edinburgh: 1793. V. 49
The Story of Jane and Joan. Mt. Horeb: 1977. V. 54

WILDE, OSCAR
After Berneval - Letters of Oscar Wilde to Robert Ross. London: 1922. V. 49; 53
The Ballad of Reading Gaol. London: 1898. V. 48; 51; 52; 53; 54
The Ballad of Reading Gaol. London: 1899. V. 51
The Ballad of Reading Gaol. New York: 1899. V. 53
The Ballad of Reading Gaol. East Aurora: 1905. V. 52
The Ballad of Reading Gaol. Greenwich: 1905. V. 51
The Ballad of Reading Gaol. London: 1924/25. V. 47; 52
The Ballad of Reading Gaol. New York: 1928. V. 48; 50; 54
The Ballad of Reading Gaol. New York: 1930. V. 48; 50
The Ballad of Reading Gaol. New York: 1937. V. 52; 53; 54

WILDE, OSCAR continued
The Ballad of Reading Gaol. 1994. V. 52
Ballade de la Geole de Reading. Paris: 1898. V. 53
Ballade de la Geole de Reading. Paris: 1951. V. 47
Berneval: an Unpublished Letter. London: 1981. V. 49
The Birthday of the Infanta. Paris: 1928. V. 54
The Birthday of the Infanta. New York: 1929. V. 48
The Complete Works. Garden City: 1923. V. 48
Complete Writings. New York: 1905-1909. V. 51
The Critic as Artist: a Dialogue. Utrecht: 1957. V. 52
De Profundis. London: 1905. V. 48; 49; 50; 51; 52; 53
De Profundis. London: 1908. V. 48; 53
De Profundis. London: 1925. V. 50
De Profundis. London: 1949. V. 54
Essays, Criticisms and Reviews. London: 1901. V. 48
Extracts from the Poems of Oscar Wilde. London: 1980. V. 53
The Fisherman and His Soul and Other Tales. London: 1929. V. 50
A Florentine Tragedy. Boston: 1908. V. 53
The Happy Prince and Other Tales. London: 1888. V. 49; 52; 53
The Happy Prince and Other Tales. London: 1913. V. 48; 51
The Happy Prince and Other Tales. Stamford: 1936. V. 49
Hellenism. Edinburgh: 1979. V. 50; 52
The House of Judgement. Utrecht: 1986. V. 52
A House of Pomegranates. London: 1891. V. 49; 51; 52; 53; 54
A House of Pomegranates... London: 1908. V. 49
The House of Pomegranates. London and New York: 1915. V. 51
An Ideal Husband. London: 1899. V. 48; 49; 51; 52; 53; 54
The Importance of Being Earnest. London: 1899. V. 50; 51
The Importance of Being Earnest. London: 1908. V. 48; 53
The Importance of Being Earnest. London: 1910. V. 49; 52
The Importance of Being Earnest. New York: 1956. V. 52; 53
Impressions of America. Sunderland: 1906. V. 48; 49; 51; 53
Intentions. London: 1891. V. 51
Intentions... London: 1894. V. 54
Intentions. Portland: 1904. V. 51
Intentions. New York: 1905. V. 51
Der Junge Fischer und Seine Seele. Zurich: 1951. V. 50
Lady Windermere's Fan. London: 1893. V. 51
Lady Windermere's Fan... Paris: 1903. V. 49; 52
Lady Windermere's Fan... London: 1973. V. 47; 52; 54
The Letters of Oscar Wilde. London: 1962. V. 50
Letters to Graham Hill. Edinburgh: 1978. V. 54
Lord Arthur Savile's Crime and Other Stories. London: 1891. V. 54
Miscellanies. London: 1908. V. 48; 53
Oscar Wilde: Graham Hill - a Brief Friendship. Edinburgh: 1982. V. 54
Phrases and Philosophies for the Use of the Young. London: 1902?. V. 52
Phrases and Philosophies for the Use of the Young. London: 1905?. V. 52
The Picture of Dorian Gray. London: 1891. V. 48; 49; 51; 52
The Picture of Dorian Gray. Vienna: 1908. V. 47
The Picture of Dorian Gray. Paris: 1910. V. 49
The Picture of Dorian Gray. London: 1925. V. 48; 51; 54
The Picture of Dorian Gray. New York: 1930. V. 52
The Picture of Dorian Gray. New York: 1957. V. 50
The Plays of Oscar Wilde. Boston: 1905. V. 51
Poems. Boston: 1881. V. 47; 48; 49; 50; 51
Poems. London: 1881. V. 48; 52
Poems. London: 1882. V. 51
The Poems... Portland: 1903. V. 53
The Poems... New York: 1927. V. 47
Poems by Oscar Wilde Together With his Lecture on the English Renaissance. Paris: 1902. V. 51
Poems in Prose and the Preface to the Picture of Dorian Gray. 1974. V. 49
Ravenna. Oxford: 1878. V. 47; 48; 51; 52; 53; 54
Reviews. London: 1908. V. 48; 53
The Rise of Historical Criticism. Hartford: 1905. V. 51
Rose Leaf and Apple Leaf L'Envoi. London: 1904. V. 51
Salome. Paris: 1893. V. 48; 49; 52
Salome. London and Boston: 1894. V. 47; 49; 51
Salome. San Francisco: 1896. V. 51
Salome. Leipzig: 1907. V. 50
Salome. London: 1907. V. 47
Salome. London: 1908. V. 48; 53
Salome. 1922. V. 47
Salome. Paris: 1922. V. 53
Salome... Paris: 1923. V. 52
Salome. New York: 1927. V. 53
Salome. San Francisco: 1927. V. 48; 51
Salome. Paris: 1930. V. 49; 54
Salome. New York: 1938. V. 52
Salome. Paris & London: 1938. V. 48; 52; 53
Salome. London: 1957. V. 52; 53
Salome. Paris: 1966. V. 51
Sebastian Melmoth. London: 1904. V. 54
Selected Poems of Oscar Wilde Including the Ballad of Reading Gaol. London: 1919. V. 50; 53
The Selfish Giant. West Burke: 1967. V. 50
The Short Stories Of... Burlington: 1968. V. 52; 54
Some Letters...to Alfred Douglas, 1892-1897 (Heretofore Unpublished). San Francisco: 1924. V. 47
The Soul of Man. London: 1895. V. 53
The Soul of Man... Portland: 1950. V. 47
The Sphinx. London: 1894. V. 47; 49; 52; 54
The Sphinx. London: 1901. V. 51
The Sphinx. London: 1920. V. 48; 49; 53; 54
Stories/Plays and Poems/ Essays and Letters. London: 1993. V. 53
To M. B. J. Hampstead: 1920. V. 53
Vera; or, the Nihilists. London: 1902. V. 50; 51
What Never Dies. Paris: 1902. V. 53
Wilde v. Whistler, Being an Acrimonious Correspondence on Art. London: 1906. V. 48
A Woman of No Importance. London: 1894. V. 47; 51
A Woman of No Importance. London: 1908. V. 48
The Works... Paris. V. 49
Works. London: 1908. V. 49; 50; 54
The Works... Paris: 1908. V. 48
The Works... London: 1908-22. V. 51
The Works... Boston & New York: 1909. V. 50
Works. London: 1969. V. 51; 52
The Young King and Other Fairy Tales. New York: 1962. V. 52

WILDE, R.
Memoir of Gabriel Beranger, and His Labours in the Cause of Irish Art and Antiquities. London: 1880. V. 47

WILDE, W. R.
Lough Corrib, Its Shores and Islands. London: 1872. V. 48

WILDE, WILLIAM ROBERT WILLS
The Closing Years of Dean Swift's Life... Dublin: 1849. V. 54

WILDENSTEIN, GEORGES
Chardin. Zurich: 1963. V. 51; 53
Chardin. Greenwich: 1969. V. 50
Chardin. Oxford: 1969. V. 51
Ingres. London: 1926. V. 52
Ingres. London: 1954. V. 51
Ingres. London: 1956. V. 52
The Paintings of Fragonard. London: 1960. V. 51; 53
Paul Gauguin. Paris: 1964. V. 54

WILDER, DANIEL W.
The Annals of Kansas. Topeka: 1875. V. 51; 54

WILDER, LAURA INGALLS
Little House on the Prairie. New York: 1953. V. 49
On the Banks of Plum Creek. New York: 1937. V. 48

WILDER, MITCHELL A.
Santos: the Religious Folk Art of New Mexico. Colorado Springs: 1943. V. 52; 53

WILDER, ROBERT
The Sound of Drums and Cymbals. London: 1974. V. 54

WILDER, THORNTON
The Alcestiad, or a Life in the Sun. New York: 1977. V. 54
The Angel That Troubled the Waters... London: 1928. V. 48
The Angel that Troubled the Waters. New York: 1928. V. 48; 51; 53; 54
The Bridge of San Luis Rey. London: 1927. V. 50; 51
The Bridge of San Luis Rey. New York: 1927. V. 47; 48; 49; 50; 53
The Bridge of San Luis Rey. London: 1929. V. 50
The Bridge of San Luis Rey. New York: 1929. V. 47; 48; 51; 52; 53; 54
The Bridge of San Luis Rey. New York: 1962. V. 48; 54
The Cabala. London: 1926. V. 50
The Cabala. New York: 1926. V. 47; 48; 50; 51
The Cabala. USA: 1926. V. 53
The Cabala. London: 1928. V. 51
The Eighth Day. New York: 1967. V. 48; 50; 51; 54
Heaven's My Destination. London: 1934. V. 47
Heaven's My Destination. New York: 1935. V. 47
The Ides of March. New York: 1948. V. 53; 54
The Long Christmas Dinner and Other Plays in One Act. New York: 1932/31. V. 48
The Merchant of Yonkers. New York: 1939. V. 47; 51
Our Town. New York: 1938. V. 51
Our Town. Avon: 1974. V. 48; 50; 52; 54
Theophilus North. 1973. V. 50
Theophilus North. New York: 1973. V. 48; 54
A Thornton Wilder Trio. New York: 1956. V. 48
The Woman of Andros. 1930. V. 50; 53
The Woman of Andros. London & New York: 1930. V. 47; 48; 54

WILDERSPIN, SAMUEL
Early Discipline Illustrated; or, the Infant System Progressing and Successful. London: 1832. V. 54

WILDMAN, JOHN
The Settle Almanack... Settle: 1840. V. 51
The Settle Almanack for the Year of Our Lord 1842. Settle: 1842. V. 53

WILDMAN, THOMAS
A Treatise on the Management of Bees. London: 1768. V. 48; 52
A Treatise on the Management of Bees. London: 1770. V. 48

WILDRIDGE, T. TINDALL
The Grotesque in Church Art. London: 1900. V. 54
Northumbria: a Repository of Antiquities of Northumberland, Cumberland, Westmorland, Durham, Yorkshire, Lancashire and the Borders of Scotland. London: 1888. V. 48; 53

WILDWOOD, WARREN
Thrilling Adventures Among Early Settlers. Philadelphia: 1861. V. 47; 51

WILENSKI, R. H.
Flemish Painters, 1430-1830. London: 1960. V. 54
Flemish Painters, 1430-1830. New York: 1960. V. 48; 50; 51; 53

WILEY, AUSTIN
The History of the Anti-Slavery Cause in State and Nation. Portland: 1886. V. 53

WILEY, CALVIN HENDERSON
Address to the People of North Carolina. Raleigh: 1861?. V. 49

WILEY, HUGH
The Prowler. New York: 1924. V. 52

WILEY, SAMUEL T.
Biographical and Portrait Cyclopedia of the Third Congressional District of New Jersey, Comprising Middlesex, Monmouth and Somerset Counties. Philadelphia: 1896. V. 47; 49; 51

WILFORD, JOHN
Memorials and Characters, Together with the Lives of Divers Eminent and Worthy Persons...from the Year One Thousand Six Hundred to the Present Time... London: 1741. V. 52

WILHELM, GOTTLIEB TOBIAS
Unterhaltungen aus der Naturgeschichte... Augsburg: 1810-14. V. 47; 52
Unterhaltungen Aus der Naturgeschichte... Augsburg: 1810-21. V. 47
Unterhaltungen aus der Naturgeschichte. Vienna: 1813. V. 48; 50

WILKES, CHARLES
Narrative of the United States Exploring Expedition During the Years 1832-42. New York: 1856. V. 53
Narrative of the United States Exploring Expedition During the years 1838-42. Philadelphia: 1845. V. 47
Narrative Of the United States Exploring Expedition During the Years 1838-42. Philadelphia: 1849. V. 50
Narrative of the United States Exploring Expedition During the Years 1838-42. Upper Saddle River: 1970. V. 48

WILKES, GEORGE
The Great Battle, Fought at Manassas, Between Federal Forces, Under General McDowell, and the Rebels, Under Gen. Beauregard, Sunday, July 21, 1861. New York: 1861. V. 48; 51
Project of a National Railroad from the Atlantic to the Pacific Ocean, for the Purpose of Obtaining a Short Route to Oregon and the Indies. New York: 1845. V. 47
Proposal for a National Rail-Road to the Pacific Ocean, for the Purpose of Obtaining a Short Route to Oregon and the Indies. New York: 1847. V. 48

WILKES, JOHN
An Essay on Woman and Other Pieces, Printed at the Private Press...1763 and Now Reproduced in Fac-simile. London: 1871. V. 49; 51
The History of England from the Revolution to the Accession of the Brunswick Line. London: 1768. V. 48
The North Briton. Dublin: 1763. V. 48
The North Briton. London: 1763. V. 53
The North Briton. Dublin: 1764-65. V. 54
The Speeches of Mr. Wilkes in the House of Commons. 1786. V. 48
The Speeches...in Parliament...29th Day of November 1774, to the Prorogation the 6th Day of June 1777. London: 1777. V. 48

WILKES, JOSEPH
To the Catholics of England. London: 1789. V. 54

WILKES, MAURICE V.
Automatic Digital Computers. New York: 1956. V. 48; 50; 52; 54

WILKES, WETENHALL
A Letter of Genteel and Moral Advice to a Young Lady. Dublin: 1741. V. 53
A Letter of Genteel and Moral Advice to a Young Lady... London: 1744. V. 47

WILKIE, FRANC B.
Davenport Past and Present: Including the Early History and Personal and Anecdotal Reminiscences of Davenport. Davenport: 1858. V. 47; 52
Pen and Power. Boston: 1888. V. 54

WILKIE, WILLIAM
Fables. London: 1768. V. 47

WILKINS, CHARLES
The History of the Iron, Steel, Tinplate and Other Trades of Wales. 1903. V. 51
The History of the Iron, Steel, Tinplate, and Other Trades of Wales. Merthyr Tydfil: 1903. V. 49
The History of the Literature of Wales from the Year 1300 to the Year 1650. Cardiff: 1884. V. 54

WILKINS, CHARLES ARMAR
Curiosities of Travel; or Glimpses of Nature. London: 1876. V. 50; 54

WILKINS, GEORGE
The Two Rectors. London: 1824. V. 47; 54

WILKINS, GEORGE HUBERT
Under the North Pole. The Wilkins-Ellsworth Submarine Expedition. New York: 1931. V. 54
Undiscovered Australia, Being an Account of an Expedition to Tropical Australia to Collect Specimens of the Rarer Native Ferns from the British Museum 1923-25. New York: 1929. V. 54

WILKINS, H. P.
Moon Maps: with Chart Showing the Other Side of the Moon Based Upon the Soviet Photographs. New York: 1960. V. 54

WILKINS, H. ST. CLAIR
Reconnoitering in Abyssinia. London: 1870. V. 52; 54

WILKINS, JOHN
The Autobiography of an English Gamekeeper. London: 1892. V. 51; 52

WILKINS, JOHN, BP. OF CHESTER
An Essay Towards a Real Character, and a Philosophical Language. (with) An Alphabetical Dictionary... London: 1668/68. V. 49
The First Book. The Discovery of a New World, or a Discourse Tending to Prove That 'Tis probable There May be Another Habitable World in the Moone. London: 1640. V. 48
The Mathematical and Philosophical Works. London: 1708. V. 48
The Mathematical and Philosophical Works... London: 1708-07. V. 51
The Mathematical and Philosophical Works... London: 1802. V. 52
Mathematical Magick. London: 1648. V. 47; 49
Mathematical Magick... London: 1691. V. 47
Of the Principles and Duties of Natural Religion. London: 1699. V. 52

WILKINS, THURMAN
Clarence King, a Biography. New York: 1958. V. 53
Thomas Moran - Artist of the Mountains. Norman: 1966. V. 54

WILKINS, W. H.
The Romance of Isabel Lady Burton. London: 1897. V. 50; 51; 52

WILKINS, WILLIAM
The Antiquities of Magna Graecia. Cambridge: 1807. V. 50
Atheniensia, or Remarks on the Topography and Buildings of Athens. London: 1816. V. 48
Indians Remaining in Florida, Etc... Washington: 1844. V. 48; 51

WILKINS, WILLIAM J.
Hindu Mythology, Vedic and Paranic. Calcutta: 1882. V. 49

WILKINSON, ANNE
Counterpoint to Sleep. Montreal: 1951. V. 47

WILKINSON, ANNE MARGARET
A Lady's Life and Travels in Zululand and the Transvaal During Cetewayo's Reign. London: 1882. V. 54

WILKINSON, CHARLES
Epitome of the History of Malta and Gozo. London: 1804. V. 54

WILKINSON, CLENNELL
Bonnie Prince Charlie. London: 1932. V. 54

WILKINSON, E. S.
The Shanghai Bird Year. Shanghai: 1935. V. 51
Shanghai Birds. Shanghai: 1929. V. 49; 52; 53

WILKINSON, GARDNER
Modern Egypt and Thebes: Being a Description of Egypt... London: 1843. V. 48; 49

WILKINSON, GEORGE BLAKESTON
South Australia: Its Advantages and Its Resources. London: 1848. V. 53

WILKINSON, GEORGE THEODORE
An Authentic History of the Cato-Street Conspiracy... London: 1820. V. 52; 53

WILKINSON, H. D.
Submarine Cable Laying and Repairing. London: 1808. V. 49

WILKINSON, HENRY
Characters of a Sincere Heart, and the Comforts Thereof, Collected Out of the Word of God... Oxford: 1674. V. 49; 51
Engines of War... London: 1841. V. 47; 49

WILKINSON, HEYWOOD & CLARK
Monograms and Heraldic Designs. London: 1890. V. 47; 50; 53

WILKINSON, HUGH
Sunny Lands and Seas. 1883. V. 52; 54
Sunny Lands and Seas... California: 1883. V. 48
Sunny Lands and Seas. London: 1883. V. 48

WILKINSON, J. B.
Laredo and the Rio Grande Frontier. Austin: 1975. V. 53

WILKINSON, J. V. S.
The Lights of Canopus... New York: 1929. V. 47; 50
The Lights of Canopus... London: 1930. V. 48

WILKINSON, JAMES
Memoirs of My Own Times. Philadelphia: 1816. V. 47

WILKINSON, JEMIMA
Memoir of...A Preacheress of the Eighteenth Century. Bath: 1844. V. 53

WILKINSON, JOHN
Quakerism Examined; in a Reply to the Letter of Samuel Tuke. London: 1836. V. 49

WILKINSON, JOHN GARDINER
The Manners and Customs of the Ancient Egyptians. London: 1878. V. 49
On Colour and On the Necessity for a General Diffusion of Taste Among All Classes. London: 1858. V. 47; 50; 51
A Popular Account of the Ancient Egyptians. New York: 1854. V. 50
A Second Series of the Manners and Customs of the Ancient Egyptians, Including their Religion, Agriculture, &c. London: 1841. V. 47
Topography of Thebes and General View of Egypt. London: 1835. V. 49

WILKINSON, JOSEPH
Worsborough: Its Historical Association and Rural Attractions. London: 1872. V. 53
Worthies, Families and Celebrities of Barnsley and the District. London: 1880. V. 53; 54

WILKINSON, NORMAN
The Dardanelles - Colour Sketches from Gallipoli. London: 1915. V. 47

WILKINSON, ROBERT
Londini Illustrata. London: 1819-25. V. 48; 51

WILKINSON, S.
The London Illustrated News Record of the Transvaal War, 1899-1900. London: 1900. V. 50

WILKINSON, SARAH
The Child of Mystery, a Novel. London: 1808. V. 50
Love and Hymen; or the Gentleman's and Ladies' Polite and Original Valentine Writer. London: 1821?. V. 50

WILKINSON, SYLVIA
Moss on the North Side. Boston: 1966. V. 49; 53; 54

WILKINSON, TATE
Memoirs of His Own Life. York: 1790. V. 48; 49; 51; 52
Memoirs of His Own Life. Dublin: 1791. V. 47
The Wandering Patentee; or, a History of the Yorkshire Theatres. York: 1795. V. 47; 49; 52

WILKINSON, THOMAS
Tours to the British Mountains, With the Descriptive Poems of Lowther and Emont Vale. London: 1824. V. 50; 52

WILKINSON, WILLIAM
English Country Houses. London & Oxford: 1875. V. 54

WILKINSON, WILLIAM CLEAVER
A Free Lance in the Field of Life and Letters. New York: 1874. V. 48

WILKS, ROBERT
Memoirs of the Life of...Containing...His Reputation on the British Stage...Adventures Among the Ladies... London: 1732. V. 47; 54

WILL, JOHN BAXTER
Trading Under Sail Off Japan, 1860-99. Tokyo: 1968. V. 54

WILL Of Aethelgifu. London: 1968. V. 50

WILL, W. C. O.
Primates, Comparative Anatomy and Taxonomy. Edinburgh: 1953-66. V. 49

WILLARD, CAROLINE MC COY WHITE
Life In Alaska. Letters of Mrs. Eugene S. Willard. Philadelphia: 1884. V. 53

WILLARD, CHARLES DWIGHT
A History of the Chamber of Commerce of Los Angeles, California: From Its Foundation, September, 1888 to the Year 1900. Los Angeles: 1899. V. 47

WILLARD, EMMA
Geography for Beginners or the Instructor's Assistant... Hartford: 1826. V. 49

WILLARD, FRANCES E.
A Wheel Within a Wheel. Chicago: 1898. V. 48; 53
Woman in the Pulpit. Chicago: 1889. V. 53

WILLARD, JOHN WARE
A History of Simon Willard, Inventor and Clockmaker. Boston: 1911. V. 53

WILLARD, MARGARET WHEELER
Letters on the American Revolution 1774-1776. Boston & New York: 1925. V. 52

WILLARD, NANCY
Childhood of the Magician. New York: 1973. V. 50

WILLARD, SAMUEL
The Franklin Family Primer. Boston: 1812. V. 48

WILLARD, THEODORE A.
The Lost Empires of the Itzaes and Mayas: an American Civilization... Glendale: 1933. V. 51

WILLARD, X. A.
Willard's Practical Butter Book. New York: 1875. V. 50

WILLCOCKS, JAMES
From Kabul to Kumassi. 1904. V. 52; 54
From Kabul to Kumassi... London: 1904. V. 51

WILLDENOW, D. C.
The Principles of Botany, and Of Vegetable Physiology. Edinburgh: 1805. V. 52

WILLEBEEK LE MAIR, HENRIETTE
Auntie's Little Rhyme Book. London: 1915. V. 50
Old Dutch Nursery Rhymes. London: 1917. V. 50

WILLEFORD, CHARLES
Cockfighter. Chicago: 1962. V. 47; 49
Cockfighter. New York: 1972. V. 48
Cockfighter Journal. Santa Barbara: 1989. V. 52; 53
Everybody's Metamorphosis. London: 1988. V. 54
Everybody's Metamorphosis. Missoula: 1988. V. 52
A Guide for the Undehemorrhoided. 1977. V. 53
A Guide for the Undehemorrhoided. Boynton Beach: 1977. V. 51; 52
High Priest of California. New York: 1953. V. 53
High Priest of California. 1987. V. 54
High Priest of California and Wild Wives. San Francisco: 1987. V. 53
Honey Gal. Boston: 1958. V. 53
Kiss Your Ass Good-bye. Miami Beach: 1987. V. 52
The Machine in Ward Eleven. New York: 1963. V. 53
New Hope For the Dead. New York: 1985. V. 48; 51; 52
Off the Wall. Montclair: 1980. V. 47; 49; 51; 52; 53
The Outcast Poets. New York: 1947. V. 50
Pick-Up. Boston: 1955. V. 53
Poontang. Crescent City: 1967. V. 53
Proletarian Laughter. 1948. V. 52
Proletarian Laughter. New York: 1948. V. 48; 50; 53
Proletarian Laughter. Yonkers: 1948. V. 51; 52
Sideswipe. New York: 1987. V. 51; 52
The Way We Die Now. 1988. V. 52
The Woman Chaser. Chicago: 1960. V. 47; 52

WILLEM I, PRINCE OF ORANGE
Apologie/Ofte Verant Woodrdinghe des Doerluchtighen Ende Hooghegebozenen... Holland: 1851. V. 49

WILLEM III, PRINCE OF ORANGE
Whereas the Necessity of Affairs Does Not Require Speedy Advice... St. James's the Three and Twentieth Day of December 1688.. London: 1688. V. 47
Whereas Upon the Late Irregular Disbanding of the Forces...Given at St. James's... One and Twentieth... December 1688. W. H. Prince de Orange, by His Highness's Command, C. Huygens. London: 1688. V. 47

WILLERT, D. J. VON
Life Strategies of Succulents in Deserts. London: 1992. V. 50; 51

WILLES, THOMAS
A Word in Season, for Warning to England... London: 1659. V. 49

WILLETT, EDWARD
Around the House. New York: 1882. V. 51
Cat's Cradle. London: 1880. V. 52
Cat's Cradle... New York: 1881. V. 51

WILLETT, MARK
An Excursion from the Source of the Wye. Chepstow: 1820. V. 50

WILLETT, MARY
A History of West Bromwich. West Bromwich: 1882. V. 49; 51; 52

WILLETT, W. N.
Charles Vincent; or, The Two Clerks. A Tale of Commercial Life. New York: 1839. V. 48

WILLETT, WILLIAM M.
A Narrative of the Military Actions of Colonel Marinus Willett, taken Chiefly from His Own Manuscript. New York: 1831. V. 49

WILLEY, BENJAMIN G.
Incidents in White Mountain History... Dover: 1856. V. 54

WILLEY, MISS
Lines to the Memory of Dr. Erastus Willey. Richmond?: 1839. V. 47

WILLEY, SAMUEL H.
An Historical Paper Relating to Santa Cruz, California... San Francisco: 1876. V. 47

WILLIAM Morris and the Art of the Book. 1976. V. 54
WILLIAM Morris and the Art of the Book. New York: 1976. V. 52

WILLIAM, OF MALMESBURY
De Gestis Regum Anglorum. (and) Historiae Novellae. London: 1887-89. V. 49
Gesta Regum anglorum,, Atque Historia Novella. Londini: 1840. V. 48
The History of the Kings of England and the Modern History. London: 1815. V. 51; 53

WILLIAM, OF NEBURGH
Guilielmi Neubrigensis Historia Sive Chonica Rerum Anglicarum, Libris Quinque. Oxford: 1719. V. 48

WILLIAM, OF WORCESTER
Itineraria Symonis Simeonis et Willelmi de Worcestre. Cantabrigiae: 1778. V. 53

WILLIAM, PRINCE OF SWEDEN
Among Pygmies and Gorillas. 1921/23. V. 48; 52
Among Pygmies and Gorillas. 1923. V. 54

WILLIAMS, A. BRYAN
Game Trails in British Columbia. New York: 1925. V. 53

WILLIAMS, A. F.
The Genesis of the Diamond. London: 1932. V. 51; 52; 53; 54

WILLIAMS, AARON
The Harmony Society, at Economy, Pennsylvania. Pittsburgh: 1866. V. 47; 54

WILLIAMS, ALFRED
Nature and other Poems. London: 1912. V. 49
A Wiltshire Village. London: 1912. V. 50

WILLIAMS, ALFRED M.
Sam Houston and the War of Independence in Texas. Boston: 1893. V. 48

WILLIAMS, AMELIA W.
The Writings of Sam Houston: 1821-1847. Austin: 1938-41. V. 52

WILLIAMS, AMES W.
Stephen Crane: A Bibliography. Glendale: 1948. V. 51

WILLIAMS, ANNA
Miscellanies in Prose and Verse. London: 1766. V. 47; 48; 50

WILLIAMS, ARTHUR ANDERSON
The Registers of Colton Parish Church, in Furness Fells. London: 1891. V. 50; 52

WILLIAMS, B. J.
Choice Stove and Greenhouse Ornamental-Leaved Plants and Choice Stove and Greenhouse Flowering Plants. London: 1870-73. V. 51

WILLIAMS, BEN AMES
The Happy End. New York: 1939. V. 48

WILLIAMS, BENJAMIN SAMUEL
The Orchid Grower's Manual... London: 1862. V. 53
The Orchid Grower's Manual. London: 1885. V. 49; 52; 54
The Orchid Grower's Manual. London: 1894. V. 51; 52
The Orchid Grower's Manual. London: 1961. V. 49; 52
The Orchid Grower's Manual. London: 1973. V. 50; 51

WILLIAMS, BUTLER
A Manual for Teaching Model-Drawing, from Solid Forms. London: 1843. V. 47; 53

WILLIAMS, C.
Zoological Gardens, Regent's Park. London: 1835. V. 52

WILLIAMS, C. K.
With Ignorance. Boston: 1977. V. 53

WILLIAMS, C. R., MRS.
The Neutral French; or, the Exiles of Nova Scotia. Providence: 1841. V. 53
Tales: National and Revolutionary. Providence: 1830. V. 53

WILLIAMS, C. W.
Observations on the Inland Navigation of Ireland and the Want of Employment for Its Population, with a Description of the River Shannon. London: 1833. V. 54

WILLIAMS, CALVIN O.
The Blob. New York: 1978. V. 53

WILLIAMS, CARL M.
Silversmiths of New Jersey, 1700-1825. Philadelphia: 1949. V. 47; 49; 51

WILLIAMS, CAROLINE RANSOM
The Decoration of the Tomb of Per-neb. The Technique and Color Conventions. New York: 1932. V. 49; 51
Gold and Silver Jewelry and Related objects. New York: 1924. V. 51; 54

WILLIAMS, CATHERINE READ ARNOLD
Biography of Revolutionary Heroes... Providence: 1839. V. 47
The Neutral French; or, the Exiles of Nova Scotia. Providence: 1841. V. 47
Original Poems, on Various Subjects. Providence: 1828. V. 54

WILLIAMS, CHARLES
The Alps, Switzerland and the North of Italy. London: 1854. V. 50
Cranmer of Canterbury. Canterbury: 1936. V. 50
Dead Calm. New York: 1963. V. 49
Descent into Hell. London: 1937. V. 47
Divorce. London: 1920. V. 52
The English Poetic Mind. Oxford: 1932. V. 48; 49
The Greater Trump. New York: 1950. V. 49
Heroes and Kings. London: 1930. V. 48
Many Dimensions. London: 1931. V. 52
Many Dimensions. New York: 1949. V. 49
Old World Scenes. Pittsburgh: 1867. V. 48
The Pathology and Diagnosis of Diseases of the Chest... London: 1840. V. 54
Poems of Conformity. London: 1917. V. 47; 50; 53
Poetry at Present. London: 1930. V. 50; 52; 53
Poetry at Present. Oxford: 1930. V. 54
The Region of the Summer Stars. London: 1944. V. 49
War in Heaven. New York: 1949. V. 49
Witchcraft. 1941. V. 47

WILLIAMS, CHARLES H.
Sidelights On Negro Soldiers. Boston: 1923. V. 54

WILLIAMS, CHARLES HANBURY
The Country Girl: an Ode. London: 1742. V. 49
An Ode from the E(arl) of B(ath) to Ambition. London: 1741. V. 49
The Odes. London: 1775. V. 49
The Odes... London: 1780. V. 47; 54
The Works...from the Originals in the Possession of His Grandson, the Right Hon. the Earl of Essex... London: 1822. V. 47

WILLIAMS, CHARLES JAMES WATKIN
An Essay Upon the Philosophy of Evidence... London: 1853. V. 54
An Essay Upon the Philosophy of Evidence... London: 1855. V. 48

WILLIAMS, CHARLES WYE
An Elementary Treatise on the Combustion of Coal and the Prevention of Smoke, Chemically and Practically Considered. London: 1858. V. 50
On Heat In Its Relations to Water and Steam: Embracing New Views of Vaporisation, Condensation and Explosions. London: 1861. V. 53

WILLIAMS, CLARA ANDREWS
The Doll's House That Glue Built. Edinburgh: 1910. V. 49

WILLIAMS, CLAYTON
Never Again... Naylor: 1969. V. 53
Never Again... San Antonio: 1969. V. 47; 51; 53

WILLIAMS, CYNRIC R.
A Tour through the Island of Jamaica, from the Western to the Eastern End in the Year 1823. London: 1827. V. 49

WILLIAMS, D. E.
The Life and Correspondence of Sir Thomas Lawrence. London: 1831. V. 50

WILLIAMS, DAVID
Egeria, or Elementary Studies on the Progress of Nations in Political Oeconomy, Legislation and Government. London: 1803. V. 51
Lectures on Politeness, Giving a Beautiful Display of Nature and Her Laws. London: 1819. V. 50
Royal Recollections on a Tour to Cheltenham, Gloucester, Worcester and Palces Adjacent in the Year 1788. London: 1788. V. 50

WILLIAMS, EBENEZER
Presentation of a Banner by the Republican Club, of North Hempstead, to the Colored Republican club, of that Town, Feb. 23, 1872. New York: 1872. V. 53

WILLIAMS, EDWARD
Iolo Manuscripts. 1848. V. 49
Virgo Triumphans: or, Virginia in Generall, but the South Part Thereof in Particular. London: 1650. V. 48

WILLIAMS, EDWINA DAKIN
Remember Me to Tom. New York: 1963. V. 54

WILLIAMS, ELISHA
The Essential Rights and Liberties of Protestants. Boston: 1744. V. 48

WILLIAMS, EMLYN
The Corn is Green: a Comedy in Three Acts. New York: 1941. V. 49

WILLIAMS, ERIC
The Negro in the Caribbean. Washington: 1942. V. 54

WILLIAMS, FLORA M.
The Glengarry McDonalds of Virginia. Louisville: 1911. V. 50

WILLIAMS, FRANCIS
A Method for More Fully Determining the Outline of the Heart by Means of the Fluoroscope... 1896. V. 54

WILLIAMS, FRANKLIN B.
The Gardyners Passetaunce c. 1512. 1985. V. 47; 54

WILLIAMS, FREDERICK LAKE
An Historical and Topographical Description of the Municipium of Ancient Verulam... St. Albans: 1822. V. 47

WILLIAMS, FREDERICK S.
The Midland Railway: Its Rise and Progress. London: 1876. V. 49

WILLIAMS, GARDNER F.
The Diamond Mines of South Africa. New York: 1902. V. 47; 52
The Diamond Mines of South Africa. New York: 1906. V. 47; 48; 50

WILLIAMS, GEORGE
Bullet & Shell. War As Soldiers Saw it. New York: 1882. V. 50; 52
The Holy City or Historical and Topographical Notices of Jerusalem, with Some Account of Its Antiquities and of Its Present Condition. London: 1845. V. 49

WILLIAMS, GEORGE H.
Report of the Senate Committee, by Senators Williams and Ferry, on the McGarrahan Bill. V. 49

WILLIAMS, GOMER
History of the Liverpool Privateers and Letters of Marque, with an Account of the Liverpool Slave Trade. London: 1897. V. 48

WILLIAMS, H. M.
The Gray Man. 1911. V. 48; 52

WILLIAMS, HARCOURT
Tales from Ebony. London: 1934. V. 47; 48

WILLIAMS, HAROLD
Medical Atlas for Attorneys. San Francisco & Rochester: 1967. V. 49

WILLIAMS, HARRY
Texas Trails, Legends of the Great Southwest. San Antonio: 1932. V. 54

WILLIAMS, HEATHCOTE
Sacred Elephant. London: 1989. V. 47

WILLIAMS, HELEN MARIA
Julia, a Novel. Dublin: 1790. V. 48
Letters Containing a Sketch of the Politics of France, from the Thirty-First of May 1793, Till the 10th of Thermidor, Twenty-Eighth of July 1794... London: 1795. V. 48; 53
Letters Containing a Sketch of the Politics of France from the Twenty-First of May, 1793, Till the Twenty-eighth of July, 1794 and of the Scenes Which Passed in the Prisons of Paris. Philadelphia: 1796. V. 50
Memoirs of Mons. and Madame du F. Boston: 1794. V. 47; 49; 50
A Narrative of the Events Which Have Taken Place in France... London: 1815. V. 47
A Narrative of the Events Which Have Taken Place in France... Philadelphia: 1816. V. 49; 50; 51; 53; 54
Poems, Moral, Elegant and Pathetic. London: 1796. V. 48
A Residence in France, During the Years 1792, 1793, 1794 and 1795. London: 1797. V. 53

WILLIAMS, HENRY
Elements of Drawing, Exemplified in a Variety of Figures and Sketches of Parts of the Human Form. Boston: 1818. V. 49
The Flax of Dream The Beautiful Years; Dandelion Days; the Dream of Fair Women; The Pathway. London: 1931. V. 51

WILLIAMS, HENRY C.
The Indian Raid in Young County, Texas, October 13, 1864. Houston: 1935. V. 49

WILLIAMS, HENRY SMITH
The History of the Art of Writing. Cambridge: 1900. V. 48
The History of the Art of Writing. Cambridge: 1910. V. 53

WILLIAMS, HENRY T.
The Pacific Tourists. Williams' Illustrated Trans-Continental Guide of Travel, the Atlantic to the Pacific Ocean. New York: 1876. V. 47
William's Pacific and Guide Across the Continent. New York: 1879. V. 48; 50; 52

WILLIAMS, HENRY WILLARD
A Practical Guide to the Study of the Diseases of the Eye; Their Medical and Surgical Treatment. Boston: 1862. V. 53

WILLIAMS, HERBERT W.
A Bibliography of printed Maori to 1900. (with) Supplement... Wellington: 1924-28. V. 49

WILLIAMS, HUGH ROSS
Gods and Mortals in Love. London: 1935. V. 48

WILLIAMS, HUGH WILLIAM
Select Views in Greece. London: 1829. V. 48
Travels in Italy, Greece and the Ionian Islands. Edinburgh: 1820. V. 48; 49; 50; 52; 53

WILLIAMS, IOLO A.
Early English Watercolours... London: 1952. V. 54
Early English Watercolours... London: 1970. V. 48
Points in Eighteenth Century Verse: a Bibliographer's and Collector's Scrapbook. London: 1934. V. 50

WILLIAMS, IZA
Santa Catalina Island. Los Angeles: 1905. V. 50

WILLIAMS, J.
The Northern Almanac for 1837, Being the First After Bissextile, or Leap Year and the Eighth of the Reign of His Present Majesty... (with) Companion to the Northern Almanac for 1837. Penrith: 1837. V. 52

WILLIAMS, J. WHITRIDGE
Obstetrics. A Text-book for the Use of Students and Practioners. New York: 1903. V. 48; 51

WILLIAMS, JAMES
Imposed Rebellion. Fresno: 1959. V. 52
Letters on Slavery from the Old World: Written During the Canvass for the Presidency of the United States in 1860. Nashville: 1861. V. 48
Memorials of the Lineage, Early Life, Education and Development of the Genius of James Watt. London: 1856. V. 48
A Narrative of Events Since the First of August 1834, by James Williams, an Apprenticed Labourer in Jamaica. London: 1837. V. 53
The Rise and Fall of the "The Model Republic". London: 1863. V. 49
The South Vindicated. London: 1862. V. 53
The Topography and Climate of Apsley Guise, in Reference to Their Influence Upon Health and Disease. London: 1858. V. 51

WILLIAMS, JAMES LEON
The Land of Sleepy Hollow and the Home of Washington Irving. New York & London: 1887. V. 48

WILLIAMS, JAMES ROBERT
Cowboys Out Our Way. New York: 1951. V. 51

WILLIAMS, JANE
The Paper People, The Origin, Rise and Progress of... London: 1856. V. 47

WILLIAMS, JOHN
The Climate of Great Britain; or Remarks on the Change It Has Undergone Particularly Within the Last Fifty Years... London: 1806. V. 50
The Eccentricities of John Edwin, Comedian. London: 1791. V. 47; 48
An Enquiry Into the Truth of the Tradition Concerning the Discovery of America. (with) Farther Observations on the Discovery of America... London: 1791/92. V. 47
The History of Gunpowder-Treason, Collected From Approved Authors... London: 1679. V. 50
The Life of the Late Earl of Barrymore. London: 1793. V. 51; 52; 53
A Missionary...in South Sea Islands. London: 1837. V. 53
The Missionary's Farewell: Valedictory Services of the Rev. John Williams Previous to the Departure for the South Seas... London: 1838. V. 54
A Narrative of Missionary Enterprises in the South Sea Islands. London: 1838. V. 47; 53
A Narrative of Missionary Enterprises in the South Sea Islands... London: 1839. V. 47; 52
New and Valuable Recipes for the Cure of Many Diseases. New York: 1828. V. 50
A Postscript to the New Bath Guide. London: 1790. V. 48; 54
The Redeemed Captive Returning to Zion. Boston: 1774. V. 47
The Redeemed Captive Returning to Zion... Boston: 1795. V. 54
The Redeemed Captive Returning to Zion... New York: 1802. V. 51
The Rise, Progress and Present State of the Northern Governments. London: 1777. V. 51; 53
Sacred Allegories; or Allegorical Poems, Illustrative of Subjects Moral and Divine. London: 1810. V. 47
A Spanish Apocalypse: The Morgan Beatus Manuscript. New York: 1992. V. 47

WILLIAMS, JOHN A.
Love. 1988. V. 51
Night Song. New York: 1961. V. 51; 52
Sissie. New York: 1963. V. 50

WILLIAMS, JOHN, BP. OF CHICHESTER
An Apology for the Pulpits... together with An Appendix... London: 1688. V. 50; 51

WILLIAMS, JOHN S.
The American Pioneer. Cincinnati: 1842-43. V. 47; 48

WILLIAMS, JONATHAN
Amen Huzza Selah. Highlands: 1960. V. 48
Amen Huzza Selah... Karlsruhe-Durlach: 1960. V. 54
Aposiopeses (Odds and Ends). Minneapolis: 1988. V. 53
Blue and Roots/Rue & Bluets: A Garland for Appalachians. Durham: 1985. V. 49
Blues and Roots/Rue & Bluets: a Garland for Appalachians. New York: 1971. V. 51
Descant on Rawthey's Madrigal - Conversations with Basil Bunting. Lexington: 1968. V. 52
Elegies and Celebrations. Highlands: 1962. V. 54
Elite/Elate Poems: Selected Poems 1971-75. 1979. V. 54
The Empire Finals at Verona. Poems. Highlands: 1959. V. 54
Epitaphs for Lorine. Penland: 1973. V. 52; 54
Five from Up T'Dale. Corn Close: 1974. V. 54
In the Azure Over the Squalor: Ransackings and Shorings. 1983. V. 54
In the Field at the Solstice: Seven Epitaphs for His Friends. Champaign: 1976. V. 47
Letters to Mencken from the Land of Pink Lichen. New York: 1994. V. 51; 52
Lullabies Twisters Gibbers Drags... Bloomington: 1967. V. 51; 53
Mahler. London: 1966. V. 47; 50
No-No Nse-Nse. Limericks. Meta-Fours...and Clerihews... Mt. Horeb: 1993. V. 51; 53
Pairidaeza. Dentdale, Cumbria: 1975. V. 48; 53; 54
Portrait Photographs. Frankfort: 1979. V. 48
Sharp Tools for Catullan Gardens. Poems. Bloomington: 1968. V. 53
Strung Out with Elgar on a Hill. Urbana: 1970. V. 52
Twelve Jargonelles from the Herablist's Notebook. 1965. Bloomington: 1965. V. 51; 53
La Vie Entre les Gadarenes (Infinity, First Not Last). Black Mountain: 1951. V. 52; 53

WILLIAMS, JOSEPH
An Essay On the Use of Narcotics and Other Remedial Agents Calculated to Produce Sleep in the Treatment of Insanity. London: 1845. V. 54

WILLIAMS, JOSEPH J.
Psychic Phenomena of Jamaica. New York: 1934. V. 53

WILLIAMS, JOSEPH S.
Old Times in the West Tennessee. Reminiscences Semi-Historic Of Pioneer Life and the Early Emingrant Settlers in the Big Hatchie Country... Memphis: 1873. V. 47

WILLIAMS, KENNETH POWERS
Lincoln Finds a General: a Military Study of the Civil War. New York: 1949-59. V. 52

WILLIAMS, L.
The Dalton Brothers in Their Oklahoma Cave. Chicago: 1893. V. 49

WILLIAMS, MARY FLOYD
History of the San Francisco Committee of Vigilance of 1851... Berkeley: 1921. V. 52; 54
Papers of the San Francisco Committee of Vigilance of 1851. Berkeley: 1919. V. 51

WILLIAMS, OSCAR
The Man Coming Toward You - A Book of Poems. New York: 1940. V. 50
New Poems: 1940 - An Anthology of British and American Verse. New York: 1941. V. 54
New Poems 1943. An Anthology of British and American Verse. 1943. V. 53

WILLIAMS, OSCAR WALDO
By the Camp-Fire in the Southwest. 1902. V. 49
Letters to J. C. Williams. Fort Stockton: 1925. V. 48; 50; 52
Pioneer Surveyor, Frontier Lawyer: Personal Narrative of...1877-1902. El Paso: 1966. V. 49

WILLIAMS, PAUL R.
The Small Home of Tomorrow. Hollywood: 1945. V. 52

WILLIAMS, R.
Bulmer's Pomona. Hereford: 1987. V. 49

WILLIAMS, R. B.
Coelenterate Biology: Recent Research on Cnidaria and Ctenophora. Dordrecht: 1991. V. 49; 50

WILLIAMS, R. H.
The Adventures of a Seventeen Year-Old Lad and the Fortunes He Might Have Won. Boston: 1894. V. 53

WILLIAMS, R. H. continued
With the Border Ruffians: Memories of the Far West, 1852-1868... London: 1908. V. 48

WILLIAMS, R. T.
The Williams' Official British Columbia Directory 1897-98. Victoria: 1897. V. 52

WILLIAMS, RICHARD
A View of the Laws Relating to Physicians, Druggists and Dentists. Philadelphia: 1884. V. 50
A View of the Laws Relating to Physicians, Druggists and Dentists. Philadelphia: 1885. V. 49

WILLIAMS, ROBERT
Vitamin B1 (Thiamin) and its Use in Medicine. New York: 1938. V. 47; 49; 54

WILLIAMS, ROBERT FOLKSTONE
Mephistophiles in England. Philadelphia: 1835. V. 48
Shakspeare (sic) and His Friends, or, "The Golden Age" of Merry England. London: 1838. V. 54

WILLIAMS, ROBERT P.
Modern and Valuable Books, for Sale Wholesale and Retail, Cornhill Square, May 21, 1819. Boston: 1819. V. 52

WILLIAMS, ROGER
A Key to the Language of America, or an Help to the Language of the Natives in that Part of America Called New England. Providence: 1827. V. 48

WILLIAMS, ROSE BERTHENIA CLAY
Black and White Orange. New York: 1961. V. 53

WILLIAMS, SAMUEL
The Natural and Civil History of Vermont. Burlington: 1809. V. 52
Sketches of the War, Between the United States and the British Isles... Rutland: 1815. V. 50

WILLIAMS, SAMUEL WELLS
A Journal of the Perry Expedition to Japan (1853-1854). Tokyo: 1910. V. 47
The Middle Kingdom... New York: 1853. V. 50; 53
The Middle Kingdom. London: 1883. V. 51
The Middle Kingdom... New York: 1883. V. 48; 51; 54
The Middle Kingdom. New York: 1898. V. 53

WILLIAMS, SIDNEY HERBERT
A Bibliography of the Writings of Lewis Carroll. London: 1924. V. 48
A Handbook of the Literature of the Rev. C. L. Dodgson. London: 1931. V. 47

WILLIAMS, STANLEY T.
The Life of Washington Irving. New York & London: 1935. V. 51

WILLIAMS, STEPHEN W.
American Medical Biography, or Memoirs of Eminent Physicians... Greenfield: 1845. V. 48; 49; 50; 51; 52; 53; 54

WILLIAMS, T. H.
Devonshire Scenery; or, Directions for Visiting the Most Picturesque Spots on the Eastern and Southern Caost from Sidmouth to Plymouth. Exeter: 1827. V. 50
Picturesque Excursions in Devonshire and Cornwall. London: 1804. V. 48; 50

WILLIAMS, TALIESIN
Cardiff Castle; a Poem. Merthyr-Tydfil: 1827. V. 48; 51; 54

WILLIAMS, TENNESSEE
Androgyne, Mon Amour. New York: 1966. V. 54
Androgyne, Mon Amour. New York: 1977. V. 48; 49; 51; 53; 54
Baby Doll. New York: 1956. V. 54
Baby Doll. London: 1957. V. 53; 54
Battle of Angels. Murray: 1945. V. 47; 51
Camino Real. New York: 1953. V. 51
Cat on a Hot Tin Roof. New York: 1955. V. 47; 52
Cat on a Hot Tin Roof. London: 1956. V. 51
Dragon Country. New York: 1970. V. 54
The Eccentricities of a Nightingale/Summer and Smoke: Two Plays. New York: 1964. V. 54
The Glass Menagerie. New York: 1945. V. 47; 48; 49; 50; 51; 52
Grand. New York: 1964. V. 54
Hard Candy... New York: 1954. V. 48; 52
Hard Candy. Norfolk: 1954. V. 54
I Rise in Flame, Cried the Phoenix. 1951. V. 49
I Rise in Flame, Cried the Phoenix. Norfolk: 1952. V. 54
In the Bar of a Tokyo Hotel. New York: 1969. V. 50
In the Winter of Cities. Norfolk: 1956. V. 50; 53
It Happened the Day the Sun Rose. Los Angeles: 1981. V. 50; 51; 54
Kingdom of Earth: The Seven Descents of Myrtle. New York: 1968. V. 54
The Knightly Quest. New York: 1966. V. 54
Memoirs. Garden City: 1975. V. 47; 54
Memoirs. New York: 1975. V. 48
The Milk Train Doesn't Stop Here Anymore. New York: 1964. V. 54
Moise and the World of Reason. New York: 1975. V. 48; 50; 51; 53
The Mutilated. New York: 1967. V. 54
Orpheus Descending, with Battle of Angels. New York: 1958. V. 54
Period of Adjustment. New York: 1960. V. 48; 51; 53
The Remarkable Rooming-House of Mme. Le Monde. New York: 1984. V. 49; 54
The Roman Spring of Mrs. Stone. New York: 1950. V. 47; 48; 50; 53; 54
The Rose Tattoo. 1950. V. 48
The Rose Tattoo. New York: 1950. V. 49
The Rose Tattoo. New York: 1951. V. 47; 53
Selected Plays. 1980. V. 50
Selected Plays. Franklin Center: 1980. V. 49
Small Craft Warnings. New York: 1972. V. 54
Steps Must Be Gentle. New York: 1980. V. 48; 51; 52; 53; 54
A Streetcar Named Desire. New York: 1947. V. 47; 48; 49; 52; 53; 54
A Streetcar Named Desire. Norfolk: 1947. V. 50
A Streetcar Named Desire. London: 1949. V. 51
A Streetcar Named Desire. New York: 1982. V. 47; 48; 50; 51
Suddenly Last Summer. 1958. V. 50
Summer and Smoke. New York: 1948. V. 47; 48; 49; 50; 52; 53; 54
Summer and Smoke. London: 1952. V. 53
Tennessee Williams' Letters to Donald Windham... Verona: 1976. V. 48; 54
The Theater of Tennessee Williams. Volume 6. New York: 1981. V. 54
The Theater of Tennessee Williams. Volume 7. New York: 1981. V. 54
Three Plays of Tennessee Williams. New York: 1964. V. 54
Un Tramway Nomme Desir. (Streetcar Named Desire). Paris: 1949. V. 53
Twenty-seven Wagons Full of Cotton... New York: 1945. V. 54
Twenty-seven Wagons Full of Cotton. Norfolk: 1945. V. 49; 50
The Two-Character Play. 1969. V. 50
The Two-Character Play. New York: 1969. V. 47; 54
The World of Tennessee Williams. New York: 1978. V. 48; 51
You Touched Me!. New York: 1947. V. 48

WILLIAMS, TERRY TEMPEST
Pieces of White Shell. New York: 1984. V. 50
The Secret Language of Snow. San Francisco: 1984. V. 54

WILLIAMS, THEODORE
Catalogue of the Splendid and Valuable Library. London: 1827. V. 48; 50

WILLIAMS, THOMAS
Ceremony of Love. Indianapolis: 1955. V. 52
The Night of Trees. New York: 1961. V. 51; 53
Oriental Field Sports... London: 1807. V. 53
Oriental Field Sports... London: 1819. V. 48

WILLIAMS, THOMAS D.
Cohesion. New York: 1982. V. 52

WILLIAMS, THOMAS WALTER
The Farmer's Lawyer... London: 1819. V. 49

WILLIAMS, URSULA MORAY
Adventures of the Little Wooden Horse. London: 1938. V. 48

WILLIAMS, W.
History of the Fire Lands, Comprising Huron and Erie Counties. Cleveland: 1879. V. 53

WILLIAMS, W. L., MRS.
Golden Years: an Autobiography. Dallas: 1921. V. 47

WILLIAMS, W. MATTIEU
Through Norway with a Knapsack. London: 1859. V. 52

WILLIAMS, W. R.
The Parliamentary History of the County of Oxford, Including the City and University of Oxford, and the Boroughs of Banbury, Burford, Chipping Norton, Dadington, Witney and Woodstock... Brecknock: 1899. V. 48; 49; 50

WILLIAMS, WALTER
Missouri, Mother of the West. Chicago and New York: 1930. V. 51

WILLIAMS, WELLINGTON
Appleton's Railroad and Steamboat Companion. Being a Travellers' Guide through the United States of America, Canada, New Brunswick and Nova Scotia. New York: 1849. V. 47
The Traveller's and Tourist's Guide Through the United States... Philadelphia: 1853. V. 50
The Traveller's and Tourist's Guide through the United States... Philadelphia: 1854. V. 47
The Traveller's and Tourist's Guide through the United States... Philadelphia: 1855. V. 47; 50
The Traveller's and Tourist's Guide through the United States... Philadelphia: 1859. V. 50

WILLIAMS, WILLIAM
The Duty and Interest of a People, Among Whom Religion Has Been Planted... Boston: 1736. V. 49
The Head of the Rock, a Welsh Landskip. London: 1775. V. 50; 54
Journal of the Life, Travels and Gospel Labours of William Williams. Cincinnati: 1828. V. 47; 50; 53
Oxonia Depicta sive Collegiorum et Aularum in Inclyta Academia Oxoniensi... London: 1732-33. V. 49
A Vocabulary of Familier (sic) Dialogues in English and Welsh... Carnarvon: 1837. V. 52

WILLIAMS, WILLIAM A.
The Journal of Llewellin Penrose, a Seaman. London: 1815. V. 53

WILLIAMS, WILLIAM CARLOS
The Autobiography of... New York: 1951. V. 50
A Book of Poems: Al Que Quiere!. Boston: 1917. V. 47
The Broken Span. Norfolk: 1941. V. 50
The Clouds, Aigeltinger, Russia, &c. Aurora: 1948. V. 51; 54
The Clouds, Aigeltinger, Russia, &c. Cummington: 1948. V. 52
The Collected Later Poems. 1950. V. 49
The Collected Later Poems... New York: 1950. V. 47; 52
The Collected Later Poems. Norfolk: 1950. V. 49; 51

WILLIAMS, WILLIAM CARLOS continued
The Desert Music. New York: 1954. V. 48; 51; 52
The Farmer's Daughters: the Collected Stories of William Carlos Williams. New York: 1961. V. 53
Flowers of August. Poems. Iowa City: 1983. V. 54
Go Go. New York: 1923. V. 53
The Great American Novel. Paris: 1923. V. 53
In the American Grain. New York: 1925. V. 49; 51; 53
In the Money: White Mule...Part II. Norfolk: 1940. V. 51; 52; 54
Journey to Love. New York: 1955. V. 51; 53
The Knife of the Times and Other Stories. Ithaca: 1932. V. 51; 52; 53
The Knife of the Times and Other Stories. New York: 1932. V. 48
Kora in Hell: Improvisations. San Francisco: 1957. V. 53
Life Along the Passaic River. Norfolk: 1938. V. 48; 51; 53; 54
Make Light of It. New York: 1950. V. 52
A Novelette and Other Poems. Paris: 1932. V. 47
A Novelette and Other Prose. Toulon: 1932. V. 48
Paterson (Book 1). New York: 1946. V. 51
Paterson (Book 1-5). New York: 1946-58. V. 47; 48; 49; 52; 53; 54
Paterson. (Book 1-5). New York: 1946/48/49/51. V. 48; 54
Paterson (Book 2). New York: 1948. V. 47
Paterson (Book 3). New York: 1949. V. 47
Paterson (Book 4). Norfolk: 1951. V. 53
Paterson (Book 5). New York: 1958. V. 50; 51; 53
The Pink Church. Columbus: 1949. V. 52
Selected Poems. New York: 1949. V. 49
Sour Grapes. Boston: 1921. V. 52; 53
Spring and All. 1923. V. 53
The Tempers: Poems. London: 1913. V. 49; 53
Two Drawings, Two Poems. 1937. V. 48; 51
Two Letters to Rene Taupin. New York: 1993. V. 53
Two Poems. 1937. V. 53
A Voyage to Pagany. New York. V. 52
A Voyage to Pagany. New York: 1928. V. 54
The Wedge. Cummington: 1944. V. 53; 54
White Mule. Norfolk: 1937. V. 48; 51; 53
Yes, Mrs. Williams. New York: 1959. V. 51

WILLIAMS, WILLIAM, LT. COL.
The Life and Times of the Duke of Wellington... London. V. 48
The Life and Times of the Late Duke of Wellington. London: 1853-56. V. 48

WILLIAMS-ELLIS, CLOUGH
Architecture Here and Now. London: 1934. V. 52
The Tank Corps. London: 1919. V. 47

WILLIAMSON, ALEXANDER
Journeys in North China, Manchuria and Eastern Mongolia... London: 1870. V. 50

WILLIAMSON, C.
A General Dictionary of Husbandry, Planting, Gardening and Vegetable Part of the Materia Medica. Bath: 1779. V. 49

WILLIAMSON, CHARLES
Description of the Genesee Country - Its Rapidly Progressive Population and Improvments. New York: 1799. V. 47

WILLIAMSON, E. M.
Confederate Reminiscences. Danville: 1935. V. 50

WILLIAMSON, G.
English Conversation Pictures of the 18th and Early 19th Centuries. V. 50

WILLIAMSON, GEORGE
Letters Respecting the Watt Family. Greenock: 1840. V. 50
Memorials of the Lineage, Early Life, Education and Development of the Genius of James Watt. Edinburgh: 1856. V. 47
Memorials of the Lineage, Early Life, Education and Development of the Genius of James Watt. London: 1856. V. 47; 50; 53

WILLIAMSON, GEORGE CHARLES
Andrew & Nathaniel Plimer, Miniature Painters, Their Lives and Their Works. London: 1903. V. 53; 54
The Book of Amber. London: 1932. V. 50
English Conversation Pictures of the Eighteenth and Early Nineteenth Centuries. London: 1931. V. 54
George Engleheart 1750-1829. London: 1902. V. 53
The Guild Hall of Guildford and Its Treasures. Guildford: 1928. V. 47
Guildford Charities, a Description of the Various Charities Appertaining to the Town and Neighbourhood. Guildford: 1928. V. 47
John Russell, R.A. London: 1893. V. 50
The Keats Letters, Papers and Other Relics in the Hampstead Public Library. London: 1914. V. 53
Lady Anne Clifford. Countess of Dorset, Pembroke and Montgomery, 1590-1676. London: 1967. V. 52
Portrait Miniatures, from the Time of Holbein, 1531 to that of Sir William Ross, 1860. London: 1897. V. 50; 53
Richard Cosway, R.A. London: 1905. V. 49
Trade Tokens Issued in the Seventeenth Century in England, Wales and Ireland by Corporations, Merchants, Tradesmen, etc. London: 1889-91. V. 47

WILLIAMSON, HAROLD F.
The American Petroleum Industry. Evanston: 1959/63. V. 53

WILLIAMSON, HENRY
The Ackymals. San Francisco: 1929. V. 48; 53
A Chronicle of Ancient Sunlight. London: 1951-69. V. 49; 53
A Chronicle of Ancient Sunlight. London: 1984. V. 50
Colfe's Grammar School, Lewisham and the Great War 1914-19. London: 1920. V. 50
The Flax of Dream. London: 1936. V. 54
A Fox Under My Cloak. London: 1955. V. 50
Genius of Friendship: T. E. Lawrence. London: 1941. V. 48; 50
The Gold Falcon or the Haggard of Love. London: 1933. V. 53
How Dear Is Life. London: 1954. V. 50
In the Woods. Llandeilo: 1960. V. 53; 54
In the Woods. Llandeilo: 1961. V. 48
The Incoming of Summer. London: 1923. V. 53
The Innocent Moon. London: 1961. V. 49; 50
The Linhay on the Downs. London: 1929. V. 51; 53
The Lone Swallows: Nature Essays. London: 1922. V. 53
Love and the Loveless. London: 1958. V. 50
The Nature of Books of Henry Williamson. London: 1945-46. V. 48
The Old Stag - Stories. London: 1926. V. 48
The Patriot's Progress. London: 1930. V. 47; 50; 51; 53
Salar the Salmon. London: 1935. V. 48
Salar the Salmon. London: 1936. V. 48; 49; 50
The Scandaroon. London: 1972. V. 50
The Star-Born. London: 1933. V. 50
The Story of a Norfolk Farm. London: 1941. V. 48; 54
Sun Brothers. Stories. New York: 1925. V. 48
Tarka the Otter. London: 1927. V. 48; 54
The Village Book. Essays and Stories. London: 1930. V. 53; 54
The Wet Flanders Plain. London: 1929. V. 47; 48; 50; 52; 54

WILLIAMSON, HUGH
The History of North Carolina. Philadelphia: 1812. V. 47
Observations on the Climate in Different Parts of America... New York: 1811. V. 47
The Plea of the Colonies, On the Charges Brought Against Them by Lord M——d, and Others, in a Letter to His Lordship. London: 1776. V. 47
Remarks on the Importance of the Contemplated Grand Canal, Between Lake Erie and the Hudson River. New York?: 1812. V. 47

WILLIAMSON, HUGH ROSS
Gods and Mortals in Love. London: 1936. V. 51

WILLIAMSON, ISAAC HALSTED
Opinion of Isaac H. Williamson, Esq. and Garret D. Wall, Esq. In Relation to the Corporate Powers of "The Trenton and New Brunswick Turnpike Company". Trenton: 1835. V. 47

WILLIAMSON, J.
Darker Than You Think. 1948. V. 48; 52
The Girl from Mars. 1929. V. 49; 54
The Humanoids. 1949. V. 49
The Legion of Space. 1947. V. 48; 52
The Legion of Time. 1950. V. 52
The Legion of Time. 1952. V. 48

WILLIAMSON, J. PINCKNEY
History of the Crater and Ten Months Siege of Petersburg Va. Petersburg?: 1907?. V. 50
Personal Rexperience of a 'Union' Horse Captured at the Wilderness. Petersburg?: 1907. V. 50
Ye Olden Tymes History of Petersburg, Virginia for Nearly 300 Years. Petersburg: 1906. V. 54

WILLIAMSON, JAMES A.
The Voyages of the Cabots and the English Discovery of North America Under Henry VII and Henry VIII. London: 1929. V. 47; 48; 49; 50; 51

WILLIAMSON, JAMES J.
Mosby's Rangers: a Record of the Operations of the Forty-Third Battalion Virginia Cavalry from Its Organization to the Surrender. New York: 1896. V. 48; 49

WILLIAMSON, JOHN
The British Angler. London: 1740. V. 47; 48; 49
The Narrative of a Communted Pensioner. Montreal: 1838. V. 48; 50; 53

WILLIAMSON, JOHN P.
An English-Dakota Dictionary. New York: 1938. V. 48
English-Dakota Vocabulary. Santee Agency, Nebraska: 1871. V. 48
Odowan: Dakota Hymns. New York: 1907. V. 51

WILLIAMSON, R. S.
On the Use of the Barometer on Surveys and Reconnaissances. (with) Practical Tables in Meteorology and Hypsometry... New York: 1868/68. V. 50
Report Upon the Removal of Blossom Rock, in San Francisco Harbor, California. Washington: 1871. V. 54

WILLIAMSON, R. T.
Diseases of the Spinal Cord. London: 1911. V. 47

WILLIAMSON, R. W.
Religion and Social Organizaition in Central Polynesia. Cambridge: 1937. V. 48; 52
Religious and Cosmic Beliefs of Central Polynesia. Cambridge: 1933. V. 48
The Way of the South Sea Savage. London: 1914. V. 52

WILLIAMSON, THOMAS
The Complete Angler's Vade-Mecum. London: 1808. V. 47; 52

WILLIAMSON, THOMAS continued
The Dominican; a Romance: of Which the Principal Traits are Taken from events Relating to a Family of Distinction... London: 1809. V. 48
Oriental Field Sports. London: 1807. V. 48; 50
Oriental Field Sports... London: 1808. V. 51; 52; 54
Oriental Field Sports... London: 1819. V. 49

WILLIAMSON, WILLIAM
Description of the Tumulus, Lately Opened at Gristhorpe, Near Scarborough... Exeter: 1827. V. 54
Description of the Tumulus, Lately Opened at Gristhorpe, Near Scarborough... Scarborough: 1834. V. 50

WILLIAMSON, WILLIAM CRAWFORD
The Recent Foraminfera of Great Britain. London: 1858. V. 52
Reminiscences of a Yorkshire Naturalist. London: 1896. V. 54

WILLICH, ANTHONY FLORIAN MADINGER
The Domestic Encyclopaedia... London: 1802. V. 49; 54
The Domestic Encyclopaedia.... Philadelphia: 1804. V. 53
Elements of the Critical Philosophy... London: 1798. V. 53
Lectures on Diet and Regimen... London: 1799. V. 50; 54

WILLINGHAM, CALDER
End As A Man. New York: 1947. V. 48; 49; 51
Geraldine Bradshaw. New York: 1950. V. 53
Rambling Rose. New York: 1972. V. 53

WILLIS, BAILY
Northern Patagonia: Characger and Resources. New York: 1914. V. 50

WILLIS, BROWNE
Notitia Parliamentaria... London: 1715. V. 51
Notitia Parliamentaria... London: 1716. V. 48
Notitia Parliamentaria... London: 1730. V. 52
Notitia Parliamentaria... London: 1730-16-50. V. 49; 53

WILLIS, CHARLES JAMES
The Pit Town Coronet: A Family Mystery. London: 1888. V. 54

WILLIS, CONNIE
Doomsday Book. New York: 1992. V. 51

WILLIS, HENRY NORTON
Biographical Sketches of Eminent Persons, Whose Portraits Form Part of the Duke of Dorset's Collection at Knole. London: 1795. V. 50; 54

WILLIS, JOHN
Mnemonica; or, the Art of Memory, Drained Out of the Pure Fountains of Art and Nature. London: 1661. V. 47

WILLIS, MATTHEW
The Mountain Minstrel; or, Effusions of Retirement. Poems. York: 1834. V. 50

WILLIS, NATHANIEL PARKER
The Album. New York: 1824. V. 47
American Scenery. London: 1840. V. 47; 48; 53
American Scenery... London: 1840-42. V. 52
Canadian Scenery. London: 1842. V. 47; 49; 50; 51; 52; 54
Mountain, Lake and River. New York: 1884. V. 49
Picturesque American Scenery. Boston: 1886. V. 53
The Poems of... New York: 1849. V. 48
The Scenery and Antiquities of Ireland. London: 1841. V. 53
The Scenery and Antiquities of Ireland. London: 1845. V. 53
The Scenery and Antiquities of Ireland. London: 1850. V. 49
Sketches. Boston: 1827. V. 52

WILLIS, ROBERT
The Architectural History of the University of Cambridge, and of the Colleges of Cambridge and Eton. Cambridge: 1886. V. 50
An Attempt to Analyze the Automaton Chess Player of Mr. De Kempelen. London: 1821. V. 48
Benedict de Spinoza: His Life, Correspondence and Ethics. London: 1870. V. 49
Remarks on the Architecture of the Middle Ages, Especially Italy. Cambridge: 1835. V. 47
The Works of William Harvey, M.D. London: 1847. V. 49

WILLIS, THOMAS
The Anatomy of the Brain... Montreal: 1965. V. 52; 53; 54
The Anatomy of the Brain. Tuckahoe: 1971. V. 48
Cerebri Anatome: cui Accessit Nervorum Descriptio et Usus. London: 1664. V. 50; 51; 52
De Anima Brutorum Quae Hominis Vitalis ac Sensitiva est, Exercitationes Duae... London: 1672. V. 53
De Anima Brutorum Quae Hominis Vitalis Ac Sensitiva est, Exercitationes Duae. Amsterdam: 1674. V. 48; 51
Diatribae Duac Medico-Philosophicae: Quarum Prior agit de Fermentatione, sive de motu Intestino Particularum in Quovis Corpore... Amsterdam: 1663. V. 47
Dr. Willis's Practice of Physick, Being the Whole Works of the Renowned and Famous Physician. London: 1684. V. 50
Opera Omnia. Geneva: 1676. V. 47
Opera Omnia, Ex Nupera Gravissimis Undequaque, Atque ad Publicam Perniciem Erroribus... Venetiis: 1720. V. 48
Opera Omnia Nitidius Quam Unquam Hactenus Edita... Venetiis: 1708. V. 47; 48; 49; 50
Pathologiae Cerebri, et Nervosi Generis Specimen in Quo Agitur de Morbis Convulsivis et de Scorbuto. Amsteoldami: 1670. V. 49; 50

WILLIS, WILLIAM
The Shakespeare-Bacon Controversy: A Report of the Trial of an Issue in Westminster Hall, June 20, 1627. Read in the Inner Temple Hall Thursday, May the 29th, 1902. London: 1902. V. 48

WILLIS, WILLIAM JOHN
Successful Exploration through the Interior of Australia, from Melbourne to the Gulf of Carpentaria, from the Journals and Letters of... London: 1863. V. 52

WILLISON, JOHN
A Fair and Impartial Testimony. Pittsburgh: 1808. V. 53

WILLIUS, FREDERICK A.
Cardiac Classics. St. Louis: 1941. V. 47; 49; 50; 51; 52
Classics of Cardiology; A Collection of Classic Works in the Heart and Circulation, with Comprehensive Biographical Accounts of the Authors. Malabar: 1983. V. 50; 52

WILLLS, WILLIAM HENRY
Poets' Wit and Humour. London: 1860. V. 48

WILLMORE, FREDERIC W.
A History of Walsall and Its Neighbourhood. Walsall: 1887. V. 53

WILLMOTT, ELLEN
The Genus Rosa. London: 1910-14. V. 48
The Genus Rosa. London: 1914. V. 47
Warley Garden in Spring and Summer. London: 1924. V. 54

WILLOCK, COLIN
The Gun-Punt Adventure. London: 1958. V. 49

WILLOCK, FRANKLIN J.
The Dalmation. New York: 1927. V. 47

WILLOUGHBY, CHARLES C.
Antiquities of the New England Indians. Cambridge: 1935. V. 50

WILLOUGHBY, EDWIN ELLIOT
The Making of the King James Bible. Los Angeles: 1956. V. 48

WILLOUGHBY, F.
The Ornithology... London: 1678. V. 47; 51

WILLOUGHBY, HARRIET
The History of France, in Rhyme. London: 1846. V. 51

WILLOUGHBY, HENRY POLLARD
The Apology of an English Landowner, Addressed tot he landed Proprietors of the County of Oxford. Oxford: 1827. V. 51

WILLOUGHBY, HOWARD
Australian Pictures Drawn with Pen and Pencil. London: 1886. V. 50

WILLOUGHBY, JOHN C.
East Africa and its Big Game. London: 1889. V. 48

WILLOUGHBY, LADY
So Much of the Diary of Lady Willoughby as Relates to Her Domestic History & to the Eventful Period of the Reign of Charles the First. London: 1844. V. 51

WILLOUGHBY, VERA
A Vision of Greece. London: 1925. V. 51

WILLOUGHBY DE BROKE, RICHARD GREVILLE VERNEY, LORD
Hunting the Fox. London: 1925. V. 49

WILLS, A.
The Eagle's Nest in the Valley of Sixt: a Summer Home Among the Alps, Together with Some Excursions Among the Great Glaciers. 1960. V. 53

WILLS, ALFRED
Wanderings Among the High Alps. 1858. V. 47
Wanderings Among the High Alps. London: 1858. V. 54

WILLS, CHARLES JAMES
John Squire's Secret. London: 1891. V. 47

WILLS, WILLIAM
An Essay on the Rationale of Circumstantial Evidence, Illustrated by Numerous Cases. London: 1838. V. 48

WILLS, WILLIAM HENRY
Old Leaves, Gathered from Household Words. London: 1860. V. 49; 54
Poet's Wit and Humour. London: 1861. V. 48; 53

WILLSHIRE, WILLIAM HUGHES
A Descriptive Catalogue of Early Prints in the British Museum. German and Flemish Schools. London: 1879-83. V. 50
A Descriptive Catalogue of Playing and Other Cards in the British Museum Accompanied by a Concise General History of the Subjects and Remarks on Cards... London: 1975. V. 50; 51
An Introduction to the Study and Collection of Ancient Prints. London: 1874. V. 49
An Introduction to the Study and Collection of Antique Prints. 1877. V. 52
An Introduction to the Study and Collection of Antique Prints. London: 1877. V. 50

WILLSON, BECKLES
The Great Company, Being a History of the Honourable Company of Merchants-Adventurers Trading Into Hudson's Bay. Toronto: 1899. V. 47; 52
The Great Company,... Being a History of the Honourable Company of Merchants-Adventurers Trading into Hudson's Bay... London: 1900. V. 48
John Slidell and the Confederates in Paris (1862-1865). New York: 1932. V. 50

WILLSON, BECKLES continued
The Life of Lord Strathcona and Mount Royal: G.C.M.G., G.C.V.O. Boston & New York: 1915. V. 54
The Life of Lord Strathcona and Mount Royal, G.M.G., G.C.V.O... London: 1915. V. 50

WILLSON, DAVID
The Impressions of the Mind: To Which are Added Some Remarks on Church and State Discipline, and the Acting Principles of Life. Toronto: 1835.. V. 54

WILLSON, DIXIE
Pinky Pub and the Empty Elephant. Joliet: 1922/28. V. 49

WILLSON, HARRY
The Use of a Box of Colours, in a Practical Demonstration on Composition, Light and Shade and Colours. London: 1842. V. 54

WILLUGHBY, FRANCIS
Ornithologiae Libri Tres... London: 1676. V. 48
The Ornithology. London: 1678. V. 51; 52
The Ornithology... London: 1687. V. 48
The Ornithology..1678. London: 1972. V. 51

WILLYAMS, COOPER
A Selection of Views in Egypt, Palestine, Rhodes, Italy, Minorca and Gibraltar. London: 1822. V. 53; 54
A Voyage Up the Mediterranean in His Majesty's Ship the Swiftsure... London: 1802. V. 49; 50; 51

WILLYAMS, JANE
Chillon; or Protestants of the Sixteenth Century. London: 1845. V. 48

WILMERDING, JOHN
A History of American Marine Painting. Boston: 1968. V. 50; 51; 53; 54

WILMERSING, LUCIUS
A Catalogue of an Exhibition of Renaissance Bookbindings Held at the Grolier Club ... New York: 1937. V. 50; 52

WILSON, A. N.
The Sweets of Pimlico. London: 1977. V. 50; 53

WILSON, A. PHILIPS
A Treatise on Febrile Diseases... Hartford: 1809. V. 52; 54

WILSON, ADELAIDE
Historic and Picturesque Savannah. Boston: 1889. V. 50

WILSON, ADRIAN
The Design of Books. London: 1967. V. 49
The Making of the Nuremberg Chronicle. Amsterdam: 1976. V. 48; 52; 53
The Making of the Nuremberg Chronicle. Amsterdam: 1978. V. 52; 54
The Medieval Mirror: Speculum Humanae Salvationis 1324-1500. Berkeley Los Angeles &: 1984. V. 52
The Nuremberg Chronicle Designs.. San Francisco: 1969. V. 54
Printing for Theater. San Francisco: 1957. V. 47; 50; 52
The Work and Play of Adrian Wilson. Austin: 1983. V. 47

WILSON, ALBAN
Sport and Service in Assam and Elsewhere. 1924. V. 52; 54
Sport and Service in Assam and Elsewhere. 1960. V. 54
Trout Fishing in Kashmir. Calcutta & Simla: 1920. V. 47

WILSON, ALEXANDER
American Ornithology. Edinburgh: 1831. V. 47; 50
American Ornithology... London & Edinburgh: 1832. V. 48; 49; 50; 54
American Ornithology... London: 1876. V. 50
The Flora of Westmorland. Arbroath: 1938. V. 54
The Flora of Westmorland. London: 1938. V. 49; 50; 52; 53
The Foresters: a Poem, Descriptive of a Pedestrian Journey to the Falls of Niagara, in the Autumn of 1804. Newtown: 1818. V. 47
The Foresters: a Poem, Descriptive of a Pedestrian Journey to the Falls of Niagara, in the Autumn of 1804. West Chester: 1838. V. 54
Some Observations Relative to the Influence of Climate on Vegetable and Animal Bodies. 1780. V. 54

WILSON, ALEXANDER, & SONS
A Specimen of Printing Types... Glasagow: 1789. V. 47; 48
Specimen of Printing Types. Glasgow: 1815. V. 51

WILSON, ANDREW
The Abode of Snow. Edinburgh: 1875. V. 54
The Abode of Snow. New York: 1875. V. 51; 53
Catalogue of Thoroughbred Short Horn Cattle, Belonging to Andrew Wilson, to be Sold at Public Auction Without Reserve, on Wednesday, August 20th, 1873, at Kingsville, Shawnee County Kansas, on Wednesday, August 20th, 1873 at Kingsville, Shawnee... Topeka: 1873. V. 49
The Ever Victorious Army': A History of the Chinese Campaign Under Lt.-Col. C. G. Gordon, C.B. R.E. and the Suppression of the Tai-Ping Rebellion. London: 1868. V. 50

WILSON, ANGUS
As If by Magic. London: 1973. V. 52
Late Call. London: 1963. V. 54
Laughing Matter. New York: 1967. V. 52
Setting the World on Fire. London: 1980. V. 50
Such Darling Dodos and Other Stories. London: 1950. V. 49
The Wrong Set and Other Stories. London: 1949. V. 54

WILSON, ARNOLD T.
Loyalties: Mesopotamia... London: 1930. V. 54
Loyalties: Mesopotamia... London: 1930-31. V. 47

WILSON, ARTHUR
The History of Great Britain, Being the Life and Reign of King James the First... London: 1653. V. 54
The Inconstant Lady, a Play... Oxford: 1814. V. 47

WILSON, AUGUST
The Piano Lesson. New York: 1990. V. 53

WILSON, AUGUSTA JANE EVANS
Inez. A Tale of the Alamo. New York: 1855. V. 49
Vashti; or "Until Death Us Do Part". New York: 1869. V. 54

WILSON, AUGUSTUS, MRS.
Parson's Memorial and Historical Library Magazine. St. Louis: 1885. V. 47; 51

WILSON BROS. & CO.
The Clifton Hydraulic Mining Co., Oro, Arizona. Report of Wilson Brothers & Co., Civil Engineeers, Philadelphia, Pennsylvania. Philadelphia: 1882. V. 49

WILSON, C. H.
The Wanderer in America, or Truth at Home... Thirsk: 1828. V. 47

WILSON, CARROLL A.
Catalogue of the Collection of Samuel Butler (of Erewhon) in the Chapin Library, Williams College, Williamstown, Mass. Portland: 1945. V. 52
First Appearance in Print of Some Four Hundred Familiar Quotations. Middletown: 1935. V. 49
Thirteen Author Collections of the Nineteenth Century and Five Centuries of Familiar Quotations. New York: 1950. V. 49; 54

WILSON, CHARLES
The Cats of Wild-Cat Hill. New York: 1947. V. 47; 51

WILSON, CHARLES HENRY
The Polyanthea; or, a Collection of Interesting Fragments, in Prose and Verse... London: 1804. V. 51
Swiftiana. London: 1804. V. 48

WILSON, CHARLES THOMAS
Uganda and the Egyptian Soudan. London: 1882. V. 50; 53

WILSON, CHARLES WILLIAM
From Korti to Khartum. Edinburgh: 1885. V. 54
Jerusalem. The Holy City. London: 1889. V. 51
Picturesque Palestine, Sinai and Egypt. London: 1880. V. 47
Picturesque Palestine Sinai and Egypt. New York: 1880-83. V. 50
Picturesque Palestine, Sinai and Egypt. New York: 1881-83. V. 47

WILSON, CHARLOTTE ELEANOR
Somersetshire Dialogues, or, Reminiscences of the Old Farmhouse at Weston-Super-Mare (in 1826). Weston-super-Mare: 1822. V. 52

WILSON, COLIN
The Age of Defeat. London: 1959. V. 51
The Mind Parasites. Sauk City: 1967. V. 50
The Outsider. London: 1956. V. 49; 50
Ritual in the Dark. London: 1960. V. 52

WILSON, DANIEL
The Archaeology and Prehistoric Annals of Scotland. Edinburgh: 1851. V. 52; 54
Chatterton: a Biographical Study. London: 1869. V. 49
Ethnical Forms and Undesigned Distortions of the Human Cranium. Toronto: 1862. V. 54
Moses an Example to Children. London: 1822. V. 50
Pipes and Tobacco; an Ethnographic Sketch. Toronto: 1857. V. 54
Prehistoric Annals of Scotland. London: 1863. V. 49; 52; 54
Prehistoric Man. Cambridge: 1862. V. 54
Prehistoric Man... London: 1876. V. 51

WILSON, DAVID
A Catalogue of the Manuscripts and Printed Books Collected by David Wilson, M.D., Glasgow. Eckersleys, Southport: 1925. V. 50; 52

WILSON, DAVID M.
Anglo-Saxon Ornamental Metalwork 700-1100 in the British Museum. London: 1964. V. 50

WILSON, DONALD ROLLER
The Dreams of Donald Roller Wilson. New York: 1797. V. 54

WILSON, DOUGLAS
Trade Winds. Sheffield: 1948. V. 54

WILSON, E.
Hetty Dorval. Vancouver: 1967. V. 47

WILSON, E. F.
Salt Spring Island, British Columbia. Victoria: 1895. V. 47

WILSON, EDITH BOLLING
My Memoir. Indianapolis: 1939. V. 47; 54

WILSON, EDMUND
The American Jitters. New York: 1932. V. 48
An Atlas of the Fertilization and Karyokinesis of the Ovum. New York: 1895. V. 54
The Boys in the Back Room. San Francisco: 1941. V. 48; 49; 52; 54
The Cold War and the Income Tax: a Protest. London: 1964. V. 48; 51

WILSON, EDMUND continued
Corrections and Comments. Iowa City: 1976. V. 52; 54
Europe Without Baedeker. Garden City: 1947. V. 54
The Forties. New York: 1983. V. 51
I Thought of Daisy. New York: 1929. V. 51
Memoirs of Hecate County. Garden City: 1945. V. 53
Memoirs of Hecate County. Garden City: 1946. V. 50
Note Books of Night. San Francisco: 1942. V. 47; 48; 51; 54
Patriotic Gore: Studies in the Literature of the American Civil War. New York: 1962. V. 53
Poets, Farewell!. New York: 1929. V. 49
The Rats of Rutland Grange. New York: 1974. V. 51
The Shock of Recognition. USA: 1943. V. 53
This Room and This Gin and These Sandwiches. New York: 1937. V. 48; 53; 54
To the Finland Station - A Study in the Writing and Acting of History. London: 1941. V. 49
Travels in Two Democracies. New York: 1936. V. 51; 54
The Triple Thinkers. New York: 1938. V. 50; 54
Wilson's Christmas Stocking. Fun for Young and Old. New York: 1930's. V. 48
The Wound and the Bow. Boston: 1941. V. 50

WILSON, EDWARD L.
The American Carbon Manual: or, The Production of Photographic Prints in Permanent Pigments. New York: 1868. V. 48
Wilson's Quarter Century in Photography. New York: 1887. V. 54

WILSON, ELIJAH N.
Among the Shoshones. Salt Lake City: 1910. V. 47

WILSON, ELIZA
New Zealand, and Other Poems. London: 1851. V. 50

WILSON, ERASMUS
The Eastern, or, Turkish Bath; With its History, Revival in Britain and Application to the Purposes of Health. New York: 1867. V. 49
An Inquiry Into the Relative Frequency, the Duration and Cause of Diseases of the Skin as Deduced from the Observation of One Thousand Consecutive Cases... London: 1864. V. 51
On Diseases of the Skin. Philadelphia: 1852. V. 47

WILSON, ERNEST H.
Aristocrats of the Trees. Boston: 1930. V. 48; 51; 52
The Cherries of Japan. 1916. V. 47
China: Mother of Gardens. Boston: 1929. V. 48; 50; 51; 53
The Lilies of Eastern Asia. London: 1929. V. 48
The Lilies of Eastern Asia... Boston: 1929/25. V. 51
Plant Hunting. Boston: 1927. V. 49; 50; 54
Plantae Wilsoniae. Cambridge: 1911-12. V. 49

WILSON, ETHEL
The Equations of Love. London: 1952. V. 54
The Equations of Love. Toronto: 1952. V. 48; 50; 53

WILSON, EUGENE E.
A Pilgramge of Anglers. Hartford: 1952. V. 47

WILSON, FRANK I.
The Battle of Great Bethel. Raleigh: 1864. V. 49

WILSON, FRANK N.
Selected Papers of Dr. Frank N. Wilson. Ann Arbor: 1954. V. 49; 54

WILSON, G. HENRY
The Eccentric Mirror... London: 1807. V. 49
The Eccentric Mirror. London: 1813. V. 52; 54

WILSON, G. MURRAY
Fighting Tanks. An Account of the Royal Tank Corps in Action. 1916-1919. London: 1929. V. 47

WILSON, G. W.
Photographs of English and Scottish Scenery. Aberdeen: 1866. V. 47; 54

WILSON, GAHAN
Eddy Deco's Last Chapter: an Illustrated Mystery. New York: 1987. V. 48
I Paint What I See. New York: 1971. V. 48

WILSON, GEORGE
Cyril, a Poem in Four Cantos and Minor Poems. 1834. V. 47
Cyril, a Poem in Four Cantos and Minor Poems. Leeds: 1834. V. 48
The Life of...Henry Cavendish, Including Abstracts of His More Important Scientific Papers and a Critical Inquiry into the Claims of all the Alleged Discoveries of the Composition of Water. 1851. V. 47
Memoir of Edward Forbes, F. R. S. 1861. V. 47
A Practical Treatise on Fines and Recoveries... London: 1780. V. 50
A Sketch of the Life of George Wilson, the Blackheath Pedestrian; Who Undertook to Walk One Thousand Miles in Twenty Days!. London: 1815. V. 50

WILSON, GORDON
Christopher North a Memoir of John Wilson. Edinburgh: 1863. V. 54

WILSON, H.
A Memorial of the Late J. D. Sedding. London: 1892. V. 51

WILSON, H. W.
Battleships in Action. London: 1925/26. V. 53
Japan's Fight for Freedom, the Story of the War Between Russia and Japan. London: 1904-06. V. 53

WILSON, HAROLD F.
The Jersey Shore. A Social and Economic History of the Counties of Atlantic, Cape May, Monmouth and Ocean. New York: 1953. V. 51
The Newfoundland Fishery Dispute, or the "French Shore" Question. Newfoundland: 1904. V. 47

WILSON, HARRIETTE
Clara Gazul, or Honi Soit qui Mal y Pense. London: 1830. V. 50

WILSON, HENRY
The Book of Wonderful Characters. London: 1869. V. 49
The Book of Wonderful Characters. London: 1870. V. 52

WILSON, HOWARD E.
Mary McDowell Neighbor. Chicago: 1928. V. 51

WILSON, J.
A Descriptive Catalogue of the Prints of Rembrandt. London: 1836. V. 49; 52; 54

WILSON, J. FARLOW
A Few Personal Recollections. London: 1896. V. 47

WILSON, J. G.
Appleton's Cyclopaedia of American Biography. New York: 1888. V. 53

WILSON, J. OLIVER
Birds of Westmorland and the Northern Pennines. London: 1933. V. 52

WILSON, JAMES
Lectures on the Blood, and on the Anatomy, Physiology and Surgical Pathology of the Vascular System of the Human Body. London: 1819. V. 49; 54
A Missionary Voyage to the Southern Pacific Ocean, Performed in the Years 1796, 1797-1798, in the Ship Duff, Commanded by Captain James Wilson. London: 1799. V. 48
The Monumental Inscription of the Churchyard, and Cemetery of S. Michael's, Dalston, Cumberland. Dalston: 1890. V. 50; 52
The Parish Registers of Dalston, Cumberland. Baptisms 1570-1678; Marriages 1570-1678; Burials 1570-1678. Dalston: 1893. V. 50
The Parish Registers of Dalston, Cumberland. Baptistms 1679-1812; Marriages, 1679-1812; Burials 1678-1812. Dalston: 1895. V. 50
The Register of the Priory of St. Bees. Kendal: 1915. V. 50; 52
The Rod and the Gun. Edinburgh: 1840. V. 49
The Rod and The Gun. London: 1840. V. 51; 52
Tournay; or Alaster of Kempencairn. Edinburgh: 1824. V. 54
A Treatise on Quadrupeds. Edinburgh: 1836. V. 47; 52
The Victoria History of the County of Cumberland. London: 1905. V. 52
The Victoria History of the County of Cumberland. London: 1968. V. 50

WILSON, JAMES GRANT
Thackeray in the United States, 1852-1856. London: 1904. V. 47; 48

WILSON, JAMES HARRISON
The Life and Services of Brevet Brigadier-General Andrew Joanthan Alexander. New York: 1887. V. 50
The Life of John A. Rawlins, Lawyer, Assistant Adjutant-General, Chief of Staff, Major General of Volunteers and Secretary of War. New York: 1916. V. 53
Under the Old Flag: Recollections of Military Operations in the War for the Union, the Spanish War, the Boxer Rebellion, Etc. New York: 1912. V. 47; 50; 52; 54

WILSON, JAMES HOLBERT
Temple Bar, the City Golgotha. London: 1853. V. 50

WILSON, JEREMY
T. E. Lawrence. 1988. V. 51

WILSON, JOB
An Inquiry into the Nature and Treatment of the Prevailing Epidemic, Called Spotted Fever. Boston: 1815. V. 47

WILSON, JOHN
Belphegor; or the Marriage of the Devil. London: 1691. V. 53
The Dramatic Works... London: 1874. V. 49
General Notice No. 522. for Restoring Lands to Market on Certain Proposed Railroads. Washington: 1854. V. 47
The Isle of Palms and Other Poems. Edinburgh: 1812. V. 50; 51
The Land of Burns. London: 1840. V. 54
The Recreations of Christopher North. Edinburgh and London: 1842. V. 47; 49
Recreations of Christopher North. London: 1860. V. 54
The Royal Philatelic Collection. London: 1952. V. 48; 49; 53
Wilson's Historical, Traditionary and Imaginative Tales of the Borders and of Scotland. London: 51
The Works of Professor Wilson Noctes Amboisianae. Edinburgh & London: 1855. V. 53; 54

WILSON, JOHN ALBERT
History of Los Angeles County, California. Oakland: 1880. V. 51

WILSON, JOHN, BOOKSELLER
Shakspeariana. Catalogue of All the Books, Pamphlets, &c. Relating to Shakespeare... London: 1827. V. 54

WILSON, JOHN LYDE
The Code of Honor; or Rules for the Government of Principals and Seconds in Duelling. Charleston: 1838. V. 49

WILSON, JOHN MAC KAY
The Land of Burns, a Series of Landscapes and Portraits, Illustrative of the Life and Writings of the Scottish Poet. London: 1840. V. 52
The Rural Cyclopaedia, or a General Dictionary of Agriculture... Edinburgh: 1847. V. 49; 52
The Rural Cyclopaedia or a General Dictionary of Agriculture. Edinburgh: 1848. V. 54

WILSON, JOHN MAC KAY continued
Tales of the Borders and Of Scotland. Gateshead-on-Tyne: 1870. V. 52; 54

WILSON, JOSEPH
A History of Mountains, Geographical and Mineralogical. London: 1807-10. V. 51

WILSON, JOSEPH T.
The Black Phalanx: A History of the Negro Soldiers of the United States in the Wears of 1775-1812, 1816-'65. Hartford: 1888. V. 47; 49; 52; 53

WILSON, JOYCE LANCASTER
The Ark of Noah. San Francisco: 1975. V. 49
The Swing. 1981. V. 52
The Work and Play of Adrian Wilson. Austin: 1983. V. 48

WILSON, LAURA
Watt Matthews of Lambshead: a Photographic Study of a man and His Ranch. Austin: 1989. V. 51

WILSON, LILLIAN M.
Ancient Textiles from Egypt in the University of Michigan Collection. Ann Arbor: 1933. V. 49

WILSON, LUCY SARAH
A Visit to Grove Cottage. London: 1823. V. 54

WILSON, MATTHEW
Infidelity Unmasked, or the Confutation of a Booke Published by Mr. William Chillingworth... 1652. V. 53
Mercy and Truth, or Charity Maintayned by Catholiques. St. Omer: 1634. V. 50

WILSON, MONA
The Life of William Blake. London: 1927. V. 47; 51

WILSON, NEILL COMPTON
Silver Stampede. The Career of Death Valley's Hell-Camp, Old Panamint. New York: 1937. V. 47
Treasure Express: Epic Days of the Wells Fargo. New York: 1936. V. 47

WILSON, O. S.
The Larvae of the British Lepidoptera and Their Flood Plants. London: 1880. V. 49; 52; 53; 54

WILSON, OBED G.
My Adventures in the Sierras. Franklin: 1902. V. 47

WILSON, R.
The Girls from Planet 5. 1955. V. 49
Martin Mar-Sixtvs. A Second Replie Against the Defensory and Apology of Sixtus the Fift Late Pope of Rome... London: 1592. V. 49

WILSON, R. E.
The Earthquakers, Overseas History of the 12th Bomb Group. Tacoma: 1947. V. 49

WILSON, R. R.
History of Grant County Kansas. Wichita: 1950. V. 48; 53

WILSON, RICHARD
Some Account of the Life of Richard Wilson... London: 1824. V. 50

WILSON, RICHARD L.
Colt an American Legend The Official History of Colt Firearms from 1836 to the Present. New York: 1985. V. 50
Short Ravelings from a Long Yarn, or Camp and March Sketches of the Santa Fe Trail. Santa Ana: 1936. V. 53; 54
Winchester, The Golden Age of American Gun Smithing and the Winchester of 1000. Cody: 1983. V. 52; 53

WILSON, ROBERT
Never Give Up; or, Life in the Lower Provinces. Saint John: 1878. V. 47

WILSON, ROBERT A.
Ben K. Green: a Bibliography of Writings By and About Him. Flagstaff: 1977. V. 47
Bibliography of Gertrude Stein. 1994. V. 52; 53
Gertrude Stein: a Bibliography. New York: 1974. V. 49
Tea With Alice. Faulkner On Fire Island. Michael and the Lions. Mushrooms. Six Favorites. New York: 1978-82. V. 48

WILSON, ROBERT THOMAS
History of the British Expedition to Egypt... London: 1802. V. 51; 53
History of the British Expedition to Egypt. London: 1803. V. 48; 52

WILSON, ROMER
All Alone. The Life and Private History of Emily Jane Bronte. London: 1928. V. 54
Red Magic. London: 1930. V. 49

WILSON, RUFUS ROCKWELL
Out of the West. New York: 1933. V. 48

WILSON, S.
1844. Albany City Guide. Albany: 1844. V. 53

WILSON, S. A. KINNIER
Neurology. London: 1940. V. 47
Neurology. Baltimore: 1955. V. 47

WILSON, S. B.
Aves Hawaiienses: the Birds of the Sandwich Islands. London: 1890-99. V. 47; 48
Aves Hawaiienses. The Birds of the Sandwich Islands. Honolulu: 1989. V. 50

WILSON, S. S.
A Narrative of a Greek Mission; or Sixteen Years in Malta and Greece... London: 1839. V. 48; 54

WILSON, SAMUEL
An Account of the Province of Carolina in America. London: 1682. V. 47; 48

WILSON, SARAH
Early Recollections, or Scenes from Nature. London: 1828. V. 49
Fruits of Enterprize Exhibited in the Travels of Belzoni in Egypt and Nubia... London: 1821. V. 48
Fruits of Enterprize Exhibited in the Travels of Belzoni in Egypt and Nubia... London: 1825. V. 48; 53
South African Memories. London: 1909. V. 50

WILSON, SELDEN L.
Recollections and Experiences, During the Civil War, 1861-1865, in the 15th Penna. Vol. Cavalry, Better Known as the Anderson Cavalry. Washington: 1913. V. 52

WILSON, T.
Lessons in Natural Philosophy for Children. London: 1850. V. 50

WILSON, THOMAS
The Art of Rheotrike. London: 1567. V. 48; 50
The Arte of Rhetorike, for the Use of All Suche as Are Studious of Eloquence... London: 1584. V. 48; 54
A Catalogue Raisonne of the Select Collection of Engravings of an Amateur. London: 1828. V. 47
A Christian Dictionary. London: 1622. V. 48
Distilled Spirituous Liquors the Bane of the Nation. London: 1736. V. 48
The Pitman's Pay, and Other Poems. Gateshead: 1843. V. 54
A Review of the Project for Building a New Square at Westminster-School. London: 1757. V. 50
The Rule of Reason Conteinying the Art of Logike. London: 1567. V. 50; 53
A Short and Plain Instruction for the Better Understanding of the Lord's Supper...for the Benefit of Young Communicants. Belfast: 1736. V. 54
Vita et Obitus Duorum Fratrum... Henrici et Caroli Barndoni (etc). London: 1551. V. 50

WILSON, THOMAS, BP. OF SODOR & MAN
An Essay Towards an Instruction for the Indians... London: 1740. V. 49
The Knowledge and Practice of Christianity: Made Easy to the Meanest Capacities. London: 1759. V. 50

WILSON, THOMAS, DANCING MASTER
The Complete System of English Country Dancing... London: 1820. V. 54

WILSON, WILLIAM
Bryologia Brittanica... London: 1855. V. 48; 53
Mathew Paxton. London: 1854. V. 50
A Missionary Voyage to the Southern Pacific Ocean, Performed in the Years 1796, 1797, 1798 in the Ship Duff... London: 1799. V. 47; 48

WILSON, WILLIAM RAE
Travels in Egypt and the Holy Land. London: 1823. V. 54
Travels in Russia. London: 1828. V. 48; 53

WILSON, WILLIAM, TOPOGRAPHER
The Post Chaise Companion; or, Travellers Directory through Ireland... Dublin: 1806. V. 51

WILSON, WILLIAMSON
Gathered Together. Poems. London: 1860. V. 54

WILSON, WOODROW
Division and Reunion 1829-1889. New York: 1893. V. 54
George Washington. New York: 1897. V. 48; 50
A History of the American People. New York: 1902. V. 49
Mere Literature and Other Essays. Boston: 1896. V. 48
The State. Elements of Historical and Practical Politics. Boston: 1889. V. 50
When a Man Comes to Himself. New York: 1901. V. 47; 53

WILSON, YORICK
The Gentleman's Modern System of Farriery, or Stable Directory... Trenton: 1811. V. 49

WILSON-HAFFENDEN, J. R.
The Red Men of Nigeria, an Account of a Lengthy Residence Among the 'Fulani...and other Pagan Tribes of Central Nigeria...Their...Customs, Habits and Religion. London: 1930. V. 53

WILTON, ANDREW
J. M. W. Turner: His Art and Life. New York: 1979. V. 53; 54

WILTON, MAURICE
The Old Love is the New. London: 1880. V. 51

WILTSEE, ERNEST A.
Gold Rush Steamers of the Pacific. San Francisco: 1938. V. 47; 48; 54
The Pioneer Miner and Pack Mule Express. San Francisco: 1931. V. 47; 48; 49
The Truth About Fremont: an Inquiry. San Francisco: 1936. V. 47; 50

WIMPEY, JOSEPH
Rural Improvements; Or, Essays on the Most Rational Methods of Improving Estates... London: 1775. V. 51

WINANS, WALTER
The Art of Revolver Shooting. New York: 1901. V. 47
Deer Breeding for Fine Heads, with Descriptions of Many Varieties and Cross Breads. London: 1913. V. 48

WINCH, HUMPHREY
Reports of... Sir Humphrey Winch... London: 1657. V. 53

WINCHELL, NEWTON H.
The Aborigines of Minnesota. St. Paul: 1911. V. 48; 51

WINCHELL, PRENTICE
Where There' Smoke. Philadelphia: 1946. V. 48

WINCHESTER, CLARENCE
Shipping Wonders of the World. London: 1936-37. V. 50

WINCHESTER, JAMES DALY
Captain J. D. Winchester's Experience on a Voyage From Lynn, Massachusetts to San Francisco, California and to the Alaskan Gold Fields. Salem: 1900. V. 49; 50; 51

WINCHESTER'S Repeating Fire Arms, Rifled Muskets, Carbines, Hunting and Target Rifles, etc., also Hotchkiss Fire Arms for Military and Sporting Use and Metallic Cartridges of All Kinds. New Haven: 1884. V. 50

WINCHILSEA, ANNE FINCH, COUNTESS OF
Miscellany Poems on Several Occasions. London: 1713. V. 47

WINCHILSEA, GEORGE JAMES FINCH HATTON, EARL OF
Flying Childers His Cruise. London: 1870. V. 49
Voices through Many Years. London: 1879. V. 49; 51

WINCHIP, G. P.
Cabot Bibliography with an Introductory Essay on the Careers of the Cabots. London: 1900. V. 51

WINCKELMANN, JOHANN JOACHIM
Critical Account of the Situation and Destruction by the First Eruptions of Mount Vesuvius, of Herculaneum, Pompeii and Stavia. London: 1771. V. 47

WINCOP, THOMAS
Scanderbeg; or, Love and Liberty. London: 1747. V. 48

WINCZA, ADA
Bush and Plains. Clinton: 1984. V. 47

WIND, HERBERT WARREN
The Complete Golfer. London: 1954. V. 52

WINDELER, B. C.
Elimus: a Story. Paris: 1923. V. 50; 51; 53

WINDHAM, DONALD
Footnote to a Friendship: a Memoir to Truman Capote and Others. Verona: 1983. V. 49
The Hitchhiker. Florence: 1950. V. 48; 51
June 26, 1988; the First Pages of a Memoir. 1992. V. 54
June 26, 1988. The First Pages of a Memoir. Verona: 1992. V. 49
Two People. New York: 1965. V. 54

WINDHAM, WILLIAM
A Plan of the Discipline for the Use of the Norfolk Militia. London: 1768. V. 47
The Speech...Delivered in the House of Commons...1801, on the Report of an Address to the Throne; Approving of the Preliminaries of Peace with the Republick of France. London: 1801. V. 54
Speeches in Parliament, to Which is Prefixed Some Account of His Life by Thomas Amyot. London: 1812. V. 51

WINDLE, MARY J.
Life in Washington, and Life Here and There. Philadelphia: 1859. V. 47

WINDON, WILLIAM
The Northern Pacific Railway; Its Effect Upon the Public Credit...(and) Develop the National Resources, and Thereby Diminish the National Burdens. Washington: 1869. V. 47

WINDSOR, EDWARD, DUKE OF
Farewell Speech of King Edward the Eighth Broadcast from Windsor Castle the Tenth Day of December, MCMXXXVI. San Francisco: 1938. V. 51
King's Story: Memoirs of H.R.H. New York: 1951. V. 53

WINDSOR Guide, Containing...The Present State of the Paintings and Curiosities in the Royal Apartments. (with) A Pocket Companion to the Royal Palaces. Windsor,: 1785. V. 50

WINDSOR, RUDOLPH R.
From Babylon to Timbuktu: a History of the Ancient Black Races Including the Black Hebrews. New York: 1969. V. 54

WINDT, H. DE
From Pekin to Calais by Land. London: 1892. V. 48

WINDUS, JOHN
A Journey to Mequinez; the Residence of the Present Emperor of Fez and Morocco, On Occasion of Commodore Stewart's Embassy Thither for the Redemption of the British Captives in the Year 1721. London: 1725. V. 51

THE WINE-Drinker's Manual. London: 1830. V. 48

WINES, E.
Two Years and a Half in the Navy; or, Journal of a Cruise in the Mediterranean and Levant, on Board of the U.S. Frigate Constellation, in the Years 1829, 1830 and 1831. Philadelphia: 1832. V. 48

WINES, ENOCH COBB
The State of Prisons and of Child-Saving Institutions in the Civilized World. Cambridge: 1880. V. 47; 48

WINFIELD, CHARLES H.
History of the County of Hudson, New Jersey, From Its Earliest Settlement to the Present Time. New York: 1874. V. 47; 49; 51

WING, CONWAY P.
1731. History of Cumberland County, Pennsylvania, with Illustrations. Philadelphia: 1879. V. 51

WING, DONALD
Short-Title Catalogue of Books, Printed in England, Scotland, Ireland, Wales and British America and of English Books printed in Other Countries, 1641-1700. New York: 1945/48/51. V. 48
Short-Title Catalogue of Books Printed in England, Scotland, Ireland, Wales and British America and of English Books Printed In Other Countries, 1961-1700. New York: 1945-51. V. 50; 51

WING, J. M.
The Tunnels and Water System of Chicago. Under the Lake and Under the River. Chicago: 1874. V. 51; 53

WING, JOHN
Geodoete Practicus Redivivus, The Art of Surveying: Formerly Publifh'd by Vincent Wing... London: 1700. V. 51

WING, SAMUEL B.
The Soldier's Story. Phillips: 1898. V. 47

WING, TALCOTT E.
History of Monroe County, Michigan. New York: 1890. V. 49

WINGATE, EDMUND
An Exact Abridgment of All Statutes in Force and Use from the Beginning of Magna Charta Untill...1675. London: 1675. V. 52

WINGATE, GEORGE W.
Through the Yellowstone Park on Horseback. New York: 1886. V. 54

WINGE, H.
The Interrelationship of the Mammalian Genera. Copenhagen: 1941-42. V. 54

WINGED Words, American Indian Writers Speak. Lincoln: 1990. V. 51

WINGET, D. H.
Anecdotes of Buffalo Bill: Which Have Never Before Appeared in Print. Clinton: 1912. V. 47

WINGFIELD, MARSHALL
General A. P. Stewart. His Life and Letters. Memphis: 1954. V. 50

WINGLER, HANS M.
The Bauhaus: Weimar, Dessau, Berlin, Chicago. Cambridge: 1969. V. 54
Oskar Kokoschka: the Work of the Painter. 1958. V. 47

WINKFIELD, UNCA ELIZA
The Female American, or, the Extraordinary Adventures of Unca Eliza Winkfield. Vergennes: 1814. V. 54

WINKLE, DANIEL VAN
Old Bergen. History and Reminiscences. Jersey City: 1902. V. 53

WINKLER, ERNEST W.
Journal of the Secession Convention of Texas, 1861. Austin: 1912. V. 49
Manuscript Letters and Documents of Early Texians: 1821-1845. Austin: 1937. V. 52

WINKLER, HANS A.
Rock Drawings of Southern Upper Egypt. Sir Robert Mond Desert Expedition. London: 1938-39. V. 48

WINKLER, WILLIAM
Journal of Secession Convention of Texas 1861. Austin: 1912. V. 49

WINKLES, B.
French Cathedrals. London: 1837. V. 47; 50; 51
Our National Cathedrals...Their History and Architecture from Their Foundation to the Modern Times, with Special Accounts of Modern Restorations... London: 1887-89. V. 50

WINKWORTH, WILLIAM
An Earnest Address to Servants. 1790. V. 47

WINLOCK, H. E.
Models of Daily Life in Ancient Egypt. Cambridge: 1995. V. 51
The Monastery of Epiphanius. New York: 1926. V. 49; 51
The Rise and Fall of the Middle Kingdom in Thebes. New York: 1947. V. 51
The Temple of Hibis in El Khauregh Oasis. Part I: Excvations. New York: 1941. V. 49; 51

WINN, GODFREY
Dreams Faded,. London: 1928. V. 47

WINNETT, FRED V.
The Excavations at Dibon (Dhiban) in Moab. New Haven: 1964-72. V. 50; 52

WINNING, HASSO VON
Pre-Columbian Art of Mexico & Central America. New York. V. 48
Pre-Columbian Art of Mexico & Central America. New York: 1968. V. 47; 50
Pre-Columbian Art of Mexico & Central America. New York: 1969. V. 47

WINNIPEG Canada. Winnipeg: 1903. V. 54

WINSEMIUS, PIERIUS
Sirius. Franekerae: 1638. V. 53

WINSHIP, GEORGE PARKER
The Journey of Coronado 1540-1542. New York: 1904. V. 54
The Journey of Francisco Vazquez de Coronado 1540-1542. San Francisco: 1933. V. 47

WINSHIP, GEORGE PARKER continued
The Merrymount Press of Boston. Vienna: 1929. V. 48
William Caxton. 1909. V. 49

WINSLOW BROS. CO.
Ornamental Iron and Bronze. Chicago: 1910. V. 50

WINSLOW, C. E. A.
Nursing and Nursing Education in the United States. Report of the Committee for the Study of Nursing Education. New York: 1923. V. 52

WINSLOW, DON
The Trail to Buddha's Mirror. New York: 1992. V. 52

WINSLOW, FORBES BENIGNUS
The Anatomy of Suicide. London: 1840. V. 48; 50; 52
On Obscure Diseases of the Brain and Disorders of the Mind. Philadelphia: 1860. V. 47; 49; 50
The Plea of Insanity in Criminal Cases. London: 1848. V. 48; 52

WINSLOW, JAMES BENIGNUS
An Anatomical Exposition of the Structure of the Human body. London: 1733. V. 48; 49
An Anatomical Exposition of the Structure of the Human Body... London: 1749. V. 49
The Anatomical Exposition of the Structure of the Human Body. Edinburgh: 1763. V. 47
Exposition Anatomique de la Structure du Corps Humain. London: 1732. V. 52

WINSLOW, L. FORBES
Man Humanity. New York: 1898. V. 53; 54

WINSLOW, OLA ELIZABETH
American Broadside Verse, From Imprints of the 17th & 18th Centuries. New Haven: 1930. V. 48

WINSLOW, W. H.
Cruising and Blocading. Pittsburgh: 1885. V. 49

WINSOR, FREDERIC ALBERT
Considerations On the Nature and Objects of the Intended Light and Heat Company. London: 1808. V. 53

WINSOR, HENRY J.
The Great Northwest A Guide-Book and Itinerary for the Use of Tourists and Travelers Over the Lines of the Northern Pacific Railroad, and the Oregon Railroad and Navigation Company and the Oregon and California Railroad. St. Paul: 1886. V. 47

WINSOR, JUSTIN
The Memorial History of Boston. Boston: 1880. V. 47
Narrative and Critical History of America. Boston & New York: 1884-89. V. 48; 49
Narrative and Critical History of America. Boston: 1889. V. 49; 50; 53

WINSOR, KATHLEEN
Forever Amber. New York: 1944. V. 49

WINSTANLEY, W.
The Hypocrite Unmask'd: a Comedy, in Five Acts. New York: 1801. V. 48

WINSTANLEY, WILLIAM
The Honour of the Taylors; or, the Famous and Renowned History of Sir John Hawkwood, Knight. London: 1687. V. 53
The Lives of the Most Famous English Poets, or the Honour of Parnassus... London: 1687. V. 49; 54

WINSTON, CHARLES
An Inquiry Into the Difference of Style Observable in Ancient Glass Paintings, Especially in England. Oxford: 1847. V. 50

WINSTON, JOHN A.
Fasten This Up In Your Place of Business! The Following Correspondence Has Recently Taken Place Between the Governor of Alabama and Henry J. Gardner, Governor of Massachusetts...Freemen of Massachusetts, Read It and Decide... Boston?: 1856. V. 48

WINSTON, W. R.
Four Years in Upper Burma. London: 1892. V. 48; 50

WINTER.. Boston: 1825. V. 47

WINTER, DOUGLAS E.
Night Visions 5. Arlington Heights: 1988. V. 48; 51
Prime Evil. 1988. V. 53
Prime Evil. West Kingston & Hampton: 1988. V. 47; 50

WINTER, FERDINAND
The Combs of All Times, From the Stone Age to the Present Day... Leipzig: 1906. V. 49

WINTER, GEORG SIMON
Bellerophon, Sive Eques Peritus. Norimbergae: 1678. V. 51

WINTER, GEORGE
A Compendious System of Husbandry... London: 1797. V. 50
Journals and Indian Paintings of George Winter, 1837-1839. Indianpolis: 1948. V. 47
A New And Compendious System of Husbandry. Bristol: 1787. V. 49

A WINTER *In Paris; or Memoirs of Madame de C****.* London: 1811. V. 54

WINTER *Poems (by) Robert Dana, Debora Greger, George O'Connell.* Lisbon: 1977. V. 54

WINTER, WILLIAM
Henry Irving. New York: 1885. V. 54
Life and Art of Edwin Booth. New York: 1893. V. 54
The Life of David Belasco. New York: 1918. V. 47
Poems. Boston: 1855. V. 51
The Poems... New York: 1909. V. 48
The Queen's Domain; and Other Poems. Boston: 1859. V. 54

WINTERBOTHAM, WILLIAM
An Historical, Geographical, Commercial, and Philosophical View of the United States of America, and of the European Settlements in America and the West-Indies. New York: 1796. V. 52
The Trial of Wm. Winterbotham, Assistant Preacher at Hows Lane Meeting, Plymouth, Before the Hon. Baron Perryn, and a Special Jury, at Exeter, on the 25th (-26th) of July, 1793 for Seditious Words. London: 1794. V. 51

WINTERBOTTOM, THOMAS
An Account of the Native Africans in the Neighbourhood of Sierra Leone... London: 1803. V. 51

WINTERFIELD, CAPTAIN
The Life, Voyages, Travels and Wonderful Adventures of Captain Winterfield, an English Officer, Who After Many Successes and Surprising Escapes in Europe and America with English Forces, Became, at Last a Distinguished Rebel Chief in Ireland. London: 1805. V. 47

WINTERICH, JOHN T.
Books and the Man. New York: 1929. V. 54
The Grolier Club 1848-1950: an Informal History. New York: 1950. V. 47; 48

WINTERNITZ, E.
Musical Instruments of the World. New York: 1966. V. 49

WINTERNITZ, MILTON CHARLES
Collected Studies on the Pathology of War Gas Poisoning. New Haven: 1920. V. 49; 50; 53; 54
Collected Studies on the Pathology of War Gas Poisoning. New York: 1920. V. 51

WINTERS, IVOR
The Magpie's Shadow. Chicago: 1922. V. 48; 52
Poems. Los Altos: 1940. V. 49
Three Poems. Cummington: 1950. V. 48; 49

WINTERSON, JEANETTE
Boating for Beginners. London: 1985. V. 51
Fit for the Future. London: 1986. V. 51
Oranges Are Not the Only Fruit. New York: 1987. V. 54
The Passion. London: 1987. V. 51

WINTERSON, JEANNETTE
Sexing the Cherry. London: 1989. V. 51; 53

WINTHER, OSCAR OSBURN
The Old Oregon Country. Bloomington: 1950. V. 51; 53
The Story of San Jose, 1777-1869, California's First Pueblo. San Francisco: 1935. V. 48

WINTHROP, ANNE
Poem. New London. V. 51

WINTHROP, JOHN
A Short Story of the Rise, Reign and Ruin of the Antinomians, Familists & Libertines, That Infected the Churches of New England... London: 1644. V. 48
Two Lectures on Comets... Boston: 1811. V. 50

WINTHROP, ROBERT C.
The Life and Letters of John Winthrop, Governor of the Massachusetts-Bay Co. at their Emigration to New England, 1630. Boston: 1864. V. 53
Speech of Mr. Winthrop of Massachusetts, on the Annexation of Texas, Delivered...Jan 6, 1842. Washington: 1845. V. 49

WINTHROP, THEODORE
The Canoe and the Saddle or Klalam and Kickatat... Tacoma: 1913. V. 54

WINTRINGHAM, TOM
English Captain. London: 1939. V. 49

WINTROBE, MAXWELL
Blood, Pure and Eloquent: a Story of Discovery of People and Of Ideas. New York: 1980. V. 50; 52

WINWOOD, RALPH
Memorials of Affairs of State in the Reigns of Q. Elizabeth and K. James I. London: 1725. V. 51

WINZET, NINIANE
Certane Tractatis for Reformatioun of Doctryne and Maneris in Scotland... MDLXII-MDLXIII. Edinburgh: 1835. V. 52

WIONI, PSEUD.
Songs of the Wye, and Poems, by Wioni. London: 1859. V. 52

WIRDIG, SEBASTIAN
Nova Medicina Spirituum: Curiosa Scientia and Doctrina... Hamburg: 1673. V. 48; 49; 50

WIRSING, ADAM LUDWIG
Abbildungen der Marmor-Arten Mamora et Adfines Lapides... Nurnberg: 1775. V. 52

WIRT, ELIZABETH WASHINGTON GAMBLE
Flora's Dictionary. Baltimore: 1830?. V. 52
Flora's Dictionary. Baltimore: 1837. V. 47

WIRT, WILLIAM
The Letters of the British Spy... Richmond: 1803. V. 47
The Letters of the British Spy. Richmond: 1805. V. 47; 50
Sketches of the Life and Character of Patrick Henry. Philadelphia: 1817. V. 47

WIRT, WILLIAM continued
Sketches of the Life and Character of Patrick Henry. Philadelphia: 1818. V. 47; 50

WIRTZUNG, CHRISTOPH
The General Practise of Physick. London: 1617. V. 47; 49; 53
The General Practise of Physick... London: 1654. V. 53; 54
Praxis Medicinae Universalis... London: 1598. V. 53

WISCHNITZER, RACHEL
The Architecture of the European Synagogues. Philadelphia: 1964. V. 53

WISCONSIN. GEOLOGICAL SURVEY
First Annual Report of the Geological Survey of the State of Wisconsin. Madison: 1854. V. 47

WISCONSIN RAILROAD COMMISSION
Opinions and Decisions of the Railroad Commission of the State of Wisconsin. Madison: 1908-12. V. 52

WISCONSIN. (TERRITORY). CONSTITUTIONAL CONVENTION
Journal of the Convention to Form a Constitution for the State of Wisconsin: Begun and Held at Madison, on the Fifth Day of October, 1846. Madison: 1847. V. 52

WISCONSIN. (TERRITORY). LAWS, STATUTES, ETC.
Laws of Wisconsin Territory, Passed by the Legislative Assembly, at the Session Thereof Commenced in Februrary A.D. 1848. Madison: 1848. V. 48

WISDOM in Miniature; or the Pleasing Instructor; Being a Collection of Sentences, Divine, Moral and Historical. London: 1819. V. 50

WISDOM in Miniature: or the Young Gentleman and Lady's Pleasing Instructor... Worcester: 1796. V. 50

WISDOM in Miniature; or the Young Gentleman and Lady's Pleasing Instructor... Coventry: 1797. V. 47; 53

WISE, FRANCIS
A Letter to Dr. Mead, Concerning some Antiquities in Berkshire. Oxford: 1737. V. 52
A Letter to Dr. Mead Concerning Some Antiquities in Berkshire. (with) Further Observations Upon the White Horse and Other Antiquities in Berkshire. Oxford: 1738-42. V. 47; 49
Nummorum Antiquorum Scriniis Bodleianis Reconditorum. Catalogus Cum Commentario Tabulis Aeneis et Appendice. Oxonii: 1750. V. 48

WISE, GEORGE
Campaigns and Battles of the Army of Northern Virginia. New York: 1916. V. 49
History of the Seventeenth Virginia Infantry. Baltimore: 1870. V. 48; 52

WISE, HENRY
An Analysis of One Hundred Voyages to and From India, China, &c. Performed by Ships in the Honble. East India Company's Service... London: 1839. V. 53

WISE, HENRY A.
Los Gringos: or, an Inside View of Mexico and California. New York: 1849. V. 47

WISE, HUGH D.
Tigers of the Sea. New York: 1937. V. 49

WISE, ISAAC M.
History of the Hebrews' Second Commonwealth with Special Reference to its Literature, Culture and the Origin of Rabbinism and Christianity. Cincinnati: 1880. V. 53
Rev. Dr. Adolph Huebsch, Late Rabbi of the Ahawath Chesed Congregation, New York. A Memorial. New York: 1885. V. 50

WISE, JENNINGS CROPPER
The Long Arm of Lee or the History of the Artillery of the Army of Northern Virginia with a Brief Account of the Confederate Bureau of Ordnance. Lynchburg: 1915. V. 49
The Military History of the Virginia Military Institute. Lynchburg: 1915. V. 47; 52
The Red Man in the New World Drama. Washington: 1931. V. 53

WISE, JOHN
The John Wise Collection of Ancient Peruvian Art. Hartford: 1937. V. 51
A System of Aeronautics, Comprehending Its Earliest in Investigations, and Modern Practice and Art. Philadelphia: 1850. V. 47; 49

WISE, JOHN R.
The First of May. A Fairy Masque. London: 1881. V. 50
The New Forest. London: 1863. V. 48; 50
The New Forest... London and Manchester: 1883. V. 52

WISE, JOHN S.
Memorial Address of Hon. John S. Wise, Delivered at the Unveiling of a Monument to the Memory of Southern Soldiers and V.M.I. Cadets Who Fell in the Battle of New Market, May 15th, 1864. Roanoke: 1895. V. 49

WISE, T. A.
Commentary on the Hindu System of Medicine. Calcutta: 1845. V. 47

WISE, THOMAS JAMES
The Ashley Library... London: 1924. V. 51
The Ashley Library. London: 1936. V. 53
The Ashley Library... London: 1971. V. 50
Between the Lines. Austin: 1945. V. 51
A Bibliography of the Writings in Prose and Verse of George Henry Borrow. London: 1914. V. 48; 54
A Bibliography of the Writings in Verse and Prose of George Gordon Noel, Baron Byron. London: 1932. V. 48
A Bibliography of the Writings in Verse and prose of George Gordon Noel, Baron Byron. London: 1932/33. V. 49
A Bibliography of the Writings in Verse and Prose of George Gordon Noel, Baron Byron. London: 1972. V. 50; 52
Bibliography of the Writings of Joseph Conrad. London: 1920. V. 51
A Bibliography of the Writings of Joseph Conrad... London: 1921. V. 54
A Browning Library. A Catalogue of Printed Books, Manuscripts and Autograph Letters by Robert and Elizabeth Barret Browning. London: 1929. V. 51
A Byron Library. A Catalogue of Printed Books, Manuscripts, and Autograph Letters by George Gordon Noel, Baron Byron. London: 1928. V. 49
A Conrad Library. London: 1928. V. 47; 49; 54
A Landor Library. A Catalogue of Printed Books, Manuscripts and Autograph Letters by Walter Savage Landor. London: 1928. V. 51
Literary Anecdotes of the Nineteenth Century. London: 1895-96. V. 53

WISEMAN, JAMES
Studies in the Antiquities of Stobi. Beograd: 1973-81. V. 50; 52

WISEMAN, NICHOLAS P. S., CARDINAL
Fabiola; or the Church of the Catacombs. London: 1855. V. 48; 50

WISEMAN, NICHOLAS P.S., CARDINAL
Lectures on the Principal Doctrines and Practices of the Catholic Church, Delivered at St. Mary's Moorfields, During the Lent of 1836. London: 1836. V. 49

WISEMAN, RICHARD
Severall Chirurgicall Treatises. London: 1676. V. 48
Severall Chirurgicall Treatises. London: 1686. V. 47

WISHART, GEORGE, BP. OF EDINBURGH
A Complete History of the Wars in Scotland; Under the Conduct of the Illustrious James Marquis of Montrose. London: 1720. V. 47; 48; 52
De Rebus Auspiciis...Caroli...Regis...Sub Imperio...Jacobi Montisrosarum (etc). Amsterdam?: 1647. V. 51
The Memoirs of James Marquis of Montrose 1639-1650. London: 1893. V. 54
Montrose Redivivus, or the Portraicture of James Late Marquess of Montrose... London: 1652. V. 47

WISHART, WILLIAM T.
Six Disquisitions on Doctrinal and Practical Theology. St. John: 1853. V. 53

WISLIZENUS, FREDERICK ADOLPHUS
A Journey to the Rocky Mountains in the Year 1839. St. Louis: 1912. V. 47; 52
Memoir of a Tour to Northern Mexico... Washington: 1846. V. 50
Memoir of a Tour to Northern Mexico. Washington: 1848. V. 47

WISSETT, ROBERT
A Treatise on Hemp, Including a Comprehensive Account of the Best Modes of Cultivation and Preparation as Practised in Europe, Asia and America. London: 1808. V. 48

WISSLER, CLARK
The Pageant of America. New Haven: 1925. V. 49

WISSMANN, HERMANN VON
My Second Journey through Equatorial Africa from the Congo to the Zambesi in the Years 1886 and 1887. London: 1891. V. 47

WISTAR, CASPAR
Dissertatio Medica Inauguralis. De Animo Demisso. Edinburgh: 1786. V. 47; 48
A System of Anatomy... Philadelphia: 1811-14. V. 50
A System of Anatomy... Philadelphia: 1817. V. 47; 48; 50

WISTAR, ISAAC
Autobiography of... Philadelphia: 1914. V. 47; 53

WISTER, FRANCIS
Recollections of the 12th U.S. Infantry and Regular Division, 1861-65. Philadelphia: 1887. V. 49

WISTER, OWEN
The Jimmyjohn Boss and Other Stories. New York: 1900. V. 52
A Journey in Search of Christmas. New York: 1904. V. 48
Lady Baltimore. New York: 1906. V. 49
Lin Mc Lean. New York: 1898. V. 52
Neighbors Henceforth. New York: 1922. V. 50
The New Swiss Family Robinson. New York: 1922. V. 52
The Virginian. New York: 1902. V. 51; 52; 53
The Virginian... New York: 1911. V. 49
The Virginian... New York: 1929. V. 48
The Virginian. Los Angeles: 1951. V. 51
The Virginian. New York: 1951. V. 50
Watch Your Thirst. New York: 1923. V. 51; 52
The Writings of Owen Wister. London: 1928. V. 50

WITCHELL, C. A.
The Fauna and Flora of Gloucestershire. Stroud: 1892. V. 54

WITCHELL, MARK EDWIN NORTHAM
An Account of the Principal Branches of the Family of Clutterbuck, from the Sixteenth Century to the Present Time. London: 1924. V. 54

WITCHER, W. C.
The Reign of Terror in Oklahoma. Fort Worth: 1925. V. 48

WITHAM, HENRY T. M.
The Internal Structure of Fossil Vegetables Found in the Carboniferous and Oolitic Deposits of Great Britain. Edinburgh: 1833. V. 50

WITHER, GEORGE
Britain's Remembrancer. London: 1628. V. 50
A Christmas Carroll: a Poem. 1915. V. 52; 54
A Collection of Emblemes, Ancient and Modern. London: 1973. V. 50

WITHER, GEORGE continued
Epithalamia, or Nuptiall Poems Upon the Most Blessed and Happy Marriage Between the High and Mightly Prince Frederick the Fifth, Count Palatine of the Rhine, etc. London: 1622. V. 48
Extracts from Juvenilia, or Poems. London: 1785. V. 53
Fair Virtue, the Mistress of Phil'arete. The Shepherd's Hunting. Bristol: 1840. V. 51
A Love Song. Concord: 1903. V. 48
The Poetry. London: 1902. V. 50
Select Lyrical Poems Written about 1622. Kent: 1815. V. 49; 51
Speculum Speculativum; or, a Considering-Glass... London: 1660. V. 54

WITHERBY, HARRY FORBES
The Handbook of British Birds. London: 1938-41. V. 48; 54
The Handbook of British Birds. London: 1943-45. V. 47; 52; 53
The Handbook of British Birds. London: 1945. V. 49
Handbook of British Birds. London: 1946 or 1948. V. 48
Handbook of British Birds. London: 1948. V. 50; 51; 52; 53
The Handbook of British Birds. London: 1949. V. 52
The Handbook of British Birds. London: 1952. V. 48
A Practical Handbook of British Birds. London: 1920-24. V. 54

WITHERING, WILLIAM
An Account of the Foxglove and Some Of its Medical Uses. Tokyo: 1950. V. 49
An Arrangement of British Plants.. Birmingham and London: 1796. V. 47; 50; 51
A Botanical Arrangement of All the Vegetables Naturally Growing in Great Britain. Birmingham: 1776. V. 51; 54
A Botanical Arrangement of all the Vegetables Naturally Growing in Great Britain... London: 1776. V. 49
A Systematic Arrangement of British Plants. Birmingham: 1812. V. 53

WITHERS, ALEXANDER S.
Chronicles of Border Warfare, or a History of the Settlement by the Whites of North-Western Virginia. Clarksburg: 1831. V. 47; 48

WITHERS, GEORGE
A Rich Store-House; or, Treasury for the Diseased. London: 1650. V. 52

WITHERSPOON, JOHN
The Dominion of Providence Over the Passions of Men. A Sermon Preached at Princeton, on the 17th of May, 1776. Philadelphia: 1776. V. 53
A Serious Inquiry Into the Nature and Effects of the Stage... New York: 1812. V. 49; 53
Some Truth, Much Wit...The Humble Confession, Declaration, Recantation and Apology of Benjamin Towne, printer in Philadelphia. Philadelphia: 1778. V. 50

WITHINGTON, MARY C.
Catalogue of Manuscripts in the Western Americana Collection Yale University Library. New Haven: 1952. V. 54

WITHINGTON, WILLIAM
Modern Ideas in Prose and Poetry, Dictated by the True Spirit. Portland: 1854. V. 52

WITKIN, JOEL PETER
Gods of Earth and Heaven. Altadena: 1989. V. 47
Joel Peter Witkin: Photographs. Pasadena: 1985. V. 47

WITKOWSKI, G. J.
Human Anatomy and Physiology...Part I. The Human Body (Neck and Trunk). London: 1870's. V. 51
Human Anatomy and Physiology...Part III. The Female Genital Organs. London: 1870's. V. 51
Human Anatomy and Physiology...Part VI. The Brain, the Cerebellum and Medulla Oblongata. London: 1870's. V. 51

THE WIT'S Album, or, Pine-apple of Literature... London: 1829. V. 48; 51; 53

THE WIT'S Magazine; or, Library of Momus. London: 1784-85. V. 51

WITSIUS, HERMAN
Miscellaneorum Sacrorum Libri IV. Trajecti ad Rhenum: 1692. V. 47

WITT, HAROLD
Family in the Forest and Other Poems. San Francisco: 1956. V. 53

WITT, JOHN
William Henry Hunt. Life & Work with a Catalogue. London: 1982. V. 50; 53

WITTENBERG, MARY THERESA, SISTER
The Machados & Rancho La Ballona: The Story of the Land and Its Ranchero Jose Agustin Antonio Machado. Los Angeles: 1973. V. 53; 54

WITTGENSTEIN, LUDWIG
Philosophical Investigations. New York: 1953. V. 51
Philosophical Investigations. Oxford: 1953. V. 50
Remarks on the Foundations of Mathematics. Oxford: 1956. V. 51
Tractatus Logico-Philophicus. New York: 1922. V. 48; 50
Tractatus Logico-Philosophicus. London: 1955. V. 51

WITTICH, JOHANN
Bericht von den Wunderbaren Bezoardischen Steinen, so Wieder Allerley Gifft Krefftiglich Dienen, und aus den Leiben der Frembden Their...(with) Von dem Ligno Guayaco, Wunderbawn, Res Nova Genandt, von der China, ex Occidentali India, von der Sarssa... Leipzig: 1592/92. V. 47

WITTIE, ROBERT
Ouranoskopia, or, a Survey of the Heavens. London: 1681. V. 54

WITTKE, CARL
The History of the State of Ohio in Six Volumes. Columbus: 1941-44. V. 52

WITTKOWER, RUDOLF
Gian Lorenzo Bernini, the Sculptor of the Roman Baroque. London: 1955. V. 49; 50; 51
Gian Lorenzo Bernini: the Sculptor of the Roman Baroque. 1981. V. 51; 53
Gian Lorenzo Bernini, the Sculptor of the Roman Baroque. Ithaca: 1981. V. 53; 54
Studios in the Italian Baroque. London: 1975. V. 54

WITTMAN, WILLIAM
Travels in Turkey, Asia-Minor, Syria and Across the Desert into Egypt During the Years 1799, 1800 & 1801... London: 1803. V. 48; 49; 51
Travels in Turkey, Asia-Minor, Syria and across the Desert Into Egypt During the Years 1799, 1800 & 1801. Philadelphia: 1804. V. 48

WITTMER, W.
Fauna of Saudi Arabia. Basel: 1979-81. V. 54

WITTON, P. H.
Views of the Ruins of the Principal Houses Destroyed During the Riots at Birmingham, 1791. London: 1792. V. 52

WITTOPKONING, D. A.
Art and Pharmacy. Deventer Holland: 1965-66. V. 47

WIVELL, ABRAHAM
An Inquiry Into the History, Authenticity & Characteristics of the Shakespeare Portraits, etc. (with) A Supplement to An Inquiry. London: 1827. V. 49

WIZLIZENUS, F. A.
A Journey to the Rocky Mountains in the Year 1839. St. Louis: 1912. V. 54

WLD, ISAAC
Travels through the States of North America, and Provinces of Upper and Lower Canada, During the Years 1795, 1796 and 1797. London: 1807. V. 47

WLLACE, HAROLD FRANK
The Big Game of Central and Western China Being an Account of a Journey from Shanghai to London Overland Across the Gobi Desert. London: 1913. V. 48

WODARCH, CHARLES
An Introduction to the Study of Conchology. London: 1820. V. 52; 53
Introduction to the Study of Conchology. London: 1832. V. 54

WODDERSPOON, JOHN
John Crome and His Works. Norwich: 1876. V. 47

WODEHOUSE, PELHAM GRENVILLE
America, I Like You. New York: 1956. V. 47
Angel Cake. Garden City: 1952. V. 48
Aunts Aren't Gentlemen. London: 1974. V. 54
Author! Author!. New York: 1962. V. 49; 50
Barmy in Wonderland. London: 1952. V. 51
Bertie Wooster Sees It Through. New York: 1955. V. 49; 51
Big Money. London: 1931. V. 47; 48; 51
Bill the Conqueror. London: 1924. V. 48; 50; 51
Bill the Conqueror. New York: 1924. V. 48; 51; 52; 53
Bill the Conqueror. New York: 1925. V. 48
Blanding's Castle and Elsewhere. London: 1935. V. 47; 49
Bring On the Girls. New York: 1953. V. 50
Bring On the Girls. London: 1954. V. 48; 53; 54
Brinkley Manor. Boston: 1934. V. 48
Brinkley Manor. Garden City: 1937. V. 47
The Brinkmanship of Galahad Threewood. New York: 1964. V. 51
The Butler Did It. New York: 1957. V. 49; 51
Carry On, Jeeves. London: 1925. V. 48; 50; 51
A Century of Humour. London: 1934. V. 49
The Clicking of Cuthbert. London: 1920's. V. 49; 50
The Clicking of Cuthbert. London: 1922. V. 48; 51
Cocktail Time. London: 1958. V. 51; 54
Cocktail Time. New York: 1958. V. 50
The Code of the Woosters. London: 1938. V. 48; 51
The Code of the Woosters. New York: 1938. V. 53
The Code of the Woosters. London: 1940. V. 49
Company for Henry. London: 1967. V. 51
The Crime Wave at Blandings. 1937. V. 50
The Crime Wave at Blandings. Garden City: 1937. V. 48
The Crime Wave at Blandings. New York: 1937. V. 51
A Damsel in Distress. New York: 1919. V. 48; 51
A Damsel in Distress. London: 1930?. V. 47
Divots. New York: 1927. V. 51
Do Butlers Burgle Banks?. London: 1968. V. 51
Doctor Sally. London: 1932. V. 48
Doctor Sally. London: 1933. V. 49; 50
Eggs, Beans and Crumpets. London: 1940. V. 47; 48; 49; 50
Eggs, Beans and Crumpets. New York: 1940. V. 53; 54
Eggs, Beans and Crumpets. London: 1949. V. 47
A Few Quick Ones. London: 1959. V. 49; 51
A Few Quick Ones. New York: 1959. V. 49; 53
French Leave. London: 1955. V. 47
French Leave. New York: 1959. V. 51
Frozen Assets. London: 1964. V. 47; 49; 50; 51
Full Moon. London: 1947. V. 48; 53
Full Moon. New York: 1947. V. 50
Full Moon. London: 1948. V. 51; 54

WODEHOUSE, PELHAM GRENVILLE continued
Galahad at Blandings. London: 1965. V. 51; 54
A Gentleman of Leisure. London: 1939. V. 48
The Girl in Blue. London: 1970. V. 48
The Gold Bat. London: 1911. V. 49; 50
Gold Without Tears. New York: 1924. V. 51
Good Morning Bill. London: 1928. V. 48; 51
The Great Sermon Handicap. London: 1933. V. 51
He Rather Enjoyed it. New York: 1925. V. 50
The Head of Kay's. London: 1924. V. 47
Heavy Weather. Boston: 1933. V. 48; 51
Heavy Weather. London: 1933. V. 47; 48; 49; 50; 54
Heavy Weather. Toronto: 1933. V. 51
How Right You Are, Jeeves. New York: 1960. V. 49
Ice in the Bedroom. London: 1961. V. 47
The Ice in the Bedroom. New York: 1961. V. 48; 51; 53
If I Were You. London: 1931. V. 48; 51
Indiscretions of Archie. New York: 1921. V. 51
Indiscretions of Archie. Leipzig: 1929. V. 54
Indiscretions of Archie. London: 1930's. V. 51
Indiscretions of Archie. London: 1935?. V. 48
The Inimitable Jeeves. London: 1923. V. 48; 51
The Intrusion of Jimmy. New York: 1910. V. 48; 49; 51; 53; 54
The Intrusion of Jimmy. New York: 1911. V. 49
Jeeves. New York: 1923. V. 48; 51
Jeeves and the Feudal Spirit. London: 1954. V. 48
Jeeves in the Offing. London: 1960. V. 47; 51; 54
Joy in the Morning. London: 1947. V. 47; 49
Laughing Gas. Garden City: 1936. V. 48; 50
Laughing Gas. London: 1936. V. 48
Laughing Gas. London: 1940's. V. 49; 50
Leave it To Psmith. London: 1924. V. 47; 49; 50
Leave It to Psmith. New York: 1924. V. 51
Leaves It to Psmith. New York: 1925. V. 48
The Little Nugget. London: 1914. V. 48
The Little Nugget. New York: 1914. V. 48; 51; 53; 54
The Little Nugget. London: 1931. V. 48
Lord Emsworth and Others. London: 1937. V. 48; 49; 51
Louder and Funnier. London: 1932. V. 53
Love Among the Chickens. New York: 1909. V. 47; 48
The Luck of the Bodkins. London: 1935. V. 47; 49; 51; 54
The Luck of the Bodkins. Boston: 1936. V. 47; 48; 49; 50
The Man with 2 Left Feet. New York: 1933. V. 48
The Mating Season. London: 1949. V. 47; 49; 50
Meet Mr. Mulliner. London: 1927. V. 47; 48; 49; 51
Meet Mr. Mulliner. Garden City: 1928. V. 53
Mike and Psmith. London: 1952. V. 48; 51
Mr. Mulliner Speaking. New York: 1930. V. 54
Money for Nothing. London: 1928. V. 48
Money in the Bank. Garden City: 1942. V. 47
Money in the Bank. Garden City: 1942. V. 47; 48; 49; 50
The Most of P. G. Wodehouse. New York: 1960. V. 50
Mostly Sally. New York: 1923. V. 48; 51
Much Obliged Jeeves. London: 1971. V. 47; 50; 51
Mulliner Omnibus. London: 1935. V. 47
My Man Jeeves. London: 1919. V. 50; 51; 52
Nothing Serious. London: 1950. V. 47; 49; 50
Nothing Serious. Garden City: 1951. V. 53
The Old Reliable. London: 1951. V. 47; 49; 50
A Pelican at Blandings. London: 1969. V. 47; 48; 49; 50; 51; 54
Performing Flea. London: 1953. V. 47; 48; 51
Pigs Have Wings. London: 1952. V. 48
Pigs Have Wings. Garden City: 1962. V. 54
The Play's The Thing. 1927. V. 50
Plum Pie. London: 1966. V. 51
The Pothunters. London: 1902. V. 51
The Prince and Betty. V. 49
The Prince and Betty. New York: 1912. V. 48; 51
Psmith in the City. London: 1910. V. 48; 51; 54
Psmith in the City. London: 1919. V. 49; 50
Psmith in the City. London: 1934. V. 48
Psmith in the City. London: 1950. V. 51
Psmith Journalist. London: 1915. V. 48; 51
Quick Service. 1940. V. 50
Quick Service. London: 1940. V. 48; 51; 52
Quick Service. New York: 1940. V. 47; 48; 49
Quick Service. Toronto: 1941. V. 51
The Return of Jeeves. New York: 1954. V. 48; 52; 54
Right Ho, Jeeves. London: 1934. V. 47; 48; 49; 50
Sam in the Suburbs. New York: 1925. V. 48; 53
Sam the Sudden. London: 1925. V. 47; 49; 50
Service with a Smile. New York: 1961. V. 54
Service With a Smile. London: 1962. V. 48; 54
The Small Bachelor. New York: 1927. V. 48; 50

Something Fishy. London: 1957. V. 49; 54
Something Fresh. London: 1926. V. 49; 50
Something New. 1915. V. 50
Spring Fever. Garden City: 1948. V. 51; 54
Spring Fever. London: 1948. V. 47; 51; 54
Stiff Upper Lip, Jeeves. London: 1963. V. 48; 51; 54
Summer Lightning. London: 1929. V. 47; 48
Summer Lightning. Toronto: 1929. V. 53
Summer Moonshine. Garden City: 1930. V. 47
Summer Moonshine. Garden City: 1937. V. 50
Summer Moonshine. New York: 1937. V. 51; 53
Summer Moonshine. London: 1938. V. 47; 49; 53
Summer Moonshine. London: 1949. V. 51
Sunset at Blandings. London: 1977. V. 48
Thank You, Jeeves. London: 1934. V. 48
Three Men and a Maid. New York: 1922. V. 48; 51
Ukridge. London: 1924. V. 48; 54
Uncle Dynamite. London: 1948. V. 48
Uncle Fred in the Springtime. New York: 1938. V. 53
Uncle Fred in the Springtime. London: 1939. V. 48
Uncle Fred in the Springtime. New York: 1939. V. 48
Very Good, Jeeves. Garden City: 1930. V. 48
Very Good, Jeeves. London: 1930. V. 48; 50
Very Good, Jeeves. New York: 1930. V. 53
The Week-End Wodehouse. 1939. V. 50
The Week-End Wodehouse. New York: 1939. V. 53
William Tell Told Again. London: 1904. V. 50
Wodehouse Nuggets. London: 1983. V. 54
Wodehouse on Golf. 1940. V. 50
The World of Psmith. London: 1974. V. 51
Yours, Plum. London: 1990. V. 51

WODHULL, MICHAEL
The Equality of Mankind, a Poem. London: 1798. V. 52
Poems. London: 1804. V. 48; 51; 54
*A Poetical Epistle to **** ******* M.A. Student of Christ Church.* London: 1761. V. 54

WODROW, JOHN
Carthon, the Death of Cuchullin, and Dar-Thula: Poems, by Ossian the song of Fingal. Edinburgh: 1769. V. 50

WODROW, ROBERT
The Correspondence. Edinburgh: 1842-1937. V. 47

WOGLOM, GILBERT TOTTEN
Parakites. New York: 1896. V. 47

WOHL, HELLMUT
The Paintings of Domenico Veneziano c. 1410-1461. 1980. V. 49

WOHL, HELMUT
The Paintings of Domenico Veneziano, c. 1410-1461. New York: 1980. V. 52; 54

WOHLVERDIENTE Ehren-Seule dem...Herrn Ernst Hertzogen zu Sachsen, Julich, Clve und Bergk... Gotha: 1678. V. 53

WOJCIECHOWSKA, MAIA
The Life and Death of a Grave Bull. New York: 1972. V. 54

WOJKOWITZ, RENE DE NEBESKY
Oracles and Demons of Tibet. The Cult and Iconography of the Tibetan Protective Deities. London: 1956. V. 48

WOLBACH, S. BURT
Etiology and Pathology of Typhus. 1922. V. 48

WOLBARST, JOHN
Polaroid Portfolio No. 1. New York: 1959. V. 49

WOLCOT, JAMES
A Poetical and Congratulatory Epistle to James Boswell, Esq. on His Journal of a Tour to the Hebrides with the Celebrated Dr. Johnson. London: 1786. V. 47

WOLCOT, JOHN
A Benevolent Epistle to Sylvanus Urban, Alias Master John Nichols, Printer... London: 1790. V. 50
The Life of George R—, a Fashionable Swindler.... London: 1817. V. 51
The Poetical Works of Peter Pindar. Philadelphia: 1792. V. 52
The Trial of Doctor John Wolcot, Otherwise Peter Pindar, Esq. for Criminal converation with the Wife of Mr. Knight, of the Royal Navy (etc.). London: 1807. V. 49
Tristia; or, The Sorrows of Peter. London: 1806. V. 48
The Works of Peter Pindar. London: 1794. V. 49
The Works of Peter Pindar... London: 1794-96. V. 51
The Works of Peter Pindar. London: 1794/6/1801. V. 53
The Works of Peter Pindar... London: 1812. V. 48; 50

WOLCOTT, ELIZA
The Two Sisters' Poems and Memoirs. New Haven: 1830. V. 52

WOLCOTT, OLIVER
An Address, to the People of the United States, on the Subject of the Report of a Committee of the House of Representatives... Boston: 1802. V. 51; 52

WOLCOTT, ROGER
A Letter to the Reverend Mr. Noah Hobart. Boston: 1761. V. 48; 53

WOLCOTT, ROGER continued
Poetical Meditations. New London: 1725. V. 54

WOLF, ABRAHAM
A History of Science, Technology and Philosophy in the 16th and 17th Centuries. New York: 1935. V. 50
A History of Science, Technology and Philosophy in the 16th and 17th Centuries... New York: 1935/39. V. 54
A History of Science, Technology and Philosophy in the 16th and 17th Centuries. London: 1950. V. 53
A History of Science, Technology and Philosophy in the Eighteenth Century. London: 1952. V. 49

WOLF, EDWIN
A Descriptive Catalogue of the John Frederick Lewis Collection of European Manuscripts in the Free Library of Philadelphia. Philadelphia: 1937. V. 48
Rosenbach: a Biography. Cleveland and New York: 1960. V. 48; 52; 54

WOLF, GARY
Who Censored Roger Rabbit?. New York: 1981. V. 52

WOLF Hunting in Lower Brittany. 1875. V. 52
WOLF Hunting in Lower Brittany. London: 1875. V. 48

WOLF, J.
The Life and Habits of Wild Animals. London: 1874. V. 49
Monograph of the Pheasants: the Original Sketches... London: 1988. V. 48; 52

WOLF, STEWART
Human Gastric Function, an Experimental Study of a Man and His Stomach. New York: 1943. V. 49; 54

WOLF, VICTORIA
Fabulous City;. London: 1957. V. 48

WOLF-Hunting and Wild Sport in Lower Brittany. London: 1875. V. 47

WOLFE
The Extraordinary Confession, Life and Singular Adventures, of Wolfe; Who was Thirty Years a Notorious Robber, Murderer and Captain of a Gang of Fifty-Three Thieves... London: 1810. V. 53
The Extraordinary Life and Singular Adventures of Wolfe, Who Was Thirty Years a Notorious Robber, Murderer and Captain of a Gang of Fifty-Three Thieves. London: 1825?. V. 47

WOLFE, BYRON B.
The Sketchbook of Byron B. Wolfe. Kansas City: 1972. V. 49

WOLFE, CHARLES
Remains. London: 1832. V. 50

WOLFE, GENE
At the Point of Capricorn. 1983. V. 49; 54
Bibliomen. New Castle: 1984. V. 52
The Boy Who Hooked the Sun. 1985. V. 48; 52
The Castle of the Otter. 1982. V. 48; 49; 52; 54
The Claw of the Conciliator. 1981. V. 48; 52
Empires of Foliage and Flower. New Castle: 1987. V. 52
Peace. New York: 1975. V. 52
The Shadow of the Torturer. 1980. V. 47; 51
The Shadow of the Torturer. New York: 1980. V. 52
The Shadow of the Torturer. The Claw of the Conciliator. The Sword of the Lictor. The Citadel of the Autarch. The Urth of the New Sun. New York: 1980-87. V. 48; 51
Soldier of the Mist. New York: 1986. V. 52
The Sword of the Lictor. 1982. V. 47; 51
The Urth of the New Sun. 1987. V. 48; 52
The Urth of the New Sun. London: 1987. V. 52
The Wolfe Archipelago. Willimantic: 1983. V. 52
Young Wolfe. 1992. V. 52

WOLFE, HUMBERT
Circular Saws. London: 1923. V. 48; 50
Cursory Rhymes. London: 1927. V. 53
Humoresque. London: 1926. V. 52
The Silver Cat and Other Poems. New York: 1928. V. 48
The Unknown Goddess. London: 1925. V. 52

WOLFE, JAMES
General Wolfe's Instructions to Young Officers... London: 1780. V. 47; 48

WOLFE, LINNIE MARSH
John of the Mountains: The Unpublished Journals of John Muir. Boston: 1938. V. 47

WOLFE, RICHARD J.
Jacob Bigelow's American Medical Botany 1817-1821. North Hills: 1979. V. 48; 53
Louis Herman Kinder and Fine Bookbinding in America. 1985. V. 52
Louis Herman Kinder and Fine Bookbinding in America. Newton: 1985. V. 48; 49; 50; 51; 53; 54
Louis Herman Kinder and Fine Bookbinding in America. Newtown: 1988. V. 53
Marbled Paper: its History, Techniques and Patterns. Philadelphia: 1990. V. 50
On Improvements in Marbling the Edges of Books and Paper. Newtown: 1983. V. 50; 52; 53; 54
The Role of the Mann Family of Dedham, Massachusetts, in the Marbling of Paper in Nineteenth Century America and in the Printing of Music... 1981. V. 47
Three Early French Essays on Paper Marbling, 1642-1765. Newtown: 1987. V. 48; 51

WOLFE, SUSAN
The Last Billable Hour. New York: 1989. V. 51

WOLFE, THOMAS CLAYTON
The Crisis in Industry. Chapel Hill: 1919. V. 53
The Face of a Nation. New York: 1939. V. 49
From Death to Morning. New York: 1935. V. 47; 48; 49; 50; 51; 52; 53; 54
From Death to Morning. London: 1936. V. 50
Gentlemen of the Press. Chicago: 1942. V. 50; 51; 52; 54
The Hills Beyond. New York: 1941. V. 49; 52; 53
Look Homeward, Angel. New York: 1929. V. 50; 51; 54
Look Homeward Angel. London: 1930. V. 47; 50; 53
Mannerhouse. New York: 1947. V. 50
Mannerhouse. New York: 1948. V. 47; 48; 49; 51; 52; 53
A Note on Experts: Dexter Vespasian Joyner. New York: 1939. V. 48; 53
Of Time and the River. London: 1935. V. 50
Of Time and the River. New York: 1935. V. 47; 52; 53; 54
Of Time and the River. New York: 1937. V. 52
The Portable Thomas Wolfe. New York: 1946. V. 54
The Story of a Novel. New York: 1936. V. 52; 53
The Web and the Rock. New York & London: 1939. V. 47; 48; 53; 54
The Web and the Rock. London: 1947. V. 51
You Can't Go Home Again. New York: 1940. V. 49; 50; 52; 53; 54

WOLFE, TOM
The Bonfire of the Vanities. Franklin Center: 1987. V. 53
The Bonfire of the Vanities. New York: 1987. V. 47; 48; 49; 50; 51; 53; 54
The Electric Kool-Aid Acid Test. New York: 1968. V. 49; 51
From Bauhaus to Our House. New York: 1981. V. 47; 50
In Our Time. New York: 1980. V. 52
The Kandy Kolored Tangerine Flake Streamline Baby. New York: 1965. V. 50; 51; 52; 53; 54
The New Journalism. New York: 1973. V. 50; 52; 53
The Painted Word. New York. V. 53
The Painted Word. New York: 1975. V. 51; 54
The Pump House Gang. New York: 1968. V. 52
The Purple Decades. New York: 1982. V. 49; 54
Radical Chic and Mau Mauing the Flak Catchers. New York: 1970. V. 52; 54
The Right Stuff. New York: 1979. V. 48; 53; 54

WOLFE, WELLINGTON C.
Men of California. San Francisco: 1901. V. 50

WOLFENSTEIN, MARTHA
A Renegade and other Tales. Philadelphia: 1905. V. 49

WOLFF, CHRISTIAN FRIEDRICH VON
A Treatise of Algebra... London: 17399. V. 48

WOLFF, JENS
Sketches and Observations Taken on a Tour through a Part of the South of Europe. London: 1801. V. 50
Sketches on a Tour to Copenhagen, Through Norway and Sweden... London: 1814. V. 47

WOLFF, JOHN
Route of the Manly Party of 1849-50 in Leaving Death Valley for the Coast. V. 53

WOLFF, JOSEPH
Narrative of a Mision to Bokhara in the Years 1843-1845 to Ascertain the Fate of Colonel Stoddart and Captain Connolly. London: 1845. V. 50
Researches and Missionary Labours Among the Jews, Mohammedans, and Other Sects... London: 1835. V. 47
Travels and Adventures of the Rev. Joseph Wolff, DD, LLD. London: 1861. V. 50

WOLFF, MARITTA
The Big Nickelodeon. New York: 1956. V. 54

WOLFF, ROBERT LEE
Nineteenth Century Fiction: a Bibliographical Catalogue... New York & London: 1981-86. V. 51; 54
Nineteenth Century Fiction: A Bibliographical Catalogue... New York: 1985-86. V. 51
Nineteenth Century Fiction: a Bibliographical Catalogue. 1993. V. 54

WOLFF, TOBIAS
Back in the World. Boston: 1985. V. 52
The Barrack's Thief. New York: 1984. V. 47; 51; 54
In the Garden of the North American Martyrs. New York: 1981. V. 52; 53
The Other Miller. Derry/Ridgewood: 1984. V. 53
The Other Miller. Derry & Ridgewood: 1986. V. 47; 54
The Other Miller. Derry & Ridgewood: 1989. V. 51
The Other Miller. 1990. V. 51; 52
The Other Miller. Derry: 1990. V. 49; 54
This Boy's Life: a Memoir. New York: 1989. V. 52
Ugly Rumors. London: 1975. V. 51; 52

WOLFF, W. J.
Ecology of the Wadden Sea. Rotterdam: 1983. V. 48

WOLFF, WERNER
Island of Death (Easter Island). New York: 1948. V. 47; 48

WOLFFLIN, HEINRICH
Principles of Art History. London: 1932. V. 50

WOLFIUS, JOANNES
Artis Historicae penvs. Basle: 1579. V. 48

WOLFLERN Chace: a Chronicle of "Days That are No More". London: 1879. V. 54

WOLLASTON, A. F. R.
Pygmies and Papuans. New York: 1912. V. 52

WOLLASTON, ARTHUR
An English-Persian Dictionary. London: 1904. V. 48

WOLLASTON, T. C.
On the Variation of Species... London: 1856. V. 48

WOLLASTON, T. V.
Catalogue of the Coleopterous Insects of the Canaries. London: 1864. V. 48; 50
Coleoptera Hesperidum, Being an Enumeration of the Coleopterous Insects of the Cape Verde Archipelago. London: 1867. V. 49

WOLLASTON, WILLIAM
The Religion of Nature Delineated... London: 1724. V. 51
The Religion of Nature Delineated. London: 1725. V. 47; 48; 50; 54
The Religion of Nature Delineated. London: 1731. V. 49
The Religion of Nature Delineated... London: 1738. V. 47
The Religion of Nature Delineated. London: 1750. V. 52
The Religion of Nature Delineated... London: 1759. V. 48
The Religion of Nature Delineated. London: 1838. V. 48

WOLLE, F.
Desmids of the United States and List of American Pediastrums. Bethlehem: 1884. V. 49; 52
Desmids of the United States and List of American Pediastrums. Bethlehem: 1892. V. 48
Diatomaceae of North America. Bethlehem: 1890. V. 49
Fresh Water Algae of the United States. Bethlehem: 1887. V. 48; 49; 50; 52

WOLLE, MURIEL SIBELL
Montana Pay Dirt A Guide to the Mining Camps of the Treasure State. Denver: 1963. V. 54

WOLLEY, J.
Ootheca Wolleyana... London: 1864-1907. V. 48

WOLLSTONECRAFT, MARY
Letters Written During a Short Residence in Sweden, Norway and Denmark. London: 1796. V. 47; 48; 53; 54
The Love Letters of Mary Wollstonecraft to Gilbert Imlay. London: 1908. V. 53
Mary, a Fiction. London: 1788. V. 50
Mary Wollstonecraft: Letters to Imlay.... London: 1879. V. 48; 50
Original Stories from Real Life... London: 1791. V. 47; 54
Original Stories from Real Life.. London: 1796. V. 54
Posthumous Works of the Author of a Vindication of the Rights of Woman. London: 1798. V. 47
Thoughts on the Education of Daughters; with Reflections on Female Conduct, in the More Important Duties of Life. London: 1787. V. 47; 53
Vindication of the Rights of Men, in a Letter to the Right Honourable Edmund Burke, Occasioned by his Reflections on the Revolution in France. London: 1790. V. 47; 48
A Vindication of the Rights of Woman. Boston: 1792. V. 47; 53
A Vindication of the Rights of Woman... London: 1792. V. 47; 48; 49; 52; 53; 54
A Vindication of the Rights of Woman... Philadelphia: 1794. V. 51

WOLOSHUK, NICHOLAS
Edward Borein, Drawings and Paintings of the Old West. Volume II: the Cowboys. Santa Fe: 1974. V. 53

WOLSELEY, FRANCES
The Story of Marlborough. London. V. 52

THE WOLSELEY Motor Vehicle Handbook, Being Hints and Directions on the Care and Management of the Wolseley Motor Vehicles. London: 1905. V. 47

WOLSELEY, VISCOUNTESS
Some of the Smaller Manor Houses of Sussex. London: 1925. V. 47
Some Sussex Byways. London: 1920. V. 54

WOLTMANN, C. VON
The White Lady and Undine. Tales from the German. London: 1844. V. 53

WOLVERTON, F. G.
Five Months' Sport in Somali Land. London: 1894. V. 54

WOLVERTON'S Atlas of Monmouth County, New Jersey. New York: 1889. V. 47

WOMACK, BOB
The Echo of Hoofbeats. A History of the Tennessee Walking Horse. Shelbyville: 1973. V. 54

WOMACK, JACK
Ambient. New York: 1987. V. 54

WOMAN. In All Ages and In All Countries. Philadelphia: 1907. V. 51

WOMAN In All Ages and In All Countries. Philadelphia: 1907-08. V. 52; 53

WOMEN Novelists of Queen Victoria's Regin: a Book of Appreciations... London: 1897. V. 53

WOMEN of Canada. Montreal: 1930. V. 50

THE WONDER Book of Freaks and Animals in the Barnum and Bailey Greatest Show on Earth. London: 1898. V. 52

THE WONDER of All Nations!!. Norwich: 1831. V. 53

WONDERFUL Adventures. A Series on Narratives of Personal Experiences Among the Native Tribes of America. Philadelphia: 1874. V. 54

THE WONDERFUL History of Virgilius the Sorcerer of Rome. London: 1893. V. 50

WONDERFUL Prophecies Being a Dissertation On the Existence, Nature and Extent of the Prophetic Powers in the Human Mind... London: 1795. V. 50

THE WONDERS of Nature and Art... London: 1768. V. 52

THE WONDERS of Nature and Art. London: 1839. V. 47

THE WONDERS of the Yosemite Valley and California. Boston: 1872. V. 50

WONG, K. CHIMIN
History of Chinese Medicine. Tientsin: 1932. V. 52

WONG-QUINCEY, J.
Chinese Hunter. New York: 1939. V. 52; 53

WOOD, A. B.
Fifty Years of Yesterdays. Gering: 1945. V. 50; 52

WOOD, ANN MARIA MICHELL
Verses and Imitations and Translations. N.P: 1842. V. 52

WOOD, ANTHONY
Athenae Oxonienses... London: 1691-92. V. 47; 48; 49
Athenae Oxonienses... London: 1721. V. 48; 49; 50; 53
The History and Antiquities of the Colleges and Halls in the University of Oxford. Oxford: 1786-90. V. 48; 50; 52

WOOD, BUTLER
Charlotte Bronte 1816-1916. A Centenary Memorial... London: 1917. V. 54

WOOD, CASEY A.
The American Encyclopedia and Dictionary of Ophthalmology. Chicago: 1913-21. V. 47
The Fundus Oculi of Birds, Especially as Viewed by the Ophthalmoscope. Chicago: 1917. V. 50; 52; 53
An Introduction to the Literature of Vertebrate Zoology. London: 1931. V. 47; 49; 50
An Introduction to the Literature of Verterate Zoology. Hildesheim: 1974. V. 52; 53; 54

WOOD, CHARLES W.
Glories of Spain. London: 1901. V. 54

WOOD, CHRISTOPHER
The Pre-Raphaelites. New York: 1981. V. 50; 53; 54

WOOD, DEAN EARL
The Old Santa Fe Trail from the Missouri River. Kansas City: 1955. V. 49

WOOD, ED
Watts...After. Aqoura: 1967. V. 54

WOOD, EDWARD J.
Curiosities of Clocks and Watches from the Earliest Times. London: 1866. V. 52

WOOD, ELLEN PRICE
Anne Hereford. London: 1868. V. 50
Bessy Rane: a Novel. London: 1870. V. 50
The Channings. London: 1862. V. 50
Dene Hollow. A Novel. London: 1871. V. 51
East Lynne. London: 1861. V. 48; 51; 52
The House of Halliwell. London: 1890. V. 50
Johnny Ludlow... London: 1880. V. 51
Johnny Ludlow. London: 1899. V. 50
Johnny Ludlow. London: 1908. V. 50
Lady Grace and Other Stories. London: 1887. V. 48; 54
Mildred Arkell. London: 1865. V. 50
Mrs. Halliburton's Troubles. London: 1862. V. 50
Oswald Cray. Edinburgh: 1864. V. 54
The Red Court Farm. London: 1868. V. 51
The Shadow of Ashlydyat. London: 1863. V. 50
The Story of Charles Strange: a Novel. London: 1888. V. 50
Verner's Pride. London: 1863. V. 47

WOOD, EVELYN
Cavalry in the Waterloo Campaign. London: 1895. V. 50

WOOD, F. J.
The Turnpikes of New England. Boston: 1919. V. 48

WOOD, GEORGE
The Dispensatory of the United States of America. Philadelphia: 1847. V. 54
The Dispensatory of the United States of America. Philadelphia: 1851. V. 49
Introductory Lectures and Addresses on Medical Subjects. Philadelphia: 1859. V. 52
Peter Schlemihl in America. Philadelphia: 1848. V. 49

WOOD, GEORGE L.
The Seventh Regiment. New York: 1865. V. 49

WOOD, H. C.
A Contribution to the History of the Fresh-Water Algae of North America. Washington: 1872. V. 50; 51; 54

WOOD, HARVEY
Personal Recollections... Pasadena: 1955. V. 49; 53

WOOD, HENRY
Change for the American Notes in Letters from London to New York. 1843. V. 49; 54
Change for the American Notes: in Letters from London to New York. New York: 1843. V. 54

WOOD, HERBERT
The Shores of Lake Aral. 1876. V. 54

WOOD, J. MAXWELL
Smuggling in the Solway and Around the Galloway Sea-Board. Dumfries: 1908. V. 50; 52; 54

WOOD, J. N. PRICE
Travel and Sport in Turkestan. 1910. V. 54
Travel and Sport in Turkestan... London: 1910. V. 51

WOOD, J. T.
Discoveries at Ephesus, Including the Site and Remains of the Great Temple of Diana. London: 1877. V. 47; 49

WOOD, JOHN
A Correct Statement of the Various Sources from Which the History of the Administration of John Adams Was Compiled... New York: 1802. V. 47
A Description of the Exchange of Bristol... Bath: 1743. V. 52
An Elementary Treatise on Sketching From Nature; With the Principles of Light and Shade, The Theory of Colours. London: 1850. V. 47; 48
A Full Exposition of the Clintonian Faction, and the Society of the Columbian Illuminati... Newark: 1802. V. 47
A Journey to the Source of the River Oxus. London: 1872. V. 48
A Manual of Perspective Being a Familiar Explanation of the Science, Including the Rule Necessary for the Correct Represnetation of Objects... Worcester: 1841. V. 48
A Manual of Perspective...for the Use of Amateurs. Worcester: 1849. V. 47
The Origin of Building; or, the Plagiarism of the Heathens Detected... Bath: 1741. V. 47
The Origin of Building: or, the Plagiarism of the Heathens Detected. London: 1753. V. 48

WOOD, JOHN GEORGE
Animate Creation. New York: 1885. V. 53
Domestic Animals of the Bible from "Bible Animals.". London: 1887. V. 50
Homes Without Hands. London: 1869. V. 47; 48
The Illustrated Natural History. London: 1860. V. 47
The Illustrated Natural History. London: 1880. V. 50; 51
The Principles and Practice of Sketching Landscape Scenery from Nature, Systematically Arranged. London: 1816. V. 53

WOOD, JOHN, GROOM TO THE KING OF SARDINIA
A New Compendious Treatise of Farriery. London: 1757. V. 47

WOOD, JOHN W.
Union and Secession in Mississppi, by the Hon. John W. Wood, the Union Member of the Mississippi State Convention Who Refused to Sign the Ordinance of Secession, or Commit Himself in Any Way to the Secession Movement. Memphis: 1863. V. 48

WOOD, JOSEPH
Reminiscences of the Late Joseph Laurence of East Keswick. Leeds: 1887. V. 50

WOOD, JOSEPHINE
Indian Costumes of Guatemala. Graz: 1966. V. 52; 54

WOOD, L. INGLEBY
Scottish Pewter-Ware and Pewterers. Edinburgh: 1907. V. 54

WOOD, LAWSON
The Box of Mrs. Books. London. V. 49
The Hamper of Mr. Books. London: 1930's. V. 54
Lawson Wood's Fun Fair. London: 1931. V. 49
The Mrs. Books. London. V. 49
The Old Nursery Rhymes. London: 1933. V. 48

WOOD, MRS.
Letters from the Irish Highlands. London: 1825. V. 51

WOOD, N.
The Ornithologist's Text-Book Being Reviews of Ornithological Works. London: 1836. V. 47

WOOD, NICHOLAS
A Practical Treatise on Rail-Roads, and Interior Communications in General... London: 1838. V. 47; 49; 52

WOOD, R. E.
Life and Confessions of James Gilbert Jenkins: the Murderer of Eighteen Men. Napa City: 1864. V. 47; 48; 49

WOOD, RAYMOND F.
California's Aqua Fria. Fresno: 1954. V. 49

WOOD, ROBERT
Les Ruines de Palmyre, Autrement Dite Tedmore Au Desert. Londres: 1753. V. 49
The Ruins of Palmyra, Otherwise Tedmor, in the Desart. (with) *The Ruins of Balbec...* London: 1753/57. V. 50

WOOD, SALLY S. K.
Ferdinand & Elmira; a Russian Story. Baltimore: 1804. V. 49; 52

WOOD, SILAS
A Sketch of the First Settlement of the Several Towns of Long-Island With their Political Condition to the End of the American Revolution. Brooklyn: 1828. V. 47; 49; 50

WOOD, T. W.
Curiosities of Ornithology. London: 1871. V. 50; 52; 53

WOOD, THOMAS
An Inquiry Concerning the Primitive Inhabitants of Ireland. London: 1821. V. 47
An Institute of the Laws of England. London: 1734. V. 47
An Institute of the Laws of England... London: 1745. V. 50
An Institute of the Laws of England... London: 1763. V. 54
A New Institute of the Imperial or Civil Law. London: 1721. V. 50; 53

WOOD, W. D.
A Partial Roster of the Officers and Men Raised in Leon County, Texas. Waco: 1963. V. 49

WOOD, WALTER
North Sea Fishers and Fighters. London: 1911. V. 50
The Northumberland Fusiliers. London: 1900. V. 51; 53

WOOD, WILLIAM
General Conchology, or a Description of Shells arranged According to the Linnean System. London: 1835. V. 52; 54
Illustrations of the Linnean Genera of Insects. London: 1821. V. 52
Index Entomolgicus...Lepidopterous Insects of Great Britain. London: 1854. V. 53
Index Testaceologicus... London: 1818. V. 48
Index Testaceologicus... London: 1828. V. 47; 54
Index Testaceologicus. London: 1856. V. 49
A Mechanical Essay Upon the Heart... London: 1729. V. 48
The Storied Province of Quebec: Past and Present. Toronto: 1931-32. V. 50
Zoography; or, the Beauties of Nature Displayed. London: 1807. V. 50; 53
Zoography; or, the Beauties of Nature Displayed... London: 1807-11. V. 53

WOOD, WILLIAM MAXWELL
Fankwei; or the San Jacinto in the Seas of India, China and Japan,. New York: 1859. V. 52

WOOD, WILLIAM NATHANIEL
Reminiscences of Big I. Charlottesville: 1909. V. 49

WOOD, WILLIAM R.
Past Years in Pickering. Toronto: 1911. V. 54

WOODALL, MARY
Gainsborough's Landscape Drawings. Boston: 1939. V. 53
Gainsborough's Landscape Drawings. London: 1939. V. 49; 51; 53

WOODALL, R. G.
The Postal History of Yukon Territory. England: 1964. V. 53

WOOD-ALLEN, MARY
What a Young Girl Out to Know. Philadelphia: 1905. V. 47

WOODARD, DAVID
The Narrative of Captain David Woodard and Four Seamen. London: 1804. V. 49; 54
The Narrative of Captain David Woodard and Four Seamen... London: 1805. V. 47

WOODBERRY, GEORGE E.
Edgar Allan Poe. Boston and New York: 1913. V. 48
History of Wood Engraving. New York: 1883. V. 50; 53
The Life of Edgar Allan Poe. Boston and New York: 1909. V. 48

WOODBRIDGE, HENSLEY C.
Jack London: a Bibliography. Georgetown: 1966. V. 51

WOODBURN, SAMUEL
Ecclesiastical Topography. London: 1811. V. 50

WOODBURY, D. P.
Sustaining Walls: Geometrical Constructions to Determine Their Thickness Under Various Circumstances. Washington: 1854. V. 49

WOODCOCK, GEORGE
Anarchism - a History of Liberation Ideas and Movements. Cleveland and New York: 1962. V. 50
The Anarchist Prince - a Biographical Study of Peter Kropotkin. London: 1950. V. 53

WOODCOCK, H. B. D.
Lilies of the World. London: 1949. V. 50
Lilies of the World... London: 1950. V. 50; 51; 53

WOODCROFT, BENNET
A Sketch of the Origin and Progress of Steam Navigation from Authentic Documents. London: 1848. V. 47; 49; 51; 53

THE WOODCUT *of To-Day at Home and Abroad.* (with) *Commentary By Malcolm C. Salaman.* London: 1927. V. 54

WOODD, HENRY
Genealogical, Heraldic and Other Records, with Tables of Founder's Kin of the Family of Woodd. London: 1886. V. 47; 53

WOODEHOUSE, JAMES
Norbury Park, a Poem... London: 1803. V. 50

WOODESON, RICHARD
Elements of Jurisprudence Treated of in the Preliminary Part of a Course of Lectures on the Laws of England. London: 1783. V. 48

WOODFIELD, DENIS B.
Surreptitious Printing in England 1550-1640. New York: 1973. V. 54

WOODFIN, A., MRS.
The History of Miss Sally Sable. London: 1757?. V. 54

WOODFORDE, JAMES
The Diary of a Country Parson... London: 1924-31. V. 51

WOODFORDE, JAMES continued
The Diary of a Country Parson... Oxford: 1926-31. V. 51
The Diary of a Country Parson. 1981. V. 47

WOODHOUSE, JAMES
Journeyman Shoemaker. Poems on Several Occasions. London: 1766. V. 50
Poems on Several Occasions. London: 1764. V. 51; 54
Poems on Several Occasions. London: 1766. V. 47

WOODHOUSE, L. G. O.
The Butterfly Fauna of Ceylon. Colombo: 1942. V. 52

WOODHOUSE, ROBERT
An Elementary Treatise on Astronomy. Cambridge: 1812. V. 52
The Principles of Analytical Calculation. Cambridge: 1803. V. 52
The Principles of Analytical Calculation. London: 1803. V. 48
A Treatise on Astronomy. Cambridge: 1821/23. V. 52

WOODHOUSE, S. C.
Miss Bounce. New York: 1903. V. 54

WOODHULL, ALFRED A.
Catalogue of the United States Army Medical Museum. Washington: 1866-67. V. 47

WOODHULL, MICHAEL
Poems. London: 1804. V. 49

WOODHULL, VICTORIA C.
The Origin, Tendencies and Principles of Government. New York: 1871. V. 50; 51

THE WOODLAWN Cemetery in North Chelsea and Malden. Boston: 1856. V. 51; 54

WOOD-MARTIN, W. G.
History of Sligo, County and Town (1603-1688). 1889. V. 48; 52

WOODRELL, DANIEL
Muscle for the Wing. New York: 1988. V. 53

WOODROFFE, JOHN GEORGE
The Serpent Power Being the Shat-Chakre-Niruana and Paduka Panchaka. London: 1919. V. 51

WOODROFFE, PAUL
Thirty Old-Time Nursery Songs. London: 1920. V. 49

WOODRUFF, DOUGLAS
Plato's American Republic. London: 1926. V. 52

WOODRUFF, EDWIN H.
A Selection of Cases on Domestic Relations and the Law of persons. New York: 1897. V. 51

WOODRUFF, ELIZABETH
Dickey Byrd. Springfield: 1928. V. 49

WOODRUFF, FUZZY
A History of Southern Football 1890-1928. Atlanta: 1928. V. 50

WOODRUFF, HEZEKIAH N.
A Sermon. Preached at Scipio, N.Y. at the Execution of John Delaware, a Native; for the Murder of Ezekiel Crane... Albany: 1804. V. 47

WOODRUFF, MICHAEL
The Trnasplantation of Tissues and Organs. Springfield: 1960. V. 51

WOODRUFF, SAMUEL
Journal of a Tour to Malta, Greece, Asia Minor, Carthage, Algiers, Port Mahon and Spain. Hartford: 1831. V. 49

WOODRUFF, SYLVESTER
A Voyage to the Island of Philosophers, by Caesario San Blas, Bachelor. 1830. V. 47

WOODRUFF, WILFORD
Leaves From My Journal. Salt Lake City: 1881. V. 47; 49

WOODRUFF, WILLIAM EDWARD
With the Light Guns in '61-'65. Little Rock: 1903. V. 47; 49

WOODS, ALVA
Intellectual and Moral Culture. Lexington: 1828. V. 50; 53

WOODS, C. E.
The Electric Automobile: its Construction, Care and Operation. Chicago & N: 1900. V. 49

WOODS, CAROLINE H.
Woman in Prison. New York: 1809. V. 53

WOODS COUNTY ABSTRACT & LOAN CO.
Information for Investors East Hill Addition to the City of Alva, Oklahoma. Alva: 1907. V. 50

WOODS, DANIEL B.
Sixteen Months at the Gold Diggings. New York: 1851. V. 47; 49

WOODS, GEORGE
An Account of the Past and Present State of the Isle of Man. London: 1811. V. 47

WOODS INVESTMENT CO.
Gold Fields of Cripple Creek. Colorado Springs: 1901. V. 49; 54

WOODS, J. E.
Geological Observations in South Australia... London: 1862. V. 52; 53

WOODS, JAMES
Recollections of Pioneer Work in California. San Francisco: 1878. V. 49; 51; 53

WOODS, JOHN
Two Years' Residence in the Settlement On the English Prairie, in the Illinois Country, United States. London: 1822. V. 47; 49

WOODS, JOSEPH
Letters of an Architect, from France, Italy and Greece. London: 1828. V. 49
Thoughts on the Slavery of the Negroes. London: 1784. V. 51; 52

WOODS, MARGARET L.
Lycris. Oxford: 1888. V. 47; 50
Songs. Oxford: 1896. V. 52

WOODS, ROBERT ARCHEY
English Social Movements. New York: 1891. V. 52

WOODS, ROBERT HENRY
Botany Bay. Dublin: 1892. V. 54

WOODS, ROBERT STUART
First Centennial of the Anglican Church in the County of Essex, with Special Reference to the History and Work of St. John's Church, Sandwich. 1903. V. 53

WOOD'S Royal Almanack for 1846. London: 1846. V. 54

WOODS, S. JOHN
John Piper Paintings, Drawings and Theatre Designs 1932-1954. London: 1955. V. 54

WOODS, STUART
Chiefs. New York: 1981. V. 51
Run Before the Wind. New York: 1983. V. 51
Under the Lake. New York: 1987. V. 49

WOODSON, CARTER GODWIN
The Negro Heads of Families in the United States in 1830, Together with a Brief Treatment of the Free Negro. Washington: 1925. V. 52
The Negro in Our History. Washington: 1927. V. 48; 53
Negro Orators and Their Orations. Washington: 1925. V. 54
The Rural Negro. Washington: 1930. V. 52

WOODSON, HENRY M.
Historical Genealogy of the Woodsons and Their Connections. Memphis: 1915. V. 52

WOODSON, R. E.
Flora of Panama. St. Louis: 1943-59. V. 47
Flora of Panama. Part 3. Fasc. 2-5. Orchidaceae Complete. New York: 1965. V. 53

WOODVILLE, WILLIAM
Medical Botany. London: 1832. V. 53; 54

WOODWARD, A. S.
Catalogue of the Fossil Fishes. London: 1889-1901. V. 47

WOODWARD, AUGUSTUS B.
Considerations on the Executive Government of the United States of America. Flatbush: 1809. V. 47
The Presidency of the United States. New York: 1825. V. 54

WOODWARD, BERNARD B.
General History of Hampshire and the Isle of Wight. London: 1870. V. 51

WOODWARD, C. M.
A History of the St. Louis Bridge: Containing a Full Account of Every Step In Its Construction and Erection, and Including the theory of the Ribbed Arch and the ... St. Louis: 1881. V. 51

WOODWARD, CHARLES L.
Bibliothica (sic) — Scallawagiana. Catalogue of a Matchless Collection of Books, Pamphlets, Autographs... New York: 1880. V. 50

WOODWARD, DAVID
The Narrative of Capt. David Woodard and Four Seamen, Who Lost Their Ship While in a Boat at Sea and Surrendered Themselves Up to the Malays in the Island of Celebes... London: 1805. V. 52

WOODWARD, E. M.
History of Burlington and Mercer Counties, New Jersey, with Biographical Sketches of Many of Their Pioneers and Prominent Men. Philadelphia: 1883. V. 49; 51

WOODWARD, E. P.
The Safeguard and Armory. Latter-Day Delusions, No. 5. Seventh Day Adventism. Portland: 1903. V. 54

WOODWARD, GEORGE E.
Woodward's Architecture and Rural Art. No. 1. 1867. New York: 1868. V. 51
Woodward's Country Homes. New York: 1865. V. 51
Woodward's National Architect. New York: 1869. V. 52

WOODWARD, GEORGE MOUTARD
Chesterfield Travestie; or, School for Modern Manners. Philadelphia: 1812. V. 50
The Fugitive and Other Literary Works, in Prose and Poetry. London: 1805. V. 48

WOODWARD, H. B.
Stanford's Geological Atlas of Great Britain. London: 1904. V. 53

WOODWARD, HEZEKIAH
The Cause, Use, Cure of Feare. Or, Strong Consolations...Cordiall at all Times... London: 1643. V. 54

WOODWARD, JOHN
An Essay Towards a Natural History of the earth, and Terrestrial Bodyes, Especialy Minerals... London: 1723. V. 47; 54

WOODWARD, JOSEPH JANIVER
Diarrhoea and Dysentery. Washington: 1879. V. 49; 50; 51; 54
The Medical and Surgical History of the War of the Rebellion 1861-65... Washington: 1870-83. V. 47; 52
The Medical and Surgical History of the War of the Rebellion, 1861-65. Washington: 1870-88. V. 47; 48; 49; 50; 52; 53; 54
Report on Epidemic Cholera and Yellow Fever in the Army of the United States During the Year 1867. Washington: 1868. V. 54

WOODWARD, JOSEPH T.
Historic Record and Complete Biographic Roster 21st Me. Volunteers with Reunion Records of the 21st Maine Regimental Association. Augusta: 1907. V. 54

WOODWARD, JOSIAH
An Account of the Societies for Reformation of Manners in England and Ireland. London: 1700. V. 47; 54
The Soldier's Monitor. London: 1722. V. 47; 51
Some Thoughts Concerning the Stage in a Letter to a Lady. London: 1704. V. 49

WOODWARD, LLEWELLYN
British Foreign Policy in the Second World War. London: 1970-76. V. 52

WOODWARD, R.
Natal Birds. Pietermartizburg: 1899. V. 49

WOODWARD, S.
An Outline of the Geology of Norfolk. Norwich: 1833. V. 51; 54

WOODWARD, SAMUEL
Reports and Other Documents Relating to the State Lunatic Hospital at Worcester, Mass. Boston: 1837. V. 47; 50; 52

WOODWORTH, JIM
The Kodiak Bear. Harrisburg: 1958. V. 53

WOODWORTH, JOHN
Cholera Epidemic of 1873 in the United States. Washington: 1875. V. 49

WOODWORTH, LIZETTE
Edgar Allan Poe: a Centenary Tribute. Baltimore: 1910. V. 51

WOODWORTH, SAMUEL
The Champions of Freedom, Or the Mysterious Chief, a Romance of the Nineteenth Century, Founded on the Events of the War, Between the United States and Great Britain Which Terminated in March 1815. New York: 1816. V. 49

WOOL, JOHN E.
Correspondence Between the Late Secretary of War and Major General John E. Wool. Washington: 1858. V. 49

WOOLAVINGTON, LORD
Sporting Pictures at Lavington Park. (and) A Supplementary Catalogue of Lord Woolavington's Collection of Paintings by Sporting Artists. London: 1927. V. 47

WOOLDRIDGE, C. W.
Perfecting the Earth. A Piece of Possible History. Cleveland: 1902. V. 50

WOOLE, F.
Fresh Water Algae of the United States. Bethlehem: 1887. V. 49

WOOLF, CECIL
A Bibliography of Frederick Rolfe, Baron Corvo. London: 1972. V. 47

WOOLF, DOUGLAS
The Hypocritic Days. 1955. V. 53; 54

WOOLF, LEONARD
Barbarians at the Gate. London: 1939. V. 49
Diaries in Ceylon 1908-1911. 1959-April 1960. V. 47
Empire and Commerce in Africa. London: 1919. V. 48
Fear and Politics. London: 1924. V. 51
Fear and Politics. London: 1925. V. 48
The Hotel. London: 1939. V. 48; 52
Hunting the Highbrow. London: 1927. V. 51
The Journey Not the Arrival Matters. London: 1969. V. 50
Quack, Quack!. London: 1937. V. 51
Socialism and Co-Operation. London: 1921. V. 52
Stories of the East. London: 1921. V. 48
Stories of the East. Richmond: 1921. V. 49

WOOLF, VIRGINIA
Beau Brummell. New York: 1930. V. 49; 50; 51; 52; 53
Between the Acts. London: 1941. V. 48; 50; 51; 52; 53
Between the Acts. New York: 1941. V. 47; 48; 49; 51; 52; 53
The Captain's Death Bed. London: 1950. V. 51; 52; 53; 54
The Captain's Death Bed. New York: 1950. V. 51; 52
Collected Essays. London: 1966/67. V. 54
The Common Reader. London: 1925. V. 48; 50; 51; 52
The Common Reader: Second Series. London: 1932. V. 49; 53
The Death of the Moth. London: 1942. V. 47; 50; 51; 53
The Death of the Moth... New York: 1942. V. 51
The Death of the Moth. 1979. V. 50
The Diaries of Virginia Woolf. London: 1977-84. V. 52; 54
The Diaries of Virginia Woolf. New York: 1977-84. V. 47; 52; 54
The Essays of Virginia Woolf. London: 1986/87/88/94. V. 52
Flush. London: 1933. V. 50; 51; 53
Granite and Rainbow. London: 1958. V. 48; 49; 50; 51; 52
A Haunted House. London: 1943. V. 49; 51; 54
A Haunted House... New York: 1944. V. 53
Hours in a Library. New York: 1958. V. 52; 54
Jacob's Room. London: 1922. V. 51
Kew Gardens. Richmond: 1919. V. 51
Kew Gardens. London: 1927. V. 47
A Letter to a Young Poet. London: 1932. V. 49; 50
The Letters... London: 1975-79. V. 48; 50
The Letters... New York: 1975-79. V. 48
The Letters. London: 1975-80. V. 48; 50; 52
The Letters... London: 1975-80. V. 47; 54
The Letters... London: 1976/80. V. 52
The Mark on the Wall. Richmond: 1919. V. 50
Mr. Bennett and Mrs. Brown. London: 1924. V. 48
Mrs. Dalloway. London: 1925. V. 53
Mrs. Dalloway. New York: 1925. V. 50
Mrs. Dalloway. Paris: 1929. V. 48; 50; 53; 54
The Moment: and Other Essays. London: 1947. V. 48; 50; 51; 52; 54
The Moment: and Other Essays. New York: 1948. V. 50; 53
Monday or Tuesday. London: 1921. V. 50; 51
Monday or Tuesday. New York: 1921. V. 53; 54
Monday or Tuesday. New York: 1921. V. 53
Monday or Tuesday. Richmond: 1921. V. 49
Night and Day. London: 1919. V. 48; 49
Night and Day. 1920. V. 50
Night and Day. New York: 1920. V. 49; 54
On Being Ill. 1930. V. 51
On Being Ill. London: 1930. V. 47; 50; 52
Orlando. London: 1928. V. 47; 49; 51; 52
Orlando. New York: 1928. V. 47; 48; 49; 51; 53
Orlando. Leipzig: 1929. V. 53
Roger Fry. A Biography. London: 1940. V. 50
Roger Fry. A Biography. New York: 1940. V. 47; 48
A Room of One's Own. London: 1929. V. 48; 51; 52; 53; 54
A Room of One's Own. New York: 1929. V. 48
The Second Common Reader. 1932. V. 50
Street Haunting. San Francisco: 1930. V. 48; 53
Three Guineas. London: 1938. V. 47; 48; 49; 50
Three Guineas. New York: 1938. V. 49
To the Lighthouse. London: 1927. V. 48; 50; 53
To the Lighthouse. New York: 1927. V. 54
Les Vagues. Paris: 1937. V. 53
Virginia Woolf and Lytton Strachey: Letters. London: 1956. V. 50; 52
The Voyage Out. London: 1915. V. 47; 50; 51; 52; 53
The Voyage Out. New York: 1920. V. 47; 49; 53; 54
Walter Sickert: a Conversation. London: 1934. V. 50; 54
The Waves. London: 1931. V. 47; 49; 52
The Waves. New York: 1931. V. 48; 50; 51
A Writer's Diary. London: 1953. V. 49; 50; 54
A Writer's Diary. London: 1963. V. 52
The Years. London: 1937. V. 48; 49; 52; 53; 54
The Years. New York: 1937. V. 48

WOOLFE, RAYMOND G.
Secretariat. Radnor: 1974. V. 53

WOOLLCOTT, ALEXANDER
Chateau-Thierry - a Friendly Guide for American Pilgrims Between the Marne and the Vesle. Paris: 1919. V. 53
Mrs. Fiske: Her Views on the Stage Recorded. New York: 1917. V. 48; 51
The Story of Irving Berlin. New York: 1925. V. 47
While Rome Burns. New York: 1934. V. 53

WOOLLEY, CHARLES LEONARD
Dead Towns and Living Men - Being Pages from an Antiquary's Notebook. London: 1920. V. 49
The Development of Sumerian Art. New York: 1935. V. 52
The Old Babylonian Period. London and New York: 1976. V. 50; 52
A Report of the Work of the Archaeological Survey of India. 1939. V. 49
The Royal Cemetery: a Report on the Predynastic and Saragonid Graves Excavated Between 1926 and 1931. New York: 1934. V. 50; 52
Ur Excavations. The Royal Cemetery. A Report on the Predynasatic and Saragonid Graves Excavated Between 1926 and 1931. 1934. V. 52
The Ziggurat and its Surroundings. Oxford: 1939. V. 50; 52

WOOLLEY, L. H.
California 1849-1913. Oakland: 1913. V. 47

WOOLLEY, ROGER
Modern Trout Fly Dressing. 1932. V. 54

WOOLMAN, JOHN
A Journal of the Life and Travels of John Woolman in the Service of the Gospel. 1901. V. 52; 54
A Journal of the Life and Travels of John Woolman in the Service of the Gospel. London: 1901. V. 48

WOOLMAN, JOHN continued
A Journal of the Life, Gospel Labours and Christian Experiences of that Faithful Minister of Jesus Christ, John Woolman... Dublin: 1776. V. 47; 51
A Journal of the Life, Gospel Labours and Christian Experiences of that Faithful Minister of Jesus Christ, John Woolman... Dublin: 1794. V. 47
Serious Considerations on Various Subjects of Importance. London: 1773. V. 51
Some Considerations on the Keeping of Negroes. Northampton: 1970. V. 48; 51
A Word of Remembrance and Caution to the Rich. Dublin: 1793. V. 54
The Works of John Woolman. Philadelphia: 1774. V. 47; 50; 51
The Works of John Woolman. Philadelphia: 1775. V. 51

WOOLNER, THOMAS
My Beautiful Lady. London: 1863. V. 48
Poems. Nelly Dale. Children. London: 1887. V. 48

WOOLNOTH, WILLIAM
A Graphical Illustration of the Metropolitan Cathedral Church of Canterbury... London: 1816. V. 47; 52

WOOLNOUGH, C. W.
The Art of Marbling, as Applied to Book Edges and Paper, Containing Full Instructions for Executing British, French, Spanish, Italian, Nonpariel... London: 1854. V. 48
The Whole Art of Marbling... London: 1881. V. 53
The Whole Art of Marbling... Leicester: 1985. V. 48

WOOLRICH, C.
Children of the Ritz. 1927. V. 53
Cover Charge. 1926. V. 53

WOOLRICH, CORNELL
The Black Curtain. New York: 1941. V. 50; 51
Deadline at Dawn. Philadelphia: 1944. V. 51
I Married a Dead Man. Philadelphia: 1948. V. 50; 51
Night Has a Thousand Eyes. New York & Toronto: 1945. V. 47; 50
Rendezvous in Black. New York & Toronto: 1948. V. 47; 48; 50
The Ten Faces of Cornell Woolrich. A Collection of Short Stories. London: 1966. V. 47

WOOLRIDGE, C. W.
Perfecting the Earth. A Piece of Possible History. Cleveland: 1902. V. 49

WOOLSON, ABBA GOOLD
Dress-Reform: a Series of Lectures Delivered in Boston, on Dress As It Affects the Health of Women. Boston: 1874. V. 54
Woman in American Society. Boston: 1873. V. 50; 51

WOOLSON, CONSTANCE FENIMORE
For the Major. London: 1883. V. 50
Rodman the Keeper: Southern Sketches. New York: 1880. V. 51; 53; 54

WOOLWARD, F. H.
The Genus Masevallia, Issued by the Marquess of Lothian chiefly from Plants in His Collection of Orchids at Newbattle Abbey. London: 1890-96. V. 52

WOOSTER, DAVID
Alpine Plants: Figures and Descriptions of Some of the Most Striking and Beautiful of the Alpine Flowers... London: 1871-72-74. V. 53
Alpine Plants: Figures and Descriptions of Some of the Most Striking and Beautiful of the Alpine Flowers. London: 1874. V. 49; 53

WOOTEN, DUDLEY G.
A Comprehensive History of Texas: 1685-1897. Dallas: 1898. V. 49; 52; 53

WORCESTER, A.
Small Hospitals. Establishment and Maintenance. New York: 1905. V. 50
Small Hospitals. Establishment and Maintenance. New York: 1985. V. 52

WORCESTER, D. C.
The Philippines Past and Present. New York: 1930. V. 51

WORCESTER, EDWARD SOMERSET, 2ND MARQUIS OF
The Century of Inventions...from the Original MS. with Historical and Explanatory Notes and a Biographical Memoir by Charles F. Paratington. London: 1825. V. 48
A Century of the Names and Scantlings of Such Inventions, as at Present I Can Call to Mind to Have Tried and Perfected. London: 1663. V. 50
A Century of the Names and Scantlings of Such Inventions, as at Present I Can Call to Mind to Have Tried and Perfected... London: 1746. V. 48; 52
A Century of the Names and Scantlings of Such Inventions, as at Present I Can Call to Mind to Have Tried and Perfected. Glasgow: 1767. V. 50

WORCESTER, JOSEPH EMERSON
A Comprehensive Pronouncing and Explanatory Dictionary of the English Language with Pronouncing Vocabularies of Classical and Scripture Proper Names. New York: 1830. V. 50

WORCESTER STATE HOSPITAL
Annual Report of the Trustees of...41st, 42nd, 44th, 60th, 61st, 65-69th, 77th, 78th, 84th, 85th. Boston: 1874-1918. V. 52

THE WORDS of the Masters: Reflections on the Fine Art of Type Design. Maple Shade: 1982. V. 47

WORDS, Weather and Wolfmen: Conversations with Tony Hillerman. Gallup: 1989. V. 52

WORDSWORTH, CHRISTOPHER
Athens and Attica: Journal of a Residence There. London: 1836. V. 53; 54
Athens and Attica: Notes of a Tour. London: 1855. V. 48; 49
Greece, Pictorial, Descriptive and Historical. London: 1839. V. 54
Greece: Pictorial, Descriptive and Historical. London: 1840. V. 48; 52
Greece: Pictorial, Descriptive and Historical... London: 1844. V. 49

WORDSWORTH, DOROTHY
Journals... London: 1897. V. 48; 50; 52; 53; 54
Journals. London: 1938. V. 52; 54
Journals... London: 1941. V. 48
Journals... London: 1952. V. 48

WORDSWORTH, G. G.
Some Notes on the Wordsworths of Peniston and Their Aumbry. Ambleside: 1929. V. 54

WORDSWORTH, WILLIAM
The Complete Poetical Works of... Boston: 1911. V. 52
A Decade of Years: Poems 1798-1807. 1911. V. 47; 54
A Decade of Years, Poems by ... Hammersmith: 1911. V. 47; 50
A Description of the Scenery of the Lakes in the North of England. London: 1823. V. 47
The Excursion, Being a Portion of the Recluse. London: 1814. V. 48; 51; 53; 54
A Guide through the District of the Lakes, in the North of England... Kendal: 1835. V. 52
Intimations of Immortality. London: 1913. V. 49
Intimations of Immortality... 1991. V. 54
Letters. Oxford: 1935. V. 49
The Letters of William and Dorothy Wordsowrth. Oxford: 1967. V. 48
The Little Maid and the Gentleman; or, We Are Seven. York: 1820. V. 47
Lyrical Ballads... London: 1798/1800. V. 48; 49; 53
Lyrical Ballads... London: 1800. V. 47; 48; 50; 52; 54
Lyrical Ballads... London: 1802. V. 53; 54
Lyrical Ballads. London: 1924. V. 52
The Miscellaneous Poems. London: 1820. V. 54
My Dearest Love. Letters of William and Mary Wordsworth 1810. London: 1981. V. 47
Ode on the Intimations of Immortality. London: 1903. V. 48; 52
Our English Lakes, Mountains and Waterfalls. London: 1864. V. 50; 51
Peter Bell, a Tale in Verse. London: 1819. V. 51
Poems. London: 1807. V. 48; 50; 51; 53; 54
Poems... London: 1815. V. 52
The Poems... London: 1845. V. 53; 54
Poems... London: 1859. V. 52
Poems... London: 1879. V. 49
Poems... London: 1892. V. 50
Poems... London: 1902. V. 47
Poems. 1973. V. 51
Poems. London: 1973. V. 49
Poems. New York: 1973. V. 54
Poems, Chiefly of Early and Late Years. London: 1842. V. 50; 51; 52
The Poetical Works... Paris: 1828. V. 53; 54
The Poetical Works. London: 1832. V. 53
The Poetical Works. London: 1836-37. V. 47; 50; 54
The Poetical Works. London: 1840. V. 54
The Poetical Works. London: 1841. V. 54
The Poetical Works. London: 1857. V. 47; 49; 50; 53
The Poetical Works. London: 1858. V. 49
The Poetical Works. London: 1874. V. 51; 53
The Poetical Works. Edinburgh: 1882-89. V. 48; 53
The Poetical Works... Edinburgh: 1886. V. 54
The Poetical Works. Oxford: 1940-49. V. 49
The Prelude. London: 1850. V. 47; 53; 54
The Prelude... New York: 1850. V. 54
The Prelude. 1915. V. 52; 54
The Prelude. Hammersmith: 1915. V. 48; 50; 51; 54
The Prelude. London: 1915. V. 49
The Prelude... London: 1926. V. 51
The Prose Works. London: 1876. V. 48; 50; 51; 52; 53
The Recluse. London: 1888. V. 53
Selected Poems. 1987. V. 52
The Sonnets of... London: 1838. V. 54
The Waggoner, a Poem. London: 1819. V. 47; 52
The White Doe of Rylstone; or the Fate of the Nortons. London: 1815. V. 49; 51; 52
Wordsworth Selected Poems. Brighton: 1987. V. 49
Wordsworth's Poems for the Young. London: 1863. V. 49
Yarrow Revisited and Other Poems. Boston: 1835. V. 47; 50
Yarrow Revisited and Other Poems. London: 1835. V. 48; 49; 51; 52; 53; 54

WORK from Common Knowledge. Guildford: 1985. V. 50; 53

WORK, JOHN
Fur Brigade to the Bonaventura: John Work's California Expedition, 1832-1833, for the Hudson's Bay Company. San Francisco: 1945. V. 47
The Journal of John Work, A Chief Trader of the Hudson's Bay Co. During His Expedition from Vancouver to the Flatheads and Blackfeet on the Pacific Northwest. Cleveland: 1923. V. 53; 54
The Journal of John Work, January to October, 1835. Victoria: 1944/45. V. 53
The Journal of John Work, January to October, 1835. Victoria: 1945. V. 54

WORK, JOHN WESLEY
Folk Song of the American Negro. Nashville: 1915. V. 50; 51

THE WORK of the Royal Engineers in the European War 1914-1919. Chatham: 1921-1926. V. 47

THE WORK of the R.S.P.C.A. Fund for Sick and Wounded Horses, an Auxiliary of the Army Vetinerary Corps. London: 1915. V. 54

WORKERS COMMUNIST PARTY
The 4th National Convention of the Workers (Communist) Party of America. Chicago: 1925. V. 52

THE WORKING Man's Companion - The Rights of Industry, Addressed to the Working-Men of the United Kingdom, by the Author of "The Results of Machinery". I - Capital and Labour. London: 1831. V. 47

THE WORKINGTON Iron and Steel Company, Limited. London: 1914. V. 50

WORKMAN, BENJAMIN
Elements of Geography, Designed for Young Students in that Science. Philadelphia: 1790. V. 53
Gauging Epitomized. Philadelphia: 1788. V. 50; 51

WORKMAN, FANNY BULLOCK
Ice-Bound Heights of the Mustagh, an Account of Two Seasons of Pioneer Exploration and High Climbing in the Baltistan Himalaya. 1908. V. 53
Peaks and Glaciers of Nun Kun, a Record of Pioneer-Exploration and Mountaineering in the Punjab Himalaya. 1909. V. 53

WORKMAN, JAMES
A Faithful Picture of the Political Situation of New Orleans... Boston: 1808. V. 47

WORKMAN, WILLIAM HUNTER
The Call of the Snowy Hispar. London: 1910. V. 54

THE WORKS of the Most Celebrated Minor Poets. London: 1749. V. 48; 50

THE WORLD Displayed: or, a Curious Collection of Voyages and Travels, Selected from Writers of All Nations. London: 1772-90. V. 51

WORLD War Records. First Division. A.E.F. Regular. Battle Maps - Charts - Sketches. (with) Map Atlas to German Documents. Washington: 1930's. V. 49

THE WORLD'S Famous Places and Peoples. New York and London: 1894-1901. V. 51

WORLEY'S Directory of Dallas, Texas 1915. Dallas: 1915. V. 47

WORLIDGE, JOHN
Dictionarium...or, a Dictionary of Husbandry, Gardening, Trade, Commerce and All Sorts of Country-Affairs. London: 1717. V. 49
Systema Agriculturae... London: 1669. V. 50
Systema Agriculturae... London: 1675. V. 52
Systema Horti-culturae; or, the Art of Gardening... London: 1700. V. 47
Vinetum Britannicum; or a Treatise of Cider and Other Wines and Drinks Extracted from Fruits Growing in This Kingdom. London: 1691. V. 47

WORLIDGE, T.
A Select Collection of Drawings From Curious Antique Gems: Most of Them in the Possession of the Nobility and Gentry of this Kingdom. London: 1768. V. 48

WORM, OLE
Museum Wormianum. Leiden: 1655. V. 47; 48

WORMALD, FRANCIS
An Early Breton Gospel Book. Cambridge: 1977. V. 51; 54
The Winchester Pssalter. Greenwich: 1973. V. 48

WORMELEY, JUDITH
The Potomac Muse. Richmond: 1825. V. 54

WORMELL, CHRISTOPHER
English Country Traditions. 1988. V. 47

WORMLEY, T. G.
Micro-Chemistry of Poisons. New York: 1867. V. 51

WORRALL, JOHN
Bibliotheca Legum... Law Books of This Realm... London: 1749. V. 49
Bibliotheca Legum... Law Books of This Realm... London: 1777. V. 50
Bibliotheca Legum...Law Books of this Realm... London: 1782. V. 50

WORRELL, JOHN
A Diamond in the Rough, Embracing Anecdote, Biography, Romance and History. Indianapolis: 1906. V. 54

WORRELL, WILLIAM H.
The Coptic Manuscripts in the Freer Collection. New York: 1923. V. 51
Coptic Texts in the University of Michigan Collection. Ann Arabor: 1942. V. 51

WORSDELL, W. C.
Principles of Plant-Teratology. London: 1915-16. V. 50

WORSHAM, JOHN HENRY
One of Jackson's Foot Cavalry: His Experience and What He Saw During the War 1861-65. New York: 1912. V. 50

WORSHAM, WILLIAM JOHNSTON
The Old Nineteenth Tennessee Regiment, C.S.A. June, 1861. April 1865. Knoxville: 1902. V. 52

WORSLEY, ETTA B.
Columbus on the Chattahoochee. Columbus: 1951. V. 50

WORSLEY, RICHARD
The History of the Isle of Wight. London: 1781. V. 47

WORSNOP, THOMAS
History of the City of Adelaide from the Foundation of the Province of South Australia in 1836 to the End of the Municipal Year 1877. Adelaide: 1878. V. 51

WORSTER, BENJAMIN
A Compendious and Methodical Account of the Principles of Natural Philosophy. London: 1730. V. 50; 54

WORTH, THOMAS
Plutarch Restorod: an Anachronatic Metempsychosis Illustrating the Illustrious of Greece and Rome. New York: 1862. V. 47; 50

WORTHINGTON, B.
Proposed Plan for Improving Dover Harbour, by an Extension of the South Pier Head, &c... Dover: 1838. V. 50

WORTHINGTON, GREVILLE
A Bibliography of the Waverley Novels. London: 1931. V. 47; 48; 50; 50; 51; 53; 54

WORTHINGTON, S.
Inland Waters of Africa; the Result of Two Expeditions to the Great Lakes of Kenya and Uganda. London: 1933. V. 54

WORTHY, ALFRED N.
A Treatise on the Botanic Theory and Practice of Medicine. Forsyth: 1842. V. 53

WORTHY PAPER CO.
A New Showing of Six Worth Papers; Roxburghe, Aurelian, Georgian, Marlowe, Dacian and Hadian. Mittineague: 1910. V. 50

WORTIS, JOSEPH
Tricky Dick and His Pals. 1974. V. 54

WORTLEY, EMMELINE CHARLOTTE ELIZABETH MANNERS STUART, LADY
Travels in the United States, Etc. During 1849 and 1850. London: 1851. V. 47
Travels in the United States, etc., During 1849 and 1850. New York: 1851. V. 47; 50; 52

WORTLEY, MARY STUART
The Story of Zelinda and the Monster, or, Beauty and the Beast. London: 1895. V. 51

WOTTON, HENRY
The Elements of Architecture. London: 1624. V. 47
Elements of Architecture... London: 1903. V. 51
Letters and Dispatches From Sir Henry Wotton to James the First and His Ministers. London: 1850. V. 48
Reliquiae Wottonianae. London: 1651. V. 48; 53; 54
Reliquiae Wottonianae... London: 1654. V. 49; 54
Reliquiae Wottonianae... London: 1672. V. 48; 50; 52
Reliquiae Wottonianae... London: 1685. V. 47
A Short View of the Life and Death of George Villiers, Duke of Buckingham... London: 1642. V. 53
The State of Christendom... London: 1657. V. 48
State of Christendom. London: 1667. V. 51; 53

WOTTON, THOMAS
The English Baronets. London: 1727. V. 48; 53

WOTTON, WILLIAM
Miscellaneous Discourses Relating to the Traditions and Usages of the Scribes and Pharisees in...Jesus Christ's Time... 1718. V. 47
A New Ecclesiasatical History of the Sixteenth Century. London: 1703-06. V. 49
Reflections Upon Ancient and Modern Learning. London: 1694. V. 53
Reflections Upon Ancient and Modern Learning. London: 1697. V. 53; 54
Reflections Upon Ancient and Modern Learning. London: 1705. V. 48; 51

WOTY, WILLIAM
The Blossoms of Helicon. London: 1763. V. 49

WOUK, HERMAN
Aurora Dawn. New York: 1947. V. 48; 51; 53
The Caine Mutiny. Garden City: 1951. V. 50
The Caine Mutiny. New York: 1951. V. 50
The Caine Mutiny. Garden City: 1952. V. 50
The Caine Mutiny... Garden City: 1954. V. 49
The Caine Mutiny. 1977. V. 50
The Caine Mutiny. Franklin Center: 1977. V. 49
The City Boy. Garden City: 1952. V. 54
Don't Stop the Carnival. Garden City: 1965. V. 54
The Hope. Boston: 1993. V. 51; 52; 53; 54
Inside, Outside. Boston: 1985. V. 50
Marjorie Morningstar. Garden City: 1955. V. 52
Marjorie Morningstar. New York: 1955. V. 48
This is My God. New York: 1959. V. 54
War and Remembrance. Boston: 1978. V. 51; 54
The Winds of War. Boston: 1971. V. 54
Youngblood Hawk. Garden City: 1962. V. 51; 54

WOYT, J. J.
Der Neu-Vermehrt-und Verbesserte Galanterie Artzt... Dresden: 1702. V. 53

WRAGG, J.
Improved Flute Preceptor or the Whole Art of Playing the German Flute, Op 6. 1818. V. 52

WRANGHAM, FRANCIS
A Charge Delivered in July 1822, at Stokesley, Thirsk and Malton to the Clergy of the Archdeaconry of Cleveland; and Published at Their Particular Desire. York: 1822. V. 52
A Few Sonnets Attempted from Petrarch in Early Life. Kent: 1817. V. 47
The Raising of Jairus' Daughter: a Poe. London: 1804. V. 48

WRATISLAW, THEODORE
Caprices. London: 1893. V. 48; 49; 51

WRATISLAW, THEODORE continued
Oscar Wilde: a Memoir. London: 1979. V. 49

WRAXALL, FREDERICK CHARLES LASCELLES
The Fife and Drum; or, Would be a Soldier. London: 1863. V. 51

WRAXALL, NATHANIEL WILLIAM, BART
The Correspondence Between a Traveller and a Minister of State, in October and November, 1792... London: 1796. V. 48
The Historical and the Posthumous Memoirs of Sir Nathaniel William Wraxall. London: 1884. V. 54
Historical Memoirs of My Own Time. London: 1815. V. 52
Historical Memoirs of My Own Time... London: 1815/1836. V. 47
The History of France, from the Accession of Henry the Third to the Death of Louis the Fourteenth. London: 1795. V. 50
Memoirs of the Courts of Berlin, Dresden, Warsaw and Vienna. London: 1799. V. 50
Memoirs of the Courts of Berlin, Dresden, Warsaw, and Vienna in the Years 1777, 1778 and 1779. London: 1800. V. 49; 53
Posthumous memoirs of His Own Time and Historical Memoirs of My Own Time. Philadelphia: 1836/37. V. 50
A Tour through Some of the Northern Parts of Europe, Particularly Copenhagen, Stockholm and Ptersburgh. London: 1775. V. 48

WRAY, LEONARD
The Practical Sugar Planter. London: 1848. V. 47; 49

WRAY, MARY
The Ladies Library. London: 1732. V. 48; 50

WREDE, FRIEDRICH W. VON
Lebensbilder aus den Vereinigten Staaten von Nordamerika und Texas. Cassel: 1844. V. 49

WREN, CHRISTOPHER
Life and Works.... London: 1903. V. 50; 51; 54
Memoirs of the Life and Works of... London: 1823. V. 47
Numismatum Antiquorum Sylloge, Populis Graecis, Municipiis, & Coloniis Romanis Cuforum, Ex Cimellarchio Editoris. Londini: 1708. V. 48
Sir Christopher Wren A.D. 1632-1723. London: 1923. V. 48; 51

WREN, PERCIVAL CHRISTOPHER
Beau Geste. New York: 1926. V. 53
Beau Geste. London: 1927. V. 54

WREN SOCIETY
Publications. Oxford: 1924-43. V. 47

WRENIUS *Vues des Nouveaux Etablissemens Publics, des Embellisemens, des Jeux et Promenades de Catherinehoff... (with) Collection de Vues de Saint-Petersbourg et de ses Environs...* St. Petersburg: 1824. V. 47

WRIFFORD, ANSON
A New Plan of Writing Copies with Accompanying Explanations... Boston: 1810. V. 49; 52

WRIGHT & DITSON
Wright and Ditson's Catalogue of Sporting Goods and Games for In and Outdoors (for 1893). Boston: 1893. V. 53

WRIGHT, A. A.
Handbook of Snakes of the United States and Canada. Ithaca: 1975. V. 54

WRIGHT, A. H.
Life Histories of the Frogs of Okefinokee Swamp, Georgia. New York: 1932. V. 53

WRIGHT, A. O.
The Confederate Sailor. Richmond: 1925. V. 49

WRIGHT, ABRAHAM
Delitiae Delitiarum Sive Epigrammatum Ex Optimis Poetis inIlla Bibliotheca Bodleiana. Oxford: 1637. V. 48

WRIGHT, ALFRED
Adventures in Servia; or the Experiences of a Medical Free Lance Among the Bashi-Bazouks, etc. London: 1884. V. 51
A Spelling Book. Cincinnati: 1825. V. 51; 53

WRIGHT, ALLEN
Chahta Leksikon. A Choctaw in English Definition. St. Louis: 1880. V. 48

WRIGHT, ALMROTH
Handbook of the Technique of the Teat and Capillary Glass Tube and Its Applications in Medicine and Bacteriology. London: 1912. V. 49; 51; 54
Studies on Immunisation and Their Application to the Diagnosis and Treatment of Bacterial Infections. London: 1909. V. 49; 51; 54

WRIGHT, ANDREW
Court-Hand Restored. London: 1879. V. 50

WRIGHT, ANNA A.
View of Society and Manners in America; in a Series of Letters from That Country to a Friend in England During the Years 1818, 1819, and 1820. London: 1821. V. 47

WRIGHT, AUSTIN TAPPAN
Islandia. New York: 1942. V. 50

WRIGHT, BARTON
Kachinas, a Hopi Artist Documentary. Flagstaff: 1973. V. 47

WRIGHT, C.
India and Its Inhabitants. Cincinnatti: 1856. V. 54

WRIGHT, CALEB EARL
Two Years Behind the Plough; or, the Experiences of a Pennsylvania Farm-Boy. Philadelphia: 1878. V. 54

WRIGHT, CHARLES
Bloodlines. Poems. Middletown: 1975. V. 47
Colophons... Iowa City: 1973. V. 52
Colophons. Iowa City: 1977. V. 53; 54
Dead Color... Salem: 1980. V. 54
Dead Color... San Francisco: 1980. V. 50; 54
The Dream Animal. Toronto: 1968. V. 51
Five Journals. New York: 1986. V. 51; 54
The Grave of the Right Hand. Toronto: 1970. V. 47
A History of Lloyd's. London: 1928. V. 49
A Journal of the Year of the Ox. Iowa City: 1988. V. 48; 51; 53; 54
Private Madrigals. Madison: 1969. V. 51; 53
The Venice Notebook. Boston: 1971. V. 51; 53
Xionia. Iowa City: 1990. V. 53
Yard Journal. Richmond: 1986. V. 52

WRIGHT, CHARLES W.
A Guide Manual to the Mammoth Cave of Kentucky. Louisville: 1860. V. 49
The Mammoth Cave, of Kentucky. Louisville: 1859. V. 47

WRIGHT, CHAUNCEY
Letters of Chauncey Wright with Some Account of His Life... Cambridge: 1878. V. 47

WRIGHT, CHRISTOPHER
Poussin Paintings: a Catalogue Raisonne. London: 1984. V. 51
Poussin Paintings: A Catalogue Raisonne. London: 1985. V. 54

WRIGHT, DANIEL
History of Nepal. Cambridge: 1877. V. 50

WRIGHT, E. PERCEVAL
The Book of Trinity College Dublin, 1591-1891. Belfast: 1892. V. 47; 50; 52

WRIGHT, E. W.
Lewis and Dryden's Marine History of the Pacific Northwest. Portland: 1895. V. 47
Lewis and Dryden's Marine History of the Pacific Northwest. 1961. V. 53

WRIGHT, EDWARD
Some Observations Made in Travelling through France, Italy &c. in the Years MDCCXX, MDCCXXI and MDCCXXIII. London: 1764. V. 54

WRIGHT, ELIZUR
A Lecture on Tobacco, Delivered in the Chapel of the Western Reserve College, Hudson, Ohio, May 29, 1832. Cleveland: 1832. V. 51; 54

WRIGHT, FRANCES D'ARUSMONT
A Few Days in Athens... New York: 1831. V. 51
Views of Society and Manners in America... London: 1821. V. 53
Views of Society and Manners in America... New York: 1821. V. 53
Views of Society and Manners in America... London: 1822. V. 50

WRIGHT, FRANK LLOYD
An American Architecture. New York: 1955. V. 47; 48; 50; 51; 52
Architecture. Man In Possession of His Earth. New York: 1962. V. 47; 51
An Autobiography. New York: 1943. V. 53
An Autobiography. London: 1945. V. 52
Buildings, Plans and Designs. New York: 1963. V. 47; 48; 50
The Disappearing City. New York: 1932. V. 48; 53
Drawings for a Living Architecture. New York: 1959. V. 48; 51; 52
The Frank Lloyd Wright Collection of Japanese Antique Prints. New York: 1927. V. 48
Frank Lloyd Wright: the Early Work. New York: 1968. V. 48
The Future of Architecture. New York: 1953. V. 53
Genius and Mobocracy. New York: 1949. V. 48; 49; 50
The Industrial Revolution Runs Away. New York: 1969. V. 48
The Japanese Print. Chicago: 1912. V. 48
The Japanese Print... New York: 1967. V. 48
The Life Work of the American Architect Frank Lloyd Wright. Santpoort: 1925. V. 52; 54
Modern Architecture, Being the Kahn Lectures for 1930. Princeton: 1931. V. 53
The Natural House. New York: 1954. V. 47; 48; 49; 50; 51; 52; 53
An Organic Architecture. London: 1939. V. 53
The Story of the Tower. New York: 1956. V. 47; 48; 50; 51; 53
The Taliesin Fellowship. Spring Green: 1933. V. 49
A Testament. London: 1957. V. 50
A Testament. New York: 1957. V. 53
V. C. Morris. 1948. V. 52
When Democracy Builds. Chicago: 1945. V. 49
The Work of... New York: 1965. V. 53

WRIGHT, GABRIEL
The Description and Use of Both the Globes, the Armillary Sphere and Orrery, Exemplified in a Large Variety of Problems In Astronomy, Geography, Dialling &c. London: 1783?. V. 48

WRIGHT, GEORGE
The Complete Bird Fancyer, or Bird-Fancyer's Recreation...Instructions for Taking, Catching, Feeding, Breeding and Rearing, all Sorts of Song Birds... London: 1790. V. 50
Dear Variety. London: 1782. V. 48
Pleasing Melancholy, or a Walk Among the Tombs in a Country Church Yard in the Stile and Manner of Hervey's Meditations... London: 1793. V. 47

WRIGHT, GEORGE NEWENHAM
Belgium, the Rhine, Italy, Greece. London: 1840. V. 54
China Illustrated, Its Scenery, Architecture, Social Habits &c. London: 1843. V. 54
China, in a Series of Views, Displaying the Scenery, Architecture and Social Habists of that Ancient Empire. London: 1843. V. 50
China It's Scenery, Architecture, Social Habits &c. London: 1840. V. 48
China, Its Scenery, Architecture, Social Habits &c. Illustrated. London & Paris: 1843. V. 53
A Guide to County Wicklow. London: 1827. V. 53
A Guide to County Wicklow. 1835. V. 50
A Guide to the Lakes of Killarney. London: 1822. V. 53
An Historical Guide to Ancient and Modern Dublin. 1821. V. 48; 49; 50; 52
Ireland Illustrated in a series of Views. London: 1829. V. 50
Lancashire. Its History, Legends and Manufactures. London: 1842. V. 47
Landscape Historical Illustrations of Scotland and Waverly Novels. London. V. 54
The Shores and Islands of the Mediterranean. London: 1840. V. 53

WRIGHT, H. E.
A History of the Adhesive Stamps of the British Isles, Available for Postal and Telegraph Purposes. London: 1899. V. 53

WRIGHT, HAROLD BELL
The Mine with the Iron Door. New York London: 1923. V. 51
The Re-Creation of Brian Kent. Chicago: 1919. V. 50

WRIGHT, HAROLD J. L.
The Etched Work of F. L. Griggs. London: 1941. V. 51
The Etchings and Drypoints of Sir D. Y. Cameron... London: 1947. V. 50

WRIGHT, HENDRICK B.
Historical Sketches of Plymouth, Luzerne Co., Penna. Philadelphia: 1873. V. 47

WRIGHT, HENRY G.
Headaches Their Causes and Their Cure. New York: 1856. V. 54

WRIGHT, HEZEKIAH HARTLEY
Desultory Reminiscences of a Tour through Germany, Switzerland and France. Boston: 1838. V. 52

WRIGHT, HORACE J.
Beautiful Flowers and How to Grow Them. London: 1909. V. 47

WRIGHT, J. E.
The Genus Tulostoma (Gasteromycetes) a World Monograph. London: 1987. V. 50; 52

WRIGHT, JAMES
The Green Wall. New Haven: 1957. V. 47; 49; 50
The History and Antiquities of the County of Rutland... London: 1684. V. 51
The History and Antiquities of the County of Rutland... 1687. V. 47; 50
Saint Judas. Middletown: 1959. V. 49
The Temple... Nimes. Worcester: 1982. V. 51
The Temples... Nimes. 1982. V. 48
Two Citizens. New York: 1973. V. 51

WRIGHT, JAY
The Homecoming Singer. New York: 1971. V. 53

WRIGHT, JOHN
The American Negotiator, or the Various Currencies of the British Colonies in America...Reduced into English Money. London: 1765. V. 47; 50

WRIGHT, JOHN BUCKLAND
The Engravings of John Buckland Wright. London: 1990. V. 47

WRIGHT, JOHN MARTIN FREDERICK
A Commentary on Newton's Principia. 1833. V. 52
A Commentary on Newton's Principia. London: 1833. V. 48; 54

WRIGHT, JOSEPH
English Dialect Dictionary. London: 1898. V. 52
The English Dialect Dictionary. 1898-1905. V. 50
The English Dialect Dictionary. London: 1898-1905. V. 47; 51; 53

WRIGHT, LEWIS
The Clifton and Other Remarkable Suspension Bridges of the World. London: 1865. V. 51
The Illustrated Book of Poultry. London: 1875. V. 49
The Illustrated Book of Poultry... London: 1890. V. 50; 53

WRIGHT, LUCY
The Gospel Monitor. Cantaerbury: 1843. V. 50

WRIGHT, M.
Svenska Faglar Efter Naturen. Stockholm: 1927-29. V. 51; 52; 54

WRIGHT, M. R.
The New Brazil. Philadelphia...London: 1907. V. 48

WRIGHT, MARCUS JOSEPH
Reminiscences of the Early Settlement and Early Settlers of McNairy County, Tennessee. Washington: 1882. V. 47
Tennessee in the War 1861-65. New York: 1908. V. 53

WRIGHT, MARTIN
An Introduction to the Law of Tenures. London: 1730. V. 54
An Introduction to the Law of Tenures. Dublin: 1750. V. 48
Introduction to the Law of Tenures. London: 1768. V. 52

WRIGHT, NATHANIEL H.
The Fall of Palmyra; and Other Poems. Middlebury: 1817. V. 47; 52

WRIGHT, PAUL R.
Abstract of the Title to Tracts...of the lands of the Mntecito Land Company. Santa Barbara: 1887. V. 47

WRIGHT, PETER
Spycatcher. New York: 1987. V. 51

WRIGHT, R. G.
The Ducks of India. London: 1925. V. 49; 52

WRIGHT, RICHARD
Black Boy: a Record of Childhood and Youth. New York: 1945. V. 48; 51
Black Metropolis. New York: 1945. V. 48
Bright and Morning Star. New York: 1941. V. 48; 51
The Color Curtain. Cleveland: 1956. V. 50; 51; 52
Eight Men. Cleveland/New York: 1961. V. 53
How "Bigger" Was Born. New York: 1940. V. 47
The Long Dream. Garden City: 1958. V. 50; 54
Native Son. New York: 1940. V. 49; 50; 52
Native Son. New York: 1941. V. 53
Pagan Spain. New York: 1957. V. 54
Twelve Million Black Voices - a Folk History of the Negro in the United States of America. London: 1947. V. 48
Uncle Tom's Children. New York: 1938. V. 54
White Man, Listen!. Garden City: 1957. V. 50; 53; 54

WRIGHT, ROBERT
The Life of Major General James Wolfe Founded on Original Documents and Illustrated by His Correspondence... London: 1864. V. 53; 54

WRIGHT, ROBERT MARR
Dodge City. The Cowboy Capital and the Great Southwest. Wichita: 1913. V. 47; 49; 52; 54

WRIGHT, SARAH E.
This Child's Gonna Live. New York: 1969. V. 53

WRIGHT, STEPHEN
Meditations in Green. New York: 1983. V. 51; 52

WRIGHT, SYDNEY FOWLER
Dream or the Simian Maid. 1931. V. 48; 52
Elfwin. 1930. V. 52
Elfwin. London: 1930. V. 48
The Island of Captain Sparrow. New York: 1928. V. 50
The World Below. Chicago: 1949. V. 52

WRIGHT, THOMAS
The Anglo-Latin Satirical Poets and Epigrammatists of the Twelfth Century. London: 1872. V. 49; 52
The Antiquities of the Town of Halifax in Yorkshire, Wherein Is Given an Account of the Town, Church and Twelve Chapels... Leeds: 1738. V. 52
Arbours and Grottos. London: 1979. V. 47
Caricature History of the Georges. London: 1867. V. 49
A Contemporary Narrative of the Proceedings Against Dame Alice Dyteler, Prosecuted for Sorcery, 1324. London: 1843. V. 51
England Under the House of Hanover; Its History and Condition. London: 1848. V. 49; 51
The Female Vertuoso's. London: 1693. V. 47
Gesta Romanorum or, Entertaining Stories Invented by the Monkds as a Fire-Side Recreation... London: 1871. V. 49
Historical and Descriptive Account of the Caricatures of James Gillray. London: 1851. V. 49
The History and Antiquities of the Town of Ludlow, and Its Ancient Castle... Ludlow: 1826. V. 50; 54
The History and Topography of the Counties of Cumberland and Westmorland. London: 1860. V. 51
Le Keux's Memorials of Cambridge: A Series of Views of the Colleges, Halls and Public Buildings, Engraved by J. Le Keux... London: 1841. V. 52
The Life of the Sir Richard Burton. London: 1906. V. 47
The Life of Walter Pater. New York & London: 1907. V. 53
Louthiana; or, an Introduction to the Antiquities of Ireland. London: 1748. V. 48
Narratives of Sorcery and Magic from the Most Authentic Sources. London: 1851. V. 48
An Original Theory of New Hypothesis of the Universe, Founded Upon the Laws of Nature and Solving by Mathematical Princples the General Phaenomena of the visible Creation. London: 1750. V. 47
Political Poems and Songs Relating to English History, Composed During the Period from the Accession of Edward III to that of Richard III. London: 1859-61. V. 49
The Political Songs of England, from the Reign of John to that of Edward II. Edinburgh: 1884. V. 52
Popular Treatises on Science Written During the Middle Ages, in Anglo-Saxon, Anglo-Norman and English. London: 1841. V. 54
The Roll of Arms of the Princes, Barons and Knights Who Attended King Edward I to the Siege of Caerlaverock in 1300. London: 1864. V. 49
The Romance of the Shoe, Being the History of Shoemaking In all Ages and Especially in England and Scotland. London: 1922. V. 49
The Royal Dictionary-Cyclopaedia, for Universal Reference... London: 1870. V. 53
Stories by an Archaeologist and His Friends. London: 1856. V. 50
Tales and Sketches: to Which is Added the Raven: a Poem. London: 1852. V. 48

WRIGHT, W. A.
Femina Now First Printed from a Unique Ms. in the Library of Trinity College, Cambridge. Cambridge: 1909. V. 54

WRIGHT, WILLARD HUNTINGTON
The Benson Murder Case. New York: 1926. V. 49; 51
The Bishop Murder Case. New York: 1929. V. 48; 49; 51; 53
Casino Murder Case. New York: 1934. V. 48; 49; 50; 51; 53
The Dragon Murder Case. New York: 1933. V. 49; 52
The Garden Murder Case. New York: 1935. V. 51
The Gracie Allen Murder Case. New York: 1938. V. 53
The Kidnap Murder Case. New York: 1936. V. 47
The Scarab Murder Case. New York: 1930. V. 51; 53
The Winter Murder Case. New York: 1939. V. 49; 51; 53

WRIGHT, WILLIAM
An Account of Palmyra and Zenobia with Travels and Adventures in Bashan and the Desert. London: 1895. V. 54
The Brontes in Ireland, or Facts Stranger than Fiction. London: 1893. V. 54
The Brontes in Ireland, or Facts Stranger than Fiction. London: 1894. V. 50
History of the Big Bonanza... Hartford: 1871. V. 52
History of the Big Bonanza... Hartford & San Francisco: 1876. V. 49
A History of the Comstock Silver Lode and Mines. Virginia City: 1889. V. 47
Plain Advice to All Classes of Deaf Persons, the Deaf and Dumb and Those Having Diseases of the Fears. London: 1826. V. 49
Snow-Shoe Thompson. Los Angeles: 1954. V. 52; 54

WRIGHT, WILLIAM G.
The Butterflies of the West Coast. San Francisco: 1905. V. 53
Colored Plates of the Butterflies of the West Coast, Being Actual Photographs, Life-Size and In all their Natural Colors. San Bernardino: 1907. V. 53

WRIGHT, WILLIAM H. K.
Journal of the Ex-Libris Society. London: 1892-1902. V. 49
West-Country Poets: Their Lives and Works. London: 1896. V. 49

WRIGHTE, WILLIAM
Grotesque Architecture. London: 1767. V. 47
Grotesque Architecture... London: 1802. V. 48

WRIGHT'S Book of Poultry. London: 1914. V. 51

WRIGHTSON, BERNI
Berni Wrightson: a Look Back. 1979. V. 47; 51

WRIGLEY, G.
Coffee. Harlow: 1988. V. 51

WRITERS Declare Against Fascism. London: 1938. V. 47

WRITERS Outside the Margin. Sudbury: 1986. V. 54

WRITERS Take Sides. Letters About the War in Spain from 418 American Authors. New York: 1938. V. 49

WRONECKI, DANIEL
New-York. Paris: 1949. V. 48

WRONG, GEORGE M.
Chronicles of Canada. Toronto: 1915. V. 50
The Rise and Fall of New France. Toronto: 1928. V. 48

WROTH, LAWRENCE C.
The Early Cartography of the Pacific. New York: 1944. V. 48
A History of Printing in Colonial Maryland 1686-1776. Baltimore: 1922. V. 48
A History of the Printed Book. New York: 1938. V. 48; 49; 51; 53

WROTH, WARWICK
Catalogue of the Coins of the Vandals, Ostrogoths and Lombards and of the Empires of Thessalonica, Nicaea and Trebizond in the British Museum. London: 1911. V. 48
Catalogue of the Imperial Byzantine Coins in the British Museum. London: 1908. V. 48
Imperial Byzantine Coins in the British Museum. Chicago: 1966. V. 48

WU, G. D.
Prehistoric Pottery in China. London: 1938. V. 51

WUNDERLICH, CAROL REINHOLD AUGUST
Medical Thermometry and Human Temperature. New York: 1871. V. 54
On the Temperature in Diseases. London: 1871. V. 51; 52; 53; 54
Das Verhalten der Eignewarme in Krankheiten. Leipzig: 1868. V. 47; 48; 50

WUNDT, WILHELM MAX
Principles of Physiological Psychology. London: 1904. V. 54

WURM, TED
Hetch Hetchy and Its Dam Railroad. Berkeley: 1973. V. 47

WURMAN, RICHARD
The Notebooks and Drawings of Louis I. Kahn. Cambridge: 1973. V. 49

WURTENBERGER, F.
Mannerism: the European Style of the 16th Century. New York: 1963. V. 53; 54

WYANDOTTE County and Kansas City, Kansas, Historical and Biographical. Chicago: 1890. V. 54

WYATT, CLAUDE W.
British Birds. London: 1894-99. V. 50

WYATT, GEORGE
A Compendious Description of a Design for a Theatre; Made in Pursuance of an Order (and Now Published Under Permission) from the Committee of Subscrbers for Carrying into Effect the Project of Erecting a Third Theatre in the Metropolis. London: 1812. V. 52

WYATT, HORACE
Malice in Kulturland. London: 1915. V. 53

WYATT, JAMES
The Life and Surprizing Adventures of James Wyatt. London: 1755. V. 49

WYATT, JOAN
A Middle Earth Album. London: 1979. V. 54

WYATT, LEO
Leo Wyatt's Little Book of Alphabets. 1985. V. 47
A Suite of Little Alphabets Engraved in Wood: Original Prints. 1988. V. 54

WYATT, MARIAN L.
A Girl I Know. Boston: 1894. V. 48

WYATT, MATTHEW DIGBY
The Art of Illuminating as Practised in Europe from the Earliest Times. London: 1860. V. 51
The Art of Illuminating as Practised in Europe from the Earliest Times. London: 1866. V. 51
Fine Art, a Sketch of its History, Theory, Practice... London: 1870. V. 52
Metal-Work and its Artistic Design. London: 1852. V. 50
Notices of Sculpture in Ivory, Consisting of a Lecture on the History, Methods and Chief Productions of the Art Delivered at the First Annual General Meeting of the Arundel Society, on the 29 June, 1855...and a Catalogue of the Specimens... London: 1856. V. 51; 54
Views of the Crystal Palace and Park. London: 1854. V. 51

WYATT, THOMAS
The Poems of Sir Thomas Wiat. London: 1913. V. 51
The Poetical Works of Sir Thomas Wyatt. London: 1866. V. 51

WYATVILLE, JEFFRY
Illustrations of Windsor Castle. London: 1841. V. 52

WYCHERLEY, WILLIAM
The Complete Works. London: 1924. V. 48; 51; 52; 54
The Country Wife. London: 1688. V. 49
The Country Wife. London: 1934. V. 54
Miscellany Poems: as Satyrs, Epistles, Love-Verses, Songs, Sonnets &c. London: 1704. V. 47; 48
The Plain Dealer. London: 1677. V. 48; 52
The Posthumous Works...in Prose and Verse. London: 1728. V. 47; 49; 53
Works. Soho: 1924. V. 52

WYCLIFFE, JOHN
Two Short Treatises, Against the Orders of the Begging Friars... Oxford: 1608. V. 54

WYCOFF, EDITH
Bibliographical Contributions from the Lloyd Library. Numbers 1-14. 1911/14. V. 52

THE WYCOFF Family in America. A Genealogy. Rutland: 1934. V. 49; 51

WYETH, ANDREW
Andrew Wyeth. Boston: 1968. V. 52
Four Seasons. New York. V. 48
The Four Seasons... New York: 1961. V. 53

WYETH, BETSY
The Stray. New York: 1979. V. 50
Wyeth at Kuerners. Boston: 1976. V. 48; 50; 53

WYETH, JAMIE
Jamie Wyeth. Boston: 1980. V. 49; 51; 54

WYETH, JOHN ALLEN
Life of General Nathan Beford Forrest. New York: 1899. V. 47; 48; 50
A Textbook on Surgery. New York: 1887. V. 54
A Textbook on Surgery... New York: 1888. V. 54
A Textbook on Surgery... New York: 1889. V. 51
A Textbook on Surgery. London: 1891. V. 54
With Sabre and Scapel. New York & London: 1914. V. 49; 50

WYETH, JOHN B.
Oregon; or, a Short History of a Long Journey from the Atlantic Ocean to the Region of the Pacific, by Land. Cleveland: 1905. V. 51

WYETH, NATHANIEL J.
The Correspondence and Journals of...1831-1836. Eugene: 1899. V. 49; 53

WYKEN, WILLIAM
Repertorium Bibilographicum: or Some Account of Celebrated British Libraries. London: 1819. V. 54

WYLD, JAMES
An Atlas of Maps of Different Parts of the World.. London: 1839. V. 48
An Atlas of Modern Geography. London: 1853. V. 48

WYLIE, ANDREW
Sectarianism Is Heresy, in Three Parts, in Which is Shewn, Its Nature, Evils and Remedy. Bloomington: 1840. V. 52

WYLIE, ELINOR HOYT
Angels and Earthy Creatures. New York: 1929. V. 49
Collected Poems. New York: 1932. V. 48
Jennifer Lorn: a Sedate Extravaganza. New York: 1923. V. 48; 53
Mr. Hodge and Mr. Hazard. New York: 1928. V. 47; 49; 51
Nets to Catch the Wind. New York: 1921. V. 49; 50; 51
The Orphan Angel. New York: 1923. V. 51

WYLIE, ELINOR HOYT continued
The Orphan Angel. New York: 1926. V. 47; 48; 49; 52; 53; 54
Trivial Breath (Poems). New York: 1928. V. 47; 49
The Venetian Glass Nephew. New York: 1925. V. 48; 51

WYLIE, PHILIP
The Big Ones Get Away. New York & Toronto: 1940. V. 47; 49
Fish and Tin Fish. Toronto & New York: 1944. V. 47; 49
Generation of Vipers. New York & Toronto: 1942. V. 49

WYLLIE, JOHN
Tumours of the Cerebellum. London: 1908. V. 47; 48; 49; 51; 52; 53

WYLLIE, ROBERT
A Letter Concerning the Union, with Sir George Mackenzie's Observations and Sir John Nisbet's Opinion Upon the Same Subject. N.P: 1706. V. 52

WYLLY, H. C.
The Border Regiment in the Great War. 1924. V. 47
From the Black Mountain to Waziristan Being an Account of the Border Countries and the More Turbulent of the Tribes Controlled by the North-West Frontier Province.... 1912. V. 54

WYMAN, MORRILL
Autumnal Catarrh (Hay Fever). New York: 1872. V. 53
Autumnal Catarrh (Hay Fever) with Illustrative Maps. New York: 1876. V. 49; 51; 54

WYMAN, WILLIAM HENRY
Bibliography of the Bacon-Shakespeare Controversy, With Notes and Extracts. Cincinnati: 1884. V. 47

WYNDAM, PERCY
Mr. Percy Wyndam's Strictures on an Imposter and Old Actress, Formerly Bet the Pot Girl, Alis, The Banker's Ahm Widow... London: 1822. V. 47

WYNDHAM, CHARLES
Sketches of Cockermouth Castle, in the County of Cumberland. Carlisle: 1845. V. 50; 52

WYNDHAM, FRANCIS M.
Wild Life on the Fjelds of Norway. London: 1861. V. 48

WYNDHAM, H. A.
The Early History of the Thoroughbred Horse in South Africa. London: 1924. V. 47

WYNDHAM, HENRY PENRUDDOCKE
A Gentleman's Tour through Monmouthshire and Wales..June and July 1774. London: 1775. V. 53

WYNDHAM, HENRY SAXE
The Annals of Covent Garden Theatre from 1732 to 1897. London: 1906. V. 49

WYNDHAM, JOHN
Consider Her Ways and Others. London: 1961. V. 52
The Day of the Triffids. London: 1951. V. 48; 49; 50; 51; 54
The Day of the Triffids. New York: 1951. V. 52
Jizzle. London: 1954. V. 51; 52
The Kraken Wakes. 1953. V. 48; 52
The Midwich Cuckoos. 1957. V. 48
The Midwich Cuckoos. London: 1957. V. 52; 53
Out of the Deeps. New York: 1953. V. 51; 52
Re-Birth. New York: 1955. V. 52
Trouble with Lichen. London: 1960. V. 52
Trouble with Lichen. New York: 1960. V. 52

WYNDHAM Lewis the Artist. London: 1939. V. 50

WYNDHAM, MARGARET
Catalogue of the Collection of Greek and Roman Antiquities in the Possession of Lord Leconfield. London: 1915. V. 52

WYNDHAM, PERCY, MRS.
The Ballad of Mr. Rook. London: 1901. V. 54

WYNN, MARCIA RITTENHOUSE
Pioneer Family of Whiskey Flat. 1945. V. 53
Pioneer Family of Whiskey Flat. Los Angeles: 1945. V. 51

WYNNE, EDWARD
Eunomus; or, Dialogues Concerning the Law and Constitution of England... London: 1785. V. 48
Eunomus; or, Dialogues Concerning the Law and Constitution of England. Dublin: 1791. V. 48

WYNNE, ELLIS
Bweledigaetheu Y Bardd Cwsc. Visions of the Sleeping Bard. Newtown: 1940. V. 54

WYNNE, JAMES
Private Libraries of New York. New York: 1860. V. 48; 50

WYNNE, JOHN
An Abridgment of Mr. Locke's Essay Concerning Human Understanding. London: 1696. V. 54
An Abridgment of Mr. Locke's Essay Concerning Humane Understanding. London: 1700. V. 49; 54

WYNNE, JOHN HUDDLESTON
Fables of Flowers, for the Female Sex. London: 1773. V. 50
The Prostitute, a Poem. London: 1771. V. 54
Tales for Youth; in Thirty Poems; to Which are Annexed, Historical Remarks and Moral Applications in Prose. London: 1794. V. 50; 52

WYNNE, JUSTINE
Alticchiero. Venice: 1787. V. 53

WYNNE, MAY
The Seven Champions of Christendom. London: 1920. V. 49

WYNNE, W. ARNOLD SMITH
St. Olave's Priory and Bridge, Herringfleet, Suffolk. Norwich: 1914. V. 54

WYNTER, ANDREW
The Borderlands of Insanity and other Allied Papers. London: 1875. V. 50
Fruit Between the Leaves. London: 1875. V. 51; 54

WYNTER, HARRIET
Scientific Instruments. London: 1975. V. 53

WYNTER-BLYTH, M. A.
Butterflies of the Indian Region. Bombay: 1957. V. 49

WYOMING.. New York: 1941. V. 53

WYOMING
Constitution of the Proposed State of Wyoming Adopted in Convention at Cheyenne, Wyoming. Cheyenne: 1889. V. 48

WYON, ALFRED BENJAMIN
The Great Seals of England, from the Earliest Period to the Present Time... London: 1887. V. 51

WYSE, HENRY T.
Modern Type Display and the Use of Type Ornament. Edinburgh: 1911. V. 48

WYSS, JOHANN DAVID
The Family Robinson Crusoe; or, Journal of a Father Shipwrecked, With His Wife and Children... London: 1814. V. 48
The Family Robinson Crusoe; or, Journal of a Father Shipwrecked, with His Wife and Children... London: 1814-16. V. 47; 52
The Swiss Family Robinson. Ipswich: 1963. V. 52; 53

WYTSMAN, P.
Genera Avium. Brussels: 1905-14. V. 51
Genera Avium. London: 1905-14. V. 50

WYVILL, CHRISTOPHER
A Letter to the Right Hon. William Pitt. York: 1793. V. 53

X

XENOPHON
Cyropaedia; or the Institution of Cyrus. London: 1728. V. 48; 50; 54
Cyrupaedia: the Institution and Life of Cyrus... Newton: 1936. V. 47; 48; 50; 51; 52
De Cyri Institutionae Libri Octo. Eton: 1613. V. 47; 49
De Cyri Institutione, Libri Octo. Philadelphia: 1806. V. 50; 52
De Cyri Minoris Expeditione, Libri VII. Romulus Amasaeus Vertit. Lyons: 1536. V. 53
Della Vita de Cyro re de Persi. Tusculano: 1527. V. 54
The Ephesian Story. London: 1957. V. 48
The Ephesian Story. Waltham St. Lawrence: 1957. V. 47; 54
The Expedition of Cyrus Into Persia. London: 1749. V. 48
History of the Affairs of Greece. London: 1760. V. 48
History of the Affairs of Greece. London: 1770. V. 49; 50
Memoirs of Socrates. Bath: 1762. V. 48
Opera Varia. V. 48
Oratio de Agesilao Rege. Oxonii: 1754. V. 53
Xenophon's Treatise of Household. London: 1550?. V. 47

Y

YABLON, G. A.
A Bronte Bibliography. 1978. V. 54
A Bronte Bibliography. London: 1978. V. 52

YADIN, YIGAEL
The Art of Warfare in Biblical Lands in Light of Archaeological Study. New York: 1963. V. 52
The Finds from the Bar Kokhba period in the Cave of letters. Jerusalem: 1963. V. 50; 52
Hazor I-IV. Jerusalem: 1958-61. V. 50
Hazor I-IV. Jerusalem: 1958-89. V. 52

YAHUDA, A. S.
The Language of the Pentateuch in Its Relation to Egyptian. London: 1933. V. 52

YALE & TOWN MANUFACTURING CO.
Album of Crane Designs. New York: 1887. V. 52

YALE UNIVERSITY
Catalog of the Yale Collection of Western Americana. Boston: 1961. V. 53

YAMADA, CHISABUROH F.
Decorative Arts of Japan. Tokyo: 1964. V. 49
Decorative Arts of Japan. Tokyo: 1965. V. 54

YAMAGUCHI, RYUJI
The Clocks of Japan. Tokyo: 1950. V. 53

YAMASHINA, Y.
A Natural History of Japanese Birds. Tokyo: 1933-41. V. 48

YAMAZAKI, AKIRA
Monograph of Plant-Dyeing Peculiar to Japan. Kanagawa: 1961. V. 48
Nippon Hand Weaves in "Kusakizome" Dyes. 1960. V. 48; 54

YAMBOO; or, The North American Slave. London: 1812. V. 48

YANCEY, BENJAMIN C.
Speech of Benjamin Yancey, Esq. of Edgefield, in Relation to the bank of the State of South Carolina Delivered...1848. Hamburg: 1848. V. 50

THE YANKEE in London; or a Short Trip to America. Philadelphia: 1826. V. 49; 52

YARNALL, M.
Catalogue of Stars Observed at the United States Naval Observatory During the Years 1845 to 1877. Washington: 1878. V. 53

YARNELL, DUANE
Auto Pioneering, a Remarkable Story of Ransom E. Olds, Father of Oldsmobile and Reo. New York: 1949. V. 54

YARON
Rendezvous with Handel. London: 1991-92. V. 54

YARRANTON, ANDREW
England's Improvement by Sea and Land to Out-do the Dutch Without Fighting, to Pay Debts without Money, to Set at Work all the Poor of England with the Growth of Our Own Lands... London: 1677. V. 54

YARRELL, WILLIAM
A History of British Birds. London: 1837-43. V. 51
A History of British Birds. London: 1837-43-45. V. 52
A History of British Birds. London: 1843. V. 48; 52; 53; 54
A History of British Birds. London: 1845. V. 49; 50
A History of British Birds. London: 1856. V. 47; 50; 54
A History of British Birds. London: 1871-75. V. 52
A History of British Birds. London: 1871-85. V. 49; 50
A History of British Birds. London: 1875-85. V. 51
A History of British Fishes. London: 1836. V. 49; 52; 53
History of British Fishes. London: 1841. V. 53
A History of British Fishes. London: 1856-59. V. 50; 52

YARROW, W.
Robert Henri, His Life & Works. New York: 1921. V. 47

YASHIRO, YUKIO
2000 Years of Japanese Art. New York: 1958. V. 49
Sandro Botticelli. London: 1925. V. 47
Sandro Botticellio and the Florentine Rennaissance. London: 1929. V. 51; 53

YATES, EDMUND HODGSON
Black Sheep. London: 1867. V. 54
Edmund Yates: His Recollections and Experiences. London: 1884. V. 47
Land at Last. London: 1866. V. 54
Running the Gauntlet. London: 1865. V. 54

YATES, FRANCES
Collected Essays. London: 1982. V. 54

YATES, GEORGE
An Historical and Descriptive Sketch of Birmingham... Birmingham: 1830. V. 51

YATES, JAMES
Thoughts on the Advancement of Academical Education in England. London: 1827. V. 49

YATES, RICHARD
Eleven Kinds of Loneliness. Boston: 1962. V. 51; 53
Revolutionary Road. Boston: 1961. V. 47; 54
William Styron's Lie Down in Darkness: a Screenplay. Watertown: 1985. V. 52

YATES, ROBERT
Secret Proceedings and Debates of the Convention Assembled at Philadelphia in the year 1787, for the Purpose of Forming the Constitution of the United States of America. Albany: 1821. V. 52

YATES, WILLIAM
View of the Science of Life; on the Principles Established... (by) John Brown, M.D., with an Attempt to Correct Some Important Errors of that Work... Dover: 1801. V. 48

YATO, TAMOTSU
Naked Festival. New York and Tokyo: 1969. V. 54
Young Samurai. New York: 1965. V. 47
Young Samurai. New York: 1967. V. 50; 52

YAU, JOHN
Notarikon. New York: 1981. V. 54

YAVNO, MAX
The Los Angeles Book. Boston: 1950. V. 47

YDE, JENS
An Archaeological Reconnaissance of Northwestern Honduras: a Report of the Work of the Tulane University Danish National Museum Expedition to Central America. Copenhagen: 1938. V. 50

YE Sneak Yclepid Copperhead: a Satirical Poem. Philadelphia: 1863. V. 47

YEARBOOK. Anno Primo (-Anno VIII) Henrici VII. London: 1508?. V. 53

THE YEARBOOK of Photography, and Photographic News Almanac for 1884(-1889). London: 1884-89. V. 50

THE YEAR'S at the Spring. London: 1920. V. 48
THE YEAR'S at the Spring. New York: 1920. V. 47; 48; 53

YEARSLEY, ANN
Poems on Several Occasions. London: 1785. V. 47
The Royal Captives: a Fragment of Secret History... Philadelphia: 1795. V. 48

YEARSLEY, IAN
The Manchester Tram. Huddersfield: 1962. V. 51; 53

YEARY, MAMIE
Reminiscences of the Boys in Gray, 1861-65. Dallas: 1912. V. 49

YEATES, W. M.
Winged Victory. London: 1934. V. 47

YEATMAN, J. P.
The Early Genealogical History of the House of Arundel...Account of the Origin of the Families of Montgomery, Albini, Fitzalan and Howard...from the Conquest of Normand. London: 1882. V. 52

YEATMAN, JAMES E.
Report on the Condition of the Freedmen of the Mississippi, Presented to the Western Sanitary Commission, Dec. 17th, 1863. St. Louis: 1864. V. 48

YEATS, JOHN BUTLER
La La Noo. Dublin: 1943. V. 52
A Little Book of Drawings. Dublin: 1971. V. 52
A Little Fleet. London: 1905. V. 50
Passages from the Letters of John Butler Yeats: Selected by Ezra Pound. Dundrum: 1917. V. 48
Sligo. London: 1930. V. 51
The Treasure of the Garden. London: 1902. V. 49

YEATS, WILLIAM BUTLER
Autobiographies. New York: 1927. V. 48; 51; 54
Beltaine: Organ of the Irish Literary Theatre... 1899-1900. V. 49; 50
Beltaine: Organ of the Irish Literary Theatre. London: 1899-1900. V. 53
A Book of Images. London: 1898. V. 51
The Bounty of Sweden: a Meditation, and a Lecture Delivered Before the Royal Swedish Academy and Certain Notes. Dublin: 1925. V. 50
The Cat and the Moon and Certain Poems. Dublin: 1924. V. 49; 53; 54
Celtic Twilight. London: 1893. V. 48; 52; 53
Collected Plays. London: 1934. V. 50; 54
The Collected Works in Verse and Prose. Stratford-on-Avon: 1903. V. 48
The Collected Works in Verse and Prose. London: 1908. V. 53
Collected Works in Verse and Prose. Stratford-on-Avon: 1908. V. 51
The Countess Kathleen. An Various Legends and Lyrics. Cameo Series. London: 1892. V. 48
The Cutting of an Agate. New York: 1912. V. 48; 51; 54
The Cutting of an Agate. London: 1919. V. 49; 53; 54
The Dawn. Grasse: 1982. V. 50
The Death of Synge, and Other Passages from an Old Diary. Dublin: 1928. V. 53
Deirdre. London: 1907. V. 47
Discoveries; a Volume of Essays. Dundrum: 1907. V. 47
Dramatis Personae... Dublin: 1935. V. 47
Early Poems and Stories. London: 1925. V. 48; 50
Early Poems and Stories. New York: 1925. V. 51; 53; 54
Eight Poems. London: 1916. V. 48; 49
Essays. London: 1924. V. 54
Essays. New York: 1924. V. 54
Essays: 1931-1936. 1937. V. 47
Estrangement: Being Some Fifty Thoughts from a Diary Kept by William Butler Yeats in the Year Nineteen Hundred and Nine. Dublin: 1926. V. 53; 54
Fairy and Folk Tales of the Irish Peasantry. London: 1888. V. 54
The Fancy. London: 1905. V. 51
Florence Farr, Bernard Shaw and W. B. Yeats. Dublin: 1941. V. 48
Four Plays for Dancers. London: 1921. V. 47; 48; 49; 52; 53
Four Plays for Dancers. New York: 1921. V. 47; 48; 53
Four Years. Churchtown, Dundrum: 1921. V. 48; 53
Full Moon in March. London: 1935. V. 47; 49; 51; 52; 54
Green Helmet and Other Poems. Churchtown, Dundrum: 1910. V. 49
The Herne's Egg... 1938. V. 54
The Herne's Egg... London: 1938. V. 47; 50; 51
The Herne's Egg... New York: 1938. V. 48
The Hour-Glass... London: 1904. V. 48; 52; 53
The Hour-Glass... New York: 1904. V. 47; 54
Ideas of Good and Evil. New York: 1903. V. 51
If I Were Four-and-Twenty. Dublin: 1940. V. 48; 53; 54

YEATS, WILLIAM BUTLER continued
In the Seven Woods... Dundrum: 1903. V. 48
In the Seven Woods. New York: 1903. V. 51; 54
Irish Fairy and Folk Tales. 1888. V. 49; 50; 54
Irish Fairy and Folk Tales. London: 1888. V. 51
Irish Fairy Tales. London: 1892. V. 51
Irish Fairy Tales. London: 1893?. V. 48
Irish Folk Tales. Avon: 1973. V. 53
Irish Folk Tales. Connecticut: 1973. V. 51
The King of the Great Clock Tower... 1934. V. 47
The King of the Great Clock Tower. Dublin: 1934. V. 50
The King of the Great Clock Tower... Dublin: 1934. V. 50; 53
The King of the Great Clock Tower. New York: 1935. V. 53
The King's Threshold... London: 1904. V. 53
The King's Threshold. New York: 1904. V. 47; 48; 52; 53
The Lake of Innesfree. London: 1924. V. 52
The Land of Heart's Desire. Chicago: 1894. V. 47
The Land of Heart's Desire. London: 1894. V. 47
The Land of Heart's Desire. Portland: 1903. V. 47
The Land of Heart's Desire. London: 1912. V. 52
Last Poems. London: 1940. V. 47
Later Poems. London: 1922. V. 48; 50
Later Poems. New York: 1924. V. 49; 54
Michael Robartes and the Dancer. 1920. V. 50
Michael Robartes and the Dancer. Dundrum: 1920. V. 48
The Mother of God. Grasse: 1982. V. 50
New Poems. Dublin: 1938. V. 47
On the Boiler. Dublin: 1938. V. 47
On the Boiler. Dublin: 1939. V. 49; 53
The Oxford Book of Modern Verse 1892-1935. Oxford: 1936. V. 48
A Packet for Ezra Pound. Dublin: 1929. V. 51; 53; 54
Per Amica Silentia Lunae. London: 1918. V. 48; 54
The Player Queen. London: 1922. V. 52
Plays and Controversies. London: 1923. V. 48
Plays and Controversies. New York: 1924. V. 54
Plays for an Irish Theatre... London: 1911. V. 54
Plays for an Irish Theatre. London: 1913. V. 51
Plays in Prose and Verse. New York: 1924. V. 54
Poems. London: 1895. V. 50
Poems. London: 1899. V. 50; 53; 54
Poems. 1901. V. 49; 50
Poems. London: 1901. V. 47
Poems. London: 1904. V. 52; 53
Poems. 1916. V. 54
Poems. London: 1922. V. 53
Poems. London: 1927. V. 54
The Poems... London: 1949. V. 48
Poems. New York: 1957. V. 51
The Poems... New York: 1970. V. 48; 51; 53
Poems 1899-1905. London & Dublin: 1906. V. 48; 49; 50; 51; 53; 54
Poems of Place. 1991. V. 48; 50
Poems of Place. Market Drayton: 1991. V. 52
Poems. Second Series. London: 1909. V. 54
The Poetical Works... New York: 1906. V. 51
The Poetical Works... New York: 1906/09. V. 49
The Poetical Works... New York: 1911-12. V. 54
The Poetical Works. New York: 1921. V. 49
Poetry and Ireland: Essays by... Churchtown, Dundrum: 1908. V. 53
Responsibilities... Churchtown, Dundrum: 1914. V. 48; 50; 53
Responsibilities... 1916. V. 54
Responsibilities... London: 1916. V. 48
Responsibilities... New York: 1916. V. 48; 53; 54
Reveries Over Childhood and Youth... Churchtown: 1915/15. V. 53
Reveries Over Childhood and Youth. Dundrum: 1916. V. 48
Reveries Over Childhood and Youth. New York: 1916. V. 53
The Secret Rose. London: 1897. V. 47; 48; 51; 52; 53
Selected Poems... London: 1929. V. 50
Selected Poems. Amsterdam: 1939. V. 47
Selected Poems... Pennsylvania: 1979. V. 50
Selected Poems. San Francisco: 1990. V. 47
Seven Poems and a Fragment. Dublin: 1922. V. 48
The Shadowy Waters. New York: 1901. V. 47; 50
Sophocles' King Oedipus. A Version for the Modern Stage. New York: 1928. V. 51
Stories of Red Hanrahan. Dundrum: 1904. V. 51; 52; 54
Stories of Red Hanrahan. New York: 1914. V. 53
Stories of Red Hanrahan... 1927. V. 48
The Tables of the Law...Adoration of the Magi. London: 1904. V. 49
Tables of the Law...The Adoration of the Magi. Stratford-upon-Avon: 1914. V. 50; 52
Three Things. London: 1929. V. 47; 49; 52
The Tower. 1928. V. 49; 50
The Tower. London: 1928. V. 47; 51; 52
The Tower. New York: 1928. V. 51
The Trembling of the Veil. London: 1922. V. 48; 49; 51; 53; 54
Tribute to Thomas Davis... Cork: 1947. V. 53
Two Plays for Dancers. Dublin: 1919. V. 51
Two Plays for Dancers. Dublin: 1929. V. 48
The Variorum Edition of the Poems of W. B. Yeats. New York: 1957. V. 53; 54
A Vision. London: 1925. V. 48; 51
A Vision. 1937. V. 49; 50
A Vision. London: 1937. V. 49; 53
The Wanderings of Oisin and Other Poems. London: 1889. V. 49; 50
Wheels and Butterflies. 1934. V. 49
Wheels and Butterflies. London: 1934. V. 48; 51
Where There is Nothing. London: 1903. V. 53; 54
Where There is Nothing. New York: 1903. V. 53; 54
The Wild Swans at Coole. New York: 1919. V. 48
The Wind Among the Reeds. London: 1899. V. 51; 53
The Winding Stair. New York: 1929. V. 48
The Winding Stair... 1933. V. 49; 50; 54
The Winding Stair... London: 1933. V. 48
The Words Upon the Window Pane. Dublin: 1934. V. 48; 51

YEH, CAROL
Houdini. Laguna Beach: 1971. V. 48

YEIVIN, S.
The Israelite Conquest of Canaan. Istanbul: 1971. V. 52

YELD, G.
Scrambles in the Eastern Graians, 1878-1897. 1900. V. 53

YELDHAM, WALTER
Lays of Ind; Comic, Satirical and Descriptive Poems... Calcutta: 1879. V. 51

THE YELLOW Book. London: 1894-96/1949. V. 52
THE YELLOW Book. London: 1894-97. V. 48; 49; 51; 52; 53

THE YELLOW Fellow Year Book. A Treatise Upon Stearns Bicycles Made by E. C. Stearns & Co., Syracuse, New York. Syracuse: 1897. V. 51

YELLOW JACKET SILVER MINING CO.
Annual Report of the Yellow Jacket Silver Mining Co. for the Year Ending June 30th, 1879. Virginia City: 1879. V. 49

THE YELLOW Witch Book. Reading & London: 1905. V. 52

YELVERTON, HENRY
The Reports of... London: 1735. V. 52

YENNE, BILL
One Foot on the Highway - Bob Dylan on tour. San Francisco: 1974. V. 50

YEOMAN, THOMAS
The Report of Thomas Yeoman, Engineer, Concerning the Drainage of the North Level of the Fens, and Outfall of the Wiesbach River. London: 1769. V. 49

YEOMANS, DAVID
The Trussed Roof: Its History and Development. London: 1992. V. 53

YERBURY, F. R.
Georgian Details of Domestic Architecture. London: 1926. V. 51; 53

YERBY, FRANK
Benton's Row. New York: 1954. V. 52
The Foxes of Harrow. New York: 1946. V. 52
The Serpent and the Staff. New York: 1958. V. 50
Tobias and the Angel. New York: 1975. V. 54

YERKES, ROBERT M.
Psychological Examining in the United States Army. Washington: 1921. V. 47; 49; 50

YERUSHALMI, YOSEF
Haggadah and History. Philadelphia: 1975. V. 50; 53

YEVTUSHENKO, YEVGENY
Selected Poems. Helsinki: 1989. V. 48
Stolen Apples. Garden City: 1971. V. 47; 54

YGLESIAS, JOSE
One German Dead. Leeds: 1988. V. 47; 48; 52

YOAKUM, HENDERSON
History of Texas... New York: 1856. V. 51; 53
History of Texas... Redfield: 1856. V. 50

YOLEN, JANE
The Lady and the Merman... Easthampton: 1977. V. 47; 49

YOM-TOV, Y.
The Zoogeography of Israel... The Hague: 1988. V. 52

YONGE, C. D.
The History of the British Navy, from the Earliest Period to the Present time. London: 1863. V. 48

YONGE, CHARLOTTE MARY
The Armourer's Prentices. London: 1884. V. 50; 54
Beechcroft at Rockstone. London: 1888. V. 53; 54
Chantry House. London: 1886. V. 51; 54
The Chaplet of Pearls; or, The White and Black Ribaumont. London: 1868. V. 47; 50; 54
The Daisy Chain; or, Aspirations. New York: 1856. V. 47
Grisly Grisell or the Laidly Lady of Whitburn: a Tale of the Wars of the Roses. London: 1893. V. 54

YONGE, CHARLOTTE MARY continued
Heartsease; or the Brother's Wife. London: 1855. V. 54
Heartsease; or the Brother's Wife. New York: 1871. V. 48; 52
The Heir of Redclyffe: by the Author of "Heartsease". Leipzig: 1855. V. 48
History of Christian Names. London: 1878. V. 50; 52
The Instructive Picture Book, or Lessons from the Vegetable World. Edinburgh: 1857. V. 51
The Instructive Picture Book or Lessons from the Vegetable World. Edinburgh: 1858. V. 49
Magnum Bonum or Mother Carey's Brood. London: 1879. V. 47; 50; 52; 54
A Modern Telemachus. London: 1886. V. 50
The Story of the Christians and Moors of Spain. London: 1878. V. 50
The Two Sides of the Shield. London: 1885. V. 50; 54
Unknown to History. London: 1882. V. 53

YORD, JAMES
Alberto Giacometti. Greenwich: 1971. V. 50

YORDAN, PHILIP
Anna Lucasta. New York: 1945. V. 50; 53

YORICK'S Meditations Upon Various Interesting and Important Subjects. London: 1760. V. 48

YORK, EDWARD, 2ND DUKE OF
The Master of the Game. London: 1904. V. 47; 52

YORK Illustrated. York: 1839. V. 50

YORKE, CHARLES PHILIP
Remarks on Some Egyptian Monuments in England. London: 1826. V. 49

YORKE, CURTIS
The Mystery of Belgrave Square. London: 1889. V. 47

YORKE, F. HENRY
Our Ducks. Chicago: 1899. V. 53

YORKE, F. R. S.
The Modern House. London: 1934. V. 49

YORKE, H. A.
Report On a Visit to America. September 19th to October 31st 1902. London: 1903. V. 49

YORKE, HENRY REDHEAD
Letters from France in 1802. London: 1804. V. 50

YORKE, JAMES
The Union of Honour Containing the Armes, Matches and Issues of the Kings, Dukes, Marquesses and Earles of England from the Conquest... London: 1640. V. 47; 51; 53
The Union of Honour Containing the Armes, Matches and Issues of the Kings, Dukes, Marquesses and Earles of England from the Conquest... London: 1641. V. 48

YORKSHIRE AGRICULTURAL AND COMMERCIAL BANKING CO.
The Deed of Settlement of the Yorkshire Agricultural and Commercial Banking Co. York: 1836. V. 49

YORKSHIRE Castles. Leeds. V. 53

THE YORKSHIRE Domesday. London: 1992. V. 51

THE YORKSHIRE-Rogue, or, Capt. Hind Improv'd; In the Notorious Life, and Infamous Death, of That Famous Highway-Man, William Nevison, Who Was Executed at York, the 15th Day of March 1684. Together with a Short Account of Several Great Robberies... London: 1684/85. V. 53

YOSHIDA, KOGORO
Tanrokubon, Rare Books of Seventeenth Century Japan. Tokyo: 1984. V. 52

YOST, KARL
A Bibliography of the Published Works of Charles M. Russell. Lincoln: 1971. V. 47; 49
A Bibliography of the Published Works of Charles M. Russell. New York: 1971. V. 52
A Bibliography of the Works of Edna St. Vincent Millay. New York: 1937. V. 54

YOSY, A.
Switzerland, As Now Divided Into Nineteen Cantons... 1815. V. 48
Switzerland, as Now Divided Into Nineteen Cantons... London: 1815. V. 54

YOUATT, WILLIAM
The Horse; with a Treatise on Draught. London: 1831. V. 49; 54
The Pig: A Treatise on the Breeds, Management, Feeding and Medical Treatment, of Swine... London: 1847. V. 49
Sheep: Their Breeds, Management and Diseases... New York: 1867. V. 50

YOULE, WILLIAM E.
Sixty-Three Years in the Oilfields. Los Angeles?: 1926?. V. 48

YOUMANS, JULIAN R.
Neurological Surgery: A Comprehensive Reference Guide to the Diagnosis and Management of Neurosurgical Problems. Philadelphia: 1973. V. 48

YOUNG & MARTEN
Illustrated General Catalogue... London: 1897. V. 52

YOUNG, A. B. FILSON
The Complete Motorist... London: 1904. V. 47

THE YOUNG African Prince; or, memoirs of Naimbanna. Boston: 1822. V. 47

YOUNG, AL
Dancing. New York: 1969. V. 48; 51

YOUNG America's ABC and Pretty Picture Book. New York: 1900. V. 53

YOUNG, ANDREW
Crystal and Flint: Poems. 1991. V. 52
The Natural History and Habits of the Salmon. London: 1854. V. 51; 52; 54
Winter Harvest. London: 1933. V. 47; 50

YOUNG, ANDREW MC LAREN
The Paintings of James McNeill Whistler. New Haven: 1980. V. 53

YOUNG, ANDREW W.
Introduction to the Science of Government and Compend of Constitutional and Civil Jurisprudence of the United States. Buffalo: 1848. V. 48

THE YOUNG Angler's Companion. London: 1850. V. 52; 53

YOUNG, ARCHIBALD
Summer Sailings by an Old Yachtsman. Edinburgh: 1898. V. 47

YOUNG, ART
Art Young's Inferno. New York: 1934. V. 50

YOUNG, ARTHUR
An Abridgment of the Six Weeks and Six Months Tour's of Arthur Young, Esq.... Dublin: 1771. V. 49
The Adventures of Emmera, or the Fair American. London: 1767. V. 54
The Autobiography of Arthur Young. 1898. V. 50
The Example of France, a Warning to Britain. Dublin: 1793. V. 50
The Example of France, a Warning to Britain. London: 1793. V. 50
The Farmer's Calendar... London: 1771. V. 49
The Farmer's Calendar... London: 1805. V. 49
The Farmer's Calendar. London: 1809. V. 48; 51; 52; 53; 54
The Farmer's Guide in Hiring and Stocking Farms... London: 1770. V. 47; 52; 53
The Farmer's Guide in Hiring and Stocking Farms. Dublin: 1771. V. 52
The Farmer's Guide in Hiring and Stocking Farms. Edinburgh: 1780. V. 51
The Farmer's Letters to the People of England... London: 1768. V. 52
The Farmer's Tour through the East of England... London: 1771. V. 47
General View of the Agriculture of the County of Essex. London: 1807. V. 52
General View of the Agriculture of the County of Norfolk... London: 1854. V. 54
General View of the Agriculture of the County of Suffolk with Observations on the Means of Its Improvement. London: 1794. V. 49; 50
General View of the Agriculture of the County of Sussex. London: 1793. V. 49; 51; 52; 53
A Six Months Tour Through the North of England... Dublin: 1770. V. 48; 49
A Six Weeks Tour through the Southern Counties of England and Wales. Salisbury: 1769. V. 52
A Six Weeks Tour through the Southern Counties of England and Wales. London: 1772. V. 47
A Tour in Ireland...1776, 1777 and 1778. London: 1780. V. 49; 50
A Tour in Ireland...1776 and 1779. 1892. V. 52
Travels During the Years 1787, 1788 & 1789. Bury St. Edmund's: 1792. V. 48; 49; 50
Travels During the Years 1787, 1788 & 1789. Dublin: 1793. V. 47; 48; 50
Travels During the Years 1787, 1788 & 1789... London: 1794. V. 47; 52

YOUNG, BENJAMIN
Harness, Horse Collars and Saddlery Catalogue 47. Milwaukee: 1910. V. 54

YOUNG, BENNETT HENDERSON
The Battle of the Thames, with a List of the Officers and Privates Who Won the Victory. Louisville: 1903. V. 47; 50; 54
Confederate Wizards of the Saddle Being Reminiscences and Observations of One Who Rode with Morgan. Boston: 1914. V. 48
The Prehistoric Men of Kentucky. Louisville: 1910. V. 53

YOUNG, BETTY LOU
Pacific Palisades: Where the Mountains Meet the Sea. Pacific Palisades: 1983. V. 50
Rustic Canyon and the Story of the Uplifters. Santa Monica: 1975. V. 52

YOUNG, BRIGHAM
Governor's Message tot he Legislative Assembly of the Territory of Utah: Delivered in Great Salt Lake City, December 15, A.D. 1857. Salt Lake City: 1857. V. 50

YOUNG, CHARLES
The Amazon and the Rio Madeira. 1861. V. 47
Night-Caps for the Babies. London: 1915. V. 49

YOUNG, CHARLES E.
Dangers of the Trail in 1865 a Narrative of Actual Events. Geneva: 1912. V. 47; 53

YOUNG, CHARLES FREDERICK
The Economy of Steam Power on Common Roads, in Relation to Agriculturists... London: 1861. V. 49

THE YOUNG Chevalier: or, a Genuine Narrative of all that Befell that Unfortunate Adventurer, from His Fatal Defeat to His Final Escape... London: 1750. V. 54

THE YOUNG Child's A B C or First Book. New York: 1806. V. 47; 48; 49

THE YOUNG Child's A, B, C; or, First Book. New York: 1816. V. 48; 49

THE YOUNG Clerk's Assistant; or Penmanship Made Easy, Instructive and Entertaining... London: 1787. V. 48

THE YOUNG Clerk's Magazine; or, English Law-Repository.... London: 1763. V. 49; 51

THE YOUNG Clerk's Vade Mecum; or, Compleat Law-Tutor. New York: 1776. V. 48; 50

YOUNG, DANIEL
Young's Demonstrative Translation of Scientific Secrets; or a Collection of Above 500 Useful Receipts on a Variety of Subjects. Toronto: 1861. V. 50; 52

YOUNG, DAVID
Lectures on the Science of Astronomy, Explanatory and Demonstrative, Which Were First Delivered, at Various Places in New Jersey in the Year 1820. Morris Town: 1821. V. 51
National Improvements Upon Agriculture in Twenty-Seven Essays. Edinburgh: 1785. V. 53
The Old Rough and Ready Almanac. 1849. Philadelphia. 1848. V. 49
The Wonderful History of the Morristown Ghost. Newark: 1826. V. 51

YOUNG, E. H.
A Bird in the Bush. 1936. V. 54

YOUNG, EDWARD
The Brothers, a Tragedy. London: 1777. V. 52
The Centaur Not Fabulous. London: 1755. V. 52; 53
The Complaint...Night Thoughts... London: 1742-43. V. 51
The Complaint...Night Thoughts... London: 1743-42-45. V. 47
The Complaint...Night Thoughts... London: 1755. V. 50
The Complaint...Night Thoughts... Newburyport: 1789. V. 52
The Complaint...Night Thoughts. London: 1797. V. 48; 49; 54
The Complaint...Night Thoughts... Berwick: 1800. V. 50
Delle Notti di Young. Siena: 1775. V. 47; 50
The Force of Religion; or, Vanquish'd Love. London: 1714. V. 51
The Instalment. To the Right Honourable Sir Robert Walpole, Knight of the Most Noble Order of the Garter. London: 1726. V. 54
Love of Fame, the Universal Passion, in Seven Characteristical Satires. Dublin: 1728. V. 48
Night Thoughts. London: 1798. V. 53
Night Thoughts... London: 1902. V. 49
Ocean. An Ode. London: 1728. V. 47
A Paraphrase on Part of the Book of Job. London: 1719. V. 48
A Poem on the Last Day. Oxford: 1713. V. 47
The Poetical Works. London: 1741. V. 47; 50
The Poetical Works... London: 1858. V. 51
Two Epistles to Mr. Pope, Concerning the Authors of the Age. London: 1730. V. 49
The Works. London: 1802. V. 50

YOUNG, EDWARD HUDSON
Our Young Family in America. Durham: 1947. V. 51

YOUNG, ELLA
Poems. Dublin: 1906. V. 51

THE YOUNG Emigrant; or Juvenile Letters from the Cape of Good Hope... London: 1823. V. 47

YOUNG, ERNEST A.
Walt Wheeler, the Scout Detective. New York: 1884. V. 52

YOUNG, FILSON
The Happy Motorist. London: 1906. V. 47
Titanic. London: 1912. V. 54

YOUNG, FRANCIS BRETT
Dr. Bradley Remembers. London: 1938. V. 52
Five Degrees South. London: 1917. V. 47
Marching on Tanga. (With General Smuts in East Africa). London: 1917. V. 47
Woodsmoke. 1939. V. 52
Woodsmoke. London: 1939. V. 53

YOUNG, FRANK C.
Across the Plains in '65. Denver: 1905. V. 47; 54

YOUNG, FRANKLIN K.
The Minor Tactics of Chess: a Treatise on the Deployment of the Forces in Obedience to Stategic Principle. Boston: 1894. V. 50

YOUNG, G. M.
Early Victorian England, 1830-1865. London: 1934. V. 49

YOUNG, G. O.
Alaskan Trophies Won and Lost. Boston: 1928. V. 53

YOUNG, GAVIN
An Inquiry Into the Expediency of Applying the Principles of Colonial Policy to the Government of India... London: 1822. V. 53

THE YOUNG Gentleman and Lady's Instructor. Lewes: 1808. V. 47; 50

YOUNG, GEORGE
A Geological Survey of the Yorkshire Coast... London: 1822. V. 48
A Geological Survey of the Yorkshire Coast... Whitby: 1822. V. 47
A Geological Survey of the Yorkshire Coast... Whitby: 1828. V. 48
A History of Whitby and Streoneshalh... Whitby: 1817. V. 47; 49
A Parody on the Song "Louisiana Low Lands". New Orleans: 1862. V. 48
A Treatise on Opium, Founded on Practical Observations. London: 1753. V. 52

YOUNG, GEORGE FREDERICK
The Medici. New York: 1925. V. 54
The Medici. London: 1930. V. 48

YOUNG, GERALD
The Witches Kitchen or the India Rubber Doctor. London: 1910. V. 48

YOUNG, GRAHAEME B.
Labrys 5. London: 1979. V. 53

YOUNG, H. H.
Conversations Between the Rabbi of the Boarding House and a Company of Intelligent Ladies and Gentlemen. St. Paul: 1893. V. 48
Saint Paul, the Commercial Emporium of the Northwest. Saint Paul: 1886. V. 48

YOUNG, HARRY
Hard Knocks... Chicago: 1915. V. 54
Hard Knocks. Portland: 1915. V. 47; 48; 49

YOUNG, HUGH W.
Leaves from the Commonplace Book of Hugh W. Young of Burghead. Elgin: 1906. V. 49

YOUNG, JAMES
A Manual and Atlas of Orthopedic Surgery Including the History, Etiology, Pathology, Diagnosis, Prognosis, Prophylaxis and Treatment of Deformities. Philadelphia: 1906. V. 54

YOUNG, JAMES REYNOLDS
Recitations at Whitmarsh Rectory. London: 1865. V. 50

YOUNG, JAMES WEBB
The Compleat Angler, or How to be an Advertising Man and Catch the Poor Fish. Copa: 1953. V. 47

YOUNG, JENNIE J.
The Ceramic Art. New York: 1879. V. 50

YOUNG, JESSE BOWMAN
The Battle of Gettysburg. New York & London: 1913. V. 50

YOUNG, JOHN
A Catalogue of the Pictures at Grosvenor House, London... London: 1820. V. 54
A Catalogue of the Pictures at Leigh Court: near Bristol; the Seat of Philip John Miles Esq. M.P. London: 1822. V. 50; 54
A Criticism on the Elegy Written in a Country Church Yard. London: 1783. V. 54
A Criticism on the Elegy Written in a Country Church Yard. Edinburgh: 1810. V. 47
Letters of Agricola on the Principles of Vegetation and Tillage, Written for Nova Scotia... Halifax: 1822. V. 52; 53

YOUNG, JOHN P.
San Francisco: a History of the Pacific Coast Metropolis. San Francisco: 1912. V. 52

YOUNG, JOHN PRESTON
The Seventh Tennessee Cavalry. Nashville: 1890. V. 49

YOUNG, JOHN R.
Memoirs of John R. Young Utah Pioneer 1847. Salt Lake City: 1920. V. 47

YOUNG, JOHN RUSSEL
Around the World With General Grant... New York: 1879. V. 48; 49

YOUNG, JOSEPH
A New Physical System of Astronomy; or, an Attempt to Explain the Operations of the Powers Which Impel the Planets and Comets to Perform Eliptical revolutions Round the Suns... New York: 1800. V. 48

YOUNG, JULIAN
A Bobbery Pack in India, with an Appendix. Calcutta: 1896. V. 47
A Memoir of Charles Mayne Young, Tragedian, with Extracts from His Son's Journal. London & New York: 1871. V. 47

YOUNG Ladies' Drawing Book, or Complete Instructor in Drawing and Colouring Flowers, Fruit and Shells... 1832. V. 52

THE YOUNG Ladies Journal. New York?: 1884/85. V. 47

THE YOUNG Lady's Book: a Manual of Elegant Recreations, Exercises and Pursuits. Boston: 1833. V. 52; 53

THE YOUNG Lady's Equestrian Manual. London: 1838. V. 47

THE YOUNG Lady's Equestrian manual. Philadelphia: 1839. V. 50

THE YOUNG Lady's Equestrian Manual. Philadelphia: 1854. V. 54

THE YOUNG Lady's Parental Monitor. Hartford: 1792. V. 53

YOUNG, LYMAN
Tim Tyler in the Jungle. Chicago: 1935. V. 49

YOUNG, M.
The Complete Instructor in Boxing, Swimming, Gymnastics, Pedestrianism, Horse Raceing, Prize Fighting, Boat Raceing and Other Sports... New York: 1881. V. 47

THE YOUNG Man's Book of Amusement. Halifax: 1839. V. 50

YOUNG, MARGUERITE
Miss MacIntosh, My Darling. New York: 1965. V. 52

YOUNG, MARY JULIA
Voltairiana. London: 1805. V. 52

YOUNG, MATTHEW
An Enquiry into the Principal Phaenomena of Sounds and Musical Strings. Dublin: 1784. V. 50

YOUNG, MOSES G.
A Condensed History of the 143d Regiment New York Volunteer Infantry of the Civil War, 1861-1865. Newburgh: 1909. V. 47

YOUNG, OTIS E.
The First Military Escort on the Santa Fe Trail, 1829 from Journals and Reports of Major Bennett Riley & Lieut. Philip St. George Cooke. Glendale: 1952. V. 48; 51; 54
The West of Philip St. George Cooke, 1809-1895. Glendale: 1955. V. 48; 50; 51; 52

YOUNG, PHILIP
History of Mexico: Her Civil Wars, and Colonial and Revolutionary Annals; from the Period of the Spanish Conquest, 1520 to the Present Time, 1847, Including an Account of the War with the United States, Its Causes and Military Achievements. Cincinnati: 1847. V. 49

THE YOUNG Reader's Instructor Being a Collection of Lessons in Prose and Verse. Doncaster: 1804. V. 52

YOUNG, ROBERT
Timothy Hackworth and the Locomotive. London: 1923. V. 49

YOUNG, ROBERT M.
The Town Book of the Corporation of Belfast 1613-1816. Belfast: 1892. V. 48

YOUNG, ROLAND
Not for Children: Pictures and Verse. Garden City: 1930. V. 52

YOUNG, S. GLENN, MRS.
Life and Exploits of S. Glenn Young World Famous Law Enforcement Law Officer. Herrin: 1924. V. 54

YOUNG Samurai. New York: 1965. V. 48

YOUNG Samurai... New York: 1967. V. 51

THE YOUNG Secretary's Polite Guide to an Episotary Correspondence in Business, Friendship, Love and Marriage. Newcastle-upon-Tyne: 1778. V. 47

YOUNG, THOMAS
An Account of Some Recent Discoveries in Hieroglyphical Literature and Egyptian Antiquities... 1823. V. 54
An Account of Some Recent Discoveries in Hieroglyphical Literature and Egyptian Antiquities. London: 1823. V. 47; 50
A Course of Lectures on Natural Philosophy and Mechanical Arts. London: 1807. V. 48
A Course of Lectures on Natural Philosophy and Mechanical Arts. 1845. V. 54
A Course of Lectures on Natural Philosophy and Mechanical Arts. London: 1845. V. 48
Miscellaneous Works of the Late Thomas Young. London: 1855. V. 49; 50
Outlines of Experiments and Inquiries Respecting Sound and Light. London: 1800. V. 48; 50; 52; 54

YOUNG, WILLIAM
Corn Trade. An Examination of Certain Commercial Principles, in Their Application to Agriculture and the Corn Trade, as Laid Down in the Fourth Book of Mr. Adam Smith's Treatise on the Wealth of Nations. London: 1800. V. 53
The History of Dulwich College Down to...1857. London: 1889. V. 47
A Journal of a Summer's Excursion by the Road of Montecasino to Naples, and from Thence Over all the Southern Parts of Italy, Sicily and Malta. 1774. V. 49
A Journal of a Summer's Excursion by the Road of Montecasino to Naples, and from Thence Over All the Southern Parts of Italy, Sicily and Malta... London: 1774. V. 52
Picturesque Architectural Studies and Practical Designs... London: 1872. V. 50; 52
Town and Country Mansions and Suburban Houses... London: 1879. V. 47; 49
The West-India Common-Place Book... London: 1807. V. 50; 53

YOUNG, WILLIAM C.
Documents of American Theater History. Chicago: 1973. V. 49

YOUNG, WILLIAM T.
Life and Public Services of General Lewis Cass. Together with the Pamphlet on the Right of Search. Detroit: 1852/c.1851. V. 54

YOUNGBLOOD, CHARLES L.
A Mighty Hunter. The Adventures of Charles L. Youngblood on the Plains and Mountains. Chicago & New York: 1890. V. 47; 54

YOUNGE, RICHARD
A Hopefull Way to Cure that Horrid Sinne of Swearing; or an Helpe to Save Swearers if Willing to Be Saved.. 1645. V. 49

YOUNGER, JOHN
On River Angling for Salmon and Trout; More Particularly as Practised in the Tweed and Its Tributaries. London: 1840. V. 51
River Angling for Salmon and Trout, with a Memoir of the Author. 1860. V. 53

YOUNGER, SCOUT
Hell on the Border - Law and the Outlaw. Milwaukee. V. 53

YOUNGHUSBAND, FRANCIS EDWARD
Among the Celestials. London: 1898. V. 49
The Heart of a Continent... 1896. V. 54
The Heart of a Continent. London: 1896. V. 52
The Heart of a Continent... 1897. V. 54

YOUNGHUSBAND, G. J.
The Relief of Chitral. London: 1895. V. 54

YOUNGHUSBAND, GEORGE
The Crown Jewels of England. New York: 1919. V. 53

YOUNGMAN, EDWARD GODFREY
Trial and Execution of Edward Godfrey Youngman...Who Was Executed at Horsemonger Lane Goal...for the Murder of his Mothea (sic)...His Two Brothers...and a Young Woman to Whome He was to Have Been Married. Norwich: 1860. V. 47

YOUNGMAN, WILLIAM ERNEST
Gleanings from Western Prairies. Cambridge: 1882. V. 49; 51; 53

YOURCENAR, MARGUERITE
The Alms of Alcippe. New York: 1982. V. 48; 51; 54

YOUTHFUL Recreations, Containing Amusements of a Day, as Spent by Master Freelove and His Companions Interspersed with Stories, Suitable Observations, Verses and Other Matters of Instruction and Entertainment. London: 1802. V. 51

YOUTH'S Assistant in Drawing; or, a Complat Drawing Book. London: 1765. V. 48

THE YOUTH'S Cabinet of Nature, for the Year... New York: 1814. V. 48

THE YOUTH'S Keepsake. New York: 1851-55. V. 52

YOYOTTE, JEAN
Treasures of the Pharaohs: the Early Period, the New Kingdom, the Late Period. Geneva: 1968. V. 49; 51

YRIARTE, CHARLES
Venice. Its History, Art, Industries and Modern Life. Philadelphia: 1900?. V. 47

YRIARTE, DON TOMAS DE
Literary Fables, from the Spanish. London: 1835. V. 51
Music, a Didactic Poem, in Five Cantos. London: 1807. V. 47

YUDOVIN, SOLOMON
Yiddisher Folks-Ornament (Jewis Folk Ornament). Vitebsk: 1920. V. 48

YUKIO, YASHIRO
Art Treasures of Japan. Tokyo: 1960. V. 49

YULE, HENRY
The Book of Ser Marco Polo the Venetian Concerning The Kingdoms & Marvels of the East. New York: 1926. V. 48

YUZON, AMADO M.
The Citizen's Poems. 1960. V. 47; 48

Y-WORTH, WILLIAM
The Brittanian Magazine; or, a New Art of Making Above Twenty-Sorts of English Wines... London: 1700. V. 47

Z

Z., A.
An Epistle to I. G. the author of a Pamphlet Entitled, "Some Account of the Free Grammar School of Highgate...With Remarks on the Origin and Nature of the Recent Inquiry Into the Management of that Institution.". London: 1823. V. 52

ZABA, ZBYNEK
The Rock Inscriptions of Lower Nubia (Czechoslovak Concession). Prague: 1974. V. 51

ZABAGLIA, NICCOLO
Castelli e Ponti...Con Alcune Ingegnose Pratche e Con La Descrizione del Trasporto Dell-Obelisco Vaticano. Rome: 1743. V. 49; 53

ZABRISKIE, FRANCIS NICOLL
History of the Reformed P.D. Church of Claverack; a Centennial Address. Hudson: 1867. V. 54

ZABRISKIE, GEORGE
A Little About Washington Irving. Ormond Beach: 1945. V. 48

ZACHARAKIS, CHRISTOS G.
A Catalogue of Printed Maps of Greece, 1477-1800. Nicosia: 1992. V. 48

ZACHARIN, GREGORY
Clinical Lectures Delivered Before the Students of the Imperial Moscow University. Boston: 1899. V. 49; 50

ZADKIEL
The Handbook of Astrology: Containing the Doctrine of Nativities. In a Form Free of All Mystery...and Learn His Own Natural Character and Proper Destiny. Volume II. London: 1863. V. 52

ZADOKS-JOSEPHUS JITTA, A. H.
Roman Bronze Statuettes fromt he Netherlands I-II. Groningen: 1967-69. V. 50; 52

ZAEHNSDORF, JOSEPH W.
The Art of Bookbinding. London: 1880. V. 52

ZAEHNSDORF LTD.
A Short History of Bookbinding and a Glossary of Styles and Terms Used in Binding. London: 1895. V. 54

ZAHAV, ARI IBN
You, Jerusalem. Jerusalem: 1939. V. 53

ZAIN, C. C.
The Brotherhood of Light Complete Course in Astrology and Metaphysics. 1920's. V. 47

ZAMIATIN, E.
My (We). New York: 1952. V. 48
We. 1924. V. 48

ZAMMIT, THEMISTOCLES
Malta. The Islands and Their History. Valletta: 1929. V. 54

THE ZAMORANAO 80: A Selection of Distinguished California Books Made by Members of the Zamorano Club. Los Angeles: 1945. V. 50; 53

THE ZAMORANO 80: A Selection of Distinguished California Books Made by Members of the Zamorano Club. New York; 1969. V. 53

ZAMORANO CLUB
The Zamorano Index to Bancroft's History of California. Los Angeles: 1985. V. 53

ZAMPETTI, PIETRO
Paintings from the Marches, Gentile to Raphael. London: 1971. V. 50; 54

ZANE Grey: the Man and His Books. New York: 1918. V. 50

ZANETTI, ANTONIO MARIA
Varie Pitture a Fresco de Principali Maestri Veneziani... Venice: 1760. V. 49

ZANGWILL, ISRAEL
The Bachelor's Club. London: 1891. V. 53
Dreamers of the Ghetto. London: 1898. V. 49; 52
The Works of Israel Zangwill. London: 1925. V. 52

ZANOTTO, FRANCESCO
Facsimile Delle Miniature Contenute...Breviario Grimani...Eseguito in Fotografiada Antonio Perini... Venezia: 1862. V. 48

ZAPF, HERMANN
Das Blumen ABC von Hermann Zapf und August Rosenberger. Frankfurt a.M: 1962. V. 47
From the Hand of Hermann Zapf. 1993. V. 51
Hermann Zapf and His Design Philosophy. Chicago: 1987. V. 51
Manuale Typographicum. Frankfurt: 1954. V. 47
Manuale Typographicum. Frankfurt & New York: 1968. V. 47
Orbis Typographicus. Thoughts, Words and Phrases on the Arts and Sciences. Kansas: 1980. V. 47; 48
Pen and Graver. Alphabets and Pages of Calligraphy. New York: 1952. V. 50; 51; 52
Poetry Through Typography. New York: 1993. V. 48
Specimen Pages from the "Manuale Typographicum.". Frankfurt: 1952. V. 47
The Standard Lay of the Case. London: 1978. V. 51
Typographic Variations... New York: 1962. V. 47
Typographic Variations. New York: 1964. V. 54
Variations Typographiques. Paris: 1965. V. 47

ZAPF'S Civilite Disclosed. Northampton: 1995. V. 54

ZAPHIRUS, PHILIPPUS
In Libros Posteriorvm Analyticorvm Aristotelis Explanatio (etc.). Venice: 1567, 1568. V. 53

ZAPPA, FRANK
The Real Frank Zappa Book. New York: 1989. V. 47; 53

ZARATE, AGOSTINO
Le Historie dello Scoprimento et Conqvista del perv... Venice: 1563. V. 50; 53

ZASIUS, JOHANN ULRICH
Catalogvs Legvm Antiqvarum. Strasbourg: 1551. V. 48

ZASLOW, MORRIS
Reading the Rocks: the Story of the Geological Survey of Canada, 1842-1972. Ottawa: 1975. V. 50

ZAVALA, LORENZO DE
Viaje a los Estados-Unidos del Norte de America. Paris: 1834. V. 50

ZAYAS, MARIUS DE
A Study of the Modern Evolution of Plastic Expression. New York: 1913. V. 50

ZEIDLER, SEBASTIAN CHRSITIAN VON
Somatotomia Anthropolgica, Seu, Corporis Humani Fabrica. Pragae: 1686. V. 47

ZEILLER, MARTIN
Topographia Franconiae. Francktfurt: 1648. V. 49
Topographia Hassiae, et Regionum Vincinarum. Francktfurt: 1655. V. 49

ZEIS, EDUARD
The Zeis Index and History of Plastic Surgery, 900 B.C.-1863 A.D. Baltimore: 1977. V. 50

ZEISBERGER, DAVID
Zeisberger's Indian Dictionary - English, German, Iroquois - the Onononondaga/ and Algonquine - The Delaware. Cambridge: 1887. V. 48; 49; 50

ZEISLER, SIGMUND
Reminiscences of the Anarchist Case. Chicago: 1927. V. 52

ZEISLOFT, E. IDELL
The New Metropolis. 1600-1900. Memorable Events of Three Centuries. New York: 1899. V. 52

ZEITLIN, IDA
Skazki - Tales and Legends of Old Russia. New York: 1926. V. 50

ZEITLINGER, HEINRICH
Bibliotheca Chemico-Mathematica... London: 1921. V. 49
Bibliotheca Chemico-Mathematica... London: 1921/52. V. 54

ZELAZNY, ROGER
The Changing Land: a Novel of Dilvish the Damned. San Francisco: 1981. V. 52
Creatures of Light and Darkness. New York: 1969. V. 47; 51
Creatures of Light and Darkness. London: 1970. V. 48; 52
The Doors of His Face, the Lamps of His Mouth and Other Stories. New York: 1971. V. 47
The Dream Master. 1968. V. 47; 49; 54
Eye of Cat. San Francisco: 1982. V. 48; 51
The Guns of Avalon. 1972. V. 48
The Last Defender of Camelot. San Francisco: 1981. V. 52
Lord of Light. New York: 1967. V. 47; 51
Nine Princes in Amber. 1970. V. 48
Nine Princes in Amber. London: 1972. V. 52
A Rhapsody in Amber. New Castle: 1981. V. 51; 52
A Rose for Ecclesiastes. 1969. V. 47; 48; 52
This Immortal. 1967. V. 54

ZELICA, the Creole; a Novel, by an American. London: 1820. V. 47

ZELLMAN, M.
American Art Analog. New York: 1986. V. 54

ZEMACH, MARGOT
Duffy and the Devil. New York: 1973. V. 48

ZENEA Y LUZ, EVARISTO
Historia de la Real Casa de Maternidad de Esta Ciudad... Havana: 1838. V. 53

ZENGER, JOHN PETER
The Trial of John Peter Zenger, of New York, Printer, Who Was Tried (in 1736) and Acquitted for Printing and Publishing a Libel Against the Government. London: 1752. V. 48

ZENO, ANNANIA
Il Cavalo Di Razza, Riconosciuto dal Segno De' Merchi Delle Piu Perfette Razze del Venetiano, Lombardia & Parte della Romagna... Venice: 1658. V. 54

ZENO, ANTONIO
In Concionem Periclis & Lepidi Ex Libro Primo Historiarum Thucydidis et Sallustii, Commentarius. Venice: 1569. V. 47; 48

ZERI, FEDERICO
Italian Paintings in the Walters Art Gallery. Baltimore: 1976. V. 49; 52

ZERN, ED
Zane Grey's adventures in Fishing. New York: 1952. V. 50

ZERNER, HENRI
The School of Fontainbleau. London: 1969. V. 48
The School of Fontainebleau... New York: 1969. V. 54

ZERVOS, CHRISTIAN
Catalan Art from the Ninth to the Fifteenth Centuries. London: 1937. V. 49; 52; 54

ZETLAND, LAWRENCE JOHN LUMLEY DUNDAS, 2ND MARQUIS OF
Lands of the Thunderholt, Sikhim, Chumbi & Bhutan. Boston and New York: 1923. V. 54
Sport and Politics Under an Eastern Sky. 1902. V. 54
Sport and Politics Under an Eastern Sky. London: 1902. V. 47
A Wandering Student in the Far East. London: 1908. V. 54

ZEUSS, J. C.
Grammatica Celtica. Lipsiae: 1853. V. 49; 50

ZEVI, BRUNO
Towards an Organic Architecture. London: 1950. V. 52

ZIEGLER, GEORGE J.
Researches On the Medical Properties and Applications of Nitrous Oxide, Protoxide of Nitrogen, or Laughing Gas. Philadelphia: 1865. V. 50

ZIEGLER, HENRY BRYAN
Six Views of Ludlow... Ludlow: 1846. V. 52

ZIEMSSEN, HUGO VON
Acute Infectious Diseases. New York: 1874. V. 49; 50; 52
Handbook of Diseases of the Skin. New York: 1885. V. 49; 54

ZIENKOWICZ, LEON
Les Costumes du Peuple Polonois, Suivis d'une Description Exacte de ses Moeurs, de ses Usages et de ses Habitudes. Paris: 1841. V. 52

ZIGROSSER, CARL
The Complete Etchings of John Marin. Philadelphia: 1969. V. 53
The Modern School. Stelton: 1917. V. 54

ZILLETTI, GIOVANNI BATTISTA
Index Librorum Omnium Iuris tam Pontificii Quam Caesarei Nomina Complectens... Venice: 1563. V. 47

ZIMMER, HEINRICH
The Art of Indian Asia: its Mythology and Transformations. New York: 1955. V. 49
The Art of Indian Asia. Its Mythology and Transformations. New York: 1964. V. 50; 54
The Art of Indian Asia. Its Mythology and Transformations. Princeton: 1968. V. 49

ZIMMER, J. T.
Catalogue of the Edward E. Ayer Ornithological Library. Chicago: 1926. V. 53
Catalogue of the Edward E. Ayer Ornithological Library. 1990. V. 53

ZIMMERMAN, E. C.
Insects of Hawaii. Honolulu: 1948-58. V. 52

ZIMMERMAN, F. B.
Henry Purcell, 1659-1695: an analytical Catalogue of His Music. London: 1963. V. 49

ZIMMERMAN, H. M.
Atlas of Tumors of the Nervous System. Philadelphia: 1956. V. 54

ZIMMERMAN, JOHANN GEORG VON
An Examination of the Advantages of Solitude... (with) A Biographical Account of the Author. London: 1805. V. 49
Select Views of the Life, Reign and Character of Frederick the Great. Dublin: 1792. V. 47
Solitude Considered with Respect to Its Influence on the Mind and the Heart. London: 1791. V. 54
Solitude Considered with Respect to Its Influence on the Mind and the Heart. London: 1799. V. 49
A Treatise on Experience in Physic. London: 1782. V. 54

ZIMMERMAN, WILLIAM
Waterfowl of North America. Louisville: 1974. V. 54

ZIMMERMANN, H.
An Account of the Third Voyage of Captain Cook Around the World 1776-1780. Toronto: 1930. V. 48
Zimmermann's Account of the Third Voyage of Captain Cook. Wellington: 1926. V. 54

ZINN, JOHANNIS GOTTFRIED
Descriptio Anatomica Oculi Humani. Gottingen: 1755. V. 49; 50
Descriptio Anatomica Oculi Humani... Gottingen: 1780. V. 54

ZINSMEISTER, H. D.
Bryophytes: Their Chemistry and Chemical Taxonomy. London: 1990. V. 50

ZIONITISCHER Weyrauchs Hugel Oder: Myrrhen Berg, Worinnen Allerley Liebliches und Wohl Riechendes Nach Apotheker Kunst Zubereitetes Rauch-Werck zu Finden...* Germantown: 1739. V. 48; 50

ZIPPER, JACOB
Theoretisch-Praktische Anweisung zu Schlosserarbeiten Nebst den Dazu Gehorigen Zeichnungen und Rissen. Augsburg und Leipzig: 1822. V. 53

ZIRANEK, SILVIA
Very Food. London: 1987. V. 53

ZIRCKEL, OTTO
Tagebuch Geschrieben Wahrend der Nordamerikanisch-mexikanischer Campagne 1847-48. Halle: 1849. V. 49

ZITTEL, K. A. VON
History of Geology and Palaeontology to the End of the Nineteenth Century. London: 1901. V. 53

ZITTLE, JOHN H.
A Correct History of the John Brown Invasion at Harper's Ferry, West Va., Oct. 17, 1859. Hagerstown: 1905. V. 49

ZOETE, B. DE
Dance and Magic Drama in Ceylon. London: 1957. V. 49

ZOGBAUM, RUFUS FAIRCHILD
Horse, Foot, and Dragoons, Sketches of Army Life at Home and Abroad. New York: 1888. V. 47; 48; 54

ZOGHEB, BERNARD DE
Le Sorrelle Bronte. New York: 1963. V. 47; 53

ZOHARY, M.
Flora Palaestina. Jerusalem: 1966. V. 47; 48

ZOLA, EMILE
L'Assonmoir. London: 1928. V. 53
The Attack on the Mill. London: 1895. V. 52
Une Campagne 1880-1881. Paris: 1882. V. 47; 50; 52
La Curee... Paris: 1881. V. 47
La Curee. Paris: 1894. V. 47
Lettre a la France. Paris: 1898. V. 54
Madeleine Ferat a Realistic Novel... London: 1888. V. 47
Nana. Paris: 1880. V. 48
Paris. Paris: 1898. V. 47
Les Rougon-Macquart, Histoire Naturelle et Sociale d'une Famille Sous le Second Empire. Paris: 1886. V. 50; 52
The Trial of Emile Zola Containing M. Zola's Letter to President Faure Relating to the Dreyfus Case and a Full Report of the Fifteen Days' Proceedings in the Assize Court of the Seine... New York: 1898. V. 52
Work. London: 1901. V. 51; 52

ZOLLICOFFER, FELIX KIRK
Speech of Felix Zollicoffer, Delivered at Nashville, June 16, 1855. Nashville: 1855. V. 48

ZOLOTOW, CHARLOTTE
Mr. Rabbit and the Lovely Present. New York: 1962. V. 49
Not a Little Monkey. New York: 1957. V. 51

ZONGHI, AURELIO
Zonghi's Watermarks. Hilversum: 1953. V. 48

ZONGMU, WANG
An Essay on Paper. V. 53

ZONGO-TEE-FOH-TCHI
Napoleon in the Other World. London: 1827. V. 47

ZONG-XUN, WANG
Bibliography of Chinese Botany. 1983. V. 53

ZOOLOGICAL SOCIETY OF LONDON
Transactions. London: 1866-1965. V. 52

THE ZOOLOLOGICAL Gardens, Regents Park. London: 1835. V. 54

ZORES, CHARLES FERDINAND
Deuxieme Partie du Recueil. Profils, Assemblages, Dispositions, Armatures, Suspensions & Entretoisages des Fers Zores. Paris: 1863. V. 53

ZORGDRAGER, CORNELIUS GIJSBERTSZ
Bloeijende Opkomst der Aloude en Hedendaagsche Groenlandsche Visschery. Amsterdam: 1720. V. 49
Bloeijende Opkomst der Aloude en Hedendaagsche Groenlandsche Visschery... Amsterdam: 1728. V. 54

ZORN, ANDERS LEONARD
Anders Leonard Zorn 1860-1920. Sweden: 1980. V. 49
Zorn Engravings... 1980. V. 52
Zorn Engravings. Sweden: 1980. V. 54

ZORN, FRIEDRICH ALBERT
Grammar of the Art of Dancing, Theoretical and Practical... Boston: 1905. V. 54
Grammar of the Art of Dancing, Theoretical and Practical. Boston: 1920. V. 49

ZORN, JOHANNES
Auswahl Schoner und Seltener Gewachse, Als Eine Forsetzung der Americanischen Gewachse. Nurnberg: 1795-96. V. 53

ZOUAVE Drill Book. French Baoynet Exercise and Skirmisher's Drill, as Used by Col. Ellsworth's Zouaves. Philadelphia: 1861. V. 47

ZOUCH, THOMAS
The Life of Isaac Walton. London: 1823. V. 54
The Life of Isaac Walton... London: 1824. V. 54
The Life of Isaac Walton... London: 1825. V. 47
The Life of Izaak Walton. London: 1826. V. 47; 49
The Works of... York: 1820. V. 54

ZOUCHE, ROBERT CURZON, BARON
Armenia: a Year at Erzeroom and on the Frontiers of Russia, Turkey and Persia. London: 1854. V. 50

ZSCHOKKE, HEINRICH
Abaellino, the Bravo of Venice: a Romance. Baltimore: 1809. V. 54

ZUCROW, SOLOMON
Women, Slaves and the Ignorant in Rabbinic Literature and Also the Dignity of Man. Boston: 1932. V. 48

ZUKOFSKY, LOUIS
A 1-12 with an Essay on Poetry... Ashland: 1959. V. 47; 51
Barely and Widely. New York: 1958. V. 48; 51
It Was. Kyoto: 1961. V. 51
An Objectivists Anthology. Dijon: 1932. V. 51
Prepositions. London: 1967. V. 50; 51
Some Time. Short Poems. Stuttgart: 1956. V. 51; 52; 53; 54
Le Style Apollinaire. Paris: 1934. V. 48; 51
A Test of Poetry. New York: 1948. V. 48

ZUNIGA, FRANCISCO
Francisco Zuniga. Mexico City: 1980. V. 48

ZUNIGA, IGNACIO
Rapida Ojeada al Estado de Sonora... Mexico: 1835. V. 47; 49

ZUNIGA, LORENZO BAUTISTA DE
Annales Eclesiastaicos i Seglares de la...Ciudad de Sevilla que Comprehenden la Olimpiada o Lustro de la Corte en ella con dos Apendices. Seville: 1747. V. 53

ZUR Feier des Einhundertjahrigen Bestandes der K.K. Hof-und Staatsdruckerei. Vienna: 1904. V. 54

ZURCHER, OTTO
Gerald Landon. New York: 1917. V. 54

ZURIEL
A Series of Lectures on the Science of Celestial Philosophy: or the Language of the Stars. London: 1835. V. 47

ZURITA Y CASATRO, GERONIMO
Indices Rerum ab Aragoniae Regibus Gestarum ab Initiis Regni ad Annum MCDX...(and) Roberti Viscardi Calabriae Ducis, et Rogerii Eius Fratris Calabriae, et Siciliae Ducis Principum Normannorum... Zaragoza: 1578. V. 53

ZWEIG, PAUL
Images and Footsteps... 1971. V. 52; 54
Images and Footsteps. Verona: 1971. V. 48
The River. 1981. V. 52; 54
The River. Verona: 1981. V. 47; 48; 49

ZWEIG, STEFAN
Amerigo: a Comedy of Errors in History. New York: 1942. V. 54
The Buried Candelabrum. New York: 1937. V. 54
Conqueror of the Seas: The Story of Magellan. New York: 1938. V. 54
The Invisible Collection. New York: 1926. V. 54
Jeremiah: a Drama in Nine Scenes. New York: 1939. V. 54
Master Builders: a Typology of the Spirit. New York: 1939. V. 54
The Right to Heresy: Castellio Against Calvin. New York: 1936. V. 54
The World of Yesterday: an Autobiography. New York: 1943. V. 54

ZYGOS Annual Editions on the Hellenic Fine Arts. Athens: 1982-85. V. 47

ZYL, JOHANNES VAN
Theatarum Machinarum Universale; of Groot Algemeen Moolen-Bock. Amsterdam: 1761.
 V. 49; 53

ZYLBERZWEIG, ZALME
Album of the Yiddish Theatre. New York: 1937. V. 49; 53